Who Was Who in America

Biographical Reference Works
Published By Marquis Who's Who

Who's Who in America

Who Was Who in America

Historical Volume (1607-1896)

Volume I (1897-1942)

Volume II (1943-1950)

Volume III (1951-1960)

Volume IV (1961-1968)

Volume V (1969-1973)

Volume VI (1974-1976)

Volume VII (1977-1981)

Who Was Who in American History—Arts and Letters

Who Was Who in American History—The Military

Who Was Who in American History—Science and Technology

Who's Who in the Midwest

Who's Who in the East

Who's Who in the South and Southwest

Who's Who in the West

Who's Who of American Women

Who's Who in Government

Who's Who in Finance and Industry

Who's Who in Religion

Who's Who in American Law

Who's Who in the World

Who's Who Biographical Record—Child Development Professionals

Who's Who Biographical Record—School District Officials

World Who's Who in Science

Directory of Medical Specialists

Marquis Who's Who Publications/Index to All Books

Travelers' Guide to U. S. Certified Doctors Abroad

Who Was Who in America®
with World Notables

Volume VII
1977-1981

MARQUIS
Who's Who

Marquis Who's Who, Inc.
200 East Ohio Street
Chicago, Illinois 60611 U. S. A.

Library of Congress Catalog Card Number 43-3789
International Standard Book Number 0-8379-0210-X
Product Code Number 030209

Distributed in the United Kingdom by
George Prior Associated Publishers
37-41 Bedford Row
London, WC1, England

Manufactured in the United States of America

Table of Contents

Preface

The publication of Volume VII of WHO WAS WHO IN AMERICA is an important step forward in the growth of a series of biographical reference books that seek to reflect both American history and the genealogical heritage of this country. Most of the sketches are of deceased biographees in *Who's Who in America.* In addition, the more recent companion volumes, the four books comprising the Marquis Regional Library, extend the scope and coverage of *Who's Who in America.* As a consequence, this volume of WHO WAS WHO IN AMERICA also contains the names of deceased Marquis biographees whose careers were of essentially regional significance and whose listings were in publications other than *Who's Who in America.*

The WAS books (to use the shortened form by which they are perhaps better known) display the distinctive characteristics that have made *Who's Who in America* both an internationally respected reference work and a household word in the country of its origin. Sketches not only were prepared from information supplied by the biographees themselves, but were approved and frequently revised by the subjects before being printed in a Marquis publication. As a result, many sketches contain personal data unavailable elsewhere. The preface to the first volume of *Who's Who in America* selected this fact as one of that volume's outstanding characteristics, and stated: "The book is autobiographical, the data having been obtained from first hand." Similarly, WHO WAS WHO IN AMERICA is also largely autobiographical. Although condensed to the concise style that Marquis Who's Who, Inc. has made famous, the sketches contain the essential facts. Inclusion of date of death and place of interment completes the sketches.

In continuing improvements introduced in previous volumes of WHO WAS WHO IN AMERICA, this volume includes sketches of some Marquis biographees known to be 95 years of age or older. Lacking current information regarding these individuals, we make such inclusions in the hope that our apologies will be accepted should errors occur. Sketches of recently deceased world notables also are included, particularly of those international figures whose careers had a direct bearing on the course of recent American history.

The result is far more than a biographical directory of some 105,000 deceased American notables within the covers of eight volumes. WHO WAS WHO IN AMERICA contains a vital portion of American history from the early days of the colonies to mid-1981. It is the autobiography of America.

Table of Abbreviations

The following abbreviations are frequently used in this book:

*Following a sketch signifies that the published biography could not be verified.

†Non-current sketches of WHO'S WHO IN AMERICA biographees who were born 95 or more years ago (see Preface for explanation).

A.A. Associate in Arts
A.A.A. Agricultural Adjustment Administration; Anti-Aircraft Artillery
AAAL American Academy of Arts and Letters
A.A.A.S. American Association for the Advancement of Science
AAC Army Air Corps
A. and **M.** Agricultural and Mechanical
AAF Army Air Force
A.A.H.P.E.R. American Association for Health, Physical Education, and Recreation
AAU Amateur Athletic Union
A.A.U.P. American Association of University Professors
A.A.U.W. American Association of University Women
AB Alberta
A.B. Bachelor of Arts
ABC American Broadcasting Company
A.,B.& C.R.R. Atlanta, Birmingham & Coast R.R.
AC Air Corps
Acad. academy; academic
ACAD Arms Control and Disarmament Agency
acct. accountant
acctg accounting
ACDA Arm Control and Disarmament Agency
A.C.L.R.R. Atlantic Coast Line R.R.
A.C.L.U. American Civil Liberties Union
A.C.P. American College of Physicians
A.C.S. American College of Surgeons
ADA American Dental Association
a.d.c. aide-de-camp
adj. adjutant; adjunct
adj. gen. adjutant general
adm. admiral
adminstr. administrator
adminstrn. administration
Adminstrv. administrative
adv. advocate; advisory
advt. advertising
A.E. Agricultural Engineer
A.E. and P. Ambassador Extraordinary and Plenipotentiary
AEC Atomic Energy Commission
AEF American Expeditionary Forces
aero. aeronautical, aeronautic
aerodyn. aerodynamic
AFB Air Force Base
A.F.D. Doctor of Fine Arts
AFL (or **A.F. of L**) American Federation of Labor
AFL-CIO American Federation of Labor and Congress of Industrial Organizations
A.F.T.R.A. American Federation TV and Radio Artists
agr. agriculture
agrl. agricultural
agt. agent
AGVA American Guild of Variety Arts
agy. agency
A & I Agricultural and Industrial
A.I.A. American Institute of Architects
AIAA American Institute of Aeronautics Astronautics
AID Agency for International Development
AIEE American Institute of Electrical Engineers
A.I.M. American Institute of Management
AIME American Institute of Mining, Metallurgy & Petroleum Engineers
AK Alaska
AL Alabama
Ala. Alabama
A.L.A. American Library Association
alt. alternate
Alta. Alberta
A & M Agricultural and Mechanical
Am. American, America
A.M. Master of Arts
A.M.A. American Medical Association
A.M.E. African Methodist Episcopal
Am. Inst. E.E. American Institute of Electrical Engineers
Am. Soc. C.E. American Society of Civil Engineers
Am. Soc. M.E. American Society of Mechanical Engineers
Amtrak National R.R. Passenger Corporation
AMVETS American Veteran of World War II, Korea, Vietnam
A.N.A. Associate National Academician
anat. anatomical
ann. annual
ANTA American National Theatre and Academy
anthrop. anthropological
A.P. Associated Press
APO Army Post Office
apptd. appointed
apt. apartment
AR Arkansas
A.R.C. American Red Cross
archeol. archaeological
archtl. architectural
Ariz. Arizona
Ark. Arkansas
ArtsD. Doctor of Arts
arty. artillery
AS Air Service
A.S.C.A.P. American Society of Composers, Authors and Publishers
ASCE American Society of Civil Engineers
ASF Air Service Force
ASHRAE American Society of Heating Refrigeration and Air Conditioning Engineers
ASME American Society of Mechanical Engineers
assn. association
asso. associate; associated
asst. assistant
ASTM American Society for Testing and Materials
astron. astronomical
astrophys. astrophysical
ATSC Air Technical Service Command
A., T. & S. F. Ry. Atchison, Topeka & Santa Fe Ry.
AT & T American Telephone & Telegraph Company
atty. attorney
AUS Army of the United States
Aux. Auxiliary
Av. Avenue
AVMA American Veterinary Medical Association
AZ Arizona

b. born
B. Bachelor
B.A. Bachelor of Arts
B.Agr. Bachelor of Agriculture
Balt. Baltimore
Bapt. Baptist
B. Arch. Bachelor of Architecture
B. & A.R.R. Boston & Albany R.R.
B.A.S. Bachelor of Agricultural Science
B.B.A. Bachelor of Business Administration
BBC British Broadcasting Corp.
BC British Columbia
B.C. British Columbia
B.C.E. Bachelor of Civil Engineering
B.Chir. Bachelor of Surgery
B.C.L. Bachelor of Civil law
B.C.S. Bachelor of Commercial Science
bd. board
B.D. Bachelor of Divinity
B.Di. Bachelor of Didactics
B.E. Bachelor of Education
B.E.E. Bachelor of Electrical Engineering
BEF British Expeditionary Force
B.F.A. Bachelor of Fine Arts
bibl. biblical
bibliog. bibliographical
biog. biographical
biol. biological
B.J. Bachelor of Journalism
Bklyn. Brooklyn
B.L. Bachelor of Letters
bldg. building
B.L.S. Bachelor of Library Science
Blvd. Boulevard
B. & M. R.R. Boston & Maine R.R.
Bn. Battalion
B.O. Bachelor of Oratory
B. & O. R.R. Baltimore & Ohio R.R.
bot. Botanical
B.P. Bachelor of Painting
B. Pd. Bachelor of Pedagogy
B.P.E. Bachelor of Physical Education
B. Py. Bachelor of Pedagogy
br. branch
B.R.E. Bachelor of Religious Education
brig. gen. brigadier general
Brit. British; Britannica
Bro. Brother
Bros. Brothers
B.S. Bachelor of Science
B.S.A. Bachelor of Agricultural Science
B.S.D. Bachelor of Didactic Science
B.S.T. Bachelor of Sacred Theology
B.Th. Bachelor of Theology
bull. bulletin
bur. bureau
bus. business
B.W.I. British West Indies

CA California
CAA Civil Aeronautics Administration
CAB Civil Aeronautics Board
CAC Coast Artillery Corps
Cal. California
Calif. California
C. Am. Central America
Can. Canada
CAP Civil Air Patrol
capt. captain
CARE Cooperative American Relief Everywhere
Cath. Catholic
cav. cavalry
CBC Canadian Broadcasting Company
CBI China, Burma, India Theatre of Operations
C.B. & Q. R.R. Chicago, Burlington & Quincy R.R. Co.
CBS Columbia Broadcasting System
CCC Commodity Credit Corporation
C.,C.,C. & St.L. Ry. Cleveland, Cincinnati, Chicago & St. Louis Ry.
CCU Cardiac Care Unit
CD Civil Defense
C.E. Civil Engineer, Corps of Engineers
CEF Canadian Expeditionary Force
C. & E.I. R.R. Chicago & Eastern Illinois R.R.
CENTO Central Treaty Organization
CERN European Organization of Nuclear Research
cert. certificate, certification, certified
CETA Comprehensive Employment Training Act
CFL Canadian Football League
C.G.W. R.R. Chicago Great Western Ry.
ch. church
Ch.D. Doctor of Chemistry
chem. chemical
Chem. E. Chemical Engineer
Chgo. Chicago
Chirurg. Chirurgical
chmn. chairman
chpt. chapter
Cia. (Spanish) Company
CIA Central Intelligence Agency

CIC Counter Intelligence Agency
Cie. (French) Company
C., I. & L. Ry. Chicago, Indianapolis & Louisville Ry.
Cin Cincinnati
CIO Congress of Industrial Organizations
Cleve. Cleveland
climatol. Climatological
clin. clinical
clk. clerk
C.L.U. Chartered Life Underwriter
C.M. Master in Surgery
C.M., St. P. & P. R.R. Chicago, Milwaukee, St. Paul & Pacific R.R. Co.
C. & N.-W. Ry. Chicago & Northwestern Ry.
CO Colorado
Co. Company
C. of C. Chamber of Commerce
C.O.F. Catholic Order of Foresters
C. of Ga. Ry. Central of Georgia Ry.
col. colonel
coll. college
Colo. Colorado
com. committee
comd. commanded
comdg. commanding
comdr. commander
comdt. commandant
commd. commissioned
comml. commercial
commn. commission
commr. commissioner
condr. conductor
conf. conference
Congl. Congregational; Congressional
Conglist. Congregationalist
Conn. Connecticut
cons. consulting, consultant
consol. consolidated
constl. constitutional
constn. constitution
constrn. construction
contbd. contributed
contbg. contributing
contbn. contribution
contbr. contributor
conv. convention
coop. (or **co.op)** cooperative
CORDS Civil Operations and Revolutionary Development Support
CORE Congress of Racial Equality
corp. corporation
corr. correspondent; corresponding; correspondence
C. & O. Ry. Chesapeake & Ohio Ry. Co.
C.P.A. Certified Public Accountant
C.P.C.U. Chartered Property and Casualty Underwriter
C.P.H. Certificate of Public Health
cpl. corporal
CPR Cardiac Pulmonary Resuscitation
C.P. Ry. Canadian Pacific Ry. Co.
C.,R.I & P. Ry. Chicago, Rock Island & Pacific Ry. Co.
C.R.R. of N.J. Central Railroad Co. of New Jersey
C.S. Christian Science
C.S.B. Bachelor of Christian Science
CSC Civic Service Commission
C.S.D. Doctor of Christian Science
C. & S. Ry. Co. Colorado & Southern Ry. Co.
C.,St.P., M. & O. Ry. Chicago, St. Paul, Minneapolis & Omaha Ry. Co.
CT Connecticut
ct. court
C.T. Candidate in Theology
C.Vt. Ry. Central Vermont Ry.
C. & W.I. R.R. Chicago & Western Indiana R.R. Co.
CWS Chemical Warfare Service
cyclo. cyclopedia
C.Z. Canal Zone
CZ Canal Zone

d. daughter
D. Doctor
D.Agr. Doctor of Agriculture
D.A.R. Daughters of the American Revolution
dau. daughter
D.A.V. Disabled American Veterans
D.C. District of Columbia
D.C.L. Doctor of Civil Law
D.C.S. Doctor of Commercial Science
D.D. Doctor of Divinity
D.D.S. Doctor of Dental Surgery
DE Delaware
dec. deceased
Def. Defense
Del. Delaware
del. delegate
Dem. Democratic; Democrat
D.Eng. Doctor of Engineering
denom. denominational
dep. deputy
dept. department
dermatol. dermatological
desc. descendant
devel. development
D.F.A. Doctor of Fine Arts
D.F.C. Distinguished Flying Cross
D.H.L. Doctor of Hebrew Literature
D. & H. R.R. Delaware & Hudson R.R. Co
dir. director
disch. discharged
dist. district
distbg. distributing
distbn. distribution
distbr. distributor
disting. distinguished
div. division; divinity; divorce proceedings
D.Litt. Doctor of Literature
D.L. & W. R.R. Delaware, Lackawanna & Western R.R. Co.
D.M.D. Doctor of Dental Medicine
D.M.S. Doctor of Medical Science
D.O. Doctor of Osteopathy
DPA Defense Production Administration
D.P.H. Diploma in Public Health
Dr. Doctor, Drive
D.R. Daughters of the Revolution
D.R.E. Doctor of Religious Education
D. & R.G.W. R.R. Co. Denver & Rio Grande Western R.R. Co.
Dr.P.H. Doctor of Public Health, Doctor of Public Hygiene
D.Sc., Doctor of Science
D.S.C. Distinguished Service Cross
D.S.M. Distinguished Service Medal
D.S.T. Doctor of Sacred Theology
D.T.M. Doctor of Tropical Medicine
D.V.M. Doctor of Veterinary Medicine
D.V.S. Doctor of Veterinary Surgery

E. East
E. and P. Extraordinary and Plenipotentiary
ECA Economic Cooperation Administration
eccles. ecclesiastical
ecol. ecological
econ. economic
ECOSOC Economic and Social Council (of the UN)
ed. educated
E.D. Doctor of Engineering
Ed.B. Bachelor of Education
Ed.D. Doctor of Education
edit. edition
Ed.M. Master of Education
edn. education
ednl. educational
EDP electronic data processing
EdS. Specialist in Education
E.E. Electrical Engineer
EEC European Economic Community
EEG electroencephalogram
E.E. and M.P. Envoy Extraordinary and Minister Plenipotentiary
EEO Equal Employment Opportunity
E. Ger. German Democratic Republic
EKG Electrocardiogram
Egyptol. Egyptological
elec. electrical
electrochem. electrochemical
electrophys. electrophysical
elem. elementary
E.M. Engineer of Mines
ency. encyclopaedia
Eng. England
engr. engineer
engring. engineering
entomol. entomological
environ. environmental
EPA Environmental Protection Agency
epidemol. epidemiological
Episc. Episcopalian
ERA Equal Rights Amendment
ERDA Energy Research and Development Administration
ESEA Elementary and Secondary Education Act
ESSA Elementary and Secondary School Act
ESSA Environmental Science Services Administration
ethnol. ethnological
ETO European Theater of Operations
Evang. Evangelical
exam. examination; examining
exec. executive
exhbn. exhibition
expdn. expedition
expn. exposition
expt. experiment
exptl. experimental

F.A. Field Artillery
FAA Federal Aviation Agency
FAO Food and Agriculture Organization (of the UN)
FBI Federal Bureau of Investigation
FCA Farm Credit Administration
FCC Federal Communications Commission
FCDA Federal Civil Defense Administration
FDA Food and Drug Administration
FDIA Federal Deposit Insurance Administration
FDIC Federal Deposit Insurance Corporation
F.E. Forest Engineer
FEA Federal Energy Administration
Fed. Federal
Fedn. Federation
Fgn. Foreign
FHA Federal Housing Administration
FL Florida
Fla. Florida
FMC Federal Maritime Commission
FOA Foreign Operations Administration
Found. Foundation
FPO Fleet Post Office
frat. fraternity
FRS Federal Reserve System
FSA Federal Security Agency
Ft. Fort
FTC Federal Trade Commission, Federal Tariff Commission

G-1 (or other number), Division of General Staff
GA Georgia
Ga. Georgia
GAO General Accounting Office
gastroent. gastroenterological
GATT General Agreement on Tariffs and Trade
G.C. & S.F. Ry. Gulf, Colorado & Santa Fe Ry. Co.
G.D. Graduate in Divinity
gen. general
geneal. genealogical
geod. geodetic
geog. geographical; geographic
geol. geological
geophys. geophysical
gerontol. gerontological
G.H.Q. General Headquarters
GmbH. (German) company
G.,M. & N. R.R. Gulf, Mobile & Northern R.R. Co.
G.,M. & O. R.R. Gulf, Mobile & Ohio R.R. Co.
G.N. Ry. Great Northern Ry. Co.
gov. Governor
govt. government
govtl. governmental

GPO Government Printing Office
grad. graduated, graduate
GSA General Services Administration
Gt. Great
G.T. Ry. Grand Trunk Ry. System
GU Guam
G.W. Ry. of Can. Great Western Ry. of Canada
gynecol. genecological

Hdqrs. Headquarters
HEW Department of Health, Education and Welfare
H.H.D. Doctor of Humanities
HHFA Housing and Home Finance Agency
HI Hawaii
H.I. Hawaiian Islands
H.M. Master of Humanics
hist. Historical
HOLC Home Owners Loan Corporation
homeo. homeopathic
hon. honorary, honorable
Ho. of Dels. House of Delegates
Ho. of Reps. House of Representatives
Hort. Horticultural
hosp. hospital
HUD Department of Housing and Urban Development
H.T. Territory of Hawaii
Hwy. Highway
hydrog. hydrographic

IA Iowa
Ia. Iowa
IAEA International Atomic Energy Agency
IBM International Business Machines Corp.
IBRD International Bank for Reconstruction and Development
ICA International Cooperation Administration
ICC Interstate Commerce Commn
I.C. R.R. Illinois Central R.R. System
ID Idaho
Ida. Idaho
I.E.E.E. Institute of Electrical and Electronics Engineers
IFC International Finance Corp.
I.G.N. R.R. International—Great Northern R.R.
IGY International Geophysical Year
IL Illinois
Ill. Illinois
Illus. illustrated
ILO International Labor Organization
IMF International Monetary Fund
IN Indiana
Inc. Incorporated
Ind. Indiana
Ind. Independent.
Indpls. Indianapolis
Indsl. industrial
Inf. infantry
Info. information
ins. insurance
Insp. inspector
Insp. gen. Inspector general
Inst. institute
Insti. institutional
Instn. institution
Instr. instructor
Instrn. instruction
Internat. international
Intro. introduction
I.R.E. Institute of Radio Engineers
IRS Internal Revenue Service
I.T.T. International Telephone & Telegraph Corporation

JAG Judge Advocate General
J.B. Jurum Baccalaureus
J.C.B. Juris Canonici Bachelor
J.C.L. Juris Canonici Lector
J.D. Doctor of Jurisprudence
j.g. junior grade
jour. journal
jr. junior
J.S.D. Doctor of Juristic Science
jud. Judical
J.U.D. Juris Utriusque Doctor: Doctor of Both (Canon and Civil) Laws
Judge Adv. Gen. Judge Advocate General

Kan. Kansas
K.C. Knight of Columbus
K.P. Knight of Pythias
K.C.S. Ry. Kansas City Southern Ry.
KS Kansas
K.T. Knight Templar
KY Kentucky
Ky. Kentucky

LA Louisiana
lab. laboratory
lang. language
laryngol. laryngological
LB Labrador
lectr. lecturer
legis. legislation, legislative
L.H.D. Doctor of Humane Letters
L.I. Long Island
lic. licensed, license
L.I. R.R. Long Island R.R. Company
lit. literary; literature
Litt. B. Bachelor of Letters
Litt. D. Doctor of Letters
L.L.B. Bachelor of Laws
L.L.D. Doctor of Laws
L.L.M. Master of Laws
Ln. Lane
L. & N. R.R. Louisville & Nashville R.R.
L.R.C.P. Licentiate Royal Coll. Physicians
L.R.C.S. Licentiate Royal Coll. Surgeons
L.S. Library Science
lt. lieutenant
Ltd. Limited
Luth. Lutheran
L.V.R.R. Lehigh Valley R.R. Co.
LWV League of Women Voters

m. married
M. Master
MA Massachusetts
M.A. Master of Arts
mag. magazine
M.Agr. Master of Agriculture
maj. major
Man. Manitoba
M.Arch. Master in Architecture
Mass. Massachusetts
math. mathematical, mathematics
MATS Military Air Transport Service
MB Manitoba
M.B. Bachelor of Medicine
M.B.A. Master of Business Administration
MBS Mutual Broadcasting System
M.C. Medical Corps
M.C.E. Master of Civil Engineering
mcpl. municipal
M.C.S. Master of Commercial Science
mcht. merchant
M.C.R.R. Michigan Central R.R.
MD Maryland
Md. Maryland
M.D. Doctor of Medicine
M.Dl. Master of Didactics
M.Dip. Master in Diplomacy
mdse. merchandise
M.D.V. Doctor of Veterinary Medicine
ME Maine
Me. Maine
M.E. Mechanical Engineer
mech. mechanical
M.E.Ch. Methodist Episcopal Church
M.Ed. Master of Education
med. medical
Med. O.R.C. Medical Officers' Reserve Corps
M.E.E. Master of Electrical Engineering
mem. member
Meml. Memorial
merc. mercantile
met. metropolitan
metall. metallurgical
Met.E. Metallurgical Engineer
meteorol. meteorological
Meth. Methodist
metrol. metrological
Mex. Mexico
M.F. Master of Forestry
M.F.A. Master of Fine Arts (carries title of Dr.)
mfg. manufacturing
mfr. manufacturer
mgmt. management
mgr. manager
M.H.A. Master of Hospital Administration
MI Michigan
M.I. Military Intelligence
Mich. Michigan
micros. microscopical
mil. military
Milw. Milwaukee
mineral. mineralogical
Minn. Minnesota
M.-K.-T. R.R. Missouri-Kansas-Texas R.R. Company
M.L. Master of Laws
M.L.D. Magister Legnum Diplomatic
M.Litt Master of Literature
Minn. Minnesota
Miss. Mississippi
MIT Massachusetts Institute of Technology
mktg. marketing
Mlle. Mademoiselle
MLA Modern Language Association
M.L.S. Master of Library Science
Mme. Madame
M.M.E. Master of Mechanical Engineering
MN Minnesota
mng. managing
MO Missouri
Mo. Missouri
Moblzn. Mobilization
Mont. Montana
M.P. Member of Parliament
M.Pd. Master of Pedagogy
M.P.E. Master of Physical Education
M.P.H. Master of Public Health
M.P.L. Master of Patent Law
Mpls. Minneapolis
M.P. R.R. Missouri Pacific R.R.
M.R.E. Master of Religious Education
MS Mississippi
M.S. Master of Science
M.Sc. Master of Science
M.S.F. Master of Science of Forestry
M.S.T. Master of Sacred Theology
M. & St. L. R.R. Minneapolis & St. Louis R.R. Company
M.,St.P. & S.S.M. Ry. Minneapolis St. Paul & Sault Ste. Marie Ry.
M.S.W. Master of Social Work
MT Montana
Mt. Mount
MTO Mediterranean Theater of Operations
mus. museum; musical
Mus.B. Bachelor of Music
Mus.D. Doctor of Music
Mus. M. Master of Music
Mut. Mutual
mycol. mycological

N North
N.A. National Academician; National Army
N.A.A.C.P. National Association for the Advancement of Colored People
NACA National Advisory Committee for Aeronautics
N.A.D. National Academy of Design
N.Am. North America
N.A.M. National Association of Manufacturers
NAPA National Association of Performing Artists
NAREB National Association of Real Estate Boards
NARS National Archives and Record Service
NASA National Aeronautics and Space Administration
nat. national
NATO North Atlantic Treaty Organization
NATOUSA North African Theater of Operations, U.S. Army
nav. navigation
NB New Brunswick
N.B. New Brunswick
NBC National Broadcasting Company

NC North Carolina
N.C. North Carolina
N.,C. & St.L. Ry. Nashville, Chattanooga & St. Louis Ry.
NCCJ National Conference of Christians and Jews
ND North Dakota
N.D. North Dakota
NDEA National Defense Education Act
NDRC National Defense Research Committee
NE Nebraska
N.E. Northeast
N.E.A. National Education Association
Neb. Nebraska
neurol. neurological
Nev. Nevada
New Eng. New England
NF Newfoundland
NFL National Football League
Nfld. Newfoundland
N.G. National Guard
NH New Hampshire
N.H. New Hampshire
NHL National Hockey League
NIH National Institutes of Health
NIMH National Institutes of Mental Health
NJ New Jersey
N.J. New Jersey
NLRB National Labor Relations Bd
NM New Mexico
N.M. New Mexico
No. Northern
NOAA National Oceanographic and Atmospheric Administration
NORAD North American Air Defense
N.O.W. National Organization for Women
NPA National Production Authority
N.P. Ry. Northern Pacific Ry.
nr. near
NRA National Recovery Administration
NRC National Research Council
NS Nova Scotia
N.S. Nova Scotia
NSC National Security Council
NSF National Science Foundation
NSRB National Security Resources Board
NT Northwest Territories
N.T. New Testament
numis. numismatic
NV Nevada
NV or N/V (Netherlands) company
N.W. Northwest
N. & W. Ry. Norfolk & Western Ry.
N.W.T. Northwest Territories
NY New York
N.Y. New York
N.Y.C. New York City
N.Y.C. R.R. New York Central R.R. Company
N.Y.C. & St.L. R.R. New York, Chicago & St. Louis R.R. Company
N.Y. N.H. & H. R.R. New York, New Haven & Hartford R.R. Company
N.Y.O. & W. Ry. New York Ontario & Western Ry.
NZ New Zealand

O Ohio
OAS Organization of American States
O.B. Bachelor of Oratory
Ob-Gyn. Obstetrics-gynecology
obs. observatory
obstet. obstetrical
O.D. Doctor of Optometry
OCDM Office of Civil and Defense Mobilization
ODM Office of Defense Mobilization
OECD Organization European Cooperation and Development
OEEC Organization European Economic Cooperation
OEO Office of Economic Opportunity
ofcl. official
OH Ohio
OK Oklahoma
Okla. Oklahoma
ON Ontario
Ont. Ontario
OPA Office of Price Administration
ophthal. Ophthalmological
ops. operations
OPM Office of Production Management
OPS Office of Price Stabilization
O.Q.M.G. Office of Quartermaster General
OR Oregon
O.R.C. Officers Reserve Corps
orch. orchestra
Ore. Oregon
orgn. organization
ornithol. ornithological
O.S.L. R.R. Oregon Short Line R.R.
OSRD Office of Scientific Research and Development
OSS Office of Strategic Services
osteo. osteopathic
O.T. Old Testament
O.T.C. Officers Training Camp
otol. Otological
otolaryn. otolaryngological
O.T.S. Officers Training School
O.U.A.M. Order United American Mechanics
OWI Office of War Information
O.-W. R.R. & N. Co. Oregon-Washington R.R. & Navigation Company

PA. Pennsylvania
Pa. Pennsylvania
paleontol. paleontological
Pa. R.R. Pennsylvania R.R.
path. pathological
P.C. Professional Corporation
Pd.B. Bachelor of Pedagogy
Pd.D. Doctor of Pedagogy
Pd.M. Master of Pedagogy
PE Prince Edward Island
P.E. Protestant Episcopal
Pe.B. Bachelor of Pediatrics
P.E.I. Prince Edward Island
P.E.N. Poets, Playwrights, Editors, Essayists and Novelists (Internat. Assn)
P.E.O. women's organization
penol. penological
pfc. private first class
PHA Public Housing Administration
pharm. pharmaceutical
Pharm.D. Doctor of Pharmacy
Pharm.M. Master of Pharmacy
Ph.B. Bachelor of Philosophy
Ph.C. Pharmaceutical Chemist
Ph.D. Doctor of Philosophy
Ph.G. Graduate in Pharmacy
Phila. Philadelphia
Philharm. Philharmonic
philol. philological
philos. philosophical
photog. photographic
phys. physical
Phys. and Surg. Physicians and Surgeons (College at Columbia U.)
physiol. physiological
P.I. Philippine Islands
Pitts. Pittsburgh
Pkwy. Parkway
Pl. Place
P. & L.E. R.R. Pittsburgh & Lake Erie R.R.
P.M. R.R. Pere Marquette R.R. Co.
P.O. Post Office
P.O. Box Post Office Box
polit. political
poly. polytechnic; polytechnical
pomol. pomological
PQ Quebec (province)
PR Puerto Rico
P.R. Puerto Rico
prep. preparatory
pres. president
Presbyn. Presbyterian
presdl. presidential
prin. principal
proc. proceedings
prod. produced (play production)
prodn. production
prof. professor
profl. professional
prog. progressive
propr. proprietor
pros. atty. prosecuting attorney
pro tem. pro tempore (for the time being)
psychiat. psychiatric
psychol. psychological
P.T.A. Parent-Teacher Association
PTO Pacific Theater of Operations
pub. public; publisher; publishing; published
publ. publication
pvt. private
PWA Public Works Administration

q.m. quartermaster
Q.M.C. Quartermaster Corps
Q.M.O.R.C. Quartermaster Officers' Reserve Corps
quar. quarterly
Que. Quebec (province)

radiol. Radiological
RAF Royal Air Force
R.C. Roman Catholic
RCA Radio Corporation of America
RCAF Royal Canadian Air Force
Rd. Road
R.D. Rural Delivery
R.E. Reformed Episcopal
REA Rural Electrification Administration
rec. recording
ref. reformed
regt. regiment
regtl. regimental
rehab. rehabilitation
Rep. Republican
rep. representative
Res. Reserve
ret. retired
rev. review, revised
RFC Reconstruction Finance Corporation
R.F.D. Rural Free Delivery
rhinol. rhinological
RI Rhode Island
R.I. Rhode Island
R.N. Registered Nurse
roentgenol. roentgenological
R.O.S.C. Reserve Officers' Sanitary Corps.
R.O.T.C. Reserve Officers' Training Corps
R.P. Reformed Presbyterian
R.R. Railroad
R.T.C. Reserve Training Corps
Ry. Railway

s. son
S South
S.A. (Spanish) Sociedad Anonima: (French) societe Anonyme
SAC Strategic Air Command
SALT Strategic Arms Limitation Talks
S.A.L. Ry. Seaboard Air Line Ry.
S.Am. South America
san. sanitary
S.A.R. Sons of the Am. Revolution
Sask. Saskatchewan
S.A.T.C. Student's Army Training Corps
Sat. Eve. Post. Saturday Evening Post
savs. savings
S.B. Bachelor of Science
SBA Small Business Administration
SC South Carolina
S.C. South Carolina
SCAP Supreme Command Allies Pacific
Sc.B. Bachelor of Science
Sc. D. Doctor of Science
S.C.D. Doctor of Commercial Science
sch. school
sci. science; scientific
SCLC Southern Christian Leadership Conference
S.C.V. Sons of Confederate Veterans
SD South Dakota
S.D. South Dakota
S.E. Southeast
SEATO Southeast Asia Treaty Organization
SEC Securities and Exchange Commission
sec. secretary
sect. section
seismol. seismological

sem. seminary
sgt. sergeant
SHAEF Supreme Headquarters, Allied Expeditionary Forces
SHAPE Supreme Headquarters Allied Powers in Europe
S.I. Staten Island
S.J. Society of Jesus (Jesuit).
SK Saskatchewan
S.J.D. Doctor Juristic Science
S.M. Master of Science
So. Southern
soc. society
sociol. sociological
SOS Service of Supply
S.P. Co. Southern Pacific Co.
spl. Southern Pacific Co.
spl. special
splty. specialty
Sq. Square
sr. senior
S.R. Sons of the Revolution
S.S. Steamship
SSS Selective Service System
St. Saint; Street
sta. station
statis. statistical
stats. statistics
S.T.B. Bachelor of Sacred Theology
Stbizn. Stabilization
S.T.D. Doctor of Sacred Theology
S.T.L. Licentiate in Sacred Theology; Lector of Sacred Theology
St.L-S.F. R.R. St. Louis-San Francisco Ry. Co.
subs. subsidiary
SUNY State University of New York
supr. supervisor
supt. superintendent
surg. surgical
S.W. Southwest

T.A.P.P.I. Technical Association Pulp and Paper Industry
Tb. Tuberculosis
tchr. teacher
tech. technical, technology
technol. technological
Tel. & Tel. Telephone and Telegraph
temp. temporary
Tenn. Tennessee
Ter. Terrace
Ter. Territory
TESL Teaching English as a Secondary Language
Tex. Texas
T.H. Territory of Hawaii
Th.D. Doctor of Theology
Th.M. Master of Theology
theol. theological
TN Tennessee
tng. training
topog. topographical
T. & P. Ry. Texas & Pacific Ry. Co.
trans. transactions; transferred
transl. transition
transp. transportation
treas. treasurer
TV Television
TVA Tennessee Valley Authority
Twp. Township
TX Texas
Ty. Territory
typog. typographical

U University
UAR United Arab Republic
U.A.W. International Union United Automobile, Aircraft, and Agricultural Implement Workers of American-AFL-CIO
U.B. United Brethren in Christ
UCLA University of California at Los Angeles
U.D.C. United Daughters of the Confederacy
U.K. United Kingdom
UN United Nations
UNESCO United Nations Educational, Scientific and Cultural Organization
UNICEF United Nations International Childrens Emergency Fund
univ. university
UNRRA United Nations Relief and Rehabiliation Administration
U.P. United Presbyterian
U.P.I. United Press International
U.P. R.R. Union Pacific R.R.
urol. urological
U.S. United States
U.S.A. United States of America
USAAF United States Army Air Force
USAC United States Air Corps
USAF United States Air Force
USAFR United States Air Force Reserve
USAR United States Army Reserve
USCG United States Coast Guard
USCGR U.S. Coast Guard Reserve
USES United States Employment Service
USIA United States Information Agency
USIS United States Information Service
USMC United States Marine Corps
USMCR U.S. Marine Corps Reserve
USMHS United States Marine Hospital Service
USN United States Navy
U.S.N.A. United States National Army
U.S.N.G. United States National Guard
USNR United States Naval Reserve
USNRF United States Naval Reserve Force
U.S.O. United Service Organizations
USOM United States Operations Mission
USPHS United States Public Health Service
U.S.S. United States Ship
USSR Union of Soviet Socialist Republics
U.S.V. United States Volunteers
UT Utah

VA Virginia
Va. Virginia
VA Veterans Administration
vet. Veteran; veterinary
V.F.W. Veterans of Foreign Wars
VI Virgin Islands
V.I. Virgin Islands
vice pres. vice president
vis. visiting
VISTA Volunteers in Service to America
VITA Volunteers in Technical Service
vocat. vocational
vol. volunteer; volume
v.p. vice president
vs. versus
VT Vermont
Vt. Vermont

W West
WA Washington
WAC Women's Army Corps
Wash. Washington (state)
WAVES Womens Reserve, U.S. Naval Reserve
W.C.T.U. Women's Christian Temperance Union
W. Ger. Federal Republic of Germany
WHO World Health Organization (of the UN)
WI Wisconsin
W.I. West Indies
Wis. Wisconsin
W. & L.E. Ry. Wheeling & Lake Erie Ry. Co.
WPA Works Progress Administration
WPB War Production Board
W.P.R.R. Co. Western Pacific R.R. Company
WSB Wage Stabilization Board
WV West Virginia
W. Va. West Virginia
WY Wyoming
Wyo. Wyoming

YK Yukon
YMCA Young Men's Christian Assn.
YMHA Young Men's Hebrew Assn.
YM and YWHA Young Men's and Young Women's Hebrew Assn.
Y. & M.V. R.R. Yazoo & Mississippi Valley R.R.
yr. year
YT Yukon Territory
Y.T. Yukon Territory
zool. zoological

Alphabetical Practices

Names are arranged alphabetically according to the surnames, and under identical surnames according to the first given name. If both surname and first given name are identical, names are arranged alphabetically according to the second given name. Where full names are identical, they are arranged in order of age—those of the elder being put first.

Surnames, beginning with De, Des, Du, etc., however capitalized or spaced, are recorded with the prefix preceding the surname and arranged alphabetically under the letter D.

Surnames beginning with Mac are arranged alphabetically under M. This likewise holds for names beginning with Mc; that is, all names beginning Mc will be found in alphabetical order after those beginning Mac.

Surnames beginning with Saint or St. all appear after names that would begin Sains, and such surnames are arranged according to the second part of the name, e.g., St. Clair would come before Saint Dennis.

Surnames beginning with prefix Van are arranged alphabetically under letter V.

Surnames containing the prefix Von or von are usually arranged alphabetically under letter V; any exceptions are noted by cross references (Von Kleinsmid, Rufus Bernhard; see Kleinsmid, Rufus Bernhard von).

Compound hyphenated surnames are arranged according to the first member of the compound.

Compound unhyphenated surnames common in Spanish are not rearranged but are treated as hyphenated names.

Since Chinese names have the family name first, they are so arranged, but without comma between family name and given name (as Lin Yutang).

Parentheses used in connection with a name indicate which part of the full name is usually deleted in common usuage. Hence Abbott, W(illiam) Lewis indicates that the usual form of the given name is W. Lewis. In alphabetizing this type name, the parentheses are not considered. However if the name is recorded Abbott, (William) Lewis, signifying that the entire name William is not commonly used, the alphabetizing would be arranged as though the name were Abbott, Lewis.

Who Was Who in America

AALTO, HUGO ALVAR HENRIK, architect; b. Kuortane, Finland, Feb. 3, 1898; s. Johan Henrik and Sally Mathilda (Hackstedt) A.; grad. architecht Tech. U. Melsinki, Finland, 1921, hon. Dr., 1949; Dr. (hon.), Princeton, 1947, Norges Tekniske Hoiskole, Trondheim, 1960. Eidgenössische Technische Hochschule, Zurich, 1963, Columbia, 1964, Technische Hochshule, Wien, 1965; m. Aino Marsic, 1925 (dec. 1949); children—Hamilkar, Johanna Alanen; m. 2d, Elissa Makiniemi, Nov. 1952. Propr. archtl. offices, Jyvaskyla, Turku, Helsinki, 1923-76; prof. architecture Mass. Inst. Tech., 1946-48; exhibited at N.Y.C., Paris, Zurich, Milan, Stockholm, Oslo, Copenhagen, Berlin, Hamburg, others. Decorated chevalier Legion of Honor (France); Prins Eugen Medalj (Sweden); Royal Gold medal of Architecture (Eng.); Kommendorskorset at Danneborgen (Denmark); medaglia d'oro della Citta de Firenze; grande officiale al merito della Repubblica Italiana; Grand Cross of Lion (Finland); recipient Jefferson medal, 1967; others. Hon. fellow A.I.A. (Gold medal 1963); hon. mem. Am. Acad. Arts and Letters, Nat. Inst. Arts and Letters, Royal Coll. Arts London, Assn. Finnish Architects, Am. Acad. Arts and Scis., Orden pour Le Merite für Wissenschaften und Künste. Home: Helsinki, Finland. Died May 11, 1976.

AARON, HAROLD ROBERT, engr., army officer; b. Kokomo, Ind., June 21, 1921; s. Walter Henry and Anna (Hogan) A.; B.S., U.S. Mil. Acad., 1943; M.A., Georgetown U., 1960, Ph.D., 1964; m. Marianne Helena Donahue, Jan. 16, 1944; children—Patricia, Jacqueline, Jeffrey, Christine, Mark. Commd. 2d lt. U.S. Army, 1943, advanced through grades to lt. gen.; co. comdr. Europe, 1944-45; service in Panama, Korea, Taiwan, Okinawa, Germany; lectr. U. Md., Korea, 1964-65, U. Va., Charlottesville, 1965-67; comdr. Spl. Forces, Pacific, 1967-69; asst. chief staff intelligence Dept. Army, 1973-77; dep. dir. Def. Intelligence Agy., 1977-79; sr. staff engr. TRW, 1979-80. Boy Scout commr., Europe, 1971-72. Decorated D.S.M. (Def. and Army), Legion of Merit with 2 oak leaf clusters, Nat. Intelligence Distinguished Service medal, Mem. Am. Polit. Sci. Assn., Internat. Inst. Strategic Studies, Assn. U.S. Army (chpt. pres. 1969-72), Gold Key Soc. Roman Catholic. Address: Annandale, Va. Died Apr. 30, 1980; buried Arlington (Va.) Nat. Cemetery.

ABBOTT, CLYDE MATTHEWS, lawyer; b. Athol, S.D., July 27, 1895; s. Amos S. and Mary E. (Matthews) A.; legal edn. Ohio State U., 1923; LL.D., Salmon P. Chase Coll., 1963; m. Marguerite V. Ballinger, Feb. 16, 1926. Tchr. pub. schs., So. Ohio, 1914-17; admitted to Ohio bar, 1923, since practiced in Cin.; mem. firm Paxton & Seasongood, 1927-76. Appeal agt. local SSS, World War II. Bd. regents Salmon P. Chase Coll., Cin., chmn., 1965-67; fellow of Pierpont Morgan Library, N.Y.C. Served with U.S. Army, 1918-19; AEF in France. Mem. Am., Ohio, Cin. bar assns., Cin. Art Museum Assn., Cin. Hist. Soc., Order of Coif, Acacia, Phi Delta Phi. Republican. Presbyn. Mason (32 deg.). Clubs: Queen City, Cincinnati Country, Travel (dir. 1952-61) (Cin.). Author: (with Robert P. Goldman) Anderson's Ohio Corporation Desk Book, rev. edits., 1956-66. Contbr. legal publs. Home: Cincinnati, Ohio. Died June 23, 1976; interred Spring Grove Meml. Mausoleum, Cin.

ABBOTT, GEORGE ALONZO, cons. chemist and toxicologist; b. Alma, Ill., July 7, 1874; s. John Baughman and Harriet, (Stuart) A.; B.S., De Pauw U., 1895, A.M. pro merito, 1896; Ph.D., Mass. Inst. Tech., 1908; LL.D., U. N.D., 1951; Sc.D. (hon.), N.D. State Coll., 1962; m. Ruth Ware, June 15, 1910; children—Marian Ware (Mrs. Russell Huxsol), Stuart Ware. Instr. chemistry Evansville (Ind.) High Sch., 1896-99, Duluth, Minn., 1899-1900, Indpls. 1900-1909; asst. prof. and chemist, expt. sta., State Coll., Fargo, N.D., 1909-10; prof. chemistry, head dept., N.D., 1910-47, prof. chemistry 1948; exchange lectr. U. Man., 1912; guest prof. Coll. City, N.Y., 1940. Spl. water cons. Nat. Resources Bd., 1937, cons., 1910; toxicologist and court witness in coroners' cases and murder trials. State del. 8th Internat. Congress Applied Chemistry, 1912. Fellow Am. Inst. Chemists, Ind. Acad. Sci.; mem. Am. Assn. Univ. Profs., Am. Chem. Soc. (mem. senate on chem. edn.; charter mem. and 1st chmn. Red River Valley sect. 1948), N.D. (charter mem.; sec. from 1910), S.D. (acad. lectr.) acads. sci. Polytechnic Soc. (charter mem. and a founder), Phi Beta Kappa (charter mem. N.D. Alpha chpt.; chpt. pres. 3 times), Sigma Xi (past pres. chpt.), Delta Kappa Epsilon. Methodist. Mason. Clubs: Kiwanis Internat. (gov. Minn.-Dakotas dist. 1940; key man and charter mem. local club; dist. trustee 1921-28; lt. gov. 1929, dist. gov. Minn.-Dak. Dist. 1930, Golden Anniv. Serv. award (Kiwanis Internat.), Fortnightly Franklin. Contbg. editor Jour. Chem. Edn. 1924-40. Author: The First Fifty Years-a History of North Dakota Academy of Science, 1958; also bulls. and articles. Chemistry bldg. named Abbott Hall, U. N.D., in his honor. Home: Grand Forks ND

ABEL, DEFOREST WILLIAMS, ins. exec.; b. Franklin, Tenn., July 19, 1890; s. Frank Asbury and Julia Ann (Mott) A.; LL.B., Cornell U., 1915; m. Grace Isabel Marshall, July 2, 1926 (dec. Sept. 1974); children—DeForest Williams, Judith Marshall. Clk. law office, Ithaca, N.Y., 1915-16; admitted to N.Y. bar, 1918; in home office and spl. agt. N.E. Gen. Accident Fire & Life Assurance Corp., Phila., 1919-20; solicitor and br. prodn. mgr. Am. Mut. Liability Ins. Co., Boston, 1920-25; with Amica Mut. Ins. Co., Providence, 1925-77, sec., asst. treas., 1933-39, dir., 1934-77, v.p., sec., 1939-40, pres., 1940-68, chmn. bd., chief exec. officer, 1968-71, hon. chmn. bd., 1971-77; sec., asst. treas., dir. Amica Credit Corp., Providence, 1936-40, pres., 1940-68, dir., 1940-77; dir. Amica Life Ins. Co., Amica Underwriters, Inc., Amica Services, Inc. Served in Q.M.C., U.S. Army, 1917-18. Republican. Conglist. Mason. Clubs: Squantum, R.I. Country. Home: Barrington, R.I. Died Apr. 1977.

ABELOW, ROBERT, lawyer; b. N.Y.C., Dec. 29, 1902; s. Joshua and Ida S. (Krieger) A.; LL.B., St. Lawrence U., 1923; m. Miriam Steinbrink, June 1, 1931; 1 son, William J. Admitted to N.Y. bar, 1924; prin. mediation officer, asst. exec. sec. Nat. War Labor Bd., Washington, 1942; exec. dir., gen. counsel N.Y. Regional War Labor Bd., 1943; partner Weil, Gotshal & Manges, N.Y.C., 1944-78. Writer, lectr. labor topics; instr. labor topics New Sch. Social Research, N.Y.C. Mem. N.Y. County Lawyers Assn., Am. Arbitration Assn. Clubs: Inwood (L.I.) Country; Harmonie (N.Y.C.). Editor-in-chief Employee Relations Law Jour. Home: New York, N.Y. Died May 2, 1978.

ABELS, HENRY, ins. exec.; b. Jasper County, Ill., Feb. 19, 1867. Hon. chmn. bd. Franklin Life Ins. Co. Home: Springfield, Ill.

ABELSON, LESTER SIDNEY, distilling co. exec.; b. Niagara Falls, N.Y., Dec. 18, 1902; s. Jacob and Celia (Kantrowitch) A.; J.D., U. Chgo., 1925; m. Hope Altman, Jan. 15, 1933; children—Stuart R., Katherine A. Admitted to Ill. bar, 1925; practice in Chgo., 1926-28; with Barton Brands, Inc., Chgo. from 1944, pres. from 1962; chmn. Barton Distilling (Can.) Ltd.; pres. Barton Internat. Corp., Ky. Distbg. Co., Inc., Barton Distillers Import Corp.; v.p. Barton Western Distilling Co.; dir. Scottish Am. Distilleries, Ltd., Ho. of Stuart Bonding Co., Ltd., Barton Distillers (Europe) S.A., Alpine Trading Co. Ltd., Peter Prime Bonding Co., Ltd., D.G. Thomas Ltd., Littlemill Distillery Co., Ltd., Bowling Bonding Co., Ltd. Clubs: Standard (Chgo.); Briarwood Country (Deerfield, Ill.). Home: Chicago, Ill. Died Nov. 5, 1980; buried Rosehill Cemetery, Chgo.

ABRAHAM, CLYDE RUSH, army officer; b. Farmington, Pa., July 17, 1883; s. Enoch Hamilton and Anna Belle (Rush) A.; B.S., U.S. Mil. Acad., 1906; grad. Inf. Sch., 1926, Command and Gen. Staff Sch., 1927, Army War Coll., 1933; m. Maude Willis, Oct. 19, 1915; 1 dau., Pauline Willis (wife of William F. Cass, U.S. Coast Guard). Commd. 2d lt. U.S. Army, 1906, and advanced through the grades to brig. gen., 1940; served on Gen. Staff, 1928-32, 1934-36, 1939; Inspector General's Dept., 1920-24, 1939-40; foreign service in Cuba, Hawaii, Panama, Puerto Rico, and with A.E.F. in France and Germany; now on duty with 5th Div., Fort Custer, Mich. Mason (32 deg.). Club: Army and Navy (Washington, D.C.). Address: Fort Hamilton, N.Y.*

ABRAHAMS, JOSEPH B., calligrapher, designer, artist; b. Grodno, Poland, July 4, 1884; s. Abraham and Anna (Popkin) A.; brought to U.S., 1890, naturalized, 1905; student Nat. Acad. Design, 1898-1905; Art Students League, 1900-05; m. Lillian Jacobs, Feb. 3, 1951. Elected mayor by 5,000 pub. sch. children in 1st sch. city of ednl. instns. of Am., 1897; newspaper reporter, art editor, spl. writer, 1900-18; editor in chief Alliance Review, 1900-1901; assistant librarian N.Y. Public Library, 1901-02; boys' club leader in social settlements N.Y.C.; sec. to the pres. Jewish Theol. Sem. Am., N.Y.C., 1902-15; sec. to the librarian Smithsonian Instn., Washington, 1902-04; specialized in art advt., hotel and theatre decoration, designed type faces for classic series, Hebrew Press, Jewish Publ. Soc., Phila., and for complete Talmund to be published in Jerusalem; Hebrew inscriptions, symbols for Temple Emanu-El, N.Y.C., stained glass windows, interiors, and decorative motifs for ecclesiastical and pub. bldgs., ex-libris, book covers, illuminations for testimonial vols.; organizer, mgr., dir.*

ABRAMS, FRANK WHITTEMORE, oil co. exec.; b. Rockville Center, L.I., N.Y., June 24, 1889; s. Zachariah and Mary Louise Abrams; C.E., Syracuse U., 1912, LL.D., 1946; E.D., (hon.), Rensselaer Poly. Inst., 1948, Northeastern U., 1950, U. Miami; D.C.S. (hon.), N.Y. U., 1950; LL.D., Lehigh U., 1952, Colgate U., 1953; H.L.D., Dickinson College, 1954; LL.D., Columbia U., Johns Hopkins University, 1955, Swathmore College., Williams also Bowdoin, 1956; married Ruth Florence Corrigan, October 15, 1915; 1 son, Frank W. Engr., Standard Oil Co. of N.J., subsidiary Standard Oil Co. (N.J.), Jersey City, 1912-20, supt., 1920-22, mgr., N.Y.C., 1922-27, dir., N.Y.C., 1927-33, pres., N.Y.C., 1933-40; dir. Standard Oil Co. (N.J.), N.Y.C., from 1940, v.p., 1944-45, chmn. bd., 1946-54, ret. Mem. task force Hoover Commn. Trustee Cooper Union Inst., Council Financial Aid to Edn., Alfred P. Sloan Found., Inc., Ford Found., Indsl. Relations Counselors, Inc.; vice chmn. bd. trustees Syracuse U. Mem. Sigma Alpha Epsilon. Presbyn. Clubs: University; Shinnecock Hills Golf. Home: Mattituck, L.I., N.Y. Died July 18, 1976.

ABRAMS, GEORGE JOSEPH, mgmt. and marketing exec.; b. Hoboken, N.J., Feb. 14, 1918; s. Leo and May (Hipp) A.; B.S. magna cum laude, N.Y. U., 1947, M.B.A., 1949; m. Mary Della Sablom, Nov. 15, 1941; 1 dau., Adele Lois. Staff writer Evening Transcript, Orange, N.J., 1934-36; asst. to advt. dir. Nat. Biscuit Co., N.Y.C., 1936-41; product advt. mgr. Whitehall Pharmacal Co., N.Y.C., 1941-46; dir. market research Eversharp, Inc., N.Y.C., 1946-47; v.p. sales and advt. Block Drug Co., Jersey City, 1947-55; v.p. in charge advt. Revlon, Inc., N.Y.C., 1955-59; pres., chief exec. officer cosmetics and toiletries div. Warner-Lambert Pharm. Co., 1959-60; v.p. corporate devel. J.B. Williams Corp., 1960-62; pres. Maradel Products, Inc., N.Y.C., 1962-65; sr. v.p. high marketing exec. William Esty Co., 1965-67; exec. v.p. Reach, McClinton & Co., 1967-69; pres. Cole Fischer Rogow, N.Y.C., 1969-71, George J. Abrams & Assos., N.Y.C., 1971-75; sr. v.p. Keyes, Martin & Co., 1975-78. Lectr. advt. mgmt. N.Y. U. Grad. Sch. Bus. Administrn., 1951-54. Trustee East Orange (N.J.) Gen. Hosp. Served as lt. (j.g.) USNR, 1942-45. Named Outstanding Young Advt. Man of Year, Assn. Advt. Men and Women N.Y., 1954, Industry's Man of Year, Bklyn. Philharmonia, 1970; recipient achievement award Advt. Club of Washington, 1958; Free Enterprise Assn. award, 1964. Mem. Advt. Club N.J. (gov. 1955), Assn. Nat. Advertisers (dir. chmn. drug and toiletry group, chmn. radio-TV com., chmn. advt. mgmt., newspaper cons.), Beta Gamma Sigma, Alpha Delta Sigma (award for advt. mgmt. 1958), Alpha Phi Sigma. Club: Pinnacle (N.Y.C.); Curzon (London). Author: How I Made a Million Dollars with Ideas, 1972; The Guilt of Michael Pagett, 1973; (motion picture) The Smartest Man in the World, 1974. Contbr. articles to trade mags., Ency. Americana. Home: West Caldwell, N.J. Died Feb. 7, 1978.

ABRAMS, HARRY NATHAN, publisher; b. London, Eng., Feb. 23, 1905; s. Morris and Millie Abrahams; student N.Y. U., N.A.D., Art Students League of N.Y.; m. Nina Bolotoff, Mar. 5, 1932; children—Michael David, Robert Elihu. Art dir., prodn. mgr. Schwab & Beatty Advt. Agy., 1928-36; art dir., prodn. mgr. Book-of-the-Month Club, Inc., 1936-47, dir., 1947-50; chmn. bd. Harry N. Abrams, Inc., art book publs., N.Y.C., 1950-77; founder, chmn. bd. Abbeville Press, Inc., art book pubs., N.Y.C., 1977-79. Home: New York, N.Y. Died Nov. 25, 1979.

ABRAMS, MAX, formerly sec.-treas., pres. Emerson Radio & Phonograph Corp. Home: New York, N.Y. Died Apr. 22, 1980.

ABRAMSON, HAROLD ALEXANDER, physician, psychiatrist, educator; b. N.Y.C., Nov. 27, 1899; s. F. Samuel and M. Rose (Richard) A.; A.B., Columbia, 1920, M.D., 1923; m. Barbara H. Smith, June 26, 1933 (div.); children—Alexandra Howland (Mrs. Atilla Orhun), Harold Alexander, Barbara Howland (Mrs. Henry A. Vanderploeg), Howland Wilson; m. 2d, Virginia Tenney, 1955. Asst. inorganic chemistry Columbia U., 1918-20; intern Mt. Sinai Hosp., N.Y.C., 1923-25; research fellow Univ. Coll., London, 1925-26; practiced medicine, from 1925—; NRC fellow Kaiser-Wihelm Inst. for Phys. Chemistry and

Electrochemistry, Berlin, 1926-27; instr. medicine Johns Hopkins 1928-29; instr. biochem. scis. Harvard, 1929-31; asso. in bacteriology and immunology Cornell U., 1934-35; asst. prof. physiology Columbia, 1935-59; former chief allergy clinic Mt. Sinai Hosp., N.Y.C.; research psychiatrist The Biol. Lab., L.I., N.Y., 1952-61; dir. psychiat. research S. Oaks Psychiat. Hosp., Amityville, N.Y.; cons. research psychiatry State Hosp., Central Islip, N.Y., after 1956; cons. Community Hosp., Glen Cove, N.Y., after 1958; former cons. Dept. Army. Vice pres. Asthmatic Children's Found.; trustee Biol. Lab., Cold Spring Harbor, N.Y., 1947-61. Served in world wars I and II; initiated 1942, and directed penicillin aerosol therapy of lungs for Tech. Div., Chem. Warfare Service, World War II; asst. chief and chief Def. Materiel; former lt. col. M.C. Res. Decorated Legion of Merit. Fellow Am. Psychiat. Assn., N.Y. Acad. Medicine, Am. Coll. Allergists (distinguished), A.A.A.S., N.Y. Acad. Sci., Am. Acad. Allergists, Am. Coll. of Chest Physicians; mem. Am. Pysiol. Soc., Am. Soc. Biol. Chemists, N.Y. County Med. Soc., Soc. for Exptl. Biology and Medicine, Alpha Omega Alpha, Epsilon Chi. Author books including: Electrokinetic Phenomena, 1934; Electrophoresis of Proteins, 1942; Dimensional Analysis for Students of Medicine, 1950; The Patient Speaks, 1956; Psychological Problems in Father-Son Relationship, 1969. Editor: Problems of Consciousness, 5 vols., 1950-54; Somatic and Psychiatric Treatment of Asthma, 1952; Neuropharmacology, 5 vols.; The Use of LSD in Psychotherapy and Alcoholism, 1967; Clinical Applications of the Ultrasonic Nebulizer, 1968; former editor-in-chief Jour. Asthma Research; former mem. editorial bd. Psychosomatic Medicine, Annals of Allergy. Contbr. tech., sci. jours. Home: Cold Spring Harbor, N.Y. Died Sept. 29, 1980; buried Meml. Cemetery, St. John's Ch., Cold Spring Harbor.

ACKERMAN, JOSEPH, ret. agrl. economist; b. Morton, Ill., July 20, 1904; s. John C. and Elizabeth (Welk) A.; B.S., U. Ill., 1929, M.S., 1930, Ph.D., 1938; social sci. research fellow in agrl. econs. Harvard, 1931-32; LL.D. (hon.), Elmhurst Coll., 1966; m. Elizabeth Jane Engstrand, Aug. 30, 1930; children—Elizabeth Ann, John Welk, Sara Jane, Allan J. Farm mgr. Citizens Nat. Bk., Decatur, Ill., 1930, 31; farm mgr., rural appraiser Decatur Farm Mgmt., Inc., 1933-34; extension work in farm mgmt. U. Ill., summer 1931, 32-33, 34-39, Farm Found., Chgo., land tenure specialist, 1939-41, asst. dir., 1941-42, asso. mng. dir., 1942-55; mng. dir., 1955-70; Ford Found. project specialist agrl. econs., New Delhi, India, 1970-73. Sec.-treas. Internat. Assn. Agr. Economists, 1952-73. Mem. at large Nat. council Boy Scouts Am.; bd. dirs. Nat. Employment Registry Agrl. Economists, 1974-75. Fellow A.A.A.S., Am. Agrl. Econ. Assn. (pres. 1954-55)); mem. Am. Country Life Assn. (pres. 1946-48), Am. Soc. Farm Mgrs. and Rural Appraisers (sec.-treas. 1939-44), Nat. Sch. Bds. Assn. (pres. 1966-67), Ill. Assn. Sch. Bds. (pres. 1958-60). Phi Eta Sigma, Alpha Zeta, Gamma Sigma Delta, Phi Delta Gamma, Farm House (nat. pres. 1948-52), Sigma Xi (asso.). Author: (with others) Town and Country Churches and Family Farming, 1956; agrl. reports, bulls. Editor: Farm and Rural Life After the War, 1944; (with others) Family Farm Policy, 1947, Agrarian Reform and Moral Responsibility, 1949. Home: Elmhurst, Ill. Died May 3, 1976.

ACKERSON, HENRY E(LIJAH), JR., lawyer; b. Holmdel, N.J., Oct. 15, 1880; s. Cornelius and Anna B. (Stilwell) A.; student Senftner Prep. Sch., N.Y. City, 1898-1900; LL.B., N.Y. Law Sch., 1900-02; m. Edith Dart Calef, Apr. 5, 1910; 1 son, Cornelius. Lectr. N.Y. Law Sch., 1902-04; admitted to N.J. State bar, Mar. 7, 1904, practiced in Keyport, under own name, to 1924; atty. Boroughs of Keyport and Keansburg, 1908-14; counsel to Bd. Chosen Freeholders Monmouth County, 1914-21; Judge Ct. of Errors and Appeals, 1919-24, Circuit Ct. Judge, 1924-47; mem. Supreme Ct. of N.J. since 1948. Pres. Peoples Nat. Bank, Keyport, 1927-41. Mem. N.J. State Senate, 1914-19. Bd. mgrs. N.J. State Home for Boys, 1924-48. Mem. Am., N.J., Monmouth County (past pres.) bar assns., Holland Soc. N.Y. (past pres.). Home: Keyport, NJ.

ACKLEY, CLARK RUSSELL, architect, clergyman; b. Lansing, Mich., Jan. 28, 1911; s. Fred D. and Edith Viola (Clark) A.; B.S. in Architecture, U. Mich., 1932; m. Gladys Alice Conklin, June 26, 1930; children—Mary Ann (Mrs. Kenneth Kirkwood Stacey), Roger Allan, Wayne Russell. Positions various archtl. firms, Lansing, 1930-36; self-employed architect, Lansing, 1936-77; ordained deacon Episcopal Ch., 1973, priest, 1977. Recipient various archtl. and pub. service awards. Mem. Am. Assn. Sch. Adminstrs., C. of C., Nat. Council Archtl. Registration Bds., A.I.A. (mem. joint com. Assn. Gen. Contractors), Am. Arbitration Bd. U. Mich. Club. Optimist. Prin. works include Mich. Nat. Guard Armory, Ingham County Jail, Muskegon Gen. Hosp. Kalamazoo County Law Enforcement Bldg., Berrien County Sheriff's Dept. and Correctional Facility. Home: Lansing, Mich. Died Dec. 30, 1977.

ACREE, JOHN THOMAS, JR., ins. co. exec.; b. St. Louis, Aug. 5, 1909; s. John and Birdie Murphy (Stewart) A.; B.A. magna cum laude, Oklahoma City U., 1930; m. Margaret Deupree, Sept. 16, 1930 (dec. Dec. 1968); children—John Thomas III, Laura Diana (Mrs. C.C. Hager), Edwin L.; m. 2d, Mary M. Turner, Jan. 24, 1970. With Lincoln Income Life Ins. Co., Louisville, 1923-79, sec.-treas., 1940-46, exec. v.p., 1946-49, pres., 1949-69, chmn. bd., 1962-79, chief exec. officer, 1969; dir. Liberty Nat. Bank & Trust Co. Pres. Old Ky. Home council Boy Scouts Am., 1957-60; chmn. region 4, 1969-72, mem. nat. exec. bd., 1969-79. Chmn. bd. trustees Lexington Theol. Sem.; trustee Am. Humanics Found., Ky. Ind. Coll. Found.; bd. dirs. Goodwill Industries Ky., Kosair Crippled Childrens Hosp. Recipient Brotherhood award Louisville and So. Ind. chpt. Nat. Conf. Christians and Jews, 1973. Mem. Ky. C. of C. (pres. 1970-71), Alpha Phi Omega (hon.). Mason (33 deg.). Home: Louisville, Ky. Died Jan. 19, 1979.

ADAMI, ARTHUR ERNEST (AD'AM-E), prof. mining engring.; b. Helena, Mont., May 2, 1886; s. Henry and Elizabeth (Maas) A.; grad. high sch., Helena, 1903; E.M., Mont. State Sch. Mines, 1907; m. Alma C. Erickson, Aug. 9, 1911; children—Jane Marie Cunningham, Arthur Ernest. Chemist, Red Metal Mining Co., 1907; chemist and assayer, Anaconda Copper Mining Co., 1908; instr. in mathematics and metallurgy, Mont. State Sch. Mines, 1908-09, instr. in surveying and metallurgy, 1909-11, asst. prof. mining engring., 1911-19, asso. prof., 1919-26, prof. 1926-56, v.p., 1928-56, acting pres., 1950-51; dean 1943-56, v.p. emeritus 1956. Mem. Am. Inst. Mining and Metall. Engrs., Mont. Soc. Engrs., American Society Engring Education, Mont. Mining Association. Republican. Episcopalian. Writer of bulletin Montana State Bur. Mines, on Location, Representation and Patenting of Mineral Lands in Montana, 1923. Home: Butte, Mont. *

ADAMS, ALONZO P., banker; b. Albany, N.Y., Feb. 28, 1882; s. Alonzo P. and Mary Elizabeth (Killip) A.; grad. Albany High Sch., 1900; m. Catherine Lois Snyder, Jan. 15, 1914; children—Alonzo P. 3d, James R., Helen Cobden. With Albany Trust Co., 1900-23; v.p. N.Y. State Nat. Bank, Albany, 1923-26; v.p. First Trust Co., Albany, 1926-34, pres. since 1934; dir. Albany Packing Co. Republican. Methodist. Mason. Club: Albany Country. Home: Slingerlands, N.Y.

ADAMS, ANNE HUTCHINSON, educator; b. Hamilton, Miss., Aug. 25, 1935; d. James Perry and Lois (Wright) Hutchinson; student Miss. State U., 1953-54; B.S., Miss. State Coll. Women, 1956; M.Ed., Duke U., 1957; Ed.D., U. Miss., 1966; postgrad. U. Ga., 1966-67; m. Charles Floyd Adams, June 27, 1959 (div.); 1 son, Charles Floyd. Elementary tchr., Atlanta, 1957-59, Tampa, Fla., 1959-60, Hattiesburg, Miss., 1960-61, Oxford, Miss., 1961-64; dir. elementary edn., Columbus, Ga., 1965-67; dir. edn. LeFlore County Sch. Dist., Greenwood, Miss., 1967-69; asso. dir. staff tng. Exemplary Early Edn. Centers, U. Tex.; mem. faculty U. Miss., 1964, U. Ga., 1966; asst. prof. spl. edn. U. Tex., Austin; asso. prof. Duke U., Durham, N.C., 1971-73, prof., 1973-80, dir. Duke Reading Clinic, 1972-80; former mem. nat. adv. bd. J. B. Lippincott Co., Internat. Textbook Co., Inc., Miss. Authority for Ednl. 1973-80, reading cons.; dir. Diagnostic and Remedial Reading Center, Columbus, 1967-80. Named Outstanding Young Woman Am., Miss. State Coll. Women, 1967; N.C. Tar Heel of Week, Raleigh News and Observer; recipient Outstanding Prof. award Duke U., 1971-72. Mem. N.C. Assn. Univ. Profs. of Reading (past pres.), Internat. Platform Assn., Phi Delta Epsilon, Alpha Delta Kappa, Pi Gamma Mu, Delta Kappa Gamma, Chi Omega. Author: The Clock Struck One; The Reading Clinic; Success in Beginning Reading and Writing; Mainstreaming Science and Mathematics; Mainstreaming Language Arts and Social Studies, Benefic Subtraction Kit; Benefic Multiplication Kit; Benefic Division Kit; Reading in Today's Society; Study Guide to Reading the Newspaper; co-author: Random House Reading Program; Benefic Addition Kit; scripts for ednl. films; sr. author Learning Abilities for Children with Handicaps; Sounds for Me; Plan Readiness Experiences Program; cons. Webster's New World Dictionary; contbr. numerous articles to profl. jours. Home: Durham, N.C. Died Nov. 14, 1980.

ADAMS, ARTHUR MERRIHEW, clergyman, sem. dean; b. Phila., Sept. 28, 1908; s. Alexander Mackie and Laura (Dickey) A.; A.B., U. Pa., 1931; Th.B., Princeton Theol. Sem., 1934; D.D., Beaver Coll., 1951; m. Margaret Baker, Oct. 23, 1934; children—Robert Merrihew, Janet Dickinson (Mrs. Henry Dana Fearon III). Ordained to ministry Presbyn. Ch., 1934; pastor Glading Meml. Presbyn. Ch., Phila., 1934-44, pastor First Presbyn. Ch., Albany, N.Y., 1945-50; Central Presbyn. Ch., Rochester, N.Y., 1950-62; prof. practical theology Princeton (N.J.) Theol. Sem., 1962-79, dean sem., 1967-79, trustee, 1955-62. Bd. dirs. Presbyn. Ministers Fund, 1952-79, chmn. bd. dirs., 1978-79; mem. United Presbyn. Council on Theol. Edn., 1957-62, 65-79; vis. prof. Pacific Sch. Religion, summer 1966. Sec. Albany chpt. A.R.C., 1947-50, bd. dirs. Rochester chpt., 1959-62; mem. County Commn. Human Relations, Monroe County, N.Y., 1959-62; trustee Princeton United Fund; bd. dirs. Vocation Agy. of United Presbyn. Ch., 1967-72. Mem. Soc. for Continuing Edn. of Ministers, Ch. Adminstrn. Soc. (founder). Club: Nassau. Author: Pastoral Administration, 1964; Effective Leadership in Today's Church, 1978. Editor: Administration In The Church, 1970. Home: Princeton, N.J. Died Sept. 9, 1979.

ADAMS, ARTHUR STANTON, educator; b. Winchester, Mass., July 1, 1896; s. Charles Stanton Grace Estelle (Newhall) A.; grad. U.S. Naval Acad., 1918; A.M., U. Calif., 1926; Sc.D., Colo. Sch. Mines (fellow in metallurgy). 1927; hon. degrees include: D.H.L., Akron U., 1959; Sc.D., U. Pa., 1961; LL.D., Denison U., 1958, Middlebury Coll., 1960, Clark U., 1961, Occidental Coll., 1962, U. Colo., 1962, U. Calif., Riverside, 1964, Evansville Coll., 1964, U. Ark., 1965, Fla. State U., 1965; m. Dorothy Anderson, Nov. 21, 1918 (dec.); 1 son, d John Stanton (dec.); m. 2d, Irene H. Smith, Apr. 14, 1956 (dec.). Tchr. Denver high schs., 1922-23; asst. prin. The Pitts Sch., Denver, 1923-25; instr. in metallurgy Colo. Sch. of Mines, 1927-28, asst. prof., 1928-30, asso. prof. mechanics, 1930-32, prof. mechanics, 1932-40, asst. to pres., 1938-40, asst. to dean engring. Cornell U., 1940-42, dir. Engring. Sci. Mgmt. War Tng. Program, 1940-42, provost, 1946-48; pres. U. N.H., 1948-51; pres. Am. Council on Edn., 1951-61; pres. Salzburg Seminar in Am. Studies, 1961-65; cons. to pres. U. N.H., 1965-68; cons. to New Eng. Center for Continuing Edn., 1968-76. Chmn. acad. adv. com. USCG Acad., 1962-67. Alderman, City of Golden, Colo., 1937-39; pres. bd. of control State Indsl. Sch. for Boys, Golden, 1937-38; chmn. Res. Forces Policy Bd., 1953-55. Trustee Brookings Instn. Served with USN, 1913-21, lt., capt., 1941-45. Decorated Legion of Merit, 1945; recipient Distinguished Service award Monticello Coll., 1960; Disting. Citizen award Daniel Webster council Boy Scouts Am., 1979. Fellow AAAS; mem. Am. Soc. Engring. Edn., Colo.-Wyo. Acad. Sci., Tau Beta Pi, Sigma Xi, Phi Kappa Phi, Sigma Nu, Kappa Delta Pi (laureate). Democrat. Episcopalian. Club: Cosmos (Washington). Author: The Development of Physical Thought (with Leonard B. Loeb), 1933; Fundamentals of Thermodynamics (with George D. Hilding), 1945. Home: Durham, N.H. Died Nov. 18, 1980; buried Arlington Nat. Cemetery.

ADAMS, ELIJAH, educator, biochemist; b. Buffalo, Jan. 14, 1918; s. Joseph and Matilda (Berkman) A.; B.A., Johns Hopkins, 1938; M.D., U. Rochester, 1942; m. Blanche Macoff, June 27, 1943; children—Margaret, Janet, Joseph, James. Intern, Strong Meml. Hosp., Rochester, N.Y., 1942-43; asst. pathology Yale U. Sch. Medicine, 1946-47, USPHS fellow in biochemistry, 1947-48; asst. resident medicine New Haven Hosp., 1948-49; Am. Cancer Soc. fellow physiol. chemistry UCLA, 1949-50; vis. investigator Lab. Hereditary and Metabolic Disorders, U. Utah, 1950-52; surgeon USPHS, biochem. research NIH, Bethesda, Md., 1952-55; asso. prof. pharmacology N.Y.U. Sch. Medicine, 1955-58; prof., dir. dept. pharmacology St. Louis U. Sch. Medicine, 1958-63; prof., chmn. dept. biochemistry U. Md. Sch. Medicine, Balt., 1963-79. Served to capt., M.C., AUS, 1943-46. Mem. Am. Chem. Soc., Am. Soc. Biol. Chemists, Phi Beta Kappa, Sigma Xi, Alpha Omega Alpha. Home: Baltimore, Md. Died Oct. 2, 1979.

ADAMS, ELMER CLEVELAND, newspaper man; b. Scotland, Ill., Dec. 20, 1885; s. Charles Best and Caroline (Osborne) A.; A.B., U. of Mich., 1908 (Phi Beta Kappa); m. Edith A. Taylor, 1912 (died, 1925); 1 son, Charles Elmer. Began writing for newspapers, in Boston, 1909; asso. editor Youth's Companion, 1911-12; Mass. state organizer for Prog. party, 1912-14; writer of text for Y.M.C.A. Ednl. Secs'. Assn. of N. America, 1914; journalism in Boston, 1915; preparing cost statements for M.C.R.R. and Interstate Commerce Commn., 1916-17; editor "Wolverines" humor column, Detroit News, 1918-27. "Random Shots" column and poetry editor since 1927. Mem. Phi Beta Kappa. Club: Intercollegiate. Author: Heroines of Modern Progress (with Warren D. Foster), 1912; Y.M.C.A. Nat. Salesmanship Course, 1915; (mag. serial) Inland Treasure, 1924; Walking in the Clouds, 1939. Contbr. to boys' and humor mags. Home: Detroit. Retired 1951.

ADAMS, FREDERICK JOHNSTONE, city planner; b. London, Eng., Dec. 8, 1901; s. Thomas and Caroline Bertha (Whirter) A.; student Royal Naval Coll. of Canada, 1917-20, McGill Univ., 1920-21, Architectural Assn. Sch., London, 1921-25; B.Arch., Columbia Univ., 1928; m. Mabel Keith Folger, Aug. 24, 1929; children—Benjamin Folger, Thomas Frederick. Came to U.S., 1925, naturalized, 1933. In archtl. and planning offices, New York, N.Y., 1928-32; head dept. of planning Mass. Inst. Tech., 1932-57, asst. prof. city planning, 1932-38, asso. prof., 1938-44, professor since 1944; Arnold W. Brunner scholarship, 1951; member firm Adams, Howard & Oppermann (formerly Adams, Howard and Greeley), city planning consultants, Cambridge, Mass. Chairman of city planning bd., Cambridge, Mass., 1943-50. U.S. del. to Conf. on Planning, Housing Com. of League of Nations, Geneva, Switzerland, 1939, to Internat. Congress on Housing and Town Planning, Hastings, Eng., 1946, to UN

Regional Conference on Housing and Community Improvement, New Delhi, India, 1954. Honorary member Peruvian Inst. of Urbanism; mem. Catholic Com. Intellectual and Cultural Affairs Am. Inst. Planners (mem. bd. govs. 1937-40; sec.-treas., 1944, 45; v.p. 1946-48, pres., 1948-49, 1949-50; editor of the Planners Journal, 1937-41; Distinguished Service Award, 1955), American Society Planning Officials (bd. dirs. 1947-50). Author: Urban Planning Education in the United States, 1954. Home: Cambridge, Mass. Died Mar. 1979.

ADAMS, JAMES CARLTON, real estate cons.; b. Spring Valley, Wis., Sept. 13, 1921; s. Elmer James and Gertrude (Anderson) A.; student Whitewater (Wis.) State Tchrs. Coll., 1939-41; B.A., U. Wis., 1946; m. Magil Evon Olson, Dec. 21, 1946; children—Kay, Jane, David. With Nat. Guardian Life Ins. Co., Madison, Wis., 1948-54, Continental Assurance Co., Chgo., 1954-66; 2d v.p., asst. treas. Washington Nat. Ins. Co., Evanston, Ill., 1967-70, treas., 1970-72, v.p., 1972-75; pres., dir. WNC Devel. Co., 1972-75; pres. James C. Adams and Co., Glenview, Ill., 1975-78. Served with AUS, 1943-45. Fellow Life Office Mgmt. Assn.; mem. Am. Inst. Real Estate Appraisers, Am. Real Estate and Urban Econs. Assn., Inst. Real Estate Mgmt. (certified property mgr.). Republican. Methodist. Mason (K.T., Shriner). Home: Glenview, Ill. Died Dec. 12, 1978.

ADAMS, JAMES DOUGLASS, lawyer; b. Lawrence, Kan., Apr. 6, 1894; s. Ephraim Douglass and May Stevens (Breakey) A.; A.B., Stanford, 1915, J.D., 1920; m. Katharine Mordock, June 28, 1924; children—Douglass Mordock, Katharine, Robert Ober, Helen Bayley, Rebecca. Admitted to Cal. bar, 1920; lawyer, clk. McCutchen, Olney & Willard, San Francisco, 1920-27, partner McCutchen, Olney, Mannon & Greene, 1927-42, McCutchen, Doyle, Brown & Enersen, 1946—. Adv. bd., past pres. Marin council Boy Scouts Am.; pres. Marin Community Chest, 1947-48; dir. Legal Aid Soc. of San Francisco. Served as res. mil. aviator, 91st Aero Squadron, 1917-19; lt. comdr. to comdr. USNR, 1943-46. Mem. Am. Law Inst., Am., San Francisco bar assns., Cal. State Bar, Atlantic Union Com., Phi Beta Kappa, Order of Coif. Republican. Episcopalian (sr. warden). Home: San Rafael, Cal.

ADAMS, JAMES S., investment banker; b. Brazil, Ind., Aug. 22, 1897; s. Orley Edwin and Mary (Nees) Adams; M.L., Ind. U., also LL.D., 1959; m. Marvelle Warne, Mar. 12, 1927 (dec.); 1 son, Peter Warne; m. 2d, Elizabeth Graham, Nov. 12, 1965. With George L. Dyer Co., N.Y.C. and Chgo., 1925-28; v.p., asst. to pres. of Johns Manville Corp., N.Y.C., 1928-34; v.p., gen. mgr. Benton & Bowles, Inc., 1934-40; exec. v.p. Colgate, Palmolive Peet Co., Jersey City, 1940-41; pres. Standard Brands Inc., N.Y.C., 1942-48; gen. partner Lazard Freres & Co., 1948-76; dir. Carter Wallace, Inc. Dir. Am. Cancer Soc., dir., pres. Research to Prevent Blindness Inc. U. Found. Div. chief, spl. cons. to chmn. WPB, World War II. Served as lt., pilot, A.C., U.S. Army, World War I. Decorated Medal for Merit World War II; Imperial Medal of Iran. Mem. Phi Kappa Psi, Tau Kappa Alpha. Republican. Clubs: Metropolitan, Links (N.Y.C.); Beach (Palm Beach, Fla.). Home: New York, N.Y. Died Oct. 1976.

ADAMS, JAMES TROY, former mining co. exec.; b. El Dorado, Ark., Jan. 2, 1921; s. Garrett Lester and Eunice (Reynolds) A.; B.S., La. State U., 1943; m. Lou Ella Williams, Oct. 24, 1943; children—James Troy, George Howard, Eunice Anne. Cost accountant Aluminum Ore Co., Bauxite, Ark., 1943-44; with Freeport Minerals Co., 1946-78, analysis and planning mgr., 1961-67, adminstrv. mgr., 1967-69, controller, N.Y.C., 1969-78, v.p., 1974-78. Bd. dirs. St. James Parish (La.) Community Action, 1968. Served to 1st lt. AUS, 1944-46. C.P.A., La. Mem. La. Soc. C.P.A.'s, Beta Alpha Psi, Beta Gamma Sigma, Phi Kappa Phi. Home: Wilton, Conn. Died June 14, 1980; buried Hillside Cemetery, Wilton, Conn.

ADAMS, JOHN MILTON, physician, educator; b. Mpls., June 7, 1905; s. Paul and Olive (Marshall) A.; B.S. cum laude, Princeton, 1929; M.D., Columbia, 1933; Ph.D., U. Minn., 1943; m. Carolyn Frances Gaston, Mar. 24, 1934; children—John Milton, Herbert G., William M. Intern pediatrics New Haven Hosp., 1933-34; intern surgery U. Minn., 1934-35, asst. prof. pediatrics, 1941-46, asso. prof., 1946-49; practice pediatrics Nicollet Clinic, Mpls., 1937-43; prof. pediatrics, U. Calif. Sch. Medicine, Los Angeles, 1950-80, chmn., 1950-64. Diplomate Am. Bd. Pediatrics (dir. 1960-66), Nat. Bd. Med. Examiners. Mem. Pediatric Research Soc. (v.p.), Am. Pediatric Soc., Am. Soc. Clin. Investigation, Am. Acad. Pediatrics, Am. Phys. Art Assn., Soc. for History of Medicine, Western Soc. Pediatric Research (pres. 1959-80), Sigma Xi, Nu Sigma Nu, Alpha Omega Alpha. Author: Newer Virus Diseases, 1960; Viruses and Colds, 1967; Multiple Sclerosis, 1977. Contbr. to Brennemann's Practice of Pediatrics (4 volumes) sci. articles nat. jours. Home: Santa Monica, Calif. Died June 30, 1980.

ADAMS, LEWIS GREENLEAF, architect; b. Lenox, Mass., Nov. 23, 1897; s. William and Alice C. (Greenleaf) A.; B.A., Yale, 1920; diplôme Ecole des Beaux Arts, Paris, 1926; m. Emeline W. Kellogg, July 23, 1921; children—Richard G., Lois K. (Mrs. Sanford Goldstone). Asso., Delano & Aldrich, architects, N.Y.C., 1920-22, 27-29; partner Adams & Prentice, architects, 1929-41, Adams & Woodbridge, 1945-73; works include All Saints Chapel, Princeton, N.J., Adirondack Mus., Blue Mountain Lake, N.Y. freshman dorm and infirmary Hamilton Coll., Clinton, N.Y., Episcopal Ch. Center, N.Y.C. Served as ensign USNR, 1918-20, as comdr. USNR, 1942-45. Mem. A.I.A., Nat. Sculpture Soc. (hon.), Groupe Americain des Architects diplomes par le Gouvernement, Century Assn., Archtl. League N.Y. (pres. 1954-55). Home: New York, N.Y. Died Nov. 29, 1977.

ADAMS, ORVAL WEBSTER, banker; b. Idaho Falls, Ida., Apr. 10, 1884; s. Orval F. and Marion (Nelson) A.; ed. Utah State Agrl. Coll., 1900-03; m. Luella Nebeker, June 1911; children—Allan Nebeker, Lane Webster, Hyrum Adams, Theodore Nebeker, Preston Geddes, Orval Webster. With 1st Nat. Bank, Logan, Utah, 1903-10; cashier Hyrum (Utah) State Bank, 1910-12; in Liverpool, Eng., 1912-14; cashier Farmers & Merchants Bank, Logan, 1914-16, Thatcher Bros. Banking Co., Logan, 1916-20; v.p. 1st Nat. Bank and Ogden Savings Bank, Ogden, Utah, 1920-21; chmn. bd., mem. exec. com. Zions First Nat. Bank; dir., mem. exec. com. Zion's Coop. Merc. Inst.; dir. Utah-Ida. Sugar Co.; mem. exec. com. Beneficial Life Ins. Co., Hotel Utah; dir. Utah Fuel Co.; dir., mem. finance com. D.&R.G.W. R.R.; dir. Mt. Fuel Supply Co. Mem. Am. Bankers Assn. (pres. 1937-38), Sigma Chi. Republican. Mem. Ch. of Jesus Christ of Latter-day Saints (auditing com.). Clubs: Alta, Salt Lake Country. Home: Salt Lake City.

ADAMS, ROLLAND LEROY, publisher; b. Huntingdon, Pa., Dec. 27, 1904; s. Lemuel B. and Carrie (Snyder) A.; student Dickinson Coll. and Law Sch., 1922-25; LL.D., Dickinson Coll. 1966; m. Pauline S. Homback, June 26, 1930; children—Nancy A. (Mrs. Donald Taylor), Marcia S. (Mrs. George L. Roehr), Mary H. (Mrs. John F. Sitzer, Jr.). Teller, 1st Nat. Bank, Newport, Pa., 1925; bank examiner, Pa., 1925-29; asst. to pres. E.P. Wilbur Trust Co., Bethlehem, Pa., 1929-30; with Bethlehem Globe Pub. Co., 1930-33, gen. mgr., 1933-52, pub., pres., 1952-67, chmn. bd., 1967-79; chmn. bd. City News Co. Bethlehem, Inc.; pres. Times Pub. Co., Quaker State Coca-Cola Bottling Co. (all Bethlehem), A.B.E. Broadcasting Co. Chmn. Bethlehem Community Chest Campaign, 1949, St. Luke's Hosp. (Bethlehem) Expansion Campaign, 1952; organizer, chmn. Northampton County Civil Def. Council, 1941-42; mem. Gov's Hosp. Study Commn., 1958-79. Trustee St. Luke's Hosp., Dickinson Coll. Carlisle, Pa. Recipient Alumni award Lehigh U., 1956; named Man of Year, Sertoma Club Bethlehem, 1965. Mem. Am., Pa. (pres. 1956; ex-officio mem. exec. com.) newspaper pubs. assns., Bethlehem C. of C., Sigma Delta Chi (hon. mem.), Sigma Alpha Epsilon. Methodist Episcopalian. Clubs: Nat. Press. (Washington); Pen and Pencil (Phila.); Saucon Valley Country, Bethlehem (Bethlehem). Founder Billy Ney scholarship for Newport (Pa.) Union High Sch. Home: Bethlehem, Pa. Died Sept. 1, 1979.

ADAMS, T(HOMAS) GORDON, mdsg. exec.; b. Butte, Mont., Feb. 26, 1906; s. Paul and Sarah (Champion) A.; ed. pub. schs., Butte; m. Myrtle Webb, June 18, 1929; children—Janet (Mrs. John David Oatman), Carol (Mrs. Frank A. Svoboda, Jr.). With F. W. Woolworth Co., from 1923, various positions, Mont., successively store mgr., Pittsburg, Kan., Fargo, N.D., Omaha and Lincoln, Neb., dist. supt., mdse. man and sales mgr., Denver, asst. regional mgr., Mpls., regional mgr., 1923-58, asst. treas., from 1955, regional mgr., Chgo., 1958-63, regional v.p. North Central div., from 1963. Mem. bd. State Street Council. Trustee Garrett Theol. Sch. Methodist (trustee, lay leader). Mason (Shriner). Clubs: Kiwanis (v.p. 1961-62), Executives (Chgo.). Home: Mt. Prospect, Ill. Died Sept. 18, 1979.

ADAMS, THEODORE FLOYD, clergyman; b. Palmyra, N.Y., Sept. 26, 1898; s. Floyd Holden and Evelyn (Parkes) A.; B.A., Denison U., 1921; B.D., Colgate Rochester Div. Sch., 1924; D.D. (hon.), U. Richmond, 1938, Coll. William and Mary, 1940, Denison U., 1940, Washington and Lee U., Baylor U., 1958, Stetson U., 1959, McMaster U., 1962, Wake Forest U., 1968; L.H.D., Hampden-Sydney Coll., 1959; LL.D., Keuka Coll., 1964; m. Esther Josephine Jillson, Feb. 26, 1925; children—Betsy Ann (Mrs. Frank K. Thompson), Theodore F., John Jillson. Ordained to ministry of Baptist Ch., 1924; pastor, Cleve., 1924-27, Toledo, Ohio, 1927-36; pastor First Baptist Ch., Richmond, Va., 1936-68, pastor emeritus, 1968-80; vis. prof. Southeastern Sem., Wake Forest, N.C., 1968-78; v.p. Baptist Young Peoples Union Am., 1925-26; mem. bd. promotion Ohio Baptist Conv., 1928-35; pres. Ohio Baptist Young Peoples Union, 1925-27. Vice pres. Bapt. World Alliance, 1947-50, mem. exec. com., 1934-80, pres., 1955-60, mem. gen. com., 1960-80; mem. fgn. mission bd. So. Bapt. Conv., 1940-50, 61-67, mem. joint com. pub. affairs. Bd. dirs. Va. Inst. Pastoral Care; bd. dirs., v.p. CARE, 1960-70; bd. dirs. Rockefeller Bros. Theol. Fellowship Program, 1961-70; trustee Council on Religion and Internat. Affairs, 1951-71, 73-80; chmn. bd. Richmond Memorial Hosp.; trustee So. Bapt. Hosp., 1950-53, U. Richmond; trustee, hon. chmn. bd. Va. Union U.; trustee Va. Baptist Children's Home, 1936-57, pres. bd. trustees, 1936-53. Recipient Upper Room citation for leadership, 1960; Nat. Brotherhood citation NCCJ, 1964. Mem. Phi Beta Kappa, Beta Theta Pi, Phi Mu Alpha, Omicron Delta Kappa. Clubs: Rotary (Richmond). Author: Making Your Marriage Succeed, 1953; Making the Most of What Life Brings, 1957; Tell Me How, 1964; Baptists Around The World, 1967. Contbr. articles to religious jours. Home: Richmond, Va. Died Feb. 27, 1980.

ADAMS, THOMAS HAMMOND, lawyer; b. Ann Arbor, Mich., Sept. 1, 1901; s. Henry C. and Bertha (Wright) A.; A.B., U. Mich., 1922; LL.B., Harvard, 1925; m. Hortense O. Miller, Sept. 24, 1927; children—Thomas Hammond, Clarissa Barlow (Mrs. Thomas C. Goad). Reporter, N.Y. Evening Post, 1921-22; admitted to Mich. bar, 1927, practiced in Detroit; of counsel to firm Hill, Lewis, Adams, Goodrich & Tait, 1933-80; lectr. Wayne U. Law Sch., 1937-47. Mem. Mich. Bd. Law Examiners, 1948-60; chmn. Nat. Conf. Bar Examiners, 1952-53, mem. council sect. legal edn. and admission to bar, 1962-73, chmn., 1972-73. Mem. Am., Mich., Detroit bar assns., Am. Law Inst., Am. Judicature Soc., Alpha Delta Phi, Delta Theta Phi, Sigma Delta Chi. Clubs: Detroit; Orchard Lake Country; Village Players Birmingham. Home: Birmingham, Mich. Died Jan. 2, 1980; buried Ann Arbor.

ADAMS, WALTER HOLBROOK, mechanical engineer; b. Worcester, Mass., Apr. 17, 1882; s. Joseph C. and Etta M. (Holbrook) A.; S.B., Mass. Inst. Tech., 1903; m. Annie Marguerite Horne, of Malden, Mass., Aug. 9, 1905. Asst. in mech. engring., Mass. Inst. Tech., 1903-5; instr. in mech. engring., Poly. Inst., Brooklyn, 1905-8; prof. mech. engring., Imperial Pei Yang U., Tientsin, China, 1908-12; prof. mech. engring., Throop Coll. of Tech., Jan., 1913-May, 1918. Mem. 1st Regt. Heavy Arty., Mass. V.M., 2 yrs. Mem. Am. Soc. Mech. Engrs., Soc. Promotion Engring. Edn. Commd. capt. Engr. Officers' Reserve Corps, Mar. 1, 1917, active duty, May, 1918—. Address: Pasadena, California. *

ADAMSON, JOY, conservationist, author, painter, illustrator; b. Troppau, Silesia, Jan. 20, 1910; d. Victor and Traute Gessner; ed. Staats Prüfung, Vienna, Austria, 1972; diploma dressmaking, 1928; student art, 1929-32, medicine, 1933-35; m. Victor von Klarwill, 1935; m. 2d, Peter Bally, 1938; m. 3d, George Adamson, 1943. Painter and illustrator 1938-80; works exhibited Nat. Museum, Nairobi, Kenya, Tryon Gallery, Nairobi, 1972, Tyron Gallery, London, Indian Tea Center, London, Natural History Mus., Los Angeles; researcher wild animals, 1956-80; author, 1958-80. Head Elsa Wild Animal appeal, U.K., 1961, U.S., 1969, Can., 1971. Recipient Gold Grenfall medal Royal Hort. Soc., 1947; award merit (Czechoslovakia); Joseph Wood Krutsch medal Humane Soc. U.S., 1971; Austrian Cross of Honour for Art and Sci., 1977. Clubs: Nanyuki, Nairobi (Kenya). Author: Born Free: a lioness of two worlds, 1960 (film 1966); Elsa, The True Story of a Lioness, 1961; Living Free, 1961, 64 (film 1971); Forever Free, 1962, 66 (film 1971); Elsa and her Cubs, 1965; The Story of Elsa, 1966; (also illustrator) The Peoples of Kenya, 1967; The Spotted Sphinx, 1969 (film 1970); Pippa the Cheetah and Her Cubs, 1970 (film 1970); Pippa's Challenge, 1972; Joy Adamson's Africa, 1972. Contbr. articles to Jour. Royal Geog. Soc., Country Life, Geog. Jour., also popular mags. Home: Naivasha, Kenya. Died Jan. 4, 1980.

ADDINSELL, HARRY MESSITER, (AD'IN-SEL), investment banker, ret.; b. Brooklyn., Apr. 14, 1886; s. Frederick and Florence (Messiter) A.; student pub. schs., Brooklyn, until 1903; m. Florence Moberly, Jan. 5, 1921 (dec. 1961); m. 2d, Ruth Gibb, Aug. 7, 1962. With New York Times, 1903, with Harris Forbes Co. (later Chase Harris Forbes Corp.), 1905-33, pres., 1931-33; chmn. exec. com. and dir. First Boston Corp. June 1934-Dec. 1947, Chairman bd., 1948-51, ret. 1951; dir. 1st Boston Corp. Served as capt., F.A., World War I. Mem. executive bd. Boy Scouts of America; mem. adv. com. Community Hosp. Trustee, treas. Cathedral St. John the Divine; dir. Episcopal Ch. Found. Mem. Mil. Order Fgn. Wars. Republican. Episcopalian (jr. warden). Clubs: Links, Downtown, Pilgrims, Brock (N.Y.C.); Piping Rock (Locust Valley); Southampton (L.I.). Home: Glen Cove, L.I.

ADDISON, JOSEPH, lawyer; b. Prince George's County, Md., July 25, 1885; s. Francis Girault and Ellen Moylan (Bowie) A.; LL.B., Georgetown U., 1908, LL.M., 1909; m. Marguerite Waring Clagett, Apr. 24, 1915; children—Katherine Duckett (Mrs. Howard Pratt Johnson), Joseph, William Baruch Clagett. Admitted to Md. bar, 1909, and began practice with firm Barton & Wilmer, Baltimore, 1909, became partner, 1919; admitted to D.C. bar, 1937, and since practiced in Washington and Baltimore, mem. firm Barton, Wilmer, Bramble, Addison & Semans; dir. Peoples Drug Stores,

Inc. Mem. Md., Baltimore, D.C. and Am. bar assns. Episcopalian. Home: Prince George's County, Md.

ADDONIZIO, HUGH J., mayor, ex-congressman; b. Newark, N.J., Jan. 31, 1914; s. Frank and Livia (Barrasso) A.; grad. St. Benedict's Prep. Sch., Newark, N.J., 1935; B.S., Forham U., 1939; student Officers Candidate Sch., Ft. Benning, Ga., 1942; LL.D., Seton Hall U., 1966; m. Doris Goodheart, July 6, 1942; children—Carol, Frank, Lois, James, Thomas, Joseph. Vice pres. A & C Clothing Co., Newark, 1939-40, 46-48; mayor City of Newark, 1962-70. Mem. 81st-87th Congresses, 11th N.J. Dist. Served with U.S. Army, 1942-46; assigned 60th Inf., 9th Div.; participated campaigns in Algiers, French Morocco, Tunisia, Sicily, Normandy, Northern France, Battle of Bulge and Rhineland; disch. with rank of capt., 1946. Awarded Bronze Arrowhead with 8 campaign stars, Bronze Star Medal combat infantryman's badge. Mem. Vets. Fgn. Wars, Am. Legion, Ninth Div. Assn. N.J. Conf. Mayors (past pres.), N.A.A.C.P., N.J. League Municipalities (trustee), Urban League. Democrat. Roman Catholic. Clubs: Lions, Unicontenational, Kiwanis, Frontiers Internat., Rotary. Home: Trenton Falls, N.J. Died Feb. 2, 1981; buried Gate of Heaven Cemetery, Hanover, N.J.

ADES, HARLOW WHITING, educator; b. Rockford, Ill., Dec. 31, 1911; s. Arthur William and Mary Weston (Thayer) A.; B.S., U. Ill., 1934, M.S., 1935, Ph.D., 1938; M.D. honoris causa, U. Uppsala (Sweden), 1975; m. Florence Hill Adams, Jan. 4, 1933 (div. May 1962); children—Helen May, Elizabeth Anne, William, Susan; m. 2d, Claire Frenkel McMillan, July 31, 1963. Asst. in physiol. optics John Hopkins Sch. medicine, 1938-39; instr. in anatomy Emory U. Sch. of Medicine, 1939-42, asst. prof. anatomy, 1942-47, prof. anatomy and chmn. dept., 1947-54, on leave of absence to serve as first annual research prof. of neurology Inst. Neurology, Northwestern U. Sch. of Medicine, 1947-48; prof. anatomy U. Tex. Southwestern Med. Sch., 1954-57; chief neurol. scis. div. USN Sch. Aviation Medicine, Pensacola, Fla., 1957-65; prof. elec. engring., prof. physiology and biophysics U. Ill., 1965-76, prof. psychology, 1968-76, prof. emeritus, 1976-77; research prof. psychology U. West Fla. Mem. Am. Assn. of Anatomists, Am. Physiol. Soc., Am. Neurol. Assn., Sigma Xi. Co-author: Structural Pattern of the Organ of Corti, 1966. Specialist in research in neurophysiology of hearing and vision and motor function, eletroencephalography in relation to aviation physiology and safety, effects of noise on inner ear sensory epithelia. Home: Pensacola, Fla. Died Oct. 12, 1977; buried Beth-El Cemetery, Pensacola.

ADESKO, THADDEUS VINCENT, judge; b. Chgo., Nov. 5, 1902; s. Walter and Angela (Rylski) A.; student U. Chgo., 1920-23; LL.B., Northwestern U., 1931; m. Clara Rutkowski, June 16, 1928; children—Paul, Alice. Admitted to Ill. bar, 1931, practiced in Chgo. until 1950; asst. judge Cook County Probate Ct., 1938-46; judge Municipal Ct., Chgo., 1950-53, Superior Ct. Cook County, 1953-60, County Ct., 1960-64; presiding judge County div. Circuit Ct. Cook County, 1964-66; justice Appellate Ct., 1966-77. Mem. Pres.'s Com. on Community Relations Service; mem. Ill. Senate, 1947-51; bd. dirs. Gen. Woods Boys' Club, Polish Welfare Assn. Mem. Am., Ill., Chgo., N.W. Suburban bar assns., Am. Judicature Soc., Advs. Soc. (past pres.), Cath. Lawyers Guild (v.p.), Polish Nat. Alliance, Polish Roman Cath. Union. Democrat. Clubs: Moose, K.C., Lions; City, Chgo. Soc., Northwestern U. (Chgo.). Home: Mount Prospect, Ill. Died Aug. 23, 1978.

ADKINS, DOROTHY C., psychologist; b. Atlanta, Ohio, Apr. 6, 1912; d. George Hoadley and Pearl (James) Adkins; B.S. in Edn., Ohio State U., 1931, Ph.D., 1937. Asst. examiner U. Chgo., 1936-38, research asso. psychology, 1938-40; chief research and test constrn. Social Security Bd., 1940-44; chief social sci. and adminstrv. testing, policy cons., chief test development sect. CSC, 1944-48; prof. U. N.C., Chapel Hill, 1948-65, chmn. dept. psychology, 1950-60; prof., research Coll. Edn., U. Hawaii, 1965-74; exec. dir. Cons. and Publishing, Inc., 1974-75. Fellow Am. Psychol. Assn. (rec. sec. 1949-52, mem. policy and planning bd. 1952-55, mem. council reps. 1953-56, bd. dirs. 1955-58, pres. div. evaluation and measurement 1952-53); mem. Psychometric Soc. (pres. 1949-50), Sigma Xi, Pi Mu Epsilon, Pi Lambda Theta. Author: Construction and Analysis of Achievement Tests, 1947; Factor Analysis of Reasoning Tests, 1952; Test Construction, 1960, 2d edit., 1974; Statistics, 1964. Asst. mng. editor Psychometrika, 1937-50, mng. editor, 1950-56, council editors, 1956-68; bd. editors, 1956-72; mem. board coop. editors Ednl. and Psychol. Measurement, 1940-75; editorial cons. Pub. Personnel Review, 1955-58. Home: Plain City, Ohio. Died Dec. 19, 1975; interred Forest Grove, Williamsport, Ohio.

ADKINS, PAUL CHARLES, thoracic surgeon; b. N.Y.C., July 21, 1925; s. Robinson Edwin and Jane Rose (Mac Shane) A.; A.B., Johns Hopkins U., 1945, M.D., 1948; m. Faith Jouvenal, Oct. 15, 1949; children—David, Mark, Paul, William. Intern, Johns Hopkins Hosp., 1948-49, asst. resident in surgery, 1949-50; resident in surgery and thoracic surgery George Washington U. Hosp., 1952-56, asst. prof. surgery George Washington U. Med. Center, 1956-59, asso. prof., 1959-66, prof., 1966-80; Lewis Saltz prof. surgery, chmn. dept., 1970-80. Served with U.S. Army, 1950-52. Recipient award as outstanding clin. prof., 1975. Diplomate Am. Bd. Surgery, Am. Bd. Thoracic Surgery (chmn. 1975-77). Mem. A.C.S., Am. Surg. Assn., Am. Assn. Thoracic Surgery, Soc. Thoracic Surgeons (pres. 1979), Halsted Soc., So. Surg. Assn., So. Thoracic Surg. Assn., Alpha Omega Alpha. Republican. Roman Catholic. Clubs: Kenwood, Cosmos, Burning Tree. Contbr. numerous articles on thoracic and cardiovascular surgery to med. publs.; asso. editor Jour. Thoracic and Cardiovascular Surgery, 1960-77. Home: Washington, D.C. Died Aug. 13, 1980.

ADLER, CHARLES, inventor; b. Balt., June 20, 1899; s. Harry and Carolyn (Frank) A.; student Johns Hopkins, 1917-20; m. Alene Steiger, June 10, 1925; children—Amalie Carol, Harry. Inventor rotating stop-sign, r.r.-highway crossing signal, Adler flasher relay, traffic sonic detector, Alder double filament incandescent lamps for r.r. signals, traffic signals and airplane nav. lights, speed control hwy. signal systems, double reflector aircraft anti-collision strobe light, aircraft flashing position-light system, aircraft studded reflector tall-light, and aircraft reflector lamp, aircraft proximity indicator, traffic-actuated traffic signal, automobile spaceometer, aircraft height light, and others; proposed 1st U.S. direct air-rail linkup at Balt.-Washington Internat. Airport. Bd. dirs. Balt.-Washington Internat. Airport, 1960-66. Recipient awards Am. Legion, CAA, USAF, USN, Nat. Aeronautic Assn., Aircraft Owners and pilots Assn. Mem. State Aviation Commn. Md., 1953-59, Md. Traffic Safety Commn. Served with S.A.T.C., 1918. Named Engr. of Year, Balt. Engring. Council, 1976. Licensed profl. airplane pilot; registered profl. engr., Md. Mem. Nat. Aeros. Assn. (life mem., nat. councillor Md.), Inst. Transp. Engrs., Soc. Automotive Engrs., Airways Engring. Soc. Guest appearances on television. Contbr. to nat. mags. Home: Baltimore, Md. Died Oct. 23, 1980; buried Druid Ridge Cemetary, Balt.

ADLER, CLARENCE, concert pianist; b. Cincinnati, O., Mar. 10, 1886; s. Leopold and Rosa (Simon) A.; student Cincinnati Coll. Music, 1899-1905, Mus.D., 1938; m. Elsa Richard, Apr. 25, 1916; 1 son, Richard. Founder, 1919, and since pianist New York Trio; appeared as soloist with many leading orchestras throughout the world; gave first Mozart Piano Concertos series in U.S., season 1942-43 at Town Hall, New York City, playing fourteen concertos with orchestra (five of fourteen performed had never been publicly played in this country); pioneer in broadcasting complete cycle of chamber music works; private teacher of music; mem. faculty Inst. of Musical Art (now Juilliard Sch.), since 1913; music editor for G. Schirmer. Founder and dir. of Karinoke, music camp at Lake Placid, N.Y. Pres., dir. Music Careers, Inc. (non-profit orgn.) Mem. Beethoven Assn. Clubs: Lotos, The Bohemians, Contbr. Musical Courier, Musical America, etc. Home: New York, N.Y. *

ADLER, JOHN HANS, economist, cons.; b. Tachov, Czechoslovakia, Nov. 16, 1912; s. August and Lilly (Beck) A.; Dr. Jur., German U. (Prague), 1937; M.A., Yale, 1940, Ph.D., 1946; m. Vilma Joan Rabl, Sept. 12, 1939; children—Catherine M. Adler Ramsey, Marcia V.; came to U.S., 1938, naturalized, 1945. Instr., Yale, 1941-42, Oberlin Coll., 1942-44; economist Fed. Res. Bd., 1944-45; dep. chief finance div. U.S. element Allied Commn. Austria, 1945-47; economist Fed. Res. Bank, N.Y.C., 1947-50; economist Internat. Bank Reconstrn. and Devel., 1950-57, econ. adviser, 1957-61; dir. Econ. Devel. Inst., 1962-67, sr. econ. adviser, 1967-68, dir. programming and budgeting dept., 1968-76, asst. to v.p. finance, 1977, mem. pres.'s council, 1972-77; sr. asso. mem. (vis. fellow) St. Antony's Coll., Oxford (Eng.) U., 1978-79. Clubs: Cosmos (Washington); Edgemoor (Bethesda, Md.); East India Sports and Public Schools (London). Author: (with H. C. Wallich) Public Finance in a Developing Country, 1951; (with E.R. Schlesinger, E.C. Olson) Public Finance and Economic Development in Guatemala, 1952; (with E.R. Schlesinger, E. Van Westerborg) The Pattern of U.S. Import Trade 1952; also articles in learned jours. Home: Chevy Chase, Md. Died Apr. 7, 1980.

ADLER, SAMUEL MARCUS, artist, educator; b. N.Y.C., July 30, 1898; s. Harris Bernard and Rose (Levy) A.; student NAD; m. Sarah Fox, June 29, 1926; m. 2d, Beverly Chesler, Nov. 7, 1974. One-man exhbns. include Joseph Luyber Galleries, N.Y.C., 1948, U. Ind., 1950, Louisville Art Center, 1950, Mint Mus., 1951, Grace Borgenicht Gallery, N.Y.C. 1952, 54, Phila. Art Alliance, 1954, U. Ill., 1959, Grand Central Moderns, N.Y.C., 1960, Babcock Gallery (2), 1962; Krannert Art Mus., Urbana, Ill., 1964, Notre Dame U., 1965, Rose Fried Gallery, N.Y.C., 1965, U. Iowa, 1966, U. Ga., 1967-68, Ripon Coll., 1969, Frank Rehn Gallery, N.Y.C., 1971, 72, 76, Addison Gallery Am. Art, 1972; exhibited numerous nat., European shows, including Art Inst. Chgo., U. Iowa, Butler Inst. Am. Art, Pa. Acad. Fine Arts, N.A.D., Corcoran Inst., Denver Art Mus., U. Ill., Va. Mus. Art, Nebr. Art Assn., Met. Mus. Art, Whitney Mus. Am. Art, San Francisco Mus. Art, galleries 18 countries Europe and Orient; meml. exhbn. Terry Dintenfass Gallery, N.Y.C., 1981; represented in permanent collections U. Notre Dame, U. Ill. (Purchase award 1952), Munson-Williams-Proctor Inst., Clearwater (Fla.) Mus., Whitney Mus. Am. Art (Purchase award 1952), S.I. Inst. Arts and Scis. (Purchase award 1962), N.Y. U., Nat. Collection Fine Arts, Newark Mus., Norfolk Mus., Joseph H. Hirshhorn Museum, Glicenstein Mus., Israel, Bklyn. Mus., Ga. Mus., U. Nebr. Mus., Syracuse U. Mus., Wichita State U., St. Lawrence U., Ill. Wesleyan U., Herbert Johnson Mus.; mem. faculty N.Y. U., 1948-72, adj. prof., 1960-72; mem. faculty U. Ga., 1967; vis. prof. U. Ill., 1959-60, U. Ga., 1967-68; guest lectr. Nat. Com. Art Edn., U. Mich., 1957, Festival Contemporary Arts, U. Ill., 1953-59, 63, N.Y. State Art Tchrs. Assn., 1958, Museum Modern Art, U. Syracuse, 1961, Washington U., 1963, U. Notre Dame, 1963, Beloit Coll., numerous other schs., museums. Juror, Ford Found., 1963. Recipient J. Henry Schiedt meml. prize Pa. Acad. Fine Arts, 1951; Patron's award Audubon Artists, 1st hon. mention 1956, 57, Medal of Honor 1960; asso. mem. Inst. Advanced Study, U. Ill., Urbana, 1964; Ford Found. grant for Artist in Residence in Mus., U. Notre Dame, 1965. Author articles. Address: New York, N.Y. Died Nov. 11, 1979; buried Kensico Cemetery, Valhalla, N.Y.

ADSHEAD, GLADYS LUCY, author; born in West Didsbury, Manchester, Eng., Apr. 25, 1896; d. James Frederick and Bertha Wilson (Groome) Adshead; grad., Froebel Ednl. Inst., Roehampton, London, Eng., 1916. Came to U.S. 1921, naturalized, 1939. Tchr. in Eng., 1916-21; organized open-air free nursery sch., Balt., 1921; tchr. The Park Sch., Balt., 1922-26; demonstration tchr. Wellesley Coll. Summer Sch., 1924; ednl. travel, Europe, 1926-27; trained apprentice tchrs., created exptl. demonstration group of five year olds The Beaver Sch., Boston, 1927-34; head nursery and primary classes Buckingham Sch., Cambridge, Mass., trained apprentice tchrs., 1934-43, tchr. summer course Nursery Tng. Sch. of Boston, 1942; head lower sch. North Shore Country Day, Winnetka, Ill., 1943-49; headmistress Charles River Sch. at Dover, Mass., 1949-59. Trustee St. Hubert's Sch. Mem. Royal Soc. Tchrs., Michaelis Guild, Ind. Sch. Assn. Mass. Episcopalian. Author: Brownies—Hush!, 1938; Something Surprising, 1940; Casco, 1943; What Miranda Knew, 1944; Seventeen to Sing, 1946; Brownies, It's Christmas, 1955; Brownies, Hurry!, 1959; Smallest Brownie's Fearful Adventure, 1961. Collected and arranged with Annis Duff An Inheritance of Poetry, 1948.*

AFIFI PASHA HAFEZ, diplomat, banker, physician; b. Egypt, 1886. Egyptian fgn. minister, 1928-29; minister to United Kingdom, 1930-33; dir. Nat. Bank of Egypt and chmn. Egyptian econ. mission to Gt. Britain, 1935; ambassador to England, 1936-38; permanent Egyptian del. to U.N.; succeeded Dr. Quo Tai-chi as the fourth chmn. U.N. security council undermonthly rotation system, 1946.*

AGAR, HERBERT SEBASTIAN, author; b. New Rochelle, N.Y., Sept. 29, 1897; s. John Giraud and Agnes Louise (Macdonough) A.; A.B., Columbia, 1919; A.M., Princeton, 1920, Ph.D., 1922; Litt.D., Southwestern U., Memphis, 1936; LL.D., Boston U., 1941; m. Adeline Scott, Feb. 6, 1918 (div. 1933); children—William Scott, Agnes; m. 2d, Eleanor Carroll Chilton, Apr. 11, 1933 (div. 1945); m. 3d, Barbara Lutyens Wallace, June, 1945. London corr. Louisville Courier-Jour., Louisville Times, 1929-34; author syndicated daily newspaper column, "Time and Tide" 1935-39; editor Louisville Courier-Jour., 1940-42; lit. editor English Rev. (London), 1930-34; spl. asst. to Am. ambassador, London; dir. Brit. div. OWI London, 1943-46; dir. Rupert Hart-Davis, Ltd., London, 1951-63. Mem. Phi Beta Kappa. Editor: (with Allen Tate) symposium Who Owns America?, 1936. Served as seaman, later chief q.m. USNR, 1917-18, lt. comdr. 1942. Clubs: National Arts, Century (N.Y.C.); Savile (London). Author: (with Willis Fisher, Eleanor Carroll Chilton) (verse) Fire and Sleet and Candelight, 1928; Milton and Plato, 1928; (with E.C. Chilton), The Garment of Praise, 1929; Bread and Circuses, 1930; The Defeat of Baudelaire (translation), 1932; The People's Choice, 1933 (Pulitzer prize for Am. History); Land of the Free, 1935; What is America?, 1936; Pursuit of Happiness, 1938; (with Helen Hill) Beyond German Victory, 1940; A Time for Greatness, 1942; The Price of Union, 1950; A Declaration of Faith, 1952; Abraham Lincoln, 1952; The Price of Power, 1957; The Saving Remnant, 1960; The Perils of Democracy 1965. Home: Sussex, England. Died Nov. 24, 1980.

AGEE, JOHN HERCULES (A'GE), telephone exec.; b. Sangamon Co., Ill., July 27, 1883; s. Edwin Hercules, and Annie (Wilson) A.; student Springfield (Ill.) Business Coll., 1902, George Washington U., 1908; LL.B., U. of Neb., 1910; m. Bertha Howard, June 21, 1911; children—Howard Hercules, Richard Wallace. Began as telephone contractor, 1904; admitted to Neb. bar, 1910; director and gen. manager, Lincoln Telephone & Telegraph Co., 1926-29, now vice-pres. and gen. mgr.; dir. Security Mutual Life Insurance Co. (Lincoln, Neb.), Securities Acceptance Corp. (Omaha), F. H. Woods & Co. (Chicago), U.S. Independent

Telephone Assn., Chicago (pres. 1937-38; mem. exec. com.). Member of Telephone Industry Advisory Committee, Communications Branch, War Production Board. Dir. Lincoln Chamber of Commerce (pres. 1931); nat. Councillor U.S. Chamber of Commerce; pres. Lincoln Community Chest, 1929-30; pres. Alumni Assn. U. of Neb., 1934-35. Trustee U. of Neb. Foundation (pres. 1940-42); Distinguished Service award, U. of Neb. and Alumni Assn., 1941. Mem. Chi Phi. Republican. Baptist. Mason (32 deg., Shriner). Clubs: Rotary, Beaux Art, Saturday Nite, Fifty-Fifty, Garden, Country. Home: Lincoln Neb.

AGHA, MEHEMED FEHMY, art cons.; b. Nicolaieff, Russia, Mar. 11, 1896; s. Yossouf and Anna (Khoroz) A.; grad. Emperor Alexander Tech. Sch., Nicolaieff, 1913; grad. in econs., Poly. Inst. Emperor Peter the Great. Petrograd, 1918; grad. Ecole Nationale des Langues Orientales Vivantes, Paris, 1923. Came to U.S., 1929, naturalized, 1936. Studio chief Paris div. Condé Nast, France, 1924-27, art dir. German edit. Vogue mag., Berlin, 1927-29; art dir. Condé Nast Publs., N.Y.C., 1929-42; dir. M. F. Agha studio, N.Y.C., 1943-70. Recipient Am. Inst. Graphic Arts medal, 1957; elected to Art Dirs. Hall of Fame, 1972. Hon. mem. Inst. Graphic Arts (pres. 1954-55). Clubs: Dutch Treat, Art Directors (life mem., pres. 1934-35) (N.Y.C.). Author monographs on graphic arts. Home: Malvern, Pa. Died May 27, 1978.

AGUINALDO, LEOPOLDO R., merchant; b. Manila, P.I., Nov. 15, 1885; s. Anastacio and Marcela (Ramos) A.; student Colegio de la Convencion de Sta. Cruz, Liceo de Manila (both of Manila) and Nagoya Polytechnic Sch. of Japan, Degree of Textile Engineer; m. Da. Andrea del Rosario, of Bulacan, Bulacan, P.I., 1911; children—Daniel, Eriberto, Francisco. Industrial Teacher, Bur. of Edn., 1909; left Bur. in same year and opened a textile factory which was shortly dissolved; then formed Aguinaldo & Sampedro, later firm incorporated under name Philippine Net Braid & Mfg. Co. of which was mgr., 8 yrs.; established firm L. R. Aguinaldo, 1921; pres. Luzon Surety Co., Inc.; v.p. Madaymon Mining & Exploration Co.; dir. Manila Railroad Co., Luzon Investment Co., Nat. Life Ins. Co. Dir. Philippine Carnival Assn., Chamber of Commerce of P.I. Home: Sampaloc, Manila.

AHL, A(UGUSTUS) WILLIAM, educator, author; b. Germany, Sept. 6, 1886; s. William and Dorothy A.; A.M., Susquehanna U., Selinsgrove, Pa., 1912; grad. Breklum Sem., Germany, 1908; Ph.D., Vanderbilt U., 1920; spl. student Peaboby Coll. for Teachers, Nashville, Tenn., 1921-22; m. Henrietta Paulsen, of Schleswig, Germany, Apr. 15, 1910; children—William G., Hildegard Dorothea. Ordained Luth. ministry, at Schenectady, N.Y., 1909; pastor Herkimer, N.Y., 1909-10, Baltimore, Md., 1910-16, Nashville Tenn., 1916-22; instr. Vanderbilt U., 1921-22; prof. Greek lang. and lit., Thiel Coll., Greenville, Pa., 1922-27; prof. Greek and ancient history, Susquehanna U., Selinsgrove, Pa., since 1927. Mem. Am. Philol. Assn., Classical Assn. of the Atlantic States, Classical League, Am. Oriental Soc., Philos. Soc. Gt. Britain, Acad. Letters and Science (Naples), Pi Gamma Mu. Author: Outline of Persian History, 1922; Bible Studies in the Light of Recent Research, 1923. Home: Selinsgrove, Pa.*

AILES, EDGAR RICH, mortgage and realty co. exec.; b. Detroit, Mar. 12, 1883; s. James William and Frances Henrietta (Bradley) A.; LL.B., U. Mich., 1904; m. Florence Serena Holt, Sept. 7, 1903; children—Edgar Holt, Serena (Mrs. Thomas P. Henry). With The Hugh Wallace Co., Detroit, 1904-09, Truscon Steel Co., Detroit, also Youngstown, O., 1909-15; asst. treas. Fenestra, Inc. (formerly Detroit Steel Products Co.), Detroit, 1915-17, sec., treas., 1917-52; v.p., dir. Detroit Mortgage & Realty Co. (formerly Contract & Investment Co.), 1933—; dir. Mfrs. Nat. Bank, Mich. Mutual Liability Co. Exec. com. Detroit Community Fund, 1946. Mem. Mich. Mfrs. Assn. (pres. 1937—), Detroit Citizens League (v.p. 1940—), Detroit Bd. Commerce (dir. 1922-23), N.A.M. (dir. 1945), Detroit Assn. Credit Men (past pres.), Phi Gamma Delta. Republican. Unitarian. Clubs: Detroit, Detroit Boat, Detroit Athletic. Home: Detroit. *

AINSWORTH, DOROTHY SEARS, educator; b. Moline, Ill., Mar. 8, 1894; d. Harry and Stella (Davidson) Ainsworth; A.B., Smith Coll., 1916, Sc.D. (hon.), 1956; M.A., Columbia, 1923, Ph.D., 1930. Tchr. phys. edn. Moline High Sch., 1916-18; instr. phys. edn. Skidmore Coll., 1925-26; instr. hygiene and phys. edn. Smith Coll., 1921-23, dir., prof. phys. edn., 1926-60, prof. emeritus, from 1960; cons. internat. affairs A.A.H.P.E.R., from 1960. Organizing chmn. 1st internat. Congress on Phys. Edn. and Sports for Girls and Women, Copenhagen, Denmark, 1949, chmn. continuing com., 1949-53, co-chmn., elected pres., 2d Congress, Paris, France, 1953, pres. London, 1957, pres. Washington, (Pres.), 1961; chmn. U.S. joint council on Internat. Affairs in Health Phys. Edn. and Recreation 1950-57; mem. U.S. Com. Pan Am. Inst. Phys. Edn., 1950-56; organizing chmn. 1st Internat. Congress on Essentials of Phys. Edn. for Youth in the Conn. Valley, 1954; chmn. com. on phys. edn. World Confedn. Orgns. Teaching Profession, 1958; U.S. specialist to South Africa, 1960. Mem. Women's Def. Council, Northampton, Mass., 1942-45; with Smith Coll. Relief Unit, Grecourt, France, 1919-20. Recipient Honor award Am. Assn. Health, Phys. Edn. and Recreation, 1949, Gulick medal, 1960; Ling Gold medal Ling Gymnastic Soc., Sweden, for work in internat. affairs, 1949; Medal of Honor by Minister Edn. French Republic, 1953; Hetherington award, highest award Am. Acad. Phys. Edn., 1962; Cross of Honor from Finnish Govt., 1961; decorated comdr. Order Merite Sportif (France), 1961; recipient Woman Conscience award Nat. Council Women, 1968. Fellow Am. Coll. Sports Medicine, Am. Acad. Phys. Edn.; mem. Am. Assn. Health, Phys. Edn. and Recreation (spl. cons. internat. relations, pres.), internat. Council Health, Phys. Edn. and Recreation (pres. 1959-65, hon. pres. 1965—), Internat. Assn. Phys. Edn. and Sports Women (past pres.), Nat. Assn. Phys. Edn. Coll. Women (pres. 1937-41, hon. life mem. 1963—), New Eng. Assn., Am. Assn. U. Women, Nat. Assn. Health Phys. Edn. and Recreation (pres. 1950), Nat. Council Women U.S.A. (3d v.p. 1958), Phi Beta Kappa. Conglist. Clubs: Smith College, Cosmopolitan, Nat. Womans Republican (N.Y.C.); College (Boston); Sulgrave (Washington). Author: The History of Physical Education in 12 Colleges for Women, 1930. Editor: Individual Sports for Women, 1944, first 4 edits. 1963; (with R. Evans) Basic Rhythms, 1957. Contbr. articles profl. mags. Home: Northampton, Mass. Deceased.

AITKEN, WEBSTER, pianist; b. Los Angeles, June 17, 1908; student Emil Sauer and Artur Schnabel. Debut, Vienna, Austria, 1929; recitals in Berline, Rome, Salzburg, London; soloist with Vienna Philharmonic Orch., Am. debut Town Hall, N.Y.C., 1935; soloist with orchs. and chamber music ensembles throughout U.S.; performed complete Franz Schubert piano sonatas London and N.Y.C., 1938; rec. artist EMS, Delos records. Mem. Am. Fedn. Musicians. Personal papers and documents housed in Webster Aitken Archive, Humanities Research Center, U. Tex., Austin. Home: New York, N.Y. Died May 11, 1981; buried Inglewood Cemetery, Los Angeles.

AKERS, ANTHONY BOYCE, lawyer; b. nr. Charlotte, Tex.; s. Ambrose B. and Margaret (Long) A.; B.A., U. Tex., 1936; LL.B., Columbia, 1949; m. Jane Pope, Nov. 28, 1942; children—Andra, Ellery Jane. Instr. pub. schs., Tex., 1936-37, Cal., 1938-39; admitted to N.Y. bar, 1950, D.C. bar, 1953, U.S. Supreme Ct. bar, 1953; pvt. practice, N.Y.C., 1950—; dep. asst. sec., then dep. under sec. internat. negotiations Office Sec. Air Force, 1951-53; dir. N.Y. State Dept. Commerce for N.Y.C., 1955-58; chmn. N.Y.C. Community Mental Health Bd., 1957-58; U.S. ambassador to New Zealand, 1961-63; of counsel Cabell, Martin, Hammer and Gallo and predecessor firm, 1967-76. Pres., Landfall Devel. Co., 1972-76. Latin Am. rep. to Inter-Am. Trade and Cultural Center, 1966. Democratic candidate for Congress, 1954, 56, 58; exec. chmn. N.Y. Citizens for Kennedy-Johnson, 1960. Served to lt. comdr. USNR, 1940-46; PTO. Decorated Silver Star medal with gold star. Mem. Assn. Bar City N.Y., Fed. Bar Council, Bar Assn. D.C., Council Fgn. Relations. Home: Palm Beach, Fla. Died Apr. 1, 1976; interred St. Columbus Cemetery, Berkley Meml. Chapel, Portsmouth, R.I.

AKERS, FLOYD DESOTO, automotive exec.; b. nr. Wabash Ind., July 3, 1895; s. Orange S. and Dilla (Bridges) A.; student Ferris Inst., Big Rapids, Mich., 1917; m. Irma Wolf, Jan. 21, 1925; children—Shirley (Mrs. S. Poli Sheahan), Tomajean (Mrs. Howard L. Jobe). Sec.-treas. Columbia Asphalt Paving Co., Columbus, O., 1917; mgr. Service Motor Truck Co. Chicago br., 1919-21; asst. br. mgr. General Motors Acceptance Corp., N.Y. City, 1922; sales rep. Cadillac Motor Car Co., Detroit, 1923-29, regional mgr., 1929-34; pres. Capitol Cadillac-Oldsmobile Co., Washington, 1934—; pres. Akers Oldsmobile-Cadillac Co., Alexandria, Va., Suburban Cadillac-Oldsmobile Co., Bethesda, Md., Capitol Parisian Motors, Inc., Washington; dir., mem. exec. com. Am. Security & Trust Co.; spl. ambassador inaugural ceremonies Pres. P.I., 1957. Served with AC, U.S. Army, 1918; chairman met. war hospitality com., chairman Washington Community War Fund, civilian mem. Naval Manpower Commn., World War II. Received Naval Meritorious Award, 1944. Chmn. Nat. Stadium Com. Member of the National Memorial Stadium Commission, National Symphony Orchestra Association. Republican. Presbyterian. Mason (32 deg., Shriner, Jester). Clubs: Burning Tree (dir., Washington); The Surf (dir.; Miami Beach); Bohemian. Home: Washington, D.C. Died Nov. 22, 1978.

AKERS, SAMUEL LUTTRELL (A'KERZ), clergyman, educator; b. Knoxville, Tenn., Aug. 2, 1898; s. Benjamin Wade and Lucy Elizabeth (Broome) A.; A.B., Univ. of Tenn., 1922, B.D., Garrett Biblical Inst., 1925, Ph.D., Yale, 1929; m. Elizabeth Meek Scott, September 2, 1931; children—Joyce Elizabeth, Sarah Ann. Pastor, Methodist Ch., Leroy, Ind., 1924-25, Lake City, Tenn., 1925-26; asso. prof. philosophy, Wesleyan Coll., Macon, Ga., 1929-30, prof. since 1930, sec. of the faculty, 1930-37, acting dean, 1937-38, dean, 1938-58, counselor and chaplain, 1958—; ordained to ministry of the Methodist Church, 1932; pastor Martha Bowman Meml. Meth. Ch., 1949-52. Chmn. ednl. adv. com. of Bibb County Returning Veterans Com., 1945-46. Mem. Am. Philos. Assn., Southern Society for Philosophy and Psychology, So. Assn. Colls. for Women (exec. bd., 1954-56), Macon C. of C. (citizenship com., 1945-46; edn. com., 1946-47). Clubs: Civitan (chmn. citizenship essay com., 1933-43, pres. 1943, chmn. bd. dirs., 1944; lt. gov. Civitan Internat. Ga. Dist., 1945-46, gov., 1946-47. Home: Macon, Ga.

AKERSON, GEORGE EDWARD, JR., broadcasting exec.; b. Mpls., Apr. 20, 1918; s. George Edward and Harriet (Blake) A.; student Harvard, 1939; m. Anne Abbott, Sept. 5, 1941; children—George Edward III, Stuart A., William N.; m. 2d, Phyllis Chadwick, May 9, 1964. With Boston-Herald-Traveler Corp., 1936-72, pres., 1963-72, chmn. bd., 1968-72; pres. WHDH Corp., 1963-79, chmn. bd., 1972-79; dir. Entron, Inc. Served to lt. col. USAAF, 1940-45. Decorated D.F.C. Mem. Bus. Com. for Arts. Home: Westport, Mass. Died May 1, 1979.

AKOLT, JOHN PATRICK, JR., lawyer; b. Denver, May 16, 1918; s. John P. and Alice (Doyle) A.; student U. Notre Dame, 1936-37, U. Colo., 1937-39; B.S. in Chemistry, U. Denver, 1940, LL.B., 1946; m. Jeanette M. Humphrey, Apr. 28, 1943; children—Janet R. (Mrs. Daily), John Patrick, III, Jerri Anne. Admitted to Colo. bar, 1946; with Akolt, Dick & Akolt, and predecessors, Denver, 1946-76, partner, 1952-76, Vice pres., sec., dir. Marr Co., Denver, 1959-76. Served with USAAF, 1941-45. Mem. Nat. Assn. Coll. and U. Attys. (exec. bd. 1968-69), Am., Colo., Denver bar assns., Chi Psi, Phi Delta Phi. Clubs: Denver Country, Denver Athletic, Gyro (pres. 1974-75) (Denver). Home: Denver, Colo. Died Aug. 24, 1976.

ALBERS, JOSEF, painter, educator; b. Bottrop, Westphalia, Germany, Mar. 19, 1888; s. Lorenz and Magdalena (Schumacher) A.; student Royal Art Sch., Berlin, 1913-15, Sch. Applied Art, Essen, 1916-19, Art Acad., Munich, 1919-20, Bauhaus, Weimar, 1920-23; A.F.D., U. Hartford, 1957, Yale, 1962, Calif. Coll. Arts and Crafts, 1964, U. N.C., 1967; Dr. phil. h.c., Ruhr. U., Bochum, W. Ger., 1967; LL.D. (hon.), Bridgeport U., 1966, York U., 1973; D. Fine Arts, U. Ill., Art Sch. Mpls., Kenyon Coll., 1969, Washington U., St. Louis, 1971, Md. Inst., 1972, Pratt Inst., Bklyn., 1975, Phila. Coll. Art, 1976; m. Anni Fleischmann, May 25, 1925. Came to U.S., 1933, naturalized, 1939. Prof. art, Bauhaus, Weimar, Dessau and Berlin, Germany, 1923-33, Black Mountain (N.C.) Coll., 1933-49, prof., chmn. art Yale, 1950-58, prof. emeritus, 1958-60, ret. as chmn., 1958, vis. critic in advanced painting, 1958-60. Work exhibited and pub., Germany, Holland, Denmark, Norway, Sweden, Switzerland, Italy, France, Czechoslovakia, Eng., U.S., Cuba, Mexico, Brazil, Chili, Venezuela, Can., Australia and Japan; tchr. lectr. univs. U.S. and fgn. countries, Mus. Modern Art, N.Y.C. Decorated comdr.'s cross Order of Merit (Germany); recipient Ada S. Garret prize Chgo. Art Inst., 1954; 3d prize $1000 exhibit Corcoran Art Gallery, 1957; Konrao von Soest Preis, Westphalia, Germany, 1958; Ford Found. fellow, 1959; Graham Found. fellow, 1962; 1964 medal Am. Inst. Graphic Arts; award for painting Internat. Exhbn., Carnegie Inst., Pitts., 1967; grand prix 3d Arts and Letters Bienal Americana de Grabada, Santiago, Chile, 1968; Graphic Arts medal Skowhegan (Maine) Sch. Painting and Sculpture, 1971; Grand prix painting Nordrhein-Westfalen, West Germany. Mem. Nat. Inst. Arts and Letters, Am. Abstract Artist. Author: Poems and Drawings, 1958, 61; Interaction of Color, 1963; Search Verses Re-Search, 1969; Formulation/Articulation, 1972; contbr. articles on art edn. to mags., books, U.S., Europe. Home: Orange, Conn. Died Mar. 25, 1976.

ALBERT, CHARLES ELWOOD, educator; b. Pen Argyl, Pa., Jan. 10, 1883; s. Urbanus and Sarah Hannah (Jones) A.; C.E., Lafayette Coll., 1908; grad. work, Pa. State Coll. and N.C. State Coll.; LL.D., Southeastern, Memphis, Tenn., 1937, Lafayette Coll., 1939; Sc.D., Davis and Elkins Coll., Elkins, W.Va., 1958; m. Jeanne Marstiller, Sept. 1, 1915; children—Charles Elwood (lieut. U.S.N.R., killed in service, May 18, 1944), Jeanne Marstiller. Teacher high sch., Pa., 1909-11; prof. mathematics, Davis and Elkins Coll., Elkins, W.Va., 1911-13; instr. in mechanics, Pa. State Coll., 1913-16; civ. engr. Camden (N.J.) Iron Works, 1916-20; instr. in mechanics, Drexel Inst. (night sch.), Phila., 1920-22; dean and prof. mathematics, Davis and Elkins Coll., 1922-35, acting pres., July 1, 1935-July 6, 1936, pres., 1936-Oct. 16, 1939, prof. physics, head dept. of engring since 1946. Pres. Bd. of Edn., Randolph County, W.Va., July 1933-July 1939. Mem. W.Va. Acad. Science (pres. 1934-35), W.Va. Soc. of Professional Engrs., Alpha Tau Omega, Chi Beta Phi. Registered Professional Civil Engr. (W.Va.). Presbyn. Home: Elkins, W.Va. *

ALBERT, EDWARD JOHN, instrument co. exec.; b. Inghams Mills, N.Y., June 20, 1882; s. Frederick J. and Martina (Pope) A.; student mining U. Toronto, 1915-17; m. Bozen B. Lukes, Apr. 20, 1908; 1 dau., Annette (Mrs. Albeck); m. 2d, Anna Mudd, Sept. 25,

1971. Salesman, Ingersoll-Rand Co., 1898-1908; sales, engring., design Canadian Allis Chalmers Co., 1908-18; sec., also gen. mgr. Thwing Instrument Co., Phila., 1918-35; gen. mgr., treas. successor co. Thwing-Albert Instrument Co., 1935-46, pres., 1946—, chmn. bd., 1957-69, also dir. Col., Pa. N.G., ret.; mem. Armory Rd. Fellow A.A.A.S.; mem. Am. Soc. for Testing and Materials (hon. life, dir., award 1961), Sci. Apparatus Makers Assn. (award 1960, pres. 1953-55, dir.), T.A.P.P.I. Instrument Soc. Am. (sr.), Am. Inst. Mining Metall. and Petroleum Engrs., Candian Inst. Mining and Metallurgy, Am. Petroleum Inst., Am. Soc. Quality Control, Soc. Exptl. Stress Analysis, Forest Products Research Soc. Clubs: Union League, Engineers (Phila.); Cricket (Germantown, Pa.). Home: Philadelphia PA 19130.

ALBRECHT, GEORGE JACOB, educator, landscape architect; b. Laurel Hill, N.Y., Aug. 8, 1908; s. Jacob and Elizabeth (Glock) A.; B.S., N.Y. State Coll. Forestry, 1930; m. Sarah Virginia Gardner, Aug. 29, 1931; children—Jessie E. (Mrs. Verner W. Clapp, Jr.), Sarah Jane (Mrs. Lawrence B. White). Tchr. tech. drawing N.Y.C. high schs., 1931-33; camp supt. Civilian Conservation Corps, Selkirk Shores State Park, N.Y., 1933-34; landscape architect Nat. Park Service, 1934-44; prof. landscape architecture, chmn. dept. State U. Sch. Landscape Architecture at Coll. Forestry, Syracuse, N.Y., 1946-68, dir. Sch. Landscape Architecture, 1968-69, emeritus dir. and prof., 1969-76; cons. in field, 1950-76. Chmn. N.Y. State Bd. Examiners Landscape Architecture, 1961-68; chmn. Onondaga County Natural Resources Council, 1955-59; mem. Onondaga Lake Sci. Council, 1965-68. Served to lt. USNR, 1944-46. Fellow Am. Soc. Landscape Architects (pres. Upstate N.Y. chpt. 1962, nat. trustee 1954-56), Am. Inst. Parks Execs.; mem. Syracuse Soc. Architects (asso.), Nat. Conf. State Parks, Am. Civic and Planning Assn. Home: Henderson, N.Y. Died May 26, 1976.

ALBRECHT, RICHARD GEORGE, city ofcl.; b. Chgo., Aug. 29, 1934; s. George W. and Mildred B. Albrecht; B.A. in Acctg., Roosevelt U., 1961; m. Susan Taylor, Sept. 3, 1960; children—Daniel, Leslie. Firefighter, Chgo. Fire Dept., 1955-61, acct. at hdqrs., 1962-63, fin. officer, 1963-72, dir. adminstrv. and fiscal services, 1972-75, dep. fire commr., 1975-78, fire commr., 1978-81; mem. adv. bd. Ill. State Fire Marshall, 1978-81; mem. Office of Ill. CD Council, 1978-81. Mem. exec. bd. Salvation Army, 1978-81, Boy Scouts Am., 1978-81; mem. exec. bd. emergency med. services commn. Chgo. Hosp. Council, 1976-81; chmn. communication com., 1979-81. Served with USN, 1957-59. Recipient Superior Public Service award City of Chgo., 1965. Lutheran. Clubs: Ill. Athletic, Chgo. Yacht, Columbia Yacht. Home: Chicago, Ill. Died Mar. 20, 1981; buried Mt. Emblem Cemetery, Elmhurst, Ill.

ALBRECHT-CARRIÉ, RENÉ, historian educator; b. Izmir, Turkey, Jan. 20, 1904; s. Ernest and Claire (Carrié) Albrecht-C.; came to U.S., 1920, naturalized, 1923; B.-ès Sc., B.-ès-L., French Lycée, Aix-en-Provence, 1920; A.B., Columbia, 1923, M.A., 1923, Ph.D. 1938; m. Eleanor Kingsley, July 23, 1932; children—Claire (Mrs. Michael Tomlinson), Pierre; m. 2d, Else Beylegaard Lorch, née Petersen, July 3, 1973. Instr. math. Coll. City N.Y., also Townsend Harris High Sch., N.Y.C., 1923-42; instr. history Queens Coll., 1942-45; prof. history Barnard Coll., 1945-69; prof. history Sch. Internat. Affairs, Columbia, 1953-69, emeritus, 1969-78. Rockefeller grantee, France, 1952-53; Fulbright lectr., Italy, 1960-61; Guggenheim fellow, 1966-67. Mem. Am. Hist. Assn. (George L. Beer prize 1938), Council Fgn. Relations, socs. French, Italian hist. studies, Am.-Italy Soc., Societé d'Histoire Moderne. Author: Italy at the Paris Peace Conference, 1938; Italy from Napoleon to Mussolini, 1950; Diplomatic History of Europe since the Congress of Vienna, 1958, 73; France, Europe and the Two World Wars, 1960; Europe Since 1815, 1962; One Europe, 1965; The Meaning of the First World War, 1965; The Concert of Europe, 1968, Britain and France: Adaptations to a Changing Context of Power, 1970; Twentieth Century Europe, 1973; Adolphe Thiers: The Triumph of the Bourgeoisie, 1977; others; contbr. over 50 articles to jours., chpts. to books. Home: New York, N.Y. Died Aug. 31, 1978; buried Ferncliff Cemetery, Hartsdale, N.Y.

ALCORN, JAMES FLOYD, dentist; b. Lapeer, Mich., May 12, 1883; s. John K. and Elmora L. (Read) A.; D.D.S., Washington U. Sch. Dentistry, 1906; m. Belva G. James, Jan. 2, 1907. Began practice in St. Louis, 1906. Pres. Mo. Bd. of Dental Examiners, 1930-36, Internat. Coll. of Dentists, 1943, Wash. U. Sch. Dentistry Alumni Assn., 1913, St. Louis Dental Soc., 1926, Xi Psi Phi, 1926. Mem. Am. Dental Assn., Mo. State Dental Assn., St. Louis Soc. Dental Science, Republican. Protestant. Mason. Contbr. articles on nutrition and dental law. Editor: Jour. St. Louis Dental Soc., Ch. State Council on Dental Health. Home: University City, Mo.

ALDEN, EDITH JARVIS, railroad exec.; b. Burlington, Ia., May 10, 1884; d. Harry Edmund and Alma Cecilia (Sellon) Jarvis; student Burlington (Ia.) High Sch., 1897-1901, Gregg Bus. Sch., Chicago, Ill., 1920-21; m. Harry Scott Alden, June 22, 1910 (dec.); 1 son, John Jarvis. Connected with C., B& Q. RR. Co., Chicago, Ill., since 1918, successively as clk, and stenographer, office of v.p., 1918-22, asst. sec., 1922-38, sec. and asst. treas. since 1938; asst. sec., Colo. and Southern Ry. Co., Ft. Worth and Denver Railway Company; secretary and assistant treasurer Burlington Truck Lines, Inc., Valier Coal Co.; asst. sec. and asst. treas. Paducah & Ill. R.R. Co. Mem. Alliance of Bus. and Professional Women of Chicago, P.E.O. Republican. Club: Altrusa (Chicago, Ill.). Home: La Grange, Ill.

ALDREDGE, GEORGE N., business exec.; b. Dallas, Tex., Sept. 21, 1883; s. George N. and Betty W. (Hearne) A.; B.S., Southwestern U., 1905; m. Rona Munger, Dec. 4, 1907. Chmn. exec. com., First Nat. Bank in Dallas (Tex.); dir. Southwestern Life Ins. Co., Dallas, Tex., Standard Brands, Inc., New York City, The Texas Co., New York City. Home: Dallas, Tex. *

ALDRICH, GEORGE DAVENPORT, investment banker; b. Marblehead, Mass., Sept. 12, 1916; s. William T. and Dorothea (Davenport) A.; B.A., Harvard, 1939, LL.B., 1942; m. Alice H. Burrage, July 6, 1940 (div. July 1970); children—Camilla, Alison; m. 2d, Lucy A. Devens, June 1971. Admitted to Mass. bar, 1947; asso. Choate, Hall & Stewart, Boston, 1946-49; asso. Inc. Investors, 1949-64, v.p., 1953-64, treas., vice chmn., dir., 1954-64; treas., dir. Inc. Income Fund, 1954-64; v.p., dir. Winslow, Cohu and Stetson, Boston, 1964-69; sr. v.p. Weiss Voisin, 1969-73; account exec. H.C. Wainwright, 1973-78; corporator Provident Instn. for Savs., Boston; dir. Pyrotector, J. Ray McDermott & Co., Inc. Bd. overseers Boys' Clubs of Boston. Served as lt. comdr. USNR, World War II. Mem. C. of C. Home: Beverly, Mass. Died Feb. 7, 1978.

ALDRICH, JOHN ABRAM, coll. prof.; b. Clifford, Ont., Can., Mar. 3, 1878; s. Aaron and Mary Jane (Boulger) A.; brought to U.S. in infancy; A.B., Albion (Mich.) Coll., 1914; M.S., U. of Mich., 1915; Ph.D., 1923; m. Clara Belle Cady, June 24, 1916; children—Lyman Cady, Clare Aaron, Jane Carrier. Dep. collector and insp. customs, Port of Sault Ste. Marie, Mich., 1903-12; began teaching at Olivet Coll., 1916; prof. physics and astronomy, Washburn Coll., Topeka, Kan., 1918-25; prof. same, Oglethorpe U., 1925-43, also dean school of Science; prof. Mathematics, Potomac State School, Keyser, W.Va., 1943-48; professor physics, Lebanon Valley College since 1948. Fellow A.A.A.S.; member American Astronomical Soc., Sigma Xi. Conglist. Has specialized in work on cepheid variables. Author: Experimental Physics, Retired June 1950. Home: Climax, Mich. *

ALDRIDGE, FREDERICK FERDINAND, environ. engr.; b. Skoghole, Finland, Jan. 6, 1912; s. Albert Ferdinand and Selma Lindstedt (Soisalo) A.; came to U.S., 1914, naturalized, 1928; B.S., Mass. Inst. Tech., 1934; M.S., Harvard U., 1941; postgrad. U.S. Army Sch. Milt. Govt., U. Va., 1943; m. Jean Cairns Miller, Nov. 3, 1934; children—Karl Ferdinand, Ann Margaret Aldridge Dahl, John Frederick Ahlfors. Constrn. supr. Cambridge (Mass.) Engring. and Sewer Dept., 1936-39; san. engr. Mass. Dept. Pub. Health, 1939-41; san. engring. officer USPHS, 1941-47, 51-64, regional sanitation dir. UNRRA, Egypt, Palestine and Greece, 1944-45, chief san. engr., 1945-46, regional cons. Nat. Housing Agy., Dallas, 1946-47, chief san. engr. Tech. Cooperation Adminstrn. Mission to Iran, 1951-53, chief program engr., India, 1954-56, asst. regional engr., program dir. USPHS, HEW, San Francisco, 1956-59, chief san. engring. services div. Internat. Health, Washington, 1959-61, chief pub. health adviser U.S. AID mission to Libya, 1961-64, san. engr., dir. water supply and pollution control program Pacific N.W. region, 1964; dir. sanitation services Seattle-King County Dept. Pub. Health, 1947-51, dir. environ. mgmt., 1965-73; chief engr. Dade County (Fla.) Dept. Pub. Health, 1974-79; lectr. environ. engring. U. Wash., 1965-73, Fla. Internat. U., 1974-79; bd. dirs. U.S. Conf. Environ. Health Adminstrs., 1966-79, chmn., 1968; mem. com. on san. engring. NRC, 1946-47; mem. Wash. Environ. Council, 1966-73, Citizens for Clean Air, 1965-73. Mem. Seattle-King County Municipal League for Better Govt., 1965-73; mem. Puget Sound and King County Comprehensive Health Planning Council, chmn. environ. task force, 1969-73. Served from 1st lt. to col. USPHS, World War II, Korea. Recipient Commendation medal USPHS, 1964; registered profl. engr., Mass., Wash., Fla. Diplomate Am. Acad. Environ. Engrs. Fellow Am. Pub. Health Assn. (governing council); mem. Am. Pub. Works Assn., Nat. Soc. Profl. Engrs., Am. Water Works Assn., Nat. Sanitation Found. (council pub. health consultants 1977-79), Am. Acad. Pub. Health Adminstrs., Inter-Am. Assn. San. Engring., Nat. Environ. Health Assn., Nat. Air Pollution Control Assn., Fla. Pub. Health Assn., Fla. Engring. Soc. Contbr. articles to profl. jours. Home: Naranja Lakes, Fla. Died June 2, 1979.

ALESSANDRO, VICTOR NICHOLAS, symphony condr.; b. Waco, Tex., Nov. 27, 1915; s. Victor and Josephine (Kemendo) A.; Mus.B., U. Rochester, 1937, Mus.D. (hon.), 1948; L.H.D., So. Meth. U., 1956; student Mozarteum Acad., Salzburg, Austria, 1937, Santa Cecilia Acad., Rome, Italy, 1938; Mus.D. (hon.), Southwestern U., 1975; m. Ruth Drisko, May 1, 1955; children—Victor Tabbut, Ruth Ann. Mus. dir. Oklahoma City Symphony, 1938-51, San Antonio Symphony Orch. and San Antonio Grand Opera Festival, 1951; guest condr. Oslo Philharmonic, 1968, Turku (Finland) Symphony, 1970, Helsinki Symphony, 1971, Nat. Radio Symphony of Portugal, 1972, others. Recipient Alice M. Ditson award Columbia, 1956, Nat. Music Council award, 1964. Mem. Internat. Alliance Theatrical and Stage Employees (hon.), Am. Fedn. Musicals (hon.), Bruckner Soc. Am. (hon.), Phi Mu Alpha (hon.). Club: Torch (San Antonio). Home: San Antonio, Tex. Died Nov. 27, 1976.

ALEXANDER, ALBERT VICTOR (VISCOUNT ALEXANDER OF HILLSBOROUGH), cabinet minister; born at Weston-super-Mare, England, May 1, 1885; son of Albert Alexander; ed. Barton Hill Elementary Sch., Bristol, and evening continuation classes; m. Esther Ellen Chapple, June 6, 1908; 1 dau., Beatrix (Mrs. Bernard Evison). With Somerset County Council Edn. Com., 1903, advancing to chief clerk of higher edn.; became sec. Parliamentary Com. of Cooperative Congress, 1920; member of parliament (Labour Party) for Hillsborough Div. of Sheffield, 1922-31 and since 1935; parliamentary sec. Bd. of Trade, 1924; first lord of the admiralty, 1929-31 and 1940-46; minister of defense, 1947-50; cr. Viscount Alexander of Hillsborough, 1950; Chancellor of Duchy of Lancaster, 1950. Decorated Companion of Honour, 1941; Freeman of Weston-super-Mare, 1943; hon. LL.D., Bristol U., 1945, Sheffield U., 1947. Baptist.*

ALEXANDER, ARCHIBALD STEVENS, lawyer; born in N.Y.C., Oct. 28, 1906; s. Archibald Stevens and Helen Tracy (Barney) A.; A.B., Princeton, 1928; LL.B., Harvard, 1931; m. Susanne Dimock Tilton, June, 1929 (dec. 1935); children—Helen Barney, Archibald Stevens, Susan Tilton; m. 2d, Jean Struthers Sears, Aug. 1937; children—Jean Sears, Emily Whitney. Admitted to N.Y. bar, 1932; asso. Carter, Ledyard & Milburn, N.Y. City, 1931-40, partner, 1940-49; pub. mem. Fgn. Service Selection Bd., State Dept., 1947; spl. report on security and personnel problems A.E.C., 1947; asst. sec., Army, 1949, under sec., 1950-52; state treasurer of New Jersey, 1954-55; director New York Casualty Co., 1941-49, Hoboken (N.J.) Land & Improvement Co., 1931-48, Hoboken R.R. Warehouse & Steamship Connecting Co., 1931-47, First Nat. Bank Hoboken, 1931-33. Mem. Borough Council, bd. edn., Bernardsville, N.J., Central Atlantic Area Bd. Y.M.C.A.; mem., vice chmn. bd. govs., Rutgers U., formerly chairman. Member New Jersey Commn. on State Tax Policy, from 1956, chmn., from 1962; dir. Free Europe Com., Inc., N.Y.C., from 1959, pres., 1959-61. Chmn. the N.J. delegation to Democratic National Conv., 1948; Dem. candidate U.S. Senate, N.J., 1948, 52; dir. volunteers for Stevenson: Kefauver (Nat. Hdqrs., 1956). Trustee N.Y. Zool. Soc., St. Paul's Sch., Concord, N.H., 1949-53, bd. mgrs. N.J. Reformatory, Annandale, N.J. 1940-49. Served as 1st lt. to lt. col., U.S. Army, active duty E.T.O. and M.T.O., 1942-45. Episcopalian. Democrat. Clubs: Links, Lunch (N.Y.C.); Somerset Hills (Somerville); Ivy (Princeton). Address: Bernardsville, N.J. Died Sept. 4, 1979.

ALEXANDER, BENJAMIN, physician, educator; b. Boston, Mar. 20, 1909; s. Harry and Ida (Shumann) A.; A.B., Harvard U., 1930, M.D., 1934; m. Marie Martha Mayer, June 25, 1937; children—Millard Henry, Judith Lee, Robert Eugene. Intern, Beth Israel Hosp., 1935, staff physician, 1939-66; teaching, traveling fellow Harvard U., 1936-38, asso. prof. medicine, 1953-66; teaching and research in medicine specializing in hematology, Boston, 1939-66, N.Y.C., 1966-78; sr. investigator N.Y. Blood Center, 1966-78; asso. dir. ednl. programs N.Y. Blood Center, 1975-78; clin. prof. medicine Cornell U., 1966-76; cons. Meml. Hosp., 1966-78; attending physician N.Y. Hosp., 1967-76. Mem. Am. Soc. Clin. Investigation, Am. Chem. Soc., Am. Soc. Biol. Chemists, Assn. Am. Physicians, Interurban Clin. Club (emeritus), Am. Acad. Arts and Scis. Contbr. articles to profl. jours. Home: New York, N.Y. Died Feb. 13, 1978.

ALEXANDER, EBEN ROY, journalist; b. Omaha, Feb. 15, 1899; s. Hollis Williams and Rosemary (Conroy) A.; A.B., St. Louis U., 1918; m. Mary Louise Webb, July 9, 1927; children—Mary Patricia (Mrs. Wm. LaMothe), Eben Roy, Rosemary Conroy, Harriet Allison (Mrs. Edward Garzero), Charles Calvert, Stephen Winthrop, Hollis Williams. Member of the editorial staff St. Louis Star, 1921-24, St. Louis Post-Dispatch, 1924-39; contributing editor, Time mag., N.Y. City, 1939, managing editor 1949-60, editor from 1960. Gunnery sergeant, U.S.M.C., 1918-19; second lieutenant, Inf. Res., U.S. Army, 1921-31; 2d lt., Air Corps, Mo. N.G., 1931; disch. as major, 1939. Mem.

Aviation Writers Assn. Club: Manhasset Bay Yacht. Home: Sands Point, L.I., N.Y. Died Oct. 30, 1978.

ALEXANDER, (EDWARD) GORDON, biologist; b. Rich Hill, Mo., Aug. 18, 1901; s. James Edward and Mary Effie (Gordon) A.; A.B., Central Coll., 1923; A.M., Princeton, 1926, Ph.D., 1931; m. Marion Frances Isely, September 2, 1926; children—Mary Anne (Mrs. Richard L. Bingham), Douglas Gordon. Asst. prof., biology, Central Coll., Fayette, Mo., 1926-28; visiting prof. biology, Chulalongkorn U., Bangkok, Siam, 1928-30; asso. prof. biology, U. Colo., 1931-39, prof., 1939-66, emeritus, from 1966, head of department, 1939-58; Fulbright lecturer Chulalongkorn U., Bangkok, Thailand, 1956-57. Fellow A.A.A.S. (elected 50-yr. mem. 1971); mem. Soc. Study Evolution, Ecol. Soc. Am., Entomol. Soc. Am., Am. Ornithol. Union, Colo.-Wyo. Acad. Scis. (pres. 1963-64), Sigma Xi. Author: Biology, 9th edit., 1970; other textbooks and articles in biology; research, ecology of mountains. Home: Boulder, Colo. Died July 31, 1971; cremated.

ALEXANDER, JOHN GORDON, lawyer; b. Buffalo, Aug. 5, 1904; s. William Gordon and Margaret (Crotty) A.; A.B., Princeton, 1926; LL.B., Harvard, 1933; m. Rachel Sheldon, Nov. 25th, 1964; children—John Gordon, Cecily. Admitted to N.Y. bar, 1933, D.C. bar, 1947; practiced in Buffalo, 1933-41, Washington, 1947-50; counsel Navy Dept., 1941-44, War Assets Adminstrn., 1944-46, gen. counsel, 1946-47; gen. counsel Nat. Prodn. Authority, Washington, 1951; asso. counsel Olin Mathieson Chem. Corp., 1953-56, asst. gen. counsel, 1956-60, sec., 1960-69. Home: Irvington, Va. Died Nov. 7, 1976; interred Christ Ch. Burial Ground, Lancaster County, Va.

ALEXANDER, LEROY MONTGOMERY, steel co. exec.; b. Slater, Mo., Nov. 17, 1906; s. Roy Ancell and May L. (Montgomery) A.; extension student U. Kan., also U. Mo. at Kansas City; m. Arlene Bertino, Jan. 1, 1941; children—Judith Lee (Mrs. Bruce J. Freshwater), Susan Lynne (Mrs. David W. Shubert), Cynthia Jane (Mrs. William P. Holmes). Mgr. sales Boltand Nut div. Sheffield Steel Corp., 1925-60; mgr. bolt and forged products Armco Steel Corp., 1960-67, dir. sales Western Mill Products, 1967-72. Bd. dirs. Kansas City (Mo.) chpt. Am. Cancer Soc. Mem. Indsl. Fasteners Inst. (exec. com. 1957-64, v.p. 1965, chmn. bd. govs. 1966-76), Am. Ordnance Assn. (dir. Midwest post). Presbyn. (ruling elder). Home: Bella Vista, Ark. Died Aug. 19, 1976; interred Benton County Meml. Cemetery, Bentonville, Ark.

ALEXANDER, NORMAN DALE, librarian; b. Lead, S.D., Dec. 8, 1929; s. George Nelson and Emma Marie A.; B.A., U. Nebr., 1956; M.A., U. Denver, 1957; M.Ed. in Adminstrn., U. So. Calif., 1973, Ph.D., 1975; m. Lois Irene Eddy, Sept. 4, 1955; children—Candace Jo, Roanne Jean, Shane Nelson. Librarian, Centralia (Wash.) Jr. Coll., 1957-58; reference librarian Mont. State U., Bozeman, 1958-62; asst. to dir. libraries U. Minn., 1962-63; head library pub. services Portland (Oreg.) State U., 1963-67; library dir. So. Oreg. State Coll., Ashland, 1967-76; library dir. Calif. Poly. State U., San Luis Obispo, 1976-79; chmn. interinstl. library council Oreg. System Higher Edn., 1973-76. Served with U.S. Army, 1948-52. Decorated Bronze Star; U.S. Office Edn. fellow, 1970-72; Carpenter Found. grantee, 1972. Mem. Am. (council 1972-74), Pacific N.W. (pres. 1975-76, hon. life mem. 1976), Oreg. (pres. 1970), Calif. library assns., Coll. and Research Libraries, Theta Chi. Republican. Presbyn. Club: Rotary. Contbr. articles to profl. jours. Home: San Luis Obispo, Calif. Died Jan. 18, 1979.

ALEXANDER, PAUL JULIUS, educator, historian; b. Berlin, Germany, May 12, 1910; s. Carl and Anna (Mauthner) A.; Dr. iur., U. Hamburg (Germany), 1932; licence en droit, U. Paris (France), 1934; Ph.D. in History, Harvard, 1940; m. Eleanor Eyck, June 21, 1938; children—Ann Margaret, Lawrence Ernest, Michael Charles. Came to U.S., 1935, naturalized, 1943. Prof. history Hobart Coll., 1945-54; prof. history, chmn. dept. Brandeis U., 1954-58; prof. history U. Mich., 1958-68; prof. history and comparative lit. U. Calif., Berkeley, 1968-77, Research analyst OSS, 1943-45. Fulbright-Hayes research fellow, Italy, 1965-66; Guggenheim fellow, 1951-52, 65-66. Author: The Patriarch Nicephorus of Constantinople, 1958; Gregorii Nysseni Opera Omnia, VO. V, 1962; The Oracle of Baalbek, 1967; Religious and Political History and Thought in the Byzantine Empire, 1978. Home: Berkeley, Calif. Died Dec. 16, 1977.

ALEXANDER, ROGER GORDON, army officer; b. Paris, Mo., Aug. 1, 1883; s. Cicero and Ellen Maria (Carter) A.; student Mo. State Univ., 1900-02; B.S., U.S. Mil. Acad., 1907; grad. Engr. Sch., 1912, grad. Army War Coll., 1920; m. Ruth Baldwin, May 22, 1917; children—Ruth (Mrs. Bradish J. Smith), Roger Gordon. Commd. 2d lt. Corps of Engrs., U.S. Army, 1907, and advanced through grades to brig. gen., July 1946; served with engr. troops, Cuba, 1907-09; at Washington Barracks and Engr. Sch., 1909-12; instr. of practical mil. engring., U.S. Mil. Acad., 1912-16; asst. in 1st U.S. Engr. Dist., New York, N.Y., 1916-17; arrived in France on Gen. Pershing's staff, June 1917; chief of G-2-C, G.H.Q., A.E.F. in charge of map service (29th engrs.) and sound and flash ranging services (74th engrs.), 1917-19; head of dept. of drawing (later dept. of mil. topography and graphics) U.S. Mil. Acad., 1920-45, acting dean, 1945-46, dean, 1946-47. Decorated Distinguished Service medal, Legion of Merit; Order of St. Michael and St. George (Great Brit.); Legion of Honor, France. Home: Goshen, N.Y. *

ALFARO, RICARDO JOAQUIN, diplomat, statesman; b. Panama, Republic of Panama, Aug. 20, 1882; s. Luis R. and Hortensia (Jovane) A.; ed. Balboa Coll. U. Cartagena, Colombia, LL.D., Nat. Faculty Law, Panama, U. So. Cal.; m. Amelia Lyons, Oct. 28, 1905; children—Victor, Ivan, Rogelio, Amelita, Yolanda. Asst. sec. foreign affairs, Panama, 1905; counselor Panama Legation, Washington, D.C., 1912; mem. Code Commn., Panama, 1913; mem. U.S. Panama Joint Land Commn., 1915; premier of cabinet of Panama, 1918-22; M.P. from Panama to U.S., 1922-30, 1933-36; 1st v.p. Rep. of Panama, 1928-30, president, 1931-32; mem. Permanent Ct. of Arbitration, The Hague, 1929—; chmn. Panama delegation Gen. Assembly, UN, 1946, 47, 48, 49; mem. Internat. Law Commn., UN from 1948, chmn., 1952-53. Founder mem. Am. Inst. Internat. Law (sec. gen. 1938—). Prof. civil law Nat. Sch. of Law, 1917-22; prof. internat. law U. Panama, 1948. Mem. bd. dirs. Gorgas Meml. Inst., Washington. Recipient numerous decorations and honors from fgn. countries in the Americas and in Europe. Mem. learned socs. in Panama and fgn. countries. Author of books, 1908—; including: Dictionary of Anglicisms, 1950; The Question of an International Criminal Jurisdiction, 1950; The Question of Definition of Aggression, 1951. Address: Panama, Rep. of Panama. *

ALFONTE, JAMES R. (AL-FONT'), army officer; born Ind., Dec. 7, 1886; grad. Q.M. Corps Motor Transport Sch., 1921, Q.M. Corps Sch., 1927, Command and Gen. Staff Sch., 1930, Chem. Warfare Sch., Field Officers Course, 1937, Army War Coll., 1938; married Mary Gates Redmond; children—Mary Gates (wife of Lt. Comdr. Harold Lee Graham, Jr.), James Morehead (lt., Field Artillery, U.S. Army, Commd. 2d lt. Inf., U.S. Army, Oct. 1911; transferred to Q.M. Corps as capt. 1920, and advanced through the grades to brig. gen., June 1942; served as major, World War I; Q.M. Generals Office since June 1942. Awarded Purple Heart; Legion of Merit, Jan. 1946. Home: Washington, D.C. *

ALGER, MARY DONLON (MRS. MARTIN J. ALGER), judge; b. Utica, N.Y.; d. Joseph M. and Mary (Coughlin) Donlon; LL.B., Cornell U., 1921; LL.D., Skidmore Coll., 1947; Litt. D., Nazareth Coll., 1951, Marquette U., 1961; m. Martin J. Alger, 1971. Admitted to N.Y. State bar 1921, since practiced in N.Y.; mem. firm Burke and Burke, N.Y.C., 1928-44. Apptd. chmn. State Indsl. Bd., N.Y., 1944, chmn. State Workmen's Compensation Bd., 1945-55; apptd. by Pres. Eisenhower judge U.S. Customs Ct., 1955, sr. judge, 1966-77. Guest West Germany govt. for tour Germany, 1952. Trustee Cornell U., 1937-77; mem. adv. council on social security 80th Congress. Mary Donlon Workmen's Compensation Fund, lectures, N.Y. Stafe Sch. Indsl. and Labor Relations, Cornell U., 1945. Dormitory at Cornell U. named in her honor. Mem. Am., N.Y.C. bar assns., N.Y. County Lawyer's Assn., Internat. Assn. Indsl. Accidents Bds. and Commns. (pres. 1948), AAUW, Fedn. Bus. and Profl. Women (rep. Rep. Nat. Conv., 1952). Republican (co-mgr. Dewey-for-Gov. campaign, 1942; nat. adv. com. Citizens for Eisenhower, 1952; N.Y. State del.-at-large, Rep. Nat. convs., 1944, 48). Club: Cosmopolitan. Home: Tucson, Ariz. Died Mar. 5, 1977.

ALGER, PHILIP LANGDON, elec. engr., educator; b. Washington, Jan. 27, 1894; s. Philip Rounseville and Louisa (Taylor) A.; B.S., St. John's Coll., Md., 1912, A.M., 1916; B.S., Mass Inst. Tech., 1915; M.S., Union Coll., Schenectady, 1920; D.Engring., U. Colo., 1968; m. Catharine E. Jackson, June 30, 1918 (dec. Sept. 1945); children—Augusta Jordan (Mrs. David C. Prince, Jr.), John Rodgers Meigs, Andrew Dugald Langdon, Ann Vogdes (Mrs. Gert Ehrlich); m. 2d, Helen Jackson Hubbell (dec. Nov. 1974). Asst. instr., research asst. Mass. Inst. Tech., 1916-17; induction motor engring. dept., alternating current engring. dept., staff asst. to mgr. engring. apparatus dept. Gen. Electric Co., 1919-51, cons. engr. motor dept., 1951-58; adj. prof. elec. engring. Rensselaer Poly. Inst., 1958-70. U.S. del. plenary meeting Internat. Electrotech. Commn., Torquay, Eng., 1938. Chmn., Schenectady Charter League which sponsored adoption city mgr. govt., 1934; dir. Mohawk Devel. Service, Schenectady Bur. Municipal Research. Served as lt., ordnance dept. U.S. Army, 1917-19. Philip L. Alger award for excellence in rotating machinery design established by Gen. Electric Co., 1981; Philip L. Alger fund in engring. ethics established by Rensselaer Poly. Inst. Fellow I.E.E.E. (Lamme medal 1958), Instn. Elec. Engrs., Am. Soc. Quality Control, ASME, A.A.A.S.; mem. Am. Ordnance Assn., Am. Soc. Engring. Edn., Nat. Municipal League, Am. Math. Soc., Newcomen Soc., N.Y. State Soc. Profl. Engrs., Am. Philatelic Soc., Société Français des Electriciens, Am. Legion, United World Federalists, Va. Soc. Cin., Sigma Xi, Eta Kappa Nu (eminent mem.), Tau Beta Pi (eminent mem.). Author: The Nature of Polyphase Induction Machines, 1951; Mathematics for Science and Engineering, 1957, also Japanese edit.; The Nature of Induction Machines, 1965; Induction Machines, Their Behavior and Uses, 1970; The Human Side of Engineering, 1972; Tales of My Life and Family, 1974; More Tales of my Life and Family, 1977; also tech. articles sci. mags. Co-author: Ethical Problems in Engineering, 1965. Co-compiler: Steinmetz-The Philosopher, 1965. Editor: The Life and Times of Gabriel Kron, 1969. Profl. papers held at Union Coll. Library, Schenectady. Home: Schenectady, N.Y. Died Sept. 24, 1979; interred Crestview Cemetery, Schenectady.

ALGREN, NELSON, author; b. Detroit, Mar. 28, 1909; B.A., U. Ill., 1931. Author: Somebody in Boots, 1935; Never Come Morning, 1942; The Neon Wilderness, 1947; The Man with the Golden Arm, 1949; Chicago City on the Make, 1951; A Walk on the Wild Side, 1958; The Chateau at Sunset, or It's a Mad World, Master Copperfield, 1959; Neon Wilderness, 1960; Who Lost an American, 1963; Notes from a Sea Diary, 1965; The Last Carousel, 1973; Short Stories in O. Henry Meml; editor: (with Jack Conroy) The New Anvil; Lonesome Monsters, 1963; works appeared Awards Vols., 1935, 41, Best Am. Short Stories (Foley), 1942-45, Story Anthology, 1933-34; contbr. short fiction to popular mags. Served with AUS, 1942-45. Nat. Inst. Arts and Letters fellow, 1947; Newberry Library fellow, 1950; recipient Nat. Book award, 1950. Home: Sag Harbor, N.Y. Died May 9, 1981.

ALLAN, FRANK NATHANIEL, physician; b. Proton, Ont., Can., Dec. 26, 1899; s. George and Margaret Jane (Ewing) A.; M.B., U. Toronto, 1922, B.Sc. in Medicine, 1924, M.D. cum laude with award of Starr Silver Medal, 1928; m. Lillian Hunter Christie, Sept. 22, 1934; 1 dau., Margaret Christie (Mrs. W. Stephen Piper). Jr. mem. staff, dept. physiology U. Toronto, 1922-25; intern Toronto Gen. Hosp., 1924-25; fellow medicine Mayo Clinic, Rochester, Minn., 1925-26, staff, 1927-32; instr. medicine Mayo Found., U. Minn., 1928-32; hon. physician New Eng. Bapt. Hosp., Boston City Hosp., New Eng. Deaconess Hosp., Boston; co-dir. med. dept. Lahey Clinic, Boston, 1932-47, exec. dir., chmn., 1948-65; asso. clin. prof. med. Boston U., 1961-72, past pres. staff assn.; clin. prof. medicine Georgetown U., 1966-72; sr. cons. U.S. FDA, 1965-77. Mem. exec. com. Internat. Congress Internal Medicine, Phila., 1958; coordinator Internat. Congress on Antimicrobial Drugs, CENTO, AID, Izmir, Turkey, 1975. Awarded Banting medal Am. Diabetes Assn., 1953. Diplomate Am. Bd. Internal Medicine. Fellow A.C.P., AAAS; mem. AMA, Greater Boston Diabetes Soc. (chmn. exec. com. 1961-63), Am. (pres. 1952-53), New Eng. (pres. 1951-52, hon. pres. 1968—, Joslin medal 1969) diabetes assns., Acad. Medicine Washington, Am. Soc. Clin. Investigation, Am. Soc. Exptl. Pathology, Endocrine Soc., Internat., Am., Mass. socs. internal medicine, Canadian Diabetic Assn. (hon.), Central Soc., Clin. Research, Academia Nacional de Medicina Buenos Aires (hon.), Sigma Xi, Alpha Omega Alpha. Conglist. (moderator Old South Ch., Boston). Clubs: Brae Burn Country, Skating of Boston (bd. govs. 1965-68). Founding editor: Diabetes jour., 1951-55, then adv. editor; editorial bd. New Eng. Jour. Medicine, 1952-68, dep. editor, 1965-66. Author med., sci. articles. Home: Boston, Mass. Died July 12, 1977.

ALLAWAY, HOWARD, editor, writer; b. Homer, Nebr., Jan. 3, 1912; s. James and Mary (Adams) A.; A.B., U. Nebr., 1933; M.Sc., Columbia, 1936; m. Jean Dix, Aug. 13, 1938; children—Elizabeth, James, Thomas. With Asso. Press, N.Y.C., 1936-40; picture editor, city editor, nat. editor, news editor PM, N.Y.C., 1940-48; asso. editor Popular Sci. Monthly, 1948-50, mng. editor, 1951-57, editor, 1957-62; mng. editor Consumer Reports mag., Mt. Vernon, N.Y., 1962-63; asst. to Sunday editor N.Y. Times, 1950-51; dep. dir., tech. publs. div. NASA, 1963-64, dep. dir. sci. and tech. info. div., 1965-66, pub. affairs officer space sci., manned flight, space applications, 1966-76. Mem. Bd. Edn. Stamford (Conn.), 1955-58; mem. bd. finance, Stamford, 1960-63. Served as lt. (s.g.) USNR, 1943-45. Recipient Exceptional Service medal NASA, 1973. Mem. Council Advancement Science Writing, Mag. Pubs. Assn. (chmn. editoral com. 1960-62), Phi Beta Kappa, Sigma Delta Chi, Kappa Tau Alpha, Tau Kappa Epsilon. Unitarian. Author: The Space Shuttle at Work, 1979. Home: Canton, Mass. Died July 31, 1980.

ALLEN, ALBERT CHARLES, exec. vice pres. United Cigar Stores; b. Rockaway, N.J., June 13, 1883; s. Thomas and Amelia (Engleman) A.; ed. high sch.; m. Claribel Kinley, of Olean, New York, May 17, 1917; children—Albert Charles, James Kinley. Exec. vice pres. United Cigar Stores Co.; pres. New York Advertising Co.; dir. Reiss Premier Pipe Co., Kaufman Bros. & Bondy, United Retail Chemists Corpn. Methodist. Clubs: Advertising, Rye Country, Westchester County. Home: Rye, N.Y.

ALLEN, BURRELL CLINTON, naval officer; b. Ottawa, Kan., Sept. 2, 1881; s. Willis Clinton and Ida (Butler) A.; grad. U.S. Naval Acad., 1901, Naval War Coll., 1929, Army War Coll., 1930; m. Selma Mertz, Oct. 22, 1907; children—Burrell Clinton (officer U.S. Navy), Willis Mertz. Commd. ensign, U.S. Navy, 1901, and advanced through the grades to rear adm.; comd. U.S.S. Sampson, U.S.S. Dent (World War I), U.S.S. Rappahannock, U.S.S. Rochester, also destroyer divisions and squadron; served as head dept. elec. engring., U.S. Naval Acad., Annapolis, Md.; with mil. govt., Guam and Nicaragua; lecturer Sch. of Mil. Govt., Stanford U.; editor, U.S. Naval Inst., 1915-16; chief of staff Western Sea Frontier, 1943-45. Decorated Navy Cross, Legion of Merit (U.S.), Pour le Merite (Nicaragua), Meriot Naval (Mexico). Mem. Naval Inst. Home: La Jolla, Calif. *

ALLEN, CLIFFORD ROBERTSON, congressman; b. Jacksonville, Fla., Jan. 6, 1912; s. Clifford Robertson and Suzanne Blake (Kelley) A.; LL.B., Cumberland U., Lebanon, Tenn., 1931; m. Nancy Louise Nelson, June 28, 1931; children—Clifford Allen, III (dec.), Suzanne Allen Puckett, Nancy Lee Allen Woods, Robert N., Patricia Ann, Allen Arnold. Admitted to Tenn. bar, 1931; tax cons., atty., accountant, Nashville 1936-60; mem. Tenn. Senate from Davidson County, 1949-50, 55-56, 57-58; met. assessor of property Nashville and Davidson County, 1960-75; mem. 94th-95th Congresses from 5th Dist. Tenn.; mem. Tenn. Tax Study Commn., 1966-67; del. Tenn. Constl. Conv., 1970. Recipient J.C. Napier award Middle Tenn. Bus. Assn., 1975; Humanitarian award Souls Unltd. Civic Club, 1976; named Hero, Consumer Fedn. Am., 1976. Mem. Tenn., Nashville bar assns., Nashville Area C. of C., Tenn. State Soc. (pres. 1977); hon. life mem. Internat. Assn. Assessing officers (pres. 1969-70; Most Valuable Mem. award 1966, McCarren award 1966). Democrat. Methodist. Clubs: Elks, Oddfellows. Home: Nashville, Tenn. Died June 18, 1978.

ALLEN, CUTHBERT EDWARD, ednl. adminstr., clergyman; b. Manchester, N.H., Apr. 28, 1906; s. Arthur Bernard and Mary Anne (McMahan) A.; A.B., Belmont Abbey Coll., 1929; M.A., Cath. U. Am., 1935; postgrad. U. N.C.; LL.D., St. Vincent's Coll., 1950. Professed as Benedictine monk, 1927, ordained priest Roman Catholic Ch., 1933; instr. history and sociology Belmont Abbey Coll., 1929-36, prof., 1936-77, rector, v.p., 1936-42, 45-47, dean, 1947-54, pres., 1956-60, vice chancellor, after 1960, now exec. v.p.; pastor, Gastonia, N.C., 1933-35. Mem. N.C. Com. on Elementary Edn., 1950-55. Mem. nat. commn. NCCJ, 1948-56; bd. dirs. ARC; chmn. Health Facilities Commn. Belmont. Recipient Silver medallion, mem. Nat. Honor Corps, NCCJ; Benemerenti Papal award for outstanding service to ch. and edn., 1975. Mem. Belmont C. of C. (dir.), So. Assn. Colls. and Secondary Schs. (mem. commn. colls. and univs. 1948-55), Colls. and Univs. N.C. (pres.), Am., Am. Cath. hist. assns., Am., Am. Cath. sociol. socs., Charlotte Philos. Soc., Delta Epsilon Sigma, Pi Gamma Mu. Clubs: Charlotte City, Gastonia Country. Author: Catholic Newspapers During Civil War, 1860-65, 1936. Address: Belmont, N.C. Died Dec. 1, 1977; interred Belmont Abbey.

ALLEN, EDWARD FRANK, editor, author; b. Newark, N.J., June 9, 1885; s. Frank R. and Jane (Ayres) A.; ed. pub. and pvt. schs.; m. Vera Reed, Oct. 27, 1915; 1 son, Bruce Reed. Reporter Ontario Repository-Messenger, Canandaigua, N.Y., 1904; began contbg. to New York Times review of books, 1906; mng. editor Bohemian Mag., 1908; pub. Book News Service, 1909; editor Travel, 1910-14, Lippincott's Mag., 1914-15, McBride's Mag., 1915-16, Travel, 1916-17. Literary adviser to Robert M. McBride & Co. Spl. rep. War and Navy Depts. Commns. on Training Camp Activities, 1917-18; editor The Nat. Marine, 1918-19 and 1920-21; publicity and literary mgr. J. B. Pond Lyceum Bur., 1919-1920; served as editor Longmans, Green & Co., pubs.; Pacific Coast rep. Longmans, Green & Co., and Payson & Clarke, Ltd.; editor The Midwest Co., pubs., 1929-32; dir. of pub. relations, The Women's Screen Guild, 1933; asso. editor of Popular Science Monthly, 1944-46; associate editor Collier's Encyclopedia, New York City, 1949-50. Compiler: A Dictionary of Abbreviations, 1946; A Pocket Treasury of Supersititions, 1948. Contbr. to The Dial, Outing, Newspaper Feature Service, Scribner's, The Century, Crty. Life. Address: N.Y.C. *

ALLEN, EDWARD WEBER, lawyer; b. Oshkosh, Wis., May 12, 1885; s. Thomas Scott and Natalia (Weber) A.; student Oshkosh State Normal Sch., 1892-1903, U. Chgo., 1903-05; J.D., U. Wash., 1909; m. Hazel Rebecca Conner, June 1, 1915; children—Natalia (Mrs. George E. McSpadden), Thomas. Admitted to Wash. bar, 1909; with Wright & Kelleher, Seattle, 1909-12; dep. pros. atty. Pacific County, mem. Hewen & Allen, 1913-14; asst. atty. gen., Washington, 1914-16; now counsel DeGarmo, Leedy, Oles & Morrison, Seattle. U.S. commr., chmn. or sec. Internat. Fisheries Commn., 1932-55; U.S. commr. Internat. Salmon Fisheries Comm. 1937-51; ex-chmn., adviser U.S. del. UN FAO, Baguio, P.I., 1948, Washington, 1948, 49; mem. Gen. MacArthur Fisheries Mission to Japan, 1949; adviser U.S. del. to Tokyo to negotiate N. Pacific Fisheries Commn. 1954-76, U.S. del. UN Fishery Conv., Rome, 1955, U.S. del. UN Conf., Law the Sea, Geneva, 1958, U.S. delegation Ottawa Fisheries between U.S., Can., Japan, 1964. Served with OSS, 1942-45. Awarded Alumnus Summa Laude Dignatus, U. Wash., 1947. Fellow Am. Bar Found.; mem. Am. (ex-chmn. internat. law sect.), Internat., Wash. (pres. 1929-30), Seattle bar assns., Pacific N.W. Trade Assn., Am. Law Inst., Am. Soc. Internat. Law, Inst. World Polity, Seattle C. of C. (chmn. Alaska com. 4 yrs.), Wash. (trustee; Capt. Gray medal 1975), Seattle (trustee) hist. socs., Bibliog. Soc. Am., Wash. S.A.R. (pres. 1937-38), Mountaineers (sec. or v.p. 16 yrs., exec. com. 1919-29), U. Wash. Law Alumni Assn. (pres. 1920-22), Japan Soc., Order of Coif (hon.), Phi Gamma Delta, Delta Chi. Republican. Episcopalian. Mason (32, Shriner). Clubs: Rainier, Mountaineers, Laurelhurst Community, China, World Trade (pres., 1954-56) (Seattle); Bohemian (San Francisco); Explorers (N.Y.C.); Cosmos (Washington). Author: North Pacific, 1936; Dancing Tails and Other Fishy Jingles, 1951; The Vanishing Frenchman, The Mysterious Disappearance of Laperouse, 1959; The Rollicking Pacific, 1972. Contbr. articles to profl. jours. Home: Seattle, Wash. Died Mar. 15, 1976.

ALLEN, EMIL WILLIAM, JR., librarian; b. Raymond, N.H., Mar. 4, 1926; s. Emil William and Thelma Mae (Brown) A.; A.B., Bowdoin Coll., 1950; M.L.S., Pratt Inst., 1952; m. Anna Marilyn Coviello, Feb. 12, 1955; children—Mark Vincent, Megan Elizabeth, Rachel Ann. With sci. div. Bklyn. Pub. Library, 1952-53, stack curator, 1953-54; chief bus. and industry div. Ferguson Library, Stamford, Conn., 1955-56; asst. state librarian N.H. Library, Concord, 1956-64, state librarian, 1964-75. Sec., N.H. Library Commn., 1964-75; chmn. New Eng. Interstate Library Compact Bd., 1967-72, treas., 1972-75; cons. S.C. State Library, 1970. Dir. Saban Electric Co. Mem. Warner Town budget com., 1962-68, 70-72, chmn., 1966-68; mem. Kearsarge Coop. Sch. Dist. planning bd., 1964-66, Kearsarge Regional Sch. Bd., 1966-69; treas. New Eng. Library Bd., 1972—, New Eng. Document Conservation Center, 1972-75; mem. Warner Cemetery Commn., 1970—; precinct commnr. Warner Village Fire Dist., 1971-72. Trustee Concord Hosp.; exec. bd. New Eng. Library Information Network, 1972-73; bd. dirs. Concord Mental Health Center, 1969-71. Served with AUS, 1944-46, USAF, 1950-51. Mem. Am. Soc. Pub. Adminstrn., Am. (council 1965-69), New Eng. (pres. 1965-66), N.H. library assns., Am. Library Trustees Assn. (v.p. 1969-70), N.H. Library Council, Audubon Soc. N.H., Warner Hist. Soc., Soc. Protection N.H. Forests, N.H. Hist. Assn., Am. Civil Liberties Union, N.H. Meml. Soc. (pres. 1967-69), Republican. Unitarian. Kiwanian (pres. Concord 1962). Club: Bowdoin of N.H. Home: Warner, N.H. Died May 1975.

ALLEN, FRANCIS V., bishop; b. Toronto, Can., June 25, 1909; s. Valentine and Martha (Malcolm) A.; ed. St. Augustine's Sem. Ordained priest Roman Cath. Ch.; asst. St. Dunstan's Parish. Toronto. 1933-34, Blessed Sacrament Parish, Toronto, 1934-35; sec. St. Augustine's Sem., 1935-36; vice chancellor in Temporalibus, 1936-41; v.p. Cath. Ch. Extension Soc., 1941-42; chancellor in Spirtaulibus, 1942-48, in Spirtaulibus et Temporalibus, 1948-51; domestic prelate, 1946; vicar delegate for religious, archidiocesan consulator, 1951-52; pastor Our Lady of Sorrows Parish. Toronto, 1952-54; aux. biship, vicar gen. archdiocese of Toronto. Home: Toronto, Ont., Can. Died Oct. 7, 1977; interred Mt. Hope Cemetery.

ALLEN, FRANK EMMETT, clergyman; b. Morning Sun, Ia., Aug. 7, 1884; s. Robert John and Grace (Wilson) A.; prep. edn., high sch., Morning Sun; A.B., Geneva Coll., Beaver Falls, Pa., 1906 (winner tri-state oratorical contest); grad. Ref. Presbyn. Theol. Sem., Pittsburgh, Pa., 1911; m. Mary Ellen Dodds, of Seattle, Wash., May 4, 1911; children—Mary Grace, Marjorie Elizabeth, Teacher of science, high sch., Sagauche, Colo., 1907, Amity Coll., College Springs, Ia., 1907-08; ordained ministry Ref. Presbyn. Ch. of N.A., 1911; pastor successively Glenwood, Minn., Superior, Nebr., and Winnipeg, Can., until 1926, Hopkinton, Ia., since 1927. Mem. Speakers' Bur. Bryan Memorial Univ. Assn., 1926. Author: Practical Lectures on the Book of Job, 1923; Evolution in the Balances, 1926; The Acts of the Apostles, 1931. Contbr. to religious publs. Home: Hopkinton, Ia.*

ALLEN, FRANK LEONARD, art edn.; b. Portland, Me., Nov. 19, 1884; s. Frank Henry and Eleanor Stather (McKinley) A.; art. edn., Mass. Sch. of Art, Sch. of Museum Fine Arts, Boston, Art Students' League, New York; studied at Harvard Univ. and in Paris, France; m. Ruth Erikssen, Mar. 14, 1912; children—Erik Halway, Eleanor Judith. Dir. of art, Pub. Schs., Saugus, Mass., 1907-09; prof. English, Imperial Higher Normal Sch., Peking (now Pieping), China, 1909-12; instr. in fine arts, Pratt Inst., Brooklyn, 1912-30; dir. art edn. Cranbrook Acad., Bloomfield Hills, Mich., 1930-32; dir. Yonkers (N.Y.) Evening Sch. Design, 1915-26; dir. art, Boothbay Studios Summer Sch. of Art, 1920-42; dir. Allen Sch. of Painting, Rockport, Mass., since 1943; dir. Sch. of Individual in Art, N.Y. City, 1932-34; head. dept. design, Mass. Sch. Art, Boston, and supervisor of vocational art edn. in industry and business, Commonwealth of Mass., since 1934. Mem. Am. Water Color Soc., Eastern Arts Assn. (pres. 1938-39); chmn. Boston Color Group, 1939-41. Republican. Episcopalian. Club: Salmagundi (New York). Home: 16 Main St., Rockport, Mass. Address: Boston. *

ALLEN, FREDERICK, clergyman; b. Pontypridd, Wales, May 30, 1885; s. Elijah Richard and Esther (Vincent) A.; brought to U.S. at age of 3 months; student Colgate U., 1905-08, Crozer Theol. Sem., 1911; D.D., Weber U., 1921; m. Florence A. Jones, Sept. 16, 1908; 1 dau., Mary Ruth. Ordained Bapt. ministry, 1911; pastor First Ch., Troy, N.Y., 1922-1943; field rep. Keuka Coll., N.Y., 1941-47; asso. minister First Bapt. Ch., Syracuse, N.Y., since 1947; pres. and executive sec. National Crime Prevention League, Inc., since 1940. Mem. New York State Bapt. Conv. (pres. 1932-36); mem. Council of Finance and Promotion of American Bapt. Conv. Republican. Baptist. Mason, Elk. Clubs: Exchange, Kiwanis, Torch. Home: Syracuse, N.Y. *

ALLEN, HARRY JULIAN, govt. ofcl.; b. Maywood, Ill., Apr. 1, 1910; s. H. Judson and Dorothy (Heins) A.; B.A. in Engring., Stanford, 1932, Engr., 1935. Research asst. Guggenheim Aero. Lab., Stanford, 1934-35; jr. engr. Shell Chem. Co., 1935-36; with NASA, and predecessor NACA, 1936-69, asst. dir. astronautics Ames Research Center, 1959-65, dir. center, 1965-69; spl. research bluntness to alleviate reentry heating problems. Recipient Sylvanus Albert Reed award Inst. Aerospace Scis., 1955; Disting. Service medal NACA, 1957; Airpower trophy Air Force Assn., 1958; Exceptional Sci. Achievement medal NASA, 1965. Fellow Am. Astronautical Soc., Meteoritical Soc., AIAA; mem. Nat. Acad. Engring., Sigma Xi. Author: High Speed Problems of Aircraft and Experimental Methods, Vol. VIII, 1961; also numerous articles, reports. Home: Palo Alto, Calif. Died Jan. 29, 1977.

ALLEN, JAMES BROWNING, U.S. senator; b. Gadsden, Ala., Dec. 28, 1912; s. George C. and Mary Ethel (Browning) A.; student U. Ala., 1928-31, U. Ala. Law Sch., 1932-33; m. Marjorie Jo Stephens, Mar. 16, 1940 (dec. Jan. 1956); children—James Browning, Mary Rebecca, Debbie Allen; m. 2d, Maryon Pittman Mullins, Aug. 7, 1964; stepchildren—J. Sanford III, John Pittman, Maryon Foster. Admitted to Ala. bar, 1935, practice in Gadsden, from 1935; mem. Ala. Ho. of Reps. from Etowah County, 1939-43; mem. Ala. Senate from Etowah, and St. Clair County, 1947-51; lt. gov. State of Ala., 1951-55, 63-67; U.S. senator from Ala., 1968-78, mem. agr., rules and judiciary coms. chmn. subcom. on separation of powers, also parliamentarian. Del. Democratic Nat. Conv., 1952. Served to lt. (j.g.) USNR, 1943-46. Home: Gadsden, Ala. Died June 1, 1978; buried Forrest Cemetery, Gadsden, Ala.

ALLEN, JAMES NORMAN, educator; b. Atlanta, Jan. 7, 1925; s. Guy Hobson and Jessie Ruth (Young) A.; student Emory U., 1942-44, 44-45; M.D. cum laude, Harvard, 1949; m. Mary Brinkley, Aug. 18, 1956; children—James Norman, Thomas Brinkley. Intern Peter Bent Brigham Hosp., Boston, 1949-50; resident, USPHS fellow dept. neurology Harvard, 1950, 52-55; instr. neurology U. N.C. 1955-56, asst. prof., 1956-60, asso. prof. neurology, biochemistry and anatomy, 1960-65; prof. medicine Ohio State U., 1965-80, Helen C. Kurtz prof. neurology, 1979-80, also dir. div. neurology. Served with USNR, Neurol. Assn. (mem. council), Am. Acad. Neurology, A.C.P., Am. Assn. Neurol. Surgeons, Am. Assn. Neuropathologists, Am. Soc. Neurochemistry, Soc. Neurosci. (chmn. Columbus chpt. 1970-71), Assn. Research Nervous and Mental Disease, Assn. Univ. Profs. Neurology, Neuropsychiat. Soc. Central Ohio, Acad. Medicine Columbus and Franklin County, Ohio Med. Assn. (sec. neurology sect. 1970-80), AMA, N.Y. Acad. Sci., A.A.A.S., Internat. Food and Wine Soc., Phi Beta Kappa, Sigma Xi, Alpha Omega Alpha. Contbr. articles to sci. jours., textbooks. Home: Columbus, Ohio. Died Mar. 31, 1980.

ALLEN, JAMES SEDDON, lawyer; b. Stamford, Conn., Aug. 31, 1885; s. Richard H. and Lizzie Connor (Walker) A.; LL.B., U. Tenn., 1907; m. Sarah Perkins, Jan. 30, 1919 (dec. Aug. 1953); children—James Seddon, Newton P., Richard H., Robert G. Admitted to Tenn. bar, 1907; with firm Armstrong, McCadden, Allen, Braden & Goodman, and predecessors, Memphis, 1932—. Pres. Chickasaw council Boy Scouts Am., 1929, Memphis U.S.O., 1943-44. Mem. Tenn. (pres. 1945-46), Shelby County (pres. 1940-41), Memphis (pres. 1940-41) bar assns., Am. Legion, Sigma Alpha Epsilon. Episcopalian (vestryman 1926—, sr. warden 1957—). Clubs: Memphis Country, Rotary (pres. 1927-28). Home: Memphis.

ALLEN, JAMES STEWART, educator; b. Henrietta, Tex., Jan. 26, 1921; s. Stayton Powell and Corrie (Walker) A.; B.A., U. Tex., 1942, M.A., 1946; Ph.D., Vanderbilt U., 1954; m. Norma McKinney, Dec. 28, 1946; children—Corrie Elizabeth, Caroline Marie. Prof. English, Arlington (Tex.) State Coll., 1947-56, Sam Houston State Tchrs. Coll., 1956-61; Carnegie fellow U. Mich., 1961-62; dean Grad. Sch., Sam Houston State Tchrs. Coll., 1962-63; asst. dir. for program Tex. Commn. Higher Edn., 1963-65; v.p. acad. affairs Marshall U., Huntington, W.Va., 1965-67; exec. dir. Assn. Tex. Colls. and Univs., 1967-71, pres., 1971-72; dean Coll. Humanities, Sam Houston State U., Huntsville, Tex., 1972-78. Mem. Assn. Higher Edn., Tex. Tchrs. Assn., Phi Kappa Sigma. Presbyn. Rotarian.

Author: Legal Education in Texas, 1965; Pluralism and Partnership: A Case for the Dual System of Higher Education, 1969. Home: Huntsville, Tex. Died Dec. 13, 1978; interred Roselawn Cemetery, Denton, Tex.

ALLEN, PAUL JAMES, educator; b. Stockbridge, Mass., Sept. 28, 1914; s. Edward Bernard and Alice (Ormes) A.; A.B., Harvard, 1936; M.S., U. Rochester, 1938; Ph.D.; U. Cal. at Berkeley, 1941; m. Mary Remsen North, Apr. 3, 1943; children—David O., Thomas D., Kathryn H. Instr., U. Pa., Phila., 1941-43; microbiologist U.S. Dept. Agr., Phila., also Salinas, Cal., 1943-46; asst. prof. botany U. Wis., Madison, 1946-52, asso. prof., 1952-59, prof. 1959-76, prof. plant pathology, 1964-76, chmn. dept. botany, 1965-70; vis. prof. botany U. Cal. at Berkeley, 1960-61. Merck post-doctoral fellow, Sheffield, Eng., 1953-54. Mem. Bot. Soc. Am., Am. Phytopathol. Soc., Am. Soc. Plant Physiologists, Am. Inst. Biol. Scis., Sierra Club, Nature Conservancy, Sigma Xi. Contbr. articles, particularly on parasitic fungi, physiology of plant disease, spore germination and devel. in fungi, to profl. jours. Home: Verona, Wis. Died Nov. 13, 1976.

ALLEN, ROBERT SHARON, writer; b. Latonia, Ky.; ed. U. Wis., U. Munich (Germany), George Washington U., U.S. Cavalry Sch., Ft. Riley, Kan., Command and Gen. Staff Coll.; m. Ruth Finney. Reporter, Capital Times, Madison, Wis.; Wis. State Jour., United Press Assn., Christian Sci. Monitor, Internat. News Service; Washington corr. Phila. Record; enlisted in U.S. Cav., promoted to 2d lt., capt. Wis. N.G.; recalled to active duty U.S. Army, July 1942, with rank of Major, Cav.; promoted to lt. col., col.; operations exec. G-2 Sect. Hdqrs. 3d Army, throughout its combat operations ETO. Decorated Silver Star, Legion of Merit, Bronze Star medal, Purple Heart, Commendation Ribbon with cluster, French Legion of Honor, Croix de Guerre with palm and gold star. Mem. Sigma Delta Chi. Clubs: National Press, Washington Press. Author: Washington Merry-Go-Round; Why Hoover Faces Defeat; More Washington Merry-Go-Round; Nine Old Men; Nine Old Men at the Crossroads; Our Fair City; Our Sovereign State: The Truman Merry-Go-Round; Lucky Forward; Co-author original daily syndicated column Washington Merry-Go-Round, 1932-42; author daily syndicated column Inside Washington, 1949-81. Contbr. to mags. Home: Washington, D.C. Died Feb. 23, 1981; buried Arlington Nat. Cemetery.

ALLEN, WALTER ALFRED, coll. prof.; born Worcester, Mass., May 25, 1886; s. Walter W. and Harriett (Rose) A.; A.B., Beloit (Wis.) Coll., 1909; Mus. B., Yale, 1917; m. Virginia Princehouse, Aug. 13, 1934. Mem. faculty Pomona Coll. since 1912 now prof. musical theory and appreciation, acting head music dept., 1947-49; organist 5th Church of Christ, Scientist, Hollywood, 1923-31, 13th Church since 1931. Home: Claremont, Calif. *

ALLEN, WARD P., fgn. service officer; b. Battle Creek, Mich., Jan. 18, 1915; s. Ward W. and Alberta J. (Mason) A.; student Battle Creek Coll., 1932-34; A.B. cum laude, U. Mich., 1936, J.D., 1939; m. A. Mildred Small, July 23, 1939; children—Judith A., W. Christopher, Jeannette E., Deborah M. Admitted to D.C. bar; atty. Dept. of Justice, 1939-42; adviser to U.S. mem. Inter-Am. Polit. Def. Commn., 1942-45; with Dept. State, 1945-74; mem. U.S. dels. Inter-Am. Conf. Maintenance of Peace, 1947, IX Internat. Conf. Am. States, 1948, UN gen. assemblies, 1946, 49, 50, 51, 52, 53, UN Commn. for India and Pakistan, 1950; 1st sec. head polit. sect. Am. embassy, Copenhagen, 1955-59, consul gen., Guayaquil, Ecuador, 1960-62; dep. U.S. rep. Council of OAS, dir. Office Inter-Am. Regional Polit. Affairs, Dept. State, Washington, 1962-67, dep. asst. sec. state for internat. orgn. affairs, 1967-71; dep. chief mission Am. embassy, Bogota, Colombia, 1971-72, Dept. State, Washington, 1972-74; exec. dir. World Population Soc., 1974-76. Mem. Am. Fgn. Service Assn., Phi Beta Kappa. Home: Alexandria, Va. Died Dec. 17, 1976; interred Highland Cemetery, South Bend, Ind.

ALLEN, WARREN DWIGHT, univ. prof.; b. San Jose, Calif., Aug. 31, 1885; s. James Monroe and Emma S. (Gage) A.; m. Esther Louise Houk, Dec. 30, 1912; 1 dau., Patricia Louise. Dean, Conservatory of Music, College of the Pacific, 1912-18; became organist Stanford U., 1918, chmn. Div. of Music, 1935, prof. of music and edn., 1937; on sabbatical leave, 1943-44; vis. prof. of music, Cornell U., 1932; now professor of musicology Florida State U.; composer of occasional anthems and organ arrangements. Mem. Music Teachers Nat. Assn. (pres. 1939-40), Am. Musicol. Soc., Am. Guild of Organists, Phi Beta Kappa. Mason. Club: The Family (San Francisco). Author: Philosophies of Music History, Our Marching Civilization, 1943; co-author: The Challenge of Education, Education During Wartime and After. Home: Tallahassee, Fla. *

ALLEN, WILLIAM FRANKLIN, ex-congressman; b. Bridgeville, Del., Jan. 19, 1883; s. William Franklin and Mollie (Smith) A.; ed. pub. schs., Seaford; m. Mary Addie Davis, of Hartly, Del., Apr. 16, 1905; children—William Franklin, Layton Robert, Doris. Telegrapher, 1901-21; fruit and produce dealer, 1921-27; pres. Allen Package Co., 1927-37; real estate operator, 1927-37; pres. Allen Oil Co., 1927-32; pres. Allen Petroleum Corpn. since 1932; member 75th Congress (1937-39), Del. at large; mem. Del. State Senate, 1925-27. Democrat. Methodist. Mason (Shriner). Clubs: Democratic(Seaford). Democratic (Wilmington). Home: Seaford, Del.*

ALLEY, NORMAN WILLIAMS, news pictures; b. Chicago, Ill., Jan. 22, 1895; s. Fred Murdo and Mary Conklin (Hooker) A.; ed. grammar and high schools, Chicago and N.Y. City; m. Wylla Kilborn, Nov. 29, 1919; children—Dexter, Noreen, Janet. Reporter and cameraman Chicago Tribune, 1911-14, Chicago American, 1915-17; covered Pancho Villa and Punitive Expdn., Mexico, 1916; served as 1st lt. comdg. photographic unit, Signal Corps, U.S. Army, on major fronts in France, 1917-19; bureau mgr., cameraman and editor since 1920; editor Internat. Newsreel, 1929-30; attempted transatlantic flight, 1932, which ended in seaplane wreck off Greenland coast; covered Japanese war in China, and took motion pictures of the bombing and sinking of the U.S.S. Panay upon which he was a passenger; flew to Europe Sept. 1939 and covered the Axis side of World War II, recording invasion of Holland, Belgium, Norway, Denmark until July 1940; returned to U.S. after fall of Paris; in South America directing newsreel activities for Hearst in cooperation with Office of Commercial and Cultural Relations between American Republics since 1941; war correspondent in Australia, 1942; landed with 1st invasion force, Gela, Sicily, 1943; landed with first invasion force at Salerno, Italy, Sept. 1943; covered Pacific fleet operations, 1944-45; staff cameraman, News of the Day Newsreel. Awarded plaque for newsreel achievement by Nat. Headliners Club, 1938. Mem. Nat. and Los Angeles press photographers assns., Internat. Photographers Assn., Am. Press Relations Assn., Chicago Press Veterans Assn., American Soc. Cinematographers, National Aero. Assn., Sigma Delta Chi. Baptist. Mason. Clubs: Press (Chicago; Los Angeles); Variety, Tent 25. Author: I Witness, 1941, autobiography. Contbr. tech. articles on camera and articles on world events to mags. Spl. camera corr. covering Edward R. Murrow's CBS-TV See It Now program, 1951-54; To South America and Around the World with Richard Nixon, from 1955; western mgr. Hearst Newsreels, Los Angeles, 1954. Home: Los Angeles Woodland Hills, Calif. Died Apr. 1, 1981.

ALLISON, FRED, prof. physics; b. Glade Spring, Va., July 4, 1882; s. Robert Clark and Rebecca Jane (Clark) A.; A.B., Emory and Henry Coll., Emory, Va., 1904; grad. study, Columbia, summer, 1905, Johns Hopkins, 1907-08, 1910-11, U. of Chicago, summer, 1909; A.M., U. of Va., 1921, Ph.D., 1922; D.Sc., Ala. Poly. Inst., 1931; LL.D. from Emory and Henry Coll., 1933; m. Elizabeth Harriet Kelly, Aug. 24, 1915; children—Elizabeth Harriet (Mrs. R. T. Comer, Jr.), Fred. Prof. physics, Emory and Henry College, 1908-20, instructor and graduate student, University of Va., 1920-22; head prof. physics, Ala. Poly. Inst., 1922-53, dean of graduate sch., 1949-53; director Auburn Research Foundation, Alabama Poly Institute, 1949-51; visiting prof. Emory and Henry Coll., 1953-55; vis. prof. physics U. Texas, summer 1955, sent as cons. in physics to Chulalongkorn U., Bangkok, Thailand, vis. professor Huntingdon Coll., 1956—; cons. Operational Research Office, A.F. Missile Development Center, summer 1957, Holloman AFB, N.M., summer 1959. Fellow Am. Phys. Soc. (chmn. S.E. sect. 1941), A.A.A.S.; mem. Ala. Acad. Sci. (pres. 1929), Phi Beta Kappa, Phi Kappa Phi, Sigma Xi; hon. mem. Ga. Acad. Science, Awarded President and Visitors' Research Prize, U. of Va., 1925; Herty Research medal, 1933. Developed magneto-optic method of analysis, by means of which discovered with co-workers Element 87, 1930, Element 85, 1931. Author: College Physics Laboratory Instructions. Home: Auburn, Ala. *

ALLISON, GEORGE BOGGS, architect; b. Naini Tal, India, 1904 (parents Am. citizens); s. Alexander B. and Amy J. (Boggs) A.; B.Arch., U. Pa., 1925, M.Arch., 1926; m. Ada A. Sandin, Sept. 6, 1936; 1 son, George Richard. Woodman fellow for European travel and study, 1928-29; with office of John Russell Pope, N.Y.C., 1929-30; mem. and gen. partner Allison, Rible, Robinson & Ziegler, Architects, and predecessor firms, 1938-77, gen. partner, 1944-77; officer A-R-R-Z, asso. group Leo A. Daly Co., 1969-72, now cons. Mem. Los Angeles County Capital Projects Appeal Bd., 1969-77. Fellow A.I.A. (pres. So. Cal. 1948, nat. honor award jury 1956, jury of fellows from 1959, chmn. 1963, past mem., past chmn. ins. trustees Cal. council); mem. Am. Arbitration Assn. (nat. panel 1953), Beta Theta Pi. Methodist. Rotarian. Club: Wilshire Town (pres. 1967) (Los Angeles). Home: Los Angeles, Calif. Died June 25, 1977.

ALLISON, JOHN H(OWARD), univ. prof.; b. East Granby, Conn., Sept. 25, 1883; s. John Alexander and Mary Elizabeth (Mack) A.; Ph.B., Yale, 1905, M.F., 1906; grad. studies U. of Minn.; m. Mabel Ann Shepard, Sept. 6, 1911 (dec. 1920); 1 son, John Howard; m. 2d, Ethel Leigh Reuber, Aug. 12, 1927; 1 dau., Mary Leigh. Began as forester and advanced to forest examiner U.S. Forest Service, 1906-12, 1918-19; prof. of forestry U. of Minn. since 1913 (on sabbatical leave, 1923-24); exchange fellow Am. Scandinavian Found., 1923-24. Sr. mem. Soc. of Am. Foresters; mem. American Assn. of University Professors, A.A.A.S., Alpha Zeta. Republican. Conglist. Mason (Shriner). Club: Campus (U. of Minn.). Home: St. Paul, Minn. *

ALLMAN, GEORGE DUDLEY, chmn. U.S. Cold Storage Corp.; b. Sturgis, Nov. 9, 1884; s. William Major and Anna (Beals) A.; grad. Raymond Ch., Chicago, Ill., 1899; m. Julia Jane Spencer, Nov. 14, 1905 (died 1937); children—Thelma, Leera, George Dudley, Robert William; m. 2d. Alice Seawright, May 7, 1938. Office boy Union Cold Storage and Warehouse Co., Chicago, 1899-1903; clk., advancing to gen. supt. Chicago Cold Storage Warehouse Co., 1903-19; gen. mgr. U.S. Cold Storage Corp., Chicago, 1919-28, v.p. and dir., 1928-43, pres. since 1943; chairman of the board of directors U.S. Cold Storage & Ice Co., U.S. Wholesale Co., Detroit; v.p. and director Wolverine Properties, Inc., Chicago, 1932, chmn. bd. since 1943; v.p. U.S. Cold Storage Co., Kansas City, MO., 1923-43, chairman of the board since 1943. Member Chicago Merc. Exchange, N.Y. Merc. Exchange, Chicago Bd. of Trade. Pres. Am. Warehousemen's Assn., 1946; mem. exec. com. Nat. Assn. Refrigerated Warehouses; mem. Am. Soc. Refrigerating Engrs., Chicago Ice Assn. Republican. Clubs: Midday, Tavern, Key, Chicago Athletic Assn., South Shore Country (Chgo.). Home: Chicago, Ill.

ALMY, GERALD MARKS, educator, physicist; b. Ewing, Neb., Apr. 24, 1904; s. Billings Grinnell and Ada (Marks) A.; B.S., U. Neb., 1924, M.S., 1926; Ph.D., Harvard, 1930; m. Ruth Virtue, July 21, 1930; children—Cynthia (Mrs. T.K. Landauer), Catherine (Mrs. P.N. Hineline). Mem. faculty U. Ill., Urbana, from 1930, prof. physics, 1943-70, head dept., 1964-70, prof. emeritus, from 1970. Fellow Am. Phys. Soc.; mem. Am. Inst. Physics, A.A.A.S., Am. Assn. U. Profs., Phi Beta Kappa, Sigma Xi. Author articles molecular spectroscopy and fluorescence, betatron devel., photonuclear processes. Home: Champaign, Ill. Deceased.

ALPERN, ANNE X., state govt. ofcl.; b. 1904; B.A., LL.B., U. Pitts. Admitted to bar, 1927; formerly judge Ct. of Common Pleas of Allegheny County, atty. gen. Pa. Mem. Am. Bar Assn. Died Feb. 2, 1981.

ALPERT, HARRY, sociologist, educator; b. N.Y.C., Oct. 12, 1912; s. Morris and Mary (Levine) A.; A.B., CCNY, 1932; Certificat de Sociologie U. Bordeaux (France), 1933; M.A., Columbia U., 1935, Ph.D., 1938; student U. Paris, 1932, U. Chgo., 1940-41; m. Anitra Fink, June 15, 1936; children—Spencer Ward, Geoffrey Philip. Instr., asst. prof. sociology CCNY, 1933-47; research cons. bur. applied social research Columbia U., 1946-48; professorial lectr., adj. prof. sociology Am. U., 1947, 1950-58; prof. sociology Yale, 1947, U. Washington, 1955, U. Va., 1977; asso. prof. sociology, chmn. dept. anthropology and sociology Queens Coll., 1948-50; research scientist social psychiatry Cornell U. Med. Coll., 1951-56; dean Grad. Sch., prof. sociology U. Oreg., 1958-64, dean of faculties, prof. sociology, 1964-71, v.p. for acad. affairs, provost, prof. sociology, 1971-76, prof. sociology, 1976-77; dir. dept. social scis. UNESCO, 1967-70; mem. Franco-Am. Commn. for Ednl. Exchange, 1967-70; mem. U.S. Nat. Commn. for UNESCO, 1971-75. Pub. opinion analyst O.W.I., 1943-44; pub. opinion, rationing statistics analyst OPA, 1944-45; analytical statistician Bur. Budget, 1945-48, 50-53; cons. USAF, research and devel. bd. Dept. Def., 1948-50, program dir. social sci. research NSF, 1953-58; fellow Center for Advanced Study in Behavioral Scis., 1963-64. Fellow AAAS, Am. Statis. Assn., Am. Sociol. Assn. (v.p. 1958); mem. Pacific Sociol. Assn. (pres. 1962-63), Am. Assn. Pub. Opinion Research (pres. 1955-56), Am. Anthrop. Assn., Population Assn. Am., Council on Acad. Affairs (chmn. 1974-75), Sociol. Research Assn. (pres. 1961), World Assn. Pub. Opinion Research, Washington Statis. Soc. (pres. 1954-55), Tocqueville Assn., Soc. Psychol. Study Social Issues, Soc. Social Study Sci. Author: Emile Durkheim and His Sociology, 1939 (Spanish edit. 1945). Editor Am. Sociol. Rev., 1960-62. Home: Eugene, Oreg. Died Nov. 7, 1977.

ALPHONSUS, BROTHER, prof. philosophy; b. Providence, R.I., Apr. 4, 1886; s. Alexander Peter and Mary (McLaughlin) Linn; student Bishop Tyler Memorial Sch., Providence, 1891-98, LaSalle Acad., Providence, 1898-1901, St. Joseph's Normal Inst., New York, 1901-03; A.B., Manhattan Coll., 1920; extension courses Coll. City of New York, Univ. of Syracuse, New York State Teachers Coll. and Brown U.; M.A., Catholic U., 1924; Ph.D., Fordham U., 1927. Mem. Brothers of the Christian Schools (F.S.C., religious order). Teacher St. Patrick's Sch., New York, 1903, in N.H., 1904-05, Hartford, Conn., 1905-07, New York City high schs., 1907-12, Syracuse Acad., 1912-15; dir. St. Joseph's Normal Inst., 1915-22; prof. philosophy and the classics, Manhattan Coll., 1924-34, dean of arts and science, 1934-42, prof. philosophy since 1942. Mem. Catholic Philosophical Assn., Assn. of Deans, Christian Brothers' Ednl. Assn. Address: 4513 Spuyten Duyvil Parkway, N.Y. City 71. *

ALSCHULER, JACOB EDWARD, lawyer; b. Aurora, Ill., July 9, 1902; s. Benjamin Philip and Lillian (Reinheimer) A.; A.B., U. Wis., 1923; J.D., U. Chgo., 1926; m. Carolyn Strauss, Jan. 11, 1927; children—Rosalie A. (Mrs. Bernard Goldstein), Benjamin Philip, George Arthur. Admitted to Ill. bar, 1926, since practiced in Aurora; partner Alschuler, Putnam, McWethy, Weiss & Weiler and predecessor firms, 1926-77. Mem. Ill. Tchrs. Coll. Bd., 1935-43. Chmn. Kane County Democratic Central Com., 1932-42. Mem. Am., Ill., Kane County (past pres.) bar assns., Am. Judicature Soc., Artus, Zeta Beta Tau (past nat. v.p.). Jewish. Mason; mem. B'nai B'rith, Elk, Moose. Clubs: Aurora Country, Union League (Aurora). Home: Aurora, Ill. Died May 23, 1977; interred Springlake Cemetery, Aurora.

ALSEVER, JOHN B., physician; b. Syracuse, N.Y., Nov. 24, 1908; s. William Dewey and Clara (Bellows) A.; A.B., Syracuse U., 1930; M.D., Harvard, 1934; m. Janet N. Gilbert, Aug. 27, 1938; children—John Dewey, Robert Nichols, Margery Bradner. Intern and asst. resident Peter Bent Brigham Hosp., 1935-37; practice internal med., Syracuse, 1937-42; instr. coll. med., Syracuse U., 1937-42; dir. transfusion service, Syracuse U. Med. Center Hosps., 1940-42; tech. dir. blood plasma sect., med. div., O.C.D., 1942-44, devel. and control civilian blood plasma reserves, U.S., establishing blood banks in 180 hosps.; dir. Civilian Blood Donor Service, ARC, 1944-46, devel. state and local blood and blood derivatives programs, distbn. surplus Army-Navy blood plasma. Served Med. O.R.C., U.S. Army, 1935-42; served as surgeon, U.S. Pub. Health Service, 1942-44, sr. surg., 1946-49, med. dir., 1949-78, dir. tng. and profl. standards, hosp. div., 1946-49, asst. chief, 1949-51; dir. blood program Health and Spl. Weapons Defense Div., Fed. Civil Def. Adminstrn., 1951-53, dep. dir., 1953-54, chief hygiene of the aging, Chronic Disease program USPHS, 1954-55, med. dir., 1949-55; med. dir. Blood Services, Scottsdale, Ariz., 1955-68, v.p. med. affairs, 1968-74, exec. v.p. med. affairs, 1974-75; med. dir. Plasma Services, 1968-75, BSP Ins. Co., Scottsdale, 1962-75; now med. cons., blood services. Diplomate Am. Bd. Internal Med. Fellow A.C.P.; mem. Am., Calif., South Central assns. blood banks, Am. Soc. Clin. Pathologists, Ariz., Phoenix pathology socs., Delta Kappa Epsilon, Nu Sigma Nu, Sigma Xi. Republican. Episcopalian. Co-author: Blood Transfusion (textbook), 1948; author sci. articles profl. jours. Home: Phoenix, Ariz. Died Feb. 22, 1978; interred All Saints' Episcopal Ch., Phoenix.

ALSPACH, RUSSELL KING, ret. army officer, educator; b. Phila., Feb. 22, 1901; s. Charles Bennett and Elizabeth (Varwig) A.; B.A., U. Pa., 1924, M.A., 1931, Ph.D., 1932; m. Sara Catharine Campion, May 10, 1924; children—Ann Jane (Mrs. James Fitzcharles), Sally Campion (Mrs. Philip Anderson). Appraisal engr., 1918-20; mem. English dept. U. Pa., 1924-42, 45-47; commd. lt. col. U.S. Army, 1947, advanced to brig. gen.; ret. 1965; prof. English, U.S. Mil. Acad., 1947-65, head dept., 1961-65; lectr. English, U. Mass., 1965-66, prof. English, 1966-71, prof. emeritus, 1971-80, head dept. English, 1967-69. Vis. prof. Grad. Sch. U. Pa., 1962-63. Served to lt. comdr. USNR, 1942-45. Mem. Modern Lang. Assn., Am. Folklore Soc. (council), Nat. Council Tchrs. English, English Inst., Coll. Conf. Communication. Club: The Army-Navy Country (Washington). Author: Poetry of the Celtic Renaissance, 1932; Irish Poetry from the English Invasion to 1798, rev. edit., 1959, 78. Co-editor: The Variorum Edition of the Poetry of W. B. Yeats, 1957, The Variorum Edition of the Plays of W.B. Yeats, 1965; Wade's Bibliography of Yeats, rev. edit., 1968; editorial staff Winston Dictionary, 1926-28, 37-39. Contbr. articles to profl. jours. Home: Amherst, Mass. Died Sept. 2, 1980; buried West Point, N.Y.

ALSTON, CHARLES HENRY, painter, sculptor, educator; b. Charlotte, N.C., Nov. 28, 1907; s. Primus Priss and Anna (Miller) A.; B.A., Columbia, 1929, M.A., 1931; m. Myra Adele Logan, Apr. 8, 1944. One man shows include Oppenheimer Gallery, Chgo., 1950, John Heller Gallery, N.Y.C., 1953-57, Feingarten Gallery, N.Y.C., 1958, Dunbarton Gallery, Boston, 1960, Gallery Modern Art, N.Y.C., 1969, Atlanta U. Center, 1972; group exhbns. include Met. Mus. Art, Whitney Mus. Am. Art, Mus. Modern Art, Pa. Acad. Fine Arts, Corcoran Gallery, Washington, Balt. Mus. Art, High Mus., Atlanta; rep. permanent collections Met. Mus., Whitney Mus., Detroit Mus., U. Neb., Atlanta U., Howard U., Art Students League, N.Y.C., IBM Corp.; executed murals Golden State Mut. Life Ins. Co., Los Angeles, 1948, Harlem Hosp., N.Y.C., 1969, Mus. Natural History, N.Y.C., 1960, Coll. City N.Y., 1960, Abraham Lincoln High Sch., N.Y.C., 1961, Harriet Tubman Jr. High Sch., N.Y.C., 1962; mosaic murals for Bronx County Family and Criminal Ct. Bldg., Bronx, N.Y., 1972; illustrator Fortune mag., 1943-77, New Yorker mag., 1937-77, Red Book, 1936-77, Colliers, 1935-77, Mademoiselle, 1940-77, others; artist-critic Mus. Modern Art, 1956-57, New Sch. Social Research, 1961-62; artist OWI, 1940-41; instr. Arts Students League, 1950-77; asso. prof. Coll. City N.Y., 1970-73, prof., 1973-77. Mem. adv. bd. Nat. Council Arts, 1968-69; artist mem. N.Y.C. Art Commn., 1970-77; mem. screening com. painting Inst. Internat. Edn., 1968; co-dir. State Dept. and Mus. Modern Art art program Brussels World Fair, 1958. Bd. dirs. Nat. Soc. Mural Painters. Served with AUS, 1943-44. Grantee Inst. Arts and Letters, 1958; recipient Lowe award painting Joe and Emily Lowe Found., 1960; DeWitt Clinton Alumni award DeWitt Clinton Alumni Assn., 1961; Thomas B. Clarke award Nat. Acad. Design, 1971; Arthur Wesley Dow fellow Columbia, 1930; Rosenwald fellow, 1938-40; bronze head of Dr. Martin Luther King commd. by Community Ch., N.Y.C., 1971; bronze head Dr. Martin Luther King in permanent collection Nat. Portrait Gallery Smithsonian Instn., Washington, 1972. Home: New York, N.Y. Died Apr. 28, 1977.

ALTER, KARL JOSEPH, archbishop; b. Toledo, Aug. 18, 1885; s. John and Elizabeth (Kuttner) A.; M.A., St. John's U., Toledo, 1902, Ph.D., 1929; student St. Mary's Sem., Cleve., 1904-10; LL.D., Notre Dame U., 1937. Ordained priest Roman Catholic Ch., 1910; pastor St. Mary's Parish, Leipsic, O., 1910-12; asst. pastor St. John's Parish, Lima, O., 1912-14, dir. Diocesan charities, 1914-29, also prof. sociology all colls. St. John's U.; dir. Nat. Sch. Social Service, Washington, 1929-31; apptd. bishop of Toledo (O.), 1931, consecrated, 1931; archbishop Cin., 1950-69; titular archbishop of Minora, 1969-77; named asst. to the Papal Throne, 1950. Asst. bishop, social action dept. Nat. Cath. Welfare Conf., 1935-42, mem. adminstrv. bd., chmn. social action dept., 1942-50, treas., vice chmn. adminstrv. bd., 1950-52, chmn. adminstrv. bd., 1952-55, 58-62, sec. adminstrv. bd., 1962-66, vice chmn. adminstrv. bd., chmn. dept. lay orgns., 1956-58; mem. central prep. commn. II Vatican Council, 1959-62; mem. Commn. for Bishops and Govt. of Dioceses, 1962-65. Home: Cincinnati, Ohio. Died Aug. 23, 1977.

ALTON, JOHN TAYLOR, clergyman; b. Gnadenhutten, O., Aug. 22, 1883; s. John and Malinda (Parrish) A.; A.B., Mt. Union Coll., 1912, D.D., 1925; S.T.B., Boston U., 1915; m. Roberta Swartz, Aug. 7, 1907; children—Ralph Taylor, Ruth (Mrs. F. Byers Miller). Member Gen. Assembly State of N.H., 1915-18; ordained deacon Methodist Ch., 1915, elder, 1917; pastor Lincoln, N.H., 1915-18, Minerva, O., 1918-20, Grace Ch., Akron, O., 1920-24; supt. Norwalk (O.) Dist. 192427; pastor Windermere Ch., Cleveland, Ohio, 1927-33, Brood St., Ch., Columbus, Ohio, 1933-35; supt. Springfield (O.) Dist., 1935-40; pastor Westwood Ch., Cincinnati, O., 1940-44; supt. Columbus Dist., 1944-50. Served as Y.M.C.A. sec., World War I, Mem. North Central Jurisdictional Conf., Methodist Church, 1940, 44, 48, mem. gen. conf., 1948; pres. bd. trustees Ohio Conf. Meth. Ch. since 1950; mem. Judicial Council Meth. Ch. since 1948; trustee Meth. Children's Home (Worthington). Mem. Theta Phi. Mason (32 deg., K.T.). Contbr. articles to ch. papers and mags. *

ALTSCHUL, FRANK, exec.; b. San Francisco, Apr. 21, 1887; s. Charles and Camilla (Mandlebaum) A.; B.A., Yale, 1908, LL.D., 1967; LL.D., Bates Coll., 1952, Columbia, 1971; m. Helen Lehman Goodhart, 1913; children—Charles II (dec.), Margaret (Mrs. Daniel Lang), Edith (Mrs. Robert C. Graham), Arthur Goodhart. Chmn. emeritus Gen. Am. Investors Co., Inc. Asso. fellow Pierson Coll., Yale, New Haven, honorary fellow University Coll., Oxford. Dir. emeritus, hon. Sec. Council on Fgn. Relations, Inc., N.Y.C.; vice chmn. Nat. Planning Assn. and chmn. internat. com. Served to capt. U.S. Army, 1917-19; A.E.F.; maj. O.R.C., 1924. Decorated officer Legion of Honor (French). Mem. Union Interalliee, La Compagnie Typographique (Paris). Clubs: Pilgrims U.S., Century Assn., Grolier, Yale (N.Y.C.); Odd Volumes (Boston); Elizabethan (New Haven); Rowfant (Cleveland); Cosmos, Army and Navy, Metropolitan, 1925 F Street (Washington). Author: Let No Wave Engulf Us, 1941. Home: Stamford, Conn. Died May 29, 1981.

ALVAREZ, WALTER CLEMENT, physician; b. San Francisco, July 22, 1884; s. Luis Fernandez and Clementina (Schuetze) A.; M.D., Cooper Med. Coll. (Stanford), 1905; postgrad. Harvard Med. Sch., 1913; m. Harriet Skidmore Smyth, Feb. 22, 1907; children—Gladys (Mrs. Al Muirhead), Luis Walter, Robert Smyth, Bernice (Mrs. Bradley Brownson). Asst. in clinic pathology, Cooper Med. Coll., 1906-07; physician Cananea, Mexico, 1907-09; internist San Francisco, 1910-25; asst. in medicine, Stanford, 1911-12; asst. in research medicine, U. Calif., 1915-16, instr., 1916-20, asst. prof., 1920-24, asso. prof., 1924-26; successively asso., head of sect. and sr. cons. Div. Medicine, Mayo Clinic, Rochester, Minn., 1926-50, emeritus, 1950-78; asso. prof. medicine Mayo Found., U. Minn., 1926-34, prof., 1934-51, emeritus; professorial lectr. medicine U. Ill. Med. Sch., 1951-52, emeritus. Trustee Josiah Macy, Jr., Found., 1930-32. First Caldwell lectr. Am. Roentgen Ray Soc. Diplomate Am. Bd. Internal Medicine, Am. Bd. Gastroenterology. Fellow A.C.P.; mem. Assn. Am. Physicians, Am. Physiol. Soc., Am. Soc. for Clin. Investigation, Soc. Exptl. Biology and Medicine, Am. Gastroenterol. Assn. (pres. 1928; Friedenwald medallist 1951), Am. Soc. Pharmacology Exptl. Therapeutics, AMA, Am. Anthropol. Assn., Am. Assn. Phys. Anthropologists, AAAS, Alpha Kappa Kappa, Sigma Xi, Alpha Omega Alpha. Republican. Club: University (Chgo.). Author: Mechanics of the Digestive Tract, 1922; The Neuroses, 1951; Danger Signals, 1953; Nervousness, Indigestion and Pain, 1954, An Introduction to Gastroenterology, 1948; Danger Signals, 1957; Live at Peace with Your Nerves, 1958; Practical Leads to Puzzling Diagnosis, 1958; Minds that Came Back, 1961; Incurable Physician, An Autobiography, 1963; Little Strokes, 1966; Nerves In Collision, 1972. Emeritus editor-in-chief Modern Medicine, also Geriatrics Syndicate med. columnist, 1951-78. Home: San Francisco, Calif. Died June 18, 1978.

ALVAREZ-TOSTADO, CLAUDIO, educator; b. Durango, Mexico, June 4, 1912; B.S., U. Ariz., 1934, M.S., 1935; Ph.D. in Chemistry, Stanford, 1939; m. 1943. Jr. research asso. chemistry and medicine Stanford, 1939-40; asst. prof. chemistry Santa Clara, 1941-44; lectr. Stanford, 1943-44, acting asst. prof., 1944-46, asst. prof. phys. sci., 1946-49, asso. prof., 1949-58, prof. phys. sci. and chemistry, 1958-78. Vis. prof. chemistry U. Mayor de San Andres, Bolivia, 1956. Research in reaction kinetics, ultracentrifugation, inorganic chemistry of silicon. Home: Nogales, Ariz. Died Dec. 16, 1980.

AMAR, HENRI, educator, physicist; b. Casablanca, July 14, 1920; s. Jacob and Zora (Elbaz) A.; B.A., B.S., Acad. Paris, 1940; M.A., U. Algiers, 1942; M.A., Ohio State U., 1948, Ph.D., 1952; m. Mary Helene Genissieux, Dec. 23, 1952 (div. 1973); children—Jacques G., Francois G., Yvette Anne; m. 2d, Paula L. Bram. Asst. prof. physics Lafayette Coll., 1952-56; sr. research physicist Franklin Inst., 1956-60; asso. prof. physics Temple U., 1960-66, prof., 1966-80, co-dir. AEC research contract, 1964-80; vis. research prof. U. Grenoble (France), 1966-67. Recipient award for excellence in teaching and research, Lindback Found., 1966. Fellow Am. Phys. Soc.; mem. Am. Assn. Physics Tchrs., A.A.U.P. (chpt. pres. 1970-73, mem. nat. council 1976—), Franklin Inst. Research and publs. on theoretical physics, magnetism and metallic alloys, differential manifolds and relativity. Home: Ambler, Pa. Died Aug. 17, 1980.

AMAZEEN, EDWARD SUTHERLAND, investment co. exec.; b. Melrose, Mass., Dec. 23, 1909; s. Edward Clifton and Evelyn Maria (Sutherland) A.; A.B. cum laude, Harvard, 1931; M.B.A., 1935; m. Elizabeth Childs Taylor, Apr. 14, 1934; children—Elizabeth Anne (Mrs. Edward R. Hammond, Jr.), Edward Sutherland, Nancy Jane (Mrs. John S. Goldthwait). Grad. sec. Phillips Brooks House Assn., Harvard, 1931-36; mgr. billing dept. Carter's Ink Co., Cambridge, Mass., 1935; with Coffin & Burr, Inc., investment bankers, Boston, 1935-41, 47-58, v.p., mgr. investment trust dept., 1947-58; co-founder Importsales, Inc., also Loire Imports, Inc., N.Y.C., 1947; with One William St. Fund, Inc., N.Y.C., 1959-65, v.p. 1962-65; dir. sales One William dept. Lehman Bros., 1960-65; v.p. dir. William St. Sales Inc. 1959-64; pres. dir. Wilmington Capital Services Corp., 1965-67; v.p. Blue Ridge Mut. Fund, 1965-67; sales. exec. Lombard, Vitalis & Paganucci, Inc., N.Y.C., 1967-72; pres., dir. Southeastern Securities Corp., Hanover, Mass., 1972-79; pres., dir. Masterpieces, Inc., Hanover, 1973-79; trustee S. Scituate Savs. Bank, Norwell, Mass.; mem. Boston Stock Exchange. Pres., trustee Woodlawn Cemetery, Everett, Mass., 1949—; mem. Hanover Housing Authority, 1974-79, chmn., 1977-79. Chmn. Republican Town Com., Hanover, 1940-58; chmn. planning bd., Hanover, 1948-60; mem. Mass. Rep. Exec. Com., 1954-59. Chmn. bd. dirs., treas. Mill Pond Rest Home, Hanover, 1970—; bd. dirs., treas. Martha's Vineyard Camp Meeting Assn., 1969—. Served to comdr. USNR, 1941-47; ETO. Mem. Nat. Assn. Securities Dealers (past chmn. New Eng. dist.), Investment Bankers Assn. Am. (past vice chmn. New Eng. group, past chmn. investment cos. com.), Investment Co. Inst. Clubs: Bond (past bd. govs.), Down Town (Boston); Harvard (N.Y.C.); Old Colony Harvard (Brockton, Mass.). Home: Hanover, Mass. Died Jan. 9, 1979; interred Woodlawn Cemetery, Everett, Mass.

AMBERSON, J(AMES) BURNS, physician; b. Waynesboro, Pa., June 8, 1890; s. James Burns and Kathcrine (Good) A.; Ph.B., Lafayette Coll., 1913, Sc. D. (hon.), 1944; M.D., Johns Hopkins Med. Sch., 1917 Sc.D. (honorary), University Pa., 1953; m. Rebecca T. Steen, Jan. 1, 1919; children—James Burns III, Mrs. Mary Priscilla Adsit. Asst. and asso. physician, Loomis Sanatorium, 1917-26, physician in chief, 1927-29; visiting physician, Herman Kiefer Hosp., Detroit, Mich., and William H. Maybury Sanatorium, Northville, Mich., 1926-27; visiting physician, chest service, Bellevue Hosp., 1927-38, vis. physician in charge, 1938-55, consultant, 1955-79; cons. physician N.Y. State Tuberculosis hosps., 1935-79, Grassland Hospital, 1939-79; cons. Bergen Pines Hosp., Paramus, N.J. Presbyn. Hosp. Asst. prof. and prof. clin. medicine Coll. Phys. & Surg., Columbia, 1927-38, prof. medicine, 1938-55, prof. emeritus, 1955-79. Master Am. Coll. Physicians; mem. Nat. Tb. Assn. (pres. 1942, Trudeau Medal 1952), British Thoracic Soc. (hon.), Am. Thoracic Soc. (pres. 1940), N.Y. TB. and Health Assn. (president 1941-46; gen. dir. 1955-65), American Clinical and Climatological Society, Association Am. Physicians, A.A.A.S., Am. Assn. Thoracic Surgery, A.M.A., Harvey Soc., N.Y. Academy Medicine (v.p.

1945-47, 55), Alpha Omega Alpha (honorary), Sigma Xi. Club: Century Assn. Home: Hillsdale, N.J. Died Dec. 3, 1979.

AMBRIDGE, D. W., paper mfr.; b. Mexico City, Mexico, Jan. 5, 1898; s. Charles Theodore and Frances (White) A.; B.Sc. in Chem. Engring., McGill U., Montreal, Can., 1923; LL.D., Waterloo Luth. U., 1962; m. Jessie Louise Barlow, June 10, 1924; children—Cicely Barlow (Mrs. N. B. Bell), Janet White (Mrs. J.M.G. Scott), Shirley Sinclair, Charlotte. Control engr. Abitibi Power & Paper Co., Ltd., Iroquois Falls, Ont., Can., 1923-27; gen. supt. Anglo-Canadian Pulp and Paper Mills, Ltd.; asst. gen. mgr. Anglo-Nfld. Devel. Co., 1927-36; asst. to pres. Ontario Paper Co., Thorold, Ont., 1936; asst. gen. mgr., v.p., 1943-46; dir. Polymer Corp., Ltd., 1942-50, pres., 1945; pres., also gen. mgr. Abitibi Paper Co., Ltd., 1946-59, pres., 1959-63, chmn. bd., 1963-68, hon. chmn., 1968-77, also hon. dir.; hon. dir. Can. Malting Co., Ltd. Served with C.F.A., 2d Div. C.E.F., World War I; dir. gen. shipbldg. br. Dept. Munitions and Supply, Ottawa, Ont., World War II. Decorated comdr. Order Brit. Empire. Councillor Nat. Indsl. Conf. Bd. Mem. Phi Delta Theta. Club: York (Toronto). Home: Toronto, Ont., Can. Died Nov. 17, 1977.

AMBROSE, LUTHER MARTIN, educator; b. Conkling, Ky., Aug. 6, 1898; s. Barton Potter and Isabelle (Carmack) A.; B.S., Berea Coll., 1920; M.A., U. Chgo., 1928; Ph.D., U. Ky., 1939; m. Edith Tutt, June 10, 1922; children—Ellen (Mrs. Harry Bleecher), Frederick, Thomas, Martin. Instr. chemistry Berea Coll., 1920-21, head sci. dept. Berea Acad., 1921-39, Billings prof. edn., Berea Coll., workshop elementary teachers, summers 1945-50, director of the rural school improvement project, 1953-55; workshop elementary tchrs. U. Ky., summers, 1940-41; tchr. trainer Inst. Inter-Am. Affairs, Paraguay, 1950-52, Internat. Coop. Adminstrn., Thailand, 1955-56; acting edn. officer U.S. Operations Mission to Thailand, 1956; edn. officer U.S. Operations Mission to Paraguay, 1957-60, City councilman, Berea, Ky., 1954-55. Served with USN, 1918-19. Mem. N.E.A., Ky. Edn. Assn., Nat. Soc. for Study Edn., Am. Soc. Curriculum Development, Assn. for Student Teaching, Phi Delta Kappa, Delta Kappa Delta, Sigma Pi Sigma. Died Feb. 3, 1981.

AMEEL, DONALD JULES, retired zoologist; b. Detroit, Apr. 24, 1907; s. Jules T. and Selma Ida (Beer) A.; A.B., Wayne U., 1928; A.M., U. Mich., 1930, Ph.D., 1933; m. Henrietta Ruth Zezula, Aug. 3, 1937; children—John Jules, Donna Ruth, George Robert. Asst. in zoology U. Mich., 1928-32, fellow, 1932-33, temporary instr., 1935-36; asso. prof. biology Augustana Coll., 1933-35; instr. zoology Kan. State U., 1937-42, asst. prof., 1942-45, prof., head dept., 1945-67. Zoologist, Kans. Bd. Agr. Fellow A.A.A.S.; mem. Am. Soc. Parasitologists, Am. Microscopical Soc. (past v.p.), Kans. Acad. Sci. (pres. 1956), Helminthological Soc. Wash., Soc. Systemic Zoology, Riley County Hist. Soc., Sigma Xi, Phi Sigma, Phi Kappa Phi, Gamma Sigma Delta. Conglist. Contbr. 42 papers to profl. jours. Home: Manhattan, Kans. Died Jan. 30, 1979.

AMERASINGHE, HAMILTON SHIRLEY, Ceylon diplomat; b. Colombo, Ceylon, Mar. 18, 1913; student Royal Coll., Colombo, 1921-30, Univ. Coll., Ceylon, 1930-34; B.A. with honours, London U., 1934. Entered Ceylon Civil Service, 1937; resident mgr. Gal Oya Devel. Bd., 1950-52; counsellor Ceylon Embassy, Washington, 1953-55; Ceylon del. 5th Com. UN Gen. Assembly 12th Session, 1957; permanent sec. Ministry Nationalized Services and Rd. Transp., chmn. Port Corp., 1958; additional permanent sec. Ministry External Affairs, 1960; sec. to Treasury, permanent sec. Ministry Finance, mem. monetary bd. Central Bank Ceylon, alternate gov. for Ceylon in Internat. Bank for Reconstrn. and Devel., 1961-63; high commr. for Ceylon in India, Ceylon ambassador to Nepal and Afghanistan, 1963; mem. Ceylon delegation to prep. meeting 2d Conf. Non Aligned Nations, Colombo, 1964; leader Ceylon delegation to Prep. Meeting Fgn. Ministers, 2d Afro. Asian Conf., Jakarta, 1964; leader Ceylon delegation, vice chmn. Ann. Session ECAFE, New Delhi, 1966; permanent rep. to UN, N.Y.C., 1967, chmn. Ceylon delegation to 22d to 25th sessions of Gen. Assembly, 1967-70, chmn. Com. Peaceful Uses of Sea-Bed and Ocean Floor beyond Limits Nat. Jurisdiction, 1966-71. Home: New York, N.Y. Died Dec. 4, 1980.

AMES, ELIZABETH, art dir.; b. Montevideo, Minn.; d. Theodore F. and Sarah (Macfarlane) Knappen; B.A., U. Minn.; D.Arts, Skidmore Coll., 1947; m. John Carroll Ames, June 19, 1918. Organized plan for hospitality to composers, writers, other artists, for purpose of working in arts, at estate of Yaddo; exec. dir. Corp. of Yaddo, Saratoga Springs, N.Y., 1924-70, exec. dir. emeritus, 1970-77, also mem. corp. Recipient Distinguished Service award Nat. Inst. Arts and Letters, 1959. Mem. Am. Assn. U. Women. Mem. Soc. Friends. Home: Saratoga Springs, N.Y. Died Mar. 28, 1977.

AMES, WALTER IRVING, lawyer; b. Perry County, Ill., Dec. 4, 1892; s. George M. and Emma (Johnston) A.; A.B., Stanford U., 1919, J.D., 1921; m. Marguerite Roberts, Apr. 22, 1922; children—Nancy (Mrs. Petersen), Robert. Admitted to Calif. bar, 1921; mem. firm Gray, Cary, Ames & Frye, and predecessor, San Diego, 1926-80. Pres. bd. Putnam Found. Mem. Am., San Diego (pres. 1932) bar assns., State Bar Calif. Republican. Home: La Jolla, Calif. Died Jan. 11, 1980.

AMOS, FRANKLYN BOOTHROYD, physician; b. Chittenango, N.Y., July 16, 1906; s. Henry Edward and Jennie Leuella (Cramer) A.; M.D., Syracuse U., 1931; M.P.H., Johns Hopkins, 1937; m. Gladys Boardman, June 26, 1930; children—Susanne (Mrs. John Williamson), Franklyn Boothroyd Jr., Sarah (Mrs. Darryl Bradt), Penelope (Mrs. Robert Purzycki). Intern Syracuse Meml. Hosp., 1931-32; gen. practice medicine, Central Sq., N.Y., 1932-35; asst. dist. health officer N.Y. State Dept. Health, Batavia, 1936-38, dist. health officer, 1938-40, asst. dir. local health services, 1940-47, dir. profl. tng., 1948-67, asst. commr., 1967-71; instr. Harvard Sch. Pub. Health, 1946-62; asso. prof. community health Albany Med. Coll., 1950-69; lectr. Columbia Sch. Pub. Health, 1956-70; adj. prof. environmental engring. Rensselaer Poly. Inst., 1961-70. Mem. nat. adv. com. on pub. health traineeships, 1956-61; spl. cons. ICA Mission to Colombia, 1956. Diplomate Am. Bd. Preventive Medicine (trustee 1968-80, vice chmn. pub. health 1969-76). Fellow Am. Coll. Preventive Medicine (vice chmn. pub. health 1969-70), Am. Pub. Health Assn. (chmn. com. profl. tng. health officers sect. 1963-68); mem. Med. Soc. State of N.Y. (chmn. com. on continuing edn. 1961-66, chmn. com. on health manpower 1966-69), Assn. Am. Med. Colls., Albany County Med. Soc., Sigma Alpha Epsilon, Alpha Kappa Kappa. Methodist. Club: University (Albany). Contbr. articles profl. jours. Address: Glenmont, N.Y. Died Feb. 13, 1980.

AMY, ERNEST FRANCIS, b. Paramatta, New South Wales, Australia, November 28, 1883; s. John and Emma (Fincham) A.; brought to U.S., 1885; B.A., Wesleyan U., Conn., 1909, M.A., 1911; Ph.D., Princeton, 1914; studied Oxford U., 1921; m. Theresa Louise Say, Sept. 2, 1915; children—John Wilbur (dec.), Jonathan Weekes. Asst. in English, Wesleyan U., 1909-11; prin. high sch., Waynesville, O., 1911-12; Charles Scribner fellow in English, Princeton, 1912-14; instr. and prof. English, Ohio Wesleyan U., since 1914; prof. of English, N.C. Coll. for Women, summers, 1927-28, Bay View Summer Sch., since 1929. Mem. A.A.U.P., Modern Lang. Assn. America, Phi Beta Kappa, Sigma Chi. Episcopalian. Author: The Text of Chaucer's Legend of Good Women, 1918. Editor: Hardy's The Mayor of Casterbridge, 1933. Contbr. philol. jours. Home: Delaware, O.*

AMY, ERNEST VALENTINE, cons. engr.; b. N.Y.C., Feb. 11, 1892; s. Ernest H. J. and Isabelle (O'Donohue) A.; E.E., Columbia, 1917; m. Jessie Marie Mercier, May 15, 1943. Engr. test dept., New York Edison Co., 1919-20; engr. research dept. Marconi Wireless Telegraph Co., 1920-21; with RCA, 1922-28, in engring. dept. design div. 1921-22, in charge first installation 2-way radio telephone (on S.S. America), 1922-23; engr. in charge Radio Relay Station, Belfast, Me., 1923-25, engr. design sect., in charge constrn. antennae, Rocky Point, L.I., 1926-27, and Bolinas, Cal., 1928; cons. engr., from 1928; dir. Mercier Realty & Investment Co. Dir. Armstrong Meml. Research Found., Inc., from 1955. Served as 1st lt. 302d Engrs., 77th Div., U.S. Army, 1917-18. Recipient Armstrong medal Radio Club of Am., Inc., 1965. Registered profl. engr., N.Y. Mem. Am. Numis. Soc., Am. Inst. Elec. Engrs., I.R.E., Soc. Am. Mil. Engrs., Radio Club Am., Theta Delta Chi. Democrat. Roman Catholic. Clubs: Columbia U. (N.Y.); Atlantic Beach (L.I.). Inventor, co-inventor of sound absorber blocks and many basic radio devices for noise reduction and radio aerial systems. Home: Atlantic, N.Y. Died Feb. 5, 1979; interred Gate of Heaven Cemetery, Mt. Pleasant, N.Y.

ANDERSEN, FRED C., window mfg. co. exec.; b. Spring Valley, Minn., Sept. 1, 1886; s. Hans J. and Mary (Cummings) A.; grad. high sch.; m. Isabel Holmes Barnhart, Nov. 28, 1919 (dec. 1937); foster children—Mrs. A. D. Hulings, Hugh J. Andersen; m. 2d, Katherine Dyer Blount, June 24, 1941. With Andersen Corp., window mfr., Bayport, Minn., 1903—, v.p., 1907-14, pres., 1915-60, chmn. bd., from 1960; chmn. bd. dir. First State Bank of Bayport; dir. First Nat. Bank, Stillwater. Pres. Andersen Found., past pres. Indianhead council Boy Scouts Am.; dir. Tozer Found., Stillwater, Minn. Recipient Silver Beaver award Boy Scouts Am. Mem. Minn. Employers Assn. (past pres.), Am. Legion. Republican. Conglist. Clubs: Rotary (past pres.); Minnesota; Minneapolis. Home: Bayport MN

ANDERSON, ADOLPH GUSTOF, coll. pres.; b. Salem, S.D., Sept. 7, 1913; s. Carl Adolph and Sigrid (Traneus) A.; B.S., U. Pitts., 1934, Ph.D. in Phys. Chemistry, 1940; student Juilliard Grad. Sch. Music, 1942-44; m. Margaret Elizabeth Laird, Nov. 25, 1937; children—Christopher Laird, Peter Traneus. Tchr. chemistry Geneva Coll., Beaver Falls, Pa., 1936-40, U. Pitts., 1940-42, City Coll. N.Y., 1942-44, 46-60; with div. war research Columbia, 1944-46; mem. faculty Hofstra U., 1960-69, prof. chemistry, 1963-69, dean New Coll., 1962-69, dir. Scandinavian Seminar, 1962-76; pres. Hartwick Coll., Oneonta, N.Y., 1969-76. Trustee Scandinavian Seminar Coll., Copenhagen, Denmark, Catskill Mountains Ednl. Center, Stamford, N.Y.; chmn. bd. Coll. Center of Finger Lakes, Corning, N.Y. Decorated Order of North Star (Sweden). Mem. A.A.A.S. Home: Oneonta, N.Y. Died Apr. 5, 1976.

ANDERSON, CLINTON PRESBA, senator; b. Centerville, S.D., Oct. 23, 1895; s. Andrew Jay and Hattie Belle (Presba) A.; student Dakota Wesleyan U., 1913-15, U. Mich., 1915-16; L.H.D. (hon.), Dakota Weslyan U., 1933; D.Agr., N.M. Coll. Agr. and Mechanic Arts, 1946; LL.D., U. Mich., St. Lawrence U., 1946, Mo. Valley Coll., 1949, U. Alaska, 1965; m. Henrietta McCartney, June 22, 1921; children—Sherburne Presba, Nancy (Mrs. Ben L. Roberts). Reporter, editor, Albuquerque, 1918-22; mgr. ins. dept. Loan & Mortgage Co., 1922-24; owner ins. agy., Albuquerque, 1925-63. Treas., State of N.M., 1933-34; mem. 77th-79th U.S. congresses from N.M. at large; sec. U.S. Dept. Agr., 1945-48; U.S. senator from N.M., 1949-73. Mem. Sears-Roebuck Found. Mem. Delta Theta Phi. Democrat. Presbyn. Mason, Elk, Rotarian (pres. Rotary Internat. 1932-33). Home: Albuquerque, N.Mex. Died Nov. 15, 1975.

ANDERSON, ERICA, documentary film maker; b. Vienna, Austria, Aug. 8, 1914; d. Edvard and Ilona Kellner; student photo school in Vienna, Austria; L.H.D. (hon.); m. Larry Collier Anderson, June 20, 1940. Came to U.S., 1940, naturalized, 1945. Documentary films on persons such as Henry Moore, Grandma Moses, Albert Schweitzer, Carl Jung, Thomas Dooley, and others in Poland, Peru, Laos, Indochina, Haiti, Belgium. Established Albert Schweitzer Friendship House and library, Great Barrington, Mass., pres. Author: World of Albert Schweitzer, 1955; The Schweitzer Album; Albert Schweitzer's Gift of Friendship. Address: Great Barrington, Mass. Died Sept. 23, 1976.

ANDERSON, ERNEST W., aero. engr., educator; b. Fargo, N.D., Aug. 23, 1905; s. George Ernest and Isabelle (Lawrence) A.; B.S., N.D. Agrl. Coll., 1926; M.S., Iowa State Coll., 1928, Ph.D., 1933; postgrad. Calif. Inst. Tech., 1934; m. Florence Evelyn McCarthy, June 12, 1928; children—James Robert, John Ernest, Mary Ellen Jill. Mem. teaching and research staff Iowa State U., Ames, from 1926, prof. math., 1947-75, prof. aero. engring., 1951-75, head dept., 1955-71, Anston Marston distinguished prof. engring. 1959-75, prof. emeritus, 1975-78; asso. Ames Lab. of AEC; owner, operator Certification Hybrid Seed Co., 1935-47. Operations analyst USAF, 1951-71. Chmn. Central Iowa Airport Authority Bd.; exec. com., bd. dirs. Iowa State U. Meml. Union. Recipient Faculty citation Iowa State U., 1964. Mem. Inst. Aeros. and Astronautics, Am. Math. Assn., Am. Soc. Engring. Edn., Soc. Indsl. and Applied Math., Aerospace Edn. Council Iowa, Osborn Research Club, Sigma Xi, Phi Kappa Phi, Pi Mu Epsilon, Tau Beta Pi. Rotarian. Home: Ames, Iowa. Died Sept. 10, 1978.

ANDERSON, FLORENCE MARY BENNETT (MRS. LOUIS FRANCIS ANDERSON), author; b. Chateaugay, N.Y., May 20, 1883; d. Henry Uberto and Elizabeth Crosby (Plaskett) Bennett; grad. Coflin Sch., Nantucket, Mass., 1897; A.B., Vassar, 1903; student Am. Sch. of Classical Studies, Athens, 1906-07; Ph.D., Columbia, 1912; m. Louis Francis Anderson June 26, 1918, (dec. November 12, 1950). Asst. in Lab. of Physics, Vassar, 1903-05; Vassar Asso. Alumnae fellow, Columbia, 1905-06; Vassar special fellow, Am. Sch. at Athens, 1906-07; instr. in Greek, Vassar, 1907-10; Babbott fellow of Vassar, Columbia, 1910-11; instr. Greek and Latin, Hunter Coll., New York, 1912-14, asst. prof., 1914-17, asso. prof., 1918 (resigned). Mem. Vigilantes (World War), Poetry Soc. America, League Am. Pen Women, Soc. for Promotion of Hellenic Studies (England), Phi Beta Kappa, Archaeol. Inst. America, Delta Kappa Gamma (honorary), American Philological Assn., Am. Assn. Univ. Women, Maria Mitchell Assn., Vassar Coll. Alumnae Assn., Nantucket Hist. Assn., Classical Assn. (Eng.). Republican. Episcopalian. Clubs: Woman's Reading, Walla Walla Art, Altrusa (hon.), Business and Professional Women (hon.). Author: Religious Cults Associated with the Amazons, 1912; An Off-Islander, 1921; The Garland of Defeat, 1927; Spindrift, 1930; Through the Hawse-Hole, 1932; A Grandfather for Benjamin Franklin, 1940; The Black Sail, 1948; Leaven For The Frontier, 1953; The Shadow of The Tower, 1955; Rebel's Daughter, 1958. also articles on art, lit., philology and archaeology. Poems and essays in magazines and anthologies. Home: Walla Walla, Wash. Died Apr. 16, 1979; buried Mountain View Cemetery, Walla Walla.

ANDERSON, FRANCIS MAURICE, lawyer; b. Providence, R.I., July 20, 1885; s. Thomas Davis and Fanny M. (Cross) A.; prep. edn., Albany (N.Y.) Acad.; A.B., Brown U., 1907; LL.B., New York U., 1912; m. Jane Woolley, July 27, 1912 (died Mar. 26, 1947); 1 dau. Margaret M. m. 2d, Elisabeth E. Dowden, July 20, 1948. With Dwight Mfg. Co., Alabama City, Ala., 1908-09; studied law with Sommer, Colby & Whiting, Newark, N.J.; admitted to bar of N.J. and to U.S. courts,

1913; practiced at East Orange, N.J., 1913-16; settlement officer Fidelity Trust Co., Newark, 1917-18; asst. chief requisition br. of Purchase, Storage and Traffic Div., Gen. Staff, U.S.A., 1918-19; sr. research asst. for Congress in fgn. and internat. law, 1919-20; apptd. spl. asst. to Dept. of State, Sept. 1, 1920, asst. legal adviser Dept. of State, 1924; prof. foreign and domestic comml. law Sch. Fgn. Service, Georgetown U., 1923-41; spl. lectr. U.S. Naval War College, Newport, R.I., 1927-31; counsel for U.S. Government, U.S.-Egyptian Arbitration (Vienna), 1931; legal adviser to Am. commr. of Turkish-Am. Claims Com. (Istanbul, Turkey), 1933-34; asst. to Am. mem. of Joint Am.-Mexican Com., 1935; counsel for Spl. Mexican Claims Commn., 1935-38, in private practice of law, 1938-40. Lt. comdr., U.S.N.R., on active duty, 1941-46. Served as chief of Balkan, Near East and Southern European sects. Naval Intelligence. Mem. Fed. Bar Assn. Republican. Baptist. Club: Brown University. Author of American and Foreign Commercial Law. Now retired. Home: R.D. 1, Bristol, N.H. *

ANDERSON, GAYLORD WEST, public health educator; b. Mpls., Dec. 31, 1901; s. Frank Maloy and Mary Gertrude (Steele) A.; A.B., Dartmouth, 1922; student Sorbonne, Paris, 1922-23, U. Zurich, 1923; M.D., Harvard, 1928, Dr. Pub. Health, 1942; m. Viola Dennis, Oct. 26, 1929; one dau., Gail Elizabeth (Mrs. Harvey Safeer). Teaching asst. chemistry Harvard, 1923-24; interne Albany (N.Y.) Hosp., 1928-29, epidemiologist, div. of communicable diseases Mass. Dept. Health, 1929-30, asst. dir., 1930-31, dir. and dep. commr. of pub. health, 1931-37; asst. in pub. health adminstrn., Harvard Sch. Pub. Health, 1931-37; exec. sec. Mass. Legis. Commn. to Investigate Pub. Health Laws and Policies, 1935-37; prof., head dept. of preventive medicine and pub. health U. of Minn., 1937-44, dir. Sch. Pub. Health, 1944-46, Mayo prof. and dir., 1946-69, dean, 1969-70, dean emeritus, 1970-79; cons. govtl. orgns. and depts.; spl. cons. to Dept. of State in missions to Brazil, Argentina, Chile and Peru, 1948, Colombia and Ecuador, 1949, Chile, 1950, Korea, 1954, for WHO to Egypt, 1953, India, Iran and Egypt, 1958. Served from maj. to col. M.C., AUS, 1942-45. Decorated Legion of Merit; comdr. Order of Hipolito Unanue (Peru); recipient Harrington award Mpls. Jr. C. of C., 1959; Sedgwick Meml. award Am. Pub. Health Assn., 1963. Diplomate Am. Bd. Preventive Medicine. Hon. fellow Royal Soc. Health (Eng.); mem. Am. Epidemiol. Soc. (pres. 1951), Am. Pub. Health Assn. (pres. 1952), Canadian (hon.) pub. health assns., Mass. Med. Soc., Am. Vet. Epidemiology Soc. (hon.), Minn. Vet. Med. Assn. (hon.), Am. Coll. Preventive Medicine, Phi Beta Kappa, Alpha Omega Alpha, Sigma Xi, Delta Omega, Alpha Chi Sigma, Phi Zeta (hon.). Conglist. Clubs: Campus; U. Minn. Alumni (Mpls.). Author: Communicable Disease Control (with M.G. Arnstein), 1941; chapter on "Regulation in Public Health" in Regulatory Administration (by Graham & Reining), 1943; Global Epidemiology (with J. S. Simmons, T.F. Whayne and H.H. Horack), 1944, Vol. II, 1951, Vol. III, 1954; chpt. on Principles of Epidemiology in Bacterial and Mycotic Infections of Man (by Dubos and Hirsch), 1965. Contbr. articles med. jours. Home: St. Paul, Minn. Died Jan. 31, 1979.

ANDERSON, GEORGE K., educator; b. Springfield, Ill., Oct. 20, 1901; s. George Everett and Mary Aletta (Kumler) A.; student Tome Sch., 1912-14, Phillips Exeter Acad., 1914-16; A.B., Harvard, 1920, A.M., 1921, Ph.D., 1925; A.M. (hon.), Brown U., 1947; Litt.D., Middlebury Coll., 1966; L.H.D., Rhode Island Coll., 1973; m. Ethel Mary Humphrey, Oct. 30, 1933; children—Margaret, John. Istr. English, George Washington U., 1924-27; mem. faculty Brown U., 1927-72, prof. English, 1947-72; chmn. dept. English, 1950-60, prof. emeritus, 1972-80; vis. prof. English, Bread Loaf Sch. English, Middlebury Coll., 1931-33; 36-37, 40-42, 44, 47-55, 57-58, 60-61, 63-75, Robert Frost prof. English, 1971, N.Y. State Tchrs. Coll., 1938-39. Guggenheim fellow, 1945. Mem. Medieval Acad. Am., Renaissance Soc. Am., New Eng. Coll. English Assn. (pres. 1968), MLA, R.I., Vt. hist. socs. Author: The Literature of England, 1936; The Generation, 1939; The Literature of the Anglo-Saxons, 1949; The World in Literature, 1950-51; English Literature from the Beginnings to 1485, 1962; The Legend of the Wandering Jew, 1965; The First Fifty Years, 1969; Schoolboy with Satchel, 1979; The Saga of the Volsungs, 1981. Contbr. chpts. to books, articles to profl. publs. Home: Providence, R.I. Died Jan. 2, 1980; buried Swan Point Cemetery, Providence.

ANDERSON, HARALD, chem. co. exec.; b. Riga, Latvia, May 3, 1926; s. Harry Siegfried and Anna Amalia (Grundins) A.; B.S., Goethe U., Frankfurt/Main, Germany, 1948; m. Aelita Arija Geske, Sept. 22, 1953; children—Ilse, Harald, David, Christine. Came to U.S., 1955, naturalized, 1966. Controller, Cancit, Caracas, Venezuela, 1949-55; pres. Inversiones El Corozo, Caracas, 1956-61, Bridgewater Realty Corp., 1968-77; adminstrv. dir. Hoechst Remedia, Caracas, 1962-64; v.p. finance Am. Hoechst Corp., Bridgewater, N.J., 1964-77, dir., 1965-77; pres. Uni-Securities Corp., 1972-77, Randex Corp., Mountainside, N.J., 1975-77, ANCO Corp., Cleveland, Tenn., 1975-77, Uni-Realty Corp., Mountainside, 1976-77; dir. Hoechst Fibers, Inc., Spartanburg, S.C., Nat. Labs. Corp., Kansas City, Mo. Lutheran. Address: Summit, N.J. Died May 22, 1977; interred Poughkeepsie (N.Y.) Rural Cemetery.

ANDERSON, HARRISON RAY, clergyman; b. Manhattan, Kan., Jan. 24, 1893; s. John B. and Joe (Ferguson) A.; B.S., Kan. State Coll., Manhattan, 1911; B.D., McCormick Theol. Sem., 1917; D.D., Coll. of Emporia, 1922; LL.D., Illinois Coll., 1943; S.T.D., Northwestern University 1943; HH.D., Coe College, Cedar Rapids, Iowa; Litt.D., Washington and Jefferson College, 1946; m. Margaret Blanchard, May 29, 1917; children—Doris Elizabeth Drake, John A., Harrison Ray. Ordained Presbyn. ministry, 1917; pastor 1st Ch., Ellsworth, Kan., 1917-21, 1st Ch. Wichita, 1921-28, Fourth Ch., Chicago, since 1928; moderator Presbytery of Wichita, 1923, Chgo., 1934; vice moderator Gen. Assembly, 1943-44; moderator 163d Gen. Assembly Presbyn. Ch., 1951-52; chmn. Com. on Ch. Union. Chaplain 103d U.S. Inf., 26th Div., AEF, two citations for conduct on field of battle. Mem. bd. mgrs. Presbyn. Hosp. Mem. Permanent Judicial Commn. Presbyn. Ch., 1928-31, Permanent Commn. on Interch. Relations, Presbyn. Ch. U.S.A. Trustee Presbyterian Home, Evanston, Illnois. President Chicago Church Federation, 1943-45. Mem. Delta Tau Delta, Theta Pi. Mason (33 deg., K.T.). Clubs: Chicago Cleric, Union League (Chicago). Author God's Way; several articles. Chaplain Dem. Nat. Conv., 1944, Rep. Nat. Conv., 1952-56. Home: Chicago, Ill. Died Oct. 18, 1979.

ANDERSON, HARRY LOY, banker, lawyer; b. Palmetto, Fla., Oct. 15, 1907; s. Harry Sigler and Margaret (Loy) A.; LL.B., Stetson U., 1928; m. Therese Vivienne Areeneaux, Oct. 10, 1935; children—Andrea, Therese, Harry Loy, Denise. Admitted to Fla. bar, 1928, D.C. bar, 1938, U.S. Supreme Ct., 1934; practiced in Ocala, Fla., 1928-34, Washington, 1942-56; pros. atty. Marion County, Fla., 1930-32; partner firm Duckett, Gill & Anderson, Washington, 1953-56, Bowie & Anderson Co., Washington, 1953-56; pres., dir. First Fed. Savs. & Loan Assn., West Palm Beach, Fla., 1958-76; dir. Riggs Bank, Washington, Fairfax County Nat. Bank (Va.), Atlantic Nat. Bank, West Palm Beach, Walker & Dunlop Co., Washington, Washington Mut. Ins. Co., Washington Life Ins. Devel. Corp., Anderson & Co., Inc., Washington, Szemco, Inc., Molecular Research, Inc. (both West Palm Beach), Fed. Home Loan Bank Greensboro, Nat. Life Ins. Co. Fla., Financial Fire & Casualty Co., Key Biscayne Bank (Fla.), Blvd. Nat. Bank, Miami, Fla.; dir., mem. exec. com. Nat. Life Ins. Co. of Fla. Bd. dirs. Fla. Indsl. Devel. Corp.; mem. S. Fla. Regional Export Expansion council U.S. dept. Commerce; mem. Small Bus. Adminstrn., Small Bus. Adv. Council for Fla.; mem. Fla. World's Fair Authority; adv. council naval affairs Sixth Naval Dist. State dir. Orange Bowl Com., Miami. Pres. elect Heart Assn. of Palm Beach, Martin counties; chmn. bd. Heart Assn. West Palm Beach. Mem. Fla. Council of 100. Treas. Fla. Kennedy-Johnson Campaign, 1960. Bd. dirs. Boys Club Am., Met. Police Boys Club, Father-Son Boys Clubs, Big Bros. Palm Beach County, Pride Halfway House, Inc., Rehab. Center for Blind; trustee St. Mary's Hosp., Palm Beach County Trust Fund; mem. exec. adv. com. Fla. Atlantic U.; adv. bd. Salvation Army, Boys' Club Palm Beach County; hon. bd. govs. Gulfstream Good-will, Recipient Pop Warner award. Mem. Fla., D.C. bar assns., Home Builders Assn. Am., Nat. Assn. Real Estate Bds., Mortgage Bankers Assn. Am., Nat. Assn. Ins. Agys., Fla. C. of C. (dir.), U.S., (legislative com.), Fla. (legislative com.), Nat. savs. and loan leagues, S.A.R., Sigma Nu. Democrat. Methodist. Mason (Shriner). Clubs: Rotary (West Palm Beach); Burning Tree, Congressional (pres. 1952-56) (Washington); Seminole, Bath and Tennis, Everglades, Beach (pres. 1974-75), Coral Beach (Palm Beach); Country of Fla.; Metropolitan (N.Y.C.). Home: Palm Beach, Fla. Died July 29, 1976.

ANDERSON, HOMER WILLARD, ednl. cons.; b. Chaseburg, Wis., Oct. 6, 1886; s. Benjamin Nathan and Emma (Engh) A.; B.A., Highland Park (Ia.) Coll., 1910; M.A., University Ia., 1915, Ph.D., 1925; m. Mabel Fretz, Feb. 19, 1918; children—Stuart Paul, Carol Engh. Teacher high sch., 1910; teacher, supt. schs., Morning Sun, Ia., 1910-13; dir. ednl. research, Dubuque, Ia., 1916-17; asst. supt. schs., Omaha, Neb., 1917-19; asst. dir. ednl. research, Detroit, Mich., 1919-23; asst. and dep. supt. schs., Denver, Colo., 1923-33; supt. schs., Omaha, 1933-40; supt. instrn. St. Louis (Mo.) Bd. Edn., 1940-42, Head of Education Section, War Finance Div., U.S. Treasury, 1942-43; supt. schs. Newton, 1943-49; lectr. Harvard, 1947-48, 1949-52; consultant school building planning since 1952; summer lectr. universities of Mich., Denver, Colo., Ia., Wis. Sch. bldg. surveys Cambridge, New Bedford, Wakefield, Taunton, Mass. First lt. statistics branch Gen. Staff, U.S. Army, 1918-19. Mem. N.E.A., Am. Assn. Sch. Administrs. (pres. 1942-43, mem. 1949 yearbook commn.), Nat. Sec. for Study Edn., Mass. State Teachers Assn., Am. Legion, Phi Delta Kappa. Republican. Mason. Clubs: Rotary, Weston Golf. Contbr. ednl. articles to mags. Address: Lakeland, Fla. *

ANDERSON, HOWARD RICHMOND, educator; b. N.Y.C., Oct. 1, 1898; s. Lars Gustav and Charlotte (Johnson) A.; A.B., Augustana Coll., 1922; A.M., U. Chgo., 1928; Ph.D., U. Iowa, 1930; m. Greta Karling, June 27, 1923 (div. 1951); children—William Howard, Douglas Gustav; m. 2d, Monica Luffman, Dec. 22, 1951; children—Monica Jane, James Stewart. Head social studies Theodore Roosevelt High Sch., Wyandotte, Mich., 1922-28; head social studies Univ. High Sch., also asst. prof. history U. Iowa, 1930-37; dir. social studies Ithaca pub. schs. and prof. edn. Cornell U., 1937-44; dir. Sch. Edn., also dir. summer sessions Cornell, 1944-46; specialist for social scis. U.S. Office Edn., Washington, 1946-48, chief instrnl. problems, 1948-51, chief for social scis., 1951-54; dean Univ. Sch., dir. summer session U. Rochester, 1954-60, provost, 1960-61; sr. cons. editor, secondary sch. dept. Houghton Mifflin-Co., Boston, 1961-71. Mem. com. edn. for dem. citizenship Nat. Assn. Secondary Sch. Principals and Nat. Council for Social Studies, 1941-45; mem. U.S. delegation to UNESCO seminar on improvement of textbooks, Belgium, 1950; mem. staff UNESCO seminar on teaching of history, France, 1951. Served as 1st sgt. inf. U.S. Army, 1917-19, AEF one yr. Decorated Croce di Guerra (Italy). Mem. Nat. Council Social Studies (pres. 1940), N.E.A., Am. Ednl. Research Assn., Nat. Soc. for Study Edn., Am. Hist. Assn., Phi Delta Kappa. Democrat. Lutheran. Co-author several books, 1931-77; The History of Our World, 1959. Editor 13th and 25th yearbooks Nat. Council Social Studies. Home: Weston, Mass. Died June 9, 1977.

ANDERSON, JACK Z., govt. ofcl.; b. Oakland, Cal., Mar. 22, 1904; s. George Howard and Susan (Brown) A.; grad. San Jose (Cal.) High Sch., 1923; m. Frances Giffen, May 15, 1926; children—Jean Elizabeth, Carol Frances, Nancy Priscilla. Orchardist, San Juan Bautista, Cal., 1923-81; mem. 76th to 82d Congresses; 8th Cal. Dist.; spl. asst. to sec. agr., 1955-56; adminstrv. asst. to the Pres., from 1956. Republican. Mason, Elk. Clubs: Sainte Claire (San Jose). Home: Hollister, Calif. Died Feb. 9, 1981.

ANDERSON, JAMES RICHARD, geographer; b. Whitaker, Ind., Nov. 20, 1919; s. Pearl and Sarah Ethel (Potter) A.; B.S. with high distinction, Ind. U., 1941, A.B. with honors, 1947; M.A., 1947; student McGill U., 1947; Ph.D., U. Md., 1950; m. Joy Elaine Worstall, Feb. 14, 1945; children—James Richard, Judyth Sue, Janine Joy, John Worstall. Asst. prof. geography U. Md., 1950-52; geographer Agrl. Research Service, Dept. Agr., 1952-60; head prof. dept. geography U. Fla., Gainsville, 1960-69; chief geographer U.S. Geol. Survey, 1972-80. Recipient Meritorious Service award U.S. Dept. Interior, 1977; Alan Gordon Meml. award Am. Soc. Photogrammetry, 1981. Mem. Assn. Am. Geographers (pres. Southeastern div. 1965-67, chmn. commn. geog. applications of remote sensing 1967-69, councilor 1969-72, 1977—, v.p. 1980-81), Fla. Soc. Geographers, Am. Geog. Soc., Nat. Council on Geog. Edn., Phi Beta Kappa, Sigma Xi, Phi Kappa Phi, Phi Delta Kappa. Baptist. Author: A Geography of Agriculture, 1970; A Geography of Agriculture in the United States Southeast, 1973. Mem. internat. com. for preparing World Atlas of Agr., 1960-75. Home: Reston, Va. Died Dec. 24, 1980; buried Forest Meadows Meml. Park, Gainsville, Fla.

ANDERSON, JOHN B(ENJAMIN), army officer; b. Parkersburg, Ia., Mar. 10, 1891; s. Carl Christian and Louise Christine Frederica (Simonsen) A.; B.S. U.S. Mil. Acad., 1914; grad. Field Artillery Sch., 1923; honor grad. Command and Gen. Staff Sch., 1925; grad. Army War Coll., 1928; m. Sue Palmer, Apr. 22, 1924; 1 dau., Sue Moore. Commd. 2d lt., U.S. Army, June 12, 1914, and advanced through the grades to maj. gen., (temp.) Aug. 4, 1942; served as capt., 6th Field Artillery, 1st Div., A.E.F., July 1917-June 1918; War Dept. Gen. Staff, 1928-32, rep. War Dept. at Internat. Conf. for revision of prisoner of war code and Red Cross Convention at Geneva, 1929. Comdg. XVI Corps since Jan. 1944. U.S. and European Theater of Operations. Home: Staunton, Va. Home: Washington, D.C. Died Sept. 1, 1976.

ANDERSON, JOSEPH PAUL, social worker, assn. exec.; b. Lorain, O., Sept. 2, 1907; s. Hilary Frank and Mary Ann (Chrulska) A.; Ph.B., John Carroll U., 1930; M.S., Western Res. U., 1932; m. Virginia Ebert, July 3, 1935; children—Joel, David. Dir. adult work and community orgn. Brashear Settlement, Pitts., 1932-34; exec. dir. Emergency Relief Adminstrn., Cambria and Somerset counties, Pa., 1934-36; sec. group work div. Health and Welfare Fedn., Pitts., 1936-39, chief tenant selection and community relations Housing Authority Pitts., 1939-41; chief leasing and occupancy div. Fed. Pub. Housing Authority, Washington, 1941-43; exec. sec. Am. Assn. Social Workers, 1943-55; exec. dir. Nat. Assn. Social Workers, N.Y.C., from 1955. Acting sec. gen. Internat. Conf. Social Work, 1947-48; social welfare cons. Dept. of State, 1948; vice chmn. coms. on program and recommendations Midcentury White House Conf. on Children and Youth, 1950; adv. com. on personnel and tng. Children's Bur., also Bur. Pub. Assistance, 1947-55; adv. com. on internat. activities to Dept. Health, Edn. and Welfare, from 1952; dir. Social Work Vocational Bur., United Community Def. Services, 1954-55; mem. nat. adv. com. White House Conf. on Aging, 1959. Mem. Nat. Council Social Work Edn. (sec. 1946-51), Health and Welfare Retirement

Assn. dir.), Nat. Legal Aid Assn. (dir. from 1953), Internat. (U.S. com.), Nat. (3d v.p. 1953-54) confs. social work. Author: Opportunities in Social Work, 1952. Home: Scarsdale N.Y. Died Oct. 28, 1979.

ANDERSON, LEWIS CALVIN, clergyman; b. Frankfort, Ind., Dec. 20, 1886; s. Thomas Martin and Anna Allen (Williams) A.; A.B., Transylvania Coll., Lexington, Ky., 1913; M.A., Coll. of the Bible, 1925, also B.D., 1926; m. Maud Ethel Foster, of Richmond, Ind., July 22, 1914; children—David Thomas (dec.), Mary Ru. Prin. Ky. Classical & Business Coll., N. Middletown, 1913-15; pastor Monte Vista, Colo., 1915-18 and 1926-29, Brownsburg, Ind., 1918-21, Springport, Ind., 1921-24; prof. N.T. lit. and interpretation, Cotner Coll., Lincoln, Neb., 1929-33, pres., 1931-33; pastor First Ch., Cheyenne, Wyo., 1934-36; head dept. of religion, Chapman Coll., Los Angeles, since 1936; pastor Monroe Street Christian Church since 1937. Chaplain Colo. Soldiers and Sailors Home, Monte Vista, Colo., 1917-18. Mem. Sigma Upsilon. Independent Republican. Mem. Disciples of Christ. Home: Los Angeles, Calif. *

ANDERSON, MARTHA FORT (MRS. FRANK HARTLEY ANDERSON), portrait painter; b. Macon, Ga., June 22, 1885; d. John Porter and Tallulah Hay (Ellis) Fort; sister of Tomlinson Fort and John Porter Fort; ed. Lucy Cobb Seminary (Athens, Ga.), Piedmont Coll. (Demorest, Ga.); studied art, Boston Mus., 1910-14, Academie Colarossi, Paris, 1914-15, Art Students League, New York, 1915-16; m. Frank Hartley Anderson, Oct. 6, 1923; children—Martha Fort, Frances Hartley. Chief of Canteen Service, S.E. Div. of Red Cross, Atlanta, Ga., 1918-19; founder, 1919, Fine Arts Dept., U. of Ala., and dir. until 1923, now co-dir. extension div. of same dept. Works: Dr. Eugene Smith, U. of Ala; Dr. Semmes, St. Paul's P.E. Ch., Richmond, Va.; Judge W. D. Ellis, Fulton County Court House, Atlanta; Bishop H. J. Mikel St. Phillips Pro-Cathedral, Atlanta; Brig. Gen. J. C. Persons, First Nat. Bank, Birmingham; etc., also mural frieze (with husband). Lakeview Library, Birmingham. Mem. Am. Assn. Women Painters and Sculptors, Birmingham Art Club. Democrat. Episcopalian. Home: Birmingham, Ala. *

ANDERSON, ROBERT NELSON, lawyer; b. Roanoke, Va., May 6, 1899; s. Thomas Gerald and Lena Stuart (Nelson) A.; A.B. cum laude, George Washington U., 1921, LL.B., 1923; m. Mary Rogers, Mar. 24, 1926; children—Mary Elizabeth, Robert Nelson, William Gerald. Admitted to Va. bar, 1922, D.C. bar, 1923; spl. atty. Office Solicitor of Internal Revenue, Washington, 1922-25; asso. law firm Humphreys & Day, Washington, also N.Y.C., 1925-32; sr. mem. firm Anderson, Lawrence & Anderson, 1932-34; spl. asst. to U.S. Atty. Gen., 1934-57, reviewing officer, legal coordinating counsel, 1957-69; mem. firm Delany, Robertson & Anderson, Washington, 1969-71; pvt. practice, Washington and Arlington, Va., 1971-76. Specialist in tax litigation for U.S. govt.; tried test cases involving constitutionality of Agrl. Adjustment Act, Civilian Conservation Corps Acts, Kerr-Smith Tobacco Act, Bankhead Cotton Control Act. Mem. Ho. Deps. representing Am. Bar Assn., 2d Internat. Conf. Legal Profession, The Hague, 1948, 3d Conf., London, 1950, 4th conf., Madrid, 1952, 5th conf., Monte Carlo, 1954; rep. Fed. Bar Assn., 7th Conf., Cologne, 1958, 8th conf., Salzburg, Austria, 1960, 9th Conf., Edinburgh, Scotland, 1962, 10th Conf., Mexico City, 1964, 11th Conf., Lausanne, Switzerland, 1966, 12th Conf., Dublin, 1968, 13th Conf., Tokyo, Japan, 1970, 14th Conf., Monte Carlo, 1972; mem. plan com. 4th Nat. Conf. Citizenship, N.Y.C., 1949, 5th, 6th, 7th, 8th, 9th confs., Washington, 1950-54; mem. atty. gen.'s Adv. Com. Citizenship, 1949-54; incorporator, dir., gen. counsel Nat. Conf. on Citizenship, 1953-76; sec. Friends of Law Library of Congress, 1953-66, pres., 1966-76; an incorporator Found. of Fed. Bar Assn., 1954. Chmn. bd. govs. Lyon Village Community House, 1961-65; chmn. of com. to organize Internat. Bar Assn. by meeting of reps. of nat. bar assns. of world, N.Y.C., 1946. Mem. Fed. (nat. pres. 1942-43; nat. council from 1949), Am. (ho. dels., rep. Fed. Bar Assn. 1944-45), Internat. (council 1947-52, 58-76, chmn. mem. com. 1952-58, 67-76), D.C., Va., Inter-Am. (del. 1st Conv. Havana, 1941) bar assns., Ilustre y Nacional Colegio de Abagados Mexico (hon.), Legal Aid Bur. D.C., Arlington Hist. Soc. (editor mag. 1956-58, pres. 1958-59), Delta Tau Delta, Phi Alpha Delta. Democrat. Methodist. Clubs: Nat. Lawyers (founder mem. 1962) (Washington); Washington Golf and Country (Arlington County, Va.). Home: Arlington, Va. Died Apr. 27, 1976.

ANDERSON, ROBERT PALMER, judge; b. Noank, Conn., Mar. 27, 1906; s. Arthur Pickett and Jessie Palmer (Ashby) A.; grad. Phillips (Andover) Acad., 1923; A.B., Yale, 1927, LL.B., 1929; m. Elizabeth Paffard, Jan. 5, 1935; children—Robert Palmer, Frederic P. Admitted to Conn. bar, 1929; pub. defender New London County, Conn., 1936-47, states atty., 1947-53; judge Superior Ct., State Conn., 1953-54; judge U.S. Dist. Ct., Conn., 1954-60, chief judge, 1960-64; judge U.S. Ct. Appeals, 2d circuit, N.Y.C., 1964-71, sr. judge, 1971-78; judge Temporary Emergency Ct. Appeals, 1972-78. Mem. State Bar Examining Com., 1936-54; mem. Conn. Senate, 1947-48. Served as comdr. USCG Res., 1942-45, capt. Res., 1955-78. Decorated Bronze Star medal; Order Brit. Empire. Fellow Jonathan Edwards Coll., Yale U. Mem. Marine Hist. Assn. (trustee). Home: Noank, Conn. Died May 2, 1978.

ANDERSON, ROSE GUSTAVA, cons. psychologist; b. Gothenberg, Nebr.; d. Mathew and Emily (Axling) Anderson; A.B., U. Nebr., 1917, M.A., 1918; Ph.D., Columbia, 1925; studied in Vienna, 1929-30. Asst. psychology U. Nebr., 1917-18; asst. psychologist Psychol. Clinic, Cleve. Bd. Edn., 1918-19; research asst., mental examiner Minn. State Bd. Control, also State Dept. Edn., 1919-23; psychologist Mpls. Child Guidance Clinic, 1925-30, psychol. lab. Boston Psychopathic Hosp., summer 1930; psychol. dir. Ednl. Adjustment Bur., Westchester County Children's Assn., 1930-32; instr. Inst. Edn. N.Y. U., 1931-32; dir. child adjustment and sch. service div., cons. to women Psychol. Service Center, N.Y.C., 1932-78, dir. Psychol. Service Center, 1942-58; edn. dir. Camp Wah-Na-Gi, Lake George, N.Y., summer 1934; instr. Tchrs. Coll. Columbia, summer, 1936-37, instr. extension div., 1940-42; instr. U. Calif. at Berkeley, summers 1940-42; v.p. Psychol. Corp., 1943-56; independent research, 1958-78. Diplomate Am. Bd. Examiners. Fellow Am. Psychol. Assn. (division pres.), Am. Orthopsychiat. Assn.; mem. N.Y. State Psychology Assn., Phi Beta Kappa. Clubs: Green Mountain; Appalachian Mountain. Co-author: Kuhlman-Anderson Intelligence Tests; Kuhlmann-Anderson Measure of Academic Potential. Author articles on test scoring methods, clin. and counseling psychology. Home: Hightstown, N.J. Died Sept. 7, 1978.

ANDERSON, ROY MARTIN, food co. exec.; b. Bklyn., June 22, 1921; s. John and Mary E. (Martinsen) A.; A.B., Duke, 1944; LL.B., Columbia, 1946; m. Mary Sievers Woody, May 28, 1944; children—Roy Martin, Susan Jane, Thomas Woody. Admitted to N.Y. bar, 1948, practiced in Hempstead until 1951; with Continental Baking Co. (name changed to ITT Continental Baking Co.), Rye, N.Y., 1951-78, v.p., 1961-78, gen. counsel, 1962-69, dir., 1964-78; pres., gen. mgr. ITT Food Products Europe, from 1969; dir. Hong Kong Food Products Mfg. Co., Ltd.; Swiss wine exporter, 1972. Served with USAAF, 1942-44. Mem. Am., Internat. bar assns., Am. Judicature Soc., Sigma Alpha Epsilon, Phi Delta Phi. Home: Palma de Mallorca, Spain. Died Mar. 11, 1978.

ANDERSON, WALTER STRATTON, retired naval officer, business executive; born Carlinville, Illinois, October 4, 1881; son of William Erasmus Preston and Nellie Douglas (Hamilton) A.; student at Blackburn Coll., 1898-99; also hon. LL.D.; B.S., U.S. Naval Acad., 1903; post grad. student Naval Ordnance, 1906-07; grad. U.S. Naval War Coll., 1921; LL.D., Blackburn; m. Virginia Miller Ewing, Oct. 12, 1909; 1 son, Walter Stratton. Commd. ensign, U.S. Navy, 1905; and advanced through the grade to vice admiral, 1945, comd. U.S.S. Yankton, 1911-12; gunnery and exec. officer Battleship Ariz. during WWI; comd. Destroyer Div. 34, 1922-24; asst. chief of staff, U.S. fleet, 1927-29; comd. U.S.S. W. Virginia, 1932-33; naval attaché, London, 1934-36; mem. U.S. del. London Naval Conf., 1935-36; comdr. Cruiser Div. 4, 1937-39; director Naval Intelligence, Navy Department, 1939-41; comdr. battleships, Pacific Fleet, 1941-42; pres. Naval Bd. of Inspection and Survey, Navy Dept., Washington, D.C., 1942-44; comdr. Gulf Sea Frontier and comdt. 7th Naval Dist., 1944-45; retired Mar. 1946. Now dir. Internat. Automatic Electric Corp. and affiliated cos., Asso. Telephone & Telegraph Co. Awarded Legion of Merit, Navy Expeditionary medal (Beirut), Mexican Campaign, 2d Nicaraguan Campaign Victory, Asiatic-Pacific, Am. Zone, Defense and World War II medals, also Navy and Marine Corps medal (U.S.), Order of Naval Merit 1st Class (Cuba); King George V Jubilee medal (Eng.); King Haakon VII Liberation Cross (Norway). Clubs: Chevy Chase, Army and Navy, Army-Navy Country (Washington); N.Y. Yacht. Contbr. articles to U.S. Naval Inst. Home: New York. *

ANDERSON, WALTER STRATTON, JR., business exec.; b. N.Y.C., Apr. 21, 1912; s. Walter Stratton and Virginia Miller (Ewing) A.; B.S., Harvard, 1933; postgrad. U. Chgo., 1949-50; m. Mary McIntire Betts, Sept. 30, 1944; children—Virginia Randolph, Thomas Stratton. Vice consul, Le Havre, France, 1937-38; with Fgn. Service Officers' Tng. Sch., Dept. State, 1939; vice consul, Johannesburg, South Africa, 1939-41, Lagos, Nigeria, 1941-42, Accra, Gold Coast, 1942; with Dept. State, 1942-43; 3d and 2d sec., vice consul, Lima, Peru, 1943-46; 2d sec., consul, London, 1946-49; with Dept. State, 1949-52; first sec., Rangoon, Burma, 1953-54, Oslo, 1954-58; asst. dir. for program ops. Internat. Ednl. Exchange Service, Dept. State, 1958-60, dep. dir. Office of Ednl. Exchange, 1960-61, dep. examiner Bd. Examiners for Fgn. Service, State Dept., 1961-62, ret.; sec. Center for Internat. Affairs, Harvard, 1962-63; v.p. GTE Internat., Inc. subsidiary Gen. Telephone & Electronics Corp., Washington, 1963-77. Adviser, U.S. del. fifth meeting Consultative Com. on Econ. Devel. in South and S.E. Asia, New Delhi, 1953; mem. Bus-Industry Polit. Action Com. Mem. Am. Fgn. Service Assn., Armed Forces Communications and Electronics Assn. Roman Catholic. Club: International (Washington). Home: Washington, D.C. Died May 10, 1977; interred Monticello, Charlottesville, Va.

ANDERSON, WILLIAM, educator; b. Mpls., Oct. 25, 1888; s. Edward and Maren (Olausen) A.; A.B., U. Minn., 1913; A.M., Harvard, 1914, Ph.D., 1917; m. Morgia DeLaittre Mansur, Dec. 28, 1915; children—Morgia Jeanette (Mrs. Howard Penniman), Marian Ruth (Mrs. Robert L. Olson). Instr. govt. Harvard, 1915-16; successively instr. polit. sci., asst. prof., asso. prof. and prof. U. Minn., 1916-57, chmn. dept. polit. sci., 1927-32, 35-47, dir. Bur. for Research in Govt., 1919-28. Mem. Social Science Research Council, 1932-36; mem. Council's Com. on Pub. Adminstrn., 1933-45, chmn. 1939-45; chmn. Council's Com. on Gov., 1941-45. Mem. Mpls. Charter Commn., 1926-36, 45-48, Minn. State Planning Bd., 1935-38, Minn. Resources Commn., 1939-43; mem. com. on fed.-state relations Commn. on Orgn. Exec. Br. Govt., 1947-48, Commn. on Intergovtl. Relations, 1953-75. Pres., Mpls. Research Bur. 1941-47. Fellow A.A.A.S.; mem. Am. Polit. Sci. Assn. (1st v.p. 1929, pres. 1942). Am. Soc. Pub. Adminstrn., Am. Assn. U. Profs., Phi Beta Kappa. Author: A History of the Constitution of Minnesota, 1921; City Charter Making in Minnesota, 1922; American City Government, 1925; The Units of Government in the United States, 1934, rev. edit., 1943; Local Government and Finance in Minnesota, 1935; American Government, 1938, rev. edit., 1946; Fundamentals of American Government, 1940; The National Government of the United States, 1946; Federalism and Intergovernmental Relations, 1946; The Nation and the States, Rivals or Partners?, 1955; Intergovernmental Fiscal Relations, 1956; Man's Quest for Political Knowledge: The Study and Teaching of Politics in Ancient Times, 1964. Editor: Local Government in Europe, 1939; Intergovernmental Relations Series, 1950-60. Contbr. to Minn. Law Rev., National Municipal Rev., Am. Polit. Science Rev., others. Home: Minneapolis, Minn. Died May 14, 1975.

ANDERSON, WILLIAM BANKS, ophthalmologist; b. Haw River, N.C., Dec. 18, 1897; s. William Holt and Mary (Banks) A.; A.B., U. N.C., 1920; M.D., Johns Hopkins, 1924; m. Mildred Everett, Oct. 18, 1927; children—William Banks, Edward Everett, Charles Alexander. Intern Union Meml. Hosp., Balt., 1924-25; resident Mass. Eye and Ear Infirmary, Boston, 1925-27; practice medicine, specializing in ophthalmology, Durham, N.C., from 1927; asso. McPherson Hosp., 1927-45; asso. prof. surgery charge ophthalmology Duke Med. Center, 1930-49, prof., chief div. ophthalmology, 1949-65, prof. ophthalmology emeritus, chief div., from 1965; cons. VA Hosp., Durham, from 1950. Mem. neurol. and sensory disease service adv. com. Neurol. and Sensory Disease Service Project Rev. Panel, HEW, 1963-64, cons. Div. Hosp. and Med. Facilities, 1968. Examining physician SSS, 1941-47. Served as 2d lt., inf. U.S. Army, 1917; with USPHS, 1943. Diplomate Am. Bd. Ophthalmology (chmn. 1965-66). Fellow A.C.S. (past chmn. adv. council for ophthalmology); mem. A.M.A. (past chmn. sci. sect. ophthalmology), So. Med. Assn. (chmn. sect. ophthalmology), N.C., Durham-Orange County med. socs., Am. Ophthal. Soc., Am. Acad. Ophthalmology and Otolaryngology (v.p.), Assn. for Research in Ophthalmology, N.C. Soc. For Research in Ophthalmology, N.C. Soc. For Prevention Blindness (chmn. med. adv. com.), N.C. Eye, Ear, Nose and Throat Soc. (past chmn.). Home: Durham, N.C. Deceased.

ANDERVONT, HOWARD B(ANCROFT), biologist; b. Canton, O., Mar. 8, 1898; s. Ernest B. and Katherine (Kuehn) A.; Sc.D., Johns Hopkins, 1926; m. Letha M. Krabill, Sept. 14, 1926; children—Barbara (Mrs. Robert E. Bowman), Carolyn, John. With lab. biology Nat. Cancer Inst., Nat. Insts. Health, Bethesda, Md., 1950—. Mem. A.A.A.S., Am. Assn. Cancer Research, Am. Soc. Exptl. Pathology, Sigma Xi. Home: Bethesda, Md. Died Mar. 11, 1981.

ANDREW, C. E., civil engr.; b. Oregon, Ill., Dec. 3, 1884; s. Daniel I. and Mary (Slagle) A.; B.S. in C.E., U. Ill., 1906; m. Genevieve Garvin, Dec. 1, 1914. Field work, bridges, 1907-08; city engr., St. Johns, Ore., 1908-12; private contractor, 1913-14; plant engr. Albina Engine and Machine Works, 1915-18; bridge designer B. R.R., 1918-19; bridge engr., State of Wash., 1920-27, State of Calif., 1928-30; prin. engr. San Francisco Oakland Bay Bridge, 1930-37, Seattle pontoon bridge; chmn. cons. bd. and prin. engr., Wash. Toll Bridge Authority since 1937; in charge of design and construction of 2d Tacoma Narrow Bridge, 1938—, design floating bridges Hoods Canal, 2d Lake Washington; cons. so. crossing San Francisco Bay, also Swan Wooster, B.C.; cons. P.R.A., U.S. Army, USN. Member American Society C.E. Clubs: University, Seattle Athletic. Contributor articles to engineering journals. Research in English walnut and pear culture in Ore. Home: Seattle.

ANDREW, JOSEPH ATKINS, lawyer; b. West Point, Ind., July 13, 1885; s. Thomas M. and Lida M. (Atkins) A.; LL.B., U. Mich., 1909; m. Eulora J. Miller, Sept. 22, 1914; children—Dorothy (Mrs. Lewis E. Morrison), Sarah (Mrs. John C. Ohaver). Admitted to Ind. bar, 1909, since practiced in Lafayette; director Purdue Bank. Mem. Ind. State Gen. Assembly, 1935-39. Mem. bd. govs. Nat. Red Cross; trustee Lafayette Home Hosp., Boy Scouts of America (Silver Beaver award); pres. Ind. State Board Public Welfare, 1945-48. Mem. Am., Ind. State, Tippacanoe Co. bar assns., Am. Judicature Soc., Sigma Chi, Phi Delta Phi. Clubs: Country (Lafayette, Ind.); Columbia (Indpls.). Home: 714 Kossuth St.

ANDREWS, CARL WILLIS, JR., ednl. cons.; b. New Bethlehem, Pa., Mar. 5, 1921; s. Carl Willis and Helen L. (Smith) A.; grad. Haverford (Pa.) Sch., 1939; B.A., Amherst Coll., 1943, L.H.D., 1968; student U. Rochester, 1950; M.A., Bucknell U., 1952; m. Margaret C. Stewart, Dec. 7, 1946; children—Stewart Scott, Margaret Lathrop, Mary Bunker. With Graybar Electric Co., 1947-49; head history dept. Allendale Sch., 1949-50; dir. admissions Friends Central Sch., Phila., 1950-58; headmaster Collegiate Sch., N.Y.C., 1959-71; v.p. for ednl. services Taylor, Lieberfeld and Heldman, Inc., N.Y.C., 1971-74; ednl. cons., 1974-79. Bd. dirs. Center Programmed Instrn., Independent Schs. Fund N.Y. Guild Ind. Schs. N.Y.; trustee Nightingale Bamford Sch.; pres. Guild of Ind. Schs. Served to 1st lt., Signal Corps, AUS, 1943-46. Ford Found. travel-study grant, 1969. Mem. Country Day Headmasters Assn., N.Y. State Assn. Pvt. Schs. (trustee), Headmasters Assn., Cum Laude Soc. (regent dist. 3). Club: University. Home: Orleans, Mass. Died Nov. 29, 1979.

ANDREWS, CLIFFORD MARTIN, ceramic products and chem. mfg. co. exec.; b. Butte, Mont., Dec. 31, 1912; s. Joseph Martin and Bessie (Veale) A.; B.S. in Ceramic Engring., U. Ill., 1934; m. Mary Savilla George, May 23, 1936; children—Robert Lee, Joseph Edwin. Ceramic engr. Altorfer Bros., Peoria, Ill., 1934-36; enameling plant supt. Ingersoll Steel & Disc div. Borg Warner Co., Chgo., 1936-38; enameling plant supt. McCray Refrigerator Co., Kendallville, Ind., 1938-42; asso. research prof. ceramic engring. U. Ill., 1942-45; tech. mgr. Internat. div. Ferro Corp., Cleve., 1945-51, mng. dir. Ferro-Brazil, Sao Paulo, 1951-56, v.p. internat. operations, Cleve., 1956-65, exec. v.p., dir., 1965-72, pres., 1972-77, also chief exec. officer; dir. Ferro-Australia, Ferro-Can., Ferro-France, Ferro-Holland, Ferro Far East Ltd. Hong Kong, Ferro-India, Ferro Far East, Inc. Japan, Ferro-Mexico, Eriez Mfg. Co., Erie, Pa., Harris Calorific Co., Cleve. Mem. Greater Cleve. Growth Assn., Cleve. Council World Affairs, Nat. Fgn. Trade Council, Am. Ceramic Soc., Keramos, Sigma Xi. Mem. Christian Ch. Clubs: Union, Chagrin Valley Country. Home: Cleveland, Ohio. Died Dec. 30, 1977.

ANDREWS, COLUMBUS, univ. prof.; b. Kings Creek, N.C., Oct. 17, 1885; s. Thomas Alvah and Edith Elizabeth (Land) A.; A.B., U. of N.C., 1927, A.M., 1928, Ph.D., 1938; m. Mary Grace Woodward, June 14, 1911; children—Alice E., Margaret A. (Mrs. Waighstill H. Avery), Emilie Anne (Mrs. Walter M. Henley, Jr.). General office work in cotton textile industry, Lenoir, North Carolina, until 1917; teacher, prin. and supt. of N.C. pub. schs., 1917-26; mem. staff Inst. for Research in Social Sciences, Chapel Hill, N.C., 1929-33; field rep. N.C. Dir. of Emergency Relief, 1933-36; regional chief Family Selection, Region IV, Farm Security Adminstrn., 1937-42; with Selective Service System, 1942; asso. prof. sociology Southeastern La. Coll., Hammond, La., 1942-46; prof. and head dept. of sociology Furman U., Greenville, S.C., 1946-54. Member Am. Sociol. Soc., Am. Acad. Polit. and Social Sci., Southern Sociol. Soc., Rural Sociological Society. Democrat. Baptist. Author: Administrative County Government in South Carolina, 1933. Address: Mineral, Va. *

ANDREWS, EDWIN CARLOS, packer; b. Penn Yan, N.Y., June 3, 1877; s. John T. and Villa (Raplee) A.; grad. Penn Yan (N.Y.) Acad., 1895, Phillips Acad., Andover, Mass., 1896; A.B., Yale, 1900; LL.B., N.Y. Law Sch., 1902; m. Mary M. Conners, Nov. 14, 1918; children—Edwin C., Peter. Engaged in operating a paper mill, flour mill and produce commn. business, 1902-07; purchased Niagara Radiator & Boiler Co., 1907, of which was pres. and treas.; now chmn. bd. and pres. Jacob Dold Packing Co.; pres. Dold Packing Co. (Omaha); v.p. Conners Contracting Co., G. W. Jennings Co.; dir. Buffalo Courier Express. Republican. Presbyterian. Clubs: Buffalo, University, Country (Buffalo); Yale (New York). Home: Buffalo.

ANDREWS, F. EMERSON, author, found. cons.; b. Lancaster, Pa., Jan. 26, 1902; s. Harry and Ellen (Wiggins) A.; A.B., Franklin and Marshall Coll., 1923, L.H.D., 1952; m. Edith Lilian Severance, July 5, 1932; children—Frank M., Peter Bruce, Bryant. Free-lance writer articles in mags. and books, 1918-78; mgr. advt. printing The Macmillan Co., pubs., 1923-26, dir. mail service dept., 1926-28; dir. publs. Russell Sage Found., 1928-56; pres. Found. Library Center, N.Y.C., 1956-67, cons., 1967-78; cons. publs. Twentieth Century Fund, 1941-56; cons. NSF, 1958-68. Mem. Tenafly Planning Bd., 1936-62; trustee Franklin and Marshall Coll., Tenafly Library Bd., Am. Inst. Graphic Arts; bd. dirs. Shell Cos. Found. Mem. Duodecimal Soc. Am. (pres. 1944-50, chmn. bd. 1950-63), Authors League Am., Phi Beta Kappa, Lambda Chi Alpha. Mem. Riverside Ch., N.Y.C. Author numerous books including: New Numbers, 1935; Philanthropic Giving, 1950; Corporation Giving, 1952; Grugan's God, 1955; Philanthropic Foundations, 1956; Upside-Down Town, 1958; Legal Instruments of Foundations, 1958; Numbers, Please, 1961; Knights and Daze, 1966; The Tenafly Public Library, A History, 1970; Foundation Watcher, 1973; Nobody Comes to Dinner, 1977. Home: Tenafly, N.J. Died Aug. 7, 1978.

ANDREWS, FRANCES M., educator; b. Scranton, Pa., May 20, 1908; d. Hugh Barr and Cora Louise (Ross) Andrews; B.Mus., Marywood Coll., 1931; M.Ed., Pa. State U., 1942, D.Ed., 1948. Dir. music Fleetville (Pa.) pub. schs., 1932-36; dir. music Abington Independent Schs., Waverly, Pa., 1936-43; dir. music State College (Pa.) High Sch., 1943-50; mem. faculty music edn. Pa. State U., 1943-65, prof., head dept. music edn., 1965-73, prof. emeritus, 1973-76. Mem. Pa. Dept. Edn. Adv. Music Com. in Arts, 1960-67; mem. nat. adv. com. Young Audiences, Inc., 1973-76; del. White House Conf. on Children, 1970. Recipient (with N.C. Deihl) U.S. Office Edn. grant, 1965-67, Pa. Dept. Edn. grant, 1966, citation of excellence Nat. Band Assn., 1972, citation for contbn. to youth arts Pa. Dept. Edn., 1972, certificate for 25 years service Pa. State U., 1972, Elizabeth Mathias award Mu Phi Epsilon, 1972, citation Music Educators Nat. Conf., 1972. Mem. N.E.A. (adviser music edn. Ednl. Policies Commn., 1959-63), Music Educators Nat. Conf. (pres. 1970-72, v.p. 1972-76, com. chmn. 1970-71, pres. Eastern div. 1961-63), Music Educators Nat. Conf., Am., Pa. ednl. research assns., Am. Assn. U. Profs., Pa. Fedn. Music Clubs (chmn. music in schs. and colls. 1955-61), Mu Phi Epsilon. Author: (with Joseph E. Leeder) Guiding Junior High School Pupils in Music Experiences, 1953; (with Clara E. Cockerille) Your School Music Program, 1953; Junior High School General Music, 1971. Editor: (songbook) Sing Together Children, 1959. Editor, contbr. Music in the Secondary Schools, 1959. Editorial asso. Jour. of Research in Music Education, 1962-68. Mem. editorial bd. Music Educators Jour., 1957-62. Contbr. articles to profl. jours. Home: State College, Pa. Died June 18, 1976.

ANDREWS, JAMES FREDERICK, communications exec.; b. Westfield, Mass., Oct. 8, 1936; s. Andrew John and Margaret Elizabeth (Mihlik) A.; A.A., St. Charles Coll., Balt., 1956; A.B. in Philosophy, St. Mary's Sem. and U., Balt., 1958, M.A. in Theology, 1960; postgrad. in Philosophy, U. Notre Dame, 1960-61, in Pub. N.Y. U., 1963-64; m. Kathleen Virginia Whalen, July 31, 1965; children—Hugh Timothy, James Courtney. Stock broker Bache & Co., South Bend, Ind., 1961-63; editor Sheed and Ward, Inc. (became subs. Universal Press Syndicate 1973, name changed to Andrews and McMeel 1979), N.Y.C., 1963-65, pres., pub., editor-in-chief, Mission, Kans., 1973-80, sec., 1973-80; mng. editor Ave Maria Mag., South Bend, 1965-67, Nat. Cath. Reporter, Kansas City, Mo., 1968-70; co-founder Universal Press Syndicate, Mission, 1970, exec. v.p., treas., dir., 1970-80, chmn. bd., 1979-80; instr. investment banking Purdue U., 1962. Recipient certificate of recognition Nat. Conf. Christians, Jews, 1967. Mem. Nat. Comics Council Nat. Cartoonist Soc., Friends of Art, Philharmonic Assn. of Kansas City, Sigma Delta Chi. Roman Catholic. Clubs: Carriage (Kansas City, Mo.); K.C., Kansas City Press; Carlton, Chgo., Atrium (N.Y.C.). Author: (with John Reedy) The Perplexed Catholic, 1967; The Citizen Christian, 1968; editor: Creative Suffering, 1970; Paul VI: Critical Appraisals, 1970; Karl Barth, 1972. Home: Overland Park, Kans. Died Oct. 19, 1980.

ANDREWS, JAMES NEWTON, paperboard co. exec.; b. Cleve., Feb. 13, 1914; s. Lloyd E. and Martha Jane (Hunt) A.; A.B., Wittenberg U., 1936; m. Janet Zieger, May 20, 1939; 1 son, James Douglas. With Ohio Boxboard Co., 1936-59; company merged with Central Fibre Products Co. and Am. Box Board Co. to form Packaging Corp. Am., 1959; exec. v.p. Packaging Corp. Am., 1959-63, pres., 1963-65, chmn. bd., 1966-70; pres. Fibre Box Assn., Chgo., 1970-77; dir. State Nat. Bank, Evanston, Ill. Bd. dirs. Wittenberg U., Springfield, O. Mem. Beta Theta Pi. Home: Wilmette, Ill. Died Dec. 18, 1977.

ANDREWS, JOSEPH C(HURCH), corp. exec.; b. New Britain, Conn., Nov. 3, 1885; s. Joseph R. and Olive (Booth) A.; A.B., Cornell, 1909; m. Bess Whitmarsh, Apr. 25, 1931; children—Emily Marguerite, Zelle Whitmarsh. Chemist The Am. Hardware Corp., New Britain, Conn., 1912, purchasing agt., 1931, v.p., 1940; retired 1952, dir. New Britain Nat. Bank, Burritt Mut. Savings Bank, New Britain Gas & Light Co., Dir. New Britain Gen. Hosp.; pres. New Britain Meml. Hosp. Conglist. Clubs: Shuttle Meadow (New Britain); Cornell (N.Y. City). Home: New Britain, Conn. *

ANDRUS, EDWIN COWLES, physician; b. Kaatsban, N.Y., Feb. 28, 1896; s. Jonathan Cowles and Margaret (De Witt) A.; A.B., Oberlin Coll., 1916, A.M., 1917, hon. Sc.D., 1941; M.D., Johns Hopkins, 1921; m. Miriam Jay Wurts, June 10, 1933. House officer Johns Hopkins Hosp., 1921-23; NRC fellow in medicine London and Vienna, 1923-25; resident physician Johns Hopkins Hosp., 1925-27; asso. in medicine Johns Hopkins Med. Sch., 1926-31, asso. prof., prof., 1931-61, prof. emeritus, 1961-78, asst. dean med. faculty, 1929-34; physician Johns Hopkins Hosp.; cons. cardiology Walter Reed Army Hosp., 1954-62. Asst. to chmn. com. med. research OSRD, 1942-44, chief div. medicine 1944-46; chmn. com. med. problems in civil aviation NRC, 1944-46, mem. com. aviation medicine, 1945-46, subcom. cardiovascular diseases, 1946-51; spl. cons. to surgeon gen. USPHS, 1946-51; chmn. cardiovascular study sect. Nat. Adv. Heart Council, 1946-51, mem. council, 1953-62; sr. spl. cons. Nat. Heart Inst., 1957-62; mem. med. exchange mission to Russia, 1961; dir. 2d Nat. Conf. Cardiovascular Disease, 1963. Bd. dirs. Passano Found., 1955-72. Mem. A.C.P. (master), Inter-Am. (council 1954-68, v.p. 1960-68), Internat. (council 1958-66) cardiological socs., Sociedad Peruana de Cardiologia (hon.), A.M.A., Am. Physiol. Soc., Am. Soc. Study Arteriosclerosis, Am. Heart Assn. (pres. 1954-55), Am. Soc. Clin. Investigation, Am. Clin. and Climatol. Assn., Assn. Am. Physicians, Med. and Chirurgical Faculty Md., A.A.A.S., Phi Beta Kappa, Sigma Xi, Alpha Omega Alpha. Republican. Clubs: Elkridge, Fourteen West Hamilton Street (Balt.). Home: Baltimore, Md. Died Mar. 26, 1978; buried Jay Cemetery, Rye, N.Y.

ANDRY, E. ROBERT, biblical scholar; b. nr. Huntingburg, Ind., Sept. 24, 1907; s. George and (Mason) A.; A.B., Butler U., 1930, A.M., 1934, B.D., 1934; Ph.D., Southern Baptist Theol. Sem., 1942; m. Oma Belle Alvey, Aug. 30, 1931; children—Robert Bruce, Oma Kathryn. Ordained to ministry of the Christian Ch., 1934, and served rural chs., in Ind., 1930-34; minister Madison, Ind., 1934-38, Downey Ave. Ch. Indpls., 1938-44; head dept. religion Coll. Liberal Arts and Scis., Butler U., also prof. Bibl. history and lit., 1944-73, prof. emeritus, 1973-80; youth leader and counselor, Ford Found. fellow, Jerusalem, 1952-53. Mem. Soc. Bilbl. Lit. and Exegesis, Am. Acad. Religion, Am. Schs. Oriental Research, Kappa Delta Rho, Tau Kappa Alpha, Phi Kappa Phi, Theta Phi. Clubs: Lions (Westfield). Microfilmed 335 manuscripts in library of Greek Orthodox Patriarchate, Istanbul, 1962 (microfilms now at Dumbarton Oaks Research Library, Washington. Home: Westfield, Ind. Died Jan. 28, 1980; buried in Westfield.

ANGELIQUE, MOTHER MARY (AN'GE-LEK), coll. dean; b. Kosciusko, Miss., Apr. 12, 1882; d. Eli S. and Nannie (Lowry) Ayres; student St. Mary's Acad., Austin, Tex., 1897-1900; A.B., Our Lady of the Lake Coll., San Antonio, Tex., 1912; A.M., Catholic U. of America, 1913; student Columbia, summers 1924-28, 30. Mem. Sisters of Divine Providence. Instr. Our Lady of the Lake Acad., 1902-11; professor English and mathematics Our Lady of the Lake College, 1911-12, professor of English, 1914-43, registrar and dean, 1913-24, dean since 1924; mem. gov. bd. of Corp. of the Sisters of Divine Providence, 1928-43, pres. since 1943 (formerly ednl. dir. and supervisor of schs.); sec.-treas. bd. of lay trustees, Our Lady of the Lake Coll., San Antonio, Tex., since 1928; elected Superior Gen. of Congregation of Sisters of Divine Providence, 1943-55; mem. of the Southern Conf. of College Deans, Co-founder and member at large of Delta Epsilon Sigma, national Catholic honor fraternity. Mem. Southern Assn. of Coll. for Women (mem. exec. com., 1933-34), Texas Association of Colls. (v.p. 1942-43), Am. Assn. U. Women, N.E.A., Cath. Philos. Soc., Delta Kappa Gamma (hon. mem.). Contbr. ednl. articles to jours. Address: San Antonio, Tex. *

ANGELL, DONALD KINNEY, found. exec.; b. Cortland, N.Y., Nov. 14, 1906; s. Walter Halbert and Harriet (Kinney) A.; B.S. in Econs., U. Pa., 1930; children—Donald, Margaret A. Griffith, Stephen; m. Madelon Cunningham, 1955; stepchildren—Mary C. Daniels, Frank Cunningham, Victoria C. Case. Editor field service State Mut. Life Ins. Co., 1930-33, asst. gen. agt., N.Y.C., 1933-37; exec. sec. U. Pa., 1937-38, asst. to dir. Bicentennial Celebration, 1939-40, asst. mgr. U. Council on Devel., 1941, dir. Houston Hall, 1941-45, gen. mgr. Council on Devel., 1945-46, sec. corp., 1946-51, v.p. charge univ. fund, sec. corp., 1951-55, v.p., asst. to pres., 1956-70; sr. v.p. U. Pa. Found., 1970-80. Bd. dirs. Phila. Civic Center, Pathway Sch. Mem. Kappa Alpha (trustee). Republican. Episcopalian. Clubs: Bachelors Barge: Union League Phila. Country, Rittenhouse, Vieques Assembly (founder). Home: Philadelphia, Pa. Died Feb. 26, 1980.

ANGERS, EUGÈNE-RÉAL (ÄN-ZHÄ'), justice of the Exchequer Court of Canada; b. Montreal, Oct. 1, 1883; s. Réal and Joséphine (Trudel) A.; B.A., College Sainte-Marie, Montreal, 1904; LL.L. Université Laval, Montreal, 1907; LL.D., Ottawa U., 1937; LL.D. (honorary), Université de Montreal, 1950; m. Germaine Tousignant, Sept. 15, 1909; children—Pierre, André, Louise, Marc, Guy, Suzanne, Françoise. Began as barrister and solicitor, Aug. 1907; read law with Campbell, Meredith, Macpherson & Hague, Montreal; advocate, Bar of Province of Que., 1907; King's counsel, 1930; began practice of law with Ernest Guimont under name of Guimont & Angers; joined firm of Brosseau, Brosseau & Tansey, 1908, which became Brosseau, Brosseau, Tansey & Angers; associated with Howard S. Ross under name of Ross & Angers, 1913; mem. firm Monty, Duranleau, Ross & Angers, and successor firms, 1921-32; justice of the Exchequer Court of Can. since Feb. 1932. Mem. L'Association St.-Jean-Baptiste, L'Alliance Française d'Ottawa, La Société des Conférences de l'Université d'Ottawa, La conference Canadienne des juristes de langue francaise d'Ottawa. Roman Catholic. Home: Ottawa, Can. *

ANGERSTEIN, THOMAS CHESTER (ANG'GER-STIN), lawyer; b. Hillsboro, Ill., Nov. 10, 1886; s. Christian W. and Mary E. (Edwards) A.; student Hillsboro High Sch., 1900-03, Illinois Coll., Jacksonville, Ill., 1903-07; U. of Ill. Coll. of Law, 1907-10; m. Naomi Canny, Nov. 5, 1924. Admitted to Ill. bar, 1910; atty. in offices of Scott, Bancroft & Stephens, 1910; asst. trial atty., Internat. Harvester Co., 1911-12, asso. commerce counsel same, 1913-14; in pvt. practice of law since 1915. Mem. Am., Ill. State and Chicago bar assns., Phi Delta Phi, Delta Sigma Rho, Order of the Coif. Republican. Presbyterian (Fourth Presbyn. Ch.). Home: Chicago, Ill. *

ANGLE, WESLEY MOTLEY, telephone, television mfr.; b. Rochester, N.Y., Dec. 17, 1882; s. Charles Edwin and Ida Jane (Motley) A.; grad. Bradstreet Prep. Sch., 1899; A.B., Harvard, 1903, A.M., 1904; m. Ann Van Vranken Warner, Nov. 24, 1909; children—Charles Edwin, Richard Warner, Eleanor (Mrs. Thomas Thacher Richmond), Janet (Mrs. E. A. Mays; dec.), George Motley. With Stromberg-Carlson Co., 1903-49, successively as cable machine operator, stockroom clerk, assembler, cost clerk, office mgr., asst. sec., asst. treas. sec., v.p., pres., chmn. of board (pres. 1934-45, chmn. 1945, hon. chmn., 1949, dir., 1914-55; dir. General Dynamics Corporation; dir. R. W. Angle Corp. (Marion, Mass.), Security Trust of Rochester. Served as capt. Quarter Master Corps, U.S. Army, as chief of purchase records branch, Office of Dir. of Purchase, Washington, D.C., 1918-19. Director, U.S.-Independent Telephone Assn., 1940-49; dir. Asso. Inds. N.Y. State, 1935-50, Nat. Assn. of Mfrs. (1941-43). Dir. Genesee Hospital; hon. director Visiting Nurse Assn. Trustee Rochester Bur. of Municipal Research; dir. Rochester Civic Music Assn., 1930-45. Trustee of Rochester C. of C. Republican. Presbyn. Clubs: Country, Genesee Valley, Harvard (N.Y.C.), Brook-Lea. Home: Rochester, N.Y. *

ANGOFF, CHARLES, author, educator; b. Minsk, Russia, Apr. 22, 1902; s. Jacob Joseph and Anna (Pollack) A.; came to U.S., 1909, naturalized, 1923; A.B., Harvard U.; Litt.D., Fairleigh Dickinson U., 1966; m. Sara F. Freedman, June 13, 1943; 1 dau., Nancy Carol Angoff Gallin. Newspaperman on Boston papers, 1923; asst. editor Am. Mercury, 1925-31, mng. editor, 1931-34, editor, 1934-35; mem. editorial bd. Nation, 1935-36; editor Am. Spectator, 1936; contbg. editor N. Am. Rev., 1938-40; Am. commentator The Living Age, 1938-40; mng. editor Am. Mercury, 1943-50; exec. editor Mercury Publs. 1950-51; adv. editor True Crime Detective, 1950-51; mng. editor Book of Wit and Humor, 1950-51; lectr. English, U. Kansas City, 1949, 50; lectr. U. N.H., 1951-61; adj. prof. English, Wagner Coll., 1955-56; prof. English, Fairleigh Dickinson U., 1954-76, chief editor Fairleigh Dickinson U. Press, 1967-76; adj. prof. lit. N.Y. U., 1958-66; advisor Jewish Book Guild, 1949-76, Marquis Biog. Soc., 1969; scholar-in-residence U. Vt., 1976, vis. prof. English, 1977-78; vis. prof. English, Yeshiva U., 1975-79. Recipient Humanitarian award Becton Soc. of Fairleigh Dickinson U. and Knights of Malta, 1973; fellow Boston U. Libraries, 1964-79; Ellis Island award for significant contbns. to adopted country, 1977. Fellow Jewish Acad. Arts and Scis.; mem. Poetry Soc. Am. (pres. 1969-72), Authors League Am., Internat. P.E.N. Author: A Literary History of the American People, vols. I and II, 1931; Palestrina, Savior of Church Music, 1944; (play) Something to Sing About (produced Pasadena Playhouse), 1940; (play) Moment Musical (produced N.Y.C.), 1943; Adventures in Heaven (short stories), 1945, 2d edit., 1970; The Book of Libel, 1946, 2d edit., 1970; When I Was a Boy in Boston (short stories), 1947, 2d edit., 1970; The Fathers of Classical Music, 1947, 2d edit., 1970; Journey to the Dawn, 1951; In the Morning Light (Daroff Fiction award), 1953; The Sun at Noon, 1955; Something About My Father and Other People, 1956; H.L. Mencken, A Portrait from Memory, 1956; Between Day and Dark, 1959; The Bitter Spring, 1961; Summer Storm, 1963; The Tone of the Twenties, 1966; The Bell of Time, 1966; Memory of Autumn (Daroff Fiction award), 1968; Memoranda for Tomorrow, 1969; (novel) Winter Twilight (Author award N.J. Assn. Tchrs. English), 1970; (novel) Season of Mists (Author award N.J. Assn. Tchrs. English), 1971; (poems) Prayers at Midnight (Author award N.J. Assn. Tchrs. English), 1971; (novel) Mid-Century, 1974; editor: Arsenal for Skeptics (pen name Richard W. Hinton), 1934; Stradivari, The Violin Maker (Helen Tinyanova), 1938; (with Joseph Hilton Smyth) The World Over, 1939; (with Leon Bryce Bloch) The World Over, 1940; (with Lawrence E. Spivak) The American Mercury Reader, 1944; The World of George Jean Nathan, 1952; (with Clarence R. Decker) Modern Stories from Many Lands, 1963, sole editor, 2d edit., 1972; The Humanities in the Age of Science, 1968; George Sterling: A Centenary Memoir, 1969; (with Myer Levin) The Rise of American Jewish Literature, 1970; William Carlos Williams, 1972; Jonathan Edwards, 1974; The Concept of Freedom as Reflected in American-Jewish Literature, 1975; (novel) Toward the Horizon, 1978; editor: The Lit. Rev., 1957-76. Home: New York, N.Y. Died May 6, 1979; buried Linden Hill Cemetery, Bklyn.

ANIGSTEIN, LUDWIK, educator, lab. dir.; b. Warsaw, Poland, Feb. 2, 1891; s. Isidore and Helen (Steinkalk) A.; Ph.D. magna cum laude, U. Heidelberg, 1913; med. diploma U. Dorpat, 1915; M.D., U. Poznan, 1923; certificate London Sch. Tropical Medicine, 1923; m. Luba Heller, Apr. 16, 1916; children—Alice Helen (Mrs. Bruce Grynbaum), Robert; m. 2d, Dorothy M. Whitney, May 2, 1958. Came to U.S. at invitation of NRC, 1939, naturalized, 1945. Head parasitology State Inst. Hygiene, Warsaw, 1919-30; lectr. pub. health State Sch. Hygiene, Warsaw, 1926-39; lectr. parasitology U. Warsaw, 1929-39; research asso. U. Calif., 1940; asso. in preventive medicine U. Tex., Galveston, 1940-42, asst. prof., 1942, asso. prof. tropical medicine, 1943, prof. preventive medicine and pub. health, 1946-70, emeritus prof. preventive medicine and community health, 1970-75; dir. Rickettsial Research Lab.; cons. geog. medicine Med. Br. Hosps.; cons. med. div. Oak Ridge Inst. Nuclear Studies. Research student in tropical medicine, Britain Colonial Service, Malay States, 1929-31; malaria expert Siamese Govt., 1931; health expert Govt. of Liberia, 1935-36. Served as med. officer, Russian Red Cross, 1915-18. Mem. malaria commn. League of Nations, 1924-39, typhus experts commn., 1937; chmn. sec. tropical pathology Internat. Congress Tropical Medicine, Amsterdam, Netherlands, 1938. Mem. UNRRA med. mission to Poland, 1946. Fellow Royal Soc. Tropical Med. and Hygiene (London), Am. Pub. Health Assn., A.A.A.S., Tex., N.Y. acads. scis., Am. Acad. Microbiology; mem. Royal Soc. Health (London), Am. Soc. Exptl. Pathology, Am. Assn. Cancer Research, Am. Soc. Tropical Medicine and Hygiene, Tex. Pub. Health Assn., Soc. Am. Bacteriologists (also Tex. br.), Soc. Exptl. Biology and Medicine, Sci. Research Soc. Am., Sigma Xi, Phi Delta Epsilon, Mu Delta. Contbr. many articles on protozoology, bacteriology, epidemiology, immunology, tropical disease to sci. jours. Specialist in research in rickettsial diseases. Home: Galveston, Tex. Died Oct. 31, 1975.

ANKENBRANDT, FRANCIS L., air force officer; b. Ill., Jan. 27, 1904; B.S., U.S. Mil. Acad., 1926; M.S., Yale, 1927: grad. Signal Sch., company officers course, 1929. Commd. 2d lt., U.S., Army, 1926, and advanced through the grades to maj. gen., 1947; transferred to A.C. (now U.S. Air Force), 1946; chief signal officer, SHAPE, 1952-54; comdr. AACS, Andrews AFB, 1954-55; dir. communications-electronics Joint Chiefs of Staff, 1955-56; mgr. def. projects RCA, DEP, Camden, N.J. Home: Naples, Fla. Died Dec. 1, 1976.

ANSPACH, CHARLES LEROY, educator, public relations cons.; b. Fremont, Ohio, Mar. 5, 1895; s. Phillip Noble and Amanda (Loose) A.; A.B., Ashland Coll., 1919, A.M., 1920, LL.D., 1944; U. Toledo Night Sch. for Execs., 1917-18; A.M., U. Mich., 1923, Ph.D., 1930; LL.D., Ferris State Coll., 1959; LL.D., U. Mich., 1966; L.H.D., No. Mich. College, 1959; Litt.D., Central Mich. U., 1959; m. Mary Fisher, Sept. 10, 1916; children—Vivian Mardele, Lillian Katherine. Registrar Ashland Coll., 1923-26; fellow U. Mich., 1926-27; dean Ashland Coll., 1926-30; head dept. of edn. Eastern Mich. Coll., 1930-34, dean adminstrn., 1934-35; pres. Ashland Coll., 1935-39, pres. emeritus, 1939-77; pres. Central Mich. U., 1939-59, pres. emeritus, 1959-77; cons. Northwood Inst., Midland, Mich.; public relations cons. Isabella Bank & Trust, Mt. Pleasant; chmn. bd. dirs. Isabella County State Bank. Mem. nat. council Boy Scouts Am., 1942-62, hon. mem., 1962-77, life mem. exec. com. Region VII; del. Mich. Constl. Conv., 1961-62; bd. dirs. Alvin Bentley Found.; bd. dirs. Mich. Soc. Mental Hygiene; chmn. Mich adv. com. Community Sch. Project, 1946-54; mem. Mich. Higher Edn. Facilities Commn., 1964-66; hon. mem. Mich. Soc. Mental Health; bd. regents Eastern Mich. U.; bd. visitors Freedoms Found.; sec., No. Mich. Econ. Devel. Council; pres., Michigan YMCA. Recipient Silver Beaver, Silver Antelope awards Boy Scouts Am.; King Christian X Liberation medal; Freedoms Found. 2d award; Kappa Delta Pi distinguished Service award; Wolverine Frontiersman award Mich. Week, 1958; distinguished service award Mich. State Fair, 1959; Merit award Northwood Inst., Alma, 1960; Disting. Service award Central Mich. U. Alumni, 1970, Mich. YMCA, 1972; Phi Kappa Delta Leadership award, 1969; A.W. Thompson Humanitarian award, 1970. Mem. Mich. Schoolmasters Club, N.E.A., Pi Kappa Delta. Mem. Brethren Ch. (pres. Nat. Home Mission Bd. 1931-37; ex-vice moderator Nat. Conf.; ex-pres. laymens orgn.). Mason (33 deg.), Rotarian. Contbr. ch. publs.; co-author Problems in Educational Sociology and a Manual of Observation Problems; author: A Voice Speaks. Contbr. Vital Speeches, Peabody Journal, School and Society. Home: Mt. Pleasant, Mich. Died Oct. 1977.

ANTHONY, ANN, coll. dean; b. Sibley, Ia., Feb. 12, 1886; d. Thomas J. and Elizabeth (Roberts) Anthony; A.B., Columbia, 1907; Pd.M., New York U., 1916, Ph.D., 1929. Elementary school teacher, 1907; asst. instr. in psychology, Hunter Coll., New York, N.Y., 1911-17, instr., 1917-25, asst. prof., 1925-28, asso. prof., 1928-37, acting dean of annex. 1933, acting dean of Bronx buildings, 1933-37, prof. and asst. dean in charge Bronx buildings, 1937-41, prof. and dean in charge Bronx bldgs., 1941-43, prof. and dean of freshmen and sophomores since 1943, dean of students since 1946. Mem. bd. dirs., Lennox Hill Settlement, 1947-50; asso. alumnae Hunter Coll., 1947. Mem. N.Y. State Assn. of Deans, N.Y. City Deans Assn., Pub. Edn. Assn., N.Y. City Colls. Personnel Assn. (pres. 1948), N.E.A., Nat. Assn. Deans of Women, Am. Assn. Univ. Profs., Administrative Women in Edn., N.Y. Adult Edn. Council. Home: N.Y. City. *

ANTHONY, CHARLES R., merchant; b. nr. Trenton, Tenn., Aug. 10, 1885; s. Zachary Cicero and Elvira Ann (Pennington) A.; student Indianola Bus. Coll., Holdenville; Dr. Laws (hon.), Oklahoma City U.; Dr. Humanities (hon.), Beth Nazarene Coll.; Ph.D. (hon.), Colo. State Christian Coll.; m. Lutie L. Mauldin, July 10, 1910; children—Helen (Mrs. Galloway), Ray T., Guy M., Betty (Mrs. Zahn), Dana (Mrs. Clasby). Organized C.R. Anthony Co., Oklahoma City, Okla., 1922, former pres. and chmn. bd., dir.; chmn. bd. Citizens Nat. Bank, Oklahoma City. Pres. United Fund, 1952; mem. Okla. State Fair Bd. Bd. dirs. Frontiers of Sci. Found. Okla.; bd. dirs., treas. YMCA; trustee Nat. Cowboy Hall of Fame and Western Heritage. Recipient Horatio Alger award, 1963; named to Okla. Hall Fame; citation Nat. Conf. Christians and Jews, 1965. Hon. mem. Telephone Pioneers Am. Club: Rotary (hon. mem.). Home: Oklahoma City, Okla. Died June 16, 1976.

ANTHONY, ROY DAVID, prof. pomology; b. Rochester, N.Y., Apr. 2, 1884; s. Daniel Macomber and Charlotte R. (Finch) A.; B.S., U. of Rochester, 1908; B.S. in Agr., Cornell U., 1910, M.S., 1913, Ph.D. in Pomology and Plant Breeding, 1920; m. Marian Salisbury, of Rochester, N.Y., Aug. 8, 1911; children—Gertrude Finch (dec.), David Salisbury. Instr. dept. pomology, N.Y. State Coll. Agr., at Cornell U., 1910-13; asso. in dept. of horticulture N.Y. State Expt. Sta., Geneva, N.Y., 1913-19; prof. pomology, in charge research in pomology, Pa. State Coll., since 1919. Mem. Depot Unit, N.G.N.Y., 1917-19. Fellow A.A.A.S.; mem. Sigma Xi, Phi Beta Kappa, Psi Upsilon, Gamma Alpha, Alpha Zeta. Republican. Unitarian. Author of numerous bulls. on fruit breeding, fruit growing, orchard fertility and fruit and vegetable storage. Home: State College, Pa.*

ANTRIM, ELBERT MANLY, business exec.; b. Rensselaer, Ind., June 30, 1885; s. James F. and Alvena B. (Bouk) A.; ed. pub. sch. and high sch., Rensselaer; m. Georgiana Gillespie, Mar. 3, 1915; 1 son, Thomas Gillespie. Began as country school teacher, 1903; sec. state mgr., Equitable Life Ins. Co., 1904-05; clerk, gen. freight office, Burlington R.R., 1905-17; with Chicago Tribune, 1917-54, traffic mgr. (Chicago Tribune and affiliated companies), 1917-27, asst. to pres., 1927-28, asst. bus. mgr., 1928-44, served as business manager 1944-54. Chairman harbors and waterways commission and member executive com., Chgo. Assn. of Commerce, 1930-36. Mem. adv. bd. Inland Waterway Corp., 1930-34. Dir. Am. Newspapers Pub. Assn. pres. Chicago Newspaper Publishers Assn., 1944-54. Republican. Home: Wilmette, Ill. *

APONTE, GONZALO ENRIQUE, physician, educator; b. P.R., July 15, 1929; s. Gonzalo and Lalita (Socorro) A.; came to U.S., 1945; B.S., Georgetown U., 1948; M.D., Jefferson Med. Coll., 1952. Intern Jefferson Med. Coll. Hosp., 1952-53, resident pathology, 1953-57; fellow Nat. Cancer Inst., Jefferson Med. Coll., 1955-57, mem. faculty, 1959-79, coordinator cancer teaching, 1960-68, asst. dir. cancer tng. program, 1968-69, prof. pathology, head dept., 1967-79, dir. clin. labs., 1967-77; research collaborator Brookhaven Nat. Lab., 1960-67. Mem. exam. com. Edn. Council Fgn. Med. Students, Nat. Bd. Med. Examiners. Served to lt. comdr. M.C., 1957-59. Markle scholar med. sci., 1960-65; recipient Lindback award Distinguished Teaching, Christian R. and Mary F. Lindback Trust, 1961; named Clin. Scientist of Year, Assn. Clin. Scientists, 1967. Mem. Coll. Am. Pathologists, Am. Soc. Clin. Pathologists, Internat. Acad. Pathology, Am. Assn. Blood Banks, Assn. Clin. Scientists, Am. Soc. Cytology, Phila. County Med. Soc., Alumni Assn. Jefferson Med. Coll. (pres. 1977-78), Sigma Xi, Alpha Omega Alpha (bd. dirs. 1977-79). Home: Philadelphia, Pa. Died June 15, 1979.

APPEL, BENJAMIN, writer; b. N.Y.C., Sept. 13, 1907; s. Louis and Bessie (Mikofsky) A.; student U. Pa., 1925-26, N.Y. U., 1926-27; B.S., Lafayette Coll., 1929; m. Sophie Marshak, Oct. 31, 1936; children—Carla, Willa Suzie, Marianna Consideration. Writer, 1929-77;

mechanic Republic Aviation Corp., Farmingdale, N.Y., 1943; with Office Civilian Def., Washington, 1943-44; spl. writer to Paul V. McNutt, chmn. War Manpower Commn., Washington, 1944-45; spl. asst. to U.S. High Commr. McNutt, Manila, Philippines, 1945-46; spl. cons. to Sec. of Interior Julius A. Krug, 1946; asso. with John Steelman, dir. Office War Mblzn. and Reconversion, 1946-47; vis. author U. Pa., spring 1974. Mem. Authors Guild Am., P.E.N. Author numerous books: Fortress in the Rice, 1951; Hell's Kitchen (short stories), 1952; Plunder, 1952, Dock Walloper (short stories), 1953; Sweet Money Girl, 1954; Life and Death of a Tough Guy, 1955; In the Klondike Gold Rush (juvenile), 1956; At The Battle for Bataan (juvenile), 1957; The Raw Edge, 1958; The Funhouse, 1959; With Cortes and Montezuma (juvenile), 1959; A Big Man, A Fast Man, 1961; A Time of Fortune, 1963; With Many Voices: Europe Talks About America, 1963: Man and Magic, 1966; Why the Russians Are the Way They Are, 1966; Why the Chinese Are the Way They Are, 1968; Age of Dictators, 1968; The Fantastic Mirror, 1969; Why the Japanese Are the Way They Are, 1973; The Devil and W. Kaspar, 1977; Hell's Kitchen (novel), 1977; Heart of Ice (juvenile), 1977; Across the Zodiac-The Story of a Wrecked Record, 1978; stories in O. Henry and O'Brien anthologies. Home: Roosevelt, N.J. Died Apr. 3, 1977.

APPLEGARTH, MARGARET TYSON, author, lectr.; b. New Brunswick, N.J., July 8, 1886; d. Henry C. and Mary (Tyson) Applegarth; A.B., U. Rochester, 1908; L.H.D., Denison U., 1942. Mem. Phi Beta Kappa. Presbyn. Author: Joy To The World, 1945; Right Here, Right Now, 1950; Men as Trees Walking, 1952; Moment By Moment, 1955; Twelve Baskets Full, 1957; Heirlooms, 1966; also articles in mags. Home: New York, N.Y. Died Oct. 30, 1976.

ARBEIT, ARNOLD ARVIN, cons. architect, artist; b. N.Y.C., Oct. 1, 1916; s. Carl and Caroline (Puretz) A.; grad. Beaux Arts Inst. Design, 1936; B.Arch., N.Y.U., 1938, M.Arch., 1940; M.A. in Edn., N.Y.U., 1955; diploma Mass. Inst. Tech., 1945; Ph.D., Burton Coll., 1965; Ed.D., Brantridge, Sussex, 1966; Sc.D., Johnson C. Smith U., 1969; m. Amelia U. Feibush, Sept. 18, 1938; 1 son, Stuart Carl David. Architect, N.Y. Navy Yard, Bur. Naval Architecture, 1935-38, Bur. Constrn., Bd. Edn., N.Y.C., 1938-43; individual practice architecture, 1950-74; mem. faculty Cooper Union, 1947-65, N.Y.U., 1952-53; prof. City Coll. Sch. Architecture, 1964-67, dir. dept. coll. planning programming services, campus planning and devel. City U. N.Y., also univ. architect; cons., regional dir. Univ. facilities, Westchester, 1967-73; instr., lectr. exhibits, Laurel Gallery, Bklyn. Mus., 8th St. Gallery, Delgado Art Mus., 1967-73; one man art shows New York every year. Mem. Mayor's Panel Architects, 1952-74; supr. Civil Def. Manhattan 2d Dist. Registered profl. architect, N.Y., N.J., Conn., R.I., Pa., Mass., Md., Vt., Nat. Council Archtl. Registration Bds. Served with Transp. Corps, AUS, 1942-46; col. U.S. Army Res., chief Monument, Fine Arts and Archives Civil Affairs, until 1967. Recipient Morse medal design N.Y.U., also Armstrong medal watercolor. Mem. A.I.A. (chmn. hdqrs. com.), N.Y. Soc. Architects (chmn. arts and architecture com.; recipient Merit award for imaginative design), N.Y. State Assn. Architects, Nat. Inst. Archtl. Edn. (chmn., trustee), Soc. Coll. and Univ. Planning, N.Y.U. Archtl. Alumni Assn. (pres.). Contbr. articles to profl. publs. Address: Scarsdale, N.Y. Died Jan. 8, 1974.

ARBUCKLE, JOHN WILLIAM, communications co. exec.; b. Indpls., Apr. 29, 1925; s. William S. and Inez (Smith) A.; B.S. in Bus. Adminstrn., Butler U., 1948; m. Maxine Demlow, Aug. 18, 1946; children—Nancy Lynn, John Richard. With Ind. Bell Telephone Co., 1949-76, v.p., sec. treas., 1968-71, v.p. ops., dir., mem. exec. com., 1971-73, pres., 1974-76, chmn. bd., 1976; v.p. ops. N.J. Bell Telephone Co., 1973-74; dir. Am. Fletcher Nat. Bank & Trust Co., Am. Fetcher Corp. Bd. dirs. Ind. Symphony Soc., Inc., United Way of Greater Indpls.; trustee Butler U., Methodist Hosp. of Ind. Served with AUS, 1943-46, 50-52. Mem. Indpls. C. of C., Newcomen Soc. N. Am., Ind. C. of C. (dir.). Presbyn. Clubs: Indpls. Athletic, Indpls. Press, Meridian Hills Country, Columbia, Crooked Stick Golf, Economic (dir.) (Indpls.). Home: Indianapolis, Ind. Died July 2, 1976; interred Washington Park Cemetery North, Indpls.

ARCHBOLD, RICHARD, mammalogist, explorer; b. N.Y.C., Apr. 9, 1907; s. John F. and May (Barron) A.; ed. pvt. schs and spl. studies at Columbia. Mammalogist, Mission Zoologique Franco-Anglo-Americaineà Madagascar, 1929-31; leader and sponsor New Guinea Expdn., 1933-34, 1936-37; leader Indisch-Amerikaansche Expeditie (in cooperation with Netherlands Indies Govt.), 1938; expdn. to Ariz., 1940; pres. Archbold Expdns., 1935-76; resident dir. Archbold Biol. Sta., 1941-76. Trustee John D. Archbold Meml. Hosp., Thomasville, Ga. Decorated officer Order Orange Nassau, 1940. Mem. AIAA, Soc. Naturalists, Ecol. Soc., German Soc. Mammalogists, Am. Soc. Mammalogists, Am. Ornithologists Union. Clubs: Explorers, Am. Alpine (N.Y.). Contbr. to sci. jours. Home: Lake Placid, Fla. Died Aug. 1, 1976.

ARCHER, ARTHUR WARD, architect; b. Spencer, Iowa, April 6, 1883; s. William Fletcher and Mary Frances (Worril) A.; B.S., U. of Ill., Urbana, Ill., 1907; traveled in Europe for study, 1913; m. Nell Boswell, Sept. 18, 1912; 1 son, Arthur Ward. Supt. of construction, U.S. Pub. Bldgs., Treasury Dept., 1909-17; practicing architect, Kansas City, Mo. since 1917; mem. Archer Cooper and Robison, architects and engrs., Commerce Bldg., Kansas City, Mo. Practice consists of residences, hosps., ind. plants, churches. Chmn. State (Mo.) Bd. Registration for Architects and Professional Engrs., Jefferson Mo.; first pres. Kansas City, Museum; bd. govs., K.C. Museum Assn.; dir. Mo. Assn. Architects. Fellow Am. Inst. Architects, 1947 (dir. Central States Dist.; pres. K.C. chapter, 1936); mem. Sigma Alpha Epsilon. Club: Country. Republican. Home: Kansas City.

ARCHER, HIRAM JOHN, lawyer, educator; b. Great Pond, Me., Oct. 15, 1878; s. John S. and Frances M. (Williams) A.; grad. Monmouth Acad., Me., 1901; student Coll. Liberal Arts, Boston U., 1901-04; LL.B., U. of Me. Law Sch., 1906; m. Helen M. Stinchfield, July 13, 1907; children—Helen F., Priscilla C., Robert S., John W., Thomas C. (lt. U.S. A.A.F. fighter pilot, killed near Kiska, Aleutians, Dec. 25, 1942), Elizabeth H. Practiced at Boston since 1906; prof. law, Suffolk Law Sch. (now Suffolk U. Law Sch.), since 1907. Trustee, clerk, dir. alumni relations. Suffolk U. Member Am. Mass. State and Boston bar assns., S.A.R., Mass. Soc. Mayflower Descendants, Theta Delta Chi. Republican. Unitarian. Mason. Home: Middleboro, Mass. *

ARCHIBALD, ARNOLD ADAMS, steel co. exec.; b. Truro, N.S., Can., Sept. 16, 1905; s. Lewis Edgar and Elizabeth May (McCallum) A.; student Truro Pub. Schs., Colchester County Acad.; Chauncy Hall Sch., Boston, 1923-24; B.S., Mass. Inst. Tech., 1930; m. Clara West Butler, Dec. 24, 1937; children—Lewis Edgar II, Roger Williams, John Baird. Came to U.S., 1923, naturalized, 1942. With Jones and Laughlin Steel Corp., Pitts., 1935-70, successibely metall. asst., asst. works metallurgist, mefall. engr., salesman, asst. to v.p., 1935-54, v.p., 1954-65, adminstrv. v.p. engring., purchasing and research, 1965-70. Served as dollar-a-year man on WPB, 1942-44, 45, Civilian Prodn. Adminstrn., 1946-47. Mem. Am. Iron and Steel Inst., Am. Iron and Steel Engrs., Am. Soc. for Metals. Clubs: Pittsburgh Athletic Assn., Duquesne (Pitts.); Union (Cleve.). Home: Corapolis, Pa. Died June 24, 1980; buried Forest Hill Cemetery, East Derrg, N.Y.

ARCHIBALD, FRED IRWIN, publisher; b. McCook, Nebr.; s. William Wallace and May (Irwin) A.; student U. Nebr. Coll. Engring., 1911-13; LL.D., Morgan State Coll., Balt., 1967; m. Edna Esther Olson, Aug. 11, 1921; 1 son, Fred John. Began career as advt. salesman, 1913; advt. mgr. Lincoln (Nebr.) Star, 1913-17, bus. and advt. mgr., sec. and treas., 1919-27; advt. dir. Omaha World Herald, 1927-31; gen. mgr. Omaha Bee-News, 1931-33; advt. dir. and asst. pub. New York American, 1934-35; pub. Omaha Bee-News, 1936-37; pres. and pub. Albany (N.Y.) Times Union, 1938-53; pub. and editorial supr. Balt. News-Post and Am., 1953-64; dir. Hearst Corp.; former v.p., dir., mem. radio and TV, finance coms. Hearst Pub. Co., Inc., Hearst Consol. Publs., Inc.; sec. Armadale Farms, Inc.; partner Archibald-Armadale Assos., ranch, New Market, Md. Mem. adv. com. Ch. Home and Hosp., Balt. Chmn. Balt. Civic Center Commn.; v.p. Md. Pub. Broadcasting Corp.; chmn. Balt. Opera Co.; chmn. Md. Higher Edn. Loan Corp.; mem. Md. Cruises Commn., Balt. Bicentennial Commn. Trustee Balt. Mus Art, United Student Aid Fund, Inc., N.Y.C. Served as lt. 346th F.A., 91st Div., 1917-18; maj. Mil. Govt. Div., U.S. Army, 1943; col. N.Y. N.G. Res. ret. Mem. N.Y. Pubs. Assn. (past pres., hon. life mem.), Chesapeake Assn. A.P. (past pres.), Am. Legion (life), Balt. Advt. Club, Sigma Alpha Epsilon, Sigma Delta Chi (past state chmn.). Episcopalian. Mason (32 deg.). Clubs: Omaha Athletic; Nat. Press (Washington); Maryland, Merchants (Balt.); Gulf and Bay (Sarasota, Fla.). Home: Baltimore, Md. Died Jan. 25, 1977; interred Lorraine Park Cemetery and Mausoleum, Balt.

ARCHIE, WILLIAM COUNCILL, educator; b. Salisbury, N.C., June 23, 1908; s. George W. and Sarah (Beard) A.; B.A., Davidson Coll., 1929; M.A., Wake Forest Coll., 1935; M.A. (Bergen fellow), Princeton, 1940, Ph.D., 1949; m. Ruth Toms Newby, Sept. 1, 1934; children—Suzanne (dec.), William Councill. Tchr. Gulf Coast Mil. Acad., Gulfport, Miss., 1929-31; tchr. Oak Ridge (N.C.) Mil. Inst., 1931-33; instr. Wake Forest Coll., 1935-38, asst. prof. romance langs., 1940-42, asso. dean, 1956-57, dean, 1957-58; asso. prof. romance langs. Duke, 1946-56, dean freshmen, 1949-51, acting dean instrn., 1951-52, asst. dean Trinity Coll., Duke, 1952-56; dean Coll. Arts and Scis., Emory U., 1958-61; dir. higher edn. State of N.C., Raleigh, 1961-65; dean Coll. Arts and Science, U. Delaware, 1965-66; exec. dir. Mary Reynolds Babcock Found., Winston-Salem, N.C., 1966-74; vis. prof. humanities, cons. Wake Forest U., Winston-Salem, 1974-79. Bd. dirs. Boys Club, Winston-Salem, 1956, Learning Inst. N.C. Bd. visitors Davidson Coll.; former trustee Warren Wilson Coll. The College Found.; chmn. bd. trustees Southeastern Council Founds., 1970-73. Served from 1st lt. to maj. Intelligence Corps, AUS, 1942-46. Decorated Merito Militar (Mexico). Mem. Am. Assn. U. Profs., Modern Lang. Assn. Am., Am. Assn. Tchrs. French, Pi Kappa Phi, Omicron Delta Kappa. Democrat. Presbyn. Clubs: Forsyth Country, Rotary (Winston-Salem); Cosmos; Torch. Home: Winston-Salem, N.C. Died Apr. 9, 1979.

ARDREY, ROBERT, author; b. Chgo., Oct. 16, 1908; s. Robert Leslie and Marie (Haswell) A.; Ph.B., U. Chgo., 1930; m. Berdine Grunewald, Aug. 11, 1960; children—Ross, Daniel. Lectr., cons. evolution human behavior, from 1963. Guggenheim fellow, 1937-38; recipient Sidney Howard Meml. award, 1940; Theresa Helburn Meml. award, 1961. Fellow Royal Soc. Lit.; mem. Phi Beta Kappa. Author: (plays) Star-Spangled, 1936, Casey Jones, 1938, How to Get Tough about It, 1938, Thunder Rock, 1939, Jeb, 1946, Sing Me No Lullaby, 1954, Shadow of Heroes, 1958, Plays of Three Decades, 1968; (screenplays) They Knew What They Wanted, 1940, Lady Takes a Chance, 1943, The Green Years, 1945, The Three Musketeers, 1947, Madame Bovary, 1948, Khartoum, 1966; (novels) Worlds Beginning, 1944, The Brotherhood of Fear, 1952; (evolutionary behavior) African Genesis, 1961, The Territorial Imperative, 1966, The Social Contract, 1970, The Hunting Hypothesis, 1976. Contbr. articles to jours. and mags. including Encounter, Science, Psychology Today, Communication. Home: Cape Town, South Africa. Died Jan. 14, 1980; buried Cape Town.

ARKUSH, ARTHUR SPENCER, editor, publisher; b. Chgo., June 22, 1925; s. Herbert Edgar and Rose (Hirsch) A.; student U. Ill., 1942-43; B.A., DePaul U., 1949; m. Betty Waldman, Mar. 20, 1948; children—Daniel Robert, Herbert Barry, Richard Mitchell. Reporter, Chgo. Sun-Times, 1948-49, asst. picture editor, 1949-53; founder, dir. Lamb Publs., pubs. TV Tab mag., 1953-56; editorial dir. Publishers Devel. Corp., pubs. Guns mag., Shooting Industry mag., Boats and Motors mag., Arts and Activities, Modern Man mag., Players Showcase mag., Skokie, Ill., 1957-58, asst. to pub., gen. mgr., 1958-62, v.p., 1962-68; v.p. Transamerican & Export News Co., 1962-68; founder, pub. Pro Football Weekly, 1968-79; pres. Pro Football Weekly, Inc., 1968-79, Pro Sports Weekley, Inc., 1969-79. Served with USAAF, 1943-46. Home: Highland Park, Ill. Died Mar. 22, 1979.

ARMSTRONG, GEORGE ELLIS, surgeon; b. Lawrence County, Ind., Aug. 4, 1900; s. Frank T. and Jennie G. (Norvell) A.; A.B., U. of Ind., 1922, M.D., 1925, LL.D., 1952; grad. Army Med. Sch., Med. Field Service Sch., 1927, Advanced Course, 1940; Command and Gen. Staff Sch., Ft. Leavenworth, Kan., 1941; m. Lillian T. Ott, Mar. 20, 1937; 1 son, George B. Intern, Letterman Gen. Hosp., San Francisco, 1925; med. officer, U.S. Army, 1926-55; asst. chief, surg., Walter Reed Hosp., 1931-35; asst. chief Surg. Service, Fort Benning, Ga., 1935-37; asst. surgeon and chief, Surg. Service, Tienstsin, China, 1937-38; chief, Surg. Service, chief, venereal disease ward, Fort Stotsenburg, P.I., 1938-39; asst. theater surgeon, CBI, Jan.-June, 1944; theater surgeon, CBI, later surgeon China Theater, 1944-46; dep. surgeon gen. with rank of brig. gen. 1947, maj. gen., 1948, surgeon gen. army 1951-55; v.p. for med. affairs N.Y. U., 1955-69, also dir. of N.Y. U. Med. Center. Mem. Pres.' Health Resources Adv. Com.; med. adv. com. MEDICO; pres. Am. Bur. for Med. Aid to China; active Am. Emergency Com. for Tibetan Refugees; bd. dirs. Am.-Philippine Sci. Found. Decorated Legion of Merit, Am. Def. Service medal, Asiatic Pacific Campaign medal with three bronze stars, World War I and II victory medals, Army Commendation medal (U.S.); Cloud Banner, Hon. Nobility medal, Legion of Honor (China); Order Crown of Italy, Order of St. Maurice and St. Lazarus, Korean Order of Mil. Merit TAEGUK, French Medaille d'Honneur du Service du Sante Militarie d'Or. Fellow A.C.S., A.C.P.; mem. A.M.A., Am. Hosp. Assn., Am. Vet. Med. Assn. (hon.), Am. Pharm. Assn. (hon.), Am. Assn. Surgery Trauma (hon.), Am. Found. Tropical Medicine (hon.), Internat. Coll. Surgeons (hon.), Am. Coll. Chest Physicians (hon.), Am. Coll. Hosp. Adminstrs. (hon.), Assn. Mil. Surgeons, Council Pan-Pacific Surg. Assn., Ind. Pub. Health Assn. (hon.), Brazilian Acad. Mil. Medicine (hon.), Nat. Resuscitation Soc. (pres.), N.Y. Medico-Surg. Soc., Nat. Health Council (dir., v.p.), N.Y.C. Hosp. Soc., Soc. Med. Cons. to Armed Forces, Nat. Bd. Med. Examiners, Phi Kappa Psi (exec. com. N.Y. U. alumni chpt.), Scabbard and Blade, Phi Rho Sigma, Alpha Omega Alpha. Mason (33 Shriner), Sojourner. Clubs: N.Y. University; Lotos. Home: Santa Rosa Beach, Fla. Died June 19, 1979; buried Osyka (Miss.) Cemetery.

ARMSTRONG, HAROLD HUNTER, lawyer; b. Morenci, Mich., Apr. 9, 1884; s. Oscar Samuel and Clara Marie (Allen) A.; A.B., U. Mich., 1905, student 1907; Detroit Coll. Law, 1906; m. Elisabeth Campbell, June 15, 1917; children—Elisabeth A. (Mrs. William Horn), Allen; m. 2d Elizabeth Wardner, July 4, 1941. Admitted to Mich. bar, 1907, and since practiced in Detroit; sec. and dir. Brown-McLaren Mfg. Co. since 1942, Grinding Supplies and Service Co., also v.p. Mem. Am. and Detroit bar assns., Phi Delta Phi. Mason. Club: Detroit Boat. Author: The Groper, 1919; Zell, 1921; For Richer for Poorer, 1922; The Red Blood,

1923. Home: Detroit.

ARMSTRONG, JESSE EVAN, educator; b. Meade Co., Ky., May 16, 1883; s. John C. and Rosa John (Wimp) A.; life diploma, Central State Normal Sch., Edmond, Okla., 1906; grad. Spaulding Commercial Coll., Kansas City, Mo., 1907; Kalamazoo (Mich.) College, 1908-09; A.B., University of California, 1916; m. Aileen Hand, of San Francisco, California, August 30, 1913 (she died Aug. 18, 1928); children—Frances Aileen, John Evan, Richard Emmet. Instr. in business schs. until 1911, Ida. State Tech. Inst., Pocatello, Ida., 1912; instr. Dept. of Commerce, U. of Calif., 1913-20; founder, 1918, and pres. Armstrong Schs. of Business Berkeley, Calif. Democrat. Baptist. Club: Commonwealth. Home: Oakland, Calif. *

ARMSTRONG, JOHN WALLACE, contractor; b. Grand Rapids, Mich., June 16, 1905; s. Wallace A. and Grace H. (Laubach) A.; B.S., U. Mich., 1926; m. Virginia C. Holler, Aug. 26, 1931; children—Margaret Ann, Gail Elizabeth. Constrn. engr. J.A. Utley Co., gen. contractors, Detroit, 1926-36; v.p. Darin & Armstrong, Inc., gen. contractor, Detroit, 1936-53, pres., 1954-75, chmn. bd., chief exec. officer, 1972-75; dir. Mich. Mut. Liability Ins. Co. Bd. dirs. Detroit YMCA, United Found., Detroit. Mem. Asso. Gen. Contractors Am. (pres. Detroit 1955-56). Club: Detroit Golf. Home: Pleasant Ridge, Mich. Died May 7, 1975.

ARNALL, PAUL MCGREW, co. exec., dir.; b. Elk Falls, Kans., Aug. 4, 1895; s. Millard F. and Mary (Dinkle) F.; student Kans. U., 1919-20, Kans. State Tchrs. Coll., 1916-17; m. Edna Chain, Oct. 14, 1922; 1 dau., Patricia Ann (Mrs. J. David Lynch). From salesman to gen. sales mgr. Graton & Knight Co., Worcester, Mass., 1920-33, Chgo. mgr., N.Y. mgr. F.A. Whitney Co., Leominster, 1933-38; gen. sales mgr., v.p. charge sales, then exec. v.p., dir. Ohio Injector Co., Wadsworth, 1938-49; v.p., general mgr. Lunkenheimer Co., Cin., 1950-51, dir., 1950-80, pres., gen. mgr., 1951-68; exec. v.p., chief exec. officer Elizabeth Gamble Deaconess Home Assn., Cin., 1968-69; trustee emeritus Central Trust Co. Mem. advisory com. Gen. Protestant Orphan Home; bd. advisors Good Samaritan Hosp., 1969-80; past pres. Greater Cin. Hosp. Council; trustee Meml. Homes Found.; past vestryman St. Thomas Episcopal Ch. Served with USMC, World War 1. Mem. Sigma Alpha Epsilon. Mason (Shriner). Clubs: Queen City, Cincinnati Country (Cin.); Commercial. Home: Cincinnati, Ohio. Died Aug. 16, 1980.

ARNASON, JON, central banker; b. Sudra-Vallholt, Skagafjordur, Iceland, Nov. 17, 1885; s. Arni and Gudrun (Thorvaldsdottir) A.; m. Sigridur Bjornsdottie, Jan. 8, 1925; children—Bjorn Jonsson, Arni Jonsson, Ingunn Jonsdottir (deceased). Mgr. export dept. Federation of Iceland Cooperative Societies, 1917-46; gen. mgr., Landsbanki Islands (Nat. Bank of Iceland), Reykjavik, since 1946, chmn. bd. dirs., 1928-46; state apptd. mem. bd. dirs. Iceland Steamship Co. since 1923; mem. bd. dirs. Union of Iceland Fish Producers, 1935-45. Mem. Fgn. Trade Commn. of Iceland Govt., 1939-48; mem. fgn. trade adv. bd. Iceland Govt. since 1948; Iceland's Governor in the bd. govs. of Internat. Bank Reconstrn. and Development, since May 1948; mem. numerous ofcl. trade delegations since 1924. Lutheran. Home: Reykjavik, Iceland.

ARNER, SAMUEL DEWALT, archaeologist; b. Vandergrift, Pa., June 17, 1900; s. George William and Elizabeth (deWalt) A.; diploma in law LaSalle Extension U.; student Bellvue Coll., Westminister, Colo.; diploma Zarephath Bible Inst. N.J.; studied poetry U. Cal. Extension; m. Violet Stewart, Apr. 2, 1935 (div. Oct. 1953); children—Paul C., David D., Jon Peter; m. 2d, Irene C. de Lopez de Santa Anna, May 31, 1957. Writer many poems pub. in various periodicals, including The Woodland Ghost, and Oteen, 1917-27; theol. articles to ch. mags., 1923-27; theol. lectr., 1926-31; Western landscape artist engaged in many expdns. to various parts of Western Am., Mexico, C.Am., S.Am. in interest of archaeol. research, from 1931; archaeol. research in Egypt, Lebanon, Israel, Turkey, Greece, 1969; founder, curator Mus. of Antiquities and Art, Cathedral City, Calif., now painting series oil portraits of famous Old West characters for mus. Pres. Taxpayers and Civic Improvement Assn. Dir. Palm Springs Republican Assembly, 1959; candidate for Congress, 1942. Trustee Desert Estate Co. Recipient award Merit for archaeol. research; diploma for distinguished achievement. Mem. Internat. Platform Assn., C. of C., Smithsonian Instn. (nat. mem.), Nat. Hist. Soc. (founding), Am. Acad. Polit. and Social Sci. (founding), Internat. Oceanographic Found., Am. Assn. Museums, D.A.V. (past chpt. comdr.), Am. Inst. Fine Arts. Presbyn. Home: Palm Springs, Calif. Deceased.

ARNETT, CAREY GEORGE, insurance pres.; b. Screven Co., Ga., July 15, 1882; s. Hamilton J. and Georgia A. (Dixon) A.; ed. pub. schs., Sylvania and Macon, Ga.; m. Lena Evans, Jan. 12, 1906. Began with N.Y. Life Ins. Co., at Savannah, Ga., 1904; agency organizer and supt. agencies, Mo. State Life Ins. Co., St. Louis, 1916-24; v.p. and agency mgr. Continental Life Ins. Co., 1924-26; apptd. mng. dir. Inter-Southern Life Ins. Co., Louisville, Ky., Apr. 1926, pres., 1926-32, and pres. its successor the Ky. Home Life Ins. Co.; dir. Mo. State Life Ins. Co. Democrat. Baptist. Mason. Club: Pendennis (Louisville). Home: Louisville, Ky. *

ARNOLD, ELLIOTT, author; b. N.Y.C., Sept. 13, 1912; s. Jack and Gertrude (Frank) A.; m. Helen Emmons (div. 1957); children—Thomas Guy, Mary Jean; m. 2d, Julie Kennedy, Sept. 1958 (div. Jan. 1961); m. 3d, Jacqueline Harris Stephens, Feb. 1961 (div. 1963); m. 4th, Glynis Johns, Oct. 1964 (div. 1973); m. 5th, Joanne Shwam, 1980. With N.Y. World-Telegram, 1934-42. Served as capt. AUS, 1942-45. Decorated Bronze Star. Clubs: Players, Lotos, Wings; American (London, Eng.). Author: Two Loves, 1934; Personal Combat, 1936; Only the Young, 1939; Nose for News, 1941; Finlandia, The Story of Sibelius, 1941; The Commandos, 1942; Mediterranean Sweep (with Richart Threulsen), 1944; Big Distance (with Donald Hough), 1945; Tomorrow Will Sing, 1945; Blood Brother, 1947; Everybody Slept Here, 1948; Deep in My Heart, 1949; Walk with the Devil, 1950; Time of the Gringo, 1953; Broken Arrow, 1954; White Falcon, 1955 (William Allen White award 1958); Flight from Ashiya (Commonwealth Club of Calif. fiction award for 1960), 1959; A Night of Watching (Commonwealth Club of Calif. fiction award 1967, NCCJ brotherhood award, Lit. Guild Selection), 1967; A Kind of Secret Weapon, 1969; Code of Conduct, 1970; Forests of the Night, 1971; The Spirit of Cochise, 1972; Proving Ground, 1973; The Camp Grant Massacre, 1976; Quicksand, 1977; also short stories, articles for mags. Home: New York, N.Y. Died May 13, 1980.

ARNOLD, HAROLD GREENE, clergyman; b. Providence, R.I., Feb. 21, 1883; s. Frederick William and Josephine (Keach) A.; prep. edn., English and Classical Sch., Providence; Ph.B., Brown U., 1905; S.T.B., Harvard Div. Sch., 1908; m. Helen Hunt Freeman, Apr. 12, 1909; children—Frederick William, Harriet, Phoebe Greene, Carolyn Freeman. Ordained ministry Unitarian Ch., 1908; pastor Bridgewater, Mass., 1908-13, Ch. of the First Parish, West Roxbury, Mass., since 1913. Mem. Alpha Delta Phi. Home: Boston, Mass. *

ARNOLD, JAMES WILLIE, lawyer; b. Statham, Ga., Aug. 25, 1884; s. James K. Polk and Sarah (Booth) A.; student Martin Inst., Jefferson, Ga., 1900-03, U. of Ga., 1903-06; LL.B., U. of Ga. Law Sch., 1921; m. Hester Aycock, Oct. 20, 1907; 1 dau., Martha Jim. With firm Griffith & Welch, cotton factors, 1906-12, mgr., 1908-12; organizer J. W. Arnold & Co., cotton shippers and exporters, 1912; retired, 1916 to devote attention to large farming interests; admitted to Ga. bar, 1921 and since in practice at Athens. Rep. candidate for U.S. Senate, 1932. Edited a polit. paper known as "The Two Party Advocate." Capt. Ga. Nat. Guard, 1908-20. Methodist. Elk, I.O.O.F. Home: Bogart, Ga.

ARNOLD, (MORRIS) LEROY, coll. prof.; b. Marshfield, Wis., May 30, 1881; s. Llewellyn A. and Frances (Smith) A.; A.B., U. of Minn., 1904; M.A., Harvard, 1905; Ph.D., Columbia, 1911; m. Kate Fairchild, 1911; children—Morris Fairchild, Elizabeth Jane. Actg. chmn. dept. of English lit., U. of Minn., 1905-06; asst. in English, Columbia, 1907-08; prof. English lit., Hamline U., since 1909. Prof. English lit., Northwestern U., summer, 1928. Mem. Mod. Lang. Assn. America. Beta Theta Pi. Clubs: University, Skylight (Minneapolis); University (St. Paul). Author: Soliloquies of Shakespeare, 1911; Wish-I-May-Wish-I-Might (play for children), 1915; Masque of Minneapolis (prize pageant), 1916; Hurry, Hurry, Hurry (comedy), 1917; Victory Pageant of Hamline U., 1918; Then and Now (comedy), 1934. Lecturer on new books and plays; also contbr. to mags. Home: Minneapolis, Minn. *

ARNOLD, SAMUEL WASHINGTON (WAT), ex-congressman; b. on farm near Downing, Mo., Sept. 21, 1879; s. Cumberland Wilson and Mary Elizabeth (Hill) A.; B.S.D., Kirksville State Teachers Coll., 1902; m. Myra Gertrude Mills, Dec. 24, 1904; children—Mary, Dorothy (wife of Dr. J. Francis Brown), Sam Mills, Alyce Carrie (wife of Dr. Russell E. Pierce). Began as teacher Coffey Sch. Dist., 1896, supt. pub. schs., Middletown, Mo., 1901-02, Atlanta, Mo., 1902-03; with St. Louis Internal Revenue office, 1903-04; retail lumber business, Atlanta, Mo., 1905-08; pres. Arnold Lumber Co. since 1908. Mem. 78th to 80th Congresses (1943-49), 1st Mo. Dist. past pres., treas. Kirksville Chamber of Commerce; dir. Southwestern Lumbermen's Assn.; mem. Sigma Tau Gamma. Republican. Presbyterian (financial sec., deacon). Mason. Club: Kirksville Rotary. Home: Kirksville, Mo. *

ARNOLD, WILLIAM H., broker, army officer; b. Dyersburg, Tenn., Jan. 18, 1901; s. Luther Coleman and Lockie (Dufford) A.; student Castle Heights Mil. Acad., Lebanon, Tenn., 1917-19; B.S., U.S. Mil. Acad., 1924; grad. Inf. School, Ft. Benning, Ga., 1928, Command and General Staff Sch., Ft. Leavenworth, Kan., 1938; m. Elizabeth Welsh Mullen, Feb. 17, 1926; children—Elizabeth, Emily (dec.), William H., Joseph C. Served in Hawaii, 1928-30, in Tiensin, China, 1934-36; detailed to Gen. Staff Corps, Sept. 1941, G-1 of IV Corps until Mar. 1942, G-3 of IV Corps until Apr. 1943; then chief of staff of XIV Corps, overseas; comdr. Americal Div., Bougainville, 1944, later Cebu, Negros, Philippines; dep. dir. plans and operations War Dept. Gen. Staff, 1946; chief budget dir. Dept. of Army, 1948; chief Joint Mil. Mission for Aid to Turkey, 1950-53; comdg. gen. U.S. Forces, Austria, 1953-55; comdg. gen. 5th U.S. Army, 1955-61; ret. as lt. gen.; partner Betts Borland & Co., Chgo., brokers, 1961-72. Mem. Ill. State Police Merit Bd., 1961-64. Decorated D.S.M. with oak leaf cluster, Silver Star, Legion of Merit with oak leaf cluster, Bronze Star with oak leaf cluster, Air Medal (U.S.) officer Legion of Honor (France), chief comdr. Legion of Honor (P.I.); Grand Gold Badge of Honor (Austria). Home: Lake Forest, Ill. Died Sept. 30, 1976; buried Fed. Cemetery, Ft. Sheridan, Ill.

ARON, HAROLD GUTHRIE (A-RON'), lawyer; b. Brooklyn, New York, Aug. 22, 1886; s. Charles Henry and Ria Beatrice (Guthrie) A.; student Brooklyn Law Sch., 1904-05, Hamilton Coll., 1905-06 (A.B., 1912, A.M., 1915); LL.B., New York Law School, 1908; m. Betsy Ritchie, Oct. 1, 1913; children—Betsy, Diana (deceased); m. 2d, Lilian Strom, Jan. 14, 1935. Admitted to N.Y. bar, 1908, later to N.J. bar and bar of Supreme Court of U.S.; in active practice of law, New York, 1908-24; chief of Property Bureau, Housing Div., U.S. Shipping Bd., 1918-19; served as special counsel Federal Land Bank, U.S. Shipping Bd. Emergency Fleet Corp., Pub. Service Commn. of N.Y., City of New York, and Special asst. to atty. gen. of U.S.; lectured on law, Hamilton Coll., 1910; prof. of law, N.Y. Law Sch., 1911-19; acquired control of Nat. Am. Bank, N.Y. City, 1926; chmn. exec. com. Internat. Germanic Trust Co., 1928-30; founded Georgic Press, pubs., East River, Conn., 1932; founded Housing Investment Fund of America, Inc., 1937, and since gen. counsel. Treas. Nat. Rep. Club, 1925-28; Rep. nominee for comptroller of City of N.Y., 1929; founder Ormond Plantation (Fla.), Leesite Diatom, Chemicals Corporation (Oak Grove, Va.). Member Assn. of Bar of N.Y.C., N.Y. State Bar Assn., Sons of the Revolution, Chi Psi, Phi Delta Phi (hon.). Tomoka Hunting Club. Clubs: Nat. Republican; Bankers (N.Y.C.). Author: The Gist of Real Property Law, 1917; Digest of New York Real Property Law, 1923; Notes on Proof—the Probative Law, 1932; Respectfully Submitted, 1932; Mortgage Problem, 1934; Democracy Answers the Dictators, 1939. Home: Madison, Conn. *

ARONSON, BORIS, artist, stage designer; b. Kiev, Russia, Oct. 15, 1899; s. Solomon and Deborah (Turfsky) A.; ed. State Art Sch., Kiev, also pvt. schs., Moscow and Kiev; student art, Moscow, Kiev, Paris; m. Lisa Jalowetz, June 5, 1945; 1 son, Marc. Came to U.S., 1923. A founder Mus. Modern Art, Kiev; in U.S. worked with Unser Theatre and Yiddish Art Theatre; designer for stage and ballet, including sets for N.Y.C. prodns.: Cabin in the Sky; Sadie Thompson; Walk a Little Faster, 1932; Awake and Sing, 1935; Detective Story; 1949; I am a Camera, 1951; The Country Girl, 1951; The Crucible, 1953; The Rose Tattoo, 1951; A View from the Bridge, 1955; The Diary of Anne Frank, 1955; Bus Stop, 1955; Hole in the Head, 1956; Orpheus Descending, 1956; The Firstborn, 1958; J.B., 1958; Do Re Mi, 1960; A Gift of Time, 1962; (for Shakespeare Theatre, Stratford, Eng.) Coriolanus, 1959; (London Eng.) Judith, 1962; Incident of Vichy, 1964; Fiddler on the Roof, 1964; Cabaret, 1966; Mourning Becomes Electra (also costumes), 1967; The Price (also costumes), 1968; Zorba, 1968; Company, 1970; (Met. Opera House) Fidelio (also costumes) 1970; Follies, 1971; Great God Brown, 1972; Creation of the World and Other Business, 1972; A Little Night Music, 1973; Tzadik, 1974. Pacific Overtures, 1976; The Nutcracker, 1976-77; commd. to do art work for Interior of Temple Sinai, Washington, 1961, also Community Center Synogogue, Sands Point, N.Y.; numerous exhbns. of paintings; represented in pvt. colls., also exhibitaed stage designs, and model with projected slides, called Painting with Light, Mus. Modern Art, 1947. Recipient Guggenheim fellowship, 1950, Am. Theatre Wing Tony award for stage designs, 1950-51; Tony award, 67, 69, 71, 72, 76, Joseph Maharam award 4 times; Brandeis U. Creative Arts award commn., 1969; New Eng. Theatre Conf. Spl. award, 1970. Mem. United Scenic Artist Union. Author: Marc Chagall, 1923; Modern Graphic Art, 1923. Home: Nyack, N.Y. Died Nov. 16, 1980.

ARPAIA, ANTHONY F(ARPAYA), railway agy. exec.; b. New Haven, Dec. 17, 1897; s. Vincent and Carolyn (deRubbe) A.; A.B., Yale, 1921, LL.B., 1923; m. Charlotte Bergen, Dec. 10, 1940; 1 dau., Judith Carol. Admitted to Conn. bar, 1923, N.Y. bar, 1924; with Chadbourne, Hunt, Jaeckel & Brown, N.Y.C., 1923-25; Am. lawyer in charge Wirth & Picard, pvt. internat. law, Berlin, Germany, 1925-27; pvt. practice, New Haven, 1927-42, 51-52; area rent dir. OPA, New Haven area, 1942-43, chief counsel, Conn., June-July 1943, state dir., 1943-45; v.p., gen. counsel Adley Express Co., Inc., 1945-51; commr. ICC, 1952-60, chmn., 1956; v.p. internat. ops. REA Express, 1960-65, exec. cons., after 1965; sec.-treas. of Frantham Corp.; lectr. in field; participant numerous seminars, confs. Mem. N.Y.C. Council on Port Devel. and Promotion, Dept. of Marine and Aviation. Bd. dirs., past v.p. New Haven Taxpayers, Inc.; past judge East Haven Ct.; past mem. New Haven Legal Aid Commn.; dir. Conn. Fedn. Planning and Zoning Agencies; chmn. Regional Planning Authority of South Central Conn.; chmn. Met. Adv. Com.; bd. dirs. Boys Village, Inc.; mem. two-way exchange fellowship com. Yale. Decorated Star Solidarity (Italy). Mem. Am. Arbitration Assn. (mem. panel), Am., Conn. State, New Haven bar assns., Am. Judicature Soc., Assn. ICC Practitioners, Am. Legion (past post comdr. New Haven), Book and Gavel Legal Soc., Yale Law Sch. Assn. (v.p.), Yale Alumni Assn. (dir.), New Haven C. of C. (dir.), U.S. C. of C., Am. Soc. Traffic and Transp. (founder mem.), Nat. Def. Transp. Assn., various alumni assns., Phi Alpha Delta, Alpha Phi Delta. Democrat. Author articles on transp. econs. and law. Home: St Petersburg, Fla. Died June 25, 1978.

ARRINGTON, JAMES HUGH, oil producer; b. Jethro, Ark., May 23, 1904; s. William H. and Laura T. (Fulks) A.; L.I., Ark. Tech. Jr. Coll., 1927; B.S., Okla. A. and M. Coll., 1930; m. Veneta C. Berry, July 5, 1930; children—Harriet V. (Mrs. Jack Griffith), Aneta N. (Mrs. Davis), Laura B. (Mrs. Luke Leon Nigliazzo, Jr.). Supt., Alix pub. schs., 1927-29; athletic coach, teacher Ripley (Ark.) High Sch., 1931-33, also partner newspaper Ripley Rev. and mgr. 2000 acre ranch; buyer Lake Carl Blackwell project, 1933-35; pres. Marco Corp., 1961-73, Amco Corp., Jim Arrington Corp.; dir. Thomas N. Berry & Co., Stillwater Nat. Bank & Trust Co. (Okla.). Mem. Okla. Ho. of Reps. from Payne County, 1942-60; chmn. Okla. Dem. Party, 1940-46; Dem. nat. committeeman for Okla., 1956-68. Mem. local council Boy Scouts Am.; hon. mem. Okla. Semi-Centennial Commn., 1956-57; ann. donor Okla. State U. Devel. Found. Hon. col. various Okla. govs.; named to Okla. State U. Alumni Hall of Fame, Ark. Tech. Alumni Hall of Distinction; recipient Okla. Bankers Assn. award for conservation farming, 1977; commendation Okla. Legislature, 1977. Mem. Mid-Continent Oil and Gas Assn., Am. Petroleum Inst., Okla. Ind. Petroleum Assn. (v.p. from 1975), Okla. Heritage Assn. (sustaining), SAR, Okla. State U. Pres.'s Club, Isaac Walton League, Stillwater, Oklahoma City chambers commerce, Oklahoma City Press Assn., Okla. Jack and Jennet Assn., Red Red Rose, Sigma Nu. Mem. Ch. of Jesus Christ of Latter Day Saints (mem. exec. bd. minerals com. from 1972, mem. ch. edn. devel. com. from 1972, chmn. oil and gas com. from 1972). Clubs: Beacon, Oklahoma City Golf and Country (Oklahoma City); Yost Lake Country (Stillwater). Home: Oklahoma City, Okla. Deceased.

ARRINGTON, WILLIAM RUSSELL, lawyer, corp. exec.; b. Gillespie, Ill., July 4, 1906; s. William Parnell and Ethel Louise (Fanning) A.; A.B., U. Ill., 1928, J.D., 1930; LL.D., Lincoln Coll., 1973; Laureate, Lincoln Acad., 1973; m. Ruth Browne, Oct. 8, 1932; children—Patricia Lee, Michael Browne, Admitted to Ill. bar, 1930, sr. mem. Arrington & Healy, Chgo., from 1944; v.p., dir., gen. counsel Combined Ins. Co. of Am. and related cos., 1939-79, sec., 1962-79, sr. gen. counsel, 1978-79; acting pres., dir. Soy Bean Products Co., 1942-45; dir. Alberto-Culver Co., 1964-79, Elkay Mfg. Co., 1964-79, Bank of Chgo., 1954-79, Am. Valuation Cons., 1974-78. Gen. atty. Ridgeville Park Dist., 1941-57; mem. Gov.'s Ill. Revenue Study Commn., 1968-69; mem. U.S. Adv. Commn. on Intergovertl. Relations, 1969-73; mem. Council State Govt., 1968-72. Mem. Ill. Ho. of Reps., 4th Senatorial Dist., 1944-54; mem. Ill. Senate, 1954-73; chmn. Ho. judiciary com., 1951-55, mem. Ill. Legis. Commn. to revise Ill. Constn. Revenue Article, 1951, mem. joint legis. commn. to revise Ill. Constn. Jud. Article, 1951-53; mem. Ill. Legis. Council, 1955-73; chmn. Ill. Legis. Audit Commn., 1957-73; mem. Ill. Revenue Laws Study Commn., 1961-63; pres. pro tem, majority leader Ill. Senate, 1964-71, Republican minority leader, 1971-73; chmn. Ill. Gen. Assembly Library Study Commn., 1975-79; mem. exec. com. Nat. Conf. State Legis. Leaders, 1965-72; bd. govs. Nat. Soc. State Legislators, 1966-72; mem. intergovtl. relations com. Nat. Legis. Conf., 1965-72; mem. Council State Govts., 1968-72; trustee Legis 50, Center for Legis. Improvement (formerly Citizens Conf. on State Legislatures), 1973; adv. com. Ill. Masonic Hosp., 1964-79; chmn., bd. mgrs. Robert R. McCormick Chgo. Boys Club, 1960-79; pres. Arrington Found., 1965-79; bd. dirs. Insts. Religion and Health, 1962-74, Found. Study of Cycles, 1962-79, Found. Research on Nature of Man, 1964-79, Chgo. Boys' Clubs, 1962-79, Mental Health Assn. Greater Chgo., 1964-72, Stone-Brandel Center, 1966-69, W. Clement and Jessie V. Stone Found., 1958-79, Evanston Hosp., United Way, Far West Regional Lab. for Ednl. Research and Devel.; bd. regents Golden Valley Luth. Coll.; mem. exec. bd. San Francisco and Viking council Boy Scouts Am.; trustee Fairview Hosp. Recipient Silver Beaver award Boy Scouts Am., 1963, Man of Year award Boys Club, 1976. Mem. NEA (life), Calif. Tchrs. Assn. (life), N.D. Edn. Assn. (life), Hayward C. of C. (life), Am. Assn. Sch. Adminstrs. (joint com. Nat. Sch. Bds. Assn.), Calif. Assn. Sch. Adminstrs., Assn. for Supervision and Curriculum Devel. (nat. bd., Calif. pres.), Nat. Soc. for Study Edn., Scholia, Phi Delta Kappa. Contbr. articles to ednl. jours. Home: Evanston, Ill. Died Oct. 3, 1979.

ARTERBURN, NORMAN FRANK, judge; b. Bicknell, Ind., May 13, 1902; s. Clay H. and Anna (Hoover) A.; A.B. cum laude, Ind. U., 1923; J.D., U. Chgo., 1926; LL.D., Vincennes U., 1971; m. Lois E. Richards, 1926 (dec.), children—Joan, Linda (Mrs. Jerry Ridgley), Faith (Mrs. Charles Nicholson); m. 2d, Loretta Vieck, Oct. 1971. Admitted to Ind. bar, 1923, practiced in Vincennes, 1927-55, mem. Arterburn & Hart, 1946-55; pros. atty. 12th Jud. Dist. Ind., 1928-30; justice Supreme Ct. of Ind., 1955-71, chief justice of Ind., 1971-79; prof. law Washburn Coll., 1926-27; vis. prof. law Ind. U., 1949, 53-54. Mem. Ind. Bd. Law Examiners, 1938-44, pres., 1944; mem. exec. council Conf. Chief Justices, 1972-74. Bd. govs. Good Samaritan Hosp. Mem. Am., Ind., Vincennes bar assns. Methodist. Mason (32 deg.). Contbr. numerous legal articles. Home: Vincennes, Ind. Died Feb. 11, 1979.

ARTZ, CURTIS PRICE, surgeon, educator; b. Jerome, O., Sept. 29, 1915; s. Curtis Emuel and Bertha Louise (Price) A.; B.A., Ohio State U., 1936, M.D., 1939; M.S. in Surgery, Baylor U., 1951; m. Kathryn Lucille Risley, 1939 (dec.); children—Susan Mitchell Okun, John, Joanne; m. 2d, Mary Nelle Entrekin, Feb. 1973. Intern, Balt. City Hosps., 1939-40; gen. practice medicine, Grantsville, W.Va., 1941-45; resident surgery Ohio State U., 1945-48; commd. capt. M.C., U.S. Army, 1948, advanced through grades to lt. col., 1956; mem. research and devel. bd. Office Surgeon Gen., Washington, 1949; asst. dir. Surg. Research Unit, Brooke Army Med. Center, Ft. Sam Houston, Tex., 1950-53; dir. Army Surg. Research Team, Korea, 1953; comdg. officer Army Surg. Research Unit, Brooke Army Med. Center, 1953-56; ret., 1956; prof. surgery U. Miss. Sch. Medicine, Jackson, 1956-63; Shrine prof. surgery U. Tex. Med. Br., Galveston, 1963-65; prof. surgery, chmn. dept. surgery Med. U. S.C., Charleston, 1965-77, Distinguished Univ. prof., 1977. Mem. surgery study sect. NIH, 1966-70; chmn. com. trauma NRC, 1967-71; chief surg. cons. VA Hosp., Charleston; cons. HEW, Army Research and Devel. Command; chmn. Lowcountry EMS Council. Trustee Health Scis. Found., Med. U. S.C. Decorated Bronze Star. Recipient Modern Medicine award, 1969; Centennial Achievement award Ohio State U., 1970; Harvey Stuart Allen Distinguished Service award, 1973; others. Mem. A.C.S. (chmn. com. trauma 1968-74, vice chmn. bd. govs. 1970-72, 2d v.p. 1977, surgeon's award 1974), Am. Assn. Surgery Trauma (pres. 1971), Am. Burn Assn. (pres. 1968-69), Am. Surg. Assn., Am. Trauma Soc. (pres. 1973), Southeastern Surg. Congress (pres. 1966-67, Distinguished Service award 1973), Soc. Univ. Surgeons, So. Surg. Assn. (Shipley award 1959, chmn. Shipley award com. 1972), AMA, Halsted Soc., Alpha Omega Alpha, Phi Delta Theta, Alpha Kappa Kappa. Episcopalian. Author: Treatment of Burns, 1957, rev. edit., 1969; Complications in Surgery and Their Management, 1957, rev. edits., 1967, 75; Research in Burns, 1964; Brief Textbook of Surgery, 1976; also chpts., articles. Patentee air-fluidized bed. Home: Charleston, S.C. Died Dec. 23, 1977.

ARVEY, JACOB M., lawyer; b. Chgo., Nov. 3, 1895; s. Israel and Bertha Arvey; ed. Crane High Sch., John Marshall Law Sch.; m. Edith Freeman, June 11, 1915; children—Erwin, Howard, Helen Sue. Began practice, Chgo., 1916; asst. state's atty. Cook County, 1918-20; mem. law firm Raber, Kostner, Herr & Arvey, 1920-25; mem. firm Arvey, Hodes, Costello & Burman and predecessors, to 1977; master in Chancery Circuit Court of Cook County, 1930-34. Chmn. bd. Marina City Bank Chgo.; dir. Republic Nat. Bank, Miami, Fla. Alderman 24th Ward, Chgo., 1923-41; chmn. Cook County Democratic Central Com.; Ill. mem. Dem. Nat. Com., 1950. Bd. dirs. Am. Israel Pub. Affairs Com., Am. Friends Tel Aviv U., Am. Com. Weizmann Inst. Sci., Eleanor Roosevelt Cancer Found., Am. ORT Fedn., Asso. Talmud Torahs Chgo. (hon.), Jewish Burial Soc. Chgo., Louis Weiss Meml. Hosp., Home for the Aged, Miami, Home for Aged, Chgo., Mt. Sinai Hosp., Miami Beach, Fla.; bd. dirs., adv. bd. Am. Friends of Hebrew U.; adv. council Brandeis U., World Jewish Congress, Synagogue Council America, Emotionally Disturbed Children; mem. Cath. Interracial Council Citizens Bd., Chgo.; adv. bd. Israeli Pub. Inst.; internat. hon. bd. Ency. Judaica Press, Inc. Hon. chmn. Israel Bonds. Served with AUS, World War II. Mem. Am., Fed., Ill., Chgo. bar assns., Am. Legion (vice chmn. distinguisihed guests com.). Mason, Elk, Odd Fellow, K.P.; mem. B'nai B'rith. Clubs: Bryn Mawr Country, Covenant (Chgo.); Westview Country (Miami); Nat. Capitol Democratic (Washington); Nat. Democratic (N.Y.C.). Home: Chicago, Ill. Died Aug. 25, 1977.

ARVEY, MARTIN DALE, educator; b. Los Angeles, Dec. 6, 1915; s. David and Bessie (Tarkovsky) A.; student UCLA, 1933-35, B.A., Berkeley, 1937; M.S., U. Idaho, 1939; Ph.D., U. Kans., 1949; m. Josette L. Arvey; children by previous marriage—William D., Richard D., Michael T. Mem. faculty U. Okla., 1949-50, Long Beach State Coll., 1953-62; spl. asst. NSF, 1962-67; prof., chmn. dept. U. of Pacific, Stockton, Calif., 1967-72; prof., chmn. dept. biology U. N.C., Charlotte, 1972-79. Served to lt. USNR, 1944-46, 50-53. Rockefeller grantee, 1962; NSF Inst. grantee, 1961, 68, 70, 71. Mem. AAAS, Am. Inst. Biol. Scis., Am. Ornithologists Union, Cooper Ornithol. Soc., Sigma Xi, Phi Sigma. Home: Charlotte, N.C. Died Jan. 29, 1979.

ASCHAFFENBURG, E. LYSLE, hotel exec.; b. St. Louis, Jan. 9, 1892; s. Albert and Elvine (Schaefer) A.; M.E., Cornell, 1913; m. Helene Bloom, Jan. 21, 1918; children—Albert Lyle, Jean; m. 2d, Josye K. Wagner, Oct. 16, 1953. Pres., mgr. Lafayette Hotel, New Orleans, 1919-27; v.p. Standard Bond & Mortgage Co., 1925-30; pres. Pontchartrain Hotel, New Orleans, 1927-80, mng. dir., 1936-80, chmn. bd., 1968-80; editorial adv. staff Hotel Mgmt., 1940-80; pres. New Orleans Little Theatre Prodns., Inc., 1946-61; chmn. bd. Le Petit Theatre du Vieux Carre, 1957-80. Bd. dirs. Fair Grounds Corp., New Orleans, 1948; bd. dirs., founder mem. Internat. House, New Orleans, 1949; bd. dirs. New Orleans Crime Commn., New Orleans Safety Council; vice chmn. Mayor's Com. on Juvenile Delinquency; pres. Met. New Orleans Safety Council, 1958. Served as 1st lt. Ordnance Corps, U.S. Army, 1917, with 82d div., France, 1918-19. Recipient Gold Plate award Internat. Food Service Mfrs. Assn., 1969. Mem. Am. (bd. govs. 1949, chmn. residential hotels com. 1948), La. (pres. 1944), New Orleans (pres. 1948) hotel assns., C. of C. New Orleans Area (dir.), Cornell Soc. Hotelmen, Confrerie des Chevaliers du Tastevin (grand officier, grand senechal New Orlenas chpt.), Hotel Sales Mgmt. Assn. (chmn. so. dist. 1951), New Orleans Opera Assn. (bd. dirs. 1944-51), Am. (mem. bd. 1966), Greater New Orleans (pres. 1966) hotel and motel assns., Shakespeare Soc. New Orleans, Maitre, Commanderie de Bordeaux, New Orleans. Home: New Orleans, La. Died Mar. 20, 1980; buried Lake Lawn Cemetery, Metairie, La.

ASCHER, CHARLES STERN, pub. adminstr.; b. N.Y.C., Apr. 20, 1899; s. Ernest and Josephine (Stern) A.; student Ethical Culture Sch., N.Y., 1904-14; A.B., Columbia U., 1920, LL.B., 1921; m. Helen Shire, May 25, 1921 (dec. Mar. 1960); children—Joan, Robert. Admitted to N.Y. State bar, 1921, Ill. bar, 1933; practiced in N.Y., 1921-25; asst. counsel War Fin. Corp., Washington, 1922; sec. and gen. counsel City Housing Corp., N.Y.C., 1926-31, mem. bd. dirs., 1940-47; sec. Pub. Adminstrn. Clearing House, Chgo., 1932-36, asso. dir. N.Y.C. office, 1952-55; sec., dir. publs. Pub. Adminstrn. Service, 1933-35; exec. dir. Nat. Assn. Housing Ofcls., 1934; sec. com. pub. adminstrn. Social Sci. Research Council, 1935-42, com. housing research, 1949-51; regional rep. of adminstr. expediter region 2 Nat. Housing Agy., 1942-47, dir. urban devel. for entire agy., 1945-46; exec. officer for program Office Dir. Gen. UNESCO, Paris, 1947-48; prof. polit. sci. Bklyn. Coll. of City U. N.Y., 1948-69, prof. emeritus and adjunct, 1969-80; chmn. dept. polit. sci., 1949-66; internat. rep. Inst. Pub. Adminstrn., 1956-78; lectr. polit. sci. U. Chgo., Columbia U., Syracuse U., Pratt Inst.; rep. at UN of Internat. Inst. Adminstrv. Sci., Internat. Union Local Authorities, Internat. Fedn. Housing and Planning, 1949-80, Inter Am. Planning Soc., 1959-80, Internat. Info. Centre Local Credit, 1965-77, Eastern Regional Orgn. Pub. Adminstrn., 1965-77, Internat. Assn. Supreme Audit Instns., 1970-74; cons. N.Y. State Dept. Health, WHO, Nat. Resources Planning Bd. in charge urban program; dir. Citizens Housing and Planning Council, N.Y.C., 1941-80, pres., 1963-64; pres. Conf. Non-govtl. Orgns. in Consultative Status with UN, 1961-63. Recipient Beck prize Columbia Law Sch., 1920. Mem. Am. Soc. Pub. Adminstrn. (past pres.), Am. Soc. Planning Ofcls. (past treas.), Soc. Internat. Devel., Am. Inst. Planners, Lambda Alpha, Phi Beta Kappa, Union of Internat. Assns., Nat. Assn. Housing and Redevel. Ofcls. (sec. internat. com. 1955-77), Nat. Acad. Pub. Adminstrn. (sec. internat. com.), Inter-Am. Planning Soc. (adv. council), Radburn Assn. (trustee 1929-32, hon. trustee 1967—), Internat. Fedn. Housing and Planning (hon.). Club: Adirondack Mountain. Author: Program Making in UNESCO; The Private Covenant in Urban Development; The Administration of Publicly-Aided Housing; contbr. articles to periodicals. Home: New York City. Deceased.

ASCOLI, MAX, writer; b. Ferrara, Italy, June 25, 1898; s. Enrico and Adriana (Finzi) A.; LL.D., U. Ferrara (Italy), 1920; Ph.D., U. Rome, 1928; m. Marion Rosenwald, Oct. 5, 1940; 1 son, Peter. Came to U.S., 1931, naturalized, 1939. Prof. jurisprudence Italian univs., 1926-31; mem. grad. faculty New Sch. for Social Research, N.Y.C., 1933-50, dean grad. faculty, 1940-41, asst. dir. cultural relations, coordinator inter-Am. affairs, 1940-42; pres. Handicraft Devel. Inc., 1944-54; editor, pub. The Reporter, 1949-68. Mem. Council Fgn. Relations. Author: Intelligence in Politics, 1936; (with Arthur Feiler) Fascism for Whom, 1938; The Power of Freedom, 1948. Editor: (with Fritz Lehmann) Political and Economic Democracy, 1938; The Fall of Mussolini, 1948; Our Times, The Best From the Reporter, 1960. Home: New York, N.Y. Died Jan. 1, 1978; buried Gate of Heaven Cemetery, Hawthorne, N.Y.

ASH, J(AMES) E(ARLE), army officer, ret.; b. Phila., Pa., Sept. 4, 1884; s. William Rambo and Julia (Cook) A.; M.D., U. of Pa., 1905; m. Marguerite Hal-Brown, Apr., 1914, children—James Earle (deceased), Signé Caroline; m. 2d Mary Catherine Udall, 1947. Intern.

Blockley Hosp., Phila., 1906-07, Phila. Hosp. for Contagious Diseases, 1907-09; pathologist State Hosp. for Insane, Norristown, Pa., 1909-13; instr. pathology Harvard Med. Sch., 1913-16; entered Med. Corps U.S. Army, 1916, and advanced through the grades to col., 1941; became dir. Army Inst. of Pathology, Washington, D.C., 1937; retired from active duty, Feb. 1947; scientific dir. Am. Registry of Pathology, Nat. Research Council, a div. of Army Inst. of Pathology, ret. July 1949; professorial lectr. in pathology George Washington U., retired. Legion of Merit. Honorable consultant to Army Med. Library. Hon. fellow Am. Coll. Dentists; emeritus fellow Coll. of American Pathologists; hon. mem. Am. Dental Soc., Am. Soc. Clinical Pathologists; mem. Am. Assn. Pathologists and Bacteriologists, Washington Acad. of Medicine, Internat. Assn. for Dental Research, Pan-Am. Assn. Ophthalmology (chmn. com. on pathology), Internat. Assn. Med. Museums (sec.-treas.), A.M.A., Assn. Mil. Surgeons, Honor Soc. of Am. Acad, Ophthalmology anl Otolaryngology, Am. Urol. Assn., Wash. Soc. of Pathologists. Author: Pathology of Tropical Diseases (with Dr. S. Spitz), 1945; also Atlas of Otolaryngic Pathology, 1940, Atlas of Dental and Oral Pathology (with Maj. J. Mann), 1940, 4th edit. (with Col. J. Bernier), 1948; Atlas of Ophthalmic Pathology (with Capt. De Coursey), 1941 (all Am. Registry of Pathology). Atlas of Orthopedic Pathology (with D. M. Angevine), 1943; Atlas of Genitourinary Pathology (with N. Friedman), 1946. Home: Bethesda, Md.

ASHBAUGH, ERNEST JAMES (ASH-BU), univ. dean; b. Blackford County, Ind., July 15, 1883; s. David and Louisa (Morris) A.; Marion (Ind.) Normal Coll., summers, 1901-04, also 1904-06; A.B., Ind. U., 1912, A.M., 1913; Ph.D., State U. of Ia., 1919; m. Tacy Hope Smith, June 30, 1907; 1 dau., Beulah Rhea. Prin. high sch., Matthews, Ind., 1906-07, supt. schs., 1907-09; same, Thomson, Ill., 1909-11; prin. high sch., Bartlesville, Okla., 1913-14; instr. in edn., Northeastern State Normal Sch., Tahlequah, Okla., summer, 1914; dir. Bur. Ednl. Service of Extension Div. State U. of Ia., 1914-21; asst. dir. Bur. Ednl. Research, Ohio State U., 1921-29; prof. edn., and dean of Sch. of Edn., Miami U., Oxford, O., since 1929. Mem. N.E.A., Am. Ednl. Research Assn., A.A.A.S., Phi Delta Kappa. Presbyn. Co-Author (with Ernest Horn): Fundamentals of Spelling, 1928; High School Speller, 1928; Junior High School Speller, 1928; Progress in Spelling, 1935. Also writer of bulls. on sch. surveys. Editor Jour. Ednl. Research. Home: Oxford, O. *

ASHBROOK, JOSEPH, editor; b. Phila., Apr. 4, 1918; s. William Sinclair and Mildred (Janney) A.; B.Sc., Johns Hopkins, 1939; M.Sc. in Astronomy, Case-Western Res. U., 1941; Ph.D. in Astronomy, Harvard, 1947; m. Martha Elizabeth Dowse, July 5, 1942; children—Catherine (Mrs. Michael S. Winer), Elizabeth (Mrs. Gerald D. Bowes), Jane, Susan (Mrs. Michael R. Humphrey). Physicist USN, Washington, 1942-45; instr. astronomy Yale, 1946-50, asst. prof., 1950-53; editor Sky Pub. Corp., Cambridge, Mass., 1953-80. Mem. Democratic Town Com., Weston, Mass., 1960-80. Mem. Am. Astron. Assn., Internat. Astron Union (commn. on variable stars, planets, history of astronomy), Am. Assn. Variable Star Observers (v.p. 1952-53), Medieval Acad. Am. Editor Sky and Telescope Mag., 1970-80. Home: Weston, Mass. Died Aug. 4, 1980.

ASHBURN, WILLARD REYNOLDS, lawyer; b. Norfolk, Va., May 26, 1899; s. Wallace Putnam and Helen Gray (Wright) A.; LL.B., U. Va., 1921; m. Elisabeth Bartee Corprew, Dec. 5, 1923; children—Willard Reynolds, Susan A. (Mrs. Joseph W. Cotten), Virginia A. (Mrs. William Lanier Hill II). Admitted to Va. bar, 1921, practiced in Norfolk, 1921-53; gen. counsel Smith-Douglass Co., Inc., 1936-50, dir., gen. counsel, 1950-53, dir., v.p., gen. counsel 1953-56, sr. v.p., 1957, pres., from 1957; dir. Bank of Va., 1946-53. Home: Virginia Beach, Va. Died May 9, 1974.

ASHBY, AUBREY LEONARD, lawyer; b. Wacousta, Mich., Apr. 13, 1886; s. Henry and Sarah Bertha (Coad) A.; A.B., Olivet (Mich.) Coll., 1908, LL.D., 1950; LL.B., N.Y.U., 1910, J.D., 1920; m. Alta Virginia Lee, Aug. 31, 1916; children—John Lee (dec.), Marjory Lee (Mrs. Joe B. Morningstar). Instr. history Prospect Heights Sch. for Boys, 1908-10; admitted to Pa. bar, N.Y. bar, Supreme Ct. U.S., various fed. cts., govt. agencies; acting sec. Sch. Commerce N.Y. U., 1911; prof. law and fiance U. Pitts., 1919-29; asst. gen. atty. Westinghouse Electric & Mfg. Co. and affiliated cos., 1911-29; v.p., gen. counsel NBC, 1929-47, counsel, 1948—; pres. Olivet Coll., 1948-50, now pres. emeritus, trustee; sec., dir. Dairy Supply and Equipment Co.; dir. Perth Amboy Evening News Co. Mem. Am., Fed. Communications, Alleghany County, N.Y. State bar assns., N.Y. County Lawyers Assn. (chmn. communications com.), Bar Assn. City N.Y., Am. Judicature Soc., Am. Acad. Air Law, Am. Acad. Polit. and Social Sci., Inst. Radio Engrs. (exec. council Am. sect. internat. com. radio), Assn. Practitioners ICC, Nat. Tax Assn., Acad. Polit. Sci., N.Y. U. Alumni Assn. Republican. Presbyn. Clubs: Siwanoy Country, Bronxville Field; N.Y. U. Faculty, Author several brochures. Mem. editorial bd. Jour. Radio Law, (Northwestern U.). Home: Bronxville, N.Y.

ASHLEY, PAUL PRITCHARD, lawyer; b. Fostoria, Ohio, July 2, 1896; s. John P. and Della (Gust) A.; student U. Calif., 1919; LL.B., U. Wash., 1925; m. Katherine Macrae Smith, Aug. 20, 1932; children—Mary Macrae, Katherine Cooper. Admitted to Wash. bar, 1926, practiced in Seattle; of counsel Foster, Pepper & Riviera, to 1979; asso. prof. bus. adminstrn. U. Wash., 1928-30; lectr. Pacific Coast Banking Sch., 1939-66. Active civic activities; co-chmn. Wash. chpt. NCCJ; pres. Seattle Symphony Orch., 1963-66, War and Community Chest, 1944, Municipal League Seattle and King County, Wash., 1958-60, Estate Planning Council, 1960; trustee World Affairs Council, Seattle Opera Assn., China Club; pres. Seattle Found., 1952-54, 56. Fellow Am. Bar Found.; mem. Am. Judicature Soc., Wash. Bar Assn. (bd. govs. 1949-52, pres. 1961), Wash. CD Council, Am. Law Inst., Am., Seattle (pres. 1941) bar assns., English Speaking Union (pres. 1942-43), Nat. Conf. Bar Pres.'s (exec. com. 1962-79, pres. 1967-68), Order of Coif, Acacia, Phi Beta Kappa, Phi Delta Phi. Clubs: Lawyers (N.Y.C.); Rainier, Coll. (pres. 1938), Harbor (Seattle). Author: Cases on Business Law, 1935; Essentials of Libel, 1948; Say it Safely, 1956, rev. 5th edit., 1976; You and Your Will, The Planning and Management of Your Estate, 1975; Oh Promise Me, But Put It in Writing, 1978; 1st editor Wash. Law Rev.; contbr. articles to legal publs. Home: Seattle, Wash. Died Feb. 5, 1979.

ASHMORE, JACK PEARCE, JR., lawyer, real estate developer; b. Graceville, Fla., June 9, 1930; s. Jack Pearce and Gracie (Flournoy) A.; A.B., Emory U., 1952, J.D., 1958; m. Margaret Blythe Posey, Nov. 1, 1957; children—Blythe Gentry, Margaret Blain. Admitted to Ga. bar, 1957; mem. firm Alston, Sibley, Miller, Spann & Shackelford, Atlanta, 1957-63; partner successor firm Alston, Miller & Gaines, 1963-65; founder, partner firm Ashmore & Boozer, Atlanta, 1965-68; founder, partner firm Sanders, Hester, Holley, Ashmore & Boozer, Atlanta, 1968-71; founder, mng. partner firm Troutman, Sanders, Lockerman & Ashmore, 1972-76; mng. partner Investment Properties, Ltd., Atlanta and Athens, Ga., 1965-76, Ashmore Bros. Properties, Atlanta, 1968-76; pres. Candler Bldg. Inc., Atlanta, 1970-76; chmn. bd. Ashmore Realty Co., Gen. Apt. Co., Peachtree Air Service, Inc., St. Simons Co., King & Prince Hotel Co.; dir. Castlewood Internat. Corp., 1st Ga. Bancshares, Inc., 1st Ga. Bank (Peoples Am. Bank Atlanta); trustee Cousins Mortgage and Equity Investments; lectr. Emory U. Sch. Law, 1959-65. Bd. visitors Emory U., 1970-72, trustee, 1972-76, mem. exec. com., 1974-76, real estate com., 1973-76. Served with AUS, 1952-55. Mem. Am., Ga., Atlanta bar assns., Mortgage Bankers Assn., Phi Delta Phi, Phi Delta Theta. Democrat. Episcopalian. Clubs: Lawyers, Commerce, Piedmont Driving (Atlanta); St. Simons Island. Home: Atlanta, Ga. Died Aug. 13, 1976.

ASHMORE, JAMES, educator; b. Russellville, Ark., Aug. 6, 1926; s. Ira Ashmore; B.S., N. Tex. State Coll., Denton, 1947, M.S. in Chemistry, 1948; Ph.D. in Biochemistry, St. Louis U., 1953; m. Lottie Holt, Jan. 27, 1948; children—David, Robert, Jane, Edward. Shering fellow Endocrine Soc., 1953-54; tutor biochem. scis. Harvard, then asst. prof. biochemistry Med. Sch., 1957-58; asso. prof. biochemistry Ind. U. Sch. Medicine, 1958-60, prof., chmn. dept. pharmacology, 1960-77; spl. research endocrine regulation metabolism, use isotopes in biology and medicine, metabolism of neoplastic tissues. Mem. Endocrine Soc., Am. Soc. Biochemistry, Am. Soc. Pharmacology and Exptl. Therapeutics, Biochem. Soc. (London), Soc. Exptl. Biology and Medicine, Central Soc. Clin. Research, Am. Diabetes Assn. Contbr. articles to profl. jours. Died July 7, 1977.

ASTOR OF HEVER, BARON (JOHN JACOB ASTOR), newspaper pub.; b. N.Y.C., May 20, 1886; s. 1st Viscount Astor and Mary Dahlgren Paul; ed. Eton College; D.Lit. (honorary degree), University London; hon. degree, McGill U.; m. Lady Violet Mary Elliot, Aug. 26, 1916; children—Gavin, Hugh, John. Chmn. Times Pub. Co., London, Eng., 1922-62, now chief proprietor Times newspaper; chmn. Phoenix Assurance Co., 1952-56, dir. until 1962; chmn. London Guarantee and Accident Co. Ltd., 1952-56, dir. until 1962; dir. Hambros Bank Ltd. Mem. Parliament for Dover div. of Kent, 1922-45; dep. lt. County of Kent, 1936-62, justice of peace, 1929-62; Mem. council of St. Dunstans, 1922-62; v.p. Royal Coll. of Music, 1934-62; chmn. Middlesex Hosp., 1938-62. Pres. Newspaper Press Fund. Commonwealth Press Union; chmn. 4th through 7th Imperial press confs. Pres. Nat. Assn. for Employment Regular Sailors, Soldiers and Airmen, 1936-62; pres. Kent council, also Fleet St. br., Brit. Legion, 1934-62. Joined 1st Life Guards, 1906; a.d.c. Viceroy of India, 1911-14; served in World War I, 1914-18; lt. col. 5th Bn. City of London Home Guard, 1940-44. Chevalier Legion of Honor, 1918. Created 1st Baron Astor of Hever, 1956. Freeman Borough of Dover. Clubs: Press (pres.); Royal Yacht Squadron (Cowes). Address: Pegomas, France. *

ASTROM, AXEL LEONARD, diplomat; b. Uleaborg, Finland, Mar. 7, 1883; s. Axel and Maria (Aström) A.; M.A., U. of Helsingfors, 1909; unmarried. Formerly educator and chief insp. business edn., Finland; apptd. dir. Foreign Office, 1919, and later engaged in diplomatic missions to various countries; E.E. and M.P. to U.S. since Feb. 1922. Decorated Comdr. White Rose (Finnish); comdr. Legion of Honor (French). Lutheran. Clubs: Metropolitan, Chevy Chase, Riding and Hunt, Congressional Country. Address: Washington, D.C. *

ATHERTON, THOMAS HENRY, architect; b. Wilkes-Barre, Pa., Jan. 16, 1884; s. Thomas Henry and Melanie (Parke) A.; A.B., Princeton, 1906; B.S., Mass. Inst. Tech., 1909; m. Mary Mish, Feb. 2, 1921; children—Mary (Mrs. Frantz), William Henry, Charles Henry. Draftsman Carrere & Hastings, 1910-11; practicing architect, 1912-53; partner Lacy, Atherton & Davis, Wilkes-Barre, since 1941; prin. projects include armories, hosps. State of Pa., War Meml. State of Pa., Varennes, France (with Paul Cret), Kirby Meml. Health Center, bldgs. Wyoming (Pa.) Sem., Kingston, Pa., also Wilkes Coll. Chmn. Community Chest; co. chmn, Civil Def. Trus. Mill Meml. Library, Wyoming Sem. Served with 109th F.A., Pa. N.G., 1914-41, ret. as col.; with U.S. Army, 1916-19; now brig. gen. ret. Decorated Croix de Guerre (Belgium), Croix de Guerre with Palm (France). Fellow A.I.A.; mem. C. of C., Vets. Fgn. Wars, Battle of Wyoming Commemorative Assn. Clubs: North Mountain, Kiwanis (pres.); Princeton (N.Y.C.), Address: Hilton Head Island, S.C. 29928. *

ATHERTON, WARREN HENDRY, lawyer; b. San Francisco, Dec. 28, 1891; s. Dwight C. and Elizabeth (Hendry) A.; LL.D., U. Pacific, 1972; m. Anne Holt, July 7, 1917 (dec.); children—Holt, Warren, Dwight Copeland, Nancy Anne; m. 2d, Marietta Monachino Cochran, Aug. 17, 1952. Admitted to Cal. bar, 1914, later practiced in Stockton; gen. counsel, dept. vets. affairs State Cal.; mem. firm Atherton & Dozier; legislative counsel Port of Stockton. Pres. Westwarehouses, Inc., Inland Harbor Storage Co., Madera Factors; vice chmn., dir. San Joaquin First Fed. Savs. & Loan Assn.; dir. Lilval, Inc., Sims Grupe Mgmt. Co., Inc., Lincoln Properties, Inc., B.F.B., Inc.; owner, operator Delta Farm. Pres. Stockton Community Chest, 1938; mem. San Francisco Bay Ports Commn., 1952-57; pres., founder Stockton Opera Assn.; mem. Nat. Security Tng. Commn., 1953-59; chmn. Stockton chpt. A.R.C., 1949-50, No. Cal. chmn. Vets for Eisenhower, 1952, 56; pres. Nat. Rep. Vets. League; past chmn. Rep. Central Com. San Joaquin County. Cons. to sec. of War, World War II. Served as pvt., Co. D., 363d Inf., 91st Div.; with A.E.F., Apr. 1918-Aug. 1919; capt., Ordnance, Feb.-Sept. 1919. Mem. Cal. State Bd. Paroles, 1933-35. Trustee Counsel for Inter-Am. Affairs, 1945-47. Pres. San Joaquin County Bar Assn., 1921; pres. Stockton C. of C., 1933-35. Mem. Am. Legion (past nat. comdr., mem. exec. com. 1937-38, 44-70, chmn. Inter-Am. affairs com. 1944-57, designated Father of G.I. Bill of 1944 by Cal. dept. 1974), Am. Bar Assn., State Bar Cal., Cal. C. of C., D.A.V. Presbyn. Clubs: Rotary (hon.), Kiwanis (pres. 1924), Commonwealth, Army and Navy; Monterey Peninsula Golf and Country. Stockton Golf and Country, St. Francis Yacht. Home: Stockton, Calif. Died Mar. 10, 1976.

ATKESON, THOMAS CONNER, educator; b. Columbia, Ala., Nov. 21, 1897; s. Clarence Lee Crawford and Annie May (Conner) A.; student So. U., 1916-17, U. Ala., 1917-18; B.S., Georgetown U., 1927, M.S. cum laude, 1928, Ph.D., 1931; m. Helen Douglas Whiting, July 20, 1920; 1 dau., Helen Douglas Atkeson Phillips. Asso. prof. accounting and bus. adminstrn. Georgetown U., 1931-32; sr. econ. analyst IRS, 1935; mem. exec. com. conf. of income and wealth Nat. Bur. Econ. Research, 1941-42, asst. to commr. internal revenue in charge research and statistics, 1945, asst. to commr. internal revenue and dir. mgmt. staff, 1946-52, asst. commr. internal revenue, 1952-54; apptd. to chair of taxation Marshall Wythe Sch. Law, William and Mary Coll., 1954-68, Chancellor's prof. taxation emeritus, 1968-79, head div. social scis., 1959-62. Mem. State Revenue Resources and Econ. Study Commn., 1968-70, commn. cons., 1970-75; pres. Williamsburg Citizens Assn. Mem. financial adv. commn. City of Williamsburg, Va., 1958-70. Dir. of Ann. William and Mary Tax Conf., Coll. William and Mary, 1954-68. Recipient Exceptional Civilian Service award Sec. of Treasury, 1954. Fellow Am. Statis. Assn.; hon. mem. Tax Execs. Inst., Inc.; mem. Pi Kappa Alpha. Episcopalian (former vestryman, sr. warden). Mason. Clubs: Rotary, Cosmos (Washington); Middle Plantation. Contbr. treatises on taxation to profl. jours.; also active participant in programs nat. tax orgns. Home: Williamsburg, Va. Died July 22, 1979.

ATKINS, OLIVER OLLIE F., photographer; b. Hyde Park, Mass., Feb. 18, 1916; s. Oliver Fraser and Annie Sally (McLeod) A., A.B., U. Ala., 1938; m. Marjorie Neola Deakin, Aug. 10, 1940; children—Randie Claire (Mrs. Shumate), Dale Ann (Mrs. Wheeler). Staff and chief photographer Birmingham (Ala.) Post, 1939-40; staff photographer Washington Daily News, 1940-42; fgn. corr. photographer, 1942-45; Washington photographer Sat. Eve. Post, Washington office, 1945-69, fgn. corr., photographer, Japan and Korea, 1951; photography columnist Washington Post, 1947-50; personal photographer to Pres. Nixon, chief White House photographer, 1969-74; v.p. Curtis Pub. Co., Indpls., 1974-77; photography 2 photo books, Washington Portrait and Potomac Portrait. Recipient Grand award, White House News Photographers' Assn., 1943; portrait award Graflex All-American Photo Contest, 1946; received citation A.R.C. for overseas service. Mem. White House News Photographers Assn. (pres. 1964, exec. com.), U.S. Senate Photographers Gallery (chmn. inaugural com.), Nat. Press Photographers Assn. (personalities award 1952; fellowship award, chmn. freedom of information com.), Am. Overseas Assn. (pres.). Author: Camera on Assignment; contbg. author-photographer: The President's Trip to China, Eye on Nixon, Summons to Greatness, The Nixon Years... Lift of Leadership; the White House Years-Triumph and Tragedy, 1977. Home: Washington, Va. Died Jan. 9, 1977.

ATKINS, PAUL MOODY, financial and mgmt. cons.; b. Boston, Apr. 3, 1892; s. Edward and Martha Moody (Williams) A.; A.B., Yale, 1914; A.M., 1915; postgrad. Armour Inst., Chgo., U. Chgo., N.Y. U.; Docteur de l'Universite de Paris, 1925; m. Genevieve Bergier, June 15, 1920; children—David Pierre, Henri Bergier, Edward Moody. Cost accountant Acme Wire Co., 1914-15, Gray & Davis, Inc., 1915; prodn. engr. Square D Co., 1916; mgmt. engr. Acme Wire Co., 1916-17; cons. engr. L.V. Estes, Inc., indsl. engrs., 1919-20; instr. mfg. U. Chgo., 1920-26; engr.-economist Ames, Emerich & Co., 1926-31; spl. liquidator securities U.S. Comptroller of Currency, 1932-37; treas. Alfred P. Sloan Found., 1937-38; v.p., dir. Grant & Atkins, Inc., 1939-40; financial and mgmt. cons., 1938-77; lectr., radio commentator on internat. affairs, 1960-77; adj. prof. bus. adminstrn. Rutgers U., 1956-62. Specialist, Am. Com. to Negotiate Peace, Paris, 1919; Am. sec. sub-com. on Czechoslovakian Affairs, Peace Conf. pub. credit com. Kemmerer Financial Mission to Peru, 1931; chief Argentina-Paraguay unit Am. Hemisphere div. Bd. Econ. Warfare, 1942; econ. adviser Ministry of Finance, Imperial Govt. of Iran, 1943-45; specialist banking and fgn. exchange Am. Mission for Aid to Greece, 1947-48; temp. banking adviser for Japan to sec. army, 1948. Trustee Internat. Coll., Beirut, 1937-42; bd. dirs. Seamen's House YMCA, N.Y.C., 1939-42. Served with U.S. Army, 1917-19; instr. U.S. Army Arty. Sch., Clermont-Ferrand, France, 1918; maj. to lt. col. M.I. Res., 1924-35. Mem. Am. Econ. Assn., Intercultural Assn., Phi Beta Kappa, Beta Theta Pi, Pi Gamma Mu. Conglist. Author 12 books in field; latest being Bank Bond Investment and Secondary Reserve Management, 1940. Contbr. numerous articles to gen., financial and indsl. jours. Home: Upper Montclair, N.J. Died Jan. 31, 1977.

ATKINS, PAUL SIDNEY, clergyman; b. Hazardville, Conn., Apr. 13, 1882; s. Isaac Alfred and Jane (Carter) A.; student Library Training Sch., Springfield, Mass., 1902-03; S.T.B., Phila. Div. Sch., 1918, D.D., 1937; m. Ethel Merrick Weishampel, June 8, 1907; children—Richard Knight, Mrs. William E. Anwyll, Mrs. Robert G. Nace, Mrs. Brantley Fuller Parker, Jr., Paul Sidney, Mrs. Robert H. Ness, Donald Craige, Carolyn Merrick. Deacon P.E. Ch., 1916, priest, 1917; curate St. Asaph's Ch., Bala, Pa., 1913-17; priest in charge Ch. of Incarnation, Morrisville, Pa., 1917-18; archdeacon, Harrisburg, 1927-29; rector St. John's Ch., York, Pa., since 1918; pres. standing com., Diocese of Harrisburg, since 1933. Canon of St. Stephen's Cathedral, Harrisburg. Pres. York City Sch. Bd., York Recreation Commn. Chmn. Central Com. on Christian Social Service of the Five Dioceses of the Episcopal Ch. in Pa. Select preacher St. Bartholomew's Ch., Ch. of the Heavenly Rest, Grace Ch., Ch. of Incarnation (N.Y. City). Mem. Pa. Pub. Charities Assn., Pa. State Conf. on Welfare. Republican. Mason. Club: Cleric (co-founder and pres.). Contbr. to various publs. Home: York, Pa. *

ATKINSON, GEORGE HERRING, contractor; b. Colorado Springs, Colo., Apr. 10, 1905; s. Guy F. and Myrtle L. (Herring) A.; A.B. cum laude in Econs., Stanford, 1926; D.Bus. Adminstrn. (hon.), U. Pacific, 1959; m. Mildred McKillican, July 28, 1926 (dec. 1967); children—Duane E., Ray N., Earl H., Lois M.; m. 2d, Lavina Parsons, Apr. 1968. With Guy F. Atkinson Co., contractors and engrs., South San Francisco, Calif., 1926-78, v.p., 1934-43, gen. mgr., 1938-64, pres., 1943-70, chmn., 1970-78; mng. dir. Mangla Dam Contractors, bldrs. hydroelectric and irrigation project in W. Pakistan, 1961-68; dir. Hyster Co., 1954-78; gen. mgr. Grand Coulee Dam constrn., 1936-38. Pres. San Mateo County Community Chest, 1949-50; mem. Gen. Conf. Methodist Ch., 1948, 52, 56, 60, 64, 66, 68, 70; vice chmn. Commn. Interjurisdictional Relations Meth. Ch., 1964-68. Pres. bd. trustees Willamette U., 1964-78; trustee Pacific Sch. Religion, Berkeley, Cal., 1944-78, San Francisco YMCA, 1945-55. Recipient Golden Beaver award The Beavers, 1965; Moles award The Moles, N.Y.C., 1966. Mem. Asso. Gen. Contractors Am. (gov. bd. 1949-67), Beavers (pres. Los Angeles 1958), Phi Beta Kappa. Republican. Clubs: Arlington (Portland, Ore.); Bankers (San Francisco). Contbr. articles in field. Home: Hillsborough, Calif. Died Feb. 13, 1978.

ATKINSON, SPENCER ROANE, orthodontist; b. Camden County, Ga., Sept. 2, 1886; s. Dean Dunwody and Sarah Hardee (Scarlett) A.; ed. Marist Coll., Atlanta, Ga., 1898-1902, Ga. Sch. of Tech., 1903-05; Southern Dental Coll., Atlanta, Ga., D.D.S., 1917; Angle Coll. of Orthodontia, Pasadena, Calif., 1920; hon. Master Dental Science, U. of Southern Calif., 1936; m. Agnes Akin, Apr. 28, 1908; children—Ruth, Ann. Practice of orthodontia since 1917; lecturer and instr. in anatomy and orthodontia, Atlanta Southern Dental Coll., 1917-24; teacher Angle Coll. of Orthodontia, 1920-28; prof. of orthodontics, dir. of grad. orthodontics, Coll. of Dentistry, U. of Southern Calif., 1936-56, prof. of dental research, Sch. of Dentistry, 1948-56, now emeritus professor clinical orthodontics; visiting prof. orthodontics, Coll. of Phys. and Surg., San Francisco, 1938-57; visiting prof. orthodontics Nat. U. of Mexico, 1937-41, of odontology since 1938; hon. prof. U. of Guadalajara (Mexico) since 1941; professor of orthodontics U. of Yucatan; prof. extaordinary La Universadid Autononia de Mexico. Hon. pres. first Medico-Dental Conference, Mexico City, 1938. Fellow Am. College Dentists, International Coll. Dentists, College of Physicians and Surgeons; certificate Am. Bd. Orthodontists; mem. Am. Dental Assn., Southern Calif. Dental Assn., Am. Assn. Orthodontists, (Ketcham Memorial award, 1953), Order of Double Aztec Eagle, Insignia Grade Republic of Mexico, Pacific Coast Assn. of Orthodontists, Sigma Alpha Epsilon, Psi Omega, Sigma Xi (hon.); perpetual hon. pres. Asociacion Mexicano de Ortodonica; hon. mem. Asociacion Guadalajara Ortodoncia. Rocky Mountain Soc. Orthodontists, German Soc. Jaw Orthopedics. Episcopalian. Club: University (Pasadena). Contbr. articles to dental jours. Home: Altadena, Cal.

ATKINSON, WALTER SYDNEY, physician; b. Parrsboro N.S., Can., Feb. 3, 1891; s. Martin G. and Emma A. (Cutten) A.; M.D. C.M., McGill U., 1914; Sc.D. (hon.), St. Lawrence U., 1958; m. Mary A. Gamble, Apr. 5, 1921; children—Jeanne G. (Mrs. Peter H. Remington), John G., Grace G. (Mrs. V. Peter Mortensen). Came to U.S., 1900, naturalized, 1920. Intern Royal Victoria Hosp., Montreal, 1914-15, Herman Knapp Meml. Eye Hosp., N.Y.C., 1915-16; charge eye dept. Canadian Gen. Hosp., Taplow, 1917-18; pvt. practice, Watertown, N.Y., 1916-66; pres. med. staff House of Good Samaritan, Watertown, 1934; asso. clin. prof. ophthalmology N.Y. U. Postgrad. Med. Sch., 1946-58, lectr., 1956-65; med. and adv. com. bur. services for blind N.Y. State Dept. Social Welfare; president Jefferson County Health Assn., Inc. Member N.Y. State Commission for the Blind. Board directors Watertown Community Chest-United Fund, Found. Diocese Central N.Y., Episcopal Ch., dir. Watertown Found., pres. until 1968. Served as capt., M.C., Canadian Army, World War I. Diplomate Am. Bd. Ophthalmology (chmn. 1953-54, cons. 1956-58). Fellow A.C.S., La.-Miss. Ophthalmology and Otolaryngology Soc. (hon.); mem. N.Y. State (sec., chmn. eye, ear, nose and throat sect. 1936-37), Jefferson County (sec. 1920-30) med. socs., Am. Ophthalmology Soc. (pres. 1957-58, recipient Howe medal 1972), Am. Acad. Ophthalmology and Otolaryngology (v.p. 1956, honor award 1952), A.M.A., N.Y. Acad. Medicine, Assn. Research Ophthalmology, N.Y. Ophthalmology Soc., Central N.Y. Eye, Ear, Nose and Throat Soc. Republican. Episcopalian (sr. warden). Clubs: Canadian (N.Y.C.); Black River Valley (Watertown, N.Y.); Port Royal Beach (Naples, Fla.). Author: Anesthesia in Ophthalmology, 1955, 2d edit., 1965; also articles. Home: Watertown, N.Y. Died Jan. 6, 1978.

ATWOOD, EDWARD VINCENT, educator; b. Buffalo, N.Y., Oct. 30, 1886; s. Henry and Mary A.; prep. edn. Wesleyan Acad., Wilbraham, Mass., 1908-11; S.B., Boston U., 1915, A.M., 1920; studied Harvard Grad. Sch.; m. Margaret Gluck, July 15, 1923. Headmaster Whitefield (N.H.) High Sch., 1915-19, Reading High Sch., 1920-24, Bacon Acad., Colchester, Conn., 1925-27. Wheeler School, North Stonington, Conn., since 1927. Served as mem. Chem. Inspector's Div., Ordnance Dept., U.S. Army, Mem. N.E.A., Sigma Alpha Epsilon. Republican. Methodist. Mason. In collaboration with wife has written and presented five operettas—"The Royal Highwayman," "Rosemary," "Mary Lou," "What Hol Knave!" and "The BeggarPrince." Home: North Stonington, Conn.*

ATWOOD, FRANK J(ARVIS), army officer, consultant; b. LeRaysville, Pa., Apr. 27, 1891; s. Hollis H. and Alice (Bosworth) A.; A.B., Wash. State Coll., 1914; B.S. and grad. work, U. Mich., 1915; grad. Coast Arty. Sch., 1921, M.I.T., 1921-23; grad. Army Indsl. Coll., Washington, D.C., 1932, Army War Coll., Washington, 1933; m. Jean McBean, 1927; children—John W., Mrs. Allie Burton, Jr.; m. 2d, Lucienne Fauchére, Feb. 8, 1964. Commd. 2d lt. AUS, 1916, advanced through grades to col., Oct. 1941; served in Coast Arty., 1916-21, Ordnance Dept., 1921-45, design Ordnance optical instruments, Frankford Arsenal, Pa., 1923-25; asso. prof. metallurgy and ordnance engring., Stanford U., Calif., 1925-29; procurement duties Office Asst. Sec. of War, 1929-32; instr. Army Indsl. Coll., 1929-32; chief, Ordnance Dept. tank and automotive testing div., Aberdeen Proving Ground, Md., 1935-37; ordnance officer Armored Brigade, Fort Knox, Ky., 1937-40; chief, arty. tank and automotive div., Ordnance Dept. tech. staff, Washington, D.C., 1940-41; chief, Rochester Ordnance Procurement Dist., 1942-45; ret. as col. U.S. Army, 1945; dir. purchases Remington Rand, Inc., New York, 1945-46, asst. v.p. and dir. procurement, inventory control and traffic depts., 1946-47, v.p., 1947-56. Mem. NDRC, 1940-42. Decorated Legion of Merit, 1946. Mem. Am. Ordnance Assn., SAR, Purchasing Agts. Assn., Sigma Xi. Mason (Shriner). Clubs: University (N.Y.C.); Army and Navy Country (Arlington, Va.); Army-Navy (Washington); Cambridge (Md.) Yacht, Cambridge (Md.) Country. Home: Cambridge, Md. Died May 1, 1979; buried Arlington (Va.) Nat. Cemetery.

AUCHINCLOSS, HUGH D., b. Newport R.I., 1897; ed. Yale, 1920, also Cambridge (Eng.) U. and Columbia U. Law Sch. Partner Auchincloss, Parker & Redpath, Washington. Bd. dirs. Boys Clubs Am., Boys Clubs Newport County. Served with USN, World War I, World War II. Mason. Home: Washington, D.C. Died Nov. 20, 1976.

AUCHINCLOSS, JAMES COATS, congressman; b. New York, N.Y., Jan. 19, 1885; s. Edgar Stirling and Maria (Sloan) A.; student Groton Sch.; A.B., Yale, 1908; m. Lee F. Alexander, 1909 (dec.); children—Douglas, Gordon; m. 2d, Vera Rogers Brown, Nov. 18, 1960. Began with Farmers Loan & Trust Co., N.Y. City; mem. N.Y. Stock Exchange, 1910-35, mem. bd. govs. 18 years. Former dep. police commr., N.Y. City; founder and served as treas., pres., chmn. bd. N.Y. Better Business Bureau. Mem. Council, Borough of Rumson, N.J. 12 years, also mayor for 3 terms; mem. 78th to 88th Congresses, 3d New Jersey Dist. Republican. Served in 7th Regt., N.Y. Nat. Guard; capt. Mil. Intelligence, World War I. Home: Rumson, N.J. Died Oct. 2, 1976.

AUER, EDWARD DANIEL, ins. exec.; b. Ft. Wayne, Ind., Feb. 8, 1903; s. Daniel and Matilda S. (Peters) A.; student Heidelberg Coll., 1922, Ind. U., 1923; m. Ione Breeden, Sept. 8, 1923; children—Daniel (dec.), Edward David. Real estate bus., Ft. Wayne, 1923-39, asst. mgr. mortgage loan dept. Lincoln Nat. Life Ins. Co., 1939-43, 2d v.p., mgr. mortgage loan dept., 1943-45, v.p., mgr. mortgage loan dept., 1945-54, v.p., 1954-58, sr. v.p., 1958-68, dir., 1947-68, chmn. investment com., 1956-68; chmn. bd. Dominion Life Assurance Co., Waterloo, Ont., Can., 1957-63, Am. States Ins. Co., Am. States Life Ins. Co., Am. Economy Ins. Co. (all Indpls.), 1963-68, Am. Union Ins. Co., N.Y., 1964-68, Superior Ins. Co., Dallas, 1965-68, Sentinel Indemnity Co., Dallas, 1965-68, Utilities Ins. Co., St. Louis, 1967-68, Preferred Fire Ins. Co., 1967-68, Western Pacific Ins. Co., Western Pacific Life Ins. Co., Seattle, 1967-68; pres. Auer Investment Co., Inc., Ft. Wayne, Sharberg Realty Corp., Ft. Wayne; v.p., dir. Auer Mortgage Co., Detroit; dir., cons. Western Res. Life Assurance Co., Clearwater, Fla.; dir. Pioneer Western Corp., Clearwater, Fla., Southwestern Investment Co., Amarillo, Tex., Theo H. Davies & Co., Ltd., Honolulu, Old Fort Industries, Inc., Ft. Wayne, Peter Eckrich and Sons, Inc., Ft. Wayne, Ft. Wayne Nat. Bank. Pres. bd. dirs. Parkview Meml. Hosp., Ft. Wayne, 1966-69; trustee DePauw U., 1965-75, chmn. investment and real estate com., 1966-75; trustee Malpas Scholarship Trust, DePauw U.; chmn. finance com. Ft. Wayne Found., Inc.; bd. dirs. Parkview Hosp., 1975. Mem. Mortgage Bankers Assn., Ft. Wayne Med. Soc. Ednl. Found., Ind. Soc. Chgo., Am. Inst. Real Estate Appraisers, Nat., Ind. and Ft. Wayne real estate bds., C. of C., Beta Gamma Sigma. Methodist. Mason (Shriner, Jester). Clubs: Country, Quest, Junto (Ft. Wayne). Home: Fort Wayne, Ind. Died Nov. 8, 1975; interred Lindenwood Cemetery, Fort Wayne.

AUER, JOHANNES A. C. FAGGINGER (OUR), clergyman, educator; b. Middelburg, Netherlands, Aug. 6, 1882; s. Willem Fagginger and Charlotte A.C. (Nonhebel) A.; B.D., Meadville Theol. Sch., Pa., 1906, D.D., 1932; studied Berlin and Heidelberg; degree in theology, U. of Amsterdam, 1910; Ph.D., Cornell U., 1924; Litt.D., Clark University, 1940; A.M., Harvard University, 1942; married Johanna Cornelia Snyder, September 16, 1913; children—Willem, Tryntje, Johanna Cornelia. Came to U.S., 1902. Ordained Unitarian ministry, 1906; pastor Hyde Park, Mass., 1908-09, of liberal chs. in the Netherlands, 1910-12, Evang. Ch., West End, Pittsburgh, 1912-15, Unitarian Ch., Wheeling, W.Va., 1915-17, Ithaca, N.Y., 1917-24; minister First Parish, Concord, Mass., 1925-29; instr., Univ. of Pittsburgh, 1913-14, Carnegie Inst. of Tech., 1914-15; prof. philosophy and church history, Crane Theol. School, Tufts Coll., 1926; asst. prof. ch. history, Theol. Sch., Harvard, 1929-30. Parkman prof. history and theology since 1930; lecturer, U. of Iceland, winter 1927; delivered Lowell lectures in theology, 1932; lecturer Internat. Congress of Liberals, Copenhagen, 1934, also at universities of Berlin and Marburg, 1935; lecturer Radcliffe Coll. Vice pres. Soc. of Netherlands Scholars in N. America. Pres. Netherlands Club of New England, Boston Chapter Queen Wilhelmina Fund;

president International University Foundation. Decorated by Queen of the Netherlands, Officer Order of Orange-Nassau, 1935; Knight, Lion of the Netherlands. Clubs: Harvard Faculty, Netherlands Club of New York (pres. since 1938); Harvard (Boston); Harvard (New York). Author: Humanism States Its Case, 1933; Humanism versus Theism (with Julian Hart). Contbr. articles Philosophy, Theology, History in periodicals. Home: Hingham, Mass.

AUGENBLICK, ROBERT LEE, trade assn. exec.; b. Newark, Apr. 20, 1911; s. Adolph and Anna (Menkes) A.; B.A., Brown U., 1931; J.D., Harvard, 1937; m. Deborah Delano Allen, Mar. 2, 1943 (dec. 1971); children—Mark, Peter, Drew, Katherine (Mrs. Stephen Somers); m. 2d, Elizabeth Rivinus Leydon, Jan. 13, 1973. Admitted to N.Y. State bar, 1938; asso. firm Sullivan & Cromwell, N.Y.C., 1937-50; mem. firm Augenblick & Frost, N.Y.C., 1951-62; gen. counsel, pres. Investment Co. Inst., Washington, 1962-77. Mem. New Hope-Solebury, Bucks County (Pa.) Sch. Bd., 1948-65. Served to maj. USAAF, World War II. Decorated Bronze Star. Mem. Am. Bar Assn. Clubs: Exchequer, Internat. (Washington); Harvard (N.Y.C. and Washington). Home: New Hope, Pa. Died Mar. 16, 1977.

AUGUR, MARGARET AVERY (AW'GER), school headmistress; b. Evanston, Ill., April 18, 1885; d. Walter Wheaton and Nellie (Avery) A.; student Univ. School for Girls, Chicago, 1901-02, Rosemary Hall, 1902-03, Bryn Mawr Coll., 1903-05, U. of Grenoble, France, 1911; A.B., Barnard Coll., 1912; student Chicago U., 1914-15, Teachers Coll., Columbia, 1928. Teacher of German Rosemary Hall, 1909-10, dean of residence, 1915-18, asso. headmistress, 1918-28; acad. dean Bradford Jr. Coll., 1928-34; headmistress Kingswood Sch. Cranbrook since 1934. Mem. Headmistresses Assn. of the East (acad. standards com., 1923, nominating com., 1942). Headmistresses Assn. of the Middle West, Alumnae Association of Bryn Mawr Coll., Nat. Assn. of Prins. Club: Women's City (Detroit, Mich.). Home: Bloomfield Hills, Mich. *

AULICK, AMOS LINDSEY (AW'LIK), clergyman; b. Falmouth, Ky., Oct. 9, 1882; s. Charles Lewis and Agnes Rebecca (Wright) A.; A.B., U. of N.M., 1912; Bachelor of Thelogy, Southwestern Bapt. Theol. Sem., 1915; A.M., Colgate U., 1921, B.D., 1922, Th.D., U. of Dubuque, 1927; m. Marie Walters Cook, Aug. 26, 1908; 1 son, Charles Cook (dec.). Ordained Ministry Bapt. Ch., 1909; pastorates at Little Rock, Ark., Earlville, N.Y., Austin, Tex., Oklahoma City, Okla., 1915-35; ednl. sec. Bapt. Student Missionary Movement, 1917-20; head of dept. of Bible and Christianity, Okla. Baptist Univ., 1935-42; pastor Central Bapt. Ch., Clovis, N.M., 1943-44; visiting prof. religious edn. Eastern New Mexico Coll. since 1944. Trustee Southern Baptist Theol. Sem. Mem. Southern Baptist Ednl. Commn., com. on Evangelism of Southern Baptist Conv. Democrat. Mason. Home: Portales, NewMexico.*

AURTHUR, ROBERT ALAN, author; b. N.Y.C., June 10, 1922; s. William and Margaret (Brock) A.; B.A. in Journalism with highest honors, U. Pa., 1946; m. Jane Wetherell, May 27, 1966; 1 dau., Kate; children (by previous marriage)—Jonathan, Gretchen, Timothy. Contbr. short stories to mags., 1948-52; free-lance TV writer, 1952-56; asso. producer Philco TV Playhouse, 1955, producer, 1956; film writer, 1957-59; producer NBC Sunday Showcase, 1959-60; v.p. Talent Assos. Ltd., 1961-62; charge prodn. United Artists TV, 1963-64; film writer, 1965-66; author Broadway prodns. A Very Special Baby, 1956, Kwamina, 1961, Carry Me Back to Morningside Heights, 1968; author screen plays Edge of the City, 1956, Warlock, 1958, Lilith, 1961, Grand Prix, 1967, For Love of Ivy, 1968, Trespass, 1971, The Nixon Recession Caper, 1972, Indians, 1974, Ending, 1975, All That Jazz, 1977; writer-dir. The Lost Man, 1968-69, Mafia at War, 1973; writer (with Reginald Rose) TV series The Jurors, 1972; columnist Hanging Out, Esquire mag. mem. faculty Sch. Arts, N.Y. U., 1975-78. Del., Internat. Writers Guild Symposium, Leningrad, USSR, 1975. Served to 1st lt. USMCR, 1942-46. Recipient Sylvania award for best original TV play, 1954, 55; Emmy award, 1955. Mem. ACLU, NAACP, Television Acad. Arts and Scis. (bd. govs. 1958-59), Actor's Studio, Writers Guild America-West, Acad. Motion Picture Arts and Scis., Dirs. Guild Am., Sigma Nu. Author: The History of the Third Marine Division, 1947; (novel) The Glorification of Al Toolum, 1952. Home: East Hampton, N.Y. Died Nov. 20, 1978.

AUSE, ORVAL HOPE, packing co. exec.; b. Kenyon, Minn., Aug. 15, 1909; s. Oscar A. and Anna (Hope) A.; student St. Olaf Coll., 1928-29; B.S., Iowa State U., 1932; M.S., U. Minn., 1934; m. Maurine Brogmus, Sept. 17, 1932; children—Orval Craig, Robert G., Marianne (Mrs. Alan Mitchell), Carol Jean (Mrs. Thomas B. Nelson). Instr. dairy industry Iowa State U., 1934-35; butter insp. Dept. Agr., 1935; with H.C. Christians Co., Chgo., 1935-70, pres., 1960-70; pres. Gt. Lakes Packing Co., Chgo., 1970-74. Pres. West Suburban council Boy Scouts Am., 1959-60, trustee, 1973-74, mem. exec. com. East Central Region, mem. nat. high adventure programs com.; pres. Oak Park (Ill.) Elementary Sch. Bd., 1945-48, Hinsdale (Ill.) Community Chest, 1953-55, Hinsdale Community House, 1955-60; v.p., mem. council Suburban Community Chest; mem. Hinsdale Plan Commn., 1962-64, Hinsdale Zoning Bd. Appeal, 1965-70. Bd. govs. Iowa State U. Found.; trustee Chgo. Met. Crusade of Mercy, 1969-72. Mem. Nat. Dairy Council (dir. 1963-67), Am. Butter Inst. (dir. 1962-68), Chgo. Dairy Tech. Soc. (pres. 1942), Am. Dairy Sci. Assn., Chgo. Assn. Commerce and Industry, Chgo. Merc. Exchange, Audubon Soc., Wilderness Soc., Izaak Walton League, Alpha Sigma Phi, Alpha Zeta. Republican. Lutheran. Clubs: Hinsdale Golf; Dairymens Country (Boulder Junction, Wis.), Adventurers; Safari International. Home: Hinsdale, Ill. Died Aug. 7, 1974; interred Bronswood Cemetery, Oak Brook, Ill.

AUSTIN, BERNARD LIGE, naval officer; b. Wagener, S.C., Dec. 15, 1902; s. Elijah Andrew and Loula Ola (Gant) A.; student The Citadel, 1918-20; B.S., U.S. Naval Acad., 1924; student U.S. Nat. War College, 1946-47, Imperial Def. Coll., 1949; LL.D., Long Island U., University Rhode Island; m. Isabella Murray Leith, Apr. 16, 1925; children—Alexandra (Mrs. Nathaniel Willis James, III), Jane Stuart (Mrs. Frank Thomas Watkins, Jr.), Isabella Leith (Mrs. William Walter Warlick, Junior). Commissioned ensign U.S. Navy, 1924, advanced through grades to vice adm., 1956; jr. officer U.S.S. New York, 1924-26; student torpedo sch., Newport, submarine sch., New London, 1926-27; submarine duty, Pearl Harbor, T.H., 1927-31; instr. physics, chemistry Naval Acad., 1931-34; comdr. submarine U.S.S. R-11, 1934-37; exec. officer presdl. yacht Potomac, 1937; press relations officer Navy Dept., 1937-40; spl. naval observer, London, Eng., 1940-41; comdr. U.S.S. Woolsey, 1942, U.S.S. Foote, Destroyer Div. 46 South Pacific, 1943, Destroyer Squadron 14, Marshall Islands campaign, 1944; operations officer Comdr. Destroyers Pacific, 1944, asst. chief staff for adminstrn. Cincpac, 1944-45; Navy mem. secretariat State, War, Navy Coordinating Com., 1945-46; Navy mem. staff Nat. Security Council, 1947-48, dep. to Joint Chiefs Staff rep. on sr. staff NSC, 1951; comdr. Service Squadron 1, West Coast, 1950, Service Squadron 3, Western Pacific, 1950-51; dep. and dir. internat. affairs div. Navy Dept., 1951-54; comdr. Cruiser Div. 2, 1954-55, dir. joint staff Joint Chiefs of Staffs, 1956-58; comdr. 2d Fleet and striking fleet, Atlantic, 1958-59; dep. chief Naval Operations for Plans and Policy, 1959-60; pres. Naval War Coll., 1960-64; chmn. Inter-Am. Def. Bd., 1964-67. Decorated Navy Cross, Gold Star, D.S.M. with gold star, Legion Merit, Bronze Star, Presdl. Unit Citation. Home: Rockville, Md. Died Aug. 21, 1979.

AUSTIN, CLEM C., mech. engr.; b. Crocker, Mo., June 2, 1882; s. Chester Y. and Elinora J. (Briggs) A.; grad. Streator (Ill.) High Sch., 1899; B.S. in M.E., U. of Ill., 1907, M.E., 1913; m. Sarah D. MacKay, Nov. 30, 1914; children—Briggs MacKay, Robert MacKay, Jane. Began with Calumet & Ariz. Mining Co., 1907; teacher of mech. engring., Purdue U., Lafayette, Ind., 1909-10; salesman Am. Hoist & Derrick Co., St. Paul, Minn., 1910-19; Union Steam Pump Co., Battle Creek, Mich., 1919; gen. mgr. Am. Asphalt Assn., St. Louis, 1920-21; sec. Mancha Storage Battery Locomotive Co., St. Louis, 1922, treas., gen. mgr., 1923-32, pres., gen. mgr. Chicago, 1932-38; gen. mgr. Mancha Storage Battery Locomotive Div., Goodman Mfg. Co., Chicago, 1938-51. Chmn. Chgo. sec. A.S.M.E., 1941-42; chmn. Nat. Group Del. Con. Am. Soc. Mech. Engrs. Mem. Washington Award Commn.; mem. Chgo. advisory com. Naval Officer Procurement; chmn. joint com. on mining machinery and equipment Dept. of Interior, Washington. Mem. Am. Soc. Mech. Engrs., Delta Kappa Epsilon. Republican. Address: Chevy Chase, Md. *

AUSTIN, FRANK STEARNS, railroad exec.; b. Lynn, Mass., Nov. 6, 1886; s. George Henry and Jennie Fisher (Stearns) A.; student Dartmouth Coll., Thayer Sch. Civil Engring., B.S., 1909; m. Constance Clapp, June 26, 1926. With Boston & Albany R.R. (N.Y. Central Co. lessee), 1909-35, engring, and supervisor tracks, 1909-17, gen. storekeeper charge supplies, 1917-27, purchasing agt., Boston, 1927-35; with N.Y.C. R.R., N.Y. City since 1935, asst. purchasing agt., 1935-40, purchasing agt., 1940-44, gen. purchasing agt., 1944-46, mgr. purchases and stores, since 1948, v.p. purchases, stores since 1948; vice pres. purchases and stores P. & L.E. R.R. Ind. Harbor Belt R.R., Chicago River & Ind. R.R. since 1948. Mem. Assn. Am. R.R.'s (chmn. purchases and stores div. 1948), Dartmouth Soc. Engrs., Newcomen Soc., Club: Union League (N.Y.). Home: Bronxville, N.Y.

AUSTIN, RICHARD BEVAN, U.S. dist. judge; b. Chgo., Jan. 23, 1901; s. Harry Plumer and Alice (Bevan) A.; Ph.B., Denison U., 1923; J.D., U. Chgo., 1926; m. Louise Crew, June 20, 1925; children—Richard William, David Crew, Robert Bevan. Admitted to Ill. bar, 1926, then practiced in Chgo.; with firm Osborne, Kline & McGurren, 1926-32; asso. Dwight H. Green, 1949-52; asst. state's atty., Chgo., 1933-47, 1st asst. state's atty., 1947-48, 52-53; judge Superior Ct. of Cook County, 1953-60; chief justice Criminal Ct. of Cook County, 1954-55, 60-61; U.S. Dist. Ct. judge, Chgo., 1961-77. Democratic candidate for gov. Ill., 1956. Mason. Club: Olympia Field Country (pres. 1970-71). Home: Flossmoor, Ill. Died Feb. 7, 1977.

AUSUBEL, HERMAN, educator; b. N.Y.C., Apr. 24, 1920; s. Harry and Rebecca (Oliner) A.; B.A., Bklyn. Coll., 1940; M.A., Columbia U., 1942, Ph.D., 1948; m. Anne Weisinger, Nov. 6, 1943; children—Kenneth, Jesse. Instr. history Columbia U., N.Y.C., 1946-49, asst. prof., 1949-55, asso. prof., 1955-63, prof., 1963-77; vis. prof. Manhattan Sch. Music, 1949-52, Yeshiva U., 1954-55, Bklyn. Coll., 1972-74; Fulbright prof. U. Manchester, 1955-56; mem. evaluation com. N.Y. State Bd. Regents. Mem. ednl. adv. bd. Seamen's Ch. Inst., 1968-69, Collegiate Sch., 1967-70, Daytop Village, 1968-77. Served with AUS, 1942-45. Recipient Distinguished Acad. Achievement award Columbia Alumni Sch. Gen. Studies, 1974. Mem. Conf. on Brit. Studies, Am. Hist. Assn. Author: Historians and Their Craft, 1950; The Late Victorians: A Short History, 1955; In Hard Times: Reformers Among the Late Victorians, 1960; John Bright, Victorian Reformer, 1966; Columbia History of the World, 1972. Bd. advisers Jour. British Studies, 1969-74, Studies in British History and Culture, 1969-77, Columbia Today, 1975-77; contbr. articles to scholarly jours. Home: New York, N.Y. Died Mar. 3, 1977.

AUXIER, GEORGE WASHINGTON, educator; b. nr. Paintsville, Johnson County, Ky., Nov. 27, 1905; s. Isaac Lincoln and Jemima Catherine (Wheeler) A.; A.B., Miami U., 1930, M.A., 1934; Ph.D., Ohio State U., 1938; postgrad. Georgetown U. Law Sch., 1941; grad. Nat. War Coll., 1957; m. Fernallen Arnold, Apr. 5, 1942; children—George Calvert, Catherine Fern, John Wheeler. Asst., dept. history Ohio State U., 1934-36; supt. survey fed. archives, Ohio State, 1936-37; research asst. Library of Congress, 1937-40; asst. editor Territorial Papers of U.S. Dept. State, 1940-1942; liaison officer Office of Censorship, 1942; hist. officer, War Dept. Gen. Staff (G-2), 1942-44, prin. policy analyst Office of Exec. Sec., WPB, 1944-45, chief policy analysis staff. bur. of demobilization, Civilian Prodn. Adminstrn., 1945-46, WPB historian and chief policy analysis and records br., 1946-47, prin. policy analyst, asst. gen. mgr.'s office, U.S. AEC, 1947, dir. gen. research and reports, program officer, and occasionally acting sec. of Nat. Security Resources Bd., Exec. Office of Pres., 1947-51; exec. sec. DPA and NPA, 1951-53, Bus. and Def. Service Adminstrn., Dept. Commerce, 1953-56; with Exec. Office of Pres., 1957-68; cons., research contractor, 1968-76; lectr. U.S. history and diplomacy Am. U., 1940-41, George Washington U., 1945-46; prof. bus. adminstrn. U. Md., 1970-76. Mem. Am. Soc. Pub. Adminstrn., Am. Polit. Sci. Assn., Am. Econs. Assn., Am., Miss. Valley hist. assns., Am. Acad. Polit. and Social Scis., Soc. Am. Archivists, Phi Alpha Theta, Beta Theta Pi. Mason. Clubs: Cosmos (Washington); Officers (Fort Leslie J. McNair); Argyle Country. Author numerous books, 1934-76. Directed preparation several moblzn. studies pub. by U.S. Govt. Home: Sun City, Ariz. Died Apr. 16, 1976; interred Sunland Meml. Park, Sun City.

AVERY, RAY LONGFELLOW, army officer (ret.); b. Manchester, N.H., July 15, 1884; s. Amariah and Anna Laura (Rexford) A.; B.S., U.S. Mil. Acad., 1908; student Arty. Sch., Fort Monroe, Va., 1911-12, Chem. Warfare Sch., Edgewood Arsenal, Md., 1925. Command and Gen. Staff Sch., Ft. Leavenworth, Kan., 1930-32, Army Indsl. Coll., 1934-35, Army War Coll., 1935-36; m. Margaret Ocheltree, Aug. 1, 1911; 1 dau., Margaret (Mrs. Del McCorkle Oden). Commd. 2d lt., Coast Arty. Corps, 1908, 1st lt., 1909, capt., 1916, maj., 1920; transferred to Ordnance Dept., 1920, Chem. Warfare Service, 1925; with Militia Bur., 1927-30; commd. lt. col., 1932, col., 1937, brig. gen., 1940; comdg. gen. Edgewood Arsenal, Md., 1940-46; retired for phys. disability, 1946. Recipient Distinguished Service Mgdal (World War II), Victory medal with 2 battle stars (World War I). Mason. Clubs: Army and Navy, Army and Navy Country (Washington). Home: Carmel By The Sea, Calif. Address: Carmel, Calif. *

AVON, EARL OF, (SIR ROBERT ANTHONY EDEN), former prime minister; b. June 12, 1897; s. Sir William and Sybil Frances (Grey) E.; student Eton; B.A. with 1st class honours, Christ Church Coll., Oxford, 1922; hon. D.C.L., Oxford, 1936, Durham 1937, Cambridge, 1938; LL.D., Cambridge, Birmingham, Leeds, Sheffield, Belfast, Toronto, Cal., McGill. Columbia, Denver, Bristol univs; m. Beatrice Beckett, Nov. 5, 1923; children—Simon (killed in action in Burma, 1945), Nicholas; m. 2d, Clarissa Spencer Churchill, Aug. 1952. Served as capt. with King's Royal Rifle Corps, as brig. mag., World War I; justice of peace, Durham County, 1923; mem. Brit. Ho. of Commons, 1923-57, leader of House, 1942-45; parliamentary pvt. sec. to the sec. of state for fgn. affairs, 1926-29; parliamentary under-sec. Fgn. Office, 1931-33; privy councillor, 1934; Lord Privy Seal, 1934-35; minister without portfolio League of Nations Affairs, 1935; sec. of state for fgn. affairs, 1935-38, 1940-45, 1951-55, for dominion affairs, 1930-40, for war, 1940; deputy prime minister, 1951-55. prime minister 1955-57. Rep. Gt. Britain at Am.

British-Russian Conf., Moscow, 1943, signer of 4-power declarn. agreed upon at that conf.; chancellor U. Birmingham. Decorated Mil. Cross; created Knight Order of Garter, 1954. Author: Places in the Sun; Foreign Affairs, 1939; Freedom and Order; Days for Decision; Full Circle, 1960; Facing the Dictators, 1962; The Reckoning, 1965; Toward Peace in Indochina, 1966; Another World, 1976. Address: Salisbury, Wiltshire, England. Died Jan. 12, 1977.

AXE, LEONARD HENRY, lawyer; b. Council Grove, Kans., Oct. 9, 1900; s. Joseph Henry and Minnie (Burdick) A.; A.B., Baker U., 1923, LL.D. (hon.), 1953; LL.B., U. Kans., 1929; S.J.D., U. Mich., 1942; m. Hermia Massey, Aug. 19, 1929. Instr. bus. law U. Kans., 1929-31, asst. prof., 1931-36, asso. prof., 1936-40, prof., 1940-57, asst. to chancellor, 1945-47, acting dean sch. bus., 1947-48, dean, 1948-57; fellow human relations, grad. sch. bus. adminstrn. Harvard, 1948; exec. dir. Kans. Dept. Adminstrn., 1953-55; pres. Kans. State Coll. of Pittsburg, 1957-65, pres. emeritus, 1965-75; dir. revenue State of Kans., 1965-67; dean of coll. Cottey Coll., Nevada, Mo., 1967-68; atty.-in-residence Schroeder, Heeney, Groff & Spies. Mem. Order of Coif, Omicron Delta Kappa, Kappa Sigma, Phi Delta Phi, Beta Gamma Sigma. Rotarian. Author: Aviation Insurance, 1931. Contbr. law publs. Home: Topeka, Kans. Died Dec. 20, 1975; interred Mt. Hope Cemetery Mausoleum, Topeka.

AXELRAD, SIDNEY, social psychologist; b. N.Y.C., May 25, 1913; s. Harris and Bessie (Ehrenworth) A.; B.S.S., CCNY, 1933; M.A., N.Y. U., 1937; D.S.S., New Sch. Social Research, 1943; postgrad. N.Y. Psychoanalytic Inst., 1948-52; m. Sylvia Brody, May 11, 1949. Research asso. N.Y. U., 1933-34, N.Y. State Tng. Sch. Boys, 1934-38; supr. N.Y.C. Bd. Child Welfare, 1938-41; fellow Rockefeller Found., 1941-42; staff Research Project on Totalitarian Communications, 1942-43; from tutor to vis. prof. grad. faculty New Sch. Social Research, 1946-54; from instr. to asso. prof. Queens Coll., 1948-60, prof., 1960, chmn. anthropology-sociology dept., 1950-64, dir. grad. studies, 1962-67, dean grad. studies, 1967-76; asso. dean grad. studies City U. N.Y., 1962-76; research cons. Social Work and Mental Health Agys., 1946-76; psychol. pediatric psychiatry service Lenox Hill Hosp., 1961-67, co-dir. child devel. research project, 1963-76. Served with USAAF, 1943-46. Decorated knight Order Merit Republic Italy. Fellow Am. Social Assn., Royal Soc. Health, A.A.A.S.; mem. Am. Psychol. Assn., Sigma Xi. Author: (with others) German Radio Propaganda, 1944; Occupational Choice, 1950; Anxiety and Ego Formation in Infancy, 1970; also articles in profl. jours. Asso. editor: Psychoanalysis and the Social Sciences, 1954-58; editorial bd. Am. Jour. Orthopsychiatry, 1957-62; co-mng. editor Psychoanalytic Study of Society, 1958-70. Home: New York, N.Y. Died Feb. 1, 1976.

AXELSON, CHARLES FREDERIC, chartered life underwriter; b. Princeton, Ill., Aug. 20, 1881; s. John F. and Anna (Pohlson) A.; prep. edn. S. Side Acad.; Ph.B., U. Chgo., 1907; C.L.U., Am. Coll. Life Underwriters, 1931; m. Katherine L. Strong, July 28, 1915; children—Charles F., Kenneth S. Agt. in Chgo., Northwestern Mutual Life Ins. Co., 1910—, now agt. emeritus. Personnel supv. War Dept., World War I; commd. maj. Adj. Gen.'s Dept. O.R.C.; mem. War Finance Com., Ill., 1943-46. Trustee U. Chgo., 1923-51, hon., 1951—; trustee Rush Med. Coll., 1925-41; trustee Inst. Current World Affairs, 1935-58, pres., 1939-57. Awarded U. Chgo. Alumni citation Useful Citizen, 1943. Mem. Nat. (exec. com. 1928-33), Ill. (pres. 1934-35), Chgo. (pres. 1926-27) assns. life underwriters, Ins. Fedn. Ill. (v.p. 1938-42), U. Chgo. Alumni Assn. (pres., chmn. alumni council 1922-24), Delta Tau Delta (pres. Chgo. alumni chpt. 1919-20), Chgo. Council Fgn. Relations, Am. Scandinavian Found., John Ericsson League. Republican. Baptist. Clubs: University, Quadrangle. Home: Chgo.

AYRES, WILLIAM LEAKE, educator; b. Gatesville, Tex., June 26, 1905; s. Matthias Leake and Myrtie (Buckley) A.; A.B., Southwestern U., 1923; postgrad. U. Tex., 1923-25, U. Vienna, 1928-29; Ph.D., U. Pa., 1927; m. Juliette Pagenstecher, Sept. 3, 1926; children—Juliette (Mrs. D. G. Spears), Dorothy (Mrs. R. G. Rutishauser), William Leake III. Nat. Research fellow, 1927-29; asst. prof. math. U. Mich., 1929-33, asso. prof., 1933-41; prof. math. Purdue U. 1941-62, head dept. math., 1941-48, asst. dean Grad. Sch. 1943-47, acting dean Sch. Sci., Edn. and Humanities, 1946-47, dean, 1947-62; v.p., provost So. Meth. U., Dallas, 1962-66, prof. math., 1962-70, Findlay prof. math. 1970-72, prof. emeritus, 1972-76. Vis. prof. U. Va., summer 1938, U. Cal. at Los Angeles, summer 1939. Mem. Ind. Commn. on Pub. Employee Retirement, 1953-54. Served as operations analyst USAAF, 1944-45. Recipient Gold Honor medal Am. Rose Soc., 1969. Mem. Am. Rose Soc. (pres. 1950-51), Am. Math. Soc. (asso. sec. 1938-46), Math. Assn. Am. (v.p. 1946-47), Phi Delta Theta. Rotarian. Author: (with C.G. Fry and H.F.S. Jonah) General College Mathematics, 1952, 60, 70. Editor: (with R.L. Wilder) Lectures in Topology, 1941. Home: Dallas, Tex. Died Jan. 22, 1976.

BABB, HOWARD SELDEN, educator; b. Portland, Me., May 14, 1924; s. Hugh Webster and Persis (Conant) B.; B.A., Kenyon Coll., 1948; M.A., Harvard, 1949, Ph.D., 1955; m. Corinna Meyer, Feb. 14, 1952; 1 son, Stephen Derek. Instr., Kenyon Coll., 1951-52; asst. instr., asso. prof. Ohio State U., 1952-65; asso. prof. U. Cal. at Irvine, 1965-67, prof., 1967-78, chmn. dept. English and comparative lit., 1969-72, 75-78. Served to lt. (j.g.) USNR, 1943-46. Author: Jane Austen's Novels: The Fabric of Dialogue, 1962; The Novels of William Golding, 1970. Editor: Essays in Stylistic Analysis, 1972. Home: Newport Beach, Calif. Died June 24, 1978.

BABCOCK, CONRAD STANTON, army officer, research inst. exec.; b. Leavenworth, Kans., Jan. 12, 1904; s. Conrad Stanton and Marion (Eells) B.; B.S., U.S. Mil. Acad., 1925; student Inst. Far Eastern Studies, U. Mich., 1937-38; m. Jadwiga Noskowiak, Nov. 12, 1928; children—Barbara, Conrad Stanton III. Commd. 2d lt. cav., U.S. Army, 1925, advanced through grades to maj. gen., 1956; mem. U.S. Army Olympic Equestrian Team, 1936; asst. mil. attaché to Ambassador Grew, Japan, 1941-42; mem. joint strategic plans com., Joint Chiefs of Staff, 1944; comdg. officer 7th Cav. Regt., 1947-48; dep. chief staff for Gen. MacArthur, 1949-50; mil. adviser to John Foster Dulles on Japanese Peace Treaty, 1950; with U.S. Mil. Mission to UN, 1951-54; adviser to Arthur Dean at Panmunjon, Korea, 1953; asst. div. comdr. 7th U.S. Inf. Div., Korea, 1954; counselor of mission U.S. Mission to UN, 1954-55; asst. div. comdr. 2d U.S. Armored Div., 1955-56, comdg. gen., 1956-57; chief Mil. Assistance Adv. Group, France, 1957-59; comdg. gen. 8th U.S. Army Corps, 1959-60; dir. Mut. Weapons Devel. Team, U.S. Mission to NATO, Paris, 1960-61; ret., 1961; dir. operational tech. div. Stanford Research Inst., Menlo Park, Calif., 1961-64, spl. asst. to pres. for mil. affairs, 1964-69, asst. to pres., 1969-76; mil. aide to Pres. De Gaulle on U.S. visit, 1961. Decorated Legion of Merit, Bronze Star with gold device, Purple Heart, Commendation Ribbon with 2 oak leaf clusters. Mem. Inst. Strategic Studies, Council Fgn. Relations. Club: Knickerbocker. Home: Carmel, Calif. Died Mar. 10, 1979.

BABCOCK, F. HUNTINGTON, corp. exec.; b. Providence, May 14, 1886; s. Albert and Sarah P. (Johnson) B.; Ph.B., Brown U., 1907; LL.B., N.Y. U., 1914; m. Dorothy Doubleday, May 14, 1915; children—Mrs. Dorothy Chapin, Sylvia (Mrs. David Weaver). Dir. Doubleday & Co., Morningside Heights, Inc. Vice pres. St. Luke's Hosp., 1952—. Clubs: University (N.Y.C.); Piping Rock (Locust Valley, N.Y.). Home: N.Y.C. *

BABCOCK, FRANKLIN, army officer; b. Stonington, Conn., Aug. 11, 1885; s. Brig. Gen. John Breckinridge and Blandina (Santon) B.; C.E., Rensselaer Poly. Inst., 1907; grad. Coast Arty. Sch., 1927, Command and Gen. Staff Sch., 1928, Army Indsl. Coll., 1937; m. Elizabeth Winslow, 1921 (died 1931); children—Anne Winslow (Mrs. James O. Rankin), Elizabeth Stanton (wife of Lt. J. Frederick Eagle, Jr.); m. 2d, Eleanor Cramer, 1932. Commd. 2d lt., Coast Arty. Corps, U.S. Army, 1910, and advanced through the grades to brig. gen., 1944; serving as dir. investigations service, Office of Inspector Gen., War Dept., Washington, D.C. *

BABCOCK, FREDERIC, author, editor, lectr.; b. Ord, Nebr., Oct. 31, 1896; s. Henry Ernest and Jennie (Powell) B.; student U. Nebr., 1913-17; m. Helen Reber, Oct. 20, 1935; children—Susan, Dian. Reporter, Nebr. State Jour., 1913-17; city editor Wyo. State Tribune, 1917-24; drama editor Denver Post, 1924-26; mem. editorial staff Seattle Times, 1926, Mpls. Journal, 1927; travel editor Chgo. Tribune, 1928-42, editor Mag. of Books, 1942-60. Mem. Pulitzer fiction award jury, 1949-51. Served with U.S. Army, World War I. Mem. Authors League Am., Orlando Art Assn., Thoreau Soc., Alpha Sigma Phi, Sigma Delta Chi. Mem. Soc. of Friends. Mason (32 deg., Shriner). Clubs: University (Winter Park, Fla.); Greater Orlando (Fla.) Press. Author: Blood of the Lamb, 1932; Hang Up the Fiddle, 1954. Contbr. to Sat. Rev., The Nation, Christian Century, N.Y. Times Book Rev., other mags. Home: Winter Park, Fla. Died May 13, 1979; buried in Wheaton, Ill.

BABER, CARROLL PRESTON (BAB'ER), librarian; b. Clifton, Kan., May 4, 1885; s. Ellis Ransom and Sarah Ellen (Perkins) B.; A.B., Campbell Coll., Holton, Kan., 1912; student Bonebrake Theol. Sem., Dayton, O., 1911-13; M.A., U. of Ill., 1927; student U. of Chicago Grad. Library Sch., summer 1937; m. Nelle Salina Spencer, June 15, 1911; 1 son, Eric Ransom. Gen. asst., U. of Ill. Library, 1919; asst. librarian, U. of Okla., 1920-26; librarian, Kan. State Teachers Coll., 1927-50, librarian emeritus since 1950, director Library School, 1928-50. Member American Library Association (chairman College Librarians of the Middle West, 1929; chmn. Normal Sch.and Teachers Coll. Librarians, 1931), Kan. Library Assn. (pres. 1932, 35), Kan. State Teachers Assn., Kan. Illustriana Soc. (life), Kappa Delta Pi, Kappa Kappa Psi. Clubs: Kansas Authors (pres. 4th Dist. 1931), Faculty, Forum (pres. 1932), Lions (Emporia, Kan.). Author: Manual of Order Department Routine for the College and University Library, 1929. Co-editor: College and Reference Library Yearbook, 1930, 31. Home: Emporia, Kan. *

BABINGTON, SUREN H., surgeon, author; A.B., U. Cal., 1922, M.D., 1925; postgrad. Cook County Grad. Sch. Medicine, Stanford, U. Cal., Harvard Med. Sch.; m. Mary Dieckmann, 1937; children—Suren F., Mary Lee, Nancy, Anne. Chief surgery Mendocino State Hosp., 1926-28; pvt. practice medicine, Berkeley, Cal., from 1928; vis. surgeon Alameda. County Instns., 1929-41, Highland Hosp., 1937-41; cons. vascular surgery Fairmont Hosp., 1941-43; staff phys. Rainbow Bridge and Monument Valley Expdns., 1934-36; mem. staff Herrick Meml. Hosp.; former mem. staff Alta Bates hosps., Berkeley, Samuel Merritt, and Childrens hosps., Oakland; chief staff, chief surgery, 1948-56, chmn. acad. council for interns and residents, 1946-56, Herrick Meml. Hosp. Med. examiner SSS, 1940-45. Founder, pres. Berkeley Med. Center; Cal. del. to Assn. Am. Phys. and Surg., 1954-56; chmn. exec. com., pres. bd. trustees Herrick Meml. Hosp. Active Boy Scouts Am. (Silver Beaver Award; mem. nat. council, mem. Region XII com.); pres. Berkeley High School P.T.A., 1966-67; pres. Berkeley YMCA, 1966-70; mem. City of Berkeley Welfare Commn., 1961-62; past v.p. Community Chest; pres. Berkeley Community Concerts Assn., 1960-71. Awarded Congl. Medal Merit, 1944-46; Pres. Cup Am. Physicians Writers Guild; Benjamin Franklin award High Twelve Internat. Community Service award Berkeley C. of C., Cal. Assembly and Senate awards; Internat. Inst. award as an outstanding immigrant to U.S. Diplomate Intern at Bd. Surgery Am. Bd. Abdominal Surgery. Fellow Internat. Coll. Surgeons (del. Internat. sci. assembly, Lima, Peru, 1946, Madrid, Spain 1952. Sao Paulo, Brazil 1954, Tokyo 1968: vice-regent Cal.; del. 4th Pan Pacific Surg. Assn., Honolulu, 1948), Am. Med. Writers Assn., Am. Med. Authors, Internat. Acad. Proctology, Am. Geriatic Soc. mem. A.M.A., Am. Soc. Abdominal surgeons (program vice chmn. 1960), Alameda County, Pan. Am. (past pres. San Francisco br., regional adminstr., nat. adv. v.p.), Cal. (ho. of dels. 1944-46) med. assns., Doctors Hist. Soc. (founder and pres.), Am. Physicians Art Assn., Am. Physicians Lit. Guild, Abraham Lincoln Fellowship (life mem.), Oakland Forum and Oakland Symphony (founding mem.), Pan Pacific Surg. Assn.; hon. mem. Peruvian Acad. Surgery and Acad. Medicine, San Paulo, Brazil, Cal. Congress P.T.A. (hon. life). Episcopalian. Mason (32 deg., Shriner). Clubs: City Commons (past pres., life dir.), Lions (past pres. Berkeley; del. Internat. conv. Nice, France, 1962, Alumni Iceland (founder, pres.), High Twelve (past pres., dir. Berkeley, internat. rep.; past pres. Cal. assn.), Cal. Writers (past pres.). Author: Human Sexual Sterilization; Management of Post-operative Pain; Surgery of Diverticulitis: Phenobarbital-Rash and other Toxic Effects; Simple Ulcers of Jejuno-eileum; Surgical Treatment of Varicose Veins and other technical and sci. publs.; Among the Navajo Indians of Arizona; Navajos, Gods and Tom-Toms; Medical Practices Among the Navajos; Juvenile Delinquents-How Come; Herrick Hospital Manual; The Boomerang that Landed a Navajo; The Mysteries of the Boomerang: Why I Could Not Quit. Home: Berkeley, Calif. Died May 8, 1975.

BABKA, JOHN JOSEPH, congressman; b. Cleveland, O., Mar. 16, 1884; s. Frank and Mary B.; LL.B., Cleveland Law Sch., 1908; married. Spl. counsel for atty. gen. of Ohio, 1911-12; 3d asst. pros. atty. Cuyahoga Co., O., 1912-16; 1st asst. pros. atty. same county, 1916-19; mem. 66th Congress (1919-21), 21st Ohio Dist. Democrat. Mem. Knights of Columbus, Elks, Moose. Home: Cleveland. *

BACH, RALPH EDWARD, publisher; b. Orange, N.J., Jan. 26, 1903; s. Edward John and Minnie (Clarke) B.; B.S., N.Y. U., 1925; m. Henrietta Steenman, July 3, 1926; children—Ralph E., Peter H. Analyst trust dept. Bankers Trust Co., N.Y.C., 1925-28; asst. mgr. trust dept. Bank of Am., 1928-29; financial writer Financial World, pub. by Guenther Pub. Corp., 1929-33, research editor, 1933-40, v.p., 1941-49, exec. v.p., 1949-55, pres., 1955-73, also dir. Mem. arbitration panel Am. Stock Exchange. Mem. N.Y. C. of C., Psi Upsilon. Clubs: Maplewood (N.J.) Country; Whitehall (N.Y.C.). Home: Short Hills, N.J. Died Jan. 26, 1973.

BACHAUER, GINA, concert pianist; b. Athens, Greece, May 21, 1913; d. John and Ersilia Bachauer; studied with Woldemar Freeman at Athens Conservatoire, with Alfred Cortot at Ecole Normale, Paris, France, later with Sergei Rachmaninoff; m. John Christodoulo, 1937; m. 2d, Alec Sherman, 1951. Debut in Athens with Nat. Symphony orchestra of Athens, 1935; toured Europe, 1937-39; gave more than 600 concerts for Allied Forces 1940-45; debut in London, Eng., 1947, in N.Y.C., 1950; annual concert tours in U.S., from 1951; tours in Can., S. Am., Australia, New Zealand, Africa, Many European countries, Israel, Cuba, P.R., Hong Kong; recipient Gold medal Athens Conservatoire, 1929, Prix d'Honneur, Internat. Music Competition, Vienna, Austria, 1933. Decorated comdr. Order of Golden Phoenix, comdr. Order of Welfare

(Greece). Home: London, England. Died Aug. 22, 1976.

BACHMAN, WILLIAM FRANCIS, nat. guard officer; b. Council Bluffs, Ia., Oct. 28, 1915; s. Robert A. and Georgia M. (Dellinger) B.; B.S., Creighton U., 1950, Master of Science, 1964; married Helen L. Brodbeck, May 27, 1944; children—William A., Richard E., Mary E. With Omaha Pub. Power Dist., and predecessor, from 1938, safety dir., 1952-59, personnel dir., from 1959. Mem. Neb. N.G., from 1934, brig. gen., from 1963; served to lt. col. AUS, 1940-46; comdr. 67th Inf. Brigade, Neb. N.G., from 1964. Exec. com. pub. utilities sect. Nat. Safety Council, from 1954; mem. Gov. Neb. Com. Traffic Safety. Mem. Omaha Safety Council (vice president), American Soc. for Personnel Adminstrn., N.G. Assn. Neb., Assn. U.S. Army (bd. dirs. Great Plains chpt.), Omaha C. of C. (armed forces com.), Am. Soc. Safety engrs., N.G. Assn. U.S., Am. Legion, Am. Soc. Tng. Directors (pres. Neb. 1959-60). Republican. Lutheran. Home: Omaha, Nebr. Died Mar. 16, 1977.

BACHNER, LESTER R., pres. Dreyfus Fund, Inc. Died Apr. 5, 1976.

BACKUS, CECIL FRANKLIN, research chemist; b. Portsmouth, Va., May 6, 1885; s. William T. and Anne Amelia (Hall) B.; U. Va., 1906; m. Alice Candee, June 12, 1935; children—Anne Hall, John Warner, Cecil Franklin. Research chemist DuPont Co., 1906-13; chem. dir. Atlas Powder Co., 1913-17; dir. development dept., 1919, now mem. bd. dirs.; partner Gillespie Meeds & Co. (mem. N.Y. stock exchange), 1920-22, Laird, Bissell & Meeds, 1923-40, John H. Gross & Co., Phila., 1946-48; dir. Electric Hose & Rubber Co., Equitable Security Trust Co., Marco Co. Served as maj. U.S. Army, 1917-18. Clubs: Wilmington (Wilmington, Del.); Chesapeake Bay Yacht (Easton, Md.); Tred Avon Yacht (Oxford, Md.). Address: Easton, Md. *

BACON, WILLIAM THOMPSON, investment banker; b. Derby, Conn., May 25, 1885; s. Daniel Hungerford and Mary Knight (Stillman) B.; B.A., Yale, 1906; married Martha Elizabeth Smith, October 4, 1920; children—William Thompson, Carter Smith and Martha Elizabeth (Mrs. Cargill MacMillan, Junior). Various positions Chgo. Trust Co., 1908-14, mgr. bond dept., 1914-16, v.p., 1916-20; v.p. Northern Trust Co., Chgo., 1920-25; co-organizer Bacon, Whipple & Co., Chgo., 1926, partner, 1926-80. Mem. bd. edn., Winnetka, 1920-34. Pres. Community Chest, 1943; trustee Hadley Sch. for Blind. Served as capt. 14th F.A., U.S. Army, 1918. Mem. Investment Bankers Assn. (bd. 1932-35). Clubs: Chicago, University, Attic, Commonwealth (Chgo.); Indian Hill (Winnetka, Ill.); Yale (N.Y.C.), Coleman Lake (Goodman, Wis.); Old Elm (Ft. Sheridan, Ill.). Home: Pompano Beach, Fla.

BADERTSCHER, J(ACOB) A. (BÄ'DER-TSCHER), prof. anatomy; b. Bluffton, O., Jan. 11, 1879; s. Matthias and Lydia (Augsburger) B.; Ph.B., Ohio U., 1909, Ph.M., 1910; Ph.D., Cornell U., 1914; m. Mary Blanche Goble, Oct. 11, 1904; children—Darwin Earl, Robert Carl (dec.). Asst. dept. of biology Ohio U., 1908-09, instr., 1909-10; asst. dept. histology and embryology Cornell U., 1910-11, instr., 1911-13, instr. anatomy Ind. U., 1914-15, asst. prof. anatomy, 1915-17, asso. prof., 1917-21, prof. anatomy, 1921-49, professor emeritus of anatomy since August 1949. Fellow Indiana Acad. Sci.; mem. Am. Assn. Anatomists, A.A.A.S., Am. Assn. Univ. Profs., Sigma Xi, Phi Beta Kappa, Phi Chi. Democrat. Methodist. Author: (articles) Peculiarity in the Mode of Entrance of the Optic Nerve into the Eyeball in Some Rodents (Proc. Soc. Exptl. Biology and Medicine, 1911), Muscle Degeneration and its Relation to the Origin of Eosinophilic Leucocytes in Amphibia (Salamandra Atra) (Am. Jour. Anatomy, Vol. XV, 1913), The Development of the Thymus in the Pig (in 2 parts) (Am. Jour. Anat., Vol. 17, 1915), The Fate of the Ultimobranchial Bodies in the Pig (Sus Scrofa) (Am. Jour. Anat., Vol. 23, 1918), The Ultimobranchial Bodies in Post-natal Pigs (Sus Scorfa) (Am. Jour. Anat., 25, 1919), Eosinophilic Leucocytes in the Thymus of Post-natal Pigs (Anat. Record Vol. 18, 1920), Results Following the Extirpation of the Pineal Gland in Newly Hatched Chicks (Anat. Record, Vol. 28, 1924). A Simple Technique for in Toto Staining of Tarsal and Sebaceous Glands (Stain Tech., Vol. 15, Jan. 1940). Home: Bloomington, Ind. *

BADGER, ERASTUS BEETHOVEN, bus. exec.; b. Boston, May 26, 1886; s. Daniel Bradford and Elizabeth Fannie (Pearson) B.; A.B., Dartmouth, 1908; m. Alice Drumngould MacShane, July 10, 1920; children—Nancy (dec.), Sally, Mary Jane. Started as apprentice in copper shop of E. B. Badger & Sons Co., founded by grandfather; v.p. and gen. mgr. E. B. Badger & Sons Co., designing engrs. and constructors of chemical and oil refining plants, Boston, 1921-24, treas. and gen. mgr., 1925-34, pres. and treas. since 1935; dir. Stone & Webster Engring. Corporation, Sanborn Company. Republican. Clubs: Country (Winchester, Mass.); Algonquin (Boston); Chemists (N.Y.C.); Dartmouth (Boston); Oyster Harbors (Osterville, Mass.). Home: Oyster Harbors, Mass.

BADGER, JAMES GOLVIN, lumber co. exec.; b. La Fontaine, Ind., Feb. 8, 1895; s. Job and Emma (Summers) B.; student Marion (Ind.) Normal, summer 1912, Ind. U., 1913, Wabash Bus. Coll., 1914; m. Charlotte Lucille Blodgett, May 29, 1918; children—James Golvin, Frank Kelly. Tchr. pub. schs., 1912-14; instr., mgr. Fitzgerald's Bus. Coll., Schenectady, N.Y., also Noblesville (Ind.) Bus. Coll., 1914-16; accounting clk., 1916-17; with Edward Hines Lumber Co., 1919-76, bookkeeper, auditor So. operations, gen. auditor, sec.-treas., v.p., 1927-54, exec. v.p., 1955-60, dir., 1957-69; past dir. Ore. & Northwestern R.R. Co.; pres., dir., So. Mineral Corp. Pres. Wilmette Sch. Bd., 1944-46. Served as 2d lt. 135th F.A., U.S. Army, 1917-19. Mem. Indiana Soc. Chgo. (v.p.), Am. Legion, S.A.R. Mason. Clubs: Union League (pres. 1957-58), Rotary (treas. 1959-60) (Chgo.); Westmoreland Country (Wilmette). Home: Evanston, Ill. Died July 14, 1976.

BADGER, THEODORE LEARNARD, physician, internist; b. Boston, Nov. 17, 1899; s. Arthur Campbell and Grace (Richardson) B.; A.B., Yale U., 1922; M.D., Harvard U., 1926; m. Alice Wetherbee, Aug. 27, 1936; children—Ann Badger Emery, Martha Badger Simpson. Intern, Mass. Gen. Hosp., 1926-27; asst. med. resident Presbyn. Hosp., N.Y.C., 1928-29; chief resident chest service Bellevue Hosp., N.Y.C., 1929-30; practice internal medicine specializing in pulmonary disease, Boston, from 1931; faculty Harvard Med. Sch., 1931-68, clin. prof. medicine, 1964-68, clin. prof. medicine emeritus, after 1968, Theodore L. Badger lectr. pulmonary disease, 1974, 75; staff Boston City Hosp., 1931-68, vis. physician, chief respiratory disease Clinic; chief staff Channing Home for Tb, Boston, 1935-58; active staff New Eng. Deaconess Hosp.; bd. consulation Mass. Gen. Hosp., 1945-76, hon. physician, 1976-80; area cons. pulmonary diseases VA, 1948-60; cons. Boston Lying-In Hosp., Peter Bent Brigham and Boston Hosp. Women and Children, Children's Hosp. Med Center; chief medicine 5th Gen. Hosp.-Harvard, 1942-44; sr. cons. in Tb. Served to lt. col. M.C., AUS, 1942-45. Diplomate Am. Bd. Internal Medicine, with certification in pulmonary diseases. Recipient Henry D. Chadwick medal Mass. Thoracic Soc., 1960, Edward Livingston Trudeau award Am. Lung Assn. Fellow A.C.P., Am. Coll. Preventive Medicine (hon.); mem. Am. Clin. and Climatol. Assn., Am. Thoracic Soc. (hon.; pres. 1957-58), Nat. Tb Assn. (dir. 1945-74, v.p. 1964-65), Mass. Tb and Health League (pres. 1966-67), Internat. Grenfel Assn. (dir. 1948-75, chmn bd. 1952-53), Mass. Thoracic Soc. (pres. 1960-62), Am. Lung Assn. Mass. (hon.), Sons and Daus. First Settlers of Newbury (Mass.) 1635. Home: Chestnut Hill, Mass. Died May 27, 1980.

BADT, HARRY ASHER (BAT), naval officer (ret.); b. Tyler, Tex., Sept. 22, 1884; s. Joseph M. and Augusta (Spiro) B.; B.S., U.S. Naval Acad., 1908; M.S., Columbia, 1916; hon. LL.D., Hobart Coll., 1944; m. Jennie Yudelevit, Jan. 10, 1926; children—Lois, Esther Ellen. Commd. ensign U.S. Navy, 1908, advanced through grades to commodore, 1944; navigator, U.S.S. Arizona, 1918-20; comdg. officer, U.S.S. Simpson, 1923-24; engring officer, U.S.S. Marblehead, 1924-26; comdg. officer of Aleutian Islands survey expedition, 1933; dir. of recruiting for U.S. Navy, 1935-37; comdg. officer, U.S.S. Tuscaloosa, 1938-40; director of enlisted personnel, U.S. Navy, 1940-42; comdt., U.S. Naval Training Center, Sampson, N.Y., 1942-46; ret. from active duty, 1947. Awarded Legion of Merit, 1946. Mason. Clubs: Army Navy Country (Washington). Home: Washington, D.C. *

BAEHR, GEORGE, physician; b. N.Y.C., Apr. 16, 1887; s. Herman and Sara (Gusky) B.; M.D., Columbia U., 1908; student exptl. pathology U. of Freiburg (Germany), 1911-12, exptl. pharmacology U. Vienna, 1912-13; D.Sc. (hon.), Mt. Sinai Sch. Medicine City U. N.Y.; m. Francine Gordon, Oct. 6, 1917; 1 dau. Barbara. Internship and research fellowship Mt. Sinai Hosp., N.Y.C., 1908-11; mem. ARC San. Commn. in Russia and Balkans, 1915-16; lt. col. M.C., U.S. Army, in command U.S. Base Hosp. No. 3, France, 1918; chief, 1st med. service, Mt. Sinai Hosp., 1927-50, dir. clin. research, 1944-50; clin. prof. medicine Columbia, 1929-50; Distinguished Service prof. Mt. Sinai Sch. Medicine, City U. N.Y., 1966-78; cons. physician La Guardia Hosp., Monmouth Meml. Hosp., Long Branch, N.J.; mem. Pub. Health Council, State of N.Y., 1935-75, chmn. 1955-69; mem. Bd. Hosps. N.Y.C., 1944-73; pres. med. dir. Health Ins. Plan Greater N.Y., 1950-57; spl. med. cons., 1957-78; adminstrv. cons. Dept. Hosps., N.Y.C., 1933-45; mem. sci. bd. Pub. Health Research Inst.; bd. dirs. mem. tech. bd. Milbank Meml. Fund; med. dir. USPHS and chief med. officer U.S. Office Civilian Def., 1941-44; del. from U.S. State Dept. to 4th, 5th and 6th Decennial Internat. Confs. to revise internat. list of causes of death, Paris, 1938-48. Trustee Community Service Soc.; bd. dirs. N.Y. State Communities Aid Assn.; mem. nat. adv. health council NIH, USPHS, 1945-50. Fellow ACP; mem. AMA, Assn. Am. Physicians, Am. Heart Assn., (hon.) Am. Hosp. Assn., Am. Pub. Health Assn. (v.p. 1952-53), Soc. for Clin. Investigation, Am. Assn. Pathologists and Bacteriologists. AAAS, N.Y. Acad. Medicine (pres. 1945-48, trustee 1950-60), Sigma Xi, Alpha Omega Alpha. Clubs: Cosmos (Washington); Players (N.Y.C.). Co-author: Cecil's Textbook of Medicine, 8th edit., 1952. Co-editor: Convalescent Care, 1940; Preventive Medicine, 1942; Medical Uses of Cortisone, 1954; Oxford Loose-Leaf Medicine, vol. IV, 1955; chmn. adv. editorial bd. Standard Nomenclature of Diseases and Operations, 1932-60. Contbr. articles to pub. health and med. jours. Home: New York, N.Y. Died Sept. 6, 1978.

BAER, JOHN M(ILLER), cartoonist; b. Blackcreek, Wis., Mar. 29, 1886; s. John Mason and Libbie Caroline (Riley) B.; A.B., Lawrence Univ., Appleton, Wis., 1909; student Federal Sch. of Art, Minneapolis, and Nat. Art Sch., Washington, D.C.; m. Estelle G. Kennedy, Dec. 28, 1910; children—John Mason, Alfred Sherman, Byron. Civil engring., 1904-10; engring. and cartooning, 1910-14; mem. 65th and 66th Congresses (1917-21), 1st N.D. Dist.; cartoonist for Labor (publ. ry. unions) since 1921; publicity dir. Union Label Trades Dept., Am. Fed. of Labor; mem. adv. bd. labor edn., Nutrition and Food Conservation Br., Food Distbn. Administrn., U.S. Dept. Agr. Recipient 1st award for best cartoon Internat. Labor Press Assn., 1963. Mem. Beta Sigma Phi. Democrat. Conglist. Club: National Press. Home: Chevy Chase, Md. 20015.

BAERG, WILLIAM J., prof. entomology; b. Hillsboro, Kan., Sept. 24, 1885; s. John and Margareta (Hildebrand) B.; A.B., U. of Kan., 1915; Ph.D., Cornell U., 1922; unmarried. Prof. entomology, U. of Ark., since 1918, also entomologist Expt. Sta. Mem. A.A.A.S., Am. Assn. Economic Entomologists, Entomol. Soc. America, Am. Assn. Univ. Profs., Sigma Xi, Gamma Alpha. Author of various bulls. Ark. Agrl. Expt. Sta.; contbr. Jour. Parasitology, Scientific Monthly, etc. Club: Fortnightly. Home: Fayetteville, Ark.*

BAETJER, HOWARD, business exec.; b. Baltimore, Md., Dec. 20, 1879; s. John George and Anna Mary (Koppelman) B.; A.B., Johns Hopkins; B.S., Mass. Inst. Tech.; unmarried. Former chmn. exec. com. Mt. Vernon-Woodberry Mills, Inc.; dir. Baltimore Nat. Bank, Turner Halsey Co. Trustee Johns Hopkins Univ. Home: Baltimore.

BAGNOLD, ENID, (LADY JONES), novelist, playwright; b. Rochester, Kent, Eng., Oct. 27, 1889; d. Col. Arthur Henry and Ethel (Alger) Bagnold; student of schools in England, Paris, Lausanne, Marburg; m. Sir Roderick Jones, July 8, 1920, (dec. Feb. 1962); children—Laurian (wife of Comte Anne-Pierre d'Harcourt), Timothy, Richard, Dominick. Author: A Diary Without Dates, 1916; The Happy Foreigner, 1920; Sailing Ships (poems), 1917; Alice and Thomas and Jane (juvenile); Serena Blandish, 1924; National Velvet (prod. as movie, TV series), 1935; The Squire (The Door of Life) 1938; The Loved and Envied, 1951; (plays) Gertie, Lottie Dundas, Poor Judas (awarded Arts Theatre Prize in co. with John Whiting), The Chalk Garden (award of merit, Am. Acad. Arts and Letters); The Last Joke (play), 1960; The Chinese Prime Minister (produced in N.Y.C. and London), 1965; (3-act comedy) Call Me Jacky, 1966; Enid Bagnold's Autobiography, 1970; Four Plays, 1971. Home: Rottingdean, Sussex, England. Died Mar. 31, 1981.

BAHL, F. J., business exec.; b. Green Co., O., 1886; s. Jacob and Jennie (Rosa) B.; m. Henrietta Knapp; 1 son, Charles Daniel. Joined Merchants Cold Storage Co., 1911, pres. since 1925; chmn. bd. Matthews Frechtling Dairy Co., Tri State Butter Co. (all Cin.), Frechtling Dairy Co., Hamilton, O., Hiland Dairy Co. Newport, Ky.; dir. Nat. Dairy Products Corp. Republican.

BAILEY, ALBERT DAVID, elec. engr., educator; b. Waterloo, Ia., Feb. 16, 1915; s. Albert Oscar and Marie (Bunger) B.; B.A., Ia. State Tchrs. Coll., Cedar Falls, 1936; B.S., Ia. State Coll., Ames, 1938; M.S., U. Ill., Urbana, 1944, Ph.D., 1954; m. Madalin Webster, June 9, 1940; children—David Alan, James Hamilton. Field engr. K.R. Brown, Cons. Engr., Des Moines, 1938-41; faculty dept. elec. engring. U. Ill., Urbana, 1941-75, prof. elec. engring. Active Arrowhead council Boy Scouts Am., 1955-75. Served from ensign to lt. (j.g.), USNR, 1944-46. Mem. I.E.E.E., Am. Assn. U. Profs., Sigma Xi, Eta Kappa Nu, Tau Beta Pi, Blue Key. Home: Champaign, Ill. Died July 1975.

BAILEY, ALFRED MARSHALL, mus. dir.; b. Iowa City, Feb. 18, 1894; s. William H. and Mary (Jelly) B.; A.B., U. Iowa, 1916; D.Sc., Norwich U., 1944; Dr. Pub. Service, U. Denver, 1954; m. Muriel E. Eggenberg, June 16, 1917; children—Beth Elaine, Patricia Jean. Mem. U.S. Biol. Survey Expdn. to Hawaiian Islands, 1912-13; naturalist-curator of birds and mammals, La. State Mus., 1916-19; rep. U.S. Biol. Survey, Alaska, 1919-21; leader Arctic expdn. Colo. Mus. Natural History, 1921-22, curator of birds and mammals, 1922-26; zoologist Abyssinian expdn., Field Mus. Natural History, 1926-27; dir. Chgo. Acad. Scis., 1927-36; dir. Denver Mus. Natural History, 1936-69, dir. emeritus, 1970-78. Expdns. to Labrador, Alaska, Mid-Pacific-Australia, also New Zealand, 1949-54, 57-58, Ecuador and Galapagos Islands, 1960, Botswana and South Africa, 1969. Fellow Am. Ornithologists

Union, AAAS. Author: Birds of Arctic Alaska, 1948; Birds of New Zealand, 1955; Birds of Colorado, 2 vols., 1965; Pictorial Checklist of Colorado Birds, 1967; Field Work of a Museum Naturalist in Alaska (1919-1922), 1971. Contbr. to Condor, Auk, Nat. Geog. Mag., Jour. Mammalogy, Natural Hist., Wilson Bull., Country Life in Am., Nature Mag., Am. Forests Life, Frontier. Home: Denver, Colo. Died Feb. 1978.

BAILEY, CONSUELO NORTHROP, lawyer; b. Fairfield, Vt. Oct. 10, 1899; d. Peter Bent Brigham and Katherine E. (Fletcher) Northrop; Ph.B., U. Vt., 1921, LL.D., 1952; LL.B., Boston U., 1925; LL.D., Cedar Crest Coll., 1956, Am. Internat. Coll. 1957; m. Henry A. Bailey, Sept. 2, 1940. Admitted to Vt. bar, 1926, Vt. Supreme Ct., 1926, U.S. Dist. Ct., 1927, U.S. Supreme Ct., 1933, U.S. Customs Ct., 1942; prosecutor City of Burlington, Vt., 1925; state's atty., Chittenden County, Vt., 1927-31; state senator 1930; sec. to U.S. senator Ernest W. Gibson, 1931-37; pvt. practice law, 1937-76; vice chmn. Vt. Rep. State Com., 1934-36; del. to Rep. Nat. Conv., 1936, 1944, delivered addresses for Rep. party, 1925-76; Rep. nat. committeewoman for Vt., 1936-73, sec. Rep. Nat. Com., 1964-72; elected to Vt. Gen. Assembly, 1950, 52, elected speaker of Assembly, 1953; lt. gov. of Vt., 1954-57; presdl. elector, 1956, 72; chmn. com. on call Rep. Nat. Conv., 1960; mem. Rep. Task Force, 1965; sec. Rep. Nat. Conv., 1968. Dir. Tuttle Law Print, Inc., Rutland, Vt. Mem. U.S. Civil War Centennial Commn., 1958, Vt. Civil War Centennial Commn., 1958; mem. nat. women's adv. com. Fed. Civil Def. Adminstrn.; mem. White House Conf. World Refugee Year, 1959; mem. Vt. Historic Sites Commn., 1970-75, Vt. Status of Women Commn., 1970-76; mem. corp. Peter Bent Brigham Hosp., Boston; mem. nat. alumni council Boston U., 1963-76; mem. alumni council U. Vt., pres. Class of 1921, 1971; mem. U.S. Post Office Adv. Bd., 1933-55; bd. Dirs. Womens Med. Coll., Phila.; mem. Calvin Coolidge Found. Recipient Distinguished Alumni Service awards Boston U., 1970, U. Vt., 1971; named Rep. Woman of Year, Nat. Fedn. Rep. Women, 1969, recipient Distinguished Service award, 1971. Vt. Bar Assn., Vt. Rose Soc. (pres.), Phi Beta Kappa, Sigma Gamma, Kappa Beta Pi. Club: Burlington Zonta Internat. (founder, first pres.). Author: Digest of Primary and Election Laws of Vt., 1928. Home: South Burlington, Vt. Died Sept. 9, 1976; interred Sheldon Cemetery (Vt.).

BAILEY, ELWOOD TEWKSBURY, lecturer; b. Somerville, Mass., Sept. 6, 1883; s. James P. and Julia (Atwell) B.; grad. high sch., Kankakee, Ill.; student U. of Neb. and Y.M.C.A. Coll., Lake Geneva, Wis. (non grad.); m. Bertha Phillippi of Omaha, Neb., Dec. 10, 1907; 1 dau., Ruth Eloise. Y.M.C.A. sec. 10 yrs.; platform lecturer since 1914; lecturer-entertainer in Europe 6 mos., World War. Mem. Internat. Lyceum and Chautauqua Assn., Alpha Theta Chi. Republican. Methodist. Mason. K.P. Clubs: Kiwanis, Sciots, Optimists, One Hundred Percent (all hon.). Home: San Diego, Calif. *

BAILEY, GEORGE WILLIAM, radio exec.; b. Quincy, Mass., May 14, 1887; s. Herbert Briggs and Alice (Brown) B.; A.B., Harvard, 1907; Sc.D. (hon.), Lawrence Coll., 1958; m. Alice Cooper, June 16, 1913; children—Mary Alice (Mrs. L.H. Montgomery), George William, Richard Briggs, Chmn. radio sect, office sci. personnel NRC, Washington, 1941-43; spl. asst. to chmn. NDRC, 1941-42; chmn. com. 1, mem. coms. 12, 13 War Communications Bd., 1942-45; asst. chief communications Mil. D.C., 1942-45; chmn. agy. com. Selective Service, 1942-45; mem. interagy. com. manpower shortages, 1945-47; chief sci. personnel office OSRD, 1944-46; exec. sec. I.R.E. (became IEEE), N.Y.C., 1946-71; owner, operator amateur radio sta. W2KH, N.Y.C., 1945-75. Adviser to dir. SSS, 1948-58; cons. telecommunications to under-sec. Dept. State, 1957-76; mem. nat. industry adv. FCC. Recipient Pres.'s certificate Merit; Edison citation N.Y. Acad. Scis. Fellow I.R.E., Radio Club Am.; mem. Armed Forces Communications, Electronics Assn. (dir., pres. 1954-56), Am. Radio Relay League (pres. 1940-52), Internat. Amateur Radio Union (pres. 1940-52), Vet. Wireless Operators Assn. (Marconi medal for service, hon.), Quarter Century Wireless Assn. (hon. life), Esperanto Assn. N. Am., Theta Delta Chi. Clubs: Harvard (N.Y.C., Boston); Cosmos (Washington). Home: Nashville, Tenn. Died Dec. 19, 1976; interred North Scituate (Mass.) Cemetery.

BAILEY, HARRY PAUL, geographer, educator; b. Allentown, Pa., Feb. 12, 1913; s. Harry D. and Grace E. (Mader) B.; B.A., U. Calif. at Los Angeles, 1939, M.A., 1942, Ph.D., 1950; m. Shirley E. Pavlicek, May 22, 1942; children—Barbara R., Marian G., Ellen L. Asso. prof., head dept. Los Angeles State Coll., 1950-51; asso. prof. U. Calif. at Los Angeles, 1952-63; prof. U. Calif. at Riverside, 1963-79, head dept. geography, 1968-70. Guggenheim fellow, 1958-59; Fulbright research scholar in New Zealand, 1959; guest prof. U. Aarhus (Denmark), 1966-67. Served to capt., Air Weather Service, USAAF, 1942-46. Mem. Am. Geog. Soc., Assn. Am. Geographers, Am. Meteorol. Soc., Sigma Xi. Home: Riverside, Calif. Died Dec. 15, 1979; buried Nat. Mil. Cemetery, Riverside.

BAILEY, NATHAN LYNCH, clergyman; b. Wilmington, Del., Oct. 5, 1909; s. Nathan and Anita Marie (Lynch) B.; diploma Nyack (N.Y.) Missionary Coll., 1931; LL.D., Asbury Coll., Wilmore, Ky., 1960; m. Mary E. Dittmar, June 26, 1931; children—Marilyn Joyce (Mrs. Dahl B. Seckinger), Anita Carrol (Mrs. Fred Henry). Ordained to ministry Christian and Missionary Alliance Ch., 1932; pastor in Mattoon, Ill., 1931-34, Windsor, Ont., Can., 1934-40, Ottawa, Ont., 1940-46; dist. supt. Eastern Canadian Dist., Christian and Missionary Alliance, 1946-60, nat. v.p. 1954-60, nat. pres., 1960-79; pres. Christian Publs., Inc., Harrisburg, Pa., 1960-72, William H. Dietz Inc., Harrisburg, 1960-72, World Relief Com., Inc., 1967-79, C&MA Found., 1962-79. Mem. Pres.'s Com. on Aging, 1961; mem. Council Devel. Assistance Services, Washington, 1976-79, pres. Alliance World Fellowship, 1975—. Trustee Nyack Coll., 1954-79. Mem. Nat. Assn. Evangelicals (exec. com. 1969-79, pres. 1976-79), Nyack Coll. Honor Soc. Home: Nyack, N.Y. Died July 10, 1979; buried Oak Hill Cemetery, Nyack.

BAILEY, PEARCE, physician; b. N.Y.C., July 22, 1902; s. Pearce and Edith Lawrence (Black) B.; diploma St. Paul's Sch., Concord, N.H., 1920; A.B., Princeton, 1924; A.M., Columbia, 1931; Ph.D., Sorbonne, U. Paris, 1933; honours course in chemistry U. London, 1936; M.D., Med. Coll. S.C., 1941; m. Georgette Dora Princess Mestchersky, July 3, 1936. Asso. dir. Psychol. Center (a founder), Paris, France, 1933-36; intern Roper Hosp., Charleston, S.C., 1941-42; resident neurology Bellevue Hosp., N.Y.C., 1942-44, vis. neuropsychiatrist, 1944-46; child neurology sect. VA Central Office, 1946-51, asst. chief psychiatry and neurology div., 1948-51, cons. regional office, Washington, 1950-51; dir. Nat. Inst. Neurol. Diseases and Blindness, 1951-60, dir. internat. neurol. research, 1960-63, spl. asst. to dir., 1963-72; attending neurologist Georgetown U., D.C. Gen. hosps., 1947-60; faculty Georgetown U., 1947-60, prof. clin. neurology, 1950-60; adv. com. Psychiatry and Neurology Service, VA Central Office, 1952-60; hon. prof. clin. neurology U. P.R. Sch. Medicine, 1963-70. U.S. del. Internat. Poliomyelitis Congress, N.Y.C., 1948, 4th Internat. Neurol. Congress, Paris, 1949 (chmn. com. for advancement neurology 1949-53); asst. sec.-gen. N. Am., 6th Internat. Neurol. Congress, 1957. Served as comdr. M.C., USNR, 1944-46. Decorated Officer de la Sante Publique, 1949; commandador El Soldel Peru, 1963. Diplomate Am. Bd. Psychiatry and Neurology. Mem. Am. Acad. Neurology (editor Newsletter 1949-62, pres. 1951-53), A.M.A., Am. Neurol. Assn., Am. Psychiat. Assn., Nat. Epilepsy Soc. (pres. 1953-54), World Fedn. Neurology (sec.-treas. gen. 1957-65), Sociedad Neurologica Argentina (hon.), Sociedade de Neurologia do Rio de Janerio (hon.), Assn. Am. Med. Colls., Am. Acad. Cerebral Palsy, Nat. Soc. Crippled Children and Adults (profl. adv. council), Easter Seal Found. (trustee), Am. Med. Writers Assn., N.Y. Neurol. Soc. (hon.), Die Deutsche Gesellschaft Für Neurologie (hon.), Japanese Soc. Neurology (hon.), Sociedad de Neurologia y Neurocirugia (hon., Montevideo, Uruguay), Washington Acad. Medicine, N.Y. Acad. Scis., Harvey Cushing Soc., Assn. Mil. Surgeons, Nat. Multiple Sclerosis Soc. (adv. bd.), Société Francaise de Neurologie (hon.), Assn. for Research Nervous and Mental Diseases, S.C. Med. Assn., Med. Soc. D.C. Author: Neurologic Rehabilitation, Handbook of Neurology (with A.B. Baker, Joe R. Brown), 1952. Editor: World Neurology; mem. editorial bd. Neurology, 1951; editorial staff Internat. Jour. Neurol. Scis. Contbr. articles to med. jours. Died June 23, 1976.

BAILEY, RICHARD PAUL, univ. dean; b. Stockton, Ill., Oct. 9, 1922; s. Parke O. and Nellie Mae (Lauer) B.; B.A., N. Central Coll., Naperville, Ill., 1943; M.A., U. Wis., 1949, Ph.D., 1959; m. Olive Jean Hughes, Dec. 21, 1943; children—Susan, Jo Ellen, Dan, Carla, Anne. Tchr. high sch., Belleville and Mansfield, Ohio, 1946-48; instr. English, Wis. State U., Oshkosh, 1949-53; research asst. Bd. Regents State Colls., Madison, Wis., 1953-59; pres. Yakima (Wash.) Valley Coll., 1959-62, Northland Coll., Ashland, Wis., 1962-68, Hamline U., St. Paul, 1968-75; dean. Gen. Coll., U. Minn., Mpls., 1975-77. Past pres. Wis. Assn. Ind. Colls. and Univs., Minn. Pvt. Coll. Council. Columnist Mpls. Star, 1972-77, Today's Edn., 1973. Trustee James Jerome Hill Reference Library, Walker Methodist Residence, Choreogram Dance Studio. Served to lt. USNR, 1943-46. Mem. United Ch. Christ. Home: St. Paul, Minn. Died Dec. 8, 1977.

BAILEY, WARREN GRANT, mgmt. cons.; b. Definance, O., Oct. 28, 1886; s. Richard S. and Elizabeth C. (Bolley) B.; grad. Ind. Bus. Coll., Marion, Ind., 1906; A.B., Ind. Central Coll., Indpls., 1914, LL.D., 1954; M.A., Ind. U., 1917; m. Lavinia Good, Sept. 6, 1910; children—Robert, Arthur. Cost accountant Oliver Plow Works, South Bend, Ind., 1910-12; sec., instr. economics Ind. Central Coll., 1914-16; asst. prof. economics, auditor Miami U., Oxford, O., 1917-18; indsl. engr. Arthur Young & Co., Chgo., 1918-20; sr. asso. mgmt. engr. Griffenhagen & Assos., Chgo., 1920-22; dir. reorgn. Canadian govt. depts., Ottawa, 1919-21; mgmt. engr., asst. dir., v.p. Business Research Corp., Chgo., cons. service to pub. utilities, banks, other orgns., 1922-36; pres., gen. mgr. O-Cedar Corp., Chgo., 1936-40; dist., regional mgr. WPB, 1941; comptroller Fruehauf Trailer Co., Detroit, 1941-43; partner A.T. Kearney & Co., Chgo., 1943-57; cons. Willow Run Labs., Univ. of Mich., 1957-61, Inst. for Science and Technology, 1961—; management cons. comml., ind. orgns. Mem. Nat. Assn. Accountants, Soc. Advancement Mgmt., Am. Mgmt. Assn., Epsilon Sigma Alpha. Methodist. Clubs: Union League, City Club (Chgo.). Co-author: Accounting Procedures for Public Utilities, 1927. Address: Evanston, Ill.

BAILEY, WILLIAM LOUIS, prof. sociology; b. Rousseau, Ont., Can., Aug. 15, 1882; s. Capt. George and Emily (Kidd) B.; student Toronto U., 1 yr.; M.A., Queen's U., 1904; post-grad. work, Cornell U., U. of Wis.; m. Edith Olivia Reid, Apr. 24, 1906; 1 dau., Florence Elizabeth. Came to U.S., 1905. Fellow Sage Sch. Philosophy, Cornell U., 1905-06, U. of Wis., 1906-07; asst. in polit. science, U. of Wis., 1907-08; acting prof. social science, U. of Colo., 1908-09, U. of Mich., 1909-10; instr. in social science, U. of Wis., 1910-13; asso. prof. social science, Grinnell (Ia.) Coll., 1913-18; prof. sociology, Northwestern U. since 1918, also lecturer Garrett Bibl. Inst.; lecturer Summer Schs., Columbia, Northwestern, etc., and many convs. and conf. bodies. Mem. Com. on Social Economic Surveys, Chicago Regional Planning Assn., also mem. City Plan Commn. of Evanston. Mem. Am. Sociol. Soc., Am. Country Life Assn., Am. Assn. Univ. Profs., Alpha Delta Kappa, Alpha Phi Zeta. Methodist. Author: Manual of Survey (with C. J. Hewitt), 1921; also articles and repts. oncommunity problems. Home: Evanston, Ill. *

BAILEY, WILLIAM STUART, constrn. co. exec.; b. Calvert, Tex., Aug. 13, 1907; s. William Stuart and Tallulah (Smith) B.; B.A., Rice U., 1930; m. Jessie Jones, Oct. 1, 1931; children—William Stuart, Margaret Elizabeth. With Jesse H. Jones Interests, Ft. Worth, 1930-42; with Fischbach and Moore, Inc., Houston, 1946-79, v.p., 1946-69, sr. v.p., 1969-72, exec. v.p., dir. corporate sales, 1972-79, also dir.; dir. MacGregor Park Nat. Bank, Houston. Bd. dirs. Air Force Acad. Found., Colorado Springs. Served with USAAF, 1942-46. Home: Houston, Tex. Died Aug. 27, 1979.

BAILLY, EDWARD CASHMAN (BA'YE), lawyer, exec.; b. St. Paul, Minn., July 26, 1886; s. Frank Cory and Margaret (Cashman) B.; A.B., Columbia Univ., 1907, LL.B., 1909; m. Elizabeth Donovan, Oct. 3, 1911; children—Margaret Donovan, Edward Cashman, Ellen Hayes. Admitted to N.Y. bar, 1909, to practice before Supreme Court of U.S., 1929, also interstate Commerce Commn. and various lower fed. courts; partner Hornblower, Miller, Potter & Earle and successor firms to and including Willkie, Owen, Otis & Bailly, 1918-41; v.p., gen. counsel, dir. Carolina, Clinchfield & O. Ry. and Carolina, Clinchfield & O. Railway of South Carolina, 1928-53; formerly counsel for bondholders' protective coms. in various railroad reorganizations. Mem. advisory com. N.Y. Foundling Hosp. Mem. N.Y. State bar assn., Soc. Colonial Wars, N.Y. State S.R., Minn. Hist. Soc., N.Y. State Hist. Assn., Columbia Alumni Assn., Soc. of Older Graduates of Columbia University, Société Genealogique Canadienne Francaise, Alpha Chi Rho (nat. v.p. 1919-21; pres. 1921-23). Republican. Catholic. Author: The Legal Basis of Rate Regulation, 1911. Clubs: University (New York); Westchester Country (Rye, N.Y.). Author: The French Canadian Background of a Minnesota Pioneer. Home: White Plains, New York. *

BAIRD, ALBERT CRAIG, univ. prof.; b. Vevay, Ind., Oct. 20, 1883; s. William John and Sarah (Hedden) B.; A.B., Wabash Coll., 1907; B.D., magna cum laude, Union Theol. Sem., 1910; A.M., Columbia, 1912; Litt.D., Wabash Coll., 1932; m. Marion Peirce, June 25, 1923; 1 dau., Mary Barbara. Instr. in English, Ohio Wesleyan U., 1910-11, Dartmouth Coll., 1911-13; prof. rhetoric and argumentation. Bates Coll., 1913-25; asso. prof. speech, State U. of Iowa, 1925-28, prof., 1928-52, prof. emeritus, from 1952; vis. prof. Fla. State U., U. Wash., U. Mo., So. Ill. U., others; prof. English, Columbia, summers, 1924, 25, 31, 37. Pres., Nat. Assn. Teachers of Speech, 1939; mem. Phi Beta Kappa, Pi Kappa Delta, Delta Sigma Rho. Episcopalian. Mason. Author: Speech Criticism (with Lester Thonssen), 1948; Argumentation. Discussion and Debate, 1950; Essentials of General Speech (with F. H. (Knower), 1952; American Public Addresses: 1740-1952, 1956; Rhetoric: A Philosophical Inquiry, pub. 1965. Editor: Representative American Speeches (annually), 1937-59; C.A. Goodrich's Select British Eloquence, 1963. Home: Iowa City, Ia. Died Mar. 18, 1979.

BAIRD, EDWIN, author; b. Chattanooga, Tenn., June 28, 1886; s. William C. and Mary (Kaylor) B.; ed. pub. schs.; m. Mildred Ward, of Chicago, Nov. 20, 1911. Contbr. to mags. and newspapers since 1906; was feature writer Chicago Daily Journal and Chicago Evening American; v.p. Real Detective Tales, Inc. Episcopalian. Author: The City of Purple Dreams, 1913; The Heart of Virginia Keep, 1916; Fay, 1923; Will-o'-The-Wisp, 1925; How to Write Detective Stories, 1932. Former editor Real Detective Magazine; editor and pub. Real America Mag.; pres., Real America, Inc. Contbr. to leading mags. Home: Chicago,

Ill.; also N.Y. City and Hollywood, Calif. *

BAIRD, FREDERICK ROGERS, lawyer; b. Chicago, Ill., Jan. 12, 1885; s. Frederick S. and Hattie E. (Rogers) B.; Ph.B., U. of Chicago, 1906, J.D., 1908; m. Ruth Miller, Feb. 11, 1911; children—Roger Allen, Russell Miller. Admitted to Ill. bar, 1908; in gen. practice, Omaha, Neb., 1908-10; house atty., Parlin and Ordendorf Co., Omaha, 1910-12, Canton, Ill., 1912-15; atty., Armour and Co., Chicago, since 1915, gen. atty., 1941-46, gen. counsel, 1946-52, dir., 1950-53, mem. exec. com., 1951-53; resident, Eng., in charge European legal matters Armour and Co., 1918-25. Trustee Armour & Co. Employee's Pension Fund. Mem. Chgo. Bar Assn., Order of the "C" (U. Chicago), Phi Gamma Delta, Phi Delta Phi. Republican. Presbyterian. Clubs: Oak Park (Ill.) Country; Crystal Downs Country (gov.) (Frankfort, Mich.); Country of Fla., (DelRay Beach). Home: River Forest, Illinois; also Lake Worth, Fla.; (summer) Crystal Downs, Frankfort, Mich. *

BAIRD, WARNER GREEN, real estate exec.; b. Chgo., Mar. 26, 1885; s. Wyllys Warner and Olivia Pomeroy (Green) B.; M.E., Cornell U., 1908; m. Julia Dole, Jan. 14, 1913; children—John Wyllys, Katharine (Mrs. Herbert Hansen), Warner Green, Olive (Mrs. Neil McKay). With Baird & Warner, Inc. (formerly Baird & Bradley), Chgo., 1911—, beginning as mgr. uptown office, successively treas., v.p., 1911-28, pres., 1928-64, chmn. bd., 1964—. Republican. Clubs: University, Commonwealth (Chgo.). Home: Geneva IL. 60134.

BAITSELL, GEORGE ALFRED (BAT'SL), prof. biology; b. Wright, Ia., Oct. 2, 1885; s. John Albert and Amanda (Clammer) B.; B.S., Central College, Pella, Iowa, 1908, LL.D., 1945; A.M., Yale Univ., 1909, Ph.D., 1914; married Dorothy Morton Horning, June 22, 1914; children—Dorothy Ann, John Morton. Secretary to president Central College, 1905-08, professor biology and chemistry, 1909-10, professor biology, acting dean, 1912-13; instructor in biology, Yale, 1914-18, asst. prof. biology, 1918-25, asso. professor, 1925-28, professor, 1928—, executive officer department biology, 1947-51, Colgate professor biology, 1947-51, emeritus; mem. corp., Marine Biol. Lab. Served as asst. physiologist, Army-Navy Gas investigation, 1917-18; capt., Chem. Warfare Service, 1918. Fellow A.A.A.S. (council 1935-55, sec. Sect. F., 1935-40, exec. com. 1947-51). Mem. American Society Zoölogists, American Society Naturalists, Amer. Soc. Anatomists, Am. Physiol. Soc., Sci. Reserach Soc. Am. (nat. treas. 1945-54), Soc. Experimental Biology and Medicine, Genetics Society, International Society of Cell Biology, Conn. Acad. Arts and Science, Sigma Xi (Nat. exec. com. 1928-38, pres. 1938-40, exec. sec. 1940-53). Baptist. Mason. Clubs: Yale, Graduates. Editor: Science in Progress Series I-IX, 1939-55; Am. Scientist, 1942-55. Editor-in-chief A.A.A.S. publs., Washington, 1949-50; sci. editor Yale U. Press, 1955—. Home: New Haven. *

BAKELESS, JOHN (EDWIN), author, editor; b. Carlisle, Pa., Dec. 30, 1894; s. Oscar H. and Sara (Harvey) B.; A.B., Williams Coll., 1918; A.M., Harvard, 1920, postgrad., 1919-26, Ph.D., 1936; D.Humanities, Bridgeport Engring. Inst., 1976; m. Katherine Little, June 16, 1920. Lit. editor, Living Age, 1921-23, mng. editor 1923-25; lit. adviser to The Independent, 1925-26; mng. editor Forum, 1926-28; editor Living Age, 1928-29; lit. editor Lit. Digest, 1937-38; lectr. journalism N.Y. U., 1927-29, instr., 1929-30, asst. prof., 1930-40, asso. prof., 1940-47, lectr. journalism, 1947-54, on grad. faculty, 1948-54; vis. instr. Harvard, summers, 1938-39, U. Colo., summer 1962; Trumbull lectr. Yale, 1948, Adams lectr. U. Mich., 1960; Gray lectr. Yale, 1964; Sproul lectr. Dickinson Coll., 1968; asst. comdt. 1031st O.R.C. Sch., New Haven, 1952-53. Guggenheim fellow, 1936-37, 46-47; Huntington Library fellow, 1968-69. Commd. 2d lt., inf., 1918, assigned as instr. Central Officers' Tng. Sch., Camp Lee; capt. Inf. Res., 1934; on active duty as capt., inf., 1940, maj., inf., 1941, maj., Gen. Staff Corps, 1942, lt. col., 1942; asst. mil. attache to Turkey, 1944; mem. Am. sect. Allied Control Commn. for Bulgaria, 1945, col., 1945. Recipient Disting. Service award Bloomsburg State Tchrs. Coll., 1953. Fellow Company Mil. Historians; mem. P.E.N., Nat. Hist. Soc. (adv. bd.). Soc. Am. Historians, Lepidopterists Soc., Res. Officers Assn., Conn. Entomol. Soc., Authors Guild, Phi Beta Kappa. Clubs: University, Harvard (N.Y.C.); Army and Navy (Washington). Author: The Economic Causes of Modern War, 1921; The Origin of the Next War, 1926; Magazine Making, 1931; Christopher Marlowe, The Man in His Time, 1937; Daniel Boone, Master of the Wilderness, 1939; The Tragicall History of Christopher Marlowe, 1942; Lewis and Clark, Partners in Discovery, 1947; Fighting Frontiersman, 1948; Eyes of Discovery, 1951; Background to Glory; Life of George Rogers Clark, 1957; Traitors, Turncoats and Heroes, 1959; The Adventures of Lewis and Clark, 1962; Spies of the Confederacy, 1970; (with Katherine Bakeless) They Saw America First, 1957, Spies of The American Revolution, 1962, Signers of the Declaration, 1969; Confederate Spy Stories, 1973. Editor: Report of Round Tables and General Conferences of the Williamstown Institute of Politics, 1932; Journals of Lewis and Clark, 1964; contbg. editor Current Lit., 1929-32; contbr. to Ency. Social Scis., Dictionary Am. Biography, Dictionary Am. History, also mags.; editorial bd. Am. Scholar (Phi Beta Kappa quar.). 1937-41. Home: Seymour, Conn. Died Aug. 8, 1978; buried Old Rosemont Cemetery, Bloomsburg, Pa.

BAKER, BRUCE ALEXANDER, advt. exec.; b. Chgo., May 21, 1913; s. John Ezra and Elisabeth (Alexander) B.; grad. Hill Sch., 1930; A.B., Princeton, 1934; m. Elizabeth Quigley, Dec. 2, 1937; children—Sandra, Bruce, Lisa, Betsy, Brion. Partner Wherry, Baker & Tilden, Inc., Chgo., 1954-60; sr. v.p. Compton Advt., Inc., 1960-65; v.p. Earle Ludgin Advt., 1965-76. Served as lt., USMC, 1944-45. Home: Lake Forest, Ill. Died Dec. 4, 1976.

BAKER, BURTON LOWELL, anatomist; b. Fife Lake, Mich., Apr. 2, 1912; A.B., Kalamazoo Coll., 1933, Sc.D. (hon.), 1958; M.S., Kans. State Coll., 1935; Ph.D., Columbia U., 1941; m. Hazel M. Hicks, 1940; children—Linda Sue, Gary Jay. Grad. research asst. in zoology Kans. State Coll., 1933-35; research fellow in medicine Columbia U., 1935-36, instr. anatomy Columbia Coll. Physicians and Surgeons, 1936-38, 40-41; Upjohn research asso., summers 1946-52; Mich. Meml.-Phoenix fellow, summers 1953-54; instr. anatomy U. Mich., Ann Arbor, 1941-45, asst. prof., 1945-47, asso. prof., 1947-52, prof., 1952-78, acting chmn. dept. anatomy, 1972, 74; cons. dept. anatomy Faculty of Dentistry, U. Recife, Brazil, 1959, Inst. Biosciences, Fed. U. Pernambuco, Recife, summer 1969. Mem. ofcl. bd. First Meth. Ch., 1943-78, chmn., 1962-65, chmn. Commn. on Edn., 1952-54, v.p. bd. trustees, 1954-57, trustee Wesley Found., 1948-52, sec., 1948, chmn. Commn. on Membership and Evangelism, 1967-70; chmn. adv. com. instl. research grants Am. Cancer Soc., 1965-66; bd. dirs. Family Service Agy., 1950-53, v.p., 1952-53; trustee Kalamazoo Coll., 1965-68. Recipient Jones, Stone and Oakley prizes Kalamazoo Coll., 1951, Henry Russell award U. Mich., 1947, Disting. Faculty award, U. Mich., 1977. Hon. prof. Fed. U. of Pernambuco, 1969. Fellow AAAS, N.Y. Acad. Scis., 1951; mem. Am. Assn. Anatomists (exec. com. 1964-68, trustee R.R. Bensley Meml. Fund 1964-72), Am. Physiol. Soc., Soc. Exptl. Biology and Medicine (sec.-treas. Mich. sect. 1957-58, 59-61, vice chmn. 1958-59), Endocrine Soc., Mich. Acad. Sci., Arts and Letters, Soc. for Study Reproduction, Sigma Xi, Gamma Sigma Delta, Phi Kappa Delta. Author: (with D.J. Ingle) Physiological and Therapeutic Effects of Corticotropin (ACTH) and Cortisone, 1953. Contbr. chpts. to books and articles to profl. jours. Asso. editor Am. Jour. Anatomy, 1957-68, mng. editor, 1968-74; mem. editorial bd. Endocrinology, 1956-60, 75-78, U. Mich. Med. Bull., 1955-59, Jour. Histochemistry and Cytochemistry, 1975-78. Home: Ann Arbor, Mich. Died Oct. 14, 1978; buried Oak Grove Cemetery, Lawton, Mich.

BAKER, D(AVID) GORDON, justice; b. Marion Co., S.C., Feb. 17, 1884; s. William Wallace and Sarah (Gordon) B.; LL.B., University South Carolina, 1905, LL.D. (honorary), 1951; married Julia Badger, April 25, 1906; children—Gordon Badger, William Wallace, David Everett. Admitted to South Carolina bar, 1905; gen. practice law, Florence, S.C., 1905-35; alderman City of Florence, 1910-12; atty. Florence Co., 1923-31; senator from Florence Co., 1919-22, mem. Ho. of Reps., 1933-35; asso. justice Supreme Ct. of S.C., 1935-44, chief justice since 1944. Mem. S.C. Bar Assn. Mason. Home: Florence, N.C.

BAKER, E(DWARD) CARLETON, consul; b. at Alameda, Cal., July 11, 1882; s. J. E. and Caroline Packard B.; B.S., U. of Cal., 1905; m. Jean Pedlar, of San Francisco, Cal., Dec. 11, 1909. Asst. in economics, U. of Cal., 1905-6; apptd. vice and deputy consul, also marshal, at Foochow, China, Jan. 5, 1906; retired as marshal, June 30, 1906, reappointed Aug. 28, 1907; vice and deputy counsul and marshal, Amoy, 1907-8, Foochow, 1908-9; transferred to Dept. of State as asst. to chief Div. of Far Eastern Affairs, Feb. 1, 1909; counsul, Antung, 1909-11, Chungking, Aug. 19, 1911-Dec., 1914, Nagasaki, Japan, Dec., 1914—Oct., 1916; consul gen., Mukden, since Oct. 1916. Presbyn. Mem. Am. Acad. Polit. and Social Science, Alpha Delta Phi. Address: Mukden, China. *

BAKER, EDGAR PARK, lawyer; b. Bronxville, N.Y., Sept. 30, 1906; s. Vernon Pell and Mabel (Park) B.; A.B., Williams Coll., 1926; LL.B., Harvard, 1929; m. Katharine Jones, June 14, 1930; children—Donald Irwin, Gordon Park, Madge. Admitted to N.Y. bar, 1930, with firm of Milbank, Tweed, Hadley & McCloy, and predecessor firms, N.Y.C., 1929-76; asst. works mgr. Clinton Engring. Works, Tenn. Eastman Corp., Oak Ridge, 1944-46. Trustee Vassar Coll., 1948-58. Mem. Am., N.Y. State, N.Y.C. bar assns., Phi Beta Kappa, Kappa Alpha. Clubs: Century Assn., University, India House, Wall Street, Williams (N.Y.C.). Home: Englewood, N.J. Died July 17, 1976.

BAKER, EDWIN LATHROP, coll. prof.; b. Jamestown, N.Y., Oct. 24, 1882; s. Mark Compton and Hattie Boone (Lathrop) B.; A.B., Trinity Coll., Conn., 1905; student at St. Stephen's Coll., Wesleyan U., Oxford U., Sorbonne, and univs. of Rome, Madrid and Athens; M.A. and Mus.B., Beaver (Pa.) Coll., 1904; unmarried. Began teaching at Beaver Coll., 1903, later at Pa. State Coll. (1915); asst. prof. Romance langs., Oberlin Coll., 1917-21; Samuel Mather prof. same, Kenyon Coll., 1921-23; head of modern langs., Browning Sch., since 1923; was with Gen. Theol. Sem., New York; prof. modern langs., N.Y. Piano Conservatory and Sch. of Allied Arts; eleven trips to Europe for travel and study; around the world, 1907-08. Mem. Modern Lang. Assn. American, Poetry Soc. America, Am. Assn. Univ. Profs., Am. Assn. Teachers of Italian, S.A.R., Phi Gamma Delta, Phi Beta Kappa. Candidate P.E. Ch., 1923. Mason (32 deg.). Address: New York, N.Y. *

BAKER, ELIZABETH BRADFORD FAULKNER, educator; b. Abilene, Kan., Dec. 10, 1885; d. Lothrop Hedge and Hattie (Bearce) Faulkner; B.L., U. of Calif., 1914; A.M., Columbia, 1919, Ph.D., 1925. Instr. in economics and dean of women, State Normal Sch., Lewiston, Ida., 1915-17; dean of women, State Normal Sch., Ellensburg, Wash., 1917-18; instr. in economics, Barnard Coll. (Columbia), 1919-26, asst. prof. since 1926. Mem. Am. Econ. Assn., Am. Assn. for Labor Legislation, Am. Assn. for Social Security, Taylor Soc., Am. Assn. Univ. Women. Clubs: Town Hall, Query (New York). Author: Protective Labor Legislation, 1925; Displacement of Men by Machines, 1933. Contbr. to economic periodicals. Home: New York, N.Y. *

BAKER, ELSIE, contralto; b. Phila., Pa., Sept. 27, 1886; d. William Drinker and Carrie Ella (Green) B.; ed. pub. schs.; unmarried. Widely known as concert singer. Home: New York, N.Y. *

BAKER, FREDERICK SHERMAN, editor, author; b. Evanston, Ill., Sept. 15, 1902; s. Frederick S. and Josephine (Turck) B.; A.B., U. Wis., 1925; postgrad. Oxford U., 1928; m. Margaret Darlington, June 27, 1925; children—Penelope (Mrs. Frank E. Mee), Priscilla Darlington Griffin, Frederick Sherman. With Appleton-Century-Crofts, 1942-45; sr. editor E. P. Dutton & Co., N.Y.C., 1946-54; v.p., editor, dir. St. Martin's Press, Inc., N.Y.C., 1955-63; adv. editor McGraw-Hill, N.Y.C., 1964-66; editor Funk & Wagnalls, N.Y.C., 1966-67. Club: Players (N.Y.C.). Author: Bradford Masters, 1949; Hidden Fire, 1955; The Making, 1966. F. Sherman Baker Collection, Mugar Meml. Library, Boston U. Home: East Hampton, N.Y. Died Apr. 8, 1976; buried Cedar Lawn Cemetery, East Hampton.

BAKER, HENRY, physician; b. Boston, May 10, 1898; s. Jacob K. and Rose (Weiss) B.; B.S., Harvard 1918, M.D., 1922. Intern Boston City Hosp., 1922-23; physician-in-chief 1st med. service Boston City Hosp., 1957-63, cons. 1st and 3d Tufts med. service, 1963-79; chief staff Jewish Meml. Hosp., Boston, 1943-79, Brookline (Mass.) Hosp., 1949-79; asso. in medicine Beth Israel Hosp., Boston, 1948-79; clin. prof. medicine Tufts U. Sch. Medicine. 1941-79. Diplomate Am. Bd. Internal Medicine. Fellow A.C.P., Am. Coll. Gastroenterology (pres. 1960-61, chmn. trustees 1961-62); hon. fellow Internat. Acad. Proctology, Hollywood (Cal.) Acad. Medicine; mem. Am., Mass. heart assns., Am., Mass. diabetes assns., Am., Mass. med. assn., Greater Boston Med. Soc. Club: New Century (pres. 1961-62) (Boston). Spl. research cholesterol and lipids, blood clotting mechanism, chemotherapy in cancer control. Home: Brookline, Mass. Died June 29, 1979; interred Mishkan Tefila Meml. Park, West Roxbury, Mass.

BAKER, HENRY MEREDITH, social service; b. Bolton, Lancashire, Eng., Sept. 17, 1884; s. John and Elizabeth (Bateson) B.; student Working Men's Tech. Coll., Melbourne, Australia, 1901-02, Glen Iris Theol. Sem., Melbourne, 1907; spl. student Drake U., 1911-13, U. of Mo., 1914-15, Sch. Social Economy, St. Louis, Mo., 1916-17, Columbia U., 1929; m. Bess Leora Kime, Mar. 15, 1913; 1 son Meredith Harry. Came to U.S., 1911, naturalized citizen. Associate field dir. Am. Red Cross, Camp Bowie, Fort Worth, Tex., 1918-19; dir. disaster relief, midwestern div. Am. Red Cross, 1919-24, nat. dir., 1924 (midwestern tornado, 1925, Fla. hurricane, 1926, rehabilitation adv. Cuban Govt., Cuba hurricane, 1926, Miss. Valley flood, 1927, Porto Rico hurricane, 1928, Long Beach, Calif., earthquake, 1933, Ohio Valley Flood, 1937). New England Forest Fires, 1947; asst. administrator. Disaster Relief, American National Red Cross. Member U.S. Ecuador Rehabilitation Commission, 1942. Mem. Calif., Ore., Wash. and Idaho State confs., of social work; also mem. Nat. Conf. Social Work. Mem. Am. Assn. of Social Workers, Family Welfare Assn. of America, Am. Acad. Polit. and Social Sciences, Am. Geog. Soc. of N.Y. Mem. Disciples of Christ Ch. Club: Commonwealth, Contbr. to mags. on subject of social relief practices. Address: Long Beach, Calif. *

BAKER, HENRY SCOTT, coll. adminstr.; b. Washington, Sept. 9, 1895; s. R. W. and Abby P. (Scott) B.; B.S., Johns Hopkins, 1917; m. Frances I. Robinson, June 6, 1925; children—Henry Scott, Ralph Robinson. With Bd. of Trade, Balt., 1920-26; investment banker, 1926-34; sec. bd. trustees Johns Hopkins, 1934-60, treas., from 1934, vice president finance, from 1960; dir. National Union Investment Co.; adv. committee Met. Branch Savings Bank of Baltimore; trust com. Equitable Trust Co. Mem. adv. investment committee Maryland Retirement System. Trustee Brown Meml. Ch. Served as capt. 313th F.A., U.S. Army, 1917-19. Mem. Family and Children's Soc. (mem. investment com.). Democrat. Presbyn. Clubs: Pemigewassett Valley Fish and Game, Johns Hopkins. Home: Baltimore. Died Mar. 4, 1981.

BAKER, HERMAN MARCUS, physician; b. Louisville, Ky., July 18, 1889; s. William Henry and Lydia (Marcus) B.; M.D., U. of Louisville, 1910; m. Grace Sleno, Apr. 30, 1913; 1 dau., Elizabeth Jeanette (wife of Dallas Fickas, M.D.). Practiced medicine, Evansville, Ind., 1910-70; consultant medicine, St. Mary's, Deaconess, Welborn Meml. Bapt. and Boehne Tuberculosis hosps.; cons. Henderson Meth. Hosp., Ind.; preceptor geriatrics St. Mary's Hosp.-Grad. Med. Center, Evansville; dir. med. service Little Sisters of the Poor, Seaton Manor; adv. Evansville Center for Med. Edn., Ind. U. Med. Sch., Disting. cons., from 1973; former pres. Ind. State Bd. of Health; former cons. medical care, U.S. Pub. Health Service; apptd. to bd. trustees Evansville Coll., 1946, named life trustee, 1972. Mem. advisory committee Am. Red Cross, 1936-46. Served in Med. Corps, U.S. Army, with A.E.F., during World War; disch. as lt. col. Recipient Disting. Service award Gov. Otis Bowen, State of Ind., 1974. Diplomate Am. Bd. Internal Medicine; fellow Am. Coll. Physicians; mem. A.M.A., Ind. State Med. Assn.j(pres. 1938; chmn. com. on med. edn. and hosps.), Evansville C. of C. (dir.). Clubs: Petroleum, Evansville Country, Contbr. to med. jours. Lectr. med. and civic groups. Home: Evansville, Ind. Died Nov. 9, 1978.

BAKER, IVAN FRANKLIN, fgn. trade cons.; b. Cedar Rapids, Nebr., Apr. 11, 1887; s. Frank N. and Etta I. (Bowers) I.; B.S. in Elec. Engring., U. Nebr., 1909; m. Lucile Atkinson, 1911; 1 dau., Helen Merle (Mrs. Robert A. Cushman). Apprentice engr. Westinghouse Electric & Mfg. Co., Pitts., 1909-10, mgr. for Japan, later mng. dir. Westinghouse Electric Co. of Japan, and dir. Mitsubishi Electric & Engring. Co., 1919-27, mgr. far east Westinghouse Electric Internat. Co., N.Y.C., 1927-29, European sales mgr., European mgr., 1929-38, industry sales mgr., sales mgr., 1938-44, co. rep., Washington, 1942-43, asst. to pres., 1944-45, treas., 1945-57, v.p., treas., 1947-52, spl. rep. of the pres. on devel. electric power programs in Far East, 1953, dir. 1940-76; dir. Constructora Nacional de Maguinaria Electrica, Spain, 1930-39; cons. War Dept., 1943, H.M. Baker Assos., 1958-76; mem. adv. com. comml. activities fgn. service Dept. State and Dept. Commerce, 1946-53; cons. Fgn. Trade Fairs, Far Eastern Div. for U.S. Dept. Commerce. Del. from U.S. Govt. to ECAFE Conf. of UN, Manila, Philippines, 1953. Mem. men's exec. com. Japan Internat. Christian U. Found. Mem. I.E.E.E. Mason (32 deg.). Home: Westfield, N.J. Died June 23, 1976; interred Fairview Cemetery, Westfield.

BAKER, JOHN W., corporation official; b. Jamaica, Vt., Jan. 10, 1886; A.B., Harvard, 1908. Pres. Philippine Refining Corp. of New York, Oil Trades Association of New York, Incorporated. Dir. Philippine-American Chamber of Commerce. Clubs: India House, Downtown Athletic (New York); Litchfield (Conn.) Country; Harvard (Boston and New York). Home: New York, N.Y. *

BAKER, MELVIN HOUSTON, mfg. executive; born Sevierville, Tenn., Aug. 11, 1885; s. Joseph and Amanda (Fox) B.; student Carson Newman Coll., Dr. Indsl. Sci. (hon.), 1953; D.Sc., U. Md., 1953, Canisius Coll., 1956; LL.D., Alfred Univ., 1956; married Frances Yeager, Apr. 19, 1920; children—Melvin H. Jr., Jevene Hope. Salesman Willer Mfg. Co., Milwaukee, Wis., 1908-12; salesman Beaver Bd. Co., 1912-14, sales mgr., 1914-22; v.p. Am. Mfrs. Foreign Credit Underwriters, 1922-24; v.p. Nat. Gypsum Co., 1925-28, pres., 1928-52, chairman bd. of dirs., 1952-65, hon. chmn., 1965-76; pres. Nat. Gypsum Co. (Can.), Ltd.; dir. Manufacturers and Traders Trust Company, Sheraton Corporation of America. Member capital expenditures committee City of Buffalo, 1959. Trustee National Safety Council since 1944. Former trustee of Art Inst. (Buffalo). Dist. chmn. com. Econ. Development, 1944-46; chmn. Buffalo com. Russian War Relief, 1943-46; chmn. exec. com. Crippled Children's Guild, 1942-76, also mem. of adv. bd.; chmn. Buffalo Redevelopment Found., Inc. Mem. adv. com. Buffalo United War and Community Fund, 1943-76. Trustee Canisius College; adv. com. Univ. Buffalo. Trustee Gen. Assembly Presbyn. Ch. in U.S.A., 1954. Fellow A.I.M.; mem. Newcomen Soc. N. Am., N.A.M. (dir. 1944-45, 52-54), Acad. Political and Social Sci., Buffalo C. of C. (pres. 1939-40), U.S. C. of C. (member board of directors 1948-49, 52-55, 56-57, v.p. 1955-56), Am. Cancer Soc. (gen. chmn. N.Y., 1956). Presbyn. Clubs: Buffalo, Buffalo Country, Metropolitan (New York). Home: Buffalo, N.Y. Died June 25, 1976.

BAKER, MICHAEL, JR., cons. engr.; b. Beaver, Pa., Feb. 18, 1912; s. Michael and Anna (Thompson) B.; B.S. in Civil Engring., Pa. State U., 1936; D.Sc., Steubenville (O.) Coll., 1954; D. Engring., Ohio U., 1956, Tri-State Coll., 1965; L.H.D., Geneva Coll., 1960; m. Myrtle E. Pitzer, Mar. 23, 1932; children—Michael III, Carl Gene, Keith Joel (dec.). Boro engr. State Coll. Pa., 1936-38; contractor, 1938-40; pres. Michael Baker, Jr., Inc., Rochester, Pa., 1940-72, chmn. bd., chief exec. officer, 1940-77; pres. Michael Baker, Jr., Air Maps, Inc., 1948-77, Beaver Valley Engring. Supplies, 1955-77; chmn. bd., chief exec. officer Michael Bake Corp., 1972-77; dir. dir. Century Nat. Bank. Pres., Pa. Registration Bd. for Profl. Engrs.; cons. engr. Schuylkill Expressway, Pa. Turnpike, Squirrel Hill Tunnel, Ft. Pitt Tunnel, Pa.-Lincoln Pkwy., pub. works devel., Saudi Arabia, Peru, Ecuador, Hashemite Kingdom Jordan, Kingdom Yemen. Past mem. Brighton Twp. Sch. Bd.; mem. Salvation Army Bd.; mem. exec. com. Boy Scouts Am.; mem. United Fund. Trustee Coll. of Steubenville, Pa. Better Hwys. Com.; pres. bd. trustees Pa. State U., 1972-76. Recipient Horatio Alger award, 1954; Sons of Italy Service award; Am. Legion Distinguished award; Silver Beaver award Allegheny council Boy Scouts Am.; Distinguished Alumnus award Pa. State U., 1958; Man of Year, Rochester C. of C., Beaver Area C. of C. Registered profl. civil engr. 48 states, C.Z., D.C., 8 Canadian provinces. Fellow Am. Soc. C.E.; mem. Nat., Pa. (Engr. of Year 1968, Beaver County chpt. 1954) socs. profl. engrs., Pi Kappa Alpha (hon.), Tau Beta Pi, Chi Epsilon, Triangle (hon.). Presbyn. Club: Duquesne (Pitts.). Home: Beaver, Pa. Died Feb. 22, 1977; buried Beaver Cemetery, Beaver, Pa.

BAKER, MILTON GRAFLY, mil. acad. adminstr.; b. Phila., Aug. 24, 1899; s. Frank Robertson and Sallie (Dimmock) B.; A.B., St. John's Coll., 1921; LL.D., Gettysburg Coll., 1939, Temple U., 1949, Norwich U., 1956, Villanova U., 1966; Pd.D., LaSalle Coll., 1955; Ed.D., Suffolk U., 1966; D.Mil. Sci., PMC Colls., 1968; L.H.D., Hahnemann Med. Sch., 1969; m. May Porter Hagenbuch, Apr. 29, 1924 (dec. Mar. 1970); 1 dau., Ann Porter (Mrs. Winslow Martin); m. 2d. Josephine Louise Redenius, Dec. 5, 1970. Pres., founder Valley Forge Mil. Acad., Wayne, Pa., 1928-76. Trustee Pop Warner Little Scholars, Inc., Phila., Cabrini Coll., Radnor, Temple U., Gen George Catlett Marshall Found., Lexington, Va., Gen. Douglas MacArthur Meml. Found., Norfolk, Va., Retina Research and Devel. Found., Phila., Inf. Mus. Assn., Nat. Armed Forces Mus. Adv. Bd., Smithsonian Instn.; adv. bd. Friends of Scheie Eye Inst., Phila.; bd. dirs. Opera Guild Greater Miami; bd. dirs.; chmn. Gettysburg Battle Centennial Commn. Chmn. U.S. nat. commn. UNESCO, 1953-55, del.-at-large, 1953-58; chmn. Commonwealth of Pa. Mil. Commn., 1952-58; chmn. Dept. Def. Res. Forces Policy Bd., 1955-57; mem. bd. Pa. Gen. State Authority, 1963-70. Chmn. inauguration Gov. of Pa., 1963, 67, Scott for Senate Com. (Pa.), 1964, 70; del. Republican Nat. Conv., 1960, 64, 68, 72. Served with U.S. Army, 1917-21; comdg. gen. Pa. N.G., 1943-46; gen. U.S. dir. Civil Def., Phila., 1941-42; commd. lt. gen., 1957. Decorated U.S.; Brazil, Nicaragua, Belgium, Ecuador, Bulgaria, France; Order Sword (Sweden); Spanish Naval Cross (Spain); Order of Merit Republic of Italy; comdr. Most Excellent Order Brit. Empire; recipient numerous awards, medals U.S. Dept. Army, Dept. Def., Dept. War; Pa. Distinguished Service medal with palm, Pa. Meritorious Service medal with palm, Pa. award for excellence in field edn., 1968; Silver medal Union League Phila., 1968. Fellow Co. Mil. Historians, Internat. Coll. Surgeons; mem. Navy League U.S. (Phila. council), Am. Ch. Union (Keble award 1970), Assn. U.S. Army (pres. 1960-63, chmn. council trustees 1964-70), Pa. Soc. S.R. (pres. 1966-67), Devon Horse Show Assn. (dir.), Phila. Horse Show (dir.), Mil. Colls. and Schs. U.S. (dir., past pres.), Mil. Order World Wars (past comdr. Pa. chpt., nat. comdr. 1950-51), Franklin Inst. Pa., Assn. Jr. Colls, Assn. Am. Colls., Old Guard City Phila., Mil. Order Loyal Legion, Saint Andrews Soc., Hist. Soc. Pa., Res. Officers Assn. U.S., N.G. Assn. U.S., Am. Legion, Radnor Hist. Assn. Valley Forge Hist. Soc., Pa. Soc. N.Y., Nat. Assn. Secondary Sch. Prins., Mil. Order Fgn. Wars, Brotherhood St. Andrew, Confrerie des Chevaliers du Tastevin, English Speaking Union, Miniature Figure Collectors Am., Washington Crossing Found., World Affairs Council. Episcopalian. Mason (32). Clubs: Union League (N.Y.C., Phila.); Capitol Hill, F Street (Washington); Army Navy, Penn (Phila.); St. Davids Golf; British Officers; Rolling Rock, Ligonier (Pa.); La Gorce Country, Surf (Miami Beach); Bald Peak Colony (N.Y.); Chesapeake (Irvington, Va.). Home: Wayne, Pa. Died July 31, 1976; interred Chapel of St. Cornelius the Centurian, Valley Forge Mil. Acad.

BAKER, RAY PALMER, ret. educator, author; b. Fonthill, Can., Sept. 21, 1883; s. Jacob Johnson and Ida Emma (Fitch) B.; B.A., U. Western Ont., 1906; Ph.M., U. Chgo., 1910; M.A., Harvard, 1914, Ph.D., 1916; LL.D., U. Western Ont., 1928; D.Sc., Rensselaer Poly. Inst., 1972; m. Mary Irene Messinger, Sept. 1, 1914; children—Mary Elizabeth (dec.), Ray Palmer, Jr., David Wolverton. Modern lang. master Highfield Sch., Hamilton, Ont., 1906-09; prof. English, Okanagan Coll., 1910-11, asst. prin., 1911-13; prof. English, Rensselaer Poly. Inst., 1915-1940, head dept. arts. sci. and bus. adminstrn., 1925-40, asst. dir., 1930-49, v.p., 1949-54, dean students, 1944-49, v.p. emeritus, 1955. Bd. govs. Union U.; trustee Albany Med. Coll., Rensselaer County Hist. Soc., Asso. Hosp. Service N.E. N.Y.; trustee Dudley Obs., pres., 1956-58; trustee Troy Pub. Library, pres., 1946-65; trustee Samaritan Hosp., pres., 1935-47; chmn. bd. Bus. History Found. Mem. Rensselaer Soc. Engrs., Newcomen Soc., Modern Lang. Assn. Am. Soc. Promotion Engring. Edn., Sigma Xi. Club: Troy. Author: A History of English-Canadian Literature—Its Relation to the Literature of Great Britain and the United States, 1920, 68; Preparation of Reports, Engineering, Scientific, Administrative Business, 1923, 2d edit. (with A.C. Howell), 1937; A. Chapter in American Education, 1924; Writing—A First Book for College Students (with William Haller), 1928. Editor: Engineering Education, 1919, 2d edit. 1928; Feathers with Yellow Gold, 1920; Sam Slick (by Thomas Chandler Haliburton), 1923; The Clockmaker (by Thomas Chandler Haliburton), 1927. Contbr. to ednl., lit. and hist. periodicals, to Dictionary Am. Biography, Columbia Course in Literature, others. Home: Averill Park NY. *

BAKER, ROBERT CALHOUN, banker; b. Everett, Pa., May 22, 1902; s. Francis and Jennie (Calhoun) B.; B.S., U. Pa., 1927. Vice pres., dir. Central Nat. Bank, Richmond, Va., 1935-45; v.p. Columbia Nat. Bank, Washington, 1945-46; v.p. Am. Security & Trust Co., Washington, 1946-49, dir., 1948-76, exec. v.p., 1949-59, pres., 1959-69, chmn. bd., 1962-76; pres., dir. Am. Security Corp., 1959-76; dir. Burlington Industries, Greensboro, N.C., Peoples Drug Stores, Inc., Washington Gas Light Co., Peoples Life Ins. Co., mem. adv. bd. Washington Mut. Investors Fund. Chmn., Nat. Capital Downtown Com. Bd. dirs. United Givers Fund; trustee Juniata Coll., Fed. City Council, George Washington U. Mem. Assn. Res. City Bankers (past dir.). Clubs: University (N.Y.C.); Chevy Chase, 1925 F St., Nat. Press, University, City Tavern, Capitol Hill, Metropolitan, Burning Tree (Washington); Everglades, Bath and Tennis (Palm Beach, Fla.), Lyford Cay (Nassau, Bahamas). Home: Washington, D.C. Died Mar. 10, 1976.

BAKER, ROSS ALLEN, prof. chemistry; b. Greencastle, Ind., Nov. 13, 1886; s. Philip Schaffner and Luemma (Allen) B.; A.B., DePauw U., Greencastle, Ind., 1906, A.M., 1907; Sc.D., 1937; Ph.D., U. of Wis., 1914; m. Helen Frederika Porter, Dec. 30, 1914; children—Philip Schaffner, Porter, Frederick Ross, Stanley Allen, Raymond Davis. Instr. science, Danville (Ill.) High Sch., 1907-08; prof. chemistry, Baker U., 1908-10; instr. chemistry, U. of Wis., 1910-14; asst. prof. chemistry, U. of Minn., 1914-17; prof. chemistry, Syracuse U., 1919-30; asso. prof. chemistry, College City of N.Y., 1930-33, prof. chemistry, 1934-50; prof. chemistry Shrivenham American U., 1945; visiting prof. chemistry U. of Hawaii, 1948-49; spl. lectr. Occidental Coll., 1950; vis. prof. U. of Ala., 1951. College representative Sci. Council of New York City, 1931-43; v.p. Fedn. of Science Teacher Associations of N.Y. City, 1943-46. Nat. counselor in chemistry Boy Scouts of America 1937-48; mem. board of trustees Drew Univ. since 1941. Mem. Gen. Assembly Y.M.C.A. of City of N.Y., 1936-39 (1st vice chairman 1940-42). Lt., later captain and maj., Chem. Warfare Service, 1917-19; comdt. U.S. Gas Sch., 1918. Fellow Am. Inst. of Chemists (nat. council 1933-40), New York Acad. of Science, A.A.A.S.; mem. Am. Chem. Soc. (nat. council, 1940-50; chmn., Syracuse sect., 1923-24; chmn. N.Y. sect. 1945), Am. Assn. Univ. Profs. (chap. pres. 1940-41), N.Y. Chem. Teachers Club (pres. 1933-34), Scabbard and Blade, Phi Beta Kappa, Sigma Xi, Gamma Alpha, Alpha Chi Sigma, Phi Kappa Phi, Beta Gamma Sigma, Delt Kappa Epsilon; hon. fellow Am. Inst. of the City of New York, 1939. Del. Internat. Union of Chemistry, The Hague, 1928; del. Internat. Congress of Chemistry, Rome, 1938. Republican. Methodist Episcopal. Asst. editor Jour. Chemical Education, 1924-25, dept. editor, 1926-37. Home: Menasha, Wis.*

BAKER, RUSSELL, lawyer; b. Portage County, Wis., Apr. 28, 1901; s. George W. and Mary (Day) B.; Ph.B., U. Chgo., 1923, J.D., 1925; m. Elizabeth Wallace, June 5, 1925; children—Wallace R., Donald, James A. Admitted to Ill. bar, 1925, D.C. bar, 1967, Calif. bar, 1971; practiced in Chgo., 1925-79; partner firm of Baker & McKenzie, specialist internat. law, 1925-79, sr. partner, 1949-79; dir., chmn. bd. 1st Pacific Bank of Chgo. adv. bd. World Tax Series, Harvard U. Law Sch. First v.p., chmn. research and law enforcement coms. Chgo. Crime Commn. Recipient citation U. Chgo. Alumni Assn., 1952, Man of Year in Internat. Trade award, 1974. Mem. Chgo. Assn. Commerce and Industry (world trade com.), Internat., Inter-Am., Am., Ill., Chgo., D.C. bar assns. Author articles legal, internat., trade, tax subjects. Home: Lake Bluff, Ill. Died Sept. 28, 1979.

BAKER, RUSSELL MONTEZ, lawyer; b. Celeste, Tex., Mar. 11, 1906; s. William Perry and Kathleen (Bolte) B.; grad. So. Meth. U., 1928; m. Ollie Marie Dedman, Aug. 26, 1927 (dec. Aug. 1979); children—Harriet Kay, Russell Montez. Admitted Tex. bar, 1929, asso. Caldwell, Gillen, Francis & Gallagher, Dallas, 1929-32; jr. partner Caldwell, Gillen, Francis & Gallagher, 1932-38; mem. firm Caldwell, Baker & Jordan, Dallas, 1938-59; later sr. mem. firm Baker &

Foreman. Research fellow Southwestern Legal Found. Fellow Am. Coll. Trial Lawyers, Tex. Bar Found.; mem. Assn. Trial Lawyers Am., Am. Judicature Soc., Law Science Acad., Law Sci. Found. of Am., Internat. Acad. Trial Lawyers, Tex. Assn. Plaintiff Attys. (pres.), Internat. (patron), Am. (nuclear energy com. 1971-73), Tex., Dallas bar assns., Am. Bd. Trial Advocates, Internat. Soc. Barristers, Delta Chi. Clubs: Dallas Athletic, Dallas Athletic Country, Cosmopolitan (internat. pres. 1950-51). Editor Am. Trial Lawyers Assn. Law Jour. Home: Dallas, Tex. Died Aug. 8, 1979.

BAKER, S. ORVILLE, educator; b. Chgo., Jan. 21, 1912; s. Max and Rae (Goldberg) B.; Ph.B., U. Chgo., 1934, M.A., 1935; Ph.D., Harvard, 1948; m. Adra Wollenweber, June 24, 1938; 1 dau., Patricia. Faculty, Carnegie Inst. Tech., 1937-40, Simmons College, 1946-47, Wellesley Coll., 1948-49, Carnegie Inst. Tech., 1949-50; faculty U. No. Ill., DeKalb, 1950-78, prof., 1955-78. Mem. Ill. Tchr. Certification Bd., 1971-78. Served from lt. (j.g.) to lt. comdr., USNR, 1942-46. Mem. Modern Lang. Assn., Am. Assn. U. Profs., N.E.A., Nat. Council Tchrs. English, Ill. Assn. Tchrs. of English (pres. 1965-66). Co-author: Horizon, 1963. Home: DeKalb, Ill. Died Dec. 15, 1978.

BAKKE, ARTHUR LAWRENCE (BÄK'KE), plant physiologist; b. Horace, N.Dak., June 26, 1886; s. Martin and Angnette (Sundt) B.; B.S., Iowa State Coll., 1909, M.S. 1911; Ph.D., U. of Chicago, 1917; m. Josephine Arnquist, Aug. 25, 1929 (deceased August 24, 1948); married 2d Jeanette Donhowe Henderson, July 19, 1952. Instructor in science, Elgin (Illinois) Academy, 1909-10; instructor in botany, IoWa State College, 1910-11, asst. prof. plant physiology, 1911-17, asso. prof., 1918-24, prof., 1925-37; research prof. Ia. Agrl. Expt. Sta. since 1938; at Desert Lab. of Carnegie Instn., Tucson, Ariz., 1913-14; collaborator and asst. pathologist U.S. Dept. Agr., 1914-17, collaborator, 1935-51; spl. research at U. of Copenhagen and Central Expt. sta., Stockholm, Sweden, 1929. Chmn. research com. North Central Weed Control Conf., 1951. Known for researches on physiology of plants. Fellow A.A.A.S., Ia. Acad. Sci.; mem. Bot. Soc. Am., Am. Soc. Plant Physiologists, Sigma Xi, Phi Kappa Phi, Gamma Sigma Delta, Gamma Alpha, Chi Phi. Lutheran. Home: Ames, Ia. *

BAKKE, CLARENCE L. (BÄK'KE), ry. exec.; b. Trail County, N.D., Sept. 24, 1886; s. Ole Peterson and Carrie (Erickson) B.; student N.D. State Normal Sch., 2 years; m. Bertha Victoria Parker, Dec. 2, 1919; children—Clarence Quentin, George Burton, Thomas Neal, Karen Amelia. Began as roundhouse laborer, C.,B.&Q. Ry. Co., 1910, becoming successively locomotive fireman, brakeman, conductor, to 1922, yardmaster, 1922-25, trainmaster, 1925-36; with C.,R.I.&P. Ry. since 1936, as terminal trainmaster, 1936-37, asst. supt., 1937, supt., 1937-40, gen. supt. since 1940; also gen. supt. Burlington & Rock Island R.R.; pres. Wichita Union Terminal Ry., Ark. and Memphis Ry. Bridge and Terminal Co.; dir. Wichita Terminal Assn. Served as capt. 5th Engrs., U.S. Army, with A.E.F., World war; now lt. col. 725th Engineers (Res.). Dir. Rock Island Hosp. Assn. Mem. Am. Assn. R.R. Supts., Am. Legion (past post comdr.), Forty and Eight (past chef de gar). Address: El Reno, Okla. *

BALDERSTON, C. CANBY, business exec.; b. Kennett Square, Pa., Feb. 1, 1897; s. John L. and Anna E. (Marshall) B.; student Pa. State Coll., 1915-17; B.S. in Econs., U. Pa., 1921, A.M., 1923, Ph.D., 1928, LL.D., 1955; LL.D., Swarthmore Coll., 1965; m. Gertrude Emery, July 18, 1922 (dec.); children—Frederick E., Robert W.; m. 2d, Ida Roberts Smedley, Nov. 21, 1942; stepchildren—Walter, Henry, Alice. Asst. prof. industry U. Pa., 1925-31, prof., 1931-54, dean Wharton Sch. Fin. and Commerce, 1941-54; gov. Fed. Res. System, 1954-66, vice chmn. bd. govs., 1955-66; pres. Leeds & Lippincott Co. (Chalfonte-Haddon Hall hotels), 1951-75, chmn., 1975-76; adj. prof. fin. Am. U., 1966-77; dir. Fed. Res. Bank of Phila., 1943-53, dep. chmn., 1949-53; dir. Security Nat. Bank, Washington, 1968-73, Ind. Sq. Income Securities, Inc., 1972-79; pres. Temporary Investment Fund, Inc., 1973-79; pres. Fed. Short-term Securities Trust, 1975-79, Chestnut St. Exchange Fund, 1976-79; chief War Dept. Wage Adminstrn. Agy., and wage adminstrn. sect. Hdqrs. Army Service Forces, 1942-45. Emeritus trustee Bryn Mawr Coll.; bd. advisers Indsl. Coll. Armed Forces, 1964-66; formerly trustee Indsl. Relations Counselors; chmn. pres., dir. Nat. Bur. Econ. Research; pres. Am. Assn. Collegiate Sch. of Bus. Chmn. investment com. Westtown Sch.; bd. mgrs. Friends Hosp. Frankford; bd. dirs. Sidwell Friends Sch., Elwyn Inst. Recipient War Dept. Exceptional Civilian Service award, 1944. Mem. Phila. C. of C. (past v.p., dir.), Am. Econ. Assn., Theta Xi, Beta Gamma Sigma (nat. pres. 1952-55). Republican. Mem. Soc. of Friends. Clubs: Varsity (U. Pa.); Franklin Inn (Phila.); Cosmos (past pres.) (Washington); Rolling Green Golf and the Ozone. Author: Managerial Profit Sharing, 1928; Profit-Sharing for Wage Earners, 1937; Group Incentives, 1930; Executive Guidance of Industrial Relations, 1935; Wage Setting Based on Job Analysis and Evaluation, 1940; co-author: Wages-A Means of Testing Their Adequacy, 1931; Management of an Enterprise, 1935; Management of a Textile Business, 1938. Home: Media, Pa. Died Sept. 9, 1979.

BALDERSTON, KATHARINE CANBY, educator, author; b. Boise, Idaho, Jan. 2, 1895; d. William and Stella Burse (Sain) Balderston; B.A., Wellesley Coll., 1916; M.A., Radcliffe Coll., Ph.D., Yale U., 1925; vis. scholar Huntington Library, 1934-35. Taught English Southern Meth. U., 1916-18, publicity sec. Southwest field office YWCA, Dallas, 1918-19; instr. lit. Wellesley Coll., from 1920, Martha Hale Shackford prof. English lit., 1942-60, prof. emeritus, 1960-79. Mem. The Johnsonians, AAUP, Phi Beta Kappa. Awarded Rose May Crawshay Prize, Brit. Acad., 1944. Editor: Collected Letters of Oliver Goldsmith, 1928; Thraliana: The Diary of Hester Lynch Thrale (later Mrs. Piozzi), 2 vols., 1942. Author: History and Sources of Percy's Memoir of Goldsmith, 1926; Census of the Manuscripts of Oliver Goldsmith, 1926. Contbr. critical articles on 18th century lit. to Modern Lang. Notes, Lit. Supplement of London Times, and other jours. Home: Wellesley, Mass. Died Nov. 21, 1979.

BALDRIDGE, EDGAR EARL, oil co. exec.; b. Ft. Worth, Nov. 19, 1904; s. Edgar Earl and Florence (Gibson) B.; student Kemper Mil. Acad., Bonneville; m. Hazel Gorman, Nov. 18, 1934; children—Martha (Mrs. John W. McMackin), Edgar Earl. Partner Baldridge, King & Nichols, McAllen, Tex., 1941-48, Baldridge & King, Inc., 1948-54; pres. Champlin Oil & Refining Co., Ft. Worth, 1954-61, chmn. bd., pres., 1961-64; chmn. exec. com. Champlin Petroleum Co.; dir. Union Pacific Corp., 1st Nat. Bank of Ft. Worth. Mem. Am. Petroleum Inst. (dir.), Mid-Continent Oil and Gas Assn. (dir.). Episcopalian. Clubs: Chicago; Fort Worth. Home: Fort Worth, Tex. Died Sept. 23, 1977.

BALDRIDGE, KENNETH FERGUSON, newspaper pub.; b. Bloomfield, Ia., May 25, 1886; s. David Franklin and Margaret Jane (Ferguson) B.; student Southern Ia. Normal and Scientific Inst., 1903-04; LL.B., Drake U., 1909; m. Katharine McClure, May 17, 1910; children—John David, Josephine. Newspaper reporter, 1903-09; pub. and editor Bloomfield Democrat since 1909; organized Central Newspaper Co., consisting of 7 So. Ia. newspapers, pres., 1930-59, chmn. bd., 1959—; postmaster, Bloomfield, 1916-24, and 1935-36, resigned to be Dem. candidate for Congress; reappointed postmaster, 1937; chmn. board dirs. Nockonwood Industries, Inc., mfrs. Chmn. Dem. Central Comm. of Davis County; chmn. Nat. Code Authority for Non-Met. Printing and Pub. Industry, 1934-35; Davis County, Ia., relief adminstr., 1933-39. Received Ia. Master Editor-Publisher award from Ia. Press Assn., 1937; Amos Award, National Editorial Association, 1950. Mem. Nat. Editorial Assn. (pres. 1934-35, Ia. Press Assn. (pres. 1925-26), Southern Ia. Press Assn. (pres. 1914), Ia. Newspaper, Inc (pres. 1928-32), Nat. Postmasters Assn. (pres. Ia. Chapter 1940-42), Sigma Delta Chi. Democrat. Mem. Disciples of Christ. Mason, K.T., Shriner, K.P., Rotarian. Author: Seven Months in Orbit. Address: Bloomfield Ia.*

BALDUF, EMERY WINFIELD, educator; b. LaCarne, Ohio, July 6, 1889; s. Friedrich and Sibylla (Schwechheimer) B.; Ph.B., Heidelberg Coll., 1910; A.M., U. Chgo., 1913, Ph.D., 1926; m. Drucilla Shroeder, Sept. 10, 1927 (div. Mar. 1933); m. 2d, Freda Juvani, July 30, 1933 (div. Aug. 1952); children—Anna-Marie, Diana Ruth. Supt. schs., Sycamore, Ohio, 1910-12; instr. German, Carleton Coll., 1913-17; ch. and sch. editor Ohio State Jour., 1919-20; sec. Coll. Arts, Philosophy and Sci., Ohio State U., 1920-22; dean, prof. Central YMCA Coll., Chgo., 1924-36; dir. adult edn. and pub. forums, Des Moines, Iowa, 1936-40; nat. dir. Fed. Union, Inc., 1940-42; head sch.-coll. sect. Bur. Spl. Operations, Office of War Info., 1942-43; head sch.-coll. sect., div. conservation and salvage War Prodn. Bd., 1943-45; co-founder, dean student services, prof. philosophy Roosevelt U., Chgo., 1945-57; adj. prof. Mexico City Coll., Hebrew Theol. Coll., Skokie. Mem. Am. Philos. Assn., Adult Edn. U.S., Am. Coll. Personnel Assn., Midwest Ednl. Secs. Assn. YMCA (pres. 1928-30), Phi Beta Kappa. Unitarian. Author: Zwei Geschichten von Johanna Spyri, 1918; (with F. W. Kaufmann) Inductive Readings in German, 1929. Home: Skokie, Ill. Died Dec. 26, 1976.

BALDWIN, DONALD R., lawyer; b. Minewaska, N.Y., Aug. 1895; s. Arthur J. and Frances (Smiley) B.; A.B., Cornell U., 1916; B.L., Columbia, 1920; m. Winifred Barrett, June 1922; children—Patricia Whipple, Joan Baldwin, Diana Dunnan. Admitted to N.Y. State bar; with Griggs, Baldwin & Baldwin, 1924-78. Pres., Grosvenor, Inc.; trustee Drew U., YMCA of Oranges. Served as 2d lt. F.A., Am. Field Service, Ambulance Corps, French Army, World War I. Home: South Orange, N.J. Died May 16, 1978.

BALDWIN, FAITH, writer; b. New Rochelle, N.Y., Oct. 1. 1893; d. Stephen Charles and Edith Hervey (Finch) Baldwin; ed. Briarcliff, Mrs. Dow's Sch., Briarcliff Manor, N.Y.; m. Hugh H. Cuthrell, Nov. 6, 1920 (dec. Aug. 1953); children—Hugh (dec.), Hervey, Stephen, Ann. Mem. guiding faculty Famous Writers Sch. Nat. sponsor, dir. Conn. Save the Children Fedn. Bd. mem. Silver Hill Found. Mem. Women's Nat. Book Assn. Author: Mavis of Green Hill, 1921; Laurel of Stoney Stream, 1923; Magic and Mary Rose, 1924; Signposts (verse), 1924; Thresholds, 1925; Those Difficult Years, 1925; Three Women, 1926; Departing Wings, 1927; Alimony, 1928; Garden Oats, 1929; The Incredible Year, 1929; Broadway Interlude (with Achmed Abdullah), 1929; Office Wife, 1930; Make Believe, 1930; Judy (juvenile), 1931; Skyscraper, 1931; Babs and Mary Lou (juveniles), 1931; Myra (juvenile), 1932; Week-End Marriage, 1932; District Nurse, 1932; Self- Made Woman, 1932; Girl-on-the-Make (with Achmed Abdullah), 1932; Beauty, 1933; White Collar Girl, 1933; Love's a Puzzle, 1933; Innocent Bystander, 1934; Honor Bound, 1934; Within a Year, 1934; American Family, 1935; The Puritan Strain, 1935; The Moon's Our Home, 1935; This Man Is Mine, 1936; Men Are Such Fools, 1936; The Heart Has Wings, 1937; Twenty-Four Hours a Day, 1937; Manhattan Nights, 1937; Enchanted Oasis, 1938; Rich Girl, Poor Girl, 1938; Hotel Hostess, 1938; The High Road, 1939; Career By Proxy, 1939; White Magic, 1939; Station Wagon, 1939; Rehearsed for Love, 1939; Something Special, 1939; Letty and the Law, 1940; Medical Centre, 1940; And New Stars Burn, 1941; Temporary Address: Reno, 1941; The Heart Remembers, 1941; Blue Horizons, 1942; Breath of Life, 1942; Five Women in Three Novels, 1942; Rest of My Life with You, 1942; Washington, U.S.A., 1943; You Can't Escape, 1943; He Married a Doctor, 1943; Change of Heart, 1944; Arizona Star, 1945; A Job for Jenny, 1945; No Private Heaven, 1946; Woman on Her Way, 1946; Sleeping Beauty, 1947; Give Love the Air, 1947; Marry for Money, 1948; They Who Love, 1948; Golden Shoestring, 1949; Lookout for Liza, 1950; The Whole Armor, 1951; Face Toward the Spring, 1956; (poems) Widow's Walk, 1954; Three Faces of Love, 1957; Many Windows, 1958; Blaze of Sunlight, 1958; Testament of Trust, 1960; The West Wind, 1962; Harvest of Hope, 1962; The Lonely Man, 1964; Living by Faith, 1964; There is a Season, 1966; Evening Star, 1966; The Velvet Hammer, 1969; Take What You Want, 1970; Any Village, 1971; One More Time, 1972; No Bed of Roses, 1973; Time and the Hour, 1974; New Girl in Town, 1975; Thursday's Child, 1976; also serials, short stories, and verse. Radio and motion pictures from books and stories; Apartment for Peggy, 1948; Second Chance, 1950; The Juniper Tree, 1952. Republican. Home: Norwalk, Conn. Died Mar. 18, 1978.

BALDWIN, FRANK BRUCE, JR., business exec.; b. Phila., Aug. 28, 1907; s. Frank B. and Julia (Reynolds) B.; B.S., Pa. State Coll., 1930, Ph.D., 1934; M.S., U. Minn., 1932; D.Sc., Drexel U., 1966, LL.D., St. Joseph's Coll., 1967; m. Eleanor Dutton, June 23, 1934; children—Frank Bruce, Nancy E. Vice pres. Baldwin Dairies, Inc., 1936-50; v.p., asst. to pres. Abbotts Dairies, Phila., 1950-60, exec. v.p., 1960-62, pres., 1963-67, v.p. Fairmont Foods Co., Omaha, 1963-67, also dir.; past chmn. bd., chief exec. officer, dir. Horn & Hardart Baking Co.; past dir. Phila. Port Corp., Cloverlay, Inc., Polychorme Corp., Provident Nat. Corp. Ritter Financial Corp., Provident Nat. Bank, Phila., Phila. Agy., Inc. Dir. courses applied dairy procedure Temple U., 1936-68; past dir. Nat. Dairy Council. Mem. Phila. council Boy Scouts Am.; past chmn. Phila. Redevel. Authority; mem. SSS; past pres., dir. Crime Commn. Phila., Inc. Chmn. bd. dirs. Phila. Heart Assn.; past bd. dirs. Phila. Indsl. Devel. Corp., Blue Cress Phila., bd. govs. Acad. Food Mdsg., St. Joseph's Coll.; past trustee Beaver Coll., Phila. Coll. Osteopathy, Pa. State U. Mem. Pa. Assn. Milk Dealers (past pres., dir.), Milk Distbrs. Assn. Phila. Area (past pres., dir.), Milk Industry Found. (past pres., dir.), Sigma Xi, Alpha Gamma Rho, Alpha Zeta, Gamma Sigma Delta. Clubs: Union League (Phila.); Seaview Country Center Hills Country; Atlantic City Country. Home: Philadelphia, Pa. Deceased.

BALDWIN, FRANK CECIL, educator; b. Providence, Oct. 4, 1900; s. Frank and Amy Elizabeth (Gill) B.; B.S., Cornell, 1923; A.M., U. of Pa., 1929; m. Anne Planten Gaillard, Dec. 27, 1928; children—Anne Gaillard, Frank Cecil, Mary Elizabeth, Nathaniel Planten. Mathematics teacher Blair Acad., Blairstown, N.J., 1926-31, Pingry Sch., Elizabeth, N.J., 1931-35; acad. dean Penn Hall Jr. Coll., 1936-40; headmaster Harrisburg (Pa.) Acad., 1940-42; sec. Cornell U. Past trustee Blair Acad. Alderman, member Common Council, City of Ithaca. Served as maj. AAC, 1942-45. Mem. Nat. Assn. Student Personnel Administrators (past president), New York State Association of Deans and Guidance Personnel (past president), also Phi Delta Kappa, Phi Kappa Psi. Presbyn. (elder). Clubs: Cornell (N.Y.C.); Torch, Rotary (pres. 1963-64) (Ithaca). Home: Ithaca, N.Y. Died Apr. 30, 1979.

BALDWIN, JOHN WILLIAM, univ. prof.; b. Alton, O., June 23, 1883; s. James Lewis and Alice Etta (Glover) B.; A.B., Lebanon U., 1911; A.M., U. of Mich., 1914; m. Margaret Pearl Bracelin, Nov. 11, 1906; children—Carl Vernon, Helen Joan Berkaw, Alice Margaret Hess, Jack Bracelin. Instr. in mathematics Lebanon U., 1911-13, U. of Mich. Mich. State Normal Coll., 1917-18; instr. and asst. prof. mathematics Detroit Jr. Coll. and Coll. City of Detroit, 1918-36; registrar Detroit Jr. Coll., Coll. City of Detroit and Wayne U., 1923-38; successively asso. prof. and prof. Wayne U. since 1938. Mem. Am. Math. Assn., Mich.

Acad. Sci. Republican. Home: Detroit.

BALDWIN, ONIAS BARBER, prof. education; b. Augusta, Kan., Nov. 12, 1882; s. Sylvanus and Jane (Barber) B.; A.B., Friends U., Wichita, Kan., 1906; A.M., U. of Chicago, 1911; studied U. of Chicago, 1917-18; U. of Kan., 1928-29, Ph.D., 1930; m. Waldena Martindale, 1908; 1 son, Alfred Lee. Prof. edn., McPherson (Kan.) Coll., 1911-14; Southwestern Coll., Winfield, Kan., 1914-18; fellow in edn., U. of Chicago, 1917-18; prof. edn., Morningside Coll., Sioux City, Ia., 1919-21; prof. edn. and dean, Friends U., Wichita, Kan., 1921-35; prof. psychology, Whittier Coll. since 1935, dean of men, 1937-48. Mem. Phi Delta Kappa. Methodist. Mason. Kiwanian. Home: Whittier, Calif.

BALDWIN, PERCY MALLET, coll. prof.; b. Nottinghamshire, Eng., July 30, 1885; s. H. Harold and Annie Elizabeth (Parker) B.; B.A., Queens' U., Kingston, Ont., Can., 1913, M.A., 1915; Ph.D., U. of Calif., 1924; m. Mary Louise Buell, June 1, 1926. Came to U.S., 1921, naturalized, 1928. Pub. sch. teacher, Western Can., 1905-12; editor Commn. of Conservation, Ottawa, Can., 1913-16 and 1919-21; teaching fellow polit. sci. U. of Calif., 1921-23; prof. history N.M. Coll. of A. and M.A. since 1925, dean of arts and sci., 1927-47. Served with Med. Corps, Canadian Army, 1916-19. Fellow N.M. Hist. Soc.; mem. Fgn. Policy Assn., Southwestern Philos. Conf. Club: Rotary (past pres.). Author: (articles) Fray Marcos de Niza's Relacion, 1926; Methodology of Social Science, 1928; Historical Note on the Boundaries of New Mexico, 1930; Technological Unemployment; Constitutional Changes in New Mexico, 1935; Conditions Required for World Peace, 1938; Short History of the Mesilla Valley; Twenty Years After, 1938; The United States and the New World Order, 1940; The 1940 Census and Legislative Reapportionment in New Mexico, 1941; Elephant Butte Dam, Mesilla, and Shalam Colony (3 titles in Dictionary of Am. History), 1943. Home: Las Cruces, N.M.

BALDWIN, R(OBERT) J(AMES), univ. prof.; born Brown City, Mich., Oct. 31, 1883; s. James and Pricilla (Peart) B.; B.S., Mich. State Coll., 1904; student U. of Mich., 1907-1908; m. Bertha Lillian Van Orden, Aug. 7, 1915; children—Dorothy Jane (Mrs. Dudley F. Straubel), Robert James, Katherine Louise (Mrs. William Anderson Zabriskie). Science teacher Traverse (Mich.) City High Sch., 1908-10; geology teacher Mich. State Coll., 1910, asst. to dean of agr., 1911-13, dir. of extension, 1913-48, retired, 1949. Mem. Epsilon Sigma Psi. Republican. Member People's Church. Home: East Lansing, Mich. *

BALDWIN, VINCENT JOHN, bishop; b. Bklyn., July 13, 1907; s. John O. and Josepha (Haefelein) B.; student Inst. Philosophy, Huntington, N.Y., 1926-28; J.C.B., Gregorian U., Rome, 1929, S.T.D., 1932. Ordained priest Roman Catholic Ch., 1931; mem. matrimonial tribunal Diocese Bklyn., 1934-49, vice chancellor diocese, 1949-53; apptd. papal chamberlain, 1948; chancellor, diocesan consultor Diocese Rockville Center, N.Y., 1957, vicar gen. diocese, 1957-62, aux. bishop, 1962-79; apptd. domestic prelate, 1959. Home: Garden City, N.Y. Died Sept. 16, 1979; buried St. John's Cemetery, Middle Village, N.Y.

BALDWIN, WILLIAM H(ENRY), pub. relations counsellor; b. Saginaw, Mich., Sept. 17, 1891; s. William H. Jr. and Ruth Standish (Bowles) B.; student Hackley Sch., Tarrytown, N.Y., Phillips Acad., Andover, Mass., A.B., Harvard, 1913; student U. of Wis.; m. Cecilia Brewster, Nov. 16, 1916; children—William H., Walter Brewster, George Lee. Began as reporter on N.Y. Evening Post, 1914-17; chief petty officer and ensign in U.S.N.R.F., World War I, in press censorship and later cable censor, Key West; raised for Fisk U. first million-dollar endowment for a Negro coll. in south; estabilished office in pub. relations, 1926; served as counsel to Fed. Trustee throughout McKesson & Robbins reorganization; active in developing pub. support for extension of Reciprocal Trade Agreements Act in 1943, 45 and 48; counsel to National Crusade for Freedom, 1950; appointed adjunct prof. New York University, 1950; Dir. of Nat. Urban League from 1914, sec. of bd. 1915-42, pres. 1942-47; trustee of Sydenham Hosp. since 1943, trustee of Fisk U. from 1923; bd. mem. Fairfield State Hosp., Conn., 1949-56; director Southern Education Foundation; dir. of Nat. Policy Com. 1944-47, United Defense Fund, United Community Defense Services; treas., Am. War Community Services, 1943-47; first sec., Am. Arbitration Assn. Charter mem. Nat. Assn. Pub. Relations Counsel (chmn. bd. 1942); mem. Fgn. Policy Assn. (dir., mem. pub. affairs com.), Internat. Pub. Relations Assn., The Silurians, Am. Legion. Clubs: Harvard. Overseas Press (N.Y.). Democrat. Unitarian. Author: The Shopping Book, 1929. Home: Kennett Square, Pa. Died May 17, 1980; buried Lakeview Cemetery, New Cannaan, Conn.

BALFOUR, MAXWELL W., corp. exec.; b. Traer, Ia., June 22, 1895; s. William and Rachel (Coulter) B.; B.A., Northwestern U., 1916; m. Marie Louise Petot, Dec. 30, 1919 (div.); 1 dau., Claude (Mrs. E. Kenneth Hadden); m. 2d, Inez Wilkinson, June 30, 1973. Aviation cadet, 1917; commd. 1st lt. AC, U.S. Army, 1918, ret. as capt., 1931; dir. aviation div. Spartan Aircraft, 1939-61, v.p. Spartan Aircraft Co., 1941-61, pres., 1961-68; pres. Minnehoma Ins. Co., Minnehoma Life Ins. Co., Minnehoma Finance Co., 1961-71, chmn. bd., 1971-77. Decorated Order Brit. Empire. Mem. Quiet Birdmen, Order Daedalians, Aero. Tng. Soc. (past pres.), Newcomen Soc., Delta Tau Delta. Clubs: University; John Evans; Army-Navy. Home: Tulsa, Okla. Died Aug. 8, 1977; interred Memorial Park, Tulsa, Okla.

BALINT, DENNIS MARTIN, lawyer; b. Cleve., Apr. 5, 1933; s. Denes M. and Julia (Czaban) B.; B.S., U. Ariz., 1955; LL.B., Western Res. U., 1958; m. Betty Sue Rogers, Oct. 17, 1964; children—Tamara, Dennis Martin, Brady, Tiffany. Admitted to Ariz. bar, 1959, Ohio bar, 1958; practice in Phoenix, 1959; partner firm Rawlins, Ellis, Burrus & Kiewit, 1963-75; lectr. Ariz. Inst. Banking 1967-75. Pres. Valley Big Bros., 1968; chmn. Phoenix YMCA bd. mgmt., 1971-75. Mem. Ariz. Acad., Phoenix Execs. Club, Phoenix Jr. C. of C., Scottsdale 20-30. Kiwanian (pres. Aurora club, Phoenix 1967). Home: Phoenix, Ariz. Died Aug. 24, 1975.

BALL, ERIC GLENDINNING, biol. chemist; b. Coventry, Eng., July 12, 1904; s. C. Sturges and Nellie (Glendinning) B.; brought to U.S., 1905, naturalized, 1919; B.S. Haverford Coll., 1925, M.A., 1926, D.Sc. (hon.), 1949; Ph.D., U. Pa., 1930; M.A. (hon.), Harvard, 1942; m. Grace L. Snavely, Sept. 10, 1927. Nat. Research fellow in medicine Johns Hopkins Med. Sch., 1929-30, instr. physiol. chemistry, 1930-33, asso., 1933-40; Internat. Physiol. Congress fellow, Rome, Italy, 1932; Guggenheim fellow Kaiser Wilhelm Inst., Berlin, Germany, 1937-38; asst. prof. biol. chemistry Harvard Med. Sch., 1940-41, asso. prof., 1941-46, prof., 1946-71, prof. emeritus, 1971-79, chmn. div. med. scis., 1951-68; ind. investigator Marine Biol. Lab., 1971-79; vis. prof. U. Brazil, 1945; Guggenheim fellow, vis. investigator Scripps Clinic and Research Found., La Jolla, Calif., 1963. Trustee Woods Hole Oceanographic Inst., 1953-57, Marine Biol. Lab., Woods Hole. Recipient Eli Lilly award in biochemistry, 1940, Cruzeiro do Sol, 1945. Fellow AAAS; mem. Am. Chem. Soc., Am. Soc. Biol. Chemistry, Biochem. Soc. Gt. Britain. Am. Acad. Arts and Scis., Nat. Acad. Sci., Soc. Gen. Physiologists, Endocrine Soc., Sigma Xi, Alpha Omega Alpha. Author: Energy Metabolism, 1973. Mem. editorial bd. Jour. Biol. Chem., 1950-60, Biochemistry, 1961-70, Biochemical Prep, 1948-56, editor-in-chief vol. 2, 1952. Contbr. to sci. and tech. jours. Home: Falmouth, Mass. Died Sept. 4, 1979.

BALL, HERBERT MORTON, lawyer, business exec.; b. Syracuse, N.Y., June 9, 1908; s. Charles and Freda (Rosenson) B.; grad. Mercersburg, (Pa.) Acad., 1925; A.B., Dartmouth, 1929; postgrad. Cornell, summer 1927; LL.B., Harvard, 1932; grad. Berlitz Sch., 1941; m. Joan Florence Cameron, June 9, 1950; children—Charles Cameron, Herbert Morton, Craig Douglas; 1 son by previous marriage, Steven. Newspaper corr., 1923-29; admitted to Pa. bar, 1932, D.C. bar, 1942, N.Y. bar, 1947, Supreme Ct. U.S., 1941; pvt. law practice, Scranton, Pa., 1932-40; v.p., gen. mgr. Blue Ribbon Co., Wilkes-Barre, Pa., 1939-40; atty.-negotiator R.F.C., Washington, 1940-42; spl. asst. to pres. Fansteel Metall. Corp., North Chicago, Ill., 1942; counsel, asst. to chmn. bd. Pal-Personna Blade Co., 1946-47; asst. gen. atty. Am. Home Products Corp., N.Y.C., 1947-51; asst. sec. to asst. gen. atty. Johns-Manville Corp., Johns-Manville Sales Corp., Johns-Manville Products, Canadian Johns-Manville Co., Ltd., 1951-52, sec., gen. atty., then v.p., gen. counsel, sec. Johns Manville Corp. until 1972, also officer or dir. numerous subsidiaries; sec. Asbestos & Danville Ry. Co., Johns-Manville Dutch Brand Products Corp.; sec., dir. Johns-Manville (Overseas) Ltd.; con. N.Y. Stock Exchange, 1972-75; sr. account exec. Georgeson & Co., N.Y.C., 1975-76. Served as lt. comdr. USNR, 1942-46; PTO. Mem. Res. Officers Assn. (v.p., dir. N.Y. Navy chpt.), Naval Order U.S., Am., N.Y. State, Lackawanna County bar assns., Assn. Bar City N.Y. Club: Dartmouth Coll. (bd. govs.) (N.Y.C.). Home: Bronxville, N.Y. Died Nov. 19, 1976.

BALL, JOHN WILLIS, lawyer; b. Jacksonville, Fla., Jan. 22, 1910; s. Philip Manville and Anna McNeill (Bullock) B.; A.B. magna cum laude, Washington and Lee U., 1932, LL.B., 1935; m. Margaret Ann Moreland, Apr. 11, 1936; children—Haywood Moreland, John Willis, Margaret Ann. Admitted to Fla. bar, 1935, practiced in Jacksonville; mem. law firm Ulmer, Murchison, Ashby & Ball, 1947-78; spl. atty. lands div. Dept. Justice, 1937-54. Mem. 5th Circuit Fed. Jud. Com., Am. Bar Assn., 1963-69. Bd. dirs. Family Consultation Service, Jacksonville. Fellow Am. Bar Found. (chmn. Fla.), Am. Coll. Probate Counsel; mem. Am. (com. jud. selection, compensation and tenure 1959-63, 69-75, chmn. 1972-75, ho. dels. 1964-67), Inst. Jud. Adminstrn., Jacksonville bar assns., Am. Judicature Soc., Am. Law Inst., Fla. Bar, Order Coif, Phi Beta Kappa, Phi Gamma Delta, Omicron Delta Kappa, Phi Delta Phi. Office: Jacksonville, Fla. Died Jan. 28, 1978; buried Evergreen Cemetery, Jacksonville.

BALL, ROBERT PEARL, physician; b. Harlan, Ky., July 14, 1902; s. Robert Lee and Sarah Margaret (Carter) B.; student Centre Coll., Danville, Ky., 1918-19, D.Sc. (hon.), 1948; M.D., U. Louisville, 1924; m. Grace Baggerly, Aug. 13, 1927; children—Robert P., Elizabeth Castleman. Intern, Louisville City Hosp., 1924-26; fellow in surgery Cleve. Clinic, 1926-28; surg. pathologist U. Louisville Sch. Medicine, 1928-30; gen. surg. practice, Louisville, 1928-32; radiologist, Chattanooga, 1932-36, Presbyn. Hosp. and Coll. Physicians and Surgeons, Columbia U., 1936-49; prof. radiology. Coll. Physicians and Surgeons, 1947, Cornell U. Med. Coll., 1949-51; radiologist-in-chief N.Y. Hosp., 1949-51; pvt. practice radiology, Baton Rouge, 1951-52; radiologist-in-chief Oak Ridge Hosp., 1952-77, also E. Tenn. Hosp. for Chest Diseases. Served to lt. col. M.C., AUS, 1942-45. Named Outstanding Physician of Year, Tenn. Med. Assn., 1974. Mem. AMA, Am. Coll. Radiology (chancellor 1945-50, v.p.), Am. Roentgen Ray Soc. (rep. on NRC 1949-51), Radiol. Soc. N. Am., N.Y. Roentgen Soc. (pres. 1950-51), N.Y. State Med. Soc., N.Y. Acad. Medicine, Harvey Soc., Brit. Inst. Radiology, Soc. Medico-Quirurgica del Guayas, Ecuador, S.A. Home: Oak Ridge, Tenn. Died Jan. 5, 1977.

BALL, WILLIAM DAVID, author, educator; b. Denver, Colo., Aug. 18, 1885; s. William and Jeanette Juliet (Sanguinette) B.; A.B., U. of Denver, 1907; A.M., 1908; special study U. of Southern Calif., 1918; m. Martha Jane Woosley, July 2, 1919; children—William David, Martha Jane. Writer of short stories and articles on aviation, hunting and farming; editor Writers' Markets and Methods, 1927-46; pres. Palmer Inst. of Authorship, 1928-46. Roman Catholic. Author: Fundamentals of Creative Writing, 1924; also photoplays. Contbr. articles and fiction to nat. mags. Home: Wofford Heights, Cal. 93285. *

BALLANTINE, JOHN H., business exec.; b. Newark, 1892; grad. Cornell U., 1915. Chmn., dir. Neptune Meter Co. Home: Delray Beach, Fla. Died July 25, 1976.

BALLARD, JOHN HENRY, business cons.; b. Bklyn., June 23, 1893; s. John and Mary (Maguire) B. With Bulova Watch Co., N.Y.C., 1909-59, beginning as office boy, becoming pres., dir.; former chmn. bd., dir. Gruen Industries, Inc.; cons. several cos.; dir. Standard Fin. Corp., Standard Prudential United Corp. Bd. dirs. Jewelry Industry Council. Clubs: Metropolitan, N.Y. Athletic (N.Y.C.). Home: New York, N.Y. Died Oct. 24, 1979.

BALLARD, RUSSELL WARD, social worker; b. Donnellson, Ill., Nov. 25, 1893; s. Elbert Suveyor and Mary (Lee) B.; Ph.B., U. Chgo., 1922, postgrad., 1922-24; m. Ethel Horn, Sept. 1, 1921; children—John Horn, William Lee. Teacher, 1921-24; dir. community recreation, 1924-25; prin. elementary sch., 1925-36; county dir. pub. welfare, 1936-41; supt. Ill. State Tng. Sch. for Delinquent Boys, 1941-43; dir. Hull House, 1943-62; part-time tchr. Roosevelt U., Chgo., 1962-70; dir. community relations Midway Tech. Inst., Chgo., 1965-70. Bd. dirs. Kobe Coll., Operation ABLE. Served as capt., inf. U.S. Army, 1917-18. Recipient Thomas and Eleanor Wright Achievement award Chgo. Commn. on Human Rights, 1960; Jane Addams medal Nat. Fedn. Settlements, 1962; Disting. Service award U. Ill. Alumni Assn., 1979. Mem. Nat. Fedn. Settlements, Nat. Conf. Social Welfare, U.S. Assn. of UN, Japan-Am. Soc. (dir.), Nat. Assn. Social Workers. Phi Delta Kappa, Kappa Sigma. Methodist. Democrat. Home: La Grange Park, Ill. Died June 4, 1980.

BALLENGER, HOWARD C., physician, educator; b. Economy, Ind., Aug., 17, 1886; s. Jacob Oscar and Rachael Jane (Osborn) B.; student Indianapolis Bus. Coll., 1906; Earlham Coll., Richmond, Ind., 1906-07, Univ. of Mich. Sch. of Medicine, 1907-10, M.D., Univ. of Indiana Sch. of Medicine, 1911; m. Bessie Taylor, Aug. 15, 1912; children—Barbara Taylor (Mrs. Henry Churchill Williams), John Jacob, Howard Charles. Interne, Methodist Hosp., Indianapolis, Ind., 1911-12; asst. to Dr. W. L. Ballenger, 1912-15; instr. in otolaryngology, Univ. of Ill. Sch. of Medicine, 1912-14, 1915-17; consultant and surgeon, section otolaryngology, U.S.P.H.S. (U.S. Marine Hosp., Chicago), 1918-22; asst. surgeon of otolaryngology, Ill. Charitable Eye and Ear Infirmary, Chicago, 1917-20; asso. surgeon, Evanston Hosp., 1918-36, surgeon since 1936; part time research, Otho S. A., Sprague Inst. of Children's Memorial Hosp., 1928-31; asso., Northwestern Univ. Med. Sch., 1930-36, asst. prof., 1936-40, asso. prof. 1940-47; prof. and chmn., dept. of otolaryngology, Northwestern Univ. Med. Sch. since 1947. Fellow Am. Laryngol. Assn., Am. Otol. Soc., Am. Laryngol., Rhinol, and Otol. Soc., Am. Acad. of Ophthalmology and Otolaryngology, Am. Coll. of Surgeons, Am. Med. Assn.; mem. Chicago Laryngol. and Otol. Soc. (past pres.). Co-author: Ballenger's Diseases of the Nose, Throat and Ear, (5th edition, 1925, 9th edition, 1947). Author: Eye, Ear, Nose and Throat (with A. G. Wippern), 1917; Otology, Rhinology and Laryngology, 1st edition, 1940, 3d edition, 1947.

Contbr. numerous articles to med. books and professional jours. Home: Winnetka, Ill.

BALLENGER, WILLIAM LEE, physician; b. near Martin, Ga., Apr. 15, 1881; s. Frank and Elizabeth (Ward) B.; M.D. Atlanta Coll. Phys. and Surgs. (now Emory Univ.), 1912; m. Ethel Angel, Aug. 30, 1917 (died 1946); 1 son, William L. Taught in med. and dental schools and colleges; in private practice of medicine, Sandy Springs, Ga., since 1914; served with Atlanta Hosp., Children's Hosp., Philadelphia and St. Luke Hosp., Cleveland. Democrat. Methodist (trustee). Odd Fellow, Mason; mem. Order Eastern Star. Address: Sandy Springs, Ga. *

BALLUDER, ERWIN, business exec.; b. St. Thomas, Virgin Islands, Sept. 4, 1893; s. Heinrich and Patricia del Carmen (Long) B.; ed. in Germany; bus. training, Spain and England; m. Carmen Schwartau, May 20, 1920 (deceased June 17th, 1961); children—Carmen (Mrs. Lawrence Read Partridge), Gerda (Mrs. Leon Thorson) (dec.). Came to the United States in 1930, naturalized, 1935. Went to Mexico, 1914; with Compania Mexicana de Aviacion, 1924-29; joined Pan.-Am. Airways, 1929, v.p. and gen. mgr. Cia Mexicana de Aviacion, Pan Am. World Airways, mgr. Western Div., Brownsville, Tex., exec. asst., N.Y. City, v.p. from 1946; dir. and v.p. Pan American Grace Airways; pres. UMCA; pres., dir. Cia Argentina Pan Am., v.p., dir. Pan Am.-Grace Airways; dir. Panair do Brazil, Intercontinental Hotels Corp. Mem. Pan Am. Soc. of U.S. (dir.), Fgn. Trade Council (dir.). Clubs: University, Country, American (Mexico City); Cloud, N.Y. Athletic, Wings (New York). Home: New Hartford, Conn. Died Oct. 16, 1979.

BALOUGH, CHARLES, automotive exec.; b. Nagylak, Hungary, 1883; grad. Inst. Tech., Budapest, 1902. Chmn. bd., dir., Hercules Motors Corp., Canton, O. Home: Hills and Dales, Canton.

BAMBERGER, CLARENCE, mining engr.; b. Salt Lake City, July 16, 1886; s. Jacob Emanuel and Bertha (Greenewald) B.; ed. Phillips Exeter Acad., 1904; M.E., Cornell U., 1908; student Royal Sch. Mines, Berlin, 1909, Ecole Supericure des Mines, Paris, 1910; m. Marie Odell, 1915; children—Marie (Mrs. Joseph E. Bernolfo, Jr.), Gloria, Clarence. Engaged in leasing operations Smuggler Mine, Aspen, Colo., Daly-Daly West Mine, Park City, Utah; mgr. Weber Coal Mine, Coalville, Utah; exploration Pioche-Delamar, Nev.; petroleum exploration, Tampico, Mexico, Ohio Copper Co., Bingham Canyon, Utah; chmn. bd. Bamberger Investment & Exploration Co.; dir., mem. exec. com. Walker Bank and Trust Co., Pres. Inter-Collegiate Assn. Amateur Athletics, 1908, mem. War Industries Bd., 1918; exec. vice chmn. War Finance com. of Utah, 1942-46. Mem. Utah Legislature, 1913; chmn. for Utah, Eisenhower for Pres., 1952. Dir. Nat. Found. for Infantile Paralysis; chmn. Utah State Hosp. for Crippled Children; mem. lay adv. bd. St. Benedict's Hosp., Ogden, Utah; nat. dir. finance com. Am. Relief for France; mem. bd. govs. A.R.C.; bd. Holy Cross Hosp., Westminster Coll.; regent, U. of Utah; mem. adv. bd. Hoover Inst. and Library; mem. Cornell U. Council; mem. nat. founders bd. Salk Inst. Biological Studies; chmn. Utah Nat. Fund for Med. Edn. Vice chairman University of Utah Medical Center. Served as capt., ordnance, U.S. Army, 1917-18. Recipient Ordre Bien Publique, 1909, also Commandre de l'orde Etoile Noire, 1961 (France). Mem. Chi Psi. Clubs: Alta; Bankers of Am.; Flat Rock. Home: Salt Lake City. *

BANE, JOHN CURRY, JR., forging co. exec., lawyer; b. Pitts., July 23, 1904; s. John Curry and Kate Gertrude (Miller) B.; A.B., Princeton, 1925; B.A., LL.B., U. Cambridge (Eng.), 1927; LL.D., Thiel Coll., 1962; m. Sally Rawstorne, July 5, 1928. Admitted to Pa. bar, 1928, since practiced in Pitts.; partner Reed, Smith, Shaw & McClay; sec. Pitts. Forgings Co. (Pa., Mich.), 1933-74, v.p., 1951-74, now dir.; v.p., sec. Greenville Steel Car Co., 1936-74, now dir.; sec., counsel Neville Chem. Co., Pitts., 1944-76, dir., 1951-76. Cons. in basic steel and iron ore disputes, WSB, 1952. Trustee Thiel Coll. Presbyn. Mason. Clubs: Pitts. Athletic Assn., Duquesne, Pittsburgh; Capitol Hill, Metropolitan (Washington); Princeton (N.Y.C.). Home: Pittsburgh, Pa. Died May 24, 1976.

BANISTER, JOHN ROBERT, librarian; b. Saginaw, Mich., Feb. 5, 1912; s. John Lansing and Agnes (Bell) B.; A.A., Bay City (Mich.) Jr. Coll., 1934; A.B., U. Mich., 1936; B.S. in L.S., U. Ill., 1937; m. Nancy Simpson, Sept. 9, 1944; 1 dau., Nancy Anne (Mrs. Edmund Alan Attebury, Jr.). Asst. reference librarian Mich. State Library, Lansing 1936-41; order librarian, tech. library TVA, 1942-44; extension librarian Lansing Pub. Library, 1944-46; regional librarian Ill. State Library, Mt. Carmel, 1946-48; pub. library cons. gen. extension div. U. Fla., 1948-50; dir. libraries Chattahooches Valley Regional Library, Columbus, Ga., 1951-77; cons. in field, 1960-80. Del. Assembly Libraries of Ams., 1946; chmn. jr. mems. round table Mich. Library Assn., 1941, Ill. Library Assn., 1946. Chmn. Muscogee County (Ga.) chpt. Am. Heart Assn., 1952, Community Services Assn. Columbus, 1956-58; bd. dirs. Columbus Symphony Guild, 1962-80, Columbus United Givers, 1957-59. Mem. Am. (council 1940-41, chmn. jr. mems. round table 1946), Ga. (v.p. 1960), Southeastern (chmn. pub. libraries sect, 1948) library assns. Presbyn. Rotarian (dir. Columbus 1963—), Club: Columbus Country. Editor: The Junior Librarian, 1939-41; The Florida Public Library News-Letter, 1948-50. Contbr. articles to profl. jours. Home: Columbus, Ga. Died Mar. 17, 1980; buried Parkhill Cemetery, Columbus, Ga.

BANKER, OSCAR H., investor; b. Moonjoosoon, Turkey, May 31, 1895; s. Harutun and Sultan (Chakujian) Sarafian; student Am. Sch. Boys, Turkey, 1911-13, YMCA Night Sch., 1915-17, U. Wis. extension, 1919-20; m. Aroosiag Rose Yacoobian, Dec. 10, 1924; children—Margaret Helen (Mrs. John Carlson), Oscar Henry, Claudia Joyce (Mrs. David Evans) and Matilda Rose (Mrs. Donald James Kuch) (twins). Came to U.S., 1913. Machine designer Racine Tool & Machine Co. (Wis.), 1915-17; successively with R&V Ordnance Co., Moline, Ill., 1918, Hamilton Beach Co., Racine, 1919-22, Bud Co., Phila., 1923-26, Clayborn Process Corp., Milw., 1926-28; formed New Products Corp., Chgo., 1930 (merged with Fawick Corp. 1959), then dir. research and devel., 1959-60; founder Bay Products Devel. Co., 1961; formed Med-E-Jet Corp., 1967, dir., to 1979; inventor automatic transmission, final drive, controls for helicopters, inoculator gun medicine, saw sharpening machine, four-color flatbed printing press, numerous others. Crusader automobile safety. Mem. Nat. Roster Sci. and Specialized Personnel, World War II. Recipient citation Automotive Old Timers, Inc., 1969. Mem. Smithsonian Assos., Nat. Geog Soc., Soc. Automotive Engrs., Automotive Old Timers (life), Field Mus. Natural History (life; nat. adv. bd.). Republican. Mason. Holder more than 300 patents in various fields. Home: Bay Village, Ohio. Died Jan. 2, 1979; buried Sunset Meml. Park, North Olmsted, Ohio.

BANNERMAN, CHARLES S., lawyer; b. Bklyn., Apr. 12, 1905; s. David Boyce and Alice (Scott) B.; B.S. Princeton, 1926; LL.B., Harvard, 1929; m. Jane H. Campbell, Sept. 17, 1938; 1 dau., Ann McDonald Bannerman Bowes. Admitted to N.Y. bar, 1931, since practiced in N.Y.C.; mng. partner Clark, Carr & Ellis, 1943-69, Casey, Tyre, Wallace & Bannerman, 1969-73; partner Francis Bannerman Sons, 1946-58, pres., 1958-68; of counsel Whitman & Ransom, 1973-76. Author: The Story of Bannerman Island, 1962; The Bannerman Catalog, 1966. Home: New York, N.Y. Died Sept. 26, 1976.

BANNERMAN, HAROLD MACCOLL, educator, geologist; b. Barney's River, N.S., Can., Apr. 9, 1897; s. Alexander and Mary (S'abella) B.; B.S., Acadia U., 1924, D.Sc., 1955; Ph.D., Princeton, 1927; A.M., Dartmouth, 1934; LL.D., St. Francis Xavier U., 1953; m. Harriet M. MacIntosh, May 1929; 1 dau., Elspeth Jean. Began career as research fellow Princeton University, 1926-27; asst. geologist Canadian Geol. Survey, 1927-30; instr. geology Dartmouth, 1927-28, asst. prof., 1928-34, prof., 1934-42; cons. econ. geology, 1931-42; geologist U.S. Geol. Survey, Washington, 1942-67, chief div. econ. geology, 1944-49, asst. chief geologist, 1949-60, associate chief geologist 1960-61, research geologist, 1961-67; mem. U.S. Materials Adv. Bd., 1957-67; adj. prof. geology Wesleyan U., Conn.; acting state geologist, Conn. Served with Canadian Army, World War I; CEF, Eng., France. Recipient United States Dept. Interior Distinguished Service Medal, 1959. Fellow Geol. Soc. Am., Am. Mineral Soc., A.A.A.S.; mem. Soc. Econ. Geologists (v.p. 1962), Am. Inst. Mining and Metall. Engrs., Arctic Inst. N.A. Club: Cosmos (Wash.). Author articles on Precambrian, econ. geology. Home: Alexandria, Va. Died Oct. 30, 1976.

BANNISTER, LEMUEL, lawyer; b. Haewsville, Ky., Sept. 17, 1887; s. Silas H. and Effie (Hennen) B.; A.B., Harvard, 1909; LL.B., 1911; m. Mary Munroe Faxon, June 28, 1915 (deceased September 8, 1964; children—Lemuel, Henry F., Richard, Ruth F. Admitted to N.Y. State bar, 1912; partner law firm Bannister, Stitt, Holloway & Krause; dir. Funk & Wagnalls Co., Inc., Funk & Wagnalls Fund, Incorporated, Wilfred Funk Incorporated, also Peters Machinery Company. Mem. Bar Assn. City of N.Y., Am. Bar Assn., N.Y. County Lawyers Assn. Clubs: Upper Montclair Country, Harvard. Home: Montclair, N.J. Died Dec. 2, 1979.

BANTA, GEORGE, JR., editor, publisher; b. Menasha, Wis., Mar. 25, 1893; s. George and Ellen Lee (Pleasants) B.; ed. Wabash Coll., 1910-11, LL.D., 1968; M.A. (hon.), Lawrence Coll., 1951; L.H.D., Franklin Coll., Ind., 1960; m. Margaret Killen, Oct. 10, 1916; children—Margaret M., George R. With George Banta Co., Menasha, 1911-77, v.p., 1916-51, pres., 1951, 54-61, chmn., 1951-54, 61-70; editor Banta's Greek Exchange, 1935-77; v.p. First Nat. Bank, Menasha, Northwestern Engraving Co. Mem. exec. com. Nat. Interfrat. Conf., 1936-39, vice chmn., 1938-39; pres. Coll. Frat. Editors' Assn., 1929-30; pres. Menasha Park Bd., 1930-35. Trustee Lawrence Coll., 1930-38, pres., 1939-43, 54-59, v.p., 1960-66; trustee Milwaukee-Downer Sem., 1935-39; bd. dirs. Valley Council Boy Scouts Am., 1928—, pres., 1939-40, mem. Nat. Council, 1949-77; bd. dirs. Wis. Hist. Found., 1962-77. Mem. Wis. Hist. Soc. (curator 1944-68, exec. com., 1946, v.p., 1947, pres. 1949-52, hon. v.p. 1968-77), Holland Soc. N.Y., Ry. and Locomotive Hist. Soc., Phi Delta Theta (nat. editor 1923-32, nat. pres. 1932-34; chmn. survey commn. 1940-50). Clubs: North Shore Golf; Ormond (Fla.) Country. Author: Typographical Tips, 1912. Assisted in editing and compiling 5 edits. Baird's Manual of Am. College Fraternities; asst. editor History of the Wisconsin Central. Contbr. to jours. Home: Menasha, Wis. Died Jan. 18, 1977.

BANTLE, LOUIS A., business exec.; b. Danbury, Conn., Oct. 14, 1906; s. Louis F. and May L. (White) B.; ed. pub. schs. Bridgeport, Conn.; m. Marie Daisenberger, Dec. 28, 1927; 1 son, Louis F. With sales dept. R. J. Reynolds Tobacco Co., 1927, U.S. Tobacco Co., 1929-72, div. mgr. N.J., 1931, dept. mgr. N.Y.C., 1938, West Coast mgr., 1942, v.p., dir., 1945-59, pres., chief exec. officer, 1959-72, dir emeritus, 1972-81; pres. House Windsor Cigar Co., from 1965; chmn. bd. Tucker-Sharp Pen Co., from 1964, B.A. Barnard Co., from 1966. Republican. Home: Larchmont, N.Y. Died Apr. 27, 1981.

BARACH, ALVAN LEROY, physician; b. Newcastle, Pa., Feb. 22, 1895; s. Nathan L. and Jennie C. (Silman) B.; student CCNY, 1912-15; M.D., Coll. Physicians and Surgeons, Columbia U., 1919; m. Frederica P. Pisek, Apr. 24, 1933; children—Jeffrey Alvan, John Paul. Intern Presbyn. Hosp., N.Y.C., 1919-20; asst. in medicine Harvard U., research at Mass. Gen. Hosp., 1920-21; asst. in Medicine Presbyn. Hosp., 1922-31; asst. in medicine. Coll. Physicians and Surgeons, Columbia U., 1922-25, instr. medicine, 1925-28, asso. medicine, 1928-35; cons. medicine Woman's Hosp., 1928-34, also asso. prof. clin. medicine Coll. Physicians and Surgeons, Columbia U., 1936, cons. medicine, from 1960; clin. prof. Presbyn. Hosp., 1952-65, then cons. medicine. Mem. Nat. Inventors Council, Dept. Commerce. Mem. M.C., World War I. Awarded bronze medal, Class I, for original investigation helium and oxygen in various types of dyspnea, A.M.A., 1936; scroll of honour for meritorious research in clin. med. and gas therapy Internat. Anesthesia Research Soc., 1936, Townsend-Harris medal CCNY, 1940, award of merit Am. Assn. Inhalational Therapists, 1960; Redway medal N.Y.C. Med. Soc., 1964; Henderson medal Am. Soc. Geriatrics, 1971; Edward Trudeau medal Am. Lung Assn., 1977; named Internist of Distinction, Soc. Internal Medicine County N.Y. Fellow Am. Coll. Chest Physicians (Coll. gold medal 1961), AMA, N.Y. Acad. Medicine; mem. Am. Soc. Clin. Investigation, Assn. Am. Physicians, Soc. Exptl. Biology and Medicine, N.Y. County Med. Soc., Am. Acad. Allergy, Trudeau Soc., Alumni Assn. Presbyn. Hosp., Alpha Omega Alpha, Omega Pi Alpha. Democrat. Jewish. Author: (with Hylan A. Bickerman) Pulmonary Emphysema, 1956; A Treatment Manual For Patients With Pulmonary Emphysema, 1969. Contbr. articles to profl. jours. Devised oxygen tent generally adopted for use in treatment of pneumonia, cardiac disease and other cardio-respiratory conditions; introduced helium as a new therapeutic gas in treatment of asthma and obstructive lesions in larynx and trachea. Home: New York, N.Y. Died Dec. 13, 1977.

BARBER, JOHN EDWIN, corp. official; b. Toledo, O., Dec. 3, 1886; s. Jason Alonzo and Ida May (Hull) B.; A.B., Yale, 1910; m. Grayson Carter Beach, Dec. 18, 1920; children—Mary Custis (Mrs. William Piper), Elizabeth (Mrs. Seeley W. Mudd II). Harris, Forbes & Co., N.Y., Phila., 1910-17; pres. First Securities Co., First Nat. Bank, Los Angeles, 1920-29; pvt. investment business, Los Angeles, 1929-32; pres. and dir. Central and South West Utilities Co. and v.p. Middle West Corp., 1932-38; v.p. Middle West Service Co., 1938-44; dir. Walt Disney Productions, Inc. With The U.S. Shipping Board in various capacities, including vice pres. Emergency Fleet Corp. and attaché Am. Peace Commn., Paris, 1917-19. Asst. to Alien Property Custodian, San Francisco, Calif., in charge of Pacific Coast activities 1942-43; also served (1942) as deputy regional mgr. Distribution Division, War Production Board. Decorated Commander Order of Crown (Italy). Assistant to Dawes Commn. on German Reparations, 1924. Vice chmn. bd. trustees Cal. Inst. Tech., Pasadena. Mem. Phi Beta Kappa, Zeta Psi. Republican. Presbyn. Clubs: California (Los Angeles); Twilight (Pasadena). Home: Pasadena, Cal. *

BARBER, SAMUEL, composer; b. West Chester, Pa., Mar. 9, 1910; s. Samuel Leroy and Marquerite McLeod (Beatty) B.; piano student Isabelle Vengerova; singing student Emilio de Gogorza; composition student Rosario Scalero; grad. Curtis Inst. Music, Phila., 1932, Mus.D., 1945; hon. doctorate Harvard, 1959. Compositions: Serenade for String Quartet, 1929; Dover Beach (for voice and string quartet, 1931; String Quartet in B minor, 1936; Sonata (for cello and piano), 1932; Overture to "School for Scandal" (for orch.), 1932; Music for A Scene from Shelley (for orch.), 1933; Symphony in One Movement (for orch., 1936; Adagio for Strings (recorded by Toscanini), 1936; Essay for

Orchestra, 1937; The Virgin Martyrs (choral), 1935; Concerto for Violin and Orchestra, 1940; Second Essay, 1942; Night Flight, 1944; Capricorn Concerto, 1944; Four Excursions (for piano, introduced by Horowitz), 1944; Cello Concerto, 1945; Medea's Dance of Vengeance (ballet for Martha Graham), 1946; Knoxville, Summer of 1915 (for voice and orch.), 1947; Piano Sonata, 1948; Souvenirs (ballet-suite for orchestra), 1953; Prayers of Kierkegaard (for chorus, soprano solo and orch.), 1954; A Stopwatch and an Ordnance Map (men's chorus and drums); Reincarnations (mixed chorus); Let Down the Bars, O Death (chorus); numerous songs including Hermit Songs, 1953; opera Vanessa, Salzburg festival, 1958, Met. Opera House, 1958; Toccata Festiva for Organ and Orchestra, 1950; Die Natali; Chorale Preludes for Christmas (for orch.), 1960; Piano Concerto, 1962; Andromache's Farewell (for soprano and orch.), 1963; Antony and Cleopatra (opera), 1966; Despite and Still (song cycle), 1968; a cappella chorus Twelfth Night, To Be Sung on the Water, 1969; The Lovers (for baritone, chorus and orch.), 1971; Fadograph of a Yestern Scene (for orch.), 1971; 3 songs for Dietrich Fischer-Dieskav: Now I have fed and eaten up the rose, A green lowland of pianos, O boundless, boundless evening, 1972; compositions performed in U.S., Europe and USSR. Recipient Prix de Rome, 1935; Pulitzer prize music for opera Vanessa, 1958, piano concerto, 1963; Guggenheim award, 1945; N.Y. Music Critics award, 1946; Gold medal for Music, 1976. Served with AUS, 1943. Mem. ASCAP (dir. 1969-81), Nat. Acad. Arts and Letters. Home: New York, N.Y. Died Jan. 23, 1981.

BARBOUR, CLIFFORD EDWARD, clergyman; b. Pittsburgh, Pa., Jan. 26, 1895; s. Alfred and Jennie (Rigg) B.; A.B., U. of Pittsburgh, 1921; B.T., Western Theol. Sem., 1922; Ph.D., U. of Edinburgh, 1927; D.D., Maryville Coll., 1933, U. of Pittsburgh, 1950; LL.D., Waynesburg Coll., 1949; m. Laura Hathaway Nye Taber, June 28, 1922; 1 son, Clifford Edward; married 2d, Alice Elizabeth Patton, Aug. 2, 1950. Ordained to ministry Presbyn. Church 1922; pastor, Herron Av. Presbyn. Ch., Pittsburgh, Pa., 1923-26, Second Presbyn. Ch., Knoxville, Tenn., 1928-51; pres. Western Theol. Seminary, Pitts., 1951-59; acting pres. Pittsburgh Theol. Seminary, from 1959; dean Tenn. Sch. Religion, U. Tenn., 1933-51; moderator Gen. Assembly Presbyn. Ch. U.S.A., 1949-50, mem. Bd., Christian Edn., 1930-37; chmn. Com. on Affairs of Handicapped, State of Pa. Member bd. Maryville Coll., St. Mary's Hosp., Knoxville; mem. Community Chest (pres. 2 yrs.). Pres. Pa. United Theol. Sem. Foundation; member board trustees Chatham College, Pittsburgh. Member Delta Tau Delta, Omicron Delta Kappa. Author: Sin and the New Psychology, 1930; Young People's Departmental Graded Material, 1930. Home: Maryville, Tenn. Died Jan. 1979.

BARBOUR, ROBERT, mfr.; b. Monmouth Beach, N.J., July 5, 1886; s. William and Julia Adelaide (Sprague) B.; M.E., Columbia, 1910; unmarried. Former pres. The Linen Thread Co., Inc.; retired Sept. 30, 1939. Mem. Am. Society Mech. Engrs. Clubs: University, Union League, Racquet and Tennis (New York).

BARCLAY, HARTLEY WADE, editor, pub., mfg. engr.; b. Gladbrook, Iowa, Dec. 3, 1903; s. Wade Crawford and May (Hartley) B.; A.B., Ohio Wesleyan U., 1924; m. Marjorie Kathleen Whitley, Feb. 16, 1924 (dec.); children—Jean Marjorie (dec.), Hartley Wade, James Crawford; m. Lois Beveridge Wilson, Oct. 28, 1967. Indsl. advt. mgr. N.Y. Times, 1952-56; pub. Tide mag., 1956-59; editor, pub. Automotive Industries, 1959-70; v.p., dir. Chilton Co., 1962-70; exec. sec. Mgmt. Research Inst.; cons. research dir. Analysis & Programming Corp., editor OEM Newsletter; cons. Taft-Pierce Mfg. Co., Marine Products Co., Henry G. Thompson & Son Co., Gen. Motors Corp.; indsl. edn. cons. Copper and Brass Research Assn.; editor Mill and Factory Mag., N.Y.; bus. writer N.Y. Times, 1947-52; editorial dir., sec. Conover-Mast Corp., 1931-42; research dir. elec. trades div. McGraw Hill Pub. Co., 1930-31; editor, pub. Automotive Industries mag., 1959-70; editor, pub. Found. Survey of Corporate and Indsl. Systems Communications, 1970; Eastern v.p., engr. Nova-Chrome, Inc.; cons. Town of Rye; lectr. U.S. Army Indsl. Coll., Washington, 1937, 38, 39, 40, 41; Mississippi Riverboat capt., 1967; aviation pilot; FAA instr. aero navigation, meteorology and regulations; lectr. ednl., govtl., engring. and bus. groups; arbitrator Am. Arbitration Assn.; sec. Am. Conf. Nat. Def. Mem. Pres.'s Com. Employment Physically Handicapped, from 1957; spl. adviser N.Y. State Legislature Select Joint Com. on Econ. Affairs. Recipient Distinguished Service award N.Y. State Soc. Profl. Engrs., 1952; named hon. mem. 25th Inf. Div. and 101st Airborne Div., U.S. Army, 1965; certified mfg. engr. Mem. CAP, Am. Ordnance Assn., Tech. Soc. Council N.Y., Edison Pioneers (asso.), Am. Inst. Indsl. Engrs., Soc. Mfg. Engrs. (founder, chmn. Westchester chpt. 1971-72, regional exam. monitor 1975-76, author, examiner 5 tech. courses for certified mfg. engrs.), Sigma Delta Chi, Phi Gamma Delta, Pi Delta Epsilon, Order of Washington (life). Republican. Episcopalian (perpetual deacon). Author: Survey of Industrial Distribution, 1931; Ford Production Methods, 1936; Labor's Stake in the American Way, 1938; The Timetable of Dictatorship, 1940; Industrial News Subjects; Public Relations Methods Manual. Editor: Hor Your Business Can Help Win the War, 1942; The Foundation Survey of Production and Sales Planning; Business News; The First Standard Manual of Public Information Procedures; The Foundation Survey of Corporate and Industrial Communications, 1970; Making Money in New York City, 1976; Preacher's Kid, 1977. Contbr. articles to Atlantic Monthly, N.Y. Times, other jours., Manchester Union Leader. Home: Port Chester, N.Y. Died Nov. 12, 1978.

BARCLAY, LORNE WEBSTER, b. in Poplar Hill, Canada, Dec. 24, 1885; s. Eli Robert Barclay and Sarah Jane B.; came to U.S., 1903; B.A., Bethany (West Virginia) College, 1906, M.A., 1907, L.H.D., 1935; B.D., School of Religions (Yale), 1909; m. Myrtle Daisey, June 20, 1912; 1 son, Leeds Webster. Dir. Madison Square Boys' Club, New York, 1909-10; with Educational Book Co. of Can., 1911-12; dir. Social Center Dept., People's Inst., New York, 1913-14; scout executive Boy Scouts America, New York, 1915-16; nat. ednl. dir. Boy Scouts America, 1917-24; v.p. Children's Foundation, Valparaiso, Ind., 1924-25; scout exec. Tampa Boy Scouts, 1926-29; jamboree exec. Am. Contingent of World Boy Scout Jamboree, England, 1929; mgr. Ore. Trail Memorial Assn., 1930; dir. Ore. Trail Centennial; became dir. Nat. Parks Assn., 1930; dir. of activities Nat. Council of Boy Scouts of America, 1934-37, dir. camping and activities since 1937, appted. nat. dir. Publs., 1941; now program dir. Long Beach Community Welfare Council. Was dir. gen. French Camp Schs. for Scouting, part of each yr., 1920, 21, 22. Decorated Cross Legion of Honor, 1921. Mem. Kappa Alpha.

BARD, HARRY, educator; b. Balt., Dec. 24, 1906; s. Rubin and Fannye (Rothenberg) B.; B.S., Johns Hopkins, 1929; M.S., Columbia, 1938; Ed.D., U. Md., 1950; LL.D., Morgan Coll., 1959, Loyola Coll., Balt., 1963; m. Eleanor Ruth Blumberg, Aug. 19, 1934; children—Fane, Robert. Tchr. pub. schs., Balt., 1926-35; supr. social studies, 1935-46; part-time instr. history, polit. sci., edn. several colls., 1939-76; asst. dir. Secondary Curriculum Bur., Balt., 1946-56; dir. instructional services Gen. Secondary Edn. Balt., 1956-59; pres. Balt. Community Coll., 1959-76. Chmn. aviation commn. Am. Council Edn., 1946-56; pres. Middle States Council Social Studies. Mem. exec. bd. Balt. Council Social Agys.; active Balt. Jr. Red Cross; mem. Nat. Conf. Christians and Jews; chmn. Mayor-City Council Commn. on Redistricting City of Balt., 1965; mem. Md. Adv. Com. on Fed. Appropriation Higher Edn. Facilities. U.S. del. to internat. seminar UNESCO, Lake Success, 1948. Mem. Md. Constl. Conv. Commn., 1966-67; del. Md. Constl. Conv., 1967-68. Trustee Middle States Assn. Colls. and Secondary Schs., 1972. Recipient Balt. YMCA Ann. Service to Youth award, 1960, Fellowship House citation in human relations, 1958, Md. State Senate citation for writings on Md. govt., 1957, Ann. Alumni award Md. State Tchrs. Coll., 1959, Balt. YMCA Youth and Govt. medal, 1960; Bard Library dedicated, 1970; recipient Prof. Harry Carman award Middle States Council for Social Studies, 1974. Mem. Citizen's Planning and Housing Assn., Md. Hist. Soc. (mem. edn. com.), UN Assn. Md. (pres. 1957-59), Assn. for Supervision and Curriculum Devel. (dir.), Nat. Council Social Studies, Am. Assn. Jr. Colls., Flag House Soc. Balt., Phi Delta Kappa. Author: Maryland, The State and Its Government, rev., 1952; Maryland Today, rev., 1961; Homework: A Guide for Secondary School Teachers, 1958; Teachers and the Community, 1952; (with H. Manakee) Active Citizenship, 1951; (with others) Citizenship and Government in Modern America, 1965; Maryland, State and Government: Its New Dynamics, 1974. Home: Baltimore, Md. Died Oct. 10, 1976.

BARD, PHILIP, physiologist, educator; b. Hueneme, Calif., Oct. 25, 1898; s. Thomas Robert and Mary Beatrice (Gerberding) B.; student Thacher Sch., Ojai, Calif., 1913-17; A.B., Princeton, 1923; A.M., Harvard, 1925, Ph.D., 1927; Sc.D. (hon.), Princeton, 1947, Washington and Lee U., 1949; Dr. honoris causa U. Católica de Chile, 1951, U. Mayor de San Marcos de Lima, 1951; LL.D., Johns Hopkins, 1968; Sc.D., Rockefeller U., 1976; m. Harriet Hunt, June 29, 1922 (dec. Apr. 1964); children—Virginia Hunt (Mrs. M.K. Johnson, Jr.), Elizabeth Stanton (Mrs. B.T. O'Connor); m. 2d, Janet Mackenzie Rioch, Jan. 25, 1965 (dec. Nov. 1974); m. 3d, Colleen Calderwood Gillis, Jan. 8, 1976. Teaching fellow in physiology Harvard Med. Sch., Boston, 1925-26, instr. physiology, 1926-28, asst. prof. physiology, 1931-33; asst. prof. biology Princeton (N.J.) U., 1928-31; prof. physiology and dir. dept. Johns Hopkins U. Sch. Medicine, Balt., 1933-64, prof. emeritus physiology, 1964-77, dean med. faculty, 1953-57; Harvey Soc. lectr., 1938; Hughlings Jackson lectr. Montreal Neurol. Inst., 1943; George Cyril Graves lectr. Ind. U., 1948. Pres., trustee Internat. Found., 1969-75; trustee emeritus Rockefeller U.; trustee Thacher Sch. Served as pvt. Ambulance Service, U.S. Army, Section 578, A.E.F., 1917-19. Recipient Jacoby award Am. Neurol. Assn., 1959; Achievement award A.C.P., 1968. Fellow AAAS, Am. Acad. Arts and Scis.; hon. mem. Facultad de Biologia y Ciencias Medicas, U. de Chile, Sociedad Médica de Santiago, Sociedad Argentina de Biología; mem. Nat. Acad. Scis., Am. Physiol. Soc. (councilor 1936-39; sec. 1939-41, pres. 1942-46, chmn. bd. publ. trustees 1959-62), Am. Neurol. Assn. (hon.), Am. Philos. Soc. (Lashley award in neurobiology 1962), Harvey Soc., Soc. for Exptl. Biology and Medicine (pres. 1959-61), NRC (3 com. on mil. medicine, World War II), Nat. Bd. Med. Examiners, 1935-46, Assn. for Research in Nervous and Mental Disease (pres. 1950), Assn. Am. Physicians, Phi Beta Kappa, Sigma Xi. Clubs: 14 W. Hamilton St., Tower (Princeton); Elkridge (Balt.); Century (N.Y.C.). Editorial bd. Am. Jour. Physiology, 1939-46; chmn. editorial bd. Physiol. Revs., 1950-53. Contbr. to physiol. and med. jours., especially on neuro-physiology; editor, contbr. Macleod's Physiology in Modern Medicine, 8th edit., 1938, 9th edit., 1941; Medical Physiology, 10th edit., 1956, 11th edit., 1962. Home: Ojai, Calif. Died Apr. 5, 1977.

BARD, RALPH A., former under-sec. Navy; b. Cleveland, O., July 29, 1884; s. George M. and Helen (Norwood) B.; B.S., Princeton U., 1906; m. Mary Hancock Spear, Feb. 23, 1909; children—Ralph A. Jr., Mrs. Thomas J. Johnson, Jr., Mrs. Martin E. Manulis, George M., II. Salesman Eversz & Company, investments, Chicago, 1906; Kennett Cown & Co., 1908-09; organizer and mem. Hitchcock, Bard & Co., Inc., 1919-25; formed and became pres. Ralph A. Bard & Co., later Bard & Co., 1925; became pres. Chicago Investors' Corp., 1928; firm consol. with Chicago Corp. 1932, vice president and director until 1934; organized Ralph A. Bard & Co., Chicago, Ill., 1934, president, 1934-41. Appointed assistant secretary of the Navy, Feb. 1941; under-secretary of the Navy, June 1944-July 1945; apptd. deputy to U.S. representative, U.N. Commn. on Conventional Armament, Mar. 1947. Served as vice pres. Chicago Council, Boy Scouts of America. Director of Military Relief, Central Div. Am. Red Cross, World War I. Trustee, Northwestern U. Clubs: Chicago, Coleman Lake, Old Elm, Attic, Commercial (Chicago); Princeton, Army and Navy, Chevy Chase (Washington, D.C.). Home: Lake Forest, Ill. *

BARFF, STAFFORD EDWARD DOUGLAS, British diplomat; b. Langstone, Eng., Dec. 26, 1909; s. Arthur Douglas and Ellen (Tebbatt) B.; student Brentwood Coll., Victoria, B.C., Can., 1928; m. Marguerite Hélène Emma Iost, July 31, 1937. Engaged in brokerage bus., Vancouver, B.C., Can., 1929-31; with Personal Service League, London, Eng., 1931-33, British Gas Light Co. Ltd., London, Philips Lamps Ltd., London, 1937-40, Ministry of Info., London, 1940-45; joined Brit. Fgn. Service, 1945; dir. Brit. Info. Services, Chgo., 1945-56; U.K. high commn., New Delhi, 1956-58; 1st sec. embassy, Washington, 1958-60; dir. press div. Brit. Info. Services, N.Y.C., 1960-62; consul Brussels, Belgium, 1962, St. Louis, 1962-64; consul gen., New Orleans, 1964-69; head Anglo-Am. scholarship sect. Assn. Commonwealth Univs., London, 1970-76. Decorated Order British Empire. Home: Hove, Sussex, Eng. Died Nov. 28, 1976.

BARGEN, J. ARNOLD, physician; b. Mountain Lake, Minn., Oct. 25, 1894; s. Jacob I. and Anna J. (Balzer) B.; student Carleton Coll., 1915-17; B.S., U. Chgo., 1918; M.D., Rush Med. Coll., 1921; M.S. in Medicine, Mayo Found., 1927; m. C. Ruth Burns, Aug. 27, 1921; children—Robert Burns, Terese Ann, Loretta Mae, Cornelia Marie, Ruth Jacqueline (dec.). Borland fellow medicine St. Luke's Hosp., Chgo., 1922-23; 1st asst. in medicine Mayo Found., 1923-27, asst. prof. 1927-29, asso. prof. 1929-48, prof., 1948-76; cons. medicine Mayo Clinic, chmn. dept. gastroenterology, 1942-60, pres. staff, 1956-60, head sect. gastroenterology Scott-White Clinic, Temple, Tex., also chmn. postgrad. tng. program in gastroenterology; dir. med. edn. Scott-White Meml. Hosp., Scott-Sherwood-Brindly Found.; med. cons. M.D. Anderson Cancer Inst., Houston; cons. gastroenterology Lackland AFB, San Antonio; clin. prof. medicine U. Cal. at Irvine, 1968-76. Med. adv. bd. Sears Roebuck Med. Found.; judge Nat. Sci. Fair, 1961, 63-65; mem. Library Bd. Rochester, Minn. Bd. Med. Examiners (pres. 1954-55). Mem. Med. Enlisted Res. Corps, World War I. Recipient J. Arnold Bargen award inaugurated by Mayo Found., 1960; Caldwell medal, 1966; Friedenwald medal, 1967. Fellow A.C.P.; mem. A.M.A. (Minn. del. ho. dels. 1948-59, mem. council on sci. assembly 1957-76, chmn. council 1962-64, Distinguished Service award 1969), Interstate Postgrad. Med. Assn. N. Am. (pres. 1964-65), Am. Gastroent. Assn. (sec. 1941-45, pres. 1950), Central Clin. Research Club, Minn. Med. Assn. (Distinguished Service medal 1959, pres. 1957), Tex. Acad. Medicine, Sigma Xi, Phi Chi. Kiwanian. Author: Chronic Ulcerative Colitis, 1968; 5 other books, numerous articles. Home: Sun City, Calif. Died Dec. 26, 1976.

BARGER, HARRY S., lawyer, investigator; b. Eddyville, Ill., Sept. 26, 1882; s. Simon S. and Nancy J. King B.; LL.B., and LL.M., Nat. Univ. Law Sch., 1913; m. Bessie Brown, Sept. 26, 1906. Admitted to D.C. bar, 1914, U.S. Supreme Court, 1917; pvt. practice, Washington, D.C., 1916-31; spl. asst. to U.S. atty. gen., 1931-33; investigator for congressional coms. and depts.

of nat. govt., since 1934, serving P.W.A., P.R. Reconstruction Administration, Gen. Accounting Office, House sub-com. investigating C.P.A., Senate campaign com., joint com. on fed. expenditures; recently investigator House com. to investigate Fed. Communication Commn. Home: Washington, D.C. *

BARING, WALTER STEPHAN, congressman; b. Goldfield, Nev., Sept. 9, 1911; s. Walter Stephen and Emilie Louise (Froehlich) B.; B.S., B.A., U. Nev., 1934, high sch. tchrs. certificate; m. Alma Geraldine Buchanan, Jan. 31, 1942; children—Walter Stephan III, William Robert, John Buchanan, Thomas Jefferson. Elected chmn. Dem. Central Com. of Washoe County, 1936; assemblyman from Washoe County to Nev. Legislature, 1936, 1942; councilman 6th Ward, Reno City Council 1947; asso. with father in Sierra Furniture Co., Reno, 1945-48; mem. 81st-82d Congress, 85th-93d Congresses, Nev. at large, chmn. pub. lands subcom. on interior com., mem. vets. affairs com. Served with USNR, 1942-45. Mem. Am. Legion. Democrat. Mason (32 deg., Shriner), Eagle; mem. Order Eastern Star. Club: Sertoma. Home: Reno, Nev. Died July 13, 1975.

BARINGER, RICHARD E., architect, artist; b. Elkhart, Ind., Dec. 3, 1921; s. Elmer E. and Lelah Marie (Carpenter) B.; B.A., Inst. Design, Chgo., 1948; B.Arch., Harvard, 1950, M.Arch., 1951; m. Caryl Dianne Zumhagen, Feb. 15, 1969. Designer P.A.C.E. Assos., Architects, Chgo., 1951-53; chief designer George Fred Keck, William Keck, architects, Chgo., 1953-55; pvt. practice architecture, Chgo., 1955-61, N.Y.C., 1961-67, St. Croix, V.I., 1967-80; exhibited paintings in one man shows at Margaret Brown Gallery, Boston, 1949, Mass. Inst. Tech., 1951, Bertha Schaefer Gallery, N.Y.C., 1962, 63, 64, Columbia, 1963, Nelson Taylor Gallery, N.Y.C., 1963, Dwan Gallery, N.Y.C., 1967, 10 Downtown, N.Y.C., 1968, Choate Sch., 1968, Notre Dame U., 1968, Inst. Design of Ill. Inst. Tech., Chgo., 1968, Island Center, St. Croix, 1970; exhibited in group shows at Cal. Palace Legion of Honor, 1949, Inst. Contemporary Art, Boston, 1951, Arts Club Chgo., 1961, U. Ill. Contemporary Am. Painting, 1963, Washington Gallery Modern Art, 1963, Albright Gallery, Buffalo, 1964, Mus. Modern Art, 1965, Am. Mus. Crafts, N.Y.C., 1967, Pickor Gallery Colgate U., 1968, White House, 1967; cons. Chgo. Plan Commn., 1954; asso. prof. architecture Ill. Inst. Tech., Inst. Design, Chgo., 1956-60; asst. prof. architecture Columbia, 1962-63; vis. lectr. painting fine arts dept. U. Pa., 1966. Chief designer Am. Nat. Exhbn. in Moscow, 1959. Mem. planning com. Lincoln Park Conservation Commn., Chgo., 1957-60; chmn. planning com. Mid North Conservation Commn., Chgo., 1957-60; mem. V.I. Planning Bd., 1973-80. Bd. dirs. St. Croix Jazz Soc. Served to capt. USAAF, 1942-45. Decorated D.F.C. with oak leaf cluster, Air medal with 6 oak leaf clusters; recipient Rome prize Am. Acad. in Rome, 1951-53, Progressive Architecture award, 1957, AIA award, 1958, Archtl. Record award, 1958. Nelson Robinson Jr. scholar Harvard, 1950, Sheldon fellow Harvard, 1951-53. Fellow Am. Acad. Rome, AIA (pres. V.I. chpt. 1975; coll. of fellows). Club: Harvard (N.Y.C.). Home: Christiansted, St Croix, V.I. Died Jan. 26, 1980.

BARKAN, HANS, ophthalmology; b. San Francisco, Calif., July 26, 1882; s. Adolph and Louise (Desepte) B.; A.B., Stanford, 1905; M.D., Harvard, 1910; grad. study in ophthalmology, Vienna, 1912-14; m. Phoebe Bunker, Oct. 20, 1916; children—Adolph William, Phoebe Sarah. Asst. in pathology, Harvard, 1910-11, instr., 1911-12; vol. asst. eye clinic, Vienna, 1912-14; practiced at San Francisco since 1914; with Stanford U. Med. Sch. as asst. instr. and asso. prof. ophthalmology, 1914-28, clin. prof. 1928-47, emeritus professor since 1947, Capt. Med. Corps. U.S. Army, 1916-18. Trustee Mills Coll. Mem. Am. and Calif. med. assns., Am. Acad. Ophthalmology and Otolaryngology, Am. Ophthal. Soc., Pacific Coast Oto-ophthal. Soc., Delta Tau Delta, Alpha Omega Alpha, Sigma Nu Sigma. Clubs: Univ. Contbr. on ophthal. subjects. Home: Stanford, Cal.

BARKER, JOSEPH WARREN, engineering cons.; born Lawrence, Mass., June 17, 1891; s. Frederick and Alice Ann (Alletson) B.; student U. of Chicago, 1909-10; B.S. in Elec. Engring., MIT, 1916, M.S., 1925; student U.S. Coast Arty. Sch., 1916-17 and 1923-24; LL.D., Bucknell U., 1940; Sc.D., Northeastern U., 1940; D.Eng., Case Sch. Applied Sci., 1942; LL.D., Union College, 1944; D. Eng., Univ. of Rochester, 1944; L.H.D., Muhlenberg College, 1945; m. Mary Metcalf Perin, June 17, 1916 (died Sept. 30, 1937); children—Beatrcie Perin (Mrs. Sidney L. Hall), John Perin; m. 2d Mary Casey Mallon, Dec. 11, 1943; 1 son, Michael Mallon. Prof. elec. engring. MIT, 1925-29; professor and head dept. elec. engring., Lehigh U., 1929-30; dean of faculty engring., Columbia U., 1930-46; on leave to serve as spl. asst. to Sec. of Navy, 1941-45; pres., Research Corp., Research Constrn. Co., Inc., 1945-47, chmn. bd. 1945-59, thereafter dir.; chmn. bd. Research-Cottrell, Inc., 1945-47, thereafter dir. Cons. NASA, from 1963. Commissioned 2d lt., U.S. Army, 1916, advanced to maj., Sept. 26, 1925; with A.E.F. in France and Germany, 1918-22. Decorated Victory medal (U.S.); Order of Prince Danilo (Montenegro); recipient U.S. Navy Disting. Civilian Service award. Fellow AIEE (v.p. 1940), AAAS (mem. exec. com. 1941, ASME (pres. 1957); mem. Bus. Equipment Mfrs. Inst. (cons. from 1960, exec. v.p. 1961-62), ASCE Am. Inst. Mining and Metall. Engrs., Illuminating Engrs. Soc. (pres. 1932-33); Am. Soc. Engring. Edn., Tau Beta Pi, Sigma Xi (acting pres. 1954, pres. 1955-56), Phi Kappa Sigma, Theta Tau. Episcopalian (warden). Mason. Clubs: Cosmos (Washington); University (New Rochelle, N.Y.); Century, (N.Y.), Westchester Country. Home: New Rochelle, N.Y. Died Dec. 10, 1975.

BARKER, LEBARON R., JR., editor; b. Plymouth, Mass., Jan. 13, 1904; s. LeBaron Russell and (Hutchins) B.; A.B., Harvard, 1926; m. Mary Pope, June 28, 1926 (div. Apr. 1933); children—LeBaron Russell, III, Randolph; m. 2d, Leslie Greenough, Sept. 14, 1934 (dec. Aug. 1939); 1 dau., Leslie Lindsay; m. 3d, Eileen Lange, Apr. 10, 1941 (div. 1950); children—Jeffery, Stephanie; m. 4th, Adeline Crankshaw, Jan. 17, 1952. Worked in advt., sales, editorial departments Houghton Mifflin & Co., 1927-43; New York editor, 1937-43; trade advt. mgr. Doubleday Doran, 1943, editor-in-chief, 1943-45, exec. editor, 1945-69, sr. editor, 1969-73. Pres. Publishers Ad Club, 1941-43; chmn. radio com., Council on Books in Wartime, 1942; v.p. Am. Inst. Graphic Arts, 1947-52. Club: Dutch Treat (N.Y.C.). Co-author: (pseud. Admiral Jettison) Addelgrams, 1934. Home: New York, N.Y. Died July 2, 1973.

BARKER, WILLIAM J., judge; b. Marietta, Ga., June 25, 1886; s. William Dobbs and Kata (Agricola) B.; LL.B., with highest honors, U. of Fa., 1916; m. Pauline Eleanor Bigham, Oct. 20, 1916; children—Pauline Eleanor (Mrs. Robert C. Parker), William Julius, Katherine Hughes. Admitted to Florida bar, 1916, and began practice in Jacksonville; judge Circuit Court of State of Fla., 1925-40; U.S. district judge, Southern Dist. of Fla., since 1940. Mem. Am. and Fla. bar assns., Phi Kappa Phi, Phi Delta Phi, Alpha Tau Omega. Mason, K.P. Methodist. Home: Tampa, Fla.

BARKER, WILLIAM JUDSON, lawyer; b. Washington, D.C., June 14, 1884; s. Charles Ralph and Catherine (Douglas) B.; student Corcoran Scientific Sch., 1901-02, George Washington U. Law Sch., 1903-07; m. Ruth Laughlin, June 1, 1915 (divorced 1933); children—Jean, Larn, Laughlin. Admitted to D.C. bar, 1908; in practice, Santa Fe, N.M., since 1916; apptd. U.S. attorney, Dist. of N.M., June 13, 1933; to spl. asst. atty. gen. of U.S., July 1, 1937. Elected Dist. Judge, First Judicial Dist., State of New Mexico, for six-year term beginning Jan. 1, 1943, resigned to enter pvt. practice 1946. Dem. State Chmn. (N.M.), 1930-33. Dem. state chmn. (N.M.), 1930-33.

BARKSDALE, JAMES ALTON, educator; b. McKenzie, Tenn., Nov. 29, 1904; s. James Monroe and Judith Ada (Esch) B.; A.B., Bethel Coll., McKenzie, Tenn., 1925, D.Litt., 1959; A.M., U. Colo., 1936; student Peabody Coll., 1927; Ed.D., U. Tenn., 1954; m. Eleanor Herrin, May 18, 1928. Tchr., prin., Charlotte (Tenn.) High Sch., 1925-35; prin. Central High Schs., Ashland City, Tenn., 1935-41, E.W. Grove High Sch., Paris, Tenn., 1941-43, Tenn. High Sch., Bristol, 1943-46; supt. pub. schs., Union City, 1946-49; dir. Tenn. Dept. Personnel, 1949-50; Tenn. commr. edn., 1950-53; pres. Cumberland Presbyn. Bd. Edn., 1951-57; acting assoc. prof. edn. U. Tenn. Coll. Edn., Knoxville, 1953-55; dean Tenn. Poly. Inst., 1955-60; adviser higher edn. U.S. Overseas Mission ICA, Ankara, Turkey, 1960-62; chief edn. adviser AID, Am. embassy, Amman, Jordan, 1963-65; prof. history Bethel Coll., McKenzie, Tenn., 1965-80, interim pres., 1969. Vis. prof. Memphis State U., summer 1967; cons. Henry County Bd. Edn. 1967-68. Del., Tenn. Ltd. Constl. Conv., 1971. Mem. Am. Assn. Sch. Adminstrs., Tenn. Edn. Assn. (pres. 1959), Tenn. Coll. Assn. (pres. 1959). Mason Rotarian. Home: McKenzie, Tenn. Died Oct. 10, 1980; interred Shiloh Cemetery, McKenzie.

BARLOW, GEORGE HERBERT, dist. judge; b. Trenton, N.J., Jan. 4, 1921; s. Richard Joseph Shaw and Jane (Fine) B.; B.A., Dartmouth Coll., 1943; LL.B., Rutgers U., 1948; m. Jane Elizabeth Thorne, Feb. 12, 1944; children—Jane Ellen, Elizabeth Thorne, George Herbert III. Admitted to N.J. bar, 1948; practiced in Trenton, 1948-53; asso. firm Moore & Moore, Trenton, 1948-53; asst. counsel law revision and bill drafting com. N.J. State Legislature, 1948-53; asst. U.S. atty. Dist. of N.J., Trenton, 1953-56; U.S. commr., Trenton, 1956-63; asso. firm Katzenbach. Gildea & Rudner, Trenton, 1956-63; judge Mercer County Ct., Trenton, 1963-66, Superior Ct. N.J., Trenton, 1966-70; judge, then chief judge U.S. Dist. Ct., Trenton, 1970-79. Served from ensign to lt. (j.g.) USNR, 1944-46. Mem. Mercer County, N.J., Fed., Am. bar assn., Am. Judicature Soc. Club: Dartmouth. Home: Trenton, N.J., Died Mar. 4, 1979.

BARLOW, HENRY MAIN, stock broker; b. Enfield, Mass., Nov. 23, 1884; s. Herbert Henry and Mary Rosilla (Main) B.; student pub. schs. of Enfield and Athol, Mass.; m. Nadine Emerson Arents, Feb. 25, 1915; children—Lorraine Emerson Kirsten, Nadine DuVal Curley, Helen Main Jennings, Barbara Ann Bissell. Clk. gen. store, later clk. N.Y. Stock Exchange firms, 1903-06; salesman, v.p., sales mgr. A.G. Hyde & Sons, cotton goods commn. mchts., N.Y.C., 1906-18; mem. Brown & Barlow, cotton goods commn. mchts. 1919-28; asso. Ludwig, Robinson Co., Tobey & Co. and Carreau & Co., 1930-36; mem. Carreau & Co., mems. N.Y. Stock Exchange, 1936-47, limited partner since 1952; mem. H. M. Barlow & Co., mems. N.Y. Stock Exchange, 1947-42; dir. Russell Bros. Towing Co., Newtown Creek Towing Co. With Squadron C. New York National Guard, 1911-16. Member New York Society Order Founders and Patriots Am. Republican. Conglist. Clubs: Brooklawn Country (Bridgeport, Conn.); Canadian, City Midday (N.Y.C.). Home: Greens Farms, Conn. *

BARMACK, JOSEPH EPHRAIM, educator; b. N.Y.C., Sept. 20, 1910; s. Louis and Pauline (Sigman) B.; B.S., Coll. City N.Y., 1930; Ph.D., Columbia, 1937; research student N.Y. Psychoanalytic Inst., 1950-55; m. Therese Mayer, 1935 (dec. 1965); children—John A., Neal H. Mem. faculty Coll. City N.Y., from 1938, prof. psychology, 1955-71, emeritus, 1972-80, chmn. dept., 1962-70; cons. med. psychology St. Luke's Hosp., N.Y.C., 1975-80; asst. project dir. Psychol. Corp, 1948-49; project dir. to asst. v.p. Dunlap & Assos., 1949-60; research asso. Inst. Def. Analyses, 1962-63; cons., 1963-80; lectr. psychiatry Columbia Coll. Phys. and Surg., 1976-80. Served to lt. col. USAAF, 1942-46. Diplomate indsl. psychology Am. Bd. Examiners Profl. Psychology. Mem. Am., Eastern psychol. assns. Reseach on physiol. effects of antihypnotic drugs on boredom, accident causation and prevention, methods of classifying behavioral sci. research, social sci. research, research planning to Dept. Def. Home: Mamaroneck, N.Y. Died May 30, 1980.

BARNARD, NILES HUTTON, educator, mech. engr.; b. Chgo., Sept. 2, 1903; s. J.T. Allen and Bernice Edna (Hutton) B.; B.S., in Ry. M.E., U. Ill., 1928, M.S., 1930, M.E., 1934; m. Rhoda Eleanor Hall, June 23, 1928; children—Roger H., Allen R., Kenneth N., Ann J. (Mrs. David M. Rau). With Ill. Steel Co., South Works, Chgo., 1920-21, I.C. R.R., Chgo., 1921-24, summers 1925-28; asso. prof. Tenn. Poly. Inst., 1930-35; instr. dept. mech. engring. U. Neb., Lincoln, 1935-36, asst. prof., 1936-40, asso. prof., 1940-48, acting chmn., 1947-48, prof., 1948-70, emeritus, 1970-79, chmn. dept., 1948-66; vis. prof. indsl. engring. State U. Ia., summers 1950-58. Pres. Lincoln Council Christian Edn., 1940-44, Lincoln Goodwill Industries, 1944-46. Registered profl. engr., Neb. Fellow Am. Soc. Quality Control (Brumbaugh award com. 1954-66), Am. Soc. M.E. (life fellow, regional v.p. 1962-66); mem. Am. Assn. U. Profs., Am. Soc. Engring. Edn., Am. Interprofl. Inst. (pres. 1961-62), Tau Beta Pi, Pi Tau Sigma (regional v.p. 1963), Sigma Tau. Methodist (asso. sec. gen. bd. lay activities 1946-47, lay leader Neb. Conf. 1945-59). Mason. Home: Lincoln, Nebr. Died Aug. 3, 1979.

BARNES, C. RANKIN, clergyman; b. Manitowoc, Wis., Mar. 23. 1891; s. Rev. Charles L. and Janet (Rankin) B.; B.A., U. Calif., 1912; B.D., Gen. Theol. Sem., 1915, S.T.D., 1955; D.D., Ch. Div. Sch. the Pacific, 1943; m. Florence Lowe, 1921 (div. 1941); m. 2d, Katharine Ross, 1942. Deacon, 1915, priest, 1916, Protestant Episcopal Church; vicar Imperial Valley Mission, El Centro, California, 1916-18; rector St. James Ch., South Pasadena, Calif., 1918-31; exec. sec. Social Service Dept. P.E. Ch., 1931-36; rector St. Paul's Ch., San Diego, 1936-47; sec. Nat. Council of Episcopal Ch., 1947-61; prof. Bloy House Theol. Sch., Pasadena, from 1962; apptd. hon. canon St. Paul's Cathedral, Los Angeles, 1937. Lectr. Ch. Divinity School of the Pacific 1939-46; pres. Gen. Theol. Sem. Alumni Assn., 1935-36. Dep. Gen. Conv. P.E. Ch., 1925, 28, 31, 37, 40, 43, 46, 52; asst. sec. House of Deputies, 1937-46, sec., 1946-61; del., asso. sec. Anglican Congress, 1954. Author: The General Convention, Offices and Officers, 1785-1950; Ethelbert Talbot, 1848-1928. Contbr. to Christianity and the Contemporary Scene, 1943. Home: San Diego, Calif. Deceased.

BARNES, CHARLES BENJAMIN, lawyer; b. Hingham, Mass., July 18, 1900; s. Charles Benjamin and Josephine Lea (Low) B.; B.S., Harvard, 1924, LL.B., 1927; m. Phoebe Washburn, June 15, 1929; children—Phoebe (Mrs. John E.Z. Caner), Josephine Lea (Mrs. John Jay Iselin), Charles Benjamin, Cornelia Bradford. Admitted to Mass. bar, 1927; asso. firm Hemenway & Barnes, Boston, 1927-80, partner, 1929-80. Dir. Allied Stores Corp., N.Y.C., Jordan Marsh Co., Boston; dir., mem. dirs. adv. com. State St. Bank & Trust Co.; former dir. Joseph Bennett Co., Boston, Washburn Co., Worcester, Mass., Scott & Williams, Laconia, N.H. Alternate del. Republican. Nat. Conv., Kansas City, 1928, Chgo., 1932. Hon. chmn. bd. overseers Peter Bent Brigham Hosp. Mem. Am. Bar Assn., Mass. Bar Assn., Bar Assn. City of Boston. Clubs: Somerset, Curtis, Knockers (Boston); Anglers (N.Y.C.); Country (Brookline, Mass.); Republican of Mass. (past dir.). Home: Chestnut Hill, Mass. Died Sept. 30, 1980.

BARNES, GEORGE BUTLER, lawyer; b. Norway, Me., Oct. 17, 1904; s. Charles Putnam and Annie (M. Richardson) B.; A.B., Ricker Classical Inst., 1922; A.B., Colby Coll., 1926, M.A. (hon.), 1946; LL.B., Harvard, 1929; LL.D., Ricker Coll., 1961; m. Ada Flora Wheeler, June 27, 1931; children—Forrest Wheeler, Ann Butler, George Butler. Admitted to Me. bar, 1929; states atty. for Aroostook County (Me.), 1933-39; mem. Ho. of Reps., 1943-47, speaker, 1945; mem. Me. Senate, 1947-53; mem. Me. Jud. Council, 1953-70. Pres. bd. trustees Ricker Classical Inst. and Ricker Coll., 1952-62; chmn. vis. com. on govt., history and econs. Colby Coll., 1950-58. Asst. appeal agt. County Draft Bd., 1943-46. Del. Republican Nat. Conv., 1952. Fellow Am. Coll. Probate Lawyers, Am. Coll. Trial Lawyers; mem. Am. (com. on credentials and admissions ho. of dels.), Me. (pres. 1954) bar assns., Am. Arbitration Assn. (nat. panel arbitrators), Delta Kappa Epsilon. Republican. Baptist. Mason, Elk. Home: Houlton, Maine. Died Aug. 8, 1979.

BARNES, JOHN LANDES, mathematical engr.; b. Haddonfield, N.J., Oct. 16, 1906; s. Eugene Howard and Naomi Grace (Landes) B.; S.B., M.I.T., 1928, S.M. in E.E., 1929; A.M., Princeton, 1930, Ph.D. in Math., 1934; m. Mabel F. Schmeiser, July 3, 1935; children—George Gared, Lynne Ries (Mrs. Small). Asst. instr., research asst. math. and elec. engring. Princeton, 1932-34; instr. elec. engring. M.I.T., 1934-35; asst. prof. math. Tufts U., 1935-39, acting chmn. elec. engring. dept., asso. prof., chmn. dept. applied math., 1940-41, prof., chmn. dept., 1941-42, 45-47; research engr. RCA Mfg. Co., 1939-40; cons. Hazeltine Service Corp., 1941-42; mem. tech. staff Bell Telephone Labs., 1942-45; cons. Raytheon Mfg. Co., 1945-47, N. Am. Aviation Corp., 1947-53, chief Guidance Aerophysics Lab., 1948-51, asso. tech. dir. electromech. dept., 1951-53; cons. Ramo-Wooldridge Corp., 1953-54; dir. control and computer lab. Missile Systems div. Lockheed Aircraft Corp., 1955; v.p. Systems Research Corp., 1955-56; founder, pres. Systems Labs. Corp., Sherman Oaks, Cal., 1956-57; pres. Systems Corp. of Am., 1957-76. Prof. engring., applied sci. UCLA, 1947-74, emeritus, 1974—; expert U.S. Dept. Transp., 1974-75. Fellow A.A.A.S., Am. Acad. Arts and Scis., AIAA (asso.), I.E.E.E., Brit. Interplanetary Soc.; mem. Am. Math. Soc., Am. Phys. Soc., Inst. Math. Statistics, Sigma Xi, Sigma Nu. Co-author: Transients in Linear Systems, 1942. Co-editor, contbr. to math. sect. Handbook of Engineering Fundamentals, 1936, 52. Home: Los Angeles, Calif. Died Oct. 1, 1976.

BARNES, KENNETH KIRTLAND, educator, agrl. engr.; b. San Jose, Calif., Nov. 16, 1921; s. Roy Merrill and Helen (Kirtland) B.; student Calif. State Poly. Coll., 1939-41; B.S. in Agrl. Engring., Ia. State U., 1947, M.S. in Agrl. Engring., 1948, Ph.D., 1951; m. Elizabeth Anderson, Aug. 24, 1946; children—Ricky Sue, Roy Merrill II. Instr., Iowa State U., 1948-50, prof., 1952-59; asst. prof. Purdue U., 1950-52; prof. agrl. engring. U. Ariz., 1959-77, head dept., 1960-71, head dept. soils, water and engring., 1972-77; spl. research mgmt. agrl. machines, machines for vegetable harvesting. Served with AUS, 1943-46. Registered profl. engr., Iowa, Calif., Ariz. Fellow Am. Soc. Agrl. Engrs. (chmn. power and machinery div. 1960-61, Pacific Coast region 1963-64, chmn. edn. and research div. 1968-69, dir. edn. and research div. 1969-71, v.p. 1971-74, pres. elect 1977), Engrs. Council for Profl. Devel. (dir. 1972); mem. Am. Soc. Engring. Edn., Nat. Soc. Profl. Engrs., AAAS, Sigma Xi, Phi Kappa Phi, Tau Beta Pi, Pi Mu Epsilon, Gamma Sigma Delta, Alpha Zeta. Co-author: Soil and Water Conservation Engineering, 3d edit., 1981; Elementary Soil and Water Engineering, 1957, 2d edit., 1971. Home: Tucson, Ariz. Died July 13, 1977; buried Evergreen Cemetery, Tucson.

BARNES, MILFORD EDWIN, physician, prof. of pub. health; b. Columbus Juction, Ia., Nov. 28, 1883; s. Rev. John Albert and Mary Emaline (Sharp) B.; A.B., Monmouth Coll., 1905; B.S., U. of Chicago, 1912; M.D., Rush Med. Coll. (U. of Chicago), 1914; certificate London (Eng.) Sch. of Tropical Medicine, 1919; Dr.P.H., Sch. of Hygiene and Pub. Health, Johns Hopkins, 1925; m. Mary Emma Robinson, Feb. 24, 1916; children—Milford Edwin, Mary Margaret. Interne Cook County Hosp. and St. Joseph's Hosp., Chicago, 1914-16; physician in pub. health work since 1916; field dir. under internat. health div. of Rockefeller Foundation, 1916-30, as director for Siam, with service also in Ceylon and Java, 1916-25, director for Siam and Straits Settlements, 1925-26; director of training station for health officers in Ohio, 1927-29, in Michigan, 1929-30; professor and head of dept. of hygiene and preventive medicine, State U. Ia., 1930-52, also dir. U., dept. health; dir. Ia. State Hygienic Lab., 1930-43, cons. dir. 1943-52; mem. Ia. State Bd. Health, 1950-55. Decorated Order of the Crown and Order of the White Elephant by King of Siam, Diplomate Am. Bd. Preventive Med. and Pub. Health. Fellow Royal Soc. Tropical Med.; (fellow) A.M.A., Am. Pub. Health Assn. (governing counsel), 1941-46); mem. A.A.A.S., Am. Soc. Tropical Med. (gov. council, 1945-49), Brit. Med. Assn., Natural Hist. Soc. of Siam, Ia., Tuberculosis Assn. (pres., 1936), Conf. of Profs. of Preventive Med. (nat. chmn., 1946-47), Alpha Omega Alpha, Sigma Xi, Delta Omega (nat. pres., 1939). Presbyterian. Contbr. articles on pub. health and preventable diseases to jours. Home: Iowa City, Ia. *

BARNES, RICHARD HENRY, educator; b. San Diego, June 29, 1911; s. Willard Gray and Nell (Tribby) B.; A.B., San Diego State Coll., 1933; Ph.D., U. Minn., 1940; m. Marjorie Ironside, Mar. 24, 1942; children—Kyle, Marjorie Anne, Lisa. Research chemist Scripps Metabolic Clinic, La Jolla, Calif., 1933-37; teaching asst., then instr., asst. prof. U. Minn., 1937-44; dir. biochem. research, asso. dir. research Sharp & Dohme Research Labs., 1944-56; dean Grad. Sch. Nutrition, Cornell U., 1956-73, James Jamison prof. nutrition, 1973-76, prof. emeritus, 1976; hon. prof. biochemistry Rutgers U., 1948-56. Adv. council Masonic Med. Research Labs., Utica, N.Y. Mem. Food and Nutrition Bd. NRC-Nat. Acad. Scis., 1969-75. Bd. dirs. Fedn. Am. Socs. Exptl. Biology, 1968-70, 72-75, pres., 1973-74. Fellow AAAS, N.Y. Acad. Scis., Am. Inst. Nutrition (pres. 1968-69), Am. Nutrition Soc.; mem. Am. Chem. Soc. (chmn. div. biol. chemistry 1951-53), Am. Soc. Biol. Chemists, Soc. Exptl. Biology and Medicine, Nutrition Soc. (Britain), Group European Nutritionists, Sigma Xi. Editorial bd. Jour. Nutrition, 1948-51, editor, 1959-69. Contbr. profl. jours. Home: San Diego, Calif. Died Nov. 16, 1978.

BARNES, ROBERT GAYLORD, assn. exec.; b. Battle Creek, Mich., Oct. 18, 1914; s. George Emerson and Myrtle Kendall (Montague) B.; grad. Haverford Sch., 1933; A.B., Princeton U., 1937, postgrad., 1938-39; Yen-ching U., 1937-38; M.A., Yale U., 1942; m. Natalie Jane Stirling, Apr. 10, 1942; children—George Emerson, Jane Stirling (Mrs. Newby). Instr. Yale, part-time 1940-42; spl. asst. to dir. European Affairs Dept. State, 1945-47, chief policy reports staff, 1948-51, dep. dir. Exec. Secretariat, 1951-52; apptd. to permanent internat. staff NATO, 1952; adviser to sec. state various internat. confs., 1949-52; dep. exec. sec. NATO, 1953-55; sec. Four Power and Nine Power confs. in Paris, 1954; dir., exec. secretariat Dept. State, 1955-56, spl. asst. mut. security affairs, 1956-59; counselor embassy, Ankara, Turkey, 1959-62, minister-counselor, dep. chief mission, 1962-64; ambassador to Jordan, 1964-66; internat. affairs adviser Mobil Oil Corp., N.Y.C., 1966-67, mgr. internat. govt. relations, 1967-73; asso. dir. Am.-Arab Assn. Commerce and Industry, 1973-74, exec. dir., 1975-77. Bd. dirs. Middle East Inst., Princeton-in-Asia. Served AUS, 1942-45. Mem. Phi Beta Kappa. Presbyterian. Club: Princeton (N.Y.C.). Home: Dobbs Ferry, N.Y. Died Oct. 24, 1977.

BARNES, VIOLA FLORENCE, prof. history; b. Albion, Neb., Aug. 28, 1885; d. Dr. Cass Grove and Isabella (Smith) Barnes; A.B., U. of Neb., 1909, A.M., 1910, LL.D., 1941; Mus.B., U. of Neb. Sch. of Music, 1913; student Harvard U., summer, 1914, U. of Wis., 1915; Ph.D., Yale U., 1919; summer work at Williamstown Inst. of Internat. Relations, 1924; research in Archives Nationales, Paris, 1925 and later (two years) research in Public Record Office and British Museum, London. Instr. history, U. of Neb., 1913-16, and summer, 1921; instr. Mt. Holyoke Coll., 1919-20, asst. prof. history, Mount Holyoke, 1920-24, asso. prof., 1924-33; asso. prof. history, Smith Coll., 1933; prof. history, Mt. Holyoke Coll., since 1933; chmn. dept. hist., 1939-42, Fellow Royal Hist. Soc.; mem. Berkshire Hist. Conf. (pres. 1933-38); Am. Hist. Assn., Miss. Valley Hist. Assn., Phi Beta Kappa, Kappa Kappa Gamma. Awarded univ. scholarship, U. of Neb., 1909-10, univ. fellowship, 1910-11, teaching fellowship, U. of Neb., 1911-13, Currier fellowship, Yale U., 1916-17; Susan Rhoda Cutler fellowship, Yale U., 1917-19; Alice Freeman Palmer memorial fellowship, Am. Assn. Univ. Women, 1926-27; John Simon Guggenheim memorial fellowship, 1930-31; Am. Council of Learned Socs. grant, 1929; Social Scis. Research Council grant, 1933, 49. Cited one of the 100 "outstanding career women" in U.S. by the Woman's Centennial Congress, Nov. 1940. Democrat. Author: The Domiinion of New England, 1923; Chapters in Commonwealth History of Massachusetts, Vols. I and II, 1928-29, and in Essays in Colonial History, 1931. Co-editor: (with Leonard W. Labaree and Stanley M. Pargellis) Essays in Colonial History, 1931. Articles in Dictionary of Am. Biography and in Dictionary of Am. History. Contbr. to mags. and hist. socs. Home: South Hadley, Mass. *

BARNES, WALTER, educator; b. Barnesville, O., July 29, 1880; s. James William and Martha Ann (Dew) B.; A.B., W.Va. U., 1905; A.M., Harvard, 1911; Ph.D., N.Y. Univ., 1930; Litt.D., W.Va. Wesleyan Coll., 1935; m. Phyllis Winchester, June 15, 1911. Teacher, prin. and supt. schs.; head dept. of English, Glenville (W-Va.) Normal Sch., 1907-14; head dept. of English and dean of Coll., Fairmont State Coll., 1914-28; prof. English, New York U., 1928-47, retired 1948. Member State Bd. Education, W.Va., 1914-20; teacher and lecturer summers, U. of Pittsburgh, U. of Pa., U. of Chicago, New York U., Univ. of Wash., Stanford U. Formerly editor of W.Va. Sch. Jour. and lit. editor W.Va. Rev. Mem. Nat. Council Teachers of English (pres. 1932-33), W.Va. Ednl. Assn. (pres. 1921), Assn. for Arts in Childhood (pres. 1938-39), Phi Kappa Psi, Phi Delta Kappa, Phi Beta Kappa. Author: English in the Country School, 1913; An Easy Primer, 1918; New Democracy in the Teaching of English, 1923; The Children's Poets, 1924; English for American High Schools, 1931; The Photoplay as Literary Art, 1936; Contemporary Children's Poetry, 1938. Contbr. chapter on language to Burton's Supervision of the Elementary Subjects, 1929. Editor: Palgrave's Golden Treasury, 1915; Types of Children's Literature, 1920; The Crisis (by Churchill), 1921; Boys Life of Mark Twain, 1929. General editor: Realm of Reading (6 volumes), 1940-41; The Teacher Speaks, 1949. Home: Fairmont, W.Va. *

BARNES, BROTHER WILLIAM HUBERT, coll. pres.; b. Portsmouth, Eng., Nov. 11, 1909; s. Thomas Joseph and Ellen Josephine (Walsh) B.; A.B., Nat. U. Ireland, 1926; Dottore in Lettere, Royal U., Rome, Italy, 1942. Entered the Congregation of Christian Bros., of Ireland, 1931; instr. St. Joseph's Coll., Ledsham, Cheshire, Eng., 1936-39; instr. Istituto Marcantonio Colonna, Rome, 1939-47; prof. English, charge dept. Iona Coll., New Rochelle, N.Y., 1947-53, chmn. dept. lang. and lit., 1952-53, trustee 1952-79, sec. bd. trustees 1953, pres., 1953-79. Home: New Rochelle, N.Y. Died Jan. 23, 1979.

BARNES, WILLIAM WRIGHT, clergyman, educator; b. Toisnot (now Elm City), Wilson County, N.C., Feb. 28, 1883; s. Wright (M.D.) and Nettie Ralph (Bridgers) B.; A.B., A.M., Wake Forest (N.C.) Coll., 1904, D.D., 1934; Th.M., Southern Baptist Theol. Sem., Louisville, Ky., 1909, Th.D., 1913; studied U. of Chicago and Columbia; m. Ethel Lee Dalrymple, Oct. 20, 1909; children— William Wright, Archibald Dalrymple. Ordained Bapt. minister, 1904; prin. pub. sch., Saratoga, N.C., 1905-06; prin. Cuban-Am. Coll. (mission sch.), Havana, Cuba, 1909-12, also pastor English-speaking portion Calvary Bapt. Ch. there; prof. ch. history, Southwestern Bapt. Theol. Sem., Seminary Hill, Texas, 1913-46; research professor in Baptist history since 1946; also stated pulpit supply various chs.; chmn. faculty, Sch. of Theology of the Seminary. Ten times elected moderator Tarrent County (Tex.) Assn. Mem. Am. Soc. Ch. History, Am. Bapt. Hist. Soc., Am. Research Soc., Sons of Confederate Vets., Tex. Bapt. Hist. Soc. (pres.), Southern Bapt. Hist. Soc. (v.p.). Mason Grand Chaplain Grand Council Royal and Select Masters of Tex., 1923; Grand Prelate Commandery of K.T. of Tex., 1941. Author: The Southern Baptist Convention—A Study in the Development of Ecclesiology, 1934. Home: Ft. Worth, Tex.

BARNETT, LINCOLN KINNEAR, author; b. N.Y.C., Feb. 12, 1909; s. Leon H. and Jessie (Kinnear) B.; A.B., Princeton, 1929; B.Litt., Columbia, 1931, M.S., 1932; m. Hildegarde Harris, Oct. 10, 1935; children—Timothy Lincoln, Robert Morgan. Reporter, N.Y. Herald Tribune, 1932-37; staff writer, war corr., asso. editor Life mag., 1937-47; contbr. leading magazines, 1947-79. Trustee Westport (N.Y.) Library Assn., 1953-79. Guggenheim fellow, 1950; recipient journalism Alumni award Columbia, 1960. Mem. SAR, Sigma Delta Chi. Club: Princeton (N.Y.C.). Author: The Universe and Dr. Einstein (Nat. Book award spl. citation 1950), 1949; Writing on Life, 1952; The World We Live In (Benjamin Franklin mag. award 1953, George Westinghouse Sci. Writing award, 1953, Christopher award 1953), 1955; The Epic of Man (Benjamin Franklin mag. award 1956), 1956; The Wonders of Life on Earth, 1960; The Treasure of Our Tongue, 1964. Home: Westport, N.Y. Died Sept. 8, 1979.

BARNEY, KEITH RICHARD, army officer; b. Springfield, Vt., July 17, 1904; s. Franklin Jr. and Julia (Hayes) B.; grad. Phillips Exeter Acad., 1921; B.S., U.S. Mil. Acad., 1926; C.E., Cornell U., 1928-29; student Army Engr. Sch., 1931-32, Indsl. Coll. Armed Forces, 1949-50; m. Frances McClymonds, June 18, 1929; 1 son, Keith Richard, Commd. 2d lt. C.E., U.S. Army, 1926, advanced through grades to maj. gen., 1956; prof. mil. sci. and tactics Mich. Coll. Mining and Technology, 1938-40; comdg. officer 1120th Engr. Group ETO, World War II; dist. engr., Kansas City, Mo., 1953-55; dir. installations Office Dep. Chief of Staff for Logistics, Dept. Army, 1955-58; div. engr., U.S. Army Engr. Div., Mo. River, 1958-60; dep. chief engrs. Dept. of Army, 1960-62; ret. 1962. Decorated Silver Star, Legion of Merit, D.S.M., Legion of Honor; Croix de Guerre with palms (France). Fellow Am. Soc. C.E. Author: History of Springfield, Vt. Home: Arlington, Va. Died Jan. 12, 1977; interred Arlington Nat. Cemetery.

BARNEY, W(INFIELD) S(UPPLY), educator; born Washington, N.H., Nov. 16, 1883; s. Supply and Mary Jane (Thissell) B.; A.B., Dartmouth Coll., 1905; student Harvard Grad. Sch., 1905-06; A.M., Hobart Coll., 1911; student U. of Grenoble, France, 1911; Ph.D., Syracuse U., 1916; m. Minnie Ola Drury, Sept. 9, 1907; children—Winfield Supply, Marshall Hobart, John Ervin, Francis Penn, Mary Elizabeth. High sch. prin., Canaan, N.H., 1905-06; instr. of physics, Hobart Coll., 1907-11, instr. Romance langs., 1911-14, prof. French, 1914-15; prof. and head dept. Romance langs., Gettysburg Coll., 1916-18; prof. and head dept. Spanish, Ohio Univ., 1918-19. Prof. and head dept. Romance langs., Woman's Coll. U. of N.C. since 1919, dir. grad. work 1923-32, asst. dir. summer sch., 1929-33. Chmn.

Southern states of Modern Fgn. Lang. Study, 1924-28. Mem. Modern Lang. Assn. Am. Nat. Fedn. Modern Lang. Teachers, Am. Assn. Teachers of Spanish, Am. Assn. Teachers French, South Atlantic Modern Lang. Assn. (founder and 1st pres. 1929-31), N.C. Edn. Assn., Sigma Alpha Epsilon (mem. nat. com. on scholarship), Phi Beta Kappa (pres.). Presbyterian (trustee). Club: Civitan. Author: Practical French Review Grammar, 1940; Corneille's Comedies as a Mirror of Polite Society in First Half of 17th Century, 1916. Editor: Merimee's Colomba, 1916; Loti's Pecheur d'Islande, 1922; Daudet's Le Petit Chose, 1925; Premier Livre de Lecture, 1928. Home: Greensboro, N.C. *

BARNHART, EARL WINGERT, commercial edn.; b. Chambersburg, Pa., Sept. 15, 1882; s. Moses Gregory and Elizabeth (Wingert) B.; grad. high sch., Stockton, Calif., and business coll.; Litt. B., U. of Calif., 1909; M.A. Teachers Coll., Columbia University, 1934; m. Emmeline Handel Nelson, of Berkeley, Calif., Jan. 4, 1909 (died Oct. 20, 1922); children—Edwin Norton, Nelson Gregory; m. 2d, Florence A. Sparks, of New York City, February 9, 1924 (died March 13, 1937); m. 3d, Regina E. Groves, of Madison, Wisconsin, July 11, 1937. Teacher high schs. and State Normal Sch., Calif., until 1913; head commercial dept. Berkeley High Sch., 1913-18; superv. coml. teacher training, U. of Calif., 1919-20; in charge coml. teacher training, U. of Calif., summers 1916-20; supervisor commercial training, 12th Dist., Fed. Bd. Vocational Edn. Rehabilitation service, 1919, 20-21; chief of Coml. Edn. Service of Bd. Vocational Edn., Washington, D.C. Feb. 15, 1921-34; chief of Commercial Edn. Service, Office of Education, Department of the Interior, since October 12, 1934; instructor Teachers Coll. (Columbia Univ.), summers 1924-34; lecturer in commercial edn., George Washington U., 1929-33, Coll. City of New York, 1933-34. Mem. Am. Vocational Assn., Nat. Fed. Coml. Teachers, N.E.A., Pi Omicron Phi, Phi Delta Kappa, etc. Republican. Mason. Home: Berkeley, Calif., and Washington, D.C. *

BARNSTEAD, WINIFRED GLEN, prof. library sci.; b. Halifax, Nova Scotia, Oct. 6, 1884; d. John H. and Harriet Tupper (Creelman) B.; B.A., Dalhousie U., 1906; unmarried. Prin. Musquodoboit Harbour Sch., Nova Scotia, 1906-07; asst. cataloguer, Princeton (N.J.) U. Library, 1907-09; chief cataloguing div., Toronto (Can.) Pub. Library, 1909-28; instr. in charge, Ontario Library Sch., 1916-17, lecturer in cataloguing, 1918-27; prof. of library science and dir. of the U. Toronto Library Sch., 1928-51, dir. emeritus since 1952. Mem. A.L.A. (membership com., Ontario rep.), Canadian Library Assn. (chmn. constitution com., com. on scholarships and bursaries), Ont. Library Assn. (v.p., mem. council, chmn. certification and constn. coms., 1st hon. pres.), Bibliog. Soc. Can. (councillor), Ont. Regional Group of Cataloguers (chairman). Club: University Women's. Contbr. articles to professional jours., leaflets and monographs on librarianship. Home: Toronto, Ont., Can. *

BARON, JOSE T., diplomat; b. Havana, Cuba, July 6, 1883; s. Carlos and Clotilde (Valdes) B.; student Colegio La Gran Antilla, Havana, 1890-92; Colegio de Belen, Havana, 1892-95; B.S., Instituto de Segunda Ensenanza, Havana, 1900; LL.D., Universidad de la Habana, 1911; m. Catherine Shea, Aug. 4, 1926; 1 dau., Catalina. Officer Dept. of Interior, Cuban Govt., Havana, 1900-09, Dept. of Agr., Commerce and Labor, 1909-10, Dept. of Communications, 1910-13; sec. to vice pres. of Cuba, 1913-17; 2d sec. Cuban Legation at Panama, 1917-18; 2d sec. of embassy, Washington, D.C., 1919, 1st sec., 1922-29; minister counselor, Washington, D.C., 1929-47; charge d'affaires ad-interim, embassy, Washington, D.C., on numerous occasions. Served as sec. of commn., 6th Internat. Am. Conf., Havana, 1928; alternate del. Cuba, Inter-Am. Economic and Financial Council, Washington, D.C., 1940; ambassador Orgn. Am. States, 1956; mem. Cuban Del., IV Inter-Am. Meeting on Consulation; rep. Commemorative Meeting, Pan-Am. Congress of 1826, Panama, 1956. Decorated Grand Officer, Nat. Order of Merit Carlos Manuel de Cespedes, 1944; Grand Officer, Nat. Order of Merit, Cuban Red Cross, 1945; Cuban Ministry of State's Distinguished Medal, 1943; Commander, National Order Al Mérito of Ecuador, 1940; Grand Cross Vasco Nuñez de Balboa, Panama. Roman Catholic. Clubs: Union (Havana); Chevy Chase (Washington). Home: Washington.

BARON, SYDNEY STUART, pub. relations and mgmt. cons. co. exec.; b. N.Y.C., May 30, 1920; s. Hyman C. and Anne (Stuart) B.; B.S., St. John's U., 1942; m. Sylvia Schreibman, Oct. 23, 1938; children—Barbara Joyce Baron Balsam, Eric, Richard, Daniel Henry. Practice as publicist, 1940-50; chmn. bd. Sydney S. Baron and Co. Inc., N.Y.C., 1952-80; dir. Shopwell Supermarkets, Inc.; pub. relations and mgmt. cons. Aluminum Co. Am., Am. Can Co., Am. Ship Bldg. Co., Atlantic Cement Co., Inc., Japan Bearing Indsl. Assn., Electronic Industries Assn. Japan, Columbia U., Commodities Exchange Inc., Panax Corp., Reliance Group, Republic of China, Republic of S. Africa, others; instr. polit. sci. N.Y. U., 1954-58; Dep. commr. N.Y.C. Dept. Marine and Aviation, 1950; dep. commr., dir. promotion N.Y.C. Dept. Commerce, 1951. Bd. dirs. Nat. Assn. Rgtarded Children, N.Y.C. Big Bros. Movement; chmn. bd. dirs. Beth Jacob Schs., N.Y.C., 1956-80; trustee Maimonides Hosp., N.Y.C. Recipient Civic Merit award N.Y.C., 1951; certificate commendation Jewish War Vets. U.S.A., 1960. Mem. A.I.M. (pres.'s council), Pub. Relations Soc. Am., U.S. C. of C., Am. Mgmt. Assn., Soc. of Silurians. Democrat. Mason. Clubs: Board Room, Lone Star Boat, Friars (N.Y.C.); Internat., George Town (Washington); Fenway Golf (White Plains, N.Y.). Author: One Whirl, 1942; Men without Humor, 1944; The Bells Ring Loudly, 1946. Contbr. numerous articles to popular mags. Producer Broadway stage shows including Tambourines to Glory. Home: Scarsdale, N.Y. Died Oct. 19, 1980.

BAROODY, WILLIAM JOSEPH, research inst. exec.; b. Manchester, N.H., Jan. 29, 1916; s. Joseph Assad and Helen (Hasney) B.; B.A., St. Anselm's Coll., Manchester, N.H., 1936, LL.D. (hon.), 1965; postgrad U. N.H., 1937-38, Am. U., 1938; m. Nabeeha Marion Ashooh, Oct. 15, 1935; children—Anne Mary (Mrs. John G. Gallagher), William Joseph, Joseph D., Helene (Mrs. Michael Payne), Michael E., Maryfran (Mrs. Patrick J. Cummiskey), Katherine Jane. Asst. statistician N.H. Unemployment Compensation Div., 1937-40, supr. fiscal, research and legislative planning sects., 1941-44; dir. statis. div. N.H. War Finance Com., 1943-44; research asso. N.H. Legislative Commn. on Disability Benefits, 1940-44; chief research and statistics div., readjustment allowance service VA, Washington, 1946-49; exec. sec. com. on econ. security U.S. C. of C., asso. editor Am. Econ. Security, 1950-53; exec. v.p. Am. Enterprise Assn. (now Am. Enterprise Inst. for Pub. Policy Research), 1954-62, pres., 1962-78; counsellor, chmn. devel. com. Am. Enterprise Inst., 1978-80. Mem. U.S. Catholic Bishops' Adv. Council, 1973-75; past mem. Am. Revolution Bicentennial Adv. Council. Bd. overseers Hoover Instn. Stanford U. 1960-80; chmn. bd. Woodrow Wilson Internat. Center for Scholars; mem. exec. com. Georgetown Center for Strategic and Internat. Studies; trustee Lehrman Inst.; bd. advisers DeSales Grad. Sch. Theology; mem. adv. council Va. Poly. Inst. and State U. at Blacksburg; bd. dirs. Herbert Hoover Birthplace Found., Near East Found., Georgetown U.; bd. cons. Nat. War Coll., 1973-75; treas., trustee Inst. for Social Sci. Research, Washington, 1957-80; trustee St. Anselm's Coll., 1957-80; adv. com. Social devel. and world peace U.S. Cath. Conf., 1976-79; vis. com. Gerald R. Ford Inst. Public Service, Albion Coll.; bd. dirs. Govt. Research Corp. Served to lt. (j.g.) USNR, 1944-45. Mem. Acad. Polit. Sci., John Carroll Soc. Clubs: K.C.; Army-Navy, Carlton, F Street (Washington); Belle Haven Country (Alexandria, Va.). Author articles on pub. policy, ecumenism, Eastern rites. Home: Alexandria, Va. Died July 28, 1980.

BARR, JOHN ANDREW, lawyer; b. Akron, Ind., Sept. 10, 1908; s. Earl Ray and Bertha (Mattix) B.; student DePauw U., Greencastle, Ind., 1925-27; LL.B., Ind. U., 1930, LL.D., 1973; LL.D., Ill. Coll., 1962; m. Louise Stentz, Oct. 28, 1933; children—John Robert, George Louis, Richard Allen, Barbara Ann. Admitted to Ind. bar, 1930, Ill. bar, 1933; in practice of law, Gary, Ind., 1930-33, 35-38, Chgo., 1933-35; with Montgomery Ward & Co., Chgo., 1938-65, v.p., sec., dir. and gen. counsel, 1949-55, pres., chmn. bd., dir., mem. exec. com., 1955-61, chmn. bd., prin. policy making officer, 1961-65; dean Grad. Sch. Mgmt., Northwestern U., 1965-75; dir. No. Trust Co., NorTrust Corp., Commonwealth Edison Co., S.C. Johnson & Son, Inc., Stewart-Warner Corp., Goldblatt Bros. Inc., Marsh & McLennan Cos., Mid-West Stock Exchange. Chmn. com. on hosp. effectiveness Dept. Health, Edn. and Welfare, 1967-68. Bd. dirs. Chgo. chpt. ARC, 1956-71, Evanston Hosp. Assn., Chgo. Hosp. Council. Recipient Distinguished Alumni service award Ind. U.; Horatio Alger award, Robins award. Mem. The Conf. Bd., Chgo. Assn. Commerce and Industry, Order of Coif, Sigma Nu, Phi Delta Phi. Episcopalian. Clubs: Economic, Chicago, Commercial, Mid-America (Chgo.); Old Elm; Indian Hill Country. Home: Wilmette, Ill. Died Jan. 16, 1979.

BARRETT, E(DWARD JOHN) BOYD, author; b. Dublin, Ireland, Oct. 29, 1883; s. John Boyd and Mary (McCarthy) B.; student Congowes Coll., Ireland, 1895-1901; A.M., National U., Ireland, 1910; Ph.D., Louvain U., Belgium, 1911; m. Anna Berkeley O'Beirne, 1931; 1 son, Eamon Boyd. Came to U.S., 1924, naturalized, 1930. Mem. British Assn. of Psychologists. Author: Shepherds in the Mist, 1949; Life Begins With Love, 1952. Contbr. to mags.; cons. psychologist. Home: Santa Cruz County, Calif. *

BARRETT, NESTOR, planning cons., journalist; b. Republic, Wash., Sept. 2, 1907; s. Thomas Francis and Catherine Elizabeth (Nestor) B.; student San Jose State Coll.; m. Margaret Mary Rose, Sept. 7, 1939; 1 stepson, Charles C. Folks. Dep. county surveyor Santa Clara County, Calif., 1927-40; planning dir. Santa Clara County Plan Commn., 1940-52; v.p. Hodges, Pierce & Co., Inc., San Francisco; partner Pierce & Co., 1952-54; photographer, columnist San Jose Mercury-News, 1941-78; instr. photography San Jose Jr. Coll., Los Gatos and Campbell, 1940-42. Mem. San Francisco Bay Area Rapid Transit Commn., 1951-57; 1st chmn. San Francisco Bay Area Council Planning Dirs. Fellow Photog. Soc. Am. (hon.; exec. v.p. 1959-63, pres. 1963-67); mem. Am. Inst. Planners (pres. Calif. chpt. 1951), Soc. Motion Picture and TV Engrs., Am. Soc. Planning Ofcls., Royal Photog. Soc. Gt. Britain (asso.), Urban Land Inst., Internat. Fedn. Housing and Town Planning. Clubs: Commonwealth, Univ. Home: San Jose, Calif. Died Nov. 12, 1978; buried Oak Hill Meml. Park, San Jose.

BARRETT, WILLIAM A., congressman; grad. Brown Prep. Sch. and St. Joseph's Coll., Phila.; 3 children. Engaged as real estate broker; mem. 79th, 81st-94th congresses from 1st Dist. Pa. Democrat. Home: Philadelphia, Pa. Died Apr. 12, 1976.

BARRIE, ERWIN SEAVER, artist, art dealer; b. Canton, O., June 3, 1886; s. Evan and Jennis Josephine (Erwin) B.; student Cornell U., 1906-10; studied landscape painting Art Inst. Chgo., 1914; m. Grace Belle Beeny, Apr. 17, 1913. Dealer Am. art, 1917—; co-founder, dir., mgr. Grand Central Art Galleries, N.Y.C., 1923—; exhbns. Art Inst. of Chgo., Grand Central Art Galleries, N.Y.C., Joslyn Art Mus., Omaha, Neb., others; works in pvt. collections The White House, Bobby Jones, Atlanta, others. Created collection Famous Golf Holes I Have Played. Dir. Am. sect. Biennial Internat. Exhbn., Venice, 1937. Recipient citation Am. Artist Profl. League. Mem. U.S. (committeeman), Am., Westchester seniors' golf assns., Greenwich Artists, Greenwich Archers, Sigma Nu. Clubs: Business Men's Art in Am. (co-founder Chgo., 1917); Royal and Ancient Golf (St. Andrews, Scotland); Tin Whistles, Pinehurst Country (Pinehurst, N.C.); Greenwich Country (gov.); Boca Raton (Fla.). Home: Greenwich CT. 06830

BARRIGER, JOHN WALKER, ry. exec.; b. Dallas, Dec. 3, 1899; s. John Walker, Jr. and Edith (Beck) B.; B.S., Mass. Inst. Tech., 1921; D.Engring. (hon.), Rose Poly. Inst., Terre Haute, Ind.; m. Elizabeth Chambers Thatcher, Sept. 25, 1926; children—John Walker, IV, Elizabeth Thatcher, Ann Biddle (Mrs. Robert R. Salyard), Stanley Huntington. With the Pa. R.R., serving principally in maintenance of way and transp. depts., 1917-27; with Kuhn, Loeb & Co., N.Y., 1927-29, Calvin Bullock & Co., N.Y., 1930-33; asso. with F.H. Prince of Boston in preparation of Prince Plan of R.R. Consolidation, 1933; chief, R.R. div., R.F.C., Washington, 1933-41; reorgn. mgr. Chgo. & Eastern Ill. R.R. Co., 1940, dir. and mem. exec. com., 1941-42; asso. dir. Div. Ry. Transport, Office Def. Transp., Washington, and Fed. mfg., Toledo, Peoria & Western R.R., 1942; v.p. Union Stockyard & Transit Co. Chgo., 1943-44; mgr. Diesel Locomotive div. Fairbanks, Morse & Co., 1944-45, reorgn. mgr., 1946; pres. Monon R.R., 1946-52; v.p. N.Y., N.H. & H.R.R. Co., 1953, Rock Island R.R., Chgo., 1953-56; pres. P. & L.E. R.R., 1956-64; pres. M.-K.-T. R.R. Co., 1965-70, chief exec. officer Boston & Me. Corp., 1971-72; spl. asst. to fed. r.r. adminstr. Fed. R.R. Adminstrn., Dept. Transp., Washington, 1973-76. Trustee Thomas Alva Edison Found. Pvt. U.S. Army, 1918. Mem. S.R., Am. Ry. Engring. Assn., Am. Soc. C.E., Am. Soc. M.E., Newcomen Soc. (trustee), Sons of Colonial Wars, Loyal Legion U.S. Republican. Presbyn. Clubs: Chicago; Racquet (St. Louis); City Tavern (Washington). Author: Super-Railroads, 1956. Contbr. articles to jours. Home: St. Louis, Mo. Died Dec. 9, 1976; interred Bellefontaine Cemetery, St. Louis.

BARRON, ALEXANDER JOHNSTON, lawyer; b. Connellsville, Pa., July 16, 1880; s. John and Margaret Clark (Johnston) B.; student Lawrenceville (N.J.) Prep. Sch., 1898; A.B., Princeton, 1902; student Harvard Law Sch., 1903-04; J.D., U. Pitts., 1905; m. Elizabeth Congdon, Sept. 26, 1907. Admitted to Pa. bar, 1905, since practiced in Pitts., now of counsel Alter, Wright & Barron; mem. bar Supreme Ct. U.S., 1909—. Sec., dir. Leechburg Mining Co., Leechburn Supply Co.; past mem., pres. Osborne Borough Council; trustee, past dir., pres. Sewickley YMCA. Served with A.E.F., France, 1918-19, in YMCA as sec. in Savoie Leave Area, as bus. mgr. Britany and Dauphine Leave Areas, div. sec. Riviera Leave Area. Mem. Am. Law Inst., Am., Pa., Allegheny County bar assns., Harvard Law Sch. Assn. Republican. Presbyn. (elder). Clubs: Law, Duquesne (Pitts.); Allegheny Country (Sewickley, Pa.); Cap and Gown (Princeton). Home: Glen Osborne Sewickley PA 15143

BARROW, ALLEN EDWARD, U.S. judge; b. Okemah, Okla., Jan. 22, 1914; s. Alfred E. and Minnie Lee (Coffelt) B.; student Okla. A&M Coll. 1935-36; B.A., U. Okla., 1936; postgrad. U. Tulsa; LL.B., Southeastern State Coll., 1942; m. Dorothy Elaine Dalton, Oct. 2, 1942; children—Allen Edward, Karla Elaine, Mary Celeste. With FBI, 1940-42; admitted to Okla. bar, 1942, also Supreme Ct. U.S.; pvt. practice, Tulsa, 1946-50, 54-62; counsel Southwestern Power Adminstrn., Dept. Interior, Tulsa, 1950-54; chief judge U.S. Dist. Ct. No. Dist. Okla., 1962-79. Adv. bd. Tulsa

Salvation Army, from 1956. Mem. bd. ARC. Served to maj. AUS, 1942-46. Recipient 1st Ann. Faculty and Alumni award U. Tulsa Coll. Law, 1975. Mem. Am., Okla. (Outstanding Service award 1959) bar assns., SAR (pres. Okla. 1954), Delta Theta Phi, Phi Eta Sigma, Sigma Chi (pres. alumni assn. 1950, Significant Sig award 1975). Democrat. Mem. Christian Ch. Home: Tulsa, Okla. Died Feb. 26, 1979.

BARROW, ROSCOE LINDLEY, educator; b. La Grange, N.C., Oct. 17, 1913; s. Zebulon Vance and Ada Elizabeth (Mewborn) B.; B.S. A.S., Lewis Inst. (now Ill. Inst. Tech.), Chgo., 1935; J.D., Northwestern U., 1938; m. Ruth Elizabeth Coberly, June 4, 1941; children—Beverly Ruth, Elizabeth Rose, Lucy Vivian, Roscoe Lindley II. Admitted to Ill. bar, 1938, Ohio bar, 1951; spl. asst. to the Atty. Gen. U.S., 1951, NLRB, 1939-40, Dept. Agr., 1940-42, O.P.A., 1942, Dept. Justice, 1945-49, 1951; staff contract termination Bur. Aero., 1944-45; prof. law U. Cin., 1949-73, acting dean, 1952-53, dean, 1953-65, Wald prof. law, 1965-73, chmn. faculty, 1970-72; vis. prof. law Hastings Coll. Law, U. Calif., 1972-73, prof. law, 1973-77. Dir. broadcast network study, FCC, 1955-57, cons., 1961-63; moderator hearings on Fairness Doctrine, Spl. House Subcom. on Investigations, 1968; cons. fed. agys.; trial examiner Ohio Civil Rights Commn., 1961-62; vis. prof. law U. N.C., summer 1962, U. Va. Law Sch., 1965-66. Served with USNR, 1942-45. Mem. Cin. Bar Assn. (pres. 1961-63). Club: Literary Club (Cin.). Author: (with Howard D. Fabing, M.D.) Epilepsy and the Law, 1956, rev. edit. 1966; (with others) Network Broadcasting, 1957. Contbr. articles to profl. publs. Home: Oakland, Calif. Died Nov. 21, 1977.

BARROWS, LUCIUS D(WELLEY), state ofcl.; b. Dover-Foxcroft, Me., Aug. 12, 1885; s. Fred D. and Ellen Louise (Dwelley) B.; student U. Me., 1903-07; m. Blanche Gordon, Sept. 3, 1913. Civil engring. student U.S. Office of Pub. Rds. and Rural Engring., 1907-08, jr. asst. engr., 1908-10; engr. clk. Mem. State Highway Dept., 1910-11, asst. state highway commr. State Me., 1911-13; asst. engr. Me. State Highway Commn., 1913-28, chief engr. since 1928. Mem. State Bd. Registration for Profl. Engrs.; sec., treas. Me. Turnpike Authority; mem. indsl. adv. counsel U. Me. Mem. Am. Soc. C.E., Me. Assn. Engrs., Good Rds. Assn., Assn. Highway Ofcls. of North Atlantic States, Sigma Alpha Epsilon. Mason (Shriner). Rotarian. Home: Augusta, Me.

BARROWS, ROBERT BREWSTER, ins. co. exec.; b. Syracuse, N.Y., Aug. 19, 1922; s. Samuel Bradford and Grace Electa (Horton) B.; grad. Mt. Hermon Sch. for Boys, 1940; B.A., Cornell U., 1948; m. Mary Kayser, Apr. 4, 1944; children—David, Barbara, Philip. With Northwestern Mut. Life Ins. Co., Milw., 1948-77, asst. mgr. residence mortgages, 1963-67, v.p. mortages, 1967-73, sr. v.p. intestments, trustee, 1973-77; trustee, pres. Northwestern Mut. Life Mortgage and Realty Investors; dir. Western Pub. Co., Wis. Electric Power Co., Allen & O'Hara Constrn. Co., Memphis. Adv. mem. Southeastern Wis. Regional Planning Commn., 1966; mem. Comprehensive Health Planning Agy., Southeastern Wis., 1971-72. Bd. dirs. Milw. Model Cities Devel. Corp., United Performing Arts Fund, U. Wis.-Milw. Found. Served with USNR, 1942-47. Mem. Mortgage Bankers Assn., Urban Land Inst. (mem. exec. council, bd. trustees 1967). Episcopalian. Club: North Shore Country (Milw.). Home: Milwaukee, Wis. Died May 20, 1977.

BARRY, CLINTON ROGERS, lawyer; b. Randolph County, Ga., Apr. 2, 1883; s. Osgood Andrew and Elizabeth Jane (Allison) B.; ed. high schs., Weatherford and Van Alstyne, Tex., until 1900; m. Corinne Leslie, Mar. 15, 1905; children—Leslie (dec.), James Allison. Began practice at Sherman, Tex., 1910; moved to McAlester, Okla., 1911; settled in Ft. Smith, Ark., 1914, and has since continued there; U.S. dist. atty., Western Dist. of Ark. since Feb. 9, 1934 to May 31, 1946; retired to reenter pvt. practice. Represented U.S. in draft appeals before draft bd. for Western Dist. of Ark., World War I. Mem. Am. and Ark. State bar assns., Sebastian Co. (Ark.) Bar Assn. (sec. 14 yrs; past pres.). Democrat. Methodist. Home: Ft. Smith, Ark.

BARRY, FRED, JR., lawyer; b. Mt. Vernon, Ohio, Mar. 2, 1920; s. Fred and Ruth (Gebhardt) B.; B.A., Kenyon Coll., 1942; LL.B., Harvard, 1949, J.D., 1969; m. Virginia Ruth Motherall, June 5, 1948; children—Douglas Alan, Barbara Anne. Admitted to Ohio bar, 1949, since practiced in Mt. Vernon; acting judge Mt. Vernon Municipal Ct., 1954-59. Chmn. bd., dir. First-Knox Nat. Bank Mt. Vernon; adv. bd. Lumbermen's Mut. Casualty Co.; dir. J.S. Ringwalt Co., Worley's, Inc., J.B. Foote Foundry Co. Trustee Kenyon Coll. Served with USAAF, 1942-45. Recipient Distinguished Service award Mt. Vernon Jr. C. of C., 1956, Outstanding Pres. award, Ohio Jr. C. of C., 1955. Mem. Am., Ohio (past mem. exec. com.), Knox County (past pres.) bar assns., Mt. Vernon Area C. of C. (past pres.), Kenyon Coll. Alumni Assn. (past pres.), Phi Kappa Sigma. Rotarian. Home: Mount Vernon, Ohio. Died Feb. 6, 1977.

BARRY, JOHN, composer; b. York, Eng., Nov. 3, 1933; s. John and Doris (Wilkinson) Prendergast; ed. St. Peter's Pub. Sch.; m. Jane Birkin, Oct. 16, 1965; 1 dau., Kate; children by previous marriage—Suzanne, Sian. Leader J. Barry 7 Pop Group; film credits include Beat Girl, Never Let Go, Mix Me a Person, The Amorous Prawn, Doctor No, From Russia with Love, The Man in the Middle, Zulu, Goldfinger (Gold Disc award), Seance in a Wet Afternoon, Four in the Morning, The Ipcress File, The Knack, Mr. Moses, Thunderball, King Rat, Born Free (Oscar award), The Chase, The Wrong Box, The Quiller Memorandum, You Only Live Twice, 1967, Deadfall, The Lion in Winter (Oscar award winner 1968); theatre credits include Passion Flower Hotel; TV credits include Elizabeth Taylor in London, Sophia Loren in Rome. Recipient Clio award, 1968. Home: London, England. Died June 1, 1979.

BARRY, JOHN G(ERALD), mining geologist; b. Boston, Mass., Apr. 9, 1884; s. William F. and Mary G. (Doyle) B.; B.S. in Mining Engring., Mass. Inst. Tech., 1907; spl. grad. work, same instn., 1916-18 and 1920; m. Alice M. Pierce, June 19, 1920; 1 son, John S(amuel). Teacher, U. of N.Dak., 1907-09, also asst. state geologist; technician Ray Cons. Copper Co., 1909-10; geol. and mining exams., U.S. and Mexico, principally under J. E. Spurr and Tonopah Mining Co., 1910-16; teacher and grad. student Mass. Inst. Tech., 1916-20; chief geologist Am. Smelting & Refining Co., 1920-24; cons. practice since 1924; pres. Tex. Coll. of Mines and Metallurgy, 1931-34; pvt. cons. practice since 1934. Mem. 2d Corps Cadets Mass. Inst. Tech., 1901-04; commd. 1st lt. of engrs., Res., Sept. 29, 1917; maj. C.W.S., July 13, 1918; lt. col., Feb. 14, 1919; in charge gas defense, C.W.S., A.E.F.; citation from Gen. Pershing. Mem. Am. Assn. Engrs., Am. Inst. Mining and Metall. Engrs., Mining and Metall. Soc. America, Soc. Am. Mil. Engrs., Am. Geog. Soc., A.A.A.S., Am. Mining Congress. Mason. Home: El Paso, Tex. *

BARSTOW, RICHARD, choreographer, prod., director; born Ashtabula, Ohio; son of Thomas Arthur and Ada Mary (Hatton) B.; studied with pvt. tutors. Began show bus. career, 1916; danced, appeared stock companies on tour, Mont., Okla., Tex., 1918-21; appeared Midnight Frolic, Chgo., 1924-25, The Palace, N.Y.C., also on tour U.S.; featured musical comedies, Australia, then movie houses U.S., London and on tour Europe, 1928-30; appeared with sister The Palace, N.Y.C., 1930-39; single dancing act Radio City Music Hall, N.Y.C., Palmer House, Chgo., 1939; choreographer motion pictures Buck Benny Rides Again, Love Thy Neighbor, Swing Fever, also road company musical Helzapoppin'; prod. Olsen and Johnson show Carnival Night Club, 1946; choreographer, prod. shows including Barefoot Boy with Cheek, Tonight at 8:30, New Faces of 1952, revival of Sally, others; choreographer Municipal Opera, St. Louis, 1948; choreographer Greatest Show on Earth, Ringling Bros. Barnum and Bailey Circus, 1949-51, full director, 1952-78; director 3 summer tent theatres simultaneously, 1957; special writer, choreographer, stager Colgate Comedy Hour, numerous other TV shows; prod., choreographer, dir. revues Shooting High, What's My Act, Toast of the Town; motion pictures include Girl Next Door, New Faces, Greatest Show on Earth, A Star is Born; staged, prod., dir. choreographed with sister Champagne on Ice, London Hippodrome, 1953; prod., wrote, dir., staged with sister Motorama shows Gen. Motors, N.Y.C. and on tour, also Powerama, Chgo., 1955; dir. Theater-in-the Round, mus. tent show, Westbury, L.I., summer 1956, 57; author, producer, dir. March of Dimes show Waldorf Astoria, N.Y.C., 1958; dir., choreographer appearances of Judy Garland, N.Y.C., Chgo., San Francisco, 1959; staged, directed Song of Norway, N.Y.C., 1959, Annie Get Your Gun, Jones Beach, L.I., N.Y., 1977-78; staged shows for Ray Price and Brenda Lee; dir., stager, choreographer Ringling Bros. Barnum & Bailey Circus, 1952-78; dir., writer 1st Symphony of Fashion, St. Louis, 1948-49; dir. summer theatres; song writer; owner RICHBAR Pub. Co., Nashville. Recipient Circus Oscar. Originated toe skate, with sister tap toe dancing on a staircase. Home: New York, N.Y. Died May 2, 1981.

BARTELMEZ, GEORGE WILLIAM, univ. prof.; b. N.Y. City, Mar. 23, 1885; s. Theodore B. and Caroline (Osten) B.; B.S., New York U., 1906; Ph.D., U. of Chicago, 1910; m. Erminnie Hollis, of Bailey's Bay, Bermuda, Mar. 31, 1912 (dec.); children—Caroline Jane, Erminnie Hollis, Theodore; m. 2d, Leila Arnold, Sept. 23, 1936. Asst. in zoölogy, New York Univ., 1906-07; fellow in zoölogy, New Univ. of Chicago, 1907-09; asso. in anatomy, 1910-11, instr., 1911-15, asso. prof. 1919-29, prof., 1929—. Mem. Am. Assn. Anatomists (2d v.p.), Am. Assn. Zoölogists, Phi Beta Kappa, Gamma Alpha; hon. fellow Chicago Gynecol. Soc. One of authors of The Nature of the World and of Man, 1926. Home: 5844 Stony Island Ave., Chicago, Ill. *

BARTH, ALAN, editorial writer; b. N.Y.C., Oct. 21, 1906; s. Jacob and Flora (Barth) Lauchheimer; Ph.B., Yale, 1929; Nieman fellow, Harvard, 1948-49; m. Adrienne Mayer, July 1, 1939; children—Flora Barth Wolf, Andrew. Reporter Beaumont (Tex.) Enterprise, 1936; editorial writer Beaumont Jour., 1937-38; Washington corr. McClure Newspaper Syndicate, 1938-41; editorial asst. Sec. Treasury, 1941-42; editor reports O.W.I., 1942-43; editorial writer Washington Post, 1943-73; vis. prof. govtl. affairs U. Calif., Berkeley, 1958-59. Recipient Sigma Delta Chi award, distinguished service Am. journalism, 1947; Am. Newspaper Guild award, distinguished editorial writing, 1948, Sidney Hillman Found., 1952; Oliver Wendell Holmes Bill of Rights award, 1964; Lasker Civil Liberties award, 1967; others. Mem. Am. Acad. Arts and Scis. Author: The Loyalty of Free Men, 1951; Government By Investigation, 1955; The Price of Liberty, 1961; Heritage of Liberty, 1965; Prophets with Honor, 1974. Contbr. articles to popular mags. Home: Washington, D.C. Died Nov. 20, 1979; buried Washington Hebrew Congregation Cemetery.

BARTH, LESTER GEORGE, biologist; b. Detroit, June 29, 1905; s. Charles and Mary (Schroeder) B.; B.A., Wayne U., 1926; M.A., U. Mich., 1928; Ph.D., U. Chgo., 1930; m. Lucena Jaeger, June 9, 1948. NCR fellow, Naples, Italy, Berlin, Germany, 1930-31; Nat. Edn. fellow U. Cal., 1941; prof. biology Columbia, from 1950; mem. staff, also trustee Marine Biol. Lab., Woods Hole, Mass. Mem. Internat. Inst. Embryology (Amsterdam), Soc. Growth and Devel., Am. Soc. Zoologists. Author: Embryology, 1950, 54; The Energetics of Development, 1954. Translator: (French) Chemical Embryology, 1950. Asso. editor Physiol. Zoology, 1945-55. Home: Woods Hole, Mass. Died Feb. 25, 1979.

BARTHES, ROLAND, author; b. Cherbourg, France, Nov. 12, 1915; s. Louis and Henriette (Binger) B.; Licencie es Lettres, Diplome d'Etudes Superieures Paris, Sorbonne. Prof. letters, fellow Nat. Center Sci. Research, Paris 1952-59; dir. d'Etudes a l'Ecole des Hautes Etudes, Sorbonne, 1962, vis. prof. Johns Hopkins, 1967. Author: On Racine, 1964; Elements of Semiology, 1967; Writing Degree Zero, 1967. Address: Paris, France. Died Mar. 26, 1980.

BARTLETT, DEWEY FOLLETT, U.S. senator, former gov. Okla.; b. Marietta, Ohio, Mar. 28, 1919; s. David A. and Jessie (Follett) B.; grad. Lawrenceville (N.J.) Sch., 1938; B.S. in Geol. Engring., Princeton (N.J.) U., 1942; m. Ann C. Smith, Apr. 2, 1945; children—Dewey Follett, Joan Chilton, Mike Hopkins. Partner, Keener Oil Co., Tulsa, 1951-71; pres. Dewey Supply Co. (Okla.), 1953-56; owner-operator ranch in Wagoner County (Okla.), 1958-64, in Tulsa County, from 1958, in Delaware County, from 1968; mem. Okla. Senate from Tulsa County, 1962-66; gov. of Okla., 1967-71; then U.S. senator until 1979. Bd. dirs. Tulsa County chpt. ARC. Served as pilot USMCR, World War II. Decorated Air medal. Mem. Ind. Petroleum Assn. Am. (dir.), Okla. Ind. Producers Assn. (dir.). Republican. Roman Catholic. Home: Washington, D.C. Died Mar. 1, 1979.

BARTLETT, FORD, engring. exec.; b. Bklyn., Aug. 28, 1905; s. Frederick Lorenzo and Isabelle Louise (Whitbeck) B.; C.E., Bklyn. Poly. Inst., 1925; m. Anna Louise Shields, Aug. 28, 1926; 1 dau., Judith (Mrs. Harvey T. Harrison). Civil engineer Frederick L. Bartlett, 1923-32; partner Howard T. Lockwood and Cletus Kessler, 1932-34; with Lockwood, Kessler & Bartlett. Inc., Syosset, N.Y., from 1934—, chmn.; chmn., dir. Viatech, Inc.; trustee Lincoln Savs. Bank. Trustee emeritus Poly. Inst. N.Y., Hofstra U. Registered profl. engr., Tenn. Fellow Am. Congress Surveying and Mapping, ASCE; mem. N.Y. State Soc. Profl. Engrs., Am. Soc. Photogrammetry, Soc. Am. Mil. Engrs., Chi Epsilon, Tau Beta Pi. Clubs: Union League, Sky; Lyford Cay (Nassau, Bahamas). Home: New York, N.Y. Died Apr. 6, 1979.

BARTON, ARTHUR GIPSON, landscape architect; b. Denver, Oct. 2, 1907; s. Archilles Arthur and Eva Viola (Campbell) B.; B.S. in Landscape Design, U. Calif., Berkeley, 1929; m. Lucile Beach Brown, Aug. 26, 1930. Draftsman Yoch & Council, 1929-30; mgr. landscape dept. Theodore Payne Nursery, 1930-35; landscape architect Los Angeles County, 1935-40; pvt. practice landscape architecture, Glendale, Calif., 1940-42; farm advisor 4-H clubs Los Angles County, 1943-46; pvt. practice gen. landscape archtl. work. Glendale, from 1946—; vis. tchr. Calif. Poly. U., Pomona; bd. dirs. Glendale Beautiful, Glendale Beautification, Los Angeles Beautiful. Scoutmaster Boy Scouts Am. Fellow Am. Soc. Landscape Architects (past pres. Calif. chpt.); mem. Calif. Council Landscape Architects (pres., bd. dirs.), Nat. Am. Soc. Landscape Architects (v.p., trustee), Calif. PTA (hon. life), Architects of Glendale (hon.), Planning and Conservation League, Save-the-Redwoods League, Calif. Roadside Council, Nat. Parks Assn., Destert Protective Council. Republican. Christian Scientist. Contbg. author Azaleas and Camellias, 1962. Designer Meml. Ct. and Fountain, Kraemer Park, Placentia, Calif., 1974. Home: Glendale, Calif. Died Jan. 28, 1980.

BARTON, GEORGE ARTHUR, sports writer, assn. exec.; b. Northfield, Minn., Feb. 20, 1885; s. George Washington and Mary Ellen (Ryan) B.; student pub. schs., St. Paul; m. Kathryn Elizabeth Riley, Sept. 17, 1908; children—George Arthur, Richard Kenneth.

Sports editor Mpls. Daily News, 1903-23; sports editor Mpls. Tribune, 1923-41, sports columnist since 1941; referee amateur, profl. boxing contests, including 24 world champions; chmn. Minn. Athletic Commn. since 1942; pres. Nat. Boxing Assn., 1952-53; mem. N.Y. Athletic Commn. Bd. Rev. Received James J. Walker award for contbn. to boxing, N.Y. Boxing Writers Assn., 1953, Silver Medallion for contbn. to boxing, French Govt., 1953; awarded trophies Mpls. C. of C., Jr. C. of C.; Distinguished Citizen award Mayor of Mpls.; Golden Gloves Writers of Am. award; Minn. Centennial athletic award. Mem. Minn. Assn. Amateur Athletic Union (pres.). Club: Minneapolis Athletic. Author: My Lifetime in Sports. Home: St. Paul.

BARTON, GEORGE SAMUEL HORACE, Canadian govt. official; b. Vankleek Hill, Ont., Can., June 29, 1883; s. John M. and Margaret Ann (Allen) B.; B.S.A., Ontario Agrl. Coll., U. of Toronto, 1907; D.Sc.A., Laval U., Quebec, P.Q., Can., 1928; m. Mabel Pauline Loveridge, 1912. Lecturer and asst. prof. of animal husbandry, Macdonald Coll., McGill U., 1907-11, prof. of animal husbandry, 1911-23, dean faculty of agr., 1923-32; dep. minister of Dominion Dept. of Agrl., 1932-48, special asst. to Minister of Agriculture since 1948. Decorated Companion Order St. Michael and St. George. Rep. for Can., Council of Food and Agr. Orgn., U.N. Vice pres. Canadian Soc. Tech. Agriculturists, 1920-23, pres., 1923-25; pres. Eastern Can. Soc. of Animal Production, 1928-30. Clubs: Rideau Curling. Canadian (Ottawa). Home: Ottawa Ont. Canada.

BARTON, ROBERT THOMAS, JR., lawyer; b. Winchester, Va., Oct. 15, 1891; s. R.T. and Getrude W. (Baker) B.; student Shenandoah Valley Acad., 1901-08; B.S., U. of Va., 1914, LL.B., 1914; m. Eleanor W. Parrish, Oct. 21, 1926; children—Robert T. III, Edith P., Eleanor R. Admitted to Va. bar, 1913; mem. Barton & Barton, Winchester, Va., 1914-16, Christian, and Barton (now Christian, Barton, Epps, Brent & Chappell), Richmond, Va., 1926-80. Past chmn. exec. com. Nat. Conf. Uniform State Laws. Served as 2d lt., Inf., Mexican Border Service, capt. F.A., 1918-19; col., AC, World War II. Decorated Legion of Merit. Former chmn. bd. visitors Med. Coll. Va. Mem. Am. (former mem. ho. dels. and bd. govs.; bd. editors for jour., chmn. gen. practice sect.), Va. bar assns., Va. State Bar (pres. 1950-51), Am. Coll. Trial Lawyers, Am. Legion (former state dept. comdr. and nat. exec. com.). Clubs: Soc. of Cincinnati, Richmond Country, Deep Run Hunt, Richmond German, Commonwealth. Author: Barton's Chancery Practice, 3d edit. 1926. Home: Richmond, Va. Died Aug. 17, 1980; buried Mt. Hebron Cemetery, Winchester, Va.

BARTON, ROGER, author, editor; b. N.Y.C., Dec. 27, 1903; s. Joseph Jewett and Olive (Pettipierre) B.; B.S. cum laude, Harvard, 1925; A.M., Columbia, 1932; m. Priscilla M. Sargent, Sept. 10, 1932; children—Seth Sargent, Deborah Ann Barton Brown. News editor Daily Herald, Passaic, N.J., 1925-27; reporter Newark Evening News, 1927-30; account exec. Daniel Starch & Staff, N.Y.C., 1930-38; pres., chmn., Barton & Goold, Inc., advt. agy., N.Y.C., 1939-40; editor Advt. Agy. (formerly Advt. & Selling), 1946-55, The Am. Printer, 1950-55; project and pub. relations dir. Alfred Politz Research, Inc., N.Y.C., 1955-57; editor Media-Scope mag., N.Y.C., 1957-65; lectr. advt. Grad. Sch. Business, Columbia, 1947-65. Editorial writer nature subjects, author column on outdoors Newark Eve. News, 1946-72, N.J. Courier-News, 1972-75, Hunterdon County Democrat, 1975-76; Am. corr. Advt. and Marketing Review, London, 1948-51, Advt. Review, London, 1953-59. Mem. Pres.'s Com. Employment Handicapped; chmn. Alexandria Twp. Environ. Commn. Served as lt. col. AUS, 1940-46. Decorated Legion of Merit (U.S.); Conspicuous Service Cross (N.Y.); Armed Forces Res. medal. Mem. S.R., Soc. Colonial Wars, Marine Corps League (hon.), Am. Marketing Assn., Nat. Conf. Bus. Paper Editors (pres.), N.J. Audubon Soc. (pres.), AAUP, Copy Research Council N.Y. (sec.-treas. 1966-67). Episcopalian. Club: Harvard (N.Y.C.). Author: (with O. D. Keep) The Quiz Book, 1927; (with Daniel Starch) Faith, Fear and Fortunes, 1934; Advertising Agency Operations and Management, 1954; How to Watch Birds, 1955; Media in Advertising, 1964; Confessions of a Bird/Watcher, 1974. Editor: Advertising Handbook, 1950; Handbook of Advertising Management, 1970. Contbr. articles on advt. to Ency. Brit., 1948-59. Home: Pittstown, N.J. Died June 17, 1976; interred Restland Meml. Park, East Hanover, N.J.

BARTON, WALTER ELBERT, lawyer; b. Wadesville, Ind., Nov. 7, 1886; s. Anson and Sophia Ann (Blackburn) B.; student Ind. State Normal Sch., 1903-05, U. of Colo., 1908-09; LL.B., cum laude, George Washington U., 1914; m. Martha R. Browning, Dec. 6, 1917 (dec.); children—Eleanor Browning, Martha Browning, Mary Ellen; m. 2d, Mrs. Isabelle Stockett Nixon, Apr. 1, 1955. Admitted to Ind. bar, 1915; practiced at Evansville until 1917, Washington, since 1920; specializes in federal taxation. Student 2d O.T.C., Ft. Benjamin Harrison, Aug.-Nov. 1917; attached to 89th Div., Nov. 1917-Mar. 1918, 164th Depot Brig., until Aug. 1918; with A.E.F., Aug. 1918-July 1919; participated in Meuse-Argonne offensive; hon. disch. as 1st lt., 1919. Sigma Phi Epsilon. Republican. Episcopalian. Mason. Clubs: University (Washington). Author: Federal Income, Estate and Gift Tax Laws, 1922; Renegotiation of Government Contracts, 1952; Estate Planning Under 1954 Code, 1957. Writer of the digest of the United States tax laws for Martindale-Hubbell Law Directory, 1924-36. Revision editor Vol. 7 on Corporations, Mertens Law of Federal Income Taxation. Contbr. articles on taxation to profl. jours. Home: Washington.

BASKERVILLE, JACK H., banker; b. Virginia, 1907; ed. U. Richmond, 1928; m. Josephine A.; children—Susan B., George T., III. Exec. v.p., sr. trust officer First & Merchants Nat. Bank, Richmond, now ret.; dir. Richmond Block, Inc., Arvonia Buckingham Slate Co. Treas., trustee Med. Coll. Va. Found. Trustee Crippled Children's Hosp., Richmond Meml. Hosp. Clubs: Kiwanis (pres., dir.), Country of Va., Downtown of Richmond (past pres.). Home: Richmond, Va. Died July 12, 1976.

BASSETT, BASIL BLAINE, prof. philosophy; b. Little Sioux, Ia., July 1, 1885; s. Linus H. and Mary Ellen (Donovan) B.; LL.B., Valparaiso Esq., 1921; Major Howell Tatum's Journal, 1921; Letters of Francis Parkman to Pierre Margry, 1923. Clubs: Century (New York), Cosmos (Washington, D.C.), Northampton (Northampton). Home: Northampton, Mass.*

BASSETT, CLAUDE OSCAR, naval officer; b. La Grace, S.D., Apr. 3, 1885; s. Samuel Smith and Katharina (Hopp) B.; S.B., U.S. Naval Acad., 1906; m. Hallie Severance, Sept. 11, 1912; children—Charles Severance, Claudia Severance (Mrs. Thomas R. Kinraide). Passed midshipman, U.S. Navy, 1906-10, serving in U.S. ships Chicago, Charleston and St. Louis, resigned, 1910; engaged in real estate bus. and mfg., 1910-17; recalled to active duty, U.S. Navy, 1917; served as aide to comdt., 13th Naval District; engineer officer U.S.S. Idaho, senior engr. officer U.S.S. Columbia, 1917-19; chief engr. steam vessels since 1919; engr. The Babcock & Wilcox Co., 1920-40; comdg. officer 2d Fleet Div., 1st Naval Dist., 1927-40; recalled to active duty, 1941; assigned as instr. naval science Mass. Maritime Academy, Hyannis, Mass., 1940-43, supt., 1943-46; present rank commodore, U.S.N.R. Decorated World War I. Am. Defense, and Pre-Pearl Harbor medals, Am. Theater Operations Ribbon. World War II. U.S. Naval Reserve Service Ribbon with star. Mem. Providence (R.I.) and Boston (Mass.) engring. socs., U.S.N.R. Officers Assn., Navy Athletic Assn., Am. Legion. Rotarian. Home: Bolton, Mass. *

BASSETT, JAMES ELIAS, ret. newspaper editor, author; b. Glendale, Calif., Oct. 18, 1912; s. James Elias and Lucille (Emerton) B.; B.A. cum laude, Bowdoin Coll., 1934; m. Wilma Moreland, June 13, 1936; 1 dau., Cynthia Ann. Reporter, Los Angeles Times, 1934-37, aviation editor, 1937-41, sci. editor, 1947-48, polit. analyst, editor, 1961, dir. editorial pages, 1963-71, asso. editor, 1971-77; polit. editor Los Angeles Mirror, 1948, city editor, 1954, asst. mng. editor, 1957. Mem. Pulitzer Prize Awards Com., 1967. Press sec. Nixon vice presdl. campaign, 1952; pub. relations dir. Republican Nat. Com., 1954; campaign mgr. Vice Pres. Nixon, 1956; campaign planning activities dir. Nixon presdl. campaign, 1960. Served to capt. USNR, 1941-45. Decorated Bronze Star medal with combat clasp. Mem. Am. Soc. Newspaper Editors, Authors League Am., Phi Beta Kappa, Psi Upsilon, Kappa Tau Alpha. Clubs: Los Angeles Press, Los Angeles Athletic. Author: Harm's Way, 1962 (made into motion picture 1965); The Sky Suspended, 1968; Commander Prince, USN, 1971; contbg. author The Warlords, 1975. Home: Malibu, Calif. Died June 26, 1978; buried at sea.

BASSETT, WALLACE, clergyman; b. Middle Grove, Mo., Dec. 31, 1884; s. Alexander Martin and Mary (Settle) B.; Ph.B., La Grange (Mo.) Coll., 1909; student Kansas City Theol. Sem., 1 yr., Newton Theol. Instn., 1 yr.; D.D., La Grange, 1916, Baylor U., 1920; m. Lottie Bounds, Dec. 25, 1906 (died Dec. 4, 1938); m. 2d, Hassie Mayfield, Oct. 10, 1940; children—Marcella Margaret (Mrs. Travis Johnson), Evelyn Elaine (Mrs. H. Bertram Smith), and Verona (Mrs. Wesley Tomlinson), Wallace (M.D.). Began preaching, 1902; ordained Bapt. ministry, 1905; pastor Sulphur Springs, Texas, 1910-15, First Ch., Amarillo, 1915-18, Cliff Temple Ch., Dallas, since 1918. President Relief and Annunity Board Southern Bapt. Conv.; trustee Baylor U., Southern Bapt. Theol. Sem. (Louisville, Ky.). President State Mission Board Texas Baptists; pres. Baptist General Conv. of Texas. Mason. Author: Beatific Verities, 1917; A Star at Midnight, 1940. Home: Dallas, Tex. *

BASSICH, J(OSEPH) B(EAUREGARD), clergyman, educator; b. New Orleans, June 2, 1885; s. Joseph Beauregard and Winifred Mary (Conway) B.; A.B., Immaculate Conception Coll., 1902; A.M., St. Louis Univ., 1918; student Paray-le-Monial, France, 1920-21; A.M., Columbia, 1931; Ph.D., Gregorian, Rome, 1931. Member Society of Jesus (Jesuits). Ordained priest, Roman Catholic Church, June 27, 1917; instructor in mathematics, Spring Hill (Ala.) College, 1909-14; teacher of math., St. Mary's Univ. High Sch., Galveston, Tex., 1918-20; asst. prof. Latin, St. Stanislaus Coll., Macon, Ga., 1921-22; asso. prof. Latin, St. Charles Coll., Grand Coteau, La., 1922-24; prin. St. John's High Sch., Shreveport, La., 1924-26, Spring Hill High Sch., 1926-29; chmn. dept. and prof. edn., Spring Hill Coll., 1931-34; prin. Jesuit High Sch., New Orleans, 1934-37; spiritual dir. of community, 1958—; professor of education Loyola University, 1937-58, regent of the College of Music, 1950-52, acting dean College of Music, 1952-54, 56-58, regent of School of Dentistry, 1942-47, mem. bd. dirs., 1942-47, recording sec., 1943-47. Gen. supervisor of studies, Jesuit High Schs., Gulf States, 1931-37; consultant Orleans Parish Sch. System since 1939. Ednl. Policies Commn., 1942-45; mem. La. State Com. on Teacher Training and Certification, 1941-52. Served as aux. military chaplain, U.S. Armed Forces, 1942-46; tech. and prof. expert, U.S. War Dept., 1943-44. Mem. A.A.A.S., Internat. Council for Exceptional Children (mem. exec. com., New Orleans chpt., 1948-50), Am. Cath. Philos. Assn., N.E.A., Southern Soc. for Philos. and Psychol., Southern Assn. of Colls. and Secondary Schs. (chmn. com. on secondary schs., 1941-42, com. on secondary schs., 1934-37, 1940-47), La. Coll. Conf. (chmn. psychol. sect., 1941-42, vice pres., 1948-49), La. Teachers Assn., Classical Assn. of N.La. (charter mem., writer of constitution and 1st v.p. 1925). Nat. Assn. for Music Therapy (pres. S. E. chpt. 1960), New Orleans Philharmonic Symphony Soc. (mem. bd. dirs. 1954, 56-58), Kappa Delta Pi, Phi Mu Alpha Sinfonia. Democrat. Club: Round Table. Address: New Orleans.

BASTION, JOSEPH EDWARD, army-officer; b. Pittsfield, Mass., Mar. 27, 1883; M.D., Georgetown U., Washington, D.C., 1906; commd. 1st lt., Med. Corps, May 1910, and advanced through the grades to brig. gen., June 1943; became corps area surgeon, 6th Corps Area (6th Service Command), Chicago, Nov. 1940; assumed command Percy Jones Gen. Hosp., Battle Creek, Mich., May 1943. Address: Battle Creek, Mich. *

BATCHELLER, WILLIS TRYON, cons. engr.; b. Joliet, Ill., Dec. 23, 1889; s. Willis Watson and Leonore (Tryon) B.; B.S. in Elec. Engring., U. Wash., 1911, E.E., 1915; m. Alice Louise Rapp, Mar. 25, 1914. Testing engr. Puget Sound Power & Light Co., 1910-11; with Seattle Light & Power System, 1912-21; pres. and chief engr. Canadian Alaska Ry. Co.; pres. and dir. Willis T. Batcheller Internat., Inc., Seattle, also N.Y.C., Washington, La Paz, Bolivia, Manila, Philippines, Saigon, Vietnam; cons. engr. hydro-electric, hydraulic and power projects or systems; served as engr. design and constrn. three 10,000 kilowatt units of Lake Union steam electric plant; 18,000 h.p. hydro-electric devel. at Cedar Falls; preliminary work and design Skagit River power project; report and survey Columbia River, at Grand Coulee, Chief Joseph power project, Columbia Basin irrigation project; engr. Nimpkish River pulp, paper and power project of Internat. Harvester Co. on Vancouver Island; engr. Quincy Valley Irrigation Dist.; engr. Columbia Basin Project; engr. Richland Atomic Energy Project, Bolsa Island nuclear power and desalting plant, Los Angeles; pioneered WEST Four Corners (N.M.) coal and power plant, Centralia (Wash.) plant; also engr. many power, irrigation and water supply and indsl. projects; cons. govt. war indsl. projects. Cons. Washington Toll Bridge Authority and State Hwy. Commn. Pres., chief engr. Canadian Alaska Ry. Co. 3300 mi. transcontinental system from Seattle, and Vancouver, B.C. to Fairbanks, Alaska. Mem. state devel. com. and indsl. com. Seattle C. of C., former chmn. Reclamation Com. Chmn. Northwest Br. Y.M.C.A., Seattle. Registered profl. engr., Wash., Ore., B.C. Mem. Am. Concrete Inst., I.E.E.E., ASME (profl. practice com., dir. Western Wash. sect. divs. on fuels, heat transfer, power, nuclear engring., energetics), S.A.R., Seattle Municipal League, Engrs. Club, Nat. Soc. Profl. Engrs. Christian Scientist. Mason (33 deg., K.T., Shriner). Contbr. engring. and financial subjects. Home: Seattle, Wash. Died Oct. 28, 1975; interred Evergreen Cemetery, Seattle.

BATCHELOR, CLARENCE DANIEL, cartoonist; b. Osage City, Kans., Apr. 1, 1888; s. Daniel L. and Lillian Eugenia (James) B.; ed. Osage City Pub. sch. and Salina High Sch., 1894-1907, Chicago Art Inst., 1907-10; m. Hazel Deyo, 1918 (dec.); m. 2d, Julie Margaret Forsyth, June 19, 1948 (dec.); m. 3rd, Allegra Summers Taylor, 1959. Staff artist Kansas City Star, 1911; free lance mag. drawings, 1914-18; cartoonist Ledger Syndicate, N.Y. Post, 1923-31; N.Y. News editorial cartoonist, 1930-69. Bronze bust J. M. Patterson; oil murals Infinity and History of Printed Word in News Bldg. Awarded $200 prize for 6 best cartoons on pub. health by A.M.A., 1912; Pulitzer prize, 1937; Nat. Headliners Plaque, 1938; Page One award, 1965. Mem. Nat. Assn. Editorial Cartoonists. Clubs: Dutch Treat, Silurian, Mile Creek, Nat. Arts. Originator automobile safety series, Inviting the Undertaker. Home and studio: Deep River, Conn. Died Sept. 5, 1977.

BATCHELOR, LEON DEXTER, horticulture; b. Upton, Mass., May 8, 1884; s. Henry J. and Margaret Elizabeth (McComb) B.; B.S., Univ. of N.H., 1907; Ph.D., Cornell U., 1911; m. Florence Brown, Sept. 4, 1912; children—Margaret Elizabeth, Martha Jane. Instr. in horticulture, Cornell U., 1907-11; horticulturist, Utah Agrl. Coll., 1911-15; asso. prof. plant breeding, U. of Calif., 1915-19, prof. orchard management, 1919-29 (with field dept. Calif. Walnut Growers Assn., Mar. 1926-Apr. 1927); dir. U. of Calif. Citrus Expt. Sta., Riverside, Calif., 1929-51, prof. horticulture since 1929. Mem. A.A.A.S., Am. Hort. Soc., Alpha Zeta. Co-editor: The Citrus Industry, Vols. 1 and 2. Address: Riverside, Calif. *

BATES, FRANCIS OLIVER, hosp. adminstr.; b. Huger, S.C., Nov. 8, 1886; s. William Jones and Caroline Amanda (Cox) B.; student Coll. of Charleston and Stokes Bus. Coll., Charleston, S.C., 1909-14; m. Mabel H. Lotz, Oct. 14, 1915; 1 dau., Caroline Addie. Bus. mgr., Roper Hosp., Charleston, S.C., 1911-12, supt. since 1912, hosp. expanding under adminstrn. from 248 to 475 beds with budget increasing from $100,000 to $1,200,000; v.p. and sec., Capital Life and Health Ins. Co., since 1936. Mem. adv. com., Crippled Children's Div., S.C. State Bd. Health, since 1940; mem. bd. trustees, Carolina Health Care Assn. (helped secure legislation and organize), Hosp. and Training Sch. for Nurses (colored), since 1935. Mem. Am. Hosp. Assn. (life; 1st v.p., 1928, 1941; trustee, 1931-34; S.C. mem. Ho. Dels., since 1940), Am. Coll. Hosp. Adminstrs. (charter; mem. bd. regents, 1933-44, remelected 1947; executive committe, 1943; vice president, since 1946), South Carolina Hospital Association (charter and helped organize; past sec.-treas., pres., trustee), Carolinas-Va. Hosp. Conf. (helped organize; pres., 1932-33; mem. exec. com. since 1926), Charleston Chamber of Commerce, Y.M.C.A., Charleston Co. Tuberculosis Assn., Southeastern Shrine Assn. (5th v.p. to pres.), N.E. Soc., Arion Soc., Friendly Soc. Democrat. Methodist (mem. bd. stewards, chmn. finance com.). Mason (32 deg., S.R., Shriner), Royal Order Jesters (dir.), Elk. Clubs: Rotary (past v.p., dir.), Rifle (Charleston). Author articles on hosp. adminstrn. Home: Charleston S.C. *

BATES, GEORGE HUBERT, state ofcl.; b. Bates City, Mo., Dec. 8, 1884; s. George Washington and Jemimah H. (Griffith) B.; student U. Mo., 1903-04; m. Ernestine Norma Comer, June 18, 1913; children—Norma E. (Mrs. William L. Spencer), George Comer, William Hubert. Asst. cashier Comml. Bank, Lexington, Mo., 1905-15; dep. co. clk. Lafayette Co., Mo., 1915-23, co. clk., 1923-33; chief clk. State Auditor's Office, 1933; supr. sales tax dept., State Mo., 1934-46; state collector Dept. Revenue, 1946-49, dir. revenue, 1949-53; state treas., 1953-57; commnr. finance, 1957—. Mem. Nat. Tax Assn., Nat. Assn. Tax Adminstrn., Nat. Assn. Suprs. State Banks, Tax Inst. Democrat. Methodist. Mason (32 deg.). Home: Jefferson City, Mo.

BATES, LEGARE, judge; b. North, S.C., Aug. 20, 1898. Judge, Richland County Ct., Columbia, S.C. Former mem. S.C. Ho. of Reps.; chmn. City Democratic Exec. Com., Columbia; trustee U. S.C. Served with Armed Forces, World War I. Mem. Am. Legion, VFW. Clubs: Elks, Palmetto. Home: Columbia, S.C. Died May 14, 1979.

BATES, MERLE BANKER, univ. ofcl.; b. Green Island, N.Y., 1892; s. William Watson and Altha Louise (Soyer) B.; ed. Syracuse U., 1912; LL.D., McMaster U., 1973; m. Marguerite Louise Eberwein, July 3, 1923; 1 son, Bruce Banker. Pres., dir. Life Savers, Ltd., Hamilton, Ont., Can., Beech-Nut Co. of Can., Ltd., Life Savers & Beech-Nut Sales Co., Ltd., 1934-58; v.p., dir. Life Savers Corp., Port Chester, N.Y., 1934-56. Chmn. bd. govs. Art Gallery, Hamilton, 1960-61; past pres. Community Chest Hamilton, Air Cadet League of Can.; mem. Nat. War Finance Com., Hamilton, 1942-43; vice chmn. bd. trustees Hamilton United Appeal, 1956-63; bd. govs., mem. exec. com. McMaster U., 1954-69, chmn. devel. fund council, 1960-63, vice chmn. finance com. (growth fund), 1964-69, asst. to pres. (fund-raising), 1969-71, cons., from 1972, hon. gov., from 1976; pres., dir. The Hamilton Found., 1960-63. Served as 2d lt. Ordnance Dept., U.S. Army, 1917-19. Awarded Royal Canadian Air Force Scroll, 1946. Mem. Assn. Nat. Advertisers (chmn. bd. U.S.A. 1926). Clubs: Hamilton Golf and Country (Ancastor, Ont.); The Hamilton. Home: Burlington, Ont., Can. Deceased.

BATES, ROBERT L(EE), univ. prof., psychologist; b. Middleway, W.Va., Nov. 7, 1886; s. William Grantham and Susan Rebecca (Smith) B.; LL.B., W.Va. U., 1912, A.B., 1916; A.M., Johns Hopkins, 1920, Ph.D., 1924; m. Laura Talbott Bosley, Dec. 30, 1914; children—Fred Talbott, Susan Elizabeth (Mrs. Dan P. Darwin). Teacher pub. sch., high sch. prin., 1916-18; research fellow, Johns Hopkins, 1920-21; asst. prof. psychology, Va. Mil. Inst., 1921-22, asso. prof., 1922-25, prof., since 1925; vis. prof. summer sessions, Duke U., 1926-27, 29-30, Arkansas U., 1928, Coll. of William and Mary, 1931-32, U. of Va., 1933; mem. Va. Mil. Inst. adminstrv. coms.; institutional rep., Rhodes Scholarship Trust. Served as 1st lt. in psych. examining service, U.S. Army, 1918-19 with San. Corps, 21 months; naturalization and claims officer, Ft. McHenry, 1919; capt., San. Reserve, 1924-34; major, lt. col., col., Va. Militia (unorganized). Fellow A.A.A.S., Am. Psych. Assn.; mem. Southern Soc. Philosophy and Psychology (mem. council, 1927-30), Va. Acad. Sci., W.Va. Hist. Soc., Baptist Hist. Soc. of Va., Va. Edn. Assn., Phi Beta Kappa, Sigma Xi, Sigma Nu. Democrat. Episcopalian. Contbr. articles to prof. jours.; patent authorized on device for making relief maps of controlled size and vertical exaggeration from two-dimensional topographical map. Home: Lexington, Va. *

BATRUS, FREDERICK EDWARD, cons.; b. Altoona, Pa., May 28, 1915, s. Elias and Elizabeth (Hallow) B.; B.S. in Econs., U. Pa., 1937; LL.B., Dickinson Sch. Law, 1940; m. Eleanor Louise Harlan, Feb. 28, 1948; children—Harlan, Carol, Elizabeth. Admitted to Pa. bar, 1940; practice in Altoona, 1940-42; atty. Post Office Dept., Washington, 1946-52, asso. gen. counsel transp., 1952-55, spl. asst. bur. transp., 1955-61, dep. asst. postmaster gen. Bur. Transp., 1961-68, asst. postmaster gen., 1968-69, exec. asst. to dept. postmaster gen., 1969-71, asst. postmaster gen. logistics and engring., 1971, asst. postmaster gen. exec. adminstrn., 1972-74, ret.; cons. U.S. Congress, 1974-75. U.S. del. Congress Universal Postal Union, Paris, France, 1947, Ottawa, Can., 1957, Vienna, Austria, 1964. Served with inf. AUS, 1942-45: ETO. Decorated Silver Star medal, Bronze Star medal, Purple Heart. Mem. Am., Fed. bar assns., Kappa Sigma. Club: Nat. Lawyers. Home: Bethesda, Md. Died June 24, 1975.

BAUDER, FREDERICK WILLIAM, educator; b. Newark, July 25, 1897; s. John and Anna M. (Boehm) B.; B.S., Worcester Poly. Inst., 1920; M.S., Stevens Inst. Tech., 1945; postgrad. Columbia U., N.Y. U.; m. Florence A. Mehne, June 24, 1922; 1 dau., Stephanie Ann. Plant chemist Cooper Chem. Co., 1920-26; prod. chemist Congoleum-Nairn Co., 1926-27; mgr. Holdt Paint Co., 1928-29; instr. in chemistry N.J. Inst. Tech., 1929-41, asst. prof., 1941-48, asso. prof., 1948-56, prof., 1956-80; owner Bauder Products, 1930-80; cons. in field; indsl. waste treatment and sewage treatment cons. Dir. Mullaly Meml. Coatings Lab., Newark Coll. Engring. Served with USN, 1918. Registered profl. engr.; cert. profl. chemist. Fellow Am. Inst. Chemists; mem. Am. Chem. Soc., Am. Soc. Engring. Edn., Fedn. Socs. for Paint Tech., Phi Sigma Kappa, Omicron Delta Kappa. Club: Masons. Contbr. articles to profl. jours. Home: Short Hills, N.J. Died Aug. 24, 1980.

BAUER, BENJAMIN BAUMZWEIGER, broadcasting co. exec.; b. Odessa, Russia, June 26, 1913; s. Maurice and Miriam (Krasnianskaya) Baumzweiger; came to U.S., 1930, naturalized, 1941; E.E., Pratt Inst., N.Y.C., 1932, U. Cin., 1937; m. Ida Weintraub, Sept. 3, 1937; children—Philip J., William Baumzweiger. With Shure Bros., Inc., Evanston, Ill., 1937-57, v.p., 1949-57; sect. head, then v.p. CBS Labs., Stamford, Conn., 1958-75; v.p., gen. mgr. CBS Tech. Center, CBS, Inc., Stamford, 1975-79; vis. prof. engring. acoustics Pa. State U.; mem. acoustical working group U.S. Navy, 1967-74; mem. Naval Studies Bd., 1976-79. Decorated chevalier Order of Star of Peace, 1979. Fellow Acoustical Soc. Am. (Silver medal 1978), IEEE, Audio Engring. Soc.; mem. Nat. Acad. Engring., Conn. Acad. Sci. and Engring. Inventor unidirectional microphone, magnetic phonograph pickup, quadraphonic sound record, quadraphonic microphone system. Home: Stamford, Conn. Died Mar. 31, 1979.

BAUER, CLYDE MAX (BOU'ER), geologist, naturalist; b. Bristol, Ind., Apr. 5, 1886; s. Reuben D., and Matilda (Sherck) B.; B.S., U. of Chicago, 1908; Ph.D., U. of Colo., 1932; m. Clara Hillix, Nov. 16, 1911; children—Bruce Foster, Dean Price, Neil Clair. Science teacher Centralia (Ill.) Township High Sch., 1908-09; prin. high sch. Florence, Colo., 1909-11; asst. geologist U.S. Geol. Survey, 1911-16; comml. geologist, Okla. and Tex., 1916-20; chief geologist Mid-Northern Oil Co. and Midwest Exploration Co., 1921-31; park naturalist, Yellowstone National Park, 1932-43; chief park naturalist, 1943-46; geol. Office of Dir., Branch of Natural Hist., Nat. Park Service, since 1946; dir. exec. sec. Yellowstone Library and Mus. Assn., 1932-46. Fellow A.A.A.S., Geol. Society Am.; mem. Am. Geophysical Union (com. on glaciers), Lincoln House of University of Chicago, Pick and Hammer Club. Baptist. Mason (32 deg., Shriner). Author: The Story of Yellowstone Geysers, 1937, 2d edit., 1945; Yellowstone—Its Underworld. Contbr. to U.S. Geol. Survey publs. and professional jours. Home: Arlington, Va.

BAUER, FRANZ KARL, physician, educator; b. Vienna, Austria, Jan. 29, 1917; s. Julius and Marianne (Jokl) B.; student U. Vienna, 1934-38, U. Geneva (Switzerland), 1938-40; M.D., La. State U., 1941; m. Marjorie Frantz Bauer (Frantz), May 29, 1943; 1 dau., Anne Kathryn. Came to U.S., 1940, naturalized, 1943. Intern Charity Hosp. La., New Orleans, 1941-42, resident, 1942; resident Los Angeles County Gen. Hosp., 1946-48, chief med. resident, 1949-50; dir. radioisotope service VA Center, Los Angeles, 1951-56; chief dept. medicine Rancho Los Amigos Hosp., Downey, Cal., 1974-76; mem. faculty Sch. Medicine, U. Cal. at Los Angeles, 1951-56, 60-65, asso. clin. prof., 1954-56, prof. medicine, 1960-65; mem. faculty, adminstrn. Sch. Medicine, U. So. Cal., 1956-60, 65-76, prof., 1965-76, also dean Sch. Medicine, 1969-74; chief outpatient clinics Los Angeles County Gen. Hosp., 1956-60, chief med. service Harbor Gen. Hosp., Torrance, Cal., 1960-65; vis. prof. Commissariat a l'Energie Atomique, dept. biology Service Hosp. Frederic Joliot, Orsay, France, 1967, Alexandra Hosp., Athens, Greece, 1962; cons. Oak Ridge Inst. Nuclear Studies, 1955. Served to maj. M.C., USAAF, 1942-46. Diplomate Am. Bd. Internal Medicine, Am. Bd. Nuclear Medicine. Fellow Soc. Tropical Medicine and Hygiene, A.C.P.; mem. Am. Fedn. Clin. Research (sec. Western sect. 1953), Soc. Nuclear Medicine (v.p. 1958), Pacific Interurban Clin. Club (chmn. 1971-72), Los Angeles Soc. Internal Medicine (pres. 1966), Western Assn. Physicians, Western Soc. Clin. Research, Soc. Exptl. Biology and Medicine, A.M.A., World Fedn. Nuclear Medicine and Biology, Alpha Omega Alpha (mem. faculty). Home: Los Angeles, Calif. Died Feb. 10, 1976.

BAUER, FREDERICK CHARLES, soil scientist; b. Blue Mound, Ill., May 7, 1886; s. Charles Remandus and Alice Kitty (Wall) B.; B.S., U. of Ill., 1909, M.S., 1918; Ph.D., U. of Wis., 1920; m. Louise Wallace Garrett, Aug. 13, 1913; children—Alice Elizabeth (Eggert), Frederick Charles, Shirley Jane (Spaeth), Miriam Louise, David Garrett. Supervisor vocational Soc. Agronomy; mem. Soil Science Soc. of Am., A.A.A.S., Sigma Xi, Gamma Sigma Delta, Gamma Alagr., Ind. Sch. System, Boise, Ida., 1909-11; asst. in soil fertility, U. of Ill., 1911-18, asso. prof. soils extension, 1920-23, chief soil experiment fields, since 1923, prof. soil fertility, since 1933. Fellow Am. pha. Presbyterian. Address: Urbana, Ill. *

BAUER, HARRY CHARLES, bibliographer dowser, library cons.; b. St. Louis, July 22, 1902; s. Emile George and Jennie Theresa (Cannan) B.; A.B., Washington U., 1927, M.S., 1929; grad. St. Louis Library Sch., 1931. Chief circulation div. library, U. Mo., 1931-34; chief tech. library TVA, Knoxville, 1934-42; asst. librarian U. Wash., 1945-46, asso. librarian, 1946-47, dir. libraries and prof. librarianship, 1947-59, prof. librarianship, 1959-67, emeritus, 1967-78, sec. faculty U. Wash., 1962-66; founder, pres. Bibliog. Dowsers America, from 1959; specialist in bibliog. dowsing, from 1966. Pres., Tenn. Credit Union League, 1941-42. Sec. Allied Arts Seattle, Inc., People's Meml. Assn., Seattle Creative Activities Center; pres. Pacific N.W. Internat. Writers Conf., 1958. Mayor, Norris, Tenn., 1940. Served to maj. USAAF, 1942-45; group intelligence officer, 98th Bombardment Group, 1942-45; col. Res. Decorated Bronze Star, Air medal, Purple Heart. Mem. Ret. Officers Assn. (affiliate pres. 1953), Mil. Order World Wars, Am., Pacific N.W., Wash., Md. library assns., Assn. Coll. and Reference Libraries, Spl. Libraries Assn., Am. Legion, VFW, English Speaking Union, Met. Opera Guild, Sigma Xi, Pi Mu Epsilon, Phi Kappa Tau, Scabbard and Blade, Oval Club. Baptist. Mason (Shriner), Kiwanian (pres. 1951). Clubs: Rainier, Faculty Men's (pres. 1948). Author: Seasoned to Taste, 1961. Joint editor: Public Administration Libraries, 1941; Columnist, Seasoned to Taste, for Wilson Library Bull., 1951-61. Editor, pub. Prose Bowl. Contbr. articles to profl. jours. Home: Bethesda, Md. Died Sept. 4, 1978.

BAUER, HARRY JOHN, corp. exec.; b. Bunker Hill, Ill., Aug. 31, 1883; s. Albert E. and Mary (Thompson) B.; student U. of Calif., 1901; LL.B., U. of Southern Calif., 1909; LL.D., University of Southern Calif., 1943; m. Mabel J. Hughes, Sept. 18, 1909; 1 dau., Dorothy-Evelyn (Mrs. Burton Rawlins). Admitted to California bar, 1909; president Spring Street Realty Co.; dir. So. Cal. Edison Co., Cal. Di Giorgio Fruit Corp. Trustee Cal. Inst. Tech., U. So. Cal. Mem. Phi. Delta Phi, Sigma Chi. Clubs: California. Bohemian, Los Angeles Country, Pacific Union; Automobile Club of Southern California (hon. chmn.); Newport Harbor Yacht. Home: Pasadena, Cal. *

BAUER, RAYMOND AUGUSTINE, educator; b. Chgo., Sept. 7, 1916; s. William Henry and Anna Barbara (Diedrich) B.; student Ill. Inst. Tech., 1936-38; B.S. with highest distinction, Northwestern U., 1943; M.A., Harvard, 1948, Ph.D., 1950; m. Alice Haugh, June 12, 1941 (dec.); 1 dau., Linda Carol (Mrs. Donald H. Sibley); m. 2d, Katharine Goldthwaite Dorr Clark, Apr. 30, 1966. Chem. analyst Crane Co., 1936-44; research asst. Harvard, 1947-48, fellow Russian Research Center, 1948-50, lectr. social psychology, research asso. Russian Research Center, 1950-55, Ford Found. vis. prof. Grad. Sch. Bus. Adminstrn., 1957-60, prof., from 1960, Joseph C. Wilson prof. until 1977. Research asso. Center for Internat. Studies, 1953-57; fellow Center for Advanced Studies in Behavioral Scis. 1955-56; asso. prof. social psychology Mass. Inst. Tech., 1955-57; cons. Nat. Goals Research Staff, The White House, 1969-70. Served as lt. (j.g.) USNR, 1944-46; Russian lang. officer. Fellow Am. Acad. Arts and Scis.; mem. Am., Eastern, Mass. (pres. 1964-66) psychol. assns., Am. Sociol. Soc., Am. Mktg. Assn., Am. Assn.

Public Opinion Research (pres. 1965-66), Phi Beta Kappa. Author: The New Man in Soviet Psychology, 1952; Nine Soviet Portraits, 1955; (with Alex Inkeles, Clyde Kluckhohn) How the Soviet System Works, 1956; (with Alex Inkeles) The Soviet Citizen, 1959; (with Ithiel Pool) American Businessmen and International Trade, 1960; (with Pool and Dexter) American Business and Public Policy, 1963; (with Gross, Biderman, and others) Social Indicators, 1966; (with S.A. Greyser) Advertising in America, 1968; (with others) Second Order Consequences, 1969; (with Scott M. Cunningham) Studies in the Negro Market, 1970; (with D. Fenn) The Corporate Social Audit, 1972; (with Robert Ackerman) Corporate Responsiveness, Text and Cases, 1975. Editor: (with K. Gergen) The Study of Policy Formation, 1968; (with M. Dierkes) Corporate Social Accounting, 1972. Home: Cambridge, Mass. Died July 9, 1977.

BAUGH, ALBERT CROLL, educator; b. Phila., Feb. 26, 1891; s. Horace L. and Margaret (Croll) Baugh; A.B., U. Pa., 1912, A.M., 1914, Ph.D., 1915; L.H.D., 1961; LL.D., Ursinus Coll., 1939; Litt.D., Franklin and Marshall Coll., 1956; m. Nita Emeline Scudder, June 20, 1925; children—William Scudder, Daniel. With U. Pa., 1912-61, beginning as asst. instr. English, prof. English, 1928-61, Felix E. Schelling Meml. professorship emeritus; vis. prof., summers, Stanford U., 1928, Duke U., 1935, 37, 39, 41, Northwestern U., 1940, U. So. Calif., 1949. Fellow Medieval Acad. Am. (adv. bd., 1939-41, clk. 1948-51, pres. fellows 1960-63, pres. 1963-66); mem. Modern Lang. Assn. Am. (editorial bd., 1930-41, 1946-51, exec. council 1943-46, 2d v.p., 1950, pres. 1952), Modern Humanities Research Assn. (pres. 1949-50), Internat. Arthurian Soc., Am. Dialect Soc. (v.p. 1951), Linguistic Soc., (exec. com., 1940-42, 46-48), Internat Fedn. for Modern Langs. and Lits. (pres. 1960-63), Am. Philos. Soc., Pa. Hist. Soc., Phi Beta Kappa. Clubs: The Franklin Inn, The Collectors. Author: (with P.C. Kitchen and M.W. Black) Writing by Types, 1924; History of the English Language, 1935, rev. edit., 1957, (with Thomas Cable) 3d edit., 1978; Literary History of England (with others), 1948, rev. edit., 1967; Chaucer, 1968, rev. edit., 1977. Editor: William Haughton's Englishmen for My Money, 1917; Schelling Anniversary Papers, 1923; (with G. W. McClelland) Century Types of English Literature, 1925; (with P.C. Kitchen) Synonymns, Antonyms and Discriminations (in New Century Dictionary), 1927; Thomas Hardy's Return of the Native, 1928; (with A.H. Quinn and W.D. Howe) The Literature of America (2 vols.), 1929; (with N.E. McClure) Essays Toward Living, 1929; English Literature; A Period Anthology (with G.W. McClelland), 1954; Chaucer's Major Poetry, 1963. Asso. editor Philol. Quar., 1934-50; Word, 1945-49. Contbr. articles to mags. Home: Philadelphia, Pa. Died Mar. 21, 1981; buried Arlington Cemetery, Drexel Hill, Pa.

BAUGHMAN, CORTLANDT CHESTERFIELD, naval officer; b. West Newton, Pa., Dec. 12, 1884; grad. U.S. Naval Acad., 1907, Naval War Coll., sr. course, 1927. Commd. ensign, U.S. Navy, 1909, advanced through grades to commodore, 1943; served in U.S. ships Maine, Wilmington, Chattanooga, Colorado, Chester, Pennsylvania, Florida, Farenholt, Arizona, Cincinnati; aide on staff mil. gov., Santo Domingo, 1916-19; asst. gov. of Samoa, and capt. of the yard, Naval Station, Tutuila, 1929-30; comd. U.S.S. New Mexico, 1939-41; capt. of the yard and comdg. officer of receiving station, Pearl Harbor, T.H., 1941-42; dir. special activities Bureau of Naval Personnel, Navy Dept., Washington, D.C., 1942-43; comdr. U.S. Naval Operating Base, Londonderry, Ireland, 1943-44; became comdr. naval operating base, Trinidad, B.W.I., Sept. 1944, retired 1946; director and branch manager Furlow and Associates Incorporated, Realtors, San Diego. Decorated Bronze Star, Navy Expeditionary, Nicaraguan Campaign, Mexican Service, Asiatic-Pacific Campaign, European-African-Middle Eastern Area Campaign and Am. Area Campaign medals, Victory Medal with silver star, Am. Defense Service Medal with fleet clasp. Died Sept. 16, 1976.

BAUGHMAN, JAMES STANLEY, business exec.; born Pittsburgh, Jan. 1, 1898; s. James D. and Ida (Graham) B.; student U. of Pittsburgh, 1918-23; m. Margaret Maeder, Apr. 3, 1926; 1 dau., Mildred. Began as accountant Guffey Gillespie Oil Co., Pittsburgh, later becoming asst. treas.; auditor Thermatomic Carbon Co., Pittsburgh, 1923-32; state mgr. Home Owners Loan Corp., Philadelphia, 1935-42, dep. gen. mgr., N.Y. City, 1942-48, gen. mgr., 1948-50; pres. Federal National Mortgage Assn. since 1950. Recipient Rockefeller Pub. Service award, 1962, Pres.'s Distinguished Fed. Civilian Service award, 1962. Mason (Shriner). Home: Washington, D.C. Died July 20, 1980.

BAUMEISTER, THEODORE, engr.; b. N.Y.C., July 19, 1897; s. Theodore and Mary L. (Wilson) B.; B.S., Cityj Coll., 1918; M.E., Columbia, 1922; m. Margaret Kilpatrick, January 23, 1925; children—Theodore III, Heard Kilpatrick, Mary Berrien Baumeister (Mrs. Murray B. Parker). Asst. Columbia, 1922, instr., 1924-31, asst. prof., 1931-38, asso. prof., 1938-41, prof., 1941-50, exec. officer, dept. mech. engring., 1941-48, Stevens prof. mech. engring., 1950-64, emeritus, 1964-79; adj. prof. mech. engring. U. S.C., 1965-70; cons. engr. Stevens & Wood, 1926-38, Am. Gas & Electric System, 1936-52, Société Edison de Milano, 1950. Gen. Pub. Utilities Corp., 1950-64, Babcock & Wilcox Co., 1950-65, S.C. Electric & Gas Co., 1952-65. Mayor's Com. on Transit Power Plants, N.Y.C., 1957-58, Consol. Coal Co., 1959-64, M.R. Scharff, 1937-41; E.I. Dupont de Nemours & Co., 1945-55, Duke Power Co., 1948-49, Brookhaven Nat. Lab., AEC, 1940-58, Central Hudson Gas & Electric Corp., 1953-64, Worthington Corp., 1955-57. Trustee Engring. Socs. Library, 1947-55, N.Y. P.E. City Mission Soc., 1954-64. Licensed profl. engr., N.Y.; chartered mech. engr., Gt. Britain. Mem. ASME (chmn. met. sect., 1936-38; chmn. power div., 1943; mem. standing com. on power test codes 1940-69), Inst. Mech. Engrs. (Gt. Britain), Am. Nuclear Soc., AAAS, Am. Soc. Engring. Edn., Carolina Plantation Soc., St. George's Soc., AAUP, Newcomen Soc., Am. Soc. Naval Engrs., Nat. Soc. Profl. Engrs., Agrl. Soc. S.C., Navy League, Air Force Assn., Sigma Xi, Tau Beta Pi, Phi Gamma Delta, Theta Tau. Episcopalian (vestryman 1959-70). Club: Carolina Yacht. Contbr. sects. to Peele's Mining Engineers Handbook, 1949; Fans, 1935; Perry's Chemical Engineers Handbook, 1949; (with Sporn and Ambrose) Heat Pumps, 1947; Kent's Mechanical Handbook, 1948; Knowlton and Fink Standard Handbook for Electrical Engineers, 1957, 68; Bonilla's Nuclear Engineering, 1957; also tech., sci. jours., Ency. Brit., Steeter's Fluid Dynamics Handbook, 1961; Perry's Engineering Manual, 1967. Editor-in-chief Standard Handbook for Mechanical Engineers (Marks'). Home: Yonges Island, S.C. Died Dec. 26, 1979; buried Trinity Ch. Cemetery, N.Y.C.

BAUMERT, ANDREW, JR., b. Philadelphia, Pa., Dec. 10, 1883; s. Andrew and Emma (Sonnehorne) B.; ed. pub. schs.; m. Jessie E. Creighton, of Phoenix, Ariz., Sept. 11, 1917. Settled at Phoenix, 1906; investments. Sec. Rep. State Com., 1916-20; chief clk. State Highway Dept., 1917-18; chmn. Commn. on State Instns., Jan.-July 1919 (abolished by law), and sec. of its successor, the Bd. of Directors of State Instns., 1919-20 (resigned); Ariz. mem. Rep. Nat. Com., 1921-24. Episcopalian. Clubs: Arizona, PhoenixCountry, Iron Springs Outing. Home: Phoenix, Ariz.*

BAVOR, HERBERT JOHN, physician; b. Cleve., Feb. 4, 1915; s. John Joseph and Frieda Julia (Fuchs) B.; B.A., Adelbert Coll., Western Res. U., 1936; M.D., Case Western Res. U., 1940; m. Winifred Caroline Woodward, Feb. 12, 1942; children—Leslie Caroline, Herbert John, Clayton Woodward, Elizabeth Frederika. Intern, Charity Hosp., Cleve., 1941-42; asst. surg. resident Deaconess Hosp., Cleve., 1941-42; chief surg. resident Crile VA Hosp., Cleve., 1946-47; practice medicine, specializing in gen. and indsl. surgery, Decatur, Ill., from 1947; mem. surg. staff Decatur Meml. Hosp., from 1947, pres. med. staff, 1953-55, chief surg. staff, 1956-58; mem. surg. staff St. Marys Hosp., Wabash Hosp.; med. dir. Wagner Castings Co., Firestone Tire & Rubber Plant, Decatur, PPG Industries Works 14, Mt. Zion, Ill., Ill. Bell Telephone, Essex Internat., Mississippi Valley Structural Steel; med. cons. CSC, 1951-61; designate surgeon Civil Service employees, from 1951; examiner Police Retirement Commn., from 1972; chmn. Ill. Blood Service Council, from 1979. Bd. dirs. Macon County chpt. ARC, from 1948, chpt. chmn., 1961-64, chmn. adv. council Midwestern Area, 1963-66, hon. chmn., from 1977; co-chmn. of vols., 1967-70, mem. com. to study Am. Blood Commn., nat. bd. govs., 1970-76, named Outstanding Vol., Heart of Ill. div., 1977-78; cons. Nat. Blood Program, 1968-70, bd. govs., 1970-76; bd. dirs. Med.-Dental Credit Union; bd. dirs. Decatur Symphony Guild, from 1974, pres., from 1976. Served to maj. M.C., AUS, 1942-46. Named Young Man of Year, Jr. C. of C., 1950. Fellow Am. Soc. Abdominal Surgeons, Indsl. Med. Assn., Internat. Coll. Surgeons; mem. A.M.A., Ill., Macon County (past. pres.) med. socs., U.S., Decatur (dir.) chambers commerce, Sigma Xi. Roman Catholic. Clubs: Country of Decatur (past dir.), Decatur. Home: Decatur, Ill. Deceased.

BAXTER, JOHN KIRKMAN, b. at Nashville, Tenn., June 4, 1882; s. William Mitchell and Mary Washington (Kirkman) B.; A.B., Harvard, 1903; m. Anita Holt, of Stockholm, Sweden, Dec. 18, 1907. Clk. U.S. Civ. Service Commn., 1903-5; sec. Isthmian Canal Service Bd., 1905-12; counsul at St. Pierre and Maracaibo, Venezuela, 1912-14; chief Div. of Civ. Affairs, Panama Canal Zone, since Apr. 4, 1914. Clubs: University (Isthmus of Panama and Washington, D.C.), Harvard (New York). Home: Ancon, Canal Zone.

BAXTER, RICHARD REEVE, judge; b. N.Y.C., Feb. 14, 1921; s. Charles Minturn and Gladys (Van Deventer) B.; A.B., Brown U., 1942, LL.D. (hon.), 1979; LL.B., Harvard U., 1948; diploma internat. law, Cambridge (Eng.) U., 1951; LL.M., Georgetown U., 1952, LL.D. (hon.), 1979; m. Harriet Nell Latson, May 29, 1943; children—Alison Lawrence, Prudence Oliver. Admitted to Mass. bar, 1948; atty. Office Gen. Counsel, Office Sec. Def., 1954; research asso. Harvard Law Sch., Cambridge, Mass., 1954-55, mem. faculty, 1955-80; prof. law, 1959-80; elected judge Internat. Ct. Justice, The Hague, Netherlands, 1979-80; head of South House, Radcliffe Coll., 1968-70; vis. prof. Cambridge (Eng.) U., 1966-67. Cons. to govt., 1955-78; counselor on internat. law Office Legal Adviser, U.S. Dept. State, Washington, 1971-72, mem. adv. panel on internat. law, 1970-75, on law of sea, 1973-78; mem. adv. com. Internat. Law Reports, 1962-80; hon. fellow Jesus Coll., Cambridge U., 1976-80. Mem. Permanent Ct. Arbitration, The Hague, 1968-75; mem. Mass. Commn. on Ocean Mgmt., 1968-71, Commn. on Marine Boundaries and Resources, 1969-71; bd. advisers law and population programme Fletcher Sch. Law and Diplomacy, 1971-78; mem. bd. Syndics Harvard Press, 1973-77, 78-79. Served to maj. AUS, 1942-46, U.S. Army, 1947-54, col. USAR, 1954-68. Decorated Bronze Star medal, Legion of Merit; recipient hon. mention Harvard Univ. Press Faculty prize, 1964. Mem. Am. Law Inst., Am. Bar Assn., Am. (pres. 1974-76, hon. v.p. 1976-80), Egyptian, Indian (hon.), Philippine socs. internat. law, Internat. Law Assn. (v.p. Am. br. 1963-80), Brit. Inst. Internat. and Comparative Law, Can. Council on Internat. Law (corr.), Am. Acad. Arts and Scis., Council on Fgn. Relations, Asocié de l'Institut de Droit Internat., Phi Beta Kappa. Clubs: Athenaeum (London); St. Botolph (Boston); Harvard (N.Y.C.). Editor: Documents on the St. Lawrence Seaway, 1960; The Law of International Waterways, 1964; (with Doris Carroll) The Panama Canal, 1965; (with F.V. Garcia-Amador and Louis B. Sohn) Recent Codification of the Law of State Responsibility for Injuries to Aliens, 1974. Editor-in-chief Am. Jour. Internat. Law, 1970-78. Home: Cambridge, Mass. Died Dec. 25, 1980.

BAY, CHARLES A., Foreign service officer; b. Columbus, Ohio, June 7, 1886; s. William Lewis and Cecelia Sarah (Radenbach) B.; student Ohio State U., 1904-05, Sorbonne, France, 1919; m. Opal Alydia Martin, July 31, 1930; children—Cecelia Sarah, Charles Alexander. Railway clerk, 1905; rep. Pa. R.R., passenger dept., Mpls., 1907-10, St. Paul, 1910-17; first lieutenant, A.E.F. (Railway Engineers), 1918-19; vice-consul, assigned Dublin, Ireland, 1920, Casablanca, Morocco, 1923, Port-au-Prince, Haiti, 1924; consul, Tampico, Mexico, 1924-26, Corinto, Nicaragua, 1926, Tientsin, China, 1927; third sec., Bangkok, Siam, 1928-29; second sec., Bucharest, Rumania, 1930, Tirana, Albania, 1931-32, Rome, 1933-34 (Dept. State 1935); consul, Sevilla, Spain, 1936-39; first sec., Mexico City, 1940; comml. attache from 1942; consul gen. at Milan, 1946-48. Chmn., Buckingham Twp. Planning Commn., 1954-58. Served as 1st lt. A.E.F. (Railway Engrs.); 1918-19. Home: Lahaska, Pa. Died June 3, 1978.

BAYAR, (MAHMUT) CELAL (BI-ÄR'MÄ-MOOT' JÄ-LÄL'), 3d pres. of Turkey; b. Umerbey, Turkey, 1884; s. Fehmi and Emine Bayar; ed. French sch. in Bursa, Turkey; married; 2 children. Active politically since 1907; exec. sec. Young Turks (Party of Union and Progress), Izmir, 1908; participated in uprising resulting in establishment of constitutional form of govt. in Turkey, 1909; dep. from Saruhan to Grand Assembly, and minister of economy, 1920, also acting fgn. minister, 1921; again minister of nat. economy, 1933; premier, 1937-39; co-founder Democratic party, 1946; pres. of Turkey since May 1950. Address: Ankara, Turkey.

BAYLESS, HERMAN ARMSTRONG, lawyer; b. Augusta, Ky., Sept. 28, 1882; s. Herman G. and Mary C. (Armstrong) B.; A.B., U. Cin., 1903, LL.B., 1905; m. Alfreda Shipley, 1914 (died 1930); 1 son, Shipley Armstrong; m. 2d Amelia Smalley, Aug. 15, 1936. Admitted to Ohio bar, 1905; asso. Morison R. Waite, Cin., 1905-16; mem. Waite, Schindel & Bayless & Schneider, prin. practice corp. and probate law; sec., gen. counsel Am. Barge Line Co., Jefferson Boat & Machine Co. Served as maj. AUS, World War I; judge adv. gen. port of embarkation, Newport News. Mem. Am., N.Y., Ohio, Cin. bar assns., Phi Delta Phi, Sigma Alpha Epsilon. Home: Cin.

BAYLIS, ADELAIDE BROOKS, bacteriologist; b. Garden City, L.I., N.Y., June 28, 1883; d. William and Adelaide E. (Brooks) Baylis; student Brearley Sch., New York, 1895-1902, N.Y. Post Grad. Med. Sch., 1921-22, Institut Prophylactique, Paris, 1922; hon. D.Sc., Univ. of Pittsburgh, 1937. Asst. in bacteriology, N.Y. Post Grad. Med. Sch., 1923-28, asso., since 1928; asso. in bacteriology, Columbia U. Coll. of Physicians and Surgeons, since 1931. Comdg. officer in N.Y., Am. Red Cross Ambulance and Motor Service, 1918-19; commd. capt. N.Y. State Home Defence, 1st woman to receive commn. in N.Y. state. Corr. Mem. Institut Prophylactique since 1924. Awarded Medaille d'Hygiene Publique by French Govt., 1926. First woman amateur fencing champion of America, 1912. Helped establish first trade sch. for Crippled children in New York, 1908. Dir. N.Y. chapter Am. Red Cross since 1921; sec. Bedford Branch Westchester Hist. Soc. since 1935. Mem. A.A.A.S., Soc. of Am. Bacteriologist, Nat. Tuberculosis Assn., Colonial Dames. Democrat. Episcopalian. Eastern Star. Clubs: Colony, Cosmopolitan, Fencers, Adirondack League (New York). Contbr. to scientific jours. Home: Bedford N.Y.

BAYLIS, CHARLES AUGUSTUS, educator; b. Portland, Ore., Apr. 2, 1902; s. Thomas Farrow and Hermine Antoinette (Weber) B.; A.B., U. Wash., 1923, A.M., 1924; Ph.D., Harvard, 1926; m. Ruth Woodruff Weage, Aug. 21, 1925; children—Thomas Arthur, William Eric. Mem. faculty philosophy dept. Brown U., 1927-48, asso. prof., 1937-48; dir. N.Y.C. Freshman Coll., Providence, 1935-37; sec. Univs. Com. on Post-War Internat. Problems, Boston, 1943-45; prof. philosophy and dept. head U. Md., 1949-52; prof. philosophy Duke, 1952-70, dir. grad. studies, 1952-56, dept. chmn., 1956-68. Mem. summer sch. faculty U. Wash., 1924, 25, 48, 62, Stanford, 1936, 60, Harvard, 1947, Pacific Philosophy Inst., 1956, 60, 64, San Jose (Cal.) State Coll., 1964. Sheldon traveling fellowship Harvard, with study in England, France and Germany, 1926-27; Guggenheim fellow and Senior Fulbright scholar Univ. Coll. Oxford, Eng., 1958-59. Mem. Am. Philos. Assn. (exec. com. Eastern div. 1940, v.p. 1954, chmn. com. on publ. 1961-64, chmn. nat. bd. 1965-67), Assn. for Symbolic Logic (sec.-treas. 1936-42, v.p. 1942-46), So. Soc. for Philosophy and Psychology (pres. 1955). Author: (with A.A. Bennett) Formal Logic, 1939; Ethics, 1958; Metaphysics, 1965. Mng. editor Symbolic Logic, 1936-42, cons. editor, 1942-75; editorial cons. The Philos. Rev., 1950-53; editorial staff Philosophy and Phenomenological Research. Mem. editorial bd. Cornell Publs. in Contemporary Philosophy, 1956-60. Research in epistemology, metaphysics, ethics and perception. Home: Durham, N.C. Died Aug. 30, 1975.

BAYLISS, CHARLES WILLIAM, mfg. exec.; b. Chicago, Ill., Apr. 7, 1882; s. William Thomas and Mary Clara (Addison) B.; ed. pub. schs., Milwaukee, Wis.; m. Mary Anne Bloomfield, Apr. 29, 1911; children—Mary Bloomfield, Margaret Addison, Charles William. In railroad work, later traveling freight agent, traveling salesman and sales mgr. Portland Cement Industry until 1910; mgr. street and road dept. Gen. Asphalt Co. (now The Barber Asphalt Corp.), 1910-19, v.p., 1919-38; pres. Artic Roofings, Inc.; dir. Glassine Paper Company, The Laguna Corp. Mason. Clubs: Bachelors Barge, Racquet, Phila. Country, Aronimink Golf, Pine Valley Golf. Home: Wayne, Pa. *

BAZZONI, CHARLES BLIZARD (BAT'ZÔ-NI), physicist; b. Newburgh, N.Y., Jan. 28, 1886; s. Charles Lewis and Marie Antoinette (Dayton) B.; B.Pd., N.Y. State Normal Coll., 1905; B.S., U. of Pa., 1911, M.A., 1913, Ph.D., 1914; Harrison research fellow (U. of Pa.) at U. of London, 1915-16; m. Edith Vera Harling, Dec. 31, 1918. Teacher science, high schs. of N.Y., 1905-07; instr. in physics, U. of Pa., 1910-19; research asst., King's Coll. (U. of London), 1916-17; asst. prof. physics, U. of Pa., 1919-21, prof. exptl. physics, 1921-38; in charge geophys. exploration, Sun Oil Co., 1925-26, chief geophysicist since 1938. Capt. Corps Engrs., U.S. Army, 1917-19; in command in field of Sound Ranging Serv., A.E.F.; major field artillery, O.R.C., 1925-40; section member National Defense Research Committee, 1942-46. Receipient President's Certificate of Merit, 1948. Fellow A.A.A.S., American Physical Society; member Franklin Institute, associate editor Journal Franklin Institute (member committee on science and arts), Assn. Exploration Geophysicists, American Seismological Society, Optical Society of America, Am. Geophysical Union, Soc. X-ray and Electron Diffraction, Sigma Xi. Awarded gold medal, Sesquicentennial Expn., Phila., 1926. Decorated Brit. Military Cross; Officer d'Acadaemie with Palms (French); citation by Gen. Pershing; Order of the Purple Heart. Episcopalian. Author: Text Book of Physics, 1920; Kernels of the Universe, 1927; Matter and Energy, 1931; contbr. Jour. Franklin Inst., Philos. Magazine, Physical Rev., etc. Experimenter in field of atomic physics, seismic, gravitational and elec. geophysical exploration. Home: Wallingford, Pa. *

BEACH, GOODWIN BATTERSON, educator; b. Hartford, Conn., Oct. 2, 1885; s. Charles Coffing and Mary Elizabeth (Batterson) B.; A.B., Harvard, 1907; M.A., Trinity Coll., Hartford, 1931; Litt.D., U. Leeds, Eng., 1953; m. Ethel Gertrude Curry, Sept. 8, 1908; children—Annabel Gertrude de Coral, Mary Goodwin (Mrs. Joseph Beach), Carol Coffin (wife of Dr. Samuel W. Root); m. 2d, Edith Agnes Durrant, Jan. 26, 1927; children—Patricia H. (Mrs. Calvin Thompson), Penelope D. (Mrs. William Mck. Chittenden). Underwriter Travelers Ins. Co., 1907-12; head brokerage firm Goodwin Beach & Co., 1912-42; lectr. in Latin, Trinity Coll.; past dir. Am. Surety Co. Chmn. Hartford Housing Authority, 1945-52; mem. Conn. Liquor Commn., 1949-53. Mem. Am. Philpl. Assn. (dir.), Classical Assn. of Eng., Am. Classical League, Classical Assn. N.E., Cath. Classical Assn., N.Y. Classical Club. Home: West Hartford Conn. *

BEACH, STEWART (TAFT), editor, writer; b. Pontiac, Mich., Dec. 17, 1899; s. Samuel Elmore and Julia (Taft) B.; B.A., U. Mich., 1922; m. Josephine Cushman, May 12, 1928; one daughter, Margaret Taft (Mrs. Stanley Glos). Special lecturer on modern poetry short story N.Y. University, 1922-24; mng. editor The Independent, 1924-28; asso. editor The Outlook and Independent, 1928-29; editor, dramatic critic Theatre mag., 1929-31; mng. editor, editor Home and Field, also House Beautiful, 1931-39; contbr. fiction leading mags., 1939-42; exec. editor This Week mag. 1947-65. Served as capt to col., U.S. Army, 1942-46, chief publs. br., bur. pub. relations War Dept. Decorated Legion of Merit, War Dept. commendation Mem. The Pilgrims, Loyal Legion, Soc. Mayflower Descendants, Phi Beta Kappa, Chi. Clubs: Century Assn., University, Coffee House, Dutch Treat (N.Y.C.); St. Botolph (Boston). Author: Short Story Technique, 1929 (play) Lend Me Your Ears (with Philip Wood), 1936. Editor: This Week's Short-Short Stories, 1953; This Week's Stories of Mystery and Suspense, 1957; Samuel Adams: The Fateful Years, 1764-76, 1965; (with Samuel Chamberlain) New England in Color, 1969, Lexington and Concord in Color, 1970. Home: New York, N.Y. Died Feb. 21, 1979.

BEADLE, ROBERT CAMERON, b. Brooklyn, N.Y., Oct. 19, 1883; s. William Irwin and Emma Leslie (Cameron) B.; ed. pvt. and pub. schs., and under pvt. tutors; unmarried. Began in employ of Spencer Trask & Co., New York, 1900; became sec. to George Foster Peabody and represented him in many philanthropic, polit. and humanitarian projects; assisted in reorgn. of Am. Stoker Co. (now Combustion Engring. Corpn.), 1916-27; was asst. to pres. Internat. Combustion Engring. Corpn. and in charge publicity same, 1919-29; organized U.S. Stoker Corpn., 1912, and v.p. until 1914; was v.p. Combustion Publishing Corpn., pres. 1920-27, and changed name, 1929, to Power Engring. & Financial Pub. Corpn., of which is pres.; dir. Internat. Pub. Relations Council, Green Engring. Co., 1924-29; pres. Robert Cameron Beadle, Incorporated; dir. and treas. Am. Stoker Co.; founder Combustion (now Engineering and Finance), 1919, and since editor; also pres. Super Power Publications, Inc.; publisher of "Achievement", new large magazine. As sec. to George Foster Peabody, planned and put into motion the demonstration at Baltimore that resulted in nomination of Woodrow Wilson as president. Vice pres. Dr. Mary Halton Endowment for Girls; formerly trustee N.Y. Infirmary for Women and Children; dir. pub. relations Broad St. Hosp. N.Y. City; formerly vice chmn. building fund com. Greenwich House Music School Settlement; vet. troop commr. Boy Scouts of America, Holy Trinity Ch., Brooklyn; first financial sec. Am. Ch. Inst. for Negroes, 1910-14. Ex-v.p. Tech. Publicity Assn., Nat. Industrial Adv. Assn., Advertising Club of New York, New York Business Publishers' Assn., Nat. Publishers' Assn., Editorial Conf. Bd.; asso. mem. Am. Soc. Mech. Engrs. Republican. Episcopalian. Clubs: Bankers, Advertising, Hempstead Country. Home: Brooklyn.

BEAL, KENNETH MALCOLM, educator; b. Salem, Mass., July 4, 1906; s. Kenneth and Annie May (Lopaus) B.; B.A., Dartmouth, 1928; A.M., Harvard, 1935; m. Rachel Weston Palmateer, Sept. 8, 1931; 1 dau., Nancy May (Mrs. James M. Keech, Jr.). Instr. English, preparatory dept. Am. U., Beirut, 1928-31; instr. French and English, Jr. High Sch., Wellesley, Mass., 1932-39; mem. faculty U. Miami (Fla.), 1939-72, prof. English, 1952-72, chmn. dept., 1959-61, chmn. div. humanities, 1960-62. Mem. A.A.U.P., Hist. Assn. So. Fla., Iron Arrow, Omicron Delta Kappa. Home: Coconut Grove, Fla. Died May 6, 1977.

BEAL, THOMAS PRINCE, banker; b. Boston, Apr. 12, 1883; s. Thomas P. and Ida (DeFord) B.; grad. Noble and Greenough Sch., Boston, 1900; A.B., Harvard, 1904; m. May Lefferts Morgan, Aug. 11, 1921; children—Judith Drew (Mrs. Herbert T. Nadai), Thomas Prince. Asst. cashier 2d Nat. Bank of Boston, 1908, v.p., 1910, pres., 1923, chmn. bd., 1950-77, later chmn. adv. com. State Street Bank and Trust Co., merger of 2d Nat. Bank and State St. Trust Co.; hon. trustee Suffolk Franklin Savs. Bank; incorporator Charlestown Savs. Bank, Boston. Trustee Mt. Auburn Cemetery. Pres. Boston Clearing House, 1943, 45, 48, 52. Republican. Episcopalian. Clubs: Somerset, Union (Boston); Country (Brookline). Home: Chestnut Hill, Mass. Died Oct. 30, 1980.

BEAL, WALTER HUBERT, mgmt. cons.; b. Toledo, Iowa; s. Albert M. (M.D.) and Carrie (Middlekauff) B.; grad. U. Ill., 1916; m. Dorothy Barratt, June 2, 1920; children—Walter Hubert, Richard Barratt. With Lycoming Mfg. Co., Williamsport, Pa., 1919, sales mgr., 1919-27, v.p., 1927-30, gen. mgr., 1930-31, became pres., 1931; pres. Auburn (Ind.) Automobile Co., 1932-34; chmn. bd. N.Y. Shipbuilding Corp., 1935-38; pres. Aviation Mfg. Corp., N.Y.C., 1938-40; mgmt. cons. Riker-Maxson Corp.; dir. Somat Corp., Pomeroy, Pa.; chmn. bd. Penn-Jersey Shipbldg. Corp., 1941-46, pres. 1942-46. Served to capt. Ordnance Dept., U.S. Army, World War I. Mem. Delta Kappa Epsilon (past nat. pres.). Presbyterian. Clubs: Merion Cricket (Haverford, Pa.); Merion Golf (Ardmore, Pa.); Racquet (Philadelphia). Home: Gladwyne, Pa. Died Mar. 3, 1976.

BEALE, JOHN ALLEN, state ofcl.; b. Rockford, Ill., Aug. 10, 1918; s. Harold Watts and Mary Agnes (Long) B.; B.S., Mich. State U., 1940; M.P.A. (Ford Found. fellow), Harvard, 1954; m. Norma Lee Resech, Apr. 3, 1948; children—Virginia, Laura, Elizabeth. Forester, Wis. Dept. Natural Resources, Madison, 1945-50, supr. forest inventory, 1950-53, supr. county forestry, 1952-54, chief state forester, 1954-68, adminstr. Dept. Conservation, 1968, dep. sec. Dept. Natural Resources, 1968-76. Vis. lectr. Soc. Am. Foresters. Trustee Menominee Indian Enterprise; bd. dirs. Friends of Univ. Symphony. Mem. Sec. Agr.'s Forestry Research Adv. Com.; pres., West High Sch. P.T.A., 1974-76; mem. Madison Civic Music Assn., 1969-76, Civil War Round Table, 1965-76. Served to capt. AUS, 1941-45. Decorated Bronze Star medal, Purple Heart with clusters. Mem. Nat. Assn. State Foresters (pres. 1964), Soc. Am. Foresters (pres. 1974-75, Distinguished Service award Wis.-Mich. sect. 1972), Nat. Assn. State Outdoor Liaison Officers (pres. 1975), Soil Conservation Soc., Alpha Gamma Rho. Conglist. (chmn. bd. trustees 1969). Mason (32 deg., Shriner). Home: Madison, Wis. Died May 27, 1976; interred Forest Hills Cemetery, Madison, Wis.

BEALS, CARLETON, author, lectr.; b. Medicine Lodge, Kans., Nov. 13, 1893; s. Leon Elverson and Elvina Sybilla (Blickensderfer) B.; B.A. cum laude, U. Calif., 1916; M.A., Columbia, 1917; postgrad. U. Madrid, 1920, U. Rome, 1922, U. Mexico, 1923; m. Carolyn Kennedy, 1956. Dir., English Prep. Inst., Mexico City, 1919; prin. Am. High Sch., Mexico City, 1919-20; instr. personal staff Pres. Carranza, 1920; lectr. N.Y. Bd. of Edn., 1924; asso. editor Mexican Folkways, 1925-37; asso. editor Latin-Am. Press Syndicate, 1933-34; pres. editorial bd. Latin-Am. Digest, 1934-36; contbg. editor, Common Sense, 1933-41, Modern Monthly, 1935-37, Current History, 1939; mem. adv. bd. Living Age, 1933-35; adv. editor Controversy, 1935; corr. in Italy, 1920-22, Mexico, 1923, 1925-28, 1930-32, 1937, 46, 61, in Central Am., 1927-28, (with Gen. Sandino in Nicaragua, 1928), Spain, North Africa, Italy, Turkey, Russia and Germany, 1929, Cuba, 1932-33, 1935, 57, 59-61, Panama, Colombia, Ecuador, Peru, 1934, 46, 61; researcher Housing Authority New Haven, 1959-60; spl. corr. N. Am. Newspaper Alliance, 1935; spl. corr. New York Post, Scottsboro Trial, Ala., 1936; mem. expdns. to Indian regions, Mexico, 1926, 1930-31; spl. corr. Argentina, Chile, Bolivia, Peru, 1946, Haiti, Cuba, 1957, 59, 60, Colombia, Brazil, Paraguay, Venezuela, Uruguay, Guiana, Trinidad, 1961; lectr. Latin-Am. Univs., 1961, Mexican-Am. relations Conf. Cause and Cure of War (Washington), 1927, Seminar on Relations with Mexico, 1925-28, 1930-31; lectr. on Central America, Nat. U. Mexico, 1928; faculty lectr. on Modern Mexico and Caribbean, U. Calif., summer, 1933, New Sch. of Social Research, 1935; chmn. Com. Jacques Romain, 1935, mem. adv. bd. Better Understanding Found.; bd. govs. Acad. Fgn. Relations. Mem. roundtable Harris Found., U. Chgo., 1951, Research Fuller F. Barnes Found., 1952-53. Recipient Bonnheim award, 1916, 1917; Bryce History prize, 1917; Best Article prize Arizona Quarterly, 1961; Nat. Acad. of Recording Arts and Scis. award, 1965. Fellow John Simon Guggenheim Found., 1931-32. Fellow Am. Geog. Soc., Soc. Am. Historians; mem. P.E.N., Fgn. Press Club (Mexico City), Pi Gamma Mu. Sponsor Nat. Gallery of the Am. Indian. Author: Mexico: An Interpretation, 1923; Rome or Death, 1923; Brimstone and Chile, 1927; Destroying Victor, 1929; Mexican Maze, 1931; Banana Gold, 1932; Porfirio Diaz: Dictator of Mexico, 1932; The Crime of Cuba, 1933; Black River, 1934; Fire on the Andes, 1934; The Story of Huey P. Long, 1935; America South, 1936; The Coming Struggle for Latin America, 1937; Glass Houses, 1938; American Earth, 1939; The Great Circle, 1940; Pan America: A Program, 1940; Rio Grande to Cape Horn, 1943; What South Americans Think of Us, 1945; Lands of the Dawning Morrow, 1948; The Long Land: Chile, 1948; Our Yankee Heritage (series), The Making of Greater New Haven, 1951, The Making of Bristol, 1954, New England's Contributions to American Civilization, 1955; Stephen F. Austin; Father of Texas, 1953; Taste of Glory, 1956; Adventure of the Western Sea, The Story of Robert Gray, 1956; John Eliot: The Man Who Loved the Indians, 1958; House in Mexico, 1958; The Brass Knuckle Crusade: The Great Know-Nothing Conspiracy, 1959; Nomads and Empire Builders, 1961; Cyclone Carry, The Story of Carry Nation, 1962; Latin America: World in Revolution, 1963; Eagles of the Andes, 1963; War Within a War, 1965; Under the Fifth Sun, Mexico Past and Present, 1965; Land of the Mayas, Yesterday and Today, 1966; The Great Crusade and its Leaders, 1968; Stories Told by the Aztecs, 1968; Great Guerrilla Warriors, 1969; The Nature of Revolution, 1970; Colonial Rhode Island, 1970; The Incredible Incas, Yesterday and Today, 1973; transl. Anti-Communism in Latin America (Juan Arevalo), 1965; collaborator: Genius of Mexico, 1931; Politics U.S.A., 1961; Bits of Silver, 1961. Contributor Ency. of Social Sciences, Ency. Brit., Book of Knowledge Ency., World Book Ency., Land and Peoples Ency., Ency. of Sexual Behavior; also to mags. Home: Killingworth, Conn. Died June 27, 1979; buried Evergreen Cemetery, Killingworth, Conn.

BEAMS, JESSE WAKEFIELD, educator; b. Belle Plaine, Kan., Dec. 25, 1898; s. Jesse Wakefield and Kathryn (Wylie) B.; A.B., Fairmount (Kan.) Coll., 1921; M.A., U. Wis., 1922; Ph.D., U. Va., 1925; Sc.D., William and Mary Coll., 1941, U. N.C., 1946, Washington and Lee U., 1949, Fla. Inst. Tech., 1969, Yale, 1976; m. Maxine Sutherland, June 16, 1931. Instr.

physics and math. Ala. Poly. Inst., 1922-23; Nat. Research fellow U. Va., 1925-26, Yale, 1926-27; instr. physics, Yale, 1927-28; asso. prof. physics, U. Va., 1928-30, prof., 1930-77, Francis H. Smith prof. physics, 1953-69, chmn. dept. physics, 1948-63. Bd. dirs. Oak Ridge Inst. Nuclear Studies, Va. Inst. Sci. Research; mem. Nat. Research Fellowship com. NRC, 1949; mem. gen. adv. com. AEC, 1954-60. Recipient Potts medal Franklin Inst., 1942; John Scott award, 1956; Lewis award Am. Philos. Soc., 1958; Achievement award U. Wichita Alumni Assn., 1959; Nat. Medal of Sci., 1968; Gold medal and citation AEC, 1972; Beams lectureship in bio-physics established in his honor U. Va. Fellow Am. Phys. Soc. (pres. 1938-39, 1958-59, 68, Beams Medal for Research established in his honor SE sect.), AAAS (chmn. sect. B, 1943), Va. Acad. Sci. (pres. 1947, Merit award), Am. Acad. Arts and Sci., Am. Optical Soc.; mem. Am. Philos. Soc. (v.p. 1960-63), Am. Physics Tchrs. Assn., AAUP, NRC (physics div. 1933-36, 37-40), Nat. Acad. Scis., Phi Beta Kappa, Sigma Xi, Sigma Pi Sigma (hon.), Raven Soc. Club: Colonnade. Contbr. numerous articles. Home: Charlottesville, Va. Died July 23, 1977; buried U. Va. Cemetery.

BEAN, ERNEST F., geologist; b. Zearing, Ia., Jan. 30, 1882; s. Cyrus P. and Marion (Brown) B.; M.Di., Ia. State Teachers Coll., 1905; A.B., U. of Wis., 1909, A.M., 1911; m. Jessie G. Gillis, June 16, 1911; children—Marion, Ernest F. Instructor in geology, University of Wisconsin, 1911-15, asst. prof., 1915-17; asst. state geologist, Wis., 1916-25, state geologist 1926-53. Member Alaska glacial expedition, 1909, 10; geologist Wis. Geol. Survey, 1911; chief of field parties, same, 1913-19; geologist in charge road material surveys, Wis., 1920-25. Fellow Geol. Soc. America; member Society Economic Geologists, The Wisconsin Academy of Science, Arts and Letters, Wisconsin Hist. Soc., Sigma Xi, Gamma Alpha. Mason. Club: University. Home: Shorewood Hills, Madison. *

BEAN, JAMES WILSON, clergyman; b. Burlington, Ia., Apr. 19, 1882; s. John Victor (M.D.) and Elizabeth Reddick (Wilson) B.; A.B., Parsons Coll., Fairfield, Ia., 1902, D.D., 1914; won scholarship of Bd. of Edn., Presbyn. Ch., U.S.A., 1903; grad. Presbyn. Theol. Sem., Omaha, Neb., 1905; S.T.B., Princeton Theol. Sem., 1906; grad. student, U. of Minn., 1924-25; m. Harriet Eleanor Rice, June 30, 1908; children—Robert Taylor, Elizabeth Frances, James Edgar. Ordained Presbyn. ministry, 1906; pastor 1st Ch., Winfield, Ia., 1906-09, Cherokee, Ia., 1909-13, Hastings, Neb., 1913-18; pres. Coll. of Emporia, Kan., 1918; pastor Dayton Av. Presbyn. Ch., St. Paul, Minn., 1918-28; First Ch., Canton, O., 1929-42, First Church, Newton, Iowa, since April 1942. President of St. Paul Council of Churches, 1923-25; chmn. Synod's Com. on Edn., 1922-28; mem. exec. com. United Charities, St. Paul, 1926-28; mem. bd. of dirs. Canton (O.) Family Service Soc. and Children's Bureau, 1932-42, mem. exec. com., 1933-41 chmn. 1939-41; pres. Canton and Stark County Ministers Assn., 1939-40. Moderator, successively of Presbyteries of Sioux City, Hastings, St. Paul (twice), Mahoning. Mem. bd. trustees, Parsons Coll. Mem. Phi Kappa Phi. Rotary, Chi Alpha. Home: Newton, Ia. *

BEAR, FIRMAN EDWARD, soil expert; b. Germantown, O., May 21, 1884; s. Ira Frank and Emma (Harris) B.; B.Sc., Ohio State U., 1908, M.Sc., 1910; studied Cornell U., summer 1912; Ph.D., U. of Wis., 1917; studied Institut Nat. Agronomique, Paris, France, 1924-25; in industrial research, Berlin, Germany, 1926-27; m. Helen Judy, July 6, 1911; children—Firman Edward, II, Robert Judy. Instr. agrl. chemistry, Ohio State U., 1908-10, asst. prof. 1910-13; prof. soils, W.Va. U., 1914-16, also in charge soil investigations; prof. agrl. chemistry and soils, Ohio State U., 1916-20, prof. soils, 1920-29; asso. in soils, Ohio Expt. Sta., 1917-29; dir. agrl. research, Am. Cyanamid Co., New York, since Apr. 1, 1929. Fellow A.A.A.S.; mem. Am. Soc. Agronomy, Am. Chem. Soc., Sigma Xi, Alpha Zeta. Republican. Conglist. Author: Soil Management, 1924, 2d edit., 1927; Theory and Practice in The Use of Fertilizers, 1929. Home: Larchmont, N.Y. *

BEARD, THEODORE HEMINGWAY, office equipment mfr.; b. Bethel, Conn., June 9, 1895; s. George Edwards and Cora Augusta (Barnum) B.; B.S., M.E. M.S., N.Y. U., 1917; m. Margaret Durant Shepard, Dec. 7, 1929; children—Constance Shepard (Mrs. Willard I. Emerson, Jr.), John Edwards, Betsy Ann (Mrs. Peter B. Salisbury). Staff engr. Columbia Graphophone Mfg. Co., N.Y.C., 1920-23, cons. mech. engr., 1923-29; with Dictaphone Corp., N.Y.C., from 1929, successively supervising eng., v.p., 1936-53, vice chmn. exec. com., dir., from 1953; dir. Bullard Corp., United Illuminating Co., Conn. Nat. Bank Co., Bridgeport Hydraulic Co.; trustee Bridgeport Peoples Savs. Bank. Served as maj. U.S. Army, 1917-20. Mem. Am. Soc. M.E., Newcomen Soc., S.A.R., Nat. Rifle Assn., Army Ordnance Assn. Republican. Conglist. Mason, Rotarian. Clubs: University Brooklawn Country (Bridgeport); Army and Navy (Washington). Home Easton, Conn. Died Oct. 7, 1978.

BEARDSLEY, CHARLES EDWARD, lawyer; b. Des Moines, Apr. 21, 1904; s. John and Anna (Wyman) B.; A.B., Stanford, 1925, J.D., 1927; m. Marian Gower, Aug. 12, 1926; children—Frances (Mrs. John L. Dee), Anna (Mrs. Thomas J. McHugh), Jane Margery (Mrs. C. A. Lemeland). Admitted to Cal. bar, 1927, then practiced in Los Angeles; sr. partner Beardsley, Hufstedler & Kemble. Mem. Am., Los Angeles (1st chmn. jr. barristers, past chmn. constl. rights com., juvenile court com.) bar assns., State Bar Cal. (chmn. com. bar examiners, bd. govs. 1950-53, pres. 1952-53), Am. Coll. Trial Lawyers, Los Angeles Jr. C. of C. (past dir.), Am. Law Inst. Clubs: Chancery, University (Los Angeles); San Marino City (past pres.), Oneonta (past pres.) (South Pasadena, Cal.). Home: San Marino, Calif. Died Aug. 6, 1975.

BEARDSLEY, RICHARD KING, educator; b. Cripple Creek, Colo., Dec. 16, 1918; s. Earl Pearson and Alice (Smith) B.; B.A. summa cum laude, U. Cal. at Berkeley, 1939, Ph.D., 1947; m. Grace Elizabeth Cornog, Apr. 1, 1942; children—Elizabeth, Kelcey, Margaret. Instr. anthropology U. Mich., Ann Arbor, 1947-48, asst. prof., 1948-53, asso. prof., 1953-59, prof., 1959-78, dir. Center for Japanese Studies, 1961-64, 72-74, 77-78, acting chmn. dept. anthropology, 1971-72. Mem. Am. adv. com. Japan Found., 1975-77. Served to lt. USNR, 1942-46. Ford Found. fellow, 1953-54, 64-65, 70-71; Guggenheim Found. fellow, 1958-59; NSF fellow, 1973-75. Mem. Am. Anthrop. Assn., AAAS, Assn. Asian Studies, Ethnol. Soc. Japan. Author: Village Japan, 1959; Twelve Doors to Japan, 1965. Editor: Japanese Culture: Its Origin and Characteristics, 1962. Home: Ann Arbor, Mich. Died June 9, 1978; buried Forest Hill Cemetery, Ann Arbor.

BEARDSLEY, WALTER RAPER, drug co., exec.; b. Elkhart, Ind., Oct. 23, 1905; s. Andrew Hubble and Helen (Brown) B.; grad. Phillips Andover Acad., 1924; B.S. with honors in Politics, Princeton, 1928; m. Marjory Buschanan, Nov. 20, 1929; 1 son, Robert. Asst. to pres. Miles Labs., Inc., Elkhart, Ind., 1929-33, v.p., 1933-47, pres., 1947-61, chmn. bd., 1961-73, chmn. finance com., 1973-76, dir., 1933-80; dir. emeritus 1st Nat. Bank. Mem. Ind. Senate, 1936-40; chmn. Elkhart County Republican Com., 1930-34; del. Rep. Nat. Conv., 1948, 52, 56, 60, 68, 72; mem. Nat. Rep. Com. from Ind., 1961-68; nat. chmn. Rep. Congl. Boosters Club, Mashington, 1971-74; mem. art adv. council U. Notre Dame; trustee Elkhart Gen. Hosp. Served as lt. col., USAAF, 1942-45. Benjamin Franklin fellow Royal Soc. Arts, London, Eng. Mem. Propietary Assn. Am. (pres. 1948-50, hon. v.p.), Nat., Ind. socs. of S.A.R., Am. Legion. Presbyn. Clubs: Princeton (Chgo.); Elcona Country, City (Elkhart); Sky (N.Y.C.). Home: Elkhart, Ind. Died Oct. 23, 1980.

BEATTIE, JAMES A., prof. chemistry; b. Louisville, Ky., July 24, 1895; s. James William and Alice (Mount) B.; B.S., Mass. Inst. of Technology, 1917, M.S., 1918, Ph.D., 1920; University of Leiden, Holland, 1922-23; m. Doris A. Bunker, July 14, 1920; children—Doris Pamela, Barbara Mount, James William. Prof. chemistry, Mass. Inst. Tech., 1938-61, professor emeritus, lecturer in chemistry, 1961-81, staff mem., security officer, Radiation Lab., 1942-46. Mem. Am. Chem. Soc., Am. Physical Soc., Am. Acad. Arts and Sciences, Alpha Chi Sigma, Sigma Xi. Awarded Nat. Research fellowship, 1921-23. Home: Belmont, Mass. Died Feb. 23, 1981.

BEATTY, C. FRANCIS, indsl. exec.; born Brooklyn, Apr. 15, 1890; s. James B. and Theodora (Drake) B.; B.S., Amherst Coll., 1912; m. Helen Corning, 1916 (died 1924); m. 2d, Gene Joy, 1926; children—Helen (Mrs. John D. Swan), C. Francis, Joy, Robert M. With refinery dept. Standard Oil Co. of N.Y., 1912-15; Knox Hat Co., N.Y. City, 1915-18, New Jersey Zinc Co., N.Y. City, 1918-26; partner F. J. Ross Co., advt. agy., 1926-28; mem. mfg. com. Standard Oil Co. of N.Y., 1928-30; v.p. and dir. Socony Spltys. Co. (subsidiary of Standard Oil Co. of N.Y.), 1930-31, pres. and dir., 1931-34; pres. and dir. Socony Paint Products Co. (subsidiary Socony-Vacuum Oil Co.), 1934-46; dir., exec. in charge indsl. relations, purchasing and paint mfg. activities Socony-Vacuum Oil Co. after 1945; v.p., dir. Mobil Oil Co., to 1955. Mem. marine coatings com. W.P.B., 1942. U.S. del. to Internat. Labor Orgn., and vice chmn. petroleum sect., Geneva, 1948, '50; Scheveningen, Holland, 1952; arbitrator Am. Arbitration Assn. after 1940; mem. Nat. Indsl. Conf. Bd. since 1947. Mem. visiting com. Harvard Sch. Pub. Health; chmn. Pawling (N.Y.) Nature Res.; mem. Cornell Lab. Ornithology, Harvard Sch. Pub. Health. Trustee Assn. Protection Adirondacks. Mem. Am. Petroleum Inst., Acad. Polit. Sci., Am. Acad. Polit. and Social Sci., N.Y. Paint, Varnish and Lacquer Assn. (pres.), Phi Delta Theta. Republican. Episcopalian. Rotarian (hon.). Clubs: Amherst, Anglers, Harvard, Union League (New York); Anglers (Phila.); Quaker Hill Country (Pawling, N.Y.); Flyfishers (London); Limestone Trout, Burlington Brook, Kon-Kapot Trout, Hammersley Lake, Islamorada Fishing. Home: Pawling, N.Y. Died Jan. 31, 1976.

BEATTY, FRANK EDMUND (BA'TE), naval officer; b. Washington, D.C., June 17, 1894; s. Frank Edmund and Anne Meem (Peachy) B.; B.S., U.S. Naval Acad., 1916; B.S. in Mech. Engring., Mass. Inst. Tech., 1922; m. Lucie Patricia Horton, Oct. 2, 1918; children—Frank J. Denis, Hugh Edmund. Commd. ensign, U.S. Navy, 1916, advanced through grades to rear adm., 1944; aide to Sec. of Navy, 1941; commdr. Aruba-Curacoa Area, 1944. Decorated Navy Cross, Navy Bronze Star, British Coronation Medal. Comdr. Order of Southern Cross (Brazil); 2 Legion of Merit, grand Comdr. Orange Nassau (with swords). Clubs: Chevy Chase, Army and Navy (Washington). Home: Belvedere, Calif. Died Nov. 12, 1976.

BEATTY, ROBERT OWEN, writer, pub., corp. exec., conservationist, editor; b. Chicago, Nov. 12, 1924; s. Vernon David and Elizabeth (Rubinkam) B.; student Shattuck Sch., 1937-41, Dartmouth, 1941-42; B.S., U. Mich., 1945, M.S., 1946; m. Louise Forbush, Feb. 23, 1946; children—Deborah, David Clarke, II, Barbara. Timber stand improvement U.S. Forest Service, 1941; research asst. fish div. U. Mich. Mus. Zoology, 1942-43; staff asst. Izaak Walton League Am., 1946-47, conservation dir., 1948-53; sec.-treas. Izaak Walton League Am. Endowment Inc., 1950-53; editor Outdoor America, 1946-53, N.W. public relations officer of Crown Zellerbach Corporation, 1953-56; assistant to president Western Kraft Corp., 1956-62, mgr. product devel., advt., pub. relations, 1958-62; asst. to pres. Electro-Sci. Industries, 1962-64; mgr. Sunset Sci. Park, Inc., 1962-65; director of public relations and advt. Boise Cascade Corp., 1965-71; 1st asst. sec. for pub. affairs HEW, 1971-72; free-lance writer travel, outdoor conservation and bus. subjects, 1945-76; pres. R.O. Beatty and Assos., Inc., book pubs., Boise, Idaho. Exec. bd. Ore.-Ida. council Boy Scouts Am.; Ida. chmn. Boys Clubs Am., 1973. Pres. Oreg. Mus. Sci. and Industry, 1961, chmn. bd., 1962; bd. dirs. YMCA; trustee Boise Galley Art. Served with USMCR, 1942-45. Mem. Pub. Relations Soc. Am., Wilderness Soc., Flyfishers Oreg. (founding mem.), Outdoor Writers Assn. Am., Ducks Unltd., Phi Sigma (hon.), Psi Upsilon. Republican. Clubs: Hillcrest Country, Rotary, San Francisco Press; Arid. Author: Idaho, 1974; co-author: Nevada, 1976; Still a Lot of Living, 1978. Home: Boise, Idaho. Died Dec. 8, 1976.

BEAUDIN, PHILIP F., business exec.; b. Canada, 1884. Vice pres., dir. White Pine Copper Co., Copper Range Co., Copper Range R.R., Copper Range Motor Bus Co. Mem. Am. Inst. Mining and Metall. Engrs. Elk. Home: Brookline, Mass.

BEAVER, J(ACOB) LYNFORD, univ. prof.; b. near Phoenixville, Pa., Aug. 25, 1882; B.E., Westchester State Normal Sch., 1900; E.E., Lehigh U., 1904, M.S., 1921; Sc.D., Harvard, 1932; m. Henrietta E. McClatchey, Mar. 29, 1910; children—Donald Payne, Margaret Walker, Mary Elizabeth, Ann Harrison. With N.Y. Fire Ins. Co., 1904-05; instr. elec. engring. U. of Pa., 1905-07; sr. instr. Drexel Inst. Tech., Phila., 1907-17; with Phila. Electric Co., 1917-18; asst. prof. elec. engring. Lehigh U., Bethlehem, Pa., 1918-24, asso. prof., 1924-37, prof. since 1937, acting head dept. elec. engring., 1941-45; vis. prof. N.C. State Coll., Raleigh since 1953. Member board Moravian Prep. Sch. Recipient distinguished service award Theta Xi, 1949. Fellow Am. Inst. E.E. (v.p.), Soc. for Advancement Sci.; mem. Am. Soc. Engring. Edn., Sigma Xi, Theta Xi (bd. dirs.), Tau Beta Pi, Eta Kappa Nu. Rep. Mem. Moravian Ch. Clubs: Torch (bd. dirs.), National Dinner (chmn. program com.). Author: Alternating Currents, 1910; Principles of Alternating Currents and Alternating Currents Machinery, 1921. Contbr. articles to profl. jours. Home: Phoenixville, Pa. *

BEAVER, SANDY, educator; b. Augusta, Ga., Oct. 5, 1883; s. Sandy and Savannah (Webb) B.; A.B., Univ. of Ga., 1903, Pd.D., 1930; traveled and studied in Europe; m. Annice Lowry, Feb. 17, 1912; children—John Lowry, Dorothy Agnes, Louise Lowry, Lucile Elizabeth. Teacher, housemaster and prin., Univ. Sch. for Boys, Stone Mountain, Ga., 1903-13; pres. Riverside Mil. Acad. since June 1, 1913; mem. bd. regents Univ. System of Ga., 1933-39. Col. and chief of staff to gov. of Ga. since 1933. Democrat. Presbyterian. Mason, K.P., Shriner. Home: Gainesville, Ga.*

BEAZLEY, SIR JOHN DAVIDSON, classical archaeologist; b. Glasgow, Scotland, Sept. 13, 1885; s. Mark John Murray and Mary Catherine (Davidson) B.; student Christ's Hosp.; M.A., Balliol Coll., Oxford Univ., 1910; honorary degrees; Litt.D., Cambridge Univ., 1927, Ph.D., Univ. of Marburg, 1927, LL.D., Univ. Glasgow, 1953, D. Litt., Univ. Durham, 1943, University Reading, 1953, Oxford University, 1956. Dr.-ès-Lettres, Univ. Lyons, 1947; hon. fellow Balliol College and Lincoln College (Oxford University); hon. student Christ Church (Oxford University); Dr.-es Lettres (hon.), University of Paris, 1960; D. Phil. (hon.), U. Thessalonike, 1963; m. Marie Henriette Bloomfield, August 13, 1919. Student, tutor Christ Church. Oxford U., 1908-25, prof. classical archaeology, 1925-56; Sather prof. U. Cal., 1949. Knighted, 1949. Recipient Petrie Medal, University of London, 1937; Kenyon medal of British Acad., 1957; Companion of Honour, 1959; Premio Feltrinelli, 1965. Fellow of British Academy, Metropolitan Museum of Art New York (hon.); fgn. mem. Am. Philos. Soc., Am. Acad.,

Archaeol. Inst. Am., Accademia Pontificia Romana, Accademia dei Lincei, Royal Danish Acad., Austrian Acad.; associé étranger Academie des Inscriptions et des Belles-Lettres; fgn. mem. Athens Acad. Author: Attic Vases in American Museums, 1918; Attic Red-figure Vasepainters, 1942, 63; Etruscan Vase-painting, 1947; Development of Attic Black-figure, 1951; Attic Black-figure Vase painters 1956; Paralipomena, 1969. Home: Oxford, Eng. *

BECHTEL, KENNETH KARL, ins. exec.; b. Oakland, Calif., July 4, 1904; s. Warren A. and Clara (West) B.; student U. Calif., 1922-23; m. Nancy Foote, Nov. 2, 1961; children by previous marriage—Peter Bechtel, Jon. With W.A. Bechtel Co., constrn. engrs., San Francisco, 1921-70, v.p., dir. 1925-45, dir., 1950-70; mem. exec. com., sr. dir. Indsl. Indemnity Co., pres. 1931-55, chmn. bd., 1955-70, chmn. exec. com., 1970-76; dir. emeritus Wells Fargo Bank. Mem. nat. exec. bd. Boy Scouts Am., 1947-74, pres. Nat. council, 1956-59, mem. adv. council, from 1974; trustee, pres. Belvedere Sci. Fund; bd. dirs. Indsl. Indemnity Found. Mem. Calif. Acad. Scis. (trustee), Calif. Hist. Soc., Nat. Audubon Soc., Beta Theta Pi. Republican. Mason (Shriner). Clubs: San Francisco Yacht (Belvedere); Bohemian, Marin Yacht (San Rafael, Calif.); Pacific Union. Home: San Francisco, Calif. Deceased.

BECHTEL, WELKER GEORGE, editor; b. Dubuque, Iowa, Mar. 1, 1902; s. George and Louise (Welker) B.; B.A., U. Dubuque, 1924; M.S., U. Chgo., 1928; postgrad. State U. Iowa, 1930, Iowa State Coll., summers 1931-32, 37, 42; m. Shirley Esther Fisher, Aug. 25, 1928; 1 dau., Marilyn (Mrs. Arnold F. Becchetti). Prof. chemistry Boone (Iowa) Jr. Coll., 1928-42; research fellow Corn Industries Research Found., N.Y.C., 1943-49; research chemist Am. Inst. Baking, Chgo., 1949-53, dir. labs., 1953-68; sci. editor Am. Assn. Cereal Chemists, Las Cruces, N.Mex., 1968-77. Fellow AAAS; mem. Am. Assn. Cereal Chemists (dir. 1965-67, William F. Geddes Meml. award 1970), Am. Chem. Soc., Sigma Xi. Contbr. articles profl. jours. Patentee corn industries viscometer. Address: Las Cruces, N.Mex. Died Dec. 14, 1977.

BECK, CLYDE, literary critic; b. Clinton Co., Ind., Nov. 16, 1884; s. Charles Benton and Inez Louise (Cokayne) B.; A.B., Earlham Coll., 1907; A.M., U. of Ill., 1916; m. Josephine Johnson, Sept. 2, 1921; children—Claudia, Mary (Mrs. Bernard Janssen). Teacher of English, German and Latin, high schs., Ind., Ill., Fla., 1908-13; instr. English composition, U. of Ill., 1914-18; reporter, city editor, Richmond (Ind.) Item, 1938; editorial staff, Indianapolis (Ind.) Star, 1919-20; state editor, Youngstown (O.) Telegram, 1920-21; lit. editor, Detroit (Mich.) News, since 1926; lecturer and radio commentator; spl. instr. in book reviewing, Wayne Univ., Detroit, since 1946. Program chmn. Friends of Detroit Public Library. Member of the Indiana Society of Chicago. Democrat. Club: Earlham (president 1938-39). Home: Detroit, Mich. *

BECK, CLYDE MCKAY, army officer (ret.), physician; b. Keatchie, La., Dec. 15, 1886; s. James Alston and Donna (McKay) B.; Ph.G.; U. of South, Sewanee, Tenn., 1906; M.D., Coll. Phys. and Surg., Memphis, 1908; m. Dorothy Brema Coors, June 29, 1909; children—Eleanor (Mrs. John Freeman Kerkam), James Alston. Practiced gen. medicine until 1917; served with 90th Div., U.S. Army, World War I, continued army career, serving at Camp Pike, Ark., 1920-21, Ft. Lewis, Wash., 1921-22, Presidio of San Francisco, 1923-25, Manila, P.I., 1926-27, Army and Navy Gen. Hosp., Hot Springs, Ark., 1928-32, Ft. Myer, Va., 1932-36, Panama Canal, 1936-38, Ft. Adams, Newport, R.I., 1938-39; prof. mil. sci. and tactics Georgetown Med. Sch., Washington, 1939-40; comdg. officer Sta. Hosp., Camp Joseph T. Robinson, Ark., 1941-42, Ashford Gen. Hosp., White Sulphur Springs, W.Va., 1942-46, Pratt Gen. Hosp., Coral Gables, Fla., 1946-47; brig. gen. retired, 1947; mgr. Kennedy V.A. Hosp., Memphis, 1948-51. Awarded Legion of Merit. Democrat. Mason. Clubs; Rotary (hon.), Senior Golfers of Virginia (hon.), Memphis Country. Home: Memphis.

BECKER, HARRY J., hosp. ins. cons., educator; b. Lincoln, Neb., Oct. 3, 1909; s. Harry J. and Julia (Hotaling) B.; A.B., U. Neb., 1933, A.M., 1941; student Columbia, 1940, N.Y. Sch. Social Work, 1937, Yale, 1940; children (by previous marriage)—Harry J., Ruth M., Martha Jane. Spl. asst. to state dir. Kan. Emergency Relief Adminstrn., hdqrs. Topeka, 1935-37; state dir. Neb. State Child Health and Welfare Services, Lincoln, 1937-41; cons. med. care adminstrn. N.Y. City Dept. Health, 1940-41, USPHS, 1941-42; dir. adminstrv. methods, med. care adminstrn. cons. Fed. Security Agy., Washington, 1942-48; dir. social security dept. United Automobile Workers-C.I.O., Detroit, 1948-57; also dir. Commn. on Financing Hosp. Care; later hosp.-med. program cons.; tchr. hosp. econs. and prepayment plan adminstrn., program in hosp. adminstrn. Northwestern U.; exec. sec. com. on spl. studies N.Y. Acad. Med.; v.p. Nat. Blue Cross Assn., also mem. faculty Sch. Adminstrv. Medicine Columbia, from 1957; prof. community medicine Albert Einstein Medical Coll.; prof. New Sch. for Social Research, Cornell Inst. Adminstrv. Med.; pres. Health Alternatives; cons. Health Services Adminstrn., N.Y.C. Mem. pension research council Wharton School of Finance. Dir. United Automobile Workers-C.I.O. Health Inst.; labor rep. bd. trustees Mich. Hosp. Service (Blue Cross), Mich. Med. Service (Blue Shield); mem. com. pensions 20th Century Fund. Author: Financing Hospital Care in the U.S.; Prepayment and the Community; Financing Care for Non-Wage and Low Income Groups; also contbr. various publs. Editor: Expanding Ambulatory Services, others. Home: Brookfield Center, Conn. Died Dec. 23, 1975.

BECKER, HENRY W(ILLIAM), retired banker; b. N.Y. City, 1885; s. William and Caroline (Andrews) B.; student pub. schs. N.Y. City, Am. Inst. Banking; m. Sadie V. E. Hancox, June 12, 1909; children—Howard H., Richard H. Asst. cashier Columbia Bank, N.Y. City, 1920-23; v.p. Mfrs. Trust Co., N.Y. City, 1943-50, ret., Sept. 1, 1950. Mem. Homefield Assn. Yonkers N.Y., Inc. Republican. Mason. Home: Yonkers, N.Y. *

BECKER, LOFTUS EUGENE, lawyer; b. Buffalo, Apr. 29, 1911; s. Rueben Ezra and Helen Mary (Gilmartin) B.; A.B. magna cum laude, Harvard, 1932, LL.B. magna cum laude, 1936; student U. Vienna, 1932-33; m. Ellen Vander Voort, Dec. 25, 1933 (div. 1961); children—Susan B. Hussein, Gretchen E., Loftus Eugene; m. 2d, Elizabeth M. Mason, May 17, 1962; 1 dau, Kathleen Elizabeth. Admitted to Hawaii bar, 1936, N.Y. State bar, 1940; asso. firm Anderson, Marx Wrenn & Jenks, Honolulu, T.H., 1936-38, Wright, Gordon, Zachry, Parlin & Cahill, N.Y.C., 1938-42; partner firm Cahill, Gordon Zachry & Reindel, N.Y.C., 1946-51; mil. advisor delegations Nuremberg War Trials; dep. dir. CIA, Washington, 1951-53; Washington partner Cahill, Gordon, Reindel & Ohl, 1953-56, resident partner European office, 1959-67; legal adviser Dept. State, 1957-59; partner firm Cahill, Gordon, Sonnett, Reindel & Ohl, N.Y.C., 1959-72; ret., 1973. Served with AUS, 1942-45. Mem. Am., Fed., D.C., N.Y. State, Hawaii, N.Y.C. bar assns. Clubs: Metropolitan (Washington); Orienta Beach and Yacht, Brook, Univ. (N.Y.C.). Home: Mamaroneck, N.Y. Died Aug. 26, 1977; interred Ferncliff Cemetery, Hartsdale, N.Y.

BECKMAN, ALDO BRUCE, journalist; b. Lima, Ill., Dec. 24, 1934; s. Aldo Henry and Mildred Maxine (Lummis) B.; B.S., Western Ill. U., Macomb, 1956; children—Theresa, Patricia, Jennifer, Mary Kay, Eugene. Writer, reporter UPI, Chgo., 1958-59; with Chgo. Tribune, from 1959, corr. Washington Bur., 1965-80, White House corr., 1970-77, bur. chief, 1977-80. Served with U.S. Army, 1956-58. Recipient Edward Scott Beck award Chgo. Tribune, 1966, 72; Alumni Achievement award Western Ill. U., 1973; Merriman Smith award, 1976. Mem. White House Corrs. Assn. (pres. 1978), Sigma Delta Chi. Methodist. Home: Arlington, Va. Died Sept. 10, 1980; buried Quincy, Ill.

BEDDINGFIELD, EDGAR THEODORE, JR., physician; b. Clayton, N.C., Mar. 5, 1923; s. Edgar Theodore and Alice Bertha (Casey) B.; student E. Carolina U., 1943, U. Mich., 1944; certificate in Medicine, U. N.C., 1946; M.D. cum laude, Harvard, 1948; m. Lorraine Morrill Moore, Aug. 22, 1947; children—Edgar Theodore III, Alice B. (Mrs. William Dean Moss, Jr.), Gladys Lorraine. Instr. pharmacology U. N.C., 1943-45; intern Walter Reed Gen. Hosp., Washington, 1948-49; founder, practicing physician Community Clinic, Stantonsburg, N.C., 1950-67; partner, practicing physician Wilson (N.C.) Clinic, 1968-77; co. physician Swift & Co., Wilson, 1958-77; mem. med. staff, med. cons. to employees Wilson Meml. Hosp., 1964-77. Dir. So. Nat. Bank, Wilson. Commr., Town of Stantonsburg, 1952-56; mem. Gov.'s Council on Aging, 1964-69; mem. Bd. Social Services, State of N.C., 1972-77, Wilson County Bd. Edn., 1971-72. Chmn. bd. dirs. Nat. Driving Center, Research Triangle Park, N.C.; bd. dirs. N.C. Schs. for Deaf, 1962-70, Am. Med. Polit. Action Com. Served to capt. M.C., U.S. Army, 1948-50. Recipient Distinguished Service awards N.C. Mental Health Assn., 1963, 70, U. N.C. Sch. Medicine, 1968; named Tar Heel of Week, Raleigh News and Observer, 1961; Edgar T. Beddingfield, Jr. High Sch. named for him. John Harvard fellow Harvard Med. Sch., 1948. Diplomate Am. Bd. Family Physicians. Mem. Inst. of Medicine, Nat. Acad. Scis., A.M.A. (del. N.C. 1966-77, vice chmn. Council on Legis. 1974-77), N.C. (pres. 1969-70), Boyleston med. socs., Sigma Xi, Phi Delta Chi, Rho Chi, Alpha Kappa Kappa, Alpha Omega Alpha. Democrat. Baptist. Mason, Kiwanian. Clubs: Aesculapian; Wedgewood Country; Willow Springs Country; Happy Valley Country. Home: Stantonsburg, N.C. Died Sept. 10, 1977; interred Stantonsburg Cemetery.

BEDE, JEAN-ALBERT, educator; b. Caussade, France, Apr. 2, 1903; s. Honore and Heloise (Aillet) B.; Agrege des Lettres, Ecole Normale Superieure, Paris, 1927; dipl., Ecole des Sciences Politiques, Paris, 1929; m. Lise Sittner, May 23, 1953 (dec. Feb. 1969). Came to U.S., 1929, naturalized, 1939. Instr., Princeton, 1929-30, asst. prof., 1930-35; asso. prof. Brown U., 1935-37; asso. prof. Columbia, 1937-45, prof., 1945-69; Blanche W. Knopf prof. French, 1969-71, emeritus, 1971-77. Guggenheim fellow, 1948-49; Fulbright teaching fellow U. London, 1964-65; vice dean Faculty Letters, Ecole Libre des Hautes Etudes, French U. N.Y., 1950-71. Dir. French translations Office War Information, N.Y.C., 1944-45. Decorated chevalier Legion d'Honneur, chevalier Palmes Academiques. Mem. Modern Lang. Assn. Am., Societe des Professeurs Francais en Amerique (past pres.). Editor: The Romanic Review, 1967-71. Contbr. sect. to Ency. Americana, from 1957; contbr. Columbia Dictionary of Modern European Lit., 1947, gen. editor rev. edit., 1971-77; gen. editor for 19th century Critical Bibliography of French Lit., 1971-77. Contbr. articles to profl. jours. Home: New York, N.Y. Died Jan. 19, 1977.

BEEBE, ALBERT EDWARD, clergyman; b. Liberty, N.Y., July 8, 1886; s. Anderson and Hester (Phillips) B.; B.A., Wesleyan U., Conn., 1913; B.D., Yale, 1915; D.D., Hamline U., 1924; m. Ruth Brown, of Brooklyn, N.Y., May 5, 1924. Ordained ministry M.E. Ch., 1913; successively pastor Nichols and Norwalk, Conn. Simpson Ch., Brooklyn, N.Y., until 1926, Calvary Ch., N.Y. City, 1926-29, First Ch., Bridgeport, Conn., since 1929. Pres. New York Methodist Preachers' Meeting, 1927. Mem. Brooklyn Clerical Union, Sigma Chi. Republican. Club: Yale. Mason (K.T.). Home: Bridgeport, Conn. *

BEEBE, RALPH A(LONZO), educator, research chemist; b. Monson, Mass., Mar. 8, 1898; s. Alonzo M. and Minnie A. (Smith) B.; A.B., Amherst Coll., 1920; Ph.D., Princeton, 1923; m. Elizabeth Wagner, July 18, 1928; children—John H., David S., Christopher. Faculty Amherst Coll., 1923-66, prof. chemistry, 1937— councilor-at-large Gordon Research Conf.; mem. vis. scientists program, div. chem. edn. Am. Chem. Soc.; researcher NIH. Fellow Am. Acad. Arts and Scis.; mem. Phi Beta Kappa, Sigma Xi. Author articles on adsorption. Home: Amherst, Mass. Died Oct. 1, 1979. 66 prof. emeritus, 1966-79; vis. prof. Carleton U., Ottawa, Can., 1966-68, Voorhees Coll., S.C., 1967-69;

BEECHER, CARL MILTON, musician; b. in La Fayette, Ill., Oct. 22, 1883; s. Charles Myron and Helen Mae (Reeve) B.; Mus. B., Northwestern U., 1908, Mus. M., 1920; studied in Europe, 1909-13; pupil of Paul Juon and Joseph Lhevinne, Berlin; unmarried. Teacher, Northwestern U., 1913-34; head dept. of music theory same, 1923-34, also administrative dir. Sch. of Music, 1924, and dean, 1930-34, retired, 1934. Mem. Am. Assn. Univ. Professors, Beta Theta Pi. Composer: Piano Concerto, Two Piano Pieces, 1908; Seven Fantasie Pieces, 1913; Trio for violin, cello, and piano, 1915; Suite for cello, 1916; Three Songs, 1922; The Jester, 1923; Two Songs, Suite for two pianos, 1924; Four Preludes, 1927. Home: Island of Moorea, Society Islands.

BEECHER, HENRY KNOWLES, physician, educator; b. Wichita, Kan., Feb. 4, 1904; s. Mary Julia (Kerley) B.; A.B., U. Kan., 1926, A.M., 1927; M.D., Harvard, 1932; M.D. (hon.) U. Lund, Sweden, 1961; children—Jonathan French, Harriet, Mary Knowles. Intern, Mass. Gen. Hosp., 1932-34, asst. resident in surgery, 1936, dir. dept. anesthesia, from 1936; research (as Moseley Traveling fellow Harvard) lab. of Prof. August Krogh, Copenhagen, 1935; Henry Isaiah Dorr prof. research in anesthesia Harvard, 1941-76; Hodgen lectr., St. Louis, 1940, Calhoun lectr., Atlanta, 1948, Kellogg lectr., Washington, 1948, Lowell lectr., Boston, 1948, Judd lectr., Mpls., 1950; exchange lectr. on anesthesia Nat. U., Colombia, 1941; Holme lectr., London, 1954, Macarthur lectr., Edinburgh, 1954, Eastman Meml. lectr., Rochester, 1954, State lectr., Turin, Italy, 1954; Alpha Omega Alpha lectr., Louisville, 1955; lectr. Oxford, Hartman Meml. Switzerland, Royal Acad. Medicine, Ireland, Gross Meml., Can., Acad. Sci., Leningrad, others, 1956. Mem. com. on Shock NRC, 1940, mem. subcom. on anesthesia, 1942-43, chmn. subcom. on anesthesia, 1946-76. Served as maj. AUS, 1943; cons. resuscitation and anesthesia MTO, 1943-45; disch. rank of lt. col., 1945; cons. to surgeon gen. U.S. Army, 1946-76, USAF, 1952-54, USN (hon.), 1953-56, USPHS, 1947-52, 57-58; mem. pharmaceology tng. com. NIH, 1958-61. Decorated Legion of Merit, Chevalier de la Legion d'Honneur (France); Knight Royal Order Dannebrog (Denmark); recipient Warren Triennial prize Mass. Gen. Hosp., 1931, 1937, plaque by Forum of Anesthetists, 1939. Diplomate Am. Bd. Anesthesiology. Fellow Royal Coll. Surgeons, A.A.A.S., Inst. Soc., Ethics and Life Scis. (hon.); mem. Internat. Soc. for Research in Anesthesia and Analgesia, A.M.A. (mem. therapeutic trials com., 1949-50, council on pharmacy and chemistry 1949, com. on med. research 1950-76), Am. Soc. Pharmacology and Exptl. Therapeutics, Soc. Clin. Investigation, Am. Soc. Anesthesiology, Mass. Med. Soc., N.Y. Acad. Sci. (life mem.), St. Louis Med. Soc. (hon. mem.), Royal Soc. Medicine London, hon., Argentina Soc. for Thoracic Surgery (hon. mem.), Am. Acad. Arts and Scis., Assn. Anaesthetists of Gt. Britain and Ireland (corr. fellow), Sociedad Nacional de Anestesiologic (fgn. corr. mem.), Swedish Soc. Anesthesiologists (hon.), Assn. Univ.

Anesthetists, Am. Surg. Assn., Sigma Xi, Alpha Omega Alpha. Author: Resuscitation and Anesthesia for Wounded Men, 1949; Experimentation in Man, 1959; Measurements of Subjective Responses: Quantitative Effects of Drugs, 1959; Disease and the Advancement of Basic Science (editor H. K. Beecher), 1959; also articles. Editor: Physiological Effects of Wounds, 1951. Home: Boston, Mass. Died July 25, 1976.

BEECHER, JOHN, poet; b. N.Y.C., Jan. 22, 1904; s. Leonard Thurlow and Isabel (Garghill) B.; student Va. Mil. Inst., Cornell U.; A.B., U. Ala., 1925; M.A., U. Wis., 1930; postgrad. Harvard, U. N.C.; L.H.D., Ill. Coll., Jacksonville, 1948; m. Barbara Marie Scholz, Aug. 16, 1955; children (by 2 previous marriages)—David, Leonard, Joan (Mrs. J. Eichrodt), Michael, Thomas Edward. Steel worker, Birmingham, Ala., 1918-19, 20-21, 23-24, 28-29; instr. English, Dartmouth, 1927, U. Wis., 1929-33; adminstr. fed. govt. agencies in South, 1934-42; staff writer N.Y. Post, 1943; chief editor Nat. Inst. Social Relations, 1946-47; mem. faculty San Francisco State Coll. (now U.), 1948-50, 77-80; lectr. English, Ariz. State U., 1959-61; poet in residence U. Santa Clara (Calif.), 1963-65; vis. prof. Miles Coll., 1966-67; poet in residence North Shore Community Coll., Beverly, Mass., 1969-71, St. John's U., Collegeville, Minn., 1970; vis. scholar Duke, 1973-75; nationwide poetry readings, 1963-79; operator Rampart Press, 1958-63. Served as officer U.S. Mcht. Marine, 1943-45. Recipient Western Books Exhbn. award, 1960, 61, 63. Fellow Fund Advancement Edn., 1951-52; fellow arts program Assn. Am. Colls., 1969-72; Nat. Endowment Arts fellow, 1976-77. Author: And I Will Be Heard, 1940; Here I Stand, 1941; All Brave Sailors, 1945; Land of the Free, 1956; Observe the Time, 1956; In Egypt Land, 1960; Phantom City, 1961; Report to the Stockholders and Other Poems, 1962; To Live and Die in Dixie and Other Poems, 1966; Hear the Wind Blow!, 1968; Collected Poems, 1974; Tomorrow is a Day, 1980; (microfilm edit.) Complete Works & Papers, 1973; recs. include To Live and Die In Dixie, 1967, Report to the Stockholders, 1977. Home: San Francisco, Calif. Died May 11, 1980; buried Los Gatos, Calif.

BEEDE, VICTOR (AUGUSTUS) (BE-DE), forester, coll. prof.; b. East Braintree, Mass., Dec. 9, 1886; s. Frank Herbert and Caroline May (Coan) B.; A.B., Yale, 1910, M.F., 1912; m. Ella Small, June 26, 1912; 1 son, John Knowlton. Asst. sec., Mass. Forestry Assn., 1912; with U.S. Forest Service, Pike Nat. Forest, Denver, Colo., 1913-14; asst. state forester, Concord, N.H., 1914-16; sec., N.Y. State Forestry Assn., Syracuse, 1916-17; asst. mgr., Timberlands Mutual Fire Ins. Co., Portsmouth, N.H., 1917-18; woods insp. and scaler, Brown Corp., Trois Pistoles, Quebec, Can., 1918-20, local mgr., Riviere du Loup, 1920-24, forester, Quebec City, 1924-31; instr. and asst. prof. of forestry, Pa. State Coll., 1931-34; visiting prof., Yale, 1934-35; asso. prof., Pa. State Coll., 1935-37, head, dept. of forestry, prof. forest mgmt., 1937-52, now emeritus. Chmn., alumni adv. council, Yale Sch. of Forestry, 1941-47; mem. Yale Alumni Bd., since 1941; vice chmn., adv. council, Northeastern Forest Expt. Sta., U.S. Forest Service, Phila., Pa. Mem. Yale Forest Sch. Alumni Assn. (pres., 1941-47), Pa. Forestry Assn. (exec. bd.), Soc. of Am. Foresters (chmn., com. on civil service, Canadian Soc. of Forest Engrs., Am. Forestry Assn., Zeta Psi, Alpha Zeta, Xi Sigma Pi, Gamma Sigma Delta. Contbr. articles to Jour. of Forestry. Professional travel in France, Germany, Switzerland, 1912, Scandinavian countries, Finland, France and Germany, 1927. Home: State College, Pa. *

BEEMAN, ELIZABETH ANN, educator; b. Barre, Vt., Aug. 12, 1916; A.B., Grinnell Coll., 1938; M.S., U. Chgo., 1939, Ph.D. in Behavior, 1947; M.A., Mt. Holyoke Coll., 1941. Asst., U. Chgo., 1941-44, asst. in biol. sci., 1944-45, instr., 1945-49, asst. prof., 1949-51; mem. sci. faculty Sarah Lawrence Coll., 1951-60; asso. prof. Mt. Holyoke Coll., 1960-70, prof. biol. scis., 1970-79. NSF faculty fellow, 1959-60. Mem. A.A.A.S., Am. Soc. Zoology, Am. Ecol. Soc., N.Y. Acad. Scis. Home: South Hadley, Mass. Died Jan. 22, 1979.

BEERS, HENRY SAMUEL, ins. co. exec.; b. New Haven, Conn., June 22, 1898; s. George Emerson and Margaret (Lowry) B.; A.B., Trinity Coll., 1918, LL.D., 1968; m. Dorothy Carpenter, Apr. 28, 1926; children—Henry Samuel, Elizabeth (Raymond), John William. Pres., Aetna Life Ins. Co., Hartford, Aetna Casualty and Surety Co., Standard Fire Ins. Co., 1956-62, chmn., 1962-63, also dir.; chmn. bd. Excelsior Life Ins. Co., Toronto, Ont., Can., 1960-63; chmn. bd. N. Am. Reins. Corp., also N. Am. Reassurance Co., 1964-70. Chmn. of Gov.'s Commn. on Unemployment Compensation, 1936; mem. Conn. State Employees' Retirement Commn., 1939-64; Chmn. bd. trustees S.S. Huebner Found. for Ins. Edn., 1958-61. Named Ins. Man of Yr. in life and fire-casualty fields Ins. Field mag., 1961; mem. Ins. Hall of Fame, 1979. Fellow Soc. Actuaries; mem. Phi Beta Kappa, Delta Psi. Episcopalian. Club: Appalachian Mountain. Home: Tucson, Ariz. Died Apr. 26, 1981.

BEERY, JOHN REPLOGLE, educator; b. Tyrone, Pa., Mar. 4, 1909; s. Charles O. and Louella (Replogle) B.; A.B., Juniata Coll., 1930, LL.D., 1951; A.M., U. Chgo., 1934; Ph.D., Columbia, 1942; LL.D., U. Miami, 1974; m. Anna Florence Stayer, June 18, 1943; 1 dau., Linda Althea. Instr. math. Martinsburg (Pa.) High Sch., 1930-32, Merchantville (N.J.) High Sch., 1932-35, Princeton (N.J.) High Sch., 1935-38; asst. secondary edn. Columbia Tchrs. Coll., summers 1938-39; asst. dir. occupational adjustment study Nat. Assn. Secondary Sch. Prins., 1939-40, asso. dir., 1940-41; asso. prof. edn. U. Miami (Fla.), 1941-46, prof. edn., from 1946, coordinator univ. guidance center, 1946-47, dean Sch. Edn., 1947-74, dean emeritus, 1974-80, dir. instrn., 1948-64; dir. instl. self-study, 1974-76. Served as capt. USAAF, 1942-45. Mem. AAAS, AAUP, Am. Coll. Personnel Assn., Am. Ednl. Research Assn., Am. Psychol. Assn., Fla. Acad. Sci., Fla. Edn. Assn., Nat. Assn. Secondary Sch. Prins., N.E.A., Nat. Vocational Guidance Assn., Phi Delta Kappa, Kappa Delta Pi. Mem. Brethren Ch. Author: Current Conceptions of Democracy, 1943; co-author The School Follows Through, 1941; Occupational Adjustment and the School 1940; Professional Preparation and Effectiveness of Beginning Teachers, 1960. Contbr. articles to ednl. jours. Home: Miami, Fla. Died Jan. 13, 1980.

BEESLEY, EUGENE NEVIN, found. exec.; b. Thorntown, Ind., Jan. 29, 1909; s. Ralph N. and Della Mae (Rinehart) B.; A.B., Wabash Coll., 1929; LL.B., Ind. U., 1943; LL.D., DePauw U., 1956, Wabash College, 1959; D.Sc., U. Toledo, 1957; Doctor of Humanities, Ind. Central Coll., 1964; D.H.L., Butler U., 1966; LL.D., Ind. U., 1966, Franklin Coll., 1973; D.B.A., Marian Coll., 1973; m. Marian L. Crehore, Oct. 23, 1931; children—Mary Louise (Mrs. Needham S. Hurst), Mark Crehore. With Eli Lilly & Co., Indpls., 1929-76, various sales, personnel and adminstrv. positions, 1929-51, v.p. 1951-52 exec. v.p., dir., 1952-53, pres., 1953-69, chmn. bd., 1969-73, now dir.; dir. Lilly Endowment, Inc., 1951-76, v.p., 1960-73, pres., 1973-76; dir. Procter & Gamble Co., Am. Fletcher Corp., Gen. Motors Corp., Pub. Service Ind. Admitted to Ind. bar, 1943. Pres., United Presbyn. Found. Bd. govs. Asso. Colls. Ind.; bd. dirs. Ind. U. Found., United Fund Greater Indpls., Inc.; trustee Wabash Coll. Mem. Am., Ind. bar assns., James Whitcomb Riley Meml. Assn., Bus. Council, Beta Theta Pi. Presbyn. (elder). Mason (33 deg., Shriner). Clubs: Indpls. Athletic, Meridian Hills Country, Columbia (Indpls); Links (N.Y.). Home: Indianapolis, Ind. Died Feb. 8, 1976.

BEESLEY, THOMAS QUINN, publicist; b. Chicago, Ill., July 17, 1885; s. Thomas and Mary Elizabeth (Quinn) B.; Litt.B., Princeton, 1912; M.A., Loyola U., 1913; post grad. study U. of Chicago, 1914; fellow, Princeton, 1915; m. Mae Geraldine McCarthy, of Dubuque, Ia., Sept. 20, 1916 (died Sept. 7, 1922); children—Thomas Quinn, II (dec.), Patricia; m. 2d Mrs. Helen Morse Longley, of South Bend, Ind., Apr. 27, 1926. Lecturer on English lang. and lit., Catholic U. of America, 1916-17; asst. to dir. gen. of civilian relief, Am. Red Cross, 1917-18, to dir. gen. of mil. relief, 1918-19; attaché to Cardinal Mercier for Red Cross during his visit to U.S., 1919. Exec. officer for Dept. of State for Am. Exec. Com., 15th Internat. Congress Against Alcoholism, Washington, D.C., 1920; staff of Secretary Colby, Oct. 1920-Mar. 1921, as asst. chief, Div. of Foreign Intelligence; staff of Sec. Hughes, Mar.-July 1921, as chief Div. of Current Information; broker of investment securities, Chicago, 1921-23; mem. editorial staff Chicago Herald and Examiner, 1923-24; dir. of publicity, Dem. Nat. Com., western hdqrs., 1924; head of dept. of advertising, Sch. of Commerce, Loyola U. since 1925; v.p., Conover-Mooney Co., advertising, Chicago, 1924-26; v.p. McCutcheon-Gerson Service, Chicago, since 1926. Dir. of publicity in campaign of Employers' Assn. of Chicago against racketeering, 1928-29; mem. exec. com. and dir. Voters Non-Partisan Assn., Chicago, since 1928. Fellow Am. Geog. Soc.; mem. Am. Soc. Internat. Law, Internat. Advertising Fed., Izaak Walton League, Am. Whig Soc. (Princeton). Catholic. Clubs: Harvard-Yale-Princeton, Medievalists (hon.), White Paper (Chicago); Nat. Press (Washington, D.C.); Advertising, Nat. Arts (New York); Tower (Princeton). Author: It's a Racket (with Gordon L. Hostetter), 1929. Home: Chicago.

BEETON, RALPH ALBERT, banker; b. Alexandria, Va., May 30, 1927; s. Frank Emerson and Anna (Vetter) B.; B.A., U. Va., 1950, LL.B., 1954; m. Virginia Elizabeth Holland, Apr. 30, 1955; children—Thomas McHarg, Sarah Elizabeth, William Trammell, Charlotte Ames. Admitted to Va. bar; pvt. practice law, Waynesboro, Va. and Arlington County, 1954-60; exec. v.p., gen. counsel First Va. Bankshares Corp., Arlington, 1960-62, pres., gen. counsel, 1962-67, pres., chief exec. officer, 1967-75, chmn., chief exec. officer, 1974-79, dir., 1957-79, also vice chmn.; dir. First Va. Bank, Larchmont Realty Mgmt., Inc. Mem. Va. Gov.'s Bus. Adv. Bd., 1967, 69, 70, Va. Ports Study Commn., 1969, Va. Hwy. and Transp. Commn., 1974-79. Bd. visitors Longwood Coll., Farmville, Va., 1968-72. Served with USNR, 1945-46. DuPont scholar U. Va., 1952-54, Marcuse scholar, 1953-54, Bennett scholar, 1953-54. Mem. Newcomen Soc., Va., Arlington County bar assns., Va. Bankers Assn. (pres. 1975-76). Methodist. Clubs: Washington Golf and Country (Arlington); Farmington Country, University of Va. (Charlottesville). Home: Potomac, Md. Died Mar. 1979.

BEFFA, HARVEY ARTHUR, brewery exec.; b. St. Louis, June 19, 1900; s. Anton and Mary (Degan) B.; student pub. schs. St. Louis; m. Henrietta Stahl, June 24, 1922; children—Harvey Arthur, Helen, Mary Etta, Daniel. Clk. Anton Beffa & Son Wrecking & Supply Co., St. Louis, 1915-20, gen. mgr., 1920-32; sec. Falstaff Brewing Corp., St. Louis, 1933-35, v.p., dir. 1935, later exec. v.p., gen. mgr., then chmn. bd., 1962-69, then chmn. exec. com.; dir. Merc. Commerce Nat. Bank. Bd. dirs. Midwest Polio Assn.; chmn. bd. trustees Shriners Hosps. for Crippled Children, also chmn. emeritus St. Louis unit. Recipient St. Louis Humanities award, 1964; named Big Brother of Year, St. Louis, 1966. Mem. Master Brewers Assn. Am. Republican. Presbyn. Mason (33 deg., Shriner; past imperial potentate). Clubs: Missouri Athletic, Glen Echo Country, St. Louis. Home: Normandy, Mo. Died Oct. 20, 1975.

BEGGS, GEORGE ERLE, JR., mfg. exec.; b. Princeton, Aug. 6, 1916; s. George Erle and Frances May (Ingalls) B.; grad. Lawrenceville Sch., 1934; B.A. in Physics, Princeton, 1938; m. Margaret Mueller, Mar. 19, 1940; children—Barbara Anne, Robert Eric. Research dept. John A. Roebling's Sons & Co., Trenton, N.J., 1938-40; with Leeds & Northrup Co., Phila., 1940-76, chmn. bd., pres., dir.; dir. Provident Mut. Life Ins. Co. Phila., 1st Pa. Corp., Carpenter Tech. Corp., NARCO Sci. Industries Inc., Cin. Milacron Inc. Bd. mgrs. Franklin Inst. With nat. def. research com. OSRD, 1942-45. Recipient President's Certificate of Merit. Fellow I.E.E.E.; Franklin Inst. (bd. mgrs.), Electric Mfrs. Club. Home: Warrington, Pa. Died Aug. 16, 1976.

BEGIN, FLOYD LAWRENCE, bishop; b. Cleve., Feb. 5, 1902; s. Peter H. and Stella (McFarland) B.; Ph.D., U. Propaganda, Rome, Italy, 1924, S.T.D., 1928; J.C.D., U. Apollinaris, Rome, 1930. Ordained priest Roman Catholic Ch., 1927; asst. rector North Am. Coll., Rome, 1928-30; diocesan sec., vice chancellor Diocese of Cleve., 1930; apptd. monsignor, 1934, domestic prelate, 1935, officialis, diocesan tribunal, 1938; diocesan dir. Nat. Council of Cath. Men, Eucharistic Congresses, 1934; vicar gen., women in religious communities; consecrate bishop of Sala and aux. bishop, Cleve., 1947; vicar gen. of cleve., 1948; pastor St. Agnes Parish, Cleve., 1949-62, bishop, Oakland, Calif., 1962-77. Mem. adminstrv. tribunal 2d Vatican Council, 1963; mem. papal commn. revision code of canon law from 1967. Home: Piedmont, Calif. Died Apr. 26, 1977.

BEGLE, EDWARD GRIFFITH, mathematician, educator; b. Saginaw, Mich., Nov. 27, 1914; s. Ned G. and Cornelia (Campbell) B.; B.A., U. Mich., 1936, M.A., 1937; Ph.D., Princeton, 1940; m. Elsie Alkin Pierce, Aug. 14, 1937; children—Cornelia, Sarah, James, Emily, Elsie, Edward, Douglas. NRC fellow, 1941-42; instr. Yale, 1942-44, asst. prof., 1944-49, asso. prof. 1949-61, dir. sch. math. study group, 1958-72; prof. math. edn. Stanford U., 1961-78. Mem. Am. Math. Soc. (sec. 1951-56), Math. Assn. Am. (Distinguished Service award 1969), AAAS, Sigma Xi, Phi Delta Theta. Home: Palo Alto, Calif. Died Mar. 2, 1978.

BEHNKEN, JOHN WILLIAM (BEN'KEN), clergyman; b. Cypress, Tex., Mar. 19, 1884; s. Rev. George William and Helen (Wunderlich) B.; jr. coll. courses, St. John's Lutheran College, Winfield, Kansas, 1897-1903; student Concordia Theological Sem., St. Louis, 1903-06, D.D., 1934; LL.D., Valparaiso University, 1953; married Gertrude Geisler, Aug. 13, 1909 (dec.); m. 2d, Hilda Grassmuck, Apr. 22, 1914 (dec.); children—Victor Louis, Ruth Lucille, John William, Donald Edward, Lester Lloyd, Lois Marie, Kenneth Wayne, Helen La Delle. Ordained minister Evang. Luth. Ch., 1906; pastor Trinity Ch., Houston, Texas., 1908-35; Luth. camp pastor, Camp Logan, Ellington Field, Ft. Crockett, 1917-18. V.p. Tex. Dist. Mo. Synod, 1920-26, pres., 1926-29; 2d v.p. Lutheran Ch. Mo. Synod, O. and other states, 1929-32; 1st v.p., 1932-35; pres. since 1935. Author: Noonday Sermons, 1926; Mercies Manifold, 1951. Contbr. theol. pubs. Home: St. Charles, Mo.

BEHR, KARL H(OWELL), investment banker; born Brooklyn, May 30, 1885; s. Herman and Grace (Howell) B.; grad. The Lawrenceville Sch., 1903; Ph.B. Sheffield Scientific Sch., Yale, 1906; LL.B., Columbia, 1910; m. Helen Newsom, March 1, 1913; children—Karl H., Peter H., James H., Sally H. Admitted to N.Y. State bar, 1910, and associated with firm of McKeen, Brewster & Morgan, N.Y. City, 1910-13; director and counsel of Herman Behr & Co., Inc., N.Y. City, 1913-28; dir. Behr Manning Corp., abrasive mfrs., since 1928; became associated with Dillon, Read & Co., Inc., investment bankers, N.Y. City, 1924, vice pres. since 1937. Dir. Interchem Corp., Witherbee Sherman Corp. Past dir. Fisk Rubber Co., Gen. Cable Corp., Goodyear Tire & Rubber Corp., Nat. Cash Register Co. Transwestern Oil Co. Mem. Squad. A Cavalry, New York, 1907-11, active Preparedness Movement, 1915-16 (an organizer and vice pres. of the Great Preparedness Parade, 1916; chmn. campaign com., Nat. Security League, 1915-16); served as capt., U.S. Army and exec. officer of Dist. D., Motor Transport Corps, 1918. Mem. U.S. Davis Cup Tennis teams, 1907-14. Episcopalian. Mem. Book and Snake Soc., Yale. Clubs: Yale, Univ., Down Town Assn., Maidstone; N.Y. City; Auorelian Honor Soc., Yale, St. Nicholas Soc. Home: New York.

BEHRE, ELLINOR H(ELENE) (BÂ'RE), coll. prof.; b. Atlanta, Sept. 28, 1886; d. Charles Henry and Emilie (Schumann) Behre; A.B., Radcliffe Coll., 1908; grad. student Tulane U., 1912-15; summer course Marine Biol. Lab., Woods Hole, Mass., 1923; Ph.D., U. of Chicago, 1918; unmarried; adopted children—Emil, Charotte. Instr., Newcomb Coll., Tulane U., 1912-15, asst. prof., 1919-20; grad. asst. U. of Chicago, 1915-18; instr. Milwaukee-Downer Coll., 1916; research asst. Carnegie Sta. for Expt. Evolution, 1918-19; asst. and asso. prof. La. State U., 1920-33, prof. zoölogy since 1933, dir. Marine Lab., 1928-46; research and advanced study Panama, 1921-22, New York U., Johns Hopkins, 1931, Friday Harbor (Wash.) Lab., 1922, U. of Indiana Museums, 1923, U.S. Fisheries and Duke U. Lab., Beaufort, N.C., 1928, 32, 48. Highlands Lab., 1949-51; vis. prof. Mt. Holyoke Coll., 1st semester, 1936; research lectureship U. Puerto Rico, Mayaguez, 1945-46; instr. Gulf Coast Research Lab., summers, 1949, 1950. Member American Society of Zoologists, American Society Ichthyologists and Herpetologists, A.A.A.S., New Orleans Acad. Sci., La Acad. Sci., Sigma Xi, Phi Kappa Phi, Sigma Delta Epsilon. Contbr. tech. articles to sci. jours. Home: Baton Rouge. *

BEILENSON, EDNA, book publisher, designer; b. N.Y.C., June 16, 1909; d. John and Anna (Beilenson) Rudolph; B.A., Hunter Coll., 1928; m. Peter Beilenson, July 20, 1930; children—Anthony C., Roger N., Elizabeth R.; m. 2d, Joseph E. Barmack, June 19, 1966 (div. 1975). Owner, Peter Pauper Press, Mt. Vernon, N.Y., 1930-81; pres. Walpole Printing Office, Mt. Vernon; free-lance designer children's books; books exhibited Fifty Books of the Year, Best Children's Books of the Year; dir., v.p. Am. Inst. Graphic Arts, 1953-57, pres., 1958-60; dir. The Goudy Soc., 1967-68, chmn. bd., 1968-74, 78-81, hon. chmn. bd., 1974-81, pres., 1975-77; pres. the Distaff Side. Recipient Goudy award Rochester Inst. Tech., 1980. Author: Festive Cookery, 1951; Recipes Mother Used to Make, 1952; ABC of Casseroles, Canapes, others (series), Holiday Cook Book Series, Simple French Cookery, Simple Italian Cookery, others; editor: Little Riddle Book, Little Quiz Book, Little Joke Book; (as Elisabeth Deane) Gift of Friendship, Gentle Thoughts, Words of Love, Gift of Prayer. Fellow Royal Soc. Arts, London; mem. Typophiles, Am. Printing History Assn. (trustee), Friends of Morgan Library. Club: Grolier. Home: New York, N.Y. Died Feb. 28, 1981.

BEINECKE, EDWIN JOHN (BI'NEK-E), business exec.; b. N.Y. City, Jan. 6, 1886; s. Bernhard and Johanna Elizabeth (Weigle) B.; ed. Philips Acad., Andover, Mass., 1901-03; grad. Yale Coll., 1907; D. II.L. (hon.), Bowdoin, 1950, Dr. Humane Letters; m. Linda Louise Maurer, Apr. 22, 1909; children—Sylvia L. (wife of Dr. John N. Robinson), Edwin John. Pres. Henry Maurer & Son, 1921-23; pres., chmn. bd. Sperry and Hutchinson Co., 1923—, chmn. until 1967, now dir.; dir. pres., chmn. U.S. Realty & Improvement Co., 1936-42; chmn. bd. Plaza Hotel Co., 1936-42; chmn. bd. George A. Fuller Co., 1941-56, dir., 1941-65; chmn. bd. Patent Scaffolding Co., 1957-61; dir. Hotel Waldorf Astoria Corp., Mfrs. Hanover Trust Co. N.Y.C. (hon.). Served as capt. construction div., U.S. Army, World War I; dep. commr. Am. Red Cross in Great Brit., World War II. Awarded Medal of Freedom. Past chmn. council fellows Pierpont Morgan Library; past chmn. trustees Yale Library Assos. Mason. Clubs: Com. of 25 (Palm Springs, Cal.); Bath and Tennis, Everglades (Palm Beach); Yale, Lawyers, Whitehall (past pres.), Regency Whist, Marco Polo, Fifth Avenue, Grolier (hon. mem.) (N.Y.C.), Blind Brook (Port Chester, N.Y.); Portland, Savile (London). Home: Cliffdale Rd., Greenwich, Conn. 06830.

BEITZEL, GEORGE BREUNINGER, bus. exec.; b. Phila., July 23, 1893; s. William Henry and Hester Jacoby (Brenner) B.; grad. U. Pa., 1916; m. Mary Elizabeth Bickley, Sept. 10, 1918; children—George Bickley, Anna Margaret. Joined Pa. Salt Mfg. Co., Phila., 1930, pres., dir., 1949-55, later spl. rep. fgn. operations; dir. Fidelity-Phila. Trust Co., Pensalt Chems. Corp., Globe Ticket Co., asst. dir. for prodn. ODM, Washington 1957-65; Cons. to ICA. Pres. bd. Delaware County Hosp.; bd. dirs. Meth. Hosp. Republican. Methodist. Mason. Clubs: Union League (Phila.); Rolling Green Golf. Died Nov. 27, 1975.

BELANGER, GUY, bishop; b. Valleyfield, Que., Can., Jan. 24, 1928; s. Raphael and Blanche (Gauthier) B.; B.A., Valleyfield Coll., 1943-47; B.Th., St. Paul Sem., Ottawa, 1949, M.A. Th., 1951; Ph.D., Angelicum U., Rome, 1953. Ordained priest Roman Catholic Ch., 1951; tchr. Valleyfield High sch., 1953-54, Valleyfield Coll., 1954-62; chaplain Montreal U., 1962-65; rector Valleyfield Coll., 1965-67; dir. gen. Valleyfield Pub. Coll., 1967-69; bishop of Valleyfield, 1969-75. Home: Valleyfield, Que. Died Oct. 15, 1975.

BELAVAL, GERMÁNICO SASTRANO, mem. Republican Nat. Com.; b. Santurce, Porto Rico, July 19, 1883; s. José S. Belaval and Concepción (Veve) B.; student Instituto Provincial, P.R., 1895-97, Instituto Cardenal Cisneros, Madrid, Spain, 1898; D.D.S., Baltimore (Md.) Coll. of Dental Surgery, 1903; student U. of Pa., 1904; m. María Luisa Mercado, of Ponce, P.R., Jan. 27, 1912; children—Germánico S., Selma, Esther. Dental surgeon since 1905; mem. Municipal Council, Ponce, P.R., 1915; mem. Insular Bd. of Elections, 1931; mem. Bd. of Commrs., San Juan, P.R., since 1931; mem. Rep. Nat. Com. since 1932; dir. Monjas Racing Corpn. Vice pres. for P.R. of Comite Internat. de Propagande pour la Pratique de la Morale Fonde sur les Lois de la Nature, London, Eng. Hon. mem. Progressive Civic League of Ponce, P.R. (dir. 1913), Freethinkers Assn., Ponce; mem. Am. Dental Assn., Am. Stomatol, Assn., Xi Psi Phi, The Roycroft Frat. Clubs: Union, Escambron Beach (San Juan). Home: Santurce, P.R.

BELCHER, DONALD RAY, financial cons.; b. Albion, Mich., Nov. 4, 1887; s. Sylvester H. and Margaret (Donald) B.; A.B., Kalamazoo Coll., 1909, LL.D., 1944; A.M., Columbia, 1915; student Sorbonne U., Paris, 1919; m. Mary Carver Williams, Aug. 9, 1921; children—Donald William, Mary (Mrs. Robert Dello-Russo), Jonathan. Tchr. math. pub. schs., 1909-10; prof. math. Hanover (Ind.) Coll., 1910-14; instr. math. Columbia, 1914-18; asst. chief statistician Am. Tel. and Tel. Co., 1919-43, asst. comptroller, 1943-44, treas., 1944-52; cons. bd. trustees U. Pa., 1957-59, Case Inst. Tech., 1961, Winterthur Corp., 1961, Lake Erie Coll., 1964, Cornell U., 1964-65. Asst. chief Office Procurement and Material, Navy Dept., 1942-43; asst. dir. U.S. Bur. Budget, 1953-55; regents prof. U. Cal., 1955-57; cons. Cleve. Mus. Natural History. Mem. N.J. Pension Survey Commn., 1930-32; mem. and approval officer N.J. Commn. for Blind, 1932-39; pres. Westfield Bd. Edn., 1939-42, 45-47; mem. Westfield Town Council, 1949-53. Trustee Nat. Music Camp, Interlochen Arts Acad. Served with A.E.F., France, World War I. Recipient Distinguished Civilian Service medal Sec. of Navy, 1944, Presdl. Certificate of Merit, 1947. Fellow A.A.A.S., Am. Statis. Assn.; mem. Am. Math. Soc., Acad. Polit. Sci. Republican. Clubs: Century Assn.; Cosmos (Washington). Author: The Board of Trustees. Home: Westfield, N.J. Died Nov. 24, 1975; interred Long Lake, N.Y.

BELCHER, PAGE, congressman; b. Jefferson, Okla., Apr. 21, 1899; s. George Harvey and Jessie (Ray) B.; student Friends U., U. Okla.; LL.D., Oklahoma City U.; m. Gladys Collins, June 16, 1922; children—Page, Carol Jean (Mrs. Clyde V. Collins). Admitted to Okla. bar, 1936, also U.S. Supreme Court, other fed. courts; ct. clk. Garfield Co., Okla., 1934-38; municipal judge, Enid, Okla., 1938; sec. to Congressman Ross Rizley, eighth dist., Okla., 1941; pvt. practice, Enid, Oklahoma. Mem. 82d to 92d Congresses from 1st Okla. dist., mem. com. on agr., ho. Republican policy com. Mem. Great Salt Plains council Boy Scouts Am. Recipient Silver Beaver award Boy Scouts Am., 1948; named to Okla. Hall of Fame, 1965. Mem. Okla. Bar Assn., Tulsa County Bar, Tulsa C. of C., Am. Legion (comdr. 1947). Methodist. Odd Fellow, Kiwanian. Club: Varsity O. Home: Tulsa, Okla. Died Aug. 5, 1980.

BELDEN, FREDERICK HESLEY, bishop; b. Watertown, N.Y., Sept. 25, 1909; s. Stacy Beardsley Denn and Emma May (Hesley) B.; B.A., Hartwick Coll., 1932; S.T.B., Gen. Theol. Sem., 1936, S.T.D., 1972; m. Dorothy Elizabeth Reumann, Nov. 26, 1936; children—David Allan, Jeffrey Owen, Patricia (Mrs. Paul Conrad Carlson), Bruce Edward. Ordained to ministry Episcopal Ch., 1935; rector Christ Ch., Duanesburg, N.Y., 1936-37, Christ Ch., Walton, N.Y., 1937-42, St. Johns Ch., Johnstown, N.Y., 1942-49, St. Pauls Ch., N.Kingstown, R.I., 1949-71; bishop coadjutor Diocese of R.I., 1971-72; bishop of R.I., Providence, 1972-79. Pres. R.I. State Council Chs., 1964-65. Trustee Gloversville (N.Y.) Library, 1943-49. Mem. Guild of Ascension (warden 1961-69). Club: University (Providence). Home: Providence, R.I. Died Nov. 4, 1979; buried Old Narragansett Ch., North Kingstown, R.I.

BELFORD, JOHN STUART, lawyer; b. Denver, May 29, 1898; s. Samuel W. and Helen (Thomas) B.; A.B., U. Nev., 1920; LL.B., Harvard, 1923; m. Marion E. Bishop, May 31, 1934; children—Frances B. (Mrs. Frederick E. Bickle), Susanah, Samuel W. Admitted to Nev. bar, 1922; practiced in Reno, from 1923; mem. firm Belford and O'Mara and predecessor firms, 1958-71; dist. judge 2d Jud. Dist., 1952-54. Mem. adv. com. on rules of civil procedure Supreme Ct. Nev., 1951-71. Mem. Am., Washoe County bar assns., State Bar Nev. (bd. govs. 1951-52), Sigma Alpha Epsilon. Republican. Mason. Club: Prospectors (Reno). Home: Reno, Nev. Died 1971.

BELKIN, SAMUEL, univ. pres.; b. Swislicz, Poland, Dec. 12, 1911; s. Solomon and Mina (Sattir) B.; rabbi, Radun Theol. Sem., 1929; Ph.D. (hon. fellow), Brown U., 1935, D.D. (hon.), 1959; student Harvard, 1934; L.H.D. (hon.), Dropsie U., 1964; m. Selma Ehrlich, Nov. 10, 1935; children—Linda Rose Schuchalter, Salo Maurice; m. 2d, Abby Polesie, Jan. 3, 1963. Came to U.S. 1929, naturalized, 1941. Instr. Greek, Yeshiva Coll. (now Yeshiva U.), N.Y.C., 1935-40, prof. Hellenistic lit., 1940-43, pres., Yeshiva U., 1943-76, instr. Talmud, 1936-40, dean of Rabbi Isaac Elchanan Theol. Sem., 1940-76; mem. N.Y. State Regents Adv. Council; publ. com. Jewish Publ. Soc. Am.; mem. commn. on chaplaincy Nat. Jewish Welfare Bd.; nat. adv. bd. United World Federalists; trustee World Acad. in Jerusalem; bd. dirs. Soc. Friends Touro Synagogue Nat. Hist. Shrine, Youth Aid, Inc., Council of Higher Ednl. Instns. in N.Y.C. Recipient Bronze medal, 1963, 75th Anniversary medal, Scroll of Distinguished Service, 1973 (all City of N.Y.). Mem. Union Orthodox Rabbis U.S. and Can., Jewish Book Council Am., Jewish Acad. Arts and Scis. (hon.), N.Y. Acad. Pub. Edn., Am. Acad. Polit. and Social Sci., Jewish Hist. Soc. (nat. adv. bd. com. of '76 bicentennial of Am. Revolution), Acad. Religion and Mental Health, Am. Assn. Jewish Edn., Am. Acad. Jewish Research (bd. fellows), Phi Beta Kappa. Author: The Alexandrian Halakhah in Apologetic Literature, 1936; Philo and Oral Law, 1940; Essays in Traditional Jewish Thought, 1956; In His Image, 1961. Contbr. to various learned publs. including Hapardes, Talpioth, Horeb, Sura. Home: New York, N.Y. Died Apr. 18, 1976.

BELKNAP, WILLIAM BURKE, educator, farmer; b. Louisville, Ky., Apr. 18, 1885; s. William Richardson and Alice Trumbull (Silliman) B.; B.A., Yale U., 1908; studied U. of Chicago, 1913-14; M.A., Harvard U., 1915; m. Helen Clark Strong, Sept. 14, 1922 (divorced 1935); children—William Burke, Jonathan Trumball, Helen Strong; m. 2d, Edith Mary Clarke, 1937. With Belknap Hardware & Mfg. Co., 1909-13, now dir.; head of economic dept. U. of Louisville, 1916-27; owner Land o' Goshen Farms, specializing in Southdown sheep, Angus cattle and Ky. saddle horses; mem. Ky. Ho. of Rep., 3 terms, 1924-28, also 1934-36. Chmn. Ky. League for British Victory. Holder of John Harvard Fellowship, 1915-16. Captain Am. Red Cross service abroad 9 mos., 1918. Trustee Berea Coll., 1914-35; mem. Nat. Com. on Inheritance Taxes, 1925; mem. bd. of govs. Council of State Governments; speaker Interstate Legislative Assembly, 1933-35; mem. Interstate Commn. on Conflicting Taxation, 1933-35. Mem. Horse and Mule Assn. America, Ky. Tax Research Assn. Former pres. Falls Cities Milk Producers Assn.; pres. Ryeland Sheep Assn., Am. Legislators Assn. (pres. 4 yrs.); hon. mem. Southdown Sheep Soc. (Eng.); mem. Am. Saddle Horse Breeders' Assn. (treas.), Nat. Tax Assn., Am. Economic Assn., Acad. Polit. Science, Ky. Hist. Soc., Filson Club, Zeta Psi, Phi Beta Kappa; fellow Royal Econ. Soc. (Eng.). Democrat. Presbyterian. Mason. Clubs: Pendennis, Arts, Country (Louisville); Yale (New York). Writer on nat. taxation. Home: Goshen, Kentucky.*

BELL, ALVIN EUGENE, clergyman; b. Mansfield, O., Apr. 10, 1882; s. Frank J. and Alice A. (Ludwig) B.; A.B., Wittenberg Coll., 1905, D.D., 1923; B.D., Hamma Div. Sch. (Wittenberg Coll.), 1908; m. Nola E. Bair, Aug. 26, 1910; children—Ruth Alberta, Paul Luther, Lois Miriam, Alvin Eugene, George Theodore. Ordained Lutheran ministry, 1908; pastor First Ch., Bryan, O., 1907-13, Glenwood Av. Ch., Toledo, 1913-52, pastor emeritus, 1952—; interim pastor Grace Luth. Ch., Phoenix, Messiah Luth. Ch. Denver, 1952-54; orgainzed First Church, Stryker, O., 1911, Augsburg, Olivet, Bethany chs., Toledo, 1914, 17. Mem. bd. Am. Missions of United Lutheran Ch. in America, 1926-34; mem. bd., Wittenberg College, 1926-55, chairman, 1938-42; chmn. Children's Bureau, Toledo, 1928-35; president Toledo Council of churches, 1919; chairman board of Hamma Divinity School 1943-48; member board Child and Family Agency of Toledo, 1930-43, vice president board, 1932-41; member executive board United Lutheran Ch. in Am., 1934-42; mem. bd. Deaconess Work, United Luth. Ch. Am., 1948-60, pres., 1950-54; official visitor United Luth. Ch. of Am. to World Council of Churches, Amsterdam, Holland, 1948. Received the Meritorious Service Award of the Wittenberg College Alumni Assn., 1941; member Toledo Community Chest Board, 1946. Club: Exchange. Author: The Word of a Woman Versus the Word of God, 1917; The Gist of the Bible, Book by Book, 1961; Words of Life and Beauty, 1941; Today's 'Good News' (daily devotions), 1953; also "Brass Tacks on the Sunday School Lesson," syndicated articles. Home: Toledo.

BELL, FRANK THOMAS, commr. fisheries; b. nr. Japan, Mo., Sept. 21, 1884; s. William Lafayette and Amy Lee (Farrar) B.; ed. pub. schs. and business coll. Began as farmer in Grant Co., Wash., 1907; real estate business, Ephrata, Wash., 1910; apartment and hotel business, Seattle, 1912-18; county commr., Grant Co., 1918-22; sec. to U.S. Senator C. C. Dill, 1922-33; apptd. U.S. commr. of fisheries, Apr. 15, 1933. Active in promoting irrigation projects, especially Columbia Basin project. Mem. Izaak Walton League. Democrat.

Methodist. Odd Fellow, Eagle. Home: Seattle, Wash.

BELL, GOLDEN WOOLFOLK, lawyer; b. Pinos Altos, N.M., Jan. 14, 1886; s. Nathaniel and Susan R. (Woolfolk) B. student Beloit College, 1903-04; B.L., Univ. of Calif., 1907; LL.B., Harvard, 1910; m. Madelyn I. Llewellyn, 1919. Admitted to California bar, 1910; member District of Columbia and Philippine bars; general practice in San Francisco, Calif., 1910-33; part-time prof., Hastings Coll. of Law, U. of Calif., 1911-30; with Commn. for Relief in Belgium, and Am. Relief Administration, New York City, 1919; special asst. to U.S. Atty. Gen., Washington, D.C., 1933-35; asst. solicitor gen., 1935-39; legal adviser to U.S. High Commr. to the Philippines, 1939-41; resigned Sept. 1941; legal div., War Prodn. Bd. and asst. gen. counsel, 1942-45; asst. gen. and gen. counsel, Surplus Property Adminstrn. and successors, 1945-46; resigned Mar. 1946. Home: Oceanside, Calif. *

BELL, GORDON HUMPHREY, corp. exec.; b. Boston, Sept. 25, 1920; s. Harold Ingersoll and Ellen Morrell (Foster) B.; student Iowa State U., 1939-42, Am. U., 1969; m. Theodora M. Clarke, June 26, 1944; children—Ellen, Laramie, Allyson, Gordon C. Divisional head for govt. sales John Morell & Co., Sioux Falls, S.D., 1950-53; v.p. Foster-Bell Co., Sioux Falls, 1953-66; asst. dir. for pvt. cooperation USIA, 1967-68, chief cultural affairs div. ICS, 1968-69, pub. affairs officer, Sydney, Australia, 1969-71; v.p., gen. mgr. Aspen (Colo.) Inst. for Humanistic Studies, 1972; pres. 1st Colo. Corp., Aspen, 1972-76; dir. Raven Industries, Inc., Sioux Falls. Pres. Zool. Soc. Sioux Falls, 1958-66. Bd. dirs. Sioux Valley Hosp., 1953-64, v.p., 1960, pres., 1961. Served with USNR, 1942-45. Recipient outstanding achievement award pub. service S.D. Sch. Mines, 1965. Address: Aspen, Colo. Died Feb. 9, 1978.

BELL, JAMES ALEXANDER, educator; b. Midway, Pa., May 26, 1882; s. James and Jane (Major) B.; Ph.B., Grove City Coll., 1908; A.B., Harvard, 1915; A.M., American U., Washington, D.C., 1923, Ph.D., 1925; LL.B., Southeastern U., 1930; m. Margaret Hood Bamford, Aug. 25, 1915; children—Virginia Marguerite, Winona Hood. Began ednl. work Washington County Pa., 1902; entered Y.M.C.A. ednl. work, 1911; Y.M.C.A. sec., A.E.F., France and Germany, January, 1918-May, 1919; now in radio broadcasting, Washington, D.C.; instr. pub. speaking, U.S. Naval School of Hosp. Adminstrn., Nat. Naval Med. Center, Bethesda, Md. Mem. Bars of District Court of U.S., D.C., Va., U.S. Supreme Ct. Mem. Phi Delta Kappa. Presbyterian. Mason. Author: Lab. Manual of English Writing (Spencer and Bell), 1917; Famous Masons, 1928; Cases on Personal Property, 1938. Author: Speaking That Wins (Randolph and Bell), 1940; Business Law, 1943. Home: Bradbury Heights, Md. *

BELL, JAMES DUNBAR, ednl. adminstr., former U.S. ambassador; b. Lebanon, N.H., July 1, 1911; s. Frank Upham and Louise (Dunbar) B.; A.B., U. N.M., 1934; A.M., U. Chgo., 1936, Ph.D., 1941; m. Helen Foy Johnstone, Dec. 4, 1934 (div. May 1960); children—James Dunbar, Diane Elizabeth, Christopher Johnstone; m. 2d, Stephanie Ann Mathews, June, 1961; children—Stephanie Susan, Jefferson Matuzic. Reporter Alburquerque Journal, 1933-34; chief statistician N. M. Dept. Public Welfare, 1936-37; instr. Gary (Ind.) College, 1939-41; analyst Office Coordinator Inter-American Affairs, 1941-42; spl. asst., Dept. Justice, 1943-44; asst. prof. Hamilton Coll., 1946-47; labor attache, counsul Am. embassy, Bogota, Colombia, 1944-46; counsul Am. embassy, Santiago, Chile, 1947, Manila, P.I., 1950; 1st sec. and consul, Am. embassy, Manila, 1951; assigned to Dept. State, Washington, 1953-55, dep. dir. Philippine and Southeast Asian Affairs, 1955, dir. Office Southwest Pacific Affairs, 1956, 1960-64; dep. chief of mission Am. embassy, Djarkarta, 1957-60; U.S. ambassador to Malaysia, 1964-69; diplomat in residence U. Cal. at Santa Cruz, 1969-70, fellow Merrill Coll., 1969-79, acting dir. Center for South Pacific Studies, 1973-74. Adviser U.S. delegation to UN Gen. Assembly, 1961. Mem. Am. delegation ILO Regional Conf., Montevideo, Uruguay, 1949. Mem. Cal. State Democratic Com., 1971-72; dist. dir. Cal. Dem. Council, 1971-72. Mem. Soc. Cin., UN Assn. (pres. Santa Cruz chpt. 1971). Club: Internat. (Washington). Home: Santa Cruz, Calif. Died Apr. 14, 1979; buried Rock Creek Cemetery, Washington.

BELL, JOHN HOWARD, educator; b. Derry, N.H., May 21, 1883; s. Samuel Howard and Etta (Nise) B.; grad. Pinkerton Acad., Derry 1901; A.B., Dartmouth, 1905; student Boston U., 1905-06; grad. summer sch. phys. edn., Harvard, 1916; student U. of Pa., 1923-25, Harvard, 1927; degree of Ed.M., Harvard Graduate School, 1929; m. Maria Beardslee Prescott, of Derry, Mar. 17, 1906; 1 dau., Harriet Prescott. Began with Nonotuck Silk Co., Florence, Mass., 1906; Walter A. Wood Mowing & Reaping Machine Co., Hoosick Falls, N.Y., 1907-10; dir. of health and physical edn., Hoosac Sch., Hoosick, N.Y., 1910-12; asst. to gen. supt. Sherwin Williams Co., Cleveland, O., 1912-14; prof. hygiene and dir. physical edn., Mich. Coll. Mines, 1914-16; dir. physical edn., Friend's Central Sch. and Elementary Systems, Phila., Pa., 1916-25; headmaster Darlington Sem. and dir. Darlington Sch. of Physical Edn., West Chester, Pa., 1925-28; now prin. Pinkerton Acad., Derry, New Hampshire. Mem. N.Y.N.G., 1908-10. Mem. N.E.A., Am. Physical Edn. Assn., N.H. State Teachers Assn., Rockingham Co. Teachers Assn., Headmasters Assn., Nat. Soc. Secondary School Principles, Phi Gamma Delta. Republican. Episcopalian. Mason. Home: Derry, N.H.*

BELL, RALPH PICKARD, shipping exec.; b. Halifax, N.S., Mar. 28, 1886; s. Andrew Mackinlay and Mary Emmerancy (Pickard) B.; B.A. and D.C.L., U. of Mount Allison, Sackville, New Brunswick, Can., 1907; m. Anna Marguerite Deinstadt, May 22, 1907 (died Mar. 17, 1943); children—Dorothy Allison Deinstadt (wife of Maj. James Isbester Maclaren, Royal Canadian Arty.), Helen Pickard (Mrs. Stuart B. Wood), Nancy Allison (wife of Robert W. Moncel, officer Canadian Army); m. 2d, Marjorie Young Smith, June 17, 1944. Salesman, Canadian Fairbanks Co., Ltd., 1907-11; sec. A. M. Bell & Co., Ltd., Halifax, N.S., 1911-14; in real estate development, 1914-17; sec. Halifax Relief Commn., 1917-19; lumber, timberlands and pulpwood business, 1919-30; fishing industry, 1927-36; in shipping since 1936, now pres. and chief owner Pickford & Black, Ltd., Halifax, N.S. With Canadian Dept. Munitions and Supplies (dollar a year man), 1940-44; apptd. dir.-gen. aircraft production Aug. 1940, later became aircraft controller, also mem. Production Board and mem. Wartime Industries Control Board; mem. Joint War Production Board of Canada and U.S.; resigned as dir.-gen., controller and mem. of foregoing boards, effective Dec. 1944. Decorated Order British Empire. Mem. Royal Canadian Air Force Benevolent Fund. Clubs: Halifax, Halifax Short Snorter, Royal Nova Scotia Yacht Squadron (Halifax); Mount Royal (Montreal); Rideau, Country (Ottawa).

BELL, ROBERT JUDSON, judge; b. Fayetteville, Ark., July 18, 1900; s. Joseph Conway and Elfie Laura (Campbell) B.; A.B., U. Okla., Norman, 1923, LL.B., 1923; m. Marjorie Narissa Walcott, Feb. 19, 1924; children—Robert Judson, Marjorie Breidenback. Admitted to Okla. bar, 1923; asst. county atty. Pittsburg County (Okla.), 1923-29; pvt. practice, 1930-40; mayor, City McAlester, Okla., 1940-42; city atty., McAlester, 1947-50, Krebs, Okla., 1950-63; chief judge 18th Judicial Dist. Ct., Eufala and McAlester, Okla., 1963-75, ret., 1975. Ex-officio judge Ct. Appeals State Okla., 1971. Bd. dirs., trustee McAlester Found., 1946-63; trustee, sec. McAlester Scottish Rite Charitable and Ednl. Assn., 1969-76, McAlester Scottish Rite Bldg. Corp., 1969-76. Served to lt. col. USAAF, 1942-45; ETO. Decorated Bronze Star; named Most Valuable Citizen McAlester, 1942; Most Valuable Mem., McAlester chpt. Navy League, 1968; recipient S. Arch Thompson Citizenship award Freedom Found. Valley Forge, 1972. Fellow Am. Coll. Trial Lawyers; mem. State Bar Okla., Pittsburg County Bar Assn. (pres. 1936), McAlester C. of C. (dir. 1946-63), Am. Legion (exec. com. 1940-63), Order of Coif, Phi Beta Kappa, Phi Delta Theta (pres. student assn. 1922-23). Democrat. Mason (33 deg. Shriner). Home: McAlester, Okla. Died July 26, 1976; interred Oak Hill Cemetery, McAlester, Okla.

BELLAH, JAMES WARNER, author; b. N.Y.C., Sept. 14, 1899; s. James Warner and Harriette Louise (Johnson) B.; A.B., Columbia U., 1923; M.A. (history), Georgetown U., 1945; student Grad. Sch. Polit. Sci., U. Pa., 1946; m. Helen Lasater Hopkins, Oct. 22, 1942 (dec.); 1 dau. by previous marriage, Ann; children—James, John, Stephen; m. Eunice Irvine Taylor Mannas, July 3, 1974. Advt. writer, 1923-25; instr. English Columbia, 1923-26, 36-37; fgn. corr. Aero Digest, Europe and Far East, 1927-28; story writer and novelist, 1923-76; v.p. Lancaster and Chester R.R.; lecture tour U.S. and Can., 1947-49; mem. 9th Global Strategy Conf., Naval War Coll., 1957; Dance Meml. lectr. Va. Mil. Inst., 1957. Mem. Cal. Civil War Centennial Commn.; nat. adv. com. Civil War Centennial Commn. Served as cpl. Co. E, 1st Provisional Tng. Regt., Fort Terry, N.Y., 1916; served as 2d lt., pilot 117th Squadron, Royal Air Force and Royal Flying Corps, 1917-19; first reserve officer called for Gen. Staff duty with 1st Div., Oct. 7, 1940; grad. command and General Staff Sch., Ft. Leavenworth, Kan., Apr. 1940; detailed to Gen. Staff Corps as 1st lt.; G-2, 80th Inf. Div., 1942-43, hdqrs. Southeast Asia Command, 1943-44, hdqrs. Army Ground Forces, 1944. Mem. crew on first regular mail plane, Pan-Am. Airways, Miami to Havana, Central America, and Panama, Feb. 19, 1929. Received pilot's license Federation Aeronautique Internationale, July 15, 1918. Decorated Legion of Merit, Bronze Star medal, Air medal, Army Commendation Pendant (U.S.); knight of grace Order St. John Jerusalem (Yugoslavia), comdr. Order St. Lazarus Jerusalem; 175th Anniversary Medal of Honor, Georgetown U. Chmn. Conn. div. Amateur Fencers League of Am. (Conn. open champion Epee 1934, v.p. of League, 1936-37 and 1937-38); mem. exec. com. Intercollegiate Aerial Assn., 1919-20. Fellow Royal Geog. Soc., Royal Asiatic Soc. Gt. Britain and Ireland; mem. Am. Legion, Soc. Colonial Wars (gov. Cal. chpt. 1969), S.R., Quiet Birdmen. Republican. Episcopalian. Clubs: Royal Air Force (London). Author twenty books, later ones including: Irregular Gentleman (autobiography), 1947; Land Actions, 1812-14, A Reconsideration, 1947; also The Valiant Virginians, The Bones of Napoleon, Seven Must Die, Rear Guard, and Soldier's Battle: Gettyburg; (screen plays) She Wore a Yellow Ribbon, The Man Who Shot Liberty Valance, The Sea Chase, Target Zero, Ten Tall Men; also dialogue for This Is Korea (John Ford), Sergeant Rutledge, A Thunder of Drums; The Journal of Colonel DeLancey, 1967. Contbr. Holiday Mag., Sat. Eve. Post, 1926-76. Donor James Warner Bellah collection books and papers to Boston U. Library. Address: Pacific Palisades, Calif. Died Sept. 22, 1976; interred VA Cemetery, Los Angeles.

BELLANCA, FRANK MERLO, airplane designer; b. Sciacca (Sicily), Italy, Nov. 16, 1882; s. Andrew and Concetta B.; student Post-Tech. Inst. of Physics-Mathematics, Palermo and Trapany, Italy, 1902-06; m. Claudia Boggiali, Dec. 8, 1906; children—Thea, Edi, Mirthe. Began experiments in aviation with brother, G. M. Bellanca, Taliedo, Milan, Italy, 1910, building first tractor bi-plane; built with brother, first monoplane of modern design, Belmont Park, Long Island, N.Y., 1912; designing and asso. Bellanca Aircraft Corpn., Staten Island, N.Y., 1927-28, production mgr., 1928-29, dir. of exptl. engring., New Castle, Del., 1929-32, v.p., 1933-35; dir. of fgn. sales, New York office, 1935-37; designed spl. gullwing long distance plane for Commercial Airplane Co., Bridgeport, Conn., 1929; in 1937 designed 4 commercial planes, single and multi-engine, and 3 mil. types, twin-engine, battleship-submarine destroyer and pursiut bomber; designer and v.p. White Aircraft, Ltd., Toronto, Can., since 1938; pres. Internat. Aircraft Trading Co., Bellanca Aircraft Mfg. Co. Inventor of twin-engine with both engines in the central line of symmetry with central line of thrust, resistance and lift passing always through, or close to, central gravity line, irrespective if one or both engines are functioning; air brakes and ailerons working on airfoil vacuum; central beam fuselage construction; hydroplane torpedo chaser; designed 2-engine helicopter, 1943; general manager and asst. to president, Bellanca Aircraft Corp., New Castle, Del., 1946; gen. mgr. Wildwood Airport, 1947; designed electronic teleflrah for wireless telephone conversation and permanent registration, 1948. Vice president, Italian People's Union. Chmn. Anti-Fascist Alliance. Catholic. Author: Military Superiority of the Airplane Over the Dirigible, a study, 1910; The Intellectual Movement of Today in Italy, 1912; Principles and Methods in the Labor Movement, 1916; The New Italian Immigration in the United States, 1919. Editor: World Labor Forum, since 1948. Sent by Industria Sportiva, Italian mag., to first aeronautical conf., Paris, 1912. Home: Forest Hills; L.I., N.Y. *

BELLINGER, FREDERICK, chem. engr.; b. New Orleans, Aug. 14, 1904; s. Lyle Frederick and Annie Beall (Dobbs) B.; B.S., Ga. Inst. Tech., 1926; M.S., Emory U., 1935; D.Eng., Yale U., 1940; m. Emma Marie Parker, July 6, 1937; 1 dau., Barbara Lynn. Chem. engr. C.W.S., U.S. Army, 1926-28; chief plants design, then chief chem. engr. Huntsville Arsenal, 1941-43; chem. engr. R & H. Chem. Co., 1928-32; self-employed, 1932-33; chem. engr. Mfrs. Cons. Engrs., 1933; market devel. Robert & Co., 1933-34; instr. chem. engring. Yale U., 1935-37; research chem. engr. Hercules Powder Co., 1937-40; from asso. prof. to prof. chem. engring. Ga. Inst. Tech., 1945-72, head chem. scis. div. engring. expt. sta., 1953-56, asst. dir. for industry, 1956-58, chief material sci. div., 1958-61, chief chem. sci. and materials div., 1961-72; cons. Chem. Corps, 1952-66; UNESCO adviser Nat. Research Center, Egypt, 1955-56; spl. cons. to Under Sec. of War on German chem. industry, 1948; dir. Civil Def. Preliminary Operation Survival Project of Ga., 1957; mem. Gov.'s Commn. Sci. Research and Devel., 1963-64. Trustee Ocean Sci. Center of Atlantic, 1969-72. Served from maj. to lt. col. C.W.S., AUS, 1943-45, 51-52; col. Res., from 1952. Decorated Legion of Merit, 1956; registered profl. engr., Ga. Fellow Ga. Acad. Sci. (treas. 1958-61, pres. 1962); mem. Inst. Am. Strategy, Am. Inst. Chem. Engrs. (life; past chmn. Atlanta sect.), Am. Chem. Soc. (life), Ga. Engring. Soc. (life; dir. 1971-73), Sigma Xi, Tau Beta Pi, Alpha Chi Sigma. Presbyn. (elder). Club: Atlanta Athletic. Contbr. Ency. Chemistry, 1958, 65. Home: Atlanta, Ga. Died Oct. 22, 1978.

BELMONT, ALAN HARNDEN, ret. orgn. exec.; b. N.Y.C., Jan. 22, 1907; s. Arthur B. and Teresa Annie (Harnden) B.; student San Diego State Coll., 1927-30; A.B., Stanford, 1931; m. Loretta Agnes Drzyeimski, May 14, 1938; children—Barbara Lenore, Alan Nicholas. Acct., Calif., 1931-36; spl. agt. FBI, 1936, assigned Birmingham, Ala., Chgo. and N.Y.C., 1936-43, in charge field office, Cin., 1943-44, asst. dir. domestic intelligence div., 1951-62, asst. to dir. charge investigations, 1961-65; exec. asst. to dir. Hoover Instn. on War, Revolution and Peace, Stanford U., 1966-69, asso. dir. for adminstrn., 1969-74. Episcopalian. Home: Mountain View, Calif. Died July 30, 1977; interred Gate of Heaven, Los Altos, Calif.

BEMB, WALTER J(ACOB) (BEM), business exec.; b. Esslingen, Germany, May 17, 1885; s. Jacob and Louise (Krimmel) B.; ed. pub. schs. of Detroit; m. Inez DeCosta, May 25, 1914. Came to U.S., 1893, naturalized, 1914. Began as automobile mechanic, with the William E. Metzger Co., Detroit, 1902; branch manager for Ford Motor Co., Detroit, 1906-08; mgr. of J. H. Brady Auto Co., Detroit, 1908-10; asst. sales mgr. of Hudson Motor Car Co., 1910-12; established Bemb-Robinson Co., Detroit distributor for Hudson Motor cars, 1912, received the dealer franchise for the Buick and Pontiac automobiles, 1924, also granted the distributorship in Mich. for Rolls Royce of England during the 1920's; mfrs. agent for Houdaille-Hershey Corp. (automobile parts), Detroit, 1926-47, v.p., dir. (charge of customer relations) since 1947; vice pres., dir. of Muskegon Motor Specialties Co., Muskegon, Mich. (subsidiary of Houdaille-Hershey Corp.); dir. Skinner Co., Ltd., Oshawa, Ontario, Can. (Canadian subsidiary). Pres. Detroit Automobile Dealers Assn., 1918. Mem. Detroit Bd. of Commerce. Republican. Presbyterian. Clubs: Bloomfield Hills (Mich.) Country; Automobile Old Timers (N.Y. City); Athletic, Gun, Recess (Detroit); Pere Marquette Rod and Gun (Baldwin, Mich.); Question, National Club. Home: Birmingham, Mich.

BEMIS, WILLIAM HAY, lawyer; b. Cleve., Mar. 3, 1897; s. Alton Adelbert and Elizabeth (Hay) B.; A.B., Dartmouth, 1918; LL.B., Western Res. U., 1922; m. Alice McNeil, Nov. 12, 1927 (dec. Oct. 1956); children—Elizabeth (Mrs. Dean C. Cameron), Rebecca (Mrs. Arthur L. Amiot); m. 2d, Wilma Suits Nye, May 6, 1961. Admitted to Ohio bar, 1921, practiced in Cleve. from 1921; mem. firm Baker Hostetler & Patterson, 1924-26, partner, 1927-70, counsel, 1970-76. Mem. Am., Ohio, Cleve. bar assns. Clubs: Country, Union (Cleve.); Highland Park (Lake Wales, Fla.). Home: Shaker Heights, Ohio. Died Sept. 17, 1976.

BENBOW, CHARLES FRANK, business exec.; b. Winston-Salem, N.C., Aug. 22, 1924; s. Charles Frank and Ruth (Harper) B.; B.S., U. N.C., 1947; postgrad. Grad. Sch. Credit and Fin. Mgmt., Amos Tuck Sch., Dartmouth, 1951, 52, 54; m. Mary Elizabeth Bexter, Sept. 13, 1947; children—Shirley, Martha, Mary. With R.J. Reynolds Tobacco Co., 1947-70, asst. credit mgr., 1948-58, asst. sec., 1956-58, credit mgr., 1958-68, treas., 1968-70, v.p., 1969-70; v.p. finance R.J. Reynolds Industries, Inc., Winston-Salem, 1970-73, sr. v.p., 1973-79, sec., 1976-79, dir., 1970-79; treas., dir. Archer Products, Inc., 1966-71; treas. Reynolds Foods, Inc., 1967-70; chmn. bd. Reynolds Leasing Co., 1969-73; dir. Monterey Transp. Co., Inc., Hatteras Income Securities, Inc., Charlotte br. Fed. Res. Bank Richmond, McLean Industries, RJR Foods, Inc. Mem. Bd. Natural and Econ. Resources N.C., 1975-79; Bd. visitors Guilford Coll., Greensboro, N.C.; mem. Bus. Com. for Arts, Inc., N.Y.C. Recipient Victory medal Joslin Diabetic Found., 1968. Episcopalian. Home: Winston-Salem, N.C. Died Oct. 1979.

BENCHER, WALTER SEAMAN, mfg. co. exec.; b. Bklyn., Jan. 21, 1917; s. Alfred and Wilhelmina (Caëmmerling) B.; student Drexel Inst., 1935, Pratt Inst., 1937, St. Johns U., 1941; m. Rita Frugoli, June 16, 1937; children—Anita, Karen, Steven. Accountant, Cities Service Oil Co., 1935-41; engr. Combustion Engring., Inc., 1941-52, asst. controller, 1952, controller, 1953-78, v.p., 1956, v.p. internat. ops., 1961-78; pres., dir. Combustion Engring. Overseas, Inc.; vice chmn., dir. Energie-und Verfahrenstechnik G.m.b.H.; dep. chmn. Internat. Combustion (Holdings) Ltd.; dir. Lummus Co., CE-rrey, SA (Mexico), Combustion Engring-Superheater Ltd., Compagnie Fonciere, Clarke Chapman Ltd., Internat. Combustion (Africa) Ltd., Combustion Chems., Inc., Franco Tosi, S.A., Stein Industrie, S.A. Cermatec, Ltd., Combustion-Stein-Astilleros, S.A., Fabricados para Construcción, S.A., Ibérica Construcciones de Aluminio, S.A., Obras Montajes e Instalaciones, S.A., Aplicaciones Téchnicas Industriales, S.A. Internat. Combustion Australia Ltd., Nat. Tank France, Ltd., Uddcomb Sweden, A.B., Ramtite Europ, CESO International, Ltd. Mem. ASME, Atomic Indsl. Forum, Soc. Profl. Engrs., Am. Inst. Mgmt., Mexican C. of C. Clubs: Union League; Wampanoag Country; Landmark; Country of Darien. Home: Milford, Conn. Died Apr 4, 1978.

BENCHLEY, BELLE JENNINGS (MRS.), zoo dir.; b. Larned, Kan., Aug. 28, 1882; d. Fred M. and Ida Belle (Orrell) Jennings; ed. high sch. and State Teachers Coll., San Diego, Calif.; corr. courses in journalism and accounting; m. William L. Benchley, June 26, 1906 (divorced); 1 son, Edward Jennings. Taught sch. 4 yrs. before marriage; with San Diego Zoöl. Garden since 1925, as bookkeeper, 1925-27, exec. sec. and head of staff since 1927; publishes a monthly mag. called Zoonooz (publ. Zoöl. Soc. of San Diego); radio speaker; has appeared in broadcasts of radio and TV shows as well as newsreels. Mem. Women's Geog. Soc. America, American Assn. Park Execs., Assn. of Zool. Parks and Aquariums (past pres.), International Union Zoo Dirs., hon. mem. Izaak Walton League, Am. Assn. University Women) (San Diego branch). Clubs: Altrusa, Pen and Brush, San Diego Press. Author: My Life in a Man Made Jungle; My Friends, The Apes; My Animal Babies; Shirley Visits the Zoo. Contbr. to Nature Mag.

BENCKER, RALPH B(UCKLEY), architect; b. Phila., Pa., Dec. 24, 1883; s. John and Mary (Bowden) B.; ed. Sch. of Industrial Arts, 1900-02, Acad. Fine Arts, 1902-03, Atelier of T-Square Club, 1903-05, Temple U., 1905-07 (all of Phila.); m. Mary G. Brendel, June 24, 1907; 1 dau., Helen Wayne. Began as draftsman in office of Wilson Eyre, architect, 1900; became connected with Price & McLanahan, 1904; admitted to partnership upon decease of Mr. Price, 1918, and title of firm changed to McLanahan & Bencker; practiced alone since June 1, 1925. Architect of bldg. representing Commonwealth of Pa. at Sesquicentennial; Wyoming Bank & Trust Co. Bldg., First Christian Ch., Tradesmen's Nat. Bank Bldg., N.W. Ayer & Son Advertising Agency Bldg., Southwestern Nat. Bank Bldg., Am. Radiator Bldg., Children's Heart Hosp., State Theatre—all Phila.; Pa. Freight Station, Chicago; Union Ry. Station, Indianapolis; Equitable Trust Co. Bldg. and M.E. Blatt Dept. Store, Atlantic City, N.J.; etc. Mem. Phila. Zoning Commn. Fellow A.I.A. (pres. Phila. Chapter); mem. Acad. Fine Arts, Pa. Mus. and Sch. Industrial Arts. Republican. Mem. First Christian Ch. Clubs: Art Club, Rotary, Philadelphia Yacht. Home: Haverford, Pa.

BENDICH, AARON, biochemist, educator; b. N.Y.C., June 18, 1917; s. Louis and Ellen (Goldberg) B.; B.S., Coll. City N.Y., 1939; Ph.D., Columbia, 1946; m. Clare Kaufman, Aug. 28, 1940; children—Arnold Jay, Stephen Zachary. Research asst. biochemistry Columbia, 1940-42, mem. sci. staff div. war research, 1943-45, research asst. bacteriology, 1946-47; part-time instr. chemistry Coll. City N.Y., 1946-48, 52, 54, 55, 59; fellow Sloan Kettering Inst., 1947-48, asst., 1948-49, asso., 1949-60, mem., from 1960, chief sect. synthesis lab., 1954-58, chief sect. organic biochemistry, from 1958, chief division of cell biochemistry. from 1969, chmn. postdoctoral studies com., 1960; faculty Sloan-Kettering div. Cornell U. Med. Sch., N.Y.C. from 1949, prof. biochemistry. from 1961. Mem. bd. sci. advisers St. Jude Children's Hosp. and Research Inst., Memphis. Fellow Am.-Swiss Found. Sci. Exchange, 1956; recipient R. Thornton Wilson award genetic and preventive psychiatry, 1960; A.P. Sloan Found. award for cancer research, 1964; Research Career award, NIH, 1964; Townsend Harris outstanding achievement award, 1974. Fellow N.Y. Acad. Scis.; mem. A.A.A.S., Am. Chem. Soc., Am. Soc. Biol. Chemists, Am. Soc. Human Genetics, Harvey Soc., Lymphoid Club, N.Y. State Soc. Med. Research, Nat. Geog. Soc., Sigma Xi. Editor Archives Biochemistry and Biophysics, from 1960. Home: Bronx, N.Y. Died Sept. 14, 1979.

BENEDEK, MARTIN HENRY, industrialist; b. Budapest, Hungary, Feb. 15, 1904; s. Adolph and Julie (Roth) B.; brought to U.S., 1908, naturalized, 1916; student public schs. N.Y.C.; m. Leonore Friedman, Jan. 19, 1935; children—Warren Donald, A. Richard, Barry Paul. Pioneer in devel. components electronic industry; with Gen. Instrument Corp., from 1955, chmn. bd., chief exec. officer, 1955-68, chmn. fin. com., dir., 1968-78. Founder Albert Einstein Coll. Medicine; pres. bd. Benedek Found., Inc. Home: Palm Beach, Fla. Died Mar. 26, 1978.

BENEDICT, DANIEL NORRIS, mfr. refrigerating and farm machinery; b. Franklin County, Pa., Jan. 23, 1882; s. Daniel Mack and Isabel Price (Norris) B.; M.E., State Tchrs. Coll., Shippensburg, Pa., 1900; m. Ethel Grace Washabaugh, Sept. 12, 1917; 1 dau., Amy Katherine (Mrs. L.D. Morrill). Sch. tchr., 1900; with Frick Co., Waynesboro, Pa., 1902—, treas. 1906-28, v.p. and gen. mgr., 1928-42, pres. 1942—; president, member board of directors Citizens Nat. Bank and Trust Co.; dir. Landis Machine Co. Trustee Waynesboro Hosp., Waynesboro Beneficial Fund Assn. Mem. Pa. Soc., Am. Soc. Refrigerating Engineers. Republican. Elk. Clubs: National Republican (N.Y.C.), Elks. Home: Waynesboro, Pa. *

BENEDICT, WILLIAM LEMUEL, surgeon; b. Springport, Ind., Feb. 13, 1885; s. Hanford and Grace D. (Lanham) B.; grad. Spiceland (Ind.) Acad., 1904; M.D., U. Mich., 1912, LL.D., 1955; m. Edith Henrietta Betz, June 2, 1914; children—Virginia Clare, Barbara Jane, Walter Hanford, John William. Demonstrator ophthalmology U. Mich. Med. Sch., 1912-13; asst. to Dr. W. R. Parker, Detroit, 1913-14; group practice medicine, Fresno, Cal., 1914-17; head ophthalmology sect. Mayo Clinic, Rochester, Minn., 1917-50, pres. staff, 1932-34, prof. opthalmology U. Minn. Grad. Sch. Med., Mayo Found., to 1950; pres. Ophthalmic Pub. Co., Chgo. Sec. gen. XVII Internat. Congress Ophthalmology, 1951; cons. Am. Bd. Ophthalmology. Mem. Am. Ophthal. Soc., Am. Acad. Ophtalmology and Otolaryngology (exec. sec., treas. 1942), A.M.A., Minn. Acad. Medicine, Sigma Xi, Phi Beta Pi. Republican. Mem. Disciples of Christ Ch. Mason. Clubs: University, Kiwanis (pres. Rochester 1923). Contbr. articles to med. jours. Home: Rochester, Minn. *

BENEDUM, PAUL GREGORY, bus. exec.; b. Cameron, W.Va., Feb. 17, 1902; s. Charles Yantis and Leota (Hicks) B.; A.B. in Metall. Engring. and Geology, Ohio State U., 1927; LL.D., Capital U., Columbus, O., 1949; D.Sc. (hon.), W.Va. Wesleyan Coll., 1951; LL.D., Waynesburg Coll., 1955, Davis and Elkins Coll., 1961, Ohio State U., 1971, Alderson Broadous, 1971; D.Hum., Salem Coll., 1963, Springfield Coll., 1972; m. Beatrice Willeen Ludwig, Apr. 17, 1928; 1 son, Paul Gregory, Jr. Geologist, Benedum-Trees Interests, 1927-30; with M.L. Benedum as head, geol. expdn. to Lake Van region, Turkey, 1930; geologist and dist. mgr., Pa., and later the Southwest, Benedum-Trees, 1930-43; pres., dir. Hiawatha Oil & Gas Co. until 1961, dir., 1961-77; pres., dir. Penn-Ohio Gas Co. until 1961, dir., 1961-77; pres., chief exec. officer, dir. Plymouth Oil Co., 1961-63; pres., dir. Bentex Oil Corp., 1963-69; pres. Benedum-Trees Oil Co., 1963-77, also dir.; v.p. Republic Pipe Line Co., dir. subsidiary cos.; dir. Pitts. Nat. Bank. Active Boy Scouts Am., recipient Silver Buffalo award. Pres., Claude Worthington Benedum Found., 1959-77; trustee Waynesburg Coll., Shady Side Acad., W.Va. Wesleyan Coll.; bd. dirs. Western Pa. Hosp., Children's Home of Pitts., Western Pa. Sch. for Blind Children; bd. dirs., treas. Fellowship Christian Athletes; bd. mgrs. Children's Hosp. Served to lt. col. USAAF, 1943-46. Decorated Legion of Merit. Mem. Nat. Petroleum Council, Mil. Petroleum Adv. Bd., Def. Services Com. of Am. Petroleum Inst., Sigma Gamma Epsilon, Kappa Kappa Psi, Delta Chi. Methodist. Clubs: Fox Chapel Golf, Duquesne, Pittsburgh Athletic Assn. (Pitts.); Gibson Island (Md.) Yacht Squadron, Bayou, Ramada (Houston); Pike Run Country (Jones Mills, Pa.); Army Navy (Washington); Laurel Valley Golf, Rolling Rock (Ligonier); Edgartown (Mass.) Yacht; Ocean Reef (Key Largo, Fla.); Naples Sailing, Naples Yacht, Port Royal Beach, Royal Poinciana Golf (Naples, Fla.); Jockey (Miami, Fla.). Home: Ligonier, Pa. Died Mar. 23, 1977; buried Homestead Cemetery, Pitts.

BENET, LAURA, author; b. Ft. Hamilton, N.Y. Harbor; d. James Walker and Frances (Nell) Rose Benet; grad. Emma Willard Sch., Troy, N.Y.; A.B., Vassar Coll., 1907 Litt.D. (hon.), Moravian Coll., Bethlehem, Pa. Settlement worker, Spring St. Settlement, N.Y.C., 1915-17; placement worker Children's Aid Soc., N.Y.C., 1917; sanitary insp. U.S. Red Cross, Augusta, Ga., 1917-19; worker St. Bartholomews House, 1924-25; sec., asst. editor book pages N.Y. Evening Post, 1927-28, N.Y. Evening Sun, 1928-29; book review editor's asst. and book review substitute, N.Y. Times, summer 1930; free lance writer, from 1930. Received medal as honor poet, Nat. Poetry Center, 1936; poems recorded at Library of Congress, 1958. Democrat. Episcopalian. Author: Fairy Bread (poems), 1921; Noah's Dove (poems) 1929; Goods and Chattels (fiction), 1930; Basket for a Fair (poems), 1934; The Boy Shelley (biography), 1937; The Hidden Valley (fiction), 1938; Enchanting Jenny Lind (biography), 1939; Roxana Rampant (fiction), 1940; Young Edgar Allan Poe (biography), 1941; Come Slowly, Eden: A Novel about Emily Dickinson, 1942; Caleb's Luck (for children), 1942; Washington Irving, Explorer of American Legend, 1944; Is Morning Sure? (poems), 1947; Thackeray of the Great Heart and the Humorous Pen (biography), 1947; Barnum's First Circus and Other Stories (for children), 1949; Famous American Poets, 1950; Coleridge, Poet of Wild Enchantment, 1952; Stanley, Invincible Explorer (biography), 1955; Famous American Humorists, 1959; In Love With Time (book of poems), 1959; Horseshoe Nails, 1965; Famous Poets for Young People, 1964; Famous English and American Essayists, 1966; Famous Storytellers, 1968; Famous New England Poets, 1970; Introductions to Classics; articles, verse to periodicals. Mem. Poetry Soc. Am., Women Poets, Craftsmen, P.E.N. Club, Pen and Brush Club (hon.). Home: New York, N.Y. Died Feb. 1979.

BENETATOS, DEMETRIOS (BE-NE-TÄ'TOS), diplomat of Greece; b. Galatz, Rumania, Sept. 9, 1884; s. Constantine and Catherine (Diamanti) B.; LL.D., Nat. U. of Athens, Greece, 1907, Sch. of Political Sciences, Paris, France, 1908-09; m. Irene E. Lykiardopouls, Jan. 22, 1928. Attaché at the State Dept. of Greece, 1910; vice-consul at Janina, 1911, Mersina (Turkey), 1912; at the State Dept., 1912-13; vice-consul at Brousse, 1914-17; dir. Gen. Consulate at Barcelona, 1917-18; sec. at the Greek Legation and consul at Paris, 1918-20, at Rhodes, 1921; consul-gen. Jerusalem, 1921-25; dir. State Dept., 1925-29; consul-gen. Jerusalem, 1929-35, Genoa (Italy), 1935, Chicago, Ill., 1937-43; resident minister, June 20, 1943, retired from active service, Aug. 1943. Decorated Orders Daniel of Montenegro, Star of Abyssina, Crown of Rumania, Saviour and Phenix of Greece, Holy Cross of the Greek Orthodox Patriareate of Jerusalem. Club: Rotary of Chicago. Home: Chicago, Ill. *

BENGEL, LAWRENCE WOODS, engring. firm exec., army officer; b. Denison, Tex., Oct. 20, 1920; s. Charles W. and Ola (Woods) B.; student Rutgers U., 1952-53, U. Wash., 1954-56; B.S. in Mil. Sci., U. Md., 1957-59; grad. Army Signal Sch., 1939, Army Command Mgmt. Sch., 1955, Army Command and Gen. Staff Coll., 1956, Army War Coll., 1960; m. Johnnie King, Mar. 17, 1946; children—John Ross, Charles Wade. Commd. 2d lt.

U.S. Army, 1941, advanced through grades to col., 1961; comdr. 74th Signal Co., 1942-45; adviser Greek Armed Forces during guerrilla warfare, 1948-50; comdr. Signal Long Lines Battalion, Japan, 1957-59; Army project officer constrn. major army communications facilities, 1950-52; mem. Office Joint Chiefs Staff, 1960-62; chief staff Army Strategic Communications Command, 1964-65; exec. mem. tech. staff Computer Scis. Corp., Falls Church, Va., 1965-72; exec. v.p. Halifax Engring. Inc., Alexandria, Va., 1972-81. Decorated Legion of Merit, Purple Heart, Army Commendation medal with oak leaf cluster; Mil. Cross (Greece). Sr. mem. I. Armed Forces Communications and Electronics Assn., Assn. U.S. Army. Elk. Home: Alexandria, Va. Died Jan. 15, 1981; buried Arlington Nat. Cemetery.

BENGTZ, TURE, artist; b. Aland, Finland, Oct. 23, 1907; s. Carl Algot and Edit Zaida (Erikson) B.; came to U.S., 1927, naturalized, 1932; diploma Sch. Museum Fine Arts, Boston, 1934, Slade Sch., London, 1934, Fontainebleau Sch., Paris, 1934; m. Lillian E. Erickson, Sept. 20, 1937; 1 dau., Lanci (Mrs. Page C. Valentine). Mem. faculty Sch. Mus. Fine Arts, Boston, 1934-69, head drawing and graphics arts dept. and human anatomy, 1941-69; asst. dir., head drawing and graphic arts dept. Berkshire Mus. Summer Sch., Pittsfield, Mass., 1947-50; propr. own summer sch. Bengtz Sch. Art, Lenox, Mass., 1951-57; dir. Art Complex, Inc., Duxbury, Mass., 1971-73; tech. illustrator radar equipment, World War II; condr. TV program Bengtz on Drawing, 1957-60; one-man exhbns. include Guild Boston Artists, 1935, Seligman Gallery, N.Y.C., 1944, White House, Braintree, Mass., 1968, Boston City Club, 1935, Tyringham (Mass.) Galleries, Abbott Acad., Andover, Mass., 1950, Swedish Hist. Soc., Phila., 1936, Shore Galleries, Boston, 1944, Duxbury Free Library, 1971, Alands Konstvänners Församling, Mariehamn, Finland, 1935; also numerous group and travelling exhbns.; rep. permanent collection Boston Mus. Fine Arts, Addison Gallery, Andover, Berkshire Mus., Seattle Art Mus., Cin. Art Mus., DeCordova Art Mus., Lincoln, Mass., Library Congress, Wiggin collection Boston Pub. Library, Fogg Mus., Cambridge, Mass., Alands Konstvänners Församling, Tel Aviv Mus., New Eng. Conservatory Music, Boston, Fitchburg (Mass.) Art Mus., also pvt. collections, designer stained glass window St. Olaf's Ch., Mariehamn, Finland 1968. Paige travelling scholar, 1933; Tiffany Found. fellow, 1940, 41; recipient 1st prize New Eng. competition Stewart Art Gallery, Boston, 1946; Palmer meml. award Nat. Acad. Design, 1944; award Soc. Am. Etchers and Engravers, 1946; Louis A. Black award Boston Printmakers, 1954, lithograph prize, 1965, Wiggin prize, 1966, Boston Mus. prize, 1965, Printmakers prize, 1969, Gendrot prize, 1969. Illustrator: White Squaw (Wheeler), 1958. Home: Duxbury, Mass. Died Nov. 10, 1973.

BENJAMIN, EDWARD B., minerals co. exec.; b. New Orleans, Nov. 18, 1897; s. Emanuel Victor and Rachel (Goldsmith) B.; A.B. magna cum laude, Harvard, 1918; L.H.D., U. Rochester, 1960; m. Blanche Sternberger, Oct. 19, 1921; children—Edward Bernard Jr., William Mente Sternberger, Jonathan Sternberger. Began in employ of family interests, 1919; past pres. E.V. Benjamin Co., Inc., Myles Salt Co., Starmount Co., Bay Chem. Co., New Orleans, Friendly Center, Inc., Greensboro, N.C.; pres. Benjamin Minerals, Inc., 1947-80. Dir. Grayson Found., donor Benjamin Awards for Restful Music. Trustee, founder (with wife) Sternberger Children's Hosp. (later Guilford Co. Welfare Center), Greensboro; mem. vis. com. dept. biology Harvard, 1953-59. Mem. export adv. com. U.S. Dept. Commerce, 1946. Mem. orgn. com. New Orleans Community Chest, New Orleans Welfare Com., 1930-32; dir. New Orleans Opera House Assn.; chmn. organizing com., 1st pres. Cultural Attractions Fund Greater New Orleans, 1960-61; pres. Community Concert Assn. New Orleans, 1960-68; mem. Nat. Bd. Morality in Media; mem. adv. com. Duke Med. Cancer Center, 1974-80. Bd. dirs. Human Betterment League N.C., U.S. Coast Guard Found., 1969-71; trustee Southwestern Legal Found. Served with Harvard R.O.T.C., 1917, Camp Lee (Va.), 1918. Clubs: Round Table, Southern Yacht, New Orleans Country (New Orleans); Merchants and Manufacturers, Greensboro Country (Greensboro); Turf and field (N.Y.C.); Royal Thames Yacht. Author: The Larger Liberalism, 1918; The Restful in Music, 1970. Contbr. articles on religion, sociology, econs., music, yachting, horse breeding to mags. Home: New Orleans, La. Died Mar. 16, 1980.

BENJAMIN, RICHARD NEWTON, mgmt. cons.; b. Phila., May 5, 1904; s. Frank Tarbell and Ida (Malone) B.; B.S. cum laude, Harvard, 1925, M.B.A., 1927; m. Linda Tabb, June 26, 1936; children—Richard Dyke, John Tabb, Thomas Bruce, Elizabeth Payne. With Stone & Webster, Inc., 1927-37, pres., 1959-71, chmn. exec. com., 1971-72, dir., 1959-75; sec. Engrs. Pub. Service Co., 1937-47; v.p. Stone & Webster Service Corp., N.Y.C., 1948-53, pres., dir., 1953-58, chmn., 1959-61; dir. Upper Peninsula Generating Co., 1953-58, dir. subsidiaries; chmn. bd., dir. Jamaica Pub. Service Co. (W.I.), 1952-65, Pub. Utilities Reports, Inc., Reddy Kilowatt, Inc., 1964-74; cons., dir. W.R. Grace & Co., N.Y.C., 1972-75; dir. Riley Co., Chgo. Bd. dirs. Inst. Gas Tech., Chgo., 1968-71. Mem. Nat. Indsl. Conf. Bd. (sr.), Am. Gas Assn. (dir. 1967-72), N.Y. Soc. Security Analysts, Soc. Gas Lighting. Clubs: Links, Recess, Harvard; Echo Lake Country. Home: Westfield, N.J. Died June 3, 1975; interred Fairview Cemetery, Westfield.

BENJAMIN, ROBERT S., lawyer; b. N.Y.C., May 14, 1909; student CCNY, 1924-28; J.D. cum laude, Fordham U., 1928-31; L.H.D. (hon.), Brandeis U., 1971; m. Jean Kortright, 1949; children—Margret Lisa Taylor, Jonathan Adam. Office boy N.Y. Film Bd. Trade, 1924; clk. law offices Phillips & Nizer, 1925, partner, 1935, gen. partner, 1938; admitted to N.Y. bar, 1931; v.p. Pathe Film Corp., 1937-41; pres. J. Arthur Rank Orgn., Inc., 1945-67, also dir.; v.p., gen. counsel Pathe Industries, Inc., Eagle-Lion Films, Inc.; v.p., gen. counsel for United World Pictures, Inc., 1945; sr. partner Phillips, Nizer, Benjamin, Krim & Ballon; chmn. United Artists Corp. 1952-69, co-chmn., 1969-74, chmn. finance com., 1974-79; dir. Transamerica Corp. Hon. trustee Carnegie Hall Corp., Am.-Israel Cultural Found.; chmn. Nat. Citizens Commn. for Internat. Cooperation Yr., 1965; vis. com. for arts Mass. Inst. Tech., 1974-79; bd. dirs. Urban League Greater N.Y.; trustee Eleanor Roosevelt Meml. Found., 1963, exec. vice chmn., 1963-66, chmn. exec. com., 1966-72, chmn. bd. Eleanor Roosevelt Inst., 1972-79. Mem. exec. com. Citizens' Com. Internat. Devel.; nat. chmn. U.S. Com. for UN, 1961-64; bd. dirs. UN Assn. U.S.A., 1961-64, chmn. nat. bd., 1963-64, pres., 1965-69, chmn. bd. govs., 1969-73, co-chmn., dir., 1973-74, chmn., 1974-75, chmn. bd. govs., 1975-79; sr. adviser U.S. delegation 21st Gen. Assembly UN, del., ambassador 22d Gen. Assembly. Elected to Electoral Coll. for Kennedy, 1960; finance chmn. adv. council Nat. Dem. Com. Vice chmn. bd. trustees Brandeis U., 1969-77, chmn., 1977-79; bd. dirs. Corp. for Pub. Broadcasting, 1968-79, vice chmn., 1973-74, chmn., 1974-77, chmn. emeritus, 1977-79; chmn. UN Devel. Corp., 1977-79. Served as a maj., Signal Corps, AUS, 1942-45. Decorated Legion of Merit; recipient Townsend Harris medal, Peace medal for 1971, Sec.-gen. UN; award for outstanding leadership in public broadcasting Harris Found., 1975. Mem. Assn. Bar City N.Y. Jewish religion (Conservative). Home: Kings Point, N.Y. Died Oct. 22, 1979.

BENNETT, BERTRAM WHITCOMB, steel co. exec.; b. Des Plaines, Ill., Jan. 10, 1899; s. Harry Thomas and Elda Pauline (Whitcomb) B.; A.B., Knox Coll., 1920; m. Mary Elizabeth Wallace, June 28, 1924 (dec. Aug. 4, 1959); 1 son, Robert W.; m. 2d, Elizabeth Ann Huser, May 20, 1961. With Benjamin Electric Co., Des Plaines, Ill., 1920-22; with Caspers Tin Plate Co., Chgo., 1922—, pres., 1938-57, chairman, 1957—, dir.; director Lafayette Steel & Aluminum Company. Trustee Knox Coll. Member National Interfraternity Council (v.p.), Beta Theta Pi (pres. 1954-57). Republican. Clubs: Chicago Athletic Assn., Lake Shore (Chgo.); Oak Park (Ill.) Country. Home: River Forest, Ill.

BENNETT, CARROL MORTIMER, financial and mgmt. cons.; b. Clarksburg, W.Va., Dec. 8, 1910; s. Clyde M. and Martha (Martin) B.; student U. Tex.; m. Elizabeth A. O'Beirne, May 29, 1937; children—Carrol Mortimer, Randolph, Barbara A., Betty J. Engr. Magnolia Petroleum Co., 1931-34; v.p., dir. Dallas, Rupe & Son, investment bankers, Dallas, 1935-55; pres., dir. Bennet, Osborn & Hall, financial, mgmt. cons., Dallas, 1955-60; v.p., dir. Middletown, Inc., Dallas, from 1945; dir. Small Business Investment Co. of S.W.; chmn. bd. Tex. Pacific Oil Co., Inc., 1956-76; dir. Distillers Corp., Gaz Marina; mgmt. cons., 1975-78; regional adminstr. Emergency Petroleum Gas Adminstrn. Mem. Nat. Petroleum Council, Dallas C. of C. (petroleum affairs com.). Presbyn. (elder). Home: Dallas, Tex. Died June 11, 1978; buried Hillcrest Cemetery, Dallas.

BENNETT, HIRAM ROCKWELL, clergyman; b. Troy, Pa., Mar. 8, 1886; s. Samuel Currier and Metta (Rockwell) B.; studnet Coll. City of N.Y., 1905-06; B.D., Gen. Theol. Sem., N.Y. City, 1913; D.D., Phila. Divinity Sch., 1940; m. Louise Arritta Youngs, September 11, 1909; one son, Hiram Rockwell. Ordained as a deacon P.E. Church, 1913, priest, 1914; rector Grace Ch. (Greenville), Jersy City, N.J., 1915-19, Trinity Ch., Asbury Park, N.J., 1919-23, Christ Ch., Williamsport, Pa., 1923-35; dean Cathedral Church of St. John, Wilmington, Del., 1935-44; rector Grace Church, Everett, Mass., 1944-51; rector Christ Ch., Towanda, 1951-56, emeritus, 1956—. Served as civilian chaplain, Camp Dix, 1918. Dir. J. V. Brown Library (Williamsport, Pa.), Lycoming County Tuberculosis Soc. President, New England branch The Clerical Union. Mem. Mediaeval Acad. America, Phi Gamma Delta. Republican. Episcopalian (hon. canon St. Stephen's Cathedral, Harrisburg, Pa., 1931-35). Mason. Author and editor: St. Paul, The Church, The Apocrypha, The Old Testament (Episcopal Lesson Series). Contbr. to mags. Home: Troy, Pa. *

BENNETT, JAMES VAN BENSCHOTEN, dir. U.S. Bureau of Prisons; b. Silver Creek, Chautauqua County, N.Y., Aug. 28, 1894; s. Rev. Edmund C. and Mary Frances (Berry) Bennett; A.B., Brown University, 1918, Doctor of Laws (honorary), 1950; LL.B., George Washington Univ., 1926; Doctor of Humanities (hon.), Springfield Coll., 1955; m. Marie Ettl, May 16, 1919 (dec. 1967); children—Edmund John, Ann Frances, Brenda; m. 2d, Olympia Stone, 1971. Apptd. asst. investigator U.S. Bur. of Efficiency, 1919, advancing to chief investigator, studied and reported on methods of various govt. agencies, 1920-23; head staff div. and sec. Personnel Classification Bd., 1923-26; investigated employment policies of Federal Prisons, 1926-28; asst. dir. Field Survey Div. Personnel Classification, 1928-29; mem. Roberts Commn. to study Panamanian Govt., 1929; cooperated with Congressional Com. investigating Federal Prisons and drafted report, 1929; apptd. asst. dir. Bur. of Prisons, 1930, commr. Federal Prison Industries, 1933; dir. U.S. Bureau of Prisons 1937-64; on 6 months leave of absence to organize civil prisons in Germany for the Am. Mil. Govt., 1945, chmn. Civilian Com. to Study Naval Confinement Procedures. Del. Internat. Prison, Congresses, Berlin, 1935, chmn. U.S. del. The Hague, 1950; sec. Nat. Parole Conf., 1939; pres. Washington Council of Social Agencies, 1941. Recipient Army Exceptional Civilian Service medal, Navy Distinguished Public Service award, Selective Service medal. Member American Law Institute, American (vice chmn. of section on criminal law), Bar Assn., Am. Prison Assn. (pres. 1939), Am. Assn. Social Workers, Soc. for Public Adminstrn., Kappa Sigma. Episcopalian. Club: Cosmos. Author: I Chose Prison, 1971; contbr. articles on prisons, criminal law, parole and probation to profl. jours. Home: Bethesda, Md. Died Nov. 1978.

BENNETT, JOHN CHARLES, army officer; banker; b. Washington, Dec. 6, 1923; s. Ivan Loveridge and Ruby (Jenrette) B.; B.S., U.S. Mil. Acad., 1945; M.A., Columbia U., 1951; M.A., George Washington U., 1964; student Emory U., 1940-41; m. Jean Hazelton MacKenzie, Sept. 8, 1945; children—Jill Anne, John Charles Jr., Judith MacKenzie, Robert MacKenzie. Commd. 2d lt. U.S. Army, 1945, advanced through grades to maj. gen., 1970; asst. prof. English, U.S. Mil. Acad., 1949-52, comdr. 4th Mechanized Div., also Ft. Carson, Colo., 1970-72, ret., 1972; dep. asst. to Gen. Alexander Haig, chief of staff to Pres. Nixon, 1973-74; v.p. El Paso Alaska Co., 1974-77; v.p. Alaska Pacific Bank, Anchorage, 1977-80. Decorated Legion of Merit with 2 oak leaf clusters, Bronze Star, Air medal with nine oak leaf clusters, D.S.M. Mem. Order Daedalians, Sigma Chi. Home: Anchorage, Alaska. Died May 4, 1980.

BENNETT, NEWCOMB BENJAMIN, JR., civil engr.; b. Sheridan, Wyo., Oct. 14, 1910; s. Newcomb Benjamin and Mabel Lillian (Haywood) B.; student Kemper Mil. Sch., 1928-29; B.S., U. Neb., 1933; m. Thelma Lee Sanders, Oct. 20, 1934; children—Newcomb Benjamin III, Becky Lou. Surveyor U.S. Bur. Reclamation, 1933-35, engr., 1942-53, chief div. project devel., 1953-59; asst. commr. for power and gen. engring., 1959-70; resident engr. Dan J. McQuaid Engring. Service, 1935-39; asst. state engr. Wyo., 1939-42; engr.-sec. Wyo. Water Conservation Bd., 1939-42; resources cons. engr., 1970-79; dir. Papago Tribal Utility Authority, 1970-79, chmn. bd., 1975-79. Former chmn. U.S. sect. Internat. Souris-Red River Engring. Bd., Internat. Waterton-Belly Engring. Bd., chmn. U.S. sect. Internat. Pembina River Engring. Bd.; former mem. adv. bd. office critical tables Nat. Acad. Scis., Nat. Research Council; former mem. exec. com. Fed. Constrn. Council; former mem. Interior Com. on Research and Devel. Recipient Superior Performance award U.S. Dept. Interior, 1958, Distinguished Service award, 1968. Fellow ASCE; mem. Sigma Alpha Epsilon. Mason. Home: Sun City, Ariz. Died Mar. 12, 1979; buried Sun City.

BENNETT, REGINALD VICTOR, clergyman; b. Ceralvo, Ky., Mar. 9, 1885; s. Sam Peyton and Naoma (Shultz) B.; A.B., Vanderbilt U., 1912; student Southern Bapt. Sem., Louisville, Ky., 1916-18, U. of Ky., summers 1931, 32; D.D., Ky. Wesleyan Coll., 1930; M.A. in Mathematics, U. of Ky., 1934; D.D., Washington and Lee U., 1934; m. Augusta Carpenter, June 20, 1912; children—Eleanor Louise, Jessica Marie, Joel Samuel, John Zebulun, Reginald Victor. Ordained to M.E. ministry, 1912; pastor Corydon, Ky., 1912-16, Beechmont Ch., Louisville, Ky., 1916-18; pres. Lindsey Wilson Coll., Columbia, Ky., 1918-32, Ky. Wesleyan Coll., 1932-37; pastor First M.E. Ch.; Campbellsville, Ky., 1937-39, First Methodist Ch., Henderson, Ky., 1939-41; dist. supt. Louisville Dist., Louisville Conf. Methodist Ch., 1941-46; pastor State St. Meth. Ch., Bowling Green, since 1946. Mem. Phi Beta Kappa, Pi Mu Epsilon. Mason. Club: Kiwanis. Home: Bowling Green, Ky. *

BENNETT, ROBERT HENRY, foods co. exec.; b. Passaic, N.J., Mar. 17, 1902; s. Frank D. and Agnes (Miller) B.; Litt.B., Rutgers U., 1923; student advanced mgmt. program, Harvard, 1950; m. Margaret Travell, Jan. 17, 1925. Sales promotion Crowell Pub. Co., 1923-24; copy, prodn. Ajax Advt., N.Y.C., 1924-26; advt. mgr. Devoe & Reynolds, N.Y.C., 1926-27; with Gen. Foods Corp., White Plains, N.Y., 1927-80, beginning as export advt. mgr., successively mdse. mgr., asst. gen. mgr. Maxwell House div., gen. mgr. Jello-O div., 1927-55, v.p., 1955-80. Home: Ridgewood, N.J. Died Jan. 6, 1980.

BENNETT, ROBERT WILLIAM, metall. engr.; b. Denver, Feb. 26, 1917; s. William J. and Augusta J. (Robson) B.; Metall. Engr., Colo. Sch. Mines, 1940; m. Geraldine Carrell, July 4, 1941; children—Robert J., Jeri Janene, Kathleen J. Welding metallurgist Caterpillar Tractor Co., 1940-42; welding research engr. Battelle Meml. Inst., Columbus, O., 1942-49, sr. tech. adviser, 1965-76; metallurgist, chief quality control engr. Alco Products, Inc., Dunkirk, N.Y., 1949-54, chief metallurgist charge welding, metall. and chem. engring., Schenectady, 1955-62, dir. research and devel. engring., 1962-63; asst. to gen. mgr., project mgr. atomic fuel div. Westinghouse Electric Corp., 1963-65. Mem. citizens adv. com. Niskayuna Pub. Schs. Registered profl. engr., Ohio. Mem. Am. Soc. Metals, Am. Soc. Testing Materials (exec. council central N.Y. dist.), Canadian Welding Bur., Am. Ordnance Assn., Pipe Fabrication Inst., Am. Welding Soc., Am. Soc. M.E. (code com. sect. IX on welding), Sigma Xi. Methodist. Odd Fellow, Mason. Author tech. papers, lectr. in field. Home: Columbus, Ohio. Died Feb. 9, 1976.

BENNETT, VICTOR A(LEXANDER), advt. cons.; b. Eng., Nov. 11, 1906; s. George Victor and Marion (Duncan) B.; student English pvt. schs.; m. Maxine Georgetta Yorty, Sept. 17, 1931 (dec. Oct. 1959); children—Duncan Yorty, Ian Yorty; m. 2d, Margaret Berryman Blanchard, November 25, 1961. American representative Great Western Ry. of Eng., 1930-35; with N.Y. Sun, 1935-37, 39-41, African Asso. Newspapers, 1937-39, Bamberger Broadcasting Co., 1941-43, Bremer Broadcasting Co., 1943-48; pres. Victor A. Bennett Co., Inc., N.Y.C., 1948-62; chmn., chief exec. officer Pritchard Wood, Inc., N.Y.C., 1962-65; pres. Bennett Assos., Inc.; partner Bennett, Newbery & Cowan, from 1966. Mem. Radio and TV Execs. Soc., St. George's Soc., Brit.-Am. C. of C. Presbyn. Clubs: Canadian, British Luncheon (N.Y.C.) American (London). Home: New York, N.Y. Died Mar. 27, 1976.

BENNETT, WILLIAM ANDREW CECIL, premier B.C.; b. Albert Co., N.B., Can., Sept. 6, 1900; s. A. H. and Mary (Burns) B.; student pub. schs., N.B., also Alberta; m. Annie Elizabeth May Richards, July 11, 1927; children—Anita (Mrs. Geoffrey H. Tozer), Russell J., William R. Pres. Bennett's Stores, Ltd., Kelowna, Westbank, Penticton, Vernon, Kamloops, B.C., from 1941; mem. B.C. Provincial House, 1941-52; elected premier, pres. exec. council Social Credit Govt., B.C., 1952, 53, 56, minister finance, 1954. Mem. Okangan Bd. Trades (past pres.). Mem. United Ch. Can. Mason (Shriner). Club: Union of Victoria. Home: Victoria, B.C., Canada. Died Feb. 26, 1979.

BENOIT, EMILE, educator, economist, author; b. N.Y.C., July 14, 1909; s. Isadore and Rosina (Freeman) Benoit-Smullyan; B.A., Harvard, 1932, M.A., 1933, Ph.D., 1938; m. Mary Louise Mincher, Mar. 13, 1936; 1 son, Jon; m. 2d, Etta Leist Fleming, Feb. 11, 1959. Mem. faculty Harvard, 1934-36, U. Ill., 1938-39, Wells Coll., 1939-42; sr. economist Dept. Labor, 1943-47; attache Am. embassy, London, 1948-51, Vienna, 1951-53; economist McGraw Hill Pub. Co., 1954-56; prof. internat. bus. Grad. Sch. Bus. and Sch. Internat. Affairs, Columbia, N.Y.C., 1956-74, prof. emeritus, sr. research asso., 1974-78. Cons., Def. Dept., UN, Dept. State, Asian Devel. Bank, Pfizer Internat. Corp.; dir. research program on econs. arms control Ford Found., Carnegie Corp., and U.S. Arms Control and Disarmament Agy.; dir. research project Effects of Nat. Def. on Devel. Econs., 1968-71. Vice chmn. Ams. for Democratic Action, 1966-69. Bd. dirs. N.Y. Friends Group, Soc. Family of Man, 1968-69; mem. adv. bd. Negative Population Growth, 1973-78. Mem. Am. Econs. Assn., Soc. Internat. Devel., A.A.A.S. Club: Harvard of N.Y. Author: Europe at Sixes and Sevens, 1961; Disarmament and the Economy, 1963; Defense and Economic Growth in Developing Countries, 1973. Editorial bd. Columbia Jour. World Bus., 1964-72, The Internat. Exec., 1962-72, Disarmament and Arms Control, 1963-78, Jour. of Arms Control, 1963-64, Jour. Conflict Resolution, 1966-78, Am. Rev. of East West Trade, 1968-72, Quar. Jour. Econs., 1975-78; editor, contbr. Disarmament and World Economic Interdependence, 1966. Contbr. chpts. to books, articles to profl. jours. Home: New York, N.Y. Died May 4, 1978.

BENSINGER, BENJAMIN EDWARD, corp. exec.; b. Chgo., Dec. 6, 1905; s. Benjamin E. and Rose (Frank) B.; Ph.B., Yale; m. Linda Galston, Nov. 28, 1929; children—B. Edward III, Roger G., Peter B. Asst. to sales mgr. Brunswick Corp. (formerly Brunswick-Balke-Collender Co.), Chgo., 1928-32, dir., 1930—, asst. sec., treas. 1932-36, gen. mgr., 1936, exec. v.p., 1937-50, pres., 1950-54, chief exec. officer, from 1954, chmn. bd., 1963-71, chmn. exec. com. until 1976, also dir.; dir. Am. Nat. Bank & Trust Co., Chgo., Inland Life Ins. Co. Mem. adv. council U. Chgo. Grad. Sch. Bus.; mem. U. Ill. Citizens Com. Bd. dirs. Michael Reese Hosp., Project Hope, Chgo. Lyric Opera, Chgo. council Boy Scouts Am.; trustee Jewish Fedn. Met. Chgo., Ill. C. of C., Chgo. Assn. of Commerce and Industry, NCCJ, U. Chgo., Michael Reese Hosp. and Med. Center, George Washington Corp., Northwestern U., asso. U. Ill.; bd. dirs., v.p. Citizens' Commn. Internat. Atlantic Salmon Found. Recipient Humanitarian award Chgo. chpt. B'nai B'rith. Mem. Art Inst. Chgo. (life), Soc. Contemporary Art, Lincoln Park Zool. Soc. (founder, life), Northwestern U. Assos., Restigouche Repàrian Assn. (chmn.). Clubs: Standard, Lake Shore Country, Yale (dir.), Commercial, Tavern (Chgo.); Tryall Ltd. (Jamaica) Home: Chicago, Ill. Died Jan. 19, 1979.

BENSON, CARL FREDERICK, ret. educator; b. Camden, Ark., Feb. 19, 1916; s. Louis Victor and Elizabeth (Walther) B.; student So. Ark. U., 1933-35; B.A., U. Tex., 1937, M.A., 1938; Ph.D., U. Ill., 1948; m. Martha Ellen Blanks, May 29, 1941; children—Stephen Louis, Katherine Ellen. Asst. prof. English, U. Ark., Monticello, 1939-41; mem. faculty U. Ill., 1941-43, 46-47; asst. prof. Auburn (Ala.) U., 1947-52, asso. prof., 1952-62, prof., 1962-74, Hargis prof., 1964-74; ret., 1974; vis. prof. N.Y. U., summer 1964. Ford faculty fellow Harvard and Mass. Inst. Tech., 1955-56; Fulbright lectr. Erlangen (Germany) U., 1960-61. Served with AUS, 1943-46; ETO. Mem. Modern Lang. Assn., South Atlantic Modern Lang. Assn. Co-author: The Idea of Tragedy, 1966, Essays for Exposition, 1977. Contbr. articles to profl. jours. Home: Auburn, Ala. Died Apr. 15, 1979.

BENSON, WILLIAM ARCHIBALD, printing co. exec.; b. Nashville, Dec. 7, 1886; s. John Thomas and Eva (Green) B.; student Vanderbilt U., 1907; m. Florence Riddle, Apr. 15, 1916; children—William Archibald, Mary (Mrs. Albert Duling, Jr.). Asst. supt. Tenn. Packing Co., 1906-07; salesman Commins-Bennett, 1907-08; partner Benson Printing Co., Nashville, now chmn. bd.; now retired; v.p., dir. Army & Navy Pub. Co., Baton Rouge, 1941-47. Mrm. Nashville Printer's Club (pres. 1914), Nashville C. of C., Sigma Chi. Clubs: Hermitage, Uptown Social, Belle Meade Country (Nashville). Home: Nashville TN. *

BENSON, WILLIAM CLARENCE, polit. scientist, author, clergyman; b. Mt. Horeb, Wis., May 18, 1884; s. Andrew and Kari (Lie) B.; A.B., St. Olaf Coll., 1906; A.M., U. of Minn., 1913; candidate of theology, Luthern Sem., St. Paul, 1910-13; student U. of Chicago, 1919-21; m. Helen Frame Stevens, Mar. 19, 1913; children—Esther, Claude, Barbara (Mrs. Gordon Taft). Prof. of history and polit. sci. St. Olaf Coll., 1913-41, prof. polit. sci. since 1941. Served as 1st lt., inf., 1918-19; maj., Chaplain Corps. U.S. Army, 1941-46. Mem. bd. edn., Northfield, Minn., 1925-30, mem. city council, 1935-41. Mem. Am. Hist. Assn., Norwegian Am. Hist. Soc., Am. Polit. Sci. Assn. Mem. Evangelical Lutheran Ch. Author: High on Manitow: A History of St. Olaf College, 1949. Home: Northfield, Minn. *

BENT, MICHAEL JAMES, bacteriologist; born San Andres, Colombia, S.A., Aug. 18, 1885; s. Amiel James and Mekila S. (Corpus) B.; ed. pvt. sch. in San Andres; normal course for tchrs., New Collegiate Sch., Kingston, Jamaica, 1907; Walden, Nashville, 1917; profl. training, Meharry Med. Coll., Nashville, 1921; Nat. Research Council fellow in bacteriology and hygiene, Columbia, 1922-24. Teacher in pub. schs., Colombia, 1911-14; now dean and prof. bacteriology Meharry Med. Coll. Diplomate Am. Bd. Preventive Medicine. Fellow Am. Pub. Health Assn.; mem. Vol. State Med. Soc., Nat. Med. Assn. U. Profs., Sigma Xi, Alpha Phi Alpha, Agora Assembly. Author numerous articles in profl. jours. since 1923. *

BENT, WILLIAM WOODWORTH, lawyer; b. Norwich, Conn., 1883; s. Martin F. and Harriet Peckham (Woodworth) B.; LL.D., Yale, 1905; m. Corrine Ethel Secor, Jan. 1, 1909; children—Laura B. Mackenzie, David W., Mary B. Benedict, Ethel B. Walsh. Admitted to Conn. bar, 1905; practiced in Bridgeport, Conn., 1905-29, 1941—; mem. Miller, Bent & Smith, 1941—; judge Probate Ct., 1929-41. Mem. Conn. Ho. of Reps., 1911; pres. Conn. Probate Assembly, 1937-39. Corporator Mechanics & Farmers Bank, 1943—, trustee, 1949—; mem. adv. com. North End Bridgeport City Trust Co., 1949—. Mem. Bridgeport C. of C. (v.p. 1942), State Bar Assn. Conn., Am., Fairfield County (v.p. 1942), Bridgeport (pres. 1940-41) bar assns. Home: Bridgeport.

BENTON, CHARLES, JR., electronic machines mfg. co. exec.; b. Verona, N.J., July 9, 1913; s. Charles and Amy (Vreeland) B.; A.B., Dartmouth, 1935; student Cades C.P.A. Sch.; exec. seminar Mass. Inst. Tech.; m. Frances Laura Sparks, Nov. 21, 1945; children—Charles III, Martha Ellen, Barbara. With Merrill Lynch, Pierce, Fenner & Beane, 1936-37; balance sheet auditor Am. Gas & Electric Corp., 1937-39; with IBM Corp., 1939-68, beginning as br. mgr., successively dist. mgr., Eastern regional mgr., asst. to v.p. charge sales, mgr. marketing programs, gen. mgr. mil. products div., 1939-59, pres. fed. systems div., 1959-62, dir. marketing and service fed. systems div., 1963-65, dist. mgr. data processing div., 1966-68; pres., chief exec. officer, exec. com. Computer Usage Corp., 1968-69; chmn. bd., pres. Gen. Information Systems Corp., 1970-72; pres. Md. Cablevision, Inc., 1970-76; owner Coastal Devel. Co., Vero Beach, Fla., 1973-76. Clubs: Congressional Country; John's Island (Fla.). Home: Vero Beach, Fla. Died Nov. 29, 1976.

BENTON, CORNING, school official; b. Newton, Mass., June 17, 1885; s. Edward Raymond and Annie Cline (Corning) B.; A.B., Harvard, 1903-07, A.M., 1908, student Harvard grad. sch., 1907-10, Columbia, 1910-11; m. Marion Ireland, June 10, 1933; 1 son, Corning. Instr. history and English, Phillips Exeter Acad., 1911-18, bus. mgr., 1918-22, treas., 1922-51; president and dir. Exeter Cooperative Bank; dir. Rockingham Nat. Bank, Exeter, N.H., Metropolitan Bldg., Inc.; trustee, N.H. State Industrial Sch. Member New Hampshire legislature, 1935-36; mem. vis. com. overseers Harvard Coll., 1955-57. Member Newcomen Soc., N.H. Hist. Society. Club: Harvard (Boston); past pres. Harvard Club of N.H. Founder Business Office Assn. Prep. Schools. Contbr. various reports on sch. management to jours. Home: Exeter, N.H. *

BENTON, EDWARD LAMAR, lawyer; b. Macon, Ga., July 27, 1906; s. Daniel Morrison and Emma Jane (Crumo) B.; LL.B., Mercer U., 1929; m. Mary Wynelle Willums, Dec. 19, 1928; children—Edward Bruce, Mary Lamar (Mrs. James W. Grimsley). Admitted to Ga. bar, 1929, then practiced in Macon; partner firm Jones, Cork, Miller & Benton, 1968-72. Mem. Am. Bar Assn., State Bar Ga., Am. Judicature Soc., Phi Alpha Delta. Methodist. Mason (32 deg., Shriner), Elk, Moose. Home: Macon, Ga. Died Feb. 8, 1974.

BENTON, JOSEPH GEORGE, physician, educator; b. N.Y.C., Jan. 20, 1915; A.B., Bklyn. Coll., 1937; M.Sc., N.Y. U., 1938, Ph.D., 1940, M.D., 1945; children—Nancy J., Elizabeth A. Intern, Bellevue Hosp., 1945-46; fellow clin. pharmacology Cornell U. Med. Sch., 1946-48; fellow rehab. med. N.Y. U. Coll. Medicine, asso. prof., also Inst. Rehab. Medicine, 1948-58; prof., chmn. dept. rehab. medicine SUNY Coll. Medicine, Downstate Med. Center, 1958-78; Distinguished Alumni lectr., 1966, N.Y. U. Coll. Medicine dean Coll. Health Related Professions, 1966-78; physiatrist-in-chief Kings County Hosp. Center, State U. Hosp.; cons. L.I. Jewish Hosp., Bklyn. State Hosp., VA Hosp., Maimonedes Hosp., Bklyn. Cumberland Med. Center, L.I. Coll. Hosp., Meth. Hosp. Recipient Distinguished Service award Am. Congress Rehab. Medicine, 1968. Mem. Am. Bd. Phys. Medicine and Rehab. Home: Brooklyn, N.Y. Died Oct. 21, 1978.

BENTON, RALPH, biologist, naturalist; b. Munich, Germany, Aug. 2, 1884; s. Frank and Harriet M. (Wheeler) B. (parents both citizens of U.S.); B.S., Mont. State Coll., 1906; B.L., U. of Cal., 1907, M.S., 1909; M.A., U. of Southern Cal., 1914; m. at Los Angeles, Cal., Imogen Benton, of Rome, Italy (parents both citizens of U.S.), Aug. 10, 1907. Asst. to U.S. examiner of surveys, Mont., 1901; instr. mil. science and tactics, Mont. State Coll., 1901-3; asst. to entomologist, Mont. Agrl. Expt. Sta., summers 1902, 03, 04; asst. in apiculture, Mont. State Coll., 1904-05; field assistant U.S. Dept. Agr., in Europe, 1905; assistant in entomology, 1905-8, instr., 1908-10, U. of Cal.; spl. insp. apiaries, Tulare Co., Cal., 1910; head of agr. nature-study, Los Angeles State Normal Sch., 1910-12; spl. lecturer on entomology, U. of Southern Cal., 1911, 12; biologist and lecturer on apiculture, Cal. Sch. of Apiculture, summer 1912; asso. prof. applied biology, U. of Southern Cal. and Venice (Cal.) Marine Biol. Sta., 1912-14; dist. insp. in charge Cal.-Ariz.-Nev. dist. U.S. Biol. Survey, 1914-18; 2d lt. inf. U.S.A., and personnel adjt., 1918-19; instr. agrl. edn., U. of Cal., 1919—. Mem. A.A. A.S., Am. Entomol. Soc., Audubon Soc., Am. Ornithologists' Union, Agassiz Assn. (western field sec.), Acad. Science of Southern Cal., Cooper Club, S.R., Mil. Training Camps Assn., American Legion, Phi Sigma Kappa. Progressive-Rep. Presbyn. Author: Practical Beekeeping, 1907; also contbr. on apiarian and other topics.

BENTONELLI, JOSEPH (JOSEPH HORACE BENTON), lyric tenor; b. Kansas City, Sept. 10, 1898; s. Oliver Horace and LaMiza (Seawell) Benton; A.B., U. Okla. 1920, Mus.B., 1921, M.A. in Modern Langs., 1941; studied with Jean de Reszk. Debut in Don Giovanni, Nice, France, Dec. 1924; created world-premieres two different operas Il Vassallo of Smareglia, Trieste, Nov. 1930, and Cecilia of Refice with soprano, Claudia Muzio, at Royal Opera House, Rome, Feb. 1934; with Chgo. Civic Opera Co., 1934; debut with Met. Opera Co., N.Y.C., Jan. 10, 1936, taking place (on 33 hrs. notice) of Richard Crooks because of latter's sudden illness, and subsequently performed many roles including first Am. presentation Puccini's Gianni Schicchi in English; tenor Met. Opera Quartet, 1936-75. Chmn., adviser dept. of voice U. Okla., Norman, 1944-75. Voted by Italian Fascist Soc. of Musicians one of Italy's four most popular tenors during 1934 season; elected Olka. Hall of Fame, 1951. Fellow Am. Inst. Vocal Pedagogy of Nat. Assn. Tchrs. of Singing (Geneva); mem. Internat. Inst. Arts and Letters (asso.), Am. Hist. Soc., Am. Biol. Assn., Am.

Nat. Opera Assn. (dir.), Pi Kappa Alpha, Phi Beta Kappa, Phi Beta Kappa Assos., Phi Mu Alpha, Phi Delta Kappa, Kappa Delta Pi, Kappa Tau Pi (one of founders). Presbyn. (elder). Mason (32 deg.), Lion, Star on 3 major radio hours of NBC, 1934 and guest on 7 other radio hours, NBC and CBS; gives yearly coast-to-coast concert tours and lecture-recitals; made first English translation of Clovis Nogueira de Sa's Brazilian novel No Delirio da Vida (In the Delirium of Living), summer 1942; on commn. from novel's author, first translation into Italian as Nel Delirio della Vita, 1943. Hon. Col. on staff of gov. of Okla. Author: Oklahoma Tenor, 1973. Home: Norman, Okla. Died Apr. 4, 1975.

BENZ, JOHN STEPHEN, economist; b. Milw., Aug. 27, 1910; s. Edward and Catherine Benz; B.Ed., Wis. State Coll.; student U. Wis. With Wis. Income Study, 1936-37, div. tax research Treasury Dept., 1938-41, SSS, 1941, Census Bur., 1947-48; assigned ECA mission to U.K., London, 1949-55, ICA mission to Pakistan, Karachi, 1955-59, to Laos, Vientiane, 1959-61; assigned Internat. Coop. Office, State Dept., 1962-64, dir. U.S. AID mission, Yemem, 1964-66, Kathmandu, 1966-68, assigned Hdqrs. AID, Washington, 1969-74, dir. office operations appraisal staff, until 1974, cons., 1974-80. Served to capt. AUS, 1942-46. Co-author: Sterling Area, An American Analysis. Address: Washington, D.C. Died Oct. 17, 1980.

BERENS, ANTHONY F(RANCIS) (BER'ENZ), priest; b. Green Bay, Wis., Jan. 16, 1884; s. Fred and Anna (Berendsen) B.; attended St. Louis (Mo.) U., 1903-10, 15-19; Teacher High Sch., St. Mary's (Kan.) Coll., 1910-15; prin. High Sch., St. Louis U., 1920-21; teacher St. Louis and Campion Coll., 1922-25; prin. and dean, St. Mary (Kan.) Coll., 1925-27; regent Med. and Dental Schs. and Coll. Nursing; dir. and sec. Marquette U. Sch. of Medicine, Milwaukee, since 1927. Mem. Society of Jesus; ordained priest, Roman Cath. Ch., 1918. President Wis. Anti-Tuberculosis Assn. Home: Milwaukee, Wis. *

BERGANTZ, JOSEPH ARTHUR, educator; b. Knoxville, Tenn., June 8, 1914; s. George Stanley and Maud Montressor (Manley) B.; B.S. in Chem. Engring., U. Tenn., 1934; M.S., U. Ill., 1937; Sc.D. (Arthur D. Little fellow), Mass. Inst. Tech., 1941; m. Joan Osborn, Apr. 24, 1943; children—Barbara (Mrs. John P.R. Moslow), William, George, James. Engring. aide TVA, Wilson Dam, Ala., 1934-36; instr. to asst. prof. Mass. Inst. Tech., 1939-42; project engr., research mgr. FMC Corp., Buffalo, 1946-60; ind. cons., Buffalo, 1960-61; prof., chmn. dept. chem. engring. State U. N.Y., Buffalo, 1961-68, asso. provost, 1969-71, acting provost engring. and applied scis., 1970-71, prof., 1972-76. Vice pres. Creative Edn. Found. Served with AUS, 1942-46. Decorated Army Commendation ribbon. Hon. research asso. Univ. Coll., London, Eng., 1968. Fellow Am. Inst. Chem. Engrs. (chmn. awards com. 1973-76, Profl. Progress award Western N.Y. sect. 1962); mem. Am. Soc. Engring. Edn. (chmn. chem. engring. div. 1965), Am. Chem. Soc., Sigma Xi, Tau Beta Pi, Phi Kappa Phi, Alpha Chi Sigma, Sigma Chi. Clubs: Buffalo, Pundit. Home: Buffalo, N.Y. Died June 5, 1976.

BERGAUST, ERIK, author; b. Baerum, Oslo, Norway, Mar. 23, 1925; B.S. in Chemistry, Frogner Gymnasium, 1943; student Oslo Handelsgymnasium, 1944; m. Jean Cameron Somers, Jan. 13, 1951; children—Christine C., Erik R., Paul R., Jane. Came to U.S., 1949, naturalized, 1956. Aviation editor Aftenposten, Oslo, 1946-48; pub. relations dir. Norwegian Aero Club, 1946-48; mgr. Thoftefly Taxiplane Co., 1948-49; free lance aviation writer, 1949-52; mgr. Norwegian Helicopter Service, 1952; project engr., tech. editor Design Service Co., 1952-54; project officer, editor Douglas Engring. Co., 1954-55; rocket engring. editor Aero Digest, 1955-56; missile sci. editor Am. Aviation, 1956; editor Missiles and Rockets mag., 1956-59, NATO Jour., 1960-62; pub., editor Space Daily, 1959, Ground Support Equipment mag. and Underwater Engring. mag., 1959-60; Washington dir. Missiles and Space mag.; pres. North Springs, Inc., 1962-64; pub. Remington & Ross, Inc., Washington. Mem. information adv. group President's Com. on Scientists and Engrs., 1957. Chmn. Republican Adv. Com. on Space and Aeros., 1962-78. Mem. Norweigan Resistance Movement, 1943, Norwegian Exile Army, 1944-45. Mem. Am. Rocket Soc. (past pres. nat. capital sect.), Aviation and Space Writers Assn., Convertible Aircraft Poineers, Environmental Writers Assn. Am. (dir. 1972-78), Authors Guild, Am. Mil. Engrs., Am. Helicopter Soc., Norsk Astronautisk Forening. Clubs: Nat. Space (founder, pres. 1957-58), Nat. Press (Washington). Mason. Author numerous books including: The Next Fifty Years of Flight, 1954; (with William Beller) Satellite, 1956; Rockets and Missiles, 1957; Rockets Around the World, 1958; (with Seabrook Hull) Rocket to the Moon, 1958; Satellites and Space Probes, 1959; Rockets of the Navy, 1959; Rockets of the Air Force, 1960; Rockets of the Army, 1960; First Men in Space, 1960; Reaching for the Stars (biography of Dr. Wernher von Braun), 1960; Rocket Aircraft, USA, 1961; Rockets to the Moon, 1961; Rockets to the Planets, 1961; Birth of a Rocket, 1961; Rocket Power, 1961; Space Stations, 1962; Saturn Story, 1962; Our New Navy, 1962; (with William O. Foss) Helicopters in Action, 1962, Coast Guard in Action, 1962; Rocket City, USA, 1963; The Next Fifty Years in Space, 1963; Marine Corps in Action, 1965; Skin Divers in Action, 1965; Illustrated Space Ency., 1965; Murder on Pad 34, 1968; Mars: Planet for Conquest, 1970; The Nuclear Ency., 1971; The Next Fifty Years On The Moon, 1973; National Outdoorsmen's Ency., 1973. Home: Falls Church, Va. Died Mar. 1, 1978.

BERGEN, EDGAR (JOHN), entertainer; b. Chgo., Feb. 16, 1903; s. John and Nellie (Swanson) Bergen; student Lane Tech. and Lakeview high schools, Chgo.; spl. student Northwestern U., 1924; m. Frances Westerman; 1 dau., Candice. Ventriloquist and magician Chautauqua circuits, summers, 1922-25; vaudeville American and European theatres and entertainer supper clubs, 1926-36; made first radio appearance, Dec. 17, 1936; creator of comedy characters Charlie McCarthy, Mortimer Snerd, Effie Klinker. Recipient Spl. Acad. Award for motion picture appearances, 1937. Mem. Soc. Cinematographers, Screen Actors Guild, Actors Equity, Delta Upsilon. Home: Hollywood, Calif. Died Sept. 30, 1978.

BERGENDOFF, RUBEN NATHANIEL, engring. exec.; b. Newman Grove, Neb., Jan. 5, 1899; s. Carl August and Emma Mathilda (Fahlberg) B.; B.S. in Civil Engring., U. Pa., 1921; m. Dorothy Lindgren, June 1, 1925; children—Raymond Carl, Robert Perry, Marjorie Ann. With N.C. Hwy. Dept., 1921-22; cons. engr. Harrington, Howard & Ash, 1922-28, Ash, Howard, Needles & Tammen, 1928-39, Howard, Needles, Tammen & Bergendoff, 1940-77; designer bridges, expressways, turnpikes in numerous states, also govt. units, pvt. corp. bldgs.; dir. Swedish Am. Savs. & Loan Assn., Grand Av. Bank, Kansas City; pres. Kansas City Commn. Internat. Relations and Trade, 1958; v.p. Downtown Com. Bd. dirs. Trinity Luth. Hosp. Recipient numerous awards for beautiful bridges Am. Inst. Steel Constrn.; award for distinguished service in engring. U. Mo., 1957; Distinguished Service award Luth. Brotherhood, 1967; named Man of Month, 1970. Mem. Am. Soc. C.E., Am. Inst. Cons. Engrs. (v.p. 1967), Mo. Soc. Profl. Engrs., Am. Ry. Engring. Assn., Am. Pub. Works Assn., Am. Soc. Testing and Materials, Theta Xi. Clubs: Kansas City, Mission Hills Country, Rotary (pres. 1956) (Kansas City); Ocean Reef (Fla.). Home: Kansas City, Mo. Died Feb. 16, 1977.

BERGER, MORROE, educator, author; b. N.Y.C., June 25, 1917; s. Morris and Frieda (Trotiner) B.; B.S.S., Coll. City N.Y., 1940; M.A., Columbia U., 1947, Ph.D., 1950; m. Paula Wainer, Mar. 7, 1943; children—Edward Morris, Kenneth Harry, Laurence Philip. Mem. faculty Princeton U., 1952-81, prof. sociology, 1962-81, chmn. dept. sociology, 1971-74, dir. program Near Eastern Studies, 1962-68, 73-77, chmn. Council on Internat. and Regional Studies, 1968-77; chmn. joint com. Near and Middle East, Social Sci. Research Council and Am. Council Learned Socs., 1963-68; cons. 20th Century Fund, 1957, Congress Cultural Freedom, 1958-61, Ford Found., 1960-63, 67-68; adv. panel on Middle East, Dept. State; pres. Am. Research Center in Egypt, 1974-78. Mem. Middle East Studies Assn. (pres. 1967). Served with AUS, 1940-45. Author: Equality by Statute, rev. edit., 1967; Bureaucracy and Society in Modern Egypt, 1957; The Arab World Today, 1962; Islam in Egypt Today, 1970; Real and Imagined Worlds: The Novel and Social Science, 1977; also articles. Editor, translator: Madame de Stael on Politics, Literature and National Character, 1964. Home: Princeton, N.J. Died Apr. 7, 1981.

BERGER, SAMUEL D(AVID), fgn. service officer; b. Gloversville, N.Y., Dec. 6, 1911; s. Harry I. and Bess (Coben) B.; Ph.B., U. of Wis., 1933, student U. of Wis., 1935-38, London Sch. Economics, 1938-39; m. Margaret Fowler, Sept. 25, 1937. Social Science Research Council fellowship, 1938; labor advisor to the Spl. Mission to Great Britain, 1942-44; first sec., Am. Embassy, London, 1945-50; on detail to the White House from State Dept., 1950-51; spl. asst. to the dir. for Security, 1951-53; counsellor Am. Embassy, Tokyo, Japan, 1953-54; counsellor of Embassy, Wellington New Zealand, 1954-58, Athens, Greece, 1958-62; U.S. ambassador to South Korea, 1961-64; dep. commandant fgn. affairs Nat. War Coll., 1964-67; dep. asst. sec. for East Asian and Pacific affairs Dept. State, 1967-80. Served as capt., AUS, 1944-45. Home: Gloversville, N.Y. Died Feb. 16, 1980.

BERGFELD, ALBERT JOSEPH, mgmt. cons.; b. St. Paul, July 15, 1910; s. Charles Daniel and May Adele (Carey) B.; grad. Antioch Coll., Yellow Springs, O., 1934; m. Elizabeth Smith Palmer, June 13, 1941; children—Charles Daniel II, Kristin Palmer, Elisabeth Pennock. With Stevenson, Jordan & Harrison, Inc., N.Y.C., 1934-62, mem. firm, 1942-62, pres., 1958-64; pres. Case and Co., Inc., 1962-76; dir. Am. Chain & Cable Co., Inc. Served to lt. USN, World War II. Clubs: Union League, N.Y. Yacht (N.Y.C.); Racquet (Chgo.). Author: (with Dr. James S. Earley, W. R. Knobloch) Pricing for Profit and Growth, 1957. Home: Stamford, Conn. Died Sept. 11, 1976.

BERGMAN, BERNARD AARON, editor; b. Chillicothe, Ohio, July 8, 1894; s. Eleazer and Carrie (Weiler) B.; B.A., Ohio State U., 1916; spl. student Universite de Poitiers, 1919; m. Sue Wells, 1922 (div. 1933); m. 2d, Frances Dellar, Mar. 17, 1933 (dec. Oct. 1965). Reporter, Chillicothe News Advertiser, 1915-16, Columbus (Ohio) Dispatch, 1917; public relations work, N.Y.C., 1919-31; mng. editor New Yorker mag., 1931-33; editor March of Events Page, Hearst Newspapers, 1933-35; successively Sunday editor, feature editor, exec. editor Phila. Record, 1935-42, also feature editor N.Y. Post, 1938; feature editor Pageant mag., 1946; dir. public relations Publicker Industries, Inc., 1947-55; editor, dir. Phila. Daily News, 1955-58; editor Jewish Exponent, Phila., 1958-61; editor Sunday mag. Phila. Bull., 1961-66, editor book div., 1966-69, book editor, 1970-80, book columnist, 1977-80; spl. instr. journalism U. Pa., 1951-52, lectr., 1960. Served as sgt. maj. U.S. Army, World War I; lt. col. USAAF, World War II. Recipient journalism award Temple U., 1956. Mem. Phi Beta Kappa, Zeta Beta Tau, Sigma Delta Chi. Democrat. Jewish. Clubs: Peale, Franklin Inn (Phila.). Author: The Smiling Corpse (with Philip Wylie), 1935. Phila. Bull. established B.A. Bergman award for outstanding lit. achievement in Greater Phila., 1974. Home: Philadelphia, Pa. Died Apr. 11, 1980.

BERGMAN, HENRY DALE, college dean; b. Newton, Ia., Nov. 22, 1886; s. Henry August and Eliza Gordon (Pickens) B.; D.V.M., Ia. State Coll., 1910; post-grad. study in physiology and pharmacology, U. of Chicago, 1911 and 1914; m. Mabel Blanche Hart, Oct. 25, 1911; 1 dau., Betty Sue (Mrs. C. R. Houghan), Asst. prof. veterinary physiology and pharmacology, Iowa State Coll., 1911-13, asso. prof., 1913-16, professor and head dept. since 1916; dean Division of Veterinary Medicine and director Veterinary Research Institute since 1943; consultant Procurement and Assignment Service, War Manpower Commn., 1942-46. Del. to Internat. Vet. Congress, London, 1930, New York, 1934, Pres. Assn. Deans Am. Colls. Veterinary Med., since 1948; mem. exec. com., Assn. Land-Grant Colls. and Univs., since 1949. Fellow A.A.A.S.; mem. Am. Vet. Med. Assn. (pres. 1938); res. sec., Iowa, 1917-21; com. unofficial buet. remedies, 1919-21; com. on edn., 1918-23; chmn. com., 1921-23; chmn. asso. com. on vet. preps., revision of National Formulary, 6th, 7th and 8th edits., 1930-45; chmn. com. on proprietary pharmaceuticals, 1927-38; rep. div. med. sciences, National Research Council, 1947-50); U.S. Livestock San. Assn., Research Workers in Animal Diseases in North America; Iowa Veterinary Medical Association (sec., 1918-23, president, 1924). Iowa Academy of Science, Sigma Xi, Phi Kappa Phi, Phi Lambda Upsilon, Phi Zeta, Gamma Sigma Delta. Sec. Mo. Valley Intercollegiate Athletic Assn., 1935-41. Republican. Presbyn. Club: Osborn Resrch. Contbr. many papers and articles to leading vet. med. jours. Home: Ames, Ia. *

BERGSON, HERBERT AUGUSTUS, lawyer; b. Boston, Jan. 14, 1909; s. Harry and Augusta (Cook) B.; student Boston Latin Sch., 1920-26; A.B., Harvard, 1930, LL.B., 1933; m. Bernice A. Weber, Sept. 22, 1933; children—Richard W., Barbara C. (dec.), Paul C., Mary K. Admitted to Mass. bar, 1933, practiced in Boston, 1933-34, Washington, 1950-77; trial atty. claims div., Dept. Justice, 1934-36, asst. chief legislation, 1936-43, chief legislation, 1945-48, cons. to atty. gen., 1946-47, acting asst. atty. gen. claims div., 1947-48, exec. asst. to atty. gen., 1948, asst. atty. gen. charge of anti-trust div., June 1948-Sept. 1950; gen. counsel O.D.M., 1951; mem. firm Bergson, Borkland, Margolis and Adler, Washington. Served as lt. USCGR, 1944-45. Mem. Am. (chmn. sect. antitrust law 1957-58), Fed. bar assns., Bar Assn. D.C. Clubs: Harvard, Army and Navy (Washington). Editor: Federal Bar Jour, 1947-48. Home: Sumner, Md. Died May 15, 1977.

BERGSTRAND, KARL JOHAN HILDING, pathologist; b. Jonkòping, Sweden, Jan. 12, 1886; s. Karl and Augusta (Holmdal) B.; student U. Uppsala, 1905-09, U. Stockholm, 1909-13; M.D., Stockholm Carol Inst., 1916; D.V.M., U. Stockholm, 1944; D.D.M., 1955; m. Elsa Bachman, Feb. 11, 1914; children—Carl-Gustaf, Anders. Asst. prof. pathology, Caroline Inst. Med. Sch., 1919-24, prof. pathology, 1924-53, dean, 1942-53; chief med. officer, Life Ins. Co., Thule, 1923-52. Mem. internal com. ins. medicine City Council of Stockholm; mem. com. orgn. Swedish Med. Schs. Bd. Nobel Found., 1942-53, chmn. medicine Nobel com., 1947-53; bd. Caroline Hosp., 1940-53, Eastman Dental Inst. Served as surgeon Swedish Navy, 1916-19. Mem. Swedish Cancer Soc. (chmn.), Acad. Nationale Medicine Buenos Aires. Author: Larobok i patologi, 1943; History of the Swedish Medical Society, 1958; also articles in field. Home: Stockholm, Sweden. *

BERGWALL, EVAN HAROLD, clergyman; b. Jamestown, N.Y., Sept. 16, 1915; s. A. Elof and Alice H. (Lund) B.; A.B., Taylor U., 1939; B.D., Yale (Tew prize 1942, Julia Archibald High scholar, Day fellow 1943), 1943; postgrad. Yale, N.Y. U., Emory U., Oxford (Eng.) U.; D.D., Asbury Theol. Sem., 1955; m. Jean Mitchell Francis, Aug. 30, 1941; children—Evan Harold, David Francis. Ordained to ministry Meth. Ch., 1941; minister Bethelship Ch., Bklyn., 1941-43, Grace Ch., Waterbury, Conn., 1943-45, Lexington Av. Ch., N.Y.C., 1945-48, High St. Ch., Muncie, Ind., 1948-49, First Ch., Kendallville, Ind., 1949-51; pres. Taylor U., Upland, Ind., 1951-59; minister Simpson Meth. Ch., Fort Wayne, Ind., 1959-67; supt. Elkhart dist. N. Ind.

Conf., 1967-73; dir. chaplaincy services Parkview Meml. Hosp., Ft. Wayne, Ind., 1973-79. Goodwill ambassador to Meth. Ch. in Germany, 1950; visitor mission stas. Meth. Ch. in Congo and Rhodesia, summer 1963, 70, 72, Middle East, 1953, 63, 70, Haiti, 1968, 70; mem. staff Ft. Wayne Counseling Center of Meth. Ch.; del. Gen. and Jurisdictional confs. Meth. Ch., 1968. Chmn. bd. Basher Home of United Meth. Ch., Goshen, Ind.; pres. bd. Bethel Meth. Home for Aged, Ossining, N.Y., 1947-48; bd. dirs. Child Care Found. Recipient Widsom award of Honor, 1970. Mem. Am. Assn. Sch. Adminstrs., NEA, North Ind. Conf. Meth. Ch., Chi Alpha Omega. Contbr. articles to religious publs. Home: Fort Wayne, Ind. Died Jan. 27, 1979.

BERK, VIOLA GREENHUT, broadcasting co. exec.; b. Cleve., Sept. 21, 1897; d. Max and Gizella M. (Edelstein) Greenhut; student Case Western Res. U., 1917-19; B.A., Stetson U., 1920; m. S. Bernard Berk, Aug. 28, 1919; children—Roger G., James L., With Summit Radio, Akron, O., 1940-77, writer, 1940-77, producer, 1940-65, pres., 1966-77; dir. WAKR Radio and WAKR-TV, Akron, 1940-77, WONE Radio, WTUE, Dayton, Ohio, 1967-77; Group One Broadcasting Co. Tex., KBOX, KMEZ, Group One Broadcasting Co.-West, KLZ, KAZY, Rogim Inc., Radio TV Center Akron Inc. Bd. dirs. Akron Gen. Hosp. Clubs: Rotary Ann; Akron City; Rosemont Country. Home: Akron, Ohio. Died Apr. 25, 1977.

BERKELEY, BUSBY (WILLIAM BERKELEY ENOS), dance dir.; b. Los Angeles, Nov. 29, 1895. Started career on N.Y. stage, later joined Warner Bros.; joined MGM, 1939. Pictures include: 42nd Street, Footlight Parade, Hollywood Hotel, Men Are Such Fools, Broadway Serenade, Strike Up the Band, Fast and Furious, Ziegfeld Girl, For Me and My Gal, Gang's All Here, Cinderella Jones, Take Me Out to the Ball Game, Two Weeks with Love, Call Me Mister, Two Tickets to Broadway, Million Dollar Mermaid, Small Town Girl, Easy to Love, Rose Marie; supr. revival of No No Nanette, N.Y.C., 1971. Address: Palm Desert, Calif. Died Mar. 14, 1976.

BERKMAN, DAVID MAYO, physician; b. Rochester, Minn., May 26, 1886; s. David Mack and Gertrude (Mayo) B.; B.S., U. of Minn., 1909, M.S., 1920; M.D., Rush Med. Coll., 1912; m. Frances Scott, June 8, 1915; children—David, Louise, Nancy, John and (twins) Helen and Ruth. Interne Presbyn. Hosp., Chicago, 1912-13; staff mem. Mayo Clinic since Nov. 1, 1913, head of sect. in medicine 1921-48, retired; asst. prof. medicine, Mayo Foundation, U. of Minn.; mem. bd. govs., Mayo Clinic; resigned. Served in Med. Corps, U.S. Army, 1917-19; maj. with A.E.F., 1 year. Fellow Am. Coll. Physicians; mem. A.M.A. Southern Minn. Med. Assn., Sigma Xi, Psi Upsilon, Alpha Kappa Kappa. Episcopalian. Home: Rochester, Minn.

BERMAN, MYRON PHILIP, paper co. exec.; b. N.Y.C., Nov. 24, 1916; s. Morris Bernard and Rose (Hecht) B.; student N.Y. U., 1934-38; m. Roslyn Rettich, Dec. 17, 1939; children—Janice Lee (Mrs. David Lawrence), Harvey Alan. Vice pres. Harlem Card & Paper Co., N.Y.C., 1938-52; pres. Berman Paper Co., N.Y.C., 1952-60; pres., chmn. bd. dirs. Saxon Industries, Inc., N.Y.C., 1960-77; dir. Can. Life Ins. Co. N.Y., Sterndent Corp., Mt. Vernon, N.Y. Vice chmn. Paper Distbn. Council, Layman's Nat. Bible Assn. Recipient Brotherhood award NCCJ. Mem. Nat. Paper Trade Assn. (bd. dirs. 1966-70). Jewish (pres. temple 1960-62). Club: Putnam Country (Mahopac, N.Y.). Home: Mahopac, N.Y. Died Aug. 1977.

BERN, HOWARD LEONARD, hotel exec.; b. Flushing, N.Y., Sept. 8, 1924; s. Benjamin Harrison and Ida (Eisenstadt) B.; B.S. in Bus. Adminstrn., Hofstra U., 1948; m. Pearl Esther Dlugatz, June 23, 1963; children—Harrison David, Miriam Susan. Owner, operator Millbrook Lodge, Kerkonkson, N.Y., 1947-55; desk clk. to v.p. and gen. mgr. Grossinger (N.Y.) Hotel, from 1955. Mem. ethics com. County of Sullivan (N.Y.), from 1970, airport commn., from 1975, zoning bd. appeals, 1972-76. Served to 2d lt. USAAF, 1943-46. Mem. Am. Soc. Assn. Execs., Hotel Sales Mgrs. Assn., Zeta Beta Tau. Jewish. Club: Masons. Home: Liberty, NY. Deceased.

BERNARD, FREDERIC HORTON, lawyer; b. Tucson, Ariz., Aug. 18, 1885; s. Allan Cunningham and Minnie (Chouteau) B.; student U. of Ariz., 1900-04, Stanford, 1904-08; m. Gwendolyn Beecher, of Tucson, Feb. 3, 1925. Admitted to Ariz. bar, 1909, and began practice in Tucson; city atty., 1917-21; U.S. dist. atty., Dist. of Ariz., by apptmt. of President Harding, Feb. 25, 1922. Mem. Am. Bar Assn., Delta Tau Delta. Republican. Elk. Clubs: Kiwanis, Old Pueblo, Tucson Golf and Country. Home: Tucson, Ariz.*

BERNHARD, JOHN HELENUS, inland navigation consultant; b. Amsterdam, Holland, Feb. 13, 1884; s. Nicholas Adrianus and Christine Maria (Henke) B.; M.E., Technical Coll., 1905; m. Dora Solosko (died Aug. 3, 1942); 1 son, Alexander Alfred; m. 2d, Leona Nelken, June 24, 1944. Came to U.S. Aug. 1905, naturalized, July 1922. Built fleet of self propelled 1000 ton river barges for movement of coal from Alabama to New Orleans; cons. engr. on inland navigation since 1917; asst. to pres. of Higgins Industries, Inc., New Orleans; consultant Commission Papaloapan de Mexico. Edited inland waterways section, Second Five Years Plan of Soviet Russia. Address: Mexico. *

BERNSTEIN, JOEL, govt. ofcl.; b. Chgo., Jan. 9, 1921; s. Fred and Lillie (Greenberg) B.; B.A., U. Chgo., 1942, M.A., 1948, Ph.D., 1956; m. Merle Anne Sloan, Sept. 14, 1946; children—Jonathan Lewis, Deborah Lynn. Prof. econs. DePaul U., 1947; U.S. fgn. econ. assistance adminstr., London, Paris, Rome, Washington and Monrovia, 1948-59; dir. AID Mission to Nigeria, 1959-64, to Seoul, Korea, 1964-67; dir. program evaluation AID, Washington, 1968-69, asst. adminstr., 1969-74; dir. Pres. Ford's Food and Nutrition Study, Nat. Acad. Scis., 1975-77, dir. studies for U.S. Govt. proposing initiatives to mobilize U.S. Sci. and Tech. for Devel., 1977-79. Served to 1st lt. AUS, 1942-46. Mem. Am. Econ. Assn., Soc. Internat. Devel., Phi Beta Kappa, Pi Lambda Phi (past pres. Chgo.). Home: Chevy Chase, Md. Died Jan. 1, 1980; buried Falls Church, Va.

BERNSTEIN, THEODORE MENLINE, editor; b. N.Y.C., Nov. 17, 1904; s. Saul and Sarah (Menline) B.; A.B., Columbia, 1924, B.Litt., 1925; m. Beatrice Alexander, Sept. 2, 1930 (dec. Jan. 1971); 1 son, Eric Menline. Mem. staff N.Y. Times, 1925-79, news editor, 1951-52, asst. mng. editor, 1952-69, founding editor internat. edit., Paris, 1960, editorial dir. book div., 1969-71, exec. editor N.Y. Times Encyclopedic Almanac, 1969-71, cons. editor, 1971-79; from asst. to asso. prof. Columbia Sch. Journalism, 1925-50; cons. U.S. Panel Ednl. Research and Devel., 1964. Mem. Authors Guild, Sigma Delta Chi. Author: (with R.E. Garst) Headlines and Deadlines, 2d edit., 1961; Watch Your Language, 1958; More Language That Needs Watching, 1962; The Careful Writer, 1965; Miss Thistlebottom's Hobgoblins, 1971; Bernstein's Reverse Dictionary, 1975; Dos, Donts and Maybes of English Usage, 1977. Cons. on usage Random House Dictionary, Am. Heritage Dictionary; columnist Bernstein on Words, N.Y. Times Spl. Features Syndicate, 1972—. Home: New York, N.Y. Died June 27, 1979.

BERNTON, HARRY SAUL, physician; b. Kurland, Jan. 15, 1884; s. Philip Goodman and Rose (Davidson) B.; A.B., Harvard, 1904, M.D., 1908; m. Rhea Van Baalan Loewenberg, Mar. 1, 1916, children—Ruth Elizabeth (dec.), William Philip, Horace Wright. Came to U.S. from Ireland, 1896, naturalized, 1913. Interne Boston City Hosp., 1908-09; with Bender Hygienic Lab., Albany, N.Y., as asst. and dir., 1909-14; prof. pathology and bacteriology, Albany Med. Coll., 1912-14; bacteriologist N.Y. State and Albany depts. of health, 1912-14; pathologist R.I. Bd. Health, 1914-18; instr. pathology, Harvard, 1915-17; chief Bur. of Preventable Diseases and dir. Biol. Labs. of Health Dept., Dist. of Columbia, 1918-19; dir. Child Welfare Soc., Dist. of Columbia, 1919-22; prof. med. jurisprudence, George Washington U., 1919-24; expert in hay fever, U.S. Pub. Health Service, 1922-25; attending specialist in allergic diseases, U.S. Vets. Adminstrn., 1925-33; lecturer of hygiene, Georgetown U., 1919-21, asso. prof., 1921-29, prof. 1929-51; clin. specialist allergy Bur. Agrl. Chemistry and Engring., Dept. Agr., since 1936. Clinical prof. medicine, Coll. Med., Howard Univ. Commd. sr. lt., U.S. Naval Res., 1918. Dir. Assn. for Prevention of Tuberculosis, Central Admitting Bur. for Hosps., Inc., Med. Dental Service Bur., Inc. Fellow A.C.P., Am. Coll. Allergy, Am. Acad. Allergy; mem. Internat. Assn. Med. Mus., Am. Assn. Bacteriol. and Pathologists, Am. Bacteriol. Soc., Med. Soc. of D.C., Biol. Soc. of Washington, A.M.A., Southern Med. Assn., Am. Assn. for the Study of Allergy (pres. 1927-28), Soc. for Study of Asthma and Allied Conditions. Awarded Fisk prize of R.I. Med. Soc. Liberal Hebrew. Clubs: Cosmos, National Press, Torch, Harvard, Clinical (Washington); Harvard (Boston). Contbr. articles on allergy to med. jours.

BERRY, FRANK B(ROWN), b. Dorchester, Mass., May 13, 1892; student Roxbury Latin Sch., 1909; A.B., Harvard, 1914, M.D., 1917; LL.D., Hahnemann Med. Coll., 1955, Jefferson Med. College, 1956; married Lois Bliss Langdon, 1959. Intern, Peter Bent Brigham Hosp., Presbyn. Hosp. of N.Y.C.; intern, later resident pathology Boston City Hosp.; resident, later vis. surgeon, dir. 1st surg. and chest surg. div., Bellevue Hosp., N.Y.C.; practice medicine, Providence, 1921-23; practice surgery, N.Y.C., 1924-54; prof. clin. surgery Columbia, 1946-54; asst. secretary health and medical affairs Dept. of Def., 1954-61, dep. asst. sec. def. for manpower-health and medical affairs, 1961-63; founder Interdepartmental Com. of Nutrition for Nat. Def. Served with M.C., U.S. Army, 1918-19, as col., M.C., AUS, 1942-46; brig. gen., ret., 1952; surg. cons. 7th Army; dep. cons. div. Surgeon General's Office. Decorated Legion of Merit; Croix de Guerre, Chevalier Legion d'Honneur (France). Mem. nat. bd. govs., ARC. Diplomate, founder mem. Am. Bd. Surgery, Am. Bd. Thoracic Surgery. Fellow A.C.S.; mem. AMA, N.Y. Med. Soc., Am., So. Pan Pacific surg. assns., Am. Assn. Thoracic Surgery, N.Y. Surg. Soc., N.Y. Acad. Med. (trustee). Episcopalian. Clubs: Metropolitan, Army and Navy (Washington); Union; Harvard; Century Assn. Home: New York, N.Y. Died Oct. 14, 1976.

BERRY, FRANKLIN HAYWOOD, lawyer, banker; b. Manahawkin, N.J., May 15, 1904; s. J. Willits and Jessie (Haywood) B.; A.B., U. Pa., 1925, LL.B., 1928; m. Eleanor Lamon, Oct. 10, 1928; 1 son, Franklin Haywood; m. Leonora Patterson, Aug. 14, 1948; children—Margaret L. (Mrs. Margaret Laird), John Sherwin, Elizabeth R. (Mrs. W.M. Collinsworth). Admitted to N.J. bar, 1928, practiced in Toms River, from 1928; partner firm Berry Summerill, Rinck & Berry and predecessor, 1933-75; pres. Beach Haven Nat. Bank & Trust Co., 1939-70, chmn. bd., 1970-75; v.p., counsel Adm. Farragut Acad., 1946-75; dep. atty. gen. N.J., 1946-48; pres. Long Beach Water Co., 1961-71; dir. emeritus First Nat. Bank Toms River. Del. N.J. Constl. Conv., 1947. Trustee Richard Stockton State Coll. Served from capt. to col. AUS, 1941-46; col. Res. (ret.). Decorated Legion of Merit, Bronze Star medal. Fellow Am. Bar Found. (life); mem. C. of C., Ocean County Bankers Assn. (past pres.), Am. (mem. ho. of dels., mem. com. on lawyers in armed forces), N.J. (past pres.), Ocean County bar assns., Judge Adv. Assn. (dir., past pres.), N.J. Soc. S.R., Holland Soc. N.Y. Presbyn. (elder). Clubs: Ocean County Lawyers (past pres.); Union League (Phila.); Little Egg Harbor and Toms River Yacht. Home: Pine Beach, N.J. Died June 16, 1975; buried Manahawkin, N.J.

BERRY, JAMES LAMPTON, fgn. service officer; b. Columbia, Miss., May 10, 1908; s. Miles Riley and Olivia Jane (Lampton) B.; B.A., U. Miss., 1929, M.A., 1931; grad. student U. Ill., 1931-32, Cowles fellow Yale, 1932-34; grad. Army-Navy Staff Coll., 1945; m. Angela Margaret Ogilvie, Mar. 8, 1945; 1 son, James Lampton. Am. vice consul. Durban. Johannesburg, Capetown, Port Elizabeth, Union South Africa, also Lourenco Marques, Portuguese East Africa, 1934-40; Am. vice consul, Calcutta, India, 1940-41; sec. to Am. commr., New Delhi, India, 1941-42, sec. to personal rep. Pres. of U.S., New Delhi, 1942-44; asst. chief Div. Middle Eastern Affairs, Dept. of State, 1945-47, spl. asst. to dir. Office Near Eastern and African Affairs, 1947-48, mem. policy planning staff, 1948-50, State Dept. adviser Air War Coll., 1950-52, mem. policy planning staff, 1952-53, dep. operations coordinator Office Under-Sec. of State, 1953-54; Am. consul gen. with rank of minister, Singapore, 1954-55; spl. asst. to dep. under-sec. state for adminstrn., 1955-56; dep. asst. sec. of state for Near Eastern, South Asian, African Affairs, 1956-58; ambassador to Ceylon, from 1958. Home: Columbia, Miss. Died Feb. 5, 1980.

BERRY, LLOYD EASON, univ. dean; b. Houston, Aug. 1, 1935; s. Joel Halbert and Fay (Eason) B.; B.A., U. N.C., 1957, M.A. (Carnegie Found. fellow), 1958; Ph.D. (Marshall scholar), Magdalene Coll., Cambridge (Eng.) U., 1960; m. Elizabeth Perry, 1955 (div. 1971); children—Susan, Lloyd, Sharon; m. 2d, Deborah J. Goss, Apr. 9, 1977. Asst. prof. English, U. Ill., Urbana, 1960-63, faculty fellow, 1962, asso. prof., then prof. English, 1963-72, asst. chancellor, 1969-72, asso. mem. Center Advanced Study, 1967-68; prof. English, dean Grad. Sch., dir. research U. Mo., 1972-77; commr. Midwest region Marshall Scholarship Com., 1969-76, chmn., 1972-76; pres. Central Renaissance Conf., 1969-70, 74—. Bd. dirs. Camp Howard, 1965-67, Nat. Acad. Arts, 1967-77, Univ. YMCA, 1969-72, Carle Hosp. Found., 1971-77, United Community Council, 1969-72, Champaign C. of C., 1971-72, Commn. on Arts, 1977. Am. Philos. Soc. grantee, 1963, 65; Henry H. Huntington Library fellow, 1965; Folger Shakespeare Library fellow, 1965; Guggenheim fellow, 1966-67; recipient Alumnus award Kinkaid Prep. Sch. Mem. MLA, Modern Humanities Research Assn., Milton Soc. (exec. com.), Renaissance Soc. Am. (adv. com.), Renaissance English Text Soc. (returning officer, mem. exec. com.), Malone Soc., Bibliog. Soc., Cambridge Bibliog. Soc. (sec. U.S. and Can.), Marshall Scholars Assn. (permanent sec.), Assn. Grad. Schs. (policy com.), Nat. Conv. Univ. Research Adminstrs., Phi Beta Kappa, Phi Kappa Phi, Sigma Tau Delta, Pi Gamma Mu, Kappa Tau Alpha, Alpha Chi. Baptist. Clubs: Cambridge-Oxford; Rotary. Author: A Bibliography of Studies in Metaphysical Poetry, 1939-60, 64; The English Works of Giles Fletcher, the Elder, 1964; John Stubb's Gaping Gulf with Letters and Other Relevant Documents, 1968; Rude and Barbarous Kingdom: Russia in the Accounts of Sixteenth-Century English Voyagers, 1968; The Geneva Bible: A Facsimile of the 1560 Edition, 1969; The Dramatic Works of George Chapman, 1970; also articles. Home: Columbia, Mo. Died Dec. 20, 1977.

BERRY, LOREN MURPHY, business exec.; b. Wabash, Ind., July 24, 1888; s. Charles D. and Elizabeth (Murphy) B.; student Northwestern U., 1909-10; LL.D., Rio Grande (Ohio) Coll.; D.C.S., Biscayne Coll., Fla.; m. Lucile Kneipple, June 9, 1909 (dec.); m. 2d, Helen Anderson Henry, Aug. 28, 1938 (dec.); children—Loren Murphy, Martha Sue Fraim, John William, Elizabeth Anne Gray; m. 3d, Ruth Heston, Apr. 21, 1976; 1 son, Leland Henry. Newspaper reporter, Wabash, Ind., Joliet, Ill., Chgo.; sold telephone directory advt., Marion, Ind., 1910, St. Louis,

Louisville, Indpls., which developed into nat. sales orgn. of L.M. Berry & Co., main office, Dayton, Ohio, now vice chmn. bd.; dir. emeritus United Telecommunications, Inc., Kansas City, Mo., 3d Nat. Bank & Trust Co., Dayton; dir. Super Food Services, Inc., Dayton, Laughter Corp., Dayton. Mem. Republican Nat. Finance Com. Trustee Jr. Achievement, Dayton, Rio Grande Coll. Mem. U.S. Ind. Telephone Pioneers (pres. 1938-39), Bell Telephone Pioneers Assn. (v.p. N.C. Kingsbury chpt. 1939-40). Episcopalian. Mason (32 deg., Shriner). Clubs: Capitol Hill (Washington); Dayton City, Engineers, Kiwanis, Dayton Country, Dayton Bicycle, Moraine Country (Dayton); Sury (gov.), Committee of 100 (v.p.), Indian Creek, Bath, Palm Bay, Jockey (Miami Beach, Fla.); Bohemian (San Francisco). Home: Dayton, Ohio. Died Feb. 10, 1980; buried Woodland Cemetery, Dayton.

BERRY, WILLIAM, psychologist; b. Manchester, Eng., Nov. 1, 1884; s. James and Charlotte (Hall) B.; B.A., U. of Alberta, 1916, M.A., 1918; Ph.D., U. of Chicago, 1922; m. Margaret McGorman Lamb, of Edmonton, Can., Sept. 23, 1914; children—Donald William, Evelyn Margaret. Came to U.S., 1920, naturalized citizen, 1926. Instr. in philosophy and psychology, U. of Alberta, 1916-20; instr. U. of Chicago, 1920-22; asst. prof. psychology, U. of Rochester, 1922-26, prof. since 1926, head of dept. since 1928. Asso. mem. Am. Psychol. Assn.; mem. Optical Soc. America, A.A.A.S., Sigma Xi. Presbyn. Club: Faculty. Home: Rochester, N.Y. *

BERRYHILL, WALTER REECE, dean of medicine; b. Charlotte, N.C., Oct. 14, 1900; s. Samuel Reece and Minnie Eugenia (Scott) B.; A.B., U. of N.C., 1921; student U. of N.C., Sch. of Medicine, 1923-25; M.D., Harvard U., 1927; D.Sc. (hon.), Davidson (N.C.) College, 1956; m. Norma Connell, Aug. 2, 1930; children—Jane Carol, Catherine Brewer. Intern Fourth Med. Service, Boston City Hosp., 1927-29; asso. prof. physiology, U. of N.C., 1929-30; resident physician Med. Service, Lakeside Hosp., Cleveland, 1930-31; instr. in medicine, Western Res. Sch. of Medicine and asst. physician Lakeside Hosp., 1931-33; asso. prof. medicine, U. of N.C. and physician University Infirmary, since 1933; dir. student Health Service, U. of N.C., since 1933, asst. dean, Sch. of Medicine, 1937-41, dean and prof. Clinical Medicine since 1941. Mem. Marine Corps, S.A.T.C., 1918. Member of Visiting Staff, The Watts Hospital, Durham, N.C. Fellow Am. Coll. Physicians; member A.M.A., So. Med. Assn., Phi Beta Kappa, Sigma Xi, Delta Sigma Phi. Club: Harvard of N.C. (pres. 1941). Contbr. to med. jours. Home: Chapel Hill, N.C. Died Jan. 1, 1979.

BERRYMAN, ROBERT BENTON, nat. resources co. exec.; b. Brookeland, Tex., Mar. 9, 1924; s. Andrew Alvin and Effie (McDaniel) B.; B.S. in Mech. Engring., Tex. A. and M. Coll., 1948; m. Mary Anne Tabb, Aug. 14, 1948. With United Gas Corp., 1948-68, asst. sec., 1958-64, sec., 1965-68; sec. Pennzoil Co. (merger United Gas Corp. and Pennzoil Co.), 1968-76. Served to 1st lt., pilot USAAF, 1943-45. Mem. Am. Gas Assn., Ind. Petroleum Assn. Am., Am. Petroleum Inst., Am. Soc. Corporate Secs. Home: Houston, Tex. Died Sept. 21, 1976; interred Forest Park Cemetery, Shreveport, La.

BERSELL, PETRUS OLOF IMMANUEL (BER-SEL'), church exec.; b. Rock Island, Ill., May 6, 1882; s. Prof. Anders O. (Ph.D.) and Uma B. (Lagerlund) B.; A.B., Augustana Coll., 1899; B.D., Augustana Theol. Sem., 1906; D.D., Augustana Coll. and Theol. Sem., 1930; hon. L.H.D., Luther Coll., Decorah, Ia., 1938; LL.D., Upsala College, East Orange, N.Y., 1945; Th.D., Uppsala Univ., Sweden, 1948; married Emelia Frideborg Bergh, Aug. 20, 1908; children—Eleanor Sara (Mrs. Earl Andersen), Ralph Bergh. Instr. in Greek, Luther Coll., Wahoo, Neb., 1899-1900; teacher pub. schs., Marquette County, Mich., 1901-03; instr. in history, Augustana Coll., 1904-05; ordained ministry, Augustana Lutheran Church, 1906; pastor Immanuel Lutheran Ch., Chicago Heights, Ill., 1906-11, Grace Luth. Ch., Chicago, 1911-13, First Luth. Ch., Ottumwa, Ia., 1913-35. Vice-pres. Ia. Conf. of Augustana Ch., 1923-28, pres., 1928-35; pres. Augustana Evangel. Lutheran Church, 1935-51; chmn. finance com., Augustana Synod, 1927-31; gen. sec. Am. Luth. Conf., 1930-34, vice-pres., 1934-36, member executive com. since 1943; member various bds. Augustana Church; mem. Bd. Fgn. Missions United Lutheran Church in America since 1936; pres. National Lutheran Council, 1941-45; councillor since 1935; chmn. Service Commn. since 1941; Luth. commr. to Europe, 1945; member commn. on Orphaned Missions, National Lutheran Council since 1948; vice del. Provisional Com., World Council of Chs., Geneva, Switz., Feb. 1946; Buck Hill Falls, Pa., 1947; mem. Central Commn. World Council Chs. since 1948; mem. exec. com. Lutheran World Fedn. since 1948; chmn. U.S. Adminstrn. Com. Luth. World Fedn., since 1948; mem. gen. bd. Nat. Council of Chs. of Christ in U.S. since 1950; v.p. Luth. Brotherhood of Am. 1918-22; v.p. and dir. Luth. Brotherhood (fraternal ins.), 1927-43, and editor official organ. "The Bond." Honorary member Minneapolis Club. Comdr. 1st Class, Royal Order of North Star (Sweden), 1948. Contbr. to ch. publs. Home: Indian Lake, Manistique, Mich. *

BERTHIAUME-DUTREMBLAY, ANGELINA, publisher; b. Montreal, Can., Mar. 27, 1886; d. Treffle and Helmina (Gadbois) Berthiaume; student Dames de la Congregation de Notre-Dame, Montreal; m. P. R. DuTremblay, Sept. 7, 1907 (dec.). Pres., gen. mgr. La Cia. de Publican de La Presse, Limitée, 1955—; pres. La. Cia. de Publication de La Patrie, Limitée, 1955—, Montreal Apartments, Ltd., L'Ile des Prairies, Limitée, Montreal. Home: Montreal, Can. *

BERTOIA, HARRY, artist; b. San Lorenzo, Italy, Mar. 10, 1915; s. Giuseppe and Maria (Mussio) B.; student pub. schs., Italy and Mich., Arts and Crafts Sch., Detroit, Cranbrook Acad. Art, Bloomfield Hills, Mich., 1937-42; m. Brigitta Valentiner, May 10, 1943; children—Mara Lesta, Val Odey, Celia Marei. Came to the U.S. 1930, naturalized, 1947. Student tchrs. Cranbrook Acad., 1938-43; development war material Evans Products Co., 1943-46; independent artist, jewelry craftsman, 1946-47; with U.S. Electronics Lab., San Diego, 1948-50; chair designer Knoll Internat., 1950-54; executed sculptural screens for Gen. Motors, New Tech. Center. Mfrs. Trust Bank N.Y., Mass. Inst. Tech. chapel; bronze sculpture View of Earth from Space, Dulles Airport, Washington, 1962; copper and bronze fountain piece Civic Center, Phila.; exhibited London Triennial, 1963, sculpture shows, Paris, 1964, Amsterdam, 1967, Zurich, 1968; ceiling sculpture Seattle 1st Nat. Bank, 1968. Recipient gold medal Archtl., League N.Y., 1955; gold medal, A.I.A., 1956; Graham Found. scholarship, 1957; Hazlett Meml. award for sculpture, 1980. Home: Barto, Pa. Died Nov. 6, 1978; buried at home.

BERTRAND, CHARLES EDWARD, railroad ofcl.; b. Pine Bluff, Ark., May 30, 1915; s. Charles L. and Kibble (Moore) B.; ed. pub. schs.; m. Ludene A. Asklund, Dec. 23, 1933; children—Cynthia Ludene, Charles Edward. With B. & O. R.R. Co., 1937; gen. mgr. Eastern region, 1960, asst. v.p. operations and maintenance, 1960-61, v.p. ops. and maintenance, 1961-78; chief exec. officer Reading Co.; pres., dir. Balt. and Ohio Stores, Inc., B.R.& P. Warehouse, Inc., Camden Warehouses, Inc., Md. Constrn. Co. of Balt., New Gauley Coal Corp., Terminal Storage Co. Washington, Toledo, Lorain & Fairport Co.; v.p., dir. numerous subsidiaries and affiliates B. & O. R.R. Co.; pres. Reading Co.; pres., chief exec. officer Del. and Hudson Ry.; dir. Central R.R. Co. Republican. Presbyn. Mason (Shriner). Home: Huntington Valley, Pa. Died Mar. 3, 1978; interred George Washington Meml. Cemetery.

BESLEY, HAROLD JOSLYN, grain expert; b. Waukegan, Ill., June 25, 1884; s. Edmund D. and Sarah A. (Joslyn) B.; B.Sc., U. of Wis., 1907; unmarried. With U.S. Dept. Agr. since 1910; in charge grain div., 1920-33; transferred to Agrl. Adjustment Administration, Aug. 1, 1933, now asst. chief field investigation section. Mem. Kappa Sigma. Home: 1105 K St. N.W. Address: Washington, D.C. *

BESSE, HARRY WILLIAM, stockbroker, investment counselor; b. Wareham, Mass., June 9, 1898; s. Frank Alden and Mary (Gammons) B.; A.B., Tufts Coll., 1920; m. Olive Brett, Jan. 11, 1927; m. 2d, Geraldine Taylor, Aug. 8, 1979. With Boston Stock Exchange, 1927-80, pres., 1946-62; with Stock Clearing Corp., Boston, 1946-62, pres., 1946-62; ltd. partner Josephthal and Co.; pres. Indamer Jamaica Inc., Holyoke Shares; dir. Allegheny Airlines; pres., dir., chmn. bd. Ventura Internat. Moderator, Town of Gilmanton (N.H.). Served as col. USAAF, 1942-46. Home Gilmanton Iron Works, N.H. Died Apr. 2, 1980; buried Gilmanton Iron Works.

BESSELL, WILLIAM WESTON, JR., army officer; b. San Juan, Puerto Rico, May 17, 1901; s. William Weston and May (Hall) B.; B.S., U.S. Mil. Acad., 1920; C.E., Rensselaer Poly. Inst., 1922, E.D., 1960; E.D., Rose Poly. Inst., 1965; grad. Command and General Staff School, 1940; m. Katherine Mary Hanratta, Aug. 29, 1922 (dec.); 1 dau., Constance; m. 2d, Lillian Stanford Touchstone, Nov. 22, 1959; stepchildren—Stanford Touchstone, Anne Touchstone Combs. Commd. 2d lt. C.E., U.S. Army, 1920, advanced through the grades to brig. gen., 1944; served in Territory of Hawaii, 1932-34; asst. to dist. engr., Zanesville, Ohio, Muskingum River Flood Control, 1935-36; officer in charge European office Am. Battle Monuments Commn., Paris, 1936-39; with Office of Chief of Engrs., 1940-42; with War Dept. Gen. Staff, Army dir. Joint War Plans Com., 1942-46; comdg. gen. Antilles Dept., San Juan, Puerto Rico, 1946-47; prof. and head dept. math. U.S. Mil. Acad., West Point, N.Y., 1946-59, dean acad. bd., 1959-65. Decorated D.S.M., Legion of Merit, Chevalier de la Legion d'Honneur (France), Hon. Comdr., Order Brit. Empire. Mem. Math. Assn. Am., Am. Statis. Assn., Soc. Am. Mil. Engrs., Nat. Council Tchrs. Math., Am. Soc. Engring. Edn., Theta Xi, Sigma Xi. Club: Army and Navy (Washington). Home: West Point, N.Y. Died Jan. 15, 1977.

BESSIN, HYMAN, corp. exec. Chmn. bd. Acklands Ltd., Eliaz Binyamina (1818) Ltd., Israel, Mindy's Ltd.; pres. B & V Mgmt. Services Ltd., Rachel Investments Ltd., Fort Garry Court Ltd., Winston Hall Ltd.; dir. Mizrachi Bank Israel. Past nat. pres. Canadian Zionist Fedn.; mem. exec. World Zionist Orgn., Canadian Found. for Jewish Edn.; trustee Bar Ilan U., Israel, Yeshiva U., N.Y.C., Shaare Tzedek Hosp., Israel; chmn. bd. Hyman Bessin Charitable Found. Home: Ottawa, Ont., Can. Deceased.

BESSIRE, DALE PHILIP, artist; b. Columbus, Ohio, May 14, 1892; s. Jules Philip and Margaret Salome (Ritzler) B.; student U. Chgo., 1910-11, Herron Art Inst., Indianapolis, 1909, 27; m. Sabina Ruth Sayer, June 30, 1913; children—Philip Dale, William Sayer, Marianne Ruth. Represented in various exhibns. Recipient numerous prizes including Psi Iota, Xi Award, 1945, Gov. Gates Purchase Award and First Landscape Award, Ind. Artists Club, Annual Exhibit, 1945; Mr. and Mrs. Charles Lynn Landscape Award, Ind. Artists Club, Annual Exhibit, 1946; Bruce C. Kixmiller prize, Hoosier Salon, 1952. Mem. Brown County Guild, Brown County Art Gallery Assn. (charter mem., sec., treas., 1926-48; pres. 1934-36, 44). Ind. Artists (1st v.p., 1944, pres., 1945-47), Hoosier Salon Assn. (Chicago), Chicago Galleries Assn., Fla. Federated Art Clubs (Manatee County Art Assn.), Ind. Soc. of Chicago, Sigma Nu. Republican. Methodist. Mason. Home: Nashville, Ind. Died Jan. 5, 1974; interred Crown Hill, Indpls.

BEST, CHARLES HERBERT, physiologist, educator; b. West Pembroke, Me., Feb. 27, 1889; s. Herbert Huestis and Luella (Fisher) B.; B.A., U. Toronto (Ont., Can.), 1921, M.A., 1922, M.D., 1925, LL.D., 1970; D.Sc., U. London (Eng.), 1928, U. Chgo., 1941, Paris, 1945, Cambridge U., 1946, Oxford U., 1947, Laval U., 1952, U. Me., 1955, Northwestern U., 1959, Laurentian U., 1971; hon. degrees univs. of Chile, Uruguay, San Marcos, Peru; Dr. Medicine h.c., univs. of Amsterdam, Louvain, Liege, 1947; LL.D., Dalhousie U., 1949, Queens U., 1950, U. Melbourne, 1952, U. Edinburgh, 1959; Hon. Dr., Central U. Venezuela, 1958; Dr. Medicine h.c., Thessaloniki, 1963, (hon.), Freie U. Berlin, 1966, Ottawa, 1972; Ph.D., Hebrew U. Jerusalem, 1971; M.D. (hon.), U. Zagreb, 1976; m. Margaret Hooper Mahon, Sept. 3, 1924; children—Charles Alexander, Henry Bruce Macleod. With U. Toronto, 1920—, fellow dept. physiology, 1920-21, research mem. Counaught Labs., 1922-32, research asso. Banting-Best Dept. Medicine Research, 1923-41, dir., 1941-67, emeritus, 1967-78, asst. prof. physiol. hygiene, 1926-29, acting head dept. physiol. hygiene, 1929-41, prof. physiology, 1929-78, head dept., 1929-65, dir. emeritus, 1967-78, grad. lectr., 1965-78; asso. dir. Counaught Labs., 1932-41. Mem. adv. com. med. research WHO, 1963-78; mem. bd. sci. dirs. Jackson Lab. Trustee Nutrition Found. Served as sgt. 70th Battery, 2d Canadian Tanks Corps, with B.E.F., World War I; dir. med. research div. Royal Canadian Navy, surgeon with rank of capt., World War II. Discoverer of insulin with F.G. Banting, 1921. Instrumental in initiation of Canadian serum project for provision of dried human serum of mil. use. Decorated knight comdr. Mil. and Hospitaller Order St. Lazarus of Jerusalem; F.N.G. Starr gold medal Canadian Med. Assn., 1936, Charles Mickle fellowship Council of Faculty Medicine, U. Toronto, 1939; Baly medal Royal Coll. Physicians, 1939; Flavelle medal Royal Soc. Can., 1950; Order Brit. Empire (civil), 1944, Legion of Merit (U.S.), 1947; King Haakon VI Cross of Liberation (Norway) 1947; comdr. Order of Crown, Belgium, 1948; John Phillips Meml. medal A.C.P., 1953; J. Howard Reber medal Phila. Metabolic Assn., 1955; Banting medal Am. Diabetes Assn.; Croonian lectr. The Royal Soc., 1955; Civic award of merit Toronto, 1958; Dale medal Soc. for Endocrinology, 1959; commemorative medal Czechoslovak Soc. Phys. Medicine, 1962; grand silver medal City of Paris, 1962; 1st Joslin medal New Eng. Diabetes Assn., 1965; Centennial medal, 1967; companion Order of Can., 1967, comdr. Order Brit. Empire; Companion of Honor, 1971; Brazil Sci. Biennal award, 1971; Gairdner Found. Internat. award, 1971. Fellow Royal Soc. London, Royal Soc. Can., Royal Soc. Edinburgh, Royal Coll. Phys. and Surg. Can., Physiol. Soc., Biochem. Soc. (Eng.), Royal Coll. Physicians (Edinburgh), Toronto Acad. Medicine (hon.), Med. Soc. London (hon.); mem. Am. Soc. Clin. Nutrition (hon.), Am. Diabetic Assn. (hon., pres. 1948, council), Brit. Diabetic Assn. (v.p.), Canadian Diabetic Assn. (hon. pres.), Am. Acad. Arts and Sci., Royal Acad. Scis., Amsterdam, Royal Soc. Medicine, Canadian, Ont. med. assns., Canadian Assn. Gastroenterology (hon.), Acad. Royal de Med. Belgique, Soc. de Farmacol., Buenos Aires, Am. (council), Canadian physiol. socs., Am. Soc. Biol. Chem., Am. Soc. Clin. Investigation, Nat. Acad. Scis. (fgn. asso.), Am. Philos. Soc., Assn. Am. Physicians, Internat. Union Physiol. Scis. (1st pres. 1953), Physiol. Soc. Gt. Britain (hon.), European Assn. for Study Diabetes (hon.), Pontificial Acad. Scis., Toronto Bd. Trade (hon.), Nu Sigma Nu (pres. hon. council 1948), Alpha Omega Alpha. Clubs: Athenaeum, Canadian (hon.), York Downs Golf (hon.). Author: (with F.G. Banting) The Internal Secretion of the Pancreas (original publ. on insulin), 1922; (with N.B. Taylor) The Physiological Basis of Medical Practice, 9th edit., 1973;

The Human Body, 4th edit., 1963; The Living Body, 4th edit.; Selected Papers of Charles H. Best, 1963; also numerous publs. on insulin, histaminase, muscular exercise, choline, carbohydrate and fat metabolism, heparin, shock. Home: Toronto, Ont., Can. Died Mar. 31, 1978; interred Mount Pleasant Cemetery, Toronto.

BEST, GORDON, advt. exec.; b. Chgo., Mar. 18, 1895; s. Herbert and Elizabeth K. (Daw) B.; student Northwestern U., 1914-15; m. Marion Burton Shapland, July 7, 1917; children—Stanley G., George H., William R., John Howard, Richard B. Copy writer McJunkin Advt. Co., 1917-24, v.p., 1924-41, pres., 1941-47; pres. Gordon Best Co., Inc., Chgo., 1947-60, chmn. bd., 1960-62; also dir. Treas., Church Home for Aged Persons, Chgo. Episcopalian. Clubs: Chgo. Federated Advertising, Church, Builders (Chgo.). Home: Kenilworth, Ill. Died Sept. 13, 1976.

BETZ, CARL, actor; b. Pitts., Mar. 9; student Duquesne U., Carnegie Inst. Tech. Profl. debut in Pitts. summer stock company; Broadway debut in The Long Watch; films include Powder River, Dangerous Crossing; TV appearances in Love of Life; The Donna Reed Show; Judd For the Defense. Served with AUS, 1942. Recipient Emmy award 1968. Died Jan. 18, 1978.

BEVERIDGE, THOMAS ROBINSON, geologist, educator; b. Sandwich, Ill., June 30, 1918; s. Merritt Hoy and Isabelle Beveridge (Robinson) B.; B.S., Monmouth Coll., 1939; B.S. in Mining Engring., Mo. Sch. Mines, 1942; M.S., U. Iowa, 1947, Ph.D., 1949; m. Nancy Mary Lytle, June 12, 1946; children—Nancy L., Mary I. Geologist Iowa Geol. Survey, 1945-47; instr. U. Iowa, 1947-49; geologist Mo. Geol. Survey, 1949-55, state geologist and dir., 1955-64; prof. geology and geophysics U. Mo. at Rolla, from 1964, chmn. dept. geology and geophysics, from 1965. Served with Ill. N.G., 1936-40; 1st lt. USAAF, 1943-45. Fellow Geol. Soc. Am.; mem. Sigma Xi. Presbyn. Home: Rolla, Mo. Died Aug. 24, 1978; buried Oak Mound Cemetery, Somonauk, Ill.

BEVERSDORF, SAMUEL THOMAS, composer, educator; b. Yoakum, Tex., Aug. 8, 1924; s. Samuel T. and Estelle M. (Hamblen) B.; Mus.B. cum laude (Hoblitzel fellow), U. Tex., 1945; Mus.M., Eastman Sch. Music, U. Rochester (N.Y.), 1946, Dr. Mus. Arts (Danforth fellow), 1959; m. Norma Iris Beeson, June 26, 1945; children—Anne Elizabeth, Paula Lynn Gabbard, Sarah Katherine, Samuel Thomas III, David Quentin. First trombonist Houston Symphony Orch., 1946-48, resident composer, 1946-48; instr. music composition U. Houston, 1946-48; bass trombonist Pitts. Symphony Orch., 1948-49; faculty Sch. Music, Ind. U., Bloomington, 1951-81, prof. music composition, 1964-81; composer-in-residence, guest prof. Bucknell U., Lewisburg, Pa., 1970-71; guest condr. Indpls. Symphony Orch., 1951, Houston Symphony Orch., 1951, Eastman-Rochester Summer Symphony Orch., 1957; world premieres include: Christmas Sonata for horn and piano, Eastman Sch. Music, 1946, Symphony No. 1, Eastman-Rochester Symphony Orch., N.Y., 1946, Reflections for small orch., Houston Symphonette, 1950, Suite on Baroque Themes for clarinet, violincello and piano, U. Houston, 1948, Mexican Portrait, Houston Symphony, 1948, Concerto Grosso, Pitts. Symphony, 1951, Quartet No. 1, Berkshire Quartet, Bloomington, Ind., 1952, Symphony for Winds and Percussion, Ind. U. Wind Ensemble, 1954, Quartet No. 2, Berkshire Quartet, Bloomington, 1956, Symphony No. 3 for Orch., Ind. U. Philharmonic Orch., 1958, Serenade for small orch., U. Tex., 1956, Sonata for Tuba and Piano, Oreg. U., 1956, Serenade for Winds and Percussion, Eastman Wind Ensemble, Rochester, 1958, The Rock (Oratorio), Bloomington, 1958, Concerto for Violin and Orch., Eastman-Rochester Symphony, 1957, Symphony No. 4, Ind. U. Philharmonic Orch., 1960, Variations for Piano, CBC, 1959, Sonata for Trumpet and Piano, Ind. U., 1962, Variations for Orch., Ind. U. Orch., 1963, Sonata for Violin and Piano, Festival of Am. Music, Rochester, 1964, Sonata for Flute and Piano, Pan Am. Festival Contemporary Music, 1965, Generation with the Torch, Bayreuth, Germany, 1965, Divertimento da Camera for flute, oboe, double bass, harpsichord, Hanover Coll., 1968, Sonata for Violincello and Piano, San Francisco Jewish Community Center, 1970; works commd.; Houston Symphony Orch., 1953, Ind. U., 1967, Cin. Symphony, 1953, Teltschik duo Pianists, 1951, Variations for Piano, B. Borzormenyi-Nagy, 1959, Houston Youth Orch., 1964, Bucknell U., 1970, Concerto for Tuba, Harvey Phillips, 1975, Sonata for Violin and Harp, Jacques Israelievitch, 1975. Served with USAAF, World War II. Recipient Disting. Served to Music award Tex. Fedn. Music Clubs, 1970. Mem. ASCAP (Spl. award 1965-79), Am. Fedn. Musicians, AAUP, Phi Mu Alpha Sinfonia, Pi Kappa Lambda. Club: Masons. Author-librettist The Rock, 1956; (operas) The Hooligan, 1964, The Metamorphosis, 1968. Transcribed various 18th Century mus. compositions for trombone and piano. Home: Bloomington, Ind. Died Feb. 15, 1981.

BEVIN, NEWTON PHILO, architect; b. East Hampton, Conn., Oct. 4, 1895; s. Samuel Mills and Julia (Williams) B., Litt.B., Princeton, 1917, postgrad., 1919; B.Arch., U. Pa., 1922; m. Elizabeth Hopkins, June 25, 1936. Architect, Milliken & Bevin, N.Y.C., 1927-44; head firm Newton P. Bevin, Architect, N.Y.C., 1944-76. Served to 1st lt. U.S. Army, 1917-18; AEF in France. Recipient Ward Melville certificate for Washington (Conn.) community improvement, 1960. Mem. A.I.A., Nat. Inst. Archtl. Edn., N.A.D. Republican. Presbyn. Club: Century (N.Y.C.). Prin. works include residences of Anderson, Mt. Kisco, N.Y., 1930, de Waal, Lexington, Ky., 1938, Shelden, Grosse Pointe, Mich., 1954, Pratt, Frijole, Tex., 1942, Whittemore, Middlebury, Conn., 1961; offices of Telanswer Phone, 1946, N.Y. Airbrake Co., 1953, Rheem Mfg. Co., 1954 (all N.Y.C.); restoration Washington Depot, Conn., 1955. Home: New York, N.Y. Died Oct. 9, 1976; buried Lakeview Cemetery, East Hampton, Conn.

BEYEN, JOHAN WILLEM, diplomat; b. Utrecht, Netherlands, May 2, 1897; s. Karel Herman and Louise Maria (Coenen B.; grad. in jurisprudence, Univ. of Utrecht, 1918; m. 2d, Margaretha Antonia Lubinka, Nov. 14, 1945; children (by previous marriage)—Karel Herman, Frederique, Jan Willem. In Ministry of Finance, 1918-23, dep. treas. gen., 1921-23; legal adviser Philips Incandescent Lamps, 1924-25; mgr. Amsterdam office Javasche Bank, 1925-27; mgr. dir. Rotterdamsche Bankvereniging, 1927-35; alternate to pres., Bank for Internat. Settlements, 1935-37; pres., 1937-40; financial dir. Lever Bros. and Unilever, Ltd. 1940-46; financial adviser Netherlands govt., from 1940; became exec. dir. Netherlands and Norway Internat. Bank for Reconstruction and Development, 1946; exec. dir. Internat. Monetary Fund, 1948; minister of fgn. affairs, The Hague, Netherlands, 1952-56; govt. Commr. for German Affairs, 1956-57; Netherlands ambassador to France, from 1958. Home: Paris, France. Died Apr. 29, 1976.

BHAKTIVEDANTA, ABHAY CHARANARAVINDA (SWAMI PRABHUPADA), author; b. Calcutta, India, Sept. 1, 1896; s. Gour Mohan and Rajani (Dasi) De; B.A., Scottish Chs. Coll., Calcutta, 1920; m. Srimati Radharani Dutt, June 1918; several children. Mgr. chem. factory, Calcutta; owner pharmacy, Allahabad, India; preacher in India, from 1954, U.S., from 1965; founder acarya of Internat. Soc. for Krishna Consciousness; spiritual master Hare Krishna Movement. Recipient title Bhaktivedanta, 1947; spiritual status of sannyas, 1959. Author: Teachings of Lord Caitanya, 1968; Sri Isopanishad, 1969; The nectar of Devotion, 1970; Easy Journey to Other Planets, 1970; Krishna Consciousness: The Topmost Yoga System, 1970; Krishna, The Supreme Personality of Godhead (3 vols.), 1970; Transcendental Teachings of Prahlad Maharaja, 1972; Krishna the Reservoir of Pleasure, 1972; The Perfection of Yoga, 1972; Beyond Birth and Death, 1972; On the Way to Krishna, 1972; Raja-vidya: The King of Knowledge, 1972; Elevation to Krishna Consciousness, 1972; Bhagavad-gita As It Is, 1972; Srimad Bhagavatam, 30 vols., 1972-77; Lord Caitanya in Five Features, 1973; Sri Caitanya-caritamrita, 17 vols., 1973-75; Krishna Consciousness: The Matchless Gift, 1974. Founder, Back to Godhead mag., 1944. Address: Bombay, India. Died Nov. 14, 1977; buried Vrindavan, Mathura, India.

BIANCHI, JOÃO A(NTONIO) DE (BE-ÄN'KE), diplomat; b. Funchal, Madeira Island, Dec. 19, 1884; s. Viscount de Valle Paraiso and Maria Conceicão Lyra; married. Began career as sec. Portuguese Embassy, London, 1915; sec. gen. Portuguese delegation to Peace Conf., Paris, 1919; spl. del. to S. Africa with rank of minister, 1922; at London as minister, counsellor; del. of Treasury, 1923-25; minister to China, 1925-29; chief of polit. and colonial dept. of Ministry for Fgn. Affairs, Lisbon, 1930-33; minister to U.S. 1933-34; ambassador to the U.S., 1944-47; sec. gen. Portuguese Fgn. Office, 1947-48; ambassador to Brazil since 1948. Decorated Grand Cross of the Order of Christ; Comdr. Order of St. Thiago of Portugal. Address: Rio de Janeiro, Brazil. *

BIBB, THOMAS WILLIAM, coll. prof.; b. Montgomery, Mo., June 28, 1884; s. Martin Luther and Mary Elizabeth (Cushman) B.; A.B. William Jewell Coll., Liberty, Mo., 1908; A.M., U. of Wash., 1926, Denny fellow, 1927-28, Ph.D., 1928; m. Mabelle Ila Dunbar, July 2, 1913; children—Martha Virginia, Thomas William. Supt. schsl, Grays Harbor County, Wash., Central Wash. Coll. of Edn., 1920-25; pres. Lewis and Clark College, 1929-38, Mo. Valley Coll., 1938-43; resigned Sept. 1943; now prof. econ. and business, Whitworth Coll. Pres. Mo. Coll. Union, 1942. Mem. Am. Palestine Com., Com. for Jewish Army of Stateless and Palestinian Jews, War Sav. Ednl. Com.; mem. Nat. Edn. Assn., Soc. Mayflower Descendants, Phi Delta Kappa, Pi Gamma Mu (provincial gov.), Sigma Nu. Republican. Presbyn. Mason. Rotarian. Author: History of Early Common School Education in Washington, 1929; (with Frederick E. Bolton) History of Education in Washington, 1934. Contbr. to ednl. jours. Address: Spokane, Wash. *

BIBERMAN, JACOB M., clothing co. exec.; b. Russia, 1884; s. Moses and Muriel (Herman) B.; brought to U.S., 1893, naturalized by Act of Congress; m. Fannie Nahin, June 9, 1908; three children. Vice chairman, treasurer, finance dir. L'Aiglon Apparel, Inc., Phila., 1961—. Jewish. Mason. Club: Green Valley Country. Home: Phila. *

BICKEL, KARL AUGUST, editor; b. Geneseo, Ill., Jan. 20, 1882; s. William August and Emily (Anderson) B.; educated Stanford University; m. Helen Madira Davis. Editor Grand Junction, Colo., Daily News, 1908-13; with United Press, 1913-35, pres., 1923-35; apptd. mem. Press Div., Office Co-ordinator Inter-American Affairs (Pan. Am. relations) Oct. 1940; mem. operating com. Ringling Mus.; mem. Fla. bd. of Parks, Historic Memorials, 1949-53. Clubs: University (Tampa, Florida); Metropolitan, Nat. Press (Wash.); Longboat (Fla.) Cabana; Sarasota (Fla.) Country. Author: New Empires-The Newspaper and Radio, 1930; The Mangrove Coast, 1941. Home: Sarasota, Fla.*

BICKFORD, FAITH, school prin.; b. Cambridge, Mass., July 15, 1882; d. Rev. Thomas and Anna Maria (Searl) B.; unmarried. Prin. Sea Pines Sch. for Girls; dir. Sea Pines Camp. Mem. New England Association Colls. and Secondary Schs., Pvt. Sch. Assn. of Boston, Progressive Edn. Assn., Mary Hemenway Alumnae Assn. (grad. dept. of hygiene and phys. edn., Wellesley Coll.), Camp Directors Association, Amy Morris Homan's Club. Author: Daddy Joe's Fiddle, 1903; Gloria, 1904. Address: Brewster on Cape Cod, Mass.*

BICKNELL, JOHN W., consultant plantation div., U.S. Rubber Co.; b. Malden, Mass., Dec. 5, 1886; s. Joseph L. and Louise (Beal) B.; A.B., Harvard, 1909; m. Florence Macdonald, Oct. 19, 1910. Mng. dir. Holland Am. Plantations Co., Si Pare Pare Rubber Co., Nederland Langkat Rubber Co., Malayan Am. Plantation, Ltd., cons. plantation div., U.S. Rubber Co., N.Y. City. Clubs: Harvard, (N.Y. City); East India and Sports (London). Home: Hopewell Jct., Dutchess County, N.Y. *

BIDDISON, PASCAL MCDONALD, cons. engr.; b. Lane, Kan., Dec. 13, 1884; s. Valeda Hull and Kate (Hawes) B.; B.S., Kan. State Coll., 1904; m. Christine M. Walker, Dec. 22, 1945. Cons. engr. in gen. practice, Dallas, 1941-42, Chicago, 1943-50, Tulsa since 1950. Served as cons. engr. on war gases U.S. Bureau of Mines, 1917-18; in Office of War Utilities, W.P.B., 1942-43. Fellow Am. Soc. M.E. Tech. Valuation Soc.; mem. Am. Inst. Mining and Metall. Enrs., Am. Gas Assn., Southern Gas Assn., Pacific Coast Gas Assn., Soc. Am. Mil. Engrs., A.A. A.S., Beta Theta Pi, Phi Kappa Phi. Registered profl. engr., Tex., Okla., and Ill. Contbr. tech. papers and articles to various publs.; also author of numerous reports of investigations relating to property values and estimates of natural gas and oil projects conducted since 1930.

BIDDLE, FRANCIS, lawyer, formerly atty. gen. of the United States; b. in Paris, France, May 9, 1886; s. of Algernon Sydney and Frances (Robinson) Biddle; brought to America in infancy; student Haverford (Pa.) Sch., 1895-99, Groton (Mass.) Sch., 1899-1905; B.A., cum laude, Harvard, 1909, LL.B., cum laude, 1911; LL.D., La Salle Coll., Boston U., 1942; Drexel Institute, Hobart and William Smith Colleges, 1943; m. Katherine Garrison Chapin, Apr. 27, 1918; children—Edmund Randolph, Garrison Chapin (dec.). Admitted to Pa. Bar, 1912; private sec. to Justice Holmes, U.S. Supreme Court, 1911-12; associate Biddle, Paul & Jayne, Phila., 1912-15, Barnes, Biddle & Myers, Phila., 1917-39; special asst. U.S. atty., Eastern Dist. Pa., 1922-26; Class C dir. Fed. Reserve Bank, 1938-39, dep. chmn., 1938-39; chief counsel Joint Com. to investigate Tenn. Valley Authority, 1938-39; judge U.S. Circuit Court of Appeals, 3d Circuit, 1939-40; solicitor general of U.S., 1940; attorney gen. of U.S., Sept. 1941-June 30, 1945; U.S. member International Military Tribunal, 1945-46. Former mem. Permanent Court of Arbitration. Admitted to practice before Supreme Court of the United States, 1927. Served in U.S. Army, Oct. 23-Nov. 29, 1918. Chmn. Phila. Branch Foreign Policy Assn., 1924-39; chmn. Nat. Labor Relations Bd., 1934-35; mem. Gov. Pinchot's Commn. on Special Policing in Industry, 1934; mem. Phila. County Board of Law Examiners, 1923-32; mem. bd. of Pub. Edn., Phila., 1936-39; chmn. national com. Am. Civil Liberties Union. Mem. Franklin Delano Roosevelt Memorial Commission; mem. bd. trustees Twentieth Century Fund (N.Y.). Hon. bencher. Inner Temple (London, England), 1946; Four Freedoms award, 1942; Order of Merit, Italy, 1954. National chmn. Ams. for Democratic Action, 1950-53; del. at large from Pa. Nat. Dem. Conv., 1944, delegate from D.C., 1952. Democrat. Mem. Am. Acad. of Arts and Sciences. Clubs: Cosmos (Washington, D.C.); Philadelphia, Legal (Phila.); Coffee House (N.Y.C.). Author: Llanfear Pattern, 1927; Mr. Justice Holmes, 1942; Democratic Thinking and the War, 1944; The World's Best Hope, 1949; The Fear of Freedom, 1951; A Casual Past, 1961; Justice Holmes, Natural Law and the Supreme Court, 1961; In Brief Authority, 1962. Contbr. to legal publs. Home: Washington also Wellfleet, Mass. *

BIDDLE, JOHN HUNTER, publisher, banker, assn. exec.; b. Everett, Pa., July 29, 1905; s. Joseph Franklin and Anna Patton (Hunter) B.; A.B., Haverford Coll., 1927; student Juniata Coll., 1961-62; m. Helen Isabella Read, Aug. 23, 1933; children—Townley (Mrs. Robert Harold Neill), Joseph F. II, John Read, Andrew Christopher Reeves, Anne Patton Hunter. Editor The Daily News, Huntingdon, Pa., 1927-36, pub., 1936-73; pres. Gazette Pub. Co., also Inquirer Printing Co., Bedford, Pa., 1936-73; v.p. Prog. Pub. Co., Clearfield, Pa., 1944-73; pres. Huntingdon Broadcasters, Inc. (Pa.), 1947; pres. WBFD, 1950-73, WAKM, Bedford, 1967-73; v.p. Niles Pub. Co. (O.), 1961-67, v.p. Apache Pub. Co., Glendale, Ariz., 1963-65; pres. Grange Trust Co., Huntingdon, 1955-58; pres., chief exec. officer successor bank Penn Central Nat. Bank, 1962-68, chmn. bd., 1969-77; chmn. bd. First Nat. Bank, Bedford, 1965-77, also dir.; sta. WDAD, Indiana, Pa. Past mem. sponsoring com. Pa. Prison Soc.; sec. Huntingdon County Tb Soc., 1933-62; pres. Pa. Tb and Health Soc., 1950-54; councillor Internat. Union Against Tb, Paris, 1953, Madrid, 1954, Moscow, 1971. Mem. Huntingdon Municipal Council, 1944-60; mem. Pa. Republican Com., 1950-68. Bd. dirs. Nat. Tb and Respiratory Disease Assn., pres., 1971-72; trustee Luth. Theol. Sem., Gettysburg, Pa., 1950-56, Pa. Correctional instn., Huntingdon, 1939-55, Grier Sch. for Girls, 1959-73. Named Newspaperman of Year Pa. Press Conf., 1956. Mem. Pa. Newspaper Pubs. Assn. (pres. 1947), Nat. Newspaper Assn. (treas. 1959-66, pres. 1967-68). Mason. Clubs: Nat. Press (Washington); Union League (Phila.); Dartmouth House (London, Eng.); Huntingdon Country; Spruce Creek (Pa.) Rod and Gun; British Club, El Campo de Golf, Real Club Nautico (Las Palmas de Gran Canaria, Spain). Home: Huntingdon, Pa. Died May 14, 1977; interred Friends Cove, Trinity Ch., Bedford County, Pa.

BIDGOOD, LEE, prof. economics; b. Norfolk County, Va., Feb. 2, 1884; s. Willis Deanes and Belle (Mackan) B.; B.A., U. of Va., 1905, M.A., 1906; LL.D., U. of Ala., 1923; D.S.C. hon(oris) c(ausa), New York University, 1950; m. Emily Smith, June 14, 1916; children—Mary Emmeline, Lee, Willis Deanes, Anne Morris. Head dept. of history and social sciences, State Normal Sch., Farmville, Va., 1906-09; fellow in economics, U. Wis., 1909-10; grad. student and asst., same, 1910-11; adj. prof. economics, U. of Va., 1911-12; instr. economics, U. of Wis., 1912-13; prof. economics, U. of Ala., since 1913, also dean Sch. Commerce and Business Adminstrn. since 1919. Mem. Am. Assn. Collegiate Schs. of Bus. (pres. 1949-50), Am. Econ. Assn. So. Econ. Assn. (past pres.), Alabama Conference of Social Work. (ex-pres.), Phi Beta Kappa, Delta Sigma Rho, Alpha Kappa Psi, Beta Gamma Sigma. Democrat. Presbyterian. Author: (with C. W. Alvord) First Explorations of the Trans-Allegheny Region, 1912; (with E. W. Gregory, Jr.) Introductory Sociology: A Study of American Society, 1939. Home: Tuscaloosa, Ala. *

BIDWELL, ABEL TROOD, naval officer; b. Bellefonte, Pa., Sept. 19, 1885; s. Henry Martin and Mary (Parker) B.; B.S., U.S. Naval Acad., 1908; M.A., Columbia U., 1915; m. Alpha Grace Hafer, Sept. 1, 1914; children—Robert Gordon, James Collins. Became midshipman, U.S. Navy, 1904, and advanced through to grades to rear adm., 1941; served as exec. officer, U.S.S. Birmingham on convoy duty, Gibraltar to Plymouth, Eng., during World War; comdr. U.S.S. Gregory, 1918-19, U.S.S. Bushnell, 1933-35, U.S.S. Chicago, 1938-39; dir. officer of personnel, Bur. of Navigation, Navy Dept., 1940; asst. chief, Bur. of Navigation, since 1940. Received Victory medal (with convoy clasp), 1917; 2d Nicaraguan Campaign medal, 1928. Club: Army and Navy (Washington, D.C.). Home: Bellefonte, Pa.*

BIELASKI, FRED, communications co. exec.; b. Washington, Feb. 28, 1898; s. Alexander and Roselle (Woodward) B.; B.S., St. John's Coll., 1916; LL.B., Columbia, 1924; m. Rosalyn Calais, Sept. 2, 1924; children—Ruth (Mrs. Frank H. Balsley), Patricia. Admitted to N.Y. bar, 1924; law clk. Simpson, Thacher & Bartlett, N.Y.C., 1923-25; pres. Standard Oil Co., Lima, Peru, 1926-27, Cia. Impulsora de Empresas Electricas, Mexico City, 1928-30; with Electric Bond & Share Co., Mexico City, 1928-30, Argentina, 1930-42; with ITT cos., Mexico City, 1945-79, v.p. indsl. and pub. relations, 1945-46, v.p., gen. mgr., 1947-50, sr. rep. Internat. Standard Elec. Corp., Mexico, 1950-60, pres., dir. Standard Electrica de Mexico, 1955-79; pres. ITT Mexico, 1968-79. Served to 2d lt., inf., U.S. Army, 1917-19, from maj. to lt. col., AUS, 1942-45. Mem. Mexican Assn. Indsl. Relations Chiefs (hon.), Am. Legion. Clubs: Bankers, Univ. (Mexico City). Home: Mexico City. Died Aug. 7, 1979.

BIENFANG, RALPH DAVID, educator; b. Jefferson, Wis., Jan. 15, 1905; s. John Matthew and Nellie (Arnold) B.; student U. Colo., 1922-23; B.S., U. Wis., 1926, M.S., 1927, Ph.D., 1929; m. Bess Irene Marriott, June 27, 1934; 1 dau., Jane Marriott B. (Mrs. James G. Harlow, Jr.). Prof., Conn. Coll. Pharmacy, 1929-30; asst. prof. pharmacognosy U. Okla., Norman, 1930-37, asso. prof., 1937-41, prof., 1941-42, prof. pharmacy, 1942-65, David Ross Boyd prof., 1965-75, emeritus, 1975. Mem. Am. Pharm. Assn., Wis. Hist. Soc., Sociedade de Farmacia e Quimica de Sao Paulo (hon.), Sociedade de Farmacia de Rio de Janeiro (hon.), Poetry Soc. Okla., Sigma Xi, Rho Chi, Phi Sigma, Kappa Psi, Alpha Sigma Phi. Lutheran. Lion. Contbg. author: Excellence in University Teaching. Writer of Poetry. Home: Norman, Okla. Died Dec. 11, 1975.

BIER, WILLIAM CHRISTIAN, clergyman, psychologist; b. Bklyn., May 1, 1911; s. Christian J. and Adelaide M. (Kraus) B.; A.B., Woodstock Coll., 1934, Ph.L., 1935, S.T.L., 1941; M.A., Fordham U., 1939; Ph.D., Catholic U. Am., 1948. Entered Soc. of Jesus, 1928; ordained priest Roman Cath. Ch., 1940; instr. dept. psychology Fordham U. Grad. Sch., 1948-51, asst. prof., 1951-55, asso. prof., 1955-66, prof., 1966-80, also chmn. dept., 1958-68, asso. acad. v.p., 1973-80. Recipient award for excellence in teaching Fordham U., 1968. Fellow Am. Psychol. Assn.; mem. Am. Cath. Psychol. Assn. (a founder), Insts. Religion and Health (profl. bd.). Editor: Pastoral Psychology Series, 1962-80. Home: Bronx, N.Y. Died March 6, 1980; buried Auriesville, N.Y.

BIERMANN, FRED, ex-congressman; b. Rochester, Minn., Mar. 20, 1884; s. Ewald and Martha (Christopher) B.; student U. of Minn., 1901-04; A.B., Columbia, 1905; student Valder Coll., 1905-06, Harvard Law Sch., 1907-08; m. Adel Rygg, Jan. 25, 1930. Editor and pub. Decorah (Ia.) Jour., 1908-31; mem. 73d to 75th Congresses (1933-39), 4th Ia. Dist.; U.S. Marshal, Northern Dist. of Ia., since 1940. Postmaster, Decorah, 1913-23, park commr. since 1923. Del. Dem. Nat. Conv., 1928, 40. Served as lieut., U.S. Army, World War. Rep. of U.S. Congress at Interparliamentary Union Conf. Paris, 1937. Pres. Decorah Chamber of Commerce, 1923. Mem. Vets of Foreign Wars, Am. Legion. Democrat. Mason, Elk. Club: Oncota Golf and Country. Home: Decorah, Ia. *

BIERWIRTH, JOHN E., bus. exec.; b. Bklyn., Apr. 21, 1895; s. Julius Carl and Nettie Gheradine (Cocks) B.; A.B., Yale, 1917; m. Alice M. Von Bernuth, May 24, 1922; children—John Cocks, Nancy Elizabeth. Vice-pres., dir. Thompson-Starrett Co., Inc., contractors, 1919-29; v.p. N.Y. Trust Co., 1929-41, pres., trustee, 1941-49; pres. Nat. Distillers & Chem. Corp., 1949-58, chmn. bd., dir., chief exec. officer, 1958-70, chmn. bd., 1970, chmn. exec. com., to 1978; pres., dir. John DeKuyper & Son, Inc.; dir. Bridgeport Brass Co., Discount Corp., Reactive Metals, Inc., Merc. Stores Co., Miliken & Co. Hon. trustee Presbyn. Hosp., N.Y.C. Served as 1st lt. with A.E.F., U.S. Army, 1917-19. Clubs: Yale, Pinnacle, Union League (N.Y.C.); Rockaway Hunting, Lawrence Beach (L.I.). Home: Cedarhurst, N.Y. Died Apr. 3, 1978.

BIGARD, ALBANY BARNEY LEON, clarinetist; b. New Orleans, Mar. 3, 1906; s. Alexander and Emanuella (Marquez) B.; student Straight Coll., New Orleans, 1919-23; m. Dorothe Edgecomb; children—Winifred, Marlene, Patricia, Barney. With King Oliver, Chgo., 1925-27, Duke Ellington, 1927-42, Freddie Slack Band, 1942-44; leader 6-piece group Barney Bigard Sextette, 1944-47; joined Louis Armstrong All-Stars Concert Group, 1947, 3 European tours, Japan and Australia; African Good Will Tour for State Dept., 1960; also recs., TV and motion pictures; joined jazz group Los Angeles, 1956; free-lance concerts, recs., club work, from 1961; coll. Lectr. jazz history, from 1969; concert tour colls. and high schs., 1971, colls., 1974-75; appeared N.Y.C.-Newport Jazz Festival, 1974-75, European Jazz Festivals, 1974, Nice Festival, 1979; appeared jazz festivals, concerts, TV, also coll. jazz seminars, 1972; composer songs, including: Mood Indigo, Clouds in My Heart, Rocking in Rhythm, Minuet in Blues, Steps Steps Up and Steps Steps Down, Stompy Jones. Recipient Silver Jazz award Esquire, 1945, 46, 48; Gold award West Coast Lamplighter, 1943, 44, 45; award Hot Club of France, 1947, 64, award Nat. Acad. Rec. Arts and Scis., 1975, award Newport Jazz Hall of Fame, 1975, 2 Grammy awards. Mem. ASCAP. Home: Los Angeles, Calif. Died June 27, 1980. Buried Holy Cross Cemetery, Los Angeles.

BIGELOW, KARL WORTH, educator; b. Bangor, Maine, May 10, 1898; s. Bert Elmer and (Annie) Florence (Worth) B.; A.B., Clark U., 1920, L.H.D., 1938; student Cornell U., 1920-21; Ph.D., Harvard U., 1929; LL.D., Parsons Coll., 1941, Moravian Coll., 1963; D.Litt., U. East Africa, 1970; m. Margaret Johnson, Sept. 15, 1921 (dec. 1960); children—Mark Hamilton (dec.), David Hall, Stephen Colton, Paul Jay. Instr. econs. Cornell U., 1920-21; tutor, instr. econs. and sociology Harvard U., Radcliffe Coll., 1921-30; asst. prof. econs. U. Buffalo, 1930-31, prof., 1931-37; headmaster Park Sch. of Buffalo, 1933-35; vis. prof. edn. Tchrs. Coll., Columbia U., 1936-37, prof., 1937-63, prof. emeritus, 1963-80, dir. Inst. for Edn. in Africa, 1962-66; dir. Commn. Tchr. Edn., Am. Council Edn., 1938-44; dir. Afro-Anglo-Am. Program in Tchr. Edn., 1960-69; vis. lectr. U. London Inst. of Edn., 1958; Inglis lectr. Harvard Grad. Sch. Edn., 1964; cons. Assn. for Tchr. Edn. in Africa, 1969-78; mem. overseas liaison com. Am. Council of Edn., 1963-73, vice chmn., 1965-69, mem. panel consultants, 1973-78; chmn. com. sent by Dept. State to study relations of Am. vol. agys. with Germany and Austria, 1950; lectr., cons. UNESCO seminar on edn. for internat. understanding, France, 1947, dir. seminar edn. and tng. of tchrs., Eng., 1948; mem. U.S. nat. commn. UNESCO, 1948-54, U.S. mem. governing bd. Inst. for Edn., Germany, 1957-61; student higher edn. and tchr. tng. in Brit. Africa, under auspices Brit. Colonial Office, U. London Inst. Edn. and Inter-univ. Council for Higher Edn. in Colonies, 1952; del. Am. Assn. Colls. Tchr. Edn. to Am. Council Edn., 1951-56, mem. com. on studies, 1954-60; mem. council U. Zambia, 1964-73. Served with USN, 1917-19. Recipient Distinguished Service medal Tchrs. Coll., Columbia, 1970. Mem. AAUP, Phi Beta Kappa, Kappa Delta Pi, Phi Delta Kappa. Co-author books including: The Improvement of Teacher Education, 1946; General Education, 1952; Education and Foreign Affairs, 1965. Mem. editorial bd. Internat. Rev. of Edn., 1955-61, Tchr. Edn. in New Countries, 1962-72. Contbr. articles on gen., tchr., and African edn. to profl. publs. Home: Temple, N.H. Died Apr. 2, 1980.

BIGGS, EDWARD GEORGE POWER, concert organist; b. Westcliff, Eng., Mar. 29, 1906; s. Clarence Power and Alice Maud (Tredgett) B.; student Hurstpierpoint Coll., 1917-24; grad. Royal Acad. Music (Thomas Threfall Organ scholar), 1929; Mus.D. (hon.) Acadia U., Can., 1963, New Eng. Conservatory Music, Oberlin (Ohio) Coll., 1974; D.F.A. (hon.), Coe Coll.; m. Margaret Allen. Came to U.S., 1930, naturalized, 1937. Toured Eng., appearing in numerous historic cathedrals, Queen's Hall, London, 1929; N.Y. debut Wanamaker Auditorium, 1932; organ recitals CBS radio, 1942-58; concert tours throughout U.S., Can., Mexico, Europe, Australia; soloist N.Y. Philharmonic, Boston Symphony, Phila. Symphony, London Philharmonic, BBC, London, Morzarteum, Salzburg, Radio Can., Detroit Symphony, Chgo. Symphony, Milw. Symphony, others. Decorated knight comdr. Order of Isabella the Catholic; recipient Hubert Kiver Organ prize, 1929; citation for services to Am. music, Nat. Assn. Am. Composers and Condrs., 1952. Fellow Royal Acad. Music (hon.), Am. Acad. Arts and Scis., Royal Coll. Organists (hon.). Contbr. articles to mus. publs. Recs. for Columbia Records. Home: Cambridge, Mass. Died Mar. 10, 1977.

BILLHEIMER, ALBERT (BIL'HI-MER), educator; b. Reading, Pa., Aug. 23, 1886; s. Thomas Charles and Emma Catherine (Ziegler) B.; A.B., Gettysburg Coll., 1906; student U. Pa., 1908-09; A.M., Princeton, 1910, Ph.D., 1918; m. Mary Ruth Bream, Sept. 9, 1914; children—Thomas William, David Albert. Instr., Gettysburg (Pa.) Acad., 1906-08; prof. Greek Gettysburg (Pa.) Coll., 1912-30; asso. prof. classics N.Y.U., 1930-42, prof. classics, 1942-51, prof. emeritus since 1951. Mem. mng. com. Am. Sch. Classical Studies, Athens, Greece, 1939-51. Member Am. Philol. Assn., Archaeol. Inst. Am. (gen. sec. 1930-32), Sigma Chi, Phi Beta Kappa, Kappa Phi Kappa, Tau Kappa Alpha, Eta Sigma Phi, Alpha Phi Omega. Presbyn. Home: Tenafly, N.J. *

BILLINGSLEY, JOHN DABNEY, army officer; b. Fredericksburg, Va., Nov. 4, 1904; s. Addison Gordon and Ellie (Leavell) B.; B.S., U.S. Mil. Acad., 1928; B.S. in Mech. Engring., M.I.T., 1933; M.B.A., Harvard, 1947; grad. Nat. War Coll., 1949; m. Margaret Elizabeth Monk, Oct. 17, 1931; children—Elizabeth C. (Mrs. William W. Hill), John Dabney. Commd. 2d lt. F.A., U.S. Army, 1928, advanced through grades to col., 1943; ordnance officer, 1932-51; comdt. Ordnancce Sch., Aberdeen, Md., 1942-43; prof., head dept. ordnance U.S. Mil. Acad., 1951. Asso. mem. bd. visitors Ordnance Tng. Command, 1955-62, Ordnance Bd., 1956-62. Decorated D.S.M., Legion of Merit with oak leaf cluster, Bronze Star. Mem. Am. Soc. Engring. Edn., Am. Ordnance Assn., Nat. Sojourners. Mason (33 deg.). Home: West Point, N.Y. Died May 23, 1976.

BILLINGTON, RAY ALLEN, historian; b. Bay City, Mich., Sept. 28, 1903; s. Cecil and Nina (Allen) B.; Ph.B., U. Wis., 1926; M.A., U. Mich., 1927; Ph.D., Harvard, 1933; M.A., Oxford U., 1953; Litt.D., Bowling Green U., 1958, U. Redlands, 1965, Adrian Coll., 1979; LL.D. (hon.), Park Coll., 1961, Occidental Coll., 1969, U. Toledo, 1970; L.H.D., Northwestern U., 1971; Clark U., 1974; m. Mabel R. Crotty, Sept. 6, 1928; children—Anne, Allen. Instr., asst. prof. history Clark U., 1931-37; asst. prof. Smith Coll., 1937-38, asso. prof., 1938-44, prof., 1944; prof. history Northwestern U., 1944-49, William Smith Mason prof. history, 1949-63; sr. research asso. Huntington Library, 1963-81; Harmsworth prof. Am. history Oxford U., 1953. Guggenheim Meml. fellow, 1943-44; Schouler lectr. Johns Hopkins, 1944; Taft lectr. U. Cin., 1954; Blazer lectr. U. Ky., 1960; Harris lectr. Northwestern U., 1975; hon. cons. Library of Congress, 1974-77. Hist. editor Dryden Press, 1949-56, Rinehart and Co., 1956-60; hist. cons. Ency. Americana, 1962-69. Trustee Newberry Library; trustee Westerners Internat., pres., 1976-77; trustee Occidental Coll.; bd. dirs. Social Sci. Research Council. Fellow Hist. Soc. Calif.; mem. Am. Studies Assn. (pres. 1959-61), Am. Hist. Assn., Orgn. Am. Historians (pres. 1962-63), Hist. Assn. Eng. and Wales (hon.), So. Calif. Agrl. History Soc., So., Western (pres. 1962-63), Wash. State (hon.) history assns., Phi Beta Kappa, Phi Beta Kappa Assos., Hermitage Frat., Sigma Delta Chi. Author: The Protestant Crusade,

1938; Westward Expansion, 1949; American History Since 1865, 1950; American History Before 1877, 1951; The Far Western Frontier, 1830-1860, 1956; Historians' Contribution to Anglo-American Misunderstanding, 1966; America's Frontier Heritage, 1966; Genesis of Frontier Thesis, 1971; Frederick Jackson Turner, 1973 (Bancroft prize 1974); America's Frontier Culture, 1977; articles. Co-author: The United States, American Democracy in World Perspective, 1947; The Making of American Democracy, 1950. Editor: The Jours. of Charlotte L. Forten, 1953; The Westward Movement in the United States, 1959; Frontier and Section, 1961; The Frontier Thesis, 1966; The Reinterpretation of Early American History, 1966; America's Frontier Story, 1969; Dear Lady: The Letters of Frederick Jackson Turner and Alice Forbes Perkins Hooper, 1970; People of the Plains and Mountains, 1973; Allan Nevins on History, 1975; Histories of American Frontiers series, 1962-81. Bd. editors Am. Heritage, 1959-62, Ariz. and West, 1959-73, Am. West, 1962-81, America: History and Life, 1964-81, Pacific Historian, 1965-81, Western Historical Quar., 1970-75. Home: San Marino, Calif. Died Jan. 10, 1981.

BIMEL, FREDERICK B., chmn. Internat. Petroleum Co.; b. Huntsville, O., 1884. Chmn. bd. and dir. Internat. Petroleum Co., Ltd.; dir. Andian Nat. Corp., Internat. Ecuadorean Petroleum Co.; ret. Jan. 1, 1947. Home: Shreveport, La.; summer home: Port Severn, Ont. *

BING, KARL ROGER, mfg. co. exec.; b. Freeport, Ill., Oct. 13, 1926; s. Henry Hans and Martha Marie (Kurth) B.; B.A., Cornell Coll., Mt. Vernon, Iowa, 1950; m. Suzanne Mooney, May 19, 1956; children—David, Kathleen. With Ray-O-Vac Co. (now div. ESB Inc.), 1950-72, nat. distbn. sales mgr., Madison, Wis., 1960-65, v.p. mktg., 1966-72; exec. v.p. mktg. Newell Cos., Inc., Freeport, Ill., 1972-74; pres. Norwood Mills, 1975-77, Newell Window Furnishing Co., 1977-81; exec. v.p. and pres. Newell Operating Cos. Served with USAAF, World War II. Home: Madison, Wis. Died Jan. 31, 1981; buried Greenwood Cemetery, Broadhead, Wis.

BINGAY, JAMES SCLATER, life ins. co. exec.; b. Seattle, Oct. 10, 1919; s. Pierson Livingston and Janet Gibson (Sclater) B.; B.A., U. Wash., 1942; grad. advanced mgmt. program Harvard, 1960; m. Margaret Anita Blackstock, Mar. 4, 1942; children—James Sclater, Janis Lynn. With Mut. Life Ins. Co. N.Y., N.Y.C., 1945-76, v.p. sales, 1962-63, sr. v.p., 1963-67, exec. v.p., from 1967, pres., chief exec. officer, to 1976; chmn. MONY Life Can., MONY Reins. Corp.; dir. Carrier Crop., N.Am. Life & Casualty Co., Hart, Schaffner & Marx; mem. advisory bd. Life Ins. Exams. N.Y. State Dept. Ins. Trustee Am. Coll.; bd. dirs. Inst. Religion and Health; chmn. N.Y. Adv. Bd. Salvation Army; chmn., trustee S.S. Huebner Found. Ins. Edn. Mem. Life Ins. Agy. Mgmt. Assn., Agy. Officers Round Table, Life Underwriters Assn. N.Y.C., Sales Execs. Club N.Y.C., Am. Council Life Ins. (dir.); Theta Chi. Clubs: Innis Arden Country (Old Greenwich, Conn.); Metropolitan (N.Y.C.); Washington Athletic (Seattle). Home: Riverside, Conn. Died July 30, 1976.

BINGER, CARL A. L., psychiatrist; b. Long Branch, N.J., Aug. 26, 1889; s. Gustav and Frances (Newgass) B.; A.B., Harvard, 1910, M.D. cum laude, 1914; m. Clarinda Garrison, June 3, 1926; children—David G., Beatrice, Katherine G. Austin teaching fellow, lectr. on history sci. Harvard, 1914; study, tng., research, 1914-33; asst. attending physician N.Y. Hosp., 1933-47, asso. attending psychiatrist, 1947-54; asst. prof. clin. med. in psychiatry Cornell U. Med. Coll. and later asst. prof. clin. psychiatry, 1933-47, asso. prof., 1947-54; cons. psychiatrist Med. Dept. Radcliffe Coll., 1954-76; hon. cons. Harvard U. Health Services, 1964-76; vis. prof. psychiatry U. Cin. Med. Coll., 1956-68; ednl. cons. Psychiat. Tng. Faculty of Mass., 1956-58; spl. cons. psychiat. unit Peter Bent Brigham Hosp., Boston; lectr. psychiatry Harvard Med. School, Boston, 1954-56; vis. psychiatrist Mass. Gen. Hosp., 1954-58, hon. physician, 1958-76; with rehab. clinic Payne Whitney Clinic, 1943-46; cons. SSS, 1943-46; cons. neuropsychiatry VA, 1955-56; rev. editor Psychosomatic Medicine, 1945-47, editor-in-chief, 1947-62, mem. editorial bd., 1962-76; dir. Mary Conover Mellon Fund for Advancement of Edn. at Vassar Coll., 1949-51; chmn. com. to study neuropsychiat. problems in Tb, VA. Served as 1st lt. M.C. (A.E.F.), U.S. Base Hosp. No. 6, 1917-19. Awarded citation by Gen. Pershing, Purple Heart; Order of St. Geoge (Greece); Mil. medal of Greece. Diplomate Am. Bd. Internal Medicine, Am. Bd. Neurology and Psychiatry. Fellow A.M.A., Am. Acad. Arts and Scis., N.Y. Acad. Medicine, Am. Psychiat. Assn.; mem. Internat. Congress on Mental Health, Internat. Com. Mental Hygiene to WHO (mem. interim governing bd., exec. com.), Nat. Com. for Mental Hygiene (bd. dirs., del. to Internat. Congress on Mental Health, Eng., Aug. 1948, gave opening address Congress 1948), Mental Health Film Bd. (pres. 1952), Am., Mass. psychoanalytic assns., Mass. Med. Soc. Clin. Investigation, Assn. Psychoanalytic Med. Assn. (pres. 1943-44), Am. Psychosomatic Soc. (pres. 1963-64; a founder), Group Advancement Psychiatry (ex-chmn. com. on pub. edn.), Harvey Soc., Am. Legion, Alpha Omega. Clubs: Harvard, Century Assn. (N.Y.C.); Sakonnet Yacht. Author: The Doctor's Job, 1945 (winner Norton award 1945); Personality in Arterial Hypertension (monograph, with others), 1945; More About Psychiatry, 1949; Revolutionary Doctor, Benjamin Rush 1746-1813, 1966; The Two Faces of Medicine, 1966; Thomas Jefferson, a Well-Tempered Mind, 1970; also sci. popular articles. Address: Cambridge, Mass. Died Mar. 1976; interred at Little Compton, R.I.

BINGHAM, JAMES LYMAN, assn. exec.; b. Brookfield, Mo., Feb. 25, 1892; s. Lyman and Carrie Elizabeth (Van Brunt) B.; A.B., U. Denver, 1916; m. Helen Hess Wright, Aug. 20, 1919; children—Barbara Ann, Betty Jean. Instr. Loveland (Colo.) High Sch., 1916-17; dir. athletics U. Denver, 1919-30; asst. to pres. Amateur Athletic Union U.S., Chgo., 1930-50. Served as lt. F.A., U.S. Army, 1917-18, Gen. mgr. track and field athletics Olympic Games Los Angeles, 1932; sec. sport com. Chgo. Centry of Progress; mem. adv. com. N.Y. World's Fair; chef de mission and asst. treas. U.S. Winter Olympic Team, St. Moritz, Switzerland, also London, 1948, asst. treas., gen. mgr., Oslo Norway, 1952; gen. mgr. U.S. Olympic Team, Helsinki, Finland, 1952. Exec. dir. U.S. Olympic Assn., 1950-65; dir. fund raising U.S. Olympic Com., 1966-68; gen. mgr. U.S. Team, 1st Pan-Am. Games, Buenos Aires, 1951; gen. mgr. U.S. Team II Pan-Am. Games, Mexico City, 1955, Olympic winter games, Cortina, Italy, 1956, Melbourne, Australia, 1956, U.S. Team III, Pan Am. Games, Chgo., 1959, U.S. Olympic Team, Rome, Italy, 1960, Pan Am. Games, Sao Paulo Brazil, 1963, Winter Olympic Games, Innsbruck, Austria, 1964; chef de mission Games of XVIII Olympiad, Tokyo, Japan, 1964. Mem. Sigma Phi Epsilon. Republican. Baptist. Mason (Shriner). Home: Montrose, N.Y. Died Mar. 9, 1981.

BINGHAM, SIDNEY HEDLEY, transp. cons.; b. N.Y.C., Aug. 12, 1894; s. William and Ada E. (Hedley) B.; LL.D., Fordham U., 1953; Ed.D. (hon.), Cath. U., Santiago, Chile, 1954; D.S. (hon.), Duquesne U., 1955, Lafayette Coll., 1955. Engr. transp. Interborough Rapid Transit Co., N.Y.C., 1915-40; asst. to chmn. N.Y.C. Bd. Transp., 1945-46; gen. supt. N.Y.C. Transit System, 1946-47, commr., 1947-49, chmn., 1950; gen. mgr. N.Y.C. Transit Authority, 1953-56, exec. dir., gen. mgr., 1954-56; cons. r.r. and rapid transit, N.Y.C., 1956-80; prin. Col. S. H. Bingham Assos., Inc., N.Y.C., to 1980; cons. Disneyland Monorail. Served with U.S. Army, 1918-19, to col. AUS, 1942-45; ETO. Decorated Purple Heart, Legion of Merit, Bronze Star (U.S.); chevalier Legion of Honor, Croix de Guerre with palm (France); Order Leopold (Belgium); knight Order Brit. Empire (Eng.); knight Royal Order North Star (Sweden); Order Al Merito Bernardo O'Higgins (Chile); rosette d'Officier de la Légion d'Honneur; recipient medal Soc. des Ingenieurs Civils de France, 1955; registered profl. engr., N.Y. Fellow Cons. Engrs. Council Washington; mem. Am. Inst. Cons. Engrs., Nat. Panel Arbitrators, Assn. Cons. Engrs. Gt. Britain, Chambres des Ingenieurs-Conseils de France, ASME, Inst. Mech. Engrs., Engring. Inst. Can., Inst. Engrs. Chile, Inst. de Engrs., Nat., N.Y. State socs. profl. engrs., Municipal Engrs. City N.Y., Inst. Transp. Gt. Britain, Soc. des Ingrs. Civils de France, Soc. Am. Mil. Engrs., Order Lafayette, Ret. Officers Assn., Friendly Sons St. Patrick. Roman Catholic. Designer Bingham Bus. Address: New York, N.Y. Died May 3, 1980.

BINKERD, ROBERT STUDEBAKER, b. Dayton, Ohio, November 7, 1882; s. Oscar William and Emma (Brown) B.; Ph.B., Yale, 1904. Sec. Municipal Voters' League, Buffalo, N.Y., 1905-08, Citizens' Union, New York, 1908-09, City Club, New York, 1909-17; asst. to the chmn. Assn. of Ry. Executives, 1917-22; vice chmn. Com. on Pub. Relations of the Eastern Railroads, 1923-27; was partner investment house Jas. H. Oliphant & Co.; v.p., dir. of sales, Baldwin Locomotive Works (Phila.), 1931-38. Clubs: Railroad, Salmagundi, Yale (New York); Racquet, Art Club (Phila.). Home: South Lee, Mass. *

BINNEY, ARTHUR FREMONT, research analyst; b. Big Rapids, Mich., Nov. 25, 1905; s. Rupert Fremont and Bessie Ruth (Westfall) B.; B.S., U.S. Naval Acad., 1928; postgrad. Harvard, 1936, Naval War Coll., 1951; LL.D., Ferris Inst., Big Rapids, Mich., 1962; m. Jean Elizabeth Shacklette, June 7, 1928; children—Douglas Craig, Elizabeth Jean (Mrs. Carol Sidney Hartley). Commd. 2d lt., USMC, 1928, designated naval aviator, 1930, advanced through grades to maj. gen., 1957; participated 2d Nicaraguan campaign, 1931-33, Central Pacific, World War II; naval attaché, C.A., 1945-48; dir. electronics div. Bur. Aero., Navy Dept., 1949-50; with 1st Marine Aircraft Wing, Korean campaign, 1951-52, comdg. gen., Western Pacific, 1956-57; comdg. gen. 2d Marine Aircraft Wing, Air Sta., Cherry Point, N.C., 1958-59; dir. Marine Corps Aviation, 1959-61, dep. comdr. Fleet Marine Force, Atlantic, 1961-63; ret., 1963; cons. Research Analysis Corp., McLean, Va., 1965-68, analyst, 1968-77. Cons., Ins. for Def. Analysis. Clubs: Army and Navy, Army and Navy Country (Washington). Home: Washington, D.C. Died May 31, 1977.

BINNS, JOSEPH PATTERSON, hotel exec.; b. Winona, O., June 28, 1905; s. Edward T. and Esther (Brackin) B.; B.S., Cornell, 1928; student Wharton Sch., U. Pa., 1924-26; m. 2d, Catherine Gregg Daumit, Dec. 17, 1955; 1 dau. (by previous marriage), Ruth Anne (Mrs. Alan Hall). Room clerk Chalfonte-Haddon Hall, Atlantic City, 1928-31; asst. mgr. Claridge Hotel, 1931-32, mgr., 1932-33, gen. mgr. Claridge Hotel, also mgr. Park Lane Apts., 1933-39; gen. mgr., dir. Stevens Hotel, Chgo., 1939-42; gen. mgr. The Palmer House, Chgo., 1946-49, The Plaza, N.Y.C., 1949; exec. v.p., gen. mgr., The Waldorf-Astoria, 1949-61; vice president Hilton Hotels Corp., 1946-62, senior vice president, 1962-65; senior vice president, dir. Statler Hotels Delaware Corp.; vice chmn., dir. Hotel Waldorf-Astoria Corp.; pres., chief exec. officer Rock-Hill Uris Corp., 1961-64; asso. Carl M. Loeb, Rhodes & Co., investment bankers, N.Y.C., 1965-80; chmn. bd. Coll. Inns Am.; dir. Ann Arbor R.R., Gen. Host Corporation; mem. the board of trustees Greenwich Savings Bank. Head task force on subsistence services Hoover Commn. Served USAAF, 1942-46; disch. as col. Air Transport Command. Decorated Legion of Merit, Croix de Guerre with palm and star, Bronze Star Medal, Am. Campaign Medal, Asiatic-Pacific Campaign Medal, European-African-Middle Eastern Campaign Medal, World War II Victory Medal. Mem. Sigma Chi. Quaker. Clubs: University (N.Y.C.); Bohemian (San Francisco). Home: New York, N.Y. Died Nov. 25, 1980.

BINZ, LEO, ret. archbishop: b. Stockton, Ill., Oct. 31, 1900; s. Michael and Thecla (Reible) B.; student Loras Coll., Dubuque, Ia., 1914-18, LL.D., 1944; A.B., St. Mary's Sem., Balt., 1919, A.M., 1920; student Sulpician Sem., Washington, 1920-21, N. Am. Coll., Rome, 1921-24; S.T.D., U. de Propaganda Fide, Rome; Ph.D., Gregorian U., 1926; LL.D., St. Mary's College, Winona, Minn., 1948, St. Ambrose Coll., 1956, Creighton U., 1962; S.T.D., Pontificium Athenaeum Angelicum, Rome, 1956. Ordained priest Roman Catholic Ch., Rome, 1924; instr. N. Am. Coll., Rome, 1924-26; asst. pastor St. Mary's Ch., Sterling, Ill., 1927-28; sec. to Bishop of Rockford, Ill., 1928-29; chancellor, Diocese of Rockford, 1929-32; pastor St. Rita's Ch., Cherry Valley, Ill., 1929-32, St. Peter's Church, Rockford, 1932-33, St. James' Church, Belvidere, Ill., 1933-36; diocesan consultor, 1932-36; sec. to Apostolic Delegation, 1936-42; chaplain, St. Rose Sch., Washington, D.C., 1938-42; titular bishop of Pinara, coadjutor bishop of Winona, Minn., and apostolic adminstr. of Winona, 1942-49; titular archbishop of Silyum, Coadjutor to the archbishop of Dubuque, Ia., 1949-54, archbishop of Dubuque, 1954-61, St. Paul, 1961, now St. Paul and Mpls.; asst. Pontifical Throne, 1954; pallium conferred, 1958, 62; consultor Commn. on Bishops and Govt. of Dioceses, 2d Vatican Council, 1962-65, mem. Post-Counciliar Commn. Bishops and Govt. of Dioceses, 1966; adminstrv. bd. Nat. Cath. Welfare Conf., 1963-75; archbishop of St. Paul and Mpls., 1975-75, ret., 1975. Episcopal chmn. dept. lay orgns., 1963-66. Home: Maywood, Ill. Died Oct. 9, 1979; buried Resurrection Cemetery, St. Paul, Minn.

BIRD, FRANCIS WESLEY, pub. utilities; b. Sligo, Ireland, Aug. 6, 1882; s. Francis and Frances (Cullen) B.; student Toronto Collegiate Inst. and Mont. State Coll.; m. Zoe Bertha Duncan, Dec. 22, 1908; children—Kathleen (Mrs. E.M. Parkin, dec.), Francis, Thomas, Philip, Virginia Lee (Mrs. P. L. MacDonald). Began as civil engr., later U.S. Geol. Survey, U.S. Reclamation Service & R.R.'s; became pres. Mont. Power Co., Butte, 1940, now chmn. bd. Clubs: Bankers of Am., Montana, Butte Country. Home: Polson, Mont. *

BIRD, J(AMES) MALCOLM, journalist; b. at Brooklyn, N.Y., Sept. 2, 1886; s. Joseph Gedney and Elizabeth (Baltz) B.; A.B., Columbia, 1913, grad. work in mathematics, Columbia, 1913-16; m. Katherine Alice Montgomery, of Louisville, Ky., Aug. 28, 1915. Asst. in mathematics, Columbia, 1914-16; instr. mathematics, Cooper Union, 1914-15; instructor in same, extension courses, Columbia, 1915-22; asso. editor Scientific American, 1916-24; mng. editor, 1924; research officer Am. Soc. for Psychical Research, 1925-31. Sec. com. of judges in the Eugene Higgins $5,000 prize contest for best popular essay on Einstein theories, 1920-21; sec. to com. of judges in Scientific American investigation of psychic phenomena, 1922-24. Author: Einstein's Theories of Relativity and Gravitation, 1921; My Psychic Adventures, 1923; Margery the Medium, 1925; Proceedings, A. S. P. R., 1926, 27, 28. Home: Scotch Plains, N.J. *

BIRD, ROBERT MONTGOMERY, med. educator; b. Charlottesville, Va., Feb. 1, 1915; s. Robert Montgomery and Caroline (Reid) B.; B.S. in Medicine, U. Va., 1937, M.D., 1939. Intern N.Y. Hosp., 1939-40, asst. resident medicine, 1940-42; fellow physiology Am. Cancer Soc., Cornell U. Med. Coll., 1946-48, from research asso. to asst. prof. physiology, 1946-50, instr. medicine, 1947-52; from asst. to physician to physician outpatients N.Y. Hosp., 1946-52; practice medicine specializing in internal medicine, N.Y.C., 1950-52; asso. prof. medicine U. Okla. Coll. Medicine, Oklahoma City, 1952-61, prof. medicine, 1961-74, prof. physiology, 1962-74, vice chmn. dept. medicine, 1961-65, asso. dean planning and devel. 1965-70, dean Coll. Medicine,

1970-74; from attending staff to cons. medicine Oklahoma City VA Hosp., 1953-74; dir. Lister Hill Nat. Center for Biomed. Communications, Nat. Library Medicine, NIH, 1974-77. Mem. constrn. sch. med. rev. com. HEW, 1967-70, cons. div. physician manpower, 1967-74; chmn. com. B instl. research program evaluation VA, 1970-71. Mem. Okla. Sci. and Arts Found., Oklahoma City Symphony Soc. Served with M.C. AUS, 1942-46. Recipient U. Okla. Regents award for superior teaching, 1969. Mem. A.C.P. (gov. Okla. 1970-74), Am. Physiology Soc., Am. Soc. Hematology, A.A.A.S., Am. Clin. and Climatol. Assn., AMA, Am. Fedn. Clin. Research, Central Soc. Clin. Research, Harvey Soc., So. Soc. Clin. Investigation, N.Y. Acad. Scis., Acad. Sigma Xi, Alpha Omega Alpha, Omicron Delta Kappa. Episcopalian. Contbr. articles to profl. jours. Home: Bethesda, Md. Died Dec. 31, 1976.

BIRD, VIGGO EDWARD, pub. utility executive; b. Copenhagen, Denmark, Apr. 29, 1885; s. Regnar Edward and Regine (Ewaldsen) B.; grad. U. of Copenhagen, 1903; B.S., Mass. Inst. Tech., 1908; m. Anita Parker, of San Francisco, Calif., Apr. 10, 1911; children—Mary Parker, Elizabeth Ewaldsen, Thora Anna, Regnar Edward. Came to U.S., 1903, naturalized, 1918. Began with Hammond V. Hayes, cons. engr., Boston, Mass., 1908-10; in engring. dept. Stone & Webster, Boston, 1910-11; supt. Fall River (Mass.) Gas Works Co., 1911-13; mgr. Conn. Power Co., New London, 1913-22, v.p. and gen. mgr., 1922-29, pres. since 1933 and dir. since 1929; exec. v.p. Hartford Electric Light Co., 1929-35, pres. since 1935 and dir. since 1926; treas., sec. and dir. New London Northern R.R.; v.p., treas. and dir. Central Vt. Transportation Co.; dir. Central Vt. Ry., Inc., Morris Plan Bank of Hartford, Phoenix Mutual Life Insurance Co., Nat. Bank of Commerce of New London; trustee Mechanics Savings Bank of Hartford, New London Savings Bank. Mem. Am. Inst. of E.E., Guild of Gas Managers (past pres.), N.E. Gas Assn. (past pres.), Am. Gas Assn., Soc. for Gas Lighting. Republican. Clubs: Hartford, Hartford Golf. Home: West Hartford. *

BIRD-MALEY, ROSE ANNA, state supt. schs.; b. Stevens Point, Wis., 1884; d. John Charles and Anna Elizabeth (Potter) Bird; grad. Cambria (Wyo.) High Sch.; B. of Ped., U. of Wyo.; m. John Thomas Maley, lawyer, of Denver, Colo., Nov. 18, 1912. Teacher rural and graded schs., Wyo.; co. supt. schs., Weston Co., Wyo., 1908-10; state supt. pub. instrn., Wyo., 1910-14. Located homestead and improved same from earnings as teacher and now owns ranch and engages in stock raising. Democrat. Catholic. Home: Cheyenne, Wyo. *

BIRDSALL, GUY HENRY, govt. ofcl., lawyer; b. Algoma, Wis., Apr. 18, 1893; s. Asa and Alice (Perry) B.; pre-legal, State Coll., Stevens Pt., Wis., 1916; J.D., Georgetown U., 1922; m. Lillian May Koken, Jan. 29, 1927; 1 dau., Marjorie (Mrs. Edwin F. Irish). Tchr. grade sch., Kewaunee Co., 1912-13; asst. prin., Blair, Wis., 1916-17; admitted to D.C. bar, 1922; supervision, rating and adjudication of claims VA, 1922-29, legislative counsel, asst. solicitor, 1930-46; asst. adminstr. for legislation and congl. liaison, 1946-56, gen. counsel, 1956-60; mem. President's Com. Employment Handicapped; legislative and legal cons. hist. and probate matters. Active Friendship Citizens' Assn., Washington and Fedn. of Citizen's Assns., 1941-45. Served with U.S. Army, 1917-19. Mem. Am. Legion, V.F.W., D.A.V. Episcopalian. Mason (33 deg., Shriner). Compiler handbooks and resumes of vets. laws. Home: Washington, D.C. Died Feb. 19, 1980; buried Columbia Gardens Cemetery, Arlington, Va.

BIRGE, RAYMOND THAYER, physicist, educator; b. Bklyn., Mar. 13, 1887; s. John Thaddeus and Caroline S. (Raymond) B.; A.B., U. Wis., 1909, A.M., 1910, Ph.D., 1914; LL.D., U. Calif., 1955; m. Irene Adelaide Walsh, Aug. 12, 1913, (dec. 1980); children—Carolyn Elizabeth, Robert Walsh. Instr. physics Syracuse U., 1913-15; asst. prof., 1915-18; instr. physics U. Calif., 1918, asst. and asso. prof., prof., 1926-55, prof. emeritus, 1955-80, chmn. dept., 1933-55; co-operating expert in Internat. Critical Tables; mem. adv. com. Office of Critical Tables. Physics Bldg. at U. Calif. at Berkeley named in his honor. Fellow Am. Phys. Soc. (v.p. 1954, pres. 1955), Optical Soc. Am., AAAS; mem. Nat. Acad. Scis., Am. Philos. Soc., Am. Assn. Physics Tchrs., Am. Inst. Physics (governing bd. 1955-58), Phi Beta Kappa, sigma Xi. Contbr. to Phys. Rev., others; research in field of spectroscopy. Home: Berkeley, Calif. Died Mar. 22, 1980.

BIRNBAUM, NATHAN, chemist; b. N.Y.C., July 14, 1907; s. Jacob and Sarah (Schutzberger) B.; B.A. cum laude, CCNY, 1929; M.A., Columbia, 1932, Ph.D., 1937; m. Jeanne D. Pancoast, Jan. 16, 1931. Mem. faculty dept. chemistry CCNY, 1929-73, beginning as fellow, successively tutor, instr., asst. prof., asso. prof., 1929-56, prof., 1956-72, chmn. dept., 1954-69. Mem. Nat. Def. Research Com., Columbia, 1941; mem. radiol. safety sect. Bikini automatic weapons test, 1946; civilian cons. to Chem. Corps, U.S. Army, 1947-49, 52-65; cons. FDA, 1965-67; mem. Nat. Com. Radiation Protection, 1950-51; chief Chem. Corps group Operation Greenhouse, Eniwetok, 1951. Served from capt. to lt. col. AUS, 1942-47, 49-52; col. Res. Decorated Army, Navy, Air Force commendation ribbons. Mem. Am. Chem. Soc., A.A.A.S., Phi Beta Kappa, Sigma Xi, Phi Lambda Upsilon. Home: Fort Lee, N.J. Died Dec. 9, 1975.

BIRON, ROBERT HENRY, JR., business exec., cons.; b. Mpls., Aug. 12, 1912; s. Robert Henry and Alice (Brugger) B.; student Carleton Coll., 1929; B.A., U. Minn., 1933, LL.B., 1935; m. 2d, Jean Machamer, Apr. 14, 1951; 1 dau., Patricia. House counsel Mpls.-Honeywell Regulator Co., 1936-43; asst. to dir. indsl. relations Consol. Vultee Aircraft Corp. (now Convair div. Gen. Dynamics Corp.), 1943-45; v.p. Northrop Aircraft, Inc., 1945-47; v.p. Transcontinental & Western Air, Inc., 1947-48; v.p. adminstrn. Convair div. Gen. Dynamics Corp., 1948-61, sr. v.p. Gen. Dynamics, 1961-64; vice chancellor for bus. and finance U. Cal. at San Diego, 1964-68; pres. Rancho LaJolla, Inc., 1968-79; v.p. La Jolla Village Corp., land devel.; dir. San Diego Gas and Electric Co.; cons. in field. Mem. Theta Delta Chi, Phi Delta Phi. Republican. Home: Rancho Santa Fe, Calif. Died Sept. 23, 1979.

BIRR, HERMAN THEODORE, stock broker; b. Oakland, Calif., June 28, 1907; s. H.T. and Elizabeth (Carstenn) B.; student U. Calif. ext., 1923-26; m. Antoinette Corniea, May 25, 1929; children—Herman Theodore III, Robert Roger. Asst. mgr. Bank of Am. (formerly Bank of Italy), 1924-30; mgr. Reinhard & Co., 1930-32; dist. mgr. Asso. Am. Distbrs., 1932-37; v.p. Bankamerica Co., 1937-45; chmn. pres. First Calif. Co., 1945-57; chmn. Blair, Rollins & Co., Inc., N.Y.C., 1951-54; v.p. Walston & Co., Inc., 1958-59; chmn. bd. Birr, Wilson & Co., Inc. (formerly Birr & Co., Inc.), 1959-71, founding chmn. bd., 1971-76. Mem. N.Y. Stock Exchange, Pacific Coast Stock Exchange; mem. Am. Stock Exchange, A.P. Giannini Scholarship Found. Mem. Calif. Hist. Soc., Beta Phi Sigma. Clubs: Commercial, Stock Exchange, Merchants Exchange, Bond (San Francisco); Wall St. (N.Y.C.); Claremont Country. Home: Piedmont, Calif. Died Aug. 4, 1976.

BISBEE, FRANK DOAN, business exec.; b. Knoxville, Tenn., Nov. 13, 1891; s. William Adolphus and Harriet Anne (Backus) B.; prep. edn., St. Paul's Sch., Concord, N.H., Harstrom Sch., Norwalk, Conn.; student U. Pa., 1911-13; m. Ella Taylor Slemons, Oct. 25, 1921; 1 son, Frank Doan. Bank runner, Fla. Nat. Bank, Jacksonville, 1912; mgr. Bisbee Bldg.; pres. Frank D. Bisbee & Co. (became Bisbee-Baldwin Corp.), office bldg. mgmt., ins., real estate, mortgage loans; chmn. bd. Bisbee-Baldwin Corp.; pres. Bisbee Investment Co.; v.p. Holly Point Devel. Co.; trustee Profit Sharing Plan of Bisbee-Baldwin Corp.; dir. Barnett First Nat. Bank, Vol. with French Ambulance Corps., 1916, 1st lt., later capt. inf., U.S. Army, World War I; ensign, USCG Aux., World War II. Former lt. col. personal staff Gov. Spessard Holland of Fla. Ex-chmn. Selective Service System, Duval County Local Board No. 5; past facility security officer Fla. under Office Civilian Def. Mem. City Council, Jacksonville, 1923-25. Vice pres., dir. Children's Home Soc.; past pres. N.E. Fla. div. Children's Home Soc.; past pres. Travelers' Aid Soc.; dir. com. Jacksonville Community Chest; past v.p. N.E. Fla. Heart Assn. Mem. S.A.R., Am. Legion, U.S., Fla., Jacksonville chambers commerce, Newcomen Soc. Eng., Camellia Soc. N. Fla. (dir.), Internat., Am. (permanent judge) camellia socs., Phi Kappa Sigma. Democrat. Episcopalian. Clubs: River, Men's Garden (dir.) (Jacksonville); Meninak, Seminole (past pres.), Fla. Yacht, Timuquana Country. Home: Jacksonville, Fla. Died Feb. 7, 1974.

BISCH, LOUIS EDWARD (BISH), neuropsychiatrist; b. Brooklyn, N.Y., Mar. 10, 1885; s. Otto George and Dorothea Louise B.; A.B., Columbia, 1907, Ph.D., 1912; M.D., Coll. Physicians and Surgeons, same, 1911; m. Henriette B. Bousquet; children—Barbara, Betty. Interne Manhattan State Hosp., N.Y. City, 1911-13; physician Clearing House for Mental Defectives, 1912-15, N.Y. Neurol. Inst., 1912-16; instr. neuropathology, N.Y. Post-Grad. Med. Sch., 1914-15; consulting neurologist, N.Y. City Children's hosps. and schs., 1913-15; lecturer and asso. in ednl. psychology, Teachers Coll., and lecturer psychology, Columbia, 1913-16; prof. of neuropsychiatry, N.Y. Polyclinic Med. Sch. and Hosp. since 1926; organizer and dir. Psychopathic Lab. N.Y. City, 1916, Mental Hygiene Clinic, Norfolk, Va., 1918-19; cons. specialist in neuropsychiatry, U.S.P.H.S. Hosp. 45, Biltmore, N.C., 1921-22; med. dir. Hillcrest Manor. Organizer, 1917, and dir. psychopathic div. 5th Naval Dist., U.S.N.R.F. until 1919. Fellow A.M.A.; mem. Eugenics Research Assn., Am. Psychiatric Assn., New York and North Carolina state medical socs., A.A.A.S., Authors' League of America, Am. Anthropol. Assn., N.Y. Acad. of Sciences, etc. Clubs: Lotos (New York); Authors' (London, Eng.). Author several books, including among the later published; Your Nerves, 1945; Cure Your Nerves Yourself, 1953, also sci. paper and contbr. to mag. *

BISHOP, ELIZABETH, poet; b. Worcester, Mass., Feb. 8, 1911; d. William Thomas and Gertrude (Bulmer) B.; A.B., Vassar Coll., 1934; LL.D., Smith Coll., 1968, Rutgers U., 1972, Brown U., 1972. Houghton Mifflin poetry fellow, 1945; Guggenheim fellow, 1947; Lucy Martin Donnelly fellow Bryn Mawr, 1951, Amy Lowell fellow, 1957; Chapelbrook Found. fellow, 1960; lectr. English, Harvard, 1970-79. Cons. poetry Library of Congress, 1949-50. Recipient Am. Acad. Arts and Letters award, 1951; Shelley Meml. award, 1952; Partisan Review fellowship, 1956; Pulitzer prize for poetry, Poems, 1956; award Acad. Am. Poets, 1964, Poetry Soc. Am., 1964; Merrill Found. award, 1969; Nat. Book award, 1970; Order Rio Branco (Brazil), 1971; Harriet Monroe award for poetry, 1974. Mem. Nat. Inst. Arts and Letters, Acad. Am. Poets (chancellor 1966-79). Author: North & South (poems), 1946; Poems, 1955; Brazil, 1962; Questions of Travel, 1965; Selected Poems, Chatto and Windus, 1967; Complete Poems, 1969; Anthology of Contemporary Brazilian Poetry, 1972; Geography III, 1977. Contbr. poems and stories to mags. and anthologies. Address: New York, N.Y. Died Oct. 6, 1979.

BISHOP, GEORGE WESLEY, JR., educator; b. N.Y.C., Jan. 13, 1910; s. George Wesley and Anna (Farrington) B.; A.B., Coll. William and Mary, 1935; M.B.A., N.Y. U., 1955, Ph.D., 1959; m. Helen Young, Dec. 22, 1942; children—Georgelen Elizabeth Kuhn, George Wesley III. With Union Carbide Corp., N.Y.C., 1935-36, U.S. Gypsum Co., N.Y.C., 1936-42; account exec., portfolio analyst Merrill Lynch, Pierce, Fenner & Smith, N.Y.C., 1947-50, 54-56, 57-59; adminstrv. asst. to dean Grad. Sch. Bus. Adminstrn., N.Y. U., 1956-57; with U. Tenn, 1959-65, asst. prof. finance, 1959-60, asso. prof., 1960-64, prof., 1964-65; prof., head dept. finance No. Ill. U., DeKalb, 1965-74; research fellow dept. history Yale, 1970-71; cons., expert witness Fed. Ct. Served with USNR, 1942-46, 50-54; capt. Res. ret. Mem. Omicron Delta Kappa, Delta Sigma Pi, Pi Kappa Alpha, Beta Gamma Sigma. Episcopalian. Author: Charles H. Dow and the Dow Theory, 1960. Editor: Charles H. Dow, Economist, 1967. Contbr. articles profl. jours. Home: DeKalb, Ill. Died Aug. 14, 1974; interred Arlington Nat. Cemetery (Va.).

BISKUP, GEORGE JOSEPH, clergyman; b. Cedar Rapids, Iowa, Aug. 23, 1911; s. Frank L. and Julia (Kuda) K.; A.B., Loras Coll., 1933; student Gregorian U., Rome, 1933-37. Ordained priest Roman Cath. Ch., 1937; curate St. Raphael's Cathedral, Dubuque, Iowa, 1937-39; faculty Loras Coll., 1939-48; head art dept. Loras Coll., 1941-48; minutante sacred congregation Oriental Ch., Vatican City, 1948-51; chancellor of Archdiocese of Dubuque, 1951-52, vicar gen., 1952-65; bishop of Des Moines, 1965-67; coadjutor archbishop of Indpls., 1967-70, archbishop, 1970-79; pastor St. Joseph's Ch., 1951-52; chaplain Mt. Loretta Convent, Dubuque, 1952-58; archdiocesan dir. Cath. Cemeteries, 1953-58, aux. bishop, 1957-65; pastor Ch. of Nativity, 1958-65. Vicar gen. Archdiocese Dubuque, 1952-65. Papal chamberlain, 1949, domestic prelate, 1951. Home: Indianapolis, Ind. Died Oct. 17, 1979; buried Calvary Cemetery Mausoleum, Indpls.

BISSELL, LOUIS G., lawyer; b. Bklyn., May 17, 1883; A.B., Princeton, 1904, A.M., 1905; LL.B., Columbia, 1910. Admitted to N.Y. bar, 1910; mem. firm Charbourne, Parke, Whiteside, Wolff & Brophy, N.Y.C.; dir. Granite City Steel Co. Mem. Assn. Bar City N.Y., Am., N.Y. bar assns. *

BISSELL, RICHARD, writer; b. Dubuque, Iowa, June 27, 1913; s. Frederick Ezekiel and Edith Mary (Pike) B.; B.S., Harvard, 1936; Litt.D., U. Dubuque, 1973; m. Marian Van Patten Grilk, Feb. 5, 1938; children—Thomas St. George, Nathaniel Gaylord, Anastasia, Samuel Pike. With Polarizing Instrument Co., N.Y., 1937; factory supt. H.B. Glover Co., Dubuque, 1938-40, supt., stylist, 1944-52, v.p., 1944-60; mate and pilot towboats Central Barge Co., 1940-44; pres. Bissell Towing & Transport Co., Dubuque, 1958-77. Recipient Antoinette Perry award for best musical play, 1954, Donaldson award for outstanding achievement in theatre, 1954-55. Holder pilot license all tonnage, Upper Mississippi and Monogahela rivers. Mem. Sons and Daus. Pioneer Rivermen, Dramatists Guild, Screen Writers Guild, New Zealand Antarctic Society (hon.). Clubs: Harvard, Lambs (N.Y.C.); Peosta Boat (Dubuque). Author: A Stretch on the River, 1950; The Monongahela, 1952; 7 1/2 Cents, 1953; High Water, 1954; Say Darling, 1957; Good Bye Ava (novel), 1960; You Can Always Tell a Harvard Man, 1962; Pursuit of the Happy Cabbage, 1964; Still Circling Moose Jaw, 1965; My Life on the Mississippi, or Why I am not Mark Twain, 1973; How Many Miles to Galena, 1968; Julia Harrington, 1913, 1969; New Light on 1776 and All That, 1975; plays: (with George Abbott) Pajama Game, 1954, (with Abe Burrows, Marian Bissell) Say Darling, 1958; contbr. short stories to nat. mags., coll. textbooks, anthologies. Home: Dubuque, Iowa. Died May 4, 1977; interred Linwood Cemetery, Dubuque.

BISSHOPP, KENNETH EDWARD, educator; b. Beloit, Wis., July 14, 1909; s. John and Maud Alice (Lufkin) B.; A.B. in Math., U. Ill., 1930; M.S. in Math., Ill. Inst. Tech., 1946; Ph.D. in Mech. Engring., 1954; m. Beatrice Lenora Ortmann, June 16, 1932; 1 son, Frederic Edward. Design calculator Fairbanks Morse and Co., 1930-32, research engr., 1934-44, cons., 1950-55; mech. engr. Sun Shipbldg. & Dry Dock Co.,

Chester, Pa., 1932-34; research engr. Armour Research Found., Chgo., 1944-48, st. engr., 1948-55; prof. mechanics Hartford Grad. Center, Rensselaer Poly. Inst., East Windsor Hill, Conn., 1955-57, prof. mech. engring., Troy, N.Y., 1957-75, chmn. dept. mech. engring., 1957-67. Mem. ASME (lectr. 1959-60), Am. Math. Soc., Am. Soc. Engring. Edn., Sigma Xi, Tau Beta Pi. Contbr. articles to profl. jours. Home: Troy, N.Y. Died June 19, 1975.

BITTNER, WALTON S(IMON), author, educator; b. Dayton, Ore., Aug. 13, 1884; s. Henry I. and Mary (Kapser) B.; A.B., Univ. Chicago, 1909, A.M., 1928, grad. work at Ind. Univ. 1930-33, at Mexico City, 1939; m. Adela K. Wohler, June 20, 1913; 1 dau., Margaret (Mrs. Robert J. Francis). Prin. Etna (Ind.) High Sch., 1907-08; instr., Spokane Coll., 1910-11, Mich. State Coll., 1911-14; sec., public welfare service, Ind. Univ., 1914-18, asso. dir., extension div., asso. prof. sociology, 1920-45, asso. dean, div. of adult edn. and public services and prof. of sociology since 1945. Asso. dir. ednl. extension U.S. Dept. Interior, Washington, D.C., 1918-19; served as mem., ad. com. of U.S.A.F.I., Joint Army and Navy Com. on Recreation and Welfare, 1941-45. Recipient Patriotic Service award by Secs. of War and Navy for work with U.S.A.F.I. Mem. A.A.A.S., Am. Sociol. Soc., Nat. Univ. Extension Assn. (sec. 1927-57), Am. Anthropol Assn., Am. Assn. Adult Edn. (council), Alpha Pi Zeta, Alpha Kappa Delta. Episcopalian. Author (with Helen Duncan): Guide to Correspondence Study, 1954; University Teaching by Mail, 1954. Editor: Bulletin, 1935-57, Proc. of Nat. U. Extension Assn., 1927-57. Home: Bloomington, Ind.*

BJORKMAN, OLAF (BYÔRK'MAN), sculptor; b. Stockholm, Sweden, July 15, 1886; s. Dr. Gustav and Augusta (Jungmarker) B.; ed. in Stockholm; studied sculpture in Paris with Bourdelle, drawing with Steinlen, anatomy at Beaux Arts Sch., and at Karolinska Inst., Stockholm. Came to U.S., 1891, naturalized, 1895. Works: The Titan, Beethoven statue, The Caress, Edgar Allan Poe and the Raven, The Song of Eternity; war memorial relief in Gustavus Adolphus Ch., New York; portrait relief of Francis Eyre Parker, at the Parker Memorial Home, New Brunswick, N.J.; portrait relief of Gustaf Stromberg, at Ardencaple Castle, Scotland; portrait relief of Miss Anne Sherwood, New York, of Mrs. Henrietta Macaulay Parker Stromberg, Parker Memorial Home, New Brunswick, N.J., of Charles A. Lindbergh, Swedish Chamber of Commerce of U.S., New York; Svea Monument, intended for Chicago; Rodin Memorial, for Paris; design for mural, The Journey of Life (135 nude figures); etc.; busts include Dr. Frank Crane, Dr. Johannes Hoving, Frank and Robert McCarter, Jr., Beethoven, Patrick Henry, Lincoln, Mrs. Olaf de Brun, Dr. F. J. Swanson, Monumental head of the Vala. Author several plays and poems. Home: New York, N.Y. *

BJORLEE, IGNATIUS (BE-ÛR'LE), educator for the deaf; b. Freeborn County, Minn., Dec. 9, 1885; s. Elias and Karen (Tostenson) B.; student public schs., Northwood, Ia.; B.S., St. Olaf Coll., Northfield, Minn., 1909, LL.D., 1933; M.A., Gallaudet Coll., Washington, 1910, L.H.D., 1943; grad. study, Columbia, 1916-18; m. Cornelia Cleophas, Feb. 19, 1916. Instr. N.Y. Instn. for Instrn. of the Deaf, 1910-18; supt. and prin. Md. State Sch. for the Deaf 1918-55. Chmn. exec. com. Conf. of Execs. of Am. Schs. for the Deaf, 1939-49; sec. Conv. Am. Instrs. of Deaf, 1920-33, pres., 1937-39; pres. Md. State Conf. of Social Work, 1926-27; pres. Francis Scott Key Council Boy Scouts of America, 1925-29; Silver Beaver Award, 1939; chmn. Certification Com. of Teachers and of Training Centers for Teachers of the Deaf, 1932-55; mem. bd. dirs. Gallaudet Coll., 1944—; chmn. Frederick County Branch. Am. Automobile Assn., 1943-55; pres. Frederick Community Chest Inc., 1945-48, gov. 34th Dist. Rotary Internat., 1929-30; chmn. Community Service Com. and mem. Aims and Objects Com. Rotary Internat., 1932-33. Chmn. N.R.A., Compliance Bd., 1933-34; chmn. Police Commn., Frederick, 1941-45; mem. OPA price panel, 1942-46. Mem. 22d Regt. Engrs. N.Y. Nat. Guards, 1913-17. Mem. Am. Assn. to Promote Teaching to Speech to the Deaf, Academy of Political Science, Pi Gamma Mu. Editor of Am. Annals of the Deaf, 1943. Home: Frederick, Md. *

BLACK, CHARLES LUNN, lawyer; b. Hillsboro, Tex., Nov. 7, 1883; s. Thomas Bradbury and Susan (Philips) B.; ed. U. of Tex., 1906-07; m. Helena Bowman, Mar. 8, 1908; children—Charles L., Elizabeth (Mrs. Robert L. Hatchett, Jr.), Thomas Bowman. Admitted to Tex. bar, 1907; practiced in Hillsboro, 1907-13, Austin, Tex., since 1913; mem. Black and Stayton. Mem. American Bar Assn., Texas Bar Assn., Travis County Bar Assn., Order of Coif (hon.). Home: Austin, Tex. *

BLACK, HENRY FRANKLIN, lawyer; b. Newport, Vt., Mar. 27, 1906; s. Harry A. and Jane M. (Gates) B.; B.S., Norwich U., 1928, LL.D., 1974; LL.B., George Washington U., 1933; m. Beatrice M. Skinner, Sept. 12, 1930; children—Harry A., Roy S. Admitted to Vt. bar, 1934; state's atty. Windsor County, Vt., 1937-41, superior judge, 1941-49; practiced in White River Junction, Vt., 1949-77; sr. partner firm Black & Plante, White River Junction, 1959-77. Lectr. med. jurisprudence Dartmouth Med. Sch., 1968-77; mem. adv. com. on civil rules Vt. Supreme Ct., 1971-77; co-chmn. trust div. Nat. Conf. Lawyers and Bankers, 1974-74. Dir., gen. counsel Vt. Mut. Fire Ins. Co., Montpelier, Vt., No. Security Ins. Co., Montpelier; dir. Twin State Fruit Corp., White River Junction, Dartmouth Nat. Bank of Hanover, N.H. Mem. Vt. Bd. Edn., 1950-53; chmn. Town of Hartford (Vt.) Planning Commn., 1958-61, town moderator, 1965-77. Corporator Mary Hitchcock Meml. Hosp., Hanover; trustee Norwich U.; mem. World Conf. Peace Through Law, 1968-77. Fellow Am. Coll. Trial Lawyers, Am. Coll. Probate Counsel, Am. Bar Found.; mem. Inter-Am., Am. (mem. ho. dels. 1961-77, bd. govs. 1975-77), Vt. (pres. 1956-57; certificate of merit 1963), Windsor County (pres. 1938) bar assns., Am. Judicature Soc., Am. Fedn. Ins. Counsel, Am. Trial Lawyers Assn., Assn. Ins. Attys. Republican. Episcopalian. Mason (Shriner), Rotarian, Elk. Author: Some Observations Relative to Vermont's Judicial System, 1956. Home: White River Junction, Vt. Died Aug. 3, 1977; interred at Norwich, Vt.

BLACKBURN, MORRIS ATKINSON, painter; b. Phila., Oct. 13, 1902; s. James Meyers and Emma (Brightly) B.; student Pa. Acad. Fine Arts; William Emlen Cresson traveling scholar to Europe, 1928, 29; m. Sarah Elizabeth Thompson, May 1, 1937; 1 dau., Patricia Joan. Faculty Bryn Mawr Coll., 1946-48, Temple U., 1948-52, Phila. Mus. Sch. Indsl. Art, 1933-40; faculty Pa. Acad. Fine Arts, 1952-79, Phila. Mus. Art, 1944-72; works exhibited U.S., France, Eng., Italy, Holland, Yugoslavia, India, Pakistan and N.Z.; represented in permanent collections: Phila. Mus. Art Acad. Fine Arts, Butler Inst. Art, Nat. Mus. Art, Washington, Carnegie Inst., Capehart Collection, Lessing J. Rosenwald Collection, Brooks Meml. Art Gallery, Clearwater Mus., Dept. State, N.J. State Mus., Del. Art Mus., Sch. Pharmacy, Temple U., Wheaton Mus., Free Library of Phila., Library of Congress, Woodmere Art Gallery, Pa. State U., U. Mont., Mus. N.Mex., U.S. embassies abroad. Recipient John Gribbel prize Phila. Print Club, 1942, Lessing J. Rosenwald prize and Mary S. Collins prize, 1950; gold medal award Pa. Acad. Fine Arts, 1946, fellowship prize, 1949, Harrison S. Morris prize, 1951, Thronton Oakley prize, 1955, Pyramid Club award, 1957; Gugenheim fellow painting and graphic art, 1952, Zimmerman prize, 1960, Artist of Year, Ocean City, N.J., 1968, Phila. Water Color Club medal of award, 1969, Dawson Meml. medal, 1973. Mem. Am. Water Color Soc., Phila. Water Color Club, Allied Artists, Audubon Soc. Home: Philadelphia, Pa. Died July 14, 1979; buried Arlington Cemetery, Delaware County, Pa.

BLACKMAN, EARL AUSTIN, clergyman; b. Kendallville, Ind., Oct. 2, 1882; s. John Austin and Myra Ellen (Herrick) B.; ed. Pratt Inst. (Brooklyn), Tri-State Coll. (Angola, Ind.), U. of Kan.; m. Eva May Morgan, of Salina, Kan., Apr. 29, 1913; children—Elouise and Lilabel (twins). Ordained ministry Christian (Disciples) Ch., 1914; pastor Chanute, Kan., 1914-23; co-minister, Linwood Boul. Ch., Kansas City, Mo., 1923-29; minister and director of Kansas City Youth Forum since 1929; sec. Am. Extension Foundation. First lt., chaplain 1st Kan. F.A., federal service, 1917; 1st lt., chaplain 130th F.A., 35th Division, 12 months with A.E.F.; hon. discharged, May 30, 1919; commd. 1st lt. chaplain 1st Kan. F.A., N.G., Mar. 17, 1921; capt., chaplain, 130th F.A., 35th Div., N.G., Dec. 1, 1922; capt., chaplain 110th engrs., 35th Div. Mo. N.G., July 2, 1924; nat. chaplain American Legion, 1921-22. Mason (32 deg. Shriner), Elk. Club: Cooperative. Known as the "Kansas Fighting Parson"; advocates participation of ministers of the gospel in established forms of amusement for the purpose of direction and control. Lecturer. Author of Boxing for Everybody. Home: Kansas City, Mo. *

BLACKWELL, ASHBY CARLYLE, educator; b. Lynchburg, Va., Aug. 4, 1896; s. Samuel Ashby and Minnie Lee (Doyle) B.; A.B., Randolph-Macon Coll., 1918; A.M., 1919; D.Sc., Morris Harvey Coll., 1941; student Princeton U., 1920-21; Ph.D., U. Chgo., 1960, Union Carbide & Carbon Chems. Co. fellow, 1957-58, 59-60; U.S. Rubber Co. Institute of Organic Chemistry fellow, 1958-59, Shell fellow in fundamental research, 1958-59, Shell fellow in fundamental research, spring 1959; m. Harriett Cazenove Purdy, Apr. 9, 1925; 1 dau., Nancy Purdy (Mrs. John Charles Allan). Instructor of mathematics at Randolph-Macon Coll., 1916-19; instr. mathematics and science, Randolph-Macon Acad., 1919-20; part-time asst. in chemistry, Princeton U., 1920-21; prof. chemistry, Morris Harvey College, from 1921, vice president, 1933-51, chairman of natural science division, 1938-41, dean, 1941-56, dean emeritus, 1956-75, coll. treas., 1942-48. Municipal recorder, Barboursville, W.Va., July 1, 1933-Aug. 31, 1935. Mem. Am. Chem. Soc. (dir. Kanawha Valley Sect., 1939 and 1942, v.chmn. fall 1940, chmn. 1941, councillor 1954-56), A.A.A.S., N.E.A., W.Va. Edn. Assn., W.Va. Assn. Higher Edn. (pres. 1947-48), W.Va. Acad. Sci. (pres.1955-56), Phi Beta Kappa, Chi Beta Phi (nat. Pres. 1924-48, hon. dir.; nat. marshal), Sigma Upsilon, Tau Kappa Alpha, Pi Gamma Mu, Sigma Xi. Democrat. Episcopalian. Mason. Club: Lions. Writer articles in field. Contbg. editor in test program Am. Chem. Soc. Home: Charleston, W.Va. Died July 7, 1975; buried Lawrenceville, Va.

BLACKWELL, JEFFERSON DAVIS, coll. president; b. Blackwell, Mo., Sept. 5, 1885; s. Aquilla and Dolly Ann (Coleman) B.; B.S., U. of Mo., 1914; A.M., Teachers Coll., Columbia U., 1923; Ph.D., Johns Hopkins U., 1929; m. Salome Love, Aug. 1, 1915; children—Edith Lucile, Harold Richard, David Jefferson. Rural teacher, Halifax, Mo., 1906-07; grade teacher, Bonne Terre, Mo., 1907-08; supt. schs., Blodgett, Mo., 1910-12; instr. State Normal Sch., Warrensburg, Mo., summer 1914; asso. prof. edn., Tex. Agrl. & Mech. Coll., 1914-17; chmn. div. of vocation edn., Tex. State Dept. of Edn., 1917-20; asst. dir. vocation edn., Pa. State Dept. Pub. Instrn., 1920-23; dir. vocational edn., Md. State Dept. of Edn., 1923-35; pres. Salisbury (Md.) State Teachers Coll., since 1935; instr. U. of Ky., summers, 1928, 30, 31 and 32. Mem. Am. Assn. Sch. Administrators, Alpha Zeta, Phi Delta Kappa, Acacia. Democrat. Presbyterian (elder). Club: Salisbury Rotary (pres. 1939-40). Author: The Organization and Supervision of Vocational Education, 1929. Home: Salisbury, Md. *

BLACKWELL, OTTO BERNARD, telephone engr.; b. Bourne, Mass., Aug. 21, 1884; s. Edwin Alston and Abbie G. (Walker) B.; B.S., Mass. Inst. Tech., 1906; m. Elsie Eldredge, July 2, 1917; children—Edwin Alston, Anne Louise. Engring dept. Am. Telephone & Telegraph Co., 1906-14, transmission and protection engr., 1914-19, transmission development engr., 1919-34; dir. of transmission development Bell Telephone Labs., Mar. 1934-June 1935, mgr. staff depts., June 1935-Dec. 1936, v.p. 1937-44; asst. v.p. Am. Telephone & Telegraph Co. 1944 to 1949. Fellow Am. Inst. E.E., Inst. Radio Engrs., Acoustical Soc. America; mem. A.A.A.S., Am. Physical Soc. Clubs: Salmagundi. Home: Plandome, N.Y.

BLACKWELL, RANDOLPH TALMADGE, govt. ofcl.; b. Greensboro, N.C., Mar. 10, 1927; s. Joe and Blanche Mary (Donnell) B.; B.S., A. and T. State U., 1949; J.D., Howard U., 1953; LL.D., Payne Coll., 1977: m. Elizabeth Knox, Dec. 24, 1954; 1 dau., Blanche Renne. Mem. faculty Winston-Salem (N.C.) State U., Ala. A. and M. Coll., 1953-62; dir. Voter Edn. Project, Atlanta, 1962-63; program dir. So. Christian Leadership Conf., Atlanta, 1963-66; dir. So. Rural Action, Inc., Atlanta, 1966-77; dir. Office of Minority Bus. Enterprise, Dept. Commerce, Washington, 1977-78, dir. Office of Minority Enterprise Program Devel., 1978-81. Bd. dirs. Martin Luther King Center for Social Change; bd. dirs. So. Rural Action, Inc. Served with AUS, 1944-45. Recipient Martin Luther King Jr. Peace Prize, 1976. Mem. NAACP, Urban League, Operation Push, So. Christian Leadership Conf. Democrat. Methodist. Co-author textbooks in field of bus. law and econs. Home: Atlanta, Ga. Died May 21, 1981.

BLADES, BRIAN BREWER, surgeon; b. Scottsville, Kan., July 4, 1906; s. Samuel Thomas and Martha Minette (Hoffmeister) B.; A.B., U. Kan., 1924-28; M.D., Washington U. Sch. Medicine, 1928-32; fellow in surgery, 1936-38; m. Virginia Layton, Jan. 1, 1932; children—Beverly, Judith, Brian. Surg. intern Henry Ford Hosp., Detroit, 1932-33; 2d (Cornell) div., Bellevue Hosp., N.Y., 1934-36; instr. clin. surgery, Washington U. Sch. Medicine, 1938-41; asst. prof. 1941; asst. surg. Barnes Hosp., Children's Hosp. and Maternity Hosp., St. Louis; vis. surgeon Mo. Pacific R.R. Hosp., St. Louis; prof. surgery emeritus George Washington U. Sch. Medicine, Washington; distinguished physician VA, 1972-77. Served as col., M.C., AUS, World War II; chief thoracic surg. sect. Walter Reed Gen. Hosp., Washington, cons. surgeon gen. in thoracic surgery, USAF. Decorated Legion of Merit (U.S.). Mem. Am. Assn. Thoracic Surgery, Assn. Surgery of Trauma, AMA, So. Med. Assn., Am. Coll. Chest Physicians, So. Surg. Assn., A.C.S., Washington Acad. Surgery, Soc. Clin. Surgery, Am. Surg. Assn., Sigma Xi, Alpha Omega Alpha, Beta Theta Pi. Editor Jour. Thoracic Surgery, 1961-77. Contbr. to current med. jours. on thoracic surgery. Home: Bethesda, Md. Died Sept. 28, 1977.

BLAIR, CHARLES STANLEY, fed. judge; b. Kingsville, Md., Dec. 20, 1927; s. Charles Edward and Beulah (Gibson) B.; B.S., U. Md., 1951, LL.B., 1953; m. Opal Linkous Whiteford, June 27, 1964; 1 stepdau., Cynthia Whiteford (Mrs. Peter Tutalo). Admitted to Md. bar, 1953; partner firm Cameron, Close, Reed & Blair, Bel Air, Md., 1961-69; mem. Md. Ho. of Reps., 1963-67; sec. state State of Md., 1967-69; chief of staff to v.p. U.S., 1969-70; U.S. judge Dist. Md., Balt., 1971-80. Republican candidate for gov. Md., 1970. Served with U.S. Maritime Service, 1945-47; to capt. AUS, 1953-56. Home: Darlington, Md. Died Apr. 20, 1980.

BLAIR, DAVID, ballet dancer; b. Halifax, Yorkshire, Eng., July 27, 1932; s. John and Zette Carolyne Elizabeth (Whiteley) B.; ed. Trinity Sch., Halifax, also Royal Ballet Sch., London; m. Maryon Lane, June 22, 1957; children—Catherine and Diana (twins). Mem. Sadler's Wells Ballet (now Royal Ballet), 1948-73, premier dancer, 1955-73; prin. roles include The Catch,

1948, Children's Corner, 1948, Capt. Belaye in Pineapple Poll, 1950-51, 59, Franz in Coppelia, 1951, Blue Bird, 1950, Red Knight in Checkmate, 1953, the miller in Three-Cornered Hat, 1953, prince in Cinderella, 1956, prince in Sleeping Beauty, 1955, prince in Swan Lake, 1955, Albrecht in Giselle, 1955, lead in premiere Prince of the Pagodas, 1957, Petroushka, 1959, Rake, 1950, Satan in Job, 1959, Colas in La Fille Mal Gardee, 1960; partner Alicia Markova in Giselle, 1957, Margot Fonteyn, 1956; U.S. tours with ballet company, 1951-52, 53, 55, 57, 60, 63, 65; choreographer Swan Lake for Am. Ballet Theatre at Met. Opera House, N.Y.C., 1967, Giselle, 1968. Decorated comdr. Order of British Empire. Home: London, England. Died Apr. 1, 1976.

BLAIR, JOHN E(DWARD), bacteriologist; b. Monroe, Me., May 30, 1899; s. John Stott and Alice Ethel (Staples) B.; A.B., Clark U., 1920; Sc.M., Brown U., 1921, Ph.D., 1923; m. Lorraine Hunter Ferguson, Sept. 6, 1923; children—Donald Ferguson, Malcolm John. Instr. biology Brown U., 1922-23; instr. bacteriology Stanford, 1923-26; head dept. bacteriology Hosp. Joint Diseases, N.Y.C., 1927-64, cons. in bacteriology, from 1964; head dept. of microbiology Roosevelt Hosp., New York City, from 1964. Chmn. internat. com. on staphylococcal phage typing Internat. Assn. Microbiol. Socs., 1958-62. Recipient Kimble Methodology Research award, 1957. Diplomate of the American Board of Microbiology. Fellow Am. Acad. Microbiology (bd. govs. 1961-64). Fellow A.A.A.S., N.Y. Acad. Medicine; mem. Am. Soc. Microbiology (sec.-treas. 1949-50, pres. 1961-62), Am. Pub. Health Assn., Internat. Assn. Microbiol. Socs. (chmn. com. on staphylococcal phage typing 1958-66). Sigma Xi. Contbr. articles sci., med. jours. Home: Oak Bluffs, Mass. Died Mar. 26, 1980; interred Oak Bluffs.

BLAIR, MORRIS MYERS, educator, clergyman; b. Chanute, Kan., Nov. 7, 1886; s. John Franklin and Anna (Myers) B.; student Drake U., 1907-09; B.S., S.W. Mo. State Coll., 1928; A.M., U. Mo., 1929; Ph.D., U. Wis., 1939; m. Corinne Brown, Dec. 27, 1916; children—John Morris, Corinne Ann, Jane, David Rufus. Ordained to ministry Christian (Disciples) Ch., 1909; pastor, Mesa, Ariz., 1910-11, Birmingham, Ala., 1912-13, Russellville, Ark., 1914-16, Little Rock, Ark., 1918-20; statistician B.F. Goodrich & Co., Akron, O., 1916-17, Merc. Trust Co., Little Rock, 1918-20; high sch. prin., Mt. Judea, Ark., 1921-26; prof. econs. and statistics Okla. A. & M. Coll., 1930-47, U. Tulsa since 1947. Mem. Am. Statis, Assn., Am. Econ. Assn., Am. Acad. Polit. and Social Sci., A.A.A.S., Okla. Acad. Sci., Southwestern Social Sci. Assn., Alpha Kappa Psi, Lambda Chi Alpha. Mem. Christian Ch. (elder). Author: Elementary Statistics, 1944; Christ, Christianity and Communism, 1950; also articles. Home: Tulsa. *

BLAIR, WILLIAM LEEPER, newspaper editor; b. Lamar, Mo., Mar. 19, 1883; s. William and Amanda (Campbell) B.; A.B., Stanford U., 1906; m. Caro Fairchild, 1909 (dec. 1953); 1 son, Alan Fairchild. Editorial work on various Southern Calif. newspapers, 1906-10; city editor Pasadena Star, 1911-17; mem. Commn. for Mexican Research, 1917-19; asso. mng. editor Pasadena Star-News, 1921-31; mng. editor and editorial columnist Pasadena Post, 1932-44; associate editor, Star-News, since 1945. Member Pasadena Bd. Education, 1929-49; member State Board of Education since 1943, pres. since 1946. Republican. Unitarian. Mason (33 deg.). Clubs: University, Twilight (Pasadena). Home: Pasadena. *

BLAKE, GEORGE H., utilities exec.; b. Harrison, N.J., 1884; grad. New York Univ., 1906. Pres., mem., exec. com., dir. Public Service Electric & Gas Co., Public Service Coordinated Transport and Public Service Interstate Transportation Co. (all Newark, N.J.); mem. exec. com., dir., West Hudson Nat. Bank of Harrison, N.J.; dir., New York & Long Branch R.R. Co. Home: West Orange, N.J. *

BLAKE, JAMES HUBERT (EUBIE BLAKE), musician; b. Balt., Feb. 7, 1883; s. John Sumner and Emma (Johnstone) B.; student Schillinger System of Composition, N.Y. U., 1949; D.H.L., Bklyn. Coll., 1973, Dartmouth, 1974; D.F.A., Rutgers U., 1974; Mus. D., New Eng. Conservatory Music, 1974; m. Marion Gant Tyler, Dec. 27, 1945. Began profl. piano career, 1901; became partner vaudeville team Sissle and Blake, 1915; collaborator Broadway show Shuffle Along, 1921, Blackbirds, 1930; mus. condr. U.S.O. Hosp. Unit, 1941-46; now active pub. appearances, recording; founder Eubie Blake Music, rec. co., 1972; appearances jazz festivals, Europe; mus. autobiography French TV. Recipient numerous honors and awards. Mem. A.F.T.R.A., A.S.C.A.P., Negro Actors Guild, Actors Equity. Mason. Composer songs including: Memories of You, You're Lucky to Me, I'm Just Wild About Harry (ofcl. campaign song H.S. Truman). Home: Brooklyn NY. *

BLAKEMORE, WILLIAM BARNETT, JR., educator, clergyman; b. Perth, Western Australia, July 22, 1912 (parents Am. citizens); s. William Barnett and Nell (Porter) B.; B.S., Washington U., St. Louis, 1933; A.M., U. Chgo., 1937, D.B., 1938, Ph.D., 1941; m. E. Josephine Gilstrap, June 2, 1942; children—William B., Josephine Jory. Tech. salesman G.S. Robins & Co., St. Louis, 1933-35; mem. counseling and directorial staff Am. Youth Found. St. Louis, 1936-40, mem. faculty, 1948-75, trustee, 1957-75; ordained to ministry Disciples of Christ Ch., 1941; instr. psychology of religion U. Chgo., 1941-43, asst. prof., 1943-48; asso. prof. practical theology, 1948-71, prof. ecumenical Christianity, 1971-75, mem. cabinet Federated Theol. Faculty, 1945-61, asst. to dean. Disciples Divinity House, 1941-45, acting dean, 1945-46, dean 1946-75, asso. dean Rockefeller Meml. Chapel, 1959-66; minister Normal Park Baptist Ch., Chgo, 1950-51. Mem. dept. pastoral services Fed. Council Chs. of Christ in Am., 1947-57; mem. bd. higher edn. Disciples of Christ, 1945-75, mem. council of agys., 1945-68, sec., 1956-58; bd. dirs. Ill. Disciples of Christ, 1950-56; mem. Disciple Panel of Scholars, 1956-62, chmn., 1958-62; mem. central com. Brotherhood Commn. on Restructure, 1961-69; del. Ch. Fedn. Greater Chgo., pres., 1967-68; del. assembly World Council Chs., New Delhi, India, 1961, Uppsala, Sweden, 1968; mem. Council Christian Unity; chmn. Dept. Ecumenical Studies, 1961-66; mem. Ill. Commn. on Ministry; del.-observer Vatican Council II, 1964, 1965; del. to 4th World Conf. on Faith and Order, Montreal, Que., Can., 1963; fraternal del. Faith and Order Commn., Bristol, Eng., 1967, Louvain, Belgium, 1971, Legon, Ghana, 1974; adviser central com. World Council of Chs., Canterbury, Eng., 1969, Addis Ababa, Ethiopia, 1971, Utrecht, 1972, Geneva, 1973, Berlin, 1974; pres. World Conv. Chs. of Christ 1974-75. Recipient Susan Colver Rosenberger prize for meritorious research U. Chgo., 1938; travelling fellow. Disciples Divinity House, 1938-39. Mem. Assn. Disciples Theol. Discussion, Am. Theol. Soc. (midwest br.), Disciples of Christ Hist. Soc., Assn. Theol. Profs. in Practical Field, N. Am. Acad. Ecumenists. Club: Quadrangle (Chgo.). Author: The Cornerstone and the Builders, 1955; A Needy One Stands Before Thee, 1956; Encountering God, 1965; The Discovery of the Church, 1966; The Bible Enlightens Our Lives, 1968; Quest for Intelligence in the Ministry, 1970. Editor of: Disciples in Illinois, 1959; mem. editorial bd. Pastoral Psychology, 1949-54; editor, contbr. The Renewal of Church, 3 vols., 1963; The Challenge of Christian Unity, 1963. Contbr. to religious periodicals. Home: Hinsdale, Ill. Died May 2, 1975.

BLAMEY, LT. GEN. SIR THOMAS ALBERT (BLA'MI), Australian Army officer; b. Wagga, New South Wales, Australia, Jan. 24, 1884; m. Minnie Millard, Sept. 8, 1908 (died 1935); 1 son. Began with Commonwealth Mil. Forces, 1906; served in World War I, 1914-18; served as chief of staff, Australian Corps, 1918, Australian Imperial Force, 1919; became dep. chief of gen. staff, Australia, 1920; Australian defense rep. in London, attached to War Office, 1922-24; 2d chief of gen. staff, Commonwealth Mil. Forces, 1923-25; chief commr. of police, Victoria, 1925-37; comdr. 3d Australian Div., 1931-37; controller-gen. of Recruiting Secretariat, Australia, 1938-39; became comdr. Australian Army Corps, 1940; apptd. comdr. Australian Forces in Middle East, 1940; apptd. dept. comdr-in-chief Brit. Forces in Middle East, 1941; returned to Australia to take command of Australian Forces in war against Japanese, and to serve under Gen. MacArthur, Mar. 1942. Awarded Distinguished Service Order; mentioned in 7 dispatches, World War I; Companion of Bath, 1919; Companion of St. Michael and St. George.*

BLANCHAR, CARROLL HENRY, utility co. exec.; b. Windsor, Wis., Apr. 3, 1912; s. John C. and Amelia (Eggleson) B.; B.A., U. Wis., 1933; C.P.A., U. Ill., 1943; grad. Advanced Mgmt. Program, Harvard U., 1951; LL.D., Franklin Coll.; m. Cecile Cunningham, Dec. 24, 1934; children—Beverly, Patricia, Thomas. Accountant, Arthur Andersen & Co., C.P.A.'s, 1933-37; auditor Commonwealth Edison Co., 1937-43; comptroller United Air Lines, Inc., 1943-52; v.p. fin. Roddis Plywood Corp., 1952-58, pres., 1958-60; pres. Pub. Service Co. of Indiana, Inc., 1960-68, chmn. bd., chief exec. officer, 1968-77, chmn. bd., 1977-80, also dir.; dir. Mchts. Nat. Bank & Trust Co., Indpls., Am. United Life Ins. Co., Indpls. Bd. govs. Asso. Colls. Ind.; bd. mgrs. Rose-Hulman Inst. Tech.; bd. dirs. Edison Electric Inst. N.Y. Mem. Ind. C. of C. (dir., officer), Alpha Kappa Psi, Beta Alpha Psi, Beta Gamma Sigma. Clubs: Union League (Chgo.); Columbia Indpls. Athletic (Indpls.); Meridian Hills Country. Home: Indianapolis, Ind. Died Mar. 16, 1980; interred Crown Hill Mausoleum, Indpls.

BLANCHARD, GEORGE WASHINGTON, ex-congressman; b. Colby, Wis., Jan. 26, 1884; s. Horace Jones and Emma (Brinker) B.; A.B., U. of Wis., 1906, LL.B., 1910; m. Helen Sherman, Nov. 5, 1910; children—George, David, Sherman. Admitted to Wis. bar, 1910, and since in practice at Edgerton; city atty. Edgerton, 1913-32; mem. State Assembly, 1924-26, State Senate, 1926-33; mem. 73d Congress (1933-35), 1st Wis. Dist. Mem. Wis. State Bar Assn. Republican. Mason. K.P. Home: Edgerton, Wis.*

BLANCHARD, HENRY G., banker; b. Purcell, Okla., Nov. 10, 1904; s. John A. and Blanche N. Blanchard; B.C.S., Drake U., 1927; m. Catherine Remus, Aug. 29, 1929; 1 son, Robert H. Cashier, Nodaway Valley Bank, Maryville, Mo., 1927-47; with Comml. Nat. Bank, Kansas City, Kans., 1947-76, chmn. bd., to 1976; dir. Republic Mut. Fire Ins. Co., Am. Royal. Pres. Kansas City (Kans.) Clearing House Assn. Treas. Kansas City (Kans.) United Funds, Cancer Soc. Wyandotte County, Kan.; pres. Kaw council Boy Scouts Am., bd. dirs., mem. exec. council region VIII. Bd. dirs. Am. Royal Hosp., Kansas City, Kans.; chmn. bd. dirs. Bethany Hosp., Kansas City, Kans.; mem. adv. bd. dirs. Baker U. Recipient Silver Beaver and Silver Antelope awards Boy Scouts Am. Mem. Am. (v.p. Kans.), Kans. (chmn. legislation com., past pres., chmn.) bankers assns., Kan. (past dir.), Kansas City (Kans.) (past pres.) chambers commerce; Delta Sigma Pi. Mason (Jester, Shriner). Home: Shawnee, Kans. Died Sept. 1976.

BLANCHARD, ROBERT WESLEY, supt. schs.; b. Newburgh, N.Y., Aug. 23, 1926; s. William Wesley and Relda Jane (Reissmann) B.; A.B., Bowdoin (Maine) Coll., 1951; Ed.M., U. Maine, 1959; Ed.D., Harvard, 1962; m. Kathryn M. Alar, June 30, 1962; children—Wade, Roberta, Daniel. Prin. high sch., prin., tchr. pub. schs., Maine, 1952-59; adminstrv. asst. to supt. Greenwich (Conn.) Pub. Schs., 1960-62; asst. supt. S. Huntington Schs., Huntington Sta., N.Y., 1962-64; supt. schs., Montclair, N.J., 1964-69, Portland, Oreg., 1969-80; mem. nat. task force on desegregation Edn. Commn. of States. Bd. dirs. Oreg. Museum Sci. and Industry, Western Forestry Center. Served with AUS, 1944-46. Mem. Council Gt. City Schs. (sec.-treas.), Am. Assn. Sch. Adminstrs., Large City Sch. Supts. Assn., Confedn. Oreg. Sch. Adminstrs., Portland C. bf C., NAACP. Clubs: City, Multnomah Athletic, Portland Golf. Author articles, monographs. Home: Portland, Oreg. Died Nov. 10, 1980; inurned Sunset Hills Meml. Park, Portland.

BLANCHET, ANTOINE ALBERT, diplomat; b. Jérémie, Haiti, Dec. 26, 1884; s. Arthur Antoine and Marie Elisabeth Ilda (Gaveau) B.; certificate, Coll. of Christian Brothers, Port-au-Prince; licentiate, Nat. Sch. of Law, Port-au-Prince, 1905; m. Henriette Laraque, of Jérémie, Dec. 12, 1912. Began practice of law at Jérémie, 1905; served as prof. law, pvt. law sch., and as insp. pub. instrn. sec. Haitian Legation, Washington, D.C., 1917-21; E.E. and M.P. from Haiti to U.S., Feb. 25, 1921—. Mem. Governing Bd. Pan Am. Union. Roman Catholic. Address: Washington, D.C. *

BLANCHFIELD, FLORENCE A., col. (ret.), Nurse Corps; b. Shepherdstown, W.Va., April 1, 1884; d. Joseph Plunkett and Mary Lavinia (Anderson) B.; student Oranda Inst., Oranda, Va., Martin Bus. Coll., Pittsburgh, Pa., U. of Calif., Columbia U.; grad. South Side Training Sch. for Nurses, Pittsburgh, Pa., 1906; post grad. Dr. Howard Kelly's Sanitorium, and Johns Hopkins Hosp. in surg. technique, operating room supervision. Served as operating room supervisor South Side Hosp., 1907, Montefiore Hosp., Pittsburgh, 1908; supt. Suburban Gen. Hosp., Bellevue, Pa., 1909-13, 1916-20 (granted military leave 1917); gen. duty, anaesthetist Ancon Hosp., Canal Zone, Panama, 1913; indsl. nurse U.S. Steel Bessemer Plant, Bessemer, Pa., 1914-15. Apptd. Army Nurse Corps, assigned Base Hosp. No. 27, Sept. 1917, in France, 1917-19; relieved from active duty, reappointed and assigned to Letterman Gen. Hosp. (San Francisco), Camp Custer (Mich.), Fort Benjamin Harrison (Ind.), 1920; instr., recreational dir., Army Sch. of Nursing Letterman Gen. Hosp., 1921; asst. to chief nurse Sternburg Gen. Hosp., Manila, 1922-24; chief nurse Camp John Hay, P.I., 1924; reported to Walter Reed Gen. Hosp., Washington, D.C., 1925; spl. duty as chief nurse Fort McPherson, Ga., 1925-29; chief nurse Jefferson Barracks, Mo., 1929-32; assigned to Fort William McKinley, P.I., 1932-34; duty in Tientsin, China, 1934-35; duty in Office Surgeon Gen., U.S., 1935-42; commd. lt. col. U.S. Army, assigned first asst. to supt. of Army Nurse Corps, 1942-43; supt. Army Nurse Corps, col., U.S. Army, 1943; ret., 1947. Awarded D.S.M., 1945. Mem. South Side Hosp. Nurses Alumnae Assn., Am. Nurses Assn. (D.C.), Nat. League of Nursing Edn. (D.C.). Ret. officers Assn. (dir.). Home: Arlington, Va. *

BLANK, SAMUEL ALLAN, lawyer; b. Phila., June 22, 1910; s. Philip and Olga (Millis) B.; B.S. in Econs., Wharton Sch. of U. Pa., 1929; LL.B., 1932; LL.D., Phila. Coll. Osteo. Medicine, 1963; m. Ruth Saler, May 19, 1938; children—Robert Saler, Jeffrey Charles. Admitted to Pa. bar, 1932, since practiced in Phila.; sr. partner firm Blank, Rome, Klaus & Comisky, and predecessor firm, from 1946; dir. Continental Bank, Indsl. Cold Storage & Warehouse Co., Title Ins. Corp. Pa., Pa. Refrigerated Terminals, Inc. Mem. Pa. Ho. of Reps. from Phila. County, 1936-37. Trustee Acad. Natural Scis., Fedn. Jewish Agys. Phila., Moss Rehab. Hosp.; former chmn. bd. Phila. Coll. Osteo. Medicine. Mem. Am., Pa., Phila. bar assns. Clubs: Philmont Country, Locust (gov. Phila.). Address: Philadelphia, Pa. Deceased.

BLANKENAGEL, JOHN CHARLES (BLAN-KE-NÄ'GEL), prof. of German; b. Germantown, Wis., Dec. 22, 1886; s. August and Lucie (Becker) B.; A.B., U. of Wis., 1908, Ph.D., 1915; grad. student U. of Toulouse, 1919, U. of Paris, 1928, U. of Munich, 1929; m. Caroline Elizabeth Jesse, June 3, 1921; 1 dau., Helen Elizabeth. Teacher high school, Stoughton, Wis., 1908-09; high school, Appleton, Wis., 1909-10; instr. German, Pomona Coll. 1911-13; fellow and asst. in German, U. of Wis., 1913-15; asst. prof. German, Goucher Coll., 1915-16, asso. prof. German, 1916-17; translator of German and French med. literature, Mayo Clinic, 1919; instr. French, U. of Mont., 1920; prof. modern langs., Franklin Coll., 1920-22; prof. German, Ohio Wesleyan U., 1922-34, Wesleyan U., Middletown, Conn., since 1934; visiting prof. German lit., U. of Chicago, summer, 1930; visiting prof. German, Coll. of the City of N.Y., summer, 1934. Served as sergt. 313th Inf. U.S. Army, 1917-19, with A.E.F. in Meuse-Argonne Sector. Treas. Ohio Coll. Assn., 1924-34. Mem. Modern Lang. Assn. of Am. (chmn. Germanic Sect., 1936; exec. council, 1940-43, v.p. 1949), N.E. Modern Lang. Assn., Am. Assn. U. Profs., Am. Assn. Teachers of German (pres., 1946), Kleist-Gesellschaft, Frankfort, Oder., Phi Beta Kappa, Omicron Delta Kappa and Phi Gamma Delta. Author: Pascal's Short Life of Christ (translated with Emile Cailliet), 1950. Contbr. articles to literary and philol. jours. Home: Middletown, Conn. *

BLANSHARD, PAUL, author; b. Fredericksburg, Ohio, Aug. 27, 1892; s. Francis George and Emily (Coulter) B.; A.B., U. Mich., 1914; LL.B., Bklyn. Law Sch., 1937; postgrad. Harvard, Columbia, Union Theol. Sem.; m. Julia Anderson, Oct. 20, 1915 (dec. 1934); children—Paul, Rufus; m. 2d, Mary W. Hillyer, Aug. 1, 1935 (dec. 1965); m. 3d, Beatrice Mayer. Ordained to ministry Conglist Ch., 1917, pastor First Ch., Tampa, 1917-18; ednl. dir. Amalgamated Clothing Workers Am., Rochester, N.Y., 1920-24; field sec. League Indsl. Democracy, 1925-33; asso. editor The Nation, 1928-29; dir. city affairs com., N.Y.C., 1930-33, commr. investigations and accounts under Mayor LaGuardia, 1934-38; admitted to N.Y. bar, 1938, practiced, 1939-41; econ. analyst, cons. Caribbean Commn. Dept. State, 1942-46; writer, 1946-80. Mem. Phi Beta Kappa, Delta Sigma Rho. Unitarian. Author: An Outline of the British Labor Movement, 1923; (with Norman Thomas) What's the Matter with New York, 1932; Democracy and Empire in the Caribbean, 1947; American Freedom and Catholic Power, 1949; Communism, Democracy and Catholic Power, 1951; The Irish and Catholic Power, 1953; The Right to Read, 1955; God and Man in Washington, 1960; Freedom and Catholic Power in Spain and Portugal, 1962; Religion and the Schools, 1963; Paul Blanshard on Vatican II, 1966; Personal and Controversial, An Autobiography, 1973; Some of My Best Friends are Christians, 1974; Classics of Free Thought, 1977. Home: St Petersburg, Fla. Died Jan. 27, 1980.

BLASINGAME, R(ALPH) U(PSHAW), agrl. engr.; b. Russell Co., Ala., Dec. 24; 1886; s. Benjamin Turner and Willie (May) B.; S.B. (C.E.), Ala. Poly. Inst., Auburn, Ala., 1908; S.B. (agr.), 1910; S.B. (agri. engring.), Ia. State Coll., 1913; m. Sue May Combs, Aug. 20, 1913; children—Robert Combs, Benjamin Paul, Ralph Upshaw. Extension agrl. engr., Ala. Polytechnic Inst., 1915-17; head, dept. agrl. engring., Pa. State Coll., 1917-51, ret.; agrl. engr. University of Puerto Rico, 1951-52; farm development engr., council in research, div. of agrl. engring., U.S. Dept. of Agr., 1934; investigator, Giant Power Survey, Pa., 1924; leader, threshing div., Grain Corp. Pa. div., 1917-18; br. head agrl. engring. dept., Shrivenham Am. U., War Dept., Shrivenham, Eng., 1945-46; spl. cons. in edn. training dept., Internat. Harvester Co., 1948; organized industry seminar, Farm Equipment Inst., 1938. Award: B. F. Goodrich award, distinguished pub. service, 1940. Fellow Am. Soc. Agrl. Engrs. (chmn. power and machinery div., 1st v.p., chmn. S., N. Atlantic sects., pres. 1935-36); mem. Alpha Zeta, Alpha Gamma Rho, Phi Kappa Phi. Methodist Co-author: The Progressive Students Course-Some Recommendations. *

BLAU, HENRY HESS, phys. chemist; b. Dayton, Ohio, May 16, 1897; s. Samuel and Lena (Bowman) B.; B.S. in Chem. Engring., Carnegie Inst. Tech., 1919; M.S. (Dupont fellow), Mass. Inst. Tech., 1920; Ph.D., U. Pitts., 1935; m. Edith Elizabeth Piersol, Sept. 9, 1924; children—Elizabeth Blau Stickney, Henry Hess, Carol Blau Perot. Research chemist Macbeth-Evans Glass Co., 1920-36, dir. research, 1925-36, asst. gen. mgr., 1927-36; research and exec. positions Corning Glass Works, 1936-41; gen. mgr. Fed. Glass Works, 1941-80, v.p., 1943-80; prof. glass sci. Ohio State U., 1945-80; v.p., dir. Fed. Glass Co.; v.p. Fed. Paper Bd. Co.; chmn. ceramic data com., com. ceramic chemistry NRC; chmn. adv. com. on ceramics Internat. Critical Tables. Served with Engrs. Res. Corps, W.W. I; Sci. cons. Joint Chiefs of Staff, 1945-46. Recipient S.B. Meyer Jr., Toledo awards in glass and ceramics Am. Ceramic Soc., Albert Victor Bleininger Meml. award, 1965; Alumni Merit award Carnegie Inst. Tech. Fellow AAAS, Am. Ceramic Soc. (hon. life mem.; chmn. Pitts. sect. 1932; chmn. glass div. 1934, treas. 1963-65), Brit. Soc. Glass Tech. (hon. Am. treas.); mem. Sci. Research Soc. Am., Am. Inst. Chem. Engrs., Am. Inst. Ceramic Engrs., Am. Chem. Soc. (life), Illuminating Engring. Soc., Keramos, German Soc. Glass Tech., Am. Legion, Sigma Xi, Phi Lambda Upsilon, Tau Beta Pi. Clubs: Univ. (Columbus); Faculty Ohio State U.; Chemists (N.Y.C.); Rotary. Author: Technology of German and Austrian Glass Industry, 1946; other publs. Patentee in field. Home: Columbus, Ohio. Died Feb. 11, 1980.

BLAUG, SEYMOUR MORTON, univ. dean; b. N.Y.C., Dec. 21, 1923; s. Charles and Rose (Grannis) B.; B.S., Columbia U., 1950, M.S., 1952; Ph.D., U. Iowa, 1955; m. Eugenia Babette Goodman, Aug. 29, 1953; children—Carla, Suzanne, Amy, Elisabeth. Instr., asst. prof. U. Ia., 1955-57, asso. prof., 1957-61, prof., 1961-74; dean, prof. pharms. U. N.C. Sch. Pharmacy, Chapel Hill, 1974-75. Served with AUS, 1943-46. Recipient Borden award, 1950, Abbott Research award, 1969. Bigelow fellow, 1950-52. Fellow Acad. Pharm. Scis.; mem. Am., N.C. pharm. assns., N.Y. Acad. Sci., Sigma Xi, Rho Chi, Phi Delta Chi. Democrat. Club: Chapel Hill Tennis. Contbg. author: Prescription Pharmacy, 1970; American Pharmacy, 1974; Remington's Pharmaceutical Sciences, 1975. Contbr. articles to profl. jours. Home: Chapel Hill, N.C. Died Nov. 19, 1975.

BLAYNEY, JAMES ROY, dentist; b. Alexis, Ill., July 28, 1889; s. James Albert and Emma C. (Mead) B.; D.D.S., Northwestern U., 1913; B.S., Lewis Inst., Chicago, 1924; M.S., Univ. of Chicago, 1928; m. Alice E. Crain, Mar. 18, 1914. Dentist in Tallula, Ill.; instructor dental pathology and therapeutics, U. of Ill., 1918-23, associate prof., 1923-31, professor, 1931-36; professor dental surgery and director Walter G. Zoller Memorial Dental Clinic, U. of Chicago, 1936-54, emeritus professor of dental surgery, 1954-80; director Evanston Dental Caries Study, 1946-80. Howard Taylor Ricketts Award 1928: John Callahan Award, 1946, Fellow Am. Acad. Oral Pathology, Am. Assn. Advancement of Science. Member International Association of Dental Research, Am. Dental Assn., Ill. (past pres.), Chgo. dental socs., Chgo. Odontographic Soc., Inst. Medicine Chgo., Xi Psi Phi (supreme pres. 1945), Sigma Xi, Omicron Kappa Upsilon. Author: Dental Materia Medica and Pharmacology, 1936. Home: Evanston, Ill. Died Nov. 22, 1980.

BLEAKLEY, WILLIAM FRANCIS (BLAK'LE), lawyer; b. Verplanck, Cortlandt, N.Y., Nov. 11, 1883; s. Angelo and Mary A. (Drennan) B.; LL.B., Cornell U., 1904; m. Anna S. Martin, June 28, 1911; children—William Francis, James Robert, Margaret Mary. Admitted to N.Y. bar, 1905; city judge of Yonkers, N.Y., 1918-22; county judge, 1922-28; judge N.Y. Supreme Court, 1928-36; resigned to run for gov. on the Rep. ticket; defeated and returned to private practice; mem. firm Bleakley, Platt, Schmidt, Hart & Fritz; member board of directors of Companion Life Ins. Co., county exec. Westchester County, 1939-41; apptd. counsel Joint Legislative Com. of State of N.Y. on Reapportionment; Moreland Commr. (apptd. by Gov. Lehman, re-apptd. by Gov. Dewey) to investigate adminstrn. of Workmen's Compensation Law. Vice-pres. Constitutional Conv., 1938. Pres. Cornell Law Assn. Mem. N.Y. State Bar Assn. (v.p. and pres. judicial sect.). Republican. Catholic. Elk, K.C. Clubs: Golf, Cornell University (New York). Home: Yonkers, N.Y. *

BLEIBTREU, JACOB, stockbroker; b. Frankfort am Main, Germany, Sept. 30, 1886; s. Nathan and Auguste (Homburger) B.; grad. Comml. High Sch., Frankfurt am Main, 1902; m. Helen Reinthaler, Oct. 27, 1924; children—John N., Ann-Louise (Mrs. Hugh Thornton). Came to U.S., 1909, naturalized, 1916. With Lazard-Speyer-Ellissen, Frankfurt am Main, 1902-09, Speyer & Co., bankers, N.Y.C., 1909-19; sr. partner Abraham & Co., N.Y.C., 1919-71, ltd. partner, 1971, hon. chmn. bd. Abraham & Co., Inc., until 1975; spl. partner Lehman Bros., Inc., to 1976. Mem. N.Y. Stock Exchange, 1921-76, gov., 1954-60. Chmn. war record bur. Greater N.Y. Jewish Welfare Bd., 1944-47; mem. com. Wall St. Fedn. Jewish Charities; chmn. Wall St. com. Am. Jewish Com. Bd. dirs., v.p. Arthritis and Rheumatism Found. of N.Y.; trustee Hillside Hosp., L.I. Served with U.S. Army, 1918-19; gen. staff 2d Army, AEF; instr. Air Force Intelligence Sch., Harrisburg, Pa., 1942-45. Mem. Am. Legion. Clubs: New York Stock Exchange Luncheon; Buttonwood (dir. sec. of club and found.); Sunningdale Country (Scarsdale, N.Y.). Home: New York, N.Y. Died Dec. 6, 1976.

BLENKO, WALTER JOHN, lawyer; b. London, Eng., Mar. 4, 1899; s. William J. and Sarah (Balman) B.; came to U.S. as infant; B.S., Carnegie-Mellon U., 1921, M.E., 1941; J.D., Duquesne U., 1924, LL.D., 1963; m. Ardis L. Jones, Sept. 15, 1921; children—Walter J., Don Balman. Admitted to Pa. bar, 1924, since practiced in Pitts. Bd. dirs. Duquesne U.; trustee Carnegie Inst., Carnegie-Mellon U. Mem. Newcomen Soc. N.Am., N.Y. Acad. Scis., Sigma Alpha Epsilon, Phi Kappa Phi, Tau Beta Pi, Pi Tau Sigma, Omicron Delta Kappa. Clubs: University, Duquesne, Fellows. Home: Allison Park, Pa. Died Nov. 6, 1978.

BLINN, CLARENCE J., judge; b. Beaver County, Pa., June 24, 1886; s. John A. and Caroline A. (Stuber) B.; prep. edn., Acad. Dept. U. of Va., 1904-05; student Law Dept. U. of Mich., 1905-07; LL.B., Yale, 1908; m. Margaret F. Davis, Aug. 23, 1911; children—John Dean (dec.), Barbara Dean, Robert Davis. In practice of law, mem. Wright & Blinn, Oklahoma City, Okla., 1909-34. Mayor of Oklahoma City. 1931-33; county judge, Oklahoma County, December 1934-Jan. 1951. Apptd. chmn. Okla. Co. Advisory Bd. for Registrants, 1940; elected chmn. Okla. County Defense Com., 1941. Chmn. Oklahoma City Dem. Central Com., 1923. Mem. Okla. State and Okla. County bar assns., Oklahoma City Chamber Commerce (past dir.); v.p. Okla. Municipal League, 1933-34. Presbyn. K.P. (Grand Chancellor, Okla., 1925-26; elected dir. and chmn. Home Board, 1937; ordained elder 1941); member D.O.K.K. (Imperial Rep., 1925-35; mem. judiciary com., Imperial Palace, 1935-39, elected Imperial Basha, Aug. 1939, Imperial Prince, Aug. 1941). Home: Oklahoma City. *

BLISS, CHESTER ITTNER, biometrician; b. Springfield, Ohio, Feb. 1, 1899; s. Chester Bradley and Henrietta (Ittner) B.; B.A., Ohio State U., 1921; M.A., Columbia, 1922, Ph.D., 1926; postgrad. Univ. Coll., London, Eng., 1933-35. Asso. entomologist U.S. Dept. Agr., New Orleans, 1926-29, entomologist, Mexico City, 1928, Whittier, Calif., 1930-33; mem. Inst. Plant Protection, Leningrad, USSR, 1935-37; biometrician Conn. Agr. Exptl. Sta., New Haven, 1940-71; biometrician Storrs (Conn.) Expt. Sta., 1940-53; lectr. Yale, 1942-67, 72; mem. Gonville and Caius Coll., Cambridge (Eng.) U., 1953-54; vis. prof. N.C. State Coll., 1946; vis. staff Commonwealth Sci. and Indsl. Research Orgn., Australia, 1961, 67, Japanes Union Scientists and Engrs., Japan, 1961, 67, Indian Statis. Inst., 1961-62, UAR Dept. Statistics and Census, Cairo, 1962. Mem. com. revision U.S. Pharmacopeia. Fellow Am. Statis. Assn. (v.p. 1943, 47), Royal Statis. Soc., A.A.A.S. (v.p. sect. U. 1958), Inst. Math. Statistics; mem. Biometric Soc. (hon. life; sec. 1947-55, pres. 1962-63, editorial bd. 1947-65), Entomol. Soc., Ecol. Soc. Am., Am. Soc. Pharmacology, Soc. Quality Control, Internat. Statis. Inst. Author: The Statistics of Bioassay, 1952; (with D.W. Calhoun) An Outline of Biometry, 1954; Statistics in Biology, Vol. 1, 1967, Vol. 2, 1970; also numerous articles. Research in statis. methods in biology, biol. assay, exptl. design in biology agr. and med. research. Home: New Haven, Conn. Died Mar. 14, 1979.

BLISS, GEORGE WILLIAM, newspaperman; b. Denver, July 21, 1918; s. William Lane and Marie (Bresnan) B.; student Northwestern U., 1938; m. Helen Jeanne Groble, June 29, 1940 (dec. June 1959); children—William R., George L., Dennis M., Marianne, Carol, Helen Jeanne; m. 2d, Therese O'Keefe, Aug. 11, 1960; 1 son, Terrence. With Chgo. Evening Am., 1937-42; with Chgo. Tribune, 1942-68, 71-78, labor editor, 1953-68, dir. investigative task force, 1971-78; chief investigator Better Govt. Assn., 1968-71, also acting exec. dir. Dir. Chgo. Tribune Task Force, 1971. Served with USNR, World War II. Recipient Edward Scott Beck award Chgo. Tribune, 1954, 58, 73; Spot News Reporting award Chgo. Newspaper Guild, 1957, A.P., 1958, 59; Pulitzer prize for local reporting, 1962, 73, 76; Jacob Scher award, 1973; News Writing award A.P. Ill., 1972, 74, A.P. Editors Assn., 1974; Inland Daily Press Assn. award, 1974; News award U.P.I., 1974. Mem. Chgo. Newspaper Reporters Assn. Clubs: Press, Ill. Athletic Assn. (Chgo.). Home: Evergreen Park, Ill. Died Sept. 11, 1978.

BLIVEN, BRUCE, editor; b. Emmetsburg, Iowa, July 27, 1889; s. Charles F. and Lilla C. (Ormsby) B.; A.B., Stanford, 1911; m. Rose Emery, May 17, 1913; 1 son, Bruce. Editorial staff San Francisco Bull., 1909-12; mag. contbr. and advt. writer, 1912-14; dir. dept. journalism U. So. Calif., 1914-16; editorial staff Printers' Ink, 1917-18; mem. editorial bd. N.Y. Globe, 1919-23, New Republic, 1923-55; N.Y. corr. Manchester Guardian, 1927-47; lectr. communication and journalism Stanford, 1956-77. Bd. dirs. Twentieth Century Fund, 1923-57. Author: The Men Who Make the Future, 1942; Preview for Tomorrow, The Unfinished Business of Science, 1953; The World Changers, 1965; Five Million Words Later (autobiography), 1970; A Mirror for Greatness, 1975. Editor: What the Informed Citizen Needs to Know, 1945; Twentieth Century Unlimited, 1950. Contbr. to Sat. Eve. Post, Ladies' Home Jour., Readers Digest, Harper's, Redbook, etc. Address: Stanford, Calif. Died May 27, 1977.

BLOCK, ADOLPH, sculptor; b. N.Y.C., Jan. 29, 1906; s. Henry and Dora (Wolpin) B.; student Beaux Arts Inst. Design, Fontainebleau Sch. Fine Arts; m. Tilda M. Frishman, June 29, 1930 (dec. Mar. 1972). Sculptor, works exhibited N.A.D., Archtl. League N.Y., Pa. Acad. Fine Arts, Whitney Mus., Jewish Mus., French and Argent Galleries, Salamagundi Club, Lever House; works installed at Bayonne (N.J.) Pub. Library, William Cullen Bryant High Sch., Morris High Sch., Queens Vocat. High Sch., Beth-El Hosp. (all N.Y.C.), Garfield Restaurant, Bklyn., Saxony Restaurant, Newark Concord Restaurant, Jamaica, L.I.; designer Spencer Grady medals Am. Chem. Soc., Karl Taylor Compton medal Am. Inst. of Physics, Long Lines Medal of Am. Tel. & Tel. Co., Allen medal Am. Soc. Human Genetics, 63d medal Soc. Medallists, bronze portrait medallions Tobacco Industry Hall Fame, bronze portrait plaque Dr. Franz J. Kallman, Columbia Presbyn. Med. Center, N.Y.C., 1967, Washington Irving medal N.Y. U. Hall Fame Series, 1968, others; designed eight 9-foot figure panels Nat. Shrine Immaculate Conception, Washington; has done bronze busts of Spinoza, Simon Barer and others; designed Nathan Hale Coin medal for Nat. Commemorative Soc., 1969, Simon Newcomb medal for N.Y. U. Hall of Fame series, 1970, Del. Fine Arts Fedn. N.Y., 1954-64, dir., chmn. sculpture, 1955-56; mem. faculty Nat. Acad. Sch. Fine-Arts, 1959-73. Tiffany Found. fellow, 1926; Fontainebleau fellow, 1927; Beaux-Arts Architects Silver medal, 1926, Beaux Arts Inst. Paris prize, 1927, 1st award for sculpture at ann. exhbns. Fontainebleau Alumni Assn., 1932, 34, 38, hon. mention for sculpture Nat. Gold Medal Exhbns., Archtl. League N.Y., 1955-56, Lindsay Morris prize, bas reliefs, Allied Artists Am., 1956, Gold Medal of Honor, 1958, 1st Lindsay Morris prize for bas relief sculpture, 1969; Lindsay Morris prize for medals, Nat. Sculpture Soc., 1958, Herbert Adams Meml. medal and citation, 1961; 1st Mrs. John Newington prize Hudson Valley Art Assn., 1960, gold medal of honor for sculpture, 1961; Henry Hering Meml. medal and citation, 1961; Harriet Mayor Meml. award for sculpture Am. Artists Profl. League, 1961; Gold Plate award Acad. Achievement, 1961; Silver medal Nat. Sculpture Soc. Ann. Exhbn., 1967, cash award for most notable service, 1970; cash award for portrait bust Nat. Arts Club, 1969. First v.p. Altruists chpt. City of Hope, 1954-56. Fellow Nat. Sculpture Soc. (rec. sec. 1953-56, sec. 1956-59, chmn. membership com., 1956-63, 1st v.p. 1959-62, pres. 1963-65); academician Nat. Acad. Design; mem. Allied Artists Am. (v.p. 1958-61, chmn. jury of selection 1958, dir. bd. govs., v.p., pres. 1964-65, Lindsay Morris Meml. prize for bas-relief 1963, Therese Richard Meml. prize for religious sculpture 1964), Internat. Assn. Plastic Arts (2d v.p. U.S. com. 1960-62), Fine Arts Fedn. N.Y. (dir. 1954-63, 70-78, chmn. sculpture), Archtl. League N.Y., Fontainebleau Alumni Assn. Editor: Nat. Sculpture Rev., 1958-73, editor emeritus, 1973-78. Home: New York, N.Y. Died Aug. 20, 1978.

BLOCK, HENRY DAVID, mathematician, engr., educator; b. N.Y.C., Feb. 22, 1920; s. Isaac and Celia (Gottschall) B.; B.S. cum laude, CCNY, 1940, B.C.E., 1943; M.S., Iowa State U., 1947, Ph.D., 1949; m. Phoebe T. Goggin, May 12, 1946; 1 son, David Lee. Exptl. flight test engr., stress analyst Goodyear Aircraft Corp., Akron, Ohio, 1943-45; aerodynamicist Fairchild Engine & Aircraft Corp., Jamaica, L.I., N.Y., 1946; teaching fellow Iowa State U., 1946-47, faculty, 1947-53; asst. prof. U. Minn., 1953-55; mem. faculty Cornell U., 1955-78, prof. theoretical and applied mechanics, 1961-78; vis. prof. applied electrophysics U. Calif. at San Diego, LaJolla, 1966-67; vis. prof. info. scis. U. Calif. at Santa Cruz, 1976; chmn. Gordon Research Conf. on Biomath., Andover, N.H., 1969-70. Recipient award Japan Soc. Promotion of Sci., 1977. Guggenheim Meml. Found. fellow for research in biomath., 1970-71. Mem. Am. Math. Soc., Math. Assn. Am., Assn. Computing Machinery, IEEE, Phi Beta Kappa, Sigma Xi, Tau Beta Pi, Pi Mu Epsilon, Phi Kappa Phi. Author: An Introduction to Tensor Analysis, 1962. Contbr. articles profl. jours. Home: Ithaca, N.Y. Died Oct. 6, 1978.

BLOCK, HERMAN BERNHARDT, exec.; b. Crawfordsville, Ind., Aug. 8, 1904; s. Morris and Frances (Goldberg) B.; student Harvard Mil. Acad., Los Angeles, 1919-20, U. Wis., 1922-25; m. Lillian Shirley Callin, Apr. 12, 1927 (dec. 1958); children—Francine Joan Shalit, Richard Morse; m. 2d, Florence Joyce Boden, May 11, 1960; 1 son, Ronald Jay. Dept. store mgmt., 1927-35; owner indsl. salvage firm, 1935-45; sales indsl. supplies, 1946-52; subcontract mgr. Merritt-Chapman & Scott Corp., 1952-54, v.p. procurement, 1956-57, exec. v.p. procurement, 1958-66, pres., 1972-80, also dir.; pres. Practical Mfg. Co., 1966-72; dir. purchasing Devoe & Raynolds Co., Inc., 1954-56. Served as lt. comdr. USNR, 1943-46. Mem. Phi Sigma Delta. Elk; mem. B'nai B'rith. Clubs: Chemists (N.Y.C.); Inverary Country (Ft. Lauderdale, Fla.); Haresfoot (U. Wis.). Home: New Fairfield, Conn. Died Oct. 26, 1980.

BLOCK, PHILIP D., JR., business exec.; b. Chgo., June 25, 1906; s. Philip D. and Celia (Leopold) B.; student Phillips Acad., Andover, Mass., 1922-24; B.S., Sheffield Sci. Sch. Yale, 1928; m. Margaret L. Selz, Nov. 28, 1934; children—Philip D., III, Andrew K. With Inland Steel Co., Chgo., 1928-77, asst. v.p., 1934-48, dir., 1942-77, hon. dir., 1977-81, became v.p. in charge raw materials, 1948, later sr. v.p., vice chmn., 1959-67, chmn. bd., 1967-71, chmn. exec. com., 1971-77; mem. exec. com. Chgo. Community Trust, 1962-78, chmn. exec. com., 1972-78; dir. Continental-Ill. Nat. Bank & Trust Co. of Chgo., 1959-72. Bd. dirs. Jewish Children's Bur., Chgo., 1930-50, Jewish Fedn. of Chgo., 1954-59; bd. dirs. United Charities of Chgo. 1939-58, pres., 1951-52; trustee U. Chgo., 1957-76, life trustee, 1976-81. Clubs: Standard, Tavern, Casino, Mid-Day, Lake Shore Country, Quadrangle, Chicago (Chgo.); Mid-America, Lyford Cay (Nassau). Home: Chicago, Ill. Died May 28, 1981; interred Rosehill Mausoleum.

BLODGETT, KATHARINE BURR, research in physics and chemistry; b. Schenectady, Jan. 10, 1898; d. George Reddington and Katharine Buchanan (Burr) Blodgett; A.B., Bryn Mawr Coll., 1917; S.M., U. Chgo., 1918; Ph.D., Cambridge (Eng.) U., 1926; D.Sc. (hon.), Elmira Coll., 1939, Brown U., 1942, Western Coll., 1942, Russel Sage Coll., 1944. Began as research worker, 1918; employed in research lab., Gen. Electric Co., Schenectady, N.Y., 1918-24, from 1926; inventor non-reflecting glass. Fellow Am. Phys. Soc.; mem. Optical Soc. Am. Club: Zonta (Schenectady). Author several articles in sci. jours. Home: Schenectady, N.Y. Died Dec. 10, 1979.

BLOEDORN, WALTER ANDREW, physician; born Platte Center, Nebraska, November 22, 1886; son of William and Wilhelmina (Henrich) B.; graduate Franklin (Neb.) Acad., 1905; M.D., Creighton U. Med. Sch., Omaha, Neb., 1909; A.B., George Washington University, 1915, A.M., 1916, D.Sc. (hon.), 1948; graduate study, New York Post Graduate Med. School, 1916-17, National Hospital, London, 1922; Allgemeines Krankenhaus, Vienna, 1922. Comdr. Med. Corps, U.S. Navy (retired); prof- essor medicine, George Washington U., dean. Sch. Medicine, med. dir. U. Hosp., until 1957; mem. adv. bd. Nat. Bank, Washington. Pres. Gorgas Meml. Inst. 1957-61. Pres. National Board Medical Examiners, 1957-60, mem. of executive committee, 1960-62. Diplomate Am. Bd. Internal Medicine. Fellow A.C.P.; mem. A.M.A., Assn. Am. Medical Colleges (pres. 1947-48), Alpha Omega Alpha, Phi Beta Pi. Clubs: Army and Navy, Army-Navy Country, Metropolitan, Burning Tree. Author monographs on medicine and contbr. to med. jours. Home: Washington. *

BLOMMERS, PAUL J., educator; b. Pella, Iowa, Mar. 5, 1910; s. John J. and Lilla (Renaud) B.; B.A., Central Coll., 1932; M.S., U. Iowa, 1936, Ph.D., 1943; m. Yvonne E. Aschenbrenner, Aug. 2, 1934 (div.); children—James J., Thomas J.; m. 2d, Frances S. Gordon, 1975. Tchr., prin. Dunlap (Iowa) High Sch., 1932-37; tchr. Shenandoah (Iowa) High Sch., 1937-38; supt. schs., Dunlap, 1938-40; research asst. U. Iowa, 1940-43, exec. sec. Exam. Service, 1943-45, registrar, examiner, 1945-47, acting dean Coll. Edn., 1947-48, asso. prof., 1948-55, prof., 1955-77, chmn. div. ednl. psychology, measurement, and statistics, 1966-77, chmn. bd. control athletics, faculty rep. to Big 10, 1947-56, chmn. research com. Coll. Edn., 1948-77. Fellow Am. Psychol. Assn.; mem. Inst. Math. Statistics, Am. Statis. Assn., Biometric Soc., Psychometric Soc., Nat. Soc. Study Edn., Am. Edn. Research Assn., Nat. Council Tchrs. Math., AAUP, AAAS, Phi Delta Kappa, Sigma Xi. Mason, Elk. Author (with E.F. Linquist) Elementary Statistical Methods, 1960, rev. edit. (with Robert A. Forsyth), 1977. Home: Iowa City, Iowa. Died Aug. 10, 1977; interred Oakland Cemetery, Iowa City.

BLONDELL, JOAN, actress; b. N.Y.C., Aug. 30, 1912; d. Edward and Kathryn (Cain) Blondell; student many schs.; m. George Barnes, Aug. 31, 1937 (div.); m. 2d, Dick Powell, June 1937 (div. 1944); children—Norman, Ellen; m. 3d, Mike Todd, 1946 (div. 1950). Mem. family vaudeville act Lost Boy, 1915-28; numerous stage appearances latest being Something for the Boys, The Rope Dancers, Come Back Little Sheba, The Time of the Cuckoo, Call Me Madam, A Tree Grows in Brooklyn, New Girl in Town, Copper and Brass, Crazy October, Dark at the Top of the Stairs, Bye Bye Birdie, Watch the Birdie, The Effect of Gamma Rays on Man-in-The-Moon Marigolds; numerous films, 1930—, latest being Unfit to Print, Model Wife, Topper Returns, Stage Struck, Larceny Lane, Lady for a Night, Blondie Johnson, Cry Havoc, Don Juan Quillgan, A Tree Grows in Brooklyn, Christmas Eve, Adventure, Nightmare Allay, The Corpse Came C.O.D., For Heaven's Sake, The Blue Veil, The Opposite Sex, Lizzie, Will Success Spoil Rock Hunter, Desk Set, This Could Be the Night, Angel Baby, Advance to the Rear, The Cincinnati Kid, Ride for Vengence, Paradise Road, Waterhole Number Three, Kona Coast, Stay Away Joe, The Phynx, Support Your Local Gunfighter, Won Ton Ton, The Dog Who Saved Hollywood; appeared on TV series Here Come the Brides, 1969-70; appeared in TV movies The Dead Don't Lie, 1975, Winner Take All, 1975, Death at Love House, 1976; numerous TV appearances on spls., series, talk shows, movies made for TV, also past radio appearances. Author: Center Door Fancy, 1972. Address: New York, N.Y. Died Dec. 25, 1979.

BLOOD, HOWARD EARL, mfr.; b. Petoskey, Mich., Feb. 26, 1886; s. Maurice Eugene and Mary Louvica (Brackett) B.; B.S., U. of Mich., 1909; m. Edith Cornelia Goodrich, June 24, 1910; children—Lorna Augusta Candler, Elizabeth Mary Davis, Martha Irene Zeder, Howard Earl. Gen. mgr. Canadian Products Div., General Motors of Can., 1919-23; gen. mgr. Detroit Gear & Machine Co. 1923-51; organized Norge Corp., pres. 1927-48; merged Norge Corp. with Borg-Warner Corp., 1929, v.p. since 1932. Dir. Mich. Mfrs. Assn., Economic Club, Detroit. Exec. officer McCook Field, Dayton, during World War I, with rank of major. Clubs: Chicago; Detroit, Detroit Athletic, Country Club of Detroit. Home: Grosse Pointe Farms Mich. *

BLOOMFIELD, MIKE B., musician; b. Chgo., July 28, 1943; s. Harold and Dorothy (Eller) B.; m. Susan Jay Smith, Sept. 4, 1962. Formerly lead guitarist with Paul Butterfield Blues Band; leader own group The Electric Flag; performed 1st annual Monterey Pop Music Festival. Home: Mill Valley, Calif. Died Feb. 15, 1981.

BLOOMGARDEN, KERMIT, theatrical producer; b. Bklyn., Dec. 15, 1904; s. Zemad and Annie (Groden) B.; B.C.S., N.Y. U., 1926; m. Kinda Lee, 1939 (dec. Aug. 1942); m. 2d, Virginia Kaye, Sept. 29, 1943 (div. Jan. 1965); children—David, John. Practice as certified pub. accountant, 1922-33; gen. mgr. Arthur Beckhardt, theatrical producer, 1933-34, Herman Shumlin, 1935-45; theatrical producer, 1945-76; produced plays include: Deep Are the Roots, Woman Bites Dog, Command Decision, Death of a Salesman (Pulitzer prize, Tony award, N.Y. Critics Circle award), The Crucible, (Tony award), Legend of Sarah, View from the Bridge, Diary of Anne Frank (Pulitzer prize, N.Y. Critics Circle award, Tony award), The Lark, Most Happy Fella (N.Y. Critics award), Autumn Garden, Another Part of the Forest, Look Homeward, Angel (Pulitzer prize, N.Y. Critics Circle award 1958), The Music Man (Tony award, N.Y. Critics Circle award 1958), The Gang's All Here, The Fighting Cock, Toys in the Attic (New York Critics Circle Award 1960), Anyone Can Whistle, The Playroom, Ilya Darling, Hot L Baltimore (N.Y. Drama Critics award 1973), The Seahorse, Equus (Tony award, N.Y. Drama Critics award 1975), Poor Murderer. Mgr., Stage Door Canteen. Mem. League N.Y. Theatres (dir.), Council Living Theatre (dir.), Am. Theatre Wing (dir.). Home: New York, N.Y. Died Sept. 20, 1976.

BLUEMEL, CLIFFORD (BLOO MEL'), army officer; b. Trenton, N.J., Nov. 9, 1885; s. John Theodore and Martha Jane Kelly (Kewell) B.; B.S., U.S. Mil. Acad., 1909; grad. Army War Coll., 1918. Advanced Course Inf. Sch., Ft. Benning, 1926; distinguished grad. Command and Gen. Staff Sch., Ft. Leavenworth, 1927; m. Elsie Gunner, Dec. 28, 1910; children—Dorothy Elizabeth, Edward. Commd. 2d lt. Inf., U.S. Army, 1909, and advanced through the grades to brig. gen. (temp.), Dec. 18, 1941. Retired with rank of brigadier general. Oct. 31, 1947. With 24th Inf., later 8th Inf., Philippines, 1912-15; with 22d Inf., Ariz., 1915-17, Ft. Hamilton, N.Y., 1917-18; with 152d Depot Brig., Camp Upton, N.Y., June-Oct. 1918, with 15th Div., Camp Logan, Tex., Nov.-Dec. 1918; demobilization officer, Camp Dix, N.J., Jan.-May 1919; with 22d Inf., Ft. Jay, 1919-20; with 42d Inf., later 33d Inf., Panama Canal Zone, 1920-23; with 11th Inf., Ft. Benjamin Harrison, 1923-25; instr. N.J. Nat. Guard, 1927-32; with Civilian Conservation Corps, Ft. Harrison, 1932-36; asst. chief staff 3d Corps Area Baltimore, 1936-40; commd. 45th Inf., Philippine Islands, July 1940. Comd. 45th Inf. (PS), July 1940-Sept. 1941; comdt., Staff Sch., Camp Allen, Baguio, P.I., Sept. 21-Nov. 14, 1941; comd. 31st Div., P.A., Nov. 18, 1941-Apr. 9, 1941; Bataan Campaign. Taken prisoner by Japanese on Apr. 9, 1942 when Bataan surrendered. Released at Mukden Aug. 10, 1945, by Russians. Decorations: Distinguished Service Cross, Distinguished Service Medal, Silver Star, Unit Citation with 2 Oak Leaf Clusters. Inf. Combat Badge. Address: Yardley, Pa. *

BLUM, BERNARD, engineer; b. Chicago, Ill., Feb. 12, 1883; s. August and Edith Sarah (Bromfield) B.; B.S., Mass. Inst. Tech., 1904; m. Lilian Elizabeth Swan Wynn, of Chicago, Aug. 8, 1908. Began with Chicago Junction Ry., 1905; with Northern Pacific Ry. since 1907, engr. maintenance of way, St. Paul, Minn., 1919-28, chief engr. since 1928. Mem. Am. Soc. C.E., Am. Ry. Engring. Assn., St. Paul Engrs. Soc. Clubs: University, St. Paul Athletic, Minnesota. Home: St. Paul, Minn. *

BLUM, E(DWARD) H(OWARD), business exec.; born Phila., Aug. 2, 1886; s. Jacob and Catherine (Hoffman) B.; ed. Central High Sch., Phila., 1905; B.S., Temple Coll., 1909; m. Elsie May Hall, Oct. 4, 1916. Blue print machine operator, The Atlantic Refining Co., Phila., 1905, chief draftsman, crude oil subsidiary, Phila., 1916-19, gen. mgr., Dallas, 1919-29, vice pres. and gen. mgr. producing subsidiary under name of Atlantic Oil Producing Co., Dallas, 1929-36, vice pres. and gen. mgr. domestic crude oil producing activities, Atlantic Refining Co., Dallas, 1936-46, gen. mgr. domestic and fgn. crude oil prodn. since 1946; director Atlantic Refining Co. since 1937, vice pres. since 1936; dir. and v.p. Atlantic Refining Co. of Cuba since 1946; pres., dir. Gulf of Maracaibo Corp. since 1946, Mara Oil Fields Corp. since 1946. Venezuelan Atlantic Refining Co. since 1946; v.p. Atlantic Refining Co. (Del.) since 1946; sec.-treas. & Tex. Salt Water Disposal Co., since 1944, dir. and mem. exec. com. since 1942; dir. Guasare Oil Co., Mid-Continent Oil and Gas Assn. Alderman, Town of Highland Park, Tex., 1946-48, mayor since 1948. Mem. Am. Petroleum Inst., Mid-Continent Oil and Gas Assn. (dir.), Am. Inst. Mining and Metall. Engrs., Dallas C. of C. Citizens' Traffic Commn., Dallas Citizen's Council. Republican. Lutheran (mem. Council of Luth. Men (past pres.). Mason. Clubs: 25 Year of the

Petroleum Industry. Brook Hollow Golf, Athletic, Country, Petroleum. Home: Dallas. *

BLUM, HAROLD F., scientist; b. Escondido, Calif., Feb. 12, 1899; s. Robert Frederick and Dora (Batschy) B.; A.B., U. Calif., 1922, grad. student Med. Sch., 1922-23, Ph.D., 1927; student Harvard Med. Sch., 1923-24; m. Mabel Muriel Gilham, Sept. 19, 1930; 1 dau., Jannet Susan. Asst. prof. U. Oreg., 1927-28; instr. Harvard Med. Sch., 1928-30; asst. prof. U. Calif., 1930-36, asso. prof., 1936-38; with Nat. Cancer Inst., USPHS, 1939-43, 47-67; prin. biophysicist Naval Med. Research Inst., 1943-45; vis. prof. dept. biology Princeton, 1947-67; prof. dept. biol. sci. State U. N.Y. at Albany, 1967-73, prof. emeritus, 1975—; vis. prof. photobiology Skin and Cancer Hosp., Temple U. Health Sci. Center, Phila., 1973—; sec. gen. Comité Internat. Photobiologie, 1951-56; asso. Columbia U. Seminar Ecology and Cultural Evolution. Trustee Marine Biol. Lab., Woods Hole, 1956-60. Served with Signal Corps, U.S. Army, 1918-19; AEF. Recipient medal U. Liege, Belgium, 1933; Finsen prize in photobiology, 1976; John Simon Guggenheim Meml. fellow, 1936, 46, 53; fellow Belgian Am. Ednl. Found., 1953; USPHS Spl. Research fellow, 1957-58. Fellow AAAS, Calif. Acad. Scis.; mem. Société Philomathique de Paris, Assn. Physiologistes (France), Soc. Gen. Physiologists (pres. 1950). Author: Photodynamic Action and Disease Caused by Light, 1941, rev. edit., 1964; Time's Arrow and Evolution, 1951, 3d edit., 1969; Carcinogenesis by Ultraviolet Light, 1959. Asso. editor Jour. Cellular and Comparative Physiology, 1956-67. Contbr. chpts., articles sci. publs. Home: Philadelphia, Pa. Died Oct. 29, 1980.

BLUMBERG, HENRY, mathematician; b. Zhagory, Russia, May 13, 1886; s. Bernhard and Yetta (Shochet) B.; brought to U.S., 1891; A.B., Columbia, 1907, A.M., 1908, fellow, 1909-10; Ph.D., Göttingen, 1912; studied U. of Chicago and univ. of Paris and Zürich; unmarried. Instr. in mathematics, U. of Neb., 1913-14, asst. prof., 1914-18; asso. in mathematics, U. of Ill., 1918-19, asst. prof., 1918-25; prof. mathematics, Ohio State U., since 1925. Asso. editor Annals of Mathematics, 1916-26, Am. Math. Monthly, 1919-20. Member A.A.A.S., Am. Math. Soc., Math. Assn. America, Sigma Xi. Awarded John Dash Van Buren prize in mathematics, 1907. Author: (with A. Barnett) A Short Course in Trigonometry. Asso. editor Zentralblatt für Math. since 1931. Contbr. articles to math. jours. Home: Columbus, OH. *

BLUMGART, HERRMAN LUDWIG, physician; b. Newark, July 19, 1895; s. David and Sophie (Hiller) B.; S.B., Harvard, 1917, M.D. 1921, Sc.D., 1962, Moseley Traveling Fellow, London and Europe, 1923; m. Margaret Stein, July 18, 1931; 1 dau., Ann. Med. intern Peter Bent Brigham Hosp., 1921-22; asst. Thorndike Meml. Lab., Boston City Hosp., 1924-28, asso. prof. medicine Harvard, 1928-46, prof. medicine, 1946-62, prof. emeritus, spl. cons. to dean of faculty Harvard Med. Sch., 1962-66; vis. physician Beth Israel Hosp., 1928-46, physician in chief and dir. med. research, 1946-62, physician in chief emeritus, to 1977; cons. Peter Bent Brigham Hosp., Harvard Health Service. Served from lt. col. to col., M.C., AUS, 1943-46. Decorated Legion of Merit with oak leaf cluster; recipient Gold Heart award, Am. Heart Assn. Diplomate Am. Bd. Internal Medicine. Fellow A.C.P. (hon. master), Am. Coll. Cardiology (hon., first James Bryan Herrick award), Indian (hon.), Spanish (hon.) cardiologic socs.; mem. Am. Soc. Clin. Investigation, Assn. Am. Physicians, Am. Physiol. Soc., Am. Acad. Arts and Scis., Soc. Cons. of World War II; A.M.A. (chmn. sect. internal medicine), Am., Mass. (past pres.) heart assns., Mass. Med. Soc., New Eng. Cardiovascular Soc. (past pres.); Harvard Med. Sch. Alumni Assn. (past pres.), Am. Nuclear Soc. (hon., recipient Pioneer award). Former editor-in-chief Circulation, Journal Am. Heart Assn.; past mem. editorial bd. New Eng. Jour. Medicine. Home: Cambridge, Mass. Died Mar. 21, 1977.

BOARDMAN, FRANCIS, govt. ofcl.; b. N.Y.C., Oct. 2, 1915; s. Francis and Anne Macdonald (Calef) B.; grad. Deerfield (Mass.) Acad., 1934; B.A., Williams Coll., 1938; m. Anne Dwight Hooker, Sept. 10, 1953; 1 dau., Pamela Dwight. Instr. English and Journalism, Am. U. Beirut, 1938-41; analyst Fgn. Econ. Adminstrn., 1942-44; comml. policy div. Middle East br. U.S. Dept. State, 1944-48, attache Am. Embassy, Ankara, Turkey, 1948-50, in Office Near Eastern Affairs, 1951-56; 1st sec., consul Am. Embassy, Beirut, 1956-59; prin. econ. officer Turkish sect., 1959-60; with Near East and S. Asia div. Export-Import Bank, 1962-76. Asst. to econ. adviser U.S. del. Paris Peace Conf., 1946. Mem. Middle East Inst. (bd. govs.), Fgn. Service Assn., Alpha Delta Phi. Episcopalian. Club: Met. (Washington). Author: Institutions of Higher Learning in the Middle East, 1961, 77. Contbr. articles to periodicals. Home: Washington, D.C. Died Dec. 20, 1976.

BOARDMAN, WILLIAM KILBOURNE, educator clinical psychologist; b. Tarboro, N.C., July 25, 1925; s. William Kilbourne and Mary Clark (Robeson) B.; student Emory U., 1943-44, postgrad., 1946-48; B.S., U. S.C., 1945; M.A., Duke, 1951, Ph.D., 1956; m. Katherine Baker Blackshear, July 24, 1951; children—William Hinton, David Robeson, Katherine Anne. Instr., Baylor U. Coll. Medicine, 1956-59, asst. prof., 1959-63; research technician II, Houston State Psychiat. Inst., 1958-60, research specialist I, 1960-63; lectr. U. Houston, 1960-61, clin. asst. prof., 1962-63; asso. prof. psychiatry Emory U. Sch. Medicine, 1963-67, asso. prof. psychology, 1965-67; dir. tng. and research for psychology Ga. Mental Health Inst., 1965-67; prof. dept. psychology U. Ga., 1967-78, dir. clin. psychology tng. program, 1975-78; individual practice psychology, 1956-78; cons. psychologist, 1957-78. Chmn., Ga. Bd. Examiners of Psychologists, 1975-78. Served to ensign USN, 1943-46; to lt., 1951-53; Korea. USPHS Predoctoral fellow, 1954-56; USPHS Research grantee, 1962-63. Diplomate Am. Bd. Profl. Psychology. Mem. Am. Psychol. Assn., Am. Group Psychotherapy Assn., Chi Phi. Research and publs. relating perception to personality and mental illness. Home: Athens, Ga. Died Jan. 22, 1978; buried Oconee Hills Cemetery, Athens.

BOAS, GEORGE, univ. prof.; b. Providence, Aug. 28, 1891; s. Herman and Sarah (Eisenberg) B.; A.B., Brown U., 1913, A.M., 1913; A.M., Harvard, 1915; studied Columbia, 1914-15; Ph.D., U. Calif., 1917; LL.D., Washington and Lee U., 1949, U. N.Mex., 1951; D.H.L., Washington College, 1959; married Simone Brangier, June 22, 1921. Began as instr. in forensics, U. Calif., 1915; with Johns Hopkins since 1921, asso. prof. philosophy, 1927-33, prof. of the history of philosophy, 1933-57, prof. emeritus of philosophy, 1957—; vis. Mellon professor philosophy U. Pitts., 1960-61; vis. prof. philosophy, U. Calif., spring 1949; Traux Lecturer Hamilton College, 1957. Served as first lieutenant U.S. Army, 1917-19; commd. lt. comdr. U.S. Naval Reserve, Nov. 1943, comdr., May 1945. Trustee Baltimore Mus. Art. Mem. Am. Philos. Assn., American Society for Aesthetics, American Academy of Arts and Sciences. Associé Académie Royale de Belgique (hon.). Author: Essays on Primitivism and Related Ideas in the Middle Ages, 1948; Wingless Pegasus, 1950; Dominant Themes of Modern Philosophy, 1957; The Inquiring Mind, 1959; Some Assumptions of Aristotle, 1959; The Limits of Reason, 1961; Rationalism in Greek Philosophy, 1961; The Heaven of Invention, 1963; Vox Populi, 1969; The History of Ideas, 1969. Translator: The Hieroglyphics of Horapollo, 1950. Editor: Romanticism in America, 1940. Home: Baltimore, Md. Died Mar. 7, 1980.

BOATWRIGHT, WALTER PUTNEY, army officer; b. Buckingham County, Va., Mar. 17, 1886; s. Walter Leake and Mary Alice (Putney) B.; student Fork Union Mil. Acad., 1902-03; B.S., Va. Poly. Inst., 1907; student Mass. Inst. Tech., 1915-16, Coast Arty. Sch., 1914, Command and Gen. Staff Sch., 1925-26; m. Gladys Sweeting Curry, June 29, 1912; children—Joan Dolores, Walter Putney. Commd. 2d lt., 1908; promoted through grades to brig. gen., 1940; served with Arty., A.E.F., 1917-19 (temp. maj. and lt. col.), participating in battles of Aisne, Marne, Oise-Aisne, Argonne. Comdg. general, Frankford Arsenal; district chief New York Ordnance District; commanding general, Office chief of Ordnance, Detroit. Awarded Purple Heart, Officer of Order of Black Star (France), Legion of Merit, Distinguished Service Medal. Clubs: Army and Navy Country (Washington), Detroit. Retired from active service Feb. 28, 1946; now vice pres. Globe Wireless, Ltd. Home: San Francisco, Calif. *

BOBLETER, LOWELL STANLEY, artist, educator; b. New Ulm, Minn., Dec. 24, 1902; s. John Edward and Alma (Dunkel) B.; student Bishop Brissman Inst., 1920-23, St. Paul Sch. Art, 1923-25; D.F.A., Sch. Asso. Arts, 1965; m. Mabel M. Wendt, Sept. 15, 1924. Dir., St. Paul Gallery and Sch. Art, 1940-42; supt. fine arts Minn. State Fair, 1942-48; prof. art. chmn. Sch. Fine Arts Hamline U., 1942-48; pres. Sch. Asso. Arts, St. Paul, from 1948; exhibited group and one-man shows at Met. Mus. Art, 1944-47, Mus. Modern Art, 1945, Carnegie Inst., 1940-42, U.S. Library of Congress, 1938-45, Nat. Gallery, 1943-45, Corcoran Gallery, 1938-47, Art Inst. Chgo., 1940-45, museums in Rome, 1938-39, Italy, 1939-40, Oslo, 1940-42, Paris, 1938-40, N.Y.C., 1938-65, Phila., 1938-60, Boston, 1938-60, Chgo., 1938-65, Denver, 1940-45, San Francisco, 1938-55, Los Angeles, 1940-47, Buffalo, 1943, New Orleans, 1945, Kansas City, 1940-50, Washington, 1938-45, Mpls., 1930-65, Balt., 1940-47, Seattle, 1940-50; represented in permanent collections Library Congress, Met. Mus. Art, Nat. Gallery Art, Pa. Acad. Fine Arts, Cal. State Library, Flint Inst. Art, Soc. Am. Etchers, Parkersburg Arts Center, Chgo. Art Inst., Smithsonian Inst., N.Y. Pub. Library, Mpls. Inst. Art, Walker Art Center, Harbor Beach Pub. Library, Chgo. Soc. Etchers. Mem. Nat. Com. for Preservation Cultural Resources, 1940-45; mem. Minn. Art. Commn., 1942-48. Recipient numerous first awards, medals in exhbns. throughout U.S. Mem. AAUP, Nat. Assn. Mus. Dirs., Coll. Art Assn., Artists Equity, Minn. Artists Assn. (pres.), Nat. Soc. Interior Designers, Am. Fedn. Art. Home: St. Paul, Minn. Deceased.

BOBST, ELMER H., pharm. co. exec.; b. Clearsprings, Md., Dec. 16, 1884; s. Isaac Walton and Alice (Holmes) B.; grad. Franklin and Marshall Acad., 1902, L.H.D., 1951; m. Ethel Rose; 1 son, Elmer Walton. Clk. drugstore, Phila., 1902-07; salesman Frederick Stearns & Co., 1907-09, F. F. Ingram & Co., 1909-10; prescriptionist George B. Evans Drug Stores, 1910-11; salesman Hoffmann-La Roche, Nutley, N.J., 1911-14; in charge sales, 1914-26, gen. mgr. and treas., 1920, v.p., pres., 1928-44; now chmn. bd. Warner Lambert Pharmaceutical Co., Incorporated, New York City. Chairman of the adv. bd. U.S. Savings Bonds, N.J. Div., Nat. Campaign for Am. Cancer Soc.; vice chmn. bd. Am. Cancer Soc., mem. nat. adv. cancer council for Nat. Cancer Inst., Nat. Inst. Health; mem. med. adv. com. CARE. Dir. Nat. Hosp. for Speech Disorders, N.Y.C., Am.-Korean Found., Tom Spies Com. for Clin. Research; chmn. bd. dirs. Gustavus and Louise Pfeiffer Research Found. Trustee Franklin and Marhall Coll., Rutgers U., Nat. Found. Med. Edn., U. Pa. Registered pharmacist. Clubs: Chemists, Drug and Chemical, Metropolitan, New York Yacht (N.Y.C.) Goats (Phila.), Montclair Golf, Essex, Down Town (Newark); Spring Lake Golf and Country, Bathing and Tennis (Spring Lake, N.J.); Pine Valley (N.J.) Golf; Everglades (Palm Beach, Fla.); Key Largo (Fla.) Anglers; Cat Cay (Cat Key, Bahamas); Havana Yacht, El Country (Havana, Cuba); Porcupine (Nassau). Home: Montclair, N.J.; and Spring Lake, N.J. *

BOCHER, MAIN ROUSSEAU, (MAINBOCHER), designer; b. Chgo., Oct. 24, 1890; s. George R. and Luella (Main) B.; student piano with Claire Osborn Reed, 1907, with Frank La Forge, 1914; student art, Chgo., 1908-09, N.Y.C., 1909-11, Munich, Germany, 1911-12; student singing with Henri Albers and Giulia Valda, 1919. With Paris studio E. A. Taylor, 1913-14; began fashion drawing, 1922; illustrator Harper's Bazaar, Paris, 1922-23; editor French Vogue, 1923-29; founder, pres. Mainbocher, Paris, 1930-39, Mainbocher, Inc., N.Y.C., 1940-76; designer WAVES uniforms, 1942, Women Marine Corps uniforms, 1951, Girl Scout uniforms, 1946, Red Cross Uniforms, 1948, Passavant Hosp. (Chgo.) nursing sch. uniforms, 1949. Served with hosp. unit, France, 1917; with U.S. Army, 1918. Illustrator: Aucassin and Nicolette, 1914; play, Tiny Alice. Address: New York, N.Y. Died Dec. 27, 1976.

BOCKES, THOMAS WILLIS (BOK'ES), lawyer; b. Central City, Neb., Mar. 20, 1885; s. George David and Ada (Howe) B.; LL.B., U. of Neb., 1908; m. Doris Lorna Corn, June 27, 1925; children—Suzann, Patricia, Thomas George. Admitted to Neb. bar, 1908; practiced at Lincoln, 1908-11; mem. firm Martin & Bockes, Central City, 1911-18; local atty. Union Pacific R.R. Co., 1911-18, asst. gen. atty., 1918-33, gen. atty. for Neb., 1933-36, asst. western gen. counsel, Jan.-Aug. 1936, gen. solicitor Eastern Dist., 1936-42, western gen. counsel since July 1942; also western gen. counsel Los Angeles & Salt Lake R.R. Co., Ore. Short Line R.R. Co., Ore.-Wash. R.R. & Navigation Co., St. Joseph and Grand Island Ry. Co., Union Pacific Coal Co. Mem. American, Neb. State and Omaha bar assns., Phi Delta Theta, Phi Delta Phi. Republican. Presbyterian. Mason. Home: Omaha, Neb.

BOCKIUS, GEORGE HAMLIN, mfg. co. exec.; b. Canton, Ohio, Jan. 24, 1895; s. Edward Graham and Florence (Hamlin) B.; M.E., Cornell, 1917; m. Irene Catherine Blake, Apr. 4, 1942. Plant engr. Gordon Tire & Rubber Co., Canton, 1919-21; draftsman Diebold, Inc., Canton, 1921-35, dir., 1930-78, dir. purchases, 1935-43, v.p., asst. gen. mgr., 1943-44, v.p., gen. mgr., 1944-45, pres., gen. mgr., 1945-52, chmn. exec. com. 1952-78; dir. Canton Nat. Bank. Trustee Aultman Hosp. Mem. C. of C., Ohio Soc. Profl. Engrs. Clubs: Canton, Brookside Country. Home: Canton, Ohio. Died May 31, 1978.

BOCKLET, CHARLES J., fin. cons.; m. Mary Byrne Mulholland; 4 children— 2 stepchildren. Chmn. bd. govs. Am. Stock Exchange, to 1964; sr. partner Bocklet, Will & Co., to 1964; fin. cons., Naples, Fla.; mgr. Naples office McCormick & Co.

BODANSKY, OSCAR, biochemist, physician; b. Elisabethgrad, Russia, Aug. 21, 1901; s. Phineas and Eva (Geiro) B.; brought to U.S., 1907, naturalized, 1923; B.A., Columbia, 1921, M.A. in Chemistry, 1922, Ph.D. in Chemistry, 1924; M.D., U. Chgo., 1938; m. Barbara Biber, May 31, 1929; 1 dau., Margery Franklin. Asst. and research asst. chemistry Columbia, 1921-25; research asso. biochemistry U. Calif., 1926-27; instr., Med. Sch. U. Tex., 1927-28, adj. prof., 1928-29, asso. prof., 1929-30; instr. pediatrics Coll. Medicine N.Y. U., 1930-37, lectr. pediatrics, postgrad. div., 1946-55; biochemist children's med. div. Bellevue Hosp., 1930-37; clin. asst. pediatrics Beth Israel Hosp., N.Y.C., 1939-40, asst. adj. attending, 1940-42, asso. attending, 1946-48; asso. prof. clin. pharmacology Sloan-Kettering Inst., 1948-51, prof. biochemistry, 1951-71, mem., chief biochemistry div., 1956-71, v.p., 1966-71, mem. emeritus, 1971-77; attending clin. biochemist, chmn. dept. biochemistry Meml. Hosp. for Cancer and Allied Diseases, N.Y.C., 1948-67, emeritus, 1967-77, dir. research tng., 1967-71; vis. clin. biochemist James Ewing Hosp., N.Y.C., 1951-67; cons. biochemistry Hosp. Spl. Surgery, 1958-71; guest investigator

Rockefeller U., 1973-77. Chmn. adv. com. on research on pathogenesis of cancer Am. Cancer Soc., 1964-69; mem. panel gen. biochemistry, com. of growth NRC, 1955-56. Served from capt. to lt. col. M.C., AUS, 1942-46; chief biochem. sect., med. div. C.W.S., 1943-45, dir. med. research, 1945-46. Decorated Legion of Merit; recipient Distinguished Service award Med. Alumni U. Chgo. Med. Sch., 1952; Alfred P. Sloan award in cancer research, 1962; Van Slyke award in clin. chemistry, 1965; Lucy Wortham James award for clin. investigations in cancer, 1973. Diplomate Am. Bd. Pathology. Mem. A.M.A., Am. Soc. Biol. Chemists, N.Y. Acad. Medicine, N.Y. State, N.Y. County med. socs., Am. Soc. Pharmacology and Exptl. Therapeutics, Soc. Exptl. Biology and Medicine, Harvey Soc., Am. Assn. Cancer Research, Coll. Am. Pathologists, Phi Beta Kappa, Sigma Xi. Author: Biochemistry of Disease, 2d edit. 1952; Biochemistry of Human Cancer, 1975. Mem. editorial bd. Anesthesiology, 1946-54, Cancer, 1950-77, Cancer Research, 1965-68, Biochem. Medicine, 1967-77; asso. editor Jour. Pharmacology, 1946-56. Contbr. articles to profl. jours. Home: New York, N.Y. Died Aug. 21, 1977; buried Westchester Hills Cemetery, Westchester, N.Y.

BODKIN, HENRY GRATTAN, lawyer; b. Olive, Calif., Mar. 20, 1886; s. John Joseph and Marian (O'Brennan) B.; B.S., St. Vincent's Coll., 1906; J.D. (hon.), Loyola U. at Los Angeles, 1928, LL.D. (hon.), 1932; m. Ruth M. Wallis, May 29, 1918; 1 son, Henry Grattan, Jr. Admitted to Calif. bar, 1910, Ariz. bar, 1920; mem. Bodkin, Breslin & Luddy, Los Angeles, since 1939; faculty mem. sch. law Loyola U. at Los Angeles, 1920-32, mem. athletic bd., 1928-38, 1946-51, chmn., 1936. Mem. Bd. Police Commrs. (Los Angeles), 1938-41, pres., 1940-41. Mem. State Bar of Calif. (mem. bd. govs., 1929-33, v.p., 1933), Native Sons of Golden West. K.C. Home: Los Angeles. *

BOECKEL, FLORENCE BREWER (MRS. RICHARD MARTIN BOECKEL), writer; b. Trenton, N.J., Oct. 20, 1885; d. Albert and Anna (Muirheid) Brewer; prep. edn., high sch., Tiffin, O., and Caroline Gerrish Prep. Sch., N.Y. City; A.B., Vassar Coll., 1908; grad. study in Paris and Dresden 1 yr.; m. Richard Martin Boeckel, of Washington, D.C., Jan. 10, 1916; children—Richard Martin, John Hart. Spl. investigator, pub. schs., Poughkeepsie, N.Y., 1910-11; feature and editorial writer, Poughkeepsie News Press, 1911-13; mem. editorial staff Vogue, 1913-14; feature writer, Baltimore (Md.) Sun, 1914-15; publicity dir., Nat. Woman's Party, 1917-20; editor The Suffragist, 1919-20; ednl. dir. Nat. Council for Prevention of War since 1921. Mem. nat. council, Nat. Woman's Party. Clubs: Nat. Woman's Press (founder), Manor. Author: Study of Occupations Open to Young Women, 1911; Through the Gateway, 1926; Across Borderlines, 1926; Between War and Peace, 1928. Home: Washington, D.C. *

BOETTCHER, ARTHUR HENRY, lawyer; b. Chgo., Nov. 10, 1886; s. Charles and Barbara (Reinel) B.; student Lewis Inst., 1904-05; LL.B., Chicago Kent Coll. Law, 1908; spl. student U. Wis., 1908-09; m. Rose Cecil Krieger, May 29, 1912; children Barbara Mary (Mrs. C. Lyman Emrich, Jr.), Stephen Arthur. Admitted to Ill. bar, 1908; practicing lawyer, specializing in patent law, Chgo., 1909—; with Brown & Williams, 1909-12; mem. Brown, Williams, Bell, Hanson & Boettcher, 1912-14, Brown, Hanson & Boettcher, 1914-17, Brown, Boettcher & Dienner, 1919-27, Brown, Jackson, Boettcher & Dienner, 1927—. Served with the flying corps, USNR 1917-18, lt. comdr. (ret.). Decorated Navy Cross (with citation for invention of pilot directing feature of bomb-sights). Mem. Am., Chgo. bar assns., Am., Chgo. (pres. 1941) patent law assns., Alpha Sigma Phi. Republican. Presbyn. Clubs: University (Chicago); Glen View (Golf, Ill.). Home: Evanston, IL. *

BOGARDUS, EMORY STEPHEN, sociologist, editor, graduate school dean; born near Belvidere, Illinois, February 21, 1882; son of Henry Brown and Eliza Maria (Stevenson) B.; A.B., Northwestern U., 1908, A.M., 1909; Ph.D., U. of Chicago, 1911; Litt.D., U. So. Cal., 1945, U. Ariz, 1960; L.H.D., U. Redlands, Cal., 1946; LL.D., Boston U., 1950; married Edith Mildred Pritchard, August 9, 1911; 1 daughter, Ruth Mildred. Fellow Northwestern U. Settlement, Chicago, 1908-09; fellow in sociology, U. of Chicago, 1909-11; asst. prof. sociology and economics U. of Southern Calif., 1911-13, asso. prof., 1913-15, prof. sociology since 1915, also organizer and first chmn. same dept.; dir. Div. of Social Work, same, 1920-37, dean, 1935-39; acting dean Grad. Sch., U. of So. Calif., 1926-27, annual research lecturer, 1937, dean, 1945-49; visiting prof. of sociology, Northwestern Univ., summer 1926; visiting prof. sociology, U. of Wash., summer 1928. Regional research dir. (Southern Calif.) Pacific Coast Race Relations Survey, 1923-25; social research dir. Boys Work Survey of Los Angeles, California, 1924-25. President of the Los Angeles Social Service Commn., 1916-18; pres. Los Angeles Chapter, Am. Assn. of Social Workers, 1923-25; mem. bd. Goodwill Industries of So. Cal., 1919-49; trustee All Nations Found., 1940-55; pres. Pacific Sociol. Soc., 1929-30; pres. Am. Sociol. Soc., 1931; mem. Phi Beta Kappa, Delta Sigma Rho, Phi Kappa Phi, Alpha Pi Zeta, Alpha Kappa Delta (nat. pres., 1924-28, and 1947), Phi Delta Kappa. Received award of merit, Northwestern University, 1933. Editor of the Journal of Sociology and Social Research, 1916-61, at University of Southern California editor annual proceedings, Pacific Sociol. Society, 1930-39; registered social worker (Calif.), 1934-49; university editor, U. of Southern Calif., 1942-45; advisory editor, Dictionary of Sociology, 1944; editor, Research News, Univ. of Southern Calif., 1945-49. Author numerous books, 1912—, latest being: Fundamentals of Social Psychology, 4th edit., 1950; The Making of Public Opinion, 1951; Principles of Cooperation, 1952, third edition, 1964, Spanish edition, 1964; Sociology Applied To Nursing (with Brethorst) 3rd edit., 1952; Sociology, 4th edition, 1954; The Development of Social Thought, 4th edit., 1960, also Spanish, Indian, Portuguese edits., 1964-65; History of Cooperation, 2d edit., 1965; The Traveler, 1956; Social Distance, 1959; Problems of Cooperation, 1960; The Explorer; Much Have I Learned, 1962; Toward a World Community, 1964; Thrice-Seven Wonders of the World, 1965; The Observer, 1966; A Forty-Year Racial Distance Study, 1967; The Wonderful World of Sonnets, 1968. Contbr. articles.

BOGARTE, MARTIN BRUCE, head master; b. Valparaiso, Ind., July 2, 1885; s. Martin Eugene and Lillian Alice (Chamberlin) B.; Valparaiso High Sch.; B.A., Valparaiso U., 1904; Purdue U., 1904-7; A.B., Columbia, 1910; m. Florence Anne Howard, of Salt Lake City, Utah, Aug. 20, 1911. Instr. mathematics, Valparaiso U., 1907-9, Horace Mann Sch., 1912-15; instr. mathematics, Terrill Sch. (for boys), Dallas, Tex., 1915-16, head master since 1916 (sch. owned jointly with brother, R. H. Bogarte). Mem. Phi Delta Kappa, Delta Tau Delta. Democrat. Mem. Disciples of Christ. Mason (32 deg. K.T., Shriner). Rotarian. Home: Dallas, Tex. *

BOGER, ROY GARLAND, educator; b. Nacogdoches, Tex., July 1, 1892; s. Green D. and Mary Pitt (Love) B.; grad. high sch., Nacogdoches, 1909; student Clebarro Coll., 1909-10; A.B., Southwestern U., Georgetown, Tex., 1913, A.M., 1929; student U. of Colo., University of Texas; LL.D., McMurry College, 1944; m. Ruth Bolton, Aug. 28, 1917; children—Ruth Bolton, Roy Garland, Betty Jane. Prof. German, athletic dir., Alexander Coll., Jacksonville, 1913-17, dean, 1915-17; prof. science, Clarendon (Tex.) Coll., 1917-18; president and prof. edn., Lon Morris Coll., 1918-23; pres., prof. edn., Weatherford Coll., 1923-36; dean, McMurry College, 1936-41; exec. secretary Southern Methodist U., 1941-42; dir. Evening Center West Texas State College, Canyon, 1942-62; psychological cons. Continental Carbon Co., from 1954; adj. prof. Amarillo (Tex.) Coll., 1962-66. Dir. Family Service Agy., Mental Health Assn., Infantile Paralysis, Amarillo Civil Service Commn. Trustee Mt. Sequoyah Assembly, Fayetteville, Ark.; president Weatherford Chamber Commerce. Pres. Tex. Jr. Coll. Oratorical Association, 1924-29, Tex. Assn. of Junior Colls., 1932-33; mem. of com. on classifying and accrediting high schools of Tex., 1932-35; county prohibition chmn., 1933; v.p. Tex. Jr. Coll. Assn., 1927-28, Tex. Jr. Coll. Athletic Assn., 1928-29; secretary-treasurer, The Association of Texas Colleges; mem. Jurisdictional Board of Edn. Meth. Church; dist. lay leader, Abilene dist.; mem. bd. of edn. Northwest Texas Meth. Conf., also mem. bd. lay activities; Dir. W. Tex. Fair Assn. Mem. (asso.) Am. Psychol. Assn.; mem. Kappa Sigma. Democrat. Methodist. Mason. Mem. Rotary (pres.), Lion's Club (pres. 1940-41). Home: Amarillo, Tex. Died Feb. 19, 1980.

BOGERT, GEORGE GLEASON, educator; b. Scotland, S.D., June 13, 1884; s. Taylor O. and Jeanette (Gleason) B.; A.B. Cornell U., 1906, LL.B., 1908; m. Lolita Eleanor Metzger, Apr. 6, 1918; children—Elizabeth E., George T., Virginia L. Admitted to N.Y. bar, 1908; admitted to Ill. bar, 1936; practiced at Elmira, N.Y., 1908-11; acting asst. prof. law Cornell, 1911-12, asst. prof., 1912-16, prof. 1916-25, dean Coll. of Law, 1921-25; prof. law U. Chgo., 1925-49, Hastings Coll. of Law, San Francisco, 1949—; mem. Whitman, Ottinger & Ransom, N.Y., 1923-24. Compliance commr. WPB, 1942-46; drafted uniform conditional sales act, uniform state law for aeros., uniform trustee's accounting act, uniform trusts act, uniform common trust fund act; commr. Uniform State Laws for N.Y., 1920-25, for Ill. 1927-49, life mem., 1949; sec. Conf. on Uniform State Laws, 1922-28. Mem. 1st O.T.C., Madison Barracks, N.Y., 1917; commd. capt. F.A., R.C., 1917; regtl. adj. 308th F.A., Camp Dix, N.J., 1917; maj. judge adv. R.C., 1917; apptd. asst. div. judge adv. 78th Div., 1917, div. judge adv., 1918; in France, 1918-19; lt. col., Judge Adv. Gen. Corps, 1919. Cited for efficient service. Pres. Am. Law Sch. Assn., 1935-36. Mem. Am., Chgo. bar assns., Phi Beta Kappa, Phi Delta Phi. Zodiac (Cornell), Sphinx Head (Cornell). Clubs: Quadrangle, Chikaming Country. Author: Trusts and Trustees, 10 vols.; Hornbook on Trusts; Case Books on Trusts and Sales. Address: (summer) Three Oaks, Mich.; (winter) San Francisco. *

BOGGS, WADE HAMILTON, clergyman; b. Liberty, S.C., Nov. 12, 1883; s. Marcus Addison and Rebecca (Smith) B.; A.B., Davidson Coll., 1907; B.D., Austin (Tex.) Theol. Sem., 1913; grad. work, U. Tex., 1910-13, Bibl. Sem. N.Y., 1922; D.D., Presbyn. Coll. of S.C., 1926; LL.D., Southwestern Coll., 1944; m. Louise Sheldon, July 7, 1915; children—Wade Hamilton, Marjorie (Mrs. Charlie H. Lovelace). Ordained to ministry of Presbyn. Ch., 1913; asst. pastor First Ch., San Antonio, Tex., 1913-14; pastor Central Ch., Shawnee, Okla., 1915-19, Arsenal Hill Ch., Columbia, S.C., 1919-26, Druid Hills Ch., Atlanta, 1926-35, First Ch., Shreveport, La., 1935-43; exec. sec. of exec. com. Christian Edn. and Ministerial Relief, Presbyn. Ch. U.S., 1943-50, exec. sec. Bd. Annuities and Relief, 1950-54, cons. Bd. Annuities and Relief, 1954-56; associate pastor Druid Hills Presbyn. Church, Atlanta, 1956-61; interim pastor First Presbyn. Ch., St. Petersburg, Fla., 1961—; moderator Presbyterian Church of the U.S., 1954-55. Mem. bd. trustees Presbyn. Coll. S.C., 1922-26, Thornwell Orphanage, 1922-26; bd. dirs. Austin Theol. Sem., 1938-43, Southwestern Coll., 1938-43, Assembly's Tng. Sch., Richmond, Va., 1944-55; Community Chest in Columbia, S.C., 1924-26, in Atlanta, 1930-34. Mem. C. of C. (dir.). Rotarian.

BOHAN, MERWIN LEE, Latin Am. cons.; b. Chgo., Jan. 21, 1899; s. Daniel Joseph and Delia (Lee) B.; ed. Am. Grammar Sch., Mexico City, 1909-13; grad. Dallas High Sch., 1916; m. Harriet Davis, Feb. 5, 1921; children—Elizabeth Rowe, Harriet Davis. Clk. Pierce Fordyce Oil Assn., Dallas, 1916, Cia. Mex. de Petroleo El Aguila, Mexico City, 1917, Am. consulate, 1919, Am. embassy, Mexico, 1920; asst. mgr. U.S. Rubber Export Co., 1920-22; with Dallas C. of C. (fgn. trade sec. and publicity mgr.), 1922-26; trade commr. U.S. Dept. Commerce, Havana, 1927, asst. comml. attache, 1927; comml. attache Guatemala, San Salvador and Honduras, 1928-31, Peru and Ecuador, 1931-33, Chile, 1933-40, Colombia, 1940-41; chief U.S. Econ. Mission to Bolivia, 1941-42; counselor of embassy for econ. affairs Am. embassy, Buenos Aires, 1942; assigned to Dept. State, 1944-45; counsellor of embassy for econ. affairs, Mexico City, 1945-49, ret. 1949; prof. internat. relations Am. Inst. Fgn. Trade, Phoenix, 1949-50; mem. U.S. delegation GATT Conf., Torquay, Eng., 1950-51; U.S. ambassador Inter-Am. Econ. and Social Council, 1951-55; U.S. commr. Joint Brazil U.S. Econ. Devel. Commn., 1952-53; ret. 1955; cons. to U.S. and internat. agys., Dept. State, AID, UN, OAS, others, 1955-72. Decorated grand cross Order of So. Cross (Brazil, 1956), grand officer Order of Quetzal (Guatemala) 1962. Mason. Author publ. Investment in Cuba. 1956; Investment in Chile, 1960. Home: Dallas, Tex. Died Nov. 23, 1975; interred Grove Hill, Dallas.

BOHLER, JOHN FREDERICK (BO'LER), prof. physical edn.; b. Reading, Pa., Apr. 14, 1885; s. John Allen and Susan (Mohn) B.; B.S. Albright Coll., Reading, Pa., 1907; student U. of Neb., 1907-08; diploma in physical edn. and athletics, Chautauqua Sch. Physical Edn. and Athletics; m. Ida Louise Hatz, Dec. 29, 1909; children—John Frederick, Robert Allen. With State Coll. of Wash., Pullman, Wash., since 1908, prof. phys. edn. and dir. athletics since 1916, track and basket ball coach and phys. dir., 1908-25. Mayor, City of Pullman, Wash., since Jan. 1, 1949. Mem. Nat. Collegiate Basket Ball Rules Com., 1915-36; mem. Am. Olympic Basket Ball Com.; sec. Pacific Northwest Collegiate Athletic Conf., 1915-26. Student R.O.T.C., Presidio, Calif., 1918; at Physical Edn. and Bayonet Sch., Princeton, N.J., when Armistice was signed; physical training dir. for the State College of Wash. Army Specialized Training Program, and the Army Air Corps C.T.D. programs, 1942-44. Member American Phys. Education Assn., Washington Edn. Assn., College Physical Edn. Assn., Nat. Edn. Assn. Republican. Methodist. Mason, Kiwanian. Home: Pullman, Wash.

BOHMBACH, STANTON MONROE, appliance co. exec.; b. Duluth, Minn., Mar. 2, 1926; s. Clifford E. and Cora S. (Monroe) B.; B.B.A., U. Minn., 1949; m. Marilyn Finch, Sept. 3, 1949; children—Paul Stanton, David Merrill, Susan Jane, James Finch. With Sunbeam Corp., Oak Brook, Ill., 1949-76, pres. internat. div., 1971-74, exec. v.p. corp., 1974, pres. Sunbeam Appliance Co., 1974-76, also responsible for Sunbeam Consumer Products Group. Served with Mil. Police, AUS, 1944-46. Mem. Internat. Trade Club, Chgo. Assn. Commerce and Industry, Sigma Alpha Epsilon. Club: Oak Park Country. Home: River Forest, Ill. Died May 9, 1976.

BOHN, ERNEST JOHN, lawyer, univ. lectr.; b. Austria-Hungary, May 12, 1901; s. Frank J. and Juliana (Kiry) B.; came to U.S., 1911, naturalized, 1920; A.B. cum laude, Adelbert Coll., Western Res. U., 1924, J.D., Law Sch., 1926, LL.D., 1951. Admitted to Ohio bar, 1926, practiced in Cleve., 1926-38; mem. Ohio Gen. Assembly, 1929-30; mem. Cleve. City Council, 1930-40; mem. Internat. Housing Commn., 1934; archtl. adv. com. Fed. Pub. Housing Authority, 1939; cons. U.S. Housing Authority, HHFA, Resettlement Adminstrn., Def. Housing div. Fed. Works Agy. Pub. Housing Adminstrn., HEW; 1st dir. Cleve. Met. Housing Authority; lectr. urban and environmental studies Case Western Res. U.; dir., organizer Regional Assn. Cleve.; bd. dirs. Nat. Housing Conf.; dir. Cardinal Fed. Savs. and Loan Assn. Cleve.; chmn. City Planning Commn. Cleve.; adv. bd. Urban Renewal Agy. Cleve.; organizer, chmn. 1st Nat. Conf. Slum Clearance, 1933; mem. Ohio Urban Devel. Commn., Midwest Regional Planning Commn.; mem. policy com., planning com. health goals and central planning bd. Cleve. Welfare Fedn.; mem. Regional Planning Commn. Cuyahoga County (Ohio); hon. v.p. Internat. Fedn. Housing and Planning, The Hague, Netherlands; exec. com. Pres. Eisenhower's adv. com. housing policies, Am. Council to Improve our Neighborhoods; mem. Nat. Action Council of Urban Am., Nat. Urban Coalition, Nat. Council on Aging, com. on housing for elderly, adv. com. housing and community devel. and housing for sr. citizens HHFA, Washington; adv. com. on retired workers UAW, Detroit; U.S. del. housing com. UN Econ. Commn. for Europe, Geneva, 1959; nat. com. White House Conf. Children and Youth, 1960, panel on phys. environment Pres.'s Commn. Nat. Goals, 1960; adminstrv. com., nat. adv. com. White House Conf. on Aging, 1961; cons. subcom. problems aged and aging U.S. Senate; mem. Ohio Gov.'s Commn. on Aging, also adv. bd. Ohio Adminstrn. Aging; mem. adv. com. Ohio Civil Rights Commn.; panel cons. on aging HEW; trustee Better Homes and Neighborhoods Cleve.; mem. Cleve. Met. Services Commn.; adv. bd., past chmn. Cath. Charities Bur.; trustee, mem. exec. com. Cath. Charities Corp.; citizens adv. com. Cuyahoga County Hosp. Bd., DePaul Infant Home, others; mem. council of Civil Def. adv. bd. St. Vincent's Charity Hosp., Garden Center, Cleve.; adv. com. Notre Dame Coll., Cleve.; chmn. Devel. Council Greater Cleve.; mem. Cuyahoga County Govtl. Consol. Com. Past pres. League Rep. Clubs of Cuyahoga County; mem. Cuyahoga County Republican Exec. Com. Past mem. vis. com. Harvard Grad. Sch. Design; mem. vis. com. Western Res. U. Sch. Applied Soc. Scis.; trustee Goodrich Social Settlement; co-founder, trustee Golden Age Center, Roadside Council; bd. dirs., past pres. Ohio Planning Conf. Cleve. Forum for Community Devel., Citizens' Action Com. on Nursing Homes; trustee Vis. Nurses Assn. Recipient numerous awards for pub. service including Archbishop Edward F. Hoban medal for distinguished service, 1964, silver medal Am. Soc. Planning Ofcls., 1966. Gov.'s award for Community action; named Outstanding Alumnus, Case-Western Res. U. Law Sch., 1972, Sr. Citizen of Year, Cuyahoga County Sr. Citizen's Council, 1972; Ernest J. Bohn Goldenage Center, named in his honor 1968; Ernest J. Bohn Tower, named in his honor, 1972. Mem. Nat. Assn. Housing and Redevel. Ofcls. (a founder, 1st pres.), Am. Soc. Planning Ofcls. (pres. 1951), Am. Inst. Planners, Adult Edn. Assn., Consumers League, Nat. Conf. Social Welfare, Cleve. Bar Assn., Western Reserve U. Law Sch. Alumni Assn. (pres. 1952). Roman Catholic. K.C. (past dist.). Club: Mid-Day. Author: (with others) A Housing Program for the U.S., 1934. Wrote and obtained passage of Ohio Housing Authority Law (1st in nation), 1933. Home: Cleveland, Ohio. Died 1975.

BOLIN, HARVEY WESLEY, former gov. Ariz.; b. Butler, Mo., July 1, 1909; s. D.S. and Margaret (Combs) B.; student Phoenix Coll.; m. Marion Knappenberger, Aug. 14, 1967; children—Wesley, William, Bruce, Thomas, Steve. Constable, W. Phoenix Precinct, 1938-43; justice of peace W. Phoenix Precinct Ct., 1943-48; sec. state State of Ariz., 1948-77, gov., 1977-78. Mem. exec. bd. Nat. Secs. of State, 1953-77; chmn. Ariz. Leukemia Fund, 1976. Named Man of Year, Boys Clubs, 1976; recipient Silver Beaver award Boy Scouts Am., Silver Antelope award. Democrat. Congregationalist. Clubs: Elks, Camelback Kiwanis, Phoenix Country. Home: Phoenix, Ariz. Died Mar. 4, 1978.

BOLLES, THOMAS DARLEY, athletic dir.; b. Willow River, Minn., Sept. 25, 1902; s. Henry Albert and Edith (Lewis) B.; A.B., U. Wash., 1926, M.A., 1936; student Harvard Grad. Sch. Arts and Scis., 1937-40; m. Catharine Hope, Sept. 3, 1936 (dec. 1968); children—Lemuel Harry, Hope Catharine; m. 2d, Doris F. Lewis, Aug. 15, 1970. Coach U. Wash. Freshmen, 1928-36; head rowing coach, Harvard, 1937-51 (from 1937-50 the Harvard Varsity crew lost only one race to Yale; 1939 and 1950 Varsity crews won the Grand Challenge Cup at Henley Regatta, Eng.; the 1947 Varsity won the Lake Washington Regatta 2000 meter sprint race, setting a world's record of 5:49), dir. Athletics, Harvard, 1951-63, dir. emeritus, 1963-78, mgr. U.S. Olympic Rowing Team, 1952, 56; chmn. U.S. Olympic Rowing Com., 1964. Served as lt. comdr. USNR, World War II. Elected to Helms Hall of Fame, 1956. Mem. Rowing Coaches Orgn. Am. (pres., 1943-46), Am. Legion, Fellowship of U.S.-Brit. Comrades, London, Mil. Order of World Wars. Republican. Methodist. Clubs: Harvard Faculty; Harvard Varsity; Carolina Country (Raleigh). Author of rowing articles included in Robert F. Herrick's Red Top, 1948. Home: Raleigh, N.C. Died Dec. 17, 1978.

BOLTON, CHARLES HOUSTON, clergyman; b. Belgreen, Ala., Sept. 13, 1886; s. Franklin Marion and Josephine (Hall) B.; student Atlanta Theol. Sem., 1912-14, Southern Bapt. Theol. Sem., 1915-17; D.D., Mercer U., 1933; L.H.D., John B. Stetson U., De Land, Florida, 1943; m. Lena Mae Painter, Sept. 20, 1904; children—Charles Houston, Elinor Lyle, Edith Annette. Ordained to ministry Baptist Ch., 1916; pastor in Kentucky, Ala. and Florida, 1916-39; associate sec. Relief and Annuity Bd., Southern Bapt. Conv., 1939-41; exec. sec.-treas. Fla. Bapt. Conv. 1941-44; pastor Riverside Baptist Ch. Miami, 1944-49; exec. sec. So. Bapt. Fdt., 1949-53; pastor 1st Ch., Avon Park, Fla., 1953—. Chmn. bd. trustees Stetson U. Democrat. Mason, Kiwanian. Address: Avon Park, Fla.

BOLTON, FRANCES PAYNE, congresswoman; b. Cleve., Mar. 29, 1885; d. Charles William and Mary Perry (Payne) Bingham; student Mannes Music Sch., N.Y.C.; LL.D., Colgate U., 1940, Ohio Wesleyan U., 1942, Fenn Coll., 1953, Oberlin Coll., 1953, Heidelberg Coll., 1954, Western Coll. for Women, Oxford, Ohio, 1957, U. Maine, 1960; L.H.D., Baldwin-Wallace Coll., 1944, Kenyon Coll., 1947, Coll. Wooster, 1948, Western Reserve U., 1944; Tuskegee Inst., 1957, Johns Hopkins, 1959, others; m. Chester Castle Bolton, Sept. 14, 1907; children—Charles Bingham, Kenyon Castle, Oliver Payne (dec.), Elisabeth (dec.). Mem. 76th to 89th Congresses, 22d Ohio Dist.; ranking Rep. mem. fgn. affairs com.; U.S. del. 8th General Assemby UN, 1953; first woman mem. Congress to head mission abroad, 1955; U.S. del. Brit.-Am. Parliamentary Conf., 1961; alt. del. NATO Parliamentary Conf., Paris, 1966; U.S. delegate Ghana Independence ceremonies, 1957; U.S. del. to Council of Europe, Strasbourg, France, 1966. Mem. Rep. State Central Com., 1938-40; vice chmn. Nat. Rep. Program Com., 1937-40; del., mem. platform com. Rep. Nat. Conv., 1956, 60, 64, 68; hon. mem. Rep. Executive Com. Cuyahoga County. Vice regent from Ohio, Mount Vernon Ladies' Assn. in charge of George Washington Nat. Shrine at Mount Vernon, Va.; trustee Lakeside Hosp.; hon. trustee Mus. African Art; bd. Sch. Advanced Internat. Studies; bd. women's Africa Com., African-Am. Inst.; adv. council Sch. Nursing of Western Reserve U. (all Cleve.); trustee U.S. Hist. Soc., Nat. Trust Historic Preservation, Lake Erie Coll., Tuskegee Inst., Meharry Med. Coll.; adv. com. Aid to African Students Phelps-Stokes Fund, Rep. Women's Com. Spl. Activities. Recipient William Freeman Snow award, 1949; M. Adelaide Nutting award, 1951; Women for Achievement Inc., nat. award, 1951; Officer French Legion of Honor, 1956; award for achievement in govt. Zonta Internat. 1956; service plaque State Dept., 1961; community service plaque V.F.W. Cleve., 1961, award, 1963; Distinguished Achievement award Nat. Assn. Colored Women's Clubs, 1963; award Operation Crossroads Africa, 1965; named hon. flight nurse U.S. Air Force, 1968, others. Hon. fellow Cleve. Medical Library Assn. Mem. D.A.R., Am. Social Hygiene Assn. (v.p., hon. mem.), Nat. League for Nursing (hon.), Soc. Women Geographers, Alumni Assn. Army Sch. Nursing, Edward Angle Soc. Orthodontia (hon.), Capitol Hill Assos. (bd.), League Women Voters, U.S. Capitol Hist. Soc.; hon. mem. Alpha Iota, Beta Sigma Phi, Delta Kappa Gamma, Phi Delta Gamma, Theta Sigma Phi. Presbyn. Clubs: Women's City (Cleve.); Women's Nat. Republican, Pen and Brush (N.Y.C.); League of Republican Women, Internat. (Washington); Women's Advt. of Cleve. (hon.). Home: Lyndhurst, Ohio. Died Mar. 9, 1977.

BOLTON, JAMES CALDERWOOD, banker; b. Alexandria, La., Apr. 17, 1899; s. James Wade and Mary (Calderwood) B.; B.S., Wharton Sch. Finance and Commerce, U. Pa., 1920; m. Frances Sample, Apr. 10, 1924; 1 dau., Frances (Mrs. Paul M. Davis Jr.). Mem. credit dept. Nat. Bank of Commerce, 1921-22; with Rapides Bank & Trust Co., Alexandria, 1922-74, asst. cashier, 1922-25, v.p., 1925-36, pres., 1936-56, chmn. bd. dirs., 1956-74; dir. Delta Cotton Oil & Fertilizer Co., Jackson, Miss. Chmn. La. Bd. Pub. Welfare, 1952-56, 60-64; chmn. Alexandria Civil Service Commn., 1944-70. Pres. La. State U. Found., 1964-65. Served with U.S. Army, World War I. Mem. Alexandria (pres. 1930-31), Alexandria-Pineville (chmn. indsl. devel. div. 1965-74) Chambers Commerce, La. (pres. 1933-34), Am. (pres. state bank div. 1935) bankers assns. Baptist (exec. bd. La. Baptist Conv. 1928-53, pres. found. 1948-59). Mason, Kiwanian. Home: Alexandria, La. Died Sept. 10, 1974; interred Greenwood Cemetery, Pineville, La.

BOLTON, WILLIAM P., congressman; born Hartford County, Md., July 2, 1885; grad. Baltimore U. Admitted to Md. bar, 1909; mem. Md. State Senate, 1946-48; mem. 81st Congress (1949-51), 2d Md. Dist. Democrat. *

BOMAR, WILLIAM PURINTON, corporate exec.; b. Lookout Mountain, Tenn., Aug. 9, 1886; s. David Terry and Anna E. (Purinton) B.; B.S., Yale, 1908; m. Jewel Nail, Nov. 2, 1915 (dec. Oct. 1965); 1 son, William Purinton; m. 2d, Portia Goulder Hamilton, July 1, 1966. With Bewley Mills, Fort Worth, 1909-57, pres., gen. mgr., 1943-57; past pres. Inland Investment Co.; chmn. bd. Chicasha Cotton Oil Co., 1961—; past chmn. bd. Houston Gen. Ins. Group; dir. Tex. Utilities Co., Tex. Electric Service Co., State Res. Life Ins. Co., Southwestern Expn. and Fat Stock Show, Flour Mills Am., Inc., Mo.-Kan.-Tex. R.R. Co. Pres. Ft. Worth Grain and Cotton Exchange, 1925. Chmn. bd. W. I. Cook Childrens Hosp., Ft. Worth, 1928—; bd. dirs. Tex. Research Found., Retina Found., Boston. Mem. Millers Nat. Fedn. (past pres.), Am. Mixed Feed Mfrs. Assn. (past pres.), Ft. Worth C. of C. Presbyn. (chmn. bd. trustees). Mason. Clubs: Ft. Worth (past pres.), Rivercrest Country (Ft. Worth). Address: Fort Worth TX. *

BONAR, JOHN STANLEY, college president; b. Rosbys Rock, W.Va., Jan. 13, 1882; s. David and Catherine Virginia (Parsons) B.; grad. West Liberty (W.Va.) State Normal Sch., 1913; attended W.Va. U.; B.S., Ohio U., 1926; m. Claudia Vaughn Jerrome, of West Liberty, Aug. 27, 1913; 1 son, John Stanley. Teacher, rural schs. Marshall Co., W.Va., 1899-1906; prin. grade sch., Benwood Junction, 1906-12, North Benwood, 1912-13; supt. schs., Cameron, 1913-19, Hinton, 1919-21; asst. state supervisor rural schs. W.Va., 1921-26; pres. West Liberty State Teachers College since 1926. Mem. N.E.A., W.Va. State Edn. Assn. Republican. Methodist. Mason, K.P. Home: West Liberty, W.Va.*

BOND, ALFRED M., business exec.; b. Detroit, Mich., May 21, 1883; s. Charles Granville Mellin and Harriet Alice (Taylor) M.; B.C.E., Tufts Coll., 1904; m. Ethel Bond, Aug. 29, 1907; children—Gertrude I. (Mrs. Joseph De Masi), Dorothy A. (Samuel McNeilly). Clerk Bond & Bond Co., Roxbury, Mass., 1904-07; a founder, with father, Climax Paper Box Co., Cambridge, Mass., 1907, treas., 1907-31, gen. mgr., 1913-31; formed Consolidated Paper Box Co., Somerville, Mass., 1931, treas. and gen. mgr. since 1931. Chmn. O.P.A. Industry Adv. Com., 1942-46, mem. W.P.B. Industry Adv. Com., 1942-44. Mem. Nat. Paper Box Mfrs. Assn. (pres.-dir. since 1944), N.E. Paper Box Mfrs. Assn. (chmn. 1943-45), Delta Tau Delta. Republican. Unitarian. Club: Winchester Country (dir. 1942-45). Home: Arlington, Mass. *

BOND, CHAUNCEY DAVID, business exec., engr.; b. York, Pa., Sept. 2, 1884; s. Allen and Mary Elizabeth (Meckley) B.; grad. York High Sch., 1903; student Y.M.C.A. night sch., York, Pa., 1907-10; m. Clara Stover, June 10, 1910. Apprentice machinist, A. B. Forquhar Co., York, Pa., 1905-09; in draughting room, Hearny Co. (now Gen. Electric), York, 1909-10; prodn. engr., Weaver Piano Co., York, 1910-11, factory supt., 1911-12, gen. supt., 1912, vice pres. and gen. mgr., 1943-49, director since 1941; cons. on acoustics, plywood and glues. Chmn. adv. bd. Pa. State Coll. Tech. Inst. Member National Piano Mfg. Assn. of Am., Inc. (past pres.), Acoustical Soc. of Am., A.A.A.S., York Engring. Soc. (past pres.), Pa. Soc. of New York. Republican. Lutheran. Clubs: Lafayette (York); Nat. Republican (New York). Contbr. artilces to trade press and tech. jours. Inventor Weaver B., and other piano improvements. *

BOND, DANIEL CARL, lawyer; b. Buffalo, Oct. 29, 1942; s. Daniel Carl and Margaret Grace (Frey) B.; A.B. with gt. distinction, Stanford, 1964; J.D., cum laude, Harvard, 1967; m. Elizabeth Lou Davis, Feb. 29, 1970; children—Lloyd Thomas, Elizabeth Margaret. Admitted to Calif. bar, 1968; practiced in Los Angeles, to 1977; asso. Gibson, Dunn & Crutcher, 1967-69; prin. Rodi, Pettker, Galbraith, Bond & Phillips, 1969-77; sec., gen. counsel Davis Communications, Inc., Los Angeles, Atlanta and Hawaii. Mem. Am., Calif., Los Angeles County bar assns., Phi Beta Kappa. Republican. Methodist. Clubs: California, Los Angeles Country. Home: Los Angeles, Calif. Died June 1, 1977.

BOND, DOUGLAS DANFORD, physician; b. Waltham, Mass., July 2, 1911; s. Earl Danford and Grace (Newson) B.; A.B., Harvard, 1934; M.D., U. Pa., 1938; fellow Inst. of Pa. Hosp., 1940-41; research fellow in physiology Harvard Med. Sch., 1941-42; D.Sc., U. Heidelberg, 1953; m. Helen Cannon, July 3, 1937; children—Peter Danford, Thomas Cannon, Sharon, Barbara. Resident psychiatry Butler Hosp., Providence, 1939-40; candidate Boston Psychoanalytic Inst., 1941-42; chief lab. psychiatry, Sch. Aviation Medicine, Randolph Field, Tex., 1942-43; chief div. psychiatry 1st Central Med. Establishment, 8th Air Force, 1943-45; Central Med. chief cons. in psychiatry Army Air Forces, Washington, 1945; prof. psychiatry Case Western Res. U. Med. Sch., Cleve., 1945-76, head dept., 1945-69, dean Med. Sch., 1959-66, dir. psychiatry Univ. Hosps. 1945-69. Expert cons. to sec. of army on personnel mgmt., 1946; cons. in psychiatry to med. dir. of VA, 1946-48. Mem. adv. bd. A.R.C., 1948-76; mem. com. neuropsychiatry NRC, 1946-51; mem. adv. com. psychiatry USPHS, 1954-59; adv. com. to dir. NIH, 1965-69; mem. bd. sci. counsellors NIMH, 1966-76; cons. on security AEC, 1974-76. Pres., Grant Found., 1966-76. Mem. Am. Psychoanalytic Assn. (sec. 1955-57), Am. Acad. Psychiatrists, Ohio Psychiat. Assn. (pres. 1952-53), A.M.A., Am. Psychiat. Assn., Am. Acad. Psychoanalysts (pres. 1975), Ohio Med. Assn., Cleve. Acad. Medicine, Med. Cons. World War II, Am. Acad. Arts and Scis. Clubs: 50 (Cleve.); Century Assn. (N.Y.C.); Harvard. Author: Love and Fear of Flying, 1952. Contbr. chpt. in Teaching Psychotherapeutic Medicine, 1948; also articles on physiology and psychiatry to publs. Home: Cleveland, Ohio. Died Oct. 30, 1976.

BOND, ELSIE M(URDOCH), social worker; b. Baltimore, Md., Sept. 25, 1884; d. Nicholas Penniman and May Campbell (Murdoch) B.; student Bryn Mawr, 1901-02; N.Y. Sch. of Social Work, 1913; honorary LL.D., Skidmore College, June 1948. Served as case supervisor, 1917-18; asst. secretary Family Welfare Soc., Baltimore (Md.), 1919-20; with Am. Relief Commn. in Roumania, 1918-19; dir. social service, A.R.C., Czechoslovakia, 1920-22; with Nat. Information Bur., Russia, 1922; asst. sec. State Charities Aid Assn., New York, 1923-48. Dir. child care, N.Y., State War Council, 1942-46; mem. and sec. N.Y. State Legislative Commn. for long-range health program, 1938-47; sec. N.Y. State Assn. Pub. Welfare Officials, 1937-48; retired. Author: Public Relief in New York State, 1937, 1938, 1939; Child Care in New York State, 1943. Home: Danbury, Conn. *

BOND, JOHNNY (CYRUS W.), singer, guitarist, comedian, composer; b. Enville, Okla., June 1, 1915; s. Rufus Thomas and Annie Mae (Camp) B.; student U. Okla., 1937-38; m. Dorothy Louise Murcer, Dec. 30, 1939; children—Sherry Louise (Mrs. Charles Weedman), Jeanne Anne (Mrs. Herman Wood), Susan Paulette Riley. Appeared on radio broadcasts in Okla., 1934-40, CBS Radio Melody Ranch with Gene Autry, 1940-56, Town Hall Party TV, Los Angeles, 1953-61, Melody Ranch TV, Los Angeles, 1964-71; rec. artist for Columbia, Capitol, Decca, Starday, Mercury. Mem. Country Music Assn. (dir.), Acad. Country and Western Music (pres., dir.). Author biographies on Gene Autry and Tex Ritter. Composer numerous songs. Home: Burbank, Calif. Died June 12, 1978.

BOND, OTTO FERDINAND, univ. prof.; b. Hopkinton, R.I., Nov. 3, 1885; s. Carlos and Emma M. (Saunders) B.; grad. David Prouty High Sch., Spencer, Mass., 1904; A.B., Clark Coll., Worcester, Mass., 1907; M.A., Ohio State U., 1912; student U. of Grenoble, France, 1908-09, U. of Chicago, 1914-16; research work, U. of Grenoble and U. of Paris, 1930-31; m. Julia Seney Hopkins, Nov. 27, 1912; children—Juliana Allison, Alan Brandon. Began as asst. prin., Robbins Sch., Norfolk, Conn., 1907; instr. fgn. langs., Racine (Wis.) Coll., 1909-11; instr. Romance langs., Ohio State U., 1911-14; fellow and asst. in Romance langs., U. of Chicago, 1914-15; adjunct prof. Romance langs., U. of Tex., 1915-20; asst. prof., U. of Chicago, 1920-24, asso. prof. Romance langs. and chmn. dept. of modern langs., 1924-34, prof. and chmn. of Romance langs. in the Coll., 1934-45, prof. and chmn. of French in the coll. 1945-50, emeritus 1951, William Rainey Harper Prof. of French in the College (for distinguished service) 1950. Director French and assistant personnel officer, War Work Council of Y.M.C.A., Southern War Dept., 1918; head of French schs. at Army Hdqrs., El Paso, Tex. and Camp Travis, San Antonio, Tex., 1917-18; instr. and examiner, A.S.T.P. U. of Chicago, 1943-44. Mem. Modern Lang. Assn. of America, Am. Assn. Univ. Profs., Fedn. of Mod. Lang. Teachers, Am. Assn. Teachers of French, A.A.A.S., Académie de Montauban of France (asso.), Scholarship Soc. of Clark Coll. Mem. United Ch. Clubs: Quadrangle, Univ. Colony. Editor of Heath-Chicago French, Spanish and Russian Lang. Series (textbooks). Author: U. of Chicago Spanish-English English-Spanish Dictionary (with Carlos Castillo). Contbr. articles on linguistic pedagogy to yearbooks and inst. publs. Home: Chgo. *

BOND, RICHMOND PUGH, educator; b. Magnolia, Miss., Sept. 16, 1899; s. Albert Richmond and Ruth (Pugh) B.; A.B., Vanderbilt, 1920; A.M., Harvard, 1923, Ph.D., 1929 (Dexter traveling fellow, 1927, 1928-29); Sterling research fellow, Yale, 1937-38; m. Marjorie Eliza Nix, Sept. 3, 1924. Instr. in English, Baylor Univ., Tex., 1921-22, Hollins Coll., Va., 1923-24, Ind. Univ., 1924-26; asst. prof. of English, U. N.C., 1929-34, asso. prof., 1934-39, prof., 1939-70, Kenan professor of English, 1970-79; prof. English summer terms, U. of Texas, Duke U., N.Y. U. honorary lecturer University Coll., London, 1949-51; spl. University lectr., U. of London, 1950-51; resident fellow Newberry Library, 1963. Lt. comdr. USNR, 1942-45. Recipient Navy Unit Commendation. Mem. MLA, Bibliog. Soc. Am., Bibliog. Soc. U. Virginia, English Assn. (London), Phi Beta Kappa. Author: English Burlesque Poetry, 1700-1750, 1932; Chesterfield: Letters and Other Pieces, 1935; English Literature, 1660-1800: A Current Bibliography, Philological Quarterly, 1938-41; Studies of British Newspapers and Periodicals from their Beginning to 1800: A Bibliography (with K. K. Weed), 1946; Queen Anne's American Kings, 1952; Studies in the Early English Periodical, 1957; New Letters to the Tatler and Spectator, 1959; The Tatler: The Making of a Literary Journal, 1971; contbr. revs. and articles. Specialist English lit. with emphasis on 18th century. Home: Chapel Hill, N.C. Died Feb. 15, 1979.

BONER, CHARLES PAUL, cons. in acoustics; b. Nocoma, Tex., Feb. 8, 1900; s. Charles Wilbur and Sally Elizabeth (Lee) B.; A.B., U. Tex., 1920, M.A., 1922, Ph.D., 1929; postgrad. (Whiting fellow) Harvard, 1927-28; m. Marian Oldfather, Sept. 9, 1930; children—Donald Stephen, Charles Randall, Richard Elwood. Tutor dept. physics U. Tex., Austin, 1920-22, instr., 1922-24, 25-27, adj. prof., 1928-35, asso. prof., 1935-36, prof., 1936-42, 45-70, dir. Def. Research Lab., 1945-65, cons. to dir. of lab., 1965-70, dean Coll. Arts and Scis., 1949-54, dean Univ., 1953-54, v.p. acad. affairs, 1954-57, exec. dir. Office Govt. Sponsored Research, 1949-54, 57-65; radio engr. A.E. Hancock Co., Austin, 1924-25; asso. dir. Underwater Sound Lab., Harvard, 1942-45; accoustical cons. in design broadcast studios, auditoriums and pub. bldgs., 1937-79; partner C.P. Boner & Assos., Austin, 1968-74; ret., 1974. Expert cons., research and devel. bd. Dept. Def., 1948-53. Recipient Naval Ordnance Devel. award, 1945; certificate of appreciation OSRD, 1945; Joint Army-Havy certificate of appreciation, 1948. Fellow Acoustical Soc. Am. (exec. council 1947-50, pres. 1963), AAAS, Tex. Acad. Sci., Audio Engring. Soc., Nat. Council Acoustical Consultants; mem. Phi Beta Kappa, Sigma Xi, Sigma Pi Sigma (hon.). Democrat. Baptist. Clubs: Town and Gown, Headliners. Editorial bd. Rev. of Sci. Instruments, 1947-49. Contbr. tech. papers to jours. Home: Austin, Tex. Died Apr. 12, 1979; buried Oakwood Cemetery, Austin.

BONHAM, JOHN HENRY, drummer; b. Redditch, Worcestershire, Eng., May 31, 1949; married; 1 son, 1 dau. Played with various rock groups including Band of Joy; with rock group Led Zeppelin, 1968-80; worldwide concert performances; performed in film Song Remains the Same, 1976; albums include: Led Zeppelin I, Led Zeppelin II, Led Zeppelin III, Led Zeppelin IV, Houses of the Holy, Physical Graffiti, Presence, In Through the Out Door. Died Sept. 26, 1980.

BONNER, WILLARD HALLAM, educator, writer; b. Lynn, Mass., May 13, 1899; s. Arthur and Josephine (Whitaker) B.; student U. Ala., 1916; A.B., Coll. of Pacific, 1920; A.M., Stanford 1921; Ph.D., Yale, 1931; m. Kathryn Cummings, Mar. 27, 1926 (dec. 1950); children—Willard Hallam, Anne Cummings; m. 2d, Elda O. Baumann, Jan. 19, 1951. Asst. in English, Stanford, 1921; instr. English, Mich. State U., 1921-22; prof. English, SUNY at Buffalo, 1922-68, James H. McNulty prof. English, 1955-68, emeritus, 1968-80, dir. grad. studies in English, 1958-67, editor univ. publs., 1923-39, 40-48. Mem. AAUP Modern Lang. Assn. Am., Phi Beta Kappa. Club: Internat. Torch. Author: Pirate Laureate, the Life and Legends of Captain Kidd, 1947; The Journals and Letters of Sarah and William Hazlitt, 1822-1831, 1959; co-editor: Letters of William Hazlitt, 1978; contbr. articles to mags. and learned jours. Home: Brunswick, Maine. Died Apr. 22, 1980.

BONNIER, AKE (BO-NI-E', O'KE), publisher; b. Stockholm, Sweden, Aug. 4, 1886; s. Karl Otto and Lisen (Josephsson) B.; grad. Högre Realläroverk, Stockholm, 1905; m. Eva B. Bachner, May 8, 1911; 1 son, Gerard Mortimer. Came to U.S., Apr. 1939. Began in father's publishing business, 1905; co-dir. and partner Albert Bonniers Förlag, publishers, Stockholm, since 1917; pres. Ahlen & Akerlund, Stockholm, since 1929; pres. Gerard Pub. Co., Inc., N.Y. City, publishers of Who (mag.), 1941-42, also editor of Who. Decorated Comdr. Order of Vasa and Knight Order of North Star (Sweden), Legion of Honor (France). Home: Gloversville, N.Y. *

BONNY, JOHN BRUCE, constrn. exec.; b. San Francisco, Feb. 8, 1903; s. Bruce and Mabel Abbey (Lewis) B.; B.S., U. Cal., 1925; m. Mary Louise McDaniels, 1923 (div. 1927); 1 dau., Jean Bruce (Mrs. McCauley); m. 2d, Dorothy Ernestine Black, May 23, 1929 (div. 1953); 1 dau., Dorothy Ann; m. 3d, Marie Womack, 1954 (dec. 1969); m. 4th, Marion Peel Crawford, 1969. Contractor Derbon Constrn. Co., Seattle, 1926-29; project mgr., supt. Morrison Knudsen Co., Inc., Boise, Idaho, 1930-34, dist. mgr., Los Angeles, 1934-47, v.p., div. mgr., 1942-47, v.p., gen. mgr. Boise, 1947-60, pres., 1960-69, chmn. bd., 1969; dir. Kaiser Cement & Gypsum, Albertson's, Inc., Boise. Mem. Moles, Beavers (pres., dir. 1970-71). Clubs: Pacific Union (San Francisco), California (Los Angeles). Author: Fifty Years of Construction Progress, 1962; author, editor: Handbook of Construction Management and Organization, 1973. Home: Boise, Idaho. Deceased.

BONOMO, JOE, publisher, mcht.; b. N.Y.C., Dec. 25, 1901; s. Albert and Esther (Juaka) B.; student pub. schs., N.Y.C., N.Y. Mil. Acad., Cornwall-on-Hudson, N.Y.; m. Ethel-Ramona Newman, Feb. 11, 1930. Stuntman, serial star Universal Pictures, Hollywood, Cal., 1925-34; lectr. on beauty, charm, health and strength, 1936—; owner mail order bus., N.Y.C., 1932-75; owner Bonomo Industries, 1932-78, Bonomo Studios, Inc., N.Y.C., 1935-78; pres., owner Bonomo Culture Inst. Winner, Modern Apollo Contest sponsored by New York Daily News, 1919. Author: (autobiography) The Strongman, 1968; numerous manuals, pamphlets, papers. Home: New York, N.Y. Died Mar. 28, 1978.

BOOKER, RUSSELL EVERETT, clergyman; b. Scottsville, Ill., Dec. 17, 1885; s. Everett Edward and Clara May (Elder) B.; student Transylvania Coll. and Coll. of the Bible, Lexington, Ky., 1904-09; private student in voice and harmony, Lexington and Los Angeles; m. Katherine Price, Sept. 9, 1916; 1 dau., Mary Russell. Ordained to ministry of Disciples of Christ Ch., 1909; asst. minister and minister of music Central Christian Ch., Lexington, 1909, First Christian Ch., Los Angeles, 1910-13; minister of music Wilshire Blvd. Christian Ch., Los Angeles, 1914; First Meth. Ch., Redlands, Calif., 1915-18; asst. to Dr. Peter Ainslie, Christian Temple, Baltimore, Md., 1919-21; ednl. dir. and minister of music Seventh Street Christian Ch., Richmond, Va., 1922; student pastor, U. of Colorado, Boulder, 1923-24; pastor Christ Ch., Manzanola, Colo., 1925; pastor First Christian Ch., Pittsfield, Ill., 1926-44; pastor First Christian Church Snow Hill, Maryland, since 1945. Pres. Ill. Disciples of Christ State Conv., 1938-39; mem. administrative bd. Ill. Christian Home for Aged, 1930-44; govt. relief administr., Pittsfield, 1930-31. Chmn. Pike County Chapter American Red Cross, 1940-42, Condr. Schubert Club, Pittsfield. Clubs: Spinet (Redlands, Calif.); Wayfarers (Pittsfield). Author of newspaper column, Friendly Talk from a Small Town Manse; composer of several anthems and songs. Home: Berlin Road, Snow Hill, Md. *

BOOKMAN, CLARENCE MONROE, social worker; b. Lancaster, O., Feb. 17, 1882; s. Fred and Katherine (Foor) B.; A.B., Otterbein, 1904, A.M., 1906, L.H. D., 1936; hon. A.M., Brown, 1927; L.H.D., U. of Cincinnati, 1929, Otterbein, 1936; m. Ethel Metz, June 26, 1907; children—Elizabeth Ann, Helen Fuhr, Barbara, John Frederick. Head dept. of mathematics Central High Sch., Columbus, O., 1909-13; with Am. Book Company, 1913-14; associate director Council of Social Agencies, 1914-16; became executive dir. Community Chest of Cincinnati and Hamilton Co., 1917, exec. vice chmn., 1936-47; chmn. exec. com., 1947-49; hon. mem. 1951; v.p. Cincinnati Guardian Bank & Savings Co., 1918-50; pres. Assn. of Community Chests and Councils, 1927-28; pres. Nat. Conf. of Soc. Work, 1931-32; asst. adminstr. Fed. Emergency Relief, 1933; mem. Relief Study Nat. Resources Planning Bd., 1939-41; exec. vice chmn. Cinn. Community Chest, 1935-47; exec. v.p. War Chest of Cinn. and Hamilton Co., 1942-46; chmn. adv. cabinet Nat. War Fund, 1942-46. Nat. Budget com.; cons. War Relief Control Bd. Episcopalian. Clubs: Queen City; Commonwealth. Author: Business Arithmetic, 1913; First Steps in Bookkeeping (with F. S. Blue), 1917; also pamphlets and articles on social service subjects. Home: Cin.

BOONE, RICHARD ALLEN, actor; b. Los Angeles, June 18, 1917; s. Kirk and Cecile (Beckerman) B.; student San Diego Army and Navy Acad., 1929-32, Stanford, 1934-37, Neighborhood Playhouse, N.Y.C., 1945-47, also Actors Studio, N.Y.C.; m. Clair McAloon, Apr. 27, 1951; 1 son, Peter. Actor, appeared in plays including Medea, 1947, MacBeth, 1949, The Man, 1950, also live TV, N.Y.C., 1947-50; motion picture actor 20th Century Fox, 1950-53, films include Halls of Montezuma, The Robe, Way of a Gaucho, Vickie, Beneath the 12-Mile Reef, Siege at Red River, The Raid, Dragnet, Man Without a Star, Ten Wanted Men, Robbers Roost, Battle Stations, Star in the Dust, Away All Boats, The Alamo, Guns of Rio Conchos, The War Lord, The Arrangement, numerous others; independent films The Raid, Lizzie; other films include War Lord, Hombre, Winter Kills, The Shootist, Big Jake, The Big Sleep, The Kremlin Letter, Madron, The Last Dinosaur, The Night of the Following Day; voice in TV cartoon spl. The Hobbit; TV series, Medic (as Dr. Konrad Styner), as Mr. Paladin in Have Gun Will Travel; The Richard Boone Show, Hec Ramsey, 1973. Served with USNR, World War II. Four times nominated for Emmy award, 1954. Mem. Acad. TV Arts and Scis., Acad. Motion Picture Arts and Scis. Tau Theta Xi. Died Jan. 10, 1981.

BOOTH, GEORGE E., broker; b. Marion, Ia., June 29, 1883; s. John Marcus and Rachel Blakesly (Ives) B.; B.S., Coe Coll., 1905; m. Josephine Duncan McKercher, Mar. 18, 1930. With Lamson Bros. & Co., grain and stock brokers, Chicago, since 1910, partner since 1919; dir. Laurel Book Co. Mason (Shriner). Clubs: Indian Hill Country, Union League, University. Home: Winnetka, Ill. *

BOOTON, JOHN ROLLER, civil engring. co. exec.; b. Luray, Va., Jan. 1, 1910; s. John H. and Pearl (Roller) B.; B.S., Va. Mil. Inst., 1930; m. Mary Daniel, Sept. 20, 1948. Structural engr. Am. Bridge Co., Ambridge, Pa., 1930-33; county engr. Civil Works Authority, Shenandoah, Va., 1933-34; works engr. E.I. DuPont de Nemours & Co., Inc., Richmond, Va., 1934-59; sr. v.p. Wiley & Wilson, Inc., Richmond, from 1960; owner thoroughbred breeding farm and racing stable. Bd. dirs. Sr. Citizens Richmond. Registered profl. engr. Va., Md., N.C., Ohio. Fellow ASME (chmn. profl. practices com. 1975-76), ASCE, Va. Assn. Professions, Nat. Soc. Profl. Engrs., Soc. Am. Mil. Engrs., Va. Thoroughbred Assn. Presbyterian. Clubs: Engrs. Richmond, Commonwealth. Home: Chester, Va. Died July 17, 1980; buried Stonewall Jackson Meml. Cemetery, Lexington, Va.

BOPP, KARL RICHARD, banker; b. Kirkwood, Mo., Feb., 1906; s. Andrew Theodore and Christina (Raaf) B.; A.B., B.S., U. Mo., 1928, M.A., 1929, Ph.D., 1931, LL.D., 1961; LL.D., Temple U., 1960, Cedar Crest Coll., 1964; m. Ruth Callies, June 12, 1931; children—Karl Richard, Joanna Ruth (Mrs. Albert V. Bear). Asst. to asso. prof. U. Mo., 1931-41; dir. research Fed. Res. Bank of Phila., 1941-47, v.p. charge research,

1947-58, pres., 1958-70, ret., 1970. Dir. Atlantic City Electric Co. Lectr. finance U. Pa., 1946-58, Princeton, 1947; faculty Stonier Grad. Sch. Banking Rutgers U., 1950-58, Central States Sch., U. Wis., 1954-58, exec. program bus. adminstrn. Columbia, 1955-58, Tech. sec. Bretton Woods Monetary Conf., 1944; spl. temporary asst. to chmn. bd. govs. Fed. Res. System, 1948. Trustee, Temple U., 1964-70. Fellow Social Sci Research Council, 1932-33, Guggenheim Found., 1939-40. Mem. Am. Econ. Assn., Am. Philos. Soc. (councillor 1961-64, sec. 1965-67), Am. Acad. Polit. and Social Sci. (dir.), Am. Statistics Assn., Phi Beta Kappa. Clubs: Cosmos (Washington); Sunday Breakfast (Phila.). Author: Agencies of Federal Reserve Policy, 1935; Hjalmar Schacht: Central Banker, 1939; also articles. Home: Sanibel, Fla. Died Feb. 24, 1979.

BORDEN, MARY (MARY BORDEN SPEARS), author; b. Chicago, Ill., 1886; d. William and Mary Borden; ed. Vassar Coll.; m. 2d, Brig. Gen. Edward Louis Spears, of London, Eng., 1918. Equipped and directed Mobile Hosp. in France, 1915-18. Decorated Legion of Honor, French Red Cross. Mem. Ch. of England. Author: The Romantic Woman, 1919; Jane, Our Stranger, 1922; Three Pilgrims and a Tinker, 1924; Jericho Sands, 1925; Four O'clock, 1926; Flamingo, 1927; Jehovah's Day, 1928; The Forbidden Zone, 1929. Home: Westminster, London, Eng. *

BORER, HAROLD PETER, shipping exec.; b. Bklyn., Oct. 4, 1892; s. Emil V. and Jennie (Newman) B.; student pub. schs.; m. Elizabeth Meyer, Jan. 25, 1916; children—Harold, Kenneth, Donald. With Cunard Steam-Ship Co., Ltd., N.Y.C., from 1910, gen. passenger mgr., 1934-45, gen. mgr. U.S., from 1945; v.p., dir. Beach Blvd. Marina Inc.; pres., dir. Twenty-Five Broadway Corp. Decorated comdr. Order Brit. Empire; knight Order of White White White Rose (Finland), Knight of Malta. Mem. N.Y. Shipping Assn. (dir.), Brit. Mcht. Navy Club (dir.), Maritime Assn. N.Y. (dir.), St. George's Soc., Pilgrims of Am. Clubs: Ponte Vedra; India House. Home: Ponte Vedra, Fla. Died Apr. 3, 1979.

BORING, OMEN KONN, univ. prof.; b. Jamestown, O., Oct. 30, 1883; s. Frank M. and Ella Francinia (Van Pelt) B.; A.B., Miami U., 1907; A.M., Ohio Wesleyan U., 1920; Ph.D., U. of Chicago, 1929; student, U. of Paris, 1904, U. of Madrid, 1904-05; m. Cora Hazel McClure, June 22, 1910; children—Catherine Louise (Mrs. William P. Cross), James McClure. Instr. French and Spanish, Miami U., 1906-09, Dayton, O., 1909-16; successively instr., asst. prof., asso. prof., prof. French and Spanish, Ohio Wesleyan U., 1916-31, prof. Spanish, since 1931. Teacher French to officers' classes, Camp Sherman, Chillicothe, O., World War I. Mem. Am. Assn. Teachers of Spanish and Portuguese, Delta Upsilon. Republican. Methodist. Author: Structural Balance in Calderon. Co-author: Series Lessons for Beginners in Spanish. *

BORLAND, HAL (HAROLD GLEN), author; b. Sterling, Nebr., May 14, 1900; s. William Arthur and Sarah M. (Clinaburg) B.; student U. Colo., 1918-20, Litt.D., 1944; B.Litt., Columbia, 1923; m. 2d, Barbara Ross Dodge, 1945; children by previous marriage—Harold (dec.), Donal, Neil (dec.), Diana (stepdau.) (Mrs. James C. Thomson, Jr.). Reporter Denver Post, 1918; asso. editor Flagler (Colo.) News, 1920-21; reporter Bklyn. Times, 1921, U.P. N.Y.C., 1921-22; with King Feature Service, N.Y.C., 1922; various positions with Salt Lake City, Carson City, Fresno, San Diego and Marshall (Tex.) papers, 1923-24; telegraph editor Asheville, N.C., 1924; publicity (Ivy Lee), 1925; pub. Stratton (Colo.) Press, 1925-26; asst. night editor Phila. Morning Sun, 1927-28; editorial writer Phila. Morning Ledger, 1929-33; lit. editor morning and evening Ledgers, Phila., 1934-37; staff writer N.Y. Times Sunday mag., 1937-43, outdoor editorial essayist N.Y. Times, Sunday editorial page, 1942—; editorial page columnist Pitts. Press, 1966—; columnist Berkshire Eagle, Pittsfield, Mass., 1958-68, 70—. Dir. non-fiction sect. Writers Conf. Rocky Mountains, U. Colo., 1955. Bd. suprs. Bartholomew's Cobble Nature Reservation, Ashley Falls, Mass., 1963—; chmn. bd. Berkshire-Litchfield Conservation Council, Inc., 1970—; mem. Gov.'s Commn. on Conservation Policy for Conn., 1970-71. Served in USNRF, 1918. Recipient Westerners' Buffalo award for best nonfiction, 1957; ann. book award Secondary Edn. Bd., 1957, Journalism Alumni award Columbia, 1962; John Burroughs award and medal, 1968; Edward J. Meeman Conservation Writing award, 1967; interpretive Naturalists award, 1973. Mem. Phi Gamma Delta, Sigma Delta Chi. Mason. Club: Century Assn. (N.Y.). Author: Heaps of Gold (verse), 1922; Rocky Mountain Tipi Tales, 1924; Valor, 1934; Wapiti Pete, 1938; What Is America? (play, with Philip Dunning), 1942; America Is Americans (poems), 1942; An American Year, 1946; High, Wide and Lonesome, 1956; How To Write and Sell Non-Fiction, 1956; This Hill, This Valley, 1957; The Amulet (novel), 1957; The Enduring Pattern, 1959; The Seventh Winter (novel) 1960; The Dog Who Came to Stay, 1961; Beyond your Doorstep, 1962; The Youngest Shepherd, 1962; When the Legends Die (novel), 1963; Sundial of the Seasons, 1964; King of Squaw Mountain (novel), 1964; Countryman: A Summary of Belief, 1965; Hill Country Harvest, 1967; Homeland, A Report from the Country, 1969; Christmas Plants, 1969; Country Editor's Boy, 1970; Borland Country, 1971; Penny, 1972; This World of Wonder, 1973; Seasons, 1973; History of American Wildlife, 1975; A Place To Begin: The New England Experience, 1976; Hal Borland's Book of Days, 1976; The Golden Circle, 1977; Twelve Moons of the Year, 1979; A Countryman's Flowers, 1981; A Countryman's Woodland, 1982; (under pseudonym Ward West) Trouble Valley, 1934, Halfway to Timberline, 1935. Editor: Our Natural World, 1965. Collaborator (with Barbara Dodge Borland) novelettes and other fiction, popular mags., 1946-56. Contbg. editor Audubon Mag., 1967—. Address: Salisbury, Conn. Died Feb. 22, 1978.

BORLAND, MAND RIVES, b. N.Y. City, Apr. 14, 1886; d. John and Constance (Rives) B.; unmarried. Fifth v.-p. and chmn. exec. council Woman's Dept. Nat. Civic Federation. Episcopalian. Club: Colony. Home: New Hamburgh, N.Y. *

BORN, MAX, physicist; b. Breslau, Germany (now Poland), Dec. 11, 1882; s. Gustav and Margaret (Kauffmann) B.; student Breslau, Heidelberg, Zurich univs.; Ph.D., Goettingen U., 1907; D.Sc. (hon.), Bristol U., Eng., 1928; M.A., Cambridge U., Eng., 1933; D.Sc. (hon.), Bordeaux U., 1948, Oxford U., 1954; Dr. rer. nat., Freiburg U., 1957, Berlin U., Frankfurt U.; LL.D., Edinburgh U., 1957; Dr. ing. (hon.), Stuttgart Tech. U., 1960; D.Sc. (hon.), Oslo U., 1961, Brussels University, 1961; Dr. rer. nat. (honorary), Frankfurt University, 1964; m. Hedwig Ehrenberg, August 2, 1913; children—Irene (Mrs. Newton - John), Margaret (Mrs. Pryce), Gustav V.R. Privat-docent, Goettingen U., 1909, prof., 1921; guest lectr. U. Chgo., 1912; prof. U. Berlin, 1915, Frankfurt University, 1919, Goettingen, 1921; guest lecturer at Massachusetts Inst. Tech., 1925; Stokes lectr. Cambridge U., Eng., 1933; guest prof. Indian Inst. Science, Bangalore, 1935-36; prof. natural philosophy, Edinburgh, Scotland, 1936-53, emeritus, 1953—. Decorated Stokes medal, Cambridge, 1934; Macdougall-Brisbane and Gunning-Victoria Jubilee prize, Royal Soc. Edinburgh, 1945, 1950; Max Planck medaille, Germany, 1948; Hughes medal Royal Soc. London, 1950; Freedom City of Goettingen, 1953; Nobel prize, 1954; Grotius Medal, Munich, 1956. Member of the Royal Society of Edinburgh, Royal Society of London; mem. acads. Berlin, Goettingen, Copenhagen, Stockholm, Moscow, Dublin, Am. Acad. Arts and Scis., Nat. Acad. Sci. Author many books and articles, mostly on theoretical physics. Home: Bad Pyrmont, Germany. *

BORTREE, LEO WILLIAMS (BÔR'TRE), physician; b. Sterling, Pa., Mar. 26, 1883; s. Eugene and Adda E. (Churchill) B.; A.B., Colo. Coll., 1906; M.D., Harvard, 1910; m. Nellie E. Cheley, Aug. 22, 1916; 1 son, David William. Capt. Med. Corps, U.S. Army, at Gen. Hosp. No. 21, Denver, Colo., 1918-19. Alumni trustee Colo. Coll., 1920-33. Fellow A.M.A.; mem. Colo. State Med. Soc. (pres. 1938), Am. Clin. and Climatol. Assn., Phi Gamma Delta, Phi Beta Kappa. Republican. Episcopalian. Mason. Elk. Home: Colorado Springs, Colo. *

BOSSHART, JOHN HENRY (BÔS'HÄRT), commr. of education; b. Rochester, N.Y., Jan. 30, 1882; s. Albert and Marie (Isler) B.; A.B., Cornell U., 1902; LL.D. (hon.) Seton Hall Coll., 1944, Upsala Coll., 1944, Princeton 1947, John Marshall Coll. of Law, 1947, Rider Coll., 1948, L.H.D., Rutgers Univ., 1944; married Fanny Perry Gillett, Aug. 14, 1907; children—Mary Frances (Mrs. H. Gordon Poole), John Henry, Robert Forbes, Lena Gillett. Prin. Shortsville (N.Y.) Union Sch., 1903-06; supt. schs., N.Y. 1906; principal Franklin Elementary Sch., Rochester, N.Y., 1906-11; East High Evening Sch., Rochester, 1910-11, Lincoln Elementary Sch., East Orange, N.J., 1911-13, Salem (Mass.) Classical and High Sch., 1913-20, Columbia High Sch., South Orange, Maplewood, N.J., 1920-27; supervising principal, South Orange-Maplewood (N.J.) pub. schs., 1927-43; state commr. edn. State of N.J. since 1943. Pres. Rochester (N.Y.) Teachers Assn., N.J. Dept. of Supts., N.J. Council of Edn., N.J. Schoolmasters Club. Pres. Nat. Council of Chief State Sch. Officers. Mem. Am. Assn. Sch. Adminstrs., N.E.A. Mason, Rotarian. Home: Maplewood, N.J. *

BOST, THOMAS CREASY, surgeon; b. Cabarrus County, N.C., Jan. 20, 1886; s. Constine McColum and Laura Genette (Hartsell) B.; student Weaver Sch., Lenoir, N.C., 1906-07, Rutherford Coll., 1907-08; M.D., George Washington U., 1915; m. Vera Elizabeth Ledwell, June 17, 1933; 1 son, Tommy M. Interne, resident surgeon, Children's Hosp., Garfield Meml. Hosp., George Washington U. Hosp., 1915-16; in charge surg. div., War Hosp., Dartford, Eng., 1916-18; chief surgeon Pryor Hosp., Chester, S.C., 1919. Practicing surgeon, Charlotte, N.C., since 1920; chief surgeon Mercy Hosp., Reenes Hosp.; attending surgeon Presbyn., Memorial Hospital, Good Samaritan hosps.; cons. surgeon U.S. Vets. Bur. since 1920. Chmn. board of health of Mecklenburg County. Capt. Royal Army Med. Corps (Eng.). Member Mecklenburg County (pres.), North Carolina, Tri-State and Southern med. socs., Am. Med. Assn. Fellow Am. Coll. Surgeons. Democrat. Methodist. Mason (32 deg.), Shriner. Clubs: Civitan, Charlotte Country. Contbr. scientific articles to med. jours. Home: Charlotte, N.C. *

BOSWELL, LORIN ALBERT, dairy exec.; b. Fort Worth, Nov. 14, 1899; s. William Edward and Margie (Huffmaster) B.; B.A., Tex. Christian U., 1937, LL.D., 1967; m. Annie Josephine Shaw, Dec. 21, 1935; children—Lorin Albert, Loretta Gayle (Mrs. Thomas P. Gordon, Jr.). Pres., Boswell Dairies, Fort Worth, 1958-63, chmn. bd., 1963-78; dir. Univ. State Bank. Past pres. Dairy Products Inst. Tex., Better Bus. Bur. Fort Worth; trustee Tex. Christian U., chmn., 1958-69; hon. chmn., pres. Van Cliburn Found., Inc., Fort Worth; pres. bd. dirs. Boswell Found. Recipient Nat. citation NCCJ, 1955. Mem. S.A.R. (past pres.), Newcomen Soc. N.Am., Internat. Assn. Ice Cream Mfrs. (nat. councillors to U.S. C. of C. 1950-57), Beta Gamma Sigma (hon.), Phi Kappa Sigma, Alpha Chi. Mem. Christian Ch. Clubs: Fort Worth (bd. govs. 1961-69), Knife and Fork (pres.), Exchange (pres.) (Fort Worth); Rivercrest Country. Author: The Wayside School, 1966; Gustavus Boswell and Descendants, 1970. Address: Fort Worth, Tex. Died Mar. 5, 1978; buried Greenwood Cemetery, Fort Worth.

BOTTORFF, ORVILLE ORIS, concert mgr.; b. Cortland, Ind., Jan. 15, 1896; s. Milas Frank and Ellen (Whitted) B.; student Northwestern U., 1915-17; m. Lillian Johnston, July 1924 (dec. 1932); m. 2d, Marguerite Zender, June 30, 1936. Rep. and circuit mgr. Redpath Chautauqua and Lyceum Bur., Chgo., 1917-28; also assisted in pioneering civic music assn., organized audience movement and Community concert assns., from 1921; audience promotional dir. Chgo. Civic Opera Co., 1928-31; with Civic Concert Service, Inc., Chgo., from 1935, successively asst. mgr., v.p., dir. and gen. mgr., pres., from 1941; founder, co-owner, v.p., dir. Nat. Concert and Artist Corp., N.Y.C., from 1941, pres., from 1949. Bd. dirs. Ft. Lauderdale Symphony Orch., Opera Guild. Pres., sr. exec. officer, mem. bd. The Broadway Theatre Alliance, Inc. Named Honorable Alumnus, Nova U. Mem. Sigma Nu. Clubs: N.Y. Athletic, Bohemians, Lotus (N.Y.C.); Town (Scarsdale); Ft. Lauderdale Yacht. Author articles trade jours. Home: Fort Lauderdale, Fla. Died Oct. 1, 1975; interred St. Mary's Cemetery, Kenton, Ohio.

BOTTORFF, ROBERT INGRAM, editor; b. Columbus, Ind., Aug. 30, 1907; s. Dean Miles and Gertrude (Eckelman) B.; A.B., DePauw U., 1929; m. Katherine Stoner, May 2, 1930 (dec. 1944); children—Peter, Katherine; m. 2d, Mary Edna Davis, Feb. 14, 1947; children—Susan, Sally. Copy editor Pacific Coast edit. Wall St. Jour., 1930-32, news editor, 1932-42, mng. editor, 1942-51, mng. editor Midwest 1955-57, exec. editor, 1957-63; v.p., gen. mgr. Dow Jones & Co., 1966-70, ret., 1970; chmn. bd. Dow Jones-Irwin, Inc., 1965-70; former vice pres. and sec. The Newspaper Fund, Inc. Mem. Alpha Tau Omega, Sigma Delta Chi. Club: Monterey Peninsula Country (Pebble Beach, Calif. Home: Carmel, Calif. Died Nov. 1, 1978.

BOUCHER, ISRAEL EDMOND, business exec.; b. Mansonville, P.Q., Can., Apr. 5, 1886; s. Israel A. and Eglae (Dalpe) B.; ed. pub. schs., Manchester, N.H.; m. Gertrude Dearborn Davis, Oct. 15, 1907 (dec. Apr. 2, 1943); children—Corinne E. (Mrs. Winton P. Simmons), Virginia G. (Mrs. Emil Mettatal), Elinor M. (Mrs. George Parsons). Came to U.S., 1891, naturalized, 1921. Millhand, Amoskeag Mfg. Co., Manchester, N.H., 1902-11, millhand and clerk, 1911-17, purchasing agent, 1917-23; selling agent, Waltham Watch Co., Waltham, Mass., 1923-44, mgr. since 1944, vice pres. since 1945. Dir. Newton-Waltham Bank & Trust Company, Waltham Watch Co., Gt. Britain and Ireland, Ltd.; incorporator Waltham Savings Bank; exec. trustee Waltham Hosp.; chmn. jewelled and non-jewelled watch com. Mem. adv. council, Made-in-America Foundation, Inc., N.Y. City. Republican. Conglist. Clubs: Union League, 24 Karat (New York); Algonquin (Boston) Home: (New York); Algonquin (Boston). *

BOUCHER, JEROME H. P., investment co. exec.; ed. Trinity Coll., Hartford, Conn.; m. Joan Murray; children—Joan Sill, Jerome H.P., David. With Harris Upham, from 1951, partner, from 1954; exec. v.p. Smith Barney, Harris Upham & Co., N.Y.C. Served with U.S. Navy, World War II. Home: New York, N.Y. Died May 15, 1976.

BOUCHER, ROGER, chemist; b. Montreal, Que., Can., Dec. 17, 1931; s. Gerard and Jeanne (Forcier) B.; B.Sc., U. Montreal, 1955, M.Sc., 1957, Ph.D. in Chemistry, 1959; m. Suzanne Descôteaux, Aug. 17, 1957; 1 dau., Lise. Dir. lab. biochemistry on hypertension Clin. Research Inst. Montreal, 1967-80; asso. mem. dept. exptl. medicine McGill U., 1968-80; titular prof. med. faculty U. Montreal, 1970-80. Recipient Archambault medal Can. Assn. Advancement Sci., 1976. Fellow Chem. Inst. Can., Royal Coll. Can., Can. Royal Soc.; mem. Soc.

Canadienne de Recherches Cliniques, Council High Blodd Pressure Research Am. Heart Assn., N.Y. Acad. Scis., Can. Soc. Endocrinology and Metabolism, Internat. Soc. Hypertension. Contbr. articles to profl. jours. Home: Laval, Que., Canada. Died Jan. 20, 1980.

BOUDREAU, FRANK GEORGE (BOO-DRO), cons. Milbank Memorial Fund; b. of Am. parents, New Glasgow, Que., Can., July 18, 1886; s. Rev. M. F. and Ann (Ward) B.; M.D., C.M., McGill University, 1910; LL.D., Glasgow University, Scotland, 1947; m. Charlotte L. Dickson, June 22, 1911; children—William F., Barbara (deceased), and Elizabeth. Epidemiologist Ohio Department of Health, Columbus, 1912-15, director Division of Communicable Diseases, 1915-17, chief Bureau of Local Health Organization, 1919-25; lecturer on pub. health, Ohio State U., 1915-16; epidemiologist statistician Health Orgn., League of Nations, 1925-30, chief Bur. of Epidemiological Intelligence and Pub. Health Statistics, 1930-37, dir. Health Orgn., 1934; exec. dir. Milbank Memorial Fund 1937-56, pres. 1956-62; member Fund's Technical Board; served U.S. Army 1917-19, major Med. R.C., 1919. Chmn. Food and Nutrition Bd. of Nat. Research Council, 1941-51; former chmn. subcom. on nutrition, OFRRO; adviser to dir. gen. of UNRRA, pres. League of Nations Assn., 1939-44; tech. sec. U.N. Conf. on Food and Agr., Hot Springs and Quebec; cons. to U.S. War Food Adminstrn.; U.S. del. Internat. Health Conf., N.Y.C., 1946, World Health Meml. Assembly, 1958; cons. U.N. Interim Commn. on Food and Agr.; Com. Study Orgn. of Peace. Mem. adv. bd. Columbia U. Inst. Nutritional Scis. Trustee N.Y. Community Trust, Population Council, Inc.; trustee Nat. Vitamin Found., pres., 1958-60; trustee Nutrition Found., Inc.; hon. trustee N.Y. Sch. Social Work. Recipient Lasker award Am. Pub. Health Assn., 1957, Sedgewick Meml. medal, 1961. Fellow Am. Pub. Health Assn., N.Y. Acad. Medicine, N.Y. Acad. Sci.; mem. State Charities Aid Assn. (trustee), Am. Inst. Nutrition (hon.). Clubs: Cosmos (Wash., D.C.); Century (N.Y.). Writer of numerous articles on epidemiology, pub. health, adminstrn., nutrition and internat. cooperation in hygiene. Made Chevalier de l'ordre de la sante publique, 1946. Home: Woodstock, N.Y.; also N.Y.C.

BOUGHTON, ALICE CAROLINE (MRS. ARTHUR B. SCHAFFNER) (BO'TUN), research and adminstrn.; b. Phila., Aug. 5, 1885; d. John W. and Caroline W. (Greenbank) Boughton; B.Sc., Columbia Teachers Coll., 1914, A.M., 1915, Ph.D. (economics), 1917; m. Arthur B. Schaffner, Jan. 12, 1935. Supt. sch. luncheon, Starr Centre, Phila., 1907-10, Home and Sch. League, 1910-15; made study of sch. feeding in Eng. and continent of Europe, 1912; expert on home economics and sch. lunches, Cleveland (O.) Edn. Survey, 1915-16; spl investigator, Bur. of Ednl. Experiments, N.Y. City, 1917; chief sect., elementary and secondary edn. Div. of Food Conservation, and chief price sect. Statis. Div. U.S. Food Administration, May 1917-June 1918; spl. expert div. of Planning and Statistics, War Industries Bd., July-Dec. 1918; with J. Walter Thompson Co., New York, 1919-24; v.p. Central Dist. Constrn. Corp., New York, 1924-26; exec. sec. Com. on Maternal Health, Acad. of Medicine, Cincinnati, 1929-31; exec. dir. Am. Birth Control League, 1931-32. Author: (books) Annual Reports of Phila. Com. on School Lunches, 1911-14; Household Arts and School Lunches (Cleveland Edn. Survey), 1916. Contbr. mags. and newspapers. Address: Chicago, Ill. *

BOUHUYS, AREND, physician, educator; b. Deventer, Netherlands, Oct. 18, 1925; s. Hendrik Willem and Minke (van der Bij) B.; M.D., U. Utrecht, 1948; D.M.S., U. Amsterdam, 1956; M.A. (hon.), Yale, 1968; m. Aleid A. Kuiper, Dec. 11, 1951 (div.); children—Jaaike M., Henriette H.; m. 2d, Fenna G. van Gulik, Mar. 23, 1956; children—Hendrik W., Margaritha J., Welmoed. Came to U.S., 1962, naturalized, 1969. Intern, Hosp U. Utrecht (Netherlands), 1948-50, chief asst. dept. physiology, 1951-52; resident medicine U. Hosp., Amsterdam, 1952-55; resident chest disease Beatrixoord Tb. Sanitarium, Appelscha, Netherlands, 1955-57; research physician Netherlands Inst. Preventive Medicine, Leiden, 1957-58; asst. prof., head lab. clin. physiology U. Hosp., Leiden, 1959-62; asst. prof. physiology and medicine Emory U., 1962-64; asso. prof. epidemiology Sch. Medicine, Yale, 1964-68, fellow J.B. Pierce Found., 1964-78, prof. medicine and epidemiology, 1968-79; dir. Yale Lung Research Center, 1971-78; prof. physiology U. Utrecht (Netherlands) 1979; NATO sci. fellow, 1961; conf. chmn. Sound Prodn. in Man, N.Y. Acad. Scis., 1966, cons. editor, 1968; conf. chmn. Airway Dynamics, Internat. Union Physiol. Sci., 1968; mem. Task Force on Environmental Health Scis. Research Planning, 1968-69; cons. WHO, 1975-78, U.S. Dept. Labor, 1978-79. Mem. governing council Conn. Air Conservation Com., 1969-72. Recipient G.C.E. Burger prize in indsl. medicine Netherlands Soc. Occupational Health, 1963; Josiah Macy, Jr. Faculty Scholar award, 1975-76. Fellow AAAS, A.C.P.; mem. Am. Physiol. Soc., Am. Thoracic Soc., Am. Soc. Clin. Investigation, Am. Fedn. Clin. Research, Am. Soc. Pharm. Exptl. Therapeutics, Société de Pathologie Thoracique du nord (France), Association des physiologistes, Sigma Xi. Clubs: Cosmos (Washington); Yale (N.Y.C.). Editor: Airway Dynamics-Physiology and Pharmacology, 1970, Lung Cells in Disease, 1976; author: Breathing—Physiology, Environment and Lung Disease, 1974; The Physiology of Breathing, 1977; mem. editorial bd. Am. Jour. Physiology, Jour. of Applied Physiology, 1966-72; mng. editor Lung-Internat. Jour. Lungs, Airways and Breathing, 1975-79. Died June 15, 1979.

BOULANGER, NADIA JULIETTE, tchr. composition, condr., lectr.; b. Paris, Sept. 16, 1887; d. Ernest and Raissa (Princess Mychetsky) Boulanger; studied Paris Nat. Conservatory; hon. Mus.D., Russell Sage Coll., Brown U., Washington Coll. Music, Harvard, Brown U., U. So. Ill. and Smith Coll. Formerly head of theory dept. Ecole Normale de Musique, Paris; came to U.S. in 1924, 35, 40, 58; was faculty mem. Longy Sch. Music, Cambridge, Mass.; instr. composition Peabody Conservatory; dir., hon. prof. Nat. Conservatory Music, Paris; prof., dir. Am. Conservatory in Fontainebleau; lectr. Radcliffe Coll., Wellesley Coll. Guest condr. Boston Symphony Orch., Royal Philharmonic, London, N.Y. Philharmonic, Phila. Orch., Washington Symphony. Decorated Officier Legion of Honor (France); Officer Arts et Letters (France); Comdr. Polonia restituta (Poland); Officer St. Charles (Monaco); Henry Hadley medal, 1949. Mem. Soc. of Authors, Composers and Editors of Music (France). Roman Catholic, Composer of songs, cello pieces, an opera in collaboration with Raoul Pugno (La Ville Morte). Contbr. to musical mags. Recordings for La va'x de son Maitu, Decca. Home: Paris, France. Died Oct. 22, 1979; buried Montmartre Cemetery, Paris.

BOULTON, LAURA CRAYTOR, ethno-musicologist, writer, lectr., filmmaker; b. Conneaut, Ohio; d. Herbert Orleans and Emma Lucy (Nottingham) Craytor; student Western Res. U.; A.B., L.H.D., Denison U.; postgrad. U. Chgo., Chgo. Musical Coll., Sorbonne, U. Paris, U. London; m. W. Rudyerd Boulton (div. 1941). Ethnologist, musicologist Straus Central African expdn. for Am. Mus. Natural History, 1929, South African expdn. for Carnegie Mus., 1930, Pulitzer Angola expdn., 1931, S.W. Indian project for U. Chgo., 1933, Straus West African expdn. for Field Mus., 1934, Mandel W.I. expdn., 1938, Crane Mexican expdn. for Mus. Modern Art, 1940, S.W. Indian expdn. for Dept. Interior, 1940; dir. coast-to-coast film and rec. project on peoples of Can. for Can. Govt., Nat. Film Bd., 1941-43, including Can. N.W. expdn., Eastern Arctic expdn., 1942; Alaskan expdn. for Dept. Interior, 1946; Haiti expdn., 1947, African expdn. for U. Calif., 1947-48, Asiatic expdn. Am. Mus. Natural History and Buffalo Mus. Sci., 1949-50; European Folk Music Survey including Balkans, for UNESCO, 1951; rec. projects as guest of govts. Spain, Portugal, Greece, Turkey, 1952-54, African-Asian expdn., 1956; expdn. to Balkans and Eastern Europe, 1957-58, Near East, 1959, South and Central Am., 1960, Harvard U.-Dumbarton Oaks Byzantine Project, 1960-68; lectr. primitive music U. Chgo., 1931-33, music faculty U. Calif., 1946-49; Coptic Music project, Ethiopia, 1966-68, Micronesia, 1976, Papua New Guinea, 1978, Polynesia, 1979; dir. Laura Boulton Collection traditional and liturgical music, Columbia U. Sch. Internat. Affairs, 1962-72, dir. research project world music, 1962-71; Disting. prof. fine arts, dir. Laura Boulton Collection World Music and Musical Instruments, Ariz. State U., 1972-77, dir. research project on world music and musical instruments, 1977-80; producer, dir. documentary films on nat. groups and primitive tribes; broadcaster radio and TV; del. numerous nat., internat. confs.; lectr. U.S. and abroad; mem. Com. African Music, UNESCO, Com. for Comparative Music, Berlin, Com. Liturgical Music, Rome; Winifred Cullis lectureship fellow English Univs., 1965. Grantee Am. Council Learned Socs., Am. Philos. Soc., Carnegie Corp., Harvard U.-Dumbarton Oaks. Fellow Am. Geog. Soc., Royal Geog. Soc.; mem. Internat. Inst. Comparative Musical Studies Berlin, Inst. Liturgical Music Rome, Asia Soc., Am. Anthrop. Assn., Am. Musicol. Soc., Internat. Folk Music Council, Internat. Council Women, Soc. Ethnomusicology, Phi Beta Kappa, Delta Omicron. Republican. Episcopalian. Rec., pub. albums with accompanying booklets: Africa Music-Rhythm in the Jungle, 1940; Indian Music of the Southwest, 1941; Indian Music of Mexico, 1942; Songs and Dances of Yugoslavia, 1952; Songs and Dances of Switzerland, 1953; The Eskimos of Hudson Bay and Alaska, 1954; Songs and Dances of Turkey, 1955; Christmas Songs of Spain, 1955; Christmas Songs of Portugal, 1955; Ukrainian Christmas Songs, 1955; Ethnic Music of Yugoslavia, 1956; French Folk Songs, 1957; author: The Music Hunter, 1969; Musical Instruments of World Cultures, 1972, rev. edit., 1975; contbr. articles to sci. and popular mags. Home: Scottsdale, Ariz. Died Oct. 16, 1980.

BOUMEDIENNE, HOUARI, pres. of Algeria; b. 1927; ed. Islamic Inst., Constantine and Cairo. Former tchr., Guelmo; promoted rebel activities Oran area, Algeria, 1955; comdr. of Wilaya, 1955-57; chief staff F.L.N., 1960-62, minister of def., ALgeria, from 1962, 1st dep. premier, 1963-65; chmn. Revolutionary Council, 1965—; prime minister, from 1965, also pres. Algeria. Address: Algiers, Algeria. Died Dec. 27, 1978.

BOURDEAUX, ROBERT MONTGOMERY, lawyer; b. Meridian, Miss., Mar. 14, 1882; s. Robert Montgomery and Caroline Maria (Walker) B.; LL.B., U. of Miss., 1903; m. Annie Wilson, of Meridian, Miss., Dec. 15, 1910; children—Robert Montgomery III, Ann Wilson, Margaret DeVane, Jeanne Walker. Admitted to Miss. bar, 1903, practicing in Meridian; mem. firm Gilbert, Bourdeaux and Venable, 1906-13; asst. atty. gen. Miss., 1919-20; circuit judge, 10th Jud. Dist., Miss., 1925-27; became U.S., dist. atty. Southern Dist. Miss., 1933; county judge Lauderdale County, Miss., since 1938. Mem. Phi Delta Theta. Democrat. Episcopalian. Home: *

BOURGET, MAURICE, Canadian senator; b. Lauzon, Que., Can., Oct. 20, 1907; s. Philippe T. and Elmire (Gosselin) B.; B.Sc. in Engring., Ecole Polytech., Montreal, 1932; m. Marguerite Cleary, Aug. 31, 1949; children—Suzanne, Louise. Engaged as cons. engr., Que., Can.; mem. Canadian Ho. of Commons from Quebec Province, 1940-62; Canadian del. to UN, Paris, France, 1951; parliamentary asst. to minister pub. works, 1953-57; del. Gen. Conf. Commonwealth Parliamentary Assn., London, Eng., 1961; joint chmn. Canadian delegation 7th meeting Can.-U.S. Interparliamentary Group, Washington, 1964; mem. Canadian Senate, 1963-80, speaker, 1963-66; called to Privy Council for Canada, 1966; dir. l'Unique Insurance Co., Quebec City. Mem. Engring. Inst. Can., Profl. Engrs. Corp. Que. Mem. Liberal Party. Catholic. K.C. Clubs: Reform, Garrison. Home: Lévis, PQ, Canada. Died Jan. 28, 1980.

BOURNE, EDWARD WALTER, lawyer; b. New Haven, June 17, 1898; s. Edward Gaylord and Annie Thomson (Nettleton) B.; A.B., Yale, 1919, postgrad. Law Sch., 1919-20; m. Margaret Watson, July 5, 1930; children—Margaret Gaylord (Mrs. Austin B. Pedersen), Susan Holdrege (Mrs. Nikolaus H. Brinkama), Edward Gaylord, Jane Thomson, James Russell. Admitted to N.Y. State Bar, 1922; asso. firm Alexander & Green, N.Y.C., 1920-29, partner firm, 1929-67, counsel, 1967-77. Served as 2d lt., F.A., U.S. Army, 1918; govt. appeal agt., Local Bd. 42, N.Y.C., 1940-43; mem. alien enemy hearing bd., No. 3, N.Y.C., 1943-45. Mem. Am., N.Y. State bar assns., Assn. Bar City N.Y., Soc. of N.Y. Hosp. (hon. gov.), Phi Beta Kappa. Republican. Episcopalian. Clubs: Century Assn., Down Town Assn., Yale (N.Y.C.); Sharon Country. Home: West Cornwall, Conn. Died July 27, 1977; interred North Cornwall, Conn.

BOUSFIELD, EDWARD LLOYD, biologist; b. Penticton, B.C., Can., June 19, 1926; s. Reginald Harker and Marjorie Frances (Armstrong) B.; B.A., U. Toronto, 1948, M.A., 1949; Ph.D., Harvard, 1954; m. Barbara Joyce Schwartz, June 20, 1953; children—Marjorie Anne, Jessie Katherine, Mary Elizabeth, Kenneth Lloyd. Invertebrate zoologist Nat. Mus. Can. (changed to Nat. Mus. Natural Scis. 1968), Ottawa, Ont., 1950-64, chief zoologist, 1964-74, sr. scientist, 1974-80. Fellow Royal Soc. Can.; mem. Ecol. Soc. Am., Am. Soc. Limnology and Oceanography, Canadian Soc. Zoologists (pres. 1979-80), Biol. Council Can., Profl. Inst. Pub. Service Can., Sigma Xi. Club: Ottawa Field-Naturalists (pres. 1959-60). Author: Canadian Atlantic Sea Shells, 1960; Shallow-water Gammaridean Amphipoda of New England, 1973. Contbr. articles to profl. jours. Home: Ottawa, Ont., Canada. Died June 25, 1980.

BOUWSMA, OETS KOLK, educator; b. Muskegon, Mich., Nov. 22, 1898; s. Joachum and Helen (Kolk) B.; A.B., Calvin Coll., 1922; Ph.D., U. Mich., 1928; Litt.D. (hon.), U. Nebr., 1975; m. Gertrude Elsie de Vries, Aug. 10, 1922; children—William James, Charles Edmond, Gretchen Ellen (Mrs. R. Bruce Emmons). Instr. English, U. Mich., 1922-28; prof. philosophy U. Nebr., 1928-65; prof. U. Tex., Austin, 1965-78; vis. prof. Smith Coll., 1949-50; John Locke lectr. Oxford (Eng.) U., 1951; pres. Western Div. Philos. Soc., 1956-57. Recipient Distinguished Alumnus award Calvin Coll., 1973. Fulbright Prof.'s Research grantee Oxford U., 1950-51; Woods Study grantee U. Nebr., London, 1956. Mem. Phi Beta Kappa. Author: Philosophical Essays; also essays in philos. jours. Home: Austin, Tex. Died Mar. 1, 1978.

BOWDEN, ROBERT JOHN, educator; b. Conemaugh, Pa., Feb. 14, 1915; s. George S. and Ora (Zimmerman) B.; A.B. cum laude, Waynesburg Coll., 1937; S.T.B., Western Theol. Sem., 1940; M.Ed., U. Pitts., 1942, Ph.D., 1946; m. Sara Catherine Klingensmith, Oct. 7, 1940; children—Robert John II, William B. Ordained minister Presbyn. Ch., 1940; pastor Smithfield & Bloomfield Presbyn. Chs., Ohio, 1940-46; dean Uniontown Center of Waynesburg Coll., 1946-50; prof. Bible and philosophy Waynesburg Coll., 1950-51, prof. English, 1951-70, chmn. dept., 1955-70, prof. religion, 1970-79, chmn. dept., 1972-79. Mem. AAUP, Greene County Hist. Soc., U.S. Power Squadrons. Republican. Presbyterian. Author: Were You There, 1963. Home: Waynesburg, Pa. Died Feb. 24, 1979; buried Plum Creek Cemetery, Pitts.

BOWDEN, WITT, historian, economist; b. Russellville, Ark., Dec. 5, 1886; s. James Newton and Dora (McAnally) B.; student Southwestern U., Georgetown, Tex., 1909-11, U. of Wis., 1912-13; A.B., U. of Colo., 1914; Ph.D., U. of Pa., 1919; m. Mary Edith Myers, June 21, 1918. Instr. in history, U. of Pa., 1914-17; instr. in history, Carnegie Inst. Tech., 1919-20; asst. prof. history U. Pa., 1920-30; lectr. summer schools Columbia University, U. Texas, U. of Tennessee; with Bureau of Labor Statistics, U.S. Dept. of Labor, 1931-51, cons., 1952—; U.S. govt. rep. Internat. Labor Conf., Geneva, 1935; govt. rep., coal mines com. Internat. Labor Orgn., 1945-51, inland transport com., 1951; del. UN Sci. Conf. on Conservation and Utilization of Resources, 1949. Served with U.S.N., 1918-19. Author of books, including: Industrial Society in England toward End of Eighteenth Century, 1924; Industrial History of the United States, 1930; various govt. bulls. and pamphlets, notably The Gift of Freedom, 1949 (trans. various foreign languages); American Labor and the American Spirit, 1954, Spanish edition, 1957. Co-author several books, including: Economic History of Europe (with Karpovich and Usher), 1937. Contbr. to periodicals, reference works and symposiums. Home: Washington. *

BOWDEY, GEORGE H(ALL), retired naval officer; b. Chapin, N.Y., Aug. 9, 1886; s. George Henry and Ella (Hall) B.; B.S., U.S. Naval Acad., 1907; m. Ethel Huton Potts, June 7, 1911 (divorced May, 1941); children—George William, Richard; m. 2d Mabel Norton Fenn, May 22, 1942. Commd. ensign U.S. Navy, 1908, advanced through grades to commodore, 1945; exec. officer, U.S.S. Minneapolis, World War I; chief of staff, U.S. Naval War Coll., 1938-40, 44-46; comdr., Naval R.O.T.C., Brown U., 1941-42; retired from active service, Mar. 10, 1946. Awarded Navy commendation ribbon for services at Naval War Coll., World War II. Mem. Preservation Soc. of Newport Co. (exec. sec.), Newport Hist. Soc. (curator of coins and medals). Protestant. Club: Rotary. Address: Newport, R.I. *

BOWEN, CAWTHON ASBURY (BO'EN), editor; b. Holly Springs, Miss., Dec. 25, 1885; s. James Asbury and Alice (Cawthon) B.; student Millsaps Coll., Jackson, Miss., 1902-04, D.D., 1927; B.A., Emory Coll., Oxford, Ga., 1906; M.A., Vanderbilt U., 1908; post-grad. study Northwestern U., summer 1921; m. Nellie Virginia Sloss, June 16, 1910; children—Sarah Virginia (dec.), Cawthon Asbury. Ordained ministry M.E. Ch., S., 1908; pastor successively Stevenson, Birmingham and Dadeville, Ala., till 1914; pres. N. Ala. Epworth League, 1912-13; prof. religious edn., Woman's Coll. of Ala., Montgomery, 1914-21, v.p., 1921; prof. religious edn., Millsaps Coll., 1921-25; chmn. Miss. Conf. Sunday Sch. Bd., 1922-30; asso. S.S. editor M.E. Ch., S. 1925-30; pres. gen. Sunday Sch. Council, 1926; mem. exec. com. and ednl. commn. Com. on Basic Philosophy and Policies, Internat. Council Religious Edn. (chmn. group lesson com.; v. chmn. ednl. program; member advisory board Standard Bible com.; chmn. com. graded series). Graded Lesson Syndicate, Leadership Training Public Assn.; sec. editorial dept. Gen. Bd. Christian Edn., M.E. Ch., S., 1930-40, exec. editor church school publs. Meth. Ch., since 1940; chmn. Miss. Conf. Bd. of Christian Edn., 1930-36; mem. Council of Churches of Christ in the U.S. Mem. Religious Edn. Assn., mem. Gen. Conference M.E. Ch., South. 1934, 38; mem. Uniting Conf. Methodist Chs., 1939; mem. Gen. Conf. and S.E. Jurisdictional Conf., Meth. Ch., 1940-48; sec. editorial div. Bd. Edn., Methodist Church, 1944; mem. exec. com. Fed. Council of Churches. Member Phi Beta Kappa, Kappa Sigma, Pi Gamma Mu, Theta Phi. Democrat. Clubs: Calumet (Vanderbilt U.), Belle Meade Country (Nashville), Author and editor various religious publs. *

BOWEN, FRANK SAYLES, JR., army officer; b. Philippine Islands, Mar. 4, 1905; B.S., U.S. Mil. Acad., 1926; grad. Inf. Sch., co., officers course, 1933, tank course, 1934, Command and Gen. Staff Sch., 1939, grad. Nat. War Coll., 1948. Commd. 2d lt., U.S. Army, 1926, and advanced through the grades to maj. gen., 1955. Chief Mil. Assistance Adv. Group, Taiwan, 1956-58, also comdr. army component U.S. Taiwan Def. Command; comdg. gen. XII U.S. Army Corps Res., Atlanta, from 1958. Decorated D.S.C. with oak leaf cluster, D.S.M. with oak leaf cluster, Silver Star with 3 oak leaf clusters, Bronze Star Medal with V device and oak leaf cluster, Air Medal with oak leaf cluster, Purple Heart with oak leaf cluster, Am. Presdl. Unit Citation with oak leaf cluster, Yangtze Patrol (Navy), Asiatic Pacific with Arrowhead, Korean Service with Arrowhead, Medal Mil. Merit (Philippine), Ulchi with Gold Star (Korean), Philippine Liberation with 2 bronze stars. Address: Columbia, S.C. Died Sept. 24, 1976.

BOWEN, HAROLD LINWOOD, bishop; born Dighton, Mass., Apr. 27, 1886; s. David Irving and Rebecca Talbot (Briggs) B.; student St. Stephens Coll., Annandale, N.Y., 1905-07; A.B., U. of Okla., 1909, B.D., Scabury Div. Sch., 1918; D.D., Seabury-Western Theol. Sem., 1934; m. Elizabeth Sherrill Cockle, Sept. 5, 1916. Ordained to ministry P.E. Church, deacon, 1910, priest, 1911; missionary work in Oklahoma, including work among students of U. of Okla., asst. St. Paul's Cathedral, Oklahoma City, and minister Chickasba, Okla., 1907-12; rector St. Martin's Ch., Omaha, Neb., 1912-14; St. Paul's Ch., Peoria, Ill., 1914-21; St. Peter's Ch., Chicago, 1921-30; rector St. Mark's Ch., Evanston, Ill., 1930-47; bishop coadjutor of Colo., 1947-49, bishop since 1949. Pres. St. Luke's Hosp. and Ch. Home (Denver), Parkview Episcopal Hosp. (Pueblo). Mem. Phi Beta Kappa, Kappa Sigma. Home: Denver. *

BOWEN, JOHN CLYDE, judge; b. Newbern, Tenn., May 12, 1888; s. William Allen and Maryette (Featherston) B.; A.B., U. Tenn., 1913; LL.B., Harvard, 1916; m. Ruth Welsh Tuttle, Sept. 1, 1961. Prin. high sch., Timberville, Miss., 1909-10; admitted to Tenn. bar, 1916, Hawaii bar, 1917, Wash. bar, 1919; practiced at Seattle; U.S. dist. judge, Seattle, 1934-78. Mem. Wash. Senate, 1931; legal adviser to Gov., 1933; mem. Columbia River Basin Commn. which promoted Grand Coulee Dam project and assisted in letting that project's first constrn. contract, 1933-34; collector IRS dist. Wash. and Alaska, 1933-34. Served with U.S. Army, 1917-18, 2d lt. F.A.R.C. Mem. Am., Wash., Seattle bar assns., Am. Legion, Maritime Law Assn. U.S., Order of Coif (hon.). Democrat. Baptist. Mason. Clubs: Rainier, Harvard (Seattle). Home: Seattle, Wash. Died Apr. 27, 1978.

BOWEN, RAY PRESTON, univ. prof.; b. Wellsboro, Pa., Jan. 31, 1882; s. Benjamin Franklin and Mary Ann (Forsyth) B.; student Bucknell U., Lewisburg, Pa., 1901-04; A.B., Harvard, 1905; A.M., Cornell U., 1915, Ph.D., 1916; student U. of Grenoble, France, 1911-12, Sorbonne, Paris, France, 1921-22; unmarried. Prin., Hill Acad., Redding, Conn., 1905-07; prof. Romance langs., Huron (S.D.) Coll., 1909-14; teaching fellow and instr., Cornell U., 1914-16; asst. prof., Syracuse U., 1916-18, asso. prof., 1920-25; head of dept. of Romance langs., Earlham Coll., Richmond, Ind., 1918-19; asso. prof., Colorado Coll., 1919-20; lecteur d'Améicain, Sorbonne, Paris, France, 1921-22; head of dept. of Romance langs., U. of Ore., 1925-47; retired since June 1947; vis. prof. Linfield Coll., McMinnville, Ore., 1947-48. Officer d'Acadé mie (Fr.). Author: The Novels of Ferdinand Fabre, 1918; The Dramatic Construction of Balzac's Novels, 1940. Home: Eugene, Ore. *

BOWERS, RAYMOND, educator, physicist; b. London, Eng., July 11, 1927 (came to U.S. 1951; naturalized 1964); B.Sc., London U., 1948; D.Phil., Oxford (Eng.) U., 1951; m. Research fellow U. Chgo., 1951-53; research physicist Westinghouse Electric Corp., 1954-60; asso. prof. Cornell U., Ithaca, N.Y., 1960-65, prof. physics, 1965-79, dep. dir. program sci., tech. and soc., 1969-73, dir. program sci., tech. and soc., 1973-78; on leave with Office Sci. and Tech., Exec. Office of President, 1966-67; vis. fellow Clare Coll., Cambridge (Eng.) U., 1972; cons. to govt. and industry, 1960-79. Fellow Am. Phys. Soc. (chmn. div. solid state physics 1974), Phys. Soc. London, AAAS (chmn. com. sci. and pub. policy 1972-75), Am. Acad. Arts and Scis. Author: Communication for a Mobile Society, 1977; also articles on physics and tech. assessment. Home: Ithaca, N.Y. Died Apr. 29, 1979.

BOWERS, RENZO DEE, author; b. Clarksdale, Mo., Nov. 9, 1883; s. R. D. and Martha J. (Chappell) B.; B.S., Okla. A and M. Coll., 1904; m. Lolla J. Adams, Apr. 19, 1911; children—Linwood M., Barbara Nell (Mrs. Alan N. Peck), Glendon D. Admitted to Okla. bar, 1905, N.M. bar, 1907, Md. bar, 1926, Supreme Ct. of U.S., 1926, Ky. bar, 1931, Ind. bar, 1939; editor in law dept., Bobbs-Merrill Pub. Co., Indianapolis, Ind., 1936-38. Editor: Chattel Mortagages and Conditional Sales (3 vols.), 1933; Bonds and Bond Securities (3 vols.), 1935. Author: Law of Waiver, 1914; Law of Conversion, 1917; Civil Process and Service, 1927; Judicial Discretion of Trial Courts, 1931. Compiler: Inaugural Addresses of the Presidents, 1929. Contbr. articles to mags. Democrat. Christian (Disciples of Christ). Address: Hagerstown, Md. *

BOWLBY, SAMUEL FISCHER, banker, bus. exec., cons.; b. La Crosse, Wis., Dec. 27, 1904; s. Samuel L. and Hulda (Fischer) B.; student Wis. Inst. Tech., 1924-26; B.S., U. Okla., 1927; m. Gertrude Amelia Hedde, Sept. 1, 1938. Former v.p. Shell Oil Co., Los Angeles; adv. dir. Bank of Calif., N.A., San Francisco; dir. Baker Oil Tools, Inc., Tetra Tech, Inc. Republican. Clubs: California, Pacific Union (San Francisco); Annandale. Home: San Marino, Calif. Died July 23, 1976.

BOWLES, ELLA SHANNON (MRS. ARCHIE RAIMOND BOWLES), author; b. Pittsfield, N.H., Jan. 9, 1886; d. Edwin Howe and Myra Estelle (Berry) Shannon; grad. N.H. State Normal Sch., Plymouth, 1905; m. Archie Raimond Bowles, June 22, 1907 (dec.); children—Mariette (Mrs. William B. Hurd, Jr.), Raimond. Teacher in public schools, New Hampshire, 1905-07; tutor for private schools; has made special study of New England antiquities and handicrafts. Research worker in New Hampshire history (special work for State of N.H.); publs. editor emeritus University N.H.; staff member Univ. of N.H. Writers' Conference. Mem. N.H. br., Nat. League Am. Penwomen, N.H. Hist. Soc., Durham Bus. and Prof. Women's Club. Mem. Christian Ch. Author: (serial) The Trail to Nemoghome; co-author (with Dorothy Towle) Secrets of New Eng. Cooking, 1947. Contbr. to Writers on Writing, 1950. Contbr. leading mags. Home: Alexandria, Va. *

BOWLES, HELOISE, journalist; b. Ft. Worth; d. Charles L. and Amelia (Harrison) Bowles; grad. Felt and Tarrent Bus. Coll.; student Tex. Sch. Fine Arts, 1938; grad. Draughn's Bus. Coll., 1939; Dr. Humanities, Nat. Christian U., 1972; children—Louis D., Ponce K. Columnist, Honolulu Advertiser, 1959-62; writer Hints from Heloise, King Features Syndicate, N.Y.C., 1962-77. Active A.R.C. Recipient Silver Lady Banshee award Headliners Club, Austin, Tex., 1964; Headliner's award, San Antonio, 1968; Howe Press award for work with blind, 1971; Trophy Internat., Perkins Sch. Blind, Boston, 1972; Internat. Ecology award, Paris, France, 1973, Mental Health trophy McLennan County Assn. Mental Health, 1973, ALMA award, Dallas, 1973; keys to city, Ft. Worth, 1965, New Orleans, 1971, Waco, Tex., 1971; Outstanding Service award San Antonio Press Club, 1966; NIRC recognition for distinguished service, 1969; numerous citations; named Woman of Achievement, Theta Sigma Phi (now Women in Communications), 1962, Ecology Woman of Yr., 1972, 73, 76. Mem. Order Eastern Star, Lady Shriner. Author: Heloise Housekeeping Hints, 1963; Heloise Kitchen Hints, 1964; Heloise All Around the House, 1965; Heloise's Work and Money Savers, 1967; Heloise Hints for the Working Woman, 1970; Heloise in China, 1972. Home: San Antonio, Tex. Died Dec. 28, 1977; buried San Antonio.

BOWLES, JOHN DAVIS, consulting engineer; b. St. Louis, Mo., June 30, 1886; s. Samuel Addison and Julia (Johnson) B.; B.S. in E.E., U. of Mo., 1909, E.E., 1910, research asst., Engring. Expt. Sta., 1909-10; m. Ethelyn May Sullivan, May 1, 1914; 1 son, John Davis; m. 2d, Grace Marie Leonard, May 11, 1926. Elec. and mech. engr., F.E. Newbery Elec. Co., St. Louis, Mo., and Chicago, Ill., 1910-13; chief engr. Mo. Pub. Service Commn., 1913-15; supt. Springfield (Mo.) Gas & Electric Co., 1915-18; mech. supt. Douglas Co., Cedar Rapids, Ia., 1918-19; engr., Federal Light & Traction Co., New York, 1919-21, chief engr., 1921-27, v.p. and chief engr., 1927-33; was also v.p. and dir. various subsidiary cos.; now cons. engr.; dir. North Sydney (N.S.) Collieries, Ltd. Mem. Am. Soc. M.E., Am. Inst. E.E. (mem. standards com), Am. Soc. of Municipal Engrs., Am. Soc. Mil. Engrs., Tau Beta Pi, Sigma Xi, Sigma Nu, Steinmetz Club. Republican. Mason. Contbr. to tech. publs. Home: Westphalia, Mo. Address: Cedar Rapids, Ia. *

BOWLES, LESTER LLEWELLYN, educator; b. Sharpsville, Ind., 1907; s. Edrite M. and Mary (Terrell) B.; student U. Notre Dame, 1933-34; A.B., Franklin Coll., 1934; M.D., Ind. Univ., 1938; m. Miriam Elleman, Sept. 2, 1933; children—Barbara Ann, James Terrell. Research asso. dept. anatomy Med. Coll. Ga., Augusta, 1938-41, asst. prof. microscopic anatomy, 1940-47, asso. prof., 1947-48, prof., 1948-72, prof. emeritus, 1972-77, chmn. dept., 1950-64, head div. microscopic anatomy, 1964-71, instr. psychiatry, 1954. Received Cadaver award for excellence in teaching, 1956, 64, 65; Alumni citation Franklin Coll., 1957. Mem. Am., Ga., County med. assns., Am. Psychiat. Assn., Ga. Acad. Sci., Am. Assn. Anatomists, Alpha Omega Alpha. Mem. Society of Friends. Author: Laboratory Exercises in Histology and Embryology, 1949; also author articles in field. Home: Augusta, Ga. Died Nov. 25, 1977.

BOWLING, JACK FRANK, artist, silversmith, naval officer; b. Bonham, Tex., July 5, 1903; s. James Frank and Nanie B. (Sparkman) B.; B.S., U.S. Naval Acad., 1927; grad. U.S. Naval War Coll., 1945; m. Evelyn Renn Fletcher, Jan. 3, 1932; 1 dau., Kathryn R. (Mrs. J. Allan Hovey). Commd. ensign USN, 1927, advanced through grades to rear adm., 1947; staff Adm. King, 1942-43; comdr. Anti-Submarine Task Force 62, North Atlantic, 1944-45; sank U-248 1945, received surrender U-805, 1945; ret., 1947; profl. artist, metal worker, 1958-79; lectr. on silver and silver work. One-man exhbns. include Honolulu Acad. Art, 1935, Lawrence Gallery, Dallas, 1937, Newport Art Assn., 1945, Colombo, Ceylon, 1946, Singapore, 1946, Manila, 1946, William Penn Meml. Mus., Harrisburg, 1972; group exhbns. include So. Printmakers, 1937, Cal. Printmakers, 1938; exhibited Mpls., 1960, Grace Cathedral, San Francisco, 1960, Pitts., 1961; represented in permanent collections Honolulu Acad. Art, Library of Congress, 1st Bapt. Ch., Bonham, Tex., Diocese of Tex., Houston, Ch. of the Holy Trinity, Phila., St. Columba's Washington, Immanual Episcopal Ch., Wilmington, Del., George Washington Meml. Chapel, Valley Forge, Pa., Christ's 1st Presbyn. Ch., Hempstead, N.Y., St. Timothy's Ch., Roxborough, Pa. Decorated Legion of Merit with V; Recipient 1st award for ecclesiastic arts, Los Angeles, 1959; cash award, San Francisco, 1960, 1st award gold or silver Woodmere Art Gallery, 1962, 63, 67, 68; Best in Show award I.P.A. Exhibit, Washington, 1971. Mem. Woodmere Art Assn., Guild Religious Architects, Stained Glass Assn. Am., Phila. Art Alliance, Phila. Mus. Art, Am.

Craftsmen's Council, Internat. Platform Assn. Episcopalian (vestryman). Clubs: Army-Navy (Washington); Print (Phila.). Address: Philadelphia, Pa. Died July 20, 1979; buried Arlington Nat. Cemetery.

BOWMAN, A. SMITH, distillery exec.; b. Lexington, Ky., Mar. 26, 1906; s. A. Smith and Katherine L. (DeLong) B.; A.B., Princeton, 1927; M.Arch., Harvard, 1931; m. Kate Hyde Scully, Nov. 17, 1945 (dec. Jan. 5, 1960); m. 2d, Mary Walker Lee, Nov. 25, 1960. Pvt. practice architecture, 1931-35; exec. A. Smith Bowman Distillery, Sunset Hills, Va., 1935-81, chmn. bd., treas. until 1981; v.p. Internat. Fueling Co., from 1967, dir., from 1961; v.p. Nat. Service Corp., from 1968, dir., from 1966; vice chmn. bd. Republic Bank and Trust Co., Herndon, Va., 1963-68; dir. emeritus 1st Am. Bank of Va. Dir. Distilled Spirits Inst., 1955-73, v.p., 1956-60, treas., 1965-71, vice chmn., 1960-65, mem. exec. com., 1971-73, (merged with Licensed Beverage Industries and Bourbon Inst. to form Distilled Spirits Council U.S. 1973); dir. Licensed Beverage Industries, 1968-71, Bourbon Inst., 1971-73; mem. exec. com. Distilled Spirits Council U.S., 1973-81. Treas., mem. exec. com. Fairfax Race Assn., from 1958, pres., from 1967; treas., trustee Fairfax Hunt, from 1956; mem. exec. bd. Nat. Capital Area council Boy Scouts Am., 1953-70, v.p. exec. bd., 1956-66, mem. adv. bd., 1970-81; bd. dirs. United Cerebral Palsy No. Va., 1954-59, United Givers Fund Nat. Capital Area, 1961-67; pres., dir. Bowman Found., 1958-74; trustee Garfield Hosp., Washington, 1954-62, v.p., 1956-62; treas., trustee Fairfax Hosp., 1956-65; trustee D.C. Presbyn. Home, 1961-68, Va. Museum Fine Arts; mem. corp. Washington Hosp. Center, from 1958; mem. Va. Hist. Landmarks Commn., 1973-81; trustee St. James (Md.) Sch., 1966-81, Landon Sch., Bethesda, Md., 1972-79, Va. Mus. Fine Arts, 1974-81. Served from lt. to lt. comdr. USNR, 1942-46. Recipient Silver Beaver award Boy Scouts Am., 1960. Mem. Hist. Soc. Fairfax County (dir. from 1957, pres. 1964-68), Fairfax County C. of C. (dir. 1959-63), Soc. of Cincinnati (standing com. 1964-67, 74-77), S.R., Mil. Order of Carabao, Va. Thoroughbred Assn. (dir. 1973-78), Nat. Steeplechase and Hunt Assn. (sr. mem. hunts com. from 1964, bd. stewards 1973-78), Am. Legion. Presbyterian (bd. deacons 1952-56, treas. 1961-62, trustee 1956-62). Clubs: Metropolitan, Nat. Press, Chevy Chase, City Tavern (gov.) (Washington); Princeton (N.Y.C.); Coral Beach and Tennis (Bermuda); Farmington Country (Charlottesville, Va.); Mill Reef (Antigua, W.I.); Rolling Rock (Ligonier, Pa.); Campus (grad. bd. trustees), Nassau (Princeton, N.J.); Springdale Hall (Camden, S.C.); Commonwealth (Richmond, Va.). Home: McLean, Va. Died May 7, 1981.

BOWMAN, EARL CASSATT (BO'MAN), prof. edn.; b. Hamilton, O., Aug. 26, 1886; s. James Douglas and Mabel (Riggs) B.; B.A., Miami U., Oxford, O., 1909; M.A., U. of Chicago, 1922; Ph.D., Ohio State U., 1928; m. Alpha Viola Ingersoll, Dec. 10, 1910; children—Max Ingersoll, Lee Douglas (dec.). Prin. Hannas Creek High Sch., Liberty, Ind., 1909-11, 1912-15; supt. of schools, Weston, O., 1911-12; life insurance agent, Liberty, Ind., 1915-16; prin. Green Township High Sch., Ridgeville, Ind., 1916-19, Monroe Township High Sch., Parker, Ind., 1919-22; prof. of edn., West Liberty (W.Va.) State Teachers Coll., 1922-23, dean, 1923-25, acting pres., 1925-26; grad. asst., Ohio State U., 1926-27; dir. student teaching, Otterbein Coll., Westerville, O., 1928; with De Pauw U., Greencastle, Ind., since 1928, as dir. student teaching, since 1928, head dept. of edn. since 1940. Mem. N.E.A. (life), Am. Assn. Univ. Profs., Am. Soc. Coll. Teachers of Edn., Nat. Assn. Supervisors of Student Teaching (pres. 1931-32), Sigma Alpha Epsilon, Phi Delta Kappa. Methodist. Club: Kiwanis. Author: Observation, Participation and Student Teaching, 1937; Living Safely (with P. F. Boston), 1938. Home: Greencastle, Ind. *

BOWMAN, GEORGE ARVENE, ret. univ. pres.; b. Galion, Ohio, May 11, 1893; s. Walter Scott and Elizabeth (Wirick) B.; A.B., Adelbert Coll., Case Western Res. U., 1917; A.M., Columbia, 1931; summer student Ohio U., 1912, 13, Ohio State U., 1914, U. Chgo., 1921, 22, Harvard, 1938; LL.D., Bowling Green U., 1945, Western Res. U., 1960, Youngstown U., 1960, Kent State U., 1963, Miami U., 1963; L.H.D., U. Akron, 1960; m. Edith Duncan, July 11, 1923. Tchr. rural sch., South Bloomfield Twp., Morrow County, Ohio, 1911; tchr. prin., supt. sch., Edison Morrow County, O., 1912-14; coach, athletic dir., tchr., prin., Zanesville, O., 1919-23; supt. schs., Chillicothe, Ohio, 1923-29, Marion, Ohio, 1929-34, Lakewood, O., 1934-41, Youngstown, Ohio, 1941-44; pres. Kent (O.) State U., 1944-63, pres. emeritus, gen. personnel cons., 1963-76. Served with C.E., USN, 1917-19. Mem. Ohio Edn. Assn. (past pres.), N.E.A. (v.p. 1944), Soc. for Advancement Edn., A.I.A. (hon.), Ohio Coll. Assn. (pres. 1959-60), Akron Adv. Council on Naval Affairs, Inter-U. Council Ohio (pres. 1952, 58, 62), Ohio Hist. Soc., Kent C. of C. (hon. life), Am. Legion, Horace Mann League, A.A.A.S., Arnold Air Soc., Pershing Rifles, Phi Delta Kappa, Kappa Delta Pi, Omicron Delta Kappa, Sigma Nu. Mem. United Ch. of Christ. Rotarian (past pres. Kent-Chillicothe chpt.; past pres., made hon. mem. Kent chpt. 1971). Home: Kent, Ohio. Died May 7, 1976; buried Standing Rock Cemetery, Kent.

BOWMAN, GROVER CHESTER, educator; b. Covington, Ind., Dec. 15, 1884; s. Herschel Volney and Cora Alice (Winders) B.; A.B., Williams Coll., 1906, L.H.D., 1955; A.M., Yale, 1912; grad. work Coluumbia, 1913-14; Ed.D., R.I. Coll. of Education, 1941; m. Mathilda Elizabeth Bullett, Nov. 27, 1907; children—Mary Elizabeth (Mrs. Irving Hartley Call), Margaret Louise (Mrs. Mario Marciano), Marion Eileen (Mrs. Lloyd Perper). Teacher in New Brighton, New York, 1906; supervising agent Connecticut State Department of schools, Seymour, Conn., 1909-12, Fairfield and Westport, Conn., 1912-18, Thompsonville, Conn., 1918-22, North Adams, Mass., 1922-36; pres. Mass. State Tchrs. Coll., 1937-55; now emeritus; instr., lecturer various coll. summer courses, 1914-36; del. and speaker before World Fed. of Edn. Assns., Oxford (Eng.), 1935. Trustee North Adams Pub. Library, 1927-33. Mem. N.E.A., Acad. of Polit. Science, Am. Sociol. Soc., Berkshire Co. Teachers Assn. (pres. 1937-38). Democrat. Conglist. Mason. Clubs: Kiwanis (North Adams). Author: The Traditional Philosophy of Education—and other essays and addresses on education. Lecturer before ednl. and civic groups. Mem. City Council, 1940-48. Home: North Adams, Mass. *

BOWMAN, RAYMOND ALBERT, educator; b. Chgo., Apr. 14, 1903; s. Wilhelm F. and Hattie (Howe) B.; B.S. in Edn., Northwestern U., 1928, M.A., 1929; B.D., Garrett Bibl. Inst., 1931; Ph.D., U. Chgo., 1935; m. Marguerite Laidley, Nov. 27, 1924; children—Donna Lee (Mrs. Victor Acevedo), Philip Keith. Faculty, Northwestern U., 1930-34; faculty U. Chgo., 1935-69, mem. Oriental Inst., 1935-69, prof., 1935-69, emeritus from 1969. Mem. Standard Bible Com. Mem. Am. Oriental Soc., Soc. Bibl. Lit. and Exegesis, Am. Assn. U. Profs., Nat. Assn. Hebrew Profs., Soc. Bibl. Lit., Am. Acad. Religion. Mason. Club: Quadrangle (U. Chgo.). Author: Aramaic Ritual Texts from Persepolis; Aramaic Tablets from Persepolis; contbg. author Interpreters Bible, 1954. Home: Chicago, Ill. Died Oct. 29, 1979.

BOWMAN, WILLIAM C., banker; b. Monroe, La., Sept. 14, 1882; s. Francis E. and Pauline (Chapman) B.; A.B., Millsaps Coll. (Jackson, Miss.), 1904; LL.B., U. of Miss., 1905; m. Alverne Madden Prescott, Sept. 11, 1953. Lawyer, Natchez, Miss., 1905-22; v.p. First Nat. Bank of Montgomery, Ala., 1922, became pres., 1929, now chmn. bd. and dir.; dir. Ala. Power Co. Mem. Miss. Senate, 1914-18. Trustee So. Research Inst. Home: Montgomery, Ala. *

BOWMER, ANGUS LIVINGSTON, educator, theatrical producer, dir., cons.; b. Bellingham, Wash., Sept. 25, 1904; s. Charles C. and Flora B.; life teaching certificate Western Wash. Coll. Edn., 1926; B.A., U. Wash., 1930, M.A., 1934; D.F.A., Lewis and Clark Coll., 1960's; hon. degree U. Portland, 1960's, Linfield Coll., 1976; m. Gertrude Bowmer, Dec. 30. Tchr., adminstr. Wash. pub. schs., 1924-30; from instr. to prof. drama So. Oreg. Coll., Ashland, 1931-70; founder Ashland Elizabethan Theatre and Oreg. Shakespearean Festival, 1935, producing dir., 1935-71, has produced all the Shakespearean plays in 125 prodns.; devel. cons. Oreg. Shakespearean Festival Assn., 1972-79. Presdl. appointee to Nat. Council Arts, 1974-79. Served with AUS, 1942-43. Recipient Distinguished Service award U. Oreg., 1961; Edith Knight Hill Meml. award for outstanding contbn. to Oreg., Portland profl. chpt. Theta Sigma Phi, 1964; Salute, Oreg. State Legislature, 1965; award for contbn. to devel. of theater in Northwest, Wash. Arts Council, 1966; Distinguished Service award Oreg. State U., 1967; Tom McCall award Oreg. Broadcasters Assn., 1975; Gov.'s Arts award, 1977; recognition by joint resolution Oreg. Legislature, 1977. Ford Found. grant for travel and study in Europe, 1960's; indoor theatre named in his honor, 1970; Alumnus Summa Laude Dignatus, U. Wash., 1976. Mem. Northwest Drama Conf. (dir. 1960-63), Internat. Inst. Arts and Letters (life fellow). Author: As I Remember, Adam, an Autobiography of a Festival, 1975. Home: Ashland, Oreg. Died May 26, 1979.

BOYD, ALBERT, corp. executive; b. Rankin, Tenn., Nov. 22, 1906; student Biltmore Coll., 1926-27, Air Corps Tech. Sch.; m. Anna Lu Oheim. Maj. gen. USAF; chief engring. officer Hawaiian Air Depot, 1941-43; air material command Wright Patterson Air Force Base, 1944-49; comdr. Air Force Flight Test Center, Edwards AFB, Calif., 1949-52; comdr. Wright Air Development Center, Wright-Patterson AFB, 1952-55; dep. comdr. Weapon Systems, Hdqrs. Air Research and Development Command, Balt., 1955-57; v.p. Westinghouse Corp., 1958-76. Decorated Legion of Merit, D.F.C., D.S.M., recipient Air Power Trophy, 1950; Octave Chanute award, 1955; Medaille de l'Aeronautique. Set world speed record, 1947. Fellow Inst. Aero. Scis., Soc. Exptl. Test Pilots. Home: Arlington, Va. Died Sept. 18, 1976.

BOYD, BERNARD HENRY, educator, clergyman; b. Mt. Pleasant, S.C., Nov. 16, 1910; s. Frank T. and Eunice (Beaty) B.; A.B., Presbyn. Coll., 1932; Th.B., M.A., Princeton, 1935; Th.D., Union Theol. Sem., 1946; m. Thelma Hicklin, Aug. 5, 1944; children—Donald Beaty, Karen Elizabeth. Ordained to ministry Presbyn. Ch., 1943; prof. Bible Presbyn. Coll., 1936-46, Davidson Coll., 1946-50; James A. Gray prof. Bibl. lit. U. N.C., Chapel Hill, 1950-75; chmn. dept. religion, 1952-60; archaeol. exploration in Israel, summers 1963-74; organizer of expedn. to Lachish, 1966; ednl. dir. Inst. Mediterranean Studies, 1965-67, archaeol. dir., 1968-75; co-dir. U. N.C.-Hebrew U. expdn. to Tell Arad, 1967, Lynn Prickett archaeol. expdn. to Lachish, 1968; ednl. dir. Archaeol. Expn. to Tell Beer Sheba, 1971-74. Lectr. Served as chaplain USN, Marines, 1943-45. Recipient Tanner Meml. award, 1956, 67, Nicholas Salgo award, 1973. Mem. Soc. Bibl. Lit. and Exegesis, Am. Acad. Religion, Am. Schs. Oriental Research, Archaeol. Inst. Am., Order Golden Fleece, Blue Key. Pi Kappa Delta. Omicron Delta Kappa. Home: Chapel Hill, N.C. Died Sept. 28, 1975.

BOYD, HOMER LEON, business exec., banker; b. Clearwater, Kan., Aug. 18, 1885; s. Frank Leslie and Elizabeth Rendleman) B.; A.B., U. Colo., 1908; student law U. Cal., 1908-09; LL.B., U. Wash., 1910; m. Norma Gertrude Floyd, Sept. 26, 1916. Note teller, mgr. bond dept. Lumbermen's Nat. Bank, Portland, Ore., 1910-14; with John E. Price & Co., investment bankers, Seattle, 1914-28, sec., 1918-28, v.p., sec., 1928-33, sec. since 1933; v.p., treas., dir. Marine Bancorporation since 1927; v.p., Marine Nat. Co., Seattle, 1928-30, pres., dir., 1930—; v. chmn. bd. Nat. Bank Commerce, Seattle, 1948, dir., 1930—. Mem. Investment Bankers Assn. Am. (bd. govs. 1934-35), Investment Bankers Conf., Inc. (chmn. dist. 1). Clubs: Rainier, Golf (Seattle). Home: Seattle. *

BOYD, HUGH NEWELL, publishing co. exec.; b. Rumson, N.J., Aug. 23, 1911; s. William Butler and Ruth (O'Day) B.; student Browning Sch., N.Y.C., 1922-26; grad. Choate Sch., 1930; student Yale, 1930-32; Litt.D., Rutgers U., 1970; m. Jean Maclachlan, 1932 (div. 1946); 1 son, William Maclachlan; m. 2d, Mary Martha Wren, Feb. 10, 1947. Various positions Home News Pub. Co., Pubs. Daily Home News, Sunday Home News, New Brunswick, N.J., 1932-42, gen. mgr. newspapers, 1946-55, pub., pres., 1955-76, chmn. bd., editorial chmn., 1976-79; dir. A.P., 1959-68. Adv. council U. Mo. Freedom of Info. Center. Mem. bur. pub. relations War Dept., 1942-43; with OSS, U.S., Eng., France, 1943-45. Recipient citation English Speaking Union, 1957. Mem. N.J. Press Assn. (pres. 1952-53, chmn. freedom of info. com. 1953-54), Internat. Press Inst. (Am. chmn. 1968), Am., Newspaper Pubs. Assn., Nat. Editorial Assn. (President's award as chmn. freedom of info. com. 1955; Amos award), English Speaking Union U.S. (nat. dir. 1958-66, exec. com. 1960-66), Council Fgn. Relations. Clubs: Metropolitan (Washington); Nassau, Bedens Brook (Princeton, N.J.); Century Assn.; Yale (N.Y.C.). Home: Princeton, N.J. Died May 13, 1979.

BOYD, JULIAN PARKS, educator; b. Converse, S.C., Nov. 3, 1903; s. Robert Jay and Melona (Parks) B.; A.B., Duke U., 1925, M.A., 1926, Litt. D., 1951; Litt.D., Franklin and Marshall Coll., 1939, Bucknell U., 1952, Rutgers U., 1956; L.H.D., Washington and Jefferson Coll., 1952, Yale, 1964, Lehigh U., 1966; LL.D., U.S.C., 1977; m. Grace Wiggins Welch, Dec. 21, 1927; 1 son, Kenneth Miles. Editor Wyo. Hist. and Geol. Soc., Wilkes-Barre, Pa., 1928-32; dir. N.Y. State Hist. Assn., 1932-34; librarian Hist. Soc. of Pa., 1935-40; librarian Princeton (N.J.) U., 1940-52, prof. history, 1952-72, prof. history emeritus, 1972-80. Decorated comdr. Brit. Empire. Mem. Am. Antiquarian Soc., Am. Philos. Soc. (pres. 1973-76) Soc. Am. Archivists, N.Y., Mass., Pa., Va. hist. socs., Am. Hist. Assn. (pres. 1964), Phi Beta Kappa. Editor: Papers of Thomas Jefferson (to comprise about 60 vols.), 1950-80. Home: Titusville, N.J. Died May 28, 1980.

BOYD, MYRON FENTON, bishop, educator; b. Shelbyville, Ill., July 19, 1909; s. Edward Pliny and Greta A. (Pierce) B.; A.B., Seattle Pacific Coll., 1932, D.D., 1949; Litt.D., Houghton (N.Y.) Coll., 1957; m. Ruth Elinor Putnam, June 28, 1932; children—Myron D. (dec.), Donald E., Darold D., Carolyn R. (Mrs. Dale Martin). Ordained to ministry Free Meth. Ch., 1931; pastor in Tonasket, Wenatchee, Mt. Vernon and Seattle, Wash., and New Westminster and Vancouver, B.C., Can., 1932-48; dir., speaker Light and Life Hour, Worldwide Radio Ministry, 1945-65; bishop Free Meth. Ch. N.Am., 1964-76, chmn. gen. missionary bd., 1964-74, pres. bd. adminstrn., 1969; prof. Greenville (Ill.) Coll., 1977-78. Recipient award for producing best all around nat. religious broadcast Nat. Religious Broadcasters, 1955. Mem. Nat. Holiness Assn. (pres. 1954-58, 68-72), Nat. Assn. Evangs. (v.p. 1968-72, pres. 1972-74), Nat. Religious Broadcasters (pres. 1954-56). Author: To Tell the World, 1964. Home: Greenville, Ill. Died July 31, 1978; interred Mt. Auburn Cemetery, Greenville.

BOYD, ROBERT OSBORNE, lawyer; b. Kennewick, Wash., July 29, 1903; s. Daniel and Ethel (Axtell) B.; A.B., Amherst Coll., 1926, M.A. (hon.), 1961; postgrad. George Washington U., 1930-33, LL.B., 1956; m. Jacqueline Zurcher, Dec. 10, 1929; 1 son, Daniel Zurcher. Admitted to Oreg. bar, 1933, practiced in Portland; counsel Oreg. Liquor Control Commn.,

1939-42; mem. emergency bds. authorized under Railway Labor Act to investigate different disputes affecting several railroads, airlines and their employees, 1948-52; neutral referee Nat. R.R. Adjustment Bd., 1948-52; mem. Nat. Mediation Board, 1954-63, chmn. board, 1956-60; arbitrator railroad and indsl. disputes, after 1962. Served with U.S. Coast Guard (TR), 1944-45. Mem. Am. (ho. dels. 1952-54), Oreg. (gov. 1946-49) bar assns., Nat. Acad. Arbitrators, English Speaking Union (pres. Portland 1953-54), World Affairs Council Oreg. (pres. 1952-53), Portland Com. Fgn. Relations (sec. 1947-54), S.A.R. (pres. Oreg. 1944), Phi Delta Theta, Delta Theta Phi. Mason. Clubs: University, Multnomah Athletic (Portland); University (Washington). Home: Alexandria, Va. Died Sept. 10, 1979.

BOYDEN, EDWARD ALLEN, educator; b. Bridgewater, Mass., Mar. 20, 1886; s. Arthur Clarke and Katherine Chipman (Allen) B.; grad. Bridgewater Normal Sch., 1907; A.B., Harvard, 1909, A.M., 1911, Ph.D. in Med. Sci., 1916; postgrad. U. Freiburg, 1911-12; m. Margaret L. Hilsinger, Nov. 12, 1913 (dec.); children—Mary Scarborough, Arthur Clarke. Asst. in zoölogy, Harvard, 1908-11; fellow in histology and embryology, Harvard Med. Sch., 1912-16, instr. in comparative anatomy, 1916-19, asst. prof., 1919-26; acting asso. prof. anatomy, Stanford U., 1921-22; asso. prof. anatomy, U. Ill. Coll. Medicine, 1926-28, prof., 1929; prof. human anatomy and head dept. U. Ala., 1929-31; prof. anatomy, U. Minn., 1931, chmn. dept., 1940, head, 1949, prof. emeritus, 1954; vis. prof. U. Wash., 1954-56, research prof., 1956-77; mng. editor Anat. Record, 1928-48. Recipient gold medal So. Minn. Med. Assn., 1937; citation for med. research Minn. Med. Assn., 1956; Distinguished Service award, Modern Medicine, 1960. Fellow Am. Coll. Chest Physicians (hon.); mem. A.A.A.S., Am. Assn. Anatomists (pres. 1956-57, Henry Gray award 1970), Am. Soc. Zoologists, Soc. Exptl. Biology and Med., Am. Physiol. Soc., Am. Acad. Arts and Scis. (50 year award 1974), Chgo. Acad. Medicine, Minn. Pathol. Soc. (pres. 1943), Hennepin County Med. Soc. (hon.), Internat. Coll. Surgeons (hon.), Sigma Xi, Nu Sigma Nu, Acacia, Ind. Republican. Unitarian. Clubs: College, Harvard (Seattle). Author: A Laboratory Atlas of the Pig Embryo; Segmental Anatomy of the Lungs, 1955. Co-author: Kosher Code of the Orthodox Jew. Am. editor: Acta Anatomica, 1945-73. Contbr. to profl. jours. Home: Seattle, Wash. Died Oct. 27, 1977.

BOYER, CHARLES, actor; b. Figeac, France, Aug. 28, 1899; m. Pat Paterson (dec.); 1 son, Michael (dec.). Made stage debut in Paris; appeared on legitimate stage in N.Y.C. and on tour, with First Drama Quartet, in Don Juan in Hell, Lord Pengo, 1962, Man and Boy, 1963; appeared on TV in Four Star Playhouse; TV series The Rogues, from 1964; appeared in numerous films, including Back Street, 1941, Hold Back the Dawn, 1941, The Constant Nymph, 1943, Gas Light, 1944, Cluny Brown, 1946, The Happy Time, 1952, Thunder in the East, 1953, Earrings of Madame De, 1954, Around the World in 80 Days, 1956, Fanny, 1961, Is Paris Burning?, 1966, Casino Royale, 1967, Barefoot in the Park, 1967, The April Fools, 1969, Madwoman of Chaillot, 1969, Lost Horizon, 1973, Stavisky, 1974. Founder, 1940, pres. French Research Found. (non-profit orgn. to provide research and French library facilities); past pres. Beverly Hills chpt. Am. Friends of France, Hollywood chpt. French War Relief. Named chevalier Legion d'Honneur; recipient Della Austria medal for performance in Lord Pengo, 1963. Address: Los Angeles, Calif. Died Aug. 26, 1978.

BOYKIN, LESTER ERNEST, govt. official; b. Lamar, S.C., Feb. 21, 1882; s. William Franklin and Harriet (McLendon) B.; B.S., Clemson Coll., 1905; LL.B., Georgetown U., 1908; m. Grace Marie Junod, Oct. 1, 1921; children—Lester Junod, June Elizabeth. Sec., U.S. Seantor A.C. Latimer, 1905-08; chief, div. of highways laws and contracts, U.S. Bur. of Pub. Roads, Dept. of Agr., 1908-39; solicitor U.S. Pub. Roads Adminstrn., Fed. Works Agency, 1939-49; solicitor U.S. Bur. of Pub. Roads, Department of Commerce, since July 1949. Admitted S.C. bar, 1908, D.C. bar, 1912. Mem. Forest Hills Citizens Assn., Georgetown U. Alumni Assn., S.C. State Soc. (Washington), Am. Assn. State Highway Ofcls., Fed. Bar Assn., Clemson Alumni Assn., Police Boys Club. Mason. Methodist. Home: Washington. *

BOYLE, ASHBY DOUGLAS, lawyer; b. Ogden, Utah, July 14, 1886; s. A. McLaren and Isabella (Douglas) B.; student U. of Utah, 1908-10; LL.B., U. of Chicago, 1912; m. Dessie Grant, Nov. 24, 1908. Missionary Latter-day Saints Ch., Germany and Switzerland, 1904-06; editor Der Stern, Zurich, Switzerland, 1906-07; asst. in German, U. of Utah, 1909-10; admitted to bar of Utah, Feb. 11, 1913; practice of law in Salt Lake City since 1913; gen. counsel Utah-Idaho Sugar Co. since 1930, Beneficial Life Ins. Co. since 1920, Utah Home Fire Ins. Co. since 1914; lecturer U. of Utah Law Sch., 1917-26. Dir. Boyle Furniture Company, Filer Seed Company. Member Utah State Bar Association. Republican. Club: Cooper Ornithological. Home: Salt Lake City, Utah. *

BOYLE, FRANCIS DENNIS, naval officer; b. Everett, Wash., July 30, 1910; s. Dennis Peter and Louise Anna (Zahler) B.; B.S., U.S. Naval Acad., 1934; postgrad. Armed Forces Staff Coll., 1952; m. Marjorie Felicite Finney, June 24, 1936; children Doris (Mrs. J.E. Whitely, Jr.), Patricia Felicite. Commd. ensign USN, 1934, advanced through grades to rear adm., 1963; comdr. U.S.S. Charr, 1944-46; instr. naval history Naval Sch., Newport, R.I., 1946-48; tech. liaison officer Bur. Ordnance, Jet Propulsion Lab., Calif. Inst. Tech., 1949-50; comdr. U.S.S. Bradford, 1950-51; br. head guided missiles research div. Bur. Ordnance, Navy Dept., Washington, 1952, 53- 54; guided missile project supr., tech. dir. Terrier guided missile project, dir. rep. chief Bur. Ordnance, Naval Indsl. Res. Ordnance Plant, Pomona, Cal., 1952-53; officer-in-charge guided missile evaluation unit 1, Operational Devel. Force, Naval Air Sta., San Diego, 1954-56; group comdr. hydrographic survey group II, comdg. officer U.S.S. Tanner, 1956-57; comdr. Naval Ordnance Missile Test Facility, White Sands Proving Ground, N.M., 1958-60; comdg. officer U.S.S. Springfield, 1960-61; asst. dir., spl. asst. to chief naval operations, Washington, 1961-62; comdr. Fleet Tng. Group, San Diego, 1962, Cruiser Destroyer Flotilla 7, 1962-63; dep. dir. Communications Satellite Project Office, Defense Communications Agy., Washington, 1963-66; chief MAAG, Norway, 1966-68; lectr. Decorated Navy Cross, Legion of Merit. Mem. Nat. Geog. Soc., Naval Inst., Naval Acad. Alumni Assn., Monterey History and Art Assn. (Laura Powers award). Home: Monterey, Calif. Died Oct. 22, 1978.

BOYNTON, RAY SCEPTER, artist; b. Whitten, Ia., Jan. 14, 1883; s. Charles Henry and Sarah Ellen (Cole) B.; grad. high sch., Strawberry Point, Ia., 1901; student Chicago Acad. of Fine Arts, 1904-07; m. Margaret Gough, of Ottawa, Can., July 25, 1919 (died Aug. 11, 1931); m. 2d, Kathleen Mains, of Coventry, Eng., May 16, 1932. Asst. prof. art, U. of Calif., since 1923; instr. drawing and painting (fresco), Calif. Sch. of Fine Arts, San Francisco. Designed and created encaustics, frescoes, decorations for various halls, offices, etc., including decorations for Council Chamber, City Hall, Spokane, Wash.; First Congl. Ch., Berkeley, Calif.; Hall for Chamber Music, Mills Coll.; fresco for Coit Memorial Tower, San Francisco; executing murals for Treasury Dept., Washington, D.C., 1935-36, etc. Awarded 1st prize San Francisco Art Assn. 55th Exhbn. Mem. bd. dirs. San Francisco Art Assn., 1931; sub. chmn. Pub. Works of Art Projects, Region 15, 1934. Mem. San Francisco Art Assn. (pres. Artists Council, also pres. Alumni Assn.), Nat. Soc. Mural Painters, Calif. Soc. Mural Artists (v.p. since 1935). Clubs: Faculty (U. of Calif.); Bohemian (San Francisco). Home: San Francisco, Calif. *

BRACE, GERALD WARNER, author, educator; b. Islip, N.Y., Sept. 23, 1901; s. Charles Loring and Louise (Warner) B.; B.A., Amherst Coll., 1922, Litt.D., 1969; M.A., Harvard, 1924, Ph.D., 1930; Litt.D., Southeastern Mass. U., 1965, U. Me., 1972; m. Huldah Laird, Dec. 3, 1927; children—Charles Loring, Gerald Warner, Barbara (Mrs. Ralph Seeley). Instr. Williams Coll., 1924-26; instr., tutor Harvard, Radcliffe Coll., 1927-30; instr. Dartmouth, 1930-34; instr., asst. prof. Mt. Holyoke Coll., 1934-39; prof. English, Boston U., 1939-68, prof. English emeritus, 1968-78; tchr. Cummington Sch., summer 1934, Writers Conf., U. N.H., summer 1953; vis. lectr. Harvard, 1955-56. Mem. Am. Assn. U. Profs., Phi Beta Kappa. Author: The Islands, 1936; The Wayward Pilgrims, 1938; Light on a Mountain, 1941; The Garretson Chronicle, 1947; A Summer's Tale, 1949; The Spire, 1952; Bell's Landing, 1955; The Age of the Novel, 1957; The World of Carrick's Cove, 1957; Winter Solstice, 1960; The Wind's Will, 1964; Between Wind and Water, 1966; The Department, 1968; The Stuff of Fiction, 1969; Days That Were, 1976, 79. Home: Belmont, Mass. Died July 20, 1978.

BRACE, RICHARD MUNTHE, educator; b. Alameda, Calif., Aug. 11, 1915; s. Albert H. and Mabel (Munthe) B.; A.B., U. Calif., Berkeley, 1936, M.A., 1937, Ph.D. (Taussig traveling fellow in Paris 1939-40), 1940; m. Joan Tilden von Schmidt, June 16, 1939; children—Geoffrey R., Pamela J. Instr. history U. Maine, 1941-43; asst. prof. history Pomona (Calif.) Coll., 1943-45; asso. prof. U. Colo., 1945-47; asso. prof. Northwestern U., 1947-57, prof. history, 1957-65; chmn. dept. history Oakland (Mich.) U., 1965-68, prof., 1969-77. History editor D. Van Nostrand & Co., 1960-68; vis. prof. history U. Calif., San Diego, 1968-69; pres. Evanston Sch. World Affairs, 1959. Recipient prize in European history Pacific Hist. Assn., 1945. Am. Council Learned Socs. fellow, 1946; Social Sci. Research Council fellow 1951, 60-61, 65; Fulbright research fellow, Paris, 1954-55; Rockefeller Found. fellow, 1964-65. Mem. Am. Hist. Assn. (Herbert B. Adams prize com. 1959-63), Soc. for French Hist. Studies (v.p. 1968), Société Française d'Etudes du XVIII Siècle. Author: Bordeaux and the Gironde 1789-94, 1947; Historical Evolution of Modern France, 1949; The Making of the Modern World, 1955; (with Joan T. Brace) Ordeal in Algeria, 1960; Algerian Voices, 1965; Morocco, Algeria, Tunisia, 1964; in progress at time of death: (with Joan Brace) a study of slavery in French colony of Martinique. Bd. editors Jour. Modern History, 1960-62; contbr. numerous papers to profl. confs. and jours. Home: Lake Orion, Mich. Died June 5, 1977; buried Hunter's Creek Cemetery, Lapeer, Mich.

BRACKEN, ARCHIE KAY, college pres.; b. Inman, Tenn., Sept. 13, 1884; s. Archie Lewis and Laura Alexander (Chaudoin) B.; student Peniel (Tex.) Coll., 1914-16; A.B., Greenville (Ill.) Coll., 1917; A.M., U. of Okla., 1925; grad. study U. of Calif. 1927; D.D., Pasadena (Calif.) Coll., 1932; m. Gertrude Humble, of Pikeville, Tenn., June 8, 1903 (died 1904); 1 son, Kyle Bruce (dec.); m. 2d, Mattie Emma Green, of Greenville, Texas, Aug. 27, 1908. Teacher rural schs., Tex., 1909-10, high sch., 1910-12, supt. grade sch., 1912-14; teacher history and English South Eastern Nazarene Coll., at Donalsonville, Ga., 1917-18; actg. pres. Peniel Coll., 1918-19; pres. Bethany-Peniel Coll., Bethany, Okla., 1920-28 and since 1930; dean Olivet Coll., Olivet, Ill., 1928-30. Pres. Bethany Chamber Commerce 3 yrs. Mem. Phi Delta Kappa. Mem. Ch. of Nazarene. Contbr. to Herald of Holiness (official organ of Ch. of Nazarene). Home: Bethany, Okla. *

BRACKMAN, ROBERT, artist; b. Odessa, Russia; s. Moyssi and Celia B.; ed. common schools, Russia; art edn., Nat. Acad. Design, N.Y.C. 1919-21; m. 2d, Frances Richard Davis, Feb. 15, 1936; children—Roberta Frances, Celia Davis. Mem. of Faculty Art Students League N.Y., from 1933, Bklyn. Inst. of Art, from 1936; Ford grant artist in residence Norfolk Mus.; art cons. USAF. Represented in permanent collections Met. Mus. N.Y.C. and others. Commd. portraits include J.D. Rockefeller, Jr., for Colonial Williamsburg (Va.), Inc., Dr. Evarts Graham, Washington U., St. Louis, John Foster Dulles for State Dept. Awarded Thomas B. Clarke prize, 1932, Saltus medal, 1941, Andrew Carnegie prize, 1965, Nat. Acad. Design; awarded Atheneum prize, Conn. Acad., 1932, Noel Flagg prize, 1936, 1st prize, 1948, Anonymous prize Art Inst. Chgo., 1929; hon. mention Carnegie Inst. Paintings in U.S., 1949; gold medal Nat. Art Club, 1950; gold medal of honor Allied Artists Am., 1952; 1st prize Laguna Beach Art Festival, 1952; Carol H. Beck gold medal Pa. Acad. Fine Arts, 1958, Salmagundi Club award, 1961; Gold Medal of Honor, Allied Artists of Am., 1966; named to Pastel Soc. Am. Hall of Fame, 1980; to Accademia Italia, 1980. Academician, Nat. Academy of Design. Mem. Allied Artists Am., Mystic Art Assn. (pres. 1951-52), Audubon Soc. Artists, Am. Water Color Soc., Conn. Acad., Wilmington Acad., New Haven Paint and Clay Club, Internat. Inst. Arts and Letters, Royal Soc. Arts (London). Home: Noank, Conn. Died July 16, 1980; buried Elm Grove Cemetery, Mystic, Conn.

BRACY, CARL CLUSTER, ednl. assn. exec.; b. Carterville, Ill., Jan. 29, 1912; s. Clyde and Ola (Stephens) C.; A.B., McKendree Coll., 1936, D.D., 1946; Th.M., Iliff Sch. Theology, 1940; LL.D., Ohio Wesleyan U., 1959; L.H.D., Ohio No. U., 1967; m. Ermal E. Hacker, Sept. 29, 1936 (div. 1967); children—Marvin Carl, Carla Elaine, Brenda Sue; m. 2d, Katherine P. Branfield. Ordained to ministry Meth. Ch.; pastor, Donnellson, Ill., 1934-36, Broomfield and Greeley, Colo., 1936-39, Faulkton and Madison, S.D., 1939-45; pres. McKendree Coll., Lebanon, Ill., 1945-49; chancellor Nebr. Wesleyan U., Lincoln, 1949-54; pres. Mount Union Coll., 1954-67; exec. dir. Ohio Found. Ind. Colls., Columbus, 1968-74, pres., 1974-77. Mem. Meth. Gen. Bd. Edn., 1948-54; del. 10th, 11th World Meth. Confs., Oslo, 1961, London, 1966. Mem. Nat. Assn. Schs. and Colls. Meth. Ch. (pres. 1961-62), Newcomen Soc. N.Am., Blue Key, Pi Kappa Delta, Alpha Psi Omega, Sigma Tau Delta, Pi Gamma Mu, Phi Kappa Phi. Rotarian. Home: Columbus, Ohio; buried Alliance (Ohio) City Cemetery. Died Aug. 22, 1977.

BRADBURN, JAMES RUPERT, mgmt. cons.; b. Los Angeles, May 31, 1911; s. Rupert H. and Alice (Hamilton) B.; B.S., Calif. Inst. Tech., 1932; M.B.A., Harvard, 1934; m. King Turnbull, Sept. 9, 1939; children—Alice, James, Kenneth. Engr., Gen. Electric Co., 1934-37, Gleason works, Rochester, N.Y., 1937-38, Eastman Kodak Co., 1938-41; exec. engr., v.p. Consol. Electrodynamics Corp., 1945-54; pres., dir. Electro Data Corp., 1954-56, gen. mgr. Electro Data Div. and v.p. Burroughs Corp., 1956-60, v.p. engring. and mfg., 1960-65, also dir.; gen. mgr. electronic data processing div., v.p. RCA Corp., 1965-68, exec. v.p., gen. mgr. information systems, 1968-71; mgmt. cons., 1971-77. Bd. dirs. Boy Scouts Am. Served to maj., ordnance dept. AUS, 1941-45. Mem. I.E.E.E., Harvard Bus. Sch. Assn., Tau Beta Pi, Eta Kappa Nu. Republican. Christian Scientist. Club: Bald Peak (Colony, N.H.). Home: Mirror Lake, N.H. Died July 4, 1977.

BRADDOCK, DANIEL MCCOY, fgn. service officer; b. Little Rock, Apr. 5, 1906; s. John Sellers and Katherine (McCoy) B.; A.B. summa cum laude, M.A., Kenyon Coll. Grambier, Ohio, 1926; student Ecole des Sciences Politiques, Paris, 1926-27; m. Marguerite Virginia Lipscomb, July 22, 1929; children—Daniel McCoy, John Lipscomb, Carolyn Anderson, Edward Sellers, Richard Scott. Vice consul, Medan, Sumatra, 1929-31; vice consul, Barcelona, Spain, 1932-34, consul, 1934; 36; 2d sec. of embassy, Caracas, Venezuela, 1937-40; consul, Porto Alegre, Brazil,

1940-43, Bahia, Brazil (including details to consulate at Belem and to embassy at Rio de Janeiro), 1943-45; asst. chief, div. of Brazilian Affairs Dept. State, 1945, chief, 1946-47, asst. chief Am. Republics Br. Chief, Div. Comml. Policy, 1947-48; 1st sec. embassy, Madrid, 1948-49; mem. U.S. del. Annecy Trade and Tariffs Conf., 1949; mem. Fgn. Service Selection Bd., 1950; conselor economic affairs, Madrid, 1950, Manila, 1952-54; dep. chmn. U.S. del. Philippine Trade Negotiations, 1954-55; counselor, dept. chief of mission, Rangoon, Burma, 1955-57; minister-counselor, dep. chief of mission, Havana, Cuba, 1957-60, career minister, from 1960, sr. fgn. insp., from 1964, acting dep. asst. sec. state for Inter-Am. affairs, summer 1961; mem. U.S. del. UN Gen. Assembly, from 1961; minister, consul gen., Sao Paulo, Brazil, 1962-67; consul gen., Bombay, India, from 1967; assigned Nat. War Coll., 1951-52. Mem. Am. Fgn. Service Assn., Phi Beta Kappa, Delta Kappa Epsilon. Clubs: Internat, DACOR, Foreign Service (Washington). Address: Washington, D.C. Died Nov. 24, 1979; buried Rock Creek Cemetery, Washington.

BRADEN, SPRUILLE, diplomat; b. Elkhorn, Mont., Mar. 13, 1894; s. William and Mary (Kimball) B.; Ph.B. in Mining Engring., Yale, 1914; hon. degree U. Buenos Aires, 1938; LL.D., Johns Hopkins, 1939, Clark U., Allbright Coll., 1946; E.D., Mont. Sch. Mines, 1947; H.H.D., Hillsdale Coll.; m. María Humeres del Solar, Sept. 5, 1915 (dec. May 1962); children—Maruja (Mrs. Luiz de Meirelles), Laurita Isolina (Mrs. John Burgess Young), William II, Patricia (Mrs. William L. Clark), Spruille; m. 2d, Verbena Victoria Williams, May 29, 1964. Miner, 1912, engring. various mining constrn. activities, 1912-20; negotiated contracts for electrification Chilean State Rys. Westinghouse Electric Co., 1920; organized Cohoe Processes, Inc., 1926; reorganized Englishtown Carpet Co. (renamed Monmouth Rug Mills Inc.), 1925-29, also dir.; organized Rehab. Corp., financing income-producing properties, 1932; dir. Am. Ship and Commerce Corp., W.A. Harriman Securities, Pa. Coal and Coke, Marion Steam Shovel Co., Kingscote Realty Corp., Capitol Theatre Corp., others; trustee, mem. exec. com. Dry Dock Savs. Bank. numerous assignments as ambassador and spl. rep. U.S. Pres., from 1935; ambassador to Colombia, 1939-42, Cuba, 1942-45, Argentina, 1945; asst. sec. state Am. Republic Affairs, 1946-47. Pres., Americas Found., 1960-66, Colombia Found., Colombian Assn. Mut. Aid. Chmn. N.Y.C. Anti-crime Com., 1951-58. Recipient decorations from many fgn. countries including grand cross of Brazil, Chile, Peru, Colombia, Bolivia, Paraguay, Haiti; grand cross Ruben Dario (Nicarague), grand cross Order of Quetzal (Gautemala), grand cross Knightly Order St. Brigitte, grand cross Cuba's Legion of Honor; many citations including Order of Lafayette Freedom award, 1962, gold medal Cubans in Exile, Eloy Alfaro grand cross L.I. U.; recipient Medal of Freedom (U.S.). Conservative. Mem. PanAm Soc. U.S. (pres. 1953-59, hon. pres., 1959-78), Inter-Am. Edn. Assn. (hon.), Chevaliers du Tastevin (grand officer), Soc. of Cincinnati (hon.), Am. Arbitration Assn. (dir., exec. com.), Navy League U.S. (life). Clubs: Met. (past pres. N.Y.C., hon. life); Nejapa Country (Managua, Nicaragua). Author: Diplomats and Demagogues-the Memoirs of Spruille Braden, 1971. Negotiated peace treaty settling Chaco War between Bolivia and Paraguay. Address: New York, N.Y. Died Jan. 10, 1978.

BRADLEY, FREDERICK MOFFAT, lawyer: b. Washington, Dec. 7, 1901; s. Thomas and Mabel W. (Moffat) B.; LL.B., George Washington U., 1923; m. Carolyn Chamberlain, June 2, 1928; children—Carol F. (Mrs. John R. Caswell), Thomas, Frederick M. (dec.). Admitted to D.C., U.S. Supreme Ct. bars; partner Hogan & Hartson, Washington, 1954-76; dir., gen. counsel Washington Loan & Trust Co., 1938-54; dir. Riggs Nat. Bank of Washington, 1954-69, now adv. dir.; counsel Renegotiation Bd., U.S. Maritime Commn., 1942-43. Trustee Corcoran Gallery Art, Washington Hosp. Center, Louise Home. Mem. Washington Nat. Monument Soc., Am. Law Inst., Am., D.C. (past chmn. com. on probate law) bar assns., Assn. Bar City N.Y., Newcomen Soc. N.Am., Phi Delta Phi, Delta Tau Delta. Episcopalian. Clubs: Alibi, Chevy Chase (past gov.), Metropolitan (past gov.), Alfalfa, Lawyers, Barristers (Washington). Home: Washington, D.C. Died Oct. 21, 1980.

BRADLEY, JAMES CHESTER, prof. entomology; b. West Chester, Pa., Feb. 11, 1884; s. Daniel Hiester and Lucy Virginia (Blanchard) B.; A.B., Central High Sch., Phila., 1903; A.B., Cornell, 1906, Ph.D., 1910; M.S., U. of Calif., 1907; married Ruth Stephens Baker, June 27, 1940. Spl. asst. entomologist State of Ga., 1909-13; asst. in entomology, later fellow, 1905-10, asst. prof., 1911-17, 1918-20, prof. entomology and curator invertebrate zoölogy, 1920-39, prof. entomology from 1939, Cornell U.; entomologist and curator Expt. Station, 1937-39, entomologist since 1939; assistant in entomology, University of Calif., 1905-06, and asst. prof. (in exchange), 1917-18. Member Internat. Commn. on Zoölogical Nomenclature, American Com. on Entomological Nomenclature, Internat. Committee Entomol. Nomenclature. Fellow A.A.A.S., Entomological Society London, Entomol. Soc. America; mem. Am. Entomol. Soc., Am. Assn. Economic Entomologists, Am. Assn. Univ. Profs., Am. Soc. Naturalists, Ecological Soc. America, Phila. Acad. Natural Sciences, Biol. Soc. Washington, Pacific Coast Entomol. Soc., Société Linnéenne de Lyon, 7th, 12th Internat. Congresses Zoölogy, Deutsche Entomologische Gesellschaft, Sociéta Entomologica Italiana, 4th, 5th, 6th, 7th Internat. Congresses of Entomology, Sigma Xi, Gamma Alpha, Pi Kappa Alpha; life mem. Société Entomologique de Belgique, also of France; corr. mem. Société Scientifique du Chile, Soc. Ent. du Chile, Soc. cientifico de Argentina. Made scientific exploration in British Columbia, 1905, 08, also various Cornell U. entomol. explorations in U.S. and in S. America, 1919-20, Central America, 1924. Scoutmaster Boy Scouts America, 1921-26. Author: Rules for Entries in Bibliographies, Supplementary to the American and British Library Associations' Catalog Rules, 1915; Insect Life (a manual for use of boy scouts); A Manual of the Genera of Beetles of America North of Mexico, 1930; A Laboratory Guide to the Study of the Wings of Insects, 1931, rev. edit., 1939; Brief Laboratory Guide and Exercises in Phylogeny, 1931. Contbr. to scientific periodicals. Home: Ithaca, N.Y. Died Feb. 25, 1975.

BRADLEY, MARY HASTINGS (MRS. HERBERT EDWIN BRADLEY), author; b. Chgo.; d. William and Lina (Rickords) Hastings; B.A., Smith Coll.; m. Herbert Edwin Bradley, June 21, 1910; children—Alice Hastings (Mrs. Huntington Denton Sheldon), Mary Lee. Fellow Royal Geog. Soc.; mem. Soc. Women Geographers, Phi Kappa Psi. Conglist. Clubs: Casino, Fortnightly, Arts, Contemporary (Chgo.). Author: Favor of Kings, 1912; Palace of Darkened Windows, 1914; Splendid Chance, 1915; Wine of Astonishment, 1919; Fortieth Door, 1919; The Innocent Adventures, 1921; On the Gorilla Trail, 1923; Caravans and Cannibals, 1926; Alice in Jungleland, 1927; Trailing the Tiger, 1929; Alice in Elephantland, 1929; Murder in Room 700, 1931; Road of Desperation, 1932; Old Chicago Stores, 1933; Unconfessed, 1934; The Five Minute Girl, 1935; Pattern of Three, 1937; A Hanging Matter, 1938; Mimi Foster, 1945; Understudy, 1946; Without Witness, 1947; Murder in the Family, 1949; Nice People Poison, 1952 (pub. Eng. 1956, Holland 1957, Die Weise Neggerin 1960, Une Viellr Touquee 1963); I Passed for White, The Story of Reba Lee, 1955. Accompanied husband on expdn. of Carl E. Akeley of Am. Mus. Natural History, into Belgian Congo for gorillas, 2d trip to Belgian Congo with husband, 1924; 1st expdn. to traverse region west of Lake Edward, in Sumatra and Indochina for tigers, 1935; 3d expdn. to Africa, studying Pygmies and Mangbetou tribes, 1930-31. Spl. corr. Coller's mag., covering Eastern, Far Eastern European and Mediterranean war zones, 1945; South African, Eastern Equatorial expdn., auspices Dept. State, 1951, Research Mexico and C.Am. Home: Chicago, Ill. Died Oct. 25, 1976.

BRADLEY, OMAR NELSON, army officer, watch co. exec.; b. Clark, Mo., Feb. 12, 1893; s. John Smith and Sarah E. (Hubbard) B.; B.S., U.S. Mil. Acad., 1915; grad. Inf. Sch. (advance course), 1925, Command and Gen. Staff Sch., 1929, Army War Coll., 1934; LL.D., U. Mo., Drury Coll., 1946, U. Ill., Harvard U., Dartmouth Coll., Northwestern U., N.Y. U., 1947, Princeton U., U. Wis., U. Calif., 1948, Columbia U., Hamilton Coll., Trinity Coll., 1949, Tex. A. and M. Coll., 1950, Cambridge (Eng.) U., U. Pitts., 1951, U. Akron, 1956, Tex. Christian U., 1972; Sc.D., St. Johns U., 1946, Lafayette Coll., 1949; Dr. Humanities, Birmingham-So. Coll., 1947; D. Eng., Rensselaer Poly Inst., 1950; Dr. Internat. Law, Pa. Mil. Coll., 1951; Dr. Mil. Sci. Norwich U., 1952; L.H.D., L.I. U., 1961; m. Mary Quayle, Dec. 28, 1916 (dec. Dec. 1965); 1 dau., Elizabeth; m. 2d, Kitty Buhler, Sept. 12, 1966. Commd. 2d lt., inf., U.S. Army, 1915, advanced through grades to gen., 1945, gen. of the Army, 1950—; comdg. gen. 2d corps, No. Tunisian campaign, 1943, Sicilian campaign, 1943, 1st U.S. Army, Normandy campaign, 1944, 12th Army Group, France, Belgium, Holland, Luxembourg, Germany campaigns, 1944-45; adminstr. vets. affairs, 1945-47; chief of staff, U.S. Army, 1948-49; chmn. U.S. Joint Chiefs Staff, 1949-53; chmn. bd. Bulova Watch, 1958-73, hon. chmn. bd., 1973—; chmn. Bulova Sch. Watch Making. U.S. rep. standing group, mil. com. NATO, 1949-53. Decorated D.S.M. with 3 oak leaf clusters, D.S.M. (Navy), Legion of Merit with oak leaf cluster, Silver Star, Bronze Star, Presdl. Medal of Freedom, D.D.S.M. (U.S.); Knight Comdr. Bath (Gt. Britain), Grand Cross Legion of Honor, Croix de Guerre with palm (France), Order Suvorov, 1st degree, Order Kutuzov (Russia), Grand Cross Couronne de Chene, Croix de Guerre (Luxembourg), Grand Cross Order of Crown, Croix de Guerre with palm (Belgium), Cross of 1939 (Czechoslovakia), Grand Cross Ouissan Alaouite; mem. Order Orange-Nassau (Netherlands). Mem. Christian Ch. Mason. Clubs: Army and Navy, Burning Tree (Washington); Hillcrest Country, Lakeside Country, Wilshire Country, El Paso Country, Coronado Country. Author: A Soldier's Story, 1951. Address: Fort Bliss, Tex. Died Apr. 8, 1981; buried Arlington Nat. Cemetery.

BRADLEY, ROBERT HOLMES, ins. exec. ret.; b. New York, N.Y., 1883; grad. Columbia Univ., 1905. Vice pres. The Prudential Insurance Co. of America. Home: Mercer, Me.*

BRADLEY, WILLIAM JOSEPH, educator; b. Bradley, Ga., Apr. 2, 1883; s. John Wiley and Mollie L. (Greer) B.; A.B., Mercer U., Macon, Gas., 1902; A.B., A.M., U. of Chicago, 1905; studied Columbia, 1910; m. Edna Blanche Gurley, Dec. 26, 1907 (died 1937); children—William Joseph, John David, Annie Blanche; m. 2d, Mrs. Anna Thomas Burden, Feb. 4, 1938. High sch. prin., 2 yrs.; head dept. economy and polit. science, N. Ga. Agrl. Coll., 1907-11; head dept. history and philosophy, Okla. Bapt. U., 1911-12; head of dept. English, Gordon Inst., Sept.-Dec. 1912; head of dept. history and English, S. Ga. State Normal Coll., 1913, head of dept. history, 1913-20; head dept. of history and govt., Okla. Bapt. U., 1920-22; head dept. polit. science and dean Sch. of Commerce, Mercer U., 1922-27, head of dept. of history, 1927-40; on leave of absence, 1940-41; resigned, 1941. Member National Council for Social Studies, American Academy Political and Social Science, Am. Research Soc., Am. Social Hygiene Assn., Nat. Municipal League, Ga. Edn. Assn. Democrat. Missionary Baptist. Mem. Sigma Nu. Mason (32 deg.). Club: Lions. Author: Plato's Conception of the Soul—Its Relation to the Worlds of Being and Becoming, 1905; also Jesse Mercer, in Dictionary of Am. Biography. Home: Round Oak, Ga. *

BRADLEY, WILMOT HYDE, geologist; b. Westville, Conn., Apr. 4, 1899; s. John Lucius and Anna Miner (Hyde) B.; Ph.B., Sheffield Sci. Sch., Yale, 1920; Ph.D. in Geology, Yale, 1927, Sc.D. (hon.), 1947; m. Catrina van Benschoten, Nov. 4, 1922; children—Ann, Penelope (Mrs. David Shavit). Geologist, U.S. Geol. Survey, 1922-69, chief geologist, 1944-59; retired, 1969; field work in Wyo., Colo., Utah, N.Y., Me. and Fla. Served with USNRC, 1918. Recipient Distinguished Service award Dept. Interior, 1958, F.V. Hayden Gold medal Phila. Acad. Scis., 1971. Mem. Nat. Acad. Scis., Am. Philos. Soc., Am. Acad. Arts and Scis., Geol. Soc. Am. (Penrose Gold medal 1972), Limnological and Oceanographic Soc., Internat. Limnological Soc., Am. Assn. Petroleum Geologists, A.A.A.S. Club: Cosmos (Washington). Contbr. profl. jours. Address: Milbridge, Maine. Died Apr. 12, 1979; buried Steuben, Maine.

BRADSHAW, AARON, army officer; b. Washington, D.C., July 1, 1894; s. Aaron and Mary Emma (Leech) B.; B.S., U.S. Mil. Acad., 1917, Oxford U., Brasenose Coll., 1919, M.I.T., 1919-20; m. Edith Gwendoline Doulton, July 1, 1919; 1 son, Robert Doulton. Commd. 2d lt., 1917, advanced through grades to maj. gen., 1943. Decorated D.S.M., Silver Star, Legion of Merit with oak leaf cluster, Bronze Star Medal, Army Commendation Medal with oak leaf cluster (United States), also decorated Officer Legion of Honor, Croix de Guerre with 2 palms, Order of the Army (France), Hon. Comdr. Order British Empire (Great Britain), Silver Medal for Valor, Cross of Knight Comdr., Sovereign Military Order Malta, Comdr. Order Crown of Italy, Patriot's Medal, Comdr. Order of SS, Maurice and Lazarus (Italy), Papal Lateran Cross. Mem. Ret. Officers Assn., Mil. Order of Caraboa. Mason. Clubs: National Press, Army-Navy, Metropolitan (Washington); The Lambs; Post Mortem. Editor USCG Jour., 1936-40. Address: Washington, D.C. Died Nov. 8, 1976.

BRADSHAW, ARMISTEAD E., banker; b. Nov. 7, 1880; s. Elisha Lenoah and Susan (Schumate) B.; grad. Seymour (Mo.) High Sch., 1898; m. Lena Hall, Nov. 5, 1903; children—Genevieve (Mrs. I. C. Parker), James (dec.), Dorothy (Mrs. George H. Gates), William H. (dec.). Teacher common schs. of Mo., 1898-1901; in banking business, 1901—, now chmn. bd., chief exec. officer Nat. Bank of Tulsa; dir. Okla. Natural Gas Co. Mason. *

BRADSHAW, MARION JOHN, clergyman, educator; b. Salem, O., Dec. 14, 1886; s. Lewis C. and Elizabeth A. (Barber) B.; A.B., Hiram (O.) Coll., 1911, M.A., 1912; studied Columbia, 1914-18; B.D., summa cum laude, Union Theol. Sem., 1917; studied Harvard, 1921-23, Marburg, Germany, summers, 1922, 24; D.D., U. of Me., 1930; m. Bessie Baumgardner, Aug. 17, 1912; children—Jane (Mrs. Alvin Aisenberg), Peter. Preacher Ada, O., 1911; ordained ministry Christian (Disciples) Ch., 1912; pastor Union Ch., Palisade, N.J., 1916-18; asst. systematic theol., Union Theol. Sem., 1917-19; prof. philosophy, Hiram Coll., 1919-20; sec. Congl. Edn. Soc., 1921; pastor Riverside Memorial Ch., Haverhill, Mass., 1922-23; prof. religious thought, Grinnell (Ia.) Coll., 1923-25; prof. philosophy of religion, Bangor Theol. Sem. since 1925; pastor Universalist chs., Guilford-Sangerville, 1930-34. Hazen lecturer, Middlebury Convocation, 1937. Lecturer on travel subjects, pub. affairs. Mem. Am. Philos. Assn., Theta Pi, Compiler of The War and Religion, 1919. Author: Third Class World, 1938; Philosophical Foundations of Faith, 1941; The Maine Land, 1941; The Nature of Maine, 1944; The Maine Scene, 1947. Home: Bangor, Me. *

BRADY, HAROLD, m. Harriet; 3 daus. Founder, Harold S. Brady Co., Chgo.; chmn. bd. U.S. Smelting Corp., Portland, Maine, Riverside Foundry, Bettendorf, Iowa. Home: Chicago, Ill. Died Dec. 31, 1976.

BRADY, ROBERT FREDERICK, elec. engr.; b. Washington, Jan. 14, 1909; s. John Frederick and Elsie Elinor (Dawson) B.; B.E.E., Catholic U. Am., 1932; LL.B., Columbus U., Washington, 1938, M.P.L., 1939; m. Mary Catherine Spillan, June 28, 1941; children—Robert Frederick, Mary Margaret, Mary Catherine (Mrs. Michael Gazarek), Mary Eileen, Francis Joseph. Admitted to D.C. bar, 1938, U.S. Dist. Ct. bar, Ct. Appeals, D.C., U.S. Patent Office, FCC; asso. John B. Brady, Washington, 1932-41; research, devel. staff engr. Office Chief Signal Officer U.S. Army, 1941-61; head electronics sect. NATO Internat. Staff, Paris, France, 1961-65; tech. adviser U.S. Army Materiel Command, Washington, 1965-70; sr. staff officer U.S. Army Advanced Materiel Concepts Agy., 1970-71; cons., 1971. Recipient Exceptional Civilian Service award, 1945, Meritorious Civilian Service award, 1958, 70. Registered profl. engr., D.C. Mem. I.E.E.E. K.C. (past grand knight). Home: Falls Church, Va. Died May 2, 1976.

BRAGG, RAYMOND BENNETT, clergyman; b. Worcester, Mass., Oct. 10, 1902; s. John Gould and Emma Rilla (Bennett) B.; student Bates Coll., Lewiston, Maine, 1921-24, Brown U., 1924-25, U. Chgo., 1926-27; grad. Meadville Theol. Sch., Chgo., Ill., 1927; Sc.D. (hon.), U. Antioquia, Medellin, Columbia, S.A., 1948; D.D., Meadville Theological Sch., 1948; m. Ilse Meyn, July 13, 1935; children—Susan Elizabeth, Kate Bennett. Ordained to ministry Unitarian Ch., 1927; pastor, Church of All Souls, Evanston, Ill., 1927-30; sec. Western Unitarian Conf., Chicago, 1930-35; asso. pastor First Unitarian Soc., Mpls., 1935-38, pastor 1938-47; exec. v.p. Am. Unitarian Assn., 1947-48; exec. dir. Unitarian Service Com., 1943-52; pastor All Souls Unitarian Ch. of Kansas City, 1952-73; instr. philosophy U. Kansas City, from 1958; asst. prof. philosophy Kans. Art Inst., 1958-79. Pres. Children's Protective Soc., Mpls., 1942-47; mem. board directors Mo. Mental Health Assn. Chmn. Foreign Policy Assn. (Mpls. br.), 1941-43. Exec. officer Italian Medical Mission (Italy) in cooperation with U.N.R.R.A., 1945. Dir. Am. Unitarian Assn. Trustee Meadville Theol. Sch.; dir. Kansas City Mental Hygiene Soc., 1953-54, pres., 1954. Mem. Kansas City Adult Edn. Assn. (v.p. 1954), Unitarian Ministers' Assn. Editor: The New Humanist, 1935-36. Author: The Humanist Pulpit (with John H. Dietrich), 1936. Contbr. reviews, articles to religious jours. Home: Kansas City, Mo. Died Feb. 15, 1979.

BRAGINTON, MARY VICTORIA, educator; b. Manson, Iowa, Mar. 15, 1901; d. George Frederick and Anna (Greenside) B.; A.B., Grinnell Coll., 1920, L.H.D., 1950; A.M., Yale, 1921, Ph.D., 1923; student univs. Burssels and Ghent, Belgium, 1925-26; Univ. of Grenoble (France), summer 1925; Am. Sch. Classical Studies, Athens, Greece, summer 1934; L.H.D. (hon.), Rockford College, 1967. Instr in Latin, Mount Holyoke Coll., S. Hadley, Mass., 1923-25; fellow Commn. for Relief of Belgium, Ednl. Found., 1925-26; asst. prof. Latin, Mt. Holyoke Coll., 1926-27; prof. Latin and Greek, Rockford (Ill.) Coll., 1927-67, dir. admission, 1945-47, acad. dean, 1949-57, dean of faculty, 1957-63, chmn. dept. fgn. languages, chmn. div. language and lit., 1963-67; vis. prof. classics U. Pacific, Stockton, Calif., 1967-73; vis. prof. classics Tulane U., 1970, 71. Bd. dirs. Kobe College Corp., Chgo. Served from lt. (j.g.) to lt. Women's Reserve. USNR, 1943-45. Emerson-Lathrop grantee, Europe, 1961-62; recipient Grinnell Coll. Alumni award, 1971; Disting. Service award Rockford Coll., 1972; Talcott Cross, Rockford Coll. Alumni Assn., 1972. Mem. Am. Philol. Assn., American Classical League, Classical Assn. Middle West and South (1st v.p., 1938, pres., 1949-50). N.E.A., Ill. Classical Conference, (vice pres. 1952-53, pres. 1953-54), AAUP, AAUW (pres. local br. 1942-43, chmn. Ill. com. status women 1959-61), Classical Soc. Am. Acad. Rome (pres. 1942). Phi Beta Kappa (sec.-treas. east central dist. 1958-64, v.p. 1964-67), Delta Kappa Gamma. Conglist. Clubs: Zonta (Rockford, Ill.); Cercle des alumni de la Foundation Universitaire (Brussels). Author: The Supernatural in Seneca's Tragedies, 1933. Contbr. articles to classical jours. Home: Rockford, Ill. Died July 26, 1973.

BRAHAM, HERBERT JACKSON, conductor; b. Brooklyn, N.Y., 1885; s. Harry and Tina (Jackson) B.; ed. in music with Phaff, Klugeschied, Sbriglia and Shakespeare, noted teachers of Europe; m. Irma N. Vogel, of Brooklyn, 1909. Associated with Henry W. Savage English Grand Opera Co., 1904-09; organizer and condr. Brooklyn Orchestral Soc. since 1917. Mem. exec. music com. Brooklyn Inst. Arts and Sciences. Methodist. Mason. Home: Brooklyn, N.Y. *

BRAIDER, DONALD TOWNLEY, author; b. N.Y.C., Apr. 30, 1923; s. Clifford Arthur and Josephine Miriam (Giglio) B.; student Swarthmore Coll., 1940-42, Rutgers U., 1943-44, Grenoble U., 1945, Merton Coll., Oxford U., 1946, Swarthmore Coll., 1946-47, Middlebury U., 1961; m. Carol Parthenia Newton, June 22, 1946; children—Christopher, Susan, Jackson. Pub. relations dir. United World Federalists, N.Y.C., 1948-49, bookseller, East Hampton, N.Y., 1953-57; head French dept. Wooster Sch., 1957-63, dir. devel., 1970-75; free lance writer, 1950-76. Del. Conn. Democratic Conv., 1972; mem. Dem. Town Com., Redding, Conn., 1972-76. Served with AUS, 1942-46. Author: Palace Guard, 1958; Putnam's Guide to the Art Centers of Europe, 1965; Color From a Light Within, 1967; Rage in Silence, 1969; Five Early American Painters, 1969; An Epic Joy, 1971; George Bellows, 1971; The Niagara, 1972; Life History and Magic of the Horse, 1973; Solitary Star: Sam Houston, 1974. Home: Cooperstown, N.Y. Died June 22, 1976.

BRAILOWSKY, ALEXANDER, pianist; b. Kiev, Russia, February 16, 1896; s. Peter and Elizabeth (Raptchinsky) B.; grad. with gold medal, Conservatoire (Kiev), 1911; studied with Theodore Leschetizky in Vienna, 1911-14; m. Felicia Karczmar, Nov. 17, 1931. Made debut in Paris, many tours of European countries; has toured U.S. since 1924, S.Am., C.Am., North Africa, Far East. First to present entire work of Chopin in cyclic form, within framework of 6 recitals, Paris (on Chopin's own piano, played only by Franz Liszt since composer's death), Brussels, Zurich, N.Y.C., Mexico City, Buenos Aires, Montevideo. Recipient Order of Knight conferred by late King Albert of Belgium; Order "Pour le Merite", by King Carol of Rumania; knight Leg. of Hon. (France), King Christian X medal (Denmark), Silver medal City of Paris, Scroll of Honor for personal contbn. to humanitarian work behalf world's refugees. Mem. Greek Orthodox Ch. Club: Bohemians (N.Y.C.). Recorded for CBS and RCA. Address: New York, N.Y. Died Apr. 25, 1976.

BRAINARD, GEORGE C., manufacturer; b. Danvers, Mass., June 1, 1885; s. John C. and Mary H. (Treworgy) B.; spl. student Northwestern U., 1906-07, Cornell U., 1907-09; m. Alice Maude Littlefield, Sept. 6, 1911 (dec.); children—Barbara (Mrs. T. J. Montgomery), George C., Elizabeth (Mrs. Daniel A. Heindel, Jr.), Edward L. Engr. with R. B. McMullen, Chicago, Ill., 1909 and 1914; with Hydraulic Pressed Steel Co., as sales engr., chief engr., factory mgr. and gen. mgr., 1914-23; with Gen. Fireproofing Co., Youngstown, O., as gen. supt., vice pres. and pres., 1923-45, now dir. and chmn. exec. com.; pres., and director Addressograph-Multigraph Corporation, 1946-52, chmn. exec. com., 1952-60, ret.; now pres. Holden Arboretum; chmn. exec. com., dir. Nat. Acme Company; chmn. bd. Fed. Reserve Bank of Cleveland, 1939-52; dir. Youngstown Sheet & Tube Co. Cleve. & Pitts. R.R. Co. Mem. bd. trustees Western Res. U. Civilian Staff expert in charge of shell forging Production Div., Ordnance Dept., U.S. Army, 1918-20; asst. dist. chief Cleveland Ordnance Dist., 1940, chief, 1950-53; chief tools div. and dep. dir. prodn. WPB, 1942. Trustee Western Res. U. Mem. Beta Theta Pi. Republican. Episcopalian. Clubs: Union, Kirtland Country, Tavern. Home: Chardon, O. *

BRAMAN, JAMES D'ORMA, savs. and loan exec., former mayor of Seattle; b. Lorimor, Iowa, Dec. 23, 1901; s. Jacob Wesley and Susie Mae (Huntzinger) B.; student pub. schs., Bremerton, Wash.; m. Margaret V. Young, Nov. 27, 1920; children—James D'Orma, Robert C. Pres. Braman Millwork Supply Co., 1920-29, Braman Mill & Mfg. Co., Inc., Bremerton, 1929-43, Braman Lumber & Hardware Co., Inc., Seattle, 1946-56; chmn. bd. Shoreline Savs. & Loan Assn., Seattle, from 1952; mem. Seattle City Council, 1954-64; mayor of Seattle, 1964-69; asst. sec. U.S. Dept. of Transp., 1969-70. Rep. Seattle to Wash. State World's Fair Commn., 1957-62; mem. Seattle Center Adv. Commn.; mem. adv. council U.S. Conf. Mayors; chmn. Puget Sound Governmental Com.; mem. nat. council, pres. Chief Seattle council Boy Scouts Am. Trustee Pacific Sci. Center Found.; trustee, mem. steering com. Century 21 Corp., 1959-62. Served to comdr. USNR, 1942-46. Recipient Silver Beaver award Boy Scouts Am., 1949. Mem. Nat. League Cities (chmn. com. transp. and communications, mem. exec. bd.), Japan-Am. Conf. of Mayors and C. of C. Presidents (exec. com.), Seattle C. of C. Republican. Mason, Kiwanian. Home: Seattle, Wash. Died Aug. 21, 1980.

BRAMMAN, WILLIAM JACOB, banker; b. St. Louis, July 14, 1885; student pub. schs.; m. Irene Clare Moore, Apr. 21, 1913. With Merchants Laclede Nat. Bank, St. Louis, 1903-29, as collector, chief clerk asst. cashier, and v.p. until bank merged with Miss. Valley Trust Co., July 1, 1929, when became v.p. and later exec. v.p. Mem. C. of C., Am. Bankers Assn., Assn. Reserve City Bankers. Past pres. St. Louis Clearing House. Mem. adv. com. R.F.C. Home: St. Louis. *

BRANCH, CLAUDE RAYMOND, lawyer; b. Providence, Jan. 9, 1886; s. John Baker and Fannie Welles (Mowry) B.; A.B., Brown U., 1907, LL.D., 1974; LL.B. cum laude, Harvard, 1911; m. Hope Shepardson Cary, Feb. 19, 1928 (div.); children—Audrey (Mrs. Stephen Smith), Cecily (Freifrau v. Gemmingen-Hornberg), Elizabeth Hilary (Mrs. Harvey Eggeman), Judith (Mrs. John L. Hart, Jr.). Admitted to R.I. bar, 1911, Mass. bar, 1932; 3d asst. atty. gen. of R.I., 1915-16; mem. Edwards & Angell, 1916-29; pres. Providence & Worcester R.R. Co., 1927-29; spl. asst. to U.S. atty. gen., 1929-32; mem. Choate, Hall & Stewart, Boston, 1932—; dir. Providence Washington Ins. Co., Peoples Trust Co.; trustee Peoples Savs. Bank. Head enforce. div. U.S. Food Adminstrn., R.I. 1917-18. Fellow emeritus Brown U. Fellow Am. Acad. Arts and Scis.; mem. Am. Law Inst., Am. R.I., Boston bar assns. R.I. Hist. Soc. (pres. 1928-29), Phi Beta Kappa (pres. R.I. Alpha 1948-49), Alpha Delta Phi. Republican. Clubs: Hope, Providence Art, Agawam Hunt. Home: Providence RI *

BRANCH, HAZEL ELISABETH, educator; b. Concordia, Kan., Oct. 1, 1886; d. Vernon H. and Luella (Brown) Branch; A.B., U. of Kan., 1908, A.M., 1912; Ph.D., Cornell, 1921; unmarried. Grad. asst., biology, Cornell, 1918-22; prof. of biology, Fairmount College, Wichita, Kan., 1922-26; prof. of zoology, U. of Wichita since 1926. Mem. A.A.A.S. (fellow), Am. Soc. Parasitologists, Am. Soc. Zoologists, Entomol. Soc. of Am., Kan. Acad. of Sci. (pres., 1931). Home: Wichita, Kan. *

BRAND, CARL FREMONT, educator; b. Greenfield, Ind., Oct. 8, 1892; s. Charles Samuel and Jessie Fremont (Davis) B.; A.B., Ind. U., 1915; A.M., 1916; A.M. Harvard, 1918, Ph.D., 1923; m. Nan Alwilda Surface, Sept. 12, 1930; children—Charles Macy, Robert Alan, Donald Edwin. Instr. history, Smith Coll., 1919-20, U. of Mich., 1921-24; asst. prof., history, Stanford U., 1924-30, asso. prof., 1930-40, prof. of history, 1940-58, emeritus professor, 1958-81; visiting prof. of history U. Cal. at Los Angeles, 1964-65. Member American Hist. Assn., Pacific Coast Conf. Brit. Studies (pres. 1960-61), Pacific Coast Br. Am. Hist. Assn. (sec.-treas., 1928-34, v.p., 1948, pres., 1949). Author: The Know Nothing Party in Indiana (serially in Ind. Mag. of History), Mar.-Sept. 1922; British Labour's Rise to Power, 1941; The British Labour Party: A Short History, 1964. Home: Stanford, Calif. Died Mar. 21, 1981.

BRAND, LOUIS, mathematician, educator; b. Cin., Sept. 27, 1885; s. Louis William and Josephine (Zingsheim) B.; Ch.E., U. Cin., 1907, E.E., 1908, A.M., 1909, Doctor of Science (honorary), 1956; Ph.D., Harvard University, 1917; m. Lulu Edith Shinkle, Aug. 14, 1915; children—Sara Josephine (Mrs. Oliver Marcy), Martha Louise (Mrs. Bruce Raymond). Head dept. mathematics and mechanics, coll. engring. U. Cin., 1919-56, head dept. mathematics, 1935-56, prof. emeritus, 1956—; Whitney vis. prof. Trinity Coll., 1956-57; M.D. Anderson professor of mathematics University of Houston, Tex., 1957—; vis. prof. University of Brazil, 1963. Fellow grad. sch. arts and scis. 1932—. Fellow A.A.A.S., Ohio, Tex. acads. scis.; mem. Am. Math. Soc., Am. Math. Assn., Sigma Xi, Tau Beta Pi, Phi Kappa Phi. Author math. textbooks, latest being Differential and Difference Equations, 1967; also articles math. jours. Home: Houston. *

BRAND, VANCE, banker, lawyer; b. Urbana, Ohio, Sept. 14, 1906; s. Charles and Louise (Vance) B.; A.B., LL.B., George Washington U.; D.Sc., Universitatis Administrationtio, Monterrey, Mexico; m. Katherine Lyon; children—Louise (Mrs. Tyler), Dixie, Joseph, Charles Vance. Admitted to Ohio, D.C., Fed. bars; gen. counsel, sec. Imported Date Assn.; gen. counsel, dir. Champaign Nat. Bank, 1935-79, pres., 1950-54; dir. Export-Import Bank, Washington, 1954-59; mem. bd., mng. dir. Devel. Loan Fund, 1959-61; chmn. Vance Brand Co. Mem., sec. citizens adv. com. U.S. Senate Banking and Currency Com.; sr. adviser Am. delegation Council OAS, Bogota, Colombia, 1960. Recipient George Washington U. Alumni achievement award in law and internat. finance, 1960. Mem. Champaign County Bar Assn. (pres.). Clubs: Metropolitan, Burning Tree (Washington); Golf (New Albany, Ohio); Rolling Rock (Ligonier, Pa.); Country of Fla. (Delray); Urbana Country. Home: Woodstock, Ohio. Died Mar. 29, 1979; buried Urbana, Ohio.

BRANDLI, HENRY EDWARD, oil exec.; b. Joplin, Mo., 1884. Vice pres., gen. mgr., dir. Cities Service Oil Co. (Pa.); pres., dir. Crew Lerick Corp. (both N.Y.C.). Petrol Corp. (Md.), Patroil Corp., Petrol Tanker Industries, Inc., Tanker Sag Harber Corp.; pres., mem. exec. com., dir. Cities Service Oil Co. of Argentina, Buenos Aires; dir. Petroleum Advs., Inc., N.Y.C., Service Oil Co., Inc. Mason (Shriner). Home: N.Y.C. *

BRANDON, J. CAMPBELL, lawyer; b. Butler, Pa., July 17, 1884; s. W.D. and Clara B. (Campbell) B.; grad. Mercersburg Acad., 1902; A.B., Princeton, 1906; student Harvard Law Sch., 1906-08; m. Kathleen Walker, June 11, 1914; children—J. Campbell, Virginia (Mrs. Carlton W. Bristol, Jr.), John W. III. Admitted to Pa. bar, 1910, U.S. Supreme Ct., 1935. Served with U.S. Army, 1917-18; AEF. Mem. Am., Pa. (pres. 1954-55), Okla., Butler County bar assns. Mason. Clubs: Butler Country; Harvard-Yale-Princeton (Pitts.). Home: Butler, Pa.; (winter) Tucson. *

BRANIGIN, ROGER DOUGLAS, gov. Ind., lawyer; b. Franklin, Ind., July 26, 1902; s. Elba L. and Zula (Francis) B.; A.B., Franklin Coll., 1923, LL.D., 1956; LL.B., Harvard, 1926; LL.D., Butler U., Ind. U., Ind. State U., Vincennes U.; m. Josephine Mardis, Nov. 2, 1929; children—Roger, Robert M. Admitted to Ind.

bar, 1926; dep. pros. atty., Franklin, Ind., 1926-29; counsel Fed. Land Bank and FCA, Louisville, 1930-38, gen. counsel, 1932-38; pvt. practice law, 1938-42, 46-65; gov. State of Ind., 1965-69; practiced in Lafayette, Ind., 1969-75. Hon. dir. Lafayette Nat. Bank, Lafayette Life Ins. Co. Past pres. Harrison council Boy Scouts Am. Chmn. Ind. Democratic conv., 1948. Trustee Franklin Coll., Purdue U., Asso. Colls. Ind., Conner Prairie Farms, Inc., Lilly Endowment, Indpls., Athenaum, Indpls. Served to lt. col. AUS, 1942-46; chief legal div., transp. corps, 1944-45. Decorated Legion of Merit. Hon. fellow Lilly Library Ind. U. Mem. Harvard Law Sch. Assn., Am. Legion, Ind. (pres. 1951-52), Am. (ho. of dels.) bar assns., Am. Coll. Trial Lawyers, C. of C. (past pres.), Am. Law Inst., Indiana Soc. of Chgo. (v.p.), Am. Counsel Assn., Am. Judicature Soc. (dir.), Newcomen Soc., Ind. Hist. Soc. (trustee), Indpls. Lit. Club, Phi Delta Phi, Phi Delta Theta. Mason, Elk. Clubs: Indianapolis Athletic Town and Gown, Press (hon. life) (Indpls.); Sagamore of the Wabash; Legal (hon. life Chgo.); Lawyers (U. Mich). Home: Lafayette, Ind. Died Nov. 19, 1975.

BRANSOM, (JOHN) PAUL, painter, illustrator; b. Washington, D.C., July 26, 1885; s. John James and Margaret (Myers) B.; ed. pub. schs., Washington, D.C.; m. Grace H. Bond of Chicago, Ill., Jan. 31, 1906. Patent draftsman, 1898-1901, then draftsman with Southern R.R., and later with Gen. Electric Co.; joined staff of New York Evening Journal in 1902 as comic artist and continued the strip "Latest News from Bugville" created by Gus Dirks; free lance illustrator of animal stories since 1906; Clubs: Water Color, Salmagundi, Dutch Treat (New York). Home: Canada Lake, N.Y. *

BRANT, IRVING NEWTON, editor, writer; b. Walker, Iowa, Jan. 17, 1885; s. David and Ruth (Hurd) B.; A.B., U. Ia., 1909; m. Hazeldean Toof, Sept. 3, 1913; children—Ruth (Mrs. Jack Davis), Robin (Mrs. Kenneth Lodewick). Reporter, later mng. editor Iowa City Republican, 1909-14; editor Clinton (Ia.) Herald, 1914-15; asso. editor Des Moines Register and Tribune, 1915-18; editorial writer and editor editorial page St. Louis Star, 1918-23; editor editorial page St. Louis Star-Times, 1930-38, contbg. editor, 1938-41; editorial writer Chicago Sun, 1941-43, fgn. corr., 1945. Cons. covering personal assistance to Sec. of Interior Ickes and Roosevelt, PWA, 1938-40; dir. Nat. Pub. Ho. Conf., N.Y.C., 1935-44; treas. Emergency Conservation Com., N.Y.C., 1930-62; mem. council Inst. Early Am. History and Culture, 1959-62; mem. adv. bd. James Madison Papers, U. Chgo.; vis. scholar U. Va., 1963-64; vis. prof. history U. Oreg., Spring 1966. Recipient E. B. MacNaughton award Oreg. affiliate ACLU, 1971; Disting. Service award U. Oreg., 1974. Mem. Soc. Am. Historians, Overseas Writers, Phi Theta Kappa, Delta Sigma Rho. Author: Dollars and Sense, 1933; Storm Over the Constitution, 1936; Enlargement of Olympic National Park, 1938; James Madison: The Virginia Revolutionist, (Vol. I), 1941; Road to Peace and Freedom, 1943; The New Poland, 1946; James Madison: The Nationalist, 1780-1787 (Vol. II), 1948; James Madison: Father of the Constitution, 1787-1800 (Vol. III), 1950; James Madison: Secretary of State, 1800-1809, (Vol. IV), 1953; James Madison: The President, 1809-1812 (Vol. V), 1956; James Madison: Commander in Chief, 1812-1836 (Vol. VI), 1961; Friendly Cove (hist. novel), 1963; The Bill of Rights: Its Origin and Meaning, 1965; James Madison and American Nationalism, 1967; The Fourth President: A Life of James Madison, 1969; Impeachment: Trials and Errors, 1972; (juvenile) The Cave of Kingarew, 1979, The Youngest Argonaut, 1979. Contbr. sect. The Madison Heritage to book The Great Rights, 1963; sect. Election of 1808 to book The History of American Presidential Elections, 1971; numerous others. Address: Eugene, Oreg. Died Sept. 18, 1976.

BRAUER, RICHARD DAGOBERT, mathematician, educator; b. Berlin, Feb. 10, 1901; s. Max and Lilly Caroline (Jacob) B.; Ph.D. summa cum laude, U. Berlin, 1925; D. Math. (hon.), U. Waterloo, 1968; D.Sc., U. Chgo., 1969, U. Notre Dame, 1974, Brandeis U., 1975; m. Ilse Karger, Sept. 17, 1925; children—George Ulrich, Fred Gunter. Naturalized U.S. citizen, 1954. Privatdozent, U. Koenigsberg (Germany), 1927-33; vis. prof. U. Ky., 1933-34; asst. Inst. for Advanced Study, Princeton, N.J., 1934-35; asst. prof. U. Toronto, 1935-43, asso. prof., 1943-46, prof., 1946-48; math. U. Mich., 1948-52; prof. math. Harvard, Cambridge, Mass., 1952-66, Perkins prof. math., 1966-71, Perkins prof. emeritus, 1971-77. Vis. prof. Nagoya U., 1959, U. Chgo., 1968-69, 74, U. Aarhus, Denmark, 1972. Gauss prof. Akademie der Wissenschaften, Göttingen, 1964. Fellow John Simon Guggenheim Found., 1941-42. Recipient Nat. Medal Sci., 1970. Mem. Royal Soc. Can., Am. Math. Soc. (Cole prize 1949; v.p. 1952-53, pres. 1957-58), Nat. Acad. Sci., Math. Assn. Am., Am. Acad. Arts and Scis., Canadian Math. Congress, Akademie der Wissenschafter Göttingen (fgn. mem.), Am. Philos. Soc. Home: Belmont, Mass. Died Apr. 17, 1977.

BRAUN, GAIUS A., business exec.; b. Wauseon, O., 1885; children—Mrs. Howard J. Werner, Samuel J. Former pres. Prosperity Co., Inc., Syracuse, N.Y.; now chmn. bd. G. A. Braun, Incorporated. Mem. Apostolic Christian Ch. Club: Lake Shore (Chgo.). Address: Syracuse, N.Y. *

BRAY, EVERETT NEWTON, mfg. exec.; b. Boston, Aug. 9, 1886; s. Mellen N. and Alice L. (Sanborn) B.; A.B., Harvard, 1909; m. Esther Ela Clapp, May 30, 1910 (dec.); children—Everett Newton (dec.), Philip Vaughan, Ruth (Mrs. Smith). Dir. Tubular Rivet & Stud Co., 1916, later vice pres., became pres., 1946, also chmn., ret. as cons. Club: Harvard (Boston). Home: N. Falmouth, Mass. *

BRAY, JOHN RANDOLPH, motion picture producer; b. Addison, Mich., Aug. 25, 1879; s. Rev. Edward A. and Sarah Priscilla (Haire) B.; student Alma (Mich.) Coll., 1895-96; m. Margaret Till, Aug. 25, 1905; 1 son, Paul A. Artist Detroit Evening News, 1901, Bklyn. Daily Eagle, 1903-04; contbr. cartoons to Life, Puck, Judge, McClure Newspaper Syndicate European humorous mags., 1905-13; invented and developed animated motion picture cartoon processes; introduced first animated cartoon in theatres, 1912; patented processes by which animated cartoons are made; organized Bray-Hurd Process Co., 1914, to issue licenses under these patents; put into this co. his three basic patents, and one patent by Earl Hurd covering an improvement; organized chmn. bd. Bray Studios Inc., 1914, to produce animated cartoons in quantity; developed and also introduced animated technical drawing, 1916. During World War I, pioneered use motion pictures to expedite tng. of draft army; made over 100 tng. films for same; have continued prodn. for Navy and Air Force since. Producer tng., ednl., comml. and documentary films. Recipient citation for patriotic civilian service to Dept. of Army, 1956, citation as animation pioneer World Retrospective on Animation, 1967. Republican. Home: Bridgeport CT *

BRAY, RICHARD MARVIN, univ. dean; b. Redvale, Colo., June 12, 1915; s. Edgar W. and Mattie Kate (Ensign) B.; B.A., U. Colo., 1938, M.A., 1939; m. Mayfield Sleeth, Oct. 15, 1938; children—Michael Edgar, Mayfield Ruth, Martha Alaetha. Dir. Denver Extension Center, U. Colo., 1939-47, Spokane Center State Coll. of Wash., 1947-54; faculty Am. U., 1954-70, prof. govt., 1958-70, asso. dean faculty, 1957-70, dean Coll. of Continuing Edn., 1964-70. Chmn. organizing com. Washington Center for Met. Studies, 1956-58; supr. Adams-Morgan Demonstration Project, prevention urban blight, 1958-60; chmn. com. on univ. ednl. policy, 1962-63; mem. com. of 100 for Federal City, chmn. subcoms. on parks and conservation; chmn. Citizens Council for a Clean Potomac, 1956-58; pres. Adult Edn. Assn. Greater Washington, 1956. Bd. dirs., exec. com. Nat. Inst. Labor Edn. Mem. Assn. U. Evening Colls., Adult Edn. Assn. U.S., Lambda Alpha, Pi Sigma Alpha, Phi Alpha Theta. Democrat. Conglist. Home: Bethesda, Md. Died May 18, 1980.

BRAYTON, DEAN FLEMING (BRAY TON), lawyer; b. Cincinnati, Feb. 9, 1884; s. Forrest W. and Martha Tullis (Pollock) B.; A.B., Ohio Wesleyan U., 1904; LL.B., U. Cincinnati, 1907; m. Aileen Maclean, June 28, 1911; children—Donald F., Nancy (Mrs. Thomas W. Harris), Susan (Mrs. John H. Lipscomb). Admitted to Ohio bar, 1906, Utah bar, 1909, Nev. bar, 1912; practicing lawyer, Cincinnati, 1906-09, Salt Lake City, since 1909; mem. Gustin, Gillette & Brayton, 1910-21, Stephens, Brayton & Bagley, 1923-26, Stephens, Brayton & Lowe, 1926-60, Brayton, Lowe & Hurley, 1960—; bd. directors Waterworks Equipment Company, and also the Crager Wire & Iron Works, Colonial Corp., Arnold Machinery Co. Chmn. Utah Supreme Ct. Com. to Draft Rules Civil Procedure and Jud. Code, 1943-51; chmn. panel 2 Utah State Appeal Bd., Selective Service. Republican candidate U.S. Rep. 2d dist. Utah, 1938. Served as 1st lt. F.A., U.S. Army; instr. Saumur Arty. Sch., 313th F.A., France, World War I. Mem. Am. and Utah State (pres. 1931) bar assns., S.A.R., Newcomen Soc., Phi Delta Phi, Alpha Tau Omega. Mason. Clubs: University, Fort Douglas, Rotary (past pres.) (Salt Lake City). Home: Salt Lake City. *

BRAZIER, CARL EDWARD (BRA'SHER), editor; b. Revere, Mass., Dec. 25, 1885; student Harvard Coll., 1904-08; m. 2d, Edith Bryant Duncan, May 18, 1934; children (by previous marriage)—Carl Edward, Donald Gerrish, Marjorie Ellen (Mrs. Folke Olsen). With Chico (Cal.) Enterprise, Sacramento (Cal.) Union, Oakland (Cal.) Tribune, 1909-19; various editorial capacities Seattle Times, 1920—. Home: Seattle, Wash. *

BREAZEALE, HOPKINS PAYNE, lawyer; b. Natchitoches, La., Oct. 16, 1886; s. Hopkins Payne and Cammila (Lachs) B.; A.B., La. Northeastern Coll., 1905; LL.B., Yale, 1910; m. Nita Sims, Nov. 22, 1916; children—Hopkins Payne, Nita Sims (Mrs. Maurice J. Wilson), Robert P. Sch. tchr., 1905-07; admitted to Conn. bar, 1910, La. bar, 1911, since practiced in Baton Rouge; sr. mem. Breazeale, Sachse & Wilson; U.S. referee in bankruptcy, 1919-45; city atty., Baton Rouge, 1924-45; dir., atty. Fidelity Nat. Bank; mem. Jud. Council 5th Circuit Ct. of Appeals 1945—. Mem. exec. com. Baton Rouge Community Chest and United Givers, Pub. Affairs Research Council La.; dir. La. Heart Assn., Inc. Mem., sec. bd. appeals SSS No. 2, 1940-47. Served as capt. 358th inf. 90th Div., U.S. Army, World War I; officer in charge Civil Affairs Pelm. Germany, 1918; participated in Preny, St. Mehielf, St. Mihiel, Meuse Argonne offensives. Decorated For Gallantry in Action. Mem. Am., Baton Rouge (pres. 1935-36), La. State (pres. 1931-32) bar assns., Nat. Assn. of R.R. Trial Counsel, Am. Judicature Soc., Am. Legion (charter mem. Nicholson post; dep. judge adv. La. dept.), Baton Rouge C. of C. (past pres.), La. Golf Assn. (past pres.), Am Counsel Assn., Baton Rouge Community Concerts, Baton Rouge Symphony Soc., Newcomen Soc., Selden Soc., U.S. C. of C. (counsellor 1940-49), La. Law Inst., Phi Delta Pi. Episcopalian (vestryman). Mason, Elk (past exalted ruler). Clubs: Baton Rouge Country (past pres.), City (Baton Rouge); Boston, Avoca (New Orleans). Author: Revenue Laws of Louisiana (with Porter), 1912; History-358th Combat Infantry, 90th Division, World War I. Home: Baton Rouge LA *

BRECHT, ARNOLD, prof. polit. science, jurisprudence and pub. finance; b. Lübeck, Germany, Jan. 26, 1884; s. Ernst Walther and Marie (Weishaupt) B.; student univs. of Bonn, Berlin, Göttingen, 1902-05; Dr. Juris Utriusque, U. of Leipzig, 1906; studied govt. and administrn. of France and Eng., 1927, of U.S., since 1933; m. Clara Ernestine Berg, Dec. 4, 1915. In-service training, province of Hanover and in Berlin, 1905-10; Judge in Lübeck, 1910; Berlin, 1914-17; sec. com. on reform penal code, 1911-13; held. high exec. positions as non-partisan official, 1910-33, in ministry of justice, 1910-18, economics, 1918, interior, 1921-27, Prussian state and finance ministries, 1927-33; Reich Chancellory, 1918-21, under 7 Reich chancellors; apptd. privy councillor, 1919; ministerial dir., 1921-33; mem. governmental com. on Fed. reform, 1928; chief del., later leading del. to Fed. Council; vice pres. Nat. Debts Commn., also of Inst. of Economy in Pub. Adminstrn.; mem. bd. trustees Postal Service and of Pub. Works Corp., 1928-33; defended democracy against Papen coup before Supreme Court, 1932; ousted from office, arrested but released, left Germany and came to U.S., 1933; now U.S. citizen. Lecturer, then chmn. dept. on pub. law, Hochschule für Politik, 1928-33; mem. grad. faculty New Sch. for Social Research, N.Y.C., 1933-54, emeritus, 1954—; guest lectr. Harvard, 1937, 40; Woodward lectr. Yale, 1944; lectr. Civil Affairs Tng. Schs. of Harvard and Yale, 1943-44. Chmn. spl. com. on comparative adminstrn. Social Sci. Research Council, 1942-44; v.p. Am. Polit. Sci. Assn., 1946; cons. to high commr. Germany, 1950, to O.M.G., Germany, summer 1948; German state sec., ret., 1953; guest prof. Heidelberg, 1952, 54, 55. Mem. research council Inst. World Affairs (N.Y.C.), 1945-54. Author: Prelude to Science, 1944; Federalism in Germany, 1945; The Political Philosophy of Arnold Brecht (collected essays), 1954; Political Theory (Woodrow Wilson award Am. Polit. Sci. Assn. 1960), 1959; also articles. Home: N.Y.C. *

BRECKINRIDGE, JOHN BAYNE, lawyer, congressman; b. Washington, Nov. 29, 1913; s. Scott Dudley and Gertrude (Ashby-Bayne) B.; A.B., U. Ky., 1937, LL.B., 1939; m. Frances Archibald, Aug. 12, 1945; children—Knight (Mrs. Stephen Osheroff), John Bayne; m. 2d, Helen Congleton, July 5, 1954. Admitted to Ky. bar, 1940; atty. anti-trust div. Dept. of Justice, 1940-41; pvt. practice of law, 1946-72; mem. Ky. Ho. of Reps., 1956-59; atty. gen. Ky., 1960-64, 68-72; mem. 93d-95th congresses from 6th Ky. Dist., mem. Agr. com., Small Bus. com., chmn. Congl. Rural Caucus, 1975-78; corp. counsel City Lexington (Ky.), 1964. Del. to White House Conf. on Children and Youth, 1960; mem. adv. com. state ofcls. AEC; past chmn. So. Interstate Nuclear Bd.; chmn. Ky. Adv. Com. Nuclear Energy, 1960-66; bd. trustees Frontier Nursing Service, Ky. Employee's Retirement System, Ky. Tchrs. Retirement System, Ky. State Law Library; commr. Nat. Conf. Commns. on Uniform State Laws, 1960-64; mem. Ky. Constitution Revision Com., 1960-62; mem. Ky. Atomic Energy and Space Authority, 1964-79, dir., 1966-67; counsel Ky. Citizens for Child Welfare, 1956-59. Bd. dirs. Ky. Welfare Assn., v.p., 1962-63; bd. dirs., vice chmn. Ky. Social Welfare Found.; chmn. Ky. Sci. and Tech. Adv. Council, 1966-68; mem. Ky. Commn. on Children and Youth, 1966-79, Ky. Health and Geriatric Authority, Ky. Turnpike Authority, Ky. Pub. Sch. Authority, Ky. State Property and Bldg. Commn., Ky. State Archives and Records Commn.; v.p., mem. operating bd. officers and exec. com. United Cerebral Palsy Assn., Inc., past asst. v.p. So. region, past pres. United Cerebral Palsy of Ky., United Cerebral Palsy of Bluegrass. Del. Democratic Nat. Conv., mem. rules com., Los Angeles, 1960. Served from 1st lt. to col., AUS, 1941-46; chief projects and indsl. licensing div. Bd. Econ. Warfare, 1941-42, asst. chief internat. div. USAFIME Hdqrs., comdg. officer Mil. Liaison Hdqrs., Albania. Recipient Distinguished Alumni award U. Ky., 1974. Mem. Am. Council for Community (past mem. exec. com., dir.), Am., Ky., Fayette County bar assns., Am. Judicature Soc. (dir. Ky.), Ky. Hist. Soc. (pres. 1962-64), Atlantic Union Com. (pres. Ky. chpt. mem. council), Nat. Assn. Attys. Gen. (chmn. com.

Office Atty. Gen., 1968-72, Wyman award, 1968-69), V.F.W., Am. Legion, Kappa Alpha (pres. Theta chpt. 1936-37). Democrat. Contbr. articles to legal jours. Home: Lexington, Ky. Died July 29, 1979; buried Lexington.

BREECE, CHARLES ALBERT (BRES), professl. engr.; b. Canal Fulton, O., Jan. 27, 1884; s. Charles Wesley and Mary Jane (Mills) B.; ed. Canal Fulton High Sch., and university extension courses in engineering, law, business, etc.; m. Georgia Alfreda Cripps, Nov. 24, 1905; children—Lynn Albert, Charles Albert. Began as switchboard repairman, Central Union Telephone Company, Akron, Ohio, 1901, and advanced to district toll wire chief; in division wire chief's office, same company, Columbus, O., 1907, and with chief engr., Indianapolis, Ind., 1907-14; gen. mgr. and auditor United Telephone Co., Bluffton, Ind., 1914-20; gen. comml. supt. Ind. Bell Telephone Co. and charge unification of Indianapolis Telephone Co. with Ind. Bell Co., 1920-22; v.p. and gen. supt. Ind. Bell Interest Cos., 1922-29, communication engr., 1929-33; mkt. and developmt. engr., 1933-49. Dir., v.p. Wheeler City Rescue Mission, Indianapolis; pres. Indianapolis Church Fedn., 1944-45; chmn. Indianapolis Census Tract Com., 1939-40, 1949-50. Registered profl. engr. Member Bell Telephone Club (president 1925), Hoosier State Chap., Telephone Pioneers of Am. (pres. 1926), Sons Am. Revolution (nat. trustee; nat. v.p. gen. 1932-33; pres. Ind. Soc. 1939); asso. mem. Ill. Soc. Order of Founders and Patriots of America. Presbyn. (edler). Mason (K.T., 32 deg., Shriner; past master, past illus. master of Council). Clubs: Columbia, Scientech, Emeritus (Indianapolis). Home: Nashville, Indiana.*

BREECH, ERNEST ROBERT, ret. industrialist; b. Lebanon, Mo., Feb. 24, 1897; s. Joseph F.E. and Martha (Atchley) B.; student Drury Coll., Springfield, Mo., 1915-17, Walton Sch. Commerce, 1918-21; C.P.A., U. Ill., 1921; LL.D., Drury Coll., U. Mo., U. Detroit, U. Mich.; D.Sc. in Bus. Adminstrn. (hon.), Bowling Green (Ohio) State U.; m. Thelma Rowden, Nov. 11, 1917; children—Ernest Robert, William Howard. Accountant, Fairbanks, Morse & Co., Chgo., 1917-20; auditor Adams & Westlake, Chgo., 1920-22; comptroller Yellow Cab Mfg. Co., Chgo., 1923-29; dir. Yellow Truck & Coach Mfg. Co., Chgo., 1927-33; gen. asst. treas. Gen. Motors Corp., N.Y.C., 1929-33, group exec., 1935-39; pres. N.Am. Aviation, 1933-35, chmn. 1933-42, v.p. charge household appliance div., aviation subsidiaries, mem. adminstrn. com., 1939-42; pres. Bendix Aviation Corp., 1942-46; exec. v.p. Ford Motor Co., 1946-55, chmn. bd., alternate chief exec. officer, 1955-60, chmn. finance com., 1960-61, dir., 1946-67; chmn. Trans-World Airlines, 1961-69, hon. chmn., dir. emeritus, 1969-78. Mem. Business Council, 1954-59, vice chmn., 1957-58, hon. mem., 1967-78. Chmn. Central Aircraft Council, Detroit, 1942-45. Mem. Anglo-Am. Council on Productivity, 1948; mem. Panel on Peaceful Uses of Atomic Energy, 1955. Hon. trustee Drury Coll. Republican. Mason (33 deg.). Clubs: Bloomfield Hills (Mich.) Country; Little Harbor (Harbor Springs, Mich.); Wequetonsing (Mich.) Golf; Paradise Valley (Scottsdale, Ariz.). Address: Detroit, Mich. Died July 3, 1978.

BREED, JAMES MCVICKAR, lawyer; b. Malone, N.Y., May 15, 1880; A.B., Amherst Coll., 1903; LL.B., N.Y. Law Sch., 1905. Admitted to N.Y. bar, 1905, since practiced in N.Y.C.; mem. firm Breed, Abbott & Morgan, Mem. Am., N.Y. State bar assns., Assn. Bar City N.Y., N.Y. County Lawyers Assn. *

BREEDIS, CHARLES, educator; b. Morrisville, Pa., Aug. 7, 1911; s. Anthony and Ottilia (Kallenberg) B.; A.B., N.Y. U., 1938; M.D., Cornell U., 1942; m. Marjorie Alberta Andresen, Feb. 17, 1968; stepchildren—Richard G., Elizabeth A., Diane P., Patricia M., Stephen A., Peter J., John K. (all McManus). Intern, Grasslands Hosp., Valhalla, N.Y., 1943; instr. U. Pa. Sch. Medicine, Phila., 1946-50, asst. prof., 1951-55, asso. prof., 1955-59, prof. pathology, 1959-79, emeritus prof. pathology, 1979-81, chmn. grad. group pathology, 1965-81, dir. pathology Div. Grad. Medicine, 1968-81. Mem. pathology study sect. USPHS, 1962-66. Served with M.C., AUS, 1944-46. Cancer research grantee USPHS, 1952-81. Mem. Am. Assn. Cancer Research, Am. Assn. Pathologists and Bacteriologists, Am. Soc. for Cell Biology, Am. Soc. for Exptl. Pathology, AAUP, AAAS, N.Y. Acad. Scis., Franklin Inst., Sigma Xi. Contbr. articles on growth and cancer to profl. jours. Home: Drexel Hill, Pa. Died Apr. 24, 1981; buried Arlington Cemetery, Drexel Hill.

BREEN, LEONARD ZACHARY, sociologist, educator; b. Chgo., Sept. 26, 1922; s. Joseph A. and Jennie (Nelson) B.; B.S., Ill. Inst. Tech., 1949; M.A., U. Chgo., 1950, Ph.D., 1956; m. Mildred A. Steinberg, June 25, 1946; children—Jeni Ann, Martha Gail, Richard Joseph. Sr. study dir. Chgo. Community Inventory, 1949-51; asst. prof. polit., social sci. Ill. Inst. Tech., Chgo., 1951-55; asst. prof. sociology U. Chgo., 1955-57; asso. prof. Purdue U., Lafayette, Ind., 1957-63, prof., 1963-77, head dept. sociology, 1967-77; asst. dean grad. sch., 1966-67. Vis. prof. sociology Indian Inst. Tech., Kanpur, U.P., India, 1964-66, U. Essex, Colchester, Eng., 1971; cons. Ind. State Commn. on Aging, Aged, 1966-77; dir. post doctoral studies Midwest Council for Social Research in Aging, 1976-77. Served with USAAF, 1942-46. Fellow Am. Sociol. Assn., The Gerontol. Soc. Author articles, chpts. on gerontology to profl. mags., books. Home: West Lafayette, Ind. Died Apr. 16, 1977.

BREER, CARL, retired engineering consultant; b. Los Angeles, California, Nov. 8, 1883; s. Louis and Julia (Buehn) B.; A.B. in Mechanical Engineering, Stanford U., 1909; hon. Master of Engring., 1933, hon. Dr. Engring., 1938; m. Barbara Zeder, Sept. 5, 1918; children—Carl Frederick, William Zeder, Robert Carlton, Thomas Carol. Apprentice Allis Chalmers Co., Milwaukee, Wis., 1909-12; supt. of plant Moreland Distillate Truck Co., Los Angeles, 1912-14; organized Acme Elec. Auto Works and part owner, 1914-16; research engr. Studebaker Corp., 1916-20; with Willys Corp., Elizabeth, N.J., 1920-21; mem. Zeder, Skelton & Breer, cons. engrs., 1921-23; exec. engr. Maxwell Motor Car Corp., 1923-25; exec. engr., dir. of research Chrysler 1925-49; engring. consultant, Chrysler Corp., 1949-52, ret., dir., 1937-53; of first Chrysler-built car in 1924. Mem. Society Automotive Engineers, Am. Society Mech. Engineers (fellow), Engring. Society Detroit, Franklin Institute, A.A.A.S., Sigma Xi, Tau Beta Pi. Clubs: Detroit, Detroit Athletic, Country, Old (Detroit); Grosse Pointe Yacht, Question, Economic (Detroit); Aero Club of Mich. Home: Grosse Pointe Park, Mich.; (winter) Pasadena, Cal. *

BREL, JACQUES, composer, lyicist, singer; b. Brussels, Belgium, Apr. 8, 1929; m.; children—Chantal, France, Isabelle. Worked in father's corrugated carton factory, 1948-53; singer-writer 1948-78; debut at Theater of the Three Donkeys, Paris, 1953, then appeared at l'Ecluse, Patachou, Olympia; toured with Sydney Bechet in provinces and N. Africa, 1955; singing tours in Paris at Alhambra, 1957, Olympia, 1958, 61, 64, 66, Bobino, 1959, USSR, 1965; radio performances in The Idiot, Lettres d'amour, also serial En attendant Madeleine; cinema performances Les Risques du metizr, 1967, la Bande à Bonnot, 1968; theatre performances L'Homme de la Mancha, Brussels and Paris, 1968; appeared in 4 films, France; wrote over 500 songs, some of which were presented in English transl. in Off-Broadway revue Jacques Brel Is Alive and Well and Living in Paris; prin. songs include: Ne me quitte pas, les Bourgeois, Mathilde, le Boribord, les Bonbons, Amsterdam, Jacky, Mon Enfance, Fils de, Les Vieux Amants, Quand on a que L'Amour, others. Home: Paris, France. Died Oct. 9, 1978.

BRENAN, RALPH BETTS, business exec.; b. St. John, N.B., Can., Nov. 20, 1901; s. Frederick Betts and Mabel Ella (Engall) B.; student pub. schs., St. John; m. Gertrude Edna Hunt, Oct. 17, 1927; children—Ralph Betts, Diana Hunt. With T.H. Estabrooks Co., Ltd., 1922-49, pres., 1938-49; mng. dir. G. E. Barbour Co., Ltd., 1949-58, pres., 1958-76, chmn. bd., 1968-76; v.p., dir. Fraser Cos. Ltd.; dir. Adm. Beatty Hotel Co., Fundy Broadcasting Co., Crush Internat., Zeller's, Ltd., Can. Cement LaFarge Ltd. Clubs: Union, Cliff (St. John); Mt. Royal (Montreal Que.). Home: Rothesay, N.B., Canada. Died Oct. 10, 1976.

BRENIZER, ADDISON GORGAS (BREN'I-ZER), surgeon; b. Charlotte, N.C., July 24, 1883; s. Addison Gorgas and Frances M. (Gilmer) B.; A.B., U. of N.C., 1903, student med. dept. same, 1904; M.D., Johns Hopkins, 1907; Dr. von Med., Heidelberg, 1908; m. Mary Richmond Harding, Apr. 9, 1913; children—Addison Gorgas, Mildred Harding, Harriet Irving. Was asst. and interne, surg. clinic, U. of Heidelberg; asst. gynecol. clinic, U. of Vienna; surgeon in charge American Hospital, Paris; practiced at Charlotte since 1911; surgeon to Presbyterian Hospital and Charlotte Sanatorium, Memorial Hospital. Former instructor in operative surgery and surgical pathology North Carolina Medical College, 1911-13. Organized hospital unit and took it to France, with 3 other units; chief of surgical service, Base Hospital No. 6 (5,000 beds), A.E.F., France, 1917-19; major and lieutenant col. Med. Corps, U.S. Army. Organized the 111th Station Hospital, Assam, India, 106th Station Hospital, Italy, World War II, now on foreign service. Fellow American College Surgeons, Southern Surg. Assn., Am. Assn. for Study of Goiter, Am. Assn. Traumatic Sur., Sigma Alpha Epsilon, Nu Sigma Nu. Presbyterian. Clubs: Kiwanis, Goodfellows. Author of many professional papers. Former lecturer on surgery, Duke Univ. Home: Charlotte, N.C. *

BRENN, HARRY ALLEN, fgn. service officer; b. Spearfish, S.D., May 4, 1903; s. Milton Lafayette and Emma (Stannus) B.; student Northern Coll. of S.D., 1920-21; B.S., U. Idaho, 1925, grad. student econs.; m. Hester Madelyn Yost, July 27, 1927; children—Harry M., Bruce M. Pvt. bus. hardware and contracting, Idaho, 1927-47; policy adviser Gen. McArthur's staff, rehabilitation of Japan, South East Asia Mineral. Development for U.S. stockpile, Singapore; dir. FOA/ICA, U.S. Operations Mission to P.I., 1953-58; dir. U.S. Operations Mission to Iran, 1958-62. Mem. Idaho Senate, 1937-40. Served from capt. to col. F.A., AUS, 1940-46; gen. purchasing agt. Occupation Forces Japan. Decorated Legion of Merit with cluster; distinguished pub. service award FOA, 1955. Clubs: Rotary Internat. (dist. gov. 1971-72, Paul Harris fellow 1972), Olympia Shrine (pres. 1967-68), Knife and Fork (pres. Port Angeles, Wash. chpt. 1968-69). Home: Sequim, Wash. Died Aug. 27, 1976; interred Ocean View Cemetery, Port Angeles.

BRENNAN, DONALD GEORGE, strategist, mathematician; b. Waterbury, Conn., Apr. 9, 1926; s. George J. and Jessie (Griswold) B.; B.S., Mass. Inst. Tech., 1955, Ph.D. in Math. (Gerard Swope fellow), 1959; m. Katie Sheldon, Oct. 11, 1969 (dec. May 17, 1975). Chief engr. radio sta. WWCO, Waterbury, 1947-49; mem. staff Crystal Research Lab., Hartford, Conn., also instr. Ward Sch. Electronics, U. Hartford, 1949-51; mem. staff Lincoln Lab., Mass. Inst. Tech., 1953-59, group leader, 1959-62; research asso. math. Mass. Inst. Tech., 1959-61; pres. Hudson Inst., Croton-on-Hudson, N.Y., 1962-64, dir. nat. security studies, 1964-80; cons. Dept. Def., State Dept., ACDA, Dept. Energy, Exec. Office Pres.; lectr. strategy, arms control, mil. policy in fgn. countries, U.S. Nat., Air, and Naval War colls., Can. Nat. Def. Coll.; dir. World Trading and Shipping Corp. Mem. Pres.'s Nat. Citizens' Commn. Internat. Coop. Year, 1965; mem. adv. council Republican Nat. Com.; bd. dirs. Com. on Present Danger. Served with AUS, 1944-47. Mem. Internat. Inst. Strategic Studies, Am. Math. Soc., Council on Fgn. Relations, Sigma Xi. Clubs: M.I.T. Faculty; Reform (London). Co-author, editor: Arms Control, Disarmament and National Security, 1961; (with others) Why ABM, 1969; mem. editorial bd. jour. Internat. Security; contbr. articles to profl. jours. Home: Irvington, N.Y. Died Apr. 18, 1980.

BRENNAN, EDWARD THOMAS, fgn. service officer; b. Toorak Australia, Feb. 28, 1921; s. William Rowley and Katherine Angel (Donovan) B.; came to U.S., 1922, naturalized, 1924; B.S. in Fgn. Service, Georgetown U., 1949; m. Denise Helen Meier, Dec. 31, 1945; children—Kevin, Denise, Edward Thomas, Peter. Joined U.S. Fgn. Service, 1941; assigned Dept. State, 1941-42, charge diplomatic courier ops. for Latin Am., South Pacific and No. Europe, 1947-50, chief couriers, 1952-53, officer charge European region, Paris, 1953-54, Frankfurt am Main, Germany, 1954-56; assigned Am. embassy, Manila, 1957-59, Tunis, Tunisia, 1959-63; dep. chief mission, counselor Am. embassy, Bangui, Central African Republic, 1963-66; assigned Nat. War Coll., Washington, 1966-67; spl. asst. internat. affairs div. plans and ops. USAF, 1967-68, asst. dep. dir. plans for policy, 1968-69, dir. Office Multilateral Policy and Programs, Dept. State, 1969-71, U.S. consul gen., Thessaloniki, Greece, 1971-75; counselor of embassy for refugee and migration affairs U.S. Mission to UN, Geneva, 1975-; alt. del. U.S. del. to 16th Gen. Conf., UNESCO, Paris, 1970; del. exec. bd. Intergovtl. Com. on European Migration, also exec. coms. UN High Commn. for Refugees, Geneva, 1976-77. Served as aviator USNR, 1942-47, 50-52. Recipient Exceptional Civilian Service commendation Dept. Air Force, 1970; Superior Service award Dept. State, 1971, 79. Mem. Am. Fgn. Service Assn., U.S. Naval Inst., Georgetown U. Alumni Assn. Clubs: Army and Navy, Am. Internat. (Geneva). Home: Bethesda, Md. Died Sept. 25, 1979.

BRENNAN, JOHN ALOYSIUS, JR., ry. co. exec.; b. Phila., Mar. 21, 1926; s. John Aloysius and Emma (Pfautz) B.; student U. Pa., 1944-48, St. Joseph's Coll., 1948-49 B.S. in Bus. Adminstrn., LaSalle Coll., 1956; m. Ruth A. Flynn, June 3, 1950; children—John Aloysius III, Lawrence Joseph. Clk. accounting dept. Pa. R.R., Phila., 1944-53, asst. head clk., 1953-57, accountant, 1957-59; accountant Trailer Train Co., Phila., 1959-61, mgr. accounting operations, 1961-65, comptroller, 1965-69, v.p., treas., 1969-71; asst. to v.p. finance Reading Co., 1972-78. Mem. Eastern Car Service Officers, So. Assn. Car Service Officers, Am. Assn. R.R.s, Nat. Assn. Accountants, Adminstrv. Mgmt. Soc., Financial Execs. Inst. Republican. Roman Catholic. Home: Oreland, Pa. Died July 30, 1978.

BRENNER, CLARENCE DIETZ, educator; b. Warren, O., Nov. 4, 1892; s. Jacob and Louisa (Dietz) B.; A.B., Princeton, 1915, A.M., 1917, Ph.D., 1926; m. Helen Robbins, 1926; children—Frederick Chandler, Richard Graham. Instr. Princeton, 1923-27; asst. prof. U. Calif., Berkeley, 1927-42, asso. prof., 1942-50, prof. French, 1950-60, chmn. dept., 1952-57. Served as lt. A.E.F., U.S. Army, 1917-19. Decorated Order of the Redeemer, Legion of Honor. Mem. MLA, AAUP, Phi Beta Kappa. Author: Eighteenth-Century French Plays (with N. A. Goodyear), 1927; L'Histoire nationale dans la tragédie française du XVIIIe siècle, 1929; Le développement du proverbe dramatique en France et sa vogue au XVIII siècle, 1937; Dramatizations of French short stories in the eighteenth century, 1947; A Bibliographical list of plays in the French language, 1700-1789, 1947. Home: Berkeley, Calif. Died Nov. 26, 1977; buried Sleepy Hollow Cemetery, Concord, Mass.

BRENNER, DANIEL, architect; b. N.Y.C., Apr. 13, 1917; s. Samuel and Yetta (Grubman) B.; B.Arch., Columbia, 1939; M.S., Ill. Inst. Tech., 1949; m. Rachael Bracken Orner, July 30, 1949; children—Ariel, Jonathan. Partner, Brenner & Turck, 1957-61; partner Brenner-Danforth-Rockwell, Chgo., 1961-77; prof.

dept. architecture Ill. Inst. Tech. Mem. A.I.A.-Am. Bar Assn. Joint Com. Design of Courtrooms and Courtroom Facilities. Chmn. Fedn. for an Open Lakefront. Trustee Mus. Contemporary Art, Chgo., Chgo. Sch. Architecture Found., Chgo. Archtl. Assistance Center. Served with Signal Corps Intelligence, AUS, 1943-46. Recipient A.I.A. citations for design excellence. Fellow A.I.A. (mem. task force rebldg. city); mem. Arts Club Chgo. Important works include Maremont Bldg., Graham Found. Hdqrs., Nat. Design Center, Old Stock Exchange Bldg., Mus. Contemporary Art, J.B. Speed Art Mus. Addition, Louisville, Spertus Mus. Judaica, Great Primate House of Lincoln Park Zoo, Auditorium Hotel Restoration, Glessner House Restoration. Home: Chicago, Ill. Died Feb. 13, 1977.

BRESCIANI-TURRONI, CONSTANTINO (BRE-SHE-Ä' NE'-TÛR-RO'NE), economist; b. Verona, Italy, Feb. 26, 1882; s. Alessandro and Erminia (Turroni) B.; law degrees, Univ. of Padova, 1902; m. Clara Lubrecht, Feb. 13, 1926. Prof. of statistics, Univ. of Palermo, 1909-12, Univ. of Genova, 1912-25; prof. of economics, Univ. of Bologna, 1925-26, Univ. of Cairo (Egypt), 1927-40, Univ. of Milano, since 1940; exec. dir., Internat. Bank for Reconstruction and Development, Washington, since 1947. Mem. of Consulta (interim Chamber of Deputies), Italy, 1945-46; chmn. of bd. of dirs., Banco di Roma. Mem. Accademia dei Lincei (Rome); corr. mem., Institut de France; council mem., Econometric Soc. (U.S.). Mem. Liberal Party. Roman Catholic. Author: Economics of Inflation, 1932. Home: Milan, Italy.

BRESS, DAVID GERALD, lawyer, educator; b. N.Y.C., June 7, 1908; s. Abraham and Elizabeth (Geto) B.; B.S., U. Va., 1928; LL.B., Harvard, 1931; m. Flora M. Lyon, Sept. 20, 1941; children—Pamela Lyon, David Gerald. Admitted to D.C. bar, 1931, since practiced in Washington; mem. firm Ginsburg, Feldman & Bress, 1969-76; U.S. atty. for D.C., 1965-69; faculty Washington Coll. Law, Am. U., 1932-52; prof. law Georgetown U. Law Sch., Washington, 1953-61, U. Va. Law Sch., 1963-64. Mem. adv. bd. dirs. Riggs Nat. Bank. Bd. dirs. Columbia Hosp., Police Boys Club; v.p. Nat. Capitol Area council Boy Scouts Am. Served as comdr. USNR, 1941-45. Fellow Am. Coll. Trial Lawyers, Am. Bar Found.; mem. Am. Bar Assn. (ho. of dels. 1957-64, chmn. com. on uniform rules evidence fed. cts. 1958-59, from 64), Bar Assn. D.C. (pres. 1957-58), Am. Jewish Com. (past pres. Washington chpt.), Am. Jud. Soc., (dir. 1966-68), Phi Beta Kappa. Jewish religion (past pres. congregation). Home: Washington, D.C. Died Mar. 10, 1976.

BRETALL, ROBERT WALTER, educator; b. Hinckley, Ill., Feb. 8, 1913; s. Walter Herbert and Ora Jane (Bastian) B.; A.B., Princeton, 1935, A.M., 1937, Ph.D. (Chancellor Green fellow), 1938; postgrad. U. Chgo., 1939-42, 53-54, Union Theol. Sem., 1942-43, 52-54, Columbia, 1952-54, Cambridge U., 1962-63; m. Patricia Hodgkinson, Aug. 30, 1954 (dec. 1972); m. 2d, Eleanor Victoria Flor, May 29, 1975. Philosophy, music editor Am. Educator Ency., 1945-47; grad. asst. in philosophy Northwestern U., 1945-46; asst. prof. philosophy and humanities U. Ariz., Tucson, 1947-52, asso. prof., 1954-64, prof. philosophy, 1964-76, emeritus, 1976-80; lectr. philosophy Wagner Coll., N.Y.C., 1952-53; vis. prof. philosophy Wash. State U., 1967-68; mem. summer colloquium in philosophy of religion Calvin Coll., 1973; cons. Princeton U. Press, Macmillan Co., Northwestern U. Press. Mem. exec. bd. So. br. Ariz. Civil Liberties Union, 1966-72, chmn. ch.-state com., 1966-67, chmn. acad. freedom com., 1967-69. Democratic precinct committeeman Pima County (Ariz.), 1970-74. Bd. dirs. Ariz. Friends Music, 1948-80. Ford Found. Faculty fellow, 1953-54. Mem. Am. Assn. U. Profs. (past pres. U. Ariz. chpt.), Am. Acad. Religion, Am. Philos. Assn., Princeton Grad. Alumni Assn., Phi Beta Kappa. Democrat. Episcopalian. Author: A Kierkegaard Anthology, 1946; The Concept of Purpose in Reformation Thought, 1973. Editor: (with Charles W. Kegley) The Theology of Paul Tillich, 1952; Reinhold Niebuhr: His Religious, Social and Political Thought, 1956; The Empirical Theology of Henry Nelson Wieman, 1963. Home: Tucson, Ariz. Died Dec. 20, 1980.

BRETSCHGER, MAX E. (BRETSH'GER), chem. engineer; b. Buchs-Zuerich, Switzerland, June 20, 1884; s. Ulrich and Seline (Schnoch) B.; student Fed. Inst. Tech., Zuerich, Switzerland, (1901-08); Ph.D., U. Zuerich, 1910; m. Julie Rose Steffen, Sept. 20, 1921; children—Alfred Max, Paul Ulrich. Came to U.S., 1926, naturalized, 1934. Plant chemist Chiozza & Cie, Cervignano, Italy, 1910-12; research chemist Ehrich & Graetz, Berlin, Germany, 1912-14; chem. engr. Chem. Fabrik Griesheim-Elektron, Griesheim am Main, Germany, 1915-18; plant mgr. Usine Electrochimique Francke, Aarau, Switzerland, 1919-26; plant mgr. Buffalo Electro-Chemical Company, Inc. (now Becco Chem. Div. Food Machinery & Chem. Corp.), Buffalo, 1926-31, v.p., 1931-52, pres., 1952—; v.p. Food Machinery & Chem. Corp., San Jose, Cal., 1952—. Member board trustees Erie County Technical Institute. Served as sci. consultant C.W.S., mission to Europe, 1945. Fellow Chem. Inst. Can.; mem. Am. Chem. Soc., Am. Inst. Chem. Engrs., Electrochem. Soc., Soc. Chem. Industry (London), Tech. Assn. Pulp and Paper Industry, Am. Soc. Testing Materials, Engring. Soc. Buffalo. Clubs: Buffalo, Buffalo Athletic, Buffalo Country, Chemists, Saturn, Rotary, Automobile. Holder numerous patents; U.S., foreign countries, particularly processes for prodn., appln. hydrogen peroxide. Home: Buffalo. *

BRETT, DOROTHY, artist; b. London, Eng., Nov. 10, 1883; d. Oliver Sylvain Baliol (Viscount Esher) and Eleanor (Van-de-Weyre) Brett; student Slade Sch. U. of London, 1917-21; unmarried. Came to U.S., 1925, naturalized. Freelance artist; has exhibited throughout U.S. Address: Taos, N.M. *

BRETT, GEORGE HOWARD, army officer; b. Cleveland, O., Feb. 7, 1886; s. William Howard and Alice (Allan) B.; E.E., Va. Mil. Inst., 1909; grad. Army Air Corps Tactical Sch., 1928; Command and Gen. Staff Sch., 1930. Army War Coll., 1936; m. Mary Devol, d. Maj. Gen. C. A. Devol, A.U.S., Mar. 1, 1916; children—Dora (Mrs. B.A. Schriever), Lucille (Mrs. John Hart Tate), Devol. Commd. 2d lt., Philippine Scouts, 1910; cavalry, 1911, aviation sect., Signal Corps, 1916, promoted through grades to lt. col., 1934; brig. gen. comdg. 19th Wing, Albrook Field, Panama, 1936-38; brig. gen. asst. chief Air Corps, chief, Material Div., Wright Field, O., 1938-39; on duty O.C.A.C., Washington, D.C., Oct. 1939; apptd. mag. gen. U.S. Army, Oct. 2, 1940; maj. gen. C.O. A.C., Apr. 1941; lt. gen., Air Corps, Jan. 1942; apptd. dep. sup. comdr. unified command S.W. Pacific area, Jan. 1942. Apptd. comdr. all American troops in Australia, Mar. 1942; comdr.-in-chief, Allied Air Forces in Australia, Apr. 1942. Mem. Am. Mission to arrange aid to Russia, 1941; spl. missions in England, Burma, China, Egypt, Australia, 1941. Comdg. gen. Caribean Defense Comd. and Panama Canal Dept., 1942; retired as C.O.A.C. with permanent rank of maj. gen. May 1945, retained as comdg. gen. CDC and PCD with rank of lt. gen.; retired. Mem. Kappa Alpha. Decorations: D.S. M., Silver Star, D.S.M. with O.L.C., Distinguished Flying Cross; Presidential citation for the New Guinea Campaign (United States); citation for Defense of Philippines (Java campaign). Clubs: Union, Panama Country (Panama); Columbia Country, Army and Navy (Washington), University (Winter Park, Florida). Holds commission as hon. comdr. and pilot in Air Force of Ecuador, Nicaragua and Brazil. Home: Orlando, Fla. *

BRETZ, J HARLEM, geologist; b. Ionia County, Mich., Sept. 2, 1882; s. Oliver Joseph and Rhoda Maria (Howlett) B.; A.B., Albion (Mich.) Coll., 1905; Ph.D., U. of Chicago, 1913; m. Fanny Challis, June 26, 1907; children—Rudolf Challis, Rhoda Irene. Asst. prof. geology, U. of Wash., 1913-14; instr. in geology, 1914-15, asst. prof., 1915; retired prof., U. of Chicago; 1946. Mem. Geol. Soc. Am., Phi Beta Kappa, Sigma Xi. Home: Homewood, Ill. Died Feb. 3, 1981.

BREWER, BASIL (BROO'ER), newspaperman; b. Rush Hill, Mo., July 22, 1884; s. Addison Lanius and Juliet B.; grad. Mo. State Teachers Coll., Kirksville, 1901; student U. Chgo., 1903-05; Dr. Journalism, Suffolk U., 1951; M.S., New Bedford Inst. Textiles and Tech., 1954; Litt.D., Calvin Coolidge College Liberal Arts, Portia Law Sch., 1957; m. Jean Armor Given, 1913; children—Given, Juliet; m. 2d, Mary Minot Caswell, Jan. 3, 1920; children—John Caswell (dec.), Alice Caswell. With Scripps-Howard newspapers, 1908-21, bus. mgr. Cincinnati (O.) Post, 1916-19; same, Cleveland (O.) Press, 1919-21; editor and pub. Omaha (Neb.) Morning and Evening Bee, 1921-24; editor, pub. and prin. owner Lansing (Mich.) Capital News, 1924-29; now publisher and controlling owner of New Bedford (Mass.) Standard-Times; controlling owner Mass. Air Industries, New Bedford; Cape Cod Standard-Times, Hyannis, Mass., radio stations WNBH and WNBH-FM. New Bedford, Mass., WOCB and WOCB-FM, West Yarmouth, Mass., president, treasurer WTEV Television, Inc. Trustee Robert A. Taft Meml. Found., Inc. Decorated Knight Officer Ancient and Most Noble Mil. Order of Christ (Portugal), 1947; Knight Order So. Cross (Brazil), 1949; Distinguished Service award for gen. reporting, Sigma Delta Chi, 1941; Pedro Francisco award Portuguese Continental Union, 1960; Brewer Hall at No. State Tchrs. Coll. dedicated in his honor, 1958; Basil Brewer Boys Town of Desert, Banning, Cal., renamed in his honor, 1960; recipient Naval Res. Surface Div. award, 1961. Elk (named hon. founder Nat. Found. for Elks 1960), Mason. Clubs: Wamsutta, Country (New Bedford); Racquet, Thunderbird (Palm Springs, Cal.). Home: New Bedford, Mass.*

BREWER, CARLOS (BROO'ER), army officer; b. Mayfield, Ky., Dec. 5, 1890; s. Lafayette and Celia (Cross) B.; student West Ky. Coll., 1905-08; B.S., U.S. Mil. Acad., 1913; grad. advance course, Field Arty. Sch., 1927, staff course Command and Gen. Staff Sch., 1928, Army War Coll., 1933; m. Grace Moore, Dec. 21, 1913; children—Carlos Breckenridge, Sherman Theodore, Robert Moore, Grace Elizabeth. Commd. 2d lt., U.S. Army, 1913; promoted through grades to maj. gen., Aug. 1942; instr. West Point, 1916-21; dir. Field Arty. Sch., 1928-32; prof. mil. science and tactics, Purdue U., 1933-37; comdg. Gen., 12th Armored Division, 1933-37. Protestant. Home: Camp Campbell, Ky. Died Sept. 29, 1976.

BREWER, NORMAN (CRAIG), JR., lawyer; b. Black Hawk, Miss., Oct. 4, 1913; s. Norman C. and Ella Hunter (Jumper) B.; A.B., U. Miss., 1935, LL.B., 1937; m. Martha Manly, Apr. 12, 1946; children—Martha, Norman III. Admitted to Miss. bar, 1937, practiced in Greenwood; sr. mem. firm Brewer, Deaton & Evans, 1958-79; city judge Greenwood, 1939-43, 47-57; commr. Yazoo-Miss. Delta Levee Dist., 1960-68, atty., 1968-79; mem. Miss. Bd. Bar Admissions, 1954-60, chmn., 1958-60. Treas., Nat. Found. Infantile Paralysis, Inc., Le Flore County, from 1948; dir. Girl Scout Campers, 1950-60; chmn. bd. Miss. Christian Missionary Soc., 1956-61; mem. adv. bd. Mt. Beulah Christian Center, Edwards, Miss., 1956-61; state pres. Conv. Christian Chs., 1957-58. Served as lt. comdr. USNR, 1942-46. Mem. Am. Coll. Probate Counsel, VFW, SAR (state pres.), Am. Legion (past comdr.), Internat. Assn. Ins. Counsel, Am., Leflore County (pres.) bar assns., Nat. Interfraternity conf. (sec., treas., v.p. 1976-78, pres. 1979), Miss. Assn. Def. Lawyers, Miss. State Bar (commr.), C. of C. (mem. exec. com.), Soc. Colonial Wars (bd. govs. state pres.), Sigma Chi (nat. pres. 1969-71), Omicron Delta Kappa, Phi Delta Phi. Mem. Christian Ch. (chmn. ofcl. bd.). Clubs: Elks, Greenwood (Miss.) Country. Home: Greenwood, Miss. Died Apr. 11, 1979; buried in Greenwood.

BREWER, RICHARD FREDERICK, JR., textile co. exec.; b. Johnson City, Tenn., Nov. 5, 1908; s. Richard Frederick and Mollie (McDonald) B.; B.S., Va. Mil. Inst., 1929; m. Anne Rorer Amis, Apr. 20, 1946; children—Richard Frederick III, Anne Amis. Supt. chem. div. N. Am. Rayon Corp., 1946-52, gen. supt., 1952-55, plant mgr., 1956-57; prodn. mgr. viscose yarn div. Beaunit Mills, Inc., 1958-59, v.p. viscose yarn prodn., research and devel., 1959-65, v.p., tech. dir. viscose, 1965-66; spl. asst. to v.p. fiber mfg. and engring. Beaunit Corp., 1966-67, dir. prodn. planning, 1967-68, tech. dir. cellulose fibers, 1968-71, dir. tech. services, fibers, 1968-72. Served to lt. col. USAAF, 1942-46; col. Res. until 1968. Decorated 4 bronze, 1 silver campaign stars, 2 Presdl. unit citations. Mem. Res. Officer Assn. (past sr. v.p. Tenn., v.p. for Air Force Tenn.). Presbyn. Clubs: Johnson City Country, Hurstleigh (Johnson City, Tenn.). Home: Raleigh, N.C. Died Oct. 9, 1977.

BREWER, WAYNE BURDETTE, rubber co. exec.; b. Findlay, Ohio, Sept. 6, 1923; s. William B. and Edna (Hurrel) B.; B.S. in Chem. Engring., Purdue U., 1944; Dr. Humanics (hon.), Findlay Coll.; m. Leola E. Karpuleon, June 27, 1946; children—Sharon, Larry, Nancy, Patricia, Michael, David. With Cooper Tire & Rubber Co., Findlay, 1946-77, exec. v.p., 1958-60, pres., 1960-77, also dir. Served to lt. (j.g.) USNR, 1943-46. Recipient Distinguished Service award Findlay Jr. C. of C.; Distinguished Engring. Alumnus award Purdue U.; Silver Beaver award Boy Scouts Am. Mem. Am. Chem. Soc., Catalyst Soc. (Purdue), Tau Beta Pi, Phi Lambda Upsilon, Omega Chi Epsilon. Mason, Kiwanian. Home: Findlay, Ohio. Died Mar. 23, 1977.

BREWSTER, JAMES, librarian; b. Groton, S.D., July 22, 1886; s. William Joseph (clergyman) and Emma (Colby) B.; Trinity Coll., Hartford, Conn., 1908; B.L.S., Albany Library Sch., Albany, N.Y., 1926; m. Jessie A. Mills, Jan. 1, 1918; children—Mary Bunce, Cynthia. Cashier Travelers Ins. Co., 1908-14; auditor Canada Steamship Lines, 1914-18 and 1919-24; with Albany Library Sch., 1914-26; head of order sect. N.Y. State Library, 1926-27; librarian Union Coll., Schenectady, N.Y., 1927-35; asst. state librarian Conn. State Library, 1935-36, state librarian since 1936. Served in U.S. Navy, 1918. Mem. Am. Library Assn., Conn. Library Assn. (pres. 1937-38), Conn. Hist. Soc., Nat'l Assn. of State Librarians 2d v.p.), Conn. Soc. Colonial Wars (sec.), Antiquarian and Landmark Soc., Soc. Am. Archivists, Society of Descendants of the Founders of Hartford, New London County Historical Society (honorary), Archives Committee of Franklin D. Roosevelt Library, Inc. Mem. Psi Upsilon. Episcopalian. Clubs: Grolier (New York) Acorn (Conn.). Home: West Hartford, Conn. *

BREWSTER, KINGMAN, lawyer, author; b. Worthington, Mass., Dec. 24, 1882; s. Charles K. and Celina S. (Baldwin) B.; A.B., Amherst Coll., 1906; LL.B., Harvard, 1911; m. Theo Urch, Aug. 11, 1930; children—Mary, Kingman, Barbara. Admitted to bars of Ore., 1911, Mass., 1913, Dist. of Columbia, 1923; mem. Brewster & McLean, 1936-38; mem. Brewster & Steiwer since Feb. 1, 1938; gen. counsel and registrar 1st Federal Land Bank, 1918; asst. counsel U.S. Shipping Bd., 1921-22; spl. counsel U.S. Bur. Internal Revenue, 1922-23; chmn. Com. on Appeals and Review, 1922-23; vice pres. Greenfield Tap and Die Co., 1919-20; pres. Millers Falls Co., 1920-21. Mem. Am. and Dist. of Columbia bar assns., Soc. of Mayflower Descendants, Sons of Am. Revolution, Phi Beta Kappa, Alpha Delta

Phi. Republican. Conglist. Clubs: Multnomah Athletic (Portland, Ore.); Metropolitan, Harvard (Washington, D.C.); Woodmont Rod and Gun (Md.). Author: Federal Tax Appeals (with G. E. Holmes), 1927; Outline of the New Deal, 1934; Distraint Under the Federal Revenue Laws, 1937. Author: 1940 Excess Profits Tax. Home: Washington. *

BREWSTER, LEO, judge; b. Fort Worth, Oct. 16, 1903; s. C. B. and Mary (Thomas) B.; LL.B., U. Tex., 1926; m. Lois Rice, Mar. 21, 1928; children—Gayle (Mrs. Ben Rollert, Jr.), Sarah (Mrs. Richard Griffith). Admitted to Tex. bar, 1926, practiced in Fort Worth; 1st asst. dist. atty., Tarrant County, Tex., 1935-39; U.S. dist. judge No. Dist. Tex. Fellow Am. Coll. Trial Lawyers; mem. Fort Worth Jr. C. of C. (pres. 1932), Am. (mem. Ho. of Dels. 1958-62), Fort Worth (v.p. 1951, pres. 1952) bar assns., State Bar of Tex. (dir. 1952-57, chmn., pres. 1958-59). Clubs: Fort Worth, Ridglea Country (Fort Worth). Home: Fort Worth, Tex. Died Nov. 27, 1979.

BREWTON, CHARLES SIDNEY, lawyer; b. Larkinsville, Ala., Nov. 9, 1913; s. Charles Spurgeon and Ora (Smith) B.; student Birmingham-So. Coll., 1932-35; LL.B., J.D., U. Ala., 1938; m. Jewell Wann, Oct. 12, 1940; children—Carol Ann, Charles Sidney. Admitted to Ala. bar, 1938; partner firm Brewton & Jones, Scottsboro, Ala., 1938-40; spl. asst. to U.S. atty. gen., 1940-43; staff dir. U.S. Senate Com. Expenditure in Exec. Depts., 1943-44; adminstrv. asst. to U.S. Senator Lister Hill, 1943-56; asso. dir. law and legislation Joint Commn. Mental Illness and Health, Cambridge, Mass., 1956-59; gen. counsel Senate Com. Small Bus., 1959-61; asst. dir. Office Emergency Preparedness, Exec. Office of Pres., 1961-69; exec. dir., gen. counsel Joint Com. on Def. Prodn., Washington, 1969-73; legal adviser U.S. Senator John Sparkman, 1969-73; practiced in Scottsboro, Ala., 1973-75. Chmn. com. arrangements Nat. Conf. Nat. Def. Exec. Res., 1965. Asst. campaign mgr. presdl. nominee Adlai E. Stevenson, 1952, 56; asst. to chmn. Presdl. Inaugural Com., 1965. Mem. Assn. Senate Adminstrv. Assts. and Exec. Secs. (past pres.), Nat. Grange, Sigma Alpha Epsilon. Clubs: President's, Nat. Democratic. Author: (with others) Action for Mental Health, 1961. Home: Scottsboro, Ala. Died July 21, 1975; interred Cedar Hill Cemetery, Scottsboro.

BRIDAHAM, LESTER museum cons., b. Denver, Aug. 30, 1899; s. Lester Burbank and Alice Gano (Beesley) B.; B.S., M.S., Mass. Inst. Tech., 1923; student Art Students League N.Y., 1928, 30, 33; postgrad. mus. adminstrn. Fogg Art Mus., Harvard, 1936-37; m. Dorothy M. Odenheimer, June 27, 1941; 1 dau., Vivian Burbank. Research Gothic sculpture, France, 1929-30; Am. Field Service Found. fellow, France, Morocco, 1931; exhibited paintings, N.Y.C., 1928, 34, Wadsworth Athenaeum, 1934, water colors Coll. Art Assn. N.Y., 1936, Mus. Modern Art, 1936, Art Students League, 1936, Art Inst., Chgo., 1946-48; represented permanent collection Denver Art Mus.; staff Art Inst. Chgo., 1938-54, head pub. relations dept., 1938-43, editor Quarterly, 1953, sec. trustees, 1954; mus. dir. La. State Mus., New Orleans, 1954, Chgo. Hist. Soc., 1956; was dir. Strathmont Museum, Elmira, N.Y.; now instr. drawing and painting Opportunity Sch., Denver; also art and history museum consultant. Served as lt. USNR, 1943-45. Mem. American Assn. Museums, Am. Assn. State and Local History, N.Y. State Hist. Assn., Coll. Art Assn., Artists Equity (dir.). Author: Gargoyles, Chimeres and the Grotesque in French Gothic Sculpture, 1930; Brief Guide to Collections Art Institute of Chicago, 1953; Guide to the Louisiana State Museum, New Orleans, 1956. Contbr. profl. publs., art mags. Home: Denver. *

BRIDGER, GROVER LEON, chem. engr.; b. Memphis, July 11, 1911; s. Grover Cleveland and May (Beckham) B.; B.S., Rice Inst., 1933, A.M., 1935; Ph.D., Iowa State Coll., 1938; m. Elizabeth Lou Everett, Aug. 2, 1941; children—Carolyn A., Susan E., Ellen E., Elizabeth L. Engaged in plant operations and research Shell Petroleum Corp., Houston, 1933-35; grad. asst., instr. chem. engring. Iowa State Coll., Ames, 1935-38, head dept. chem. and mining engring., also in charge chem. engring. divs. Engring. Expt. Sta. and Ames Lab. of AEC, 1947-55; instr. chem. engring. Rice Inst., 1938-39; project leader and chief of process devel. div. TVA, Wilson Dam, Ala., 1939-47; prof. chem. engring. Ga. Inst. Tech., Atlanta, 1964-78, dir. Sch. Chem. Engring., 1968-78. Cons. chem. engr., 1947-78, dir. agrl. chem. research Davison Chem. Co. Balt., 1955-57, W.R. Grace & Co., 1957-64; cons. on devel. of recently discovered phosphate deposits in So. Rhodesia (visited area in 1948, 50); Smith-Mundt appointee to N.Z. to survey fertilizer prodn. problems summer 1951. Registered profl. engr., Iowa, Ga., Md. Fellow Am. Inst. Chem. Engrs.; mem. Am. Soc. Engring. Edn., Am. Chem. Soc., Sigma Xi, Tau Beta Pi, Phi Kappa Phi, Phi Lambda Upsilon. Baptist. Author: Development of Processes for Production of Concentrated Superphosphate, TVA Chem. Engring. Report No. 5 (book-length bull.), 1949. Contbr. articles tech. jours. Patentee in field. Home: Atlanta, Ga. Died Nov. 3, 1978.

BRIDGMAN, CHARLES SIMMONS, educator, psychologist; b. Rochester, N.Y., Jan. 24, 1913; s. George A.and Eleanor (Simmons) B.; A.B., Union Coll., 1934; M.S., Brown U., 1936; Ph.D., U. Rochester, 1938; B.S., Ohio State U., 1940; m. Marjorie Deninger, July 22, 1938; children—Charles P., George J., Katherine A., Joan C. From instr. to asso. prof. physiol. optics Ohio State U., 1938-48; prof. psychology U. Wis., Madison, 1953-74, chmn. dept. psychology U. Wis. Extension, 1950-74, and Center System, 1950-71. Mem. Am. Psychol. Assn., Psychonomic Soc., Am. Optical Soc., Am. Acad. Optometry. Spl. research in vision, behavioral cybernetics, applications indsl. psychology. Home: Madison, Wis. Died Oct. 30, 1974.

BRIGGLE, CHARLES GUY, judge; b. Rushville, Ill., Jan. 27, 1883; s. Rice T. and Mary E. (Thompson) B.; LL.B., U. of Ill., 1904; m. Mary Ethel Stites, Dec. 15, 1908; children—Charles G., Jean., (Mrs. Stanley Thomas). Began practice at Springfield, 1904; master in chancery, Circuit Court, 10 yrs.; elected judge Circuit Court, 1927, term of 6 yrs.; judge U.S. Dist. Court, So. Dist. of Ill., since 1932. Mem. Phi Kappa Sigma, Phi Delta Phi, Coif. Republican. Presbyn. Mason, Elk. Home: Springfield, Ill.

BRIGGS, CHARLES WILLIAM, lawyer; b. Cairo, Iowa, July 30, 1887; s. Edward Samuel and Lucy Maria (Weaver) B.; A.B., U. Iowa, 1909; LL.B., Harvard U., 1913; m. Lois Ione Johnson, June 3, 1922; children—Warren Marshall, Edward Samuel, Charles William. Admitted to Iowa bar, 1912, Minn. bar, 1919; practicing lawyer, Wapello, Iowa, 1913-17, pros. atty., 1914-17; mem. firm Briggs and Morgan, Inc. and predecessors, St. Paul, 1919-78; counsel Weyerhaeuser Co., 1940-78; dir., mem. exec. com. First Trust Co. St. Paul. Chmn. exec. com. Timber Industries Com. on Timber Valuation and Taxation. Served as capt., inf., U.S. Army, World War I; AEF in France; lt. col. inf. Res., 1932-46. Recipient award Forest Industries Com. on Timber Valuation and Taxation, 1974; Distinguished Service award Forest Farmers Assn., 1975. Mem. Minn., Am. (taxation com.) bar assns., Am. Judicature Soc., Am. Interprofl. Inst., Am. Polit. Sci. Assn., NAM (tax revision com. tax sect.), Nat. Hist. Soc., Liberty Lobby (policy com.), Am. Soc. Internat. Law, Fgn. Policy Assn., Delta Sigma Rho. Republican. Congregationalist. Clubs: Masons; Minn., Athletic, Informal (St. Paul). Contbr. articles to profl. jours. Home: Saint Paul, Minn. Died Oct. 17, 1978.

BRIGGS, ELLIS ORMSBEE, writer, U.S. ambassador; b. Watertown, Mass., December 1, 1899; s. James and Lucy (Hill) B.; A.B., Dartmouth, 1921, LL.D., 1955; LL.D., Bowdoin Coll., 1959, Colby Coll., 1965, Ricker Coll., 1965, Nasson Coll., 1966; m. Lucy Barnard, May 26, 1928; children—Lucy, Everett. Instr. Robert Coll., Constantinople, 1921-23; contbr. articles mags., 1923-25; joined fgn. service, 1925, after jr. service Peru, Liberia, Cuba, Chile and Washington, apptd. ambassador 1945-62, to Dominican Republic, 1944, to Uruguay, 1947, to Czechoslovakia, 1949, to Korea, 1952, to Peru, 1955, to Brazil, 1956, to Greece, 1959, to Spain, 1961; minister-counselor, Chungking, China, 1945; dir. Office Am. Republics Affairs, 1945-47, apptd. career ambassador, 1960; vis. prof. U. S.C. Inst. Internat. Relations, 1965. Recipient Medal Freedom for meritorious services as ambassador to Korea, 1955; Ann. award The Americas Found., 1966. Republican. Clubs: Metropolitan, Chevy Chase (Washington); University, Brook, Century (N.Y.C.). Author: Shots Heard Round the World, 1957; Farewell to Foggy Bottom, 1964; Anatomy of Diplomacy, 1968; also numerous mag. articles. Home: Hanover, N.H. Died Feb. 22, 1976; interred at Topsfield, Maine.

BRIGGS, JOSEPH HAMILTON, corp. exec.; b. Chicago, Nov. 14, 1886; s. Robert and Sarah (Conley) B.; student Northwestern; m. Kate Gemler, June 1, 1910; children—Lorraine (Mrs. Steve Toth, Jr.), Donald. Chairman of executive committee and director H. M. Byllesy & Co., Incorporated; director and mem. exec. com. Continental Foundry & Machine Co.; dir. Chicago, S. Shore & S. Bend R.R.; Interstate Bakeries Corp. Clubs: Mid-Day (Chicago); Wall Street, Recess (N.Y. City). Home: Highland Park. *

BRIGGS, STEPHEN FOSTER, mfg. exec.; b. Watertown, S.D., Dec. 4, 1885; s. Stephen Albro and Flora Dyer (Foster) B.; B.S., South Dakota State College, 1907, D.Sc. (honorary), 1956; married Beatrice Branch, Feb. 10, 1910; children—Stephen Albro, Barbara (Mrs. Robert P. McCulloch), John Newton, James Branch. Co-founder Briggs & Stratton Corp., 1909, organized Outboard Motor Corp., 1929 (merged with Johnson Motor Co., 1936), became Outboard, Marine & Mfg. Co., 1936, chmn. bd. dirs. from 1936; chmn. bd. dirs. Continental-Diamond Fibre Co., 1951-55. Fellow Royal Society of Arts. Member of the National Audubon Soc., Am. Ornithologists Union, Photog. Soc. Am. Home: Naples, Fla. *

BRIGHAM, DWIGHT STILLMAN, corp. exec.; born Worcester, Mass., Aug. 24, 1886; s. John S. and Nellie J. (Spurr) B.; A.B., Harvard, 1908; m. Marion Brittan Shattuck, June 26, 1909; children—Nancy B. (Mrs. John B. Hawes), Mary S. (Mrs. Benjamin Fisher, Jr.). Pres. and dir. Keyes Fibre Co., Waterville, Me., 1935-51, chmn. bd. dirs., 1954-61. Served as lt. col., Engrs., World War I. Republican. Episcopalian. Clubs: Union, Brookline Country, Cumberland, Harvard. Home: Newton Center, Mass. *

BRIGHAM, FRANCIS GORHAM, physician; b. Flushing, L.I., N.Y., Sept. 27, 1882; s. Dana Bullard and Frances (Slade) B.; B.S., Colgate U., 1905, D.S., 1931; M.D., Harvard, 1909; m. Helen Greeley McKissock, Oct. 1, 1913; children—Francis Gorham, Harriet Dickson. Physician out-patients' dept., Mass. Gen. Hosp., Boston, Mass., 1911-25; phys. House of Good Samaritan, 1912-26; visiting phys. N.E. Deaconess Hosp., 1913, on permanent staff, 1926, physician in chief since 1935; physician in chief Palmer Memorial Hospital, 1935-45. First lt. Med. Corps; later capt. and maj., World War. Trustee N.E. Deaconess Hosp. Assn. Fellow Am. Coll. Physicians; member A.M.A., Mass. Med. Soc., Delta Kappa Epsilon, Phi Beta Kappa. Republican. Unitarian. Clubs: Harvard; Country. Home: Chestnut Hill, Mass. *

BRILL, LEONARDO, conductor; b. Bucharest, Roumania, Aug. 29, 1883; s. Albert and Selma (Fischer) B.; grad. Conservatory of Music, Bucharest, 1901; Vienna Conservatory, 1904; studied under Prof. Carl Flesch and Prof. Grun; m. Gladys Greenough, of Spokane, Wash., July 10, 1913; children—Joan Jacqueline, Leonardo. Came to U.S., 1908, naturalized citizen, 1918. Condr. Spokane Symphony Orchestra since 1911, also leader Davenport Hotel Orchestra. Home: Spokane, Wash. *

BRIM, ORVILLE GILBERT, univ. prof.; b. Latchie, O., Aug. 18, 1883; s. Gilbert Burchell and Elizabeth Amelia (Hahn) B.; B.Sc., Valparaiso (Ind.) U., 1907; studied Harvard, 1909-10; M.A., Teachers Coll. (Columbia), 1911; Ph.D., Columbia, 1920; m. Mary Helen Whittier, June 29, 1912; children—Betty, Lois Whittier, Mary Agnes, Orville Gilbert. Prin. high sch., Berne, Ind., 1907-09; head dept. edn., Miss. Normal Coll., Hattiesburg, Miss., 1912-15, Winthrop Coll., Rock Hill, S.C., 1915-17; prof. rural edn., Cornell U., 1920-23; became prof. elementary edn., Ohio State U., 1923; retired. Y.M.C.A. war work in France and Italy, 1917-19. Mem. N.E.A., Nat. Soc. for Study of Edn., Phi Delta Kappa. Democrat. Protestant. Author: Rural Education, 1923; The Teaching Personnel (with others), 1923. Home: Lakeville, Conn.*

BRIMSON, ALICE W. S., missionary sec.; b. LaFayette, Ind., Apr. 19, 1884; d. William George and Susan Hunt (Smith) Brimson; B.A., Smith College, 1905; student U. of Chicago Divinity Sch.; M.A., Sch. of Social Service Administration, U. of Chicago, 1927; unmarried. Began as sec. Christian Americanization, Woman's Am. Bapt. Home Mission Soc., 1919-26; pres. Baptist Missionary Training Sch., Chicago, 1926-37; exec. sec. Woman's Am. Bapt. Home Mission Soc., 1937-46; retired since June 1, 1946. Trustee Mather Sch., Beufort, S.C. Mem. Phi Kappa Psi. Republican. Baptist. Has written many leaflets and articles on missionary work pub. by Am. Bapt. Pub. Soc. Home: Chicago. *

BRIN, FANNY FLIGELMAN, b. Berlad, Roumania, Oct. 20, 1884; d. John and Antoinette (Friedman) Fligelman; brought to U.S. when 3 months old; B.A., U. of Minn., 1906; m. Arthur Brin, of Minneapolis, Minn., Mar. 19, 1913; children—Rachel, Howard Baer, Charles Fligelman. Taught in high school, 1906-12. Mem. National Council of Jewish Women (past president; national chairman dept. of international relations and peace). Mem. National Women's Committee for Mobilization for Human Needs; mem. Nat. Com. of Conf. on Cause and Cure of War; mem. exec. com. Conf. on Jews and Christians. Mem. League of Women Voters, Women's Internat. League for Peace and Freedom, Hadassah, Phi Beta Kappa. Jewish religion. Clubs: Womans, College Women's (Minneapolis). Home: Minneapolis, Minn. *

BRINDLEY, GEORGE VALTER (BRIND'LE), surgeon; b. Auburn, Tex., Jan. 8, 1886; s. George Goldthwaite and Mattie (Hanes) B.; student Grandview (Tex.) Jr. Coll., 1903-06; M.D., U. Tex., 1911; m. Arabella Owens, Mar. 5, 1913; children—George Valter, Clyde Owens, Hanes Hanby. Intern Scott and White Hosp., Temple, Tex., 1911-12, mem. staff, 1911—; practice medicine and surgery, 1911—; lectr. med. sch. U. Tex., 1945-49, asst. dean, prof. surgery postgrad. sch. medicine Temple div., 1951—. Fellow A.C.S. (gov.; bd. regents); mem. Tex. Surg. Soc., So. Surg. Assn., A.M.A., Tex. Med. Assn. (past pres.), also the American Cancer Society (past president). Rotarian. Contbr. med. articles profl. publs. Home: Temple, Tex. *

BRINGHURST, JOHN HENRY, civil engr.; b. Houston, Tex., Oct. 11, 1885; s. John Henry and Minnie (Abercrombie) B.; B.S. in C.E., U. of Mich., 1910; m. Alma Cheatham, of Clarksville, Tex., Sept. 30, 1909.

Various engring. positions, 1910-13; instr. and asst. prof. civ. engring., U. of Mich., 1913-16; asso. prof. civ. engring., Johns Hopkins, 1916-19; dean Drexel Inst. since May 15, 1919. Mem. Soc. for Promotion Engring. Edn.; asso. mem. Am. Soc. C.E., Kappa Alpha. Democrat. Episcopalian. Mason. Club: City (Phila.). Home: Lansdowne, Pa. *

BRINK, JOSEPH ANDREW, JR., educator, cons., indsl. exec.; b. Kansas City, Mo., July 8, 1925; s. Joseph Andrew and Agnes Julia (McDonald) B.; B.S., Denver U., 1947, M.S., 1948; Ph.D., Purdue U., 1953; m. Dorothy E. Shea, Apr. 30, 1955. Research engr. Denver Research Inst., 1948-49; instr. Purdue U., West Lafayette, Ind., 1949-53, asst. prof. chem. engring., 1953-54; research engr. Monsanto Co., Everett, Mass., 1954-57, St. Louis, 1957-59, supr. and engring. devel. mgr., 1959-69, mgr. devel. and tech. Monsanto Enviro-chem. Systems, St. Louis, 1969-70, devel. dir. 1971-73; prof. chem. engring. Wash. State U., Pullman, 1974-79, chmn. dept. chem. engring., 1973-79; cons. various industries and govt., 1968-79; pres., chmn. bd. Brink & Assos., Inc., consultants, engrs., scientists, Moscow, Idaho, 1975-79; sr. projects v.p., dir. Am. Carbon and Chem. Corp., 1975-76. Served with USNR, 1944-46. Recipient Gaston DuBois award Monsanto Co., 1957; Distinguished Engring. Alumnus award Purdue U., 1972; Outstanding Engring. Alumnus award Denver U., 1973. Fellow Am. Inst. Chemists; mem. Am. Chem. Soc., Am. Inst. Chem. Engrs., AAAS, Air Pollution Control Assn., ASME, Sigma Xi, Omega Chi Epsilon. Contbr. articles to profl. jours. Patentee in field. Inventor, Brink Mist Eliminator for air pollution control, 1960. Home: Moscow, Idaho. Died Mar. 15, 1979.

BRINKLEY, STERLING G(ARDNER), univ. prof.; b. Quitman, Ga., Nov. 22, 1884; s. Sterling Gardner and Roberta Florence (Smith) B.; A.B., Emory Coll., 1907; B.D., Vanderbilt U., 1912; A.M., Columbia, 1920, Ph.D., 1925; m. Margaret Beadle, June 29, 1914; children—Ruby Margaret, Sterling Gardner. Teacher, Ga. high schs., 1907-09; teacher, Coll. and Middle Sch., Soochow U., China, 1912-18, prin. Soochow U. Middle Sch. No. 2, Shanghai, 1918-19, prof. edn., Soochow U., 1921-23; prof. psychology and edn., Ill. Coll., 1924-25; asst. prof. edn., Emory U., 1925-29, asso. prof. 1929-35, prof. since 1935. Mem. Ga. State Council on Teacher Edn., 1936-41; pres. Atlanta Scoutmaster's Club 1935. Mem. Ga. Edn. Assn., N.E.A., Nat. Assn. Secondary Sch. Prins., Nat. Assn. Coll. Teachers of Edn., A.S.C.D., Am. Forestry Assn., Nat. Geographic Soc., Philosophy of Edn. Soc., Alpha Epsilon Upsilon, Phi Beta Kappa, Kappa Phi Kappa, Phi Delta Kappa. Methodist. Author: Values of New Type Examinations in the High School, 1924; English Mastery Tests: Silent Reading. Forms S, T, U. and V., 1923; contbr. articles to ednl. jours. etc. Home: Atlanta, Ga. *

BRINTON, HOWARD HAINES, ret. educator; born West Chester, Pa., July 24, 1884; s. Edward and Ruthanna Haines (Brown) B.; B.A., Hayerford (Pa.) Coll., 1904, M.A., 1905; M.A., Harvard, 1909; Ph.D., University of California, 1925; Litt.D., Haverford College, 1950; married Anna Shipley Cox, July 23, 1921; children—Lydia Shipley, Edward, Catherine Morris, Joan Mary. Instr. Friends Boarding Sch., Barnesville, O., 1906-08, Pickering Coll., Newmarket, Ont., Can., 1909-15; prof. mathematics, Guilford (N.C.) Coll., 1915-19, acting pres., 1917-18, dean, 1918-19; publicity dir. Am. Friends Service Com., 1919-20; dir. of child feeding in plebiscite area, Upper Silesia, 1920-21; prof. physics, Earlham Coll., 1922-28; prof. religion, Mills Coll., 1928-36; dir. Pendle Hill Grad. Sch. for Religious and Social Study, 1936-52, emeritus since 1952; acting dir. and lecturer, 1934-35. Swarthmore lecturer, London, Eng., 1931; research fellow and lecturer, Woodbrook Coll., Selly Oak Coll., Eng., autumn 1931; lecturer in philosophy Haverford Coll., 1932, 45, 49; William Penn lecturer, Phila., 1932, 38; lecturer in history religion, Bryn Mawr Coll., Pa., 1934, 36; Dudleian lecturer, Harvard University, 1949. Del. World Council of Churches, Amsterdam, 1948. Rep. Am. Friends Service Com. in Japan since 1952. Mem. Am. Theol. Soc., Am. Philos. Assn., Phi Beta Kappa. Mem. Soc. of Friends. Author several books, latest: A Guide to Quaker Practice, 1943; Critique by Eternity, 1943. Editor and contbr., Byways in Quaker History (studies in memory of William I. Hull), 1944, The Quaker Doctrine of Inward Peace, 1948; Prophetic Ministry, 1950; The Pendle Hill Idea, 1951; Frignds for 300 Years, 1952. Contbr. religious articles. Home: Wallingford, Pa. *

BRISTOL, LEE HASTINGS, JR., ch. orgn. exec.; b. Bklyn., Apr. 9, 1923; s. Lee Hastings and Elizabeth (Wigton) B.; A.B., Hamilton Coll., 1947; postgrad. Grad. Inst. Internat. Studies, Geneva, Switzerland, U. Geneva, also Conservatoire de Musique, Geneva, 1947-48; L.T.C.L., Trinity Coll. Music, London, 1947; H.H.D., Los Angeles Conservatory, 1955; Litt.D., Webber Coll., 1957; Mus.D., Dickinson Coll., 1957; LL.D., Mo. Valley U., 1961, Findlay Coll., 1961; Mus.D., Combs Coll. Music, 1965; L.H.D., Hobart and William Smith Colls., 1965, Temple U., 1966; Ped. D., Ricker Coll., 1968; LL.D., Hamilton Coll., 1968; D.F.A., Westminster Choir Coll., 1969; m. Louise Wells, May 20, 1950; children—Elizabeth, Henry Platt, Sara, Lee Hastings III. Asst. to pres. Bristol-Myers Co., N.Y.C., 1948-49, home research staff, dir. products div., 1951, asst. advt. mgr., 1951-52, advt. mgr., 1952-56, dir. pub. relations, 1957-62; stage mgr. TV prodn. dept. NBC, 1949-50; trainee Doherty, Clifford, Steers & Shenfield, Inc., advt., 1950-51; pres. Westminster Choir Coll., Princeton, N.J., 1962-69, pres. emeritus, 1976-79; vice chmn., exec. sec. Joint Commn. on Ch. Music of Episcopal Ch., 1969-73; Cathedral Colleague Cathedral St. John the Divine, N.Y.C., 1975; dir. Laymen's Movement for a Christian World, Rye, N.Y., 1949-58, pres., 1954-55; mem. faculty Creative Problem-Solving Inst., State U. N.Y. at Buffalo, 1956-69; chmn. Greater N.Y. campaign Assn. for Help Retarded Children, N.Y.C., 1957-59, hon. chmn., 1959-60; co-chmn. nat. campaign Am. Nurses Found., 1960-61; hon. faculty U.S. Army Mgmt. Sch., Ft. Belvoir, Va., 1960-61; dir. Atlantic Corp., Newark, from 1961. Del. Gen. Conv. Episcopal Ch., 1973, 76. Mem. regional pub. relations adv. com. YMCA, 1959-61. Trustee, organist All Saints' Ch., Bay Head, N.J., 1947-79, Creative Edn. Found., Buffalo, 1955-70; (pres. 1960-68); bd. dirs. N.Y. Philharmonic Symphony Orch., 1966-79; trustee Berkeley Div. Sch., New Haven, 1956-62, 65-70, Westminster Choir Coll., 1957-70, Miss Mason's Sch., 1958-69, Princeton Pub. Library, 1960-61, Princeton Chamber Orch., 1964-66; bd. advisers Edward W. Root Art Center, Hamilton Coll., Clinton, N.Y., 1958-68, Bay Head, N.J. Chapel, 1963, Presser Found., 1969-72, 77-79, Diocese of N.J. Music Commn., 1969-76, Hamilton Coll., 1971-79, Union Theol. Sem., 1971-72, Pine Manor Jr. Coll., 1972, John Jay and Eliza Watson Found., 1969-79, Lillia Babbitt Hyde Found., 1970-79; council Royal Sch. Ch. Music, from 1972; v.p. Met. Opera Nat. Council, 1975-79. Recipient Outstanding Civilian Service award Dept. Army, 1962, Bishop of N.J. Medal of Honor, 1966, Partner in Edn. award Salem Coll., Man of the Year award Greater Princeton C. of C., 1969; decorated comdr. Order St. John of Jerusalem, 1973, Knight of Grace Order St. Lazarus, 1974. Fellow Royal Sch. Ch. Music, 1969. Fellow Hymn Soc. Am. (exec. com. 1948-79); mem. Am. Guild Organists (nat. council 1964-67), Am. Bible Soc. (trustee 1968-71), N.J. Hist. Soc. (trustee 1968-76), Pilgrims of U.S., Pub. Relations Soc. Am., Royal Coll. Organists, Phi Beta Kappa, Sigma Phi, Alpha Delta Sigma. Episcopalian (lay reader 1943-79, vice chmn. laymen's work Province II, 1959-64). Clubs: Century Assn., University (N.Y.C.); Nassau (Princeton, N.J.); Bay Head (N.J.) Yacht; Manasquan River Golf (Brielle, N.J.); Bedens Brook (Skillman, N.J.). Author: Hymns for Children and Grown-ups, 1952; Seed for a Song, 1958; Developing the Corporate Image, 1960; More Power To You, 1975; The Big Picnic, 1975; Renewal from Within, 1977. Composer anthems, sacred music, collections of songs. Contbr. articles and music to profl. jours. Home: Princeton, N.J. Died Mar. 11, 1979.

BRISTOW, GWEN, author; b. Marion, S.C., Sept. 16, 1903; d. Louis Judson and Caroline Cornelia (Winkler) Bristow; A.B., Judson Coll.; student Anderson Coll. and Sch. of Journalism, Columbia U.; m. Bruce Manning, Jan. 14, 1929 (dec.). Newspaper reporter 10 yrs. Author: Invisible Host, 1930, reprinted as the Ninth Guest, 1975; Gutenberg Murders, 1931; Two Make Twenty-two, 1932 (all 3 titles with Bruce Manning); Deep Summer 1937, Handsome Road, 1938, This Side of Glory, 1940 (with background chpts. pub. as Plantation Trilogy, 1962); Tomorrow Is Forever, 1943; Jubilee Trail, 1950; Celia Garth, 1959; Calico Palace, 1970; Golden Dreams, 1980. Home: Encino, Calif. Died Aug. 17, 1980; interred Garden of Memories, New Orleans, La.

BRITAIN, KENNETH EDWARD, cons. engr.; b. Dallas, Dec. 12, 1910; s. Tristam A. and Margaret Eula (Overton) B.; student Tex. A & M U., 1942, U. Houston, 1951-54, U. Ga., 1969, U. Alaska, 1970; m. Cleo Heavrin, Mar. 28, 1936; 1 dau., Cleo Ann. Insp., Tex. Hwy. Dept., 1929-36; draftsman United Gas Pipeline Co., 1936-37; asst. chief engr. Pure Oil Co., 1937-48; chief engr. Howe & Wise, cons. engrs., Houston, 1948-51; project engr. Tenn. Gas Transmission Co., 1951-56; project mgr. Trans-Can. Pipelines Ltd., 1956-58; chief engr. Midwestern Gas Transmission Co., 1958-60; asst. chief engr. Tenn. Gas Pipeline Co., 1961-75; cons. engr. Polargas Project, Can., 1975-76; mem. adv. com. Internat. Pipeline Tech. Conv., 3 years; mem. Nat. Gas Industry Tech. Com. for Ocean Devel., 1967-68. Del. Tex. Democratic Conv., 1972. Registered profl. engr., Tex., 19 others states, also 2 provinces Can.; certified Nat. Council State Engring. Examiners. Life fellow ASCE (chmn. exec. com. pipeline div. 1966-70, certificate appreciation 1970, Stephen D. Bechtel Pipeline Engring. award 1976), Am. Congress Surveying and Mapping (citation Tex. sect. 1965); fellow Tex. Engring. Found., Soc. Am. Mil. Engrs.; mem. Nat., Tex. (pres. San Jacinto chpt. 1973-74, 4 citations) socs. profl. engrs., Houston Engring. and Sci. Soc. (life), Tex. Link-Order of Engr. (founder 1977), Nat. Rifle Assn. (life). Baptist. Clubs: Bayou Rifles Gun (life), Tennwood Country (life), Elkins Lake Country, Masons, Shriners. Contbr. papers to tech. jours.; co-designer Atascocita Bridge, 1950; assisted in design of 1st offshore structure in Gulf of Mexico, 1937. Home: Houston, Tex. Died Apr. 29, 1979.

BRITSCH, CARL CONRAD, architect; b. Archbold, O., Apr. 12, 1889; s. Hans George and Anna (Kutzli) B.; B.A., Carnegie Inst. Tech., 1916; m. Leone F. Northway, June 4, 1920; children—Virginia Marie (Mrs. R.J. Hollister), James Arthur. Pvt. practice of architecture, Toledo, 1923-27; partner Britsch & Munger, 1927-55, Britsch, Macelwane, Poseler & Lubeck, Toledo, 1955-74; projects include numerous schs., chs., hosps., coll. bldgs. for Bowling Green State U., Ohio No. U., Toledo U., Nat. Am. Legion hdqrs., Washington. Chmn. Downtown Toledo Planning Com. Served with U.S. Army, World War I. Recipient 1st prize in drawing, six 1st prizes in water color, art shows in N.W. Ohio. Fellow A.I.A. (pres. Toledo 1944-45); mem. Architects Soc. Ohio (pres. 1951-52), Church Archtl. Guild Am., Toledo Fedn. Art Socs. (pres. 1952-53), Toledo C. of C., Am. Legion. Methodist. Mason (32 deg.). Clubs: Torch, Lions. Author: (hist. novel) The Sound of the Hammer, 1963; also articles on travel, architecture. Home: Sylvania, Ohio. Died Dec. 19, 1974.

BRITT, LAURENCE, VINCENT, clergyman, educator; b. San Francisco, Apr. 30, 1912; s. Laurence and Alice L. (Boyle) B.; A.B., U. Detriot, 1933; M.A., Loyola U., 1939; S.T.L., West Baden Coll., Ind., 1944; Ph.D., U. Minn., 1954. Joined Soc. of Jesus, 1933, ordained priest Roman Catholic Ch., 1943; tchr. St. Ignatius High Sch., Cleve., 1937-40, Loyola U., 1943; dean freshmen Loyola U., Chgo., 1946-47, dean Coll. Arts and Scis., 1954-56; dean Coll. Arts and Scis., U. Detroit, 1956-59, pres., 1960-66; prof. edn., dir. acad. counselling John Carroll U., Cleve., 1966-67, dean Coll. Arts and Scis., from 1967. Trustee Xavier U. Mem. N.E.A., Assn. Am. Colls., Jesuit, Nat. Cath. ednl. assns., Alpha Kappa Psi, Phi Delta Kappa. Alpha Sigma Nu, Alpha Delta Gamma. Home: Cleveland, Ohio. Died Nov. 15, 1980.

BRITT, STEUART HENDERSON, market research co. exec., cons.; b. Kingdom of Callaway, June 16, 1907; s. A.T. and Katherine (Henderson) B.; student Washington U. (St. Louis), Columbia sch. law; A.B., Washington U., St. Louis, 1931, M.A. in Psychology, 1932; Ph.D. in Psychology (Inst. Human Relations fellow), Yale, 1935; m. Marion M. Hansell, June 1, 1936. Admitted to Mo. bar, 1929, N.Y. bar, 1936, U.S. Supreme Ct., 1936, U.S. Ct. Appeals for D.C., 1937; research asst. Columbia U. Inst. Ednl. Research, 1935-36; asst. prof. psychology George Washington U., prof. psychology Mount Vernon Sem., Washington, 1936-42; civilian wartime work, Washington, 1941-43, exec. dir. Office Psychol. Personnel, NRC, sec. Emergency Com. in Psychology, exec. sec. Com. on Wartime Requirements for Specialized Personnel; expert cons. Nat. Resources Planning Bd. and War Manpower Commn.; exec. positions McCann-Erickson, N.Y.C., 1945-51; v.p. Needham, Louis & Brorby, Inc., Chgo., 1951-56; adminstrv. v.p. Earle Ludgin & Co., Chgo., 1956-57 prof. marketing Grad. Sch. Mgmt., Northwestern U., Evanston, Ill., 1957-75; pres. Britt and Frerichs Inc., mktg. research firm, Chgo., 1971-77, Britt Mktg., 1977-79. Westinghouse Ann. Sci. Talent Search, 1942-60; cons. editor McGraw-Hill series advt. and marketing, 1951-64; editorial dir. Marketing Sci. Inst., 1967-68; producer ann. Advt. Age Creative Workshop, 1958-70. Lectures and Seminars European Countries, Asian Countries, Australia, New Zealand. Served from lt. to lt. comdr. USNR, 1943-45, comdr.-in-chief Hdqrs. U.S. Fleet. Recipient Alumni citation Washington U., 1959; mem. Hall of Fame in Distbn., 1963, Wisdom Hall of Fame, 1970. Diplomate Indsl. Psychology, Am. Bd. Examiners in Profl. Psychology. Fellow A.A.A.S., Am. Psychol. Assn. (pres. div. consumer psychology 1963-64), Am. Sociol. Assn., Am. Acad. Advt.; mem. Am. Marketing Assn., Phillipine Marketing Assn., ESOMAR in Europe. Clubs: Cosmos (Washington); Yale (N.Y.C.); University (Chgo.); University, Canal Shores Golf (Evanston); Kenilworth. Author, editor 15 books including: Social Psychology of Modern Life, 1941, rev. 1949; (with I. Graeber) Jews in a Gentile World, 1942; Selected Readings in Social Psychology, 1950; (with D.B. Lucas) Advertising Psychology and Research, 1950; The Spenders, 1960 (Spanish edit. 1961); (with D.B. Lucas) Measuring Advertising Effectiveness, 1963 (translated into German, Dutch, Italian, Japanese); (with Harper W. Boyd, Jr.) Marketing Management and Administrative Action, 1963 (translated into German), rev. 1968, 73, 77; Consumer Behavior and the Behavioral Sciences, 1966; Do Advertising Agencies Train Trainees?, 1968; Consumer Behavior in Theory and in Action, 1970; Psychological Experiments in Consumer Behavior, 1970; Marketing Managers Handbook, 1973; Psychological Principles of Marketing and Consumer Behavior, 1978; also numerous articles. Developed and edited 51 books in 3 book series. Bd. editors Jour. Marketing, 1947-57, editor, 1957-67. Home: Wilmette, Ill. Died Mar. 15, 1979.

BRITTEN, CLARENCE R., business exec.; b. Jersey City, N.J., Feb. 10, 1882; s. Edwin F. and Mary (Huson) B.; student Stevens Sch., Hoboken, N.J.; Stevens Inst. Tech., Hoboken, N.J.; m. Mildred Rose Wilson, Dec. 6, 1920; 1 son, Wilson Allan. Began as plant mgr., Monroe Calculating Machine Co., Orange, N.J., 1937, treas., 1940-47, sec. since 1947; retired, May, 1947; dir. Savings Investment Trust Co., East Orange, N.J.; own business as management cons. since 1947. Dir. and treas., Y.M.C.A. of the Oranges, N.J.; commr. Pension Fund, Essex County, N.J.; mem. State Bd. of Mediation; vice chmn., Republican Finance Com., N.J.; chmn., Orange Rationing Bd., 1941-45. Mem. Soc. for Advancement of Management, Am. Soc. Mech. Engrs., Nat. Assn. Cost Accountants, Controllers Inst. Am., S.A.R., Holland Soc. of N.Y. Republican. Episcopalian. Clubs: Rotary of the Oranges, Essex (Newark, N.J.), Maplewood Country. Address: Maplewood, N.J. *

BRITTEN, EDWARD BENJAMIN, composer; b. Lowestoft, Eng., Nov. 22, 1913; s. Robert Victor and Edith Rhoda (Hockey) B.; student Gresham's Sch., Holt and Royal Coll. of Music, London, Eng. Engaged in work on documentary films, 1934-35; free lance composer for films, radio and theater, 1934-76; came to U.S., 1939; returned to Eng., 1942; concert tour U.S. with tenor Peter Pears, 1949. Decorated Companion of Honour. Order of Merit; recipient Aspen award, 1964. Mem. Ch. of England. Composer. Orchestra: Sinfonietta; Soirees Musicales and Matinees Musicales (2 suites after Rossini); Mont Juic (with Lennox Berkeley); Canadian Carnival; Sinfonia da Requiem; Young Person's Guide to the Orchestra, string orchestra; Simple Symphony; Variations on a Theme by Frank Bridge; Prelude and Fugue; chamber music: Phantasy; Suite; Six Metamorphoses after Ovid; String Quartets Nos. 1 and 2, Lachrymae; Golden Sonata; organ: Prelude and Fugue on a Theme of Vittoria, Missa Brevis; concerti: Piano Concerto; Violin Concerto; Diversion; Scottish Ballad; Cello Symphony; piano: Holiday Dairy; Introduction and Rondo alla Burlesca; Mazurka Elegiaca; chorus: A Boy Was Born; Our Hunting Fathers (text W.H. Auden); Ballad of Heroes; Hymn to St. Cecilia; Ceremony of Carols; Rejoice In the Lamb (text Christopher Smart); Festival Te Deum; Saint Nicolas Cantata; Spring Symphony; Five Flower Songs; I Lov'd A Lass; Lifi Boy; Advance Democracy; Ballad of Little Musgrave; A Wedding Anthem; Cantata Academica; War Requiem; A Hymn of St. Columba; Cantata Misercordium; vocal: Friday Afternoons; On This Island; Les Illuminations, (text Rimbaud); Seven Sonnets of Michelangelo; Holy Sonnets of John Donne; Canticle I (Text Francis Quarles); Canticle II (text from Chester Miracle play); Canticle III (Still Falls the Rain-E. Sitwell), 1954; Nocturne; Serenade; The Birds, Fish in the Unruffled Lakes; Under the Abject Willow; Mother Comfort; Charm of Lullabies; 3 Vols. of Folk Song arrangements (Brit. Isles and France); realisations of Purcells vocal and instrumental works; operas; Peter Grimes (polled 1st choice in Metropolitan Opera Broadcasts, 1948); Rape of Lucretia; Beggar's Opera (after Gay); Albert Herring; Let's Make An Opera (The Little Sweep); Billy Budd; Gloriana (presented for Coronation of Queen Elizabeth, 1953); The Turn of the Screw, 1954; The Prince of the Pagodas (3 act ballet); Noye's Fludde (opera), 1958; A Midsummer Night's Dream, 1960; Notturno (piano), 1963; Nocturnal (guitar), 1964; Curlew River (opera), 1964; Suite for Cello Solo, 1965; Gemini Variations, 1965; Songs and Proverbs by William Blake, 1965; Voices for Today, 1965; The Poet's Echo, 1965; The Burning Fiery Furnace (opera), 1966; the Golden Vanity, 1966; the Building of the House (overture), 1967; Second Suite for Cello, 1967; the Prodigal Son (opera), 1968; Children's Crusade, 1969; Suite for Harp, 1969; Owen Wingrave (opera), 1970. Home: Aldeburgh Suffolk England. Died Dec. 4, 1976.

BRITTON, RALPH BURTON, business exec.; b. Gananoque, Ont., July 9, 1884; s. Charles Edwin and Marian (Holland) B.; student Upper Can. Coll., 1901-05; m. Ethel Margot Van Riper, Sept. 30, 1916; children—Russel Hubert, Marian Holland (wife Dr. Nicholas Preston), Gordon Reginald. Came to U.S., 1916, naturalized, 1941. Sales engr. Canadian Fairbanks-Morse, Torono, Ont., 1906-10; sec.-treas. Cowan & Britton Mfg. Co., Ltd., Garanoque, Ont., 1911-15; with Stanley Works, New Britain, since 1916, prodn. supervision, 1916-21, sales mgr., 1921-26, div. mgr., 1926-42, v.p. since 1942; dir. Stanley Works of Can., 1938-48, Pressed Metal Ins., 1948-51. Chmn. integrating com., small arms div. War Dept., 1941-43. Clubs: Shuttle Meadow Country (New Britain); Canadian (N.Y.C.), Essex (Conn.) Yacht. Home: New Britian, Conn. *

BROADBENT, SAM ROBERT, mgmt. cons.; b. St. Louis, Sept. 23, 1898; s. Samuel and Hermine (Karberg) B.; B.S. in Forestry, U. Mo., 1920; M.F., Yale, 1922; m. G. Isabelle Jackson, Dec. 18, 1926. With Laurentide Pulp & Paper Co., 1921; with U.S. Forest Service, 1922-39, alternate chief div. operations, 1937-39; with Bur. of Budget, 1939-68, chief commerce and transp. div., 1965-68. Cons. Hoover Commn. Reorgn. Fed. Govt., 1948. Served with U.S. Army, 1918. Recipient Commendation for Outstanding Service during tornado at Gainesville, Ga., 1936; Citation of Merit, Nat. Civil Service League. Mem. Soc. Am. Foresters (sr.), Am. Forestry Assn. (asst. treas. 1962-73), Kappa Sigma. Club: Cosmos (pres. 1960, treas. 1962-75, treas. Found. 1969-73, chmn. trustees 1974-75). Address: Washington, D.C. Died Jan. 4, 1981.

BROCK, WILLIAM ELIHU, coll. dean; b. Blackwell, Okla., Aug. 10, 1914; s. Zedekiah Clark and Bertha Elisabeth (King) B.; student Park Coll., 1933-35; A.B., Wichita State U., 1937; postgrad. La. State U., 1937-39; D.V.M., Kans. State U., 1944; M.S., Okla. State U., 1955; Ph.D., U. Okla., 1958; doctor honoris causa U. San Carlos (Guatemala), 1967; m. Alice Lee Massey, Sept. 30, 1939; 1 dau., Lina Lee. Operator dairy farm, Monitor, Ore., 1939-40; veterinarian, Oregon City, Oreg., 1944-49; prof. vet. medicine, Okla. State U., Stillwater, 1949-78, dean coll. vet. medicine, 1970-78. Chief of party AID contract Okla. State U., Guatemala 1965-67; mem. steering com. Okla. Regional Med. Program, 1970-72. Recipient commendation Okla. Senate, 1965; Outstanding Contbn. award Okla. Vet. Med. Assn., 1966; Sigma Xi lectr. Mem. Am., Okla. vet. med. assns., U.S. Animal Health Assn., Sigma Xi, Phi Kappa Phi, Phi Zeta. Democrat. Presbyn. Rotarian. Patentee vaccine against anaplasmosis. Home: Stillwater, Okla. Died Mar. 8, 1978; interred Mausoleum, Wichita, Kans.

BROCK, WILLIAM EMERSON, JR., candy mfr.; b. Clarksville, Tenn., Nov. 5, 1903; s. William Emerson and Miriam (Acree) B.; grad. McCallie Sch., Chattanooga, 1921; Washington and Lee U., 1925; student Babson's Inst., Babson Park, Mass.; L.H.D. (hon.), U. Chattanooga, 1969; m. Myra Peggy Kruesi, Apr. 5, 1928; children—William Emerson III, Paul Kruesi, Frank Acree. Chmn. bd. Brock Candy Co., Chattanooga; pres. Century Co., Chattanooga; dir. Provident Life & Accident Ins. Co. (both Chattanooga). Past chmn. confectionary industry div. Com. Econ. Devel. Chmn. organizing com. United Fund Greater Chattanooga, also mem. exec. com. Chmn. trustee U. Chattanooga; founding dir. Community Found. Greater Chattanooga; trustee McCallie Sch., Dr. E. Stabley Jones Found. Recipient Liberty Bell award Chattanooga Bar Assn., 1965; Man of Year award Chattanooga Kiwanis Club, 1966; Human Relations award NCCJ, 1972; Distinguished Alumnus award McCallie Sch., 1976. Mem. Nat. Confectionary Assn. (past v.p., dir.), Nat. Soc. S.A.R. (N.C. chpt.), Sigma Chi. Presbyn. (elder, tchr.). Clubs: Mountain City, Lookout Mountain Fairyland (Chattanooga). Home: Lookout Mountain, Tenn. Died June 1, 1979.

BROCK, WILLIAM MEGRUE, banker; b. Cin., Aug. 24, 1884; s. J. Harry and Virginia E. (Megrue) B.; ed. pub. schs., Cin. With Gem City Savs. Assn., Dayton, O., 1904—, chmn. bd., 1965—; pres. Home Av. R.R. Co., Dayton, 1940—; dir. Dayton Power & Light Co., 1947—; bd. dirs., vice chmn. bd. FHLB, Cin., 1936-56. Mem. local Draft Bd., World War II; pres. Dayton Better Bus. Bur., 1925. Pres. Dayton Art Inst., 1942. Recipient SSS medal, 1945. Mem. U.S. Savs. and Loan League (pres. 1945), Ohio Bldg. Assn. League (pres. 1935). Republican. Methodist. Home: Dayton OH *

BROCKWAY, LAWRENCE OLIN, educator, chemist; b. Topeka, Kan., Sept. 23, 1907; s. Paul Lemon and Kate (Weed) B.; B.S., U. Neb., 1929, M.S., 1930; Ph.D., Calif. Inst. Tech., 1933, research fellow, 1933-37; Guggenheim fellow Oxford, Royal Inst., 1937-38; m. Hazel Klein, Sept. 30, 1932; 1 dau., Doris Marie. Asst., asso. prof. U. Mich., 1938-45, prof., 1945-79. Recipient award in pure chemistry Am. Chem. Soc., 1940. Mem. Am. Chem. Soc. A.A.A.S., Am. Assn. U. Profs., Am. Crystallographic Assn., Electron Microscope Soc. Am. Home: Ann Arbor, Mich. Died Nov. 17, 1979.

BROCKWAY, LOUIS NEWELL, business exec.; b. Clinton, N.Y., Mar. 1, 1897; s. William Henry and Sarah Ann (Boone) B.; A.B., Hamilton Coll., Clinton, N.Y., 1917; m. Germaine Downward, June 15, 1923. With advt. dept. Scribner's Mag. (Chas. Scribner's Sons), 1919, Eastern advt. mgr., 1920-23, advt. mgr., 1923-26; advt. mgr. The American Mercury, (Alfred A. Knopf, Inc.), 1926-30; account exec. Young & Rubicam, New York, N.Y., 1930-39, asst. account supervisor, 1939, v.p. and account supervisor, 1939-43, exec. v.p., 1943-61, director, from 1943, chmn. exec. com., 1958-60; cons. Nat. Ednl. TV and Radio Center, from 1960. Trustee Hamilton Coll. Served as lt., inf., 78th Div., 1917-19, France, 1918-19. Mem. Advt. Council (chmn. 1956-58), Am. Assn. Advt. Agencies (chmn. 1951-52), Delta Kappa Epsilon. Independent Presbyn. Clubs: Union League, Delta Kappa Epsilon (New York); Indian Harbor Yacht (Greenwich, Conn.). Home: Greenwich, Conn. Died Mar. 23, 1979.

BROD, RUTH HAGY, TV producer, journalist; b. N.Y.C., May 31, 1911; d. Abraham and Jeanette (Rapaport) Fleischman; student Crane Jr. Coll., 1928; Mus.B., Chgo. Coll. Music, 1929; m. Anatol Frikin, 1929 (dec.); dau., Sybil Joan (Mrs. Robert Lefferts); m. 2d, Lewis Hagy, 1932 (dec.); m. 3d, Ed Albert Thomas Brod, May 28, 1954. News reporter N.Y. Graphic, Chgo. Daily Am., Chgo. Daily Times, Chgo. Daily News, also radio reporting; TV editor Gen. Fedn. Women's Clubs mag. The Clubwoman; Western editor Macfadden movie and radio mags., Hollywood, 1936-38; spl. feature writer, byline reporter Phila. Ledger, 1938-41; publicity dir. United Way Chest campaigns, also mem. women's adv. bd. exec. com. U.S. Savs. Bond div. U.S. Treasury, 1942-46; women's editor Phila. Bull., then founder, dir. Civic Service Bur., founder, dir. Phila. Bull. Forum, also radio, TV, from 1946; producer, moderator Coll. News Conf., from 1952; pres. Ruth Hagy Prod. and News Service, N.Y.C., from 1962; Far East corr. NBC, Radio Press Internat., others. Dir. pub. information Job Orientation in Neighborhoods, City N.Y., U.S. Dept. Labor; columnist, feature writer for N.Am. Newspaper Alliance - Women's News Service. Sponsor for Atlantic Council of U.S.; v.p. for Women's affairs United Shareholders Am. Nat. vice chmn. 10th anniversary com. NATO. Mem. nat. bd. Women's Med. Coll., Damon Runyon Meml. Fund; women's adv. bd. Am. Heritage Found. Recipient numerous awards. Mem. Am. Women Radio and Television Radio and Television Corrs., U.S. Nat. Student Assn. (nat. finance chmn., sr. adviser). Clubs: Overseas Press (chmn. youth and student activities, organizer dir. 4th ann. coll. editors conf. sponsored by Readers Digest) (N.Y.C.); Am. Women' Newspaper, Women's Nat. Press (Washington). Home: New York, N.Y. Died May 9, 1980.

BRODERICK, HENRY, business exec.; b. Mpls., Oct. 12, 1880; s. Lawrence and Mary (Cronin) B.; student pub. schs., Mpls.; m. Mary Barclay, Oct. 1901 (dec.). Founder, Henry Broderick, Inc., 1911, pres., 1911—; pres., dir. Henry Broderick Investment Co.; pres. Realty & Leasehold Co., Boston Drug Co.; sec. 1941 Corp.; dir. Seattle 1st Nat. Bank, New World Life Ins. Co., Seattle Baseball Club; trustee J.C. Silverton Trust. Mem. Prison Parole Bd., 1929-33. Trustee Seattle U. Republican. Roman Catholic. Clubs: Rainier Tennis, Washington Athletic, Press, Harbor. Author: The Shoveler, 1932; The Commandment Breakers of Walla Walla, 1933; Early Seattle Profiles. Home: Seattle WA *

BRODIE, BERNARD, educator emeritus, author; b. Chgo., May 20, 1910; s. Max and Esther (Bloch) B.; Ph.B., U. Chgo., 1932, Ph.D., 1940; m. Fawn McKay, Aug. 28, 1936; children—Richard M., Bruce R., Pamela B. Instr., Dartmouth, 1941-43; asso. prof., dir. grad. studies internat. relations Yale, 1945-51; sr. staff mem. RAND Corp., 1951-66; prof. U. Calif. at Los Angeles, 1966-77, prof. emeritus, 1977-78; vis. prof. Nat. War Coll., 1946, bd. cons., 1955-57; tech. expert UN Conf., San Francisco, 1945. Bd. dirs. Found. Research Psychoanalysis, Los Angeles, 1965-68. Served to lt. USNR, 1943-45. Recipient Gold medal Argentine Naval War Coll., 1948. Fellow Inst. Advanced Study, Princeton, 1940-41; Carnegie reflective year fellow, Paris, 1960-61; 50th ann. Faculty Research lectr. U. Calif. Los Angeles, 1975. Fellow Am. Acad. Arts and Scis. Author: Sea Power in the Machine Age, 3d edit., 1968; A Guide to Naval Strategy, 5th edit., 1965; The Absolute Weapon, 1946; Strategy in the Missile Age, 2d edit., 1965; (with Fawn M. Brodie) From Cross-Bow to H-Bomb, 2d edit., 1973; La Guerre Nucleaire, 1965; Escalation and the Nuclear Option, 1966; War and Politics, 1973. Home: Pacific Palisades, Calif. Died Nov. 24, 1978.

BRODIE, FAWN MCKAY, biographer, historian; b. Ogden, Utah, Sept. 15, 1915; d. Thomas E. and Fawn (Brimhall) McKay; B.A., U. Utah, 1934; M.A., U. Chgo., 1936; m. Bernard Brodie, Aug. 28, 1936; children—Richard, Bruce, Pamela. Sr. lectr. history U. Calif., Los Angeles, 1968-70, prof., 1971-77; author: No Man Knows My History - The Life of Joseph Smith the Mormon Prophet, 1945, Thaddeus Stevens - Scourge of the South, 1959, (with husband) From Crossbow to H-Bomb, 1961, The Devil Drives - A Life of Sir Richard Francis Burton, 1967, Thomas Jefferson - An Intimate History, 1974; Richard M. Nixon; The Shaping of his Character, 1981. Recipient medal in history Commonwealth Club of Calif., 1959; named Fellow of Year, Utah Hist. Soc., 1967, Woman of Year, Los Angeles Times, 1975; Alfred A. Knopf fellow, 1943; recipient Ann. prize Berkshire Conf. Women Historians, 1975, Merit Honor award U. Utah, 1976. Mem. Am. Hist. Assn. Editor: Route from Liverpool to Great Salt Lake Valley, 1962, The City of the Saints, 1963; contbr. articles to N.Y. Times mag., Ency. Brit. Home: Pacific Palisades, Calif. Died Jan. 10, 1981.

BRODIE, GANDY, artist; b. N.Y.C., May 20, 1924; s. Max and Minnie (Tau) B.; m. Jocelyn Levine, Jan. 25, 1955; 1 son, Shane. One-man show Krasner Gallery, N.Y.C.; exhbns. include Kootz Gallery, N.Y.C., Durlacher Gallery, N.Y.C., Saidenberg Gallery, N.Y.C., represented in permanent collections Mus. Modern Art, Whitney Mus., Jewish Mus., N.Y.C., Park Av. Synagogue, N.Y.C., Phillips Collection, Washington, Balt. Mus. Art, Chrysler Mus., Provincetown, Mass., Mass. Inst. Tech., Sarah Lawrence Coll., Gloria Vanderbilt Mus. (purchase fund), Longview Found. (Purchase award 1960, 61), Mint Mus., Charlotte, N.C.; art faculty New Sch. Social Research, 1967; artist-in-residence Hollins Coll., 1968; vis. scholar Wash. State Colls., 1968-69; asso. prof. Gandie Brodie Sch. Fine Arts, Carnegie Mellon U., Newfane, Vt. Winner Mark Twain Contest, 1958; recipient Ingram Merrill Found. award, 1962; Nat. Arts Council award, 1968; Guggenheim fellow, 1968-69; Wash. Cultural Enrichment grantee, 1969. Home: West Townshend, Vt. Died Oct. 22, 1975.

BRODSKY, NATHAN, univ. dean; b. Phila., Sept. 22, 1916; s. Alfred and Pauline (Sennett) B.; B.S. with honors, Temple U., 1937; postgrad. U. Pa., 1938-40; Ph.D. in Econs., Am. U., 1959; m. Margaret Sara McStay, Dec. 27, 1946; children—James Alfred, David Arthur, Barbara Ann. Social worker Pa. Dept. Pub. Assistance, 1937-40; successively chief Brit. Dominions and India br. and chief procurement coordination br. UNRRA, 1946-48; chief policy div. office of distbn., dep. chief office of distbn., dep. vice-chmn. for supply mgmt. Munitions Bd., 1948-52; dep. dir. Def. Supply Mgmt. Agy., 1952-53; asst. dir. cataloging, standardization and inspection Dept. Def., 1954-57; dir. research and spl. projects Office Sec. Def., 1957-66, dir. edn. programs and mgmt. tng., 1966-73, acting dep. asst. sec. def. for edn., 1968-70, 72; dean Coll. Continuing Edn., Am. U., Washington, 1973-75; comdg. officer Moblzn. detachment, 1961-63, chmn. Def. Logistics Mgmt. Tng. Bd., 1963-66, chmn. Def. Logistics Research Conf., 1965. Vis. lectr.; cons. intergovtl. relations subcom. U.S. Ho. of Reps., 1949-52; mem. Interagy. Council on Internat. Ednl. and Cultural Affairs, 1966-73, Fed. Interagy. Com. Edn., 1968-73, Nat. Adv. Council on Extension and Continuing Edn., 1966-73; assisted Hoover Commn. Task Force on Fed. Supply, 1948. Served as 2d lt. to col., AUS, 1941-46. Decorated Bronze Star medal; recipient Civilian Meritorious Service medal Sec. of Def., 1970, 73. Mem. Am. Econ. Assn., Acad. Polit. Sci., Am. Polit. Sci. Assn., Inst. Mgmt. Sci., Washington Operations Research Council. Contbr. articles in bus. and econ. jours. Home: Arlington, Va. Died Oct. 7, 1975.

BROGDEN, WILFRED JOHN, psychologist; b. Sydney, Australia, May 6, 1912; s. John and Elsie May (Taylor) B.; came to U.S., 1914, naturalized, 1926; student So. Meth. U., 1929-32; A.B., U. Ill., 1933, Ph.D., 1936; NRC fellow Johns Hopkins Sch. Medicine, 1936-37; m. Elinor Taylor Davis, Sept. 8, 1935; children—Penelope, Ann. Research asst. in psychiatry Johns Hopkins Sch. Medicine, 1937-39; asst. prof. psychology U. Wis., 1939-43, asso. prof., 1944-46, prof. psychology, from 1946, asst. dean Grad. Sch., 1947, asso. dean, 1951-58. Vis. lectr. U. Rochester, summer 1942, Harvard, summer 1946. Active research applied psychology panel NDRC, 1942-45 (awarded presdl. certificate of appreciation, 1947); expert cons. to sec. nat. def., 1947-54; mem. sub-panel on sensory functions Research and Dev. Bd., 1947-48, chmn., 1948, mem. panel on human engring. and psychophysiology, 1948-54; mem. div. anthropology and psychology NRC, 1948-52, chmn. com. fellowship selection procedures. Mem. profl. adv. com. on human resources USAF, 1948-50. Fellow A.A.A.S., Am. Psychol. Assn. (pres. div. physiology and comparative psychology 1949; sec. div. theoretical and exptl. psychology 1948); mem. Am. Assn. U. Profs., Psychonomics Soc. (organizing com. 1960; governing bd. 1960-63, chmn. 1962), Soc. Exptl. Psychology, Midwestern Psychology Assn., Sigma Xi. Contbr. articles to sci. jours. Home: Madison, Wis. Died 1973.

BROIDA, HERBERT PHILIP, physicist; b. Aurora, Colo., Dec. 25, 1920; s. Theodore D. and Lucy (Shatz) B.; B.A. in Physics, U. Colo., 1944; M.A., Harvard U., 1945, Ph.D., 1949; m. Ina Burnes, Aug. 8, 1948; children—John Phillip, Allison Burnes. Instr. physics Wesleyan U., Middletown, Conn., 1944-45; teaching and research fellow Harvard U., 1945-49; research asso. Georgetown U. Sch. Medicine, 1957-63; sect. chief, program coordinator Nat. Bur. Standards, Washington, 1949-63, physicist, 1976-77; chmn. evaluation panel optical physics div., 1973-75; prof. physics U. Calif., Santa Barbara, 1963-78, dir. Quantum Inst., 1973-78; mem. com. comparative evaluation of trace gas techniques for detection explosives Research Triangle Inst.; com. atomic and molecular physics NRC-Nat. Acad. Sci.; mem. Santa Barbara Environmental Quality Adv. Bd., 1974-76; cons. in field. Guggenheim fellow, 1952-53; sr. fellow NSF, 1959-60; recipient Flemming award U.S. Jr. C. of C., 1956; Broida Hall of Physics, U. Calif. at Santa Barbara, named in his honor. Fellow Am. Phys. Soc. (vice chmn. div. electron and atomic physics 1978, Broida prize named in his honor), AAAS, Optical Soc. Am.; mem. Combustion Inst., Am. Assn. Physics Tchrs., Western Spectroscopy Assn. Co-author: Formation and Trapping of Free Radicals, 1960. Contbr. profl. jours. Home: Santa Barbara, Calif. Died Apr. 9, 1978.

BROKENBURR, ROBERT LEE, state senator, lawyer; b. Phoebus, Va., Nov. 16, 1886; s. Benjamin F. and Mary Elizabeth (Baker) B.; grad. Hampton Inst., 1906; LL.B., Howard U., 1909, LL.D., 1956; m. Alice J. Glover, June 28, 1911; m. 2d, Nettie W. Hightower, Nov. 27, 1947. Admitted to Ind. bar, 1910, since practiced in Indpls.; chmn. bd. Madam C. J. Walker Mfg. Co., 1945—; ex-alternate U.S. rep. UN Gen. Assembly; dir. Community Surveys, Inc., Flanner House Homes, Inc.; mem. Ind. state senate, 1940-48, 52—. Dir. Central Ind. council Boy Scouts Am.; dir. met. bd. YMCA, Indpls., 1949-58, elected v.p. 1954; trustee Indpls. YMCA, 1957—; dir. YMCA of Ind., 1924, sec., 1943-47, 1st v.p., 1949-58; del. nat. council YMCA, 9 yrs. Rep. candidate for superior ct. judge Marion County, Ind., 1958; sec. Ind. Rep. State Conv., 1958. Recipient 3d Ann, Stephen S. Wise Meml. citation, Indpls. chpt. Am. Jewish Congress; Outstanding Alumnus award Hampton Inst., 1949; Mason of Year award Grand Lodge of Ind., 1956. Mem. Am., Nat., Ind., Indpls. bar assns. Mem. A.M.E. Zion Ch. Mason (33 deg.). Home: Indpls. *

BROMAGE, ARTHUR WATSON, educator; b. East Windsor, Conn., Feb. 27, 1904; s. William George and Emma Irene (Bower) B.; B.S., Wesleyan U., 1925, A.M., Harvard, 1926, Ph.D., 1928; m. Mary Cogan, July 5, 1928; 1 dau., Susanna Sarah (Mrs. John Paterson). Asst. in govt. Harvard, 1926-28, instr., 1928-29; instr. U. Mich., Ann Arbor, 1928, asst. prof. polit. sci., 1929-31, asso. prof., 1931-38, prof., 1938-74, emeritus, 1974-79, chmn. dept. polit. sci., 1961-64. Cons. Mich. Commn. of Inquiry into County, Twp. and Sch. Dist. Govt., 1931-33; mem. Nat. Municipal League Com. on County Govt., 1932-42; leader roundtable on local govt. Va. Inst. Pub. Affairs, 1936; sec. Mich. Commn. on Reform and Modernization Govt., 1938-39; chmn. exec. bd. Ann Arbor Citizens Council, 1942-43; mem. city council Ann Arbor, 1949-53; Mich. Commn. on Inter-govtl. Relations, 1954-55; adv. mem. Mich. Legislative Interim Com. on Intergovtl. Relations, 1954-55; mem. Mich. Commn. on Annexation, 1962-63, Mich. Commn. on Local Govt., 1970-71. Mem. exec. com. Coll. Lit., Sci. and Arts, U. Mich., 1948-49, 67-70; v.p. Midwest Conf. Polit. Scientists, 1963-64. Served to lt. col. AUS, 1943-45. Mem. Am. Polit. Sci. Assn. (exec. council 1944-46), Am. Soc. Pub. Adminstrn., Nat. (council 1953-60), Mich. (v.p. 1952, hon. life) municipal leagues, Internat. City Mgrs. Assn. (hon.), Inst. Pub. Adminstrn. (exec. com. 1947-64), Survey Research Center U. Mich. (exec. com. 1947-52), Delta Sigma Rho, Phi Beta Kappa, Phi Kappa Phi. Author: American County Government, 1933; (with T.H. Reed), Organization and Cost of County and Township Government, 1933; State Government and Administration in the United States, 1936; Manager Plan Abandonments, 1940; Introduction to Municipal Government and Administration, 1950; On the City Council, 1950; A Councilman Speaks, 1951; Councilmen at Work, 1954; Political Representation in Metropolitan Agencies, 1962; Urban Policy Making: The Council-Manager Partnership, 1970. Contbr. articles to jours. Home: Ann Arbor, Mich. Died Feb. 9, 1979.

BROMLEY, BRUCE, lawyer; b. Pontiac, Mich., Mar. 20, 1893; s. Peter Brewater and Sarah Suydam (Ditmas) B.; A.B., U. Mich., 1914, LL.D. (hon.), 1949; LL.B., Harvard, 1917; LL.D. (hon.), Union U., Schenectady, 1958; m. Esther Baldwin, May 10, 1922; children—Stephen Baldwin, Peter Brewster, Bruce (dec.), Sarah Suydam (Mrs. Cory B. Kilvert). Admitted to N.Y. bar, 1920; asso. firm Cravath, Swaine & Moore, N.Y.C., 1923-26, partner, 1926-49, 50—; asso. judge N.Y. State Ct. Appeals, 1949; Sterling lectr. Yale Law Sch., 1933-38, 46-47; dir. IBM Corp. Mem. Lawyers Com. for Civil Rights Under Law, 1963-80, N.Y.C. Mayor's Bd. Ethics, 1961-80, Nat. Com. Study Antitrust Laws, 1953-80. Fellow Am. Coll. Trial Lawyers; mem. Am., N.Y. bar assns., Met. Trial Lawyers Assn. Home: New York, N.Y. Died Jan. 30, 1980.

BROMMAGE, CLAUDE STILSON, interior designer; b. Ovid, Mich., July 31, 1908; s. Edward and Stella (Stilson) B.; student Western Mich. State U., Kalamazoo, 1929, Art Inst., 1930-33; m. Alice M. Weaver, 1930 (div. 1933). With Marshall Field & Co., Chgo., 1933-38; mgr. home furnishings dept. Miller and Paine, Lincoln, Nebr., 1938-68, coordinator home furnishings and interior design studio and contract sales, 1968-73; propr. Claude S. Brommage Interiors, Tucson, 1973-79. Dir. supple for ARC, MTO, 1944-46. Served with AUS, 1942-44. Fellow Am. Soc. Interior Designers (v.p. 1958-62, dir. 1956-62), Nebr. Art Assn., Tucson Mus. Art, Nat. Travel Club. Republican. Christian Scientist. Club: Elks. Author travel articles. Home: Tucson, Ariz. Died June 20, 1979; buried Maple Grove Cemetery, Ovid, Mich.

BRONK, DETLEV W., scientist, educator; b. N.Y.C., Aug. 13, 1897; s. Mitchell and Marie (Wulf) B.; A.B., Swarthmore Coll., 1920; postgrad. U. Pa., 1921; M.S., U. Mich., 1922, Ph.D., 1926; recipient over 55 hon. degrees from univs. and colls.; m. Helen A. Ramsey, Sept. 10, 1921; children—John Everton Ramsey, Adrian, Mitchell Herbert. Mem. univ. faculties, 1921-49; pres. Johns Hopkins, 1949-53; pres. Rockefeller U., N.Y.C., 1953-68, pres. emeritus, 1968-75. Coordinator research Air Surgeons Office, Hdqrs. Army Air Forces, 1942-46, vice chmn. Nat. Adv. Com. Aeros., 1948-58. Held 12 endowed named lectureships, 1938-75; dir. Johnson Research Found., U. Pa., 1929-49; chmn. NRC, 1946-50; pres. Nat. Acad. Scis., 1950-62; chmn. bd. NSF, 1956-64; mem. Pres.'s Sci. Adv. Com., 1956-63; cons.-at-large, 1963-75; chmn. Panel on Internat. Sci., 1957-63; vice chmn. N.Y. State Sci. and Tech. Found., 1965-68, chmn., 1968-75; pres. N.Y. Hall of Sci.; mem. Inter-Am. com. on sci. and tech. OAS, 1969-75; mem. N.Y. State Pub. Health Council, 1972-75. Trustee Atoms for Peace Awards, Renssalaer Poly. Inst. (chmn. bd. 1966-71), Tulane U., U. Pa., Bucknell U., Haifa U., Marine Biol. Lab., Johns Hopkins, Population Council, Protein Found., Rockefeller Bros. Fund, Sloan-Kettering Inst. Served as ensign U.S. Naval Aviation Corps, 1918-19. Decorated officer Order Brit. Empire; recipient award for exceptional civilian service, 1946, Longacre award Aero. Med. Assn., 1948, Priestley award Dickinson Coll., 1956; Gold medal Internat. Ben Franklin Soc., 1958; medal Soc. Promoting Internat. Sci. Relationships, 1959, Gold medal Holland Soc., 1961, George Washington award Hungarian-Am. Soc., 1962, Franklin medal Franklin Inst., 1962; Presdl. Medal of Freedom, 1964; Pub. Welfare medal Nat. Acad. Scis., 1964; Nat. Sci. medal, 1969; Lehman award N.Y. Acad. Sci., 1974. Fellow A.A.A.S. (pres. 1952); mem. or hon. mem. many Am., fgn. prof. socs. (sometime officer several). Baptist. Clubs: N.Y. Yacht, University, Century, Lotos (N.Y.C.); Rittenhouse (Phila.); Maryland (Balt.); Seal Harbour Yacht; Cosmos (Washington); Athenaeum (London, Eng.). Home: New York, N.Y. Died Nov. 17, 1975.

BRONSON, ROY A., lawyer; b. Los Angeles, July 20, 1889; s. Edward D. and Mabel S. (Knox) B.; A.B., U. Santa Clara, 1912, A.M., 1913, LL.B., 1914; m. Clarisse Caspers, Feb. 16, 1916 (div.); children—Jean (Mrs. John E. Miller), Margery (Mrs. Stephen S. Townsend), Claire (Mrs. Van S. Trefethen); m. 2d, Lola Jones Rankin, Oct. 8, 1949. Admitted to Cal. bar, 1914, practiced in San Francisco; founder, sr. partner firm Bronson, Bronson & McKinnon, 1927-77; dir. various corps. Pres. Cal. Safety Council, 1949. Pres. adv. bd. Mary's Help Hosp. Fellow Am. Bar Found.; mem. Internat., Am. (ho. of dels. 1952-58, 62-63, chmn. traffic ct. program), San Francisco (past pres.) bar assns., Am. Judicature Soc. (past dir.), Am. Law Inst., Western States Bar Conf. (past pres.). Republican. Roman Catholic. Clubs: Bohemian, Commercial, World Trade, San Francisco. Home: Walnut Creek, Calif. Died June 12, 1977.

BROOK, ALEXANDER, artist; b. Bklyn., July 14, 1898; s. Onufri and Eudoxia (Gelescu) B.; student Art Students League, 1915-19; m. Peggy Bacon, May 4, 1920 (div. 1940); children—Belinda, Alexander Bacon; m. 2d, Gina Knee, Dec. 22, 1944. Awards: Logan medal and purchase prize ($2,500), Chgo. Art Inst. 1929; 2d prize, Lehman award, 29th annual, Carnegie Inst., Pitts., 1930; Temple gold medal 126th annual Pa. Acad. Fine Arts, Phila., 1931; fellowship in painting Guggenheim Found., N.Y.C., 1931; 1st prize Los Angeles Mus., 1934; Gold medal Am. Sect. Internat. Expn., Paris, 1937; 1st prize and special merit award 17th Annual Expn. of Advt. Art, N.Y.C., 1937; 1st prize, Am. painting, Worcester, Mass., 1938; medal of award San Francisco Art Assn., 1938; 1st prize 38th Annual, Carnegie Inst., 1939; Beck gold medal Pa. Acad., 1948; Benjamin Altman 2d prize N.A.D., 1957, 60. Represented in permanent collections Metropolitan Mus., N.Y.C.; Bklyn. Mus.; Art Inst. Chgo.; Carnegie Inst., Pitts.; U. Neb.; William Nelson Gallery, Kansas City, Mo.; Wadsworth Atheneum, Hartford, Conn.; Mus. Modern Art, N.Y.C.; Newark (N.J.) Mus., Boston Mus.; Toledo (Ohio) Mus., Ann Arbor (Mich.) State U.; De Young Mus., San Francisco Mus.; Corcoran Gallery, Washington; Albright Gallery, Buffalo; City Art Mus., St. Louis; Whitney Mus. of Am. Art, N.Y.C., Ogunquit (Maine) Mus. Art. Mem. Nat. Inst. Arts and Letters, N.A.D. (Gold medal 1950). Home: Sag Harbor, N.Y. Died Feb. 4, 1980.

BROOKS, BURROW PENN, dean; b. Altus, Ark., Jan. 30, 1886; s. William Joshua and Fannie Jeannie (Brooks) B.; A.B., Union U., Tenn., 1906; M.A., Peabody Coll., 1932; student Columbia U., 1920-21; m. Olive Kirby, July 10, 1907 (died 1935); children—Alice Frances (Mrs. William R. Crudup), William Robert (dec.); m. 2d, Mary Wilkinson Hutton, Aug. 7, 1937; children—Mildred Hutton, Burrow Penn. Principal Wagoner High School, Wagoner, Oklahoma, 1906-07, Mississippi Methodist Conference Training School, Montrose, Miss., 1907-11; superintendent Shubuta (Miss.) Pub. Schs., 1911-16; prin. Hattiesburg (Miss.) High Sch., 1916-18; supt. Belzoni (Miss.) Pub. Sch., 1918-36; financial sec. Miss. State Coll., 1937-40, dean Sch. of Edn., dir. instrn. and dir. Summer Sch., 1940-57, retired; dean Wood Junior College, 1957—. Member of State High School Accrediting Commn. since 1940, Miss. Jr. Coll. Commn. since 1940. Mem. State Dept. Council on Education since 1949. Mem. exec. com. Commn. on Curricular Problems and Research, Southern Assn. of Colls. and Secondary Schools, since 1942; Army-Navy rep. for 4th area Command at Miss. State Coll. since 1942; mem. Miss. Edn. Assn. (exec. com. 1933-36), N.E.A., Dept. of Superintendence, Alpha Tau Omega, Phi Delta Kappa, Starkville Chamber of Commerce. Democrat. Methodist. Club: Rotary (dist. gov. Rotary Internat. 1935-36). Contbr. to Miss. Ednl. Advance. Collaborator: Ethics in Teaching Profession, 1941. Asso. editor of New Orleans Christian Advocate since 1942. Home: State College, Miss. *

BROOKS, CLYDE, physician; b. Paris, Mo., Aug. 30, 1881; s. Evan Sandifer and Malvina (Kennedy) B.; A.B., U. of Missouri, 1905; Ph.D., U. of Chicago, 1911; M.D., Rush Medical Coll., Chicago, 1913; LL.D., U. of Alabama, 1928; m. Camilla Purcell Tharp, Sept. 5, 1912. Student asst. U. of Mo., 1905; fellow in physiology, U. of Chicago, 1906; instr. physiology and pharmacology,

Washington U., 1907; asst. in exptl. medicine, U. of Chicago, 1908; instr. physiology and pharmacology, 1910, asst. prof., 1911, U. of Pittsburgh; prof. and head Dept. Physiology, Physiol. Chemistry and Pharmacology, Ohio State U., 1915-20; prof. of physiology and pharmacology and dean, 1920-28, prof. physiology and pharmacology, also lecturer on internal medicine, 1928-31, Sch. of Medicine, U. of Ala.; prof. physiology and pharmacology, La. State U. Med. Center, New Orleans, 1931-45; dean, prof., head dept. physiol. and pharmacology, Essex Coll. Med. and Surg., Newark, N.J., since 1945. Research work, War Dept., 1917-18, as consulting physiologist, and organizer and dir. of a unit at Ohio State Univ. Fellow Am. Coll. Physicians, A.M.A.; mem. Pan Am. Med. Assn., Am. Rheumatism Assn., A.A.A.S., Am. Physiol. Soc., Am. Soc. Pharmacology and Experimental Therapeutics, Sigma Xi, Gamma Alpha, Phi Beta Pi and Phi Beta Kappa, fraternities; founder Gorgas Medical Society. Mem. Christian (Disciples) Ch. Rotarian. Club: Audubon Golf. *

BROOKS, EDWARD HALE, assn. dir.; b. N.H., Apr. 25, 1893; s. Edward Waite and Mary Frances (Hale) B.; B.S. in Civil Engring., Norwich (Vt.) U., 1916, M. Mil. Sci., LL.D.; grad. F.A. Sch., 1922, Command and Gen. Staff Sch., 1934, Army War Coll., 1937; Doctor Mil. Sc., Pa. Mil. Coll.; m. Beatrice Leavitt, Nov. 29, 1917; children—Elizabeth Allen (Mrs. R. Potter Campbell, Jr.), Maj. Edward Hale, Jr., A.C. (dec.). Served as capt. 1st Vt. Cav., 1915-16; commd. 2d lt., cav., U.S. Army, Aug. 1917 and advanced through grades to lt. gen., 1948; participated in Second Battle of Marne, Aisne-Marne, San Mihiel and Meuse-Argonne offensives; with Army of Occupation, Nov. 1918-July 1919, transferred to F.A., 1920; served in Philippines, 1926-28; chief, statistics branch, War Dept. Gen. Staff, 1939-41; artillery officer, Armored Force, 1941-42; comdg. gen. 11th Armored Div., Aug. 1942-Mar. 1944, 2d Armored Div., England, Normandy, Belgium Mar. 1944-Sept. 1944, comdg. gen. V Corps, Luxembourg, Germany Sept. 1944-Oct. 1944, comdg. gen. VI Corps, France, Germany, Austria Oct. 1944-May 1945; accepted surrender of German 19th Army, Innsbruck, Austria, May 5, 1945; later dep. comdg. gen. 3d Army, Atlanta; comdg. gen. Antilles Dept., San Juan, Puerto Rico; comdg. gen., U.S. Army Caribbean. Asst. chief of staff, G-1, Personnel, Dept. Army, Wash.; comdg. gen. 2d Army, Ft. Meade, Md. 1951-53; exec. dir., Assn. Mil. Coll. and Sch. U.S., 1953-64. Corporator, New Hampshire Savings Bank. Exec. bd. Daniel Webster council Boy Scouts Am. Decorated D.S.C., D.S.M. with oak leaf cluster. Legion of Merit with oak leaf cluster. Silver Star with oak leaf cluster, Bronze Star, officer Legion of Honor, Croix de Guerre with two palms (France); grand officer Netherlands Order Orange-Nassau; Mil. Order 1st Class, Army Republic of Chile; officer Order of the Crown, Croix de Guerre with Palm (Belgium); Abdon Calderon, 1st class, Republic of Ecuador. Mem. Soc. of Cincinnati, Assn. U.S. Army (council trustees 1959-65). Home: Concord, N.H. Died Oct. 10, 1978; buried Arlington Nat. Cemetery.

BROOKS, JOSHUA TWING, congressman; b. Edgeworth, Pa., Feb. 27, 1884; Ph.B., Sheffield Scientific Sch. (Yale), 1908; m. Ruth Walker, of Pittsburgh, Pa.; children—Bertha Bennett, Ruth Walker. Connected with Carnegie Steel Co. and Franklin-Park Foundry Co., until 1918; later treas. Woodings Forge & Tool Co. until 1928; then head Pittsburgh Sales Co., ry. supplies and steel; mem. 73d and 74th Congresses (1933-37), 30th Pa. Dist. Served in quatermaster div., U.S.A., World War. Democrat. Address: Sewickley, Pa.*

BROOKS, PHILIP COOLIDGE, archivist, ret. library dir.; b. Washington, Jan. 14, 1906; s. Franklin E. and Sara (Coolidge) B.; B.A., U. Mich, 1928; M.A., U. Calif., 1930. Ph.D., 1933; m. Dorothy H. Holland, Feb. 12, 1938; 1 son, Philip Coolidge. Teaching and traveling fellow U. Calif., 1929-33; teaching asst. George Washington U., 1933-34; bibliographer Am. Hist. Assn. 1933-35; exam., staff officer, chief archivist records br. Nat. Archives, 1935-48, 50-53; records officer Nat. Security Resources Bd., 1948-50; chief fed. records center Gen. Services Adminstrn. San Francisco, 1953-57; dir. Harry S. Truman Library, GSA, 1957-71; sec. Harry S. Truman Library Inst., 1957-71, mem. bd., 1972-77; cons. oral history Nat. Archives and Records Service, 1971-77. Vis. lectr. U. Panama, 1954; records mgmt. adviser Republic Panama, ICA, 1954-55. Mem. adv. bd. Nat. Trust for Historic Preservation, 1970-71; mem. Ariz. Hist. Adv. Commn., 1974-77. Recipient Distinguished Service award Gen. Services Adminstrn., 1967; Outstanding Achievement award U. Mich., 1972. Fellow Soc. Am. Archivists (sec. 1936-42, pres. 1949-51); mem. Am. Hist. Assn., Am. Assn. State and Local History, Jackson County Hist. Soc. (v.p. 1960-71). Orgn. Am. Historians, Methodist. Author: Diplomacy and the Borderlands, 1939, 70; Public Records Management, 1949, rev. 1961, El Manejo de Archivos y Documentos, 1955; Research in Arhives, 1969. Contbr. articles, revs. to hist., archival jours. Home: Sun City, Ariz. Died July 25, 1977; interred Evergreen Cemetery, Colorado Springs, Colo.

BROOKS, ROBERT ANGUS, mus. ofcl.; b. Calcutta, India, Oct. 16, 1920 (parents U.S. citizens); s. Milton and Mabel (Spence) B.; A.B. summa cum laude, Harvard, 1940, M.A., 1941, Ph.D., 1949; m. Jane S. Kochmann, Jan 2, 1943; children—Alison Spence (Mrs. John Yellen), Roger Angus, Camilla Jane. Jr. fellow Soc. Fellows, Harvard, 1942, 46-48, instr., 1949-51; research asso., v.p., dir. Harbridge House, Inc., Boston, 1951-65, pres., 1969-71; asst. sec. of army for installations and logistics, 1965-69; dep. under sec. Smithsonian Instn., 1971-72, asst. sec., 1972-73, under sec., 1973-76. Mem. Nat. Adv. Council on Minority Bus. Enterprise, 1969-71. Served to capt. USAAF, 1942-46; PTO. Mem. Am. Philol. Assn., Phi Beta Kappa Episcopalian. Clubs: Harvard (Boston); Cosmos (Washington). Author numerous articles, poems, plays, reports, essays; narrator various recs. Home: Washington, D.C. Died Apr. 11, 1976; buried Mt. Auburn Cemetery, Cambridge, Mass.

BROOKS, THOMAS DUDLEY, school adminstrn.; b. Percy, Miss., Jan. 18, 1882; s. Ambrose Dudley and Minnie (Watson) B.; A.B., Baylor U., 1903; A.M., U. of Chicago, 1920, Ph.D., 1921; m. Elizabeth Oberthier, Dec. 27, 1905. Teacher and prin. pub. and high schs., Tex., until 1906; supt. pub. schs., Hillsboro, 1906-16; pres. Southeastern State Normal Sch., Okla., 1916-19; prof. sch. administration, Baylor U., 1921-32, also dean summer sch.; dean Sch. of Arts and Sciences and of Grad. Sch., Agrl. and Mechanical Coll. of Tex., 1932-47; dean emeritus and professor of education, since 1947. Member City Commn. and mayor, City of Waco, 1928-30. Mem. commn. and staff of Tex. Ednl. Survey, 1923. Democrat. Baptist. Mason. Rotarian (gov. 41st Dist. Rotary Internat. 1931-32). Home: College Station, Tex. *

BROOKS, WHITNEY LAWTON, banker; b. Torrington, Conn., Dec. 13, 1918; s. Charles Kenneth and Laura Marana (Brooks) Lawton; grad. Kent Sch., 1937; B.A., Williams Coll., 1941; postgrad. Grad. Sch. Banking, Rutgers U., 1952; m. Nancy Pierson Hirose, May 7, 1945 (div. 1964); children—Marguerite, Marana; m. 2d, Elizabeth Pringle Campbell, June 11, 1966; stepchildren—Mary, Elizabeth. With Brooks Bank & Trust Co., Torrington, 1941-79, successively treas., 1952-61, exec. v.p., 1961-68, chmn. bd., 1968-70, merged with Colonial Bank & Trust Co., Waterbury, Conn., 1970, sr. v.p., 1970-79, also dir.; corporator Torrington Savs. Bank; v.p., dir. sec. Burns, Brooks & McNeil, Inc., ins., Torrington. Chmn. Conn. Hist. Commn., 1956-66, vice chmn., 1966-79; mem. N.E. adv. com. Nat. Archives, 1971-79; treas. N.W. Conn. council Girl Scouts U.S.A., 1964-79; chmn. Wolcottville Sch. Soc., 1967-79; vice chmn. Conn. Am. Revolution Bicentennial Commn., 1974-79; mem. adv. com. Litchfield Historic Dist., 1977-79; lt. col. First Litchfield Arty., 1963-79. Bd. dirs., treas. Litchfield County Credit Bur.; treas. Hillside Cemetery Assn.; trustee, sec.-treas. Torrington Library; corporator Maria Brooker Meml. Clinic; bd. overseers Old Sturbridge (Mass.) Village. Served with AUS, 1943-46. Mem. Torrington Hist. Soc. (dir. 1945-79, pres. 1960-79), Litchfield Hist. Soc. (dir. 1961-79), Antiquarian and Landmarks Soc. Conn. (dir. 1971-79). Republican. Episcopalian. Clubs: Sanctum, Litchfield County University; Williams (N.Y.); Waterbury (Conn.); Officers (Hartford). Home: Litchfield, Conn. Died May 14, 1979.

BROOKS, WILEY GLEN, college pres.; b. Adelphia, O., Oct. 24, 1886; s. Leonadis Culver and Adelina Humphrey (Alford) B.; student Fairfield Union Acad., Pleasantville, O., 1901-02, Baker U., Baldwin City, Kan., 1903-05; B. Edn., Neb. State Teachers Coll., Peru, Neb., 1911; A.B., York (Neb.) Coll., 1910; A.M., Columbia, 1915; Ph.D., State U. of Ia., 1936; m. Etha Nell Crabill, Aug. 21, 1912; children—Mary Jane Alford, Helen Jean. Supt. schs., Caldwell, Ida., 1910-13, Plattsmouth, Neb., 1913-18, Nebraska City, Neb., 1918-22, York, Neb., 1922-25, Burlington, Ia., 1925-37; pres. and trustee Ill. Wesleyan U., 1937-40; research asst., Inst. Ednl. Research, Teachers Coll., Columbia, 1940-41; pres. Neb. State Teachers Coll., Chadron, since July 1, 1941; visiting lecturer in ednl. adminstrn., summer sch., U. of Pittsburgh, 1940. Mem. N.E.A. (life), Am. Assn. Sch. Adminstrs., Ia. State Teachers Assn. (pres. 1936-37), Am. Council of Edn., Phi Kappa Phi, Delta Tau Delta, Phi Delta Kappa. Republican. Methodist. Mason (32 deg., K.T.). Club: Rotary of Chadron (past pres. Burlington, Ia., club). Home: Chadron, Neb. *

BROPHY, FRANK CULLEN, banker, rancher; b. Bisbee, Ariz., Nov. 16, 1894; s. William Henry and Ellen (Goodbody) B.; grad. Phillips Acad., Andover, 1913; A.B., Yale, 1917; m. Sallie Ropes Blake, May 3, 1919; children—Alice Blake (Mrs. John T. McChesney), William H., Anthony Blake, Sallie Cullen (Mrs. George J.W. Goodman), Frank C., Mary Kathleen, James M.R. Dir. Ariz. Central Bank, Flagstaff, No. Ariz. Securities Co., Los Angeles, 1923-27; dir., exec. v.p. Phoenix Nat. Bank, Phoenix Savs. Bank & Trust Co., 1923-30; dir., pres. Bank of Douglas (Ariz.), 1935-55, chmn. of Douglas, Phoenix, 1955-59; pres. Phoenix Date Co., 1927-55, Gen. Grocery Co., 1941-58, Gen. Sales Co., 1943-58, PM Sales Co., 1957-78, Libbey Fruit Packing Co.; owner, operator Babacomari Ranch, Elgin, Ariz., 1937-72, El Fresnal Ranch, Aguga Prieta, Sonora, Mexico, 1942-48. Mem. nat. council John Birch Soc., 1961-78. Trustee St. Joseph's Hosp., Barrows Neur. Inst., 1952-68, Brophy Coll. Prep. Dir. Am. Inst. for Fgn. Trade, 1946-55. Founder Maricopa County Taxpayers Assn.; mem. Ariz. State Fair Commn., 1938-40; chmn. Ariz. Racing Commn., 1949-53, mem., 1970-74; Ariz. Semicentennial Com., 1960. Mem. adv. bd. For Am., 1955; nat. bd. Campaign for 48 States, 1956. Decorated comdr. Sovereign Order of St. John of Jerusalem, Knights of Malta. Clubs: University (Seattle); Athletic (Los Angeles); Old Pueblo (Tucson); Phoenix Country. Author: Arizona Sketch Book. Contbr. articles to Commonweal, Cath. World, Ariz. Hwys. Home: Phoenix, Ariz. Died Feb. 3, 1978.

BROPHY, GERALD B., ret. lawyer; b. Yonkers, N.Y., Nov. 12, 1901 s. Patrick F. and Mary E. (Renahan) B.; A.B., Columbia, 1924, LL.B., 1926. Admitted to N.Y. State bar, 1927, Cal. bar, 1957; asso. firm Chadbourne, Parke, Whiteside, Wolff & Brophy and predecessors, N.Y.C., 1926-34, partner, 1934-55; dir. N. Am. Aviation, Inc., Los Angeles, 1940-42, 46-61, gen. counsel, v.p., 1955, sr. v.p., 1958-61, sr. counsel, 1961-66; dir. Oppenheim Collins & Co., Inc., 1935-42, Gen. Aniline & Film Corp., 1948-53. Spl. cons. to U.S. sec. of state, 1950-51. U.S. rep. Internat. Civil Aviation Orgn., Montreal, 1945-46; chief, U.S. delegation North Atlantic Air Conf., Dublin (Eire), 1946; cons. to U.S. delegation Gen. Assembly of Internat. Civil Aviation Orgn., 1947; mem. adv. council Congl. Aviation Policy Bd., 1948. Served as maj., later col. USAAF, 1942-45; col. USAF Res., 1945-53. Decorated Legion of Merit. Mem. Bar Assn. City of N.Y., Am., N.Y. State bar assns., Psi Upsilon, Phi Delta Phi. Roman Catholic. Club: University (N.Y.C.). Home: Bronxville, N.Y. Died Dec. 25, 1978.

BROPHY, JOHN, labor union official; b. St. Helen, Lancanshire, Eng., Nov. 6, 1883; s. Patrick and Mary (Dagnall) B.; self-educated; m. Anita Anstead, Aug. 13, 1918; children—Philip Noel, Jacqueline Anstead. Began as coal miner, 1895; labor union official since 1916; pres. of Dist. 2, United Mine Workers of America, 1917-27; officer Congress of Industrial Organizations since 1935; mem. United Steelworkers Union. treas. C.I.O. community service com. Mem. Nat. War Labor Bd.; mem. President's Com. on Fair Employment Practices, Home: Washington. *

BROSIO, MANLIO, Italian senator, ambassador; b. Turin, Italy, July 10, 1897; s. Edoardo and Fortunata (Curadelli) B.; Law Degree, Turin U., 1920; m. Clotilde Brosio, Oct. 1, 1936. Practice of law, Turin, Italy, 1922-43; mem. Liberal Party, central sec. Liberal Revolution movement, 1922-25, sec.-gen. Party, 1944-45; mem. underground Nat. Liberation Com., 1943-44; minister without portfolio, Bonomi Govt., 1944; v.p. Council of Ministers, Parri Govt., 1945; minister def., 1945-46; ambassador to Moscow, 1947-51; Italian ambassador, London, 1952-54, U.S., 1955-61, France, from 1961; senator Italian Republic, from 1972, chmn. Liberal faction Italian Senate; mem. nat. council, nat. directorate Liberal Party. Served with Alpini Corps, Italian Army, 1915-18. Contbr. profl. jours. Home: Torino, Italy. Died Mar. 14, 1980.

BROSSARD, EDGAR BERNARD (BROS'SÁRD), chmn. tariff commn.; b. Oxford, Ida., Apr. 1, 1889; s. Amable Alphonse and Mary Catherine (Hobson) B.; B.S., Utah Agrl. Coll., 1911, LL.D., 1954; in Europe as missionary and pres. French Mission, Church of Jesus Christ of Latter-Day Saints (Mormon), 1911-14; M.S., University of Minnesota, 1917; student Grad. Sch., Cornell, 1917-18; Ph.D., U. of Minn., 1920; m. Laura P. Cowley, Aug. 25, 1915. Instr. mathematics, Utah Agrl. Coll., 1909-10; economist U.S. Tariff Commn., 1923-25; mem. U.S. Tariff Commn. 1925-59, chmn., 1930, 53-59, member interdepartmental com. on trade agreements and chairman committee reciprocity information; on ofcl. business for U.S. Tariff Commission in 13 principal European countries, summer, 1927, 9 countries, summer 1938. Mem. U.S. Govt.'s Interdeptl. Com. on Scientific and Cultural Cooperation; on official business for Com. in Mexico, Central and S. Am., Cuba, spring, 1946; U.S. alternate del., U.N. 2d Preliminary Conf. on Trade and Employment, Geneva, Switzerland, summer 1947; U.S. alternate del. U.N. Conference on Trade and Employment, Havana, Cuba, winter 1947-48; U.S. del. Internat. Trade Agreements Negotiations (GATT), Geneva, Switzerland, 1956. Mem. American Economic Assn., American Farm Economic Assn., Pub. School Assn. of Dist. of Columbia, Nat. Grange, Phi Kappa Phi, Alpha Zeta, Pi Kappa Alpha. Republican. Mem. Ch. of Jesus Christ of Latter Day Saints (Mormon). Club: Inquirendo. Author of bulls. and addresses on economics of agr., tariffs, world trade, etc. Home: Washington, D.C. Died 1980.

BROUGHAM, ROYAL, newspaperman; b. St. Louis, Sept. 17, 1894; s. Herbert David and Mattie (Brewer) B.; ed. pub. schs.; Litt.D., Biola Coll., LaMirada, Calif.; m. Alice Swanson, Apr. 14, 1915 (dec.); 1 dau., Alice May. Reporter Post-Intelligencer, Seattle, 1911, mng. editor, 1925, asso. editor. Founder Royal Brougham Found. Mem. Sigma Delta Chi. Clubs: Rotary, Wash.

Athletic, Seattle Yacht. Home: Seattle, Wash. Died Oct. 30, 1978.

BROUILLETTE, J(OSEPH) W(ALTER), SR., educator; b. Marksville, La., Mar. 30, 1898; s. Romulus M. and Blanch (Laborde) B.; Diploma, La. Normal Coll., 1918; B.S., George Peabody Coll., 1923, Ph.D., 1937; A.M., La. State U., 1932; m. Thelma Brown, Aug. 31, 1923; children—Joseph Walter, Janice Lou, Jean Martha. Prin. elementary school, Glencoe, La., 1917, Echo, La., 1919; prin. Port Barre (La.) High Sch., 1920-28; asst. supt. and supervisor instrn., St. Landry Parish, Opelousas, La., 1928-35; elementary state sch. supervisor and dir. audio-visual edn., also asso. supervisor Negro edn. and dir. teacher edn. and certification La. State Dept. Edn., 1935-40, 1942-44; dir. teacher edn. Miss. State Coll., 1940-42; dir. Gen. Extension div. La. State Univ. from 1944; teacher summer sessions, La. State Normal Coll., La. State Univ., from 1944; summer lecturer, Haiti, 1944. Served as pvt., U.S. Army, 1918. Asst., Survey Miss. Study Higher Edn., also S.C. Survey Instns. Higher Edn., 1945-46; spl. cons. La. Legislative Committee on Educational Survey, 1947-48; F.O.A. educational consultant Vietnam, Laos, and Cambodia, 1954; bd. dirs. La. State U. Found., La. State U. Anglo-Am. Art Mus. Recipient General Education Board fellowship, George Peabody Coll., 1931-32. Mem. Nat. U. Extension Assn. (pres. 1952-53, mem. exec. com.), Can.-U.S. Com. on Edn. (co-sec., mem. exec. com. 1937), La. Edn. Assn. (pres. elementary dept. 1926-30; chmn. research com. 1934-35), American Association of Land Grant Colls. and State Universities (chmn. council gen. extension 1959), So. Rural Life Council (mem. exec. com.), Phi Delta Kappa. Democrat. Roman Catholic. Club: Rotary. Co-author: (monographs) Teaching Foreign-Speaking Beginners How to Read and Speak English, 1925; A Comparative Study of the School Progress of Foreign-Speaking and English-Speaking Children in Early Elementary Grades, 1925. Co-author: Education and Rural Living in the South '47. Editor: Education in Louisiana, A Study, 1948. Mng. editor: Ednl. Outlook, 1926-35. Home: Baton Rouge, La. Died Mar. 26, 1978.

BROUN, MAURICE, naturalist; b. N.Y.C., Aug. 27, 1906; ed. pub. schs.; D.Sc., Muhlenberg Coll., 1952, Albright Coll., 1976; m. Irma Knowles Penniman, Jan. 15, 1934. Ornithol. work with Edward H. Forbush, 1927-29; pioneer devel. Pleasant Valley Sanctuary, Lenox, Mass., 1929-31; research asso. Austin Ornithol. Research Sta., South Wellfleet, Mass., 1931-34; curator Hawk Mountain Sanctuary, Kempton, Pa., 1934-66. Served with USNR, 1943-45. Recipient Conservation award Am. Motors Corp., 1965. Fellow, hon. mem. Delaware Valley Ornithol. Club; hon. mem. Rochester Acad. Sci.; elective Mem. Am. Ornithologists Union; mem. Am. Fern Soc., Wilson Ornithol. Soc. Author: Index to North American Ferns, 1938; Hawks Aloft, The Story of Hawk Mountain, 1949. Contbr. to Birds of Massachusetts and Other New England States, 1929; also numerous other books and profl. jours. Home: New Ringgold, Pa. Died Oct. 2, 1979.

BROUSE, ARTHUR H., banker; b. Strang, Neb., Aug. 22, 1886; s. Francis T. and Caroline (Baxter) B.; student Riverside Bus. Coll., 1905; m. Mary Meharg, Mar. 26, 1908; 1 son, Harold. Bookkeeper Nat. Bank of Riverside, Calif., 1907-15, cashier, 1915-18; inspector Bank of Italy, San Francisco, 1918-20, asst. cashier, Los Angeles, 1920-25, br. mgr., 1925-29, vice pres. in charge personnel, 1929-31; v.p. and dist. mgr. Bank of America, 1931, v.p. and mgr. San Bernardino br., 1932-37; exec. v.p. Nat. Bank of Washington, Tacoma, 1937-41, pres. since 1941. Mem. city planning commn., Tacoma. Mem. C. of C. Elk. Mason (Shriner). Club: Rotary. Home: Tacoma, Wash. *

BROWER, ALONZO BLAINE, physician; b. Amity, Ohio, June 5, 1884; s. Joseph S. and Nancy E. (Hern) B.; A.B., U. of Mich., 1908, M.D., 1910; m. Florence Giles, Aug. 27, 1913, one son, Bruce M. Interne, U. of Mich. Hospital, 1909-10, physician, Calumet & Hecla Mining Co., 1910-11, city physician, Dayton, O., 1912-15; in gen. practice of medicine, 1911-22; specialist in internal medicine since 1922. Mem. sr. med. staff, Miami Valley Hosp., St. Elizabeth's Hosp.; med. consultant, Nat. Mil. Home; cardiologist, Miami Valley Hosp.; mem. bd. trustees, dir. med. sect., Miami Valley Hosp. Served with A.E.F., 1918-19. Recipient Alfred Stengel Memorial award, 1953. Certified by Am. Bd. of Internal Medicine, 1937. Mem. Montgomery Co. Med. Soc. (pres. 1923-24), Ohio State Med. Assn., Am. Med. Assn., Am. Coll. Physicians (2d v.p., 1946), bd. regents), Med. Past President's Assn. (pres.), Central Soc. of Clin. Research, Am. Heart Assn., Assn. for Study of Internal Secretions, Phi Kappa Sigma, Phi Rho Sigma. Republican. Baptist. Mason. Club: Moraine Country. Home: Dayton.

BROWN, ALANSON CHARLES, shoe mfr.; b. St. Louis, Mo., Sept. 21, 1882; s. Alanson D. and Ella G. (Bills) B.; ed. Western Mil. Acad., Alton, Ill.; m. May Stegall, of Jackson, Tenn., Jan. 30, 1905; children—Alanson C., Helene C., Rhoda Elizabeth, Elbert. With Hamilton-Brown Shoe Co., established by father, since beginning of active career, became pres., 1914, now v.p. Baptist. Home: Clayton, Mo. *

BROWN, ALLYN LARRABEE, judge; b. Norwich, Conn., Oct. 26, 1883; s. Lucius and Hannah M. (Larrabee) B.; grad. Norwich Free Acad., 1901; A.B., Brown U., 1905, LL.D., 1938, Wesleyan University, 1950; student at Harvard University Law School, 1905-07; married Marion M. Brown, June 4, 1913; children—Allyn Larrabee, Frances Hannah. Admitted to Conn. bar, 1909; mem. firm Brown & Perkins, Norwich, Conn., 1909-21; mayor City of Norwich, 1916-18; mem. State Senate, 1921; judge Conn. Superior Court, 1921-35; asso. justice Conn. Supreme Court 1935 to March 10, 1950; chief justice since March 10, 1950. Trustee Brown Univ., Norwich Free Acad., Mansfield State Training Sch. Dir. Norwich Savings Soc. Republican. Baptist. Home: Norwich, Conn. *

BROWN, ARVIN HARRINGTON, JR., judge; b. Los Angeles, Nov. 21, 1917; s. Arvin Harrington and Kathleen Alberta (Maw) B.; A.B., Stanford U., 1939; J.D., U. So. Calif., 1947; m. Kathleen O'Connor, May 12, 1946; children—Kathleen Ellen Brown Lowery, Arvin Harrington, Michael B., Gregory T. Admitted to Calif. bar, 1948; asso. firm Gibson, Dunn & Crutcher, Los Angeles, 1948-49, Moss, Lyon & Dunn, Los Angeles, 1949-50, 52-57; partner firm Luce, Forward, Hamilton & Scripps, San Diego, 1958-66, Brown, Schall & Stennett, San Diego, 1967-70; asso. justice High Ct., Trust Ter. of Pacific Islands, 1970-78; instr. trial techniques U. San Diego Law Sch., 1966-70. Served to capt. inf. AUS, 1941-45, to maj. Judge Adv. Gen. Corps, 1950-52. Mem. Phi Delta Phi, Zeta Psi. Home: Ponape, Eastern Caroline Islands. Died Mar. 19, 1978; buried at Fort Rosecrans, San Diego, Calif.

BROWN, B(ENJAMIN) WARREN, sociologist; b. Janesville, Wis., Dec. 20, 1885; s. William Fiske and Hila Mandana (Bennett) B.; A.B., Beloit (Wis.) Coll., 1907; grad. study in sociology, U. of Chicago, 1913-16; m. Marjorie Waterman Gregory, 1913; 1 dau., Barbara Frances. Instr., high sch., Sparta, Wis., 1907-08; instr. Fargo (N.D.) Coll., 1909-10, prof. economics, 1910-11, dean, 1911-14; asst. to Prof. C. R. Henderson, U. of Chicago, 1915; research asst., Internat. Prison Commn., and instr., Grad. Sch., U. of Chicago, 1916-17; survey sec., Council Ch. Bds. of Edn. in U.S., 1917-20, asso. sec., 1921; asso. editor Christian Education, 1924-26; exec. sec. Liberal Arts Coll. Movement. Editor Liberal Arts Coll. Bulletin. Director ednl. survey of Presbyn. Church in U.S., 1926-28; dir. surveys in edn. for M.E., S., Bd. of Edn., since 1928. Mem. Delta Sigma Rho, Sigma Chi, Phi Beta Kappa. Baptist. Writer of monographs and reports, including Social Groups, 1926; A Statistical Survey of Illinois Colleges, 1918; Education Under Church Auspices, 1918; A Symposium on the Christian College, 1923; Report of the Survey of Educational Work and Responsibility of the Presbyterian Church in the U.S., 1927. Editor Presbyterian mag. "Pageant," 1938. Home: Chicago. *

BROWN, BRUCE K., mgmt. cons.; b. Columbus, Ohio, May 4, 1899; s. B. Frank and Anna S. (Lotspiech) B.; B.S., U. Ill., 1918, M.S., 1920; m. Antoinette Turner, July 19, 1919; children—Janet, Bruce K. With Burgess Labs., Madison, Wis., 1920-23, Comml. Solvents Corp., Terre Haute, Ind., 1923-27; admitted to Ill. bar, 1937, Ind. bar, 1925, D.C. bar, 1937, U.S. Supreme Ct. bar, 1930; practiced patent law, N.Y.C., 1928-29; with Standard Oil Co. of Ind., Chgo., 1929-41, gen. mgr. research and devel., 1938-41, v.p., dir., 1945-49; pres. Pan-Am. So. Corp., 1949-56; pres., chief exec. officer Petroleum Chems., Inc., 1956-60; bus. cons.; former chmn. bd., chmn. exec. com., dir. Murphy Corp., El Dorado; dir. Ingram Corp., New Orleans. Asst. dep. petroleum coordinator, Washington, 1941-45, chmn. mil. petroleum adv. bd., 1947-50; mem. Nat. Petroleum Council; dep. adminstr. Petroleum Adminstrn. for Def., Washington, 1950-52. Trustee Dillard U. Served as 2d lt., inf. U.S. Army, 1918. Republican. Methodist. Clubs: Pickwick, Petroleum (New Orleans). Author: A Survey of Nitrocellulose Lacquers, 1926; Oil Men in Washington, 1965; Committee Structures, 1965. Home: New Orleans, La. Died Mar. 2, 1980; interred Hope Mausoleum, St. John Cemetery, New Orleans.

BROWN, CAREY HERBERT, engr.; b. Rural Dale, O., May 2, 1886; s. James Abram and Frances Martha (Bethel) B.; student U. Chgo., 1903-06; B.S., U.S. Mil. Acad., 1910; student Army Engr. Sch., 1910-12, Command and Gen. Staff Sch., 1929-30; m. Walda Taylor McLaughlin, Nov. 29, 1911 (dec. Jan. 1914); 1 son, Herbert W.; m. 2d, Derryle Elizabeth Law, Nov. 30, 1918; children—Carey Herbert, Alston Law. Asst. engr. commr. D.C., 1919-22; engr. Nat. Capital Park and Planning Commn., 1925-29; dir. Civic Improvement Assn., Rochester, N.Y., 1930-33; engr., exec. Eastman Kodak Co., 1934-54, engr., then works mgr. Holston Ordnance Works, Kingsport, Tenn., 1942-45. Dir. civil and mil. engring. Engr. Sch. U.S. Army, 1922-25; chmn. tech. bd. rev. U.S. Pub. Works Adminstrn., 1933-34; past chmn. Engring. Manpower Commn., Engrs. Joint Council, Task Force on Navigation, Engrs. Joint Council; mem. task force on water resources and power Second Hoover Commn.; civil engring. adv. bd. Norwich U. Mem. bd. Rochester Gen. Hosp., Otetiana council Boy Scouts. Served 2d lt. to col., C.E., U.S. Army, 1910-30. Fellow Am. Soc. C.E. (dir. 1956-58, 62-63, v.p. 1962-63), Am. Soc. M.E. mem. Rochester C. of C. (trustee), Tau Beta Pi, Sigma Alpha Epsilon. Episcopalian. Author articles on engring. subjects. Home: Scottsville, N.Y. *

BROWN, ELI HUSTON, III, lawyer; b. Frankfort, Ky., Nov. 5, 1906; s. Eli Huston and Rose McKnight (Crittenden) B.; B.A., Princeton, 1929; LL.B., Harvard, 1933; LL.D., U. Louisville, 1967; m. Mavin Hamilton, Apr. 27, 1935 (dec. 1967); children—Mavin Hamilton, Eli Huston, IV. Admitted to Ky. bar, 1934; atty. Fed. Land Bank, Louisville, 1934-35; 2d asst. U.S. atty., Western Dist. Ky., 1935-37, 1st asst., 1937-38, U.S. dist. atty., 1938-45; now sr. partner Brown, Todd & Heyburn. Dir. Liberty Nat. Bank & Trust Co. Chmn. of com. Ky. Center Performing Arts; mem. Louisville and Jefferson County Air Bd., 1971-74. Trustee U. Louisville, 1948-70, acting pres., 1950-51, chmn. bd. trustees, 1949-51, 62-66. Mem. Am., Ky., Louisville bar assns. Democrat. Episcopalian. Clubs: Century, Harvard-Princeton (N.Y.C.); Wynn-Stay; River Valley; Gulfstream Bath and Tennis (Fla.). Home: Louisville, Ky. Died May 14, 1974.

BROWN, EMILY CLARK, economist; b. Mpls., Oct. 15, 1895; d. Edward J. and Mary (Fullerton) Brown; A.B., Carleton Coll., 1917; M.A., U. Chgo., 1923, Ph.D., 1927. Research asst. United Typothetae of Am., 1920-25; Social Sci. Research Council fellow, 1927-28; asst. prof. Wellesley Coll., 1929-32; asst. prof. to prof. Vassar Coll., 1932-61; operating analyst NLRB, 1942-44. Mem. Indsl. Relations Research Assn., AAUP, Assn. for Comparative Econ. Studies. Author: Book and Job Printing in Chicago, 1931; From the Wagner Act to Taft-Hartley (with Harry A. Millis), 1950; Soviet Trade Unions and Labor Relations, 1966. Home: Minneapolis, Minn. Died Oct. 13, 1980.

BROWN, FELIX HARRY, publishing co. exec.; b. Rostok, Austria, July 23, 1908; s. Max and Irma (Wlaschin) Braun; came to U.S., 1938, naturalized, 1943; student Columbia U., 1940-42; LL.B., N.Y. Law Sch., 1952; m. Edith B. Arndt, Aug. 18, 1966; children—Susan (Mrs. E. James Lieberman), Judith (Mrs. Barry Greif). Pub. accountant, N.Y.C., 1942-53; admitted to N.Y. bar, 1952; with Book-of-the-Month Club, Inc., N.Y.C., 1953-78, v.p., treas., 1966-73, exec. v.p., treas., 1973-75, exec. v.p., 1975-78, dir., 1969-78. C.P.A., N.Y. Mem. Am. Inst. Accountants, N.Y. State Soc. C.P.A.'s, New York County Lawyers Assn. Died Jan. 7, 1978.

BROWN, FREDERICK FERNANDO, clergyman; b. Glenville, N.C., Nov. 27, 1882; s. Horace Alonzo and Dorcas Elizabeth B.; prep. edn., Skyland Inst., Asheville, N.C., and Mars Hill (N.C.) Coll.; B.A., Wake Forest (N.C.) Coll., 1908, M.A., 1909, D.D., 1925; Th.M., Southern Bapt. Theol. Sem., Louisville, Ky., 1912, Th.D., 1913; LL.D., Carson Newman College, 1951 H.H.D., Lincoln Memorial University, 1951; married to Nona Lee Dover, April 12, 1914; children—Nona Lee, Ailene Virginia, Imogene, Fred Maxey, Mary Elizabeth. Ordained ministry Baptist Ch., 1913; pastor Harrodsburg and Frankfort, Ky., and Sherman, Tex.; pastor First Ch., Knoxville, Tenn., since 1921. Exec. sec. promotion com. Southern Bapt. Conv., 1931-32; pres. Southern Baptist Conv., 1933. Trustee Carson-Newman Coll., Jefferson City, Southeastern Baptist Seminary, East Tenn. Baptist Hosp., dir. Tenn. Baptist Orphange, Franklin, Tenn. Mem. exec. com. Bapt. Tenn. State Conv. Mason. Kiwanian (hon.). Author: This Is My Church, 1929. Home: Knoxville, Tenn. *

BROWN, FREDERICK NATHAN, JR., architect; b. Providence, Dec. 9, 1899; s. Frederick Nathan and Mary Woodhull (Coombs) B.; student R.I. Sch. Design, 1916-19, Brown Prep. Sch., Phila., 1919-20, U. Pa., 1920-23; m. Helen May Brakenwagen, June 28, 1924; children—Helen Mary (Mrs. Ralph Vernon Boyens), Frederick Nathan III. Architect, Jackson, Robertson & Adams, 1923-31; gen. practice architecture, Providence, 1931-41; architect War Dept., 1942-46; asso. architect Charles A. Maguire & Assos., Boston, Providence, 1946-54; specifications writer Perry, Shaw, Hepburn & Dean, Boston, 1954-66; head dept. graphics New Eng. Tech. Inst. of R.I., 1966-72, drafting instr., 1966-72. Mem. A.I.A. (emeritus mem.; asso. editor R.I. chpt.), Constrn. Specification Inst., U. Pa. Gen. Alumni Soc., Boston Philatelic Soc., R.I. Philatelic Soc. Conglist. Mason. Home: Warwick, R.I. Died June 13, 1977; buried Swan Point Cemetery, Providence, R.I.

BROWN, GEORGE SCRATCHLEY, air force officer; b. Montclair, N.J., Aug. 17, 1918; s. Thoburn Kay and Frances (Scratchley) B.; student U. Mo., 1936-37; B.S., U.S. Mil. Acad., 1941; grad. Nat. War Coll., 1957; m. Alice Colhoun, May 19, 1942; children—Dudley K., Daniel W., Susanah B. Commd. 2d lt. U.S. Army, 1941, advanced through grades to gen., 1968; comdr. 62d Troop Carrier Group, Washington, 1950-51, 56th Fighter Interceptor Wing, Air Def. Command, Mich., 1951-52, 1952, 3525th Pilot Tng. Wing, Ariz., 1953-56,

Eastern Transport Air Force, McGuire AFB, N.J., 1963-64, Joint Task Force 2, Sandia Base, N.M., 1964-66; dir. operations 5th Air Force, Korea, 1952-53; exec. to chief staff USAF, 1957-59; mil. asst. to sec. def., 1959-63; asst. to chmn. Joint Chiefs Staff, Washington, 1966-68; comdr. 7th Air Force PACAF, Saigon, 1968-70; comdr. Air Force Systems Command, Andrews AFB, Md., 1970-73; Air Force Chief of Staff, 1973-74, chmn. joint chiefs of staff, 1974-78. Decorated D.S.C., Silver Star, Legion of Merit with two oak leaf clusters, D.F.C. with one oak leaf cluster, Bronze Star, Air medal with three oak leaf clusters, D.S.M. with 3 oak leaf clusters, numerous fgn. decorations. Died Dec. 5, 1978.

BROWN, HENRY BEDINGER RUST, investment banker; b. Pitts., Feb. 13, 1926; s. Stanley Noel and Elizabeth Fitzhugh (Rust) B.; A.B., Harvard U., 1947; m. Betsey Jean Smith, Mar. 27, 1954; children—Peter, Alexander, Elizabeth, Harriet. Asst. v.p. 1st Nat. City Bank, N.Y.C., 1954-64; 2d v.p., mgr. securities dept. Tchrs. Ins. and Annuity Assn., N.Y.C., 1964-67; partner Brown & Bent, Investment Bankers, N.Y.C., 1968-81; chmn. Res. Fund, Inc., 1970-81, also dir. Served with USN, 1945-46. Club: Harvard (N.Y.C.). Address: New York, N.Y. Died Feb. 3, 1981.

BROWN, HOMER S., lawyer, judge; b. Huntington, W.Va., Sept. 23, 1896; s. William Roderick and Maria Wiggins (Rowlett) B.; grad. Va. Union U., also hon. degree; LL.B., U. Pitts., 1923, also hon. degree; hon. degree Lincoln U., Va. State Coll.; m. Wilhelmina Byrd, 1927; 1 son, Byrd Rowlett. Admitted to Pa. bar; practiced in Pitts.; judge Allegheny County Ct., from 1949, 5th Jud. Dist. Superior Ct., 1956—57, Allegheny County Common Pleas Ct., 1957-77; mem. Pa. Ho. of Reps., 1934-50. Active civil rights leader; pres. NAACP, Pitts., 1924-48. Served with U.S. Army, 1 yr. Named most outstanding legislator (2). Mem. Allegheny Bar Assn. Democrat. Home: Pittsburgh, Pa. Died 1977.

BROWN, HUGH AUCHINCLOSS, elec. engr., author; widower; children—Samuel C., Hugh Auchincloss. Pres., Columbia U.'s Grand Army of the 49th St Era. Mem. A.A.A.S. Author: Cataclysms of the Earth. Home: Douglaston, N.Y. Died Nov. 9, 1975.

BROWN, JAMES VINCENT, oil exec.; b. Lawrence, Mass., Feb. 6, 1896; s. Fred H. and Mary Ann (Guilfoyle) B.; grad. McIntosh Comml. Sch., 1921, Bentley Coll. Accounting and Finance, 1924; student St. Bonaventure Coll.; m. Jeanie Small Murray Eaton, Sept. 22, 1925; children—Martha (Mrs. John L. Murphy), Florence (Mrs. James J. Vaughn, Jr.), Harriett (Mrs. Lynton E. Gilbreath), James Webster, Vincent Murray, Elizabeth Anne (Mrs. Borland Bardell). Accountant, office mgr. Murray Bros. Co., Lawrence, 1919-24; instr. accounting McIntosh Comml. Sch., 1924; agt. U.S. Internal Revenue, Washington, Pitts., Bradford, Pa., 1924-29; pub. accountant, tax specialist, Bradford, 1929-52; comptroller Healey Petroleum Corp., Bradford, 1929-41; petroleum specialist U.S. Tariff Commn., 1941-42; petroleum econs. analyst Ind. Petroleum Assn. Am., Washington, 1942-46, chmn. cost com., mem. tax policy com. supply and demand com. of assn., dir., 1953; partner, mgr. Healey Ins. Agy., Bradford, 1941-45; exec. sec., treas. Nat. Petroleum Council, Washington, 1947-62; pres., dir. Brown Realty Corp., from 1938, Ella Oil Corp., 1940-48, Le Suer Oil Corp., 1940-48; treas., dir. Terminal Bldg. Corp, 1930-62, Moody, Karl & Wintermantel, Inc., 1938-45; dir. Haas Dobson, Inc., participant in Allegheny Land & Mineral Co., oil and gas production, W.Va., from 1959. Sec.-treas. nat. crude oil industry adv. com. OPA, 1945-46; mem. requirements panel and domestic civilian demand com. Mil. Petroleum Adv. Bd., 1947-51. City treas., Bradford, 1930-31; town commr., Bethany Beach, Del., 1960-62. Trustee, corporator Bentley Coll., from 1964. Mem. bd. govs. Port St. Lucie (Fla.) Country Club Home and Plan Owner's Assn., 1964-70. Served as cpl. A.A.F., 1918. Fellow Baker Vanguard Soc., Bentley Coll.; mem. Am. Petroleum Inst., Ind. Petroleum Assn. Am., Interstate Oil Compact Commn. (vice chmn. econ. adv. com. 1946-50), Mid-Continent Oil and Gas Assn. (econ. adv. subcom. to depletion com.), Internat. Platform Assn., St. Andrews Soc. of Fla., Omega Beta Omega (charter). Clubs: National Press (Washington); Ocean Beach; St. Lucie Country. Author articles to profl. jours. Home: Port St Lucie, Fla. Deceased.

BROWN, JO BAILY, lawyer; b. Owen Co., Ky., Nov. 7, 1886; s. Knox and Adeline Crittenden (Watson) B.; A.B., Centre Coll., 1907; LL.B., U. Pittsburgh, 1912; m. Helen May Blish, Dec. 25, 1919; children—Knox, Louise Joslin (Mrs. Ronald Porter), Helen Elizabeth. Admitted to Pa. bar, 1912 and since practiced in Pittsburgh; intelligence agt. State Dept., 1918; tech. adv. indsl. property, patents, trade marks, copyrights Peace Commn., Paris, 1919; U.S. del., v.p. Internat. Union Protection Indsl. Property, The Hague, 1925. Mem. President's com. investigation patent office practice, 1923-24, mem. patent adv. panel AEC, 1957-59. Trustee Centre College, Danville, Ky., 1940-44. Recipient Kettering award Patent, Trademark and Copyright Found., 1961. Mem. Am. Law Inst., Am. (pres. 1936-38) and Pittsburgh (pres. 1942-43) patent law assns., Am. (chmn. patent sect. 1932-34), Pa. State and Allegheny Co. bar assns., Beta Theta Pi, Phi Alpha Delta. Clubs: Cosmos (Washington); Duquesne, Oakmont, Field (Pittsburgh). Author numerous articles relating to patent law. Home: Pittsburgh. *

BROWN, JOHN ANTHONY, coll. pres.; b. Harrisburg, Pa., July 15, 1918; s. John Anthony and Agnes (Smith) B.; A.B., Temple U., 1943; M.A., U. Chgo., 1945; LL.D., Westminster Coll., 1962; L.H.D., Ursinus Coll., 1962; LL.D. Tarkio (Mo.) Coll., 1967; Litt.D., Rider Coll., 1969; L.L.D., St. Louis U., 1972; m. Franceline Harrison, 1943 (div. 1972); children—Barbara, John Anthony III, Philip, David; m. 2d, Nancy McClanahan, June 14, 1973. Prodn. editor Time, Inc., 1943-48; asst. prof. polit. sci. Temple U., 1948-54, dean of men, 1952-55, asst. to pres., 1955-60; v.p. pub. affairs and finance Occidental Coll., 1960-63; v.p. plans and resources George Washington U., 1963-64, v.p., dean faculties, 1964-66; pres. Lindenwood Coll., 1966-73; cons. in higher edn., 1973-75; pres. Muskingum Coll., New Concord, O., 1975-78. Cons. higher edn. N.Y. State Legislature, 1964; cons. Acad. Ednl. Devel., 1965-68; mem. ednl. evaluation team in Brazil, AID, 1964; cons. Ford Found., Bogota, Colombia, 1965; pres. Ind. Colls. and Univs. of Mo., 1969-72, Seven Colls. Consortium of Mo., 1968-70; exec. com. Mo. Colls. Fund; adv. com. on accreditation and instnl. eligibility U.S. Office of Edn., 1971-73; pres. St. Louis Council World Affairs, 1974-75; writer, broadcaster CBS radio series Governments of Man, 1959-63; host TV series Q.E.D. Capital, 1964-65, Washington Profile, 1965-66. Bd. dirs. Fed. Union, Washington, World Affairs Council, St. Louis, Vis. Nurses Assn. St. Louis, Good Samaritan Hosp., Zanesville, Ohio. DuBois fellow polit. sci. Princeton, 1947-48; Fund for Advancement Edn. Faculty fellow, 1951-52. Mem. A.A.U.P., Am. Polit. Sci. Assn., Am. Alumni Council. Club: University (Washington). Columnist Daily Jeffersonian, Cambridge, Ohio, 1976-78. Home: New Concord, Ohio. Died Feb. 16, 1978.

BROWN, JOHN NICHOLAS, real estate exec.; b. New York, N.Y., Feb. 21, 1900; s. John Nicholas and Natalie Bayard (Dresser) B.; grad. St. George's Sch., Newport, R.I., 1918; A.B., magna cum laude, Harvard, 1922, A.M., 1928; LL.D. (hon.), Ripon College, 1947, Tufts College, Trinity College, Rhode Island State Coll., 1948; m. Anne Seddon Kinsolving, Oct. 18, 1930; children—Nicholas, John Carter, Angela Bayard. Pres., Counting House Corp.; trustee Providence Instn. for Savings; asst. sec., of Navy for air, 1946-49; chmn. Sealol, Inc.; dir. Gorham Mfg. Co. First chmn. R.I. State Planning Bd. Served in U.S. Navy, 1918. Trustee, R.I. Found., Butler Hosp., Byzantine Inst., Am. Sch. for Classical Studies at Athens, St. George's Sch.; fellow and mem. advisory and exec. com. Brown U., also chmn. building and planning com.; mng. com. John Carter Brown Library (Brown U.); regent Smithsonian Instn. Del. Gen. Conv. P.E. Ch., 1925, 28, 31, 34, 37, 43, 46, 49, 52, 58; standing committee Diocese R.I. Adviser cultural matters U.S. Group Control Council, Germany, 1945. Recipient Joseph Henry medal for leadership Smithsonian Instn., 1975. Hon. member AIA, Mass. Hist. Soc.; mem. Mediaeval Acad. Am. (treas.), Am. Philos. Society, Phi Beta Kappa. Democrat. Clubs: New York Yacht, Harvard (New York City); Eastern Yacht, Tavern, Harvard (Boston); Newport Country, Reading Room, Clambake, Spouting Rock Beach, Newport Yacht, Ida Lewis Yacht (Newport); Hope, Agawam Hunt, Providence Art (Providence). Home: Providence, R.I. Died Oct. 9, 1979; buried Providence.

BROWN, JOHN WILLIAM, public health director; b. Lockhart, Texas; March 25, 1885; s. Rev. Alanson and Catherine Elizabeth (Moore) B.; M.D., Vanderbilt Univ. School of Medicine, 1910; M.P.H., Johns Hopkins Sch. of Pub. Health and Hygiene, 1924; m. Katherine Laurence Adams, June 4, 1913; children—John William, Eoline, Alanson. Gen. practice of medicine, 1911-17; served in U.S. Army, Camp McArthur, Waco, Tex., Philippines and China, 1917-20; city health officer, El Paso, Tex., 1920-26; gen. practice, Marfa, Tex., 1926-32; state health officer Tex., 1932-36; dir. of pub. health, Houston, 1937-41. On active duty as sr. surgeon U.S. Pub. Health Service, dir. Comanche County Health Unit, Lawton, Okla., since Oct. 1941. Mem. Am. Med. Assn., Am. Pub. Health Assn., Harris County Med. Soc., Delta Omega. Mason. Home: Lawton, Okla. *

BROWN, (HERMAN) LARUE, lawyer; b. Louisville, Ky., Dec. 17, 1883; s. George Herman and Nelly (LaRue) B.; A.B., Harvard, 1904, LL.B., 1906; m. Dorothy Browning Kirchwey, Nov. 23, 1915; 1 dau., Eleanor LaRue (dec.). Mem. Brown, Field & McCarthy, Boston. Assistant reporter of decisions, Mass Supreme Ct., 1908; chmn. Mass. Minimum Wage Commn., 1912-14; spl. counsel Mass. Pub. Service Commn.; spl. counsel for U.S. in Shoe Machinery and other Sherman Act and Clayton Act cases, 1914-22; asst. atty. gen. of U.S., 1918-19; gen. solicitor U.S.R.R. Administration, 1919-21, spl. counsel, 1921-25; counsel truck div. Nat. Automobile Chamber of Commerce, 1926-33; counsel to the federal and state authorities in prosecution of banking frauds, 1932-34; chmn. Laundry and Retail Stores Minimum Wage Bds., 1936, Jewelry Bd., 1939; Hotel and Restaurant Bd., 1941; mem. Jewelry Industry Com., Wages and Hours Act, 1940. Consultant Office of Defense Transportation, 1942; spl. rep. of the Atty. Gen. of U.S., and asst. to the Ambassador, U.S. Embassy, London, England, 1943-46. Vice chmn. Public Franchise League; vice chmn., Regional Loyalty Bd. 1947-53; A.D.A. (chmn. Mass. chpt. 1953-55); pres., Voluntary Defenders Com., Incorporated; chmn. Massachusetts Defenders Committee, 1960-62, 1965-66; chmn. Friends of Framingham Reformatory, 1948-52; mem. bd. trustees Civic Edn. Found., Inc. Mem. Atty. Gen.'s Adv. Com. on Civil Rights, 1958-62. Member American, Boston (chmn. committee on the Bill of Rights 1956—) bar assns. Democrat. Mason. Home: Boston. *

BROWN, LEO CYRIL, clergyman, economist, educator; b. Stanberry, Mo., Apr. 28, 1900; s. Edward P. and Mary (Wallace) B.; A.B., St. Louis U., 1926, A.M., 1928, S.T.L., 1935; A.M., Harvard, 1938, Ph.D., 1940; LL.D. (honoris causa), Loyola U., Chgo., 1970. Entered Jesuit Order, 1921; priest, Roman Cath. Ch., 1934; Wertheim fellow Harvard, summer, 1940; instr. econs. Regis Coll., Denver, 1940-41; asst. in econs. St. Louis U., 1930-35, instr. 1942-43, asst. prof., 1943-45, asso. prof., 1945-49, prof. econs., from 1949, dir. labor sch., 1942-47, acting regent sch. law, 1948-49, dir. Inst. Social Order, 1947-62; research asso. Cambridge (Mass.) Center of Social Studies, 1965-68. Arbitrator and permanent umpire labor agreements, from 1942; pub. mem. War Labor Bd. VII, 1943-45; public mem. WSB VII, 1945, IX, 1951-52; mem. Atomic Energy Labor-Mgmt. Relations Panel, 1953-68, chmn. of panel, from 1968. Trustee St. Louis U., 1949, 54, 56-64, council regents, deans, 1944-63; trustee Marquette U. Mem. Nat. Acad. Arbitrators (nat. pres. 1960), Am., Cath. (pres. 1949) econ. assns. Author: Union Policies in the Leather Industry, 1947; Impact of New Labor Law on Union-Management Relations, 1948. Editor social sci. area Cath. Ency., 1963-65; subject of book: (Gladys W. Groenberg) Labor Peacemaker: The Life and Works of Father Leo C. Brown, S.J., 1981. Home: St. Louis, Mo. Died May 3, 1978.

BROWN, MONTREVILLE JAY, lawyer; b. Morris, Minn., June 13, 1884; s. Calvin Luther and Annette (Marlow) B.; A.B., U. Minn., 1907, LL.B., 1909; m. Minnie Stinchfield, Nov. 19, 1910; children—Alice Katherine (widow of Hawley Sanford, dec.); Louise (Mrs. Robert James Christianson), Margaret Annette (Mrs. Conley Brooks), Joanne (Mrs. Theodore Douglas Wright). Admitted to Minn. bar, 1909; practiced in Bemidji, 1909-18; city atty., 1917-18; asst. atty. gen. Minn., 1918-23, also mem. State Securities Commn., 1918-21; instr. Minn. Coll. Law, 1921-31; mem. Oppenheimer, Hodgson Brown, Baer & Wolff, St. Paul, since 1923; counsel Minneapolis St. Paul Met. Airports Commn. since 1944; spl. counsel City of Minneapolis in street car fare hearings before R.R. and Warehouse Commn. of Minn. Mem. Draft Bd., Beltrami Co., World War I; appeal agt. Draft Bd. 3, Ramsey Co., World War II. Mem. Am., Minn. and Ramsey Co. bar assns., Alpha Delta Phi, Phi Delta Phi. Congregationalist. Mason (grand master, Grand Lodge of Minnesota, 1933). Clubs: Somerset Country, Athletic (St. Paul). Home: St. Paul. *

BROWN, MOREAU DELANO, banker; b. N.Y.C., Mar. 30, 1905; s. Thatcher Magoun and Caro Lord (Noyes) B.; student St. Paul's Sch., Concord, N.H., 1917-22; B.A., Yale, 1926; m. Alice Cordelia Barbour, Oct. 8, 1927; children—Alice Cordelia, Moreau Delano. With Brown Bros. & Co. and successors Brown Bros. Harriman & Co., from 1928, clk., N.Y.C., 1928-34, Phila., 1934, mgr. Phila., 1935-39, partner, from 1939; sec., dir. Beaver Mgmt. Corp.; dir. Leeds & Northrup Co., Phila. Reins. Corp., Fidelity Mut. Life Ins. Co., Magee Carpet Co., SKF Industries, Inc., Phila.; bd. mgrs. Western Savs. Fund Soc. of Phila.; mem. Phila-Balt.-Washington Stock Exchange. Chmn. bd. trustees Moore Coll. Art, Phila., Robert Coll. Am. Coll. for Girls, Istanbul; vice chmn. Southeastern Pa. chpt. A.R.C.; dir. Phila. Maritime Mus.; bd. dirs. Union Theol. Sem. N.Y.C., Children's Aid Soc. of Pa., Grenfell Assn. of Am., Community Services of Pa. Mem. Wolf's Head Soc. Phi Beta Kappa, Alpha Delta Phi. Clubs: Philadelphia, Racquet, Yale (Phila.); Merion Cricket (Haverford); Edgartown Yacht; Corinthian Yacht; New Bedford Yacht; N.Y. Yacht. Home: Haverford, Pa. Died Oct. 19, 1974.

BROWN, NELSON COURTLANDT, forester; b. S Orange, N.J., Mar. 1, 1885; s. Ashbel Greene and Lucinda Ann (Van Duyne) B.; B.A., Yale, 1906, M.F. 1908; Forest Engineer (honorary) from Biltmore, 1952 m. Alice Virginia Baker, Aug. 23, 1911. With U.S Forest Service, in Mont., Wash., Fla., and Ala 1908-11; prof. forest utilization, N.Y. State Coll. of Forestry, Syracuse, N.Y., 1912-17; mem. U.S. Trad Commn. in Europe, 1917-18; civilian engr. with A.E.F in France and Spain, 1918; apptd. spl. adviser t Czecho-Slovak Republic on management of crow forests, Dec. 1919; partner, mgr. Am. Woods Expo

Assn., New York, 1919-22; prof. in charge forest utilization, N.Y. State Coll. Forestry, since 1921, acting dean, 1928-30, retired 1951 as prof. emeritus; now forestry cons. Mem. N.Y. State Reforestation Commn.; co-ordinator C.C.C., 1933; chairman War Council, Syracuse and Onondaga Co., 1943-44; forestry adv. to Pres. F.D. Roosevelt, 1929-45; chief Forestry Div., Allied Control Commn. Italy Rome, 1945. Studied forestry developments in Europe, 1937, 39. Mem. Onondaga County Park Bd. Ex-pres. Syracuse Salvation Army Bd.; mem. Soc. Am. Foresters, A.A.A.S., Am. Wood Preservers' Assn., Am. Forestry Assn., Assn. Yale Class Secs., Sigma Xi, Delta Theta Sigma, Phi Kappa Phi, S.A.R. (ex-pres. Syracuse chapter). Decorated Knight Crown of Italy, 1922. Presbyn. Clubs: Yale (New York); Rotary (Syracuse); Onondaga Golf. Author: Forest Products, Their Manufacture and Use, 1919; The Lumber Market in Italy and Reconstruction Requirements, 1919; The Lumber Market in Spain and Portugal, 1920; American Lumber Industry, 1923; Logging—Principles and Practices, 1934; General Forestry, 1935; Logging—Transportation, 1935; Timber Products and Industries, 1937; Lumber Manufacture, 1947; Logging, 1949; Forest Products, 1950. Co-author: Elements of Forestry (with F. F. Moon), 1914. Contbr. many miscellaneous professional, scientific and popular articles on forestry, lumber and forest products. Home: Syracuse, N.Y.; summer; Milford, Pike County, Pa. *

BROWN, PEMBROKE HOLCOMB, educator; b. Rockford, Ill., Apr. 26, 1885; s. Thomas Henry and Caroline Elizabeth (Holcomb) B.; A.B., U. Ill., 1915, M.A., 1917, Ph.D., 1923; m. Florence Maud Coerper, June 26, 1919. Asst. prof. econs. U. Ill., 1925-37, asso. prof., 1937-41, prof. econs. since 1941. Mem. Am. Finance Assn., Am. Econ. Assn., Phi Beta Kappa, Beta Gamma Sigma, Alpha Kappa Psi, Beta Alpha Psi, Pi Kappa Lambda. Episcopalian. Mason. Home: Champaign, Ill. *

BROWN, REVELLE WILSON, ry. official; b. Carlyle, Ill., Aug. 5, 1883; s. Porter W. and Mary (Randall) B.; ed. pub. schs. and Carlyle High Sch.; m. Carolyn Holdener, Dec. 9, 1903; children—Mary Mrs. Vickery, Pauline (Mrs. John F. Deems), Ralph W. Began as laborer, Ill. div., B.&O. R.R. Co., 1901-02, fireman, 1902-05, engr., 1905-10; air brake instr., supt. motive power, Cincinnati, O., asst. road foreman of engines, Ill. div., successively, 1910-11; engr., Ill. div., 1911-12; asst. road foreman of engines, engr., Ill. div., road foreman of engines, Indianapolis, 1912-14; supervisor locomotive operation, 1914-15; road foreman of engines, Toledo div., trainmaster, Wellston div., 1915-16; trainmaster, Toledo div., 1916-17; asst. supt., O. div., 1917-19, supt., 1919-21; supt. Connellsville div., 1921-23, Cumberland div., 1923-26; gen. supt., Md. dist., 1926-30; gen. mgr., C. R.R. Co. of N.J., 1930-31; v.p. and gen. mgr., 1931-35; v.p. in charge operation and maintenance, Reading Co. and C. R.R. Co. of N.J., 1935-41; pres. L.V. R.R. 1941-44; pres. Reading Co. since 1944; vice pres. Pa.-Reading Seashore Lines; dir., mem. exec. com. Lehigh & Hudson River Ry. Company, Pennsylvania Company for Banking and Trusts; mgr. Philadelphia Savings Fund Soc., director, C. R.R. of New Jersey, Fidelity Mutual Life Ins. Co., Mutual Fire, Marine & Inland Ins. Co. Chmn. com. on pub. relations Eastern R.R. Presidents Conf. Mem. Pa. Soc., Newcomen Soc., U.S. and Pa. Chamber Commerce. Clubs: Union League (Philadelphia and Chicago); Railroad and Machinery, Railroad, Recess, Traffic (New York); Pine Valley Golf, Racquet, Country (Philadelphia). Home: Barclay Hotel, 18th and Rittenhouse Sq.

BROWN, RICHARD FARGO, found. exec.; b. N.Y.C., Sept. 20, 1916; s. Percy Melville and Hazel (Wyatte) B.; A.B., Bucknell U., 1940; postgrad. N.Y. U., 1940-42; M.A., Harvard, 1948, Ph.D., 1952; m. Polly Story, Dec. 19, 1941 (dec. 1967); 1 son, Michael Fargo; m. 2d, Jane Hoag, 1968; children—Richard S., Tracy E.M., Wyatt K. Teaching fellow Harvard, 1947-49, vis. prof. fine arts, 1954; research scholar, lectr. Frick Collection, N.Y.C., 1949-54; chief curator Los Angeles County Mus., 1955-62; dir. Los Angeles County Mus. Art, 1962-66, also trustee; head dept. art County Los Angeles, 1961-66; dir. Kimbell Art Found., Ft. Worth, 1966-79. Trustee Mus. Western Art, Ft. Worth. Mem. Cal. Arts Commn. Served with USNR, 1942-46. Decorated Order Arts and Letters (France). Bacon-Rich travelling fellow Harvard, 1949. Mem. Coll. Art Assn. Am. (pres., dir.), Am. Assn. Art Mus. Dirs. (sec.-treas., exec. com., pres. 1970-71), Am. Assn. Museums (council), Western Assn. Museums (pres.), Nat. Council on Arts, Phi Beta Kappa. Home: Fort Worth, Tex. Died Nov. 6, 1979.

BROWN, RICHARD PARKE, corp. exec.; b. Wichita, Kan., Feb. 25, 1912; s. John Wesley and Golda Leona (Dodds) B.; A.B., Washburn Coll., 1934; B.D., Colgate-Rochester Div. Sch., 1938; M.A., Cornell, 1939; m. Marcie Geraldine Williams, Aug. 20, 1932; children—Barbara Christine (Mrs. Jack McFarland), Suzanne Louise (Mrs. Henry). Dir. personnel relations Mesta Machine Co., 1946-51, dir. indsl. relations, 1954-63, v.p. finance, 1963-68, exec. v.p., 1968-75, also dir.; v.p., dir. O. Hommel Co., Asko Industries, Inc.; dir. Chester Engrs., Inc., Forsyth Engring. and Machine Corp. Adv. mem. Pan-Am. Internat. Monetary Fund. Dir. Community Fund, Pitts. Fellow Soc. Advancement Mgmt. (dir., past pres. Pitts.); mem. Am. Mgmt. Assn., Pitts. Personnel Assn. (dir., past pres.), Pa. Assn. for Blind, Psychol. Services Pitts. (pres., dir.), Fgn. Policy Assn., Indsl. Relations Research Assn., Sigma Alpha Epsilon. Clubs: University, Cornell, Duquesne (Pitts.); University (Washington). Author: The Development of Public Sentiment Against Child Labor, 1910-35; The Development of Industrial Democracy, 1900-40; The Human Factor in Industry; articles in field. Home: Pittsburgh, Pa. Died June 30, 1975.

BROWN, ROBERT CARLTON (BOB BROWN), auth June 14, 1886; s. Robert Carlton and Cora Lovi B.; ed. U. of Wis., 1904; married; children—Co Carlton. Contbr. stories and serials to mags. zilian American (Rio de Janeiro, Brazil), 1919 Kappa Pi, Psi Upsilon. Author: What Happened t The Remarkable Adventures of Christoph Poe, 19 jonary, 1915; 1450-1950, 1929; The Readies, 19 Globe-Gliding, 1930; Nomadness, 1931; Words, 1931; Gems, 1931; Demonics, 1931; Readies for Bob Brown's Machine, 1931; You Gotta Live, 1932; Let There Be Beer! 1932.*

BROWN, SPENCER WHARTON, geneticist, educator; b. Vermillion, S.D., Nov. 26, 1918; s. J. Maughs and Lillian (James) B.; B.A., U. Minn., 1938; postgrad. U. Mo., 1938-41; Ph.D., U. Cal. at Berkeley, 1942; m. Roberta Marie Schuknecht, Jan. 6, 1939 (div., 1958). Asst. prof. botany U. Ga., 1943-45; asso. in genetics U. Cal. at Berkeley, 1945-46, instr., 1946-48, asst. prof., 1948-54, asso. prof., 1954-60, prof. genetics, 1960-77. Guggenheim fellow, 1956-57. Mem. Am. Soc. Naturalists, Genetics Soc. Am. (sec.-gen. XIII Internat. Congress Genetics), Internat. Genetics Fedn. (pres. from 1973), Bot. Soc. Am., Am. Assn. U. Profs., Phi Beta Kappa, Sigma Xi. Contbr. articles to profl. jours. Address: Berkeley, Calif. Died June 10, 1977.

BROWN, STANLEY DOTY, lawyer; b. New York, N.Y., March 8, 1885; s. Robert I. and Clarissa (Doty) B.; A.B., Cornell U., 1905, LL.B., 1908; m. Margaret Jenks, Oct. 23, 1920; children—Georgia Jenks, Margaret, Katharine. Admitted to New York bar, 1908; mem. firm Sackett, Chapman and Stevens, 1914-20, Sackett, Chapman, Brown and Cross, 1920-46, Brown, Cross, and Hamilton, since 1947; sec. dir. New York Herald Tribune, Inc.; gen. law practice specializing in newspaper law. Served as capt., F.A., U.S. Army, 1917-19. Home: Scarsdale, N.Y. *

BROWN, W(ILLIAM) NORMAN, indologist; b. Baltimore, Md., June 24, 1892; s. George William and Virginia Augusta (Clark) B.; student Prep. Sch., Hiram (O.) Coll., 1905-07, Hiram Coll., 1907-08; A.B., Johns Hopkins, 1912, fellow, 1913-15, Ph.D., 1916; Harrison research fellow, U. of Pa., 1916-19, Litt.D. (honorary degree), 1963; Johnston scholar, Johns Hopkins, 1919-22; studied Sanskrit at Benares, India, 1922-23; D.Litt. (honorary), University of Madras, 1957, University of Michigan, 1965, Jadavpur U., 1970; Jnana-Rana-Kara, W. Bengal Government Sanskrit Coll., Calcutta, 1961; m. Helen Harrison, June 29, 1921; children—Norman, Ursula (Mrs. J.H. Perivier). Acting head of Sanskrit dept., Johns Hopkins, 1921-22, asso. in Sanskrit, 1925-26; professor Sanskrit, University of Pennsylvania, 1926-66, prof. emeritus, 1966-75, chairman South Asia regional studies, 1947-66; editor Jour. of Am. Oriental Society, 1926-41; fellow on the John Simon Guggenheim Memorial Foundation, 1928-29; curator of Indian art, Phila. Mus. Art, 1931-54; curator Oriental sect. U. Pa. Museum, 1942-50; pres. Am. Inst. Indian Studies, Poona, India, 1961-71. Successively cadet U.S. Naval Aviation Corps, cryptographer with Mil. Intelligence Bur. and spl. agt. with U.S. Naval Intelligence, 1918; Office of Strategic Service Wash., 1941-45. Recipient G.V. Watumull Distinguished Achievement award in Indology, 1967. Fellow Royal Asiatic Soc. (London); hon. fellow Asiatic Soc. (Calcutta), Bhandar-Kar Oriental Research Inst. (Poona), Deccan Coll. (Poona), Kuppuswauri Research Inst. (Madras); mem. of the Am. Philosophical Soc., American Oriental Soc. (pres. 1941-42), Linguistic Soc. Am., Assn. Asian Studies (pres. 1960-61), Royal India, Pakistan and Ceylon Soc. (London), Phila. Oriental Club, Phi Beta Kappa, Delta Upsilon. Author: The Story of Kalaka, 1933; Miniature Paintings of the Jaina Kalputras, 1934. Manuscript Illustrations of the Uttaradhyayana Sutra, 1941; The United States and India and Pakistan, 1953, 2d rev. edit., 1963, (with Kitle), 3d edit., 1972; The Saundaryalahari, 1958; The Vasanta Vilasa, 1962; The Mahimnastava, 1965; Man in the Universe, 1966; several other publs. prior to 1940. Editor, part author: India, Pakistan, Ceylon, 1951, 2d rev. edit., 1963. Contbr. to learned and popular pupls. Home: Moylan, Pa. Died Apr. 22, 1975.

BROWN, W. SHELBURNE, coll. pres.; A.B., Pasadena Coll., 1940, M.A., 1942, D.D., 1960; Ed.D., U. So. Calif., 1969. Pastor in Carson City, Nev., Banning, Calif. and Alhambra, Calif., 1942-54; dist. supt. Los Angeles, Ch. of Nazarene, 1952-64; pres. Point Loma Coll., San Diego (formerly Pasadena Coll.), 1964-78. Address: San Diego, Calif. Died Oct. 3, 1978.

BROWN, WARNER, prof. psychology; b. Greensboro, Ga., Feb. 9, 1882; s. Jacob Conklin and Alida Robins (Warner) B.; A.B., U. of Calif., 1904, A.M., 1905; Ph.D., Columbia, 1908; m. Jessie Milliken, of San Francisco, Calif., June 25, 1908; children—Frederick Hosmer (dec.), Ellen. Asst. in psychology, U. of Calif., 1904-06; asst. in philosophy, Columbia, 1906-07, in psychology, 1907-08; instr. in psychology, U. of Calif., 1908-13, asst. prof., 1913-20, asso. prof., 1920-23, prof. since 1923; asso. dean Coll. Letters and Science, 1926-27, 29. Fellow A.A.A.S.; mem. Am. Psychol. Assn., Soc. Exptl. Psychologists, Western Psychol. Assn., Nat. Inst. Psychology. Home: Berkeley, Calif.

BROWN, WILLARD COWLES, illuminating engr.; b. Glens Falls, N.Y., Mar. 17, 1895; s. Willard Wilson and Kate (Cowles) B.; B.S., Va. Mil. Inst., 1914, E.E., 1925; B.S., Harvard, 1916; B.S., Mass. Inst. Tech., 1916; m. Alice Lynd Harshaw, Dec. 11, 1919 (dec. Sept. 1966); children—Willard C., Eleanor; m. 2d, Dorothy Bowman, Mar. 17, 1967. Asso. prof. elec. engring. Va. Mil. Inst., 1916-17; with Nela Park Engring. Dept., Gen. Elec. Co., 1920-42, charge gen. lighting, 1936-42, mgr. application engring., lamp div., 1948-55, mgr. lighting edn., Cleve., 1955-60. Am. del., dir. secretariat on lighting practice Internat. Commn. on Illumination, Netherlands, 1939, dir. secretariat, Paris, 1948, Stockholm, 1951; v.p. Internat. Com. on Illumination, 1959-63. Served with USN, 1917-20, USNR, 1942-45; capt. Res. ret. Fellow Illuminating Engring. Soc. (pres. 1941-42, bd. govs. Mission chpt., recipient Gold medal 1960); mem. Cleve. Engring. Soc. (pres. 1957-58), Naval Supply Officers Assn., English Speaking Union, Navy League, Alpha Tau Omega. Republican. Episcopalian. Clubs: Army and Navy (Golden Circle) (Washington); Santa Barbara Channel City, Men's Garden. Address: Santa Barbara, Calif. Died Apr. 14, 1979; buried Arlington Nat. Cemetery.

BROWN, WILLIAM ROBERTSON, educator; b. Leander, Tex., Nov. 7, 1886; s. Timothy Alvin and Mary (Robertson) B.; A.B., U. of Tex., 1907; A.M., Harvard, 1915, Ph.D., 1917; m. Emma Wales, Oct. 6, 1915. Mem. faculty English dept. Western Mich. Coll. since 1917. chmn. dept. since 1946. Mem. Phi Beta Kappa. Home: Kalamazoo, Mich.

BROWN, WYOURN D., army officer; born S.C., June 23, 1899; B.S., U.S. Mil. Acad., 1918; grad. F.A. Sch., Basic Course, 1920. Command and Gen. Staff Sch., 1937. Commd. 2d lt. F.A., 1918, and advanced through the grades to brig. gen., Feb. 1943; served on Gen. Staff Corps, 1941-42. Died Apr. 3, 1981.

BROWNE, BENJAMIN PATTERSON, coll. chancellor; b. Wiscasset, Maine, Jan. 25, 1893; s. Benjamin Randall and Lena Evelyn (Patterson) B.; student Harvard, summer 1924, Boston U., summers 1926, 27, Sch. Theology, 1928-30, Andover-Newton Sem., 1930-32; D.D., Eastern Baptist Theol. Sem., Overbrook, Pa., 1947, William Jewell Coll., 1962; L.H.D., Hillsdale Coll., No. Bapt. Theol. Sem., 1963; Litt.D., Ottawa U., 1961; Ed.D., Judson Coll., 1967; m. Rachel Eunice Sprague, Apr. 3, 1915; children—Rachel Sprague Browne Diggs, Priscilla Alden Browne Wagner, Benjamin Judson, Marcia Carol. Ordained to ministry Baptist Ch., 1912; pastor Corliss St. Ch., Bath, Maine, 1912-16, Essex St. Ch., Bangor, Me., 1916-21, 1st Baptist Ch., Rockland, Me., 1921-28 (pres. Maine United Baptists Ministers Conf., 1926), 1st Baptist Ch., Winchester, Mass., 1928-32, 2nd Baptist Ch., Holyoke, Mass., 1932-41 (pres. No. Baptists Ednl. Soc., 1941-42); dir. promotion Mass. Baptist Conv. hdqrs. Tremont Temple, Boston, 1941-44; exec. sec. Pa. Baptist Conv., Phila., 1944-47; editorial exec. Christian publs. of Bd. of Edn. and Pubsl. Am. Bapt. Conv., Phila., 1947-62, pres. Am. Bapt. Conv., 1962-63, also pres. Asso. Ch. Press; pres. No. Bapt. Theol. Sem., 1959-64; founder, pres. Judson Coll., Elgin, Ill., 1962-66, chancellor, 1967-76; pres. Christian Writers Conf., 1948; exec. dir. Nat Christian Author's Guild. Trustee Lincoln Acad. Republican. Mason. Author: Let There Be Light, 1956; The Writers Conference Comes to You, 1956; Techniques of Christian Writing, 1959; Signal Flares, 1960; Gateway to Morning, 1961; Tales of Baptist Daring, 1962; Illustrations for Preaching, 1975; (booklets) Meaning of Church Membership, 1944, Martyrs of Christ, 1945, Magnificent Men, 1946. Compiler and editor: Christian Journalism for Today, 1952. Staff editor Mass. Baptist Bull., 1941-44, editor The Penn Baptist 1944-47, The Baptist Leader, 1947-62. Home: Alhambra, Calif. Died Aug. 3, 1976; interred Bluff City Cemetery, Elgin, Ill.

BROWNE, MARGARET FITZHUGH, artist; b. Boston, Mass., June 7, 1884; d. William Maynadier and Cordelia Brooks (Fenno) Browne, student Boston Latin Sch., 1899-1903, Mass. Normal Art Sch., 1904-09, Sch. of Boston Mus. Fine Arts, 1910. Began career as portrait painter, 1910; art editor Boston Evening Transcript, 1919-20; mem. Grand Central Galleries, New York. Has painted many portraits of prominent men and women. Received special award at the national exhibition of the Society for Sanity in Art, Chicago, 1941. Apptd. mem. Art Commn. of City of Boston, 1937-42. Mem. North Shore Arts Assn. (president 1934-36), Connecticut Academy of Fine Arts, National Association Women Artists, Springfield (Illinois) Art

Assn., Springfield (Mass.) Art League, Newport (R.I.) Art Assn., Boston Art Club, Copley Soc. of Boston, Allied Artists of America, N.E. Branch Soc. Sanity in Art (pres. since 1939). Author: Portrait Painting, 1933. Home: Boston. *

BROWNE, WALTER LYMAN, newspaper editor; b. Minneapolis, Minn., July 31, 1885; s. Glen Walter and Nina (Sturtevant) B.; prep. edn., high sch. and business coll.; student U. of Ore., 1904-08; m. Ethel M. Dowling, of Butte, Mont., July 17, 1917; children—Glen Walter, Adelaide, Robert Dowling. Began newspaper work with The Billings (Mont.) Gazette, 1908; reporter and assistant city editor, Butte Miner, 1909-16; reporter Butte Daily Post, 1916-17; mng. editor Billings (Mont.) Gazette, 1917-20, and since 1921; sec. The Gazette Printing Co. Trustee and publicity dir. Nat. Custer Memorial Assn. Republican. Elk, K.C. Club: Billings Commercial. *

BROWNELL, ROY EDMUND, lawyer; b. Metamora, Mich., Sept. 18, 1883; s. Edmund and Lexy (Copeman) B.; LL.B., U. of Mich., 1907; m. Chandler Begole, Nov. 15, 1922; 1 son, Edmund Begole. Admitted to Mich. bar, 1907, and since practiced in Flint; sr. partner Brownell & Gault; pros. atty. Genesee County, 1916-20; commr. State Bar of Mich. (the integrated bar organized by act of legislature 1935), term 1936-40. Dir. and sec. Charles Stewart Mott Foundation; mem. bd. dirs. Continental Dept. Stores, Inc., U.S. Sugar Co., Northern Ill. Water Co., Ill. Water Service Co., St. Louis County Water Co., Wayne-Oakland Bank, Long Island Water Co., Michigan Chem. Co. Pres. Mich. State Bar Assn., 1934-35, Flint C. of C., 1922. Republican. Home: Flint, Mich. *

BROWNELL, WILLIAM ARTHUR, college dean; b. Smethport, Pa., May 19, 1895; s. Fred William and Hattie Adelaide (Foote) B.; A.B., Allegheny Coll., Meadville, Pa., 1917, LL.D., 1942; A.M., U. Chgo., 1923, Ph.D., 1926; postgrad. U. Ill., 1923-25; m. Kathryn Kahn, Dec. 21, 1924; children—Florence Dyer (dec.), Kathryn, Carol Anne. High sch. tchr. 1917, 1919-22; ins. salesman, 1918-19, instr. ednl. psychology, U. Ill., 1923-25; teaching fellow U. of Chicago, 1925-26; asst. prof. rural education, Cornell U., 1926-27; asst. prof. ednl. psychology, U. of Mich., 1927-28; prof. ednl. psychology, George Peabody Coll., Nashville, 1928-30; prof. ednl. psychology, Duke, 1930-49, Northwestern U., 1949-50; dean school edn. U. Cal. at Berkeley 1950-62; summer teacher U. Chgo., U. Tex.; vis. prof. Edn., U. of Puerto Rico, 1941. Served at Camp Jackson, S.C., Camp Taylor, Louisville, Ky., Camp Stanley, Tex.; 2d lt. 45th F.A., U.S. Army, 1918. Consultant Civilian Pre-Induction Training Br., Army Service Forces, 1943. Mem. A.A.A.S. (vice pres.; chmn., sect. Q, 1947), Nat. Council Tchrs. Math. (mem. Post-War Planning Commn.), Am. Ednl. Research Assn. (pres. 1939), pres. Div. of Psychol. Edn., 1947, Am. Psychol. Assn., Nat. Soc. Study Edn. (dir. 1942-48 and since 1950), National Council Coll. Teachers Edn., Nat. Council Com. Arithmetic, A.A.U.P. (council, 1941-43), Phi Beta Kappa, Kappa Delta Pi, Kappa Phi Kappa, Delta Sigma Rho, Phi Delta Theta, Phi Delta Kappa. Democrat. Episcopalian. Author: Development of Children's Number Concepts in the Primary Grades, 1928; (monograph—with L. B. Stretch) Effect of Unfamiliar Settings on Problem Solving, 1931; Learning as Reorganization (monograph with others), 1939; Arithmetic in Grades I and II (monograph), 1941; Learning the Multiplication Combinations (monograph), 1943; Meaningful vs. Mechanical Learning (monograph) 1948. Daily Life Arithmetics—Grades 1-8 (with G. T. Buswell and Lenore John); Living Arithmetic (text); Review Arithmetics (for Armed Forces Institute); co-author math. and other year books. Home: Berkeley, Calif. Died May 24, 1977.

BROWNING, GORDON, ex-gov. Tenn.; b. Carroll Co., Tenn., Nov. 22, 1889; s. Jas. H. Browning and Melissa A. (Brooks) B.; B.Sc., and Pg.B., Valparaiso U., 1913; LL.B., Cumberland U., 1915, LL.D. (hon.), 1936; m. Ida Leach, Nov. 11, 1920. Admitted to Tenn. bar, 1915, and began practice at Huntingdon; Chancellor 8th Tenn. Chancery Div., 1942-49; mem. 68th to 73d Congresses (1923-35), 8th Tenn. Dist.; gov. of Tenn., 1937-39, 1949-53. Enlisted in Tenn. Nat. Guard, June 1917; commd. 2d lt. U.S. Army, July 25, 1917 and assigned to 114th Field Arty., 30th Div.; 1st lt., Nov. 23, 1917; capt., May 10, 1918; served with A.E.F. 10 mos.; participated in battles at St. Mihiel, Argonne, Woevre; honorably discharged Apr. 1919; served with U.S. Army, 1943-Feb. 17, 1947; overseas 3 yrs. in European theatre, dep. head, G-5, Belgium-Luxembourg Mission; dir. Mil. Govt. Bremen Enclave; lt. col. Decorated Legion of Merit (U.S.), Order Brit. Empire (Eng.), Order Orange-Nassau (Netherlands), Order Adolph-Nassau (Luxembourg), Order Leopold and Order of Crown (Belgium); memorabilia and documents of Gov. and Mrs. Browning housed in Gordon Browning Room, McKenzie (Tenn.) Meml. Library. Methodist. Mem: Tenn. Bar Assn., Am. Legion, VFW. Club: Masons (32d deg.). Home: Huntingdon, Tenn. Died May 23, 1976; buried Oak Hill Cemetery, Huntingdon.

BROWNLEE, WILLIAM ALLEN, banker; b. Bonham, Tex., Sept. 23, 1885; s. William Whitfield and Fay (Allen) B.; student pub. schs. Bonham; m. Frances Hunt, Dec. 10, 1919; children—Mary Frances, James Whitfield, Joanne, Robert Edward; married second Bernice Chapman, 1949. Executive vice pres. Nat. Bank of Tulsa (Okla.), 1933-57, president, 1957-60, vice chairman board, 1960—. Director Tulsa Philharmonic Soc., Tulsa Y.M.C.A.; dir. Tulsa Community Chest. Mem. Res. City Bankers Assn. Clubs: Tulsa, Southern Hills Country. Home: Tulsa. *

BRUCE, BRYSON, naval officer; b. Garden Grove, Ia., Mar. 20, 1886; s. Bryson and Mary Ann (Liddle) B.; B.S., U.S. Naval Acad., 1907; M.A., Columbia U., 1914; m. Louise Frances Downs, Feb. 18, 1911; children—Louise Frances (wife of Comdr. Morton Sunderland, U.S.N.), Betty Dunlevy (wife of Lt. Comdr. Neil E. Harkleroad, U.S.N.). Commd. ensign, U.S. Navy, Sept. 1906; promoted through grades to rear adm., 1941. ret. 1946. Awarded Mexican, China and World War campaign medals. Mem. Am. Soc. Naval Engrs., U.S. Naval Acad. Alumni Assn., Newcomen Society. Episcopalian. Club: Army and Navy Country (Washington) Racquet, Engineers Club (Phila.). Home: Arnold, Md. *

BRUCE, DAVID K. E., diplomat; b. Balt., Feb. 12, 1898; s. William Cabell and Louise Este (Fisher) B.; student Princeton, U. Va., U. Md.; m. Ailsa Mellon; 1 dau., Audrey (dec.); m. Evangeline Bell; children—Alexandra (dec.), David, Nicholas. Admitted to Md. bar, 1921, practiced in Balt., 1921-25; vice consul U.S. Fgn. Service, Rome, 1926-28; engaged in bus. and farming, 1928-40; chief rep. in Gt. Britain for A.R.C., 1940; with OSS, 1941-45, dir., ETO, 1943-45; asst. sec. of commerce, 1947-48; chief ECA Mission to France, 1948-49; U.S. ambassador to France, 1949-52; under sec. of state, 1952-53; apptd. spl. U.S. observer at interim com. of European Def. Community, 1953; spl. Am. rep. to European High Authority for Coal and Steel, 1953-54; ambassador to Fed. Republic Germany, 1957-59, to Great Britain, 1961-69; U.S. rep. to Vietnam Peace Talks, Paris, 1970-71; chief U.S. Liaison Office, Peoples Republic of China, Peking, 1972-74; ambassador to NATO, Brussels, 1974-75. Mem. Md. Ho. of Dels., 1924-26, Va. Ho. Dels., 1939-42. Served with U.S. Army, 1917-20, AUS, 1942-45. Awarded mil. decorations by U.S., Gt. Britain, France, Poland, Norway, Denmark, Czechoslovakia. Democrat. Episcopalian. Author: Revolution to Reconstruction, 1938. Home: Washington, D.C. Died Dec. 5, 1977.

BRUCE, JAMES, ret. bus. exec.; b. Balt., Dec. 23, 1892; s. William Cabell and Louise Este (Fisher) B.; Litt.B., Princeton, 1914; LL.B., U. Md., 1916; m. Ellen McHenry Keyser, May 24, 1919; children—Ellen Bruce Terry, Louise Este. Mem. 1st Plattsburg Camp, 1915; pvt. to maj., U.S. F.A., 2d Div. Staff 1st Army, 1917-18; mil. aide to Pres. Wilson, also asst. mil. attaché Italy, also rep. Versailles Peace Treaty, Montenegro and Albania, 1919; v.p. Chase Nat. Bank, 1926-31; pres. Balt. Trust Co., 1931-33; fin. adv. to bd. dirs. Home Owners Loan Corp., Washington, 1933-34; v.p. Nat. Dairy Products Co., 1935-47; ambassador to Argentina, 1947-49; 1st dir. Mut. Def. Assistance Program, 1949-50; dir. Am. Airlines, Inc., Am. Hawaiian S.S. Co., AVCO Mfg. Co., Chem. Bank & Trust Co., Fruehauf Trailer Co., Kraftco, Technicolor, Inc., Comml. Credit Co., Fed. Home Loan Bank of N.Y., Gen. Am. Investors, Md. Casualty Co., Revlon, Inc., Republic Steel Co. Vice chmn. United Hosps. Fund, 1946. Decorated Order of Merit (Italy); Medal Militaire (France). Mem. Am. Legion, VFW. Democrat. Episcopalian. Mason (Shriner, 32 deg.), Moose. Clubs: Maryland (Balt.); Brook, Links, Links Golf, Racquet and Tennis. Author: Those Perplexing Argentines. Home: New York, N.Y. Died July 17, 1980; buried Baltimore, Md.

BRUCE, JOHN MARKEY, physician; b. New Orleans, Apr. 13, 1917; s. Charles Tiffany and Margaret Lillian (Markey) B.; M.D., La. State U., 1951; M.P.H., Tulane U., 1955; m. Irma D. Weisdorffer, Feb. 19, 1941; children—Elizabeth Bruce Voelker, David, Margaret Bruce Camin, Gregory, Melody. Intern Hotel Dieu Hosp., New Orleans, 1951-52; asst. dir. Jefferson Parish health unit Dept. Health, Gretna, La., 1953; regional health officer local health units Western La., 1956-57; sect. chief, div. preventive medicine La. Dept. Health, New Orleans, 1957-66, dir. div. local health services, 1966-67; med. dir. East La. State Hosp., Jackson, 1967-74; dir. State Div. Health, New Orleans, 1974-77; ret., 1977. Served with USAAF, World War II. Diplomate Am. Bd. Preventive Medicine, Fellow Am. Coll. Preventive Medicine; mem. Delta Omega. Home: Metairie, La. Died Oct. 21, 1978.

BRUCE, WILLIAM CONRAD, ret. publishing co. exec.; b. Milw., Jan. 17, 1882; s. William George and Monica (Moehring) B.; A.B., Marquette U., 1901, M.A., 1905, LL.D., 1956; LL.D., Mt. Mary Coll., 1954. Editorial asst. Am. Sch. Bd. Jour., 1902-10, asst. editor, 1910-52, editor, 1952-67; v.p. mng. editor Bruce Pub. Co., Milw., 1914-52, pres., 1952-60, chmn. bd., 1961-68; chmn. Am. State Bank, Milw., 1959-61. Sec. bd. govs. Mt. Mary Coll., Milw., 1941-63; mem. lay bd. advisers Misericordia Hosp., Milw., 1952-60. Mem. Nat. Council Schoolhouse Constrn. (hon. mem., sec., 1922-37). Home: Wauwatosa WI. *

BRUCHHAUSEN, WALTER, judge; b. Bklyn., May 29, 1892; s. Hugo and Anne (Dietrich) B.; LL.B., N.Y. U., 1912; m. Lois Thayer, June 12, 1943; 1 dau., Alice. Admitted to N.Y. bar, 1919, since practiced in N.Y.C.; mem. firm Duncan & Bruchhausen, 1919-42, Cadwalader, Wickersham & Taft, from 1942; U.S. dist. judge, 1953-76; chief judge U.S. Dist. Ct. for Eastern Dist. of N.Y., 1959-62, then sr. judge. Mem. N.Y. State Jud. Council, 1950-53. Served with mil. at Mexican Border, also World War I. Mem. Bklyn. Bar Assn. (past pres.), Brooklyn Heights Assn. (past pres.). Mason (33 deg.). Home: Brooklyn, N.Y. Died Oct. 11, 1976; interred Greenwood Cemetery, Brooklyn.

BRUCKER, HERBERT, writer, editor; b. Passaic, N.J., Oct. 4, 1898; s. Carl and Adele (Balthasar) B.; A.B., Williams Coll., 1921, LL.D., 1964; B. Litt., Columbia, 1924, L.H.D., 1963; Pulitzer traveling scholar, 1924; L.H.D., Colby Coll., 1960; D. Litt., U. Hartford, 1965; m. Sydney Seabury Cook, Feb. 6, 1926 (dec. Apr. 1950); children—Christopher, Sydney (Mrs. James Sowles), Thomas; m. 2d, Mrs. Elizabeth Spock Dominick, Aug. 10, 1951; 2 stepsons, William F., Anthony Dominick. Reporter, Springfield (Mass.) Union, 1923, World, N.Y.C., 1925-26; mem. editorial staff World's Work, 1926-27, Rev. of Revs., 1927-32; asst. to dean Columbia Sch. Journalism, 1932-44, asst. prof. journalism, 1933-35, asso. prof., 1935-42, prof., 1942-44; chief media div., asso. chief Bur. Overseas Publs., OWI, 1942-43; asso. editor Hartford Courant, 1944-47, editor, 1947-66; dir. profl. journalism fellowships Stanford, 1966-69; syndicated newspaper columnist, 1968-77. Served with USN, 1918. Recipient John Peter Zenger award U. Ariz., 1959. Mem. Am. Soc. Newspaper Editors (pres. 1963-64), Am. Council Edn. for Journalism (pres. 1959-63), Chi Psi, Sigma Delta Chi. Episcopalian. Author: The Changing American Newspaper, 1937; Freedom of Information, 1949; Journalist: Eyewitness to History, 1962; Communication Is Power: Unchanging Values in a Changing Journalism, 1973. Address: Avon, Conn. Died Apr. 5, 1977.

BRUENING, HEINRICH, univ. prof.; b. Muenster, Germany, Nov. 26, 1885; s. Friedrich Wilhelm and Bernhardine (Beringhoff) B.; ed. U. of Munich, U. of Strassburg, U. of Bonn (Ph.D.), London Sch. of Economics; LL.D., Brown U., 1937; hon. A.M., Oxford U., 1938. Came to U.S., 1935. Prussian Ministry of Welfare, 1919-21; polit. and econ. advisor to Christian Trade Unions, 1921-30; member German Reichstag, 1924-33; chancellor German Reich, 1930-32; lecturer Oxford Univ., 1937-38; lecturer, Harvard, since 1937, Littauer prof. of pub. administrn. since 1939. Served in German Army during World War. Decorated Iron Cross, 2d and 1st class. Roman Catholic. *

BRUGMAN, FRANCIS ALBERT (BRUG'MAN), oculist and aurist; b. Iowa City, Ia., Jan. 20, 1885; s. John Albert and Mary Theresa (Barry) B.; M.D., State U. of Ia., 1909; m. Mable V. Shalla, Sept. 15, 1909; 1 dau., Mary Jean. Physician and surgeon, Minot, N.D., 1909-10; resident surgeon Ill. Charitable Eye and Ear Infirmary, Chicago, 1911-12; oculist and aurist, Minot, N.D., 1913-23, Seattle, Wash., since 1924; partner Drs. Würdemann and Brugman. Served as lt. Med. Corps, U.S. Army, 1918-19; capt. Med. Reserve, 1920-30. Mem. A.M.A., Wash. State Med. Soc., King County Med. Soc., Puget Sound Acad. Ophthalmology and Otolaryngology (sec. 1929-33, pres. 1934), Pacific Coast Oto-Ophthal. Soc., Am. Legion (post comdr. 1923). Democrat. Catholic. Clubs: College, Washington Athletic, Stillaguamish Country, Lake Washington Saddle, I Club (U. of Ia.). Contbr. (with Dr. H. V. Wurdemann) chapter on eye injuries in Modern Trends in Ophthalmology; also to med. jours. Home: Bellevue Wash. *

BRUMBAUGH, DAVID EMMERT, lumber co. exec.; b. Martinsburg, Pa., Oct. 8, 1894; s. Moses R. and Sarah Florence (Stuard) B.; ed. pub. schs., North Woodbury Twp., Pa., Summer normal school Martinsburg, Pa., and Internat. Corr. Schs., Scranton Pa.; D.C.S. (hon.), Franklin and Marshall Coll.; m. Carolyn L. Acker, Oct. 29, 1919; children—D. Robert Sumner E., Carol and Carolyn (twins). Engaged ir banking bus., Claysburg, Pa., 1914-77; partner Queen Lumber Co., from 1921; established D. Emmer Brumbaugh Ins. Agy., 1920; chmn. bd. Central Pa. Nat Bank; dir. Penn State Mut. Ins. Co., Johnstown; mem 78th Congress from 23d Pa. Dist., 79th Congress, 22 Pa. Dist.; sec. of banking Commonwealth of Pa 1947-52; former state senator Pa., 30th Dist. Chmn Blair County S.S.S. Bd. No. 1, Hollidaysburg, Pa 1941-43; chmn. Blair County chpt. A.R.C. 1934-62 now mem. exec. com. Trustee Pa. Indsl Sch Huntingdon, Pa., Cedar Crest Coll., Altoona Hosp Served as pvt. 33d Div., U.S. Army, World War Citation from Hood Coll., Frederick, Md. Mem V.F.W., Am. Legion, 40 and 8, Pa. Soc. of N.Y. Mason (32 deg., Shriner, Jester). Republican. Clubs: Unio

League (Phila.); Blairmont Country (Hollidaysburg); Iron Masters Country (Roaring Spring, Pa.). Address: Claysburg, Pa. Died Apr. 22, 1977.

BRUMLEY, ALBERT EDWARD, music pub., composer; b. Spiro, Okla., Oct. 29, 1905; s. William Sherman and Sarah Isabelle (Williams) B.; student Hartford (Ark.) Mus. Inst., 1926-30; m. Goldie Edith Schell, Aug. 30, 1931; children—Bill, Albert Edward, Tom, Bob, Jack, Betty (Mrs. Billy John Pockrus). Pres., Brumley/Hartford Interprises, Powell, Mo., 1926-43. Circuit clk., recorder of deeds, McDonald County, Mo., 1942-44. Mem. Nashville Songwriters Assn.'s Hall of Fame, Gospel Music Assn. Hall of Fame, Country Music Hall of Fame. Mem. Ch. of Christ. Composer over 600 gospel and religious songs. Address: Powell, Mo. Died Nov. 15, 1977; interred Fox Cemetery, Powell.

BRUMLEY, CORWIN H., optical co. exec.; b. Pelham, N.Y., 1923; student Mass. Inst. Tech., 1944. Sr. v.p. Bausch & Lomb, Inc., Rochester, N.Y. Home: Penfield, N.Y. Died July 9, 1978.

BRUN, ANTOINE EDMOND, educator; b. St. Cannat (B du R), France, Dec. 31, 1898; s. Antoine Marius and Marie (Villecrose) B.; B.Sc., U. Marseille, 1921, M.S. (fellowship nat. competitive test), 1923; D. Scis., Paris, 1934; m. 1923. Prof. spl. courses Lycée Nice, 1923-30, Parisian Lycée, 1930-42; lectr., then prof. fluid mechanics Faculté des Sciences de Paris, 1942-70, hon. prof., 1970-79; dir. Laboratoire d'Aérothermique, 1942-70, hon., 1970-79, prof. Ecole Nationale Superieure de l'Aéronautique, 1942-70. Mem. Armed Forces, 1917-19. Decorated officer Legion of Honor; comdr. Mil. Merit (Brazil); comdr. Palmes Académiques, Medaille de l'Aeronautique, Laureate Acad. Scis. Fellow Royal Aero. Soc., Am. Inst. Aeros. and Astronautics (hon.), Am. Astronautical Soc. (hon.); fgn. asso. Nat. Acad. Scis. (U.S.), Internat. Astronautics Acad. (v.p.), Société Francaise d'Astronautique (pres. 1960-62), Internat. Astronautical Fedn. (pres. 1960-62), Société Francaise des Thermiciens (pres. 1964-65), Société Météorologique de France (pres. 1959), Société des Ingénieurs Civils de France (pres. 1969), Acad. Scis. (Institut de France); mem. Internat. Center for Heat and Mass Transfer (pres. sci. council 1969-74), Com. on Consequences of Stratospheric Flights (pres. 1972-77), Acad. Scis. and Arts of Serbia. Author articles and books on aerodynamic heating, convection, icing of aircraft, aerosols, fluid mechanics. Died Nov. 4, 1979.

BRUNDAGE, PERCIVAL FLACK, consultant; b. Amsterdam, N.Y., Apr. 2, 1892; s. William Milton and Charlotte (Flack) B.; A.B. cum laude, Harvard, 1914; D.Sc., N.Y. U. Partner Price Waterhouse & Co., N.Y.C., 1930-54, cons., 1958-79; pres., dir. 56 Pine St. Inc., N.Y.C., 1944-54; dep. dir. Bur. of Budget, 1954-56, dir., 1956-58, cons., 1958-60. Dir. Montclair Community Chest 1950-54; dir. Nat. Bur. Econ. Research, 1942-67, pres., 1954, hon. dir., 1967-79; chmn. Unitarian Devel. Fund Campaign, 1959-62. Dir., treas. People to People Health Found., Inc., Atlantic Council U.S.; treas. Internat. Movement for Atlantic Union. C.P.A., N.Y., N.J., Mass. Mem. Internat. Assn. Religious Freedom (pres. 1952-55), Fed. Union, Inc. (dir.), Unitarian Service Com. (dir. 1949-54), Am. Unitarian Assn. (dir. 1942-48), N.Y. C. of C. (chmn. exec. com. 1952-54), Am. Inst. Accountants (pres. 1948-49), Council Fgn. Relations, Fgn. Policy Assn., UN Assn., Washington Inst. Fgn. Affairs. Clubs: Century Assn., Harvard (N.Y.C.); Hillsboro (Florida); Gulf Stream Golf (Florida); Chevy Chase (Md.); Metropolitan, City Tavern Assn. (Washington). Author: The Bureau of the Budget, 1970. Home: Pompano Beach, Fla. Died July 16, 1979.

BRUNNIER, HENRY J. (BRU-NER), structural engr.; b. Manning, Ia., Nov. 26, 1882; s. Martin and Maroline (Meyer) B.; B.C.E., Iowa State Coll., 1904, C.E., 1913; m. Ann Weideman, Oct. 2, 1905; 1 son, Henry J. Jr. (dec.). Structural detailer, bridges and indsl. plants, Am. Bridge Co., Pittsburgh, Pa., 1904-05; structural designer, power-houses and allied structures, New York Edison Co., 1905; structural engr., reconstruction United Railroad properties in San Francisco, Ford-Bacon and Davis Co. of New York, N.Y., 1906-08; priv. practice as structural engr. and cons. engr. on construction, San Francisco, Calif., since 1908; served as spl. consultant on foundation problems to Western Sugar Co. (San Francisco), Gray's Harbor Pulp and Paper Co. (Hoquiam, Wash.), for numerous large buildings in various western cities; cons. engr. low level Broadway tunnels between Alameda and Contra Costa counties; cons. engr. on construction of buildings for earthquake safety to bd. of edn., San Francisco, San Rafael, Redwood City and San Leandro (Calif.), Helena (Mont.), U. of Calif. and Pedro Corcuera y Mier Estate (Mexico, D.F.). Mem. cons. bd. engrs. San Francisco—Oakland Bay Bridge Project. In cooperation with Rudolph Wig, organized and managed concrete ship dept. U.S. Emergency Fleet Corp., World War I; engr. for U.S. Navy, U.S. Army in numerous bases, communications and fortification structures in Calif. and Canal Zone, World War II; pres. Calif. Bd. Registration for Civil Engrs., 1931-32; West of Twin Peaks Improvement Clubs Council, 1926-29. Mem. Calif. Major Highway Development Co.; vice chmn. San Francisco Traffic Survey Com. Recipient several honors nat. and fgn. profl. societies; Ernest E. Howard award Am. Soc. C.E., 1965; Officier de l'Ordre de la Couronne, Belgium; Officier de la Legion d'Honneur, France. Member American Automobile Assn. (past pres.), Am. Soc. C.E. (hon. mem., past pres. S.F. sect.), Pacific Assn. Cons. Engrs. (past pres.), Structural Engrs. Assn. No. Calif. (past pres., hon.), Structural Engrs. Assn. So. Cal. (hon.), Structural Concrete Inst., Calif. State Automobile Assn. (past pres.; chmn. hwy. com.), San Francisco C. of C. (past v.p.), Cardinal Guild, Chi Epsilon, Tau Beta Phi. Mason. Clubs: Engineers (past pres, hon. mem.) (San Francisco), Rotary (past pres. San Francisco, past pres. internat.). Awarded Marston Medal, Ia. State Coll., 1941. Home: San Francisco. *

BRUNO, GUIDO (PEN NAMES "MAUDE MARTIN" AND "MILDRED MEEKER"), editor, author; b. in Bohemia, Oct. 15, 1884; grad. Royal Gymnasium, Prague, 1898; post-grad. work, univs. of Prague, Vienna and Gratz; m. Ragna Pauluda Jacobsen, of Christiania, Norway, Aug. 10, 1909. Came to U.S., 1906; formerly editorial writer, spl. corr. European papers, dramatic critic and war corr.; editor Greenwich Village (semi-monthly devoted to art and lit.), Bruno's Chap Books (monthly), Bruno's Weekly; owner Bruno's Garrett (art gallery). Club: New York Press. Author: The Dutch-German Branch of the Washington Family, 1912; Lincoln as Seen by the Caricaturists of His Time, 1913. Lecturer on lit. subjects and art. Home: New York *

BRUNO, HARRY A., public relations counsel; b. London, Eng., Feb. 7, 1893; s. Henry A. and Annie (Thompson) B.; ed. Action County Sch., Portland Coll., London, Eng., Montclair (N.J.) High Sch.; D.Aviation Mgmt., Embry-Riddle Aero. U., 1975; m. Nydia de Sosnowska, Jan. 18, 1930; m. 2d, Evelyn Denny Witten, Jan. 6, 1972. Came to U.S., 1907, naturalized, 1928. Advt. mgr. Montclair (N.J.) Herald, 1914-15, Am. Press, N.Y., 1916-17; local sales mgr., N.Y. City Car Adv. Co., 1919; publicity dept., Mfrs. Aircraft Assn., 1920; sales and advt. mgr., Aeromarine Airways, Inc., 1921-22, v.p., 1923; partner H.A. Bruno, R.R. Blythe and Assos., pub. relations, 1923-34; owner H.A. Bruno and Assos., 1934-70; pres. H.A. Bruno and Assos., Inc., 1953-68, chmn., 1968-69; asst. to head of div. of contract distbn. OPM, dir. of Def. Specials for WPB, Washington, 1941-42. Acted as personal rep. for Adm. R.E. Byrd, Col. Charles A. Lindbergh, Wiley Post, Harold Gatty, Dr. Hugo Eckener, Lincoln Ellsworth, Jacqueline Cochran; chmn. Pub. Relations Adv. Com. to USAF, 1949-54; mem. selection com. Aviation Hall of Fame, Dayton, 1976-78. Mem. nat. adv. council Embry Riddle Aero. U., Daytona Beach, Fla. Bd. govs. Flight Safety Found. Served with Royal Flying Corps., Can., 1917. Recipient Glidden trophy N.Y. Aero Club, 1921; diploma d'honneur, Ligue Internationale des Aviateurs, 1930; McGough Meml. Award A.S. Post 501, Am. Legion, 1950, Frank M. Hawks Meml. award, 1973; Cross of Lorraine (France), 1951; Elder Statesman of Aviation award Nat. Aero. Assn., 1962; Gen. William Mitchell medal Aviation Writers Assn., 1951; Exceptional Service Award, USAF, 1953, Hap Arnold award Gen. Arnold chpt. Air Force Assn., 1968; Distinguished Service Mktg. award Sales Execs. Club N.Y.; named to Aviation Hall of Fame. Founder mem. Airplane Owners and Pilots Assn.; mem. Aviation Space Writers, Air Force Assn., Navy League, Silurians, Am. Legion, Internat. Platform Assn., Quiet Birdmen (founder), Early Birds, Internat. Assn. Chiefs of Police (asso.), Air Force Hist. Soc. (trustee), Broadcast Pioneers. Democrat. Baptist. Clubs: Wings (founder, hon. life mem.), N.Y. Athletic (life), Lotos (pres. 1951-62, hon. pres. 1962-67, pres. emeritus 1968-78), Sales Execs. (founder); Adventurers (pres. 1948), N.Y. Yacht (N.Y.C.); Overseas Press; Sky. Author: Wings Over America, 1942. Contbr. articles to mags. Home: Montauk, N.Y. Died Mar. 21, 1978.

BRUNS, FRANKLIN RICHARD, JR., museum curator; b. N.Y.C., May 25, 1912; s. Franklin Richard and Anna Sophie (Feuring) B.; ed. pub. schs.; m. Priscilla Ann Garfield, Oct. 24, 1936; children—Priscilla Lee (Mrs. Edwin G. Sando), Franklin Richard III, James Harold, Katharine Ann. Stamp editor N.Y. Sun, 1932-50, N.Y. World Telegram and Sun, 1950-52; syndicated stamp and coin columnist, 1951-79; asso. curator div. philately Smithsonian Instn., 1951-57; dir. div. philately Post Office Dept., 1957-62; initial curator Cardinal Spellman Philatelic Mus., Weston, Mass., 1962; engaged in pvt. industry, 1962-72; asso. curator div. postal history Smithsonian Instn., 1972-79; mem. Assay Commn., 1973; philatelic adviser and agt. Republic Liberia, 1947-52. Mem. Postmaster General's Citizens Stamp Adv. Com., 1957-62, 71-79. Trustee Cardinal Spellman Philatelic Mus., Regis Coll., Weston, Mass. Mem. Am. Philatelic Congress (pres. 1944-47, editor 1952, 55, hon. council 1959-79; Service award 1969), Collectors Club N.Y.C. (gov. 1944-53, sec. 1944-48, editor 1942-48), Collectors Club Washington (hon. life), Soc. Philatelic Americans (v.p. 1963-65, sec. bd. 1970-74, dir. 1974-79; Lagerloef award 1972, H.L. Lindquist award 1974), Am. Philatelic Soc., Am. Numis. Assn., Am. Air Mail Soc. (hon. life), Combined Philatelic Exhbn. Chicagoland (hon. life). Mason. Home: Takoma Park, Md. Died Mar. 24, 1979; buried Woodlawn Cemetery, N.Y.C.

BRUNSTING, LOUIS ALBERT, physician, educator; b. Grand Rapids, Mich., July 7, 1900; s. Albert L. and Kate (Bolt) B.; student Calvin Coll., 1917-18, Grand Rapids Jr. Coll., 1918-19; M.D., U. Mich., 1924; M.Sc., Mayo Found. U., 1929; m. Lena J. Pleune, 1923 (dec. Nov. 1967); children—Anna Lea (Mrs. Franklin Earnest, III), Louis Albert (dec.), Carl David, Linda Jane; m. 2d, Kathryn Chabot, Sept. 28, 1969. High sch. sci. tchr., Grandville, Mich., 1919-20, gen. practitioner, Nashville, Mich., 1925-26; staff cons. dermatology and syphilology Mayo Clinic, 1930-77; prof. dermatology and syphilology Mayo Found., U. Minn. Grad. Sch., 1950-65; pvt. practice as cons. in dermatology, 1965-77; ret., 1977; civilian cons. indsl. dermatosea USPHS, 1947-53. Mem. Minn. Bd. Parks and Recreation, 1940-47. Served with inf. SATC, U.S. Army, 1918. Diplomate Am. Bd. Dermatology. Mem. A.M.A. (residency rev. com. on dermatology and syphilology), Am. Dermatology Assn. (hon. mem., sec. 1948-53, pres. 1953-54), Minn., Chgo. (pres. 1956) dermatol. socs., Soc. Investigative Dermatology, Am. Acad. Dermatology (rep. Am. Bd. Dermatology 1958-61), Minn. Med. Assn. (chmn. com. on syphilis and social diseases), Sigma Xi, Phi Chi; hon. mem. Austrian, German, Yugoslav, Brazilian, Polish, Venezuelan dermatol. socs., Brit. Assn. Dermatology, Royal Soc. Medicine; corr. mem. Swedish, Dutch, French dermatol. socs., dermatol. socs. of Israel, Argentina, Norway, Denmark. Presbyn. Mem. adv. panel on dermatology U.S. Pharmacopoeia. Contbr. articles to profl. jours. Home: Sun City, Ariz. Died Oct. 9, 1980.

BRUNTON, FREDERIC KEMBLE, metallurgical engr.; b. Leadville, Colo., Apr. 17, 1886; s. David William and Katherine May (Kemble) B.; ed. St. John's Military Acad., Delafield, Wis., 1902-5, Colo. Sch. of Mines, 1905-7; McGill U., Montreal, Can., 1907-9; m. Edith Merz Hasley, of Anaconda, Mont., Nov. 6, 1909. Began as asst. engr. of tests, Anaconda Mining Co., May, 1909; asst. supt. British Columbia Copper Co., Ltd., since Oct., 1912. Progressive. Mem. Am. Inst. Mining Engrs. (life), Kappa Sigma, W.W.G. Home: Anaconda, B.C. *

BRUSON, HERMAN ALEXANDER, chemist; b. Middletown, Ohio, July 20, 1901; s. Samuel J. and Rebecca (Arnovitz) B.; B.Sc., MIT, 1923; D.Sc., Fed. Poly. Inst., Zurich, Switzerland, 1925; D.Sc. (hon.), New Haven U., 1980; m. Virginia Haber, Mar. 30, 1929; children—Rita, Dorothy, Barbara. Sect. editor Chem. Abstracts, 1937-60; asso. prof. organic chemistry Temple U., 1939-48; Priestly lectr. Pa. State Coll., 1944; with Olin Mathieson Chem. Corp., New Haven, 1952-66, v.p. research chem. div., 1960-66, chem. cons., 1966-81; chem. research specializing petroleum-based chems. U.S. rep. to OECD Plastics Com., 1967. Recipient Pioneer award in creative chemistry N.A.M., 1965; Wisdom award Honor, 1970; Eli Whitney award for contbns. to sci. Conn. Patent Law Assn. Mem. Société de Chimie Industrielle, Am. Chem. Soc. (chmn. New Haven 1953, award for creative invention 1977, Gold medal for creative invention 1977, Maurice Chamberland award 1981), AAAS, Am. Inst. Chemists (Pioneer award 1966), Chemists Club N.Y. Club: Graduate (New Haven). Author: Cvanoethylation, chpt. in Organic Reactions, 1949. Contbr. articles to profl. jours. Holder 400 U.S. and fgn. patents; discovered oil additive enabling Allied tanks to function in cold weather. Home: Woodbridge, Conn. Died May 31, 1981; buried New Haven.

BRYAN, ALVIN WESLEY, dental educator; b. Marcus, Ia., Apr. 4, 1884; s. Oliver Schrader and Nancy Emmeline (Woodford) B.; D.D.S., State U. of Ia., 1911; m. Gertrude Lucretia Riggs, Oct. 2, 1907; children—Marjorie Anne, Clarys Jeanette. Began practice of dentistry, 1911; instr. in operative dentistry, State U. of Ia., 1912-17, asst. prof. dental therapeutics, 1917-24, prof. and head dept. of pathology and therapeutics, 1924-52, dean Coll. of Denistry, 1932-52. Fellow Am. Coll. Dentists (president 1939), A.A.A.S., N.Y. Acad. Dentistry; mem. Am. Dental Assn., Internat. Assn. Dental Research, Am. Acad. of Periodontology (president 1938), American Assn. Dental Schools (pres. 1944, 1945, vice pres., 1943), Iowa State Dental Society (vice-president 1935; president 1938), Iowa Academy of Science. Sigma Xi, Delta Sigma Delta. Republican. Methodist. Clubs: Kiwanis, Triangle. Contbr. tech. articles to mags. Home: Iowa City, Ia. *

BRYAN, FREDERICK VAN PELT, judge; b. Bklyn., Apr. 27, 1904; s. Frederick J. and Mary Elizabeth (van Pelt) B.; A.B., Columbia, 1925, LL.B., 1928; m. Denise Frances Farquharson, Apr. 4, 1945; children—Antonia Denise (Mrs. Woodfin Camp III), Neville Johanna Farquharson (Mrs. William H. Peltz). Admitted to N.Y. bar, 1929; asso. firm Spence, Hopkins & Walser, N.Y.C., 1928-33; asst. corp. counsel, City, N.Y., 1933-37, 1st asst. corp. counsel, 1938-42; mem. firm Saxe, Bacon, O'Shea & Bryan, N.Y.C., 1946-56; mem. State Commn. to Study Orgnl. Structure Govt. City

N.Y., 1953-54; counsel Temporary Commn. Cts. of State N.Y., 1954-56; U.S. dist. judge So. Dist. N.Y., 1956-78, sr. judge, 1972-78. Republican candidate for Congress, 18th Congl. Dist. N.Y., 1946; chmn. N.Y. State Eisenhower Clubs, 1952. Bd. dirs. Child Care Center, 1940-69, Windham Child Care, 1969-78; trustee Columbia, 1961-76, trustee emeritus, 1976-78; trustee Brit. Am. Ednl. Found. Served with USAAF, 1942-45, col.; dep. chief staff 2d Air Div., 8th Air Force, col. Res. ret. Decorated Legion of Merit (U.S.); officer Order Brit. Empire (Gt. Britain); Croix de Guerre with palm (France). Fellow Am. Coll. Trial Lawyers; mem. Columbia U. Alumni Fedn. (pres. 1951-55), Am., N.Y. State bar assns., Assn. Bar City N.Y., Am. Judicature Soc. (dir. 1968-70), Inst. Jud. Adminstrn., Am. Law Inst., The Pilgrims, St. George's Soc., Phi Delta Phi, Delta Upsilon. Presbyn. Club: Century (N.Y.C.). Home: New York, N.Y., also Wingdale, N.Y. Died Apr. 19, 1978.

BRYAN, GEORGE SLOAN, naval officer; b. Scotland Neck, N.C., Dec. 23, 1884; s. George Washington and Nellie (Hawkins) B.; A.B., U.S. Naval Acad., 1906; m. Mary Frances Littell, Nov. 20, 1919; children—George Sloan, William Littell. Commissioned ensign, U.S. Navy, 1906; promoted through grades to captain, 1929, rear admiral, 1942; commander of U.S.S. Maryland, 1935-36; chief of staff Scouting Force, 1936-37; hydrographer of the U.S. Navy since 1938. Trustee Woods Hole Oceanographic Inst. Awarded Navy Cross and Victory medal. Fellow Am. Geog. Soc. Baptist. Club: Army and Navy (Washington). Home: Washington. *

BRYAN, JOHN BUCKLEY, engr.; b. N.Y.C., June 30, 1896; s. James Joseph and Bridget Aloysius (Buckley) B.; B.S., Columbia, 1921, A.B., 1921; C.E., Harvard, 1923, M.S., 1924; m. Helen Winona Mooney, Oct. 20, 1928; children—Helen Winona, John Buckley, Michael James. Field engr. and constrn. supt. United Engrs. and Constructors, 1924-33; N.Y. State prodn. mgr. Fed. Home Owner's Loan Corp., 1933-35; dir. Fed. Works Adminstrn., Westchester, Orange, Putnam, Duchess and Rockland cos., N.Y. State, 1935-36; chief engr., exec. dept. N.Y. State, 1936-41, dir. state budget, 1941-42; exec. v.p. L. Bamberger & Co., Newark, 1943-49; corporate engr. R. H. Macy & Co., Inc., 1949-50, corporate v.p. for engring. and constrn., 1950-77; also director Garden State Plaza Corp., Bam Properties, Inc., L & K Properties, Inc. Pres., chmn. bd. Cotton Point Assn., Lake George, N.Y. Chmn. Postwar Pub. Works Planning Commn., Automotive Rationing Commn., 1941-42; mem. Salary Standardization Bd., Fiscal Affairs Investigating Commn., 1941-42. Licensed profl. engr. and land surveyor, N.Y. Served as aviator, U.S. Navy, World War I. Mem. Am. Arbitration Assn., Harvard Engring. Soc. (past pres.), Kappa Sigma (past grand master). Clubs: Kex (Harvard); Harvard (N.Y. City); Canoe Brook Country (Summit, N.J.). Home: Summit, N.J. Died Jan. 20, 1977.

BRYAN, PAUL E(ASTERLING), prof. law; b. Boston, Ga., Sept. 7, 1884; s. Robert Burns and Rebecca Anna (Easterling) B.; A.B. magna cum laude, Emory U., 1907; A.M. (classics), LL.B., Yale, 1916; S.J. D., Harvard (Fairchild fellow), 1932; student, summers, U. of Chicago, 1910-11, Columbia, 1916; m. Isabel Reynolds Mawha, Sept. 1, 1923; children—Isabel Reynolds (Mrs. Robert Rodney Stone, Jr.), Paul Easterling. Admitted to bar Atlanta, 1916. Instr. modern lang., dir. athletics, Stamford Coll., Tex., 1907-10; Prussian exchange teacher, Stettin, and Muenster, Westphalia, 1912-13; prof. law, Lamar sch. of law, Emory U., Atlanta, 1916-18, and since 1921, intermittently acting dean; vis. prof. law, U. of Ga., summers, 1939, 1948; filed amicus curiae brief in Ga., Supreme Ct., in Ga. dual-gov. litigation, 1946, which prevailed in Court. Dir. Gen. Securities Corp., Home Bldg. & Loan Assn. (both Atlanta). Vice chmn. U.S. Wage Stabilization Bd., 1951-53. Mem. Ga. and Atlanta bars, Alpha Tau Omega, Phi Delta Phi, Omicron Delta Kappa, Phi Beta Kappa. Democrat. Methodist. (chmn. ofcl. bd.). Contbr. to Dictionary of Am. Biography, revs. in ours. Home: Atlanta. *

BRYANT, DANIEL PENNINGTON, van and storage co. exec.; b. Waukegan, Ill., Sept. 28, 1908; s. Daniel and Emma (Dempcy) B.; A.B., Stanford, 1931, J.D., 1934; m. Noel Walster, Dec. 25, 1932; children—Rachel, Dan W., David W. Admitted to Cal. bar, 1934; mem. firm Chase, Barnes & Chase, Los Angeles, 1934-43; v.p., sec. Bekins Moving & Storage Co., Los Angeles, 1943-45, gen. mgr., 1945-57, pres., 1957-68, chmn. bd., chief exec. officer, 1968-75; chmn. bd., chief exec. officer The Bekins Co., 1968-73, hon. chmn., 1973-75; dir. Bank of Am. Nat. Trust & Savs. Assn., Pacific Tel & Tel. Co., Pacific Lighting Co., Olga Co., Calif. Life Corp., Transit Mixed Concrete Co. Sr. fellow, vis. prof. Woodrow Wilson Found. Trustee Occidental Coll., Los Angeles, Haynes Found., Milo W. Bekins Found.; past trustee Com. Econ. Devel.; regent ct. of honor Forest Lawn Meml. Park, Glendale, Calif.; mem. corp. Conf. Bd. Decorated knight Order St. Lazarus of Jerusalem. Mem. Nat. Furniture Warehousemen's Assn. (past pres., dir.), Mchts. and Mfrs. Assn. Los Angeles (past pres., dir.), U.S. (past dir.), Los Angeles (dir., past pres.) chambers commerce. Conglist. Clubs: California, Bohemian, Lincoln (past pres.). Home: San Marino, Calif. Died Feb. 3, 1975; interred Forest Lawn Meml. Park, Glendale, Calif.

BRYANT, JOHN MYRON, elec. engr.; b. East Templeton, Mass., July 10, 1877; s. John Artemus and Clara Swan (Hale) B.; B.S., in E.E., Worcester Poly. Inst., 1901, E.E., 1909; M.S., U. of Ill., 1911; m. Lucinda Jane Rice, Aug. 18, 1904; 1 dau., Kathryn Hale (Mrs. F. B. Menger). Engring. dept. Gen. Electric Co., 1901-03; instr., asst. prof. and associate prof. elec. engring., U. of Ill., 1903-14; also practiced as cons. engr.; prof. elec. engring., U. of Tex., 1914-28; also pres. Academic Bd. U.S. Army Sch. of Mil. Aeronautics, same univ., and chmn. Bd. of Control of War Schs., U. of Tex.; had charge of edn. of over 14,000 men for Army, World War; prof. elec. engring., Univ. of Minnesota and head of department, 1928-46, professor emeritus, electrical engineering since 1946; president board Lightning and Transients Research Institute, Minneapolis since 1946. Fellow A.A.A.S., Am. Inst. E.E.; mem. American Soc. for Engring. Edn., Illuminating Engring. Soc., Sigma Xi, Tau Beta Pi, Eta Kappa Nu, Kappa Eta Kappa, Acacia. Methodist. Mason (32 deg.). Clubs: Campus, Engineers (Minneapolis). Author: Alternating Current Circuits (with J. A. Correll), 1925; Alternating Current Machinery (with Prof. E. W. Johnson), 1936; Elements of Utility Rate Determination (with R. R. Hermann), 1940; numerous professional papers. Home: St. Paul, Minn. *

BRYNILDSSEN, YNGVAR, corp. exec.; b. Fredrikstad, Norway, May 19, 1905; s. Bjarne and Margit (Bramer) B.; brought to U.S., 1907, naturalized, 1911; student Northwestern, 1930; m. Alletta Elizabeth Mathison, Apr. 27, 1926; children—Joy Mathilda (Mrs. L.F. Draper, Jr.), Jack Peter. Bank examiner State of Ill., 1930-33; examiner RFC, 1933-36; exec. v.p. Home Fed. Savs & Loan Assn., Chgo., 1936-39; v.p. Gen. Mortgage Investments, Inc., 1940-42; asst. treas. Stewart-Warner Corp., 1945-47; v.p., dir. finance Best Built Co. of Ill., Chgo., 1947-51, 53-77; chmn. bd. pres. Guardian Savs & Loan Assn., 1964-77; dep. adminstr. Small Def. Plants Adminstrn., Washington, 1952, adminstr., 1953; v.p., dir. Community Savs. & Loan Assn., Chgo.; dir.-at-large Fed. Home Loan Bank, Chgo. Mem. bd. Tb Inst. Chgo. and Cook County, pres., 1966-67; trustee Ill. Masonic Med. Center, 1970-77. Served as lt. comdr. USNR, 1942-45. Mem. Am. Legion. Mason (32 deg., Shriner; past potentate Medinah Temple). Home: Evanston, Ill. Died Oct. 19, 1977.

BUBIER, ROBERT HARVEY, city ofcl.; b. Hartford, Conn., June 12, 1927; s. Sylvester Breed and Ruth (Harvey) B.; A.B. in Journalism, U. Miami, 1951; m. Rosemary Theresa Brogan, July 26, 1951; children—Debra Ruth, Michelle. Personnel technician City of Ft. Lauderdale (Fla.), 1956-59, acting dir. recreation, also asst. city mgr., 1961-62, city mgr., 1963-76. Dir. Civil Def., Ft. Lauderdale, 1964-76. Bd. dirs. United Fund, YMCA, Swimming Hall of Fame. Served with USN, 1943-46, USAF, 1951-53, 61-62. Recipient Good Govt. award Ft. Lauderdale Jr. C. of C., 1967; Sales and Marketing Execs. award, 1969. Mem. Internat. City Mgrs. Assn. (regional v.p. 1972-76), Fla. (dir.), Broward Co. (pres.) leagues of municipalities, Fla. City and County Mgmt. Assn. (pres. 1972-73), Air Force Assn. (pres. chpt. 1972-73), Am. Legion, Sigma Delta Chi, Sigma Chi. Episcopalian (vestryman). Rotarian, Elk. Home: Fort Lauderdale, Fla. Died July 2, 1976.

BUCHANAN, ARCHIBALD C., judge; b. Tazewell, Va., Jan. 7, 1890; s. A. Beauregard and Nannie E. (Chapman) B.; A.B., Hampden-Sydney Coll., 1910; LL.B., Washington and Lee U., 1914, LL.D., 1949; m. Ollie McCall, Dec. 18, 1915; children—Sara (Mrs. Herbert Silvers) (dec.), Archibald C. Admitted to Va. bar, 1914; gen. practice state and fed. courts, 1915-27; mem. law partnership, Chapman, Peery and Buchanan, Tazewell, Va., judge 22d jud. circuit of Va., 1927-46; justice Supreme Ct. Appeals of Va., 1946-69; mayor, Tazewell, Va., 1917-21; commr. of accounts, Tazewell County, 1919-27; mem. Jud. Council Va., 1928-32; chmn. com. of judges to fix salaries of trial justices of Va. and their clerks, 1942-46; com. of Judiciary of Va. State Bar, 1941-46. Recipient Algernon Sydney Sullivan Medallion, 1950. Trustee Hampden-Sydney Coll., 1928-69, Mary Baldwin Coll., Staunton, Va., 1948-62. Mem. Am. Bar Assn., Va. Historic Soc., Va. Bar Assn., Pi Kappa Alpha, Phi Delta Phi, Phi Beta Kappa. Democrat. Presbyn. (elder). Clubs: Tazewell County Country, Rotary, Commonwealth. Home: Tazewell, Va. Died May 3, 1979; buried Maplewood Cemetery, Tazewell.

BUCHANAN, JAMES HERMAN, corp. exec.; b. Venus, Tex., Mar. 13, 1898; s. William W. and Modene (Boots) B.; student E. Tex. Normal Coll., 1912-14; m. Helen L. Lawrence, Dec. 10, 1919; children—Barbara (Mrs. John C. Bachmann). Chmn. bd., dir. Crescent Corp., N.Y.C., 1965-76; v.p., dir. Taylor Internat. Corp., Miami, Fla.; 1966-76. Served with U.S. Navy, World War I. Republican. Mason. Club: La Gorce Country (Miami Beach). Home: Miami Beach, Fla. Died Nov. 5, 1976.

BUCHANAN, M(ARION) L(YNN), agriculturist; b. El Dorado, Kans., Oct. 17, 1913; s. Orlando and Bertha (Ashenfelter) B.; grad. El Dorado Jr. Coll., 1932; B.S., Okla. A. and M. Coll., 1935; M.S., W. Va. U., 1937; student U. of Wis., 1939-41; m. Lucye Nell Yates, Oct. 2, 1935; children—Arthur, Lynnel, David. Instr. in animal husbandry W.Va. U., 1937-39; univ. fellow U. of Wis., 1940-41; asso. prof. animal husbandry U. of Ga., 1941-42; asst. prof. animal husbandry U. of Ida., 1942-43; agrl. development agt. Great Northern Ry., Great Falls, Mont., 1943-44; asso. prof. animal husbandry N.D. Agrl. Coll., 1945-46, chief div. animal industry from 1946. Mem. Am. Soc. Animal Prodn., Am. Genetic Assn., Columbia Sheep Breeders Assn. (sec. 1945), Alpha Zeta, Sigma Xi. Methodist. Home: Glyndon, Minn. Died Sept. 10, 1976.

BUCHANAN, ROBERT EARLE, bacteriologist; b. Cedar Rapids, Ia., Mar. 27, 1883; s. John and Josephine (Hall) B.; B.S., Ia. State Coll., Ames, Ia., 1904, M.S., 1906; Ph.D., U. of Chicago, 1908; D.Sc. Rutgers U., 1954, Ia. State U., 1958; m. Estelle D. Fogel, Jan. 5, 1910; 1 son, Joseph Hall. Prof. bacteriology, Iowa State University, Ames, Iowa, 1908—, head department of bacteriology, 1910-45, dean indsl. science, 1914-19, dean Grad. Coll., 1919-48, now dean emeritus; director of Iowa Agricultural Experiment Sta., 1933-48, research prof., 1948; guest prof. Goethe U., Frankfurt, Germany, 1949-50. Mem. Indian-Am. Commn. on Agr. in India, 1956; pres. bacteriol. sect. Internat. Bot. Congress, Cambridge, 1930; pres. sect. on agrl. bacteriology, Internat. Microbiological Congress, London, 1936; a v.p. Internat. Microbiol, Congress, New York, 1939; mem. Internat. Com. on Bacteriol. Nomenclature, 1930— (life); chmn. Internat. Bacteriol. Judicial Commn., 1939—; member agricultural board Nat. Research Council; member Committee of Nine, agr. expt. sta. orgn. and policy, Assn. Land-Grant Colleges and Univs.; mem. administrative com., Inter-Am. Inst. Agrl. Scis. Mem. agr. commn. Depts. of State and Agr., to Arab countries, 1946; Agrl. Mission of Food and Agrl. Orgn. to Greece, 1946; mem agrl. adv. com. U.N. com. for Arab refugees in Near East, 1949. Sectional president 5th International Congress of Microbiology held at Rio de Janeiro, 1950. Fellow A.A.A.S., Iowa Academy Science (president 1935-36); member Soc. Am. Bacteriologists (hon., pres. 1918, life mem.), Am. Chem. Soc., Soc. Gen. Microbiology of Great Britain (hon.), Sigma Xi, Phi Kappa Phi, Phi Lambda Upsilon, Gamma Sigma Delta. Presbyn. Contbr. to Microbiology, 1911, 17, 21. Editor Ia. State Coll. Jour. of Sci., 1926-36, 50—; editor for gen. bacteriology Biological Abstracts, 1926—; editor Internat. Jour. Systematic Bacteriology, 1951—. Chmn. editorial bd. Internat. Code Nomenclature of Bacteria. Home: Ames, Ia. *

BUCHOLTZ, CARL (BUK'HOLTZ), railroad official; b. Baltimore, Md., Mar. 21, 1883; s. William and Alma (Hoen) B.; studied under Col. R. M. Johnson, Baltimore, 1891-94; student Loyola Coll., 1894-99; unmarried. Clerk in leaf tobacco business, 1899-1901, law office, 1901-02; machinist apprentice to supervisor of track B.&O.R.R. Co., 1902-08; maintenance of way insp. to div. engr. M.P.R.R., 1910-14; asst. engr. through grades to asst. gen. mgr. Erie R.R. Co., 1915-27, gen. mgr., 1927-32; gen. mgr., later v.p. and general manager Virginia Ry., 1933-34, pres. 1934-44; retired May 9, 1944. Mem. Am. Ry. Engrs. Assn., Railway Signal Assn., Newcomen Soc. Clubs: Princess Anne Country, Virginia Beach (Va.). Home: Baltimore County, Md. *

BUCK, EUGENE EDWARD (GENE BUCK), producer, song writer; b. Detroit, Mich., Aug. 8, 1885; s. George William and Katherine (McCarthy) B.; ed. U. of Detroit (non-grad.); studied art, Detroit Art Acad.; m. Helen Falconer, Oct. 2, 1919; children—Eugene Falconer, George William. Principal librettist for Ziegfeld Follies and Frolics since 1912, and writer of themes and songs for 30 productions of same; wrote "Zig Zag" for London Hippodrome, 1917; collaborated in an operetta with Augustus Thomas and Mischa Elman, in comedy with Ring Lardner and in songs and lyrics with Victor Herbert, Jerome D. Kern, Raymond Hubbell, Rudolf Friml and others. Mem. bd. The Am. Dramatists. Mem. American Society Composers, Authors and Publishers (director, consultant, adviser; president 1924-42), Authors League America (council; executive committee). Democrat. Catholic. Clubs: Dutch Treat (mem. bd. of govs.), The Players, Lambs (New York); Bohemian (San Francisco, Calif.); Nat. Press, Alfalfa (Washington); North Hempstead Country, Soundview Country. Writer: (songs) Hello Frisco; Tulip Time; 'Neath the South Sea Moon; Garden of My Dreams; Lovely Little Melody; No Foolin'; Maybe; Someone-Someday-Somewhere; also many more—about 500 in all; producer of "Yours Truly," 1926; "Take the Air," 1927; "Ringside," 1928. Home: Kensington, Great Neck, N.Y. *

BUCK, GEORGE H., business exec., cons. engr.; b. Eliot, Me., Dec. 22, 1894; s. A.O. and Sophie (Simpson) B.; B.S., U. Pa., 1918; m. Loretto Reavey, Sept. 10, 1927; 1 son, George H. Partner Buck, Seifert & Jost, Englewood Cliffs, N.J., 1936-76; pres., dir. Hackensack

Water Co., Weehawken, N.J., Spring Valley (N.Y.) Water Co., Inc.; dir. Hudson Trust Co. Served as pvt. C.A.C., 1917. Mem. Delta Kappa Epsilon. Episcopalian. Clubs: Downtown Assn. (N.Y.C.); Cosmos (Washington). Died June 3, 1976.

BUCK, PAUL HERMAN, educator; b. Columbus, Ohio, Aug. 25, 1899; s. Henry John and Adele (Kreppelt) B.; A.B., Ohio State U., 1921, A.M., 1922; A.M., Harvard, 1924, Ph.D., 1930; LL.D., Coe Coll., 1946, Ohio State U., 1946, Colby Coll., 1952, Brown U., 1953; Litt.D., Harvard, 1946, Princeton, 1947; L.H.D., Western Res. U., 1956; Sheldon Traveling fellow, London and Paris, 1925-26; m. Sally Burwell Betts, Dec. 21, 1927. Instr. history, Harvard U., 1926-36, asst. prof., 1936-39, asso. prof., 1939-42, prof., 1942-69, dean faculty, 1942-53, provost, 1945-53, dir. univ. libraries, 1955-64, Carl II. Pforzheimer univ. prof., 1958, Univ. prof. Am. history, 1965-69, univ. prof. emeritus, 1969-78. Mem. adminstrv. com., Dumbarton Oaks, 1944-53, chmn., 1952-53; mem. civilian adv. com. USN, 1945-47; bd. dirs. Center for Advanced Study in Behavioral Scis., 1952-69, chmn., 1960-69; chmn. Role of Edn. in Am. History, 1957-69; mem. com. on financing higher edn. and research Rockefeller Found., 1949-53. Trustee High Altitude Obs., Boulder, Colo., 1952, Smith Coll., 1952-62, Harvard Yen Ching Inst., 1945-53, Teachers Ins. and Annuity Co., 1954-58, Ednl. Testing Service 1956-58. Recipient Pulitzer prize in history, 1938; Ohioana Career medal, 1957; decorated chevalier Legion Honor (France); comdr. Order Phoenix (Greece). Mem. Am. Hist. Assn., Mass. Hist. Soc., Miss. Valley, So. hist. assns., Am. Agrl. Soc., Phi Beta Kappa, Kappa Sigma. Episcopalian. Clubs: Odd Volumes, Tavern, Harvard (Boston); Harvard (N.Y.); Faculty (Cambridge). Author: The Road to Reunion, 1937; Libraries and Universities, 1964. Co-author: General Education in a Free Society, 1945; Nature and Needs of Higher Education, 1953. Editor: The Social Sciences at Harvard, 1965. Bd. editors Jour. So. History, 1941-47. Contbr. to hist. jours. and Dictionary Am. Biography. Home: Cambridge, Mass. Died Dec. 23, 1978; interred at Columbus, Ohio.

BUCKLEY, JOHN, lawyer; b. Stafford Springs, Conn., May 12, 1885; in infancy lost both parents; grad. Hitchcock Free Acad., Brimfield, Mass., 1904; LL.B., U. of Me., 1907, LL.M., 1908; m. Grace Robinson Gaylord, Dec. 10, 1930. Was admitted to bar of Conn., 1910, and began practice at Hartford; mem. Conn. Ho. of Rep., 1909-10; clk. Conn. Ho. of Rep., 1915-16, Senate, 1917; sec. Rep. State Com., 1916-21; alternate del. Rep. Nat. Com., 1916; exec. sec. to Gov. Marcus II. Holcomb, 1917-20; mem. Conn. Ho. of Rep., 1921-22 (chmn. com. on judiciary and Rep. floor leader); U.S. atty., Dist. of Conn., by apptmt. of President Coolidge, Sept. 24, 1924, and reapptd. by same, Feb. 1928; now mem. Buckley, Creedon & Gallivan; dir. South End Bank & Trust Co., Hartford. Served as maj. U.S. Army, 1917-19; assigned as draft exec. for State of Conn. Apptd. chmn. Liquor Commn. by gov. of Conn., also as mem. Commn. under Liquor Control Act, enacted by legislature of Conn. Trustee Conn. University. Mem. Am. and Conn. State bar assns. Mason. Home: Union, Conn. *

BUCKNER, G(ARRETT) DAVIS, chemist; b. Lexington, Ky., May 17, 1885; s. Garrett Davis and Mary (Martin) B.; B.S., U. of Ky., 1908; Ph.D., Princeton, 1912; studied at Pasteur Inst. and Alliance Francaise, Paris, France, 1922, and Oceano-graphic Inst., Monaco, 1923; m. Sarah Gibson Chenault, Oct. 29, 1914; children—Sarah C., G(arrett) Davis, Mary Martin. Food chemist Ky. Experiment Sta., Lexington, Ky., 1908; chemist Sterling Sugar Factory, Franklin, La., 1909; asst. instr. in chemistry, Princeton, 1909-12; research chemist Ky. Experiment Sta., 1912-27, research prof. in charge of Animal Nutrition since 1927. Official U.S. del. World Poultry Congress, Rome, 1933, and Leipzig, Germany, 1936. Mem. A.A.A.S., Ky. Acad. of Sci., Soc. of Animal Production, Poultry Sci. Assn., Soc. Biol. Chemistry, Research Club of Univ. of Ky. (pres. 1929), Univ. of Ky. Alumni Assn. (pres. 1929-31), Am. Chem. Soc. (pres. Lexington sect. 1917), Kappa Alpha, Omicron Delta Kappa, Phi Beta Kappa, Sigma Xi. Episcopalian. Clubs: Rotary, Lexington Country. Author many scientific articles, principally on nutrition. Address: Lexington, Ky. *

BUDD, JOHN M., railroad exec.; b. Nov. 1907; s. Ralph and Georgia (Marshall) B.; B.S., Yale, 1930, grad. work, 1 yr. Began as chainman, G.N. Ry., summer 1926, asst. to elec. engr., 1930-31, asst. trainmaster, div. supt., various locations, 1933-42, asst. gen. mgr., lines east of Williston, N.D., 1945-47, v.p. operating dept., 1949-51, pres., 1951-70; chmn., chief exec. officer Burlington No. Inc., 1970-71, chmn. finance com., 1971-72, ret. 1972, dir.; pres. Chgo. and Eastern Ill. R.R., 1947-49. Served as lt. col. Mil. Ry. Service, Africa, Italy, France and Germany, AUS, 1942-45. Home: Inver Grove Heights, Minn. Died Oct. 25, 1979.

BUDDINGTON, ARTHUR FRANCIS, geologist; b. Wilmington, Del., Nov. 29, 1890; s. Osmer Gilbert and Mary Salina (Wheeler) B.; Ph.B., Brown U., 1912, Sc.M., 1913; Ph.D., Princeton U., 1916; hon. Sc.D., Brown, 1942; m. Jene Elizabeth Muntz, Sept. 10, 1924; 1 dau., Elizabeth Jene. Instructor Brown University, 1917 and 1919; petrologist, geophysical laboratory, Carnegie Inst., 1919-20; asst. prof. geology, Princeton University, 1920-26, asso. prof., 1926-32, professor, 1932-59, Blair prof. geology emeritus, 1959-81; chairman of department, 1936-50; temporary geologist U.S. Geol. Survey, from 1919, N.Y. State Mus., 1916-41; guest lectr. India Sci. Congress and Geol. Survey, 1957. Served as private Aviation Sect., Signal Corps, and sergt. 1st class Chem. Warfare Service, U.S. Army, 1918. Fellow Geol. Soc. Am. (councillor 1939-42, v.p. 1943, 47, Penrose medalist 1954), Soc. Econ. Geologists, Am. Geophysical Union (pres. volcano sect. 1941-44), American Acad. Arts and Sciences (fellow), Am. Mineral. Soc. (councilor 1936-40, pres. 1942; Roebling medalist, 1956), Am. Philos. Soc., Nat. Acad. of Sciences, A.A.A.S., Internat. Geol. Congress (del. of U.S. State Dept., London, 1948, Algiers, 1952). Methodist. Contbr. articles to jours. on geology. Asso. editor Am. Jour. Sci., from 1950. Home: Princeton, N.J. Died Dec. 29, 1981.

BUESS, CHARLES MERLYN, chemist, educator; b. Forest, Ohio, Apr. 22, 1922; s. Charles Amos and Jessie Katherine (Benning) B.; B.S., Ohio State U., 1942; M.S., Western Res. U., 1946; Ph.D., U. So. Calif., 1950; postdoctoral fellow Northwestern U., 1949-51; m. Anita Durand, June 7, 1953; children—Alice Katherine Buess Fisher, Charles Louis, Ann Lynn Buess Livington, Zoe Bell Chemist, NACA, Cleve., 1943-46; asst. prof. U. Ga., Athens, 1951-56; asso. prof. U. Ky., Lexington, 1956-57; asso. prof. U. So. Calif., Los Angeles, 1957-61; prof. chemistry Wichita (Kans.) State U., from 1961; vis. sr. scientist Jet Propulsion Lab., Pasadena, Calif., 1966. Fellow AAAS, Am. Inst. Chemists; mem. Am. Chem. Soc., Chem. Soc. (London), Kans. Acad. Sci., Phi Beta Kappa, Sigma Xi, Phi Kappa Phi, Phi Lambda Upsilon. Contbr. articles to profl. jours. Home: Benton, Kans. Died Jan. 7, 1980; buried Hueston Cemetery, Forest, Ohio.

BUFF, CONRAD, artist; b. Speicher, Switzerland, Jan. 15, 1886; s. Conrad and Anna (Bruderer) B.; student Sch. Arts and Crafts, St. Gallen, Switzerland, 1900-03, pvt. art sch., Munich, Germany, 1903; m. Mary Marsh, July 7, 1922; children—Conrad, David Marsh. Came to U.S., 1905, naturalized, 1933. Represented by lithographs in permanent collections of Brit. Mus., London, Met. Mus., N.Y.C., also murals. Recipient purchase prize Los Angeles Mus., 18th Annual Exhbn. of Paintings and Sculpture, for painting Westward, 1937; second award in painting L.A. Municipal Exhbn., 1948. Mem. Am. Artists Group. Co-author, illustrator: Dancing Cloud (on Navajo Indians), 1936; Kobi (on Switzerland), 1939; Dash and Dart, 1942; Big Tree, 1946; Peter's Pinto, 1949; The Apple and The Arrow, 1951; Magic Maize, 1953; Hurry Skurry and Flurry, 1955; Hah-Nee, 1956; Elf Owl, 1958; Trix & Vix, 1960; Forest Folk, 1962; Kemi (Friends of Library award U. Cal. at Irvine 1968), 1966; The Colorado; River of Mystery, 1968. Home: Laguna Hills CA. *

BUHLER, JOHN EMBICH, ret. coll. dean; b. Marion, Ind., June 28, 1908; s. Jesse Thurman and Ethel Claire (Pillars) B.; D.D.S., Ind. U., 1935; m. Ruth Zike, Jan. 24, 1940; children—Karen Ann (Mrs. Lawrence Douglas Wilkerson), John Embich. Intern, Ind. U. Med. Center and Dental Sch., 1935-36, instr. clin. dentistry and oral histology-pathology, 1936-37, instr. clin. oral surgery and oral histology, 1937-42; asso. prof. clin. oral surgery, sec. to faculty Temple U., 1942-48, prof., chmn. dept. oral diagnosis, 1947-48; dean Emory U. Sch. Dentistry, Atlanta, 1948-61; exec. v.p. Hanau Engring. Co., Inc., Buffalo, 1961-64; dean Coll. Dental Medicine, Med. U. S.C., 1964-71, dean emeritus, 1971-76; cons. dental div. Office Surgeon Gen., Dept. Army, 1954-61; cons. to chief dental officer USPHS, 1945-48, dental dir. Res. Dir. Fund for Dental Edn., 1954-61. Fellow Am. Coll. Dentists; mem. Am. Assn. Dental Schs. (sec. 1946-50, pres. 1954-55, exec. com. 1946-55), Am. Dental Assn. (council on dental edn. 1955-61), Ga., S.C. dental assns., Omicron Kappa Upsilon, Delta Sigma Delta. Episcopalian. Home: Charleston, S.C. Died Apr. 18, 1976; interred Charleston, S.C.

BUHRMAN, PARKER WILSON (BUR'MAN), b. Botetourt County, Va., Sept. 5, 1885; s. Joseph Blaine and Sarah Elizabeth (Lemon) B.; student Randolph-Macon Acad., Front Royal, Va., 1904-06; A.B., Randolph-Macon Coll., Ashland, Va., 1910; LL.B., Washington and Lee University, 1916. Teacher of high school at Martinsburg, West Virginia, 1911-12; admitted to Virginia bar, 1916, and practiced in Botetourt County, 1916-18; appointed U.S. consul, Malmo, Sweden, 1918, consul and member Inter-Allied Trade Commission for Finland, Helsingfors, Finland, 1919-20; consul, Cieba, Honduras, 1920-21, Surabaya, Java, 1921-23, Aleppo, Syria, 1923-25; detailed to Department of State, 1935, chief of Passport Division, 1927; consul, Berlin, 1928-29; consul and judge ex-officio, Am. Consular Court, Casablanca, Morocco, 1930-34; consul at Cologne, Germany, 1935; consul gen. Libson, Portugal, 1935-37, Sydney, Nova Scotia, 1937-38, Basel, Switzerland, 1939-40, consul gen. Glasgow, Scotland, 1940; consul gen., Belfast, Northern Ireland, 1940-43. Assigned Dept. of State, 1943. Representative Dept. of State in visits to prisoner of war camps. Sec. to mission U.S. Polit. Advisor on German Affairs, Supreme Hdqrs., Allied Expeditionary Force, 1945; polit. adviser 3d Army; consul gen., Munich; consul general, Bratislava, Czechoslovakia 1946, Gdansk, Poland, 1947; retired Sept. 1948. Mem. Kappa Alpha, Phi Delta Phi, Pi Gamma Mu. Methodist. Clubs: University, Nat. Press; Lotos (New York). Home: Raleigh, N.C. *

BULAND, GEORGE LEONARD, lawyer; b. Greenwood, Wis., Apr. 6, 1897; s. George L. and Bertha E. (Mason) B.; A.B., Reed Coll., 1916; LL.B., Columbia, 1919; m. Anne D. Shea, Sept. 10, 1924; children—Nan (Mrs. Peter Koerner), George. Editor, Columbia Law Rev., 1917-19; practiced in Portland, Ore., 1919-30; partner firm Dey, Hampson & Nelsen, 1923-30; lectr. Northwestern Coll. Law, 1926-30; pres. Kalama State Bank (Wash.), 1923-30; editor Ore. Law Rev., 1927-30; asst. gen. counsel S.P. Co., N.Y.C., 1930-44, eastern gen. counsel, 1944-45, asso. gen. counsel, 1945-47, gen. counsel, 1948-50, v.p., gen. counsel, 1951-63; dir. Pacific Fruit Express Co., 1935-44 (pres. 1943-44); St. Louis Southwestern Ry. Co.; dir., exec. com. So. Pacific Co., various subsidiaries, 1953-69; counsel Severson Werson, Berke & Melchior, 1963-75. Hon. trustee Reed Coll., Portland; bd. visitors Stanford Law Sch. Served in USN, 1918. Recipient medal for conspicuous service Columbia U., 1955. Mem. Am., Ore. bar assns., State Bar Cal., C. of C. Clubs: Commonwealth, Family, Pacific Union (San Francisco); Menlo Country (pres.) (Redwood City). Author publs. in field. Home: Palo Alto, Calif. Died Dec. 10, 1975.

BULKELEY, MAX M., lawyer; b. Knox County, Ill., Sept. 29, 1883; s. James C. and Sarah C. (Copley) B.; LL.B., U. of Denver; m. Sue V. Burkett, July 21, 1913; children—James B., Robert A. Admitted to Colo. bar, 1908, and practiced law in Wray, mem. firm Bulkeley & Snydal, 1908-1947; U.S. dist. atty., Colo., since 1947. Active in Red Cross and Boy Scout orgns. Mem. Am., Colo. and 13th Jud. Dist. bar assns., Phi Delta Phi, Delta Alpha Epsilon. Democrat. Christian Scientist. Odd Fellow, Elk, Rotarian. Home: Denver. *

BULKLEY, EDWIN MUHLENBERG, JR., investment broker; b. Englewood, N.J., Sept. 13, 1903; s. Edwin Muhlenberg and Lucy (Kidder) B.; student Hill Sch., Choate Sch., Occidental Coll.; m. Marianne Dodge, 1924 (div. 1941); 1 dau., Joan (Mrs. Edward B. deSelding); m. Maud Oberman, Nov. 9, 1969. With Spencer Trask & Co., N.Y.C., 1924-68, partner, 1937-68. Clubs: Gulf Stream Golf, Bath and Tennis, Yacht (Delray Beach, Fla.); Wianno (Mass.). Home: Delray Beach, Fla. Deceased.

BULL, DANIEL F., corp. exec.; b. Grand Forks, N.D., 1886; s. George and Elizabeth Hults (McBride) B.; graduate Univ. of N.D., 1906, Dr. of Comml. Science (honorary), 1952; married Rosamond E. Leland, 1910; children—Daniel F. and Webster M. (deceased), Rosamond E. Howe, David F. Constrn. engr., 1908-18; asst. gen. mgr., The Cream of Wheat Corp., 1921-40, pres. and gen. mgr., 1940-59, chairman of the bd. of directors, 1959—; director Household Finance Corp., First Nat. Bank, Northern Pacific Railway, First Bank Stock Corporation, Minnesota and Ontario Paper Company. In charge of constrn. Curtis Bay Ordnance Depot, Mo., Field Signal Sch., Camp Meade, Md., 1918-19. Clubs: Minneapolis (pres. 1943), Woodhill, Lafayette, Minneapolis Rotary (pres. 1925). Mason. Home: Wayzata, Minn. *

BULLARD, EDWARD CRISP, physicist; b. Norwich, Norfolk, Eng., Sept. 21, 1907; s. Edward John and Eleanor Howes (Crisp) B.; B.A., Cambridge U., 1929, Ph.D., 1932, Sc.D., 1948; m. Margaret Thomas, July 25, 1931 (div. Jan. 23, 1974); children—Belinda, Emily, Henrietta, Polly; m. 2d, Ursula Curnow, June 17, 1974. Demonstrator in geodesy Cambridge U., 1931-35, reader in exptl. geophysics, 1945-48; research fellow Royal Soc., 1936-43; exptl. officer Brit. Admiralty, 1939-45; prof. physics Toronto U., 1948-49; dir. Nat. Phys. Lab., Teddington, Middlesex, Eng., 1950-55; fellow Caius Coll., Cambridge, 1956-57, fellow Clare Coll., 1957-60, asst. dir. research Cambridge U., 1956-60, reader in geophysics, 1960-64, prof. geophysics, 1964-74; prof. Scripps Instn. Oceanography, U. Calif. at San Diego; fellow Churchill Coll., Cambridge, 1960-80; dir. IBM (U.K.), 1964-75. Created knight, 1953; recipient Day medal Geol. Soc. Am., 1959; Agassiz medal Nat. Acad. Sci., 1965; gold medal Royal Astron. Soc., 1965; Wollaston medal Geol. Soc. London, 1967; Vetlesen Prize, 1968. Mem. Geophys. Union (Bowie medal 1975, Ewing medal 1978), Royal Soc. London (Hughes medal 1953, Royal medal 1975), Royal Astron. Soc., The Phys. Soc. (Chree medal 1956), Cambridge Philos. Soc., Geol. Soc., London, Geol. Soc. Am., Am. Acad. Arts and Scis., U.S. Nat. Acad. Sci. (fgn. asso.); fgn. mem. Am. Philos. Soc. Home: La Jolla, Calif. Died Apr. 3, 1980.

BULLARD, SELLAR, corp. dir.; b. Liberty, N.M., Apr. 23, 1886; s. Edward D. and Marie (Sellar) B.; B.S., U. Cal., 1906; m. Bessie B. Smith, Oct. 8, 1910; children—Carol (Mrs. Bullard Nugent), Barbara (Mrs. Charles A. Storke), Jean (Mrs. John R. Holmes).

Investment banker Hitchcock & Co., Chgo., 1910-34; v.p., dir. Marquette Cement Mfg. Co., Chgo., 1922-26; retired, 1935; dir. Chgo. Mill & Lumber Co., Sunbeam Corp. (both Chgo.), Sherman P. Stow Co. (Goleta, Cal.); adv. com. Security First Nat. Bank, Santa Barbara. Pres. Santa Barbara Botanic Gardens; trustee Cottage Hosp., Santa Barbara, Santa Barbara Found. Mem. Alpha Tau Omega. Republican. Episcopalian. Clubs: Chicago, Mid-day (Chgo.); Santa Barbara. Address: Goleta, Cal. *

BULLEN, KEITH EDWARD, applied mathematician, educator; b. Auckland, New Zealand, June 29, 1906; s. George Sherrar and Maud (Burfoot) B.; M.A., U. New Zealand, 1928, B.Sc., 1930; M.A., U. Melbourne (Australia), 1945; Ph.D., U. Cambridge (Eng.), 1937. Sc.D., 1946; D.Sc., U. Auckland, 1963, U. Sydney, 1975; m. Florence Mary Pressley, May 15, 1935; children—John Edward, Anne. Master, Auckland Grammar Sch., 1926-27; lectr. math. Auckland U., 1928-39; sr. lectr. math. Melbourne U., 1940-45; prof. applied math. U. Sydney (Australia), 1946-71; spl. lectr. math. physics Hull (Eng.) U. Coll., 1933; Einstein Meml. lectr. Australian Inst. Physics, 1959, Harricks lectr., 1963. Pres. Internat. Assn. Seismology and Phsics Earth's Interior, 1954-57; v.p. Internat. Sci. Com. Antarctic Research, 1958-62, Internat. Union Geodesy and Geophysics, 1963-67; chmn. Australian nat. com. for I.G.Y., 1955-60. Sr. Univ. scholar pure and applied math. U. New Zealand, 1925; Strathcona exhibitioner St. John's Coll., Cambridge U., 1932-33; Lyle medallist Australian Nat. Research Council, 1951; Found. fellow Australian Acad. Sci., 1953; Walter Burfitt prizeman Royal Soc. New South Wales, 1953, Hector medalist, Royal Soc. New Zealand, 1952; Flinders lectr., medallist Australian Acad. Sci., 1969; Pontifical Academician, 1968 Gold medallist Royal Astron. Soc. London, 1974. Fellow Royal Soc. London, Am. Geophys. Union (William Bowie medallist 1961); corr. Geol. Soc. Am. (Arthur Day medallist 1963); fgn. hon. mem. Am. Acad. Arts and Scis.; fgn. asso. Nat. Acad. Sci.; hon. fellow Royal Soc. New Zealand; fgn. and commonwealth mem. Geol. Soc. London. Author books articles, chpts. in field. Home: Sydney, N.S.W., Australia. Died Sept. 23, 1976.

BULLITT, ORVILLE HORWITZ, banker; b. Cape May, N.J., July 30, 1894; s. William C. and Louisa G. (Horwitz) B.; B.S., U. Pa., 1915, L.H.D., 1970; m. Susan B. Ingersoll, Nov. 15, 1916. Partner W.H. Newbold's Son & Co., 1926-43; pres., dir. Beaver Coal Co.; then pres., dir. Beaver Mgmt. Corp.; formerly dir. Fidelity Bank, Westmoreland Coal Co., Va. Coal & Iron Co., Stonega Coal & Coke Co., Central Pa. Nat. Bank, Muskogee Co., Kans. Okla. & Gulf R.R.; formerly trustee Phila. Saving Fund Soc., Penn Mut. Life Ins. Co. Founder, pres., dir. Asso. Hosp. Service, Phila.; life trustee U. Pa.; pres., chmn. bd. Phila. Orch. Assn., 1938-68, dir., 1933-79; pres., mgr. Hosp. of Univ. Pa., 1931-61; trustee Phila. Mus. Art; treas., dir. Fairmont Park Art Assn., 1943-73; chmn., dir. Acad. Music, Phila.; chmn. U. Pa. Press. Participant Univ. Museum discovery Sybaris. Served with AEF, France, 1917-19. Author: Search for Sybaris, 1969; For the President, 1972. Home: Ft Washington, Pa. Died July 29, 1979.

BULLOCK, JOHN RICE, lawyer; b. Covington, Ky., July 16, 1906; s. John R. and Harriet (Dulaney) B.; A.B., U. Ky., 1928; LL.B., Yale, 1930; LL.D., U. Cin., 1963; m. Marion McDonell, 1937; children—Arden Marion (Mrs. William H. P. Robertson), John McDonell. Admitted to Ky. bar, 1930, Ohio bar, 1931; asso. firm Taft, Stettinius & Hollister, 1930-36, partner, 1936-79. Sec., dir. Coca-Cola Bottling Corp. and subsidiaries; dir. 1st Nat. Bank of Cin., also various corps. Trustee Bethesda Hosp., trustee Cin. Symphony Orch., pres. 1957-61; v.p. Cin. Inst. Fine Arts; chmn. United Fine Arts Fund, Cin., 1952; chmn., pres. Community Chest and Council of Cin. Area, Inc., 1966-67; chmn. Cincinnatians United for Good Schools, 1967-68. Mem. U. Ky. Alumni Assn. (pres. 1948), Am., Ohio, Cin. (pres. 1969) bar assns., Phi Beta Kappa, Delta Tau Delta. Republican. Episcopalian. Clubs: Cincinnati Country, Queen City, Optimists, Commercial (Cin.) Ryland Lakes Country. Recess, Commonwealth, Gyro. Home: Cincinnati, Ohio. Died Jan. 25, 1979; buried Spring Grove Cemetery, Cin.

BUNDESEN, RUSSELL, lawyer; b. Chgo., May 23, 1912; s. Herman N. and Rega R. (Russell) B.; student Lake Forest (Ill.) Coll.; B.S., Northwestern U., 1933, J.D., 1936; m. Jayne McGahey, Nov. 22, 1947; children—Lynne, Karine (Mrs. Jim Baltzell), Brian. Admitted to Ill. bar; partner firm Smith, Bundesen, White & Raynor, 1943; practice law, 1943-64; partner firm Ehrlich, Bundesen, Friedman & Ross, 1963-65, Ehrlich, Bundesen, & Cohn, 1965-71, Ehrlich, Bundesen, Broecker & Sproger, Chgo., 1971-77. Mem. Chgo. (bd. mgrs. 1965-67, chmn. membership 1970-71), Ill. State (chmn. sect. family law 1966-67, bd. govs. 1974-77), Am. (chmn. divs. news judging 1972, TV judging 1973-74) bar assns., Chgo. Bar Found. (pres. 1970-72), Am. Acad. Matrimonial Lawyers (pres. chpt. 1975—), Am. Judicature Soc., Assn. Trial Lawyers Am., Ill. Trial Lawyers' Assn., Nordic Law Club (pres. 1971-72). Contbr. articles to profl. jours. Home: Chicago, Ill. Died May 8, 1977.

BUNKER, JOHN WYMOND MILLER, educator, dean; b. Toungoo, Burma, July 10, 1886; s. Alonzo and Louisa Augusta (Bradbury) B.; A.B., Brown University, 1909, A.M., 1910, Ph.D., 1912; Sc.D., 1949; married Helen Frances Crawshaw, August 31, 1912; children—Helen Bradbury (Mrs. J. K. Ross), Margaret Bradbury (Mrs. R. P. Curtis), Barbara Adams (Mrs. W. J. Finney). Instructor in sanitary biology Harvard University, 1911-15; assistant professor of physiology and biochemistry, Mass. Inst. of Tech., 1921-24, asso. prof., 1924-28, prof. since 1928; dir. of biol. research labs., 1936-40, in charge biophysics and biol. engring., 1937-40, dean Graduate School, 1940-52, emeritus. Supervisor of atomic civilian defense in Mass., 1950. Served as private to 1st lt., Mich. Nat. Guard, 1916-19; maj. San. Reserve, 1924-39. Fellow Am. Acad. of Arts and Scis. (sec. 1948), A.A.A.S.; mem. Am. Soc. for Engring. Edn., Sigma Xi, Alpha Chi Sigma, Delta Omega, Delta Tau Delta. Republican. Unitarian. Author: Personal Hygiene for Nurses (with C. E. Turner), 2d edit., 1929. Contbr. numerous papers to jours. Home: Belmont, Mass. *

BUNTEN, WILLIAM ANDREW, surgeon; b. Pawnee City, Nebr., Aug. 22, 1896; s. William Muir and Mary M. (Milligan) B.; student Grinnell Coll., 1916-18; B.Sc., U. Nebr., 1920, M.D., 1922; fellow surgery Mayo Clinic, 1927-29; m. Elsa Louise Boesel, July 17, 1923; children—John A., William Andrew. Intern Univ. Hosp., Omaha, 1922-23, house surgedn, 1922; gen. practice, Worland, Wyo., 1923-27; chief subdiv. neurosurgery Grace Hosp., Detroit, 1929-30; cons. neurosurgery Providence and Woman's Hosp., Detroit, 1929-30; propr. Bunten Clinic, Cheyenne, Wyo., 1932-58; pres. staff Meml. Hosp., Cheyenne, 1943; surgeon U.P. R.R., 1938-48, dist. surgeon Employees Hosp. Assn., 1948-73; chief staff DePaul Hosp., Cheyenne, 1962, chief surgery, 1959-61, mem. exec. com., 1956-66. Mem. med. adv. bd. Wyo. SSS, 1940-45. Fellow Internat. Coll. Surgeons (regent for Wyo.), A.M.A. (del. 1952-56, pres. conf. presidents, 1952, bd. dirs. grass roots conf. 1947-52, mem. joint commn. on accreditation hosps. 1956-65, mem. council med. edn. 1954-64; v.p. 1965-66), Wyo. (pres. 1945), Laramie County (pres. 1938) med. socs.; sr. fellow Southwest Surg. Congress; mem. Am., Western assns. ry. surgeons, World Med. Assn. (chmn Wyo.), Phi Rho Sigma Presbyn. (elder). Rotarian. Contbr. numerous articles in figld. Home: Cheyenne, Wyo. Died July 30, 1979; buried Bethel Cemetery, Cheyenne.

BURCHAM, WILLIAM DAVID (BÛR'CHAM), mining engr.; b. Washington County, Ind., June 10, 1884; s. James Fayette and Isabella (Lusk) B.; ed. Stanford U., 1904-10; m. Ruby Richardson, Apr. 22, 1917; children—William Jackson, Richard Lusk, Ruby June. Engr. and accountant Presidio Mining Co., 1910-13; mill supt. for same company, 1913-15; partner and mgr. Study Butte Mining Co., Study Butte, Tex., 1915-19; pres. and gen. mgr. Mariscal Mining Co., 1919-27; pres. and mgr. Brewster Quicksilver Consol. Mining Company, Tex., 1927-35; superintendent Pacific Syndicate, 1942-43, Esperado Mines since 1943. Commr. Brewster County, Tex., 1922-40. Vice-pres. for Tex. of Nat. Quicksilver Producers Assn.; mem. com. on natural resources Tex. Centennial; dir. of mineralogy West Tex. Scientific and Hist. Soc.; mem. Am. Inst. Mining Engrs. Republican. Mason (32 deg.). Contbr. articles on quicksilver industry. Home: Alpine, Texas.*

BURCHARD, JOHN ELY, archtl. historian, critic and cons.; b. Marshall, Minn., Dec. 8, 1898; s. James Clark and Sidonie (Schupp) B.; student U. Minn. Coll. Liberal Arts, 1915-17, Coll. Medicine, 1917; S.B. in Archtl. Engring., M.I.T., 1923, S.M., 1925; L.H.D. (hon.), Union Coll., 1953; D.Architecture (hon.) U. Mich., 1956; m. Marjorie Walker Gaines, Sept. 7, 1926; children—John Ely, Marshall Gaines. With Bemis Industries Housing Co., 1926-35; prof., dir. Albert Farwell Bemis Found., M.I.T., 1938-48, dean sch. humanities and social sci., from 1948-64, then dean emeritus; Canadian Hazen lectr., 1953; Lowell Inst. lectr. Boston Mus. Fine Arts, 1955; vis. prof. U. Calif., 1954, 55, 64-68, acting head dept. design, 1965-66, acting dean Coll. Environmental Design, 1966-67; Mellon vis. prof. environmental design, 1967-68; Thomas Jefferson vis. prof. U. Va., 1969; cons. on aesthetics Bay Area Rapid Transit Dist.; lectr., Iran, Pakistan, India, 1962; studied new German architecture as guest of Fed. Republic, 1963; cons. Graham Found. for Advanced Studies in Fine Arts, 1955-60. Various posts OSRD, 1940-46, ending as chief div. 2 and dep. chief Office Field Services; mem. Am. delegation to France and Norway on higher edn., 1957; mem. Kawana (Tokyo) Conf. on Sci. and Modern Civilization, 1960. Mem. adv. bd. U.S. Mcht. Marine Acad., Kings Point, N.Y., 1953-60, chmn., 1956-57; mem. Yale Council Com. on Library, 1949-58, Princeton U. adv. council of library, 1949-55; trustee Mt. Holyoke Coll., 1951-61, mem. exec. com., 1953-61; mem. com. to visit grad. sch. design Harvard, 1953-59; trustee Boston Mus. Fine Arts, 1957-60. Recipient Presdl. medal for Merit, 1948; U. Minn. outstanding achievement award, 1960; Thomas Jefferson Meml. medal Architecture, 1969; decorated officier de l'Ordre des Arts et des Lettres (France). Fellow Am. Acad. Arts and Scis. (pres. 1954-57, bd. editors Daedalus 1958-73); mem. A.I.A. (hon.). Author: (with others) The Evolving House, 3 vols., 1933-36; (with Oscar Handlin) The Historian and the City, 1963; (with A. Bush-Brown) The Architecture of America, 1961; The Voice of the Phoenix, Post-war Architecture in Germany, 1966; Bernini Is Dead?: Architecture and the Social Purpose, 1976. Editor, annotator; Mid-Century; The Social Implications of Scientific Progress, 1950. Contbr. chpts. to Planning the University Library Building, 1949, Religious Faith and World Culture, 1951, The Individual and Liberal Education, 1952, The Metropolis in Modern Life, 1954, Symbols and Society, 1954, The Metropolitan Enigma, 1967. Home: Boston, Mass. Died Dec. 25, 1975; buried Tewksbury, Mass.

BURDELL, EDWIN SHARP, ednl. cons.; b. Columbus, Ohio, Feb. 2, 1898; s. William Frederick and Jennie Nottingham (Kelsey) B.; student Asheville (N.C.) Sch., 1911-15, Chaucey Hall Sch., Boston, 1915-16, Mass. Inst. Tech., 1916-20, Harvard Grad. Sch. Bus. Adminstrn., 1920-21; A.M., Ohio State U., 1929, Ph.D., 1934, D.L. (hon.), 1954; Litt.D. (hon.), Pratt Inst., 1960; m. Emma Metthea Mathiasen, Apr. 2, 1927; children—Karla Kelsey Burdell Basaran, Mary Metthea Burdell Keane. Banking, 1922-24; traveling and writing in Europe, Mex., C. Am., 1924-27; grad. study and teaching Ohio State U., 1928-34; mem. Ohio Commn. on Unemployment Ins., 1932; dir. Sch. for Unemployed, Ohio State U., 1932; state adminstr. for Emergency Edn. in Ohio, 1933-34; prof. sociology and dir. summer sch. Mass. Inst. Tech., 1934-38, dean humanities, 1937-38; dir. Cooper Union for Advancement Sci. and Art, N.Y., 1938-51, pres., 1951-60, pres. emeritus, 1960-78; pres. Middle East Tech. U., Ankara, Turkey, 1960-62; cons. Cranbrook Found., Bloomfield Hills, Mich., 1962-78; dean Rollins Coll., Winter Park, Fla., 1963-66, dean emeritus, 1975-78; co-chmn. Can.-U.S. Commn. on Edn., 1958-60; dir. Regional Plan Assn., 1957-60; chmn. AIA Commn. for Survey Edn. and Registration, 1949-54. Bd. dirs. Central Fla. Red Cross, 1963-78; trustee Winter Park Meml. Hosp., 1969-78. Served as 2d lt., inf., AUS, World War I; capt. USCGR, 1960-78. Decorated King Christian X medal of Liberation, 1946; Knight Cross of Dannebrog (Danish), 1951. Vice chmn. Zoning Bd. Columbus, 1923-34; chmn. Municipal Housing Bd. Columbus, 1933-34; mem. Mass. Bd. Prison Industries, 1935-38; chmn. com. on housing Community Service Soc., 1948, trustee, 1942; trustee Am.-Scandinavian Found.; mem. USCG Acad. adv. com., 1956-60. Fellow Am. Sociol. Soc.; mem. AIA (hon.), Am. Inst. Interior Designers (hon.), Am. Inst. Planners, Am. Soc. Nat. Recreation and Parks Assn. (dir. lay div.), Sigma Chi, Phi Beta Kappa. Episcopalian. Clubs: Century (N.Y.C.); Univ. (Winter Park, Fla.). Contbr. articles to jours. Home: Maitland, Fla. Died Aug. 28, 1978; interred Columbus, Ohio.

BURDEN, WILLIAM DOUGLAS, naturalist; b. Troy, N.Y., Sept. 24, 1898; s. James Abercrombie and Florence Adele (Sloane) B.; A.B., Harvard, 1922; M.A., Columbia, 1926; grad. Naval Aviation Tng. School, 1918; m. Katharine Curtin White, Aug. 1924 (div. 1939); children—Wendy (Mrs. Edw. Morgan), William Douglas, Andrew White; m. 2d, Elizabeth Chace Gammack, Jan. 26, 1940; 1 son, Christopher; m. 3d, Jeanne Wight Booth, Apr. 26, 1971. Began in diamond mine, Brazil, 1921; collecting expdn. Far East, Am. Mus. Natural History, 1922-23, exploration, Nicaragua, 1924, led expdn. to capture dragon lizards of Komodo, 1926, started dept. exptl. biology, later animal behavior, 1928; producer Red Indian documentary film The Silent Enemy, 1928-29; pres., dir. Burden Pictures, Inc., 1928-31; pres., dir. Marineland of Fla., Inc., 1937-61; chmn. bd. Surluga Gold Mines, Ltd., 1962-68, hon. chmn., 1968-78. Trustee Am. Mus. Natural History, 1926-61, asso. benefactor, 1927-78, hon. trustee; trustee N.Y. Zool. Soc., 1938-41; mem. governing bd. Marineland Research Lab. Mem. Gov.'s Scenery Preservation Commn., 1970-78; chmn. bd. trustees Vt. Wildland Found., 1966-78. Cons. OSS, Wright Field, Dayton, O., 1944; responsible investigator com. med. research Office Sci. Research and Devel., 1945, assigned Joint Target Group, War Dept. Mem. Sigma Xi. Clubs: Harvard Travellers, Explorers (hon. mem.). Author: Dragon Lizards of Komodo, 1927; Look to the Wilderness, 1960; various articles nat. mags. Address: Charlotte, Vt. Died Nov. 14, 1978.

BURDETT, ALLEN MITCHELL, JR., army officer; b. Washington, Aug. 25, 1921; s. Allen Mitchell and Margaret (Briscoe) B.; B.S., U.S. Mil. Acad., 1943; grad. Inf. Sch., 1951, Command and Gen. Staff Coll., 1953, Armed Forces Staff Coll., Norfolk, Va., 1955; Army War Coll., 1959; M.A., George Washington U., 1965; m. Antoinette Salley, Apr. 19, 1948; children—Allen Mitchell III, William M., Margaret B., Douglas N. Commd. 2d lt. U.S. Army, 1943, advanced through grades to lt. gen., 1973; asst. prof. mil. sci. and tactics Ga. Inst. Tech., 1947-50; S3 and bn. exec. officer 508th Airborne Regtl. Combat Team, 1951-52; inf. bn. comdr., regtl. exec. officer 31st Inf., 7th Inf. Div., 1953-54; G1 and G2, 7th Inf. Div., 1954; army rep. Office of Comdt. USAF Acad., 1955-58; dir. Combat Devels. Office, dep. asst. comdt. Army Aviation Sch., 1960-62; exec. officer to asst. sec. army, 1962-65; comdg. officer 11th Aviation Group, 1st Cav. Div., 1965-66; mil. asst. Office Dir. Def. Research and Engring., 1966-68; asst. div. comdr. 101st Airborne

Div., 1968-69; comdg. gen. 1st Aviation Brigade, 1969-70; dir. Army Aviation, Office Asst. Chief of Staff for Force Devel., Dept. Army, 1970; comdg. gen. U.S. Army Aviation Center and comdt. U.S. Army Aviation Sch., Ft. Rucker, Ala., 1970-73; comdg. gen. III Corps and Fort Hood (Tex.), 1973-75; comdg. gen. 5th U.S. Army, Ft. Sam Houston, Tex., 1975-78; ret., 1978. Decorated D.S.M. with oak leaf cluster, Silver Star with oak leaf cluster, Legion of Merit with oak leaf cluster, D.F.C. with oak leaf cluster, Bronze Star with V and 2 oak leaf clusters, Air medal with 24 oak leaf clusters, Army Commendation medal, Air Force Commendation medal, Purple Heart, Combat Inf. badge, Vietnamese Gallantry Cross with palm. Mem. Army Aviation Assn. Am., Assn. Grads U.S. Mil. Acad., Assn. U.S. Army, Soc. of Cincinnati, Order of Daedalians. Home: San Antonio, Tex. Died July 8, 1980.

BURGER, RUDOLPH E., pub. utilities exec.; b. Galena, Kan., May 28, 1883; s. Samuel and Dora Burger; B.S. in Elec. Engring., U. of Mo., 1907; m. Frances Paperte, June 15, 1920; Children—Rudolph E., Milan R. Apprentice engr. Denver Gas & Electric Co., 1907-09; operating mgr. all pub. utilities of Cities Service Co., New York, 1920, later becoming gen. mgr. Cities Service Power & Light Co., pres. 1941-46; pres., gen. mgr., chmn. bd. Ohio Pub. Service Co., 1945-50; vice pres., director Portsmouth Gas Co. (Ohio); public utilities consultant, N.Y.C.; director and consultant Ohio Edison Co.; power plant on Ohio River at Dilles Bottom, O., was given name of R.E. Burger Power Plant, 1944. Fellow American Inst. of Elec. Engrs.; member American Gas Association Tau Beta Pi, Sigma Chi. Clubs: Engineers, Bankers of America, Sands Point Golf (N.Y.). Home: Sands Point, L.I., N.Y. *

BURGESS, GEORGE VAN TRUMP, cons. engr.; b. Pitts., Mar. 13, 1903; s. George Heckman and Harriet (Van Trump) B.; B.S., Yale, 1925; E.D. (hon.), Case Inst. Tech., 1950; m. Helen G. Steers, June 6, 1930; children—Claire Louise (Mrs. Burt W. Phillips), George Van Trump. Field clk. Eire R.R., Wanaque, N.J., 1925-26; resident engr. G., M. & N. R.R., Jackson, Miss., 1926-27; field engr., structural designer Dwight P. Robinson & Co. at Am. Rolling Mill Co., Middletown, O., 1927-29; constrn. mgr. F.H. McGraw & Co., N.Y.C., 1929-31; accoustical cons. engr. Elec. Research Products, Inc., N.Y.C., 1931-34, v.p., 1934-38, comml. relations mgr., 1938-41; gen. mgr. Gen. Service Studios, Long Island City, N.Y., sr. staff engr. Coverdale & Colpitts, N.Y.C., 1941-42, partner, 1943-69. Mem. Am. Inst. Cons. Engrs. Home: Rye, N.Y. Died May 1979.

BURGESS, MERRILL CHARLES, pub. co. exec.; b. Mpls., May 28, 1893; s. Henry Guilford and Pauline (Langenbach) B.; student Minn. Sch. Bus., 1912; D.B.A. (hon.), Hamline U., 1977; m. Gladys Steptoe Linnell, Aug. 26, 1916; children—Linnell Guilford, Barbara Jean. Asst. sales mgr. Janney, Semple, Hill & Co., Mpls., 1912-18; founder, pres. Burgess-Beckwith, Inc. (became div. Burgess Pub. Co. 1973), Mpls., 1918-79, chmn. bd., chief exec. officer, 1975-79; founder, pres. Burgess Pub. Co., Mpls., 1932-75, chmn. bd., chief exec. officer, 1975-79; founder, pres., Burgess House, mail order co., Mpls., 1950-60; pres. Am. Automobile Assn., Mpls., 1965-70. Mem. Direct Mail Mktg. Assn., Mail Advt. Service Assn. Internat. (pres. 1946-47), C. of C. of Mpls. (v.p. 1947-50). Republican. Methodist. Clubs: Kiwanis (pres. Mpls. club 1947). Home: Minneapolis, Minn. Died June 6, 1979.

BURGESS, WARREN RANDOLPH, banker, govt. ofcl.; b. Newport, R.I., May 7, 1889; s. Isaac Bronson and Ellen (Wilbur) B.; A.B., Brown U., 1912, LL.D. 1937; Ph.D. Columbia U., 1920; LL.D. (hon.), U. Rochester, 1948, Bowdoin Coll., 1959, U. Calif., 1962; m. May Ayres, May 17, 1917 (dec. July 1953); m. 2d, Helen Hamilton Woods, Mar. 5, 1955; children—Leonard Randolph, Julian Ayres. With Fed. Res. Bank, N.Y.C., 1920-38, dep. gov., 1930-36, v.p., 1936-38; vice chmn. Nat. City Bank of N.Y. 1938-48, chmn. exec. com., 1948-52; chmn. bd. City Bank Farmers Trust Co.; dir. Discount Corp., Internat. Banking Corp., U.P.R.R. Royal-Liverpool Group Ins. Cos. in U.S.; dep. to Sec. Treasury, 1953-54, undersec. of Treasury, 1955-57; U.S. permanent rep. on NATO, 1957-61; Regent prof. U. Cal. at Berkeley, 1962. Served as maj., asst. acting chief of statistics br. Gen. Staff World War I. Fellow Brown U. Trustee Robert Coll. Tchrs. Coll., (Columbia). Chmn., N.Y. State War Finance Com., 1943-44. Pres., Per Jacobsson Found. Decorated comdr. Légion d'Honneur (France). Fellow Am. Statis. Assn. (pres. 1937), Acad. Polit. Sci. (trustee, pres. 1939), Am. Hist. Assn., N.Y. State Bankers Assn. (pres. 1940-41, Res. City Bankers Assn. (pres. 1952), Am. Bankers Assn. (chmn. econ. policy Commn., 1940-44, pres., 1944-45, chmn. com. public debt policy, 1946-47); mem. Internat. C. of C. (chmn. monetary com. 1946-47), Atlantic Treaty Assn. (chmn. 1961-63, vice chmn. 1963—), Atlantic Council U.S. (chmn. 1971), Am. Econ. Assn., Am. Philos. Soc., Fgn. Policy Assn. (dir.), Delta Upsilon, Phi Beta Kappa. Clubs: Metropolitan (Washington); Century Assn., University, River, Chevy Chase, Cosmos. Author: Trends of School Costs, 1920; The Reserve Banks and the Money Market, 1927, rev. edits. 1936, 46. Editor: Interpretations of Federal Reserve Policy (by Benjamin Strong), 1930; (with James R. Huntley) Europe and America—The Next Ten Years. Contbr. articles to profl. jours. Home: Queenstown, Md. and Washington. Died Sept. 16, 1978; buried Arlington Nat. Cemetery.

BURGREEN, DAVID, educator; b. N.Y.C., Aug. 1, 1917; s. Max and Minnie (Dresner) B.; B.C.E., Coll. City N.Y., 1943; M.Aero. Engring., Bklyn. Poly. Inst., 1947, Ph.D., 1950; m. Lillian Mandel, Apr. 6, 1941; children—Vicki Joan, Bruce Lawrence, Rosalind Susan, William Scott. Adv. engr. atomic power div. Westinghouse Electric Corp., 1950-51; engring. specialist Asso. Nucleonics Co., 1951-56; cons. engr. United Nuclear Corp., 1956-65; prof. mech. engring. Poly. Inst. of N.Y., 1966-79. Served to lt. (j.g.) USNR, 1943-47. Mem. ASME, ASCE, Am. Nuclear Soc., AIAA, Sigma Xi, Tau Beta Pi. Author books and papers in field. Home: J.:maica, N.Y. Died Nov. 30, 1979.

BURGSTAHLER, HERBERT JOHN (BÛRG'STÄL-ER, clergyman, educator; b. Buffalo Lake, Minn., Nov. 24, 1886; s. John Andrew and Martha Mary (Burkhardt) B.; A.B., U. of Minn., 1913; S.T.B., Boston U., 1915, LL.D., 1930; D.D., Syracuse, 1923; m. Alice Mabel Wolf, June 24, 1909; children—Cyrus Herbert, Faith Adelle. Ordained ministry M.E. Ch., 1915; pastor Bell Congl. Ch. and Minnehaha M.E. Ch., Minneapolis, Minn., 1909-13, Greenwood (Mass.) Union Ch., 1913-15, Lake Harriet M.E. Ch., Minneapolis, 1915-17, Central Park Ch., St. Paul, Minn., 1917-21, First Ch., Rochester, N.Y., 1921-25, Plymouth Ch., Buffalo, N.Y., 1925-27; pres. Cornell Coll., Mt. Vernon, Ia., 1927-39; pres. Ohio Wesleyan U. 1939-47, chancellor, 1947-55, pres. emeritus. Mem. Phi Beta Kappa, Delta Sigma Rho, Kappa Delta Pi, Omicron Delta Kappa. Republican. Mason. Rotarian. Author: How to Raise Funds for Schools and Colleges. Home: St. Petersburg, Fla. *

BURHOP, WILLIAM CHARLES (BÛR'HOP), clergyman; b. at Fraser, Mich., Oct. 21, 1884; s. William and Marion Elizabeth (Searle) B.; student Concordia Coll., Milwaukee, Wis., 1900-04, Concordia Theol. Sem., St. Louis, 1905-08; grad. student Johns Hopkins U., 1916-17, Columbia U., summer, 1923, U. of Chicago, 1924-25; m. Julia Mueller, June 23, 1909; children—Ruth Ada (Mrs. Ralph Siemon), Waldemar William, Esther Julia (Mrs. Arnold Lehmann). Teacher Zion Lutheran Elementary School, Palmyra, Mo., 1904-05; ordained to Lutheran ministry, 1908; pastor St. Paul's Ch., Kansas City, Mo., 1908-12, Redeemer Ch., Baltimore, 1912-17; prof. English, Concordia Coll., Ft. Wayne, Ind., 1917-26, pres., 1926-37; pastor Calvary Lutheran Univ. Ch., Madison, Wis., since 1937. Contbr. articles to church papers and theological magazines. Translator: (from the German) selected Lenten sermons of Dr. G. Stoeckhardt, published 1945. Address: Madison, Wis. *

BURKE, EDWARD NOLAN, bank exec.; b. Orange, N.J., Sept. 5, 1918; s. John I. and Marie (Burke) B.; A.B., Columbia, 1940; student Harvard Bus. Sch., 1943-44; m. Marjorie Madden, Nov. 9, 1941; children—Elizabeth, David. Exec. trainee R.H. Macy & Co., N.Y.C., 1940-41; with advt. dept. Procter & Gamble Co., 1941-43; with Newark News, 1946-71, bus. and financial editor, 1957-69, mem. editorial bd., 1969-71; pub. information officer 1st Nat. State Bank N.J., Newark, from 1971, then v.p. in charge public relations and advt. Served with USNR, 1943-46; PTO. Mem. Phi Beta Kappa. Club: Bond of N.J. Home: Orange, N.J. Died Feb. 6, 1978; buried St. John's Cemetery, Orange.

BURKE, ELLEN COOLIDGE, librarian; b. Alexandria, Va., May 10, 1901; d. Henry Randolph and Rosella (Trist) Burke; B.A., Catholic U. Am., 1938, M.A., 1943. With Alexandria Library, 1939-69, successively cataloguer, reference, 1st asst. library dir., 1948-69. Ellen Coolidge Burke Br. Library dedicated in her honor, Alexandria, 1968. Mem. Va. Library Assn., Va. Council Human Relations, Common Cause, League Women Voters, Montecello Assn., Historic Alexandria Found. (charter). Roman Catholic. Club: Zonta. Home: Alexandria, Va. Died Dec. 29, 1975.

BURKE, MELVILLE, theatrical producer; b. St. Louis, Mo., Nov. 4, 1884; s. William and Mary (Radcliff) B.; A.B., Washington U., 1907; postgrad. work, Harvard, 1908; unmarried. Dramatic dir. for college theatricals, civic pageants, etc., 1909-14; dir. Art Theatre, St. Louis, 1915-16; mgr. and dir. Municipal Theatre, Northampton, Mass., 1916-18; mgr. and dir. Lyric Theatre, Hamilton, Ont., Can., 1918; dir. Schubert Theatre, Minneapolis, Minn., 1919-22; gen. dir. Stuart Walker Co., New York, 1923—. Dir. Gilbert Emery's "Episode," Bijou Theatre, New York, and Kenneth Webb's "One of the Family"; dir. Elitch Garden Repertory Co., Denver, Colo. Mem. Kappa Alpha. Republican. Unitarian. Home: 35 W. 64th St. Address: New York, N.Y. *

BURKE, THOMAS JOHN M., clergyman, univ. dean; b. Boston, Nov. 19, 1920; s. Thomas J. and Agnes (Cahill) B.; A.B., Boston Coll., 1944, M.A., 1945; licentiate in theology Weston Coll., 1952; certificate dramatics Fordham U., 1946; Ph.D., N.Y. U., 1962. Joined Soc. of Jesus, 1938, ordained priest Roman Cath. Ch., 1951; religion editor America, 1953-54; dir., asso. editor Jesuit Missions, N.Y.C., 1954-63; dir. pub. relations Fairfield (Conn.) U., 1963-66, dean grad. sch. corporate and polit. communication, 1964—, dir., founder Center for Advancement Human Communication, 1964—. Coordinator, author TV series Face of the World, 1958-59. Trustee Human Resources Inst., Westport, Conn. Mem. Pub. Relations Soc. Am., Am. Soc. Pub. Adminstrn., Internat. Communication Assn., N.Y. Soc. Gen. Semantics, Am. Acad. Polit. and Social Scis., F.C.P.R. Assn., Marquis Biog. Library Soc. (adv.), Soc. for Edn. in Film and Television, Jesuits in Communication Internat. Editor, contbr.: Beyond All Horizons, 1957; Sinews of Love, 1961; Mary and Modern Man, 1954. Address: Fairfield, Conn. Died Mar. 10, 1981.

BURKHALTER, GEORGE LEWIS, mfg. co. exec.; b. Metter, Ga., Sept. 23, 1922; s. George Lewis and Henrietta (Pierce) B.; LL.B., Mercer U., 1948, A.B., 1949; m. Miriam Amerson Worsham, July 15, 1972; 1 dau. (by previous marriage) Sandra. Admitted to Ga. bar, 1949; pvt. practice law, Macon, 1949-50; spl. agt. FBI, Phila., N.Y.C., 1950-52; with Bibb Mfg. Co., Macon, 1952-78, asst. credit mgr., 1952-56, asst. sec., credit mgr., 1956-62, credit mgr., sec., 1962-78; v.p., sec. Star Chems., Inc., Macon, Ga. Served to 1st lt. USAAF, 1942-45; ETO. Decorated D.F.C., Air medal with three oak leaf clusters. Mem. Ga. Assn. Credit Mgmt. (dir. past pres.). Clubs: Masons (33 deg.), Shriners, Moose, Kiwanis. Home: Macon, Ga. Died Apr. 23, 1978.

BURKHARD, SAMUEL, educator; b. Roseland, Neb., May 5, 1883; s. Daniel and Hannah (Snyder) B.; A.B., Goshen Coll., 1911; student Union Theol. Sem., 1911-12; A.M., Columbia, 1912; student U. of Chicago, summers 1912, 19; Ph.D., N.Y. U., 1930; m. Elsie Byler, Aug. 14, 1913; children—Charles Austin, Olin Eugene, Samuel Merton, Raymond Kenneth. Teacher, Jewish Orphan Asylum, 1912-15; teacher edn. Bethel Coll., 1916-19; head, dept. edn. Bluffton Coll., 1919-21; prof. edn. Ariz. State Coll., Tempe, 1921-54, prof. emeritus, 1954—, head dept. edn., 1930-54; edn. cons. Lincoln Found., 1954-55; tchr. summer sessions U. of Hawaii, 1935, N.Y. U., 1944, U. of So. Calif., 1946. Mem. city council, Tempe. 1932-50; lectr. on social issues. Mem. Am. Assn. U. Profs., Philosophy of Edn. Soc., John Dewey Soc., Phi Delta Kappa, Kappa Delta Pi. Conglist. Author: Work Book in the Philosophy of Education, 1950: A Guide to the Study of Social Relations, 1948. Home: Tempe, Ariz. *

BURKHART, WILLIAM H., soap co. exec.; b. Warren, Pa., Apr. 26, 1899; s. Louis H. and Elizabeth (Hoddle) B.; B.S., U. of Pa., 1921; m. Frantzes Dinsmoor, Feb. 27, 1922; 1 dau., Diane Dinsmoor. Tech., management exec. Procter & Gamble Co., 1921-25; management exec. Gold Dust Corp. and Hocker Products Corp., 1925-39; management exec. Lever Brothers Co. 1939, prodn. v.p. 1949, dir. 1949, exec. com. 1950, exec. v.p., 1953-55, pres., 1955-59, chmn. bd., 1958-64; chmn. bd. Thomas J. Lipton, Inc., Lever Brothers, Ltd., Toronto, 1959-64, Thomas J. Lipton, Limited, Toronto, Ont., 1961-64. Served USNR, 1918-21. Mem. Soc. Chem. Industry, Alpha Chi Rho, Alpha Chi Sigma. Clubs: University (N.Y.C.); Sleepy Hollow Country, Algonquin (Boston). Home: New York, N.Y. Died July 31, 1976.

BURLAGE, HENRY MATTHEW, educator, pharmacist; b. Rensselaer, Ind., May 23, 1897; s. Max and Mary Anne (Linzbach) B.; A.B., Ind. U., 1919; A.M., Harvard, 1921; Ph.G., B.S., Purdue, 1924, D.Sc., 1961; Ph.D., U. Wash., 1929; m. Alleda Virginia Robb, Dec. 29, 1925; 1 son, Robb Kendrick. Austin teaching fellow Harvard, 1919-20; instr. pharmacy and pharm. chemistry Purdue, 1921-24, asso. prof., 1929-31; instr. pharmacy U. Wash., 1924-27; asso. prof. drug analysis and insp. Ore. State Bd. Pharmacy, 1927-29; prof. pharmacy U. N.C., 1931-47; prof. pharmacy and pharm. chemistry U. Tex., 1947-71, prof. emeritus, 1971-78, dean, 1947-62. Registered pharmacist in Tex. Fellow AAAS; mem. Am. (council 1961-64, hon. pres. 1966-67), Tex. (treas. 1966-68) pharm. assns., Am. Chem. Soc., Am. Assn. Colls. Pharm. (mem. exec. com. 1959-60, pres. 1960-61), Phi Beta Kappa, Sigma Xi, Phi Kappa Phi, Rho Chi, Kappa Psi, Alpha Chi Sigma, Phi Lambda Upsilon. Mason (K.T.). Author: Study Guide to Essential Literature of Pharmacy, rev. 1969; (with M.L. Jacobs) Index to the Plants of North Carolina with Reputed Medicinal Uses, 1959; Index to the Plants of Texas with Reputed Medicinal and Poisonous Properties, 1968; also other lab. manuals. Editor: Orientation to Pharmacy, 1959; Physical and Technical Pharmacy, 1963; Experiments in Physical and Technical Pharmacy, 1968; The Wild Flowering Plants of the Highland Lakes Country of Texas, 1973; (with Robb Burlage) The Four Walls of Pharmacy, 1974. Home: Austin, Tex. Died Oct. 6, 1978.

BURLEIGH, CECIL, violinist, composer; b. Wyoming, N.Y., Apr. 17, 1885; s. Lewis Edward and Nellie (Babcock) B.; studied with Anton Witek, Max Grunberg and Hugo Leichtentritt, Berlin, 1903-05; studied with Emile Sauret and Felix Borowski, Chicago

Musical Coll., 1906-08, with Leopold Auer, New York City, 1919-21. Hon. doctorate in music (for composition) from Am. Conservatory of Music, Chicago, 1938; m. 2d, Jessie Meredith Jennings, May 25, 1940. Instr., U. of Mont., 1914-19; concert work, New York City, 1919-21; head violin and composition depts., U. of Wis., from 1921. Mem. Sinfonia, Nat. Assn. of Composers and Conductors, Bohemians (N.Y. City), Am. Soc. of Composers, Authors and Publishers, Pi Kappa Lambda. Compositions: 35 piano works; full orchestra, Mountain Pictures, and Evangeline. Home: Madison, Wis. Died July 28, 1980.

BURLESON, ELIZABETH (MRS. GAMEWELL DAVID BURLESON), author; b. Kerrville, Tex., Nov. 2, 1912; d. Edward Elijah and Mary (Sproul) Morriss; student U. Tex., 1932-33, San Antonio Coll., summer 1936, Trinity U., nights 1949-50; m. Gamewell David Burleson, May 17, 1951. Tchr. pub. schs. rural Tex., 1932-36; with USAF, 1941-53, edn. specialist, 1952-53. Recipient Cokesbury award Tex. Inst. Letters, 1965, Gold Spur award Western Writers Am., 1968. Baptist. Club: Cactus Study (Junction). Author: A Man of the Family, 1965; Middl'un, 1968; Eline Ranch in Texas (German trans. A Man of the Family), 1970 Home: Kerrville, Tex. Died Oct. 2, 1979; buried Sunset Cemetery, Kerrville.

BURLINGHAM, CHARLES, lawyer; b. N.Y.C., June 8, 1884; s. Charles C. and Louisa (Lawrence) B.; A.B., Harvard, 1906, LL.B., 1908; m. Cora Weir, Apr. 2, 1929; 1 son, Charles. Admitted to N.Y. bar, 1908, since practiced in N.Y.C.; partner firm Burlingham, Underwood & Lord, and predecessors, from 1912, now counsel. Trustee Community Service Soc. N.Y.C., 1936-67, sec., 1942-67. Mem. N.Y. State Bar Assn., Assn. Bar City N.Y.; Maritime Law Assn. U.S. Democrat. Episcopalian (past vestry). Home: New York City NY *

BURLINGHAM, MRS. GRACE SEMPLE, b. St. Louis, Mo., Aug. 3, 1882; d. Edward Humphrey and Mary Olivia (Hart) Semple; ed. pvt. schs.; m. Louis H. Burlingham (M.D.), of St. Louis, Sept. 19, 1921. Formerly mem. Rep. Nat. Com.; 1st v.p. Girl Scouts of America; mem. President's Planning Com. White House Conf. on Child Health and Protection; mem. Com. on Pub. Health Administration. Episcopalian. Home: St. Louis, Mo. *

BURMESTER, HARRY FREDERICK, banker; b. San Francisco, May 17, 1903; s. Henry D. and Erna (Hesse) B.; student Coll. of Pacific, U. Cal.; LL.D., Baldwin-Wallace Coll.; D.Sc., Fenn Coll.; D.C.S., Cleve. State U.; m. Edna Jensen, Aug. 17, 1924; 1 dau., Maren (Mrs. R.B. Houghton); m. 2d, Margarete Allen, June 27, 1975. Vice pres. Union Commerce Bank, Cleve., 1938-43, sr. v.p., 1943-56, pres., 1956-68, dir., chmn. exec. com., 1968-69; dir. Samuel Moore & Co., Steel Improvement & Forge Co. Bd. dirs. Fenn Ednl. Found. Mason (33 deg., Shriner, K.T., Jester). Clubs: Shaker Heights Country, Pepper Pike Country, Union (Cleve.); Fifty. Home: Cleveland, Ohio. Died Nov. 6, 1979.

BURMESTER, HENRY FINCH (BUR'MES-TER), editor; b. Grantsville, Utah, June 11, 1884; s. Theodore and Maria (Finch) B.; student U. Utah, 1902-03; M. Humanities, Long Beach State College, 1957; m. Betty Corey, Jan. 6, 1931. In newspaper work since 1903; formerly asso. Salt Lake Herald, Butte (Mont.) Miner, Seattle Times, Post-Intelligencer, San Francisco Examiner and Chronicle, Asso. Press, Los Angeles Times, Denver News; exec. editor Long Beach (California) Press-Telegram, 1943-52; editor, 1952—. Member of advisory board of Long Beach State College, 1951; member State College Council, 1951. Mem. Long Beach C. of C. (pres. 1924-25). Clubs: Rotary (pres. 1949), Pacific Coast (Long Beach). Author verse and prose. Home: Long Beach, Cal. *

BURN, HARRY THOMAS, lawyer, banker, orgn. ofcl.; b. Niota, Tenn., Nov. 12, 1895; s. James LaFayette and Febb King (Ensminger) B.; studied law with lawyers, 1919-23; m. Ellen Folsom Cottrell, Feb. 14, 1937; 1 son, Harry Thomas. Admitted to Tenn. bar, 1923; practice in Rockwood, 1923-27, Sweetwater, 1927-50; pres., chmn. 1st Nat. Bank & Trust Co., Rockwood, 1950-77; sr. v.p. Belted Galloway Soc., Inc., 1967-77. Mem. S.A.R., 1931, treas. gen., 1962-64, pres. gen., 1964-65, Minute Man award, 1962. Mem. Tenn. Ho. of Reps. from McMinn County, 1919-23, Tenn. Senate from 7th Dist., 1949-53; mem. Tenn. Planning Commn., 1952-72; del. Tenn. Constl. Conv., 1953, 59, 65, 71. Mem. Am., Tenn. bar assns. Republican. Presbyn. Clubs: Burns (Atlanta); Civitan (pres. Rockwood 1960-61). Home: Niota, Tenn. Died Feb. 19, 1977; interred New Cemetery, Niota.

BURNAM, JOSEPH E(DWARD), prof. mathematics; b. Platte Co., Mo., Oct. 11, 1883; s. Jesse H. and Margaret I. (Jackson) B.; student Scranton (Tex.) Acad., 1904-08; A.B., Simmons Coll., 1913; M.A., U. of Tex., 1920, grad. student, 1923-24; summer student U. of Colo., 1929, U. of Ia., 1930; m. Opha Jobe, Dec. 30, 1909; children—Edwin, Paul Wayne. Pub. sch. teacher, Tex., 1904-05, 1906-07 and 1909-12; instr. Latin and mathematics Simmons Coll. (now Hardin-Simmons U.), Abilene, Tex., 1913-24, prof. and head dept. of mathematics, 1925-56. Served as ground instr. navigation, motors and meteorology, U.S. A.A.F., 1941-44. Fellow Tex. Acad. of Sci.; mem. Am. Math. Soc., Math. Assn. of Am. (Tex. sect.). Independent. Baptist. Home: Abilene, Tex. Retired. *

BURNAP, GEORGE, landscape architect; b. Hopkinton, Mass., Nov. 28, 1885; s. Charles Russell and Elizabeth (Cerry) B.; B.S., Mass. Inst. Tech., 1906; M.A., Cornell U., 1910; fellow Am. Acad. in Rome; Diplômé in City Planning, U. of Paris, 1923. Instr. landscape design, Cornell U., 1908-10; landscape architect of pub. bldgs. and grounds, Washington, D.C., 1910-16; originator of city plans, park systems, park designs for Washington, D.C., St. Joseph, Mo., Omaha, Neb., Council Bluffs, Ia., Granville, N.Y., Hagerstown, Md., Petersburg, Va., Greenwood, S.C., and elsewhere. City planning consultant, Civic Center, Washington, D.C. Mem. Société des Urbanistes Diplômés, Paris. Clubs: Nat. Press (Washington, D.C.); Technology (New York); University (Chicago). Author: Landscape Architecture (Vol. 1), 1916. Address: Paris, France. *

BURNELL, NATHANIEL ALANSON, army officer; b. Westbrook, Me., Sept. 13, 1897; s. John Phinney and Lottie (Lawrence) B.; B.S., U.S. Mil. Acad., 1919; student Command and Gen. Staff Coll., Ft. Leavenworth, Kan., 1938, Army War Coll., Washington, 1939; m. Adene Harriet Soelberg, June 30, 1921; 1 dau., Anne Louise. Commd. 2d lt. U.S. Army, 1919, advanced through grades to maj. gen.; various assignments Ft. Monroe, Va., Ft. Flagler, Wash., Ft. Mills (Corregidor), P.I., Ft. Winfield Scott, Cal., Ft. Randolph, C.Z., Ft. Eustis, Va.; mem. War Dept. Gen. Staff, 1940-42; comdr. 52d A.A.A. Brigade, Europe, 1943-46; appointed assistant chief of staff G4, Second Army, 1948-49; chief army sect. MAAG, Netherlands, 1950-51; chief MA AG, Belgium and Luxemburg, 1951-54; comdg. gen. 1st A.A. Regional Command, 1954-57, ret., 1957. Decorated Legion of Merit, Bronze Star medal (U.S.); Order of Merit Adolphe of Nassau, Croix de Guerre (Luxemburg); Order of Leopold II with palm, Croix de Guerre with palm (Belgium); Croix de Guerre (France). Mason. Home: Edgewater, Md. Died June 27, 1976; buried Arlington Nat. Cemetery.

BURNES, JAMES ALTON, educator; b. Boston, Jan. 2, 1921; s. Charles D. and Dora (Appel) B.; B.S. in Econs., Wharton Sch. U. Pa., 1942; LL.B., Harvard, 1944; LL.M., Boston U., 1949; D.Phil., Magdalen Coll., Oxford U., 1958; m. Olga E. Pillau, Aug. 9, 1950; 1 dau., Bettina Danielle. Asso. prof. law U. Miami, 1948-51, prof. 1951-62, also dean Law Sch., 1957-61; prof. law U. Fla., Gainesville. Mem. Mass. Bar Assn., Fla. Bar. Home: Hillsboro Beach, Fla. Died June 6, 1979.

BURNET, DAVID, ex-commr. internal revenue; b. Cincinnati, Oct. 22, 1886; s. William Bromwell and Caroline (Neff) B.; ed. pub. schs., under pvt. tutors and in bus. coll.; m. Agnes West, June 19, 1913; children—William Bromwell, Thornton West, David Staats. Began, 1908, as shipping clk., Lion Buggy Co., Cincinnati; with Lawrence Mendenhall Co., Cincinnati, 1908-17; business mgr. Builders Exchange, 1918; with War Dept., 1918-19, as construction expert and as auditor income tax unit; internal revenue agt. Cincinnati Div., 1919-22, in charge at Cincinnati, 1922-29, at Boston, Mar.- July 1929; dep. commr. in charge income tax unit, Washington, D.C., 1929-30; commr. internal revenue, 1930-33. Republican. Presbyn. Home: Charlottesville, Va.*

BURNETT, CHESTER ARTHUR (HOWLIN' WOLF), Delta blues singer, guitarist, harmonica player; b. West Point, Miss., June 20, 1910; m. Lillie Jones, Mar. 14, 1964; 2 children—Barbara, Betty Jean. Formed blues group, 1948; rec. artist Chess Records; later propr. Chess Producing Co., Chgo.; 1st hit record, Moanin' at Midnight, 1951; numerous public concert appearances until Dec. 1975. Mem. Broadcast Music Inc. Home: Chicago, Ill. Died Jan. 10, 1976; buried Oak Ridge Cemetery, Hillside, Ill.

BURNEY, VIRGIL DAN, diversified industry exec.; b. Ft. Worth, May 12, 1927; s. William Homer and Grace (Carter) B.; student Tex. Christian U., 1944-45, 47-49; LL.B., So. Meth. U., 1953; m. Diane Owen King, July 14, 1962; children—Kendall King, King Carter. Admitted to Tex. bar, 1953, N.Y. bar, 1958, U.S. Supreme Ct. bar, 1967; asst. supr. joint agreements Atlantic Refining Co., Dallas, 1953-57; asso. firm White & Case, N.Y.C., 1957-62; with LTV Corp., Dallas, 1962-74, gen. counsel, 1966-74, sec., 1966-69, v.p., 1967-70, sr. v.p., 1970-74; v.p., gen. counsel LTV Aerospace Corp.; v.p., gen. counsel, dir. Jones & Laughlin Industries, Inc., LTV Wilson Industries, Inc. Served with USNR, 1945-46, 50-51. Mem. Am., N.Y. State, Tex., Dallas bar assns., Am. Soc. Corporate Secs. (pres. Dallas region 1969-70), Internat. Law Assn., Phi Alpha Delta. Home: Dallas, Tex. Died May 21, 1974; interred Hillcrest Cemetery, Dallas.

BURNHAM, JOSEPH ANDREW, retail co. exec.; b. Berryville, Ark., Mar. 11, 1920; s. Joseph Andrew and Tommie (Wade) B.; B.S., U. Ark., 1941; postgrad. Inst. for Mgmt., Northwestern U., 1955; m. Ruth Merrifield Drover, Sept. 26, 1943; children—Bruce, Stephen, Philip, Gregory, Ann. With Marshall Field & Co., various positions, 1948-77, exec. v.p., gen. mgr. Chgo. stores, 1970-71, exec. v.p. operations, 1971-74, pres., 1974-77, chmn., chief exec. officer, 1977—, also dir.; dir. Harris Trust & Savs. Bank, Standard Oil (Ind.). Trustee Community Hosp., Geneva, Ill., Rush-Presbyn.-St. Luke's Med. Center, Chgo.; pres., chief exec. officer Orchestral Assn., Chgo.; trustee U. Chgo. Served to lt. USNR, 1942-46. Mem. Econ. Club Chgo. Republican. Conglist. Clubs: Chicago, Commercial, Casino. Home: Batavia, Ill. Died Oct. 10, 1977; buried West Batavia Cemetery.

BURNS, DEAN CARL, surgeon; b. Petoskey, Mich., Dec. 19, 1896; s. Dean Samuel and Emma Caroline (Bohm) B.; Sc.B., U. Chgo., 1919; M.D., Rush Med. Coll., 1922; postgrad. Harvard, 1930, Columbia, 1932; m. Marcella Ann Whalen, Oct. 29, 1930; children—Ann Emma (Mrs. John Behan), Mary Juanita Burns McKee, Dean Daniel. Asst. in dept. materia medica Rush Med. Coll. 1919-21; lectr. chemistry and toxicology Presbyn. Hosp. Tng. Sch., Chgo., 1921; mem. resident staff St. Luke's Hosp., Chgo., 1921-23, chief of resident staff, 1923; practiced in Petoskey, 1923-78; attending surgeon, v.p. Petoskey Hosp., 1923-78; med. dir., chief of staff Little Traverse Hosp., Petoskey, 1939-60, mem. active staff, 1939-78; founder, dir. Burns Clinics (now Burns Clinic Med. Center), 1938-78; surgeon for P.M. and Pa. rys.; mem. archtl. commn. for constrn. No. Mich. State Sanatorium. Mem. State Cancer Control Com., 1946-78, Mich. Coordinating Council for Pub. Higher Edn., 1962-78. Pres. bd. trustees North Central Mich. Coll., from 1958; trustee Mich. YMCA, 1970-78; pres. Mich. Assn. Community-Jr. Coll. Governing Bds. Recipient Outstanding Community Service award Jr. C. of C., 1963; Distinguished Citizen award Lake Superior State Coll., 1973; Distinguished Service award Mich. Community Coll. Assn., 1972; Certificate of Commendation, Mich. State Med. Soc., 1972. Served in Med. R.C., 1918-19, World War. Fellow A.C.S. (Mich. regional com. on fractures and other traumas, councilor Mich. chpt.), Royal Soc. Health (Gt. Britain); mem. A.M.A., A.A.A.S., N.Y. Acad. Scis., Am. Cancer Soc. (state exec. com., trustee Mich. div.), Mich. Arts, Sci. and Letters, Internat. Coll. Surgeons, Mich. Med. Soc., No. Mich. Med. Soc., Internat. Platform Assn., Tau Kappa Epsilon, Phi Beta Pi. Republican. Episcopalian. Mason. Clubs: Petoskey, Petoskey Country; University (Chgo.); Walloon Lake Country. Contbr. articles to med. jours. Home: Petoskey, Mich. Died Feb. 9, 1978.

BURNS, JAMES HENRY, army officer; b. in N.Y., Sept. 13, 1885; B.S., U.S. Mil. Acad., 1908; grad. Army Industrial Coll., 1926, Army War Coll., 1927. Commd. 2d lt., U.S. Army, Feb. 14, 1908; promoted through grades to col., Ordnance Dept., Oct. 19, 1918; apptd. maj. gen., Oct. 1, 1940; apptd. exec. officer, Div. of Defense Air Reports, Office of Exec. Management, 1941; apptd. chief of army ordnance, Apr. 1942; retired Dec. 1944. Address: Washington, D.C. *

BURNS, JAMES MATTHEW, labor official; b. Johnstone, Scotland, Mar. 25, 1881; s. Matthew and Agnes (McDonald) B.; ed. grammar sch., Johnstone; m. Nellie Josephine Galvin, Nov. 29, 1906; children—Mary J., James J., Agnes C., Josephine (dec.), Robert, Elinor. Came to U.S., 1895, naturalized citizen, 1902. Began as sheet metal worker, ry. shops, Readville, Mass., 1909; internat. rep. Sheet Metal Workers International Assn., 1917-26; sec. Ry. Employes Dept., Am. Federation of Labor since 1926. Mem. Baltimore Agreement Commn. Democrat. Catholic. Home: Chicago, Ill. *

BURNS, RAYMOND JOSEPH, detective agy. exec.; b. Columbus, O., Mar. 25, 1886; s. William J. and Annie M. (Ressler) B.; student Ohio State U., 1905-06; m. Gladys Sykes, Apr. 9, 1907; 1 son, William J. With William J. Burns Internat. Detective Agy., Inc., from 1909, pres., 1948-55, chmn. bd. 1954-64, chmn. exec. com., 1964-70, also dir. Mem. Ohio Soc. N.Y., Delta Chi. Clubs: Union League, N.Y. Athletic, Sky, Cloud (dir. N.Y.C.); Sleepy Hollow Country (Scarborough, N.Y.); Lyford Cay (Nassau, B.W.I.). Home: New York, N.Y. Died July 7, 1977.

BURNS, ROBERT HOMER, educator; b. Laramie, Wyo., Aug. 23, 1900; s. Otto Lyle and Adelaide (Barton) B.; B.S.A., U. Wyo., 1920; M.S., Ia. State Coll., 1921; Ph.D., U. Edinburgh, Scotland, 1930-31; m. Agnes Millar, Mar. 4, 1925; children—Margaret Adelaide (Mrs. Page), Robert Lyle, Agnes (Mrs. Rainwater), Eleanor (Mrs. Higgins). Research, faculty animal husbandry N.M. A.&M. Coll., 1921-22; research, resident, extension faculty animal husbandry, U. Ariz., 1922-24; faculty U. Wyo. from 1924, head wool dept. 1948, chief of party Wyo. U. contract to Afghanistan, U.S. Operations Mission A Kabul 1956-58; head wool sect. bur. agrl. econs. Dept. Agr. Washington, 1937-39; carpet wool cons. China-U.S. Agrl. Mission, 1946; livestock cons., mission to Iran Overseas Cons., Inc., 1949; dir. agrl. program in Iran

1965-69; chmn. forum, also livestock com. Albany Co. Farm Bur. from 1947; sec. livestock com. Wyo. Farm Bur.; tech. com. Nat. Columbia Sheep Breeders' Assn.; insp. Nat. Targhee Sheep Breeders' Assn.; chmn. Western Regional Wool Marketing Research Project. Chairman of J.A. Hill Memorial Scholarship Trust, from 1951. Recipient Univ. Wyo. Alumni Association Distinguished Alumni award, 1962. Mem. Am. Soc. Animal Prodn., Am. Legion, Sigma Xi, Alpha Tau Omega, Alpha Zeta, Lambda Sigma Delta (historian from 1960). Kiwanian. Author: Ranch History, 1954; Wyoming's Pioneer Ranches. Contbr. articles profl. publs. Home: Laramie, Wyo. Died June 14, 1973.

BURNS, VINCENT GODFREY, poet, lectr., writer; b. Bklyn., Oct. 17, 1893; s. James H. and Katherine (Rossberg) B.; B.S., Pa. State Coll., 1916 (John W. White prize fellowship); A.M., Harvard, 1917; B.D., Union Theol. Sem., 1922; postgrad. Columbia, 1922-24; m. Edna Rodenberger, June 15, 1924; 1 dau., Barbara; m. 2d, Katherine Howard, Aug. 21, 1945; 2 sons, Vincent Howard, Victor David. Ordained to ministry Congl. Ch., 1920; successively pastor of City Park Chapel (Presbyn.) Bklyn. South Congl. Ch., Pittsfield, Mass., Central Christian Ch., N.Y.C., until 1929, pastor Union Ch. (Community), Palisade, N.J., 1929-36; leader Log Cabin Shrine, 1936-79; pastor Community Ch., Washington, 1953-79; spl. lectr. U. Kan., 1952-53, U. Wis., 1953-54; radio artist (as Bobby Burns, poet of the air), recitalist (chiefly poetry) and lectr. Founder Young Am. Patriots, 1970. Served to lt. U.S. Army, 1918; grad. Saumur F.A. Sch.; served on staff of Gen. Foote, 163d F.A. Brigade. Chmn. bd. Ft. Lee Pub. Library, N.J. Recipient Gold medal Freedoms Found., 1958; named poet laureate of Md., 1962; founder Poet Laureate's Com. of 100. Mem. Internat. Platform Assn. (poet laureate), Composers, Authors and Artists Am. (pres. chpt.), Vets. World War I, Md. Poetry Soc. (pres. 1964), Am. Legion, Alpha Zeta, Delta Sigma Rho, Phi Kappa Phi. Mason, Odd Fellow, Jr. O.U.A.M. Founder Nat. Poetry Clubs, Santa Barbara Theatre Guild. Club: Rockland County Golf (Nyack, N.Y.). Author: The Master's Message for the New Day, 1926; (with brother Robert Burns), I am a Fugitive from a Georgia Chain Gang, 1932; I'm in Love with Life, 1933; Female Convict, 1934; Heavenly Vision, 1939; Out of These Chains, 1942; I Am My Brother's Keeper (play) 1942; Heart on Fire, 1963; also author (brochures) Fosdick and the Fundamentalists, Health Is Life; Redwood and Other Poems, 1952; World on Fire (play), 1962; poem A Nation Prayed (awarded Freedoms Found. Gold Medal), 1953; America, I Love You, 1957; Vagabond's Luck, 1958; Flame Against The Night (poems), 1960; Poetry for Young Americans, 1962; Maryland's Revolutionary Hero, story of Col. Tench Tilghman, 1963; Memories and Melodies of Maryland, 1964; Still Life (poems), 1969; Red Fuse on a World Bomb, 1969; The Sunny Side of Life (poems), 1970. Editor: The Red Harvest (verse), 1930, Youth Dreams (mag.); The Rainbow (poetry mag.); An American Poet Speaks, 1965; Four Tests of a Loyal American, 1966; Thirteen Songs, 1967; The Man Who Broke a Thousand Chains, 1968; Songs of the Free State Bards, 1968; Ballads of the Free State Bard, 1968; Poetry Is Fun, 1971; The Story of Old Glory (anthology), 1972; New Light in the Lindbergh Kidnapping Mystery, 1973; Secrets of Eternal Youth (poems), 1973; To You, America, on Your 200th Birthday (poems), 1975; editor, The Rainbow; asso. editor, Poetry Caravan. Contbr. to mags. Public address Four Fundamentals of American Idealism (Freedoms Found. top honors, George Washington Gold medal, 1955). Home: Annapolis, Md. Died Feb. 3, 1979; buried Memorial Cemetery, Annapolis, Md.

BURNS, WILLIAM JOSEPH, mgmt. services firm exec., former hotel exec.; b. N.Y., Apr. 15, 1915; s. Edward R. and Elizabeth (Donovan) B.; m. Lee Lefton, October 1964. Assistant to v.p. Hilton Hotels, 1945-49; v.p., gen. mgr. Chicagoan Hotel, 1949-53; gen. mgr. Pick-Congress Hotel, Chgo., 1953-60; v.p. hotel div. Pick Hotels Corp., 1960-62, v.p., gen. mgr. Pick Hotels Corp., Chgo., 1963-65, executive vice pres., 1965-68; exec. dir. operations Playboy Clubs Internat., from 1968; founder, pres. Heritage Mgmt. Service, Cleve., until 1980. Bd. advisers Statler Found.; bd. govs. Culinary Inst.; trustee LaRabida Sanitarium, Chgo. Served from pvt. to maj., AUS, 1940-45. Decorated Bronze Star with cluster. Mem. Am. Hotel and Motel Assn. (pres.), Ill. (dir.), Greater Chgo. (past pres., chmn. bd.) hotel assns. Roman Catholic (dir.). Club: Illinois Athletic (past pres.). Home: Cleveland, Ohio. Died Sept. 27, 1980.

BURNSIDE, CAMERON, portrait painter; b. London, Eng. (Am. parents), July 23, 1887; s. Thomas and Elizabeth (Mulholland) B.; ed. Colet Court and St. Paul's Sch., London, Eng.; m. Irene Cochran, Dec. 27, 1927. Official artist for Am. Red Cross, 1918-19. Exhibited: Royal Acad., Royal Inst. (London), salons in Paris, Nat. Acad. (New York), Pa. Acad. Held one-man exhbns. at Paris, The Hague, Washington, D.C. Represented in collections of French govt. and in England, France and U.S. Portraits painted for Am. Philos. Soc., Phila. Bar Assn., Yale Univ., Jefferson Med. Coll., Pa. Univ., Phipps Inst., Bok Foundation Sch. Received silver medal Panama Pacific Expn., San Francisco, Calif., gold medal Expn. Coloniale, Marseille, France. Officer Order of Nichan Iftikhar. Societaire Société Nationale des Beaux Arts, Paris. Mem. Am. Water Color Soc., Phila. Water Color Club. North Shore Art Assn., Gloucester Soc. of Artists. Studied orchestral composition in London, Paris, Salzburg and in Brussels under Paul Gilson. Home: Philadelphia, Pa. *

BURNSTAN, ROWLAND, business exec.; b. Scranton, Pa., Nov. 9, 1901; s. Arthur H. and Lucie (Rowland) B.; B.S., Lafayette Coll., 1925, A.M., 1926, LL.D., 1961; Ph.D. (traveling fellow Western Europe), Columbia, 1929; postgrad. Heidelberg U., Germany, 1930-31; Sc.D., Chgo., 1938; m. Naomi Sloan, Oct. 19, 1929; children—Rowland, Alex Sloan. Comml. work, S.Am., 1926-27; research economist N.Y. State Tax Commn., 1927-28; research in comml. geography, Tunis and Algeria, N. Africa, 1929-30; economist N.Y. State Commn. for Revision Tax Law, 1930; lectr. econs., Heidelberg, Germany, 1930-31; economist U.S. Dept. Commerce, asso. editor Survey of Current Bus., 1931-32; dir. marketing research Armour & Co., Chgo., 1932-33; mem. J.O. McKinsey & Co., Chgo., 1933-35; bus. mgr. Chgo. Times, 1935-37; lectr. econs. U. Chgo., 1933-37; prof. econs. Carleton Coll., Northfield, Minn., 1937, chmn. dept., 1941; dir. aero. div. Mpls.-Honeywell Co., 1941-43; pres. Lawrence Aero. Corp., 1943-50; dir. Sch. Aero. Electronics, U. Minn., 1941-43; pres. Indian Motorcycle Co., 1944-45; dir. European operations Pepsi-Cola Corp., mng. dir., Pepsi-Cola de France, 1950-54; pres., dir. Borg-Warner Internat. Corp., 1954-61; asst. sec. commerce Dept. Commerce, 1961-62; pres. Indsl. Relations Counselors, Inc., 1962-64; chmn. York Shipley, Ltd. (Eng.), Euromat A.G. (Switzerland), Federated Purchaser Corp.; chmn., dir. Borg & Beck do Brasil (Brazil); dir. B.W.I. Panama (Panama), Borg-Warner A.G. (Switzerland), Freymon (Spain), Matfroid S.A., Fiby S.A. (France), Torque, Wobron (Argentina), Yorkaire Py. (Australia), Skofel Italiana, S.R.L. (Italy), Henninger Internat. (Germany), First Fed. Savs. & Loan Assn. (Chgo.), Colonial Trust Co. (N.Y.C.). Treas., World Fedn. for Mental Health, 1965-70; mem. adv. com. Minn. Inst. Govtl. Research; rep. N.Y. State at Nat. Tax Assn., 1929; mem. League of Nations Commn. to Study Orgn. of Peace. Trustee Chgo. Med. Sch., Meadville Theol. Sem., U. Chgo.; bd. dirs. Unitarian Service Com., Nat. Tb Assn. Decorated chevalier Legion d'Honneur (France); commendador del Orden Merito Civil (Spain); recipient Man of Year award in internat. relations, Chgo., 1961. Fellow Royal Econ. Soc.; mem. Am. Econ. Assn., Acad. Polit. Sci., A.A.A.S., Inst. Aero. Sci. (asso.); mem. Nat. Aero. Assn., Am. Mgmt. Assn. (v.p., dir., council, steering com.), N.Y. Acad. Medicine, Royal Aero. Soc. Eng., Nat. Fgn. Trade Council, Phi Gamma Delta. Unitarian. Mason. Clubs: University, Congressional Country (Washington); University (N.Y.C.); Nassau (Princeton, N.J.). Author books on taxation, other econ. subjects (pub. English, German); articles on aeros., fgn. bus. Home: Princeton, N.J. Died Dec. 15, 1977.

BURPEE, DAVID, seedsman; b. Phila., Apr. 5, 1893; s. Washington Atlee and Blanche (Simons) B.; student Cornell U., 1913; D.Sc. (hon.), Bucknell U., 1959, Del. Valley Coll. Sci. and Agr., 1972; m. Lois Torrance, July 18, 1938; children—Jonathan, Blanche Elizabeth (Mrs. Michael R. Dohan). Asst. to father in seed bus., Phila., 1914; chief exec. officer W. Atlee Burpee Co., 1915-70, dir., untill 1977. Hon. dir., Del. Valley Coll. Sci. and Agr., Doylestown, Pa., Bucknell U.; bd. dirs. Welcome House, Doylestown, Pa.; former dir. emeritus Abington Meml. Hosp. Recipient Gold seal Nat. Council State Garden Clubs, 1964; Am. Home Achievement medal, 1964; Gold medal for outstanding contbn. to horticulture Men's Garden Club Los Angeles, 1974; certificate of appreciation Men's Garden Club of Delaware Valley, 1975; Liberty Hyde Bailey medal Am. Hort. Soc., 1978; cert. of appreciation All-Am. Selections. Mem. Am. Seed Trade Assn. (dir., past pres.), Soc. War 1812, Canadian Soc. Phila. (hon. life pres.), English-Speaking Union, Pa. Soc. N.Y. (v.p.), Pa. S.R., Am. Hort. Council (citation 1958), Royal Hort. Soc., Nat. Sweet Pea Soc. Gt. Britain (Henry Eckford Meml. medal 1963), Scottish Nat. Sweet Pea Soc., Société Nationale d'Horticulture de France, Newcomen Soc. N.A., Phila. Soc. Promoting Agr. (Agrl. award 1950), Men's Garden Clubs Am., Quaker City Farmers Club, Delta Mu Delta (hon.), Alpha Zeta (hon.), Delta Upsilon. Republican. Clubs: Union League (v.p. 1933-35), Racquet (Phila.); Hillsboro (Fla.). Plant breeder; created, introduced new hybrid flowers, vegetables. Home: Doylestown, Pa. Died June 24, 1980; buried Doylestown Cemetery.

BURRELL, BERKELEY GRAHAM, assn. exec.; b. Washington, June 12, 1919; s. Hayward G. and Fannie (Miles) B.; student Howard U., 1941-43; D. Arts (hon.), Va. Coll., Lynchburg; m. A. Pat Robinson, June 10, 1951; 1 son, Berkeley Graham. Co-owner Burrell's Superb Cleaners, Washington, from 1946; pres. Burrell Industries; partner Graham Assos.; lectr. Coll. Urban Studies, Howard U., Morgan State Coll., Fisk U., Vanderbilt U., Am. U.; pres. Nat. Bus. League, Washington, from 1962; cons. urban affairs Coopers & Lybrand, Washington; also adviser U.S. Presidents. Trustee research Found. Doctor's Hosp.; mem. Joint Council Econ. Edn., Robert R. Moton Inst.; chmn. mgmt. com. Moton Conf. Center; bd. advisers Council Fin. Aid to Edn.; bd. dirs. Daniel H. Williems U., Corp. for Blacks in Pub. Broadcasting; mem. Research Council for Small Bus.; sr. warden St. Mary's Episcopal Ch., Washington; pres. St. Mary's Ct. Housing Devel. Corp. Served with AUS, World War II, Korea. Named One of 100 Most Influential Blacks in Am., Ebony Mag., 1971-77. Author: (with John Seder) Getting It Together: Black Businessmen in America, 1971. Editorial bd. Black Forum; also syndicated columnist. Home: Washington, D.C. Died Aug. 31, 1979.

BURRELL, LOOMIS, mfr.; b. Little Falls, N.Y., July 31, 1872; s. David Hamlin and Louisa (Loomis) B.; B.S., Pa. Mil. Coll., 1892, D.Sc., 1961; Ph.B., Yale, 1894; m. Lois Watson Wing, June 20, 1912 (dec.); children—Lilian Wing (Mrs. Edwin M. Fisher), Elizabeth Loomis (Mrs. William Slater Barkentin, Jr.) (dec.), Jean (Mrs. G. Dickinson). Various positions with D.H. Burrell & Co., manufacturers of dairy machinery equipment and supplies, 1895-1919, D.H. Burrell & Co., Inc., 1919-28; chmn. bd. Cherry-Burrell Corp. 1928-54; pres. Herkimer Co. Trust Co., 1941-48, chmn. bd. 1948-63; v.p., dir. Reed Tissues Corp., 1929-61, Mohawk Valley Paper Co., Burrows Paper Corp.; mgr. N.Y. Tng. Sch. for Girls, 1908-09; cons. U.S. Pub. Health Service, 1932-37. Del. to World's Diary Congress, Berlin, 1937. Dir. Auburn Theol. Sem., 1908-55, Little Falls Pub. Library, 1910-57. Recipient award for services to dairy industry from Cornell Dairy Sci. Assn., 1952. Republican. Presbyn. Home: Little Falls, N.Y. Died Nov. 11, 1975.

BURRIS, JOSEPH JENNINGS, lawyer; b. Aberdeen, S.D., Dec. 29, 1913; s. Joseph Henry and Lura Stella (Jennings) B.; A.B., Stanford, 1936, J.D., 1940; m. Patricia A. Burris; children—Joseph Steven, Susan Dirksen. Admitted to Calif. bar, 1942; practice in Los Angeles, from 1942; mem. firm Burris, Lagerlof, Swift & Senecal, 1953-80. Dir. Stauffer Chem. Co., Raffles, Inc. Chmn., Stanford Athletic Bd., 1961-65; asst. sec. Orthopaedic Hosp., Los Angeles Orthopaedic Found., Los Angeles Orthopaedic Med. Center, Crippled Children's Hosp. Trustee Ind. Colls. So. Calif.; chmn. bd. overseers Hoover Instn. on War, Revolution and Peace, Stanford U.; trustee, mem. exec. com., chmn. bd. Pacific Legal Found.; trustee Eisenhower Med. Center; mem., chmn. bd., exec. com. bd. trustees Republican Assos. Served to lt. commdr. USNR, World War II. Mem. Am., Calif., Los Angeles County (mem. exec. com. law office mgmt. sect.), Wilshire bar assns., Phi Delta Theta, Stanford Alumni Assn. (pres. 1952-53), Stanford Law Soc. So. Calif. (pres. 1957-58), Stanford Assos. (bd. govs. 1954-60), Pasadena-Foothill Tennis Patrons Assn. (bd. govs.), Los Angeles World Affairs Council, Town Hall Calif. (bd. govs., pres.). Clubs: Annandale Golf (Pasadena); Los Angeles, Stanford (pres. 1948-50) (Los Angeles); Buck (bd. dirs. 1955, chmn. 1955-57) (Stanford); Bohemian (San Francisco); FLint Canyon Tennis. Home: Flintridge, Calif. Died Mar. 28, 1980; interred Forest Lawn, Glendale, Calif.

BURRISS, STANLEY WILLIAM, aircraft mfg. co. exec.; b. Bklyn., July 15, 1910; s. Charles Scott and Elwine (Dreyer) B.; B.S., Newark Coll. Engring., 1938, D.Eng., 1964; postgrad. nuclear physics Los Alamos Lab., 1948-49, radar and electronics Bowdoin Coll., Mass. Inst. Tech., 1943, math. and electronics City Coll. N.Y., 1942; m. Maria Sartori, Oct. 25, 1958; 1 son, Richard S. With Los Alamos Sci. Lab., 1946-53, chief of staff to test dir. Operation Greenhouse, 1950-51, comdr. sci. task group Operation Ivy, 1952; project analyst Oriole project Patrick AFB, Glenn L. Martin Co., 1953-54, dir. Polaris missile system, 1956-61; v.p., gen. mgr. Missile Systems div. Lockheed Missiles & Space Co., Sunnyvale, Calif., 1961-69, pres., 1969-75; v.p. Lockheed Aircraft Corp., 1961-69, group v.p., 1969-79. Served to lt. comdr. USNR, 1943-46. Recipient Certificate of Appreciation sec. Army, 1953, Meritorious Pub. Service award U.S. Navy, 1961, Edward F. Weston Distinguished Alumnus award Newark Coll. Engring., 1962. Fellow Am. Inst. Aero. and Astronautics, Royal Aero. Soc.; mem. Nat. Acad. Engring., Am. Ordnance Assn., Navy League. Home: San Jose, Calif. Died Mar. 22, 1979.

BURRITT, MAURICE CHASE, dir. agrl. extension; b. Hilton, N.Y., Feb. 4, 1883; s. Stephen Day and Anna (Chase) B.; Genesee Wesleyan Sem.; B.S.A., Cornell, 1904-8, M.S.A., 1910; m. Estella May Buell, of Bergen, N.Y., Aug. 9, 1911. Farming, Hilton, N.Y., 1902—. Scientific asst., U.S. Dept. Agr., Washington, 1908-11; editor New York Tribune Farmer, 1911-13; county agt. leader, N.Y. State Coll. Agr., Cornell U., 1914-17; v.-dir. extension, same, 1917—. Prominent in organizing Farm Bur. and agrl. extension system in N.Y. State. Mem. Grange, N.Y. State Hort. Soc., Monroe Co. Farm Bur., Sigma Phi Sigma, Alpha Zeta, Heb-Sa. Republican. Methodist. Club: Rotary. Author: Apple Growing, 1915; The County Agent and the Farm Bureau, 1922. Home: Ithaca, N.Y. *

BURROUGHS, CLYDE HUNTLEY (BÛR'OZ), b. Vassar, Mich., Feb. 17, 1882; s. Leander H. and Katherine (Reeves) B.; ed. pub. and high schs.; studied art at Detroit Mus. of Art and in galleries of Europe; m. Edith Gibson, Sept. 17, 1907. With Detroit Museum of

Art (now Detroit Inst. Arts) since 1901, sec. and curator, 1913-20, sec. 1920-46, retired, 1946; now sec. emeritus. Mem. Assn. Art Museum Dirs. (ex-pres.), Am. Assn. Museums (councillor). Episcopalian. Home: Detroit, Mich. *

BURROUGHS, WILBUR GREELEY, geologist; b. Shortsville, N.Y., Dec. 7, 1886; s. Joseph B. and Emma (Greeley) B.; A.B., Oberlin Coll., 1909 (Phi Beta Kappa), A.M., 1911; Ph.D., Cornell U., 1932; m. Mavis Marian Reynolds, Aug. 31, 1922. Asst. geologist on Ohio State Geol. Survey, 1912-14; ednl. work, geologic and financial investigations, since 1914. Founded, 1920, dept. of geology at Berea Coll., Ky., for people of Appalachian Mts., and prof. geology, Berea Coll., 1920-56, filling Shaler chair, 1923-56, emeritus professor, 1956—; professor of geology and geography, Chautauqua 19(New York State) Summer Schs. for 23 seasons; geological and geographical work, 1921—; geologist Ky. Geol. Survey, 1922-32, 42-48; cons. geologist, 1956—. Fellow Royal Geog. Soc. (Egn.); mem. S.E. div., Assn. Am. Geographers, Ky. Acad. Sci. (v.p. 1925; pres. 1926), Phi Beta Kappa, Sigma Xi, Phi Kappa Phi, Sigma Gamma Epsilon, various humane socs. Presbyn. Author numerous publications on geology and geography of Ky., and on coal mining, including: Coal Mining in the U.S., 1921; Geography of Kentucky (for govt. publ., The American Guide); geology text for Berea Coll. sci. survey course. Contbr. New Internat. Ency., 1917; also contbr. to mining and sci. jours. Author, collaborator govt. geol. maps of Ky. and Ohio. Explored and mapped prehistoric strongholds of Indian Fort Mt. and Basin Mt. in Ky. Address: Berea, Ky.

BURROWS, J(AMES) AUSTIN, coll. prof.; b. Dubuque, Ia., Mar. 5, 1885; s. James Hogarth and Emily Elizabeth (Conzett) B.; B.S., Ill. Wesleyan U., 1906; M.S., Ia. State Coll., 1922, Ph.D., 1925; m. Martha Gertrude Bolton, Aug. 18, 1914; s. James Austin Jr., David Bolton, Robert Gordon. High sch. sci. teacher, Marengo, Ia., 1907-09, Sioux City, Ia., 1909-10, Dubuque, Ia., 1910-12, Paducah, Ky., 1912-13, Des Moines, Ia., 1913-18; instr. chemistry Ia. State Coll., 1918-25; asst. prof. chemistry U. of N.D., 1926-29; asso. prof. Okla. A. and M. Coll., 1929-39, prof. of chem. 1939-50, emeritus, head freshman chem., 1929-47. Boy Scout councilman. Mem. Am. Chem. Soc., Okla. Acad. Sci., Phi Gamma Delta, Sigma Xi, Phi Kappa Phi, Phi Lambda Upsilon. Presbyterian. Mason. Author: Semimicro Laboratory Exercises in General Chemistry, 1942. Contbr. articles on inorganic chemistry to Jour. of Am. Chem. Soc. Home: Stillwater, Okla. *

BURROWS, MILLAR, clergyman, educator; b. Cincinnati, O., Oct. 26, 1889; s. Edwin Jones and Katharine Douglas (Millar) B.; B.A., Cornell U., 1912; B.D., Union Theol. Sem., 1915; Ph.D., Yale U., 1925, D.D., 1961; D.D., Oberlin Coll., 1960, Brown U., 1961; m. Irene Gladding, July 6, 1915; 1 s., Edwin Gladding. Ordained ministry Presbyn. Ch., 1915; pastor of rural ch., Tex., 1915-19; rural supervisor for Tex., Interchurch World Movement, 1919-20; coll. pastor and prof. Bible, Tusculum Coll., 1920-23; asst. prof. Bibl. lit. and history of religions, Brown, 1925-29, asso. prof., 1929-32, prof. and chmn. dept., 1932-34; prof. Biblical theology, Yale U. Div. Sch., 1934-58; chmn. dept. Near Eastern languages and literatures, Yale Grad. Sch., 1950-58, prof. emeritus, 1958-80; vice chmn. Standard Bible Com., 1958-63; visiting professor religion, Am. U. of Beirut, Syria, 1930-31; director Am. Sch. of Oriental Research, Jerusalem, 1931-32, 47-48. Member American Academy of Arts and Sciences, Soc. Bibl. Literature and Exegesis (pres. 1954), Am. Middle East Relief Inc. (pres. 1954-56), Nat. Assn. Bibl. Instrs., National Council of Religion in Higher Edn., Am. Oriental Soc., Phi Beta Kappa. Conglist. Author: Outline of Biblical Theology, 1946; Palestine is Our Business, 1949; The Dead Sea Scrolls, 1955; More Light on the Dead Sea Scrolls, 1958; also articles periodicals. Editor: The Dead Sea Scrolls of St. Mark's Monastery. Address: Winter Park, Fla. Died 1980.

BURROWS, WILLIAM, bacteriologist; b. New Haven, Mar. 6, 1908; s. William and Winifred Elizabeth (Johnson) B.; B.S., Purdue U., 1928; M.S., U. Ill., 1930; Ph.D., U. Chgo., 1932; m. Margaret Pound, June 24, 1931; 1 dau., Mary. Gen. Edn. Bd. fellow, 1935-37; research asst. U. Chgo., 1932-35; asst. prof., 1937-42, asso. prof., 1942-47, prof. microbiology, 1947-73, emeritus, 1973-78; responsible investigator Office Sci. Research and Devel., 1942-46, U.S. Army Research and Devel. Command, 1963-73, USPHS, 1946-49, 53-73, biol. div. chem. corps U.S. Army, 1950-60; cons. Argonne Nat. Lab.; mem. WHO, expert adv. Panel Cholera. Recipient Ricketts prize, 1932. Fellow A.A.A.S., Am. Acad. Microbiology; mem. Chgo. Hist. Soc., Am. Soc. (Microbiology (hon.), Am. Assn. Immunologists, Soc. Ill. Microbiologists (pres. 1949), Sigma Xi, Gamma Alpha, Sigma Alpha Epsilon. Republican. Episcopalian. Clubs: Literary, Quadrangle (Chgo.). Author: Textbook of Microbiology, 20th edit., 1973; Cholera, 1974; research papers med. jours. Mem. editorial bd. Am. Med. Dictionary. Home: Cobden, Ill. Died Nov. 15, 1978; buried Elmwood Cemetery, Litchfield, Ill.

BURSON, GEORGE ALLEN, JR., farm coop. exec.; b. Camilla, Ga., Mar. 3, 1917; s. George Allen and Eugenia (Ivey) B.; B.S. in Agrl. Engring., U. Ga., 1940; m. Elizabeth McRanie, July 20, 1946; children—Jane Elizabeth, Charles Allen. With Cotton Producers Assn. (name now Gold Kist Inc.), Atlanta, 1946-78, v.p. agri-services, 1969-72, exec. v.p., chmn. exec. com., 1972-77, pres., 1977-78; vice chmn. bd. CF Industries, Inc., Long Grove, Ill., 1974-78; bd. dirs. Nat. Council Farmer Coops., Washington; v.p. Ga. Agribus. Council; mem. C&S Agribus. Adv. Bd. Trustee, Reinhardt Coll. Served with U.S. Army, 1941-45. Decorated Bronze Star. Methodist. Clubs: Atlanta Farmers (dir.), Rotary, Capital City, Druid Hills Country (Atlanta). Home: Decatur, Ga. Died Oct. 5, 1978.

BURT, KATHARINE NEWLIN, author; b. Fishkill-on-Hudson, N.Y., Sept. 6, 1882; d. Thomas Shipley and Julia Maria (Onderdonk) Newlin; ed. at home and at Miss Mackie's Sch., Newburgh, N.Y.; kindergarten course, Munich, Germany; m. Maxwell Struthers Burt, Feb. 9, 1913 (dec. Aug. 29, 1954); children—Nathaniel, Julia Bleecker. Episcopalian. Author: Close Pursuit, 1947; Still Water, 1948; Strong Citadel, 1949; Escape from Paradise, 1952. Fiction editor, Ladies' Home Jour. Home: Southern Pines, N.C.; also Moran, Wyo. *

BURT, LAURA, actress; b. Ramsey, Isle of Man, Sept. 16, 1882; d. Capt. Brown and Ann Lloyd (Welsh) B.; ed. Am. Acad. Dramatic Arts, New York; m. Henry Stanford, actor, Mar. 2, 1902 (died 1921). Became Am. citizen, 1924. As a child played as "star" in "Blue Jeans," 14th St. Theatre, New York, 1890, and played Madge in "In Old Kentucky," Eng. and U.S., 1890-93; appeared in "The Heart of the Klondyke," "A Dangerous Maid," as Helen of Swabia, in "Dante," in "Louis XI," etc.; played as co-star with Sir Henry Irving, and co-star with her husband in "Dorothy Vernon of Haddon Hall"; created rôle of Nurse in "Damaged Goods"; has appeared in various Shakespearean roles. Address: New York, N.Y. *

BURT, RICHARD LAFAYETTE, educator, physician; b. Springfield, Mass., Dec. 7, 1915; s. Lafayette and Theresa (Maines) B.; B.S., Springfield Coll., 1938; Sc.M., Brown U., 1940, Ph.D., 1942; M.D., Harvard, 1946; m. Regina Meed, June 27, 1942; children—Jonathan M., Duncan T., Deborah D., Priscilla M. Research fellow Harvard, 1942-43; intern U.S. Navy Hosp., Chelsea, Mass., 1946-47; asst. resident obstetrics and gynecology N.C. Baptist Hosp., 1949-52, chief resident, 1952-53; mem. faculty Bowman Gray Sch. Medicine, 1949—, prof. obstetrics and gynecology, 1958—, chmn. dept., 1966—; cons. NIH, 1964-68; research prof. USPHS, 1960-64. Served to lt. (j.g.) USNR, 1946-49. Mem. Am. Gynecol. Soc., Soc. Gynecol. Investigation, Endocrine Soc., St. Atlantic Assn. Obstetricians and Gynecologists, Am. Diabetes Assn., A.M.A., N.C. Soc. Obstetricians and Gynecologists, Sigma Xi, Alpha Omega Alpha. Author papers in field. Mem. editorial bd. Obstetrics and Gynecology, 1966—. Home: Clemmons, N.C. Died Dec. 15, 1978; buried Clemmons Meml. Gardens, Clemmons, N.C.

BURT, RUSSELL JEFFORDS, lawyer; b. Charleston, W.Va., Jan. 2, 1886; s. Benjamin R. and Lillian Allen (Jeffords) B.; B.A.; m. Hilda J. Corwin, June 23, 1913 (dec. Dec. 1926); children—John C., Ben R.; m. 2d, Adelaide Wise, Jan. 27, 1928 (dec. Feb. 8, 1972); 1 son, Richard J. Admitted to Ohio bar, 1910; with firm Goulder, Day, White, Garry & Duncan, Clev., 1910-12; practice in Canton, O., 1912—; partner firm Amerman, Burt & Jones, 1957—. Tchr. corp. law William McKinley Law Sch., Canton, 1928-32; dir. Peoples-Mchts. Trust Co., Canton, 1958-66. Fellow Am. Coll. Trial Lawyers; hon. mem. Ohio Bar Assn; mem. Delta Upsilon. Republican. Home: Canton OH *

BURTNER, CHARLES ALLEN, community devel. rep.; b. White Post, Va., Mar. 18, 1929; s. William Dorsey and Golda Virginia (Dearmont) B.; diploma Randolph-Macon Acad., 1947; B.A., Randolph-Macon Coll.; m. Janet Ellen Flora, Dec. 12, 1959; children—Tamsey Leigh, Sydney Ann, Tiffaney Ellen. Reporter, advt. salesman South Boston News & Halifax County Record-Advertiser, South Boston, Va., 1952-54; sports editor, spl. assignment reporter Waynesboro (Va.) News-Va., 1954-57; exec. sec. Bedford (Va.) County C. of C., 1957-60; dir. pub. relations Charlotte (N.C.) C. of C., 1960-62; dir. New River Indsl. Commn., 1962-66; v.p., sec. Lynchburg (Va.) C. of C., 1966-68; exec. mgr. Greater Richmond (Va.) C. of C., 1968-74; community devel. rep. Va. Div. Devel., 1974-79. Bd. dirs. Better Bus. Bur. Richmond, 1968-74. Mem. Va. Assn. C. of C. Execs. (pres. 1968-70), Va. C. of C. (indsl. com. 1966-74), Pi Delta Epsilon. Club: Downtown (Richmond). Home: Richmond, Va. Died Apr. 24, 1979.

BURTNESS, HAROLD WILLIAM, railroad exec.; b. Chgo., Nov. 16, 1897; s. Theodore and Marie (Rone) B.; student Met. Bus. Coll., 1915-16, LaSalle Extension U., 1920-21; m. Grace M. Reinholtzen, Aug. 16, 1924; children—Roger William, James Harold. Clk., C., B.&O. R.R., 1914; clk., stenographer, sec. to mgr. Star Union Line, later gen. freight agt., traffic mgr. Pa. R.R., 1915-22; sec. to pres., chmn. bd. C.G.W. R.R. Co., 1922-33; sec. to chmn. Western Assn. Ry. Execs., 1925-30; asst. to pres., sec. C.G.W. R.R. Co., 1933-41, in charge transp. div. operating dept.; v.p., dir. 6 subsidiary cos. C.G.W. R.R., pres. Gt. Western Coal Co., 1934-78; v.p. C.G.W. R.R., 1941-46, pres., dir., chmn. exec. com., 1946-48; chmn. bd. Luth. Mut. Life Ins. Co., 1965-78; dir. Kansas City Terminal Ry. Co., St. Paul Union Depot Co., Minn. Transfer Ry. Co. Mem. 1st Div. Nat. R.R. Adjustment Bd., 1949-78. Pres., Bethesda Home for Aged. Pres. bd. trustees Luth. Deaconess Home and Hosp. Mem. Am. Assn. R.R. Supts. Republican. Lutheran. Clubs: Union League, Chicago. Home: Oak Park, Ill. Died May 26, 1978.

BURTON, FRANK, cons. engr.; b. Detroit, Mich., July 24, 1886; s. Clarence Monroe and Harriet Jane (Nye) B.; B.S., U. of Mich., 1907; m. Bernice Mary Landon, Aug. 29, 1913. Insp. R.R., 1907; chemist 1907-10; engaged as consulting chemist, 1910-12; research engr. Gen. Motors Corp., 1912-13; structural engr. dept. of bldg., City of Detroit, 1913-17; chief engr. dept. of bldg. and safety engring., Detroit, 1919-20; chief engr., Donaldson & Meier, Detroit, 1920-21; commr. dept. of bldg. and safety engring., Detroit, 1921-26; indsl. cons. engineer since 1926; chmn. bd. Burton Abstract & Title Co.; pres. Burton Mortgage Bond Co. Served as capt. Signal Corps. U.S. Army with A.E.F., 1917-18; with Chief of Engrs. U.S. Army, construction of war plants, 1941-43. Hon. member and ex-pres. Building Officials Conference; member Detroit Engring. Society (ex-pres.), Tau Beta Pi, Sigma Xi. Mason. Wrote bldg. codes for cities of Flint, Wyandotte, Lansing, Dearborn, Detroit, Mich., and Minneapolis, Minn.; contbr. of articles to tech. mags. Home: Detroit. *

BURTON, HARRY PAYNE, editor; b. Cleveland, O., Jan. 20, 1886; s. Alfred Payne and Minnie Eliza (Payne) B.; student Western Reserve U. and Kenyon Coll.; m. Katherine Kurz, of Cleveland, Aug. 6, 1910; children—Harry Payne, Pamela Huckstep, Richard Ronald St. John. Began as reporter, Cleveland Press, later spl. traveling corr.; joined Newspaper Enterprise Assn., Chicago, 1912, and served as New York corr. 2 yrs., asso. editor, war corr. in Europe (also for Scripps newspapers and United Press), 1914-15, later with same orgn. in U.S.; became editor McCall's Magazine, 1921; then editor Cosmopolitan Magazine. Episcopalian. Club: Nat. Arts. *

BURTON, JOE WRIGHT, editor, clergyman; b. Miles, Tex., Sept. 7, 1907; s. William Thomas and Martha Ellen (Davison) B.; A.B., Hardin-Simmons U., 1929, D.D., 1946; Th.M., Southwestern Bapt. Theol. Sem., Ft. Worth, 1932; postgrad. U. Mo. Sch. Journalism, summer 1940; m. Lula Grace Williams, Sept. 9, 1931; children—Mary Lu (Mrs. H. David Smith), John Williams, Robert Henry. Ordained to ministry Bapt. Ch., 1928; pastor Thornberry Ch., nr. Wichita Falls, Tex., 1933, Big Lake, 1934-35; sec. edn. So. Bapt. Conv. Home Mission Bd., Atlanta 1936-45, sec. So. Bapt. Conv., 1947-65, sec. family life dept. Bapt. Sunday Sch. Bd., Nashville, 1946-66, also editor Home Life, 1947-72; hist. researcher and writer for So. Bapt. Conv., 1973-75; pastor Munich (West Germany) Bapt. Ch., 1972-73. Preacher home revivals, evangelistic meetings throughout South; condr. Clin. Study Sch. Pastoral Care, Winston-Salem, 1968, Inst. Advanced Pastoral Studies, Detroit, 1970, family study tours, No. Europe, 1952, Near East, 1955, Israel 1969, Europe, 1971. Recipient citation from Lambda Lambda Lambda for distinctive service in religious journalism, 1947. Author: Missionary Illustrations, 1938; Epochs of Home Missions, 1945; Prince of the Pulpit, 1946; The Church and Family Life, 1948; Tomorrow you Marry, 1950; Family Life—A Bible View, 1964. Editor 42 vols. pub. by Home Mission Bd., 1936-45; Altar fires for Family Worship, 1954; So. Bapt. Family Life quar. 1954-60; Light From Above, 1968. Home: Nashville Tenn. Died May 6, 1976.

BURTON, JOHN FLACK, plastic surgeon; b Wicklyffee, Ky., July 10, 1897; s. Leslie D. and Martha (Flack) B.; A.B., Okla. U., 1918; B.S., 1921; M.D. COlumbia U., 1923; m. Naomi McCasland, May 5 1925; children—John Flack (dec.), James Leslie; m. 2d Barbara Jean Cook Iselin, June 21, 1962. Intern 1st surg div. Bellevue Hosp., N.Y.C., 1923-24; gen. practice in Tex., 1924-29; mem. faculty Okla. U. Med. Sch., from 1931, clin. prof. surgery, after 1940; founder, 1st chie dept. plastic surgery Okla. U. Med. Center, 1932, med dir. plastic surgery sect.; cons. Will Rogers VA Hosp also Bur. Family Service of HEW; attending surgeo Okla. U., St. Anthony's, Mercy, Baptist, Presbyn Mid-West City hosps.; surg. cons. Okla. Dept. Pub Welfare. Founder mem., v.p. Okla. Blue Shield Plan pres. Okla. U. Sooner Scholarship Trust Plan; bd. dir. Okla. Soc. Crippled Children, 1958; adv. bd. Goodwi Industries Oklahoma City, 1958-59. Diplomate Am Bd. Plastic Surgery. Fellow A.C.S.; mem. AMA (h dels. 1949-56, council med. service 1956-63, chm 1962-63, chmn. com. indigent care 1956-62, Okla. Me Assn. (past pres.). Republican. Congregationalis

Clubs: Rotary; Doctors Dinner, Men's Dinner, Beacon, Touchdown (Oklahoma City). Author sci. papers. Hoe: Eufaula, Okla. Died Dec. 11, 1979.

BURTON, WILLIAM MERIAM, ex-pres. Standard Oil Co.; b. Cleveland, Nov. 17, 1865; s. Erasmus D. and Emeline (Meriam) B.; A.B., Western Reserve U., 1886; Ph.D., Johns Hopkins, 1889; m. Kean Woodruff, Dec. 27, 1911 (deceased). Entered employ of Standard Oil Co., as chemist, 1889; promoted to gen. supt., 1895; v.p. Standard Oil Co. of Ind., 1915-18, pres., 1918-27. Awarded Willard Gibbs medal, by Amer. Chem. Soc., 1918, Perkins medal, Soc. Chem. Industry, 1921. Mem. Alpha Delta Phi. Republican. Home: Pasadena, Calif. *

BUSCH, ALFRED H., corp. exec.; b. Chgo., 1919; ed. U. Wis., 1942; LL.B., De Paul U., 1947. Sec. Stewart-Warner Corp., 1953-59, sec.-treas., 1959-64, v.p., sec.-treas., 1964-77, sr. v.p., sec.-treas., 1977-79, sr. v.p., treas., 1979, also dir. Home: Chicago, Ill. Died Nov. 2, 1979.

BUSCH, BONNIE (BOOSH), author; b. Washington, D.C., Jan. 21, 1884; d. Wilbur Fisk and Josephine C. (Shutt) Melbourne; ed. pvt. schls. in America and Europe; studied music in Europe; m. Clarence Marshall Busch, Nov. 19, 1904 (divorced 1935); children—Clarice, Marshall, Leslie Melbourne; m. 2d, R. Vincent Jackson, 1935. Built and equipped the Christian Hospital for Negroes at Miami, Fla.; mem. bd. N.J. Children's Home, Trenton, N.J.; mem. Authors' League America, League Am. Pen Women (nat. president, 1929-30), Nat. Inst. Social Sciences; hon. mem. Am. Woman's Association (New York), Poets of Great Britain. Clubs: Miami Woman's City (president 1931); Washington (Washington, D.C.); American Woman's (Paris). Author: Morality Court, 1920; Out of the Middle West, 1921; His Mortgaged Wife, 1923; Eager Vines, 1925; Progressive Marriage, 1925; Where the Wind Listeth, 1929; Waiting, 1934. Co-author: Red Fog, 1929. Contbr. short stories to mags. Wrote words and music of song "The Afterglow." Home: Coral Gables, Fla. *

BUSCHMAN, LEONARD VICTOR, clergyman; b. McGirks, Mo., Sept. 15, 1893; s. Kasten D. and Lydia (Mellies) B.; B.A., Westminster Coll., Fulton, Mo., 1915, D.D., 1928; M.A., Princeton, 1918; postgrad. Princeton Theol. Sem., 1918; m. Lillian Martin, Oct. 16, 1918. Ordained to ministry Presbyn. Ch., 1918; pastor First Presbyn. Ch., Woodbridge, N.J., 1918-25, Tyler Pl. Presbyn. Ch., St. Louis, 1925-29, Central Presbyn. Ch., Buffalo, 1929-41, Central Presbyn. Ch., Summit, N.J., 1941-58, pastor emeritus, from 1958; asso. minister First Congl. Ch., Sarasota, 1961-63. Mem. Bd. Christian Edn. U.P. Ch. U.S.A.; regional rep. Presbyn. Found. Mem. Beta Theta Pi. Republican. Mason, Rotarian. Club: Ivy League (pres. Sarasota). Home: Sarasota, Fla. Deceased.

BUSH, EDITH LINWOOD, educator; b. Everett, Mass., Sept. 15, 1882; d. Rev. Richard Perry and Emma Linwood (Paine) Bush; A.B., Tufts College, 1903, Litt.D., 1942; student at Radcliffe College, Boston University. Teacher of mathematics, secondary schs., 1903-18; principal high school, Provincetown, Massachusetts, 1918-20; instructor mathematics, Tufts College, 1920-22, assistant professor, 1922-26, professor mathematics and dean, Jackson Coll. for Women, Tufts Coll. since 1926. Mem. Assn. Math. Teachers, Assn. Deans of Women, Am. Assn. Univ. Women, Phi Beta Kappa, Chi Omega. Republican. Universalist. Clubs: College (Boston); Research (Mayflower descendants), (Provincetown). Home: Provincetown, Mass. *

BUSHER, JOHN JOSEPH, judge; b. Cleve., Aug. 19, 1882; s. John and Elizabeth (Barry) B.; LL.B., Cleve. Law Sch., 1923; m. Mary Agnes Spellman, Nov. 26, 1914; children—Mary Elizabeth, John Thomas, Margaret Jane. Admitted to Ohio bar, 1923; dep. clk. criminal br., Common Pleas Ct. of Cuyahoga Co., O., 1913-21, clk. room 1, 1922-32; bond commr., 1921; clk. Common Pleas and Ct. of Appeals, 1933-39; judge Municipal Ct. Cleve-, 1940-46, chief justice since 1946. Mem. Ohio State, Cuyahoga Co., Cleve. bar assns. Home: Cleve. *

BUSHNELL, ASA SMITH, athletic adminstr.; b. Springfield, O., Feb. 2, 1900; s. John Ludlow and Jessie Manton (Harwood) B.; grad. The Hill Sch., 1917; B.S., Princeton, 1921; student law sch., Columbia, 1922; LL.D., Syracuse U. 1955, Hobart and William Smith Colls., 1965; Pd.D., St. John's U., 1961; m. Thelma Lucille Clark, Feb. 11, 1924 (dec. 1972); children—Asa S., Barbara C. (Mrs. John C. Leonard). Teller Morris Plan Bank, Springfield, 1922-23, dir., 1924-25; treas., office mgr. Direct Products Co., 1924-25; editor Lagonda Pub. Co., 1924, Princeton (U.) Alumni Weekly, 1925-30; founder Princeton Athletic News, 1932, editor, 1932-37; grad. mgr. athletics Princeton, 1927-37, acting dir. athletics, 1942-44; commr. Eastern Coll. Athletic Conf., 1938-70, cons., 1970-71. Apprentice seaman USNR, 1918. Dir. sports sect. Office Coordinator Inter-Am. Affairs, 1941-42; mem. Nat. Com. on Phys. Fitness, 1942-44; asst. to dir. schs. and tng. br. OSS, 1944; spl. cons. athletic br. Spl. Services Div., U.S. Army, 1944-45. Originator Princeton Invitation Track Meet, 1934, dir., 1934-38. Sports adv. com. N.Y. World Fair, 1939, 64. Sec. Nat. Football Found. and Hall Fame, Inc., 1948-51, 70-75; dir., 1952-75. Recipient Olympic Torch, U.S. Olympic Com., 1966; Austrian Olympic medal, Austria, 1966; Distinguished Service award from Princeton Class of 1921, 1955; Sportsmanship Brotherhood award, 1954; Touchdown Club award, 1957; meritorious service award N.Y. Track Writers Assn., 1958; named to Helms Athletic Found. Rowing Hall Fame, 1958; James Lynah Meml. award Eastern College Athletic Conf., 1959; distinguished service award Del. Valley chpt. Football Found., 1967; Madison Square Garden Hall of Fame, 1967; James Corbett Meml. award Nat. Assn. Coll. Dirs. Athletics, 1969; Helms Athletic Found. Commrs. and Athletic Dirs. Hall Fame, 1970. Mem. Amateur Athletic Union of U.S. (gov.), Nat. Coll. Athletic Assn. (exec. com. 1943-44, 1947-51; dir. TV program 1952-70, cons. 1970-72). Collegiate Commrs. Assn. (pres. 1947-52), S.R., U.S. Olympic Com. (asst. treas. 1936-37, mem. exec. com. 1937-45, 65-71, sec. 1945-65), Order Founders and Patriots Am. Episcopalian (vestryman). Club: University Cottage (gov.). Editor: 1948 and 1952 U.S. Olympic Book. Co-contbr. sects. on football in Ency. Brit. and Collier's Ency. Home: Princeton, N.J. Died Mar. 22, 1975.

BUSKIN, MARTIN, journalist; b. Bklyn., July 9, 1930; s. Harry and Frances (Drimmer) B.; A.B., N.Y. U., 1951; m. Saundra Rosman, June 3, 1956; children—Linda, Randi. Reporter, Newsday, Garden City, N.Y., 1953-55, copy editor, 1955-59, feature editor, 1959-61, edn. editor, 1962-76. Cons. U.S. Office Edn. Served with AUS, 1951-53. Recipient 1st prize for outstanding coverage local edn. issues Edn. Writers Assn., 1964, 65, 1st prize for outstanding columns on brotherhood Nat. Conf. Christians and Jews, 1966. Mem. Edn. Writers Assn. (pres.), Nat. Council for Advancement Edn. Writing (vice chmn.). Author: (with Howard Hagler) Great Moments in Sports, 1968; Parent Power: A Candid Guidebook to Help You Get the Most Out of Your Child's School, 1975. Contbr. to Naked Came The Stranger, 1969. Contbr. articles profl. jours. Home: Commack, N.Y. Died Feb. 8, 1976.

BUSSEY, HENSON ESTES (BUS'E), engineer; b. Columbus, Ga., Dec. 31, 1884; s. William Wallace and Charlotte Luella (Estes) B.; grad. University High Sch., Birmingham, Ala., 1902; E.E. and M.E., Ala. Poly. Inst., Auburn, Ala., 1904; m. Adele Johnston Bussey, June 24, 1911; 1 child, William Wallace II. With Gen. Electric Co., hdqrs. Schenectady, N.Y., since 1904, with testing dept., 1904-05, constrn. engr., 1905-06, dist. engr. since 1906, now in charge all engring. of the co. in Southeastern states. Fellow Am. Inst. E.E. (v.p. 1923-25); mem. Sigma Alpha Epsilon. Home: Atlanta, Ga. *

BUSTAMANTE, WILLIAM ALEXANDER, prime minister Jamaica; b. 1884. Soldier, policeman, journalist, organized Bustamante Trade Union; leader Jamaica Labour Party, 1943—; mem. Ho. of Reps. for Claredon South; minister communications Exec. Council, 1944-53, chief minister, 1953-55, prime minister, 1962—. Commr. Brit. sect. Caribbean Commn., 1950-55. Address: Kingston, Jamaica. *

BUSWELL, JAMES OLIVER, JR., clergyman, educator; b. Burlington, Wis., Jan. 16, 1895; s. James Oliver and Emeline (Porter) B.; B.A., U. Minn., 1917; M.A., U. Chgo., 1924; B.D., McCormick Theol. Sem., 1923; D.D., Dallas Theol. Sem., 1927; LL.D., Houghton College, 1936; Ph.D., N.Y. U., 1949; m. Helen Spaulding, May 20, 1918; children—Jane Alice, James Oliver III, Ruth Helen, John William. Ordained to ministry Presbyterian Ch. of U.S.A., 1918; pastor Perseverance Ch., Milw., 1919-22, Grace Reformed Ch., Bklyn., 1922-26; president Wheaton (Ill.) Coll., 1926-40; prof. systematic theology and apologetics, Faith Theol. Sem., Wilmington, Del., 1940-47; pres. Shelton Coll., Ringwood, N.J., 1941-56; dean Grad. Sch. Theology, Covenant Coll. and Sem., St. Louis, 1956-70; split from Presbyn. Ch. of U.S.A., 1936, to co-found Presbyn. Ch. Am., part of which became known as Reformed Presbyn. Ch., Evang. Synod. Chaplain, 140th Inf., U.S. Army, World War; citation in 35th Division, general order following Meuse-Argonne drive. Member Am. Philos. Soc., Am. Sci. Affiliation, Soc. Bibl. Lit., Evang. Theol. Soc., AAAS, Pi Gamma Mu. Author: Problems in the Prayer Life, 1928; Lamb of God Series; The Philosophies of F. R. Tennant and John Dewey, 1950; Thomas and the Bible; Being and Knowing: An Introduction to Philosophy, 1960; Systematic Theology, Vol. 1, 1962, Vol. II, 1963. Home: Saint Louis, Mo. Died Feb. 3, 1977; buried Quarryville, Pa.

BUTCHER, WILLIAM LEWIS, banker; b. Newark, Aug. 31, 1907; s. William Lewis and Mae (Lewis) B.; A.B., Williams Coll., 1928; grad. Rutgers Sch. Banking, 1939; m. Aimee Tweedy, May 24, 1929 (dec. 1967); children—Gayle (Mrs. Foster Nichols), Lynne (Mrs. Merrell Mays Clark), Tweedy (Mrs. Derek Lee Tattersall); m. 2d, Kathleen R. Cox, Jan. 20, 1968; children—Abigail, Thomas, Coletta Cox. Exec. sec. Zeta Psi Frat., N.Y.C., 1929-35; v.p. Central Trust Co., Cin., 1935-46; exec. v.p. County Trust Co., White Plains, N.Y., 1946-57, pres., 1957-60, chmn. bd., 1960-72; dir. County Trust. Bank of N.Y. Co., Inc., Dictaphone Corp. Faculty, Rutgers Sch. Banking, 1949-58. Mem. N.Y. State Met. Transp. Authority. Trustee Pace Coll.; bd. dirs. White Plains Hosp., N.Y. Sch. for Deaf, Burke Found., Westchester County Assn., Westchester Med. Center Found. Mem. Zeta Psi. Episcopalian. Mason. Clubs: Westchester Hills Golf (White Plains); Shenorock (Rye, N.Y.); University, Williams (N.Y.C.); Club at Point O'Woods (N.Y.). Home: White Plains, N.Y. Died Nov. 29, 1976.

BUTLER, EDWARD FRANCIS, lawyer; b. N.Y.C., Mar. 10, 1909; s. William and Katherine (Mahan) B.; B.S., U.S. Naval Acad., 1929; LL.B., Harvard, 1933; m. Maybelle McManus, June 23, 1934; children—Michael, Katherine (Mrs. Claiborne H. Johnson, Jr.), Norah, Martha. Admitted to N.Y. bar, 1934, practiced in N.Y.C.; partner firm Conboy, Hewitt, O'Brien & Boardman, 1946-79; spl. asst. to atty. gen. Dept. Justice, 1942. Mem. N.Y.C. Commn. Health Services, 1959-61. Trustee St. John's Hosp., Cath. Med. Center Bklyn. Served to comdr. USNR, 1942-46. Mem. Assn. Bar City N.Y., Am., N.Y. bar assns., Nat. Assn. R.R. Trial Counsel, Knights of Malta. Roman Catholic. Clubs: Down Town Assn., Downtown Athletic, Harvard (N.Y.C.); Westchester Country (Rye, N.Y.). Home: New York, N.Y. Died May 29, 1979.

BUTLER, G(EORGE) PAUL, author, editor; b. Chester, Pa., Oct. 23, 1900; s. William Austin and Katherine Maud (Anthony) B.; A.B., Lawrence Coll., 1923; Ph.D., Milton U., 1929; A.M., U. So. Calif., 1932; postgrad. Drew U. Theol. Sem., Columbia; LL.D., Atlanta Law Sch., 1971; m. Erica Helene Bracher (dec.); children—George Paul II, Eric and Renate (twins), Joylan; m. 2d, H. Jean Stanko. Ordained to ministry Meth. Ch., 1923; pastor, Wis., N.J., staff N.Y. Times, 1924-27; head English dept., West Side YMCA Schs., N.Y.C., 1924-27; head dept. history, Silver Bay Sch., 1928-29; prof. constl. history, lectr. Southwestern U., Los Angeles, 1929-38; English faculty Los Angeles Jr. Coll., 1932-38; head dept. English lit. Chapman Coll., Los Angeles, 1936-38; editor, mgr. books, chs., Schs., religious and book editor N.Y. Mirror, 1938-63. Research in lit., rare books, history Bibliotheque Nationale de Paris, Shakespeare Library, Stratford-on-Avon, Library Brit. Mus., U. Strassbourg, U. Heidelberg, U. Geneva, League of Nations, Vatican libraries, Bodleian Library, U. Oxford (Eng.); lectr. books, life today. Recipient Freedoms Found. citation, 1956; certificate Nat. Conf. Christians and Jews, 1956; USAF citation, 1956. Mem. Author's Club N.Y. Author, editor: Best Sermons, vols. I-XII, 1943-75 (1st world wide anthologies contemporary preaching, selected from 58 countries); Butler's South America, 1960; Butler's Mexico, 1960; Butler's Caribbean, 1960; Butler's Europe, and the Mediterranean, 1973; Butler's The Orient, Hawaii, The Pacific and Round The World, 1975; Contbr. numerous articles to profl. jours., book revs. Address: Cape Coral, Fla. Deceased.

BUTLER, PAUL TEMPLE, physician; b. Springboro, Pa., Dec. 11, 1858; s. Hiram and Lydia Eliza (Temple) B.; M.D., Eclectic Med. Inst., Cincinnati, O., 1881; m. Rose Hyat, 1888 (now dec.); children—Mary (dec.), Ben H., Paul T. (killed in World War); m. 2d, Charlotte Gertrude Wheeler, Aug. 3, 1893; children—Esther (Mrs. A. Leon Sikkenga), Robert Bruce, Donald Wheeler. Began teaching school, 1874; practice of medicine and surgery, Manchester, Ia., 1881-82, Alamo, Mich., 1882-1907, Kalamazoo, Mich., 1902-33, Orlando, Fla., since 1924. City commr., Kalamazoo, Mich., 4 terms. Mem. U.S. Bd. of Appeals, World War. Mem. A.M.A., Mich. Med. Soc., Kalamazoo Acad. of Medicine, Kalamazoo, Mich., and Orlando, Fla., chambers of commerce. Mason. Contbr. on hernia, snakes and snake poison, obstetrical subjects, etc. Home: Orlando, Fla. *

BUTLER, SHEPPARD, editor; b. Highland Park, Ill., July 9, 1883; s. Nathaniel and Florence Reeves (Sheppard) B.; student Coburn Classical Institute, Waterville, Me., 1895-99; A.B., Colby Coll., 1903; A.M., U. of Chicago, 1904; m. Bertha Ballou, Jan. 4, 1909; m. 2d, Martha McElliott, July 29, 1925. Mem. editorial staff Chicago Tribune, 1905-09, 1915-24 (dramatic critic, 1921-24); with Chicago Record Herald, 1909-15, Sunday editor, 1912-15; asso. editor Liberty Magazine, 1924-28, exec. editor, 1928-31, asso. editor, 1931-42; asso. editor Redbook Magazine, 1943-48, mng. editor since 1948. Mem. Phi Beta Kappa, Delta Kappa Epsilon. Home: Larchmont, N.Y. *

BUTLER, T. J., bldg. materials mfr.; b. Austin, Tex., May 25, 1884; s. Michael and Mary J. Butler; student jr. coll.; m. Hazel O. Butler, Feb. 14, 1924; children—T.J., Martin, Mary Jo (Mrs. W. Douglas Cooper). Pres., dir. Elgin-Butler Brick Co., Austin, Teci Prodn. Co. Mem. Structural Clay Products Inst. Washington (dir.), Clay Products Assn. S.W. (pres., dir.). Roman Catholic. K.C. Clubs: Austin, Austin

Country. Home: Austin TX *

BUTLER, THOMAS CLIFTON, chain food store exec.; b. Granville, N.Y., Nov. 14, 1900; s. Thomas A. and Agnes T. (Matthews) B.; student Green Mt. Coll., 1917; LL.D., St. Joseph's Coll., Phila., 1965; m. Helen V. Woods, Oct. 15, 1927; children—Robert C., Norman W. With Grand Union Co., 1918-77, sec.-treas., 1946-58, v.p., treas., 1958-60, pres., 1960-66, chief exec. officer, 1960-68, chmn., 1966-68, chmn. bd., 1968-74, chmn. emeritus, 1974-77; dir. First Nat. Bank N.J.; bd. mgrs. Bloomfield Savs. Bank (N.J.). Mem. N.J. Ednl. Facilities Authority; mem. borough council Glen Ridge, N.J., 1948-54, mayor, 1954-58. Bd. dirs. Better Bus. Bur. Met. N.Y., N.J. area Boy Scouts Am.; Trustee Nat. Conf. Christians and Jews, chmn. exec. com. N.J. region; trustee Acad. Food Mktg., St. Joseph's Coll., Marymount Coll.; chmn. bd. trustees Hosp. Service Plan (Blue Cross) N.J. Recipient Nat. Brotherhood award NCCJ, 1960; Meier Merchandising award Advt. Club N.Y., 1964; Human Relations award Am. Jewish Com., 1965; Freedoms Found. George Washington medal, 1967. Mem. N.J. C. of C. Clubs: Serra (West Essex, N.J.); Glen Ridge Country. Home: Glen Ridge, N.J. Died Oct. 30, 1977.

BUTTELMAN, CLIFFORD VINCENT, association exec.; b. Mankato, Minn., Apr. 8, 1886; s. Rev. John Henry and Margaret Ethel (Purdie) B.; ed. Ferris Inst., Big Rapids, Mich.; m. Eulalia Snyder, Feb. 26, 1913. With Big Rapids (Mich.) Evening Bulletin, 1906-08, exec. sec. Music Educators Nat. Conf. (dept. of N.E.A.) 1930-55, emeritus, 1955—, dir. publs., 1955—, mng. editor of assn. pubs.; Music Educators Jour., 1930—; practicing cons. in orgn. engring.; instr. in advt. sales correspondence, etc., Kalamazoo, Coll., Y.M.C.A., Parsons Bus. Coll., 1920-24. Mem. adv. com. on music Dept. of State, 1941-45; mem. sub-com. on music Army and Navy Com. on Welfare and Recreation, 1941-45; Music Teachers Nat. Assn. (exec. com. 1934-44), Nat. Interscholastic Music Activities Commission, American Musicological Society, Federation Music Clubs, Phi Mu Alpha. Republican. Methodist. Mason. Club: Ill. Athletic (Chicago). Editor of Boston (Mass.) Rotary Club Bulletin, 1925-27, organizing chmn. Jackson (Mich.) Rotary Club, 1915. Contbr articles to music mags, educational and trade jours. Home: Horton, Mich. *

BUTTERFIELD, RICHARD JOSEPH, TV sta. exec.; b. N.Y.C., Jan. 23, 1924; s. Robert Edwin and Catherine Eleanor (Morrissey) B.; student Syracuse U., 1945-47; m. Virginia P. Grace, Jan. 14, 1950; children—Catherine, Elizabeth, D'arcy, Richard Joseph, Virginia. With CBS TV, N.Y.C., 1947-55; gen. mgr. Sta. WARD-AM-TV, Johnstown, Pa., 1955-57; sta. mgr. Sta. KCRG AM-TV, Cedar Rapids, Ia., 1957-58; sta. mgr. Sta. KMSP-TV, Mpls., 1958-67, Sta. WHDH-TV, Boston, 1967-73; gen. mgr. KOIN-TV, Portland, Ore., 1973-78. Served with USAAF, 1941-45. Decorated Purple Heart. Mem. Nat. Assn. Broadcasters, Ore. Assn. Broadcasters, CBS Radio Affiliate (bd. dirs. 1975-76), Ad Club Am. Club: Portland Execs. Home: Lake Oswego, Oreg. Died Sept. 9, 1978.

BUTTERFIELD, VICTOR LLOYD, educator; b. Kingston, R.I., Feb. 7, 1904; s. Kenyon Leach and Harriet (Millard) B.; grad. Deerfield Acad., 1923; B.A., Cornell U., 1927, M.A., 1928; Ph.D., Harvard, 1936, LL.D., 1961; M.A. (hon.), Wesleyan U., 1942, L.H.D., 1967; LL.D. (hon.), Brown U., 1943, Amherst Coll., 1944, Williams Coll., 1944, Lawrence Coll., 1947, Columbia, 1954, Tulane U., 1957, Mount Allison (Can.), 1958, Dartmouth, 1967; Litt.D., Bowdoin Coll., 1955; L.H.D., Trinity Coll., 1946, U. Hartford, 1959, Boston Coll., 1965; D.Sc., Union U., 1961; m. Katharina Geyer, June 11, 1928; children—Margot (Mrs. Robert Siekman), Daniel Kenyon. Tchr. English, Deerfield Acad., 1928-29, Riverdale Sch., N.Y.C., 1929-31; instr. philosophy Lawrence Coll., 1934-35; dir. admissions Wesleyan U., Middletown, Conn., 1935-41, dean freshmen, 1938-41, asso. dean, 1941-42, acting pres., 1942-43, pres., 1943-67, pres., emeritus, 1967-75. Chmn., Conn. Commn. Selection for Rhodes Scholarships, 1946-49; chmn. com. faculty fellowships Fund for Advancement of Edn., Ford Found., 1951-54, study assignment ednl. situation in Near East, 1952-53; mem. coll. grants adv. com. Ford Found., 1955; mem. New Eng. Bd. Higher Edn., 1955-61; mem. vis. com. Harvard Divinity Sch., 1956-61, Philosophy Dept., Harvard, 1962-65; v.p. New Eng. Colls. Fund, Inc., 1958-60; cons. Ford Found. Humanities and Arts Program, 1960; mem. com. plans and objectives for higher edn. Am. Council of Edn., 1962-65; mem. adv. council Danforth Grad. Fellowship Program, 1963-65; mem. Nat. Com. on Accrediting Adv. Commn. to Study Influence on Higher Edn., 1963; mem. commn. coll. and soc. Assn. Am. Colls., 1966-69, mem. com. on liberal learning, 1966-69, chmn. spl. com. liberal studies, 1965-75; chmn. bd. selection E. Harris Harbison Award for Gifted Teaching, Danforth Found., 1967-69; cons. liberal studies Ford Found., 1969-75; mem. council Coll. Arts and Scis., Cornell U., 1958—; cons. Acad. for Ednl. Devel., 1969-70; pres. Nat. Council on Religion in Higher Edn., 1949-56, fellow, 1927-61. Alumni trustee Cornell U., 1946-51; trustee Edward W. Hazen Found., 1947-67; bd. regents U. Hartford, 1959-63; trustee Deerfield Acad., 1956-75, Wilbraham Acad., 1957-65, New Coll., 1965-75. Carnegie Corp. grantee, 1939, 52. Fellow Soc. for Religion in Higher Edn. (bd. dirs. 1962-75); mem. Am. Acad. Arts and Scis., Phi Beta Kappa, Beta Theta Pi. Club: University. Author: The Life of the Teacher, 1954; The Faith of a Liberal College, 1955; Counter Attack in Liberal Learning, 1966; numerous essays. Home: Middletown, Conn. Died Nov. 19, 1975; interred Wildwood Cemetery, Amherst, Mass.

BUTTERWORTH, JULIAN SCOTT, physician; b. Iowa City, Sept. 24, 1910; s. Julian Edward and Veta (Scott) B.; A.B., Cornell U., 1932, M.S. in Chemistry, 1933, M.D., 1937; Med.Sci.D., Columbia, 1942; m. Marjorie Moore, June 6, 1942; children—Barbara, David Scott. Intern, resident N.Y. Post Grad. Hosp., 1937-39, Mellville fellow cardiology, 1939-41; pvt. practice, N.Y.C., 1941-76; asso. prof. medicine N.Y. U. Sch. Medicine, 1949-76; mem. staff Bellevue, Univ. hosps. Served to maj. USAAF, 1942-45. Diplomate Am. Bd. Internal Medicine (cardiovascular diseases). Fellow A.C.P.; mem. Am. Heart Assn. (award of merit 1959, Gold Heart award 1965, pres. 1961-62), A.M.A. (Frank Billings Gold medal 1953), Sigma Xi. Author: Cardiac Auscultation, 1960. Died Mar. 26, 1976.

BUTTON, ROBERT YOUNG, lawyer, former state ofcl.; b. Culpeper, Va., Nov. 2, 1899; s. John Young and Margaret Agnes (Duncan) B.; LL.B., U. Va., 1922; m. Kathleen Mary Antoinette Cheape, Aug. 20, 1931; children—Kathleen Margaret (Mrs. L.H. Ginn), Robert Young. Admitted to Va. bar, 1922; practice in Culpeper, 1922-61, 70-77; atty. gen. Va., 1962-70. Dir. Mut. Fire Ins. Co. Loudoun, Mchts. Grocery Co. Culpeper, 2d Nat. Bank Culpeper, Central Hardware Co. Mem. Va. Commns. on Pub. Edn., 1954, 59, Potomac River Commn., 1958, Va. Bd. Edn., 1945-60, Va. Parole Bd., 1942-45. Mem. Va. Senate, 1946-61. Trustee Jamestown Corp. Fellow Am. Coll. Trial Lawyers, Am. Judicature Soc., Va. State Bar (council 1950-56), Am., Va., Richmond City, Culpeper County bar assns. Democrat. Baptist. Mason, Rotarian. Clubs: Culpeper Country; Commonwealth (Richmond). Home: Culpeper, Va. Died Sept. 1, 1977; buried Culpeper Masonic Cemetery, Culpeper, Va.

BUTTRICK, GEORGE ARTHUR, clergyman, educator; b. Seaham Harbour, Northumberland, Eng., Mar. 23, 1892; s. Tom and Jessie (Lambert) B.; grad. Lancaster Ind. Theol. Coll., Manchester, 1915, Victoria U. (honors in philosophy), 1915; D.D., Hamilton Coll., 1927, Middlebury Coll., 1930, Miami U., 1934, Princeton U., 1940, Harvard U., 1960, Grinnell Coll., 1963; Bucknell U., 1965; S.T.D., Yale U., 1932, Columbia U., 1944, Northwestern U., 1963; LL.D., Bethany Coll., 1940, Davidson Coll., 1970; Litt.D., Albright Coll., 1940; L.H.D., Wooster Coll., 1967; m. Agnes Gardner, June 27, 1916; children—John Arthur, George Robert, David Gardner. Ordained to ministry Congl. Ch., 1915; pastor 1st Union Congl. Ch., Quincy, Ill., 1915-18, 1st Congl. Ch., Rutland, Vt., 1919-21, 1st Presbyn Ch., Buffalo, 1921-27, Madison Ave. Presbyn. Ch., N.Y.C., 1927-54; Jessup lectr. Union Theol. Sem., N.Y.C., 1937-54; preacher to univ., Plummer prof. Christian morals Harvard U., 1954-60, emeritus; Harry Emerson Fosdick vis. prof. Union Theol. Sem., N.Y.C., 1960-61; prof. preaching Garrett Theol. Sem., Northwestern U., 1961-70; vis. prof. Vanderbilt U. Div. Sch., 1970-71; vis. lectr. Louisville Presbyn. Theol. Sem. and So. Bapt. Theol. Sem., Louisville, 1972-80; Joseph Cook lectr. various fgn. countries, 1951-52; William Belden Noble lectr. Harvard U., 1962; vis. prof. Chgo. Theol. Sem., 1962, Union Theol. Sem., Richmond, Va., 1963, 74, 76, Agnes Scott Coll., 1965; vis. lectr. Scripps Coll., So. Calif. Sch. Theology, 1966, Davidson Coll., 1970; past pres. Fed. Council Chs. Christ in Am. Recipient Gutenberg award Chgo. Bible Soc., 1966. Mem. Am. Acad. Arts and Scis. Author: The Parables, 1925; Jesus Came Preaching, 2d edit., 1970; Prayer, 1942; Christ and Men's Dilemma, 1946; So We Believe, So We Pray, 1951; Faith and Education, 1952; Sermons Preached in a University Church, 1959; Biblical Thought and the Secular University, 1960; Christ and History, 1963; God, Pain and Evil, 1966; The Beatitudes, 1968; The Power of Prayer Today, 1970; gen. editor: The Interpreter's Bible, 12 vols., 1952; editor: The Interpreter's Dictionary (4 vols.), 1959. Home: Louisville, Ky. Died Jan. 23, 1980; buried Charleroix, Mich.

BYERLY, PERRY, educator, seismologist; b. Clarinda, Ia., May 28, 1897; B.A., M.A., Ph.D., U. Cal., 1920-21, postgrad., 1921-24; LL.D., U. Cal. at Berkeley, 1966; children—Perry Edward, David Donald; m. 2d, Lillian Lizee, 1941. Instr. physics U. Nev., 1924-25; successively instr., asst. prof., asso. prof., prof. seismology U. Cal., 1925-64, chmn. dept. geol. scis., 1949-54, dir. emeritus seismographic stas., prof. emeritus. Guggenheim fellow, 1929, 52; Smith-Mundt Act lectr. Nat. U. Mexico, 1954; Condon lectr. U. Ore.; Sr. Fulbright scholar U. Cambridge (Eng.), 1960-61. Fellow Royal Astron. Soc., Geol. Soc. Am., Am. Geophys. Union, Internat. Assn. Seismology and Physics of Interior of Earth (pres. 1960-63), mem. Am. Acad. Arts and Scis., NRC, Washington Acad. Scis., Nat. Acad. Scis. (chmn. sect. geophysics 1957-60, chmn. panel seismology and gravity Internat. Geophys. Year 1956-58), Earthquake Engring. Research Inst., Seismol. Soc. Am. (hon., recipient medal 1975). Author: Seismology, 1942. Contbr. articles profl. jours. Home: Oakland, Calif. Died Sept. 26, 1978; inurned Chapel of Chimes, Oakland, Calif.

BYRD, BENJAMIN FRANKLIN, physician, med. dir.; b. Brookhaven, Miss., May 15, 1886; s. James Quitman and Isabel (Felder) B.; B.S., Miss. Coll., 1906; M.D., Vanderbilt 1916; m. Ida Muriel Brister, May 27, 1909; children—Frances Brister (dec.), Benjamin Franklin. Asst. chemist Vanderbilt Med. Sch. Nashville, 1913-17, acting prof. physiology and pharmacology, 1918-21; asst. med. dir. Nat. Life & Accident Ins. Co., Nashville, 1919-39, med. dir. since 1939. Chmn. med. bd. Tenn. Valley Authority and Tenn. State Tchrs. retirement systems. Fellow A.M.A.; mem. Am. Life Conv. (sec. med. sect. since 1933, chmn. since 1951), Nashville Acad. Medicine, Tenn. State, Davidson Co. med. socs., Middle Tenn. (past pres.), Am. (assembly mem.) heart assns., Tennessee State Heart Association (pres. 1953-55), Nashville C. of C. (hon. mem. bd. govs.), English Speaking Union, Am. Pub. Health Assn., Am. Diabetic Soc., Y.M.C.A. Bapt. (deacon). Mason (32 deg., Shriner). Clubs: Exchange (past pres.), Belle Meade Country (Nashville). Home: Nashville, Tenn. *

BYRNE, EUGENE HUGH, prof. history; b. Baraboo, Wis., Nov. 16, 1882; s. Thomas D. and Catherine (Monroe) B.; B.L., University of Wisconsin, 1903, fellow in history, 1909-10, Ph.D., 1915; Harrison fellow history, University of Pa., 1910-11; Guggenheim Fellow, 1930; m. Janet Macdonald, Dec. 22, 1913; children—Horace, Wayne. Engaged in business, 1903-09; instr. history, Amherst, 1911-12; apptd. instr. history, U. of Wis., 1912, prof. 1922-31, also chmn. course in humanities; prof. history, Barnard Coll. (Columbia), 1931-49, retired. Engaged in resrch. archives of Genoa, Italy, 5 periods, 1911-30. Mem. Col. House Commn. of Inquiry for the Near East, 1918. Mem. Mediaeval Acad. America, American Historical Assn., Wis. Hist. Soc., Am. Catholic Hist. Assn., Academy Political Science, Economic History Assn., Chi Psi; honorary mem. Societa Ligure di Storia Patria. Clubs: Century (New York), Au Sable Country. Catholic. Author: Genoese Shipping in the 12th and 13th Centuries, 1930; also special articles on medieval trade and commercial instns. Home: Princeton, N.J., also Keene, N.Y. *

BYRNE, JAMES MACGREGOR, fgn. service officer; b. Oyster Bay, N.Y., Aug. 18, 1909; s. James and Helen (MacGregor) B.; student St. Paul's Sch.; A.B., Harvard, 1931, LL.B., 1934; m. June Beakes, Nov. 27, 1946; children—Moyra (by previous marriage), Jill, Jaird, James MacGregor. Admitted to N.Y. bar, 1937; clk. with law firm, 1934-35; mem. Harvard-Columbus expdn., 1939-40; spl. asst. to Am. ambassador, Buenos Aires, 1941-45; fgn. service officer, 1946-64; assigned successively Bern, Dept. of State, Washington, Addis Ababa, Ethiopia, Tunis; asst. chief aviation div. Dept. of State, 1958-60, deputy coordinator of senior seminar in foreign policy Foreign Service Institute, 1960-62; mem. U.S. Mission to NATO, 1962-64. Member Association Bar City New York, Council Fgn. Relations N.Y. Club: Century Assn. (N.Y.C.). Home: Chevy Chase, Md. Died Nov. 30, 1979; buried Rock Creek Cemetery, Washington.

BYRNE, MIRIAM, author; b. Chicago, Jan. 13, 1884; d. James and Hannah (Elliott) B. Librarian Cook Co. (Ill.) Hosp., keeper of med. statistics and clin. records. Author: The Would-Be Witch, 1906; House of the Red Fox, 1907. Home: Chicago. *

BYRNES, HAZEL WEBSTER, institute ofcl.; b. Charles City, Ia., July 29, 1886; d. Abel Blinn and Susannah (Haines) Webster; B.A., Ia. State Tchrs. Coll., 1910; student U. Ia., 1925; M.A., Columbia, 1935; m. Frank Lloyd Byrnes, Jan. 1, 1912. Formerly faculty mem. state colls., Cedar Falls, Ia., Peru, Neb., Mayville, N.D., state librarian, Bismarck, N.D., 1948-65; asst. dean, research asst. Inst. Lifetime Learning, Long Beach, Cal., 1965—. Guest instr. U. Nev. Mem. joint nat. com. N.E.A.-A.L.A., 5 yrs.; del. Internat. Fedn. Library Assns., Rome, Italy, 1964. Mem. A.L.A. (mem. state council (9 yrs.), Adult Edn. Assn. U.S., N.E.A., Adminstrv. Women in Edn., Nat. League Am. Pen Women, Am. Assn. U. Women, P.E.O., Delta Kappa Gamma. Methodist. Club: Zonta. Author and editor numerous articles. Home: Petersburg, N.D.; Long Beach, Cal. *

BYRON, GOODLOE EDGAR, congressman; b. Williamsport, Md., June 22, 1929; s. William D. and Katharine (Edgar) B.; B.A., U. Va., 1951; J.D., George Washington U., 1953; m. Beverly Barton Butcher, Dec. 20, 1952; children—Goodloe Edgar, Barton Kimball, Mary McComas. Admitted to Md. and D.C. bars, 1953; law clk. to Judge Andrew Hood, D.C. Municipal Ct. Appeals, 1954; practice law, Frederick, Md., from 1958, county atty., 1959-62; mem. Md. Ho. of Dels., 1963-66, Md. Senate, 1967-70; mem. 92d-95th Congress from 6th Dist. Md. Legal adviser Frederick County San. Commn., 1960-66, Frederick County Planning

Commn., 1960-63; chmn. Md. Planning and Zoning Law Study Commn., 1967-70. Pres. Young Democratic Clubs Md., 1961-62. Mem. Md. Hist. Trust, 1963-78, Appalachian Trail Nat. Adv. Council, 1969-78; bd. visitors Md. Sch. for Deaf, 1964-78. Served from 1st lt. to capt. U.S. Army, 1955-58. Mem. Frederick Hist. Soc. (pres. 1962), Frederick County Bar Assn. Episcopalian. Mason (Shriner), Elk, Eagle, Red Man, Optimist. Club: Lewistown Ruritan. Home: Frederick, Md. Died Oct. 11, 1978; buried Antietam Nat. Cemetery, Sharpsburg, Md.

CABOT, CHARLES CODMAN, lawyer; b. Brookline, Mass., Nov. 22, 1900; s. Henry Broomfield and Anne Macmaster (Codman) C.; A.B., Harvard, 1922, LL.B., 1925; m. Ellen P. White, July 1, 1929; children—Charles Codman, Walter M. Admitted to Mass. bar; practice in various Boston offices; partner firm Ropes, Gray, Best, Coolidge and Rugg, 1933-43; asso. justice Mass. Superior Ct., 1943-47; partner firm Herrick, Smith, Donald, Farley and Ketchum. Sec. U.S. Strategic Bombing Survey, 1945. Chmn. Greater Boston United War Fund campaign, 1943; moderator, former chmn. Bd. Selectmen, Dover, Mass.; chmn. bd. dirs. Mass. Bay Transp. Authority, 1966-69; participant various charitable, civic and polit. enterprises. Trustee New Eng. Center Hosp., Milton Acad.; overseer Harvard Coll., 1944-50. Served as pvt. USMC, World War I. Mem. Mass., Boston bar assns. Home: Dover, Mass. Died Aug. 28, 1976.

CABOT, JOHN M., U.S. ambassador; b. Cambridge, Mass., Dec. 11, 1901; s. Godfrey Lowell and Maria (Buckminster) Moors C.; A.B. magna cum laude, Harvard, 1923; B.Litt., Brasenose Coll., Oxford, Eng., 1925; LL.D., Tufts U. (hon.), 1956; D.Fgn. Service (hon.), Suffolk U., 1966; m. Elizabeth Lewis, Apr. 2, 1932; children—Majorie Moors (Mrs. Antonio Enriquez-Savignac), John G.L., Lewis Pickering, Elizabeth Tracy (Mrs. Bogislav von Wentzel). Became U.S. fgn. service officer, 1926; vice consul, Callao-Lima, Peru, 1927-28; 3d sec., Dominican Republic, 1929-31, Mexico, 1931-32; 3d sec. and 2d sec., Rio de Janeiro, Brazil, 1932-35; 2d sec., The Hague, Netherlands, 1935-38; sec., Stockholm, Sweden, 1938-39, Guatemala, 1939-41; asst. chief div. Am. Republics, Dept. State, 1942, chief div. Caribbean and Central Am. affairs, 1944; counselor of embassy, Buenos Aires, Argentina, 1945-46, Belgrade, Yugoslavia, 1947; apptd. career minister, 1948; consul gen., Shanghai, China, 1948-49; minister to Finland, 1950-52; ambassador to Pakistan, 1952-53; asst. sec. of state for Inter-Am. affairs, 1953-54; U.S. A.E. and P. to Sweden, 1954-57; ambassador to Colombia, 1957-59, Brazil, 1959-61, Poland, 1962-65; dep. comdt. Nat. War Coll., 1965-66; lectr. Fletcher Sch. Law and Diplomacy, Tufts U., 1967-68; tech. officer U.S. delegations to Dumbarton Oaks, Mexico City and San Francisco Confs.; del. Conf. Am. States, Caracas, Venezuela, 1954. Decorated Grand Cross Order of So. Cross (Brazil). Mem. Am. Acad. Arts and Scis. Clubs: Metropolitan, Chevy Chase, University (Washington); Brook (N.Y.C.); Somerset (Boston). Author: The Racial Conflict in Transylvania, 1926; Toward Our Common American Destiny, 1955. Home: Washington, D.C. Died Feb. 1981.

CABOT, SAMUEL, mfg. chemist; b. Brookline, Mass., Apr. 30, 1884; s. Samuel and Helen Augusta (Nichols) C.; grad. St. Mark's Sch., Southborough, Mass., 1902; A.B., Harvard, 1906; student Mass. Inst. Tech., 1909; m. Nancy Graves, 1909; children—Samuel, Helen C. Lyman, Nancy C. Walton, Elizabeth C. Cochran. Mfg. chemist at Boston, 1906; past pres. Samuel Cabot, Inc.; pres. N.E. Felt Roofing Works; dir. Sulpho Napthol Co. Served as maj. 303d Inf., 1917-19. Fellow A.A.A.S., Am. Inst. Chemists; mem. Soc. Chem. Industry, Am. Chem. Soc., Delta Psi. Republican. Unitarian. Clubs: Tavern (Boston); The Country (Brookline). Home: Jamaica Plain, Mass.

CADBURY, HENRY JOEL, educator; b. Phila., Dec. 1, 1883; s. Joel and Anna Kaighn (Lowry) C.; A.B., Haverford Coll., 1903, Litt.D., 1933; A.M., Harvard, 1904, Ph.D., 1914; D.D., U. Glasgow, 1937; LL.D., Whittier Coll., 1951, Swarthmore Coll., 1954; L.H.D., Howard U., 1959, Earlham Coll., 1967; m. Lydia Caroline Brown, June 17, 1916; children—Elizabeth (Mrs. John K. Musgrave, Jr.), Christopher Joel, Warder Henry, Winifred (Mrs. Martin M. Beer). Asso. with Haverford Coll. 1910-19, Harvard, 1919-26, Bryn Mawr Coll., 1926-34; Hollis prof. divinity Harvard, also Dexter lectr. Bibl. lit., 1934-54, now emeritus; lectr. Pendle Hill, Wallingford, Pa., 1954-72, Haverford Coll., 1954-63; adj. prof. Temple U., 1962-66; sec. Am. Schs. Oriential Research, 1934-54; dir. Andover-Harvard Theol. Library, 1938-54; Lowell lectr., Boston, 1935, 53, Carew lectr. Hartford Sem., 1935; Shaffer lectr. Yale Div. Sch., 1946; Samuel A. Crozer lectr. Crozer Sem., 1953; Edward Cadbury lectr. U. Birmingham, 1956; Swarthmore lectr. at London Yearly Meeting, 1957. Chmn. bd. dirs. Bryn Mawr Coll., 1956-68. Mem. Am. Friends Service Com. (chmn. 1928-34, 1944-60; hon. chmn. 1960—, engaged child-feeding in Germany, summer 1920; commr. to Eng., winter 1941); mem. Am. Standard Bible Com., 1930-72. Fellow Am. Acad. Arts and Scis.; hon. mem. Oxford Soc. Hist. Theology; mem. Am. Oriental Soc., Soc. Bibl. Lit. (sec. 1916-33, pres. 1936; del. Am. Council Learned Socs., 1929-50), Am. Antiquarian Soc., Am. Philos. Soc., Studiorum Novi Testamenti Societas (pres. 1958-59), Phi Beta Kappa. Mem. Soc. of Friends. Pacifist. Author books including: The Making of Luke-Acts, 1927; George Fox's Book of Miracles, 1948; Letters to William Dewsbury, 1948; The Book of Acts in History, 1955; John Woolman in England, 1971; Friendly Heritage, 1972; Narrative Papers of George Fox, 1972; also articles on history of Quakerism, Bibl. subjects. Editor Annual of Am. Schs. of Oriental Research, 1927-32. Home: Haverford PA.

CADDICK, WILLIAM ANDREW, newspaper exec.; b. Avalon, Pa., Jan. 3, 1904; s. William Alfred and Susie (Millar) C.; B.S., U. Pitts., 1927; m. Kathleen McKain, Aug. 22, 1930; 1 son, George Lewis. Accountant, Barnes & Co., C.P.A.'s, Pitts., 1927-35; treasury agt. U.S. Treasury Dept., Terre Haute and Evansville, Ind., 1935-43; pub. accountant Caddick and Co., Evansville, 1943-54; partner Caddick, Gaither & Hortin, C.P.A.'s, Evansville, 1954-65; treas., dir. Evansville Courier, Inc., 1952-67, pres., dir., from 1967, also chmn. bd.; treas., dir. Evansville Printing Corp., 1963-67, chmn. bd., from 1968; treas., dir. Central Evansville Improvement Corp., 1963-67; sec., dir. Hercules Mfg. Co., Henderson, Ky., from 1959; sec., dir. Henderson Trailer Co., Colonial Mfg. Co. Treas., adv. bd. St. Mary's Hosp. Sec., trustee Downtown Evansville, Inc.; bd. dirs. Evansville Mus. Fine Arts and Sci. C.P.A., Ind., Ky., Ill. Mem. Nat. Assn. Accountants, Am. Soc. C.P.A.'s, Ind. Soc. C.P.A.'s, Evansville Petroleum Club. Episcopalian. Kiwanian, Elk. Clubs: Evansville Country, Evansville Kennel; Central Turners; Metropolitan Dinner (pres.). Home: Evansville, Ind. Died Apr. 1, 1980.

CADE, C(LAUDE) M(ARSHALL), coll. prof.; b. Capac, Mich., Aug. 29, 1885; s. Marshall M. and Anzonetta B. (Churchill) C.; B.S., Mich. State Coll., 1907, C. E., 1913, A.M., 1930; m. Agnes Hunt, July 10, 1915; children—William, Jane (Mrs. H.S. Huber), Richard. Instr., Purdue U., 1907-08; field officer U.S. Coast and Geodetic Survey, Washington, 1908-13; instr. civil engring. Mich. State Coll., 1913-16, asst. prof., 1916-23, asso. prof., 1923-37, prof. civil engring., 1937-52, emeritus; lectr. engring. San Diego (Cal.) State Coll.; cons. and asst. engr. City Lansing, 1917-25, Mich. Dept. Conservation, 1926; civil engring. consultant since 1916. Served as state rep. U.S. Coast and Geodetic Survey, 1932-34; mem. joint boundary survey, commn., Mich., Wis., Minn., 1948-49. Served as lt. col., U.S. Army, 1941-42. Mem. Vets. Fgn. Wars (hon.), Tau Beta Pi. Mason (life mem.). Home: East Lansing, Mich.

CADIEUX, MARCEL, Canadian diplomat; b. Montreal, Que., Can., June 17, 1915; s. Romeo and Berthe (Patenaude) C.; B.A., Andre Grasset Coll. (Can.), 1936; Licentiate Laws, U. Montreal, 1939; postgrad. McGill U., 1939-40; LL.D. univs. Montreal, 1964, Poitiers (France), 1966, Ottawa, 1968; m. Anita Comtois, Jan. 21, 1956; children—Francois, Rene. Called to Que. bar, 1939, named Queen's counsel, 1962; with Canadian Dept. External Affairs, Ottawa, Ont., 1941-44, London, Eng., 1944-45, Brussels, Belgium, 1945-47, head personnel div. Ottawa, 1948-51, Paris, France, 1951-54, Hanoi, Vietnam, 1954-55, head UN div., Ottawa, 1955-56; asst. under-sec. state for external affairs, legal adviser, Ottawa, 1956-60; dep. under-sec., legal adviser, 1960-64, under-sec., 1964-70; Canadian ambassador to U.S., Washington, 1970-75; prof. pub. internat. law Faculty of Law, U. Ottawa, 1956-63. Mem. UN Internat. Law Commn., 1961-66. Bd. govs. Nat. Film Bd. Can., 1958-69. Decorated companion Order of Can.; recipient Vanier gold medal Inst. Pub. Adminstrn. Can., 1969, Outstanding Achievement award of Pub. Service, 1969. Mem. Royal Soc. Roman Catholic. Clubs: Metropolitan, Chevy Chase (Washington); Rideau (Ottawa). Author: Le Ministere des Affaires Exterieures, 1949; Premieres Armes, 1950; Embruns, 1951; Le Diplomate Canadien, 1962; also articles. Home: Ottawa, Ont. Died Mar. 19, 1981.

CADIGAN, ROBERT JAMES, journalist; b. Mt. Vernon, N.Y., Jan. 22, 1912; s. Edward J. and Christina (Lindblom) C.; A.B., Swarthmore Coll., 1934; M.A., U. Chgo., 1942; Litt.D., Waynesburg Coll., 1950; H.L.D., U. Dubuque, 1956; LL.D., Carroll Coll., 1958; m. Rosemary Cowden, June 24. 1936; children—Kevin, Robert, Rosemary, Tchr. Amherst (Mass.) High Sch., 1935; chmn. English dept. Friends' Central Sch., Phila., 1935-44; free-lance mag. writer, 1944-45; asso. editor Holiday Mag., 1945-47; gen. mgr. Presbyn. Life Mag., 1947-79, editor, 1954-72; editor A.D. Mag., 1972-79; pres. Asso. Ch. Press, 1955-57. Served AUS, 1945. Mem. Phi Delta Kappa. Presbyn. Editor: (with H.H. Giles), Playwrights Present, 1942; September to June, 1942. Contbr. to popular mags. and tech. jours. Home: Swarthmore, Pa. Died Sept. 27, 1979.

CADOGAN, ALEXANDER GEORGE MONTAGU (KĂ-DUG'AN), Brit. govt. ofcl.; b. England, 1884; ed. Eton Sch. and Balliol Coll., Oxford U.; m. Lady Theodosia Gosford; 4 children. Began as attaché, Constantinople, Turkey, 1909; served in fgn. office, 1912, 14, at Vienna, Austria, 1913; apptd. 1st sec., 1919, and counsellor, 1928, doing special work with League of Nations, particularly in the Manchurian dispute; became minister to China, 1934, ambassador, 1935-36; served as deputy under-sec. of state, Foreign Office, 1936-38; became permanent under-sec. of state, 1938; attended Churchill-Roosevelt sea meeting, Aug. 1941. Decorated Companion of Bath, Knight Comdr. of St. Michael and St. George.*

CADY, GILBERT HAVEN (KA'DE), geologist; b. Chicago, Ill., Dec. 18, 1882; s. Martin Everts and Helen Louise (Howard) C.; B.A., Northwestern U., 1905, M.A., 1911; studied Yale, 1909-10, U. of Ill., 1910-11; Ph.D., U. of Chicago, 1917; m. Marian Adelia Denmark, July 26, 1906; children—Ruth Louise (Mrs. George H. Adams), Gilbert Haven (dec.), Mary Virginia (Mrs. Elmer F. Johnson), John Allan (dec.). Served on staff of State Geol. Survey of Ill., most of time, 1907-19; with exploration expdn. into Western Yunnan, China, 1919-20; prof. geology and head dept., U. of Ark., 1920-26; sr. geologist State Geol. Survey of Ill. since 1926, and head of coal div. since 1931. Mem. Geol. Soc. America, Am. Inst. Mining and Metall. Engrs., Soc. Econ. Geologists, A.A.A.S., Ill. Acad. Sciences, Ill. Mining Inst., Inst. of Fuel (London), Ill. Geological Soc., Pan-Am. Inst. Mining Engring. and Geology. Sigma Xi, Phi Beta Kappa, Delta Upsilon. Methodist. Club: Chaos. Author bulls. and repts. on geology and coal resources of Ill., etc. Home: Urbana, Ill.

CAEMMERER, H(ANS) PAUL, (KEM'MER-ER), author, historian, city planning consultant; born at Chandlerville, Illinois, June 24, 1884; son of Reverend Martin and Elizabeth (Schieferdecker) C.; A.B., George Washington U., 1916, A.M., 1917; LL.B., Georgetown U., 1924; special work, Wittenberg College, 1926; Ph.D., American U., 1938; architectural engring, Columbia Tech. Institute. 1943; m. Alice Louise Bailey, Aug. 16, 1932. Railway mail clerk, 1904-06; clerk Post Office Dept. (Washington, D.C., 1906-17, stenographer office of postmaster general, 1917-19; clk. Nat. Commn. of Fine Arts, 1919-20, asst. to sec., 1920-22, sec., 1922-54. Mem. Am. Planning and Civic Assn., Columbia Hist. Soc. (past pres.), Washington Bldg. Congress, Nat. Geog. Soc., Nat. Council Historic Sites and Bldg., Archaeol. Institute of America (life member). Lutheran. Author: Washington, The National Capital, 1932; Origin and Development of Washington, 1939; The Sesquicentennial of the L'Enfant Plan, 1940; The Sesquicentennial of the United States Capitol, 1943; Architects of the Capitol, 1945; History of the Gospel Mission, Washington, D.C., 1945; Our National Capital, 1946; Historic Washington, 1948; Life of Pierre Charles L'Enfant, 1950; Topographic Features of the Plan of Washington, 1952; The Corps of Engineers and The Capital City, 1953. Contbr. hist. articles to mags. Home: Alexandria, Va.

CAFFREY, DONALD JOHN, entomologist; b. Brooklyn, N.Y., Nov. 17, 1886; s. John Francis and Mary Abbie (Treacey) C.; grad. high sch., Gardner, Mass., 1905; B.S., Mass. Agrl. Coll., Amherst, 1909, grad. study, 1909-10; B.S., Boston U., 1909; m. Laura Mae Couture, of Toledo, Ohio, January 29, 1934. Assistant entomologist, Conn. Agrl. Expt. Sta., 1910-13; same, U.S. Dept. Agr., research on cereal and forage insects, in southwest, Colo. and Calif., 1913-17, on wire-worms in Md., 1917-18, successively asst. entomologist, asso. entomologist, entomologist, sr. entomologist, in charge European corn borer research, 1918-34; asst. chief div. of truck crops and garden insects, Bur. of Entomology and Plant Quarantine, U.S. Dept. Agr., since Mar. 1, 1934. Mem. Am. Assn. Econ. Entomologists, Entomol. Soc. America, Entomol. Soc. Washington. Catholic. Club: Cosmos. Contbr. to Jour. Econ. Entomology. Home: Washington, D.C.

CAIN, ARTHUR LEONARD, lawyer; b. Cleve., Oct. 20, 1924; s. Charles Arthur and Margaret Angeline (Beitel) C.; B.S., Case Inst. Tech., 1945; J.D., Western Res. U., 1950; m. Marjorie Louise Yonker, Dec. 20, 1945; children—Jeanne (Mrs. Larry Thomas Layne), Calvin, David. Admitted to Ohio bar, 1950, also U.S. Supreme Ct. bar; mem. firm Cain & Henn, Cleve. Councilman, Lakewood City, Ohio, 1963-67; mem. bd. edn., Strongsville, 1969-73; mem. Lakewood Planning Commn., 1955-62, chmn., 1960-62; Republican ward leader, Lakewood, 1950-68; chmn. Am. Party Ohio, 1970-77; vice chmn. Am. Party U.S., 1972-76; exec. vice chmn. Am. Independence Party, 1975-77. Served with USNR, 1942-46, 51-52. Mem. Strongsville C. of C. Mason. Home: Strongsville Ohio. Died July 17, 1977.

CAIN, JAMES MALLAHAN, newspaperman; b. Annapolis, Md., July 1, 1892; s. James William and Rose Cecilia (Mallahan) C.; A.B., Washington Coll., Chestertown, Md., 1910, A.M., 1917; m. Florence Macbeth, 1947. Mem. staff Balt. Am., 1917-18, Balt. Sun, 1918-23; prof. journalism St. John's Coll., Annapolis, 1923-24; editorial writer N.Y. World, 1924-31; mag., syndicate, and moving picture work, from 1931. Served as pvt. 1st class, Hdqr. Troop, 79th Div., A.E.F., 1918-19; editor-in-chief Lorraine Cross, ofcl. newspaper 79th Div., 1919. Democrat. Author: Our Government (sketches), 1930; (novels) The Postman Always Rings Twice, 1934, (play, 1936);

Double Indemnity, 1936; Serenade, 1937; Career in C Major, 1938; The Embezzler, 1940; Mildred Piece, 1941; Love's Lovely Counterfeit, 1942; Three of a Kind, 1943; Past All Dishonor, 1946; The Butterfly, 1947; Sinful Woman, 1947; The Moth, 1948; Jealous Woman, 1950; Galatea, 1953; The Root of His Evil, 1954; Mignon, 1962; The Magician's Wife, 1965; Rainbow's End, 1975; The Institute, 1976. Address: Hyattsville, Md. Died Oct. 27, 1977.

CAIN, JOSEPH ALEXANDER, artist, educator; b. Henderson, Tenn., May 27, 1920; s. Thomas Watson and Rose Anna (Wimberly) C.; B.F.A., U. Calif. at Berkeley, 1947, M.F.A., 1948; m. Mabe Louise Barton, Aug. 21, 1945; 1 dau., Jonizo. One-man shows include Centennial Mus., Corpus Christi, Tex., 1950, Richmond Art Center, 1951, Tex. Coll. Arts and Industries, 1952, Little Theatre, Corpus Christi, 1956, Victoria, Tex., 1957, Southwestern U., Georgetown, Tex., 1961, Incarnate Word Coll. San Antonio, 1961, Legoa Duncan Gallery, N.Y.C., 1963, U. Oreg., 1964, Williamantic (Conn.) State Coll., 1965, Laguna Gloria Austin, Fine Arts Library, Jersey City, 1968, Art Community Center, Corpus Christi, 1977, others; exhibited in over 700 group shows including Ahda Artz Gallery, Nat. Arts Club, N.A.D., Lynn Kottler Gallery, Am. Acad. and Inst. Arts and Letters, Richmond Art Center, La Jolla Art Center, Otis Art Inst., Oakland Art Mus., Palm Springs Desert Mus., Witte Mus., Dallas Mus. Fine Art, Houston Mus. Fine Arts, Art Mus. of South Tex., Chapman Gallery, Burch Wademan Mus., El Paso Mus., Beaumont Mus., Rosenberg Gallery, Abilene Fine Arts Mus., Butler State U., Brooks Meml. Mus., Birmingham Mus., Montgomery Mus., Cleve. Mus., Smithsonian Instn., Mus. of N.Mex., Pa. Acad. Fine Art, Sarasota Art Assn., Grand Central Galleries, Petite Gallerie, N.Y.C., Los Angeles County Mus., other museums, galleries U.S., Mexico, France, Japan, Can. tchr. art Corpus Christi High Sch., 1948-50, W.B. Ray High Sch., 1950-65, Corpus Christi Fine Arts Colony Workshops, Cain Studio, Corpus Christi; prof. art Delmar Coll., Corpus Christi, 1965-80; art editor Corpus Christi Caller-Times, 1955-73, critic, 1955-80; rep. permanent collections including Collection Contemporary Tex. Art, Michael M. Engel, M. Grubacher, Inc., Seton Hall U., Del Mar Coll., Goliad Library Rosenberg Gallery, Beaumont Mus., others; exhbn. casein paintings on nat. tour Old Bergen Art Guild, 1964-66, acrylic paintings on tour Old Bergen Art Guild, 1967-80; executed mosaic murals Spohn Hosp., Buccaneer Bowl, 1961. Mem. Corpus Christi Municipal Art Commn., 1968-72, chmn., 1972-73; mem. Corpus Christi Bicentennial Commn., 1973-80. Served to capt. USMCR, 1942-46, 50-52; col. Res. Recipient over 250 awards including Gold medal Seton Hall U., 1958; Sarah Goode award, 1963; Phila. Water Color Club prize Pa. Acad. Fine Arts, 1965; Purchase award Calif. show Nat. Watercolor Soc., 1969; Southwestern Mo. Mus. Assn. Purchase, 1973, top purchase First S.T.A.L. Nat. Exhbn., Shreveport, La., 1973; Juror's award of merit Central Pa. Festival Art Del Mar Coll. faculty devel. grantee, 1977-78. Fellow Royal Soc. Arts (London); mem. South Tex. Art League (pres. 1970-71), Tex. Watercolor Soc. (regional dir. 1958-80, 3d v.p. 1964-66), Tex. Fine Arts Assn. (regional dir. 1957-80, v.p. 1977-78), Sarasota, Miss. art assns., Calif., Ala., Nat. (hon. State rep.) watercolor socs., Corpus Christi Art Found., Nat. Soc. Painters in Casein (Grumbacher 1st award 1965), Nat. Artists and Art Patrons Soc. Contbr. articles to publs. Home: Corpus Christi, Tex. Died Sept. 8, 1980; buried Seaside Meml. Park and Mausoleum, Corpus Christi, Tex.

CALDER, ALEXANDER, sculptor; b. Phila., July 22, 1898; s. Alexander Stirling and Nanette (Lederer) C.; M.E., Stevens Inst. Tech., 1919; m. Louisa James, Jan. 17, 1931; children—Sandra, Mary. Devised Wire Sculpture, Paris, 1927, Stabiles, 1931, Mobiles, 1932, Constellations, 1943, gongs, towers, 1951; numerous one-man exhbns.; represented in numerous collections. Awarded 1st prize for non-Italian sculptor Biennale di Venezia, 1952; 1st prize sculpture Internat. Exhbn. Contemporary Painting and Sculpture, Pitts., 1958. Mem. Nat. Inst. Arts and Letters (Gold Medal award 1971). Address: Roxbury, Conn. Died Nov. 11, 1976.

CALDWELL, HARRY BURKHEAD, agrl. ins. co. exec.; b. Woodsfield, O., Nov. 23, 1908; s. Oliver F. and Elizabeth (Burkhead) C.; Dr. Humanities, N.C. State Coll., 1962; m. Margaret Virginia Hood, Apr. 3, 1930; children—Harry Burkhead, Robert Hood. Dir. orgn. and edn. N.C. State Grange, 1929-37, master, 1937, 47-61; sec.-treas. N.C. Grange Mut. Ins. Co., 1935-71, pres., treas., 1971; chmn. exec. com. Nat. Grange, 1951-67, chmn. fgn. relations com., 1939, agrl. com., 1938, 42, 47, legislative com., 1943, co-op. com., 1945, transp. com., 1948; del. Internat. Fedn. Agrl. Producers, Rome, 1953, Lafayette, Ind., 1957, Dublin, Ireland, 1963. Mem. interim agrl. adv. com. U.S. Dept. Agr., 1953; chmn. Nat. Agrl. Adv. Commn., 1961-65. Mem. N.C. Adv. Budget Commn., 1949-53, planning bd., 1942-43; exec. dir. Farm Labor Commn., N.C., 1943; mem. N.C. Tax study Commn., 1965-66, 67-68, Food and Fiber Commn., 1966-67, Commn. Study Revenue Structure of State. Exec. sec. N.C. Good Health Assn., 1946-47; mem. United Forces for Edn., 1947-61; pub. dir. Blue Cross Hosp. Savs. Assn., 1948-62. Recipient Distinguished Service award Faculty of U. N.C. Sch. Medicine, 1957. Mem. Am. Agrl. Assn. (chmn. cotton adv. com.), Nat. Planning Assn. (trustee 1944-45), N.C. Farmers Coop. Council of N.C. (exec. v.p.), N.C. Milk Producers Fedn. (dir.), Farmers Coop. Exchange (dir.), Tobacco Assos., Inc., Gamma Sigma Delta (hon.), Alpha Zeta (hon.). Baptist (v.p. gen. bd. 1951). Home: Greensboro, N.C. Died Mar. 4, 1980.

CALDWELL, IRENE CATHERINE SMITH, clergywoman, educator; b. Sublette, Kans., Aug. 29, 1908; s. O. Herbert and Eva L. (Henage) Smith; B.A., Northwestern State Coll., Okla., 1930; M.A., U. Okla., 1936; B.Th., Anderson (Ind.) Coll., 1939; M.A., Oberlin Sch. Theology, 1945; Ph.D., U. So. Calif., 1959; m. Mack M. Caldwell, Dec. 16, 1944. Prof. Warner Meml. U., Eastland, Tex., 1930-32; tchr. Cherokee (Okla.) High Sch., 1932-38; ordained to ministry Ch. of God, 1939; exec. sec. nat. bd. Christian edn. Ch. of God, 1939-45; chmn. dept. Christian edn. Warner Pacific Coll., Portland, Oreg., 1945-66, Anderson (Ind.) Coll. Sch. Theology, 1966-73; chmn. dept. Christian edn. Warner So. Coll., Lake Wales, Fla., 1973-79. Del. World Council Christian Edn. Assembly, Toronto, 1950, Lima, Peru, 1971. Bd. dirs. Community Action Council Madison County, Ind., 1967-73. Recipient Distinguished Service award Anderson Coll. Sch. Theology, 1973. Grantee World Council Chs., U. West Indies, 1968. Mem. Religious Edn. Assn. Author: Solving Church School Problems, 1944; Our Concern Is Children, 1948; Teaching That Makes a Difference, 1950; Adults Learn and Like It, 1955; Responsible Adults in the Church School Program, 1961; Basics for Communication in the Church, 1971; Teacher as Evangelist, 1972. Home: Lake Wales, Fla. Died Apr. 4, 1979.

CALDWELL, RALPH MERRILL, cons. cereal breeding; b. Brookings, S.D., June 27, 1903; s. Peter and Margaret (Christie) C.; B.S., S.D. State U., 1925; M.S., U. Wis., 1927, Ph.D., 1929; m. Margaret Dunlap, Sept. 12, 1931; 1 dau., Janet Harriet (Mrs. Ralph W. Storts). Asst. botany U. Wis., 1925-28; state leader in barberry eradication in Wis., U.S. Dept. Agr., 1928-30; agt. plant pathology U.S. Dept. Agr., Purdue U., 1930-31, asso. pathologist, 1931-37, chief, dept. botany and plant pathology Purdue U. Agrl. Expt. Sta., 1937-50, head dept. agrl. botany Purdue U., 1943-50, head dept. botany and plant pathology, 1950-54, prof. plant pathology, 1937-71, cons. cereal breeding DeKalb Agrl. Research Inc. from 1971. Fellow A.A.A.S., Am. Soc. Agronomy, Am. Phytopath. Soc. (treas.; bus. mgr. Phytopathology 1944-46, nat. councilor-at-large 1964-66); mem. Ind. Acad. Sci., Sigma Xi, Gamma Alpha, Phi Sigma, Alpha Zeta. Clubs: Rotary International, University (Lafayette); Torch. Editor: Phytopathology, 1954-57. Contbr. sci. papers profl. jours. Breeder disease and insect resistant wheat and oats and barley varieties. Home: West Lafayette, Ind. Deceased.

CALDWELL, ROBERT GRANVILLE, public official; b. Bogota, Colombia, Aug. 31, 1882, of Am. parents; s. Milton Etsil and Susanna (Adams) C.; B.A., Coll. of Wooster, 1904; Ph.D., Princeton, 1912; m. Edith Jones, 1915; children—Alice Wyman, Robert Granville, Janet. Instr., Forman Coll., India, 1904-06, Huron Coll., 1907-08, Coll. of Wooster, 1908-10; fellow in history, Princeton, 1910-12; prof. politics and economics, Coll. of Wooster, 1912-14; asst. prof. history, Rice Inst., 1914-19, prof. Am. history, 1919-33, dean, 1918-33; E.E. and M.P. to Portugal, 1933-37, to Bolivia, 1937-39; dean of humanities, Mass. Inst. of Tech. from 1939; chmn. cultural program with Latin America, Coordinator's Office, Nat. Defence Council, 1940-42; mem. gen. adv. com. Cultural Div., Dept. of State, 1941-43; visiting prof. of Latin Am. instns., Fletcher Sch. of Diplomacy, 1940-47; cultural officer Am. Embassy, Buenos Aires, 1948-52, Mexico City, 1952-54; U.S. mem. Inter-Am. Com. for Cultural Action, from 1954. Mem. Am. Hist. Assn., Phi Beta Kappa. Author: Lopez Expdns. to Cuba, 1915; A Short History of the American People, Vol. I, 1925, Vol. II, 1927; James A. Garfield—Party Chieftain, 1931; Role of the Parties, 1933; also articles on history and politics. Contbr. to Dictionary of Am. Biography. Home: Fishkill, N.Y. Died May 8, 1976.

CALDWELL, ROBERT TATE, lawyer; b. Taylor County, Ky., May 7, 1882; s. James Thomas and Annie (Read) C.; B.S., Centre Coll., Danville, Ky., 1903; student Centre Coll. Law Sch., 1906-08; m. Virginia B. Hoge, Dec. 27, 1916 (dec. 1962); m. 2d, Ruth Turner, 1963. Admitted to Ky. bar, 1908; instr. and coach, Selma Military Inst., 1908-10; practiced in Louisville, 1910-14; assistant atty. gen. for Ky., 1914-16; chmn. Ky. Workmen's Compensation Bd. (author of Ky. Workmen's Compensation Act), 1916-18; private practice, Ashland, Ky., since 1919; mem firm Caldwell & Hughes. Enlisted Field Arty., 1918; commd. capt., Nov. 1918. Adviser U.S. delegation Internat. Labor Conf., 1935; mem. Nat. Conf. of Commrs. Uniform State Laws (1944-50). Trustee Pikeville Coll. Mem. regional adv. conf. NLRB.; mem. Ky. All Industries Wage Bd., Ky. Adv. Com. on Nuclear Energy. Mem. Am., Ky. (pres. 1934, 35), Boyd County bar assns., Kappa Alpha (Southern), Order of Coif. Democrat. Presbyterian. Address: Ashland, Ky.

CALDWELL, SARAH CAMPBELL, educator; b. Newton Co., Ga., Dec. 31, 1904; d. Robert Walker and Mary Mabel (Patrick) Campbell; B.S., Woman's Coll. of Georgia, Milledgeville, 1928; Litt.D. (honorary), Akron University, 1952; Ped.D. (honorary), Bowling Green State U., 1953; m. Leslie Godfrey Caldwell, Aug. 21, 1935 (dec. 1965); 1 dau., Arline. Primary teacher, Sparta, Ga., 1923-25; critic, demonstrator Normal Tng. Sch., Atlanta, 1925-27, Ashley Hall, Charleston, S.C., 1927-29; primary tchr., Akron, 1929-31, high sch. tchr., 1931-54; teacher Roswell Kent Junior High Sch., Akron, 1954-63. Rep. N.E.A. dept. classroom tchrs., World Orgn. Teaching Profession meeting, Berne, Switzerland, 1949, head N.E.A. delegation 6th assembly, Copenhagen, Denmark, 1952; del. 7th Gen. Conf. UNESCO, Paris, 1952; chmn. delegation U.S.A. educators VI Congress Am. Educators, Montevideo, Uruguay, 1957; mem. Ednl. Policies Commn., 1950-54, 55-59, chmn., 1953-54; mem. Def. Adv. Com. on Women in the Services, 1954-57; mem. adv. com. on edn. Internat. Coop. Adminstrn., 1954-57; ednl. counselor, old master program Purdue U., 1962. Recipient Outstanding Service to Pub. Edn. citation Classroom Tchrs. Assn. N.Y., 1955; named Woman of Year, Akron Interclub Council Bus. and Profl. Women, 1948. Mem. World Confedn. of Orgns. of Teaching Profession (exec. com. from 1953, observer 8th Gen. Conf. UNESCO, Montevideo 1954), N.E.A. (pres. 1952-53). Malta Union Tchrs. (hon. pres.), League Women Voters, Bus. and Profl. Women's Club, Delta Kappa Gamma, Kappa Kappa Iota, Kappa Delta Pi; hon. life mem. Nat., Ohio congresses parents and tchrs., All Ceylon Union of Tchrs. Home: Akron, Ohio. Died Dec. 30, 1976.

CALDWELL, WILLIAM T., JR., chemist, educator; b. Pawtucket, R.I., May 29, 1895; s. William T. and Maria Louise (Pownall) C.; A.B., Princeton, 1915, grad. student, 1915-16; A.M., Yale, 1917, Ph.D., 1923; m. Rose Mary McGinness, Aug. 13, 1921; children—William T., 3d, Margaret, Mary Rose. Grad. asst. at Yale, 1916-17; Bureau of Mines, Chem. Warfare Sect., 1917-18; instr. Temple U., Phila., 1919-23, asso. prof., 1924-25, prof. chemistry and chmn. dept. chemistry, 1926-42; dean Coll. of Liberal Arts and Sciences, Temple U., 1942-61; v.p. dir. Research Inst. of Temple U., 1946-61. Mem. Am. Chem. Soc., AAAS. Author: Organic Chemistry, 1943. Home: Red Bank, N.J. Died June 30, 1976.

CALHOON, THOMAS BRUCE, educator; b. Columbus, Ohio, Dec. 15, 1926; s. Clair Henry and Virginia (Powell) C.; B.A., Ohio State U., 1948, Ph.D., 1952; m. Carmen Louise Day, June 11, 1950; children—Kenneth, Kay. Instr. physiology Ohio State U., 1951-52, asso. prof., 1963-66, prof., 1966-67; asst. prof. physiology Med. Coll. S.C., 1952-60, asso. prof., 1960-63; asst. dean basic sci. affairs U. Louisville Sch. Medicine, 1970-72, asst. dean curricular affairs, 1972-75, asso. dean, from 1975, prof., chmn. physiology and biophysics, from 1967; guest lectr. MSF Summer Inst. in Biomed. Engring. Sci., 1972, 73; vis. prof. physiology U. Tenn., 1970; vis. prof. anatomy and physiology Ind. U., 1971. Prin. investigator USPHS grant, 1959-66, United Fund S.C., 1960-63, Central Ohio Heart Assn. grant, 1965-67, Ky. Heart Assn. grant, 1968-71. Recipient Distinguished Tchr. award Ohio State U., 1966, Outstanding Freshman Tchr. awards U. Louisville Sch. Medicine, 1968, 71-75. Mem. Am. Physiol. Soc., A.A.A.S., Assn. Am. Med. Colls., Am. Inst. Biol. Scis., N.Y., Ohio acads. scis., Am. Heart Assn., Sigma Xi. Contbr. articles to profl. jours. Home: Louisville, Ky. Deceased.

CALHOUN, ARTHUR WALLACE, college prof.; b. Dayton, Pa., Jan. 29, 1885; s. Noah Franklin (M.D.) and Sara Nancy (White) C.; A.B., U. of Pittsburgh, 1906; A.M., U. of Wis., 1913; student summer quarter, George Peabody Coll. for Teachers, Nashville, Tenn., 1915; Ph.D., Clark U., 1916; m. Mildred Alice Tourtellot, of Hopkinton, Ia., Aug. 31, 1916; children—Donald Wallace, Robert Allan. Prof. English and philosophy, New Windsor (Md.) Coll., 1906-07; prof. Latin and history, St. Petersburg (Fla.) High Sch., 1907-09; instr. German and history, Fla. State Coll. for Women, 1910-11; prof. social science, Lenox Coll., Hopkinton, Ia., 1912-13, Maryville (Tenn.) Coll., 1913-15; asst. prof. social science, Clark Coll., and lecturer on sociology, Clark U., 1916-18; asst. prof. sociology, U. of Ky., 1918-19; prof. sociology, Ohio State U., summer session, 1919; ednl. dir. Tri-State Co-operative Assn., Pittsburgh, Pa., 1919-20; lecturer on co-operation, Rand Sch. of Social Science, N.Y. City, 1920-21; prof. commerce, Grove City (Pa.) Coll., 1921-22; prof. of history, Ala. Coll., summers 1923, 24; teacher social economics, Brookwood Labor Coll., 1923—, dir. of studies, 1924—. Author: Social History of the American Family, 3 vols., 1917-19; The Worker Looks at Government, 1927. Home: Brookwood, Katonah, N.Y.

CALHOUN, WILLIAM LOWNDES, naval officer; b. Palatka, Fla., July 13, 1885; s. Benjamin Putnam and Julia Catherine (Petermann) C.; g.g.s. of John C. Calhoun, U.S. senator from S.C., v.p. U.S.; B.S., U.S. Naval Acad., 1906; U.S. Naval War Coll., 1929-30; m. Margaret Young McCoy Anderson (niece Admiral E. A. Anderson, U.S. Navy, g.d. Dr. W. A. Anderson,

Yale, 1835), Jan. 31, 1911; children—William Lowndes, Jr., John Caldwell, Elizabeth Kirk (niece adopted as daughter; wife of Warren Welch, U.S. Navy); married 2d, 1st Lt. Rosalie Oneschuk, A.N.C., February 10, 1946; 1 son, Alexander Oneschuk. Commd. ensign, U.S. Navy, 1908, and advanced through the grades to rear adm., 1938. Command U.S.S. Rochester, 1932-33, U.S.S. California, 1937-38, chief of staff and aide Comdr. Battleships, Battle Force, 1938-39, Naval War Coll., 1939-40, comdr. Base Force U.S. Fleet, since 1940; comdr. Service Force, Pacific, 1942-45; commander South Pacific Force to October 23, 1945; vice adm. since Feb. 27, 1942. Decorated Victory medal with submarine clasp, World War; medal 2d Nicaraguan Campaign; Yangste River Medal, 1932; Am. Defense Service medal; Asiatic Pacific Area Campaign medal; Legion of Merit (gold star); 3 combat stars South Pacific Campaign; designated to wear Navy Combat V. Episcopalian. Clubs: Army-Navy (Manila); Brooklawn Country; Johnathan (Los Angeles). Home: Coronado, Calif.

CALL, ASA VICKREY, life ins. co. exec.; b. Los Angeles, Oct. 28, 1892; s. Joseph Harry and L'Dora (Vickrey) C.; student U. So. Calif., 1914, LL.D. (hon.), 1946; LL.D. (hon.), U. Calif., Los Angeles, 1960, U. Redlands (Calif.), 1955, Pepperdine U., Los Angeles, 1972; m. Margaret Fleming, May 23, 1917; children—Thomas F., Richard W., Janet Call Burby. Admitted to Calif. bar, 1914; partner firm Call & Call, Los Angeles, 1914-27, Call & Murphy, Los Angeles, 1928; with Pacific Mut. Life Ins. Co., Los Angeles, 1933-78, pres., 1942-56, chmn. bd., 1956-64, chmn. bd. dirs. exec. com., 1964-67, hon. chmn., 1967-78, also dir., mem. exec. com.; dir., mem. exec. com. Calif. Portland Cement Co., Cyprus Mines Corp.; dir. Asso. So. Investment Co., Standard Oil of Calif., N.Am. Aviation; hon. dir. Western Bancorp. Chmn., then hon. chmn. Music Center Operating Co., Los Angeles, 1971-72; trustee U. So. Calif., 1929-78, chmn., 1958-60. Named knight of St. Gregory, Vatican, 1967; recipient Achievement award U. So. Calif., 1965. Clubs: Los Angeles Country, California (Los Angeles); Pacific Union (San Francisco). Home: Beverly Hills, Calif. Died June 17, 1978.

CALLERY, MARY, sculptor; b. N.Y.C., June 19, 1903; d. James Dawson and Julia (Welch) Callery; student Art Students League, 1924-28; m. Frederic R. Coudert, Jr., June 23, 1923; 1 dau., Caroline (dec.); m. 2d, Carlo Frua de Angeli, May 7, 1934. One-woman shows art Curt Valentin Gallery, 1944, 47, 50, 52, 55, Arts Club, Chgo., 1945, Galerie Mai. Paris, 1949, Margaret Brown Gallery, 1951, Galerie Cahiers d'Art, Paris, 1954, B.C. Holland Gallery, Chgo., 1968, Daniel Morris Gallery, Detroit, 1968, 69; also exhbn. Knoedler & Co., 1957, 61, 62-64; commns. include Laughlin Children's Center, Sewickley, Pa., Internat. Expn., Brussels, 1958; public commns. include 3 hanging birds, Aluminum Co. Pitts., also portrait heads, R.K. Mellon-Fairless, Pitts., 3 hanging stars and moons Standard Oil N.J. (Exxon), N.Y.C.; grille in pub. sch., N.Y.C.; relief Bklyn. Ct. House; sculpture arch Lincoln Center Opera; work rep. Mus. Modern Art, Mus. Fine Arts Toledo, Mus. Fine Arts Cin., Mus. Fine Arts San Francisco, Addison Gallery, Andover, Atheneum, Hartford, Mus. Fine Arts, Richmond, Va., Mus. Fine Arts Phila., Whitney Mus. Fine Arts, also numerous pvt. collections. Address: Paris, France. Died Feb. 12, 1977.

CALLIMANOPULOS, PERICLES GRIGORIOS, shipping line exec.; b. Patras, Greece, Oct. 20, 1892; s. Gregory and Catherine (Sevastopoulos) C.; student schs., Patras, also pvt. study; m. Anna Sismanoglou, Feb. 19, 1931; children—Catherine, Mary, Gregory, Donna. Jr. clk. J. S. Coulis & Co., Alexandria, Egypt, 1911-13, br. mgr., 1913-18; ship broker, Piraeus, Greece, 1918-24, coal mcht., shipowner, 1924-79; dir. Fenton Steamship Co., Ltd., London, 1933-45, mng. dir., from 1945; founder, pres. Hellenic Lines, Ltd., 1934-79. Decorated knight comdr. Royal Order George I of Greece, 1954; Gold medal of merit Mcht. Marine, Greece, 1959; medal of St. Mark of the Patriachate Alexandria; also decorated by govts. of Italy, Jordan and Netherlands. Clubs: Whitehall Luncheon (N.Y.C.); Indian Harbor Yacht (Greenwich, Conn.); Westchester County (Rye, N.Y.). Home: Greenwich, Conn. Died Sept. 20, 1979; buried Piraeus, Greece.

CALLOWAY, AUGUSTUS JAMES, JR., utilities exec.; b. Texarkana, Tex., June 24, 1908; s. Augustus James and Alice Ann (Hawkins) C.; A.B., U. Mich., 1936; postgrad. Washington and Jefferson U., 1943-44; m. Mary Frances Billups, May 31, 1937; children—Augustus James III, Brian Joseph. Letter carrier Fed. Govt., 1936-37; investigator Welfare Dept., Detroit, 1938-40; comml. rep. Mich. Bell Tel. Co., Detroit, 1940-43, 46-50, mgr. pub. office, 1950-55, 57-61, staff rep. comml. personnel, 1955-57, mgr. bus. office, 1961-62, mgr. pub. relations, 1962-63, asst. mgr. customer relations, 1963-64, mgr. customer relations, 1964-67, dir. community affairs, 1967-71, asst. v.p. urban affairs, 1972-73. Mem. Trade Union Leadership Council, 1962-77. Bd. dirs. San Antoine YMCA, 1958-59, chmn. com. mgmt., 1958-60; chmn. Ambassador Bridge dist. Boy Scouts Am., 1961-63, recipient Silver Beaver award, 1973; mem. exec. com. Family Services Met. Detroit, 1964-77; v.p. Mich. United Fund, 1965-77; mem. Detroit Community Council, 1951-52, pres., 1953-55, mem. exec. com., 1954-56; mem. Detroit Council Polit. Edn., 1965-77. Trustee Mich. Coll. Osteo. Medicine, 1966-71, Burton Mercy Hosp.; bd. dirs. Delta Sigma Theta Home for Girls, 1967-71; bd. govs. Wayne State U., 1969-76, chmn., 1971-74. Served with USAAF, 1943-45. Recipient posthumous disting. service award Detroit chpt. NAACP; scholarship fund established in his name Wayne State U., 1977. Mem. Inst. Black Elected Ofcls., Booker T. Washington Bus. Assn. (pres. 1957-58), Alpha Phi Alpha, Sigma Pi Phi. Democrat. Optimist. Home: Detroit, Mich. Died Aug. 29, 1977; interred Woodlawn Cemetery, Detroit.

CALVERLEY, EDWIN ELLIOTT (KAL'VER-LE), prof. Arabic and Islamics; b. Philadelphia, Pa., Oct. 26, 1882; s. Benjamin Franklin Sr. and Ida (Reeves) Calverley; A.B., Princeton Univ., 1906, A.M., 1908; grad. Princeton Theol. Sem., 1909; Ph.D., Hartford Sem. Foundation, 1923; m. Eleanor Jane Taylor, M.D., Sept. 6, 1909; children—Grace Taylor (Mrs. C. Hans Evans). Elizabeth Reeves, (Mrs. Evan Lawn) Eleanor Taylor. (Mrs. Chas. H. Schafer) Ordained to ministry of Presbyterian Church of U.S.A. at Phila., 1908; missionary in Arabia of Reformed Church in America, 1909-30; prof. of Arabic and Islamics, 1937-51. Mem. Royal Asiatic Soc., Mediaeval Acad. of America, Royal Central Asian Society, Am. Oriental Soc., Oriental Soc. of the Hartford Sem. Foundation (secretary), Linguistic Society of America, Phi Beta Kappa; member Committee on Arabic and Islamic Studies of the American Council of Learned Socs., 1938-47, mem. com. on Near Eastern Studies, 1948-50; trustee v.p., mem. exec. com. Am. Research Center in Egypt; trustee Am. Univ., Cairo, Egypt, since 1939. Mem. Reformed Ch. in America. Author books. Editor: The Muslim World, 1947-52; dept. editor for comparative religion New Schaff-Herzog Ency. of Religious Knowledge. Member com. Versions of the Am. Bible Soc., 1938. Instr. in Intensive courses in Arabic at Columbia Univ. summers of 1942 and '43. Visiting prof. at Amer. Univ. at Cairo, Egypt, 1944-45. Home: Hartford, Conn.

CAMACHO, CARLOS GARCIA, gov. of Guam; b. Agana, Guam, Nov. 16, 1924; s. Felix M. and Antonia C. (Garcia) C.; student Aquinas Coll., 1947-50; D.D.S., Marquette U., 1954; m. Lourdes Duenas Perez, May 15, 1955; children—Carlos Anthony, Felix James, Thomas John, Mary Margaret, Ricardo Jose, Francis Gerard, Victor Charles. Mem. dental staff Guam Meml. Hosp., 1952-53, Cath. Med. Center, 1953-56, 58-69; appt. gov. of Guam by Pres. Richard M. Nixon, 1969-71, became Guam's 1st elected gov., 1971-74. Senator 8th Guam Legislature, 1964-66. Served as capt., Dental Corps, U.S. Army, 1956-58. Republican. Roman Catholic. K.C. (4 deg.). Address: Agana, Guam. Died Dec. 6, 1979.

CAMBERE, ARA ANGELE, investment banker; b. N.Y.C., Nov. 7, 1911; s. Haroutioun A. and Leontine (Canzuch) C.; B.S. in Econs., Wharton Sch. of U. Pa., 1933; m. Marion S. Quinn, Jan. 31, 1942 (dec. Mar. 1968); children—Yvonne, Mary-Frances (Mrs. G. Peter Mumbach), Peter, Kathleen (Mrs. Henry Muller), John, Richard; m. 2d, Francesca P. Cuzzi, 1971. Mem. promotion dept. N.Y. Sun, 1933-35; mem. buying dept. Hayden, Stone & Co., 1936-49; v.p., dir. Mfrs. Capital Corp., N.Y.C., 1949-51; pres., dir. Berry Motors, Inc., Corinth, Miss., 1951; v.p., dir. Oliver Steel & Iron Corp. Pitts., 1951-55; asst. to pres. Stewart-Warner Corp., Chgo., 1955-60; partner Hayden, Stone & Co., 1960-62; exec. v.p., dir. Hayden, Stone, Inc., N.Y.C., 1962-65, pres., dir., mem. exec. com., 1965-68, vice chmn., dir., mem. exec. com., 1968-70; chmn. bd. Haywood Mgmt. Corp., 1969-71; sr. v.p. Hornblower & Weeks, Noyes & Trask Inc., 1971-78; dir. Integrated Resources, Inc. Republican. Roman Catholic. Clubs: Duquesne (Pitts.); Chicago, Bond (Chgo.); Harbor View, Bond, Veterans 7th Regiment (N.Y.C.). Home: Bronxville, N.Y. Died Oct. 28, 1978.

CAMBIAIRE, CÉLESTIN PIERRE (KAM-BE-ÂR'), univ. prof.; b. Averyron, France, Dec. 22, 1883; s. Célestin and Victorine (Lebrou) C.; student Coll. of Bordeaux, France, 1896-1900; A.B., U. of Lille, France, 1901; Ph.B., U. of Paris, France, 1902; A.M., U. of Mo., 1922; grad. student U. of Chicago, summer 1922; Ph.D., State U. of Ia., 1925; unmarried. Came to U.S., 1904, naturalized, 1909. Instr. Forest High Sch., Dallas, Tex., 1918-19, Grubbs Coll., Arlington, Tex., 1910-20; instr. foreign lang., Sch. of Mines, U. of Mo., 1920-23, asst. prof., 1923-27; asst. prof. Romance langs., U. of Louisville, Ky., 1927-30; prof. Greek and Latin, Williamette U., Ore., 1930-31; head foreign langs. dept., Lincoln Memorial U., Harrogate, Tenn., 1931-33; professional lecturer in Romance langs., Univ. of Minn., 1934-35. Instr. Romance languages, College of the City of New York, since 1935. Officier d'Academie, conferred by French Govt. for work in edn., 1932, Officier de l'Instruction Publique, 1937. Member Modern Language Assn. of America, Am. Assn. Univ. Profs., Beta Pi Theta (grand pres. since 1927). Democrat. Author: Influence of Edgar Allan Poe in France, 1927; Fleurs d'Amérique (original poems in French, Spanish and English), 1927; Black Horse of Apocalypse, 1932; Le Probléme de la Prohibition, 1932; East Tennessee and West Virginia Mountain Ballads, 1934; My Rosary of Dreams (orig. poems), London, 1935; Le Rôle de la France Dans l'Expansion des Etats-Unis, 1935; (booklet) Louis Philippe in 18th Century America, 1946. Contributor of articles, also poems, book revs., to publications including Romanic Review, French Rev., Modern Lang. Notes, Revue France-Amérique, Bulletin Internat. du Vin, Louisville Herald-Post, Knoxville Sunday Jour., Claiborne Progress. Artes y Letras, etc. Composer: (songs) Down the Nile to Old Cairo; Give Me Youth and the World Is Mine. Poems have appeared in several anthologies. Contbr. poems to The Poet. Home: New York, N.Y.

CAMBRIDGE, GODFREY, comedian; b. N.Y.C., Feb. 26, 1933; s. Alexander and Sarah Cambridge; grad. Hofstra Coll.; student Coll. city N.Y.; student dramatic coaches. First profl. appearance in off-Broadway prodn. Take a Giant Step, 1956; Broadway appearances include Nature's Way, Detective Story, Lost in the Stars, The Blacks, Purlie Victorious, The Living Promise, A Funny Thing Happened on the Way to the Forum, How to be a Jewish Mother; film appearances include The Last Angry Man, Gone Are The Days, Purlie Victorious, The Troublemaker, The President's Analyst, The Busy Body, The Biggest Bundle of Them All, Bye Bye Braveman, Cotton Comes to Harlem; numerous TV appearances including Jack Paar show; recording artist for Epic Records; nightclub and coll. campus appearances. Recipient Obie award, 1961. Author: Put Downs and Put-Outs, 1967; also articles. Address: Ridgefield, Conn. Died Nov. 29, 1976.

CAMDEN, AUBREY HEYDEN, educator; b. Bedford Co., Va. July 28, 1886; s. Horsley Barnes and Willie Thomas (Campbell) C.; grad. Fork Union Mil. Acad., 1907; grad. U. of Richmond, 1911; m. Bessie Robert Wheat, of Bedford Co., Sept. 12, 1911; 1 son, Aubrey Snead. Instr. mathematics Fork Union Mil. Acad., 1911-12; prin. West End High Sch., Alexandria, Va., 1912-13; became connected with Chatham Training Sch., 1913, as prof. mathematics and dean; pres. Hargrave Military Academy since 1918. Democrat. Baptist. Home: Chatham, Va.

CAMERER, C(LYDE) B(RADLEY), naval med. officer (ret.); b. Kinmundy, Ill., Aug. 20, 1882; s. John Douglas and Annetta Adelaide (Bradley) C.; M.D., St. Louis Univ. Sch. Med., 1909; student, U.S. Naval Med. Sch., Washington, D.C., 1909-10, N.Y. Postgrad. Med. Sch., 1923-24; grad., Naval War Coll., 1935; m. Martha Louise Steuber, May 22, 1910. Entered U.S. Navy as Med. Officer, Oct. 12, 1909, advanced through grades to Rear Adm., 1945; with Root Commn. to Russia, 1917; Bgd. Surg. 3rd. Prov. Bdg., U.S.M.C., 1917-19; Med. Officer in Command, U.S. Naval Hosp., Canacao, P.I., 194041; Dist. Med. Officer, 9th Naval Dist., 1944, 14th Naval Dist., 1945-46; specialized in eye, ear, nose and throat work, 1913-46; ret. from active service, Nov. 1, 1946. Engaged in Red Cross work. Awarded Legion of Merit, World War II, Nicaraguan campaign, Mexican campaign, Haitian, China campaign medals, Am. and Asiatic area medals, Victory medals, (World Wars I & II), Marine Corps Expeditionay medal, and others. Fellow A.C.S.; mem. A.M.A., Nat. Sojourners, Mil. Order of World Wars, Nat. Geog. Soc., Alpha Kappa Kappa (charter mem. Alpha Mu chapt.). Protestant. Mason. Clubs: Jonanthan (Los Angeles), 4 Service (San Diego). Author numerous medical and historical articles. Home: San Diego, Calif.

CAMERON, BASIL, conductor; b. Reading, Eng., Aug. 18, 1885; ed. Grammar Sch., Tiverton, Eng., 1892-96, Hochschule für Musik, Berlin, Germany, 1901-03; unmarried. Founder, and first condr. Torquay Municipal Orchestra, at Torquay, Eng., 1912-15 (Wagner Centenary Festival, Apr. 1913, Strauss Festival, Apr. 1914); condr. Hastings Municipal Orchestra, 1923-30, Harrogate Municipal Orchestra, 1924-30, Royal Philharmonic Society's concerts, at London, 1928-31, Liverpool Philharmonic Soc., 1930, Prague Philharmonic Orchestra, at Prague, Czecho-Slovakia, 1930, B.B.C. Symphony concerts, at London, 1928-33, San Francisco Symphony Orchestra, 1930-32, Seattle (Wash.) Symphony Orchestra since 1932. Enlisted in 13th Batt., London Regt., 1915; gazetted as 2d lt., 1917; served in France, 1917-18; wounded in action at Bullecourt, Aug. 26, 1918. Mem. Church of England. Clubs: Savage (London, Eng.); University (Seattle). Address: Seattle, Wash. *

CAMERON, GEORGE GLENN, educator; b. Washington, Pa., July 30, 1905; s. William Byers and Elizabeth (Smith) C.; student Washington and Jefferson Coll., 1923-25; A.B., Muskingum Coll., New Concord, Ohio, 1927, Litt.D., 1952; A.M., U. Chgo., 1930, Ph.D., 1932; Ph.D. (hon.), U. Teheran, 1974; m. Frances Thomas, June 25, 1932 (dec. Aug. 1955); children—Thomas W., Douglas R.; m. 2d, Margaret F. Bell, Aug. 18, 1956; children—Elizabeth B., Mary M. Traveling fellow Oriental Institute, U. Chgo., 1930-32, instr. Oriental langs., asst. prof. of ancient Oriental hist., 1933-45, asso. prof., 1945-48; prof. of Near Eastern cultures, dept. Near Eastern studies U. Mich., 1948-75, emeritus, 1975-79, chmn. dept., 1948-69; annual prof., Baghdad Sch. of Am. Schs. of Oriental Research, organizer expdn. to Bisitun inscription of Darius, 1948-49; dir. U. of Mich. expdn. to the Near East, 1951; Haskell lectr. Oberlin College, 1954; Fulbright research scholar U. Göttingen, Germany, 1956-57. Decorated Order of Homayoun 2d class (Iran), 1949. Mem. Am. Oriental Soc. (pres. Midwest br. 1952-53), Am. Hist. Assn., Archaeol. Inst. America. Author: History of Early Iran, 1936, repub., 1971, also French trans.; Persepolis Treasury Tablets, 1948. Editor of posthumous work of Edward Chiera, They Wrote on Clay, 1938, trans. into French, German, Danish, Dutch; Am. Jour. of Semitic Langs. and Lits., 1940-41, Jour. of Near Eastern Studies, 1940-48. Home: Ann Arbor, Mich. Died Sept. 15, 1979.

CAMERON, J. WALTER, fruit canner; b. Canton, Mass., June 6, 1896; s. Colin Campbell and Mary E. (Pond) C.; student pub. schs., Brookline, Mass.; m. Frances H. Baldwin, July 17, 1924; children—Colin Campbell, Mary Ethel. With Street & Smith Pub. Co., Boston 1920-21. Hearst's Internat. mag., Boston, 1921-23; Advertisers Pub. Co., Honolulu, T.H., 1923-24; foreman Haleakala Ranch, Maui, T.H., 1924-26; mgr. Haleakala Pineapple Co., 1926-33; chmn., dir. Maui Pineapple Co. Ltd., 1933-76, Haleakala Dairy, Inc.; gen. mgr., pres., chmn. Alexander & Baldwin Inc., 1957-62; pres., dir. Haleakala Ranch Co., Ltd., Maui Electric Co., Ltd., Maui Pub. Co., Ltd., dir. Sheraton Corp. Hawaii, Hawaiian Telephone Co., Bank of Hawaii, Hawaiian Airlines Ltd. Chmn. mgmt. adv. com. Maui County Hosp. System, 1970-76; mem., chmn. mng. com. Kula Sanitorium, 1930-68. Served from 2d lt. to capt. U.S. Army, 1917-19. Mem. Hawaiian Sugar Planters Assn. (exec. com.), Pineapple Growers Assn. Hawaii. Clubs: Maui Country; Pacific (Honolulu); Pacific Union (San Francisco). Address: Kahului Maui, Hawaii. Died Jan. 2, 1976.

CAMM, FRANK, army officer; b. Lynchburg, Va., Jan. 8, 1895; s. John and Katherine (Ambler) C.; Va. Polytechnic Inst.; LL.B., Univ. of Va., 1917; grad. Saumur Field Artillery Sch., France, 1918, Camp St. Maur Tractor Artillery Sch., Paris, France, 1918, F.A. School, Fort Sill, Okla., 1924, Command and Gen. Staff Sch. (special course), 1941 (div. officer's course), 1942; m. Felicia Beall Taylor, June 3, 1921; children—Frank Ambler (U.S. Army), William Taylor, John Cary, Felicia Beall. Commd. 2d lt., F.A., U.S. Army, 1917, and advanced through the grades to brig. gen., 1951; served with the 55th Arty. (C.A.C.), 1918, France; regulating Sta. H, France and Germany, 1919; Instr. mil. sci. Harvard U., 1926-30; 17th Field Arty., Fort Bragg, N.C., 1930-34; adj. 13th F.A. Brigade, Schofield Barracks, Hawaii, 1934-36; prof. mil. sci. and tactics Xavier U., Cin., 1936-40; 28th Field Artillery and commander 56th Field Artillery, Fort Jackson, S.C., 1941-42; exec. officer 78th Div. Arty., Camp Butner, N.C., 1942-43; comdr. 15th F.A. Brigade, Fort Bragg, 1943; XIII Corps Arty., Camp Picket, Va., 1943; 78th Div. Arty., U.S., Eng., France, Belgium and Germany, 1943-46; 31st A.A.A. Brigade, Esslingen, Germany, 1946; spl. field rep. and dir. for Germany, Office of Foreign Liquidation Commr., Bad Orb, Germany, 1946-47; dep. for combat arms, general staff U.S. Army, 1948-50; asst. chief career management div., dept. of army, 1950-51; chief of military assistance advisory group, U.S. Embassy, Lisbon, Portugal, 1951-53, ret., 1953. Participated in campaigns: Meuse-Argonne, Aisne-Marne, 1918; Ardennes (Battle of the Bulge), Rhineland (Ramegen Bridge), Central Germany, 1944-45. Decorated Legion of Merit, Bronze Star Medal with oak leaf cluster, Commendation Ribbon (U.S.), Legion of Honor, Croix de Guerre with palm (France). Mem. Va. Law Review, Raven Society, Scabbard and Blade (hon.), Va. Alumni Assn., U.S. Armed Forces Assn., Am. Cancer Soc. (chmn. 3 years). Home: Monroe, Va. Died Dec. 16, 1976; buried Arlington Nat. Cemetery.

CAMP, JOHN M., mfg. exec.; b. Franklin, Va., Apr. 4, 1885; s. Paul D. and Ella (Cobb) C.; B.S., Va. Mil. Inst., 1905; A.M., U. Va., 1907; m. Mary Webb; children—Mary V. (Mrs. Charles L. Smith, Jr.), John M., Olive W. (Mrs. Lawrence M. Johnson). With Camp Mfg. Co., 1907-50, dir., 1913-56, v.p., gen. mgr. to 1956; treas., dir. Chesapeake-Camp Corp., 1938-43; dir. Union Bag-Camp Paper Corp., 1956—; officer, dir. several other corps. Bd. supervisors, Southampton County, Va., 1937—; director of lumber and wood products NRA, 1950-52. Pres. Va. Mil. Inst. Found., 1950—; bd. dirs. Va. Mil. Inst., 1942-50. Recipient diploma of distinguished merit Virginia Military Institute, 1960. Member Virginia Manufactures Association (president 1945-47), Va. Mil. Inst. Alumni Assn. (pres. 1948-50). Baptist. Clubs: Franklin Rotary; Commonwealth (Richmond, Va.); Princess Anne Country (Virginia Beach, Va.). Address: Franklin, Va.

CAMP, WILLIAM BACON, govt. ofcl.; b. Greenville, Tex., Nov. 25, 1913; s. William Hille and Marguerite (Bacon) C.; student Tex. Mil. Coll., 1932, Baylor U., 1933; m. Lida Eileen Conner, Nov. 23, 1947. With U.S. Office Comptroller, 1937-73, comptroller of currency, 1967-73; mem. faculty Stonier Sch. Banking, Rutgers U., from 1962. Mem. Christian Ch. (chmn. trustees, elder). Rotarian. Home: Rockville, Md. Died Nov. 13, 1975.

CAMPBELL, ALEXANDER, editor, author; b. Edinburgh, Scotland, Oct. 19, 1912; s. Alexander Maclean and Elizabeth (Morgan) C.; came to U.S., 1961; M.A. with first honours in Econs., Edinburgh U., 1934; m. Jane Young Lowe Shand, June 8, 1937; children—Morgan Brand, Kenneth Maclean, Lesley Ann. Editorial writer Scotsman Edinburgh, 1935-37, East London (South Africa) Daily Dispatch, 1937-42; asst. to editor The Star, Johannesburg, South Africa, 1942-50; bur. chief for Time-Life, Johannesburg, 1950-54, New Delhi, India, 1954-56, Tokyo, Japan, 1956-60, Middle East, 1960-61; Washington corr. The Economist, London, Eng., 1961-63; mng. editor New Republic, 1964-71; mem. editoral bd. Toronto (Ont., Can.) Daily Star, from 1970; editor Fin. Times of Can., Montreal, Que.; internat. affairs writer U.S. News and World Reports, 1973-77. Recipient award outstanding accomplishment fgn. corr. Sigma Delta Chi, 1954. Mem. Overseas Writers. Author: The Heart of Africa, 1954; The Heart of India (Overseas Press Club Am. award, 1959), 1958; The Heart of Japan, 1961; Unbind Your Sons, 1970; The Trouble With Americans, 1971. Home: Toronto, Ont., Can. Died Jan. 13, 1977.

CAMPBELL, ARTHUR BERL, banker; b. Tulsa, Jan. 28, 1914; s. George Albert and Edna (Summers) C.; B.S., U. Utah, 1950; grad. mgmt. and indsl. engring. Rensselaer Poly. Inst., 1952; m. Thelma Jean Canfield, Apr. 10, 1935; 1 son, Robert Arthur. Enlisted U.S. Navy, 1931, advanced through grades to comdr., 1959; ret., 1959; with First Nat. Bank Ariz., Phoenix, 1959-77, v.p., cashier, 1967-77. Bd. dirs. Family Service Phoenix, 1961-67, pres., 1966; bd. dirs. Metro Phoenix Nat. Alliance Businessmen, chmn., 1974; bd. dirs. Phoenix United Way. Mem. Phoenix C. of C., Valley Forward Assn., Navy League U.S. (pres. Ariz. 1966, nat. dir. 1966). Founder monthly econ. bull. profile of Ariz., 1963. Home: Phoenix, Ariz. Died July 1977.

CAMPBELL, CECIL RAYMOND, retail drug co. exec.; b. Gilman Ill., Aug. 17, 1907; s. Jason R. and Gerturde (Baker) C.; student U. Wis., 1926-30; M.B.A., U. Chgo., 1945; m. Jean C. Bartholomy, Apr. 27, 1935; children—Robert S., Charles R., James C. asst. buyer Mandel Bros. Dept. Store, Chgo., 1930-31; partner Anderson & Campbell Real Estate, Chgo., 1932-33; with Walgreen Co., Chgo., 1934-70, v.p., treas., dir. until 1970; dir. Mickelberry's Food Products Co. Mem., past pres. U. Chgo. Exec. Program; exec. com. U. Chgo. Grad. Sch. Bus.; pres. Cancer Research Fund; U. Chgo. Mem. Ill. C. of C. (past dir.), Urban Land Inst., Beta Gamma Sigma. Clubs: Executives, Economist (Chgo.); North Shore Country (Glenview); Chicago Curling (past pres.) (Northbrook, Ill.); Pere Marquette Rod and Gun (Mich.), La Quinta Country (Calif). Home: Glenview, Ill. Died Feb. 15, 1981.

CAMPBELL, ED HOYT, congressman; b. Battle Creek, Ia., Mar. 6, 1882; s. Romeo Hoyt and Hattie (Powell) C.; grad. high sch., Battle Creek, 1900; LL.B., State U. of Ia., 1906; m. Esta Fein, Oct. 24, 1913 (died Apr. 4, 1931); 1 son, Ed. Admitted to Ia. bar, 1906, began practice Battle Creek; mem. firm Campbell & Campbell; also farm operator. Served as pvt., inf., U.S.A., World War. Mayor of Battle Creek, 1906-11; mem. Ia. Ho. of Rep., 1911-13, Ia. State Senate (pres. pro tem. 1924-26), 1920-28; mem. 71st and 72d Congresses (1929-33), 11th Ia. Dist. Mem. Ia. State Bar Assn., Am. Legion, Phi Delta Phi. Republican. Presbyn. Mason (Shriner), Odd Fellow, K.P., O.E.S. Home: Battle Creek, Ia.

CAMPBELL, FRANK LESLIE (KAM'BEL), scientist; b. Philadelphia, Pa., September 5, 1898; s. Andrew Jackson and Esther Margaret (Williams) C.; student Haverford Coll., 1916-17; B.S. in Ch.E., Univ. of Pa., 1921; M.S., Rutgers Univ., 1924; D.Sc., Harvard, 1926; m. Elizabeth Mildred Boyd, Oct. 8, 1921 (dec. Jan. 25, 1946); children—Drew B., Lucile E.; m. 2d, Ina Mae Lee, April 17, 1947. Asst. prof. biology N.Y. U., 1926-27; entomologist Bur. of Entomology and Plant Quarantine, Washington, 1927-36; prof. entomology Ohio State U., 1936-43; editor The Scientific Monthly (A.A.A.S.), 1943-48; exec. sec., div. biology and agr. Nat. Research Council, from 1953. Fellow A.A.A.S.; mem. A.I.B.S. (exec. dir. 1953-55), Entomol. Soc. Am., Am. Chem. Soc., Washington Academy of Sciences (president 1959), Entomological Society Washington (president 1957). Clubs: Cosmos, Torch (pres. 1952-53) (Washington). Contbr. tech. articles on toxicology of insecticides and insect physiology. Home: Washington, D.C. Died July 13, 1979.

CAMPBELL, GEORGE MURRAY, railroad exec.; b. Cincinnati, O., Jan. 30, 1896; s. George Hollister and Lillian Townsend (Lytian) C.; student Leal's Sch. for Boys, Plainfield, N.J., 1908-13; Gilman Country Sch., Baltimore, Md., 1943-45; B.S., University of Mass., 1920, LL.D., 1955; married Irene Ivers Smith, June 17, 1922; children—Frederick Hollister, Edward Carleton, Anna May. College field agent and alumni sec. Univ. of Mass., 1920; with B. & O. R.R., since 1916 (except during service World War I), beginning as timekeeper, filled various clerical positions, traffic dept., 1921-23, freight rep., Baltimore, 1923, traveling indsl. agent, Pittsburgh, 1924-25, dist. freight rep., Jacksonville, Fla., 1925-29, dist. freight agent, Toledo, O., 1929-30, northwestern freight agent, Minneapolis, Minn., 1930-33, asst. gen. freight agent, Washington, D.C., 1933-37, asst. coal traffic mgr., Baltimore, 1937-38, coal traffic mgr., 1938-43, gen. freight traffic mgr., Baltimore, 1943-46, vice pres., exec. rep., Chicago, B. & O. R.R. and Baltimore & Ohio Chicago Terminal Railroad, 1946-61. Member of the Chicago Crime Commission. Served with the third Officers Training Corps, Plattsburgh, N.Y., 1918. Vice pres. Goodwill Industries (Chicago), Travelers Aid Soc., chmn. Mayor's Com. for Rehabilitation, Chgo. Trustee Burr and Burton Sem., Manchester, Vt., Glenwood Sch. for Boys (Ill.). Mem. Taxpayers Fedn. Ill., Soc. Colonial Wars, Phi Sigma Kappa (pres. found.). Republican. Conglist. Mason. Clubs: Executives, Commercial, Chicago, University, Adventurers' (Chgo.). Home: Winnetka, Ill. Died Dec. 8, 1979.

CAMPBELL, H(ARRY) BRUA, lawyer; b. Middletown, Pa., Dec. 16, 1885; s. Harry Brua and Annie (Nisley) C.; B.S., Gettysburg Coll., 1906; LL.B., Harvard, 1910. Admitted to N.Y. bar, 1912, U.S. Supreme Ct., 1920; law clk. Pierce & Greer, N.Y.C., 1910-20, mem. firm, 1920-52; past dir. Ann Arbor R.R. Co., N.J., Ind. & Ill. R.R. Co., Lake Erie & Ft. Wayne R.R. Co., Detroit & Western Ry., Mainistique & Lake Superior R.R. Co., Menominee & St. Paul Ry. Co., Ann Arbor Boat Co., Wabash Motor Transit Co. Served as 2d lt. inf., U.S. Army, 1917-19, A.E.F., 1918-19. Mem. Bar Assn. City N.Y., Phi Beta Kappa, Sigma Chi. Republican. Club: Union (N.Y.C.). Author: Legal Aspects of Transfer of Securities, 1920. Home: N.Y.C.

CAMPBELL, HARRY, consular service; b. Harper, Kan., Aug. 10, 1885; s. I. P. and Jessie (Graham) C.; Fairmount Coll., Wichita, Kan., 1903-05; A.B., U. of Kan., 1907; unmarried. In employ Bur. of Edn. and Bur. of Customs, P.I., 1908-15; apptd. v. consul at Singapore, Straits Settlements, July 14, 1915; apptd. consul, Oct. 18, 1915; on detail at Singapore, 1915-17, Penang, Apr.-July 1917, Singapore, July 1917-May 1918; consul at Soerabaya, Java, 1918-20; at Dept. of State, Washington, Dec. 1920-Feb. 1921; consul at Asuncion, Paraguay, Feb. 9, 1921-Sept. 1923, at Iquique, Chile, since 1923. Mem. Phi Gamma Delta. Home: Wichita, Kan.

CAMPBELL, HAYWARD, JR., research labs. exec.; b. Abbeville, La., Apr. 30, 1934; s. Hayward and Elodie (Simms) C.; B.S., So. U., 1954; M.S., U. Iowa, 1961, Ph.D., 1962; m. Thomasine McMillan, Dec. 26, 1959; children—Janet Michelle, Jennifer Hilary. Dept. head, biol. assay devel. Lilly Research Centre, Ltd., Eng., 1963-65, mgr. biol. devel., 1965-66, head ampoule pilot plant, 1966-68, head pharm. research, 1968-69, dir. product devel., 1969, dir. immunizing biologicals research and devel., 1969-71, mng. dir., 1971-73; dir. personnel sci. and medicine Lilly Research Labs., Indpls., 1973-74, exec. dir., 1974-76, v.p., 1976-78. Bd. dirs. Flanner House of Indpls., Boys Club, Marion County Cancer Soc. Served with M.S.C., AUS, 1954-56. Recipient Distinguished Alumni award U. Iowa, 1977. Mem. Am. Soc. Microbiologists, Sigma Xi. Presbyterian. Home: Indianapolis, Ind. Died Oct. 5, 1978.

CAMPBELL, IAN, geologist; b. Bismarck, N.D., Oct. 17, 1899; s. Dugald and Agnes (Gilkison) C.; A.B., U. Oreg., 1922, A.M., 1924; Ph.D., Harvard, 1931; Univ. fellow, Northwestern U., 1923-24; m. Catherine Robbins Chase, Sept. 16, 1930; 1 son, Dugald Robbins. Asst. prof. geology La. State U., 1925-28; instr. mineralogy and petrography Harvard, 1928-31; mem. faculty Calif. Inst. Tech., Pasadena 1931-78, prof. petrology, 1946-59, exec. officer div. geol. scis., 1952-59, research asso. in geology, 1959-70, prof. emeritus, 1970-78; state geologist, chief Calif. Div. Mines and Geology, 1959-69; dir. Calif. Dept. Conservation, 1966-67; mem. adv. council U. Calif. Inst. Marine Resources, 1962-68; commr. Am. Commn. on Stratigraphic Nomenclature, 1962-68; sec. Calif. Geothermal Resources Bd., 1967-69; research asso. geology Carnegie Instn. of Wash., 1932-38; mem. div. war research U. Calif., 1944-46; vis. com. geol. scis. Harvard Bd. Overseers, 1970-78, chmn., 1975-78; cons. geologist, 1926-59, 70-78; mem. Calif. Bd. Registration for Geologists, 1969-78, pres., 1972-74. Served with U.S. Army, 1917-19; AEF. Del. of 3 sci. socs. to 18th Internat. Geol. Congress, Gt. Britain, 1948; del. to 23d Internat. Geol. Congress, Prague, 1968, 25th, Australia, 1976. Recipient Scholarship Found. award, Am. Fedn. Mineral Socs., 1969. Mem. Am. Assn. Petroleum Geologists (Pub. service award 1973), Assn. Am. State Geologists (editor 1960-63, pres. 1965-66), Am. Assn. U. Profs. (nat. council 1957-60), Am. Inst. Mining and Metall. Engrs. (exec. com. San Francisco sect. 1961-70, chmn. 1967, Hardinge award 1962), Mineral. Soc. Am. (pres. 1962), Am. Geol. Inst. (pres. 1961, dir. 1955-64), Calif. Acad. Scis. (trustee 1960-76, research asso. geology 1969-78, sec. 1970-71, pres. 1971-75), Geol. Soc. Am. (councillor 1951-55, asso. editor 1963-67, pres. 1968), Le Conte Geol. Soc. (pres. 1963-64), Soc. Econ. Geol., A.A.A.S. (pres. Pacific div. 1957-58), Branner Geol. Soc. (pres. 1938), Am. Geophys. Union,

Assn. Engring. Geologists (hon.), Geochem. Soc., Nat. Assn. Geology Tchrs., Internat. Union Geol. Scis. (U.S. com. 1961-65), Soc. Mining Engrs. (western vice-chmn. 1966-69), Am. Inst. Prof. Geologists (Ben H. Parker Meml. medal 1970), Laymen's League, 91st Div. Assn., Phi Beta Kappa, Sigma Xi, Gamma Alpha, Unitarian. Clubs: Athenaeum, Commonwealth, Engineers (San Francisco). Mason. Asso. editor Am. Mineralogist, 1954-57. Contbr. articles to geol. jours. Home: San Francisco, Calif. Died Feb. 11, 1978.

CAMPBELL, JOHN PATRICK, artist, cartoonist; b. Belfast, Ireland, Mar. 7, 1883; s. William Henry and Catherine (Canmer) C.; ed. St. Malachy's Coll., Belfast, Castleknock Coll., Dublin; unmarried. Began as illustrator and cartoonist, Dublin, 1900; later drew cartoons for New Age (London), Ulster Guardian, Nomads Weekly, etc., and illustrations for books, Celtic legends, etc.; art dir. Ulster Lit. Theatre, Ireland, 1904-13, also producer of plays in London, Manchester, Dublin and other cities of Great Britain and Ireland; came to America, 1912; art dir. Irish Historic Pageant, prod. New York, May, 1913; prod. play "The Drone," at Auditorium, Baltimore, Belasco Theatre, Washington, Daly's Theatre, New York. Exhibited at Franco-British Exhbn., London; Brussels Exhbn.; St. Louis Exhbn., 1906; Ulster Arts Club Exhbn., Belfast, annually; Nat. Arts Club, etc. Mem. Belfast Art Soc., Irish Lit. Soc. (London), Irish Texts Soc. (London), Irish Arts and Crafts Soc. Prominent in creating the artistic, lit., musical and dramatic awakening in Ireland; founder and dir. Irish Theatre of America; identified with Veritas Photoplay Co., Cincinnati, O. Address: New York, N.Y.

CAMPBELL, L. MERLE, retired banker; b. Emlenton, Pa.; Sept. 17, 1886; s. Joseph A. and Lucy A. (Bell) C.; student Pa. State Normal Sch.; m. Ada McFeeters, Mar. 20, 1908; children—Geraldine (Mrs. Charles A. Perry), Gretchen (Mrs. William H. Liddle). Chmn. emeritus N.W. Pa. Bank & Trust Co., Oil City; dir. McCoy Natural Gas Co., Oil City Scarcroft Securities, Ltd., Toronto, Monongahela Connecting R.R., Aliquippa & So. R.R. Co., Cuyahoga Valley Ry. Co., Peoples Bldg. & Loan, Oil City. Past sec. banking Commonwealth Pa. Mason (32, Shriner). Clubs: Wanango Country, Oil City. Home: Oil City PA.

CAMPBELL, LEVIN H., JR., corp. exec.; b. Nov. 23, 1886; B.S., U.S. Naval Acad., 1909; LL.D. (hon.), U. of Ark.; m. Lucille Chapman Woods, 1913; 1 dau., Virginia (Mrs. George Francis Fox, III). Transferred to U.S. Army and commd. 2d lt. coast arty., 1911; promoted through grades to lt. gen., 1945; chief of Ordnance, 1942-46; v.p. International Harvester Company, 1946, became executive vice president, 1947. Decorated D.S.M. (Oak-Leaf Cluster) (Army), D.S.M. (Navy); Cross French Legion of Honor (officer), Knight Comdr. Most Excellent Order Brit. Empire; Crozier, Harrison and Jones medals. Mem. A.S.M.E., Am. Ordnance Assn. (pres.). Author: Industry-Ordnance Team, 1946. Home: Annapolis, Md.

CAMPBELL, NEIL, geologist; b. Medicine Hat, Alta., Can., Apr. 27, 1914; s. Duncan and Ruth (Wilson) C.; B.Sc. in Mining Engring., U. Alta., 1937; postgrad. Queen's U., 1938-39; Ph.D., Mass. Inst. Tech., 1943; LL.D., U. Alta., 1970; m. Eunice Engle Hull, Oct. 1, 1944; children—Alan N., John I., Laura Ruth. Sr. geologist Cominco Ltd., 1937-56, supt. exploration, 1957-64; chief geologist Cominco Am., Inc., Spokane, 1965-68; cons. geologist, Spokane, 1968-78; pres. Silvermont Inc., 1969-78. Registered profl. engr., Wash. Fellow Royal Soc. Can.; mem. Geol. Soc. Am., Soc. Econ. Geologists, Canadian Assn. Profl. Engrs., Am. Assn. Petroleum Geologists, Am. Inst. Metall. Engrs., Canadian Inst. Mining and Metallurgy (Barlow Meml. gold medal 1947), Sigma Xi. Contbr. articles to profl. jours., chpts. to vols. on field and econ. geology. Prin. geol. projects include Pine Point zinc, Con gold, Wedge copper, Vanscoy potash mines to Can., Magmont lead mines Mo. Home: Spokane, Wash. Died July 12, 1978; buried Medicine Hat, Alta., Can.

CAMPBELL, NICHOLAS JOSEPH, JR., petroleum co. exec.; b. Jersey City, N.J., Apr. 22, 1915; s. Nicholas Joseph and Clara Agnes (Zimmermann) C.; A.B., St. Vincent Coll., 1937, LL.D., 1965; J.D., Harvard, 1940; m. Katherine Mary Hickey, Apr. 10, 1944; 1 dau., Mary (Mrs. Patrick A. Caldwell). Mgr. law dept. Creole Petroleum Corp., Caracas, 1951-56, v.p., dir., N.Y.C., 1956; asso. gen. counsel Exxon Corp., N.Y.C., 1956-62, sr. v.p., dir., 1965-66, 71-76; dir. Esso Internat., Inc., N.Y.C., 1957-62; dir. Toa Nenryo Kogyo K.K., Tokyo, 1963-64; dir., pres. Esso Standard Sekiyu K.K., Tokyo, 1962-64; dir., chmn. Esso Africa, Inc., London, 1968-70; dir., pres. Esso Europe, Inc., London, 1966-70. Mem. adv. com. Center for Strategic and Internat. Studies Georgetown U.; bd. dirs. Am. Ditchley Found.; trustee Elizabeth Seton Coll., 1972-78, Teagle Found., 1972-78, Conf. Bd., 1976-78, Am. Arbitration Assn., 1975-78. Served to maj. USAAF, 1942-46. Mem. Nat. Planning Assn. (trustee), Am. Bar Assn., Am. Judicature Soc., Internat. Bar Assn., Acad. Polit. Sci., Am. Petroleum Inst. Contbr. articles to profl. jours. Home: Crestwood, N.Y. Died July 22, 1978.

CAMPBELL, ROBERT FARISS, lawyer; b. Cleburne, Tex., June 25, 1890; s. Clark Calhoun and Annie Juriah (Fariss) C.; student U. Tex., 1914; m. Genevieve Atkinson Carver, Mar. 12, 1918 (dec.); 1 son, Robert Fariss. Admitted to Tex. bar, 1914, practiced in Houston; mem. Andrews, Kurth, Campbell & Jones, attys. Served as 1st lt. 131st F.A., U.S. Army, 1917-19. Mem. Am., Houston bar assns., Phi Delta Theta, Phi Delta Phi. Democrat. Episcopalian. Mason. Clubs: River Oaks Country, Petroleum (Houston). Home: Houston, Tex. Died Aug. 14, 1976.

CAMPBELL, ROY ENGLISH, business exec.; b. Danville, Ill., July 20, 1885; s. Thomas Jefferson and Luella (English) C.; LL.B., U. of Minn., 1908; m. Willa C. Scobey, June 19, 1913; 1 dau., Elizabeth Campbell Palmer. Asst. atty. gen., State of Washington, 1910-16; with law firm, Donworth, Todd & Higgins, 1917-25; exec. v.p., chmn. bd. Arden Farms Co., since 1925. Dir., Washington Mut. Savs. Bank, dir., Puget Sound Power & Light Co. Trustee, Seattle Chamber of Commerce; mem. American Bar Assn., Washington State Bar Assn., Beta Theta Pi. Reoublican. Presbyterian. Clubs: Rainier, Seattle Golf. College. Washington Athletic. Home: Edmonds, Wash.

CAMPBELL, STANLEY HOWARD, univ. adminstr.; b. Front Royal, Va., June 16, 1906; s. Charles P. and Mary (Reller) C.; B.A. in Bus. Adminstrn., Pa. State U., 1932; m. Louise Will, Nov. 11, 1932; children—Thomas W., Richard W. Mem. staff Pa. State U., 1932-69, dir. housing and food service, 1960-61, v.p. bus., 1962-69, ret., 1969. Mem. Nat. U. Extension Assn. (dir. 1955-58), Eastern (mem. exec. com.), Nat. assns. coll. and univ. bus. officers, Acacia. Mason, Elk. Address: Naples, Fla. Died Apr. 9, 1980.

CAMPBELL, STEWART, mining engr.; b. Palisade, Nev., July 3, 1883; s. Neil and Catherine (Campbell) C.; B.S. in Mining Engring., U. of Idaho, 1907; m. Agnes C. Davis, Aug. 4, 1915; children—Norman Davis, Helen Shirley, Eugene Stewart. Engr. Idaho Consol. Mines Co., Minnie Moore Mine, Bellevue, Ida., 1907-09, Garfield Gulch Mining Co., July-Oct. 1909; contracting (principally mining), 1909-10; pvt. practice in mining engring. at Haily, Ida., 1910-21; elected insp. of mines, State of Ida., Nov. 1920, and 5 times reelected. Mem. Ida. legislature, 1913; served as 1st lt. engrs., U.S. Army; hon. disch. Jan. 10, 1919. Mem. Am. Inst. Mining and Metall. Engrs. Republican. Elk. Author of 23d-34th annual repts. Ida. Mining Industry, 1921-32. Consulting mining engineering. Home: Boise, Ida. *

CAMPBELL, STUART BLAND, lawyer; b. Wytheville, Va., Apr. 14, 1888; s. Archibald A. and Susie (Stuart) C.; A.B., Hampden-Sydney Coll., 1906; LL.B., U. of Va., 1910; m. Mary Rebecca Miles, Sept. 30, 1915; children—Stuart Bland, Martha Susan. Admitted to Va. bar, 1910, and began practice at Wytheville; commonwealth's atty. of Wythe County, 1911-16; pres. First Nat. Farmers Bank, Wytheville, Wytheville Hotel Corp., Wytheville Bldg. & Loan Assn. Chief yeoman U.S.N.R.F., during World War. Mem. Va. Representative Commrs. on Uniform State Laws, Va.; pres. Bd. Bar Examiners; mem. exec. com. Nat. Conf. Bar Examiners. Rep. Wythe County, Va. Gen. Assembly 1942-46. Recognized as outstanding lawyer of 50 yrs. practice Am. Bar Found., 1961. Member American Bar Assn. (mem. ho. of dels. 1938-58), Va. Bar Assn. (chmn. exec. com. 1934-35; pres. 1935-36), Am. Judicature Soc., Am. Law Inst., Raven Soc., Order of Coif, Phi Beta Kappa, Kappa Sigma. Democrat. Presbyn. Club: Commonwealth (Richmond, Va.). Home: Wytheville, Va. Died Nov. 17, 1973.

CAMPBELL, WILLIAM BURNSIDE, clergyman, educator; b. Garrard Co., Ky., Feb. 16, 1886; s. Hiram Barkley and Nannie (Burnside) C.; student, Transylvania U., Ky., 1905-06; A.B., Ky. Wesleyan Coll., 1908; Vanderbilt U., 1908-09; D.D., Wofford Coll., Spartanburg, S.C., 1921; m. Ruth Robb Finney, of Nashville, Tenn., Oct. 6, 1909. Ordained ministry M.E. Ch., S., 1909; pastor Walton, Ky., 1909, Williamstown, 1910-13, Georgetown, 1913-14, Maysville, 1914-19; Pres. Ky. Wesleyan Coll., 1919-24; pastor St. Paul's Ch., Parkersburg, W.Va., 1924-28, Highland Ch., Ft. Thomas, Ky., since 1928. Mem. Sigma Chi. Democrat. Past pres. Kiwanis. Home: Ft. Thomas, Ky.

CAMPIOLI, MARIO ETTORE, architect; b. Parma, Italy, Sept. 3, 1910; s. Marcello and Genevieve (Pesci) C.; student Columbia Sch. Architecture, 1930; B.Arch., N.Y. U., 1937; m. Margaret Giordano, May 28, 1933; children—Genevieve (Mrs. Irwin W. Kemp), Elizabeth (Mrs. J.R. Lovewell), Margaret (Mrs. Wesley W. Dement), Carl Michael. Asso., Dwight James Baum, architect, N.Y.C., 1928-39; prodn. mgr. Eggers & Higgins, architects, N.Y.C., 1940-49; dir. architecture Colonial Williamsburg, Inc., 1949-57; asso. Alfred Easton Poor, architect, N.Y.C., 1957-59; asst. architect of U.S. Capitol, 1959-80. Mem. bd. archtl. consultants Old Georgetown Act, Washington Commn. Fine Arts, 1965-71; bd. consultants U.S. Capitol Hist. Soc., 1966-81; mem. Fairfax County History Commn., 1971-81; mem. editorial adv. bd. Capitol Studies, U.S. Capitol Hist. Soc., 1976-81. Recipient Water Color award, Morse prize N.Y. U., 1932; medal in design Soc. Beaux Arts Architects, 1935; Michaelangelo award in architecture Sons Columbus in Am., 1970; Nat. Capitol award D.C. Council Engring. and Archtl. Socs., 1972. Fellow A.I.A.; mem. Am. Registered Architects (hon.), Soc. Archtl. Historians, Producers' Council (hon.), Nat. Sculpture Soc. (allied profl.). Home: McLean, Va. Died Jan. 8, 1981.

CANADAY, WARD MURPHEY, advt., housing financing, automobile mfg. co. exec.; b. New Castle, Ind., Dec. 12, 1885; s. Miles Murphey and Sarah Helena (Smith) C.; student U. Colo., 1903-05; A.B., Harvard, 1907; LL.D., Toledo U., 1945; H.H.D. Wooster (Ohio) Coll., 1967; m. Mariam Louise Coffin, June 15, 1912; 1 dau., Doreen Damaris (Mrs. Lyman Sptizer, Jr.). Advt. mgr. Hoosier Kitchen Cabinet Co., New Castle, 1907-16; pioneered time payment plan, 1907; advt. mgr. to dir. Willys-Overland Co., Toledo, 1916-21, chmn. bd. Willys-Overland Motors, Inc. (now Overland Investment Corp.), 1936-46, chmn. finance com., 1946-53, chmn. bd., from 1949, pres., 1950-63; dir. State St. Research & Mgmt. Co., Boston. Asst. in orgn. 1st automobile credit co., 1917; organizer U.S. Advt. Corp., Toledo, 1921, pres., from 1921; organizer Dealers' Finance Co. (automobile), 1925, later merging with Comml. Credit Co., Balt., dir., until 1961; apptd. chmn. orgn. rep. group Toledo bank depositors during crisis 1933; promoted passage Nat. Housing Act, 1933; asst. adminstr., dir. pub. relations FHA, 1933, 35. Mem. War Industries Bd., Non-War Constrn. Div., World War I; dir. devel. and prodn. of mil. vehicle later trademarked Jeep, World War II; U.S. co-chmn. Caribbean Commn., 1948-52; mem. bd. Nat. Indsl. Cont. Bd. Bd. dirs. Toledo Area Med. Coll. and Found., Fund for Peaceful Atomic Devel.; chmn. bd. trustee Toledo U. Endowment Found.; trustee Toledo Mus. Art, Archaeol. Inst. Am.; hon. trustee Green Mountain Horse Assn.; chmn. bd. trustees Am. Sch. Classical Studies, Greece; pres. Friends of Toledo U. Library. Decorated comdr. Order of Orange Nassau; Grand Cross Order of Phoenix (Greece); named hon. citizen City of Athens (Greece); recipient Eloy Alfaro medal, Cross Eloy Alfaro. Mem. Am. Ordnance Assn. (dir.). Unitarian. Clubs: Toledo Country, Inverness Country, Harvard (Toledo); Harvard (Vt.); Bohemian (San Francisco); Harvard, Recess. Economic, Brook, Explorers (N.Y.C.); 1925 F Street, Metropolitan, Nat. Press (Washington); Lake Placid (N.Y.); Detroit Athletic; Tennis, Country (St. Croix, V.I.); Lakota, Country (Woodstock, Vt.). Home: Ottawa Hills, Ohio. Died Feb. 27, 1976.

CANDELL, VICTOR, artist; b. Budapest, Hungary, May 11, 1903; s. Adolph and Esther (Fuchs) C.; m. Clara Steiner, 1927. Came to U.S., 1922, naturalized, 1927. Profl. artist, 1924-77; exhibited French galleries, 1928-31; mem. Whitney Art Project, 1934; mem. fine arts sect., art project WPA, 1936; exhibited Met. Mus. Art, Art Inst. Chgo., Albany Art Inst., U. Ill., Audubon Painters Soc., Whitney Mus. Art; executed mural for govt. of Iraq bldg., N.Y. Worlds Fair, 1939; rep. pvt. collections and collections of U.S. Govt., Met. Mus. Art, Corcoran Gallery Art, Washington, Newark Art Mus., U. Neb. Galleries, Montclair Mus. Art, Inst. Art and Letters, Whitney Mus. Am. Art, Carnegie Inst., Munson-Williams-Proctor Inst. (Utica, N.Y.), Brandeis U., Krannert Mus., Urbana, Ill., Tex. U. Mus., Austin, Notre Dame (Ind.) U. Coll.; lectr. tchr., art, 1941-77; mem. faculty Bklyn. Mus. Sch. Art, 1946-54, Cooper Union, 1954-68; asst. prof. art N.Y. U., from 1969; tchr. Silvermine Coll. Art, from 1961; vis. instr. Ohio U., 1951, Cranbrook Acad., 1958; guest critic Columbia Sch. Painting, 1952, 54; co-founder, dir. Provincetown (Mass.) Workshop, 1959-77. Recipient award Mus. Modern art exhbn., 1940, 2 awards U.S. Treasury, 1942, 1st prize drawing 30th Annual, Bklyn. Soc. Arts, 1st prize painting 34th Ann., 1950, Artists prize in painting 10th Ann., Audubon Artists, 1952, Emily Lowe prize, 1956, Lamont award for painting, 1961; Silver Mine Guild painting prize New Eng. Ann., 1968. Mem. Artists Equity Assn. (dir.), Allied Mems. Edward McDowell Assn., Provincetown Art Assn. (trustee), Audubon Artists (dir., Silver medal 1973). Home: New York, N.Y. Died Feb. 15, 1977.

CANDLER, ASA WARREN, lawyer; b. Atlanta, Aug. 30, 1914; s. Asa W. and Hattie Lee (West) C.; A.B., U. Ga., 1936; LL.B., Emory U., 1938; m. Elaine M. Davidson, Oct. 21, 1939; children—Gail Mary, Asa Warren III, David McDowell. Admitted to Ga. bar, 1938, since practiced in Atlanta; mem. firm Candler, Cox, Andrews & Hansen and predecessors, 1946-76; spl. agt. FBI, 1939-40; spl. asst. atty. gen., Ga., 1940. Sec. Pershing Point Pharmacy, Inc., Paragon Service Co. Inc., Reeder & McGaughey, Inc., Marler Oil Co.; dir. Palmer, Inc. Served to col. USAAF, 1941-45; brig. gen. Res. ret. Decorated Legion of Merit. Mem. Am., Ga. (bd. govs.), Atlanta (past pres.) bar assns., Am. Legion. Clubs: Touchdown (past pres.), Peachtree Racket (past pres.), Atlanta Athletic (bd. dirs.), Lawyers of Atlanta (past pres.) (Atlanta). Home: Atlanta, Ga. Died Nov. 18, 1976.

CANE, MELVILLE HENRY, lawyer, poet; b. Plattsburg, N.Y., Apr. 15, 1879; s. Henry William and Sophia (Goodman) C.; A.B., Columbia, 1900, LL.B., 1903; m. Florence Naumburg, Dec. 23, 1909;

children—Katherine (Mrs. Paul Marcus), Mary (Mrs. Arthur Robinson). Admitted to N.Y. bar, 1903; mem. firm Ernst, Lowenstein & Cane, and successors, N.Y.C. from 1905, then Ernst, Cane, Berner & Gitlin; specialized in copyright law, allied fields. Awarded medal for conspicuous alumni service Columbia, 1933; Columbia U. Medal for excellence in law, poetry, 1948. Mem. Assn. Bar of N.Y.C., Poetry Soc. Am. (Gold medal 1971). Author poetry including: A Wider Arc, 1947; Making a Poem (prose), 1953; And Pastures New, 1956; Bullet-Hunting 1960; To Build A Fire, 1964; So That It Flower, 1966; All and Sundry (autobiography), 1968; Eloquent April, 1971; The First Firefly, 1974; Snow Toward Evening, 1974. Co-editor: The Man from Main Street, 1953; The Golden Year, 1960. Contbr. articles, fiction and verse to leading mags. Home: New York, N.Y. Deceased.

CANFIELD, LEON H(ARDY), educator, historian; b. Binghamton, N.Y., Oct. 3, 1886; s. Andrew and Phebe (Hardy) C.; A.B., Syracuse U., 1908; Ph.D., Columbia University, 1913; LL.D., Fairleigh Dickinson University, 1956; married Luella Kinyon, Aug. 31, 1908 (dec.); children—Leon (dec.), Edith (Mrs. H. Gaylord); married 2d, Estelle R. Hess, Dec. 17, 1955. Instr. history Coll. City N.Y., 1909-42, head dept. evening, summer sessions, 1923-35; supr. history Townsend Harris, 1917-42; master history, head upper sch. Brunswick Sch., Greenwich, Conn., 1943-46; head dept. social sci. Fairleigh Dickinson Coll., 1947-56, prof., 1950-56, prof. emeritus, 1956—, dir. gen. studies, 1951-56, retired (leave of absence), 1956. Mem. Am. Hist. Assn. Author: The Early Persecutions of the Christians, 1913; The United States in the Making (with others), 1937; The Making of Modern America, 1950, 66; The Presidency of Woodrow Wilson: Prelude to a World in Crisis, 1966. Home: Ridgewood, N.J.

CANNON, BROWN W., food co. exec.; b. Denver, June 16, 1916; s. Hugh Brown and Margaret (Reynolds) C.; A.B., Stanford U., 1938; M.B.A., Harvard, 1940; m. Charla Gates Apr. 9, 1941; children—Brown W., Charles G., Reynolds G. With Beatrice Foods Co., Denver and Chgo., 1940-75, v.p. and dist. mgr., from 1948. exec. v.p., until 1975, also dir.; dir. United Bank of Denver, United Bank of Colo., Pub. Service Co. of Colo., Van Schaack & Co. Commr. Colo. Commn. Higher Edn. Trustee Nat. Jewish Hosp. and Research Center. Served as lt., USNR, 1942-45. Mem. Mountain States Employers Council (dir.), Zeta Psi. Rotarian. Home: Denver, Colo. Died Aug. 8, 1975; interred Fairmount Mausoleum, Denver.

CANNON, GEORGE W., mfr.; b. Springfield, Ill., Aug. 10, 1883; s. John C. and Alice (Flynn) C.; m. Irene Purtell, Oct. 27, 1909; children—George W., Jr., Bernice A. (Mrs. Wm. H. Nicholls), Margaret M. (Mrs. John F. Fredericks), William J. With Campbell, Wyant & Cannon Foundry Co., Muskegon, Mich., since 1908, v.p., 1908-44, pres. since 1944, chmn. of bd., 1947. Home: North Muskegon, Mich.

CANNON, HOWARD HENRY, lawyer; b. Lyons Falls, N.Y., June 26, 1903; s. George C. and Joanna (Cassidy) C.; A.B., Hamilton Coll., 1923; LL.B., Harvard, 1927; m. Marion E. Schermerhorn, Aug. 31, 1929; children—Mary Ellen (Mrs. N. Austin Weston), Elizabeth A. (Mrs. Frank E. Gump). Admitted to N.Y. bar, 1927, practiced in Syracuse; asso. Bond, Schoeneck & King, 1927-45, partner, 1945-79. Sec., dir. A.E. Nettleton Co.; dir., mem. exec. com. Lincoln First Bank Central, 1937-77. Mem. vis. com. Harvard Law Sch., 1961-67; chmn. com. Harvard Law Sch. Fund, 1953-76, Harvard Law Sch. Sesquicentennial Fund Upstate N.Y., 1966-70. Bd. dirs. Blue Shield of Central N.Y., Inc., 1954-74; bd. dirs. N.Y. Higher Edn. Assistance Corp., 1957-73, chmn., 1961-65; trustee Ct. of Appeals Library; treas., bd. dirs. J. Stanley Coyne Found.; pres., trustee Cogar Found., Inc. Recipient Man of Year award for community service Greater Syracuse C. of C., 1966; Bell Ringer award Hamilton Coll. Fellow Am. Bar Found.; mem. Am., N.Y. State (past sect. chmn., mem. exec. com.), Onondaga County (Distinguished Lawyer of Year award 1975) bar assns., Am. Judicature Soc., Greater Syracuse C. of C. (past pres.), Harvard Law Sch. Assn. Upstate N.Y. (past pres.). Democrat. Roman Catholic. Clubs: University, Onondaga Golf and Country, Century (Syracuse). Home: Syracuse, N.Y. Died Mar. 20, 1979.

CANNON, LEGRAND, JR., author; b. New Haven, Conn., Dec. 1, 1899; s. LeGrand and Florence (Pond) C.; Ph.B., Yale U., 1920; M.B.A., Harvard U., 1922; m. Jeannette Peabody, Dec. 30, 1922; children—Jeannette, LeGrand, 3d, Winthrop, Margaret. Author: A Mighty Fortress, 1937; The Kents, 1938; Look to the Mountain, 1942; Come Home at Even, 1951. Home: New Haven, Conn. Died Dec. 12, 1979.

CANNON, ROBERT M., army officer; b. Utah, Aug. 16, 1901; B.S., U.S. Mil. Acad., 1925; grad. Air Corps Primary Flying Sch., 1927, F.A. Sch., battery officers course, 1931, Command and Gen. Staff Sch., 1938; attended Basic Airborne Course, 1948; m. Jo Riter; children—Jo Anne, Robert. Commd. 2d lt., U. S. Army, 1925, and advanced through the grades to lt. gen., 1957; comdg. gen. 82d Airborne Div., Ft. Bragg, N.C., 1948-51; spl. asst. to the Joint Chiefs of Staff, 1955-57; dep. comdr. in chief, chief staff U.S. Army, Pacific, Ft. Shafter, Hawaii, 1957-59; comdg. gen. 6th U.S. Army, 1959-61. Decorated Distinguished Service medal, Bronze Star, Air medal, Combat Infantryman's badge, Comdr. Brit. Empire, Order Cloud and Banner (Republic of China). Rated parachutist and gliderman. Address: San Francisco, Calif. Died Sept. 3, 1976.

CANTAROW, ABRAHAM, biochemist, educator; b. Hartford, Conn., Jan. 27, 1901; s. Joseph and Helen (Karp) C.; student Tufts Coll., 1917-20; M.D., Jefferson Med. Coll., 1924, D.Sc. (hon.), 1968; m. Elizabeth Stern, Aug. 1, 1932; 1 dau., Ellen. Intern Jefferson Med. Coll. Hosp., 1924-27, resident instr., asst. prof., asso. prof. medicine Jefferson Med. Coll., 1927-45, prof. biochemistry, head dept., 1945-66, prof. biochemistry emeritus, 1966-79; biochemist Jefferson Med. Coll. Hosp., 1932-45, asst. physician, 1936-45; research planning officer Nat. Cancer Inst., Bethesda, Md., 1966-75, spl. cons., 1975-79; cons. in biochemistry Bur. Medicine and Surgery, U.S. Navy, from 1947. Mem. study sect. NIH, 1960-64. Recipient Silver medal U. Helsinki, 1963, Sci. award Phi Lambda Kappa, 1963. Mem. Am. Assn. Cancer Research (dir., pres. 1969), Am. Physiol. Soc., Am. Soc. Pharmacology Exptl. Therapeutics, Endocrine Soc., A.A.A.S., Soc. Exptl. Biology and Medicine, Phila. Biochemists Club, Sigma Xi, Alpha Omega Alpha. Author: Textbook of biochemistry, 1954; Clinical Biochemistry, 1932; Clinical Endocrinology, 1954; Calcium Metabolism, 1932; Lead Poisoning, 1940. Mem. editorial bd. Metabolism. Home: Washington, D.C. Died Sept. 1, 1979.

CANTRELL, JOHN HOWARD, lawyer, bus. exec.; b. Dardanelle, Ark., July 17, 1898; s. John Marion and Martha Jane (Bearden) C.; A.B., U. Okla., 1921, LL.B., 1924; m. Lucille Josephine Farish, June 6, 1925; 1 son, John Edward. Admitted to Okla. bar, 1924; with firm Biddison & Campbell, Tulsa, 1924-34; gen. counsel Southwestern Bell Telephone Co., Oklahoma City, 1934-54; v.p., gen. counsel C.R. Anthony Co., Oklahoma City, 1954-60; with firm Cantrell, Douglass, Thompson & Wilson, Oklahoma City, 1960-75; of counsel Thompson, Thompson, Harbour, Nance & Selfph, Oklahoma City, 1975-80. Mem. Oklahoma City Charter Revision Com., 1954. Served with USMC, 1918-19; AEF. Fellow Am. Coll. Trial Lawyers (Okla. chmn. 1970-71), Am. Bar Found. (Okla. chmn. 1970-71); mem. Am. (state del. 1942-46), Okla. (pres. 1941-42), Oklahoma County (pres. 1938), Tulsa County (pres. 1931) bar assns., Oklahoma City C. of C. (chmn. govtl. relations div. 1954), Am. Legion, Order of Coif, Phi Delta Phi, Sigma Alpha Epsilon. Methodist. Rotarian. Club: Beacon. Home: Oklahoma City, Okla. Died Apr. 19, 1980; buried Rose Hill Cemetery, Oklahoma City.

CANTWELL, CONAN, lawyer; b. Corsicana, Tex., July 2, 1907; s. James William and Ada (Westmoreland) C.; A.B., U. Kans., 1928, LL.B., 1930; m. Pauline Bramlette, July 28, 1937; children—Carolyn, Conan, Nancy Lawrence. Admitted to Tex. bar 1930; practice in Dallas, 1936-77; mem. firm Jackson, Walker, Winstead Cantwell & Miler; spl. dist. judge, 1934. Past chmn. grievance com. Fifth Congl. Dist of Tex. Served to lt. USNR, World War II. Fellow Am., Tex. bar founds.; mem. Am., Tex., Dallas (pres. 1958) bar assns., Am. Judicature Sec., Tex. Surveyors Assn., Phi Delta Phi, Beta Theta Pi. Clubs: Dallas Petroleum, Brookhollow Golf, (Dallas). Author publs. in field. Home: Dallas, Tex. Died Jan. 21, 1977; interred Hillcrest Meml. Park, Dallas.

CANTWELL, ROBERT EMMETT, author; b. Little Falls (now Vader), Wash., Jan. 31, 1908; s. Charles James and Nina Adelia (Hanson) C.; student U. Wash., 1924-25; m. Mary Elizabeth Chambers (dec.); children—Joan McNiece (Mrs. George Stolz), Betsy Ann (Mrs. Walter Pusey III), Mary Elizabeth (Mrs. Lars-Erik Nelson); m. 2d, Allison Semmes Joy (div.); m. 3d, Eva Stolz, Oct. 3, 1978; stepchildren—Patricia C., William John, Louis George, Eva Susan, Mary Anne and Charles Hanley Gilleran. Plywood factory veneer clipper operator, Hoquiam, Wash., 1925-29; contbr. to publs., 1929-35; editorial staff Time, 1935-36, Fortune, 1937; asso. editor Time, 1938-45; lit. editor Newsweek, 1949-54; editorial cons. Sports Illustrated, N.Y.C., 1956-61, sr. editor, 1961-73, spl. contbr., 1973-78. Mem. Battery A. 248th Coast Arty., Wash. N.G., 1925-26. Mem. N.Y. Hist. Soc., N.Y. Geneal. and Biog. Soc., Sigma Delta Chi. Author: Laugh and Lie Down, 1931; The Land of Plenty, 1934; Nathaniel Hawthorne: The American Years, 1948; American Men of Letters, 1956; Alexander Wilson, Naturalist and Pioneer, 1961; The Real McCoy: the Life and Times of Norman Selby, 1971; The Hidden Northwest, 1972. Home: New York, N.Y. Died Dec. 8, 1978.

CAPEHART, HOMER EARL, former U.S. senator; b. Algiers, Ind., June 6, 1897; s. Alvin Thomas and Susan (Kelso) C.; ed pub. schs.; m. Irma Viola Mueller, Jan. 19, 1921; children—Homer Earl, Thomas (dec.), Patricia Louise. Salesman Burton-Paige Mfg. Co., Chicago, 1919-20; special rep. J. I. Case Plow Works Co., Racine, Wis., 1920-21; with Baker-Capehart Co., advt. agency, Green Bay, Wis., 1922-23; sales mgr. Sanford Bros., Chattanooga, Tenn., 1923-24, Holcomb & Hoke Mfg. Co., Indianapolis, Ind., 1925-27; pres. The Canehart Corp., mfrs., Fort Wayne, 1927-32; v.p. The Wurlitzer Co., Cin. and North Tonawanda, N.Y., 1933-40; chmn. of board, Packard Mfg. Co., Indpls.; owner Capehart Farms, Washington, Ind. Served in 12th Inf. and Q.M Dept., U.S. Army, 1917-19. Elected U.S. Senator from Ind., 1944 50, 56. Mem. Am. Legion, Elk. Republican. Lutheran. Mason (32 deg., Shriner). Clubs: Union League (Chicago); Columbia, Rotary, Meridian Hills Country (Indianapolis); National Republican (New York); Rotary (hon. life), Washington Country (Washington, Ind.); Contemporary, Executives, Variety, Press, Nat. Press, Army and Navy, Burning Tree (Washington). Home: Indianapolis, Ind. Died Sept. 3, 1979; buried Crown Hill Cemetery, Indpls.

CAPELLE, HENRY THEODORE, investment co. exec.; b. Loyal, Wis., Sept. 10, 1917; s. Henry Edward and Emma Elizabeth (Helmke) C.; student Wis. State U., 1939-42; B.S. in Mining Engring., Mo. Sch. Mines, 1947; m. Marion Hulda Reineking, Dec. 25, 1942; children—Stephen Henry, Kathryn Jean, Helen Christine. With Shell Oil Co., 1947-69, engring. geologist, mgr., Wichita, Kan., Wichita Falls, Tex., Ardmore, Okla., Midland, Tex., Houston, 1947-66, regional mgr. Tex. and N.M. charge gas dept. and prodn., Houston, 1967-69, v.p. gen. mgr. Blue Dolphin Pipeline Co. div. Shell, Houston, 1966-69; sr. v.p. charge gas div. Coastal States Gas Producing Co., Corpus Christi, Tex., 1969-71, pres. subsidiaries Lovaca Gathering, S. Tex. Natural Gas Gathering, Tex. Southeastern Gas, 1971-74, mem. exec. com., dir. parent co., 1971-74, sr. v.p., dir. Coastal States Gas Corp., 1972-74, energy cons., 1974-77; pres., dir. Capolle/Davies Investments Inc., 1975-77, Creative Internat. Inc., 1975-77. Guest lectr. Shell Mgmt. Sch., Galveston, Tex., 1963-66. Chmn., regional forum on offshore gas handling, Natural Gas Processing Assn., 1966-67. Mem. long range planning com. City of Houston, 1966-67. Served to capt. USAF, 1942-46; PTO. Mem. Nat. Alliance of Bus. Men (jobs. mgr. Houston 1967-68), Am. Petroleum Inst. (v.p. electric logging div. 1952), Presbyn. (ruling elder 1962-64). Home: Houston, Tex. Died May 28, 1977.

CAPITMAN, WILLIAM GARDINER, educator, social scientist; b. N.Y.C., Nov. 2, 1921; s. H. and B. (Rykus) C.; A.B., U. Cin., 1942; postgrad. Georgetown U., 1944, U. Brisbane, Australia, 1945; M.A., Columbia, 1947; J.D., N.Y. U., 1950; m. Barbara Baer, July 2, 1948; children—Andrew William, John Amson. Pres., Center for Research in Mktg., Inc., 1957-75; prof. bus. policy Fla. Internat. U., Miami, 1973-75.; vis. prof. Yale U. Sch. Organizational Scis., U. Pitts. Grad. Sch. Bus. Sr. cons. Mktg. Sci. Inst.; cons. Senate Com. on 1970 Census; cons. commn. on advt. and TV, FTC. Chmn., The Thoughtful People, N.Y.C., 1970-75. Bd. dirs. Sr. Citizens, Inc., Environment; Pitts., Peekskill C. of C., 1959-62. Served with CIC, AUS, 1942-46. Decorated Purple Heart. EPA Research grantee, 1973-75; Research scholar Yale, 1971. Mem. Authors League, Am. Acad. Social and Polit. Sci., Coll. Mgmt. Tech., Inst. Mgmt. Sci., Acad. Mgmt. Clubs: Yale, Miami Yacht (Miami); Vineyard Haven Yacht. Author: Advertising and Purchase Behaviour, 1959; Projections of the Negro Population, 1965; Everyone's Legal Adviser, 1966; Panic in the Boardroom, 1973. Home: Miami Beach, Fla. Died July 29, 1975.

CAPLAN, HARRY, univ. prof.; b. Hoag's Corners, N.Y., Jan. 7, 1896; s. Jacob and Sarah (Tolchin) C.; A.B., Cornell U., 1916, A.M., 1917, Ph.D., 1921; Litt.D., Wesleyan U., 1967. Grad. scholar in archeology and comparative philology, Cornell U., 1916-17, grad. fellow in Latin and Greek, 1917-18; instr. pub. speaking, Cornell U., 1919-23, in classics, 1924-25, asst. prof. classics, 1925-30, prof. classics, 1930-67, chmn. dept., 1929-46, Goldwin Smith prof. classical langs. and lit. 1941-67, emeritus, 1967-80. Vis. prof., summers, U. Wis., 1925, U. Mich., 1932, Northwestern U., 1938, Stanford, 1942, 48, U. Chgo., 1945, Columbia, 1946; fellow Center for Advanced Studies, Wesleyan U., 1962-63, 64; Andrew Mellon vis. prof. U. Pitts., 1967-68; Walker Ames vis. prof. U. Wash., 1968; Ziskind vis. prof. Brandeis U., 1968-69; vis. prof. U. Minn., 1969, Stanford, 1969, U. Ill., 1970-71; asst. editor Quar. Jour. Speech, 1923; joint editor Cornell Studies in Classical Philology. Served with U.S. Army during World War, 1918-19. Fellow Mediaeval Acad. Am.; mem. Am. Philol. Assn. (pres. 1955), Speech Assn. Am., Renaissance Soc. of Am., Modern Lang. Assn. Am., Linguistic Soc. Am., Am. Assn. U. Profs., Classical Assn. of Eng. and Wales, Phi Beta Kappa, Phi Eta Sigma, Delta Sigma Rho, Phi Delta Kappa, Phi Kappa Phi. Fellow John Simon Guggenheim Meml. Found., 1928-29 (studying medieval rhetoric in libraries of Europe), also 1956. Jewish religion. Author and editor: Gianfrancesco Pico della Mirandola On the Imagination, 1930; Mediaeval Artes Praedicandi, 1934; Medieval Arts praedicandi—A supplementary Hand-List, 1936; Rhetorica ad Herennium, 1954; (with H. H. King) Pulpit Eloquence-English, 1955; Pulpit Eloquence-German, 1956; Of Eloquence (edited by Anne King and Helen North), 1970. Contbr. articles and revs. in fields of classical and medieval lit. Home: Ithaca, N.Y. Died Nov. 29, 1980.

CAPLAN, LOUIS, lawyer; b. Sept. 15, 1886; s. David and Rachel C.; LL.B., U. Pitts., 1912, LL.D., 1966. Admitted to Pa. bar, 1912, since practiced in Pitts.; mem. firm Sachs & Caplan, 1919-45. Dir. May, Stern & Co., Keystone Bank, Pitts. Bd. dirs. Action Housing Pitts., 1957-76; pres., bd. dirs. Louis J. and Mary E. Horowitz Found., to 1972; bd. govs. (hon.) Hebrew Union Coll.-Jewish Inst. Religion, Cin.; trustee Pitts. United Jewish Fedn., 1956-58, Leon Falk Family Trust, Lehman-Epstine Trust, Halpern Found. Past pres., hon. pres. J.M. Gusky Hebrew Orphanage and Home of Western Pa.; bd. dirs., past nat. v.p., chmn. exec. bd. Am. Jewish Com., pres., 1961-62, hon. pres., from 1962, Louis Caplan Center on Group Identity and Mental Health established, 1977. Served as 1st lt., Q.M.C., U.S. Army, 1918-19; alien enemy hearing officer, World War II. Recipient award NCCJ; Louis Caplan Human Relations award given annually by Pitts. chpt. Am. Jewish Com.; Louis Caplan lectures in law established in his honor U. Pitts. Law Sch.; Louis Caplan vis. lectureship Jewish law founded in his honor Hebrew Union Coll.-Jewish Inst. Religion; named Man of Year, Jewish War Vets. Post 49, Pitts., 1961. Mem. Am., Pa., Allegheny County (pres. 1954) bar assns., 3d Circuit Fed. Jud. Conf., Am. Law Inst. Home: Pittsburgh, Pa. Died Dec. 16, 1978.

CAPLENOR, DONALD, botanist, univ. dean; b. Smith County, Tenn., Feb. 10, 1922; s. John W. and Daisy (Purnell) C.; student Cumberland U., 1943-44; B.S. in Biology, George Peabody Coll. Tchrs., 1948, M.A., 1949; Ph.D., Vanderbilt U., 1954; summer student U. Chgo., 1959-60, Cal. Inst. Tech., 1961; m. Sue Cooksey, June 9, 1946; children—Deborah Kay, Terry Michael, Donna Sue (Mrs. Allen Pahmeyer). Instr. biology George Peabody Coll. Tchrs., 1949-51, Vanderbilt U., 1951-53; asso. prof. biology, chmn. dept. Ga. Tchrs. Coll., 1953-55; asso. prof. George Peabody Tchrs. Coll., 1955-57, prof., chmn. div. sci. and math., 1963-66; prof. biology, chmn. dept. Millsaps Coll., 1957-63; dean Coll. Arts and Sci., prof. biology Tenn. Tech. U., 1966-70; dean faculty, prof. biology U. Ala., Huntsville, 1970-72; dean Sch. Liberal Arts, prof. biology U. Tenn., 1972-73; dean undergrad. studies Tenn. Technol. U., 1973-76, asso. v.p. for research, dean instrnl. devel., 1976-79; biologist USPHS, summer 1957. NSF sci. faculty fellow, summers 1959-61. Mem. Tenn. Acad. Scis. (sec. 1955-57, editor jour. 1965-70), Ecol. Soc. Am., Bot. Soc. Am., Assn. Southeastern Biologists, Sigma Xi, Beta Beta Beta, Alpha Epsilon Delta, Omicron Delta Kappa. Contbr. articles to profl. jours. Home: Cookeville, Tenn. Died Apr. 7, 1979; buried Crestlawn Meml. Cemetery, Cookeville.

CAPP, AL, cartoonist, columnist; b. New Haven, Sept. 28, 1909; s. Otto and Matilda (Davidson) C.; student Pa. Acad. Fine Arts, Museum Fine Arts, Boston; m. Catherine Wingate Cameron; children—Julie Ann (Mrs. Julian Cairol), Catherine Jane (Mrs. Michael Pierce), Colin C. Author Comic strips Li'l Abner, also columnist N.Y. Daily News Syndicate; daily syndicated radio-TV commentator. Home: Boston, Mass. Died Nov. 5, 1979.

CAPPS, RICHARD BROOKS, physician; b. Chgo., Mar. 14, 1906; s. Joseph A. and Christy (Brooks) C.; B.S. magna cum laude, Princeton, 1927; M.D., Harvard, 1931; m. Mary F. Grulee, July 8, 1930; 1 son, Richard Brooks. Intern Mass. Gen. Hosp., Boston, 1931-33; asst. resident Thorndike Meml. Lab., Boston City Hosp., 1933-35; practice medicine specializing in internal medicine, Chgo., from 1936, asso. prof. medicine Northwestern U., 1953-57; asso. clin. prof. medicine U. Ill., 1957-62, clin. prof., from 1962; sr. attending physician Presbyn.-St. Lukes Hosp., Chgo., pres. staff, 1962-64, 66-67. Dir. Chgo. Blue Cross Plan. Served as lt. col. M.C., AUS, 1942-46. Diplomate Am. Bd. Internal Medicine in cardio-vascular disease. Fellow A.C.P.; mem. Am. Assn. Study Liver Disease (treas. 1954-57, pres. 1959), Soc. Med. Consultants Armed Forces, Am. Assn. Physicians, Am. Soc. Clin. Investigation, Central Soc. Clin. Research, Am. Clin. and Climatical Assn. (mem. council 1948-53; v.p. 1962-63), Constantinian Med. Soc., Chgo. Inst. Medicine (bd. govs. 1950-55, 69-72), Chgo. Soc. Internal Med. (pres. 1954), Am., Chgo. (bd. govs. 1952-57) heart assn., Am. Therapeutic Soc. (mem. council 1962-64), A.M.A., Chgo. Zool. Soc. (gov.), Phi Beta Kappa, Sigma Xi, Alpha Omega Alpha. Clubs: Commonwealth, Economic, University, (Chgo.); Commercial, Old Elm. Contbr. articles to profl. jours. Home: Chicago, Ill. Died Dec. 25, 1976.

CAPRANO, JULIUS JOHN, corp. dir.; b. N.Y.C., Feb. 25, 1885; s. Charles and Edna (Hopt) C.; student pub. schs., N.Y.C.; m. Kathryn Gough, Oct. 1, 1943. Ret. v.p. Girard Trust Corn Exchange Bank, Phila.) dir. City Stores Co., N.Y.C., Roberts Filter Manufacturing Company, also of Bankers Securities Co., Home Life Insurance Company of America (all Phila.); director Girard Trust Corn Exchange Bank. Clubs: Racquet, Union League. Home: Philadelphia.

CAPSHAW, HULON, former judge; b. Cookeville, Tenn., June 2, 1891; s. Robert Byrd and Alice (Whitson) C.; grad. Peabody Coll., 1911; A.B., U. Tenn., 1913; scholar Columbia, 1914-16, LL.B., 1916. Admitted to N.Y. bar, 1916, bar U.S. Supreme Ct., 1926; with Cravath & Henderson, 1916-18, Olney & Comstock, 1919-21; pvt. practice, 1921-28; mem. Capshaw & Capshaw, 1928-29; judge N.Y. City Magistrates Cts., 1929-40. Served to ensign USNRF, World War I. Mem. N.Y. So. Soc. (sec. 1926-29), Tenn. Soc. in N.Y. (pres. 1935-37), Pilgrims of U.S., S.R., N.Y. Soc. Mil. and Naval Officers World War, Kappa Alpha (pres. nat. conv. Louisville 1929). Episcopalian. Mason. Clubs: University (non-resident), Kappa Alpha (Southern) (pres. 1926-34), Down Town (non-resident), Laymen's of Cathedral of St. John the Divine (pres. 1935-37). Home: Cookeville, Tenn. Died Jan. 5, 1977.

CAREY, ARCHIBALD J., JR., clergyman, judge; b. Chgo., Feb. 29, 1908; s. Archibald J. and Elizabeth (Davis) C.; student U. Chgo., 1925-27; B.S., Lewis Inst., 1928; B.D., Northwestern U., 1932; J.D., Chgo. Kent Coll. Law, 1935; D.D., Wilberforce U., 1943; LL.D. (hon.), John Marshall Law Sch., 1954; m. Hazel Harper, Jan. 1, 1931; 1 dau., Carolyn Eloise. Ordained to ministry A.M.E. Ch., 1930; pastor Woodlawn Ch., Chgo., 1930-49; pastor Quinn Chapel, 1949-67, minister emeritus, 1967-81; admitted to Ill. bar., 1936, practiced in Chgo.; mem. Prescott, Taylor, Carey & Cooper; judge Circuit Ct. of Cook County, 1966-78, 80-81; dir., past pres. Ill. Fed. Savs. & Loan Assn. Elected alderman 3d Ward, Chgo., 1947, 51. Chmn. Pres.'s Com. on Govt. Employment Policy, 1957-61, vice chmn., 1955-57; mem. U.S. delegation 8th Gen. Assembly UN, 1953. Rep. nominee 1st Ill. Dist., U.S. Congress, 1950. Received 1st prize oratorical contest Chgo. Daily News, 1924; Edmund W. Burke law scholarship, 1935. Mem. Alpha Phi Alpha (past pres.). Home: Chicago, Ill. Died Apr. 20, 1981; buried Lincoln Cemetery, Chgo.

CAREY, CHARLES IRVING, lawyer; b. Westmoreland Co., Va., Apr. 2, 1884; s. William Jett and Maria Louisa (Eichelberger) C.; A.B., William and Mary Coll., Williamsburg, Va., 1905; LL.B., Washington and Lee U., Lexington, Va., 1909; m. Arline Smith, Oct. 29, 1914; children—Charles Irving, William Hart, Jack Smith. Admitted to Va. bar, 1909, Ga. bar, 1909, Fla. bar, 1924, also to practice before federal courts and Supreme Court of U.S.; sr. partner Carey & Harrison, St. Petersburg, Fla., since 1934; mem. Fla. legislature, 1933. Former trustee Darlington Prep. Sch. for Boys, Rome, Ga. Mem. Am. Fla. State and Pinellas County bar assns., St. Petersburg Bar Assn. (pres. 1927), Phi Beta Kappa Assos., Phi Delta Phi, Phi Beta Kappa, Theta Delta Chi. Episcopalian. Kiwanian. Home: St. Petersburg, Fla.

CAREY, WILLIAM NELSON, civil engr.; b. St. Paul, Minn., July 13, 1887; son of Andrew John and Bridget (Shaughnessy) C.; student University of Minnesota, 1913; specialized pvt. edn.; m. Mary Helen Wade, Oct. 14, 1914; children—William Nelson, Thomas Wade, John Wade, David Hood. Jr. engr., War Dept., River and Harbor work, 1913-17; pvt. engring. practice, St. Paul, Minn., 1919-23; asst. city engr. and city engr., St. Paul, Minn., 1923-33; Minn. State engr. for P.W.A.; P.W.A. project engr. on design and constrn. Minneapolis-St. Paul sewerage works, 1933-37; in pvt. engring. practice, W. N. Carey and Associates, St. Paul, Minn., 1938-40; exec. sec. Am. Soc. C.E., 1945-55, sec.-emeritus. Mem. bd. direction Engring. Found., United Engring. Trustees, Engring. Socs. Library, Engrs. Joint Council. Served as capt., later maj., engrs. corps, A.U.S., with combat div. French front, then asst. engr. 7th corps, Army of Occupation, Germany, 1917-19; col. corps of engrs. in immediate charge of design and constrn. army camps and air fields in Fla. and S. Ga., 1941-42; spl. duty chief Engr., Fed. Works Agency, Washington, D.C., 1942-45. Mason (Scottish Rite). Clubs: Engineers of New York, Contributor of various technical papers principally in highway and airport design field. Recipient official personal citation for meritorious mil. service connected with engring. work performed 1942-45. Home: Vero Beach, Fla. Died May 9, 1980; interred Arlington (Va.) Meml. Cemetery.

CARGILL, FRANK VALENTINE, publications exec., editor; b. Port Huron, Mich., Mar. 31, 1885; s. William Rice and Luvia (Powers) C.; student, courses Sch. Commerce, Northwestern, 1906-12, 1932-34; m. Muriel Wilson, Aug. 8, 1916 (dec.); m. 2d, Mildred Hanson; children—William Rice, III, Barbara Ruth. Subscription mgr. Jour. A.M.A., 1906-08, established biog. records of physicians, 1909-12, field orgn. work A.M.A., 1912-16, dir. membership records and circulation jour., also nine other publs., 1951—; editor Am. Med. Dir., 1909—, established supplement Report Service, 1927—; circulation mgr. Todays Health, formerly Hygeia, 1923-53. Mem. Circulation Round Table of Chgo., Direct Mail Assn., Med. Soc. Exec. Conf. Republican. Mason (Shriner). Author numerous articles on direct mail, also in med. jour. Home: Highland Park, Ill.

CARGILL, JAMES NELSON, advt. exec.; b. Portsmouth, Va. Oct. 15, 1914; s. Woodson Hughes and Barbara (Revels) C.; B.S. in Arch., Va. Poly. Inst., 1936; m. Frances Virginia McDaniel, Sept. 9, 1939; children—James Nelson, Nancy (Mrs. Brian Vachon), Sally Page, Anne (Mrs. James Baker). Office mgr. Comml. Credit Co., Miami Fla., 1937-41; sales mgr. Richmond Oil Equipment Co. (Va.), 1946-48; exec. v.p. Cabell Eanes, Inc., Richmond, 1948-50; founder Cargill, Wilson & Acree, Inc., Richmond, 1950, pres., 1950-65, chmn. bd., 1965-79; dir. Summitt Container Corp.; chmn. bd. dirs. Summitt Alsop & Elliott, Ltd. Past bd. dirs. United Givers Fund, Richmond chpt. ARC. Served to lt. col. AUS, World War II. Decorated Legion of Merit, Bronze Star (U.S.); Croix de Guerre (France and Belgium); named Advt. Man of Year, Richmond Advt. Club, 1961. Mem. Am. Assn. Advt. Agys. (past nat. bd. dirs.), Richmond Sales and Mktg. Execs. (past pres.), Richmond C. of C., Va. Poly. Inst. Alumni Assn. (past dir.), Omicron Delta Kappa. Kiwanian. Clubs: Commonwealth, Country of Va. (Richmond) Indian Creek Country. Home: Deltaville, Va. Died Feb. 24, 1979.

CARGILL, OTTO ARTHUR, lawyer; b. Viola, Fulton County, Ark., Feb. 26, 1885; s. John E. (M.D.) and Anna (Mize) C.; ed. high sch., Salem, Ark., and coll. at Mountain Home, Ark.; m. Delia Arnold, May 2, 1905; children—Otha (Mrs. Harold F. Westcott), Oklahoma (Mrs. Edgar Hood), Otto Arthur, Ollie Burns. Settled in Oklahoma City, 1912; street car conductor, later mem. police dept.; studied law at night sch.; admitted to bar, 1916; county atty. Oklahoma County, 1919-20; mayor of Oklahoma City, 1923-27; member of law firm Cargill & Cargill; pres. Cargill Oil & Gas Co. Mem. bd. dirs. Oklahoma C. of C. Mem. Am., Okla. bar assns., Internat. Academy of Trial Lawyers. Democrat. Baptist. Mason (32 deg., Shriner), Odd Fellow, Elk. Woodman. Club: Oklahoma. Author of "Spare Moments," "Fratricide." Lecturer. Home: Oklahoma City.

CARHART, RAYMOND T., educator, audiologist; b. Mexico City, Mexico, Mar. 28, 1912; s. Raymond Albert and Edith (Noble) C.; A.B., Dak. Wesleyan U., 1932; M.A., Northwestern U., 1934, Ph.D., 1936; m. Mary Ellen Westfall, Aug. 2, 1935; children—Richard Alan, Robert Noble, Raymond Edgar; m. 2d, Jeanette Davis Grunig, Mar. 31, 1973. Instr. speech re-edn. Northwestern U., 1936-40, asst. prof., 1940-43, dir. Edn. Deaf and Hard of Hearing, 1942-55, asso. prof., 1943-47, prof. audiology 1947-75, asst. prof. otolarynology, 1948-52, prof., 1952-75; instr. 2d Internat. Course in Audiology, Stockholm, 1950; cons. U.S. Army, 1946-52; com. on hearing NRC, 1948-52; cons. com. on conservation of hearing Am. Acad. Opthalmology and Otolaryngology, 1944-65; cons. audiology VA, 1955-61. Mem. nat. adv. council Nat. Inst. Neurol. Diseases and Stroke, NIH, 1965-69; dir. Am. Bd. Examiners in Speech Pathology and Audiology, 1960-61. Served as capt. Med. Adminstrv. Corps, U.S. Army, acoustic physicist, Deshon Gen. Hosp., Pa., 1944-46. Recipient award of merit Am. Acad. Opthalmology and Otolarynology, 1960; Research Career award Nat. Inst. Neurol. Diseases and Stroke, 1963; Alumni medal Northwestern U., 1974. Fellow Am. Speech and Hearing Assn. (pres. 1957), Am. Acad. Ophthalmology and Otolaryngology (hon.), Acoustical Soc. Am., Otosclerosis Study Group, Am. Triological Soc., Am. Otol. Soc. Author articles in profl. publs. Research on psychophysis of hearing loss, hearing aids, edn. of the acoustically handicaped, training non-med. specialists in audiology. Home: Wilmette, Ill. Died Oct. 2, 1975.

CARLSON, ESKIL CONSTANTINE, lawyer; b. Des Moines, Ia., Mar. 14, 1885; s. John Peter and Anna Brita (Swanson) C.; LL.B., Drake U., 1908; LL.M., Yale U., 1909; LL.D., Augustana Coll. and Theol. Sem., 1938; m. Helen O. Walder, Sept. 25, 1915; children—Helen Christine, Constance Ann. Admitted to Iowa bar, 1909; asst. city solicitor, Des Moines, 1910-14, city solicitor, 1914-16, municipal judge, 1916-18, city solicitor, 1925-29; mem. firm Lappen & Carlson, Des Moines, 1919-50; prof. practice, Drake Law Sch., 1920-1942; mem. State Board of Edn. of Iowa, 1931-35; mem. finance com. Augustana Synod since 1928. Served with Y.M.C.A. (A.E.F.), France, June 1918-May 1919. Pres. Des Moines Y.M.C.A. 15 yrs.; mem. exec. com. and past pres. North Central Area Y.M.C.A.; mem. council, mem. bd., mem. World com. and past pres. Nat. Council Y.M.C.A. (U.S.); pres. U.S.O. Council of Iowa; chmn. Asso. Services, Am. Forces, Des Moines Group. Mem. Am. and Iowa State bar assns., Am. Judicature Soc. Republican. Lutheran. Mason, Odd Fellow. Contbr. articles to Lutheran Companion and Augustana Quarterly. Home: Des Moines, Ia.

CARLYON, JAMES THOMAS (KÄR-LI'ON), religious educator; b. Ontario, Can., Feb. 18, 1884; s. Richard and Elizabeth Ann (Bray) C.; A.B., Mo. Wesleyan Coll., 1904, D.D., 1920; S.T.B., Boston U., 1908; A.M., Harvard, 1912, S.T.M., 1918; Ph.D., U. of Chicago, 1926; m. Florence J. Mason, Aug. 6, 1914; children—Marian Elizabeth, Alice Janette, Richard Dean. Brought to U.S., 1886. Ordained ministry M.E. Ch., 1905; pastor various chs., 1904-18; prof. of New Testament, Iliff. Sch. of Theology, Denver, 1918-36; prof. of Christian doctrine, Southern Meth. U., Dallas, since 1936. Co-author: Fruits of Faith, 1950. Author: My Favorite Sermons, 1950. Contbr. to religious jours. Home: Dallas.

CARMER, CARL, author; b. Cortland, N.Y., Oct. 16, 1893; s. Willis Griswold and Mary (Lamson) C.; Ph.B., Hamilton Coll., Clinton, N.Y., 1914, Ph.M., 1917; M.A., Harvard U., 1915; Litt.D., Elmira Coll., 1937, Susquehanna U., 1944; L.H.D., Hamilton Coll., 1941; LL.D., U. Buffalo, 1962; m. Elizabeth Black, Dec. 24, 1928. Instr. in English, Syracuse U., 1915-16, U. Rochester, 1916-17; chmn. pub. speaking dept. Hamilton Coll., 1919; asst. prof. English, U. Rochester, 1919-21; asso. prof. U. Ala., 1921-24, prof., 1924-27; columnist New Orleans Morning Tribune, 1927; asst. editor Vanity Fair, 1928-29, Theatre Arts Monthly, 1929-33; pres. Boscobel Restoration, Inc. Bd. overseers Coll. of Virgin Islands, 1963. Served as 1st lt. F.A., World War I. Recipient merit award Am. Assn. State and Local History, patriotic achievement medal Order Founders and Patriots of Am. Fellow N.Y. State Hist. Assn. (v.p.); mem. MacDowell Assn., P.E.N., Poetry Soc. Am., Authors Guild of Authors League Am., P.E.N., Poetry Soc. Am., N.Y. State Folklore Soc. (v.p.), Soc. Am. Historians (bd. dirs.), Nat. Assn. Student Personnel Adminstrs., Am. Acad., Victorian Soc. in Am. (bd. dirs.), Hudson River Conservation Soc. (1st v.p.), Phi Beta Kappa, Psi Upsilon. Presbyn. Clubs: Pilgrims, Century. Author: Stars Fell on Alabama, 1933; Listen for a Lonesome Drum, 1936; The Hudson, 1939; Dark Trees to the Wind, 1949; Windfall Fiddle, 1950; The Susquehanna, 1955; The Screaming Ghost, 1956; My Kind of Country, 1966; The Farm Boy and the Angel, 1970. Editor: Rivers of America Series; The Regions of America Series; The Tavern Lamps Are Burning; The Drummer Boy of Vincennes, 1972; The Loyal Pirates, 1975. Address: Irvington-on-Hudson, N.Y. Died Sept. 11, 1976.

CARMICHAEL, HUGH THOMPSON, psychiatrist, psychoanalyst, educator; b. Peterborough, Ont., Can., Feb. 10, 1898; s. Duncan Nevin and Jessie Eliza (Nevin and Jessie Eliza (Bolster) C.; M.D., C.M., Queen's U., Kingston, Ont., 1923; M.S., U. Minn., 1931; m. Charlotte L. Greenwood, June 27, 1923; children—William Greenwood, Donald Keith, Charlotte Elizabeth; m. 2d, Carolyn G. Ruhland, July 10, 1937; children—Sandra Jennifer, Peter John Hugh. Came to U.S., 1926, naturalized, 1932. Pvt. practice medicine, Omemee, Ont., 1924-26; fellow internal medicine and neurology Mayo Found., Mayo Clinic, 1927-30; sr. fellow neuropsychiatry and instr. neuropathology Albany Med. Coll., 1930-31; asso. neuropsychiatrist, 1930-31; jr. physician to chief psychiatrist research service Worcester (Mass.) State Hosp., Meml. Found. for Neuroendocrine Research, 1931-35; psychiatrist Neuropsychiat. Inst. and Hosp. of Hartford (Conn.) Retreat, 1935, instr. to asst. prof. psychiatry U. Chgo., 1935-43; Rockefeller fellow Inst. Psychoanalysis, Chgo., 1936-40; asso. attending physician Cook County Psychopathic Hosp., 1939-40, 42; asso. prof. psychiatry U. Ill., 1943-47, prof., 1947-52, clin. prof., 1952-61, prof. psychiatry, 1961-66, prof. emeritus, dept. psychiatry, 1966-80; dir. office continuing edn. for psychiatrists Am. Psychiat. Assn., Washington, 1967-74; on leave as professorial lectr. psychiatry U. Chgo. Sch. Medicine, 1960, 61; cons. psychiatry Surgeon Gen. U.S. Army, 1960; adv. com. psychiatry and neurology service VA Dept. Medicine and Surgery, 1960-64; asso. dir. psychiat. div. Ill. Neuropsychiat. Inst., 1943-52; attending psychiatrist Research and Edn. Hosps., Chgo., 1943-66; attending psychiatrist Chgo. Meml. Hosp., 1943-51, hon. staff, 1951-54; courtesy staff Inst. Psychiat. and Psychosomatic Research and Tng., Michael Reese Hosp., 1954-67. Mem. Joint Com. on Mental Illness and Health, 1955-61, trustee, 1955-57; commr. Joint Commn. on Accreditation of Hosps., 1958-67, treas., 1963-67; sr. cons. continuing edn. br. Nat. Inst. of Mental Health, 1966-67; adv. bd. Med. Specialities, Inc., 1958-65, mem. com. on standards, 1962-65, chmn., 1963-65, exec. com., 1963-65; mem. White House Conf. on Aging, 1971. Served with C.E.F., 1917-18. Recipient Vestermark prize, 1974. Diplomate Am. Bd. Psychiatry and Neurology (dir. 1957-65, v.p. 1963-64). Fellow Am. Psychiat. Assn. (life; v.p. 1963-64), Am. Orthopsychiat. Assn. (life), Am. Coll. Psychiatrists, Am. Coll. Psychoanalysts (2d v.p. 1974), Eastern Psychoanalytic Assn.; mem. A.M.A. (council on mental health 1953-61), Chgo., D.C. med. socs., A.A.A.S., World Med. Assn., Central Neuropsychiat. Assn., Am. Psychoanalytic Assn. (life; exec. council 1954-56), Am. Psychosomatic Soc. (life), Ill. (pres. 1956-57), Washington psychiat. socs., Chgo. (life; pres. 1952-54), Washington (life) psychoanalytic socs., Inst. Medicine Chgo., Chgo. Neurol. Soc. (pres. 1952), World Fedn. Mental Health (asso.), Internat. Psychoanalytic Assn., Alumni Assn. Mayo Found., Group Advancement Psychiatry (exec. com. 1956-58), Am. Assn. U. Profs., Canadian Psychiat. Assn. (life), Sigma Xi. Author: Prospects and Proposals: Lifetime Learning for Psychiatrists (with Regan and Small), 1972. Contbr. tech. articles to profl. jours. Home: Washington, D.C. Died Feb. 23, 1980.

CARMICHAEL, OLIVER CROMWELL, JR., business exec.; b. Birmingham, Ala., Mar. 10, 1920; s. Oliver Cromwell and Ruth Mae (Crabtree) C.; A.B., Vanderbilt U., 1940; LL.B., Duke, 1942; M.A., Columbia, 1951, Ph.D., 1953; m. Ernestine Morris, Sept. 28, 1946; children—Carmen Murphy, Oliver Cromwell III, Ernestine Morris, Stanley Clark. Admitted to Tenn. bar, 1942, Ind. bar, 1948; asst. gen. counsel Assos. Corp. N. Am., S. Bend, Ind., 1946-49, chmn. bd., from 1960; chmn. bd. Marshall County Bank & Trust Co., Plymouth, Ind., FBT Bancorp, Inc., South Bend, Bremen State Bank (Ind.). dir. W.R. Grace & Co. Gen. chmn. Com. Higher Edn. No. Ind.; past mem., chmn. Commn. Higher Edn. for Ind., Ind. Forums pres. Citizens Nat. Com. Higher Edn.; del. 29th Gen. Assembly UN, 1974. Bd. dirs. United Community Services, S. Bend; trustee Converse Coll., Spartanburg, S.C., Vanderbilt U., U. Notre Dame; bd. dirs. Vanderbilt U. Med. Center. Treas., Republican Nat. Com.; mem. exec. com. Rep. Nat. Finance Com. Served to lt. USNR, 1942-46. Mem. Phi Beta Kappa, Order of Coif, Omicron Delta Kappa. Republican. Presbyn. Clubs: Ocean (Delray Beach, Fla.); Pickwick (Niles, Mich.); New York Athletic; Country of Florida. Home: South Bend, Ind. Died Aug. 3, 1976.

CARMICHAEL, PATRICK HENRY, clergyman, school dean; b. Goodwater, Ala., May 4, 1889; s. Daniel Monroe and Amanda (Lessley) C.; Ph.G., Mercer U., 1909; B.S., U. of Ala., 1915; certificate, Princeton Theol. Sem., 1918; Ph.D., N.Y. Univ., 1931; hon. D.D., Southwestern Coll., Memphis, Tenn., 1930; Litt.D., Davidson (N.C.) Coll., 1937; m. Mary McPhail Partridge, Aug. 16, 1917; 1 dau., Miriam Willena. Pharmacist, 1909-12; ordained Presbyterian ministry, 1918; moderator of the Presbytery of Birmingham, Synod of Ala., 1925; prof. English Bible and religious edn., Columbia Theol. Sem., Decatur, Ga., 1933-38; dir. leadership edn. Presbyn. Church in U.S., 1938-47. Dean faculty, professor religious education, Gen. Assembly's Training Sch., Presbyn. Church U.S., ret. 1959; lectr. Princeton Theol. Sem., 1959-60; guest minister, Tuscaloosa, Ala., Portsmouth, Newport News, Va., other cities, 1960-74. Mem. Internat. Council Religious Edn. from 1942 (chmn. com., Cycle Graded Lesson Series 1941-47); mem. dept. research and edn., commn. on prison chaplains, Fed. Council of Chs. of Christ in Am., from 1943, mem. Am. Council on Edn., 1943-45; mem. com. on promotion, Presbyn. Ch. in U.S., 1945-46; chmn. sub-com. extension edn. and relationship to institutions, Leadership Training Publishers Association (sec.-treas., 1940-45); mem. exec. com. leadership sect., Internat. Council of Religious Edn., from 1943; chmn. leadership sect., 1946-49; mem. Cooperative Pub. Assn., 1946-48. Mem. Am. Assn. Schs. Religious Edn. (chmn. accreditation commn.), Presbyn. Ministers Assn. Richmond (pres. 1956), Jasons (U. Ala.), Phi Beta Kappa, Kappa Delta Pi, Phi Delta Kappa, Pi Gamma Mu. Democrat. Book rev. edit., Presbyn. of the South, 1937-44. Clubs: Torch, Rotary (Richmond). Author: (brochure) Discovering a Strategy for Christian Service to the Uprooted Peoples in War Industry Areas; co-author: Basis of World Order. Author-editor: Understanding the Books of the Old Testament. Editor: Understanding the Books of the New Testament. Contbr. articles and book revs. to religious jours. Home: Richmond, Va. Died Feb. 1977.

CARNEY, MABEL, college prof.; b. Carthage, Mo., Jan. 14, 1885; d. James and Elizabeth Jane (Lyon) C.; grad. high sch., Marseilles, Ill., 1901; diploma State Normal Sch., DeKalb, Ill., 1909; B.S., Teachers Coll. (Columbia), 1918, M.A., 1919. Teacher rural schs., Ill., 1902-06; critic teacher Western Ill. Normal Sch., Macomb, Ill., 1906-09; dir. rural edn., State Normal Sch., Cheney, Wash., 1910-11, Ill. State Normal U., Normal Ill., 1911-14; state supervisor high sch. training, Minn., 1914-17; asso. prof. rural edn., Teachers Coll. (Columbia), since Sept. 1917. Mem. N.E.A., Am. Country Life Assn., Nat. Community Center Assn., Ill. State Grange. Universalist. Author: Country Life and the Country School, 1912. Home: New York, N.Y.

CARNEY, ROBERT GIBSON, educator, dermatologist; b. Ann Arbor, Mich., Apr. 25, 1914; s. Robert John and Frances (Gibson) C.; A.B., U. Mich., 1935, M.D., 1939; m. Dorothy Ann Briscoe, June 18, 1939; children—Robert Gibson, Patricia Lee (Mrs. Hentzel), Kathleen Ann (Mrs. Hill), Margaret Lou (Mrs. Ryan). Intern U. Iowa Hosps., 1939-40, resident dermatology, 1940-43; mem. faculty U. Iowa Med. Sch., Iowa City, 1947-76, prof. dermatology, chmn. dept., from 1961. Mem. com. revision U.S. Pharmacopcia. Served with USNR, 1943-46. Mem. Am. Dermatol. Assn., Am. Acad. Dermatology, Soc. Investigative Dermatology, AMA, Iowa Dermatol. Soc., Phi Beta Kappa, Alpha Omega Alpha. Author: Dermatology for the Student and Physician. Home: Iowa City, Iowa. Died Nov. 4, 1976.

CARNOVSKY, LEON (KÄR-NOV'SKE), prof. library science; b. St. Louis, Mo., Nov. 28, 1903; s. Isaac and Jennie (Stillman) C.; A.B., U. of Mo., 1927; student St. Louis Library Sch., 1927-28 (certificate in librarianship); Ph.D., U. of Chicago, 1932; m. Marian Satterthwaite, Aug. 25, 1939. Gen. asst. St. Louis Pub. Library, 1927-28; asst. to librarian, Washington U., St. Louis, 1928-29; instr. Grad. Library Sch., U. of Chicago, 1932-36, asst. prof. library science, 1936-41; asso. prof., 1941-43, prof. since 1943, asst. dean 1942-45, associate dean and dean of students, 1945-47; associate director Survey of Westchester County, N.Y., Libraries, 1935, Survey of Mich. State Library, 1937, survey of Chicago Public Library, 1938; dir. Appraisal Study of Cleveland Public Library, 1939; member of U.S. Education Mission to Japan, 1946. Pres. Assn. of Am. Library Schs., 1942-43; mem. American Library Association, Am. Library Inst., Am. Assn. Univ. Profs., Phi Beta Kappa, Alpha Pi Zeta. Club: Quadrangle. Author: Library Service in a Suburban Area (with E. A. Wight), 1936; Libraries and Readers in the State of New York (with D. Waples), 1939; A Metropolitan Library in Action (with C. B. Joeckel), 1940. Editor, The Library in the Community (with L. Martin), 1944. Managing editor The Library Quarterly. Home: Oakland, Calif. Deceased.

CAROTHERS, NEIL, economist; b. Chattanooga, Sept. 19, 1884; s. Neil and Asenath (Wallace) C.; B.A., U. Ark., 1906; Rhodes Scholar, Oxford (Eng.) U., 1904-07, diploma in econs., 1907; Ph.D., Princeton, 1916; m. Eileen Hamilton, Aug. 11, 1917; children—Neil III, Hamilton, Stuart. Instr., later asst. prof. econs. U. Ark., 1907-14; asst. prof., preceptor in econs. and finance Princeton, 1916-19; econ. expert Dept. State, 1919-20; engaged in banking, N.Y.C., 1920-23; prof. econs., dir. Coll. Bus. Adminstrn., Lehigh U., Bethleham, Pa., 1923-36, organizer, acting head dept. indsl. engring., 1925-27, Macfarlane prof. econs., dean Coll. Bus. Adminstrn., 1936-49, emeritus, 1949—. Econ. adviser Republican vice presdl. candidate, 1936; econ. adviser Rep. Nat. Campaign Com., 1943-44; dir. econ. survey of canning industry in U.S., 1939-41; dir. survey of pineapple transp., 1942; spl. investigations of Hawaiian industries, 1945; condr. program econ. edn., Gen. Electric Co., 1948-49. Chmn. Selective Service Appeal Bd., 1940-45. Gen. economist UN Civil Assistance Command, 8th Army, Korea, 1952, also personal adviser to Unified Command, rep. Combined Econ. Bd., Korea, 1952; v.p. Economists' Nat. Com. on Monetary Policy. Served as 1st lt. Aviation Sect., Signal Corps, U.S. Army, 1917-18; captain Gen. Staff, 1919. Recipient award Freedoms Found., 1951. Mem. Am. Econ. Assn., Newcomen Soc. Eng., Pacific Coast Numismatic Soc. (hon. life), Scabbard and Blade, Phi Beta Kappa, Omicron Delta Kappa, Alpha Kappa Psi, Kappa Sigma. Presbyn. Author: (with others) Economic Agengies of the World War (U.S. War Dept.), 1920; Fractional Money, 1930; Experimenting with Our Money, 1935; Silver in America, 1936; Synopsis of Basic Economic Factors, 1948. Contbr. to periodicals; radio commentator. Address: Princeton, N.J.

CARPENTER, CARLOS CLAY, prof. plant sci.; b. Kalona, Ia., Oct. 17, 1885; s. El Dorado and Matilda Ann (Manatt) C.; student Ottawa U., 1903-07, Kan. State U., 1909-10; B.S., Colo. State U., 1914; student U. of Calif., 1916; M.S., Syracuse U., 1923; student Cornell U., 1924; m. Pearl Ebaugh, May 27, 1911; children—Hope (Mrs. McCully), William, James, Constance. Sci. teacher and athletic coach Mt. Lincoln High Sch., Palisade, Colo., 1912-13; asst. state forester, Colo., 1913-14, U.S. Forest Service, Fremont Exp. Sta., 1914; high sch. instr. sci. and athletic coach, Walla Walla, Wash., 1914-17, St. Joseph, Mo., 1917-18; prof. plant sci. Syracuse (N.Y.) U. since 1918, chmn. sci. div. since 1948, athletic adv. bd. since 1928. Dept. farms and markets, N.Y. state, 1926-28; dir. rural activities, N.Y. Temporary Emergency Relief Adminstrn., 1935-37; exec. vice pres. N.Y. Rural Rehabilitation Corp., 1935-39; Syracuse U. rep. to N.Y. governor's marketing com., 1927-28. Fellow A.A.A.S.; mem. Am. Genetics Assn., Nat. Geographic Soc., Sigma Xi (chapter pres. 1933-34). Independent Republican. Protestant. Club: Faculty of Syracuse U. Author of articles, Appletufts (Bot. Gazette, 1923), Key to Commercial Apples (1925), Vitamins in Fungi (Sci. 1940), B2 Vitamins in Soil (Sci. 1944). Holder of patents on plant vitalizer, 1927, and Syr Petrie Dish, 1938. Home: Syracuse.

CARPENTER, FARRINGTON REED, lawyer, cattle breeder; b. Evanston, Ill., Aug. 10, 1886; s. Edward Farrington and Mary Belle (Reed) C.; Litt.B., Princeton, 1909; LL.B., Harvard, 1912; m. Eunice Pleasant, of Kan., Aug. 28, 1920; children—Edward Farrington, Rosamond, Willis Vincent. Partner Carpenter & White, Hereford cattle breeders, Hayden, Colo., 1907; admitted to Colo. bar, 1912; sr. partner Carpenter & Videon, Hayden; county atty. Routt County, 1920-28; dist. atty. 14th Jud. Dist., 1928-32; mgr. Dawson Cattle Co., Director of Grazing, U.S. Dept. of Interior, 1934-38. Served in World War, 19 mos. Mem. Am. Bar Assn. Republican. Conglist. Club: University (Denver). Home: Hayden, Colo.

CARPENTER, GEORGE WAYLAND, missionary, church exec.; b. Greenfield, N.Y., Jan. 6, 1901; s. Daniel William and Mary Edith (Carr) C.; B.S., Union Coll., Schenectady, 1921, D.D., 1943; B.D., Colgate Rochester Div. Sch., 1925; M.A., Yale, 1936, Ph.D., 1937; m. Isabel Frances West, July 6, 1937. Ordained to ministry Baptist Ch., 1925, apptd. missionary Am. Bapt. Fgn. Missionary Soc., 1925; tchr., Kimpese, Belgian Congo, 1926-29, 30-35; ednl. sec. Congo Protestant Council, 1937-48; mng. dir. Central Protestant Lit. Agy. and Press, Leopoldville, 1940-52; Africa sec. div. fgn. missions Nat. Council Chs. Christ in U.S., 1953-57, mem. exec. com. dept. internat. affairs; sec. Internat. Missionary Council, 1957-61; sec. div. world mission and evangelism World Council Chs., 1961-65; exec. chmn. Coordinating Com. Christian Broadcasting, from 1963; cons. div. overseas ministries Nat. Council Chs. Trustee Phelps-Stokes Fund; pres. North Warren Bd. Edn., 1973-74; founder, charter mem., trustee Horicon Hist. Soc. Mus. Decorated Gold medal Ordre Royal du Lion, chevalier Ordre Royal du Leopold II (Belgium). Founding fellow Africa Studies Assn.; mem. Council Fgn. Relations, Internat. Fellowship. Reconciliation. Author: Highways for God in Congo, 1952; The Way in Africa, 1958; Encounter of the Faiths, 1967. Home: Brant Lake, N.Y. Died May 1, 1976.

CARPENTER, JAY ARNOLD, mining engr.; b. Beloit. Ia., May 12, 1883; s. Edwin Elisha and Mary Elizabeth (Miller) C.; B.S. cum laude, U. of Nev., 1907, E.M., 1911; m. Florence Bender, Dec. 22, 1909; children—Elizabeth, Clayton. Began as surveyor and assayer, Tonopah, Nev., 1907; instr. and asst. prof. metallurgy, Mackay Sch. of Mines, Reno, Nev., 1908-10; mill supt. West End Consolidated, Tonopah, 1910-16, mine foreman, supt. and mgr. of Nev. mines, 1916-20; prof. mining, S.D. Sch. of Mines, 1921-22; supt. Randsburg Silver Mining Co., 1922-23; pres. Insulex Co., 1924-25; industrial engr. Pacific Portland Cement Co., 1925-26; cons. engr., Los Angeles, 1920-26; prof. mining, Mackay Sch. of Mines, U. of Nev., 1926-39; dir. Mackay Sch. of Mines, Nev. State Bureau of Mines retired 1951; cons. engr. since 1951. Mem. American Institute of Mining and Metallurgical Engrs. (chmn. Nev. sect. 1927-34; chmn. nat. com. on student relations, 1934-36), Member State Planning Bd., 1939-50. Nevada Consultant Metals Reserve Co., 1942-44. Phi Sigma Kappa. Presbyterian. Contbr. of engring. and mining articles to mags. Home: Reno, Nev.

CARPENTER, MONTE CUTLER, bldg. material mfg. exec.; b. Cedar City, Utah, Nov. 12, 1916; s. John Cutler and Annie (Levanger) C.; student U. Utah, 1937; m. Cecilia Ada Young, Sept. 15, 1938; children—Anne, Stephanie, Mary Leslie, Christine. Mdse. mgr. U.S. Gypsum Co., 1949-57; nat. mdse. mgr. Montgomery Ward & Co., 1958-65; v.p. bldg. materials div. Flintkote Co., White Plains, N.Y., 1965-71, exec. v.p., 1971-76, pres., from 1976, also dir.; dir. Compania Indsl. de Mexicali, Polymer Bldg. Systems. Mem. nat. adv. bd. Goodwill Industries Am.; bd. dirs. Goodwill Industries Conn. Served with USNR, 1945. Mem. Nat. Home Improvement Council (past pres.), Asphalt Roofing Mfrs. Assn. (dir., past pres.), Que. Asbestos Mining Assn. (dir.) Gypsum Assn., Portland Cement Assn. (dir.), Asphalt and Vinyl Asbestos Tile Inst. Republican. Clubs: Knickerbocker Country (past pres., trustee); Canadian, Metropolitan (N.Y.C.). Home: Dallas, Tex. Deceased.

CARPENTER, RHYS, author, archeologist; b. Cotuit, Mass., Aug. 5, 1889; s. William Henry and Anna Morgan (Douglass) C.; A.B., Columbia, 1908, Ph.D., 1916; B.A., Balliol Coll., (Oxford U., Eng.), 1911. M.A., 1914; Litt.D., Rutgers U., 1941; studied Am. Sch. Classical Studies, Athens, Greece, 1912-13; m. Eleanor Houston Hill, Apr. 23, 1918. Instr. classical archeology, 1913-15, asso., 1915-16, asso. prof., 1916-18, prof., 1918-55, prof. emeritus, 1955-80, Bryn Mawr Coll.; dir. Am. Sch. Classical Studies, Athens, Greece, 1927-32, 46-48, vis. prof., 1956-57; in charge Classical Sch., Am. Acad., Rome, 1939-40; Sather prof. classical lit. U. Cal., 1945. Served as 1st lt. M.I. Staff, AUS, 1918-19; attached Am. Commn. to Negotiate Peace, Paris, 1919. Mem. Am. Philos. Soc., Archeol. Inst. Am., Phila. Oriental Club, Am. Philol. Assn., Linguistic Soc. Am., Phi Beta Kappa; hon. mem. Greek Archaeol. Soc. German Archaeol. Inst., Austrian Archeol Inst., Hispanic Soc. Am. Corr. mem. Pontifical Roman. Acad. Archaeology. Author: Folk Tale, Fiction Saga in the Homeric Epics, 1946; others; also profl. articles in jours. Home: Chester Springs, Pa. Died Jan. 2, 1980.

CARPENTER, SAMUEL THEODORE, educator, cons. engr.; b. Montpelier, O., Sept. 2, 1906; s. Otto A. and Bernice (Brownwell) C.; B.C.E., Ohio State U., 1930, C.E., 1935, M.S., 1939; m. Mary Nofzinger, Mar. 31, 1934; 1 dau., Shirley Marie. Instr. Swarthmore (Pa.) Coll., 1935-39, asst. prof., 1939-42, asso. prof., 1942-46, prof., chmn. civil engring. dept., 1946-64, chmn. dept. engring., 1964-72; pvt. cons. engr., 1932-77. Council mem. Engring. Coll. Adminstrv. Council; bd. visitors Sch. Engring., U. Pitts. Mem. Swarthmore-Rutledge Union Sch. Bd. Mem., chmn. Swarthmore Planning Commn., 1971-77. Named Engr. of Year, Del. County chpt. Pa. Soc. Profl. Engrs., 1967; recipient Centennial Distinguished Alumnus award Ohio State U., 1970. Registered profl. engr., Ohio, Pa. Mem. Am. Soc. Engring. Edn., Am. Soc. C.E., Soc. for Exptl. Stress Analysis, Sigma Xi, Tau Beta Pi, Sigma Tau, Triangle. Rotarian. Author: Structural Frameworks (with C. T. Morris), 1943; Structural Mechanics, 1960. Contbr. articles to engring. jours. Home: Swarthmore, Pa. Died Jan. 28, 1977.

CARPENTER, WALTER SAMUEL, JR., industrialist; b. Wilkesbarre, Pa., Jan. 8, 1888; s. Walter S. and Belle (Morgan) C.; prep. edn., Wyoming Sem., Kingston, Pa., 1902-06; student Cornell U., 1906-10; m. Mary Wootten, June 3, 1914; children—Walter Samuel III, John W., Edmund N. II. With E.I. du Pont de Nemours & Co., Wilmington, Del., 1909-75, v.p., 1919-40, pres., 1940-48, chmn., 1948-62, hon. chmn., 1962-75; dir. Christiana Securities Co. Trustee emeritus Wyoming Sem., Kingston, Pa.; past pres. U. Del. Trustees. Methodist. Clubs: Wilmington, Wilmington Country; Fisher's Island (N.Y.). Home: Wilmington, Del. Died Feb. 2, 1976.

CARR, CHARLES HARDY, U.S. judge; b. Coahoma, Miss., Aug. 18, 1903; s. Charles Hardy and MaiBelle (Landers) C.; A.B., Vanderbilt U., 1925; LL.B., Yale, 1926; m. Margaret Applewhite, Aug. 1, 1936; foster sons—Darrell V. Cole, James Applewhite Cole. Admitted to Tenn. bar, 1926, Calif. bar, 1931, U.S. Supreme Ct. bar, 1937; practice law, Memphis, 1926-29, Los Angeles, 1931-33, 40-43, 46-62; asst. U.S. atty. for Los Angeles, 1933-36; spl. asst. to atty. gen. U.S., 1936-40; U.S. atty. So. Dist. Cal., 1943-46; judge U.S. Dist. Ct., Los Angeles, from 1962. Instr., Southwestern U., Los Angeles, 1930-31. Mem. regional loyalty bd. U.S. Civil Service Commn., 1949-52. Mem. Am., Internat. (patron) bar assns., Phi Alpha Delta, Kappa Alpha. Clubs: Oahu Country, Outrigger Canoe (Honolulu). Home: Beverly Hills, Calif. Died Mar. 1976.

CARR, EARL INGRAM, surgeon; b. Auburn, N.Y., Feb. 11, 1886; s. of Clayton F. and Fannie (Ingram) C.; M.D., University of Michigan, 1910; Sc.D., Cleary College, 1958; was married to Ruth Smith, November 8, 1916; children—Fannie (deceased), Charlotte (Mrs. J. Woodward Roe). Mem. surgical staff, surg. intern, asst. surg. (gen., g.u., oral), Univ. Hosp., U. Mich., Ann Arbor, 1909-11; asst. physician, Ontanogon Mines, 1911-12; asst. surg., Copper Range Hosp., Copper Range R.R. Co., 1912-13; began pvt. practice, limited to surg., 1914; chief cons. surg. Mich. Dept. Health; chief surg. penal instns. of Mich., 1921-26; founder and surg. Orthopedic Clinic of Lansing, 1923-27; now cons. surg. St. Lawrence Hosp. (past chief surg.); cons. surg. Edward W. Sparrow Hosp. (past sec. of staff, past chief surg., past chief of staff); cons. surgeon Ingham Med. Hosp.; cons. to r.r.'s, ins. cos. Dir. Detroit Mortgage & Realty Co. Pres. and trustee, Mich. Foundn. for Med. and Health Edn., Inc.; trustee Mich. Health Council; chmn. Ingham Med. and Sci. Trust, 1952-60. Recipient medal award for distinguished service in cancer control, 1951, service certificate, 1960, Am. Cancer Soc.; service citation Ingham County Med. Soc., 1961. Diplomate Internat. Bd. Surgery. Fellow A.C.S., Acad. Internat. Medicine (counsellor 1960—), A.M.A., Internat. Coll. Surg. (founder, trustee, chmn. bd. trustees 1960, v.p. United States sect. 1962, gov. 1963—, dir. Hall of Fame and Museum, co-chmn. 1960, chmn. 1961—, recipient plaque 1966). Dir. Am Cancer Soc., Mich. Div. Inc. (mem. exec. com., med. chmn.), Mich. Med. Service, Inc. (past chairman medical advisory board). Member of Detroit Acad. Surgery, American Assn. Indsl. Phys. and Surg., Mich. Assn. Indsl. Phys. and Surgeons (past pres.), Mich. State Med. Soc. (past 1st v.p., past chmn. surg., Distinguished Health Service award 1963), Ingham County Med. Soc. (past pres.), Gorgas Memorial Institute Tropical and Preventive Medicine, American Arbitration Assn., Citizens Hist. Assn. (life), Internat. Sch. History Surg. and Related Scis. (hon. mem.), Nu Sigma Nu. Conglist. Clubs: Union League of Michigan (honorary life); Michigan Union (life), University of Michigan Emeritus (Ann Arbor); Sportsmans Club of Michigan; various local clubs. Earl Ingram Carr award, created by National Conference Rural Health, A.M.A., 1960. Home: Lansing, Mich.

CARR, JAMES KENNEDY, cons. engr.; b. Redding, Calif., Jan. 15, 1914; s. Francis and Mary (Kennedy) C.; B.S. in Civil Engring., U. Santa Clara (Calif.), 1934, D.Eng. (hon.), 1968; m. Katherine Kergan, Oct. 14, 1939; children—Mary (Mrs. William Chapman), Ann (Mrs. Gene Dallosto), Susan (Mrs. Michael Taylor), Margaret (Mrs. Dino Boito). Engr. with WPA, geol. surveyor Dept. Interior, Shasta County (Calif.) Surveyor's Office, city engr.'s office, Redding, 1934-36; with Bur. Reclamation, Dept. Interior, 1936-51, planning, constrn. and operations dir. Shasta Dam, 1936-40, Keswick Dam, 1945-51, Orland Project, 1945-51, dir. studies Trinity and Feather River projects, 1945-51, dist. mgr. all activities in Calif. north of Sacramento, 1946-51; engring. cons. com. interior and insular affairs U.S. Ho. of Reps., 1951-53; asst. gen. mgr. Sacramento Municipal Utility Dist., 1953-61; under sec. Dept Interior, Washington, 1961-64; gen. mgr. pub. utilities City-County of San Francisco, 1964-70; dir. San Francisco Internat. Airport, 1970-73; dir. aviation County of Sacramento, 1973-76; cons. engr., Sacramento, 1976-80. Chmn. Calif. Water Commn., 1959-61. Bd. regents U. Santa Clara, 1959-65. Registered profl. engr., Calif., D.C. Fellow ASCE (Civil Govt. award 1964); mem. Sacramento C. of C., Airport Operators Internat. (pres. 1973), Tau Beta Pi. Clubs: Rotary, K.C. Home: Sacramento, Calif. Died Sept. 4, 1980; buried Calvary Cemetery, Sacramento.

CARR, JOHN DICKSON, author; b. Uniontown, Pa., 1906; ed. Hill Sch., Haverford Coll.; m. Clarice Cleaves, 1931; 3 children. Writer of mystery fiction, 1930-77; lived in Eng., 1931-48; worked with Adrian Conan Doyle on life of Sir Arthur Conan Doyle, 2 yrs.; now a leading authority on Sir Arthur Conan Doyle. With BBC, Eng., World War II. Mem. Baker Street Irregulars. Clubs: Savage, Garrick (London). Author (also under pseudonyms Carr Dickson, Carter Dickson), Life of Sir Arthur Conan Doyle, 1949; Bride of Newgate, 1950; Devil in Velvet, 1951; Behind the Crimson Blind, 1952; Poison in Jest, 1952; Waxworks Murder, 1952; Nine Wrong Answers, 1952; Eight of Swords, 1953; Cavalier's Cup, 1952; Third Bullet, 1954; Captain Cut-Throat, 1955; The Dead Man's Knock, 1958; Fire Burn; Fear is the Same; Patrick Butler for the Defense; Scandal at High Chimneys; The Arabian Nights Murder; The Burning Court; In Spite of Thunder, 1960; Most Secret, 1964; Blind Barber; Case of the Constant Suicides; Corpse in the Waxworks; Dark of the Moon, 1967; House of Satan's Elbow, 1967; Castle Skull, 1968; Pappa La-Ba, 1968; Crooked Hinge; Death Watch; Emperor's Snuff Box; Four False Weapons; Ghosts' High Noon; Hag's Nook; It Walks By Night; Lost Gallows; Mad Hatter Mystery; Men Who Explained Myster-ies; The Problem of Green Capsules; To Wake the Dead. Home: Mamaroneck, N.Y. Died Feb. 27, 1977.

CARR, OSCAR CLARK, JR., cotton producer, church exec.; b. Memphis, Aug. 4, 1923; s. Oscar Clark and Blanche (Busby) C.; student Cornell U., 1941-42; B.S. with distinction, U.S. Naval Acad., 1945; D.C.L., Berkeley Div. Sch. at Yale, 1972; L.H.D., Cuttington Coll., Liberia, 1975; m. Billie Fisher, June 21, 1950; children—Oscar Clark, Blanche Busby, Palmer Scott, John T. Fisher, Elane Tucker. Pres. Carr Planting Co., cotton producer, Clarksdale Miss., 1948-77; partner Carr-Fisher Realty, 1964-77; organized First Nat. Bank Clarksdale, 1964, chmn. bd., 1964-70; chmn. bd. Samelson Cigar Co., 1964-68; pres. Holiday Inn of Clarksdale, 1957-71; mem. exec. com. Planters Oil Mill, N. Delta Congress; dir. John T. Fisher Motor Co. Pres. Planters Club Coahoma County, 1953; bd. dirs. Cotton Council Internat., 1965-68; king Memphis Cotton Carnival, 1956; pres. Delta Council 1961. Pres. Episcopalian Laymen of Miss; 1963; del. Episcopalian Gen. Conv., 1967, 1969, 70; mem. standing com. Episcopal Diocese Miss., 1967-71; participant Am. Assembly, 1969, 73; mem. Presiding Bishop's Renewal Commn., 1965-66; mem. Joint Commn. on Ch. in Human Affairs; v.p. exec. council Episcopal Ch. for Devel., 1971-77. Del. Democratic Nat. Conv., 1968; chmn. Mississippians for Robert Kennedy, 1968; mem. Miss. Dem. Exec. Com., 1968-71. Trustee St. George's Episcopal Day Sch., 1958-64, Hutchinson's Sch., All Saint's Sch., Okolona Coll., 1962-67, Episcopal Ch. Found., 1971-77; mem. president's council Southwestern U.; vice chmn. bd. trustees Berkeley Divinity Sch., Yale, 1973. Served to lt. (j.g.) USN, 1945-47. Mem. Nat. Cotton Council Newcomen Soc., Psi Upsilon. Club: Princeton of N.Y. Home: New York, N.Y. Died Nov. 5, 1977.

CARR, ROBERT KENNETH, educator, author; b. Cleve., Feb. 15, 1908; s. Clifford A. and Sue (Stewart) C.; A.B., Dartmouth, 1929, A.M., Harvard, 1930, Ph.D., 1935; LL.D., Dartmouth, Concord, Ohio Wesleyan U., 1960, U. Pitts., 1962, Ripon Coll., 1967, Denison U., 1970; m. Olive Grabill, Aug. 25, 1933; children—Norman Stewart, Elliott Grabill, Robert Clifford. Mem. dept. govt., also dir. bur. municipal research U. Okla., 1931-37; mem. dept. govt. Dartmouth, 1937-59; Parker prof. of law and polit. sci. 1948-59, dir. Great Issues course, 1955-57; Guggenheim fellow, 1954-55; pres. Oberlin (Ohio) Coll., 1960-70; research scholar Am. Council Edn., 1970-73; exec. dir. Southeastern Mass. Coll. Consortium, 1974-77. Cons. U.S. Civil Rights Commn., 1959; mem. adv. com. higher edn. HEW, 1967-68; exec. sec. Pres.'s Com. on Civil Rights, 1947. Mem. Hanover Sch. Bd., 1943-52. Exec. com., trustee Carnegie Found. Advancement Teaching, 1964-70; trustee Am. Council Edn., 1964-67; mem. vis. com. dept. govt. Harvard, 1965-70; acad. adv. bd. U.S. Naval Acad., 1969-71; bd. visitors Mass. Maritime Acad., 1973-79. Fellow Am. Acad. Arts and Scis.; mem. Am. Polit. Sci. Assn. (council 1949-51), AAUP (council 1952-53, 2d v.p. 1956-58, gen. sec. 1957-58, chmn. acad. freedom and tenure com. 1958-60), New Eng. Polit. Sci. Assn. (pres. 1955-56), Phi Beta Kappa. Clubs: Century (N.Y.C.); Cosmos (Washington). Author: The Supreme Court and Judicial Review, 1942; Federal Protection of Civil Rights, 1947; American Democracy in Theory and Practice (with others), rev. edit., 1977; The Unamerican Activities Committee, 1952; Collective Bargaining Comes to the Campus, 1973. Home: Oberlin, Ohio. Died Feb. 21, 1979; interred Oberlin, Ohio.

CARREIRO, JOSEPH ALVAREZ, educator, indsl. designer; b. Cambridge, Mass., Mar. 13, 1920; s. Camillo A. and Maria (Borges) C.; B.S., Mass. Coll. Art, 1950; postgrad. Cranbrook Acad., 1947-48, Harvard, 1951-53; m. Dorothy Rita Bellefleur, Nov. 22, 1947; children—Joel, Christine, Donald, Anthony, Suzanne, Michele, Amanda. Instr. dept. housing and design Cornell U., Ithaca, N.Y., 1950-54, prof., chmn. dept., 1965-78; chmn. dept. design and environ. analysis, 1965-68, chmn. design and environ. analysis dept., 1968-75; dir. indsl. design dept. Phila. Coll. Art, 1954-60, dir. indsl., interior and dimensional design depts., 1960-63, dean faculty, 1963-65; pres. Carreiro Design Asso., Carreiro Indsl. Designers; lectr. on indsl. design edn. in U.S., Bauhaus, German Democratic

Republic, 1978. Mem. planning com. Design in Govt. Conf., Dept. Agr., Washington, 1964; mem. planning com. Role of Crafts in Edn. Conf., HEW, Washington, 1964-65; chmn. Fulbright Com. design div. Inst. Internat. Edn., 1963-65; ednl. cons. All-Union Research Inst. Indsl. Design, USSR, 1976. Bd. dirs. Nat. Corp. Housing Partnerships. Recipient Nat. Design Div. award Am. Ceramic Soc., 1964. Nat. Endowment for the Arts grantee for nat. study of design edn. in U.S. Mem. Indsl. Design Edn. Assn. (past pres.), Indsl. Designers Soc. Am. (bd. govs.), Am. Assn. Housing Educators (v.p., chmn. edn. com.). Coll. Art Assn., N.E.A. Author: (with Steven Mensch) Building Blocks: Design Potential and Constraints. Project dir., research publ. The New Building Block: A Report on the Factory-Produced Dwelling Module. Home: Ithaca, N.Y. Died Oct. 15, 1978; buried Ithaca.

CARRELL, ORA W. (KAR'REL), clergyman, educator; b. Waukee, Ia., May 1, 1883; s. George B. and Harriet (Jones) C.; grad. high sch., Union, Ia., 1903; A.B., Penn. Coll., Oskaloosa, Ia., 1908; grad. student U. of Ia., 1908-09; B.D., Hartford Theol. Sem., 1915; m. Golda O. Ruan, June 22, 1912. Pastor Bloomfie:d Friends Ch., Oskaloosa, Ia., 1907-08, Muscatine, 1908-12, Allen's Neck, Mass., summer 1913, Fall River, Mass., 1914, 15; field sec. Ia. Yearly Meeting of Friends, 1915-18; pastor Central City, Neb., and head dept. of religion, Neb. Central Coll., 1918-21; pres. Neb. Central Coll., since 1921. Mem. Bd. of Edn. Five Years'. Meeting of Friends in America; mem. Am. Friends Service Com.; mem. Neb. Assn. Ch. Colleges (pres. 1948-49). Clubs: Commercial, Lions. Home: Central City, Neb.

CARRIGAN, JOHN WILLARD, fgn. service officer; b. San Francisco, Calif., Sept. 27, 1908; s. Clarence and Anna (Sperry) C.; student Orley Farm, Harrow, Eng., 1917, Institut Sillig, Vevey, Switzerland, 1919-25, Phillips Exeter Acad., 1925-27; A.B., Harvard, 1931; m. Frances Miller Little, July, 1933. Foreign service officer, from 1932; vice counsul, Vigo, Spain, 1933, Funchal, Madeira, 1935; 3d sec. of legation and vice consul, Managua, 1935; 3d sec. of embassy, Mexico City, 1938; became asst. chief, div. of Mexican Affairs, Dept. of State, 1944, chief, 1944-46; first sec. embassy, San José, Costa Rica, Jan. 1946-47; 1st sec., counselor embassy, Caracas, Venezuela, 1947-50; assigned to Dept. of State and Nat. War Coll., 1950-51; spl. asst. for Mut. Def. Assistance Program and counselor Am. Embassy, Lisbon, Portugal, 1951-54; consul gen., Dhahran, Saudi Arabia, 1954-57; faculty advisor Air Univ., Maxwell AFB, Ala., 1957-60; sr. evaluator Office Insp. Gen. and Comptroller Mut. Security Affairs, Dept. State, Washington, 1960-61, fgn. assistance insp., spl. asst. Office Insp. Gen. for Fgn. Assistance, from 1961. Home: Washington, D.C. Deceased.

CARRINGTON, JOHN CLAIBORNE, minerals co. exec.; b. San Antonio, Sept. 7, 1912; s. John Baron and Zula Lee (Gaddis) C.; Princeton U., 1933; grad. Advanced Mgmt. Program, Harvard U., 1950; m. Elizabeth Meusebach, June 21, 1935; children—Elizabeth Bierman, Judith Green. With Akron (Ohio) Times Press, 1933-38, Carl Byoir Assos., N.Y.C., 1938-39; with Freeport Minerals Co., N.Y.C., 1939-78, v.p., then sr. v.p., 1952-74, exec. v.p., dir., 1974-78. Treas. Eastern region Met. Opera Nat. Council; pres. bd. trustees Hewitt Sch., N.Y.C. Mem. Harvard Advanced Mgmt. Assn. N.Y. (dir.). Clubs: Princeton, Coffee House (N.Y.C.); Argyle (San Antonio). Home: New York, N.Y. Died May 4, 1978.

CARROLL, DANIEL REYNOLDS, newspaper editor; b. Long Island City, N.Y., Nov. 13, 1886; s. John Warren and Mary (Reynolds) C.; ed. pub. and high schs.; m. Cora Mae Tiddle, of Albany, N.Y., Apr. 25, 1924. Began newspaper work with New York Sun, 1907; with Albany (N.Y.) Times Union, 1915, news editor, 1915-17; war corr. New York Herald, World War; mng. editor Albany Times Union, 1919-28, also v.p., 1924-28. Democrat. Catholic. Home: West Lebanon, N.Y.

CARROLL, GORDON, author, editor; b. Balt., Apr. 29, 1903; s. Charles Gordon and Elizabeth (Swann) C.; grad. Balt. Poly. Inst., 1920; student U. Md., 1921-23; m. Phyllis Oliver Fechtig, Sept. 6, 1926; children—Gordon, Robert McHenry. Reporter, editor various met. newspapers, 1924-34; mng. editor Am. Mercury, 1934-38; sr. editor Reader's Digest, 1938-41; editor publs. Office Civilian Def., 1942; editor Time, Inc., 1943-45; exec. editor Coronet, 1945-48, editor in chief, 1948-52, pub., 1952-55; dir. Famous Writers Sch., Westport, Conn., 1958-70; pres. Ltd. Edits. Club, Westport. Home: Weston, Conn. Died Jan. 11, 1978.

CARROLL, JAMES MATTHEW, lawyer, arbitrator, utility exec.; b. Springfield, Mass., Dec. 9, 1908; s. Alfred Joseph and Margaret E. (Cruse) C.; A.B. magna cum laude, Holy Cross Coll., 1931; LL.B., Yale, 1934; m. Ruth Madelyn Crowe, Feb. 14, 1942; children—James Matthew, Deborah V. (Mrs. Stephen C. Effler), Kathleen M., Nancy C. Admitted to Mass. bar, 1934; asst. city solicitor Springfield, 1938-39, city solicitor, 1940-43; spl. counsel SEC, Phila., 1944-46; spl. asst. to U.S. atty., Los Angeles, 1945; commr. Mass. Dept. Pub. Utilities, 1949-51; counsel, sec. Am. Bosch Arma Corp., 1951-55; asst. gen. counsel Boston Edison Co., 1956-63, v.p., gen. counsel, 1963-74, also dir.; practice law, arbitrator. Incorporator, Cath. Scholarships for Negroes, 1946. Mem. Am., Mass., Hampden County, Boston bar assns. Democrat. Roman Catholic. Home: Wellesley Hills, Mass. Died Oct. 25, 1978.

CARROLL, LOREN, fgn. service officer, editor; b. Scanlon, Minn., Mar. 5, 1904; s. John and Mary (Noonan) C.; m. Sheila M. Baker, May 9, 1949; children—Alexander, Nicholas. Various positions newspapers 1924-33; corr. Internat. News Service, Europe, 1933; city editor N.Y. Herald Tribune, European edit., 1934-37; fgn. editor, Newsweek, N.Y., 1940; chief OWI Psychol. Warfare Operations, Western Europe, hdqrs. London, 1942-43; press attache Am. Diplomatic Mission Algiers, Am. embassy, Paris, 1944; chief Paris bur. Newsweek, 1945-51; pub. affairs officer attached to NATO, Paris, France, 1952-56; U.S. consul-gen., Que., 1956-60, Palermo, Sicily, Italy, 1960-64; editor Fgn. Service Jour., Washington, 1964-78. Author: Wild Onion, 1930; Conversation Please, 1939. Home: Chevy Chase, Md. Died Oct. 21, 1978.

CARROLL, PENN LEARY, naval officer; b. oinden, La., Feb. 17, 1886; s. George Stephens and Lavilla (Tompkins) C.; B.S., U.S. Naval Acad., 1909; M.S., Columbia, 1916; M.S.E.E., Mass. Inst. Tech., 1917; M.S., Harvard, 1917; m. Mary Belle Hobson, Nov. 4, 1912; children—Eleanor Hobson, George Peyton, Katharine C. Wallace. Commd. ensign U.S. Navy, 1911, advanced through the grades to commodore, U.S. Navy, 1945; participated in World War I and II; retired from active duty, Nov. 30, 1947; Dept. of State visiting prof. Instituto Tecnologico de Monterrey, Monterrey N.L., Mexico, 1949-51, prof. and asst. to pres. since 1951. Awarded Legion of Merit, Bronze star, Chinese Order of Merit. Member American Society of Engring. Edn., Inst. Elec. Engrs., Soc. Naval Engrs. Protestant. Clubs: Army and Navy, Army-Navy Country (Washington); Internat. Rotary. Home: Monterrey, Mexico.

CARROLL, WILLIAM ERNEST, prof. animal husbandry; b. Orderville, Utah, Nov. 8, 1882; s. Charles William and Susan Amelia (Snyder) C.; B.S., Utah Agrl. Coll., Logan, 1909; M.S., U. of Ill., 1911, Ph.D., 1914; m. Lenore Ure, Sept. 1, 1915; children—William Robert, Marjorie. Prof. animal husbandry, Utah Agrl. Coll., 1911-25, and dean Sch. of Agr., 1937-38; prof. swine husbandry, U. of Ill., 1925-37, 1938-51, emeritus, head dept. animal husbandry, 1939-47; asso. dir. Ill. Agr. Exptl. Station, 1947-51; professor and acting head, dept. animal husbandry Utah State Agricultural College, Logan, Utah. Served as captain Sanitarv Corps, United States Army, with A.E.F., 1918-19. Fellow A.A.A.S.; mem. Am. Soc. of Animal Production (pres. 1934), Phi Lambda Upsilon, Sigma Xi, Phi Kappa Phi, Gamma Sigma Delta. Member of Congl. Church. Author: Producing Farm Livestock (with 4 others), 1932; Swine Production (with J.L. Krider), 1950. Contbr. to farm mags., agrl. explt. sta. bulls., and sci. jours. Home: Urbana, Ill.

CARR-SAUNDERS, ALEXANDER, retired; born in Reigate, Eng., Jan. 14, 1886; s. James and Flora Ann (Tower) Carr-S.; student Eton Coll., 1899-1903; M.A., Oxford, 1911, M.A., Cambridge, 1940, Lit.D., 1961; LL.D., Glasgow, 1945; Litt.D. (honorary), Dublin, 1947; Hon. dr. en Droit, Univ. Grenoble, 1949; D.Litt. (hon.), Malaya, 1950; LL.D. (honorary:, Columbia, 1954, Natal, 1954; D.Sc. (honorary), London Univ., 1959; married Teresa Molyneux-Seel, Mar. 9, 1929; children—Edmund, Flora, Nicholas. Prof. social scis. U. Liverpool, 1923-37; dir. London Sch. Econs. 1937-56. Hon fel. Peterhouse, Cambridge. Knight British Empire. Capt. Royal Army Service Corps, 1914-18. Fellow British Acad. Author: The Population Problem, 1922; Social Structure of England and Wales, 1928; The Professions, 1933; World Population, 1936; Social Conditions in England and Wales, 1958; New Universities Overseas, 1961. Home: London, Eng.

CARRUTH, LAURENCE ADAMS, entomologist, educator; b. Mansfield, Mass., June 11, 1907; s. Charles Mason and Sarah Millicent (Cole) C.; B.S., Mass. Agrl. Coll., 1929; M.S., S.D. State Coll., 1931; Ph.D., Cornell U., 1935; m. Wynne Eleanor Caird, June 26, 1937; children—James Charles, Susan Wynne (Mrs. J.J. Ellington). Entomologist, N.Y. State Agr. Expt. Sta. (Cornell U.), 1935-49; prof. entomology, entomologist Agr. Expt. Sta., U. Ariz., 1949-73, prof. emeritus, 1973-78, head dept., 1949-67, head dept. emeritus, 1967-78. Fellow AAAS; mem. Entomol. Soc. Am., Sigma Xi. Home: Tucson, Ariz. Died Dec. 26, 1978.

CARRY, CHAMP, mfg. co. exec.; b. Lockport, Ill., May 31, 1896; s. Joeph Carles and Arabella C. (Dill) C.; M.E., Cornell U., 1918; m. Marion Osborne, Oct. 14, 1922; children—Marion (Mrs. Jerome Rich), June (Mrs. Irving Seaman, Jr.). Began in shops of Haskell & Barker Car Co., mfrs. freight cars, 1919; with Pullman Car & Mfg. Corp., 1922-32; v.p., 1929-32; v.p. Pullman Co., 1932-41, exec. v.p., 1941-46; pres. Pullman-Standard Car Mfg. Co., 1946-50; pres. Pullman, Inc., 1950-61, chmn. bd., 1961-66, hon. chmn. bd. dirs., 1966-70, also dir. Lt. 18th F.A., 3d Div. U.S. Army, World War I. Decorated D.S.C. Clubs: Chicago, Chicago Commonwealth, Onwentsia, Commercial, Old Elm, Shoreacres, Links (N.Y.C.). Home: Lake Forest, Ill. Died Aug. 15, 1979.

CARSON, ALBERT BEN, educator; b. Sedalia, Mo., Aug. 10, 1913; s. Albert Edwin and Alice Ben (McGee) C.; A.B., Colo. Coll., 1935; M.B.A., Northwestern U., 1937; Ph.D., U. Nebr., 1943; m. Ruth Bradley, Dec. 24, 1937; children—Mary Beth, Nancy Jean. Instr. accounting Morningside Coll., 1937-38, U. Nebr., 1938-43; accountant Kaiser Co., Inc., 1943-45; asst. prof. accounting U. Utah, 1945-47; accountant Beesley, Wood and Co., C.P.A.'s, Salt Lake City, 1946-47; faculty U. Calif. at Los Angeles, 1947-73, prof. accounting, 1958-73, prof. emeritus, 1973-79, vice chmn. dept. bus. adminstrn., 1957-65, acting asso. dean Sch. Bus. Adminstrn., 1958-59. Fulbright lectr., Australia, summer 1962; vis. prof. Ariz. State U., 1965-66, Australian Nat. U., Canberra, 1968. Mem. Educator-Cons. Com. to Comptroller Gen. U.S., 1959-64. C.P.A., Utah. Mem. Am. Accounting Assn. (dir. research 1959, pres. 1961), Am. Inst. C.P.A.'s, Beta Theta Pi, Alpha Kappa Psi. Co-author: College Accounting, 5th-10th edits., from 1951; author: The Public Accounting Profession in California, 1956. Contbr. articles to profl. jours., to Accountants' Cost Handbook, 2d edit., 1960; also Ency. Brit. Home: Laguna Hills, Calif. Died Aug. 31, 1979.

CARSON, NORMA BRIGHT, editor; b. Phila., Jan. 7, 1883; d. Joseph C. and Emma (Moore) Bright; grad. Girls High Sch., Phila., 1901; m. Robert Carson, June 20, 1906; children—Robert Bright, Dorothy Bright. Editor The Book News Monthly, Phila., 1906-18; assn. lit. editor Phila. Press, 1918-20; mng. editor Photo-Play World, 1918-20; editor The Photo Drama Magazine, 1920-21; managing editor The Republican Woman, 1923-36; editor The Clubwoman's Journal since 1935; apptd. magistrate City of Phila., 1932; apptd. chief of juvenile div., Crime Prevention Bureau, City of Phila., Feb. 1936; apptd. supervisor of policewomen, crime prevention div., Phila. Bur. of Police, 1941; apptd. chief women's div., Phila. Bur. of Police, 1950. Presbyn. Author: ten books, 1905-18. Founder, editor The Phila. Policewoman, 1947. Home: Philadelphia.

CARSON, RALPH MOORE, lawyer; b. Indpls., Aug. 22, 1896; s. Oliver Howard and Mary (Dowdigan) C.; A.B., U. Mich., 1917, J.D., 1923, LL.D., 1959; B.A. (Rhodes scholar), Oxford U., 1922; m. Cécile Bellé, Oct. 14, 1928; 1 son, Jean-Philippe (dec.). Admitted to N.Y. bar, 1926; with Davis Polk & Wardwell, and predecessor law firms, N.Y.C., 1923-77, partner firm, 1935-77. Served with USNRF, 1918. Mem. Oxford Union Soc. (pres. 1922), Am., N.Y. County bar assns., Bar Assn. City N.Y., Phi Beta Kappa, Delta Sigma Rho. Clubs: Downtown Assn., Century Assn. (N.Y.C.); Univ. of Mich. Lawyers; Everglades (Palm Beach, Fla.). Editor: Jurisprudence in Action, 1953. Contbr. articles to legal periodicals. Home: Pawling, N.Y. Died Apr. 16, 1977.

CARSON, RUSSELL MACK LITTLE, Adirondackian authority; b. Glens Falls, N.Y., June 20, 1884; s. Charles Herbert and Katherine Luella (Little) C.; grad. Glens Falls Acad., 1901; m. Mary Isabelle Goodman, May 28, 1910 (died July 14, 1939); children—Shirley Elizabeth, Samuel Goodman, Charles Herbert II; m. 2d, Ann Elizabeth Tymchyn, June 21, 1946. Ins. business, Glens Falls, 1901; head Carson Ins. Agency, 1915-46; pres. Carson-Duffy Agency, Incorporated, since Jan. 1946; president Joints Lime Co., State Association Service, 1938-40; v.p. Glens Falls Savs. & Loan Assn., spl. cons. on ins. to Army Exchange Service, 1942. Capt. Co. K, 105th Inf., N.Y. Nat. Guard, 1918-24; mem. Bd. of Edn., Glens Falls, N.Y., 1925—, president, 1937-41; director Glens Falls Tree Commission, 1936—. Trustee Assn. for Protection of Adirondacks (sec. 1938-39). Mem. N.Y. State Conservation Dept. Advisory Council, 1931. Member National Association Ins. Agents (chmn. com. on commns; past dir., chmn. finance com.), N.Y. State Assn. Local Agents (chairman committee on pub. property Ins., 1936-38, pres., 1939-40, exec. com. 1934-50, nat councillor, 1940-42; nat. state dir. 1941-45 and 1948-49; chmn. conf. and co-ordination committee, since 1946; chairman National Councillors in Eastern Underwriters Assn. Territory, 1940-42; mem. Business Development Office Advisory Council, 1941-42, Adirondack Improved Trail Soc., N.Y. States Com. on 50 Years of Conservation (exec. com. 1935), N.Y. State Sch. Bds. Assn. (chmn. spl. com. on ins. and bonding since 1934), pres., 1940-41 past dir. N.Y. State Ins. Fedn.; chmn. Warren Co. Highway Safety Committee; member Regents Commission on State Aid for Education, 1939-40, Regents Advisory Council on Buildings and Grounds, 1941-42; executive com. Nat. Council of State Sch. Bd. Assns., 1941. Vice pres. Adirondack Historical Museum. Mem. The Wilderness Society, New York State Archeological Society, New York State Wildlife Week Com., Glens Falls Ins. Club (pres. 1932-33). Awarded President's Citation N.Y. State, 1948, Nat., 1949, assns. ins. agents; citation Ohio

State Assn. Ins. Agents, 1950. Republican. Methodist; trustee Christ Church, Glens Falls. Mason (past master). Clubs: Adirondack Mountain (pres. 1930-31), Glens Falls Rotary (pres. 1936-37), Camp Fire of Am., Adirondack Loj. Author: Peaks and People of the Adirondacks, 1927; (with Lawrence Daw and Orrin Terry) An Insurance Program for the Guidance of School Boards, 1936; A Mount Marcy Anthology, 1937. Editor High Spots, 1935. Contbr. on Indian occupancy of Adirondacks to mags. and newspapers. Home: Glen Falls, N.Y.

CARSON, WILLIAM WALLACE, professor history; born Canton, N.C., Aug. 28, 1886; s. Julius Lafayette and Mary (Williamson) C.; A.B., Wofford Coll., 1907; A.M., Trinity Coll., 1908; Ph.D., U. of Wis., 1914; m. Luella Lucile Haskins, 1916; 1 dau., Mary Frances. Began teaching at Central Coll., Fayette, Mo., 1908; prof. history and politics, Morningside Coll., Sioux City, Ia., 1913-16; prof. polit. science and history, and head dept. of polit. science, DePauw U., 1916-27, head dept. of history and polit. science, 1927-38, head dept. history since 1938, chmn. div. of social science, 1933-36. Mem. Am. Hist. Assn., Miss. Valley Hist. Assn., Am. Assn. Univ. Profs., Kappa Alpha (Southern), Phi Beta Kappa (hon.). Methodist. Home: Greencastle, Ind.

CARSWELL, D. B., marine consultant; b. Paisley, Scotland, Aug. 3, 1884; s. Allan B. and Elizabeth (Ballantyne) C.; ed. Paisley Tech. Coll. and Manchester Tech. Coll. (both Eng.); m. Charlotte Lyon, Sept. 27, 1913; children—Kathleen Wallace Ballantyne (Mrs. W. Rowan Simpson), Elizabeth Ballantyne (Mrs. John Y. Carlyle). Mech. engr. since 1899; mech. training, 1899-1904; marine engring. at sea, 1905-08; in drawing office, Henry Simon, Ltd., Manchester, Eng., 1908-09, asst. works mgr., 1909-13; chief engr. Deloro Mining and Reduction Co., Can., 1913-15; supt. Detroit (Mich.) Shipbuilding Co., 1915-19, asst. gen. mgr., McDugal Duluth Shipbuilding Co., Duluth, Minn., 1919-21; supt. engr., Canadian Nat. Steamship Co., 1921-27; gen. mgr. and vice pres. Canadian Vickers, Montreal, Can., 1928-33; dir. gen. of shipbuilding and repairs for Can., hdqrs. Ottawa, Ont., Can. Decorated Order British Empire. Vice pres. Inst. Marine Engs. (London). Fellow, Soc. Consulting Marine Engrs. and Ship Surveyors. Member Society Naval Architects and Marine Engrs. (U.S.). Mason. Clubs: Beaconsfield Golf, Mount Stephen (Montreal). Home: Montreal, Que., Can. *

CARTER, ALAN, musician; b. Greenwich, Conn., July 29, 1904; s. Herbert Swift and Mabel (Pettit) C.; student Taft Sch., Watertown, Conn., 1920-22, Mannes Music Sch., N.Y.C., 1922-23, Conservatory of Music, Cologne, Germany, 1923-24; Mus.D. (hon.), U. Vt., 1955; m. Marianne Townsend, May 18, 1926; children—Joan Pettit, Alan Peter; m. 2d, Barbara Kent, July 7, 1934; children—Timothy, Eric, Kent, Thayer. Musician, 1923-75; founder, condr. Vt. State Symphony Orch.; mem. musical faculty Middlebury Coll., 1939-69, chmn. music dept., 1955-69; music dir. Vt. Symphony Orch. Assn., Inc.; dir. Composers' Conf. and Chamber Music Center, Middlebury Coll., 1946-50, Bennington (Vt.) Coll., 1950-72, Johnson State Coll., 1972-74; pres., dir. Chamber Music Conf. and Composers' Forum of East, Bennington Coll., 1975. Served as capt. U.S. Army, music officers Hdqrs. 4th Service Comd., Atlanta, 1942-44; Hdqrs. 1st Service Comd., Boston, 1943-44. Recipient Alice M. Ditson condr.'s award Columbia U., 1968; Gov.'s award for excellence in the arts Vt. Council on Arts, 1972. Contbr. articles on music and music edn. Home: Middlebury, Vt. Died Sept. 21, 1975.

CARTER, BOYD GEORGE, educator, writer; b. Duffield, Va. May 8, 1908; s. James David and Viola (Fraley) C.; student U. Toulouse (France), 1926-27; A.B., Coll. William and Mary, 1929; A.M., U. Ill., 1933, Ph.D., 1937; postgrad. U. Iowa, summer 1942; m. Mary Eileen Barry, June 16, 1965; With AP, summer 1929; tchr. Beaver High Sch., Bluefield, W.Va., 1929-31; grad. asst. U. Ill., 1931-37; instr. U. Idaho, 1937; asst. prof. U. Wyo., 1938; prof., chmn. dept. modern langs. Coe Coll., 1939-45; prof. U. Nebr., 1945-59, chmn. dept. Romance langs, 1950-56; prof. So. Ill. U., 1959-67, U. Mo., Columbia, 1967-76; vis. prof. U. Iowa, 1977; scholar in residence, adj. prof. Romance langs. Tex. Tech. U., 1978-80; lectr. Mexico City, 1962, Managua, Nicaragua, 1967; mem. adv. com. project Mass. Council Public Schs., 1959-67. Decorated Palmes Académiques (France). Mem. MLA. Am. Assn. Tchrs. French (pres. West Central chpt. 1948-50), Am. Assn. Tchrs. Spanish and Portuguese, Latin Am. Studies Assn., 82d Airborne Div. Assn. (hon.), Mexican Acad. (corr.), C-47 Club (hon.), John G. Neihardt Corral of Westerners, Phi Beta Kappa, Phi Kappa Phi, Omicron Delta Kappa, Phi Sigma Iota, Phi Kappa Tau. Author: (with C. G. Rowe) A French Review Grammar, 1948; Manuel Gutiérrez Nájera: estudio y escritos inéditos, 1956; Las revistas literarias de Hispanoamérica, 1959; En torno a Gutiérrez Nájera, 1960; (with Joan L. Carter) Manuel Gutiérrez Nájera florilegio crítico-conmemorativo, 1966; La Revista de Americá de Rúben Darió y Ricardo Jaimes Freyre, 1967; Historia de la literatura hispanoamericana a través de sus revistas, 1968; (with Mary Eileen Carter) Manuel Gutiérrez Nájera, Plato del diá, 1972; Divagaciones y fantasías: Crónicas de Manuel Gutiérrez Nájera, 1974; Editor: Those Devils in Baggy Pants (Ross S. Carter), 1951, 2d, rev. edit., 1979; German Review Grammar (D. F. Allison), 1965; advisory editor Prairie Schooner, 1949-59; contbr. articles, stories, poetry to periodicals. Home: Clintwood, Va. Died Dec. 18, 1980.

CARTER, EDGAR BROCK, research cons.; b. Elkinsville, Ind., Apr. 22, 1886; s. Tobe Wilford and Nannie Elizabeth (Brock) C.; A.B., U. Ind., 1911; m. Susie Field Huffines, June 4, 1914 (dec. 1918); 1 son, John Robert; m. 2d, Ruth Ann Cheney, June 17, 1922; 1 dau., Carol Ruth (Mrs. H. Dale Clark). Analytical, cons. chemist Landon C. Moore, Dallas, 1911-15; dir. biol. lab. Swan-Myers Co., Indpls., 1915-20, dir. sci. work, 1920-31; with Abbott Labs., North Chicago, 1931—, bd. dirs., 1935-52, asso. dir. research 1942-46, exec. dir. research, asst. sec., 1946-52, now cons. Chmn. sub-com. sterile products, mem. exec. rom. U.S. Pharmacopoeia Revision Com., 1950-60; pres. Highland Park (Ill.) Social Service Com., 1938-40. Fellow Am. Pub. Health Assn., A.A.A.S., Am. Inst. Chemists, Royal Soc. Health; mem. Am. Chem. Soc., Am. Pharm. Assn., Am. Soc. for Microbiology, Sigma Xi, Alpha Chi Sigma. Presbyn. (elder:. Mason (32), Kiwanian. Club: Chemists. Author chpt. in Drug. Research and Development, 1948. Home: Miami FL. 33157

CARTER, JAMES MARSHALL, judge; b. Santa Barbara, Calif., Mar. 11, 1904; s. James Madison and Belle A. (Hicks) C.; A.B., Pomona Coll., 1924; postgrad. Harvard Law Sch., 1924-25; J.D., U. So. Calif., 1927; LL.D., U. San Diego, 1962; m. Dorothy Freeland, 1927; 1 dau., Joan F.; m. 2d, Ruth Doty, Sept. 17, 1938; m. 3d, Bina Cheney, Dec. 30, 1953. Admitted to Calif. bar, 1928, and practiced in Los Angeles, 1928-40; dir. State Dept. Motor Vehicles for Calif., 1940-43; chief asst. U.S. atty. So. Dist. Calif., 1943-46, U.S. atty., 1946-49; U.S. dist. judge, 1949-67; judge ninth circuit U.S. Ct. of Appeals, from 1967, sr. circuit judge, from 1971, judge Temporary Emergency Ct. Appeals, from 1975; chmn. Calif. State Hwy. Traffic Adv. Com. to War Dept., 1941-42; mem. Commn. on Interstate Cooperation, State of Calif., 1941-42, Interstate Commn. on Crime, 1941-42, mem. gov.'s council, 1940-42. Mem. various coms. Jud. Conf. of U.S., mem. com. to celebrate Bicentennial, 1975-76; mem. adv. council judges Nat. Council Crime and Delinquency. Bd. dirs. Fed. Jud. Center, 1968-71. Mem. Am. Bar Assn., Inst. Jud. Adminstrn., Order of Coif, Phi Kappa Phi, Sigma Tau, Phi Alpha Delta, Ephebian Soc. Democrat. Eagle, Elk. Home: San Diego, Calif. Died Nov. 18, 1979.

CARTER, JAMES R., corp. exec.; b. Newton, Mass., July 14, 1907; s. Hubert Lazell and Edith Harriet (Adams) C.; grad. Worcester Acad., 1925; student Harvard, 1925-29, Harvard Bus. Sch. 1932-33; m. Placidia White, Apr. 2, 1954. With Townsend, Anthony & Tyson, stockbrokers, 1930-32, Am. Pulp & Paper Assn., 1933-34; with Nashua Corp. (N.H.), 1934-79, chmn., dir., until 1979; dir., chmn. bd. Nashua Copycat Ltd. (Eng.); dir. N.E. Electric System, Cabot Corp., Boston. Chmn. bd. visitors Whittemore Sch. Bus. and Econs., U. N.H. Served as lt. col. USAAF, 1942-46. Mem. Am. Mgmt. Assn., Sons Colonial Wars. Clubs: Brook (N.Y.C.); Union (Boston). Home: Santa Barbara, Calif. Died Aug. 12, 1979.

CARTER, MOTHER MAYBELLE, folk singer; b. Nickelsville, Va., May 10, 1909; d. Hugh Jack and Margaret Addington; m. Ezra J. Carter, 1925; children—June (Mrs. Johnny Cash), Anita, Helen. Mem. of performing group The Carter Family, 1927-78; albums recorded include Wildwood Flower, Keep on the Sunnyside, Wabash Cannonball (Grammy award song Will the Circle be Unbroken); other albums for United Artists, Columbia, Victor, Smash, Kapp, Liberty; appearance at Newport (R.I.) Folk Festival, 1965; regular on Johnny Cash TV show, 1969-72. Elected to Country Music Hall of Fame by Country Music Assn., 1971; recipient Am. Music award as mem. of Country Music Group of Yr., 1973. Home: Madison, Tenn. Died Oct. 23, 1978; buried Woodlawn Cemetery, Hendersonville, Tenn.

CARTER, OLIVER JESSE, judge; b. San Francisco, Apr. 7, 1911; s. Jesse W. and Tiny E. (Gish) C.; student Stanford, 1928-32; LL.B., U. Calif., 1935; m. Hildur Emlyn Westlind, Oct. 11, 1941, (dec. Dec. 1969); 1 dau., Karin Westlind; m. 2d, Mary D. Wallace, Apr. 18, 1970. Admitted to Calif. bar, 1936; asso. Carter, Barrett, Finley & Carlton, 1936-38; asst. dist. atty. Shasta County, 1938-39; partner Carter, Barrett & Carlton, 1940-41, pvt. practice, 1941-50; mem. Calif. Senate, 5th Senatorial Dist., 1941-49; U.S. dist. judge, then chief judge No. Dist. Calif., from 1950. Sec., Shasta County Democratic Central Com., 1941-48; vice chmn. Calif. State Central Com. for 2d Congl. Dist., 1948; chmn. Dem. State Central Com. Calif., 1948-51. Mem. Hastings Coll. Law Alumni Assn. U. Cal. Presbyn. Elk. Home: San Francisco, Calif. Died June 14, 1976; interred Trinity Alps, Calif.

CARTER, SARA, singer; b. Flatwoods, Va., July 21, 1898; m. A.P. Carter, June 18, 1915 (div. 1932); children—Gladys, Janette, Joe; m. 2d, Coy Bayes, 1939 (dec. 1976). Mem. Carter Family mus. team; songs first recorded 1927; albums include Great Original Carter Family; Mid the Green Fields of Virginia, A Collection of Favorites, The Famous Carter Family, Great Original Recordings, Home Among the Hills, Great Sacred Songs, others; also TV appearances Named to Country Music Hall of Fame Country Music Assn., 1970. Address: Lockeford, Calif. Died Jan. 8, 1979.

CARTER, WORRALL REED, naval officer (ref.); b. aboard Storm King, Pacific Ocean, Jan. 11, 1885; s. Charles John and Clarissa (Reed) C.; B.S., U.S. Naval Acad., 1908; A.M., Columbia, 1915; m. Mary Ambler Willcox, July 2, 1912; children—Worrall Reed, Thomas Hamlin Willcox, Charles John (killed in combat, France), Mary Cary. Commd. ensign U.S. Navy 1908, and advanced through grades to commodore, 1944; comdr. U.S. Naval Sta., Guantanamo, Cuba, 1938-40, naval service squadron (Adm. Nimitz's secret floating support of Pacific fleet in drive across central Pacific), World War II; ret. from active duty, 1947. Awarded D.S.M., Legion of Merit, various area medals. Mem. U.S. Naval Inst. Protestant Episcopal. Club: Army Navy (Washington). Home: Yarmouth, Me.

CARTLEDGE, GROVES HOWARD, chemist; b. Gainesville, Ga., Feb. 10, 1891; s. Samuel Jackson and Louisa (Burns) C.; A.B. and A.M., Davidson (N.C.) Coll., 1911, Sc.D., 1937; Ph.D., U. of Chicago, 1916; m. Matilda S. Witmer, June 6, 1918; children—Matilda Roberts, Louisa Burns. Prof. chemistry, Presbyn. Coll. of S.C., 1913-17; asso. prof. chemistry, Davidson Coll., 1917-18; 2d lt. Chem. Warfare Serv., 1918-19; chief chemist Island Refining Corp., New York, 1919-20; asso. prof., later prof. and dir. of coll. work in chemistry, Johns Hopkins, 1920-31; prof. chemistry and head dept. U. of Buffalo, 1931-45; head materials dept. Curtiss-Wright Research Lab., 1943-45; dean of faculty and prof. of chemistry, King College, Bristol, Tenn., 1946-51; a group leader Oak Ridge Nat. Lab., 1951-61, cons., 1961-71. Mem. Am. Chem. Soc. (Herty gold medal 1967, Lind lectureship 1971), Nat. Assn. Corrosion Engrs. (Whitney award 1966), Phi Beta Kappa, Sigma Xi. Democrat. Presbyn. Home: Brevard, N.C. Died June 9, 1980.

CARTTER, ALLAN MURRAY, educator; b. Westfield, N.J., June 17, 1922; s. Allan Murray and Bertha Louise (Baker) C.; A.B., Colgate U., 1946; A.M. Yale, 1949, Ph.D., 1952; m. Marietta S. Macklin, June 26, 1943 (div. May 1972); m. 2d, Jill Warburg Maass, Mar. 30, 1973. Instr. econs. Colgate, 1946-48; from asst. prof. to asso. prof. econs. Duke, 1952-57, prof., dean Grad. Sch., 1959-62; v.p. Am. Council on Edn., 1963-66; chancellor N.Y. U., 1966-72; program asso. Ford Found., 1957-59; sr. research fellow Carnegie Commn. of Higher Edn., 1972-74; prof. higher edn., dir. lab. for research on higher edn. U. Cal. at Los Angeles, 1974-76. Mem. Inter-Univ. Com. Econ. Devel. of South, 1960-64; dir. Commn. Plans and Objectives for Higher Edn., 1963-66; com. grad. sch. Yale, 1966-70; mem. Pres.'s Econ. Survey Team, Indonesia, 1961-62; mem. task group on manpower Pres.'s Sci. Adv. Com., 1963-64, mem. Commn. on Human Resources, 1963-70, N.Y. Gov.'s Council Econ. Advisers, 1968-72; mem. vis. com. Harvard Grad. Sch., from 1973, Nat. Bd. on Grad. Edn., 1972-75; v.p.-treas. Higher Edn. Research Inst., 1973—. Bd. dirs. Tchrs. Ins. Annuity Assn., 1967-71, Theol. Fund, 1966-72. Served with U.S. Army, 1942-45. Mem. Am. Econ. Assn., AAAS, Indsl. Relations Research Assn. Clubs: Cosmos (Washington); Century (N.Y.C.). Author: Redistribution of Income in Postwar Britain, 1955; Theory of Wages and Employment, 1959; An Assessment of Quality in Graduate Education, 1966. Co-author: Economic Survey of Indonesia, 1962; Labor Economics, 1967. Editor: American Universities and Colleges, 1964; Assuring Academic Progress Without Growth, 1975. Home: Beverly Hills, Calif. Died Aug. 4, 1976.

CARTUN, WALTER PAUL, mfg. co. exec.; b. Cleveland Heights, Ohio, Jan. 15, 1916; s. Paul O. and Gertrude (Bauer) C.; B.Sc., Ohio State U., 1937; M.B.A., Harvard, 1939; m. Lavette S. Watterson, Jan. 17, 1941; children—David, William (dec.), Richard. With Gen. Electric Co., 1936-62; v.p. Westinghouse Air Brake Co., 1962-69; pres. Railroad, Friction Products Corp., 1966-69; exec. v.p. Emhart Corp., from 1969, also dir. Vice pres. Pitts. C. of C., 1966-69; v.p. Jr. Achievement Southwest Pa., 1963-69. Trustee Indsl. Health Found., Pitts. Served to lt. USNR, 1941-45. Decorated Commendation ribbon. Mem. Soc. Advancement Mgmt. (Profl. Mgr. citation 1965; regional v.p. from 1970), Inst. Mgmt. Scis. Home: Avon, Conn. Deceased.

CARTY, JOHN VICTOR, utility exec.; b. N.Y.C., Apr. 12, 1904; m. Edna M. Lynch, 1928 (dec.); m. 2d, Ruth E. Riddle, 1960. With Ohio Water Service Co., 1935-76, v.p., sec., 1945-52, exec. v.p., 1952-63, pres., treas., 1963-69, chmn. bd., 1969-76, also dir. Mem. Am. Water Works Assn., C. of C. Kiwanian. Club: Youngstown. Home: Sarasota, Fla. Died May 17, 1976; interred Prayer Garden, Pine Shores Presbyn. Ch., Sarasota, Fla.

CARTY, WALTER VINCENT, pub. relations exec.; b. Boston, Jan. 22, 1927; s. John and Mary Ellen (Moran) C.; B.S., Boston Coll., 1951; postgrad. Harvard, 1952; m. Sally Clarke, Sept. 14, 1957; children—Mary Ellen, Elizabeth Seton, Jennifer Jane, Michael Clarke, Thomas More. Corr., Boston Herald-Traveler, 1948-50; columnist, editor Boston Pilot, 1950-52; reporter-writer Time-Life Publs., N.Y.C., 1952-54; asso. editor Curtis Publs., N.Y.C., 1954; with John Moynahan & Co., Inc., N.Y.C., 1955-72, pres., 1968-72; sr. v.p. Hill and Knowlton, Inc., N.Y.C., 1972-77. Lectr. A.M.A., N.Y. U.; chmn. spl. communications seminar N.Y. U., 1972, 73, 74, San Francisco, 1975. Capt., United Fund of Larchmont, 1967-70. Bd. dirs. Mens Club, St. Augustines, Larchmont, 1963-66. Served with USNR, 1944-46. Mem. Pub. Relations Soc. Am. (program chmn. N.Y. chpt. 1962, 64, 68, program chmn. nat. conf. Atlanta 1970, dir. N.Y. chpt. 1969, pres. 1971-72, chmn. counselors sect. 1973-74). Contbr. articles to profl. jours. Home: Larchmont, N.Y. Died June 17, 1977; buried Nantucket, Mass.

CARV, LUCIAN, writer; b. Hamlin, Kan., Jan. 1, 1886; s. Charles Preston and Myra Treat (Pugsley) C.; student U. of Wis., 1902-06 except 1 yr. Beloit (Wis.) Coll., 1905, U. of Chicago, 1907-08; m. Augusta Stromme, 1906; children—Lucian, Peter, Michael. Instr. English, Wabash Coll., Crawfordsville, Ind., 1908-10; reporter Chicago Tribune, 1910-12; lit. editor Chicago Evening Post, 1913-14; acting editor The Dial, Chicago, 1914; with Collier's Weekly, 1916-17; staff corr., 1918-19. Author: (novels) The Duke Steps Out; One Lovely Moron; The Duke Comes Back; The Little Champion; Second Meeting. Contbr. to mags. Home: Colebrook, Conn. *

CARVER, EDGAR M., manufacturing consultant; b. Morton, Ind., October 22, 1886; s. Oliver Morton and Lucy Belle (Marshall) C.; B.S. in Mech. Eng., Purdue, 1909, M.E., 1915; m. Avelyn Parks, Oct. 21, 1917; 1 dau., Carolyn. With Dodge Mfg. Co., power transmission machinery, Mishawaka, Ind., since July 15, 1909, beginning as draftsman, has served as salesman, gen. supt. and since 1927, v.p. and dir. Served as lt. and capt. U.S. Army, Ordnance Div. Chicago, 1917-19. Republican. Presbyterian. Mason. Club: South Bend Country. Home: South Bend, Ind.

CARY, WILLIAM HOLLENBACK, gynecologist; b. Barton, N.Y., Aug. 13, 1883; s. William Ezra and Estella (Hollenback) C.; student Owego (N.Y.) Free Acad., 1897-1901, Syracuse U. Coll. of Medicine, 1901-05; m. Donna Feederle, of Akron, O., Oct. 18, 1913. Interne Nursery and Child's Hosp., New York, 1905-06, Brooklyn (N.Y.) Hosp., 1906-08; specialist in gynecology and obstetrics since 1908; research work in human sterility since 1913, asso. attending gynecologist and obstetrician Lying-In Hosp. of Cornell Med. Center since 1936. Fellow Am. Coll. Surgeons; mem. Am. Med. Assn., N.Y. Obstetrical Soc., Brooklyn Gynecol. Soc., Nat. Com. on Maternal Health (dir.), N.Y. Co. Med. Soc. Ind. Republican. Methodist. Author: Sterility and Conception (with C. G. Child), 1931; chapter on "Sterility," Nelson Loose-Leaf Living Surgery. Contbr. to med. mags. Home: New York.

CASE-BLECHSCHMIDT, DOROTHY (KAS'BLEK'SHMIT), surgeon; b. Ithaca, Mich., Apr. 9, 1885; d. Marcus A. and Harriet (Helms) Case; prep. med., Battle Creek (Mich.) Coll., 1903; M.D., Women's Med. Coll. of Pa., Phila., Pa., 1907; post grad. work, clinics—London, Berlin, Berne and Geneva during 1911; m. Dr. Jules Blechschmidt, Sept. 14, 1910; 1 dau., Helen Harriet. Asso. clinical prof. of gynecology, Women's Med. Coll. of Pa., Phila., 1916-22, asst. in gen. surgery to Dr. Deaver, 1922-24; asst. gynecologist, Woman's Hosp., of Phila., 1923-27, chief in general surgery, 1927-28; chief in gynecology at Doctors Hospital, Philadelphia, also chief of cancer prevention, breast clinic, at Doctors Hosp., Phila. chief in gen. surgery, 1927-38, cons. surg. since 1938. Chmn. of Pub. Health, Phila. Fed. of Women's Clubs and allied orgns. Fellow Am. Coll. Surgeons, A.M.A.; mem. Phila. County and Pa. State med. societies, Nat. Woman's Med. Assn. Republican. Lutheran. Clubs: One Hundred of Phila. (dir.), Contemporary, Phila. Music, Art Alliance, Women's Univ., Philomusician (Phila.:. Lectures on Cancer of the Breast, Cancer of the Uterus, Appendicitis, Duodenal Ulcer, Cholecystitis, Psychology of Drinking, The Liver's Budget, Women after 40, Backache in Women, Music and Medicine, Our Children. Home: Philadelphia. *

CASEY, DANIEL EDWARD, association exec.; b. Auburn, Me., Aug. 29, 1882; s. M. A. and Josephine (Coughlin) C.; A.B., Holy Cross Coll., Worester, Mass., 1906; LL.B., Georgetown U., Washington, D.C., 1909; m. Marie Baker; 1 dau., Rita. With Dept. of Commerce, 1909-16, as chief of dept. ed. div., and during World War I, served as liaison officer with other govt. depts., also govt. wartime agencies; editor in chief El Comercio export publs., New York City, 1922-26; dir. public relations Am. Taxpayers Assn., Business Mens Tax Advisory Com. and Nat. Council of State Legislatures, 1927-34; exec. vice pres. and sec. Am. Taxpayers Assn. since 1935. Dir. foreign trade dept. Sch. of Foreign Service and Business Administrn., Georgetown Univ., Washington, D.C., since 1924. Clubs: National Press, Manor Country (Washington). Author: Handbook on Taxation, 1931; also numerous pamphlets and articles relating to taxation. Home: Washington. *

CASEY, LAWRENCE B., bishop; b. Rochester, N.Y., Sept. 6, 1905; s. Joseph L. and Agnes M. (Switzer) C.; student St. Andrew's Minor Sem., Rochester, 1919-24, St. Bernard's Theol. Sem., Rochester, 1924-30. Ordained as priest Roman Cath. Ch., 1930; vice chancellor Diocese of Rochester, 1932-46; pastor Holy Cross Ch., Rochester, 1946-52; rector Sacred Heart Cathedral, Rochester, 1952; titular bishop of Cea and aux. to bishop of Rochester, 1953-66; bishop, Paterson, N.J., 1966-77. Home: Paterson, N.J. Died June 15, 1977.

CASEY, LORD RICHARD GARDINER, former gov.-gen. Australia; b. Brisbane, Queensland, Australia, Aug. 29, 1890; s. Richard Gardiner and Evelyn Jane (Harris) C.; student Melbourne U., 1908-09; B.A., Trinity Coll., Cambridge, Eng., 1913; LL.D., Bates Coll. (Me.), 1941, Birmingham U. (Eng.), 1943, Mich. State U., 1958, Monash U., Victoria, Australia, 1966, U. Tasmania, 1966, U. Papua, New Guinea, 1967, Australian Nat. U., 1969; D.Sc., U. New South Wales, 1966, U Sydney (Australia), 1968; D.Engs., Newcastle U., 1967; m. Ethel Marian Sumner Ryan, June 24, 1926; children—Jane Alice Camilla (Mrs. Murray Wynne Macgowan), Richard Charles Donn. Liaison officer Australian Govt. and Fgn. Office, London, 1924-31; mem. Australian Ho. of Reps. for Corio, 1931-40, for Latrobe, 1949-60; asst. fed. treas., 1933-35; fed. treas., 1935-39; rep. Australia at London Conf. on Conduct of War, 1939; minister for supply and devel., 1939-40; minister to U.S.A., 1940-42; minister state resident in Middle East, mem. War Cabinet U.K., 1942-43; gov. Bengal, 1944-46; fed. pres. Liberal Party Australia, 1947-49; minister for works and housing, 1949-51, for supply and devel., 1949-50, for nat. devel., 1950-51; minister charge Commonwealth Sci. and Indsl. Research Orgn., 1950-60, part-time mem. exec., 1960-65; minister external affairs, 1951-60; gov. gen. Commonwealth Australia, Canberra, 1965-69. Served to maj. Gen. Staff, 1914-18. Created life peer, 1961, knight Noble Order Garter, 1969. Hon. fellow Australian Inst. Mgmt., Royal Australian Coll. Surgeons, Royal Australian Chem. Inst., Royal Australian Inst. Architects, Royal Melbourne Inst. Tech.; hon. mem. Instn. Engrs. Australia, Australian Planning Inst. Author: An Australian in India, 1947; Double or Quit, 1948; Friends and Neighbours, 1954; Personal Experience 1939-46, 1962; The Future of the Commonwealth, 1963; Australian Father and Son, 1965. Home: Victoria, Australia. Died June 17, 1976; buried Mt. Macedon, Victoria.

CASHMAN, ROBERT, coll. adminstr.; b. Sioux Falls, S.D., Jan. 12, 1886; s. Leonard M. and Nettie Ione (Brown) C.; student pub. schs. Sioux Falls, S.D.; LL.D., Bradley U., 1950; m. Virginia M. Linn, Oct. 10, 1911; children—Robert L., Anne F. (Mrs. Robert M. Van Vakenburgh); m. 2d Zelma C. Siau, Sept. 1, 1935; children—Chappell F., Majoree L. (Mrs. Geo. F. Rung, Jr.). Grocery bus., 2 yrs.; with Mut. Life Ins. Co. of N.Y., 3 yrs.; bus. mgr. World's Internat. Sunday Sch. assns., 12 yrs.; sales mgr. pub. firm, 3 yrs.; bus. mgr. Chgo. Theol. Sem., 1923-51, asst. treas., asst. sec. bd. dirs., 1924-52, v.p. in charge development program since 1951. Nat. chmn. to raise $1,200,000 for pensions of aged ministers and widows of Congl. Christian denomination, 1942-47; Pres. bd. trustees Congl. and Christian Conf. of Ill.; moderator Gen. Council Congl. Christian Chs., Claremont, Cal., 1952-54; former moderator Chgo. Assn. Congl. Christian Chs.; dir. Kobe (Japan) Coll. Corp. Member Congregational Christian Church. Clubs: Congregational (past pres.), Union League (Chgo.). Author: The Business Administration of A Church, 1937; The Finances Of A Church, 1949; also articles religious mags. Home: Chicago. *

CASSADY, RALPH, JR., educator; b. Vallejo, Cal., Dec. 30, 1900; s. Ralph L. and Caroline (Luchsinger) C.; B.S., U. Cal. at Berkeley, 1924, M.S., 1927, Ph.D., 1930; m. Dorothea Jatho, Aug. 13, 1927; children—Ralph III, John Michael, Peter William, Patricia Anne. Teaching fellow econs. U. Cal. at Berkeley, 1926-27; instr. econs. Princeton, 1927-28; engaged in study prodn. costs Paramount Pictures, 1928-29; asst. prof. marketing U. Minn., 1930-36; successively asst. prof., asso. prof., prof. emeritus U. Cal. at Los Angeles, 1936-78, dir. bur. bus. and econ. research, 1949-68; vis. prof. U. Western Australia, 1963. Mem. price policies com. Social Sci. Research Council, 1942-51, Hall of Fame in distbn. Boston conf. on distbn., 1954; del. Internat. Econ. Assn. Fisheries Roundtable, Rome, Italy, 1956; cons. study world tuna markets for FAO, Japan, summer 1961, mem. panel experts on fisheries devel., 1962-78; cons. traditional market study, Oaxaca, Mex., 1965-72. Vice pres., dir. Friends of Soochow U., Taiwan, 1963-78. Recipient Am. Marketing Assn. Nat. award, 1952. Mem. Am. Econ. Assn., Am. Anthrop. Assn. Episcopalian. Author: (with H.J. Ostlund) The Retail Distribution Structure of the Small City; (with W.C. Waite) The Consumer and the Economic Order; (with Wylie L. Jones) The Changing Competitive Structure in the Wholesale Grocery Trade; The Nature of Competition in Gasoline Distribution at the Retail Level; Price Making and Price Behavior in The Petroleum Industry; Competition and Price Making in Food Retailing; Price Warfare in Business Competition; (with Ralph Cassady III) The Private Antitrust Suit in American Business Competition; Auctions and Auctioneering; Exchange by Private Treaty, 1973. Mem. editorial bd. Jour. of Marketing, 1940, 1944-46, mng. editor, 1946-48, editor-in-chief, 1949-51. Contbr. articles to bus. and econ. jours. Home: Los Angeles, Calif. Died Feb. 22, 1978.

CASSIDY, HÉLÈNE MONOD, educator; b. Pontarlier, France, Apr. 24, 1909; d. Victor and Germaine (Bouvier) Monod; came to U.S., 1926, naturalized, 1940; A.B., Tusculum Coll., 1928; diplôme de professeur de Français à l'étranger, Sorbonne, Paris, 1928; M.A. (1st Internat. fellow), Oberlin Coll., 1930; postgrad. (fellow), Bryn Mawr Coll., 1930-31; Ph.D., U. Mich., 1938; m. Frederic Gomes Cassidy, Dec. 26, 1931; children—Frederic Monod, Victor Monod, Claire Monod, Michael Monod. Instr. French, Shipley Sch., Bryn Mawr, Pa., 1930-31; prof. English, Coll. Lucie Berger, Strasbourg, France, 1935-36; instr. French, Univ. Coll. West Indies, Jamaica, 1951-52, lectr., 1959; instr. U. Wis., Madison, 1960-62, lectr., 1962-68,asso. prof., 1968-72, prof., 1972-80; cons. TV, Madison Pub. Schs., 1961-62; program devisor Sta. WHA-TV, Madison, 1960-62; tchr. NDEA Inst., Madison, 1960. Pres French House, 1962-76. Am. Philos. Soc. grantee, 1970; decorated chevalier de l'Ordre du e(rite, 1979. Mem. Modern Lang. Assn., Am. Assn. Tchrs. French, Internat. Soc. for 18th Century Studies, Société française des Etudes du 18e Siècle, Société des Palmes Académiques (chevalier 1967, officier 1969), Soce(té des Amis de Sèvres. Author: L'Abbé le Blanc, 1941; La Jamaïque, 1952; (with Julian Harris) Petites Conversations, 1956, 60; Nouvelles Conversations, 1961, Conversations d'Aujourd'hui, Pensée et Littérature françaises; Anthology of 18th Century French Plays, 1973; Jérome Lalande, Journal d'un Voyage en Angleberre 1763, 1980. Home: Waunakee, Wis. Died June 12, 1980.

CASTANO, GIOVANNI, artist; b. Gasperina, Calabria, Italy, Oct. 2, 1896; s. Joseph and Maria Therese (Procopio) C.; brought to U.S., 1904; art edn. under Philip L. Hale, Leslie P. Thompson, Huger Elliott, F.M. Lamb, Henry James and at Museum of Fine Arts, Boston, 1916-21; m. Josephine Caruso, Feb. 6, 1926; children—John Elvira (Mrs. Carlo Palmerio), Marie (Mrs. John Robert Lothrop). Works are represented in Pub. Library, Brockton, Mass., Springfield (Mass.) Art Assn. Painter stage settings Boston Opera House; scenic artist and designer Cin. Grand Opera, 1922-27; executed murals First Baptist Ch., Covington, Ky., Mercy Acad., Cin., Met. Theatre, Boston, 1927; painter all stage scenery for Town Hall, Peterborough, N.H., 1936; decorated St. Peter's Church, Boston, 1936; also recently painted individual portraits; restorer Albert Herter murals, Ho. of Reps., Boston. Decorated cavaliere Ordine al Merito Della Repubblica Italiana; recipient hon. mention Pa. Acad. Fine Arts, 1918, Springfield Art Club, 1926; Mass. gov.'s plaque for restoration of mural in State House, Boston, 1971. Mem. Accademia Tiberina (Rome, Italy). Republican. Roman Catholic. Clubs: Art (Boston, Cin., Brockton). Address: Needham, Mass. Deceased.

CASTELLANOS ARTEAGE, DANIEL, Uruguayan lawyer, diplomat, senator; b. Montevideo, Uruguay, Dec. 21, 1882; s. José María and Lucía (Arteaga) C.; LL.D., U. de Montevideo, 1907; m. Maria Cibils Larravide. Mem. nat. commn. on edn., 1909; sec. Council for Protection of Delinquents and Minors, 1911-15; prof. history U. de Montevideo, 1916-28; sec. to Presidency of the Republic, 1927-30; minister plenipotentiary to Spain and Portugal, 1930-39, Gt. Britain, 1939-42; nat. senator since 1942; minister fgn. affairs, 1948-49. Decorated Grand Cross Mérito Naval (Spain), Knight Order Gustav Vasa (Sweden). Address: Montevideo, Uruguay. *

CASTLE, ALFRED LOWREY, lawyer, business exec.; b. Honolulu, T.H., Mar. 18, 1884; s. William Richards and Ida Beatrice (Lowrey) G.; student Oahu Coll., Hotchkiss Sch., A.B., Harvard, 1906, LL.B., 1908; m. Ehelinda Schaefer, Dec. 8, 1908; children—Alfred Lowrey (dec.), Gwendolyn, William Donald. Practised in Honolulu with father's firm, Castle & Withington, later with Robertson, Castle & Anthony; dep. commr. in Siberia for Am. Red Cross, 1918; field dir. for Hawaii and spl. rep. for Japan, Hawaii, China, and Philippines for Red Cross; rep. terr. legislature, 1911, senator, 1915-17; served on Honolulu Bd. of Supervisors; pres. Honolulu Rapid Transit Co., Ltd., Honolulu Gas Co., Ltd.; manager of his father's estate; director in numerous Hawaiian corporations. Past president Hawaiian Tennis Assn. (won singles championship: 1908, 1910, 1911, 1917; and doubles: 1911, 1916, 1919, 1920, 1921, 1922, 1924; pitcher on Harvard baseball team. Clubs: FoFox, Varsity, Hasty Pudding, D.K.E., Institute of 1770, Thayer Law of Harvard, Pacific,

University, Havard, Beretania Tennis, Hawaii Polo and Racing. Home: Honolulu. *

CASTLE, RALPH, C.S. lecturer; b. Beckenham, Kent, Eng., Apr. 24, 1886; s. Ralph Waldo and Ethel Frances (Ridler) C.; student Holy Trinity, London; m. Gwendolin Mary Sheppard, July 3, 1909; children—Richard Geoffrey, Christopher. Came to U.S., 1914, naturalized, 1918. Financial staff C.S. Monitor and Wall St. Jour., 1919-22; asst. advt. mgr. C.S. Monitor, 1922-27, Pacific Coast mgr., 1927-33; practicing Christian Scientist, San Francisco, since 1933, wartime minister, 1941-47; elected to bd. lectureship The Mother Ch., First Ch. of Christ Scientist, Boston, 1947. Served as ensign, U.S.N.R.F., 1917-19. Home: Marin County, Cal.

CASTLE, WILLIAM, motion picture dir.; b. N.Y.C., Apr. 24, 1914; m. Ellen Castle; children—Georgiana, Terry. Former actor, asst. dir. N.Y. stage; dialogue dir. Columbia Pictures; producer Universal Pictures, 1964-65, Paramount Pictures, 1966; motion pictures include Chance of a Lifetime, When Strangers Marry, Mark of the Whistler, Voice of the Whistler, The Crime Doctor's Warning, Texas, Brooklyn and Heaven, Johnny Stool Pigeon, Undertoe, The Fat Man, Hollywood Story, Cave of Outlaws, It's a Small World (also screen play), Fort Ti, Serpent of the Nile, Drums of Tahiti, Battle of Rogue River, Iron Glove, Saracen Blade, Charge of the Lancers, Masterson of Kansas, The American, New Orleans Uncensored, Gun That Won the West, Duel on the Mississippi, Houston Story, Uranium Boom, The American; producer, dir. Macabre, House on Haunted Hill, Tingler, 13 Ghosts, Homicidal, The Old Dark House, 13 Frightened Girls, Straight-Jacket, The Night Walker, I Saw What You Did, Let's Kill Uncle, The Spirit is Willing, Busy Body, Project X, Shanks; producer Rosemary's Baby, Riot, Bug; producer, dir. TV show Men of Annapolis. Address: Beverly Hills, Calif. Died May 31, 1977.

CASWELL, WILBUR LARREMORE, clergyman; b. Hackensack, N.J., June 15, 1883; s. Alanson Wadsworth and Carrie Elisabeth (Schwarz) C.; B.A., Columbia, 1906; grad. Gen. Theol. Sem., 1909; unmarried. Deacon, 1909, priest, 1910, P.E. Ch.; curate St. Mary's Ch., Mott Haven, N.Y., 1909; asst. minister St. Thomas's Ch., N.Y. City, 1910-16; rector St. Thomas's Ch., Mamaroneck, N.Y., 1916-23; asst. minister St. Thomas's Ch., N.Y. City, 1923-25; rector St. Paul's Ch., Yonkers, N.Y., since 1925. Mem. New York Churchmen's Assn., Phi Beta Kappa. Author: (plays) The Quest of Sir Galahad, 1914; No Room at the Inn, 1916; Christmas in the Heart, 1918; The Upsettin' o' Panther Mountain, 1921. Clubs: The Club, Rectory Club, Fortnightly, Westchester Clericus. Editorial writer The Churchman, and conductor column "Gargoyles"; contbg. editor The Chronicle. Home: Yonkers, N.Y.

CATE, CURTIS WOLSEY, teacher; b. Boston, Dec. 5, 1884; s. Martin Luther and Martha Gertrude (Curtis) C.; grad. Roxbury Latin Sch., 1903; A.B., Harvard, 1907, A.M., 1908; m. Katharine S. Thayer, of Lancaster, Mass., June 30, 1924. Teacher, Marienfeld Sch., Riverside, Calif., 1908-09, Thacher Sch., Ojai, Calif., 1909-10, Santa Barbara Sch., Carpinteria, Calif., since 1910, headmaster since 1910, also trustee. Episcopalian. Clubs: Harvard (New York); Union (Boston). Home: Casitas Rd., Carpinteria, Calif.

CATION, WILLIAM RITCHIE, banker; b. Peoria, Ill., Apr. 5, 1883; s. John and Janet Rae (Waugh) C.; student Bradley Poly. Inst., Peoria, 1897-1901; m. Catheryne E. Finch, of Detroit, Mich., Aug. 14, 1918; 1 dau., Barbara Finch. Began as clk. Central Nat. Bank, Peoria, Ill., 1902, asst. cashier, 1904-13; fruit grower, 1914-15; chief clk. First & Old Detroit Nat. Bank, 1916-17; cashier Detroit Br. of Federal Reserve Bank of Chicago, 1918-23, mng. dir., 1923-34; pres. Guardian Depositors Corpn., May 7, 1935-July 1936, now dir.; with Van Grant & Co. since 1937. Attached to Detroit office of treas. of Am. Red Cross, 1917. Republican. Presbyn. Club: Detroit. Home: Grosse Pointe, Mich.

CATLETT, FRED WAYNE, lawyer; born at Wellsville, Ohio, February 10, 1882; s. John Chadwick and Julia Frances (Abbey) C.; A.B., magna cum laude, Harvard, 1904, A.M., 1905; LL.B., 1907; m. Florence Gertrude Chase, September 14, 1907; children—Dorothea Lucile, Fred Wayne, Jr., Virginia (Mrs. Edward F. Rudolph). Admitted to Massachusetts State and Washington bars, 1907; assistant in government, Harvard, 1905-07; secretary to mayor of Seattle, 1911-12; lecturer in municipal govt. Harvard U. and Radcliffe Coll., 1913; asst. prof. law, U. of Wash., 1914-18; practiced at Seattle, 1907-34; and since 1942; mem. firm of Catlett, Hartman & Jarvis; general counsel Puget Sound Dist. for N.Y. Life Ins. Co., 1918-34, and since 1942, The Prudential Insurance Co. of America; mem. Fed. Home Loan Bank Bd., Washington, D.C., 1934-42; dir. Home Owners' Loan Corp.; trustee Federal Savings and Loan Ins. Corp. (acting mgr. 1934-35). Trustee, Seattle Municipal League, Am. Counsel Assn. Mem. Am., Wash., Seattle bar assns. (sec. 1924), English Speaking Union (pres. 1944-46), Phi Delta Phi. Republican. Conglist. Mason. Clubs: Harvard, Seattle Table, Loyal Knights of Round Table, Rainier, Broadmoor Golf.

CATLIN, GEORGE EDWARD GORDON, philosopher, educator; b. Liverpool, Eng., July 29, 1896; s. George E. and Edith K. (Orton) C.; B.A. summa cum laude (triple prizeman), Oxford U., 1920, M.A., 1924; Ph.D., Cornell U., 1924; m. Vera Brittain, July 24, 1925 (dec. 1970); children—John, Shirley; m. 2d, Linda Tassi, Apr. 16, 1971. Prof. politics Cornell U., 1924-35; asso. with Harold Laswell of Yale in devel. of quantitative polit. sci., 1935-56; Bronman prof. polit. sci., chmn. dept. McGill U., 1956-60, now emeritus; found. lectr. Calcutta (India), Peking (China) univs., 1948; Goethe Centenary lectr. Heidelberg (Germany) U., 1949; Kierkegaard Commemoration lectr. Copenhagen (Denmark) U., 1949; Weil Lectr. U. N.C., 1957; Tagore Centenary lectr. London Royal Soc. Arts; lectr. Yale, 1937, U. Calif. at Berkeley, 1953; Walker-Ames lectr. U. Wash., 1963. Spl. adviser late Wendell Willkie, 1940, Arthur Greenwood, dep. leader Brit. Labour Party, 1930-41, Harold Wilson, leader Labour Party, 1970-79; pioneer (with Walter Lippmann) proposal for Atlantic community, 1941; draftsman declaration in support Indian independence, 1943. Twice nominated to exec. com. Brit. Labour Party. Created knight, 1970; decorated comdr. grand cross Order of Merit (Germany). Fellow Royal Soc. Lit.; mem. Fabian Soc. (exec. com.), Am. and Brit. Commonwealth Assn. (co-founder), World Acad. Arts and Scis. (v.p.), Instituto Estudios Politicos (Spain) (hon.), Anglo-German Assn. (v.p.), Popular TV Assn. U.K. (v.p.), Inst. Strategic Studies, Internat., Am., Brit., Canadian polit. sci. assns., Am., Brit. social assns., Union Mondlale des Europeens (nat. pres., internat. v.p.). Author: Science and Methods of Politics, 1926 (Spanish transl.); Principles of Politics, 1930; History of the Political Philosophers, 1939 (Spanish transl.); One Anglo-American Nation, 1941; (with Vera Brittain) Above All Nations, 1947 (German transl.); On Political Goals, 1957; In the Path of Mahatma Gandhi (German transl.); The Atlantic Community, 1959; Systematic Politics, 1962 (Japanese transl.); Applications, 1963; The Grandeur of England and the Atlantic Community, 1966 (U.S. title: The Stronger Community;) The Atlantic Commonwealth, 1969. Co-editor (with H.G. Wells, Arnold Bennett, others) The Realist, 1929-30. Home: Lyndhurst, Hampshire, England. Died Feb. 8, 1979; buried Milverton Churchyard, Warwickshire, Eng.

CATTON, BRUCE, writer, editor; b. Petoskey, Mich., Oct. 9, 1899; s. George R. and Adella M. (Patten) C.; student Oberlin Coll.; Litt.D. (hon.), Md., Wesleyan, Dickinson colls., 1955, Oberlin, Lincoln colls., 1956, Harvard, Syracuse, Northwestern, Olivet univs., 1957, Ill., Western Mich. colls., 1958; LL.D. (hon.), Knox Coll., 1958; D.L.C. (hon.), Union Coll., 1956; m. Hazel H. Cherry, Aug. 16, 1925; 1 son, William Bruce. Reporter, Cleve. News, Boston Am., later with Cleve. Plain Dealer; became spl. writer, Washington corr. for Newspaper Enterprise Assn., Washington; asso. dir. info. WPB, 1942, dir., 1943; dir. info. Dept. Commerce, 1945-46; spl. asst. to sec. commerce, 1948. Recipient Pulitzer Prize for hist. work, 1954; Nat. Book award, 1954; non-fiction award for The Coming Fury, Ohioana Library Assn., 1962; Presdl. Freedom medal, 1977. Mem. Am. Acad. Arts and Letters. Presbyterian. Author: The War Lords of Washington, 1948; Mr. Lincoln's Army, 1951; Glory Road, 1952; A Stillness at Appomatox, 1953; U.S. Grant and the American Military Tradition, 1954; Banners at Shenandoah, 1955; This Hallowed Ground, 1956; America Goes to War, 1958; Grant Moves South, 1960; The Coming Fury, 1961; (with William Catton) Two Roads to Sumter, 1963; Terrible Swift Sword, 1963; Never Call Retreat, 1965; Grant Takes Command, 1969; Waiting for the Morning Train, 1972; Gettysburg: The Final Fury, 1974; Michigan: A Bicentennial History, 1976; (with William Catton) The Bold and Magnificent Dream, 1978. Editor: Am. Heritage Mag., 1954-59, sr. editor, 1959-78. Home: New York, N.Y. Died Aug. 28, 1978; buried Benzonia, Mich.

CAULEY, JOHN ROWAN, newspaper corr.; b. Rushville, Ind., Apr. 25, 1908; s. Thomas S. and Mary Ann (Kelly) C.; student Rockhurst Coll., Kansas City, Mo., 1926-28, D.H.L. (hon.); B.J., U. Mo., 1932. Pub. weekly newspaper The Summit News, Kansas City, Mo., 1933-36; mem. staff Kansas City (Mo.) Star, 1936-76, news editor, 1954, fgn. affairs editor Washington bur., 1957-64, chief bur., 1964-76. Recipient Pro-Meritis award Rockhurst Coll., 1960. Mem. A.P. Mng. Editors Assn. (dir. 1953-54). White House Corrs. Assn., John Carroll Soc. (gov.), Sigma Delta Chi. Roman Catholic (usher). Clubs: Kansas City Press (pres. 1950), Nat. Press (bd. govs.), Gridiron (Washington). Home: Kansas City, Mo. Died May 17, 1976.

CAULFIELD, LEO PATRICK, lawyer; b. Preston County, W.Va., May 29, 1885; s. Patrick Francis and Mary Alice (Mattingly) C.; A.B., Rock Hill Coll., Ellicott City, Md., 1906; LL.B., U. Va., W.Va., 1913. Admitted to W.Va. bar, 1913; dep. county clk., Harrison County, W.Va., 1908-10, dep. sheriff, 1912-17; now partner firm Steptoe & Johnson, offices Clarksburg and Charleston, W.Va., also Washington. Mem. Am., W.Va., Harrison bar assns., W.Va. State Bar, Phi Kappa Psi. Democrat. Roman Cath. Elk. Home: Clarksburg.

CAVANAGH, JEROME PATRICK, lawyer, former mayor; b. Detroit, June 16, 1928; s. Sylvester J. and Irene (Timmins) C.; Ph.B., U. Detroit, 1950, J.D., 1954; m. Kathleen M. Disser; children—Mark, Patrick, David, Mary Therese, Christopher, Philip, Jerome C., Elizabeth Angela, Kathleen Mary. Admitted to Mich. bar, 1954; practiced in Detroit, 1954-62, from 70; mayor of Detroit, 1962-70. Past pres. U.S. Conf. Mayors, Nat. League Cities. Mem. Am., Detroit bar assns., State Bar Mich. Home: Ann Arbor, Mich. Died Nov. 27, 1979.

CAVERT, SAMUEL MCCREA, clergyman, ch. exec.; b. Charlton, N.Y., Sept. 9, 1888; s. Walter I. and Elizabeth (Brann) C.; B.A., Union Coll., 1910, D.D., 1935; M.A., Columbia, 1914; B.D., Union Theol. Sem., 1915; D.D., Lawrence Coll., 1928; LL.D., Ohio Wesleyan U., 1942; D.D., Yale, 1948, Princeton, 1951, Kalamazoo Coll., 1956; Th.D., U. Goettingen, 1948; L.H.D., Am. U., 1951; Litt.D., Park Coll., 1952; m. Ruth Miller, Nov. 14, 1918 (dec. Feb. 1920); 1 dau., Mary Ruth (Mrs. Harold A. Ramsey); m. 2d, Ruth Twila Lytton, June 28, 1927. Sec., student YMCA, 1910-12, also instr. Greek, Union Coll.; ordained Presbyn. ministry, 1915; asst. systematic theology Union Theol. Sem., 1915-16; fellow Union Theol. sem., Orient, 1916-17; asst. sec. Gen. War-Time Commn. Chs., 1917-18; 1st lt., chaplain U.S. Army, 1918-19; sec. Com. on War and Religious Outlook, 1919-20; asso. sec. Fed. Council Chs. Christ in Am., 1920, gen. sec., 1921-50; gen. sec. Nat. Council Chs. Christ in U.S.A. 1951-54; exec. sec. World Council Chs., 1954-57; William Henry Hoover lectr. Christian Unity, 1958; del. World Conf. of Chs., Jerusalem, 1928, Oxford, Edinburgh, 1937, Utrecht, 1938, Lund, 1952, New Delhi, 1961, Geneva, 1966, Uppsala, 1968. Chmn., Com. on Arrangements for First Assembly of World Council, Amsterdam, Holland, 1948; Protestant liaison ofcl. between German chs. and Am. Mil. Govt. authorities, U.S. Zone Occupation, 1946. Vice chmn. bd. dirs. Union Theol. Sem., 1948-66; trustee Union Coll., hon. chancellor, 1945. Mem. Pres. Roosevelt's Adv. Com. for Polit. Refugees; chmn. com. on ch. center UN, 1963-65; trustee Christian Century Found.; exec. dir. Interch. Center, N.Y.C., 1963-64. Mem. Phi Beta Kappa, Kappa Alpha. Democrat. Clubs: Century (N.Y.C.); Siwanoy Country (Bronxville, N.Y.). Author: Securing Christian Leaders for Tomorrow, 1926; The Adventure of the Church, 1927; On the Road to Christian Unity, 1961; The American Churches in the Ecumenical Movement: 1900-1968, 1968; Church Cooperation and Unity in America, 1970; (part author or editor) The Church and Industrial Reconstruction, 1920; Christian Unity: Its Principles and Possibilities, 1921; The Teaching Work of the Church, 1923; (with Henry P. Van Dusen) The Church Through Half a Century, 1936. Chmn. adv. bd. Religious Book Club, 1958-68; editorial bd. Religion (quar.); sr. editor Pulpit Digest, 1958-68. Home: Bronxville, N.Y. Died Dec. 21, 1976.

CAZAYOUX, FRANCIS EARLE, glass exec.; b. New Roads, La., Dec. 15, 1903; s. Jean Albert and Leonore (LeJeune) C.; student Baton Rouge Coll. Bus., 1921-23; pvt. study Internat. Accountants Soc., Columbia Extension, Alexander Hamilton Inst.; m. Margaret Yost, Oct. 27, 1928 (dec.). With Standard Oil Co. of Ohio, 1926-27, Toledo Sugar Co., 1927; joined Libbey-Owens-Ford Glass Co., Toledo, 1927, comptroller, treas., 1946-56, v.p. finance, from 1955, exec. v.p., from 1964, also dir.; chmn. Modern Pattern & Plastics, Inc., from 1966; director Libbey-Owens-Ford Export Co., Bogardus, Wilson, Ltd., Vancouver, B.C., Ornamental Bronze Co., Ltd., Vancouver, Nat. Bank of Toledo. Bd. dirs. Toledo chpt. A.R.C., 1957-61, Toledo Community Chest, 1953-61. Dir. Toledo Mus. Art. Mem. N.A.M., Financial Execs. Inst., Am. Mgmt. Assn., Nat. Assn. Accountants, Toledo C. of C. (dir., treas. 1949-51). Mason. Clubs: Rotary, Inverness, Toledo (trustee 1958-61), Toledo Country (dir. from 1963) (Toledo); Carranor Hunt and Polo. Home: Toledo, Ohio. Died Apr. 1, 1978.

CECIL, ARTHUR BOND (SIS'EL), surgeon, urologist; b. Millersville, Md., May 8, 1885; s. Leonidas and Helen Sinclair (Owens) C.; student Anne Arundel Acad., St. John's Coll. Prep. Sch., 1900-01; B.S., St. John's Coll., 1905; honor grad. Johns Hopkins Med. Sch., 1909; grad. U.S. Naval Med. Sch., 1910; m. Mary Wrightson Caulk, July 24, 1913; children—Arthur Bond, Duncan Cameron Walton; married 2d, Henrietta Alice Smith, August 12, 1938; children—Anne Arundel, Henrietta Alice, Josephine, William Hodgdon. Resigned from United States Navy to become assistant to Doctor Hugh H. Young, 1911; resident urologist at Johns Hopkins Hospital, 1912-13; removed to Los Angeles, Calif., 1913; attending urologist Hosp. of Good Samaritan; chief dept. urology Good Hope Clinic and Hosp. Foundation; chief sect. of urology Los Angeles

County Gen. Hosp., 1932-36; prof. urology Sch. Med. Evangelists, 1932-36; dir. Good Hope Clinic and Hosp. Foundation. Lieut. comdr. Med. Reserve Corps, U.S. Navy. Fellow Am. Coll. of Surgeons; mem. Am., Calif. State, Southern Calif., and Los Angeles County med. assns., Pacific Coast Surg. Assn., Am. Urol. Assn., Am. Assn. of Genito-Urinary Surgeons, Los Angeles Symposium Soc., Soc. of Colonial Wars, S.A.R., Soc. War of 1812, Phi Sigma Kappa; hon. mem. Omaha Mid-West Clinical Soc. Republican. Episcopalian. Author of many pub. addresses and papers on urol. surgery; contbr. chpts. to Cabot's System of Urology, Campbell's Urology and Pediatric Clinics of North America. Home: Los Angeles.

CELLER, EMANUEL, former congressman; b. Bklyn., May 6, 1888; s. Henry H. and Josephine (u-ller) C.; A.B., Columbia, 1910, L.L.B., 1912; LL.D., Yeshiva U., 1971, Bklyn. Coll.; m. Stella B. Baar, June 30, 1914 (dec.); children—Jane B. (Mrs. Sydney B. Wertheimer), Judith C. (dec.). Admitted to N.Y. State bar; practiced in N.Y.C., 1912-81; mem. Weisman, Celler, Spett, Modlin & Wertheimer; organizer Bklyn. Nat. Bank; dir. Fischbach & Moore, Inc.; mem. 68th-91st congresses from 10th N.Y. dist., author Fed. Register Act, Fgn. Trade Zone Act, India Immigration and Naturalization Act, Celler-Kefauver Anti-Merger Act, Celler Civil Rights Acts of 1957, 60, 62, 65, 70, others. Mem. Commn. on Revision Fed. Ct. Appellate System. Mem. Am. Jewish Com., Am. Jewish Congress; pres. Am. Red Mogen David. Mem. com. platforms and resolutions Democratic Nat. Conv. 1944, 48, 52, 56, 60; del. N.Y. State Dem. convs. Hon. bd. dirs. Jewish Family Welfare Soc.; bd. dirs. Brookdale Hosp., Bklyn.; trustee Jewish Nat. Found. Decorated Order Republic Guatemala; award and medallion of chevalier, commendature Order Merit Republic of Italy; recipient Alexander Hamiltion medal Columbia U.; Emmanuel Celler U.S. Dist. Ct. House in Bklyn. named in his honor by U.S. Congress. Mem. Am. (state com. sect jud. administrn.), County, Bklyn. bar assns., Columbia Alumni Assn. (N.Y.C.). K.P.; mem. B'nai B'rith. Club: Unity (Bklyn). Author (autobiography) You Never Leave Brooklyn. Home: West Brooklyn, N.Y. Died Jan. 15, 1981.

CÉSAR, ALEJANDRO, diplomat; b. Granada, Nicaragua, Mar. 27, 1886; s. Octaviano and Margarita (Chamorro) C.; LL.D., Universidad de Oriente, Granada, 1906; M.D., U. of Paris, 1915; m. Maria Benard, of Granada, July 14, 1920. Formerly prof. Physiology, U. of Granada; served with Med. Corps, French Army, during World War; del. from Nicaragua to 2d Pan-Am. Scientific Congress, 1916; E.E. and M.P. from Nicaragua to U.S., 1920-21 and since 1927. Mem. Am. Inst. Internat. Law, Anatom. Soc. Paris; asso. mem. Med. Soc. Washington, D.C. Catholic. Address: Washington, D.C.

CHADWICK, E. WALLACE, lawyer; born Vincennes, Indiana, January 17, 1884; s. William Burtch and Margaret (Moore) Chadwick; A.B., Univ. of Pa., 1906, LL.B., 1910; married Alice Cambern. President judge, Orphans Court of Delaware County, 1945. Mem. 80th Congress (1947-49), 7th Pa. Dist. Mem. law firm Chadwick, Curran, Petrikin & Smithers, Chester, Pa. President J. Lewis Crozier Library; director Delaware County National Bank. Member Delaware County Bar Assn. (past pres.), Phi Beta Kappa, Republican. Clubs: Chester Rotary, Union League of Phila. Home: Delaware County, Pa.

CHAFFEE, EMORY LEON, physicist; b. Somerville, Mass., Apr. 15, 1885; s. Emory Franklin and Belle Genevieve (Carter) C.; S.B., Mass. Inst. Tech., 1907; A.M., Harvard, 1908, Ph.D., 1911 (Bowdoin Prize); m. Alice Nampson, Mar. 25, 1924. Instr. physics and elec. engring., Harvard, 1911-17, asst. prof. physics, 1917-23, asso. prof., 1923-26, prof., 1926-35, Gordon McKay prof. physics and communication engring. since 1935. Mem. exec. com. of Internat. Scientific Radio Union. Fellow Am. Acad. Arts and Sciences, Am. Physical Soc., Am. Inst. Radio Engrs. (v.p. 1925); mem. Tau Beta Pi, Sigma Xi. Author: Physical Laboratory Manual, 1914; Theory of Thermionic Vacuum Tubes, 1933. Writer numerous articles in physics and engring. jours. Home: Belmont, Mass.

CHALIAPIN, BORIS, painter; b. Russia, 1907; came to U.S., 1935; s. Feodor Chaliapin; studied art in Russia and France; m. Helcia Davidson; 1 dau., Irina Chaliapin Murphy. Artist specializing in portraits; best known for more than 400 covers for Time mag., 1940's-60's; subjects included Sergei Rachmaninoff, William Scranton, George Meany, others; in addition to portraiture, work included figure paintings, landscapes, pencil sketches, pictures of opera settings; exhibited 1-man show sponsored by USIA, Moscow, 1975; work represented in Nat. Portrait Gallery of Smithsonian Instn., Washington. Home: Easton, Conn. Died May 18, 1979.

CHALKER, LLOYD TOULMIN, Coast Guard officer; b. Mobile, Ala., Dec. 4, 1883; s. James Humphrey and Zide (Bowers) C.; grad. U.S. Coast Guard Acad., 1906; grad. Naval Air Station, flight instrn., 1935; m. Aline Brooks Risque, Apr. 11, 1908; 1 dau., Aline Beverly (Mrs. James Hartwell Hopkins Hunter). Commd. ensign, U.S. Coast Guard, 1906, and advanced through grades to rear admiral, 1942; served as chief personnel officer, 1931-34; chief aviation officer, 1936-40; assistant comdt. since Jan. 1, 1942. Tech. adviser to Am. del. at Internat. Conf. on Private Air Law, Brussels, Belgium, 1938; observer on initial flight of Pan-Am. Airways seaplane, Yankee Clipper, from Baltimore to Azores, Portugal, France, England, Ireland and return, Mar.-Apr. 1939. Awarded World War I medal with escort clasp and star. Home: Chevy Chase, Md.

CHALLINOR, MERCEDES C(RIMMINS) (MRS. DAVID CHALLINOR), mem. bd. dirs. A.R.C.; b. N.Y. City, June 13, 1885; d. John D. and Lily L. (Lalor) Crimmins; grad. Convent of the Sacred Heart, Manhattanville, N.Y., 1903; m. David Challinor, June 12, 1919; children—David, Jr., Mary (Mrs. William Ewing, Jr.). Dir. canteen service A.R.C., Orly, France, 1918-19, mem. bd. dirs. N.Y. chapter, 1933-50, Darien chapter since 1948, mem. nat. bd. since 1949. Chmn. Com. for Blind of Poland since 1948; exec. chmn. Greater N.Y. War Fund, 1941-42. Address: Noroton, Conn.

CHAMBERLAIN, ERNEST BARRETT, ednl. consultant; b. Oberlin, O., Jan. 22, 1883; s. William Benton and Emily Elizabeth (Peck) C.; A.B., Oberlin Coll., 1904; A.M., 1906; student Union Theol. Sem., New York, N.Y., 1907-09; B.D., Oberlin Theol. Sem., 1910; student Oberlin Conservatory of Music, 1910-12, U. of Wis., 1915-16; m. Gladys Taber, June 26, 1912; 1 son, Thomas Taber; m. 2d, Katharine Butler Kane, Feb. 1, 1935. Teacher, Chillicothe (O.) High Sch., 1904; teacher English, Oberlin Acad., 1906-07; teacher history of music, Knox Coll., Galesburg, Ill., 1912-14, U. of Wis., 1915-18; teacher history, McBurney Sch., New York, N.Y., 1920-23; dir. publicity, pub. relations and fund-raising programs for schools, colleges and philanthropic institutions, 1923-37; dir. pub. relations, 1938-40; ednl. consultant since 1940. Dir. mass singing, A.E.F., 1918-19, State of Va., 1919-20. Mem. com. on pub. service Secondary Edn. Bd. Mem. Am. Acad. Polit. and Social Science, Assn. of Am. Colls., Phi Beta Kappa, Cum Laude Soc. Club: University Glee (New York). Author: Our Independent Schools, 1944. Home: New York, N.Y.

CHAMBERLAIN, RICHARD HALL, physician, educator; b. Jacksonville, Fla., May 25, 1915; s. William Douglas and Lucille (McKowen) C.; A.B., Centre Coll., 1934; M.D., U. Louisville, 1939; postgrad. U. Pa., 1940-42. Asst. instr. radiology U. Pa., Phila., 1940-46, instr., 1946-47, asso., 1947-48, asst. prof., 1948-50, asso. prof. 1950-52, prof., 1952-75, chmn. dept. radiology, 1961-75; cons. in radiology USPHS, 1968-73. Mem.nat. adv. council radiation USPHS, 1958-60, chmn. med. x-ray adv. com., 1964-68; chmn. radiology tng. com. Nat. Inst. Gen. Med. Scis., 1966-69; mem. com. on pathologic effect of atomic radiation NRC-Nat. Acad. Sci., 1957-63; sr. adviser Internat. Commn. on Radiol. Units; mem. Nat. Council Radiation Protection; mem. expert adv. panel radiation WHO, 1964-75; U.S. ofcl. del. UN Sci. Com. on Effects Atomic Radiation, 1963-75. Trustee Asso. Univs., Inc., 1963-70. Diplomate Am. Bd. Radiology, Fellow Am. Coll. Radiology (v.p. 1964-65, Gold medal 1969); mem. A.M.A., Radiol. Soc. N. Am. (Gold medal 1971), Am. Radium Soc., Am., Phila. (past pres.) roentgen ray socs. Home: Philadelphia, Pa. Died Dec. 4, 1975.

CHAMBERLAIN, THOMAS GASSNER, lawyer; b. Auburn, Calif., June 25, 1892; s. Louis Lee and Sarah (Gassner) C.; A.B., U. Calif., 1915; J.D., Calif. Sch. of Jurisprudence, Berkeley, 1917; m. Gertrude Geoghegan, Oct. 21, 1944. Asst. to U.S. commissioner of reclamation conduction land settlement investigation, Calif., 1915; teaching fellow in polit. science, U. Calif., 1915-17; admitted to Calif. bar, 1917, and began practice at San Francisco; member of firm of Chamberlain Willi and Ouchterloney. Served as 2d lt., 1st lt. and capt. U.S. Army, 1917-18; with 1st Div. Arty., A.E.F., at Verdun, Chateau-Thierry, etc.; settled in N.Y.C., 1919; with ex-President William H. Taft in speaking tour of U.S. for League to Enforce Peace, discussing foreign policy of U.S., 1919-20; also conducted tour of Calif. for Hoover campaign, later nat. tour for Pro-League Republicans, 1920; incorporator of cotton cooperative marketing assns. throughout South, negotiating loans of over $100,000,000 from banks and War Finance Corp., 1922-23; mem. Finance Com. of Nat. Republican Com., 1928; speaking tour U.S.; gen. counsel and dir. Pacific Egg Producers Cooperative, Inc., Taber & Co., Inc., Sunrise Egg Producers Cooperative, Inc., Am. Lyric Theater, Inc.; pres., Mark Twain Co.; gen. counsel. trustee N.Y. Infirmary, Booth-Ferris Found., Estate of Samuel L. Clemens (Mark Twain); counsel Sun-Maid Raisin Growers, Washington Coop. Egg and Poultry Assn., Sunland Sales Coop. Assn., Calif. Peach & Fig Growers Assn., Poultry Producers of Central Calif., Gordon Baking Co. Dir. League of Nations Assn.; mem. Internat. Com. of YMCA. Bd. dirs. Met. Opera Assn. Mem. Am. Bar Assn., New York Law Inst., N.Y. C. of C., Phi Delta Phi, Kappa Sigma. Episcopalian. Mason. Clubs: The Pilgrims; Lawrence Beach; Everglades, Bath and Tennis (Palm Beach, Fla.); Skytop (Pa.); University, Sleepy Hollow Country, Downtown Athletic, Metropolitan, Metropolitan Opera, Rotary of N.Y. Author: Land Settlement Conditions in California, 1915; Why We Fought, 1919; The Geneva Institute of International Relations, 1925; Disarmament, The International Debts. Contbr. to Scripps Howard Newspapers. Home: New York, N.Y. Died May 9, 1978.

CHAMBERLAIN, WILLIAM E., charitable orgn. exec.; b. N.Y.C., Jan. 9, 1909; s. William Edgar and Mary Alice (Craswell) C.; grad. Salvation Army Sch. for Officer's Tng., 1927; D.H.L. (hon.), Syracuse U., 1975; m. Ethel Turner, Apr. 25, 1931; children—Alice Chamberlain Baxendale, Jean Chamberlain Mosher, Roberta Chamberlain Schofield, Carol Chamberlain Appleby. With Salvation Army, 1927-80, youth club dir., city comdr., div. comdr., dir. operations Greater New York, N.Y.C., 1963-66, territorial comdr. Carribbean and Central Am. terr., 1967-69, territorial comdr. So. states, 1969-74, nat. comdr., N.Y.C., 1974-80. Mem. Nat. Assn. Social Workers, Acad. Certified Social Workers, Nat. Conf. Social Welfare, Am. Protestant Health Assn., Christian Children's Fund. Club: Rotary (N.Y.C.). Home: Asbury Park, N.J. Died Mar. 24, 1980.

CHAMBERLIN, CLARENCE DUNCAN, aviator; b. in Denison, Iowa, November 11, 1893. Made record non-stop flight, in the monoplane Columbia, with C. A. Levine as passenger, from Roosevelt Field, N.Y., to Eisleben, Germany, a distance of 3,911 miles, in 42 hours and 31 minutes, June 4-6, 1927. Author: Record Flights, 1928. Home: Teterboro, N.J. Died Oct. 30, 1976.

CHAMBERLIN, GEORGE LEONARD, paper co. exec.; b. Churchville, Pa., Jan. 20, 1915; s. John Elbert and Josephine (Nestor) C.; grad. George Sch., 1933; A.B., U. Pa., 1937; m. Helen Kramer, July 14, 1939; children—Craig Frederick, Holly. Fin. and Gen. mgmt. Gen. Electric Co., 1937-61; v.p. Bell & Howell Co., 1961-65; v.p., controller Scott Paper Co., 1965-80; controller, dir. Brunswick Pulp & Paper Co., 1966-80. Bd. govs., exec. com. Eastern div. Pa. Economy League, 1972-80. Mem. Financial Execs. Inst., Am. Paper Inst., Pa. C. of C. (dir., mem. exec. com., chmn. finance com.), Phi Beta Kappa. Home: Media, Pa. Died Sept. 16, 1980; buried Churchville, Pa.

CHAMBERLIN, JOSEPH WEBB, newspaper exec.; b. Dallas, Feb. 16, 1913; s. Charles and Marie (Lamb) C.; A.B., Stanford, 1934; m. Jean Richardson, Oct. 28, 1944 (div.); children—Carol Jill, Joseph Scott, Leslie, Wendy; m. 2d, Nancy P. Reineman, Oct. 17, 1972. Sales engr. E. I. duPont de Nemours & Co., Inc., 1935-39; partner Fitzpatrick and Chamberlin, pubs. advt. reps., 1940-54; account exec. Young & Rubicam, advt., 1954-61; vice chmn. bd., chief exec. officer, dir. Million Market Newspapers, Inc., N.Y.C., 1961-76; ret., 1976. Mem. endowment fund raising com. Stanford. Calif. dir. Wilkie Vols., 1940. Served to lt. (s.g.) USNR, 1942-45. Decorated Bronze Star. Mem. Am. Mgmt. Assn. Clubs: Sky (N.Y.C.); Wee Burn Country (Darien, Conn.). Home: Rancho Santa Fe, Calif. Died Sept. 22, 1977.

CHAMBERLIN, WELLMAN, cartographer; b. Phila., Feb. 15, 1908; s. Leroy and Rose Charlton (Wellman) C.; B.A., Antioch Coll., 1932; m. Anne Carter Waller, Oct. 8, 1938; children—Robert Wellman, John Charlton, David Waller. With Nat. Geog. Soc., 1935-71, chief cartographer, 1964-71; originator Chamberlin trimetric projection, which allows the mapping of entire continents with minimum distortion, 1947. Club: Cosmos (Washington). Author: The Round Earth on Flat Paper, 1947. Inventor Nat. Geog. world globe, 1961. Home: Waterford, Va. Died July 4, 1976; buried Quaker Graveyard, Waterford.

CHAMBERS, ARTHUR WOODBURNE (CHAM'BERZ), lawyer; b. Toms River, N.J., Dec. 8, 1886; s. Elias H. and Mary Louise (Camberne) C.; student Rutherford Institute, 1902-06; LL.B., Yale U., 1909; m. Winifred Langdale Smith, June 10, 1916 (died 1928); children—Arthur Woodburne, Gordon Phelps, Marshall Hale; m. 2d, Maude Wedmore Barton, Jan. 20, 1931; step-daughters, Beverly Barton (Mrs. Randolph V. Hall), Barbara Barton (Mrs. Elwin R. Lindsey). Admitted to Conn. bar, 1909; practiced in New Haven since 1909; mem. law firm Chambers & Chambers; sec. to Congressman John Q. Tilson, 1912; sec. Civil Service Commn., New Haven, 1915-23; judge City Court of New Haven, 1923-25; trustee and chmn. of bd. Nat. Savs. Bank, New Haven; pres. State Prison and Parole Board, 1946-55. Member of New Haven Grays and 2d Conn. Inf., 1910-16; 1st lt. and batn. adj., Mexican border service, 1916; 1st lt. inf., Conn. State Guard, 1940-42. Mem. Am., Conn. State and New Haven County (chairman grievance committee, 1933-56), bar assns.; S.A.R. (pres. 1931), New Haven Chamber of Commerce (dir. 1929-31), Am. Judicature Soc., Yale Law Sch. Alumni (mem. exec. com.), Phi Alpha Delta. Republican. Baptist. Mason (32 deg., K.T., Shriner). Clubs: Kiwanis, Graduate, Quinnipack. Home: New Haven, Conn.

CHAMBERS, PAUL LAURENCE DUNBAR, JR., jazz bassist; b. Pitts., Apr. 22, 1935; s. Paul Laurence Dunbar and Margaret (Eccles) C.; m. Ann Williams,

June 20, 1952 (div. 1961); children—Eric, Renee, Pierre; m. 2d, Myra Greenspan, Feb. 24, 1962. Tech. dir. Cass Tech. High Sch., Detroit, 1951; bassist for Paul Quinichette Quartet, 1954, Benny Green Quintet, 1954, Miles Davis Quintet, 1955-61, Wynton Kelly Trio, 1961-65; recording artist for Columbia, Riverside, Blue Note, Vee-Jay records. Recipient New Star award Downbeat mag., 1957; 1st place Jazz Poll, 1958. Died Jan. 4, 1969.

CHAMBLISS, ROLLIN, sociologist, educator; b. Plains, Ga., July 17, 1902; s. James R. and Henrietta L. (Davison) C.; A.B., U. Ga., 1927; M.A., Harvard, 1941, Ph.D., 1943; m. Amy Carlson, May 21, 1939; children—Carlson, John. Asso. prof. U. Ga., 1946-48, prof. 1948-62; prof. sociology U. Hartford (Conn.), from 1962. Fulbright vis. prof. Finland, 1955-56, Pakistan, 1959. Served with AUS, 1936-39, 41-46. Fellow Am. Sociol. Assn.; mem. So. Sociol. Soc. (v.p.), Phi Beta Kappa, Phi Kappa Phi. Author: Social thought from Hammurab: to Comte, 1954; The Nature of Man, 1961; Meaning for Man, 1966. Contbr. articles to profl. jours. Home: West Hartford, Conn. Died Sept. 4, 1980; buried Mt. Auburn Cemetery, Cambridge, Mass.

CHAMPION, GOWER, choreographer, dancer; b. Geneva, Ill., June 22, 1919; s. John W. and Beatrice (Carlisle) C.; student pub. schs., Los Angeles; m. Marjorie Celeste Belcher, Oct. 5, 1947 (div. 1972); children—Gregg, Blake. Early dancing appearances with Jeanne Tyler as Gower and Jeanne, west coast night clubs, also N.Y.C.; appeared Broadway mus. revues including Streets of Paris, Lady Comes Across, Count Me In, 1939-41; appeared with Marjorie Bell (Marjorie Celeste Belcher) as Marge and Gower Champion, N.Y.C. debut in Hotel Plaza, 1947; night club tours, 1948; staged dances for Broadway revue Small Wonder; choreographer Lend an Ear, Hollywood, film Girl Most Likely, 1956; TV Chevy Show, Jack Benny Show, Screen Dirs. Playhouse, G.E. Theatre: weekly show Admiral Broadway Revue, Dumont NBC-TV Ngtwork, 1949; appeared with Bing Crosby in motion picture Mr. Music, Paramount, 1950; movies include Show Boat, Lovely to Look At, Everything I Have is Yours, 1952, Give the Girl a Break, 1952; various nightclub, TV appearances, including TV show Toast of the Town, 1953, GE Theatre, 1957, Dinah Shore Show, 1958, Telephone Hour, 1959, We Four, 1960; appeared in Three for Tonight; producer, dir. Acad. Awards Show, 1969; choreography and directing Bye, Bye, Birdie (Tony award 1961), Hello, Dolly (Tony award 1964), Carnival, I Do I Do, Three Bags Full, Sugar, 1972, Irene, 1973; on Broadway in The Act, 1978; 42d Street, 1980. Served with the USCG, World War II; transport duty, also toured with mus. show Tars and Spars. Recipient Donaldson, Dance mag., Antoinette Perry awards for creation best dances on Broadway; Tony award for best dir. musical, choregrapher The Happy Time, 1967-68. Mem. Screen Dirs. Guild. Address: Los Angeles, Calif. Died Aug. 25, 1980.

CHANDLEE, GROVER C., coll. prof.; b. Delta, Pa., Sept. 5, 1884; s. Samuel and Elizabeth Ann (Barton) C.; Ph.B., Franklin and Marshall Coll., 1907, hon. D.Sc., 1943; M.S., Pa. State Coll., 1913; M.A., Columbia U., 1922, Ph.D., 1925; unmarried. Instr. Pa. State Coll., 1907-10 (indsl. work in chemistry 1910-11), asst., asso. and full prof., 1912-21, head dept., 1921-49; acting dean, Grad. School, 1933-34; prof. emeritus Pennsylvania State Coll. since 1949; prof. chemistry, Univ. of South Carolina, 1949-50; U.S. Army University, Shrivenham, England, 1945; vis. prof. chemistry Univ. of Hawaii, 1952-53. Served in World War I. Mem. Am. Chem. Soc., Phi Kappa Phi, Phi Lambda Upsilon, Sigma Xi, Phi Kappa Sigma, Alpha Chi Sigma. Club: Chemists (N.Y.). Contbr. to chemical mags. Home: Conestoga, Pa.

CHANDLER, ALBERT R., prof. philosophy, author; b. Norwich, Conn., May 25, 1884; s. Charles E. and Frances E. (Brown) C.; prep. edn. Norwich Free Acad.; A.B., Dartmouth Coll., 1908, A.M., 1909; A.M., Harvard, 1911, Ph.D., 1913; student univs. of Marburg and Göttingen, Germany, 1911-12; m. Alice T. Wing, 1921 (died 1935); children—Charles W., Margaret F.; m. 2d, Mary M. Shields, 1938. Asst. in philosophy, Harvard, 1912-13, instr., 1913-14; asst. prof. philosophy, Ohio State University, 1914-25, prof., 1925-51, professor emeritus since 1951; visiting associate professor philosophy, New York University, 1924. Served with Am. Ambulance Hosp. (Neuilly) and Am. Red Cross in France and Italy, 1917-19. Mem. Am. Philos. Assn., Am. Psychol. Assn., Am. Soc. for Aesthetics, Phi Beta Kappa. Conglist. Author: Beauty and Human Nature, 1934; Bibliography of Psychological Aesthetics (with E. N. Barnhart), 1938; Larks, Nightingales and Poets, 1938; The Clash of Political Ideals, 1940; Rosenberg's Nazi Myth, 1945. Home: Columbus, O.

CHANDLER, CAROLINE A., physician, writer juvenile books; b. Ford City, Pa., Dec. 7, 1906; d. Andrew Hartupee and Lucile Isobel (Brown) C.; student U. Pitts., 1924-27; B.A., Barnard Coll., Columbia, 1929; M.D. cum laude, Yale, 1933. Research fellow pediatrics Harvard Med. Sch., asst. med. service Children's Hosp., Boston, 1934-36; asst. in bacteriology and immunology Harvard Sch. Pub. Health, 1936-37; asst. in bacteriology, research fellow obstetrics Harvard Med. Sch., vol. asst. in bacteriology, Boston Lying-In Hosp., 1937-39; research fellow pediatrics Johns Hopkins, 1939-41, instr. preventive medicine, 1941-43; asst. dispensary pediatrician Johns Hopkins Hosp., 1939-41, asst. dispensary pediatrician, 1939-41, asst. visiting pediatrician, 1941-43, asst. prof. preventive medicine, instr. pediatrics Med. Sch., 1946-53, asst. prof. pediatrics 1953-72, prof. emeritus, 1972-79; instr. mental hygiene, 1960-72; cons. community mental health Nat. Inst. Mental Health, NIH; med. counselor Coll. Notre Dame of Md., 1951-56; med. dir. Family and Children's Soc., Balt., 1954-57; chief Div. Maternal and Child Health, Md. Dept. Health, 1957-59, chief Office Mental and Child Health, 1959-79; chief demonstrations sect. Nat. Inst. Mental Health, 1963, chief child mental health sect. community research and services br., 1964-66, chief Center for Studies Mental Health of Children and Youth, Bethesda, Md., 1966-68; cons. infant rearing study Children's Hosp., Washington, 1968-79. Cons. project head start Office Child Devel., 1968-72, Plays for Living, N.Y.C., 1968-72; staff Children's Bur., Dept. Labor, 1943-44; med. columnist Cath. Woman's World, 1939-42. Commd. surgeon (Res.) USPHS, 1944, sr. srugeon, 1949, med. dir., 1965-79. Lena Lake Forest fellow. Nat. Fedn. Bus. and Profl. Women's Clubs for research on influenzal meningitis, 1936. Diplomate Nat. Bd. Med. Examiners U.S., Am. Bd. Pediatrics. Am. Bd. Preventive Medicine and Pub. Health. Fellow Am. Acad. Pediatrics, Soc. for Pediatric Research, Am. Pub. Health Assn., Am. Coll. Preventive Medicine, Royal Soc. Health (Gt. Britain), Am. Orthopsychiat. Assn.; mem. Am. Psychiat. Assn., Balt. Urban League, Authors League Am., Md. Assn. for Mental Health, St. Clement Soc., Phi Beta Kappa, Sigma Xi. Democrat. Roman Catholic. Clubs: 16 East Hamilton St., John Hopkins. Author: Susie Stuart, M.D., 1941; Susie Stuart. Home Front Doctor, 1943; (with Marion L. Faegre) Your Child From One to Six, rev. edit., 1945; Dr. Kay Winthrop, Intern. 1947; Famous Men of Medicine, 1950; Famous Modern Men of Medicine, 1965, (with others) Early Child Care-The New Perspectives, 1968, (with Sharon H. Kempf) Nursing as a Career, 1970. Contbg. editor child health Farm Jours., Farmer's Wife, editorial bd., Yale Jour. Biology and Medicine, 1931-33. Contbr. World Book Ency., sci. and med. jours. Address: Bethesda, Md. Died Dec. 18, 1979.

CHANDLER, H. DALAND, architect; b. Boston, Mass., Jan. 23, 1884; s. Francis Ward and Alice (Daland) C.; grad. Groton Sch., 1902; A.B., Harvard, 1906; Mass. Inst. of Tech., 1906-09, Ecole des Beaux Arts, Atelier Duquesne, Paris, 1909-12; m. Ellen Bancroft Dalton, June 11, 1925. Associate partner Allen & Collens, 1921-25; in independent practice since 1925. Capt. Coast Arty. Corps, World War I; Ft. Standish, Boston Harbor, A.D.C., Maj. Gen. Wm. Crozier, Clarence R. Edwards. Fellow A.I.A., (past dir.); past pres., Boston Soc. of Architects. Past mem. Mass. Bd. of Registration of Architects. Clubs: Harvard (Boston), Architectural (Boston). Home: Boston.

CHANDLER, HENRY PORTER, lawyer; b. Indian Orchard, Mass. Mar. 19, 1880; s. John Henry and Abbie White (Smith) C.; student Leland Stanford Jr. U., 1896-98; A.B., Harvard, 1901; J.D., U. Chgo., 1906; m. Helen Firman Mack, Mar. 24, 1907 (dec. Nov. 1930); 1 dau., Margaret Mack (Mrs. Myles F. Gibbons); m. 2d, Olive Hull, Nov. 28, 1931. Instr. English, U. Chgo., 1901-04, sec. to pres., 1904-06; admitted to Ill. bar, 1906; practiced law, 1906-39; mem. law firm Tolman & Chandler, 1931-39; dir. Adminstrv. Office U.S. Cts., 1939-56, ret.; cons. territorial cts. Hawaii, 1957; cons. judical adminstrn., ct. systems, from 1957; 1st ct. adminstr. State of Ill., 1959-60. Mem. permanent commn. on inter-ch. relations Presbyn. Ch. U.S.A., 1938-53. Mem. Am. Law Inst., Am. (chmn. mcpl. law sect. 1938-39), Ill., Chgo. (pres. 1938-39), Fed. bar assns., Phi Delta Phi. Clubs: Union League (pres. 1932-33), City (pres. 1923-25), Chgo. Lit. (Chgo.); Cosmos (Washington). Author: Some Major Advances in the Federal Judicial System, 1922-1947, 1963. Contbr. to legal periodicals. Home: Bethesda, Md. Died Dec. 12, 1975.

CHANDLER, PORTER RALPH, lawyer; b. Buffalo, May 11, 1899; s. Porter and Mary (Wadsworth) C.; grad. St. Mark's Sch., 1917; A.B., Harvard, 1920; B.A., Oxford U., 1923, B.C.L., 1924, M.A., 1950; LL.D., St. John's U., 1952, Manhattan Coll., 1956; m. Gabrielle Chanler, July 8, 1924 (dec. Oct. 1958); children—Joseph, Mrs. Judith Chandler Houston, David, Mrs. Mary Chandler Jackson. Admitted to N.Y. State bar, 1924; spl. asst. to atty. gen. U.S., 1924-26; asst. U.S. atty. So. Dist. N.Y., 1926-28; with law firm Davis Polk & Wardwell, N.Y.C., 1929-70, partner, 1938-70. Mem. bd. higher edn., N.Y.C., 1952-70, chmn., 1966-69. Served as pvt. U.S. Army, 1918; lt. col. USAAF, 1942-45. Mem. Assn. Bar City N.Y., Am. Bar Assn., N.Y. County Lawyers Assn., Guild of Catholic Lawyers (past pres.). Republican. Roman Catholic. Knight of Malta. Home: New York, N.Y. Died Nov. 6, 1979.

CHANEL, GABRIELLE (BONHEUR), fashion designer; b. nr. Issoire, Auvergne, France, 1883. Began early career as milliner; creator simplicity of style for women's fashions in hats and dresses, 1920-38, 54—; mfr. textiles, costume jewelry; inventor and mfr. perfume. Address: Paris Ier, France. *

CHANTER, WILLIAM GEORGE (CHANT'ER), clergyman, educator; b. New Carlisle, Province of Quebec, Can., July 29, 1884; s. Charles Frederick and Julia (Ford) C.; came to U.S., 1900; grad. Wilbraham (Mass.) Acad., 1910; B.A., Wesleyan Univ. (Conn.), 1914, M.A., 1915; S.T.B., Boston Univ. School Theology, 1918; M.A., Harvard Univ., 1920; D.D., Lawrence College, 1930; unmarried. Ordained, M.E. ministry, 1916; pastor Upton, Mass., 1914-16, Cliftondale Ch., Saugus, Mass., 1918-19; Frank D. Howard fellow, Boston U. Sch. Theology, 1919-20; mem. faculty Wesleyan U., 1920-41, prof. ethics and religion, 1922-41; dean of freshmen, 1927-28, dean of Univ., 1930-35; pastor College Church, 1928-41, Broadway Meth. Church, Somerville, Mass., 1941-42; visiting prof., Drew Theological Seminary, Madison, N.J., 1942-43, prof. of English Bible since 1943. Army sec. Y.M.C.A., with Indian Expeditionary Force in Mesopotamia, 1916-17. Mem. Am. Philos. Assn., Nat. Assn. Biblical Instrs., N.E. Conf. of the Methodist Church, Phi Beta Kappa, Phi Nu Theta. Awarded British Great War Medal. Spl. contbr. Zions Herald, Boston, 1939-46. Author: A Self Worth Having, 1938; The Prophets, 1946. Home: Madison, N.J.; (summer) W. Yarmouth, Mass.

CHANTRY, ALLAN J(OSEPH) (CHAN'TRE), naval officer (ret.); b. Malvern, Ia., Apr. 15, 1883; s. Allan Joseph and Harriet Adelaide (Rains) C.; A.B., U.S. Naval Acad., 1906; M.S. in naval architecture, Mass. Inst. of Tech., 1910; hon. D.Sc. Drexel Inst. of Tech., 1943; m. Edna Starr Scott, Jan. 1, 1910; children—Carolyn Carol, Helene (dec.). Commd. ensign U.S. Navy, 1908, advanced through grades to rear adm., 1938; head, design div., bur. of construction and repair (now bur. of ships), U.S. Navy Dept., Washington, 1936-39; mgr. Navy Yard, Phila. Pa., 1939-45; retired from active service, 1946. Awarded Legion of Merit; Order of the Brit. Empire with rank of comdr.; Order of Oange-Narssau with rank of grand officer (Netherlands); Order of the So. Cross with rank of great officer (Brazil); numerous other U.S. decorations for world war service. Mem. Soc. of Naval Architects and Marine Engrs., Naval Hist. Soc., Sigma Chi. Episcopalian. Clubs: Chevy Chase (Md.), Phila. (Pa.). Home: Radnor, Pa.

CHAPIN, EDWARD YOUNG, JR., banker; b. Chattanooga, Aug. 10, 1897; s. Edward Young and Elise (Hutcheson) C.; B.S. in Econs., U. Pa., 1918; m. Dorris Inman Carter, Dec. 6, 1921; children—Edward Young III, Mary Lynn (Mrs. W.T. Patten), Dorris (Mrs. J.R. Wells). With Am. Nat. Bank & Trust Co., 1919-72, pres., 1948-57, chmn. exec. com., 1957-72, then adv. dir.; v.p., dir. Rock City Gardens. Hon. trustee Benwood Found.; trustee Crystal Found., Maclellan Found., Chattanooga Tb Sanitorium Assn., Forest Hills Cemetery Assn. Mem. Beta Theta Pi. Presbyn. Clubs: Lookout Mountain Fairyland, Mountain City, Lookout Mountain Golf; Royal Poinciana Golf (Naples, Fla.), Naples Yacht. Home: Lookout Mountain, Tenn. Died June 5, 1976; buried Forest Hills Cemetery, Chattanooga, Tenn.

CHAPIN, SLOCUM, travel agy. exec.; b. Quincy, Mass., May 12, 1913; s. Charles Mathews and Helen Marguerite (Slocum) C.; student Peoples Acad., Morrisville, Vt., 1928-30, Tilton (N.H.) Sch., 1930-32, Dartmouth, 1932-35; m. Elaine Hunt, Oct. 20, 1933; 1 son, John; m. 2d, Joan Igou, Aug. 18, 1937; children—David (dec.), Joan, Michele; m. 3d, Jane Daly, Mar. 4, 1961. Guest relations NBC, N.Y.C., 1933-35; pres. Broadcast Builders, Inc., Hanover, N.H., 1935-36; asst. sales promotion mgr. World Broadcasting System, Inc., N.Y.C., 1936-37; salesman Radio Sta. WOC, Davenport, 1937-41; sales mgr. Radio Sta. WKBN, Youngstown, O., 1941; gen. mgr. Radio Sta. WSTC, Stamford, Conn., 1941-42; with Am. Broadcasting Co. (then Blue Network, Inc.), 1942-66, Eastern sales mgr. for TV, 1948-51, v.p. charge ABC owned TV Stas. 1951, v.p. charge sales TV Network, 1954, v.p. charge sales Western div., 1958-64, v.p. exec. relations, 1964-66; pres. Adventures Unlimited, agts. for travel at Abercrombie & Fitch, N.Y.C., 1966-75. Mem. Camp Fire Club Am., Broadcast Pioneers, Psi Upsilon. Club: Explorers. Home: New York, N.Y. Died Nov. 15, 1975; buried Montpelier, Vt.

CHAPLIN, CHARLES SPENCER, actor, writer, composer; b. London, Eng., Apr. 16, 1889; both parents in theatrical bus., student pub. schs., London; m. Mildred Harris; 1 son (dec.); m. 2d, Lita Grey; children—Charles Spencer, Sydney; m. 3d, Paulette Goddard (div. 1942); m. 4th Oona O'Neill, June 16, 1943; children—Geraldine, Michael, Josephine, Victoria, Eugene, Jane, Annette-Emily, James. Identified with theater at 7 years old, employed in vaudeville and legitimate playhouses; first appearance was as Billy with William Gillette, in Sherlock Holmes; came to U.S. with vaudeville act, 1910. Screen debut, 1914, with Keystone Film Co.; with Essanay Co., 1915;

Mutual Film Corp., 1916; signed with new First Nat. Exhibitors' Circuit to make eight two-reel pictures for $1,000,000, 1917; began as producer with constrn. of own motion picture studios at Hollywood, Calif., starring in and directing prodns. of his own creation; then playing and producing own pictures, distributed by United Artists Corp. of which he was founder member; latest productions Limelight, 1952, Monsieur Verdoux, 1947; directed film Great Dictator, 1940, A Countess from Hong Kong, 1967; also revived musical and sound version The Gold Rush, 1942; Special Acad. award for contributions to film industry, 1972; Acad. award for musical score of Limelight, 1973; created Knight, 1975. Mem. Société des Beaux Arts, Paris, ASCAP. Decorated chevalier Legion of Honor (France). Co-recipient (with Dmitri Shostakovich) of world peace prize of World Peace Council, 1953. Clubs: Lambs (New York); Tuna (Catalina). Author: Charles Chaplin: My Autobiography, 1964. Home: Vevey, Switzerland. Died Dec. 25, 1977.

CHAPMAN, CEIL, fashion designer; b. N.Y.C., Feb. 19, 1912; d. William and Elizabeth (Doyle) Mitchell; student parochial schs.; m. Peter Fitzgibbon; 1 son, Peter; m. 2d, Samuel Chapman (div.); m. 3d, Thomas G. Rogers, Dec. 1, 1951. Vice pres. Samuel Chapman Inc.; pres. Ceil Chapman Enterprises. Received Mademoiselle merit award, 1946; Am. Fashion Critics' award, 1946; named one of ten best designers Fashion Trade; recipient Foley's Golden Year Designer award; Wilshire Award, May Col; awards for fashion design John Wanamaker, Suawbridge & Clothier, Phila. Fashion Group, others. Home: New York, N.Y. Died July 13, 1979.

CHAPMAN, CHARLES FREDERIC, editor, yachtsman; b. Norwich, Conn., Jan. 4, 1881; s. Charles Billings and Mary (Warburton) C.; M.E., Cornell U., 1905; m. Alice May Armstrong, 1909; 1 dau., Mary Campbell (Mrs. Robert H. Watts). Editor, bus. mgr., pub. Motor Boating, now pub. Mem. bd. trustees, Village of Plandome, L.I., 1928-40, acting mayor, police commr., fire commr., water commr., 1947-55. Recipient Ole Evinrude Boating Found. award for contbn. recreational boating, 1955. Mem. U.S. Power Squadron (chief comdr. 1946-47). Clubs: Manhasset Bay Yacht (commodore 1941-44) Port Washington, N.Y.); Larchmont (N.Y.) Yacht; Essex (Conn.) Yacht; University, New York Athletic (N.Y.C.). Home: Essex, Conn. Died Mar. 21, 1976; buried Essex.

CHAPMAN, GILBERT W., bus. exec.; b. Woodmere, L.I., May 24, 1902; s. Henry Otis and Harriet M. (Murphey) C.; B.S., Sheffield Sci. Sch., Yale, 1924; LL.D., Roanoke Coll., 1959; m. Katherine Bright, Mar. 21, 1925 (dec. 1949); children—Harriet W. (Mrs. H. Worthington Kalt), Gilbert W.; m. 2d, Elizabeth Fuller (former Mrs. Charles B. Goodspeed), Oct. 28, 1950. With engrng. staff Am. Water Works & Electric Co., 1924-27, asst. treas., 1927-35, treas., 1935-43, v.p., 1943-47, pres., 1947-48; v.p. charge finance Yale & Towne Mfg. Co., 1948-49, pres., 1949-60, ret., 1960; then pres., dir. Sutton Place South Corp. Hon. bd. dirs. Lincoln Center Performing Arts; hon. trustee N.Y. Public Library. Clubs: Racquet and Tennis (N.Y.C.); St. Anthony's (Yale U.). Home: New York, N.Y. Died Dec. 16, 1979.

CHAPMAN, JOHN HERBERT, Canadian dept. adminstr.; b. London, Ont., Can., Aug. 28, 1921; s. Lloyd Poole and Kathleen Saunders (Allen) C.; B.Sc. in Radio Physics with honors, U. Western Ont., 1948; M.Sc. in Physics, McGill U., 1949, Ph.D. in Physics, 1951; LL.D. (hon.), Laurentian U., 1967; D.Eng. (hon.) Waterloo U., 1969; m. Marian Christine Holmes, Sept. 3, 1949; children—Margaret, Paula, John Sheila, Ann. Dep. chmn. sci. Def. Research Bd., Ottawa, Ont., 1949-68; asst. dep. minister space program Dept. Communications, Ottawa, 1968-79. Served with RCAF, 1940-45. Recipient Charles Chree medal and prize Phys. Soc. and Inst. Physics, London, 1967. Fellow Royal Soc. Can. (pres sci. sect. 1972-73), IEEE, Canadian Aero. and Space Inst. (recipient McCurdy award 1967); mem. Canadian Assn. Physicists, Am. Geophys. Union, Assn. Profl. Engrs. Ont. (recipient Engring medal, 1966). Anglican. Club: Cityview Curling. Editor: Upper Atmosphere and Space Programs in Canada, 1967. Contbr. articles in field to profl. jours. Home Ottawa, Ont., Canada. Died Sept. 28, 1979.

CHAPMAN, OSCAR LITTLETON, lawyer, former sec. of interior; b. Omega, Va., Oct. 22, 1896; s. James Jackson and Rosa Archer (Blount) C.; ed. Randolph-Macon Acad., Bedford, Va., 1918, U. Denver, 1922-24, U. N.M., 1927-28; LL.B., Westminister Law Sch., Denver, 1929; LL.D., Colo. State Coll. of Edn., Augustana Coll., Howard U., 1949, U. Denver, 1951, Western State Coll. Colo., 1961; m. Olga Pauline Edholm, December 21, 1920 (dec.); m. 2d, Ann Kendrick, Feb. 24, 1940; 1 son, James. Asst. chief probation officer Juvenile Ct., Den., 1922-24, chief, 1924-27; admitted to Colo. bar, 1929; apptd. asst. sec. of interior, 1933; apptd. under sec. of interior, 1946; sec. of interior, 1949-53; mem. law firm Chapman, Duff & Paul, Washington. Bd. overseer Coll. of V.I. Served with U.S. Navy, 1918-20. Mem. Am. Legion, Phi Alpha Delta. Democrat. Methodist. Home: Washington, D.C. Died Feb. 7, 1978; buried Arlington Nat. Cemetery.

CHAPMAN, ROBERT HETT, textile mfg. co. exec.; b. Middlesboro, Ky., Feb. 13, 1895; s. James Alfred and Rachel (McMaster) C.; M.E., Cornell U., 1917; dr. Textile Industries Clemson Coll., 1951; m. Sarah Elizabeth Lipscomb, June 29, 1918 (dec. Aug. 1947); children—Sarah Elizabeth (Mrs. Thomas Samuel Means, Jr.), Robert Hett; m. 2d, Laura Noell Carr, Sept. 2, 1948. Partner charge mech. engring. dept. J.E. Sirrine & Co., Greenville, S.C., 1919-37; v.p., asst. treas. Inman Mills (S.C.), 1937-64, dir., 1937-76, chmn. bd. dirs., 1965-76; dir. Citizens and So. Nat. Bank of S.C. Chmn. bd. Inman-Riverdale Found. Served as ensign USNR, 1917-19. Registered profl. engr., S.C. Mem. Am. Soc. M.E., Chi Psi. Democrat. Presbyn. Clubs: Piedmont, Spartanburg Country. Home: Spartanburg, S.C. Died Aug. 27, 1976.

CHAPPELEAR, E(DGAR) S(TRATTON), banker; born Zanesville, O., Jan. 12, 1886; s. Charles Francis and Mildred (Stratton) C.; ed. Phillips Exeter Acad., Exeter, N.H., 1903-05; A.B., Dartmouth Coll., 1909; M.B.A., Harvard, 1911; m. Margaret Elizabeth Lacy, July 12, 1930; 1 dau., Joan Margaret. With Bankers Trust Co. since 1911, auditor, 1921-25, comptroller, 1925-27, v.p., 1927-51; dir. Credit-America Corp., West African Constructors, Ltd., Am. Cotton Supply Corp. Mem. War Industries Bd., 1917-18. Mem. adv. com. Nat. Cotton Council of America. Mem. Newcomen Soc. of Eng. (Am. treas.), Pilgrim Soc., Delta Tau Delta. Presbyterian. Clubs: India House, Harvard (New York). Home: N.Y.C.

CHAPPELL, CLOVIS GILLHAM (CHAP'PEL), clergyman, author; b. Flatwood, Tenn., Jan. 8, 1882; s. Wm. B. and Mary C.; prep. edn., Webb Sch., Bell Buckle, Tenn.; student Duke U., 1902-03, Harvard, 1904-05; D.D., Duke U., 1920, Centenary College of La., 1920; D.Litt., Birmingham-Southern Coll., 1936; m. Cecil Hart, April 15, 1908; children—Clovis Gillham, Bob Hart. Ordained ministry M.E. Ch. S., 1908; pastor successively Polytechnic, Tex., Gatesville, Tex., Epworth Ch., Oklahoma City, Okla., Highland Park, Dallas, Tex., Mount Vernon Place Ch., Washington, D.C., First M.E. Ch., Memphis, Tenn.; later pastor First M.E. Ch., Houston, Tex.; pastor First Ch., Birmingham, 1932-36, St. Luke's M.E. Ch., S., Oklahoma City, 1936-41, Galloway Memorial Meth. Ch., Jackson, Miss., 1941-45, First Ch., Charlotte, N.C., 1945-49; retired since 1949. Author: The Village Tragedy, 1921; Sermons on Bible Characters, 1922; More Sermons on Bible Characters, 1923; Sermons on New Testament Characters, 1924; Sermons on Old Testament Characters, 1925; Home Folks, 1926; Familiar Failures, 1927; Christ and the New Woman, 1928; Men That Count, 1929; The Sermon on the Mount, 1930; Sermons from the Psalms, 1931; Sermons from the Parables, 1933; Sermons on the Lord's Prayer, 1934; Special Sermons, 1936; Sermons from the Miracles, 1937; Ten Rules for Living, 1938; Values That Last, 1939; The Road to Certainty, 1940; Faces About the Cross, 1941; Feminine Faces, 1942; Sermons from Revelation, 1943; Living Zestfully, 1944; If I Were Young, 1945; And the Prophets, 1946; Questions Jesus Asked, 1948; When the Church Was Young, 1950; Annointed to Preach, 1951; The Seven Words, 1952; In Parables, 1953; Meet These Men, 1956; Sermons From Job, 1957; Sermons from Simon Peter, 1959; The Cross Before Calvary, 1960; Living with Royalty, 1962; Surprises of the Bible, 1967. Home: Waverly, Tenn.

CHAPPELL, SIDNEY LOVETT, army officer; b. Washington, D.C., July 22, 1886; s. John W. and Ida M. (Adamson) C.; M.D., George Washington U., 1909; m. Florence B. Thornton, June 4, 1913. Intern Casualty Hosp., Washington, 1909-10; intern and resident physician, Children's Hosp., Washington, 1910-11. Commd. 1st lt., M.C.Res., U.S. Army, 1911, 1st lt., M.C., U.S. Army, 1913, and advanced through grades to brig. gen., 1945; retired as brig. gen., 1946. Awarded Legion of Merit, 1946. Fellow American College Physicians, American Bd. Psychiatry and Neurology; mem. A.M.A., Am. Psychiatric Assn. Mason. Address: Washington.

CHARLES, CLAYTON HENRY, educator, sculptor; b. Goodman, Wis., Sept. 11, 1913; s. Clayton Henry and Mabel (Wilkins) C.; B.A., U. Wis., 1938, M.A., 1939; m. Madelene Johnson, Aug. 5, 1939; children—Steven, David, Nancy. Asst. prof. art U. Ala., 1939-41; asso. prof., chmn. dept. art Meredith Coll., Raleigh, N.C., 1941-43; asst. dir. Milw. Art Inst., 1946-47; asso. prof., chmn. dept. art, dir. Art Hall, Beloit Coll., 1947-51; prof., chmn. dept. art U. Miami (Fla.), 1951-76. One man shows U. Ala., 1939, N.C. State Art Soc., 1942, Beloit Coll., 1949, Robinson Gallery, Miami Beach, 1951, Barry Coll., Miami, 1958, Rudolph Galleries, Coral Gables, 1961; rep. permanent collections Milw. Pub. Library, U. Wis., Beloit Coll., N.C. State Art Soc., Milw. Hosp., Peabody Coll. Vice pres. Mental Health Served as lt. (j.g.), USNR, 1943-46. Recipient 1st prize for sculpture Wis. Painters and Sculptors, 1950, Art Inst. medal Milw. Art Inst., 1949; 1st prize Asso. Fla. Sculptors, 1961. Mem. Coll. Art Assn., Artists Equity, Asso. Fla. Sculptors (v.p.). Home: Miami, Fla. Died Sept. 1, 1976.

CHARLOT, JEAN, muralist; b. Paris, France, Feb. 7, 1898; s. Henri and Anna (Goupil) C.; educated pub schs. and art schs.; D.F.A. (hon.), Grinnell Coll., 1946; LL.D., St. Marys Coll., 1956; m. Dorothy Zohmah Day, May 26, 1939; children—Ann Maria, John Pierre, Martin Day, Peter Francis. Mural painting for Mexican gov., 1922-26; archeol. studies in Yucatan, Carnegie Instn., Washington, 1926-29; painter, lectr. and art tchr., U.S., 1929-79; held more than 100 one-man shows murals in N.J., Iowa, N.C., Ga.; exhibited Salzburg and Vienna, 1978, 79; recent murals, Notre Dame U., St. Mary's Coll., Ind., Des Moines Art Center, Christ the Good Shepherd Ch., Lincoln Pk., Mich., St. Sylvester Ch., Kilauea Kauai, Hawaiian Village Hotel, Walkiki, Des Moines Art Center; sculpture includes panels for chapel doors Punahou Sch., Honolulu, 1971, bas-reliefs St. John's Evangelist Ch., Mililani, Oahu, ceramic statues Hanalei, Kauai, 1969, Ala Moana Hotel, Honolulu, 1971, multi-media sculpture Moanalua Intermediate Sch., Honolulu, 1972-73, Maryknoll Sch., Honolulu, Christ and the Samaritan Woman, Honolulu, 1978, Madonna and Child, 1979, Damien, Wailuku, Maui, 1980; instr. Art Students League, U. Iowa, U. Calif., Columbia, U. Ga., Black Mountain Coll., Smith Coll.; head Fine Arts Sch., Colorado Springs, 1947-49; prof. art U. Hawaii, 1949-66, emeritus, sr. specialist East-West Center, 1967-79; Ryerson lectr. Yale U., 1948; summer tchr. U. Notre Dame (Ind.), 1955-56. Served as arty. officer French Army, World War I. Recipient award of merit Honolulu chpt. Nat. Soc. Arts and Letters; Freedom award Sertoma Club, 1979; Maryknoll Art Center named for him; State of Hawaii Order of Distinction for Cultural Leadership, 1977; Benjamin Franklin fellow Royal Soc. for Encouragement Arts Manufactures and Commerce, 1972. Fellow in perpetuity Met. Mus. Art; Guggenheim fellow, 1945-47. Nat. dir. Artists Equity. Mem. Am. Inst. Graphic Arts (v.p. 1947), Soc. Am. Etchers, Gravers, Lithographers and Woodcutters, Hawaiian Hist. Soc. Author: Art-Making from Mexico to China, 1950; Dance of Death, 1951; foreword to Towards a People's Art, 1977. Contbr. articles to mags. and periodicals in Mexico and U.S. Executed over 60 murals since 1922, latest being Ch. St. Francis Xavier, Naiserelagi, Fiji, 1962-63, Jefferson Hall, East West Center, Honolulu, 1967, Grace Episcopal Ch., Hoolehua, Molokai, 1967, United Pub. Workers Bldg., Honolulu, 1970-75, Leeward Community Coll., Honolulu, 1974. Author or illustrator over sixty-five books and portfolios, latest being Mexican Art and the Academy of San Carlos, 1875-1915, 1963; Mexican Mural Renaissance, 1963; Three Plays of Ancient Hawaii, 1963; Jean Charlot: Posada's Dance of Death, 1964; The Timid Ghost (by Anita Brenner), 1966; Mowentihke Chalman, 1969; Spoken Hawaiian (by Samuel H. Elbert), 1970; Jose Clemente Orozco El Artista en Nueva York, 1971; An Artist on Art, 1972; Picture Book II, 1973; Two Hawaiian Plays, 1976; Jean Charlot's Prints, 1976; Popular Art: The Example of Jean Charlot, 1978; Cartoons Catholic from the brush and brain of Jean Charlot, 1978; A First Book (Zohmah Charlot), 1980. Home: Honolulu, Hawaii. Died Mar. 20, 1979.

CHASE, HARVEY DURELL, coll. adminstr.; b. Kilgore, O., Apr. 12, 1884; s. Harvey Sweat and Sarah Jennie (Ruse) C.; student Ohio Northern U., 1901-03; B.A., Ohio Wesleyan U., 1914; M.A., Ohio State U., 1915; grad. asst. U. of Chicago, 1923-24; m. Dora Dean Slates, June 15, 1915; 1 dau., Kathleen Iola (Mrs. Paul Y. Burns). Pub. school teacher, Carroll Country, Ohio, 1903-07; chmn. dept. biology Culver Stockton Coll., 1915-17; chmn. dept. biology U. Tulsa, 1917-28, chmn. dept. zoology, 1928—, counselor to men, 1936-42, prof. emeritus, 1954—. Fellow Okla. Acad. Sci. (past pres.), A.A.A.S.; mem. Am. Genetics Assn., Alpha Sigma Phi, Pi Gamma Mu, Sigma Xi. Presbyterian. Home: Tulsa, Okla.

CHASE, ILKA, author, actress; b. N.Y.C.; d. Frank D. and Edna (Allaway) Chase; ed. pvt. schs., nr. N.Y.C. and Paris; m. Louis Calhern, 1926 (div.); m. 2d, William B. Murray, July 13, 1935 (div.); m. 3d, Norton Sager Brown, 1946. Appeared in over 20 Broadway prodns. including The Animal Kingdom, Revenge with Music, The Women; motion pictures including Miss Tatlock's Millions, Johnny Dark, Big Knife, Ocean's 11; radio programs, Luncheon at Waldorf, Penthouse Party, Ilka Chase Program; TV appearances Glamour-Go-Round, Fashion Magic; guest appearance on dramatic programs including Cool Million, 1972. Author: Past Imperfect, 1942; In Bed We Cry, 1943; I Love Miss Tilli Bean, 1946; Free Admission, 1948; New York 22, 1951; Always in Vogue (with Edna Woolman Chase), 1954; The Island Players, 1956; Three Men on the Left Hand, 1960; The Carthaginian Rose, 1961, Elephants Arrive at Half-Past Five, 1963; Second Spring and Two Potatoes, 1966; Fresh from the Laundry, 1967; Varied Airs of Spring, 1969; Around the World and Other Places, 1970; Sounds of Home, 1971; Worlds Apart, 1972; The Care and Feeding of Friends, 1973; also syndicated weekly newspaper column. Address: New York, N.Y. Died Feb. 15, 1978.

CHATELAIN, LEON, JR., architect; b. Washington, Mar. 8, 1902; s. Leon and Bertha (Aeschbacker) C.; student George Washington U., 1927; m. Mary Wysong, Feb. 14, 1945; children—Leon, Jo Ann (adopted), Edward Russell (adopted). Asso., Waddy B. Wood, 1927-30; pvt. archtl. practice, Washington, 1930-56; partner Chatelain, Gauger & Nolan, 1956-70, Chatelain, Samperton & Nolan, Washington, 1970-75. Pres., D.C. Bd. Registrars and Examiners of Architects, 1962-65; chmn. Nat. Commn. Archtl. Barriers, 1966-68. Chmn., Nat. Employ the Physically Handicapped Week; pres. Crippled Children's Soc., 1955, Met. Police Boys' Club, 1954; chmn. D.C. Council on Human Relations, 1958-60, Benjamin Franklin Found., 1957-79. mem. exec. com. Pres.'s Com. Employ the Handicapped; pres. Nat. Soc. Crippled Children and Adults, 1967-69; sec. Heroes. Bd. dirs. YMCA, Washington; trustee George Washington U., Bullis Sch. Recipient medal Conseil Superior, award for community service Wash. Pub. Relations Soc., 1962; F. Stuart Fitzpatrick medal, 1966; Benjamin J. Latrobe Outstanding Architect award, 1966; Pres.'s Distinguished Service award; Das Grosse Verdienstkreuz (West Germany), 1968. Fellow Constrn. Specifications Inst., Royal Archtl. Inst. Can. (hon.), Philippines (hon.), New Zealand (hon.), Am. (past pres. Washington chpt., nat. treas. 1954-46, nat. pres. 1956-58, chmn. finance com.) insts. architects; mem. Archtl. Soc. Colombia (hon.), Royal Inst. Brit. Architects (hon.), Ch. Archtl. League Am., Bldg. Research Inst. (gov., pres. 1961), Nat. Acad. Scis.-NRC, N.Y. Archtl. League, Wash. Bldg. Congress (pres. 1945-46), Wash. Bd. Trade (pres. 1948-49, Man of Year award 1962). Mason (Shriner), Kiwanian. Clubs: Union Interalliee (Paris, France); Cosmos, Columbia Country, Capitol Hill, City Tavern, Arts, Congressional Country, University. Home: Washington D.C. Died May 6, 1979; buried Ft. Lincoln Cemetery, Washington, D.C.

CHAWNER, LOWELL JENKINS, fgn. service officer; b. El Modena, Cal., Oct. 14, 1896; s. John and Mary E. (Jenkins) C.; student Whittier Coll., 1915-16; A.B., Occidental Coll., 1921; C.E., Cornell U., 1931; Univ. fellow, Columbia, 1934-35; A.M., Harvard, 1951, Ph.D., 1954; LL.D., Korea U., 1957; m. Lucia Mary Soulé, Sept. 3, 1930; children—Priscilla Mary, Lucia Martha, Grace Atwater (Mrs. John Bowles), Lydia Ann (Mrs. John Detrick). Instr. civil engring. Cornell U., 1923-24, McMullen research fellow, 1930-34; asst. prof. econs. Occidental Coll., 1924-30; with U.S. Dept. Commerce, 1935-42, chief div. econ. research, bur. fgn. and domestic commerce, 1937-41, spl. asst. to sec. commerce, 1942; sr. econ. analyst CIA, 1947-53; staff Council Econ. Advisers, 1954-55; staff ICA, Dept. State, 1955-61; econ. adviser, asst. dir. U.S. Operations Mission to Korea, 1955-58, dep. dir., 1959-60; vis. prof. fgn. trade Coll. Bus. Administration Univ. Washington, Seattle, Wash., 1960-71. Served from pvt. to sgt. U.S., Army, 1917-18; AEF in France; from maj. to col., AUS, 1942-46. Decorated Legion of Merit. Mem. Am. Econ. Assn., Royal Econ. Soc., Phi Kappa Phi. Presbyn. Club: Cosmos (Washington). Home: Laguna Hills, Calif. Died Nov. 23, 1979.

CHENERY, CHRISTOPHER TOMPKINS (CHEN'ER-I), corp. exec.; b. Richmond, Va., Sept. 16, 1886; s. James Hollis and Ida Burnley (Taylor) C.; student Randolph-Macon Coll.; B.S. in Engring., Washington and Lee University, 1909; LL.D., Randolph Macon College, 1964; m. Helen Clementina Bates; children—Hollis Burnley, Margaret Emily, Helen Bates. Chmn. bd. So. Natural Gas Co., now chmn. emeritus; dir. Offshore Company. Trustee Washington and Lee Univ. Served as capt., later maj., engrs., U.S. Army, World War I. Mem. Am. Soc. C.E., New England Geneal. Soc., Acad. Polit. Sci., Am. Waterworks Assn., Inc., Newcomen Soc., N.Y. So. Soc., Va. Hist. Soc., Va. Thoroughbred Assn., Phi Beta Kappa, Phi Delta Theta, Phi Beta Kappa Assos., Omicron Delta Kappa. Clubs: City Midday, Jockey, Madison Sq. Garden, Turf and Field, Recess, Pinnacle (N.Y.C.); American Yacht, Shenorock Shore (Rye, New York); Pelham Country, Boulder Brook, Union League, Deep Run Hunt, Country of Virginia, Commonwealth. (Richmond); Metropolitan (Washington); Mt. Brook (Birmingham, Ala.); Blind Brook (Purchase, N.Y.); Everglades. Home: Pelham Manor, N.Y.

CHENEY, EDWARD RICE, fgn. service officer; b. LaCrosse, Wis., July 1, 1927; s. Moses Edward and Florence A. (Dahl) C.; B.A., Harvard, 1949; M.A., 1951; m. Sally Drew Leavitt, Dec. 28, 1948; children—Dorothy, Margaret, Edward, Thomas. Joined U.S. Fgn. Service, 1952; vice consul, Penang, Malaya, 1952-54; 2d sec., consul, The Hague, Netherlands, 1955-59; fiscal and fin. economist State Dept., 1960-64; 1st sec., consul, Managua, Nicaragua, 1964-67; consul, Bombay, India, 1967-70; fiscal and fin. economist State Dept., 1970-73; econ.-comml. counselor, Lima, Peru, 1973-75, Manila, Philippines, 1976. Served with USAF, 1945-47. Home: Sunapee, N.H. Died Sept. 13, 1976; buried Winchester, Va.

CHENEY, SHELDON WARREN, author; b. Berkeley, Cal., June 29, 1886; s. Warren and May Lucretia (Shepard) C.; A.B., U. Cal., 1908; m. Maud Meurice Turner, Apr. 2, 1910 (dec. Feb. 1934); children—John Turner, Elizabeth, Michael Sheldon; m. 2d, Martha Candler, Nov. 27, 1934 (dec. Nov. 1973). Art critic various newspapers and mags., 1910-16; founder Theatre Arts Mag., 1916, editor, 1916-21; freelance writer, 1921-22, 1926-75, contbr. numerous mags.; with Equity Players (The Actors' Theatre), N.Y.C., 1922-25; hon. fellow in art Union Coll., 1937-40; lectr. univs. and art museums, 1935-47. Served in War Camp Community Service, 1918-19. Fellow Royal Soc. Arts, London, Eng.; mem. Authors League Am., Soc. Am. Historians. Club: Players (N.Y.). Author: The New Movement in the Theatre, 1914; The Open Air Theatre, 1918; A Primer of Modern Art, 1923; The Art Theatre, 1925; Stage Decoration, 1927; The Theatre: Three Thousand Years of Drama, Acting and Stagecraft, 1929, rev. and enlarged edit., 1972; The New World Architecture, 1930; Expressionism in Art, 1934; Art and the Machine (with Martha Candler Cheney), 1936; A World History of Art, 1937; The Story of Modern Art, 1941; Men Who Have Walked With God, 1945 (pub. in German as Von Mystischen Leben); A New World History of Art, 1956; Sculpture of the World: A History, 1968; collected and edited Isadora Duncan's papers, pub. as The Art of the Dance. Contbr. to Ency. Brit., The New Caravan, other encys. and symposia. Home: Berkeley, Calif. Died Oct. 17, 1980.

CHERRINGTON, BEN MARK, educator; b. Gibbon, Neb., Nov. 1, 1885; s. George Whittington and Laura Ida (Frick) C.; A.B., U. Neb., 1911, LL.D., 1946; M.A., U. Cal., 1922; Ph.D., Columbia, 1934; Ps.D, U. Denver, 1953; m. Edith Mary Harper, June 28, 1924; children—Anne Mary, Stevens, Benjamin Mark. Gen. sec. U. Cal. YMCA, 1911-17; coach, U. Cal., 1915-17; nat. sec. student YMCA, 1919-26; dir. Social Sci. Found., U. Denver, 1926-51; prof. internat. relations, 1926—, chancellor, 1943-46; dir. Denver Regional office Inst. Internat. Edn., 1951-68; cons., 1968—. Adviser to U.S. delegation 8th Internat. Conf. Am. States, Lima, Peru, 1938; chief Div. of Cultural Relations, Dept. State, 1938-40; asso. cons. to U.S. delegation UN Conf., San Francisco, 1945; mem. U.S. Nat. Commn., UNESCO matters, 1946-51, vice chmn., 1951. Trustee Carnegie Endowment for Internat. Peace. Recipient citation U.S. Dept. State, 1967; Malcolm Glenn Wyer award Denver Adult Edn. Council, 1965; Civis Princeps award, Regis Coll., 1969. Named hon. mem. Order Brit. Empire, 1956. Fellow Colo.-Wyo. Acad. Sci. (pres. 1949-50); mem. Am. Polit. Sci. Assn. (exec. council, 1948-50), Colo.-Wyo. Social Sci. Assn., Council Fgn. Relations, Am. Acad. Polit. Sci., N.E.A., Am. Assn. for Adult Edn. (pres. 1950-51), Delta Sigma Rho, Kappa Delta Pi, Phi Beta Kappa, Phi Kappa Psi. Conglist. Rotarian. Clubs: Mile High, Country (Denver); Cosmos (Washington). Author: The British Labor Movement, 1921; Methods of Education in International Attitudes, 1933. Co-author: Role of Higher Education in World Affairs, 1950; Outlook for Freedom Then and Now-1926-51; others. Contbr. to religious, social sci. and ednl. jours. Home: Denver CO. 80218

CHESTER, ALLAN GRIFFITH, educator; b. Phila., Jan. 13, 1900; s. Howard Griffith and Laura (White) C.; A.B., U. Pa., 1922, A.M., 1924, Ph.D., 1930; m. Ama June Warder, June 15, 1933 (dec. May 1943); m. 2d, Florence Foerderer Koch, Feb. 8, 1946. With dept. English, U. Pa., from 1923, successively instr., asst. prof., asso. prof., prof., from 1953, Felix E. Schelling prof. English lit., 1967-70, emeritus, 1970-76, chmn. grad. dept., 1946-48, 54-56, 60-62, chmn. dept. English, 1962-66, dir. Navy V-12 English program, 1943-45. Mem. Modern Lang. Assn. (editorial cons.), Modern Humanities Research Assn., Mediaeval Acad. Am., Renaissance Soc. Am., Nat. Council Tchrs. Eng., Phila. Council Tchrs. English (pres.), Shakespeare Soc. Am., Phi Beta Kappa, Sigma Nu. Club: Franklin Inn (Phila.). Author: Thomas May, Man of Letters, 1595-1650, 1931; Hugh Latimer, Apostle to the English, 1954; (with C.C. Butterworth) George Joye, Translator of the Scriptures, 1960. Editor: The Bible: Selections from the Old and New Testaments, 1953; Shakespeare, Henry IV, Part II (The Pelican Shakespeare), 1956; The Sermons of Hugh Latimer, 1965. Contbr. articles to profl. jours. Home: Conshohocken, Pa. Died Nov. 25, 1976.

CHIANG, YEE, author, educator; b. Kiukiang, China, June 14, 1903; s. Ho An and Hsiang-Lin (Tsai) C.; B.A., Nat. Southeastern U., Nanking, China, 1924; postgrad. London (Eng.) U., 1934-35; m. Tseng Yung, June 3, 1924; children—Chien Fei, Hsiao Yen, Chien-Lan. Came to U.S., 1955, naturalized, 1966. Lectr., Chinese Sch. Oriental and African Studies, London U., 1933-38; head Chinese sect. Wellcome Mus., London, 1938-49; mem. faculty Columbia, N.Y.C., from 1955, asso. prof. Chinese, 1959-70, prof., from 1970. Curator Chinese ethnology Peabody Mus., Salem, Mass., from 1956. Emerson fellow in poetry Harvard, 1958-59; recipient Sr. Specialist award East-West Center, Hawaii, 1967; named hon. mayor of Oklahoma City, 1969. Fellow Royal Soc. Arts London; mem. Am. Acad. Arts and Scis. Author books including: A Chinese Childhood, 1940; The Chinese Eye, 1935; Chinese Calligraphy, 1938; The Silent Traveller in New York, 1950; The Silent Traveller in Boston, 1959; The Silent Traveller in San Francisco, 1964; The Silent Traveller in Japan, 1971. Home: New York, N.Y. Deceased.

CHICHESTER, CASSIUS MONCURE (CHI'CHES-TER), lawyer; b. Fairfax, Va., Mar. 25, 1882; s. Daniel McCarty and Agnes Robinson (Moncure) C.; A.B., William and Mary Coll., 1902; LL.B., U. of Va., 1907; m. Roberta Kyle Pleasants, June 30, 1917 (died 1918); 1 son, Robert Kyle Pleasants; m. 2d, Virginia Archer Page, Nov. 8, 1924; children—Richard Henry Lee, Randolph Bolling Conway, Virginia Archer Page. Instr. in law, U. of Virginia, 1907-09; law partner Wise & Chichester, later Pollard, Wise & Chichester, Richmond, 1909-17; asso. prof. law, T. C. Williams Law Sch., U. of Richmond, 1913-36; gen. counsel State Corp. Commn., Va., 1923-34; dir. securities div. State Corp. Commn., 1934-41. Dir. Div. of Statutory Research and Drafting, Commonwealth of Virginia, since 1941. Sec. Va. advisory legislative council since 1941. Mem. commn. for revision of Virginia code, since 1946; mem. Virginia State Planning Board, 1941. Associate member Nat. Conf. of Commrs. on Uniform State Laws since 1941, mem. since 1943. Mem. Va. State Bar Assn. (sec.-treas., 1921-41), Phi Beta Kappa, Kappa Alpha (So.), Raven Soc. of U. of Va. Democrat. Episcopalian. Clubs: Richmond German, Country Club of Va. Home: 1605 Park Av., Richmond, Va.

CHILCOTT, JAMES CLEMENS, pharm. mfr.; b. Bangor, Me., July 19, 1897; s. Langdon S. and C. Lillian (Eaton) C.; A.B., Dartmouth, 1920; m. Ruth Hackney, Apr. 5, 1941; children—Barbara, Joan, Diane. Advt. exec. N. W. Ayer & Son, N.Y.C., 1920-28; pres. Chilcott Labs., Inc. (formerly The Maltine Co.), Pharm. Mfrs., 1928-52; vice chmn. Warner-Lambert Pharm. Co., N.Y.C., from 1952. Trustee Columbia Coll. Pharmacy. Mem. S.R. Clubs: University, (N.Y.C.); Morris County Golf. Home: New Vernon, N.J. Died Nov. 23, 1980.

CHILDRESS, FRANCIS BROWN, investment banker; b. Valdosta, Ga., July 18, 1897; s. Parks Monroe and Judson (Jones) C.; student pub. schs.; m. Miranda Watson Yerkes, Nov. 30, 1926; 1 dau., Frances Ann (Mrs. Lewis S. Lee). Various positions Citizens Bank, Valdosta, Fed. Res. Bank of Atlanta, Treasury Dept. 6th Fed. Res. Dist., Atlanta, 1914-17; with Atlantic Nat. Bank, Jacksonville, Fla., 1919-32, v.p., 1925-32, pres. investment affiliate Atlantic Nat. Co., 1928-32; propr. Childress & Co., investment banking, Jacksonville, 1932-77. Chmn. finance and financial adv. subcom. Jacksonville Com. of One Hundred, 1952-61; pres. Francis and Miranda Childress Found. Bd. dirs., mem. exec. com. St. Luke's Hosp., 1961—; bd. dirs. Jacksonville area Community Chest-United Fund; bd. dirs. Children's Home Soc. of Fla., 1930-77, v.p., 1939-63. Served with USNRF, World War I. Episcopalian. Clubs: Seminole (pres. 1946-47), Timuquana Country, Fla. Yacht, River, Ponte Vedra, Friars, Ye Mistic Revelers (Jacksonville). Home: Jacksonville, Fla. Died Apr. 15, 1977.

CHILDS, RICHARD SPENCER, orgn. exec., publicist; b. Manchester, Conn., May 24, 1882; s. William Hamlin and Nellie (Spencer) C.; grad. Poly. Prep. Sch. Bklyn., 1900; B.A., Yale, 1904; LL.D., Lehigh U., 1972; m. Grace P. Hatch, June 15, 1912 (dec. 1961); children—Virginia, Mary, Nancy Jane (dec.). With The Erickson Co., N.Y., 1904-18; gen. mgr. Bon Ami Co., 1911-20; dept. mgr. A. E. Chew Co., 1921-28, asst. to pres., 1928-47; dir. Am. Cyanamid Co.; exec. v.p. Lederle Labs., Inc., 1935-44; chmn. Nat. Municipal League, 1947—. Served as asst. U.S. War Dept., 1918. Recipient La Guardia Meml. Assn. award, 1954; Am. Judicature Soc. Jubilee award, 1964. Mem. Nat. Municipal League (past pres.), Am. Proportional Representation League (past pres.), Citizens Union (chmn. 1941-50), Inst. Pub. Administrn. (chmn. 1948-60), Am. Museum Health (pres. 1947-48), Phi Gamma Delta. Republican. Presbyn. Club: City (pres. 1928-40). Author: Short Ballot Principles, 1911; Civic Victories, 1953; First 50 Years of the Council, Manager Plan, 1965; Unfinished Political Reforms, 1977. Initiator city manager plan and short ballot movement. Home: Brooklyn NY. *

CHILLINGWORTH, CHARLES FREDERICK, JR., naval officer; b. Honolulu, Mar. 6, 1903; s. Charles Frederick and Anna Victor ia (Stratemeyer) C.; grad. U.S. Naval Acad., 1925; grad. Nat. War Coll., Washington, 1950; m. Virginia Beauchamp Etnier, Sept. 26, 1932. Commd. ensign U.S.N., 1925, advanced through grades to rear adm., 1952; comdr. U.S.S. Preble-Dewey-Renshaw-Desdiv 100-Desron 50, 1940-44, U.S.S. Rochester, 1952; comdr. mil. sea transport service, eastern Atlantic Mediterranean area, 1952-53; vice adm. USN ret. 1956; pres. Wyndham Hills Corp., Petren Products, Inc. (both York, Pa.). Decorated Legion of Merit 2 awards, Bronze Star 3 awards, Commendation Ribbon. Died Mar. 4, 1976.

CHIRIBOGA VILLAGOMEZ, JOSÉ R., diplomat; b. Quito, Ecuador, Feb. 11, 1911; s. Miguel Chiriboga and Ines Villagómez; Ph.B., Colegio San Gabriel; J.D., Universidad Central, Quito; m. Fanny Barba G., Mar. 12, 1937; children—Hernán, Enrique; married second to Norma Peters Beacom. Under-sec. govt., Ecuador, 1938-40, sec. gen. pub. adminstrn., 1940-43; senator of Republic, 1943-44; mayor, City of Quito, 1948-52; Liberal-radical candidate for pres., Ecuador, 1952; ambassador to U.S., Washington, 1953-60; minister of foreign relations of Ecuador, from 1960. Secretary Commn. on Comparative Legislation. Decorated by govts. of Cuba, Venezuela, Holland; Grand Cross of Merit (Ecuador); Grand Cross Order Sebastian of Benaleazar; named hon. citizen, all dists. of Ecuador. Mem. Ateneo de Cultura of Ecuador. Assn. Municipalities of Ecuador (pres.), Hall Ecuadorean Culture. Lawyers (pres.). Lions (Quito). Home: Quito, Ecuador. Died Mar. 5, 1981.

CHITTENDEN, FAYETTE DUDLEY, rubber co. exec.; b. New Haven, Aug. 11, 1902; s. George Dudley and Ellen (Rossiter) C.; B.S., Yale, 1923, Ph.D., 1926; m. Helen Dickinson, Nov. 11, 1932; children—Ann (Mrs. Cunningham), Jane (Mrs. Harry P. Hopkins, Jr.). Mem. staff research center U.S. Rubber Co., Passaic, N.J., Providence plant, 1926-42, staff Naugatuck (Conn.) chem. div., 1942-60, co. v.p., gen. mgr. chem. div., 1960-64, sr. v.p. tech. and mfg., 1964-68; with Oxford Mgmt. and Research Center, Uniroyal Inc., Middlebury, Conn., 1968-75. Mem. Am. Chem. Soc. Clubs: Graduate (New Haven); Pine Orchard (Conn.) Yacht and Country. Home: Branford, Conn. Died Sept. 17, 1975.

CHITTUM, JOHN WILLIAM, educator, chemist; b. Wapello, Iowa, July 19, 1901; s. John Hefner and Ida Mae (Davis) C.; B.S., Iowa Wesleyan Coll., 1922, Sc.D., 1961; Ph.D., U. Chgo., 1924; m. Alma Pearl Spencer, Aug. 22, 1924; children—John Raymond, Edith Eileen (Mrs. Earl Cornelius), Roger Dean. Instr., Eddyville (Iowa) High Sch., 1922-23; prof. physics Wesleyan Coll., 1924-27; prof. chemistry Olivet (Mich.) Coll., 1928-29; mem. faculty Coll. Wooster (Ohio), from 1929, prof. chemistry, from 1938, chmn. dept., from 1959, Brown prof., from 1959. Mem. Wooster City Sch. Bd., 1958-61. Mem. gen. conf. Methodist Ch., 1956, 60, 64, 66, 68, 70, 72, 76, also mem. nat. bds. and commns. Recipient Alumni Certificate Merit, Iowa Wesleyan Coll., 1956. Mem. Am. Chem. Soc., Fedn. Am. Scientists, Ohio Acad. Scis., Soc. Social Responsibility in Sci., Sigma Xi. Author lab. manuals. Editor: (with Roy I. Grady) The Chemist at Work, 1940. Home: Wooster, Ohio. Died May 31, 1980.

CHIU, ALFRED KAIMING, librarian; b. Chinhai, Chekiang, China, Mar. 11, 1898; s. Lienfang and Feng (Wang) C.; A.B., Boone U., 1922, A.M., 1927; Ph.D., Harvard, 1933; m. Hui-chun Huang, July 1, 1923; 1 dau., May-i; m. 2d, Yu Tseng, Aug. 24, 1939; children—Chuang-i, Hsuan-i, Hua-i, Wei-i. Librarian, Amoy U., 1922-24; adv. Chinese Library Assn., 1924-46; custodian Chinese and Japanese books Harvard, 1927-30; chief research fellow Peiping Inst. Social Scis. Academia Sinica, 1930-31; librarian Chinese-Japanese library Harvard-Yenching Inst., 1931-65, hon. curator rare books Harvard-Yenching Library, 1965-77, lectr. Chinese lit., 1936-65; univ. librarian, prof. Chinese U. Hong Kong, Kowloon, 1966-70. Vis. prof., curator, cons. Oriental collection Walter Library, U. Minn., 1965-68; cons. East Asian library material Boston Mus. Fine Arts, 1940-64, Far Eastern books U. Cal. Library, Berkeley, 1947, cataloging Far Eastern books A.L.A., 1954-68. Mem. Am. Oriental Soc., Far Eastern Assn., Spl. Libraries Assn. Author textbooks on classification; also sect. on agr. in China (MacNair, UN series). Contbr. articles to profl. mags., publs. Home: Cambridge, Mass. Died Nov. 13, 1977; buried Mt. Auburn Cemetery, Cambridge, Mass.

CHOATE, ROBERT ALONZO, educator, musician; b. Anna, Ill., Oct. 22, 1910; s. Robert Melvin and Mary Ellen (Coffman) C.; student U. Ill., 1928-30; Mus.B. Cornell, Mt. Vernon, Ia., Mus.D., 1953; Mus.M., Northwestern U., 1939; student Wash. State Coll., 1940-42; Ed.D. Stanford, 1950; study music with Harold Baltz, Horace Whitehouse, Walter Stulz, Horace Miller; m. Helen Lucille LeMaster, Aug. 5, 1939; children—Mary Lucie, Robert Benjamin, John Gardner. Tchr. music pub. schs., Toledo, Ia., 1935-37; supr. music pub. schs., Polo, Ill., 1936-38; minister music First Presbyn. Ch., Spokane, Wash., 1939-42; dir. music edn. pub. schs., Spokane, 1939-42, Oakland Cal., 1942-50, Evanston, Ill., 1950-52; minister music St. John's Presbyn. Ch., Berkeley, Cal., 1942-50; mem. editorial bd. Music Educators Jour., 1948-50, chmn. bd. 1950-54; vis. prof. Northwestern U., chmn. dept. music edn., dir. placement sch. music, 1950-52; summer faculty U. Cal., Stanford; dean coll. music Boston U., 1952-54; dean school of fine and applied arts, 1954-60, now prof. music. Dir., cons. Manhattanville Music Curriculum project, 1964; dir. Tanglewood Symposium, 1967, New Eng. Opera Theatre, 1953; mem. Boston com. Friends of Albert Schweitzer, 1953-60; chmn. music com. Boston Arts Festival, 1955-59. Trustee, mem. exec. com. Boston Opera Group; bd. dirs. Mass. Council for Humanities. Mem. Wash. Music Educators Assn. (pres. 1940-42), Cal. Sch. Suprs. Assn. (chmn. 1944-48), Music Educators Nat. Conf. (com. Latin Am. music, com. internat. relations. bd. dirs. 1946-50, exec. com. 1948-50 pres. 1954-56, chmn. publs. com. 1964-75), Nat. Assn. Schs. Music (grad. commn.), Oakland Symphony Assn. (bd. dirs.). N.E.A., Am. Musicological Soc., Am. Assn. U. Profs., Am. Guild Organists, Boston Chamber Music Soc. (pres. 1963-66), Phi Delta Kappa, Phi Mu Alpha, Pi Kappa Lambda. Presbyn. Mason. Co-author: Music of Our Time, 1969; sr. author Music Texts-New Dimensions in Music, 1970. Editor: Music of China, 1947; Music of Latin America, 1947; Music In American Society, 1968; editorial bd. Jour. Aesthetic Edn., 1966—. Contbr. profl. publs. Home: Newtonville, Mass. Died Jan. 1975.

CHOPE, HAROLD DELOS, physician, educator; b. King City, Cal., Mar. 25, 1904; s. John Edward and Nellie M. (Rickard) C.; A.B., Stanford, 1926, M.D., 1931; M.P.H. cum laude, Harvard, 1933, Dr. Pub. Health cum laude, 1940; m. Marjorie Ann Campbell, Aug. 3, 1929; children—Cecille (Mrs. Raymond Whittle) (dec.), Peter. Intern, Stanford Hosp., 1930-31, resident, 1931-32; practice medicine, specializing in preventive medicine, San Mateo, Cal., 1948-70; research instr. dept. preventive medicine Stanford, 1929-31, instr., 1931-32, clin. prof. Sch. Medicine, 1955-69, emeritus, 1969-76; chief Bur. Epidemiology, St. Louis City Health Dept., 1933-34; asst. dir. Cal. Health Dept., 1934-35; health officer, Newton, Mass., 1935-40; dir. field tng. unit, instr. dept. pub. health adminstrn. Harvard, 1935-40, asso. pub. health adminstrn. Sch. Pub. Health, 1940-41; lectr. Simmons Sch. Pub. Health Nursing, 1936-41; mem. staff internat. health div. Rockefeller Found., Sao Paulo, Brazil, 1941-44; asst. dist. health officer San Joaquin Dist., Stockton, Cal., 1944-48; lectr. Pub. Health Adminstrn. U. Cal. at Berkeley, 1947-70; dir. Dept. Pub. Health and Welfare, San Mateo, 1948-70. Pres., Cal. Conf. Local Health Officers, 1955; pres. Cal. Conf. Local Mental Health Dirs., 1960-61; mem. Regional Water Pollution Control Bd., 1949-51; mem. State Hosp. Adv. Council, 1950-61; chmn. health, hosp. adv. bd. County Suprs. Assn., 1956-69; cons. community services com. Nat. Inst. Mental Health, 1959-60, chmn., 1961, chmn. tng. com., 1963-76; chmn. Bay Area Regional Health Facilities Planning Com., 1962-64; mem. State Adv. Com. Pub. Med. Care for Children, 1962-76; mem. Gov.'s Adv. Com. Mental Health, 1963-65; mem. Gov.'s Study Commn. Mental Retardation, 1963-65; mem. Nat. Com. Community Health Services, 1963-76; mem. San Mateo County Commn. on Aging, 1962-76. Bd. dirs. Nat. League Nursing. Recipient Bronfman prize for pub. health achievement, 1963. Diplomate Am. Bd. Preventive Medicine. Mem. Am. Assn. Pub. Health Ofcls., Am. Cancer Soc. (dir. San Mateo County chpt.), Cal. Acad. Medicine, Cal. Med. Assn. (mem. sci. bd. 1969-76, mem. adv. panel on preventive medicine and pub. health), Am. Pub. Health Assn. (editorial bd. 1969-76), San Mateo County Med. Soc., Western Hosps. Assn., Phi Beta Kappa, Alpha Omega Alpha, Delta Omega. Bd. editors; Pub. Health Reports, 1957-60. Contbr. articles to profl. jours. Home: Belmont, Calif. Died Apr. 25, 1976.

CHRISMAN, ALLEN SIMPSON, physician; b. Greensboro, N.C., July 18, 1906; s. John Riley and Jane (Watlington) C.; B.S. in Medicine, U. N.C., 1928; M.D., Harvard, 1930; grad. Submarine Sch., 1931, Naval War Coll., Newport, R.I., 1951; m. Eleanore Meta Krekeler, Dec. 21, 1935; children—Jane, Allan. Commd. lt. (j.g.) M.C., USN, 1930, advanced through grades to rear adm., 1958; submarine med. officer, 1931-38; staff Submarine Force Atlantic, 1944-45, 51-52; exec. officer naval hosps., Bainbridge, Md., 1945-46, Camp Lejeune, N.C., 1947-50; dir. personnel Bur. Medicine and Surgery, Washington, 1952-56; comdg. officer Naval Hosp., San Diego, 1956-61, dep. surgeon gen. USN, 1961-64; asso. med. officer Am. Nat. Red Cross, Washington, 1964-67, sr. med. officer, 1967-78. Diplomate Am. Bd. Preventive Medicine. Fellow Am. Coll. Preventive Medicine; mem. A.M.A., Phi Beta Kappa, Phi Kappa Sigma, Phi Chi. Home: Bethesda, Md. Died Apr. 18, 1978.

CHRISTEN, ARNOLD BUHL, lawyer; b. Iowa City, Iowa, Oct. 14, 1915; s. William and Marie Margaret (Hatsfeldt) C.; B.S., U. Iowa, 1938; J.D., Georgetown U., 1942; m. Hedwig Gaetcke, May 12, 1979; children—Carol Sue, Madeleine C. Glennon, Lee Arnold. Admitted to D.C. bar, 1942; practiced in Washington, 1946-80; partner firm Fisher, Christen & Sabol, and predecessors, 1946-80; founding dir. Nat. Patent Devel. Corp., 1958-80; pres., dir. A.P. Originals, Ltd., 1962-80, Pureco, Ltd., 1962-80. Served to lt. USNR, 1942-45, Decorated Commendation ribbon (2). Mem. Am., Fed. bar assns., Am. Patent Law Assn. (chmn. patent office affairs com. 1950, copyright com. 1951, employment com. 1952-54, treas. 1953-54), Am. Chem. Soc. Club: Nat. Aviation Washington). Home: Annapolis, Md. Died July 27, 1980; buried St. Anne Cemetery, Annapolis.

CHRISTENSEN, ERWIN OTTOMAR, art, curator; b. St. Louis, June 23, 1890; s. Otto and Ida (Schnuhr) C.; B.S., U. Ill., 1914; M.Arch., Harvard, 1916, M.A., 1927; m. Edna Florance, Aug. 14, 1937; children—Hilde Marie (Mrs. Edward F. McGrath), Edith Anne (by previous marriage), James Erwin, Judith Florance. Instr. art history Ohio State U., 1915-19, U. N.D., 1919-26, Syracuse U., 1934-36, U. Pa., 1937-39, Am. U., 1945-46; asst. dir. Isabella Stewart Gardner Mus., Boston, 1928-31; dir. edn. work Am. Fedn. Arts, Washington, 1931-34; curator decorative arts and index Am. design Nat. Gallery Art 1940-60; dir. publs. and research Am. Assn. Museums, Washington, 1960, consultant, from 1964. Served in Aerial Photography, Aero Section, Number 84, 1918-19. Member Washington Ethical Soc. Author: Popular Art in the U.S., 1948; The Index of American Design, 1950, 2d edit. 1959; Early American Wood Carving, 1952; Primitive Art, 1955; The Hist. Western Art, 1959; Am. Crafts and Folk Arts, 1964; A Pictorial History of Western Art, 1964; A Guide to Art Museums of the United States; also articles profl. jours. Home: Lanham, Md. Died Jan. 7, 1976.

CHRISTENSEN, PAUL WALTER, mfg. exec.; b. Phila., Aug. 14, 1901; s. John C. and Marie (Jensen) C.; B.S. in Mech. Engring., Purdue U., 1923; m. Lucy M. Sickler, Oct. 6, 1923 (dec.); 1 son, Paul Walter; m. 2d, Elizabeth Leynan, July 5, 1968. Time study engr. Cin. Milling Machine Co., 1923; with Cin. Gear Co., 1924-78, pres., 1941-58, chmn., 1958-78; pres. Cin. Steel Treating Co., 1958-78; dir. Cin. & Suburban Bell Telephone Co., Lukenheimer Co., Gen. Air Conditioning Corp. Bd. dirs., v.p. Boys' Clubs Cin., Inc.; bd. dirs. Bethesda Hosp., United Appeal; chmn. bd. Cin. Symphony Orchestra; nat. bd. dirs. Boy's Clubs Am.; trustee Dean Herman Schneider Found. Mem. Am. Gear Mfrs. Assn. (past pres.). Home: Cincinnati, Ohio. Died Feb. 3, 1978.

CHRISTIAN, DAVID ELWYN, govt. ofcl., diplomat; b. Woodland, Mich., Apr. 4, 1915; s. Forest B. and Nora (Witwer) C.; B.A., Mich. State U., 1937; m. Yolande Shell, July 4, 1940 (dec. 1974). With War Manpower Commn., 1942-47, Council Econ. Advisors, 1947-50, Nat. Security Resources Bd., 1950-51, Dept. State, 1951-54, Dept. Labor, 1955-68; dep. asst. sec. labor for manpower, 1962-64, asst. manpower adminstr., 1964-66; mem. U.S. Mission to Orgn. Econ. Coop. and Devel., head social affairs div., Paris, France, 1968-73; cons. econ. planning to Malaysia and Brazil. Home: Washington, D.C. Died May 12, 1981.

CHRISTIAN, STUART GRATTAN, lawyer; b. Richmond, Va., Aug. 15, 1883; s. George Llewellyn and Emeline (Dudley) C.; B.A., Hampden-Sydney Coll., 1904; LL.B., U. Va., 1907; m. Lightfoot T. Sims, Mar. 30, 1916; children—Raleigh Colston, Stuart Grattan. Admitted to Va. bar, 1907; mem. firms, Christian Gordon and Christian, at Richmond, 1924-42, Christian and Lamb, 1942-55, Buford, Christian, Huntley and Scott, 1945-56, Christian, Marks, Scott and Spicer, 1956—; chmn. standing com. Mut. Assurance Soc. Va. Mem. Richmond Bar Assn. (pres.), Va. Hist. Soc. (exec. com.), U. Va. Alumni Assn. (pres.), Va. Mus. Fine Arts, Chi Phi, Phi Delta Phi. Clubs: German (v.p.), County of Virginia (pres.), Commonwealth (pres.) (Richmond). Home: Richmond.

CHRISTIE, HENRY GEORGE FREDERICK, newspaperman; b. Singapore, Aug. 22, 1883; s. Lt. Col. Walter Henry and Elizabeth (Blurton) C.; student Tonbridge Castle, Kent, Eng., 1891-96; Neuenheim Coll., Heidelberg, Germany, 1896-99; Royal Mil. Acad., Woolwich, Eng., 1899-1900. Commnd. Royal Field Arty., 1900, served in Eng. and India; trans. to Indian Army, 1904; active service in France and Belgium, German and Portuguese E. Africa, N.W. frontier of India; retired 1920; came to Can., 1920; wrote fiction; began newspaper work, 1926, as asso. editor The Saint John Telegraph Journal and The Evening Times-Globe, editor since 1943. Recipient 5 war medals. Served on provincial and city library commns. Mem. Saint John Bd. of Trade. Mem. Ch. of Eng. Clubs: Union and Eclectic, Saint John. Home: Rothesay, N.B.

CHRISTY, FRANCIS TAGGART, lawyer; b. Scranton, Pa., July 23, 1897; s. Arthur H. and Annie S. (Taggart) C.; B.S., Dartmouth, 1918; LL.B., Harvard, 1921; m. Catherine Virginia Damon, June 14, 1922; children—Arthur Hill, Francis Taggart. Admitted to N.Y. bar, 1923, since practiced in N.Y.C.; partner Murray, Aldrich & Webb, 1930-31, Milbank, Tweed, Hope & Webb, 1931-34, Christy & Perkins, 1944-60, Christy, Perkins & Christy, 1960-63, Christy, Bauman & Christy, 1963-65, Christy Bauman, Frey & Christy, 1965-68, Christy, Frey & Christy, 1968-76, Christy & Viener, 1976-79. Sec., dir. Rockefeller Center, Inc., 1928-39, v.p., 1934-39; v.p., sec., dir. Underel Holding Corp., 1929-39; pres. dir. Center Restaurants, Inc., 1933-39, Rockefeller Center Warehouses, Inc., 1936-39; pres., dir. Dodeca, Inc.; dir. Ameaster Internat. Corp., Am. Eastern Corp., Am. Eastern S.A.I., Barr. & Barr, Inc.; former dir. North Am. Philips Corp. Hon. trustee Bklyn. Inst. Arts and Scis.; bd. dirs. Community Funds, Inc.; mem. N.Y.C. Art Com., 1955-68; mem. dist. com. New York Community Trust. Decorated officer Order of Oranje Nassau (Netherlands). Mem. Am., N.Y. State bar assns., Assn. Bar City of N.Y. Unitarian. Clubs: University,

Rockefeller Center Luncheon, Century (N.Y.C.); Mastigouche F. & G. (Can.). Author: The Transfer of Stock, 1929, 5th edit., 1972. Home: Wilton, Conn. Died July 22, 1979.

CHRISTY, HARLEY HANNIBAL, naval officer; b. Circleville, O., Sept. 18, 1870; s. John W. and Rachel M. C.; grad. U.S. Naval Acad., 1891; m. Helen Manuel, Sept. 4, 1895; children—Gladys Pallas (Mrs. Gladys Crawford), Dorothy Helen (wife of J. B. Will, U.S. Navy), Marjory Yvonne (wife of W. T. Clement, U.S.M.C.) (dec.). Ensign, U.S. Navy, June 30, 1893; promoted through grades to rear adm., Nov. 27, 1924. Comd. U.S.S. Salem, East Coast, Mexico, 1914; commd. U.S.S. San Diego, escorting troop convoys, 1917-18, until that vessel was sunk by enemy mine July 19, 1918; comd. U.S.S. Wyoming in the Grand Fleet at end of war and present at surrender of German High Seas Fleet; comdt., U.S. Naval Air Station, Pensacola, Fla., 1919-23; comd. U.S.S. California, flagship of Battle Fleet, 1923-24; in command Control Force, U.S. Fleet, 1925-27; apptd. comdt. 15th Naval Dist. and Naval Operating Base, Panama Canal Zone, Aug. 1927; comdr. Battleship Div. 3, U.S. Fleet, 1929, Battleship Div. 4, 1930; comdt. 8th Naval Dist., 1931-33; mem. Gen. Bd., Navy Dept., 1933; pres. Naval Examining Bd., Washington, D.C., Dec. 27, 1933-Oct. 1, 1934 (retired). Decorations: campaign medals, West Indies, 1898, Philippines 1899-1903, Mexican, 1914; D.S.M., World War; Grand Official d'Avis (Portugal); Abdon Calderon, 1st Class (Equador). Mem. Am. Soc. Naval Engrs., Naval Inst. Episcopalian. Club: Army and Navy (Washington, D.C.). Address: Washington, D.C.

CHUBB, ROBERT WALSTON, lawyer; b. Bklyn., May 13, 1894; s. Percival and Louise (Walston) C.; A.B. cum laude, Harvard, 1915; LL.B., Columbia, 1920; m. Irene Sylvester, May 18, 1918 (dec. 1953); children—Louise, Robert Walston, Elliott; m. 2d, Louise Langenohl, Dec. 4, 1953. Admitted to Mo. bar, 1917, N.Y., 1920; asst. gen. counsel War Finance Corp., 1921-24; spl. counsel RFC, 1932; practice in N.Y.C., 1920-21, St. Louis, 1924-77; partner firm Lewis, Rice, Tucker, Allen & Chubb, 1929-77. Trustee St. Louis Merc. Library Assn., World Affairs Council St. Louis; pres. Open Space Found. Served as capt. U.S. Army, 1917-19; AEF, France. Recipient Profl. Merit award Columbia Law Sch. Alumni Assn., 1970. Mem. Am., St. Louis bar assns., Phi Delta Phi. Democrat. Clubs: Noonday, Missouri Athletic (St. Louis); Crystal Downs Country (Frankfort, Mich.). Home: Saint Louis, Mo. Died Oct. 13, 1977.

CHURCH, ALBERT THOMAS, naval officer (ret.); b. Idaho City, Ia., Apr. 6, 1882; s. Frank Forrester and Mary Elizabeth (Barry) C.; B.S., U.S. Naval Acad., 1905; postgrad. course in marine engring., 1909-11; m. Marion Gibson, May 18, 1911; children—William Campbell Gibson, Albert Thomas. Commd. ensign, U.S. Navy, 1907, and advanced through grades to rear admiral, 1938; retired, 1945. Awarded spl. letter of commendation, Legion of Merit. Mech. engr. and naval architect. Mem. Mil. Orders of World War. Roman Catholic. Clubs: Army and Navy, New York Yacht; Elks. Home: Annapolis, Md.

CHURCH, DONALD (EISENBREY), transp. cons.; b. Reno, Feb. 25, 1904; s. James Edward and Florence (Humphrey) C.; A.B., U. Nev., 1926; A.M., U. Calif., 1929; Ph.D., U. Mich., 1939; postgrad. Columbia; m. Pearl Dee Friedman, June 16, 1929; 1 son, Russell Miller. Asst. labor commr. State Nev., Carson City, 1926-27; bus. research analyst Bur. Bus. Research, Met. Life Ins. Co., N.Y.C., 1929-34; research fellow Brookings Instn., Washington, 1936-37; head statistics dept. Coll. Commerce Ohio U., Athens, 1937-41; prin. analyst transp. div. Bur. Fgn. and Domestic Commerce, Washington, 1941; chief transp. sect. Office Civilian Supply, WBP, 1941-42; chief research and statistics br. hwy. div. Army Transp. Corps, 1942-44; chief research and analysis sect., processed foods br. OPA, 1944-45, chief supply and requirements div. sugar br., 1945-47; cons. on transp. P.O. Dept., 1947; transp. economist in charge transp. research Bur. Agrl. Econs., 1947-51; chief transp. div. Bur. Census, 1951-72; cons. transp. statistics, 1972-79; professorial lectr. geography George Washington U., Washington, from 1962; planner, dir. 1st census of transp. in U.S., 1963. Recipient award Nat. Assn. Travel Orgns., 1958; Silver medal for meritorious fed. service for planning and directing 1st census transp. U.S. Dept. Commerce, 1965; Research award for pioneering research Efforts in Census Transp., Travel Research Assn., 1968. Mem. Am. Statis. Assn., Am. Mktg. Assn., Transp. Research Forum, Hwy. Research Bd. Author: Speed Methods of Statistics, 1940. Home: Sun City, Ariz. Died Feb. 15, 1979; buried Sunland Meml. Park, Sun City.

CHURCH, GAYLORD, naval officer; b. Meadville, Pa., Aug. 14, 1885; s. Alfred Gaylord and Alice Lillian (Mosier) C.; student Allegheny Coll., Meadville, Pa., 1902-05; B.S. (with distinction), U.S. Naval Acad., 1909; C.E., Rensselaer Poly. Inst., 1913; grad. Naval War Coll., Newport, R.I., 1920; m. Bess V. Rist, Oct. 26, 1912; 1 son, Gaylord, IV. Began as midshipman, 1905; commd. ensign, 1911, and advanced through the grades to rear admiral, 1942; afloat U.S.S. Connecticut, 1909, U.S.S. New York, 1910-11; transferred to staff, Civil Engr. Corps, 1913; served at Naval Station, Pearl Harbor, 1913-14; Navy Yard, Phila., 1915-17; Naval Mine Depot, 1919; Submarine Base, New London, Conn., 1920-21; Submarine Destroyer Base, Astoria, Ore., 1921-24; Navy Yard, Puget Sound, Wash., 1924-26; Naval Station, Canal Zone, Panama, 1926-28; Bureau of Yards and Docks, 1928-32; Naval Station, Cavite, P.I., 1932-34; Navy Yard, Portsmouth, N.H., 1934-37; Navy Yard, Phila., 1937-42; superintending civil engr., Area I, II and III, since 1942. Received 2 letters of commendation from Sec. of Navy; Victory medal with Silver Star; Sharpshooter medal with Expert Bar, Assn. mem. Am. Soc. Civil Engrs.; mem. A.A.A.S., Sigma Xi, Delta Tau Delta. Mason (K.T., 32 deg.). Clubs: Army and Navy (Manila, P.I.); Army and Navy (Washington, D.C.). Address: Washington, D.C. *

CHURCH, I. W., lawyer; b. Menomonee Falls, Wis., Aug. 23, 1884; A.B., Lawrence U., 1906; LL.B., Columbia, 1911. Admitted to Mont. bar, 1911; now partner firm Church, Harris, Johnson & Williams, Great Falls, Mont. Mem. Selective Service Bd., World War I; appeal agt. Selective Service, World War II. Mem. Bd. Sch. Trustees, Cascade County, 1932-42, chmn., 1937-42. Mem. Mont., Cascade County bar assns., Phi Alpha Delta, Delta Sigma Rho. Rotarian (gov. 1928-29). *

CHURCH, JAMES MARION, educator; b. Worcester, Mass., Sept. 25, 1903; S. Frank LeGrand and Mary (Andrews) C.; B.A., William Jewell Coll., 1925; postgrad. Harvard, 1925-27; Ph.D., Pa. State U., 1933; m. Dorothy Borden, June 3, 1933; children—Larry Borden, Thomas Marion, James Andrews. Lab. asst. in chemistry William Jewell Coll., 1923-25; Austin Teaching fellow Harvard, 1925-27; instr. chemistry Allegheny Coll., 1927-28, Drexel Inst., 1928-30; chemist and devel. engr. Monsanto Chem. Co., St. Louis, 1932-40; mem. faculty Columbia, 1940-79, successively asst. prof., asso. prof. 1940-53, prof., 1953-72, prof. emeritus, 1972-79, acting chmn. dept. chem. engring., 1970-71; vis. scientist Stanford Research Inst., Menlo Park, Cal., 1968. Mem. Bd. Edn., Tenafly, N.J., 1959-65, pres., 1964-65. Recipient Distinguished Alumni award William Jewell Coll., 1955. Mem. Am. Chem. Soc. (chmn. I & C.E. div. 1959, councillor 1958-62, 64-79; Scroll of Honor, I. & C.E. div. 1963), Am. Inst. Chem. Engrs., Soc. Plastics Engrs., Sigma Xi, Alpha Chi Sigma, Phi Kappa Phi, Phi Lambda Upsilon (nat. sec. 1945-54, nat. pres. 1954-57. Distinguished Nat. Service award 1962, Harold C. Urey award Gamma chpt. U. Cal. 1975). Presbyn. (elder). Author articles profl. jours. Contbr. to tech. books. Patentee in field. Home: Tenafly, N.J. Died Aug. 1, 1979.

CHURCH, WILLIAM FARR, educator; b. Monmouth, Ill., Dec. 13, 1912; s. Henry Ward and Helen (Farr) C.; A.B., Allegheny Coll., 1934; M.A., Harvard, 1935, Ph.D., 1939; m. Margaret Kathleen Lovelock, Aug. 4, 1947; children— Barbara Monica, David Edmund. Instr. history Gettysburg Coll., 1940-41; instr. history U. Ky., 1941-42, asst. prof., 1946; faculty Brown U., 1947-77, prof., 1951-77, Munroe, Goodwin, Wilkinson prof. history, 1959-77. Guggenheim fellow, 1946-47, 54; Nat. Endowment for Humanities sr. Fellow, 1967. Served with AUS, 1942-45, Mem. Am. Hist. Assn., Soc. French Hist. Studies, Am. Assn. U. Profs., Phi Beta Kappa. Author: Constitutional Thought in Sixteenth Century France, 1941; Richelieu and Reason of State, 1972; Louis XIV in Historical Thought, 1976. Editor: The Greatness of Louis XIV, 1959; The Influence of the Enlightenment on the French Revolution: Creative, Disastrous or Non-Existent?, 1964; The Impact of Absolutism in France, 1968. Contbr. articles to profl. jours. Home: Rumford, R.I. Died Nov. 4, 1977.

CHURCHILL, EDWARD PERRY, zoologist; b. Allerton, Ia., July 19, 1882; s. Edward Payson and Flavilla Ann (Kellogg) C.; A.B., State U. Ia., 1907; Ph.D., Johns Hopkins, 1916; m. Nellie Arlene Lewis, Aug. 12, 1908; adopted dau., Marjorie C. (Mrs. Marjorie C. Fibikar). Prin. high schs. in Ia., 1907-12; asst. in zoology State U. Ia., 1912-13, Johns Hopkins, 1913-15, fellow in zoology, 1915-16; in charge shellfish investigations U.S. Bur. Fisheries, 1916-20; asst. prof. zoology U. S.D., 1920-22, prof., 1926—. Mem. S.D. Acad. Scis., Am. Soc. Zoologists, Soc. Colonial Wars, Phi Beta Kappa, Sigma Xi. Republican. Conglist. Mason (K.T., 32 deg.). Author: Life History of Blue Crab, 1919; Zoeal Stages of Blue Crab, 1942; The Least of These; (with W.H. Over) Fishes of South Dakota, 1933; Three Thousand Coyotes and I (memoirs), 1961. Home: Vermillion SD 57069. *

CHU TEH (GEN.), army officer, dep. premier People's Rep. of China; b. 1886; ed. Yunnan Acad., and univs. Berlin and Göttingen. Engaged in Communist polit. activities from early years; became comdr.-in-chief Communist Forces, 1930. Chinese 8th Route Army, 1937, 18th Group Army, 1946; comdr.-in-chief Chinese People's Liberation Army, also vice chmn. People's Mil. Council, and Central People's Govt., 1949—; vice chmn. People's Republic of China, 1953—. Mem. central com. Communist Party of China. Address: Peiping, China.*

CIAMPAGLIA, CARLO, mural painter; b. Italy, Mar. 8, 1891; s. Natale and Benelde (Delmonaco) C.; diploma Cooper Union, N.Y.C., 1917; student N.A.D., N.Y.C., 1909-15; m. Annette Paltrinieri, Sept. 7, 1920 (dec.); m. 2d, Rosalie Woodbury, May 22, 1969. Came to U.S. 1891, naturalized, 1919. Mural painter, from 1924; made designs for Masonic Temple, Scranton, Pa., ceiling Chgo. Tribune Bldg., niches and ceilings Slovak Girls Acad., Danville, Pa.; decorations Ct. House, Sunbury, Pa., residence Frank Potter, Rome, N.Y.; decorations in mosaic Fairmont Mausoleum, Newark, in tiles Green Hill Farm swimming pool, Phila.; murals in residence David Milton, N.Y.C., Tex. Centennial Expn., 1936, Dallas, in Adminstrn., Transp., Foods, Agr. and Live Stock bldgs.; designed murals Foods Bldg., N.Y. World's Fair, 1939, residence Theodore Kiendl, Bronxville, N.Y., Anzio (Italy) Meml. for Am. Battle Monuments Commn.; painting purchased by Cranbrook Found., Bloomfield Hills, Mich., 1939; painted mural Isaly Dairy Plant, Youngstown, O., 1940. Former instr. in life class Cooper Union Art Sch., life drawing Traphagen Sch. Fashion, N.Y.C. Am. Acad. in Rome fellow in painting. Recipient portrait prize at Plainfield Exhbn., 1951. Academician, N.A.D.; mem. Allied Artists Am., Alumni Am. Acad. in Rome. Address: Middle Valley, N.J. Died Sept. 18, 1975.

CITRON, WILLIAM MICHAEL, lawyer; b. New Haven, Conn., Aug. 29, 1896; s. Benjamin L. and Dora (Newmark) C.; A.B., Wesleyan U., 1918; LL.B., Harvard Law Sch., 1921. Mem. Conn. State Legislature (Dem. floor leader), 1927-29 and 1931-33; mem. Conn. Old Age Pension Commn., 1932-33; clk. State Senate, 1933; corpn. counsel city of Middletown, 1928-34; mem. 74th and 75th Congresses (1935-39), Conn. at large. Mem. Am. Legion. Home: Middletown, Conn. Died June 7, 1976.

CLACK, ROBERT WOOD, educator; b. Clear Lake, Ia., June 9, 1886; s. William Rollinson and Sarah Adda (Wood) C.; A.B., Grinnell (Ia.) Coll., 1907, A.M., 1908; student U. Chicago, summer 1909, North China Union Language Sch., 1912-14, U. Mich., summers 1937, 38, 39, extension, 1938-39; D.Sc., Alma Coll., 1952; m. Edith Gordon, Mar. 21, 1911; children—Gordon, Constance (Mrs. F. M. Fisher), Douglas, Llywelyn, Roderick, Wynne. Ordained to ministry Congl. Ch., 1924; prof. mathematics and astronomy, Alma (Mich.) Coll. since 1924, registrar, 1928-43. Served as exec. sec., Central Chili Famine Relief Orgn., 1921-22; Chinese rep., Internat. Olympics Com., 1919-21. Mem. Math. Assn. Am. (pres. Mich. sect., 1931-32), Mich. Assn. Collegiate Registrars (pres. 1932-33), Mich. Intercollegiate Athletic Assn. (dir. 1928-50), Am. Council, Inst. Pacific Relations, Far Eastern Assn., Poetry Soc. Mich. (charter mem., sec.-treas. 1935-38), Phi Beta Kappa. Author books including: Anthology of Chinese Poetry; Outline History of East Asia, 1952. Reads colloquial Mandarin and literary work in Chinese and Japanese. Home: Alma, Mich.

CLAFLIN, AVERY, composer, bus. exec.; b. Keene, N.H., 1898; grad. Phillips Exeter Acad.; grad. Harvard; studied piano with John P. Marshall, composition with Erik Satig and Archibald T. Davison. Business Career with French Am. Banking Corp., rising to pres.; ret. Served with Am. Field Service and French Red Cross, World War I. Composer: (operas) The Fall of Usher, 1921, Hester Prynne, 1932, La Grande Bretèche, 1947; (for orch.) Moby Dick Suite, 1929; (oratorio) Mary of Nazareth; (for orch.) Fishhouse Punch; (for string orch.) Teen Scenes; Four Pieces for Orchestra; (for orch.) Larghetto and Shuffle; (chorus) Lament for April 15, also symphonies, piano concerto, ballet, chamber music, Hon. dir. Composers Recordsings, Inc. Home: Greenwich, Conn. Died Jan. 9, 1979; interred Mt. Wollaston Cemetery, Quincy, Mass.

CLAFLIN, WILLIAM HENRY, III, securities exec.; b. Boston, Jan. 27, 1920; s. William Henry and Helen (Atkins) C.; A.B., Harvard U., 1941; m. Nancy Allis, Feb. 21, 1942; children—William H. IV, Josephine D., Prentice W., Edward A., Elaine Y. With Tucker, Anthony & R.L. Day, Inc., Boston, 1946-80, gen. partner, 1948-75, pres., 1975-78, chmn., 1978-80; chmn. Tucker, Anthony Mgmt. Corp.; mem. corp. Suffolk Franklin Savs. Bank. Treas., Belmont Hill Sch.; treas., mem. exec. com. Mass. Eye and Ear Infirmary; bd. govs. Mus. Sci. Boston; bd. govs., exec. com. New Eng. Aquarium; trustee, chmn. fin. com. Wheaton Coll., Norton, Mass.; gen. chmn. United Way of Mass. Bay, 1965. Served to maj. U.S. Army, 1941-45. Mem. Investment Banks Assn. Am. (nat. gov. 1962-64), Nat. Assn. Securities Dealers (nat. chmn. 1961), Bond Club Boston, Boston Investment Club. Republican. Unitarian. Clubs: Somerset, Country, City, Delphie, Boston Madison Sq. Garden, Tavern. Home: Belmont, Mass. Died Feb. 5, 1980.

CLAGETT, HENRY B., air force officer (ret.); b. Fort Wayne, Mich., Dec. 19, 1884; s. John Rozier and Cornelia M. (Black) C.; B.S., U.S. Mil. Acad., 1906; grad. Air Corps Tactical Sch., 1923, Army Indsl. Coll., 1936; m. Mary G. Steacy, June 4, 1921; children—Jean (Mrs. H. G. Thorne, Jr.), Louise L. (Mrs. J. W. Guerin),

Henry B. Commd. 2d lt., 1906, advanced through grades to brig. gen. Episcopalian. Club: Army-Navy (Washington and Manila, P.I.). Address: Wichita Falls, Tex.

CLAIBORNE, JAMES ROBERT (KLA'BERN), ex-congressman; b. St. Louis, June 22, 1882; s. James R. and Fannie (Moore) C.; LL.B., U. of Mo., 1907; m. Louise Minnis, November 26, 1919; children—Mrs. Martha Ann Hyland, James R. Admitted to Missouri bar, 1907, and since in practice at St. Louis, Mo., now member of law firm of Bishop, Claiborne & Heneghan. Lecturer St. Louis U. Law Sch. for 10 yrs. Dem. candidate for circuit judge, St. Louis, 1924; mem. 73d Congress (1933-35), Mo. at large, and 74th Congress (1935-37), 12th Mo. dist. Home: University City, Mo. *

CLAIR, MILES NELSON, cons. civil engr.; b. Lickdale, Pa., Sept. 1900; s. Harry Monroe and Victoria (Sussana) C.; B.S. in Engring., Drexel Inst. Tech., 1921, D.Eng. (hon.), 1960; S.M. in Civil Engring., Mass. Inst. Tech., 1923; m. Carolyn Florence Green, June 16, 1928; children—Cynthia Yorke (Mrs. Stan Norkin), Valierie de Luce (Mrs. John D. Stelling), Ardith Monroe. Positions with constrn. orgn. in field and office, 1919-22; asst. instr. Mass. Inst. Tech., 1923-24; instr. civil engring. Drexel Inst. Tech., 1924-25; with Thompson & Lichtner Co., Inc., Brookline, Mass., 1925-81; pres., 1949-81; projects include civilian and mil. airports; spl. lectr. Mass. Inst. Tech., Northeastern U., Harvard. Mem. Am. Com. on Large Dams; mem. bldg. code com. City of Boston, 1936-65; air transp. com. New Eng. Council, 1958-62; adv. com. bldg. U.S. C. of C., 1960-81; mem. mayor's adv. com. on pub. bldgs., Newton, Mass., 1960-64; mem. U.S. State Dept. People to People Commn. to S. Am., 1973. Adv. bd. South End Boys Club, Boston, 1940-81; nat. councillor U.S.O., 1957-81: pres. Salvation Army Assn. Greater Boston, 1958-61; mem. Mass. Com. on Children and Youth, 1964-81. Recipient Bronze Keystone medal Boys Club Am., 1958; citation of achievement City of Phila., 1961; Man and Boy awards Boys CLub Am. and Salvation Army, 1963; Howard Coonley medal U.S.A. Standards Inst., 1968; Others award Salvation Army, 1973; named hon. col. Salvation Army Assn., 1967. Fellow Am. Soc. C.E. (pres. New Eng. sect. 1948; chmn. standards com.), S.A.R. (life); mem. Am. Soc. for Testing Materials (pres. 1961-62), Am. Concrete Inst. (dir. 1940, hon. mem.), Am. Standards Assn. (v.p. 1961-62, dir.), Boston Soc. Civil Engrs. (Herschel prize 1950, Ralph W. Horne Fund award 1966, pres. 1954-55, constrn. standards bd. 1950-81), Boston Aero. Club, Nat. Aero. Assn., Phi Kappa Phi, Tau Beta Pi. Mason. Author numerous tech. papers. contbr. articles to tech. publs. Pioneered devel. ready-mixed concrete, light-weight aggregates, precast concrete, constrn. quality control of use of compacted fills for bldg. founds. Home: Waban, Mass. Died Jan. 28, 1981; buried Forest Hills Cemetery; Jamaica Plain, Mass.

CLAIR, RENE, motion picture writer, dir.; b. Paris, France, Nov. 11, 1898; student Lycee Montaigne, Lycee Louis le Grand, Paris; Dr. honoris causa, Cambridge U. (Eng.), 1956, Royal Coll. Art (Eng.), 1967; m. Bronja Clair, 1925; 1 son, Jean Francois. Writer, newspaperman, 1919-22, writer, dir. motion pictures, including: Paris oui dort, 1923; Entr'acte, 1924; The Italian Straw Hat, 1928; Sous les Toits de Paris, 1930; Le Million, 1931; A Nous la Liberte, 1932; The Ghost Goes West, 1936; I Married a Witch, 1942; Le Silence est D'or, 1947; Les Belles de Nuit, 1953; Les Grandes Manoeuvres, 1955; Porte des Lilas, 1957; Les Ftes Galantes, 1965; and others. Served with French Red Cross, 1917. Decorated Legion of Honor (France). Mem. Academie Francaise. Author: Adams, 1926; Reflexion Faite, 1951; La Princesse de Chine, 1951; Comedies et Commentaires, 1959; Cinema d'Hier Cinema d'aujourd'hui, 1970. Home: Neuilly sur Seine, France. Died Mar. 15, 1981.

CLANCY, ROBERT H., ex-congressman; b. Detroit, Mich., Mar. 14, 1882; s. Owen and Helen (Reardon) C.; A.B., U. of Mich., 1907; studied law same univ. 1 yr.; unmarried. Formerly newspaper reporter; sec. to Congressman F. E. Doremus, 1911-13; sec. to E. F. Sweet, asst. sec. of commerce, Washington, D.C., 1913-17; U.S. Customs appraiser for Mich., 1917-22; mgr. U.S. War Trade Bd. at Detroit during World War; also chief insp. in Mich. for Med. Corps of War Dept. and asst. recruiting officer Aviation Div. in Detroit; mem. 68th and 70th to 72d Congresses (1923-25, 1927-33), 1st Mich. Dist. Mem. U. of Mich. Alumni of Detroit. Republican. Clubs: K.C., Elks, Detroit Yacht; Nat. Press (Washington). Home: Detroit, Mich.

CLARK, ANDREW GILES, mathematician; b. Evansville, Ind., Feb. 18, 1900; s. Andrew Jackson and Frances Elizabeth (Giles) C.; A.B., U. Colo., 1921, A.M., 1922, LL.D. (hon.), 1964; postgrad. U. Ill., 1931-32, U. Calif., 1939-40; m. Orpha Mae Spielman, June 10, 1923; children—Kathryn Clark Bourne, Andrew James, Frances Clark Barrie. Instr. mathematics, U. Wyo., 1922-23; mem. faculty Colo. A. and M. Coll. (now Colo. State U.), 1923-65, prof. mathematics, 1940-65 head dept., 1942-45, dean of the faculty, 1952-65; statis. cons. to AAF, 1944-45; statis. cons. from 1932. Andrew G. Clark Social Sci. Bldg. dedicated at Colo. State U., 1977. Mem. Nat. Collegiate Athletic Assn. (regional v.p., 1946-47), Math. Assn. Am., Am. Statis. Assn., Inst. Math. Statistics, Sigma Xi. Contbr. articles on math. statistics and applications. Dir. and supervisor collegiate athletics on both regional and nat. basis. Home: Fort Collins, Colo. Died Dec. 13, 1979.

CLARK, ANTHONY MORRIS, art historian, museum exec.; b. Phila., Oct. 12, 1923; s. Theobald Forstall and Dorothy (Nevin) C.; B.S., Harvard, 1945; student painting in N.Y.C., Italy, Greece, Denmark, Switzerland and Eng., 1945-54. Faculty asst. Salzburg Seminar of Harvard, 1950; conservation asst. Mus. Art, R.I. Sch. Design, 1953; field worker Byzantine Inst., Istanbul, 1954; sec. of mus., editor Mus. Notes, Mus. Art, R.I. Sch. Design, 1955-59; David E. Finley fellow Nat. Gallery Art, 1959-61; curator paintings and sculpture Mpls. Inst. Arts, 1961-63, acting dir., 1963, dir., 1963-73; chmn. dept. European paintings Met. Mus. Art, N.Y.C., 1973-75; adj. prof. fine arts N.Y. U., 1975-76; paintings exhibited Phila. Art Alliance, 1948, Mus. Art, R.I. Sch. Design, 1954; spl. research 18th century paintings in Rome; Roman Baroque and Neoclassical art. Art adv. panel Internal Revenue Service, subpanel for conservation N.E.A. Decorated comdr. Order Royal North Star (Sweden); comdr. Order Merit (Italy). Mem. Socio Benemerito of Amici dei Musei di Roma, Archaeol. Inst. Am., ICOM, Am. Assn. Museums, Coll. Art Assn. Am. (dir. 1970-73), Intermus. Conservation Assn. (pres. 1966-67, 70-73), Am. Fedn. Arts, English Speaking Union, Drawing Soc. (nat. com.). Club: Athenaeum (London, Eng.). Author: The Age of Canova, 1957; also numerous articles. Mem. consultative com. Art Quar.; editorial bd. 18th Century Studies; conseil de direction Gazette des Beaux-Arts. Home: New York, N.Y. Died Nov. 22, 1976.

CLARK, AUGUSTA F(ARNUM), educator; b. Malden, Mass., Nov. 9, 1883; d. Albert Warren and Mary Whittredge (Dodge) Farnum; A.B., Boston U., 1907; A.M., Columbia, 1943; m. Myron H(enry) Clark, Oct. 7, 1909; children—Eugene Whittredge, Philip Farnum. Teacher of French, Leominster (Mass.) High Sch., 1907-09; acting dean of women Boston U., 1943-45. Pres. bd. Y.W.C.A., Reading, Pa., 1933-36; mem. bd. dirs. Boston Y.W.C.A., Boston Univ. Women's Council, Boston Univ. Women Grad. Club (past pres.); mem. bd. trustees Boston Univ. Mem. Mass. Soc. Univ. Edn. of Women, Nat. Assn. Deans of Women, Am. Assn. Univ. Women, Kappa Kappa Gamma. Republican. Conglist. (pres. Andover Dist., Congl. Women's Work, 1929-31; Mass. chmn. edn. 1937-39; chmn. Mass. Congl. Women's Work, 1939-42). Home: Andover, Mass.

CLARK, CARROLL D., sociologist; b. Minneapolis, Kans., Jan. 10, 1898; s. Rolla M. and Elva (Chapin) C.; A.B., U. Kans., 1922, M.A., 1925; Ph.D., U. Chgo., 1931; m. Pearl L. Holland, July 18, 1923; children—Chapin D., DeEtta Jean, Ruby Lorain. Taught school, Ashland, Kans.; supt. schs., Wakefield, Kans., 1922-24; sociol. cons. to Gov. Alfred M. Landon's State Planning Bd., 1933-36; prof. and chmn. dept. sociology U. Kans., 1933-62, prof. sociology, 1962-68, prof. emeritus, 1968-78. Research fellow in human relations Harvard 1945-46 (on sabbatical leave from U. Kans.); vis. prof. various summer sessions Cornell U., U. Oreg., U. Idaho; condr. weekly broadcast on sociomusicology of jazz music over KANU, U. Kans. FM Sta., 1957-59. Served with U.S. Army, 1917, 53d Regt. Coast Arty., in France; as capt. 1942, maj., 1944, USAAF. Fellow Am. Sociol. Assn.; mem. Kans. Conf. Social Work (pres. 1934), Soc. Study Social Problems, S.W. (pres. 1939), Mid-West (pres. 1941) sociol. socs., N.Y. Acad. Scis., Kans. Adult Edn. Assn., AAUP, Phi Beta Kappa, Phi Delta Kappa, Phi Mu Alpha. Club: Old and New (Lawrence, Kans.). Author books, also articles in various sociol. jours. Home: Lawrence, Kans. Died Jan 1, 1978; buried Pioneer Cemetery, Lawrence.

CLARK, DONALD SHERMAN, educator; b. Springfield, Mass., Dec. 27, 1906; s. Webster Clifton and Lilla (Sherman) C.; B.S., Cal. Inst. Tech., 1929, M.S., 1930, Ph.D., 1934. Mem. faculty Cal. Inst. Tech., 1934-76, prof. phys. metallurgy, 1951-72, prof. emeritus, 1972-76, dir. placements, 1934-72; cons. in in field, 1934-76; spl. research dynamic properties metals and alloys. Mem. Am. Soc. Metals (pres. 1956, trustee 1938-40, 55-58; Edward DeMille Campbell lectr. 1953), Am. Soc. Testing and Materials (Templin award 1949, Dudley medal 1951), Western Coll. Placement Assn. (dir. 1963-66), Am. Soc. M.E., Am. Welding Soc., A.A.U.P., Am. Soc. Engring. Edn., Sigma Xi, Tau Beta Pi (pres. 1962-66), Pi Tau Sigma. Author: Engineering Materials and Processes, 3d edit., 1959; (with W.R. Varney) Physical Metallurgy for Engineers, 2d edit., 1962. Home: Pasadena, Calif. Died Oct. 2, 1976.

CLARK, ELIOT CANDEE, artist; b. N.Y.C., Mar. 27, 1883; s. Walter and Jennie (Woodruff) C.; ed. pub. and high schs., N.Y.; self taught in art; m. Elizabeth Trowbridge Egleston, Apr. 5, 1922; m. 2d, Margaret Winslow Fowler, July 8, 1944. Formerly tchr. Art Students' League, N.Y.C.; tchr. Savannah Art Club, 1924-25. Represented in N.Y. Water Color Club at 9 and in Nat. Acad. at 13 years of age; residence and travel abroad, 1904-06; painting trip in Painted Desert in Ariz., 1926, 35, in Himalayas, travel and study in India, 1937-38. Splty. landscape; exhibited in important annual exhbns.; retrospective exhibited mus. of U. Va.; exhibited Savannah Telfair Acad., 1977; represented in Md. Inst., Muncie (Ind.) Inst. Dayton (Ohio) Mus., Fort Worth Mus., Met. Mus., N.Y.C., others; retrospective exhbn. (1905-75) U. Va. Mus., 1975; "Rolling Country," purchased by Woodrow Wilson, "Winds of Destiny," Ranger Fund Purchase, N.A.D., 1922; represented in several permanent collections. Recipient Third Hallgarten prize N.A.D., 1912; Edgar Davis prize San Antonio, 1929, Nat. Academician, 1944; Burton Bush prize Allied Artists, 1950; Spl. exhbn. Paintings of India, Iranian Inst., N.Y.C., 1947. Mem. council India Inst.; mem. council N.A.D., 1946-48, corr. sec., 1948-56, pres., 1956-59, mem. awards jury, 1962; ex-officio trustee Met. Mus., 1956-59. Bd. dirs. City Center Art Gallery, N.Y., Fine Arts Fedn. N.Y. Fellow Met. Mus.; mem. Allied Artists Am. (pres. 1948-52, certificate of merit 1972), N.Y. Soc. Painters; chmn. adv. com. Fine Arts East and West Assn.; mem. Internat. Inst. Arts and Letters, N.Y. Water Color Club, Am. Watercolor Soc. (pres. 1921-23, hon. pres. from 1967), League N.Y. Artists, Artists' Fund Soc., Conn. Acad. Fine Arts, Union Internationale des Beaux Arts et des Lettres; Nat. Sculpture Soc. (hon.). Clubs: Century Assn., Salmagundi Club (hon. mem.), Nat. Arts of N.Y. (life mem; gov., mem. exec. com., 1942; chmn. com. on painting). Author: Alexander Wyant (2 vols.), 1916; John Henry Twachtman, 1924; J. Francis Murphy, 1927; Theodore Robinson, 1979; History of the National Academy of Design, 1954. Contbr. articles to mags.; N.Y. art critic of studio London. Address: Charlottesville, Va. Died May 19, 1980; buried Monticello Meml. Gardens, Charlottesville.

CLARK, EUGENE AUGUSTINE, coll. pres.; b. Washington, D.C., July 21, 1883; s. Daniel and Maria (Robinson) C.; A.B., Williams Coll., 1908; grad. Miner Normal Sch., Washington, D.C., 1909; A.M., Columbia U., 1924; hon. Ed.D., Morgan State Coll., Baltimore, 1940; m. Mabel Johnson, Dec. 24, 1912; 1 son, Eugene Augustine. Teacher elementary schs., Washington, 1909-14; teacher, Miner Normal Sch., 1914-20, prin., 1921-26; asst. supt. in charge elementary schs., Washington, D.C., 1926-30; pres. Miner Teachers Coll., since 1930. Mem. exec. bd. Catholic Charities, Assn. for Study of Negro Life and History; consultant Ednl. Policies Commn. of N.E.A.; chmn. Interstate Teacher Edn. Conf.; mem. bd. control Eastern Assn. of Professional Schs. for Teachers. Mem. Omega Psi Phi. Roman Catholic. Home: Washington, D.C. *

CLARK, FRANK DONALD, coll. dean; b. Wellington Kan., Jul 15, 1913; s. Frank Dan and Nan (Daugherty) C.; student Friends U., Wichita, Kan., 1931-32; B.S., Kan. State Tchrs. Coll., 1936; M.A., State U. Ia., 1938; postgrad. U. Mich., 1941; m. Evelyn Lorene Madison, June 28, 1939; 1 dau., Candy Sue. Actor, Globe Theatre Repertory Co., Dallas summer 1936; instr. speech and drama Kan. State Tchrs. Coll., 1936-38; instr. speech and drama Parsons (Kan.) Jr. Coll., 1938-40; head speech and drama dept. Amarillo (Tex.) Coll., 1940-44; radio news editor KFDA, Amarillo, 1944-46; asst. prof. broadcasting U. Okla., Norman, 1946-55, asso. prof. drama, 1955-61, acting dean Coll. Fine Arts, 1959-61, dean, prof. drama, 1961—. Pres. S. W. Theatre Conf., 1961-62; coordinator adv. panels Okla. Arts and Humanities Council, 1964-75. Mem. Nat. Council Fine Arts Deans (past chmn.), Nat. Council Arts in Edn. (dir.). Home: Norman, Okla. Died Nov. 7, 1975.

CLARK, GEORGE MCMURRY, banker; b. Christiana, Tenn., Oct. 8, 1902; s. Henry Harvey and Bessie Robinson (Jacobs) C.; student Branham-Hughes Mil. Acad., 1918-21, Vanderbilt U., 1921-22; Cumberland U., 1924; m. Mary Evans Shelton, Feb. 28, 1931; 1 son, George McMurry, Jr. Prin., Murray High Sch., Rutherford County, Tenn., 1922-23; cashier Pioneer Bank, 1924-30; exec. sec. Consumers Bankers Assn., 1930-34; exec. v.p. Pioneer Bank, 1934-36 pres., 1937-59, chmn. bd., 1959-79; pres. Consumer Bankers Assn., 1947-50. Mem. Yacutan Exploring Soc. (pres. under water archeology), Pi Kappa Alpha. Presbyterian Clubs: Mountain City, Fairyland, Golf and Country. Originator Efficiency Audit, technique for measuring bank efficiency (while chmn. Com. on Operations of Consumer Bankers Assn.), 1947; orginator and financer of artificial insemination program in dairy devel. (while mem. Agrl. Com. Chattanooga C. of C.). Home: Chattanooga, Tenn. Died Sept. 1, 1979.

CLARK, GRENVILLE, lawyer; b. N.Y.C., Nov. 5, 1882; s. Louis Crawford and Marian de Forest (Cannon) C.; A.B., Harvard, 1903, LL.B., 1906, LL.D., 1951; LL.D., Princeton, 1951, Dartmouth, 1953; m. Fanny Pickman Dwight, Nov. 27, 1909; children—Mary Dwight, Grenville, Louisa Hunnewell; m. 2d, Mary Brush, January 1, 1965. Admitted New York State bar, 1906, began practice with Carter, Ledyard & Milburn, N.Y.C.; mem. Root, Clark & Bird, and successor firms, 1909-46; counsel to Cleary, Gottlieb, Steen and Hamilton, 1954. A founder Mil. Tng. Camps Assn., 1915-16; chmn. Nat. Emergency Com. for Selective Service, 1940-41; chmn. Citizens Com. for Nat. War

Service, 1944-45. Served from maj. to lt. col. Adj. Gen.'s Dept., U.S. Army, 1917-18. Decorated D.S.M.; awarded Theodore Roosevelt Meml. Medal, 1940; gold medal Am. Bar Assn., 1959; 2d Ann. Publius award N.Y. Met. Com. of United World Federalists, 1965. Member of Pres. and Fellows Harvard College, 1931-50; member American Bar Association (chairman committee bill of rights 1938-40), Assn. Bar City of N.Y., N.Y. Law Inst., United World Federalists (v.p.), Phi Beta Kappa. Clubs: Century, Downtown Assn., Somerset Author: A Plan for Peace, 1950; (with L. B. Sohn): World Peace through World Law, 1958, rev. edit., 1960; also articles on civil govt., world orgn. and legal subjects. Home: Dublin, N.H. Died Jan. 12, 1967.

CLARK, HENRY WADSWORTH, shipping executive; b. Wrangell, Alaska, Apr. 11, 1899; s. Willoughby and Georgianna (Choquette) C.; student Phillips-Exeter Acad., 1917-18; A.B. magna cum laude, Harvard, 1923, A.M., 1928; m. Evelyn Rockwell, Oct. 18, 1946. Dir. of athletics and history instr., Harvard, 1927-37; dir. of athletics and history prof., Lafayette Coll., 1937-41; field rep., Fed. Security Agency, 1941-42; gen. mgr., Alaska Development Bd., Juneau, 1946; v.p. and gen. mgr. Pacific Maritime Assn., San Francisco, 1946-50, pres., 1950-52; Washington rep. Alaska Steamship Co. from 1952. Commd. major, U.S. Army, 1942; charge Army athletic program for spl. services div., serving in every theatre of war; commd. col., 1944; released to Res. rank of col., 1946. Awarded Legion of Merit, 1946. Mem. Nat. Arctic Soc. Nat. Defense Transportation Association, Phi Beta Kappa. Clubs: Harvard (N.Y. City); University, Propeller of U.S. (San Francisco). Author: A History of Alaska, 1930; Alaska the Last Frontier, 1936. Home: Silver Spring, Md. Died Mar. 23, 1976.

CLARK, MRS. J. C. (MILAM AVA BERTHA), home economics; b. Macon, Mo., Nov. 27, 1884; d. Ancil and Mary Louisa (McGinnis) Milam; Ph.B., U. of Chicago, 1910, A.M., 1911; student summers, Columbia and U. of Chicago; married J.C. Clark, Nov. 1, 1952. Teacher in pub. sch., 1902-04, pvt. sch., 1904-07; instr. home econ. dept., Ia. State Coll., 1911; asst. prof. domestic science, Ore. State Coll., 1911-16, prof. household science, 1916-17, dean of home econ., 1917-32; dean and dir. home econ., Ore. State System of Higher Edn., 1932-46, dean home economics, 1946-50; home economics expert and technical assistant, Mission FAO, United Nations to Syria, Iraq, 1951-52; on leave of absence to do research and introduce home economics at Yenching U., Peiping, China, 1922-24; served as cons. in home economics in colleges of China, Japan and Korea, 1931-32; on leave to serve as consultant to home economics depts. in 9 colls. in China and Korea, conferred with ednl. leaders in Japan, Siam, 1948; mem. ednl. survey Commn. of Philippines under auspices of Fgn. Missions Conf. N. Am. Dir. home economics for Ore., World War I; nutrition chmn. for Ore., World War II. Mem. Home Econ. Assn., Phi Kappa Phi, Omicron Nu. Author: A Study of Student Homes of China, 1928; (with Donald P. Cottrell) Schools and Colleges in the Philippines, A Report, 1948. Home: Corvalles, Ore.

CLARK, JAMES ANTHONY, petroleum historian, author; b. Abita Springs, La., Sept. 7, 1907; s. Edward Arlie and Laura (Page) C.; student Lamar Tech. Coll., 1927; m. Estelle Walton, Apr. 8, 1934. News writer, 1927-39; gen. mgr. Beaumont Natural Gas Co., 1939-41; Washington corr., 1946-48; with Glenn H. McCarthy Corp., Houston, 1948-51. Bd. dirs., founding mem. Energy Research and Edn. Found.; trustee Houston Mus. Natural Sci. Served with AUS, 1941-46; PTO. Decorated Bronze Star; recipient 1st ann. journalistic award Am. Assn. Petroleum Geologists, 1972. Mem. Authors Guild. Roman Catholic. Clubs: Nat. Press, Headliners. Author: (with Michel T. Halbouty) Spindletop, 1952, 72, The Last Boom, 1972; (with Weldon Hart) The Tactful Texan, 1958; Three Stars for the Colonel, 1954; A Geography of Oil, 1959; A Biography of Robert Alonzo Welch, 1963; The Chronological History of the Petroleum and Natural Gas Industries, 1963; Founders of the Oil Industry, 1967; Marrs McLean: A Biography, 1969. Home: Houston, Tex. Died Apr. 5, 1978.

CLARK, JAMES H., business exec.; b. El Paso, Tex., Aug. 29, 1909; s. John Milton and Esther (Compton) C.; student Washington and Lee U., 1927-29, U. Fla., 1929-30, U. N.Y., 1930-31; m. Lillian Bell, May 18, 1935; 1 son, James H. Asso. Lee Higginson Co., N.Y.C., 1930-32, Lawrence Marks & Co., 1932-39; partner Duff & Phelps, 1940-50; asso. Murchison Bros., Dallas, 1951-58; chmn. exec. com. Phila. Suburban Water Co., Bryn Mawr, Pa.; dir. Phila. Suburban Corp., Bryn Mawr, Pa., Oil Field Rental Service Co., Houston. Trustee Dallas Mus. Fine Arts. Served as lt. comdr. USNR. Clubs: Brook Hollow Golf, Petroleum (Dallas). Home: Dallas, Tex. Died July 23, 1979.

CLARK, JAMES LIPPITT, b. Providence, R.I., Nov. 18, 1883; s. Herbert Willis and Ella Amanda (Brown) C.; ed. pub. schs.; student R.I. Sch. of Design; D.Sc., W.Va. Wesleyan Coll., 1933; m. Sadie Harfield, June 16, 1918. Lecturer, animal sculptor, taxidermist, explorer, big game hunter and motion picture engr.; dir. of preparation and installation American Museum of Natural History; director emeritus since January 1949; president James L. Clark Studios, Incorporated; pres. James L. Clark Industrial Exhibits, Inc. Mem. Morden-Clark Asiatic Expdn., 1926-27, and of Carlisle-Clark African Expdn., 1928; leader O'Donnell-Clark African Expdn., 1931; co-leader Fleischmann-Clark Expedition to Indochina, 1936; co-leader McConnell-Clark Wyoming Expdn., 1937; leader Central African Expdn. of the Am. Museum of Natural History, Nov. 1947-May 1948. Fellow N.Y. Zool. Soc.; mem. S.A.R., Nat. Sculpture Soc., Am. Com. Internat. Wild Life Protection; mem. Nat. Court Honor, Boy Scouts. Clubs: Ends of the Earth, Boone and Crockett, Camp Fire Club of America (pres. 1929-31), Anglers (hon.), Larchmont Business Men's (hon.). Author: Trails of the Hunted. Contbr. to Asia, Field and Stream, Forest and Stream, etc. Awarded Speyer Memorial prize in sculpture, N.A.D., 1930; gold medal of honor Camp Fire Club of Am., 1950; Silver Buffalo, Boy Scouts Am., 1951; hon. life mem. Adventurers Club of N.Y., 1955. Spl. cons. AAF Materiel Command, Wright Field, Ohio, 1942-43. Home: N.Y.C.

CLARK, JEROME BAYARD, congressman; b. Elizabethtown, N.C., Apr. 5, 1882; s. John Washington and Catharine Amelia (Blue) C.; ed. Davidson (N.C.) Coll. and U. of N.C.; m. Helen Purdie Robinson, June 2, 1908; children—Martha Holton, Jerome Bayard, Herman Robinson, Helen Purdie. Admitted to N.C. bar, 1906, and began practice at Elizabethtown; pres. Bank of Elizabethtown, 1910-22; moved to Fayetteville, N.C., 1920; mem. firm Dye & Clark. Mem. N.C. Ho. of Rep., 1915; presdl. elector, N.C., 1916; chmn. Dem. Exec. Com., Bladen County, N.C., 10 yrs.; mem. N.C. State Dem. Com. 10 yrs.; mem. N.C. State Judicial Conf., 1924-28; mem. 71st and 72d Congresses (1929-33), 6th N.C. Dist., and 73d to 80th Congresses (1939-49), 7th N.C. Dist.; mem. Rules Com.; retired, 1949. Mem. Pi Kappa Alpha. Presbyterian. Mason, K.P., Elk. Club: Fayetteville Country. Home: Fayetteville, N.C.

CLARK, JOHN BUNYAN, educator; b. Hamilton, Ala., June 6, 1884; s. Henry Turner and Missouri Ann (Carpenter) C.; B.S., Ala. Poly. Inst., 1907; A.M., Vanderbilt, 1910; A.M., Harvard, 1911; grad. student Columbia U.; Ph.D., New York U., 1926; grad. student University of Michigan, summer, 1932, University of Chicago, summer, 1939; married Lillie Pearce, 1911; 1 son, John B., Jr. High Sch. prin., u. lectr. and prof.; prof. history and dean Mercer University, 1929-41; pres. Tennessee College for Women, 1942-46; head dept. citizenship and history, Lincoln Meml. U., 1946-53; vis. prof. social sci. Austin Peay State Coll., 1953-54. Recipient Sullivan award for distinguished citizenship, 1953. Sec., v.p., pres. Ala. History Tchrs. Assn. Mem. Am. Assn. U. Profs., So., Tenn. (corr. sec.), E. Tenn. hist. assns., Ga. Edn. Assn., Ga. Soc. Archaeology, Blue Key, Phi Eta Sigma, Sigma Pi, Kappa Delta Pi, Pi Gamma Mu, Sigma Mu, Lions Club; v.p., later pres. Assn. Ga. Colls.; v.p. and pres. Academic Deans' Conference Southern Colleges and Universities. Baptist. Democrat. Author: Populism in Alabama; Outline of U.S. History; Alabama Government. Reproduced Adiel Sherwood's Gazetteer of Ga. (1827). Contbr. on social science; Dictionary of Am. History. Address: Nashville.

CLARK, JOHN DAVIDSON, economist; born Ft. Collins, Colo., Sept. 26, 1884; s. Gibson and Frances Amanda (Johnson) C.; A.B., U. of Neb, 1905; LL.D., same, 1938; LL.B., Columbia, 1907; Ph.D., Johns Hopkins, 1931; m. Joyce Broady, June 24, 1908; children—Robert Gregory, John Broady. Began practice of law, 1907; prof. econs. U. Denver, 1931-34; U. Neb., 1934-37; lectr. econs., U. of Denver, 1937-41; prof. of economics, dean of Coll. of Business Administration, U. of Neb., 1941-46; mem. Council of Econ. Advisers 1946-52. Mem. of the Wyoming legislature 1941; member Wyoming Council of National Defense, 1941; Nebraska State Development Committee 1944-45; dir. Am. Nat. Bank of Cheyenne, 1919-46; dir. Omaha Br., Fed. Reserve Bank, 1941-46. Del. Democratic Nat. Conv., Baltimore, 1912. Advisor U.S. Senate Com. on Govt. Reorganization, 1937-39. Pres. Am. Finance Assn., 1943. Mem. Am. Econ. Assn., Phi Beta Kappa, Phi Delta Phi, Chi Phi, Beta Gamma Sigma. Democrat. Episcopalian. Elk. Author: The Federal Trust Policy, 1931. Home: Cheyenne, Wyo.

CLARK, KENNETH WILLIS, educator; b. N.Y.C., Jan. 11, 1898; s. Willis Henry and Jennie (Knapp) C.; grad. cum laude Peddie Sch. (valedictorian), 1920; A.B. (Runk scholar 1920-21), Yale, 1924; B.D., Colgate-Rochester Div. Sch., 1927; Ph.D. (fellow in N.T.), U. Chgo., 1931; D.D., U. Glasgow, 1968; m. Adelaide Emeline Dickinson, July 23, 1925. Ordained to ministry No. Bapt. Conv., 1926; pastor, Holley, N.Y., 1926-27, Webster, 1927-28; instr. N.T., div. sch. Duke, 1931-37, asst. prof., 1937-42, asso. prof., 1942-45, prof., 1945-79, Junaluska summer sch. (affiliated with Duke), 1936-39, 41; vis. prof. Shaw U., 1941-42, Garrett Bibl. Inst., summer 1945, Duke, summers 1944, 46, 47, 52, U. Manchester (Eng.), 1954-55; Fulbright scholar to Eng., 1954-55, Greece, 1961-62; lectr. John Rylands Library, 1954, U. Salonica, U. Thessaloniki, 1961-62; acting dir., ann. prof. Am. Sch. Oriental Research, Jerusalem, 1949-50; dir. microfilm expdn. Greek Patriarchal Library, Jerusalem, 1949-50; gen. editor expdn. to St. Catherine's Monastery, Mt. Sinai, 1950; cons. Library of Congress, 1950-52. Del. Pauline Pilgrimage in Greece, 1951, Meth. Ecumenical Conf. in Oxford, Eng., 1951; guest lectr. Studiorum Novi Testamenti Societas in Oxford, 1951, Brit. Soc. for O.T. Studies, 1952, Internat. Congress on Four Gospels, Oxford, 1957, Internat. Conf. Patristic Studies, Oxford, 1959, Internat. Congress Orientalists, Moscow, 1960, Internat. Congress Byzantine Studies, Ochrid, 1961; exec. com. Internat. Greek N.T. Project, co-dir., exec. editor; lectr. U. Marburg, 1955; rep. World Methodist Conf., 1956; tech. advisor Office Chief Chaplains USAF. Mem. Studiorum Novi Testamenti Societas (Gt. Britain), Western N.C. Meth. Conf., Soc. Bibl. Lit. (sec. 1946-50, pres. 1964-65), Conf. Secs. of Am. Council Learned Socs., So. Humanities Conf., Am. Acad. Religion, Archaeol. Inst. Am. (lectr. 1951), Am. Assn. U. Profs., Conf. Pres. Deans and Profs. Meth. Theol. Schs., Phi Beta Kappa, Pi Gamma Mu, Beta Theta Pi. Methodist. Author: Codex 2401—The Theophanes Praxapostolos, 1934; A Descriptive Catalogue of Greek New Testament Manuscripts in America, 1937; Eight American Praxapostoloi, 1941; New Testament Manuscript Studies (in collaboration), 1950; Checklist of Manuscripts in St. Catherine's Monastery, 1952; Checklist of Manuscripts in the Greek Orthodox Patriarchate and the Armenian Patriarchate in Jerusalem, 1953; The Gentile Bias and Other Essays, 1979. Adv. bd. editor The New Peak Commentary. Mem. editorial bd. Novum Testamentum, Jour Bibl. Lit. Contbr. scholarly and religious publs., including Interpreter's Bible, Interpreters Dictionary of Bible, Peake's Commentary. Home: Durham, N.C. Died July 27, 1979.

CLARK, LEROY WALTER, prof. of mechanics; b. Nassau, N.Y., Sept. 4, 1882; s. Frank Ward and Lucinda Minerva (Coons) C.; C.E., Rensselaer Poly. Inst., Troy, N.Y., 1906; m. Bertha Louise Sybrandt, June 13, 1907; 1 dau., Martha Leland (Mrs. Wilbur E. Kidder). Instr. in mechanics, Rensselaer Poly. Inst. 1906-13, asst. prof., 1913-21, prof., 1921-39, William Howard Hart prof. of rational and tech. mechanics and head dept. mechanics, 1939-50; emeritus; structural designing with Penn Steel Co., 1911-13; cons. engr. in structural, sanitary and concrete engring. Lt. comdr. Civil Engr. Corps, Naval Reserve. Mem. Am. Soc. Civil Engrs., Am. Soc. Testing Materials, Soc. Promotion Engineering Education, American Welding Society, Soc. Engineers of East New York, Sigma Xi, Tau Beta Pi. Republican. Presbyterian. Club: Adirondack Mountain. Author: Mechanics for Engineers, 1928; Analysis of Indeterminate Structures, 1937. Home: Troy, N.Y.

CLARK, MALCOLM EMERY, coast guard officer; b. Cambridge, N.Y., Oct. 14, 1923; s. Emery and Delia Harriet (Perry) C.; B.S., U.S. Coast Guard Acad., 1946; Naval Engr., M.I.T., 1954; m. Anne C. Rook, June 8, 1946; children—Alan R., Cynthia A., Evan B., Steven E. Commd. ensign U.S. Coast Guard, 1946, advanced through grades to rear adm., 1975; served in various duties ashore and afloat, 1948-60, including comdr. Loran Sta., Umnak, Alaska, 1948-49; chief sect. naval engring. 9th Coast Guard Dist., Cleve., 1960-64; chief maintenance br. Naval Engring. Div., Coast Guard Hdqrs., Washington, 1964-68; head dept. applied sci. and engring. U.S. Coast Guard Acad., 1968-72, supt. acad., 1977-81; indsl. mgr. Coast Guard Yard, Curtis Bay, Md., 1972-73; dep. chief Office Engring., U.S. Coast Guard, Washington, 1973-75, chief, 1975-77. Decorated Meritorious Service medal with gold star. Mem. Am. Soc. Mil. Engrs. (dir.), Soc. Naval Architects and Marine Engrs., Am. Soc. Naval Engrs., U.S. Naval Inst., Southeastern Conn. C. of C. (dir. 1977-81). Club: Rotary (New London, Conn.). Home: New London, Conn. Died Jan. 24, 1981.

CLARK, PAUL FRANKLIN, bacteriologist; b. Portland, Me., May 9, 1882; s. Jotham Franklin and Martha Ella (Dresser) C.; Ph.B., Brown U., 1904, A.M., 1905, Ph.D., 1909; studied Johns Hopkins Med. Sch., 1913-14; student, Institut Pasteur, Brussels, Belgium, and Molteno Inst. Parasitology, Cambridge, England, 1923; m. Alice Edith Schiedt, Sept. 28, 1911; children—Eunice W., Edith S. (dec.), Rebecca F., Arnold F. Asst. in biology and bacteriologist, Brown U., 1904, 09; asst. bacteriologist, State Bd. of Health, Providence, R.I., 1905-07; fellow, asst., asso., Rockefeller Inst. for Med. Research, New York, 1909-14; asso. prof. bacteriology, Univ. of Wis. Med. Sch., 1914-18, prof., 1918-52, emeritus 1952. Cons. bacteriologist, C.W.S., 1918. Fellow A.A.A.S.; mem. Soc. Am. Bacteriologists (pres. 1938). Soc. Exptl. Biology and Medicine, Soc. Exptl. Pathology, Am. Assn. Immunology, Alpha Tau Omega, Sigma Xi, Phi Beta Pi. Democrat. Conglist. Club: University. Home: Madison, Wis.

CLARK, RICHARD ELIJAH, clergyman, univ. prof.; b. Pittsboro, N.C., Feb. 22, 1882; s. Nathan Stedman and Betty (Wortham) C.; A.B., Wake Forest Coll., 1910;

A.M., U. of Pa., 1913; B.D., Crozer Theol. Sem., 1913; grad. student U. of Chicago, 1914; Ph.D., U. of Pa., 1915; post-grad. work, U. of N. Carolina, summers 1930, 31; m. Mattie Vivian Griffin, June 23, 1915; children—Edward, Jefferson, Julian, Mattie Lucille (Mrs. H. W. Johnson), Benjaman Robert. Supervising prin. Rural Retreat (Va.) high sch., 1918-19; prof. history and social sci., Juniata Coll., 1920; head dept. econ. and business adminstrn., Olivet Coll., 1920-21; head dept. econ. and business administrn., Centre Coll., 1921-23; dean, Chowan Coll., 1923-24; prof. history and Bible, 1924-25; head dept. polit. sci., Coker Coll., 1925-26; pastor, First Bapt. Ch., Cheraw, S.C., 1926-30; head dept. sociology, John B. Stetson Univ. since 1930. Exec. bd. mem. local chapter Am. Red Cross. Mem. Fla. Acad. Scis., Southern Sociol. Soc., Am. Assn. Univ. Profs., Am. Acad. Polit. and Social Sci., Pi Gamma Mu. Democrat. Baptist. Mason. Home: De Land, Fla.

CLARK, SHERMAN EDWARD, banker; b. Indpls., July 13, 1928; s. Sherman Ephriham and Mildred Cora (Sullivan) C.; certificate in advanced mgmt. Harvard U., 1977; m. Margaret Amanda Padgett, July 16, 1949; children—Coleen, Colette, Dennis, Constance, Kevin, Keith, Catherine, Casey. Nat. bank examiner Comptroller of Currency, Washington, 1949-54, 63-70; asst. v.p. Peoples Nat. Bank, Lawrenceburg, Ind., 1954-63; exec. v.p. Soc. Corp., Cleve., 1970-78. Mem. Am. Inst. Banking, Assn. Bank Holding Cos. Roman Catholic Clubs: Lakewood Country, Clevelander, Elks, K.C.; Harvard (N.Y.C.). Home: Westlake, Ohio. Died May 15, 1978.

CLARK, THOMAS WINDER YOUNG, lawyer; b. Maryville, Tenn., Feb. 26, 1892; s. Lindley Daniel and Maria Elizabeth (Young) C.; B.S. with honors, Earlham Coll., 1918; LL.B., George Washington U., 1921; m. Aurie Marion Austin, Oct. 1, 1938; children—Joann Clark Austin, Robert H.A. Admitted to D.C. bar, Md. bar, 1922, U.S. Supreme Ct. bar, 1925; examiner U.S. Patent Office, 1914-18; with firm Brown, Marshall, Brune & Parker, 1921-25; individual practice law, 1925-35; partner firm Samuels & Clark, 1935-44; individual practice, Balt., 1944-78. Mem. Soc. of Friends,; treas. Balt. Yearly Meeting Friends, 1929-64; mem. mission bd. Five Years Meeting Friends, 1930-70, mem. exec. council, 1960-65. Trustee Miles White Beneficial Soc., from 1930, sec., 1930-73. Mem. Am. Patent Law Assn , Md. Bar, D.C. Bar. Home: Baltimore, Md. Died Sept. 12, 1978; buried South China, Maine.

CLARK, TOM C., asso. justice U.S. Supreme Ct.; b. Dallas, Sept. 23, 1899; s. William H. and Jennie (Falls) C.; ed. Va. Mil. Inst., 1917-18; A.B., U. Tex., 1921, LL.B., 1922; hon. degrees from 30 Am. colls. and univs.; m. Mary Ramsey, Nov. 8, 1924; children—William Ramsey, Mildred (Mrs. Thomas R. Gronlund), Tom C. (dec.). Admitted to Tex. bar, 1922, U.S. Supreme Ct. bar, 1932; asso. firm Clark & Clark, Dallas, 1922-27; civil dist. atty. Dallas County, Tex., 1927-33; partner firm McGraw and Clark, Dallas, 1933-37; joined Dept. Justice, 1937, asst. atty. gen. charge antitrust div. 1943, asst. atty. gen. charge criminal div., 1943-45; atty. gen. U.S., 1945-49; asso. justice U.S. Supreme Ct., 1949-67. Chmn. adv. com. Nat. Commn. on Reform Fed. Criminal Laws; organizer, pres. Nat. Conf. on Citizenship; mem. President's Commn. for Observance Human Rights Year, 1968, also chmn. law com.; dir. Fed. Jud. Center, 1968-70. Mem. at large nat. council Boy Scouts Am. Served with 153d Inf. U.S. Army, World War I. Recipient Silver Buffalo award Boy Scouts Am., 1960, Silver Beaver award, 1962, Distinguished Eagle Scout award; Gold medal Am. Bar Assn., 1962; 1st Distinguished Service award Am. Judicature Soc., 1962, Justice award, 1967; Pres.'s Key, Loyola U., Chgo.; Distinguished Alumnus awards Ex-Students Assn. U. Tex., 1962, U. Tex. Sch. Law, 1964; St. Thomas More award U. San Francisco, 1966; award merit N. Am. Judges Assn., 1970; Furtherance of Justice award Nat. Dist. Attys. Assn., 1967, award of merit Nat. Conf. Law Revs., 1968, Big Bro. award Nat. Conf. on Citizenship, 1950, Mr. Sam award Touchdown Club; citations for civil rights work Am. Legion, Army-Navy Union, Nat. Catholic Vets. Assn.; 1st Chai award B'nai B'rith, 1974; medallion Marshall-Wythe Sch. Law, 1974. Fellow Am. Coll. Trial Lawyers (hon.), Inst. Jud. Adminstrn. (pres. 1966-68); mem. Am. Judicature Soc. (chmn. bd. dirs. 1967-69), Nat. Coll. State Trial Judges (hon. life; chmn. bd. dirs. 1963-71), State Bar Tex., Am. (chmn. sect. jud. adminstrn. 1958-59, chmn. joint com. for effective adminstrn. of justice), Dallas, D.C., Fed. (pres. 1944-45) bar assns., Am. Legion (Distinguished Service medal 1967), V.F.W. (Loyalty Day award 1964), Philos. Soc. Tex., Order of Coif (hon.), Phi Alpha Delta (supreme vice justice 1964-68), Delta Tau Delta (pres. 1966-68). Democrat. Presbyn. (elder). Mason (33 deg., Shriner), Rotarian (hon.), Eagle (life). Clubs: University, Chevy Chase, Exchange (life), Alfalfa, Burning Tree, National Lawyers (Washington); Post Mortum; City of Dallas (hon.). Home: Washington, D.C. Died June 13, 1977; Buried in Dallas.

CLARK, WESLEY PLUMMER, educator; b. Chesterfield, Va., Apr. 5, 1882; s. Plummer Barzillai and Martha Ann (Belcher) C.; B.A., U. of Richmond, Va., 1903, M.A., 1904; student U. of Grenoble, 1920, U. of Montpellier, France, 1921; Ph.D., U. of Chicago, 1928; m. Anna Clark Henderson, June 26, 1912; children—John Wesley, Robert Kenley, Eleanor Henderson (Mrs. Norman S. Bent), Martha Carson (Mrs. James C. Gasser). Instr. Jacksonville (Tex.) Coll., 1904-06, Simmons Coll., Abilene, Tex., 1906-07. Colgate U., 1910-12; prof. Latin and Greek, Coll. of William and Mary, 1912-20; prof. and chmn. dept. classical langs., Mont. State U., Missoula, since 1921, dean Grad. Sch. since 1946; vis. prof. Greek, U. of Chicago, 1927-28. Mem. Am. Philol. Assn., Am. Assn. Univ. Profs., Am. Fedn. Teachers, Classical League of Am., Classical Assn. of Pacific States, Missoula C. of C. Ind. Democrat. Author: (articles) Benefactions and Endowments in Greek Antiquity (Abstracts of Theses, U. of Chicago Humanistic Series, Vol. 6), Vergil's Gods (Classical Weekly, Nov. 15, 1948), also series, The Learning and the Teaching of Foreign Languages (Mont. Edn.). Home: Missoula, Mont.

CLARK, WILLIAM BURT, exec.; b. Brooklyn, N.Y., Dec. 15, 1884; s. William Joshua and Mary Alice (Collins) C.; ed. Brooklyn High Sch. Sec. to pres. of Wells Fargo & Co., 1911-18, asst. sec., 1913-18; asst. to pres. and asst. sec. Am. Ry. Express Co., 1918-28, v.p. and treas., 1928-29; v.p. and treas. Ry. Express Agency, Inc., since 1929; also v.p. and treas. Ry. Express Agency of Calif., and Va., and Ry. Express Motor Transport, Inc., of Ind. Mason (Scottish Rite, Shriner). Clubs: New York Athletic, Lawyers (N.Y. City). Home: Ridgewood, N.J. *

CLARK, WILLIAM VAN ALAN, business exec.; born Long Branch, N.J., Dec. 7, 1887; s. William V. and Mary Vanderbilt (Spader) C.; student Adelphi Acad., Brooklyn 1905; M.E., Cornell, 1909; m. Edna McConnell, July 26, 1917; children—Hays, William Van Alan, James McConnell. Engr., Consolidated Gas Co. of N.Y., 1909-11, Astoria Light, Heat & Power Co. of N.Y., 1911-14, Brooklyn Union Gas Co., 1914-18, U.S. Shipping Bd. Emergency Fleet Corp., 1918-19; with Avon Products, Inc., chairman board, from 1943; dir. Rockland Nat. Bank. Vice pres. Rockland County council Boy Scouts of Am. Mem. Am. Chem. Soc. Republican. Presbyn. Mason. Clubs: Chicago (non-resident mem. Chgo.); University, Union League, Cornell (N.Y. City); Rotary (hon. mem., Suffern, N.Y.). Home: Suffern, N.Y. Died Oct. 14, 1976.

CLARKE, DWIGHT L., insurance exec.; b. Berkeley, Calif., Nov. 2, 1885; s. James L. and Myrtie E. (Williams) C.; student U. Cal.; LL.D. (hon.), Loyola U., Los Angeles, 1954; married Edna M. Willcox, October 24, 1916; 1 son, Edmund W. Clerk and assistant trust officer, Union Trust Co., San Francisco, California, 1906-11; assistant secretary Savings Union Bank and Trust Co., 1911-16; asst. mgr. and trust officer, Security Trust Co., Bakersfield, Calif., 1916-22, v.p. and mgr., 1927; v.p. and mgr. San Joaquin Valley Securities Co., 1923-27; with United Security Bank and Trust Co. and successors, including Bank of America, Nat. Trust and Savings Assn., v.p. and mgr. Bakersfield Branch, 1927-32, exec. v.p., Los Angeles, 1932-36; exec. v.p. and dir. Occidental Life Ins. Co., Los Angeles, Calif., 1936-43, pres., dir., 1944-50, chmn. adv. council, dir., 1951-53, dir.; dir., mem. exec. com. Citizens National Bank, Los Angeles; chairman of the board Allied Bldg. Credits, Inc., Los Angeles; dir. Bishop Oil Co., Producers Cotton Oil Co. Fresno, Producers Cotton Oil Co., Ariz. Treas. Community Redevelopment Agency of Los Angeles, 1953—. Pres. Am. Life Conv., 1947; sec. Cal. Rand Silver, Inc., 1919-30. Mem. Cal. Hist. Soc. (trustee, 2d v.p.), Hist. Soc. So. Cal. (dir.). Clubs: California, Zamorano (Los Angeles). Home: Los Angeles.

CLARKE, NORRIS JAY, ret. corp. exec.; b. Cleveland, Aug. 29, 1883; s. Jay Newton and Pauline (Doll) C.; ed. public schools and high schools, Cleveland, O.; m. Kathern McKee Pearson, June 24, 1907 (dec.); children—Kathleen (Mrs. Kenneth D. Mann), Marguerite (Mrs. Dudley P. Felt). Clerk, Bourne-Fuller Co., Cleveland, O., 1897-1904, sales mgr., Pittsburgh, Pa., 1904-11; sec. and mgr. of sales, later vice pres. and gen. mgr., Upson Nut Co., Cleveland, 1911-19; pres. Lake Erie Bolt & Nut Co., Cleveland, 1919-29; exec. vice pres. Lamson & Sessions Co., Cleveland, 1929-30; vice pres. in charge of sales, Republic Steel Corp., Cleveland, 1930-45; sr. v.p., 1945-49. Served as maj., U.S. Army Ordnance Corps, World War I. Dist. chief, Cleve. Ordnance Dist., Dept. of Army, 1948-49. Mem. Cleve. C. of C. (past v.p.). Mason. Clubs: Union, Pepper Pike (Cleve.); Duquesne, (Pitts.); Gulf Stream Golf, Gulf Stream Bath and Tennis (Delray Beach, Fla.); Gatineau Fish and Game (Point Comfort, Que.); Everglades (Palm Beach, Fla.). Home: Cleve.

CLAUSER, MILTON U., engr.; b. Kansas City, Mo., May 25, 1913; s. Claude H. and Celeste U. (Horton) C.; B.S., Calif. Inst. Tech., 1934, M.S., 1935, Ph.D., 1937; D. Engring., Purdue U., 1967; m. H. Virginia Randall, July 30, 1937; children—Milton John, Marilyn Ann. Engr. Douglas Aircraft Co., Calif., 1937-50; prof. head Purdue U. Sch. Aeros., 1950-54; dir. aerodynamics and structures guided missile research div. Ramo Wooldridge Corp., 1954-55, v.p., dir. phys. research lab. Space Tech. Labs., 1955-60; pres., chmn. bd. Clauser Tech. Corp., Torrance, Calif., 1960-62, cons., 1962-65; dir. research and engring. support div. Inst. Def. Analysis, Arlington, Va., 1965-66; dir. internat. devel. Communication Satellite Corp., Washington, 1966; dir. Lincoln Lab., Mass. Inst. Tech., 1967-70; provost, acad. dean Navy Postgrad. Sch., Monterey, Cal., 1970-74, dean emeritus, 1974-80. Cons. aircraft nuclear propulsion Gen. Electric Co.; cons. space systems adv. com. NASA Space Program Adv. Council, 1971-74; cons. Nat. Engring. Sci. Co., Draper, Gaither & Anderson, Cyberdata, Peterborough (Ont.) Utilities Commn., Emerson Electric Mfg. Co., St. Louis, Communications Satellite Corp., Hughes Research Lab., Litton Systems in Calif.; tech. adv. panel on aeros. asst. sec. def.; sci. adv. bd. USAF, 1956-59; mem. research com. elec. energy systems NASA, 1959-62; cons. ARO, Inc., 1950-54, USN, MIT Ops. Evaluation Group, 1961-64; mem. rev. com., reactor engring. div. Argonne Nat. Lab., 1961-64; mem. Mercury ad hoc com. Pres.'s Sci. Adv. Com., 1961, mem. space sci. panel, 1961-63; mem. adv. com. Project Agile, Advanced Research Projects Agy., 1967-69; mem. observers, div. adv. group Air Force Electronics Systems Div., 1967-70; mem. adv. bd. for regional conf. New Eng. Econ. Research Found., 1970; mem. lab adv. bd. for air warfare Naval Research Adv. Com., 1969-70. Mem. research and devel. adv. task force Nat. Adv. Commn. on Criminal Justice Standards and Goals, 1971; pres. Aguajito Property Owners Assn., 1975-77; advisor to Monterey County Planning Dept., 1976-78. Recipient Distinguished Pub. Service medal Dept. of Def., 1972, Superior Civilian Service medal Dept. of Navy, 1972. Fellow Am. Inst. Aeros. and Astronautics (mem. ground testing com., council); mem. Am. Acad. Arts and Scis., AAAS, Internat. Astronautics Fedn., Tau Beta Pi, Sigma Xi, Sigma Gamma Tau. Mem. editorial bd. Jour. Def. Research, 1968—. Contbr. articles to tech. publs. Research on sailboat hull performance. Home: Carmel, Calif. Died Jan. 26, 1980.

CLAXTON, JOHN WILBERT, clergyman; b. Richmond, Ont., Can., June 30, 1901; s. Edwin and Eva Nina (Graham) C.; B.A., Queen's U., Kingston, Ont., 1923; M.A., McGill U., Montreal, 1927; B.D., United Theol. Coll., Montreal, 1927; fellow Union Theol. Sem., N.Y.C., 1927-28; D.D., Defiance Coll., 1940; m. Elizabeth Field Laughton, June 6, 1933 (dec. June 1966); children—Edwin John and George Laughton (twins); m. 2d, E. Francealia Heuhs, July 1, 1970. Ordained to ministry United Ch. of Can., 1927; asst. minister Asbury M.E. Ch., Watertown, N.Y., 1928-29; asso. minister First Congl. Ch., Detroit, 1929-31; minister First Congl. Ch., Manistee, Mich., 1931-36; pres. Defiance (Ohio) Coll. 1936-43; minister Union Congl. Ch., Green Bay, Wis., 1943-52, Plymouth Congl. Ch., Lansing, Mich., 1952-67; asso. sec. Nat. Assn. Congl. Chs., 1962-70, dean, exec. sec. Congl. Found. for Theol. Studies; interim minister First Congl. Ch., Los Angeles, 1970-72. Pres., Congl. Summer Assembly, Frankfort, Mich.; minister (summer) Little Stone Ch., Mackinac Island, Mich., 1948-76; mem. com. on ministry Mich. Congl. Conf.; chmn. Lansing Christmas Parade Com.; v.p. Greater Lansing Council Chs.; pres. Lansing Ministerial Assn., mem. Nat. Commn. on Ministry Congl. Chs., 1948-54; moderator Central Assn., Congl. Chs.; mem. chmn. publs. Nat. Assn. Congl. Chs. Mem. Gov.'s Commn. Hwy. Safety. Bd. dirs. Lansing YMCA. Republican. Rotarian. Author: Facets of Our Faith. Contbr. articles to mags. Home: Treasure Island, Fla. Died Oct. 3, 1976; buried Mackinac Island, Mich.

CLAY, HENRY, economist; b. Nienwerck, Germany, May 9, 1883 (parents Brit. subjects); s. James Henry and Elizabeth (Bulmer) C.; B.A., Oxford, 1906, M.A., 1912; D.Sc. (hon.), Cape Town, 1929; m. Gladys Priestman, May 10, 1910. Oxford U. tutor workers' ednl. classes, 1909-21, fellow New Coll., 1919-21; prof. econs. Manchester U., 1922-30; econ. adviser Bank of Eng., 1930-44; warden Nuffield Coll., Oxford, 1944-49, ret. 1949. Hon. fellow Nuffield Coll. and U. Coll., Oxford. Hon. mem. Am. Econ. Assn., Am. Philos. Soc.; fgn. hon. mem. Am. Acad. Arts and Scis. Home: Oxford, Eng.

CLAY, LUCIUS DUB, army officer, corp. exec.; b. Marietta, Ga., Apr. 23, 1897; s. Alexander Stephen and Frances (White) C.; B.S., U.S. Mil. Acad., 1918; m. Marjorie McKeown, Sept. 21, 1918; children—Lucius D., Frank B. Commd. 2d lt. U.S. Army, 1918, advanced through grades to gen., 1947; instr. Officers Tng. Sch. (Engrs.), 1918; with Engr. troops, 1918-24; instr. in civil and mil. engring. U.S. Mil. Acad., 1924-28; river and harbor assignments; U.S. rep. Permanent Internat. Naval Conf., Brussels, 1934; on Gen. MacArthur's staff in Philippines, 1937; in charge of constrn. Red River Dam, Denison, Tex., 1938-40; in charge of def. airport program CAA, 1940-41; asst. chief of staff for Materials Service of Supply; apptd. dep. dir. for war programs, Dec. 1944; dep. to Gen. Eisenhower, 1945; dep. mil. gov. Germany (U.S.), 1946; comdr. in chief U.S. Forces in Europe and mil. gov. U.S. Zone, Germany, 1947-49, ret., 1949; personal rep. of Pres. Kennedy (with rank ambassador) in Berlin, 1961; chmn. bd., chief exec.

officer Continental Can Co., 1950-62, dir., mem. exec. com. until 1970; sr. partner Lehman Bros., 1963-73; chmn. bd. Fed. Nat. Mortgage Assn., 1970-71. Decorated D.S.M. with 2 oak leaf clusters, Legion of Merit, Bronze Star, many other U.S. and fgn. decorations, hon. degrees and other awards. Trustee Presbyn. Hosp., N.Y.C., Tuskegee Inst.; hon. mem. Bus. Council, Washington; former chmn. bd. Free Europe, Inc. Fellow Am. Acad. Arts and Scis.; mem. ASCE (recipient 1st Pres.'s award 1976; Hoover medal), Soc. Am. Mil. Engrs., Permanent Internat. Nav. Congress. Clubs: Army and Navy, Links, Univ., Blind Brook, Pinnacle (N.Y.C.); Bohemian (San Francisco); Eastward Ho! Country. Author: Decisions in Germany, 1950; Germany and the Fight for Freedom. Died Apr. 16, 1978; buried West Point, N.Y.

CLAYBOURN, LESLIE WILLIAM, mech. engr., inventor; b. Albert Lea, Minn., June 13, 1883; s. John Bethel and Ellen (Clink) C.; student tech. course in drafting and mech. engring., private courses in art and spl. course in photography; m. Emily Louise Herkenroder, May 20, 1925; children (by previous marriage)—Bona Zoe, Clayton Carlton. Portrait photographer, Sioux City, Ia., 1900-04; official photographer Omaha Gunning System, 1904-06; pres. Model & Electro-Plating Co., Winona, Minn., 1907-12, Dubuque (Ia.) Art Mfg. Co., 1912-14; development engr. Printing Machinery Co., Cincinnati, 1914-18; v.p. and dir. operation Menasha Printing & Carton Co., Menasha, Wis., 1918-21; pres. Claybourn Process Corp., Milwaukee, 1921-37; cons. engr. C. B. Cottrell & Sons Co., Claybourn Div., since 1937; exec. v.p., dir. operations J. W. Clement Co.; to Jan. 1945; organized L. W. Claybourn, Inc., Chicago; president, v.p. Member 122d Division Minnesota State Militia, serving as hosp. steward, Lake City, Minn., 1901-04. Received Modern Pioneer award, Mass. Inst. Tech., 1940. Hon. life mem. Internat. Printing Pressmen and Assts. Union of North America; hon. life mem. San Francisco, Milwaukee, Boston, Cincinnati, Buffalo, Seattle and Los Angeles Craftsmans assns.; mem. Research Electrotype and Photo-Engraving assns., Menasha Chamber of Commerce (ex-pres.). Republican. Mason (32 deg., K.T., Shriner). Clubs: Ill. Athletic (Chicago); Milwaukee Athletic, Pine Lake Yacht Club; Buffalo (Buffalo); Graphic Arts (New York). Author: The Printer in the Future, 1932. Contbr. to printing jours.

CLAYTON, CHRISTINE B., dean of home economics; b. Salt Lake City, Utah, Jan. 29, 1884; d. Dirk and Alida (DeHaan) Bockholt; B.S., Utah St. Agr. Coll. and U. of Utah, 1915; student U. of Chicago, summers, 1924, 29; M.S., U. of Minn., 1927; grad. study Columbia U.; m. Alma C. Clayton, June 18, 1903 (divorced 1908); children—Alida (Mrs. Fred DuBois Hogan), Loretta Ann (Mrs. Anthon Hunter Lunt). Teacher home economics, Jordan High Sch., 1915-19, Branch Agr. Coll., 1919-22; nutritionist, extension service, Utah State Agrl. Coll., 1922-24, asst. prof., resident teacher foods and nutrition, 1924-27, prof., 1927-43, dean sch. home econ., 1929-43; vis. prof. nutrition, Temple Univ., Phila., since 1944. Nutritionist, Utah State Defense Council, 1941-44. Fellow Laura Spelman Rockefeller Fund. Mem. Nat. Home Econ. Assn., Am. Assn. Univ. Women, Nat. Edn. Assn., Penn. Edn. Assn., Phila. Dietetic Assn., Phi Kappa Phi, Phi Upsilon Omicron, Omicron Nu, Chi Omega. Home: Phila., Pa.; and New York, N.Y.

CLAYTOR, GRAHAM, public utility exec.; b. Bedford, Virginia, Dec. 20, 1886; s. Graham and Marion Orville (Bell) C.; student Va. Poly. Inst., 1902-06; m. Gertrude Harris Boatwright, Feb. 19, 1908; children—Graham IV, Robert Buckner, Richard Anderson. Student engr. Gen. Electric Co., Lynn, Mass., 1906-07; engring. supt. and mgr. Roanoke Ry. & Electric Co. and Lynchburg (Va.) Traction & Light Co., 1907-17; chief engr. Am. Electric Power Co., Phila., 1923-24, gen. mgr., 1925-26; v.p., dir., mem. exec. com. Am. Gas & Electric Co., N.Y. City; v.p. Ohio Power Co. since 1940, also dir.; v.p. and dir. various other utility cos.; president Indiana Franklin Real Estate Company. Served as captain Q.M.C., U.S. Army, 1917-18. Fellow Am. Inst. of E.E. Democrat. Episcopalian. Clubs: Railroad and Machinery (N.Y. City); Country (Roanoke, Va.); Army and Navy (Washington). Home: New York.

CLEARY, GEORGE EDWARD, lawyer; b. Platteville, Wis., Nov. 7, 1890; s. Thomas L. and Ada Jane (Grindell) C.; B.A., U. Wis., 1911, LL.B., 1914; m. Lulu M. Rundell, Nov. 21, 1915; 1 dau., Elizabeth Ann; m. 2d, Frances Power, July 2, 1936; 1 son, George Edward. Assessor incomes, Platteville, 1914-16; prof. law U. Mont., 1916-18; sec. adv. tax bd. Bur. Internal Revenue, 1919; mem. firm Root, Clark, Buckner & Ballantine, N.Y.C., 1926-45, firm Cleary, Gottleib, Steen & Hamilton, N.Y.C., 1946-74, of counsel, 1974-81. Mem. Order of Coif, Phi Beta Kappa, Beta Gamma Sigma. Republican. Roman Catholic. Clubs: Univ., Harbor View (N.Y.C.). Home: New York, NY. Died Mar. 26, 1981.

CLEAVER, J. BENJAMIN, lawyer; b. Dixon, Ill., Sept. 2, 1898; s. Joseph Brierton and Violet May (Canfield) C.; student U. Ill., 1922-23; J.D., Chgo.-Kent Coll. Law, 1926; m. Helen Louise Haas, Sept. 25, 1926; children—Helen Louise (Mrs. Robert K. Smither), Joseph B. Admitted to Ill. bar, 1926; practiced in Chgo., 1929-70; ret. as partner firm Kirkland, Ellis, Hodson, Chaffetz & Masters, Chgo. Mem. Am., Ill., Chgo. bar assns., Delta Theta Phi. Republican. Presbyn. Club: Exmoor Country (Highland Park). Home: Northbrook, Ill. Died Nov. 26, 1976; buried Riverview Cemetery, Oregon, Ill.

CLEAVES, HERBERT MARTIN, assn. exec.; b. Lowell, Mass., Feb. 27, 1911; s. William S. and Blanche (Blake) C.; A.B., Harvard, 1933; m. Barbara Morrison, March 6, 1936 (dec. Mar. 1963); children—Deborah, Craig, Linda; m. 2d, Madolyn Wood, May 16, 1964; With the sales dept. Aetna Life Ins. Co., 1933-34, Am. Tissue Mills., 1934-36; with Gen. Foods Corp., 1936-71, beginning in sales areas. successively nat. sales mgr. Diamond Crystall Salt div., marketing mgr. asso. products div., gen., v.p.-marketing, 1961-64, sr. v.p., 1964-71, dir., 1960-71; vice chmn. Council Better Bus. Burs., N.Y.C., 1970-79. Dir., trustee Nutrition Founds., Inc., 1965-70; chmn. nat. marketing adv. com. Dept. Commerce, 1969-70. Mem. Grocery Mfrs. Am. (dir. 1960-70), Newcomen Soc. Clubs: Harvard (New Canaan, Conn.); Norwalk (Conn.) Yacht; Harvard (N.Y.C.); Portland (Me.) Yacht; International (Washington). Home: North Palm Beach, Fla. Died Sept. 10, 1979; buried Pemaquid, Maine.

CLEBORNE, GUY MILLER, steel co. exec.; b. Bridgeport, Conn., Jan. 20, 1927; s. Edmund B. and Mary (Miller) C.; grad. Phillips Exeter Acad., 1944; B.S., Yale, 1947; m. Ruth Larrabee, Nov. 29, 1952; children—Keith D., Guy E., Rockwell J. With Wallingford Steel Co. (Conn.), 1948-65, v.p. gen. mgr. sales, 1960-65; treas. Allegheny Ludlum Steel Corp., Pitts., 1965-80, v.p., 1974-80. Originator, dir. 1st United Fund, Wallingford, 1959; mem. nat. adv. council United Fund, 1960-65; past head fund drives ARC, Am. Cancer Soc., YMCA, Wallingford. Mem. Wallingford Bd. Finance, 1958-61. Served to capt. USMCR, 1944-46, 51-52. Named Man of Yr., Wallingford Jr. C. of C., 1961. Mem. Am. Iron and Steel Inst. Home: Pittsburgh, Pa. Died Apr. 5, 1980.

CLEETON, GLEN URIEL, psychologist; b. Green City, Mo., July 2, 1895; s. Zina A. and Dora (Ransom) C.; B.S. NE Mo. State U., Kirksville, 1917; M.A., U. Iowa, 1923; m. ces Terry, Apr. 12, 1914; children—Mary F. (Mrs. R. Glenna R. (Mrs. W.F. Nesbit), Alan R., Merle M. Pr Park (Mo.) Schs., 1915-16; supt., Ellington (Mo Park (Mo.) Schs., 1915-16; supt., Ellington (Mo 1917-18, Hilton Twp. (Iowa) Schs., 1918-22; instr. prof. psychology Carnegie-Mellon U., 1923-26, head dsl. edn., 1926-35, prof. graphic arts, head dept. mgmt., 1935-42, asst. dir. div. Humanities and Social Scis., 1942-44, dean, 1944-63, spl. asst. to pres., 1963-65; cons. psychologist pvt. practice, 1939-80. Chief psychol. examingrs U.S. Army Induction Sta., Pitts., 1942-43. Fellow Am. Psychol. Assn. (diplomate in indsl. psychology); mem. Sigma Xi, Phi Kappa Phi, Epsilon Pi Tau. Club: Masons. Author books including: Executive Ability: Its Discovery and Development, 1946; Making Work Human, 1949; General Printing, 1953; The Story of Carnegie Tech., 1965. Cons. editor McGraw-Hill Book Co., N.Y.C., 1961-78. Contbr. articles on psychological measurement and indsl. selection to tech. jours. Home: Allison Park, Pa. Died June 22, 1980.

CLELAND, HANCE H., business exec.; b. Campbell Hill, Ill., Oct. 4, 1884; s. James and Mary Jane (Carson) C.; B.S. Central Normal Coll., Danville, Ind., 1906, LL.B., 1906; m. Ethel Christine Anderson, June 24, 1914; children—Grace Elizabeth, John Alexander, Hance H. Asst. Atty. Gen., State of Washington, 1916-19, mem. Public Service Comm., 1919-24; private law practice, 1924-38; pres. Calif. Ore. Power Co., Medford, Ore., 1938-41; pres. San Diego Gas & Electric Co., 1941-46, chmn. bd., 1946-49, ret. Pres. San Diego City and Co. War Chest, 1942, San Diego Chamber of Commerce, 1943-44, Pacific Coast Elec. Assn., 1944-45. Republican. Presbyterian. Clubs: San Diego, Country (San Diego), Cuyamaca; San Diego-California (pres. 1945). Home: San Diego, Calif.

CLELAND, JAMES T., clergyman; b. Yoker, Scotland, July 8, 1903; s. James and Margaret G. (Curdie) C.; M.A., Glasgow U., 1924, B.D., 1927, D.D. (hon.), 1956; S.T.M., Union Theol. Sem., 1928, Th.D., 1954; D.D. (hon.), Davidson Coll., 1951; m. Alice Mead, Sept. 7, 1932. Came to U.S., 1931, naturalized, 1941. Ordained to ministry Presbyn. Ch. U.S.A., 1938; instr., then asst. prof. and asso. prof. of religion Amherst Coll., 1931-45; became prof. preaching and preacher to the univ., Duke, 1945, James B. Duke prof. of preaching, 1954-68, dean of the chapel, 1953-73, cons. to chapel, 1973-78; vis. prof. preaching Union Theol. Sem., N.Y.C., summers 1948, 55, 62, Pacific Sch. Religion, Berkeley, Calif., summer 1951; Frederic Rogers Kellogg lectr. Episcopal Theol. Sch., 1953; Hoyt lectr. Union Theol. Sem., 1955; Peyton lectr. So. Meth. U., 1956; Zimmerman lectr. Luth. Theol. Sem., 1956; Thomas White Currie lectr. Austin Presbyn. Sem., 1958; Wells sermons lectr. Tex. Christian U., 1959, 69; Perkins lectr. First Meth. Ch., Wichita Falls, Tex., 1961; Warrack lectr. theol. colls. four Scottish univs., 1964. Mem. Phi Beta Kappa, Alpha Omega Alpha. Club: Cosmos (Washington). Author: The True and Lively Word, 1954; Wherefore Art Thou Come?, 1961; Preaching to Be Understood, 1965; He Died As He Lived, 1966; also articles in various publs. Home: Durham, N.C. Died Nov. 14, 1978; inurned Duke U. Chapel Crypt, Durham.

CLEMENT, SAMUEL AVERETT, naval officer (ret.); b. Callands, Va., Aug. 15, 1884; s. H.C. and Harriett (Morrison) C.; student, Va. Polytechnic Inst., 1901-03; B.S., U.S. Naval Acad., 1907; grad., Naval War Coll., 1934, 39; m. Agnes Marshall Taliaferro, Feb. 23, 1910 (dec. 1937); m. 2d Louise Leyendecker, July 23, 1938 (dec. 1946); 1 son, Samuel Averett. Commd. ensign U.S. Navy, 1909, advanced through grades to commodore, 1943, served 1st Chinese revolution, 1911-12, Nicaraguan revolution, 1927, World War I with Atlantic fleet; chief of staff, Caribbean Sea Frontier, 1942; comdr. Am. forces (including U.S. Army, Navy, Air Force, Coast Guard and Dutch Army), Aruba, Dutch West Indies, 1942-44; ret. from active service, 1945. Episcopalian. Clubs: Golf and Country (Danville, Va.), Hamilton (Brooklyn, N.Y.). Home: Danville, Va.

CLENDENIN, GEORGE MOREY (KLEN-DEN-IN), former pub. exec. and govt. ofcl.; b. Springfield, Ill., Jan. 29, 1883; s. Henry Wilson and Mary (Morey) C.; student U. of Ill., 1902-05; m. Nell Oller, June 1, 1921. Admitted to Ill. bar, 1905; engaged in practice of law, 1905-07; reporter State Register Pub. Co., Springfield, Ill., 1907-12, advt., 1912-14, mng. editor, 1914-19, business mgr., 1919-27, pres. and pub., 1927-42, retired from newspaper, May 1942; apptd. dist. rent officer, Office of Price Adminstrn., 1942; now with Office of Housing Expediter until 1953. Democrat. Conglist. Elk. Mason. Clubs: Illini, Sagamo (Springfield, Ill.); Union League (Chgo.). Home: Springfield, Ill. 62707.

CLERKIN, JAMES JOSEPH, JR., telephone co. exec.; b. New Britain Conn., June 4, 1923; s. James Joseph and Lillian (Seipel) C.; B.S. in Mech. Engring., Worcester Poly. Inst., 1944; M.B.A., Harvard, 1947; m. Theresa D. Vadnais, June 30, 1945; 1 dau., Patricia Ann. With Theo. Gary & Co., and subsidiaries, 1947-56; v.p., dir. Continental Telephone Co. and subsidiaries, 1952-56; with Comptometer Corp., 1956-61; pres. Gen. Telephone & Electronics Internat. Corp., N.Y.C., 1961-64; exec. v.p. telephone operations Gen. Telephone and Electronics Corp., 1964-75; also dir.; dir. Allied Products Corp., Genesco, Inc. Trustee Worcester Poly. Inst. Served with USNR, 1944-45. Mem. Harvard Bus. Sch. Assn., Worcester Poly. Inst. Alumni Assn. Clubs: Harvard of New York; Wee Burn Country (Darien, Conn.); University (N.Y.C.). Home: Darien, Conn. Died Nov. 20, 1975.

CLEVELAND, GEORGE GILBERT, banker; b. Malden, Mass., Oct. 18, 1907; s. Charles G. and Anna (Harverty) C.; B.B.A., Boston U., 1935; m. Grace Halliday Macdonald, Oct. 15, 1938; 1 dau., Susan E. With Provident Instn. Savs., Boston, from 1928, sr. v.p., 1969-72, corporator, 1961-80, trustee, 1972-80; v.p. Bankers Data Processing Inc., Boston, 1962-72. Served with AUS, 1943-45. Home: West Dennis, Mass. Died May 8, 1980; buried Yarmouthport, Mass.

CLIFFORD, JAMES LOWRY, educator; b. Evansville, Ind., Feb. 24, 1901; s. George S. and Emily (Orr) C.; A.B., Wabash Coll., 1923, L.H.D., 1956; B.S., Mass. Inst. Tech., 1925; Ph.D., Columbia, 1941; Litt.D. (hon.), Evansville Coll., 1955; L.H.D., Ind. U., 1963, Lehigh U., 1972; m. Virginia Iglehart, Aug. 31, 1940; children—Emily Orr, James Townley, Joseph Holt. Gen. mgr. Young Car Co., Evansville, 1926-28; English master Evans Sch., Tucson, 1929-32; Cutting traveling fellow Columbia, 1935-36; from English instr. to asso. prof. Lehigh U., 1937-44; asso. prof. English, Barnard Coll., 1945-46; prof. English, Columbia, 1946-69, William Peterfield Trent prof. English, 1964-69, emeritus, 1969-78. Guggenheim fellow 1951-52, 65-66; research in Eng., 1958-59. Editor Johnsonian News Letter; sec. English Inst. 1946; chmn. 18th century groups Modern Lang. Assn., 1944, 46. Fellow Royal Soc. Lit. (London); mem. Johnson Soc. (pres. Lichfield, Eng. 1958-59; hon. v.p. London), P.E.N., Am. Soc. for Eighteenth Century Studies (pres. 1972-73), Phi Beta Kappa, Phi Gamma Delta. Presbyn. Author: Hester Lynch Piozzi (Mrs. Thrale), 1941; Young Sam Johnson, 1955; From Puzzles to Portraits: Problems of a Literary Biographer, 1970. Editor: Dr. Campbell's Diary, 1947; Johnsonian Studies 1887-1950. A Survey and Bibliography, 1951, rev. and expanded (with D.J. Greene), 1970; Eighteenth Century English Literature: Modern Essays in Criticism, 1959; (with Louis A. Landa) Pope and His Contemporaries, 1949; Biography as an Art, 1962; Peregrine Pickle (Tobias Smollett), 1964; Man Versus Society in Eighteenth-Century Britain, 1968. Adv. editorial bd. Yale Boswell edit., also Wesleyan U. edit. Works of Henry Fielding, Yale Johnson edit. Contbr. articles to profl. jours. Home: New York, N.Y. Died Apr. 7, 1978.

CLIFFORD, JOHN FENN, hotel exec.; b. New Haven, Aug. 31, 1915; s. Daniel J. and Marguerite J. (Kelley) C.; student Holy Ghost Apostolic Coll., Cornwell Heights, Pa., 1932; m. Rita Clendenen, Sept. 23, 1939; children—John Fenn, Kathleen M. Clifford Keating, Margaret Clifford Collins. With The Taft, New Haven, 1933-42; v.p., gen. mgr. The Gotham Hotel, N.Y.C., Hollywood (Fla.) Beach Hotel, 1963-66; pres., gen. mgr. Ariz. Biltmore, Phoenix, 1966-70; pres. Flagler Systems, Inc., owners, operators The Breakers Hotel, Palm Beach, Fla., 1970-80; trustee Am. Hotel Found. Recipient Bus. Leadership award Palm Beach Daily News, 1975. Mem. Am. Hotel and Motel Assn. (Resort Exec. award 1975), Fla. Hotel and Motel Assn., Palm Beach County Hotel and Motel Assn., N.Y.C. Hotel Assn., Hotel Sales Mgmt. Assn., Palm Beach C. of C., West Palm Beach C. of C. Roman Catholic. Clubs: Skal, Rotary (Palm Beach). Home: Palm Beach, Fla. Died Oct. 17, 1980.

CLIFFORD, JOHN MCLEAN, lawyer; b. Salt Lake City, Dec. 9, 1904; s. William Ernest and Margaret M. (McLean) C.; student U. Utah, 1923-25; J.D., Southwestern U., 1930; m. Lucetta Penrose Brown, June 10, 1925; 1 dau., Patricia Lou (Mrs. Frank Jordan). Admitted to Calif. bar, 1930, D.C. bar, 1939; v.p. NBC, Inc., N.Y.C., 1953-54, adminstrv. v.p., 1954-56, exec. v.p., 1956-61, v.p. RCA, 1961-62; exec. v.p. Curtis Pub. Co., Phila., 1962-64, pres., dir., 1964-68; counsel Brazelton, Clifford, Smith & Oksner, 1968-79; dir. Beehive Internat., Salt Lake City. Mem. D.C., Calif. bar assns. Home: Santa Barbara, Calif. Died Mar. 10, 1979.

CLIFFORD, PHILIP GREELY, lawyer; b. Portland, Me., Sept. 11, 1882; s. William Henry and Ellen Greely (Brown) C.; A.B., Bowdoin Coll., 1903; law study, Harvard, 1904-05; m. Katharine Hale, Oct. 11, 1905; children—Margaret Ellen, Matilda Greely (Mrs. Wm. H. Clifford, 3d), Ann (Mrs. Howard H. Dana). Admitted to Maine bar, 1907, and practiced since at Portland; treas., dir. and clerk W. H. Clifford Co.; dir., treas. and gen. mgr. J. B. Brown & Sons; also mem. board of dirs. Anderson, Adams Co., Fern Park Land Corp. Mem. Legal Advisory Bd., Portland, World War. Trustee Portland Pub. Library; mem. board overseers Bowdoin Coll. Mem. Am., Me. State and Cumberland County bar assns., Me. Hist. Soc. (trustee), Portland Soc. Art, Portland Soc. Natural Hist., Psi Upsilon. Phi Beta Kappa. Democrat. Clubs: Cumberland, Portland Yacht (Portland). Author: Nathan Clifford, Democrat, 1922; Romances of 1903. Contbr. fiction to mags Home: Portland, Me.

CLIFT, DENISON HALLEY, writer, motion picture dir.; b. San Francisco, Calif., May 2, 1885; s. Nathaniel and Esther Elizabeth (Castell) C.; A.B., Stanford, 1907; m. Lillian Gardner Sturgiss, Aug. 16, 1907; children—Edwin Sturgiss (dec.), Catherine Esther. Editor Overland Monthly, 1907; advertising expert, San Francisco, 1908-17; writer magazine stories, also of motion picture scenarios for Paramount Pictures, Fox Film Corpn., Cecil B. DeMille, Metro-Goldwyn-Mayer, since 1917; motion picture dir., Hollywood, London. Mem. Acad. Motion Picture Arts and Sciences. Republican. Clubs: University (Los Angeles); Hollywood Athletic; Beach (Santa Monica, Calif.). Author: Guns of Galt, 1927; Man About Town, 1932; The Mighty Thing, 1933; I Belong To You, 1933; Ogpu, 1933; also (plays) The Woman Disputed, prod. New York, 1926; Scotland Yard, prod. New York, 1929; The Moon is Red, prod. London, 1934. Motion picture dir. of This Freedom, A Bill of Divorcement, A Woman of No Importance, Mystery of the Mary Celeste, Atlantic Cable, The Romance of Madame Tussaud, etc. Contbr. to Collier's Red Book, Youth's Companion, etc. Home: Beverly Hills, Calif.

CLIFTON, ERNEST SMITH, educator; b. Darlington, S.C., July 31, 1914; s. Thomas and Rosa (Smith) C.; B.A., U. Va., 1935; M.A., La. State U., 1937, Ph.D., 1940; student U. Cologne, Germany, 1938, U. Heidelberg, 1939; m. Eula Clyde Miller, Aug. 27, 1940; children—Frank, Ernest, Gail, Patricia. Sch. prin., Johnsonville, S.C., 1935-36; tchr. English, North Tex. State U., Denton, 1939-49, dir. dept. English, 1950-76, chmn. div. humanities, 1957-65. Mem. Tex. Folklore Soc. (past v.p.), Tex. Conf. Coll. Tchrs. English (pres. 1969), South-Central Modern Lang. Assn. (chmn. gen. linguistics sect.), Modern Lang. Assn. Am. AAUP, Nat. Council Tchrs. English, Coll. English Assn., Conf. Coll. Composition and Communication, Phi Beta Kappa, Phi Kappa Phi. Home: Denton, Tex. Died Dec. 27, 1979.

CLIFTON, LEONARD LEROY, dean; born at Geneseo, Ill., Jan. 14, 1889; s. William M. and Mary Elizabeth (Black) C.; A.B., U. of Okla., 1916; A.M., U. of Chicago, 1934; Ph.D., Colo. State Coll. of Edn., Greeley, Colo., 1941; LL.D., Oklahoma City U., 1961; m. Ethel Helen Deckard, May 26, 1923; children—Helen Eloise, Charles William. Began as sch. teacher, Tonkawa, Okla., 1907; supt. of schools, Washington, Oklahoma, 1919-23, Tipton, Okla., 1923-33 and 1935-37; dean, Southeastern Teachers Coll., Durant, Okla., 1933-35; became dean Huntingdon Coll., Montgomery, Ala., 1937; adminstrv. dean Oklahoma City U., dir. tchr. education, head dept. edn.; dir. Evening Coll., Oklahoma City Southwestern Coll. Director Travelers Aid Soc.; dir. Ala. War Chest. Mem. Ala. Edn. Assn., N.E.A., Assn. Collegiate Registrars, Am. Statis. Assn., Nat. Soc. Coll Teachers of Edn., Kappa Delta Pi, Phi Delta Kappa. Mason (Shriner, K.T.). Club: Lions (past pres.) (Montgomery, Ala.). Address: Oklahoma City, Okla. Died June 30, 1976.

CLINE, ARTHUR RAYMOND, lawyer; b. Barr Mills, Ohio, Aug. 20, 1898; s. Alvin Arthur and Clara (Froelich) C.; student Coshocton County (O.) Normal Sch., 1916-17; A.B., Ohio State U., 1923, J.D., 1925; m. Christine D. Wippel, Sept. 2, 1924. Tchr. rural schs., Ohio, 1917-18; brakeman Pa. R.R., 1920; supt. maintenance and repair Athens County (O.) Dept. Hwys., 1925-28; admitted to Ohio bar, 1925; practice in Toledo from 1928; mem. Cline, Bischoff and Cook Co., L.P.A., from 1941. Sec., dir. Dundee Truck Line, Inc., Funk Motor Transp., Inc., Auto-Tronic Control Co., Dundee Motor Express, Inc., Airport Mobile Homes, Inc.; v.p., dir. Progress Nat. Bank, Toledo, 1965-73. Chmn. Toledo Citizens Com. Lake Erie Water Works, 1938, mem. citizens adv. com. constrn., 1938-41, exec. chmn. dedication com., 1941; mem. Toledo City Plan Commn., 1937-74, chmn., 1941-74; mem. Lucas County (O.) Plan Commn., 1941-74, chmn., 1942-74; chmn. coordination com. Toledo Regional Plan for Action, 1963-74. Trustee U. Toledo, 1967-75, trustee emeritus, from 1975. Served with U.S. Army, 1918-19. Recipient Alumni Citizenship award Ohio State U., 1977; Disting. Lawyer award U. Toledo Coll. Law Alumni Assn., 1979. Mem. Am., Ohio (v.p. 1942-44), Toledo (past pres.), Lucas County (past pres.) bar assns., Am. Soc. Planning Ofcls. (life), Ohio State U. Alumni Assn. (life), Toledo C. of C. (past trustee), Am. Legion (life), Sphinx, Gamma Eta Gamma. Methodist. Mason (33 deg., Shriner). Clubs: Toledo, Maumee River Yacht (life) (Toledo); South Side Toledo Exchange (past pres.), High Twelve. Home: Toledo, Ohio. Deceased.

CLINE, EARL, lawyer; b. Weeping Water, Neb., Dec. 18, 1886; s. William T. and Emma F. (Meloy) C.; student Peru State Tchrs. Coll., 1905-07, U. Neb. Coll. Law, 1910-12, U. Mich. Coll. Law, 1916; LL.D. (hon.), U. Neb., 1966; m. Mildred Holland, Sept. 4, 1919. Tchr. high sch., 1907; prin. high sch., Sidney, Neb., 1907-09; supt. schs., Geneva, Neb., 1913-15, Nebraska City, Neb., 1915-16; with law firm Pitzer, Cline & Tyler, Nebraska City, 1917-22; mem. Hall, Cline & Williams, Lincoln, 1922-42, Cline, Williams & Wright, 1942-51, Cline, Williams, Wright & Johnson, 1951-76, now Cline, Williams, Wright, Johnson & Oldfather. Bd. regents U. Neb., 1925-37. Trustee U. Neb. Found., pres., 1954-55. Served as capt. 89th Div., U.S. Army, 1917-19; wounded in action St. Mihiel offensive, 1918. Decorated Order of Purple Heart. Recipient Distinguished Service award U. Neb., 1946. Mem. Am., Neb., Lincoln bar assns., Am. Legion (state comdr. 1919), Phi Kappa Psi, Phi Delta Phi. Republican. Methodist. Mason. Club: Country (Lincoln). Home: Lincoln, Nebr. Died Mar. 15, 1976; buried Wyuka Cemetery, Lincoln.

CLINGMAN, CHARLES, bishop; b. Covington, Ky., Jan. 19, 1883; s. Charles and Mary Ellen (Hartsough) C.; A.B., Kenyon Coll., 1905, L.H.D., 1931, grad. Va. Theol. Sem., Alexandria, 1908, D.D., 1928; D.D., U. of the South, 1928; m. Elizabeth Florence Core, Oct. 21, 1909; 1 son, Robert Core. Deacon, 1907, priest, 1908, P.E. Ch.; rector St. Paul's Ch., Newport, Ky., 1908-13, Ch. of the Incarnation, Dallas, Tex., 1913-18, Trinity Ch., Houston, Tex., 1918-24, Ch. of the Advent, Birmingham, Ala., 1924-36; elected bishop Diocese of Ky., Jan. 24, 1936. In Red Cross Service, World War. Dep. to Gen. Conv. P.E. Ch. 7 times to 1934. Chmn. Dept. Pub. Welfare, Birmingham and Jefferson County, 1933-34; mem. bd. dirs. Birmingham Community Chest; chmn. St. Mark's Sch. for Negroes (Birmingham). Mem. bd. Regents, U. of the South; bd. trustees, Va. Theological Seminary. Mem. Psi Upsilon. Republican. Mason (32 deg.). Club: Pendennis. Address: Louisville, Ky.

CLIPPINGER, ROY, ex-congressman; b. Fairfield, Ill., Jan. 13, 1886; s. Anthony Clinton and Eliza Belle (Donahey) C.; ed. pub. schs. of White Co., Ill.; m. Verna Essery, May 31, 1917; children—Earl E., John L. With Norris City Record, Norris City, Ill., 1896 to 1909; editor and pub. Carmi Democrat Tribune since 1909; mem. 79th and 80th Congresses (1945-49), 24th Dist. of Ill.; mgr. White County Bridge Commn.; dir. Am. Toll Bridge Assn. Pres. Carmi Hosp. Assn.; founder and chmn. Bd. Greater Weeklies, New York, N.Y. Mem. Am. Press Assn. (bd. pubs.), Ill. Press Assn. (past pres.) Carmi Chamber of Commerce (founder and past pres.), Am. Red Cross (chmn. White County chapter). Republican. Methodist. Mason (32 deg., Shriner), Elk. Club: Union League (Chicago). Home: Carmi, Ill. *

CLOCK, HENRY HARRIMAN, lawyer; b. Hampton, Iowa, Mar. 8, 1908; s. Ralph H. and Maude H. (Harriman) C.; student Stanford, 1925-28, Southwestern Law Sch., 1929-30; m. Frances Terry, Aug. 28, 1932; children—Philip T. (dec.), Ralph, Edwin. Admitted to Calif. bar, 1931; practice in Long Beach, 1931-76, in Los Angeles, 1931-38; partner firm Clock, McWhinney & Clock, 1931-38, Clock, Waestman & Clock, 1938-71; pvt. practice, 1971-76. Chmn. adv. bd. Bank Am., 1955-66; dir. Farmers and Merchants Bank, Long Beach, Angeles Abbey; officer, dir. Fenwick, Inc., Westminster Meml. Park Cemetery, Mortuary in Westmininster Meml. Park; dir. various small corps. Past pres. Boys Clubs Long Beach, past mem. nat. bd. dirs. Boys Clubs Am.; pres. Long Beach Area council Boy Scouts Am., 1963-64; campaign chmn., pres. Long Beach Community Chest, 1958; campaign chmn. various capacities Greater Los Angeles area Community Chest and United Way; mem. Los Angeles County Health Adv. Commn., 1963-66, Calif. Health Planning Council, 1966-69, Long Beach Marina Adv. Com., 1962-65; chmn. Long Beach Harbor Commn.; adviser Jr. League Long Beach, 1966-70; chmn. Greater Long Beach YMCA capital fund drive, 1974-75; bd. dirs. Long Beach Grand Prix Assn. Mem. Los Angeles County Republican Central Com., 1934-38, 64-68; mem. exec. com. Calif. Rep. Central Com. Bd. dirs. Meml. Hosp. Med. Center, Long Beach, pres. 1962-63; bd. dirs. Meml. and Children's Med. Center Found., pres., 1972-73; mem. chancellor's assos. Calif. State Univs. and Colls., 1972-76; bd. visitors Stanford Sch. Law; mem. president's asso. Calif. State U., Long Beach.; bd. dirs. numerous other charitable orgns. Recipient Golden Boy and Man award Long Beach Boys Club, 1960; Brotherhood award Long Beach chpt. NCCJ, 1971; Outstanding Salesman of Yr. award Long Beach Sales and Marketing Execs., 1973; Outstanding Citizens of Yr. award Long Beach Elks, 1973; Boss of Year award Legal Secs. Assn., 1976. Fellow Am. Coll. Probate Counsel; mem. Am., Calif., Los Angeles County, Long Beach (dir. 1947-50, 62-76, pres. 1965) bar assns., Am. Judicature Soc., Am. Bar Found. Clubs: Virginia Country (pres. 1945-46), Long Beach (pres. 1947), Internat. City, Yacht, Petroleum (Long Beach); Thunderbird (Palm Springs, Calif.); Tuna (pres. 1965) (Avalon, Calif.); Marlin (San Diego); Balboa Angling San Joaquin Gun (Newport Beach); Southern Calif. Tuna; Light Tackle Marlin. Author articles various subjects. Home: Long Beach, Calif. Died Nov. 21, 1976; interred Westminster Mausoleum, Westminster, Calif.

CLOCK, JOHN G., lawyer; b. Hampton, Ia., Feb. 26, 1896; s. Henry A. and Susan M. (Reeve) C.; student U. So. Calif. Law Sch., 1915-19; m. Blanche Dorsett, Sept. 30, 1922; children—Rosemary (Mrs. John Sadler), Carolyn (dec.). Admitted to Cal. bar, 1920, since practiced in Long Beach; mem. Clock, Waestman and Clock. Served in U.S. Army, 1917-19. Fellow Am. Bar Found.; mem. Am., Los Angeles County (trustee 1939-42), Long Beach (pres. 1943) bar assns., Am. Judicature Soc., Am. Counsel Assn., State Bar Cal. (bd. govs. 1945-48; v.p. 1948), Am. Coll. Probate Counsel (pres. 1950-51, regent), So. Cal. Golf Assn. (dir. 1941-50, pres. 1946), Cal. Golf Assn. (sec.-treas. 1946, pres. 1950), U.S. Golf Assn. (exec. com.; pres. 1960-61), Delta Theta Phi. Mason (32 deg.). Republican. Clubs: Royal and Ancient Golf (St. Andrews, Scotland); Virginia Country (pres. 1950). Home: Long Beach, Calif. Deceased.

CLOETE, STUART, author; b. Paris, France, July 23, 1897; s. Laurence and Edith Margaret (Park) C.; student Paris schs. and Lancing Coll.; Sussex, Eng.; m. Mildred Ellison, Apr. 6, 1940. Served in Brit. Army as mem. Coldstream Guards, 1914-25, and wounded in action, 1916 and 1918; ranching in South Africa, 1925-35; visited U.S., 1937; writing for several yrs., publishing first novel in 1937. Trustee South Africa Found. Mem. Internat. Platform Assn. Mem. Ch. of Eng. Clubs: Guards, Savage (London); Coffee House, Explorers, Nat. Arts (N.Y.C.). Author: Turning Wheels, 1937; Watch For the Dawn, 1939; Yesterday is Dead, 1940; The Hill of Doves, 1941; The Young Men and the Old, 1941; Congo Song, 1943; Against These Three; The Third Way; Curve and the Tusk, 1952; The African Giant, 1955; Mamba, 1956; The Mask, 1957; Gazella, 1958; The Soldier's Peaches and Other African Stories, 1959; The Fiercest Heart, 1960; The Silver Trumpet, 1961; West With the Sun, 1962; Rags of Glory, 1963; The Looking Glass, 1963; The Thousand and One Nights of Jean Macque, 1965; The Honey Bird, 1965; The Abductors, 1966; The Writing on the Wall, 1967; South Africa Land and People, 1968; How Young They Died, 1969; Three White Swans, 1971; A Victorian Son, 1971; The Gambler, 1973; More Nights of Jean Macque, 1975. Contbr. to mags. Home: South Africa. Died Mar. 21, 1976.

CLOKE, HARVEY WALTON, pub. relations and advt. exec.; b. Hazelton, Pa., Aug. 12, 1919; s. Harvey Raymond and Viola Mary (Walton) C.; A.B., Bucknell U., 1942; m. Janet Alden House, July 24, 1943; m. 2d, Marjorie Mitchell Smith, Dec. 18, 1960; 1 stepdau., Martha Carol Smith. Mng. editor Lewisburg (Pa.) Jour., 1940-42; financial writer, legislative corr. Asso. Press, 1943-45; financial corr. N.Y. Times, Phila. and Washington burs., 1945-50; coordinator pub. relations Kaiser Industries Corp. and affiliates, 1950-63; sr. v.p. Barnet and Reef Assos., Inc., N.Y.C., 1963-64; v.p. pub. relations and advt., corporate officer Am. Can Co., N.Y.C., 1964-68; v.p. pub. relations and advt., also corporate officer Rockwell Internat., Pitts., 1968-75; Washington editor Finance mag., 1948-50. Bd. dirs. Advt. Council; mem. Nat. Advt. Rev. Bd. Past exec. bd. U.S. nat. com. UNESCO. Mem. Pub. Relations Soc.

Am. (past pres., mem. accreditation bd.), Am. (past pres.), Internat. pub. relations assns., Assn. Nat. Advertisers (dir.), Pub. Relations Found. (dir.), N.A.M. (pub. relations council), Aerospace Industries Assn. (chmn. exec. com., pub. affairs council), Lambda Chi Alpha, Sigma Tau Delta, Phi Delta Epsilon. Clubs: Nat. Press, Internat., Nat. Aviation (Washington); Fox Chapel, Pitts. Field, Pitts. Press, Duquesne, Racquet (Pitts.); Overseas Press, Pinnacle (N.Y.C.); Bel Air Country (Los Angeles). Home: Pittsburgh, Pa. Died Sept. 13, 1975.

CLOUGH, WILLIAM PLUMMER, JR., (CLUF), surgeon; b. Hanover, N.H., May 19, 1911; s. William Plummer and Bertha (Ross) C.; student Tabor Acad., 1929-30; A.B., Dartmouth, 1934, student med. sch., 1933-35; M.D., Columbia, 1937; m. Louise Brokaw, June 25, 1938; children—William Plummer, John Francis, Nancy. Intern Newton (Mass.) Hosp., 1937-38; surg. house officer Boston City Hosp., 1938-40; house officer Boston Lyin-In Hosp., 1940-41; practice surgery, New London, since 1941. Pres. planning bd., New London, 1943-47. Fellow A.C.S.; mem. A.M.A., New Eng. Gynecol. and Obstet. Soc., N.H., Merrimack Co. (pres.) med. socs., N.H. Surg. Soc. (pres. 1956-57). Club: New London Outing, (pres.). Home: New London, N.H. Died Nov. 5, 1976.

CLURMAN, HAROLD EDGAR, stage dir., critic; b. N.Y.C., Sept. 18, 1901; s. Samuel Michael and Berth (Saphir) C.; student Columbia U., 1919-21; diplome U. Paris, 1923; D. Lit. (hon.), Bard Coll., 1958; D.F.A. (hon.), Carnegie Inst. Tech., 1963, Boston U., 1963, Ripon Coll., 1963. Actor, stage mgr., play reader, 1924-31; co-founder Group Theatre, N.Y.C., 1931-41, mng. dir., 1937-41; film producer, dir. 20th Century Fox, Paramount, RKO, 1941-46; critic of arts Tomorrow Mag., N.Y.C., 1946-52; theatre critic New Republic, N.Y.C., 1949-52, The Nation, N.Y.C., 1953-80; guest theatre critic London Observer, 1959, 63; exec. cons. Repertory Theatre of Lincoln Center, N.Y.C., 1963-64; Sunday theatre critic World-Jour.-Tribune Sunday Mag., N.Y.C., 1966-67; dir. numerous plays, including: The Member of The Wedding, N.Y.C., 1949-50 (Donaldson award for direction 1950), also Awake and Sing, Golden Boy, Ladies of the Corridor, Bus Stop, The Waltz of the Toreadors, A Touch of the Poet; dir. The Iceman Cometh (in Japanese), State Dept., Tokyo, summer 1968; vis. prof. theatre Hunter Coll., from 1964; Andrew Mellon lectr. in drama Carnegie Inst. Tech., 1963; chmn. Brandeis U. Arts Commn.; guest lec- tr., vis. prof. numerous Am. univs. Decorated chevalier Legion of Honor (France); recipient George G. Nathan prize English depts. Cornell, Princeton and Yale univs., 1958; medal of Achievement, Brandeis U., 1976. Mem. Soc. Stage Dirs. and Choreographers. Club: Players. Author: The Fervent Years, 1945; Lies Like Truth, 1958; The Naked Image, 1966; On Directing, 1968; The Divine Pastime, 1974; All People Are Famous, 1974; Ibsen, 1977; contbr. articles to popular mags., including N.Y. Times, Harper's Bazaar, Partisan. Home: New York, N.Y. Died Sept. 9, 1980.

COATS, MARION (MRS. CLIFFORD L. GRAVES), educator; b. Eton, N.Y., Aug. 2, 1885; d. Albert B. (D.D.) and Dilla Marie (Woodworth) C.; A.B., Vassar, 1907; studied Yale, 1910-11; M.A., Radcliffe Coll., 1912, post-grad. work, 1911-15; post-graduate work, Columbia U., 1929-32; m. Clifford L. Graves, of Bronxville, N.Y., July 4, 1929. Began teaching at Miss Kimball's School, Worcester, Mass., then Oxford Sch., Hartford, Conn., 1909-10; prin. Ferry Hall, Lake Forest, Ill., 1915-18; prin. Bradford Acad., 1918-27; pres. Sarah Lawrence Coll., Bronxville, N.Y., 1927-29. Chmn. Experiential Groups, N.Y. City, 1931. Mem. Nat. Assn. Principals of Schs. for Girls (pres. 1919-22), Am. Assn. Univ. Women, Am. Women's Assn. of New York, Women's City Club of N.Y. City, Kappa Delta Phi, Phi Beta Kappa. Home: Harpursville, N.Y.

COBB, CULLY ALTON, editor, printing corp. exec.; b. Prospect, Tenn., Feb. 25, 1884; s. Napoleon Bonaparte and Mary Agnes (Woodward) C.; B.S., Miss. Agrl. & Mech. Coll. (now Miss. State U.), 1908; D.Sc., Clemson U., 1937; m. Byrdie Ball, Dec. 23, 1910 (dec.); children—Cully Alton, David Alexander; m. 2d, Lois Dowdle, Aug. 24, 1934. Supt. high sch. Buena Vista, Miss., 1908-10; state agt. Miss. Agrl. and Mech. Coll., in charge boys' agrl. club work, 1910-19, also asst. dir. extension work in Miss.; editor and dir. So. Ruralist, 1919-30; pres. Ruralist Press, Inc., Atlanta. Dir. cotton div. AAA, 1933; served as mem. printing industry com. WPB. Mem. agr. com. U.S. C. of C. Bd. govs. Agrl. Hall of Fame, 1964. Mem. Ash Kahn Crew (hon. soc. printing industry Am.); recipient Distinguished Service award Printing Industry of Atlanta, 1958, citation for distinguished service Printing Industry Am., 1962; Patron Excellence award Miss. State U., 1965. Mem. Nat. Boys' and Girls' Club Com. from 1923, Unit of Value Stabilization Com. created by Am. Farm Bureau Fed. Mem. Atlanta C. of C. (chmn. agrl. com., livestock com.), Ga. Printers Assn. (pres.), Atlanta Master Printers Club (pres. 1944), Am. Agrl. Editors Assn. (pres. 1923-28), Country Life Assn. (dir.), Printing Industry Am. (past pres. union employer sect.), Omicron Delta Kappa (hon.). Democrat. Baptist. Mason (32 deg.). Rotarian. Organized first sch. of Miss. system of agrl. high schs., and first internat. stock judging contests; as pres. Am. Agrl. Editors' Assn., conducted agrl. study tours to Europe, Can. and Mexico. Home: Decatur, Ga. Died May 7, 1975.

COBB, JAMES BLAINE, lawyer, union ofcl.; b. Durham, NC., Nov. 12, 1903; s. James and Mary (Cox) C.; B.S., Howard U., 1926, LL.B., 1947; m. Leona M. Cobb, Sept. 2, 1926; children—James W., Bessie Cobb, Howard, Joan. Staff Library of Congress, 1926-31; clk. Post Office Dept., 1931-53; admitted to D.C. bar, 1948, since practiced in D.C.; with Nat. Alliance of Postal Employees, 1931-61, pres., 1953-61. Mem. Urban League, N.A.A.C.P., D.C. Bar Assn., Omega Psi Phi. Mason, Elk. Home: Washington, D.C. Died Jan. 11, 1979.

COBB, LEE J., actor; b. N.Y.C., Dec. 9, 1911; s. Benjamin Jacob and Kate (Neilecht) C.; student Coll. City N.Y.; m. Helen Beverly, Feb. 6, 1940; m. 2d, Mary Hirsch, July 1957. Actor, dir. Pasadena Community Playhouse, 1931-33; mem. Group Theatre, N.Y.C., 1935-40, appeared Group prodn. Golden Boy, London, Eng., 1938; appeared in title role Broadway prodn. Death of a Salesman, The Emperor's Clothes; on screen from 1937; numerous motion pictures include: The Moon is Down, 1943; Song of Bernadette, 1945; Anna and the King of Siam, 1946; Boomerang, 1947; Captain from Castile, 1948; Call Northside 777, 1948; But Not For me, 1959; The Trap, 1959; Green Mansions, 1959; Exodus, 1960, How the West Was Won; Come Blow Your Horn, 1963; The Man Who Loved Cat Dancing, 1973; appeared on TV series The Virginian, the Young Lawyers. Mem. Actors Equity Assn., Screen Actors Guild, Am. Fedn. Radio Artists, Nat. Aero. Assn., Aircrafts Pilots and Owners Assn., Civil Air Patrol. Address: Beverly Hills, Calif. Died Feb. 11, 1976.

COBB, META R., occupational therapist; b. Saginaw, Mich., Jan. 30, 1886; dau., John Jacob Rupp and Betty Nienstedt Rupp; attended Nat. Park Seminary, Forest Glenn, Md., Miss Bennett's Sch., Irvington on Hudson, N.Y., 1899-1904; m. Humphrey Cobb, Sept. 15, 1923. Began occupational therapy training 1917; served mil. hosps, 1917-21, asst. exec. sec., American Occupational Therapy Assn., 1923-33, exec. sec., 1938-48. Republican. Presbyterian. Author: Betty Blake, O.T., (with Edith M. Stern), 1940, Joan Chooses Occupational Therapy (with Holland Hudson), 1944. Clubs: Cosmopolitan (N.Y.). Home: New York.

COBB, ROGER BURNHAM, ret. utility exec.; b. Kingston, R.I., July 21, 1914; s. George Robert and Ethel (Burnham) C.; B.A., St. John's Coll., Annapolis, Md., 1933; B.E., Johns Hopkins, 1935; m. Millicent Allen, June 14, 1939; 1 son, Allen R. Engr. Iroquois Gas Corp., Buffalo, 1937-43, supt., 1944-53, v.p., 1953-63, sr. v.p., 1963-76, dir., 1965-76. Bd. dirs. Jr. Achievement, from 1958, pres., 1960; bd. dirs. United Taxpayers League, 1962-75; mem. Buffalo Bd. Safety, 1963-66. Mem. Buffalo Area C. of C., Ellicott Club Assn., Automobile Club Buffalo (dir. 1964-67), S.R. Home: Buffalo, N.Y. Deceased.

COBB, STANWOOD, author, lectr., educator; b. Newton, Mass., Nov. 6, 1881; s. Darius and Laura Maria (Lillie) C.; A.B., Dartmouth, 1903; A.M., Harvard, 1910; m. Ida Nayan Whitlam, 1919. Tchr. Nautical Prep. Sch., 1904; instr. English and Latin, Robert Coll., Constantinopel, Turkey, 1907-10; pvt. teaching, Washington, 1910-12; touring Europe, Sargent's Travel Sch. for Boys, 1912-13; traveling tutor, 1913-14; head English dept. St. John's Coll., Annapolis, Md., 1914-15, Asheville (N.C.) Sch. for Boys, 1915-16; instr. English and history U.S. Naval Acad., 1916-19; founder, 1919, and prin. Chevy Chase Country Day Sch., until 1961; founder, dir. Mast Cove Camp, 1926-61; editor Avalon Press, 1963—; Nat. lectr. Bahai World Faith, 1964—; lectr. Green Acre Bahai Summer Sch., Eliot, Me., St. Elizabeths Hosp., Washington. Founder, 1919, and chmn. exec. com. Progressive Edn., Assn. (pres. 1927-30). Mem. Phi Beta Kappa. Clubs: Cosmos, Authors (founder, pres.), Harvard. Author: The Real Turk, 1914; Ayesha of the Bosphorus, 1915; The Essential Mysticism, 1918; Simla a Tale in Verse, 1919; The New Leaven, 1928; The Wisdom of Wu Ming Fu, 1931; The Genius Within You, 1932; Security for a Failing World, 1934; New Horizons for the Child, 1934; Patterns in Jade of Wu Ming Fu, 1935; Character-A Sequence in Spiritual Psychology, 1938; The Way of Life of Wu Ming Fu, 1942; Symbols of America, 1946; The Donkey or the Elephant, 1951; Tomorrow and Tomorrow, 1951; What is Man, 1952; Sage of the Sacred Mountain, 1953; Magnificent Partnership, 1954; What is God, 1955; What is Love, 1957; The Jade Necklace of Lin San Kwei, 1958; Islamic Contributions to Civilization, 1963; Poems to Live By, 1968; Life with Nayan, 1969; Radiant Living, 1970; Wings of the Spirit, 1971; Memories of Abdul Baha, 1972; Scientific Study of the Hand, 1973; Thoughts on Education and Life, 1975. Co-editor: World Order, 1935-42; editor Baha'i mag., 1923-35. Contbr. articles to mags. Home: Chevy Chase MD also Eliot ME. *

COBB, W. R., banker; b. Owen County, Ky., Nov. 7, 1883; s. Lewis and Mary (Sidebottom) C.; student Georgetown (Ky.) Coll.; m. Mary Sandford, Mar. 15, 1908. With Citizens Fidelity Bank & Trust Co., Louisville, since 1907, vice pres. since 1919; dir. Am. Creosoting Co. (and affiliates), Glenmore Distilleries Co., Fed. Chemical Co., Louisville Builders Supply Co., W. M. Cissell Mfg. Co. (Louisville). Clubs: Pendennis, Louisville Country. Home: Louisville.

COCHRAN, BURT, advt. exec.; b. Metropolis, Ill., Feb. 5, 1898; s. William Phares and Sarah Effie (Jones) C.; A.B., U. Kan., 1921; m. Jessie-Lee Wyatt, Jan. 14, 1922; 1 son, Burt. Ad writer, salesman Dallas News and Evening Jour.; asst. advt. mgr. Foreman & Clark, 1921; copywriter, account exec. Ferry-Hanley Advt. Co., 1922-26; account exec. H. K. McCann Co. (now McCann-Erickson, Inc.). San Francisco, 1926-27, mgr. Seattle office, 1927-36, Chgo. office, 1936-38, mgr. So. Cal. operations, 1941-59; v.p. McCann-Erickson, Inc., 1945-58; exec. v.p., partner Stebbins & Cochran, advertising. Los Angeles, 1958; partner McNeil, McCleery & Cochran, 1959-61; Burt Cochran, Advt., marketing communications service, from 1961; dir. Bell Brand Foods. Ltd., Los Angeles. Mem. pub. relations com. Boy Scouts Council of Greater Los Angeles, California. Served as 2d lieutenant inf., U.S. Army, World War I. Mem. Am. Assn. Advt. Agencies (past mem. bd., vice chmn. So. Cal. chpt.), Friends of Huntington Library, So. Cal. Symphony Assn., Pasadena Art Museum, also member of the Conquistadores del Cielo, Sigma Nu, Alpha Delta Sigma, Sigma Delta Chi. Clubs: Greater Los Angeles Advertising (past mem. bd.), California, Men's Garden, Sales Execs. (Los Angeles). Home: La Canada, Cal. Died Oct. 23, 1979.

COCHRAN, HAMILTON, author; b. Phila., Sept. 9, 1898; s. Rev. Joseph Wilson and Helen V. (Scudder) C.; student Swarthmore Prep. Sch., 1914-17; A.B., U. Mich., 1922; m. Enid C. D. Slee, Apr. 18, 1925; children—Enid Clare (Mrs. R.N. Taylor), Susan H. (Mrs. S.C. Swanson), Margaret Ellen (Mrs. Garret C. Miller). Engaged in advt. and editorial work, including 2 years in Eng. handling advt. for Am. and Brit. firms, 1931-32; commr. pub. welfare for islands of St. Thomas and St. John, govt. Virgin Islands of U.S., 1932-33; advt. work for Standard Oil Co. N.J., 1933-36; sales promotion and sales tng. work for Tradeways, Inc., N.Y.C., 1936-40; advt. work for R. H. Donnelley Corp., N.Y.C., 1940-44; automotive marketing mgr. Saturday Eve. Post, Phila., 1944-60; advt. dir. Curtis Circulation Co., 1960-62; v.p. Stanley Pub. Co., Chgo., 1962-64, cons., free-lance writer 1965-77. Served in USCG, 1917-19. Decorated World War medal. Fellow Co. Mil. Historians; mem. Am. Legion, Delta Sigma Pi. Republican. Episcopalian. Author books including: Rogue's Holiday, 1947; Blockade Runners of the Confederacy, 1958; Pirates of the Spanish Main, 1961; Dram Tree, 1962; Noted American Duels, 1963; Freebooters of the Red Sea, 1965; Scudders in the American Revolution, 1976. Contbr. 3 anthologies poetry; articles and fiction. Established native handicraft industries in Virgin Islands and created markets for them in U.S. Home: Wallingford, Pa. Died July 27, 1977.

COCHRAN, HERBERT GREEN, judge; b. Farmington, Del., Apr. 15, 1885; s. Frederick J. and Dora (Hoffecker) C.; A.B., Dickinson Coll., Carlisle, Pa., 1908; Rhodes scholar, Oxford U., Eng., 1908-11; student University of Virginia, 1911-12; m. Jeannette Payne Tabb, April 5, 1941. Admitted to Virginia bar, 1912, and began practice at Norfolk; pub. defender, Norfolk, 1916-17, 1920-23; spl. asst. city atty., 1919-20; substitute judge Juvenile and Domestic Relations Court, 1923-25, judge since 1925; mem. Roper & Cochran. Pres. Norfolk Council of Social Agencies; pres. Va. State Conf. of Social Work, 1930; trustee Norfolk Community Fund; v.p. Va. Interracial Commn., 1931-32; pres. Norfolk Interracial Commn.; mem. White House Conf. on Child Health and Protection, 1931; mem. delinquency and juvenile court com. of Virginia Advisory Legislative Council; member adv. committee of the National Council of Juvenile Court Judges. Became pres. Norfolk Day Nursery in 1928; mem. Va. Com. for Selection Rhodes Scholars. Dir. Little Theatre of Norfolk since 1929. Mem. Am., Va. State and Norfolk-Portsmouth bar assn., Am. Law Inst., Nat. Probation Assn. (dir.), Am. Acad. Polit. and Social Science, Nat. Econ. League, Phi Beta Kappa, Phi Kappa Psi, Phi Delta Phi. Democrat. Methodist. Compiler: Norfolk City Code of 1920. Home: Norfolk.

COCKE, CHARLES FRANCIS (KOK), banker; b. Roanoke, Va., June 10, 1886; s. Lucian Howard and Lelia Maria (Smith) C.; A.B., U. of Va., 1908; student U. of Va. Law Sch., 1908-10; m. Francis Tilghman Mingea, October 1, 1914; 1 daughter, Lelia Smith (Mrs. William B. Bagbey). Admitted to Virginia bar, 1910, and since practiced in Roanoke; sr. member Cocke, Hazlegrove & Shackelford, retired Jan. 1947; pres., First Nat. Exchange Bank, Roanoke, 1938-56; chairman board, 1955-64, director, 1927-64; director of Peoples Federal Savings & Loan Association, Chesapeake &

Potomac Telephone Co. of Va. Served as 2d lt. Air Service, 1917-19. Mem. Virginia State Library Bd., 1945-54. President bd. trustees Hollins (Va.) Coll.; trustee Roanoke Hosp., Va. Mus. Fine Arts. Mem. Am. and Virginia State Bar Assn., American Bankers Assn. (v.p. 1950-51; pres. 1951-52), Va. Bankers Assn. (pres. 1948-49), Am. Legion (dept. comdr. for Va., 1919), Sigma Chi, Phi Delta Phi, Alpha Kappa Psi. Democrat. Episcopalian (chancellor Diocese of S.W. Va. 1919-61). Clubs: Commonwealth (Richmond), Shenandoah, Roanoke Country, Rotary (Roanoke); University (N.Y.C.). Author: Parish Lives of Diocese of Southwestern Va. and So. Va. Home: Roanoke.

COCKE, ERLE, SR., banker, ry. exec.; b. Lee County, Ga., June 26, 1895; s. Isaac Perry and Minne (Huff) C.; grad. Dawson (Ga.) High Sch., 1911; B.S., U. Ga., 1915; m. Elise Meadows, Dec. 9, 1917; children—Aline (Mrs. Eugene P. Cofeld, Jr.), Erle. Banking, mfg. and farming, Dawson and Macon, Ga., 1920-31; sec.-treas. and exec. officer, bd. regents Univ. System of Ga., 1932-33; mgr. Atlanta agy., R.F.C., 1934-38, R.F.C. Mortgage Co., Atlanta area, 1936-38, C.C.C., Atlanta area 1934-39; gen. chmn. Roosevelt Homecoming, 1935; state dir. Nat. Emergency Council, 1936-38; v.p. Fulton Nat. Bank, 1938-42, exec. v.p., 1942-45, pres., 1945-54, vice chmn. bd., chmn. exec. com., 1954-57; pres. Atlanta Clearing House, 1947, 51; dir. Fed. Deposit Ins. Corp., 1957-60, chmn., 1960-63, dir.; v.p., dir. Central of Ga. Ry. Co.; cons. So. Ry. Systems; dir. Citizens Bank Md., Am. Bank Atlanta, Gen. Acceptance Corp., financial observer Bretton Woods Conf. inaugurating World Bank & World Fund, del. ann. meetings, 1958, 61. Mem. Ga. Senate, 1927-28. Trustee Com. for Econ. Devel. Served as lt. AEF, World War I. Mem. Am. Legion (nat. vice comdr., 1922-23), Ga. (chmn. fed. legislative com., other offices), Am. (v.p. 1955-56, pres. 1956-57) bankers assns., Nat. Indsl. Conf. Bd., Soc. Indsl. Realtors (award bd.), Nat. Planning Assn. (nat. council), Newcomen Soc., Ga. Agrl. and Indsl. Devel. Bd. (adv. com. 1944-45), Internat. C. of C. (trustee U.S. council), Alpha Tau Omega. Baptist. Clubs: Capital City, Piedmont Driving (Atlanta); Nat. Press (Washington). Home: Atlanta, Ga. Died Oct. 7, 1977.

COCKLEY, WILLIAM BARNEY, lawyer; b. Lexington, O., Dec. 20, 1883; s. William W. and Mary U. (Beverstock) C.; A.B., Ohio State U., 1904, LL.B., 1908; S.J.D., Harvard, 1915; m. Katharine Ann Jones, June 20, 1914; children—William B., Jr., Eben Hoyt, Katharine Ann (Mrs. John F. Schindler), Rollin Beverstock. Admitted to O. bar, 1908; mem. faculty Ohio State U. Law Sch., 1908-17, prof. law, 1915-17; partner firm Jones, Day, Cockley & Reavis, and predecessor firms, Cleveland, since 1919. Mem. Am., Ohio and Cleveland bar assns., Phi Beta Kappa, Order of the Coif. Club: Union. Home: Lexington,

COCKRELL, MONROE FULKERSON, banker; b. Dallas, Tex., Dec. 15, 1884; s. Alexander and Ettie (Fulkerson) C.; ed. Va. Mil. Inst., Lexington, Va.; m. Nadine Steele, Nov. 2, 1910; children—Nancy Cockrell O'Reilly, Monroe Alexander. Teacher, Am. lit. and Spanish, 1907; bank examiner, State of Missouri, 1918; chief examiner, Fed. Reserve Bank, Kansas City, Mo., 1920; mgr., Kansas City Mo., Clearing House Assn., 1921; with Continental Ill. Nat. Bank & Trust Co., 1923-50, v.p., 1933-50. Chmn. Chgo. Regional Renegotiation Bd., 1952-53. Clubs: Glenview Golf; Caxton, Civil War Round Table; The Westerners. Home: Evanston, Ill.

COE, FRED HAYDEN, TV and theatre producer, film dir.; b. Alligator, Miss., Dec. 23, 1914; s. Frederick Hayden and Annette (Harroll) C.; student Peabody Coll. for Tchrs.; student fine arts, Yale; children—John Hayden, Laurence Anne, Sue Anne, Samuel Hayden; m. 2d, Joyce Beeler, Aug. 1, 1952. Producer, dir. NBC-TV, 1947-57, Philco-Goodyear Playhouse, Mr. Peepers, Producer's Showcase, CBS-TV, Playhouse 90, 1957-60; theatrical prodns. (N.Y.C.); 1945-79; Trip to Bountiful, Two For the Seesaw, The Miracle Worker, All The Way Home, Gideon, A Thousand Clowns, Wait Until Dark; Fiddler on the Roof, Promenade All; dir. Night Watch; motion picture prodns.: The Left Handed Gun, The Miracle Worker, A Thousand Clowns (also dir.), Me Natalie (also dir.). Recipient Peabody award, 1952-53. Died Apr. 29, 1979.

COE, MAXWELL A(LANSON), business executive; born Omaha, Nov. 10, 1883; s. Charles Alanson and Jessie Price (Fell) C.; student Mass. Inst. Tech., 1902-06; m. Ethel M. Norton, Apr. 20, 1914; children—Charles Norton, Maxwell Duncan. Vice pres. The Stanley Works, New Britain, Conn., since 1932, dir. since 1938; gen. mgr. Stanley Tools (div. of Stanley Works) since 1929. Dir. The Savs. Bank New Britain, Shinner Chuck Co. Mem. Phi Beta Epsilon. Conglist. Clubs: Technology (N.Y. City); Shuttle Meadow (New Britain). Home: New Britain, Conn.

COFFIN, VINCENT BROWN, university official; b. Middletown, Conn., Feb. 7, 1897; s. Seward V. and Della M. (Brown) C.; Bachelor of Arts, Wesleyan University, 1919, H.H.D. (hon.), 1959; LL.D. (hon.), U. Hartford, 1967; m. Gertrude Emily Rush, Sept. 16, 1922; children—S. Rush, Jane V.; m. 2d, Mary Catherine Hitchcock, Nov. 13, 1943. Agent Provident Mutual Life Ins., Utica, N.Y., 1920-22, asst. gen. agt., Albany, N.Y., 1920-27; teacher life ins. course N.Y. U., summer 1926-27, asso. prof. and dir. life ins. training, 1927-28; dir. edn. Penn Mutual Life Ins., Phila., Pa., 1928-31; supt. agencies Conn. Mutual Life Ins., Hartford, Conn., 1931-37, 2d vice pres., 1937-40, v.p. and supt. agys., 1940-46, vice president, 1946-50, sr. v.p., 1950-58; chancellor University of Hartford, from 1959. Dir. Life Ins. Sales Research Bur., 1938-41 (chmn. bd., 1940, chmn. exec. com. 1941). Former dir., vice pres. Hartford Coll. Ins. (merged with U. of Conn.); dir. Inst. Living; corporator Am. Sch. for Deaf, Hartford Hosp.; campaign chmn. Greater Hartford Community Chest, 1952, pres., 1953-55; vice pres. National Travelers Aid Assn., 1951-56, pres., 1956-58, bd. chmn., 1958-80; sec., United Community Funds and Councils of Am., also bd. mem., mem. exec. com.; pres. New Eng. Community Chests and Councils, 1957-59. Mem. Ct. Common Council, City of Hartford, 1957-80. Mem. bd. trustees American College of Life Underwriters, Wesleyan U. Recipient Russell Meml. Award, 1954. Mem. Life Underwriters Assn. (v.p. Utica, 1922, pres. Albany, N.Y., 1927, sec.-treas. N.Y. State, 1924-28); dir. Life Agencies Officers, 1942-45, Hartford C. of C., 1941-44. Ind. Republican. One of founders, 1st pres. Sales Mgrs. Club of Hartford. Clubs: Hartford Golf; University (N.Y.). Author: Sensible Selling, 1933, More Sensible Selling. Contbr. to ins. jours. Home: Hartford, Conn. Died Mar. 6, 1980.

COFFMAN, CHARLES F., newspaper editor; b. Fond du Lac, Wis., Mar. 25, 1886; s. Adelbert and Mary E.; grad. high sch., Fond du Lac; m. Georgeanna G. Birge, June 22, 1910. Began as reporter Fond du Lac Daily Reporter, 1904, city editor, 1906-10, mng. editor since 1910 (merged with Daily Commonwealth, 1926, and since published as Fond du Lac Commonwealth Reporter); vice-pres. Reporter Printing Co. Mem. Council Nat. Defense, World War. Mem. NRA State Recovery Board. Pres. Wis. A.P., 1930-31, Wis. Daily League, 1932-34. Mem. Fond du Lac Assn. Commerce (dir.), Y.M.C.A., Sigma Delta Chi, K.C., Elk. Clubs: Rotary, Twilight, Forum, (Fond du Lac); Milwaukee Press, Milwaukee Athletic. Mem. Civilian Defense Council of Fond du Lac. Home: Fond du Lac, Wis. *

COFFMAN, L. DALE, lawyer, educator; b. Delta, Iowa, Aug. 28, 1905; s. Ralph Gideon and Georgia (Green) C.; B.A., State U. Iowa, 1926, J.D., 1928; LL.M., Harvard, 1929, S.J.D., 1935; m. Helen Crouch, Dec. 31, 1925; 1 dau., Georganne. Practiced law with Sargent Gamble & Read, Des Moines, 1928-31; prof. law U. Nebr., 1931-37; counsel Gen. Electric Co., Schenectady, 1937-46; dean Sch. Law, Vanderbilt U., 1946-49; dean Sch. Law, U. Calif. at Los Angeles, 1949-57, prof. law, 1957-73, prof. law emeritus, 1973-77; chief cons. Commn. on Govt. Security, 1956-57; arbitrator in labor-mgmt. disputes. Fellow Am. Bar Assn.; mem. Order of Coif, Phi Delta Phi, Phi Beta Kappa, Kappa Sigma. Republican. Conglist. Mason. Clubs: Harvard, Lincoln, Riviera Country, Los Angeles Athletic, California Yacht. Editor: Cases on Nebraska Trial Practice, 1933. Contbr. articles to law publs. Home: Pacific Palisades, Calif. Died Aug. 31, 1977; buried Rose Hills Meml. Park, Whittier, Calif.

COGGESHALL, JAMES, JR., investment banker; b. N.Y.C., June 4, 1896; s. James and Hannah Elizabeth (Harrington) C.; B.S., Harvard, 1918, student law sch.; m. Esther Clarke, Aug. 15, 1918; children—John Clarke (dec.), Timothy, Caroline Frothingham (Mrs. Joseph Clark Segar), James Wells, Clarke. With First Boston Corp. 1919-72, pres., 1947-62, dir., 1934-72; dir. Colonial Equity Fund. Bd. dirs. Colonial Fund, Boston; mem. adv. com. Colonial Growth Fund, Colonial Income Fund, Boston. Trustee Cape Cod Hosp. Clubs: Bond, Harvard (N.Y.). Home: Barnstable, Mass. Died May 15, 1976.

COGLEY, JOHN, editor; b. Chgo., Mar. 16, 1916; s. John Francis and Anne (Geenty) C.; A.B., Loyola U., Chgo., 1947; Licentiate in Philosophy, U. Fribourg (Switzerland), 1949; D. Litt. (hon.), St. Martin's Coll., 1962; m. Theodora Schmidt, Apr. 6, 1942; children—Terence, Ann, Christopher, Joan, Paul, Mark. Editor, Today Mag., 1946-48; exec. editor Commonweal, 1950-55; religious news editor N.Y. Times, 1965-66; exec. staff Fund for the Republic, 1956-64; editor The Center Mag., 1967-75; sr. fellow and asso. Center for Study of Democratic Instns., 1967-75. Vis. lectr. U. Cal. at Santa Barbara, 1970-75, Ind. U., 1972; mem. selection bd. Dept. State, 1962. Mem. campaign staffs John F. Kennedy, 1960, Eugene McCarthy, 1968. Trustee Council on Religion and Internat. Affairs, 1956-70. Served with USAAF, 1942-45. Recipient award for coverage of Vatican Council, Catholic Press Assn., 1965. Author: Report on Blacklisting, 1956; Religion in a Secular Age, 1969; Catholic America, 1973; A Canterbury Tale, 1976. Editor: Religion in Am., 1958; Natural Law and Modern Society, 1963. Contbr. to Ency. Britannica 15th edit., New Cath. Ency. Died Mar. 28, 1976.

COHAN, AVERY BERLOW, educator; b. Boston, July 12, 1914; s. Max Joseph and Elizabeth (Berlow) C.; A.B., Cornell U., 1934; A.M., Columbia, 1942, Ph.D., 1959; m. Margaret Ann Kelley, Jan. 20, 1948; children—Beth Neal, Judith Kelley, Kevin Berlow, Peter Marshall. Research asst. Nat. Bur. Econ. Research, 1943; research asso. N.A.M., 1944-45; attache Dept. State, Berne, Switzerland, 1945-48, Stockholm, Sweden, 1949-51; resident rep. Econ. Com. Europe, Geneva, Switzerland, 1951-53; sales Top Co., Boston, 1953-56; teaching asso. Harvard, 1956-57; mem. faculty U. N.C., 1957-77, prof. finance, 1961-77, chmn. grad. studies bus. adminstrn., 1962-67; on leave as chief ins. br., cons. UN Conf. Trade and Devel., Geneva, Switzerland, 1968-69; cons. Nat. Bur. Econ. Research, 1961-69; vis. prof. IMEDE Mgmt. Devel. Inst., Lausanne, Switzerland, 1964-65; Mills Bee Lane vis. prof. finance U. Ga., 1973-75. Dir. Key Co., Greensboro, N.C. Bd. govs. Durham Acad., 1967-69. Mem. Am., So. econ. assns., Am., So. (v.p. 1974-75, pres.-elect 1975) finance assns., Inst. Mgmt. Scis., Am. Statis. Assn., Fin. Mgmt. Assn. (dir. 1975-76), Beta Gamma Sigma. Club: Chapel Hill Country (treas. 1963). Author: Cost of Flotation of Long Term Corporate Debt Since 1935, 1961; Yields on Corporate Debt Directly Placed, 1967; Financial Decision-Making—Theory and Practice, 1971; Case Problems in Financial Decision Making, 1972; The Risk Structure of Interest Rates, 1973; also articles. Book rev. editor Jour. Finance, from 1974. Home: Chapel Hill, N.C. Died Feb. 22, 1977.

COHEN, JESSE, ret. city ofcl.; b. Albany, N.Y., Apr. 13, 1885; s. Isaac and Josephine (Gratz) C.; student Albany (N.Y.) Bus. Coll., 1899-1900; m. Florence Feldman, Jan. 27, 1922; children—Richard Isaac, Janice Carol. Stenographer to N.Y. State historian, 1900-07, N.Y.C. tax dept., 1907-45; asst. to pres. tax dept., 1945-46; adminstrv. asst. tax dept., N.Y.C. 1946-53. Man of Year, Met. Council, Nat. Fedn. Temple Brotherhoods, 1957. Mem. Nat. Fedn. Temple Brotherhoods (past pres.), Union Am. Hebrew Congregations (mem. exec. bd.) N.Y. Fedn. Reform Synagogues (exec. bd.), Jewish Chautauqua Soc. (exec. bd.), Synagogue Council of Am. (treas.), Central Conf. Am. Rabbis, Albany Soc. of N.Y. Democrat. Jewish religion. Mem. Temple Beth Emeth. Home: Uniondale, L.I., N.Y.

COHEN, MANUEL FREDERICK, lawyer; b. Bklyn., Oct. 9, 1912; s. Edward and Lena (Kartzmar) C.; B.S. in Social Scis., Bklyn. Coll., 1933; LL.B. cum laude, St. Lawrence U., 1936, LL.D., 1962; LL.D., Babson Inst. Finance, 1968; L.H.D., Hebrew Union Coll. 1969; m. Pauline Grossman, Apr. 20, 1940; children—Susan D. (Mrs. Borman), Jonathan W. Research asso. 20th Century Fund, 1933-34; admitted to N.Y. bar, 1937; practiced in N.Y.C., 1937-42; with SEC, 1942-69, chief counsel div. corp. finance, 1952-59, adviser to commn., 1959-60, dir. div. corp. finance, 1960-61, commr. 1961-69, chmn., 1964-69; mem. Wilmer, Cutler, & Pickering, 1969-77. Lectr. law George Washington U. Law Sch., 1958-77; mem. council Adminstrv. Conf. U.S., 1961-69, pub. mem. 1974-77; mem. adv. bd. Bur. Nat. Affairs. Recipient Rockefeller Pub. Service award, 1956, Nat. Civil Service League Career Service award, 1961; Brotherhood award Nat. Conf. Christians and Jews. Mem. Am. Acad. Polit. and Social Sci., Am., Fed., N.Y., Interam., Internat., D.C. bar assns., Am. Soc. Internat. Law, Am. Law Inst., Am. Judicature Soc., Acad. Polit. Sci., Société Royale D'Economic Politique de Belgique, Practicing Law Inst. (nat. bd. advisers, chmn. Commn. Auditors' Responsibilities). Clubs: Cosmos, Internat., Woodmont Country. Contbr. articles to profl. jours. Home: Bethesda, Md. Died June 16, 1977.

COHN, HERMAN MICHAELS, neckwear mfr.; b. Rochester, N.Y., Dec. 28, 1886; s. Herman C. and Lillie (Michaels) C.; Ph.B., U. Rochester, 1907; m. Terese Hoffman, Jan. 30, 1919, children—Howard, Catherine (Mrs. Abraham L. Hertzel). Pres. Superba Cravats, Inc., Rochester, N.Y., 1929-56, chairman of the board, 1956—; director of the Lincoln Rochester Trust Co., 1942—, Haloid Co., 1946—, Fashion Park, Inc., 1951-53. Trustee Rochester Museum Arts & Scis., 1944—, U. Rochester, 1952—. Chmn. Industry com. N.R.A., 1934. Pres. Genesee Hosp., 1944-46; dir. Jewish Home for Aged, 1951-53, Rochester Hosp. Fund; hon. chmn. exec. com. Rochester br., Am. Jewish Com., 1953—. Dir. Rochester Community Chest, Inc., 1937—, Rochester chpt. A.R.C., 1940-58; pres. Rochester Council Boy Scouts Am., 1939-41; dir. JYM and WA, 1922-53. Served as ensign, USN, 1917-19. Mem. C. of C. (pres. 1943, trustee, 1939—). Club: Rochester. Home: Rochester.

COHRS, WALTER LOUIS, lawyer; b. Chicago, Dec. 23, 1892; s. Diederich Fred and Mary (Hellberg) C.; LL.B., John Marshall Law Sch., Chicago, 1916; m. Elizabeth Scholle, July 29, 1936; children—Mary Virginia, James Calvin, John Scholle, Walter Louis, Nancy Irene. Various clerical positions, Chicago Title & Trust Co., 1908-16; admitted to Ill. bar, 1917; asso. as atty. with various concerns, 1917-20; asst. mgr. real estate loan dept., First Nat. Bank of Chicago, 1920-31, v.p., real estate loan dept., 1931-58; private practice of law, 1958-77. Served as first lieutenant in A.E.F.,

1917-19. Mem. American and Chicago bar assns., Am. Legion, Delta Theta Phi. Republican. Clubs: Mid-Day, Athletic (Chicago); Indian Hill Country (Winnetka). Home: Winnetka, Ill. Died Jan. 22, 1977.

COINER, RICHARD TIDE, JR., air force officer; b. Washington, Sept. 2, 1910; s. Richard and Emily (Hall) C.; B.S., U.S. Mil. Acad., 1932; m. Helen Lanier Nix, Feb. 22, 1936; children—Richard Tide III, Beverly Nix, William Lanier. Commd. 2d lt., U.S. Army, 1932, advanced through grades to maj. gen., 1956; exec. to asst. sec. of war for air, 1941-43; commd. 397th Bomber Group, ETO, 1943-45; RAF Staff Coll., 1946; Hdqrs. U.S. Air Force Europe, 1946-49; dep. dir. div. mil. application AEC, 1949-51; dep. comdr., field command, Armed Forces Spl. Weapons Project, 1951-54; asst. dep. chief of staff Operations for Atomic Energy, Hdqrs. USAF, 1954-58, asst. chief staff, Air and Spl. Operations, SHAPE, 1958-61; comdr. Hdqrs. 9th Air Force, 1961-63; dir. trans. Hdqrs. USAF, 1963-66; chmn. bd., dir. Nix Profl. Bldg. Corp., Nix Hosp. Inc., Nix Garage Inc. Mem. Nat. Def. Transp. Assn., Nat. Rifle Assn., Izaak Walton League (life mem.). Episcopalian. Clubs: The Argyle, San Antonio Country (San Antonio); Army and Navy (Washington). Home: San Antonio, Tex. Died Nov. 15, 1980.

COKER, CHARLES WESTFIELD, mfg. exec.; b. Hartsville, S.C., Aug. 15, 1906; s. Charles Westfield and Carrie (Lide) C.; A.B., U. S.C., 1928, LL.D., 1958; postgrad. Harvard Sch. Bus., 1929-30; m. Elizabeth Howard, Oct. 23, 1931; children—Charles Westfield, Fitzlee Howard. With Sonoco Products Co., 1930-78, v.p., exec. v.p., 1934-61, pres., 1961-70, chmn. bd., 1970-78; dir. Sonoco Products Co. of Canada, Ltd., Brantford, Ont., Bank of Hartsville, Hartsville Oil Mill, J. L. Coker & Co., Sonoco de Mexico, S.A., Mexico City, T.P.T. Ltd., Romiley, Eng., Coker's Pedigreed Seed Co., Columbia, Newberry & Laurens R.R., S.C. Nat. Bank; Carolinas adv. bd. Am. Mut. Liability Ins. Co. Regional exec. com. Boy Scouts Am.; chmn. bd. trustees Coker Coll. Mem. Composite Can and Tube Inst. (v.p.), N.A.M., Newcomen Soc., Soc. Colonial Wars, Pi Kappa Alpha, Omicron Delta Kappa. Mason, Rotarian. Club: Lotos, Metropolitan (N.Y.C.). Home: Hartsville, S.C. Died Oct. 3, 1978.

COLBERT, SISTER MARY COLUMKILLE, coll. pres.; b. Ireland, Mar. 12, 1884; d. Michael and Alice (Kenniry) Colbert; A.B., Catholic U. of Am., 1913, A.M., 1914, Ph.D., 1923; student U. Minn., summer, 1927, Columbia U., summer, 1928, U. Mexico, summer, 1944. Tchr. high sch., 1905-11, 14-17; inst. Latin, Incarnate Word Coll., 1917-21, became pres. and prof. classical langs., 1923, chmn. bd. dirs. Mem. Tex. Edn. Commn., 1930-34, Conf. of Catholic Women's Coll., 1931-35. Mem. Am. Philol. Assn., Am. Classical League, Nat. Catholic Ednl. Assn. (com. on reorgn. 1934-36; exec. com. of Coll. and Univ. Dept. 1938-42), Tex. State Tchrs. Assn., Texas Council on Tchr. Edn. Author: The Syntax of the De Civitate Dei of St. Augustine, 1923. Address: San Antonio, Tex. Died Oct. 5, 1976.

COLBURN, JOSEPH BRADLEY, lawyer; b. Washington, Apr. 10, 1902; s. William Edward and Frances (Augusterfer) C.; LL.B., George Washington U., 1924; m. Grace Harris, Feb. 28, 1931; 1 dau., Carolyn Ann. With U.S. Consular Service, London, Eng. 1919-20; admitted to D.C. bar, 1924; with U.S. Tarriff Commn., 1924-28; pvt. practice law, N.Y.C., Washington, from 1929; partner firm Barnes, Richardson & Colburn, N.Y.C., Washington, from 1935; rep. U.S. Customs Ct. in Matter of Spector, 1959. Mem. Am. (chmn. com. customs law), Inter-Am., Internat. bar assns., Assn. Customs Bar (dir.). Home: Port Washington, N.Y. Died Dec. 1980.

COLBY, CARROLL BURLEIGH, author; b. Claremont, N.H., Sept. 7, 1904; s. Melvin Forrest and Stella Adella (Whitcomb) C.; grad. Sch. Practical Art (now Art Inst. Boston), 1925; m. Lila Margaret Thoday, Nov. 29, 1928; children—Susan (Mrs. Robert S. McKanna), Fred Melvin. Free-lance illustrator and author, 1925-37; editor Air Trails and Air Progress mags., 1937-43; aviation editor Popular Sci. Monthly, 1943-46; free-lance writer, author, illustrator, 1946-77; camping editor Outdoor Life mag., 1958-75; lectr. writing books, mil., space, history, conservation, camping, wildlife. Past mem. Briarcliff Manor (N.Y.) Bd. Trustees, also Planning Commn.; past fire commr., also mem. hook and ladder and rescue co.; capt. spl. patrolmen Briarcliff Manor Police Dept. Past pres. Briarcliff Manor Library Bd. Mem. USAF aux., 1942-77, lt. col. Recipient Freedom Found. award, 1973. Mem. Aviation Space Writers Assn. (a founder 1937), Outdoor Writers Assn. Am. (past bd. dirs.), Adventurers Club, Camp Fire Club Am., S.A.R., Company Mil. Historians, Soc. Am. Travel Writers, Arctic Circle Club. Author over 100 published books, including Colby Books for Boys. Home: Briarcliff Manor, N.Y. Died Oct. 31, 1977; buried Claremont, N.H.

COLBY, WILLIAM GEORGE, educator; b. Henry County, Ill., Feb. 4, 1907; s. William Davis and Fannie Jane (Vail) C.; B.S., U. Ill., 1929; M.Sc., Rutgers U., 1932, Ph.D., 1934; m. Dorothy Axford, Oct. 27, 1934; children—Dorothy Louise (Mrs. John B. Hall), William George, Jonathan Axford, Thomas Vail. Agronomist, Soil Erosion Service, 1935-36; research prof. agronomy U. Mass., 1936-50, prof., head dept., 1950-64, research prof. agronomy, dept. plant and soil sci., 1964-74. Fulbright vis. research prof., Japan, 1965. Mem. Am. Soc. Agronomy, Soil Sci. Soc. Am., Sigma Xi. Rotarian. Home: Amherst, Mass. Died Dec. 13, 1975.

COLCLOUGH, OSWALD S., educator; born at Monroeton, Pa., Nov. 19, 1898; son of Rev. William Frederic and Sara Cooper (Guy) C.; B.S., U.S. Naval Acad., 1920; LL.B., George Washington U., 1935, Sc.D., 1961; LL.D., Muhlenberg Coll., 1945, Dickinson Coll. Law, 1958; m. Kathleen Bain, June 1, 1922; children—Eugenia (Mrs. F. A. F. Cooke), Dorothy (Mrs. George Bruns), Sara Kathleen (Mrs. John F. Dolan). Rear admiral in USN; judge adv. gen., 1945-48; vice-adm. USN (ret.); prof. law George Washington U. 1949-64, emeritus, 1965-81, dean law sch., 1949-53, dean of faculties, 1953-64, emeritus, 1964-81, acting dean law sch., 1956-58, acting pres., 1959-61, 64-65, provost, 1961-64; admitted D.C. bar; dir. Hazeltine Corp. Mem. Atomic Energy Labor-Mgmt. Relations Panel, from 1953; v.p., chmn. exec. com. Nat. Capital Downtown Com., from 1959; mem. Nat. Council Urban Affairs, Inc.; trustee Wash. Center Met. Studies, from 1959. Dir. Patent, Trademark and Copyright Research Inst. Decorated Legion Merit with Gold Star, Chevalier Legion Honor, other mil. decorations; recipient Jefferson medal N.J. Patent Law Assn., 1959. Mem. Am., D.C., Fed. bar assns., Maritime Law Assn. U.S., Newcomen Soc., Nat. Security Indsl. Assn. (hon. life), U.S.S. N.C. Battleship Assn., Judge Advs. Assn., Phi Delta Phi, Order of Coif. Clubs: Army and Navy, Army-Navy Country (Washington). Home: Chevy Chase, Md. Died Jan. 26, 1981.

COLCLOUGH, WILLIAM FREDERIC, printing co. exec.; b. Elkland, Pa., July 10, 1905; s. William F. and Sara (Guy) C.; A.B., Lehigh U., 1925; J.D., U. Pa., 1930; m. Olga Fabian, May 17, 1947. Admitted to Pa. bar, 1930, N.Y. bar, 1932; with Sullivan & Cromwell, N.Y.C., 1930-40; asst. to pres. Am. Bank Note Co., N.Y.C., 1940-41, 45-49, sec., 1945-49, v.p., 1949-52, pres., 1952-65, chmn., 1957-70, chief exec. officer, 1952-70. Mem. Town of Hurley (N.Y.) planning Bd. Trustee Lehigh U. Served from pvt. to maj. AUS, 1941-45. Decorated Bronze Star medal. Mem. Phi Beta Kappa, Phi Delta Phi, Theta Delta Chi. Episcopalian. Clubs: University, Lehigh (N.Y.C.). Home: West Hurley, N.Y. Died Sept. 23, 1976.

COLCORD, JOANNA CARVER (KAWL'KUD), social worker; b. at sea, Mar. 18, 1882; d. Capt. Lincoln Alden and Jane French (Sweetser) Colcord; brought to U.S. in 1884; B.S. cum laude, U. of Me., 1906, M.S., 1909, hon. M.A., 1932; certificate, N.Y. Sch. of Social Work, 1911; unmarried. Began as chemist, Agrl. Explt. Sta., Orono, Me., 1906; asst. dist. sec. New York Charity Organization Soc., 1911, supt. of district work, 1914-25; on leave of absence as field rep. Am. Red Cross, to Virgin Islands, 1920-21; general sec. Minneapolis Family Welfare Assn. and lecturer U. of Minn., 1925-29; dir. charity orgn. dept. Russell Sage Foundation, New York, 1929-45. Member adv. council Govt. of Virgin Islands, U.S. Dept. of Interior; pres. Minn. Conf. of Social Work, 1929. Mem. Am. Assn. of Social Workers, Phi Kappa Phi, Phi Beta Kappa, Alpha Omicron Pi. Democrat. Conglist. Co-editor: The Long View, 1930. Author: Broken Homes, 1919; Emergency Work Relief (with Kurtz and Koplowitz), 1932; Cash Relief, 1936; Songs of American Sailormen, 1938; Your Community, 1939; Sea Language Comes Ashores, 1945. Home: Searsport, Me.

COLDWELL, COLBERT, realtor; b. Durango, Colo., Apr. 11, 1883; s. Nathaniel and Ellen (Robinson) C.; student U. Calif., class of 1906; m. Johanna Leaton, Aug. 30, 1905. Realtor, property management, Coldwell Banker & Co., San Francisco, since 1903, also Los Angeles, Oakland, San Mateo; dir. Cal. Packing Co.; adv. dir. Wells Fargo Bank, Dir. San Francisco Real Estate Bd., 1917-22, pres., 1921-22. Trustee Children's Hospital. Director San Francisco Chamber of Commerce, 1921-25, president, 1923-25; dir. Cal. C. of C., 1925-35. Republican. Clubs: Pacific Union, Bohemian, Golf. Home: San Francisco.

COLE, ALPHAEUS PHILEMON, artist; b. Jersey City Heights, N.J., 1876; s. Timothy and Annie (Carter) C.; preparatory education in Italy and France; studied under Benjamin Constant and Jean Paul Laurens at Julian Acad., Paris; Elève des Beaux Arts. Paris; m. Margaret Ward Wamsley, August 15, 1903; m. 2d, Anita Rio Higgins, April 1962. Portrait painter; has painted numerous portraits, including Dr. Jessica Cosgrave, Pres., Finch Junior College, Engraver at Work, water color portrait, Bklyn. Museum, Dr. Alfred B. Butts presented to Univ. Miss. Recipient various awards including: Laymenber's prize Salmagundi Club, 1943; Archer M. Huntington award, Hudson Valley Art Assn., 1956; prize for Oil Allied Artists Am., 1972. N.A.; pres. N.Y. Water Color Club, 1931-41, when club merged with Am. Water Color Soc.; mem. Grand Central Art Gallery Assn., Allied Artists Am. (pres. 1952-53; hon.), N.A.D. (council), Old Lyme Art Assn. Clubs: Nat. Arts, Salmagundi. Author: Timothy Cole, Wood Engraver (with Margaret Ward Cole), 1936. Home: New York City NY also Ole Lyme CT. *

COLE, ARTHUR CHARLES, prof. Am. history; b. Ann Arbor, Mich., Apr. 22, 1886; s. Harry Loomis and Pauline (Kuster) C.; B.A., U. of Mich., 1907, M.A., 1908; Ph.D., U. of Pa., 1911; m. Ethel Sleight, 1907 (dec.); children—Arthur C., Beth Elaine. Asst. in Am. history, U. of Mich., 1907-08; instr. Shortridge High Sch., Indianapolis, 1908-09; Harrison fellow in history, U. of Pa., 1909-11; Harrison sr. fellow for research, same univ., 1911-12; instr. history, 1912-15, asso., 1915-17, asst. prof., 1917-20, U. of Ill.; prof. Am. history, Ohio State U., 1920-30; prof. history, Western Reserve, 1930-44, chmn. div. history, 1931-44, prof. history, Brooklyn Coll., 1944-56, prof. emeritus, 1956-76, chmn. dept., 1950-56; vis. prof. history, U. of Wis., 1928-29, Columbia U., 1941, 1948-49. Associate editor of American Hist. Review, 1928-34; mng. editor Miss. Valley Hist. Review, 1930-40. Fellow Soc. American Historians. Member American Historical Association (Justin Winsor prize, 1912), Mississippi Valley Historical Assn. (pres., 1941-42), Econ. History Assn., Phi Beta Kappa. Author several books on Am. history. Editor: Constitutional Debates of 1847 (Vol. XIV, Collections of Ill. State Hist. Library), 1919; also many hist. articles. Chmn. academic freedom Com. Am. Civil Liberties Union, 1950-54. Home: Naples, Fla. Died Feb. 26, 1976.

COLE, CHARLES WOOLSEY, author; b. Montclair, N.J., Feb 8, 1906; s. Charles Buckingham and Bertha Woolsey (Dwight) C.; A.B., Amherst Coll., 1927, L.H.D., 1942, LL.D., 1960; A.M., Columbia, 1928, Ph.D., 1931, LL.D., 1954; LL.D. Wagner Coll., 1946, Wesleyan U., 1946, Williams Coll., 1946, Doshisha U., 1953, Emerson Coll., 1964; Litt.D., Hamilton Coll., 1948; Sc.D., Clarkson Coll., 1948; L.H.D., U. Mass., 1951, Trinity Coll., 1953; LL.D., Am. Internat. Coll., 1952; m. Katharine Bush Salmon, Aug. 29, 1928 (dec. 1972); children—Elizabeth (Mrs. Hugh M. Hamill, Jr.), Katharine (Mrs. John C. Esty, Jr.); m. 2d, Marie Greer Donahoe, May 15, 1974. Instr. history Columbia 1929-35; travelling fellow Social Sci. Research Council Paris, 1932-33; asso. prof. econs. Amherst Coll., 1935-37. George D. Olds prof. econs., 1937-40; vis. lectr. econs. Yale, 1938-39; prof. history, Columbia, 1940-46; pres. Amherst Coll., 1946-60, pres. emeritus, 1960-78; v.p. Rockefeller Found., 1960-61; U.S. ambassador to Chile, 1961-64; editor Macmillan Career Books. Chief Service Trades Br. Retail Trade, services div., OPA, 1942, regional price exec., N.Y. region, 1942-43; mem. teaching staff, Navy Sch. Mil. Govt. and Adminstrn., Columbia, 1943-44; lectr. Army Sch. Mil. Govt., Charlottesville, Va., 1943-44; mem. faculty Manhattan Sch. Music, 1944-46. Mem. Nat. security orgn. com. of Commn. on Orgn. of Exec. Br. Govt., 1948; selective service sci. adv. com., 1948-51. Trustee Charles E. Merrill Trust. Decorated grand cross Order of Merit (Chile); grand officer Order of Morazán (Honduras). Mem. Am. Acad. Arts and Scis., Am. Hist. Assn. (council 1947-50), Council Fgn. Relations, Phi Beta Kappa, Delta Kappa Epsilon, Delta Sigma Rho. Conglist. Clubs: Century, Anglers (N.Y.C.); Seattle Golf, University (Seattle). Author: French Mercantilist Doctrines Before Colbert, 1931; Colbert and a Century of French Mercantilism, 2 vols., 1939, 64; Economic History of Europe (with S.B. Clough), 1941, French Mercantilism, 1683-1700, 1943; History of Europe (with C. J. H. Hayes and M. Baldwin), 1949; (with C.J.H. Hayes and M. Baldwin) History of Western Civilization, 1962-67; (with S.P. McCutchen and H.W. Bragdon) A Free People, The United States in the Formative Years, 1970, A Free People, The United States in the Twentieth Century, 1970; History of a Free People, 1973. Home: Seattle, Wash. Died Feb. 6, 1978; buried Wildwood Cemetery, Amherst, Mass.

COLE, DAVID L., lawyer; b. Paterson, N.J., May 1, 1902; s. Nathan and Ethel (Feldman) C.; B.S., Harvard, 1921, LL.B., 1924; LL.D., Fairleigh Dickinson U., 1964; m. Helen M. David, Oct. 8, 1925; children—Elizabeth, Morrill J., Charles T. Admitted to N.Y. bar, 1925, N.J. bar, 1926, practiced in Paterson, 1926-78; mem. firm Cole, Berman & Garth, 1932-78; mem. city counsel Paterson, 1952. Active in labor relations as counsel for employer groups in textile industry 1926-42; dir., counsel Comml. Nat. Bank, 2d Nat. Bank, Paterson, 1937-49. Chmn., N.J. State Bd. Mediation, pub. mem. 2d region War Labor Bd., 1943-45, chmn. steel and iron ore panels, 1943; chmn. No. Textile Commn., 1945-46; impartial chmn. numerous labor contracts; chmn. presdl. bd. inquiry Bituminous Coal Industry, 1948, 50, Longshore Industry, 1953, 68; mem. or chmn. Pres.'s Emergency Bd. on dispute between r.r.'s and 16 unions representing non-operating employees, 1948, 52, Ry. Express Co., 1949, Am. Airlines Pilots, 1951, Eastern Air Lines pilots and flight engrs., 1958; gov. Nat. Acad. Arbitrators, 1948-52, pres. 1951-52, chmn. conciliation panel N.Y.C. Transit, 1961-65, transit fact finding bd., 1950, 57, N.J. Gov.'s pub. service electric cases; mem. Pres.'s Steel Industry Bd., 1949; dir. Fed. Mediation and Conciliation Service, 1952-53; chmn. N.J. Gov.'s Com. on Pub. Utility Strike Legislation, 1954; chmn., sec. labor's adv. com. on atomic energy, 1955-78; cons. ILO,

Geneva, 1955, 56, 64; mem. Pres.'s Labor-Mgmt. Adv. Com., 1961-65, N.Y. Gov.'s Com. Pub. Employee Relations, 1966-68; chmn. Pres.'s Commn. Indsl. Peace, 1973-74; N.Y.C. Mayor's rep. newspaper labor dispute, 1966; pub. mem. Kaiser Steel Long-Range Com.; vis. prof. Cornell U., 1954-55; Kestenbaum lectr. Harvard, 1962. Trustee Carnegie Endowment for Internat. Peace; pres., bd. dirs. Shapiro Found. Recipient N.J. award Nat. Conf. Christians and Jews, 1954; medal Commonwealth of Pa. 1956. Mem. Am. Arbitration Assn. (medal 1955, dir.). Jewish religion. Clubs: Harvard (N.Y.C.); Preakness Hills Country (pres., trustee 1937-42). Author: The Quest for Industrial Peace, 1963. Home: Paterson, N.J. Died Jan. 25, 1978.

COLE, EDWARD N., automobile mfg. co. exec.; b. Marne, Mich., Sept. 17, 1909; s. Franklin Benjamin and Lucy Catherine (Blasen) C.; student Grand Rapids Jr. Coll., 1927-29; B.S., Gen. Motors Inst., Flint, Mich., 1933; D.Eng., Lawrence Inst. Tech.; D.Sc., Wayne State U.; D.Engring., Mich. State U., U. Mich., Widener Coll.; LL.D., Akron U., Eastern Mich. U.; Dr. Pub. Service, Detroit Inst. Tech., 1973; m. Dollie Ann McVey, Dec. 11, 1964; children—Anne Murray, Robert Michael Joseph, Edward N.; children by previous marriage—David, Martha. With Gen. Motors Corp., Detroit, 1933-77, beginning as lab. asst. Cadillac Motor Car div., successively lab. technician, technician and designer, engr., chief design engr., ordnance equipment, asst. chief engr., chief engr., works mgr., plant mgr. Cadillac-Cleve. Tank plant, chief engr. and gen. mgr. Chevrolet Motor div., Detroit, group v.p. charge Car and Truck divs. Gen. Motors, then exec. v.p. corp. charge operations staff, 1965-67, pres., chief operating officer, 1967-74, ret., 1974, past mem. 6 policy groups, also chmn. exec. and adminstrn. coms.; chmn. Internat. Husky, Inc., Bloomfield Hills, Mich., 1974-77; dir. Consumers Power Co., Rocket Research Corp., Bank Commonwealth, Am. Seating Co. Dir., past pres. Detroit Area council Boy Scouts Am.; pres. bd. dirs., chmn. Detroit United Found.; trustee Mich. Heart Assn., Detroit Grace Hosp., Detroit Inst. Tech., Siena Heights Coll., Mayo Found., Environ. Research Inst. Mich.; gov. United Way Am.; chmn. Gen. Motors Inst., 1962-65. Mem. Soc. Automotive Engrs., Nat. Indusl. Pollution Control Council, Nat. Acad. Engring. (treas.), Am. Soc. Metals (distinguished life mem.), Engring. Soc. Detroit, Am. Def. Preparedness Assn., Greater Detroit Bd. Commerce, Motor Vehicle Mfrs. Assn. U.S. (vice chmn.), Sigma Xi, Tau Beta Pi, Pi Tau Sigma, Delta Sigma Pi. Clubs: Detroit Athletic, Recess, Economic (Detroit); Bloomfield Hills (Mich.). Died May 2, 1977.

COLE, HAROLD HARRISON, educator; b. Waterloo, Wis., Feb. 11, 1897; s. Clarence E. and Hattie (White) C.; B.S., U. Wis., 1920; M.S., U. Calif. at Davis, 1925; Ph.D., U. Minn., 1928; LL.D., U. Calif., 1965; m. Jessie I. Cliff, May 1, 1929 (dec. 1952); 1 son, Cliff H.; m. 2d, Cynthia Clegg, Mar. 2, 1955; 1 dau., Nancy. Asst. prof. animal husbandry U. Calif. at Davis, 1928-43, prof., 1943-78, chmn. dept., 1952-60, faculty research lectr., 1943. Chmn. subcom. bloat Com. Animal Health, 1944-54; com. on beef NRC, 1959-60; range land utilization adv. com. Calif. Bd. Forestry. Recipient Morrison award Am. Soc. Animal Prodn., 1952. Mem. Am. Assn. Anatomists, Soc. Exptl. Biology and Medicine, Endocrine Soc., Am. Dairy Sci. Assn., Am. Soc. Animal Prodn. (asso. editor Jour. 1943-45), A.A.A.S., Am. Soc. Animal Sci. (subcom. on use hormones in livestock prodn. 1972-76, Animal Physiology and Endocrinology award 1963), Soc. Study Reprodn. (editor Biology of Reprodn. 1968-70, Carl G. Hartman award 1974), Sigma Xi. Club: Commonwealth (San Francisco). Co-editor: Reproduction in Domestic Animals, 2 vols., 1959, 68; Animal Agriculture, 1974; editor: Introduction to Livestock Production, Including Dairy and Poultry, 1962, 66; Gonadotropins: Their Biological and Chemical Properties and Secretory Control. Contbr. articles to profl. jours. Home: Davis, Calif. Died May 28, 1978.

COLE, HAROLD NEWTON, dermatologist; b. Shingle House, Pa., Feb. 28, 1884; s. Charles Henry and Jessie Adelaide (Newton) C.; Ph.B., Bucknell U., Lewisburg, Pa., 1906, hon. Sc.D., 1918; M.D., Western Res. U., 1909; m. Hazel Louise Knapp, Aug. 21, 1914; children—Dorothy Cornelia, Barbara Ann, Harold Newton. In practice of dermatology and syphilology since 1912; demonstrator in dermatology and syphilology, Western Reserve U., 1912-14, instr. dermatology, 1914-16, asso., 1916-18, asst. prof., 1918-21, asso prof., 1921-26, asso. clin. prof., 1926-36, clin. prof. since 1936. Acting surgeon with U.S.P.H.S. in charge of work against venereal diseases in Ohio, 1917-19; ex-mem. surgeon general's Adv. Com. on Syphilis since 1922. Ex-mem. Am. Bd. Dermatology and Syphilology; mem. A.M.A. (sec. sect. dermatology and syphilology 1920-22, chmn. 1923; ex-mem. council pharmacy and chemistry), Am. Dermatol. Assn. (pres. 1933-34), Deutsche Dermatologischen Gesellschaft, Am. Radium Soc., Central States Dermatol. Soc., Cleveland Dermatol. Soc., Phi Beta Kappa, Alpha Omega Alpha, Sigma Xi, Nu Sigma Nu, Sigma Chi; corr. mem. Danish Dermatol. Soc., Associacion Argentina de Dermatologia Y Sifilologia, Societas Dermatologica Hungarica, Sociedade Brasileria de Dermatologica e Sifilografia. The British Assn. of Dermatology and Syphilology. Republican. Baptist. Mason (32 deg.). Clubs: Rowfant, The Shaker Heights Country. Contbr. articles on dermatology and syphilology. Mem. editorial bd. Archives of Dermatology and Syphilology. Home: Shaker Heights.

COLE, PATIENCE BEVIER, writer; b. Nicollet, Minn., Feb. 13, 1883; d. Samuel A. and Ida M. (Harkins) Bevier; B.Litt., Ohio Wesleyan U., 1904; studied U. of Kan., 1 term, 1905; m. Robert J. Cole, of New York, June 1, 1907; children—Edward Clay, Calvert Hubbard. Contbr. short stories to mags. Author: Dave's Daughter, 1913. Editor woman's page, New York Sun, 1916-20; advertising, Realart Pictures Corpn., 1920-22, v.p. Advertisers' Service Corpn., 1923-24, Phoebe Cole Publicity Bureau, 1924-29; staff New York World since 1929. Home: Forest Hills, L.I.

COLE, ROBERT FRANKLIN, ret. govt. ofcl., author; b. Kaufman, Tex., Dec. 16, 1883; s. William Dale and Flora Tennessee (Corley) C.; student LaSalle U., Chgo., 1920-22; m. Dorothy Vera Shatel, July 16, 1914; 1 dau., Sara Jane. Miner, Ariz., Nev., 1900-04; locomotive fireman, engr., S.P. Co., Sparks, Nev., 1904-17; mem. Nev. Indsl. Commn., ex-officio labor commnr. 1917-20; dir. Nev. State Employment Service, 1920-26; chief div. adminstrn. U.S. Bd. Mediation, 1926-34, field mediator, 1934-37, 49-55, exec. sec., 1937-48, ret. 1955. Dir. Shenandoah Corp., Miami, 1955—. Del. nat. conv., Brotherhood Locomotive Fireman and Enginemen, Washington, 1908, St. Paul, 1910, Denver, 1913. Mem. Dist. Bd., Nev. Selective Service, World War I. Mem. inaugural com. for receptions govs., distinguished guests, inauguration Pres. Hoover, 1929, Pres. Roosevelt, 1933. Hon. del. Nev. Pacific Coast Conf., League of Nations promotion, 1919. Mem. Nev. Dem. State Central Com., 1916-18. Recipient testimonials from Pres. Wilson, Gov. Boyle of Nev., Pres. Eisenhower. Certificate of Merit, Inst. Am. Genealogy; Nat. Mediation Bd., 1955; resolution Nev. State Assembly, 1955. Mem. Sons. Confederate Vets., S.A.R., Va., Pa., St. Augustine (Fla.) hist. socs., Inst. Am. Genealogy, Washington Philatelic Soc., Nat. Geographic Soc., Nat. Assn. Retired Civil Service Employees, Retired Railroad Employees. Democrat. Methodist. Club: Texas (Washington). Author: Richard Cole, 1805-1892, 1941; Ten and Twenty Poems, 1955. Address: Miami, Fla.

COLE, WILLIAM R., (COZY COLE), musician; b. East Orange, N.J., Oct. 17, 1909; s. Reuben and Carrie (Johnson) C.; student Wilberforce U., 1927-30, Juilliard Conservatory Music, 1941; m. Evalena Kiggins, July 18, 1951. With Benny Carter Orchestra, 1934-37, Cab Calloway Orchestra, 1939-42, Raymond Scott Orchestra, 1942-44; actor stage play Carmen Jones, 1944-47; with Benny Goodman's Band, 1945-47, Louis Armstrong, 1949-52; sec., v.p. Gene Krupa and Cozy Cole Music Sch., Inc., N.Y.C. Recipient citation of merit Muscular Dystrophy Assn. Am., Inc., 1956. Mem. Nat. Jazz Frat. (dir.). Mason. Home: Bronx, N.Y. Died Jan. 29, 1981.

COLEAN, MILES LANIER, cons. economist; b. Peoria, Ill., Aug. 4, 1898; s. William Henry and Frances (Putman) C.; student U. Wis., 1916-17; B. Arch., Columbia, 1922; m. Marion Feltman, Jan. 21, 1925; 1 dau., Mary Katherine (Mrs. E.D. Etherington). Asso. with R.H. Dana, architect, N.Y.C., 1922-24, Holabird & Root, Chgo., 1925-29; mem. Cowles, Colean, Architects, Chgo., 1929-34; tech. dir. FHA, 1934-37, asst. administr., 1937-40; dir. housing survey Twentieth Century Fund, 1940-42; v.p. Starrett Bros. & Eken, Inc., 1942-44; cons. constrn., finance, from 1944; chmn. Investors Central Mgmt. Corp., 1956-75, hon. chmn., 1975-80; econ. adviser Mortgage Bankers Assn. Am., from 1945; adviser Central Mortgage & Housing Corp. Can., 1945-55; dir. Walker & Dunlop, Inc. Chmn., Am. delegation 16th Internat. Congress on Planning and Housing, Mexico City, 1938; mem. Central Housing Com., 1936-40; cons. Adv. Com. on Nat. Def., 1940, Nat. Resources Planning Bd., 1942; bd. govs. Nat. Assn. Housing Ofcls., 1934-42; adviser on housing Senate and House Postwar Policy and Planning Coms., 1944-46; mem. bus. research adv. com. U.S. Bur. Labor Statistics, 1947-60, chmn., 1953-54; mem. Adminstrn. Bd. Urban Land Use and Housing Studies of Columbia, 1947-49; mem. adv. com. U.S. Bur. Budget, U.S. Census on constrn., housing statistics, 1949-50; mem. Pres.'s Com. on Housing Policies and Programs, 1953; mem. bldg. research adv. bd. NRC, 1950-57; staff Nat. Bur. Econ. Research, 1947-50; chmn. adv. com. housing inventory Bur. Census, 1956; chmn. adv. com. for 1960 housing census Bur. Census, Dept. Commerce; chmn. adv. com. on constrn. statistics Bur. Census, 1960-68; chmn. Pres.'s Task Force on Urban Renewal, 1969-70. Trustee Fed. City Council, 1954—. Recipient Columbia U. medal, 1943. Fellow A.I.A., A.A.A.S., Am. Statis. Soc.; mem. Nat. Assn. Bus. Economists, Conf. Bus. Economists (chmn. 1960). Episcopalian (warden, vestryman). Clubs: Metropolitan, Chevy Chase, Cosmos (Washington). Author: Can America Build Houses?, 1938; Housing for Defense, 1940; The Role of the Housebuilding Industry, 1942; American Housing: Problems and Prospects, 1944; Stabilizing the Construction Industry, 1945; Impact of Government on Real Estate Finance in the United States, 1950; (with Robinson Newcomb) Stabilizing Construction: The Record and Potential, 1952; Renewing Our Cities, 1953; Mortgage Companies and Their Place in the Financial Structure, 1962; (with R.J. Saulnier) The Federal Land Bank System and the Real Estate Lending Activities of the Farmers Home Administration, 1962; A Backward Glance, An Oral History: The Growth of Government Housing Policy in the United States, 1934-75. Editorial adviser Architectural Forum, House and Home mags., 1944-64, House Beautiful mag., 1944-68; contbg. editor Savs. Bank Jour., 1959-61. Contbr. to periodicals. Home: Washington, D.C. Died Sept. 16, 1980.

COLEFAX, PETER, bus. cons.; b. London, Eng., Mar. 22, 1903; s. Arthur and Sibyl (Halsey) C.; student Eton Coll., 1916-20; B.A., M.A., Oxford, 1921-24; m. Elda Garbe Cook, Aug. 23, 1957; 1 son (by previous marriage), Michael; stepchildren—Barbara (Mrs. Willard E. Fay), Penny (Mrs. William J. Gemar). Came to U.S., 1924, naturalized. With N.Y. Times, 1924-25, Edward B. Smith & Co. (now Smith, Barney & Co.), N.Y.C., 1925-29; Am. rep. Guinness Mahon & Co., London, Eng., 1929-32; with Cyrus J. Lawrence & Sons, N.Y.C., 1932-34; with Am. Potash & Chem. Corp., N.Y.C., 1934-45, Los Angeles, 1945-69, dir., 1935-69, sec.-treas., 1935-41, v.p., sec.-treas., 1941-44, v.p., sec., 1944-45, exec. v.p., sec., 1945-46, exec. v.p., 1946-47, pres., 1947-63, chmn., 1960-68, chief exec. officer, 1963-68; cons.; dir. Kerr-McGee Corp.; adv. dir. Security Pacific Nat. Bank; dir. New Perspective Fund, Inc., Investment Co. Am. Trustee Santa Barbara Mus. Art. Clubs: California (Los Angeles); Birnam Wood (Montecito). Home: Montecito, Calif. Died Mar. 3, 1979.

COLEGROVE, KENNETH WALLACE, educator; b. Waukon, Ia., Oct. 8, 1886; s. Chauncey Peter and Winifred Della (Mack) C.; diploma Ia. State Tchrs. Coll., 1905; A.B., State U. Ia., 1909; Ph.D., Harvard, 1915; Litt.D. (hon.), Columbia, 1945; m. Louise Burrows Funkhauser, Jan. 5, 1923; 1 dau., Marian Louise (Mrs. John H. Blankenship); m. 2d, Gladys Marie Chadsey St. John. Lectr. history Mt. Holyoke Coll., 1913-16; asst. prof. European history Syracuse (N.Y.) U., 1916-19; asso. prof. polit. sci. Northwestern U., 1919-26, prof., 1926-52; prof. polit. sci. Queens Coll., 1953-54; editor-in-chief Inst. Fiscal and Polit. Edn., N.Y.C., 1954-58; prof. history and polit. sci. C.W. Post Coll., L.I. U., 1959-69; sr. research asso. Center for Study of the Presidency, N.Y.C., from 1970. Mem. Bd. Personnel Examiners, U.S. Dept. Labor, 1933; chmn. Evanston chpt. Com. to Defend Am. by Aiding the Allies, 1940-41; cons. OSS, Washington, 1943-45; polit. cons. Gen. MacArthur Hdqrs., Tokyo, Japan, 1946. Trustee, Upper Iowa U. Mem. Am. Soc. Internat. Law, Am. Council Learned Socs. (del. 1952-55), Am. Hist. Assn., Am. Polit. Sci. Assn. (sec.-treas. 1935-47), Alpha Pi Zeta. Methodist. Clubs: Faculty House, Columbia University (N.Y.C.); University (Evanston). Author several books including: International Control of Aviation, 1929; Militarism in Japan, 1936; The American Senate and World Peace, 1944; Democracy versus Communism, 1957; (with Hall Bartlett) The Menace of Communism, 1962. Editor European Economic and Political Survey (Paris), 1929. Contbr. articles to profl. jours. Home: N.Y.C. Died Jan. 3, 1975.

COLEMAN, BERTRAM, investment banker; b. Phila., 1920; ed. Yale, 1942. Co-chmn. exec. com., dir. Drexel-Harriman-Ripley, Inc.; dir. B.V.D. Co., Wyomissing Corp., Western Sav. Bank, Abitibi Paper Co., Ltd., Susan Thomas, Inc., Rockowan Bros.; trustee Greenfield Real Estate Investment Trust. Home: Bryn Mawr, Pa. Died Oct. 28, 1976.

COLEMAN, ELLIOTT, author, educator; b. Binghamton, N.Y., Sept. 26, 1906; s. Benjamin Archibald and Jennie (Galbraith) C.; B.A., Wheaton (Ill.) Coll., 1928; postgrad. Princeton Theol. Sem., 1933; diaconate Gen. Theol. Sem., N.Y.C., 1941. Master, Asheville (N.C.) Sch., 1928-32, 34-40; with Henry Holt & Co., 1942-43, Doubleday & Co., 1944-45; faculty Johns Hopkins, from 1945, prof. English writing, from 1960, dir. writing seminars, from 1946. Hon. mem. Phi Beta Kappa. Author: (poems) An American in Augustland, 1940, A Glass Darkly, 1952, 33 Night Sonnets, 1955, Mockingbirds at Fort McHenry, 1963, Broken Death, 1964, Rose Demonics: 1936-66, 1967; The Oxford Poems of Elliott Coleman, 1977; (prose) The Golden Angel: Papers on Proust, 1954. Translator: (Georges Poulet) Studies in Human Time, 1956-59, Proustian Space, 1977. Editor: Poems of Byron, Keats and Shelley, 1968; One Hundred Poems, 1972; (poems) The Tangerine Birds, 1973; In the Canyon, 1974. Home: Baltimore, Md. Died Feb. 22, 1980.

COLEMAN, J. T., clergyman; b. Anna, Ill., Aug. 27, 1883; s. James Marshall and Arminda (Hatley) C.; ed. Carbondale (Ill.) State Teachers College, Valparaiso (Ind.) U., U. of Ill. and Vanderbilt U.; m. Ida Underwood, of Goreville, Ill., Apr. 25, 1909; children—Agatha, Reba, Helen. Ordained ministry Cumberland Presbyn. Ch., 1908; now pastor First Ch. Nashville, Tenn.; built chs. at each of five charges. Republican. Mason, Odd Fellow, Woodman. Address: 9th and McGavock Sts., Nashville, Tenn.

COLEMAN, JOHN A., stock broker, civic worker; b. N.Y.C., Dec. 24, 1901; s. John A. and Nora (O'Connor) C.; student Holy Trinity Sch., 1907-15; LL.D., Manhattan Coll., Niagara U., St. Anselm's Coll., Notre Dame U., Fordham U., Manhattanville Coll., Marymount Coll., Syracuse (N.Y.) U.; D.C.S., Holy Cross; Ph.D. in Bus. Adminstrn., Providence Coll.; m. Ann Meehan, June 7, 1930; children—John A., Thomas, Mary Ann (Mrs. Harry C. Hagerty, Jr.). Floor page N.Y. Stock Exchange, 1916; mem. N.Y. Curb Exchange, 1923-24; mem. N.Y. Stock Exchange, 1924-77, gov. 1938-43, 48-77, vice chmn. bd., 1941-43, chmn., 1943-47; partner Adler, Coleman & Co.; dir. Chrysler Corp., Mfrs. Hanover Trust Co., East River Savs. Bank, N.Y. Telephone Co; chmn. exec. com. Am. Broadcasting-Paramount Theatres; dir. Gen. Aniline & Film Corp. Pres. bd. N.Y. Foundling Hosp.; trustee Cath. U. Am., Washington, Altman Found., Alfred E. Smith Meml. Found. Exec. Chmn. Cardinal's Com. of Laity. Trustee Cath. Charities, Inc. Decorated knight St. Gregory the Great; knight of the Order of Malta (pres.-master); Grand Cross Equestrian Order Holy Sepulchure; recipient Cath. Action medal St. Bonaventure's Coll., Saint Vincent de Paul, St. John's U., Bklyn.; Brotherhood award Nat. Conf. Christians and Jews, Papal Chamberlain, 1957. Mem. Friendly Sons of St. Patrick (past pres.). Clubs: Athletic, Manhattan (N.Y.C.); Bathing and Tennis, Spring Lake (N.J.) Golf and Country. Home: New York, N.Y. Died Feb. 23, 1977.

COLEMAN, RALPH PALLEN, JR., editor, pub., financial exec.; b. Chestnut Hill, Pa., May 26, 1923; s. Ralph Pallen and Florence (Haeberle) C.; A.B., U. Pa., 1946, M.B.A., 1948; m. Jean Louise Kilpatrick, Sept. 10, 1949; children—Ralph Pallen III, Richard Carleton. Editor indsl. publs., 1943-69; founder, editor, pub. Over-The-Counter Securities Rev., 1951-80, Listed Securities Jour., 1961-70; editor, pub. Over-The-Counter Securities Handbook, 1954-72; Over-The-Counter Spl. Reports, 1958-80, Over-The-Counter Newsletter, 1963-80, New Issues, 1968-72, Over-The-Counter Directory, 1979. Founder, pres., treas., dir. Over-The-Counter Securities Fund, Inc., 1955-80; pres. Rev. Pub. Co., 1951-80; pres., treas., dir. Rev. Mgmt. Corp., 1955-80. Founder Pa. Hall of Fame, 1971, pres., 1971-80. Served with USCGR, 1944-45. Mem. Nat. Assn. Over-The-Counter Cos. (founder, exec. dir. 1973-80), Huguenot Soc. Pa. Republican. Presbyn. Home: Jenkintown, Pa. Died Oct. 28, 1980; buried George Washington Meml. Perk, Plymouth Meeting, Pa.

COLEMAN, ROWLAND HENRY, arms mfg. ofcl.; b. Mystic, Conn., June 7, 1909; s. William Harold and Edna (Wilcox) C.; A.B., Bucknell U., Lewisburg, Pa., 1929, L.L.D., 1965; m. Esther Keim, May 31, 1930; children—Rowland Henry, William Harold II. Div. advt. mgr. E. I. duPont de Nemours & Co., Wilmington, Del., 1929-37; advt. mgr. Remington Arms Co., Inc., Bridgeport, 1937-41, dir. sales promotion div., 1941-44, asst. dir. sales, 1944-49, dir. sales, 1949-51, v.p., dir. sales 1951-54, v.p., asst. gen. mgr., 1954-63, pres., gen. mgr., 1963-74, dir., 1963-76; hon. dir. Conn. Nat. Bank; trustee, mem. exec. com. People's Savs. Bank. Chmn. bd. trustees Bucknell U.; trustee Bridgeport Hosp., N. Am. Wildlife Found. Mem. Am. Ordnance Assn. (past v.p., dir.), Am. Hardware Mfrs. Assn. (past pres.), Wildlife Mgmt. Inst., Nat. Rifle Assn. (patron), Ducks Unltd., Field Trial Gunners Guild, Nat. Skeet Shooting Assn., Amateur Trap Shooting Assn., Sigma Alpha Epsilon, Tau Kappa Alpha. Republican. Conglist. Mason. (32 deg., Shriner). Clubs: Pequot Yacht; Aubichwi Gun, Brooklawn Country, Fairfield Country, Aspetuck Fish and Game (Fairfield); Ekwanok Country (Manchester, Vt.); Ocean Reef, Cara Sound Country (North Key Largo, Fla); Yacht, (N.Y.C.). Home: Fairfield, Conn. Died July 15, 1976; buried Oaklawn Cemetery, Fairfield, Conn.

COLEMAN, SYLVAN CLARENCE, financial exec.; b. San Francisco, Aug. 29, 1905; s. William W. and Rose (Loewy) C.; B.S., U. Calif., 1926; M.B.A., Harvard, 1928; m. Louise MacNamara, Oct. 17, 1941. With E.F. Hutton & Co., N.Y.C., 1928—, mgr. research div., 1931-35, mgr. fgn. dept., 1935-38, gen. partner, 1938-62, chmn., chief exec. officer E.F. Hutton & Co. Inc., 1962-70, cons., 1970-81; dir. Am. Internat. Group, Inc., Petroleum & Resources Corp., Continental Telephone Corp., Scudder Duo-Vest, Inc., Scudder Duo-Vest Exchange Fund, Inc. Mem. Navy Dept. and War Dept. Price Adjustment Bd. office undersec. USN, Washington, 1942-45. Chmn. E.F. Hutton Found.; bd. dirs. Fountain House Inc., Manhattan Eye, Ear and Throat Hosp., Am. Cancer Soc.; bd. dels. U. Calif. at Berkeley Found.; hon. trustee Am. Mus. Natural History. Mem. Beta Gamma Sigma (chmn. dirs. table). Republican. Clubs: Univ., Deepdale Golf. Home: New York, N.Y. Died Apr. 15, 1981.

COLEMAN, WILLIAM CARLTON, mfg. and transp. exec.; b. McEwen, Tenn., Sept. 4, 1898; s. William H. and Donna (Daniel) C.; B.S., Southwestern U., Georgetown, Tex., 1919; student U. Tex.; m. Elizabeth Murphy, Oct. 25, 1922; children—William Carlton, James Wilburn, Joan Elizabeth (Mrs. Cushman S. Radebaugh, Jr.), Richard Thomas. Prof. history and English, MacFarren Jr. Coll., Martin, Tenn., 1920-21; salesman So. Coal Co., Memphis, 1921-24; sales mgr. Randall Fuel Co., Atlanta, 1925-29; dist. mgr. Koppers Coal Co., Atlanta, 1929-35, Cin. div., 1936-41; dist. mgr. Northwestern div. Koppers Eastern Gas & Fuel Assn., Chgo., 1941-53; v.p., dir. Milw. & Suburban Transp. Co., 1953-76, Indpls. Transit System, Inc.; pres., dir. Mid Empire Corp., 1953-76; dir. Monon Coal Co., Chgo. & Indpls. Coal Co., Inc., Monon Realty Co.; dir., exec. com. Monon R.R.; dir. Can. Javelin Ltd., Gateway Industries, Inc., Midland Transp. Corp., Louisville Transit Co. Served as aviator USN, World War I. Home: Milwaukee, Wis. Died July 15, 1976.

COLEMAN, WILLIAM SMITH, army officer; b. Iva, S.C., Jan. 29, 1919; s. Clifford Dean and Leon (Smith) C.; B.S., Clemson (S.C.) Coll., 1939; postgrad. Command and Gen. Staff Coll., 1951-52, Army War Coll., 1959-60; M.A., George Washington U., 1966; m. Ruth Ducworth, Dec. 19, 1942; children—Susan C. (Mrs. David A. Fedor), Nancy C. (Mrs. Robert H. Hart), William Smith, Mary L. Commd. 2d lt. U.S. Army, 1942, advanced through grades to maj. gen., 1970; S-3 and exec. officer 1st Bn. 8th Cav. Regt., 1949-50, S-3 and exec. officer 8th Cav. Regt., 1950; comdg. officer 2d Bn., 8th Cav. Regt., 1950-51; instr. tactical dept. Inf. Sch., 1952-55; sr. Army adviser Alaska N.G., 1955-57; mem. Joint Secretariat, Office Joint Chiefs of Staff, 1957-59; staff officer Plans Div., Joint Staff, CINCPAC, 1960-63; comdg. officer 2d Brigade, 1st Armored Div., 1963-64, chief of staff 1st Armored Div., 1964-65; staff officer Inst. Advanced Studies, Army Combat Devels. Command, 1965-66; dir. course I and internat. relations studies, faculty Army War Coll., Carlisle Barracks, Pa., 1966-67; asst. div. comdr. 1st Inf. Div. U.S. Army, Vietnam, 1967-68; dep. asst. chief of staff, J-3, U.S. Army Vietnam and RF/PF, USMACV, 1968, asst. div. comdr. 1st Inf. Div., U.S. Army, Vietnam, 1968; dep. comdg. gen., Ft. Jackson, S.C., 1969-70, comdg. gen., 1970-72; chief Army adv. group, Vietnam, 1972-73; comdr. Army Readiness Region VI, 1973-74; ret., 1974. Decorated D.S.M. with oak leaf cluster, Silver Star medal with 3 oak leaf clusters, Legion of Merit with oak leaf cluster, D.F.C. with oak leaf cluster, Bronze Star medal with V device, Air medal with 38 oak leaf clusters with V device, Joint Service Commendation medal, Army Commendation medal with 3 oak leaf clusters, Combat Inf. badge; Order Brit. Empire; Vie tnamese Cross of Gallantry with palm, Republic of Vietnam Armed Forces Honor medal 1st Class. Mem. Greater Columbia C. of C. (dir.), Assn. U.S. Army, Mil. Order World Wars. Mason. Home: Columbia, S.C. Died July 25, 1977.

COLES, ALBERT LEONARD, lawyer; b. Bridgeport, Conn., Nov. 8, 1909; s. Joseph and Margaret (Lennon) C.; B.A., Yale, 1931, LL.B., 1933; m. Eileen M. Pelath, 1946; children—Kevin A., Matthew A., Brigid M., Albert L., Mary Norah. Admitted to Conn. bar, 1933, also the U.S. Dist. Ct., Ct. Appeals, U.S. Supreme Ct.; practice of law, Bridgeport, 1933-78; mem. Coles, O'Connell, Dolan and McDonald, 1942-78; pros. atty. city ct. Bridgeport, 1941-43, judge, 1945-47, 49-51; atty. gen. Conn., 1959-63; judge Conn. Superior Ct., 1963-65. Dir. United Illuminating Co., So. New Eng. Telephone Co.; Corporator, trustee People's Savs. Bank. Senator, 22d Dist. of Conn., 1939-47, majority leader, 1941; Democratic chmn. Bridgeport, 1952-55. Bd. dirs. Park City Hosp. Fellow Am. Coll. Trial Lawyers; mem. Phi Beta Kappa. K.C. Home: Bridgeport, Conn. Died Dec. 18, 1978.

COLLACOTT, ROBERT HOVER, former oil co. exec., child welfare ofcl.; b. Painesville, O., Aug. 30, 1897; s. Harry R. and Mary (Hover) C.; A.B., Cornell U., 1919; m. Margaret Oliver, Sept. 7, 1929; children—May O. (Mrs. Robert S. Targett), Chatharine H. (Mrs. Richard DeWitt). With Standard Oil Co., Cleve., 1920-69, dir. pub. relations, 1955-62, spl. asst. to pres., 1962-69; pres. Jos. Dyson & Sons, Inc.; dir. Akron Nat. Bank, Steere Enterprises, Inc. (both Akron). Chief petroleum products pricing OPA. World War II; mem. Nat. Indsl. Conf. Bd. Pres., Child Welfare League Am., 1962, 64, v.p., 1964—; pres. Cleve. Council World Affairs, 1962-64, chmn., 1964-69; v.p. Family Services Assn. Am., 1956-62; pres. Family Service Assn. Cleve. 1958-60, trustee, 1950-76; mem. Cleve. Sr. Council, 1957-76; chmn. Cleve. Better Bus. Bur., 1959-61, trustee, 1954-76; vice chmn. Ohio U. Council Econ. Edn.; mem. adv. council Coll. Arts and Scis., Univ. council, chmn. administrv. bd., pres library assos. devel. com. Cornell U., Ithaca, New York; mem. Clergy-Econ. Edn. Found. Trustee Akron Gen. Hosp., Lake Erie Coll.; bd. dirs. Ohio Citizens Council Health and Welfare, 1958-76, Nat. Conf. Social Welfare, 1962—. Mem. N.A.M., Am. Mgmt. Assn., Am. Econ. Assn., U.S., Ohio chambers commerce, Cleve. Engring. Soc., Am. Acad. Polit. and Social Scis., Newcomen Soc., N.A.M., English Speaking Union. Republican. Episcopalian. Clubs: Union, Cornell, Mid-Day, Philosophical (past pres.). University, City (Cleve.); City (Akron); University, Cornell (N.Y.C.). Home: Mentor, Ohio. Died Nov. 24, 1976.

COLLADAY, EDGAR BERGMAN (KOL'LA-DA), brig. gen.; b. Madison, Wis., Jan. 8, 1885; s. Forrest Henry and Charlotte (Keenan) C.; B.S., U. of Wis., 1909; grad. Army Gen. Service Sch., 1928, Army War Coll., 1930, Army Industrial Coll., 1933; m. Mary Clare Waring, Apr. 21, 1917; 1 son, Edgar Bergman. Commd. 2d lt. Coast Arty., 1910 and promoted through various grades to brig. gen., Oct. 1940; foreign duty since Sept., 1941. Decorated D.S.M., Legion of Merit with Oak Leaf Cluster. Episcopalian. Mason. Clubs: Army and Navy (Washington, D.C.), Chevy Chase (Md.). Home: Burlingame, Calif.

COLLADAY, THOMAS, army officer; b. Mich., Mar. 17, 1882; commd. 2d lt., Inf., Mich. Nat. Guard, Mar. 24, 1908, advancing through the grades to brig. gen., June 1940; Fed. service, Jan. 1941; command of 63d Inf. Brigade, 32d div., in training, Camp Livingston, La., since 1941. Address: Camp Livingston, La.*

COLLETT, FREDERICK GEORGE, b. Camden, N.Y., Jan. 9, 1885; s. Joseph George and Margaret (Near) C.; ed. spl. course, Syracuse U.; mil. course, U. of Calif., 1917; pvt. study; married. Made study of Indian conditions in Calif., 1910-11; organized, 1912; Indian Bd. of Cooperation of which is exec. officer; organized Indians of Calif. into auxiliaries to Indian Board of Cooperation; successful in securing many favorable decisions from state and federal courts, including right of Indians to attend pub. schools, and citizenship for 25,000 Calif. Indians, also securing nat. and state legislation for their welfare; editor and business mgr. Calif. Indian Herald. Democrat. Conglist.

COLLEY, ROBERT H. (KOL'LE), oil official; b. Bridgeport, Conn., June 15, 1886; s. William Edgar and Ruth (Smith) C.; ed. pub. schs.; m. Mabel Louise Smith, Oct. 1, 1908 (dec.).; 1 dau., Mrs. E. K. Twining, m. 2d, Esther Louise Smith, June 30, 1921. Treas. Superior Oil Corp., 1920-26; asst. treas. Atlantic Refining Co., 1926-29; treas. 1929-37, v.p. 1936-37, became president, 1937, chairman of the board since 1952; chairman of board, Keystone Pipe Line Co.; vice pres. Atlantic Pipe Line Co.; dir. First National Bank of Phila., American Petroleum Inst. Trustee Nat. Foundation for Infantile Paralysis. Entered U.S. Army Sept. 1917; attended O.T.C., Camp Devens, Mass., and French Artillery Sch., Saumur, France; participated in Battles of St. Mihiel and Meuse-Argonne as 2d lt. 307th F.A. Clubs: Union League (Phila.). Home: Wayne, Pa.

COLLIER, NEIL REX, journalist; b. Washington, Sept. 20, 1897; s. Harry Lee and Maude (Hicks) C.; student George Washington U., 1916-18; m. Pauline L. Palmer, Oct. 1, 1919; children—Elaine (dec.), Neil Rex (dec.), William Lee, Jack Wayne. Reporter, Washington Herald, 1919, Washington Post, 1919-20, Evening and Sunday Star, 1920-23, asst. city editor, 1924, asst to mng. editor, 1939-40, editorial writer, 1940-62; author syndicated newspaper strip War on Crime, 1938-39; collaborated with Phillips Lord in first authenticated series of radio dramatizations of FBI cases, 1937. Student-officer, U.S. Naval Aviation, 1918, commd. Vol. Naval Res., 1927, active duty, 1942-45; Office Pub. Relations, Navy Dept., and 1st Navy Dist.; capt. USNR, 1945. Mem. U.S. Naval Inst., Am. Mus. Natural History, Robert E. Lee Meml. Found., Ret. Officers Assn. Home: Arlington, Va. Died Jan. 21, 1978.

COLLIER, PAUL STANLEY, trade assn. cons.; b. Durant, Ia., Mar. 28, 1890; s. Durbin Burton and Lydia (Schreckengast) C.; A.B., U. Ia., 1911, M.A., 1912; Ph.D., Columbia 1915; m. Fannie A. Koch, Mar. 6, 1917; children—Gretchen Koch, Paul Stanley. Investigator, N.Y. State Factory Investigating Commn., 1913-15; research N.Y. Bur. Municipal Research, 1915-16; sec. Oneonta (N.Y.) C. of C. and sec.-mgr. Retail Lumber Dealers Assn. State N.Y., 1916-21; sec.-mgr. Northeastern Retail Lumbermens Assn., Rochester, N.Y., 1922-49, exec. v.p., 1949-61, cons., 1961-76; sec. mgr. Merchandising Council of Retail Lumber Dealer Assns., 1932-38; sec. and councillor Retail Lumber Bldg. Material Code Authority, 1933-35; sec., treas. Merchandising Inst. Nat. Retail Lumber Dealers Assn., Inc., 1938-65; treas. Merchandising Inst., Nat. Lumber and Bldg. Material Dealers Assn., Inc., 1965-76; dir. Northeastern Homes Found. 1940-76; pres. and chmn. adv. bd. Am. Trade Assn. Execs., 1933-35, chmn. com. ethics and standards, 1935-37. Mem. Rochester, U.S. chambers commerce, Am. Acad. Polit. and Social Sci., Citizens Hist. Assn., S.A.R., Phi Beta Kappa, Delta Sigma Rho. Episcopalian. Mason. Rotarian. Clubs: Rochester, University, Advertising, The Monroe Golf and Country (Rochester, N.Y.). Editor: Hand Book for Lumber and Building Material Dealers, 1920; Decisions Under the Anti-Trust Laws, 1935. Author: Minimum Wage Legislation in Australasia, 1915; How the Lumber Code Affects the Lumber Distributor, 1934; The Changing Picture of Recovery and its Challenge to Associations, 1934; What Is a Trade Association Executive, 1936; Is the Price Too High, 1947. Pub. Law of the Construction Industry, 1943. Editor and pub. The Lumber Cooperator Jour., 1917-61, chmn. editorial bd., 1961-76. Contbr. to jours. and publs. Home: Rochester, N.Y. Died Oct. 28, 1976.

COLLINGE, ROBERT JOY, opera dir.; b. New Bedford, Mass., Apr. 23, 1928; s. Robert Bakewell and Claire Frances (Lovejoy) C.; B.S., R.I. Coll. Edn., 1949. Tchr. math secondary schs., Mass. and Md., 1949-62;

gen. mgr. Balt. Opera Co., 1962-80; pres., co-founder OPERA Am., Inc., 1970-75. Trustee, Nat. Opera Inst. Devel. new concept ednl. opera prodn., 1972-77. Decorated cavalieri dell'Ordine al Merito della Repubblica Italiana, 1976. Home: Baltimore, Md. Died May 22, 1980.

COLLINS, ARDEN LEROY, hosp. adminstr.; b. Chillicothe, O., Apr. 21, 1920; s. John Edward and Roxsey (Dickenson) C.; B.S., Ohio State U., 1943, postgrad., 1946; postgrad. Wayne State U., 1952, U. Chgo., 1960-61; m. Elizabeth Jean Harness, Aug. 1, 1946; children—Dianna (Mrs. Kurt Kiesling), Elizabeth (Mrs. Brian Blazy), Theresa (Mrs. Michael O'Nele), Mary. Grad. asst. Ohio State U., 1946; corrective therapist VA Hosp., Louisville, 1946-47, chief corrective therapist, rehab. coordinator, Dearborn, Mich., 1947-57; rehab. coordinator Hines VA Hosp., Maywood, Ill., 1957-65; asst. hosp. dir. trainee Research VA Hosp., Chgo., 1966, asst. hosp. dir., Grand Island, Neb., 1967; dir. bldg. mgmt. service VA Central Office, Washington, 1968-72; dir. VA Hosp., Canandaigua, N.Y., 1972-76. Mem. exec. bd. Rochester Regional Med. Group, Canandaigua Bicentennial Com. Served to capt. AUS, 1943-46; ETO. Mem. Am. Assn. Rehab. Dirs. and Coordinators (nat. pres. 1966), Assn. Mil. Surgeons, Canandaigua C. of C., Scabbard and Blade, Phi Kappa Tau. Methodist. Kiwanian. Died June 23, 1976.

COLLINS, CLEM WEIZELL, C.P.A.; b. Bloomfield, Arkansas, July 7, 1883; son of Andrew Thomas and Sarah Ann (Franks) C.; B.C.S., U. of Denver, 1911, B.S., 1933; m. Marie Harker, June 23, 1917; children—Clem Wetzell, Virginia Putnam, Harker. C.P.A., Colo., 1912, Calif., 1923; prof. accounting, mem. exec. com. U. of Denver Sch. Commerce, 1918-45, asst. dean 1933-36, dean 1936-45; mgr. revenue, City and Co. of Denver, 1923-31; regional adminstr. Office of Price Administration, Jan. 1942-Feb. 1944; ex-chmn. State Bd. of Accountancy of Colo.; mem. President's Loyalty Review Bd.; consultant United States Department of the Interior. Served as capt. Q.M.C. dir. Inter-Bureau Unit, World War I. Past pres. Am. Inst. Accountants, Colo. Soc. C.P.A.'s; mem. Am. Legion, Acacia, Omicron Delta Kappa, Delta Pi Epsilon. Past pres. Denver Council of Boy Scouts of Am., Big Brother Movement. Dem. Mason (32 deg., Shriner, past potentate El Jebel); mem. Jr. Order U.A.M. Clubs: Denver, Kiwanis (past pres., past district gov.); Cosmos. Author books on accounting and appraising. Home: Denver.

COLLINS, DENNIS ALPHONSUS, fgn. service officer; b. Hamler, O., July 24, 1920; s. Paul Alphonsus and Marie Catherine (Dietrick) C.; student DeSales Coll., 1939-40, U. Md., 1951; m. Mary Anne Della, Aug. 14, 1948; children—Delia Mary, Dennis Alphonsus, Kenneth Paul, Kathleen Marie. Dep. dir. div. finance, Office Central Field Commr. for Europe, Fgn. Liquidation Commn., 1946-49; asst. econ. commr. ECA mission to Denmark, 1949-50, auditor, asst. fiscal dir. Office Spl. Rep. for Europe, ECA, 1950-54; chief fiscal sect. and mgmt. budget sect. Am. embassy, Paris, France, 1954-57; dep. dir. Office Finance, Dept. State, Washington, 1957-60, dir. Regional Finance Center, Dept. State, Paris, France, from 1961, 2d sec., 1954-57, 1st sec., from 1961. Served to maj. AUS, 1941-46. Home: Washington, D.C. Died Sept. 15, 1979.

COLLINS, HENRY, retired insurance exec.; born Eng., Jan. 7, 1883; s. John Henry and Elizabeth (Richardson) C.; ed. Kings College, London; m. Belle Johnson Manahan, 1906; children—Barbara E., Marjorie B. U.S. mgr. The Ocean Accident & Guarantee Corp. since 1930; pres. Columbia Casualty Co., N.Y. City, 1930-47; retired June 30, 1947; dep. mgr. Comml. Union Assurance Co. since 1938. Home: Knoll Rd., Tenafly, N.J.

COLLINS, JOSEPH DORSEY, surgeon; b. Edinburg, Shenandoah County, Va., Feb. 3, 1884; s. George Thomas Dorsey and Emma Davis (Hutchinson) C.; ed. Washington and Lee U., 1899-1901; M.D., Med. Coll. of Va., Richmond, Va., 1905; m. Julia Crump Cottrell, Apr. 7, 1910. Practiced at Portsmouth, Va., 1906—; cons. surgeon; chmn. department of surgery Portsmouth General Hospital. Formerly mem. Board of Visitors, Medical College of Va. Member Founders Group of American Board of Surgery. Fellow A.M.A., American College Surgeons, American Association for the Surgery of Trauma, Southern Surg. Assn., Southeastern Surg. Congress; mem. Southern Med. Assn., Med. Soc. Va., Seaborad Med. Soc., Norfolk County Med. Soc. (past pres.). Democrat. Episcopalian. Mason (32 deg., Shriner). Home: Portsmouth, Va.

COLLINS, LEROY PIERCE, army officer (ret.); b. Troy, N.Y., Mar. 4, 1883; s. Leroy Morey and Clara (Bonesteel) C.; student Union Coll., Schenectady, 1901-04; grad. Gen. Service Sch., 1924, Army War Coll., 1925, Naval War Coll., 1926; Sc.D., Union Coll., 1942; m. Constance E. Jones; children—Howard P., (dec.) Leroy P., Constance E. Enlisted as private U.S. Army, Aug. 4, 1904; served with Troop K, 15th Cav. as private, corpl., sergt., 1904-07; commd. 2d lt., field arty., 1907, advanced through the grades to brig. gen., 1941. Awarded Victory medal for World War I; Legion of Merit, Bronze Star, World War II. Mem. Phi Gamma Delta. Presbyterian.

COLLINS, MARY LOVE, lawyer; b. Loveville, Pa., June 3, 1882; d. Winfield and Amelia (Rider) Love; ed. prep. sch., Conway Hall; A.B., Dickinson Coll., 1902, A.M., 1908, L.H.D., 1952; U. Chgo.; LL.B., U. of Ky. Law Coll. 1915. Teacher wills and adminstrn., U. of Ky., Coll. of Law, 1918; atty. solicitor's office, Bur. of Internal Revenue, 1919-20, Formerly mem. Acad. Social and Polit. Science, Am. Polit. Science Assn., Am. Bar Assn.; mem. D.A.R., Chi Omega (pres. 1910-52; administrative councilor since 1952), Phi Beta Kappa, Phi Delta, Phi Beta. Author: Human Conduct and the Law. Co-author: Eminent Women, 1949. Edited Public Services of Women's Organizations, 1951; A Dynamic Freedom (phamphlet), 1953. Address: Cin.

COLLINS, THOMAS HIGHTOWER, newspaperman, author; b. Cedartown, Ga., Nov. 26, 1910; s. Clifford Augustus and Fannie Lou (Hightower) C.; student U. Ga., 1929-31, Ga. State Coll., 1931-35; m. Beulah Blagden Stowe, Apr. 6, 1946; children—Carol, Kent, Paul, Todd. Reporter, DeKalb New Era, Decatur, Ga., 1932-35; copyreader, picture editor Atlanta Jour., 1935-40; copyreader, writer Louisville Courier-Jour., 1940-42; copyreader Chgo. Daily News, from 1942, feature editor, 1946-59, asst. mng. editor, 1959-60, mng. editor, 1960-61, exec. editor, 1961-62. Served to lt. (s.g.) USNR, 1944-46. Episcopalian. Author: The Golden Years, An Invitation to Retirement, 1956; The Complete Guide to Retirement, 1970; syndicated column, The Golden Years, 1948-78; (pseudo Paul Hightower) syndicated column The Senior Forum, from 1952. Address: Chapel Hill, N.C. Died June 25, 1978.

COLLINSON, JOSEPH BRUERD, mfg. co. exec.; b. Raymond, Ohio, Dec. 11, 1914; s. Alfred O. and Jennifer L. (Bruerd) C.; B.S., Ohio State U., 1938; m. Jean Crayton, May 31, 1939; children—Jeffrey, Jill. Mgr., Arthur Young & Co., Tulsa and Cleve., 1948-51, partner, 1951-55, partner, Chgo., 1957-59; v.p. Soc. for Savs., Soc. Nat. Bank, Cleve., 1956-57; v.p., treas. Textron Inc., Providence, 1959-63, exec. v.p., 1963-74, pres., 1974-80, chmn., chief exec. officer, 1978-80, also dir.; dir. Old Stone Bank, Allied Chem. Corp., Textron, United Mut. Ins. Co., Amstur, Property Capital Trust, Allendale Ins. C.P.A., Okla., Ohio, Ill., Mich. Clubs: R.I. Country, Turks Head (Providence); John's Island (Vero Beach, Fla.). Home: John's Island, Fla. Died Feb. 21, 1980.

COLLVER, CLINTON, security analyst; b. Clinton, Wis., May 27, 1886; s. Dr. Clarence Walker and Amy (Gillis) C.; student U. of Wis., 1904-07; B.C.S., New York Univ., 1908, M.C.S., 1911; m. Nathalia Swanson, of Madison, Wis., Jan. 21, 1912; 1 dau., Hulda Nathalia. On editorial staff Wall Street Journal, 1907-08; pub. accountant with Haskins & Sells, Everett Audit Co. and Lybrand Ross Bros. & Montgomery, 1909-11; served as member editorial staff of System Magazine, 1912; N.Y. mgr. Brookmire Economic Service, 1912-13; editorial staff, Iron Age, 1913-14; dean Baltimore Sch. of Commerce Accounts and Finance, 1915-16; security expert Moody's Investors Service, 1916-18; mgr. investment dept. Lyman D. Smith & Co. (now Walter J. Fahy & Co.), 1918-29; with Russell Miller & Co. since 1929; dir. Gowin United Cos., Am. Securities Service, Am. Executives Inst., N.J. Bond & Shareholding Corporation, Internat. Shopping Service. Fellow Royal Econ. Soc.; mem. Am. Assn. Security Analysts (pres. since 1925), Am. Econ. Assn., Acad. Polit. Science, Am. Acad. Polit. and Social Science, American Statis. Association, Alpha Kappa Psi. Presbyn. Mason. Club: Nat. Press (Washington). Author: How to Analyze Industrial Securities, 1917; Industrial Securities, 1922; The Choice of Stocks, 1924. Co-Author: Trading and Investing, 1925. Contbr. to mags. and newspapers. Home: New York.

COLMER, WILLIAM MEYERS, former congressman; b. Moss Point, Miss., Feb. 11, 1890; s. Henry and Anna S. (Meyers) C.; student Millsaps Coll., Jackson, Miss., 1910-14; m. Ruth Miner, Sept. 17, 1917; children—William Meyers, James Henry, Thomas Warren. Sch. tchr., 1914; admitted to Miss. bar, 1917; county atty. Jackson County, 1921-27; dist. atty. 2d Dist. of Miss., 1928-33; mem. 73d to 92d Congresses, 5th Miss. Dist., chmn. house rules com. Served with U.S. Army, 1918-1919. Mem. Am. Legion, 40 and 8, Pi Kappa Alpha. Democrat. Methodist. Mason, Woodman, Rotarian. Home: Pascagoula, Miss. Died Sept. 11, 1980.

COLMERY, HARRY WALTER, JR., investment banker; b. Topeka, Kan., Jan. 10, 1924; s. Harry Walter and Minerva (Hiserodt) C.; A.B., Dartmouth, 1949; student U. Va. Law Sch., 1949-50; m. Sallie Morphy, Oct. 19, 1955; children—Sarah E., Scott G., Katherine E. Partner, William R. Staats & Co., 1953-79; sr. v.p. charge Western div. Glore, Forgan, Wm. R. Staats, Inc., 1965-66, exec. v.p., dir. charge Western div., 1966-79; dir. Dymo Industries, Mut. Exploration Funds, Inc. Cal. Financial Corp., Security Savs. & Loan, Pioneer Nat. Life Ins. Co., Regency Life Ins. Co. Bd. govs. Pacific Coast Stock Exchange. Served with USMCR, 1942-46, maj., 1950-52. Decorated D.F.C., Air medal, Clubs: San Francisco Stock Exchange, Los Angeles Athletic, California, Pacific Union (Los Angeles). Home: Pasadena, Calif. Died Aug. 23, 1979.

COLUM, PADRAIC, poet, dramatist; b. Longford, Ireland, Dec. 8, 1881; s. Padraic and Susanna (MacCormack C.; Litt.D., Columbia, 1958, Trinity Coll. (Dublin Ireland), 1958; m. Mary Gunning Maguire, 1912 (dec.). Came to U.S., 1914. Mem. Acad. Irish Letters (pres.), Am. Acad. Arts and Letters. Roman Catholic. Author: Wild Earth (poems), 1907; A Boy in Eirinn, 1913; Three Plays, 1916; The King of Ireland's Son, 1916; The Adventurers of Odysseus and the Tale of Troy; The Boy Who Knew What the Bird Said, 1918; The Girl Who Sat by the Ashes, 1919; The Children of Odin, 1920; The Boy Apprenticed to an Enchanter, 1920; The Golden Fleece, 1921; The Children Who Followed the Piper, 1922; Castle Conquer, 1923; Dramatic Legends (poems), 1922; The Island of the Mighty, At the Gateways of the Day (Hawaiian Stories), 1924; The Voyagers, The Forge in the Forest, The Bright Islands (Hawaiian Stories), 1925; The Road Round Ireland, 1926; Creatures (verse); The Fountain of Youth, 1927; Balloon, a comedy in four acts; Orpheus Stories from the Mythologies of the World, 1929; Poems, 1932; A Half-Day's Ride and A Book of Essays, 1932; The Big Tree of Bunlahy (stories), 1933; The Legend of Saint Columbia, 1935; The Story of Lowry Maen (narrative poem), 1937; Where The Winds Never Blew and the Cocks Never Crew, 1940; The Frenzied Prince, 1943; Anthology of Irish Verse, 1948; A Treasury of Irish Folklore, 1954; The Flying Swans, 1957; Arthur Griffith and the Origins of the Irish Free State, 1958; Our Friend James Joyce, 1958; Legends of Hawaii, 1960; Ourselves Alone, 1960; Poet's circuits (collection of poems of Ireland), 1960; Roofs of Gold (poetry anthology), 1964; The Stone of Victory (anthology own children's poems), 1966. Recipient Acad. Am. Poets award, 1952; Gregory medal Irish Acad. Letters, 1953; Regina medal Cath. Library Assn., 1961; Boston Arts Festival Poet, citation 1961; Georgetown U. 175th Anniversary Medal of Honor, 1964. Address: New York City NY.

COLWELL, ARCHIE TRESCOTT, cons. engr.; b. Yankee Jims, Calif., July 30, 1895; s. George A. and Sarah (Jones) C.; B.S., U.S. Mil. Acad., 1918; grad. U.S. Army Engrs. Sch., 1920; Eng. D. (hon.), Case Inst. Tech., 1953; m. Sallie M. Tuttle, Sept. 23, 1920; children—Marion (Mrs. J. O. Findeisen, Jr.), Sallie Lucile Smith. Began career as sales engineer Steel Products Co. (later became Thompson Products, Inc., now named TRW, Inc.), 1922-30, employed as chief engineer, 1930-31, director of engring., 1934-37, dir., from 1939, corp. v.p. charge engring., 1937-60, cons., 1960-68; dir. Rand Devel. Corp., Ferro Corp., Harris-Intertype Corp. Trustee, Fenn Coll. Fellow Inst. Aero. Scis., Inst. Mech. Engrs. (Eng.), Royal Aero Soc. (Eng.); mem. Soc. Automotive Engrs. (life, past pres., chmn. finance com.), Cleveland Engineering Soc., Cleveland Technical Socs. Council (past pres.). Republican. Clubs: Union, Country, Pepper Pike (Cleve.); The Recess, Detroit Athletic (Detroit). Home: Cleveland, Ohio. Died Dec. 18, 1979.

COLWELL, ARTHUR RALPH, SR., physician; b. Chgo., July 8, 1897; s. Lewis William and Grace (Stryker) C.; S.B., U. Chgo., 1919; M.D., Rush Med. Coll., 1921; Nat. Research Council fellow, Harvard, 1928-29; m. Jeane Haskins, Sept. 1, 1921; children—Arthur Ralph, John Amory, Elizabeth (dec.), Mary Ann (Mrs. Nitchie). Practice medicine specializing in internal medicine, Chgo., 1923-49; chmn. dept. medicine, Irving S. Cutter prof. medicine Northwestern U. Med. Sch., Chgo., 1950-65, prof. emeritus medicine, 1965-78; attending physician Northwestern Meml. Hosp., Chgo., 1950-78. Recipient Banting Meml. medal and award Am. Diabetes Assn. 1952, 68. Fellow A.C.P.; mem. Assn. Am. Physicians A.M.A., Am. Diabetes Assn. (pres. 1951), Central Soc. Clin. Research, Sigma Xi, Beta Theta Pi, Nu Sigma Nu Alpha Omega Alpha. Club: Big Foot Country (Fontana Wis.). Author: Diabetes in General Practice, 1948 Types of Diabetes Mellitus and Their Treatment, 1949 Home: Evanston, Ill. Died June 4, 1978.

COMAR, CYRIL LEWIS, phys. biologist, educator; b Dudley, Eng., Mar. 28, 1914; s. David and Berth (Simon) C.; B.S., U. Calif. at Berkeley, 1936, postgrad food tech., 1937-38; Ph.D., Purdue U., 1940; m Mildred Cashin, Aug. 7, 1939; children—Anne Patricia Thomas Allan, Louise Elaine. Came to U.S., 1923 naturalized, 1941. Prof. biophysics U. Tenn., 1948-54 lab. dir., research coordinator U. Tenn.-AEC agr research program. Oak Ridge, 1948-54; chief biomed research Oak Ridge Inst. Nuclear Studies, 1954-57; di lab. radiation biology, prof. radiation biology Cornell U 1957-60, head dept. phys. biology, 1960-75, pro emeritus, 1975-79; dir. environ. assessment. dep energy analysis and environment div. Electric Powe Research Inst., Palo Alto, Calif., 1975-79; cons. pro Stanford U. Med. Sch., 1976-79; cons. biology an medicine div. AEC, Oak Ridge Inst. Nuclear Studie

atomic energy and agr. FAO, also USPHS. Mem. U.S. delegation Conf. on Peaceful Uses Atomic Energy, Geneva, 1955; mem. com. effects atomic radiation on agr. and food supplies Nat. Acad. Sci., 1956; cons. effects atomic radiation UN Sci. Com., 1956-58; cons. FAO to UNESCO Conf. Radioisotopes Sci. Research, Paris, 1957, WHO Conf. on Radiochem. Methods of Analysis, Geneva, 1958; dir. internat. tng. courses on use radiosotopes in biol. research FAO, 1959, 62, 65, 70; cons. Nat. Center Radiol. Health, USPHS, 1967—, Nat. Adv. Radiol. Health Council, 1967; cons. environmental health scis. div., USPHS, 1968—; mem. nat. adv. com. radiation to surgeon gen. Chmn. adv. com. Fed. Radiation Council, 1966—. Recipient Borden award, 1968; spl. award Am. Nuclear Soc., awarded posthumously, 1980. Mem. Am. Soc. Biol. Chemists, A.A.A.S., Soc. Nuclear Medicine, Am. Vet. Med. Assn., Am. Chem. Soc., Am. Inst. Nutrition, Soc. Exptl. Biology and Medicine, Radiation Research Soc., Am. Soc. Animal Prodn., Sigma Xi, Phi Lambda Upsilon, Gamma Sigma Epsilon, Gamma Alpha. Author: Radioisotopes in Biology and Agriculture, Principles and Practice, 1955. Editor: Atomic Energy and Agriculture, 1957; (with F. Bronner) Mineral Metabolism, An Advanced Treatise, 3 vols., 1960-69. Contbr. articles to profl. jours. Home: Atherton, Calif. Died June 11, 1979.

COMBS, JOSIAH HENRY, author, lecturer; b. at Hazard, Perry Co., Ky., Jan. 2, 1886; s. John Wesley and Clementina (Cody) C.; diploma, W.C.T.U. Sch., Hindman, Ky., 1905; A.B., Transylvania U., Lexington, Ky., 1911; unmarried. Teacher Latin and Romance langs., in Ky., Tenn. and Okla., since 1911; was prof. Romance langs., Okla. N.E. State Normal Sch. Lecturer on Ky. Highlanders, Folk-Lore, Dialect of the Southern Mountains, and Old Ky. Mem. Am. Folk-Lore Soc., Am. Dialect Soc., Ky. Folk-lore Soc., Authors' League, Sigma Upsilon, Mem. M.E. Ch., S. Author: A Syllabus of Kentucky Folk-Songs, 1911; The Kentucky Highlanders, 1913; All That's Kentucky, 1915; The Language of Our Southern Highlanders, 1915; Lèse Majesté, 1919; The Siege of Larisbury Court, 1920. Collector of folk-songs and of poetry relating to the various states. Contbr. to mags. Home: Hindman, Ky.

COMBS, LEE, JR., lawyer; b. Valley City, N.D., Nov. 25, 1905; s. Lee and Mabel (Osher) C.; B.A., Harvard, 1926; J.D., U. So. Cal., 1929; m. Evelyn Hefner, Feb. 25, 1929; children—David (dec.), Donald (dec.), Deanna (dec.), Lee Hefner (dec.), Margaret Evelyn (Mrs. Michael Chumo, Jr.). Admitted to Cal. bar, 1929, also U.S. Supreme Ct. bar; practice in Los Angeles, 1929-51, Beverly Hills, 1951-71, Los Angeles, 1971-76. Pres., dir. So. Cal. Com. Olympic Games. Co-founder, trustee Belair (Cal.) Town and Country Sch., 1949-52; pres. Lee Hefner Combs Meml. Found., 1960-76, also dir.; trustee Harvard Sch., 1959-64; asso. U. So. Cal., 1961-76. Mem. Am. Judicature Soc., Am., Cal., Los Angeles County, Beverly Hills (bd. govs. 1952-59, pres. 1956) bar assns., U. So. Cal. Alumni Assn., U. So. Cal. Law Alumni Assn. (pres.), Brit. Interplanetary Soc., Am., Cal. (v.p. 1960-61, dir. 1959-61) revenue assns., Am. Horse Show Assn., Am. Philatelic Assn., Skull and Dagger. Episcopalian. Mason (Shriner). Clubs: Bel Air Bay, Exchange (founding pres.), Stock Exchange (Beverly Hills); Flintridge (Cal.) Riding. Home: Los Angeles, Calif. Died Aug. 5, 1976.

COMBS, WILLIAM HOBART, educator, adminstr.; b. Bloomfield, Ind., Oct. 5, 1896; s. James E. and Nellie (Mays) C.; A.B., Ind. U., 1924, A.M., 1926; Baldwin fellow U. Cin., 1926-27; Ph.D. (Harrison fellow), U. Pa., 1933; m. Elizabeth J. Edington, Apr. 15, 1916; children—Robert G., Joan E. (Mrs. Wm. Rudman), Hilda Ann (dec.). Tchr. pub. schs. in Ind., 1914-25; asso. prof. Berea Coll., Ky., 1928-30; instr. U. Tenn., 1931-38; cons. Tenn. State Dept. Pub. Welfare, 1938; asst. prof. to asso. prof. history and polit. sci., prof. and head dept. pub. adminstrn., Mich. State U., 1938-49, adminstrv. asst. to pres. charge acad. affairs, 1947-67, dean all-coll. div., 1949-56, dean univ. services, 1956-67, sec. of faculties, 1959-67, prof. and dean emeritus, 1967, dir. archives, asst. dean continuing edn. Coll. Arts and Letters, part-time, 1967-79. Mem. Commn. on Modernization and Reform of Govt. in Mich., 1938-39; mem. Constl. Revision Study Commn., 1942; mem. tech. staff Tax Study Adv. Commn., 1945-46; mem. Mich. Inst. of Local Govt., 1948-79; bd. dirs. Midwest Inter-Library Corp., 1949-66, chmn., 1957-58; mem. council Center for Research Libraries, 1966-67; project dir. Mich. Joint Legislative Com. Reorgn. State Govt., 1950; staff dir. Mich. Constl. Conv. Prep. Commn., 1961; co-dir. research and drafting Mich. Constl. Conv., 1961-62. Mem. Internat. City Mgrs. Assn., Mich. Acad. Arts, Letters and Sci., Soc. Am. Archivists, Am. Records Mgmt. Assn. (Mid-Mich. chpt.). Conglist. Mason. Club: University. Author: (with W.E. Cole, A. D. Mueller and C.P. White) Constitutional Problems in Tennessee, 1937; (with W. E. Cole) Tennessee A Political Study, 1940. Contbr. articles to Am. Polit. Sci. Rev., Tenn. Law Rev., Nat. Municipal Rev., Bull. Nat. Tax Assn. Home: East Lansing, Mich. Died Apr. 6, 1979.

COMEY, DAVID DINSMORE, environ. research exec.; b. Cin., Dec. 21, 1934; s. Harold Dean and Jane (Dinsmore) C.; grad. with high honors Phillips Exeter Acad., 1952; B.A. magna cum laude, Princeton, 1956; children—Sean, Sarah. Asst. prof. Osteuropa Institut, U. Fribourg, Switzerland, 1961-63; dir. Research Inst. on Soviet Sci., research asso. Center for Internat. Studies, Cornell U., 1963-69; dir. research div. Schickel Environ. Devel. Co., 1969-70; dir. environ. research Bus. and Profl. People for the Pub. Interest, Chgo., 1970-76; pres. Citizens for Better Environment, 1976-79. Mem. cooling water studies panel U.S. EPA, 1972-76, mem. toxic substances adv. com., 1977-79; mem. steering com. C-SELM Project, U.S. Army, 1970-72; mem. utility conservation panel Fed. Energy Adminstrn.; mem. U.S. Nuclear Proliferation and Safeguards Panel, 1976-77; mem. nat. energy policy impacts panel Office Tech. Assessment, U.S. Congress, 1977; mem. energy study panel Nat. Council Chs., 1977-79. Recipient First Ann. Environ. Quality award EPA, 1974, Ford Found. fellow, 1959-61. Anglican. Author: Incident at Browns Ferry, 1975. Home: Chicago, Ill. Died Jan. 5, 1979.

COMLEY, ARTHUR M., lawyer; b. Bridgeport, Conn., June 1, 1883; s. William H. and Lucy I. (Nicholson) C.; A.B., Yale, 1907, LL.D., 1910; m. Emilie L. Schwab, June 12, 1918. Admitted to Conn. bar, 1910, since practiced in Bridgeport, sr. partner Pullman, Comely, Bradley & Reeves, and predecessor firm, since 1919; also mem. Pullman, Comley, Marshall & Parker, Greenwich, Conn.; judge Bridgeport City Ct., 1920-21; v.p., trustee, mem. exec. com. Bridgeport People's Savs. Bank since 1948; pres. Hart Realty Co. since 1935. Mem. Conn. State Park and Forest Commn., 1942-48. Mem. Am., Conn., Bridgeport bar assns. Clubs: University, Algonquin, Brooklawn Country. Home: Fairfield.

COMPTON, JAMES C., ret. jurist; b. Fayetteville, Ark., Dec. 19, 1886; LL.B., Cumberland U., 1908, J.D., 1951; LL.D., Eastern N.M. U.; m. Bessie Johnson; children—Helen, James C., Ben. Admitted to N.M. state bar, 1909; served as dist. atty, 9th Jud. Dist. of N.M.; judge 9th Jud. Dist., 1941-47; apptd. to N.M. Supreme Ct., 1947, elected for 8 yr. term, 1948, 56, 64; ret. 1973. Home: Santa Fe NM. *

COMSTOCK, DANIEL FROST, physicist, engineer; b. Newport, R.I., Aug. 14, 1883; s. Ezra Young and Nellie Preston (Barr) C.; S.B., Mass. Inst. Tech., 1904; studied U. of Berlin, 1905, U. of Zürich, 1905-06, U. of Basel, 1906, Ph.D., studied U. of Cambridge, Eng., 1906-07, under J. J. Thomson; m. Joan Barton, June 30, 1925; children—Daniel Frost, Charles Barton. Apptd. to teaching staff, Mass. Inst. Tech., 1904, instr. in theoretical physics, 1905-10, asst. prof., 1910-15, asso. prof., 1915-17; directed scientific work on development of means for detection of hostile submarines, World War I, president Comstock & Wescott, Inc., Engrs. 1912-14; v.p. Kalmus, Comstock & Wescott, Inc., engrs., 1914-25; dir. of scientific work on, and principal inventor of the process for producing Motion Pictures in natural color known as the Technicolor process, developed by Kalmus, Comstock & Wescott, Inc., for the Technicolor Motion Picture Corp., during 1914-25; v.p. Technicolor Motion Picture Corp., 1918-25; pres. Comstock & Wescott, Inc., 1925-67, chairman of the board, 1967—; engaged almost exclusively with research and development on war projects during World War II; now engaged in industrial research. Pres., treas., dir. Stator Co., co-inventor of new refrigeration process owned by same. Member National Advisory Council to Committee on Patents, Ho. of Reps., 1939. Fellow Am. Academy Arts and Sci., Am. Physical Society; mem. Am. Chemical Society. Club: St. Botolph (Boston). Author: Nature of Matter and Electricity (with L.T. Troland), 1917. Contbr. original research articles on modern theory of electricity and optics to Am. and English tech. jours. Home: Sheraton Commander Hotel, Cambridge, Mass.

CONANT, FREDERIC WARREN, Airplane exec.; b. Santa Barbara, Calif., Feb. 8, 1892; s. Frank A. and Anna (Heath) C.; C.E., Cornell U., 1914; m. Dorothy Davis, June 29, 1918; children—Peter, Michael Richard. Civil engr. Union Sugar Co., 1914-17; engaged in building construction as individual contractor, 1921-33; with Douglas Aircraft Co., Inc., since 1933, became v.p., 1940, sr. vice pres., 1945, vice chmn. bd., 1957. sr. v.p. mfg., from 1958. Enlisted in F.A., 1917; served as 2d lt. Inf., later capt. Engring. Corps, 1917-21. Clubs: St. Francis Yacht, Cruising of America, Los Angeles Yacht. Home: Hollywood, Calif. Died Apr. 24, 1974.

CONANT, HARRISON JOSIAH, library cons.; b. Southbridge, Mass., June 8, 1882; s. Harrison Johnson and Ellen Lucy (Bennett) C.; A.B., Amherst Coll., 1904; A.M., Columbia, 1906, LL.B., 1907; m. Bess Butterfield, Sept. 14, 1909; 1 dau., Ruth (Mrs. Frank Follett). Admitted to New York bar, 1907, gen. practice of law New York City, 1907-10, Montpelier, Vt., 1910-17; Vt. exec. clerk, 1910-11; sec. Montpelier Chamber of Commerce, 1914-15; farmer 1917-22; Vt. legislative reference bur. Librarian, 1922-52, State Librarian, 1925-52; cons. State Library since 1952; chmn. Vt. pub. records commn., 1943-52. Sec. Vt. Commn. to revise the statutory law of Vt., 1945-48. Mem. Nat. Assn. State Libraries (pres. 1927), Vt. Bar Assn. (sec. 1926-52), Phi Beta Kappa. Republican. Contbr. to mags. Home: Montpelier, Vt.

CONANT, JAMES BRYANT, educator, former U.S. ambassador; b. Dorchester, Mass., Mar. 26, 1893; s. James Scott and Jennet Orr (Bryant) C.; A.B., Harvard, 1913, Ph.D., 1916; also numerous hon. degrees; m. Grace Thaver Richards, Apr. 17, 1921; children—James Richards, Theodore Richards. Prof. chemistry Harvard, 1919-33, pres., 1933-53, pres. emeritus; U.S. high commr. for Germany, 1953-55; U.S. ambassador to Fed. Republic Germany, 1955-57; condr. studies through Carnegie Corp. N.Y. grants Am. Pub. High Sch., 1957-62, Edn. of Am. Tchrs., 1962-63. Chmn. Nat. Def. Research Com., 1941-46; dep. dir. OSRD, 1941-46; mem. gen. adv. com. AEC, 1947-52; ednl. adviser to Ford Found., Berlin, Germany, 1963-65. Served CWS, U.S. Army, 1917-18. Author: On Understanding Science, 1947; Education in a Divided World, 1948; Science and Common Sense, 1951; Modern Science and Modern Man, 1952; Education and Liberty, 1953; The Citadel of Learning, 1956; Germany and Freedom, 1958; The American High School Today, 1959; The Revolutionary Transformation of the American High School, 1959; The Child, The Parent, and the State, 1959; Education in the Junior High School Years, 1960; Slums and Suburbs; A Commentary on Schools in Metropolitan Areas, 1961; The Education of American Teachers, 1963; Two Modes of Thought, 1964; Shaping Educational Policy, 1964; The Comprehensive High School, 1967; Scientific Principles and Moral Conduct, 1967; My Several Lives, 1970; (with N. H. Black) a high sch. chemistry textbook; also other textbooks on organic chemistry. Editor: Harvard Case Histories in Experimental Science, 2 vols., 1957. Address: New York, N.Y. Died Feb. 11, 1978; interred Mt. Auburn Cemetery, Cambridge, Mass.

CONDON, MARTIN J., III, business exec.; b. Pelham Manor, N.Y., Dec. 11, 1908; s. Martin J. and Shirley (Cummins) C.; A.B., Princeton, 1932; H.H.D., Southwestern U., 1958; m. Alice Berry, Feb. 22, 1936; children—Alice, Katherine, Louisa, Frances, Martin. Joined Am. Snuff Co. (now Conwood Corp.), 1933, pres., 1949-74, chmn. bd., 1974-77, also dir.; dir. Union Planters Nat. Bank, Memphis, Schering-Plough Corp., Bloomfield, N.J., Cavenham Ltd., London, Eng., Generale Occidentale, Paris, France. Trustee Garrison (Md.) Forest Sch. Served as lt. USNR, 1943-45. Mem. Nat. Indsl. Conf. Bd. (dir.), NAM (past v.p., dir.), Tenn. Mfrs. Assn. (past pres., dir.), U.S. Indsl. Council (past pres., dir.), Newcomen Soc., Phi Beta Kappa. Episcopalian. Clubs: Brook (N.Y.C.); Memphis Country, Hunt and Polo, Tennessee (Memphis); Ivy (Princeton, N.J.). Home: Memphis, Tenn. Died Dec. 28, 1977; buried Meml. Cemetery, Memphis, Tenn.

CONE, FAIRFAX MASTICK, advt. agy. exec.; b. San Francisco, Feb. 21, 1903; s. William H. and Isabelle F. (Williams) C.; grad. U. Cal., 1925; LL.D., Mundelein Coll., 1961; m. Gertrude Kennedy, June 29, 1929; 1 dau., Mary Mastick (Mrs. Richard H. O'Riley). With San Francisco Examiner, 1926-29, copywriter and account exec. Lord & Thomas, advt. agy., San Francisco, 1929-38, v.p. and mgr., 1938-40, v.p. in charge creative work, N.Y.C., 1941, exec. v.p. mgr. Chgo. office, 1942; with Emerson Foote and Don Belding, organized Foote, Cone & Belding Dec., 1942, chmn. exec. com., 1942-48, chmn. bd., 1942-51, pres., 1951-57, chmn. exec. com., 1957-66. Mem. Chgo. Bd. Edn., 1961-63. Bd. dirs. Community Fund Chgo., 1940-63; chmn. bd. trustees U. Chgo., 1963-70; trustee Chgo. Ednl. TV, 1961-70, Com. for Econ. Devel.; chmn. 1960 Crusade of Mercy, Berkeley fellow U. Cal. Recipient Distinguished Service in Advt. medal Syracuse U., U. Mo. Address: Chicago, Ill. Died June 21, 1977.

CONE, JOHN CARROLL, airline exec.; b. Snyder, Ark., July 4, 1893; s. Jesse H. and Anne (Edwards) C.; student Ouachita Coll., 1906-10; LL.D. (hon.), U. Ark., 1942; m. Virginia Cuniff, Apr. 27, 1945; children—Virginia Carol, John Caroll and William Randall. Engaged as automobile distributor, Ark., 1913-17, 1919-20; asst. sec. State Ark., 1920-21, state auditor, 1921-25; aircraft mfr. 1925-30; dir. aeros., Ark. 1930-32; asst. dir. Bur. Air Commerce, Washington, 1933-36; advisor to U.S. on European aeronautics, 1936-37; mgr. Atlantic div. Pan Am. Airways, 1937-39, asst. v.p., Washington, from 1939. Vice chmn. finance com. Dem. Nat. Com. 1948. Mem. Am. Legion, Inst. Aeronaut. Scis., Nat. Aeronautic Assn. Clubs: Wings, Sleepy Hollow Country (New York); Congressional Country, Metropolitan, Touchdown, 1923 F Street, Army and Navy (Washington); Little Rock (Ark.). Home: Washington, D.C. Died Aug. 11, 1976.

CONEL, JESSE LEROY (KON'EL), prof. anatomy; b. Mt. Auburn, Ill., Jan. 31, 1883; s. William Rockwell and Estelle (Murphy) C.; A.B., Millikin U., Decatur, Ill., 1912; A.M., U. of Ill., 1913; Ph.D., 1916; m. Helen Mary Boughton, Oct. 18, 1917; 1 dau., Harriet Ames. Instr. in anatomy, N.Y. Univ. and Bellevue Hosp. Med. Sch., 1916, asst. prof., 1919, asso. prof., 1920; asso. prof.

Tufts Coll. Med. Sch., 1921-23; asso. prof. Boston U. Sch. of Medicine, 1923-27, prof. anatomy, 1927-48, head dept. of anatomy, 1944-48; now prof. emeritus; research fellow in pathology, Harvard Med. Sch., 1936-38, research asso. since 1938; research associate in pathology Children's Hosp. and the Infants' Hosp., Boston. Mem. Am. Assn. of Anatomists, Am. Assn. of Univ. Profs., Tau Kappa Epsilon, Gamma Alpha, Sigma Xi, Kappa Delta Pi, Phi Delta Kappa. Episcopalian. Contbr. to anat. jours. Writer monographs on postnatal development of human cerebral cortex. Home: Newton, Mass.

CONGDON, LEON ABEL, chemist; b. Owego, N.Y., May 8, 1885; s. Daniel Olney and Frances Estelle (Scott) C.; B.S., Syracuse U., 1908; M.S., Colgate, 1916; m. Mabel Beatrice Piers, of Fargo, N.D., June 19, 1912. Chemist, N.J. State Expt. Sta., 1909-10; chemist and food and drug insp., N.D. State and Govt. Expt. Sta., 1910-14; chief of State Div. of Food and Drugs, Kan. State Bd. of Health, Topeka, May, 1914-Nov., 1917. Commd. capt., Sanitary Corps N.A., Nov. 1917. Was state hotel commr. of Kan., 1915-17. Has made extensive researches on foods. Mem. Am. Chem. Soc., Kan. Acad. Science, Kan. Pharm. Assn. Mason (K.T.), Odd Fellow. Author: Fight for Food, 1916; also numerous bulls. and articles on chem. and food subjects. Home: Topeka, Kansas.

CONGER, N., dean of edn.; b. Smithville, Tenn., Aug. 21, 1882; s. William P. and Ellen (Foster) C.; B.S., Ohio U., 1917; A.M., Columbia, 1921, PhD., 1929; m. Gladys Pelton, Dec. 25, 1920; 1 dau., Florence Ellen. Teacher in common schs., 1905-09; dir. County Normal Sch., New Vienna, O., 1914-15; dir. Psychol. Clinic, Warren, O., 1917-19; dir. dept. edn., Sue Bennett Memorial Sch., London, Ky., 1919-21; dir. training sch., Southeastern State Teachers Coll., Durant, Okla., 1921-28; dir. of personnel, Okla. Agrl. and Mech. Coll., Stillwater, 1929-30; dir. teachers training, State Dept. of Edn., Okla., 1930-35; dean Sch. of Edn., Okla. Agrl. and Mech. Coll. since 1935, now dean emeritus and professor of education. Member State Jr. Coll. Committee, N.E.A., Okla. Edn. Assn., Phi Delta Kappa, Kappa Delta Pi. Joint author: Drill Book in Arithmetic, 1925; First Steps in Curriculum Building, 1927; Graded Steps in Arithmetic, 1933; Series of Arithmetic Work Books, Grades 1 to 8, 1934. Home: Stillwater, Okla.

CONGLETON, RICHARD J., lawyer; b. Newark, July 25, 1905; s. Jerome T. and Jesse (Tobin) C.; B.S., Princeton, 1928; LL.B., Rutgers U., 1931; m. Margaret Hedden, June 23, 1930 (dec.); children—Margaret Jane (Mrs. James R. Lacey), Richard J., William G.; m. 2d, Melba Coutsonikas, Jan. 20, 1968. Admitted to N.J. bar, 1931, D.C. bar, 1969; asso. McCarter & English, Newark, 1931-37; partner Congleton & McLaughlin, Newark, 1937-42; first asst. prosecutor Essex County, N.J., 1946-48; partner Shanley, Congleton & Fisher, Newark, 1948-52; prosecutor Essex County, 1950-52; gen. atty. Prudential Ins. Co. Am., Newark, 1952-65, sr. v.p., 1965-70. Served with USAAF, 1942-46. Mem. Am., N.J., Essex County (pres. 1954-55), Fed. bar assns., Assn. Life Ins. Counsel, Rutgers Law Sch. Alumni Assn. (pres. 1952). Home: Arlington, Va. Died Jan. 26, 1976.

CONIGLIARO, SALVATORE ALFRED, electronics co. exec.; b. N.Y.C., Sept. 17, 1924; s. Anthony and Mary (Yodice) C.; B.E.E., Poly. Inst. Bklyn., 1949, M.E.E., 1954; m. Sarah Billitteri, July 20, 1945; children—Maryann, Anthony, Peter. With Sperry Rand Corp., 1949-80; mgr. Polaris program Sperry Gyroscope Co., Great Neck and N.Y.C., 1961-64, group mgr. programs, 1964-66, v.p. systems mgr., 1966-67, v.p., gen. mgr. Sperry Systems Mgmt. div., Great Neck, 1967-71, pres. Sperry div. Great Neck, 1971-80. Mem. pres.'s advisory council Poly. Inst. N.Y., 1974-80, trustee, 1974-80. Mem. Navy League (life), IEEE (sr.), Inst. Nav., Am. Soc. Naval Engrs.; Nat. Security Indsl. Assn. (trustee 1971-80, exec. com. 1971-80), Nat. Alliance Businessmen (chmn. L.I. Met. Area chpt. 1975-80). Clubs: Huntington (N.Y.) Crescent, Deepdale Golf and Country (N.Y.). Devel. and prodn. Sparrow I missile, Polaris submarine nav. systems, devel. integrated avionic systems, deep submergence electronic systems. Home: Huntington, N.Y. Died Mar. 23, 1980; buried St. Patrick's Cemetery, Huntington.

CONN, HAROLD JOEL, soil bacteriologist; b. Middletown, Conn., May 29, 1886; s. Herbert William and Julia Maria (Joel) C.; Ph.B., Wesleyan U., Conn., 1908; Ph.D., Cornell U., 1911; m. Anna Carter Mansfield, Jan. 5, 1916; children—Jean Elizabeth, Herbert William. Soil bacteriologist since 1908; asst. in soil technology, N.Y. State Coll. of Agr., until 1911; asso. bacteriologist, N.Y. Agrl. Expt. Sta., 1911-20; chief research 1920-48, now emeritus. Chmn. Biol. Stain Commission, 1922-44, president since 1944. Fellow A.A.A.S.; member Soc. Am. Bacteriologists (chmn. com. on bacteriol. technique 1920-47, pres. 1948), Beta Theta Pi, Sigma Xi, Phi Beta Kappa. Presbyn. Author: Bacteriology (with H. W. Conn), 1923; Biolog. stains (with others), 1925, 29, 36, 40, 46; Lab. Guide in Gen. Bacteriology, 1927; Hist. of Staining, 1933; Staining Procedures, 1943. Editor: (also part author) Manual of Methods for Pure Culture Study of Bacteria, 1923, 26, 30, 36. Editor of Stain Technology (pub. by Biol. Stain Commn.). Home: Geneva, N.Y.

CONNALLY, BEN C., judge; born Marlin, Texas, Dec. 28, 1909; s. Tom and Louise (Clarkson) C.; A.B., U. of Tex., 1930, LL.B., 1933; LL. M., Harvard, 1934; m. Sarah Nell Allen, Sept. 27, 1937; children—Tom, Louise. Admitted to bar. Tex., 1933; practiced as mem. firm Sewell, Taylor, Morris & Connally, Houston, 1934-42, Butler & Binion, 1945-49; U.S. district judge, southern district of Texas, 1949-75, sr. judge. Served with USAAF, 1942-45. Mem. Am., Tex. and Houston bar assns. Methodist. Home: Houston, Tex. Died Dec. 3, 1975.

CONNELL, FREDERICK MARTIN, mining engr.; b. Spencerville, Ont., Can., Sept. 9, 1884; s. Martin and Sarah (Bennett) C.; B.S., Queen's U., 1906, LL.D., 1950; m. Amy Florence Milne, 1912 (dec.); children—John Martin, Elizabeth (Mrs. John E. Kennedy); m. 2d, Cicely J. Burge, 1950. Chmn., dir. Conwest Exploration Co., Ltd.; pres., dir. Central Patricia Gold Mines, Ltd. Metals, controller, Can., 1939-45. Decorated Order Brit. Empire. Mem. Assn. Profl. Engrs. Ont., Canadian Inst. Mining and Metallurgy. Mason. Clubs: York, National, Rosedale Golf, Toronto Hunt (Toronto); Mount Royal (Montreal); Mining (N.Y.C.). Home: Toronto, Canada.

CONNELL, LOUIS FRED, coll. prof.; b. Mt. Vernon, Ark., Oct. 2, 1883; s. Christopher C. and Sarah (Maddox) C.; Diploma N. Tex. Normal Coll., 1907; A.B., N. Tex. State Teachers Coll., 1924; A.M., Univ. Tex., 1925; grad. study, Univ. Wis., summer 1935; m. Hazel Price, Sept. 4, 1912; children—Louis Fred, Sarah Frances (Mrs. Frederick Norton Wells). Teacher of math., Hamlin (Tex.) High Sch., 1907-08; teacher math. and science, Honey Grove (Tex.) High Sch., 1909-11, prin., 1912-17, supt. of schs., 1920-24; registrar and asso. prof., Tex. Coll. of Arts and Industries, 1925-27, prof. and chmn. dept. economics and sociology since 1927, asso. dean, 1929-34, dir. div. of arts and scis. since 1947; summer sch. teacher, N. Tex. State Teachers Coll., 1921-24. Mem. Am. Assn. Univ. Profs., Southwestern Political and Social Sci. Assn. Tex. State Teachers Assn. (life mem.). Democrat. Presbyterian. Home: Kingsville, Tex.

CONNELLY, BERNARD CHAMBERLIN, fgn. service officer; b. Rock Island, Ill., May 3, 1908; grad. Phillips Exeter Academy; A.B., Princeton, 1930; married; three children. Appointed clerk for the Am. consulate, Trieste, 1931, vice consul, 1931-32; assigned Fgn. Service Sch., 1932; vice consul, Sydney, Australia, 1932, Melbourne, 1933; vice consul, 3d sec., Bucharest, 1936; vice consul, Karachi and Kabul, 1937-41; 3d sec., vice consul, Lima, 1941, 2d sec., vice consul, 1941-46, 2d sec., consul, 1946; assigned Dept. State, 1946-49; 1st sec., Pretoria, 1949-51; consul, Zagreb, 1951-54, Lyon, France, 1954-57; assigned Dept. State, from 1957. Died Feb. 7, 1977.

CONNELLY, MARC (MARCUS COOK), playwright; b. McKeesport, Pa., Dec. 13, 1890; s. Patrick Joseph and Mabel Fowler (Cook) C.; ed. Trinity Hall, Washington, Pa., 1902-07. Reporter Pitts. newspapers and writer of humorous column Pitts. Gazette Times; contbr. verse, articles and short stories (O. Henry award 1930) to mags; former prof. playwrighting Yale. Past pres. Author's League of Am., Nat. Inst. Arts and Letters. Mem. exec. com. U.S. nat. commn. for UNESCO. Clubs: Coffee House, Players; Savage (London). Author: The Wisdom Tooth (play), 1926; The Green Pastures (Pulitzer award), 1930; A Souvenir from Qam (novel), 1965; Voices Offstage (memoirs), 1968; A Stitch in Time (comedy), 1977; co-author: Dulcy, To the Ladies, Merton of the Movies, Beggar on Horseback, The Farmer Takes a Wife, other plays, several musical comedies. Address: New York, N.Y. Died Dec. 21, 1980.

CONNELLY, MATHEW J., sec. to pres. of U.S.; b. Clinton, Mass., Nov. 19, 1907; grad., Fordham U., 1930; married. In stock brokerage bus., New York, N.Y., 1930-33; with Western Union Telegraph Co., 1933-34; with Fed. Emergency Relief Adminstrn., Boston, Mass., 1935; with div. of investigation, Works Progress Adminstrn., 1935-38; mem. appropriations com., U.S. House of Reps., 1939; mem. spl. com. to investigate campaign expenditures, U.S. Senate, 1940; mem. spl. com. to investigate Nat. Defense Program, 1941-44; exec. sec. to v.p., Jan. 1945; sec. to pres. from April 1945. Home: Cicero, Ill. Died July 10, 1976.

CONNER, BENJAMIN F., business exec.; b. 1884. Dir. Gray Mfg. Co., Hartford, Conn., Phoenix State Bank & Trust Co., Hartford; pres. and dir. Colta Mfg. Co. Home: West Hartford.

CONNER, NORVAL WHITE, coll. adminstr.; b. Blacksburg, Va., Sept. 18, 1905; s. William George and Virginia (Thomas) C.; B.S., Va. Poly Inst., 1925, M.E., 1926; M.S., Ia. State Coll., 1930; m. Margaret Prentis Miller. Engr., Atlantic Ice Co., Coatesville, Pa., 1926-27, Lukens Steel Co., Coatesville, 1927-28; research engr. Ia. State Coll.; instr. mech. engring. Va. Poly. Inst., Blacksburg, 1928-29, asst. prof. applied mechanics, head aeronautics, 1930-37; asst. prof. engr. mechanics N.C. State Coll., Raleigh, 1937-38, asso. prof., 1938-44, prof. fluid mechanics, 1944-47, prof. mech. engring., head design div. 1947-51, dir. engring. research, 1951-67, asst. dean for research, from 1967. Mem. Am. Soc. M.E. (sec.-treas. Raleigh sect.; hon. chmn. student br.; sec. Region IV 2 years), Am. Soc. for Testing Materials (mem. council, vice chmn. Middle Atlantic dist.), Am. Soc. Engring. Edn. (pres. Southeastern sect.), Am. Ordnance Assn. (bd. dirs.), N.C. Soc. Engring., Sigma Xi, Phi Kappa Phi, Tau Beta Pi, Pi Tau Sigma, Sigma Chi. Presbyn. Clubs: Engineers (Raleigh), Executives. Contbr. to Engineer Experiments Sta. Bull. Home: Raleigh, N.C. Deceased.

CONNER, SABRA, author; b. Normal, Ill., Apr. 9, 1884; d. Samuel and Sara Elizabeth C.; student U. of Chicago, A.B. and A.M., U. of Ore.; unmarried. Began as teacher pub. schs., 1902; writer of hist. novels since 1927. Mem. Christian Ch. Eastern Star. Mem. Woman's Professional League. Author: The Quest of the Sea Otter, 1927; Sweet Water Trail, 1928; Captain Red Legs, 1930; Fighting Starrs of Oregon, 1932. Home: Portland, Ore.

CONNOLLY, DONALD HILARY, former army officer; b. Fort Mojave, Ariz., Feb. 11, 1880; s. Thomas Worthington and Mary Alice (Kiser) C.; student U. Cal., 1905-06; B.S., U.S. Mill. Acad., 1910; student Engr. Sch. of Application, 1911-12, Command and Gen. Staff Sch., 1922-23, Army War Coll., 1928-29; m. Grace Hollingsworth Baxter, Sept. 16, 1916 (dec. Sept. 1963); children—Donald Hilary, Thomas Worthington. Joined C.E. U.S. Army, 1910; fgn. service in Canal Zone, Philipines, France, Iran, and Iraq; mem. War Dept. Gen. Staff, 1916-22, in charge Memphis River and Harbor Dist., 1923-28, instr. Command and Gen. Staff Sch., Fort Leavenworth, Kan., 1929-34; in charge Civil Works Adminstrn., Los Angeles, 1934, Chicago River and Harbor Dist., 1934-35, WPA, So. Calif., 1935-39; comdr. 2d Engrs., Fort Logan, Colo., 1939-40, adminstr. civil aeronautics Dept. Commerce, Washington, 1940-41; with Hdqrs. USAAF, Washington, 1942; comdr. Persian Gulf command, 1942-44; dep. Army-Navy Liquidation Commn., 1945, fgn. liquidation commn., 1945-48; ret. maj. gen.; dir. Balt. dept. aviation, 1948-56. Decorated D.S.M., Legion of Merit; Order of Suvorov (Russia); Order of Homayoon (Iran); hon. companion Order of Bath (British). Mem. Am. Soc. C.E., Soc. Am. Mil. Engrs., Am. Legion, Newcomen Soc. of Eng. Democrat. Mason. Clubs: Army and Navy, Army, Navy Country (Washington); Gibson Island (Md.). Home: Gibson Island MD 21056

CONNOLLY, PAUL RAYMOND, lawyer; b. Balt., June 28, 1922; s. Paul Raymond and Loretta (Barry) C.; A.B. cum laude, Loyola Coll., Balt., 1943; LL.B., Georgetown U., 1948, LL.M., 1952; m. Mary Catherine Garvey, June 26, 1948; children—Mary Tressa, Paul Brian, Margaret Carroll, Sheila Barry, Michael Ignatius, Peter Christopher. Admitted to Md. bar, 1948, D.C. bar, 1949; mem. firm Hogan & Hartson, Washington, 1948-66, partner, 1956-66; partner firm Williams, Connolly & Califano, 1967-78; adj. prof. Georgetown U. Law Sch., 1956-65. Mem. adv. council Practicing Law Inst.; mem. Jud. Conf. D.C. Circuit, 1954-78. Trustee Pub. Defender Service, D.C., 1969-78. Served to lt. (j.g.) USNR, 1943-46. Fellow Am. Coll. Trial Lawyers; mem. Am. (council sect. litigation 1973-75, chmn. 1976-77), D.C. (v.p. 1958, dir. 1959-61), Md. bar assns., Internat. Assn. Ins. Counsel (exec. com. 1967-69), Am. Judicature Soc., Barristers, Lawyers and Counsellors, John Carroll Soc. (chmn. bd. govs. 1967-69, pres. 1969-70), Delta Theta Phi, Alpha Sigma Nu. Democrat. Roman Catholic. Clubs: Metropolitan, George Town, Internat. Nat. Lawyers (Washington); Chevy Chase, Burning Tree; Mid-Ocean (Bermuda). Home: Washington, D.C. Died July 13, 1978; buried St. Gabriel's Cemetery, Potomac, Md.

CONNOR, CHARLES WILLIAM, govt. ofcl.; b. Leith, Pa., Oct. 11, 1883; s. Charles and Jane (Musgrove) C.; student Pa. State Coll.; m. Agnes Turnbull, Oct. 17, 1907; 1 son, Charles William. Mgr. mining div. Armco Steel Corp., Montcoal, W.Va., 1927-50; v.p. Colcord Coal Sales Co., Charleston, W.Va., 1943-50; adminstr. Defense Solid Fuels Administration since 1950. Member American Institute of Mining and Metall. Engineers, Am. Mining Congress, W.Va. Mining Inst. Republican. Meth. Elk, Mason (32 deg., K.T., Shriner). Clubs: Rotary, Press (Charleston, W.Va.). Home: Washington, also Charleston, W.Va.

CONNOR, FRED (WALLACE), naval officer (ret.); b. Augusta, Me., Feb. 25, 1885; s. Fred Elsworth and Etta May (Haskell) C.; student special course George Washington U., 1916; m. Geralde Smith, May 1, 1924. Enlisted as apprentice, U.S. Navy 1902, commd. ensign, 1917, and advanced through grades to capt., 1942; retired with rank of rear admiral, 1946. Recipient Mexican Campaign ribbon, World War I (victory) with submarine bar, Commendation ribbon awarded by comdr. in chief Pacific; Bronze Star Medal (V) Iwo Jima, Sec. of Navy Citation ribbon. Republican. Home: Honolulu, T.H.

CONNORS, C(HARLES) H(ENRY), horticulturist; b. New Brunswick, N.J., July 2, 1884; s. William Henry and Martha Matilda (Steinert) C.; B.Sc., Rutgers Coll., 1913, Ph.D., 1928; m. Jennie Roberta Wark, Oct. 10, 1916; 1 dau. Roberta Elizabeth. With N.J. Agrl. Expt. Sta. since 1913; with Rutgers U. since 1920, prof. and research specialist in ornamental horticulture since 1932. Reported relation of soil reaction to color in hydrangeas, 1922; reported on heredity in peaches and sterility in peaches, 1919. Mem. Middlesex Council, Boy Scouts of America (vice pres. 1917). Recipient Silver Beaver from Boy Scouts of America; gold medal Dahlia Soc. of N.J. for service; bronze medal Garden Club of N.J. Fellow A.A.A.S.; mem. Am. Soc. for Hort. Science, Am. Genetics Assn., Am. Hort. Council, Sigma Xi, Pi Alpha Xi. Alpha Sigma Phi. Democrat. Mem. Dutch Reformed Ch. Mason. Club: Kiwanis. Author: Chemical Gardening for the Amateur (with V. J. Tiedjens), 1940; Grounds for Living (with others), 1946. Contbr. on hort. subjects to bulls., mags. and jours. Home: Highland Park, N.J.

CONSIDINE, ROBERT BERNARD, newspaperman; b. Washington, D.C., Nov. 4, 1908; s. James William and Sophie (Small) C.; ed. Gonzaga High Sch., George Washington U.; m. Mildred Anderson, July 21, 1931; children—Michael Riley, Robert Barry, Dennis Joel, Deborah Joan. Corr. sports, drama, writer Sunday features Washington Post, 1930-33; sports editor, editorial and feature writer Washington Herald, 1933-37; syndicated sports columnist, trial reporter, feature writer N.Y. Am., during 1937 was transferred to Mirror and Internat. News Service, 1938; war corr. Internat. News Service, England, 1943, CBI theatre, 1945, Korea, 1950. Recipient George R. Holmes Memorial Award, 1947; Catholic Writers Guild and Catholic Inst. of the Press Awards, 1949, Lasker Award 1952; Overseas Press Club awards for best fgn. correspondence, 1957-58; Named to Deadline Club/Sigma Delta Chi Hall of Fame, 1975. Mem. Sigma Alpha Epsilon, Sigma Delta Chi. Roman Catholic. Knight of Malta. Clubs: Dutch Treat, Overseas Press (past pres.), Nat. Press (Washington), Artists and Writers. Author: MacArthur the Magnificent, 1942; (with Capt. Ted W. Lawson) Thirty Seconds over Tokyo, 1943; (with Sammy Schulman) Where's Sammy, 1943; (with Gen. Jonathan M. Wainwright) Gen. Wainwright's Story, 1946; (with Babe Ruth) The Babe Ruth Story, 1948; Innocents at Home, 1951; Panama Canal, 1952; Man Against Fire, 1955; Christmas Stocking, (with Bill Slocum) Jack Dempsey Story; (with W. R. Hearst, Jr. and Frank Conniff) Ask Me Anything-Our Adventures with Krushchev; The Brink's Robbery; It's All News to Me—A Reporter's Deposition; asst. Harold E. Stassen, Stanislaw Mikolajczyk and Robert E. Stribling in prep. their books, 1948; motion picture originals: Church of the Good Thief, Ladies Day, The Beginning or the End, The Babe Ruth Story, Hoodlum Empire. Contbr. fiction and articles to nat. mags., 1944-75. Home: New York, N.Y. Died Sept. 25, 1975.

CONSTABLE, STUART, architect, landscape architect, pub. ofcl.; b. Columbus, Ohio, Sept. 9, 1900; s. Thomas Gibson and Francis M. (Whisner) C.; B.S., Ohio State U., 1922; M. Landscape Architecture, Harvard, 1927; m. Margaret Joyce Cottingham, Sept. 9, 1922; children—John Stuart (dec.), Thomas Gibson II. Pvt. practice St. Petersburg, Fla., and Stamford, Conn., 1924-35; chief designer Dept. Parks City N.Y., 1936-55, exec. officer, 1955-60; acting commnr. N.Y.C. Planning Commn., 1950-60, N.Y.C. Art Commn., 1949-55; v.p. operations N.Y. World's Fair 1964-65 Corp., 1960-66; pres. C & T Enterprises, Ft. Lauderdale, 1966-72; cons. 1st hdqrs. UN, Jones Beach State Pkwy. Authority and N.Y. State Power Authority, also James Found. of St. James, Mo., Dorado, P.R. Winner Bklyn. War Meml. Competition, 1945. Mem. Am. Security Council, Alpha Gamma Rho. Clubs: Surf (Wrightsville Beach, N.C.); Cape Fear Country (Wilmington, N.C.). Home: Wilmington, N.C. Died Sept. 11, 1979; buried National Cemetery, Wilmington.

CONSTABLE, WILLIAM GEORGE, art historian, author; b. Derby, Eng., Oct. 27, 1887; ed. Slade Sch., London, Eng.; M.A., Cambridge (Eng.) U. Former asst. dir. Nat. Gallery, London, dir. Courtauld Inst. Art, U. London, Slade prof. Cambridge U., curator paintings Boston Mus. Fine Arts, lectr. Yale U. New Haven. Decorated chevalier Legion of Honor; commendatore Crown of Italy; officer Ordre Arts and Lettres, France. Fellow Soc. Antiquaries, Internat. Inst. Conservators (past pres.); mem. Art Workers Guild, Goldsmiths Co., Am. Acad. Arts and Scis. Author: English Painting 17th and 18th Centuries; The Painters Workshop; Canaletto and Art Collecting in the U.S. Contbrs. articles to profl. jours. Home: Cambridge, Mass. Died Feb., 1976.

CONVERSE, JOHN MARQUIS, surgeon; b. San Francisco, Sept. 29, 1909; s. George Marquis and Adele (Clot) C.; student Ecole Gerson, 1920-24; A.B., Lycee Janson de Sailly, 1928; M.D., U. Paris (France), 1935; D.honoris causa, U. Bordeaux (France), 1978; m. Sheila Paull-Delany, Nov. 12, 1932; 1 son, John Marquis; m. 2d, Veronica Balfe Cooper, June 27, 1964. Surgeon-dir. clinic reconstructive plastic surgery of face Manhattan Eye, Ear and Throat Hosp., N.Y.C., 1952-75, chmn. dept. plastic surgery; Lawrence D. Bell prof. plastic surgery N.Y. U. Sch. Medicine, dir. Inst. Reconstructive Plastic Surgery, N.Y. U. Med. Center, from 1957; cons. VA Hosp., N.Y.C.; med. cons. Armed Forces. Served as maj. French Army, North Africa, 1943-44, AUS, 1944-46. Decorated Croix de Guerre with palms; comdr. Legion of Honor, comdr. Order Sci. Merit (France). Diplomate Am. Bd. Plastic Surgery. Fellow A.C.S., Am. Soc. Plastic and Reconstructive Surgeons (spl. citation 1978), Am. Assn. Plastic Surgeons (hon. citation 1976), Am. Acad. Ophthalmology and Otolaryngology, N.Y. Acad. Medicine; hon. fellow Spanish, Venezuelan, Uruguayan, Brazilian, Japanese plastic surgery socs.; mem. Internat. Soc. for Advancement Microbiology (vice chmn. 1976), Soc. Rehab. Facially Disfigured (v.p. from 1951, founder), N.Y. Acad. Scis., Purkinje Soc. Czechoslovakia (hon.), Brit. Assn. Plastic Surgeons; French Soc. Plastic and Reparative Surgery (corr.), Transplantation Soc. (founder, pres. 1968). Author: (with Dr. V.H. Kazanjian) Surgical Treatment of Facial Injuries, 3d edit., 1974, also numerous sci. articles. Editor: Reconstructive Plastic Surgery, 2d edit., 1977. Address: New York, N.Y. Died Jan. 31, 1981.

CONWAY, CARL FREDERICK, lawyer; b. Garner, Ia., Sept. 16, 1906; s. Charles Robert and Emma (Hoeft) C.; B.A., Coe Coll., 1929; J.D., U. Ia., 1931; m. Edith Marietta Fisher, July 16, 1941; 1 dau., Roberta. Admitted to Ia. bar, 1931, practiced in Osage; mem. firm Conway & Casey; county atty. Mitchell County, 1935-58. Dir. Home Savs. & Loan Assn., Osage. Served with AUS, 1942-45; PTO. Mem. Am., Ia. (bd. govs. 1953-58, pres. 1959-60), Mitchell County bar assns., Am. Legion (past post comdr.), Phi Kappa Tau, Phi Delta Phi. Republican. Lutheran. Rotarian (pres. Osage 1948-49). Home: Osage, Iowa. Died May 26, 1978.

COOK, CECIL NEWTON, lawyer; b. Lufkin, Tex., Feb. 14, 1905; s. William Newton and Mattie (Stanley) C.; LL.B., U. Tex., 1926; m. Donalda Maxine Lamb, Jan. 7, 1944; children—James Randolph, Richard Nash. Admitted to Tex. bar, 1926; practice in Fort Worth, 1926-34, Houston, 1934-80; asst. dist. atty., 1926; asso. Coates & Mastin, 1927-28; partner Phillips, Trammell, Chizum, Price & Estes, 1929-34, Cook & Walker, 1935, Kayser, Liddell, Benbow & Butler, 1936-40, Cook, Blake, McCormick & Dickson, 1941-44, Butler, Binion, Rice, Cook & Knapp, 1945-80. Lectr., Southwestern Legal Found., Dallas, Am. Bar Assn. N.Y.C. Spl. asst. atty. gen. Tex., 1954; chmn. bd. Houston Law Rev., Inc., 1970-77. Pres. Houston Civic Music Assn., 1951. Trustee Edna Gladney Home, Fort Worth, S. Tex. Coll. Law, Houston (chmn.), Gray Found. Fellow Am. Bar Found., Tex. Bar Found; mem. Am., Tex. (past chmn. mineral sect.). Houston (past pres.) bar assns., Tex. Juridical Inst. (trustee 1973-80), Am. Law Inst., Phi Kappa Psi, Phi Delta Phi. Baptist (chmn. bd. deacons). Clubs: Houston Country, Petroleum, Ramada, Houston (dir. 1970-73, v.p. 1973-74) (Houston). Contbr. articles to legal jours., Mid-Century Law. Home: Houston, Texas. Died Aug. 12, 1980.

COOK, HOWARD NORTON, artist; b. Springfield, Mass., July 16, 1901; s. Frank Chester and Annie (Norton) C.; studied Art Students League, N.Y.C., 1919-21; m. Barbara Latham, May 27, 1927. Commd. to do war industry paintings Office Emergency Adminstrn., Norfolk, Va., 1942, guest prof. art, U. Tex., 1942-43, U. N.Mex., summers 1947, 60, U. Calif., 1948; guest instr. Colo. Springs Fine Arts Center, 1949; tchr. painting Mpls. Sch. Art, 1945, 50, guest artist, 1950; leader war art unit C.E., U.S. Army, PTO, 1943; war artist corr. Collier's mag., 1943-44; guest artist Scripps Coll., 1951, Washington U., St. Louis, 1954-55, Highlands (N.Mex.) U., summer 1957; artist-in-residence Roswell (N.Mex.) Mus. and Art Center, 1967-68. Exhbn. war paintings, watercolors, Rehn Galleries, 1945, oil paintings of N.Mex., winter 1949; paintings of N.Y., Alexandre Rabow Galleries, San Francisco, 1955; war paintings Roswell Mus. and Art Center, 1968; paintings of the City, Grand Central Moderns, N.Y.C., 1951, 56, Grand Central Moderns, Collages exhbn., 1960, 64, Phila. Art Alliance, exhbn. collages 1961, paintings, collages Colorado Springs Fine Arts Center, 1961; paintings Governor's Gallery, Santa Fe, N.Mex., 1977; retrospective paintings exhbns. Rosequist Galleries, Tucson, 1962, Raymond Burr Galleries, Beverly Hills, Calif., 1962, Roswell Mus. and Art Center, 1975, 76; retrospective exhbn. graphics Prakapas Gallery, N.Y.C., 1976; exhbn. prints and watercolors Bethesda (Md.) Art Gallery, 1977, 78; executed fresco murals law library, Springfield, Mass., 1934, Fed. Bldg., 1936, Pitts., Alamo Plaza P.O. Lobby, San Antonio, 1937-39. Mem. regional and nat. jury Am. Painting Today, Met. Mus. illustrator in woodcut, pen and ink on Forum (6 years), Harper's Century, Scribner's, Survey Graphic, Nation mags.; executed frescoes, 2 tempera murals, U.S. Post Office, Corpus Christi, Tex., 1941; mural paintings; commn. Mayo Clinic, Rochester, Minn., 1952-53; circuit exhbn. 20 pastels, 25 Museums U.S., 1951, 52, 53; 20 pastels Grand Central Moderns, 1952, oil of New York, 1951; represented by etchings, woodcuts, lithographs, drawings and water colors in U.S. and fgn. museums including Met. Mus., Whitney Mus. Am. Art, Mus. Mod. Art, N.Y. Pub. Library (N.Y.C.), Art Inst. Chgo., Fogg Art, Mus. Work in graphic arts awarded 9 prizes, 1929-37; Mrs. Henry F. Noyes award to Exodus etching Soc. Am. Etchers, 1946; represented in 50 Prints of Year for 5 years; several awards including 6th purchase award, Artists for Victory Exhbn., Met. Mus., N.Y.C., 1942; Painting Purchase award Denver Art Mus., 1950; Mark Rothko Found. award, 1951; Fleisher Meml. Purchase Painting, Phila., 1952; Tupperware purchase award, 1956; 1st award oil painting Tucson Art Assn., 1958; purchase awards drawings Mus. N.Mex., Dallas Museum Fine Arts, Nat. Acad. Design, 1958; 1st purchase award paintings Oklahoma City Art Ann., Am. Ann.; Oakes purchase award, Collage-Taos Art Assn.; Samuel F. B. Morse Gold medal Nat. Acad. Design; Grand award oil painting N.Mex. State Fair, 1964; Logan medal in graphics Art Inst. Chgo.; Gold medal mural painting Archtl. League N.Y.; N.Mex. Gov.'s award for Excellence in Fine Arts, 1979. Mem. Graphic Class N.A.D.; life mem. Art Student's League of N.Y. Contbr. articles to Survey-Graphic, Jr. Red Cross, Forum, Am. Mag. Art, Springfield (Mass.). Republican. Author-illustrator; Sammis Army (juvenile picture book), 1943; Road from Prints to Frescoes (autobiography), 1942. Home: Santa Fe, N.Mex. Died June 24, 1980.

COOK, ORVAL R., aero. industry exec.; b. West Union, Ind., July 27, 1898; s. Owen E. and Eliza A. (Mathas) C.; B.S., U.S. Mil. Acad., 1922; student Air Service Advanced Flying Sch., 1924, Air Corps Engrng. Sch., 1930, Air Corps Tactical Sch., 1938; grad. Command and Gen. Staff Sch., 1939; m. Minna Edwards, Sept. 11, 1925; children—Peyton E., Orval E., Benjamin H. Commd. 2d lt., Air Service, U.S. Army, 1922, advanced through grades to gen., USAF, 1954; dep. comdr-in-chief U.S. European Command. 1954-56; ret.; pres., gen. mgr. Aerospace Industries Assn. Am., Washington, 1957-80; dir. U.S. Life Ins. Co., Washington. Decorated Legion of Merit, DS.M. with cluster; Legion of Honor (France); Order of Merit (Italy). Asso. fellow Inst. Aero. Scis. Home: Falls Church, Va. Died Mar. 18, 1980; buried Arlington Nat. Cemetery.

COOK, ROBERT CECIL, educator, author; b. Fayette, Ala., July 6, 1903; s. James Alfred and Athea (McKelvey) C.; B.S., Miss. State, 1924; A.M., Columbia, 1933, Ed.D., 1942; m. Bonnibel Wood, June 30, 1926; children—Robert Cecil, Rhetta Louise (Mrs. R.T. Dodder). Tchr. and prin. of high schs., 1924-29; dir. U. High Sch., dir. tchr. edn., asso. prof. edn. U. Miss., 1929-41, dean Sch. Edn., dir. summer session, prof. secondary edn., 1941-42; pres. Miss. So. Coll., 1945-54; v.p., gen. mgr. Jackson (Miss.) State Times, 1955; pres. Southeastern Life Ins. Co., 1955-70; dir. Univ. and Coll. Press of Miss., 1970-73; pres. Educators' Biog. Press, Hattiesburg, 1973-79. Dist. chmn. Boy Scouts Am.; mem. Miss. Econ. Council; chmn., State Library Commn., 1968-72, Miss. Ednl. TV Commn. Trustee, Insts. of Higher Learning. Served 39th Brigade Coast Arty., Anti-Aircraft, Seattle, Dec. 1942-Oct. 1943; staff officer, A.S.T.P., Stanford U. Oct. 1943-Dec. 1944. Chief, curriculum and advisement sects. Army Edn. Program, U.K. Base Hdqrs. ETOUSA, 1944-45. Recipient Outstanding Citizen award, Hattiesburg, 1948. Fellow AAAS; mem. Ciceronian Circle, Newcomen Soc., Phi Delta Kappa, Alpha Tau Omega, Pi Kappa Pi, Omicron Delta Kappa. Episcopalian. Mason, Rotarian. Club: Country. Author: McGowah Place and Other Memoirs; Mist over the Delta. Editor Who's Who in American Education, 1928-68; Current Science Rev., 1926-28; Presidents in American Colleges and Universities, 1934-68; Leaders in American Science, 1953-68. Home: Hattiesburg, Miss. Died Mar. 6, 1979; buried Highland Cemetery.

COOK, SAMUEL HENRY, educator; born Brunswick, Ga., Feb. 9, 1887; s. Samuel Henry and Virginia Madison (Ralston) C.; A.B., Davidson (N.C.) Coll. 1909, A.M., 1910, hon. Pd.D. 1929; unmarried. Began as instr. gymnastics, Davidson Coll., 1910; teacher Berry Schs., Mt. Berry, Ga., 1911-18 dean, 1918-27, acting pres., from 1951; head dept. phys. scis., professor of mathematics and dean of Berry College, 1927, acting president, registrar, from 1936. Mem. Davidson Coll. Alumni Council. Served in U.S. Army, World War. Mem. Am. Math. Soc., Am. Legion, Omicron Delta Kappa, Democrat. Presbyterian. Clubs: Honor, Varsity, Georgian, X Club. Address: Mount Berry, Ga. Died Aug. 7, 1975.

COOK, THOMAS IRA, polit. scientist; b. Suffolk, Eng., Mar. 31, 1907; s. Frederick and Martha (Pell) C.; student Dover (Eng.) Coll., 1921-25; B.Sc. in Econs., London Sch. Econs., London U., 1928; Ph.D., Columbia, 1937; m. Anne Peloubet, June 21, 1930 (dec.); children—Penelope Anne, Jennifer Taft; m. 2d, Anne Crystal. Came to U.S., 1930. Instr. econs. Acadia U., Wolfville, N.S., 1929-30; instr. govt., Columbia, 1930-36; asst. prof. polit. sci. U. Cal. at Los Angeles, 1936-39; asso., later prof. polit. sci. U. Wash., 1939-49; vis. prof. social scis. U. Chgo., 1948-49; vis. prof. polit. sci. Johns Hopkins, 1949-50, prof. polit. sci., 1950-66, chmn. dept., 1961-64; H.Y. Benedict prof. U. Tex. at El Paso, 1966-76. Asst. dir. wage stblzn. div. 12th regional WLB, 1942-44. Mem. Am. Polit. Sci. Assn. (exec. council 1943-45), Am. Assn. U. Profs., Northwest Polit. Sci. Assn. (acting pres. 1947-48). Author: History of Political Philosophy from Plato to Burke, 1937; Democratic Rights versus Communist Activity, 1954; Power Through Purpose, 1954. Editor: John Locke, Two Treatises of Government, 1947. Mem. editorial bd. Western Polit. Quar., 1948-50. Home: El Paso, Tex. Died Aug. 10, 1976.

COOKE, EDMUND FRANCIS, lawyer, ex-congressman; b. Prescott, Ariz., Apr. 13, 1885; s. John H. and Mary (Goodman) C.; ed. pub. schs.; m. Jennie O. Swanson, June 29, 1908; children—Eileene J., John H., Richard T. Admitted to N.Y. bar, 1910, and since in practice at Buffalo. Mem. N.Y. State Assembly, 1922-28; mem. 71st and 72d Congresses (1929-33), 41st N.Y. Dist. Admitted to practice before Supreme Court of U.S., 1939. Republican. Home: Alden, N.Y.

COOKE, JAMES NEGLEY, JR., drug and pharm. mfr.; b. Pitts., Mar. 12, 1908; s. James Negley and Mary (Miller) C.; grad. Salisbury (Conn.) Sch., 1928; student Princeton, 1932; m. Frances Ann Bonfoey, May 2, 1931; children—Diann Bonfoey Coombs, James Negley III; m. 2d, Nancy Reynolds, Dec. 23, 1941; children—Peter Reynolds, Christopher Creighton. Salesman Monroe Chem. Co., Quincy, Ill., 1931-32; mgr. Monroe Chem. Co., Ltd., London, Eng., 1932; sales mgr. Monroe Chem. Co., N.Y.C., 1933-34; gen. mgr. Wells & Richardson Co., Burlington, Vt., subsidiary Sterling Drug, Inc., 1935-40, The Cummer Products Co., also The Molle Co., Bedford, Ohio, subsidiary Sterling Drug Inc., 1940-43; divisional v.p. Cummer Products Co. div. Sterling Drug, Inc., Brattleboro, Vt., 1943-50; dir. marketing Sterling Drug, Inc., N.Y.C., 1950-56, v.p., 1956-72, sr. v.p., 1972-74, dir., 1960-74, adv. dir., 1974-76, pres. Glenbrook Labs. div., 1958-72; past v.p., dir. Mt. Mansfield Co., Stowe, Vt., Mad River Glen Ski Area, Waitsfield, Vt.; v.p. d'Con Co., Inc., subsidiary Sterling Drug, Inc., N.Y.C., 1957-78. Hon. dir. Brattleboro Meml. Hosp.; mem. bd., past chmn. Brand Names Found., N.Y.C.; bd. dirs. Topnotch at Stowe, Vt.; past trustee Holderness Sch., Plymouth, N.H.; trustee, vice chmn. bd. U.S. Ski Ednl. Found. Inc., Park City, Utah, 1972-78; past pres., hon. v.p., bd. dirs. Proprietary Assn. Mem. U.S. Eastern Amateur Ski Assn. (past dir.; chmn. N.Y. com. U.S. Ski Team Fund 1969-78). Clubs: Princeton, Amateur Ski (N.Y.C.); Stowe Country, Mt. Mansfield Ski (Stowe); Cap and Gown (Princeton, N.J.); Pinnacle (N.Y.C.). Home: Stowe, Vt. Died Aug. 2, 1978; buried Stowe, Vt.

COOKENBOO, JOHN B., gas co. exec.; b. Wharton, Tex., 1910; ed. South Tex. Coll., 1943. Sr. v.p. adminstrn. and finance Houston Natural Gas Corp., 1967-69, exec. v.p., 1969-71, vice chmn. bd., 1971-73, past dir.; v.p., dir. Oasis Pipe Line Co.; dir. Houston Pipe Line Co., H.N.G. Petrochems. Co., Valley Gas Transmission Co., Valley Pipe Lines, Inc., Liquid Carbonic Corp., Intratex Gas Co., HNG Oil Co. Mem. Am. Inst. C.P.A.'s, Financial Execs. Inst. Club: Petroleum (Houston). Home: Houston, Tex. Died Nov. 8, 1977.

COOKSON, FRANK BARTON, educator; b. Wigan, Eng., Sept. 27, 1912; s. William and Hannah (Barton) C.; came to U.S., 1913, naturalized, 1939; B.Mus., Northwestern U., 1935, M.Mus., 1936; Ph.D., Eastman Sch. Music, 1947; m. 2d, Sandra Palmer, June 17, 1961; children (by previous marriage)—Julie (Mrs. Denis Jones), Christine (Mrs. David Wheelock); 1 son by present marriage, Matthew Barton; stepchildren—Karla Wentzel, Ingrid Wentzel. Mem. faculty Northwestern U., 1939-62, prof., chmn. dept. theory and composition, 1951-62, mng. editor Ednl. Music mag., 1936-53; organist, choir dir. chs. in Ill., 1934-62; v.p. Ednl. Music Bur., 1953-63; v.p. Frederick Charles Pub. Co., 1959-62; prof. U. Conn., 1962-77, dean Sch. Fine Arts, 1962-67. Mem. Conn. Commn. on Arts, 1965-77. Mem. bd. edn. Regional High Sch. 11, Conn., 1965-67. Mem. Nat. Council Fine Arts Deans, Phi Mu Alpha, Pi Kappa Lambda. Co-author, gen. editor: Creative-Analytical Theory of music, vols. 1 and 2, 1948-49. Composer over 60 choral compositions. Home: Storrs, Conn. Died Feb. 2, 1977.

COOLEY, ARTHUR EDWARD, lawyer; b. Cloverdale, Calif., Jan. 22, 1882; s. John Buckingham and Elizabeth N. (Elliott) C.; A.B., Stanford U., 1903, LL.B., 1904; m. Ethel McLean, Oct. 15, 1914 (died 1934); children—Florence Elizabeth, Arthur Crawford; m. 2d, Frances R. Hudson, Feb. 1, 1936. Admitted to Calif. bar, 1903, Supreme Ct. of U.S. bar, 1920; practiced law in San Francisco since 1904; sr. mem. firm Cooley, Crowley, Gaither, Godward, Castro & Huddleson; member of the board of directors of Healy Tibbitts Constrn. Co., S. & L. Subdivision. Incorporated, H. R. Basford Company, Michel & Pfeffer Iron Works, Inc., Pacific Indemnity Co.; pres. Cooley Ranch, Inc.; owner livestock ranch Calif. Mem. Delta Upsilon, Phi Delta Phi. Clubs: Bohemian, San Francisco Commercial. Home: San Francisco.

COOMBE, REGINALD GORTON, banker; b. N.Y.C., Jan. 27, 1895; s. Thomas Gorton and Lydia (Daikers) C.; cum laude Groton Sch., 1914; B.A., Yale, 1918; m. Philena Hope Lincoln, May 22, 1922; children—Patricia, Philena Emily (dec.), Hope Lincoln. Salesman Bonbright & Co., 1919-20; sec. in office of William Rockefeller, 1920-23; sales exec. Brown Bros. & Co., 1923-27; partner Edward B. Smith & Co., and successor, Smith Barney & Co., N.Y. City, 1927-39; v.p. Hanover Bank, N.Y.C., 1939-55, sr. v.p., 1955-58; cons. Laurance S. Rockefeller and Rockefeller Bros. Fund, 1958-76; dir., mem. exec. com. Gen. Security Assurance Co., First New Haven Nat. Bank; dir. U.S. Borax & Chem. Corp. Trustee, mem. exec. com., pres. Sloan-Kettering Inst. for Cancer Research; trustee, mem. exec. com., chmn. finance com. Meml. Sloan-Kettering Cancer Center. Mem., former pres. Yale U. Council; asso. fellow Davenport Coll.; dir. Boys' Club in Greenwich; dir. Nat. Assn. Mental Health, trustee Research Found. Lt. USNRF, 1917-18. Recipient Yale medal for distinguished service, 1954. Rep. Episcopalian. Clubs: Field (Greenwich, Conn.); Wings, Links, Century Association, Rockefeller Center Luncheon (N.Y.C.); Graduate Club Assn. (New Haven). Home: Greenwich, Conn. Died May 2, 1976.

COOMBS, EDWIN SEEGER, JR., beverage exec.; b. Kansas City, Mo., June 9, 1926; s. Edwin Seeger and Grace Marion (Winegar) C.; student U. N.C., 1945, 46; B.A., U. of South, 1948; m. Georgi Culliton, Mar. 3, 1953; children—Craig Edwin, Carolyn Ainsworth, Scott Michael. Account exec. Ayer Baker Advt., Seattle, 1955-60; div. advt. mgr. Carling Brewing Co., Tacoma, 1961-64, div. sales mgr., 1964, Western div. mktg. dir., 1965-67, Western div. v.p., 1967-69; pres. Rainier Brewing Co., Seattle, from 1969, also chief exec. officer; dir., v.p. Rainier Cos., Inc., 1970-71, pres., dir., from 1971. Mem. Puget Sound adv. com. Wash. State U., from 1970; bd. dirs. Evergreen Safety Council; officer, bd. dirs. Econ. Devel. Council of Puget Sound. Served with USNR, 1944-46; to lt. (j.g.) USCGR, 1950-51. Mem. Seattle C. of C. (dir.). Clubs: Washington Athletic, Broadmoor Golf, Rainier (Seattle). Home: Bellevue, Wash. Died 1980.

COON, CARLETON STEVENS, anthropologist; b. Wakefield, Mass., June 23, 1904; s. John Lewis and Bessie (Carleton) C.; A.B. magna cum laude, Harvard U., 1925, A.M., 1928, Ph.D., 1928; m. Mary Goodale, 1926; children—Carleton S., Charles Adams; m. 2d, Lisa Dougherty Geddes, 1945. Field work, anthrop. research, North Africa, Balkans, Ethiopia, Arabia, 1925-34, discovered remains of Aterian fossil man, in N. Africa, 1939; successively instr., asst. prof., asso. prof., prof. anthropology Harvard, 1934-48, on leave, 1942-45; curator ethnology, prof. anthropology Univ. Mus., Phila., 1948-63, research curator in anthropology, from 1963; research asso. in ethnology Peabody Mus., Harvard, from 1968; cons. Scott-Foresman and Co., Chgo.; mem. com. on scientific personnel NSF, 1961-64, Smithsonian Com. on Fgn. Currency, 1965-70; led archeological expdn. which discovered Hotu man, Iran, 1951; expdn. to Afghanistan, 1954, Syria, Central Africa, 1955, India, 1956-57, Alakaluf Indians, Chile, 1959, Morocco, 1962-63, discovering Jebel Ighoud man No. 2, Sierra Leone, 1965; Chad and Libya, 1966-67. Spl. asst. Dept. State, 1942-43. Served to maj. AUS (OSS), 1942-45; NATOUSA. Decorated Legion of Merit, 1945; recipient Viking Medal in Phys. Anthropology, 1952, Gold medal Phila. Athenaeum, 1962, Gold medal Harvard Travelers Club, 1972. Mem. Assn. de la Libération Francaise du 8 Novembre (hon.), Nat. Acad. Sci., Am. Anthrop. Assn., Am. Assn. Phys. Anthropologists (pres. 1962-63), Am. Acad. Arts and Sci., Honneur Assn. de la Liberation Française du 8 Nov. 1942, Phi Beta Kappa, Sigma Xi. Conglist. Clubs: Explorers (fellow) (N.Y.C.); Cosmos (Washington); Franklin Inn (Phila.); Harvard (Boston). Editor: Dixon Memorial Volume for Peabody Museum (Harvard), 1943; author: Tribes of Rif, 1931; Flesh of the Wild Ox, 1932; The Riffian, 1934; Measuring Ethiopia, 1935; Races of Europe, 1939; Principles of Anthropology (with Eliot D. Chapple), 1942; A Reader in General Anthropology, 1948; Races (with Garn and Birdsell), 1950; The Mountains of Giants, 1950; Cave Explorations in Iran, 1951; Caravan, 1951; The Story of Man, 1954; The Seven Caves, 1957; The Origin of Races, 1962; The Living Races of Man, 1965; Yengema Cave Report, 1968; The Hunting Peoples, 1971; Racial Aptitudes, 1979; contbr. articles to anthrop. jours., mags., Ency. Brit. Panelist, What in the World, TV show, 1949-64. Home: Gloucester, Mass. Died June 3, 1981.

COONS, ALBERT HEWETT, med. scientist; b. Gloversville, N.Y., June 28, 1912; s. Albert Selmser and Marion (Hewett) C.; A.B., Williams Coll., 1933, Sc.D., 1960; M.D., Harvard, 1937; Sc.D., Yale, 1961, Emory U., 1969; m. Phyllis Watts, Dec. 27, 1947; children—Elizabeth Schuyler, Susan Wakefield, Hilary, Wendy, Albert Hewett. House officer Mass. Gen. Hosp., Boston, 1937-39; asst. resident physician Thorndike Meml. Lab., Boston City Hosp., 1939-40; research fellow medicine Harvard, 1939-40, research fellow bacteriology, immunology, 1940-47, on leave 1942-46, instr., 1947-48, asso., 1948-50, asst. prof., 1950-53, vis. prof., 1953-70, prof., from 1970; research fellow med. scis. NRC, 1940-42; career investigator Am. Heart Assn., from 1953; cons. USPHS, 1956-62; Harvey lectr., 1957. Served to maj. M.C. AUS, 1942-46. Recipient Kimble Methodology award, 1958, Lasker award, Am. Pub. Health Assn., 1959, Paul Ehrlich award (Germany), 1961, Passano award, 1962, T. Duckett Jones Meml. award, 1962, Gairdner Found. award (Can.), 1962; Emil v. Behring prize (West Germany), 1966; Albion O. Bernstein M.D. award N.Y. State Med. Soc., 1973; Boerhaave medal U. Leyden, 1974. Fellow A.A.A.S., Am. Acad. Arts and Scis.; mem. Soc. Am. Bacteriologists, Soc. Exptl. Biology and Medicine, Nat. Acad. Scis., Am. Assn. Immunologists (pres. 1960-61), Am. Rheumatism Soc., Histochem. Soc. (councillor 1952-56, pres. 1964-65), Sigma Xi, Phi Delta Theta. Clubs: Harvard (Boston); Brookline (Mass.) Country. Asso. editor Jour. Immunology, 1956-61, editor, 1961-65; asso. editor Jour. Histochemistry and Cytochemistry, 1958-75; adv. editor Jour. Exptl. Medicine, 1963-70. Home: Brookline, Mass. Deceased.

COONS, SHELDON R., business counselor; b. Wilkes-Barre, Pa., Jan. 12, 1895; s. Joseph D. and Ella (Constine) C.; ed. pub. and pvt. prep. schs., Wilkes-Barre; m. Esther Merrill, 1920; 1 son, Sheldon (mem. Eighth Air Force; killed, ETO, June 8, 1945) m. 2d, Elizabeth R. Kearney, 1933; children—Deirdre K., Joseph D. Began Fowler, Dick & Walker, Wilkes-Barre, 1912, advt. mgr., 1914-17; sales mgr. Lipman, Wolfe and Co., Portland Ore., 1918-19; publicity and sales dir. Gimbel Bros., N.Y.C., 1919-28, gen. mdse. mgr. and v.p., Gimbel Bros., Inc., 1928-31; exec. v.p. and dir. Lord and Thomas, advt., 1931-40; gen. bus. counselor, 1941-79. Founding mem., past chmn., dir. Better Bus. Bur. of N.Y. Vice chmn., trustee Mt. Sinai Hosp., N.Y.C.; founder, trustee, vice chmn. Mt. Sinai Med. Sch., N.Y.C.; chmn. bd. trustees Mt. Sinai Med. Center, N.Y.C., 1976-77; bd. govs. Arthritis Found. N.Y. Clubs: Century Country, Lotos. Author distbn. and econ. studies. Address: New York, N.Y. Died Sept. 21, 1979.

COOPER, THOMAS FRANKLIN, naval med. officer; b. Windsor, Mo., May 28, 1899; s. Thomas Lee and Lorena (Kidwell) C.; A.B., U. Mo., 1922; M.D., Jefferson Med. Coll., 1924; m. June Scurlock, Dec. 25, 1925; children—Thomas Lee, Jane Calvert. Commd. lt. (j.g.), asst. surgeon, M.C., USN, 1924, advanced through gradgs to rear adm., 1952; intern U.S. Naval Hosp., San Diego, Cal., 1924-25; sr. med. officer U.S.S. Brooklyn, 1939-40; sr. med. officer U.S.S. Atlanta (sunk during battle of Guadalcanal), 1942; requirements officer material div., Bklyn., 1942-45; force med. officer Staff Comdr. Service Force, Pacific Fleet, 1945-47; med. officer in command U.S. Naval Med. Supply Depot, Oakland, Cal., 1947-48; exec. officer U.S. Naval Hosp., Phila., 1948-50; comdr. Naval Hosp., Great Lakes, Ill., 1950-52; dist. med. officer First Naval Dist., Boston, 1952-53; asst. chief Bur. Medicine and Surgery for Planning and Logistics, Navy Dept., Washington, 1953-55; insp. gen. (med.) Bur. Medicine and Surgery, 1955-56; comdg. officer Nat. Naval Med. Center, Bethesda, Md., from 1956. Decorated Bronze Star Medal, with Combat V, Presdl. Unit Citation. Fellow A.C.S.; mem. A.M.A., Mil. Order World Wars, Assn. Mil. Surgeons U.S., Alpha Kappa Kappa. Died June 3, 1976.

COOPER, TOM RICHARDSON, advt. exec.; b. Denver, Nov. 14, 1909; s. Elmer A. and Clara S. (Richardson) C.; A.B., Stanford, 1931; M.B.A., Harvard, 1933; m. Marion T. Dirr, Nov. 26, 1937; children—Peter Dirr, Tom Richardson. Formerly v.p. and mgr. Los Angeles office J. Walter Thompson; chmn. bd. Steedman, Cooper & Busse, Inc., San Francisco. Mem. Zeta Psi. Home: Aptos, Calif. Died Jan. 13, 1979.

COOPER, WILLIAM SKINNER, ecologist; b. Detroit, Mich., Aug. 25, 1884; s. David Mack and Caroline (Skinner) C.; B.S., Alma (Mich.) Coll., 1906; D.Sc., 1930; Ph.D., U. of Chicago, 1911; m. Dorothy Grace Shearer, Dec. 18, 1920; children—David Shearer, Elizabeth Russell (Mrs. William Tracy Maeck). Asst. in plant ecology, Summer School of Brooklyn Inst., Cold Spring Harbor, 1907; lecturer in plant ecol., Stanford, 1914-15; instr. botany, U. of Minn., 1915, prof., 1929-51, professor emeritus since 1951. Fellow A.A.A.S., Geol. Society of Am., Arctic Inst. of N. Am., Am. Geographical Soc.; mem. Ecological Soc. America (v.p. 1927; pres. 1936), British Ecol. Soc., Botanical Soc. of Am., Am. Geophysical Union, Assn. American Geographers, Minn. Acad. of Science (pres. 1937), American Soc. Naturalists, Société Linnéenne de Lyon, Sigma Xi, Gamma Alpha. Presbyn. Clubs: Explorers, Skylight. Author: The Broad-Sclerophyll Vegetation of California, 1922; The Late Wisconsin and Post-glacial History of the Upper Mississippi River, 1935; An Introduction to Plant Ecology. Contributor about 35 articles on plant ecology and glacial geology. Four scientific expdns. to Glacier Bay, Alaska, 1916, 21, 29, 35. Home: Minneapolis.

COORS, HENRY G(EORGE) (COORS), judge; b. Las Vegas, N.M., Feb. 20, 1885; s. Henry G. and Alice Louise (Seewald) C.; A.B., Ky. Mil. Inst., 1903; LL.B., U. Mich., 1907; m. Corinne Noel, Sept. 9, 1910 (dec. 1933); m. 2d Rowena Shook, Nov. 2, 1934; children—Henry George, IV, Kenneth Shook, Rowena. Admitted to N.M. bar, 1907; practiced in Las Vegas,

1907-09, Clovis, 1909-13, Albuquerque, 1913-41; sr. dist. judge, Albuquerque, 1942-51, also Middle Rio Grande conservancy dist. judge; asst. U.S. dist. atty., 1913-21; elected justice Supreme Ct. of N.M., 1951; pres. Clovis Nat. Bank, 1911-12; chmn., dir. bd. dirs. First Nat. Bank in Albuquerque, 1933-41. Mem., pres. bd. regents U. N.M., 1931-35. Mem. Bernalillo Co. Tax Payers Assn. (past pres.), Phi Gamma Delta. Presbyn. Elk (past exalted ruler). Clubs: Kiwanis (past pres.); Albuquerque Country (past pres.). Home: Santa Fe, N.M.

COOTNER, PAUL HAROLD, educator, economist; b. Logansport, Ind., May 25, 1930; s. William David and Rose (Singer) C.; B.S. magna cum laude, U. Fla., 1949, M.A., 1950; Ph.D., Mass. Inst. Tech., 1953; m. Cathryn Mae Marcho, Dec. 2, 1962; 1 son, Joshua David Marcho. Ford teaching intern Brown U., 1955-56; research asso. Resources for the Future, Inc., 1956-59; mem. faculty Mass. Inst. Tech., 1959-70, prof. finance, 1966-70; cons. to govt. and industry, 1959-78; Ford Found. distinguished vis. prof. finance Harvard Bus. Sch. 1969-70; C.O.G. Miller prof. finance Grad. Sch. Bus. Stanford (Cal.) U., 1970-78. Served with AUS, 1953-55. Ford Found. faculty fellow, 1965-66. Mem. Am. Econ. Assn., Am. Finance Assn., Phi Beta Kappa. Jewish. Co-author: Retail Banking in the Electronic Age, 1977. Editor: The Random Character of Stock Market Prices, 1964. Home: Stanford, Calif. Died Apr. 16, 1978.

COPELAND, MELVIN THOMAS, director research; b. Brewer, Me., July 17, 1884; s. Salem Dwight and Livonia Estelle (Pierce) C.; A.B., Bowdoin, 1906, hon. Sc.D., 1931; A.M., Harvard, 1907, Ph.D., 1910; m. Else Helbling, June 25, 1912; children—Elsie Marie, Martha. Instr. in economic resources, Harvard, 1909-10; instr. in economics, New York U., 1911-12; instr. in comml. orgn., Harvard, 1912-15, asst. prof. marketing, 1915-19, prof. since 1919, George Fisher Baker professor of administration, 1950, also dir. Bur. Business Research, 1916-26, director business research since 1942. Member Massachusetts Commission on Cost of Living, 1916-17; sec. Commercial Economy Bd., Council of Nat. Defense, Washington, D.C., 1917-18; exec. sec. Conservation Div. War Industries Bd., 1918; sec. research com. Nat. Council Cotton Mfrs., 1919; chmn. Mass. Com. on Postwar Readjustment, 1941-46; mem. Purchase Policy Advisory Committee, U.S. War Dept., 1943; chmn. Jury Harvard Advt. Award, 1925-31. Mem. bd. of overseers Bowdoin Coll., 1934-47, trustee since 1947. Chmn. Adv. Council, U.S. Senate Trade Policies Com., 1947; chmn. bd. trustees, Aero. Research Foundation, since 1947. Fellow American Statistical Association; member American Economic Assn., Beta Theta Pi. Founding member Phi Beta Kappa Assn., 1942. Awarded David A. Wells prize, Harvard, 1912; Assn. medal, Nat. Assn. Cotton Mfrs., 1921. Republican. Conglist. Author: Cotton Manufacturing Industry of U.S., 1912; Problems in Marketing, 1920; Principles of Merchandising, 1924; Raw Material Prices and Business Conditions, 1933; International Raw Commodity Prices and the Devaluation of the Dollar, 1934; A Raw Commodity Revolution, 1938. Joint author: Merchandising of Cotton Textiles-Methods and Organization, 1933; The Board of Directors and Business Management, 1947. Editor: Business Statistics, 1917. Commentator: Harvard Business Reports, 1927-31. Home: Annisquam, Mass.

CORBET, DARRAH, bus. exec.; b. Brookville, Pa., Nov. 19, 1884; s. Charles and Mary A. (Darrah) C.; student Kiskiminetas Springs Sch., Saltsburg, Pa., 1899-1902; Ph.B., Yale, 1905, M.E., 1909; married Katherine Trumbull, Feb. 7, 1917 (dec.); children—Darrah (dec.), Katherine (Mrs. John S. Carey), Ann Trumbull (Mrs. Irving Clark, Jr.). Draughtsman Charles C. Moore & Co., San Francisco, 1906-09, sales engr., Seattle, 1909-20, asso. mgr. Seattle office, 1920-29; pres., dir. Smith Cannery Machines Co., Seattle, 1929, now chmn.; dir. Lakeview Cemetery Assn.; sec.-treas., dir. Morden Machines Co., Portland, Ore., 1931—; dir., mem. exec. com. Nat. Bank Commerce; dir. Boeing Airplane Co., Marine Bancorp., Puget Sound Power & Light Co. Dir. Seattle Symphony Orchestra Association. Mem. NAM, Wash. Metal Trades, Inc., Wash. Employers, Inc., Yale Assn. Wash., C. of C., Sigma Xi. Mason (Shriner). Clubs: Rainier, Seattle Golf, Rotary, College, Monday. Home: Seattle

CORBETT, ELIZABETH, author; b. Aurora, Ill., Sept. 30, 1887; d. Richard W. and Isabelle Jean (Adkins) Corbett; AB., U. Wis., 1910. Mem. Phi Beta Kappa, Alpha Gamma Delta. Author: many books since 1916, latest of which are Immortal Helen, 1948; Eve and Christopher, 1949; The Duke's Daughter, 1950; Portrait of Isabelle, 1951; The Richer Harvest, 1952; in Miss Armstrong's Room, 1953; Our Mrs. Meigs, 1954; Family Portrait, 1955; The Head of Apollo, 1956; Professor Preston at Home, 1957; The Crossroads, 1957; The President's Wife, 1958; Hamilton Terrace, 1960; The Wainwright Inheritance, 1960; Hidden Island, 1961; The Paige Girls, 1962; The Distant Princess, 1963; The Heart of the Village, 1963; Lisa Kennerley's Husband, 1964; Anniversary, 1964; The Continuing City, 1965; The Crossroads, 1965; The Old Callahan Place, 1966; Harry Martin's Wife, 1967; Ladies Day, 1968; The Three Lives of Sharon Spence, 1969; Hotel Belvedere, 1970; Sunday at Six, 1971. Home: New York, N.Y. Died Jan. 24, 1981; buried Arlington Cemetery, Milw.

CORBETT, HIRAM STEVENS, former Rep. nat. committeeman; b. Tucson, Ariz., Sept. 13, 1886; s. Johnston Knox and Elizabeth (Hughes) C.; grad. high sch., Tucson, 1907; grad. Belmont Preparatory School, Belmont, Calif.; m. Dorothy Udall, of Tucson (divorced); 1 son, J. Knox; m. 2d, Ruth Weissinger, of Jeffersonville, Ind., Oct. 24, 1925; 1 dau., Ruth Elizabeth. Driver, J. Knox Corbett Lumber & Hardware Co., Tucson, 1907, yardman, 1908-09, mgr., 1910-19, pres. and gen. mgr. since 1919. Former chmn. Tucson Rep. Central Com., Pima Co. Rep. Central Com., Ariz. Rep. State Com. (2 terms); mem. Rep. Nat. Com., Ariz., 1929-32. Pres. Tucson Chamber Commerce, Tucson Sunshine Climate Club. Presbyn. Mason (K.T.), Elk. Clubs: Old Pueblo, Tucson Country, El Rio Country (Tucson). Home: Tucson, Ariz.

CORCORAN, CHARLES ROBERT, pub. relations co. exec.; b. N.Y.C., Aug. 16, 1909; s. Peter J. and Lydia (Purcell) C.; student Fordham U., Columbia, Pratt Inst.; m. Isabel Birney, Oct. 12, 1935 (dec.); m. 2d, Ruth Joan Finnegan, Nov. 9, 1940; children—Mary (Mrs. Frank Ehmann), Jean (Mrs. Paul Schott), Charles A., Ruth Ann (Mrs. Stephen Howley), Lucile. With Manhattan Life Ins. Co. of N.Y., 1928, mgr. new bus., mgr. Chgo. br. office, supt. agys., N.Y.C., 1938-43; v.p. Livermore & Knight Co., Providence, 1943-46; dir. sales promotion Equitable Life Assurance Soc. U.S., 1946-53, 2d v.p. sales promotion, sales devel., 1953-59, v.p. advt. and publs., 1959-60, v.p. advt., publs. and press relations, 1960-65, v.p. and chmn.'s staff, 1965-68, v.p. advt. and graphics and spl. assignments, 1968-69; exec. v.p. Comml. Communication Corp., N.Y.C., 1969-71; pres. Concoran Assos., N.Y.C., 1971-78. Nat. coordinator U.S. Labor Dept. and Advt. Council, 1966-72. Chmn. pub. relations, chmn. spl. devel. St. Mary's Sem.; bd. govs. Human Resources Center; co-chmn. devel. com., mem. N.Y. council Hofstra Coll., Fordham Prep. Sch.; trustee Loretto Heights Coll., Denver, 1967-71. Mem. Life Advertisers Assn. (mem. exec. com. 1958-59, treas. 1959, founder Gotham group), Life Underwriters Assn., Life Ins. Agy. Mgmt. Assn., Pub. Relations Soc. (chmn. pub. service com. N.Y. chpt. 1961-62, chmn. workshop com. 1962, pres. N.Y. chpt. 1968-69, dir. 1963-70). Author: Search for a Sign; contbg. author P.R. for life Insurance, Handbook of Advertising Management, others. Contbr. articles to profl. jours. Home: Huntington, N.Y. Died July 1978.

CORDELL, HARRY WILLIAM (KOR-DEL'), prof. economics; b. Moundsville, W.Va., July 21, 1883; s. Allan A. and Mary B. (Rock) C.; Ph.B., Tri-State Coll., Angola, Ind., 1907; Ph.B., Hiram (O.) Coll., 1908; M.A., U. of Chicago, 1915; grad. study, 1915-17; Ph.D., Ohio State U., 1930; m. Alta M. Girkins, Jan. 1, 1909; children—Vernon Earle, Edward William, Walter (dec.). Ordained ministry Disciples of Christ, 1908; pastor Harrisburg, Pa., and Cincinnati, O., until 1913; instr. economics, State Coll. of Washington, 1917-19, asst. prof., 1919-21, asso. prof., 1921-22, prof., 1922-28, head of dept. of economics and business adminstrn., 1920-27; univ. fellow, Ohio State U., 1927-28, asso. prof. marketing since 1928. Mem. Am. Marketing Assn., Phi Kappa Phi. Mason (K.T.), Kiwanian. Author: Installment Credit in the Retail Furniture Trade, 1930. Home: Columbus, O.

CORLETT, ALLEN N., lawyer; b. Cleve., Sept. 3, 1904; s. Lynnus George and Jennie (Lindsey) C.; A.B., Western Res. U., 1926, LL.B., 1929; m. Dorothy Wilhelmy Weaver, Jan. 15, 1943; children—Mary Anne (Mrs. Robert J. Rotatori), Marsha (Mrs. Joseph C. Sarakaitis), Sister M. Jennifer, Ursuline, Allen N. Admitted to Ohio bar; practiced in Cleve.; mem. firm Roudebush, Brown, Corlett & Ulrich Co. Mem. Ohio Ho. of Reps., 1931-32; mem. Cuyahoga County Republican Exec. Com., 1946-78; mem. Ohio Senate, 1947-48; mem. Presdl. Electoral Coll., 1953. Served to capt. USNR, World War II; PTO. Mem. Am., Ohio, Cleve. (past mem. exec. com.) bar assns., Am. Trial Lawyers Assn., Res. Officers Naval Services (past nat. v.p.), Alpha Tau Omega. Mason. Clubs: Cleve. Athletic (past dir.); Shaker Heights Country. Home: Shaker Heights, Ohio. Died Dec. 8, 1978.

CORLEY, FRANCIS JOSEPH, clergyman, educator; b. St. Louis, Nov. 11, 1909; s. John Louis and Beulah Madeleine (Hayes) C.; student Marquette U., 1934-35; A.B., St. Louis U., 1933, M.A., 1938, S.T.L., 1941. Joined Soc. of Jesus, 1927, ordained priest Roman Catholic Ch., 1940; instr. theology and history St. Louis U., 1942-45, research asso. Inst. Social Order, 1945-58, editor Social Order, 1947-58, asst prof., 1958-61, asso. prof., 1961-72, chmn. library bd., 1963-72. Ford Found. grantee, Viet-Nam, S.E. Asia, 1956-57. Mem. Am. Oriental Soc., Am. Hist. Assn., Assn. for Asian Studies, Am. Friends of Vietnam (nat. com.), Royal Asiatic Soc. (Malaya), Am. Assn. U. Profs., Societe des Etudes Indochinoises (Saigon). Author: Viet-Nam Since Geneva, 1959; (with R.J. Willmes) Wings of Eagles, 1941, 67. Mem. internat. editorial adv. bd. S.E. Asia, Internat. Quar. Home: Saint Louis, Mo. Died Oct. 10, 1972.

CORNELIUS, DAVID WILLIAM, prof. physics; b. Linton, Ind., Apr. 28, 1885; s. William Fletcher and Alice Victoria (Osborn) C.; A.B., DePauw U., 1906; Ph.D., U. of Ill., 1912; m. Orrelle Fidlar of Terre Haute, Ind., Aug. 17, 1912. Asst. in physics, DePauw, 1905-06; instr. physics, Purdue U., 1906-08; grad. student and asst. in physics, U. of Calif., 1908-10; fellow U. of Ill., 1910-12; prof. physics and engr., Ottawa U., 1912-13; acting asst. prof. physics and astronomy, U. of Kan., 1913-15; research, U. of Wis., summer 1915; instr. physics, U. of Mo., 1915-17; prof. physics, Alma Coll., 1917-20; prof. physics, U. of Mich., summer 1920; prof. physics, U. of Chattanooga, since 1920. Fellow A.A.A.S. (life); mem. Am. Physical Soc., Am. Assn. Univ. Profs., Tenn. Acad. Sciences (pres. 1930), Am. Assn. Physics Teachers, Theta Alpha Phi, Alpha (hon. scholastic), Phi Gamma Delta, Sigma Pi Sigma (nat. v.p.), (former nat. v.p.; now mem. exec. com.), Pi Gamma Mu. Republican. Methodist. Mason. Author: (brochures) Velocity of Electrons in the Photo-electric Effect, as a Function of the Wave-Length of the Light; A Liquid High Resistance as a Substitute for a Bronson Resistance. Lecturer on scientific subjects. Home: Signal Mountain, Tenn.

CORNELIUS, MARTY, artist, art therapist; b. Pitts., Sept. 18, 1913; d. James Alvin and Ethel (Lewis) Cornelius; B.A., Carnegie-Mellon U., 1935; student Pitts. Playhouse, 1938-39; student art therapy orientation, VA Hosp., Menningers, Topeka, 1954; studied art with Reginald Marsh, N.Y.C., Samuel Rosenberg, Pitts.; m. J.F. Fitzpatrick (div.). Formerly writer and designer Aluminum Co. Am.; later with Jos. Horne Co., Pitts.; exhibited annually, 1937-72; profl. artist, therapist tchr., head diagnostic art clinic VA Hosp.-Neuro-Psychiat. Hosp., Pitts.; demonstrator art of painting in oil through Horne's advt. dept., 1955, 56; prof. freshman drawing, painting and design dept. Fine Arts Coll., Carnegie Inst. Tech., 1959-60; employed by U.S. Govt., 1954-72; on TV series WQED ednl. TV stas., Pitts., 1962; exhibited Carnegie Inst. Pitts., Pa. Ann., summers 1959-73, Westmoreland County Mus. Art, Greensburg, Pa., 1964, Painting in U.S. exhibit Carnegie Inst., 1947-50, Ogunquit Art Center (ann.), Ohio U., Audubon Artists, N.Y.C., ann. show Asso. Artists of Pitts., from 1937 (awarded prizes 1939, 46, 47, 48, 49, 53, 55), Contemporary Am. Painting Whitney Mus. of Art, N.Y.C., Nat. Biennial Contemporary Painters, Corcoran Gallery, Washington, 1941, 47, Palace of Legion of Honor, San Francisco, 1949; represented in permanent collections 100 Friends Pitts. Art, 100 Friends Latrobe Art, New Bethlehem High Sch., pvt. collections, Latrobe, Pa., Danville, Va., Mercy Hosp., Pitts., Mus. Modern Art, N.Y.C.; regional painting, sculpture exhibit Westmoreland County Mus. Art, Greenburg, Pa., 1963, 65, 67; Asso. Artists Pitts., 1938-79; 3 Rivers Arts Festivals through Carnegie Inst. and Mus. Recipient prizes Martin Leisser Sch. Design, Pitts., 1946, 48, Butler Inst., Youngstown, Ohio, 1948, Asso. Artists Pitts. Exhibit, Carnegie Inst., Pitts., 1953, Garden Club Allegheny Co., 1947, 55, also numerous local show prizes and awards. Has served several juries and panels. Registered Med. Rehab. Therapists. Fellow Internat. Inst. Arts and Letters; mem. Pitts. Tchrs. Assn., Asso. Artists Pitts. (dir. 1939-40), Western Pa. Conservancy, Kappa Kappa Gamma (award for individual alumnae achievement in art 1952). Free lance profl. artist, painter, illustrator, art therapist; illustrations in Pittsburgh, The Story of An American City (Stefan Lorant), 1964. Address: Ligionier, Pa. Died Oct. 21, 1979.

CORNELIUS, OLIVIA SMITH, author; b. Pittsburgh, July 23, 1882; d. George Carson and Jennie (Prosser) Smith; ed. private schools, Atlanta, Ga., and Phila., and Adrian (Mich.) Coll.; m. Harry Allen Cornelius, of Ardian, Mich., Oct. 9, 1901. Author: The Eyes at the Window, 1911; The Persian Tassel, 1913. Home: Pittsburgh.

CORNELL, HERBERT WATSON (KOR-NEL'), civil service legal cons.; b. Phila., Dec. 26, 1884; s. Watson and Mary Ella (Hurtt) C.; student U. of Pa., 1904-07; A.B., U. of Colo., 1908; LL.B., George Washington U., 1919; m. Ruth Dunlap Paul, Nov. 4, 1913; children—Paul Watson, Marian Whiting (Mrs. Hugh C. Cutler). Prin. Blue Rapids (Kan.) High Sch., 1908-09; chief examiner and sec. Colo. Civil Service Commn., 1909-12; tech. examiner U.S. Civil Service Commn., 1912-20; admitted to Wis. bar, 1920; asst. chief examiner and sec. City Civil Service Commn., Milw., 1920-24, chief examiner, 1924-55, retired; vice pres. Civil Service Assembly of U.S. and Canada, 1926-27, elected to life membership in 1951; chmn. Central States Regional Conf. of Civil Service Commns., 1929-31. Hon. curator in Astronomy Milw. Public Museum. Member Wis. Industrial Relations Assn., Milwaukee Astron. Soc., Wis. Archaeol. Soc., Wis. Geol. Soc., Wis. Friends of Native Landscape, Am. Soc. Pub. Administrn., Franklin Inst., Rittenhouse Astronomical Soc., Milw. County Historical Soc., Am. Astron. Soc., Midwest Assn. Polit. Scientists, Delta Tau

Delta, Delta Sigma Rho. Republican. Presbyn. Club: Milwaukee City. Contbr. articles on civil service and conservation to periodicals. Home: Phila.

CORNFIELD, JEROME, educator, statistician; b. N.Y.C., Oct. 30, 1912; s. Samuel and Jenny (Horen) C.; B.S., N.Y. U., 1933; postgrad. Columbia, 1933-34, U.S. Dept. Agr. Grad. Sch., 1936-38; m. Ruth June Bittler, July 6, 1937; children—Ann, Ellen. Statistician, U.S. Dept. Labor, 1934-47; statistician NIH, 1947-58, 60-67; prof. Johns Hopkins, 1958-60; prof. U. Pitts., 1968-72, George Washington U., 1972-79; tchr. Columbia, Am. U., U. Mich., Stanford, U. Oslo. Recipient Superior Service award Dept. Health, Education and Welfare, 1967. Mem. Am. Statis. Assn. (pres. 1974), Inst. Math. Statistics, A.A.A.S., Am. Epidem. Soc. (pres. 1972), Biometric Soc., Am. Heart Assn., Washington, Va. acads. sci. Contbr. articles profl. jours. Home: Great Falls, Va. Died Sept. 17, 1979.

CORNMAN, JAMES WELTON, educator; b. Phila., Aug. 16, 1929; s. Ralph Miller and Rose (Scharfe) C.; grad. Haverford Sch., 1947; A.B., Dartmouth, 1956; M.A., Brown U., 1957, Ph.D., 1960; m. Elizabeth Marie Pedrotty, Feb. 2, 1955; children—Deborah, Julie, Diane, Elizabeth. Instr. philosophy Ohio State U., 1960-63; asst. prof. philosophy U. Rochester, 1963-65, asso. prof., 1965-67; asso. prof. philosophy U. Pa., Phila., 1967-69, prof., 1969-78, chmn., 1970-72. Andrew Mellon postdoctoral fellow, 1965-66; NSF grant, 1968-70, 71-73; Am. Council Learned Socs. fellow, 1970-71; John Simon Guggenheim fellow, 1974-75. Author: Metaphysics, Reference and Language, 1966; (with K. Lehrer) Philosophical Problems and Arguments, 2d edit., 1974; Materialism and Sensations, 1971; Perception, Common Sense, and Science, 1975; Skepticism, Justification and Explanation, 1980. Home: Wayne, Pa. Died May 31, 1978.

CORRINGTON, JOHN W., investment banker; b. Alexander, Ill., 1898; ed. U. Ill., 1923, Harvard Grad. Sch. Bus. Adminstrn., 1924. Gen. partner Paine, Webber, Jackson & Curtis, Chgo., until 1966. Home: Naples, Fla. Died Jan. 1979.

CORRINGTON, JULLAN DANA, biologist; b. Hot Springs, Ark., Dec. 22, 1891; s. Joe W. and Jessie W. (Knox) C.; A.B., Cornell U., 1913; Ph.D., 1925; m. Veronica Elisabeth Flicke; children—Mariette, Paul. Asst. zoölogy, Cornell U., 1915-16, curator of Mus., 1916-17 and 1919-20; asst. prof. biology, U. of S.C., 1921-22, prof. zoölogy, 1922-26; asst. prof. zoölogy, Syracuse U., 1926-30; asso. prof. biology, Drew U., 1930-31; dir. ednl. service Frank A. Ward Found. Natural Science, U. Rochester, 1931-36; prof. biology, Washington Coll., 1936-44; asst. prof. zoology, U. Miami, 1944-45, asso. prof., 1945-47, prof., from 1947, department chairman, 1953-57. Traveled and studied in Europe, 1913-14; mem. N.Y. State Bd. of Regents, biology com., 1929-31; sec. Md. Dept. of Research and Edn., 1941-44; pres. Md. Assn. Biol. Teachers, 1942-44. Served as 2d lt., U.S. Army, 1918. Fellow, A.A.A.S.; mem. N.Y. Micros. Soc., Am. Soc. Amateur Microscopists (founder, sec. 1939-44, president, 1944-50), Southeastern Assn. Biol., Fla. Acad. Sci. (v.p. 1949), Sigma Xi, Phi Beta Kappa, Omicron Delta Kappa, Alpha Phi Omega, Beta Beta Beta, Alpha Epsilon Delta, Phi Delta Sigma, Scabbard and Blade. Author: Adventures with the Microscope, 1934; Working with the Microscope, 1941; Exploring with Your Microscope, 1957. Writer biological studies and contributer to periodicals. Dept. editor Nature Magazine, 1937-59, Bios, from 1954, Natural History, from 1950. Address: Coral Gables, Fla. Deceased.

CORROON, RICHARD FRANCIS, lawyer; b. Bklyn., Aug. 5, 1913; s. James Francis and Katherine (Larkin) C.; A.B., Yale, 1935; LL.B., Harvard, 1938; m. Nancy Elms, Dec. 7, 1940; children—Nancy (dec.), Ellen (Mrs. Eric C. Petersen), Kate (dec.), Polly (Mrs. Kenneth Ratner). Admitted to N.Y. bar, 1939, Del. bar, 1946; with firm Miller, Owen, Otis & Bailey, N.Y.C., 1938-42; partner firm Potter Anderson & Corroon, and predecessors, Wilmington, Del., 1946-78; v.p. Corroon & Black Corp.; dir. Wellington Fund, Windsor Fund, Exeter Fund, Gemini Fund, W.L. Morgan Growth Fund, Wellsley Income Fund, Ivest Fund, Westminster Bond Fund, Trustees' Equity Fund, Explorer Fund, Qualified Dividend Portfolio, Qualified Dividend Portfolio II, Warwick Municipal Bond Fund; trustee Whitehall Money Market Trust, 1st Inclex Investment Trust. Mem. Del. Bd. Bar Examiners, 1951-66; vice chmn. Del. Corp. Law Revision Com., 1964-67. Mem. bd. edn., Wilmington, 1949-53; pres. Diocesan Bd. Edn., Wilmington, 1966-68; mem. Catholic Social Services Wilmington, 1960-66. Bd. dirs. Del. Curative Workshop, 1950-56; trustee Del. Art Mus., 1969-78, St. Francis Hosp., Wilmington, 1973-78. Served to lt. comdr. USNR, 1942-46. Decorated Purple Heart. Fellow Am. Coll. Trial Lawyers; mem. Am., Del. (pres. 1975-76) bar assns., Assn. Bar City N.Y., Am. Law Inst. Home: Wilmington, Del. Died Jan. 15, 1978.

CORT, STEWART SHAW, steel co. exec.; b. Duquesne, Pa., May 9, 1911; s. Stewart Joseph and Carolyn Myrtilla (Schreiner) C.; B.A., Yale, 1934; M.B.A., Harvard, 1936; LL.D., Moravian Coll., Bethlehem, Pa., 1967, Lehigh U., 1969; m. Elizabeth Fiske Brumilier, Apr. 15, 1961. With Bethlehem Steel Corp., from 1937, asst. gen. mgr. sales, 1960-61; v.p., Pacific Coast div., 1961-63, pres., dir., 1963-71, chmn. bd., chief exec. officer, from 1971; dir. Continental Ill. Nat. Bank & Trust Co. of Chgo., Industrias Penoles, S.A., Conill Corp., Mem. exec. com. Yale Devel. Bd.; trustee Princeton Theol. Sem., Com. Econ. Devel., Blair Acad.; chmn. Radio Free Europe Fund. Decorated grand comdr. Order African Redemption (Liberia). Mem. Am. Iron and Steel Inst. (hon. v.p., recipient Gary medal 1975), Am. Inst. Steel Constrn. Steel Service Center, Institute, Advt. Council (industries adv. com.), C. of C. U.S. (nat. task force on econ. growth and opportunity), Internat. Indsl. Conf. (U.S. Council), Newcomen Soc., Pa. Soc. Club: Economic (N.Y.). Home: Bethelhem, Pa. Died May 1980.

CORY, ERNEST NEAL, entomologist; born Alden, N.Y., Aug. 13, 1886; s. Azro J. and Marie (Matheson) C.; B.S., U. of Md., 1909, M.S., 1913; Ph.D., American U., 1926; m. Elizabeth Elder, Oct. 31, 1911; children—Ernest Neal, William Robert, Jean Marie. Asst. entomologist, Md., 1909-11; instr. Md. Agrl. Coll. (now U. of Md.), 1911-12, asst. prof. 1912-13, asso. prof. entomology and zoölogy, 1913-14, prof. entomology, asst. dir. extension, U. of Md., 1914; exptl. sta. and state entomologist, 1914-57, emeritus prof.; chief of party U. Md.-ICA, Brit. Guiana, 1956-57. Gold Medal Achievement in Orchidology, Am. Orchid Soc. Treas. Am. Assn. Econ. Entomologists, 1936-53, pres., 1946-47; sec.-treas. Eastern Plant Bd., 1925-56; pres. Nat. Shade Tree Conf., 1940; pres. Wash. Entomol. Soc., 1942. Mem. Am. Orchid Soc. (life mem., sci. adviser), Entomol. Soc. Am. (hon.), Md. Nurserymen's Assn. (life), Nat. Capital Orchid Soc. (hon.), Sigma Xi, Omicron Delta Kappa, Phi Kappa Phi, Kappa Alpha. Episcopalian. Mason. Club: Cosmos. Author bulls., leaflets and contbns. sci. jours. Home: College Park, Md. Died Jan. 1979.

CORY, HERBERT ELLSWORTH, univ. prof.; b. Oct. 8, 1883; s. Benjamin H. and Ella Frances (Cook) C.; A.B., Brown U., 1906; Ph.D., Harvard, 1910; m. Ethel Duncan Morton, Oct. 10, 1922 (died 1932); m. 2d, Mary Ellen Austin, May 6, 1933-five children (adopted)—Michael, Brigid, Mary Sharon, Anthony, James. Was assistant professor of English, U. of Calif., 1910-18; mem. War Labor Policies Bd., Washington, D.C., 1918; research in psychology and biology, Johns Hopkins, 1918-22, lecturer in aesthetics, 1922-23; prof. liberal arts, U. of Wash., since 1923; lecturer in Christian Culture Series Assumption Coll., Windsor, Ont., May 1941; editor U. of Calif. Chronicle, 1912-14; studied, Columbia U., summers 1921, 22. Awarded deSmet medal by Gonzaga Univ., 1940, Moraga Crest by St. Mary's Coll., 1942. Elected to Gallery of Living Catholic Authors, 1942. Mem. bd. dirs. House of Good Shepherds, Seattle. Mem. Am. Assn. Univ. Profs., Am. Philos. Soc., Research Soc. U. of Wash., A.A.A.S., Mediaeval Acad. of America, John Henry Newman Hon. Soc., Holy Name Soc., St. Vincent de Paul Soc., Pi Gamma Mu, Phi Sigma Kappa. Catholic. Knights of Columbus. Clubs: Athenian (Oakland, Calif.); Faculty (U. of Wash.). Author: Edmund Spenser, a Critical Study, 1917; Essays in Exposition, 1918; The Intellectuals and the Wage Workers, 1919; The Emancipation of a Free Thinker, 1941; The Religious Significance of Beauty in Nature and Art, 1947. Contbr. to The Dial, The Forum, Jour. Philosophy, Jour. Internat. Ethics, Publ. Modern Lang. Assn., U. of Calif. Pub. in Lit. and Philology, Mod. Lang. Notes, Mod. Philology, Thought, The Modern Schoolman. Home: Seattle, Wash. *

CORY, MERTON M(AINE), engr., coll. teacher; b. Nashua, N.H., Aug. 18, 1882; s. Sidney Lawrence and Fannie Eugenia (Jones) C.; B.S., U. of N.H. 1908, E.E., 1913; M.S., U. of Mich., 1933; m. Mona Mae Manning, May 3, 1909 (died Sept. 26, 1926); m. 2d, Ethel Carolina Whitney, Dec. 17, 1927. With engring. dept., City of Nashua, N.H., 1902-08; sales engr., Am. Radiator Co., Boston, Mass., 1909; student test course, Gen. Elec. Co., Lynn, Mass., 1909-11; elec. engr., Janesville Elec. Co., Wis., 1911; investigator, Milwaukee Elec. & Ry. Co., Wis., 1912; prof. elec. engring. Mich. State Coll. 1912-49; chmn. bd. appeals, City of East Lansing, Mich.; mem. adv. com. Lansing Auto Club (A.A.A.). Fellow Am. Inst. Elec. Engrs. (past chmn. Mich. sect.); member, Michigan Engineering Society, Engineering Society of Detroit, Alpha Tau Omega, Tau Beta Pi (nat. pres.). Republican. Clubs: Lansing Engring. (past pres.), Mich. State Coll. Faculty (past pres.). Author of mag. articles, notes and outlines for instructional purposes. Home: East Lansing, Mich.

COSGROVE, JOHN C., banker, coal operator and cons. engr.; b. Houtzdale, Pa., Apr. 28, 1886; s. Patrick B. and Zaidee M. (Schoff) C.; prep. edn. St. Vincent's Coll.; grad. short course in mining, Pa. State Coll., 1905; m. Florence M. Neff, July 7, 1909; children—Pat B., F. Elizabeth, Margaret L., John C. Organizer By-Products Coal & Coke Co., 1906, Hastings Coal & Coke Co., 1907, Grazier Coal Mining Co., 1913, and was gen. mgr. of each; organizer, 1911, and pres. Lenox Coal Co.; dir. Federal Reserve Bank of Phila., 1922-34; past pres. Johnstown Chamber of Commerce and Farmers Bank & Trust Co., Johnstown, Pa.; past president West Virginia Coal & Coke Co.; partner Cosgrove and Mylander; dir. several cos. Treas., Smoky Mountain Village, Inc. Bd. dirs. Clearwater Beach Civic Center, Clearwater Beach Assn.; trustee Chapel by the Sea. Registered Engr. Pennsylvania. Mem. American Inst. M.E., Am. Mining Congress, Newcomen Soc. of Eng. (hon.), Phi Delta Theta (finance commr.). Mason (Shriner). Clubs: Rotary, Clearwater (Florida) Yacht; Bachelors (Johnstown). Author articles on coal, research and travel. Address: Clearwater, Fla. Died Feb. 23, 1978.

COSGROVE, ROBERT, govt. official; b. Tea Tree, Tasmania, Dec. 28, 1884; s. Michael T. and Mary Ann (Hewitt) C.; student Richmond and Hobart Tasmania public schs.; m. Gertrude A. Geappen, Jan. 10, 1911; children—Gladys Lillian, Mary Irene, Robert James, Henry Edward. Mem. House of Assembly, Denison since 1919; Govt. Whip, July, 1926, June, 1928. Opposition Whip and Magistrate for the Terr., 1930; hon. minister, June-July, 1934; Minister for Agr., 1934-39; Premier and Treas. of Tasmania since 1939; minister in charge of Hydeo-Electric dept. 1939-48; minister for Edn., 1948. Mem. Commercial Travellers' Assn. Club: Royal Autocar. Address: Hobart, Tasmania.

COSTELLO, JOHN MARTIN, congressman; b. Los Angeles, Calif., Jan. 15, 1903; s. Martin and Mary (McNeilis) C.; A.B., Loyola U., Los Angeles, 1922, A.M., 1923, LL.B., 1924; unmarried. Admitted to Calif. bar, 1924; teacher Los Angeles secondary schs., 1924-25; Dem. candidate for 73rd Congress; mem. 74th to 78th Congresses (1935-45), 15th Calif. Dist. General Counsel, Washington Office of Los Angeles Chamber of Commerce. Mem. Native Sons of the Golden West. Mem. Knights of Columbus, Elks. Home: Washington, D.C. Died Aug. 28, 1976.

COSTELLO, JOSEPH A., bishop; S.T.D., LL.D. Ordained priest Roman Catholic Ch., 1941; titular bishop Choma and aux. bishop Newark, 1962-78. Address: Belleville, N.J. Died Sept. 22, 1978.

COSTELLO, WILLIAM FRANCIS, physician; b. Binghamton, N.Y., Jan. 22, 1884; s. Frank and Elizabeth (McGowan) C.; M.D., U. Buffalo, 1907; m. Mary Loughlin, June 16, 1914 (dec. Dec. 1950); children—John, Elizabeth (Mrs. James Lowe); m. 2d, Mary Kelly, Feb. 9, 1955. Intern St. John's Hosp., Long Island City, 1907-09; pvt. practice medicine, Dover, N.J., 1910—; med. dir. St. Claire's Hosp., Danville, N.J., 1953—; mem. staff Dover Gen. Hosp. Pres. Dover Bd. Health, 1922-60. Vice pres. Dover Trust Co. Recipient Edgar J. Ill award Acad. Medicine No. N.J., 1960—. Served to 1st lt., M.C., U.S. Army, 1918. Mem. A.M.A. (v.p., N.J. del.). Home: Dover, N.J.

COTE, RAYMOND HENRI, educator; b. Quebec, Que., Can., June 25, 1923; s. Albert Emile and Emilienne Marie-Ange (Simard) C.; B.A., Laval U., 1944, B.Sc. in Chemistry (NRC Can. scholar), 1949, Ph.D. (Canadian Industries Ltd. scholar), 1952; m. Therese Blouin, Aug. 6, 1949; children—Raymonde, Gaëtan Annette, Francoise, Dominic, Isabelle. Research asst. Inst. Pasteur, Paris, France, 1952-54, Lister Inst., London, Eng., 1954-58; mem. faculty Laval U., Quebec, 1958-77, prof. biochemistry, 1967-77. Canadian Industries Ltd. scholarship, Beit Meml. fellow, London, 1955-58; NRC-Med. Research Council grantee, from 1959. Mem. Brit. Chem. Soc., Brit. Biochem. Soc., Canadian Soc. Immunology, N.Y. Acad. Scis. Roman Catholic. Address: Giffard, Que., Canada. Died Mar. 25, 1977.

COTNER, THOMAS EWING, educator, govt. ofcl.; b. Dallas, Oct. 26, 1916; s. Thomas Ewing and Nina D. (Crawford); student North Tex. Agrl. Coll., 1933-35; B.A., Baylor U., 1937; M.A., U. Tex., 1939, Ph.D. (grad. fellow 1939-40, 41-42), 1947; m. Jeanne Booth, Dec. 26, 1941; children—Thomas Ewing III, Zachary B., George R. Tchr. history Brownwood (Tex.) High Sch., 1937-39; dir. hist. div. Tex. Meml. Mus., Austin, 1939-40; instr. history U. Tex., summer 1940, Latin-Am. history Tulane U., 1940-41, polit. sci. George Washington U., 1948-52; with internat. div. U.S. Office Edn., HEW, Washington, 1942-43, 46-79, dep. asso. commr., 1962-65, dir. div. internat. exchange and tng., 1965-75, chief internat. services and research br., 1975-79; mem. U.S. del. XXIX Internat. Conf. on Pub. Edn., Geneva, Switzerland, 1966; U.S. mem. of council Bur. Internat. Edn., Geneva. Mem. Falls Church (Va.) Sch. Bd., 1966-69. Served to lt. USNR, 1943-46. Recipient Superior Service award, other commendation Office Edn.; Medal of Merit Belgian Govt., 1957. Mem. Am. Hist. Assn., Acad. Polit. Sci., Comparative and Internat. Edn. Soc., Phi Kappa Sigma, Alpha Chi. Author: The Political and Military Career of Jose Joaquin de Herrera, 1792-1854, 1949; International Educational Exchange: A Selected Bibliography, 1961. Editor: Essays in Mexican History, 1958. Home: Falls Church, Va. Died Dec. 1, 1979; buried Oakwood Cemetery, Falls Church.

COTTERILL, ROBERT SPENCER, coll. prof.; b. Battle Run, Ky., Aug. 12, 1884; s. Francis Marion and Jane Eliza (Spencer) C.; B.A., Ky. Wesleyan Coll., Winchester, Ky., 1904; M.A., U. of Va., 1907; Ph.D., U. of Wis., 1918; m. Mabel Lola Howe, July 13, 1907. Prof. history and Latin, Ky. Wesleyan Coll., 1910-14; prof. history, Western Md. Coll., Westminster, Md., 1915-20, also dean of men, 1918-20; prof. history, U. of Louisville, 1920-28, head of dept., 1923-28; prof. history, Florida State U., 1928-52, prof. emeritus, chair So. history and Americanism, 1931-50, research prof. history, 1950-52; vis. prof. U. Ga., 1953; vis. prof., summers, Ky. U., 1925, 45-47, George Washington U., 1926, U. Pa., 1927, U. of Cin. 1928, 30, U. of Va., 1937; research, London, 1935. Mem. Mississippi Valley Historical Assn., Southern Hist. Assn. (v.p. 1946-48), pres. since 1948), American Assn. Univ. Profs., Tallahassee Historical Society (pres. 1941-43), Phi Alpha Theta. Democrat. Episcopalian. Author several books since 1917, the latest on Southern Indians, 1953; also contbr. articles to history magazines and reviews. Member editorial bd. Miss. Valley Hist. Review, 1926-29; editor Filson Club Quarterly, 1926-28; editorial bd. Journal of So. History, 1939-43. Home: Tallahassee.

COTTON, EMILE LOUIS, real estate broker; b. Elwood, Ind., May 15, 1899; s. Emile N. and Mary (Schach) C.; student Ind. U., 1918-19; A.B., U. Chgo., 1923; m. Mildred Galloway, Aug. 12, 1925; 1 son, Emile Louis. Tchr. jr. high sch., Elwood, 1923-24; real estate and landscaping bus., Miami, Fla., 1925-30; tchr. Dade County Sch. System, 1930-33; prin. Kendall (Fla.) Sch., 1933-37, South Miami Sch., 1937-43; real estate broker, South Miami, 1943-75; pres. E.L. Cotton, Inc., 1949-75, South Miami Investment Co., 1950-75; dir. First Nat. Bank of South Miami, South Miami Fed. Savs. & Loan Assn. Bd. dirs. Cancer Inst. Miami, 1959-65, v.p., 1962-65; trustee U. Miami, 1959-75. Served as pvt. U.S. Army, 1918. Mem. Nat. Assn. Real Estate Bds., Kendall-Perrine Realty Bd., South Miami Dist. C. of C. (dir. 1945-66), Musicians Club Am. (dir. 1960-75), Alpha Sigma Phi. Methodist. Mason, Rotarian (dir. 1953-55, 64-65). Home: Miami, Fla. Died Aug. 31, 1975.

COTZIAS, GEORGE C., research physician; b. Canea, Crete, Greece, June 16, 1918; s. Constantin and Katherine (Strumpuli) C.; came to U.S., 1941, naturalized, 1952; student Nat. U., Athens, 1935-40; M.D. cum laude, Harvard, 1943; Sc.D. Med. Sci. (hon.), Catholic U. Santiago (Chile); D.Sc. (hon.), Med. Coll. Pa., St. John's U.; m. Betty Ghinos, June 30, 1951; 1 son, Constantin G. Intern, then resident Peter Bent Brigham and Mass. Gen. hosps., Boston, 1943-46; asst. Rockefeller Inst., 1947-52; sr. scientist, head physiology div. Brookhaven Nat. Lab., Upton, N.Y., 1953-75; prof. neurology Mt. Sinai Med. Sch., 1970-75; prof. medicine U. State N.Y. at Stony Brook, 1970-75, Cornell Med. Coll., 1974-77; attending physician N.Y. Hosp., 1974-77, Meml. Hosp. for Cancer, 1975-77, Rockefeller U. Hosp., 1974-77; mem. Sloan-Kettering Inst. for Cancer Research, 1975-77; adj. prof. Rockefeller U., 1974-77. Served with Royal Greek Army, 1940-41. Decorated comdr. Greek Royal Order Phoenix; recipient Albert Lasker award clin. med. research, 1969, Gold medal AEC, 1972, Borden award Assn. Am. Med. Colls., 1972, Oscar B. Hunter award, 1972, A.C.P. award, 1974. Fellow Am. Acad. Arts and Scis., N.Y. Acad. Sci.; mem. Nat. Acad. Scis., Assn. Am. Physicians, Am. Soc. Clin. Investigation, Am. Physiol. Soc. Home: New York, N.Y. Died June 13, 1977.

COUCHMAN, GAYLORD M., educator; b. Popejoy, Ia., Sept. 11, 1906; s. Thomas B. and Elsie (Davidson) C.; B.A., Des Moines U., 1927; B.D., McCormick Theol. Sem., 1934; D.D., U. Dubuque, 1945; m. Esther Dunkerton, July 29, 1935; children—Barbara (Mrs. George French), Carol (Mrs. James Cramer), Mary (Mrs. John Beerling), John. Ordained to ministry Presbyn. Ch., 1934; served as pastor in Grimes, Ia., 1934-36, Lake City, Ia., 1936-39, Boone, Ia., 1939-43, Westminster Presbyn. Ch., Dubuque, Ia., 1943-53; pres. U. Dubuque, 1953-68, bd. dirs., 1946-53, also vice chmn. exec. com., dir. ch. relations Theol. Sem., U. Dubuque, 1968-71, pres. emeritus, 1971. Mem. bd. nat. mission, past chmn. council theol. edn., United Presbyn. Ch. U.S.A.; past pres. Presbyn. Coll. Union; chmn. bd. dirs. Assn. Theol. Faculties Ia., Inc. Mem. City Council, Dubuque, 1968-71, mayor, 1971. Bd. dirs. Ia. Coll. Found. Mem. Ia. Coll. Pres. Assn. (past pres.), Ia. Assn. Colls. and Univs., Am. Assn. Sch. Adminstrs., N.E.A., Ia. Assn. Pvt. Colls. and Univs. (chmn., pres. pro tem). Rotarian. Home: Dubuque, Iowa. Deceased.

COUDERT, ALEXIS CARREL, lawyer; b. NY.C., June 3, 1914; s. Frederic R. and Alice Tracy (Wilmerding) C.; B.A., Yale, 1935; LL.B., Columbia, 1938; m. Allison Moore, June 8, 1936 (div. 1961); children—Alexis Tracy, Allison Pierce; m. 2d, Cora Craddock Amory Kirby, Apr. 7, 1961. Admitted to N.Y. bar, 1938; law asst. to justice U.S. Supreme Ct., 1938-30; mem. Coudert Bros., N.Y.C., 1942-80; prof. law Columbia U., 1949-56, acting dir. Parker Sch. Fgn. and Comparative Law, 1949-55, trustee, 1946-80; chmn. Unity Fire & Gen. Ins. Co., Gen. Security Assurance Corp., Urbaine Life Ins. Co.; dir. Dime Savs. Bank N.Y., Pellon Corp., French-American Banking Corp., IMS Internat., Inc., Michelin Tire Corp. U.S. rep. to Internat. Com. Comparative Law, 1951-55. Bd. dirs. N.Y. Eye and Ear Infirmary, 1949-80; pres. Humanities Fund, Inc., 1965-72; sec., dir. Brez Found., 1940-64, pres., 1965-72; bd. dirs. Alfred Jurzykowski Found., 1960-80, pres., 1970-80. Decorated chevalier Legion of Honor, chevalier Ordre de Sante Publique (France). Mem. Am. Assn. Comparative Study of Law, Inc. (pres. 1955-60, 65-71), Assn. Bar City N.Y., Am., New York County, N.Y. State bar assns., Am. Fgn. Law Assn. (pres. 1959-63), Am. Soc. Internat. Law, Internat. C. of C. (exec. com. U.S. council). Clubs: Piping Rock (Locust Valley, N.Y.); Yale, Sky (bd. govs.) (N.Y.C.); Paris-American (pres. 1972-76). Home: New York, N.Y. Died Nov. 2, 1980.

COULTER, CHARLES WELLSLEY, prof. sociology; b. Lampton, Ont., Can., Feb. 14, 1884; s. John and Mary (Black) C.; B.A., U. of Toronto, 1908; B.D., Victoria Coll., 1910; M.A., Yale, 1910, Ph.D., 1914; studied U. of Chicago, summer, 1917; m. Gladys Rowse, June 22, 1910; 1 dau., Vivian McFadden. Ordained ministry Canadian Meth. Ch., London, Ont., 1909; asst. prof. Western Res. U., 1914-23; prof. sociology Ohio Wesleyan U., 1923-34, head department on sociology U. N.H., 1935-53; visiting professor sociology 1953-54. Investigator race relations, Cleveland Mayor's War Board, 1918-20; recreational dir. Cleveland Foundation, 1919; spl. investigator, Hiram House Social Settlement, Cleveland, 1928. Visiting prof. to univs. of Union of S. Africa under Carnegie Corp., 1929-30; sociol. investigator for Nat. Industrialization Survey of Central Africa, 1932-33; supervisor unemployment study Nat. Research for N.H., 1936-37; mem. N.H. Bd. Prisons, N.H. Bd. of Parole, 1950-53; mem. edn. bd. Am. Econs. Found. since Mem. Am. Sociol. Soc. Delaware C. of C. (pres.), Consu Instn. of Am., Inc. (dir.), Text Research and Educatio (dir.), Golden Rule Farm Homes (dir.), Phi Gamma Mu, P Kappa, Alpha Tau Omega, Alpha Kappa Delta. Republican. author several sociol. publs. Contbr. to mags. Home: Dade City, Fla.

COULTER, GLENN MONROE, lawyer; b. Syracuse, N.Y., Aug. 8, 1894; s. Fred and Florence Lucretia (Mills) C,; grad. Yates Poly. Inst., Chittenango, N.Y., 1911; A.B., U. Mich., 1916, J.D., 1920, LL.D., 1958; m. Doris McDonald, Sept 1, 1922; childred—Thomas Edward and Patricia Stoddard (twins). Admitted to Mich bar, 1920, since practiced in Detroit; counsel Hill, Lewis Adams, Goodrich & Tait. Pres. United Community Services Met. Detroit, 1950-54; trustee Detroit YMCA; bd. dirs. United Found; chmn. exec. com. War Chest of Detroit, 1944-46. Served to maj. U.S. Army Ambulance Service, 1917-19. Fellow Am. Bar Found. (past treas.); mem. Am. (past treas.; past chmn. com. on admissions and credentials, profl. ethics, scope and correlation, past state del. of Mich.), Detroit (pres. 1942-43, vice chmn. legal aid bur.) bar assns., Am Judicature Soc., U.S.A.A.C. Vets. Assn. (nat. comdr. 1929-30), U. Mich. Alumni Assn. (nat. pres. 1950-52), Am. Coll. Probate Counsel (regent), Mich. Hort. Soc. (trustee, 1st v.p.), Detroit Hist. Soc., Phi Beta Kappa Assos., Scribes, Phi Beta Kappa, Theta Chi (past v.p. nat. bd. trustees), Phi Delta Phi. Clubs: Paul Bunyan, Prismatic (pres. 1956-57) (Detroit). Author profl. articles. Lectr., writer stained glass and mosaics. Home: Grosse Pointe Farms, Mich. Died Nov 5, 1974.

COULTER, KIRKLEY SCHLEY, govt. ofcl.; b. Nashville, July 26, 1914; s. John L. and Phoebe E. (Frost) C.; B.A., Am. U., 1935, postgrad., 1935-37, 60-62, M.A., 1963; postgrad. U. Wis., 1936, Columbia, 1940-41; m. Irene Maria B. Prazmowski, Aug. 16, 1945; 1 step-dau., Barbara M. Mem. staff Senator Hugh Butler, Nebr., 1941-42, 46-47, adminstrv. asst., legislative asst., 1947-53; chief clk., staff dir. Senate Com. on Interior and Insular Affairs, 1953-54; asst. to undersec. interior, 1954-55; asst. dir. Office Territories, Dept. Interior, 1955, dep. dir., 1955-57, legislative adviser, 1957-60; chief div. internat. comml. relations U.S. Tariff Commn., Washington, 1960-62; minority economist antitrust and monopoly subcom. U.S Senate Judiciary Com., 1963-73. Joint founder, joint co-chmn. Arlingtonians for a Better County, 1955. Chmn. Republican exec. com. Arlington County, 1954. Served to 1st lt. AUS, 1942-46. Recipient Founders' award Am. Council Polish Cultural Clubs, 1979. Mem. Am. Econ. Assn., Omicron Delta Kappa, Pi Gamma Mu, Alpha Tau Omega. Episcopalian. Home: Falls Church, Va. Died July 9, 1980.

COUNIHAN, EDWARD AUGUSTINE, JR., judge; b. Cambridge, Mass., Aug. 2, 1882; s. Edward Augustine and Mary Louise (Long) C.; student Cambridge Latin Sch., 1900, A.B., Harvard, 1904, LL.B., 1906; m. Susan A. Collins, Jan. 15, 1913 (died 1919); children—Edward A., Paul G. Admitted to Mass. State bar, Feb., 1906, and began practice in Cambridge; pres. Cambridge Fed. Savings & Loan Assn. since 1935; special justice, Cambridge Dist. Court, 1921-49; asso. justice, Mass. Supreme Judicial Court since 1949. Mem. Mass. State Senate, 1919-20. Mem. sch. com., City Cambridge, 1910-16; mem. city council, 1916-20; chmn Cambridge com. pub. safety, 1941-49; chmn. Cambridge centennial com., 1945-46. K.C. Elk. Club: Harvard of Boston. Home: Cambridge, Mass.

COUNSELMAN, THEODORE BENTON, mining cons.; b. N.Y.C., Dec. 10, 1889; s. Thomas Hart Benton and Jessie D'Ella (Peebles) C.; E.M., Columbia, 1910; m. Eleanor Crabbe Eayres-Gardner, June 10, 1914; children—Theodore Benton, Edward Gardner, Revere G., Eleanor R. (Mrs. Carl Oxholm, Jr.). With Inspiration Copper Co., 1911-12, Cananea Consol. Copper Co., 1912-13, 15, Ariz. Copper Co., 1912-15, Miami Copper Co., 1915-16, Mesabi Iron Co., 1916-23; sales engr., 1924-27; with Dorr Co., 1928-55; partner, sec.-treas., v.p., dir. Behre Dolbear & Co., Inc., sr. cons., 1968-76. Recipient Egleston medal Columbia, 1966, Robert H. Richards award Am. Inst. Mining Engrs., 1967. Mem. Am. Inst. Mining, Metal and Petroleum Engrs. (v.p. 1953-57, dir. 1952-57, exec. com. 1954-57), Mining and Metall. Soc. Am. (council 1960-61), Engrs. Joint Council (dir. 1955-61, exec. com. 1956-61), Columbia Alumni Fedn. (dir. 1961-62), Delta Tau Delta. Republican. Episcopalian. Mason (Shriner). Clubs: Mining (gov. 1962-64, v.p. 1963), Columbia University (N.Y.C.); Shinnecock Yacht, Quogue (N.Y.). Contbr. articles to profl. jours. Inventor various ore dressing, roasting furnaces, synthetic rubber processing machines. Home: Newtown Square, Pa. Died July 6, 1976.

COUSINS, C(LARENCE) E(DWIN), educator; b. Salem, Mass., Oct. 14, 1884; s. Charles and Ada (Ballard) C.; A.B., Tufts Col l., 1906; A.M., U. Wisconsin, 1911; married Ruby I. Watts, June 11, 1925 (deceased February 1955). Employed as instr. Tufts Coll., 1906-07, Case Sch. Applied Sci., 1907-08; U. Mich., 1908-09; instr. U. Wis., 1909-17, asst. prof., 1917-18; asso. prof. State U. Ia., 1918-47, prof., head Romance lang. dept., 1947-53, prof. emeritus, 1953—. Mem. Am. Assn. U. Profs., Modern Lang. Assn. Home: Iowa City, Ia.

COUSINS, SOLON BOLIVAR, JR., clergyman; b. Luthersville, Ga., Nov. 13, 1885; A.B. and D.D., Mercer U.; grad. student U. of Edinburgh; m. Hattie Llewellyn Glausier; 1 son, Solon Bolivar, 3d. Has been teacher of Latin and Greek, Locust Grove (Ga.) Inst., and asso. prof. English, Mercer U. Served following pastorates—First Bapt. Ch., Montezuma, Ga., First Ch., Waynesboro, Ga., Liberty Ch., Liberty, Mo.; First Ch., Columbus, Ga.; Second Ch., Richmond; prof. of Bible, U. of Richmond. Former pres. Bapt. Gen. Assn. of Va.; mem. Bapt. Bd. of Missions and Education, Foreign Mission Bd., Southern Bapt. Conv. Mem. Sigma Nu. Home: Richmond, Va. *

COVALT, DONALD A., physician; b. Muncie, Ind., Nov. 11, 1906; s. Elmer F. and Maude (Fallis) C.; student DePauw U., 1924-27; B.S., Ind. U., 1932, M.D., 1933; m. Anna Mary Aloisi, Aug. 1, 1959; 1 dau., Maude Helen. Rotating intern Cleve. City Hospital, 1933-34; gen. practice, Muncie 1934-42; asst. med. dir. Med. Rehab. Service VA, 1946-47; asso. dir. Inst. Rehab. Medicine, N.Y. U. Med. Center, also prof. phys. medicine and rehab., N.Y. U. Sch. Medicine, 1947-77; chief convalescent tng. div. Office Air Surgeon, Hdqrs. USAF, 1944-45, cons. phys. medicine and rehab., 1951-53; cons. phys. medicine and rehab., VA, 1950-56; mem. med. adv. com. Social Security Adminstrn., 1955-61. Past mem. N.Y. State Bd. Med. Examiners. Recipient Mark A. Light award World Com. on Employment of the Handicapped, 1961. Served to lt. col. M.C., USAAF, 1943-45. Diplomate Am. Bd. Phys. Medicine and Rehab. (exam. bd.). Mem. AMA, N.Y. County, N.Y. State med. socs., Am. Acad. Compensation Medicine (pres. 1959-60), Nat. Rehab. Assn. (W.F. Faulkes award 1954), Am. Congress Rehab. Medicine (pres. 1960-61), N.Y. Acad. Medicine. Contbr. articles profl. jours., chpts. in books. Home: Westport, Conn. Died Oct. 30, 1977.

COVAULT, CLARENCE HARTLEY (KO-VAWLT'), veterinarian; b. Troy, O., Mar. 1, 1886; s. William Alonzo and Mary Elizabeth (Miller) C.; student Nat. Normal U., Lebanon, O., 1904-05; grad. Ohio State U., 1911; m. Kathryn Hyde, May 20, 1912; 1 dau., Evelyn (Mrs. William H. Thompson). Practiced veterinary medicine, Springfield, O., 1911-13, Akron, O., 1914-17; field veterinarian Agrl. Commn. of Ohio, 1913; asst. prof. vet. medicine, Ia. State Coll., 1917-21, asso. prof., 1921-29, prof. and head of dept., 1929-36, head dept. and dir. of clinics, 1936-51. Mem., A.A.A.S., Am. and Ia. Vet. med. assns., Phi Kappa Phi, Phi Zeta, Gamma Sigma Delta. Methodist. Club: Kiwanis. Home: Ames, Ia.

COVERDALE, JOHN WALTER, b. Clinton Co., Ia., Apr. 4, 1883, s. Elijah Anthony and Sarah Jane (Jepson) C.; prep. edn. high sch., Delmar, Ia., student Ia. State Coll., 1902-05; m. Elsie Helen Grindrod, of Delmar, Jan. 1906; 1 son, John Walter, Jr. Farming in Clinton Co., Ia., since 1906; county agt. leader, Ia. State Coll., 1912-19; sec. Ia. Farm Bur. Federation, 1919-20; sec. Am. Farm Bur. Federation, 1920-24; sec.-treas. Grain Marketing Co., Chicago, 1924-25; gen. manager animal and plant food div., Rath Packing Co., Waterloo, Ia. Mem. Am. Inst. Agr. (exec. bd.), Nat. Com. on Agr. and Electricity (ex-chmn.), Nat. Live Stock and Meat Bd. (ex-dir.), Nat. Com. Boys' and Girls' Club Work (exec. com.), Gamma Sigma Delta. Republican. Methodist. Mason (K.T.), Kiwanian (past pres.). Home: Waterloo, Ia.

COWAN, LOUIS G., pub. co. exec., communications exec.; b. Chgo., Dec. 12, 1909; s. Jacob J. and Hetty (Smitz) C.; Ph.B., U. Chgo., 1931; Litt.D., Emerson Coll.; m. Pauline Spiegel, Aug. 7, 1939; children—Paul, Geoffrey, Holly, Liza. Pres., Louis G. Cowan Co., pub. relations, 1931-41, Louis G. Cowan, Inc., radio and TV prodns., 1946-55; v.p. creative services CBS, Inc., 1955-58, pres. CBS TV Network, 1958-59; dir. Morse Communication Research Center, Brandeis U., Waltham, Mass., 1961-65; dir. Spl. Programs, Grad. Sch. Journalism, Columbia, N.Y.C., 1965-76; pres., editor Chilmark Press, Inc., 1962-76; chmn. publs. and adv. bd. Partisan Rev.; chmn. pub. com. Columbia Journalism Rev. Pres. Broadcast Inst. N. Am. Nat. chmn. Weiner Oral History Library, Am. Jewish Com. Trustee Internat. Broadcast Inst. Cons. radio sect. Bur. Public Relations, War Dept., 1941-43; dir. Voice Am., chief N.Y.C. office Overseas O.W.I., 1943-45. Mem. Council on Fgn. Relations, A.A.A.S., Zeta Beta Tau. Clubs: Tavern (Chgo.); Lotos, Columbia (N.Y.C.). Home: New York, N.Y. Died Nov. 18, 1976.

COWDEN, ROY W(ILLIAM), educator; b. Fredonia, N.Y., June 27, 1883; s. David Henry and Ida May (Litch) C.; A.B., U. of Mich., 1908; A.M., Harvard, 1909; m. Florence Mabel Kerr, July 28, 1909; 1 dau., Jean Elizabeth (Mrs. William L. Hindman, Jr.). Mem. faculty, U. of Mich., since 1909, prof. of English since 1935. Dir. of Hopwood awards since 1934. Mem. Modern Lang. Assn., Nat. Council Teachers of English. Home: Ann Arbor, Mich.

COWELL, JOSEPH GOSS, painter, sculptor; b. Peoria, Ill., Dec. 4, 1886; s. Benjamin and Mary Anna (Goss) C.; student Bradley Coll., 1902-06, U. of Ill., 1907-08, Art Students League (New York), 1908-09, Sch. of the Mus. of Fine Arts (Boston), 1909-12, County Council Sch. of Arts and Crafts (London), 1914-15, Academie Julien (Paris) 1920; B.S., Bradley University, 1943; m. Helen Parkhurst, Mar. 26, 1913; children—Jean, Mark. Artist, sculptor, painter of murals and designer of memorial windows and ch. altars; mem. faculty Mass. Sch. of Art, 1922-27; asso. dir. Boston Designers Art Sch., 1927-33; creative therapy and research, Boston State Hosp., 1933-39; dir. Nat. Art Sch., Washington, D.C., 1940-42, dean, now dean emeritus; with Office of Strategic Services, 1942-43; Navy Hydrographic Office, Washington, 1943-57, now retired. Murals and portraits in public bldgs.; other works include portrait Lahiri Mahasaya, wall painting, AUM, Adavita Temple, Washington; Temple Alter Painting, Jhargram, India; Windows, altars, mural and sculpture St. Mary's Cathedral, Peoria; triptych, Fourth Presbyn. Ch. (Chicago); sculptures, Memorial Park (Wrentham, Mass.); altar decorations, National Cathedral, Washington, D.C.; portraits in Australia, England. Illustrations in Gray's Anatomy. Served as sargeant in Tank Corps, A.E.F., U.S. Army, 1919-20. Mem. Am. Soc. Photogrammetry, Nat. Geog. Soc., A.A.A.S., Advaita. Episcopalian. Mason. Contbr. to profl. publs. Home: Wrentham, Mass.

COWGILL, JAMES JOSEPH, educator; b. Ronan, Mont., Mar. 20, 1914; s. James Daniel and Kathryn (Salchert) C.; B.S. in Chemistry, M.S., Gonzaga U., 1939, M.A. in Philosophy, 1940; S.T.L., Alma Coll., Los Gatos, Cal., 1946; Ph.D. in chemistry, U. Notre Dame, 1957. Ordained priest Roman Catholic Ch., 1945; mem. faculty Seattle U. from 1950, head dept. physics, 1956-67, prof. physics from 1960, dir. NSF summer Inst. from 1963, acting dean Grad. Sch., 1967-68, asso. dean, 1968-70, dean from 1970, trustee, 1958-65, dir. research and instl. devel. from 1968. Bd. dirs. Jesuit Research Council Am., 1962-69, first v.p. Council Priests Archdiocese of Seattle. Mem. Am. Chem. Soc., Soc. Research Adminstrs., Nat. Council U. Research Adminstrs., N.W. Sci. Assn., Am. Assn. Physics Tchrs., A.A.A.S., Sigma Xi. Address: Seattle, Wash. Deceased.

COWIE, ALEXANDER, educator; b. St. Paul, Mar. 8, 1896; s. George G. and Mary (Hanrahan) C.; A.B., U. Minn., 1919, A.M. 1920; Ph.D., Yale, 1930; m. Elspeth Nicolson, Sept. 3, 1926; children—Alan, Gwendolen. Instr. English, U. Ill., 1920-22, Univ. Minn., 1922-23; instr. Wesleyan U., 1924-27, prof. English since 1949; vis. lectr. Trinity Coll., 1941, Ohio State U., summer 1941, U. Minn., 1945, Univ. Pa., 1949; lectr. Am. lit. for Dept. State (Smith-Mundt Act), Gothenburg, Lund univs., Sweden, 1951-52. Served with 872d Aero Squadron, U.S. Army, World War I. Mem. Modern Lang. Assn., Coll. English Assn., Phi Beta Kappa. Author: John Trumbull; Connecticut Wit, 1936; The Yemassee, 1937; The Rise of the American Novel, 1948; American Writers Today, 1956. Contbr. Lit. History of U.S., 1948; also articles profl. publs., popular mags. Home: Middletown, Conn. Died Nov. 3, 1978; cremated.

COWLES, RUSSELL, painter; b. Algona, Ia., Oct. 7, 1887; s. Gardner and Florence (Call) C.; A.B., Dartmouth, 1909; L.H.D., 1951; D.F.A. (hon.), Grinnell Coll., 1944; m. Eleanor Stanton, 1928 (div. 1954); m. 2d, Nancy Cardozo Egleson, 1954. Exhibited in most leading nat. exhbns., works in permanent collections Dartmouth Coll., Whitney Mus., N.Y.C., U. Wichita, Mpls. Inst. Art, Pa. Acad. Fine Arts, Swope Gallery, Des Moines Art Center, Blandon Gallery, Denver Art Mus., Santa Barbara Mus., Addison Gallery, Va. Mus. Ency. Brit. Collection and others, Prix de Rome, Am. Acad. in Rome, 1915-21. Club: Century Assn. of N.Y. Home: New Milford, Conn. Died Feb. 23, 1979.

COWLEY, WILLIAM HAROLD, educator; b. Petersburg, Va., May 28, 1899; s. William Frederick and Elizabeth (Maddock) C.; A.B., Dartmouth Coll., 1924; Ph.D., U. Chgo., 1930; LL.D., Hamilton Coll., 1938, St. Lawrence U., 1943; L.H.D., Hobart Coll., 1939; Litt.D., Union Coll., 1940; m. Jean McCampbell, Sept. 8, 1934; children—Virginia, Ellen McCampbell. With Bell Telephone Labs., N.Y.C., 1924-25; adminstrv. staff U. Chgo., 1927-29; research asso., asst. prof. psychology Bur. Ednl. Research, Ohio State U., 1929-34, asso. prof., 1934-35, prof., 1935-38; pres. Hamilton Coll., 1938-44, prof. higher edn. Stanford, 1945-68, David Jacks prof. higher edn., 1954-68, emeritus, 1968-78; George A. Miller vis. prof. U. Ill., 1959; Fulbright scholar Eng., 1951-52. Home: Palo Alto, Calif. Died July 22, 1978.

COWLING, HERFORD TYNES, photographic engr., movie producer, explorer; b. Nansemond County, Va., Aug. 20, 1890; s. John Phillips and Caroline Weaver (Tynes) C.; student George Washington U., 1912-13; m. Virginia Hardin, Jan. 14, 1927. Chief photographer U.S. Reclamation Service, 1909-16; traveled extensively in U.S., Canada and Mexico, 1913-16; headed cinematographic expdn., 1917, to Formosa, Philippines, Indo-China, Siam, Dutch East Indies, Australia, Tasmania, China, Japan, New Zealand and South Sea Islands, producing semi-ednl. and travel motion pictures; chief cinematographer and tech. dir. for Paramount—Burton Holmes Travel Films; technical director Teaching Films Department, Eastman Kodak Co., 1927-32; official photographer Century of Progress, Chicago, 1933; supervised of motion picture production of Emergency Conservation Works, Washington, D.C., 1934; tech. dir. div. of motion pictures and sound recording, U.S. Nat. Archives, Washington, July 1, 1935-Mar. 15, 1937; technical assistant to administrator, National Unemployment Census, Washington, D.C., 1937; sr. administrative assistant Commerce Dept., 1938-40, then chief of photographic services U.S. Dept. Labor. Prod. motion pictures of Europe, 1919, including France, Belgium, Germany, Austria, Switzerland, Czecho-Slovakia, Italy, also Algeria, Tunisie, Tangier, Morocco, Sicily, Spain, Egypt, Palestine, Constantinople, Cuba and Mexico, 1921; expdn. to British East Africa, Uganda, Congo and The Sudan, filming big game hunting, 1922; India, Kashmir, Tibet, 1923-24; China war corr., Sept.-Nov. 1924; made moving pictures in Tibet of its people and customs; produced motion picture of coronation of Maharaja of Kashmir, 1926. Served in Army Air Forces, Jan. 1941-Dec. 1946; col. Air Reserves from Dec. 1946; col., Air Corps; chief operations, photographic services, A.M.C., A.A.F., Wright Field (Ohio). Mem. Federal Photog. Society (president, 1915-16), Am. Soc. Cinematographers, Am. Soc. Photogrammetry, Soc. Am. Archivists, Air Forces Assn., Am. Legion, Post No. 200, Dayton, Soc. of Motion Picture Engrs., S.A.R., Internat. Photographers; fellow Royal Photog. Soc., Great Britain. Mason. Clubs: Explorers; Army-Navy Country, Army and Navy (Washington); Engineers (Dayton, O.). Home: Arlington, Va. Died Oct. 15, 1980.

COX, ARTIMUS WARD, dept. store exec.; b. Red Knob, W.Va., Aug. 18, 1885; s. Mark and Mary (Bradley) C.; ed. pub. schs., W.Va.; m. Narcie G. Payne, May 6, 1908; children—Sybal (Mrs. Harold L. Vannetta), Wilbur E., Mildred (Mrs. Cox Bostwick), Ward (dec.). Founder, mgr. A.W. Cox Dept. Store Co., Clendenin, W.Va., 1909-14; co-founder Diamond Dept. Store Co., Charleston, W.Va., 1927, v.p., 1927-56, chmn. bd., 1956—; pres. A.W. Cox Dept. Store Co., Charleston, 1914—, Interstates Investment Corp., Charleston, 1929—, Elkana Co., Charleston, 1957—. Mem. bd. missions Meth. Episcopal Ch. South, 1922-39, treas. W.Va. Conf., 1922-34. Chmn. trustees Morris Harvey Coll., 1932-62. Named Hon. Alumnus, Morris Harvey Coll., 1954, W.Va. Layman of Year, M.E. Ch., 1956. Democrat. Mason, Rotarian. Home: Charleston, W.Va.

COX, EARL L., business exec.; b. 1905; grad. Rider Coll., 1926; married. With Fernald & Co., Phila., until 1956; treas., dir. Chem. Leaman Tank Lines, Inc., Downington, Pa., 1956—. Died 1974.

COX, EDWIN, chem. engr.; b. Richmond, Va., Sept. 20, 1902; s. Edwin Piper and Sally Bland (Clarke) C.; B.S. in chem. engring., Va. Mil. Inst., 1920, M.S. in chemistry, 1920; m. Virginia Bagby DeMott, May 19, 1927; 1 son, Edwin. With Va.-Carolina Chem. Corp., 1920-57, v.p., 1949-57; pvt. practice chem. engr., chemist, Aylett, Va., from 1958; pres. Tobacco By-Products and Chem. Corp.; partner Edwin Cox Assos., Richmond; mem. adv. com. Va. Bicentennial. Trustee Va. Inst. Sci. Research. Personal Aide five Va. Govs., 1926-50. Pres. Va. Hist. Soc. Served to col. Inf., AUS, 1940-46, comdg. officer 176th inf., Joint Chiefs of Staff Secretariat, SHAEF, operational control I.G. Farben, 1945; brig. gen. Va. N.G. Decorated Legion of Merit, Bronze Star medal, Army Comm. Ribbon with oak leaf cluster; recipient Distinguished Service award Va. sect. Am. Chem. Soc., 1951; Gold medal award Am. Inst. Chemists, 1965; Distinguished Service award Va. Mil. Inst., 1974; Chem. Engring. Achievement award. Registered profl. engr., Va., N.Y. Fellow A.A.A.S., Am. Inst. Chemists; mem. Am. Chem. Soc., Am. Inst. Chem. Engrs., Va. Acad. Sci., Mil. Order World Wars, Soc. Colonial Wars, Nat. Soc. Profl. Engrs., S.R., Jamestown Soc. (past gov.). Democrat (past chmn. 3d dist. com., past sec. Va. State Com.). Episcopalian (lay reader). Knight of Malta. Clubs: Commonwealth, Richmond; Chemists (N.Y.C.). Author articles in chem. and hist. jours. Patentee in field. Address: Aylett, Va. Died Feb. 22, 1977.

COX, GERTRUDE M., statistician; b. Dayton, Iowa, Jan. 13, 1900; B.S., Iowa State U., 1929, M.S., 1931, D.Sc. (hon.), 1958; postgrad. U. Calif., Berkeley, 1931-33. Asst. Iowa State Coll., 1933-39, asst. prof., 1939-40; prof., head dept. exptl. statistics N.C. State Coll., 1940-49, prof., dir. Inst. Statistics, N.C. State U., Raleigh, 1944-60; dir. statistics research div. Research Triangle Inst., Research Triangle Park, N.C., 1959-64, sr. statis. advisor, 1966-71; program specialist U. Cairo, Egypt, 1964-65; cons. Rockefeller Found., Thailand, 1970-71; cons. in statistics, 1971-78; collaborator U.S. Dept. Agr., 1941-50, 54-60; mem. adv. com. statis. policy U.S. Bur. Budget, 1956-61; mem. adv. com. NIH, 1959-64; mem. panel HEW Office of Edn., 1963-64. Recipient Watauga medal N.C. State U., 1977. Fellow Am. Pub. Health Assn., AAAS, Inst. Math. Statistics, Am. Statis. Assn. (pres. 1956), Royal Statis. Soc. (hon.); mem. Nat. Acad. Sci., Internat. Statis. Inst. (treas. 1955-61), Internat. Biometric Soc. (hon. mem., pres. 1968-69), Sigma Xi, Gamma Sigma Delta, Phi Kappa Phi, others. Home: Raleigh, N.C. Died Oct. 17, 1978.

COX, IGNATIUS WILEY, clergyman, educator; b. Washington, D.C., June 20, 1883; s. James Herman and Mary Genevieve (Schark) C.; ed. Mt. St. Mary's Coll., Md.; studied philosophy and theology, Woodstock (Md.). Coll., A.B., 1908, A.M., 1909; Ph.D., Fordham, 1922. Joined Soc. of Jesus (Jesuits), 1902; ordained priest R.C. Ch., 1917; prof. poetry and rhetoric, Boston Coll., 1909-14, prof. philosophy, 1919-21; prof. philosophy, Fordham, 1921-25, student counselor, 1923-25. Dir. in Eastern U.S. of Knights of the Blessed Sacrament, 1921-25; editor Pilgrim (quarterly) 1925; editor Jesuit Missions (nat. mission monthly) since 1927. Mem. N.E. Assn. Schs. and Colls., Philos. Assn. Eastern Jesuits. Author: Ontology (textbook on philosophy), 1923. Lecturer and preacher. Address: New York, N.Y.

COX, LAURIE DAVIDSON, college president; b. Londonderry, N.S., Can., Aug. 18, 1885; s. George Wilbert and Evangeline (Davidson) C.; brought to U.S., 1894; A.B., Acadia Univ., Wolfville, N.S., 1903; S.B. in Landscape Architecture, Harvard, 1908; D.Sc. honoris causa, Acadia Univ., 1931; m. Gretchen Smith Sanborn, Sept. 7, 1910; children—Barbara Sanborn, Laurie Davidson, Priscilla De Lanie. Asst. city engr., Boulder, Colo., 1909; asso. of T. Glenn Phillips, in landscape architecture, Detroit, Mich., 1909-11; landscape engr. Los Angeles (Calif.) Park Commn., 1911-14; designed Exposition Park, Lincoln Park, Griffith Park, Municipal Conservatory-all at Los Angeles; asst. prof. landscape architecture, N.Y. State Coll. of Forestry, 1914-18, prof., 1918-46; pres. New England Coll. Henniker, N.H., since 1947; head dept. landscape and recreational management; also pvt. practice. Constrn. supt., U.S. Shipping Bd. under John Nolen, city planner, World War. Landscape architect to Central N.Y. State Park Commn. since 1926. Designer of grounds and bldgs., Selkirk Shores, Green Lakes, Chenango Valley, Gilbert Lake, Chittenango Falls, Clark Reservation (all state parks, N.Y.); resident landscape architect Reconnaissance Survey Green Mountain Parkway for U.S. Nat. Park Service, 1934. Mem. bd. govs. Nat. Conf. State Parks since 1942. Fellow Am. Soc. Landscape Architects; mem. Sigma Alpha Epsilon. Head coach Syracuse U. lacrosse team, 1916-31, winning World's title in Eng., 1923; coach "All America" lacrosse team representing U.S. Intercollegiate Lacrosse Assn. in internat. series with Canada, 1930, 34, 35; head coach All America lacrosse team winning "Flannery Cup" in internat. series with England, in England, 1937; brought Oxford-Cambridge lacrosse team to U.S. for Am. tour, 1922, 26, 30. Selected All American Lacrosse Team for U.S. Intercollegiate Lacrosse Assn. annually, 1922-44. Editor Intercollegiate Lacrosse Guide, 1922-34. Author numerous tech. publs. and papers on park design and maintenance.

COX, ORMOND LEE, naval officer; b. Rix Mills, O., Oct. 16, 1883; s. Samuel Gregory and Martha Jane (Herron) C.; B.S., U.S. Naval Acad., 1905; student Engring. Post Grad. Sch., Annapolis, 1909-11; m. Ethel Merriam, Nov. 16, 1910; children—Marion (Mrs. Hollis B. Idleman), Dorothy (Mrs. Henry O. Redue, Jr.), Jane (Mrs. Tracy C. Miner, Jr.), Helen (Mrs. Daniel C. Park). Commissioned ensign U.S. Navy, 1907, and advanced through the grades to rear admiral, 1938; engineer officer on U.S.S. Nevada, 1916-18, Navy Yard Charleston, S.C., 1918-21; Design Div. Bureau of Engring., Navy Dept., Washington, D.C., 1922-25; Div. and Fleet Engr., Battle Fleet 1925-27; Head of Design Div. Bureau of Engineering, 1927-32; dir. U.S. Engring. Expt. Station, Annapolis, Md., 1933-39; supervisor of shipbuilding, Newport News, Va., since 1939.

Episcopalian. Author: Naval Turbines (with Miles A. Libbey), 1924. *

COX, PHILIP WESCOTT LAWRENCE, educator; b. Malden, Mass., July 25, 1883; s. Alfred Elmer and Annie Adelaide (Bell) C.; B.A., Harvard, 1906, M.A., 1920; Ph.D., Columbia, 1925; grad. student U. of N.H., 1907; m. Ruth Dillaway, July 17, 1909; children—Philip Westcott Lawrence, Edward Dillaway, Nancy Ryder, Kenneth Faulkner (dec.). Asst. instr. in botany Harvard, 1905; tchr., and ednl. adminstrv. positions, 1905-20; headmaster Washington School of N.Y., 1920-22; prin. high sch. dept. Lincoln Sch. of Teachers Coll., New York City, 1922-23; prof. edn. New York Univ., 1923-49, emeritus prof. 1949-72. Member National Education Assn. (ex-president dept. elementary education), National Association of Secondary Sch. Principals (ex-v.p.), National Soc. Coll. Teachers of Education (chmn. editorial com. 1937), Teachers' Ins. and Annuity Assn. (nominating com., 1926-27), Boy Scouts America (nat. council from 1930), Marthas Vineyard Assn., Kappa Sigma, Phi Delta Kappa, Kappa Delta Pi, Pi Gamma Mu. Clubs: Harvard (Martha's Vineyard); The Greeks (Maplewood). Author six books, 1925-38; Basic Principles of Guidance (with J. C. Duff and Marie McNamara), 1948; (with Blaine E. Mercer) Education in Democracy, 1961. Asso. editor The Clearing House. Contbr. chpts. High School Curriculum (H. R. Douglas, editor), 1947. Home: Vineyard Haven, Mass. Died Nov. 1975.

COX, RICHARD FERGUSON, army officer (ret.); born Graceville, Minn., Feb. 26, 1886; s. William and Rebecca (Mills) C.; M.E., U. of Minn., 1908; grad. Coast Arty. Sch., 1915, 26. Command and Gen. Staff Sch., 1927, Army War Coll., 1930, Naval War Coll., 1935, 1936; m. Ann French, Oct. 1, 1913; 1 son, Richard French. Commd. 2d lt., Coast Arty. Corps, U.S. Army, 1910, advanced through grades to brig. gen., 1940; retired Feb. 1944. Mem. Sigma Psi, Tau Beta Pi. Episcopalian. Mason. Address: St. Petersburg, Fla.

COX, ROY WESLEY, grain handling exec.; b. Elsmore, Kan., Jan. 8, 1884; s. Henry W. and Jennie S. (Ritter) C.; student Baker U., 1902-03; m. Irene E. Swanson, May 23, 1906 (dec. 1954); children—Claire (Mrs. M. C. Detter), Joyce (Mrs. H. E. Schaulis), Royal Rockwell, Jane (Mrs. William J. Ball), Jacquelyn I. (Mrs. J. P. McFadden); m. 2d Hazel S. Richards, May 2, 1955. Tchr. pub. schs., Allen Co., Kans., 1904-05; editor Elsmore (Kan.) Enterprise, 1905-06; postmaster, Elsmore, 1906-08; mgr. Burgner-Bowman Lumber Co., Elsmore and Savonburg, Kan., 1907-13; propr. Cox Broom Corn & Hay Co., Savonburg, 1913-19; propr. grain elevators, Elsmore, Moran, Piqua, Bayard, Kan., 1919-56 Mayor, Elsmore, 1919-22; highway commr., 1939-47, dir. highways, 1947-51. Chmn. rep. state com., mem. Rep. Nat. Com., 1953-54. Mem. C. of C. Republican. Methodist. Mason. Address: Iola, Kan. Retired.

COY, OWEN COCHRAN, univ. prof.; b. Farragut, Ia., Apr. 16, 1884; s. Rev. Charles Fremont and Lucia May (Cochran) C.; Ph.B., Coll. of Pacific, 1907; M.A., Stanford, 1909; Ph.D., U. of Calif., 1918; m. Hazel Broderick, June 18, 1913; children—Glenn Broderick, Barbara May, Margaret Elma, Clyde Francis. Asst. in history, Stanford, 1908-09; head of history dept., Eureka (Calif.) High Sch., 1909-13; asst. in history, U. of Calif., 1914-15; with Calif. Hist. Survey Commn., 1915-23, dir. and archivist, 1919-23; dir. Calif. State Hist. Assn. since 1923; prof. history, Univ. of Southern Calif., since 1925, chmn. dept., 1935-38, curator of history Los Angeles Museum, 1926-29; mem. bd. govs. of the Museum since 1932; member bd. dirs. Museum Associates since 1938. Executive sec. Calif. War History Com. and historian Calif. State Council of Defense, 1918-19. Lecturer in Am. history, Mills Coll., Jan.-May 1922. Mem. Am. Hist. Assn., Am. Assn. Univ. Profs., San Diego Hist. Soc., Hist. Soc. of Southern Calif., Ore. Trail Memorial Assn., Phi Kappa Phi, Phi Alpha Theta, Alpha Pi Zeta, Pi Gamma Mu; fellow Pacific Geog. Soc. Republican. Methodist. Author: Guide to County Archives of California; The Care and Use of County Archives, 1921; California County Boundaries; Genesis of California Counties, 1923; California's Constitutions (with Herbert C. Jones), 1930; Gold Days, 1929; The Great Trek, 1931; The Humboldt Bay Region (1850-1875), 1930; California, Our Home State (a geography), 1936; also articles on Calif. history and archives. Editor: Architectural History of Mission San Carlos Borromeo, 1921; California History Nugget; Physical and Political California (a map), 1936. Editor and compiler; Pictorial History of California, 1925. Home: Los Angeles. *

COYLE, VINCENT JOHN, former hotel exec.; b. Phila., Jan. 27, 1900; s. John J. and Mary A. (Donnell) C.; degree in structural engring., Pratt Inst., Bklyn., 1921; m. Honora Frawley, Feb. 12, 1928 (dec.); children—Vincent Joseph, Christina D.; m. 2d Dorothy Knoepke, May 19, 1941; stepchildren—Lois and E. Christian Stengel. Sales engr. Atlantic Terra Cotta Co., 1921-25; constrn. engr. Trinity Placer Mines, Inc., 1925-26; structural engr. Calvin Morris Constrn. Co., 1926-30; mng. dir. Carlyle Hotel, N.Y.C., 1930-38, Hampshire House, 1938-46; became v.p., mng. dir. Essex House, 1946. Decorated Ordre Merite d'Agricole (France); recipient Grand Medaille d'Argent, City of Paris. Mem. Am., Internat. hotel assns., Hotel Sales Mgrs. Assn., Les Amis d'Escoffier Soc. (pres.), Hotel Assn. N.Y.C. (1st v.p.). Club: Baltusrol Golf (Springfield, N.J.). Home: Springfield, N.J. Died Aug. 14, 1978.

COYNE, ROBERT WILLIAM, trade assn. exec.; b. Bangor, Me., Feb. 26, 1904; s. Patrick Henry and Mary F. (Nichols) C.; LL.B., George Washington U., 1925; m. Rose Marie Guglberger, Apr. 14, 1934; 1 son, Robert William. Admitted to Mass. and Me. bars, 1926; spl. investigator, then asst. dist. supr. U.S. Treasury and Dept. of Justice, 1925-39; nat. field dir. War Bond program, 1940-46; exec. dir. Am. Theatres Assn., also Theatre Owners Am., 1946-48; spl. counsel Council Motion Picture Orgns., 1950-58; pres. Distilled Spirits Inst., Washington, 1959-77; cons. DISCUS, 1973—. Mem. Gamma Eta Gamma. Democrat. Roman Catholic. Clubs: Metropolitan (N.Y.C.); Nat. Press, Nat. Democratic, (Washington); Variety, Laurel Turf. Home: Washington, D.C. Died Jan. 8, 1977.

COZIER, J. KENNETH, lumber co. exec.; b. Aurora, Neb., Sept. 23, 1901; s. Melvin W. and Mary Cathorine (Robbins) C.; B.S.C., U. Nebr., 1924, D.H.L. (hon.); postgrad. N.Y. U., 1925; m. Mary Katherine Towie, Oct. 12, 1926 (dec. 1973); children—John Kenneth, Charles Towle, Nancy Cozier Whitcomb; m. 2d, Elizabeth Fackler Herrick, 1975. Salesman. Chgo. Mill & Lumber Co., 1925-30; pres. Cozier Corp., Cleve., Curtis Cos., Inc., Clinton, Iowa. Past mem. industry adv. com. OPS, WPB. Past mem. Health and Rehab. Allocation Com., Cleve.; mem. adv. com. Ohio Bur. Services for Blind; mem. nat. adv. com. Nat. Center for Deaf-Blind Youths and Adults; past mem. Ohio Gov.'s Council on Vocat. Rehab.; past mem. Commn. on Standards for Agys. Serving Blind; past trustee Case Work Council and Health Council of Cleve. Welfare Fedn.; trustee U. Nebr. Found., Am. Found. for Blind, Inc., Nat. Accreditation Council for Agys. Serving the Blind, Ohio Soc. for Prevention Blindness; trustee, past pres. Cleve. Soc. for Blind. Recipient Distinguished Service award U. Nebr. Alumni Assn., 1955, 50 Year Alumni Achievement award, 1974; Distinguished Service award Cleve. Welfare Fedn.; Distinguished Service award, Alfred Allen award Am. Assn. Workers Blind; Distinguished Service award Nat. Accreditation Council for Agys. Serving the Blind and Visually Handicapped, Inc., 1974; Nat. Migel medal for outstanding vol. work in field for blind Am. Found. Blind, 1975. Mem. Nat. Wooden Box Assn. (pres. 1950-51, past trustee), Delta Tau Delta, Beta Gamma Sigma (Distinguished Service award) Alpha Kappa Psi. Mem. Plymouth Ch. (trustee). Clubs: The Country, Union, University. Home: Shaker Heights, Ohio. Died Jan. 13, 1978.

COZZENS, JAMES GOULD, author; b. Chgo., Aug. 19, 1903; s. Henry William and Bertha (Wood) C.; grad. Kent (Conn.) Sch., 1922; student Harvard, 1922-24, Litt.D., 1952; m. Bernice Baumgarten Dec. 31, 1927. Author: Confusion, 1924; Michael Scarlett, 1925; Cockpit, 1928; The Son of Perdition, 1929; S.S. San Pedro, 1931; The Last Adam, 1933; Castaway, 1934; Men and Brethren, 1936; Ask Me Tomorrow, 1940; The Just and the Unjust, 1942; Guard of Honor, 1948; By Love Possessed, 1957; Children and Others, 1964; Morning Noon and Night, 1968; A Flower in Her Hair, 1974; A Rope for Dr. Webster, 1976. Home: Stuart, Fla. Died Aug. 9, 1978.

CRABTREE, JOHN ICKERINGILL, photographic and motion picture research; b. Clayton le-Moors, Lancashire, Eng., Mar. 27, 1891; s. John and Ann (Fish) C.; B.Sc., honors in chemistry, Victoria U., 1912, M.Sc., 1913; came to U.S., 1913, naturalized, 1924; m. Ruth S. Crabtree. Research chemist Eastman Kodak Co., 1913-16, founder photog. chemistry dept., chief photographic chemist, 1916, asst. supt., 1929. Instr. School of Aerial Photography, World War I. Fellow Soc. Motion Picture and Television Engrs. (past pres.; Progress Medal award 1952), Royal Inst. Chem., Gt. Britain and Ireland, Royal Photographic Society, A.A.A.S., Soc. Photog. Engrs. Photog. Soc. America (Jour. award 1949, Progress Medal Award, 1956); mem. of the Am. Chem. Soc., Optical Soc. of Am., Acad. of Motion Picture Arts and Sciences, Am. Standards Assn. (chmn. com. photographic processing PH4, from 1950); hon. member Kodak Camera Club. Awarded Progress Medal by French Photographic Soc., 1924; Journal award, Soc. of Motion Picture Engrs., 1944; Henderson award, Royal Photographic Soc., 1944; awards on display at Eastman Kodak Co.; records of work at Library of Congress. Wesleyan Methodist. Club: University (Rochester). Author tech. books, contbr. profl. jours.; holder 35 U.S. patents. Home: Middlesex, N.Y. Died July 24, 1979.

CRAFT, JAMES PRESSLEY, clergyman, educator; b. Hartwell, Ga., June 14, 1885; s. John Franklin and Ellen (Goss) C.; S.B., Mercer U., Macon, Ga., 1906; Thayer scholar, Harvard, 1908-09, A.M., 1909; Th.G., Southern Bapt. Theol. Sem., Louisville, Ky., 1912, studied U. of Chicago, summer 1920; m. Edith Galphin, of Hartwell, Ga., June 29, 1910; children—James Pressley, Edith. Teacher acad. and pub. schs., Ga., until 1910; ordained ministry Bapt. Ch., 1912; pastor Louisville, Ga., 1912-16, Swainsboro, 1916-17, Shellman, 1918-19; prof. Shorter Coll., Rome, Ga., 1919-21; pres. Averett Coll. (Jr.) for Young Women, Danville, Va., 1921-27; pres. Hardin Coll., Mexico, Mo., 1927-28; pastor South Broad Bapt. Ch., Rome, Ga., 1929-36; prin. Lyerly High Sch., since 1937. Elected moderator Floyd County Bapt. Assn., 1936. Mem. Kappa Alpha. Democrat. Home: Lyerly, Ga.

CRAIG, ALLEN THORNTON, educator; b. Marion, Ala., Aug. 5, 1904; s. Edgar Montgomery and Vivia (Roark) C.; A.B., U. Fla., 1927, A.M., 1928; Ph.D., U. Iowa, 1931. Instr. math. U. Fla., 1929-30; asso. in math. U. Iowa, 1931-33, asst. prof., 1933-38, asso. prof., 1938-45, prof. math. 1945-70. Served as mem. research group M. Nat. Def. Research Com., 1942. Served to lt. comdr. USN, 1942-46. Mem. Am. Math Soc., Math Assn. Am. Fellow Inst. Math. Statistics (sec.-treas. 1935-38, v.p. 1939-41). Author (with R. V. Hogg): Introduction to Mathematical Statistics, 1959, 3d edit., 1970. Mem. editorial bd. Annals of Mathematics Statistics, 1938-50. Contbr. tech. articles in math. theory of statistics to profl. jours. Home: Dade City, Fla. Died Nov. 27, 1978; buried Dade City Cemetery.

CRAIG, BURT J., sec.-treas., trustee; b. Detroit, Mich., Aug. 7, 1885; s. John G. and Harriet (Henry) C.; ed. pub. and pvt. sch.; m. Everil M. Stone, June 17, 1908; 1 daughter. Accountant, Ford Motor Co., 1907-08, sec., 1918-43, v.p., treas., treas., 1943-46, sec.-treas., trustee, Ford Foundation since 1946; director Mfrs. National Bank. Republican. Mason. Clubs: Detroit, Detroit Athletic, Detroit Golf; Surf (Miami Beach, Fla.). Home: Detroit, Mich.

CRAIG, CLAYTON BION, church dir.; b. Watertown, S.D.; s. Bion Sidney and Sarah Ann (Bigelow) C.; A.B., U. S.D., 1925; postgrad. Harvard, 1925-26; B.A., Oxford U. (Rhodes scholar), 1929, M.A., 1935; m. Ethelbelle Alle Taylor, Dec. 17, 1931. Tchr. social scis. pvt. sch. N.Y.C., 1930-31; asst. to gen. mgr. and sales mgr. mfg. firm, Cin., 1931-36; entered pub. practice Christian Sci., 1936, authorized tchr., 1940; C.S. com. on publ. for Ohio, 1941-45; C.S. lectr., 1945-48; bd. dirs. First Ch. of Christ Scientist, Boston, 1948-73. Mem. English Speaking Union, Delta Tau Delta, Delta Sigma Pi, Tau Kappa Alpha, Theta Alpha Phi. Mason (32 deg., K.T., Shriner). Home: Laguna Hills, Calif. Died Aug. 2, 1978.

CRAIG, JOHN WILLIAM, elec. mgr., bus. cons.; b. Troy, Ohio, Feb. 2, 1907; s. John Wesley and Julia (Conrad) C.; BS. in Mech. Engring., U. Dayton, 1929; m. Thelma G. Stevens, Aug. 22, 1928 (dec.); 1 dau., Judith Craig Wilhoit (dec.); m. 2d, Marguerite Schott, Sept. 6, 1975. Engr. Frigidaire div. Gen. Motors Corp., 1929-37; v.p., gen. mgr. Crosley div. Avco Mfg. Corp., 1937-53; pres. Aluminum Industries, Inc., 1953-54; v.p. RCA, 1954-55; v.p., gen. mgr. Elec. Appliance div. Westinghouse Electric Corp., Mansfield, O., 1955-62, v.p., gen. mgr. spl accounts, 1963; vp., dir. Hupp Corp. Cleve., 1963-65; v.p. Admiral Corp., Chgo., 1965-69, exec. v.p., dir., 1969-74; bus. cons., 1974-80. Recipient Navy Bur. Ordnance Devel. award. Mem. Am. Soc. Refrigerating Engrs., Hist. and Philos. Soc. Ohio, Newcomen Soc. N.Am. Republican. Roman Catholic. Club: Cincinnati. Home: Cincinnati, Ohio. Died Aug. 4, 1980; buried Casstown, Ohio.

CRAIGHILL, RICHARD STARR, naval officer; b. Oakmont, Pa., Aug. 27, 1909; s. James Rutherford and Ellen Wattles (Lee) C.; student George Washington U., 1926-28; B.S., U.S. Naval Acad., 1932; grad. Naval War Coll., 1950; m. Virginia Drewry Jones, June 24, 1939; children—Richard Starr, Virginia Drewry, William Sebrell. Commd. ensign U.S. Navy, 1932, advanced through grades to rear adm., 1960; served with Atlantic, Pacific, 6th and 7th fleets in U.S.S. Pennsylvania, 1932-34; assigned U.S.S. New Orleans, 1934-36, U.S.S. Badger, 1936-38, U.S.S. Blakeley, 1939-40, U.S.S. Patterson, 1940-42, U.S.S. Blue, 1942; staff comdr. 7th Fleet, 1942-43; comdr. U.S.S. Drayton, 1943-44; assigned U.S.S. Little Rock, 1948-49; staff comdr. battleship cruiser Atlantic Fleet, 1952-53; comdr. U.S.S. Salamonie, 1953-54, U.S.S. Bremerton, 1957-58; comdt. 15th Naval Dist., 1960-62; comdr. amphibious group 2, Atlantic Fleet, 1962-63; dir. politico-mil. policy div. Office Chief Naval Operations, 1963-64, asst. chief naval operations, 1964-65; comdr. Caribbean Sea Frontier, comdt. 10th Naval dist., comdr. Antilles Def. Command, 1965-70. Decorated Legion of Merit, Silver Star, Bronze Star with combat V, various campaign and service ribbons. Mem. Soc. Lees of Va., Theta Delta Chi. Episcopalian. Rotarian. Club: Army-Navy Country (Washington). Home: Atlanta, Ga. Died Feb. 7, 1980.

CRAIGMILE, CHARLES S., mfg. exec.; b. La Grange, Ill., Sept. 29, 1892; s. David Francis and Mary Louise (Holt) C.; student U. Ill., 1910-13; m. Nellie Marie Truby, Mar. 15, 1924; children—Winston Charles, David Francis, Donald Holt. Elec. engr. Dolese & Shepard Co., 1913-15, Belden Mfg. Co., Chgo., 1915-18, chief insp., 1919, gen. foreman, 1920, plant supt., 1921, gen. foreman, 1922-23, asst. gen. supt., 1924-27, gen. supt., 1928-34, v.p., 1935-41, exec. v.p.,

1942-48, pres., 1948-63, chmn. bd., chief exec. officer, 1963-65, hon. chmn., from 1965, dir. Dir. Greater Chgo. Safety Council from 1936, pres., 1939-42; dir. Jr. Achievement of Chgo., Inc., 1949-52, Chgo. Adv. Council, 1952-55; trustee Village of Hinsdale, Ill., 1949-52, president of the village, 1953-56. Served as 1st lieutenant, 331st F.A., 86th Div., U.S. Army, 1917-19; with A.E.F., 5 mos. Mem. Am. Mgmt. Assn. (v.p. 1933-34, dir. 1944-47, 1950-52) Ill. Mfrs. Assn. (dir. 1950-53, chmn. 1958, member of the advisory board from 1959), Associated Employers Ill. (dir., from 1939, v.p. 1939-45, pres. 1946-53; chmn. exec. com., 1953-57), Nat. Metal Trades Assn. (nat. pres. 1952-53, mem. adminstrv. council 1945-53), Employers Assn. (dir., from 1941, pres. 1944-45; adv. council, 1949-53, exec. council, 1954-56), N.A.M. (dir., 1956-58), Tau Kappa Epsilon. Republican. Conglist. Clubs: Executives (vice pres. 1939-41), Commercial, University (Chgo.); Hinsdale (Ill.) Golf (pres. 1942-44); Illinois Senior Golf (pres., 1955-56). Home: Hinsdale, Ill. Died Apr. 30, 1977.

CRANDALL, ARTHUR BERT, lawyer; b. Thompson, Ohio, Sept. 13, 1918; s. Bert G. and Lena (Pomeroy) C.; BA., Hiram Coll., 1940; LL.B Western Res. U., 1948; m. Mary Alice Gibbons, Oct. 3, 1947; 1 son, Douglas A. Clk., B.G. Crandall Co., Thompson, O, 1935-40; tchr. econs., asst. coach Auburn (Ohio) High Sch., 1941-42; admitted to Ohio bar, 1948, since practiced in Painesville; legal counsel, dir. Lake County Fed. Savs. & Loan Assn. Dir., clk. Lake County Bd. Elections, 1952-65; clk., mem. Painesville Twp. Bd. Edn. 1953-76, pres., 1971-75. Mem. Republican Central Com., 1964-80. Vice pres., trustee Lake County Mental Health Clinic. Served with USNR, 1942-46; PTO. Recipient Distinguished Alumni award Hiram Coll., 1973. Mem. Am., Ohio, Lake County (past pres.) bar assns., Hiram Coll. Alumni Assn. (pres.), Painesville Jr. C. of C. (pres. 1950, dir.). Methodist (trustee, del. Eastern Ohio conf. 1975, 76, 77, 78). Rotarian. (past pres.). Moderator Legal Adviser radio program, 1954-74. Home: Painesville, Ohio. Died July 3, 1980; buried Riverside Cemetery, Painesville, Ohio.

CRANDALL, HARRY WELLS, army officer, corporation executive; b. Annapolis, Maryland, August 26, 1898; s. Charles Albert and Elizabeth (Lindenborn) C.; B.S., U.S. Mil. Acad., 1925; m. Ada Elizabeth Wilson, Oct. 8, 1927; children—Nancy M. (Mrs. P. T. Maddocks), Harry Wilson (U.S. Army), Stephen Charles Albert. Commd. 2d lt. inf., U.S. Army, 1925, advanced through grades to maj. gen., 1956; finance officer 6th Inf. Div., 1940-42, XIII Corps, 1942-45; finance officer U.S. Mil. Acad., 1947-50, treas., 1953-54; assigned Pacific, 1950-52; asst. chief finance, U.S. Army, 1954-56, chief finance, 1956-58. Mem. Army Finance Assn. (pres.). Episcopalian. Clubs: Fort Myer Officers, Fort McNair Officers'. Home: Alexandria, Va. Died Mar. 18, 1978; interred Arlington Nat. Cemetery.

CRANDON, CHARLES HENRY, wholesale druggist; b. Acushnet, Mass., Nov. 9, 1886; s. Philip Howland and Emma (Winslow) C.; ed. New Bedford, Mass. High School; married Agnes Conoly, April 3, 1919; children—Patricia (wife of Donald H. Randell), Philip Howland. Salesman, 1905; organizer, president, The Crandon-Hunter Co., wholesale drugs, 1916-25; pres. Crandon Wholesale Drug Co., 1935-43; v.p. and dir. First Nat. Bank of Miami; pres. and dir. The Cranter Corp.; pres. Fairchild Tropical Garden. Member Dade County Commission. 20 years; organizer and chmn. Dade Co. Park Dept., 1930-48, Dade Co. Bd. Health, 1943-48; chmn. Dade Co. Finance Com., Dade Co. Port Authority; v.p. Asso. Industries Fla., Am. Shore and Beach Preservation Assn. Private, 66th Balloon Co., World War I. Trustee U. of Miami. Mem. Miami Civic Music Assn. (pres.), Dade County Tuberculosis Assn. (exec. com.). Mason (K.T.). Clubs: Kiwanis (dir.); Biscayne Yacht (Miami). New $6,000,000 park on Biscayne Key named in his honor. Home: 3600 Red Rd., Coral Gables, Fla. Address: Miami, Fla. *

CRANE, BOB EDWARD, actor; b. Waterbury, Conn., July 13, 1928; s. Alfred T. and Rosemary (Senich) C.; grad. high sch.; m. May 20, 1949 (div. June 1970); children—Robert David, Deborah Ann, Karen Leslie; m. 2d, Patricia Olson, Oct. 16, 1970; 1 step dau., Melissa Suzanne; 1 son, Robert Scott. Broadcaster radio sta. WLEA, Hornell, N.Y., 1950, WBIS, Bristol, Conn., 1951, WICC, Bridgeport, Conn., 1951-56, KNX, Hollywood, Calif., 1956-65; actor Donna Reed Show, ABC TV, 1963-65; appeared as Col. Hogan in Hogan's Heroes, CBS-TV, Hollywood, 1965-71; TV series The Bob Crane Show, 1975; profl. musician, drummer with Conn. Symphony, 1944-46, various dance bands East and West coasts; appeared in motion pictures Return to Peyton Place, 1963, Mantrap, 1963, Wicked Dreams of Paula Shuutz, 1967, Walt Disney prodns. Super-Dad, 1972, Gus, 1976; lead (with Helen Hayes and Lillian Gish) in TV version of Arsenic and Old Lace, 1968; sub host for Johnny Carson, Merv Griffin shows; host Bob Crane Show, NBC-TV, 1975. Served with Conn. N.G., 1948-50. Emmy award nominee for role of Hogan on Hogan's Heroes, 1965, 66. Mem. Screen Actors Guild, Am. Fedn. Musicians, AFTRA, Actors Equity, Acad. Motion Picture Arts and Scis., TV Acad. Arts and Scis. Address: Beverly Hills, Calif. Died June 29, 1978.

CRANE, ROYSTON CAMPBELL, cartoonist; b. Abilene, Tex., Nov. 22, 1901; s. Royston Campbell and Mamie (Douthit) C.; student Hardin-Simmons U., 1918-19, U. Tex., 1919-22, Chgo. Acad. Fine Arts, 1920; L.H.D. (hon.), Rollins Coll.; m. Evelyn Hatcher, Feb. 8, 1927; children—Nancy (Mrs. Gerard Arthur), Marcia (Mrs. Charles W. Starcher III). With art dept. Fort Worth Record, 1919; reporter Austin (Tex.) Am., 1921-22; art dept. N.Y. World, 1922-24; cartoonist-writer newspaper strip, Wash Tubbs-Captain Easy, 1924-43, Buz Sawyer, King Features Syndicate, 1943-77. Recipient commendation from sec. navy as war corr., 1946; Reuben award Nat. Cartoonists Soc., 1950; Gold Medal award for distinguished pub. service U.S. Navy, 1957; Silver Lady award from Banshees as outstanding cartoonist of year, 1961; Best Story Strip award Nat. Cartoonists Soc., 1966; Yellow Kid award for distinguished career as cartoonist Salon, Internazionale dei Comics, Lucca, Italy, 1974; John Young award for unique accomplishments. Mem. Nat. Cartoonists Soc., Navy League U.S., Phi Kappa Psi, Sigma Delta Chi. Club Orlando Country. Address: Orlando, Fla. Died July 8, 1977; cremated.

CRANMER, H. JEROME, educator, economist; b. Morristown, N.J., June 2, 1920; s. Horace K. and Elizabeth (Fletcher) C.; A.B., Drew U., 1947; A.M. Columbia, 1949, Ph.D., 1955; m. Margaret E. Welch, June 21, 1947; children—Carol Anne, Susan Kinney, Charles Nelson, Thomas Fletcher. Mem. faculty Drew U., 1949-80, prof. econs., chmn. dept., 1958-80; cons. in field, 1957-80. Served to capt. AUS, 1942-46. Mem. Am. Econ. Assn., Am. Fin. Assn., Econ. History Assn., N.J. Council Econ. Edn. Author: New Jersey in the Automobile Age, 1964; also articles. Home: Madison, N.J. Died 1980.

CRATSLEY, EDWARD KNEELAND, coll. adminstr., educator; b. Warren, Ohio, Sept. 10, 1914; s. John Carlisle and Carolyn (Kneeland) C.; A.B., Coll. of Wooster, 1936; M.B.A., Harvard, 1938, D.C.S., 1943; m. Mary Jane Payton, Sept. 4, 1937; children—John Christopher, David Bruce. Research asst. Harvard Grad. Sch. Bus. Adminstrn., 1938-39, instr. accounting, 1939-41; comptroller, asst. prof. bus. adminstrn. St. Lawrence U., Canton, N.Y., 1941-47, sec., 1942-43, comptroller, prof. bus. adminstrn., 1947-50; v.p., prof. econs. Swarthmore (Pa.) Coll., from 1950, acting pres., 1965-66, 69, 72-73. Del. in edn. 9th Internat. Mgmt. Congress 1951; mem. N.Y. Milkshed Price com., 1947-49, Commn. on Higher Instns., Middle States Assn. Colls. and Secondary Schs., 1952-58, v.p., 1962, pres. 1963. Mem. Swarthmore Borough Council, 1962-69. Trustee Phila. Coll. Art, 1960-76, Coll. Entrance Exam. Bd., 1966-70; bd. dirs. Univ. City Sci. Center, from 1969. Mem. Nat. Assn. Coll. and Univ. Bus. Officers (dir. 1960-65), Nat. Assn. Ednl. Buyers, Eastern Assn. Coll. and Bus. Officers (pres. 1958), Phi Beta Kappa. Republican. Presbyn. Rotarian. Clubs: Springhaven; Seaview Country. Home: Swarthmore, Pa. Died June 15, 1978 buried Warren, Ohio.

CRAVEN, AVERY ODELLE, educator; b. Warren County, Ia., Aug. 12, 1886; s. Oliver and Mary E. (Pennington) C.; A.B., Simpson Coll., 1908, LL.D., 1936; M.A., Harvard, 1914; Ph.D., U. Chgo., 1923; Litt.D., Simpson Coll., 1946, U.S.C. 1961; D.H.L., Tulane U., 1952, Wayne State U., 1957, Purdue U., 1969; M.A., Cambridge U., 1952; m. Grace Greenwood Oct. 2, 1914 (dec. 1936); 1 dau., Jean Greenwood; m. 2d, Georgia D. Watson, Sept. 26, 1938. Prof. history Coll. of Emporia (Kan.), 1920-22; asst. prof. Mich. State Coll., 1923-24; asst. prof. U. Ill., 1924-26, asso. prof., 1926-28; asso. prof. U. Chgo., 1928-29, prof. Am. history 1929—. Distinguished Fgn. prof. U. Sidney, Australia, 1947; Pitt. prof. Am. history and instns. Cambridge U., 1952-53; lectr. Am. Seminar, Salzburg, 1953, 54; fellow Downing Coll., Cambridge, 1952-53; vis. prof. U. Cal., U. Colo., U. N.C., U. So. Cal., Northwestern U., U. Wis., Western Mich. U.; Distinguished fgn. lectr. Am. Studies Com., Japan, 1967. Cons. Library of Congress; mem. Civil War Centennial Commn., 1958—, Ill. Lincoln Sesquicentenial Commn., 1959—. Mem. So. Hist. Assn. (pres. 1952), Orgn. Am. Historians (pres. 1963-64), Am. Agrl. Soc. (past pres.), Phi Beta Kappa. Co-author: Sources of Culture in the Middle West; author several books including: The United States, Experiment in Democracy, 1947; Coming of the Civil War-The Rise of Southern Nationalism, 1953; Civil War in the Making, 1815-60, 1959; Ending of the Civil War, 1968. Contbr. articles to profl. jours. Home: Dune Acres Chesterton Ind. Died Jan. 21, 1980.

CRAVEN, JAMES BRAXTON, JR., judge; b. Lenoir, N.C., Apr. 3, 1918; s. James Braxton and Katherine Simmons (Covington) C.; A.B., Duke, 1939, postgrad. Law Sch., 1946; LL.B., Harvard, 1942; children—James Braxton III, Stephen K., Elizabeth Bible; m. 3d, Susan A. Schatzel, Aug. 6, 1973. Admitted to N.C. bar, 1946; solicitor Burke County Criminal Ct., 1947; asst. U.S. atty., Charlotte-Asheville, 1948-52; became judge Superior Ct. of N.C., 1956; U.S. judge Western dist. N.C., 1961-66; U.S. circuit judge 4th Circuit Ct. Appeals, 1966-77; vis. prof. constl. law U. N.C. Law Sch., summers 1967, 70, 74; vis. prof. fed. cts. U. Tex. Law Sch., summer 1968. Del., Southeastern Jurisdictional Conf., Methodist Ch., 1956, 60, 64, Gen. Conf. Meth. Ch., 1964. Trustee, Duke, from 1972. Served from ensign to lt., USNR, 1942-46. Mem. Am., N.C. (v.p. 1959-60), Burke County bar assns., Am. Judicature Soc., Order of Coif, Phi Beta Kappa, Omicron Delta Kappa. Home: Asheville, N.C. Died May 3, 1977.

CRAVEN, MARGARET, author; b. Helena, Mont., Mar. 13, 1901; d. Arthur John and Clara Emily (Kerr) Craven; A.B. with gt. distinction, Stanford, 1924. Editorial writer, columnist San Jose (Calif.) Mercury, 1924-28; contbr. short stories to Ladies Home Jour., Colliers mag., others, 1928-41, Saturday Evening Post, 1941-62; author (novel) I Heard the Owl Call My Name, 1967, Walk Gently This Good Earth, 1977 (Daughter of Mark Twain award); Again Calls the Owl, 1980; The Home Front, 1981. Home: Sacramento, Calif. Died July 19, 1980.

CRAVEN, WESLEY FRANK, educator; b. Conway, N.C., May 19, 1905; s. Wesley Frank and Elizabeth (Turner) C.; A.B., Duke U., 1926, M.A. 1927; Ph.D., Cornell U., 1928; m. Helen G. McDaniel, May 31, 1932; children—Nancy Elizabeth, Betty Morris. Instr. history N.Y. U., 1928-30, asst. prof., 1930-37, asso. prof., 1937-40. prof., 1940-50; Edwards prof. Am. history Princeton, 1950-64, George Henry Davis '86 prof. Am. history, 1964-73, emeritus, 1973-81. Served from maj. to lt. col. AUS, AAF, 1943-46. Decorated Legion of Merit. Mem. Am. Hist. Assn., Colonial Soc. Mass., Mass., Va. hist. socs., Am. Antiquarian Soc., Phi Beta Kappa, Delta Sigma Phi. Author: Dissolution of the Virginia Company, 1932; Introduction to History of Bermuda, 1938; The Southern Colonies in the Seventeenth Century, 1949; The Legend of the Founding Fathers, 1956; New Jersey and the English Colonization of North America, 1964. Co-editor: The Army Air Forces in World War II, vols. I-VII, 1948-58; The Colonies in Transition, 1660-1713, 1968; White, Red, and Black: the Seventeenth-Century Virginian, 1971. Home: Princeton, N.J. Died Feb. 10, 1981.

CRAVER, ARTHUR WILLIAM, univ. prof.; b. Brooklyn, Pa., Oct. 20, 1884; s. Charles Manning and Alice (Tewksbury) C.; A.B., Cornell U., 1907; student Johns Hopkins, 1927-31; unmarried. Instr. in English, Beloit (Wis.) Coll., 1908-11; asst. prof. of English, Miami Univ., Oxford, O., 1911-19, asso. prof., 1919-31, prof. of English since 1931. Mem. Modern Lang. Assn. of Am., Am. Assn. Univ. Profs. Home: Oxford, O.

CRAWFORD, JOAN, actress, soft drink co. exec.; b. San Antonio, Mar. 23, 1908; ed. schs. Kansas City; student Stephens Coll., Columbia, Mo.; m. Douglas Fairbanks, Jr., June 3, 1929 (div.); m. 2d, Franchot Tone, Oct. 11, 1935 (div.); m. 3d, Phillip Terry, July 21, 1942 (div.); m. 4th, Alfred Nu Steele, May 10, 1955 (dec. Apr. 1959); children—(adopted) Christina, Christopher, Cynthia, Cathy. Appeared as dancer on stage as Lucille Le Sueur; entered movies in 1926; starred in following films: Our Dancing Daughters; Our Blushing Brides; Untamed; Our Modern Maidens; Paid; Laughing Sinners; Possessed; Grand Hotel; Rain; Dancing Lady; The Gorgeous Hussy; The Bride Wore Red; Mannequin; Forsaking All Others; No More Ladies; The Last of Mrs. Cheyney; Ice Follies of 1939; The Shinning Hour; The Women; A Woman's Face; They All Kissed the Bride; Above Suspicion; Reunion in France; Hollywood Canteen; Mildred Pierce; Humoresque; Daisy Kenyon; Flamingo Road; The Damned Don't Cry; Harriet Craig; Goodbye, My Fancy; This Woman Is Dangerous; Sudden Fear; Torch Song; Johnny Guitar; Female on the Beach; Queen Bee; Autumn Leaves; The Story of Esther Costello; The Best of Everything; What Ever Happened to Baby Jane; The Caretakers; Strait Jacket; I Saw What You Did; Berserk; Trog. Dir., Pepsi-Cola Co., Purchase, N.Y. Recipient Acad. award for role in Mildred Pierce, 1945. Hon. fellow Brandeis U. Author: (with Jane Kesner Ardmore) A Portrait of Joan, 1962; My Way of Life, 1971. Died May 10, 1977; buried Ferncliff Cemetery, Hartsdale, N.Y.

CRAWFORD, MORRIS DE CAMP, b. N.Y. City, Sept. 23, 1882. Formerly research asso. Am. Mus. Natural History, later research asso. in textiles for Mus. of Science and Industry of Rosenwald Foundation; now research editor Fairchild Publications. Author: Peruvian Textiles, 1915; Peruvian Fabrics, 1915; The Heritage of Cotton, 1924; The Comeback (novel), 1925. Address: New York, N.Y.

CRAWFORD, RALSTON, artist; b. St. Catharines, Ont., Can. Sept. 25 1906; s. George Burson and Lucy (Colvin) C.; brought to U.S., 1910, naturalized citizen; student Otis Art Inst., Los Angeles, 1927. Pa. Acad. Fine Arts, Phila., 1927-30, Barnes Found., 1928-30, Breckenridge Sch., Columbia, others; m. Margaret Stone, Oct. 17, 1932; children—James Ralston, Robert Frederick; m. 2d, Margaret Elizabeth Frank, Feb 5, 1942; children—Neelon Frank, John Colvin. Began career with Walt Disney, 1927; painter, lithographer, etcher, photographer, illustrator; tchr. drawing, painting Cinn. Art. Acad., Buffalo Sch. Fine Arts, Art Sch. of

Bklyn. Mus., U. Minn., La State U., U. Colo., New Sch. Social Research, N.Y.C., Honolulu Acad. Art; asso. prof. dept. art Hofstra Coll., Long Island, 1960-62; photographic research cons. New Orleans Jazz Archives, Tulane U., Photog. studies Indian cave temples, 1945; art observer Bikini atom bomb test, 1946; exhibited nationally and internationally in group shows; one man shows include Md. Inst. Art. Balt., Flint (Mich.) Inst. Arts, Seattle, Portland art museums, Howard U., Honolulu Acad. Arts, Santa Barbara Mus., Milw. Art Inst., St. George's Gallery, London, U. Minn., San Francisco Mus., U. Nebr., Wesleyan U., Creighton U., Omaha, Century Assn., N.Y.C., and others; represented in permanent colls. U. Ga., Ala. Poly. Inst., Butler Mus. Am. Art, Whitney Mus. Am. Art, Duke U., N.Y. Pub. Library, Vassar Coll., Walker Art Center, Library Congress, Met. Mus. Art. Mus. Modern Art. N.Y.C., Cin. Art Mus., Toledo Art Mus., others; Ford Found. vis. artist U. Nebr., 1965; vis. artist U. Ill., 1966; commd. spl. art program U.S. Dept. Interior, 1969. Articles, Illustrations, numerous mags. and jours.; work featured in Richard B. Freeman's The Lithographs of Ralston Crawford, 1962. Clubs: Century Assn., Coffee House, Players, St. Andrew's Soc. Home: New York, N.Y. Died Apr. 27, 1978.

CRAWLEY, GEORGE E(DWIN) (CR-AW-LEY), sugar exec.; b. Brooklyn, Mar. 19, 1886; s. Edwin Fitzroy and Anna Frances (Mooney) C.; grad. Horace Mann Sch., 1904; M.E., Columbia, 1908; m. Esperanza Rionda, June 29, 1921; children—George Edwin, Esperanza Rionda, Charles Albert. With The Francisco Sugar Co., N.Y. City, since 1914, dir. since 1924, pres. and mem. exec. com. since 1949; dir. Cia. Azucarera Elia, Cia. Azucarera Cespedes. Mem. Am. Soc. M.E., Assn Ex-Mems. Squadron A, Beta Theta Pi. Tau Beta Pi. Club: Columbia University. Home: N.Y. *

CREAMER, WALTER J(OSEPH), educator; b. Penobscot, Me., Mar. 3, 1896; s. Walter J. and Lena (Wardwell) C.; B.S., U. of Me., 1918, E.E., 1921, A.B., 1923; married Mildred M. French, August 17, 1930; one son, Dustin Walter. Assistant in Bell Telephone Laboratories N.Y. City, 1918-19; instructor in drawing, University of Me., 1919-20, instr. in elec. engring., 1920-22, asst. prof., later asso. prof., 1922-27, asso. prof. elec. communication, 1927-38, prof. communication engring., 1938-61, emeritus, 1961-77, asst. to dean, College of Tech., later acting dean, 1923-27, dir. of Freshman Week, 1927-41, head dept. electrical engring., Univ. Me., from 1945. Mem. Electricians Examining Bd., State of Maine, 1961-71. Fellow Am. Inst. E.E.; mem. Am. Soc. for Engring. Edn., Inst. Radio Engrs. (sr. mem.), Tau Beta Pi, Phi Kappa Phi, Eta Kappa Nu. Universalist. Author: Elements of Electrical Engineering, 1948; Communication Networks and Lines 1951. Contbr. various technical studies pub. by Electrical Engineering, Journal Inst. Radio Engrs., U. of Maine; and contbr. to popular tech. mags. Home: Bangor, Maine. Died Apr. 23, 1977.

CREEDY, FREDERICK, elec. engring. research; b. London, Eng., Mar. 27, 1883; s. Frederick and Annie Arabella C.; grad. (with honors) Imperial Coll. of Science and Technology, London, Eng., 1904; m. Eveline Louise Gough, June 10, 1914; children—Phyllis Eveline, John Alan, Richard Frederick. Teacher mathematics, London U., 1905; elec. designer, Westinghouse Engring. & Mfg. Co., Pittsburgh, Pa., 1907-09; chief elec. engr. B. F. Sturtevant Co., Boston, 1909-11; cons. engr., London, 1912-29; became research asso. prof. in elec. engring., Lehigh, 1929; engring. war work for Canadian Govt., 1941-46; spl. lectr. U. Toronto, 1952-53; inventor, cons. engr. Awarded Ayrton Premium, 1923, by Instn. Electric Engrs.; Prix Montefiore, 1925. Author books, the latest being: The Next Step in Civilization, 1955; contbr. tech., econ. and philos. jours. Address: Toronto, Ont., Can.

CREEKMORE, EDWARD FITZGERALD, cotton merchant; b. Van Buren, Ark., Sept. 29, 1885; s. Renfrow B. and Emily (Lynch) C.; ed. pub. schs. of Van Buren; m. Elizabeth Otilla Holland, Jan. 6, 1915; children—Edward Fitzgerald, Saralee C. (wife of Capt. I.G. Peters). With Lesser-Goldman Cotton Co., Van Buren, Ark., 1902-12, mgr. plant at Fort Smith, Ark., 1912-18; pres. E.F. Creekmore & Co., Fort Smith, Ark., 1918-30; pres. The Cotton Stabilization Corp., 1931-34; gen. mgr. Am. Cotton Coop. Assn., New Orleans, 1930-40; former chmn. bd. E.F. Creekmore & Co., Inc., New Orleans; now partner E.F. Creekmore Ltd.; dir. Hibernia Nat. Bank New Orleans Cotton Exchange. Dir., past pres. New Orleans Cotton Exchange; pres. Okla. Cotton Exchange, 1918-19. Bd. dirs. Eye, Ear, Nose and Throat Hosp., Fair Grounds Corp., Audubon Park Commn. Mem. Am. Cotton Shippers Assn. (dir.). Clubs: Boston, New Orleans Country (New Orleans). Home: New Orleans.

CREEVY, CHARLES DONALD, physician; b. Minneapolis, Minn., Feb. 5, 1902; s. Charles Burt and Berdella (Serface) C.; B.S., U. of Minn., 1924, M.B., 1926, M.D., 1927, M.S., 1930, Ph.D., 1931; m. Alice Youngberg, Aug. 15, 1932; children—Donald Charles, Michael Hugh. Intern, Lane Hosp., San Francisco, Calif., 1926-27; fellow in surgery, U. of Minn., 1927-30, instr. in surgery, 1930-32, asst. prof., 1932-37, prof. surgery (urology) from 1937, asst. dean of med. sch., 1939-44, prof. surgery (urology); dir. division of urology. Recipient Charles Bolles Bolles Rogers Bowl for disting. service to local medicine. Mem. Minn. and Am. med. assns., Am. Urol. Assn., Am. Assn. Genito-urinary surgeons, Minn. Acad. Medicine, Urosurgical Soc., Clin. Society Genito-Urinary Surgeons, Sigma Xi, Theta Delta Chi, Nu Sigma Nu. Home: Minneapolis, Minn. Died Jan. 31, 1977.

CREIGHTON, HENRY JERMAIN MAUDE, chemist; b. Dartmouth, N.S., Mar. 2, 1886; s. Henry Dolby and Helen James (Robson) C.; B.A., Dalhousie U., 1906, M.A., 1907, LL.D., 1948; M.Sc., U. Birmingham (Eng.), 1909; student U. Heidelberg (Germany), 1909-10; D.Sc., Fed. Polytech. Zurich, Switzerland, 1913; Sc.D., Swathmore Coll., 1957; m. Jean Hamilton Walker, June 21, 1916; children—Robert, Rosamond (Mrs. Seymour J. Ettman). Came to U.S., 1912. Lectr. chemistry Dalhousie U., 1911; instr. chemistry Swarthmore Coll., 1912-13, asst. prof., 1913-24, asso. prof., 1924-27, prof. 1927-52, emeritus prof.; head chemistry dept., 1927-49; cons. in electrochemistry; on leave of absence with Manhattan Project at Columbia U., 1943-46. Recipient Longstreth medal, 1918, Potts Gold medal, 1939, Modern Pioneer award, 1940, Acheson Gold medal and prize, 1946; War Research medallion Columbia, 1946. Rep., Electrochem. Soc. on Research Com. Am. Electroplaters' Soc. 1948-51. Mem. A.A.A.S., Am. Chem. Soc. (chmn. Phila. sect. 1940-41), Electrochem. Soc. (v.p. 1936-38, pres. 1939-40), Chem. Soc. (London), Soc. Chem. Industry, Faraday Soc., Franklin Inst. (chmn. com. on sci. and arts, 1918; mem. Franklin medal com., 1922-52, chmn. 1933), Nova Scotian Inst. Sci., N.Y. Acad. Sci., Chem. Inst. Can., Phi Beta Kappa (hon.), Sigma Xi (chmn. nat. lectureship com. 1938-43). Clubs: Chemists Men's Faculty of Columbia U. (N.Y.); University (Montreal); Halifax Royal Nova Scotia Yacht Squadron; English-Speaking Union, Royal Commonwealth Soc., Over-Seas League (London, Eng.). Author: Principles of Electrochemistry, 4th edit., 1943. Home: Glen Margaret, N.S., Can. Died 1975.

CREIGHTON, JOHN WALLIS, educator and clergyman; b. Creighton, Mo., Jan. 16, 1882; s. Marcus Anthony and Mary Adella (Wallis) C.; A.B., Westminster Coll., 1904; Ph.D., U. of Mo., 1917; LL.D., Coll. of Wooster, O., 1936; m. Lois Jameson, Sept. 14, 1910; children—Mildred (Mrs. Frank M. Barry), Ruth (Mrs. Charles E. Campbell Jr.), John Wallis, Robert Jameson, Joseph Riggs. Missionary Presbyn. Ch. Fgn. Missions to China, 1907; prin. Boys Boarding Sch., Yeung Kong, China, 1908-15; prin. True Light Middle Sch. (girls), Canton, 1917-28; prof. of missions and comparative religion, Coll. of Wooster, 1928-34; pres. Hastings (Neb.) College, 1934-43; independent and advanced study of economic problems of Far East, 1943-44; pastor First Presbyn. Ch., Maryville, O., 1944-45; prof. economics, Westminster Coll., Pa., 1944-46; prof. chmn. dept. history, dir. summer session, 1947, chmn. dept. of history, polit. sci., sociology, 1950-52; interim pastor Westminster Presbyn. Ch., Pitts., 1952-53. Dir. Hackett Med. Coll. and Union Theological College, Canton, 1923-28, Canton Hosp., 1926-28; pres. Am. Assn. of South China, 1923-25; chmn. ednl. com. Council of Presbyn. Missions in China, 1925-28. Mem. Am. Oriental Soc., Am. Assn. Univ. Profs., Am. Econ. Assn., Econ. Hist. Assn., Am. Hist. Assn., Kappa Alpha. Democrat. Home: Pitts.

CRESKOFF, JACOB JOSHUA, cons. engr.; b. Belz, Russia, Mar. 30, 1900; s. Louis and Tillie (Lerner) C.; brought to U.S., 1905; grad. Gratz Coll., Phila., 1919; B.S. in C.E., Towne Sci. Sch. (U. Pa.), 1922; m. Mildred Blumenthal, Mar. 16, 1935; children—Stephen, Ruth. Made investigation of Washington Monument for spalling and aseismic qualities; cons. to depts. of U.S. Govt. on design of earthquake-proof bldgs., and on rec. and analysis of structural vibrations, including aeronautical structures; devised first practical dynamic system of aseismic design; method of distbn. of wind and earthquake forces to walls and columns; method of using site vibrations as check on geol. findings; method of using periods of vibration of structures as guide to end fixities and to detect invisible damage; v.p. Vacuum Concrete Corp., 1938-42, 46-50; resident v.p. McCloskey & Co., 1942-46; pres. Thermo-Fluid Corp., 1950-59, Vacuum Concrete Corp. of Am., 1959-69; chmn. bd. Aerovac Corp., 1969-72; guest prof. Grad. Sch. Engring., Villanova U., 1962-72. Served in Engrs. S.A.T.C., U.S. Army, 3 months, 1918; lt. comdr. Civil Engr. Corps, USNR, from 1938. Citation, Distinguished Engr. U. Pa., 1955. Fellow Am. Concrete Inst. Jewish. Author: Dynamics of Earthquake Resistant Structures, 1934. Contbr. on engring. subjects. Home: Wynnewood, Pa. Died Aug. 18, 1979.

CRESSE, WADSWORTH, banker; b. Green Creek, N.J., 1883. President and trust officer First National Bank and Trust Co., Woodbury, N.J.; dir. Pitman (N.J.) Nat. Bank & Trust Co., People's Bldg. & Loan Association, New Jersey Bell Telephone Company. Member national board of field advisers Small Bus. Adminstrn., Region III, Phila. Mason (Shriner). Home: Woodbury, N.J.

CRESSMAN, PAUL LEROY, dir. Bur. of Instrn.; b. Springtown, Pa., Apr. 29, 1893; s. George Landis and Clara Arabella (Meyers) C.; grad. State Teachers Coll., Kutztown, Pa., 1912; B.S., U. of Pittsburgh, 1925; grad. work, Columbia; Ed.D., Pa. State Coll., 1934; m. Lenora Grace LeClaire, June 24, 1916; children—Claire Marie, Hazel Irene, Paul LeRoy. Grade teacher and elementary sch. prin., Lehighton, 1912-15; head of arts dept., State Normal Sch., Bloomsburg, Pa., 1915-18, high sch., Uniontown, Pa., 1918-20; cabinet trade instr., Academy High Sch., Erie, Pa., 1920-21; dir. vocational edn., Erie City Sch., Pa., 1921-24; supervisor and later dir. of industrial edn., State Dept. Public Instrn., Pa., 1924-34, dir. Bureau of Instruction from 1936; asst. supt. pub. instrn., Michigan, 1934-36; instr. summer school, U. of Pittsburgh, 1924, 25, Pa. State Coll., 1928-35. Mem. N.E.A., Am. Vocational Assn., Am. Assn. of Sch. Adminstrs., Pa. State Edn. Assn., Iota Lambda Sigma, Phi Delta Kappa, Kappa Phi Kappa. Methodist. Contbr. to ednl. jours. Home: Mechanicsburg, Pa. Died Feb. 2, 1975.

CRICHTON, JOHN HENDERSON, assn. exec.; b. Padroni, Colo., Mar. 4, 1919; s. John Henderson and Lyda (McClain) C.; B. Journalism, U. Mo., 1940; m. Zula Miller, Nov. 24, 1939; children—John Michael, Kimberly, Douglas Christopher, Catherine. With newspapers, Colo., Mont., 1940-41; with Advt. Age Mag., Chgo., 1941-42, N.Y.C., 1946-62, editor, 1958-62; pres. Am. Assn. Advt. Agencies, Inc., N.Y.C., 1962-77. Mem. adv. com. U.S. council Internat. C. of C.; mem. commerce info. adv. com. Dept. Commerce; sec., dir. Advt. Council; dir. Traffic Audit Bur. Mem. nat. adv. council Hampshire Coll. Bd. dirs. Advt. Research Found. Served to lt. (j.g.) USNR, 1944-46. Mem. U.S. C. of C., Am. Mktg. Assn. Clubs: Lake (New Canaan); Union League, Sky, Economic (N.Y.C.); Metropolitan (Washington); Norwalk Yacht. Author: (with W. H. Mullen) The New Competition, 1956. Home: New Canaan, Conn. Died Dec. 27, 1977; buried New Canaan.

CRIKELAIR, ROBERT JOHN, paper co. exec.; b. Green Bay, Wis., Nov. 27, 1916; s. Frank L. and Alma (Stenger) C.; student St. Norbert Coll., DePere, Wis., 1934-36; B.A., U. Wis., 1938; grad. exec. devel. program U. Ill., 1960; m. Adeline Seidel, Jan. 30, 1943; children—Martha (Mrs. George Wohlford III), Frank, Robert, Linda, Daniel, Lisa. With Haskins & Sells, C.P.A.'s, N.Y.C. and Chgo., 1938-46; with Kimberly-Clark Corp., Neenah, Wis., 1946-79, asst. comptroller, 1961-63, comptroller, 1963-70, staff v.p. administrv. services, 1970-73; v.p., treas. Kimberly-Clark Internat. Services Corp., 1973-79; former dir. Twin City Savs. & Loan Assn. Campaign chmn. Neenah-Menasha Community Chest, 1954, bd. dirs., 1955-60. Served to maj. USAAF, 1941-45; ETO. C.P.A., Ill., Wis. Mem. Financial Execs. Inst. (dir Milw. chpt.), Am. Paper Inst. (past chmn. financial mgmt. com.), Sigma Nu, Beta Alpha Psi. K.C. (past grand knight Neenah-Menasha). Home: Amersham Bucks England. Died Sept. 1979.

CRISS, MABEL LEONE, ins. co. exec.; b. Ia.; John W. and Jessie B. (Flanders) Chambers; m. Dr. C.C. Criss (dec.). Founder (with Dr. C.C. Criss) Mut. Benefit Health & Accident Assn., 1909, now dir. personnel and planning; co-founder United Benefit Life Ins. Co., Omaha, 1926, dir. personnel and planning. 1st v.p., 1948-78; also dir. Mem. planning com. City of Omaha. Bd. dirs. Children's Meml. Hosp., Clarkson Meml. Hosp. First woman recipient award for outstanding mgmt. Nat. Office Mgmt. Assn., 1951. Home: Omaha, Nebr. Died Mar. 19, 1978.

CRISS, NELL LOUIS, ins. exec.; b. Sac City, Ia., Aug. 13, 1886; s. James L. and Villa (Wadell) C.; M.D., Creighton U., 1912. With Mutual Benefit Health & Accident Assn., 1910, treas., sr. v.p., med. dir., dir., 1923—. v.p., med. dir., United Benefit Life Ins. Co., 1926—(now Mut. of Omaha Ins. Co.). Mem. Am. Legion. Clubs: Happy Hollow, Omaha Athletic, Elks. Home: Omaha, Neb.

CRITES, AURE BRIAN, physician; b. Enterprise, Kan., May 19, 1893; s. Rev. Thomas Daniel and Cynthia Belle (Carpenter) C.; A.B., Coe Coll., 1916; D.O., Central Coll. of Osteopathy, 1919; M. D., Kansas City U. of Physicians and Surgeons, 1920; grad. study N.Y. Eye and Ear Infirmary, 1925-26, also at London, Eng., 1928, and U. of Vienna, 1931; Sc.D. (hon.), Coll. of Osteo. Physicians and Surgeons, Los Angeles, 1956; m. Helen M. Smith, Feb. 14, 1918; m. 2d, Gail Alexander, July 11, 1936. Practiced in Kansas City, Mo., from 1920, specializing in eye, ear, nose and throat; past pres. Lakeside Hosp. staff; prof. ophthalmology, Kansas City Coll. of Osteopathy and Surgery; post-grad. prof. and surgeon Conley Clin. Hosp.; former chief of staff Osteopathic Hosp. Fellow Osteopathic Coll. of Ophthalmology and Otorhinolaryngology. Mem. examining bd. for certifying osteopathic splsts. Mem. Phi Sigma Gamma (past pres., named Doctor of Yr. 1961). Mem. United Brethren Ch. Mason (Scottish Rite, Shriner). Club: Blue

Hill Golf and Country. Contbr. to professional jours. Home: Crystal River, Fla. Died Jan. 28, 1980.

CROCKER, MICHAUX HENLY, ins. co. exec.; b. Greensboro, N.C., Apr. 13, 1908; s. Thomas Henly and Annie (Michaux) C.; student U. N.C., 1925-26, 53-54; m. Mary Walker Schenck, Jan. 21, 1933; children—Michaux Henly, Walker Crocker Caudle. With Jefferson Standard Life Ins. Co., Greensboro, N.C., 1926-73, treas., 1956-73, v.p., 1964-73; dir., v.p. Jefferson-Pilot Broadcasting Co., Charlotte, N.C., 1953-73, Jefferson-Pilot Broadcasting Co. of Va., Richmond, 1968-73, N.C. Broadcasting Co., Greensboro, 1952-73; dir., pres., treas. Jefferson-Carolina Corp., Greensboro, 1966-72; dir., pres. Mgmt. Devel., Inc., Chapel Hill, N.C., 1964-66. Finance chmn. Downtown Com., Greensboro, 1962-64, Greensboro Bond Campaigns, 1964, 68; co-chmn. Com. to Establish William J. Graham Chair, U. N.C., 1966. Mem. Greensboro City Council, 1965-67. Served with USMCR, 1943-45. Mem. Soc. Cin., Phi Kappa Sigma. Democrat. Episcopalian. Home: Greensboro, N.C. Died Apr. 20, 1977; buried Greensboro.

CROCKER, SAMUEL E. M., assn. exec.; b. Fitchburg, Mass., Dec. 10, 1882; s. George H. and Emma Louise (Miller) C.; grad. Groton (Mass.) Sch., 1903; special student Harvard, 1931-32, U. of Maryland, 1 yr.; m. Gladys Thomas, June 11, 1907; children—Samuel E. M., Wethered Thomas (officer U.S.M.C.), Carol (Mrs. Carrington Clark), Malcolm, Quentin, Gladys T. (wife of Lt. John Swasey, U.S.N.R.). Paper maker, Crocker Burbank & Co., Boston, Mass., 1903-11, became vice pres., 1911; with Nat. Red Cross, Washington, D.C., 1921-23; with Dept. of Commerce, Washington, D.C., 1923-26; engaged in farming, Stockbridge, Mass., 1926-30; psychologist, Boston and New York, 1931-41; exec. dir. Joint Army and Navy Com. and asst. to vice chmn., Washington, D.C., 1941-44; nat. vice pres. Navy League since 1942; consultant to Sonotone Corp. since 1944. Mem. common council and alderman, Fitchburg, Mass., 1914-17. Served with State Guard of Mass., 1917-19. Mason (32 deg.). Clubs: Nantucket (Mass.); Beverly (Mass.) Yacht. Home: Boston, Mass.

CROCKER, TEMPLETON, scientific research; b. San Francisco, Calif., Sept. 2, 1884; s. Charles Frederick and Jennie (Easton) C.; grad. Westminster Sch., Simsbury, Conn., 1903; A.B., Yale, 1908; unmarried. Research in South Seas, Galapagos Islands, for Calif. Acad. Sciences, 1932; Solomon Islands for Bishop Museum, Honolulu, 1933, Eastern Polynesia, Pitcairn and Easter Islands for Am. Museum of Natural History, 1934-35, Lower Calif. and west coast of Gulf of Calif. for Dr. William Beebe, New York Zoölogical Society, 1936, Hawaii, Tongareva, Samoa for American Museum Natural History, 1936-37. Decorated Chevalier Legion of Honor (France). Fellow Royal Geographical Soc.; mem. Am. Museum Natural History, N.Y. Zoöl. Soc., Field Museum, Calif. Acad. Sciences, S.A.R., Native Sons of the Golden West, Soc. Mayflower Descendants. Republican. Episcopalian. Clubs: Pacific Union, Bohemian (San Francisco); The Brook (N.Y. City); St. James', Royal Automobile, Authors (London). Author: The Cruise of the Zaca, 1933. Author of libretto of opera Fay-Yen-Fah. Home: San Francisco, Cal.

CROFT, A(RTHUR) C., publisher; b. Cleve., May 26, 1890; s. John Henry and Lucetta (Shirk) C.; ed. pub. schs. Cleve., m. Christine Marquis, Sept. 9, 1920; 1 son Noyes. With A.W. Shaw Co. Inc., pubs., Chgo., 1912-28, McGraw-Hill Pub. Co., Inc., N.Y.C., 1928-36, dir. circulation, from 1937; chmn. bd. Nat. Foremen's Inst., New London, Conn., 1937-75; dir. Am. Arbitration Assn., 1950-75; pres. A.C. Croft, Inc., Aim Co., Inc.; pub. Personnel Jour. Republican. Home: Santa Barbara, Calif. Died Sept. 6, 1975; buried Santa Barbara Cemetery.

CROHN, BURRILL BERNARD, physician; b. N.Y.C., June 13, 1884; s. Theodore and Lean (Baum) C.; B.A., Coll. City N.Y., 1902; M.D., Columbia University, 1907; m. Rose Blumenthal, June 30, 1948; children—Ruth Dickler, Dr. Edward B. Practice of medicine, 1911—, specializing internal medicine, 1920—; cons. gastroenterology Mt. Sinai Hosp., N.Y.C., Columbia U., 1946—. Recipient Townsend Harris medal Coll. City N.Y., 1949, Friedenwald medal for gastroenterology, 1951. Mem. Am. Gastroenterological Assn. (past pres.). Home: N.Y.C.

CROMBIE, DAVID JOSEPH, airline exec.; b. Hartford, Conn., May 5, 1915; s. David H. and Ida (Vannie) C.; A.B., Fordham U., 1938, M.A., 1940; m. Frances O'Brien, Aug. 31, 1940; children—David A., Michael F., Timothy J., Alison E., Nicholas E., Pamela A., Jean F. Instr. Fordham U., 1938-41; with Underwood Corp., N.Y.C., 1941-59, beginning as engr., successively factory mgr., v.p. mfg., v.p. indsl. relations, v.p. adminstrn.; sr. v.p. adminstrn. Trans World Airlines, N.Y.C., 1960-80. Chmn. trustees Rosary Coll. Mem. Fordham U. Alumni Assn. Clubs: University (N.Y.); Innes Arden Country. Home: Stamford, Conn. Died Mar. 22, 1980; buried Mt. St. Benedict Cemetery, Hartford.

CROMER, VOIGT RHODES, clergyman, coll. cons.; b. Rhodhiss, N.C., July 31, 1906; s. Joseph Lee and Lillie Mae (Rhodes) C.; A.B., Lenoir Rhyne Coll., 1925, D.D., 1947, L.H.D., 1967; A.M., U. S.C., 1927; B.D., Lutheran Theol. So. Sem., Columbia, S.C., 1928; S.T.M., Hartford Sem. Found., 1929; postgrad. Union Theol. Sem., N.Y.C., 1939; LL.D., Gettysburg Coll., 1956; m. Sara Elizabeth Dreher, Aug. 17, 1932; children—Elizabeth Rhodes (Mrs. Robert Carswell), Rebecca Ruth (Mrs. Richard Campbell). Ordained to ministry Lutheran Ch., 1928, served pastorates in Summerville, S.C. (St. Lukes), 1929-30, Lincolnton, N.C. (Emmanuel), 1930-36, Concord, N.C. (St. James), 1936-41, Hickory, N.C. (Holy Trinity), 1941-47; pres. United Evang. Luth. Synod of N.C., 1947-49; pres. Lenoir Rhyne Coll., 1949-67, pres. emeritus cons. 1967-80, trustee, 1936-47, mem. devel. bd., 1969-80; v.p. Howell Mfg. Co., Cherryville, N.C., 1950-80. Mem. bd. social missions United Luth. Ch. Am., 1948-60, mem. bd. Am. missions, 1960-62; mem. exec. council Luth. Ch. in Am., 1962-70; commr. United Luth. Ch. in Am. to Joint Commn. on Luth. Unity, to Nat. Luth. Council, 1948-54; pres. Conf. Ch.-Related Colls. So., 1954-55; pres. Luth. Ednl. Conf. Am. 1955; chmn. Catawba County chpt. A.R.C., 1942-45. Recipient Lenoir Rhyne Distinguished Alumnus award, 1966; Nat. Luth. Brotherhood award, 1967. Mem. NEA, Assn. Sch. Adminstrs. Clubs: Hickory Rotary (dir., past pres. Lincolnton club), Catawba Valley Executives (pres. 1970-71). Contbr. to synod publs. Home: Hickory, N.C. Died May 31, 1980.

CROMWELL, HARVEY, univ. dean, author; b. Wanette, Okla., Aug. 16, 1907; s. Sheldon Winfield and Martha Jane (Hibbard) C.; B.S., Okla. East Central Coll., 1930; M.A., U. Okla., 1940; Ph.D., Purdue U., 1949; m. Mattie Lou Patterson, June 10, 1931; children—Harvey, Betty Jane (Mrs. Henry D. Lawrence). High sch. instr. speech and math., Okla., 1929-33; agt. Met. Life Ins. Co., Oklahoma City, 1933-37; instr. speech El Reno (Okla.) High Sch. and Jr. Coll., 1938-40; head dept. speech McMurry Coll., 1940-42; coordinator instr. tng. USAF, Sheppard Field and Amarillo, Tex., 1942-44; instr., debate coach Purdue U., 1944-49; prof. speech Miss. U. for Women, 1949-75, head dept., 1949-66, dir. program for superior students, 1961-64, dean Grad. Sch., 1966-75, dean instrn., 1967-69, dir. research, 1969-75; vis. prof. speech No. Mich. U., 1950, 53, U. Miss., 1951, 54, U. Southwestern La., 1955-59, N.Mex. Highlands U., 1960, Stamford U., 1962, Miami-Dade Coll., 1969. Cons. spl. edn., chmn. regional screening com. Miss. Dept. Edn., 1954-69; mem. coordinating coms. neurol. and sensory div. project Miss. Bd. Health, 1964-65; mem. Pres.'s Com. Employment of Handicapped, 1966-77; mem. Miss. Vocat. Rehab. Planning Com., 1967-69. Mem. Nat. Forensic League, Miss. (pres. 1952, exec. council 1951-64), So. (exec. council 1951-52, 67-69) speech assns., Speech Assn. Am. (legis. assembly 1958-61), Assn. So. Deans, Pi Kappa Delta (nat. pres. 1959-61), Tau Kappa Alpha, Phi Kappa Phi. Democrat. Baptist. Author: An Oral Approach to Phonetics (with C.R. Van Dusen), 1969; A Compact Guide to Parliamentary Procedure, 1966, 73; Working for More Effective Speech, 1955; Suggestions for the Beginning Course in Speech, 1956; Student Guide and Instructor's Guide for Speech I and II, 1957; (with A.H. Monroe and L.S. Winch) Interview Problems, 1946. Contbr. articles profl. jours. Home: Columbus, Miss. Died Dec. 28, 1977.

CRON, ROLAND SPUHLER, gynecologist; b. Manistee, Mich., May 19, 1892; son of Fred W. and Amelia (Spuhler) Cron; B.S., U. Mich., 1914; M.D., 1917; M. Florence Schroeder, November 14, 1925; children—James Grant, Judith Elizabeth. Intern, U. of Michigan Hosp., 1917-18; resident, New York (N.Y.) Lying-in-Hosp., 1919-20; instr. gynecology and obstetrics, U. of Mich., 1920-21, asst. prof., 1921-23; prof. and head dept. obstetrics and gynecology, Marquette U., from 1938, mem. staff Milwaukee City Hosp.; cons. staff Columbia, Milw. County hosps. With U.S.A. Med. Res. Corps, 1918. Diplomate Am. Bd. Obstets. and Gynecology. Fellow A.C.S., Am. Gynecological Society; mem. Am. Assn. Obstetricians and Gynecologists, Milwaukee, Chgo, gynecol. Socs., Central Assn. Obstetrics and Gynecology, Wisconsin Soc. Obstetrics and Gynecol., Milwaukee Acad. of Medicine, Phi Rho Sigma. Clubs: University (Milwaukee), Rotary Contbr. of articles to profl. jours. Home: Milwaukee, Wis. Died Sept. 12, 1978.

CRONAN, RICHARD J., lawyer; b. 1886; B.A., City Coll. N.Y.; LL.B., N.Y. U. Admitted to N.Y. bar, 1909, since practiced in N.Y.C. Mem. Am. Bar Assn. Address: N.Y.C. *

CRONIN, ARCHIBALD JOSEPH, author; b. Cardross, Scotland, July 19, 1896; s. Patrick and Jessie (Montgomerie) C.; M.B., B. Chir. and M.D., Glasgow; D.Litt., Bowdoin U., Lafayette Coll.; m. Agnes Mary Gibson, 1921; children—Vincent Archibald, Patrick, Robert Francis Patrick, Andrew James. Began as doctor of medicine, in South Wales, 1919, later practiced in London, 1930; became med. insp. mines for Great Britain, 1924; author, 1930-81. Life gov. Sussex Gen. Hosp.; mem. Fischer Com.; mem. of Council of Authors Soc. Author: Hatters Castle, 1931; Three Loves, 1932; Grand Canary, 1933; The Stars Look Down, 1935; The Citadel, 1937; Jupiter Laughs (3-act play), 1940; The Keys of the Kingdom, 1941, The Green Years, 1944; Shannon's Way, 1948; The Spanish Gardener, 1950; Adventures in Two Worlds, 1952; Beyond this Place, 1953; A Thing of Beauty, 1956; The Northern Light, 1958; The Judas Tree, 1961; A Song of Sixpence, 1964; A Pocketful of Rye, published in 1969. Clubs: Links, University (N.Y.C.). Home: Montreux, Switzerland. Died Jan. 6, 1981.

CROOK, WELTON JOSEPH, metall. cons.; b. Melbourne, Australia, Feb. 1, 1886; s. William Joseph and Grace (Cooper) C.; student Scotch Coll., Melbourne, 1898-1904, Melbourne Sch. Mines, 1906-07; A.B., in Mining and Metallury, Stanford, 1911, E.M., 1919; Dr.Ing., Bucharest, 1936; m. Maud L'Anphere, 1911. Came to U.S., 1908, naturalized 1927. Chemist and assayer Dept. Mines and Water Supply, Victoria, Australia, 1907-08; asst. in metallurgy Stanford, 1910; chief chemist Pacific Coast Steel Co., 1911-13; prof. metallurgy S.D. State Sch. Mines, 1913-17; metall. chemist U.S. Bur. Mines, 1915; metallurgist and chief chemist Pacific Coast Steel Co., 1917-19, metallurgist and chief insp., 1919-20, chief metallurgist, 1920-21, cons. metall. engr. 1922-30, coöp. analyst U.S. Bur. Standards from 1920; cons. engr. U.S. Bur. Mines, 1922; cons. metall. engr., from 1922; prof. metallurgy Stanford, from 1921, now metall. cons. dept. applied earth scis. Served as 2d, later 1st lt., Commonwealth Mil. Forces, Australia, 1904-07; with Cal. N.G., 1912-13, with M.C., S.D. N.G., 1913-14; attended O.T.C., Presidio, San Francisco, 1917; maj., 1927-39; specialist Res., U.S. Army, lt. col., 1939-42; col. Ordnance Dept., U.S. Army, 1942-46; tech. officer, officer in charge engring. dept. and steel casting div. Rock Island (Ill.) Arsenal; now col. AUS retired. Decorated Legion of Merit, Am. Def. Service medal, Letter of Commendation. Registered profl. engr., Nev., Cal. Mem. Am. Inst. Mining Metall. and Petroleum Engrs., Am. Soc. Metals, N.Y. Acad. Scis., Sigma Xi, Theta Xi, Tau Beta Pi. Republican. Mason. Author: Tables of Arc Spectrum Lines, 1934; Metallurgical Spectrum Analysis, 1935; Recherches Expérimentales sur la Constitution Mineralogique et sur l'Action Chimique des Scories d l'Acier, 1936; Abacus Arithmetic, 1958; The Vreeland Spectrograph, 1968. Contbr. articles to tech. publs. Spl. metall. studies at Scoala Politechnica, Bucharest, Rumania, 1935-36. Address: Stanford, Calif. Died Mar. 13, 1976.

CROOKER, JOHN HENRY, lawyer; b. Mobile, July 15, 1884; s. Norman W. and Margaret J. (Kelton) C.; m. Marguerite Malsch, Dec. 31, 1913; children—John Henry, Robert W. Admitted to Tex. Bar, 1911; judge inferior ct., Houston, 1911-14; dist. atty., Houston, 1914-17; mem. firm Fulbright & Crooker, Houston, and successor firm, Fulbright, Crooker, Freeman, Bates & Jaworski, Houston, 1919—, now of counsel. Dir. First City Nat. Bank, Houston. Served as maj., div. judge adv., 16th Div., U.S. Army, 1918-19. Episcopalian (past sr. warden, vestryman). Mason (grand master Tex. 1934-35). Home: Houston TX.

CROPLEY, MARSHALL F(REEMAN), transportation exec.; b. San Jose, Calif., May 26, 1882; s. Charles C. and Henerietta (Abel) C.; student San Jose Bus. Coll., 1901-02; m. Gladys Weston Thomas, Feb. 12, 1912; children—Henerietta E., Janice C. Stenographer Rock Island Ry., San Francisco, 1904-06; cashier Alaska Pacific Steamship Co., San Francisco, 1906-15; gen. agt., Pacific Steampship Co., San Francisco, 1915-17, asst. gen. frt. agt., 1917-20, asst. mgr., 1920-21, mgr., 1921-23, asst. freight traffic mgr., 1923-25; asst. frt. traffic mgr., Matson Navigation Co., San Francisco, 1925-30, frt. traffic mgr., 1930-47, v.p. 1947-51, asst. to pres. since 1951. Mason (Shriner). Clubs: Bohemian, California Golf, Rotary (San Francisco); Pacific (Honolulu). Home: San Francisco.

CROSBY, BING (HARRY LILLIS), actor; b. Tacoma, Wash., May 2, 1904; s. Harry Lowe and Catherine C.; student Gonzaga U., Spokane, Wash., 1914-24, Ph.D. (hon.), 1937; m. Wilma W. Wyatt, Sept. 29, 1930 (dec. 1952); children—Gary Evan, Dennis Michael, Philip Lang, Howard Lindsay; M. 2d, Olive Grandstaff (Kathryn Grant), Oct. 24, 1957; children—Harry Lillis III, Mary Frances, Nathaniel Patrick. Began career as a singer with dance bands, 1925-30; broadcasting with Columbia System, 1931-35, NBC 1936-57; entertained U.S. servicemen, World War II; with A.B.C. 1947-49; with Columbia, from 1950; screen actor with Paramount Prodns., Inc., from 1931; appeared in over 50 films including Here Is My Heart, Pennies From Heaven, The Road To Singapore, Road to Zanzibar, Birth of the Blues, Holiday Inn, Road to Morocco, Star Spangled Rhythm, Going My Way, Bells of St. Mary's, Welcome Stranger, Blue Skies, Road to Rio, The Emperor Waltz, Mr. Music, Here Comes the Groom, Little Boy Lost, White Christmas, Country Girl, Anything Goes, Stage Coach. Pres. Bing Crosby Ltd. Recipient Academy Award, 1944, William D. Richardson Meml. Trophy for contbns. to game of golf, 1950. Roman Catholic. Clubs: Bel-Air Country, Friars (N.Y.C.). Author: Call Me Lucky (autobiography),

1953. Founder Crosby Nat. Pro-Am Golf Tournament; sold over 300,000 records including songs Silent Night and White Christmas. Died Oct. 14, 1977.

CROSBY, LUCIUS OSMOND, JR., corp. exec.; b. Bogue Chitto, Miss., Oct. 6, 1907; s. Lucius Olen and Margaret Henrietta (Reed) C.; grad. Jefferson Mil. Coll., Washington, Miss., 1926; B.S. in Commerce, U. Miss., 1931; children—Dorothy Lynn (Mrs. Lynn Crosby Gammill), Lucius Osmond III. Employee relief adminstr. and farm mgr. Goodyear Yellow Pine Co., Picayune, Miss., 1931-33, personnel and farm mgr., 1934-35; v.p. in charge sales and mfg. Crosby Lumber & Mfg Co., 1936-41, v.p., dir., 1936-66; pres. gen. mgr. Crosby Forest Products Co., Picayune, 1941-78, also dir.; chmn., dir. Pearl River Valley R.R. Co. Pres. Pine Burr Area council Boy Scouts, 1955-57, exec. bd. nat. council, regional chmn., 1958-62, chmn. nat. com. on exploring, 1963-69; past dir. state, local YMCA; past dir. So. States Indsl. Council. Chmn. 6th Congl. Dist., Miss. Citizens for Eisenhower Commn., 1957; mayor, City Picayune, 1957-61. Past trustee New Orleans Bapt. Theol. Sem. Recipient citizen of year award, Picayune, 1948; Man of the Year in Tung award, 1960; Silver Beaver, Silver Antelope, Silver Buffalo awards Boy Scouts Am. Mem. N.A.M. (past dir.). Am. Tung Oil Assn., Tung Oil Research and Devel. League (dir.), Miss. Forestry Assn. (v.p. 1950-58), Nat. Tung Oil Marketing Coop. (dir.), Pan-Am Tung Research and Devel. League (pres. 1964-67), Sigma Chi, Baptist. Mason Home: Picayune, Miss. Died Dec. 24, 1979.

CROSLAND, CLAYTON EDWARD, college pres.; b. Selma, Ala., July 25, 1886; s. Edward Davidson and Marie Antoinette (Goodwin) C.; B.A., Howard Coll., Birmingham, Ala., 1907; Rhodes scholar, Oxford U., Eng., 1910-13, B.A., 1913; studied univs. Göttingen, München, Marburg and Paris; m. Ida Holly, of Abbeville, Ala., Aug. 19, 1914. Ednl. sec., Southern Bapt. S.S. Bd., Nashville, Tenn., 1907-10; pres. Southeast Ala. Agrl. Coll., 1913-14; dir. of Assemblies, Peabody Coll. for Teachers, Nashville, Tenn., summer 1941; pres. Fork Union (Va.) Mil. Acad. 1914-17; pres. Averett Coll. for Young Women, Danville, Va., 1917-21; asso. pres. Ward-Belmont Coll., Nashville, Tenn., 1921-23; pres. and supt. Columbia Mil. Acad., Columbia, Tenn., since 1923. Mem. Psi Delta. Democrat. Baptist. Mason (K.T.). Clubs: Kiwanis, Century (Columbia). Lecturer on ednl. and Chautauqua subjects. Address: Columbia Military Academy, Columbia, Tenn.

CROSLAND, DAVID WOOLLEY, JR., circuit judge, lawyer; b. Montgomery, Ala., Aug. 26, 1909; s. David Woolley and Virginia (Burton) C.; student U. of South, 1930; J.D., U. Ala., 1932; m. Marie Virginia Denegre, Oct. 24, 1931; 1 son, David Woolley, III. Admitted to Ala. bar, 1932, practiced in Montgomery; prosecutor, asst. judge City Ct., 1955-63; dist. atty. 15th Jud. Circuit, Montgomery, 1963-75. Dir. Farmers Nat. Life Ins. Co., Peoples Ins. Co.; v.p. Security Life Ins. Co.; instr. Montgomery and Ala. Police Acads. Mem. Downtown Unltd.; v.p. Ala. Fedn. Humane Soc., 1970; active Ala. Mental Health Assn. Tax assessor Montgomery County, 1941-55; asst. clk. Ala. Ho. of Reps., 1956-63. Bd. dirs. Montgomery Fellowship Houses. Served to lt. USNR, World War II; PTO. Mem. Pioneers of Montgomery (trustee); Ala. Dist. Attys. Assn. (pres. 1971). Kiwanian (dir. 1969). Composer, editor: A Picture History of Montgomery, 1962. Home: Montgomery, Ala. Died Nov. 27, 1975.

CROSS, CLEVELAND ROSELLE, lawyer; b. Denver, Colo., May 19, 1882; s. Roselle Theodore and Emma Asenath (Bridgman) C.; A.B., Oberlin (O.) Coll., 1903; grad. study U. of Wis., 1903-04; LL.B., Western Reserve, 1907; m. Ruth Adah Savage, Nov. 11, 1908; children—Robert Alden, Caroline Murdock. Admitted to Ohio bar, 1907, and practiced since at Cleveland; with Fackler, Wilcox & Morris, 1907, Hitchcock, Morgan & Fackler, 1908-12; mem. Hitchcock, Morgan, Fackler & Cross, 1912-15, Wilkin, Cross & Daoust, 1915-27, Garfield, Cross, MacGregor, Daoust and Baldwin, 1927-41; now member firm Cross, Knight & Miller; president Colonial Savings & Loan Co.; mem. executive com. Land Title Guarantee & Trust Co.; trustee Northwestern Mut. Life Ins. Co. Pres. Cleveland Municipal Research Bur., 1924-27; pres. Cleveland Welfare Fed., 1926-28; trustee Cleveland Community Fund, 1924-31; mem. Lakewood Bd. of Edn., 1920-32. Trustee Oberlin Coll. (mem. exec. com.), Cleveland Mus. Natural History; former trustee Hathaway Brown Sch. for Girls. Mem. American Bar Assn., Ohio State Bar Assn., Cleveland Bar Assn., Cleveland Chamber Commerce, Phi Alpha Delta Fraternity. Republican. Congregationalist. Mason. Clubs: Westwood Country, Clifton. Home: Lakewood.

CROSS, JOHN STORRS, cons.; b. Birmingham, Ala., Sept. 18, 1904; s. Thomas C. and Elise Fairfax (Troy) C.; student McCallie Sch. for Boys, Chattanooga, Marion Mil. Inst., Ala.; B.S. in Elec. Engring., Ala. Poly. Inst., 1923; m. Ruth Fuller, Dec. 23, 1932; children—John Fuller, Claude Christopher. Exptl. engring. lab. Studebaker Corp., Detroit, 1923-24; staff Realty Trust Co., U.S. Mortgage Bond Co., Detroit, 1924-26; constrn. supt. S.S. Kresge Co., 1926-27; asst. resident engr. S.C. Hwy. Dept., 1927; survey chief Mich. Hwy. Dept., 1928-30; staff Dept. Interior Nat. Park Service, 1931-41, successively design engr. water systems San Francisco office, field engr. in charge constrn. Hot Springs Nat. Park, then chief survey design and road div., asst. chief engring. Washington office; asst. chief telecommunications div. Dept. State, 1946-58; commr. FCC, 1958-63; pres. Cross Communication Cons., 1963-76. Chmn. U.S. delegation Internat. Meeting on Marine Radio Aids to Nav., N.Y.C., New London, Conn. 1947, Internat. Radio Consultative Com., Warsaw, Poland, 1956, Maritime VHF Radio Telephone Conf., The Hague, Netherlands, 1957. Served from lt. comdr. to capt. USN, 1942-46. Decorated Legion of Merit. Clubs: Manor Country (Norbeck, Md.); Congressional Country (Potomac, Md.). Home: Bethesda, Md. Died Nov. 8, 1976; buried Eureka Springs, Ark.

CROSS, LESLIE (FRANK), journalist; b. Milw., May 12, 1909; s. James L. and Zoe S. (Windfelder) C.; student Beloit Coll., 1927-28; m. Helene Catherine O'Keeffe, Mar. 9, 1929; children—Dion Leslie, James O'Keeffe. Reporter, copy editor Milw. Leader, 1929-38; copy editor New Milw. Leader, 1938-39; copy editor, news editor, asst. to editor, columnist Milw. Post, 1939-41; sec. Wis. Guardian Pub. Co., 1940-41; reporter, copy editor Milw. Jour., 1941-46, exchange editor, writer, 1946-51, columnist, book editor, 1951-77. Recipient 1st Bookfellow of Year award Bookfellows of Milw., 1966; decennial award Wis. Com. Nat. Library Week, 1967; Distinguished Service award Soc. Midland Authors, 1969, Distinguished Service award Council for Wis. Writers, 1974; Distinguished Service award Friends of Lit., 1976. Mem. Soc. Midland Authors, Nat. Book Critics Circle, Council Wis. Writers, Sigma Delta Chi. Club: Milw. Press. Author: Written in Wisconsin, 1972. Contbr. articles mags. Home: Milwaukee, Wis. Died July 3, 1977; cremated.

CROSS, PAUL CLIFFORD, chemist, educator, research adminstr.; b. Bruin, Pa., July 19, 1907; s. Henry Anderson McLean and Catherine P. (Smith) C.; B.S., Geneva Coll., 1928, Sc.D., 1963; M.S., U. Wis., 1930, Ph.D., 1932; M.S. ad eundum, Brown U., 1942; Sc.D., Waynesburg Coll., 1963; m. Sara Agnes Groves, June 18, 1932; children—Carroll Edward, Robert Henry, Beverly Jane, Elizabeth Ann. Alumni research fellow U. Wis., 1932-33; nat. research fellow Calif. Inst. Tech., 1933-35; Carnegie Found. fellow Stanford, 1935-36, asst. prof., 1936-38; asso. prof. Brown U., 1938-42, prof., 1942-49, dir. Metcalf Research Lab., 1946-49, chmn. chemistry dept., 1947-49; prof., exec. officer dept. chemistry U. Wash., 1949-61; pres., chief exec. officer, trustee Mellon Inst., Pitts., 1961-67, v.p. for research Carnegie-Mellon U., 1967-71, cons. to pres., 1971-72, bd. dirs. Mellon Inst., 1961-67, trustee Carnegie-Mellon U., 1967-73; pres. emeritus Mellon Inst. Carnegie-Mellon U., 1973-78. Lectr. summers Harvard, 1941, 46, U. Wis., 1952; cons. weapons systems evaluation group Dept. Def., summer 1953; cons. Wright Air Devel. Center, summers 1954, 55; cons. various govt. agys.; dep. research dir. Underwater Research Lab., USN Woods Hole Oceanographic Inst., 1943-44, research dir., 1944-46. Bd. dirs. San Diego Opera Assn., 1977-78, Scripps Meml. Hosp. Found., 1977-78; Duquesne U.; trustee Geneva Coll., Carnegie-Mellon U., Woods Hole Oceanographic Inst. Recipient Life G Alumni award Geneva Coll., 1958. Fellow Am. Phys. Soc., Am. Acad. Arts and Sci., AAAS, Am. Chem. Soc. (dir.-at-large 1967-71; Pitts. award 1971); mem. Spectroscopy Soc. Pitts., Pa. Soc., Western Pa. Conservancy, Phi Beta Kappa, Sigma Xi, Alpha Chi Sigma, Gamma Alpha, Phi Lambda Upsilon. Club: Lomas Santa Fe (Solana Beach, Calif.). Author: (with E.B. Wilson, Jr., J.C. Decius) Molecular Vibrations, 1955; (with H.C. Allen, Jr.) Molecular Vib-Rotors, 1963. Contbr. numerous articles to profl. publs. Home: Solana Beach, Calif. Died Sept. 20, 1978.

CROSSLEY, MOSES LEVEROCK (KROS'LE), chemist; b. of Am. parents at Saba, Dutch West Indies, July 3, 1884; s. John George Everett and Frances Antoinette (Johnson) C.; Ph.B., Brown University, 1909; Sc.M., 1910, Ph.D., 1911, Sc.D., 1944; Sc.D., Wesleyan U., 1947; m. Elise Emeline McCausland, Jan. 1, 1914; 1 son, Evan McCausland. Instr. chemistry Brown U., 1909-11; asso. prof. chemistry William Jewell College, Liberty, Mo., 1911-13; same, Wesleyan University, Middletown, Conn., 1913-18; head of dept., 1914-18; chief chemist, Calco Chem. Co., Bound Brook, N.J., 1918-36, research dir., 1936-39; research dir. Calco Chem. Div., American Cyanamid Co., 1939-41, Am. Cyanamid Co., 1941-49, ret.; research consultant since 1949; honorary research specialist Bur. of Biological Research, Rutgers University, since 1949. Member board of trustees Union Junior College, Brown U. Fellow N.Y. Acad. Scis.; mem. Inst. of Chemists (pres., 1924-26 and 1934-36; awarded Inst. gold medal, 1947), Am. Chem. Soc., The Faraday Soc., Soc. Chem. Industry, A.A.A.S., Am. Inst., New York City, Chem. Soc. (London), Associated Alumni of Brown Univ. (pres., 1945-47), Plainfield Art Association, Sigma Xi, Sigma Nu, Alpha Chi Sigma. Received "Brown Bear" award, 1940. Republican. Episcopalian. Clubs: Chemists, Brown University (New York), East Chop Country, Vineyard Haven Yacht. Collaborated in Chemistry in Industry, 1925; contributor chapter to National Research Council's Annual Survey of American Chemistry, 1930, 31. Research and discoveries in dyes and pharmaceuticals, cancer research. Home: Plainfield, N.J. Retired, 1953.

CROSTHWAIT, STANLEY WOOD, mgmt. cons.; born Greenfield Center, N.Y., Dec. 24, 1898; s. Edwin R. and Maud E. (Rodgers) C.; B.S., George Washington U., 1928; student American U., 1937; m. Richie Weir, July 1, 1922; children—Stanley W., Betty J. (Mrs. William Saffell), Richard E. Clerical and adminstrv. duties, Bur. of Ordnance, Dept. of Navy, 1916-21; various administrative and personnel assignments with depts. and burs. 1921-41; exec. officer in charge of all adminstrv. activities, Petroleum Adminstrn. for War, 1941-42; dir. of supply, Bur. of Reclamation, 1946-54, asst. commr., 1954-58; pvt. practice mgmt. cons., Hyattsville, Md., 1958-76. Served enlisted man, U.S. Navy, World War I; entered active duty, U.S. Air Force, 1942; served in New Guinea, Luzon, Ryukyus, and Western Pacific; disch. to Air Force Res., rank of col., Jan. 1946. Awarded Am. Campaign, World War II victory, Bronze Star (Oak Leaf cluster), Asiatic Pacific campaign (4 Bronze battle stars), medals; recipient distinguished service award Dept. of Interior, 1958. Mem. Phi Sigma Kappa, Quiet Birdman. Holder comml. pilots license. Address: Coral Springs, Fla. Died Dec. 23, 1976.

CROW, CHARLES ROHRER, JR., educator; b. Braddock, Pa., June 27, 1908; s. Charles Rohrer and Mary Donaldson (Wilson) C.; A.B., U. Pitts., 1930, M.A., 1931, Ph.D., 1948. Faculty, U. Pitts., 1933-73, Distinguished Service prof., 1970-73, emeritus, 1973. Served with AUS, 1942-45. Mem. Modern Lang. Assn. Am., Phi Beta Kappa, Delta Tau Delta. Episcopalian. Contbr. articles on Henry James and Shakespeare to profl. jours. Home: Pittsburgh, Pa. Died Feb. 10, 1976.

CROWDUS, WILLIAM W., lawyer; b. St. Louis, May 22, 1899; s. James Caldwell and Elizabeth Grice (Elliott) C.; LL.B., Washington U., 1922; m. Virginia Deane Garrett, Feb. 12, 1927; children—Susan Deane (Mrs. Forrest E. Heacock), William Warren II. Admitted to Mo. bar, 1922; pvt. practice William W. Crowdus, St. Louis; instr. med. jurisprudence Washington U. Sch. Medicine, 1937-62; interim U.S. atty. Eastern Dist. Mo., 1953. Vice pres. Mo. Inst. Adminstrn. Justice; pres. Jefferson Nat. Expansion Meml. Assn., 1949-59, 66-68, chmn. bd., 1968-74; mem. U.S. Terr. Expansion Meml. Commn. Pres. The Lighthouse for the Blind. Mem. Am. Bar Assn. (ho. dels. 1946-48), Am. Judicature Soc., St. Louis (pres. 1942-43), Mo. (gov. 1944-47) bar assns., Phi Delta Phi. Clubs: Noonday, University (St. Louis). Contbr. profl. jours. Home: St Louis, Mo. Died Jan. 24, 1974.

CROWE, JAMES ROGER, rice planter; b. Lanes Ferry, Tenn. Apr. 11, 1895; s. Bennett and Emma (Kirkpatrick) C.; student Highland Park Coll.; m. Hazel Price Davis, Jan. 10, 1917; 1 dau., Patricia (Mrs. Lewis M. Gravis). Pres., Roger Crowe Farms, Inc.; dir. 1st Nat. Bank, Ark. La. Gas Co.; rice planter, 1918-79. Chmn. Ark. Game and Fish Commn.; Stuttgart (Ark.) City Council, 1928-30, Sch. Bd., 1930-36, Ark. Bd. Finance, 1936-40. Trustee Ducks Unltd., Inc. of Am., 1948-79; chmn. bldg. com. Stuttgart Meml. Hosp. Mem. Stuttgart C. of C. Mason (Shriner, K.T.). Clubs: Little Rock Country, Little Rock; Stuttgart Country. Home: Stuttgart, Ark. Died June 7, 1979.

CROWE, PHILIP KINGSLAND, diplomat, conservationist; b. N.Y.C., Jan. 7, 1908; s. Earl and Kathleen McClellan (Higgins) C.; ed. U. Va., 1932; m. Irene Pettus, June 21, 1937; children—Phillippa, Irene, Mary; m. 2d, Suzanne Norregaard, Nov. 26, 1975; 1 dau., Clara. Reporter, N.Y. Evening Post, 1933; chief customers dept. Milmine Bodman, broker, N.Y.C., 1934-35; explorer, hunter big game, French Indo-China, 1935-37; dir. travel advt. Life mag., 1937-38; advt. staff Fortune mag., 1938-41, 44-48; spl. rep. ECA, China, 1948-49; ambassador to Ceylon, 1953-56; U.S. del. ECAFE Conf. UN, 1954; spl. asst. to sec. state, 1957-59; U.S. ambassador to Union of South Africa, 1959-61, Norway, Oslo, 1969-73, Denmark, Copenhagen, 1973-75. Leader, Wildlife Mission to Near East, 1963, S. Am., 1964, Far East, 1965, Middle East, 1966, Central Am., 1967, South Africa, 1968. Mem. bd. adv. Sch. Advanced Internat. Studies, Johns Hopkins. Trustee Fletcher sch. law and diplomacy Tufts U., Fgn. Service Ednl. Found.; bd. dirs. World Wildlife Fund, African Wildlife Leadership Found. Served lt. col. USAAF, 1941-44, chief intelligence OSS, CBI. Decorated Bronze Star (U.S.); Order of Yun-Hui (Republic of China); officer French Legion Honor; grand ofcl. Mil. Order Christ; Portugal, 1963; Grand Cross St. Olav (Norway). Fellow Royal Asiatic Soc., Royal Geog. Soc.; mem. Council Fgn. Relations, Soc. Colonial Wars, Huguenot Soc., St. Nicholas Soc., Soc. Cin., Ex-mems. Assn. Squadron A (N.Y. N.G.) Am. Com. for Internat. Wildlife Protection, Tobique Salmon Club, Atlantic Salmon Assn., Internat. Order St. Hubert. Clubs: Racquet and Tennis, Explorers, Brook, Anglers, Century Assn., Bonne and Crocket (N.Y.C.); Lokota; Round Table, Country (Woodstock, Vt.); Harvard Travellers (Boston); Hill (Ceylon); Dacor House, Metropolitan (Washington); Boodles,

Flyfishers, Whites (London); Rand (Johannesburg) South Africa; Chesapeake Bay Yacht (Easton, Md.); Norske Selskab, Royal Norwegian Yacht, Linge (Oslo); Tobique Salmon (Can.); Royal Shooting, Royal Danish Yacht (Copenhagen). Author: Sport is Where you Find it, 1953; Diversions of a Diplomat in Ceylon, 1957; Sporting Journeys, 1966; The Empty Ark, 1967; World Wildlife-the Last Stand, 1970; Out of the Mainstream, 1970. Address: Easton, Md. Died Oct. 16, 1976.

CROWTHER, BOSLEY, journalist; b. Lutherville, Md., July 13, 1905; s. F. Bosley (Leisenring) C.; student Woodberry Forest Sch.; B.A., Princeton, 1928; m. Florence Marks, Jan. 20, 1933; children—Bosley, John M., Jefferson H. Joined news staff N.Y. Times, 1928, as gen. reporter, rewrite man, served as asst. drama editor, 1932-37, asst. screen editor, 1937-40, screen critic and editor, 1940-68, critic emeritus, 1968; cons. Mem. N.Y. Film Critics (past chmn.). Contbr. articles on motion pictures to mags. Recipient Screen Dir. Award, 1953. Club: Century (N.Y.C.). Author: The Lions Share, 1957; Hollywood Rajah, 1960; The Great Films, 1967. Home: White Plains, N.Y. Died Mar. 7, 1981.

CROY, MAE BELLE SAVELL (MRS. HOMER CROY), writer; b. Molino, Fla., July 26, 1886; d. John Henry and Rhoda (Strickland) Savell; ed. pvt. schs.; m. Homer Croy, of Maryville, Mo., Feb. 7, 1915. Clubs: Pen and Brush, City. Author: 1000 Shorter Ways Around the House, 1916; 1000 Things A Mother Should Know, 1917; 1000 Hints on Flowers and Birds, 1917; 1000 Hints on Vegetable Gardening, 1917; A Red Letter Day (play); also magazine writer. Home: Forest Hills Gardens, L.I., N.Y.

CRUMMEY, JOHN D., corp. exec.; b. Chgo., Mar. 18, 1878; son David C. and Addie (Bean) C.; ed. Stanford Univ.; LL.D., Coll. of the Pacific, 1951; m. Vivan Gelatt, Mar. 26, 1901; (deceased); children—Beth C. (Mrs. Chinchen), Faith C. (Mrs. Paul L. Davies), D. Clifford, Marie C. (Mrs. R. F. Foster), J. Delbert; m. second, Caroline Hughes Harban, Jan. 2, 1952. Asso. FMC Corp., San Jose, Cal., and predecessor cos., from 1901, pres., dir., 1928-40, chmn. bd., 1940-56, hon. chmn., 1956-76, also dir., past pres., now hon. trustee U. of Pacific; bd. dirs., hon. pres. San Jose YMCA. Methodist (bd. publs. 1936-60, now hon. mem. bd.). Mason. Rotarian. Home: San Jose, Calif. Died Nov. 19, 1976.

CRUMP, JAMES IRVING, author, editor; b. Saugerties, N.Y., Dec. 7, 1887; s. William Russell and Emma F. (Peters) C.; ed. public and private schools, and at Erasmus Hall, Columbia University; m. Marguerite Duryea Whitney, Apr. 4, 1910; children—Margaret Whitney, James Irving. Asso. editor Edison Monthly, 1912-14; editor Boys' Life (Boy Scout mag.), 1918-23; mag. editor Pictorial Review, May 1923—Aug. 1924; editor of Boys' Life since 1935. Member Ulster County Society of N.Y., Omega Gamma Delta, Republican. Baptist. Clubs: Town Hall, Players. Author: Conscript 2989, 1918; Boys' Book of Firemen, 1919; Boys' Book of Policemen, 1920; Boys' Book of Mounted Police, 1921; Boys' Book of Railroads, 1922; Og, Son of Fire, 1922; Boys' Book of Forest Rangers, 1923; Boys' Book of Arctic Exploration, 1924; Og, Boy of Battle, 1925; Boys' Book of the U.S. Mails, 1926; Boys' Book of Airmen, 1927; Boys' Book of the Coast Guard, 1928; Mog, the Mound Builder, 1931; Boys' Book of Fisheries, 1932; "Making" the School Newspaper, 1933; Newsreel Hunters, 1933; (with Capt. C.D. Woodyatt), Creole Wench, 1933; also The Great War Series for Boys (5 vols.); Adventures in Birdland (5 vols.); Boy Scout Fire Fighters; Cloud Patrol Series (3 vols.); Boys' Book of Cowboys, 1934; Og, of the Cave People, 1935; Our Police, 1935; Our Airmen, 1936; Our G-men, 1937; Our Firemen, 1938; Our Airliners, 1940; Out of the Woods, 1941; Our U.S. Secret Service, 1942; Our U.S. Marines, 1943; Oil Hunters, 1947. Editor: Boys' Life Dog Stories, 1949; Boys' Life Adventure Stories, 1950; Boys' Life Scout Stories, 1952; Our Tanker Fleet, 1952; Our Army Engineers, 1953; The Birdsong Boys, 1955; Our State Police, 1955; Our Merchant Marine Academy-Kings Point, 1958. Contbr. fiction to mags., also radio dramatizations and original stories for motion pictures. Freedoms Found. award for article Ragged Rabble. Home: Oradell, N.J. Died July 3, 1979.

CRUMP, JOHN DAVID, wholesale drug exec.; b. West Point, Miss., Aug. 30, 1885; s. Stephen Alexander and Lelia (Cook) C.; student Emory U.; m. Jennie Riley, June 18, 1913; children—Joseph Riley, Helen Cook, Crump Cutler. State and co. tax collector, 1910-24; wholesale druggist J.B. Riley Drug Co., 1919-28, McKesson & Robbins, Inc., 1928-46, regional v.p. S.E. region since 1944; dir., chmn. trust com. First Nat. Bank & Trust Co., Macon, Ga.; dir. Macon Fed. Savs. & Loan Assn. Pres. bd. pub. edn. Bjbb Co., Ga. Episcopalian. Elk. Club: Rotary. Home: Macon, Ga.

CUBBISON, DONALD CAMERON, army officer; b. Harrisville, Pa., May 8, 1882; s. James Newton and Mary (Kerr) C.; B.S., U.S. Mil. Acad., 1904; Mounted Service Sch., Fort Riley, Kan., 1909-10; Army Sch. of the Line, 1920-21; General Staff Sch., 1921-22; Army War Coll., 1926-27; m. Lucile Abrams, Dec. 29, 1908; children—Donald Cameron, Rose Anne (Mrs. J. Arch Butts, Jr.), Gordon. Commd. 2d lt., U.S. Army, 1904, and promoted through the grades to brig. gen., 1938; served as capt. major, lt. col. and col. with 7th F.A., with A.E.F. on Western Front, France, 1917-19; comdg. 11th F.A. Brigade, 1939; comdt. Field Arty. Sch., Fort Sill, Okla., 1940-41; maj. gen. U.S. Army, Jan. 1941; comdg. First Div., Feb. 1941-June 1942; comdg. Field Arty. Replacement Center, Fort Bragg, N.C., 1942-46, retired. Decorated D.S.M. (U.S.); Officer Legion of Honor, Croix de Guerre with palm (France), Legion of Merit. Episcopalian. Club: Army and Navy Country (Washington, D.C.). Home: Carmel, Calif.

CUDDIHY, PAUL R., chmn., Funk & Wagnalls Co., until 1965. Served with USCG, World War II. Died Jan. 7, 1980.

CUETO, MANUEL RICHARD, ins. co. exec.; b. Bklyn., May 27, 1906; s. Maximo and Emilia (Garcia) C.; student New Utrecht Sch., Bklyn., 1920-24; m. Cathleen Annabelle Pennell, May 9, 1936; children—John Manuel, Anthony Richard. With N.Y. Life Ins. Co., N.Y.C., 1924-72, successively actuarial supr., asst. actuary, asso. actuary, actuary, 2d v.p. and actuary, 1944-62, v.p. charge electronic planning and devel., 1962-65, v.p. charge electronic operations and planning, 1965-72. Cons. electronic applications for regulations N.Y. Ins. Dept.; mem. Presdl. com. on mgmt. of computers in fed. govt., 1964-68; chmn. Industry Adv. Com. Automation. 1972-76. Fellow Soc. Actuaries; mem. Acad. Actuaries, Assn. Computing Machinery, Actuaries Club N.Y., Internat. Congress Actuaries. Contbr. articles in field. Home: Manhasset, N.Y. Died May 11, 1979; interred Hartsdale, N.Y.

CULBERTSON, HUGH EMMETT, lawyer; b. at Havana, Huron Co., O., Apr. 15, 1882; s. Elihu and Ida (Gregory) C.; grad. Milan (Ohio) High Sch.; studied law in offices of King & Ramsey, Sandusky, O.; LL.B., Ohio State U., 1905; m. Flora Nell Paul, of Milan, O., Mar. 17, 1906. Began practice at Sandusky, 1905, with Judge Grayson Mills; in same yr. became editor on staff of Laning Law Book Co., Norwalk, O.; law writer on staff of Lawyers' Coöperating Pub. Co., Rochester, N.Y., 1907-12; resumed practice, Loudonville, O., Jan. 1, 1912. Mayor of Milan, 1907-8 (resigned). Democrat. Presbyn. Odd Fellow. Author: Medical Men and the Law, 1913. Address: Loudonville, O.

CULBERTSON, JOHN GIFFEN, born in Knox, Pa., Sept. 3, 1883; s. Albert and Lavina (Moats) C.; Pa. State Coll., 1906; post-grad. work in mining engring., 1907; unmarried. Power plant constrn. work until 1910; pres. and mgr. Wichita Motors Co., Wichita Falls, Tex., 1910-22. Del. Rep. Nat. Conv., Chicago, 1920; Rep. candidate for gov. of Tex., 1920. Mem. Nat. Foreign Trade Council, Sigma Alpha Epsilon, etc.; fellow Am. Geog. Soc. Presbyn. Mason (32 deg., Shriner). Club: Dallas Athletic. Traveled in S. America, 1922-23, crossing continent alone from mouth of Amazon to Lima, Peru; extensive travel, Ecuador, 1925; in all countries of S. America, 1926, year of 1927 in Africa, visiting all colonies of the Guinea Coast and doing extensive big game hunting in French Cameroon and Congo.*

CULBERTSON, WALTER LEROY, petroleum co. exec.; b. Dederick, Mo., July 29, 1918; s. Alfred and Ethel Ida (Belong) C.; B.S. in Mech. Engring., Kans. State U., 1939; m. Wanda Marian Atkins, Sept. 30, 1940; children—Philip, Robert. With Phillips Petroleum Co., Bartlesville, Okla., from 1939, sr. v.p. corp. planning and budgeting. Mem. ASME, Nat. Soc. Profl. Engrs., Am. Inst. Chem. Engrs. Republican. Mem. Christian Ch. (Disciples of Christ). Club: Bartlesville Hillcrest Country. Home: Bartlesville, Okla. Died July 12, 1980.

CULHANE, FRANK JAMES, investment co. exec.; b. Chgo., Feb. 25, 1923; s. Frank O. and Lillian (Kearney) C.; B.S., U. Notre Dame, 1948, J.D., 1950; m. Mary Seng, Aug. 16, 1947; children—James, Michael, Cathy, Ann, Patricia. Admitted to Ill. bar, 1950; tax accountant, auditor Arthur Andersen & Co., Chgo., 1950-55; asst. treas. Formfit Co., Chgo., 1955-57, treas., 1957-63; pres. Formintern div. Genesco, Inc., Chgo., 1963-64, group v.p. Genesco, Inc., Nashville, 1964-67, mem. bd. gov., corp. dir. Genesco of Can., Conf. San Remo Treviso, Italy; v.p., treas. Hart, Schaffner & Marx, Chgo., 1967-71; sr. v.p. fin. and adminstrn. Ozite Corp., Libertyville, Ill., 1971-72; v.p., treas. GL Corp. and Refco Group, Chgo., 1973-77, also dir.; dir. Formfit Founds., Ltd., London, Eng., Formfit-France, S.A. (Paris), Formfit Pty. Ltd. Sydney, Australia, Rock River Savs. & Loan Assn., Rockford, Ill.; Treas., Village Park Forest Ill. 1954-57. Served as lt. (j.g.) USNR, 1944-46, to lt., 1951-52. Recipient Superior Achievement Recognition award Genesco, Inc., 1963. Mem. Chgo. Bar Assn., Internat. Trade Club Chgo. (sec. 1969, v.p. 1970). Clubs: Caymanas Golf (Jamaica, W.I.); Chicago Athletic Assn.; Michigan Shores (Wilmette, Ill.). Home: Winnetka, Ill. Died Nov. 1977.

CULLEN, STUART CHESTER, physician; b. Milton Junction, Wis., Jan. 31, 1909; s. Archibald H. and Myrtle E. (Killam) C.; A.B., U. Wis., 1931, M.D., 1933; m. Caroline Swannell, June 25, 1932; children—Carol Lynn, Bruce Frederick. Intern Mulnomah County Hosp, 1933-34; resident Bellevue Hosp., 1936-38; chmn. div. anesthesiology, prof. surgery State U. Iowa, 1938-58, mem. bd. control athletics, 1946-58; prof. anesthesia U. Calif. Med. Center at San Francisco, 1958-73, emeritus, 1974-79, chmn. dept. anesthesia, 1958-66, asso. dean Sch. Medicine, 1963-66, dean, 1966-70. Mem. med. mission to Austria sponsored by WHO and Unitarian Service Com., 1947, India, 1953; sr. instr., organizer internat. course anesthesiology, Copenhagan, WHO, 1950-52, 54, 58, 62; cons. WHO, Middle East, 1962. Mem. Belvedere City Council, 1974; mayor City of Belvedere, until 1979, bd. dirs. Bay Area Air Pollution Bd., 1976, Marin County Employment and Tng. Commn., 1974. Recipient Distinguished Service award Am. Soc. Anesthesiologists. Diplomate Am. Bd. Anesthesiology. Mem. AMA, San Franciso Med. Soc., Am. Soc. Anesthesiologists, Am. Soc. Pharmacology and Exptl. Therapeutics, Soc. Exptl. Biology and Medicine, N.Y. Acad. Medicine, Central Surg. Assn., Royal Coll. Surgeons London (hon. fellow faculty anesthetists), Osterreichische Gesellschaft fur Anesthesiologie, Nordisk Anestesiologisk Foresning, Alpha Omega Alpha. Author: Anesthesia in General Practice, 1946; (with E.G. Gross) Medical Emergencies, 1949; (with C.P. Larson) Essentials of Anesthetic Practice, 1974. Editor: Year Book of Anesthesia, 1961-69. Home: Belvedere, Calif. Died Aug. 11, 1979.

CULLEY, FENTON BAYARD, company dir.; b. Franklin, Va., Jan. 30, 1885; s. Harry Randolph and Nannie O. (Britt) C.; B.S., The Citadel, 1906; m. Emily Gale Britt, Dec. 22, 1909; children—Bayard J., Laurens S., Donnell R., John B., Charles deB., Nancy (Mrs. George Edward Waehler). Dir., mgr. Augusta Ry. & Electric Co. (Ga.), to 1953; pres. So. Ind. Gas & Electric Co., Evansville, Ind., to 1953, nor dir.; dir. Peoples Savs. Bank, Interstate Finance Co., and assos. Bd. trustees Evansville Coll. Mem. Evansville C. of C. (pres.). Mason (Shriner). Home: Evansville, Ind. *

CULLITY, BERNARD DENNIS, educator; b. Havre, Mont., Nov. 9, 1917; s. Eugene Dennis and Elizabeth (Dougherty) C.; B.Engring., McGill U., 1940; M.S., U. Minn., 1943; Sc.D., Mass. Inst. Tech., 1947; m. Elizabeth Kercheval, Jan. 31, 1953. Instr. metallurgy Mont. Sch. Mines, 1940-42, U. Minn., 1942-43; group leader Manhattan Project, Mass. Inst. Tech., 1943-45; postdoctoral fellow Ecole des Mines, Paris, France, 1947-48; sci. liaison officer Office Naval Research, Am. Embassy, London, England, 1948-49; mem. faculty U. Notre Dame, from 1950, prof. metallurgy, from 1959. Fellow Am. Soc. for Metals; mem. Am. Inst. Mining, Metall. and Petroleum Engrs., Inst. Metals, Am. Crystallographic Assn., Sigma Xi. Author: Elements of X-Ray Diffraction, 1956; Introduction to Magnetic Materials, 1972. Home: South Bend, Ind. Died Mar. 26, 1978; buried Cedar Grove Cemetery, Notre Dame, Ind.

CUMMIN, GAYLORD CHURCH, municipal finance specialist; b. Dayton, O., Oct. 9, 1882; s. Robert Irvin and Ellen Pearson (Church) C.; grad. Steele High Sch., Dayton, 1900; C.E., Cornell U., 1904; m. Hazel Edith Carr, of Dayton, May 1, 1912; children—Robert Irvin, Edith, Elizabeth Carver. Ry. and other civil engring. work until 1912, city engr., Dayton, O., 1912-13, 1914-15; asst. engr. Miami Conservancy Dist., 1913-14; city manager, Jackson, Mich., 1915-17, Grand Rapids, 1917-18; asst. to pres. Kelsey, Brewer & Co., Grand Rapids, 1918-19; consultant with Inst. for Pub. Service, N.Y. City, 1919-23; civic consultant; organizer Municipal Securities Service; municipal credit specialist, Reynolds & Co.; consultant to various taxpayers assns.; mem. consulting staff Nat. Industrial Conf. Bd. Author of A Critical Analysis of State Debts and articles on municipal finance in American City, Nat. Municipal Rev., Savings Bank Jour., Barron's Weekly, etc. Episcopalian. Home: Greenwich, Conn.

CUMMING, CHARLES GORDON, clergyman, educator; b. Westville, N.S., Can., Apr. 21, 1885; s. Rev. Robert (D.D.) and Corinna (Grant) C.; B.A., Dalhousie Coll., 1905; U. of Chicago, 1907-8; B.D., Union Theol. Sem., 1911; studied in Germany, 1911-13; Ph.D., Columbia, 1919; m. Minnie Lenore Smith, of Sydney, N.S., Jan. 12, 1915. Teacher Presbyn. Theol. Coll., Trinidad, B.W.I., 1905-7; pastor Trinidad, 1913-16; ordained ministry Can. Presbyn. Ch., 1915; instr. O.T. Union Theol. Sem., 1916-19; prof. O.T. lang. and lit., Bangor Theol. Sem., 1920—. Author: Assyrian and Hebrew Hymns of Praise, 1921. Home: Bangor, Me.

CUNEO, GILBERT ANTHONY, lawyer; b. St. Marys, Pa., June 29, 1913; s. George L. and Cunigunda (Jaeger) C.; A.B., St. Vincent Coll., Latrobe, Pa., 1934, LL.D. (hon.), 1974; LL.B., Harvard, 1937; m. Mary Rita Garrigan, Nov. 18, 1944; 1 dau., Mary Kathleen. Admitted to N.Y. bar, 1938, D.C. bar, 1953, U.S. Supreme Ct. bar, 1947; practiced in N.Y.C., 1937-42, 46; mem. Armed Services Bd. Contract Appeals, Washington, 1946-58; mem. firm Sellers, Conner & Cuneo, Washington, 1958-78. Served with AUS, 1942-46. Mem. Am. Bar Assn. (chmn. pub. contracts div., adminstrv. law sect. 1962-64, chmn. sect. public contract law 1968-69), D.C. Bar Assn., Fed. Bar Assn., N.Y. County Lawyers Assn., Am. Judicature Soc. Roman Catholic. K.C. Clubs: Cosmos, Columbia Country, Metropolitan, Nat. Lawyers, University (Washington). Author: Government Contracts Handbook, 1962. Contbr. articles to profl. jours.; lectr. on govt. contracts. Home: Sumner, Md. Died Apr. 12, 1978; buried Gate of Heaven Cemetery, Washington, D.C.

CUNEO, JOHN F., printer and binder; b. Chgo., Dec. 24, 1885; s. Frank and Amelia (Gondolfo) C.; ed. Chicago Latin Sch.; grad. Univ. Sch., Chgo.; student Yale, 1904-06; m. Julia Reed Shepherd, June 24, 1930; children—John F., Jr., Consuela. Became pres. of John F. Cuneo Co., 1907; pres. The Cuneo Press, Inc., of Chgo., N.Y.C., Kokomo, Ind., Phila., Milw., Boston, 1919-77; former chmn. exec. com. Nat. Tea Co.; former dir. Continental Ill. Nat. Bank, Chgo. Served as asso. chief Poster Div., Information and Ednl. Service, Dept. Labor, Washington, World War I; mem. Nat. War Labor Bd., World War II. Decorated Knight Equestrian Order Holy Sepulchre Jerusalem, Knight St. Sylvester of Gt. Cross with Grand Cross, Knight of Malta. Roman Catholic. Clubs: The Cloud Club, Yale Club, Recess Club, Bankers (New York); Chicago Athletic Assn., Chicago Golf, The Tavern, Racquet (Chicago); Knollwood (Lake Forest). Home: Libertyville, Ill. Died Apr. 30, 1977.

CUNNINGHAM, BESS VIRGINIA, prof.; b. Bethesda, O., Mar. 15, 1882; d. William Work and Virginia (Gorby) C.; B.S., U. of Toledo, O., 1917; A.M., O. State U., 1921; Ph.D., Columbia, 1923; unmarried. Teacher in pub. schs., Toledo, O., 1903-17; supervisor kindergarten dept., State Teachers Coll., San Francisco, Calif., 1917-19; dir. kindergarten dept., State Teachers Coll., Greeley, Colo., 1919-20; research and teaching asst. teachers coll., Columbia U., 1921-22, Grace Dodge fellow, 1922-23, exec. sec. Child Development Inst., 1923-24, asst. prof. edn. and supervisor of ednl. clinic, 1924-26, asso. prof. edn., teachers coll., 1926-34; asso. prof. edn. U. of Toledo, O., 1936-38, prof. edn. since 1938. Fellow Am. Psychol. Assn., A.A.A.S.; mem. Alpha Chi Omega, Kappa Delta Pi, Delta Kappa Gamma. Republican. Author: Family Behavior (Saunders, 1936-awarded Parents Magazine Medal, 1937); Psychology for Nurses, 1946; Pintner-Cunningham Primary Test (with R. Pintner), 1923. Home: Toledo.

CUNNINGHAM, CHARLES CREHORE, mus. ofcl., found. exec.; b. Mamaroneck, N.Y., Mar. 7, 1910; s. Stanley and Esther Lowell (Burnett) C.; A.B., Harvard U., 1932; B.A. diploma Courtauld Inst., London (Eng.) U., 1933; Arts D. (hon.), U. Hartford, 1959; L.H.D. (hon.), DePaul U., 1970; m. Eleanor Lamont, June 27, 1932 (dec. May 1961); children—Charles Crehore, Priscilla, Thomas Lamont, James Stanley; m. 2d, Elinor Gregory, June 19, 1962 (dec. Dec. 1977). Asst. curator paintings Mus. Fine Arts, Boston, 1934-41; dir. Wadsworth Atheneum, Hartford, Conn., 1946-66; dir. Art Inst. Chgo., 1966-72; chief curator Sterling and Francine Clark Art Inst., Williamstown, Mass., 1972-77; pres. Internat. Council Museums Found., 1977-79; lectr. Williams Coll. grad. program in the fine arts. Mem. vis. com. Smith Coll., Williams Coll.; 1st chmn. Conn. Commn. Arts, 1964-66; hon. trustee Wadsworth Atheneum, Hartford; trustee Berkshire Art Assn. Served as lt. comdr. USNR, World War II. Decorated Bronze Star, Commendation Ribbon for combat duty aboard aircraft carriers; Order of Merit, Republic of Italy; Benjamin Franklin fellow Royal Soc. Arts, London. Mem. Assn. Art Mus. Dirs. (hon.; pres. 1958), Internat. Council Museums (chmn. U.S. nat. com. 1970-72), AIA (hon.), Am. Soc. Interior Designers (hon.), Archeol. Inst. Am., Am. Fedn. Arts (trustee), Coll. Art Assn., Internat. Inst. Conservation of Works of Art, Am. Assn. Museums. Republican. Episcopalian. Clubs: Century Assn. (N.Y.C.); Harvard (N.Y.C.); Taconic Golf, Williamstown. Author: Modern French Painting and Drawing in Art Institute of Chicago, Japanese edit., 1970; Jongkind and the Pre-Impressionists: Painters of the Ecole Saint-Simeon, 1978; co-author: Rembrandt After 300 Years, 1969; editor: Art in New England, 1939; The Elegant Academics, 1974; contbr. Art in Am., Art News, Art Quar. Home: Williamstown, Mass. Died June 17, 1979.

CUNNINGHAM, DAVID F., bishop; b. Walkerville, Mont., Dec. 3, 1900; ed. St. Michael's Coll., Toronto, Ont., Can., St. Bernard's Sem., Rochester, N.Y., also Cath. U. Am. Ordained priest Roman Cath. Ch., 1926; titular bishop Lampsacus and auxiliary of Syracuse, 1950-70, bishop of Syracuse, 1970-79. Address: Syracuse, N.Y. Died Feb. 22, 1979.

CUNNINGHAM, JAMES HUTCHINGS, army officer; b. Mass., June 15, 1886; s. Charles E. and Marilla (Griffin) C.; B.S., U.S. Mil. Acad., 1908; m. Ann Gifford Cunningham; 1 son, Lt. Col. James H., Jr. (air corps; killed in airplane accident). Commd. 2d lt. coast arty., U.S. Army, 1908, advanced through grades to brig. gen. 1940; comdg. harbor defenses, Puget Sound, since 1940.

CUNNINGHAM, JESSE, librarian; b. Lebanon, Ind., May 24, 1882; s. William Alexander and Mary Catherine (Sieks) C.; student Ind. U., 1901-05; A.B., U. of Neb., 1906; L.S.B., N.Y. State Library Sch., 1910; m. Else Miller, June 1912; m. 2d, Grace Norwood, June 1919; children—Jane (Mrs. John Dancy McDowell), June (Mrs. William R. Crawford), Virginia (Mrs. Oscar Chapleau). Asst., Ind. U. Library, 1901-05; reference asst., U. of Neb. Library, 1905-06; law librarian, U. of Neb., 1906-07; asst., N.Y. State Law Library, 1908-11; asst. and municipal reference librarian, St. Louis Pub. Library, 1911-12; librarian, U. of Mo. Sch. of Mines Library, 1912-16; librarian, Pub. Library, St. Joseph, Mo., 1916-25; librarian Camp Grant, Rockford, Ill., 1918; librarian, Cossitt (Pub.) Library, Memphis, Tenn., since 1925. Dir. and sec. Memphis Open Air Theatre Assn.; dir. and sec.-treas. National Civic Operetta Association, dir. and sec. Memphis Symphony Society, Mem. A.L.A. since 1909; Mo. Library Assn., 1912-16 (sec.-treas., pres., on exec. board 1915-16), Tenn. Library Assn. since 1925 (pres. 1926-29), Southeastern Library Assn. since 1925, Delta Tau Delta. Democrat. Club: Hatchie Coon Hunting and Fishing (dir. and sec. treas.). Home: Memphis.

CUNNINGHAM, MAURICE PATRICK, educator; b. Nicholson, Pa., Aug. 27, 1913; s. James Joseph and Anna (Finan) C.; A.B., U. Calif. at Berkeley, 1938, Ph.D., 1941; m. Regina Marie Conley, June 17, 1941; children—Ann Margaret, Patrick Myles. Instr. classics Stanford, 1945-46, Smith Coll., 1946-47, Yale, 1947-49; mem. faculty Lawrence U., Appleton, Wis., 1949-78, prof., 1960-78, Hiram A. Jones prof. classics, 1960-78; vis. prof. U. Mich., 1959-60, 67, U. Wis. at Madison, 1972, Trinity Coll., Hartford, Conn., summers 1963, 64. Am. rep. Thesaurus Linguae Latinae, Munich, Germany, 1967-72. Mem. Am. Philol. Assn., Am. Inst. Archeology, Classical Assn. Middle West and South, Classical Assn., Phi Beta Kappa. Mem. editorial bd. Classical Philology, 1970-78. Contbr. articles to profl. jours. Home: Appleton, Wis. Died Feb. 25, 1978; buried St. Mary's Cemetery, Appleton.

CUNNINGHAM, PAUL JAMES, news corr.; b. New Rochelle, N.Y., Aug. 13, 1917; s. Paul James and Mary Ada (Morris) C.; B.A. in Journalism, U. Minn., 1946; m. Maaike A. van Haren; children—Paul James, McAllister M., Meredith M., Marieka, Ian. Reporter, Mpls. Star, 1946-48, KSTP-TV, 1948-49; corr. NBC, N.Y.C., from 1949, producer Today Show and various documentaries, also corr., London, Eng., network news corr., N.Y.C. Served with USAAF, 1941-45. Recipient Albert Laskar award for med. journalism. Democrat. Roman Catholic. Home: New Canaan, Conn. Died Jan. 12, 1981; buried Lakeview Cemetery, New Canaan.

CUNNINGHAM, WILLIAM PILPEL, lawyer, educator; b. Boston, Oct. 11, 1922; s. William Hayes and Mildred G. (Pilpel) C.; grad. Phillips Exeter Acad., 1940; A.B., Harvard, 1944, LL.B., 1948; m. Dorothy A. Havey, Dec. 9, 1950; children—Steven, Janet. Admitted to Mass. bar, 1948, Md. bar, 1954; asso. firm Brown, Field & McCarthy, Boston, 1948-50, Haussermann, Davison and Shattuck, Boston, 1951-53; teaching fellow Harvard Law Sch., 1953-54; mem. faculty U. Md. Sch. Law, Balt., 1954-76, prof. law, 1960-76, dean, 1962-75. Mem. Md. Bd. Commrs. on Uniform Laws, from 1965; mem. Com. To Revise Md. Code, 1970-76; chmn. Bd. of Ethics, Balt. City, 1967—. Served with USAAF, 1943-45. Mem. Am., Md. (exec. dir., dir. continuing legal edn. 1960-62) bar assns. Home: Lutherville, Md. Died Oct. 20, 1976.

CURME, GEORGE OLIVER, JR., indsl. research chemist; b. Mount Vernon, Iowa, Dec. 24, 1888; s. George Oliver and Caroline Chenoweth (Smith) C.; B.S., Northwestern U., 1909, D.Sc. (hon.), 1933; postgrad. Harvard, 1909-10; Ph.D., U. Chgo., 1913, D.Sc. (hon.), 1954; student U. Berlin, 1913-14; m. Lillian Hale, June 29, 1916; children—Katharine Hale (Mrs. Randolph C. Neely), George Oliver III, Mary Ellen (Mrs. Charles P. Cooper, Jr.), Florence Louise (Mrs. Richard C. Horton), John Henry. Indsl. research chemist Mellon Inst., 1914, conducting research on organic synthesis based on natural hydrocarbons, on behalf of cos. which later became units of Union Carbide and Carbon Corp.; became chief chemist, Carbide and Carbon Chems. Corp., Inc. to commercialize results of preceding research, with plants near Charleston, W.Va., 1920, v.p. and dir. research, 1929-44, v.p., 1944-51; v.p. Union Carbide and Carbon Research Lab., Inc., 1938-52, chmn. bd., 1952-54; v.p., dir. Carbide and Carbon Chems. Ltd., 1944-55; v.p. research Union Carbide Corp. (formerly Union Carbide & Carbon Corp.), 1951-55, dir., 1952-61. Chandler medalist, 1933, Perkin medalist, 1935, Elliott Cresson medalist, 1936, Willard Gibbs medalist, 1944; recipient Nat. Modern Pioneer award, 1940. Mem. Am. Chem. Soc., Am. Inst. Chem. Engrs., Soc. Chem. Industry, AAAS, Nat., N.Y. acads. sci., Phi Beta Kappa, Sigma Xi, Sigma Alpha Epsilon, Phi Lambda Upsilon. Clubs: Chemists, University (N.Y.). Home: Charlottesville, Va. Died July 28, 1976; buried Martha's Vineyard, Mass.

CURRAN, JEAN ALONZO, physician; b. Ironwood, Mich., Jan. 12, 1893; s. Charles William and Emma Florence (Conley) C.; A.B., Carleton Coll., Northfield, Minn., 1916, LL.D., 1951; M.D., Harvard, 1921; m. Frances Rose, Aug. 5, 1923; children—Jean Alonzo, William Sheldon, Robert Theodore. Intern, Brooklyn Hosp., 1921-23; med. missionary Am. Bd. Mission Hosp., Fenchow, Shansi and Tungchow, Chili, China, 1923-30; instr. medicine N.Y. U. Coll. of Medicine, Cornell Med. Coll., 1931-33; exec. N.Y. Com. on Study Hosp. Internships and Residencies, 1934-37; dean L.I. Coll. Medicine, 1937-42, pres., 1942-51; dean State U. of N.Y. Coll. Medicine at N.Y.C., 1951-54, prof. history medicine, 1954-63, emeritus, 1963-77; expert cons. Office Surgeon Gen., Dept. Army, 1948-67; cons. hist. research Harvard Sch. Pub. Health; cons. WHO, 1955-56; survey med. edn. Philippines; cons. Yonsei U. Coll. Medicine and Severance Hosp., Seoul, Korea, 1963. Trustee, sr. cons. Bingham Assos. Fund of Mass., 1957-77, Yonsei U. Coll. Medicine-China Med. Bd. N.Y., 1961, 63; trustee N.E. Center Hosp., 1948-77; pres. Cambridge Mental Health Assn., 1970-72; chmn. Joseph Garland Meml. Fund of Boston Med. Library, 1973-77. Diplomate Am. Bd. Internal Medicine. Fellow Am. Coll. Physicians; mem. A.M.A., N.Y. Acad. Medicine, Alpha Omega Alpha. Clubs: Harvard (Boston). Author works including: Founders of Harvard School Public Health, with Biographical Notes, 1909-1946, 1970. Home: Cambridge, Mass. Died Jan. 16, 1977.

CURRENS, FREDERICK HAWLEY, coll. dean, author; b. Carthage, Ill., Dec. 25, 1882; s. James Nathaniel and Josephine (Hawley) C.; A.B., Coe Coll., Cedar Rapids, Ia., 1904, A.M., 1907; Ph.D., U. of Neb., 1921; m. Winona Peregrine, Aug. 1, 1905; children—Martha (Mrs. LaVerne King), James (M.D.), Ruth (Mrs. William B. Waterman), Mary Alice (dec.). Prin. Corning (Ia.) Acad., 1904-08; prof. of chemistry, Lenox (Ia.) Coll., 1908-09, Bellevue Coll., Neb., 1909-10; prof. of chemistry, U. of Omaha, 1910-12; instr. in chemistry, U. of Neb., 1912-13; head of chemistry and physics dept., Western Ill. State Teachers Coll., Macomb, since 1913, dean of coll. since 1923, of grad. sch. since 1950, chmn. of grad. com. since 1942. Mem. Ill. Tchrs. Coll. Faculties (chmn. executive committee 1932), Illinois Academy of Science, Pi Gamma Mu, Sigma Zeta, Phi Delta Kappa. Presbyterian. Mason. Club: Kiwanis of Macomb (pres. 1931; dist. chmn. underprivileged child committee, Kiwanis Internat., 1931). Author: Brief Chemistry Text on Qualitative Analysis, 1924; Universal Laboratory Manual in Elementary Chemistry, 1924, Joint author General Chemistry-Miner Series, 1920, and General Chemistry for College Students, 1939. Home: Macomb, Ill.

CURRIE, GEORGE WASHINGTON, coll. prof.; b. Jasonville, Ind., Mar. 22, 1885; s. Lawrence and Martha (Mitten) C.; A.B., Indiana U., 1908, A.M., 1911, Ph.D., 1924; studied U. of Chicago, 1911-15; m. Rose Blanche Bryan, Dec. 28, 1918; children—Robert Bryan, Julian Edward, Margaret Jeanne, Donald Beck, Richard Allen. Principal schs., Cynthiana, Ind., 1908-09; supt. schs., Forest, Ind., 1909-11; instr. Latin and Greek, Hedding Coll., Abingdon, Ill., 1911-12, U. of Wyo., 1913-15; acting prof. Latin, Hendrix Coll., Conway, Ark., 1918-19; prof. Latin and Greek, Birmingham Southern Coll., 1920-39; prof. Latin and Greek, Millsaps Coll. since 1939; summer instr. Teachers Coll., Denton, Tex., 1929, 30, Bowling Green, Ky., 1931, 32; instr. Latin, Indiana Univ., summer, 1935. Mem. Classical Assn. Middle West and South, Am. Classical League; hon. mem. Eta Sigma Phi, Pi Gamma Mu, Phi Beta Kappa, Theta Chi. Democrat. Methodist. Author: (brochure) The Military Discipline of the Romans from the Founding of the City to the Fall of the Republic, 1928; (brochure) A Bachelor's Apology (verse), 1929; Contemporary American Poets (edited by Horace C. Baker), 1930. Editor: "Nuntius," official mag. of Eta Sigma Phi, 1937-39. Sculptor of Hendrix Coll. World War Memorial, also plaques for various colleges and for Classical League. Home: Jackson, Miss.

CURRIE, GILBERT ARCHIBALD, congressman; b. Midland Co., Mich., Sept. 19, 1882; s. Dougald and Flora C.; LL.B., U. of Mich., 1905; m. Charlotte B. Chapman, of Midland, Mich., Oct. 3, 1907. Mem. Mich. Ho. of Rep., 1909-14 (speaker 1913-14); mem. 65th and 66th Congresses (1917-21), 10th Mich. Dist.; Republican. Home: Midland, Mich. *

CURRIE, JAMES NIMROD, chemist; b. Jasonville, Ind., Oct. 21, 1883; s. Lawrence and Martha (Mitten) C.; A.B., Ind. U., 1908, M.A., 1909, hon. LL.D., 1931; Ph.D., U. of Wis., 1912; m. Martha Bailey, Apr. 12, 1919; children—Ellen Louise, John Bailey. Instr. chemistry, Ind. U., 1908-09, U. of Ore., 1909-10, U. of Wis., 1910-12; chem. research, dairy div., U.S. Dept. Agr., 1912-17; industrial research in biol. chemistry since 1917; now with Chas. Pfizer & Co., Inc., Brooklyn. Fellow A.A.A.S.; mem. Am. Chem. Soc., Soc. Am. Bacteriologists. Sigma Xi. Methodist. Home: Brooklyn.

CURRIE, WILLIAM MARK, manufacturing exec.; b. Port Perry, Ont., Can., Jan. 1883; s. William M. and Christina V. (McGill) C.; engring. student Toronto U.; m. Olive K. Hodgins, 1905; children—William G., Katharine C. (Labatt), John M. Successively engr. Westinghouse Electric Corp., Pitts.; engr. Internat.

Harvester Co., Hamilton; prodn. engr. Steel Co. of Can.; v.p., gen. mgr. Burlington Steel Co.; pres. Currie Products, Ltd., since 1920; dir. Nat. Gypsum Co. (U.S.), Dingwal Shipping Co., Ltd. Home: Hamilton, Ont. Can.

CURTIN, FRANK DANIEL, educator; b. Crafton, Pa., Nov. 10, 1905; s. Daniel Francis and Clara (Schlessman) C.; B.A., U. Pitts., 1927, M.A., 1929; Ph.D., U. Chgo., 1939; m. Mary McKenna, Sept. 16, 1941; children—Daniel, Jeremy, Hugh, Elizabeth. Instr. English, U. Pitts., 1929-38; instr. English, Cornell U., 1938-42; asst. prof. English, St. Lawrence U., Canton, N.Y., 1942-45, asso. prof., 1945-47, prof., 1948-71, prof. emeritus, 1971-78, chmn. dept., 1948-71; asso. prof. English, Washington and Jefferson Coll., 1947-48. Ford fellow, 1953-54; Ford Humanities grantee, 1970. Mem. AAUP, MLA, Omicron Delta Kappa. Contbr. books, articles profl. jours. Home: Glenshaw, Pa. Died Dec. 28, 1978; buried Pitts.

CURTIS, CHARLES EDGAR, ins. exec.; b. Wadsworth, Ohio, Sept. 18, 1900; s. Charles A. and Flora (Loomis) C.; A.B., U. Mich., 1922; LL.B., Western Res. U., 1926; m. Elizabeth Ames, Dec. 21, 1929; children—Nancy (Mrs. Charles Deering Stocking), Elizabeth Ann (Mrs. David Cohn). Admitted to Ohio bar, 1926; assistant general counsel Ohio Farmers Insurance Company, Ohio Farmers Indemnity Co., LeRoy, O., 1931-39, gen. counsel, 1939-57, exec. v.p., 1956-57, pres. from 1957, dir.; chmn. Citizens Bank, Wadsworth; director, mem. executive com. Underwriters Adjusting Company, Chicago; dir. Underwriters Salvage Co. Mem. committee on laws National Board Fire Underwriters, N.Y.C. Mem. Am., Ohio (chmn. ins. sect. 1940) bar assns., Order of Coif, Beta Theta Pi. Mason. Home: Westfield Center, Ohio. Died Oct. 5, 1976; interred in Wadsworth.

CURTIS, EDWARD GILLMAN, lawyer; b. Somerville, Mass., Dec. 11, 1886; s. Edward Bissell and Mary Augusta (Colson) C.; student Worcester Acad., 1903-05; A.B., Harvard, 1909, LL.B., 1912; m. Mary Helen Seelbach, Oct. 28, 1920; children—Mary Gilman (Mrs. John R. Brooks), Anne Raquet (Mrs. J. Wayne Fredericks), Eleanor Colson (Mrs. Jan S. F. van Hoogstraten), Edward Morey. Admitted to Massachusetts bar, 1912, New York bar, 1922; law practice, Boston, 1912-17; apptd. spl. asst. to Atty. Gen. U.S., in charge def. of U.S. in patent litigation, 1919-21; pvt. practice law, specializing in patents, N.Y. City, since 1922; sr. mem. Curtis, Morris & Safford since 1948. Mem. Bronxville (N.Y.) Sch. Bd., 1940-43. Trustee Worcester (Mass.) Acad., 1945-48. Served as 1st lt. Ordnance, U.S. Army, Europe and U.S., 1917-19; maj. to lt. col. Res. Corps. Mem. Am. Legion (post comdr. 1931), Am. Bar Assn., New Eng. Soc., Sigma Alpha Epsilon. Mason (K.T.). Clubs: Union League, Harvard (N.Y. City); Am. Yacht (Rye, N.Y.). Home: Bronxville, N.Y.

CURTIS, HARRY ALFRED, chemical engr.; b. Sedalia, Colo., Feb. 16, 1884; s. Frederick A. and Lydia A. (Cramer) C.; grad. Douglas Co. High Sch., Castle Rock, 1904; B.S., U. of Colo., 1908, M.A., 1910, Sc.D., 1930; Ph.D., U. of Wis., 1914, Sc.D., 1937; m. Irene Hall, May 14, 1911; children—Jeanne Carol, Patricia May. Instr., later prof. chemistry, U. of Colo., 1908-17; prof. chemistry, Northwestern U., 1919-20; chief chemist, later plant supt. Internat. Coal Producing Corpn., Irvington, N.J., 1920-21; gen. mgr. Clinchfield Carbocoal Corpn., South Clinchfield, Va., 1921-23; chief of nitrogen survey, U.S. Dept. Commerce, 1923-24; prof. chem. engring., 1923-30, and chmn. Dept. of Chem. Engring., 1929-30, Yale U.; chmn. div. of chemistry and chem. technology, Nat. Research Council, 1930-31; dir. of research for Vacuum Oil Co., 1931-33; became chief chem. engr., Tenn. Valley Authority, 1933. Mem. President Coolidge's Muscle Shoals Commn. Mem. Colo. N.G., 1915-17; Mexican border service 3 mos., 1916; capt. ordnance, U.S.A., World War, assigned to nitrate div. of ordnance and engaged in chem. engring. Mem. Am. Inst. Chem. Engrs. (v.p.), Am. Chem. Soc., A.A.A.S., Sigma Nu, Alpha Chi Sigma. Clubs:Chemists' (New York); Cosmos (Washington, D.C.).*

CURTIS, HUGH EVERETT, JR., journalist, educator; b. Rock Island, Ill., June 19, 1907; s. Hugh Everett and Mary Augusta (Dart) C.; B.A., Grinnell Coll., 1931; m. Martha Page Hippee, Sept. 26, 1934; children—Hugh Everett III, Sara Easton. Asst. circulation mgr. Better Homes and Gardens mag., 1931-34; editorial asst. Successful Farming mag., 1934-35, asso. editor charge farm structures and housing, 1935-43, mng. editor charge structures and electricity, 1943-50; mng. editor Better Homes and Gardens mag., 1950-52; editor, 1952-60; editorial cons., dir. services div. Webb Pub. Co., St. Paul, 1960-62; prof., dean Sch. Journalism, Drake U., Des Moines, 1962-69, prof. mag. journalism, 1969-73, dean and prof. emeritus, 1973-79, Drake lectr. Named Hon. Iowa Farmer, Future Farmers of Am., 1937. Mem. Indsl. Editors, Future Farmers Am., Assn. for Edn. in Journalism, Phi Beta Kappa, Kappa Tau Alpha, Sigma Delta Chi, Omicron Delta Kappa. Episcopalian. Clubs: Embassy, Pow Wow, Advertising (Des Moines). Home: Des Moines, Iowa. Died Oct. 13, 1979.

CURTIS, LEWIS PERRY, historian, educator; b. Southport, Conn., Nov. 3, 1900; s. Roderick Perry and Louisa (Wells) C.; B.A., Yale, 1923, Ph.D., 1926; m. Jeanet Ellinwood Sullivan, Dec. 26, 1929; children—Lewis Perry, Nancy Ellinwood (Mrs. Michael D. Padnos). Mem. faculty Yale, 1927-69, Colgate prof. history, 1967-69. Traveling fellow Am. Council Learned Socs., 1931-32; Guggenheim fellow, 1941-42. Mem. Am. Hist. Assn. Editor: Letters of Laurence Sterne, 1935, 1965; Gibbon's Paradise Lost in the Age of Johnson, 1949; Intellectual Aristocracy in Eighteenth-Century England in Curtis and H.W. Liebert, Esto Perpetua, 1963; Chichester Towers, 1966; Anglican Moods of the Eighteenth Century, 1966. Home: New Haven, Conn. Died Apr. 8, 1976.

CURTISS, JOHN HAMILTON, mathematician; b. Evanston, Ill., Dec. 23, 1909; s. David Raymond and Sigrid Sofia (Eckman) C.; A.B., Northwestern U., 1930; S.M., State U. Ia., 1931; Ph.D., Harvard, 1935. Instr. John Hopkins, 1935-36; instr. Cornell U., 1936-39, asst. prof., 1939-43; asst. to dir. Nat. Bur. Standards, 1946-47, chief Applied Math. Labs., 1947-53; vis. lectr. Harvard, 1953; sr. scientist, adj. prof. math. Inst. Math. Sci., N.Y.C., 1953-54; exec. dir. Am. Math. Soc., 1954-59; prof. math. U. Miami (Fla.), 1959-75, chmn. dept., 1959-61. Served to lt. comdr. USNR, 1943-46. Recipient medal of award Dep. Commerce. Fellow A.A.A.S., Inst. Math. Statistics (past v.p.), Am. Statis. Assn.; mem. Am. Math. Soc., Phi Beta Kappa, Sigma Xi. Author: Introduction to Functions of a Complex Variable, 1977. Founder, editor Nat. Bur. Standards Applied Math. Series, 1946-53; editor various Nat. Bur. Standards, Am. Math. Soc. symposia vols. Contbr. numerous articles to tech. publs. Home: Miami, Fla. Died Oct. 13, 1977.

CURTS, MAURICE EDWIN, naval officer; b. Flint, Mich., Mar. 25, 1898; s. Edwin James and Minnie Elwood (Quirk) C.; B.S., U.S. Naval Acad., 1919; S.M. in Elec. Engring., Harvard, 1928; m. Nina Irvine, Aug. 16, 1919 (dec. Nov. 1965); children—Robert, Daniel; m. 2d, Fayette Purcell Hobbs, Jan. 1967 (dec. Nov. 1970); m. 3d, Martha Ferneding. Commd. ensign U.S. Navy, 1919, advanced through grades to adm., 1955; with Naval Research Lab., 1936-38, comdr. U.S.S. Case, 1938-39; communication officer U.S. Fleet, 1939-44; comdr. U.S.S. Columbia, 1944-45; chief of staff 1st Carrier Task Force, Pacific Fleet, 1945; comdr. Cruiser Div., 1946; chief Navy Gen. Plans, 1947-48; comdr. operational devel., 1949-50; asst. chief of Naval operations, 1951-53; comdr. cruisers, destroyers, Pacific, 1953-55; dep. comdr. in chief Pacific Fleet, 1955-57, comdr. in chief, 1958; comdr. Western Sea Frontier, comdr. Pacific Res. Fleet, 1958-60; dir. telecommunications policy Dept. Def., Washington, 1960-65; ret., 1965. Decorated Navy Cross, Silver Star, Bronze Star, Purple Heart; recipient Commendation for Radar Devel. Home: Rancho Santa Fe, Calif. Died Feb. 16, 1976; buried Arlington Nat. Cemetery.

CURTS, PAUL HOLROYD, educator; born DeKalb, Ill., July 3, 1884; s. John Lawrence and Clara Adele (Holroyd) C.; B.A., Yale, 1905, M.A., 1907, Ph.D., 1909; grad. study, U. of Berlin, 1911-12; M.A. adeundem, Wesleyan U., 1920; m. Marian Huntting Bradley, June 26, 1915; children—Holroyd Bradley, Marjorie Huntting. Instr. in German, Yale, 1907-08; instr. in German, Wesleyan U., 1909-11, asso. prof., 1912-20, professor, 1920-52, Marcus L. Taft professor, 1935-52, professor emeritus since 1952, acting registrar, 1925-26; professor of German, Institute for Ausländer, U. of Berlin, July-August, 1931, 34, 36; lecturer in German, Conn. College for Women, 1932-33. Served as dollar a year man, Govt. censorship and secret service, 1917-18; mem. mil. com. Wesleyan R.O.T.C., 1917-18; chairman of instructors of principles of flying at the Navy Pre-Flight School, Wesleyan, 1943-44. Pres. Middlesex County Council Boy Scouts of Am., 1942-44 (received Silver Beaver award). Member council, Bridgehampton, L.I., N.Y., 1959—. Mem. Modern Language Assn. America, American Association Teachers of German, Am. Assn. University Profs., Phi Beta Kappa, Sigma Xi, Pi Delta Epsilon, Psi Upsilon. Republican. Presbyn. Author: A Short German Grammar, 1933; Readings in Scientific and Technical German, 1935; Basic German, 1938; Einführung in die Chemie, 1938; Lebensbilder aus der deutschen Geschichte, 1939. Simplizissimus, 1945; Basic German, revised, 1946; Parzival, 1948; Allerlei Menschen (with F. H. Reinsch), 1949; Hebbel's Herod and Mariamne (metrical translation), 1950. Editor: Wesleyan U. Alumni Record, 8th edit., 1952; Basic German, 3d edition, published, 1952; German Science Grammar (with Van de Luyster), 1955. Editor, contbr.: Bridgehampton's Three Hundred Years, 1956; The Bridgehampton Tercentenary Celebration, 1957. Home: Bridgehampton, L.I., N.Y.

CUSHMAN, AUSTIN THOMAS, merchandising exec.; b. Albuquerque, 1901; s. Charles Otis and Lena (Hughes) C.; student N.M. Mil. Inst., grad. U. Cal.; m. Paula Paiver, 1926; 1 son, John. With Sears, Roebuck & Co., 1931-67, successively salesman boys wear, Oakland, mgr. San Francisco, Oakland stores, gen. mgr., mgr. Cal. dist., gen. mgr. Los Angeles area, 1931-49, v.p. charge Pacific Coast ty., 1949-62, mem. bd., 1950-78, chmn. bd., chief exec. officer, 1962-67; mem. bd. Bank of Am., Allstate Ins. Co., Am. Hosp. Supply, Simpson-Sears Ltd., First Nat. Bank Chgo., Bell & Howell Co., Dun & Bradstreet, Gen. Cable Corp. Mem. bd. Boy Scouts Am.; trustee Com. Econ. Devel., Nat. Indsl. Conf. Bd.; chmn. bd. trustees Savs. and Profit Sharing Pension Fund of Sears, Roebuck & Co., 1967-78. Clubs: Chicago, Commercial, Mid-America, Old Elm, Annandale Golf, Racquet (Chgo.), California. Home: Chicago, Ill. Died June 13, 1978.

CUSUMANO, STEFANO, painter; b. Tampa, Fla., Feb. 5, 1912; s. Ignazio and Rosa (Albano) C.; student Cooper Union, 1928-29, Met. Art Sch., 1930-32; m. Antoinette Ferrari, Aug. 16, 1939; children—Noelle (Mrs. Louis Marak), Peter Anthony. Tchr. painting Cooper Union, 1954-75, N.Y. U., 1951-75; one-man shows include Montross Gallery, N.Y.C., 1942, George Binet Gallery, N.Y.C., 1946, 47, 48, 50, Passedoit Gallery, N.Y.C., 1953, 56, 57, 59, Mari Gallery, Woodstock, N.Y., 1962, Gallery 63, N.Y.C., 1963, 64, Phila Art Alliance, 1948, Woodmere Art Gallery, Phila., 1950, Tampa Art Inst., 1949, Ore. State Coll., 1951, Wash. State U., 1951, Gallery 63, Rome, Italy, 1964, T. Dintenfass Gallery, N.Y.C., 1967, 68-69, Tweed Mus. Art, Duluth, Minn., 1971, 72; Pa. Acad. Fine Arts, Phila., 1972; nat. exhbns. include Mus. Modern Art, Whitney Mus., U. Ill., Pa. Acad., Corcoran Gallery, Carnegie Inst., Am. Inst. Arts and Letters, numerous others; represented in permanent collections Nat. Gallery, Butler Inst. Am. Art, Youngstown, Ohio, Met. Mus. Art, Whitney Mus., Bklyn. Mus., Phila. Mus., Newark Art Mus., Pensacola (Fla.) Art Mus., U. Ill., Wesleyan U. Ill., Johns Hopkins, Joslyn Art Mus., Omaha, Tweed Mus. Art, Krannert Mus. Art, Champaign, Ill. Recipient Ford Found. Purchase prize, 1962; Childe Hassam award Am. Inst. Arts and Letters, 1968, 71; Dillard Purchase award, Weatherspoon Mus., 1969. Address: New York, N.Y. Died Nov. 18, 1975.

CUTHBERT, FREDERICK ALEXANDER, design cons., landscape architect, urban planner; b. Welland, Ont., Can., May 7, 1902; s. William Francis and Euphemia Margaret (Oliphant) C.; came to U.S., 1908, naturalized, 1938; A.B., U. Mich., Ann Arbor, 1926, M. Landscape Design, 1928; m. Elva Mettert, Jan. 1, 1924; children—Peter, Ann (Mrs. William F. Bauman), Priscilla (Mrs. Gary M. Haynes). Tchr., Oreg. State Coll., 1928-42, U. Oreg., 1932-42; charge subregional office Nat. Housing Agy., Portland, Oreg., 1942-46, asst. regional rep., Seattle, 1946-47, dep. regional rep. Office of Housing Expeditor, 1947; head dept. landscape arch. and urban planning U. Oreg., 1947-68, dean Sch. Architecture and Allied Arts, 1968-71; ret., 1971; cons. League of Oreg. Cities, 1933-40; cons. Nat. Resources Planning Bd., 1941-42; mem. environ. impact study team Portland Internat. Airport, 1972; mem. King County (Wash.) Design Commn., 1968-78; chmn. Eugene (Oreg.) Renewal Agy. Design Review Team, 1972-78; mem. Oreg. State Capitol Planning Commn., 1971-73; chmn. advisory com. Alton Baker Park, Eugene, 1973-76; mem. Master Plan Com. for Mt. Pisgah Regional Park, Lane County, Oreg., 1974-78. Lake Forest (Ill.) Found. Architects and Landscape Architects scholar, 1928; Fulbright research scholar to New Zealand, 1952-53; recipient profl. honor award Oreg. Park and Recreation Soc., 1973. Fellow Am. Soc. Landscape Architects (past chmn. council fellows, past bd. trustees, honor award for service Oreg. chpt. 1975); mem. Am. Inst. Planners (past bd. govs., mem. bd. examiners), AAUP (past pres. U. Oreg. chpt.), Eugene Round Table (past pres.), Eugene Very Little Theatre (past pres.). Republican. Contbr. articles on planning and landscape design to profl. jours. and mags. Home: Eugene, Oreg. Died Sept. 14, 1978.

CUTHBERTSON, GEORGE RAYMOND, mgmt. cons., educator; b. Liberty, Mo., June 23, 1910; s. William Nancy R. (Shepherd) C.; B.A., William Jewell Coll., 1931, LL.D. (hon., 1964; M.A., Harvard, 1933, Ph.D., 1935; m. Mary Louise Archer, Sept. 3, 1931; children—Nancy (Mrs. Frank H. Halley), George Raymond, David Archer. Teaching fellow Harvard, 1931-35, research asst., 1935-36; research chemist U.S. Rubber Co., 1936-50, asst. dir. devel. Tire Div., 1951, factory mgr. Los Angeles tire plant, 1952-1953, prodn. mgr. all tire plants, 1953-1955, asst. gen. mgr., 1955-1956, became v.p., gen. mgr. Tire div., 1956, then v.p. research and devel. U.S. Rubber Tire Co. div. until 1963, tech. dir. textile div., 1963-70; mgmt. cons., 1970-79; prof., acting chmn. engring. mgmt. dept. U. Mo., 1971-73; devel. synthetic rubber tires, 1941-45. Mem. Am. Mgmt. Assn., Am. Chem. Soc., Mo. Acad. Sci., Harvard Assn. Chemists, Rolla C. of C., Kappa Alpha, Theta Chi Delta, Sigma Pi Sigma, Alpha Chi Sigma. Baptist. Club: Oak Meadow (Rolla). Patentee in field. Home: Rolla, Mo. Died Mar. 31, 1979.

CUTLER, IVAN BURTON, educator; b. Salt Lake City, Jan. 11, 1924; s. Ralph and Virginia (Burton) C.; B.S., U. Utah, 1947, Ph.D., 1951; m. Beth Ashton, June 6, 1945; children—Coy Cutler Hogan, Claudia Cutler Van Orden, Christopher A., Raymond A., Bonita Cutler Hughes, Connie, Ralph A., Willard A., Louise, Paul A. Instr. ceramic engring. U. Utah, Salt Lake City, 1951-52, asst. prof., 1952-56, asso. prof., head dept.

ceramic engring., 1956-79, prof., 1959-67, prof. mech. engring., 1965-79; vis. prof. ceramic engring. U. Ill., 1967-68. Chmn. Gordon Research Conf., 1965; liaison scientist Office Naval Research, London, Eng., 1972-73; mem. Internat. Inst. for Sci. of Sintering, Internat. Com. on Reactivity Solids. Served to ensign USNR, 1944-46, Fellow Am. Ceramic Soc., mem. Brit. Ceramic Soc., Sigma Xi, Phi Kappa Phi, Tau Beta Pi. Home: Centerville, Utah. Died Sept. 26, 1979.

CUTLER, JOSEPH A., business exec.; b. Dodgeville, Wis., Nov. 29, 1886; s. Joseph and Letitia (Carson) C.; B.S., U. Wis., 1909; m. Bernice Jacobs, August 29, 1925; children—Patricia, Joseph A. Instr. engring. U. Wis., 1909-12; sales engr. Johnson Service Co., 1912-21, dist. mgr., 1921-28, v.p. in charge sales, 1928-38, pres., 1938-61, chmn., 1961—. Dir., v.p. U. Wisconsin Found.; director Country Day Sch. Mem. Am. Soc. Heating and Ventilating Engrs.(life), Am. Soc. Mil. Engrs., Milw. Engring. Soc. Clubs: Rotary (dir.), Milwaukee Athletic, University (Milw.). Home: Milwaukee.

CUTLER, LELAND WHITMAN, surety bonds; b. Colusa, Calif., Jan. 14, 1885; s. George Leland and Elda (Durham) C.; A.B., Leland Stanford Jr. U., 1906; m. Ethel Pierce, Oct. 3, 1916; children—Jane Le, Leland Whitman, Mary Ellen. Began as newspaper reporter, 1906; in mfr. brick and clay products, 1907-09; in ins. and surety bond business since 1909; v.p., dir. Fidelity & Deposit Co. of Md., Am. Bonding Co. of Baltimore, over 20 yrs.; former chmn., now hon. chmn. San Francisco World Trade Authority. Served as campaign chmn. San Francisco Community Chest, 2 terms. Trustee Stanford U. (v.p., bd.); trustee Stanford Kindergarten Trust (president bd.). President of the San Francisco Chamber of Commerce 3 terms. Pres. San Francisco Bay Expn., 1939. Republican. Mem. Disciples of Christ Church. Clubs: Commercial, Pacific Union, Family (ex-pres., dir.). Author: Once Upon A Time; America is Good to a Country Boy. Home: San Francisco.

CUTTING, CHARLES SUYDAM, naturalist; b. New York, N.Y., Jan. 17, 1889; s. Robert Fulton and Helen (Suydam) C.; prep. edn. Groton Sch., 1903-09; A.B., Harvard, 1912; m. Helen McMahon, 1932, Trustee Robert F. Cutting Estate from 1913; field work on expdns. to Central Asia for Am. Museum Natural History, Field Museum of Natural History, Chicago Pitt River Museum of Oxford, Eng. Trustee Am Museum Natural History, New York Zoöl. Soc. Ho fellow Field Museum of Natural History, Chicago. Served as 1st lt., U.S. Army during World War; with A.E.F. in France 15 months. Performed active duty abroad as lt. col., U.S. Army. Decorated Croix Noire (French), Croix de Guerre with Gold Star, Honorary Comdr. Most Excellent Order of British Empire. Member of Bombay Natural History Society, Royal Geog. Soc., Royal Central Asia Soc. (all Brit.); Himmalyan Club. Republican. Episcopalian. Clubs: Knickerbocker, Brook, Racquet (New York). Author: The Fire Ox and Other Years, 1940; also series of articles pub. by Am. Museum Natural History. Home: Bernardsville, N.J. Died Aug. 1972.

CUTTING, FULTON, educator; b. N.Y.C., Dec. 27, 1886; s. Robert Fulton and Helen (Suydam) C.; grad. Groton Sch., 1905; A.B., Harvard, 1909, A.M., 1910, M.E., 1911, Sc.D., 1915; M.S. (hon.), Stevens Inst. Tech., 1954, Sc.D., 1959; m. Mary J. Amory, June 22, 1914; children—Mary Josephine, Justine Bayard, Robert (dec.), Grace Minot. Chmn. Colonial Radio Corp., Buffalo, 1926-45; prof. physics Stevens Inst. Tech., 1947—, also asst. to pres., trustee, 1954—. Served with Bur. Aircraft Prodn., World War I; operational research staff Office Chief Signal Officer, ALSOS Mission, World War II. Mem. Inst. Radio Engrs. (past pres.). Home: N.Y.C.

DAANE, GILBERT LEONARD, born in Grand Rapids, Michigan, May 30, 1886; s. Hubert and Mary (Witters) D.; prep. edn., high sch. and bus. coll., Grand Rapids; student Mich. State Coll., E. Lansing, 1904-05; m. Mamie Blocksma, June 15, 1909; children—Gilbert Warren, Mary Elizabeth Davidson, James Dewey. Teller, Commercial Savings Bank, Grand Rapids, 1905-10; cashier, Mich. Exchange Pvt. Bank, 1910-17; v.p. and cashier, Grand Rapids Savings Bank, 1917-23, became pres., 1923; chmn. bd. Peoples Nat. Bank Grand Rapids, 1933; resigned to enter pvt. bus., 1935; now dir. and treas. Davidson Mfg. Corpn., Chicago, Ill.; v.p. Breen-Halladay Fuel Co., Grand Rapids, Mich. Republican. Mem. Christian Ref. Ch. Clubs: Rotary, Blythefield Country (Grand Rapids); Elk Rapids Golf (Elk Rapids, Mich.). Homes: Grand Rapids, Mich.; and Chicago, Ill.; (summer) Elk Rapids, Mich.

DACK, GAIL MONROE, physician, educator; b. Belvidere, Ill., Mar. 4, 1901; s. John Henry and Cora May (McAllister) D.; B.S., U. Ill., 1922; Ph.D., U. Chgo., 1927, M.D., 1933; m. Martha Pierson Bowsfield, Dec. 25, 1926; children—John Colvin, Carol Jean. Instr. hygiene, bacteriology U. Chgo., 1925-29, asst. prof., 1929-37, asso. prof. bacteriology, 1937-46, prof., 1946-66, prof. emeritus microbiology, 1966-76, dir. Food Research Inst., 1946-66; prof. Food Research Inst. U. Wis., 1966-71. Cons., FDA, USPHS, Army. Chmn. Nat. Research Council Com. Foods, 1951-54; chmn. com. on microbiology Nat. Acad. Sci., NRC, from 1958; mem. cons. panel Robert A. Taft San. Engring. Center, from 1956; adv. bd. Lobund Inst., 1956-64. Served as medical cons., chief safety div. Camp Dietrick, Md., 1943-46. Recipient Ricketts' prize U. Chgo., 1925; Exceptional Performance of Duty citation Sec. War, 1946; Babcock-Hart award Inst. Food Technologists, 1956; Pasteur award Soc. Ill. Bacteriologists, 1957. Mem. Q.M. Food and Container Inst., Soc. Exptl. Biol. and Med., Soc. Am. Bacteriologists (pres. 1953, chmn. adv. com. to chief chem. corps, from 1955), Central Society Clin. Research, A.A.A.S., Am. Pub. Health Assn., Food Technologists, Soc. Ill. Bacteriologists, WHO (expert adv. panel environmental sanitation), Research and Devel. Assos. (chmn. bd.), Am. Acad. Microbiology, Sigma Xi, Gamma Alpha, Alpha Omega Alpha. Author: Food Poisoning, 1949, 3d edit., 1956. Home: Elgin, Ill. Died June 21, 1976.

DACSO, MICHAEL MIHALY, physician, educator; b. Tovaros, Hungary, June 25, 1909; s. Laszlo and Hedvig (Bauer) D.; M.D., Royal Hungarian U. of Budapest, 1934; m. Magda Rona, June 6, 1936; 1 son, Clifford. Came to U.S., naturalized. Research asso Municipal Research Inst. for Rheumatic Diseases, Budapest, 1934-40; intern, then resident Goldwater Meml. Hosp., N.Y. U. Med. Div., 1941-44, asso. vis. physician in medicine, 1945-52, dir. Rehab. Medicine Service, 1949-68, cons., 1968-75, pres. med. bd., 1967-68; cons. Manhattan State Hosp., Wards Island, N.Y., 1964-67; vis. physician Bellevue Hosp., N.Y. U. div., 1947-68; attending physician Univ. Hosp., N.Y. U. Med. Center, 1945-68, staff physician Inst. Rehab. Medicine, 1948-68; cons. Mary Manning Walsh Home, 1951-75; mem. med. adv. bd. Peabody Home, 1962-75; attending physiatrist Mt. Sinai Hosp., 1968-72; med. dir. Daus. of Jacob Geriatric Center, 1972-75; clin. asst. in medicine N.Y. U. Sch. Medicine, 1944-47, asst. prof. clin. rehab. medicine, 1948-54, asso. prof., 1954-58, asso. prof. rehab. medicine, 1958-63, prof., 1963-68; prof. health scis. Hunter Coll., City U. N.Y., 1968-73, dean Inst. Health Scis., 1968-72; prof. rehab. medicine Mt. Sinai Sch. Medicine, City U. N.Y., 1968-72, prof. community medicine, 1969-75. Chmn. sub-com. on med. care Mayor's Adv. Com. for Aged, N.Y.C., 1955-58; mem. Nat. Adv. Com. on Chronic Disease and Health of Aged, 1957-59; cons. gerontology br. Dept. Health, Edn. and Welfare, 1963-64, cons. rehab. medicine div. direct health services, 1967-68, chmn. med. research study sect. Social and Rehab. Service, 1969-75; mem. adv. com. on health careers City U. N.Y., 1966-75; cons. City U. N.Y. Feasibility Study on Proposed Inst. Health Scis. in cooperation with Hunter Coll. and Mt. Sinai Sch. Medicine, 1967-68; mem. Health Resources Commn. Task Force, N.Y. Dept. Health, Albany, 1968-75; mem. Nat. Joint Practice Commn., 1973-75. Mem. med. adv. com. N.Y. County chpt. Nat. Multiple Sclerosis Soc.; mem. tech. adv. com. Community Service Soc., 1955; mem. adv. com. Pub. Health Nursing Project, 1959; co-chmn. health exec. com. on aging Community Council Greater N.Y., 1960; mem. tech. adv. com. Found. for Med. Tech., 1962; mem. project adv. bd. Goodwill Industries Greater N.Y., 1968-75. Vice pres., bd. dirs. Nat. Council on Aging; trustee Sirovich Day Center; bd. govs. Human Resources Center, Albertson, N.Y. Recipient AFL-CIO Dist. 65 award for services to aged, 1959, Japan Rehab. Assn. scroll for contbn. to process in rehab. medicine in Japan, 1966, Meritorious Services diploma City of N.Y. Dept. Hosps., 1969. Diplomate Hungarian Bd. Phys. Medicine, Am. Bd. Phys. Medicine and Rehab. Fellow A.C.P., Am. Pub. Health Assn.; mem. Am. Congress Rehab. Medicine, Am. Acad. Phys. Medicine and Rehab. (past pres.), A.M.A., N.Y. State and County Med. Soc., Assn. Am. Med. Colls., Am. Semmelweis Sci. Soc., Pub. Health Assn. N.Y.C. (dir.), Mexican Soc. Phys. Medicine and Rehab., Internat. Soc. Electromyographic Kinesiology, Am. Geriatric Soc., Assn. Tchrs. Preventive Medicine, Asso. editor Am. Lecture Series. Editorial bd. Jour. Chronic Diseases, 1954. Contbr. articles to profl. jours. Home: Roslyn, N.Y. Died Oct. 11, 1975.

DAGGETT, ELEANOR NINA, author; b. Chama, N.M., May 21, 1919; d. Arthur George and Mattie Clare (Taylor) D.; grad. Spanish-Am. Normal Sch., El Rito, N.M., 1935; student corr. schs. U. N.M., 1966; Oswell A. Washburn, Oct. 22, 1938; 1 dau., Rochelle (Mrs. Joseph D. Genre). Corr. New Mexican, 1967-74; free lance naturalist, author. Mem. North Central N.M. Comprehensive Health Planning Council. Bd. dirs. N.M. Wildlife Fedn. Mem. N.M. Ornithol. Assn., Nat. Wildlife Fedn. Presbyn. Mem. Order Eastern Star. Author: Nature Trek column, 1968-74; History of Chama, 1973. Contbr. articles to profl. jours. Home: Chama, N.Mex. Died Feb. 28, 1974.

DAGGETT, WINDSOR PRATT, writer, lecturer; b. Auburn, Me., Apr. 9, 1884; s. Russell and Eliza Catherine (Hunt) D.; prep. edn., Edward Little High Sch., Auburn; Ph.B., Brown U., 1902; studied expression under Leland Powers and Dr. S. S. Curry, Boston; studied phonetics under William Tilly, Columbia U.; unmarried. Prof. pub. speaking, U. of Me., 1907-18; editor Spoken Word Dept., Billboard, 1921-26; lecturer on phonetics, U. of Wis., summers, 1925-27; lecturer on dramatic diction, Am. Laboratory Theatre, New York, 1925-27; teacher of phonetics and public speaking, Jewish Inst. of Religion, New York, since 1926. Mng. dir. Naples (Me.) Repertory Theatre, summer 1933; head of drama and speech dept., New York Sch. of Vocal Art, Carnegie Hall, 1933—. Mem. Shakespeare Assn. America (bd. dirs.), Phi Gamma Delta. Republican. Episcopalian. Author and publisher of The Spoken Word Course with Phonographic Records and Phonetic Script, 1924.

DAHL, ROLAND J(OHN), business exec.; b. Providence, July 23, 1907; s. John Albert and Linnea W. (Bjorklund) D.; B.S., U. of Mich., 1930; m. Anne Klopsic, June 2, 1934; 1 dau., Meredith Anne. Professional service representative E. R. Squibb & Sons, division of Mathieson Chemical Corporation, now Olin-Mathieson Chemical Corporation, N.Y.C., 1930-39, product sales mgr., 1940-42, mgr. product development, 1943-45, dir. product development, 1946-47, vice pres. and dir. development, 1947-49, v.p. research and development, 1949-52, v.p., dir. research adminstrn., 1952-55. v.p., dir. research and development, 1955-64, vice president for Scientific Affairs, from 1964; pres. Stiexel Research Inst.; cons. drug research adminstrn. Mem. Am. Chem. Soc., Assn. Research Directors. American Pharmaceutical Association. A.A.A.S., Society Chemical Industry. N.Y. Acad. Scis. Clubs: Whippoorwill Golf, New York Athletic. Chemists (N.Y.); Pine Valley Golf. Home: Southbury, Conn. Died Dec. 15, 1978.

DAHLBERG, EDWARD, author; b. Boston, July 22, 1900; s. Saul Gottdank and Elizabeth Dahlberg; student U. Cal., 1922-23; B.S. in Philosophy, Columbia, 1925; m. Julia Lawlor, June 13, 1967. Began writing novels in Monte Carlo, 1926; lived and wrote in London and Paris, 1926-28. Author: (novels) Bottom Dogs, 1930 (trans. into Spanish and pub. in Chile, 1940); From Flushing to Calvary, 1932; Kentucky Blue Grass, 1932; Those Who Perish, 1934; (literary criticism) Can These Bones Live, 1941, Sing O Barren (foreward by Herbert Read), 1947; Flea of Sodom, 1950; The Sorrows of Priapus (illustrated by Ben Shahn), 1957; Can These Bones Live (illus. by James Kearns), 1960; (with Sir Herbert Read) Truth Is More Sacred, 1961; Because I Was Flesh (autobiography), 1964; Alms for Oblivion; The Anxious Years; Moby Dick An Hamitic Dream; Reasons of the Heart, 1965; Cipango's Hinder Door, 1965; Edward Dahlberg Reader, 1967; Epitaphs of our Times, The Letters of Edward Dahlberg, 1967; The Leafless American, 1967; The Carnal Myth, 1968; The Confessions of Edward Dahlberg, 1971; The Complete Sorrows of Priapus, 1972; The Gold of Ophir, 1972. Contbr. Fortnightly Rev., Poetry, New Republic, The Nation, also Holiday Mag., New Directions Annual, N.Y. Times, Tomorrow, Prose Mag. several others. Carolyn Benton Cockefair prof. U. Mo. at Kansas City, 1964-65, prof. lang. lit., 1966-77; prof. Columbia, 1968. Recipient Longview Found. award; award Nat. Found. on Arts and Humanities. Rockefeller grantee, 1965, 66; Ariadne Found grantee; grantee CAPS, Nat. Endowment Arts. Mem. Inst. Arts and Letters. Home: Santa Barbara, Calif. Died Feb. 27, 1977.

DAILEY, JAMES A., b. Ossining, N.Y., Apr. 3, 1884; ed. public schools, Packard Commercial Sch., and New York Prep. School, N.Y. City; m. Alice L. McGarr, of Auburn, N.Y., Nov. 2, 1911. Sec. to Herbert L. Satterlee, gen. counsel M.,K.&T. Ry., N.Y. City, 1905-11; with N.Y.C.R.R., 1911-35; sec. to gen. claims atty., N.Y.C.R.R., 1911-20, chief clk. to same, 1920-23, with pension bur., 1923-35, sec. pension bur. and bd. of pensions, 1925-35; apptd. mem. R.R. Retirement Bd., Washington, D.C., 1935-38, representing employers. Home: Washington.

DAILY, HARRY PARKER, lawyer; b. Ft. Smith, Ark., Aug. 26, 1886; s. John Calhoun and Jane Eliza (Lanigan) D.; A.B., Stanford U., 1907; studied law same univ.; m. May Speer, Nov. 1, 1911; children—John Speer, Agnes May (dec.), Jane. Admitted to Ark. bar, 1907 and since pripracticed at Ft. Smith; sr. partner Daily & Woods; city atty., Ft. Smith, 1913-17; atty. for First Nat. Bank since 1917, Merchants Nat. Bank since 1925; dir. Ballman-Cummings Furniture Co., Ark. Valley Trust Co. Mem. bd. dirs. Ft. Smith Sch. Dist., 1918-22, Chamber of Commerce, 1919-35; mem. Ark. State Bd. of Edn., 1925-26. Mem. Am. Bar Assn., Ark. State Bar Assn. (pres. 1931-32), Phi Beta Kappa, Phi Delta Phi, Delta Upsilon. Democrat. Episcopalian. Elk. Contbr. to law publs. Home: Smith, Ark.

DAKIN, EDWIN FRANDEN, author; b. Hannibal, Mo., Dec. 19, 1898; s. Horace Edwin and Elmore (James) D.; A.B., Washington U., 1921; unmarried. Asso. editor Commerce and Finance (weekly), 1922-26; with Ivy Lee Associates, N.Y. City, 1926-28; pub. relations counsellor to Harmon interests, 1928-32, Inst. of Aerodynamic Research since 1932. Servgd with Washington U. Ambulance Corps, A.E.F., 1917-19.

Mem. Phi Beta Kappa, Pi Kappa Alpha. Author: Mrs. Eddy—The Biography of a Virginal Mind, 1929. Home: New York, N.Y. Died Mar. 26, 1976.

DAKIN, ROGER, editor; b. Gloucester, Mass., May 27, 1905; s. John Arthur and Gertrude (Brinnick) D.; student pvt. schs.; m. Helen Craig Smith, Sept. 6, 1929 (dec. June, 1953); m. 2d, Alexandra Lewandowska, Sept. 9, 1954. Rewrite man New York Telegram, 1929-33; rewrite, asst. city editor N.Y. Daily News, 1933-40; asst. mng. editor P M, 1940-43; asso. editor Woman's Home Companion, 1943-52, editor Collier's, 1952-55; editorial mgr. Gen. Foods, 1956-62, asso. dir. pub. relations, 1962-64, mgr. editorial and publs., 1964-70. Home: West Lebanon, N.H. Died Aug. 28, 1978.

DALE, HARRISON CLIFFORD, comptroller; b. Lyon, Mass., Mar. 7, 1885; s. Alvin Clifford and Helen Mary (Worthen) D.; A.B., Harvard, 1907, A.M., 1908, student 1907-10; LL.D., Coll. of Ida., 1945, Whitman Coll., 1946, Miami U., 1952; m. Beulah May Garrard, June 5, 1916; children—Mary, Harrison Clifford (dec.), Paul Worthen, Winthrop Garrard. Asst. prof. history, Utah Agrl. Coll., 1910-12; instr. history, Wash. U., 1912-15; prof. polit. science, U. of Wyo., 1915-20; prof. economics and polit. sci. since 1920; dean sch. of business adminstrn. U. of Ida., 1925-28; same, Miami U., Oxford, Ohio, 1928-37; pres. Univ. of Idaho, 1937-46; comptroller, Reed Coll., 1946-50, ret., 1950. Wyo. state dir. of speakers Victory Loan Campaign, 1919; cons. economist div. of Review, NRA, 1935. Mem. Alpha Tau Omega, S.A.R. Episcopalian. Author: The Ashley-Smith Explorations and the Discovery of a Central Route to the Pacific, 1822-1829, 1918. Home: Marine Route, Coeur d'Alene, Ida. Ret.

DALE, PAUL NEWTON, lawyer; b. Cherry Creek, N.Y., Sept. 12, 1883; s. Wesley Wilson and Ella Frances (Taylor) D.; A.B., Ohio Wesleyan U., 1905, LL.B., Harvard, 1911; m. Margaret Emerson Eames, Nov. 25, 1914; children—David Eames, Gordon Eames, Stanley Emerson. Admitted to Ill. bar, 1912, and since practiced in Chicago, mem. firm of Dale, Lytton, Haffner & Grow. Mem. Am., Ill. and Chicago bar assns., Phi Beta Kappa, Phi Kappa Psi. Methodist. Republican. Mason. Clubs: Harvard (Chicago); Westmoreland Country (Wilmette, Ill.). Home: Evanston, Ill.

D'ALELIO, GAETANO FRANCIS, educator, chemist, inventor; b. Charlestown, Mass., Dec 26, 1909; s. Severino and Francesca (Polcari) D'A.; A.B., Boston Coll., 1931; Ph.D., Johns Hopkins, 1935; m. Josephine Marie McCarthy, Sept. 5, 1932; children—Denny F., Ellen F., Jane M. d'Alelio Paine, William A. Asso. chemistry Boston Coll. Grad. Sch., 1935-36; dir. plastic research Gen. Electric Co., Pittsfield, Mass., 1936-39, dir. research devel. and control labs., 1939-41, mem. mgrs. staff, 1941-43; dir. research Pro-phy-lac-tic Brush Co., Florence, Mass., 1943-44, v.p., 1944-46; mgr. high polymer research Indsl. Rayon Corp Cleve., 1946-47; asst. dir. research Koppers Co., Inc., Pitts., 1947-49, v.p., mgr. research, 1949-54; head dept. chemistry U. Notre Dame, 1955-60, research prof., 1960-75, emeritus prof., 1975-80; indsl. cons., 1955-80; dir. Dal-Mon, Inc., Cleve., 1959-80. Cons. to referee bd. chmn. branch office prodn. research and devel., WPB, 1942; mem. adv. panel to com. Q.M. problems NRC, 1943; cons war research Manhattan project Columbia, 1944, Naval 1 dir., coordinator Gen. Electric lab. research on plast rocket launchers; cons. U.S. Army Chem. Corps Engring. Command, 1959-61; mem. Research adv. com. on materials NASA, 1961-62, apptd. polymer expert cons. to NASA, 1963-66; mem. labs. com. Franklin Inst., Phila., 1963-71; mem. vertically integrated coupling program USAF, Wright-Patterson AFB, O., 1966-69. Bd. dirs. Aeolian Choral Soc., South Bend. Recipient certificate of merit Air Force Systems Command, 1975. Fellow Am. Inst. Chemists, A.A.A.S., N.Y. Acad. Scis.; mem. Nat. Acad. Scis. (com. radiation preservation of food 1965-80), Am. Chem Soc., Textile Inst., Am. Assn. U. Profs., Ind. Acad. Sci., Chem. Soc. London, Am. Inst. Chem. Engrs., Assn. U.S. Army, Armed Forces Chemical Assos., Hist. Sci. Soc., Acad. Applied Scis., Phi Beta Kappa, Sigma Xi, Phi Lambda Upsilon. Republican. Roman Catholic. Clubs: University (South Bend, Ind.); Kiwanis (dir. 1946) Duquesne (Pitts.). Author: (with R. L. Guile) Laboratory Manual of Synthetic Plastics and Resinous Materials, 1942; A Laboratory Manual of Plastics and Synthetic Resins, 1943; Experimental Plastics and Synthetic Resins, 1946; Fundamentals of Polymerization, 1952. Editorial bd., asso. editor Jour. Macromoleular Sci.-Chemistry, 1968-80. Contbr. articles to profl. publs. Patentee in field; inventor secret radar insulation and sulfonated styrene-type and crosslinked acrylic acid-type ion exchange resins. Home: South Bend, Ind. Died Aug. 30, 1980; buried Cedar Grove Cemetery, Notre Dame, Ind.

DALEY, EDMUND LEO, army officer; b. Worcester, Mass., Nov. 1, 1883; s. John and Katherine Elizabeth (Martin) D.; B.S., with honors, U.S. Mil. Acad., 1906; grad. Engineer Sch., 1910, Army Field Engineer Sch., 1916 (honor grad.), Army War Coll., 1936; m. Beatrix Ottillie Koehler, Sept. 11, 1906 (died Sept. 17, 1928); children—Edmund Koehler, John Phillips, Donal Martin. Commd. 2d lt. Corps of Engrs., U.S. Army, 1906, and advanced through grades to maj. gen. in 1940; in Philippine Islands, 1908-09; instr. dept. of engring., U.S. Mil. Acad., 1911-15; dist. engr. and officer in charge ry. operations, Laredo, Tex., 1916-17; instr. 1st Engr. O.T.C., Vaucouver Barracks, Wash., 1917; lt. col. with 310th Engrs., Camp Custer, Mich., 1917-18; col. 55th Engrs., en route to France, July 1918; comdg. 6th Engrs. and div. engr. 3d Div., Aug. 1918-Feb. 1919 (participated in Marne-Vesle, St. Mihiel and Mèuse-Argonne offensive and march into Germany); sect. engr. to reconstruction, France, Feb.-Aug. 1919; with mission to Armenia, 1919-20; prof. practical engring., U.S. Mil. Acad., 1920-22; with Hoover Relief, Russia, 1922; dep. Red Cross commr., Smyrna disaster, 1922-23; dist. engr., Pittsburgh, Pa., 1923-26; asst. to chief of engrs., Washington, D.C., 1926-30; mem. San Francisco Bay Bridge Commn., 1929-30; asst. to div. engr. Upper Miss. Valley Div., 1930-33, div. engr., same, 1933-35; dist. engr., 1st N.Y. Dist., 1936-37; div. engr., North Atlantic Div., New York, 1937-38; comdg. 1st C.A. Dist., Boston, 1938-39; dept. comdr. Puerto Rican Dept., 1939-41; comdg. 5th Army Corps, April 1, 1941-May, 1942; dep. dir. Civilian Protection, New York State, May 1942-45; dep. dir. Div. Vets. Affairs, N.Y. State since 1945. brigadier general, retired October 1, 1942. Decorated D.S.M., Silver Star (U.S.); Officier de Merite Agricole (France); Gold Crown of the Saviour (Greece). Mem. Am. Soc. Civil Engrs., Soc. Am. Mil. Engrs. Roman Catholic. Clubs: Army and Navy (Washington, D.C.); Army and Navy Country (Va.); West Point Army Mess; Fort Orange (Albany, N.Y.). Contbr. to tech. jours. Home: Fort Orange Club

DALEY, JOHN (BUD) JOSEPH, JR., lawyer; b. Jacksonville, Fla., Dec. 14, 1938; s. John Joseph and Alberta (Register) D.; B.S.C., Spring Hill Coll., 1961; J.D., Fla. State U., 1969; LL.M., U. Ga., 1971; m. Carolyn Frances Schnauss, Feb. 6, 1965; children—Caroline, Jacqueline, Katherine. Tchr., coach Bishop Kenny High Sch., Jacksonville, 1965-66; admitted to Fla. bar, 1969, Fed. bar, 1974, U.S. Supreme Ct. bar, 1974, others; law clk. to Judge Bryan Simpson, U.S. Ct. Appeals, 1969-70; part-time teaching scholar U. Ga. Law Sch., 1970-71; asst. U.S. atty. Dept. Justice, Jacksonville, 1971-75, chief asst. U.S. atty, 1975-78, Middle Dist. Fla., 1979-80, interim U.S. atty., Middle Dist. Fla., 1978-79; mem. firm Corrigan and Moore, Jacksonville, 1979-80, Holland & Knight, Bartow, Fla., 1980. Mem. Bishop Kenny High Sch. Bd. Served to capt. USMC, 1961-64. Mem. Am. Bar Assn., Fed. Bar Assn., Fla. Bar Assn., Jacksonville Bar Assn., Jacksonville YMCA, Phi Kappa Phi. Roman Catholic. Home: Bartow, Fla. Died Oct. 24, 1980.

DALEY, RICHARD JOSEPH, mayor Chgo.; b. Chgo., May 15, 1902; s. Michael and Lillian (Dunne); LL.B., DePaul U., 1933; m. Eleanor Guilfoyle, June 23, 1936; children—Patricia, Mary Carol, Eleanor, Richard, Michael, John, William. Admitted to Ill. bar, 1933. Democratic mem. Ill. Ho. of Reps., 1936-38; Ill. Senate 1939-46; dir. Revenue for State Ill., 1948-50; clk. Cook County, 1950-55; mayor Chgo., 1955-76. Chmn. Democratic Party Cook County. Bd. dirs. Valentine Boys Club; St. Joseph Home of Friendless, Fellowship House. Chmn., Bridgeport Area Boy Scouts Am. Mem. Am., Ill., Chgo. bar assns., U.S. Conf. Mayors (pres. 1959). K.C., Moose, Elk. Home: Chicago, Ill. Died Dec. 20, 1976.

DALGETY, GEORGE S., appraiser and lecturer; b. at Port Dalhousie, Ontario, Canada, April 7, 1884; s. George Harris and Emily (White) Dalgety; graduate Genesee Wesleyan Seminary, Lima, N.Y., 1907; student Northwestern U., 1907-08; A.B., Ky. Wesleyan Coll., Winchester, 1910; m. Mildred Luse, of West Liberty, Ia., Nov. 22, 1916; children—Jean Luse, Myrtle Ruth, George S. Head of dept. English and pub. speaking, Ky. Wesleyan Coll., 1908-11, Dak. Wesleyan U., Mitchell, S.D., 1911-13; v.p. and field mgr. Redpath Chautauqua System, N.Y. and N.E., 1913-19; campaign dir. with Ward, Hill, Pierce & Wells, N.Y. City, 1919-21; exec. sec. Northwestern U. Alumni Assn., 1921-23; asst. business mgr. Northwestern U., 1923-35; lecturer Redpath Chautauqua System, 1913-19. With War Camp Community Service, 1918-19. Clubs: University (Evanston); Shawnee Country (Wilmette, Ill.). Contbr. articles to various publs. Home: Evanston, Ill.

DALLDORF, GILBERT, pathologist; b. Davenport, Iowa, Mar. 12, 1900; s. Julius and Hulda (Leisner) D.; B.S., State U. Iowa, 1921; M.D., N.Y. U., 1924; D.Sc., Bowdoin Coll., 1953; D., U. Freiburg (Germany), 1957; m. Frances Elizabeth Barnhart, Apr. 6, 1926; children—Elizabeth (Mrs. Robert Martin), Frederic. Rotating intern Norwegian Hosp., Bklyn., 1924-25; fellow pathology Pathológisches Inst., Freiburg, 1925-26; pathologist N.Y. Hosp., N.Y.C., 1926-29; instr. pathologic anatomy Cornell Med. Coll., 1926-32; pathologist Grasslands Hosp., Valhalla, N.Y., 1929-43; dir. labs. and research Westchester County, 1943-45; dir. div. labs. and research N.Y. Dept. Health, Albany, 1945-57; dir. research Nat. Found., 1958-59; mem. Sloan-Kettering Inst., Walker Lab., 1959-68; prof. pathology Sloan Kettering div. Cornell U. Med. Coll., 1960-68; chmn. Brown Hazen Fund Research Corp., N.Y.C. Commn. on Plasma Blood Research Inst. Recipient Fisher Meml. award, 1955; Distinguished Service award Coll. Medicine, N.Y. U., 1956; Lasker Award, 1959; medal N.Y. Acad. Medicine, 1964. Diplomate Am. Bd. Pathology. Mem. A.A.A.S., Am. Assn. Immunologists, A.M.A., Am. Soc. Exptl. Pathology, Assn. Am. Physicians, Nat. Acad. Sci., N.Y. Acad. Medicine, N.Y. Assn. Pub. Health Labs., N.Y. Med. Soc., Soc. Exptl. Biology and Medicine, Am. Epidemiological Soc. Club: Century Assn. Home: Oxford, Md. Died Dec. 21, 1979.

DALTON, CARTER, lawyer; b. Greensboro, N.C., Nov. 9, 1884; s. Robert Frank and Caroline Blackwell (Sparrow) D.; grad. high sch., Greensboro, 1902; Ph.B., University of North Carolina, 1906; LL.B., Harvard University, 1909; m. Mary Drew Land, Oct. 8, 1913; children—Mary Drew Ingram (Mrs. Pace Fuller), Mrs. J. H. Lumpkin, Robert Frank III. Admitted to N.C. bar, 1908, practicing at Greensboro, 1909; moved to High Point, 1913; pres. and general counsel Snow Lumber Co., Dalton Realty Company; chmn. bd. Southern Webbing Mills. Judge City Court, High Point, 1915-17; mem. N.C. Ho. of Rep., 1917; High Point Pub. Library; chmn. bd. trustees High Point Meml. Hosp.; chmn. dirs. Fort Pierce Memorial Hospital; member board trustees Pungo Dist. Hosp., Belhaven Pub. Library. Mem. Am. and N.C. State bar assns., Harvard Law School Assn., Newcomen Society, High Point Chamber of Commerce (past pres.), Beta Theta Pi. Democrat. Presbyn. Mason. Clubs: Rotary (past pres.), Harvard of N.C. (past pres.). Home: Ft. Pierce, Fla.

DALTON, MARSHALL BERTRAND, ins. exec.; b. Woodfords, Maine, Jan. 7, 1893; s. Charles B. and Josephine (Lamson) D.; S.B., Mass. Inst. Tech., 1915; Dr. Engring., Worcester Poly. Inst., 1958; m. Lydia Boardman White, June 15, 1916; children—Meralyn, Nadylis. With Liberty Mut. Ins. Co., advancing to v.p., 1916-34; pres., dir. Boston Mfrs. Mut. Ins. Co., 1934-58, chmn. bd., 1958-65, hon. chmn., 1965-74; mem. bd., chmn. exec. com. Arthur D. Little Co., 1962-65; hon. chmn. Arkwright-Boston Mfrs. Mut. Ins. Co., 1974-76. dir. emeritus, Ludlow Corp.; hon. dir. Lumber Mut. Fire Ins. Co. Mem. corp. Northeastern U.; hon. trustee New Eng. Bapt. Hosp.; life mem. corp. Mass. Inst. Tech.; trustee Willard Bass Park Assn., Monadnock Community Hosp., Peterborough, N.H.; trustee emeritus, past pres. Gov. Dummer Acad.; bd. overseers Crotched Mountain Rehab. Center, Greenfield, N.H. Fellow Am. Acad. Arts and Scis.; mem. Newcomen Soc. Eng., M.I.T. Alumni Assn. (past pres.), Phi Gamma Delta (past nat. pres., trustee ednl. found.). Clubs: Commercial (Boston); Dublin (N.H.) Lake. Home: Peterborough, N.H. Died Mar. 29, 1976; buried Peterborough.

DALTON, VAN BROADUS, oral surgeon; b. Burkesville, Ky., July 25, 1885; s. Lafayette and Elmira (Norris) D.; student Bethal Coll., Russelville, Ky., 1901-02, Auburn (Ky.) Mil. Acad., Auburn, 1902-03; D.D.S., Ohio Coll. Dental Surgery, Cin., 1907; m. Anna Stone, Dec. 16, 1914 (dec. 1950); children—Dorothy Fay (Mrs. J. H. Platz), William (dec.), Van Broadus (dec. 1931). Began career as demonstrator in operative clinics. Ohio Coll. of Dental Surgery, 1907, prof. orthodontia, exodontia and anaesthetics, 1908-20; asst. dir. dental dept., Cin. Gen. Hosp., 1920-21; mem. med. staff, Children's Hosp., Cin. 1917-19; engaged in pvt. practice, 1916—; hon. staff Bethseda Hosp.; sr. staff Christ Hosp.; cons. staff Good Samaritan Hosp. Mem. mouth hygiene council Cin. Pub. Health Fedn.; Cin. and Hamilton Co. exec. council Am. Cancer Soc. Diplomate Am. Bd. Oral Surgery. Fellow Am. Coll. Dentists; mem. Am. Dental Assn., Am. (past pres.), Gt. Lakes, Cin. (past pres.) socs. oral surgeons Am. Acad. History Dentistry (past pres.) Am. Assn. History of Medicine, Ohio Acad. History Medicine, Ohio State (past pres.), Cin. (past pres.) dental socs., Ohio State Archaeol. and Hist. Soc., State Hist. Soc. Mo., Acad. Medicine Cin. (asso.), Fedn. Dentaire Internationale (asso.), T.I. Way Dental Forum (hon.), Psi Omego (hon.). Clubs: Kenwood Country (life mem.), Cuvier Press, Automobile, The Cincinnati (Cin.). Author: Essentials of Orthodontia, 1914; The Genesis of Dental Education in the United States, 1946; also sci. and clin. articles for profl. publs. Address: Cincinnati, OH.

DALY, GEORGE JOSEPH, garment mfg. co. exec.; b. Phila., Jan. 26, 1919; s. George Joseph and Frances (Denzler) D.; B.A. in Fin. with honors, Wharton Sch., U. Pa., 1942; m. Marjorie Colleen Bishop, June 1946 (dec. 1972); 1 dau., Colleen Bishop; m. 2d Barbara Snow Kamanski, July, 1974. Spl. cons. to Sec. of Army, Washington, 1952-54; with Elgin Nat. Watch Co. (Ill.), 1954-61, exec. v.p., 1956-60, pres., chief exec. officer, 1960-61, also dir.; with Dart Industries, Los Angeles, 1961-73, exec. v.p. profit planning, 1961-69, exec. v.p., 1969-73, also dir.; exec. v.p. fin. and adminstrn., mem. exec. com. Levi Strauss & Co., San Francisco, 1973-80, also dir.; dir. Revell, Inc., Dorsey Corp., Bunker Hill Income Securities Inc., Vidal Sassoon, Inc., Shaklee Corp., Endowments, Inc., Bond Portfolio for Endowments, Inc. Chmn. bd. trustees Dominican Coll. of San Rafael, 1977-80, chmn., 1979-80; mem. adv. bd. Calif. Dept. Econ. and Bus. Devel., 1978-79, Sch. Sci., U. Santa Clara, 1979-80; v.p., bd. dirs. San Francisco

Bay Area council Boy Scouts Am., 1978-80; fire commr. City of Belvedere (Calif.), 1979-80. Served to capt. USAAF, 1942-46, as capt. U.S. Army, 1952. Decorated D.S.C. with 2 oak leaf clusters. Mem. Fin. Execs. Inst., Fin. Officers No. Calif., Newcomen Soc. Am. Clubs: Family, Mt. Tamalpais Racquet, San Francisco Yacht (dir., treas. 1979), Commonwealth, Belvedere Tennis. Home: San Francisco. Died 1980.

DALY, JAMES, actor; b. Wisconsin Rapids, Wis., Oct. 23, 1918; s. Percifer Charles and Dorothy Hogan (Mullen) D.; student U. Wis., 1933, State U. Ia., 1935-36, Carroll Coll., 1937-38; B.A., Cornell Coll., 1941, D.F.A., 1956; m. Hope Newell, Feb. 21, 1942; children—Pegeen, Tyne, Glynn, Timothy. Broadway debut in Born Yesterday, 1946; other theatrical appearances include Virginia Reel, 1947, Man and Superman (tour), 1948-49, The Cenci, 1950, The Devil's Disciple, 1950, Major Barbara, 1950-51, Billy Budd, 1951, Mary Rose, 1951-52, St. Joan, 1951, Miss Julie, 1956, Glass Menagerie, 1956, Back to Methuselah, 1957, This is Goggle, 1958, Handful of Fire, 1958, JB, 1959-60, Period of Adjustment, 1960-61, The Advocate, 1963, The White House, 1964, Who's Afraid of Virginia Woolf?, 1965, Camelot, 1965, A Moon for the Misbegotten, 1965, A Thousand Clowns, 1966, The Trial of the Catonsville Nine, 1970; summer stock roles with Port Players, Oconomowoc, Wis., 1948-50, Lakewood Theater, Skowhegan, Me., 1951, Bucks County Playhouse, New Hope, Pa., 1954, 62-63; with State Dept. tour to Germany to open Congress Hall in Berlin, 1957; films include The Court Martial of Billy Mitchell, 1955, The Young Stranger, 1957, I Aim at the Stars, 1960, Planet of the Apes, 1968, The Five Man Army, 1970, The Resurrection of Zachary Wheeler, 1971, Wild in the Sky (Black Jack), 1973; major TV appearances, 1947-78, including roles in series Foreign Intrigue, 1953-54, Hallmark Hall of Fame show in Give Us Barabbas, Ominbus role in Henry Adams, and Armstrong Circle Theatre role in Cross and the Dragon, star series, Medical Center, 1970-76. Served as ensign USNR, World War II. Recipient Daniel Blum Theatre World award, 1951; Emmy award as outstanding actor in supporting role in Eagle in a Cage, Hallmark Hall of Fame, 1966. Mem. A.F.T.R.A., Screen Actors Guild, Authors Guild, Actors Equity Assn. Died July 2, 1978.

DALY, WILLIAM JEROME, JR., publishing co. exec.; b. N.Y.C., Dec. 22, 1915; s. William Jerome and Ursula (Miller) D.; A.B., Fordham U., 1937, J.D., 1940; m. Joe Ann Godown, Jan. 25, 1958. Admitted to N.Y. bar, 1940, D.C. bar, 1948; asso. firm Baar, Bennett & Fullen, N.Y.C., 1940-42; asst. sec. Capital Transit Co., Washington, 1946-49; sec., counsel U.S.-Italy Conciliation Commn., Rome, 1949-51; pvt. practice law, N.Y.C., 1951-53; sec. gen. counsel Prentice-Hall, Inc., 1967-76; sec., gen. counsel, dir. Bur. Bus. Practice, Center for Applied Research in Edn., Greenvale Editorial Services, N.Y. Inst. Finance, Parker Pub. Co., The Pren-Hall Corp., Sylvan Properties; sec., gen. counsel Goodyear Pub. Co., Inst. Bus. Planning, Living Color Financial Displays, Prentice-Hall Can. Ltd., Prentice-Hall Internat., Reston Pub. Co., Winthrop Pubs., Prentice-Hall S.E. Asia Ltd. Served with USNR, 1942-46. Mem. Copyright Soc. U.S.A., N.Y. County Lawyers Assn., Am. Arbitration Assn. (nat. panel 1974-76), Assn. Am. Publishers (lawyers com. 1971-76), Delta Theta Phi. Clubs: The Lawyers, Traffic (N.Y.C.). Editor in chief Fordham Law Rev., 1939-40. Home: Brooklyn, N.Y. Died Oct. 14, 1976.

DALZELL, ROBERT DUFF, lawyer; b. Allegheny Co., Pa., Aug. 27, 1882; s. John and Mary Louise (Duff) D.; A.B., Yale, 1905; LL.B., George Washington U., 1909; m. Alice McFarlane, Apr. 14, 1915; children—Robert Duff, William Sage (dec.), Kathleen Alden. Admitted to Pa. bar, 1910, since practiced in Pitts.; mem. Dalzell, Pringle, Bredin & Martin. Home: Pitts.

DAM, CARL PETER HENRIK, biochemist; b. Copenhagen, Denmark, Feb. 21, 1895; s. Emil and Emilie (Peterson) D.; M.S. in Chem., Poly. Inst., 1920; DSc. in Biochemistry, U. of Copenhagen, 1934; D.Sc. (hon.), St. Louis U., 1965; m. Inger Olsen, July 15, 1924. Came to U.S., 1940. Instr. in chemistry Sch. Agr. and Vet Medicine, Copenhagen, 1920-23; instr. in biochemistry U. Copenhagen, 1923, asst. prof., 1928, asso. prof., 1929-41; prof. biochemistry Tech. U. Denmark, Copenhagen, 1941-65 (appointment in absentia), emeritus prof biochemistry, 1965-76; sr. research asso. in biochemistry U. Rochester (NY.), 1942-45; asso. mem. Rockefeller Inst., 1945-48; head biol. div. Danish Fat Research Inst., 1956-62. Recipient Christian Bohr award in physiology for discovery of vitamin K, 1939; Nobel prize in physiology and medicine (joint award), 1943; Honorary fellow Royal Society (Edinburgh); fellow Am. Inst. Nutrition; mem Soc Exptl. Biology and Medicine, Am. Soc. Biol. Chemistry, Danish Nutrition Soc., (pres. 1967-70), Internat. Union Nutritional Scis. (hon. pres.), Chem Soc. and Biological Soc. (Copenhagen), Swiss Chem. Soc., Royal Danish Acad. Scis. and Letter, Danish Acad Tech. Scis. Lectr. U.S. and Can., under auspices of Am.-Scandinavian Found 1940-41, 49; in Copenhagen, 1946-76. Contbr. many papers relating to vitamins, lipids, nutrition, blood coagulation, formation of gallstones to sci Jours. of U.S and Europe. Home: Copenhagen, Denmark. Died Apr 17 1976.

DANA, MARSHALL NEWPORT, newspaper editor; b. Washington County, O., Oct. 17, 1885; s. Rev. Watson and Margaret Elizabeth (Riley) D.; student Denison Univ., Granville, O., 1902-05; LL.D., Whitman and Linfield colleges, 1935; Litt.D., Oregon College of Edn., Monmouth, 1946; m. Nora Valentine Carl, Jan. 1, 1910; children—Marjorie Elizabeth, Marshall Norman, Mary Lois (Mrs. Hudson Lothian). Began as newspaperman on Evening Herald, Dayton, O., 1905; with Advertiser, Huntington, W.Va., 1905-07, Gazette, Charleston, W.Va., 1907, Dispatch, Huntington, 1908, Star, Kansas City, Mo., 1908-09; with Oregon Daily Journal, Portland, since 1909, asso. editor, 1918-38, editor of editorial page, since 1938. Regional adviser and regional chairman Public Works Administration, 1932-36. Pres. Pacific Advertising Clubs Assn., 1927-28; pres. Nat. Reclamation Assn., 1931-34; pres. Philharmonic Soc., 1939-42; mem. bd. trustees Linfield Coll., mem. Ore. Econ. Council, Ore. State Game Commn. 1932; mem. Battleship Oregon Commn., dist. chmn. Nat. Resources Bd., 1933-36. Mem. Am. Soc. Newspaper Editors. Democrat. Baptist. Co-author: More Power to You, 1934. Contbr. articles to jours. Home: Milwaukie, Ore.

DANA, SAMUEL TRASK, educator, dean emeritus; b. Portland, Maine, Apr. 21, 1883; s. John W. and Martha O. (Fessenden) D.; A.B summa cum laude, Bowdoin Coll., 1904, Sc.D., 1930; M.F. summa cum laude (hon.), Yale, 1907, Sc.D., 1953; Sc.D. (hon.), Syracuse U., 1928; LL.D. (hon.), U. Mich., 1953; m. Ruth Merrill, Aug. 7, 1915; children—Harriet M. (Mrs. William R. Carroll), George W. Successively forest asst., asst. chief Offices Silvics and Forest Investigations, forest economist, asst. chief br. of research, U.S. Forest Service, 1907-21, dir. Northeastern Forest Expt. Sta., 1923-27; forest commr., Me., 1921-23; prof. forestry, dean Sch. Forestry and Conservation, U. Mich., 1927-50, dean Sch. Natural Resources, 1950-51, Filibert Roth univ. prof. forestry, 1951-53, chmn. div. biol. scis., 1948-51, emeritus, 1953-78; cons. forest edn., policy, econs., 1953-78. Mem. Hoover Commn. on Reorgn. Exec. Br. of Govt., 1948-49, forest research adv. com. U.S. Dept. Agr., 1953-58; co-chmn. sect. utilization and development land resources Mid-Century Conf. Resources for Future, 1953; vice-chmn. com. natural resources and conservation Commn. Intergovtl. Relations, 1954; mem. Outdoor Recreation Resources Rev. Commn., 1958-62; program com. World Forestry Congress, 1959-60; rep. U.S. Dept. Agr., Gen. Assembly Internat. Inst. Agr., Rome, Italy, 1926, Soc. Am. Foresters and Yale, Internat. Forestry Congress, 1926, Dept. State, Latin-Am. Forestry Commn., Caracas, Venezuela, 1955. Served as capt., gen. staff, U.S. Army, 1917-18. Recipient 1st Disting. Service award Am. Forest Products Industries, 1961; medal for outstanding service in internat. forestry 6th World Forestry Congress, Madrid, 1966. Fellow Soc. Am. Foresters (pres. 1925-26; dir. study forestry edn. 1959-78; editor-in-chief jour. 1928-30, 42-46; Sir William Schlich Meml. medal 1956); hon. mem. Am. Forestry Assn. (dir. 1935-53, v.p. 1949-51, hon. v.p. 1933, 54-57, 59-78; award for outstanding services in conservation of natural resources 1954, 1st John Aston Warder award 1975), Soc. Forestry Suomi (Finland), Ecuadorian Inst. Natural Scis.; fgn. mem. Finnish Acad. Sci.; mem. Mich. Acad. Sci., Arts and Letters, Phi Beta Kappa, Sigma Xi, Phi Kappa Phi (pres. Mich. 1935), Phi Sigma (hon.), Xi Sigma Pi, Psi Upsilon. Unitarian. Club: Ann Arbor (Mich.) Rotary (pres. 1941-42; chmn. dist. conf. 1941). Author: Forest and Range Policy—Its Development in the United States, 1956; (with others) California Lands-Ownership, Use and Management, 1958; Minnesota Lands-Ownership, Use, and Management of Forest and Related Lands, 1961; also bulls., articles. Editor: History of Activities in the Field of Natural Resources, University of Michigan, 1953. Contbr. to Ency. Brit. Home: Alexandria, Va. Died May 8, 1978.

DANE, NATHAN, II, educator; b. Lexington, Mass., May 24, 1916; s. Francis Smith and Annie (Edmands) D.; A.B., Bowdoin Coll., 1937; M.A., U. Ill., 1939, Ph.D., 1941; m. Caroline Maxine Anderson, Apr. 2, 1942; children—Nathan III, Caroline Anderson, Joseph Anderson. Instr. Latin, Oberlin Coll., 1941-42; mem. faculty Bowdoin Coll., 1946—, prof. classics, 1954, Winkley prof. Latin, 1963-80. Served with AUS, 1942-46. Mem. Am. Philol. Assn., New Eng. Classical Assn. (pres. 1963-64), Phi Beta Kappa, Psi Upsilon. Author: Introduction to Languages and Literatures of Greece and Rome, 1952. Home: South Harpswell, Maine. Died Jan. 20, 1980.

DANE, WALTER ALDEN, lawyer; b. Newport, Vt., Feb. 4, 1882; s. Olin S. and Mabel (Robinson) D.; A.B., Univ. of Vt., 1903; student George Washington U. Law Sch., 1906-08; LL.D., Norwich U., 1937; m. Bertha A. Aldrich, Sept. 16, 1907; children—Barbara, Harriet F., Helen R. Confidential sec. to U.S. sec. of Navy, 1907-08; admitted to Mass. bar, 1912, since practiced Boston; mem. Dane, Howe & Brown; special counsel Christian Science Orgn., Boston; director, general counsel John Hinckley & Son Co.; dir. counsel E. C. Schirmer Music Company; counsel, sec. Bon Marche Dry Goods Co. Member of the bar of the U.S. Supreme Court. Trustee of Newton-Wellesley Hospital, Children's Hosp., Boston. Charter member World Peace Through Law Center. Member Am., Mass. bar associations, Phi Beta Kappa, Delta Psi; asso. mem. Assn. Bar City of N.Y. Republican. Conglist. Mason (32 deg.). Clubs: Dorset Field, Union, Brae Burn Country. Home: Newton Center, Mass.

DANENBERG, LEIGH, former newspaper pub.; b. N.Y.C., Sept. 23, 1893; s. Ury and Bertha (Filer) D.; student Townsend Harris Hall, 1906-09; A.B., N.Y. U.,1913; postgrad. Columbia Sch. Journalism, 1914; m. Nina Sutherland Purdy, 1920; m. 2d, Elsie Nicholas, June 23, 1928 (div.); children—Shirley, Dale, Leigh, Elsa Ann, Darryl Ann; m. 3d, Anne Bridge, May 22, 1965. Reporter, N.Y.C., Washington, San Francisco newspapers, 1914-17; free lance corr. in Germany, 1921-23; editor Norwalk Sentinel, 1923-29; pres., treas. Bridgeport Herald Corp., 1930-69; pub., editor Bridgeport (Conn.) Sunday Herald, 1930-65. Cons. in India on staff U.S. ambassador Chester Bowles, 1952-53. Served as staff sgt. M.C., AUS, 1917-18; cons. Fgn. Econ. Adminstrn. ETO, 1944-45. Clubs: Nat. Press, Overseas Press. Home: Westport, Conn. Died Dec. 3, 1976.

DANFORTH, CHARLES HASKELL, univ. prof.; b. Oxford, Me., Nov. 30, 1883; s. James and Mary Files (Haskell) D.; A.B., Tufts coll., 1908, A.M., 1910, Sc.D., 1941, Ph.D., Washington U., St. Louis, 1912; m. Florence Wenonah Garrison, June 24, 1914; children—Charles Garrison, Alan Haskell, Donald Reed. Fellow, Tufts Coll., 1908, instr. in biology, 1910-11; fellow, Harvard Med. Sch., 1910-11, lecturer in anatomy, 1929-30; instr. in anatomy, Washington U., 1908-14, associate, 1914-16, associate prof., 1916-22; associate prof. anatomy, Stanford, 1922-23, prof., 1923-49, dept. exec., 1938-49, emeritus since 1949. Mem. A.A.A.S. (v.p. and chmn. sect. H., Anthropology, 1932, pres. Pacific division, 1950-51), Am. Assn. Anatomists (exec. com., 1927-31, 2d v.p. 1936-38), Western Soc. of Naturalists (pres., 1942-44), Soc. Exptl. Biology and Medicine (v.p., 1941-43; editorial bd. of Proceedings, 1936-42), Am. Soc. Zoölogists, Genetic Soc. Am., Am. Soc. Human Genetics (v.p. 1951-52), Soc. Study Evolution, American Anthrop. Assn., California Acad. of Medicine, California Academy Sciences, Nat. Acad. Sciences, American Association of Physical Anthropologists, American Philosophical Society, Delta Upsilon, Phi Beta Pi, Sigma Xi, Phi Beta Kappa, Alpha Omega Alpha. Asso. editor: Sex and Internal Secretions, 2d edit., 1938; Am. Jour. Phys. Anthropology, 1927-42; Anatomical Record, 1928-48. Mem. editorial bd., Growth, 1940-49, Excerpta Medica, Sect. 1 since 1946. Home: Stanford, Calif.

DANIEL, JAMES MARTIN, JR., hosp. adminstr.; b. Greenville, N.C., Sept. 4, 1915; s. James M. and Ellen L. (Garrett) D.; A.B., Duke, 1936, grad. course in hosp. adminstrn., 1938; m. Virginia Elizabeth Skinner, Nov. 9, 1940; children—James Martin III, Elizabeth S. Asst. sec.-treas. Hosp. Care Assn., Durham, N.C., 1938-40; asst. supt. James Walker Meml. Hosp., Wilmington, N.C., 1940-43; adminstr. Rockingham Meml. Hosp., Harrisonburg, Va., 1943-46; supt. Columbia Hosp. of Richland County, Columbia, S.C., 1946-70; asst. coordinator S.C. Regional Med. Program, 1970-78. Dir. Blue Cross S.C., 1950-71, Graphic Communications, Milw., 1959-70. Chmn. bd. dirs. Richland County area council Boy Scouts Am.; bd. dirs. A.R.C., Harrisonburg, Va., Richland County Crippled Children's Assn.; mem. hosp. adv. council S.C. Bd. Health, 1947-71, chmn., 1965-68, chmn. licensing com. hosp. adv. council, 1947-65; bd. dirs. Va.-Carolina Hosp. Conf., 1948-60; bd. dirs., pres. Hosp. Data Center S.C., 1968-70. Fellow Am. Coll. Hosp. Adminstrs. (chmn. membership div. bd. credentials); mem. Am. (ho. dels. 1950-60, bd. trustees 1960-63; chmn. coms. and councils; del. at large ho. of dels. 1968-72), S.C. (pres. 1948, bd. trustees, past treas.) hosp. assns., Jr. C. of C., (sec.-treas., pres. elect). Episcopalian (vestryman). Rotarian. Lion (past pres.). Clubs: Civitan (past v.p.), Forest Lake Country. Home: Columbia, S.C. Died Feb. 4, 1978; buried St. Michael and All Angels Epis. Ch. Churyard, Columbia, S.C.

DANIEL, JOHN LAURENCE, chemist; b. in Prince Edward County, Va., July 22, 1882; s. William G. and Marie Louise (Jordan) D.; A.B., Hampden-Sydney (Va.) Coll., 1902; M.A., Washington and Lee U., Lexington, Va., 1905, grad. student, 1908-10; grad. student U. of Chicago, summers 1907, 08; m. Kathleen Kirkpatrick, June 18, 1914; children—Kathleen Laura (Mrs. William Monroe Spicer), John Laurence (dec.), Elizabeth Kirkpatrick. Teacher Greenbrier Presbyterial Sch., 1902-03, Mt. Clinton (Va.) Prep. Sch., 1903-04; headmaster Donald Fraser Sch., Decatur, Ga., 1905-08; chemist, development dept. Western Electric Co., New York, 1910-12; with Ga. Sch. Tech. since 1912, successively as instr., asst. prof., asso. prof., prof. of chemistry and head dept., vice dean div. of grad. studies. Fellow A.A.A.S., mem. Am. Chem. Soc., Am. Assn. Univ. Profs., Ga. Acad. of Science, Alpha Chi Rho, Alpha Chi Sigma, Phi Kappa Phi, Phi Beta Kappa,

Omicron Delta Kappa. Presbyterian. Author: Theory of Analysis (with W. C. Whitley), 1940; Calculations of Analytical Chemistry, 1941. Home: Decatur, Ga. *

DANIEL, ROLLIN AUGUSTUS, JR., surgeon; b. Union Point, Ga., June 14, 1908; s. Rollin Augustus and Mary (Frazer) D.; B.A., Vanderbilt U., 1930, M.D., 1933; m. Ann Kelley, Jan. 5, 1939; children—Ann, Rollin Augustus III; m. 2d, Enid L. Carney, June 15, 1976. Intern Vanderbilt U. Hosp., Nashville, 1933-34, resident, 1934-38; asst. resident surgeon Barnes Hosp., St. Louis, 1934-35; asst. prof. surgery Vanderbilt U. Sch. Medicine, 1941-47, asso. prof. surgery, 1947-51, prof. surgery, 1951-54, prof. clin. surgery, 1954-78; chief surg. service St. Thomas Hosp., 1962-66, chief dept. surgery, 1970-78; cons. thoracic surgery VA Hosp., Nashville, 1946-78. Diplomate Am. Bd. Surgery, Am. Bd. Thoracic Surgery (chmn. 1966-67, sec.-treas. 1968-73). Fellow A.C.S.; mem. Middle Tenn. Heart Assn. (past pres.), Vanderbilt U. Alumni Assn. (bd. dirs), Am., Surg. Assn., Soc. Clin. Surgery, Am. Assn. Thoracic Surgery, Soc. Univ. Surgeons (past sec.), Am., So., Tenn. med. assns., Nashville Surg. Soc. (past pres.), Nashville Acad. Medicine (past pres.). Baptist. Club: Belle Meade Country (Nashville). Home: Nashville, Tenn. Died Dec. 1, 1978; buried Mt. Olivet Cemetery, Nashville.

DANIEL, RUBY KATHRYN, ophthalmologist; d. Robert Harry and Beulah May (Fite) Daniel; M.D., Baylor U., 1928; M.S., U. Minn., 1938. Intern at Lane-Stanford Teaching Hosp., San Francisco, 1928-29; Intern in ophthalmology, U. Chgo. clinics, 1932-33, asst. resident in ophthalmology, 1933-34; fellowship in ophthalmology, Mayo Clinic Found., Rochester, Minn., 1934-36; mem. teaching staff and asso. in ophthalmology, Pieping, (China) Union Med. Coll. (Rockefeller Found.), 1936-37; vis. prof. ophthalmology, Women's Med. Coll. of Vellore (South India), 1937; 1st asst. ophthalmology, Mayo Clinic, 1938-39; asst. clin. prof. ophthalmology, Southwestern Med. Found., Dallas, 1943-78; practice medicine specializing in ophthalmology, Dallas, 1939-78; chief med. cons. Lighthouse for the Blind. Diplomate Am. Bd. Ophthalmology. Fellow A.C.S., Internat. Coll. Surgeons; mem. A.M.A., A.A.A.S., Am., Dallas (past pres.) acads. ophthalmology and otolaryngology, So. Clin. Soc., Dallas County Med. Soc., Alumni Assn. U. Chgo. (life), Alumni Assn. Mayo Found., Mortar Bd. Methodist. Clubs: Brook Hollow Golf, Knife and Fork, Coll. Women's Writers (Dallas). Has initiated and incorporated 2 philanthropic organizations for salvaging eyes and rehab. after eye difficulties (pres. both orgns.). Author: Allergy and Cataracts. Contbr. numerous articles to profl. jours. Home: Dallas, Tex. Died Feb. 13, 1978.

DANIELIAN, NOOBAR RETHESOS, economist; b. Constantinople, Turkey, Sept. 12, 1906; s. Réthésos and Anne (Papazian) D.; A.B., Harvard, 1928, M.A., 1929, Ph.D., 1932; m. Grace A. Apelian, Aug. 28, 1936; children—Sandra Elizabeth, Ronald Lawrence. Came to U.S., 1923, naturalized, 1928. Instr. dept. econs. Harvard, 1929-35; financial, utility expert FCC, 1935-38; dir. St. Lawrence survey U.S. Dept. Commerce, 1939-43; dir. program staff Fgn. Econ. Adminstrn., 1943-44; cons. Office Sec. Commerce, Office Undersec. State, 1944-45; v.p. Gt. Lakes-St. Lawrence Assn., 1949-52, pres., 1952-65; mem. adv. bd. U.S. St. Lawrence Seaway Devel. Corp., 1961-66; editor, pub. The Heartland, 1953-56, Port Cons., Detroit, 1955-56; econ. adviser, Lorain, O. 1955-59. Recipient Certificate of Merit, Amvets, 1955. Mem. Internat. Econ. Policy Assn. (pres. 1957-74), Am. Econ. Assn., Am. Acad. Polit. Sci., Nat. Assn. Bus. Economists, Phi Beta Kappa. Episcopalian. Clubs: Congressional Country (Bethesda, Md.); Detroit; Harvard (N.Y.C.); Harvard, National Press, Metropolitan and International (Washington). Author: The St. Lawrence Survey (7 vols.), 1941. Editor: U.S. Balance of Payments, an Appraisal of U.S. Economic Strategy, 1966; U.S. Balance of Payments, A Reappraisal, 1968; U.S. Balance of Payments: From Crisis to Controversy, 1972. Contbr. to profl. publs., mags. Home: Potomac, Md. Died May 12, 1974.

DANIELS, CLARENCE WHITE, mfg. exec.; b. Worcester, Mass., May 12, 1884; s. Fred Harris and Sarah (White) D.; Met.E., Columbia Sch. of Mines, 1910; m. Janet Wellman, July 27, 1910; children—Jeanne, Clarence W., Jr., Priscilla. Foreman Anaconda Copper Co., Great Falls, Mont., 1910-13; plants engr., Norton Co., Worcester, 1914-49, ret. June 1, 1949, now dir. and mem. exec. com. Trustee Meml. Hosp. of Worcester. Mem. Am. Soc. M.E. Clubs: Worcester, Tatnuck Country, Worcester County Republican. Home: Worcester, Mass. *

DANIELS, JOSEPH, prof. mining engring.; b. N.Y. City, Aug. 8, 1884; s. Louis and Rose (Miller) D.; S.B., Mass. Inst. Tech., 1905; M.S., Lehigh U., 1908, E.M., 1933; m. Gladys M. Fletcher, July 31, 1914; children—Martha Dorothy Prideaux, Gladys Ruth Wienker, Josephine Gayman. Mining engr. Dominion Coal Co., 1905-07; asst. prof., prof. mining engring. and metallurgy U. Wash., 1911-54, emeritus, 1954—; coöperative investigations with N.W. expt. sta. U.S. Bur. of Mines, 1917-54, cons. engr., 1939-54; prof. mining engring. Punjab College Engineering and Technology, Lahore, Pakistan, 1955-56. Chairman Military Survey Board, State of Washington, 1917-18, World War, also assistant to State Fuel administrator; Washington State Planning Council, Coal and Industrial Minerals Committee, 1934-43. Fellow A.A.A.S.; member American Institute Mining and Metall. Engrs., Am. Soc. for Metals (War Products Advisory Com., 1942-43), Am. Soc. for Engineering Edn., Canadian Inst. Mining and Metallurgy, Tau Beta Pi, Sigma Xi, Acacia. Conglist. Author of various bulls. relating to coal deposits, coking industry and mineral resources of the Pacific Northwest. Home: Seattle.

DANIELS, WORTH BAGLEY, physician; b. Raleigh, N.C., Apr. 8, 1899; s. Josephus and Addie Worth (Bagley) D.; grad. St. Albans Sch., 1916; A.B., U. N.C., 1920; M.D., Johns Hopkins, 1924; D. Sci., Georgetown U., 1962; m. Josephine Poe January, Sept. 3, 1923; children—Worth Bagley, Derick. Intern Bellevue Hosp., N.Y.C., 1925-26, house physician, 1926-27; pvt. practice internal medicine, Washington, 1927-42, 46-74; instr. phys. diagnosis George Washington Med. Sch., 1927-30; instr. medicine Georgetown Med. Sch., 1927-33, clin. prof. medicine, 1933-64, emeritus clinical prof. medicine, 1964-78; jr. attending physician Emergency Hosp., Washington, 1928-30, sr. attending physician 1930-58; sr. attending physician Washington Hosp. Center, 1958-61, sr. adv. physician, from 1961, trustee; med. cons. Walter Reed Gen. Hosp., 1946-47; sr. cons. in medicine Mt. Alto VA Hosp., 1947-53; sr. cons. internal medicine to surgeon gen. U.S. Army, from 1950. Trustee Johns Hopkins, 1954-57; regent Nat. Library Medicine, chmn., 1957-58, 61-62. Served from maj. to col. AUS, 1942-46. Diplomate Am. Bd. Internal Medicine. Master A.C.P.; mem. Assn. Am. Physicians, Am. Clin. and Climatol. Assn. (past pres.), Am., D.C. med. assns., Soc. Med. Cons. to Armed Forces (past pres.), Alpha Omega Alpha. Democrat. Episcopalian. Clubs: Alfalfa, Alibi, Metropolitan. Home: Washington, D.C. Died June 6, 1978.

DANIELSON, STIG, investment co. exec.; b. Goteborg, Sweden, Mar. 17, 1918; s. Tholw and Anna (Davidson) D.; grad. U. Commerce, Goteborg, 1940; Pub. Accountant, 1944; m. Sonja Engblad, 1969; children—Mona Christine (Mrs. Ingemar Iletorp), Ann Chatrin (Mrs. Lars Gustavii), Bjorn Christer. Accountant, J.E. Stenbergs Revisionsbyra AB, Goteborg, 1939-48, part owner, 1948-55, sole propr., 1956-59; exec. v.p., dir. Tirfing Steamship Co., Inc., 1959-69; pres., dir. Investment AB Skansen Leionet, 1964-76, AB A.K. Fernstroms Granitindustrier, 1968-76, Kullgrens Enka AB, 1969-76; chmn. Elektriska Svetsnings AB; dir. AB Custos, Stockholm, Swedish Am. Line, Swedish East Asia Co., Tirfing Steamship Co., AB Aritmos, Helsingborg, Simon Edstrom AB, Malmo, Svenska Granitindustri AB, Karlshamn, Rederi AB Goteborg-Frederikshavn-Linjen, AB Aug. Leffler & Son, Skanshus AB, AB Skepps-och Fiskeritillbehor, Swedish Orient Line. Decorated knight comdr. Vasa Order. Rotarian. Clubs: Royal Bachelors, Royal Yacht. Home: Goteborg, Sweden. Died Apr. 12, 1976.

DANKMEYER, THEODORE ROGNALD, lawyer; b. Balt., Feb. 19, 1903; s. Charles and Caroline Antonia Genevieve (Ohle) D.; J.D., U. Md., 1924; m. Anne Virginia Burrier, July 31, 1928; children—Anne Elizabeth (Mrs. Samuel Hopkins), Gretchen D. Stock, Theodore Rognald. Admitted to Md. bar, 1924; mem. firm Niles, Barton & Wilmer, specializing admiralty and shipping law, Balt., 1938-76, Editor-in-chief, pres. Am. Maritime Cases, Inc., 1952-76. Mem. com. to revise admiralty rules to conform to amendment to Fed. Rules of Civil Procedure. Bd. dirs. Lutheran Hosp. of Md., Inc., Sch. of the Chimes (handicapped children). Mem. Am. Judicature Soc., Am., Md., Balt. bar assns., Maritime Law Assn. U.S., Inter-Am. Bar Assn., Navy League U.S., Md. Hist. Soc., Md. Bar Found. (charter), Johns Hopkins Assos., Engring. Soc. Balt., Delta Theta Phi. Democrat. Lutheran. Mason. Clubs: Propeller of U.S.; University (life mem.); Merchants, 14 W. Hamilton St., Johns Hopkins (Balt.). Home: Baltimore, Md. Died Apr. 4, 1976.

D'ANTONI, JOSEPH STEVEN, physician, ret. corp. exec.; b. New Orleans, Sept. 3, 1907; s. Salvador and Mary (Vaccaro) D'A.; M.D., Tulane U., 1932; m. Helen Skelly, Oct. 19, 1933 (dec.); children—Maura Ann, Joseph Steven, Patrick Skelly. Intern Charity Hosp., New Orleans, 1932-33, asst. vis. physician, 1934-38, vis. physician, 1938-47, sr. vis. physician, 1947-54; instr. lab. clin. medicine, Tulane U., 1933-35, instr. dept. medicine, 1933-40, instr. dept. tropical medicine, 1935-40, asst. prof., 1940-43, asso. prof., 1943-46, prof. clin. tropical medicine, 1946-56, lectr. dept. tropical medicine and hygiene, 1957-79; head, div. tropical medicine, Lakeshore Hosp., New Orleans, 1946-49; vis. physician Baptist Hosp., New Orleans, 1950-79; dir. Standard Fruit & S.S. Co., 1950-72, med. dir., 1951-53, pres., 1953-64, chmn. bd., 1954-70, hon. chmn. bd., 1971-72; chmn. bd. Structural Systems Corp., New Orleans; pres. Harbor Banana Distbrs., Long Beach, Cal. Dir. Internat. Trade Mart, New Orleans; mem. bd. commrs. Port of New Orleans, 1967-71, pres., 1970. Fellow A.C.P., A.A.A.S., Am. Soc. Tropical Medicine (pres. 1947-48); mem. A.M.A., Am. Soc. Parasitologists, Am. Acad. Tropical Medicine, La. State, Orleans Parish med. socs., Nat. Malaria Soc., So. Med. Assn. Home: New Orleans, La. Died May 23, 1979.

DANTZIG, TOBIAS (DANT'ZIG), author, prof. mathematics; b. Shavli, Russia, Feb. 19, 1884; s. Samuel and Augusta (Demont) D.; ed. High Sch., Shavli, and U. of Paris; Ph.D., Ind. U., 1916; m. Anna Ourison, 1908; children—George Bernard, Henry Poincaré. Came to U.S., 1910, naturalized, 1917. Instr. Ind. U., 1914-18; mathematician War Dept., U.S. Army, 1917-18; instr. Columbia, 1918-19, Johns Hopkins, 1919-20; cons. mathematician New York and Baltimore, 1920-26; prof. math., U. of Maryland, 1926-46, retired since 1946; head dept. math., 1936-46. Mem. Am. Math. Soc. Author: Number, the Language of Science, 1930, 3d rev. edit., 1939; Aspects of Science, 1937; The Story of Geometry, 1940. Contbr. to math. jours. Home: Los Angeles, Calif.

DANZANSKY, JOSEPH BAER, lawyer, corp. exec.; b. Washington, May 16, 1914; A.B., George Washington U., 1934, J.D., 1936. Admitted to D.C. bar, 1936, U.S. Supreme Ct. bar, 1947; sr. partner firm Danzansky & Dickey, Washington, 1941-64; pres., chief exec. officer Giant Food Inc., Washington, 1964-77, chmn. bd., from 1977; dir. Chesapeake & Potomac Telephone Co., Nat. Bank of Washington. Pres. Washington Bd. Trade, 1971, 76. Mem. Am. Bar Assn., Bar Assn. D.C., Omicron Delta Kappa, Phi Eta Sigma. Home: Washington, D.C. Died Nov. 8, 1979.

DANZIGER, FREDERICK SIMON, lawyer; b. N.Y.C., Apr. 15, 1911; s. Ernst and Martha (Bachmann) D.; BA., Harvard, 1930; LL.B, Yale, 1936; m. Louise Paskus, June 24, 1935; children—Richard Martin, Frederick Michael. Admitted to NY. bar, 1936, since practiced in N.Y.C.; mem. firm Oppheimer, Haiblum & Kupfer, 1936-40; partner Silberfeld, Danziger & Bongou, 1940-80. Dir. Amerace Corp., Superior Mfg. & Instrument Corp Trustee Altro Rehab. Services, Inc. Served to maj. USAAF, 1942-45. Decorated Air medal. Mem. Assn Bar City N.Y Am. Bar Assn., N.Y. County Lawyers Assn. Home: White Plains, NY. Died Nov. 15, 1980.

D'ARCY, MARTIN CYRIL, clergyman, writer; b. Bath, Eng., June 15, 1888; s. Martin Valentine and Madoline (Keegan) D'A.; M.A. (Locke scholar 1917, Green Moral Philosophy prize 1922), Oxford U., 1916; D.D., Gregorian U., Rome, Italy, 1923; D.Litt. (hon.), Georgetown U., 1935, Fordham U., 1940, Marquette U., 1950, Nat. U. of Ireland, 1955. Entered Soc. of Jesus, 1906, ordained priest Roman Cath. Ch., 1921; lectr. philosophy Oxford U., 1926-45, master of Campion Hall, Oxford, 1932-45; provincial of English Province, Soc. of Jesus, 1945-50; lectr. at Fordham U., Notre Dame U., Georgetown U., 1939-40, 41-42, 50, 54-56, 58-59; Danforth lectr. Cornell U., 1959; Roman Cath. rep. on BBC 1936-45; lectr. for Brit. Council on Humanities in Italy, Spain, Portugal, Malta; conventual chaplain Knights of Malta. Mem. Royal Coll. Lit.; hon. mem. Am. Acad. Arts and Scis. Clubs: Athenaeum (London). Author: The Mass and the Redemption, 1926; Thomas Aquinas, 1932; The Nature of Belief, 1933; Death and Life, 1942; The Problem of Pain, 1943; The Mind and Heart of Love, 1945; Communism and Christianity, 1957; The Meeting of Love and Knowledge, 1958; The Meaning and Matter of History, 1959; No Absent God, 1962; Of God and Man, 1964; Dialogue with Myself, 1966; Facing The People, 1967; Humanism and Christianity, 1969; Facing the Truth, 1969. Address: London, England. Died Nov. 20, 1976; buried St. Mary's Catholic Cemetery, London.

DARDEN, COLGATE WHITEHEAD, JR., pres. U. Va.; b. Southampton Co., Virginia, Feb. 11, 1897; A.B., U. of Va.; M.A. and LL.B., Columbia; Carnegie fellowship, Oxford U. In practice of law in Va.; mem. Va. Gen. Assembly, two terms 1930-33; mem. 73d Congress (1933-35), Va. at large, 74th, 76th and 77th Congresses (1935-37, 1939-41, resigned to run for gov.), 2d Dist. Va. Gov. of Va., for term expiring Jan. 1946; apptd. vice chmn. Navy's Civilian Adv. Com., 1947; pres. U. Va., 1947-59. Mem. Bd. Cons. to Pres. on Mut. Security, Fgn. Intelligence. Mem. Ho. of Reps. 2d Dist. Va., 1932-36, 38-41. U.S. del. 10th Session of Gen. Assembly of UN. Mem. bd. of visitors U.S. Naval Acad., 1936 and 1939. Served with U.S. Marine Corps, also French Army, World War I. Democrat. Home: Norfolk, Va. Died June 9, 1981.

D'AREZZO, JOSEPH PAUL, bus. exec.; b. Providence, July 18, 1917; s. Louis and Erminia (Perillo) D'A.; B.S, U.S. Naval Acad., 1940; M.S Johns Hopkins, 1949; m. Helen Iwinski, Dec. 11, 1943; children—Carol, Vivian, Paul William, Mark Louis. Served with US Navy, 1934-40; commd. officer U.S. Army, 1940, advanced through grades to lt. col., Arty. Corps; mem. Army Gen. Staff, 1953-55, active Res., 1955-71, brig gen Res.; divisional vp. AMF Inc Alexandria, Va., 1955-57, divisional v.p., dir. planning, spl. asst. to pres., 1957-60, v.p., 1960-80, group exec., elec. products group, 1961-80, coordinator counter trade bus. with 3d World markets, 1980-81. Decorated Legion of Merit. Mem. Am. Ordnance Assn. Club: Army and Navy (Arlington, Va.). Home: Alexandria, Va. Died Feb. 2, 1981; buried Arlington Nat. Cemetery.

DARKEN, LAWRENCE STAMPER, phys. chemist; b. Bklyn., Sept. 18, 1909; s. William Henry and Gertrude Ann (Stamper) D.; A.B., Hamilton Coll., 1930; Ph.D., Yale, 1933; m. Margaret Elizabeth FitzGerald, Sept. 6, 1939; children—Joanne Savage, Mary Cummins, Lawrence Stamper, William Henry II, Marjorie Beth, Edward Reynolds. With U.S. Steel Corp., 1935-71, dir. fundamental research, 1962-71; prof. earth and mineral scis. Pa. State U., 1972-78; instr., adj. prof. Poly. Inst. Bklyn., 1942-53. Recipient Francis J. Clamer award Franklin Inst., 1966. Fellow N.Y. Acad. Scis., A.A.A.S., Metall. Soc., Am. Soc. Metals (Gold medal 1971), Royal Soc. Arts; mem. Nat. Acad. Scis., Am. Inst. Mining, Metall. and Petroleum Engrs. (recipient Robert W. Hunt Silver medal 1967), Am. Chem. Soc., Phi Beta Kappa, Sigma Xi, Lambda Chi Alpha. Author: (with R. W. Gurry) Physical Chemistry of Metals, 1953; also numerous articles. Home: Boalsburg, Pa. Died June 7, 1978; buried Boalsburg Cemetery.

DARLEY, WARD, physician, educator; b. Denver, Oct. 30, 1903; s. Ward and Mary (Bolles) D.; A.B., U. Colo., 1926, M.D., 1929, LL.D., 1958; D.Sc., Colo. Coll., 1954, U. Nebr., 1956, N.Y. Med. Coll., 1965, U. Ill., 1965, Brown U., 1966; LL.D., Loyola U., 1965, Northwestern U., 1965, U. N.M., 1966; m. Pauline Braiden, Apr. 29, 1930; children—Donna Jean, Ward Braiden. Intern and resident U. Colo. Sch. Medicine and Hosp., 1929-31; pvt. practice of medicine, Denver, 1931-44; asso. prof. medicine, U. Colo. Sch. Medicine, 1944-46, prof., 1946-56, dean, 1945-48, v.p. univ., dean dept. medicine, 1949-53, pres., 1953-56, pres. emeritus, 1973-79, vis. prof. medicine, 1965-73, prof. medicine emeritus, 1973-79; exec. dir. Assn. Am. Med. Colls., 1957-65. Mem. bd. cons. div. medicine and public health Rockefeller Found., 1952-53; Western Interstate Commn. Higher Edn., exec. commr. Colo., 1951-56; med., ednl. sci. adv. council Nat. Fund Med. Edn., 1953-55; bd. visitors Air U., USAF, 1955-58; trustee Nat. Merit Scholarship Corp., 1955-63. Named one of ten most influential leaders in med. edn. Council Med. Edn. of AMA, 1979. Home: Laguna Hills, Calif. Died June 28, 1979.

DARR, LESLIE ROGERS, U.S. judge; b. Jasper, Tenn., Nov. 8, 1886; s. Joseph A. and Rebecca Jane (Rogers) D.; student Pryor Inst., Jasper, 1904-08; LL.B., Cumberland U., 1909; m. Barbara Raulston, June 10, 1912; children—Barbara Katherine (Mrs. Don Hastings), Leslie Rogers. Admitted to Tenn. bar, 1910, practiced law at Jasper, Tenn., 1910-26; judge 18th Circuit of Tenn., 1926-39; U.S. dist. judge, Eastern and Middle dists. of Tenn., 1939-61; sr. United States judge for Eastern district Tennessee, 1961—. Democrat. Methodist. Mason (32 deg. Shriner). Clubs: Civitan, Lookout Mountain, Fairyland. Home: Chattanooga, Tenn.

DARRAH, DAVID HARLEY, newspaperman; b. Lloydsville, O., May 27, 1894; s. Harley Howard and Anna Jane (McFarland) D.; Ph.B., Akron Municipal U., 1917; m. Simone Jane Heller, Nov. 8, 1921. Reporter Akron Beacon Jour., Cleveland Leader and Cleveland Plain Dealer, 1912, 13; with Am. Ambulance Field Service in France in 1917; later enlisted in U.S. Army at Soissons, France, Oct. 1, 1917; night editor Paris edition of Chicago Tribune, 1919-22, mng. editor, 1922-26; asst. corr. in London of Chicago Tribune, 1926-27, chief corr. Rome Bur. of same, 1927-33; traveling corr. in Europe, 1933-35; made 18,000 mile journey through South Am. countries during 1930-31 revolutionary period; expelled by Mussolini from Italy, June 1935; chief London corr. Chicago Tribune Foreign News Service, Aug. 1935-Mar. 1940; war corr. with Franco armies in Spanish civil war, 1936, 37, 38, Battle of France, May, June 1940; cor. with Vichy govt., July 1940-Nov. 1942; seized by Germans, interned Baden-Baden, Germany, Dec. 1942-March 1944; after repatriation to United States on Gripsholm, returned France, Sept. 1944, and served as war corr. and chief Paris bur. of Tribune until Apr. 1946; spl. assignments 1946-54. Madrid corr., 1955-68. Author: Hail Caesar, 1936; Conspiracy in Paris, 1953. Home: Biarritz, France. Died Mar. 29, 1976.

DARROW, RICHARD WILLIAM, pub. relations cons.; b. Champaign County, O., Sept. 24, 1915; s. Ben H. and Frances (Carter) D.; B.A. cum laude, Ohio Wesleyan U., 1936; m. Nelda Darling, Sept. 17, 1938 (div. Sept. 1975); children—William Richard, John Harrison; m. 2d, Suzanne Jane Tillman, Sept. 21, 1975. Reporter, circulation promotion Daily Citizen, Urbana, O., 1933-34; reporter Internat. News Service, Washington, 1935; reporter, aviation editor, asst. city editor Columbus (O.) Citizen, 1936-41; mgr. pub. relations Curtiss-Wright Corp., Columbus, 1941-43, asst. dir. pub. relations, Buffalo, 1943-44, N.Y.C., 1944-45; asst. to pres. Am. Meat Inst., Chgo., 1945-46; dir. pub. relations Glenn L. Martin Co., Balt., 1946-52; v.p. Hill & Knowlton, Inc., N.Y.C., 1952-55, exec. v.p., 1955-66, pres., 1966-71, chmn. bd., chief exec. officer, 1971-76. Mem. Scarsdale (N.Y.) Recreation Council, 1956-63, vice chmn. 1958-62; chmn. Scarsdale Youth Relations Com., 1966-67; mem. Com. for Second Regional Plan Met. N.Y., 1966-68. Mem. nat. exec. bd. Boy Scouts Am., 1962-76, mem. exec. com., 1966-76, nat. chmn. pub. relations, 1962-68, chmn. communications com., 1968-71, chmn. internat. relations com., 1972-76, chmn. pub. relations Greater N.Y. councils, 1959-66, chmn. camping com., 1966-71, v.p., 1970-76, chmn. camp devel. com., 1971-73, v.p., 1973-76, chmn. world scout pub. relations com. Mem. village bd. trustees, police commr., Scarsdale, N.Y., 1967-71, mayor, 1971-73. Hon. dir. White Plains Hosp.; trustee Ohio Wesleyan U., 1957-76, chmn., 1968-72; bd. dirs. Regional Plan Assn., 1968-76. Chmn. civilian vol., pub. relations adv. commn., U.S. Mil. Acad., 1960-76. Named Outstanding Young Man Balt., 1950; Pub. Relations Profl. of Yr., Pub. Relations News, 1971; recipient TWA aviation writing awards, 1940, 41; Latin Am. pub. relations award, 1947; Silver Beaver award Boy Scouts Am., 1963. Silver Buffalo award, 1966, Distinguished Eagle award, 1969; Bronze Wolf award World Scout Assn., 1975; Bronze Tamaraw award, 1974, Silver Tamaraw award, 1975; Outstanding Civilian Service medal U.S. Army, 1972; Scarsdale Town Club medal, 1973; Scarsdale bowl, 1974. Mem. Ohio Wesleyan U. Alumni Assn. (pres. 1954-56), Pub. Relations Soc. Am. (nat. exec. com., 1958, v.p. counselors sect. 1962-63, pres. N.Y. chpt. 1953-55); Aviation Writers Assn., Assn. Petroleum Writers, Am. Petroleum Inst., Ohio Soc. N.Y. (trustee 1954-57, 62-65, v.p. 1957-59), Phi Beta Kappa, Phi Gamma Delta (sect. chief 1958-61), Omicron Delta Kappa, Pi Delta Epsilon, Pi Sigma Alpha. Mem. Dutch Ref. Ch. Clubs: Union League, Overseas Press, N.Y. Athletic, Cloud (N.Y.C.); Nat. Press, Carlton, Burning Tree (Washington); Blind Brook (Port Chester, N.Y.); Winged Foot (Mamaroneck, N.Y.); Scarsdale (N.Y.) Town (gov. 1960-67, pres. 1964-65). Co-author: Dartnell Public Relations Handbook, 1965. Home: New York, N.Y. Died Mar. 20, 1976.

DART, DONALD EDWARD, advt. exec.; b. Aurora, Ill. July 5, 1932; s. Edward and Glenna Mae (Hartless) D.; B.S. in Pharmacy, U. Ill., 1955; m. Joan Frances Bennett, Aug. 21, 1965; children—Christel, Sydney, Scott, Salesnan Upjohn Co., Chgo., 1957-60, Fenwal Labs., Chgo., 1960-65; account supr. DF Fitzsimmons, Inc., N.Y.C., 1965-67; exec. v.p. advt. Sieber & McIntyre, Inc., Chgo., 1967-80. Served with USN, 1955-57. Mem. Midwest Pharm. Advertisers Club (past pres.), Chgo. Athletic Assn. Home: Kenilworth, Ill. Died Aug. 27, 1980; buried Calvary Cemetery, Evanston, Ill.

DASHER, GEORGE FRANKLIN, college pres.; b. Edwardsburg, Mich., Jan. 12, 1882; s. Henry and Sarah Amelia (Arney) D.; grad. high sch., Kalamazoo, Mich., 1899; B.S., Kalamazoo Coll., 1904; B.S., U. of Chicago, 1905; LL.D., Georgetown (Ky.) Coll., 1921; m. Lucy Grubbs Orndorff, of Russellville, Ky., 1912 (died 1918); children—John Orndorff, Dorothy Arney; m. 2d, Arvilla Henrietta Ginsburg, of Rio Janeiro, Brazil, Oct. 15, 1921; children—George Franklin, Mary Emily. Mem. faculty, Des Moines (Ia.) Coll., 1904-08; prof. chemistry and biology, Bethel Coll., Russellville, Ky., since 1908, elected treas., 1916, pres. since 1918. Chmn. Four-Minute Men, Logan Co., Ky., 1917-18. Organizer Russellville Bapt. Ch., supt. S.S., deacon since 1916; mem. bd. Bapt. Edn. Soc. of Ky. Mem. Mu Delta Sigma, Rotary Internat. Democrat. Home: Russellville, Ky.

DASPIT, LAWRENCE RANDALL, naval officer; b. Houma, La., Oct. 18, 1905; s. Joseph Arthur and Katherine (Randall) D.; student La. State U., 1922-23; B.S., U.S. Naval Acad., 1927; grad. U.S. Naval Postgrad. Sch., 1936; M.S., U. Cal. at Berkeley, 1937; m. Charlotte Brown, Mar. 10, 1934; 1 son, Frank; m. 2d, Marjorie Walsh, May 17, 1947; children—Caroline, Dana, Peter. Commd. ensign U.S. Navy, 1927, advanced through grades to rear adm., 1954; assigned various ships and naval stations, 1927-43; comdg. officer U.S.S. Tinosa, 1943; with submarine bldg. div. Bur. Ships, 1944-45; comdr. Submarine Div. 102, 1945; chief staff officer Submarine Tng. Command Pacific, 1945; tng. and material officer Submarine Force Pacific, 1946; head program br. Office Naval Research, 1946-47; comdr. Submarine Squadron 4, 1947-48; head submarine br. Office Chief Naval Operations, 1948-50; chief staff to comdr. Submarine Force, U.S. Pacific Fleet, 1951-52; comdg. officer U.S.S. Los Angeles, 1952-53; chief navy sect. Mil. Assistance Adv. Group, Japan, 1953-54; navy dep. Armed Forces Spl. Weapons Project, 1955-56; comdr. Cruiser Div. 6, 1956-57, Task Group 7.3 and Navy Dep. Joint Task Force 7, 1957; dir. underseas warfare div. Office Chief Naval Operations, 1958-59; comdr. submarine force U.S. Atlantic Fleet, 1960, dep. comdr., 1960-62, comdt. 6th Naval Dist., 1962-65; comdt. Armed Forces Staff Coll., 1965-67; exec. sec. engring. div. Nat. Acad. Scis., 1967-73. Decorated Navy Cross, Legion of Merit, Bronze Star (2) with Combat V, Letters of Commendations (4) 1 with Combat V, Presdl. Unit Citation. Home: Arlington, Va. Died May 19, 1979.

DAU, FREDERICK JENSEN, air force officer, mfg. co. exec.; b. Fresno, Cal., Mar. 18, 1907; s. Christian Jensen and Mary (Jensen) D.; B.S., U.S. Mil. Acad., 1928; B.S. in Civil Engring., U. Cal., 1932; student Army Engring. Sch., 1932-33, Army-Navy Staff Coll., 1945; m. Susan Childress King, July 5, 1929 (dec.); 1 dau., Susan Thorne (Mrs. Thomas Julian Fannon); m. 2d, Helen Singer, Oct. 24, 1969. Commd. 2d lt., C.E., U.S. Army, 1928, advanced through grades to maj. gen. USAF; with 14th Engrs., P.I., 1928-31; asst. prof. mil. sci. and sci. and tactics Mich. Coll. Mining and Tech., 1934-37; research and devel., Wright Field, O., 1937-41, Ft. Belvoir, Va., 1941-43; intelligence duty Chief Engrs., also gen. staff War Dept., 1943-45, hdqrs. China Theater, 1945-46; asst. mil. attache, China, 1946-48; dir. program standards and cost control, hdqrs. USAF, Washington, 1949-52; asst. for materiel coordination Air Materiel Command, 1952-54, dir. supply and services, 1954-59; ret. 1959; with Champion Papers, Inc., Hamilton, O., 1959-67, v.p., until 1964, exec. v.p., 1964-67; sr. v.p., dir. U.S. Plywood-Champion Papers, Inc., 1967-68, exec. v.p., from 1968. Dir. Sargent Industries, Inc., Huntington Park, Cal. Trustee Logistics Mgmt. Inst., Washington, 1961-80. Decorated Legion of Merit with 2 oak leaf clusters (Army), D.S.M.; Order of Yun Hui (China), others. Home: Williamsburg, Va. Died May 2, 1980.

DAUBER, CLARENCE ANDREW, mech. engr.; b. Cleve., Feb. 17, 1904; s. Henry John and Hannah (Behnke) D.; B.S., Case Inst. Tech., 1926; postgrad. U. Mich. Grad. Sch. Bus. Adminstrn., Columbia Grad. Sch. Bus. Adminstrn.; m. Catherine Mary Yeagle, July 15, 1933; children—Judith Ann (Mrs. Grady Guye), Debora Claire (Mrs. John D. Mosher), James Henry. Participated design major pipeline for transporting coal; with Cleve. Electric Illuminating Co., 1928-61, dir. civil and mech. engring., 1953-61; with Charles T. Main, Inc., Boston, from 1961, former pres.; partner Uhl, Hall & Rich; past dir. Atomic Power Devel. Assos.; past trustee High Temperature Reactor Devel. Assos. Vis. Com. Arnold Arboretum, Harvard. Past mem. bd. govs. Cleve. Engring. and Sci. Center; past vice chmn. prime movers com. Edison Electric Inst.; bd. dirs. Morgan Meml. Goodwill Industries. Registered profl. engr., Mass., Ohio, N.Y., Va., Pa., Mich., Wis., Md., N.H., Conn., Vt., W.Va., N.C., Fla., Colo. Fellow Am. Soc. M.E.; mem. I.E.E.E. (sr.), Am. Inst. Cons. Engrs., Engring. Soc. New Eng., Engrs. Club N.Y., Engrs. Club Boston, Sigma Xi, Tau Beta Pi, Zeta Psi. Conglist. (sr. deacon). Club: University (Boston). Home: Boston, Mass. Died Dec. 6, 1975.

DAUGHERTY, ROBERT LONG (DÄ'ER-TI), professor mech. engring.; b. Irvington, Ind., Sept. 14, 1885; s. John H. and Myrta (Burger) D.; grad. Throop Poly. Inst., 1904-05; A.B., Stanford U., 1909, M.E., 1914; m. Lora B. Moss, July 5, 1910 (died 1931); 1 dau., Anita Elizabeth; m. 2d, Marguerite Rayner, Oct. 15, 1932. Assistant in hydraulics and mechanics, Stanford U., 1907-09, instr. mech. engring., 1909-10; asst. prof. hydraulics, Cornell U., 1910-16; prof. hydraulic engring., Rensselaer Poly. Inst., 1916-19; prof. mech. and hydraulic engring., Calif. Inst. Tech., 1919-56, professor emeritus, July, 1956—; regional advisor Engineering, Science, Management War Tng. U.S. Office Edn., 1940-45. Vice-chmn. bd. of dirs. City of Pasadena, 1927-29, chmn., 1929-31; mem. Air Pollution Control Hearing Bd., Los Angeles Co. Pres. bd. Throop Meml. Ch., Pasadena, 1921-24; chmn. Joint Tech. Socs. of Los Angeles, 1921-22; fellow American Society of Mechanical Engineers (mgr., 1925-28; v.p. 1928-30). Member Los Angeles Engineering Council (president 1932-33), Sigma Xi and Tau Beta Pi fraternities. Clubs: Gnome, Twilight. Author: Fluid Mechanics, 1953, others. Home: Pasadena, Cal.

DAUGHTON, RALPH HUNTER, ex-congressman; born Washington, D.C., Sept. 23, 1885; ed. pub. and private schools, Washington, D.C. and Md.; LL.B. and LL.M., National U., Washington; m. Susan Taggart. Engaged in practice of law; represented city of Norfolk in Gen. Assembly of Va. 1933-44; resigned to fill vacancy 78th Congress (1943-45); mem. 79th Congress (1945-47), 2d Va. Dist. Democrat. Chmn. Va. State Boxing and Wrestling Commn. Pres. Piedmont League of Professional Baseball Clubs. Methodist. Mason, Elk, K.P. Club: Norfolk Lions (charter mem.). Home: Norfolk, Va.

D'AULAIRE, INGRI (MRS. EDGAR PARIN D'AULAIRE), artist, author; b. Kongsberg, Norway, Dec. 27, 1904; d. Per and Line Ueland (Sandsmark) Mortenson; student Kongsberg High and Jr. Coll., 1918-23, Kunstindustriskolen, Oslo, 1923-24, Hans Hoffman Sch. of Art, Munich, 1924-25, Academi Lhote-Pola Gauguin and Scandinavian, Paris, 1925-29; m. Edgar Parin d'Aulaire, July 24, 1925; children—Per Ola, Nils Maarten. Came to U.S., 1929, naturalized, 1940. Artist, painter, specializing in childrens portraits, until 1931; author, illustrator (with husband) children's books, 1931-80. Recipient Caldecott medal for book Abraham Lincoln as best picture book of year A.L.A., 1940, Regina medal Cath. Library Assn., 1970. Author, illustrator: (with Edgar Parin d'Aulaire) The Magic Rug, 1931; Ola, 1932; Ola and Blakken, 1933; Conquest of the Atlantic, 1933; The Lord's Prayer, 1934; Children of the Northlights, 1935; George Washington, 1936; East of the Sun and West of the Moon, 1938; Abraham

Lincoln, 1939; Animals Everywhere, 1940; Leif the Lucky, 1941; The Star Spangled Banner, 1942; Don't Count Your Chicks, 1943; Wings for Per, 1944; Too Big, 1945; Pocahontas, 1946; Nils, 1948; Foxie, 1949; Benjamin Franklin, 1950; Buffalo Bill, 1952; The Two Cars, 1954; Columbus, 1955; The Magic Meadow, 1958; d'Aulaires' Book of Greek Myths, 1962; d'Aulaires' Norse Gods and Giants, 1967; d'Aulaires' Trolls, 1972; The Terrible Troll Bird, 1976. Home: Georgetown, Conn. Died Oct. 24, 1980.

DAUPHIN, CLAUDE LE GRAND MARIA EUGENE, actor, writer; b. Corbell, France; Aug. 19, 1903; s. Franc Nohan and Madeleine Dauphin; ed. Sorbonne and Inst. des Beaux Arts, Paris, France; m. Norma Eberhardt, May 21, 1955. Set designer for Comedy Française, Paris, 1923-31; dir. Claude Dauphin Theatre Co., Paris, 1945-50; Broadway appearances include No Exit, 1947, The Happy Time, 1950, Janus, 1956, Clerambard, 1958, Deadly Game, 1959, Giants Sons of Giants, 1962, The Full Treatment, 1962; appearances plays in France include: Une Femme Libre, 1932, Adam, 1938, La Soif, 1949, Adorable Julia, 1962; Hedda Gabler, 1963; also all plays by Henry Bernstien, 1933-39; appeared in Death of a Salesman, 1967, Battle of Ink, 1967, Voyage for Two, 1967, Barbarella, 1968; The English Lover of Marguerite Duras, 1969; motion pictures include 16 American, 5 British and 70 French. Served to lt. French Army, World War II; mem. Free French Army. Decorated Legion of Honor, War Cross, Medal of de Gaulle. Address: Oakhurst, N.J., also Paris, France. Died Nov. 17, 1978.

DAUTEN, CARL ANTON, educator; b. St. Louis, June 2, 1913; s. Paul Martin and Louise (Heyer) D.; A.B., Washington U., 1936, A.M., 1939, Ph.D., 1944; m. Dorothea Hoeman, July 18, 1942; children—Thomas, Jane, Mary. Prodn. control chemist Nat. Lead Co., St. Louis, 1937-38; prof. bus. adminstrn. Shurtleff Coll., Alton, Ill., 1940-44; sr. adminstrv. asst. U.S. CSC, Detroit, 1942; prof. econs., acting treas., bus. mgr. Mo. Valley Coll., Marshall, 1944-45; asst. prof. bus. adminstrn. U. Ark., 1945; mem. faculty Washington U., St. Louis, 1945-76, prof. finance, banking, 1952-76, dir. doctoral program Grad. Sch. Bus. and Pub. Adminstrn., 1960-63, asso. provost, 1962-64, vice chancellor adminstrn., 1964-67, vice chancellor, asso. provost, 1967-69, exec. vice chancellor, 1969-76. Dir. Concordia Pub. House, 1965-76, chmn. bd., 1971. Chmn. edn. commn. Council Lutheran Chs. Greater St. Louis, 1961-65, bd. dirs., 1961-65. Mem. adv. bd. Concordia Sem. Research Center, 1963-69. Mem. Phi Beta Kappa, Beta Gamma Sigma, Omicron Delta Kappa. Author: Business Finance, 1948, 2d edit., 1956; Business Fluctuations and Forecasting, 1954; Financing the American Consumer, 1956; (with M. Welshans) Principles of Finances, 1958, 2d edit., 1964, 3d edit., 1970, 4th edit., 1975; Consumer Finance Companies in a Dynamic Economy, 1959; Business Cycles and Forecasting, 2d edit., 1961, 3d edit. (with L. Valentine), 1968, 4th edit., 1974, 5th edit., 1978; The Role of the Mississippi-Missouri River Systems in the Development of the St. Louis Region, 1961. Asso. editor Jour. Finance, 1956-59. Home: St. Louis, Mo. Died Sept. 17, 1976.

DAVENPORT, RAYMOND RIPLEY, life ins. co. exec.; b. Bellevue, Tex., Feb. 26, 1904; s. Green W. and Josephine (Russell) D.; B.A., So. Meth. U., 1931; m. Rosa Mae Wilson, Sept. 28, 1925; children—Francha, Diane, Raymond Ripley. Sch. supt. to 1933; with Southwestern Life Ins. Co., Dallas, from 1933, successively agt., sales dir., asst. agy. dir., v.p., agy. dir., 1933-62, exec. v.p., vice chmn. bd., 1962-69, mem. exec. com., dir. Chmn. agy. sect. Am. Life Conv. 1963-64, C.L.U., 1941. Mem. Life Ins. Agy. Mgmt. Assn. (pres. 1954-55). Home: Dallas, Tex. Deceased.

DAVES, DELMER LAWRENCE, motion picture dir., writer, producer; b. San Francisco; s. Arthur Lawrence and Nan (Funge) D.; grad. Los Angeles Polytechnic, 1922; Stanford U., 1927; m. Mary Lou Lender, July 11, 1938; children—Michael Lawrence, Deborah Lou, Donna Lee. Started as property-boy, 1927; actor and writer, 1928; dir.-writer Warner Bros., 1943-58, dir. producer, writer, 1959-67; dir., writer Twentieth Century-Fox, 1949, producer, 1954; pres. Diamond D Prodns.; regents lectr. U. Calif. at San Diego; homages to film maker, Paris, France, Palais Chaillot, Oberhausen, Germany, Stanford U. Recipient Western Heritage Wrangler award Nat. Cowboy Hall of Fame, 1975. Mem. Producers Guild of Am., Dirs. Guild of Am. (nat. bd.), Stanford Assos., Am. Fedn. of Art, Mus. of Modern Art, Museum of Natural History, Mineral Society of Am., Writers Guild of Am., Motion Picture Acad. Arts and Scis. (gov.), Sigma Alpha Epsilon, Phi Delta Phi. Republican. Episcopalian. Author numerous screen plays; dir. films, writer, producer films including Destination Tokyo, The Red House, Dark Passage, Task Force, Bird of Paradise, Drum Beart, Jubal, The Last Wagon, A Summer Place, Parrish, Susan Slade, Rome Adventure, Spencer's Mountain, Youngblood Hawke; dir. Pride of the Marines, Broken Arrow, 3:10 to Yuma, Cowboy, Kings Go Forth, The Hanging Tree, Demetrius & The Gladiators; screen plays include: Flirtation Walk, Shipmates Forever, Love Affair, Stage Door Canteen, An Affair to Remember. Home: Los Angeles, Calif., also La Jolla, Calif. Died Aug. 17, 1977.

DAVID, BERT ALISON, army officer, bus. exec.; b. Lehighton, Pa., July 4, 1924; s. Bert B. and Florence (Fritch) D.; student Pa. State U., 1942-43; B.S., U.S. Mil. Acad., 1946; grad. Command and Gen. Staff Coll., 1956, Armed Forces Staff Coll., 1961, Indsl. Coll. Armed Forces, 1965; M.S., George Washington U., 1965; m. Shirley Fagan, June 8, 1946; children—Bert Alison, Scott C., Jon R., Lance B. Commd. 2d lt. U.S. Army, 1946, advanced through grades to maj. gen., 1971; platoon leader, co. comdr. 24th Inf. Regt., Japan, 1947-49; mem. regtl. and div. staff during Korean conflict; instr. Air Command and Staff Coll., Maxwell AFB, Ala., 1956-57; personnel staff officer Dept. Army, 1957-60; dep. comdr. 1st bn. 7th Inf., 1961-62; dep G3 Hdqrs. VII Corps, Germany, 1963-64; dep. dir. Joint Actions Office Dept. Chief of Staff, Logistics, Washington, 1966-67; comdg. officer 2d Brigade, 9th Inf. Div., Vietnam, 1967-68; asst. dep. chief of staff for logistics Hdqrs. U.S. Army, Europe, 1968-69; asst. div. comdr. 3d Inf. Div., Germany, 1969-70; comdg. gen. 1st ROK Army Detachment, KMAG, sr. adviser 1st ROK Army, Korea, 1970-71, chief army sect. Joint U.S. MAG, 1971-72; comdr. U.S. Army Tng. Center Inf. and Ft. Dix, 1972-74; comdr. U.S. Army Base Command Okinawa, 1974, U.S. Army Garrison Okinawa, 1974-75; asst. dep. chief of staff for logistics Dept. Army, 1975-77; engaged in bus., 1977-79. Decorated D.S.M., Silver Star, Legion of Merit with 3 oak leaf clusters, Bronze Star, Air medal with 7 oak leaf clusters, Army Commendation medal, Gallantry Cross with palm, Combat Inf. badge. Mem. Am. Legion, World War II, Korean and Vietnam last man clubs, Assn. U.S. Army, West Point Alumni Assn., ICAF Alumni Assn., Army Athletic Assn. Clubs: Masons, Elks. Home: Lehighton, Pa. Died Jan. 28, 1979.

DAVID, CHARLES WENDELL, college prof., librarian; b. Onarga, Ill., Mar. 20, 1885; s. Charles and Alvira (Harper) D.; student Northwestern U., 1905-08; B.A., Oxford U., Eng., 1911; A.M., U. of Wis., 1912; Ph.D., Harvard, 1918; Dr. of Letters, U. of Pennsylvania, 1955; married Mary Virginia Martin, Sept. 11, 1918 (died 1936); m. 2d, Margaret Florence Simpson, May 27, 1939; children—Charles Newbold, George Alfred Lawrence. Teaching fellow, U. of Wis., 1911-13; instr. history, U. of Wash., Seattle, 1915-18; asso. prof. European history, Bryn Mawr Coll., 1918-27, prof., 1927-1940, Marjorie Walter Goodhart prof. of history, 1940-46; also prof. of history and dir. of libraries, U. of Pa., 1940-55, emeritus, 1955—; dir. Longwood Library, Kennett Sq., Pa., 1955-61, Eleutherian Mills Hist. Library, Greenville, Dela., 1961; asst. to pres., dir. library development, Mystic Seaport, Conn., 1962—; chmn. bd. dirs. Union Library Catalogue of the Phila. Met. Area, 1936-40, and 1949-58. Mem. Am. Hist. Assn., Mediaeval Acad. of Am., Am. Assn. of Rhodes Scholars, A.L.A., Bibliography Society of America, Phi Delta Theta. Clubs: Franklin Inn, Philobiblon, Grolier. Rhodes Scholar, Oxford from Ill., 1908-11. Republican. Episcopalian. Author: Robert Curthose Duke of Normandy, 1920; De Expugnatione Lyxbonensi (The Conquest of Lisbon), 1936. Narratio de Itinere Navali Peregrinorum Hierosolyman tendentium et Silviam capientium, A.D. 1189, 1939. Editor: Planning The University Library Building (with John E. Burchard and Julian P. Boyd), 1949; Changing Patterns of Scholarship and the Future of Research Libraries (with Rudolf Hirsch), 1951; Journey to France and Spain, 1801 (Victor Marie du Pont), 1961. Home: Mystic, Conn.

DAVID, WILLIAM M(ORRIS), business exec.; b. Philadelphia, Pa., Mar. 14, 1886; s. Edward M. and Martha F. (Knight) D.; student Germantown Friends Sch.; B.S., U. Pa., 1906; m. Frances A. Cutler, June 6, 1914; children—Nellie C., Edward M., William M., Clifford C., F. Louise. In Trust Company work since 1906; with The Pennsylvania Co., Phila., since 1910, v.p. since 1930, senior v.p. since 1950; dir. Greenwich Real Estate Co., D.S. & H. Craig, Inc., Alden Park Corp. and subsidiaries; pres. and dir. W. Laurel Hill Cemetery Co. since 1936. Treasurer and director Phila-Camden Social Service Exchange, treasurer and director Phila. Council of Churches. Pres. Phila. Corporate Fiduciaries Assn., 1946-48. Republican. Presbyn. Club: Union League (Phila.). Home: Philadelphia.

DAVIDSOHN, ISRAEL, physician; b. Tarnopol, Austria, Apr. 20, 1895; s. Jacob and Rachel (Halpern) D.; M.D., U. Vienna, 1921; postgrad. U. Berlin, 1921-23; D.Sc., Chgo. Med. Sch., 1964; m. Clara Freud, Oct. 10, 1923; children—Ellen Doris, Samuel James. Came to U.S., 1923, naturalized, 1930. Pathologist, dir. labs. Mt. Sinai Hosp., Phila., 1925-30; dir. dept. pathology Mt. Sinai Hosp., Chgo., 1930-65, dir. dept. exptl. pathology, 1965-79; prof. dept. pathology Chgo. Med. Sch., 1947-74. Cons., Armed Forces Inst. of Pathology, Washington. Pres. Am. Bd. of Pathology, 1964-65. Recipient Morris H. Parker award Chgo. Med. Sch., 1956; John Elliott award Am. Assn. Blood Banks, 1958; joint award for distinguished services to socs. and to Am. pathology Am. Soc. Clin. Pathologists and Coll. Am. Pathologists, 1966. Mem. A.M.A., Chgo. Inst. Medicine, Am. Soc. Clin. Pathologists (pres. 1951-52; Ward Burdick award 1954), Ill. (pres. 1951), Am. (pres. 1952-53) assns. blood banks, Coll. Am. Pathologists (gov. 1956-58), Chgo. Pathol. Soc. (hon. mem.). Author and co-author med. books. Asso. editor Am. Jour. of Clin. Pathology. Home: Chicago, Ill. Died Dec. 3, 1979; buried Mt. Mayrio Cemetery, Chgo.

DAVIDSON, ARTHUR OLE, coll. pres.; b. Hancock, Minn., Sept. 27, 1910; s. Andrew and Rosella (Flom) D.; A.B., Luther Coll., Decorah, Iowa, 1931, L.H.D., 1975; M.A., U. Minn., 1938; Ed.D., Harvard U., 1952; LL.D., Hartwick Coll., 1965; Litt.D., Wagner Coll., 1976; m. H. Corinne Hellie, Dec. 29, 1948; children—Karen Flom, Daphne Loe. Elementary, jr. and high sch. prin., Iowa, 1931-38; high sch., prin.-supt. schs., Sleepy Eye, Minn., 1938-40; supt. schs., Springfield, Minn., 1940-41; chmn. edn. dept. Luther Coll., 1941-48, v.p., 1954-61; chmn. dept. edn. Dartmouth, 1948-54; lectr. Grad. Sch., U. Minn., summers 1951-56; pres. Wagner Coll., S.I., 1961-75. Served to comdr. USN, World War II. Home: Hanover, N.H. Died Nov. 18, 1979; buried Pine Knolls Cemetery, Hanover.

DAVIDSON, DAVID W., dept. store exec.; b. 1905; married. With Marshall Field & Co., 1924-72, v.p., 1956-57, sr. v.p. and asst. gen. mgr., 1957-64, exec. v.p., gen. mgr., dir. Chgo. area stores, 1964-72, gen. mgr. Frederick & Nelson div., Seattle, 1969-71. Home: Wilmette, Ill. Died Aug. 21, 1979.

DAVIDSON, HAROLD PRESCOTT, educator; b. N.Y.C., July 19, 1908; s. Harold Sidney and Christine (Bruce) D.; B.A., Pomona Coll., 1929; M.A., Claremont Coll., 1932; postgrad. U. So. Calif.; m. Rosalie Evelyn Cleek, Aug. 30, 1929; children—Douglass Sidney, Malcolm Bruce. Head music dept. Emerson Jr. High Sch., Pomona, Calif., 1929-36; dir. All-City P.T.A. Chorus, Pomona. 1932-36; master tng. tchr. Claremont Coll., 1931-36; head music dept. Calif. State Poly. U., 1936-73, also dir. coll. glee clubs, vocal ensembles, bands; adjudicator, guest condr. San Luis Obispo County Choral Festival, 1957. Active fund raising drives Boy Scouts Am., Salvation Army, A.R.C. H.P. Davidson Music Center at Calif. Poly. State U. named in his honor, 1973. Mem. ASCAP, Coll. Music Soc., Phi Delta Kappa, Alpha Gamma Sigma. Republican. Presbyterian. Club: Rotary (past pres. San Luis Obispo). Composer: (choral works for men's glee club) Pardon for Puns, 1950, Collections of Ballads, 3 sets, 1955, arrangement Mussorgsky's Hopak, 1959, Derby Ram, 1955; (coll. songs) Ride High You Mustangs, 1947, All Hail Green and Gold, 1936, Poly Memories, 1960; Love's Delights, 1964; Miserete Meus, Dei (for women's voices), 1965; others. Home: San Luis Obispo, Calif. Died Jan. 21, 1977.

DAVIDSON, HERBERT COOLIDGE, utility exec.; b. Melrose, Mass., May 19, 1883; s. Herbert Elbridge and Sarah Frances (Coolidge) D.; B.A., Harvard, 1904; m. Anne Lemira French, April 24, 1907; 1 son, Herbert. Asso. with Consolidated Edison Co. of New York, Inc., since 1913, successively controller, 1920, asst. sec. 1923, sec. 1924, v.p. and chief accounting officer since 1938, trustee since 1943, mem. exec. com. since 1946; v.p. New York Steam Corp. Home: Montclair, N.J., and Rye Reach, New Hampshire. *

DAVIDSON, J. EDWARD, merchant; b. Schenectady, N.Y., Apr. 19, 1901; s. Fred and Harriet (Rosenzweig) D.; A.B., Harvard, 1921; student Harvard Sch. Bus. Adminstrn.; m. Bernice Rosenbaum, June 6, 1925; children—Bernice Frances, Anne Elizabeth. Buyer, R. H. Macy & Co., N.Y. City, 1922-28, merchant counselor, 1928-33, vice pres., 1933-36; pres. Wm. Hengerer Co., Buffalo, 1936-38; James McCreery Co., N.Y. City, 1938-45; chmn. bd. Bloomingdale Bros., N.Y. City, 1947-63; independent business consultant, 1945-47. Dir. Associated Drygoods Corp., 1940-46, Federated Dept. Stores from 1947. Home: New York, N.Y. Died Apr. 21, 1980.

DAVIDSON, SIDNEY WETMORE, lawyer; b. Augusta, Ga., Dec. 30, 1894; s. William Treat and Carolin Amelia (Wetmore) D.; grad. Lawrenceville Sch., 1912; B.A., Yale, 1916, J.D., 1918; LL.D., Tufts Coll., 1952, Pratt Inst., 1965; L.H.D., Bates Coll., 1960; m. Mary Alice Hooker, June 24, 1916; children—Jean Hooker (Mrs. Horace A. Fay), Sidney Wetmore, Katharine Douglas (Mrs. John S. Walker), Robert Treat Hooker, Alice Hooker (Mrs. John O. Outwater), Louise Treat (Mrs. Donald Heyneman). Admitted to N.Y. bar, 1920; asso. with firm Carter, Ledyard & Milburn, N.Y.C., 1920-45, mem. firm, 1929-45; mem. firm Gasser, Hayes & Davidson, 1945-49, Davidson Dawson & Clark, 1949-74, counsel, 1974-79; partner firm Brown & Ives, Providence; ret. trustee Bklyn. Savs Bank; dir. Globe Newspaper Co., Boston, Affiliated Publs. Inc., Boston; ret. mem. adv. bd. Chem. Bank N.Y Trust Co. Mem. fed. alien enemy hearing bd., eastern dist., N.Y., 1942-45. Trustee Lawrenceville Sch. Bingham Asso. Fund (for advancement of medicine) Bethel, Me., N.E. Med. Center Hosp., Boston, (hon chmn.), Bklyn. Inst. of Arts and Sci., Gould Acad (emeritus), Bethel, Me., Pratt Inst. (emeritus); former chmn. Bklyn. Mus.; hon. chmn. exec. com. Yale Law Sch. Assn.; former trustee Packer Collegiate Inst (Bklyn.). Served with USNR, 1918-19. Mem. Am

N.Y. State bar assns., Bar Assn. City of N.Y., Corbey Court, Zeta Psi, Phi Delta Phi. Unitarian. Clubs: Century Assn., Downtown Assn., University, Yale (N.Y.C.); Rembrandt (Bklyn.); Elihu, Graduates (New Haven); Saratoga (N.Y.) Reading Room. Home: Brooklyn Heights, N.Y., also Sebec Lake, Maine. Died Oct. 27, 1979; buried Lawrenceville, N.J.

DAVIE, EUGENIE MARY (MRS. PRESTON DAVIE), civic and polit. leader; b. N.Y.C.; d. Adolph and Emily (Stevens) Ladenburg; ed. Westover Sch., pvt. tutors; m. Preston Davie, May 31, 1930; Finance chmn. N.Y. Rep. State Com., 1933-34; del. Rep. Nat. Conv., 1936; chmn. Landon Vols., Eastern Seaboard States, women's div. Rep. Nat. Com.; chmn. women's auxiliary N.Y. Rep. County Com., 1946-61, 1st v.p., 1958-64; mem. Rep. Nat. Finance Com., 1962-74; mem. exec. com. N.Y. Rep. State Com.; alternate del. Rep. Nat. Conv., 1960; asst. treas. Robert A. Taft Nat. Finance Com., 1952. Mem. bd. regents Nat. Library Medicine, 1958-60; trustee, mem. exec. com. Taft Meml. Found., 1955-64; chmn. Robert A. Taft Inst. of Govt., 1961-75, also trustee, mem. exec. com.; trustee L.I. U., 1964-69; chmn. hospitality com. N.Y. state Pavilion World's Fair, mem. N.Y. State Commn. of the Fair, 1962-63; trustee Adelphi Coll., 1945-51. Chmn. civilian operating com. Army Emergency Relief, 2d Service Command, 1942-44; dir. vols. Army Personnel Affairs Div., Mil. Dist. No. 1, 1944. Decorated Gold Cross of Merit (Poland), cross in grade of dame Order of St. Dennis of Zante (Greece). Mem. D.A.R., Daus. of Cincinnati, Am. (bd. v.p. 1955-57), N.Y. (hon. chmn. bd. dirs. from 1966) heart assns. Episcopalian. Clubs: Women's Nat. Rep. (past bd. dir.). Colony. Contbr. articles on politics to newspapers, other publs. Home: New York, N.Y. Died Sept. 19, 1975.

DAVIES, JULIEN TOWNSEND, lawyer; b. N.Y.C., Aug. 13, 1895; s. Julien Townsend and Marie Rose (de Garmendia) D.; Ph.B. cum laude, Yale, 1917, LL.B. cum laude, 1922; m. Faith de Moss Robinson, June 26, 1920 (div. 1933); children—Julien Townsend, Faith Robinson (Mrs. George R. Le Sauvage, Jr.), John Robinson (dec.); m. 2d Marie O'Connor Quinn, July 7, 1933 (div. 1960); m. 3d, Ida Pasquali, May 20, 1960. Admitted to N.Y. bar, 1924, practiced N.Y.C.; partner Davies, Hardy, Ives & Lawther and predecessor firms, 1928-71. Trustee, Village Flower Hill, Nassau County, N.Y., 1937-40, mayor, 1940-44. Served as ensign, chief gunner's mate U.S. Navy, 1917-19. Mem. Order of Coif, Sigma Xi, Delta Psi. Club: St. Anthony. Home: New York, N.Y. Died Aug. 20, 1978.

DAVIES, PAUL LEWIS, banker; b. Cozad, Neb., July 27, 1899; s. Robert and Emma Estella (Bennison) D.; student U. Cal. at Berkeley, 1917-21, Harvard Sch. of Bus., 1921-22; m. Faith Crummey, Oct. 2, 1926; children—Paul Lewis, Nancy (dec.), Judith. Clk., Nat. Bank of Commerce, 1922; asst. cashier, asst. v.p., and v.p. Am. Trust Co., 1923-28; v.p., treas., exec. v.p. and treas., pres. Food Machinery & Chem. Corp. (now FMC Corp.), 1928-56, chmn. bd., chief exec. officer, 1956-66, dir., chmn. exec. com., 1966-67, sr. dir. and dir., 1967-72, sr. dir. emeritus, 1972; sr. mng. dir. Lehman Bros., N.Y.C., 1966-73. Mem. Bus. Council; hon. trustee Com. Econ. Devel. Founding dir. Stanford Research Inst.; adv. bd. U. Cal. Sch. Bus. Adminstrn. Served U.S. Army, 1918. Mem. Smithsonian Inst. Assos. (dir.), Alpha Sigma Phi. Methodist. Mason. Clubs: Sainte Claire (San Jose, Cal.); Pacific Union, Bohemian (San Francisco); Links (N.Y.C.); Cypress Point (Pebble Beach, Cal.). Home: San Jose, Calif. Died Nov. 25, 1975.

DAVIES, RAY, mng. editor; b. Charleston, Ill., Apr. 20, 1899; s. David Hugh and Jessie Leota (Gerard) D.; A.A., Blackburn Coll., 1922; A.B., State U. Iowa, 1924, grad. study, 1927-28; m. Sylvia Jane Freeland, Nov. 19, 1919; 1 dau., Helen Elizabeth (Mrs. Bernard L. Waren); m. 2d, Mary Alice Munsell, Nov. 30, 1939. Asst. dean men State U. Iowa, 1925-28; dean Drake U., 1928-34; research exec. Gen. Marketing Counselors, Inc., N.Y.C., 1934-36; personnel exec. Sears, Roebuck & Co., Chgo., 1936-43; dir. personnel Western Auto Supply Co., Kansas City, Mo., 1943-52, v.p., 1952-62; mng. editor The Personnel Administrator, from 1962, editor, 1960-65; Ia. State dir. student relief Fed. Emergency Relief Adminstrn., 1933-34; mem. Pres.'s Conf. Tech. and Distbn. Research for Benefit Small Bus., 1957, Conf. Indsl. Safety, 1960. Served pvt., Inf., U.S. Army, 1918. Mem. Internat. Artists Soc. (exec. sec. 1931-34, chmn. bd. trustees, 1934), Am. Legion, Boy Scouts of Am. (nat. adv. com. 1932-36), Am. Soc. Personnel Adminstrn. (dir.; exec. com.; v.p. 1957-58), Nat. Affairs Com. (vice chmn. from 1957), Acad. Political Sci. (life member), Am. Personnel and Guidance Assn. (life member), Am. Coll. Personnel Assn., Nat. Vocational Guidance Assn., Am. Mgmt. Assn., U.S., Mo. State (mem. bd., chmn. labor relations council), Kansas City C.'s of C., N.A.M., Alpha Phi Omega. Elk. Author treatises. Home: Ft. Collins, Colo. Died Nov. 30, 1978; cremated.

DAVIES, RHYS, author; b. Rhondda, Wales, Nov. 9, 1901; s. Thomas Rhys and Sarah Ann (Lewis) D.; ed. Porth County Sch., Wales. Decorated Order Brit. Empire. Author: The Withered Root, 1927; A Pig in a Poke, 1931; Count Your Blessings, 1932; The Red Hills, 1932; Love Provoked, 1933; Honey and Bread, 1935; The Things Men Do, 1936; A Time to Laugh, 1937; Jubilee Blues, 1938; Under the Rose, 1940; Tomorrow to Fresh Woods, 1941; The Black Venus, 1944; The Trip to London, 1946; The Dark Daughters, 1947; Boy With a Trumpet, 1949; Marianne, 1951; The Painted King, 1954; Collected Stories, 1955; The Perishable Quality, 1957; The Darling of Her Heart, 1958; Girl Waiting in the Shade, 1960; The Chosen One, 1967; Print of A Hare's Foot, 1969; Nobody Answered The Bell, 1971; Honeysuckle Girl, 1975; also articles. Died Aug. 21, 1978.

D'AVIGDOR-GOLDSMID, HENRY JOSEPH, banker; b. June 10, 1909; s. Sir Osmond Elim d'Avigdor-Goldsmid; M.A. Balliol Coll., Oxford (Eng.) U., 1938; m. Rosemary Margaret Horlick, 1940; one dau. Alderman of Kent, 1951, justice of peace, 1949; high sheriff, 1953; mem. Parliament for Walsall South, from 1955; Parliamentary pvt. sec. to minister housing and local govt., 1955-56; chmn. Anglo Israel Bank Ltd., 1961; chmn. Pergamon pres. from 1969 Mem. Conservative Party. Clubs: White's, Carlton, St. James, Portland, (London). Home: Tonbridge, Kent, England Died Dec. 9, 1976.

DAVILA, CHARLES ALEXANDER, diplomat; b. Rumania, Dec. 1, 1886; s. Alexander Carol and Hortense Keminger (de Lippa) D.; university edn.; grad. in law. Served as mem. Parliament, Rumania; E.E. and M.P. to U.S. since Oct. 1929. Address: Washington, D.C. *

DAVIS, BENJAMIN BERNARD, lawyer; b. Lithuania, 1902 (parents Am. citizens); s. Max and Dora (Flaxman) D.; student U. Colo., 1918-19; Ph.B., J.D., U. Chgo., 1923; m. Janice Muller, Dec. 23, 1931; 1 son, Muller Davis. Law clk. Charles E. Erbstein, Chgo., 1921-23, asso., 1923-27; admitted to Ill. bar, 1923; partner Socrates & Davis, 1927-33, mem. firm. Socrates, Davis & Cohen, 1933-37; pvt. practice law, 1937-46; asso. in practice with William C. Boyden, Chgo., from 1946; partner law firm Davis, Jones & Baer. Mem. Am., Ill., Chgo. bar assns. Jewish religion. Clubs: Tavern, Lakeshore Country. Home: Chicago, Ill. Died Dec. 26, 1977.

DAVIS, CHAMPION MCDOWELL, ret. ry. ofcl.; b. nr. Hickory, N.C., July 1, 1879; s. Robert Burns and Cornelia (Nixon) D.; ed. pub. schs.; ScD., The Citadel, 1952. Beginning as messenger Wilmington & Weldon R.R. (now S.C.L.R.R.), 1893, became successively clk., stenographer freight rate clk., chief rate clk., to 1902, chief clk. traffic dept., 1902-06, asst. gen. freight agt., 1906-11, gen. freight agt. lines south of Charleston, S.C., 1911-16, gen. freight agt. entire system, 1916-18; mem. so. freight traffic com. U.S. R.R. Adminstrn., 1918-20, so. freight rate com., representing so. rail and water carriers, 1920; asst. freight traffic mgr. A.C.L. R.R., 1921-25, freight traffic mgr., 1925-28, v.p. traffic, 1928-39, v.p. all depts., 1939, exec. v.p., 1940-42, pres., 1942-57, ret., 1957; former dir. Jefferson Standard Life Ins. Co. Dir. U.S. C. of C., 1949-52, former mem. governing bd. Nations Business. Mem. nat. council P.E. Ch., 1946-52; trustee Cape Fear Tech. Inst., Wilmington, N.C.; former trustee Episcopal Radio-TV Found., P.E. Theol. Sem. Va., N.C. Ednl. Radio and Television Commn.; chmn. bd. trustees Cape Fear Meml. Hosp., Inc., Wilmington, N.C.; dir. emeritus Episcopal Ch. Found.; founder and prin. donor Champion McDowell Davis Charitable Found., 1963, Cornelia Nixon Davis Nursing Home, Porter's Neck Plantation. Served as pvt. and cpl. 2d Regt., N.C. Inf., Spanish-Am. War, 1898, later with 2d N.C. State Guard; resigned as capt., 1901. Mem. United Spanish War Vets. (comdr.), N.C. Soc. Cin., N.Y. So. Soc., Am. Soc. Traffic and Transp. (charter mem.), Am. Ry. Engring. Assn., Am. Assn. Passenger Traffic Officers (hon.) Transp. Assn. Am., Newcomen Soc. Episcopalian. Clubs: Cape Fear, Cape Fear Country (Wilmington, N.C.); Surf (Wrightsville Beach, N.C.); Wilmington Press. Home: Wilmington, N.C. Died Jan. 30, 1975.

DAVIS, CHARLES HUBBARD, state supreme ct. justice; b. Fairfield, Ill., Jan. 7, 1906; s. Horace Hubbard and Helen M. (Decker) D.; A.B., U. Ill., 1928; J.D., U. Chgo., 1931; m. Ruth Peugh, Oct. 19, 1935; children—Jean, Joan, Martha (Mrs. Russell Dearing), Mary (Mrs. John Daday), Ruth (Mrs. Thomas Hazen), John Jay, and Thomas C. Admitted to Ill. bar, 1931, practiced in Rockford, 1931-55, mem. firm Thomas & Davis, 1945-55; justice Ill. Supreme Ct., 1955-60, 70-76, chief justice, 1957-58; mem. firm Thomas, Davis and Kostantacos, 1960-65; justice 2d Dist. Ill. Appellate Ct., 1965-70. Past pres., dir. Winnebago Farm Sch. for Boys. Mem. Am., Ill., Winnebago County bar assns., Am. Coll. Trial Lawyers, Phi Delta Phi. Republican. Conglist. Mason (Shriner). Home: Rockford, Ill. Died Feb. 22, 1976.

DAVIS, CHARLES MALCOLM, banker; b. Roslyn, N.Y., July . 24, 1918; s. Charles Palmer and Jane (Hopkins) D.; B.S., N.Y. U., 1941; m. Ann Kes, Nov. 14, 1942 (div. 1973) children—Susan K., Craig M., Bruce, Grant; m. 2d, Mildred W. Oschwald, Feb. 15, 1974. With Fed. Res. Bank of N.Y., 1935-41; asso. First Nat. City Bank (formerly First Nat. Bank City of N.Y.), 1946-55, asst. cashier, 1948-50, asst. v.p., 1950-52, v.p., 1953-55; v.p. Fidelity Union Trust Co., Newark, 1955-58, sr. v.p., 1958-60, pres., 1960-69, chmn., chief exec. officer, from 1969, chmn. bd., also dir.; chmn. bd. Fidelity Union Bancorp.; former chmn. Allied Bank Internat.; dir. Allied Bank Internat. Pennwalt Corp., Pub. Service Electric & Gas Co., Newark, Prudential Ins. Co. Am., R.H. Macy & Co. Chmn. bd. trustees Newark Mus. Served to capt. AUS, 1942-46. Mem. Beta Gamma Sigma. Episcopalian. Clubs: Essex, Down Town, Somerset Hills Country, Baltursrol Golf, Links. Home: Morristown, N.J. Died June 5, 1980.

DAVIS, DAVID LYLE, banker; b. Pawnee City, Neb., Jan. 25, 1885; s. John and Emma Jane (Tracy) D.; grad. high sch., Lincoln, Neb., 1903; student U. of Neb., 1906-07; m. Georgina MacDougall, Apr. 6, 1912; children—John MacDougall, David Tracy, Donald Campbell. Began with Bank of Union, Neb., 1902; served part time with Columbia Nat. Bank, Lincoln, later with First Nat. Bank, 1907-09; with Northwest Trust and Safe Deposit Co., Seattle, Wash., 1909-17, advancing to asst. cashier; identified with Federal Reserve Bank of San Francisco since 1917, as cashier branches at Portland, Ore., Salt Lake City, Utah, Seattle, Wash., and mng. dir. Spokane Br., 1926-38; managing director Portland Branch, 1939-46, vice president, 1947-50. Member Alpha Tau Omega. Mason (Shriner). Home: Mercer Island, Wash.

DAVIS, DON A(BNER), business exec.; b. Stephenville, Tex., May 22, 1882; s. Marion Gabriel and Mary Alice (Daily) D.; ed. pub. schs.; m. Frances Louise Phillips, of Kansas City, Mo., Apr. 19, 1929; children—Don A., Jr., Carroll Phillips, Noel Norman. With Western Auto Supply Co., Kansas City, Mo., since 1915, chmn. bd. since 1937. Clubs: Kansas City, Mission Hills Golf (Kansas City, Mo.); Indian Creek, Bath (Miami Beach, Fla.). Home: Kansas City, Mo.

DAVIS, DONALD GOODWIN, JR., educator; b. Stoneham, Mass., Aug. 23, 1932; s. Donald Goodwin and Elizabeth (Fowler) D.; B.A., Wesleyan U., Middletown, Conn., 1954; Ph.D., Harvard, 1957; m. Janet M. Alford, June 26, 1954 (dec. June 1974); children—Donna Lee, Barbara Elizabeth, Scott Jeffrey. Mem. faculty Ga. Inst. Tech., Atlanta, 1957-59; asso. prof. chemistry La. State U., New Orleans, 1959-63, prof., from 1963, chmn. dept., 1960-64, dean Grad. Sch., 1965-69. Sci. adviser FDA, 1965-73. Vice pres. New Orleans Sci. Fair, 1967-73. Mem. Am. Chem. Soc., Electrochem. Soc., A.A.A.S., N.Y. Acad. Sci., Phi Beta Kappa, Sigma Xi. Contbr. articles in field to profl. jours, reference books. Home: New Orleans, La. Died Oct. 9, 1977.

DAVIS, MRS. FOSTER BOWDLE, assn. exec.; b. Lima, Ohio, Sept. 22, 1882; d. Alexander and Annette (Burton) Noble (raised by George H. and Mary Louise Long); ed. pub. schs. of Lima; m. Foster Bowdle Davis, June 15, 1902; 1 dau., Eve Louise Price. Nat. pres. Service Star Legion, Inc., Baltimore. Home: Baltimore.

DAVIS, FRANKLIN MILTON, JR., army officer, legal office adminstr.; b. Malden, Mass., July 19, 1918; s. Franklin M. and Florence (Cummings) D.; B.A., U. Mass., 1940; M.A., George Washington U., 1963; m. Erma Stuart Alvord, July 18, 1942; children—Stephen W. (dec.), Nathaniel A. Commd. 2d lt. U.S. Army, 1940, advanced through grades to maj. gen., 1969; with 18th Airborne Corps and 3d Armored Div., Europe, World War II; mem. faculty U.S. Army War Coll., 1960-62; mem. Army Gen. Staff, 1968-71; comdg. gen. 199th Light Inf. Brigade, Vietnam, 1968; dir. mil. personnel policies Hdqrs. Dept. Army, Washington, 1969-71; comdt. Army War Coll., 1971-74; ret., 1974; adminstr. Steptoe & Johnson, law offices, Washington, 1974-79. Decorated D.S.M., Legion of Merit, D.F.C., Bronze Star, Purple Heart (U.S.); Order Merit 5th Class (Vietnam). Fellow Co. Mil. Historians; mem. Nat. Muzzle Loading Rifle Assn., Internat. Brotherhood Magicians, Theta Chi. Author: Come as a Conqueror, 1967. Home: Arlington, Va. Died May 4, 1981; buried Arlington Nat. Cemetery.

DAVIS, HAL CHARLES, labor union exec.; b. Pitts., Feb. 27, 1914; s. Harry J., Sr., and Tillie (Reitzel) D.; student Duquesne U., 1931-32, 50; m. Blanche L. Faulkner, 1932 (dec. 1961); children—Joyce (Mrs. Raymond Smith), Ruth (Mrs. George Ayres); m. 2d, Marion Gray, Feb. 16, 1963. Profl. musician, percussionist, 1934-48; staff musician radio sta. KDKA, Pitts., 1943-48; pres. Pitts. local Am. Fedn. Musicians, from 1948, internat. pres., N.Y.C., from 1970. Exec. dir. Pitts. Central Labor Union Com. Polit. Edn., 1956-65; mem. exec. bd. Allegheny County Labor Council, 1952-65; v.p. Pa. AFL-CIO, 1952-71, mem. nat. exec. council, 1976-78; Presdl. appointee Nat. Council on Arts. Mem. bd. Allegheny County Port Authority, 1958-70. Bd. dirs. St. John's Hosp., Pitts., 1951-70; mem. Pa. Council on Arts, 1956-70. Served with USMC, World War II. Home: Brielle, N.J. Died Jan. 11, 1978.

DAVIS, HALLAM WALKER, prof. English; b. Poseyville, Ind., Oct. 17, 1884; s. John B. and Lute (Walker) D.; grad. high sch., Princeton, Ind., 1902; A.B., Ind. U., 1909; A.M., Columbia, 1913; m. Jessie Hedden, Dec. 28, 1910; 1 dau., Helen Louise. Prin. high sch., Poseyville, 1903-05; supt. schs., Fort Branch, 1909-13; instr. in English, Kansas State College, 1913-14, asst. prof., 1914-16, asso. prof., 1916-18, prof. since 1918; also head of English dept. since 1921. Exec. sec. U.S. Food Adminstrn. in Kan., 1917. Mem. Nat. Council Teachers of English, Kan. Assn. Teachers of English (pres. 1922-23, 1931-32), Kan. Editorial Assn., Phi Kappa Phi, Sigma Delta Chi, Sigma Phi Epsilon, Phi Mu Alpha. Republican. Clubs: Am. Coll. Quill, Kan. Author's. Author: Self-Improvement in English, 1925; The Column, 1926. Contbr. editorials to mags.; condr. Sunflower Column (humor) in Kansas Industrialist since 1916. Home: Manhattan, Kan. *

DAVIS, HARWELL GOODWIN, coll. pres.; b. Marengo County, Ala., Nov. 23, 1882; s. Thomas Wyley and Mary Kate (Goodwin) D.; grad. South Ala. Inst., 1901; LL.B., U. of Ala., 1903, LL.D., 1939; m. Lena Vail, Dec. 15, 1917; children—Harwell Goodwin, Betty Vail, Dorothy Frances. Began practice at Thomasville, Ala., 1903; moved to Gadsden, 1909; asst. atty. gen. of Ala., 1915-17; resigned to attend 1st O.T.C., at Ft. McPherson, Ga.; commd. capt. inf., Aug. 15, 1917, and assigned as comdr. Co. B, 327th Regt., U.S. Army; arrived in France, Apr. 1918; maj., Oct. 11, 1918; wounded in action at Argonne-Meuse offensive; cited by Gen. Pershing ',,for gallantry in action"; hon. discharged, May 29, 1919; apptd. spl. asst. atty. gen., Ala., Dec. 1, 1919; state fuel administrator, Oct. 1920-Feb. 1921; atty. gen. of Ala., 2 terms, 1921-27; apptd. collector of internal revenue, Dist. of Ala., July 1933; pres. Howard Coll., Birmingham, Ala., since July 1, 1939. Pres. So. Assn. Bapt. Colls. and Schs., 1949-51. Codifier Ala. agrl. code and Ala. ednl. code, 1927. Maj. J.A.G., Ala. Nat. Guard, 1919; later lt. col.; judge adv. 31st Div. Mem. Phi Beta Kappa, Omicron Delta Kappa, Phi Delta Phi, Kappa Phi Kappa, Kappa Delta Pi. Dem. Missionary Bapt. Mason, Odd Fellow, K.P. (Past Grand Chancellor). Woodman. Home: Birmingham, Ala.

DAVIS, HOWARD, lawyer; b. Otoe, Nebr., Feb. 5, 1907; s. Howard Orlando and Lydia Louise (Paap) D.; student Oklahoma City U., 1923-24; B.A., Okla. U., 1927; LL.B., 1931; m. Dorothy Kennedy, Nov. 4, 1937 (div. Oct. 1940); 1 dau., Lucy E. (Mrs. Charles A. Rey); m. 2d, Ruth Caldwell, June 27, 1944 (dec. Dec. 1975); 1 son, Howard Caldwell; m. 3d, Helen Robbins LaFollette, Oct. 10, 1976. Admitted to Okla. bar, 1931; with firm Shirk, Danner & Phelps, Oklahoma City, 1931-32; pvt. practice, Oklahoma City, 1932-36; mem. legal HOLC, 1936-37, Continental Oil Co., 1937-48; with firm Bulla and Bynum, Oklahoma City, 1948-50; mem. Kerr, Davis, Irvine, Krasnow, Rhodes & Semtner, Inc., and predecessor firms, Oklahoma City, 1950-80. Mem. Am., Okla. (chmn. real property com. 1968-71) bar assns., Oklahoma City C. of C., Alpha Sigma Phi. Clubs: Men's Dinner, Lions. Methodist. Home: Oklahoma City, Okla. Died May 13, 1980.

DAVIS, JAMES BURNAM, devel., investment and m b. Lilly, Ill., July 22, 1909; s. Charles William a Eliza (Rutherford) D.; Conservation fellow Harvard, MA, 1966, m. Delpha Lee Payne, Mar. 24, 1931; chil Carol Anne, Patricia Louise; m. 2d, Mary Martha Ban 28, 1949. High sch. tchr., Maysville, Ky., 1929; tchr., basketball coach, Washington, Ky., 1929-30; economi Instn., 1934; economist, adminstrv. officer, agricul Dept. Agr., 1935-43; prin. agriculturist, chief pro operations E. Central region AAA. 1943; chief marketing div. E. Central region Prodn. and Marketing Adminstrn., 1946-47, agriculturist Prodn. and Marketing Adminstrn., 1947-51, chief program devel. and operating methods, 1951, acting chief Pakistan br. TCA, 1951-52; sr. fgn. affairs officer specializing S. Asia, TCA, ICA, 1952-56, dep. chief agriculturist US. Tech. Coop. Mission to India, 1956-58, staff ICA, Washington, 1958-60; chief food and agr. officer AID, Lagos, Nigeria, 1961, Iran, 1965, Afghanistan, 1966, dep. asso. dir., Vietnam, 1968, asso. dir., 1969-73; mgmt. and evaluation cons., Europe, Asia, Africa, Latin Am.; now devel., investment and mgmt. cons. Served from lt. (j.g.) to lt. USNR, 1943-46. Methodist. Home: Falls Church, Va. Died July 3, 1979; interred Woodlawn Mortuary, Nashville, Tenn.

DAVIS, JEROME, educator, sociologist; b. Kioto, Japan, Dec. 2, 1891 (parents Am. citizens); s. Jerome Dean and Frances (Hooper) D.; A.B., Oberlin Coll., 1913, D.D., 1933; grad. Union Theol. Sem., 1920; M.A., Columbia, 1919, Ph.D., 1922; LL.D., Hillsdale, 1933; D.Litt., Fla. So.U., 1947; m. Mildred Rood, July 20, 1920; children—Frances Elizabeth (dec.), Helen Patricia, Wilfred Grenfell. Tchr. evening extension courses, Mpls., sec. civic work Mpls. Civic and Commerce Assn., 1913; lectr. extension courses, N.Y.C., 1914; sec. to Dr. Wilfred Grenfell, Labrador, 1915; Russian war work, 1916-18 (acting in charge 1917-18); surveyed Russian in Am. for Inter-Ch. World Movement, 1919-20; lectr. Am. Soc. for Extension Univ., Gilder fellow Columbia, 1920-21; asst. prof. sociology Dartmouth, 1921-24; Gilbert L. Stark chair practical philanthropy Yale Div. Sch., 1924-37; dir. work in prisoner-of-war camps for all Can. representing world's com. YMCA 1940-43; was corr., lectr., from 1943. Vis. prof. Hiram Coll., 1947-48, U. Colo., 1950, Fisk U., 1954. Pres., Am. Fedn. Tchrs., 1936-39; head Peace Mission to Europe, 1949; spl. investigation co-ops., Scandinavia, 1950; spl. mission to Soviet Union, 1943, spl. investigations Europe, 1947-49; head Am-European Seminar touring maj. countries Europe, 1960-62, 64, 66, 68, group profs. around world, 1967, Peace Seminar of 50 profs., tchrs., Europe, 1969, 70, 71, Internat. Peace Mission 30 profs., Europe, summer 1966; leader distinguished group to China, 1973, group profs. to Finland, Czechoslovakia, USSR, Eng., 1973; dir. Peace Mission to Europe, summer 1959; investigator conditions coal fields W.Va., 1923, conditions in Russia, summer 1926, 27, 32; exec. dir. Promoting Enduring Peace; Paine Found. lectr. to theol. sems., 1952; vis. prof. Internat. Christian U., Japan, 1965; leader educators seminar to China, 1975. Del. Democratic Nat. Conv., 1940. Chmn., Conn. State Legislative Commn. on Jails, 1931-39; pres. Eastern Sociol. Conf., 1936-37; v.p. speakers research com. UN; mem. Nat. Social Service Commn. Congl. Chs. (exec. com.), Social Service Commn. Fed. Council of Chs. Trustee Oberlin Coll. Mem. Am. Social Soc. (com. on internat. relations, 1922-24), Am. Econ. Assn., Nat. Conf. Social Work, AAUP, Loyal Legion, Alpha Chi Rho, Conglist. Club: Cosmos (Washington). Author books including: Introduction to Sociology, 1927; Readings in Sociology, 1927; Contemporary Social Movements, 1930; Labor Problems in America, 1940; Character Assassination, 1950; Peace, War and You, 1952; Religion In Action, 1956; On the Brink, 1959; Citizens of One World, 1961; World Leaders I Have Known, 1963; Disarmament A World View, 1964; A Life Adventure for Peace, 1967; Peace or World War III, 1969. Contbr. to periodicals. Home: Brookeville, Md. Died Oct. 19, 1979.

DAVIS, JIM, actor; b. Edgerton, Mo., Aug. 26; grad. William Jewell Coll.; m. Blanche. Former salesman, manual laborer; appeared in numerous movies, including: The Fabulous Texan, The Romance of Rosy Ridge, Red Stallion in the Rockies, California Passage, Iron Mistress, Last Stagecoach West, Winter Meeting, High Flying Low, One Little Indian, Bad Company, The Parallax View, Monty Walsh, The Choirboys; regular on TV series: Stories of the Century, 1954-55, Rescue 8, 1958, The Cowboys, 1974, Dallas, 1978-81; appeared in TV films: The Trackers, Deliver Us From Evil, The Smokeaters, Satan's Triangle, Stone, Just a Little Inconvenience; numerous other TV appearances. Served with USCG. Home: Northridge, Calif. Died Apr. 26, 1981.

DAVIS, JOHN C., JR., physician; b. Pottstown, Pa., June 13, 1886; s. John C. and Mary Gould (Meigs) D.; M.D., Jefferson Med. Coll., 1908; m. Elizabeth S. Henderson, Oct. 25, 1920. First lt. and asst. surgeon, U.S.N., 1913-14; asso. prof. of Medicine, Jackson Med. Coll.; attending phys. Jackson Hosp.; consulting phys., Southwestern Gen. Hosp.; hematologist French Hosp. Fellow Coll. Physicians Phila., A.M.A. Soc. Author: Clinical Hematology, 2d edit., 1930; Surgical Hematology (in Harrison's System of Surgery), 1933; Principals and Practice of Physical Diagnosis, 3d edit., 1936; Diseases of the Blood (in Hall's System of Therapeutics): Secondary Anemia (in Sabin's Cyclopedia of Practice of Medicine). Home: Chicago, Ill. *

DAVIS, JOHN EISELE, rehab. specialist; b. New Britain, Pa., Aug. 16, 1895; s. Thomas Sculi and Annie (Eisele) D.; student law Richmond U., 1913-14; A.B., Washington Coll., Chestertown, Md., 1918, A.M., 1920, D.Sc., 1945; m. Lillian Hicks, June 18, 1920; 1 son, John Eisele. Active 25 years in study recreational therapy for mentally ill, developer pioneering techniques; as chief athletics assisted in orgn. atheltic activities for VA; chief corrective phys. rehab. VA, 1946-77, sr. phys. dir. VA Hosp., Perry Point, Md., 1923-77; cons. to state hosps., rehab. services; founder Assn for Phys. and Mental Rehab., pres. assn., 1957-58, past exec. dir.; organizer (with aid Karl Menninger) sch. for therapists VA Hosp., Topeka. Fulbright lectr. U. Oslo, Norway; Exec. dir. Nat. Rehab. Tng. Inst., 1969-77; nat. cons. Dept. Health, Edn. and Welfare, 1969-77; cons. in rehab. to Dept. Health, Edn. and Welfare, VA, U.S. Govt.; project dir. Research Grant on Voluntarism Dept. Health, Edn. and Welfare, 1971. Mem. Pres.'s Com. on Employment Handicapped. Chmn. bd. Nat. Rehab. Tng. Inst. bd visitors and govs. Washington Coll. Recipient award as founder Assn. for Phys. and Mental Rehab., Chgo., 1947. Fellow A.A.H.P.E.R.; mem. Am. Congress Phys. Medicine (asso.), Am. Occupational Therapy Assn., Research Council on Problems of Alcohol, Assn. Mil. Surgeons U.S., N.P. Anonymous (chmn. com. pub. edn.), Am. Legion, V.F.W., D.A.V., Assn. Phys. and Mental Retardation (chmn. com. mental retardation), Sigma Phi Epsilon. Baptist. Mason. Author: Play and Mental Health; Principles and Practice of Rehabilitation, rev. edit., 1947; Recreational Therapy; Clinical Applications of Recreational Therapy, 1952; Recovery From Schizophrenia, the Roland Method, 1957; Recreational Therapy: A New Social Science, 1975; The Role of the Physical Educator in the Rehabilitation of the Mental Retardee, 1975; also articles. Home: Rehoboth Beach, Del. Died April 1977.

DAVIS, JOHN H., JR., cons., educator; b. Cumberland County, Va., July 16, 1901; s. John Henry and Susan Beverly (Morton) D.; B.S., M.A., Davidson Coll., 1924; Ph.D., U. Chgo., 1929; m. Emma Caroline Adcock, June 2, 1931; children—Emma Virginia, Susan Morton. Asso. prof. biology Davidson Coll., 1925-27, 28-30; prof. biology Presbyn. Coll., 1930-33, Southwestern Coll., Memphis, 1935-41; research asso. Carnegie Instn., Washington, summers 1936-40, Fla. Geol. Survey, 1941-48; vis. prof. botany U. Va. Mountain Lake Lab., 1941, 43, 45, 47; prof. botany U. Fla., 1946-69, emeritus, 1969-78; ecology cons., 1969-78; vis. prof. Auckland U. Coll., New Zealand, 1950, U. Mandalay, Burma, 1958-60, Nat. Taiwan U., Taipei, 1964-65. Mem. Ecol. Soc. Am., Assn. Southeastern Biologists, Fla. Acad. Sci., Phi Beta Kappa, Sigma Xi, Phi Sigma, Gamma Sigma Epsilon, Sigma Upsilon. Democrat. Presbyn. Author: Natural Features of Southern Florida; Forests of Burma; Influences of Man upon Coast Lines, The Role of Mangroves, others; also survey reports, bulls. Home: Gainesville, Fla. Died Jan. 27, 1978.

DAVIS, JOHN STAIGE, physician; b. Charlottesville, Va., Sept. 13, 1900; s. John Staige and Volunnia (Staples) D.; B.A., U. Va., 1921, M.D., 1925; student London Sch. Tropical Medicine; m. Camile Ruth Cole, 1930 (div. 1937); children—John Staige IV, Camiile Ruth; m. 2d, Florence Roome, 1940 (dec. 1943); m. 3d, Margaret Diggins, Nov. 1943 (div. 1952); children—Paul Staige, Roslyn Staige, Elaine; m. 4th, Mary Benzell, Jan. 19, 1954 (div. Nov. 1970); m. 5th, Tolly English Baruch, Mar. 4, 1972; 1 stepson, Frank W. Clark. Intern St. Luke's Hosp., N.Y.C., 1925-27, attending physician, 1931-77, chief arthritis clinic, 1932-70; asst. resident Rockefeller Inst., N.Y.C., 1927-28; practice internal medicine, N.Y.C., 1929-77; asso. attending physician Bellevue Hosp., 1947-77; cons. physician Southampton-Midtown hosps. Chmn. bd. Dathol Corp. Chmn. med. sect., dir. N.Y. Bd. Trade; chmn. health and safety council Manhattan chpt. Boy Scouts Am. Trustee, v.p. People to People Program U.S.A. Served to col. M.C., AUS, 1942-45; col. Res. Fellow A.C.P., N.Y. Acad. Medicine; mem. Harvey Soc., Assn. Mil. Surgeons U.S., Am. Rheumatism Assn., Mil. Order Fgn. Wars, St. Hubert Soc. Am. (pres.), Raven Soc., Navy League (v.p. Montauk), Med. Strollers N.Y., Mil. Order World Wars, Sons of Confederate Vets., Phi Beta Kappa, Sigma Xi, Alpha Omega Alpha, Delta Kappa Epsilon, Phi Rho Sigma. Clubs: University, Touchdown, Adventurers; (pres.), Club Limited, Camp Fire Club Am., Assn. Am. Sportsmen, Deep Sea (fleet surgeon, v.p.), Boone and Crockett, Governors Island Officers Open Mess. Home: New York, N.Y. and Scottsville, Va. Died Sept. 11, 1977.

DAVIS, JOHN WARREN, educator; b. Milledgeville, Ga., Feb. 11, 1888; s. Robert Marion and Katie (Mann) D.; student U. Chgo., 1911-13; A.B., Morehouse Coll., Atlanta, 1911, A., 1920, LL.D., 1965; D.Litt., State Coll., Orangeburg, S.C., 1931; LL.D., Wilberforce U. 1939, Howard U., 1940, Va. State Coll., Morgan State Coll., 1952, Harvard U., 1953; D.CL., U. Liberia (W. Africa), 1956, H.HD, 1960; H.H.D., W.Va. State Coll., 1956; LL.D., Central State Coll. (Ohio), 1965, Shaw U., 1967; m. Bessie Rucker, Aug. 24, 1916 (dec.); children—Constance Rucker (dec.), Dorothy Long; m. 2d, Ethel McGhee, Sept. 2, 1932; 1 dau., Caroline Florence. Tchr., Morehouse Coll., Atlanta, 1911-15, registrar, 1914-17; exec. sec. 12th St. br. YMCA, Washington, 1917-19; pres. W.Va. State Coll., 1919-53, pres. emeritus, 1953-80; U.S. dir. Tech. Coop. Adminstrn., Monrovia, Liberia, 1953-54; mem. U.S. Nat. Commn. for UNESCO, 1960-62; mem. U.S. Fgn. Service Selection Bd., 1962; spl. dir. dept. tchr. info. and security NAACP Legal Def. and Ednl. Fund, Inc., 1953-73, cons., 1973; dir. talent study Phelps-Stokes Fund, 1956; spl. dir. Herbert Lehman Edn. Fund, 1964; mem. Hoover's Orgn. on Unemployment Relief, Nat. Adv. Com. on Edn. of Negroes; mem. Nat. Land Grant Coll. Survey Staff, 1928, Nat. Adv. Com on Edn., 1929 mem. Commn. on Instns. of Higher Edn. of N. Central Assn. of Coll., 1936-48; mem. exec. com. N. Central Assn. Colls. and Secondary Schs., 1947; mem. NEA Com for Dgf. of Democracy Through Edn., 1945-52 chmn., 1950-52; mem. N. Central Assn. Com. on Evaulation of Accrediting Procedures, 1948; mem. Na Sci. Bd., NSF, 1950-56; mem. U.S. Office of Edn. Wartime Commn. Bd. dirs. Englewood (N.J.) Hosp. trustee Shaw U., Bergen County (N.J.) Community Coll., African-Am. Inst. Decorated grand officer Orde Nat. Honor of Merit Haiti, 1948; grand comdr. Orde Star Liberia, W. Africa, 1936; recipient James Weldon Johnson Citizenship award, 1963; granted Harmo Award in Edn., 1926. Mem. N.Y 5tate Colonizatio Soc., Am. Soc. African Culture, NEA, Assn. Tchrs in Colored Schs. (pres. 1928), Center for Study o Presidency, Pub. Mems. Assn. Fgn. Service Officer (v.p.), Nat. Freedom Day Assn. (v.p. 1948—), Phi Beta Kappa, Sigma Pi Phi, Republican. Baptist. Clubs Masons (33 deg.), Shriners. Home: Englewood, N.J. Died July 12, 1980; cremated.

DAVIS, M. EDWARD, physician, educator; b. Cheyenne, Wyo., Oct. 27, 1899; s. Max and Dora (Flaxman) D.; student U. Colo., 1916-19; B.S., U. Chgo., 1920; M.D., Rush Med. Coll., 1922; postgrad. Berlin, Vienna, 1927-28; fellow Carnegie Instn. of Embryo, 1933-34; m. Jeannette Sanger, July 12, 1927; children—Barbara Adele, M. Edward. Intern, Los Angeles Gen. Hosp., 1922-23; resident obstetrician Chgo. Lying-in Hosp., 1925-27; staff Chgo. Lying-In Hosp., U. Chgo Clinics; Instr. obstetrics Northwestern, 1929-30; asst. prof., obstetrics and gynecology U. Chgo., 1930-34, asso. prof., 1934-42, prof., 1942-66, prof. emeritus, 1966-78, Joseph Bolivar DeLee prof. obstetrics and gynecology, 1947-66, chief of service Chgo.-Lying-in Hosps., chmn. dept. obstetrics and gynecology, 1954-66; cons. Chgo. Bd. Health, 1966-67; cons., asst. dir. Am. Coll. Obstetrics and Gynecology, 1967-68. Recipient Rubin award Am. Soc. for Study Sterility, 1960. 1st Gold Medal award Barren Found., 1961. Diplomate Am. Bd. Obstetrics and Gynecology. Hon fellow History Medicine Soc Tulane; fellow A.C.S., Am. Fertility Soc. (v.p. 1965-66), Chgo. Gynecol. Soc., Am. Coll. Obstetricians and Gynecologists, Am. Fertility Soc., Inst. Medicine Chgo. (acad.); hon. mem. Sociedade de Obstetrcia e Ginecologia de Brasil, Sociedad Cubana de Obstet. y Ginecol., Sociedad de Obstet. y Ginecol. de Veneguela, A.F.A. King Obstet. Soc. of George Washington U., Honolulu. Obstet. and Gynecol. Soc.; corr. mem. Sociedad Latino Americana para el Estudio de la Esterilidad; mem. Am. Gynecol. Soc. (v.p. 1965-66), Am. Assn. Parenthood Physicians (pres. 1965-66), Soc. Gynecologic Investigation, Endocrine Soc., A.M.A. (Gold medal for work on ergot 1935), Soc. Exptl. Biology and Medicine, Am. Soc. Pharm. and Exptl. Therapeutics, Central Soc. Clin Research, Internat. Corrs. Soc. Obstetricians and Gynecologists. Author: DeLee's Obstetrics for Nurses, 1944, 47, 51, 57, 62, 66; Have Your Baby Keep Your Figure, 1963. Editor: Cancer of the Uterus (English editor), 1963, Jour. Fertility and Sterility 1957-70; editorial bd. Geriatrics, Aoga Cytologica, Psychosomatics, Exerpta Medica, Current Therapy, Ob-Gyn News, 1967-78, Jour. Reproductive Medicine, Lying-in. Contbr. articles to profl. jours. Home: Winnetka, Ill. Died Feb. 6, 1978.

DAVIS, MAUDE (BENNETT), prof. edn. and psychology; b. Waxahachie, Tex., Feb. 22, 1883; d. William Ausburn and Amanda Jemima (Bennett) Davis; ed. Ferris Inst., 1896-1900; A.B., Trinity U., 1918; A.M., U. of Chicago, 1921; student, U. of Colo., 1917, Columbia Teachers Coll. (summers), 1929-44; unmarried. Teacher, rural and high schs., 1900-09; teacher, Waxahachie High Sch., 1909-19; asst. prof. edn., Tex. State Coll. for Women, 1921-23; dean of women, 1923-45; asst. prof. edn., Trinity U., 1923-37, chmn. dept. of edn. and psychology 1939-42, dir. of counselling, 1942-45, prof. edn. and psychology, since 1945; lecturer, ednl. and mental hygiene; vis. prof. edn. and psychology, N.M. Highlands U., 1936-42; cons., Bexar County (Tex.) Mental Hygiene Soc., 1944-46. Child Guidance Inst., San Antonio, Tex., 1945-47. Mem. Tex. Assn. of Deans of Women (pres. 1930-32), Parent Teachers Assn., Am. Assn. of Univ. Women (organized Ellis County br., 1940, pres., 1940-42, pres. San Antonio br., 1944-46), Tex. State Teachers Assn., N.E.A., Tex. Mental Hygiene Soc., D.A.R., Tex. State Psychology Assn., San Antonio Hist. Soc., Presidents Club (San Antonio), Pi Lambda Theta, Pi Gamma Mu, Delta Kappa Gamma. Democrat. Presbyterian. Author: Citizenship Programs for Texas State Federation Clubs, 1922; contbd. articles to mags. Home: San Antonio, Tex.

DAVIS, MAXINE (MRS. JAMES MARSHALL MCHUGH), writer; b. Terre Haute, Ind.; d. Maxwell and Rose Davis; m. James Marshall McHugh, Apr. 3, 1943. Newspaper reporter for N.Y. World, United Press Assn., Detroit Free Press, 1924-28; proprietor syndicate, Capital News, 1926-30; free lance writer from 1932. Author: The Lost Generation, 1936; They Shall Not Want, 1937; Woman's Medical Problems, 1945; Through the Stratosphere, 1946; Facts About Menopause, 1951; The Sexual Responsibility of Woman, 1956; Sex and the Adolescent, 1958, 2d edit., 1968; How to Get the Most Out of Your Best Years, 1960; Every Woman's Book of Health, 1961; Sexual Responsibility in Marriage, 1963; Hope for the Childless Couple, 1963. Contbr. to nat. mags. Home: Washington, D.C. Died 1979.

DAVIS, MEYER, musician; b. Ellicott City, Md., Jan. 10, 1899; s. Sol and Rose (Benjamin) D.; student George Washington U., 1914-16; m. Hilda Emery, June 17, 1917; children—Virginia, Garry, Emery, Marjorie. Head Meyer Davis' Music, soc. dance orchs., from 1915; pres. Meyer Davis' Music, Inc.; performed Presdl. inaugural balls, numerous White House appearances. Clubs: Nat. Press (Washington); Lotos, Lambs, Friars, Dutch Treat (N.Y.C.). Home: New York, N.Y., also Sorrento, Maine. Died Apr. 5, 1976.

DAVIS, MORGAN JONES, geologist; b. Anson, Tex., Nov. 19, 1898; s. John Wesley and Gabrella (Jones) D.; student Tex. Christian U., 1916-18; B.A. in Geology, U. Tex., 1925; student Harvard Grad. Sch. of Bus. Adminstrn., 1947; D.Eng. (hon.), Colo. Sch. Mines, 1954; m. Veta Clare Moore, Aug. 8, 1926; children—Morgan J., Jr., James H. Worked on Tex. cattle ranch, 1915-16; engr., later asst. supt., Tulsa Spavinaw Water Project, 1921-24; became geologist Humble Oil & Refining Co., 1925; with Nederlandsche Kolonidale Petroleum Maatschappij, geologist in Java, resident geologist producing fields, Sumatra, Indonesia, 1929-34; with Humble Oil & Refining Co. (name now Exxon U.S.A.), 1934, chief geologist, 1941, mgr. exploration dept., 1946, dir. in charge exploration, 1948, v.p., 1951-56, exec. v.p., 1956-57, pres., 1957-61, chmn. board, chief exec. officer, 1961-63; dep. chmn. bd. dirs. Fed. Res. Bank of Dallas, 1961-63; cons., dir. First City Nat. Bank, Houston. Bd. trustees Kinkaid Sch., Houston; mem. vis. com. Grad. Sch. Bus. Adminstrn., Harvard, 1963-68; adv. council Geology Found., U. Tex. Bd. dirs., past pres. Nat. Space Hall of Fame. Recipient Distinguished Service award, Tex. Mid-Continent Oil and Gas Assn., 1960. Mem. Philos. Soc. Tex., Houston Geol. Soc. (life), Tex. Hist. Assn., Am. Assn. Petroleum Geologists (pres. 1952-53; Sidney Powers award distinguished achievement 1972), Assn. Profl. Geol. Scientists, Am. Petroleum Inst. (dir.), Mid-Continent Oil and Gas Assn., Am. Geog. Soc., Am. Inst. Mining, Metall. and Petroleum Engrs. Tex. Acad. Sci., Am. Geophys. Union, Geol. Soc. Am. (pres. 1968-69), Sigma Iota Epsilon, Delta Kappa Epsilon, Sigma Gamma Epsilon. Mason. Clubs: Harvard Business School, Houston Country, Ramada, River Oaks, Petroleum, Bayou (Houston); Boston (New Orleans); Mill Reef (Antigua, W.I.); St. Charles Bay Hunting (Rockport, Tex.); Twenty-Five Years of Petroleum Industry (pres. 1963). Home: Houston, Tex. Died Dec. 31, 1979; buried Claremore, Okla.

DAVIS, NORRIS GARLAND, educator; b. Bartlett, Tex., Feb. 15, 1916; s. Emet Graves and Jennie (Shults) D.; student John Tarleton Coll., 1933-35; B.J., U. Tex., 1937, M.J., 1938; postgrad. U. Wis., 1941-43; Ph.D., U. Minn., 1954; m. Edith Bess Pennington, June 3, 1939; children—Dan Garland, Dana Bess. Reporter Corpus Christi (Tex.) Caller-Times, 1938-40; instr. Tex. A.&M. Coll., College Station, 1940-41; asst. prof. journalism U. Tex., Austin, 1946-55, asso. prof., 1955-62, prof., 1962-81, chmn. journalism dept., 1965-76, asso. dean Sch. Communication, 1976-79. Bd. dirs. Tex. Student Publs. Mem. pub. relations com. Tex. div. Am. Cancer Soc., 1963-65. Served with AUS, 1943-46. Recipient Teaching Excellence award U. Tex. Students Assn., 1961, Teaching Excellence award, Piper Found., 1963, Friend of Tex. Press award, 1976, Tex. Daily Newspaper Assn. award, 1977. Mem. Internat. Council Indsl. Editors (pres. Austin chpt. 1966-67), Assn. Edn. Journalism, Southwestern Journalism Congress (pres. 1970-71), Tex. Journalism Edn. Council (pres. 1977-78), Sigma Delta Chi, Kappa Tau Alpha (nat. pres. 1977-78). Author: The Press and the Law in Texas, 1956; (with others) Modern Journalism, 1962. Contbr. articles to profl. jours. Home: Austin, Tex. Died Apr. 15, 1981.

DAVIS, ORLANDO CHESTER, librarian; b. Lowell, Mass., May 23, 1884; s. Orlando J. and Josie (Gould) D.; A.B., Dartmouth, 1907; m. Anna May Wilson, Apr. 28, 1909; children—Dorothy (Mrs. Elwood E. Gaskill) (dec.), Carol (Mrs. Edward F. Hamilton, Jr.), Marian W. (Mrs. George S. Laaff). Head cataloger, Dartmouth Coll. Library, 1907-10, reference librarian, 1909-10; librarian Pub. Library, Waltham, Mass., 1910-22, East Chicago, Ind., 1923-24, Hammond, Ind., 1925-26, Bridgeport, Conn., 1926-34; chief librarian div. Home Reading and Community Services, Pub. Library, Boston since 1934. War service under A.L.A., southern mil. camps and France, 1918-19. Mem. A.L.A., ex-pres. Ind. Library Assn., Conn. Library Assn., Sigma Alpha Epsilon. Clubs: Appalachian Mountain. Home: West Medway, Mass.

DAVIS, PAUL M., banker; b. Tullahoma, Tenn., June 2, 1882; s. Maclin H. and Christina D.; ed. Webb Sch., Bell Buckle, Tenn.; Branham & Hughes Sch., Springhill, Tenn.; Stanford U.; m. Augusta Shwab, 1909; children—Paul, Peter. Identified with business enterprises, Nashville, since beginning of active career; now adv. dir. Nashville Industrial Corp.; hon. chmn. First Am. Nat. Bank; dir. Eastern Airlines, Inc. Mem. Delta Kappa Epsilon. Episcopalian.

DAVIS, RALPH MARSHALL, clergyman; b. Omaha, Gallatin County, Ill., Apr. 13, 1886; s. Samuel M. (banker) and Phoebe Cordelia (Gregg) D.; A.B., Mo. Valley Coll., Marshall, Mo., 1908, D.D., 1922, LL.D., 1946; grad. San Francisco Theol. Sem., 1911; B.D., 1916; S.T.M., Harvard, 1918; M.R.E., Boston U., 1922; married Mary Ruth Purcell, November 29, 1906; children—Mary Cordelia (wife of Lieutenant David Joyce, A.A.F.), Ralph Marshall, Jr. Ordained ministry of Presbyterian Church, 1911; pastor successively Westminster Church, San Francisco, First Church, Colton, California, Fourth Church, Boston, Massachusetts, First Church Saint Louis until 1922, Hyde Park Ch., Chicago, 1922-29, Ch. of the Covenant, Erie, Pa., 1929-37, 1st Ch., Oakland, Calif., 1937-49. Mem. commission on home Federal Council of Chs. of Christ. Chmn. Commn. on Marriage and Divorce and Re-marriage of Gen. Assembly Presbyn. Ch., U.S. Army. Mem. special staff of preachers to Purdue Univ. since 1927; mem. bd. of dirs. Western Theol. Sem., Pittsburgh, Pa. Moderator Presbytery of San Francisco. Member Pi Gamma Mu. Republican. Mason (32 deg., Shriner, K.T.). Clubs: Commonwealth (San Francisco), Lions, Outlook, Sequogah Country. Special preacher to Great Britain, 1931. Collaborator in "Twenty-Four Views of Marriage," "Music of the Gospel," "Convocations for Worship." Home: Winters, Calif.

DAVIS, RAYMOND EARL, civil engineer; b. Gorham, Me., June 13, 1885; s. Charles and Elizabeth (Gray) D.; B.S. in C.E., U. of Me., 1911, C.E., 1914; M.S., U. of Illinois, 1916; D.Eng. U. of Maine, 1936; m. Lola Hazel McCrum, Aug. 17, 1910; children—Priscilla Joan, Raymond Earl. Started as topographer, 1906; prof. civ. engring. and dir. engring. materials lab., U. Cal., 1926-52, dir. and prof. civil engring. emeritus, 1952—; consulting engr. numerous public and pvt. projects, including TVA, C.E., U.S. Army, U.S. Bur. Reclamation Royal Irrigation Dept. Thailand, AEC, USN. Served as 1st lt. U.S. Engr. Corps, World War I. Directed or served on Advisory Committees of several War Research Projects, World War II. Twice awarded Wason medal by Am. Concrete Inst. for most meritorious paper, 1931 and 1934, also Construction Practice award for notable contribution to art of concrete constrn. 1948; Turner gold medal, 1952; Frank E. Richart award, Am. Soc. Testing Materials, 1960; Walter C. Voss award, American Society for Testing Materials, 1962, award of merit, in 1964. Fellow of the A.A.A.S., Am. Soc. C.E.; mem. Am. Congress on Surveying and Mapping, Structural Engrs. Association of Cal., Am. Soc. for Testing Materials, Am. Soc. Engring. Edn., Am. Concrete Inst. (past pres., hon. mem.), Sigma Xi, Tau Beta Pi, Delta Sigma Chi, Chi Epsilon, Sigma Nu. Clubs: Bohemian, Commonwealth, Engineers (San Francisco); Faculty (Berkeley); East Bay Engineers, Claremont Country (Oakland). Author or co-author several textbooks; tech. articles to jours. Home: Berkeley, Cal.

DAVIS, SMITH BURCHFIELD, utility exec.; b. Lincoln, Neb., July 5, 1916; s. Oak E. and Adelia (Smith) D.; A.B., U. Neb., 1946, M.A., 1947; m. Mary Bullock, June 10, 1942 (div. 1951); 1 dau., Ann Davis (Mrs. James Kuhlman); m. 2d, Jean Eversden, Oct. 29, 1953. With comptrollers dept. Douglas Aircraft Co., 1940-45; grad. asst. U. Neb., 1947; asst. dir. sales promotion Tension Envelope Corp., Kansas City, Mo., 1947-48; with So. Cal. Edison Co., Los Angeles, 1948-75, comptroller, 1962-75, v.p., 1963-64, financial v.p. 1964-75; dir. Electric Systems Co., Asso. So. Investment Co., Energy Services, Inc., Mono Power Co. Bd. dirs., v.p. Cal. Taxpayers Assn.; former chmn. investor relations com. Edison Electric Inst. Adviser, U. Cal. at Los Angeles Grad. Sch. Bus.; mem. adv. bd. Inst. Pub. Utilities, Mich. State U. Bd. dirs. United Way, Los Angeles; investment bd. Children's Hosp., Los Angeles. Mem. Pacific Coast Elec. Assn. (treas.), Financial Execs. Inst., Financial Mgmt. Assn., Nat. Fedn. Financial Analysts, Los Angeles Soc. Security Analysts, Los Angeles Town Hall, World Affairs Council, Los Angeles C. of C., S.A.R. (past pres., dir. Los Angeles), Treasury Assos. Los Angeles, Delta Upsilon, Sigma Upsilon. Clubs: Downtown Investment (pres.), Los Angeles (dir.). Home: Pasadena, Calif. Died July 12, 1975.

DAVIS, STEPHEN SMITH, educator; b. Phila., Oct. 24, 1910; s. Stephen Smith and Rosa Elizabeth (Norris) D.; B.S. in Mech. Engring., Howard U., 1936; M.S. in Mech. Engring., Harvard, 1947; m. Aileen Priscilla Harris, June 25, 1938; 1 son, Stephen Harris. Mem. faculty Howard U., 1938-77, prof. mech. engring., 1938-77, head dept., 1962, dean Sch. Engring. and Architecture, 1964-70; mech. engr. Nat. Bur. Standards, 1943-45; cons. Naval Ordnance Lab., 1953-63. Mem. D.C. Bd. Appeals and Rev., 1959-77; vice chmn. D.C. Redevel. Land Agy., 1967-75; past vice chmn. Joint Bd. on Sci. Edn., Met. Washington; active Boy Scouts Am. Registered profl. engr., D.C., Md. Mem. ASME, Am. Soc. Engring. Edn., AAAS, Washington Acad. Sci., Nat. Soc. Profl. Engrs., D.C. Soc. Profl. Engrs., Tau Beta Pi. Club: Cosmos (Washington). Inventor holding patent flexible wind-tunnel nozzle; developer equipment for air-to-sea missiles. Home: Washington, D.C. Died Jan. 15, 1977.

DAVIS, TINE WAYNE, grocery chain exec.; b. Gamaliel, Ark., Jan. 8, 1914; s. William Milton and Ethel (Chase) D.; student U. Fla., 1933-34, U. Idaho, 1934-35; doctorate Embry-Riddle Aero. U.; L.H.D. (hon.), Bethune-Cookman Coll.; H.H.D. (hon.), Rush Coll.; m. Eunice Chandler, Dec. 5, 1936; children—Dianne Davis Latimer, Tiona Davis Duke, Tine Wayne. Sr. v.p., dir., mem. exec. com. Winn-Dixie Stores, Inc.; regional dir., pres. Winn-Dixie Montgomery, Inc., Winn-Dixie La., Inc., Winn-Dixie Tex., Inc.; v.p. V.M.S., Inc.; dir. Central Bank Montgomery, Central Bancshares of South, Am. Heritage Life Ins. Co., Jacksonville, North Ala. Broadcasters, Huntsville. Bd. dirs. Ala. Safety Council, Kinder Care Learning Centers. Recipient Service to Agr. award Ala. Bur. Fedn. Mem. Airplane Owners and Pilots Assn., Quiet Birdmen, Fla. Air Pilots Assn., OX 5 Club, Ala. Sheriff's Boys and Girls Ranches (life),

Sigma Chi. Presbyterian. Clubs: Louisville Kiwanis (hon.), Montgomery Country, Audubon Country, River. Home: Montgomery, Ala. Died Aug. 6, 1980.

DAVIS, W(ARREN) JEFFERSON, lawyer; b. Front Royal, Va., Mar. 17, 1885; s. Capt. George C. and Sarah Maude D.; B.Sc., George Washington U., 1911; LL.B., Georgetown U., 1911; post-grad. work, Univ. of Va.; LL.D., Keonigsberg University, Germany, 1928; m. Beatrice Merrill, 1923; m. 2d, Ione Dismukes, 1927. Admitted Cal. bar 1913; former counsel U.S. Internat. Aviation Congress, Prague; spl. asst. mil. attache Am. embassy, Berlin; formerly active Cal. N.G. Mem. bd. regents U. Am. Former mem. several assn. and govtl. coms. concerned with aeronaut. laws, uniform laws; commr. on Uniform State Laws for California; chairman Calif. Commn. on Uniform State Laws, chmn. Labor Bd. of Motion Picture Industry; mem. Gov.'s Com. on Intergovernmental Cooperation, Gov.'s Cooperation Commn., Calif. Commn. on Interstate Cooperation; mem. Federal-State Law Enforcement Conf., Washington, Aug. 1940. Specialist in radio and aeronautical law; founder first exchange fellowship in air law between European and Am. univs. Col. U.S. Army Res. Mem. Am. Academy of Public Affairs (president), American Law Inst. (life), profl. assns., Phi Sigma Kappa, Phi Delta Phi, Pi Gamma Mu. Officer Order of the Crown (Italy), 1922; Officer Legion of Honor (France), 1927. Christian Scientist. Mason (K.T., Shriner). Clubs: University, Aero, Country, Athletic (Los Angeles); Army and Navy (Washington, D.C.); Aero Club of America. Author of several books 1930—, including: The Supremacy of the Constitution, Aeronautical Law, Laws of Air Carriers; Law of the Land, 1962; also articles in mags., jours., and for newspaper syndicates. Co-author: Dream Becomes a Nightmare—The United Nations Today, 1964; Supreme Law or Supreme Court Which?—Judicial Revolution in the Warren Court, 1965. Aero. legal cons.

DAVIS, WALTER ALLISON, univ. pres.; b. Princeton, Ind., Apr. 9, 1882; s. John Howard and Laura Frances (Hickrod) D.; A.B., Ind. U., 1907, A.M., 1913; m. Pearl Bunting, of Bicknell, Ind., Aug. 2, 1910 (died July 23, 1921); 1 son, Howard Bunting; m. 2d, Arleigh Bunting, Aug. 26, 1931. Teacher of history, principal high schools and supt. schs., Bicknell, 1907-11; supt. schs., Covington, Ind., 1912-18; dir. ednl. activities Army Y.M.C.A., Southern Dept., World War; ednl.-vocational training consultant, Eighth Army Corps, 1920-21; prof. edn., Vincennes U., 1923-24, pres. since 1924. Mem. N.E.A., Ind. Teachers' Assn., Phi Delta Kappa, Sigma Pi. Republican. Presbyn. Mason. Rotarian. Home: Vincennes, Ind.

DAVITT, THOMAS EDWARD, educator; b. Adrian, Mich., May 6, 1904; s. Thomas James and Anna (Howley) D.; A.B., U. Detroit, 1932; MA, St. Louis U., 1936, Ph.D., 1950. Joined S.J.; asst. prof. jurisprudence St. Louis U., 1947-53, asso. prof., 1953-54; asso. prof. Marquette U., 1954-60, prof. jurisprudence, 1960-80. Cons., Nat. Endowment for Humanities, 1972-80. Guggenheim fellow for research European Legal Centers, 1956-57; Am. Philos. Soc. grantee, 1960-62. Mem. Am. Arbitration Assn. (nat. panel arbitrators). Author: The Nature of Law, 1951; The Elements of Law, 1959; The Basic Values on Law-A Study of the Ethico-Legal Implications Psychology and Anthropology, 1968; Ethics in the Situation, 1970, Adv. editor Am. Jour. Jurisprudence, 1955-80. Home: Milwaukee, Wis. Died Aug. 10, 1980; buried Calvary Cemetery, Milw.

DAWLEY, ERNEST J., army officer; b. Wis., Feb. 17, 1886; M.A., U. of Wis.; B.S., U.S. Mil. Acad., 1910. Commd. 2d lt., F.A., U.S. Army, and advanced through the grades to brig gen., 1940; retired, 1947. Decorated D.S.M., Silver Star. Home: Robles del Rio, Calif.

DAWSON, CONINGSBY (WILLIAM), author; b. High Wycombe, Buckinghamshire, Eng., Feb. 26, 1883; s. Dr. William James and Jane (Powell) D.; grad. honor history schs., Merton Coll. (Oxford U.), Eng., 1905; m. Helen, d. Peter Campbell, 1918. Came to America, 1905; spl. work for English newspapers on Canadian affairs; at Taunton, Mass., 1906-10; lit. adviser to George H. Doran Pub. Co., New York, 1910-13. Joined the Canadian 1st Div. at the front as lt. F.A., 1916, and served till end of the World War; lectured in U.S. 1 month, 1917, after having been wounded; made study of Am. mil. preparedness in France under British Minister of Information, winter 1918; rejoined the Canadians spring of 1918 and was wounded in Sept.; lectured in U.S. under British Mission Nov. and Dec. 1918; returned to Eng. to make study of European reconstruction problems; lectured in every state of the Union on the results of the war, 1919-20; at request of Herbert Hoover visited stricken areas of Central and Eastern Europe and reported thereon. Fellow Royal Geog. Soc. Author of many novels since 1906, latest of which is Tell Us of the Night (with John Barton Browne), 1941. Co-editor: (with father) The Readers' Library, 1908. Home: Santa Monica, Cal.

DAWSON, DAVID HAIGH, chemist; b. Phila., Sept. 3, 1908; s. Josiah and Anne (Haigh) D.; B.S. in Chem. Engring., Drexel U., 1930, M.S., 1931; Ph.D., Ohio State U., 1933; D. Eng. (hon.), Drexel U., 1947; m. Ann Fox, Aug. 25, 1933; children—Ann Elizabeth, David Bruce, Thomas Michael. Teaching asst. Ohio State U., 1930-33; research chemist Krebs Pigment & Color Corp., Balt., 1933-35; research supr. pigments dept., E. I. du Pont de Nemours & Co., Wilmington, Del., 1935-44, asst. dir. research, 1944-46, dir. sales, 1946-48, asst. gen. mgr., 1948-51, asst. gen. mgr. fabrics and finishes dept., 1951-53, asst. gen. mgr. textile fibers dept., 1953-55, v.p., mem. exec. com., 1955-73, dir., from 1955; chmn. bd. The News Jour. Co., 1973-76, Chem. Industry Trade Adviser, 1973-76. Fellow AAAS; mem. Am. Chem. Soc. Home: Chadds Ford, Pa. Died Dec. 18, 1976.

DAWSON, JOHN ALBERT, investment dealer, religious ofcl.; b. Chgo., Sept. 3, 1904; s. John Henry and Ida Louise (Hellman) D.; student Northwestern U., 1925-27; LL.D. (hon.) Alderson-Broaddus Coll.; m. Annie Joe Howel, Mar. 24, 1934; children—Ann (Mrs. Myron Stanton), Mary MacKinnon Dawson, John H. Gen. partner John A. Dawson & Co., Chgo., 1931-79; mem. Midwest Stock exchange, Chgo., 1950-79. Past world chmn. men's dept., mem. exec. com. Bapt. World Alliance; past pres. Chgo. Bapt. Assn., Am. Bapt. Conv., Am. Bapt. Assembly, Green Lake, Wis. Mem. Chgo. Crime Commn.; mem. at large Nat. council Boy Scouts Am. Trustee Central Bapt. Children's Home, Bapt. Home and Hosp., Maywood, Ill., Bapt. Theol. Union (U. Chgo.), No. Bapt. Theol. Sem., Oakbrook, Ill; chmn. trustees Judson Coll., Elgin, Ill. Mem. Nat. (trustee), Ill. (past pres.) socs. S.A.R., Soc. Mayflower Descs. in Ill. (gov. 1960-63), Navy League U.S., Soc. Colonial Wars, Phi Kappa Sigma. Republican. Club: N Men's (Northwestern U.). Home: Wilmette, Ill. Died Oct. 20, 1979; buried Rosehill Cemetery, Chgo.

DAWSON, LYLE RAMSAY, educator; b. Long Point, Ill., Apr. 21, 1904; s. Marcus and Jessie (Ramsay) D.; Ed.B., Ill. State Normal U., 1928; M.S., U. Ill., 1932; Ph.D., U. Ia., 1935; D.Sc., U. Ky., 1971; m. Lucile Sanders, Aug. 11, 1926; 1 dau., Venita Lu. Science tchr. high schs., Ill., 1929-34; acting head dept. chemistry State Tchrs. Coll., Eau Claire, Wis., 1935-36; asst. prof. chemistry U. Omaha, 1936-37; research chemist Universal Atlas Cement Co., 1937-39; asst. prof., asso. prof., prof. chemistry La. Poly. Inst., 1939-43; research chemist and group leader Metall. Lab., U. Chgo., 1943-45; prof. phys. chemistry U. Ky., 1945-70, distinguished prof., 1956-70, head dept. chemistry, 1945-65, acting dean grad. sch., 1954-56, 60-61. Mem. Oak Ridge Council, 1950-58. Fellow A.A.A.S., Am. Inst. Chemist; mem. Am. Chem. Soc., Electro-chem. Soc., Ky. Acad. Sci., Am. Assn. U. Profs., Sigma Xi, Phi Lambda Upsilon, Kappa Delta Pi, Kappa Mu Epsilon, Alpha Chi Sigma, Omicron Delta Kappa. Democrat. Presbyn. Mason, Kiwanian. Clubs: Informal, Torch. Contbr. profl. publs. Home: Lexington, Ky. Died Apr. 16, 1976; interred Lexington Cemetery.

DAY, ALBERT M., state conservation exec.; b. Humboldt, Nebr., April 2, 1897; s. John Breese and Laura (Thayer) D.; B.S., U. Wyo.; children—Doris Jeane Day Evans, Richard Thayer, John Kendall. Began as field biologist, U.S. Biol. Survey, 1918; biol. survey in Wyo. in control of predatory animals and rodents to protect livestock and crops, 1920-30; asst. chief (supervising throughout U.S. Predator and Rodent Control, Washington, 1930-35, chief 1935-38; chief div. Federal Aid in Wildlife Restoration, promoting improved game mgmt. in cooperation with all states, P.R., V.I., 1938-42; liaison officer between Fish and Wildlife Service, and War, Navy and other govt. agencies, Washington, D.C., 1942-43; asst. dir. Fish and Wildlife Service (govt. wildlife conservation agency), Dept. of Interior, Chgo., 1943-46; dir. Fish and Wildlife Service, 1946-53, asst. to dir., 1953-55; dir. wildlife research Arctic Inst. N.A., 1955-58; dir. Oreg. Fish Commission, 1958-60; exec. dir. Pa. Fish Commission, 1960-64; adv. UN conf. on law of the sea; adv. N. Pacific Fisheries Commn.; apptd. adminstr. Def. Fisheries Adminstrn., 1950; mem. Pacific Marine Fisheries Commn., Internat. Pacific Salmon Fisheries Commn., 1947-54; mem. Pa. State Water Bd., Pa. Water and Power Resources Bd. Cpl. AUS, World War I. Mem. Wildlife Soc., Am. Forestry Assn., Nat. Audubon Soc., Am. Wildlife Inst., Am. Soc. Mammalogists, Am. Fisheries Soc., Izaak Walton League (nat. dir.), A.A.A.S., Internat. Assn. Game, Fish and Conservation Commn. Sigma Xi. Clubs: Explorers, Cosmos (Washington). Author: North American Waterfowl, 1949; Making a Living in Conservation: A guide to outdoor careers, 1971. Contbr. articles to mags. Home: Camp Hill, Pa. Died Jan. 21, 1979; buried Rolling Green Cemetery, Camp Hill.

DAY, BENJAMIN MULFORD, lawyer; b. North Plainfield, N.J., Jan. 24, 1886; s. Benjamin M. and Martha E. (Hanna) D.; grad. Hamilton Inst., N.Y., 1905; LL.B., N.Y. U., 1907, LL.M., 1908. Admitted to N.Y. bar, and began practice in N.Y.C. Sec. com. on indsl. Interests and relations of Constl. Conv., State of N.Y., 1915; sec. Mayor's Com. on Nat. Def., 1917; chief dep. collector internal revenue, N.Y., 1921-25; apptd. commr. of immigration, Ellis Island, 1926, re-apptd. 1930, resigned, 1931; apptd. mem. N.Y.C. Alcoholic Beverage Control Bd., 1933. Pres. N.Y. Young Republican Club and sec. Nat. Republican Club. Capt. Mil. Intelligence Div., U.S. Army, 1917-19. Sec. judicial sect. of Am. Bar Assn., 1934; pres. N.Y. Soc. for Prevention of Crime, 1940, 41, 42. Mem. English-Speaking Union of U.S., Pilgrims of U.S., St. Nicholas Soc. of N.Y., Colonial Soc. of Pa., Phi Delta Phi. Baptist. Clubs: National Republican, City, University. Home: New York City NY.

DAY, DOROTHY, social activist, journalist, publisher; b. Bklyn., Nov. 8, 1897; d. John J. and Grace (Satterlee) Day; student U. Ill., Urbana, 1914-16; 1 dau., Tamar Teresa. Reporter, columnist Socialist Call, N.Y.C., 1916-17; mem. staffs The Masses mag., N.Y.C., 1917, Liberator mag., N.Y.C., 1918, Chgo., 1921; probationary nurse Kings County Hosp., Bklyn., 1918-19; feature writer New Orleans Item, 1922; script writer Pathé Films, Hollywood, Calif.; writer Commonweal mag., 1932; co-founder, co-pub. (with Peter Maurin) Catholic Worker Newspaper, N.Y.C., 1933, now pub.; co-founder (with Peter Maurin) St. Joseph's House of Hospitality, N.Y.C., 1934, numerous other houses and farms for poor and homeless, 1933-80. Recipient Laetare medal U. Notre Dame, 1971; Melcher Book award, 1972. Roman Catholic. Author: From Union Square to Rome, 1938; House of Hospitality, 1939; On Pilgrimage, 1948; The Long Loneliness, 1952; Thérèse, 1960; Loaves and Fishes, 1963; On Pilgrimage: The Sixties, 1972. Address: New York, N.Y. Died Nov. 29, 1980.

DAY, PAUL L(OUIS), govt. ofcl., biochemist; b. Grants Pass, Ore., Dec. 26, 1899; s. Marcus Charles and Adella (Scott) D.; A.B., Willamette U., 1921; M.A., Columbia, 1923, Ph.D., 1927; LL.D. (honorary), University of Ark., 1960; m. Mildred Garrett, June 22, 1922; children—Peggy Day Leppmann, Dorothy Day Ciarlo. Began career as instructor chemistry Columbia Junior College, Milton, Ore., 1921-22; prof. chemistry Mont. Wesleyan Coll., Helena, 1923-25; asst. in chemistry Columbia, 1925-27; prof., head biochemistry, sch. medicine U. Ark., 1927-58, asst. dean grad. sch., 1956-58; sci. dir. U.S. Food and Drug Adminstrn., Dept. Health, Edn. and Welfare, 1959-61; scientific adminstr., extramural programs, NIH, 1962. Mem. sci. adv. com. Nat. Vitamin Found., 1953-56. Nutrition Found., Inc., 1960-62; biochemistry member of Natl. Bd. of Med. Examiners 1953-56; mem. food and nutrition bd. NRC. 1953-59; chmn. sub-com. on nutrition of lab. animals NRC Agrl. Bd. Mem. governing bd. Inst. Lab. Animal Resources, 1955-58. Served as pvt. U.S. Army, 1918. Recipient Mead Johnson Vitamin B Complex award Am. Inst. Nutrition, 1947; Midwest award in chemistry St. Louis sect. Am. Chem. Soc., 1948, S.W. regional award Am. Chem. Soc., 1952. Mem. A.M.A. (affiliate), Am. Inst. Nutrition (pres. 1953), Am. Chem. Soc. (chmn. central Ark. sect. 1952), Am. Soc. Biol. Chemists, So. Soc. Clin. Research (founder mem.), Soc. Exptl. Biology and Medicine, A.A. A.S. (council 1957-61), Sigma Xi (pres. Ark. 1956), Alpha Omega Alpha (hon.). Methodist (former steward and trustee). Author research papers in sci. and med. jours. Mem. editorial bd. Jour. of Nutrition, 1948-52, Proc. Soc. Exptl. Biology and Medicine, 1952-53, Proc. Animal Care Panel, from 1958. Home: Bethesda, Md. Died Feb. 1, 1980.

DAY, PRICE, former newspaper editor; b. Plainview, Tex., Nov. 4, 1907; s. John Walter and Zillah (Price) D.; A.B., Princeton, 1929; m. Alice Alexander, Dec. 28, 1931; children—Anthony, Joseph, Thomas, James. Cartoonist and occasional writer free lance, N.Y. and Fla., 1929-35; writer mag. fiction Sat. Eve. Post, Colliers, and others, 1935-41; city editor Fort Lauderdale (Fla.) Times, 1942; war corr. Balt. Sun, Mediterranean-ETO, 1943-45, fgn. and field corr., 1945-60; editor-in-chief Balt. Sun papers, 1960-75. Recipient Pulitzer prize for internat. reporting (articles on independence in India), 1949. Democrat. Home: Baltimore, Md. Died Dec. 9, 1978.

DAY, SAMUEL H., foreign service; b. Quincy, Calif., Sept. 7, 1886; B.S., U. of Calif., 1910, J.D., 1912. Admitted to Calif. bar, 1912, and practiced law, 1912-17; capt., U.S. Army, with A.E.F., 1917-19; tech. asst. Inter-Allied Rhineland Commn., 1919; with elec. company, 1919-21; entered Bureau of Foreign and Domestic Commerce, 1921; mgr. Phila. office, 1924-27; trade commr., Johannesburg, S. Africa, 1927-30; comml. attaché, Pretoria, 1930-37; home office, 1937-39; consul, Toronto, 1939-42; comml. attaché, Pretoria, since Apr. 1912.

DEAN, HERBERT R., insurance exec.; b. Providence, R.I., Sept. 8, 1882. V.p. and dir., Starkweather & Shepley, Inc., Providence; sec. and dir., Shepley Land Co., Providence; dir. Starkweather & Shepley, New York, Starkweather & Shepley, Inc., Ill., Starkweather & Shepley, Inc., Mass. Enlisted in R.I. militia, May 25, 1899; capt. Troop A cav., R.I. N.G.; Mexican Border, 1916; major cav. R.I. N.G., Oct. 20, 1917; major 304th cav. Fed. Service, Jan. 21, 1918; major 43d F.A., Aug. 15, 1918; col. 305th cav., March 26, 1923; brig. gen. 68th F.A. Brigade, Apr. 18, 1930; adj. gen. State of R.I.,

Feb. 5, 1931-Feb. 18, 1941; reentered Fed. Service Oct. 16, 1940; brig. gen. State Dir. Selective Service for R.I., to Oct. 29, 1945; maj. gen. (ret.) R.I. N.G., Feb. 13, 1946. Awarded Distinguished Service Medal, R.I. Mil. Cross. Trustee Butler Hosp. Corp. Home: Providence, R.I.

DEAN, JOEL, found. exec., bus. economist; b. Vershire, Vt., Oct. 5, 1906; s. Benjamin Angus and Eloise (Partridge) D.; A.B., Pomona Coll., 1927; M.B.A., Harvard, 1929; Ph.D., U. Chgo., 1936; hon. degrees Stockholm (Sweden) Sch. Econs., 1959, Pace Coll., 1964, U. Torino (Italy), 1966; m. Phyllis van Dyk, June 24, 1939 (dec. Mar. 1963); children—Joel, Gretchen, Gillian, Jurrien. Dir., Inst. of Statistics and asst. prof. U. Chgo., 1939-45; price exec. OPA, Washington, 1941-42, dir. fuel rationing div., 1942-44; prof. bus. econs. Columbia U., 1945-69, prof. emeritus, 1969-79; pres. Joel Dean Assos.; pres. Joel Dean Found. Fellow Nat. Assn. Bus. Economists; mem. Am. Econ. Assn., Financial Execs. Inst., Am. Marketing Assn. (dir.; Nat. award), Beta Gamma Sigma. Clubs: Century Association (N.Y.C.). Author: Statistical Determination of Cost, 1936; Cost Behavior and Price Policy (with others), 1942; Managerial Economics, 1951; Capital Budgeting, 1951; Statistical Estimation of Cost, 1975; (with others) Handbook of Industrial Engineering and Management, 2d edit., 1971; (with others) The Corporate Merger, 1966; (with others) Measuring the Investment Performance of Pension Funds, 1969; (with others) Handbook of Modern Marketing, 1970; (with others) Conglomerate Mergers, 1970; Statistical Cost Estimation, 1978; Decision Economics, 1979. Past bd. editors Jour. Indsl. Econs., Jour. Marketing. Home: Hastings-on-Hudson, N.Y. Died Feb. 14, 1979.

DEAN, JOHN LADD, lawyer; b. Rollersville, Ohio, Mar. 26, 1905; s George Cook and Lone (Ladd) D.; A.B, Ohio Wesleyan U., 1926; LL.B., Case Western Res. U., 1930; m. Margaret Blakely, Aug. 16, 1930; children—J. Thomas, Dorothy Lone Dean Floridis. Admitted to Ohio State bar, 1930, Fed. bar 1931 practiced in Cleve., 1930-80; partner firm Hahn, Loeser, Freedheim, Dean & Wellman, 1940-80; mem. exec. com. past dir. Carling Brewing Co., Carling, O'Keefe Ltd.; dir., sec. Nat. Telephone Supply Co.; past v.p., gen. counsel, mem. exec. com., dir. Ohio River Co.; past trustee, mem. exec. and audit coms. Eastern Gas & Fuel Assos. Mem. Citizens League Cleve. Past mem. exec. com., past trustee Christian Residences Found.; exec. com trustee St. Luke's Hosp.; past chmn. Assos., trustee Ohio Wesleyan U. Fellow Am. Bar Found.; mem. Am. (ho. of dels. 1971-72), Ohio (council dels. 1950-53, 70-80), Cuyahoga County, Cleve. (pres. 1970-71) bar assns., Chi Phi, Phi Delta Phi, Delta Sigma Rho. Republican. Methodist (trustee) Mason. Clubs: Union, Midday, Rowfant (Cleve.); Sette of Odd Volumes (London, Eng.). Home: Cleveland Heights, Ohio. Died Feb. 2, 1980; buried Evergreen Cemetery, Painesville, Ohio.

DEAN, PAUL MARSHALL, chemist, educator; b. Newcastle, Pa., Mar. 24, 1885; s. Marshall H. and Mary Irene (Cox) D.; A.B., U. of Colo., 1908, A.M., 1911; Ph.D., U. of Ill., 1916; research College de France, 1924-25; m. Cleophile Bell, June 4, 1912; 1 son, Paul Marshall. Science teacher, Golden (Colo.) High Sch., 1908-09; chemist, Western Chem. Mfg. Co., Denver, 1909-10; instr., U. of Colo., Boulder, 1911-13, 1915-16, asst. prof., 1917-20, asso., prof., 1920-23, prof. of chemistry since 1923, head, dept. chemistry, since 1943. Mem. Am. Chem. Soc., A.A.A.S., Am. Assn. Univ. Profs., Sigma Xi, Alpha Chi Sigma. Home: Boulder, Colo.

DEAR, WILLIAM RICHARD, physician; b. Hamilton, Loudon County, Va., Dec. 7, 1883; s. John William and Mary (Rogers) D.; M.D., U. of Pa., 1906; honor grad. Army Med. Sch., 1909, advanced course, 1926; grad. Sch. of Pub. Health, U. of Pa., 1931; m. Greta Marion Tibbetts, June 2, 1909; children—Richard Hamilton Briarlie (officer Army Med. Corps), Frances Brooke. Interne Emergency Hosp., Washington, D.C., 1906-07; licensed to practice medicine, Washington, D.C., 1908; commd. 1st lt., Med. Corps, 1908; advanced through the grades to brig. gen., 1941; comdr. Med. Replacement Training Center, Camp Pickett, Va., 1941-43; Comdg. Gen. Northington Gen. Hosp., Tuscaloosa, Ala., Nov. 20, 1943-Apr. 1946, Fellow American College Surgeons; mem. American Medical Association (member of house of delegates from the U.S. Army). Awarded Legion of Merit, 1946. Horatio C. Wood Undergrad. Med. Soc. (U. of Pa.), Alpha Mu Pi Omega.

DE ARAUJO CASTRO, JOAO AUGUSTO, Brazilian diplomat; b. Rio de Janeiro, Brazil, Aug. 27, 1919; s. Raimundo and Carmen (Viveiros de Castro) de Araujo Castro; LL.B., Niteroi Sch. Law (Rio de Janeiro), 1941; honoris causa degree, Nat. War Coll. (Brazil), 1963; m. Miriam Saint-Brisson, July 1, 1943; children—Carmen Saint-Brisson, Luiz Saint-Brisson, Silvia Saint-Brisson. Vice consul Brazilian consulate, San Juan, P.R., 1943-44, Miami, 1944, N.Y.C., 1944-48; assigned Ministry External Affairs, 1949-51; 2d sec. Brazilian Permanent Mission to UN, N.Y.C., 1951-53; 1st sec. Brazilian embassy, Rome, Italy, 1953-57; head polit. cultural dept. Ministry External Relations, Govt. Brazil, 1957-58, head dept. Internat. orgns., 1961, minister external relations, 1963-64; minister counselor Brazilian embassy, Tokyo, Japan, 1959-61; ambassador to Greece, Athens, 1964-66, to Peru, Lima, 1966-68, to U.S., Washington, 1971-75; perm. rep. to UN, N.Y.C., 1968-71. Chmn. delegation to Conf. on Trade and Devel., UN, 1964, to Conf. of 18 Nations Com. on Disarmament, Geneva, Switzerland, 1968. Served to 2d lt. Brazilian Army, 1940-41. Decorated grand officer decorations Army, Navy, Aeronautical Merit; Grand Cross Mexico, Bolivia, Peru, Greece, Yugoslavia; grand cross Order Rio Branco, Brazil; grand officer Order Orange Nassau, Netherlands, Order Merit (Italy), Rising Sun (Japan). Home: Washington, D.C. Died Dec. 9, 1975.

DEARSTYNE, HOWARD BEST, photographer; b. Albany, N.Y., Aug. 2, 1903; s. Charles and Lottie (Best) D.; A.B., Columbia, 1925, postgrad., 1925-28; diploma, Bauhaus, Dessau, Germany, 1932; postgrad. Bauhaus, Berlin, 1932-33; m. Barbara Louise Timmins, Oct. 5, 1946 (dec. 1973). Archtl. designer Wallace K. Harrison and J.A. Fouilhoux, N.Y.C., 1935-39, Raymond Loewy and Antonin Raymond, 1940-41; exhibited photography one man shows Va. Mus. Fine Arts, 1951, Art Inst. Chgo., 1962, U. Mich. Art Mus., 1962, Bloomfield (Mich.) Art Assn., 1963, U. Mich. Extension Service and Grad. Study Center, Dearborn, 1963, Andrew Dickson White Mus. Art, Cornell U., 1963, Grand Rapids Art Gallery, 1963, Twentieth Century Gallery, Williamsburg, 1963, Randolph Macon Woman's Coll., Lynchburg, 1963, Hollins Coll., 1963, Peninsula Arts Assn., Newport News, 1964, Richmond Profl. Inst., 1964, Longwood Coll., 1964, Howard U., 1964, Krannert Art Mus., U. Ill., Urbana, 1964, U. Tex., Austin, 1964, Tex. A. and M. U., 1964, Ariz. State U., 1965, U. Utah, 1965, U. Oreg., 1965, Ft. Worth Art Center, 1965, M. H. DeYoung Meml. Mus., San Francisco, 1966, U. Okla., 1966, Mills Coll., 1966, Ill. Inst. Tech., 1967, Tex. Technol. Coll., 1967, Wheaton Coll., Norton, Mass., 1967, Fisk U., 1968, Grand Valley State Coll., Allendale, Mich., 1968, Spelman Coll., Atlanta, 1968, Bird in Hand Galleries, Alexandria, Va., 1972, 73, Sander Gallery, Washington, 1977; exhibited group shows 2d Armory Exhbn., N.Y.C., 1945, Mus. Modern Art Shows, 1946, 50, 51, 57, 58,-59, 60, 62, Los Angeles County Mus., 1950, George Eastman House, 1959, 63-64, Photokina, Cologne, Germany, 1970, Photo Expo 71, Chgo.; faculty Black Mountain Coll., N.C., 1941-42; resident architect, tchr. arch. Lawrence Coll., Appleton, Wis., 1943-44; head dept. design Cranbrook Acad. Art, Mich., 1944-46; faculty Coll. William and Mary, 1946-57; asso. prof. dept. arch. Ill. Inst. Tech., 1957-71; asst. archtl. records editor Colonial Williamsburg, 1946-56. Fellow Graham Found. Advanced Studies Fine Arts, 1969. Mem. A.I.A., Coll. Art Assn. Am., Soc. Archtl. Historians (past dir.), Assn. Collegiate Schs. Arch. (past Com. chmn.). Author: (with A. Lawrence Kocher) Colonial Williamsburg/Its Buildings and Gardens, 1949, Shadows in Silver-A Record of Virginia, 1850-1900, 1954. Asso. editor Inland Architect, 1967-68, Translator: (with Hills Rebay) Point and Line to Plane, 1947, The Non-Objective World, 1959. Contbr. articles to mags. Home: Alexandria, Va. Died Mar. 7, 1979; buried Nat. Meml. Park, Falls Church, Va.

DEASY, MARY MARGARET, author; b. Cin., May 20, 1914; d. William P. and Clara L. (Woelfel) Deasy; Mus.B., Coll. Conservatory Music, U. Cin., 1935. Mem. Authors Guild. Author: The Hour of Spring, 1948; Cannon Hill, 1949; Ella Gunning, 1950; Devil's Bridge, 1952; The Corioli Affair, 1954; The Boy Who Made Good, 1955; O'Shaughnessy's Day, 1957; The Celebration, 1963; also numerous short stories. Address: Cincinnati, Ohio. Died May 14, 1978.

DE BAUFRE, WILLIAM LANE (DE-BO-FRE'), mech. engr.; b. Baltimore, Md., Apr. 19, 1883; s. William H. and Kate (Maidlow) De B.; diploma, Baltimore Poly. Inst., 1903; E.E., Lehigh, 1907, M.E., 1909, M.S., 1919; m. Elizabeth Kirchgessner, Mar. 10, 1906; 1 dau., Ruth Marie. Teacher Baltimore Poly. Inst., most of time, 1903-12, advancing to head of dept. of engring.; mech. engr. U.S. Naval Engring. Expt. Sta., Annapolis, 1912-19; prof. mech. engring., U. of Neb., 1919-27, also chmn. of dept.; cons. engr. and mem. bd. helium engrs., U.S. Bur. Mines, 1921-26; tech. adviser and head of tech. research dept. of Internat. Combustion Engring. Corp., 1926-31; chmn. dept. of engring. mechanics, University of Nebraska, since 1931, director Engineering, Science, and Management War Training, 1941-45, acting chairman mechanical engineering department, 1942-45; consultant on liquefaction and separation of gases. Numerous patents on regenerative system of evaporation, process for separating helium from natural gas, repurifying helium, separating oxygen and nitrogen from atmospheric air, steam boilers, etc. Fellow A.A.A.S., Am. Soc. M.E., Am. Assn. Univ. Profs. (pres. for 1947 of University of Nebraska chapter), national director Am. Interprofessional Inst. (Lincoln), 1946-50, Nebraska Engineering Society, Lincoln Chamber of Commerce, Newcomen Soc., Theta Xi, Tau Beta Pi, Sigma Xi, Sigma Tau, Pi Tau Sigma. Club: Lincoln Engineers. Author: Engineering Mechanics: Part I, Statics, Part II, Dynamics, 1948. Contributor many tech. papers on thermodynamics, heat transfer, flow of fluids, combustion and steam generation. Home: Lincoln, Neb. *

DEBLER, ERDMAN B., consulting engr.; b. Beatrice, Neb., Jan. 8, 1885; s. Carl Ferdinand and Maria (Kuhn) D.; B.S. in C.E., U. of Neb., 1907; 1 dau., Dorothy Lavane (Mrs. Edwin Melvin Powers). Various minor engring. work on railroad location and contrn., 1904-07; office engr. Arnold Co., Denver, Colo., 1908; asst. gen. mgr. Denver Reservoir Irrigation Co., 1909-10; engr. with Sam Brown, Jr., & Son, Chicago, 1910-15; railroad valuation for Interstate Commerce Commn., 1915-17; asst. engr. maintenance of way, U.P. R.R. Co., 1918; with U.S. Bureau of Reclamation, 1918-47, hydraulic engr., 1918-40, dir. project planning 1941-43, regional dir., 1944-47; cons. engr., in pvt. practice since 1948. Mem. Am. Soc. Civil Engrs., Am. Geophysical Union, Colo. Soc. Engrs., Sigma Xi. Address: Denver, Colo.

DE CAPRILES, MIGUEL, educator, lawyer; b. Mexico City, Mexico, Nov. 30, 1906; s. Abraham M. and Cristina Treserra de C.; came to U.S., 1920, naturalized, 1932; B.S. cum laude, N.Y. U., 1927, A.M., 1931, J.D., 1935; also post-grad. work law; m. Dorothy Hafner, Sept. 22, 1938; children—Thomas, Cristina. Adminstrv. officer, N.Y. U., 1927-42, mem. faculty econs. dept., 1928-42, on leave of absence, 1942-45, mem. law faculty 1945-74, emeritus, 1974-81, dir. Inter-Am. Law Inst., 1947-57, asso. dean Law Sch., 1948-63, vice dean, 1963-64, dean, 1964-67, v.p., sec., gen. counsel univ., 1967-74, dir. office instnl. research and ednl. planning, 1953-56; prof. law Hastings Coll., U. Cal. at San Francisco, 1974-81; admitted to N.Y. bar, 1936, U.S. Supreme Ct. bar, 1964; counsel to bd. trustees, Hofstra Coll., 1936-38; spl. asst. to atty. gen., war div., U.S. Dept. Justice, 1942-45; vis. prof. U. Cal., 1949, Stanford, 1950. Cons. N.Y. Joint Legislative Com. Study Revision Corp. Laws, 1959-73; treas. Inst. Jud. Adminstrn. 1952-74. Active in amateur fencing, U.S. Olympic Com., mem. U.S. Olympic and Internat. Teams, 1932-51; winner of several nat. championships, 1931-47; pres. Amateur Fencers League of Am., 1949-53; pres. Pan Am. Fencing Confedn., 1956-60, 71-75; pres. Fedn. Internationale d'Escrime, 1961-64; mem. exec. com. Pan Am. Sports Orgn., 1967-81; chief U.S. mission Olympic Games, Mexico City, Mexico, and Grenoble, France, 1968. Decorated comdr. Ordre du Mérite Sportif, 1963 (France); Silver medal Olympic Order, 1975; recipient Alumni Meritorious Service award N.Y. U., 1938. Mem. Assn. Bar City N.Y., Am., Inter-Am. N.Y. State bar Assns., Internat. Law Assn., Am. Soc. Internat. Law, Am. Econ. Assn., Am. Acad. Polit. and Social Sci., Am. Fgn. Law Assn., Am. Assn. Comparative Study of Law (pres. 1960-65), Phi Beta Kappa Assos. Clubs: Century, New York University, Fencers. Co-author: New York University Self Study, 1956; author Modern Financial Accounting, 1962. Contbr. econ. and legal publs. Home: San Francisco, Calif. Died May 24, 1981.

DE CARLO, CHARLES, multi-industry exec.; b. N.Y.C., Sept. 2, 1919; s. John and Bertha (Cervenka) de C.; evening student N.Y. U. Grad. Sch. Bus. Adminstrn.; m. Esther M. Nicholson, June 3, 1944; children—Deborah, (Mrs. Daniel R. Thompson), Barbara, Charles, Valerie. With Reynolds & Co., N.Y.C., 1936-50, security analyst, 1941-50; with Jones & Laughlin Steel Corp., from 1950, treas., 1967-72, dir. treasury services, 1972-76; dir. employee benefit trust adminstrn. LTV Corp., from 1976. Served with AUS, 1942-45. Mem. N.Y. Soc. Security Analysts. Republican. Episcopalian. Clubs: Duquesne, Royal Oaks, Lancers. Home: Dallas, Tex. Deceased.

DECHERT, ROBERT, lawyer, govt. ofcl.; b. Phila., Nov. 29, 1895; s. Henry Taylor and Virginia Louise (Howard) D.; grad. Lawrenceville (N.J.) Sch., 1912; A.B., U. Pa., 1916, LL.B., 1921, LL.D. (hon.), 1958; U.S. Army student, St. John's Coll., Oxford (Eng.) U., 1919; m. Helen Hope Wilson, May 24, 1922 (dec. Oct. 22, 1950); children—Peter, Hope (Mrs. Michael C. Mitchell), Marian Godey (Mrs. Donald F. Dixon); m. 2d, Helen Branson, Dec. 1, 1951. Admitted to Pa. bar, 1921, and began practice at Phila.; asso. Hepburn, Dechert & Norris, 1921-27; mem. faculty U. of Pa. Law Sch., 1923-42; v.p., counsel Penn Mut. Life Ins. Co., 1927-30, counsel, 1930-48, gen. counsel, 1949-56, 59-65, trustee, 1959-69; mem. firm Dechert, Price & Rhoads, Phila., 1930-68; dir. Fidelity Bank, Phila., 1932-57, 59-71; gen. counsel Dept. Def. Washington, 1957-59. Cons., Office Gen. Counsel, ECA, 1949-50; mem. Pa. Bd. Law Examiners, 1933-39, 70-72. Trustee, U. Pa., 1928-75; mem. Bd. of Law, 1928-74, chmn., 1952-56, mem. library adv. bd., 1956-74, chmn., 1956-65, mem. Bd. of Social Work 1945-68, chmn., 1945-52, chmn. Ednl. Policy Com. 1959-67, mem. Bd. Wistar Inst. of Anatomy and Biology, 1967-72; trustee Lawrenceville (N.J.) Sch., 1929-71; bd. dirs. YMCA Phila., 1936-74, pres. 1947-50; bd. dirs. United Fund Phila. 1930-72, gen. campaign chmn. 1942; chmn. Asso. Services for Armed Forces, Inc., 1950-51; mem. bd. govs., mem. corp. U.S.O., 1951-70, chmn. exec. com., 1951-55; bd. dirs., mem. exec. com. United Def. Fund, 1951-55; chmn. J. C. Brown Library Assos., Providence, 1962-65; pres. World Affairs Council Phila. 1963-65. Served to capt., U.S. Army, World War I. Decorated D.S.C. Mem. Am. (ho. of dels. 1948-49, 51-55), Pa. (ho.

of dels. 1966-69), Phila. bar assns., Ins. Fedn. Pa. (dir., pres. 1947-49), Assn. Life Ins. Counsel (pres. 1946-47), S.R., Order of Coif, Phi Beta Kappa, Delta Psi. Republican. Episcopalian. Club: Philadelphia. Contbr. articles, publs. in field of law, ins. and rare Am. books. Home: Gladwyne, Pa. Died Nov. 8, 1975.

DE CHIRICO, GEORGIE, artist; b. Volos, Thessaly, Greece, July 10, 1888; s. Evaristo and Gemma de Chirico; studied with pvt. art tchrs.; grad. Polytechnic Inst., Athens, 1906; student Acad. Fine Arts, Munich; m. Isabella Far. Painter townscapes, Italy and Paris; exhibited Salon des Independants, 1913; founded metaphysical school with Carlo Carra, Italy, 1917; designed sceneery and costumes, ballet and operatic prodns.; other work includes lithographs, murals, book illus., fabric designs; paintings include Melancholy, 1912, Delights of the Poet, 1913, Lassitude of the Infinite, 1913, Joye and Enigmas of a Strange Hour, 1913, Anxious Journey, 1913, The Square, 1913 (still life) Turin, Spring, 1914, Portrait of Guillaume Apollinaire, 1914, Inconsistencies of the Thinker, 1915, Hector and Andromache, 1916, Evangelical Still Life, 1917, Metsphysical Interior with Waterfall, 1918, Roman Villa and Knights, 1922, Autoritratto, 1924. Author: Gustave Courbet, 1925; Piccola Trattatodi Technica Pittorica, 1928; (novel) Hebdomeros, 1929; (autobiography) Memorie della mia Vita, 1945; Commedia dell'arte moderna, 1945. Home: Rome, Italy. Died Nov. 20, 1978.

DECKER, FRANK NORTON, lawyer; b. Three Rivers, Onondaga Co., N.Y., Feb. 14, 1882; s. James Lyttle and Emmie Avisa (Bruce) D.; LL.B., Cornell, 1905; m. Helen Dorance Ohlman, of Denver, Colo., Nov. 26, 1926; 1 son, Frank Norton. Admitted to N.Y. bar, 1905; in practice Phoenix, N.Y., Black Hills, S.D. and Gallatin Valley, Mont., 1905-10, Syracuse, N.Y., since 1910; has specialized in estate, corpn. and real estate law since 1920; pres. and treas. Decker Bldg., Inc., Clinton-Noxon, Inc. Trustee and sec. St. Joseph Hosp.; pres. Onondaga Co. Holstein-Friesian Club, Inc. Mem. N.Y. State and Onondaga Co. bar assns., S.A.R. Republican. Presbyn. Mason (32 deg., Shriner). Club: Cornell (Syracuse). Wrote and pub. "Kriemhild Herd—A Chapter in Holstein History," and other pamphlets and articles on bovine breeding and scientific subjects. Home: Syracuse, N.Y.

DECKER, GEORGE HENRY, ret. army officer; b. Catskill, N.Y., Feb. 16, 1902; s. Gordon H. and Mary (Napier) D.; B.S., Lafayette Coll., Easton, Pa., 1924; grad. Inf. Sch., Ft. Benning, Ga., 1932, Command and Gen. Staff Sch., Ft. Leavenworth, Kan., 1937; D.Sc., Lafayette Coll., 1953; LL.D., St. Peters Coll., 1959; Litt. D., Pa. Mil. Coll., 1961; m. Helen E. Inman, June 2, 1926; children—Jane E., James I. Commd. 2d lt. inf. U.S. Army, 1924, advancing through the grades to gen., 1956; served with 26th Inf., Plattsburgh, N.Y., 1924-28, 35th Inf., Schofield Barracks, Hawaii, 1928-31, 29th Inf., Ft. Benning, Ga., 1932-35, 7th Inf., Vancouver Barracks, Wash., 1935-36, 10th Inf., Ft. Thomas, Ky., 1937-40, 39th Inf., Ft. Bragg, N.C., 1940; hdqrs. 9th Div., Ft. Bragg, 1940-41; hdqrs. I Corps, Columbia, S.C., 1941; mem. War Dept. Gen. Staff, 1941-42; dep. chief of staff 3d Army, San Antonio, Tex., 1942-43; dep. chief of staff 6th Army, 1943-44, chief of staff 6th Army, May 1944-Jan. 1946; dep. comdr. and chief of staff U.S. Army Pacific, 1946-48; comdg. gen. 5th Inf. Div., July 1948-Mar. 1950; budget officer Dept. of Army, 1950-52, comptroller, 1952-55; comdg. gen. VII Corps, 1955-56; dep. comdr. in chief European Command, 1956-57; comdr. in chief UN Command, comdr. U.S. Forces, Korea, comdg. gen. 8th U.S. Army, 1957-59; vice chief staff U.S. Army, 1959-60, chief staff, 1960-62, ret., 1962; pres. Mfg. Chemists Assn., 1963-69. Decorated Distinguished Service Medal with oak leaf cluster, Silver Star, Legion of Merit, Bronze Star (U.S.); also decorations from govts. of Argentina, Colombia, France, Germany, Greece, Italy, Korea, Peru, Philippines, Thailand, Venezuela. Mem. Phi Gamma Delta. Episcopalian. Mason. Home: Washington, D.C. Died Feb. 6, 1980.

DECKER, GEORGE NIXON, corporate exec.; b. Springfield, Mass., Sept. 27, 1914; s. George Henry and Mary (Nixon) D.; student Rochester (N.Y.) Sch. Commerce, 1932-33, Ohio U., 1934-35, Niagara U., 1935-37; m. Rosemary Agnes Charlotte Morgan, Apr. 8, 1939; children—Sharon Lee (Mrs. James Williams), Robert Charles. Accountant, Van Vechten Milling Co., Rochester, N.Y., 1937-38; self employed grain broker Decker Grain Co., Rochester, 1938-40; supr. gen accounting IBM Corp., Rochester, 1940-43; successively asst. comptroller, comptroller, v.p., first v.p. Kellogg div. Am. Brake Shoe Co., Rochester, 1943-59, pres. Kellogg div., Oxnard, Cal., 1959-62, pres. Abex Corp. Group Aerospace Cos., Oxnard, 1962-70; pres., chief exec. officer Ventura Internat., Inc., Oxnard, 1971-81, also dir.; dir. Travel City, Inc., Sherman Oaks, Calif.; v.p., dir. Coastal Pipco Co., Oxnard, 1973-81, Athletic Supply Co. Hawaii, Ltd., Honolulu, B. F. Schoen, Inc., Honolulu, 1976-81. Active in County Republican Club. Mem. Fin. Execs. Inst. Club: Las Posas Country. Home: Camarillo, Calif. Died Oct. 18, 1981.

DECKER, WILLIAM C., business exec.; b. York, Pa., Dec. 26, 1900; s. Jacob E. and Laura (Flinchbaugh) D.; B.S., Pa. State Coll., 1922; postgrad. Columbia, 1924-25; M.B.A., Harvard, 1927; LL.D. (hon.), Alfred U., 1950; D.Eng. (hon.), Clarkson Coll. Tech., 1956; children—Thomas, Karen (Mrs. David Gonin). Chem. engr. Western Elec. Co., 1922-25; sales engr. Brown Co., 1927-30, sales mgr., 1930, treas., 1936, controller, 1939, v.p. 1941; pres., dir. Corning Glass Works, 1946-61, chief exec. officer, 1957-60, chmn. bd., chief exec. officer, 1961-64, chmn. exec. com., 1964-65, hon. vice chmn. bd., 1966-71, hon. chmn. bd., 1971-76, also dir.; dir. Pitts. Corning Corp. Mem. U.S. Commn. on Coinage. Trustee Corning Glass Works Found., Am. Friends of Bahamas Found., Eisenhower Coll. Recipient Distinguished Alumnus award Pa. State U., 1955. Clubs: Links, University (N.Y.C.); Corning Country; Elmira (N.Y.) Country; Augusta Nat. Golf; Lyford Cay (Nassau, Bahamas); Everglades (Palm Beach, Fla.). Home: Corning, N.Y. Died Dec. 9, 1976.

DE CREEFT, JOSE, sculptor; b. Guadalajara, Spain, Nov. 27, 1884; s. Mariano and Rosa (Champane) de C.; student sculpture Augustine Querol Studio, Madrid, 1900-04, Academie Julien, Paris, France, 1905-07, Maisons Greber, Paris, 1911-14; m. Alice Carr, May 15, 1928; children—William, Nina; m. 2d, Lorraine Helen Goulet, Nov. 12, 1944; 1 dau., Dona Maria. Came to U.S. 1929, naturalized, 1940. First exhibited Seattle Art Museum, 1929; exhbns. also include annually at Georgetta Passedolt Gallery, N.Y.C., 1936-49, also Fine Arts Pavilion N.Y. World's Fair, 1964, White House Festival of Arts, Washington, 1965, Kennedy Galleries, N.Y.C. 1969, 70, 72, 73, 74; one-man retrospective New Sch. for Social Research, Art Center, 1974; tchr. sculpture Art Students League, 1944-48, 57—; tchr. New Sch. Social Research, N.Y.C., 1932-48, 57-60, Norton Sch. of Art, West Palm Beach, Fla., winters 1948-49, 50-51, Skowhegan (Me.) Sch. Painting and Sculpture, summers 1948-49. Commd. Alice in Wonderland 16 foot Bronze group, N.Y., 1957, ceramic mural Bronx Municipal Hosp. Center, 1961, mosaic Bronx Municipal New Nurses Residence and Sch., 1961, bronze relief Pub. Health Lab., Bellevue Hosp., N.Y.C., 1966; represented in permanent collections Met. Art. Mus., Whitney Mus. Am. Art, Mus. Modern Art, Phila. Mus. Art, Bklyn. Mus., Pa. Acad., Seattle Art Mus., Smithsonian Instn., Vatican. Recipient 1st prize for sculpture (Torso) Acad. Julien, 1906, Met. Mus. Art (Maternity, granite), 1942, Gold Medal Pa. Acad. (head of Rachmaninoff, beaten lead), 1945; anonymous prize (figure, Maturity), Audubon Artists, 1956, gold medal, 1954, first prize, 1957; award Nat. Sculpture Soc., 1969; commd. Poet by Fairmont Park Art Assn., 1950; Ford Found. award, retrospective exhibit, 1961; decorated Orden de la Isabella Católica (Spain). N.A. Fellow Nat. Sculpture Soc., Sculptor's Guild, Fedn. Modern Painters and Sculptors; mem. Acad. Arts and Letters, Artists' Equity (dir.), Audubon Artists (dir.). Books about: Jose de Creeft, by Jules Campos, 1949; The Sculpture Jose de Creeft, 1972. Home: New York City NY.

DEEGAN, THOMAS JOSEPH, JR., mgmt. adviser; b. Bklyn., July 11, 1910; s. Thomas Joseph and Bertha (Berckmeier) D.; A.B., Fordham U., 1934, L.H.D., 1964; LL.D., U. Tampa, 1963, L.I. U., 1964; m. Alice Russell, Dec. 30, 1939; children—Mavoureen Maura, Thomas Joseph 3d, Deirdre Gael (dec.), Christopher, Timothy John, Michael Nicholas, Mary Angela, Cecily Ann. Engaged as reporter for N.Y. Times, 1932-38; pub. relations bus., 1938-42; pub. relations officer to Gen. R.W. Johnson, 1942-43; dir. pub. relations Am. Airlines, 1944-45; with C. & O. Railway, 1946-54, v.p., 1949-54, also dir. mem. exec. com.; v.p., dir. mem. exec. com. Alleghany Corp., 1954-59; v.p. staff NY Central Railroad, 1954-57; chmn. Thomas J. Deegan Co., Inc., mgmt. counsel to corps., N.Y.C., 1957-73; chmn. TJD Mgmt. Services Corp., N.Y.C., 1973-75; chmn. the Deegan Group, Ltd., 1975-77; chmn. exec. com. Sydney Baron & Co.; vice chmn., dir., mem. exec. com. Interpub., Inc., 1966-68; dir. Fifth Av. Assn., Av. of the Ams. Assn., Am. Information Services Inc.; dir., mem. exec. com. Bank of Commerce. Founder, chmn. exec. com. N.Y. World's Fair 1964-65 corp.; v.p. Nat. Museum of Racing, Inc. Mem. Adv. bd. N.Am. sect. Vatican Radio. Bd. dirs. Saratoga Center for Performing Arts, U.S.O., Boy's Club Am., Boy Scouts Am.; bd. visitors U.S. Naval Acad., 1962-65; trustee John Fitzgerald Kennedy Library, Alfred E. Smith Found. Decorated Knight Grand Cross Holy Sepulchre, Knight Malta. Mem. Marketing Execs. Soc. (past pres.), Friendly Sons Saint Patrick, Soc. Silurians, Sigma Delta Chi. Clubs: Racquet and Tennis, Hemisphere (N.Y.C.). Home: New York, N.Y. Died Nov. 16, 1977.

DEENER, DAVID RUSSELL, coll. adminstr.; b. Weverton, Md., Jan. 8, 1920; s. Russell Marcellus and Josephine (Main) D.; B.A., U. Pitts., 1941, M.A., 1948; Ph.D., Duke, 1951; m. Helen Ruth Buchner, Jan. 30, 1943; children—Karen Lee (Mrs. David Depp), Helen Jane (Mrs. Charles Johnson). Adminstrv. asst. War Dept., 1941-42; instr. U. Pitts., 1946-48; part-time instr. Duke, 1948-50, research asso., 1951-52, exec. sec. Commonwealth Studies Center, also vis. asso. prof., 1957-58; mem. faculty Tulane U., 1952-76, prof. polit. sci., 1957-76, chmn. dept., 1964-66, dean Grad. Sch., from 1966, also provost, from 1967; head dept. polit. sci. Newcomb Coll., 1960-64, acting dean, 1965-66. Cons. Brookings Instn., 1951, Inst. Pub. Adminstrn., 1960-61, Nat. Inst. Mental Health project, 1960-67; editorial adviser Hauser Press, 1958-76. Mem. New Orleans Met. Area Com., 1966-76; adv. com. fgn. relations U.S. State Dept., 1969-73; chmn. Council Grad. Schs. in U.S., 1972; mem. U.S. Edn. Commn. Task Force on Grad. Edn., 1973-76; mem. com. visitors Vanderbilt U. Grad. Sch.; pres. elect Assn. Grad. Schs., 1974-75. Bd. visitors U.S. Army Transp. Sch., Ft. Eustis, Va. Served to lt. USNR, 1942-45. Mem. Am. Soc. Internat. Law (v.p. 1964-65), Am. Polit. Sci. Assn., Phi Beta Kappa. Democrat. Mem. Ch. of Brethren. Club: Cosmos (Washington). Author: The United States Attorneys General and International Law, 1957; also articles. Editor, contbr.; Canada-United States Treaty Relations, 1963, de Lege Pactorum, 1970. Home: New Orleans, La. Died Sept. 19, 1976.

DEFALCO, LAWRENCE MICHAEL, bishop; b. McKeesport, Pa., Aug. 25, 1915; s. Rosario and Margret (Desmone) DeF.; student St. Vincent's Coll., Latrobe, Pa., 1933-35, St. John's Mission Sem., Little Rock, 1935-42; J.C.L., Gregorian U., Rome, Italy, 1955. Ordained priest Roman Catholic Ch., 1942; asst. pastor St. Patrick's Fort Worth, 1942-52, pastor, 1962; asst. pastor Sacred Heart Cathedral, Dallas, 1952; vice chancellor Dallas-Fort Worth Diocese, 1952-55, sec. Marriage Tribunal, 1955-62; pastor Our Lady Perpetual Help Ch., Dallas, 1956-62; bishop of Amarillo, Tex., 1963-79. Home: Amarillo, Tex. Died Sept. 22, 1979; buried Llano Cemetery, Amarillo.

DEFRIES, ROBERT DAVIES, physician; b. Toronto, Can., July 23, 1889; s. Thomas William and Agnes (Lumsden) D.; M.B., University of Toronto, 1911, M.D., 1913, diploma pub. health, 1914; LL.D., U. Saskatchewan, 1955; Dr. P.H., University of Montreal, 1959. Member staff Connaught Med. Research Labs., U. Toronto, Can. (formerly Antitoxin Lab.), from 1915, successively asst., asst. dir., asso. dir., 1915-40, dir., 1940-55, dir. emeritus, cons., 1955-75; faculty dept. hygiene and preventive medicine U. Toronto, 1917-55, successively lectr. hygiene, asst. prof., asso. prof., prof., 1947-55, asso. dir. Sch. of Hygiene, 1925-40, dir., 1940-55, prof., head dept. epidemiology and biometrics, 1928-47, prof., head dept. pub. health adminstrn., 1947-55. Mem. Dominion Council Health, Ottawa, 1940-62. Served as capt. Canadian Army M.C., 1916-18. Decorated Officer Order Brit. Empire, 1943, Comdr., 1945; recipient Lasker award in pub. health adminstrn., 1955. Specialist bacteriology and pub. health Royal Coll. Phys. and Surg. of Can.; diplomate Am. Bd. Pub. Health. Fellow Soc. Med. Officers of Health of Gt. Britain (hon.), Am. Pub. Health Assn.; mem. Canadian, Ont. med. assns., Acad. Medicine of Toronto. Editor Canadian Jour. Pub. Health. Home: Toronto, Ont., Can. Died Oct. 25, 1975.

DE GHIKA, GEORGE (DE-GI'KA), Hungarian minister; b. Hungary, Apr. 1, 1882. With Imperial and Royal Austro-Hungarian Ministry of Foreign Affairs, Vienna, 1905-06; attaché Austro-Hungarian Consulate, Belgrade, 1906, temporarily with Legation, Belgrade, to 1910; vice consul, Milan, 1910-12; vice consul, then consul, Hamburg, 1912-18; consul gen., Hamburg, 1918-27, N.Y., 1927-39; E.E. and M.P. to Japan, 1939-41; E.E. and M.P. of Hungary to U.S. since 1941. Decorated Austro-Hungarian War Cross; Grand Officer Royal Hungarian Order of Merit; 1st Class Japanese Order of Sacred Treasure; 1st class of Chu Kuo, Order of Manchukuo. Mem. Museum of Natural History, Audubon Soc., Entomol. Soc. (all N.Y. City); also several European sci. socs. Home: Washington, D.C.

DE GOWIN, ELMER LOUIS, physician; b. Cheboygan, Mich., Sept. 27, 1901; s. Frank Louis and Nora Eulalia (Dickes) DeG.; A.B., U. Mich., 1923, M.D., 1928; m. Laura Evelyn Meader, June 21, 1924; 1 son, Richard Louis. Intern Cleve. City Hosp., 1928-29, asst. resident, 1929-30; instr. internal medicine U. Mich., Ann Arbor, 1930-32; mem. med. faculty U. Iowa, Iowa City, 1932-80, prof. internal medicine, 1950-69, prof. emeritus, 1969-80; dir. Blood Transfusion Service Iowa, 1939-66; sec. subcom. blood substitutes NRC, 1940-46, mem. com. blood and blood derivatives, 1948-51; tech. cons. blood plasma sect. Office CD, 1942-44; mem. adv. bd. health services A.R.C., 1947-51. Recipient Billings Gold medal A.M.A., 1939. Diplomate Am. Bd. Internal Medicine. Fellow A.C.P. (gov. Iowa 1965-71); mem. AAUP (nat. council 1956-59), Assn. Am. Physicians, Am. Soc. Clin. Investigation, A.A.A.S., Internat. Soc. Hematology. Club: University Athletic. Author: (with J.B. Alseer and R.C. Hardin) Blood Transfusion, 1949; (with R.L. DeGowin) Bedside Diagnostic Examination, 1965. Home: Iowa City, Iowa. Died Aug. 31, 1980; interred Oakland Cemetery, Iowa City.

DE GUIGNE, CHRISTIAN, III, chem. corp. exec.; b. San Mateo, Calif., Aug. 26, 1912; s. Christian and Marie Louis (Elkins) de G.; student Gunnery Sch., Washington, Conn., Hun Sch., Princeton, N.J., 1930-32, Harvard, 1932-33; m. Eleanor Christenson, July 27, 1935; children—Christian IV, Charles. With Stauffer Chem. Co. and subsidiaries, San Francisco

1934-79, v.p., dir., pres., chmn., 1953-79; dir. Bank of Calif., Pacific Tel. & Tel. Co. Bd. dirs. Stanford Research Inst.; chmn. bd. of govs. Internat. Sci. Found. Clubs: Pacific Union, Bohemian (San Francisco); Burlingame (Calif.) Country; Capitol Hill (Washington); Racquet and Tennis, The Brook (N.Y.); Jockey, Travelers (Paris). Home: San Mateo, Calif. Died Oct. 5, 1979.

DE HAAS, J. ANTON (DE-HÄS'), prof. internat. relationships; b. Amsterdam, Holland, Feb. 3, 1883; s. J. de Haas, Jr., and Antonia Bémond de H.; B.A., Stanford Univ., 1910, Ph.D., 1915; M.A., Harvard Univ., 1911; LL.D., Northeastern Univ., 1947, Univ. of New Mexico, 1948; D.C.S., Bryant College, 1947; m. Hazel Carus, 1915 (died 1922); 1 dau., Hazel; m. 2d, Emily Louise Haver, 1922. Came to U.S., 1904, naturalized citizen, 1917. Instr. in economics, Stanford, 1913-15; agt. Calif. Immigration Commn. in Calif., Utah and Europe, 1914; adj. prof. business administration, U. of Tex., 1915-17; examiner for Fed. Trade Commn., summer 1917; prof. commerce, Ohio State U., 1917-18; lecturer summer sch., Columbia, 1918; prof. fgn. trade, U. of Wash., 1918-19; prof. handels-technick, U. of Rotterdam, Holland, 1919-21; prof. fgn. trade New York U., 1921-27; became William Ziegler prof. of internat. relationships, Grad. Sch. Bus. Adminstrn., Harvard, 1927; prof. internat. relationships Claremont (Calif.) Mens Coll. since 1947; lecturer at Columbia U., 1930-32, U.S. Naval War Coll., Newport, R.I., since 1928; prof. summer schools, also lectr., leader round table internat. relations. Chairman American delegation to World Federation of Educational Association, Tokyo, 1937; Henry Todd lecturer of Dept. of Edn., State of Mass., 1938-39. Chmn. Summer Inst., Leyden Univ., 1939, Colo. State Teachers Colo., 1940. Huydenkoper-Kidder lecturer, Allegheny Coll., 1938. Capt. U.S. Army, 1918. Decorated Comdr. Order of Orange-Nassau (Holland), 1939, Knights of the Order of Boyaca (Colombia), 1946. Consultant to War Dept. 1942, to Office of Coordinator of Inter-Am. Affairs, 1942-43. Organizer Sch. of Commerce, Bogotá, Colombia, 1942. Chmn. Econ. Sect. of Netherlands Postwar Study Group. Mem. Am. Econ. Assn., Royal Econ. Society (Eng.), Instituut voor Economische Geschriften, and Vereeniging voor de Staathuishoudkunde en de Statistiek (Holland), Alpha Kappa Psi, Beta Gamma Sigma. Unitarian. Club: Harvard (New York). Author of several books latest of which are: Our Allies: the Netherlands East Indies, 1942; Looking Ahead to Peace, 1942. Asso. editor: World Affairs; Knickerbocker Weekly. Contbr. to several books. Home: Alamosa Av., Claremont, Cal.

DEJONG, GERRIT, JR., educator; b. Amsterdam, Holland, Mar. 20, 1892; s. Gerrit and Lijda Marianna (Kuiper) de J.; came to U.S., 1906, naturalized, 1913; A.B., U. Utah, 1920, A.M., 1925; postgrad. Nat. U. of Mexico, summer 1921, U. Munich (Germany), 1926-27; Ph.D., Stanford, 1933; m. Rosabelle Winegar, Sept. 14, 1911; children—William Gerrit (dec.), Belle Felice (Mrs. Dean E. Van Wagenen), Nola Eloise (Mrs. Clyde E. Sullivan), Carma Rose (Mrs. Richard L. Anderson); m. 2d, Thelma Bonham, Sept. 28, 1951. Pvt tchr., music (piano and organ), 1910; instr. music and langs. Murdock Acad., Beaver, Utah, 1916-18; instr. modern langs. Latter-day Saints U., Salt Lake City, 1919-25; asso. prof. modern langs. Brigham Young U., Provo, Utah, 1925-27, prof., 1927-78, dean Coll. Fine Arts, 1925-59. Dir. Centro Cultural Brasil-Estados Unidos, Santos, Brazil, 1947-48. Mem. gen. ch. music com. Ch. of Jesus Christ of Latter-day Saints; gen. bd. Deseret Sunday Sch. Union, 1933-68. Univ. fellow, Stanford, 1931-32; recipient Karl G. Maeser Distinguished Teaching award Brigham Young U., 1960, Distinguished Service award, 1967. Fellow Utah Acad. Scis., Arts and Letters (past pres.; award distinguished services 1953; David O. McKay Humanities award 1972); mem. Modern Lang. Assn. Am., Am. Assn. Tchrs. Spanish and Portuguese, Am. Musicol. Soc., Internat. Soc. Musicologists. Republican. Author: The Elements of Musicality in the Literary and Critical Works of Otto Ludwig; Greater Dividends from Religion, 1950; Living the Gospel, 1957; The Testimony of President H. J. Grant, 1965; The Gospel Today, 1966; Four Hundred Years of Brazilian Literature, 1969; Truth and Light, 1973; Eternal Progress, 1974. Composer choral, orchestral, and chamber music. Home: Provo, Utah. Died Sept. 26, 1978; buried Provo City Cemetery.

DELAFIELD, EDWARD COLEMAN, broker; b. Westhampton Beach, L.I., N.Y., July 10, 1877; s. Maturin Livingston and Mary Coleman (Livingston) D.; A.B., Princeton, 1899; m. Margaretta Stockton Beasley, Apr. 30, 1900; children—Maturin Livingston, II, Margaretta Stockton, Edward C., Mary; m. 2d, Clelia C. Benjamin, Feb. 4, 1928; children—Clelia, Walter Benjamin, Cynthia. Vice pres. and pres. Franklin Trust Co. from 1914, merged with The Bank of America, May 1, 1920, of which was pres.; dir. and mem. exec. com. City Bank Farmers Trust Co.; resigned as v.p. City Bank Farmers Trust Co., 1937; became sr. partner stock exchange firm Delafield & Delafield; trustees Greenwich Savs. Bank; dir. Cerveceria Corona, Inc., and Cerveceria Nacional Dominicana, Inc. Trustee, Sloan Kettering Inst. Served as maj., later lt. col. 9th C.A.C., N.Y.G.; reserve list Oct. 8, 1919, Col. Finance Dept. U.S. Army, ret. Mem. N.Y. State Mil. Rifle Teams, Nat. matches, 1918-19. Decorated knight comdr. Order Crown of Italy. Bd. dirs. Delafield Family Assn. Fellow Corp. N.Y. Bot. Gardens, Am. Mus. Nat. History; mem. A.A.A.S., N.Y. Hist. Soc. (patron), Pilgrims Soc., Soc. of Colonial Wars, Soc. of the Cincinnati, Soc. War of 1812, St. Nicholas Society, S.R., N.Y. Soc. of Mil. and Naval Officers World War I, N.Y. Geneal. and Biol. Soc. (life), N.Y. Zool. Soc. (life), Soc. Descendants Signers of Declaration of Independence, Descendants of Colonial Lords of Manors in America, Brooklyn Institute of Arts and Science (life). Republican. Episcopalian. Clubs: Union, Down Town, Contemporary, Onteora (dir.). Home: Sarasota, Fla. Died April 21, 1976; buried Woodlawn Cemetery, Bronx, N.Y.

DELANO, PRESTON, ex-comptroller of currency; b. Phoenix, Mich., Apr. 2, 1886; s. M. Abbot and Ellen V. (Bennett) D.; entered Harvard, transferred to Stanford; A.B., Stanford U., 1909; m. Ruth Small, May 24, 1922. Gen. mgr. Calif. & Ore. Coast R.R. Co., 1914-17; mgr. Calif. office, Twohy Bros. Co. (engrs. and contractors), 1919-22; investment counselor, 1923-33; served as general manager Home Owners Loan Corporation, 1934-35; governor Fed. Home Loan Bank System, 1935-38; financial adviser to Federal Home Loan Bank Board, 1936-38; director Federal Deposit Insurance Corporation since 1938; comptroller of the currency, 1938-Feb. 1953. Commd. 2d lt., U.S. Army, Apr. 1917, 1st lt., Dec. 1917; regimental staff capt., Sept. 1918, with A.E.F.; hon. disch., July, 1919. Mem. Quadrangle, Sigma Sigma. Phi Delta Phi. Democrat. Clubs: Chevy Chase (Washington); Brook, India House (N.Y.C.). Home: Chevy Chase, Md.

DE LA TORRE BUENO, REY, classic guitarist. Home: Haddam, Conn. Died Jan. 15, 1980.

DELATOUR, HUNTER L., lawyer; b. Bklyn., Jan. 16, 1887; s. George L. and Rebecca S. (Holcomb) D.; LL.B., N.Y. Law Sch., 1906, LL.D., 1964; m. Margery Dohrman, June 1, 1915; children—Hunter L., Robert J. Admitted to N.Y. bar, 1909; practice law, Bklyn., now mem. firm Delatour & Miller; chmn. adv. com. Title Guarantee & Trust Co., from 1950; trustee King's County Trust Co., 1955-67; pres. N.Y. Law School, 1962-66. Trustee Village Thomaston, Great Neck, N.Y., from 1934; mem. town bd. No. Hempstead, N.Y., 1934-38; mem. Ethics Com. County Nassau, from 1964; Dir. Legal Aid Soc. of Nassau County, from 1952. Fellow Am. Bar Assn.; mem. N.Y. State (pres. 1954), Nassau (pres. 1943), Bklyn. (pres. 1943-46) bar assns., Assn. Bar City N.Y., Great Neck Library Assn. (pres. 1947-51), New Eng. Soc. of Bklyn. (pres. 1935-37). Episcopalian (chancellor of diocese 1953-72, mem. standing com. of diocese, & trustee of estate). Club: Brooklyn. Home: Great Neck. N.Y. Died May 20, 1976.

DE LA VALLEE-POUSSIN, C., educator; b. Louvain, Belgium, 1886; student Coll. of Josepites, Louvain, Coll. of Jesuites, Mons., Belgium; studied U. of Louvain, 1889-1901; m. Dhanis Marie, 1906; children—Jean-Marie, Anne-Marie, Paul, Charles, Agnes. Prof. U. Louvain. Fgn. asso. mem. Nat. Acad. Sci., Am. Acad. Arts and Scis.*

DELBRUCK, MAX, scientist; b. Berlin, Germany, Sept. 4, 1906; s. Hans and Lina (Thiersch) D.; Ph.D., U. Göttingen 1930; m. Mary Bruce, August 2, 1941; children—Jonathan, Nicola, Tobias and Ludina. Came to the United States, 1937, naturalized, 1945. Albert Billings Rudock Prof. biology Calif. Inst. Tech., 1947-77, prof. emeritus, 1977-81. Recipient Nobel prize in physiology and medicine, 1969. Mem. Nat. Acad. Sci. Address: Pasadena, Calif. Died Mar. 10, 1981.

DE LEEUW, HENDRIK, journalist, author; b. Amsterdam, Netherlands, July 18, 1891; s. Gerrit and Estelle (van Gelder) de L.; attended Amsterdam S. and H.; m. Bess Bogel, Oct. 11, 1931. Came to U.S., 1912, naturalized, 1923. Began career as world traveler, 1912; sent by Firestone Tire & Rubber Co. to Far East as spl. rep., 1920-28; chmn. Queen Wilhelmina Fund for Bklyn., Queens, L.I., 1940; joined OWI as head Netherlands sect., 1942. Made expdns. to Dutch Borneo, Surinam, Netherlands Guiana, with film records of travels, used for lectr. purposes; gave series TV lectures on WNBT; radio commentator NBC, WOR, WMCA, WEVD, WNYC, from 1930. Mem. Am. Acad. Polit. Sci., A.R.C. (life), L.I., N.Y. hist. socs., Brooklyn Heights Assn., Soc. Am. Travel Writers. Author: Crossroads of the Java Sea, 1931; Crossroads of the Caribbean Sea, 1935; Crossroads of the Zuider Zee, 1938; Crossroads of the Buccaneers, 1937; Java Jungle Tales, 1934 (juvenile); Cities of Sin, 1933; Sinful Cities of the Western World, 1934; Flower of Joy, 1939; Peewee the Mousedeer, 1943 (juvenile); History of Colonies; American Morals, A Survey and a Report, 1949; Fallen Angels, 1953; Crossroads of the Mediterranean, 1954; The Underworld Story, 1955; Conquest of the Air, 1959; Fallen Angels, 1960; From Flying Horse to Man in the Moon, 1963. Contbr. mags., sci. and travel publs., newspapers and syndicates. Home: Brooklyn, N.Y. Died July 23, 1977.

DE LEMOS, PEDRO JOSEPH (DA-LA'MOS), former art dir.; b. Austin, Nev., May 25, 1882; s. Frank Ignacio and Mary Josephine (de Bethancour) deLemos; grad. Calif. Sch. of Fine Arts (U. of Calif.), 1910; student Harry Stuart Fonda, Emile Gremke, at Art Students' League, New York, and Columbia U.; m. Reta A. Bailey, Aug. 19, 1907; children—Margaret Alva, Esther Ruth, Marie Josephine. Prof. design, U. of Calif., 1913-14; acting dir. San Francisco Inst. of Art, 1915, dir., 1916-18; dir. Museum and Art Galleries, Stanford University, 1918-46; surveyed and collected Mexican handicrafts in Mexico, 1947; collected New Mexican native Spanish handicrafts, 1947; made survey to state and private school art education in Louisiana and Alabama, 1948. Editor in chief School Arts Mag. since 1919. Exhibited Corcoran Art Gallery, Washington, D.C.; Art Inst. Chicago; Pa. Acad. Fine Arts, Phila.; Delgado Art Gallery, New Orleans; San Francisco Expn., 1915; Stanford U. Art Gallery; Oakland Municipal Art Gallery. Hon. mention for etchings, San Francisco Exposition; gold medal California Exposition, 1917; 1797-1799 Spanish portrait, Governor Don Gayoso de Lemos, La. State Museum, New Orleans. Chief dir. of Am. Art Aid; pres. Carmel Art Assn., 1927-28; dir. Calif. Soc. Etchers; pres. Allied Art Guild of Calif., 1930-32; elected fellow Royal Soc. of Art, England, 1934. Mem. Planning Com. of 7th Internat. Congress for Art Edn., 1935; art lecturer Stanford Univ., summer 1935 and spring 1936; leader and lecturer, Far Eastern Art and Culture Travel Sch., 1936. Adv. mem. Com. U.S. Spl. Services Div., Army Service Forces, N.Y., 1944. Mem. Eastern, Western and Pacific arts assns., Hispanic Soc. of Am. Author: Applied Art, 1921; Color Cement Handicraft (with R. A. Lemos), 1922; Indian Decorative Designs, 1926; Oriental Decorative Designs, 1927; Art Ages, 1929; Artists Scrap Book, 1929; Modern Art Portfolios, 1930; The Art Teacher, 1931, rev. edit., 1946; Indian Arts, 1932; Textile Decorating, 1935; Mexican Arts and Crafts, 1935; Art Metal Crafts, 1937; Guatemala Art Crafts, 1941; Creative Art Crafts, 1943; Creative Art Crafts, Book 2, 1945, Book 3, 1948. Engaged in survey and collection Mexican arts and crafts, 1931, 1946. Japanese and Chinese arts and crafts, 1935-36. Home: Palo Alto, Calif.

DELEON, ROBERT ANDREW, mgmt. cons.; b. Oakland, Cal., Oct. 14, 1950; s. Alfred Vernon and Mona (Young) DeL.; student Morehouse Coll., 1966-68, Columbia U., 1968-70; m. Diahann Carroll, May 25, 1975; children—Monica Kelli, Suzanne Patricia. Reporter-editor Newsday, Garden City, N.Y., 1968-71; guest writer Atlanta Constn., 1969-70; asst. editor Ebony mag., Chgo., 1971; mng. editor Jet mag., Chgo., 1971-75; exec. v.p. Pacific Consultants, Berkeley, Cal., 1975-77. Adj. instr. journalism Columbia Coll., Chgo., 1973-74. Sec. bd. dirs. United Bd. for Coll. Devel., Atlanta; adv. bd. Independent Found., Washington. Editor: Yearbook, Morehouse Coll., 1968. Home: Beverly Hills, Calif. Died Mar. 30, 1977.

DELGADO, FRANCISCO AFAFI, Philippine diplomat; b. Bulacan, Philippines, Jan. 25, 1886; s. Nemesio and Manuela (Afan) D.; LL.B., Ind. U., 1907, LL.D. (hon.), 1945; LL.M. cum laude, Yale, 1908; m. Rosario Montenegro, Feb. 11, 1915; children—Rosario (Mrs. Milan A. Bendik), Concepcion, Arturo. Law clk. exec. bur. Philippine Govt., 1908-10, chief legal div., 1910-13; practice of law, Manila, 1913—; founder, sr. partner firm Delgado, Flores, Macapagal & Dizon, 1937—; professorial lectr. Coll. Law U. Philippines, Far Eastern U., Philippine Law Sch., U. Manila, others, 1920-41; mem. Philippine Legislature from 1st Dist. Bulacan, 1931-34; resident commnr. to Washington, 1934-36; justice Philippine Ct. Appeals, 1936-37; mem. Philippine Senate, 1951-57; A.E. and P., permanent rep. Philippine Mission to UN, 1958—, chmn. delegation 14th session, 1959, v.p. Gen. Assembly, 1959, vice chmn. interim com. Gen. Assembly, 1960. Philippine rep. to numerous internat. meetings, UN committees; vice chmn. UN Commn. Human Rights, 1960; commnr. U.S.-Philippine War Damage Commn., 1946-51. Decorated comdr. Philippine Legion of Honor. Mem. Am. (first Filipino active mem.), Philippine (pres. 1938-50) bar assns., Assn. de Veteranos de la Revolucion (bd. dirs.), Filipino-Am. Assn. (pres. 1950-57), Theta Nu Epsilon. Mason (33 deg., Shriner; lt. grand comdr. Philippine Supreme Council Scottish Rite, 1951). Clubs: Yale Cosmopolitan (co-founder, 1st sec.) (New Haven; Wack Wack Golf and Country, Overseas Press, Army and Navy (Manila). Home: Forest Hills, L.I., N.Y.

DELLER, ALFRED, singer; b. Margate, Kent, Eng., May 31, 1912; s. Thomas William and Mary (Cave) D.; ed. secondary schs., Eng.; Mus.D. (hon.), U. Leicester; D.Litt. (hon.), U. Kent; m. Kathleen Margaret Lowe, June 5, 1937; children—Mark, Simon, Jane. Lay-clk. Canterbury Cathedral, 1940-47; vicarchoral St. Paul's Cathedral, 1947-61; soloist inaugural concert BBC program. Third, 1946; formed vocal ensemble Deller Consort, 1950; title role Oberon premier performance Britten's opera A Midsummer Night's Dream, 1961; solo concert tours U.S., 1955, 57, 59, 62, Deller Consort tours U.S., 1964, 66, 69; European festival performances include Edinburgh, York, Aldeburgh, London, Vienna, Holland, Royal Danish, Strasbourg.

Hon. music adviser U. Kent. Decorated Order Brit. Empire. Mem. Inc. Soc. Musicians, Assn. English Singers and Speakers, Royal Acad. Music (hon.). Club: Catch of Am. (pres.). Address: Kent, England. Died July 16, 1979; buried Boughton Aluph Churchyard, Ashford.

DE LONG, B(ERTON) H(ENRY), metallurgist; born Taylor, N.Y., Aug. 16, 1885; s. Willis H. and Bertha A. (Brown) DeL.; A.B., Cornell U., 1909; student, State Normal Sch., Cortland, N.Y., 1904; m. Nellie E. Bean, Aug. 16, 1911 (died 1923), m. 2d, Irene M. Boyer, June 18, 1925; children—William B., Charles B. (died 1937), Margaret E. (Mrs. George Nordblom), Allen R. Chemist, Stanley Works, 1909-10; asst. metallurgist, Carpenter Steel Co., 1910-15, metallurgist, chief metallurgist, 1915-45, v.p., tech. dir., since 1945; dir., Reading-Fed. Savings & Loan Assn. Mem. Am. Iron and Steel Inst. (N.Y. City), Iron and Steel Inst. (London, Eng.), A.A.A.S., Am. Soc. for Testing Materials, Soc. of Automotive Engrs., Inc. Methodist. Elk. Club: Kiwanis. Home: Berks Co., Pa.

DE MADARIAGA, SALVADOR, author; b. Coruña, Galicia, Spain, July 23, 1886; student Coll. Chaptal, Paris, Ecole Nationale Superieure des Mines, Ecole Polytechnique; Dr. (hon.), U. Arequipa, Lima Poitiers, Princeton, Liege, Lille; m. Constance Archibald, 1912. With Railway Co. of No. Spain, 1911-16; tech. attaché Spanish delegation, League Nations conf., Barcelona, 1921, mem. secretariat, Geneva, Switzerland, 1921, head disarmament sect., 1922-27; prof. Spanish lit., Oxford U., 1927; Spanish ambassador, Washington, 1931 Paris 1932; Guard Cross Order of Republic (Spain), White Lion (Czechoslovakia), Order of Merit (Chile), Order of Jade in Gold (China). Merit (Hungary), Bogota (Colombia), White Rose (Finland) Legion of Honor (France), Aztec Eagle (Mexico), Order of the Sun (Peru); gold medallist, Yale; fellow Exeter Coll. Mem. Acad. Moral and Polit. Sci. Madrid, Acad. Scis., Letters and Arts of Belgium. Author: The Heart of Jade, 1942; Spain, 1943; Visitors Beware, 1945; Hernan Cortes, 1948; Bolivar; 1951; also plays, poetry, essays. Address: Oxford, Eng.

DEMING, CLYDE LEROY (DEM'ING), surgeon, univ. prof.; b. Cornish, N.H., Aug. 18, 1885; s. Herbert and Nellie Ida (Hilliard) D.; student Kimball Union Acad., 1901-05; A.B., Bowdoin Coll., 1910; M.D., cum laude, Yale, 1915; D.Sc., Bowdoin Coll., 1935; m. Evelyn Dorice Kimball, Apr. 4, 1925; children—Herbert Everett, Joan, Doris. Interne New Haven Hosp., 1915-17, faculty, sch. medicine Yale, 1921—, clin. prof. urology, 1932—; chief urologist, New Haven Hosp.; attending surgeon, New Haven Dispensary (affiliated with Yale Univ.); cons. urologist Meriden Hosp., Griffin Hosp., Windham Community Memorial Hosp., Inc. Capt. R.O.T.C. Trustee Kimball Union Academy, president board of trustees, 1962. Fellow Am. College Surgeons; mem. Am. Med. Assn., Am. Urol. Assn. (sec. 1935-42, pres. 1944-46), N.E. Urol. Assn. (pres. 1935-36), Am. Assn. Genito-Urinary Surgeons (pres. 1948-49), Clinical Society of Urology (president 1951) Western Urological Soc. (honorary), Internat. Urol. Assn., N.E. Surg. Soc., Conn. State (pres. 1962-63), New Haven County med. socs., New Haven Med. Soc., Yale Med. Soc., Asso. Phys. of Long Island, N.Y. (hon.), Sigma Xi, Theta Delta Chi, Nu Sigma Nu, Alpha Omega Alpha. Awarded Ferris anatomy prize, 1912, Parker prize and Sharing Key's prize, 1915. Republican. Conglist. Clubs: Faculty, Graduates, Lawn, Mory's (all in New Haven). Home: Hamden, Conn.

DEMOREST, DANA JAMES (DEM'O-REST), prof. metallurgy; b. Marysville, O., Aug. 21, 1882; s. Louis B. and Sarah Frances (Marshall) D.; B.Sc. in chemistry, Ohio State U., 1907; m. Margaret Christine Wiltsee, 1907 (dec.); 1 dau., Margaret Frances. Chemist with U.S. Bureau Mines, 1907, with U.P. R.R., 1908; asst. prof. metallurgy, Ohio State U., 1909-12, prof., since 1912; also consulting practice. Served as maj. in Chem. Warfare Service, U.S. Army, in charge poison gas plant, Edgewood (Md.) Arsenal, World War. Mem. Am. Chem. Soc., Am. Electrochem. Soc., Am. Soc. for Testing Materials, Am. Inst. Mining and Metall. Engrs., Am. Soc. for Metals, Soc. for Promotion Engringn. Edn. Republican. Methodist. Mason. Author: Metallurgical Analysis. Home: Columbus, O.

DEMOREST, WILLIAM JENNINGS, ret. real estate exec.; b. N.Y.C., Apr. 18, 1890; s. Henry C. and Annie (Lawrie) D.; student Trinity Sch.; M.E., Columbia, 1913; H.H.D., Piedmont Coll., 1961; m. Wealthy Albro Lewis, June 29, 1918; children—Dilys (Mrs. Samuel F. Peirce), William Jennings, Annie Lawrie (Mrs. Spencer M. Hurtt), Carolyn A. (Mrs. T.H. Tenney, Jr.). With Whitney Co., 1914; sec., v.p. Cushman & Wakefield, Inc., 1919-30; v.p. Wm. A. White & Sons, N.Y.C., 1939-43, pres., 1943-63, vice chmn., chmn. exec. com., 1964-72; v.p., dir. Coliseum Exhbn. Corp., 1955-72; past. dir., mem. finance com. Home Life Ins. Co.; past trustee, mem. mortgage com. Greenwich Savs. Bank of N.Y. Past gov., sec., v.p. Real Estate Bd. of N.Y., pres., 1935-36; dir. Citizens Housing and Planning Council Realty Adv. Bd. on Labor Relations, 1934-37, Citizens Budget Com., 1935; vice chmn. adv. com. World's Fair, 1939; gen. chmn. Met. Fair Rent Com., 1945-48; chmn. bldg. com. Interch. Center, 1955-59; mem. finance com. Com. Econ. Devel., 1962. Chmn. Community Chest drive, Rye, N.Y., 1937. Mem. zoning bd. appeals, Rye, 1944-56; past mem. Mayor's Com. for Removal Elevated Structures, N.Y.C.; mem. finance com. Bd. Nat. Missions, United Presbyn. Ch. U.S., 1933-55; past gov. 42d Street Property Owners Assn. Bd. mgrs. Jerry McAuley Cremorne Mission; trustee Columbia U. Club Found., Univ. Devel. Com., Columbia. Served to capt. U.S. Army, World War I. Mem. Inst. Real Estate Appraisers, Soc. Older Grads. Columbia U. (pres.), Laymen's Movement for a Christian World (dir.), C. of C. State N.Y., Huguenot Soc., Pilgrims U.S., St. Andrews Soc., Psi Upsilon. Presbyn. (elder; pres. bd. trustees). Clubs: University, Columbia University (gov.) (N.Y.C.); Apawamis; Misquamicut (Watch Hill, R.I.). Home: Rye, N.Y. Deceased.

DEMPSEY, JAMES CHARLES, rear adm. U.S. Navy; b. Eastport, Md., 1901; s. James Patrick and Mary Elizabeth (Conroy) D.; grad. U.S. Naval Acad., 1931; m. Audrey Emanuel; 2 sons, 2 daus. Commd., U.S. Navy, advanced through grades to rear adm.; comdr. submarine S-37, PTO, 1942; served in numerous command positions including comdr. Mil. Sea Transp. Service, Atlantic, Bklyn.; ret., 1970. Decorated Navy Cross, Gold Star. As comdr. of Spearfish, he rescued the last Americans in fall of Corregidor, evacuation later fictionalized in movie Operation Petticoat. Died July 9, 1979.

DENIG, ROBERT LIVINGSTON (DEN'IG), Marine Corps officer; b. Clinton, N.Y., Sept. 29, 1884; s. Robert Gracy and Jean Livingston (Hubbard) D.; ed. Manlius Prep. Sch.; student U. of Pa., 1903-05, grad. Marine Corps Sch. of Application, Annapolis, 1905; m. Maud Broumel King, 1907; children—Robert Livingston (U.S. Marine Corps), James Livingston (U.S. Marine Corps). Commd. 2d lt., U.S. Marine Corps, Sept. 29, 1905, and advanced through the grades to brig. gen. June 1, 1940; served as capt. and maj. in command of 17th Co., 5th Marines, 1st Batt., 30th Inf., 3rd Div., 2d Batt., 6th Marines, 2d Div., 3d Batt. 9th Inf., A.E.F., Aug. 5, 1917 to Nov. 27, 1918; now dir. Marine Corps Div. of Pub. Relations. Decorated D.S.C., Navy Cross, Purple Heart, Victory medal with 5 clasps, Am. Defense Service medal with bronze star; Legion of Honor, Croix de Guerre with bronze star, Croix de Guerre with palm, Fourragere (France); Presidential Medal of Merit (Nicaragua). Home: Washington, D.C.

DENMAN, HARRY, church sec.; b. Birmingham, Ala., Sept. 26, 1893; s. William Henry and Hattie (Leonard) D.; A.B., Birmingham Southern Coll., 1921, A.M., 1930; D.D., Athens (Ala.) Coll., 1936; unmarried. With Tenn. Coal, Iron & R.R. Co. in various positions, 1904-15; sec. Birmingham Sunday Sch. Assn., 1915-19; ch. mgr. First Meth. Ch., Birmingham, 1919-38; exec. sec. Bd. of Evangelism, Meth. Ch., Nashville, 1939-64. Mem. Gen. Conf., M.E. Ch. South, 1934, 38; mem. Uniting Conf. Meth. Ch., 1939; mem. Gen. and Jurisdictional Confs., Meth. Ch., 1940, 52, Jurisdictional Conf. Meth. Ch., 1944, 48; chmn. com. on evangelism World Meth. Council. Mem. Omicron Delta Kappa. Address: Nashville, Tenn. Died Birmingham, Ala., Nov. 8, 1976.

DENNING, WILLIAM IRA, official of Post Office Dept.; b. Jones Co., Ga., Aug. 1, 1883; s. Benjamin F. and Martha J. (Wheeler) D.; George Washington U., 1908-10, LL.B., 1913; m. Eugenia Bennie Meeks, of Griswoldville, Ga., June 25, 1906. Rural letter carrier, 1903-5; ry. postal clk., 1905-7; clk. bur. of 2d asst. postmaster gen., 1907-14; supt. Div. of Equipment, 1914-15; supt. Div. Equipment and Supplies, Jan. 15-Sept., 1915; chief clk. Post Office Dept., 1915-17; gen. supt. ry. mail service, 1917-21; supt. office of spl. asst. to atty. gen., Post Office Dept., May 5, 1921—. Mem. inter-departmental bd. on coastal communications (1916-17). Admitted to D.C. bar, 1913. Democrat. Methodist. Mason (32 deg.). Home: Washington, D.C.

DENNIS, CHARLES LESLIE, Labor union exec.; b. Beardstown, Ill., June 21, 1908; s. Charles Eugene and Mae Anna (Preckwunkle) D.; ed. pub. schs., Ill.; m. Harriet Huseby, Nov. 25, 1950; children—Leslie E., Carol (Mrs. James McGraw), Marilyn (Mrs. Edward Brink), Jeffrey. With biscuit factory, Chgo., 1921-26; freight handler C.&N.W. Ry., 1926; mem. Brotherhood Ry., Airline and Steamship Cks., 1926-78, internat. v.p., 1959-63, internat. v.p., 1959-63, internat. pres., 1963-76; gen. chmn. C.&N.W. Ry. System Bd. Adjustment, 1940-57; v.p. A.F.L.-C.I.O., from 1969; chmn. r.r. retirement com. Congress Ry. Unions, from 1969; chmn. Conf. Transp. Trades, from 1968; mem. gen. council Internat. Transp. Workers Fedn. Nat. Common Productivity, from 1974. Co-chmn. labor div. United Settlement Appeal. Vice pres. Eugene Debs Found. Home: Des Plaines, Ill. Died July 29, 1978.

DENNIS, JOHN PURNELL, corp. ofcl.; b. Preston, Md., Nov. 18, 1898; s. Jesse T. and Belle V. (Harrison) D.; A.B., Princeton, 1920; m. Irene Keeler, Oct. 13, 1934; children—John P., Nancy Elizabeth, Robert H. Asst. gen. freight agt. N.P. Ry., 1921-36, asst. to freight traffic mgr., 1936-39, asst. to v.p. traffic, 1939-42; traffic mgr. Texaco, Inc., N.Y.C., 1942-54, from 1956; coordinator def. transportation ODM, Washington, 1954-56. Mem. Transportation Assn. Am., Nat. Indsl. Traffic League, Assn. ICC Practitioners. Clubs: Traffic of N.Y. (pres. 1954); Traffic of Chicago; Princeton (N.Y.C.); Scarsdale Golf. Home: Scarsdale, N.Y. Died Nov. 3, 1978; interred Preston, Md.

DENNIS, LAWRENCE, writer; b. Atlanta, Dec. 25, 1893; s. George and Mary (Smith) D.; student Phillips Exeter Acad., 1913-15; A.B., Harvard, 1920; m. Eleanor Simson, 1933 (div.); children—Emily (Mrs. Dermot Harvey), Laura (Mrs. Mark Dollard); m. 2d, Mrs. Dora Shuser Burton. In U.S. diplomatic service 1920-27, serving in Port au Prince (Haiti), Bucharest (Rumania), Managua (Nicaragua), Tegucigalpa (Honduras); was charge d'affaires for periods in Rumania, Honduras, Nicaragua; condr. peace conf. and first phase Am. Intervention in Nicaragua, 1926, during revolution; assigned to Am. embassy, Paris, June 1927, when resigned to enter banking; with J. & W. Seligman & Co., bankers, N.Y.C., 1927-30; brokerage business E.A. Pierce & Co., N.Y.C., 1936-39; writer from 1930; propr., editor and pub. The Weekly Fgn. Letter, N.Y.C., 1939-43, Appeal to Reason (weekly news analysis), from 1946. Served at Plattsburg, 1915-17, commd. 2d lt. U.S. Army, Aug. 1917; served in A.E.F., 1918-19; hon. disch. as 1st lt., Aug. 1919. Club: Harvard (N.Y.C.). Author: Is Capitalism Doomed? 1932; The Coming American Fascism, 1936; The Dynamics of War and Revolution, 1940; A Trial on Trial (with Maximillian J. St. George), 1946; Operational Thinking for Survival, 1968. Home: Garnerville, N.Y. Died Aug. 20, 1977; buried Washington Mountain Cemetery, Becket, Mass.

DENNIS, WAYNE, psychologist, author; b. Washington County, O., Sept. 1, 1905; s. Samuel R. and Mary V. (Fox) D.; A.B., Marietta Coll., 1926; A.M., Clark U., 1928, Ph.D., 1930; Social Sci. Research Council fellow, Yale, 1936-37; m. Marsena Anne Galbreath, Mar. 19, 1928 (dec. July 1965); children—Mary, Anne, James Gill; m. 2d, Margaret Wallihan Hudson, Mar. 18, 1970. Asst. prof. U. Va., 1929-42; vis. prof. Clark U., 1937-38; prof., head dept. psychology La. State U., 1942-46, U. Pitts., 1946-51; prof. psychology Bklyn. Coll., 1951-70, chmn., 1951-62; exec. officer doctoral program gen. psychology U. City N.Y., 1962-64, vis. prof. Am. U. of Beirut, 1955-56, 58-59, 74-75. Served as lt. USNRF, 1943-46; head Human Engring. sect. Spl. Devices div. Office of Naval Research. Fellow Am. Psychol. Assn., Interam. Soc. Psychology, Gerontol Soc., Soc. for Research in Child Devel.; mem. Eastern Psychol. Assn., Phi Beta Kappa, Sigma Xi. Author: The Hopi Child, 1940; Group Values Through Children's Drawing, 1966; Children of the Creche, 1973. Co-author: Current Trends in Psychology, 1947. Current Trends in Social Psychology, 1948; Current Trends in Industrial Psychology, 1949; Current Trends in the Relation of Psychology to Medicine, 1950; Current Trends in Psychological Theory, 1951. Editor: Readings in Child Psychology, 1951, rev., 1963; Readings in the History of Psychology, 1948, Readings in General Psychology, 1949, (with Ihsan Al-Issa) Cross Cultural Studies of Behavior, 1970; Historical Readings in Developmental Psychology, 1971 (with Margaret W. Dennis) The Intellectually Gifted: An Overview, 1976. Editor Psychol. Bull., 1953-58. Home: Doswell, Va. Died July 21, 1976; buried Doswell.

DENNISON, DAVID MATHIAS, theoretical physicist; b. Oberlin, O., Apr. 26, 1900; s. Walter and Anna (Green) D.; A.B., Swarthmore Coll., 1921, D.Sc. (hon.), 1950; Ph.D., U. Mich., 1924; m. Helen Lenette Johnson, Aug. 28, 1924; children—Edwin Walter, David Severin. Gen. Edn. Bd. fellow, Inst. for Theoretical Physics, Copenhagen, Denmark, 1924-26; Guggenheim fellow, 1940; prof. physics U. Mich., 1935-66, Harrison M. Randall prof. physics, 1966-70, emeritus, 1970-76, chmn. dept., 1955-65, Henry Russell lectr., 1952; cons. OSRD, 1942-45. Recipient Distinguished Faculty Achievement award, 1963; named Hon. Citizen of Tours, France, 1975; U. Mich. Physics-Astronomy Bldg. named in his honor, 1976. Fellow Am. Phys. Soc., Am. Optical Soc.; mem. Nat. Acad. Scis., Phi Beta Kappa, Sigma Xi, Phi Kappa Phi. Research in theory of infra red spectra, molecular structure, specific heat of hydrogen. Home: Ann Arbor, Mich. Died Apr. 3, 1976; buried Forest Hills Cemetery, Ann Arbor.

DENNISON, ROBERT LEE, ret. mil. officer; b. Warren, Pa., Apr. 13, 1901; s. Ludovici Waters and Laura Florence (Lee) D.; B.S., U.S. Naval Acad., 1923; M.S., Pa. State Coll., 1930; D.Eng., Johns Hopkins, 1935; m. Mildred Fenton Mooney Neely, May 10, 1937; children—Lee, Robert Lee. Commd. ensign USN, 1923, advanced through grades to adm., 1959, served with Atlantic, Pacific and Asiatic fleets, commd. U.S.S. Ortolan, 1935-37, U.S.S. Cuttlefish, 1937-38, U.S.S. John D. Ford, 1940-41, U.S.S. Missouri, 1947-48; mem. joint war plans com. Joint Chiefs of Staff, 1944-45; asst. chief of naval ops. for polit.-mil. affairs, 1945-47; naval aide to Pres. of U.S., 1948-53; comdr. Cruiser Div. 4 U.S. Atlantic Fleet, 1953-54; dir. Strategic Plans Div. asst. chief naval ops. for plans and policy, Office Naval Ops., 1954-56, 58; mem. joint strategic plans com. Join

Chiefs of Staff; comdr. First Fleet, U.S. Pacific Fleet, 1956-58; comdr.-in-chief US Naval Forces, Eastern Atlantic and Mediterranean, 1959-60, Atlantic and U.S. Atlantic Fleet. Supreme Allied Comdr. Atlantic, 1960-63; chief of staff of comdr. submarines, East Australia and Comdrs. Allied Naval Forces, East Australia, 1942; chief of staff Amphibious Forces U.S. Pacific Fleet, 1942-43; chief staff to comdr. 9th Amphibious Forces, 1943. Decorated D.S.M., Legion of Merit; Gold Star in lieu of 2d Legion of Merit; Am. Def.; Asiatic-Pacific Area, 2 Stars, Philippine Def. with Star: Navy Unit Commendation (U.S.S. Pennsylvania); Navy Occupation Service medal (European Clasp), Nat. Def. Service medal; Army Distinguished Unit Citation (Philippines) Am. Area; World War II Victory (U.S.); Order of Brit. Empire; Grand officer Order Naval Merit (Brazil); comdr. Order Crown (Belgium); comdr. Legion of Honor (France); Grand Cross Order of Orange-Nassau (The Netherlands), Grand Cross Mil. Order of Aviz (Portugal). Mem. Sigma Xi. Clubs: New York Yacht; Metropolitan, Chevy Chase, Army Navy (Washington). Home: Washington, D.C. Died Mar. 14, 1980.

DENNY, HENRY WADHAMS, chemist; b. Pittsfield, Mass., Jan. 2, 1886; s. James and Charlotte Ives (Wadhams) D., Jr.; B.S., Worcester Poly. Inst., 1908; m. Elizabeth P. Frazee, Sept. 27, 1910; Chemist, N.J. State Dept. Health, Trenton, N.J., 1908-15, chief chemist, 1915-17; dir. of research Schoenhoffen Co., Chicago, 1917-20; gen. mgr. Sugola Co. of Am., Orange, N.J., 1920-24; research technologist Sun Maid Raisin Growers Assn., Fresno, Calif., 1924-26; mgr. sales development Commercial Solvents Corp., N.Y. City, 1926-37, vice pres. in charge sales, 1937-50, director, 1943-50. Mem. Soc. Chem. Industry, Am. Chem. Soc., Sigma Alpha Epsilon. Democrat. Conglist. Home: Trenton, N.J.

DENNY-BROWN, DEREK ERNEST, physician; b. Christchurch, New Zealand, June 1, 1901; s. Charles and Marian F. (Denny) Denny-B.; M.B., U. New Zealand, 1924, M.D., 1946; Ph.D., Oxford U. (Beit Research fellow), 1928; A.M. (hon.), Harvard, 1943; LL.D., Wayne State U., 1959, U. Glasgow, 1970; D.Sci., Otago U., N.Z., 1969; m. Sylvia Summerhayes, Mar. 17, 1937; children—Bruce Charles, Martin John, Myles Robert, John Summerhayes. Came to U.S., 1941, naturalized, 1952. House officer, registrar, later vis. physician Nat. Hosp. Nervous Diseases, London, Eng., 1928-41; neurologist St. Bartholomews Hosp. and Coll., London, 1935-41; prof. neurology Harvard, 1941-46, James Jackson Putnam prof. neurology, 1946; dir. neurol. unit. neurologist-in-chief Boston City Hosp., 1941-67, pres. med. staff, 1966; chief sect. neurophysiology N.E. Primate Research Center, 1967-72. Chmn. bd. cons. Nat. Inst. Neurol. Disease and Blindness, 1965-66. Served with Royal Army M.C., 1939-41, India Burma, 1945-46, advancing from maj. to brig. gen. Decorated officer Order Brit. Empire; Order Unanue (Peru). Recipient Sherrington medal Royal Soc. Medicine (London), 1962; Jacoby award Am. Neurol. Assn., 1968; Modern Medicine award for distinguished achievement, 1965. Fogarty scholar-in-residence NIH, 1972-73. Fellow Royal Coll. Physicians; hon. fellow Royal Soc. Medicine London, Coll. Physicians S. Africa; hon. mem. Canadian, German, Mexican, Peruvian neurol. socs.; mem. Physiol. Soc., Am. Neurol. Assn. (past pres.), Assn. Am. Physicians, Assn. Brit. Neurologists, Mass. Med. Soc., Boston Soc. Psychiatry and Neurology (past pres.), Am. Assn. Neuropathologists (past pres.), Phila. Neurol. Soc. (hon.), Neurol. Soc. Paris (hon.), Swiss Neurol. (corr. mem.). Author articles and books. Home: Cambridge, Mass. Died Apr. 20, 1981.

DENSLOW, THEODORE NORTH, educator; b. Rutland, Vt., July 4, 1882; s. Herbert McKenzie and Anna Mary (Olmsted) D.; grad. Hotchkiss Sch., Lakeville, Conn., 1900; A.B., Trinity Coll., Hartford, Conn., 1904; m. Josephine Stewart, of Washington, D.C., Sept. 18, 1909; children—Theodore North, Stewart. Successively teacher Abingdon Friends' Sch., Jenkintown, Pa., Wilson Sch., Fishkill-on-Hudson, N.Y., Yeates Sch., Lancaster, Pa., Riverdale (N.Y.) Sch., Woodland Sch., Phoenicia, N.Y., and Nashotah (Wis.) House until 1912; salesman for Robt. H. IngerIngersoll & Bro., 1912-16, sales mgr., 1917; free lance salesman, 1918; teacher, Woodland Sch., 1918-20; free lance salesman, 1920-21; instr. in Greek, Nashotah House, 1921-26; headmaster Donaldson Sch., Ilchester, Md., since 1926. Address: Ilchester, Md.

DENT, L. BRUCE, savs. bank exec.; b. Niagara Falls, N.Y., Dec. 20, 1921; s. Louis F. and Alice Amelia (Winter) D.; student pub. schs., Niagara Falls; m. Marian Fribert, Feb. 5, 1944; children—Lorraine Dent Gorman, Christine Dent VanDriel, Bruce F. With Power City Trust Co., Niagara Falls, 1939-44, IRS, Niagara Falls, 1944-56; with Permanent Savs. Bank (formerly Niagara Permanent Savs. and Loan Assn.), Niagara Falls, 1956-80, sec., 1960-65, pres., 1965-80; chmn. bd., 1973-80; dir. Datek, Inc., Sta. WHLD; v.p., mem. exec. com. Erie Niagara Indsl. Devel. Corp.; past mem. N.Y. State Banking Bd. Mem. council Niagara U.; bd. dirs. Old Fort Niagara Assn. Mem. Niagara Falls Clearing House Assn. (pres. 1977), Savs. Bank Assn. N.Y. State, Nat. Assn. Mut. Savs. Banks, Niagara Falls Area C. of C. (dir.). Clubs: Niagara, Niagara Falls Country; Buffalo. Home: Niagara Falls, N.Y. Died Jan. 18, 1980.

DENT, LOUIS LINTON, lawyer; b. Salem, Mo., May 30, 1911; s. Louis and Elizabeth Bell (Dye) D.; J.D., U. Mo., 1934; m. Lorena W. Rice, Nov. 10, 1938; 1 son, Thomas. Admitted to Ill. bar, 1934; pvt. practice, Chgo., 1934-78; partner firm Dent, Hampton & McNeela, 1970-78. Mem. Park Ridge (Ill.) Zoning Bd., 1958-62. Mem. Am., Ill., Chgo. bar assns., Delta Theta Phi. Republican. Methodist. Clubs: Union League, Masons (Shriner). Home: Park Ridge, Ill. Died Dec. 1978; buried Mt. Emblem Cemetery, Elmhurst, Ill.

DERICK, CLARENCE GEORGE, chemist; b. Sutton, Quebec, Can., Oct. 29, 1883; s. Wesley Talmage and Emma Delia (Ryan) D.; S.B., Worcester Poly. Inst., 1906; M.S., U. of Ill., 1909, Ph.D., 1910; m. Edith Lillian Blowe, Aug. 27, 1907; children—Clarence George, Kenneth Earl, William Blowe, Edith Dawne, Hazel Gertrude (dec.), Lincoln, Goldie L., June Phyllis. Reseaarch asst. to Prof. Moore, Mass. Inst. Tech., 1906-07, to Prof. W. A. Noyes, U. of Ill., 1907-08; asst. in organic chemistry, 1908-10, asso., 1910-13, asst. prof., 1913-16, U. of Ill.; dir. of research, Schoellkopf Aniline & Chem. Co., Inc., Buffalo, N.Y., 1916-17. Nat. Aniline & Chem. Co., Buffalo, 1917-21; v.p. By-Products Steel Corp., Buffalo, 1924-25; pres. Derick Laboratories, Inc., Buffalo, since 1925; cons. practice. Consulting chemist Bur. of Mines, at Edgewood Arsenal br., Buffalo, during World War, in charge research on mustard gas. Mem. Nat. Research Council, 1919-22. Fellow A.A.A.S., Am. Inst. of Chemists; mem. Am. Chem. Soc., Sigma Xi, Phi Lambda Upsilon. Republican. Contbr. upon organization of chemical research; articles dealing with chemistry in organic and physical fields; patents in dye and zinc salts fields. Home: Sewaren, N.J.

DERIEUX, JAMES CLARKSON, writer; b. Spartanburg, S.C., Dec. 13, 1891; s. William Thomas and Lottie (Bookhart) D.; ed. Richmond Coll. Acad.; Suffolk (Va.) University Sch.; A.B., Furman U., 1912; LL.D. (hon.), Presbyn. Coll., S.C., 1942; m. Janie W. Gilreath, Mar. 14, 1922; children—Justin Derieux New, Samuel. Mng. editor Greenville Daily News, 1915-17; war work in France, 1917-19; secretary to governor of S.C., 1919-21; reporter on The Globe, New York, 1922; joined editorial staff American Magazine, 1922, mng. editor, 1925-31; asso. editor The State, Columbia, 1938-42; state dir. Office of Price Administration, South Carolina, May 1942-Mar. 1943, regional administrator of Southeastern region, Atlanta, Ga., 1943-44, deputy administrator O.P.A.; in charge of field operations (Washington, D.C.), 1944, asst. to adminstr., Nat. O.P.A., 1945; asso. editor Colliers, 1945, chief Washington bur. 1949-54, sr. editor Washington office Crowell-Collier Pub. Co., represented Collier's and Woman's Home Companion, 1954-57; writer articles in polit. and other fields; cons. office Emergency Planning, Exec. Offices Pres., Washington, 1963-71. Mem. Pi Kappa Phi. Clubs: Keswick (Va.) Country, Keswick Hunt: Nat. Press. Co-author: Ladies, Gentlemen, and Editors, 1960; White House Sailor, 1962. Home: Cismont, Va. Died Sept. 9, 1978.

DE ROCHEMONT, LOUIS CHARLES, motion picture producer; b. Chelsea, Mass., Jan. 13, 1899; s. Louis L. G. and Sarah Wilson (Miller) de R.; ed. pub. schs., Winchester, Mass., Naval Aviation School, Mass. Inst. Tech., and Naval Cadet Sch., Harvard 1917-18; L.H.D., U. N.H., 1944, Bates College; m. Virginia Shaler, Sept. 12, 1929; children—Louis, Virginia. Served as line officer, U.S. Navy until resignation, 1923; on staff Internat. Newsreel, 1923-27; asst. editor Pathé News, 1927-29; dir. and producer Twentieth Century-Fox; Joined TIME Inc., 1934; co-founder, 1st producer The March of Time, 1934-43; directed and produced The Ramparts We Watch, 1940; producer: The Fighting Lady, 1944 (spl. award from N.Y. film critics); The House on 92d Street, 1945; 13 Rue Madeline, 1946; Boomerang, 1946; Lost Boundaries (received eleven major awards), 1949; The Whistle at Eaton Falls, 1951; Walk East on Beacon, 1952; Windjammer; The Roman Spring of Mrs. Stone, 1960; Parions Francis; pres. Louis de Rochemont Assos., Inc.; The Earth and its People (integrated series ednl. film.) 1948; Martin Luther, 1953; Animal Farm, 1954; Cinerama Holiday, 1955. Decorated Order of St. Olav, 1959. Recipient Acad. Award for best documentary, 1944; decorated Order of Liberation, King Haakon of Norway, 1948. Home: Newington, N.H. Died Dec. 23, 1978.

DERONDE, PHILIP (DE-ROND), b. Englewood, N.J., Dec. 31, 1882; s. Abram and Harriet (Coe) D.; grad. Westminster Sch., Simsbury, Conn., 1900; student Princeton; m. Marie Dardess, Sept. 17, 1910; children—Philip Henry, Albert. Organizer, 1913, later pres. Oriental Navigation Co.; formerly pres. Colonial Trust Co. and Phoenix Securities Corp.; formerly mem. N.J. Infantry, N.J. Cavalry and Pa. Inf., Nat. Guard. Served in France during World War as officer U.S. Navy and Marine Corps. Consul of Paraguay and col. Paraguayan Army. Served in France, 1939-40, as capt. 12th Regt., French Foreign Legion, and only officer of that regiment to survive death or capture, having escaped, wounded, to England following the French Armistice. Mem. Am. Museum Natural History, Metropolitan Museum Art, Sons of Revolution, N.Y. Soc. Officers of the World War. Presbyterian. Clubs: Nat. Golf Links of America, Racquet and Tennis. Address: 1939 Avda Alvear, Buenos Aires and Quinta Nanawa, Asuncion del Paraguay.

DERRICK, LELAND EUGENE, coll. dean; b. Hollis, Okla., Apr. 14, 1901; s. Joseph Edward and Ada (Magee) D.; B.A., U. Tex., 1926, M.A., 1930, Ph.D., 1940; m. Delia May Thomas, Apr. 14, 1923; children—Leland Eugene, Gus Wilburn. Prin. Sherwood (Tex.) Pub. Sch., 1922-24, supt., 1924-25; with S.W. Tex. State Coll. (new S.W. Tex. State U.), 1926-71, instr., asst. prof., asso. prof., 1926-40, prof. English, 1940-80, dir. dept., 1954-58, v.p. and dean Grad. Sch., to 1971, acting pres. coll., 1968-69. Served to maj. USAAF, 1942-45; lt. col., 1951-52. Mem. Coll. English Assn. (pres. Tex. div. 1958-59), Coll. Tchrs. English (dir. Tex. Conf. 1956-59), Assn. Tex. Grad. Schs. (pres. 1961-62), Am. Legion. Methodist. Mason, Rotarian. Home: San Marcos, Tex. Died Jan. 3, 1980.

DESAUTELS, PIERRE G., airline exec.; b. Montreal, Can., Dec. 16, 1907; s. Joseph Theodore and Marie (Marechal) D.; grad. St. Mary's Jesuit Sch., Montreal, 1925; student McGill U., 1925-28, U. So. Cal., Los Angeles, 1940-42; m. Lytle R. P. Dickinson, Nov. 16, 1935; children—Marc Pierre, Philippe Joseph. With Johnston & Ward, 1927-37; investment counselor, 1937-43; with Trans World Airlines, Inc., from 1943, officer and v.p. nat. accounts. Bd. dirs. Woodside Heights Assn. Clubs: Travellers (Paris, France); Stock Exchange (San Francisco); Traffic (N.Y.C.). Home: LaJolla, Calif. Died Aug. 1977.

DESCHLER, LEWIS, parliamentary cons.; b. Chillicothe, Ohio, Mar. 3, 1905; s. Joseph Anthony and Lillian Louise (Lewis) D.; student Miami U., Oxford Ohio, 1922-25; LL.D., 1963; student George Washington U., 1925; M.P.L., J.D., Nat. U., 1932, LL.D., 1947; m. Virginia A. Cole, Jan. 18, 1931; children—Lewis II, Joan Mari (Mrs. Eddy). Apptd. messenger at speakers table U.S. Ho. of Reps., 1925; admitted to D.C. bar, 1934, U.S. Supreme Ct. bar, 1937; asst. parliamentarian U.S. Ho. of Reps., 1927, parliamentarian, 1928-74, parliamentary cons. to speaker, 1974-76. Asst. sec. Am. Group of Interparliamentary Union Conv., London, July 1930. Recipient Gov.'s award, Ohio, 1970; 1st Ann. John W. McCormack award of excellence, 1970; Man of Year award Doormen's Soc., 1973. Mem. Delta Tau Delta (Distinguished Service award 1964). Author: Deschler's Procedure in the U.S. House of Representatives, 1974; Deschler's Rules of Order, 1976; Deschler's Precedents of the U.S. House of Representatives, 1976. Editor: House Rules and Manual, 1929-73. Home: Bethesda, Md. Died July 12, 1976; buried in Chillicothe.

DESHA, LUCIUS JUNIUS (DE-SHA'), prof. chemistry; b. Cynthiana, Ky., June 14, 1883; s. Jack and Mary Walton (Broadwell) D.; prep. edn., high sch., Cynthiana; A.B., Washington and Lee U., 1906; Ph.D., Johns Hopkins, 1909; m. Mary Forrester, Sept. 14, 1911; children—Julia Forrester, Lucia, Mary Walton. Chemist Tenn. food and drug inspection, Nashville, 1909-12; prof. chemistry, U. of Tenn. Coll. of Medicine, Memphis, 1912-20, acting dean, 1917; capt. Sanitary Corps, U.S. Army, in France, Dec. 1917-Jan. 1919; prof. chemistry, Washington and Lee U. since 1920, dean 1946-47. Member of American Chemical Soc., Soc. Chimique de France, Phi Beta Kappa, Phi Kappa Sigma, Omicron Delta Kappa. Unitarian. Author: Organic Chemistry, 1936. Co-Author: (with L. H. Farinholt) Experiments in Organic Chemistry, 1938. Articles in Jour. Am. Chem. Soc., etc. Home: Lexington, Va.

DE SIEYES, JEAN (DE-SE-YES'), dir. French Am. Banking Corp.; b. Valence, France, Aug. 23, 1884; s. Raoul and Marie (d'Indy) deS.; LL.D., U. of Paris, France, 1906; married Elizabeth Sharp, 1948. Came to the United States, 1919. Inspector of the Banque de France, Paris, 1910-22; v.p. French Am. Banking Corp., New York, 1922-26, pres. 1926-45, chmn. 1945-57, became hon. chmn., 1957, now dir. Decorated Officer French Legion of Honor; Croix de Guerre. Club: Knickerbocker (N.Y.C.). Home: N.Y.C.

DESMOND, ALTON HAROLD, educator; b. Springfield, Vt., Aug. 3, 1922; s. Harold Michael and Louisa (Hilliard) D.; B.S., Hartwick Coll., 1949; Sc.M., Brown U., 1951, Ph.D., 1954; m. Dorothy Ann Garfield, Apr. 23, 1945; 1 dau., Jane Carol. Faculty zoology George Washington U., 1953—, prof., 1963-77, chmn. dept. biol. scis., 1969-77; cons. McGraw Hill Pub. Co., Indian Govt. Civil Service Commn., Bur. Higher Edn. Div. Grad. Programs of Dept. Health, Edn. and Welfare; mem. biology sect. NSF Panel for Evaluating NSF Fellows, 1962. Bd. dirs., chmn. Arlington (Va.) Ballet Workshop, 1960-69. Served with USCGR, 1942-46. Recipient F.W. Miller award Hartwick Coll., 1949. Eli Lilly fellow, 1952-53. Fellow Am. Acad. Forensic Sci.; mem. A.A.A.S., Am. Soc. Zoologists, Am. Micros. Soc., Am. Assn. U. Profs., Am.

Soc. Cell Biologists, Sigma Xi. Home: Annandale, Va. Died Apr. 27, 1977.

DETGEN, EDWARD JOSEPH, corp. ofcl.; b. N.Y.C., Nov. 17, 1911; s. Richard Joseph and Mary Josephine (Bannon) D.; B.S., Georgetown U., 1934; m. Benedicta Gannon, Sept. 10, 1938; children—John Peter, Mildred Mary, Edward Joseph, Virginia Lambert. Chief spltys. div. U.S. Dept. Commerce, 1939-42; dir. containers div. WPB, 1943-45; sales mgr. Owens-Corning Fiberglas Corp., 1945-54, v.p., gen. sales mgr., 1954-58; v.p., gen. mgr. home bldg. products div., 1958-66, v.p. nat. affairs, 1966-76, dir. Courtesy Assos. Life trustee Nat. Housing Center; chmn. Indsl. Energy Users Forum; bd. dirs. Action. Mem. Producers Council (dir.), Nat. Sales Execs., Home Improvement Council (dir.), Air Force Assn., Am. Ordnance Assn., Nat. Security Indsl. Assn., Washington Indsl. Round Table, Bus.-Govt. Relations Council. Clubs: Chevy Chase, International (Washington). Home: Bethesda, Md. Died July 31, 1978.

DETLEFSEN, JOHN A. (DET'LEF-SEN), physiology, genetics; b. Norwich, Conn., Sept. 12, 1883; s. George Detlef and Augusta (Nadolny) D.; Cambridge Latin Sch., 1898-1902; A.B., Dartmouth, 1908; A.M., Harvard, 1910, S.D., 1912; m. Ruth Sarah Atwell, June 18, 1914; children—John Detlef, Ruth Henrietta (Mrs. Leslie E. Rasmussen). Austin teaching fellow in zoology, Harvard, 1908-12; asst. professor genetics 1912-18, associate professor of genetics, 1918-19, prof., 1919-22, U. of Ill.; prof. genetics, Wistar Inst. Anatomy, Phila., 1922-25; in charge sect. on mouth hygiene, Phila. Hosp. and Health Survey. Statistical analyst. Federal Educational Projects, eight counties of Pa., 1939-40. Consultant, Office of Civilian Supplies, Washington, D.C., 1941; Pa. State supervisor Statistics, Office of Price Adminstrn., 1942; dep. chief statistics, War Production Bd., Washington, D.C., 1943-45; executive secretary Committee of Automotive Industry for Joint Intelligence Objectives Agency, Joint Chiefs of Staff, 1945-46; chief of scientific personnel, medical and pharmaceutical studies in Europe, Dept. Commerce, 1946-48; supervisor of evaluation of German documents, plans, records, etc., Dept. Commerce, 1948; specialist in univ. edn. and administrn. U.S. Allied Commn., U.S. Forces in Austria, 1949-50. Director of Police Sch. of Eastern Pa., 1935. Asso. editor in chief Biol. Abstracts, 1925. Member of White House Conf. on Child Health and Protection. Fellow A.A.A.S.; mem. Am. Soc. Zoölogists, Am. Soc. Naturalists, Am. Genetic Assn., Internat. Assn. Dental Research, Philadelphia Mouth Hygiene Assn. (exec. dir. since 1928), Ky. Acad. Sciences (hon.), Phi Beta Kappa, Sigma Xi, Phi Gamma Delta. Chevalier Order of Dannebrog. Author: Studies on Cavy Species Cross, 1914. Contbr. to Our Present Knowledge of Heredity, 1926; also contbr. on heredity, species crosses, physiology, med. and dental biometry and etiology. Home: Waynesboro, Va.

DETWEILER, HERBERT K(NUDSEN), physician; b. Kitchener, Ont., Sept. 24, 1886; s. Samuel S. and Emma Louise (Knudson) D.; student Galt Collegiate Inst., 1900-06; M.B., U. Toronto, 1914, M.D. cum laude, 1916; m. E. Velyian Williamson, June 29, 1918; children—Joyce Alexandra, Alan Gregory. Lectr. bacteriology U. Toronto Med. Sch., 1914-19; asso. prof. medicine, 1936-49; asso. medicine, attending physician Toronto Gen. Hosp., also cons. physician, 1949—; physician-in-chief Toronto Western Hosp., 1936-49, cons. physician, 1949—; cons. physician for Wellesley Hospital, Toronto, Canada. Fellow A.C.P. (1st v.p. 1957-58), Royal College Physicians (Can.). Clubs: Royal Canadian Yacht (commodore 1950-52), York (Toronto). Home: Bolton, Ont.

DEUTSCH, EBERHARD PAUL, lawyer; b. Cin., Oct. 31, 1897; s. Gotthard and Hermine (Bacher) D.; student Tulane U., 1924-25; J.D. (hon.), U. Messina (Sicily), 1943; m. Rhea Loeb, Aug. 1, 1929 (dec. Mar. 1961); 1 son, Brunswick G. Admitted to La. bar, 1925, since practiced in New Orleans; spl. asst. to atty. gen. U.S. on Texas City Disaster litigation, 1950-53; prin. legal adviser to Gen. Mark W. Clark in Mil. Adminstrn. of Austria, 1945-46, also chmn. Allied Legal Directorate; dir. The Vernon Bank; chmn. Dixie Ship Repair Co. Bd. dirs. Isaac Delgado Mus., New Orleans. Lt. F.A., U.S. Army, 1917-19, col., Gen. Staff Corps, 1942-46. Decorated Silver Star, Bronze Star, Legion of Merit, Purple Heart; Gold Cross of Merit (Austria); Croix de Guerre with palm and fourragere. Mem. Internat., Fed., Am. (chmn. admiralty and maritime law com. 1961-62, chmn. com. peace and law through UN 1962-63, 65-68, chmn. com. law treaties 1967; mem. com. abuse of process, com. marine resources, council sect. internat. and comparative law), La. (chmn. com. law reform), New Orleans bar assns., Assn. Bar City N.Y., Am. Judicature Soc. (dir. 1935-56), Maritime Law Assn., Am. Soc. Internat. Law, Met. Crime Commn., Miss. Valley Assn., New Orleans Philharmonic Symphony Soc., Notaries Assn. New Orleans, Tulane Alumni Fund, Indian Soc. Internat. Law, Am. Arbitration Assn., Am. Civil Liberties Union, Am. Soc. Legal History, Assn. Average Adjusters, Assn. Am. Indian Affairs, Assn. U.S. Army, Bur. Govt. Research, Consular Corps New Orleans (hon consul gen. Republic Austria), Escoffiers, Fgn. Relations Assn. (dir.), France Amerique de la Louisiane. Grand Consistory La., Information Council of Ams., Internat. Legal Aid Assn., La. Free Enterprise Assn., La. Assn. Def. Counsel, La. Civil Service League, La. Hist. Soc., La. U. Found., Research Fellows Southwestern Legal Found., Assn. ICC Practitioners, Bd. Trade, C. of C., Alumni Assn. Tulane U., Scribes, Athence Louisianais, Audubon Soc., Confrerie des Chevaliers du Tastevin, English Speaking Union, Fellowship U.S.-Brit. Comrades, Heroes of '76, Hon., Order of Blue Goose Internat., Order of Lafayette Inter-Am. Bar Assn., Le Petit Theatre du Vieux Carre, Met. New Orleans Safety Council, Mil. Govt. Assn., Mil. Order World Wars, Nat. Aero. Assn., Nat. Geog. Soc., Opera House Assn., Zool. Soc., Res. Officers Assn., Selden Soc., Council for a Better La., Internat. Soc. Mil. Law, Shakespeare Soc. New Orleans, Internat. Law Assn., Nat. Trust Historic Preservation (mem. nat. devel. com.), Nat. Waterways Conf., V.F.W., Vets. World War I U.S., U.S. Internat. Sailing Assn., Blue Key, 33d Div. War Vets. Assn., Phi Delta Phi. Mason (Shriner, Sojourner), Elk; mem. B'nai B'rith. Clubs: Army and Navy, Insurance, International House, (dir. and mem. of exec. com.), Press, University, Athletic, Knife and Fork, Petroleum, Round Table, Southern Yacht, Mariners, Opera (New Orleans); Downtown Athletic (N.Y.C.); Petroleum (Houston); Propeller U.S.; Skyriders; City (Baton Rouge); National Lawyers (Washington); Tulane Side Lines; Lamplighter; Plimsoll. Editor: The Internat. Lawyer. Home: New Orleans, La. Died Jan. 17, 1980.

DEVANE, DOZIER A(DOLPHUS) (DE-VAN), judge; b. near Lakeland, Fla., Aug. 2, 1883; s. Edward Jasper and Alice Victoria (Collins) DeV.; student Fla. State Coll., Tallahassee, 1904-05; LL.B., Washington and Lee U., Lexington, Va., 1908; m. Pauline Wilson, Aug. 11, 1909; children—Ruth Elizabeth (Mrs. Duane Barclay Wilson), Dozier Adolphus. Admitted to Fla. bar, 1908; practiced in Tampa, 1908-18; county atty. Hillsboro County, 1913-14; counsel to Fla. R.R. Commn., 1918-20; rate atty. Am. Telephone & Telegraph Co., 1920-22; gen. counsel Chesapeake & Potomac Telephone Co. and asso. cos., 1922-30; practiced law in D.C., 1930-33; solicitor Federal Power Commn., Washington, D.C., 1933-38; reentered pvt. law practice Orlando, Fla., 1938; mem. DeVane, Andrews & Patterson; apptd. U.S. dist. judge. Northern and Southern Districts of Fla., 1943, Northern dist. 1947. Mem. Phi Kappa Sigma, O.D.K., Phi Beta Kappa. Democrat. Presbyterian. Home: Tallahassee, Fla.

DEVEREUX, FREDERICK LEONARD (DEV'E-RA), b. Washington, July 19, 1882; s. Frank Nicholas and Caroline Elizabeth (Gheen) D.; A.B., Gonzaga Coll., 1902, M.A., 1903; LL.B., Georgetown U., 1906, Ph.D., 1917; m. Francis Beardsley Clark, Nov. 20, 1912 (died Mar. 2, 1922); children—Frederick Leonard, Elizabeth Clark (Mrs. Matson Holbrook); married second, Margaret Green Dargan, January 13, 1938. Traffic manager for the Chesapeake & Potomac Telephone Co., Washington, 1903-09; auditor disbursements Bell Telephone Co. of Pa., Phila., 1909-11; auditor Am. Tel. & Tel. Co., N.Y. City, 1911-19; gen. auditor Northwestern Bell Telephone Co., Omaha, Neb., 1919-22; sales mgr. Bell Telephone Securities Co., N.Y. City, 1922-23, v.p., 1923-29; gen. mgr. Elec. Research Products, Inc. (subsidiary of Western Electric Co.), 1929-31; v.p. Erpi Picture Consultants, Inc., 1932-38. Served as major, Q.M.C., later col., Purchase, Storage and Traffic Div., Gen. Staff, U.S. Army, World War; col. O.R.C., 1921-39, now on hon. retired list; chairman Westchester County Defense Council, 1941, and dir. Civilian Protection, 1942. Trustee Village of Bronxville, N.Y., 1923-38, mayor, 1939-42. Spl. Asst. to chief of Tank-Automotive Center, U.S. Army, 1942-45; dep. dir. econ. div. U.S. Group Control Council for Germany, 1945-46; spl. mission to Japan and Korea, 1946; spl. asst. U.S. Mil. Gov. of Germany, 1947-48; dir. Massing of the Colors Assn.; mem. arbitration panel N.Y. Stock Exchange, 1939-42. Chmn. Westchester County Recruiting Com. for Citizens' Mil. Tng. Camps since 1924; pres. Bronx Valley Boy Scout Council, 1926; mem. New York Elec. Soc. (v.p. 1929), Telephone Pioneers of America, Am. Legion (past comdr. Bronxville Post), Quartermasters Assn. U.S. Army (v.p. 1919-28), Mil. Order World War (sr. vice comdr. N.Y. chpt. 1927), N.Y. Soc. Mil. and Naval Officers, Reserve Officers Assn. (v.p. for N.Y. 1923), Companion Ordnance Assn., Fgn. Policy Assn. Awarded medal for exceptional civilian service by War Dept. Republican. Roman Catholic. Club: Metropolitan (Washington). Author: (with others) The Educational Talking Picture; The Strings of Shotford. Originated and developed the talking picture for ednl. use. Contbr. to ednl. and tech. mags. Home: Farneffold, Callan, Va.

DEVEREUX, HELENA TRAFFORD (MRS. JAMES FENTRESS), found. cons.; b. Phila., Feb. 2, 1885; d. Arthur Trafford and Betsy (Blyton) Devereux; ed. Phila. Normal Sch., Temple U., U. Pa.; m. James Fentress (dec.). Founder, dir. Devereux Schs., in Devon, Berwyn, Paoli, Malvern, Glenmore (all Pa.), Santa Barbara, Cal., Atlanta, Ga., Tex., Mass., Conn. and Ariz.; adminstrv. cons., trustee bd. cons. to Devereux Found., which operates Devereux Schools for Dynamic Edn., also Dr. G. Henry Katz Research and Tng. Dept. and Dr. Clinton P. McCord Psychiat. Library. Named hon. citizen Tex. Hon. fellow Am. Physchiat. Assn. (life mem.), Phila. Assn. Psychoanalysis (affiliate), Psychoanalytic Soc. Phila. (affiliate), Am. Assn. Mental Deficiency (hon. life), P.E.O. Sisterhood, Delta Kappa Gamma (hon.). Address: Devon, Pa. Died Nov. 17, 1975.

DEVERS, JACOB LOUCKS, army officer; b. Sept. 8, 1887; s. Philip Kissinger and Ella (Loucks) D.; B.S., U.S. Mil. Acad., 1909; grad. Command and Gen. Staff Sch., 1925, Army War Coll., 1933; hon. Dr. U. of Nancy, France, 1945; LL.D., Williams Coll., 1946; Dr. Mil. Sci., Norwich U., 1947; D.H.L., York Coll., 1974; m. George Hays Lyon, Oct. 18, 1911; 1 dau., Frances L. Devers Graham; m. 2d, Dorothy C.B. Ham, 1975. Commd. 2d lt. F.A., U.S. Army, 1909, advanced through grades gen., 1945. Began as battery officer 4th F.A., 1909; instr. mathematics, U.S. Mil. Acad., 1912-16, instr. tactics, 1919-24, grad. mgr. athletics, 1936-38, exec. fiscal officer, 1938-39; service in France and Germany, 1919; various F.A. tng. assignments, 1920's and 30's; comdg. officer 16th F.A., 1934-36; chief of staff Panama Canal Dept., 1939-40; chief of Armored Force, 1941; comdg. gen. E.T.O., 1943, N.A.T.O. U.S.A., 1944; dep. supreme allied comdr., Mediterranean, 1944; comdg. gen. 6th Army Group, 1944-45, Army Ground Forces, 1945-48, chief Army Field Forces, 1948-49; retired Sept. 1949; mng. dir. A.A.A. Found. for Traffic Safety, 1950; tech. asst. to pres. Fairchild Engine & Airplane Corp., 1951-59. Chief mil. adviser U.N. mission to India and Pakistan, June-Dec. 1951, negotiations to settle Kashmir affair, Europe, Sept. 1952; chmn. Am. Battle Monuments Commn., 1959-69. Decorated D.S.M. with 2 Oak Leaf Clusters, Navy D.S.M., Bronze Star, World War I Victory medal with Fgn. Service Clasp, European-African-Middle East Campaign medal with 6 Bronze Service Stars, World War II Victory medal (U.S.); Knight Comdr. Order of Bath (Brit.); Grand Officer Legion of Honor, Croix de Guerre with palm (French); also decorations from Brazil, Poland, Chile, Egypt, Belgium, Mexico; recipient George C. Marshall medal, 1965, Benjamin F. Castle meml. award, 1976. Clubs: Army Navy, Cosmos (Washington). Home: Washington, D.C. Died Oct. 15, 1979; interred Arlington Nat. Cemetery.

DE VILLAFRANCA, GEORGE WARREN, educator; b. Meriden, Conn., Nov. 21, 1923; s. Jose Francisco and Ruth (Pease) de V.; B.S., Yale U., 1948, Ph.D., 1953; m. Suzanne E. Crane, July 26, 1947 (dec. Nov. 1960); children—Suzanne C., Ruth P., George W.; m. Diana E. Fetter, Dec. 28, 1974. Instr., R.I. State Coll., 1948; faculty zoology Smith Coll., 1951-77, prof. 1963-77, Gates prof. biol. scis., 1974-77, asst. to pres., 1961-66, 77, chmn. dept. biol. scis., 1968-72. Cons. NSF, 1968. Served with USAAF, 1943-46. Lalor Found. fellow, 1953, 56; Am. Cancer Soc. fellow, 1954-55. Mem. Am. Soc. Zoologists, Biophys. Soc., Soc. Gen. Physiologists, Am. Soc. Biol. Chemists, AAAS, Sigma Xi. Home: West Cummington, Mass. Died Dec. 25, 1977; buried West Cummington.

DEVINE, GREGORY S., ry. exec.; b. Rahway, N.J., Mar. 20, 1906; s. Gregory and Mary (Barry) D.; student St. Viator's Coll., Northwestern U. Medill Sch. Journalism; m. Ursula Baumann, Dec. 27, 1933; children—Barry, Jon, Suzi; v.p. coal traffic and devel. Chesapeake & Ohio Ry. Co., 1957-60, sr. v.p., 1960-63, exec. v.p., 1963-64, pres., 1964-71, dir., mem. exec. com., 1964-71, chief exec. officer, 1966-71, chmn. exec. com., 1971-81; pres., dir., chief exec. officer Balt. & Ohio R.R. Co. until 1971, chmn. bd., 1971-81; bd. dirs. Western Maryland Ry. Co., Western Pocahontas Corp., Washington & Old Dominion R.R., Nicholas, Fayette & Greenbrier Rd., Lake Erie Coal Co., Kanawha-Ohio Corp., Ft. St. Union Depot Co. Dir. Nat. Coal Policy Conf. Mem. Assn. of Am. RRs. Clubs: Chicago Athletic; Sky, Pinnacle (N.Y.C.); Union, Pepper Pike, Westwood Country, Clifton (Cleve.). Home: Cleveland, Ohio. Died Feb. 7, 1981.

DEVISSCHER, CHARLES, judge, International Court of Justice; b. Belgium, Aug. 2, 1884; s. Charles and Augusta (Fieve) DeV.; Doctor honoris causa Univs. of Paris, Nancy and Montpellier; m. Helen Mertens, May 10, 1910. Prof. of law (pub. internat. law and conflict of laws), Univ. of Ghent, 1911-30, Univ. of Louvain, 1930-37; elected judge of Permanent Court of Internat. Justice, 1937; judge Court of Internat. Justice since Feb. 1946. Mem. Belgian Govt. (minister without portfolio), 1944-45; head polit. com. of the Underground, 1942-44. Decorated Great Cross of the Order of the Crown of Belgium. Mem. Royal Acad. of Belgium, Inst. de France. Roman Catholic. Home: Brussels, Belgium.

DE VORE, NICHOLAS, editor; b. Enon, O., May 19, 1882; s. Elcharles Arthur and Ida (Gray) de V.; ed. prep. sch. of Union Christian Coll., 1895-96; Bucknell U., 1895-97; Central Coll. Phys. and Surgeons (Indianapolis), 1900-03; m. Jessie Monteze Jay, 1909 (div.); m. 2d, Louise Starr Conrad (dec.); children—Nicholas (major United States Air Force), Louise Starr (Mrs. Carl Payne Tobey); m. 3d, Olivette Cartier, 1936, (divorced); m. 4th, Blanche March Holdsworth, 1943. Mng. editor, Richmond (Ind.)

Enterprise, 1897-99; various work 1899-1926; mgr. musical and lit. research, Nat. Broadcasting Co., 1926-32; editor, The Musician, 1935-1948. Pres. Astrologic Research Soc.; founder Am. Musical Fellowship. Mason (K.T.). Episcopalian. Editor: Songs for Everyone, 1936; Piano Pieces for Everyone, 1938. Composer of songs, piano and violin pieces, anthems. Author: Ency. of Astrology (Philos. Library), 1947; New Frontiers of Psychology, 1949. Home: Orlando, Fla.

DEVRIES, LOUIS, coll. prof.; b. Bremen, Germany, May 21, 1885; s. Edward and Gesine (Dauelsberg) DeV.; came to U.S., 1891, naturalized, 1901; A.B., Central Wesleyan Coll., 1907; A.M., Northwestern U., 1908, Ph.D., 1918; student U. of Berlin, U. of Leipzig, U. of Ill., Columbia U., U. of Mich., U. of Chicago; m. Anna Brahms, July 11, 1912; children—Margaret Elizabeth, Donald Ketchem, Louise, Harold Arvidson. Professor of modern languages, Iowa State College, Ames, Iowa, since 1913. Member Phi Kappa Phi fraternity. Author textbooks, also German and French dictionaries, including: Essentials of Reading German (with A.P. Kehlenbeck), 1953; English-German Technical and Engineering Dictionary, 1953. Editor: Sandeau, Mademoiselle de la Seiglière, 1924; Bordeaux, La Maison, 1930; (with Laura Towne) Mérimée, Carmen, 1932; (with H.E. Biester) Poultry Diseases, 1943. Home: Ames, Ia.

DEVYVER, FRANK TRAVER, educator; b. Mt. Vernon, N.Y., May 14, 1904; s. Frank Oscar and Lillian Adith (Buchanan) deV.; A.B., Oberlin Coll., 1926, M.A., 1927; M.A., Princeton, 1930, Ph.D., 1935; m. Marion Anna Roth, June 28, 1928; 1 dau., Virginia Harriet. Research asst. in labor problems Inst. Research in Social Scis., U. Va., 1928-30; instr. econs. Princeton, 1930-35; instr. Duke U., 1935, asst. prof., 1937, asso. prof., 1939, prof. econs., 1942-74, prof. emeritus, 1974—, univ. disting. service prof., 1978—, chmn. dept. econs. and bus. adminstrn., 1957-64, vice provost, 1960-69, sec.-treas. Center for Comparative Fulbright lectr. U. Sydney Law Sch., 1956-57, U. Western Australia, 1964; vis. prof. U. Natal, summers 1964, 67; vis. lectr. Monash U., Australia, 1969, 72, 74; disting. vis. prof. Davidson Coll., fall 1979; trustee Joint Council Econ. Edn., 1962-70; part-time supr. merit examinations, State of N.C. 1938-56. Indsl. relations and personnel dir. Erwin Mills, Inc., Durham, N.C., 1942-55; v.p., 1945-55. Trustee Watts Hosp., Durham, N.C., 1967-71; mem. Durham County Hosp. Commn., 1971-78. Mem. Econ. History Assn., So. Econ. Assn. (pres. 1960-61), Indsl. Relations Research Assn., Phi Beta Kappa. Democrat. Presbyn. Home: Durham, N.C. Died May 11, 1980.

DEWAR, HENRY HAMILTON HAL, investment banker; b. Chgo., Mar. 26, 1902; s. Hamilton and Mary (Kinney) D.; A.B., U. Tex., 1923; m. Hallie Ball, Oct. 14, 1927; children—Robert Ball, Hallie Ball (Mrs. George Heyer), Marion Cooke (Mrs. Michael Bell). Engaged as employee of Guaranty Co. of N.Y., 1923-24, J.E. Jarratt Co., San Antonio, 1924-29; mgr. bond dept. Alamo Nat. Co., 1929-31; partner Dewar, Robertson and Pancoast, San Antonio, 1932-67, Hornblower & Weeks-Hemphill, Noyes, San Antonio, 1967-70. Chmn. Tex. Dist. Investment Bankers Conf., 1938-39; mem. Nat. Com. of Securities Industry for War Financing, 1942; mem. financial adv. com. Com. for Econ. Devel., 1945. Mem. N.Y. Stock Exchange, 1949-67, gov., 1958-61; mem. Am. Stock Exchange, 1949-67; mem. Assn. Stock Exchange Firms (bd. govs. 1950-52); mem. finance dept. com. U.S. C. of C.; mem. investment banking div. Voluntary Credit Restraint Com. Trustee; mem. bd. govs. S.W. Research Inst., 1954-75, vice chmn., 1962-66. Pres. United Fund of San Antonio, 1957; mem. Tex. Commn. on Higher Edn. (vice chmn. 1956-60); mem. Tex. Bd. of Edn. Investment Adv. Com., 1960; mem. Commn. on Goals for South Higher Edn., 1961; mem. So. Regional Edn. Bd., 1966-75. Mem. Investment Bankers Assn. Am. (v.p. 1944-48, pres. 1948-49, gov. 1943-50), Tex. Investment Bankers Assn. (pres. 1931-32), Nat. Assn. Securities Dealers (mem. bd. govs. and exec. com. 1940-42, chmn. 1942), Delta Tau Delta, Beta Gamma Sigma. Clubs: San Antonio Country, Order of Alamo, Argyle (San Antonio), Racquet and Tennis (N.Y.C.); Bohemian (San Francisco). Deceased. Home: San Antonio, Tex. Died July 2, 1975.

DEWDNEY, SELWYN HANINGTON, aboriginal art researcher; b. Prince Albert, Sask., Can., Oct 22 1909; s. Alexander Daniel and Alice Ashwood (Hanington) D.; B.A U. Toronto (Ont), 1931; postgrad. Ont. Coll. Edn., 1932; Asso. with Honors, Ont. Coll. Art, 1936; m. Irene Maude Donner, Oct. 3, 1936; children—Donner, Alexander Keewatin, Peter North, Christopher. High sch. tchr. sci., art, English, London, Ont., 1936-45; psychiat. art therapist Westminster Hosp., London, 1953-72; research asso. dept. new world archaeology Royal Ont. Mus, Toronto, 1966-79; sr. asso., co-founder Can. Rock Art Research Assos., Thunder Bay, 1969-79; lectr. on aboriginal art Ont. Coll. Art, 1975-79. Trustee, founding mem. Western Ont. Therapeutic Community Hostel, 1970-72. Research grantee Royal Ont. Mus., Quetico Found., Toronto, 1957-79, Glenbow-Alta. Inst., Calgary, 1960-72, Nat. Mus. Man, Ottawa, Ont., 1964-67, Can. Council, Ottawa, 1968-70. Author: (novel) Wind Without Rain, 1946; The Map that Grew, for children, 1960; Indian Rock Paintings of the Great Lakes, 1962; Sacred Scrolls of the Southern Ojibway, 1975; They Shared to Survive, 1975; (novel) Christopher Breton, 1978. Home: London, Ont. Canada. Died November 18, 1979; cremated.

DEWEERD, HARVEY A., hist. and def. cons.; b. Holland, Mich., Sept. 21, 1902; s. Walter and Gertrude (Arendsen) DeW.; A.B., Hope Coll., 1924; M.A., U. Mich., 1925, Ph.D., 1937; m. Nellie Kole, Aug. 5, 1926; children—Mary Jane, Evelyn K. Instr. Colo. State Coll., 1925-26; asst. prof. Mich. State Coll., 1926-28, Wittenberg Coll., 1928-29; asst., later asso. prof. Denison U., 1929-41; vis. asst. prof. U. Mich., 1939; vis. asso. prof. U. Mo., 1940, prof. from 1946, chmn. dept. history 1950-53; mem. Inst. Advanced Study, Princeton, N.J., 1941-42; cons. Rand Corp., 1952, 68-79, stall mem., 1953-67; cons. USAF, 1974-76. Served to lt. col., AUS, 1942-46; historian Operations Div., War Dept. General Staff, 1945-46. Mem. Am. Hist. Assn., Soc. Am. Historians, Am. Mil. Inst., AAUP, Assn. Author: Great Soldiers of the Two World Wars, 1941; Great Soldiers of World War II, 1944; World War II; A Concise History (with Roger Shugg), 1946; President Wilson Fights His War, 1968. Presbyn. Editor: Selected Speeches and Statements of General George C. Marshall, 1945; field editor: W. W. Norton & Co., N.Y.C., 1940-48. Home: Pacific Palisades, Calif. Died Nov. 22, 1979.

DEWEY, CHARLES SCHUVELDT, banker; b. Cadiz, O., Nov. 10, 1880; s. Albert B. and Louise (Schuveldt) D.; student St. Paul's Sch., Concord, N.H., 1896-1900; Ph.B., Yale, 1904; m. Suzette deM. Hall, Dec. 20, 1905 (dec. Dec. 1956); children—Suzette D. (Mrs. Frederick Alger) (dec.), Charles S., Louise (Mrs. Edward B. Smith), A. Peter (dec.); m. 2d, Elizabeth Zolnay Smith, June 3, 1959. Vice pres. No. Trust Co., Chgo., 1920-24; asst. sec. treasury charge fiscal affairs, 1924-27; financial adviser Republic Poland, 1927-31; dir. Bank of Poland, 1927-31, hon. life dir.; v.p. Chase Nat. Bank, 1945-50; agt. gen. Joint Congl. Com. Fgn. Econ. Cooperation, 1946-50; mem. Washington Nat. Monument Soc., 1960-81. Nat. treas. A.R.C., 1927, chmn. D.C. chpt., 1957-61, now mem. exec. com.; pres. Washington Hosp. Center, 1951-57; mem. adv. com. Export-Import Bank of Washington, 1947. Mem. U.S. Ho. of Reps. from 9th Dist. Ill., 1941-45. Served with USNRF, 1917-19. Decorated grand officer Legion of Honor (France); grand comdr. Polonia Restituta (Poland); grand comdr. Crown of Rumania; grand comdr. Order St. Sava (Yugoslavia). Mem. S.A.R., Delta Psi. Republican. Episcopalian. Clubs: Society of Cincinnati, Chevy Chase, Metropolitan, Alibi (Washington). Home: Washington, D.C. Died Dec. 25, 1980; buried Arlington Nat. Cemetery.

DEWEY, EDWARD RUSSELL, found. exec.; b. Elmira, N.Y., May 2, 1895; s. Edward Wilkins and Harriet (Russell) D.; S.B. cum laude, Harvard, 1920; m. Elenore Stratton, Sept. 22, 1922; children—Barbara, Edward; m. 2d, Catherine Doak, Feb. 13, 1935. Dir. Found. for Study of Cycles, 1940-67, exec. v.p., 1963-67, vice chmn., 1967-69, 73-78; pres., 1969-73; adj. research prof. acad. disciplines U. Pitts., 1965-78, co-dir. Center for Interdisciplinary Cycle Research, 1970-78; adminstr. Comité international de Recherche et d'Etude de Facteurs d l'Ambiance, association internationale á but scientifique, Brussels, 1968-78. Fellow World Acad. Art and Sci.; mem. Soc. Biol. Rhythm, AAAS, N.Y. Acad. Scis., Internat. Soc. Biometeorology, Soc. Mayflower Descs. Clubs: Faculty (Pitts.); Cosmos (Washington); Harvard (Pitts). Author: (with E.F. Dakin) Cycles: The Science of Prediction, (with Og Mandino) Cycles: Mysterious Forces That Trigger Events, Cycles: Selected Writings. Editorial bd. Jour. Interdisciplinary Cycle Research, from 1970. Contbr. articles to profl. jours. Home: Oakmont, Pa. Died Feb. 6, 1978.

DEWING, HENRY BRONSON, educator; b. Westminster, Conn., Mar. 2, 1882; s. Stephen and Eva Victoria (Lincoln) D.; B.A., U. of Calif., 1903, M.A., 1905; Ph.D., Yale U., 1908; L.H.D. from Bowdoin College, 1928; m. Eunice Dewing, 1910; children—Charles Edward, Elizabeth Ogden, Henry Lincoln (dec.), Stephen Bronson. Teacher of classics, high sch., Berkeley, Calif., 1904-06; instr. in Greek, Yale, 1907-08, in classics, Princeton, 1908-10; prof. Latin and dean Robert Coll., Constantinople, Turkey, 1910-16; asst. prof. classics, Princeton, 1916-18; sec. and commr. Am. Red Cross Mission to Greece, 1918-20; asst. prof. classics, Princeton, 1920-22; asso. prof. ancient langs., U. of Tex., 1922-23; prof. Greek, Bowdoin Coll., 1923-28; pres. Athens (Greece) Coll., 1927-31; visiting prof. ancient and modern langs., Colorado Coll., 1932-35; visiting prof. Latin, U. of N.C., 1935-36. Mem. Abracadabra, Phi Beta Kappa. Presented medal of Military Merit and Cross of the Savior, by Greece, 1920. Address: Princeton, N.J.

DEWITT, ROSCOE PLIMPTON, architect; b. Dallas, Feb. 18, 1894; s. Edgar A. and Imogene (Walker) DeW.; A.B., Dartmouth, 1914, M.A. (hon.), 1937; M.A. in Architecture, Harvard, 1917; m. Elizabeth Boyd Newcomb, 1943; children by previous marriage—Sylvia Louise (Mrs. Tom Ferguson), Elizabeth Frances (Mrs. Julian Acker). Architect, Parkland, Meml. Hosp., Neiman Marcus Preston Center, Neiman Marcus Dallas, Wynnewood Housing Project, Wynnewood and Preston Center Shopping Centers, Woodrow Wilson, Sunset high schs., So. Meth. U. adminstrn. bldg., stadium and library, Highland Park Meth. Ch. and High Sch., also schs. at Galveston, Harlingen, Temple, Denison, and other cities in Tex., Pampa (Tex.) Post Office, Sam Rayburn Library, Bonham, Tex., Carswell AFB Hosp., Sheppard AFB Hosp., Mil. Housing Project, Laughlin AFB, St. Vincent's Med. Center, Jacksonville, Fla., legislative garage, remodeling the Cannon House Office Bldg., D.C.; asso. architect extension of East front of Capitol, restoration of original Senate and Supreme Ct. chambers and James Madison Meml. Bldg. of Library of Congress, Washington, Mus. of Fine Arts, Dallas, Fed. Housing Group, Dallas, Robin Hood and Avion Village housing projects, Bay Front Med. Center, St. Petersburg, Fla.; office bldgs. Nat. Cash Register Co., Dallas, Republic Ins. Co., Los Angeles, Dallas, N.Y.C., St. Paul Hosp. Chapel, Convent and Clinic, Dallas, Presbyn. Hosp., Sub-acute Hosp. and Profl. Bldg., Dallas, Doctor's Found. Hosp., Dallas; asso. architect Hotel Dieu Hosp., New Orleans. Mem. adv. bd. Tex. Commn. on Arts and Humanities. Bd. dirs. Dallas Civic Opera. Served as 2d lt., capt. C.A.C., U.S. Army, World War I; capt. to lt. col. C.A.C., World War II. Fellow A.I.A. (past pres. Dallas chpt.), Soc. Am. Registered Architects; asso. personal mem. Am. Hosp. Assn.; mem. Internat. Hosp. Fedn., Am. Fedn. Arts, Tex. Soc. Architects, Soc. Am. Mil. Engrs., Royal Soc. Arts, Am. Assn. Hosp. Planning, Phi Deta Theta. Clubs: Dallas Country, Brookhollow Golf, City (Dallas); Harvard (N.Y.C.); Cosmos (Washington). Home: Dallas, Tex. Died Nov. 2, 1975.

DEXTER, DAVID LAWRENCE, educator, physicist; b. Ashland, Wis., July 2, 1924; s. Stephen T. and Mildred (Carlstrom) D.; B.S. in Math., Mich. State U., 1947; M.S., U. Wis., 1948, Ph.D. in Physics, 1951; m. Doris Grigsby, Sept. 4, 1948; children—Cecily, Diane, Philip (dec.), Jefferson, Pamina, Melanie. Research asso. U. Wis., 1950-51, U. Ill., 1951-52; cons. U.S. Naval Research Lab., 1952; prof. Inst. Optics and Physics, U. Rochester (N.Y.), 1952-81; vis. prof. U. Alexandria, 1960-61, U. Genoa, 1962-63, U. Rome, 1969-70; cons. numerous cos. and govt. agys. Served with USAAC, 1943-46. Recipient 1st Frank Isakson prize for outstanding contbns. to field of optical effects in solids, 1980. Fellow Am. Phys. Soc.; mem. Sigma Xi, Phi Kappa Phi, Pi Mu Epsilon, Sigma Pi Sigma. Author: (with others) Excitons; X-Ray Studies of Materials. Contbr. numerous articles to research publs. Research in solid state theory. Home: Rochester, N.Y. Died Mar. 29, 1981.

DEZENDORF, JAMES CORKISH, lawyer; b. Portland, Oreg., June 7, 1910; s. James N. and Hattie (Corkish) D.; LL.B., U. Oreg., 1932; m. Nancy Bennett Richards, Apr. 10, 1940; children—Elizabeth Ann, James Nelson, Lee Richards. Admitted to Oreg. bar, 1932, practiced in Portland; partner Dezendorf, Spears, Lubersky & Campbell and predecessor firms, Portland. Sec., dir. Nicholas Ungar, Inc., Beebe Co., Inc., Domestic Indsl. Gas. Co.; dir. MacDonald Andrews Co., Inc., Portland; v.p., dir. Chicona Farms, Inc., The Gile Investment Co. Mem. Nat. Conf. Commrs. Uniform State Laws, 1941-78, chmn. exec. com., 1955-57, pres., 1957-59; mem. U.S. delegation The Hague Conf. on Pvt. Internat. Law, 1960, 64, 68, 72; mem. Am. delegation to 2d Diplomatic Conf. on Internat. Sale of Goods, The Hague, 1964; Am. rep. Internat. Inst. for Unification of Pvt. Law, Rome, 1959, 63, 68; mem. U.S. delegation Diplomatic Conf. on Internat. Will, 1973; mem. adv. com. U.S. Sec. State on Pvt. Internat. Law, 1959-78; mem. permanent editorial bd. on Uniform Comml. Code, 1959-78. Trustee Inst. for Ct. Mgmt. Mem. Internat., Am., Multnomah bar assns., Ore. State Bar, Am. Law Inst. (dir.), Am. Judicature Soc. Clubs: Arlington, Astoria Golf and Country, Multnomah Athletic, Racquet, University, Waverley Country. Home: Portland, Oreg. Died Jan. 29, 1978.

D'HERMANOY, ALICE (STAGE NAME), soprano; b. Brussels, Belgium, Jan. 18, 1885; d. Jean Baptiste and Marie Therese (Gilson) Saintenoy; ed. in Belgium; m. 2d, Charles Henri Lauwers, May 4, 1921; 1 son, Marcel Hermans (by 1st marriage). Début in Brussels, 1910; sang in Liege, Covent Garden (London), Cairo 3 seasons, Geneva 4 seasons; with Chicago Civic Opera Co. since 1921. Naturalized citizen of U.S. Red Cross nurse in Switzerland, World War. Catholic. Home: Chicago, Ill.

DHONAU, CHARLES OTTO (DO-NAU), educator; born Cincinnati, Mar. 23, 1886; s. Charles Henry and Lillie Sarah (Gampper) D.; ed. pub. schs., Cincinnati; m. Edna Horn, Mar. 5, 1910; children—Charles John, Robert H. Trained as mortician, 1904-07; became prof. Cincinnati Coll. of Embalming, 1907 (introduced new teaching programs and calendar yr. courses), asst. to pres., 1907, pres. and dean, 1909; dir. North Side Bank & Trust Co., 1945. Dir. Cincinnati-Hamilton Co. chpt.

A.R.C., 1917-48, now hon. life dir. Mem. Nat. Assn. Coll. of Mortuary Sci. (pres. 1947-49), Nat. Fedn. Pvt. Sch. Assns. (gov. 1949-52), A.A.A.S., Nat. Funeral Dirs. Assn., Cin. C. of C. Episcopalian (sr. warden; lay reader since 1923). Mason. Clubs: Rotary (trustee Camp for Crippled Children since 1952), Kenwood country, Cincinnati (Cincinnati). Author of numerous books including Manual of Case Analysis, Personalities in Funeral Management; also articles profl. jours. Home: Cin.

DIAMOND, LEO AARON, lawyer; b. N.Y.C., Jan. 8, 1906; s. Morris Isaac and Sadie (Klugman) D.; Ph.B., U. Chgo., 1927, J.D. cum laude, 1929; m. Dora Sniderman, June 16, 1932 (dec. Oct. 1975); children—Diane (Mrs. Norman Bernstein), Joseph, Gail (Mrs. David M. Schwartz). Admitted to Ind. bar, 1929, Ill. bar, 1931, N.Y. State bar, 1944, D.C. bar, 1954; practiced in Ind. and Ill., 1929-34, N.Y.C., 1944-80; spl. asst. to chief counsel IRS, Washington, 1939-43; partner firm Austin, Diamond & Margolius, N.Y.C.; asso. prof. law Rutgers U. Law Sch., 1953-56; lectr. law N.Y. U., 1953-56, Practising Law Inst., 1943-73. Contbg. editor, Mertens Law of Fed. Income Taxation, 1953-60. Contbr. articles to profl. jours. Home: Chevy Chase, Md. Died May 5, 1980.

DIAMOND, MARTIN, educator; b. N.Y.C., Dec. 19, 1919; s. George and Rose (Desowitz) D.; A.M., U. Chgo., 1952, Ph.D., 1956; L.H.D., Hartford U., 1968; m. 2d, Ann Stuart Sheldon, Mar. 7, 1970; children—Katherine, Thomas, Diane Claire Sheldon. Instr., asst. prof. Ill. Inst. Tech., 1952-55; from lectr. to asst. prof. U. Chgo., 1952-58; faculty Claremont Men's Coll. and Claremont Grad. Sch., 1958-71, Wohlford prof. Am. polit. instns., 1963-71; prof. polit. sci. No. Ill. U., Dekalb, 1971-77. Mem. Nat. Adv. Council Am. Revolution Bicentennial Adminstrn., 1975-77. Served with U.S. Mcht. Marine, 1943-45. Center Advanced Study Behavioral Scis. fellow, 1960-61; Rockefeller fellow, 1963-64; Relm Found. fellow, 1966-67, Woodrow Wilson Internat. Center for Scholars fellow, 1974-75. Mem. Am., Midwestern polit. sci. assns. Author: (with W.M. Fisk, H. Garfinkel) The Democratic Republic, 1966, 2d edit., 1970; (with others) Essays in Federalism, 1961. Editor: (with M. Frisch) The Thirties: A Reconsideration, 1968. Home: Geneva, Ill. Died July 22, 1977.

DIAZ, JOAQUIN BASILIO, educator; b. Arecibo, P.R., Apr. 15, 1920; s. Joaquin Diaz de Haro and Juanita (Reina) D.; student Washington and Jefferson Coll., 1936-38; A.B., U. Tex., 1940; Ph.D., Brown U., 1945; m. Eleanore Ursillo, Sept. 30, 1944; children—Joan Marguerite, Ronald P. Asst. prof. math. Carnegie Inst. Tech., 1946-47, Brown U., 1947-50; research asso. Inst. Fluid Dynamics and Applied Math. of U. Md., 1950-51, asso. research prof., 1951-56, research prof., 1956-66; vis. prof. math. Mass. Inst. Tech., 1956-57; prof. math., chmn. dept. U. Calif. at Riverside, 1966-67; Albert Einstein prof. sci. and math. Rensselaer Poly. Inst., 1967-78. Cons. A.E.C., 1951-56, Naval Ordnance Lab., 1955-68; mem. com. basic research, advisory to U.S. Army Research Office, Nat. Acad. Sci.-NRC, 1964-70; mem. com. math., adv. to Office Naval Research, NRC, 1968-71. Mem. Am. Math. Soc. (council 1966-68), AAUP, Phi Beta Kappa, Sigma Xi. Asst. editor of proc. Am. Math. Soc., 1949-52, proc. Conf. Differential Equation, U. Md., 1955; mng. editor proc. contbns. to Partial Differential Equations, 1962-66; editor proc. Symposium on Fluid Dynamics and Applied Math., 1961; editorial bd. Jour. Math. and Mechanics, Ind. U., 1966-68, Applicable Analysis; an Internat. Jour., from 1970. Home: Loudonville, N.Y. Died June 16, 1978.

DICK, FAIRMAN ROGERS, banker; b. Philadelphia, Pa., Aug. 7, 1885; s. Evans Rogers and Elizabeth (Tatham) D.; prep. edn., St. Paul's Sch., Concord, N.H.; A.B., Harvard, 1907; m. Gladys Roosevelt, Nov. 25, 1913 (died Nov. 2, 1926); m. 2d, Mrs. Elise Urquhart Duggan, Dec. 28, 1928. Began in investment bond bus., 1908; ltd. partner Dick & Merle-Smith, investment bankers, N.Y. City; dir. B.&M. R.R., Atlas Assurance Co. Ltd., New York local board. Trustee Seamen's Bank for Savings. Mem. S.A.R. Mem. Squadron A, National Guard, N.Y., 1908-14; sergt. 1st Aero Co., National Guard, N.Y., 1916-17; served as capt. F.A., U.S.A., later maj., 1917-18. Clubs: Knickerbocker, Harvard, Piping Rock, Boone and Crockett, Down Town Assn. Home: Locust Valley, L.I., N.Y.

DICKERSON, CECIL HARROD, M.D.; b. Conway, Ark., Oct. 5, 1883; s. George Douglass and Sallie (Richardson) D.; A.B., Hendrix Coll., Conway, 1906; M.D., Washington U., 1910; m. Nina Martin, Nov. 25, 1914; children—Cecil Harrod, William Martin. Physician, Conway, Ark., since 1910; owner Doctors' Clinic, Physicians' and Surgeons' Pharmacy, both Conway. Served as med. mem. Federal Appeal Bd., Little Rock, Ark., during World War. Mem. A.M.A., Ark. State and County med. socs., Conway Chamber Commerce. Former pres. Rotary Club. Democrat. Methodist. Mason (32 deg.). Club: Conway Country. Home: Conway, Ark.

DICKERSON, JULIAN DOUGLAS, steel co. exec.; b. Willow Grove, Pa., Oct. 2, 1909; s. Edgar H. and Miriam (Marshall) D.; B.S. in Metall. Engring., Lehigh U., 1931; student exec. mgmt. Columbia, 1957, Businessmen's Conf. Internat. Understanding, American University, Washington, D.C., 1962; m. Edith Talbott, Mar. 2, 1935; children—Elizabeth M., Lee T. Chief metallurgist Republic Steel Corp., Buffalo, 1940-53; with Crucible Steel Co. of Am., Pitts., 1953-61, v.p. operations, 1958-61; assistant mgr. fgn. mgmt. dept. Koppers Co., Inc., 1961-62; general manager of operations Erie Forge & Steel Corporation, Erie, Pennsylvania, 1962-66; v.p. mfg. Chromium Mining and Smelting Corp., Montreal, Que., Can., 1966-67. Served with the Army United States, World War II. Mem. Am. Brit. iron and steel insts., Am. Ordnance Assn., Am. Soc. Testing Materials, Am. Inst. M.E., First Iron Works Assn., Chautauqua Lake Assn. (1st v.p, dir.). Republican. Presbyn. Clubs: Beaver Valley Country (Beaver Falls, Pa.); East Aurora (N.Y.) Country; Duquesne (Pitts.); Aviation Country of Erie. Home: Ashville, N.Y. Died Dec. 6, 1979.

DICKERSON, ROY ERNEST, social worker, author, lecturer; b. Versailles, Indiana, April 3, 1886; s. Charles Lincoln and Ida May (Harrell) C.; LL.B., Univ. of Denver, 1909; LL.M., George Washington U., Washington, D.C., 1910; m. Hallie Helen Hobbs, June 5, 1922; 1 son, Roy Hobbs. Admitted to Colo. bar, 1909; in practice at Denver, 1910-16; supervisor George W. Clayton Coll. for Boys, Denver, 1916-17; with Y.M.C.A. as boys' work sec., gen. sec., asso. state sec., World War; on staff Internat. Com., Y.M.C.A., 1917-23; nat. survey Mexican boy life, 1920-21; dir. of activities internat. hdqrs., Grand Council Order De Molay, Kan. City, 1923-40; consultant Am. Social Hygiene Assn., U.S.P.H.S., 1940-41; asst. dir. Div. Social Protection, Federal Security Agency, 1941; exec. dir. Cincinnati Social Health Society since 1941; associate dir. American Institute Family Relations. Acting asso. prof. Teachers College, Univ. of Cincinnati. Formerly volunteer probation officer under Judge Ben B. Lindsey, 2 years; mem. Am. Delegation 1st World Conf. Y.M.C.A. Workers With Boys, Portschach, Austria, 1923; mem. com. boys' work, recreation and phys. edn., White House Conf. on Child Health and Protection, 1929-30; dir. seminar, 3d World Conf. Y.M.C.A., Toronto, Can., 1931; cons. Nat. Conf. on Edn. for Marriage and Family Social Relations, New York City, 1934, conf. of Christian Youth Council of North America, Lakeside, O., 1936; YMCA World Conference Older Boys, Paris, 1955; cons. World Youth Conf. World Alliance YMCA, 1960, scout commr.; dir. Nat. Council on Family Relations, 1949-52 (chmn. sect. on edn. for family life, 1951-52); mem. Mid-Century White Conf. on Children and Youth; mem. bd. govs., exec. com. Adv. Council Hamilton County Juvenile Court; mem. bd. mgrs., department family life Nat. Council Chs., cons. Nat. Conf. on the Church and Social Welfare, 1955, 57; mem. Cin. Citizens Com. on Youth; mem. com. on high sch. youth of Nat. Council YMCA, P.T.A. (social hygiene chmn., mem. State bd. mgrs. Ohio State Congress, 1946-47, cons., 1948—. Hon. Legion of Honor, De Molay. Fellow A.A.A.S., Am. Pub. Health Assn., Royal Soc. Health (London); mem. Nat. Assn. Social Hygiene Executives (pres. 1950-56), Am. Social Health Assn. (mem. bd. dirs.; hon. life mem.), Nat. Conf. Family Relations, Kappa Sigma. Awarded Alumni prize, University of Denver (Law Sch.). Presbyn. (elder). Mason (32 deg., Knight Templar). Club: Torch. Author numerous books, 1919—, latest being: Sex and Sense, 1951; Pre-Induction Health Education Manuel (with Esther Sweeney), 1952; Into Manhood, 1954; also syndicated series, Understanding Myself. Contbr. gen. publs., jours. Address: Cin.

DICKEY, RAYMOND ROOSEVELT, lawyer; b. Washington, June 10, 1917; s. Raymond B. and Rose (Maxwell) D.; student George Washington U., 1934-36; LL.B., Southeastern U., 1940; m. Hilda Finch (div. 1975); children—Susan Jean (Mrs. Leslie Bonde), Diane, David Raymond, Douglas Finch, Christopher Bruce; m. Margaret Stevenson Lynch, Aug. 23, 1975. Admitted to D.C. bar, 1940, also U.S. Supreme Ct.; expert antitrust div. Dept. Justice, 1938-40; trade regulation, then Washington editor Research Inst. Am., 1940-42; partner Dickey & Dickey, 1940-42; editor in chief Modern Plastics mag., 1942-43; mgr. plastics div. Monroe Auto Equipment Co. (Mich.), 1943-44; partner firm Buckley & Danzansky, Washington, 1945-47; chief counsel U.S. Senate Small Bus. Com. 1947-49; spl. adviser to U.S. Ambassador Harriman under Marshall Plan, Paris, 1949-50; partner firm Danzansky & Dickey, Washington, 1950-53, 54-69; gen. counsel USIA, 1953-54; sr. partner firm Danzansky, Dickey, Tydings, Quint & Gordon, 1969-80, Dickey, Study Anti-trust Laws, 1953-55. Treas., dir., counsel San J panel USIA, 1954; pub. mem. inspection team USIS, Laos, Roadman & Dickey, 1980-81; mem. Atty. Gen.'s Com. to Study Anti-trust Laws, 1953-55. Treas., dir. counsel San Juan (P.R.) Racing Assn., 1954-81. Pub. mem. fgn. service selection panel USIA, 1954; pub. mem. inspection team USIS, Laos, 1971; chmn. real estate adv. com. SEC, 1972; bd. dirs. Met. Washington Bd. Trade, 1971-81, chmn. Human Devel. Bur., 1976, gen counsel, 1977-81. Served with AUS, 1943. Mem. Delta Tau Delta. Republican. Episcopalian. Clubs: Nat. Lawyers, Nat. Press, Internat. 1925 F St. (Washington); Dorado Beach Golf and Tennis (P.R.) Home: Washington, D.C. Died Feb. 20, 1981.

DICKEY, UBERTO M., business exec.; b. Long Lake, Minn., 1876. Vice pres., dir., Northern Commercial Company; honorary vice president of Scott Paper Co.; mem. bd. directors Marine Bank Corp., Pacific Am. Fisheries, Inc., Pacific Nat. Bank, Puget Sound Power & Light Co. Home: Seattle.

DICKINSON, EDWIN WALTER, artist, painter; b. Seneca Falls, N.Y., Oct. 11, 1891; s. Edwin Henry and Emma Sofia (Carter) D.; professional art student Pratt Inst., Art Students League of N.Y., Nat. Acad. of Design, 1910-13; pupil of William M. Chase and Chles W. Hawthorne, 1912-14; studied in Paris, 1919-20; m. Frances Foley, Oct. 31, 1928; children—Helen F., Edwin C. Instr. painting and drawing Buffalo Fine Arts Acad., 1915; instr. Art Student League of N.Y., 1922-23 and since 1945; instr. Stuart School, Boston, 1940-41; instr. Assn. for music and art on Cape Cod, 1942; instr. Art Inst. of Buffalo, 1939; instr. Cooper Union, 1945-49, Art Sch. Bklyn. Museum 1949-78, Columbia, 1957. Exhibited The Carnegie Internationals, Mus. of Modern Art, Luxembourg Mus., Paris, 1920. Had one-man exhbns. Albright Art Gallery, Buffalo, 1926; Wood Meml. Gallery, Rochester, 1940; Farnsworth Mus., Wellesley Coll., 1941; Passedoit Gallery, N.Y.C., 1936-43; Mus. Modern Art. Represented in permanent collections Mus. Modern Art, Bowdoin Coll., Albright Art Gallery, Mus. of Fine Arts (Springfield, Mass.), Met. Mus. of Art, N.A.D., others. Served as radio operator U.S. Navy, 1917-19. Awarded 2d Altman prize by Nat. Acad. Design, 1929, 1st prize portrait, 1949, grant for art, Nat. Inst. of Arts & Letters, 1954, Medal for Art, The Century Assn., 1956; Benjamin Altman prize for landscape, 1958; Medalist Brandeis U., 1959, Artists Fellowship, 1962; Ford Found. grant for art, 1959; Brevoort-Eickenmeyer prize Columbia Univ., 1965. Mem. Nat. Institute Arts and Letters (v.p.), Fed. Modern Painters and Sculptors, Artists Equity Assn., N.A.D., Am. Acad. Arts and Letters. Clubs: The Beachcombers (Provincetown, Mass.); The Patteran (Buffalo). Home: New York City, N.Y. Died Dec. 2, 1978; cremated.

DICKINSON, FRANK WATT, dean emeritus; born Howells, Neb., Feb. 12, 1886; s. Reuben and Alice (Parsons) D.; A.B., U. of Neb., 1911, A.M., 1912; Sage scholar in philosophy, Cornell U., 1912-13; Ph.D., U. of Chicago, 1929; Dr. Humane Letters, U. Denver, 1953; married Minnie Funke, Aug. 12, 1914; children—Richard Funke, Edward Henry, David James. Professor philosophy and education and head of dept., Kingfisher (Oklahoma) College, 1913-17, also dean of College of Liberal Arts, 1915-17; prof. philosophy and head of dept. U. of Denver, 1917-50, dean coll. arts and sci., 1950-53, prof. emeritus, dean emeritus coll. arts and scis. since 1953, assistant dir. Summer School, 1934-35, 36, 37; teacher, Denver Community Training Sch. for Religious Edn., 1920-24. Mem. Neb. State Militia, 1905-07. Mem. American Philos. Assn. (member exec. com. Western Div. 1939-40), Colo. Schoolmasters Club. Methodist. Home: Denver.

DICKINSON, SIDNEY EDWARD, painter; b. Wallingford, Conn., Nov. 28, 1890; s. Charles Henry and Mary Lord (Thorn) D.; studied under George Bridgman and William M. Chase, Art Student's League, New York, and under Douglas Volk, Nat. Acad. Design; m. Mary Watson, August 1, 1928; children—Thorn Watson, Nathaniel Rogers. Instr. Art Students' League, 1919-20 and from 1943; instr. New Sch. of Design, 1924-26, Nat. Acad. Design, 1928-30, 1939-42. Represented in permanent collection, Corcoran Gallery, Washington, D.C., by Portrait of the Artist; Art Inst. Chgo., Unrest; City Art Museum, St. Louis, The Young Painter; Houston Art Mus., Portrait of the Artist; Davenport Municipal Gallery, Mary; The Allentown (Pa.) Museum, Mary and The Studio; portrait of Mrs. High, High Mus. Art, Atlanta; portrait Samuel H. Kress, Nat. Gallery, Washington; also represented permanent collection Dallas Mus. Awarded 3d Hallgarten prize NAD, 1917; Phila. prize Pa. Acad. Fine Arts, 1923; Popular prize Corcoran Gallery, 1924; 1st Hallgarten prize NAD, 1924; Beck gold medal Pa. Acad. Fine Arts, 1924; Bronze medal, Allied Artists Am., 1929; Walter Lippincott prize Pa. Acad., 1931; 1st prize Nat. Arts Club, 1932; Maynard portrait prize NAD, 1933; 1st Altman prize NAD, 1936; medal of honor Allied Artists Am., 1937; Maynard portrait prize NAD, 1938; Carnegie prize NAD, 1942. A.N.A., 1921, N.A., 1927; hon. mention Carnegie Inst., 1948; Century Assn. medal, 1959. Mem. Allied Artists Am., Nat. Inst. Arts and Letters, Century Assn., Lotos Club. Home: Windsor, Vt. Deceased.

DICKINSON, WILLIAM BOYD, govt. ofcl., newspaper editor; b. Kansas City, Mo., May 18, 1908; s. William Boyd and Alice G. (Hillman) D.; A.A., Kansas City Jr. Coll., 1927; A.B., U. Kans., 1929; Nieman fellow Harvard, 1939-40; m. Aileen Robinson (dec.); m. 2d, Joan S. Younger; children—William Boyd III, Beverly Dickinson Albertson, Theresa Joan, Rosalind Alice Dickinson Babcock, Diana Mary. Reporter Kansas City Star, 1929-30; with U.P.I.,

1930-49, successively mgr. burs., Denver, Mpls., N.Y.C., bus. rep., Chgo., news editor, London, S.W. Pacific mgr. and war corr., 1930-47, fgn. news editor, N.Y.C., 1947-49; with Phila. Evening and Sunday Bull., 1949-78, news editor, Washington bur. chief, asso. city editor, 1949-56, asst. mng. editor, 1956-59, mng. editor, 1959-69, exec. editor, 1969-73; mem. U.S. Privacy Protection Study Commn., 1975-77. Mem. Asso. Press Mng. Editors Assn. (past pres.), Am. Soc. Newspaper Editors (dir.), Phila. Press Assn., Sigma Delta Chi, Delta Tau Delta. Clubs: Nat. Press (Washington); Franklin Inn, Peale (Phila.). Home: Philadelphia, Pa. Died Sept. 12, 1978.

DICKSON, EVELYN WIGHT (MRS. CARROLL J. DICKSON), civic worker; b. Bklyn., Dec. 16, 1899; d. J. Sherman and Ida (Robins) Wight; student Bryn Mawr Coll., 1916-18; m. Carroll J. Dickson, Sept. 27, 1932; 1 dau., Patricia D. Tappan. Chmn. Bklyn. chpt. ARC. Nurses Aides, 1942-45; dir. Vis. Nurses Assn. Bklyn., 1946-70; dir. Bklyn. Inst. Arts and Scis., 1948-78; governing com. Bklyn. Children's Mus., 1948-78, chmn. com., 1960-68; sec. finance chmn. Nursing Service Com. for Civil Def., Greater City N.Y., 1952-55; chmn. Sch. Nursing Com., L.I. Coll. Hosp., Bklyn., 1952-54; governing mem. Bklyn. Acad. Music, 1955-67; women's com. chmn. Boston Symphony Orch. Concerts in Bklyn., 1955-58; dir. State League Nursing, 1956-58. Mem. Nat. Council Women U.S., 1956-59. Club: Civitas of Bklyn. (pres. 1953-55). Address: Brooklyn, N.Y. Died Nov. 21, 1979.

DICKSON, FRANK DAKE, surgeon; b. Pittsburgh, Pa., Nov. 11, 1882; s. Thomas C. D.; M.D., U. of Pa., 1905; m. Mrs. Mary Crowe Neal, July 30, 1922; 1 dau. Prof. clin. surgery, Univ. of Kansas Med. Sch.; orthopedic surgeon St. Luke's and Kansas City Gen. hosps., Providence Hosp., Kansas City, Kan. Fellow Am. Coll. of Surgeons; mem. Am. and Mo. State med. assns., Am. Orthopaedic Assn., Am. Surgical Assn., Western Surg. Assn., Am. Acad. Orthopaedic Surgeons, Internat. Orthopaedic Assn., Southern Surg. Assn., Internat. Surg. Assn. Republican. Episcopalian. Author: Posture In Relation to Health. Co-author: Functional Disorders of the Foot. Home: Kansas City, Mo.

DICKSON, THOMAS WYATT, univ. prof.; b. Raeford, N.C., Nov. 3, 1884; s. Albert Pickett and Frances Wyatt (DeVane) D.; A.B., U. of N.C., 1907, A.M., 1909; Ph.D., Johns Hopkins, 1913; m. Kathryn Braddy, Aug. 19, 1910; m. 2d, Irene Cadzow, Nov. 4, 1938. Instr. in Latin, Notre Dame of Maryland, 1912-13, Syracuse U., 1913-14; prof. Greek, Theil Coll., Greenville, Pa., 1914-19; asso. prof. Latin, Syracuse U., 1919-30, prof., 1930-50, ret. Republican. Presbyn. Home: Syracuse, N.Y.

DIECKHOFF, HANS HEINRICH (DEK'HOF), German ambassador to U.S.; b. Strassburg, Alsace, Dec. 23, 1884; s. Heinrich and Anna (Siebler) D.; studied law at univs. of Lausanne, Oxford, Munich, Berlin, Strassburg; J.D., U. of Marburg; m. Eva Jenke, of Constantinople, Sept. 1, 1917; 1 dau., Charlotte. Attache, Fgn. Office, Berlin, 1912, German Legation, Tangiers, Morocco, 1914, German Embassy, Constantinople, 1916-18, Fgn. Office, Berlin, 1919; German consulate gen. Valparaiso, Chile, 1920-31; counselor of Legation, Lima, Peru, 1921, Prague, Czechoslovakia, 1921-22; counsellor or Embassy, Washington, D.C., 1922-27, London, 1927-30; at Fgn. Office, Berlin, in charge Anglo-Saxon Dept., 1930-35, in charge Polit. Dept., 1935-36, in charge Undersecretary of State's duties, 1936-37; German ambassador to U.S. since May 1937. Served as lieut. German Army, Western Front, Eastern Front, Mesopotamia, 1914-16. Decorated with Iron Cross; awarded decorations from various countries. Clubs: Metropolitan, Burning Tree (Washington, D.C.). Address: Berlin, W. Germany.

DIEFENBAKER, JOHN GEORGE, prime minister Can.; b. Grey County, Ont., Can., Sept. 18, 1895; s. William Thomas and Mary Florence (Bannerman) D.; B.A., U. Sask., 1915, M.A., 1916; LL.B., 1919; LL.D., McMaster U., Dartmouth, McGill U., U. B.C., U. N.B., St. Mary's U., Wesleyan U., Laval U., U. Punjab, U. Delhi, U. Toronto, Royal Mil. Coll., Ont., U. Montreal, Mich. State U., Princeton, Assumption U., Wayne State U. Meml. U., St. Johns, Nfld., U. Alta.; Dr. Sacred Letters, Victoria Coll, Toronto; D.C.L., U. Western Ont., Mount Allison U., Depauw U., Acadia U., U. Sask., Bishop's U., Litt.D., Dropsie Coll.; D.Hum., Okla. U., m. Edna May Brower, June 29, 1929 (dec. 1951); m. 2d, Olive Evangeline Freeman Palmer, 1953 (dec. Dec. 1976). Called to Sask. bar, 1919, B.C., 1951, Alta., 1954, Upper Can. (Ont.), 1959; created King's Counsel, Sask., 1929, Ont., 1959; practiced in Prince Albert, Sask., 1922-57; Mem. Queen's Privy Council Can., 1957-79, Imperial Privy Council, 1957-79. Active polit. field, 1925-79; elected mem. Ho. of Commons, 1940, 45, 49, 53, 57, 58, 62, 63, 68, 72, 74; prime minister Can., 1957-63; leader of Opposition, 1963-67. Adviser Canadian Conservative Party of UN orgn., San Francisco, 1945; Canadian Parliament del. chmn. Parliamentary Assn. Conf. Ottawa, 1943, del., Bermuda, 1946, New Zealand, Australia, 1949; mem. NATO Parliamentary Conf., Paris, 1955. Hon. freeman City of London (Eng.); hon. fellow Bar Ilan U., Israel. Chancellor U. Sask. Served as lt. C.E.F., overseas, 1916-17. Decorated Companion of Honour. Fellow Royal Soc. Arts, Royal Soc. Can., Royal Archtl. Inst. Can.; mem. Canadian Bar Assn. (v.p. 1934-42), Law Soc. Man. (hon.), Law Soc. Upper Can. (hon. bencher), Illustre Nacional Colegio de Abogados (hon.), Gray's Inn (hon. bencher). Baptist. Mem. Progressive Conservative Party. Mason (33 deg., Shriner). Kiwanian. Author: One Canada; the Tumultuous Years, 1977. Address: Ottawa, Ont., Canada. Died Aug. 16, 1979.

DIEFFENBACH, RUDOLPH, dir. of biol. studies; b. Westminster, Md., Dec. 25, 1884; s. Ferdinand Albert and Jeannette Rix (Frankforter) D.; student Baltimore (Md.) City Coll., 1901-05; B.F., Biltmore (N.C.) Forest Sch., 1908; m. Anne Louise Molitor, Oct. 17, 1922; children—Karl Christian, Albert Woodson, Rudolph Jacob, Ann, Philip and Paul (twins). Began as junior forester, U.S. Forest Service, 1908, detailed to western U.S. on land classification and forest boundary surveys; dep. forest supervisor, Nev. Nat. Forest, 1910-12; organizer and dir. cadastral surveys of nat. forests in White, Ozark and Appalachian mts., 1912-20; in charge examination and appraisal land for nat. forests in eastern U.S., 1920-24; forest and land valuation engr. since 1924, valuation engr. since 1929, principal valuation engr. since 1941; biol. survey, Fish and Wildlife Service, since 1939; in charge acquisition Upper Miss. River Wild Life and Fish Refuge and Bear River Migratory Bird Refuge, 1925; organizer and dir. appraisal and acquisition of land for nation-wide system of wild life refugees since 1929; sec. Migratory Bird Conservation Commn. since 1930; chief div. Lands, coordinator River Basin Studies, 1945. Sr. mem. Soc. Am. Foresters, mem. The Wildlife Society. Unitarian. Mason. Author of tech. handbooks on surveys, examination and valuation of lands, etc., pub. by Dept. of Agr. Home: Bethesda, Md.

DIEHL, WALTER STUART (DEL), naval officer; b. Jonesboro, Tenn., Dec. 3, 1893; s. William Polk and Lydia (Showalter) D.; B.S. in Elec. Engring., U. of Tenn., 1915; grad. study in aeronautical engring., Mass. Inst. Tech., May-Sept. 1918; m. Zulime Summers, Mar. 21, 1923; children—Zulime Whitney, Walter Colburn. Engr. The Fulton Co., Knoxville, Tenn., 1915-17; enlisted in U.S. Navy, Aug. 1917; Aviation Ground Sch., Mass. Inst. Tech., Nov. 1917-Feb. 1918; flight training, Pensacola, Feb.-May 1918; commd. ensign U.S. Naval Reserve, July 1918, lt., U.S. Navy, 1920, comdr., 1938, capt., 1942; specialist on airplane design and research and applied aerodynamics. Mem. aerodynamics com. and several sub. coms. Nat. Adv. Com. for Aeronautics. Fellow Institute of Aeronautical Sciences; mem. Am. Rose Soc., Tau Beta Pi. Mason (32 deg.). Clubs: National Sojourners, Potomac Appalachian Trial. Author: Engineering Aerodynamics, 1928 and 1936. Contbr. to tech. jours. Home: Washington, D.C. Died Nov. 21, 1976.

DIEHM, VICTOR CHRISTIAN, broadcasting exec.; b. Sparrows Point, Md., Nov. 7, 1902; s. Christian O'Brien and Mary (Hackman) D.; student U. Md., 1925, Peabody Conservatory Music, 1925; Dr. Art of Oratory, Staley Coll., 1954; m. Hazel Virginia Loose, Dec. 19, 1936; children—Elizabeth Anne (Mrs. Richard I. Bernstein), Victor Christian. Entered radio broadcasting in Balt., 1926; with Steinman Group, Lancaster, Pa., 1931-46; owner WAZL and WVCD-FM, Hazleton, Pa., 1946-80; formed Vic Diehm Radio Group, 1948, operated radio stas. in Biddeford, Me., Boston, Allentown, Pa., Meadville, Pa., Tallahassee, Fla., 1948-60; pres., chief exec. officer MBS, N.Y.C., 1969-72; v.p. Pocono Downs Raceways, Inc. Mem. Pa. Indsl. Devel. Authority, 1955-80; Pa. lay del. Nat. Am. Cancer Soc. Bd., 1971-80. Candidate Pa. Senate, 1966. Past trustee Bloomsburg (Pa.) State Coll. Recipient Coronet Mag. award for outstanding pub. service, 1950, VFW Nat. award for distinguished local service, 1962, Bronze medal ACS; named Pa. Broadcasters ambassador of good will; Vic Diehm Day in Pa. proclaimed by gov., Nov. 6, 1969, also day in his honor, June 10, 1972. Mem. Nat. (dir.), Pa. (past pres.) assns. broadcasters, Radio Advt. Bur. (chmn. 1963-64), Pa. C. of C. (past pres.). Methodist. Mason (Shriner, Jester), Elk, Kiwanian. Home: Conyngham, Pa. Died Aug. 17, 1980.

DIEKHOFF, JOHN SIEMON, educator; b. Ann Arbor, Mich., Oct. 23, 1905; s. Tobias Johann Casjen and Julia Catherine (Schacht) D.; A.B., U. Mich., 1926, M.A., 1927; postgrad. Oxford U., 1927-28; Ph.D., Western Res. U., 1937; L.H.D., Rutgers U., 1959; m. Vera Ethel Johnston, Dec. 20, 1929. Instr. rhetoric U. Mich., 1928-29; instr. English, Oberlin Coll., 1929-40; asst. asso. prof. English, Queens Coll., 1940-51; dir. Center for Study Liberal Edn., Chgo., 1951-53; prof. edn., dir. instnl. research Hunter Coll., 1953-56; dean Cleve. Coll., Western Res. U., 1956-63; prof. higher edn. U. Mich., Ann Arbor, 1963-65; prof. English, asso. dean faculty Western Res. U., Cleve., 1965-67, acting dean Grad. Sch., 1967; vice provost Case Western Res. U., 1967-70, prof. emeritus, 1970-76; vis. lectr., prof., univs. Louisville, Mich., Chgo. Research cons. bd. higher edn., N.Y.C., 1947, 50; mem. commn. trends in edn. Modern Language Assn., 1954-57, mem., chmn., 1965-70; cons., staff asso. N.Y. state com. White House Conf. Edn., 1956; mem. governing bd. Center Study Liberal Edn. for Adults, 1956-59; mem. commn. colls. and univs. North Central Assn., 1958-65. Served from pvt. to capt. AUS, 1943-46. Rockefeller Found. fellow humanities, 1948-49. Mem. Modern Lang. Assn., Milton Soc. Am. (pres. 1957-58), Coll. English Assn., Nat. Council Tchrs. English, Theta Chi, Phi Delta Kappa, Phi Kappa Phi. Author: Milton on Himself, 1939; Milton's Paradise Lost, A Commentary, 1946; Democracy's College, 1950; The Domain of the Faculty, 1956; (with Marjorie B. Smiley) Prologue to Teaching, 1959; A Maske At Ludlow, 1968; (with Ida Long Rogers) Private Higher Education in Tennessee, 1970. Editorial bd. Prose Works of John Milton, 1948-62, 65-76. Home: Shaker Heights, Ohio. Died Aug. 20, 1976.

DIEMAND, JOHN ANTHONY, insurance; b. Phila., Pa., Jan. 19, 1886; s. Francis and Margaret (Elchele) D.; student Girard Coll., Phila., 1894-1908; LL.D., Jefferson Med. Coll. and Med. Center, 1951, Bucknell U., 1955, St. Joseph's Coll., 1956, U. Pa., 1957; D.Sc. in Commerce, Drexel Inst. Tech., 1951; Doctor of Science, Habnemann Medical College, 1960; m. Mabel Cameron, June 30, 1909; children—Christine Cameron (Mrs. H. W. Kuehn), John Anthony. Stenographer Phila. Casualty Co., 1904-10; Fidelity & Deposit Co., 1910-13; Surich Gen. Accident & Liability Ins. Corp., 1913-28; Home Indemnity Co., 1928-33; exec. v.p. Indemnity Ins. Co. of North America, 1933-41; v.p. Ins. Co. of North America, 1938-41, pres., 1941-61, chmn. bd., chief exec. officer, 1961-64, former chmn. exec. com. dir.; chmn. bd., chmn. exec. com., chief exec. officer Life Ins. Co. N. Am., 1961-74; pres., dir. Old Phila. Redevel. Corp., dir. Phila. Electric Co., Central Penn. Nat. Bank, Phila. Saving Fund Soc. Trustee Abington Meml. Hosp.; trustee Temple U., Girard Coll., Williamson Free Sch. of Mech. Trades. Recipient George Henry Ryne award Fedn. Ins. Counsel, 1936; Isaiah Van Sant Williamson award, 1957; Powell award, 1959; Nat. award Nat. Conf. Christians and Jews, 1955; Gold Medal award Pennsylvania Society, 1959. Republican. Mem. Ref. Ch. Clubs: Union League, Racquet (Phila.); Drug and Chem., India House (N.Y.); Rittenhouse. Home: Buckingham, Pa. Died Aug. 11, 1974.

DIENNER, JOHN ASTOR, patent lawyer; b. Elkhart, Ind., Sept. 22, 1886; s. Christian King and Susan (Christophel) D.; ed. pub. schs., Elkhart; B.S. in Elec. Engring., Purdue U., 1910, E.E., 1913, hon. Dr. Engring, 1939; LL.B., George Washington U., 1913; studied patent law Georgetown U., M.L.D., 1913; LL.D., John Marshall Law Sch. Chgo., 1960; m. Pearl J. Calhoun, July 27, 1915; children—John Astor, Jr., Ann Calhoun. Began in employ of Home Telephone Co., 1904; with signal dept., N.Y. Central R.R., 1903-06; Union Switch & Signal Co., 1908-09; with Gen. Electric Co., 1910; asst. examiner U.S. Patent Office, 1910-14; practiced law with Brown, Hanson & Boetteher, 1914-19; mem. Brown, Boettcher & Dienner, 1919-27; mem. firm Brown, Jackson, Boettcher & Dienner, 1927-69, Johnson, Dienner, Emrich, Verbeck & Wagner, 1969-79. Dir. Purdue Research Found. (Lafayette, Ind.); mem. patent adv. panel, AEC, 1960. Mem. Patent Office Adv. Com., 1960; del. of U.S. to Conf. for Revision of Internat. conv. for Protection of Indsl. Property by negotiation of a new treaty, London, 1934; accredited rep. of U.S. to German Govt. for Berlin Congress of AIPPI, 1936. Apptd. by Sec. Hopkins, spl. counsel for Dept. of Commerce to present evidence on the U.S. Patent System before the Temp. Nat. Econ. Com., 1939; cons. Dept. of Commerce, 1942-43; mem. penicillin adv. com. for OSRD, 1944; spl. lectr. John Marshall Law Sch., 1941-67, trustee, 1960-68. Fellow Royal Soc. London; mem. Newcomen Soc. London, Am. Inst. of Chemists, Am. Inst. E.E., Chgo. Patent Law Assn. (pres. 1936), Am. Patent Law Assn. (pres. 1945), Am. Bar Assn. (chmn. patent sect., 1942-43), Internat. Assn. for Protection of Indsl. Property (mem. bd. dirs. 1934-35, pres. 1935-43), Am. Judicature Soc., Acad. Polit. Sci. (life), Franklin Inst., Western Soc. Engrs., Nat. Rifle Assn. (life), Delta Tau Delta (life mem. pres. Chgo. Alumni chpt. 1938), Phi Delta Phi, Tau Beta Pi, Eta Kappa Nu (hon.). Republican. Episcopalian. Clubs: Union League Chgo.; University (Evanston). Home: Evanston, Ill. Died Apr. 29, 1979.

DIES, EDWARD JEROME, author, publicist; b. nr. Springfield, Oreg., May 23, 1891; s. Allen and Martha (Hilton) D.; ed. pub. schs. and under pvt. tutor; studied finance and economics two years; m. Mareeta Cole, May 29, 1912; 1 son, Douglas. Corr. United Press Assn., 1910-11; staff corr. A.P., 1911-19; reported anti-govt. activities, World War; spl. writers Canadian govt., Canadian rys. and Hudson's Bay Co., 1920-21; publicity advt. counsel Chgo. Bd. of Trade, 1922-35; owner and editor Nat. Syndicate Service, officer and pub. relations adviser to various corps. and assns., 1922-79; econ. cons. to industries. Dir. Fedn. of Am. Bus., 1931-33; mem. bd. govs. Nat. Farm Chemurgic Council, 1941-55; mem. Cereal Industries Com. of Fed. Food Adv. Bd., 1942-43; mem. nat. panel of arbitrators, Am. Arbitration Assn., N.Y., 1948-79. Fellow Royal Econ. Soc., London, Internat. Inst. Arts and Letters; mem. Huguenot Soc., Am. Acad. Polit., Soc. Sci., Am. Econ. 1948-79, Am. Soc. Internat. Law, Authors League Am.,

Soc. Midland Authors, S.R., Hereditary Order Descs. of Colonial Govs., Pi Gamma Mu. Episcopalian (vestryman). Clubs: Union League (mem. bd. of dirs. 1938-41) (Chgo.); Nat. Press, Capitol Hill (Washington); City Tavern (Georgetown). Author: The Wheat Pit, 1925; Solving the Form Riddle, 1926; The Plunger, 1929; Skylines (short history arch.), 1930; Where Trade Tides Converge (Brochure), 1930; Der Speculant (hist. novel pub. in Germany), 1931; Street of Adventure, 1935; Soybeans: Gold From The Soil, 1942; Titans of The Soil, 1949 (pub. in various Oriental langs. through Dept. State); Behind the Wall Street Curtain, 1952. Contbr. to gen., financial and bus. mags. Home: Arlington, Va. Died June 17, 1979; interred St. John's Ch., Washington.

DIEZ DE MEDINA, EDUARDO, ambassador; b. La Paz, Bolivia, Feb. 8, 1882; s. Federico and María (Lértora) Diez de M.; ed. U. of La Paz; m. Etelvina Guachalla, of La Paz, Bolivia, July 12, 1906; children—Fernando, Raul, Maria Hortensia, Gabriela. Began as asst. undersec. of state, Bolivia, 1898; successively undersec., acting sec. and sec. of state until 1923; minister to Paraguay, 1918, Uruguay, 1919, Argentina, 1924, Chile, 1926, Peru, 1927; E.E. and M.P. to U.S., Washington, D.C., since 1928. Author of 20 books, chiefly on internat. relations. Address: Washington, D.C.

DI FALCO, SAVERIO SAMUEL, judge; b. Italy, July 26, 1906; s. Antonino and Rose (Bonanno) Di F.; came to U.S., 1907, naturalized, 1909; B.C.S., N.Y. U., 1928; LL.B., 1930; m. Emma G. Sutera, Nov. 22, 1936; children—Anthony, Elisa. Admitted to N.Y. state bar, 1930; atty. for U.S. Govt., 1935-39; mem. City Council, N.Y.C., 1941-48; justice Supreme Ct., 1st Judicial Dept., 1948-56; surrogate Surrogate's Ct., N.Y.C., 1956-78, adminstrv. judge, 1967-78. Nat. chmn. Nat. Italian-Am. League to Combat Defamation, Inc., 1959-78. Del., N.Y. State Constl. Conv., 1967. Bd. dirs. Verrazzano Coll. Found., Italian Hosp.; trustee N.Y. Inst. Tech.; chmn. bd. govs. Columbus Citizens Com., Young Mens Philanthropic; mem. adv. bd. Columbus Hosp. Recipient Benjamin N. Cardozo award Anti-Defamation League of B'nai B'rith, 1970, Rapallo award Columbian Lawyers Assn., 1966, Interfaith Achievement award Am. Jewish Com., 1972. Mem. Am. Bar Assn., New York County Lawyers Assn., Nat. Coll. Probate Judges, N.Y. State Surrogates Assn. (chmn.), N.Y. U. Law Alumni Assn. (dir.), Am. Justinian Soc. of Jurists (dir., pres. 1974). Contbr. articles to profl. jours. Home: New York, N.Y. Died June 28, 1978.

DILL, CLARENCE C., lawyer; born Fredericktown, Ohio, September 21, 1884; s. Theodore Marshall and Amanda (Kunkel) Dill; B.L., Ohio Wesleyan, 1907; married Mabel Dickson, 1939. Newspaper reporter, Cleveland, 1907; teacher in high school, Dubuque, Iowa, 1907-08, Spokane, Washington, 1908-10; admitted to Wash. bar, 1910, and practiced in Spokane; dep. pros. atty., Spokane County, 1911-13; mem. 64th and 65th Congresses (1915-19), 5th Wash. Dist.; mem. U.S. Senate, 2 terms, 1923-35; practiced law, Spokane and Washington; spl. asst. to Atty. Gen., Dept. of Justice, since 1946. Member Phi Kappa Psi. Odd Fellow, Elk, Moose. Mason. Author books and articles. Home: Spokane.

DILLINGER, JOSEPH ROLLEN, educator, physicist; b. Carbondale, Ill., May 20, 1916; s. Isaac Roland and Minnie (Etherton) D.; B.Ed., So. Ill. U., 1938; Ph.D. in Physics, U. Wis., 1947; m. Martha J. Freeman, June 6, 1942; children—James R., Ellen M., Thomas E. Mem. staff radiation lab. Mass. Inst. Tech., 1941-46; mem. faculty U. Wis., 1947-75, prof. physics, 1960-75. Mem. Am. Assn. Physics Tchrs. (treas. 1962-66). Research on photoelectric and thermionic emission; devel. power pulse generators and gas discharge tubes; low temperature physics. Home: Madison, Wis. Died Nov. 16, 1975; buried Carbondale, Ill.

DILLON, CLARENCE, banker; b. San Antonio, Tex., Sept. 27, 1882; s. Samuel and Bertha (Steenbock) D.; A.B., Harvard, 1905; m. Anne McEldin Douglass, Feb. 4, 1908. Associated with Newport Mining Co. and Milwaukee Coke and Gas Co., 1905-08; abroad, 1908-10; pres. Milwaukee Machine Tool Co., 1910-12; mem. firm Wm. A. Read & Co., bankers, New York since 1916, head of the firm since 1920, firm named changed to Dillon, Read & Co., 1921. Asst. to the chmn. War. Industries Bd., at Washington, D.C., World War. Awarded Order of the Crown (Belgium), 1921; grand officer Polonia Restituta with Star (Poland), 1925; Commander Order of Crown (Italy), 1927; Officer, 1935, Comdr., 1938, Legion of Honor (France).

DILLON, PAUL WASHINGTON, mfg. exec.; b. Sterling, Ill., June 3, 1883; s. Washington Moorehead and Sarah Jane (Martin) D.; student Shattuck Mil. Acad., Faribault, Minn., 1901-03; m. Crete Blackman, Nov. 16, 1904 (dec.); children—Crete Blackman (Mrs. John W. Bowman) (dec.), Margaret (Mrs. Goddard), Washington Martin. With Northwestern Steel & Wire Co. (formerly Northwestern Barb Wire Co.), dir., 1909-80, pres., 1920-38, 40-51, treas. 1921-48, chmn. bd., 1938-79, chmn. emeritus, 1979-80; dir. Northwestern Products Corp., Sterling, Ill. Served as capt. U.S. Army, World War I. Presbyn. Clubs: Rock River Country (Sterling); Union League (Chgo.). Home: Sterling, Ill. Died Feb. 25, 1980; buried Riverside Cemetery, Sterling.

DILLON, ROBERT E., corp. exec.; b. Titusville, Pa., Oct. 31, 1904; s. John T. and Catherine F. (Hanley) D.; student Amherst Coll.; m. Marion A. McNulty, June 29, 1926; children—Robert E., James M. Pres., chmn. bd. Lake Erie Engring. Corp., Buffalo; chmn. United Steel of Am., Inc., N.Y.C., Mapes & Sprowl Steel Co., Union, N.J., Am. Steel & Aluminum Corp., Cambridge, Mass., also Hartford, Conn.; chmn. dirs. trust investment com., dir., mem. exec. com. Marine Midland Trust Co., Dunlop Tire & Rubber Corp. Mem. Temp. Emergency Relief Adminstrn. N.Y. State, 1930-33; chmn. Erie County Emergency Relief Bd., 1931-35; cons. Def. Plant Corp., Washington, 1942-43; mem. NLRB, 1942-45; adv. bd. Rochester Ordnance Dist. Mem. Buffalo council N.Y. State Commn. Human Rights; pres. Children's Aid Soc., Soc. Prevention Cruelty to Children Erie County, 1958-68; chmn. Buffalo finance com. Amherst Coll.; chmn. pub. relations Child Welfare League Am. Inc., N.Y.; trustee Millard Filmore Hosp., D'Youville Coll., Erie Community Coll., St. Bonaventure U.; finance bd. Children's Hosp., Buffalo. Pres. The Robert E. Dillon Found. Mem. Am. Ordnance Assn. (dir.), Archaeol. Inst. Am. (pres. Western N.Y.), Psi Upsilon. Clubs: Buffalo; Saturn, Metropolitan (N.Y.C.); Cumberland (Portland, Me.). Home: Buffalo, N.Y. Died May 26, 1980.

DILLON, THEODORE HARWOOD, army officer; b. Center Valley, Ind., Jan. 6, 1884; s. Lewis Finley and Eva May (Craven) D.; B.S., U.S. Mil. Acad., 1904; m. Susan Elston Baxter, Sept. 6, 1911. Commd. 2d lt., Corps of Engrs., U.S. Army, 1904; asst. to dir. of public works, Cuba, 1907-08; mil. surveys, Philippine Islands, 1909-11; in charge constrn. Dalles-Celilo Canal, Ore., 1912-14; supt. of Gatun Loeks and in charge Locks Div. and elec. engr., Panama Canal, 1915-17; comdg. 37th Engrs. and dep. chief engr., 1st Army, A.E.F., France, 1918; tech. adviser and dep. chief, War Damages Bd., Am. Peace Commn., 1919; prof. elec. engring., Mass. Inst. Tech., 1920-24; prof., Harvard Business Sch., 1925-26; div. mgr. and asst. to pres., United Fruit Co., 1927-36; dir. publs. and pub. relations, Carnegie Inst. of Washington, 1939-43; recalled to active duty, U.S. Army, as col. Q.M. Corps, 1941; advanced to brig. gen., Feb. 5, 1942; dep. chief, Transportation Div., War Dept., 1942-43; inactive list since June 1943; prin. Edgartown Schs., 1944-47; dep. chief Engring. Div., Atomic Energy Commn., 1948; chmn. Lab. Constrn. Planning Bd., A.E.C., Los Alamos, N.M., 1948-49. Received Distinguished Service Medal, Legion of Merit. Fellow Am. Acad. Arts and Sciences. Home: Edgartown, Mass.

DIN MOHOMED, Pakistan diplomat; b. Gujranwala, Pakistan, Dec. 2, 1886; s. S. Saleh Mohomed; M.A., LL.B., LL.D. Lawyer, pres. Municipal Corp., Gujranwala, Pakistan; mem. Legislative Council, Punjab; judge High Ct., LaHore; mem. Indian DeLimitation Com.; chmn. Air Transport Licensing Bd. of India; mem. Punjab Boundary Commn.; gov. Sind; adviser Kashmir affairs Govt. of Pakistan with rank cabinet minister, 1955—. Home: Gujranwala, West Pakistan.

DINES, LLOYD LYNE (DINZ), univ. prof.; b. Shelbyville, Mo., Mar. 29, 1885; s. Henry Bascom and Martha Lyne (Duncan) D.; A.B., Northwestern U., Evanston, Ill., 1906, A.M., 1907; Ph.D., U. of Chicago, 1911; LL.D., University of Saskatchewan, 1946; unmarried. Instructor, Columbia Univ., 1911-13; asso. prof. mathematics, U. of Arizona, Tucson, 1913-14; asst. prof. mathematics, U. of Saskatchewan, Can., 1914-19, prof., 1919-33, dean, 1930-33; prof. and head dept. of mathematics, Carnegie Inst. Tech., 1933-45, emeritus since 1945; visiting prof. Univ. of Saskatchewan, 1945-46; Smith College, 1946-47, Northwestern University since 1947. Member American Mathematics Society, Mathematics Association of America, A.A.A.S., Royal Soc. of Can., Societé Mathematique de France, Circolo Matematico di Palermo, Phi Beta Kappa, Sigma Xi, Phi Kappa Phi. Club: Riverside Country (Saskatoon, Can.). Author many articles for math. jours. and addresses before math. orgns. Address: Quincy, Ill.

DINKLAGE, RALPH DIETRICH, lawyer; b. Cologne, Germany, July 4, 1906; s. Herman and Leonie (Schreiber) D.; came to U.S., 1930, naturalized, 1937; student Cologne U., 1925-26, Heidelberg U., 1926-27; Ph.D., Bonn U., 1930; postgrad. Columbia, 1936-37; LLB., Fordham U., 1936; m. Lisbeth Adam, Aug. 18, 1930; children—Ingolf, Siegrun; m. 2d, Rosemarie Kasslack, Mar. 7, 1975. Individual practice as chem. cons., N.Y.C., 1930-32; admitted to N.Y. bar, 1937; asso. patent law firm Louis Burgess, 1933; partner firm Burgess & Dinklage, N.Y.C., 1939-57; sr. partner firm Burgess, Dinklage & Sprung, N.Y.C., 1957-73, legal counsel, 1973-80, officer Stemmler Bros. Mem. U.S. German C. of C. (charter mem.). N.Y. County Lawyers Assn., Am. Patent Law Assn., N.Y., D.C. bar assns., N.Y. Patent Law Assn. Home: Clearwater, Fla. Died Apr. 26, 1980.

DINNING, ROBERT JOHN, meat packing industry; b. Stratbroy, Ont., Can., May 9, 1884; s. John and Jane (Irvine) D.; ed. pub. schs. of Ontario; m. Margaret S. Bentley, Oct. 26, 1910; children—Margaret I., John B., Dorothy E. With Merchants Bank of Canada and Bank of Montreal, 1902-24; chmn. Alberta Liquor Control Bd., 1924-36; financial advisor, Edmonton, 1936-42; pres. Burns & Co., Ltd., Calgary, Alberta, since 1945, Palm Dairies, Ltd., since 1943, Woodland Dairy, Ltd. (Edmonton), since 1946; v.p. Consolidated Fruit Co., Ltd., Calgary since 1943; director several corporations. Member Anglican Ch. Mason (Shriner). Clubs: Ranchmen's, Renfrew, Rotary. Home: Alberta, Can.

DINSMORE, RAY PUTNAM, engring. mgmt. cons.; b. Tewksbury, Mass., Apr. 24, 1893; s. Hiram Putnam and Susan (Toye) D.; B.S. in Chem. Engring., Mass. Inst. Tech., 1914; D.Eng. (hon.), Case Sch. Applied Sci., Cleve., 1940; m. Violet Cowie, Sept. 24, 1919; children—Ruth H. (Ayers), Ray Putnam. Tech. staff, Goodyear Tire & Rubber Co., Ohio, 1914-16, asst. chemist, Can., 1916-19, chief chemist, Calif., 1919-21, chief chemist, research dir., Ohio, 1921-32, asst. factory mgr., 1932-39, mgr. devel. dept., 1940-43, v.p., 1943-61, dir., 1960-64, cons., 1961-67. Asst. dep. rubber dir., 1942-43, organized synthetic rubber research and devel. program for govt. and industry. Pres. Nat. Adv. Council for Gifted, 1961-63. Term mem. Mass. Inst. Tech. Corp., 1954-59; trustee Kent State U., 1959-66, trustee emeritus, 1973. Recipient Colwyn Medal awarded by Inst. Rubber Industry, 1948; Charles Goodyear medal, Am. Chem. Soc., 1955. Pres. Am. sect. Sociéte de Chimie Industrielle, 1958, chmn. bd. dirs., 1959. Fellow Am. Inst. Chemists, Inst. of Rubber Industry (Brit.), Am. Inst. Chem. Engrs. (chmn. profl. devel. com.; recipient Founder's award 1964), AAAS; life mem. Am. Chem. Soc. (councilor 1922-25, chmn. Akron sect. vice chmn. rubber div., 1925-26, chmn. rubber div., 1926-27); mem. Am. Inst. Chemists (pres. 1955, 56; chmn. bd., 1956-57), Royal Soc. Arts (Eng.), N.Y. Acad. Scis., Agr. Research Inst. (bd. govs. 1954-59), Ohio Acad. Scis., Soc. Automotive Engrs., Alpha Chi Sigma. Clubs: Chemists, Akron University (life mem.), Portage Country (hon. mem.). Contributed numerous articles on rubber to sci. mags.; lectr. rubber industry, 7th Found. lectr. Instn. Rubber Industry econ. and phys. aspects of GR-S modifications, 1952. Home: Akron, Ohio. Died Oct. 26, 1979.

DIRKS, EDWARD, business exec.; b. Indianapolis, Ind., Nov. 24, 1883; s. Gerd and Fanny (Leerkamp) D.; ed. pub. schs. of Wayne Township; m. Anna L. Bloemker, Apr. 17, 1907; children—Mildred L. (Mrs. Loew), Helen L., Edward F. Purchased retail grocery and meat market, Nov. 10, 1910, Irvington, near Indianapolis, Ind. and since has operated bus. Mem. Evangelical and Reformed Ch. (2d vice pres. of Nat. Gen. Synod, since 1944). Mem. Nat. Assn. Retail Grocers. Vice pres. Wheeler City Rescue Mission. Republican. Mason (Scottish rite). Club: Rotary. Home: Indianapolis.

DIRLAM, ARLAND AUGUSTUS, architect; b. Somerville, Mass., Oct. 17, 1905; s. Frederick William and Lena Scafe (Charlton) D.; B.S., Tufts, 1926, L.H.D., 1953, M.Arch., Harvard, 1929, traveling fellow, 1929-30; spl. courses Ecole des Beaux Arts, Am. Acad. Rome: Doctor Fine Arts (hon.), Simpson Coll., 1968; LL.D., Union Coll., 1972; m. Catherine V. Price, Dec. 16, 1933 (dec. July 1966); m. 2d, Grace Raymond Baker, Oct. 27, 1967. Architect, Mass., 1931-79, specializing church and coll. architecture; pres. Arland A. Dirlam, Inc., Boston, 1956-79; projects include Gordon Coll. and Divinity Sch., Wenham (Mass.) Library, also buildings for Tufts U., U. N.H., Colby Jr. Coll., Lawrence Acad., Green Mountain Jr. Coll., Interfaith Chapel for Mentally Ill at Warren (Pa.) State Hosp.; designed War Meml. Tower at Cathedral Pines; lectr. architecture Boston U., Inst. Social and Religious Studies N.Y.; tech. adviser bur. ch. bldg. Nat. Council Chs. Christ Am.; dir. Wesleyan Assn.; corporate mem. Morgan Meml. Dir. Marblehead Trust Co. Bd. dirs. Marblehead Scholarship Found.; trustee, incorporator New Eng. Deaconess Hosp., New Eng. Bapt. Hosp.; trustee Union Coll., Barbourville, Ky. Registered architect, Mass., R.I., Iowa, Conn., Maine, Vt., N.H., N.Y., Va. Served as lt. comdr. USNR, World War II; mem. Fgn. Liquidations Commn., 1945. Recipient distinguished service key Tufts Coll., J. Harleston Parker gold medal Boston Soc. Architects, 1952, 1st prize Religious Arts Guild Am. Unitarian Assn., hon. mention award Ch. Archtl. Guild Am., 1954. Corp. mem. Open Ch. Found. Fellow Internat. Inst. Arts and Letters; mem. Am. Soc. Ch. Arch. (dir.), A.I.A., Ch. Archtl. Guild Am. (dir., past pres.), Boston Soc. Architects, Mass. Assn. Architects, Beaux Arts Inst. Design, Marblehead Hist. Soc. (dir.), Marblehead Arts Assn. (v.p.), Newcomen Soc., Am. Arbitration Assn., Alpha Tau Omega, Tau Beta Pi. Republican. Methodist. Mason (33 deg.). Clubs: Harvard, Boston Tufts (past pres.), Boston Yacht (Boston). Contbr. relgious mags.

Home: Marblehead, Mass. Died June 20, 1979; buried Waterside Cemetery, Marblehead.

DIRSTINE, PEARL H. (DUR'STEN), coll. dean; b. Thornville, Mich., Sept. 15, 1886; s. Elias Thomas and Isabel (Sutton) D.; Ph.G., Valparaiso (Ind.) U., 1905; D.V.S., State Coll. of Washington, 1912, B.S., 1916; grad. work Stanford, 1921; m. Jet E. Evans, July 3, 1909; children—Philip Hugh, Donald Evans; m. 2d, Belle Wenz, June 30, 1937. Pharmacist, 1905-10; instr. in physiology and materia medica, State Coll. of Washington, 1912-15, asst. prof., 1915-17, prof. and head of Sch. of Pharmacy, 1917-24, dean, Sch. of Pharmacy since 1924; Employed in professional prescription stores, summers 1918-30; head of Finch Memorial Hosp., State Coll. of Wash., 1927-37. Mem. Athletic Commn., 1920-24; mem. Health Commn., 1917-27, head, 1927-37. Lecturer, British Columbia Summer Sch. for Pharmacists, Vancouver, B.C., 1942-44. Chmn. dist. 7, Am. Assn. Coll. of Pharmacy and Bds. of Pharmacy, 1939. Mem. Am. Pharm. Assn. (sec. practical pharmacy sect. 1927, chmn. 1929), Am. Assn. Colls. of Pharmacy (mem. library com., 1939-42; com. curriculum standards 1943; com. standards and membership 1944; com. on 5 yr. curricula (1944), Nat. Assn. Bds. Pharmacy and Am. Assn. Colleges Pharm. Dist. No. 7 (mem. curriculum standards com., 1943; chmn. spl. com. on bldg. plans and equipment, 1946-47), Am. Pharm. Assn., Am. Assn. U. Profs., Wash. State Pharm. Assn. (dist. gov. 1935), Northwest Science Assn., Pullman (Wash.) Chamber of Commerce, Kappa Psi, Phi Kappa Phi, Rho Chi (mem. nat. exec. com. grand council, 1946), Phi Sigma. Mason (Shriner, K.T.), Knight of Pythias. Contbr. numerous articles to professional and trade jours. Home: Pullman, Wash. *

DISKIN, MICHEL ANGELO, lawyer; b. Scottdale, Pa., Jan. 10, 1884; s. Thomas and Mary (Halleron) D.; grad. high sch., Scottdale; LL.B., U. of Notre Dame, 1907; m. Florence Dinegan, of San Jose, Calif., Nov. 25, 1912; 1 dau., Florence. Admitted to Nev. bar, 1908, and began practice at Goldfield; atty. gen. of Nev., term 1923-26, inclusive. Democrat. Catholic. Home: Carson City, Nev. *

DISNEY, DORIS MILES (MRS. GEORGE J. DISNEY), writer; b. Glastonbury, Conn., Dec. 22, 1907; d. Edward Lucas Hart and Elizabeth Anne (Malone) Miles; ed. pub. schs., Conn.; m. George J. Disney, June 19, 1936 (dec.); 1 dau., Elizabeth Miles. Democrat. Roman Catholic. Club: Woman's. Author: books among which: Family Skeleton, 1949 (Crime Club publs.) Fire at Will, 1949; Look Back on Murder, 1950; Straw Man, 1951; Heavy Heavy Hangs, 1952; Do Unto Others, 1953; Prescription: Murder, 1953; The Last Straw, 1954; Room for Murder, 1955; Driven to Kill; Unappointed Rounds, Method in Madness, My Neighbor's Wife, Black Mail; Dark Lady, 1960; Mrs. Meeker's Money, 1961; No Next of Kin; Shadow of A Man; At Some Forgotten Door; The Magic Grandfather; the Chandler Policy, 1972; They Say Miss Bessie Lewis Disappeared, 1972; Do Not Fold, Spindle or Mutilate, 1972; Trick or Treat, 1972. Home: Farmington, Conn. Died Mar. 8, 1976.

DITTMAN, MARION MARTHA, editor; b. Chgo., Feb. 24, 1909; d. Ernest C. and Lydia (Karau) Dittman; B.A., M.A., Northwestern U. Formerly editor North Shore News; editorial room staff U. Chgo. Press; editor trade books Rand McNally & Co.; sr. editor Childcraft, Field Enterprises Ednl. Corp., Chgo.; former mng. editor pub. dept. A.L.A., Chgo.; free-lance editorial cons., now ret. Mem. Chgo. Children's Reading Round Table, Women's Nat. Book Assn., Classical Club of Chgo., Midland Authors, Chgo. Council on Foreign Relations, Alumna Am. Sch. Classical Studies (Athens, Greece), Phi Beta Kappa, Delta Zeta. Home: Chicago, Ill. Died Nov. 28, 1976.

DIX, WILLIAM SHEPHERD, librarian; b. Winchester, Va., Nov. 19, 1910; s. William Shepherd and Loula (Henson) D.; B.A., U. Va., 1931, M.A., 1932; Ph.D., U. Chgo., 1946; LL.D., U. Fla., 1967; Litt.D., Washington Coll., 1971; m. Jane Griffin, June 6, 1935; children—William S., Griffin, Martha. Master Darlington Sch. Boys, 1932-39; instr. English, dir. com. on private research Western Res. U., 1940-42; instr. English, Williams Coll., 1942-44; research asso. Radio Research Lab., OSRD, Harvard, 1944-46, instr. English, 1946-47; asst. prof. English, Rice Inst., 1947-48, asso. prof. and librarian, 1948-53; librarian Princeton, 1953-56, librarian and lectr. in English, 1956-78. Chmn. U.S. Nat. Commn. UNESCO, 1959-61; mem. U.S. delegation Gen. Conf. UNESCO, Paris, 1958, vice chmn. delegation, 1960, del., Manila conf., 1961; del. Asian Am. Assembly, Kuala Lumpur, 1963; mem. Govt. Adv. Com. Internat. Book and Library Programs, 1967-69; adv. council Assn. of Am. Univ. Presses, Nat. Commn. on New Technol. Uses of Copyrighted Works, 1975-78; adv. council on grad. edn. U.S. Office Edn.; cons. Ford Found.; adv. council numerous univ. libraries. Bd. dirs. Council on Library Resources, Inc., H.W. Wilson Co., vice chmn. bd. dirs. Franklin Book Programs, Inc. Recipient Melville Dewey award, 1969; Lippincott award, 1971. Mem. Am. (pres. 1969-70, chmn. internat. relations bd.), N.J. (recipient Distinguished Service award 1969) library assns., Assn. Coll. and Reference Libraries, Assn. Research Libraries (chmn. 1962), Phi Beta Kappa. Presbyn. Clubs: Grolier, Century (N.Y.C). Author: The Amateur Spirit in Scholarship, 1942; The Princeton University Library in the Eighteenth Century, vol. 40 of The Princeton University Library Chronicle. Contbr. articles profl. jours. Home: Princeton, N.J. Died Feb. 22, 1978.

DIXON, DEAN, conductor; b. N.Y.C., 1915; grad. Juilliard Sch. Music, Columbia U., also student with Albert Stoessel; m. Baroness Mary Mandelen. Juilliard Fellowship in conducting, 1936-39; Rosenwald Fellowship, 1945-47. Has appeared as conductor of many leading orchestras in U.S. and Europe, including N.Y. Philharmonic Symphony, N.Y. Chamber Orch., Nat. Symphony Orch., N.B.C. Symphony, Boston Symphony, Goteborg Symphony in Sweden (of which he has been resident condr.), Rundfunk Symphony Orch., Hessian Radio Orch. Recorded in works by Schubert, Tchaikovsky. Address: Frankfurt/Main, German Federal Republic. Died Nov. 3, 1976.

DIXON, OWEN, chief justice High Court of Australia; b. Melbourne, Australia, Apr. 28, 1886; s. Joseph William and Edith Annie (Owen) D.; student Hawthorn Coll., Melbourne to 1904; M.A., LL.B., U. of Melbourne, 1909; LL.D. (hon.), Harvard, 1958; D.C.L. (hon.), Oxford, 1958; m. Alice Crossland Brooksbank, Jan. 8, 1920; 2 sons, 2 daus. Called to Bar of Victoria, 1910, practised as counsel in Melbourne till 1929; Kings Counsel, 1922; acting judge of the Supreme Court of Victoria, 1926; justice of High Court of Australia since 1929; chief justice of the High ct. since 1952; E.E. and M.P. for Australia at Washington, 1942-44; United Nations rep. India and Pakistan for Kashmir Dispute, 1950. Served as chmn. Central Wool Com., chmn. Shipping Control Bd., chmn. Marine War Risks Ins. Bd., chmn. Allied Shipping Consultative Council, chmn. Marine Bd., World War II. Decorated Knight Comdr. St. Michael and St. George, 1941; Knight Grand Cross St. Michael and St. George, 1954; apptd. Privy Councillor (U.K.), 1951; recipient Henry Howland Prize, Yale Univ., 1955. Home: Melbourne, Victoria, Australia.

DIXON, ROBERT GALLOWAY, JR., educator; b. Canajoharie, N.Y., Apr. 24, 1920; s. Robert Galloway and Ruth Beverly (Spencer) D.; A.B. summa cum laude, Syracuse U., 1943, Ph.D., 1947; Ford Found. Faculty fellow, Stanford, 1951-52; J.D. with highest honors, George Washington U., 1956; m. Claire Bracken, July 31, 1948; children—Janet, Barbara, Laurie. Instr. to asso. prof. govt. and politics U. Md., 1946-56; admitted to D.C. bar, 1956; asso. prof. law George Washington U., 1956-60, prof. law, 1960-75; asst. atty. gen. Office of Legal Counsel, Justice Dept., 1973-74; Daniel Noyes Kirby prof. law Washington U., St. Louis, 1975-80; vis. prof. law U. Va., 1980. Cons. Constl. Convs. N.Y., 1966-67, Pa., 1967, Md., 1968, Ill., 1970, Nat. Commn. on Reform of Fed. Criminal Laws, 1969-71; cons. Nat. Endowment for Humanities, 1975-80, NSF, 1979-80; mem. adv. bd. for improving mgmt. in govt. Com. for Econ. Devel., 1970-72; council mem. Adminstrv. Conf. of U.S., 1973-74, conf. mem., 1974-80; advisor U.S. Civil Service Commn., 1976-78; spl. lectr. Princeton, 1968, Southwestern Legal Found., So. Meth. U., 1968, 71, Cornell U., Brigham Young U., 1975, U. Mo., 1978; organizer, chmn., moderator lecture series, 1978-79, subsequently pub. in Washington U. Law Quar. Recipient Alumni Achievement award George Washington U., 1978. Ford Found. travel study grantee, 1971-72. Rockefeller Found. fellow, 1964-65, Nat. Endowment for Humanities Sr. fellow, 1971-72. Mem. Am. (mem. council adminstrv. law sect. 1975-78), Fed. (former mem. council) bar assns., Am. Polit. Sci. Assn., Assn. Am. Law Schs. (chmn. com. on Supreme Ct. decisions 1966-67), Order of Coif, Phi Beta Kappa. Presbyterian. Author: Democratic Representation (Woodrow Wilson Found. Book award), 1968; Social Security Disability and Mass Justice: An Emerging Problem in Welfare Adjudication, 1973; Standards Development in the Private Sector: Thoughts on Interest Representation and Procedural Fairness, 1978; Contbr. articles to profl. jours. Home: Clayton, Mo. Died May 5, 1980.

DOANE, D(UANE) HOWARD, professional farm manager; b. near Mexico, New York, July 30, 1883; s. Duane George and Nettie (Powell) Doane; B.S. in Agriculture, University of Missouri, 1908, M.S., 1909; m. Eureth R. Grant, of Shelbina, Mo., Nov. 7, 1911; children—Charles Earl, Helen. Scientific asst. Office of Farm Management, U.S. Dept. Agr. (except for a few mos.), 1906-15; state leader of farm advisers for Mo., jointly employed by U.S. Govt. and U. of Mo.; prof. farm management, U. of Mo., 1912-16; mgr. field div. of farm loan dept. Miss. Valley Trust Co., St. Louis, 1916-19; mgr. The George Begley, Jr., Farms, Poplar Bluff, Mo., 1919-20; owner Doane Agricultural Service. Conglist. Charter mem. Mo. Chapter Alpha Zeta. Mem. Am. Soc. Farm Mgrs. and Rural Appraisers (1st pres.), Farm House Fraternity (ex-pres.). Author: Sheep Feeding and Management, 1912; also bulletins. Pres. Interstate Agrl. and Industrial Congress, St. Joseph, Mo., 1914; mem. bd. govs. Nat. Farm Chemurgie Council; chmn. Mo. Farm Chemurgie Council. Club: Kiwanis (ex-pres.). Home: St. Louis, Mo.

DOBBINS, CRIS, business exec.; b. Denver, Jan. 8, 1904; s. George S. and Julia Josephine (Spillane) D.; B.B.A., U. Denver, 1927, LL.D., 1967; m. Elvira Mae Bjork, Oct. 19, 1930; children—Christopher, Michael A., Felicity Anne. Asst. sales mgr. Colo., Portland Cement Co., Denver, 1930-41, sales mgr., 1941-43; asst. to pres. Ideal Cement Co., Denver, 1943-44, v.p., gen. mgr., 1944-48, exec. v.p., gen. mgr., 1948-52, pres., 1952-67; chmn., pres. Ideal Basic Industries, Inc., 1968-70, chmn., chief exec. officer, 1970-71, dir., chmn., 1971-79; dir. Brown Palace Hotel Co., United Banks Colo., Inc., United Bank Denver, N.A., Colo. & So. Ry. Co., Ideal Corp. Chmn., trustee Boettcher Found.; trustee Denver Mus. Natural History; bd. dirs. Air Force Acad., Central City Opera House Assn., Conf. Bd.; bd. dirs. Am. Mining Congress, pres. 1968-71; pres., treas., bd. dirs. Dobbins Found. Mem. adv. bd. Denver Area council Boy Scouts Am.; mem. Nat. Indsl. Pollution Control Council, chmn. bldg. materials subcouncil, 1970. Mem. Most Venerable Order Hosp. St. John of Jerusalem, Alpha Kappa Psi, Beta Gamma Sigma (hon.). Republican. Episcopalian. Clubs: Denver Athletic, Denver, Denver Country; Pacific-Union (San Francisco; Burlingame Country (Calif.); Garden of the Gods (Colorado Springs, Colo.); Chicago; Eisenhower Golf (life, Air Force Acad.); Wigwam; Mile High; Tower; Balboa (Mazatlan, Mexico). Home: Denver, Colo. Died June 16, 1979.

DOBBINS, GAINES STANLEY, clergyman, educator; b. Langsdale, Miss., July 29, 1886; s. Charles Wesley and Letitia (Gaines) D.; B.A., Miss. Coll., Clinton, 1908; Th.D., So. Bapt. Theol. Sem., Louisville, Ky., 1914; M.A., Columbia, 1925; D.D., Miss. Coll., 1918, LL.D., 1947; m. May Virginia Riley, Dec. 1909; children—Gaines Stanley, Riley Franklin, Charles Austin. Ordained Baptist ministry, 1913; pastor Gloster, Miss., 1914-15, New Albany, Miss., 1915-16; mem. editorial staff So. Bapt. Sunday Sch. Bd., 1916-20; prof. religious edn. and ch. adminstrn., So. Bapt. Theol. Sem., 1920-56, treas., 1933-42, acting pres., 1950-51, dean Sch. Religious Edn., 1953-56; distinguished prof. ch. adminstrn. Golden Gate Bapt. Theol. Sem., Mill Valley, Calif., 1956-66; lectr. Samford U., Birmingham, Ala., 1967; guest lectr. prof. Ruschlikon Bapt. Sem., Zurich, Switzerland, Instituto Filadelfia, Rivili-Turin, Italy, Nigerian Bapt. Theol. Sem., Ogbomosho, So. Bapt. Theol. Sem. Chmn. commn. Bible study and membership tng. Bapt. World Alliance, 1955-66. Recipient Mullins award for Distinguished Denominational Service, So. Bapt. Theol. Sem., 1966, Gaines Dobbins chair of ch. adminstrn. named in his honor, 1976; Distinguished Service award Coll. Chaplains, Atlanta, 1972, others. Mem. Am. Acad. Polit. and Social Sci. Author 33 books, later ones are: Building Better Churches, 1947; Understanding Adults, 1948; Evangelism According to Christ, 1949; The Churchbook, 1951; Winning the Children, 1953; Building A Better Sunday School, 1957; The Years Ahead, 1959; A Ministering Church, 1960; Guiding Adults in Bible Study, 1960; The Church at Worship, 1962; Great Teachers Make a Difference, 1965; Learning to Lead, 1968; The Improvement of Teaching, 1973; Good News to Change Lives, 1976; Zest for Living, 1977, also brochures and tapes on religious topics. Contbr. Bapt. Sunday Sch. Bd., Nashville. Home: Birmingham, Ala. Died Sept. 22, 1978.

DOBZHANSKY, THEODOSIUS, educator; b. Nemirov, Russia, Jan. 25, 1900; s. Gregory and Sophie (Voinarsky) D.; grad. U. Kiev, 1921; D.Sc. (hon.), U. Sao Paulo, Brazil, 1943, Coll. Wooster (O.), 1945, U. Munster (Germany), U. Montreal (Can.), 1958, U. Chgo., 1959, U. Sidney, Australia, 1960, Oxford (Eng.) U., 1964, Louvain U., 1965, Columbia, 1964, Kalamazoo Coll., 1965, Clarkson Coll. Tech., 1965, U. Mich., 1966, U. Syracuse, 1967, U. Cal. at Berkeley, 1968, U. Padua (Italy), 1968, Northwestern U., 1968; D.H.L. (hon.), U. Cal., 1968, Wittenberg U., 1970, St. Mary's Coll., 1971, Rennes (France) U., 1974, Sorbonne, Paris, 1975; m. Natalie Sivertzev, Aug. 8, 1924; 1 dau., Sophie. Came to U.S., 1927, naturalized, 1937. Asst. prof. zoology Polytechnique Inst., Kiev, 1921-24; lectr. genetics U. Leningrad, 1924-27; fellow int. edn. bd., 1928-29; asst. prof. genetics Cal. Inst. Tech., 1930-36; prof., 1936-40; prof. zoology Columbia, 1940, later DaCosta prof. zoology; prof. Rockefeller Inst., N.Y.C., 1962-71; adj. prof. U. Cal. at Davis, 1971-79; exchange prof. U. São Paulo, Brazil, 1943, 48-49. Recipient G. Elliott prize and medal Nat. Acad. Sci., Kimber prize, 1958; Guggenheim fellow, 1959; recipient Nat. Medal of Science, 1964; Addison Emery Verrill medal, 1966; Distinguished Achievement in Sci. award Am. Mus. Natural History, 1969. Mem. Nat., Royal Danish, Royal Swedish, Brazilian acads. scis., Academia dei Lincei, Italy, Royal Soc., London, Eng., Am. Philos. Soc. (past pres.), Am. Soc. Zoologists, Am. Soc. Genetics, Am. Soc. Naturalists, Am. Soc. for Study Evolution. Author: Genetics and Origin of Species, 1937, 3d edit., 1951; Evolution, Genetics and Man, 1955; Mankind Evolving, 1962; Biology of Ultimate Concern, 1967; Genetics of the Evolutionary Process, 1970; Genetic Diversity and Human Equality, 1973. Address: Davis, Calif. Died Dec. 19, 1975.

DODDS, HAROLD WILLIS, univ. pres.; b. Utica, Pa., June 28, 1889; s. Samuel and Alice (Dunn) D.; A.B., Grove City (Pa.) Coll., 1909; LL.D., 1931; A.M., Princeton, 1914, LL.D., 1957: Ph.D., U. Pa., 1917; LL.D., Yale, 1933, Dickinson U., Am. U. Rutgers U., N.Y. U., Harvard, Williams Coll., 1934, U. Cin., 1935, U. Pa., 1936, Dartmouth, 1937, Purdue U., 1938, Tulane U., 1941, Tusculum, 1945, U. N.C., 1946, Oberlin Coll., 1947, Toronto U., 1947, Washington and Lee U., 1949, U. Glasgow, 1951, Brown U., 1954, U. Cal., U. Mich., McGill U., 1955, Dropsie Coll., Colgate U., 1957, U. B.C., 1958, U. Manchester, 1959, U. N.B., Centre Coll., 1963; D.C.L., U. Pitts., 1957; D. Social Sci., Laval U., 1952; Litt.D., Columbia, 1934, Hahnemann Med. Coll., 1937, U. Hawaii, 1949; L.H.D., Hobart Coll., 1936, Bucknell U., 1958; H.H.D., Coll. Wooster, 1938; m. Margaret Murray, Dec. 25, 1917. Instr. econs., Purdue U., 1914-16; exec. sec. U.S. Food Adminstrn., Pa., 1917-19; asst. prof. polit. sci. Western Res. U., 1919-20; sec. Nat. Municipal League, 1920-28, editor Nat. Municipal Rev., 1920-33; prof. politics Princeton, 1927-34, pres. univ., 1933-57. Electoral adviser Govt. Nicaragua, 1922-24; tech. adviser pres. Tacna-Arica Plebiscitary Commn., 1925-26; chief adviser pres. Nat. Bd. Elections Nicaragua, 1928; cons. Cuban Govt. in election law and procedure, 1935. Chmn., Pres.'s Com. on Integration Med. Services of Govt., 1946; mem. Pres.'s Adv. Commn. on Universal Tng., 1947; chmn. task force on personnel, 2d Hoover Commn., 1954-55; chmn. Am. delegation Anglo-Am. Conf. on Refugee Problem, Bermuda 1943. Named comdr. Order of King Leopold, 1937. Mem. Am. Acad. Arts and Scis., Am. Philos. Soc., Phi Beta Kappa. Presbyn. Clubs: Athaeneum (London, Eng.); Century, Princeton (N.Y.C.); Nassau (Princeton). Author: Out of This Nettle. . .Danger, 1943; The Academic President—Educator or Caretaker?, 1962; also numerous articles, surveys and reports in polit. sci. Home: Princeton, N.J. Died Oct. 25, 1980; buried Princeton Cemetery.

DODDS, JESSE TRUESDELL, clergyman; b. Grand Rapids, Mich., Mar. 12, 1882; Hamline U., 1905-07; B.Litt. and A.B., Ohio Wesleyan U., 1909; D.D., Hedding Coll., Abingdon, Ill., 1922, Carthage (Ill.) Coll., 1929; m. Almina Ulland, Aug. 29, 1906; children—Phyllis Loraine, Philip Ulland. Ordained ministry M.E. Ch., 1904; pastor successively at Wadena, Minneapolis, Fergus Falls (all Minn.), Moline, Ill., Monmouth, Ill., Paris, Ill., Maywood, Ill., 1936-45; pastor St. Charles, Ill., since July 1945. Republican. Mason (32 deg., K.T.). Rotarian. Home: St. Charles, Ill.

DODGE, ERNEST STANLEY, museum dir., writer; b. Trenton, Maine, Mar. 18, 1913; s. George Flint and Beatrice Marion (Dolliver) D.; spl. student anthropology Harvard, 1937-38; M.A (hon.), Marlboro Coll.; D.Litt., Boston U.; D.H.L., Salem State Coll., 1979; m. Irene Doucette, Dec. 23, 1938; children—Rebecca Ann, Ernest Stanley; m. 2d, Elisabeth Shrigley Wheeler, Nov. 24, 1965. Mus. asst. Peabody Mus. of Salem, Mass., 1931-37, asst. curator, 1937-43, curator, 1943-46, asst. dir., 1946-50, dir., 1950-80; Lowell lectr., 1962; sr. specialist East-West Center, 1968. Guggenheim fellow, 1960-61. Trustee, past pres. Ropes Mem.; trustee Penobscot Marine Mus., Fruitlands Mus., Merrimack Textile Mus., Funds for Edn. in Liberia; councillor Essex Inst.; past adviser Eleutherian Mills-Hagley Found., Mystic Seaport, Woodbridge House, Oxford Coll. Barges Preservation Trust. Fellow Am. Acad. Arts and Sci., Royal Anthrop. Inst., Royal Geog. Soc.; mem. Mass. Hist. Soc., Colonial Soc. Mass., Am. Folklore Soc., Am. Antiquarian Soc., Am. Ethnol. Soc., C. of C. (dir. 1953-55, 66-68), Soc. History Discoveries (pres. 1965-67), Am. Soc. Ethno History (pres. 1966-67), Soc. Colonial Wars. Unitarian. Club: Odd Volumes (Boston). Author: Gourd Growers of the South Seas, 1943; Northwest By Sea, 1961; New England and the South Sea, 1965; Beyond the Capes, 1971; Thirty Years of American Neptune, 1972; The Polar Rosses, 1973; Islands and Empires, 1976; Hawaiian and Other Polynesian Gourds, 1978; also sci., hist. and popular articles. Editor: The American Neptune. Home: Salem, Mass. Died Feb. 9, 1980.

DODGE, WASHINGTON, investment adviser; b. San Francisco, Sept. 23, 1907; A.B., Yale, 1929; m. Helen K. Hubbard, 1932; m. 2d, Helen M. Brown, 1941. Financial editor Time mag. and editorial assignments for Archtl. Forum and Fortune mags., N.Y.C., 1929-33; pub. relations Barrett Co., 1933-37; author bus. commentary, Washington Dodge's Letter, 1937-57; investment adviser, 1937-74; partner Arthur Weisenberger & Co., mem. N.Y. Stock Exchange, 1941-44, Roberts, Rutter & Co., 1944-69; v.p. Clark Dodge & Co., 1969-72. Mem. Native Sons Golden West, Skull and Bones, Alpha Delta Phi. Club: Racquet and Tennis (N.Y.C.). Home: New York, N.Y. Died Dec. 1974.

DODGE, WENDELL PHILLIPS, editor, explorer, ethnologist; b. Manchester, N.H., Aug. 12, 1883; s. Arthur Pillsbury and Elizabeth Ann (Day) D.; student Chgo. Art Inst., Chgo. Musical Coll., Chase Sch., N.A.D., Art Students League (N.Y.); civil engring., N.Y. U., 1903-06; m. Clothilde Beatrice Masson, June 23, 1908; children—Wendell Phillips (dec. May 25, 1947), Richard William. Numerous engring., indsl., comml., reportorial assignments, 1905-13, including covering Thaw Murder trial for N.Y. Evening World; founder, propr. The World Wide News Service, 1913, gen. mgr. mng. editor; contbr. to mags., U.S. and fgn.; founder-dir. Am. Theater in Paris, 1929; presented Maurice de Fe'raudy, vice dean de la Comédie Française in only Am. appearance, 1924; produced several plays, 1919-32; directed Mlle. Lucienne Boyer, Escudero, Nikita Balieff, 1934; London Intimate Opera Co., N.Y.C. and Can., 1937-38; produced Explorers TV Program sta. WNBT, N.Y.C., 1949. Explored Dead Sea, and site Gomorrah in Jordan Valley, Syrian and Red Deserts, 1901; excavated mounds of Balawat, east of Mosulate site of Ninevah, also vicinity of Baghdad; excavations at tomb of Cyrus on Plain of Pasargadae, 1900-01; circumnavigated world on sq. rigger, 1902; organized and directed P'an Ku Exploration and Exhbn. Co., Far East and Near East expdns., 1939. Hon. v.p., dir. dirs. Nat. Sesqui-Centennial Com., 1926; gen. chmn. David Belasco Centennial Celebration, 1953—. Mem. Am. adv. bd., Yenching U., Peiping, China. Served to lt. comdr. USNR, ret. 1939. Fellow Royal Geog. Soc. (London); Egyptian Geographical Soc. (Cairo); mem. several profl. assns. Clubs: Lambs, Explorers (past dir.), Army and Navy, Circumnavigators; The Silurians. Completed History of Bahai Revelation and Ency. of Religion begun by father. Author several books and plays, latest: Sweeney Todd, 1959; Short History of the Arctic, 1963; series on exploration; also articles; contbr. articles on shipbuilding and shipping to New Internat. Year Book, 1946, 51—; The Book of Knowledge (articles on explorations of the year, 1951—); editor, author: Dictionary of Geographical Discoveries, 1959. Editor Marine News, 1943-50; editor Explorers Jour., 1945-54; Circumnavigators Log, 1953, 62-63. Address: New York City NY. *

DOERING, CARL RUPP, univ. prof.; b. Phila., 1889; M.D., Baylor U., 1921; D.Sc., Johns Hopkins, 1924. Mem. faculty Harvard U. Sch. of Pub. Health. Fellow Am. Acad. Arts and Sciences. Address: Boston, Mass. Died Mar. 28, 1976.

DOFT, FLOYD SHELTON, biochemist; b. Griswold, Iowa, May 19, 1900; s. Edgar William and Sarah Elizabeth (Shelton) D.; A.B., Simpson Coll., 1921, Sc.D., 1952; Ph.D., Yale, 1926; m. Frances Pauline Fisk, Nov. 26, 1935; one stepson, Leon W. Research asst. Yale, 1923-24, Cheney fellow, 1924-26, traveling fellow guest at Carlsberg Lab., Copenhagen, Denmark, 1926-27; asst. in physiology Harvard, 1927-29; Eli Lilly fellow Yale, 1929-31; instr. in biochemistry and exptl. pathology U. Rochester, 1931-37; mem. staff NIH, 1937-62, chief biochemistry and nutrition lab., asst. dir. Exptl. Biology and Medicine Inst., 1947-50, acting dir., 1950-51; asso. dir. in charge research Nat. Inst. Arthritis and Metabolic Diseases, 1951-53, dir., 1953-62, cons., 1962-78; vis. prof. Einstein Coll. Medicine, 1962-66. Sci. adv. com. Vitamin Found., 1954-57, Nutrition Found., 1956-63, Nat. Better Bus. Bur., 1958-78; mem. nat. adv. council Monell Chem. Senses Center, U. Pa., 1968-71; chmn., devel. council Simpson Coll., 1961-66; v.p. bd. trustees Biol. Abstracts, 1963-65; mem. food and nutrition bd. NRC, 1962-66; chmn. adv. com. on research Bur. Comml. Fisheries, 1963-66. Organizer, mem. U.S. Sci. Mission to USSR, 1960. Served with U.S. Army, 1918. Recipient D.S.M., USPHS, 1962. Diplomate Am. Bd. Nutrition. Fellow Am. Inst. Chemists, A.A.A.S., Washington Acad. Scis.; mem. Nat. Assn. Standard Med. Vocabulary (cons. 1962-78), Internat. Union Nutrition (U.S. nat. com. 1961-65, vice chmn. 1961-63), Am. Chem. Soc., Am., Internat. socs. hematology, Soc. Am. Inst. Nutrition (pres. 1960-61), Exptl. Biology and Medicine, Am. Soc. Biol. Chemists, Wash. Acad. Medicine, Am. Rheumatism Assn., Pan Am. Med. Assn. (N. Am. v.p. nutrition), Nat. Trust Hist. Preservation, Sigma Xi, Delta Upsilon, Epsilon Sigma, Gamma Alpha, Alpha Chi Sigma. Clubs: Cosmos, Farmington Country (Charlottesville). Asst. editor: Nutrition Reviews, 1944-47; asso. editor Jour. Nutrition, 1951-55. Contbr. numerous articles to various sci. jours. Home: Chevy Chase, Md. Died May 25, 1978; buried Upstate N.Y. Cemetery.

DOLBEAR, SAMUEL HOOD (DOL'BER), cons. mining engr.; b. Somerville, Mass., Dec. 6, 1886; s. Amos Emerson and Alice Jeannette (Hood) D.; spl. and summer courses Tufts Coll., 1901, 04-06; student Clark University, Worcester, Massachusetts, 1904, M.Sc. (honorary), 1939, D.Sc. (honorary), 1962; m. Inza Snowden Jordan, May 31, 1941. In charge constrn. soda-ash plant Cal. Trona Co. (now Am. Potash & Chemical Co.), 1906-09; pres. Am. Steel Bar Mfg. Co., 1913-14; Pacific Coast cons. Am. Refractories Co., 1914-20; pres. Piedra Magnesite Co., Cal., 1917-18; operated chrome, magnesite and manganese mines in Cal., Ore., Ariz., 1916-20; pres. Selective Treatment Co., Ltd., 1922-31; engaged in research and development beneficiation of asbestos ore in Can.; exam. mines in Korea, 1936; pres. Wright Dolbear Co., Inc., engrs. and geologist, N.Y., Toronto and San Francisco, 1937-43; pres. Behre Dolbear and Company, Incorporated, mining engineers and geologists, 1944-61, consultant, 1961—, engaged in mineral exams., geol. and econ. studies in U.S., Can., Mexico, China, Philippines, Burma, Turkey, Cuba, Haiti, Central and S.A. Adv. Com. and cons. U.S. Bur. of Mines, 1937-40; mining engr. cons. Cal. State Div. of Mines, 1944-45, making statewide study of postwar outlook for mine operations and employment in state mineral industries; mineral advisor Provisional Gov. Republic of Korea, 1945; tech. advisor Chinese Nationalist Gov. study reserves, development and mechanization of tin mines, Yunan, natimony mines, Hunan and Tungsten mines, Kiangsi Provinces, 1946-47; tech. adviser on minerals Burma Gov., 1948, Gov. of Haiti, 1949; cons. Govt. of Denmark, 1958; lectr. U. So. Cal., 1943. Trustee Clark U., 1940-61, vice chmn. trustees, 1959-60. Hal Williams Hardinge award, outstanding achievement, Am. Inst. Mining and Metall. Engrs., 1960. Mem. Am. Inst. Mining and Metall. Engrs. (1st chmn. indsl. minerals div. 1935), Soc. Econ. Geologists, Mining and Metall. Soc. American, Am. Mining Congress, Kappa Phi. Clubs: Mining (New York City, New York); Cosmos (Washington, Dist. Columbia). Author: Economic Mineral Resources of California, 1945; also 75 tech. papers and bulls. Editor Ind. Minerals and Rocks, 1937-47. Patentee 35 U.S. and fgn. metall. processes and equipment. Home: N.Y.C.

DOLLAHON, JAMES CLIFFORD, coll. dean; b. Roswell, N.Mex., Sept. 27, 1930; s. Robert Wentworth and Annie (Calloway) D.; B.S., N.Mex. State U., 1952; M.S U.Fla., 1956, Ph.D., 1958; m. Mary Kathryn Floyd, July 17, 1954; children—Grace Ann, James Floyd. Research asst. U. Fla., 1954-58; asst. prof. animal sci. Miss. State U., 1958-60; asst. prof. genetics U. Wis. River Falls, 1960-62, chmn. dept. animal sci., 1962-64, dean Coll. Agr., 1964-80. Treas. Horses A to Z Inc., 1971-80; mem. task force on edn. in agr. and renewable resources Nat. Acad. Sci., 1976-77. Bd. dirs. Wis. Federated Youth Found., v.p., 1971-80. Served with USAF, 1952-54. Mem. Am. Soc. Animal Sci., Am. Genetics Assn., Am. Assn. Univ. Agrl. Adminstrs. (chmn. 1975-80), Sigma Xi, Phi Delta Kappa, Alpha Zeta, Phi Sigma, Gamma Sigma Delta, Sigma Alpha Epsilon. Methodist. Home: River Falls, Wis. Died May 23, 1980; buried Roswell, N.Mex.

DOLLARD, JOHN (DOL-ERD), psychologist; b. Menasha, Wis., Aug. 29, 1900; s. James E. and Ellen (Brady) D.; A.B., U. Wis., 1922; A.M., U. Chgo., 1930, Ph.D., 1931; M.A. (hon.), Yale, 1952; m. Victorine Day, Nov. 28, 1930 (div. 1959); children—Julie (Mrs. R. B. Bradford), John Day, Victorine, Peter Day; m. second, Joan Ganis Palance, Dec. 23, 1961. Secretary Memorial Union Building Com., U. Wis., 1923-26; asst. to the pres. U. Chgo., 1926-29; Social Sci. Research Council fellow in social psychology, Germany, 1931-32; research work Inst. Human Relations, Yale, 1932-52, prof. psychology, 1952-69, prof. emeritus, 1969-81; fellow Berkeley Coll.; expert cons. to Sec. of War, 1942-45. Pres. Conn. Mental Health, 1949-52. Served as pvt. U.S. Army, 1918. Certified profl. psychology, 1947. Fellow Am. Psychol. Assn. (diplomate in clin. psychology), A.A.A.S., Am. Acad. Arts and Scis.; mem. W. New Eng. Psychoanalytic Soc., Phi Beta Kappa, Sigma Xi, Alpha Tau Omega. Clubs: Lawn, Mory's Assn. (New Haven); Century Association, Coffee House, Yale (New York City); Cosmos (Washington, D.C.). Author of ten books including: Caste and Class in a Southern Town, 1937; Social Learning and Imitation (with N.E. Miller), 1941; Personality and Psychotherapy (with N.E. Miller), 1950; Steps in Psychotherapy (with Frank Auld, Jr. and Alice M. White), 1953; Scoring Human Motives (with Frank Auld, Jr.), 1959. Home: New Haven, Conn. Died Oct. 8, 1981.

DOLLARD, STEWART EDWARD, coll. ofcl.; b. Chgo., Sept. 14, 1905; s. Joseph A. and Josephine (Kelley) D.; student St. Mary of the Lake Sem., Mundelein, Ill., 1924-25; A.B., St. Louis U. 1928, A.M., 1930, Ph.D., 1934; S.T.L., St. Mary's Coll., St. Marys, Kan., 1937. Entered Soc. of Jesus, 1925. Instr. in philosophy, West Baden Coll., West Baden Springs, Ind., 1937-42, asso. prof., 1942-46, asso. dean, 1941-46; dean Grad. Sch., Loyola U., Chgo., 1946-65, dir. grad. students, 1965-75. Mem. Jesuit Ednl. Assn., Nat. Cath. Ednl. Assn., Assn. Am. Colls., Am. Cath. Philos. Assn. Home: Chicago, Ill. Died Dec. 5, 1975; buried All Saints Cemetery, Des Plaines, Ill.

DOLLEY, JAMES CLAY, economist, educator; b. Lebanon, Ill., Sept. 29, 1900; s. James Clay and Mary (Turnley) D.; A.B., McKendree Coll., 1919; A.M., U. Ill., 1923; Ph.D., U. Calif., 1928; m. Lois Dee, July 5, 1921; 1 dau., Norma Lee. High sch. instr. and athletic coach, Sparta, Ill., 1919-20, Granite City, Ill., 1920-22, Harrisburg, Ill., 1923-26; teaching fellow econ. U. Calif., 1926-28; asst. prof. bus. adminstrn. U. Tex., 1928-29, asso. prof. banking and investments, 1929-35, prof., from 1935, v.p., prof. banking, 1945-52, acting pres., 1952-53, v.p. for fiscal affairs, 1955-60, vice chancellor fiscal affairs, 1960-66; econ. adviser Fed. Res. Bank, Dallas, Tex., 1943-44, dir. research, 1944-45; dir. Austin Nat. Bank, 1935-76, pres., 1953-54. Pres., United Fund of Austin, 1954-55. Chmn. Franklin Lindsay Student Aid Fund, 1961-76. Mem. Am. Econ. Assn., Royal Econ. Soc. (Eng.), Southwestern Social and Polit. Sci. Assn., Am. Finance Assn. (v.p. 1940-41), Economists Nat. Com. Monetary Policy, Newcomen Soc., Nat. Coll. Athletic Assn. (v.p. 1937-41),

Southwestern Athletic Conf. (pres. 1943-44), Financial Analysts Fedn. (v.p. 1966-67), Beta Gamma Sigma, Delta Sigma Pi. Club: Artus. Author: Principles of Investment, 1940. Contbr. articles to nat. econ. publs. Home: Austin, Tex. Died July 28, 1977; buried Meml. Park, Austin.

DOLVE, ROBERT M., dean, sch. engring.; b. Portland, N.D., July 26, 1883; s. Helge N. and Ragnhild (Nestoss) D.; student, Bruflat Academy, 1897-99; B.S., North Dakota Agricultural College, 1905; M.S., Cornell University, 1919; m. Blance Moyer, Aug. 18, 1915; children—Robert Moyer, Philip Curtis, Mary Margaret. Instr. agrl. engring., N.D. Agrl. Coll., 1906-08, asst. prof., 1908-10, prof., 1910-12, asst. prof. mech. engring., 1912-15, prof., 1915-26, dean of engring. since 1926; in charge Student Army Training Corps ednl. program, N.D. Agrl. Coll., during World War I. In charge E.S.M.W.T. courses and ednl. dir. A.S.T.P., also A.S.R.T.P., N.D. Agrl. Coll., during World War II. Now chmn. E.C.P.D. Guidance committee for North Dakota. Licensed professional Engr. Mem. Am. Soc. Mech. Engrs., Am. Soc. for Engring. Edn., Nat. Soc. Professional Engrs., N.D. Soc. Professional Engrs., Phi Kappa Phi, Theta Chi, Sigma Phi Delta, Tau Beta,Pi, Pi Tau Sigma, Acacia. Mason (Shriner). Home: Fargo, N.D.

DOMINICK, PETER HOYT, ambassador, former U.S. senator; b. Stamford, Conn., July 7, 1915; s. Gayer G. and Eleanor (Hoyt) D.; A.B., Yale, 1937; J.D., 1940; m. Nancy Parks, July 12, 1940; children—Peter Hoyt, Michael P., Lynne B., Alexander S. Admitted to N.Y. bar, 1940, Colo. bar, 1946; asso. Carter, Ledyard & Milburn, N.Y.C., 1940-42, White & Holland, Denver, 1946-47; partner Holland & Hart, 1947-61; atty., Cherry Hills, Colo., 1947-56; mem. Ho. Reps., Colo. Gen. Assembly, 1955-58, 58-61; mem. 87th Congress 2d Dist. Colo., 1961-63; U.S. senator from Colo., 1963-75; ambassador to Switzerland, 1975. Past officer, past trustee Denver Art Mus.; trustee Arapahoe County Mental Health Center. Served from aviation cadet to capt. USAAF, 1942-46. Decorated Air medal with cluster, D.F.C. Mem. Am., Colo., Denver bar assns., V.F.W., Res. Officers Assn. Episcopalian. Kiwanian. Home: Englewood, Colo.; buried Fairmount Cemetery, Denver.

DOMONKOS, ANTHONY NICHOLAS, physician, educator; b. South Bend, Ind., May 29, 1912; s. Anton and Justina (Godollei) M.; student Northwestern U., 1930-32; M.D., Kiralyi Magyar Pazmany Peter Tudomanyegyetem, Budapest, Hungary, 1939; m. Dorothy E. Parrish, June 7, 1940; 1 dau., Dita. Intern Univ. Hosp., Budapest, 1937-39, Conemaugh Valley Meml. Hosp., 1940-41; grad. student dermatology Columbia Coll. Phys. and Surg., 1946-49; asst. dermatologist Vanderbilt Clinic, 1946-49; attending dermotologist Presbyn. Hosp., N.Y.C., 1969-77, cons., 1977-79; clin. prof. dermatology Columbia Coll. Phys. and Surg., 1969-77, prof. emeritus, 1977-79; mem. staff Doctors Hosp., N.Y.C., 1966-79. Mem. subcom. drug efficiency study NRC-Nat. Acad. Sci., 1966-68. Served to maj., M.C., USAAF, 1942-46. Decorated Bronze Star; medal Order Cristobal Columbo (Dominican Republic), 1967; Semmelweis medal, 1976; recipient George Washington award Am. Hungarian Found., 1977. Fellow A.C.P; mem. N.Y. County, N.Y. State med. socs., AMA, Am. Acad. Dermatology and Syphilology, Am. Acad. Dermatology (v.p. 1966, bd. dirs. 1965-68, chmn. spl. course dermatologic X-ray physics and treatment 1966-70), Met., N.Y. State dermatol. socs., Am-Hungarian Med. Assn. (chmn. sci. program 1965, v.p. 1967), N.Y. Acad. Medicine (chmn. sec.-treas. sect. dermatology 1967-68), World Med. Assn., Soc. Investigative Dermatology, Am. Dermatol. Assn. (treas. from 1967, pres. 1978), Internat. Soc. Tropical Dermatology; hon. mem. Iranian Soc. Dermatology and Venereology, Brit Assn. Dermatology, Israeli Dermatologic Soc.; corr. mem. Soc. Venezolana de Dermatologia, Australasian Coll. Dermatologists, Verereologia y Leprologia. Author, co-author 3 textbooks on dermatology, also sci. articles. Home: New York, N.Y. Died May 26, 1979.

DONAHEY, WILLIAM, artist; b. Westchester, Ohio, Oct. 19, 1883; s. John C. and Catherine Letitia (Chaney) D.; ed. pub. schs., Cleveland Sch. of Art; m. Mary Augusta Dickerson, of N.Y. City, Aug. 16, 1905. Began as artist on Cleveland Plain Dealer, 1903; now artist and writer children's features for newspapers, mags. and books. Mem. Am. Press Humorists, Soc. Midland Authors. Author: The Teeny Weenies, 1917; The Teenie Weenie Primar, Adventures of the Teenie Weenies, 1920; Down the River With the Teenie Weenies, 1921; The Teenie Weenie Man's Mother Goose, 1921; The Teenie Weenies Under the Rose-Bush, 1922; The Teenie Weenies in the Wildwood, 1923; 1923 Primer; Alice and the Teenie Weenies, 1927. Home: Chicago, Ill.

DONAVIN, KIRKWOOD HARRY, steamship exec.; b. Delaware, O., June 16, 1886; s. George Barclay and Edith Sophronia (Jones) D.; grad. N.Y. Mil. Acad., 1903; student Ohio State U., 1904; grad. U.S. Naval Acad., 1908; m. Dorothy Waln Morgan Draper, June 7, 1910; children—Kirwood Montrose, Patricia Stansfield (Mrs. Seymour D. Owens). Commd. ensign, U.S. Navy, 1908, and advanced through grades to lieut. comdr.; officer U.S.N.R. since 1920; operating mgr. Internat. Mercantile Marine Co., N.Y. City and San Francisco, 1920-37; asst. to pres. South America Moore McCormack Lines & Pacific Coast mgr., 1938-44; spl. rep. Todd Shipyards Corp. for Latin Am., 1944-46; exec. dir., U.S. Inter-American Council since 1947. Republican. Episcopalian. Club: Army and Navy (Washington). Home: Washington.

DONDINEAU, ARTHUR, educator; b. Pinnebog, Mich., Nov. 5, 1886; s. Peter and Lydia (Cartwright) D.; grad. Central State Teachers Coll., Mt. Pleasant, Mich., 1909; A.B., Univ. of Mich., 1914, A.M., 1915, fellow, 1915-16; summer grad. study Univ. of Chicago, 1916-17, Harvard, 1934, Wayne Univ., 1932-36; LL.D., Central Mich. Coll. Edn., 1946; m. Marguerite Bilton, Aug. 8, 1916; children—Elaine, Elizabeth (Mrs. Robert Roy). Engaged as teacher and principal of high school Kalkaska, Mich., 1909-11; prin. high school, Hart, Michigan, 1911-14; supt. schs., 1915-16; supt. schs. Grand Haven, Mich., 1916-21; supervisor social studies, Detroit, 1921-24, asst. dir. instrn., 1924-25; asso. dean Detroit Teachers Coll., 1925-28; supervising dir. instrn., 1928-33, spl. edn., 1933-41; asst. supt. schs., Detroit, 1941-45, supt., 1945-56. Dir. United Found., Boys Clubs Detroit, Fgn. Policy Assn., N.E.A., Am. Assn. Sch. Adminstrs., Internat. Council Exceptional Children, Am. Polit. Sci. Assn., Mich. Edn. Assn., Mich. Schoolmasters; Mich. Council of Social Work, Detroit Bd. of Commerce, Phi Delta Kappa, Mu Sigma Pi. Republican. Conglist. Mason (K.T.), Rotarian. Club: Noontide. Author: several books, latest (with James B. Edmonson and Mildred Letton Wittick) Civics for Youth, 1946; Civics for Americans (with others), 1959. Home: Detroit.

DONEGAN, ALFRED WILLIAM, consular service; b. Huntsville, Ala., Mar. 3, 1883; student U. of Va., 1 yr., law dept. same, 3 yrs., in Austria, 1904-05; m. in Brünn, Austria, 1905; children—Alfred, Marguerite, Edgar, Dorrit. Apptd. consular agt., Brünn, Austria, May 10, 1905; dep. consul-gen. Budapest, 1908; v. and dep. consul, Algiers, 1909; dep. consul-gen., Montreal, Can., 1910; consul Magdeburg, Germany, 1910-17; duty with Am. Legation, Berne, Switzerland, 1917; detailed to Zurich, 1919; assigned to Königsberg, 1921, to Patras, Greece, 1923; consul at Munich, Germany, 1925-31, Bucharest, 1931-33, Basel, 1933—.

DONNELL, FORREST C., lawyer, gov. Mo.; b. Quitman, Mo., Aug. 20, 1884; s. John Cary and Barbara Lee (Waggoner) D.; A.B., U. Mo., 1904, LL.B., 1907, LL.D., 1960; LL.D., Westminster Coll., Mo., 1941; m. Hilda Hays, Jan. 29, 1913; children—Ruth, John Lanier. Admitted to Mo. bar, 1907, practiced in office of Selden P. Spencer, St. Louis, 1907-11; mem. Spencer & Donnell, 1911-25, Spencer, Donnell & McDonald, 1925-28, Holland, Lashly & Donnell, 1928-33, Donnell & McDonald, 1933-41; gov. of Mo., 1941-45; U.S. senator from Mo., 1945-51; pvt. practice law, St. Louis, 1951-56; mem. firm Donnell, Schoenbeck & Donnell, St. Louis, 1956-67, Donnell, Schoenbeck & La Tourette, 1967; individual practice law, 1967-80. Pres. Assn. Young Republicans Mo., 1916; chmn. bd. mgrs. Mo. Sch. for Blind, 1931-34; former trustee State Hist. Soc. Mo.; chmn. bd. Downtown Y.M.C.A., 1932-35; mem., former chmn. St. Louis adv. bd. Salvation Army; pres. Mo. Sunday Sch. Council Religious Edn., 1929-31; pres. St. Louis City Evangelization Union of M.E. Ch., 1930-34; former chmn. St. Louis World Court Com.; del. from Mo. to Gen. Conf. Methodist Ch., Atlantic City, 1932. Trustee Jefferson Nat. Expansion Meml. Assn. Mem. Am. Bar Assn. (mem. first ho. of dels.; chmn. sect. com. on coordination of state and local bar assns., 1936-37; mem. com. Am. citizenship 1934-35; mem. com. legal aid, 1920-28, etc.), Mo. Bar, Am. Law Inst., Assn. Bar City N.Y., Bar Assn. St. Louis, Mo. Acad. Squires, Order of Coif, Phi Beta Kappa, Kappa Sigma, Phi Delta Phi. Republican. Methodist. Mason (33 deg., past grand master of Grand Lodge Mo.; dep. for Mo. of Scottish Rite 1937-39). Clubs: Noonday, Scottish Rite (St. Louis). Home: St. Louis, Mo. Died Mar. 3, 1980.

DONOVAN, BERNARD EUGENE, supt. schs.; b. Bklyn., Nov. 17, 1910; s. Bernard J. and Emily (Eisemann) D.; B.Ped., Maxwell Tchrs. Coll., N.Y.C., 1930; M.A., N.Y. U., 1934, Ed.D., 1957; LL.D. (hon.), St. Francis Coll., Bklyn., 1966; m. Jane C. Fennell, July 24, 1939; children—Michael, Mary, Anne, Eileen. With N.Y.C. Bd. Edn., from 1930, dep. supt., 1961-63, exec. dept. supt., from 1963; vis. profl. Bklyn. Coll., L.I. U., Yeshiva U., R.I. U., Stanford. Served to comdr. USNR, World War II. Mem. N.E.A., Am. Assn. Sch. Adminstrs., N.Y. Acad. Pub. Edn. Home: Saratoga Springs, N.Y. Died Oct. 27, 1979.

DONOVAN, JAMES ALPORT, JR., govt. ofcl.; b. Buffalo, May 25, 1916; s. James Alport and Laura S. (Hickok) D.; B.A. with honors in German, Yale, 1937, postgrad. Grad. Sch., 1937-40; postgrad. (Am. Council L.S. fellow) Linguistic Inst., U. Mich., summer 1938; m. Abbie Daggett Morse, July 18, 1939 (div.); children—Peter Morse, Patrick James; m. 2d, Katherine Cohn Bang, 1973. Translator, spl. agt. FBI, 1941-46; with State Dept., 1946-80, with security office, 1946-49, with Bur. Ednl. and Cultural Affairs, 1950-80, staff dir. U.S. Adv. Commn. Internat. Ednl. and Cultural Affairs, 1960-72, staff dir. Adv. Com. on Arts, 1960-63, staff dir. Govt. Adv. Com. on Internat. Book and Library Programs, 1962-71, dir. spl. projects staff, 1972-73, history project Bur. Ednl. and Cultural Affairs, 1973-78; archivist, historian Internat. Communications Agy., 1978-80; instr. German, George Washington U., 1947-49. Mem. Alexandria (Va.) Sch. Bd., 1961-67; chmn. Alexandria Adv. Com. Adult Edn., 1964-67. Trustee Greater Washington Ednl. TV Assn., 1954-67. Recipient Meritorious Service award State Dept., 1959. Mem. Soc. Former Spl. Agts. FBI, Thoreau Soc., Samuel Butler Soc. (founder, editor newsletter 1978), Oral History Assn., Soc. Historians Am. Fgn. Relations, Fed. Govt. Micrographics Council. Unitarian. Clubs: Yale, George Washington U. (Washington). Contbr. articles to profl. jours. Home: Washington, D.C. Died Oct. 31, 1980.

DONOVAN, JAMES NORTON, financial exec.; b. Toronto, Ont., Can., Aug. 28, 1921 (parents U.S. citizens); s. James Michael and Cornelia (Smith) D.; B.S., U. Calif. at Berkeley, 1947; M.B.A., 1949; m. Mary Elizabeth Carter, Dec. 6, 1944; 1 dau., Elizabeth Lathrop. Accountant, Houston, Cossar & Bartlett, Toronto, 1940-42; pub. accountant McLaren, Goode, West & Co., San Francisco, 1947-52; chief accountant, asst. controller Varian Assos., Palo Alto, Calif., 1952-57, treas., 1957-78. Served with USNR, 1942-44; USMCR, 1944-46. C.P.A., Calif. Mem. Am. Inst. C.P.A.'s. Home: Menlo Park, Calif. Died June 1, 1978; buried Alta Mesa Meml. Park, Palo Alto.

DONOVAN, JOHN CHARLES, JR., physician, educator; b. Scranton, Pa., Nov. 15, 1919; s. John Charles and Catherine Mary (Sullivan) D.; student U. Notre Dame. 1938-41; M.D., Rochester Sch. Medicine, 1945; m. Margaret Wood, May 24, 1947; children—Margaret Ann, John Charles III. Intern New Haven Hosp., 1945-46; resident obstetrics and gynecology Strong Meml. Hosp., Rochester, N.Y., 1946-50, staff, 1950-76; instr. obstetrics and gynecology U. Rochester, 1950-54, asst. prof., 1954-66, asso. prof., 1961-66, prof., 1966-76; cons. obstetrician gynecologist Genesse Hosp., Highland Hosp., Rochester, N.Y.; Fellow Am. Gynecol. Soc., Am. Assn. Obstetricians and Gynecologists Club: Oak Hill Country. Contbr. articles to med. jours. Home: Pittsford, N.Y. Died Jan. 5, 1976.

DONWORTH, CHARLES TENNEY, judge; b. Seattle, Feb. 15, 1892; s. George and Emma Laura (Tenney) D.; grad. Phillips Andover Acad., 1910; A.B., Yale, 1914; LL.B., U. Wash., 1916; m. Evelyn Carey, Feb. 5, 1918 (dec. 1934); children—Charles Carey, Mary Evelyn (Mrs. Lincoln Wayland Craighead); m. 2d, Dorothy Lee Griffin, Dec. 28, 1945. Admitted to Wash. State bar, 1916, practiced in Seattle, 1916-49, mem. firm Donworth, Donworth & Smith, 1942-49; asst. corp. counsel Seattle, 1920-23; judge Supreme Ct. of Wash., 1949-67, pro tem judge, intermittently, 1968-71, chief justice, 1956-57. Served as 1st lt., inf. U.S. Army, 1917-19. Recipient Carkeek prize U. Wash. Law Sch., 1916. Mem. Am., Seattle (pres. 1934) bar assns., Am. Judicature Soc., Phi Delta Phi, Order of Coif. Club: Rainier (Seattle). Home: Olympia, Wash. Died June 10, 1976.

DOOLEY, JAMES A., justice; b. Chgo., Aug. 7, 1914; s. James A. and Agnes (Dowling) D.; grad. cum laude Loyola U. (Chgo.), 1935, J.D., 1937; LL.B., Clark Coll., 1951; m. Virginia Proesel, Feb. 19, 1955; 1 dau., Virginia A. Admitted to Ill.'bar, 1937; practiced in Chgo., 1937-78; mem. firm James A. Dooley, 1941-76; justice Ill. Supreme Ct., 1976-78. Pres. James A. Dooley Found., Chgo., 1956-78. Chmn. bd. trustees Clark Coll., from 1955; trustee Loyola U., 1964-78. Recipient Medal of Excellence Loyola Law Sch. Alumni, 1976, Founder's Day award Loyola U., 1975. Fellow Internat. Acad. Trial Lawyers (dir. 1954-78, pres. 1960-61); mem. Am., Ill., Chgo. bar assns., Assn. Trial Lawyers Am. (pres. 1953-54), Ill. Trial Lawyers Assn. (pres. 1951-55), Law Sci. Acad. Am. (pres. 1960, gold medal award 1970), Internat. Acad. Law and Sci. Author: Modern Tort Law, Editor: Trial Mag., 1973-74. Home: Chicago, Ill. Died Mar. 5, 1978.

DOOLING, JOHN FRANCIS, JR., U.S. judge; b. Bklyn., June 13, 1908; s. John Francis and Anna Clothilde (Conlan) D.; A.B. cum laude, St. Francis Coll., Bklyn., 1929; LL.B. magna cum laude, St. Johns U., 1932, Harvard, 1934; m. Marie Dorothea Elizabeth Bernard, Apr. 24, 1937; children—Julienne (Mrs. Eugene B. Nann), Deborah (Mrs. Paul P. Fitzgerald), Peter, Ann, Marie. Admitted to N.Y. bar, 1934; with firm Sullivan & Cromwell, N.Y.C., 1934-61; U.S. judge Eastern Dist. N.Y., 1961-81. Trustee Vassar Coll., 1965-69. Mem. Am. Law Inst., Assn. Bar City N.Y. (chmn. com. state legislation 1951-53, com. cts. superior jurisdiction 1957-60). Home: Brooklyn, N.Y. Died Jan. 12, 1981.

DORAN, EARL D., corp. exec.; b. Spokane, Wash., 1886. Pres., dir. Doran Co.; dir. First Nat. Bank, Am.

Mail Line (all in Seattle). Home: Seattle.

DORAN, EDWIN BEALE (DO-RAN'), univ. prof.; b. Loudon, Tenn., Oct. 11, 1885; s. Edwin Wortham and Florence Emily (Beale) D.; B.S., U. of Ill., 1906, M.S., 1929; m. Cornelia Anne Denham, Aug. 13, 1913; 1 son, Edwin Beale. Intermittent employment as machinery expert for Internat. Harvester Co., U.S., France, Algeria, Argentina; farm experience, 1908-11; instr., La. State U., 1911, prof. and dept. head, since 1919. Mem. of bd. of dirs. Community Chest; vice pres. Boy Scout Council; vice pres. Campus Y.M.C.A. Mem. Am. Soc. of Agrl. Engrs. (sec. and pres. of S.W. sect.), Phi Kappa Phi, Alpha Zeta, Alpha Gamma Rho. Received Silver Beaver Award of Boy Scouts of Am. Democrat. Presbyterian. Author: Laboratory Manual in Elementary Land Drainage and Terracing, 1932. Home: Baton Rouge.

DORR, GOLDTHWAITE HIGGINSON, lawyer; b. Newark, Oct. 21, 1876; s. John Van Nostrand and Nancy (Higginson) D.; A.B., Harvard, 1897; J.D., Columbia, 1904; m. Virginia Elbert, Sept. 18, 1905 (dec. Jan. 1963); children—Russell Higginson, John Van Nostrand II, Katharine Goldthwaite. Admitted to bar, N.Y., 1904; lectr. Harvard, 1899, Columbia U. Law Sch., 1906-14; engaged in practice law, N.Y., from 1904; asst. U.S. atty., N.Y., and spl. asst. to U.S. atty.-gen. Dept. of Justice at various times from 1906-21; acted as expert for President Hoover's Commn. on Law Observance in U.S., 1930-31; counsel cotton textile industry in NRA code formulation and adminstrn.; engaged in gen. econ. survey of Turkey for Turkish govt., 1934; adviser Nfld. govt. as to econ. survey of Nfld., 1940; v.p., dir., gen. counsel Dorr Co., Inc., chmn. bd. Cotton Textile Inst., 1935; withdrew from practice to act as spl. asst. to sec. of war, 1942; returned to practice in N.Y.C., 1945; mem. firm Mudge, Rose, Guthrie & Alexander. Alternate to Sec. War, Cabinet Com. on Palestine, 1946; cons. to sec. of state, 1947; Am. del. to Internat. Refugee Council, 1948; cons. War Dept. on Germany, 1948-49, Japan, 1950; mem. med. services com. Hoover Commn. on Orgn. of Exec. Br. of Govt.; rep. Dept. Def. Council of Fgn. Ministers, Paris, 1949; Am. rep. Tripartite Conf. Migration Problems, Paris, 1950, guest of Italian govt. for consultation thereafter. Bd. dirs. Near East Found.; chmn. bd. Robert Coll., 1952-55; past chmn. Am. Sch. Prehistoric Research; fellow Am. Bar Found.; vis. com. dept. anthropology, also Peabody Mus., Harvard. Served as seaman, U.S. Navy, Spanish-Am. War; asst. dir. munitions, War Dept., World War I. Awarded D.S.M., Medal of Merit. Mem. Am. Acad. Polit. Sci., Am. Bar Assn., Assn. Bar City N.Y., Am. Ordnance Assn., Bus. Hist. Soc., Municipal Art Soc., Soc. Bus. Adv. Professions. Clubs: Harvard, Century Assn., Downtown Assn. (N.Y.C.); Cosmos, Metropolitan (Washington). Home: Carmel, N.Y. Died Dec. 7, 1977.

DORRANCE, CHARLES, fuel exec.; b. Meadville, Pa., Mar. 12, 1883; s. James Ford and Elizabeth Wilson (Dick) D.; ed. Wyoming Sem., Kingston, Pa.; Yale U.; E.M., Lehigh U., 1907; m. Florence Waring, Feb. 25, 1921. Pres., dir. W. Va. Coal & Coke Corp.; dir. Ohio River Co. Home: Cincinnati. *

DORSCHEL, QUERIN PETER, lawyer; b. Green Bay, Wis., Feb. 8, 1898; s. Peter Frank and Pauline (Schumacher) D.; B.S., Marquette U., 1920; LL.B., U. Chgo., 1934; m. Philemene Connell, 1927; m. 2d, Gertrude Reiss Corbett, Feb. 21, 1939. Pvt. practice pub. accounting, auto financing, Milw., Chgo., 1920-32; admitted to Ill. bar, 1934; counsel, sec. Ill. Power & Light Corp. and subsidiaries, 1934-39; partner firm Schiff, Hardin & Waite, Chgo., 1939-79. Lay trustee Loyola U.; bd. advs. Cath. Charities, Archdiocese of Chgo. Mem. Am., Ill., Chgo. bar assns. Clubs: Chicago, University, Glen View Country, Tucson Country. Home: Chicago, Ill. Died Feb. 26, 1979.

DORSEY, CAM DAWSON, lawyer; b. Atlanta, Ga., Feb. 1, 1882; s. Rufus Thomas and Sarah Matilda (Bennett) D.; B.S., U. of Ga., 1903; LL.B., Columbia, 1907; m. Minnie Wynn Adams, Dec. 4, 1909; children—Samuel Adams, Rufus Thomas (dec.), Cam Dawson, Roy Adams. Admitted to Ga. bar, 1904, and since practiced in Atlanta; member Dorsey & Dorsey; atty. U.S. Shipping Bd., Emergency Fleet Corp., 1918; dist. counsel of same for southeastern states, 1919-21; standing master in chancery U.S. Dist. Court Northern Dist. of Ga., 1920-29 (resigned); commr. on uniform state laws 1932-41 (resigned); director of Rhodes, Incorporated, and Affiliates. Pres. Fulton County Board of Edn., 1930-33; treasurer and trustee U. of Georgia Foundation. Mem. Am. and Ga. bar assns., Soc. Colonial Wars, Columbia U. Alumni Assn. (v.p.), U. of Georgia Alumni Society (president 1942-43), Phi Delta Phi, Sigma Alpha Epsilon. Democrat. Methodist. Club: Piedmont Driving. Home: Atlanta.

DORSEY, JOHN MORRIS, psychiatrist, educator; b. Clinton, Iowa, Nov. 19, 1900; s. Edward William and Anna Elizabeth (Looney) D.; A.B., U. Iowa, 1925, M.D., 1925, M.S., 1927; m. Mary Louise Carson, Oct. 26, 1926; children—John Morris, Edward Carson. Intern, U. Iowa Hosps., 1925-26; resident psychiatrist U. Iowa, State Psychopathic Hosp., instr. psychiatry, 1926-28; asst. dir. Mich. State Psychopathic Hosp., 1928-35; asso. prof. U. Mich. Med. Sch., 1933-38, lectr. postgrad. medicine, 1938-48; cons. psychiatrist Wayne County Juvenile Ct., Detroit, 1929-35, 37-50; tng. psychiatrist Children's Center, Detroit, 1938-48; psychiatrist, head Wayne State U. Mental Hygiene Service, 1938-40, chmn. dept. psychiatry, 1946-61, also professorial lectr.; psychiatrist Purdue U. Sch. Survey Com.; dir. Child Guidance Div., Children's Fund of Mich., 1945-54, Univ. Prof., Wayne State U., 1961-71. Ednl. dir. Children's Center, 1944-50; med. dir. McGregor Center, hosp. for rehab. and health edn.; chief cons. neurology and psychiatry, Dearborn VA Hosp.; staff physician Harper Hosp.; psychiatrist Children's Hosp.; chmn. dept. psychiatry Detroit Receiving Hosp. Rockefeller Found. grantee, 1935-37. Mem. Highland Park Bd. Edn. (pres. 1944, 50, 54); mem. City-County Mental Health Bd. Trustee Luella Hannan Meml. Home, John Scudder Found. for Old People. Commd. 1st lt. Med. Res. Corps. Diplomate Am. Bd. Psychiatry and Neurology. Mem. AMA, Am. Psychiat. Assn., Am. Psychol. Assn., Am. Psychopathol. Assn., Am. Assn. Mil. Surgeons, AAAS, Am. Psychoanalytic Assn., Mich. Soc. Neurology and Psychiatry (pres.), Am. Med. Writers Assn., Am. Coll. Psychoanalysis, U. Mich. Research Club, Sigma Xi, Alpha Kappa Delta, Nu Sigma Nu, Sigma Chi, Alpha Omega Alpha. Republican. Clubs: Torch, Detroit Boat, Prismatic (Detroit); Ann Arbor Golf and Outing. Author: The Foundations of Human Nature, 1935; The Use of the Psycho-Analytic Principle in Child Guidance Work, 1949; (with Walter H. Seegers) Living Consciously: The Science of Self; Illness or Allness, 1965; American Government, 1969; Psychology of Emotion, 1971; Psychology of Language, 1971; Psychology of Political Science, 1973; Psychology of Ethics, 1974; An American Psychiatrist in Vienna, 1935-37, And His Sigmund Freud, 1976; The Psychic Nature of Physiology, 1976; Selected Essays, 1976; posthumous publ.: University Professor John M. Dorsey. Editor: The Letters of Thomas Jefferson and his Personal Physician Robley Dunglison; The Growth of Self-Insight (Franklin Lecture Series). Contbr. to Modern Marriage, 1950; also to jours. Home: Highland Park, Mich. Died Aug. 6, 1978; interred Woodlawn Cemetery, Detroit.

DORSEY, MONTGOMERY, lawyer; b. Denver, Sept. 11, 1900; s. Clayton Chauncey and Marguerite (Montgomery) D.; student Hotchkiss Sch., Lakeville, Conn., 1915-18; A.B., Yale, 1922; LL.B., Denver U., 1925; m. Margaret Owen, Nov. 25, 1935. Admitted to Colo. bar, 1925; practice of law with Hughes & Dorsey, Denver, 1925-79; chmn. bd. Nat. Bank of Denver, 1957-75; dir. Rio Grande Industries, Inc., Denver & Rio Grande Western R.R. Co. Bd. dirs., pres. A.V. Hunter Trust; chmn., trustee Laurence Phipps Found.; trustee Mabel Y. Hughes Charitable Trust. Mem. Am., Colo., Denver bar assns. Clubs: Denver, Country, Athletic, 26 (Denver); Mile High; Garden of Gods (Colorado Springs). Home: Denver, Colo. Died May 25, 1979.

DOSTAL, CHARLES ANTOINE, corp. exec.; b. Paris, France, Dec. 9, 1883; s. Antoine Robert and Augustine (Brassart) D.; student Smith Acad., St. Louis, 1904; student Bryant Stratton Bus. Sch., St. Louis, 1906; m. Margaret Lewis, Dec. 20, 1913; children—Betty J. (Mrs. Howard J. White), Chas. L., Philander L. Apprentice, Westinghouse Electric Corp., Pittsburgh, 1907, salesman, St. Louis office, 1909-13, mgr. lamp div. Southwest dist., 1915-21, Northwest dist., Chicago, 1921-29; vice pres. and gen. sales mgr. Am. Flyer Mfg. Co., Chicago, 1929-31; regional sales mgr. merchandising div. Westinghouse Electric Corp., hdqrs., Chicago, 1931-39, Pacific coast dist. mgr., San Francisco, 1939-43, became v.p., San Francisco, 1943. Mem. Pacific Coast Elec. Assn. Episcopalian. Mason. Clubs: Bohemian, Electric (San Francisco); Rotary (past pres.) (Chicago). Home: Burlingame, Calif. *

DOUGHERTY, JAMES HENRY, educator; b. Fayettee, Mo., Jan. 5, 1901; s. James Lee and Minnie (White) D.; B.S., Northeast Mo. State Coll., 1925; Ph.D., U. Mo., 1933; m. Elizabeth Estelle Hurtt, Aug. 10, 1927; children—James Henry, Charles Raymond. Tchr., prin. Mo. elem. schs., 1918-22; prin. New Franklin (Mo.) pub. schs., 1923-25, supt., 1925-27; supt. Ashland (Mo.) pub. schs., 1927-30; asso. supt. Columbia (Mo.) pub. schs., 1932-37; prof. edn. Christian Coll., Stephens Coll., 1932-37; prof. edn. U. Mo., summers 1931-40; asso. prof. Tex. Christian U., 1937-40, prof., 1940-41; prof., chmn. dept. elementary edn. N. Tex. State U., 1941-78; cons. Mo. Dept. Curriculum Study, 1936-37, Johnson, Anderson and Wilbarger counties (Tex.), 1946-53, Sherman, Denison and Plano (Tex.) pub. schs., 1952-66. Mem. Tex., Nat. elem. sch. prins., Assn. Suprs. and Curriculum Devel., N.E. Mo. State Tchrs. Assn. (v.p.), Denton C. of C., Kappa Delta Pi, Phi Delta Kappa. Mem. Christian Ch. Kiwanian (dir. 1957-59, 1969-78). Author: Elementary School Organization and Management, 1936, rev. edit., 1950; Some Facts Concerning Teaching of Arithmetic, 1933; Guide to Healthful Living in Elementary Schools, 1946; Natural Phenomena as Explained by Children, 1966. Home: Denton, Tex. Died Apr. 21, 1978; interred Roselawn Meml. Cemetery, Denton.

DOUGHERTY, JAMES L(AWRENCE), lawyer; b. Piper City, Ill., Dec. 25, 1886; s. John B. and Mary Agnes (Power) D.; St. Bede Coll., Peru, Ill., 1901-03; A.B., St. Viator Coll., Bourbonnais, Ill., 1908; Catholic U., Washington, D.C., 1908-10; LL.B., Loyola U., Chicago, 1911; m. Grace Kilday, Oct. 11, 1922; 1 dau., Mary Ellen. Clerk, First Nat. Bank of Chicago, 1910; abstracter and examiner of titles, Real Estate Title and Trust Co. Chicago, 1911-12; admitted to Ill. bar, 1911, and practiced at Kankakee as mem. Granger, Dougherty & Nourie, 1912-17; mem. Dougherty & Dougherty, Sioux Falls, S.D., 1920-22; successively counsel, asst. gen. counsel and gen. counsel War Finance Corp., 1922-32; also counsel Federal Farm Loan Bd., 1928-31, and successively counsel and asst. gen. counsel, R.F.C., 1932-47, gen. counsel, 1947-51, ret.; exec. sec. Steel Products Warehouse Association since 1952; dir. The Trust Co. of N.J. 1st lt. inf., U.S. Army, 1917-1918; seriously wounded in action, July 18, 1918. Awarded Order of the Purple Heart. Mem. Am. Bar Assn., Federal Bar Assn.; Am. Legion. Catholic. Home: Washington.

DOUGHERTY, JOHN L., newspaper editor; b. Bradford, Pa., May 24, 1918; s. John L. and Edith (Larson) D.; B.A., Alfred U., 1939; postgrad. (Nieman fellow) Harvard U., 1956; m. Mary Louise Hoag, June 19, 1944; children—Brian M., Ann E., Martha L. Reporter, Salamanca (N.Y.) Republican Press, 1935-39; with Rochester (N.Y.) Times-Union, 1939-80, telegraph editor, 1952-56, city editor, 1956-62, asst. mng. editor, 1962-66, mng. editor, 1966-79; mng. editor Rochester Democrat & Chronicle, 1979-80; discussion leader Am. Press Inst., 1961-80; prof. journalism U. Rochester, 1975-80. Trustee Alfred U., 1977-80. Served to 1st lt. U.S. Army, 1942-47. Decorated Bronze Star. Mem. Soc. Nieman Fellows, N.Y. State AP Assn. (pres. 1970), AP Mng. Editors Assn. (treas. 1978-80), Sigma Delta Chi. Home: Rochester, N.Y. Died May 11, 1980; buried Holy Sepulchre Cemetery, Rochester.

DOUGLAS, HELEN GAHAGAN (MRS. MELVYN DOUGLAS), author, lectr.; b. Boonton, N.J., Nov. 25, 1900; d. Walter and Lillian Rose (Mussen) Gahagan; student Barnard Coll., 1920-22; D.C(L. (hon.), Ind. State U., Terre Haute, 1974; LL.D. (hon.), Marlboro (Vt.) Coll., 1975; m. Melvyn Douglas, Apr. 5, 1931; children—Peter Gahagan, Mary Helen. Actress, N.Y.C., starred in plays including Young Woodley, 1925, Enchanted April, 1925, Trelawney of the Wells, 1926, Tonight or Never, 1930, Mary Queen of Scotland, 1934, First Lady, 1952; opera concert singer, poetry reader, 1952-62; recorded Great American Poetry for Caedmon Records; singer European tour, 1928-30, 37; star motion picture She, 1935; mem. 79th to 81st congresses from 14th dist. Calif., mem. fgn. affairs com., co-author McMahon-Douglas Bill; U.S. del. UN Gen. Assembly, 1946; sec. Gahagan Dredging Corp., 1953-69; mem. nat. adv. com. WPA, 1939; del. of Jane Addams Peace Assn. to Soviet-Am. Women's Conf., Moscow, USSR, hon. co-chmn. Women's Internat. League for Peace and Freedom, 1964; mem. Nat. Adv. Com. on Farm Labor, 1958-72; mem. adv. council Sch. Social Work, Columbia U., 1963-73; personal rep. of Pres. Johnson with rank spl. ambassador to inauguration Pres. V.S. Tubman, Liberia, 1964; bd. dirs. Harlem Sch. Arts, N.Y.C., 1967-70, Music Therapy Center, 1969; mem. nat. adv. council Fedn. Orgns. for Profl. Women, 1974; bd. sponsors Women's Lobby, Inc., 1973; del. Dem. Nat. Conv.; Dem. Nat. committeewoman from Calif., 1940; vice chmn. Dem. State Central Com., chmn. women's div., 1941-44. Named Woman of Year, N.Y. Hadassah, 1945, 1 of 12 Outstanding Women of Year, Nat. Council Negro Women, 1945; 2d Ann. Eleanor Roosevelt Humanities award, Phila., 1964; Louise Waterman Wise award nat. womens div. Am. Jewish Congress, 1968; award from women's orgn. Stephen Wise Free Synagogue, 1973; honored by ACLU, N.J., 1974, (with husband) ACLU, Los Angeles, 1974. Mem. Nat. Women's Trade Union League Am. Author: The Eleanor Roosevelt We Remember, 1963. Address: New York, N.Y. Died June 28, 1980.

DOUGLAS, LLOYD VIRGIL, bus. educator; b. Brandon, Iowa, Aug. 4, 1902; s. Delbert G. and Dora E. (Lizer) D.; B.S., State U. Iowa, 1923, A.M., 1928, Ph.D., 1936; postgrad. Iowa State Coll., summer 1925; m. Grace A. Waddell, Aug. 26, 1925 (dec.); m. 2d, Virginia V. Marston, Aug. 4, 1973. High sch. bus. tchr., Jefferson, Ia., 1923-25; head dept. bus. edn. U. No. Iowa, 1937-70, prof. emeritus, 1970-78; summer grad. lectr. Okla. A. and M. Coll., 1941, State U. Iowa, 1946, 72, State U. Colo., 1949, U. Wis., 1950, Northwestern U., 1951; recruiting specialist 8th U.S. Civil Service Dist., St. Paul, 1942; supr. U.S. Naval Tng. Sch., Ind. U., 1942-44; distinguished prof. Mich. State U., summer 1958; vis. prof. No. Ill. U., 1970-71. Chmn. practical arts com. Iowa Secondary Sch. Coop. Curriculum Program, 1946-48; chmn. Iowa research com. United Bus. Edn.

Assn. Bus. edn. curriculum cons. Iowa secondary schs.; mem. Nat. Policies Commn. Bus. and Econ. Edn. Recipient John Robert Gregg award, 1960; Representative Citizen award Cedar Falls C. of C., 1966. Mem. N.E.A. (bd. 1950-53), United Bus. Edn. Assn. (pres. 1953-54), North Central Bus. Edn. Assn. (pres. 1967, distinguished service award 1971), Nat. Bus. Tchrs. Assn. (bd. 1942-48, v.p. 1949), Internat. Soc. Bus. Edn. (council, 1948-49), Nat. Assn. Bus. Tchr. Tng. Instns. (dir. 1941-43), Central Comml. Tchrs. Assn. (pres. 1940), Future Bus. Leaders Am. (trustee 1957-67), Am. Vocat. Assn. (research com.), Ia. Edn. Assn., Ia. Bus. Edn. Assn. (pres. 1947-48), Cedar Falls C. of C. (pres., 1945-47), Pi Omega Pi (nat. pres. 1941-44, nat. organizer, 1944-46), Delta Pi Epsilon (nat. research awards com., 1945-48), Phi Delta Kappa, Kappa Delta Pi. Lion (pres. 1949-50). Author: (with others) Modern Business, 1948; Business Education, 1963; other textbooks. Contbr. profl. mags. and yearbooks. Home: Cedar Falls, Iowa. Died July 12, 1978; buried Iowa City.

DOUGLAS, PAUL HOWARD, educator, U.S. senator; b. Salem, Mass., Mar. 26, 1892; s. James Howard and Annie (Smith) D.; A.B., Bowdoin Coll., 1913; A.M., Columbia, 1915, Ph.D., 1921; postgrad. Harvard, 1915-16; LL.D., MacMurray Coll., Bates Coll., DePaul, St. Ambrose, Lake Forest Coll., William and Mary U., Oberlin Coll., New Sch. for Social Research, Bowdoin Coll., U. Rochester, Knox Coll., Bryant Coll., Bucknell U., Amherst; Litt.D., Rollins Coll.; L.H.D., Lincoln Coll., U. So. Ill., U. Ill.; m. Dorothy S. Wolff, 1915 (div. 1930); children—Helen (Mrs. Paul Klein), John, Dorothea (Mrs. Robert John), Paul; m. Emily Taft, 1931; 1 dau., Jean (Mrs. Ned Bandler). Instr. econs. U. Ill., 1916-17; instr. asst. prof. econs. Reed Coll., Portland, Ore., 1917-18; asso. prof. econs. U. Wash., 1919-20; asst. prof. indsl. relations U. Chgo., 1920-23, asso. prof., 1923-25, prof. econs., 1925-48; U.S. senator, 1949-66; faculty New Sch. Social Research, N.Y.C., 1966-69. Vis. prof. Amherst Coll., 1924-27, Indsl. relations work with Emergency Fleet Corp., 1918-19; acting dir. Swarthmore Unemployment Study, 1930; sec. Pa. Commn. on Unemployment, 1930; econ. adviser N.Y. Commn. on Unemployment 1930; Guggenheim fellow, 1931; mem. Ill. Housing Commn., 1931-33; mem. Consumers' Adv. Bd. NRA, 1933-35, Adv. Com. to U.S. Senate and Social Security Bd. on Fed. Social Security System, 1937; chmn. Pres.'s Commn. on Urban Problems, 1967-68. Del.-at-large Democratic Nat. Convs., 1948, 52, 56, 64, 68; alderman 5th ward Chgo. City Council, 1939-42. Chmn. bd. trustees Freedom House, 1967-69. Served from pvt. to lt. col. USMC, 1942-46. Decorated Bronze Star. Recipient Sidney Hillman award, 1957; John F. Kennedy award Cath. Interracial Council, 1970. Fellow Econometric Soc., Am. Acad. Arts and Scis.; mem. Am. Econ. Assn. (pres. 1947), Am. Statis. Assn., Am. Philos. Soc., Phi Beta Kappa, Delta Upsilon. Unitarian. Quaker. Clubs: Federal City (Washington); Chicago Literary. Author: American Apprenticeship and Industrial Education, 1921; (with others) Worker in Modern Economic Society, 1923; Wages and the Family, 1925; (with others) Adam Smith (1776-1926), 1928; Real Wages in the United States (1890-1926), 1930; Economy in the National Government, 1952; America in the Market Place, 1966; Standards of Unemployment Insurance, 1933; The Theory of Wages, 1934; Controlling Depressions, 1935; Social Security in the United States, 1936; Ethics in Government, 1952; In Our Time, 1968; In the Fullness of Time, 1972; co-author: Movement of Real Wages (1926-28), 1930; The Problem of Unemployment, 1931. Contbr. to Am. Econ. Rev., Jour. Polit. Economy, Polit. Sci. Quar., others. Home: Washington, D.C. Died Sept. 24, 1976.

DOUGLAS, WILLIAM ORVILLE, asso. justice U.S. Supreme Ct.; b. Maine, Minn., Oct. 16, 1898; s. William and Julia Bickford (Fiske) D.; B.A., Whitman Coll., 1920, LL.D., 1938; LL.B., Columbia, 1925; M.A. (hon.), Yale, 1932; LL.D., Wesleyan U., 1940, Washington and Jefferson Coll., 1942, Coll. William and Mary, 1943, Rollins Coll., 1947, Nat. U., 1949, New Sch. for Social Research, 1952, U. Toledo, 1956, Bucknell U., 1958, Dalhousie U., 1958, Colby Coll., 1961; m. Mildred Riddle, Aug. 16, 1923; children—Mildred Riddle (Mrs. Norman T. Read), William Orville; m. 2d, Mercedes Hester, Dec. 14, 1954 (div. 1963); m. 3d, Joan Martin, Aug., 1963 (div.); m. 4th, Cathleen Heffernan, July, 1966. Instr. high sch. Yakima, Wash., 1920-22; admitted to N.Y. bar, 1926; practiced in N.Y.C., 1925-27; mem. law faculty, Columbia, 1925-28, Yale, 1928-34; bankruptcy studies, Yale Inst. Human Relations and U.S. Dept. Commerce, 1929-32; sec. com. on bus. of fed. cts. Nat. Commn. on Law Observance and Enforcement, 1930-32; dir. protective com. study SEC, Washington, 1934-36, commr. and chmn., 1936-39; asso. justice U.S. Supreme Ct., 1939-75; ret., 1975. Served as pvt. U.S. Army, 1918. Mem. Royal Geog. Soc. (London), Phi Beta Kappa, Beta Theta Pi, Phi Alpha Delta, Delta Sigma Rho. Democrat. Presbyn. Mason. Clubs: Himalayan (Delhi, India); University (Washington); Overseas Press. Author various law case books; also Of Men and Mountains, 1950; Strange Lands and Friendly People, 1951; Beyond the High Himalayas, 1952; North from Malaya, 1953; An Almanac of Liberty, 1954; We The Judges, 1955; Russian Journey, 1956; The Right of the People, 1958; Exploring the Himalaya, 1958; West of the Indus, 1958; My Wilderness: East to Katahdin, 1960; My Wilderness: The Pacific West, 1961; A Living Bill of Rights, 1961; Democracy's Manifesto, 1962; The Anatomy of Liberty, 1963; Mr. Lincoln and the Negroes, 1963; Freedom of the Mind, 1963; A Wilderness Bill of Rights, 1965; The Bible and the Schools, 1966; Farewell to Texas, 1967; Towards a Global Federalism, 1968; Points of Rebellion, 1969; International Dissent, 1970; Holocaust or Hemisphere Cooperation, 1970; The Three Hundred Year War, 1972; Go East Young Man: The Early Years, 1974; Go East Young Man: The Court Years, 1980. Contbr. numerous articles to law jours. Home: Goose Prairie, Wash. Died Jan. 19, 1980.

DOUGLASS, LATHROP, architect; b. Kansas City, Mo., Sept. 5, 1907; s. Willard R. and Floyd (Smith) D.; A.B., Yale, 1929, B.F.A. with honors, 1932; student Fontainebleau (France), 1931; m. Dorothy Duncan Howe, Sept. 10, 1937 (dec. 1976); children—Rebecca Lanier, Lathrop Howe. Site planner, designer, 1934-39; housing control architect N.Y. State Housing Bd., 1940-41; asst. chief engr. charge design Army Middle East Repair Bases, 1942-43; practicing architect, planning cons., from 1945; works include office bldgs., regional shopping centers, urban redevel. in U.S., S. Am., Europe; Creole Bldg. and Luz Electrica Bldg., Caracas, Venezuela; Esso bldgs., Paris, France, Bogota, Colombia, Antwerp, Belgium, Rome, Italy (cons.); Cross County Center, N.Y., Tysons Corner Center, Washington, Plaza Las Americas, San Juan, P.R., Parly 2 and La Belle Epine, Paris; new town centers of Creteil and Pontoise (France); Chapel Square Redevel., New Haven, Main Pl. Redevel., Buffalo, Greenwich (Conn.) Sta. Plaza; cons. AEC, 1951-52, Esso A.G., Hamburg, Germany, others. Lectr., Internat. Council Shopping Centers. Mem. internat. bd. Temple Understanding; past bd. dirs. N.Y. Bd. Trade; mem. pub. adv. panel Fed. Bldgs. Program, 1966-68. Recipient 1st Medal award Festival Internat. d'Architecture, Paris, 1956. Fellow A.I.A. (dir. N.Y. chpt. 1958-62, treas. 1966-67, v.p. 1967-68, pres. 1968-69); mem. Nat. Inst. Archtl. Edn. (treas. 1961-63 trustee), N.Y. State Assn. Architects. ASCE, St. Nicholas Soc., Huguenot Soc., Sigma Xi (asso.). Clubs: University, Yale (N.Y.C.); Bellehaven (Greenwich). Author mag. articles; illustrator geology textbooks. Home: Greenwich, Conn. Died Jan. 21, 1981.

DOUGLASS, RAYMOND DONALD, educator; b. Gorham, Me., Dec. 29, 1894; s. Edward K. and Josephine (Chick) D.; A.B., U. Me., 1915, A.M., 1916. Sc.D., 1943; Ph.D., Mass. Inst. Tech., 1931; m. Ollave Norton, Feb. 2, 1918; children—Charlotte (Mrs. Willard Mott), Eleanor, Marjorie (Mrs. Charles Humphreys). Prin. high sch., Mass., 1916-17; sub-master, high sch., N.H., 1917-18; successively instr., asst. prof., asso. prof., prof. math. Mass. Inst. Tech., 1919-78. Mem. bd. examiners Math. Coll. Exam. Bd. Cons. Chem. Warfare Service, Nat. Def. Research Com. Bd. dirs. Boston Center for Adult Edn., Adult Edn. Council of Greater Boston; chmn. bd. Mt. Ida Jr. Coll.; adv. bd. Salvation Army Greater Boston. Served with U.S. Navy, 1918-19; cons. Chem. Warfare Service, from 1930; state coordinator Mass., 1941-43, war man-power bd. Mass., 1941-46; war tng. programs, 1941-45; cons. camouflage sect., N.D.R.C., 1943-45. Recipient citation Army Signal Corps, commendation N.D.R.C., The Charles Francis Park Gold medal. Mem. Am. Math Assn., Am. Math. Soc., Am. Soc. Engring. Edn., Mass. Coaches Assn., Mass. Track and Field Ofcls. Assn., Phi Beta Kappa, Sigma Xi, Delta Tau Delta. Republican. Mem. Methodist Ch. Mason (grand comdr. Grand Commandry of K.T. 1962). Clubs: Bellingham Navy; Gridiron (Greater Boston); Five-O (Cambridge, Mass.); Lexington Minute Men. Author: Calculus and its Applications, 1947; Elements of Nomography, 1947; Graphical Mathematics sect. of Engineers Handbook, 1950; Analytic Geometry, 1950; Encyclopedia of Science and Technology (nomography). Home: Belmont, Mass. Died Oct. 15, 1978; buried Mt. Auburn Cemetery, Cambridge.

DOWD, LAURENCE PHILLIPS, educator; b. Ft. Monroe, Va., Oct. 21, 1914; s. William Stuart and Julia (Phillips) D.; B.A., U. Wash. 1938; M.A., U. Hawaii, 1939; Ph.D., U. Mich., 1954; m. Juliet Irene Rudolph, Sept. 7, 1938; children—William L. (dec. 1965), Richard S., Judith I. (Mrs. Stewart Rush). With Lewers & Cooke, Ltd., Honolulu, 1939-40; instr. to asso. prof. U. Wash., 1940-41, 46, 50-55; lectr., dir. Mich. Bus. Execs. Research Conf. of U. Mich., 1957-60; prof. world bus., also dir. Center for World Bus. of San Francisco State U., 1960-71, prof. world bus., 1970-79, prof. emeritus, 1979-80; vis. prof. U. Oreg., 1969-70, Kinki U., Osaka, Japan, 1974, Inst. Internat. Studies and Tng., Japan, 1980; Fulbright prof. Kobe U., Japan, 1955-57. Cons. Far East Trade Promotion, Port of Seattle, 1955-57; trustee Wash. State Internat. Trade Fair, 1950-55; cons. trans-Pacific trade research project Bur. Bus. Research of U. Hawaii, 1962-64. Served from 2d lt. to maj., U.S. Army, 1941-45. Mem. Internat. Mgrs. Assn. San Francisco (pres. 1979), Acad. Internat. Bus., Phi Beta Kappa, Beta Gamma Sigma, Phi Kappa Phi. Author: The European Economic Community; Implications for Michigan Business, 1961; Principles of World Business, 1965; Introduction to Export Management, 1977. Editorial review bd. of Jour. Marketing, 1958-73. Home: Burlingame, Calif. Died Apr. 24, 1980.

DOWDY, ANDREW HUNTER, physician; b. Longwood, Mo., Nov. 24, 1904; s. Nathaniel M. and Emma (Patterson) D.; A.B., Central Coll., 1929; M.D., Washington U., 1931; D.Sc., Central Coll., 1957; m. Helen M. Brandes, Aug. 28, 1930; children—Andrew Hunter, Robert Alan. Intern internal medicine Henry Ford Hosp., Detroit, 1931-34, intern radiology 1934-36, resident radiology, 1936-37; instr., later prof., chmn. dept. radiology, chief radiologist sch. medicine and dentistry U. Rochester, 1937-48, dir. AEC project, 1946-48; dir. Manhattan project, 1943-46; chmn. dept. radiology sch. medicine, U. Calif. at Los Angeles, 1948-66, prof., from 1948, emeritus, chief radiation biology div. AEC 1948-55, cons., 1955-62. Mem. panel appraisers Handbook Biol. Data, 1950; mem. radiol. safety adv. com. Calif. State Disaster Council, 1950-56, chmn. subcom. radiation exposure; mem. civil def. Calif. State Evaluation Bd. 1951-55. Recipient Certificate of Appreciation for work on gas gangrene U.S. Army-Navy, 1948. Diplomate Am. Bd. Radiology (certificate of appreciation 1963), Pan-Am. Med. Assn. Fellow A.A.A.S., Am. Coll. Radiology (gold medal 1970); mem. Am. Thermographic Soc. (charter), nat., state, local gen. and spl. med. assns. Author many publs. in field cancer theraphy and research, radiology and radiation biology. Home: Laguna Hills, Calif. Died Feb. 20, 1977; buried Pacific View Meml. Park, Newport, Calif.

DOWDY, GEORGE WINSTON, merchant; b. Youngsville, N.C., Mar. 10, 1904; s. Norman Austin and Cora Agnes (Wicker) D.; student pub. schs.; m. Ruth Virginia Crowell, Sept. 29, 1929; children—George Winston, Ruth Crowell. Salesman, then dept. mgr., asst. in buying Belk-Leggett Co., Durham, N.C., 1919-25, asst. mgr., Danville, Va., 1925-27; mgr., treas. Belk's Dept. Store, Concord, N.C., 1927-33; gen. mgr. Belk Bros. Co., Charlotte, N.C., 1933-68, exec. v.p., 1953-68, chmn. bd., 1968-80, also dir.; chmn. bd. Belk Stores Services, Inc., 1969-80; dir. Belk Stores Reciprocal Ins., First Union Nat. Bank N.C., Belk-Doughton Co. (Elkin, N.C.), Belk-Hudson Co. (Orangeburg, S.C.); exec. com. The Belk Stores. Mem. U.S. Trade Commn. to Italy, 1956. Decorated French Order Merite Commercial, 1957; named North Carolinian of Year, Alpha Kappa Psi, 1954, Retailer of Year N.C. Mchts. Assn., 1957; recipient Algernon Sidney Sullivan award Queen's Coll., 1954; Silver Beaver award Boy Scouts Am. Mem. Charlotte C. of C. (past pres., dir., exec. com.), Nat. Retail Mchts. (pres. 1958, dir. N.C. 1963-80, gold medal 1964), N.C. (past pres.), Charlotte (past pres.) mchts. assns., Alpha Kappa Psi. Methodist. Mason (Shriner). Clubs: Charlotte Country, Charlotte City, Good Fellows (dir.) (Charlotte). Home: Charlotte, N.C. Died Apr. 21, 1980; buried Oakwood Cemetery, Concord, N.C.

DOWELL, DUDLEY, ins. exec.; b. Little Rock, Aug. 24, 1903; s. Martin L. and Sallie E. (Pearson) D.; grad. Little Rock High Sch.; LL.D., U. Ark., 1948; LL.D., U. Portland; H.H.D., Rollins Coll.; m. Elizabeth Smith, Dec. 4, 1926; children—Dudley, Dana. Clk. N.Y. Life Ins. Co., Little Rock, 1921-25, cashier, Jackson, Miss., 1925-27, asst. mgr., Little Rock, 1927-29, mgr., Butte, Mont., 1929-36, mgr., Seattle, 1936-39, supr. Allegheny dept., Pitts., 1939-41, insp. of agys., 1941, supt. agys. 1941, supt. agys., home office, 1941, asst. v.p., 1942, v.p. 1943-45, v.p. in charge agys., N.Y.C., 1945-54, exec. v.p., 1954-62, pres., 1962-69, dir., 1958-79, chmn. exec. com., 1959-69; mem. adv. bd. dirs. Worthen Bank & Trust Co., Little Rock. Mem. devel. council U. Ark. Med. Scis., Little Rock. Pres., Little Rock Underwriters Assn., 1928, Butte Life Underwriters Assn., 1936, Seattle Mgrs. and Gen. Agts. Assn., 1937, Life Ins. Agy. Mgmt. Assn., 1948. Episcopalian. Clubs: Eden Isle Country (Heber Springs, Ark.); Capitol (Little Rock). Home: Heber Springs, Ark. Died Aug. 16, 1979.

DOWLING, NOEL THOMAS, prof. law; b. Ozark, Ala., Aug. 14, 1885; s. Angus and Laura Lavinia (Boswell) D.; A.B., Vanderbilt U., 1909; A.M., Columbia University, 1911, LL.B., 1912, LL.D., (honorary), 1954; married Elizabeth Brown Molloy, June 19, 1918; children—Janet Cameron Brown, Elizabeth Molloy. Asst. Legislative Drafting Research Fund, Columbia, 1912-14, 16-17; prof. law U. Minn., 1919-22; asso. prof. of law Columbia, 1922-24, professor of law, 1924-30, Nash professor law, 1930-46, Harlan Fiske Stone prof. of constl. law, 1946-54, emeritus, 1954—; acting prof. law Stanford U., 1925; visiting prof. law, U. of Va., 1940; major, judge advocate, United State Army, World War I; mem. com. apptd. by sec. of navy, 1943, and board, 1945, to prepare "report on the organization, methods and procedure of naval courts, with recommendations." Chmn. Mayor's fact finding bd. N.Y. City bus strike, 1941. Navy's Distinguished Pub. Service Award, 1948. Trustee and sec. Acad. Polit. Science, 1936-46. Trustee and vice chmn. Nat. Child Labor Com., 1930-42; trustee Riverside Ch., N.Y. (v.p. 1941-45, pres. 1945). Dir. Brit. division Am. Univ. Union, London, 1928-29. Mem. Am., bar assn., Assn. Bar City of New York, Am. Law Inst., Phi Beta Kappa, Sigma Alpha Epsilon. (member of the supreme council and editor The Record, 1918-20). Clubs: Century, Mens

Faculty (Columbia U.) (N.Y.). Editor: Cases on Constitution-at Law, 1931. Joint editor: Cases of Conflict of Laws, 1936-41; Cases on Public Utilities, 1926, 36; American Constitutional Law, 1954. Author: The Judicial Function in Federal Administrative Agencies (with Joseph P. Chamberlain and Paul B. Hays), 1942. Contbr. articles in law revs. Home: Jeffrey Center, N.Y.

DOWLING, WALTER, former U.S. ambassador, educator; b. Atkinson, Ga. Aug. 4, 1905; s. Walter and Alice (Benton) D.; A.B., Mercer U., 1925; LL.D., Seoul Nat. U., 1959, Mercer U., 1961, U. Md., 1962; m. Alice Jernigan, Dec. 17, 1930; children—Patricia Dowling (Mrs. Philip Winterer), Michael. Bank clk., 1925-29; sec., 1929-31; fgn. service officer, 1932-63, vice consul Oslo, 1932-36, Lisbon, 1936-38, 3d sec., Rome, 1938-41, 2d sec. and vice consul, Rio de Janeiro, 1941-44, fgn. service officer Office U.S. Rep., Adv. Council for Italy, 1944, 2d sec. and consul, Rome, 1945, asst. chief div. So. European affairs Dept. State, 1945-47, asso. chief, 1947-49, acting chief, 1949, counselor of legation, Vienna, 1949, U.S. dep. high commr. for Austria, 1950, rank of minister, 1952, dep. high commr. for Germany, 1953, minister Am. embassy, Bonn, 1955-56, ambassador to Korea, 1956-59, asst. sec. state for European affairs, 1959, U.S. ambassador to West Germany, 1959-63, career ambassador, 1962; dir. gen. Atlantic Inst., Paris, 1963-69, bd. govs., 1963-77; vis. prof. polit. sci. Mercer U., 1970-77. Chmn. internat. council Mus. Modern Art, N.Y.C., 1964-69; bd. dirs. Nat. Carl Schurz Assn., Phila., 1964-77, Historic Savannah Found., 1970-72; trustee Telfair Acad., 1972-76. Recipient Grand Cross of Merit, Fed. Republic Germany, Gold Badge Order of Merit (Republic of Austria). Mem. Atlantic Council U.S. (gov. 1969-77), Council Fgn. Relations, SAR, Pi Kappa Alpha. Episcopalian. Clubs: Metropolitan (Washington); Oglethorpe (Savannah, Ga.). Home: Savannah, Ga. Died July 1, 1977; buried Bonaventure Cemetery, Savannah.

DOWNER, SAMUEL FORSYTHE, bus. cons., receiver and trustee in bankruptcy; b. Monongahela, Pa., Aug. 12, 1918; s. Eliphalet Kern and Elizabeth (Forsythe) D.; B.S.C. cum laude, Ohio U., 1940; postgrad. Harvard Grad. Sch. Bus. Adminstrn., 1945, grad. Advanced Mgmt. Program, 1964; m. Jessie Cooper, Aug. 24, 1940; children—Benita D. Rountree, Philip Stuart. Office, credit mgr. Jessop Steel Co., Washington, Pa., 1942-44, asst. to pres., 1946-47, asst. gen. sales mgr., 1947-48; resident rep. Burroughs Corp., Colorado Springs, Colo., 1948-56; chmn. Puffer Merc. Co., Colorado Springs, 1951-53; asst. v.p. Exchange Nat. Bank, 1956-57, v.p. 1957-60; sec. Continental Can Co., N.Y.C., 1960-64; v.p. finance LTV Aerospace Corp., Dallas, 1965-72; bus. cons., 1972-78; gen. partner Properties Ltd.; mng. agt. Creditors Trust, Hill Properties Ltd. Nat. bd. govs., Am. Nat. Red Cross, 1954-60; chmn. bd. trustees Colorado Springs Child Guidance Clinic, 1953; vis. com. Coll. Bus. Adminstrn., Ohio U., 1963-66. Served with USNR, World War II; PTO. Recipient Exceptional Service award USAF. Mem. Def. Orientation Conf. Assn. (dir.), Am. Pub. Health Assn. (nat. adv. com. on finance), Assn. U.S. Army (adv. bd. dirs., v.p.), Colo. Soc. C.P.A.'s (recognition), Omicron Delta Kappa. Home: Dallas, Tex. Died May 5, 1978; buried Dallas, Tex.

DOWNEY, STEPHEN WHEELER, army officer; b. Sacramento, June 1, 1916; s. Stephen Wheeler and Edith (Jennings) D.; student N.M. Mil. Inst., 1931-36; B.A., Stanford, 1939; m. Dorothy May Wilder, Sept. 6, 1947; 1 dau., Dianne. Commd. 2d. lt. Cav. Res., 1937, U.S. Army, 1939, advanced through grades to maj. gen., 1967; served in SHAPE Hdqrs., 1958-61, 62-64; comdr. 4th Armored Div., 1968-70; faculty Army War Coll., 1955-58; chief of staff Central Army Group NATO, 1970-72; ret., 1972. Decorated D.S.M., Silver Star, Legion of Merit with 4 oak leaf clusters, Bronze Star, Army Commendation medal, Purple Heart. Mem. Phi Gamma Delta. Home: Coronado, Calif. Died June 5, 1976.

DOWNING, H(AROLD) H(ARDESTY), educator; born Lexington, Ky., Nov. 29, 1886; s. William Franklin and Mary Elizabeth (Hardesty) D.; B.C.E., U. of Ky., 1908; M.S., U. of Chicago, 1916, Ph.D., 1929; m. Lilla Bentz Ott, Nov. 25, 1908; children—Dorothy Mae (Mrs. John R. DeMoisey), Hallie (Mrs. John P. Meyers, Jr.). Began as asst. engr., Lockland, O., summer 1907, Indian Refining Co., Georgetown, Ky., summer 1908; vis. prof. U. of Ala., summers 1928, 30, 31, 32; instr. U. of Ky., 1908-10, asst. prof., 1910-27, associate professor, 1927-31, professor since 1931, head department of mathematics and astronomy, 1947-52, coach of tennis teams, 1922-46, and since 1952; member of staff on development of teaching materials. Army Inst., Ind. University, summer 1942. Mem. Am. Math. Soc., Math. Assn. Am., A.A.A.S., Am. Assn. Univ. Profs., Omicron Delta Kappa, Phi Delta Kappa, Sigma Xi, Tau Beta Pi, Pi Mu Epsilon, Pi Kappa Alpha. Democrat. Mem. Disciples of Christ Ch. (elder). Author: A Brief Course in Analytic Geometry (with P. P. Boyd), 1947. Contbr. notes and revs. to sci. jours. Home: Lexington, Ky.

DOWNS, WILLIAM RANDALL, JR., news corr.; b. Kansas City, Kans., Aug. 17, 1914; s. William R. and Katherine Lee (Tyson) D.; A.B., U. Kans., 1937; m. Rosalind Gerson, Dec. 18, 1946; children—William R., Karen Louise, Adam Michael. Began career as fgn. corr. United Press, London, 1939-42; with CBS, 1942-62, in Moscow, 1943; war corr. Europe and Far East, 1944-46, Bikini Atomic Test, 1946, Berlin, 1948-50, Korean War, 1950, Washington, 1950-53, Rome, 1953-56, diplomatic corr., 1956-62; free-lance writer, 1962-63; corr. ABC News, 1964-78. Recipient Headliners award, 1945; Overseas Press Club award for best fgn. radio reporting, 1949. Mem. Overseas Writers. Clubs: Nat. Press, Overseas Press. Contbr. to various publs., including Newsweek, This Week mag. Home: Chevy Chase, Md. Died May 3, 1978.

DOYLE, ARTHUR JOSEPH, steel co. exec.; b. Cleve., Aug. 28, 1908; s. Arthur Leo and Kathryn (Sullivan) D.; ed. privately; m. Helen L. Holloway, June 26, 1937; children—Charles J., Mary Lorine (Mrs. Gerald L. Sauter), Ann (Mrs. J. Orin Anderson). With Youngstown Steel Door Co., Cleve., 1937-79, v.p., 1958-66, pres., 1966-72, chmn., 1972-79; v.p. subsidiary Camel Sales Co., Cleve., 1951-65, pres., 1965-66; pres. subsidiary Camel Co. Ltd., Cleve., 1962-79. Mem. Cleve. Advt. Club. Clubs: Chicago Athletic Assn.; Youngstown (O.); Union, Clevelander, Cleveland Athletic (Cleve.); Mt. Stephen (Montreal, Que., Can.). Home: Gates Mills, Ohio. Died Jan. 1979.

DOYLE, EDWARD ALLEN, clergyman, dean; b. Columbia, S.C., July 14, 1914; s. Alexander Calhoun and Lillian Catherine (Allen) D.; B.A., Georgetown U., 1935; student St. Charles Coll., Grand Coteau, La., 1935-38, Spring Hill Coll., 1938-40; S.T.L., St. Mary's Coll., 1947; Ph.D., Cath. U. Am., 1953. Ordained priest Roman Cath. Ch., 1946; tchr. St. Charles Coll., Grand Coteau, La., 1940-41; dir. dramatics Jesuit High Sch., New Orleans, 1940-43; dean faculties, sch. arts and scis. Loyola U., New Orleans, 1952-65, bd. dirs., 1952-66, acad. v.p., 1965-66; dir. studies New Orleans Province Jesuit Ednl. Assn., Ponchatoula, La., 1966-67, prin. Jesuit High Sch., New Orleans, 1967-68, pres.-prin., 1968-71, pres. 1974-74; pastor Immaculate Conception Ch., 1974-76, ret.; superior Jesuit Residence, New Orleans, 1977-79. Mem. La. com. commn. on secondary schs. So. Assn. Colls. and Schs., mem. central reviewing com., 1969, policies com., 1970-79; mem. secondary sch. commn. Jesuit Ednl. Assn., 1969-79; mem. Archdiocesan Adv. Council, New Orleans, 1969-79. Bd. trustees Spring Hill Coll., Mobile, Ala; bd. dirs. Citizens for Advancement of Pub. Edn., 1965-66; rep. Nat. Cath. Edn. Assn., 4th Nat. Conf. Citizenship, 1950; chmn. Conf. Acad. Deans So. States, 1959. Pres. New Orleans Children's Bur., 1956-57. Served as lt. O.R.C., U.S. Army. Mem. Jesuit Ednl. and Lit Soc. (dir. higher edn. New Orleans province 1959-61), Assn. Collegiate Deans, Assn. Deans Jesuit Colls., Assn. Higher Edn. NEA, Soc. Advancement Edn., Nat. Soc. Study Edn., Blue Key, Alpha Sigma Nu, Kappa Delta Pi, Delta Epsilon Sigma. Author: The Status and Functions of the Departmental Chairman of Colleges of Liberal Arts, 1952; chpt. in Functions of The Dean of Studies in Higher Education, 1957. Address: New Orleans, La. Died Dec. 29, 1979; buried Grand Coteau, La

DOYLE, WILSON KEYSER, evangelist; b. Balt., Jan. 3, 1903; s. W. Harvey and Edith (Griffith) D.; A.B., U. N.C., 1924; Ph.D., Johns Hopkins, 1936. Instr. polit. sci. U. Ala., 1936-43; research asso. U. Va., 1945-47; head dept. pub. adminstrn., Fla. State U., 1947-49, dean sch. pub. adminstrn., 1949-59; mem., founder Gospel Witness Assn. Tech., con. to Commn. To Study Hospitalization of Indigents in Va., 1945; mem. Com. Va. Adv. Legislative Council, 1945; tech. cons. to joint house and senate tax survey com. State of Fla., 1949, League of Va. Counties, 1945-47, Fla. Legislative Com. on Govtl. Reorgn., 1949; Fla. Adv. Council County Officers and Employees, 1951, gov. of Fla., 1949-51; chmn. steering com. of Joint Legislative Com. on Fees Compensation, and Duties of County Officers, 1952-53; ednl. adviser Fla. Girls State, Boys State, 1950-59; cons. to Fla. Council Higher Edn., 1954-56. Gov.'s Com. on Fiscal Affairs, 1955; cons. mem. industry adv. com. Fla. Devel. Commn., 1955-59. Mem. Phi Beta Kappa. Author: Independent Commissions in the Federal Government, 1939; co-author: The Government and Administration of Florida, 1954. Editorial bd. Jour. Politics, 1954-56. Address: Greenwood, Va. Died Aug. 12, 1977; interred Greenmount Cemetery, Baltimore, Md.

DOZER, DONALD MARQUAND, educator; b. Zanesville, Ohio, June 7, 1905; s. Perley Walter and Minnie Bell (Marquand) D.; A.B. Coll. Wooster, 1927; A.M., Harvard, 1930, Ph.D., 1936; postgrad. Ohio State U., summers 1927, 28; m. Alice Louise Scott, Aug. 2, 1941 (dec. Oct. 1972); children—Charles, Jane, Hilary. Tchr. history and debating Wooster (Ohio), High Sch., 1927-29; asst. history dept. Harvard and Radcliffe Coll., 1930-34; instr. history Boston U., 1934-35; jr. archivist Nat. Archives, Washington, 1936-37, instr. history U. Md., 1937-42; research analyst Coordinator of Info., OSS, 1941-43; liaison officer Office Lend-Lease Adminstrn., 1943-44; fgn. trade analyst FEA, 1944; research analyst and asst. chief div. Am. Republics Analysis and Liaison, Dept. State, 1944-47, acting chief, div. research for Am. Republics, Office Intelligence Research, 1947-49, coordinator spl. intelligence project involving Latin Am. area for Joint Chiefs of Staff in Office of Intelligence Research, 1949-51, asst. to chief Div. Hist. Policy Research, Hist. Div., Office of Pub. Affairs under asst. sec. pub. affairs, 1951-56; Dept. State rep. spl. conf., Panama, C.Z., 1948; asst. tech. sec. U.S. delegation 9th Internat. Conf. Am. States, Bogotáa, Colombia, 1948. Lectr. Strategic Intelligence Sch., Nat. Mil. Establishment, Washington, 1949-51; lectr. Latin Am. area study program dept. internat. relations and orgn. and dept. history Am. U., Washington, 1949-59; cons. on Latin Am., Brookings Instn., 1950-51; lectr. dept. history Coll. Spl. and Continuation Studies, U. Md. and Montgomery Jr. Coll., Takoma Park, Md., 1956-59; asso. prof. history U. Calif. at Santa Barbara, 1959-64, prof., 1964-72, prof. emeritus, 1972-80. Vis. prof. internat. studies Am. Grad. Sch. Internat. Mgmt., Glendale, Ariz. and Universidad Autóonoma de Guadalajara, 1973; cons. Center for Strategic Studies, Georgetown U., 1964, 66-67, Viviendas Financiadas Argentinas, S.A., 1979-80; Internat. Investment and Devel. Corp., Phoenix, 1979-80, cons. asso. Center for Internat. Bus., Pepperdine Coll.; vis. prof. internat. relations Inst. for Internat. Studies and Tng., Boeki Kenshu, Japan, 1975; vis. lectr. Universidad Francisco Marroquin, Guatemala, 1976; chmn. Emergency Com. to Save U.S. C.Z., 1974-80. Past mem. alumni bd. Coll. Wooster; vice chmn. Jane B Dozer Dept Romance Langs and Lit U Wash.

DOZIER, JAMES CORDIE (DO'ZHER), soldier; b. Galivants Ferry, Horry Co., S.C., Feb. 17, 1885; s. John Henry and Julia Marie (Best) D.; father of Huguenot descent; student Wofford College, Spartanburg, South Carolina, 1 year; m. Margaret Tullulah Little, June 10, 1920; children—Major James C., Tech. Sergt. Donald Preston. Began bus. career employ Butler Brothers, New York City, 1908; with National Union Bank, Rock Hill, South Carolina, later sec. State Bd. Pub. Welfare, Columbia; apptd. adj. gen. S.C., 1926, elected same office 8 terms, 1926-53, also dir. civil defense under act of Gen. Assembly. Served on Mexican border with S.C. Nat. Guard, 1916; commd. 2d lt. July 13, 1917, 1st lt. Dec. 5, 1917; served overseas 11 mos. with 118th Inf., 30th Div., U.S. Army; wounded in shoulder, Oct. 8, 1918; hon. disch., Apr. 19, 1919. Returned to S.C. after World War. Cited "for conspicuous gallantry and intrepidity above and beyond the call of duty". Recipient of the Congressional Medal of Honor from the United States; Military Cross (British); Croix de Guerre and medal, also Chevalier Legion of Honor (French); War Cross (Italian); medal (Portuguese); medal (Montenegrin); Purple Heart (U.S.) Motion picture, "The Price of Peace", made under auspices U.S. Govt., shows Lt. Dozier in act of charging a nest of machine guns. Mem. Bd. of Visitors Citadel, Charleston. Mem. Am. Legion, Forty and Eight, Disabled Am. Vets, Vets of Foreign Wars. Democrat. Presbyterian. Mason. Rotarian. Address: Columbia, S.C.

DRAGONETTE, JESSICA, soprano; born of Am. parents, orphaned at early age; studied music writing under Nicola Montani; student of music at Georgian Court Coll., Lakewood, N.J., under Dr. Mary Beatrice; coached for early radio work by Estelle Liebling. Married Nicholas Meredith Turner, June 28, 1947. Became a pioneer radio artist, work including Shakespearean roles, 1-act plays, light opera, concert type broadcast; was featured on first internat. broadcast; made concert debut, 1937, and appeared in recitals throughout U.S., Canada and Hawaii, also as soloist with New York Philharmonic, Philadelphia Symphony, Chicago Symphony and many other orchestras; appeared in principal role of numerous operettas; now divides work between concert stage and radio and television; sometime lecturer Town Halls of America. Awarded Army and Navy Wings, for war service, Silver Medal, U.S. Treasury Dept. for Bond Selling; Pro Pontifice et Ecclesia Cross, Lady of Grand Cross of Equestrian Order of Holy Sepulchre of Jerusalem (Pope Pius XII); medal of the Knot of Isabella (Spain); Queen of Radio award for 8 consecutive years. Author: Faith Is A Song (autobiography); pub. vols. religious selections, Ave Maria. Address: New York, N.Y. Died May 18, 1980.

DRAKE, CARL JOHN, entomologist; b. Eagleville, O., July 28, 1885; s. William L. and Alice A. (Shippy) D.; student Heidelberg Acad., Tiffin, O.; B.S., B.Pd., Baldwin-Wallace Coll., 1912; grad. work Ohio State U., 1913-17 and 3 summers, Ph.D., 1921; unmarried. Grad. asst. in zoölogy and entomology, Ohio State U., 1913-14, asst., 1914-15, instr., 1915-17; instr. in zoölogy, Baldwin-Wallace Coll., summers, 1912-15; instr. in entomology, Syracuse U., 1917-18, asst. prof., 1918-20, prof. 1920-22; research entomologist, Fla. Expt. Sta., summer, 1918; research entomologist, Miss. Agrl. Expt. Sta., summer, 1921; prof. zoölogy and entomology, also head of dept., Ia. State Coll. Agr. and Mech. Arts, and entomologists, Ia. Expt. Sta., since 1922; state entomologist of Ia. since 1922; head Tucura (grasshopper) Commn. to Argentina, S.A., Nov. 1938 to Jan. 1939. Fellow A.A.A.S., Am. Entomol. Soc., Ohio Acad. Science: mem. Am. Assn. Econ. Entomologists (v.p. 1926), Am. Soc. Parasitologists, Am. Entomol. Soc., Fla. Entomol. Soc., Brooklyn Entomol. Soc.,

Entomol. Soc. Washington, Biol. Soc. Washington, Ia., Acad. Science, S. Calif. Acad. Sciences, Sigma Xi, Gamma Sigma Delta, Phi Kappa Phi. Member National Plant Board, 1935-42; chmn., 1941-42; chmn. Central States Plant Bd., 1945-46. Author of many articles and bulletins on econ. and taxonomic entomology. Hemiptera. Club: Ames Golf and Country. Home: Ames, Ia. *

DRAKE, HENRY LEE, psychologist; b. Savannah, Ga., Sept. 22, 1906; s. Henry Lee and Esther J. (Steinman) D.; B.A., Ind. U., 1928; M.B.A. in Econs., U. Pa., Phila., 1929; postgrad. C.G. Jung Inst. for Analytical Psychology, Switzerland, 1948; M.A. in Philosophy, U. So. Calif., 1949; Ph.D. in Psychology U. Calcutta (India), 1953; m. Sarane G. Robinson, Sept. 4, 1963; children by previous marriage—Jerome H., Adrienne A. Dir., Empire Life Ins. Co., Indpls., 1933-48, v.p., mem. finance com., 1935-48; pvt. practice psychotherapy, Los Angeles, 1950-78. Vice pres., Philos. Research Soc., Los Angeles, 1950-78; lectr. in field; mem. conf. on voluntary controls of internal states Menninger Found., Topeka, Kan., 1966, 68; cons. in field. Bd. dirs. Myers Clinic and Neuropsychiat. Found., Pasadena, Calif., 1964-78. Mem. Am., Calif. State, Los Angeles County, Indian psychol. assns., Los Angeles Soc., Psychoanalytical Psychology, Assn. Transpersonal Psychology, Soc. Clin. and Exptl. Hypnosis, Am. Philos. Assn., AAAS, Group Psychotherapy Assn. So. Calif. (dir. 1964-66). Author: The People's Plato, 1958; (with others) The Basic Ideas of Man, 1953, Studies in Consciousness, 1954; Pythagarus Introductory Essay, 1970; The Secret Teachings of All Ages: An Encyclopedic Outline of Masonic, Heometic, Oabbalistic and Rosicrucian Symbolic Philosophy, 1975. Contbr. articles to profl. jours. Home: Los Angeles, Calif. Died Nov. 7, 1978.

DRAKE, J(AMES) FRANK, mfr.; b. Pittsfield, N.H., Sept. 1, 1880; s. Nathaniel Seavey and Mary A. R. (Green) D.; prep. edn., Kimball Union Acad., Meriden, N.H.; A.B., Dartmouth, 1902; Master Comml. Sci., Amos Tuck Sch., 1903, LL.D., 1952; married Mildred Chase, July 25, 1907 (dec. Aug. 1954); children—Ruth, Virginia, James Frank, Constance. Sec. Bd. of Trade, Springfield, Mass., 1903-08; sec. Phelps Pub. Co., Springfield, 1908-14, treas. and dir., 1914-18; asst. to pres. Gulf Oil Corp., Pittsburgh, Pa., 1919-23; pres. Standard Steel Car Co. and subsidiary companies, 1923-30; chmn. bd. Pullman, Inc., 1930-31; pres. Gulf Oil Corporation, 1931-48, chairman bd., 1948-53, chmn. exec. com., 1953-55, past director; pres. dir. Standard Car Finance Corporation dir. Rockwell Manufacturing Company, Dieector Nat. Indsl. Conf. Board (chmn. 1945-47); mem. Petroleum Industry War Council, 1941-45; Common Council, Springfield, 1908-12, pres. 1910-12. Commd. maj. Ordnance Dept., U.S. Army, June 1918; served as comdg. officer finance div. Pittsburgh Dist.; lt. col. Mar. 25, 1919; hon. disch., June 3, 1919. Mem. Am. Philatelic Soc., S.A.R., Soc. Colonial Wars, Order of Founders and Patriots of America, Am. Legion, Military Order World War, American Society of the French Legion of Honor, Theta Delta Chi. Republican. Episcopalian. Clubs: University, Duquesne, Pittsburgh Golf, Fox Chapel Golf (Pittsburgh); Rolling Rock (Ligonier, Pa.); Cosmos (Washington); University (N.Y.C.). Home: Pittsfied, N.H. Died Dec. 20, 1976.

DRAKE, M(ILES) ELLIS, univ. pres.; b. Oswayo, Pa., Mar. 16, 1901; s. Watson Llewellyn and Ella (Ellis) D.; A.B., Alfred University, 1925; A.M., Syracuse U., 1928; Ph.D., American U., 1932; LL.D., Hartwick, 1954; married Marie Hunt, June 27, 1929; children—Jeanne Marie (Mrs. F.T. Allen, Jr.), Meredith Anne (Mrs. Arthur L. Hurst, Junior). Instructor of history and political sci. Alfred U., 1926-28, asst. prof., 1928-30, asso. prof., 1932-34, prof. and chmn. dept., 1934-42, dean of men, 1934-46, dir. summer sch., 1942-48, dean Coll. Liberal Arts, 1946-48, acting pres., 1948-49, pres., 1949-67. Chairman Empire State Foundation of Liberal Arts Colleges, 1956-57. Trustee Alfred University, 1948-79; trustee, vice chmn. Coll. Center of the Finger Lakes, 1961-79. Mem. Am. Hist. Assn., Pi Gamma Mu, Pi Delta Epsilon, Delta Sigma Phi, Blue Key. Republican. Episcopalian. Clubs: Rotary (Hornell, N.Y.); University (N.Y.). Home: Skaneateles, N.Y. Died Feb. 28, 1979.

DRAPANAS, THEODORE, educator, physician; b. Buffalo, Feb. 20, 1930; s. Thomas and Anastasia (Tsiros) D.; M.D., U. Buffalo, 1952; m. Arlene Ann Thrun, June 25, 1954; children—Carol Ann, Mark Thomas, Wendy. Intern, resident surgery E.J. Meyer Meml. Hosp., Buffalo, 1952-58; asst. prof. surgery State U. N.Y., Buffalo, 1959-64; prof. surgery U. Pitts. Sch. Medicine, 1964-68; Henderson prof., chmn. dept. surgery Tulane U. Sch. Medicine, 1968-75; practice medicine, specializing in surgery, New Orleans, 1968-75; surgeon-in-chief Tulane div. Charity Hosp. of La. Mem. bd. examiners Am. Bd. Surgery; mem. com. on trauma Nat. Acad. Scis.-NRC, 1969; mem. surgery study sect. NIH, 1969-73; mem. adv. com. on trauma Surgeon Gen.'s Office, Dept. Army, 1970-75; mem. surgery adv. com. FDA, 1971. Served with M.C., U.S. Army, Res. Recipient Gold Key award as outstanding man of year Buffalo Jr. C. of C., 1961. Mem. A.C.S., Am., Central, So. surg. assns., Soc. U. Surgeons (pres. 1973-74), Soc. Clin. Surgery, Soc. Vascular Surgery, Am. Assn. Thoracic Surgery, Am. Assn. Surgery of Trauma, A.A.A.S., Internat. Soc. Surgery, James IV Assn. Surgeons, Assn. Am. Med. Colls. (rep.), Phi Beta Kappa. Editor: Surgery, 1971-75. Contbr. articles profl. jours. Home: New Orleans, La. Died June 24, 1975.

DRAPER, ARTHUR STIMSON, editor and writer; b. Brooklyn, N.Y., Sept. 3, 1882; s. John H. R. and Florence A. (Velzor) D.; B.S. in M.E., New York U., 1905, hon. M.A., 1925; m. Frances W. Gibb, of Staten Island, N.Y., Apr. 30, 1908; children—Arthur Gibb, Dorothy Frances. Began as reporter New York Tribune, 1905, and continued with same paper as night city editor, 1908-10, pvt. to editor, 1910-13. Sunday editor, 1913-15, London correspondent and European manager, 1915-25; assistant editor New York Herald Tribune, 1926-33; editor Literary Digest, 1933-35; with Dept. of Labor, Washington, D.C., 1937. Clubs: Psi Upsilon, The Players; North Middlesex Golf (London). Home: Chestertown, N.Y.

DRAPER, DELBERT MORLEY, lawyer; b. Moroni, Utah, May 7, 1884; s. Riley Newton and Margaretta (Morley) D.; A.B., U. Utah, 1911; student U. Calif., 1915-16; m. Frances Mary Rogers, June 6, 1912; children—Courtney Rogers (dec.), June Katharine, Margaret Ruth, Frances Mary (dec.), Gloria Mildred, Delbert Morley. Instr. Latter Day Saints U., Salt Lake City, 1911-15; prin. Beaver Co. High Sch., Milford, Utah, 1915-16, Spanish Fork (Utah) High Sch., 1916-17; chief dep. treas. State of Utah, 1917-19; admitted to Utah bar, 1919; asst. atty. gen., State of Utah, 1919-21; in pvt. practice law, Salt Lake City since 1921; lectr. in bus. law, U. Utah, 1922-46; wrote Ins. Code (with Neil Olmstead) enacted by Utah State Legislature, 1947. Dir. OPS for Utah, 1951-52, regional director, Denver, Colorado, since 1952. State dir. Four Minute Men, World War I; pub. panel mem. regional War Labor Bd., World War II. Democrat (mem. state Central Com., chmn. 1932-42). Mem. Phi Delta Theta, Tau Kappa Alpha, Phi Delta Phi. Mem. Ch. of Latter Day Saints. Clubs: Ambassador, Knife and Fork, Aztec. Home: Denver.

DRAPER, FLOYD S(TANLEY), lawyer; b. Fulton, N.Y., Oct. 17, 1893; s. Russell J. and Emily Ena (Pearman) D.; LL.B., Valparaiso U., 1915, LL.D., 1954; m. Winnie Courtney, Sept. 16, 1916; 1 son, John Marshall. Admitted to Ind. bar, 1915; judge Appellate Ct. of Ind., 1943-51; justice Supreme Ct. of Ind., 1951-55; pvt. practice Gary, Ind., 1955-80. Home: Gary, Ind. Died Mar. 20, 1980.

DRAPER, GEORGE WILLIAM, II, judge; b. Easton, Pa., Aug. 10, 1920; s. George William and Grace (Collins) D.; LL.B., Howard U., 1947; LL.M., N.Y. U., 1948; m. Bessie Carrolle Thornton, Sept. 6, 1940; children—George William III, Thornton Collin, Wesley Robert. Admitted to Mo. bar, 1950, also U.S. Supreme Ct.; asst. prof. law Lincoln U. Law Sch., St. Louis, 1948-50; mem. firm Witherspoon, Lewis & Draper, St. Louis, 1950-52; asst. circuit atty. Office Circuit atty., St. Louis, 1952-55; mem. Draper & Martin, St. Louis, 1955-57; chief trial asst. circuit atty. Office Circuit Atty., St. Louis, 1957-60; asst. atty. gen. chief criminal appeals div., Mo., 1960-64; dir. legal services St. Louis Human Devel. Corp., also instr. Washington U. Law Sch., 1964-65; chief counsel Office Met. Devel., Dept. Housing and Urban Devel.; dep. exec. dir., gen. counsel Equal Employment Opportunity Commn.; asso. judge Superior Ct. D.C., 1972-76. First pres. Tamarack Triangle Civic Assn., Silver Spring, Md., 1966-76. Mem. Mo., St. Louis bar assns., Lawyers Assn. Mo., NAACP (life), Sigma Delta Tau, Alpha Phi Alpha. Democrat. Episcopalian. Home: Silver Spring, Md. Died July 16, 1976; buried Md. Nat. Meml. Park, Laurel.

DRAPER, PAUL AUGUSTUS, wool merchant; born Canton, Mass., Aug. 31, 1886; s. Charles Norris and Martha (Gill) D.; student Mass. Inst. Tech., 1903-04; A.B., Harvard, 1907; m. Marjorie C. Elmes, Nov. 18, 1910; children—Phyllis, Donald. Wool merchant, Boston; dir. Rexall Co., Ins. Co. of N.A., D. & H. R.R., Eastern S.S. Co. Republican. Unitarian. Clubs: Seigniory (Can.); Harvard (Boston). Home: Canton.

DRAPER, WARREN FALES, executive medical officer; b. Cambridge, Mass., Aug. 9, 1883; s. William Burgess and Carrie Maria (Drew) D.; prep. edn. Waban (Mass.) Sch. for Boys, 1900-02; A.B. Amherst Coll., 1906, D.Sc., 1945; M.D., Harvard, 1910; m. Margaret Gansevoort Maxon, Apr. 6, 1910; children—Warren Fales, Anne Gansevoort. Commd. asst. surgeon, U.S. Pub. Health Service, 1910, passed asst. surgeon, 1914, surgeon, 1920, asst. surgeon gen. in charge div. domestic quarantine, 1922-31; health commr. of Va., 1931-34; in charge extra cantonment sanitation, Camp Lee, Petersburg, Va., 1917-18, Newport News, Va., Aug.-Sept. 1918; asst. surgeon gen. in charge div. personnel and accounts, 1934-39; dep. surgeon gen., 1939-47, ret.; maj. gen. charge pub. health br. Supreme Hdqrs. Allied Expdnry. Force, 1944-45; asst. v.p. for health services Am. Nat. Red Cross, 1946-48; exec. med. officer United Mine Workers of America Welfare and Retirement Fund since 1948. Alternate mem. Civilian Health and Medical Adv. Council, Office Assistant Secretary of Def., 1956—. Decorations: Distinguished Service Medal (U.S.); Companion of the Bath (Brit.); Officer Legion of Honor, Croix de Guerre with Palm, Officer Order of Public Health (France); Officer Order of Leopold II (Belgium); Grand Officer Order of Orange-Nassau (Netherlands). Former professorial lectr. on pub. health adminstrn. George Washington U., Jefferson Med. Coll., Phila.; lectr. pub. health U. Mich., Johns Hopkins U. Mem. Nat. Bd. of Med. Examiners, 1940-48. Mem. pub. health adv. com. Commonwealth Fund, 1925-46. Diplomate Am. Bd. Preventive Medicine. Member A.M.A. (house of delegates, 1924-46; former chairman sect. on preventive and industrial medicine and public health; charter member and former member Council on Industrial Health, Com. on Coordination of Medical Activities), mem. American Public Health Association (former mem. governing counsel; former chmn. health officers sect.); hon. life mem. Internat. Soc. of Med. Health Officers, Conf. State and Provincial Health Authorities of N.A., Assn. Mil. Surgeons (pres. 1946-47); mem. Smith-Reed-Russell (hon. med. soc. George Washington U.), Sigma Xi, Omega Alpha Omega. Club: Cosmos (Washington). Episcopalian. Author many published articles on pub. health adminstrn. and preventive medicine. Home: Arlington, Va.

DREA, WILLIAM FRANCIS (DRA), radiologist, oral surgeon; b. Cambridge, Mass., Sept. 5, 1885; s. Kieran and Julia Ann (Dunn) D.; D.M.D., Harvard, 1909; m. Rhoda Worthington Smith, June 24, 1919 (dec.); 1 d., Charlotte Elizabeth. Dentistry practice, Boston and mem. faculty Harvard Dental Sch., 1910-15; practice oral surgery, Colorado Springs, since 1917; X-ray diagnosis since 1921; instructor and lecturer on X-rays, Colorado Coll., 1922-41; research asso. Colo. Found. for Research in Tuberculosis, 1928-52, asso. research dir. since 1952; mem. staff Glockner-Penrose Hosp. (dir. research in tuberculosis lab.), Memorial Hosp.; courtesy staff St. Francis Hosp. Recipient James J. Waring award for work in Tb, 1956. Fellow A.A.A.S.; mem. A.M.A., Am. Chem. Soc., N.Y. Acad. Scis., Colo. Archeol. Soc., Am. Dental Assn., Harvard Dental Alumni Assn., Colo.-Wyo. Acad. Sci., Delta Epsilon. Clubs: Cheyenne Mountain Country (Broadmoor, Colo.); Rocky Mountain Harvard. Author: (with Anatole Andrejew) The Metabolism of the Tubercle Bacillus. Contbr. articles to profl. jours. Engaged in research on tubercle bacilli. Home: Colorado Springs, Colo.

DREES, WILLEM, prime minister of the Netherlands; b. Amsterdam, Holland, July 5, 1886; s. Johannes Michiel and Anna Sophia (van Dobbenburgh) D.; student High Sch. of Commerce, Amsterdam, 1903; LL.D. (honorary), University of Maryland; m. Catharina Hent, July 28, 1910; children—Johannes, Willem, Anna Sophia. Began as bank clk., 1906; later, stenographer for Amsterdam Municipal Council, then for the States Gen., The Hague; elected chmn. Social Dem. party local, 1911; mem. The Hague Municipal Council, 1913; became alderman, 1919; elected mem. 2d Chamber of States Gen., 1933, on Social Dem. ticket; became chmn. of his party, 1939, serving until invasion of the Netherlands by German Army; imprisoned at Buchenwald, October, 1940-Oct. 1941; when released became active in Central Com. in underground as pres. Fatherland's Com.; also active in Central Com. of Resistance Movement; mem. Bd. of Reliable Men to discuss reparations when nation would be liberated; vp. and minister of social affairs 1945-48; premier in Coalition Govt., 1948—. Home: Netherlands.

DREIER, THOMAS, writer, lecturer; b. on farm near Durand, Wis., May 5, 1884; s. Lawrence and Delia (Maloney) D.; ed. parochial sch. and Durand (Wis.) High Sch.; grad. 1902; also studied for the R.C. priesthood; m. Blanche E. Nowell, Dec. 24, 1914. After graduation from high school led a vagabond life, specialty salesman in Colo. and northern Wis., bartender, confectioner, millhand, barber, waiter, "devil" and foreman of print shop; reporter Menomonie (Wis.) Times, 1904-06, Madison (Wis.) Democrat and Wisconsin State Journal, 1907; business manager Sheldon Univ. Press (Chicago) and mng. editor Business Philosopher, 1908-09; editor The Caxton, Pittsfield, Mass., Jan.-July 1910; editor The Blackbone Monthly, Aurora, Ill., and mng. editor "Human Life," Boston, 1910; edited The Printing Art, Cambridge, Mass. Head of The Thomas Dreier Service, advertising, Boston. Author: Devil of Fear, 1910; Human Chemicals, 1910; Heroes of Insurgency, 1910; Vagabond Trail, 1913; The Silver Lining, 1923; Sunny Meadows, 1933; The Mountain Road, 1935; Men—and the Power of Print, 1936; The Religion of a Vagabond, 1946; We Human Chemicals, 1948. Home: Melvin Village, N.H.; also St. Petersburg, Fla.

DRESSER, LOUISE, actress; b. Evansville, Ind., Oct. 5, 1882; d. William and Ida (Kerlin) D.; ed. at Evansville and Indianapolis; m. John Gardner, of Louisville, Ky., 1908. Toured as "Ernie," in Cal., 1902; appeared in

"About Town," Herald Sq. Theatre, New York, Aug., 1906; later played in "The Girl Behind the Counter," "The Golden Widow," "A Matinee Idol"; toured in "A Lovely Liar," 1911; toured in vaudeville, 1912; in "Potash and Perlmutter," 1913-14; Cohan Revue, 1915; Potash and Perlmutter in Society, 1916; Cordelia Blossom, and Have a Heart, 1917; tour of vaudeville with Jack E. Gardner, 1918-19.*

DRESSER, ROBERT BARTLETT, lawyer; b. Savannah, Ga., Dec. 28, 1880; s. Henry Bartlett and Mary Isadore (Griggs) D.; grad. Phillips Exeter Acad., 1898; A.B., Yale, 1902; LL.B., cum laude (editorial bd. law rev. 1904-05), Harvard, 1906; m. Ruth Greene, Nov. 29, 1919; m. 2d, Edna M. Clark, Nov. 12, 1971. Admitted to Mass. bar, 1906, R.I. bar, 1910; practiced in Providence, 1909-76; mem. firm Edwards & Angell, 1915-71, counsel, 1971-76. Trustee estate of Frank A. Sayles, 1927-71; dir. Sayles Finishing Plants, Inc., Moshassuck Valley R. R. Co., Spl. Fabrics, Inc.; hon. dir. Indsl. Nat. Bank. Mem. com. to revise R.I. Corp. Laws, 1918-20; mem. nat. com. Taxpayers Com. to End Fgn. Aid, Washington; adv. bd. Com. Constl. Govt., N.Y.C. Del. Republican Nat. Conv., 1936, 44, 48. Fellow Am. Bar Found.; mem. Am. Bar Assn., N.A.M. (past bd. dirs.). Soc. Mayflower Descendants, S.A.R., Soc. Colonial Wars, Order Founders and Patriots Am. Episcopalian. Mason. Clubs: Yale (N.Y.C.); Hope, Agawam Hunt, Turks Head (Providence). Author numerous articles on nat. issues. Home: Providence, R.I. Died Sept. 25, 1976; interred Swan Point Cemetery, Providence.

DRIFTMIER, RUDOLPH HENRY, agrl. engr.; b. Clarinda, Ia., Mar. 10, 1898; s. John Frederick and Mary (Handorf) D.; student Grinnell (Ia.) Coll., 1915-17; B.S. in agrl. engring., Iowa State Coll., Ames, 1920; M.S., Kan. State Coll., Manhattan, 1926; A.E., Kan. State Coll., Manhattan, 1929; m. Helen Spry, June 30, 1920; children—John Frederick (dec.), Betty Jo, Helen, Rudolph Henry. With Kan. State Coll., as instr. to prof. agrl. engring., 1920-30; prof. and head dept. agrl. engring., U. Ga., 1930-65, Alumni Found. disting. prof. emeritus, emeritus head dept. agrl. engring., 1965-79, chmn. div., 1950-65; supervising engr. Regents Univ. System of Ga., 1935-46; head dept. plant operations, U. Ga., 1943-45; appointed Alumni Foundation. Distinguished professor by U. Ga., 1957; farm buildings editor The Progressive Farmer, 1945-51, Engring. consultant E.C.A. Spl. Mission to France, 1950. Pres. Clarke County Board of Edn., 1956-60. Served as private, 67th C.A.C., U.S. Army, with A.E.F., 1918-19. Former mem. Manhattan (Kan.) City Planning Commn. Recipient Cyrus Hall McCormick medal engring. achievement in agr., Am. Soc. Agrl. Engrs., 1957, Massey-Ferguson ednl. medal, 1965; Am. Acad. of Achievement award, 1966; named Engr. of Distinction, Engrs. Joint Council, 1970. Fellow Am. Soc. Agrl. Engrs. (life; pres. 1944-45), Ga. Acad. Sci. Mem. Am. Soc. Engring. Edn., So. Assn. of Agrl. Engring. and Vocation Agrl. Educators (regional admin. dir. 1946), Am. Legion (former post comdr.), Sigma Tau, Gamma Sigma Delta (Ga. sr. scientist 1962), Alpha Zeta (Ga. agr. man of year award 1963), Phi Kappa Phi, Delta Sigma Phi. Dem. Presbyterian. Clubs: Gridiron, Rotary (Athens). Contbr. to jours. Home: Athens, Ga. Died Oct. 30, 1979; buried Athens.

DRIGGERS, J(AMES) CLYDE, coll. pres.; b. Ft. Green, Fla., Jan. 10, 1917; s. Uria Alonzo and Mary (Stephens) D.; B.S.A., U. Fla., 1938, Ph.D., 1949; m. Doris Esther McCullough, Aug. 25, 1940; children—David Alonzo, Billie Kay, Stephen Gause, James McCullough. Instr. poultry husbandry U. Fla., 1939-40, asst. prof., 1946-49, asso. prof., 1949-55, prof., 1955-57; chmn. poultry div. U. Ga., 1957-64; pres. Abraham Baldwin Coll., 1964-75. Served with AUS, 1941-46; col. Reserves. Mem. Poultry Sci. Assn., World's Poultry Sci., Assn. So. Agrl. Workers (past chmn. poultry sect.), Ga. Poultry Fedn., Sigma Xi, Gamma Sigma Delta (past pres. U. Ga. chpt.), Alpha Tau Alpha, Alpha Gamma Rho (grand 1st v.p.), Alpha Zeta (high censor), Kappa Kappa Psi, Gamma Sigma Epsilon, Sigma Delta Psi, Sabres, Fla. Blue Key. Democrat. Methodist. Clubs: Rotary (pres.) (Tifton, Ga.); F (U. Fla.). Home: Tifton, Ga. Died Apr. 29, 1975.

DRINKARD, ALFRED WASHINGTON, JR., agrl. research; b. Appomatox, Va., Jan. 10, 1883; s. Charles Milton and Mary Ann (Martin) D.; B.S., Va. Poly. Inst., Blacksburg, Va., 1906, M.S., 1908; Ph.D., Cornell, 1913; unmarried. Record clerk in horticulture, Va. Agrl. Expt. Station, Blacksburg, 1906-08, asst. horticulturist, 1908-12, associate horticulturist, 1912-16, director of station, 1916-46, assistnat director sta. 1946-48, ret. 1948. Mem. Blacksburg Board of Trade (pres. 1916-19); mem. Va. Water Power and Development Commn., 1924-26. Fellow A.A.A.S.; mem. Va. Acad. Science, Am. Assn. Univ. Profs., Va. State Hort. Soc. (dir. 1917-23), Science Club (Blacksburg), Grange. Democrat. Baptist. Mason, Odd Fellow, Redman. Club: Music. Contbr. articles on results of sci. research. Home: Raleigh, N.C.

DRISCOLL, FREDERICK JOSEPH, constrn. contractor; b. Bklyn., July 12, 1901; s. George Francis and Harriet (Hannigan) D.; grad. Fordham Prep. Sch., 1918; LL.D., Boston Coll., 1953, Fordham U., 1958; m. Dorothy Katherine Cornell, Apr. 23, 1924; children—Dorothy Anne (Mrs. Carlo D. Cella, Jr.), Frederick Joseph, John Henry. With George F. Driscoll Co., N.Y.C., 1919-77, sec., 1922-28, v.p., 1928-31, treas., 1931-77, pres., 1941-77; pres. George F. Driscoll Co. of Venezuela, 1941-59; treas., pres. Moccia Constrn. Corp.; trustee Kings County Lafayette Trust Co., Bklyn., Greater N.Y. Savs. Bank. Chmn. bd. trustees Bricklayers Pension Fund, 1951-77; trustee Mason Tenders Pension Fund, 1955-77, Mary Immaculate Hosp., Jamaica, N.Y.C., 1955-58, Fordham U., 1958-67. Mem. Bldg. Contractors and Mason Builders Assn. (past pres.), Bldg. Trades Employers Assn. (past pres.). Clubs: Wheatley Hills Golf (East Williston, N.Y.); Lawrence Beach (Atlantic Beach, N.Y.); The Moles (N.Y.C.). Home: Kew Gardens, N.Y. Died Feb. 3, 1977.

DRISCOLL, HUGH MACPHERSON, banker; b. St. Paul, July 27, 1898; s. Alfred E. and Isabelle (Scott) D.; B.A., Princeton, 1921; m. Margaret Burton, Oct. 17, 1936; children—Hugh MacPherson, David Burton. Trainee, accountant Nat. City Bank of N.Y., 1921-23; mgr. credit dept., asst. cashier, asst. v.p. Blvd. Bridge Bank of Chgo., 1924-33, asst. v.p., v.p. successor Nat. Blvd. Bank of Chgo., 1933-49, exec. v.p., dir., 1949-65, vice chmn., 1962-65; vice chmn. Civic Center Bank & Trust Co., Chgo., 1966-70, now vice-chmn. bd.; pres., dir. 1st Nat. Bank Blue Island, 1970-79; vice chmn., chief exec. officer, dir. Union Nat. Bank Chgo., 1971-79; dir. Inland Newspapers, Market Centers, Inc., Smith-Bucklin & Assos., Tastee Freez Industries, Inc. Active Chgo. Community Fund, Boy Scouts; pres., dir. Off-the-Street Club of Chgo., 1936-79. Trustee, v.p. Wesley Meml. Hosp., from 1942, Northwestern Meml. Hosp., 1972-79; trustee, pres. Chgo. M.E. Ch. Aid Soc.; pres. bd. trustees of Haris Schools. Served as 1st lt. inf., U.S. Army, World War I. Mem. Robert Morris Assos. (past pres., dir.), Methodist (chmn. bd. trustees). Clubs: Chicago Yacht (dir.), University, Economic, Arts (treas., dir.), Bankers (Chgo.); Rotary. Home: Evanston, Ill. Died July 14, 1979.

DROLET, GODIAS JOSEPH, health cons., med. statistician; b. St. Pie, Que., Can., July 6, 1882; s. Charles and Laura (Barbeau) D.; student St. Ann's Acad., N.Y.C., 1896-1900, Columbia, 1900-02, 12-13, Cooper Union, 1902-03, N.Y. U., 1911-12, Univ. and Bellevue Hosp. Med. Coll., 1915; m. Margaret Murphy, June 2, 1912; children—Charles M., John J., Thomas D., Francis K., Louis G., Robert C. Chief clk. Bur. Financial Studies, Credit Lyonnais, Paris, 1903-05; statistician Trudeau San., 1906-08, Tb div. Bellevue Hosp., N.Y.C., 1909-17, Com. Prevention Tb, Rockefeller Found., 1917-19; with N.Y. Tb and Health Assn., Inc., 1919—, acting dir., 1933-35, asst. dir., 1937-49, dir. Tb div., 1953-55, cons. adminstrv. service, 1956—; chmn. Council Tb and Health Assns., Greater N.Y. State, 1962-64; mem. Assn. Tb Clinics Greater N.Y., 1919-48; past staff mem. Bellevue-Yorkville Health Demonstration; cons., statician Tb San. Conf., Met. N.Y., 1926-53, com. neighborhood health devel. Health Dept., N.Y.C., 1929-47; dir. analysis Los Angeles County chest x-ray survey, 1950. Pres., mem. bd. mgrs. Queensboro Tb and Health Assn.; past pres., bd. dirs. Queensboro Council Social Welfare; mem. research com. census tract tabulations N.Y.C. Welfare Council, 1940; adv. com. future populations tech. adv. com. rezoning plan City Plan Commn.; mem. Neighborhood Health Devel., Inc. Del. 8th Am. Sci. Congress, Washington. Served as 1st lt., A.R.C., France, 1918. Recipient Will Ross award Nat. Tb Assn., 1963; Golden Plate award Am. Acad. Achievement, 1964. Fellow Royal Soc. Health, Am. Pub. Health Assn., Am. Geog. Soc.; mem. N.Y. Acad. Medicine, N.Y. Acad. Scis., N.Y. Diabetes Assn. (co-organizer), Am. Statis. Assn., Am. Epidemiological Soc. (charter mem.), Am. Mus. Health, Nat. Cancer Found. (charter mem.). Roman Catholic. K.C., Alhambra. Contbr. papers, monographs to tech. lit. Home: Flushing, L.I., N.Y.

DROSTE, EDWARD PHILIP, educator; b. Godfrey, Ill., Apr. 27, 1902; s. August Carl and Lena (Lueking) D.; B.S., Shurtleff Coll., 1924, LL.D., 1954; Ed.M., Harvard, 1941; postgrad. U. Wis., Washington U., St. Louis; m. Roberta Elise Megowen, Dec. 25, 1929 (dec. 1969); children—Adele Louise (Mrs. James H. Cunningham), Carl Sanders; m. 2d, Katherine L. Holmgreen, Nov. 27, 1970. Tchr. math. and sci., head coach Saunemin (Ill.) High Sch., 1924-26, Western Mil. Acad., 1926-41; asst. mgr. Rancho Mesa Verde for Boys, Colo., summers 1926-28; headmaster Howe (Ind.) Mil. Sch., 1941-48, Elgin (Ill.) Acad., 1948-54; dir. studies Tex. Mil. Inst., San Antonio, 1954-64, headmaster, acting pres., 1964-66, pres., 1966-70, pres. emeritus, 1970-78. Treas. Ind. Schs. Assn. Central States, 1953-54, Ind. Sch. Assn. Southwest, 1965-66; pres. Tex. Prep. League, 1967-69, Pres. Elgin Civic Music Assn., 1950-53, San Antonio Rock and Lapidary Soc., 1964, 71. Mem. Shurtleff Coll. Alumni Assn. (pres. 1932), Assn. U.S. Army, S.W. Gem and Mineral Soc., Council Internat. Relations. Episcopalian (vestryman; past chmn. sch. bd.). Lion (pres. Howe club 1945-46), Rotarian (pres. Elgin club 1952-53). Kiwanian. Clubs: Argyle; Harvard of San Antonio; Torch Internat. Men's Garden. Originator potential achievement rate system guidance, 1941. Home: San Antonio, Tex. Died Oct. 25, 1978.

DRUKKER, DOW HENRY, JR., business exec.; b. Passaic, N.J., June 4, 1903; s. Dow Henry and Helena (Deunhower) D.; B.S., Mass. Inst. of Tech., 1925; m. Margaret Adams, Feb. 4, 1926 (div. Nov. 1971); children—Joan, Dow Henry; m. 2d, Margaret Joos, Nov. 30, 1971. Pres., Union Bldg. & Constrn. Corp., 1940-76; pres., dir. Drukker & Co., 1955-76; pres. Marion Co., Inc., 1956-76; sec. Bleachery and Printing Co., Carlton Hill, N.J., 1932-60; v.p., pub. The Herald-News, Passaic-Clifton, N.J., 1942-56; v.p. Union Bldg. & Investment Co., 1936-56, N.J. Broadcasting Co., Paterson, N.J., 1942-56. Commr., Port N.Y. Authority, 1953-58. Trustee, Stevens Inst. Tech., from 1955; gov. Passaic Gen. Hosp. Mem. Phi Sigma Kappa. Clubs: Upper Montclair Country, Skytop, Poinciana; Beach (Palm Beach, Fla.). Died Nov. 18, 1976.

DRUMMOND, CHESTER ARTHUR, clergyman; b. Waterbury, Conn., Mar. 14, 1882; s. Charles and Jenny Lind (Legge) D.; grad. Meadville (Pa.) Theol. Sch., 1906; S.T.B., Tufts Coll.; m. Muriel Joy Carey, Mar. 30, 1910; 1 son, Norman Carey. Ordained ministry Unitarian Ch., 1906; successively pastor, Norwell, Mass., Littleton, Mass., Somerville, Mass., New Orleans, La.; became pastor Channing Ch., Newton, Mass., 1921; now minister emeritus at large for Benevolent Fraternity of Unitarian Chs. of Boston, serving as incumbent of Unitarian Congl. Society of Grafton (Mass.); dir. Ministers Mutual Life Ins. Co. Served as overseas sec. A.E.F., World War I. Dir. Parker Memorial, Boston. Republican. Mason. Author and dir. numerous religious dramas and pageants. Home: Sherborn, Mass.

DRUMMOND, HARRY ROBERTS, educator; b. Bismarck, N.D., Oct. 8, 1886; s. Richard William and Anna (Roberts) D.; A.B., Hobart Coll., Geneva, N.Y., 1908 (Phi Beta Kappa); M.A., Columbia U., 1937; m. Frances Aurelia Loghry, June 7, 1911. Instr. St. John's Mil. Sch., Salina, Kan., 1908-11; sr. master, St. Alban's Sch., Washington, D.C., 1911-15; headmaster Kearney (Neb.) Mil. Acad., 1915-22; asst. headmaster Shattuck Sch., Faribault, Minn., 1922-36; Horace Mann School for Boys, New York, 1937; asst. to supt. Northwestern Mil. Acad., Lake Geneva, Wis., 1937-39; asst. headmaster Shattuck School, Faribault, Minn., 1939-43; with Millbrook Sch., Millbrook, N.Y., since Aug. 1943. Episcopalian. Address: Millbrook, N.Y.

DRURY, NEWTON B., conservationist; b. San Francisco, Apr. 9, 1889; s. Wells and Ella Lorraine (Bishop) D.; B.L., U. Cal., 1912, LL.D. (hon.), 1947; m. Elizabeth Frances Schilling, June 29, 1918; children—Betty (Mrs. Austin L. Edwards), Newton, Hugh Wells. Reporter on San Francisco and Oakland newspapers, 1906-11; instr. in English, asst. prof. in forensics, sec. to pres., U. Calif., 1912-18; partner in Drury Co., advt. agency and pub. relations counsel, San Francisco, 1919-40; sec. Save-the-Redwoods League, 1919-40, 59-71, pres., 1971-75, chmn. bd. dirs., 1975-78; exec. Calif. Park Commn., 1929-40; mem. adv. bd. Yosemite Nat. Park, 1938-40; dir. Nat. Park Service, 1940-51; chief Div. State Parks, Calif., 1951-59. Regional trustee Mills Coll., Oakland, Calif., 1941-43; research Asso. Carnegie Instn. of Washington, 1938-43. Served as 2d lt., Air Service, U.S. Army (aerial observer Balloon Corps), 1918-19; 1st lt. Air Service Res., 1919-22. Recipient Conservation award Trustees of Public Reservations, Boston, 1940; Pugsley medal Am. Scenic and Historic Preservation Soc., N.Y., 1940; Hutchinson medal Garden Club of America, 1945; Conservation award U.S. Dept. Interior, 1968; medal Calif. Hist. Soc., 1975; named Alumnus of Year, U. Calif. at Berkeley, 1943. Mem. Sierra Club (hon. v.p.), Am. Soc. Landscape Architects (hon.), Soc. Am. Foresters (hon.). Club: Faculty (U. Calif.). Home: Berkeley, Calif. Died Dec. 14, 1978.

DRYE, JOHN WILSON, JR., lawyer; b. Van Alstyne, Tex., May 28, 1900; s. Wilson and Elizabeth (Cave) D.; student Valparaiso U., 1917-18, U. Mich., 1918; LL.B., Washington and Lee U., 1920, LL.D., 1956; m. Loraine Caldwell, Oct. 26, 1926; children—Robert Caldwell, Anne Elizabeth. Admitted to N.Y. bar, 1922; asso. Larkin, Rathbone & Perry, 1920-29, partner same and successor firms Rathbone, Perry, Kelley & Drye and Kelley, Drye, Newhall, Maginnes & Warren, 1930, now Kelley, Drye & Warren; dir. Park 81st Corp., Security Reins. Corp., Ltd. Pres. Juilliard Mus. Found.; bd. dirs. Juilliard Sch., Planting Fields Found., Met. Opera. Mem. Am., N.Y. State, N.Y.C., N.Y. County bar assns., Sigma Chi. Methodist. Clubs: Knickerbocker, Nassau Country, Racquet and Tennis (N.Y.C.); Burlington (Vt.) Country. Home: New York City, N.Y. Deceased.

DUBACH, ULYSSES GRANT, educator; b. Wathena, Kan., Nov. 9, 1880; s. Fred and Margaret (Hautzenrader) D.; A.B., Ind. U., 1908; M.A., Harvard, 1909; Ph.D., U. Wis., 1913; LL.D., Willamette U., 1952; L.H.D., Lewis and Clark College, 1958; married Ida Castleberry, August 12, 1909; 1 daughter, Helen (dec.). Tchr. rural sch., Kan., 1902; supt. schs., Kan., 1905-07; faculty prep. sch. Okla. U., Tonkawa, 1909-11; prof. polit. sci. Ore. State Coll., 1913-47, dean men, 1924-47;

prof. polit. sci. Lewis and Clark Coll., Portland, since 1947. Trustee Found. for Econ. Edn., Inc. Mem. Am., Western polit. sci. assns., Sigma Phi Epsilon, Alpha Kappa Psi, Phi Kappa Phi, Blue Key. Republican. Methodist. Mason. Club: City (Portland). Contbr. articles mags., profl. jours. Address: Portland, Ore.

DUBLIN, LOUIS ISRAEL, statistician; b. Kovno, Lithuania, Nov. 1, 1882; s. Max and Sarah (Rosenzweig) D.; brought to U.S., 1886; B.S., Coll. City of N.Y., 1901; Ph.D., Columbia, 1904; m. Augusta Salik, Apr. 5, 1908; children—Elizabeth, Mary, Thomas, Amos. Instr. math., Coll. City of N.Y., 1901-08; statistician Met. Life Ins. Co. since 1911, 2d v.p. 1944. Lecturer on vital statistics, Yale. Fellow Am. Pub. Health Assn. (pres. 1932); fellow Am. Statis. Assn. (pres. 1924), Population Assn. Am. (pres. 1935-36. Author: Mortality Statistics of Insured Wage Earners and Their Families, 1919, Health and Wealth, 1928; Family of Thirty Million, 1943; Health Progress, 1936-45. Collaborator (with Lee Frankel and Miles Dawson) Workingmen's insurance in Europe, 1910; (with Lee K. Frankle) Principles of Life Insurance, 1911; (with A. J. Lotka) The Money Value of a Man, 1930; To Be or Not To Be—A Study of Suicide (with B. Bunzel), 1933; Length of Life (with A. J. Lotka), 1936; Twenty-five Years of Health Progress (with A. J. Lotka), 1937; monographs, papers, addresses on vital statistics, and pub. health. Editor: Population Problems in the United States and Canada, 1926; The American People—Studies in Population, 1936. Home: Westport, Conn.

DUBNOFF, BELLE, ednl. adminstr., social service worker; B.A., U. Cal., 1933; M.A., Whittier Coll., 1940; postgrad. Claremont Coll. Social case worker Eureka Benevolent Soc., San Francisco, 1933-34, State Relief Assn., Cal.; tchr. Pasadena (Cal.) and Los Angeles pub. schs., 1940-58; part-time psychologist El Retiro Sch. for Girls, 1949-58; founder, dir. Dubnoff Sch. for Ednl. Therapy, 1948-62, North Hollywood, Cal., 1962-77. Marriage, family and child counselor Dept. Profl. and Vocational Standards, State of Cal.; mem. staff Kennedy Child Study Center, Reiss-Davis Child Study Center, Cedars-Sinai Hosp., San Fernando Valley (Cal.) Comprehensive Community Mental Health Center; cons. state psychologist to Fairview State Hosp. Sch.; cons. to various sch. dists. in Cal.; lectr. dept. spl. edn. U. So. Cal., Los Angeles; lectr. dept. child psychiatry Long Beach (Cal.) State Coll., San Fernando Valley Coll., N.J. City State Coll.; prof. U. Nev., summer, 1971. Mem. Adv. Bd. Blind Children's Center, Los Angeles. HEW grantee, 1969-70, Andrew Norman Found. grantee, 1968. Fellow Am. Orthopsychiat. Assn.; mem. Council for Exceptional Children (western regional rep.), Internat. Council of Psychologists, Cal. Assn. Sch. Psychologists and Psychometrists, Am., Western, Cal., Los Angeles County psychol. assns., Am. Group Psychotherapy Asns., Pi Lambda Theta. Author: See What I Can Do, 1957; Look I'm Reading, 1958. Contbr. articles on spl. edn. for children with learning disabilities to profl. publs. Home: North Hollywood, Calif. Died Jan. 16, 1977.

DUBOC, RAY B., ins. exec.; b. Brookings, S.D., Feb. 1889; s. Albert M. and Julia P. (Denison) D.; ed. pub. schs., Oskaloosa, Ia.; m. Fern Miller, Nov. 27, 1919. Pres. Western Ins. Securities Co. of Kansas City, 1925-72, also chmn. bd.; chmn. bd. Western Fire Ins. Co., Western Casualty & Surety Co., Ft. Scott, Kans. Mason, Rotarian (pres. 1947-48). Clubs: Kansas City, Mission Hills Country, (Kansas City). Home: Kansas City, Mo. Died Sept. 2, 1974.

DUBS, ADOLPH, fgn. service officer; b. Ill., Aug. 4, 1920; B.A., Beloit Coll., 1942; student Georgetown U., 1946-48; m.; 1 dau., Lindsay Jane. Asst. to dir. tng. Navy Sch., 1948-49; assigned Dept. State, 1949-50; resident officer, Frankfurt, Germany, 1950-52; 2d sec., vice consul, Monrovia, Liberia, 1952-54; 2d sec., vice consul, Ottawa, Can., 1954-55, consul, 2d sec., 1955-57; Russian lang. area tng. Fgn. Service Inst., 1957-58, Harvard, 1958; internat. relations officer, Dept. State, 1959-61; 1st sec., consul Am. embassy, Moscow, USSR, 1961; assigned Nat. War Coll., 1963-64; chief polit. sect. Am. embassy, Belgrade, Yugoslavia, 1964-65 counselor of embassy for polit. affairs, 1965-68; country dir. Soviet Union affairs State Dept., Washington, 1968-72, assigned Sr. Seminar in Fgn. Policy, 1972; minister-counselor Am. embassy, Moscow, 1972-74; diplomat-in-residence Southwestern U., Memphis, 1974-75; dep. asst. sec. for Near East and South Asian affairs Dept. State, 1975-79. Chmn. Internat. Sch. Bd. of Belgrade. Served to lt. (s.g.) USNR 1942-46. Died Feb. 14, 1979.

DUCE, LEONARD ARTHUR, educator; b. Princeton, Ont., Can., May 26, 1909; s. Richard Robinson and Mary Alice (Hey) D.; A.B., McMaster U., 1928, B.Th., 1930, B.D., 1931; S.T.M., Andover Newton Theol. Sem., 1937; Ph.D., Yale, 1946; m. Irma Harriet Gynn, Aug. 9, 1933; children—Robert Arthur, David Alan (dec.). Ordained to ministry Baptist Ch., 1931; pastor, Midland, Ont., Can., 1931-36; asst. pastor First Ch., Needham, Mass., 1936-37; pastor Montowese Ch., North Haven, Conn., 1938-42, Chandler, Mo., 1945-47; prof. hist. theology Central Bapt. Theol. Sem., 1943-45, prof. philosophy William Jewell Coll., 1942-49, chmn. dept. philosophy, 1947-49, dean coll., 1945-49; prof. philosophy and chmn. dept. Baylor U., Waco, Tex., 1949-60, asst. dean, 1949-55, asso. dean Grad. Sch., 1955-56, dean, 1956-60; dean Grad. Sch., Trinity U., 1960-74; pres., headmaster Tex. Mil. Inst., 1974-76; vis. prof., adminstrv. cons. Hong Kong Bapt. Coll., 1958-59; vis. lectr. theology U. So. Cal., summer 1946; instr. aerial nav. and naval history Naval Flight Sch., William Jewell Coll., 1942-44. Commr., San Antonio Housing Authority, 1961-68. Chmn. orgn. and extension com., Waco dist. Boy Scouts Am., 1950; chmn. Waco Social Welfare Council, 1957. Bd. dirs. Goodwill Industries of San Antonio, Ecumenical Center Religion and Health, Tex. Council Crime and Delinquency. Hon. fellow Am. Coll. Hosp. Adminstrs., Am. Acad. Med. Adminstrs.; Adminstrs.; mem. A.A.A.S., Texas Assn. Grad. Schs. (pres. 1960-61), Vis. Tchrs. Assn. Tex. (chmn. adv. council), Am. Studies Assn. Tex. (pres. 1963-64), Am. Philos. Assn., Southwestern Philos. Conf. (pres. 1963), Tex. Social Welfare Assn. (pres. 1961-63), Nat. Assn. Housing and Redevel. Ofcls., NEA (Dept. Higher Edn.), AAUP, Am. Conf. Acad. Deans, Beta Beta Beta. Rotarian. Contbr. articles to religious, social work, edn., hosp. adminstrn. and other jours. Home: San Antonio, Tex. Died June 9, 1979; interred San Antonio, Tex.

DUDLEY, LOUISE, educator; b. Georgetown, Ky., Nov. 15, 1884; d. Richard Moberley and Mary (Henton) D.; A.B., Georgetown Coll., 1905; Ph.D., Bryn Mawr, 1910; research student Bibliothèque Nationale, Paris, 1908-09, Oxford U., Michaelmas term, 1909. Instr. English, Mt. Holyoke Coll., 1910-11; head English dept., Stephens Coll., Columbia, Mo., 1913-14, and since 1919; prof. English lit., Lawrence Coll., Appleton, Wis., 1914-18; acting dean of women, Stephens Coll., 1921-22; acting dean of faculty, same, 1923. Social worker in French munition camps, under Y.W.C.A., 1918-19. Mem. advisory bd. Women's Edn. Work, Northern Bapt. Conv. Mem. Modern Lang. Assn. America, Nat. Council Teachers of English, English Assn. (Gt. Britain), Mo. State Teachers' Assn., Am. Assn. Univ. Women. Baptist. Author: Egyptian Elements in the Legend of the Body and Soul, 1911. Translator: Anglo-Saxon Christian Poetry, 1914. Address: Columbia, Mo.

DUERKSEN, WALTER JACOB, univ. dean; b. Enid, Okla., Feb. 21, 1907; s. Jacob and Helen (Friesen) D.; Mus.B., U. Wichita, 1931; Mus.M., Northwestern U., 1938; student Juilliard Conservatory, Columbia Tchrs. Coll., summer 1945; m. Virginia Kilbourn, June 5, 1938; children—Walter Kilbourn, Mary Virginia. Dir. instrumental music Wichita State U., 1931-72, chmn. dept. music, 1944-72, dean Sch. Music, 1949-72, dean Coll. Fine Arts, 1961-70, Univ. prof., spl. asst. to pres., 1970-72. Wichita Symphony Soc. Mem. Music Educators Nat. Conf., Music Tchrs. Nat. Assn., Am. Assn. U. Profs., Phi Mu Alpha, Kappa Kappa Psi. Conglist. Author pamphlet on coll. bands. Home: Wichita, Kan. Died Oct. 25, 1980.

DUFEK, GEORGE JOHN, naval officer; b. Rockford, Ill., Feb. 10, 1903; s. Frank and Mary (Wachuta) D.; B.S., U.S. Naval Acad., 1925; grad. Flight Tng. Sch., 1933; student Indsl. Coll. Armed Forces, 1947; LL.D., Carleton Coll.; L.H.D., LeMoyne Coll.; D.Sc., Rockford (Ill.) Coll., m. Muriel Thomson Bones, 1947; children—Mary Ellen (Mrs. Bellit), Barbara Bones (Mrs. Phillips), George John, David Frank. Commd. ensign USN, 1925, advanced through grades to rear adm., 1955; assigned U.S.S. Maryland, 1925-27; asst. navigator, asst. communications officer U.S.S. Canopus, 1927-28; aviator U.S.S. Concord, 1933-36; navigator U.S.S. Saratoga, 1936-38; exec. officer U.S.S. Lexington, 1938-39; navigator U.S.S. Bear, flagship Antarctic Devel. Project, 1939; assisted constrn. devel. new naval air sta., Jacksonville, Fla., 1940; spl. U.S. Naval observer for aviation, London, 1942; sr. naval aviator, invasion North Africa, 1942; assisted devel. invasion plans for So. France; comdr. U.S.S. Bogue, 1944; comdg. officer naval air base, Ominato, Japan, also air transport service terminal nr. Tokyo, 1945; staff Naval Regulations Bd., Washington, 1946; chief staff officer on expdn. to establish weather bases northern Polar Regions, 1946; comdr. eastern group Task Force 68, to develop unknown coast line between Palmer Peninsula and Little Am. comdr. Task Force 80 to supply existing weather stas. and establish new stas. nr. North Pole, 1947; mem. logistics planning sect. Joint Chiefs Staff, Washington, 1949-50; comdr. U.S.S. Antietam, 1951; head spl. Antarctic Planning Group, Washington, 1954; comdr. logistic and operational task force Naval Operation Deepfreeze, 1955-59; 1st Am. at geographic South Pole, 1956; ret., 1959; dir. Mariners Mus., Newport News, Va., 1960-73. Decorated Legion of Merit with 2 gold stars, Antarctic Expdn. medal; Distinguished Service medal with gold star (U.S.); Comdr. Order of Crown (Belgium); Hon. Companion Order of Bath (Eng.); Croix de Guerre, Legion of Honor (France); recipient Andre Medal, Swedish Geog. Soc., 1959. Mem. Am. Soc. Naval Engrs., Nat. Geog. Soc. (Hubbard medal 1959), Am. Geophys. Union. Clubs: James River Country; Army-Navy, Explorers. Author: Operation Deep Freeze; Through the Frozen Frontiers, 1959. Home: Newport News, Va. Died Feb. 10, 1977; buried U.S. Naval Acad. Cemetery, Annapolis, Md.

DUFF, C(ARL M(ATHIAS), prof., civil engr.; b. Versailles, Mo., Dec. 5, 1884; s. David Campbell and Karolina Katharina (Gattermeyer) D.; S.B. (C.E.), U. of Colo., 1910, S.M., 1912; m. Mary Ruth Shank, Aug. 3, 1915; 1 dau., Betty Ann (Mrs. Robert Pearce Hawthorne). Instr. drawing, mathematics, U. of Colo., 1910-13, field engr., survey for hydro-electric project, 1910-11; draftsman, designer, railroad structures, 1912; field engr., erection, bldgs., bridges, 1913-16; agrl. work, 1916-19; asst. prof. applied mechanics, U. of Neb., 1920-24, computer tractor testing, 1920, asso. prof., 1924-29, prof., 1929-35, prof. engring. mechanics, since 1935; paving inspector Neb. Dept. of Pub. Works, 1921, asst. testing engr., 1922-24, testing engr., 1924-29; testing engr., Neb. Dept. Roads and Irrigation, 1929-42. Mem. Am. Soc. Civil Engrs., Am. Soc. Testing Materials, Am. Concrete Inst., Am. Soc. Engring. Edn., Am. Assn. U. Profs., Neb. Acad. of Sciences, Neb. Engring. Soc., Sigma Xi (pres., Neb. chapter, 1944-45), Tau Beta Pi, Sigma Tau. Republican. Methodist. Mason. Clubs: Rotary, Lincoln Engrs. Contbd. journs. Home: Lincoln, Neb.

DUFFY, CHARLES BAIN, lawyer; b. Point, Pleasant, W.Va., May 27, 1900; s. William Marion and Emma Frances (Fisher) D.; LL.B., U. Okla., 1922; m. Vala Gladys Solf, Aug. 23, 1922; children—Virginia (Mrs. Albert Miles Donnell), Dorothy (Mrs. James Edward Work). Admitted to Okla. bar, 1922; practiced in Ponca City, Okla.; partner Duffy & Johnson; asst. county atty. Kay County, Okla., 1925-26. Mem. Okla. Senate, 1934-46; commr. uniform state laws, 1953-57. Govtl. appointee Okla. Acad. for State Goals; bd. dirs. Heritage House. Served as sgt. 81st aero. squadron U.S. Army, World War I. Mem. Am. Legion (state comdr. 1946-47), U. Okla. Dad's Assn. (pres. 1947-48), Am. (ho. of dels. 1955-56), Okla. (pres. 1955) bar assns., Delta Tau Delta, Phi Delta Phi. Rotarian (pres. Ponca City 1954, dist. gov. 1959-60). Home: Ponca City, Okla. Died Mar. 18, 1979.

DUFFY, FRANCIS RYAN, judge; b. Fond du Lac, Wis., June 23, 1888; s. Francis Fee and Hattie (Ryan) D.; A.B., U. Wis., 1910, LL.B., 1912, LL.D., 1952; LL.D., DePaul U., Chgo., 1955; m. Louise Haydon, Jan. 26, 1918; children—Ann Louise, Francis Ryan, Haydon Robertson, James Hamilton. Practiced law, Fond du Lac, 1912-33; mem. U.S. Senate, 1933-39; judge U.S. Dist. Ct. 1939-49, U.S. Ct. of Appeals, 7th Circuit, 1949-78, chief judge, 1954-59, sr. U.S. circuit judge, 1966-78. Served to maj. Motor Transport Corps., U.S. Army, World War I. Recipient Alumni award U. Wis. Law Sch., 1968. Mem. Am. Legion, Phi Alpha Delta, Delta Sigma Rho. Democrat. Elk, K.C. Club: Milwaukee Athletic. Home: Milwaukee, Wis. Died Aug. 16, 1979; buried Fond du Lac.

DUGGAN, WILLIAM REDMAN, fgn. service officer, educator; b. Durango, Colo., Feb. 11, 1915; s. William Edward and Pansy (Redman) D.; student Western State Coll., Gunnison, Colo., 1933-35; A.B., U. Notre Dame, 1938, M.A., 1939; postgrad. Boston U., 1955-56; m. Florence Olive Jewell, Aug. 30, 1952; 1 son, David W. Field office mgr. Social Security Bd., 1940-44; joined U.S. Fgn. Service, 1944; vice consul, Durban, South Africa, 1944-47, Vancouver, B.C., Can., 1948-50; 2d sec., consul, Copenhagen, Denmark, 1951-55; polit. liaison officer U.S. del. UN Gen. Assembly, 1956-57; officer-in-charge West African Affairs Dept. State, 1957-58; consul gen., Dar-es-Salaam, Tanzania, 1958-62; mem. Policy Planning Council Dept. State, 1962-67; consul gen., Durban, S. Africa, 1967-71; prof. polit. sci. Willamette U., Salem, Oreg., 1972-79; mem. Oreg. Ednl. Coordinating Commn., 1975-77. Del., Democratic Nat. Conv., 1976. Recipient meritorious award Dept. State, 1963, Distinguished Service award, 1971. Mem. Explorers Club, African Studies Assn., Am. Polit. Sci. Assn., Am. Fgn. Service Assn. Roman Catholic. Author: Socioeconomic Profile of South Africa, 1973; What is a Canadian, 1977; co-author Tanzania and Nyerere, 1976; pub. posthumously: Our Neighbors Upstairs: The Canadians, 1979; contbr. articles to profl. jours. Home: Salem, Oreg. Died July 11, 1977; buried at sea.

DUGGER. ROBERT WELLFORD, agrl. implement corp. exec.; b. East St. Louis, Ill., Oct. 31, 1910; s. Wellford Eugene and Elva (Whitaker) D.; student U. Miami (Fla.), 1930-31, Washington U., St. Louis, 1932-33; m. Eugenia Barklage, Feb. 1, 1938; 1 son, Walter Edward. Asso., Broderick & Smith, labor relations cons's., St. Louis, 1938-42; dir. labor relations Caterpillar Tractor Co., 1942-43, Midland Steel Products Co., 1943-49, Wyandotte Chem. Co., 1949-50; dir. indsl. relations Motor Products Co., 1950-55, Motor Wheel Corp., 1955-62; v.p. corp. relations J.I. Case Co., 1962-70; v.p. indsl. relations Tenneco, Inc., Houston, 1970-75, ret.; asso. prof. Walsh Coll., Canton, Ohio. Bd. dirs. Houston Urban League, Curative Workshop, Racine, Wis., Racine Vocat. Sch.; adv. bd. Racine Salvation Army; pres. bd. trustees Canton Regional Transit Authority. Mem. Mfrs. Assn. Racine (bd. govs.). Clubs: Masons, Shriners. Home: Canton, Ohio. Died June 6, 1980; buried Forest Hill Cemetery, Canton.

DUKE, CHARLES MARSDEN, army officer; b. Jacksonville, Tex., June 24, 1917; s. Charles Henry and Bess (Butler) D.; B.S., U.S. Mil. Acad., 1939; M.S., Cal. Inst. Tech., 1947; grad. Command and Gen. Staff Coll., 1951, Armed Forces Staff Coll., 1955, Indsl. Coll. Armed Forces, 1959; m. Vernice Lang Jones, June 27, 1942; children—Charles Marsden, Allyson Lang. Commd. 2d lt., C.E., U.S. Army, 1939, advanced through grades to maj. gen., 1967; chief U.S. Hydrographic Office, Managua, Nicaragua, 1942-44; with intelligence div. Gen. Headquarters, 1945-46; instr., then asst. prof., dept. mil. arts and engring. U.S. Mil. Acad., 1947-50; sr. staff adviser constrn. and maintenance of installations Army Hdqrs., Heidelberg, Germany, 1951-54; spl. adviser to chief of engrs., 1956-58, dist. engr. U.S. Army Dist., N.Y., also supr. N.Y. Harbor, 1959-62; asst. chief staff G4 (Logistics) I Corps, Korea, 1962-63; engr. commr. D.C., 1963-66; comdg. gen. 18th Engr. Brigade, Dong Ba Thin, RVN, 1967, U.S. Army Engr. Command U.S. Army Vietnam Engr., Long Binh, RVN, 1967-68; chief engr. U.S. Army, Vietnam, comdg. gen. Engr. Troops, Vietnam, 1968-71. Mem. D.C. Pub. Service Commn.; past chmn. Washington Met. Area Transit Commn.; past pres. Met. Washington Council Govts.; past gov. Washington Bldg. Congress. Mem. exec. bd. Nat. Capital Area council Boy Scouts Am., 1963-66; bd. dirs. Met. Police Boys' Club. Decorated D.S.M., Legion of Merit, Bronze Star, Air medal with bronze oak leaf cluster, Army Commendation medal. Registered profl. engr., D.C. Fellow Am. Soc. C.E.; mem. Soc. Am. Mil. Engrs., Nat. Soc. Profl. Engrs., Newcomen Soc., West Point Soc., Indsl. Coll. Armed Forces, Cal. Inst. Tech. alumni assns., Assn. U.S. Army, Hon. Order Ky. Cols., Assn. Grads. U.S. Mil. Acad. Methodist. Clubs: Army and Navy; Army and Navy Country. Home: Fairfax, Va. Died Aug 21, 1976.

DULL, FLOYD NORMAN, business executive; b. Toledo, Ohio, December 17, 1883; s. Norman R. and Elva F. (Brailey) D.; student pub. schools, Toledo; m. Daisy Myrtle Gordon, Feb. 23, 1904; children—James G., Helen Esther (Mrs. Franklin A. Seward), Lola Myrtle (Mrs. Charles P. Woods), Virginia Marie (Mrs. Malcolm Poignand), Floyd Norman. Office boy, later clerk Kirk Mfg. Co., Toledo, 1894-1900; clerical work Home Telephone Co., 1900-07, sec., later purchasing agent, Detroit, Mich., 1907-12; special agent, Detroit and Cleveland, later asst. mgr., mgr. Travelers Insurance Co., New York City, 1912-22; resident v.p. Commercial Casualty Co., 1922-30; became v.p. Eastern dept. N.Y. City Continental Casualty Co., Chicago, Ill., 1930; dir. and mem. exec. com. N.Y. Board of Trade (past pres.); became v.p. Best Bldg. Co., New York City, 1932; pres. Preferred Accident Insurance Co. of N.Y., 1947-51; rep. Orvis Bros. & Co., investments, 1951. Director Greater New York Safety Council. Member Ins. Fedn. N.Y., N.Y. State Chamber of Commerce, Insurance Soc. of N.Y. Republican. Mason, Elk. Clubs: Bankers, Drug and Chemical (N.Y. City). Home: Rutherford, N.J.

DUMOND, DWIGHT LOWELL, educator; b. Kingston, Ohio, Aug. 27, 1895; s. James Francis and Laura (Bell) D.; A.B., Baldwin-Wallace Coll., 1920, L.H.D.; M.A., Washington U., 1928; Ph.D., U. Mich., 1929; D.Litt., No. Mich. U., 1965; m. Irene Margaret Hettel, June 6, 1921; children—Jack Wesley, Caryl-Bell. Acting prof. history Ohio Wesleyan U., 1929-30; asst. prof. history U. Mich., 1930-35, asso. prof., 1935-39, prof., 1939-76; Commonwealth Found. lectr. U. Coll., London, 1938-39; Distinguished vis. prof. No. Mich. U., summer 1965, Howard U., 1965-66; O'Connor prof. Am. instns. Colgate U., 1968-69. Served with A.E.F., 1917-19. Recipient Disting. Achievement award U. Mich., 1963. Mem. Soc. Am. Historians, Am. (com. on teaching history in schs. and colls. 1943), Miss. Valley (exec. com. 1939-40, pres. 1948-49), So. (bd. editors, 1935) hist. assns., Mich. Acad. Arts, Scis. and Letters. Mason. Club: Research (U. of Mich.). Author books including: The Secession Movement, 1931; Roosevelt to Roosevelt, 1937; A History of the United States, 1942; America in Our Time, 1947; Black Mother: the Years of the African Slave Trade, 1961; Antislavery: Crusade for Freedom in America, 1961 (recipient Anisfield-Wolf award); America's Shame and Redemption, 1965. Editor pubs. including: Letters of James Gillespie Birney, 1831-1857, 2 vols., 1938. Home: Ann Arbor, Mich. Died May 30, 1976.

DUNBAR, OSCAR H., lawyer, banker; b. Jonesport, Me., Nov. 20, 1882; s. Horace M. and Abbie (Drisko) D.; LL.B., U. Me., 1906; m. Theresa M. Rogers, Oct. 25, 1905; children—Arline T. (Mrs. S. Donald Graves, dec.), Kendall H., Helen L., Roger P. (died in service of his country), Ethel M. Brown. Admitted to Me. bar, 1906; asst. atty. gen. State Me., 1915-16; commr. Sea and Shore Fisheries, 1917-18; mem. Me. State Bd. Bar Examiners, 1932-47; co. atty., Washington City, Me., 1935-36; mem. Me. Ho. of Reps., 1913, Me. State Senate, 1943, 45, 47; pres. Machias Savs. Bank, Machias, Me., since 1950, Del., 3d Congl. Dist., Dem. Nat. Conv., 1924; del.-at-large Me., Rep. Nat. Conv., 1948. Mem. Me. State Bar Assn. (pres. 1949-51). Mason (32 deg., Shriner), Red-Man, Eastern Star. Home: 6 Drisko St. Office: 10 Center St., Machias, Me.

DUNBAR, PAUL BROWN, ret. govt. ofcl.; b. Lebanon, Pa., May 29, 1882; s. Rev. William H. and Jennie (Chamberlain) D.; B.S., Gettysburg Coll., 1904, M.S., 1906; Sc.D., 1937; Ph.D., Johns Hopkins, 1907; m. Alice L. Davison, Sept. 7, 1910; children—Lucy (Mrs. John W. Bisselle), Emilie (Mrs. Stanley E. True), Jane C. (Mrs. Romolo D. Tedeschi). Chemist, bur. chem., U.S. Dept. Agr., 1907-25, asst. chief, 1925-27; asst. chief Food and Drug Adminstrn., Dept. of Agr., 1927, designated asst. commr. of food and drugs upon transfer of Food and Drug Adminstrn. to Fed. Security Agency, 1940, asso. commr. 1942-44, commr., 1944-51. Member Am. Chem. Soc., Assn. Food and Drug Ofcls. U.S., Assn. Ofcl. Agrl. Chemists, Phi Delta Theta, Phi Beta Kappa. Home: Chevy Chase, Md.

DUNCAN, ALEXANDER EDWARD, ret. comml. banker; b. nr. Louisville, May 27, 1878; s. John Thomas and Ida (Smith) D.; ed. Louisville Male High Sch.; m. Flora Ross, Apr. 11, 1900 (died June 20, 1936) 1 dau., Elizabeth Duncan Yaggy; m. 2d, Mrs. E. Everett Gibbs (Anne Ranson), Mar. 16, 1940. Began as bank clk. at Louisville, 1896; clerk Jungbluth & Rauterberg, Louisville, 1897-99; mem. Ross & Duncan, Crestwood, Ky., 1900-02; spl. and gen. agt. Ocean Accident & Guaranty Corp., Cincinnati, 1903-06; gen. agent at Baltimore for Am. Credit-Indemnity Co., 1907-09; organized, 1909, and pres., dir. until 1912, Manufacturers' Finance Co., Balt., Md. Organized, 1912, and pres., dir. Comml. Credit Co., Balt., chmn. bd., 1916-54, founder chairman, 1954-64, ret. mem. Robert Garrett & Sons, investments, 18 mos., 1916-17; reorganized Humphreys Mfg. Co., Mansfield, O., 1917, merged 1956 into and dir. Borg Warner Corp., Chicago; director Am. Credit Indemnity Co. N.Y., Mercantile Safe Deposit & Trust Co. (both Baltimore, Maryland). General chairman Y.M.C.A. War Work campaign (Baltimore), 1917, and for United War Work campaign, 1918; pres. Community Fund of Baltimore, 1929-31; gen. chmn. Balt. Red Cross War Fund, 1943. Adv. bd. Women's Hosp., Children's Hosp., Inc., Keswich-Home for Incurables. Republican. Episcopalian. Clubs: Bachelors Cotillon, Maryland, Elkridge, Merchants, Center (Balt.). Home: Balt.

DUNCAN, JOSEPH S., inventor, mfr.; b. nr. Pittsburgh, Pa., Apr. 5, 1858; s. Joseph S. and Mary E. (Guy) D.; ed. pub. schs. of Allegheny County, Pa.; m. Adelaide V. Yockey, Feb. 9, 1888. Engaged in business since 1881, formerly in Ia. and the Dakotas; invented the addressograph, 1893, and settled in Chicago same yr. to mfr. same; pres. Addressograph Co., 1896-1926. Republican. Presbyterian. Mason (K.T., Shriner). Mem. Franklin Inst., Art Inst. Chicago (life), Chicago Hist. Soc. Clubs: Union League, Chicago Motor, Chicago Athletic, South Shore Country (Chicago); Los Angeles Country. Home: Chicago. *

DUNGAN, SEXTON WILLIAM, investments and rentals; b. Marion, Smyth Co., Va., Oct. 13, 1882; s. William Patton and Alice Maria (Sexton) D.; grad. high sch., Marion; student Emory and Henry Coll. 2 yrs., U. of Tenn. 2 yrs.; m. Dixie B. Sisk, of Saltville, Va., June 28, 1924; children—Sexton William, Frank Edward II. With Whiting Lumber Co., Elizabethton, Tenn., 1903-04; an organizer, 1904, Standard Grocery Co., Elizabethton, of which became pres. and gen. mgr. (retired 1926); sr. partner and mgr., with 2 bros., as Dungan Bros., investments and rentals; dir. Builders Supply Co., Doe River Overall Co., Mountain Spring Water Co. Mem. com. of three that secured location of Am. Bemberg, and Am. Glanstoff corpns. at Elizabethton. Mem. Chamber Commerce, Elizabethton (ex-pres.). Col. on staff of Gov. Ben W. Hooper, 1909-13. Democrat. Mem. M.E. Ch., S. Mem. Phi Gamma Delta. Clubs: Rotary, Am. Bemberg-Glanstoff; Johnson City Country. Home: Elizabethton, Tenn.

DUNGLINSON, GEORGE, JR., ry. official; b. Cockermouth, Cumberland, Eng., July 3, 1882; s. George and Margaret Hannah (Huddart) D.; came to U.S., 1889; B.S., Ala. Poly. Inst., 1904; m. Marie Boyd, Oct. 17, 1911; 1 dau., Mary (Mrs. Franklin K. Day, Jr.). Mining engr. Goodwill & Bramwell, 1904-08; mem. and later chmn. car allotment commn. Norfolk & Western Ry., Bluefield, W.Va., 1908-17, asst. to gen. mgr., 1917-20, mgr. fuel dept., 1920-36, asst. v.p., Roanoke, Va., 1936-38, v.p. traffic, 1938-49, exec. v.p., 1949-52, chmn. development com. since 1952; director First National Exchange Bank, Roanoke, Bailey Lumber Co., Bluefield, W.Va., Kentucky Cardinal Coal Corp., Cardinal, Ky. Mem. Kappa Sigma. Democrat. Episcopalian. Clubs: Roanoke Country, Shenandoah (Roanoke).

DUNHAM, CHARLES LITTLE, physician; b. Evanston, Ill., Dec. 28, 1906; s. William Huse and Margaret (Little) D.; B.A., Yale, 1929; M.D., U. Chgo. (Rush), 1933; m. Lucia Elizabeth Jordan, June 22, 1932; children—George Stuart, Carol Jordan, Sara Gale. Intern internal medicine U. Chgo. Clinics, 1933-34; asst. resident medicine New Haven Hosp., 1934-35; asst., sch. medicine, U. Chgo., 1936-43, instr., 1943-46, asst. prof. medicine, 1946-49; asst. chief med. br. AEC, 1949-50, chief med. br., div. biology and medicine, 1950-54, dep. dir. div., 1954, dir., 1955-67; chmn. div. med. scis. Nat. Acad. Scis.-NRC, Washington, 1967-72. Mem. Nat. Council on Radiation Protection, 1965-73, WHO Expert Adv. Panel on Radiation; vis. com. med. dept. Brookhaven Nat. Lab., 1969-73; primate research adv. com. NIH, 1971-75. Served as capt. M.C., U.S. Army, 1943-46. Recipient U.S. AEC Distinguished Service award, 1957. Mem. Soc. Nuclear Medicine, AMA, N.Y. Acad. Sci., Am. Nuclear Soc., Health Physics Soc. (dir. 1964-67), Radiol. Soc. N. Am., Am. Rheumatism Assn., AAAS, Radiation Research Soc. (pres. 1969-70), Acad. Medicine Washington, Inst. Medicine Chgo., Sigma Xi, Nu Sigma Nu, Delta Kappa Epsilon. Clubs: Cosmos, Internat. (Washington); Elizabethan (Yale U.). Home: Washington, D.C. Died Dec. 7, 1975; interred Thomaston, Maine.

DUNHAM, ETHEL C(OLLINS), physician; b. Hartford, Conn., Mar. 12, 1883; d. Samuel G. and Alice (Collins) Dunham; A.B., Bryn Mawr Coll., 1914; M.D., Johns Hopkins, 1918; D.Sc., Trinity College, Hartford, Conn., 1957. House officer pediatrics Johns Hopkins Hosp., 1918-19; asst. resident New Haven Hosp., 1919-20; instr. pediatrics sch. medicine, Yale, 1920-24, asst. prof., 1924-27, asso. clin. prof., 1927-35, lectr. clin. pediatrics, 1935-50; attending pediatrician New Haven Hosp. and Children's Community Center, New Haven, 1920-34, Grace Hosp., 1928-30; med. cons. Child Welfare Assn., 1933-35; med. officer in charge neonatal studies U.S. Children's Bur., New Haven, 1927-34; acting dir. div. maternal and child health U.S. Children's Bur., Dept. Labor, Washington, Feb.-June 1935, dir. div. research child development, 1935-40, cons. pediatrics, 1940-42; med. cons. World Health Orgn., Geneva, Switzerland, 1949-52. Bd. mem. Dept. Pub. Welfare, State of Conn., 1932-34, U.S. Civil Service Commn. Fair Employment Bd., 1948-49; alumnae dir. Bryn Mawr (Pa.) Coll., 1937-42. Recipient Elizabeth Blackwell citation, 1952; John Howland medal Am. Pediatric Soc., 1957. Diplomate Am. Bd. Pediatrics. Fellow Am. Acad. Pediatrics (chmn. Conn. 1930-34); mem. Am. Pediatric Soc., Am. Pub. Health Assn., Sigma Xi. Author: Premature Infants—A Manual for Physicians, 1948; also articles med. jours. Home: Cambridge, Mass.

DUNHAM, LAWRENCE BOARDMAN, criminologist; b. West Newton, Mass., July 18, 1882; s. Edward Francis and Annie Sherry (Boardman) D.; grad. Volkmann Sch., Boston, Mass., 1900; Ph.B., Yale U., 1904; LL.B., N.Y. Law Sch., 1907; m. Margaret Vryling Putnam, June 10, 1915; children—Lawrence Boardman, William Putnam, Margaret Van Vryling. Admitted to N.Y. bar, 1907; mng. clk., law office of Whitridge, Butler & Rice, N.Y. City, 1908; in pvt. practice, N.Y. City, 1908-13; dep. police commr., N.Y. City, 1913-17; mem. staff Laura Spelman Rockefeller Memorial, 1925-27; dir. Bureau of Social Hygiene, 1928-34; tech. adviser to Am. delegation, Geneva Conv. for Limitation of Manufacture of Narcotic Drugs, 1931; became exec. officer personal staff of Mayor LaGuardia, 1934; apptd. city magistrate, N.Y. City, Apr. 1935, justice Court of Domestic Relations, N.Y. City, Sept. 1935. Served as maj. U.S. Army, 1918-19, intelligence officer, Signal Corps, War Coll. and port of embarkation, Hoboken. Commd. major in Army of U.S., July 1942, detailed as member General Staff Corps, promoted to lt. col., 1943. Mem. Delta Phi, St. Elmo Club (Yale). Democrat. Unitarian. Clubs: Yale, Riverdale, St. Andrews Golf. Home: N.Y.

DUNHAM, ROWLAND WARREN (DUN'AM), coll. dean; b. Melrose, Mass., Apr. 18, 1885; s. Edward Payson and Grace Maria (Goudy) D.; grad. New Eng. Conservatory of Music, Boston, 1908, Am. Conservatory, Fontainebleau, France, 1923; m. Ruth Terwilliger, June 16, 1920; children—Robert Scott, Martha Janice. Church organist, 1906-27; instr. Ohio Wesleyan U., 1921-24; asso. editor, The Am. Organist, since 1924; became dean Coll. of Music, U. Colo., 1927. Now emeritus; Am. Guild Organists dist. examiner since 1938; v.p. Nat. Assn. Sch. Music; chmn. choral and organ sect. Music Teachers Nat. Assn. Fellow Am. Guild Organists, 1917; mem. Colo. Schoolmasters Club, Phi Mu Alpha, Elk. S.A.R., Clubs: Rotary, Colorado University Faculty. Composer: Communion Service in D, 1908, and choral compositions. Contbr. to The Etude, The Music jour., Consumers Research, The Diapason. Home: Boulder, Colo. *

DUNHAM, WALTER LEE, industrial financing; b. in Corry, Pa., Feb. 16, 1882; s. Sherman Burt and Emma (Ford) D.; ed. high sch.; m. Maud Van Wormer, Feb. 6, 1906; married 2d, Jean McCaughna, May 1943. Former vice-president Highland Park (Detroit, Mich.) State Bank; v.p. Dime Savings Bank, Detroit, 1920-23, 1st Nat. Bank of Detroit, 1923-27; formerly pres. Detroit Savings Bank; pres. Walter L. Dunham Co., Inc.; past pres., dir. Better Business Bur.; v.p. and dir. Gen. Foundry & Mfg. Co. (Flint, Mich.), Bostick Foundry Co. (Lapeer, Mich.) Served as pvt., United States Vols., Spanish-Am. War, active duty in Porto Rico. Mem. Am. Bankers Assn. (mem. commerce and marine com.), Mich. Bankers Assn., Reserve City Bankers Assn. Pres. Detroit Clearing House Assn.; pres. Better Business Bur. of Detroit; vice president, Detroit Board of

Commerce, also mem. tax com. same and of Nat. Economic League for Mich.; mem. bd. dirs. R.F.C., 1949-50. Republican. Presbyn. Clubs: Bankers, Detroit, Detroit Country. Author: Banking and Industry in Michigan, 1929. Home: Arlington, Va.

DUNKLE, JOHN LEE (DUNK'L), coll. pres.; b. Deer Run, W.Va., Nov. 4, 1884; s. Newman Greenberry and Genina Margaret (Dahmer) D.; grad. Shepherd Coll. State Normal Sch., Shepherdstown, W.Va., 1907; B.S., W.Va. U., 1912; M.A., Columbia, 1917; m. Mary Henrietta Taylor, Apr. 19, 1919; children—Dorothy Lee, John Lee. Teacher, elementary schs., Pendleton County, W.Va., 1899; prin. high sch., La Follette, Tenn., 1907-08; supervisor schs., Edray Dist., Marlinton, W.Va., 1909-10; prin. high sch., Keyser, W.Va., 1912-14; supervisor town schs., Port Deposit, Md., 1914-16; dir. teacher training Md. State Normal Sch., Towson, 1917-23; prin. Md. State Normal Sch., Frostburg, 1923-35; pres. Md. State Teachers Coll., Frostburg, 1935-45; retired 1945. Mem. N.E.A., Am. Assn. Teachers Colls., Nat. Soc. for Study Edn., Phi Delta Kappa. Democrat. Episcopalian. Mason. Rotarian. Home: Frostburg, Md.

DUNLAP, MAURICE P., consular service; b. Toledo, O., Dec. 9, 1882; s. Thomas and Anna (Pratt) D.; B.A., Princeton, 1912; M.A., Columbia University, 1913; m. Dorothea Storm Gregersen, June 13, 1934; m. 2d, Mary Desirée Uline, June 30, 1943. Began as editor with Bowles Newspaper Syndicate, 1904-06; with Philippine civil service, 1907-14; editorial work, U.S. Dept. Agr., 1913-15; consul at Stavanger, Norway, 1915-17, Copenhagen, Denmark, 1917-18, at Odense, Denmark, 1918, Copenhagen, 1919-20, Malmo, Sweden, 1920, Copenhagen, 1921, Bangkok, Siam, 1922-33, Port au Prince, Haiti, 1924-27, Stockholm, Sweden, 1927-32, Dundee, Scotland, 1932-35, Bergen, Norway, 1936-41; retired 1942; sec. in the Diplomatic Service, 1937; lecturer on Norse civilization and contributor to magazines. Fellow Soc. of Antiquaries of Scotland; mem. Viking Soc. of London, Phi Beta Kappa. Author: Stories of the Vikings, 1923; Viking Knights, 1933. Address: Minnehaha County, S.D.

DUNMORE, EARL WILLIAM, business exec.; b. Utica, N.Y., 1886; Pres., dir. Mutual Box Board Co., Utica Knitting Mills; v.p., dir. Homestead Savs. & Loan Assn., Comml. Warehouse Corp.; dir. Utica Mut. Ins. Co., Mpls. Knitting Works. Mason. Home: New Hartford, N.Y.

DUNN, CHARLES ALFRED, naval officer; b. Oct. 14, 1885; completed postgrad. course in elec. engring.; entered U.S. Navy, July 1903; advanced through the grades to rear admiral, Dec. 1940. Awarded special letter of commendation by Navy Dept. for service during World War I.

DUNN, COLON H., educator, elec. engr.; b. Galena, Kans., June 12, 1921; s. Perry Leo and Nellie (Derfelt) D.; B.S., John Brown U., 1942; M.S., Rensselaer Poly Inst., 1953; m. Sibyl Ruth Rife, May 20, 1943; children—James, Frank, David, Diane. Instr. elec. engring. U. N.H., 1942-44; elec. engr. Naval Ordnance Lab., 1944-46; from instr. to asst. and asso. head dept. elec. engring. Rensselaer Poly Inst., 1947-59; prof. elec. engring. Wichita (Kans.) State U., 1959-75, chmn. elec. engring., 1961-64, 65-69, acting dean engring., 1964-65. Registered profl. engr., Kans. Mem. Am. Soc. Engring. Edn. (vice chmn. Kan.-Neb. sect. 1962-63, chmn. 1963-64, mem. energy conversion com. 1971-75), IEEE (tech. chmn. Wichita sect. 1959-60, program chmn. 1963-64, sec.-treas. 1964-65), Wichita Power Engring. Industry and Gen. Applications Group (pres. 1971-73), Am. Nuclear Soc. (chmn. Wichita sect. 1972-73), Sigma Xi (v.p. Rensselaer chpt. 1957-58, pres. 1958-59), Eta Kappa Nu (faculty adviser 1966—, nat. dir. 1975), Phi Kappa Phi, Tau Beta Pi. Author: Electrical Measurements Manual. Home: Wichita, Kans. Died Dec. 3, 1975; buried White Chapel Meml. Gardens, Wichita.

DUNN, EDWARD K., investment banker; b. Balt., June 15, 1899; s. Charles Irwin and Emily Oliver (Shiff) D.; A.B., Princeton U., 1922; m. Anne Butler, Nov. 24, 1931; children—Anne Butler, Edward K., Pierce Butler. Asst. cashier Mchts. Nat. Bank and First Nat. Bank, Balt., 1923-29; partner Robert Garrett & Sons, Balt., 1929-74, sr. partner, 1954-64, chmn. exec. com., 1964-70; ltd. partner, Alex. Brown & Sons, Balt., 1974-79; dir. and mem. exec. com. Colonial Stores, Inc., 1933-73, Comml. Credit Co., 1954-75, Md. Shipbuilding & Drydock Co.; v.p. and dir. Nat. Food Products; dir. Provident Savs. Bank, 1940-70, Humphrey Mfg., Carey Machinery & Supply Co., 1948-76, Green Mt. Cemetery, 1962-76. Trustee Gilman Sch., 1925-79, pres. bd. trustees, 1949-56; trustee and pres. bd. Evergreen House Found., Thomas Wilson Sanitarium; trustee Union Meml. Hosp., Ralph C. Heller Found., Anna Emory Warfield Found. Served with USN, 1918; lt. col. A.C., AUS, 1942-45. Decorated Legion of Merit. Clubs: Md., Bachelors Cotillon, Elkridge (Balt.); Brook (N.Y.C.); Ivy (Princeton); Yeamans Hall (Charleston, S.C.); Cedar Point Ducking. Home: Baltimore, Md. Died Jan. 1, 1979.

DUNN, FAYETTE SMITH, lawyer, elevator co. exec.; b. Maryville, Mo., Oct. 31, 1903; s. Samuel Orace and Carrie Eliza (Smith) D.; A.B., U. Mich., 1925; J.D., Northwestern U., 1928; m. Mildred Ingeborg Lidell, June 30, 1939. Admitted to Ill. bar. 1928, N.Y., 1936; practice law; Chgo., 1928-55, N.Y.C., 1936-60; sec. Otis Elevator Co., N.Y.C., 1951-64, gen. counsel, 1960-64, pres., dir., 1964-68, chmn. bd. 1968-70, chmn. finance com., 1970-79; dir. Irving Trust Co. N.Y., Gen. Cable Corp., N.Y.C. Mem. Commerce and Industry Assn. N.Y. (dir.). Clubs: University, India House, Pinnacle (N.Y.C.); Ekwanok Country (Manchester, Vt.). Home: New York, N.Y. Died Dec. 11, 1979.

DUNN, JAMES ARTHUR, coll. prof.; b. Richmond, Mo., March 19, 1886; s. James Elmore and Emily Oliver (Brown) D.; A.B., U. of Mo., 1908, A.M., 1909; m. Robbie Pipkin, May 22, 1913; children—Robbie Emily (wife of Dr. Grady Siske), Eleanor Joyce (Mrs. Charles W. Lloyd). Prin., Norborne (Mo.) High Sch., 1909-10; supt. Lawson, Mo. schs., 1910-11; head dept. of Latin and Greek, Southeast Mo. Teachers Coll., 1911-21; co-head dept. of English, Hastings (Neb.) Coll., 1921-23; asst. prof. of English, Woman's Coll., U. of N.C., 1923-24, asso. prof., 1924-25, prof. of English from 1925. Mem. Sigma Chi. Home: Greensboro, N.C. Died Nov. 25, 1977.

DUNN, KENNETH, mining co. exec.; b. Manchester, Eng., Apr. 21, 1921; s. William Warwick and Elizabeth (Williams) D.; grad. Manchester schs.; m. Freda Tomkinson, Oct. 12, 1939; children—Patricia (Mrs. Michel Charbonneau), Joyce (Mrs. Peter McGill). Corp. finance mgr., treas. Rio Algom Mines Ltd., Toronto, 1962-65; v.p. Finance Atlas Steel Co., Welland, Ont., 1965-68; controller Falconbridge Nickel Mines Ltd., Toronto, Ont., Can., 1968-77; dir. Falconbridge Internat. Ltd., Kiena Gold Mines Ltd., Toronto Mines Services, Ltd., others. Served with Brit. Army, 1939-46. Clubs: Ontario (Toronto). Home: Scarborough, Ont., Canada. Died Sept. 7, 1977.

DUNN, ROSS JOSEPH, lawyer; b. Toronto, Ont., Can., July 10, 1913; s. Alfred Michael and Mary (Morrison) D.; B.A., U. Toronto, 1933. M.A., 1934; postgrad. Osgoode Hall Law Sch., 1934-37; m. Margaret Hynes, Nov, 4, 1939; children—Mary Estelle (Mrs. Peter Wiley), Michael, Brian, Paul, David, Stephen. Called to Ont. bar, 1937; created Queen's counsel, 1957; asso. McMilan, Binch Toronto, 1937-48, partner, 1948-77. Dir., mem. exec. com. Algoma Steel Corp., Ltd., Ft. Lakes Power Co. Ltd.; v.p., dir. Butterworth & Co. (Can.), Ltd.; dir. Canadian Motorways, Ltd., Sun Alliance Ins. Co., E.S.B. Can. Ltd., Ft. Lakes Power Corp. Ltd., Penguin Books (Can.) Ltd., Bearium Metals Can. Ltd. Bd. dirs. Social Planning Council Met. Toronto, 1959-64, 65-70, vice chmn. bd., 1961-64, v.p., 1966-68. Bd. dirs. Nightingale Sch. Nursing, 1960-74. Served to lt. Royal Canadian Navy, 1943-45. Mem. Motor Carriers Lawyers Assn., Canadian Bar Assn. (council 1969-71, 75-77), Canadian Tax Found., Delta Chi. Clubs: National, Royal Canadian Yacht, Granite (Toronto), Beaumaris Yacht (Muskoka). Home: Toronto, Ont., Canada. Died June 17, 1977.

DUNN, WILLIAM LEWIS, coll. dean; b. Lake Village, Ark., Oct. 18, 1914; s. William Lewis and Ruth Sheldon (Dewey) D.; A.B., U. Ill., 1936; Ph.D., U. Wis., 1941; m. Eleanor Majorie Tisdel, June 8, 1940; children—Carol Ruth, Janet Marjorie (dec.). Instr. in chemistry, Cornell Coll., Mt. Vernon, Iowa, 1941-43; asst. prof. chemistry, 1943-45; prof. chemistry Colo. State Coll. Edn., 1945-49; acting chmn., div. scis., 1947-48; dean coll. Lake Forest (Ill.) Coll., 1949-62, v.p., 1962, provost and dean of faculty, 1962-74. Mem. Phi Beta Kappa, Alpha Chi Sigma. Home: Libertyville, Ill. Died June 1, 1977.

DUNNER, JOSEPH, educator, author; b. Fuerth, Bavaria, Germany, May 10, 1908; s. Samuel and Ella (Laske) D.; student U. Berlin, 1927-30; A.M., U. Frankfurt-Main, 1932; Ph.D., U. Basel, 1934; research fellow Internat. Inst. Social Research, 1930-35, Brookings Instn., 1936-37; m. Ruth Anita Bevan. Fgn. corr. under names Germanicus, Alexander Roth, for Swiss Press and Deutsche Freiheit, Saarbruecken, 1933-35; nat. lectr., cons. refugee problems Am. Jewish Joint Distbn. Com., United Jewish Appeal, 1937-42; fellow, research asso. N.Y. U., 1942-43; lectr. Sch. Overseas Adminstrn., Harvard, 1943-44; chief, intelligence sect. OWI, London, 1944-45, head press control sect. info. control, Munich, Germany, 1945-46; prof. polit. sci. Grinnell Coll., 1946-63, chmn. dept., 1946-58, dir. Inst. Internat. Affairs, 1946-58; Fulbright vis. prof. U. Freiburg (Germany), 1963-64; David Petegorsky prof. polit. sci. and internat. relations Yeshiva U., N.Y.C., 1964-74, prof. emeritus, 1974-78. Trustee Inst. Mediterranean Affairs; bd. dirs. Am. Friends Hebrew U., Am. Council for World Freedom. Decorated Order of Quissam Alaouite Cherifien by Sultan of Morocco, 1954; recipient Outstanding Service award Jewish War Vets. U.S. Mem. Polit. Sci. Assn., Internat. Polit. Sci. Assn. Author books including: The Republic of Israel, Its History and Its Promise, 1950; Democratic Bulwark in the Middle East, 1953; Baruch Spinoza and Western Democrary, 1955; Zu Protokoll Gegeben, 1970; co-author: American Experiences in Military Government in World War II, 1948; Internationalism and Democracy, 1949; Constitutions and Constitutional Trends since World War II, 1951; The Palestine Refugee Problem, 1959; editor, co-author: Major Aspects of International Politics, 1948, Dictionary of Political Science, 1964; Handbook of World History, 1967; Case Studies on Human Rights and Fundamental Freedoms, 1975. Died Aug. 24, 1978.

DUNNING, JAMES HENRY FITZGERALD, chem. co. exec.; b. Balt., Aug. 26, 1902; s. H.A. Brown and Beatrice Garelle (Fitzgerald) D.; student Balt. City Coll., 1916-20; A.B., Johns Hopkins, 1924, Ph.D., 1927; m. Mary Frances McPherson, Mar. 27, 1926; children—James Henry Fitzgerald (dec.), Betty Carey (Mrs. Dushane Patterson). With Hynson, Westcott & Dunning, Inc., Balt., 1925-74, sec.-treas., 1932-45, gen. mgr., 1941-74, pres., 1945-74; dir. Equitable Trust Co. Co-chmn. nat. resources com. Johns Hopkins, 1966-81, trustee univ., 1960-66, 67-81, mem. campaign com., 1967-81, fund bd., 1968-81, chmn. trustees' com. for applied physics lab.; chmn. Johns Hopkins U. Alumni Roll Call, 1950. Bd. dirs. Am. Found. Pharm. Edn., 1961-81, Keswick (home for incurables), Balt. Mem. Am. Chem. Soc. (chmn. Md. 1934-35), AAAS, Am. Pharm. Assn. (council 1958-61), Am. Drug Mfrs. Assn. (pres. 1955-56), Pharm. Mfg. Assn. (dir. 1958—), Johns Hopkins Chem. Alumni Assn. (pres. 1952-54), Johns Hopkins Alumni Assn. (pres. 1954-56), Newcomen Soc. N. Am., Sigma Xi, Phi Gamma Delta, Omicrom Delta Kappa. Clubs: Baltimore Country, Elkridge, Johns Hopkins (Balt.). Author articles profl. jours. Home: Cockeysville, Md. Died Feb. 14, 1981; interred Druid Ridge Cemetery Mausoleum.

DUNNINGTON, JOHN HUGHES, ophthalmologist; b. Farmville, Va., Jan. 12, 1894; s. Walter Grey and India Wycliffe (Knight) D.; A.B., Hampden-Sydney Coll., 1911, LL.D., 1952; M.D., U. Va., 1915; m. Genevieve Richards Parker, Nov. 26, 1919; 1 dau., Jean Parker (Mrs. Jean Cullen). Intern S.I. Hosp. 1915-17, Manhattan Eye, Ear and Throat Hosp., N.Y.C., 1917-18; asst. surgeon N.Y. Eye and Ear Infirmary, 1920-26, sr. asst. surgeon, 1927-28; adj. asst. vis. surgeon, eye service Bellevue Hosp., 1926-28; attending ophthalmologist Presbyn. Hosp. and Vanderbilt Clinic, 1929-32, asst. dir. and attending ophthalmologist, 1934-38, clin. dir. and attending ophthalmologist, acting dir., eye service and attending ophthalmologist, 1942-44, dir. Inst. ophthalmology, and attending ophthalmologist, now cons; instr. ophthalmology U. and Bellevue Hosp. Med. Coll., 1922-28, lectr., 1928-29; asst. prof. ophthalmology, N.Y. Postgrad. Med. Sch. and Hosp., asso. in ophthalmology Coll. Phys. and Surg., Columbia, 1928-30, asst. prof. ophthalmology, 1930-35, asso. prof. ophthalmology, 1936-37, asso. clin. prof. ophthalmology, 1938-39, prof. ophthalmology, 1940-59, prof. emeritus, 1959-77. Chmn. Am. Bd. Ophthalmology, 1950-52. Served as 1st lt. M.C., U.S. Army, 1918-19. Fellow A.C.S.; mem. A.M.A., Am. Ophthal. Soc., (pres. 1950-51), Am. Bd. Opthalmology, N.Y. Acad. Med. (chmn. 1936-37), N.Y. Opthal. Soc., N.Y. State Med. Soc., N.Y. Acad. Scis., A.A.A.S., Am. Acad. Opthalmology and Otolaryngology (pres. 1958-59), Med. Soc. County N.Y., Phi Beta Kappa, Chi Phi, Phi Rho Sigma. Democrat. Presbyn. Clubs: The Virginians, Union (N.Y.C.); Nantucket Yacht. Home: New York, N.Y. Died Oct. 18, 1977.

DUPEE, FREDERICK WILCOX, educator, author; b. Chgo., June 25, 1904; s. Leroy Church and Frances (Wilcox) D.; student U. Chgo., 1922-23; Ph.B., Yale, 1927; postgrad. English, Columbia, 1940-43; Litt.D., Bard Coll., 1965; m. Barbara Hughes, June 24, 1946; children—Joanna, Anthony. Instr. English, Bowdoin Coll., 1927-29; editorial bd. Miscellany 1929-32; lit. editor New Masses, 1936; editorial bd. Partisan Rev., 1937-41; instr. English, Columbia, 1940-44, asst. prof., 1948-51, asso. prof., 1951-57, prof., 1957-71, prof. emeritus, 1971-79; asst. prof. Bard Coll., 1944-48. Vis. prof. U. Lille (France), 1952, Harvard, 1957; faculty Salzburg (Austria) Seminar Am. Studies, 1966; Beckman vis. prof. U. Calif. at Berkeley, 1974; vis. prof. Stanford, 1975. Guggenheim fellow, 1951-52. Mem. P.E.N., Delta Kappa Epsilon. Author: Henry James, 1951; The King of the Cats and other essays, 1965. Editor: The Question of Henry James, 1945; Selected Letters of Charles Dickens, 1960; (with George Stade) Selected Letters of E.E. Cummings, 1969. Home: Carmel, Calif. Died Jan. 19, 1979.

DUPONG, PIERRE, statesman; b. Heisdorf, Luxembourg, Nov. 1, 1885; s. Henry and Marie Catherine (Binsfeld) D.; law student U. of Paris, U. of Berlin, U. of Fribourg (Switzerland); Docteur en droit, 1910; m. Sophie Schroeder, May 27, 1915; children—Marie-Thérèse, Lambert, Jean, Henriette. Admitted to Luxembourg bar, 1911, and since practiced law in Luxembourg; deputy for Canton of Capellen, Dist. of the South, Party of the Right, since 1915; dir. gen. of finances, labor and social prevision in Ministry Bech, 1926-27; minister, 1936-37; minister of state, president of govt. (central adminstrn., finances, armed forces and pub. assistance) since 1937. Christian Socialist. Roman Catholic. Home: Luxembourg.

DUPRÉ, MARCEL, organist, composer; b. Rouen, France, May 3, 1886; ed. Nat. Conservatoire de Musique, Paris. Made 1st pub. appearance at Elbeuf Ch., 1894; became organist Ch. of St. Vivien, Rouen, 1898 (aged 12); temporary organist Notre Dame, 1916-20; asst. at St. Sulpice, Paris, 1920, organist, 1934—; prof. organ and improvisation Nat. Conservatoire, 1926-54, dir. conservatoire, 1954-56; became gen. dir. Am. Conservatory in Fontainebleau, 1947; tours of Eng., from 1920, U.S., from 1922, world tour, 1939. Recipient Grand Prix de Rome, 1914; decorated Legion d'Honneur; hon. dr. Pontifical Inst. Rome. Composer works including 2 organ symphonies, many other organ works, 2 symphonies and concerto for organ and orch., works for piano and organ, De Profundis for Voices, organ and orch. Author: Traite d'improvisation a l'orgue, 1925; Methode d'orgue. Address: Meudon (Seine-et-Oise), France. *

DURANT, THOMAS MORTON, educator, physician; b. Evanston, Ill., Nov. 19, 1905; s. Harry S. and Ida Ridgway (Hair) D.; B.S., U. Mich., 1928, M.D., 1930; Sc.D., Franklin and Marshall Coll., 1964; m. Jean Margaret deVries, June 25, 1929; children—John Ridgway, Carol Christine, Catherine Elizabeth. Intern U. Mich. Hosp., 1930-32; instr. internal medicine U. Mich., 1932-35; asos. physician Desert Sanatorium So. Ariz., Tucson, 1935-36; asst. prof. Med. Sch. Temple U., 1936-38, asso. prof., 1938-46, prof. clin. medicine, 1946-56, prof., head dept. medicine, 1956-66, prof., 1966-73, emeritus, 1973-77. Ventnor Found. lectr., Weisbaden, Germany, 1956; vis. physician Phila. Gen. Hosp., 1947-77; cons. cardiology U.S. Vets. Hosp., Phila.; cons. U.S. Naval Hosp., Phila., USAF. Mem. bd. examiners Am. Bd. Internal Medicine, chmn. bd., 1957-59; chmn. drug research bd. NRC, 1968-70. Recipient Strittmater award, Phila., 1964; Distinguished Alumnus award U. Mich. Med. Sch., 1970; Distinguished Tchr. award A.C.P., 1972. Fellow A.C.P. (master 1970); gen. chmn. ann. meeting 1955, pres. 1964-65), Am. Coll. Cardiology; mem. Assn. Am. Physicians, AMA, Am. Heart Assn. (dir.), Phila. County Med. Soc. (dir.), Coll. Physicians Phila. (pres. 1961-64), Am. Fedn. Clin. Research (pres. 1945), Am. Clin. and Climatol. Assn., Sigma Xi, Alpha Omega Alpha, Alpha Kappa Kappa, Beta Theta Pi. Clubs: Merion Golf, Interurban Clinical. Mem. editorial bd. Am. Heart Jour.; asso. editor Am. Jour. Med. Scis. Address: Gladwynne, Pa. Died June 21, 1977.

DURANT, WILLIAM JAMES, author; b. Nbrth Adams, Mass., Nov. 5, 1885; s. Joseph and Marie (Allors) D.; B.A., St. Peter's Coll., Jersey City, 1907, M.A., 1908; Ph.D., Columbia, 1917; m. Ariel Kaufman, Oct. 31, 1913; children—Ethel Benvenuta, Louis R. Prof. Latin and French, Seton Hall Coll., South Orange, N.J., 1907-11; dir. Labor Temple Sch., N.Y.C., 1914-27; instr. philosophy Columbia, 1917; prof. philosophy U. Cal., Los Angeles, 1935. Recipient Huntington Hartford Found. award creative writing. Mem. Nat. Inst. Arts and Letters. Author: Philosophy and the Social Problem, 1917; The Story of Philosophy, 1926; Transition, 1927; The Mansions of Philosophy, 1929; The Case for India, 1930; Adventures in Genius, 1931; A Program for America, 1931; On the Meaning of Life, 1932; The Tragedy of Russia, 1933; The Story of Civilization: Part I, Our Oriental Heritage, 1935; Part II, The Life of Greece, 1939; Part III, Caesar and Christ, 1944; Part IV, The Age of Faith, 1950; Part V, The Renaissance, 1953; Part VI, The Reformation, 1957; (with Ariel Durant) Part VII, The Age of Reason Begins, 1961; The Age of Louis XIV, 1963, The Age of Voltaire, 1965, Rousseau and Revolution, 1967 (Pulitzer prize 1968); The Lesson of History, 1968, Interpretations of Life, 1970; The Age of Napoleon, 1975. Address: Los Angeles, CA. *

DURANTE, JIMMY (JAMES FRANCIS), comedian; b. N.Y.C., Feb. 10, 1893; s. Barthelmeo and Rosa Durante; ed. schs. of N.Y.C.; m. Jeanne Olsen, 1916 (dec. 1943); m. 2d, Margie Little, Dec. 1960; 1 dau., CeCe Alicia. First worked in father's barbershop, then as photoengraver; piano player, Coney Island at age of 17 years; organized 5 piece band, 1916; opened Club Durante with Eddie Jackson and Lou Clayton as partners (Lou Clayton is credited with coining the famous nickname, Schnozzola); the partners later formed comedy team, Clayton, Jackson and Durante, playing in night clubs, 1930; made Broadway debut at Loew's State Theatre, 1927, in Show Girl (Ziegfeld), 1928, The New Yorkers (Cole Porter), 1930; appeared in Hollywood pictures: Get Rich Quick Wallingford; The Cuban Love Song; Her Cardboard Lover; The Passionate Plumber; and others; returned to N.Y.C., and starred with Ethel Merman in Strike Me Pink, 1934; motion pictures also include: Student Tour; George White's Scandals; Land Without Music; Carnival; Start Cheering; Sally, Irene and Mary; Music For Millions; On an island with You; Roadhouse Nights, Two Girls and a Sailor, Two Sisters From Boston, Ziegfeld Follies, This Time for Keeps, The Great Rupert, Yellow Cab Man, The Milkman, Jumbo, It's a Mad, Mad, Mad, Mad World; appeared at Paladium, London, 1936; in Broadway musicals: Jumbo, 1936, Red, Hot and Blue, 1937; entertainer at Copacabana, N.Y.C. night club, 1943; began on radio and had own show to 1950, when entered TV Nov. 1950; TV shows include: All Star Revue, 1951, Colgate Comedy Hour, Texcao Star Theater, Club Oasis, others; TV spl. Jimmy Durante Meets the Seven Lively Arts, 1965, Jimmy Durante Presents the Lennon Sisters, 1969; alternate guest-host The Hollywood Palace. Recipient Peabody award for radio-TV performance, 1951. Home: Beverly Hills, Calif. Died Jan. 29, 1980; interred Holy Cross Cemetery, Culver City, Calif.

DURBIN, FLETCHER MCCULLOUGH, b. Anderson, Ind., Apr. 25, 1880; s. Winfield T. and Bertha (McCullough) D.; ed. Lawrenceville (N.J.) Sch.; Williams Coll., 1904; m. Hazel West, Nov. 20, 1907; children—Elinor West, Winfield T. II. Engaged in constrn. and operation of electric rys., Ind., 1903-10; ry. mgr. J. G. White & Co., New York, 1911; mfg. business, N.Y. City, 1912-15; v.p. Sefton Mfg. Corp., Chicago, 1915-27; pres. National Assn. Folding Box-makers, 1924-25; pres. Paperboard Industries Assn., 1925-27; director First Investors Co. of Illinois. Served as 2d lt. U.S. Vols., Cuba, 1898, Ind. Nat. Guard, 1899-1904. Mem. Local Draft Bd. 143, 1942-47. Formerly trustee Seabury-Western Theol. Sem., Chgo.; trustee The Bishop and Trustee of the P.E. Church Diocese Chgo.; Cook County School of Nursing. Mem. American Society Mech. Engrs. Military Order Loyal Legion, Ind. Soc. of Chicago (pres. 1927). Republican. Episcopalian. Clubs: Chicago, Saddle and Cycle, Commercial (Chgo.); Williams (N.Y.C.). Home: Chgo.

DURDEN, CHARLES, clergyman; b. Moseley, Eng., Sept. 5, 1882; s. John and Emily (Oldacre) D.; 3d, 2d and 1st class certificates, Brit. Army Schs., Curragh, Ireland; grad. Woodstock (Can.) Coll., 1907; A.B., William Jewell Coll., Liberty, Mo., 1913, A.M., 1915; D.D., Shurtleff Coll., Alton, Ill., 1921; m. Ethel Elizabeth Wilson, June 3, 1908; children—Dorothy Ethel, Charles Henry, John Kenneth, Thomas Edward, Samuel Percy. Came to U.S., 1907, naturalized, 1918. Ordained ministry Baptist Ch., 1907; pastor Harbor Beach, Mich., 1907-09, then successively at St. Joseph, Mo., Galesburg and Bloomington, Ill.; pastor First Bapt. Ch., Omaha, Neb., 1930-39, Cavalry Baptist Church, Pasadena, 1939-41. Member board of mgrs. Mo. Baptist Assn., 1915-17; mem. state exec. com. Ill. Bapt. Conv., 1922-28 (chmn. dept. of ministry 1927); State executive committee, Nebraska, 1930-39; 1st v.p. American Baptist Foreign Missionary Society, 1934-36, pres., 1938-39; vice-president of Ministers Council, 1935-36 and since 1941; mem. Council on Finance and Promotion, 1934-37, chmn. administrative com., 1935—all of Northern Bapt. Conv.; state evangelist for Southern Calif. Bapt. Conv., 1941-43; pastor Calvary Baptist Church, Salem, Ore., 1944-49, 1st Baptist Church, Astoria, Oregon, since 1950, Oregon Baptist State Board since 1945. Mem. Royal Army Ordnance; British Army, 4 years; served as chaplain 1st lt. U.S. Res., 1918. Mem. bd. trustees, Sioux Falls Coll., Central Bapt. Sem.; mem. bd. govs. Community Chest, Omaha; mem. bd. edn., Neb. Bapt. Student Council, and Campfire Bd.; chmn. exec. com. Oregon Bapt. Conf.; chmn., Neb. Re-employment Service; chaplain Omaha Central Labor Union. Republican. Mason (32 deg., Shriner). Club: Kiwanis. Address: Astoria, Ore.

DURFEE, JAMES RANDALL, judge; b. Oshkosh, Wis., Nov. 3, 1897; s. Thomas H. and Mary (Rossiter) D.; student Huron (S.D.) Coll., 1917, 20; LL.B., Marquette U., 1926; m. Mona Burns, July 17, 1933; children—Mary (Mrs. David Clarke), James Randall, John. Admitted to Wis. bar, 1926; practiced in Antigo, 1927-51; dist. atty. Langlade County, Wis., 1928-32; ct. commr. 10th Jud. Circuit, 1934-50; commr. Pub. Service Commn. Wis., 1951-53, chmn., 1953-56; chmn. CAB, Washington, 1956-60; judge U.S. Ct. Claims, Washington, 1960-77, sr. judge, 1972-77. Served with U.S. Army, AEF, 1917-19. Mem. Am., Wis., D.C. bar assns., Am. Legion, Delta Theta Phi. Home: Washington, D.C. Died Oct. 29, 1977.

DURHAM, PHILIP CALVIN, educator; b. Portland, Ore., Feb. 7, 1912; s. Darr Henry and Greta (Phillips) D., B.S., Linfield Coll., 1935; M.A., Claremont Grad. Sch., 1946; Ph.D., Northwestern U., 1949; m. Jeanne Frances Grandy, June 15, 1955; 1 dau., Darrann. Faculty, Elmhurst Coll., 1949-51; faculty U. Cal., Los Angeles, 1953-77; prof. English, 1966-77. Served as 1st lt. USMCR, 1942-45. Recipient Edgar award Mystery Writers Am., 1964. Am. Council Learned Socs. fellow, 1952-53. Fulbright fellow, 1955-56, Guggenheim fellow, 1960-61. Fellow Am. Philos. Soc.; mem. Modern Lang. Assn., Am. Lit. Group, Am. Studies Assn., Western Writers Am. Democrat. Club: U. Cal. at Los Angeles Faculty. Author: (with Taunu Mustanoja) America Fiction in Finland, 1960; Down These Mean Streets a Man Must Go; Raymond Chandler's Knight, 1963; (with E.L. Jones) The Negro Cowboys, 1965. Home: Santa Monica, Calif. Died Mar. 27, 1977.

DURR, CLIFFORD JUDKINS, lawyer; b. Montgomery, Ala., Mar. 2, 1899; s. John Wesley and Lucy (Judkins) D.; A.B., U. Ala., 1919; B.A. in Jurisprudence, Oxford (Eng.) U., 1922, M.A., B.C.L., 1964; m. Virginia Heard Foster, Apr. 5, 1926; children—Ann Patterson (Mrs. Walter A. Lyon), Lucy Judkins (Mrs. F. Sheldon Hackney), Virginia Foster, Lulah Johnston (Mrs. Richard V. Colan). Admitted to Ala. bar, 1923, Wis. bar, 1924, D.C. bar, 1948; mem. firm Rushton, Crenshaw & Rushton, Montgomery, 1922-23, Fawsett, Smart & Shea, Milw., 1923-24, Martin, Turner & McWhorter, Birmingham, Ala., 1925-33; asst. gen. counsel RFC, 1933-41; gen. counsel, dir. Def. Plant Corp., v.p., dir. Rubber Res. Corp., 1940-41; commr. FCC, 1941-48; pvt. practice law, Washington, 1948-50, Montgomery, 1952-64. Lectr., Am., Brit. univs.; Regents lectr. theatre arts UCLA, 1966. Served with U.S. Army, 1918. Rhodes scholar, 1918; recipient Variety award, 1946, Sch. Broadcasters award, 1947, Page One award Am. Newspaper Guild, 1948, Lasker Civil Liberties award N.Y. Civil Liberties Union, 1966. Life mem. Inst. Edn. by Radio; mem. Phi Beta Kappa, Sigma Alpha Epsilon. Democrat. Presbyn. Contbr. articles to profl. jours.; contbr. books. Address: Wetumpka, Ala. Died 1975.

DURRANT, STEPHEN DAVID, educator; b. Salt Lake City, Oct. 11, 1902; s. Stephen Thomas and Martha (Harman) D.; student Weber Coll., 1925-26; A.B., U. Utah, 1929, M.A., 1931; student U. Minn., 1931-32, U. Calif., Berkeley, 1933, 38-39; Ph.D., U. Kans., 1950; m. Sylvia Jane Burt, Dec. 21, 1933; children—Sue Marilynn, Stephen Carl. Asst. zoology U. Utah, 1929-31; ranger Zion Nat. Park, summer 1931; asst. zoology U. Minn., 1931-32; faculty U. Utah, 1932-75, prof. zoology, 1952-71, emeritus, 1971-75; supr. mosquito abatement Salt Lake City, 1935-36; field dir. U.S. Bur. Fisheries, 1934; instr. zoology U. Kan., 1945; field dir. Upper Colo. River Devel.-U. Utah Ecol. Researches in coop. with Bur. Reclamation on Glen Canyon project, 1958, Flaming Gorge project, 1959, Navajo project, 1960, Curacanti project, 1961. Mem. Wildlife Soc., Soc. Systemic Zoology (pres. Pacific sect. 1965), Biol. Soc. Washington, AAUP, Utah Acad. Arts, Sci. and Letters, Am. Soc. Mammalogists (dir. 1950-55, pres. 1961-62, hon. mem.), Sigma Xi, Phi Sigma, Phi Kappa Phi. Author: Mammals of Utah, Taxonomy and Distribution, 1952; also articles. Home: Salt Lake City, Utah. Died Nov. 11, 1975.

DURYEE, SAMUEL SLOAN, lawyer; b. N.Y. City, Nov. 18, 1893; s. Joseph Rankin and Margaret Elmendorf (Sloan) D.; A.B., Yale, 1917; LL.B., cum laude, Fordham, 1923; m. Mary Ballard, Aug. 18, 1917; children—Samuel Sloan, Nina. Admitted to N.Y. bar, 1924; mem. Parker, Duryee, Benjamin, Zunino and Malone and predecessor firms, 1943-79; vice pres., and dir. Aglic Investing & Management Co., Inc.; chmn. adv. bd. Zurich Ins. Co.; dir. First Nat. City Trust Co., Aero Associates Incorporated, Zurich Life Insurance Company, also Am. Guarantee & Liability Ins. Co., 333 E. 68th St. Corp.; treas., dir. Linn and Paul Fenimore Cooper Found. Chief tax amortization sect. Office Undersec. of War, 1941; chmn. Tax Amortization Bd., 1941-42. Trustee, past pres. St. John's Guild, also N.Y. Soc. for Relief Ruptured and Crippled (Hospital for Spl. Surgery); mem., pres. bd. trustees Groton sch.; past chmn. Yale Alumni Fund, mem. Yale Alumni Bd. Served as 2d lt. 10th F.A., Conn. N.G., 1916; capt. 302d F.A., AEF, 1917-19. Asso. fellow Trumbull Coll., Yale; mem. Am. Bar Assn., Am. Judicature Soc., Assn. Bar City N.Y., Friendly Sons of St. Patrick, Am. Legion, Holland Soc. Clubs: Yale, Coffee House, Century (New York City); Highlands Country (Garrison); Elizabethan, Graduates (New Haven). Home: New York, N.Y. Died Apr. 29, 1979.

DUSENBERRY, WILLIAM HOWARD, educator; b. Carmichaels, Pa., June 6, 1908; s. William Smith and Edith Agnes (Miller) D.; A.B., Waynesburg Coll., 1932, Litt.D., 1975; A.M., U. Mich., 1936, Ph.D., 1941. Tchr., Carmichaels area pub. schs., 1932-38; instr. history Fresno State Coll., 1942; instr. history U. Cal. at Los Angeles, 1946-48; asso. prof. history U. Pitts., 1948-61; prof. history, chmn. history dept. Waynesburg Coll., 1962-73, liaison officer between Waynesburg Coll. and Regional Council Internat. Edn. Served to maj. USAAF, 1942-46. Mem. Am., Pa., Greene County hist. assns., Agrl. Hist. Soc., Conf. on Latin-Am. History, Warriors Trail Assn., Latin-Am. Studies Assn., SAR. Author: The Mexican Mesta: Administration of Ranching in Colonial Mexico, 1963; The Waynesburg College Story, 1849-1974, 1975. Home: Waynesburg, Pa. Died Mar. 29, 1979.

DUTCHER, FRANCIS EDWARD, bldg. products co. exec.; b. Vancouver, B.C., Can., Oct. 24, 1909; s. Bert Elroy and Eva (McQuay) D.; student St. Petersburg Jr. Coll., 1929-30; B.S. in Bus., Miami U., Oxford, O., 1932; m. Nancy Jane Callander, Mar. 6, 1937; children—Barbara Ann (Mrs. Justin Kimball), Nancy Odette (Mrs. Peter Strohmeier). Came to U.S., 1914, naturalized. With Johns-Manville Sales Corp., 1933-73, v.p., sales mgr. dealer bldg. products, N.Y.C., 1958-59, v.p., gen. mdse. mgr. bldg. products div., 1959-61, sr. operating v.p. bldg. materials divs. Johns Manville Corp., N.Y.C., from 1961; now v.p. Johns-Manville Fiber Glass, Inc., Denver, also dir., pres. Johns-Manville Products Corp.; mem. adv. com. Chem Bank, N.Y.C. Bd. dirs. Producers Council. Served to lt USNR, 1943-46. Mem. Nat. Mineral Wool Assn. (pres 1961), Mineral Fibre Asbestos-Products Bur. (chmn exec. com.), Asphalt Roofing Mfrs. Assn. (past chmn exec. com.). Clubs: Union League (N.Y.C.); Tokeneke

(Darien, Conn.). Home: Darien, Conn. Died May 25, 1973.

DUTCHER, RAYMOND ADAMS, biochemist; b. Raymond, S.D., Mar. 28, 1886; s. Paul and Susie (Adams) D.; B.S., S.D. State Coll., 1907, M.S., 1910; M.A., U. of Missouri, 1912; grad. study U. of Ill. and U. of Minn.; D.Sc., Univ. of Puerto Rico, 1936; D.Sc. (hon.), South Dakota State College, 1948; m. Mary Marguerite Wright, Sept. 14, 1912; children—Adams Wright, Rachel Mary. Instr. S.D. State Coll., 1907-10, U. of Mo., 1910-12, U. of Ill., 1912-13; asst. prof. Ore. State Coll., 1913-17; asst. and asso. prof. agrl. biochemistry (nutrition), U. of Minn., 1917-21; head of dept. agrl. and biol. chemistry, Pa. State Coll., State Coll., Pa., since 1921. Oberlaender fellow Carl Schurz Foundation (Germany), 1934. Served as capt., food and nutrition div., Sanitary Corps, U.S. Army, Camp Meade, Md., 1918. Mem. Land Grant Coll. Advisory Com. on Vitamin Research; mem. White House Conf. on Child Health and Protection; mem. Research Adv. Com. Farm Chemurgie Council, 1935. Sci. cons. Field Intelligence Agency Tech. (Germany), 1945. Mem. Food and Nutrition Bd., Nat. Research Council. Mem. and counselor at large Inst. of Food Technologists; mem. General Board of Dairy Research. Fellow A.A.A.S.; mem. Am. Inst. Nutrition, Am. Chem. Soc. (chmn. biochem. div.), Soc. for Exptl. Biology and Medicine Am. Soc., Biol. Chemists (chmn. vitamin terminology com.), Pa. Acad. Science, N.Y. Acad. Science, Brit. Biochem. Soc., Sigma Xi, Gamma Sigma Delta, Alpha Zeta, Phi Lambda Upsilon, Alpha Chi Sigma, Theta Chi, Acacia, Phi Kappa Phi. Republican. Presbyterian. Mason. Clubs: Centre Hills Country (State College); Chemists (New York). Co-author: Chemistry in Agriculture, 1926; Introduction to Agricultural Biochemistry (with D. E. Haley), 1932. Home: State College, Pa.

DUTTON, HENRY POST, educator, consultant in management; b. Holland, Mich., Dec. 29, 1885; s. Charles Selwyn and Mary (Post) D.; student Hope Coll., Holland, Mich.; B.S. in Elec. Engring., U. of Mich., 1914; m. Lucy May Broceus, Sept. 5, 1914; children—John Coatsworth, Mary Lou. Instr. in factory management, Northwestern U., 1914-17, asst., later asso. prof., 1917-24, prof., 1924-43; prof. industrial engineering Illinois Institute Tech., 1934-51, chmn. indsl. engring. div., 1937-47, dean evening division, 1938-45. Associate editor, Factory Management and Maintenance (monthly mag.), 1927-36; sr. asso. Griffenhagen & Assos., 1950-52. Pres. Hendersonville Welfare Council, 1954-58. Member Society for Advancement Management, Academy of Management, Delta Sigma Pi. Republican. Kiwanian. Author: Factory Management, 1924; Business Organization and Management, 1925; Principles of Organization, 1931. Home: Hendersonville, N.C.

DU VIGNEAUD, VINCENT, educator; b. Chgo., May 18, 1901; s. Alfred Joseph and Mary Theresa (O'Leary) duV.; B.S., U. Ill., 1923, M.S., 1924, Sc.D., 1960; Ph.D., U. Rochester, 1927, Sc.D., 1965; Sc.D., Yale U., N.Y.U., 1955; St. Louis U., 1965, George Washington U., 1968; m. Zella Zon Ford, June 12, 1924; children—Vincent, Marilyn Renée Brown. Asst. biochemist Phila. Gen. Hosp., asst. biochemist U. Pa. Grad. Sch. Medicine, 1924-25; teaching asst. Sch. Medicine U. Rochester, 1925-27; NRC fellow Johns Hopkins Med. Sch., 1927-28, Kaiser Wilhelm Inst., Dresden, Germany, U. Edinburgh Med. Sch., UCH Med. Sch., London, 1928-29; asso. dept. chemistry U. Ill., 1929-30, asst. prof., 1930-32; prof., head dept. biochemistry George Washington U. Sch. Medicine, 1932-38; prof., head dept. biochemistry Cornell U. Med. Coll., N.Y.C., 1938-67; emeritus prof. biochemistry, 1967-78; prof. chemistry Cornell U., Ithaca, N.Y., 1967-78; lectr. various univs. Mem. Health Research Adv. Council City N.Y., 1958-62; nat. adv. arthritis and metabolic diseases council NIH, 1960-64; trustee Rockefeller U. Recipient Hillebrand prize Chem. Soc. Washington, 1936; Borden award for Research in Med. Scis., 1947; Lasker award Am. Pub. Health Assn., 1948; 1Merit award for War Research, 1948; John Scott award, 1954; Sci. award Am. Pharm. Mfrs. Assn., 1955; Passano Found. award, 1955; Nobel prize in Chemistry, 1955; Chandler medal, 1956; Nutrition Found. 20th Anniversary award, 1961; 7th Ann. Hon. Lecture award Albany Med. Coll., 1963; A.C.P. award, 1965; Eli Lilly award Endocrine Soc., 1967. Fellow Am. Acad. Arts and Sciences, Royal Soc. Edinburgh (hon.), Chem. Soc. London, Royal Soc. Scis. Upsala (hon.), Royal Inst. Chemistry (London); mem. Am. Inst. Nutrition (Mead Johnson vitamin award 1943, Osborne and Mendel award 1953), Am. Soc. Biol. Chemistry (pres. 1951-52), Am. Chem. Soc. (council at large 1943, chmn. N.Y. sect. 1943, Nichols medal N.Y., sect. 1945, Willard Gibbs medal Chgo. sect. 1956), Soc. Exptl. Biology (past chmn. bd.), Harvey Soc., Am. Philos. Soc., Nat. Acad. Scis. (chmn. sect. biochem. 1958-60), N.Y. Acad. Sci., Washington Acad. Medicine, Xi, Alpha Chi Sigma, Phi, Lambda Upsilon, Sigma Alpha Omega Alpha (hon.). Club: Chemists' (hon., N.Y.C.). Contbr. articles to sci. jours. Home: Ithaca, N.Y. Died Dec, 11, 1978.

DVORAK, AUGUST, educator; b. Glencoe, Minn., May 3, 1894; s. Joseph and Maud (Pulkrabek) D.; A.B., U. Minn., 1920, Ph.D., 1923; m. Hermione Louise Dealey, Sept. 8, 1921; children—Hermione Elizabeth Rice, Andrey Louise Snow, Dealey Ann Legett. Tchr. elementary schs., 1911-15, high school, 1920-23; assistant professor of education, Univ. of Washington, 1923-29, associate professor 1929-37, prof. since 1937, also dir. ednl. research, 1938-42; dir. Carnegie Found. Investigation of Typewriting, 1933-42, dir. admissions research, 1947-52, asst. dir. div. counseling and testing services, from 1956. Served 1st Minn. F.A., 1915-17; with U.S.N.R.F., 1918-19; served as lt. comdr., U.S.N.R., 1942-45, commander, 1947-57, capt., from 1957. Assigned to research NRC com. on artificial limbs, 1946-1947. Mem. Sigma Xi, Sigma Delta Psi, Phi Delta Kappa. Author books including: Scientific Typewriting—Standard Keyboard Edition (with N.L. Merrick, W.L. Dealey and G.C. Ford), 1947. Contbr. to ednl. mags. Specialist in time and motion study, visual edn. and tng. films. Home: Seattle, Wash. Died Oct. 9, 1975.

DVORNIK, FRANCIS, clergyman, educator; b. Chomyz, Czechoslovakia, Aug. 14, 1893; s. Francis and Frances (Tomeckova) D.; student Classical Gymnasium, Kromeriz, Moravia; D.D., Faculty of Theology, Olomouce, 1920, student Charles U., Prague, diploma Ecole des Sciences Polit., Paris, 1923; D.ès Lettres, Sorbonne, Paris, 1926; D.Litt. (hon.), London, St. Procopius Coll., Fairleigh Dickinson U. Came to U.S., 1948, naturalized, 1954. Ordained priest, 1916; prof. ch. history Charles U., Prague, 1928; dean faculty theology, 1935; Schlumberger lectr. Coll. of France, Paris, 1940; Birbeck lectr. Cambridge U., 1946; prof. Byzantine history, Dumbarton Oaks, Harvard U., 1949-75. Decorated knight French Legion of Honor. Fellow Brit. Acad., Am. Acad. Arts and Scis. of Boston; mem. Royal Hist. Soc. London, Am. Medieval Acad., Royal Belgian Acad. Author: Les Slaves, Byzance et Rome an IXs., 1926; St. Gregoire el Decap, et les Slaves, 1926; St. Wenceslas, Duke of Bohemia, 1929; Les Légendes de Constantine et de Méthode, 1933; National Churches, 1944; The Photian Schism, 1948, French edit., 1950, Italian edit., 1952; The Making of Central and Eastern Europe, 1949, 2d edit., 1974; The Slavs, Their Early History and Civilization, 1956; The Idea of Apostolicity in Byzantium, 1958; The Ecumenical Councils, 1961; The Slavs in European History and Civilization, 1962; Byzance et la Primunaté Romaine, 1964, English, German edit., 1966; Early Christian and Byzantine Political Philosophy, 1966; Byzantine Missions Among the Slavs, 1970; Origins of Intelligence Services, 1974. Home: Washington, D.C. Died Nov. 4, 1975.

DWIGHT, HERBERT BRISTOL, prof. elec. machinery; b. Geneva, Ill., Sept. 8, 1885; s. William Cecil and Ruth Augusta (Bristol) D.; prep. edn., high sch., Picton and Toronto, Ont.; student Toronto U., 2 yrs.; B.Sc., McGill U., D.Sc., 1924; m. Violet Constance Beryl Marshall, 1916; children—Julia Constance, Barbara Bristol, Margaret Ruth, Edith Louise, Beryl Cecilia Marshall. Elec. engr. with Can. Westinghouse Co., Hamilton, Ont., 1909-25; cons. engr. New Brunswick Power Commn., 1925; prof. elec. machinery, Mass. Inst. Tech., since 1925. Fellow Am. Inst. Electrical Engrs. Congregationalist. Author: Transmission Line Formulas, 1913; Constant-Voltage Transmission, 1915; Tables of Integrals and other Mathematical Data, 1934; also various papers pub. by tech. socs. Home: Newton, Mass.

DWORSCHAK, LEO FERDINAND, clergyman; b. Independence, Wis., Apr. 6, 1900; s. Matthew and Katherine (Theisen) D.; ed. St. John's Prep., Collegeville, Minn., A.B., St. John's U., 1922, S.T.B., St. John's Sem., 1925; LL.D., Loras Coll. Ordained priest Roman Catholic Ch., 1926; asst. St. Anthony's Ch., Fargo, N.D., 1926-35; sec. to bishop Fargo, 1929-35; chancellor Diocese Fargo, 1935-39, vicar gen., 1939-46; apptd. coadjutor bishop Rapid City, S.D., 1946; consecrated bishop, 1946; aux. bishop of Fargo, 1947-60, bishop, 1960-70, ret., 1970. Apptd. hon. Papal Chamberlain to Pope Pius XII, 1939, domestic prelate by Pope Pius XII, 1941. K.C. Home: Fargo, N.D. Died Nov. 5, 1976.

DWYER, ROBERT J., archbishop; b. Salt Lake City, Aug. 1, 1908; s. John C. and Mabel (Maynard) D.; M.A., St. Patrick's Sem., 1936; Ph.D., Cath. U. Am., 1941. Ordained priest Roman Cath. Ch., 1932; monsignor, 1950; rector Cathedral of the Madeleine, Salt Lake City, 1948-52; promoted to see of Reno, Nev., May 1952, consecrated Aug. 1952, installed in Reno Cathedral, Aug. 27, 1952; archbishop, Portland, Ore., 1967-76; editor Intermountain Catholic Register, 1934-38, 42-46, 50-52; supt. schs. Diocese of Salt Lake City. Mem. Utah State Hist. Soc. (v.p.). Author: The Gentile Comes to Utah, 1941. Home: Portland, Oreg. Died Mar. 24, 1976.

DYER, BRAINERD, educator; b. Wheaton, Ill., Nov. 9, 1901; s. Frank and Mabel (Puckey) D.; A.B., Pomona Coll., 1923; A.M., Harvard, 1925, Ph.D., 1932; m. Karin Elise Anderson, Aug. 14, 1936; children—Karin Elise, Martin Brainerd. Instr. history Dartmouth, 1926-27, 1929-30; Francis Parkman fellow Harvard, 1927-28, teaching fellow, 1928-29; asso. UCLA, 1930-32, instr., 1932-35, asst. prof., 1935-41, asso. prof., 1941-47, became prof. and chmn. dept. history, 1947, prof. history emeritus, to 1980; Fulbright lectr. Am. history U. Helsinki, 1955-56. Recipient resolution Calif. Legislature, 1969. Mem. Am. (br. pres. 1967), Miss. Valley So. hist. assns., Phi Beta Kappa, Delta Chi, Phi Delta. Club: Lincoln. Author: Public Career of William M. Evarts, 1933; Zachary Taylor, 1946. Home: Los Angeles, Calif. Died Apr. 27, 1980; interred Inglewood Park Cemetery.

DYER, GEORGE BELL, writer; b. Washington, Apr. 12, 1903; s. George Palmer and Dorothy (Bell) O.; Ph.B., Yale, 1925; M.A., U. Pa., 1948, Ph.D., 1950; m. Charlotte Leavitt, June 26, 1930. Ins. salesman, 1926; reporter San Francisco Examiner, 1929-30; free lance writer, 1930-78; faculty U. Pa., 1947-50, Army Gen. Sch., 1950-52; instr. U. Pa. Grad. Sch. Arts and Scis., 1955-67, Yale, 1957-58. Co-founder, Dyer Inst. Interdisciplinary Studies, New Hope, Pa., 1952. Served as 2d lt. to maj. AUS, 1940-47, lt. col., 1947-53. Decorated Bronze Star. Fellow Co. Mil. Historians, Am. Mil. Inst. (trustee, life); mem. Nat. Rifle Assn. (life), Soc. Am. Mil. Engrs. (life) Zeta Psi, numerous others. Club: Cosmos (Washington). Author books including: The Three-Cornered Wound, 1931; The Five Fragments, 1932; A Storm Is Rising, 1934; The Catalyst Club, 1936; The Long Death, 1937; Adriana, 1939; The People Ask Death, 1940; XII Corps, Spearhead of Patton's Third Army, 1947; (with Charlotte Leavitt Dyer) The Beginnings of a U.S. Strategic Intelligence System in Latin America, 1950; A Century of Strategic Intelligence Reporting, 1954; A Strategic Intelligence Lesson, 1955; The World Analyst, 1958; Estimating National Power and Intentions, 1960; Exercises on an Assumption of Violence, 1962; dir. numerous spl. exercises related to ritualization of war project, including The Warsaw Story (TV title, The Cruelest War), 1965, Jersey Parallel I, 1964, II, 1967, Second Battle of Valcour Island, 1969; Second March to Quebec, 1975; Upper Makefield Day, 1975-76. Home: New Hope, Pa. Died Nov. 8, 1978.

DYER, JOHN PERCY, univ. dean; b. New Albany, Miss., June 24, 1902; s. Walker Waddell and Margaret Clementine (Snipes) D.; A.B., Bryson Coll., 1925; B.S., Peabody Coll., 1926, M.A., 1930; Ph.D., Vanderbilt U., 1932; m. Frances Margaret Thaxton, Aug. 30, 1935. Instr. State Techrs. Coll., Florence, Ala., 1926-32; asst. prof. Univ. System Ga., 1934-36; head social sci. dept. Armstrong Coll., 1936-39; account exec. radio sta. WSAV, 1939-41; state price exec. OPA, 1941-45; v.p., gen. mgr. radio sta WDAR, 1945-48; prof. history, dean Univ. Coll., Tulane U., 1948-72; dir. Center for Study Liberal Edn. for Adults. Fulbright lectr. U. Liverpool (Eng.), 1962-63. Mem. Assn. U. Evening Colls. (pres. 1954-55), So. Hist. Assn., Civil War Round Table, Kappa Delta Pi, Omicron Delta Kappa. Presbyn. Rotarian. Author: Fightin' Joe Wheeler, 1941; The Gallant Hood, 1950; Ivory Towers in the Market Place, 1956; Tulane University: A History, 1966. Contbg. author: The Education of American Businessmen, 1959. Contbr. articles mags. and encys. Home: New Orleans, La. Died Oct. 5, 1975.

DYER, RUTH OMEGA (MRS. SMITH JOHNS WILLIAMS), author; b. Herndon, Va., Sept. 6, 1883; d. Elisha and Mildred Haris (Johnson) Dyer; grad. Central High Sch., Washington, D.C., 1900, State Normal Sch., Farmville, Va., 1902; Columbia University, summer sessions, 1904, 1905; M.A., Columbia, 1930; m. Smith Johns Williams, of Charleston, South Carolina, September 9, 1914. Teacher, primary grades, Roanoke, Va.; director normal dept. Gate City (Va.) High Sch., 1908-09; primary critic teacher, Ga. Normal Sch., Milledgeville, 1909-13; supervisor of Training Sch., Ark. State Normal Sch., Conway, 1913-14, teacher Memminger High Sch., Charleston, S.C., since 1922. Methodist. Author: Correlated Lesson in Language and Occupation Work, 1914; The Sleepy-Time Story Book, 1915; That's Why Stories, 1916; Cut Out Book, 1916; Day-Time Story Book, 1917; What Happened Then Stories, 1918; Snippy-Snappy and Velvet Paw, 1918; The Little People of the Garden, 1922; The Adventures of The Ink Spots, 1923. Home: Charleston, S.C.

DYKE, KEN REED, pub. relations, advt. exec.; b. N.Y.C., Mar. 12, 1897; s. James Henry and Laura (Reed) D.; grad. Speyer Sch., 1912; grad. Ethical Culture Sch., N.Y.C., 1912-16; m. Valerie Edmonds Young; 1 son, David Kimball Dyke. Advt. writer U.S. Rubber Co., N.Y.C., 1919-26, asst. advt. mgr., 1926-28; sales promotion and advt. dir. Johns-Manville Corp., N.Y.C., 1928-33; dir. advt., Colgate-Palmolive Peet Co., N.Y.C., 1933-36; eastern sales mgr. Nat. Broadcasting Co., N.Y.C., 1937-38, dir. sales promotion and research, 1938-41, adminstrv. v.p., 1946-49; v.p. on charge pub. relations and publicity Young & Rubicam, N.Y.C., 1949-58, v.p. internat. div., 1960; sr. v.p. Smith, Dingwell Assos., N.Y.C., 1960-80, treas. Dir. Children's Village. Chief bur. campaigns OWI, Wash., 1942. Served with U.S. Army, 1918-19; with A.E.F. in France and Germany; res. officer 107th Inf., 1922-28; maj., 1943; lt. col., 1943-44; col., 1944-45; brig. gen., 1945-80; chief civil information and edn. sect. GHQ SCAP, Tokyo, Japan, 1945-46; now brig. gen. U.S.

O.R.C.; mem. adv. com. First Army. Decorated World War I Victory medal (2 battle clasps), German Occupational medal, Am. Theatre, Pacific Theatre (5 battle stars), Philippine Liberation medal, Phillipe Distinguished Service Star, D.S.M., Legion of Merit, 1945; Conspicuous Service Cross (N.Y. State). Chmn. bd. Assn. Nat. Advertisers, 1936-37; dir. Mil. Govt. Assn. Mem. Am. Assn. for UN (dir.), Japan Soc. (dir.), Grand Jury Assn. (dir.), Mil. and Naval Officers World Wars, Res. Officers Assn. U.S. Alpha Delta Sigma (nat. pres. 1937-38). Clubs: Circumnavigators, Union (N.Y.C.). Home: New York, N.Y. Died Jan. 17, 1980.

DYKSTRA, JOHN ALBERT, clergyman; b. Grand Rapids, Mich., June 10, 1886; s. Jacob and Cornelia (Van den Berg) D.; A.B., Hope Coll., Holland, Mich., 1909, D.D., 1924; student at Princeton Theological Seminary and Princeton University, 1909-10, New Brunswick Theological Seminary, 1910-12; m. Irene Joanna Staplekamp, July 30, 1913; children—John Dean, William Dwight. Ordained to ministry of Reformed Ch. in America, 1912; pastor, First Ch., Catskill, N.Y., 1912-18, Hamilton Grange Ch., New York, N.Y., 1918-19, Central Ch., Grand Rapids, Mich., since 1919; minister at The Hague, The Netherlands, summer 1928. Vice-pres. Gen. Synod of Reformed Ch. in America, 1938, pres. 1939, also mem. Bd. of Domestic Missions and pres. advisory council; mem. Fed. Council of Chs. of Christ in America, 1924-30; pres. Grand Rapids Ministerial Assn., 1926; member executive committee, Board Domestic Missions; mem. bd., Mich. Temperance Foundation. Vice-pres. bd. trustees Hope Coll., 1935-39, pres. since 1939. Decorated Knight of Order of Orange (Nassau), 1950. Mem. Fraternal Soc. of Hope Coll. Republican. Club: Rotary (Grand Rapids). Author: Heavenly Days, 1944. Contbr. to religious jours. Home: Grand Rapids, Mich.

DYOTT, GEORGE M(ILLER) (DI'OT), explorer; b. N.Y. City, Feb. 6, 1883; s. Geo. Richard and Caroline (Miller) D.; E.E., Faraday House, London, Eng., 1906; m. Persis Stevens Wright, 1928; children—Richard Burnaby, Mark Hamilton, Michael Stevens. Formerly gold prospector in Calif. and Alaska; built and flew aircraft U.S. and England, 1910-13. Served Royal Naval Air Service (British), World War I; retired with rank of wing commander. Has since made many expeditions to South America and other parts of the world; regarded as an authority on South America; expdn. for Roosevelt Memorial Assn. to authenticate Col. Theodore Roosevelt's findings on River of Doubt, another into Xingu country (central Brazil) for Royal Geog. Soc. (Eng.) to search for Col. Fawcett and his lost party; discoverer volcano in Ecuador; experimented in the cultivation of oil-bearing nuts for commercial purposes, Ecuador, 1937. Now associated with British Ministry of Supply. Trapper of wild animals. Donor baby elephants, tigers, leopards, bears, etc. (caught in Assam, India) to London Zoo, 1925, N.Y. Zoö. Park, 1930; ethnol. specimens to Pitt Rivers Mus., Oxford, Eng., Municipal Mus., Gothenburg, Sweden, Mus. of Am. Indian, New York. Prod. motion pictures "Hunting Tigers in India" and "Savage Gold" (experience with head-shrinking Indians, Ecuador). Prospected for uranium, Ecuadorian and Andes Mountains, winters 1948-49. Lecturer in Europe, America. Author: Silent Highways of the Jungle; Trail of the Unknown; Man Hunting in the Jungle; (juvenile) Nip and Tuck (translated into Braille). Home: Merrick, New York.

EAGLE, DEAN, newspaperman; b. Corbin, Ky., Mar. 16, 1914; s. James C. and Terrie (Masters) E.; A.B., Berea Coll., m. Mary Lucille Sewell, Sept. 14, 1936; children—Linda Joan, Cynthia Deane. Asst. sports editor Louisville Courier-Jour., 1945-53; sports editor Louisville Times, 1953-68, Louisville Courier-Jour., 1968-73. Mem. exec. com. Berea (Ky.) Coll. Mem. Nat. Turfwriters Assn. (past pres.), Sigma Delta Chi (past pres.). Democrat. Mem. Christian Ch. Club: Big Spring Country (Louisville). Author: Never Say Die. Contbr. to Am. People's Ency. Yearbook. Home: Louisville, Ky. Died Apr. 21, 1973.

EAGLE, JOHN FREDERICK, physician, educator; b. N.Y.C., July 16, 1917; s. J. Frederick and Margery (Brown) E.; B.A., Yale, 1940; M.D., Columbia, 1943; m. Elizabeth Babcock, Aug. 29, 1943; children—John Frederick III, Anne Stanton, J. Breckenridge, Sally King, Franklin Babcock, Elizabeth Winslow. Intern Babies Hosp., N.Y.C., 1947-49; resident, then chief resident Children's Hosp., Buffalo, 1949-51; asso. prof. pediatrics U. Buffalo Med. Sch., 1951-55; dir. pediatrics St. Luke's Hosp., N.Y.C., 1956-63; asso. prof. pediatrics Columbia Coll. Phys. and Surg., 1963-67, asst. dean, 1963-67; prof. pediatrics N.Y. Med. Coll., 1967-77, dean, 1967-73. Mem. N.Y.C. Health Research Council, 1968-77, N.Y.C. Bd. Health, 1972—; asst. health commr. City of N.Y., 1975-77. Served to capt. M.C., AUS, 1944-47. Diplomate Am. Bd. Pediatrics. Mem. Am. Acad. Pediatrics, Soc. Pediatric Research, Med. Soc. County N.Y., AMA, N.Y. Acad. Medicine, Associated Med. Schs. of Greater N.Y. (pres.), Century Assn. Home: New York, N.Y. Died Mar. 30, 1977.

EAKIN, ROBERT EDWARD, educator; b. LaGrande, Oreg., Jan. 23, 1916; s. Robert S. and Netta (Kiddle) E.; B.S., Oreg. State U., 1937. M.A. (Standard Brands fellow), 1939; Ph.D. (Standard Brands fellow), U. Tex., Austin, 1942; m. Esther Aline, Oct. 13, 1940; children—Timothy, Patrick, Michael, Kelly. Research biochemist Nutrition Clinic, Hillman Hosp., Birmingham, Ala., 1941-42; research asso. U. Cin. Med. Sch., 1941-43; asst. to full prof. chemistry U. Tex., Austin, 1946-79; cons. Eli Lilly & Co., Clayton Biochemical Found. for Research. Served with USNR, 1943-46. Mem. Am. Assn. Biol. Chemists, Am. Chem. Soc., A.A.A.S., Phi Lambda Upsilon, Sigma Xi, Phi Kappa Phi, Phi Delta Theta, Presbyn. Author: (with others) Biochemistry of the B Vitamins, 1951. Home: Austin TX.

EARLE, WALTER KEESE, lawyer; b. St. Louis Park, Minn., Aug. 15, 1886; s. Oliver and Emma (Laycock) E.; A.B., Harvard University, 1910; m. Charlotte Fellowes Harding, June 9, 1914 (deceased on October 27th, 1964); children—Anne French (Mrs. Roy R. B. Attride, dec.), Morris, Margaret Wood, Louise Harding (Mrs. A. Worthington Loomis). Admitted to N.Y. bar, 1913; asso. Cary & Carroll, N.Y.C., 1914-18, partner, 1918; partner Shearman & Sterling, 1919—; N.Y.C. Mgr. N.Y. Inst. Edn. of Blind, 1934—; curator, v.p. Whaling Mus. Soc., Cold Spring Harbor, N.Y., 1944—; chmn. Zoning Bd. of Appeals, Village Oyster Bay Cove. Mem. Assn. Bar City N.Y., Am., N.Y. bar assns. Democrat. Episcopalian (sr. warden). Mason. Clubs: Century, Union, Down Town Assn. (N.Y.C.); Cold Spring Harbor Beach. Arthor articles whales, whaling, legal and hist. subjects; History of Shearman & Sterling. Home: Oyster Bay, N.Y.

EARLY, ROBERT EMIL, ins. co. exec.; b. Chgo., Dec. 15, 1917; s. U.S. Grant and Gertrude Ida (Minkley) E.; A.A., Pasadena Jr. Coll., 1937; B.S., U. So. Cal., 1939; LL.B., Drake U., 1941; m. Margaret Emily Jones, June 21, 1942. Sales supr. Curtis Pub. Co., 1936-40; admitted to Cal. and Ia. bars, 1941; adjusters Farmers Ins. Group, 1942, 1st v.p., 1955, pres., exec. dir.; mem. Early, Maslach, Boyd & Leavey (formerly Early, Maslach, Foran & Williams), Los Angeles, from 1946. Trustee Thomas and Dorothy Leavey Found., Drake U.; chmn. bd. councilors U. So. Cal. Law Center. Served with USNR, 1943-46. Mem. Internat. Assn. Ins. Counsel, Phi Nu Delta, Delta Theta Phi. Elk. Clubs: Cal., Wilshire Country (Los Angeles); Annandale Country (Pasadena, Cal.). Home: Pasadena, Calif. Died Aug. 26, 1976.

EASLEY, JAMES STONE, lawyer; b. Halifax, Va., Apr. 7, 1885; s. Robert Holt and Louisa Edmonia (Gilmer) E.; grad. Va. Mil. Inst., 1904; LL.B., U. Va., 1907; m. Margie Glen Kyle, Nov. 10, 1909; children—Bertha Glen (Mrs. R. Gordon Finney), Louise Gilmer (Mrs. Paul C. Edmunds, III). Admitted to Va. bar, 1907, since practiced in Halifax and South Boston; commonwealth atty. Halifax Co., 1920-29; mem. Easley, Edmunds & Vaughan since 1945; dir. Chesapeake & Potomac Telephone Co. of Va. Mem. House of Dels. of Va., 1918-20; mem. Va. State Senate, 1929-31; exec. mgr. War Finance Com. of Va., 1943-45. Pres. Patrick Henry Meml. Found. since 1944; mem. bd. visitors Va. Mil. Inst. (pres. 1949-50), Stuart Hall. Mem. Am., Va. State (pres. 1949-50) bar assns., Va. C. of C. (pres. 1940-42), Va. Mil. Inst. Alumni Assn. (pres. 1939-41). Episcopalian. Mason (Shriner). Clubs: Sportsmans, Golf (Halifax Co., Va.). Home: Halifax.

EASLICK, KENNETH A(LEXANDER), dentist, educator; b. Ridgeway, Mich., Sept. 12, 1893; s. Schuyler Colfax and Rosa (Pilbeam) E.; A.B., U. Mich., 1917, D.D.S., 1928, A.M., 1936; m. Mercie Marie Van Aken, Apr. 3, 1920; 1 son, David Kenneth. With prodn. dept. Reynolds Spring Co., Jackson, Mich., 1920-24; instr. clin. dentistry U. Mich., 1928-34, dir. Children's Clinic since 1930, instr. operative dentistry, 1934-37, asst. prof., 1937-42, asst. prof. pub. oealth dentistry, sch. pub. oealth, 1941-42, asso. prof. pedodontics, pub. health dentistry, 1942-45, prof. dentistry and public health dentistry, from 1945, now prof. emeritus; dental cons. USPHS, 1948-79; cons. preventive dentistry surgeon gen. USAF, 1956-60. Mem. adv. com. U.S. Children's Bur., 1948-53; mem. Mich. State Adv. Council Health, 1945-60, chmn., 1960-79; mem. Gov.'s Pub. Health Study Commn., 1956-58, cov.'s Task Force of Public Health, 1959. Served with U.S. Army Ambulance Service, 1917-19; detached service with French Army, Avocourt Sector, Verdun Sector, Soissons Offensive, Oise-Aisne Offensive and French Army of Occupation nr. Mainz Bridgehead. Decorated Croix de Guerre with 2 citations (France). Recipient Service award Am. Bd. Dental Pub. Health, 1972, Centennial award Am. Pub. Health Assn., 1972, Pedodontic Great award Found. Am. Soc. Dentistry for Children, 1973, Brookdale award Am. Dental Assn., 1974. Diplomate Am. Bd. Pedodontics, also Am. Bd. Dental Pub. Health. Fellow A.A.A.S.; Am. Coll. Dentists, Am. Pub. Health Assn. (governing council 1953-56); mem. Am. Assn. Dental Schs., Mich. Soc. Dentistry Children, Am. Pub. Health Assn., Mich. Assn. Professions, Mich. Assn. Pub. Health Dentists and Hygienists, Am. Dental Assn. (council on dental health 1945-53; mem. Inter-Assn. Com. Health 1949-79, cons. council dental health 1953-79), Mich. State Dental Assn. (council health and edn. 1940—, mem. editorial bd. 1957-79, sec. Mich. dental service corp. 1958-79), Washtenaw County Soc. (pres. 1931), Am. Soc. Dentistry Children (chmn. Am. Bd. Pedodontics 1959-60, exec. sec. 1939-42), Internat. Assn. Dental Research, Am. Assn. Pub. Health Dentists, Am. Acad. Pedodontics (pres. 1952, editor 1953-79, chmn. nomenclature com. 1956-79), Mich. Pub. Health Assn., La Sociedad Dental de El Salvador (hon.), Sociedad Odontologia Cubana (hon.), Sociedad Cubana de Odontologia Infantil (hon.), U.S. Army Ambulance Service Assn., Northwestern U. Alumni Assn. (hon.), Delta Sigma Delta (life), Phi Kappa Phi, Omicron Kappa Upsilon, Delta Omega. Club: Univ. Mich. (Ann Arbor). Author: Report Writing in Dentistry (with others), 1951; American Board of Dental Public Health: The First Twenty-two Years, 1975; contbr. articles to profl. jours.; editor: Dental Caries: Mechanism and Present Control Technics as Evaluated at the University of Michigan Workshop 1948; The Practice of Dental Public Health, 1956; co-editor: Practice Administration for the Dentist, 1955; Communicating in Dentistry, 1974; editorial bd. Dentistry-A Digest of Practice, 1940-48; editorial chmn. Report-Writing in Dentistry, 1959. Home: Ann Arbor, Mich. Died Dec. 21, 1979.

EASON, THADDEUS WINSTON, oil co. exec.; b. Marlow, Okla., Sept. 7, 1904; s. T.T. and Anna (Lee) E.; student Prep. Sch. Kan. 1923, Notre Dame U., 1923-25, Okla. U., 1925-26, Babson Inst. 1927-28; m. Ada Sohlberg, Jan. 30, 1929 (dec.); 1 dau., Virginia Lee (Mrs. John G. Weinmann). Pres. T.T. Eason & Co. (Del.), 1949-77; chmn. bd. Eason Oil Co., Oklahoma City, 1955-70, chmn. bd., 1970-77; partner Wave Drilling, Inc. Mem. pres.'s council U. Okla., Phillips U., Enid, Okla. Mem. Okla. Legislature, 1933, 37. Bd. dirs. Oklahoma City Mental Health Assn., Okla. Eye Found.; trustee Frontiers Sci. Found.; indsl. adv. bd. Okla. A. and M. Coll.; pres., treas., mem. bd. trustees Okla. Art Center. Mem. Okla. Ind. Petroleum Assn. (dir. 1965-77), Phi Delta Theta. Democrat. K.C. Clubs: Tres Vidas (Acapulco, Mexico); Oklahoma Golf and Country, Men's Dinner, Economic (past treas., dir.), Beacon, Petroleum (Oklahoma City). Home: Oklahoma City, Okla. Died Mar. 6, 1977.

EASTHAM, JAMES SAVILLE, lawyer; b. Metchuen, Mass., Aug. 7, 1897; s. William Wilson and Elizabeth (Saville) E.; A.B., Brown U., 1919; LL.D., 1969; LL.B., Harvard, 1922; m. Marcia Dana Hill, Aug. 21, 1924; children—William Eaton, John Perry, James Dana, Nancy Elizabeth. Admitted to Mass. bar, 1922; with Ropes, Gray, Boyden & Perkins, Boston, 1922-23; partner, Rowell, Clay & Eastham, Lawrence, Mass., 1924-29; gen. counsel Eastern Gas & Fuel Assos., Boston, 1930-64, sec., 1940-64, v.p., 1958-64, former sec., clerk, gen. counsel subsidiaries, former v.p., dir. Conn. Coke Co., New Haven; former pres., dir. Virginian Corp.; pvt. practice law, Andover, Mass.; asst. atty. gen. Commonwealth of Mass., 1927-30; chmn. Bd. of Appeals under Zoning Law, Andover, 1936-58. Trustee Brown U., 1945-52, trustee emeritus, 1952-77; trustee, past pres. Methuen Meml. Music Hall; dir. Silver Bay Assn. Mem. Andover Hist. Soc. Am. Law Inst., Mass. Audubon Soc., Boston Bar Assn., Am. Forestry Assn., Am. Legion, Phi Beta Kappa (past pres. R.I.), Phi Beta Kappa Assn. (life), Delta Sigma Rho, Delta Upsilon. Episcopalian. Mason. Clubs: Union, Brown (Boston); University, Harvard (N.Y.C.); Lawrence Monday Night, Appalachian Mountain, Adirondack Mountain. Address: Andover, Mass. Died Apr. 25, 1977.

EASTUS, CLYDE OTIS, lawyer; b. Cleburne, Tex., Nov. 19, 1886; s. Jefferson Franklin and Junnie Marie (Wilkinson) E.; ed. high sch. and Burnetta Coll., Venus, Tex.; m. Lily Dwyer, Jan. 5, 1909. Admitted to Tex. bar, and in practice at Fort Worth; became U.S. dist. atty. Northern Dist. Tex. July 1, 1933. Mem. Fort Worth, Dallas, Texas State, Am. and Federal bar assns. Democrat. Presbyn. Elk, Woodman. Clubs: Meadow Brook Country, University (Fort Worth), Dallas Athletic (Dallas), New York Athletic (N.Y. City). Home: Fort Worth, Tex. *

EASTWOOD, RICHARD TRUMAN, med. adminstr.; b. Pawnee County, Nebr., Nov. 19, 1912; s. Frank Wesley and Elizabeth (Wilkinson) E.; A.B., Tarkio (Mo.) Coll., 1936; M.A., U. Nebr., 1939; Ph.D. in Econs. (Richard T. Ely scholar 1939-40), U. Wis., 1954; m. Elizabeth Comer, Apr. 5, 1942; children—Elizabeth Ann, Barbara Jean. Tchr. Maysville (Mo.) High Sch., 1936-38; grad. asst. U. Nebr., 1938-39; instr. econs. U. Ala., 1939-43; asst. supr. engring., sci. and mgmt. war tng. program, 1941-43, asst. prof. mgmt., then asso. prof., 1946-54, dir. commerce extension service 1946-51, prof. econs., 1954-62, dir. Birmingham Center 1951-58, asso. dean extension div., 1956-58, exec. dir univ. affairs in Birmingham, 1958-62; exec. v.p. Tex Med. Center Inc., Houston, 1962-80, dir.; v.p., sec. Tex Med. Center, Housing Inc., 1964-80. Cons. NIH 1961-80. Chmn. Com. Aging Jefferson County, Ala. 1954, 59-60; mem. Ala. Gov.'s Adv. Com. Planning fo White House Conf. on Aging, also del., 1961; mem steering com. Houston Community Health Services Self Study. Dir. Jefferson County Coordinating Council Social Forces, 1956-62; fiscal agt., sec., chmn. adv. group regional adv. com. Regional Med. Programs in Texas; mem. spl. com. on cardiac replacement Nat. Heart Inst. Bd. dirs. Tarkio Coll.; pres. Med. Benevolence Found., 1976-80; bd. dirs. Rice Center Design and Research, 1976-80; v.p. South Main Center Assn., Houston, 1976-80. Served to lt. USNR, 1943-46. Am. Christian Palestine Com. scholar for study tour Middle East, 1955. Mem. Soc. Advancement Mgmt. (pres. Ala. 1953-54), Nat. Univ. Extension Assn. (sec. evening div. 1958-59), Am., So. econ. assns., Indsl. Relations Research Assn., Houston C. of C., Alpha Kappa Psi, Phi Beta Pi. Presbyn. (permanent theology com. Gen. Assembly 1962-65, mem. candidates ordination exam. com. 1976-80). Home: Houston, Tex. Died Jan. 14, 1980; buried Meml. Oaks Cemetery, Houston.

EATHER, EDGAR, judge; b. Eureka, Nev., Sept. 14, 1886; s. Henry and Jane (Simms) E.; m. Rose Tognoni, 1917; children—Hazel (Laiolo), Norma (Croft), Gloria (Silva), Margie (Kofler). Co. recorder and auditor Eureka, Nev., 1910; dist. atty., 1923-29; dist. judge Nev., 1930-46; chief justice Supreme Ct. Nev. 1947-48, asso. justice 1949-53, chief justice, 1953, now asso. justice. Mem. Am., Nev., Washoe bar assns., Am. judicature Soc. Elk, Rotarian. Home: Reno, Nev.

EATON, CYRUS STEPHEN, industrialist and banker; b. Nova Scotia, Can., Dec. 27, 1883; s. Joseph Howe and Mary Adelle (McPherson) E.; student Amherst Acad., Woodstock Coll.; A.B., McMaster U., Toronto, Can., 1905; D.C.L., Acadia U., N.S., 1946; LL.D., Mount Allison U., Sackville, N.B., Can., 1957, Bard Coll., N.Y., 1958, Charles U., Czechoslovakia, 1960, U. Sophia, Bulgaria, 1961; m. Dec. 29, 1907 (dec.); children—Margaret G. (dec.), Mary Adelle (Mrs. Fay A. Le Fevre), Elizabeth Ann (Mrs. Lyman H. Butterfield), Anna Bishop, Cyrus Stephen, Augusta Farlee (Mrs. Farlee E. Hume), MacPherson; m. 2d, Anne Kinder Jones, 1957; 1 step dau., Alice Ewing Jones. Came to U.S., 1900, naturalized citizen, 1913. Held earliest business position with John D. Rockefeller, Sr.; subsequently associated with East Ohio Gas Co.; later organized Canada Gas & Electric Corp.; in 1912 began extensive activity in Am. utility industry, and formed Continental Gas & Electric Co., which consolidated a number of electric and gas companies in the Am. west; joined Otis & Co., 1916; principal middlewestern business assn. has been with steel, rubber and paint industries; in 1925 reorganized and became chmn. Trumbull Steel Co.; in 1929, with W. G. Mather, formed Cliffs Corp. (now Cleveland-Cliffs Iron Co.); holder substantial interest in six important iron and steel cos.; organized Republic Steel Corp., 1930; led in formation and reorgn. many other middlewestern companies; past dir. Republic Steel, Inland Steel, Youngstown Sheet & Tube and other companies, including Cleve. Trust Co. and Nat. Acme Co. in Cleve.; mem. banking house Otis & Co.; chmn. bd., dir. Steep Rock Iron Mines, Ltd., C. & O. Ry.; dir., past chmn. Detroit Steel Corp.; dir. Cleveland-Cliffs Iron Co., Sherwin-Williams Co., Cleve. Electric Illuminating Co., Kansas City Power & Light Co., Baltimore and Ohio Railroad Co. Trustee Denison U., U. Chgo., Case Inst. Tech., Cleve. Mus. Natural History. Elector Hall of Fame, dir. Cleve. Met. Park Bd., 1930-39. Fellow Am. Acad. Arts and Scis.; mem. Am. Council Learned Socs., Am. Acad. Polit. and Social Sci., Royal Norwegian Acad. Scis., Can. Shorthorn Assn., Am. Hist. Assn., Am. Philos. Assn., Am. Shorthorn Breeders Assn. Author: The Third Term Tradition, 1940; Financial Democracy, 1941; The Professor Talks to Himself, 1942; Investment Banking Competition or Decadence?, 1944; A New Plan to Reopen the U.S. Capital Market, 1945; The Engineer as Philosopher, 1961; others; also numerous articles and speeches in field. Clubs: Union, Mayfield, Chagrin Valley Hunt, Summit Hunt; Royal Nova Scotia Yacht Squadron; Glenelg Fishing (N.S.), Chester Yacht: Liverpool Yacht; Metropolitan (N.Y.). Home: Acadia Farms Northfield OH

EATON, ERNEST RISLEY, physician; b. Melbourne, Australia, March 15, 1885; s. George and Annie (Risley). E.; A.B., George Washington U., 1910; grad. Crozer Theol. Sem., 1913; M.D., N.Y. Med. Coll., 1919; m. Mable Thaw Littell, 1913 (divorced 1920); children—Ernest Risley II, Charles (killed in action in Italy, April 18, 1945), Hamilton; m. 2d, Carolyn Mellon, 1921 (died, 1936); 1 son, William Mellon; m. 3d, Mary Caroline Watson, Oct. 4, 1939. Came to U.S. 1906, naturalized 1918. Interne Flower Hosp., N.Y. City, 1919-20; practice of medicine, N.Y. City since 1920; asso. prof. medicine N.Y. Med. Coll., since 1930; asso. attending phys. and chief arthritis clinics, Flower and Fifth Av. Hospital; cons. Metropolitan Hospital. Brigade surgeon, New York Naval Militia, 1938-40. Served with Medical Enlisted Reserve Corps, United States Army, 1918-19; lieutenant comdr., Med. Corps, U.S.N.R., 1931, comdr., 1938, capt., 1942; served Southwest Pacific, Europe; discharged 1946. Resumed practice, October 1946. Mem. Am. Rheumatism Assn., A.M.A., New York Academy of Medicine, American Society Tropical Medicine. Assn. Mil. Surgeons, Sigma Chi, Phi Alpha Gamma, Phi Chi. Clubs: Univ. (N.Y.); Cadaceus Legion. Contbr. articles on chronic arthritis to med. jours., essays on literary and mil. subjects. Home: New York, N.Y.; also Brewster, N.Y.

EATON, JAMES ROBERT, educator; b. Bluffton, Ind., Nov. 1, 1902; s. James B. and Aldula (Baumgartner) E.; B.S. in Elec. Engring., Purdue U., 1925, Ph.D., 1942; M.S. in Elec. Engring., U. Wis., 1938; m. A. Ruth Sergeant, Sept. 16, 1929; 1 son, James Robert. Engr., Consumers Power Co., Jackson, Mich., 1925-37; instr., U. Wis., 1938-40; mem. faculty Purdue U., 1940-71, now emeritus prof. elec. and nuclear engring. Vis. prof. U. Alaska, spring 1967, 69-70, 72-74; cons. in field. Registered profl. engr., Ind. Alaska. Mem. I.E.E.E., Am. Soc. Engring Edn., Sigma Xi, Tau Beta Pi, Eta Kappa Nu, Kappa Eta Kappa, Acacia. Baptist. Mason. Author: Beginning Electricity, 1952; Electrons, Neutrons and Protons in Engineering, 1966; Electric Power Transmission Systems, 1972; also articles. Home: West Lafayette, Ind. Died May 19, 1976.

EATON, ORVILLE LEE, librarian; b. Thayer, Kan., July 15, 1912; s. Arthur L. and Della (Peterson) E.; B.S., Kan. State Coll., 1938, M.S., 1940; Ph.D., U. Kan., 1946; B.L.S., U. Chgo., 1948; m. Alta Moynihan, Oct. 5, 1935. Techr. elementary schs., Kan., 1930-36, tchr. English, Joplin, Mo., 1938-40; instr U. Kan., 1940-42; editor, writer Command and Gen. Staff Coll., Ft. Leavenworth, Kan., 1943-46; dir. libraries U. Kansas City (Mo.), 1946-50; librarian, head dept. library sci. Kan. State Coll., Emporia, 1950-58, dir. grad. div., 1953-58; prof. head dept. library Central Mich. U., 1958-70, prof., 1970-74, chmn. dept. library sci., 1970-74. Mem. A.L.A., Mich. Library Assn. (chmn. coll. sect. 1965-66), Mich. Edn. Assn., North Central Assn. (coordinator 1957-62), Sigma Tau Delta, Phi Delta Kappa, Alpha Beta Alpha. Contbr. articles to profl. jours. Home: Mt Pleasant, Mich. Died June 18, 1974.

EATON, RAMONE STANLEY, assn. exec.; b. Alexandria, Va., Aug. 29, 1907; s. George H. and Irene M. (Beach) E.; student Southeastern U., Washington, 1925-26, George Washington U., 1928, U. Ga., 1931; m. June L. Clark, Jan. 16, 1933; children—June Elaine, Lyndle Stanley. Dir. pub. recreation, Alexandria, 1926, phys. edn., YMCA, Washington, 1927; field rep. 1st aid and life saving A.R.C., 1928-39, asst. nat. dir., 1st aid and life saving, 1937-40, dir. roll call, 1940-41, adminstrv. asst. mgr. N. Atlantic area, 1941-43, mgr. Eastern area and Pacific area, 1943-48, v.p., 1940-70, sr. v.p., 1970-80. Lectr. ecology and youth problems. Mem. Pub. Relations Soc. Am., Am. Canoe Assn., Phi Pi Phi, Alpha Sigma Phi. Episcopalian. Rotarian. (gov.). Clubs: Nat. Press (Washington); Toe-H. Contbr. to recreation, camping, canoeing and safety edn. publs. Home: Bryson City, N.C. Died Apr. 29, 1980.

EATON, ROBERT S., business exec.; b. Norwich, N.Y., June 10, 1883; s. Robert D. and Maria E. (Smith) E.; B.E., U. Pa., 1906; m. Mildred Cable, 1921; children—Constance E., Elizabeth M.; married 2d, Christina Murray, 1941. Dir. Norwich Pharmacal Co., 1910—; chmn. bd., 1938-56, mem. exec. com., 1956—, chmn. exec. com., 1956-61, hon. chmn. bd. dirs., 1961—; chmn. bd. Nat. Bank & Trust Co. Norwich; president Norwich Securities Corporation; director Utica Mutual Ins. Co., Dunco Realty & Equipment Corporation, Victory Markets, Incorporated, Victory Chain, Incorporated, Chenango & Unadilla Telephone Corp., Preferred Mut. Fire Ins. Co. Trustee Norwich YMCA; dir. Norwich Cemetery Assn. Elk, Mason, Rotarian. Home: Norwich City, N.Y.

EAVES, HETTIE DAWES, shipbuilding co. exec.; b. Throckmorton, Tex., Apr. 30, 1920; d. Grady William and Margaret (MacKeichan) Dawes; B.B.A., N. Tex. State U., 1940; m. Norman Eustis Eaves, May 31, 1953. Accountant, Red River Ordnance Depot, Texarkana, Tex., 1941-42; bookkeeper Avondale Shipyards, Inc., New Orleans, 1942-47, supr. gen. accounting, 1947-49, comptroller, 1949-59, treas., 1959-68, exec. v.p. fin. and adminstrn., 1968-73, exec. v.p. adminstrn., 1973-78; dir. Fed. Res. Bank Atlanta (New Orleans br.), New Orleans Pub. Service, Inc., S. Central Bell Telephone Co. Bd. dirs. S. Central council Girl Scouts U.S.A., 1954-57, St. Mary's Dominican Coll., 1973-77, New Orleans Philharmonic Symphony, 1973-78. Recipient Leadership award New Orleans YWCA, 1976; Outstanding Citizen award Inst. Human Understanding, 1976. Presbyterian. Club: Propeller (gov. 1968-70). Home: New Orleans, La. Died June 2, 1978.

EAVES, ROBERT WENDELL, ret. educator; b. Rutherford County, N.C., Nov. 23, 1903; s. Robert Wells and Della (Biggerstoff) E.; A.B., U. N.C., 1928; A.M., George Washington U., 1933, Ed.D., 1940; summer schs., Tchrs. Coll., Columbia, 1933, 34, Johns Hopkins, 1929, U. Va., 1930; m. Ruth Anderson, June 24, 1931; 1 son, Robert Wendell. Instr. elementary edn. Tchrs. Coll. Columbia, summer 1937, 38, Appalachian State Tchrs. Coll., Boon, N.C., 1939, Syracuse U., 1945, George Washington U., 1949-50, U. Mich., summers, 1950, San Francisco State Coll., 1951, 1956; chmn. com. and editor How to Know and Use Your Community, Dept. Elementary Sch. Prins., N.E.A., 1941, mem. and chmn. editorial com., 1942-45, exec. sec., then exec. sec. emeritus, cons. Dept. Elem. Prins., from 1950; prof. edn. George Mason Coll. of U. Va., Fairfax, until 1974, emeritus, 1974-79. Sec. edn. com. President's Hwy. Safety Conf., 1946-50; sec. Nat. Commn. on Safety Edn., N.E.A., 1944-50; exec. officer Nat. Conf. on Sch. Transp., Jackson's Mill, W.Va., 1948; exec. dir. Nat. Conf. on Driver Edn., 1949; mem. planning and adv. bd. Nat. Aviation Edn. Council, 1953-79; mem. Pres.'s Citizens Com. on Fitness and Youth, 1957-79; mem. Pres.'s Com. on Employment of Handicapped; faculty U. Hawaii, summers 1958, 60, 65, Ill. So. U., summer, 1961, U. So. Calif., summer 1962, U. P.R., summer 1963, U. N.C., 1964; edn. cons. AID, Dominican Republic, 1962; mem. edn. com. People to People Program. Mem. U.S. Civil Service Bd. Examiners. Recipient distinguished service award President's Hwy. Safety Conf., 1951. Trustee Joint Council Econ. Edn., 1956-59. Mem. N.E.A. (life), Dept. Elem. Sch. Prins., George Washington U. Alumni Assn. (gov. 1964-79), Phi Delta Kappa (Distinguished award 1976). Contbr. articles to ednl. publs. Home: Arlington, Va. Died Jan. 16, 1979; buried Warrenton, Va.

EBENSTEIN, WILLIAM, educator; b. Austria, May 11, 1910; s. Samuel and Gittel (Goldapper) E.; LL.D., U. Vienna, 1934; student U. London, 1934-36; Ph.D., U. Wis., 1938; m. Ruth Barbara Jaburek, Dec. 17, 1938; children—Phillip, Robert, Andrew, Alan. Came to U.S., 1936, naturalized, 1942. Fellow in econs. U. Wis., 1936-37, research asso. in law, 1937-38, instr. polit. sci., 1938-40, asst. prof. polit. sci., 1940-43, asso. prof., 1943-46; asso. prof. politics Princeton, 1946-49, prof. politics 1949-62, Ford fellow, 1953-54; prof. polit. sci. U. Calif., Santa Barbara, 1962—; 76; in charge UNESCO project Methods in Polit. Sci., Paris, 1948. Mem. Am. Polit. Sci. Assn., Hans Kelsen Inst. (Vienna). Author: Fascist Italy, 1939; Great Political Thinkers, 1951; Introduction To Political Philosophy, 1952; Modern Political Thought, 1954; Today's Isms, 1954; Political Thought in Perspective, 1957; Two Ways of Life: The Communist Challenge to Democracy, 1962; Totalitarianism: New Perspectives, 1962. Co-author: American Democracy in World Perspective, 1967; American Government in the Twentieth Century, 1968. Home: Santa Barbara, Calif. Died Apr. 28, 1976.

EBERHARD, ROBERT GEORGES, educator; b. Geneva, Switzerland, June 28, 1884; s. Eugene P. and Antoinette Louise (Eberhard) E.; student Lycee Montaigne, France, Pratt Inst., N.Y. City, Ecole des Beaux Arts, France; B.F.A., Yale, 1921, M.A., 1934; m. Nora J. Sullivan, 1910; children—Eugene P., W. Burke. Sculptor until 1926; teacher Yale Sch. Fine Arts, 1917-52, chmn. sculpture dept., 1934-52; now retired and renewed practice of sculpture; curator of scuplture Yale Gallery Fine Arts, 1932. Decorated Kim Tien, Annam, 1913; Officer d'Academie, France, 1926; Officer Instruction Publique, France, 1929. Mem. Nat. Sculpture Soc. (chmn.; recipient Herbert Adams Meml. Medal 1954). Clubs: Yale (N.Y.C.); Graduates, Paint and Clay (New Haven). Address: Newcastle, Me.

EBERHARDT, HOMER CHRISTIAN, state judge; b. Banks County, Ga., Oct. 31, 1904; s. Linton W. and Josephine (Wheeler) E.; B.S. U. Ga., 1925; LL.B. Mercer U., 1927; m. Ruby Jones, Oct. 14, 1931 (dec. July 1958); children—Gretchen (Mrs. Wilby C. Coleman) (dec.), Jan (Mrs. McCurdy); m. 2d, LaForrest Smith, Aug. 1, 1959. Admitted to Ga. Bar, 1927; practiced law, Valdosta, 1928-61, sr. partner Eberhardt, Franklin, Barham & Coleman, 1958-61; judge Ga. Ct. Appeals, 1961-74, presiding judge, 1972-74. Mem. Ga. Bd. Bar Examiners, 1958-61; mem. rules com. Supreme Ct. Ga., 1957-61. Mem. Valdosta Bd. Edn., 1948-61. Trustee, Mercer U. Fellow Am. Coll. Probate Counsel; mem. Am. Bar Assn. (appellate judges conf.), Ga. (pres. 1960-61), Valdosta Bar Assn., Atlanta Bar Assn., So., Ga., Valdosta, Atlanta hist. socs., High Mus. Art. Methodist. Elk, Mason. Home: Lake Park, Ga. Died Jan. 6, 1975.

EBERMAN, PAUL WILMOT, educator; b. Centerville, Pa., July 5, 1917; s. Gregg Franklin and Alta Alma (Allison) E.; B.S., N.Y. State Coll. Tchrs., Buffalo, 1938; M.A., N.Y. U., 1942; Ph.D., U. Chgo., 1950; summer student Syracuse U., 1941, Cornell U., 1940; children—Paul Wilmot, Kirk Galliford, Margo Ann, Karen Marie; m. 2d, Nina Renee Nikolenko, Jan. 19, 1968. Tchr. math. Bergen (N.Y.) Consol. Sch., 1938-39, R.K. Toaz Jr. High Sch., Huntington, N.Y., 1939-43; instr. N.Y. State Coll. Tchrs., Buffalo, 1946-48; instr., teaching fellow U. Chgo., 1948-49; mem. faculty U. Wis., 1949-63, prof. edn., 1956-63, asso. dean Sch. Edn., 1958-63, dir. elementary lab. sch., 1949-51; dean Coll. Edn., Temple U., Phila., 1963-73, prof. edn., 1973-78; vis. summer prof. Emory U., 1956, U. Chgo., 1958, U. Hawaii, 1961. Team leader U. Wis. tchr. edn. project, N. Nigeria for AID, 1962-63. Served to lt. Air Corps, USNR, 1943-46. Mem. Nat., Pa. edn. assns., Higher Edn. Assn., Am. Ednl. Research Assn., Am. Assn. Sch. Adminstrs., Phi Delta Kappa, Kappa Delta Pi, Kappa Kappa Kappa. Contbr. articles to profl.

jours., author reports. Co-author: The Elementary School, 1956. Home: Philadelphia, Pa. Died Nov. 4, 1978; buried Sunset Cemetery, Berkeley, Calif.

ECCLES, MARRINER STODDARD, financier, bus. exec.; b. Logan, Utah, Sept. 9, 1890; s. David and Ellen (Stoddard) E.; student Brigham Young Coll., 1905-09; LL.D., U. Utah, 1943, Utah State U., 1963; m. May Campbell Young, July 9, 1913; children—Marriner Campbell (dec.), Mrs. Eleanore May Steele, John David; m. 2d, Sara Madison Glassie, Dec. 29, 1951. Organized Eccles Investment Co., a holding co. for interests in family estate, 1916, v.p., gen. mgr. until 1929, pres., 1929-71; pres. First Nat. Bank of Ogden and Ogden Savs. Bank, and successor banks, 1920-34; organizer First Security Corp., owning and operating banks in Utah, Idaho and Wyo., pres., 1928-34, chmn., 1952-75, hon. chmn., 1975-77; chmn. First Security Bank of Utah, Nat. Assn., 1955-70, sr. dir.; hon. chmn. Amalgamated Sugar Co.; hon. chmn. Utah Internat. Inc. Asst. to Sec. Treasury, 1934; gov. Fed. Res. Bd., 1934-36; bd. govs. Fed. Res. System, 1936-51, chmn. bd. govs., 1936-48; mem. bd. Econ. Stblzn., 1942-46; U.S. del. to Bretton Woods Conf., 1944; mem. nat. adv. council on Internat. Monetary and Financial Problems, 1945-48; adv. bd. Export-Import Bank, 1945-48; mem. Nat. Commn. Money and Credit, 1958-61, World Population Emergency Campaign; trustee emeritus Am. Assembly, 1959-77; sponsor Atlantic Council, 1962-77; mem. Nat. Com. on U.S.-China Relations; mem. exec. com. Nat. Citizens Com. Concerned About Deployment of ABM. Elector Hall of Fame, 1940—. Bd. dirs. Planned Parenthood World Population. Mem. Utah Bankers Assn. (pres. 1924-25), Sigma Chi. Clubs: Pacific Union, World Trade, Commonwealth, Golf (San Francisco); Eldorado Country (Palm Springs, Calif.; The Country (Salt Lake City); Chevy Chase Country, Burning Tree (Washington); Pauma Valley Country (Pauma Valley, Calif.) Author: Beckoning Frontiers. Home: Salt Lake City, Utah. Died Dec. 18, 1977; interred Sunset Lawn Mausoleum, Salt Lake City.

ECKERT, SAMUEL BALTZ, oil co. exec.; b. Phila., Dec. 24, 1884; s. Samuel and Josephine (Baltz) E.; M.E., Cornell U., 1908; m. Agnes Musser, 1914 (died 1916); 1 dau., Josephine S.; m. 2d, Mildred Longstreth, 1939. Chief engr. Marcus Hook Refinery, Sun Oil Co., 1909-12, gen. sales mgr., 1912, v.p., since 1927; dir. Sun Shipbuilding & Dry Dock Company. Served as maj., comdg. 17th Aero Squadron attached to B.E.F., 1917-18. Republican. Episcopalian. Clubs: Racquet, Corinthian Yacht, Gulph Mills Golf, Merion Cricket. Home: Haverford, Pa.

ECKHART, HAROLD, banker; b. nr. DeSoto, Wis., Sept. 13, 1886; s. George W. and Hannah (Hewey) E.; A.B., U. Wis., 1912; m. Ruby A. Giesse, July 10, 1912; children—Alan, Edith Robin (Mrs. Frederick Jones), Gerald; m. 2d Ella H. Meyer, Oct. 7, 1940. Staff mem. Wis. R.R. Commn. (now Pub. Service Commn.), 1911-18; joined Harris Trust & Savs. Bank, Chicago, 1918, asst. sec., 1926, sec., 1926-36, in charge trust dept. since 1928, v.p. since 1934; pres., dir. Dermott Land & Lumber Co.; v.p., dir. Selma (Ark.) Timber Co.; dir. Vapor Heating Corp., Roth Rubber Co., Ace Foundry Co., Vapor Car Heating Co. of Can., Ltd., Texsteam Corp. Pres.; dir. Citizens Assn. of Chicago; trustee Provident Hosp. and Tng. Sch. Mem. Am. Bankers Assn. (exec. com. trust div.), Am. and Chicago bar assns. Clubs: Union League, Bankers (Chicago); Westmoreland Country (Wilmette, Ill.); Country (Wickenburg. Ariz.). Home: Evanston, Ill. *

ECKSTEIN, ALEXANDER, educator; b. Novisad, Yugoslavia, Dec. 9, 1915; s. Simon and Erna (Weber) E.; B.S., U. Calif., Berkeley, 1939, M.S., 1941, Ph.D. (SSRC fellow), 1952; m. Ruth Rubinstein, Feb. 16, 1947; 1 son, Robert. With FAO of UN, 1946-49, 50-51; area research fellow SSRC, 1949-50; sr. economist Dept. State, 1951-53; lectr. econs., research asso. East Asian Research Center, Harvard, 1953-59; Xerox prof. internat. econs. U. Rochester, 1959-61; prof. econs. U. Mich., Ann Arbor, 1961-76, dir. Center for Chinese Studies, 1967-69, dir. Chinese Econ. Studies Project, 1975-76; policy adviser to Sec. State, 1966-68; Rockefeller vis. research prof. Brookings Instn., 1974-75. Mem. SSRC-Am. Council Learned Socs. com. for study contemporary China, 1959-66; mem. SSRC com. on economy of China, 1961-69; mem. Internat. Com. for Chinese Studies, 1963-64; bd. mem. Nat. Com. on U.S.-China Relations, Inc., 1966-76, vice chmn., 1968-69, chmn., 1970-72. Served with M.I., AUS, 1943-46. Decorated Bronze Star medal; recipient research grants Am. Council Learned Socs., 1959-60, NSF and Rockefeller Found., 1960-62, SSRC, 1963-64, 66-67, Arms Control and Disarmament Agy., Washington, 1966-68. Inter-Univ. fellow for advanced field tng. in Chinese, 1958-59. Mem. Am. Econ. Assn., Assn. Asian Studies (past dir.), Assn. for Study Soviet-Type Econs. (past mem. exec. com.), Assn. for Study Comparative Econs. (pres. 1974), Econ. Hist. Assn., Econs. Club of Detroit. Jewish. Author: (with others) Prospects for Communist China, 1954, Moscow-Peking Axis, 1957; The National Income of Communist China, 1962; Communist China's Economic Growth and Foreign Trade, 1966; China's Economic Development: The Interplay of Scarcity and Ideology, 1975; China's Economic Revolution, 1977. Editor: (with Walter Galenson and T.C. Liu) Economic Trends in Communist China, 1968; China Trade Prospects and U.S. Policy, 1970; Comparison of Economic Systems: Theoretical and Methodological Approaches, 1971; Quantitative Measures of China's Economic Output, 1980. Contbr. articles to profl. jours. Home: Ann Arbor, Mich. Died Dec. 5, 1976.

EDDISON, WILLIAM BARTON, cons. mech. engr.; b. Irvington, N.Y., Mar. 22, 1889; s. Charles and Mary Elizabeth (Barton) E.; M.E., Columbia, 1912; m. Mary Corbin, Oct. 19, 1915; children—Mary Corbin (Mrs. E. Sohier Welch, Jr.), John Corbin, William Barton, Lee Corbin (dec.), E. Anne (Mrs. Stanford H. Brainerd). Asst. engr. Ingersoll Rand Co., 1912; asst. instr. mech. engring. dept. Columbia, 1913-15; with Surface Combustion Co., 1915-17, chief engr., 1916-17; cons., indsl. engr. Chas. E. Richardson & Co., 1919-22; cons. engr., Irvington-on-Hudson, N.Y., 1924-51; pres. Irvington Nat. Bank and Trust Co., 1945-55. Chmn. bd. trustees Irvington Public Library, 1926-59; pres. Tappan Zee Mental Health Center, 1960-67, also hon. life mem.; hon. life mem. N.E. Harbor Fleet; hon. life mem. bd. Maine Sea Coast Missionary Soc. Served as lt. (j.g.) USNRF, World War I; instr. USN Gas Engine Sch., later attached to engring. div. U.S.S. New Mexico. Recipient Edward Longstreth Medal of Merit for invention Franklin Inst., 1921, Silver Beaver award Boy Scouts Am., 1942, Trinks Indsl. Heating award, Pitts., 1956. Fellow ASME; mem. Alpha Delta Phi. Clubs: Ardsley, Ardsley Country (hon. life mem.). Patentee in indsl. furnaces, clock industry and automatic balancing processes fields. Developed means for controlling furnace atmosphere. Home: Bridgeport, Conn. Died Jan. 1, 1980; buried Tarrytown, N.Y.

EDDY, CORBIN THEODORE, metall. engr.; b. Lake Linden, Mich., Apr. 17, 1904; s. Samuel and Georgie (Duquette) E.; B.S., Mich. Coll. Mining and Tech., E.M., 1926, M.S., 1927, Ph.D., 1934; student U. Calif., 1927; spl. investigations Inst. für Eisenhüttenkunde of Technische Hochschule, Aachen, Germany, 1932; m. Helen Marie Perreault, June 12, 1941; children—Corbin Theodore John, Anthony Thomas, Mary Magdalen. Lab. instr. metallurgy, Mich. Technol. U., Houghton, 1926, instr. metall. engring., 1927-30, asst. prof. metall. 1930-32, assoc. prof., 1932-40, prof. metall. engring., 1940-70, emeritus prof., 1970-77, head dept., 1940-59, dir. metall. engring, research, 1940. Cons. engineer in processing and prodn. metallurgy. Recipient McNair Award, 1930, Alfred Noble Prize, 1932. Mem. AIME, Am. Soc. Metals, Am. Foundrymen's Assn., A.A.A.S., Am. Soc. Engring. Edn., Lake Superior Mining Inst., Phi Kappa Phi, Theta Tau, Tau Beta Pi, Alpha Sigma Mu. Author: The Constitution Diagram in Physical Metallurgy, 1938; Fundamental Principles in Physical Metallurgy, 1940. Contbr. to tech. and sci. jours. Home: Hancock, Mich. Died July 8, 1977.

EDDY, FRANCIS ROLLIN, clergyman; b. Wolcottville, Ind., Aug. 1, 1882; s. Rollin and Samantha (Bozer) E.; student Houghton Sm., 1901-04; D.D. (hon.), Houghton Coll., 1937; m. Edith Rigsbee, Aug. 1, 1906. Ordained to ministry Wesleyan Meth. Ch., 1906, preacher since 1901; pastor Ind. Conf. Wesleyan Meth. Ch., 1904-19, Sunday sch. sec., 1919-28; demon. evang. Home Missions Wesleyan Meth. Ch., 1928-31; gen. Sunday sch. sec., editor Wesleyan Meth. Ch., 1931-35, pub. agt. since 1935; pres. Wesleyan Meth. Gen. Conf., 1939-47, v.p. since 1947. Trustee Houghton Coll., Miltonvale Coll., Central Coll., Marion Coll.; gen. treas. Wesleyan Meth. Pub. Assn., Wesleyan Meth. Missionary Soc., Wesleyan Meth. Ednl. Soc. Home: Syracuse.

EDDY, GERALD ERNEST, state govt. ofcl.; b. Lansing, Mich., Sept. 20, 1907; s. George Raymond and Eva (Hill) E.; B.S., Mich. State U., 1930; M.S., U. Mich., 1932; D.Sc. (hon.), Wayne State U., 1961; m. Mary Louise Lipka, Sept. 14, 1932; children—Catherine Ann (Mrs. Edwin A. Puchis), Susan Elizabeth (Mrs. William Kelly). With State of Mich., 1933-71, dir. conservation, 1951-64, state geologist, 1964-71, environ. and geol. cons., 1971-77. Chmn., Mich. Water Resources Commn., 1965-66; mem. Great Lakes Commn., 1955-64; ofcl. rep. Gov. Mich. on Interstate Oil Compact Commn., 1946-71. Served to capt. ordnance dept. AUS and USAAF, 1942-45. Recipient Career Service award Am. Soc. Pub. Adminstrn., 1962; Gov. Mich. Service Appreciation certificate, 1964. Fellow Geol. Soc. Am.; mem. Am. Assn. Petroleum Geologists, Internat. Assn. Fish, Game and Conservation Commrs., Mich. Acad. Sci., Mich. Basin Geol. Soc., A.A.A.S. Home: Lansing, Mich. Died May 24, 1977.

EDEN, FRANK ERNEST, clergyman; b. Burton-on-Trent, England, Nov. 21, 1885; s. Frederick William and Ellen (Baldwin) E.; student Harvard Law Sch., 1907-09, Rochester (N.Y.) Theol. Sem., 1909-12; LL.B., Hamilton Coll., Chicago, Ill., 1918, D.C.L., 1928; grad. student U. of Denver, 1927; m. Mary Ella Kipp, Apr. 1, 1919; 1 dau., Mary Jane (Mrs. William Harold Dimbley), Ordained ministry Bapt. Ch., 1912; pastor First Ch., Mansfield, Pa., 1912-17, First Ch., Pueblo, Colo., 1917-20, Broadway Ch., Denver, 1920-28; missionary Am. Bapt. Fgn. Mission Soc. at Rangoon, Burma, as pastor Immanuel Ch., instr. Bapt. English High Sch., 1929-34; pastor City Park Ch., Denver, 1934-38; instr. dept. of religion, Colo. Woman's Coll., Denver, 1936-38; dir. of evangelism, Pacific Coast Area, Am. Bapt. Home Mission Soc., since 1938. Missioner, University Christian Mission, 1938. Mem. bd. Colo. Bapt. State Conv.; pres. bd. trustees Judson Coll., Rangoon, 1932; pres. Burma Mission Conf., 1930-32. Mem. Denver Ministers Assn. (pres. 1924). Mason (32 deg.). Author of "Evangelism and Christian Education: Partners." Contbr. to Gospel from the Mountains, 1936; also contbr. articles on missions to jours. Author of hymns "The Eternal Savior," "The Precious Savior." Home: Portland, Ore. *

EDGAR, ALVIN RANDALL, educator; b. Eldora, Ia., Jan. 11, 1903; s. Fred John and Blanche (Foster) E.; B.A., Upper Ia. U., 1924, Mus.D. (hon.), 1948; M.A., State U. Ia., 1935; m. Mildred Lane, Nov. 7, 1925; children—Joyce Elaine (Mrs. Alvin F. Bull), Margaret Ann (Mrs. Donald McWilliams). Tchr. instrumental music pub. schs., Ia., 1924-35; condr. symphony orch. Ia. State U., 1935-72, band dir., 1935-48, prof. music, 1948-73, prof. emeritus, 1973-75, head dept. music, 1948-61; frequent vis. prof. clinics and music festivals; adjudicator music contests. Recipient Faculty citation Ia. State U. Alumni Assn., 1962. Mem. Ia. Bandmasters Assn. (pres. 1938), Coll. Band Dirs. Nat. Assn. (pres. 1949), Music Educators Nat. Conf., Ia. Music Educators Assn., Ia. Music Tchrs. Assn. (pres. 1958-60), Phi Mu Alpha (province gov., exec. com. 1948-58). Rotarian (dist. gov. 1948). Home: Ames, Iowa. Died Oct. 26, 1975.

EDGAR, EARL EUGENE, univ. ofcl.; b. Dwight, Ill., Feb. 12, 1914; s. Earl Edward and Hazel (Losee) E.; A.B., DePauw, U., 1935; M.A., U. Nebr., 1937; student U. Wis., 1937-38; Ph.D., U. Cin., 1940; m. Joan Louise Dodds, May 29, 1944, children—Eric Reed, Ellen Louise, Earl Edward. Asso. prof. philosophy Culver-Stockton Coll., 1940-42; with wage stblzn. div. VI Regional War Labor Bd., 1942-45; instr. social scis. U. Chgo., 1945-46; asso. prof. philosophy Kans. State Coll., 1946-48, prof., 1948-61, asso. dir. Inst. of Citizenship, 1948-51, acting dir., 1951-53, head dept. gen. studies, 1953-61; prof. edn. Pa. State U. at University Park, 1961-67; dean Grad. Sch., prof. philosophy Youngstown (Ohio) State U., 1967-70, v.p. acad. affairs, 1970-80. U.S. specialist grant Internat. Ednl. Exchange Program, Dept. State; cons. gen. edn., India, 1958. Fellow Philosophy of Edn. Soc.; mem. Am. Philos. Assn., Am. Assn. . Profs., Phi Kappa Phi, Phi Delta Kappa. Home: Boardman, Ohio. Died Feb. 24, 1980; buried Manhattan, Kans.

EDGCOMB, LESLIE, steel co. exec.; b. Limington, Me., 1886; s. Loring S. and Etta (Rich) E.; student U. Me., 1905-09; m. Edythe M. Allison, 1910; children—Helen Louise, Leslie. Exec. v.p. Edgar T. Ward Co., 1924; pres. Edgcomb Steel Co., Phila., 1924—. Mem. Am. Steel Warehouse Assn., Phila. C. of C. Clubs: Duquesne (Pitts.); Philadelphia Country. Home: Cynwyd, Pa.

EDGE, JOSEPH H(ENRY), church official; born Humboldt, Ia., Sept. 20, 1888; s. Joseph and Elizabeth Ann (Webb) E.; A.B., Morningside Coll., Sioux City, Ia., 1913, D.D., 1930; S.T.B., Boston U., Sch. of Theology, 1916; D.Sc. in Education, Boston Univ., 1945; m. Mary Elizabeth Mackey, Apr. 19, 1916 (dec. May 16, 1970); children—Mary Elizabeth (Mrs. R. L. Kammerud), Eleanor Jean (Mrs. V. M. Yahne), Joseph Matthew. Ordained to ministry of the M.E. Ch., 1916; pastor at Luverne, Ia., 1916-18, Belmond, 1918-21, Spirit Lake, 1921-26, Rockwell City, 1926-28; dist. supt. Sheldon Dist., Northwest Ia. Conf., 1928-34; pastor Algona, Ia., 1934-37; pres. Dakota Wesleyan U., Mitchell, S.D., 1937-46; asso. sec. Gen. Bd. of Evangelism, dir. Dept. of Organization and Administration, Meth. Ch., Nashville, Tenn., 1946-61; vis. minister West End Ch., Nashville, 1962-78. Delegate to Methodist General Conference, Atlantic City, 1932, Kansas City, Missouri, 1944; delegate Meth. Jurisdictional Conf., Minneapolis, Minn., 1944; president South Dakota associated Church-Related Colleges, 1942-46; mem. General Bd. Education, 1944-48; pres. Dak. Conf. Bd. Edn., 1937-46. Trustee Morningside Coll., 1928-37, Meth. Hosp., Sioux City, Ia., 1928-37; mem. Fed. Council Churches in Am., 1932-36. Mem. N.E.A., S.D. Ednl. Assn., Newcomen Soc., Pi Gamma Mu, Phi Kappa Phi. Republican. Mason (K.T.), Rotarian. Home: Nashville, Tenn. Died June 19, 1978.

EDGERTON, GLEN EDGAR, ret. army officer, cons. engr.; b. Parkerville, Kan., Apr. 17, 1887; son John Edgar and Alice (Green) E.; B.S., Kansas State Coll., 1904, C.E., 1916, Dr. Engring., 1944; B.S., U.S. Military Academy, 1908; graduate Engr. School, U.S. Army, 1910; hon. grad. Command and Gen. Staff, 1924, married to Cordelia Irene Hessin, December 8, 1914 (deceased September 1958); children—Bruce Wilds Postlethwaite, Diana Trent. Commd. lt. Corps of Engrs

U.S. Army, 1908, and advanced through the grades to maj. gen., 1942; asst. engr. Panama Canal, 1908-09; chief engr. Alaska Rd. Commn., 1910-15; lt. col. 5th Engrs., col. comdg. 214th Engrs. and div. engr. 14th Div. during World War; dist. engr. U.S. Engr. Dept., Jacksonville, Fla., 1919; dir. of Sales War Dept., 1921-23; chief engr. Federal Power Commn., 1925-29; asst. prof. of engring., U.S. Mil. Acad., 1930; dist. engr. U.S. Engr. Dept., Rock Island, Ill., 1930-33; asst. to chief of engrs., U.S. Army, 1933-36; engr. of maintenance, Panama Canal, 1936-40; gov. Panama Canal, 1940-44; dir. material ASF, 1944-45; asso. adminstr. War Assets Adminstrn., 1946; dir. U.N.R.R.A. in China, 1946-47; pres. beach erosion bd. Dept. Army, 1948-49; exec. dir. Com. on Renovation of Executive Mansion, Washington, 1949-52; president, chairman bd. dirs. Export-Import Bank, 1953-55; cons. engr. Suez Canal Company, and others, from 1952. Decorated Legion of Honor (France), Brilliant Star (China), Mexican Punitive Expdn. and World War Campaign medals, D.S.M., Legion of Merit (U.S.), Polonia Restituta Krzyz Walecznych (Poland), Vasco Nañez de Balboa (Panama), Condor of Andes (Bolivia), Abdón Calderón (Ecuador), Comdr. Order of British Empire (Great Britain). Fellow Royal Geographical Society of London; mem. Am. Soc. C.E. (hon.), Am. Inst. Elec. Engrs., Soc. Am. Mil. Engrs., Phi Kappa Phi. Clubs: Chevy Chase, Army and Navy, Alfalfa (Washington); Union (Panama). Contbr. tech. articles to jours. Home: Washington, D.C. Died Apr. 9, 1976.

EDGINGTON, RALPH, oil co. exec.; b. Delaware, O., Aug. 3, 1905; s. Robert Clinton and Clara Isabelle (Rouse) E.; B.A., Mont. U., 1927; LL.B., J.D., U. So. Cal., 1931; m. Ethel Loretta Jones, Sept. 8, 1928; children—Arlis (Mrs. James Whiffen), Lyn (Mrs. Kenneth W. Kendrick). Admitted to Cal. bar, 1931; practiced in Los Angeles, 1931-42; pres. Edgington Oil Co., Long Beach, Cal., 1942-76; dir. Edgington Oxnard Refinery, Edoco Tech. Products, Sahuaro Petroleum & Asphalt Co. Mem. Sigma Chi, Phi Alpha Delta. Republican. Methodist. Clubs: Virginia Country (Long Beach); California, Jonathan (Los Angeles). Home: Los Angeles, Calif. Died Oct. 12, 1976.

EDINGTON, WILLIAM EDMUND, educator; b. Rantoul, Ill., Dec. 8, 1886; s. Robert and Caroline (Wolpert) E.; A.B., Indiana State Normal Sch., 1909; student U. of Chicago, 1912-13, U. of Colorado, 1913-14; A.M., U. of Illinois, 1919, Ph.D., 1921; m. Hazel Carolyn Binford, Aug. 31, 1919; children—William Francis, John Bentley (dec.). Instr. in mathematics and physics, Brazil (Ind.) High Sch., 1909-11; faculty Purdue U., 1922-30, associate prof., 1927-30; prof. and head of dept. of mathematics and astronomy DePauw U., 1930-53, emeritus prof. mathematics and astronomy, 1953—; Margaret Pilcher vis. prof. math. Coe Coll., 1955-57. Served as sergt. 1st class, meterol. sect., Signal Corps, U.S. Army, 1918; comdg. officer Putnam County Squadron, Civil Air Patrol, since 1945. Mem. bd. dirs. Greencastle Orphans Home since 1942. Recipient Silver Beaver award from Boy Scouts of America, 1941; Distinguished Service Citation from Pi Kappa Phi, 1934. Recipient Citizenship Medal of Vets. Foreign Wars, for service to colored people, 1946. Fellow A.A.A.S., Ia. Acad. Sci.; mem. Am. Math. Soc. Math. Assn. Am. (chmn. Ind. sect. 1937), Am. Assn. Univ. Profs., Ind. Acad. Science (press sec. 1930-34 and 1938-41; vice pres. 1935; pres. 1937), Phi Beta Kappa, Sigma Xi, Pi Kappa Phi (nat. scholarship chmn. since 1925), Alpha Phi Omega. Presbyterian. Club: Rotary (pres. 1946-47). (Greencastle). Author articles in mathematics and science. Home: East Franklin St., Greencastle, Ind.

EDLUND, SIDNEY WENDELL, mgmt. cons.; b. Bklyn., June 1, 1890; s. Claudius and Emma (Anderson) E.; A.B., Cornell U., 1913; m. Mary Garlichs, May 5, 1922; children—Timothy Wendell, Carol Minturn. Mgr. methods unit Standard Oil Co. (N.J.), 1919-24; sales mgr. Nat. Blank Book Co., 1925-27; gen. sales mgr. William A. Rogers, Ltd., 1928-30; pres. Pine Bros, Inc., 1931-38, Life Savers, Inc., 1934-38; partner Sidney Edlund Assos., Doylestown, Pa., 1939—; dir. Greenwich Workshop, Inc., World Authors, Inc. Founder, dir. Man Mktg. Clinics, 1939-65. Served with U.S. Army, 1917-19. Recipient Mgmt. Cons. award for excellence, 1979. Mem. Soc. Profl. Mgmt. Cons. (founding mem.), Inst. Mgmt. Cons., Sales Execs. Club N.Y., Sales and Mktg. Execs. S.W. Conn. Republican. Episcopalian. Clubs: Cornell (N.Y.C.); Innis Arden Golf. Author numerous books. Home: Doylestown, Pa. Died Mar. 22, 1979.

EDMONDS, THOMAS SECHLER, lawyer; b. Chgo., Oct. 21, 1899; s. Howard Owen and Mary Addison (Sechler) E.; student Phillips Exeter Acad., 1914-18, Northwestern U. Law Sch., 1922-23; A.B., Harvard, 1922; J.D., U. Chgo., 1925; m. Elizabeth Fenley, Feb. 1, 1930; 1 son, Howard Owen. Admitted to Ill. bar, 1925; law clk. McCulloch & McCulloch, Chgo., 1925-26; partner firm Gordon, Buckley & Edmonds, 1941-53, Edmonds & Linneman, 1953-56, Ashcraft, Ashcraft and predecessor, 1957-76. Mem. Am., Ill. (pres. 1955-56), Chgo. bar assns., Delta Tau Delta. Republican. Episcopalian. Clubs: Indian Hill (Winnetka, Ill.); University, Attic, Law, Legal (Chgo.). Home: Wilmette, Ill. Died Jan. 25, 1976.

EDMONDSON, JOHN PRESTON, lawyer, publisher; b. Radford, Va., Feb. 28, 1903; s. Reese Thompson and Elnora (Shumate) E.; A.B., Va. Mil. Inst., 1924; LL.B., U. Va., 1929; m. Mary Dickson Cooke, May 28, 1938; children—Mary Royster (Mrs. Richard M. Cherouny), Eleanor Reese (Mrs. Charles J. Currie), Frances Cooke (Mrs. David T. Sargent). Admitted to N.Y. bar, 1929; atty., sec., mem. bd. 20th Century Fox Film Corp., 1929-42, dir., exec. com., audit com., 1969-74, chmn. pension com., 1969-78; exec. v.p., dir. E.P. Dutton & Co., Inc., N.Y.C., 1946-68; Past pres., mem. bd. edn., Scarsdale, N.Y. Chmn. bd. trustees Mary Baldwin Coll., Staunton, Va., Cape Henry Sch., Inc., Virginia Beach, Va. Served from 1st lt. to col. USAAF, 1942-45. Decorated Legion of Merit, Croix de Guerre. Mem. Am. Book Publs. Council (treas., mem. bd.). Clubs: Princess Anne Country (Virginia Beach, Va.); Scarsdale Golf; University (N.Y.C.); Publishers' Lunch. Home: Virginia Beach, Va. Died Mar. 14, 1978.

EDMONSON, JAMES BARTLETT, educator; b. Parkersburg, Ia., Dec. 28, 1882; s. James Bartlett and Nancy Jane (Sloan) E.; A.B., University of Michigan, 1906, A.M., 1910; Ph.D., U. Chicago, 1925; D.SC., Wayne U., 1951; married Bess Chase, August 26, 1914; children—Jane Elizabeth Lewis, Donald Chase. Teacher, high school, Ionia, Mich., 1906-07; prin. high sch., Hillsdale, Mich., 1907-09, Benton Harbor, 1910-11, Jackson, 1911-14; insp. high schs. and prof. secondary edn., U. of Mich., 1914-27; instr. Univ. of Chicago, summer quarters, 1922 and 23. Dir., Div. of Univ. Inspection of High Schs., 1927-29; dean Sch. Edn., U. Mich., 1929-52, ret. Pres. N. Central Assn. of Colls. and Secondary Schs., 1931-32, sec., 1925-31; chmn. Nat. Conf. of Officers of Standardizing Agencies, 1928-29; mem. State Teachers' Retirement Board, 1915-29 (ex-pres.): mem. exec. com. Am. Council Edn., 1943-46; co-chmn. Canada-U.S. Com. on Edn., since 1944. Mem. N.E.A., State Teachers' Assn., Mich. Schoolmasters' Club (ex-pres.), Nat. Soc. Coll. Teachers of Edn., Nat. Assn. High Sch. Inspectors (ex-sec., ex-pres.), Nat. Com. on Research in Secondary Edn. (chmn. 1925-31, Mich. Council Edn. (chmn. 1934-37), Phi Delta Kappa, Kappa Phi Kappa, Phi Kappa Phi, Pi Gamma Mu. Mem. Nat. Commn. on Emergency in Education, 1933-35, Ednl. Policies Commn. 1935-43, Horace Mann League (national president, 1947-48). Mem. Com. on Accreditation, Am. Assn. Colls. Teacher Edn.; commr. N. Central Assn. Colls. and Secondary Schs. (mem. commn. on colls. and univs. 1948). Presbyn. Author textbooks, and books on ednl. adminstrn., latest: Civics for Youth (with Arthur Dondineau and Mildred Setton), 1946; also articles on ednl. subjects. Home: Ann Arbor.

EDSALL, GEOFFREY, physician; b. Phila., Jan. 28, 1908; s. David Linn and Margaret Harding (Tileston) E.; M.D., Harvard, 1934; m. Helen Fogle, Aug. 13, 1935; 1 son, Richard Anthony. Intern, Mass. Gen. Hosp., 1934-36; research fellow Harvard, 1936-39, instr. bacteriology and immunology, med. and pub. health schs., 1940-47, asst. prof. pub. health bacteriology, pub. health sch., 1947-49, vis. lectr., 1949-60, prof. applied microbiology, 1960-72, emeritus, 1972—; asst. dir., div. biologic labs. Mass. Dept. Pub. Health, 1939-42, dir., 1942-49, supt. State Lab. Inst., 1960-72; prof. microbiology and head dept. Boston U. Sch. Medicine, 1949-52; prof., head dept. microbiology London Sch. Hygiene and Tropical Medicine, 1972-75, emeritus, 1975—; dir. immunology div. Walter Reed Army Inst. Research, 1951-56, tech. dir. research of communicable and parasitic diseases, 1956-60; dir. commn. on immunization Armed Forces Epidemiol. Bd., 1952-63; vis. prof. microbiology U. Calif., 1955; spl. cons. WHO, 1953, 55, 59, 63-80, mem. expert panel immunology, 1963-80, cons. Surgeon Gen., U.S. Army, 1960-72, USPHS, 1963-72; adv. com. immunization practices USPHS, 1963-70, adv. com. on quarantine, 1965-66. Mem. subcom. on blood O.D.M., 1951-52; del. U.S. Pharmacopeial Conv., 1950, mem. revision com. U.S. Pharmacopeia, 1960-65; mem. U.S. del. 13th World Health Assembly, 1960; mem. bd. sci. counselors, div. biologies standard of NIH, USPHS, 1968-72, chmn., 1971-72; mem. rev. panel bacterial vaccines and toxoids FDA, 1973-79, cons., 1973-80; Sydney Rubbo Meml. orator, Australia, 1974; lectr. Mex., Venezuela, Colombia, India, Australia, Switzerland, Germany; mem. Joint Com. Vaccination and Immunization U.K., 1972-78; chmn. Internat. Conf. Tetanus, Senegal, 1975. Trustee Bergey Manual Trust, 1957-65. Recipient Lemuel Shattuck award, 1971. Diplomate Am. Bd. Preventive Medicine (founder mem.), Am. Bd. Microbiology. Fellow A.A.A.S., Am. Acad. Arts and Scis., Am. Pub. Health Assn. (sec. lab. sect. 1947-48, chmn. 1950), Royal Soc. Tropical Medicine and Hygiene; mem. Am. Soc. Tropical Medicine and Hygiene, Brit. Soc. Immunology, Infectious Disease Soc. Am., A.M.A. (mem. council on drugs 1960-62), Am. Epidemiol. Soc., Am. Soc. Microbiol. (pres. N.E. br. 1950, 62), Am. Assn. Immunologists (councillor 1947-49, pres. 1950), Internat. Epidemiol. Assn., Internat. Assn. Biol. Standardization (council 1967-78), Delta Omega. Editor-in-chief Jour. Immunology, 1948-54, mem. editorial bd., 1954-59; editorial bd. Jour. Biol. Standardization, 1973-78; contbr. articles to profl. publs. Home: University Hills, Calif. Died Aug. 11, 1980.

EDSON, PETER, former editor; b. Hartford City, Ind., Feb. 8, 1896; s. Charles Bloomfield and Mary (Drayer) E.; A.B., Wabash Coll., 1920, D.H.L., 1971; A.M., Harvard, 1925; m. Dorothy Ann Shulze, Oct. 13, 1936 (dec. Aug. 1957); m. 2d, Joyce Beatty, Nov. 8, 1958; children—Mary, Margaret, Michael Peter. Sunday editor Fort Wayne News Sentinel, 1921, asst. Sunday editor Boston Post, 1924-25, Sunday editor New Haven Register, 1926, Pitts. Press, 1927; editor Every Week mag., 1927-31; editor-in-chief N.E.A. Service, Inc., Cleve., 1932-41; Washington columnist N.E.A. Service newspapers, 1941-63; cons. Sch. Internat. Studies, Johns Hopkins, 1964-70. Trustee, Wabash College, 1955—. Recipient Sigma Delta Chi award for Washington corr., 1946, Raymond Clapper award for newspaper writing, 1948, Headliners award for nat. reporting, 1953. Served as lt. inf., U.S.A., 1917-19. Mem. Phi Beta Kappa, Sigma Delta Chi (charter mem. Washington Journalism Hall of Fame 1971), Phi Gamma Delta. Presbyn. Clubs: Cosmos, National Press, Overseas Writers (Washington). Home: Washington, D.C. Died July 14, 1977; buried Oak Hill Cemetery, Washington.

EDWARDS, AUSTIN SOUTHWICK, psychologist; born Oswego, N.Y., Mar. 2, 1885; s. Thomas Henry and Hannah Maria (Southwick) E.; grad. high sch., Oswego, 1902; classical diploma, Oswego Normal and Practice Sch., 1906; B.S., Columbia, 1908; M.A., U. of Minn., 1910; Ph.D., Cornell U., 1912; m. Miriam Pope, Jan. 26, 1918; 1 son, Austin Southwick. Mem. faculty U. of Minn., 1912-16; prof. psychology, U. Ga., 1916-54, prof. emeritus, from 1954; dir. U. Ga. Clinic; engaged cons. and clinical psychology. Psychol. examiner U.S. Army, Sept., 1917-Sept., 1919; chief psychol. examiner, Camp Jackson, Columbia, S.C.; morale officer, chief edn. service, Ft. Bayard, N.M. Mem. Board of Examiners in Psychology, 1951-53. Fellow Am. Assn. Applied Psychologists, Am. Psychol. Assn.; mem. Southern Soc. Philos. and Psychol. (pres. 1926-27), Am. Assn. Univ. Profs., Ga. Psychol. Assn. (pres. 1949), U. of Ga. Science Club, sec. treas. Ga. Acad. of Sci., 1941-52; pres. N.E. Ga. Council Boy Scouts of America, 1940-43, Sigma Xi, Phi Delta Kappa, Gamma Alpha; fellow A.A.A.S. Presbyterian. Mason. Author several books in psychology. Contbr. articles in psychology journals. Inventor, portable ataxiameter, portable finger tromometer. Home: Athens, Ga. Deceased.

EDWARDS, CHARLES PETER, govt. official; b. Dodleston, Chester, Eng., Dec. 11, 1885; s. Peter and Sarah Elizabeth (Hughes) E.; radio engr., Arnold Tech. Sch., Chester, Eng.; m. Ethel Maud Dickieson, Oct. 30, 1911. Jr. engr. English Marconi Co., London, Eng., 1905-06; engr. Canadian Marconi Co., Montreal, 1906-09 gen. supt. of radio of Canadian Govt., 1909-36; dir. of air services br., Dept. of Transport, 1936-41, dep. minister of dept. since 1941; dir. Trans-Can. Air Lines. Trustee Canadian Nat. Rys. Securities Trust. Chmn. Lighthouse Bd. of Can. Served as lt.-comdr. Royal Canadian Naval Volunteer Res., 1914-18. Decorated Order of the British Empire, 1918. Companion of the Most Distinguished Order of St. Michael and St. George, 1946. Reeve of the Village of Rockcliffe Park, Ottawa, 1933-37. Fellow Inst. of Radio Engrs. (past vice pres.). Mem. Engring. Inst. of Can. (ex-councillor), Assn. Professional Engrs. of Ontario (ex-councillor). Mem. Anglican Ch. Club: Royal Ottawa Golf, Rideau. Home: Ontario, Can. *

EDWARDS, CORWIN D., educator, economist, editor; b. Nevada, Mo., Nov. 1, 1901; s. Granville Dennis and Ida May (Moore) E.; A.B., U. Mo., 1920, B.J., 1921; B.Litt., Oxford (Eng.) U., 1924; Ph.D., Cornell U., 1928; m. Janet Morris Ward, Dec. 20, 1924; children—Ward Dennis, Corinne Jennifer; m. 2d, Gertrud Greig, Feb. 15, 1948. Instr. econs. Cornell U., 1924-26; from instr. to asso. prof. econs. Washington Sq. Coll., N.Y. U., 1926-33; economist, chief price sect., asst. dir. and tech. dir. Consumers Adv. Bd., NRA, 1933-35, coordinator trades practice studies sect., div. rev., 1935-36; prin. economist div. indsl. econs., President's Com. Indsl. Analysis, 1936; econ. adviser, asst. chief economist FTC, 1937-39; econ. cons., chmn. policy bd. anti-trust div. Dept. Justice, 1939-44; chief staff Am. Tech. Mission to Brazil, 1942-43; head Mission Japanese Combines, 1946; cons. Dept. State, 1943-48; prof. econs. Northwestern U., 1944-48; dir. bur. indsl. econs. FTC, 1948-53; Pitt prof. Am. Instns., Cambridge (Eng.) U., 1953-54; prof. econs. U. Va., 1954-55; prof. govt. and bus. U. Chgo., 1955-63; prof. econs. U. Oreg., 1963-71; mem. U.S. del. ECOSOC, 1951, rep. on ad hoc com., 1952-53; mem. Consumers Adv. Council, 1967-69; mem. com. on legal aspects of computerized info. systems, 1971-72. Recipient Rhodes scholarship Oxford U., Rhodes-Clay scholarship U. Mo.; Citation of Merit, U. Mo., 1969; Veblen-Commons award Assn. for Evolutionary Econs., 1978. Mem. Am. Econ. Assn., Phi Beta Kappa. Democrat. Author: Economic and Political Aspects of International Cartels, 1944; Maintaining Competition, 1949; Big Business and the Policy of Competition, 1956; The Price Discrimination Law, 1959; Cartelization in Western Europe, 1964; Trade Regulations Overseas, 1966; Control of Cartels and Monopolies, an Internat. Comparison, 1967; Studies of Foreign Competition

Policy and Practice, Vol. I, The United States, 1976; American Antitrust Policy Toward Conduct by Powerful Enterprises, 1977; co-author: Economic Behavior, 1931; Economic Problems in a Changing World, 1939; A Cartel Policy for the United Nations, 1945; Report of Mission on Japanese Combines, 1946. Fgn. editor Antitrust bull., 1970-78. Contbr. articles to profl. jours. Address: Lewes, Del. Died Apr. 20, 1979; interred, Columbia, Mo.

EDWARDS, DAYTON J(AMES), med. educator; b. Otisfield, Me., Sept. 7, 1882; s. Dominicus J. and Lottie (Gage) E.; B.S., U. Me., 1906; Ph.D., Columbia, 1913; m. Grace C. Telford, June 28, 1911 (dec.); 1 son, Seymour (dec.). Asst., instr. U. Me., 1906-08; asst. zoology Columbia, 1908-09; instr. physiology Coll. City N.Y., 1913-17; asst. prof. physiology Cornell U. Med. Coll., 1918-22, asso. prof., 1922-50, prof. emeritus, 1950—, asst., asso. dean, 1936-50, sec. faculty, 1950-59, acting dean, 1953-54. Mem. A.A.A.S., Am. Physiol. Soc., Harvey Soc., Soc. Exptl. Biology and Medicine (pres. 1931), Phi Beta Kappa, Sigma Xi, Phi Kappa Sigma. Contbr. articles profl. publs. Home: Charlottesville, Va.

EDWARDS, FRANK WILLIAM, profl. engr.; b. Williamsburg, Iowa, Aug. 10, 1905; s. Walter Ernest and Bertha Ethel (Stover) E.; B.S., U. Iowa, 1928, M.S., 1930, C.E., 1944; m. Harriet Margaret Williams, June 3, 1928; children—Doris Ann (Mrs. Rodger W. Davenport), Carolyn (Mrs. Charles W. Soderberg). Asst. engr., then engr. in charge dist. Mgmt. & Engring. Corp., 1928-32; research asst. U.S. Bur. Agrl. Engring., 1932-33; gauge reader, later prin. engr. several dists. U.S. C.E. and Panama Canal, War Dept., 1933-43, 45-46; asst. prof. civil engring. Pa. State Coll., 1943-44, asso. prof., 1944-45; prof. civil engring. Carnegie Inst. Tech., 1946-48; dir. dept. civil engring. Ill. Inst. Tech., 1948-53; mgr. Chgo. office Stanley Engring. Co., cons. engrs., 1953-64, v.p., dir., 1961-64; pres. Limbaugh Engring. & Aerial Surveys, Inc., Albuquerque, 1964-66; pres., dir. Limbaugh Engrs., Inc., 1965-70, cons., dir., 1970-73; cons. Bovay Engrs., Inc., 1970-73, St. Lawrence Seaway Devel. Corp. Gen. mgr. Centennial of Engring., 1952, Inc.; adv. bd. Coll. Engring., U. Idaho. Recipient Ill. award Ill. Soc. Profl. Engrs. Fellow Am. Soc. C.E. (pres. Ill. sect. 1953, life mem.); mem. Am. Soc. M.E. (life), Am. Soc. Engring. Edn., Nat. (life, nat. dir. 1959-64), Ill. (pres. Chgo. chpt. 1952, state pres., 1958-59, named hon. mem. 1965), N.Mex. socs. profl. engrs., Sigma Xi, Theta Tau (exec. council 1948-52), Tau Beta Pi, Omicron Delta Kappa, Chi Epsilon. Elk. Author: articles engring. jours. Home: Albuquerque, N.M. Died Oct. 31, 1976.

EDWARDS, HIRAM W(HEELER), physicist, asso. prof.; b. Spring Valley, Minn., Sept. 1885; s. Frank V. and Kate I. (Farmer) E.; student, Carlton Coll., 1903-05; B.S., Univ. of Calif., 1908, Whiting fellow in physics, 1910-11, Ph.D., 1911; m. Vena Tomlin, July 21, 1911; children—Tomlin (Mrs. E. Cary Brown), Phyllis Q., Warren Wheeler. Prof. physics, Baylor Univ., 1911-12; dir. of sci., Fresno (Calif.) State Normal, 1912-18; supervisor of teacher training in sci., U. of Calif., 1919-22, asst. prof. of physics, 1922-24, asso. prof., 1924-43; cons. physicist, Pancro Mirrors, Inc., Los Angeles, since 1938; dir. of relations with other Calif. schs. for U. of Calif., since 1936; asso. prof., U. of Calif., Berkeley, since 1943, acting dir. of admissions, 1943-44. Adminstrv. bd. mem., Lick-Wilmerding Schs., San Francisco; on bd. of trustees, Calif. Soc. Secondary Edn. Served in World War I as insp. of instruction, U.S. Ground Sch. of Mil. Aeronautics, and head lecturer, U.S. Sch. Radio Electricians, 1918. Honored by establishment of Hiram W. Edwards scholarship in physics, Calif. Assn. Ind. Secondary Schs. Mem. Am. Phys. Soc., Optical Soc. of Am., Am. Assn. Physics Teachers, Calif. Com. for Study of Edn. (sec.-treas.), Phi Delta Kappa, Sigma Xi. Republican. Conglist. Author: Analytical and Vector Mechanics, 1934. Patents on high speed vacuum oil pump, aluminum magnesium alloys for high quality mirrors. Home: Berkeley, Calif.

EDWARDS, KATE FLOURNOY, portrait painter; b. Marshallville, Ga.; d. Judge Joseph Asbury and Emma (Miller) Edwards; student Price's Coll., Nashville, Tenn.; Art Inst. Chicago; pupil of Lucien Simon, Paris. Winner 1st prize, Southeastern Fair Exhbn., at Atlanta, Ga., 1916; 1st prize, Atlanta Art Assn. Exhbn., 1921. On premanent exhbn.; portrait of Judge Philip P. Barbour, in Capitol, Washington, D.C.; portrait of Dr. John Bascom Crenshaw, Ga. Sch. of Tech.; of Gov. M. B. Wellborn. Federal Reserve Bank, Atlanta; of Dr. W. H. Emerson, Ga. Sch. of Technology, Atlanta; of Dr. John E. White, Wake Forest (N.C.) Coll.; of Judge Cincinnatus Peeples, Fulton County Courthouse; Atlanta, Ga.; of Dr. Robert J. Sprague, Rollins Coll., Fla.; of Dr. Kenneth G. Matheson, Ga. Sch. of Tech., Atlanta; of Miss Mary Lyndon, U. of Ga. (Athens); of Dr. J. Sprole Lyons, First Presbyn. Ch., Atlanta. Ga.; of Gen. Henry Lewis Benning, Headquarters Building, Fort Benning, Ga.; of Mrs. Elizabeth Forrest Day, City Library, Dayton, Wash.; of Mr. Lawrence Wood (Chip) Robert, Jr., Georgia School of Technology, Atlanta, Ga.; Joseph LeConte, U. of Ga., Athens; Miss Martha Hardaway, Wesleyan Conservatory, Macon, Ga.; Miss Mary Du Pont, Wesleyan Conservatory; Dr. Richard Orme Flinn, North Av. Presbyn, Ch., Atlanta, Ga.; Prof. Arthur H. Armstrong and Dean W. Vernon Skiles, Ga. Sch. of Tech.; Mr. Columbus Roberts and Dr. Spright Dowell, Mercer Univ., Macon, Ga.; Maj. John S. Cohen, U. of Ga., Athens, Ga.; Mr. Stewart Fleming, 4th Nat. Bank, Columbus, Ga.; Miss Thyrza Askew, Westminster Sch., Atlanta; Dr. A. B. Calhoun, Calhoun Library, Atlanta; Judge Henry R. Bryan, Craven Co. Courthouse, N.C.; Gen. Blanton Winship, Governor's Palace, Puerto Rico; Dr. Wm. V. Gardner, 1st Presbyn. Ch., Dr. J. B. Green, Columbia Theol. Sem. (both Atlanta); Dr. John Fairlie, U. Ill.; Mrs. Nannally Johnson, Johnson Sch., Columbus, Ga.; Dr. James Paullin, Atlanta (former pres. A.M.A.); picture "Out of Work." High Museum of Art, Atlanta; "Miss Lucy," Orlando (Fla.) Art Gallery; Mrs. A. B. Burrus, Decatur-De Kalb Library, Decatur; also several recent portraits permanently exhibited, Mem. Soc. Colonial Dames, Art Assn. (Atlanta), Southern State Art League, Assn. of Ga. Artists. Home; Atlanta, Ga. Died May 23, 1980.

EDWARDS, PAUL CARROLL, newspaper editor; b. Knightstown, Ind., Feb. 11, 1882; s. Joel Barlow and Sarah Elizabeth (Emery) E.; student Stanford U., 1902-06; m. Georgina Lyman, Oct. 27, 1909; children—Paul Carroll, Carroll. Began as reporter Indianapolis News, 1898; reporter, later city editor, San Francisco News, 1908; editor Dallas (Tex.) Dispatch, 1910-11, 1916-19; editor Houston (Tex.) Press, 1911-16; editor-in-chief southwestern group Scripps-Howard Newspapers, 1919-22; editor-in-chief Calif. Scripps-Howard Newspapers, 1922-31; editor San Diego (Calif.) Sun, 1925-33; asso. editor San Francisco News, 1933-56. Trustee Stanford U. Club: Commonwealth (pres. 1941-42). Home: Los Altos, Cal.

EDWARDS, RAY LEE, educator; born Forest Grove, Ore., Nov. 12, 1885; s. Darius Lyman and Mary Imogene (Houghton) E.; A.B., Oberlin Coll., 1908; B.S., Ohio Wesleyan University, 1909; A.M., Ohio State Univ., 1911; Ph.D., University of Iowa, 1925; D.Sc., Denison University, 1963; married Winifred Julia Knight, August 23, 1911; children—Jean Alice (Mrs. Mason Quebedaux), Lawrence Knight, Harold Houghton. Science teacher, 1908-10; prof. physics, Park Coll., Parkville, Mo., 1911-26; asst. instr. physics, U. of Chicago, summers, 1921-23; instr. physics, U. of Ia., 1924-25; prof. and chmn. dept. physics, Miami U., Oxford, O., 1926-56, emeritus, 1956—; visiting professor Ohio State U., summer 1942, University of Illinois, summer 1951, Colo. U., 1956-57, Beloit College, 1957-59; lectr. physics Duke U., 1959-61; guest professor Trinity U., San Antonio, 1961-62; vis. prof. Harvey Mudd Coll., 1962—. Fellow Ohio Acad. Sci. (v.p. 1933, 43, 48); mem. Am. Phys. Soc., Am. Assn. Physics Tchrs., A.A.A.S., Sigma Xi, Gamma Alpha. Presbyn. Asso. editor Am. Jour. Physics, 1945-47. Has pub. original research in mechanics, liquid viscosities, and magnetism; articles on teaching physics. Received Oersted Medal for notable contbns. to teaching of physics, 1945, mechanics, liquid viscosities, and magnetism. Home: Houston.

EDWARDS, SHERMAN, composer-lyricist; b. N.Y.C.; s. Nathan and Rae (Rosenblat) E.; B.A. in History, N.Y. U.; postgrad. Cornell U.; m. Ingrid Secretan; children—Valerie, Keith. Pianist for Lisa Kirk, Eddie Fisher, Mindy Carson; pianist jazz concerts, composer, lyricist 1776, 1969. Served with USAAF, 1942-46. Recipient Drama Critics award, 1969, Outer Circle award, 1969, Antoinette Perry awards as composer and lyricist, 1969, Christopher award, 1973. Mem. A.S.C.A.P., Am. Guild Authors and Composers, Dramatists Guild, Am. Fedn. Musicians. Composer: For Heaven's Sake, Dungaree Doll, Broken Hearted Melody, See You in September, Wonderful Wonderful, Johnny, Get Angry. Mem. N.J. Hist. Soc. Home: Boonton Manor, N.J. Died Mar. 30, 1981; buried Kensico Cemetery, Valhalla, N.Y.

EDWARDS, WALTER ALDEN, corp. exec.; b. Logansport, Ind., Mar. 15, 1913; s. Edwin Jathan and Edna Mae (DeWitt) E.; student Purdue U., 1931-32; B.S., Ind. U., 1937; m. Elizabeth Knowlson, July 17, 1943; children—DeWitt, Timothy. Asst. to exec. v.p. Pullman-Standard Car Mfg. Co., Chgo., 1937-42, sales exec., 1945-50; mgr. govt.-industry relations dept. Owens-Illinois Glass Co., Toledo, 1950-53, Washington rep., 1954-58; dep. dir. containers and packaging div., spl. asst. to dir. NPA, also asst. adminstr. Bus. and Def. Services Adminstrn., U.S. Dept. Commerce, 1953-54, dep. asst. sec. commerce for domestic affairs, 1958-61, asst. sec. of commerce, 1961; exec. Chrysler Corp., Washington, from 1961. Served as lt. comdr. USNR, 1942-45. Clubs: University (Chgo.); Army and Navy, Congressional Country, Burning Tree (Washington). Home: Millboro Springs, Va. Died Oct. 26, 1978.

EDWARDS, WARD BLOWERS, coll. pres.; b. Troupsburg, N.Y., June 21, 1885; s. Charles Perry and Mary Livonia (Blowers) E.; A.B., Wake Forest (N.C.) Coll., 1912; M.A., Columbia, 1920; m. Cinderella Stanley, of Northampton Co., N.C., July 26, 1916. Prin. high sch., Grifton, N.C., 1912-15, Jackson, N.C., 1915-18; supt. schs., Weldon, N.C., 1918-24; dean Chowan Coll., 1924-26, pres. since 1926. Democrat. Baptist. Mason. Home: Murfreesboro, N.C.

EDWARDS, WILLARD ELDRIDGE, originator The Perpetual Calendar; b. Chatham, Mass., Dec. 11, 1903; s. Arthur Robbins and Mabel Hallett (Eldridge) E.; student Mass. Inst. Tech., 1922-26; B.S., U. Okla., 1929; M.S., Litt. D., Jackson Coll., 1960, M.A., 1961; m. Dorothy L. Shiell, June 13, 1942; children—Willard Eldridge, Annabelle (dec.), Arthur, Geraldine. Originator The Perpetual Calendar, 1919, officially endorsed by Legislature, Hawaii, 1943, Commonwealth Mass., 1952, introduced in each Congress, from 1943, in over 350 cities in 100 fgn. countries, on 9 world tours 1928, 52, 56, 60, 62, 66, 68, 72, 74; proposed by Congl. resolution and bill as ofcl. calendar U.S., also for adoption by all nations; writer, lectr., from 1922; research engr. Radio Corp. Am., N.Y.C., 1926-28; elec. engr., Alexander Aircraft Co., Colorado Springs, 1929; radio engr. trans-Pacific radio-telephony Am. Tel. & Tel. Co., Denver, also Dixon, Cal., 1929-33; radio engr. radio stas., KFI-KECA, 1933-40; elec. engr. Lockheed Aircraft Co., Burbank, Cal., 1940-41; elec. engr. 9th region CAA, Honolulu, 1946-49, 14th Naval Dist., Pearl Harbor, 1949-65; ret., 1965; corrosion cons., 1953-75. Served as lt. comdr. USN, 1942-46, electronics engr. Pacific Islands, USN, ret. Registered profl. engr. Mem. Internat. Platform Assn., Soc. Am. Mil. Engrs., I.E.E.E., A.A.A.S., Nat. Assn. Corrosion Engrs., Hawaiian Astron. Soc., Honolulu Meml. Soc. (pres.), Sigma Chi, Tau Omega, Alpha Sigma Delta, Alpha Eta Rho. Mason (32 deg.). Clubs: Kokua, Toastmasters, Pearl Harbor Officers, Wollaston (Mass.) Yacht, Los Serranos (Cal.) Country. Author: The Perpetual Calendar, 1943; American Samoa, 1949; Origin of Christian Time, 1955; Underground Corrosion and Cathodic Protection, 1956. Asso. editor: The American Rationalist. Contbr. articles to profl. publs. Licensed comml. airplane pilot; originator Presidents Day and proposal of Monday (3-day) holidays that became legal in 1971; obtained legislation renaming Hoover Dam, 1947. Home: Honolulu, Hawaii. Died Aug. 15, 1975.

EDWARDS, WILLIAM HENRY, lawyer; b. Providence, Dec. 5, 1898; s. Seeber and Sarah Estella (Gurney) E.; grad. Moses Brown Sch., 1915; A.B., Brown U., 1919, LL.D., 1965; J.D. cum laude, Harvard, 1921; D.H.S. (hon.), Providence Coll., 1967; LL.D., U. R.I., 1967; m. Mabel Potter, June 18, 1921 (dec. Jan. 1969); children—Knight, Louise (Mrs. Charles E. Saul); m. 2d, Mary Rita McGinn, Sept. 8, 1969. Admitted to R.I. bar, 1922, Mass. bar, 1943, also U.S. Supreme Ct., other U.S. cts.; practiced in Providence, 1922-68; asso. Edwards & Angell, 1922-29, mem., 1929-68, counsel, 1969-76. Mem. R.I. Juvenile and Dist. Ct. Commn. 1939; chmn. R.I. Adv. Com. on Aging, 1972-74; chmn. bd. appeal R.I. SSS, 1940-42; mem. Family Ct. Commn., 1956-58; chmn. R.I. selection com. Rhodes Scholarship candidates, 1957-68; chmn. Commn. Revision R.I. Constn., 1961-63. Pres. United Fund R.I., 1955-56; mem. nat. bd. dirs. Planned Parenthood-World Population, 1965-71, hon. mem., 1971-75, bd. advisers, 1975-76; hon. mem. bd. R.I. affiliate; nat. trustee NCCJ; hon. dir. R.I. Philharm. Orch.; sec. R.I. Sch. Design, 1931-68, trustee, 1933-68, life trustee emeritus, 1968-76; trustee, past pres. Providence Lying-In Hosp.; trustee Vassar Coll., 1935-43; trustee Brown U., 1938-44, trustee emeritus, 1944-76; mem. pres.'s council Providence Coll.; chmn. bd. trustees Lincoln Sch., 1948-52, Moses Brown Sch., 1953-57; pres. R.I. Coll. Found., 1973-74. Served with U.S. Army, 1918; with USNR, 1942-45; lt. comdr. Res. (ret.). Recipient Roger Williams award for community service Greater Providence C. of C., 1974. Fellow Am. Bar Found.; mem. Am. Bar Assn., R.I. Bar Assn. (pres. 1958-59, exec. com. 1930-33, 1956-60), Mass. Bar Assn., Am. Law Inst., Am. Coll. Trial Lawyers, Assn. Bar City N.Y., Am. Judicature Soc., Council Fgn. Relations, ACLU, Selden Soc., Nat. Mcpl. League (mem. council), Phi Beta Kappa (pres. R.I. Alpha chpt. 1955-57), Alpha Delta Phi. Democrat. Congregationalist. Clubs: University, Art, Agawam, Turk's Head, Hope (Providence); Century, Harvard (N.Y.C.). Contbr. articles various publs. and book revs. Home: Providence, R.I. Died Sept. 1, 1976.

EDY, JOHN N(ORTH) (E'DI), b. Kimswick, Mo. Nov. 20, 1883; s. William John and Grace Lenor (North) E.; B.S., in civil engring., U. of Mo., 1905, C.E. 1909; A.M. in polit. science, U. of Calif., 1927; studen Stanford U., 1928-30; m. Mary Jane Brown, Feb. 14 1907; 1 son, John North. Engring. work, Mo., 1905-08 county-highway engr., Butler County, Mo., 1908-09 dep. county surveyor, Yellowstone County, Mont 1909-10; chief insp., asst. city engr., Billings, Mont 1910-16; road engr. and county engr., Yellowston County, Mont., 1916-18; asst. chief engr., later chie engr., State Highway Dept., Mont., 1918-23; city mgr Berkeley, Calif., 1923-30, Flint, Mich., 1930-31, Dalla Tex., 1931-35; asst. dir. U.S. Bur. of the Budge Washington, D.C., 1935; city mgr., Toledo, O 1936-39; exec. asst. and budget officer, office of th administrator, Federal Works Agency, Washingto D.C., October 1, 1939-May 1, 1942; assista commissioner of the Federal Public Housing Authorit May 1, 1942-January 1943; city manager, Housto

Tex., 1943-45; pres. and gen. mgr. Industrial Road Equipment Corp. since 1946. Registered professional engineer. Lecturer on public management, Stanford U., 1928-30; instr. municipal govt. and adminstrn., Southern Meth. U., 1933-34; lecturer pub. management and budgetary practice Am. University, 1940-41. Mem. Am. Soc. Civil Engrs., Internat. City Mgrs. Assn. (pres. 1927-28), Nat. Municipal League (hon. v.p.), Sigma Chi. Independent Democrat. Presbyterian. Mason (32 deg.). Contbr. articles on public management to journals. Home: Houston.

EELLS, DAN PARMELEE, bus. exec.; b. Cleveland, Ohio, September 24, 1884; s. Howard P. and Alice (Overton) E.; grad. Cornell Univ.; m. Anita Van Dyke, Sept. 7, 1912; children—Anna Camp Schroeder, Maud Wilson, Elinor Weisse, Anita Van Dyke, Alice McLesky. Treas., Bucyrus Co., 1910-27, Export Dept., 1914-27; second v.p., Bucyrus Co., 1924-27; in charge export dept. Bucyrus-Erie Co., 1928-33, v.p. 1927-45, dir. 1911-52; chmn. bd., Basic Refractories, Inc.; dir. and mem. exec. com. Medusa Portland Cement Co.; dir. H. H. Camp Co. Head of a div. of Milwaukee Co. Community Fund, 3 yrs. Clubs: University of Milwaukee, Milwaukee Country, Milwaukee (Milwaukee); Cornell (New York). Home: Milwaukee.

EGAN, JOHN TAYLOR, architect, ex-govt. ofcl.; b. N.Y.C., Nov. 27, 1890; s. John Joseph and Mary (Godley) E.; ed. Columbia Sch. of Architecture, 1910-14; m. Alma Murphy, June 1, 1927; children—Catherine, Adrian. Gen. practice of architecture with N.Y. architects, 1914-18, 19-22; registered architect, N.Y. State, 1922; pvt. practice in architecture, 1922-35; sr. architect, Farm Security Adminstrn., 1935-38; prin. housing project planner, U.S. Housing Authority, 1938-39; regional dir. for New York, Fed. Pub. Housing Authority (formerly U.S. Housing Authority), 1939-44, asst. commr. for project management, 1944-47; asst. commr. for program operations, Pub. Housing Adminstrn. (formerly Fed. Pub. Housing Authority), 1947, commr., 1948-53; mem. Holden, Egan, Wilson and Corser, architects and planners, from 1954. Served USAAF, 1918. Mem. A.I.A. Democrat. Roman Catholic. Home: Glen Cove, Md. Died July 13, 1978; interred St. Mary's Cemetery, Flushing, N.Y.

EGBERT, LAWRENCE DEEMS, lawyer; b. St. Paul, Feb. 1, 1897; s. John Paul and Anna Louise (Deems) E.; A.B., U. Mich., 1919; postgrad. Harvard, 1919-21, Acad. Internat. Law, The Hague, 1923; Dr. en Droit summa cum laude, Faculté de Droit, U. Paris, 1926; m. Evelyn Loretta Forsyth, July 18, 1922; children—Lawrence, John, Charles. Instr. internat. law U. Ill., Northwestern U., 1927-34; asst. to Law Librarian of Congress, Washington, 1935-36; specialist on comml. treaties and fgn. comml. policies U.S. Tariff Commn., 1936-41; admitted to D.C. bar, 1941; asst. chief central info. div. OSS, 1941-43; commd. maj. AUS, 1943, advanced to lt. col., 1945; ret., 1949; lectr. law faculty U. Paris, Nat. Sch. Adminstrn., Paris, Johns Hopkins; mem. exec. staff U.S. chief counsel Nuremberg trial Nazi War Criminals, 1945-46; research coordinator State Dept., 1950-60; Latin Am. specialist with office internat. confs. State Dept., 1960-61; coordinator law conf., Brazil, 1961; disarmament researcher Atlantic Research Corp., Washington, 1962; research dir. World Peace through Law Center, 1963-67; adj. prof. internat. law Am. U., 1949-65; asst. sec.-gen. Congress of Comparative Law, The Hague, Holland, 1937. Orgn. rep. Rome Food Conf., 1974; mem. Task Force on U.S. Food Policy. Decorated Croix de Guerre (France); Order of Leopold II (Belgium). Mem. Inter-Am. (exec. sec. Havana conf. 1941), Fed. (asso. editor 1936-43) bar assns., Am. Soc. Internat. Law, Pi Sigma Alpha, Phi Alpha Delta. Club: Cosmos (Washington). Author: Reference Manual Latin-American Commercial Treaties (in English, Spanish), 1940; Law Dictionary; English, Español, Français, Deutsch; also numerous articles. Editor: World Peace Through Law-The Athens World Conference, 1964, The Washington Conference; Nuremberg Trial Record, 1946-47. Address: Chevy Chase, Md. Died Feb. 5, 1977.

EGGER, ROWLAND ANDREWS, educator, research adminstr.; b. Denison, Tex., Apr. 12, 1908; s. Ernest Linwood and Martha Aldora (Harmon) E.; A.B. cum laude, Southwestern U., 1926, LL.D., 1959; A.M., So. Meth. U., 1927; Ph.D., U. Mich., 1933; m. Gretchen Lee Savin MacIlwaine, Jan. 5, 1932 (dec. April 1952). Instr. govt. So. Methodist U., 1926-28; univ. fellow U. Mich., 1928-29; instr. politics Princeton, 1929-31; tech. cons. State of N.J., 1930-31; asso. prof. polit. sci., dir. bur. pub. adminstrn. U. Va., 1931-36, prof., 1936-64, chmn. Woodrow Wilson dept. fgn. affairs, 1956-64, dept. polit. sci., 1957-64, Edward R. Stettinius prof. fgn. affairs, 1962-64, acting dean faculty, 1962-63; prof. politics and pub. affairs Princeton, 1964-72, prof. emeritus, 1972-79; John Goodwin Tower prof. Southwestern U., 1972-73; Eugene McElvaney prof. So. Meth. U., 1973-77; cons. Inst. Govt., U. Va., 1977-79. Exec. officer Joint Com. on Pub. Adminstrn., Brussels, Belgium, 1935-36; vis. prof. internat. orgn., adminstrn. Columbia, 1947-48; vis. prof. Harvard, 1961, Nat. U. Argentina, 1967, U. Amsterdam, 1970; cons. White House, UN, U.S. Bur. Budget, U.S. Dept. Agr., UNESCO, Commn. on Orgn. Exec. Br. of Govt., dir. Budget, Commonwealth of Va., 1939-42; adminstv. and financial adviser Pres. Bolivia, 1942; gen. mgr., dir. Corporación Boliviana de Fomento, 1942-45, dir. and U.S. rep., 1945-47; spl. rep. President U.S. to Govt. Bolivia, 1961-62; asso. dir. Pub. Adminstrn. Clearing House, 1951-53; adminstrv. adviser Prime Minister Pakistan, 1953; Near East rep. Ford Found., 1954-56; mem. UN Adminstrv. Tribunal, 1949-51. Mem. bd. overseers vis. com. grad. sch. pub. adminstrn. Harvard, 1954-60; vice chmn., bd. trustees Inter-U. Case Program, 1956-74. Decorated officer Order Leopold (Belgium), knight comdr. Order of Condor (Bolivia); comdr. Order Cedars (Lebanon); recipient Haldane prize Royal Inst. Pub. Adminstrn., 1960. Sr. fellow Social Sci. Research Council, 1958-59. Mem. Royal Inst. Pub. Adminstrn., Am. Soc. Pub. Adminstrn., Am., Soc. polit. sci. assns., Internat. Inst. Adminstrv. Scis. (mem. council adminstrn., exec. com.), Nat. Acad. Pub. Adminstrn., Acad. Polit. Sci., S.A.R., Raven Soc., Phi Beta Kappa, Pi Kappa Alpha. Clubs: Farmington Country; Nassau (Princeton); Princeton (N.Y.); Cosmos (Washington, D.C.). Author: (with J.E. Gates) Municipal Ownership of Electrical Undertakings, 1937; Organization of Peace at the Administrative Level, 1945; (with Weldon Cooper) Research, Education and Regionalism, 1949; Improvement of Public Administration in Pakistan, 1961; Social and Economic Development of Bolivia, 1962; President and Congress, 1963; The President of the United States, 1967; Le Métier de Président, 1970; O Presidente dos Estados Unidos, 1974. Editor, Internat. Rev. Adminstrv. Scis., 1968—. Contbr. various revs. on govt. and adminstrn. Home: Charlottesville, Va. Died July 9, 1979; buried Charlottesville.

EGGERS, OTTO R., architect; b. N.Y.C., Aug. 4, 1882; ed. Cooper Union, 1900-02, Hornbostel Atelier, 1902-12, LeBrun scholar, 1912. Designer, John Russell Pope, 1909-22, mem. firm, 1922-37; partner Eggers & Higgins, N.Y.C., 1937—. Registered architect, N.Y. Fellow A.I.A.; mem. N.A.D., Brit. Royal Soc. Arts. Prin. works include: Marshall Field Estate, Huntington, L.I., 1925; First Presbyn. Ch., New Rochelle, N.Y., 1929; Nat. Gallery, 1941; Jefferson Meml. (award of Merit Washington Bd. Trade), 1943; Nat. Fire Ins. Co., Hartford, Conn., 1948; Stepinac High Sch., White Plains, N.Y. (certificate of Merit, N.Y. State Assn. Architects), 1948; Archtl. Center, N.Y. U. Author: Sketches of Early American Architecture, 1922.

EGGLESTON, ALBERT HORACE, clergyman; b. Sheffield, Eng., May 11, 1886; s. John Thomas and Eliza Ann (Levitt) E.; student Firth Coll., Eng.; Sheffield U., Eng.; m. Ruth Elizabeth Stobbs, Sept. 2, 1911; children—Donald Austin, Hilda Margaret; came to U.S., 1911, naturalized, 1930. Ordained ministry Presbyn. Ch., 1911; pastorate successively at Emerick, Ponca, Madison, Superior, North Platte, Neb., and 1st Presbyn. Ch., Kansas City, Mo.; pastor Emmanuel Presbyn. Ch., Long Beach, Calif., to 1944; retired. Trustee Kansas Convalescent Home. Contbr. to religious jours. Lecturer on art and literature. Home: Long Beach, Calif.

EGGLESTON, JOHN WILLIAM, former judge; b. Charlotte C.H., Va., June 18, 1886; s. David Quinn and Sue (Daniel) E.; student Hampden-Sydney Coll., Va., 1902-04; B.A., Washington and Lee U., 1906; M.A., 1907, LL.B., 1910, LL.D., 1949; m. Ella Carrington, Oct. 15, 1912; children—Mary (Mrs. W. Perry Moore, Jr.), Suzanne (Mrs. William W. Simpson), Eleanor Carrington (dec.). Tchr., Washington and Lee U., 1906-07, 1908-10, McGuire's Prep. Sch., Richmond, Va., 1907-08; admitted to Va. bar, 1909; practiced at Norfolk, Va., 1910-35; mem. firms Baker & Eggleston; Hughes, Vandeventer & Eggleston; Vandeventer, Eggleston & Black; mem. Va. State Senate, 1932-35, chmn. legislative com. which drafted Alcoholic Beverage Control Act; justice Supreme Ct. Appeals of Va., 1935-58, 1969-76, chief justice, 1958-69, ret., 1969. Mem. Va. State Bar Assns., Va. Hist. Soc., Order of Coif, Phi Beta Kappa, Omicron Delta Kappa, Phi Delta Phi, Kappa Sigma. Democrat. Presbyn. Clubs: Princess Anne Country (Virginia Beach); Virginia (Norfolk). Home: Norfolk, Va. Died May 18, 1976.

EGLESTON, NATHANIEL H., army officer; b. N.J., Feb. 13, 1884; A.B., Williams Coll., Mass., 1906; LL.B., N.Y. Law Sch., 1908; comd. 2d lt. Cav., N.Y. Nat. Guard, Mar. 1915; 1st lt., Fed. service, July 1917; capt., 1918; maj. Cav., N.Y. Nat. Guard, 1921, advanced to brig. gen. May 11, 1933; in Fed. Service, Feb. 1941, in command of 102d Coast Arty. Brigade (antiaircraft), Camp Stewart, Ga. Awarded Silver Star Citation with Oak Leaf Cluster, Purple Heart, World War I. Address: Camp Stewart, Ga. *

EGLEVSKY, ANDRE, ballet dancer; b. Moscow, Russia, Dec. 21, 1917; s. Eugene Petrovitch and Zoe Alexievna (Obraszoff) E.; studied ballet with Maria Nevelska, Nice, France, 1928, Volinine, Paris 1930, N. Legat, London, 1934, also Fokine, Egorova, Kchessinska; m. Leda Anchutin, Dec. 27, 1938; children—Andre, Paul, Marina. Came to U.S., 1937, naturalized, 1943. Mem. corps de ballet col. de Basil Ballet Russe, 1933, 1st dancer, 1934-35, partner Davilova, Toumanoua Baronova; with Leon Woitzekowsky Ballet, Rene Blum Ballet de Monte Carlo, 1935, under Fokine, 1936-37; joined Balanchine Am. Ballet, 1935; appeared Dwight Deere Wiman mus. The Great Lady, 1938; with Leonide Massine Ballet Russe De Monte Carlo, 1938-42, on tour Ballet Theater, U.S., S.A., 1942-44; with Marquis de Cuevas Ballet Internat., Massine Ballet Russe Highlights, 1944-46; with original Ballet Russe, 1946, Maruquis de Cuevas Grand Ballet, 1947; with N.Y.C. Ballet, until 1958; operator, owner sch. dancing, Massapequa, N.Y., 1958-77; artistic dir. Eglevsky Ballet Co. L.I.; prodns. include Coppelia, Sleeping Beauty, Cinderella, Nutcracker, toured with Hudson Valley Philharmonic; tchr. Sch. Am. Ballet. Co-choreographer: pas de trois for Pa. Ballet, Dance Repertory Co., N.C. Dance Theatre. Address: Massapequa, N.Y. Died Dec. 4, 1977.

EHRLICH, MELVIN JOSEPH, lawyer; b. Chgo., Aug. 20, 1895; s. Samuel Davis and Theresa Judith (Ohrenstein) E.; J.D., Chgo.-Kent Coll. Law, 1917; m. Kathleen Sawers, Apr. 25, 1936; children—Susan, Martha Judith. Admitted to Ill. bar, 1917; real estate title examiner Chgo. Title & Trust Co., 1919-27; practice in Chgo., 1927-76; partner firm Ettelson, O'Hagan, Ehrlich & Frankel, 1955-76; thcr. Lane Evening High Sch., 1921-27; lectr. John Marshall Law Sch., 1928-30. Served with USNRF, 1917-19. Mem. Chgo. Bar Assn. Mason (Shriner). Home: Chicago, Ill. Died Nov. 16, 1976.

EHRMANN, WINSTON WALLACE, sociologist, coll. provost; b. Reno, May 17, 1912; s. Emil Ernest and Imogene (Irwin) E.; student Mass. Inst. Tech., 1930-31; B.S., Yale, 1934, Ph.D., 1938; m. Sarah Margaret Berlin, Sept. 13, 1934; children—Gretchen (Mrs. Bruce Maclachlan), Sally (Mrs. Andrew Baggs). Indsl. engr. U.S. Rubber Co., 1935-36; asst. prof. U. Fla., 1938-40, asso. prof., 1940-46, prof. sociology, 1946-59; prof. sociology Colo. State U., 1959-62; asso. sec. AAUP, Washington, 1962-66; prof. sociology Cornell Coll., Mt. Vernon, Iowa, 1966-77, dean of coll., 1969-75, provost, 1970-77; tech. cons. White House Conf. on Children and Youth, 1960; vis. lectr. Ind. U., 1951, Miss. State Coll. for Women, 1955, Goddard Coll., 1963, Sch. Medicine U. Calif., 1967, Okla. State U., 1968, Ind. State U., 1970. Served from 1st lt. to col., C.E., AUS, 1941-46. Decorated Bronze Star. Fellow Am. Sociol. Assn.; mem. AAUP (mem. council 1960-63, asso. editor Bull., 1962-66), Iowa Sociol. Soc. (pres. 1968-69), Phi Beta Kappa. Author: Premarital Dating Behavior, 1959. Asso. editor: Am. Sociol. Rev., 1960-63. Contbr. articles to profl. jours. Home: Mount Vernon, Iowa. Died June 20, 1978; buried Mt. Vernon.

EIBLING, HAROLD HENRY, ednl. cons.; b. Dola, O., Aug. 5, 1905; s. Henry W. and Sarah (Stanyer) E.; B.S., Ohio No. U., 1926, Ped.D. (hon.), 1959; M.A., Ohio State U., 1932, Ph.D., 1950; D.Sc. in Edn. (hon.), Mt. Union Coll., 1953; LL.D., Miami U., Oxford, O., 1963; m. Evelyn Agner, Aug. 14, 1929; children—Judith Anne, Stephen Harold, David Michael. Tchr., prin., supt. Liberty Twp. Sch., Findlay, O., 1926-36; supt. Maumee (O.) Pub. Schs., 1936-47, Elyria (O.) Pub. Schs., 1947-49; asst. supt. schs., Akron, O., 1949-50; supt. schs., Canton, O., 1950-56, Columbus, O., 1956-71; edn. cons., 1971-76. Dir. Columbus Savs. & Loan, City Nat. Bank. Bd. dirs. Franklin County chpt. A.R.C.; trustee Ohio No. U. Recipient Educator's medal Freedoms Found., 1963; Liberty Bell award Columbus Bar Assn., 1964; Boss of Year award Jr. C. of C., 1964; Supt. of Year award Ohio Edn. Assn., 1966; Distinguished Citizen awards Pub. Relations Soc. Am., 1968, Columbus Dental Soc., 1969; honor citation Ohio legislature, 1969. Mem. Assn. Sch. Adminstrs. (pres. 1970-71), Columbus C. of C. (dir.), Central-Ohio Tchrs. Assn. (pres. 1959). Presbyn. Mason (33 deg.). Clubs: University (pres.), Rotary (pres.). Co-author history textbooks: World Background for American History, 1968; Our Country, 1969; Great Names in American History, 1968; The Story of America, 1969; History of Our United States, 1969; Foundations of Freedom, 1973; Challenge and Change, 1973; United States History, 1974. Contbr. articles to ednl. jours. Home: Columbus, Ohio. Died Jan. 2, 1976.

EICHELBERGER, CLARK MELL, assn. exec.; b. Freeport, Ill., July 29, 1896; s. Joseph Elmer and Olive (Clark) E.; student Northwestern U., 1914-17, U. Chgo., 1919-20; LL.D., Kalamazoo Coll., 1964, So. Ill. U., 1967, Haverford Coll., 1968; m. Rose Kohler, Oct. 6, 1924. Lectr. nat. and internat. affairs Radcliffe Chautauqua System, Washington, 1922-27; dir. Mid-West office League of Nations Assn., 1927-34; nat. dir. League of Nations Assn., later Am. Assn. for UN, now UN Assn. U.S., 1934-64, v.p. 1964-68; temp. appointment League Nations Secretariat, 1938. Commn. to Study Orgn. of Peace, 1939-64, chmn., 1964-68, exec. dir., 1968-74, hon. chmn., 1974—. Dir. Commn. to Defend Am. by Aiding the Allies, 1940-41; cons. to State Dept., 1942-43; cons. Am. del. San Francisco Conf., 1945. Served with U.S. Army and A.E.F., 1917-19. Decorated chevalier Legion of Honor (France), 1934; recipient Man of Peace award UN: We Believe orgn., 1973. Presbyn. Club: Cosmos (Washington). Author: The United Nations Charter;

What Was Done at San Francisco; UN: The First Ten Years, 1955; UN: The First Fifteen Years, 1960; UN: The First Twenty Years, 1965; UN: The First Twenty-Five Years, 1970; Organizing for Peace: A Personal History of the United Nations, 1977. Chmn. drafting com. New the Environment, The Reform of Legal Institutions, 1972. Home: New York, N.Y. Died Jan. 26, 1980.

EICHELBERGER, FREDERICK OTHO (IKE'-L-BUR'-GER), ex-city ofcl.; b. Dayton, O., Aug. 3, 1883; s. Daniel Arthur and Anna Neil (Crum) E.; ed. public schs. Dayton; m. Olive Manning, Jan. 30, 1907; children—John Frederick, Robert Manning (deceased). Pvt. practice of engring. and r.r. constrn., Dayton, O., 1901-06; staff engrs. office City of Dayton, 1906-12, 1st asst. city engr., 1912-15, city engr., 1915-20, dir. pub. service, 1920-21, city mgr., 1921-48. Member Nat. Municipal League, Internat. City Mgrs. Assn., S.A.R., Y.M.C.A. Republican. Protestant. Mason (33 deg., Shriner). Clubs: Engrs. (past pres.), Auto City (Dayton, O.). Home: Dayton.

EIGES, HERBERT M., lawyer; b. Elmira, N.Y., Nov. 29, 1904; s. Isaac and Lena Phillips E.; LL.B., U. Mich., 1927; Admitted to Mich. bar, 1927, since practiced in Mich.; partner firm Karbel, Eiges, Rothstein & Karbel, Detroit; sec. Detroit Temperature Engrs., Livonia, Mich., also dir.; sec. Foamade Industries, Inc., Royal Oak, Mich., also dir.; counsel Mich. Men's Apparel Assn. Served with USAAF, 1942-43. Mem. Am., Mich., Detroit bar assns., Am. Arbitration Assn., Am. Judicature Soc. Home: Southfield, Mich. Died Sept. 1978.

EIMERS, HOWARD GORDON, ins. co. exec.; b. Milw., June 28, 1926; s. Edward and Hilda (Brushaber) E.; B.S. in Bus. Adminstrn. with distinction, Northwestern U., 1950; M.A. in Math., U. Mich., 1951; m. Joyce Elsie Taylor, Jan. 14, 1950; children—Dennis John, Paul Timothy, David James. Actuary, Am. Life & Accident Ins. Co. Ky., 1951-53; with Washington Nat. Ins. Co., Evanston, Ill., from 1953, actuary, 1958-62, chief actuary, 1962-63, v.p., 1963-69, actuary, 1963-71, sr. v.p., 1969-80, also dir.; v.p., dir. Washington Nat. Corp.; chmn. bd. Washington Nat. Life Ins. Co. N.Y. C.L.U. Fellow Am. Acad. Actuaries, Soc. Actuaries, Life Mgmt. Inst.; mem. Beta Gamma Sigma, Alpha Tau Omega. Home: Northfield, Ill. Died Mar. 25, 1980.

EISELEY, LOREN COREY, author, anthropologist; b. Lincoln, Nebr., Sept. 3, 1907; s. Clyde and Daisy (Corey) E.; A.B., U. Nebr., 1933; A.M., U. Pa., 1935, Ph.D., 1937; Social Sci. Research Council postdoctoral fellow Columbia and Am. Mus. Natural History, 1940-41; numerous hon. degrees; m. Mabel Langdon, Aug. 29, 1938. Mem. Morrill Paleontol. Expdns. U. Nebr., 1931-33, U. Pa. and Carnegie Expdn. to Southwest, 1934, Smithsonian Expdn. No. Colo., 1935; asst. prof. sociology and anthropology U. Kans., 1937-42, asso. prof., 1942-44; prof. sociology and anthropology, head dept. Oberlin (Ohio) Coll., 1944-47; vis. prof. anthropology Columbia, summers 1946, 50, U. Calif., Berkeley, summer 1949, Harvard U., summer 1952; prof. anthropology U. Pa., 1947-59, chmn. dept., 1947-59, provost, 1959-61, prof. anthropology and history of sci., chmn. dept. history of sci., 1961-63, Benjamin Franklin prof. anthropology and history of sci., 1961-77, curator of Early Man U. Pa. Mus., 1948-77, mem. U. Pa. Mus. archaeol. survey Mont., 1973. Host, narrator prize-winning ednl. series NBC-TV, 1966-68; mem. com. interrelationships of pleistocene research NRC, 1947-50, vice chmn. Div. of Psychology and Anthropology, 1950-52; fellow Center for Advanced Study Behavioral Scis., Stanford, Calif., 1961-62; mem. Presdl. Task Force Conservation Natural Beauty, 1965; adv. bd. nat. parks Dept. Interior, 1966-72, council mem., 1972-77; mem. coll. electors Hall Fame for Gt. Americans; mem. adv. bd. Center for Advanced Study in Religion and Sci. Bd. dirs. Samuel S. Fels Found. Research grants Wenner-Gren Found. Anthropology, 1952-53; Guggenheim Found. fellow, 1963-64; recipient Page One award Newspaper Guild Phila., 1960, Phila. Arts Festival award, 1962, Phila. Art Alliance medal achievement, 1967; Distinguished Nebraskan award, 1974. Fellow Am. Acad. Arts and Scis., AAAS (v.p., chmn. sect. L, 1969, mem. Westinghouse sci. awards com.); mem. Am. Assn. Phys. Anthropologists, Am. Anthrop. Assn. (v.p. 1948), Soc. for Am. Archaeology, Phila. Anthrop. Soc. (pres. 1948), Am. Philos. Soc., Nat. Inst. Arts and Letters, World Acad. Arts and Scis., Phi Beta Kappa, Sigma Xi. Author: The Immense Journey, 1957; Darwin's Century, 1958 (Nat. Phi Beta Kappa sci. award, Athenaeum of Phila. lit. award, 1958); The Firmament of Time, 1960 (John Burroughs Asso. medal 1960; Lecomte du Noûy award 1961); The unexpected Universe, 1969; The Invisible Pyramid, 1970; The Night Country, 1971 (Athenaeum of Phila. lit. award); Notes of an Alchemist (verse), 1972; The Innocent Assassins (verse), 1973; The Man Who Saw Through Time, 1973; All The Strange Hours (autobiography), 1975; posthumous books include: Another Kind of Autumn, 1977; The Star Thrower, 1978; Darwin and the Mysterious Mr. X, 1979; All the Night Wings, 1979; also articles and verse in popular mags. Co-editor: An Appraisal of Anthropology Today, 1953; Home: Wynnewood, Pa. Died July 9, 1977.

EISENDRATH, MAURICE NATHAN, rabbi; b. Chgo., July 10, 1902; s. Nathan Julius and Clara (Oesterreicher) E.; A.B., U. Cin., 1925, LL.D., 1957; rabbi, Hebrew Union Coll., Cinc., 1926, D.D., 1945; LL.D., Brown U., 1964; m. Rosa Brown, Nov. 24, 1926 (dec. July 1963); m. 2d, Rita Hands, June 1964; stepchildren—Linda, Charles. Rabbi, Charleston, W.Va., 1926-29, Holy Blossom Temple, Toronto, Cin., O., 1943-46; pres. Union Am. Hebrew Congregations, from 1946, pres. for life, from 1952, rep. to Synagogue Council Am. Bd. govs. Hebrew Union Coll.-Jewish Inst. Religion; bd. dirs. Nat. Jewish Welfare Bd.; vice chmn. Am. bd. World Jewish Congress; mem. theologian's com. Am. Assn. for Internat. Office of Edn.; v.p. World Union for Progressive Judaism; nat. co-chmn. commns. on religious orgns. Nat. Conf. Christians and Jews; mem. nat. council Joint Distbn. Com. Campaign; mem. Nat. Community Relations Adv. Council; mem. exec. bd. Central Conf. Am. Rabbis. Author: The Never Failing Stream, 1939; Can Faith Survive, 1958. Contbr. to Dimensions, American Judaism, Jewish Layman. Deceased.

EISENHOWER, MAMIE GENEVA DOUD, wife former Pres. U.S.; b. Boone, Ia.; Nov. 14, 1896; d. John Sheldon and Elivera M. (Carison) Doud; ed. Miss Wolcott's Sch.; L.H.D. (hon.), Colo. Woman's Coll., 1946; LL.D. (hon.), St. Joseph Coll., 1959; m. Dwight David Eisenhower, July 1, 1916; 1 son, John Sheldon Doud. Hon. pres. Girl Scouts of Am. Hon. mem. Woman's Med. Coll. of Pa. Decorated Order of Malta, Italy, 1952, Cavalier Order of So. Cross, Brazil, 1946, Grand Cross Order of Honor and Merit, Cuba, 1953. Mem. Daus. of Colo., Ia. Hist. Soc. (hon.), Distinguished Daus. Pa., D.A.R., Army and Navy Union Aux., Daus. Cin. (hon.). Republican. Presbyterian. Home: Gettysburg, Pa. Died Nov. 1, 1979.

EISTER, ALLAN WARDELL, sociologist, educator; b. Upper Sandusky, Ohio, Feb. 10, 1915; s. Allen Bertram and Helen Louise (Wardell) E.; A.B., DePauw U., 1936; M.A., Am. U., 1937; Ph.D., U. Wis., 1945; m. Dorothy M. Zulick, Jan. 2, 1948; children—Karen E., David A. Faculty Hood Coll., 1944-46, So. Meth. U., 1946-53; mem. faculty Wellesley Coll., 1953-79, prof. sociology, 1962-79, chmn. dept., 1960-65, 71-74, 77-79; Albert J. Beveridge fellow, 1936-38; Fulbright lectr. U. Karachi (Pakistan), 1959-60; vis. fellow All Souls Coll., Oxford, 1967. Faculty fellow Ford Found., 1952-53; grantee Am. Philos. Soc., 1959-60; grantee joint com. Near and Middle East studies Social Sci. Research Council and Am. Council Learned Socs., 1959-60; grantee Am. Assn. Middle East Studies, 1963, 65. Fellow Am. Sociol. Assn. (life mem.), life mem. Am. Acad. Polit. and Social Sci.; mem. Eastern Sociol. Soc., Mass. Sociol. Assn., Soc. Sci. Study Religion (pres. 1976-77), Assn. for Sociology of Religion (asso. editor Sociol. Analysis 1978-79), Phi Beta Kappa. Mem. Soc. of Friends. Author: The U.S. and the A.B.C. Powers, 1889-1906, 1950; Drawing Room Conversion: A Sociological Account of the Oxford Group Movement, 1950. Editor: Changing Perspectives in the Scientific Study of Religion, 1974. Home: Wellesley, Mass. Died Mar. 22, 1979; interred at Easton, Pa.

ELBERT, ROBERT GEORGE, business exec., retired; b. Frederick, Md., Jan. 22, 1886; s. George Cleveland and Emma C. (Bruer) E.; ed. High Sch. and Frederick (Md.) Coll.; m. Marian C. Bourne (dau. Commodore Frederick G. Bourne), Sept. 6, 1922; 1 dau., Patricia Bourne. Asso. with Boomer-DuPont hotel interests, in publicity and promotion depts., 1912-17, and following the World War; with Peabody Houghteling & Co., investments, N.Y. City, 1923-25; former pres. and chmn. bd. Aeolian Co. and Internat. Holding Co.; pres. and dir. Oakbourne Corp.; dir. Aeolian Am. Corp.; Former mem. advisory bd. Central Hanover Bank & Trust Co. (Plaza br.), N.Y. City; mem. Business Advisory Council, U.S. Dept. Commerce (former chmn. Air Commerce Planning and Merchant Marine coms.; mem. Aviation Advisory Bd.), 1933-39; served on industrial bd., NRA, 1933-35; assisted in organizing Nat. Emergency Bd., 1934; served on President's Allotment Bd., 1935. Served as lieutenant, aviator U.S. Army, World War I; now colonel, U.S. Army Air Force. Has made extensive studies of social welfare activities, public works, etc., in foreign countries. Episcopalian. Clubs: Metropolitan (N.Y. City); Nassau Country; Garden City Golf; The Creek (L.I.); 1925 F St (Washington, D.C.); Surf, Indian Creek, Country (Miami Beach, Fla.); Chevy Chase (Md.); Burning Tree (Bethesda, Md.); Palmetto (Aiken, S.C.). Author: Unemployment and Relief, 1934; An Answer to the Townsend Plan (pamphlet), 1936. Home: Elbourne, Manhasset, L.I.; and Elbourne, Aiken, S.C.

ELBERT, WILLIAN JOSEPH, distbn. co. exec.; b. Bklyn., Nov. 30, 1916; s. Jacob J. and Kathryn (Sheerin) E.; B.B.A., Coll. City N.Y., 1936; m. Anna H. Hoddersen, July 4, 1942; children—William J., Robert E. Accountant, Price, Waterhouse & Co., N.Y.C., 1936-47; treas. Swanee Paper Corp., N.Y.C., 1947-58; sec.-controller Stahl-Meyer, Inc., N.Y.C., 1959-61; financial cons., N.Y.C., 1961-63; dir. corporate accounting Foremost Dairies, Inc., San Francisco; v.p., controller Foremost-McKesson, Inc. (merger Foremost Dairies, Inc. and McKesson & Robbins, Inc.). Served to 1st lt. AUS, 1943-46. C.P.A., N.Y. Mem. Am. Inst. C.P.A.'s, N.Y., Calif. socs. C.P.A.'s. Mason (Shriner). Clubs: Olympic, World Trade, Mchts. Exchange (San Francisco). Home: San Francisco, Calif. Died June 19, 1980.

ELDER, ALBERT LAWRENCE, nutrition inst. dir.; b. Lexington, Ill., June 19, 1901; s. George Clinton and Ann (Rowlands) E.; A.B., U. Ill., 1923, M.S., 1925, Ph.D., 1928, D.Sc., 1962; m. Ruth Dixon, Aug. 31, 1925; children—Louise (Mrs. Marshall Gillispie), John. Research instr. Oberlin Coll., 1928-30; asst. prof., then prof. Syracuse U., 1930-41; dir. research Corn Products Co., 1944-59, co-ordinator research, 1959-61; director Corn Products Institute Nutrition, from 1961. Research medicinal chems., proteins, starches. Head chem. adviser WPB, 1941-44. Mem. Research and Devel. Assos. Food and Container Inst. (pres. 1951-53), Am. Chem. Soc. (pres. 1960), A.A.A.S., America Inst. Chemists, Inst. Food Technologists, Soc. Chem. Industry, Indsl. Research Inst., NRC, Sigma Xi, Sigma Pi, Alpha Chi Sigma, Phi Lambda Upsilon. Clubs: Chemists (Chgo. and N.Y.C.). Author: Demonstrations and Experiments in General Chemistry, 1937; Laboratory Manual of General Chemistry, 1941; Textbook of Chemistry, 1941. Home: LaGrange, Ill. Died June 16, 1976.

ELDER, OMAR FRANKLIN, JR., lawyer, broadcasting and film co. exec.; b. Atlanta, May 24, 1919; s. Omar Franklin and Marielen (Hargrove) E.; A.B. with honors, Emory U., 1940; LL.B., Harvard, 1943; m. Betty Anne Nyman, Nov. 16, 1946; children—Betty Anne, Omar Franklin III. Asso. O'Brien, Driscoll & Raferty, N.Y.C., 1946-47; admitted to N.Y. bar, 1947; with ABC, N.Y.C., 1947-64, beginning as atty., successively asst. sec. 1951-56, asst. gen. counsel, 1953-59, sec., 1956-59, v.p., 1959-64, gen. counsel TV network, 1959-61, gen. atty., 1961-64; asst. sec. Am. Broadcasting Paramount Theatres, Inc., ABC Radio Network, Inc., Blue Network Co., Inc.; sec., dir. ABC TV Center Co., Inc., Fine Arts Enterprises, Inc., ABC-TV Network Services of Mich., Inc.; sec. WXYZ, Inc., Detroit, Allegheny Broadcasting Corp., Pitts.; atty. Metro-Goldwyn-Mayer, Inc., 1964-69, CBS, Inc., 1970-80. Served from ensign to lt. USNR, 1942-46. Mem. Am., Fed. Communications bar assns., Assn. Bar City N.Y., Radio and TV Execs. Soc. (dir., v.p., sec.), Acad. TV Arts and Scis., Internat. Radio and TV Soc., N.Y. Southern Soc., Chi Phi. Clubs: Harvard, Athletic (N.Y.C.); Piedmont Driving, Capital City (Atlanta). Home: Greenwich, Conn. Died Apr. 13, 1980; buried Putnam Cemetery, Greenwich.

ELDER, (JAMES) WALTER, congressman; b. Grand Prairie, Tex., Oct. 5, 1882; s. John F. and Amanda (Martain) E.; ed. Baylor U., Tex., 1895-01; m. Ida Moffett, of Ruston, La., Dec. 3, 1904. Admitted to La. bar, 1903; mem. firm of Sholars, Elder & Benoit, Monroe, La.; former partner of Gov. L. E. Hall; served as mayor of Farmerville, La.; mem. La. State Senate, 25th Dist., 1908-12; mem. 63d Congress (1913-15), 5th La. Dist.; Democrat. Baptist. Mason, K.T. Clubs: Country (Monroe, La.), Army and Navy (Washington). Home: Monroe, La.

ELDRED, MYRTLE MEYER (ELD'RED), writer; b. Lincoln, Neb., Sept. 10, 1885; d. William Mendel and Harriet Ann (Miller) Meyer; student U. of Chicago, summer 1921, Teachers' Coll. (Columbia), summer 1922 and winter 1929; m. William Merte Eldred, Sept. 11, 1907 (divorced 1920); children—Janice Meyer (Mrs. Walter Morris), Harriet Ann (Mrs. Raymond Thompson), William M. (dec.), Philip David. Newspaper columnist since 1918; now conducts syndicated column "Your Baby and Mine." Mem. Child Study Assn. (New York), Nat. Council of Family Relations (New York), Child Study Group (Des Moines), Ia. League for Planned Parenthood (Des Moines), Family Social Service, Travellers Aid, Raymond Blank Memorial Hospital Guild; member League for Women Voters. Democrat. Clubs: Iowa Writers', Des Moines Women's. Author: For the Young Mother (with Helen Cowles Le Cron), 1921; Your Baby and Mine, 1931; (a new) Your Baby and Mine, 1951. Home: Des Moines, Ia.

ELDRIDGE, FRANCIS REED, commercial expert; b. Haddonfield, N.J., May 28, 1889; s. Francis Reed and Viola (League) E.; grad. Baltimore City Coll., 1908; student George Washington U. (non-grad.); m. Kathleen Sanzo, Nov. 16, 1912; children—Francis Reed, Karin Monica, Richard Adams, Patricia Darling. Student interpreter, Am. Embassy, Tokio, Japan, 1909-11; dep. consul gen. and interpreter, Yokahama 1911-12; asst. sec. and treas. Nipponophone Co., Ltd. Japan, 1912-14; with Swift & Co., packers, Columbia and Augusta, Ga., 1914-18; chief Far Eastern Div. of Bur. Foreign and Domestic Commerce, under Dept. of Commerce, 1918-26; asst. registrar, later registrar China Trade Act Cos., 1922-25; vice pres. Asiatic Selling Co., Ltd., 1926-27; New York comml. agent Dept. of Commerce, 1927; executive v.p. Am. Mfrs. Export Assn., 1930. Professor of foreign trade, New

York U. Sch. of Commerce, 1930; head Japanese Dept. Columbia Univ. Extension, 1933; chief Commercial Intelligence Div., 1934; Internat. editor, U.S. Dept. of Commerce, Washington, 1939; chief statistician U.S.C.G., 1940, historian, 1943; spl. activity with defense effort, 1951. Major O.R.C., Military Intelligence Div., Gen. Staff, U.S. Army, 1922-31; lt. comdr., U.S. Coast Guard, 1943-46. Mem. Am. Econ. Assn. Episcopalian. Mason. Author several books since 1921, latest: Science Can Wage Peace (General Semantics), 1949. Home: Washington, D.C. Died Nov. 28, 1976.

ELKINS, EARL COOK, physician; b. Spearfish, S.D., Sept. 19, 1904; s. William Scott and Harriet (Cook) E.; B.S., Buena Vista Coll., 1927, M.D., George Washington U., 1933; m. E. Elizabeth Williams, Jan. 25, 1935; children—Elizabeth Ann (Mrs. Ronald Rosanove), E. Robert, Thomas W., Joan G. Intern, Central Dispensary and Emergency Hosp., Washington, 1933-34, asst. resident surgeon, 1934-35; fellow Mayo Found., Rochester, Minn., 1935-39, prof. phys. medicine and rehab., 1961-69; cons. sect. phys. medicine and rehab. Mayo Clinic, Rochester, 1939-69, head sect., 1958-65, sr. cons., 1965-69, emeritus, 1969-77. Chmn., Am. Registry Phys. Therapists, 1953-68. Mem. Minn. Adv. Council Hosp. Constrn., 1955-73. Diplomate Am. Bd. Phys. Medicine and Rehab. (sec.-treas.). Fellow A.C.P.; mem. A.M.A., (sec. sect. phys. med. 1957-63), Am. Congress Phys. Medicine and Rehab. (pres. 1948-49; Distinguished Service Key award 1955), Am. Acad. Phys. Medicine and Rehab., Alumni Assn. Mayo Found., Sigma Xi. Author numerous articles in field. Home: Rochester, Minn. Died Apr. 5, 1977; interred Oakwood Cemetery, Rochester.

ELL, CARL STEPHENS, educator; b. Staunton, Ind., Nov. 14, 1887; son Jacob and Alice (Stephens) E.; A.B., De Pauw U., 1909; S.B., Mass. Inst. Tech., 1911, M.S., 1912; Ed. M., Harvard, 1932; Sc.D., De Pauw U., 1935; LL.D., Tufts Coll., 1948, U. R.I., 1955, Emerson Coll., 1956; L.H.D., Boston Univ., 1952; D.Sc. in Edn. (hon.), Northeastern Univ., 1959; m. Etta May Kinnear, June 10, 1913; 1 dau., Dorothy. Dean Sch. Engring., Northeastern U., 1917-40, v.p., 1925-40, pres., 1940-59, hon. chancellor, president emeritus, 1959-81; director Arkwright Mutual Insurance Co.; corporator Charlestown Savs. Bank. Mem. corporation, trustee N.E. Deaconess Hosp., Northeastern University. Fellow Am. Soc. Arts and Scis.; mem. Am. Soc. Engring. Edn., Engring. Socs. N.E., N.E. Assn. Colls. and Secondary Schs., Boston Soc. Civil Engrs., Chamber of Commerce, Society for Advancement of Education, Tau Beta Pi, Phi Beta Kappa, Delta Upsilon. Phi Delta Kappa. Methodist. Mason. Clubs: Union, Algonquin, University, Brae Burn Country. Home: Newtonville, Mass. Died Apr. 17, 1981.

ELLENBERGER, HOWARD BOWMAN (EL'EN-BER-GER), univ. prof.; b. Dallas, Ia., Nov. 15, 1882; son Daniel P. and Julia M. (Yambert) E.; B.S.A., Ia. State Coll., 1905; M.S., Cornell U., 1915, Ph.D., 1917; m. Priscilla Flatt Mills, Dec. 29, 1910. Began as herdsman in Ill. and Minn., 1903-04; asst. supt. Sinnissippi Farms, Ill., 1905; foreman of horse barns in Ill., 1906; supt. farms in Mo., 1907-12, in Ia., 1913; instr., Cornell U., 1914-17; specialist dairy mfg., Vt. Dept. Agr., summers 1915-17; asso. prof. animal and dairy husbandry, U. of Vt., 1917, prof. and head dept., 1918-48. Visited agrl. coll. in each State of U.S., 1929-30. Chmn. N.E. Governors' Dairy Advisory Bd. and adminstr., Boston Milk Market Area, 1931-33. Organized Vt. Dairy Plant Operators and Mgrs. Assn. (exec. sec. 1921-41, now honorary sec.). Mem. Am. Dairy Science Assn. (chmn. eastern div. 1926; prodn. sec., 1930; pres. nat. assn. 1931; dir. 1940-43), Am. Soc. Animal Prodn. (North Atlantic vice-pres., 1936; chmn. North Atlantic branch), Sigma Xi, Alpha Zeta.

ELLENBOGEN, FRANKLYN, lawyer; b. N.Y.C., Oct. 4, 1904; s. Joseph and Mary (Weiss) E.; LL.B., N.Y. Law Sch., 1925; m. Molly Berman, Feb. 10, 1928 (dec. 1979); children—Franklyn (dec.), Marjorie. Admitted to N.Y. bar, 1925; individual practice, N.Y.C., 1932-54; partner firm Ellenbogen & Klein, N.Y.C., 1954-79, Burns, Jackson, Miller, Summit & Jacoby, N.Y.C., 1979; sec. Soundesign Corp., Jersey City. Mem. Bar Assn. City N.Y. Democrat. Jewish. Home: New York, N.Y. Died Nov. 11, 1979.

ELLENSTEIN, MEYER C., lawyer, ex-mayor; b. New York, N.Y., Oct. 15, 1886; s. Max and Libby (Bzuroff) E.; D.D.S., Columbia U., 1912; LL.B., N.J. Law Sch., 1925; m. Hilda Hausner, Mar. 15, 1913 (div. Sept. 22, 1943); children—Miriam (Mrs. Richard Proskauer), Ruth (Mrs. Ralph Wahl), Robert; m. 2d, Ruth Tlusty, Sept. 25, 1943. Shoe clerk, 1901-09; in practice of dentistry, 1912-25; admitted to N.J. bar, 1926; in practice of law, Newark, 1926-32 and since 1941; mayor of Newark, 1933-41; dir. dept. public works, City of Newark, since May 1945. Home: 19 Lyons Av.

ELLIMAN, DOUGLAS LUDLOW, real estate broker; b. Flushing, N.Y., May 24, 1882; s. William and Mary Lawrence (Bogert) E.; student Berkeley Sch., N.Y., 1897-98, Cutler Sch., N.Y., 1898-99; m. Theodora Trowbridge, Oct. 20, 1900; children—Douglas Trowbridge, George Trowbridge, Ludlow; m. 2d, Katherine Scales Moon, Dec. 9, 1929; children—Mary Lawrence, Edward Scales. Clk. Vermilye & Co., bankers, 1899-1903; broker and officer Pease & Elliman, 1903-11; organized Douglas L. Elliman & Co., Inc., 1911, now chmn. bd., dir.; organizer, pres., dir. Douglas L. Elliman Brokerage Corp.; v.p., dir. Midtown Underwriters, Inc., Underhill Soc., 58th and Park Av., Incorporated; member board of trustees Greenwich Savs. Bank and numerous bldg. projects, N.Y.; ex-pres. Real Estate Bd. of N.Y., Inc. Served as ensign U.S.N.R.F., 1918. Member St. Nicholas Society, St. George Soc., Commerce and Industry Assn. Mem. Real Estate Bd. N.Y.; adv. com. Ladies Christian Union. Mem. N.Y. Bldg. Congress (life), Nat. Assn. Real Estate Bds., Pilgrims U.S., Mil. Order World Wars, USNR Officers Assn., Am. Legion, Navy Leagues U.S. (dir.). Methodist. Clubs: Racquet and Tennis, Piping Rock. Home: N.Y.C.

ELLIMAN, GEORGE TROWBRIDGE, mgmt. cons.; b. N.Y.C., Dec. 17, 1905; s. Douglas Ludlow and Theodora Polhemus (Trowbridge) E.; grad. St. Paul's Sch., 1923; A.B. magna cum laude, Princeton, 1928; grad. Nat. War Coll., 1958; m. Natica De Acosta, June 4, 1931; 1 son, Peter Bogert. With Doubleday, Doran & Co., 1928-33; advt. mgr. Sat. Rev. Lit., 1933-36; with Butler & Baldwin, real estate, N.Y.C., 1936-39; with U.S. govt. agys. engaged in def. and war work, 1939-42; exec. dir. Office Fgn. Liquidation, State Dept., 1945-48; asst. dir. tech. assistance div. ECA, 1948-51; dir. fgn. div. NPA, 1951-52; adviser fgn. activities Dept. Commerce, 1952-59; joined U.S. fgn. service, 1959; comml. attache Am. Embassy, Rome, 1959-64; dir. internat. activities staff Bus. and Def. Services Adminstrn. U.S. Dept. Commerce, 1964-69, dir. U.S. mission on trade and indsl. devel. to Ireland, Portugal, 1966-67, spl. asst. ILO affairs, also mem. U.S. delegation to ILO, 1967-69, mem. selection bd. Fgn. Service, 1969; self-employed cons. mgmt., The Plains, Va., 1969-77. Served to lt. comdr. USNR, 1942-45. Home: The Plains, Va. Died Jan. 19, 1977; buried Warrenton, Va.

ELLINGSON, HAROLD VICTOR, physician; b. Parker, Idaho, Feb. 26, 1913; s. Ole and Katherine (Friel) E.; B.S., U. Idaho, 1935; M.S., U. Wis., 1936, Ph.D., 1939, M.D., 1941; M.P.H., Johns Hopkins, 1946; m. Frances J. Kadulski, Nov. 18, 1944. Intern Wis. Gen. Hosp., Madison, 1941-42; commd. 1st lt. U.S. Army, 1942; trans. to USAF, 1949; advanced through grades to col., 1956; comdr. USAF Med. Service Sch., 1959-62; comdr. Sch. Aerospace Medicine, 1963-66: re., i96o; prof., chmn. dept. preveniive meoicine Ohio State U., Columbus, 1966-77, prof. emeritus, 1977-79. Decorated Legion of Merit with oak leaf cluster, Air medal. Diplomate Am. Bd. Preventive Medicine (past sec.-treas.). Fellow Am. Coll. Physicians; mem. Am. Coll. Preventive Medicine (past pres.), Aerospace Med. Assn., A.M.A. (past sect. chmn.), Internat. Acad. Aviation and Space Medicine, Am. Pub. Health Assn., Phi Beta Kappa, Sigma Xi, Sigma Chi. Contbr. to Cecil-Loeb Textbook of Medicine, 1974, articles to profl. jours. Home: Columbus, Ohio. Died Oct. 23, 1979.

ELLIOTT, DABNEY OTEY, army officer; b. Sewanee, Tenn., Oct. 13, 1890; grad. U.S. Mil. Acad., 1914; commd. 2d lt., engr. corps, June 1914, and advanced through the grades to brig. gen., June 1943; made dir. Strategic Logistics Div., hdqrs., Services of Supply (Army SerVice Forces), Washington, D.C., July 1942; overseas assignment, Apr. 1943; comdg. gen. Army Service Forces Training Center, Ft. Leonard Wood, from Dec. 1944. Decorated Legion of Merit with oak leaf cluster; comdr. Order of the British Empire. Club: Army and Navy (Washington, D.C.). Home: Glenview, Ill. Died June 20, 1976.

ELLIOTT, G(EORGE) R(OY), coll. prof.; b. London, Ont., Can., Dec. 31, 1883; s. Joseph and Ann Eliza (Coyne) E.; A.B., U. of Toronto, 1904; Ph.D., U. of Jena, Germany, 1908; Litt.D., Bowdoin Coll., 1925; L.H.D. (honorary), Tufts University, 1955; married Alma Lee Wilkins, September 20, 1910; children—Richard Lee (dec.), Jane Proudfoot (Mrs. Walter Fischer), Ann Catherine (Mrs. Stephen Kleene). Came to U.S., 1908, naturalized, 1912. Instructor in English, University of Wisconsin, 1908-13; prof. of English, Bowdoin College, 1913-25; professor of English, Amherst College, 1925-50, professor of English emeritus since 1950. Literary critic since 1910. Awarded gold medal for gen. proficiency, U. of Toronto, 1904. Mem. Modern Lang. Assn. of Am., Renaissance Soc. Am. Mem. Guild of Scholars in the Episcopal Church. Author several books including: Scourge and Minister (a study of Hamlet), 1951; Flaming Minister, 1953; Dramatic Providence in Macbeth, 1958. Contbr. periodicals and jours. Home: Bunganuc Rd., Brunswick, Me.

ELLIOTT, GEORGE PAUL, author, educator; b. Knightstown, Ind., June 16, 1918; s. Paul R. and Nita (Gregory) E.; B.A., U. Calif. at Berkeley, 1939, M.A., 1941; D.H.L., St. Lawrence U., 1971; m. Mary Emma Jeffress, Jan. 18, 1941; 1 dau., Nora Catherine. Instr., then asst. prof. English, St. Mary's (Calif.) Coll., 1947-55, 62-63; asst. prof. Cornell U., Ithaca, N.Y., 1955-56; asst. prof. Barnard Coll., 1957-60; lectr. U. Iowa, 1960-61; prof. English, Syracuse U., 1963-80. Mem. corp. Yaddo Found., 1965-80. Recipient Albert Bender grant-in-aid, 1951; fellow Fund Advancement Edn., 1953, Hudson Rev., 1956; Guggenheim fellow, 1961, 70; Ford fellow, 1965; award Nat. Inst. Arts and Letters, 1969. Mem. P.E.N. Author: (novels) Parktilden Village, 1958; David Knudsen, 1962; In the World, 1965; Muriel, 1972; (short stories) Among the Dangs, 1961; An Hour of Last Things, 1968; (essays) A Piece of Lettuce, 1964; Conversions, 1971; (poems) Fever and Chills, 1961; From the Berkeley Hills, 1969; Reaching, 1979. Editor: Fifteen Modern American Poets, 1956; Types of Prose Fiction, 1964. Home: Syracuse, N.Y. Died May 3, 1980; cremated.

ELLIOTT, GRACE LOUCKS, educator; born at Alverton, Pa., Feb. 19, 1891; d. John Lyman and Sarah Jane (Hunsberger) Loucks; A.B., Findlay (O.) Coll., 1910; student Nat. Training Sch., Y.W.C.A., N.Y., 1916-17; M.A., Teachers Coll. and Union Theol. Sem., Columbia U., 1924; Ph.D., Columbia U., 1936; LL.D. (honorary), Hood College, Frederick, Md., 1952; m. Harrison S. Elliott, June 24, 1927; children—David Loucks, Donald Harrison, Margaret Jean. Teacher, Findlay (O.) Coll. Acad., 1911-12, East Huntington High Sch., Alverton, Pa., 1912-14, Irwin (Pa.) High Sch., 1914-16; Nat. student sec., Y.W.C.A., at Dallas, Tex., 1917-20, New York, 1920-25; lecturer and conf. leader in colls. and univs., chs., social agencies, and youth orgns., since 1930; mem. faculty Union Theol. Seminary summer school, 1936-43; nat. pres. Y.W.C.A., 1940-43; mem. Nat. Bd., YWCA, 1930-43, became gen. sec., 1943; vis. prof. Wells Coll., 1954-55; pres. Beirut Coll. for Women, Lebanon, 1958-59. Mem. Kappa Delta Pi, Methodist. Author several books. Contbr. to ednl., social and religious jours. Home: New York, N.Y. Died Aug. 4, 1979.

ELLIOTT, HAROLD HIRSCH, mfg. exec.; b. Rockford, Ill., Aug. 12, 1886; s. James Hirsch and Anna (Fox) E.; student Lewis Inst., 1900-03, St. John's Mil. Acad., Delafield, Wis., 1904-06; m. Hazel Goss, Oct. 30, 1915; children—Louise Caroline, Harold H. Salesman James H. Hirsch & Co., Chgo., 1907-10; exec. Ill. Life Ins. Co., 1910-17; pres., treas. Halsam Products Co., mfrs. toys, embossed wood products, Chgo., 1917-46, chmn., dir., 1946—; chmn. Goss Printing Press Co., 1937-55. Comdg. officer Lake Mich. area Temp. Res., USCG, 1942-45. Republican. Mason (K.T., Shriner). Clubs: Chicago Athletic, Sheridan Shore Yacht, Chicago Yacht (Chgo.); Glen View (Ill.) Golf. Home: Glencoe, Ill.

ELLIOTT, OWEN N., lawyer; b. Marion, Ia., Mar. 13, 1886; s. Herbert I. and Martha (Owen) E.; A.B., Coe Coll., Cedar Rapids, Ia., 1907; LL.B., U. of Ia., 1910; m. Leone Lorimor, Nov. 12, 1929. Admitted to Ia. bar, 1910; city atty., Cedar Rapids, Ia., 1916-24. Pres. Owen and Leone Elliott Inc., charitable trust. Mem. Internat., Am., Ia. bar assns., Acacia, Phi Beta Kappa, Phi Delta Phi. Mason (32, Shriner), Elk. Clubs: Pickwick, Country, Embassy (Cedar Rapids). Home: Cedar Rapids, IA.

ELLIOTT, ROBERT CARL, educator; b. Indpls., Nov. 23, 1914; s. Robert Carl and Lucy (Woodbridge) E.; A.B., Wabash (Ind.) Coll., 1936; M.A., Columbia, 1937; Ph.D., Brown U., 1946; m. Mary Curtin, May 19, 1945. Instr. English, U. Hawaii, 1937-39, 41; from instr. to prof. English, Ohio State U., 1946-64; prof. English, U. Calif. at San Diego, 1964-81, chmn. lit. dept., 1968-71. Served to lt. USNR, 1942-46. Decorated Bronze Star. Guggenheim fellow, 1962-63, 72. Mem. Am. Acad. Arts and Scis., Modern Lang. Assn., A.A.U.P. (pres. Ohio State U. 1963-64)., Internat. Assn. U. Profs. English, P.E.N., Phi Beta Kappa. Author: The Power of Satire: Magic, Ritual, Art, 1960; The Shape of Utopia, 1970; also articles. Home: La Jolla, Calif. Died Apr. 13, 1981.

ELLIOTT, ROBERT HARE EGERTON, physician, educator; b. Flushing, N.Y., Sept. 9, 1906; s. Robert Hare Egerton and Fannie (Bogert) E.; grad. magna cum laude, Kent (Conn.) Sch., 1924; B.S., Princeton, 1928; M.D., Columbia, 1932, Med. Sc.D. in Surgery, 1938; spl. research fellow Cambridge (Eng.) U., 1933; m. Mary Amelia Turnbull, Nov. 20, 1935; children—Mary Stewart (Mrs. E.T. Fogarty), Robert Hare Egerton, Susan Anthony. Surgery intern Presbyn. Hosp., 1933-35, surg. resident, 1935-38, asst. surgery, 1941-46, clin. dir. NRC study contaminated wounds and burns, 1942-45, asst. attending surgeon, 1946-49, asso. attending surgeon, 1949-52, chief East surg. service, 1952-66, attending surgeon, 1952-72, asst. v.p., 1966-72, ednl. cons. health scis., 1972-77, also cons. in surgery; asst. surgery Vanderbilt Clinic, 1938-41, asst. chief clinic surgery, 1941-46, chief clinic surgery 1946-50; asso. attending surgeon Columbia div. Bellevue Hosp., 1949-52; civilian cons. surgery Sta. Hosp., U.S. Mil. Acad., 1949-66; cons. surgery Southhampton (N.Y.) Hosp., 1956-60, Harlem Hosp., 1964-67; mem. faculty Columbia Coll. Physicians and Surgeons, 1938-72, prof. clin. surgery, 1965-72, asso. dean Faculty Medicine, 1966-72; sec., 1970; ednl. cons.

health scis. Pace U., N.Y.C., 1972-74. Lewis Linn McArthur lectr. Frank Billings Found., Inst. Medicine, Chgo., 1947; mem. interdisciplinary com. on health manpower utilization and tng. N.Y. Met. Regional Med. Program, 1970-72, asso. dir. for health manpower, 1974-76. Chmn. dept. Christian social relations Episcopal Diocese N.Y., 1961-62, mem. council, 1958-62, mem. standing com., 1962-66. Bd. dirs. Nat. Assn. Practical Nurse Edn. and Service, 1969-73, mem. exec. com., 1971-74; trustee Georgica Assn., 1973-76; past trustee Fieldston Property Owners, Inc. Decorated comdr. Am. Soc. Most Venerable Order St. John Jerusalem, 1970. Diplomate Nat. Bd. Med. Examiners, Am. Bd. Surgery. Fellow A.C.S.; mem. A.O. Whipple Surg. Soc. (past pres.), Soc. Univ. Surgeons, N.Y. Acad. Medicine, N.Y. Surg. Soc., Am. Thyroid Assn., Soc. Alumni Presbyn. Hosp. (past pres.), Phi Beta Kappa, Alpha Omega Alpha. Episcopalian (vestryman, former sr. warden); Clubs: Riverdale Yacht, Century Assn. Contbr. to profl. jours. Home: Wainscott, N.Y. Died June 10, 1977; buried Wainscott.

ELLIOTT, WILLARD BUFORD, educator; b. Osborn, Mo., Jan. 6, 1923; s. Willard Monroe and Maude Hamer (Hartford) E.; B.A., N.W. Mo. State Coll., 1943; M.S., State U. Iowa, 1948, Ph.D., 1950; m. Helen Elizabeth Brand, July 25, 1946 (dec. July 1967): children—fimothy Brand, Alan Hartford, Olive Margaret; m. 2d, Rosemary Waite Eskridge, July 25, 1968; 1 dau. Caroline Mieke; stepchildren—Etta Mary Eskridge, Paul Burdette Eskridge. Instr. biochemistry U. Buffalo Sch. Medicine, 1950-53, asst. prof., 1953-62; asso. prof. State U. N.Y. at Buffalo, 1962-67, prof., 1967-80. Cons. biochemistry Meyer Meml. Hosp. div. Erie County Lab., Buffalo, 1951-58; asst. Laboratorium voor Physiologische Chemie, U. Amsterdam, 1957-58; NSF-CSIR scientists exchange visitor, India, 1977. Served to lt. (j.g.) USNR, 1944-46. Recipient Research Career devel. awards USPHS, 1961-70. Mem. A.A.A.S., Am. Assn. Clin. Chemists, Am. Chem. Soc., Am. Soc. Biol. Chemists, Internat. Soc. Toxinology, Soc. Applied Spectroscopy. Asso. editor Preparative Biochemistry, 1971—; mem. editorial council Toxicon, 1977. Home: Buffalo, N.Y. Died Feb. 27, 1980.

ELLIOTT, WILLIAM YANDELL, author; b. Murfreesboro, Tenn., May 13, 1896; s. William Yandell and Annie Mary (Bullock) E.; A.B., Vanderbilt U., 1917, A.M., 1920; certificate Sorbonne, Paris, France, 1919; D. Phil. (Rhodes scholar), Balliol Coll., Oxford (Eng.) U., 1923; LL.D.; m. Barbara Foster, June 28, 1923; childreWilliam Yandell (dec.), Paul Pinkerton Foster, Charles James Fox Wharton; m. 2d, Mary Louise Ward, Aug. 26, 1936; children—Ward Edward Yandell, David William Penn. Instr., Vanderbilt U., 1919-20, U. Cal., 1923-24, asst. prof., 1924-25; lectr. and tutor govt. dept., asst. prof., Harvard, 1925-29, asso. prof., 1929-31, prof., 1931-63, prof. emeritus, 1963-79, Williams prof. history and govt., 1942, dir. summer sch., 1950-60; Univ. prov. Am. U., Washington, 1963-69, prof. emeritus 1969-79; Buell G. Gallagagher Distinguished vis. prof. Coll. City N.Y., 1968-79. Cons. Pres.'s Com. on Adminstn. Mgmt., 1936, Nat. Adv. Def. Commn., 1940, Office Prodn. Mgmt., 1941, Ho. of Reps. Spl. Com. on Postwar Econ. Policy and Planning, 1945-46; cons. sec. state, 1958-63; mem. Senator Tydings mission to Philippines, 1945; dir. Stockpile and Transp. Div., WPB, 1942-44, vice chmn. Civilian Requirements, 1944-45; staff dir. House Select Com. Fgn. Aid, 1947-48, Ho. Com. Fgn. Affairs, 1947-49; asst. dir. O.D.M., 1951-53; mem. planning bd. Nat. Security Council 1953-57. Served to 1st lt., 114th Field Arty., 30th Div. A.E.F. World War I. Mem. Bus. Council (hon. mem., conf. nat. orgn.), Phi Beta Kappa, Sigma Chi. Mem. Disciples of Christ. Author books in field of polit. sci., including Pragmatic Revolt on Politics; New British Empire; Need for Constitutional Reform. Editor, The British Commonwealth at War, 1943; Western Political Heritage (with N. A. McDonald), 1949; American Foreign Policy; Organization and Control, 1952; Political Economy of the Foreign Policy of the United States, 1955; Television's Impact on American Culture, 1956; Education and Training in the Developing Countries: Foreign Aid, 1966. Co-author: The Idea of Colonialism, 1958; The Secretary of State, 1960; The U.S. and the UN, 1961. Home: Haywood, Va. Died Jan. 9, 1979; buried Murfreesboro, Tenn.

ELLIS, AILEEN VIRGINIA, librarian; b. Cranberry, N.C.; d. Cale Donald and Josephine Juanita (Hyder) Ellis; A.B. summa cum laude, Milligan Coll., B.S., Peabody Coll., M.A., 1958; postgrad. Fla. State U., 1966-68. Librarian, Maxwell AFB, 1958-63; staff librarian Robins AFB, Ga., 1963-66; base librarian Eglin AFB, Fla., 1966-70, chief library br., 1970—. Historian, Montgomery Little Theatre, 1962-63. Recipient Outstanding award Dept. Air Force, 1970, 71, 72. Mem. Am., Ala., Southeastern (vice chmn., chmn.-elect spl. libraries sect. 1976-78), W.Fla. (v.p. 1970-72), Fla. library assns., Spl. Libraries Assn. (pres. Ala. chpt. 1972-74, sec.-treas. mil. librarians div. 1973-74), A.A.U.W. (v.p. Fla. div. 1970-72), D.A.R., Hist. Soc. Okaloosa and Walton Counties. Republican. Presbyn. Club: Lake Lorraine Country (Shalimar, Fla.). Indexer: Ala. Librarian, 1963-70. Home: Shalimar, Fla. Deceased.

ELLIS, BROOKS FLEMING, geologist; b. Jonestown, W.Va., Aug. 2, 1897; s. Leander A. and Harriet E. (Fleming) E.; A.B., Marietta Coll. 1923, Sc.D. (hon.), 1953; M.S., N.Y. U., 1929, Ph.D., 1932; postgrad. Yale and Columbia; m. Nell L. Reed, Dec. 25, 1920 (dec. Apr. 1966); m. 2d, Alice Gilman, Aug. 2, 1966. Instr. Sci. W. Va. high schs., 1923-26, N.Y., 1927-29; instr. geology, N.Y. U., 1930-36, asst. prof., 1936-43, asso. prof., dept. chmn., 1943-46, prof., dept. chmn. 1946-58, prof., dept. chmn., dept. head all-univ. dept., 1958-66, prof. emeritus, 1966—; adj. prof. geology Rutgers U. of N.J., 1966-70; curator micropaleontology Am. Mus. Natural History, 1941-44, curator and chmn. micropaleontology, 1944-67, curator emeritus, 1967-76; instr. Bklyn. Coll. (evening), 1933-39; dir. Am. Mus. Research Project on Foraminifers, 1930-41. Dir. Equitable Petroleum Corp. Served with U.S. Navy, 1917-19. Fellow A.A.A.S., Am. Geog. Soc., Geol. Soc. Am.; mem. Paleontol. Soc., Soc. Econ. Palentologists and Mineralogists, Am. Assn. Petroleum Geologists (pres. Eastern sect. 1956-57), Soc. Study Evolution, Schweizerische Palaontolgische Gesellschaft, Société Geologique Suisse, Deutschen Geologische Gesellschaft, Deutsche Palaontologische Gesellshaft, Société Geologique de France, Am. Geophys. Union, Am. Polar Soc., Phi Beta Kappa, Sigma Xi. Clubs: Explorers, Centurions. Author: (with A.R. Messina) Catalogue of Foraminifera, 69 vols., Catalogue of Ostracoda, 29 vols.; (with A.R. Messina) Catalogue of Index Larger Foraminifera, 3 vols.; (with A.R. Messina, Richard Charmatz, Lilly Ronai) Catalogue of Index Smaller Foraminifera, 3 vols. Co-founder Micropaleontology (quar.), 1955. Home: St. Marys, W.Va. Died July 11, 1976.

ELLIS, CLYDE TAYLOR, lawyer, cons.; b. nr. Garfield, Ark., Dec. 21, 1908; s. Cecil Oscar and Minerva Jane (Taylor) E.; B.S. in Bus. Adminstrn., U. Ark., 1958; m. Izella Baker, Dec. 20, 1931; children—Patricia Suzanne, Mary Lynn; m. 2d, Camille W. Fitzhugh, Sept. 23, 1966. Supt. schs., Garfield, Ark., 1920-34; admitted to Ark. bar, 1933, practiced in Garfield and Bentonville; gen. mgr. Nat. Rural Electric Coop. Assn., Washington, 1943-67; mem. Nat. Water Commn., Washington, 1968-70; profl. asst. to Senator John L. McClellan, 1971-80. Spl. cons. to Sec. of Agr. Mem. Ark. Gen. Assembly, 1933-34, Ark. Senate, 1935-36; mem. 76-77th congresses from 3d Ark. Dist. Mem. Nat. Capitol Democratic Club. Served with USNR, World War II. Mem. Am., Ark., Washington bar assns. Democrat. Episcopalian. Mason. Clubs: Cosmos, Congressional Country (Washington). Author: Giant Step, 1967. Home: Chevy Chase, Md. Died Feb. 9, 1980; buried Arlington Nat. Cemetery.

ELLIS, DONALD JOHNSON, trumpeter, arranger, composer; b. Los Angeles, July 25, 1934; s. Evert Ezra and Winston E. (Johnson) E.; Mus.B., Boston U., 1956; postgrad. U. Calif. at Los Angeles, 1963-64; m. Constance Cynthia Coogan, July 28, 1961 (div. Nov. 1971); children—Brav Johnson, Tran Robert. Trumpet player with numerous orchs., 1952-66, including Glenn Miller, 1956, Charlie Barnet, Maynard Ferguson, 1958-60; numerous recs. with own groups, 1960-66; leader Don Ellis Orch., from 1965; soloist Nat. Symphony Orch., Washington, 1962, N.Y. Philharmonic Orch., 1963-64, Los Angeles Philharmonic, 1967; performed Los Angeles Music Center with Stan Kenton Neophonic Orch. in original composition Synthesis, 1966; tours U.S., Europe; rec. artist Candid, Prestige, Pacific Jazz, Columbia, MPS/BASF, Atlantic records; numerous TV appearances including pilot Movin On, NBC series Doctor's Hosp. Recipient 1st Pl. award Internat. Jazz Critics Poll, 1962; Grammy award for Theme from The French Connection (best instrumental arrangement), 1972; Disting. Alumni award Boston U., 1978; Rockefeller grantee Center Creative and Performing Arts State U. N.Y., Buffalo, 1964-65. Mem. A.S.C.A.P., Nat. Acad. Rec. Arts and Scis. Author: Rhythm, New Rhythm Book, Quartet Tones; mus. drama Future: Tense!!; composer works including Reach, a cantata, 1968; music for Shirley McLaine Spl., 1977; movie score Moon Zero Two, The French Connection, Kansas City Bomber, Seven-Ups, Man Belongs to the Earth, French Connection II, Deadly Tower, Ruby, Assault on Paradise, Natural Enemies. Home: Los Angeles, Calif. Died Dec. 1978.

ELLIS, GEORGE C(ARRINGTON), farm exec.; b. Oakland, Cal., Sept. 25, 1886; s. Felix D. and Kate S. Ellis; A.B., U. Cal., 1903; m. Ruth A. Smith, June 13, 1913. Pres. dir. Sorosis Fruit Co., Oakland, 1915—; sr. v.p., dir. Stauffer Chemical Co., also gen. mgr. West End Chemical Co. div. Home: Oakland.

ELLIS, LEWIS ETHAN, educator; b. Otisco, N.Y., Sept. 9, 1898; s. Lewis Martin and Catherine Louise (Henderson) E.; A.B., Syracuse U., 1920; A.M., U. Chgo., 1924, Ph.D., 1927; m. Helen Elizabeth Breckenridge, Sept. 5, 1931; children—Ethan Breckenridge, Robert Walter. Instr. history Emory U., 1920-23, Purdue U., 1927-28; asst. prof. Rutgers U., 1928-40, asso. prof., 1940-47, prof., 1947-63, chmn. dept. history, 1951-53, 54-57, Voorhees prof., 1954-63, prof. emeritus, 1963-77. Author: A History of the Chicago Delegation in Congress, 1823-1925, 1931; Reciprocity, 1911; A Study in Canadian-American Relations, 1939; Print Paper Pendulum: Group Pressures and the Price of Newsprint, 1948; A Short History of American Diplomacy, 1951; Newsprint: Producers, Publishers, Political Pressures, 1960; Frank B. Kellogg and American Foreign Relations, 1925-29, 1960; Republican Foreign Policy, 1921-33, 1968; also articles and revs. profl. jours. Home: Piscataway, N.J. Died Oct. 15, 1977.

ELLISON, DANIEL, congressman; b. Feb. 14, 1886; A.B., Johns Hopkins, 1907; LL.B., U. of Md., 1909; unmarried. Admitted to Md. bar, 1909, and since practiced in Baltimore; mem. Baltimore City Council, 1923-42; mem. 78th Congress (1943-45), 4th Md. Dist. Republican. Mem. Am., Md. and Baltimore bar assns. Home: Baltimore, Md. *

ELLSWORTH, DONALD WILLIAM, investment counselor; b. Meredith, N.H., June 3, 1895; s. Perry Alvin and Annie (Foss) E.; S.B., Harvard, 1918; m. Ruth Elizabeth Mesmer, Apr. 24, 1926; children—Donald Bruce, Nancy E. (Mrs. Edward J. Walsh). With Gen. Electric Co., 1918-22, AT&T, 1922-25; asst. editor, then editor The Annalist, N.Y. Times Co., 1925-40 Wall St. corr. London (Eng.) Observer, 1928-40; with Nat. Indsl. Conf. Bd., 1940-42; v.p., then sr. v.p., exec. v.p. E.W. Axe & Co., Inc., Tarrytown, N.Y., 1942-68, econ. officer, also dir., to 1977; pres. Axe Sci. Mgmt. Corp.; chmn. Axe-Houghton Stock Fund; dir. Axe-Houghton Fund B, Axe Securities Corp. Served with F.A., U.S. Army, World War I. Mem. N.Y. Soc. Security Analysts. Baptist. Mason. Clubs: Coveleigh (Rye, N.Y.); Harvard of Westchester. Home: North Tarrytown, N.Y. Died Feb. 8, 1977; interred Kensico Cemetery, Valhalla, N.Y.

ELMENDORF, JOHN VAN GAASBEEK, former coll. pres.; b. South Orange, N.J., Sept. 9, 1916; s. Arthur Raymond and Frances (Johnson) E.; grad. Choate Sch., 1933; A.B., U. N.C., 1937, M.A., 1947, Ph.D., 1951; A.M., Brown U., 1961; m. Mary Tillery Lindsay, Dec. 27, 1937; children—Calvin Lindsay, Susan Johnson. Prin., Pottsville (Ark.) High Sch., 1937-38; instr. French and German, Hopkins Grammer Sch., New Haven, 1939-41; instr. French and Spanish, Putney (Vt.) Sch., 1941-43; dep. commr. for Europe, Am. Friends Service Com., 1946; grad. instr. French and Spanish, U. N.C., 1946-49; exec. dir. Mexican-Am. Inst., Mexico City, 1950-52; v.p., dean faculty prof. linguistics Mexico City Coll., 1953-61; v.p. Brown U., Providence, 1961-65; pres. New Coll., Sarasota, Fla., 1965-72; mem. faculty, cons. Goddard Coll., 1972-80. Exec. bd. Anglo-Am. Com. for UN, 1957-61; mem. exec. com. R.I. Equal Opportunity Council. Bd. dirs. Providence Country Day Sch., Internat. House of R.I., Am. Sch. Found., 1955-61; pres. trustees Mexico City Acad., 1959-61. Served with AUS, 1943-46; ETO. Decorated Bronze Star medal with 3 oak leaf clusters. Mem. Linguistic Soc. Am., Phi Beta Kappa (v.p. Mexico 1955-61). Democrat. Mem. Soc. of Friends. Clubs: Field, Bird Key Yacht (Sarasota, Fla.). Home: Washington, D.C. Died Feb. 10, 1980.

ELMER, MANUEL CONRAD, sociologist; b. Monroe, Wis., Dec. 5, 1886; s. John and Anne (Denier) E.; S.B., Northwestern Coll., Naperville, Ill., 1911; A.M., University of Ill., 1912; Ph.D., Univ. of Chicago, 1914; H.H.D., Marietta College, 1954; married June Maud Ashley, Sept. 3, 1914; children—Anne-June Strong, Patricia Ashley Appel, Glaister Ashley. Began as prof. of sociology and economics, Fargo (N.D.) Coll., 1914-16; asso. prof. sociology and dir. sociol. surveys, University of Kansas, 1916-19; asso. prof. sociology and social work, U. of Minn., 1919-26; prof. sociology and head of dept., U. of Pittsburgh, since 1926, and dir. graduate div. social work, 1932-38; John Hay Whitney, prof. Western College for Women, Oxford, O., 1957-58; visiting professor sociology Howard Coll., 1964. Member of American Sociological Society, Kappa Delta Pi, Pi Gamma Mu, Delta Sigma Phi. Presbyterian. Author books including: Sociology of the Family, 1945; Cultural Changes in Venezuela, 1953; First Steps in Social Research, 1954; Contemporary Social Thought, 1956; Timber, 1961; The Passing of the Red Tablecloths, 1965; also many monographs. Home: Edgewood, Pitts.

ELSON, SAM, lawyer; b. N.Y.C., Dec. 25, 1908; s. Alex and Sarah (Reichick) E.; A.B., Washington U., St. Louis, 1927, LL.B., 1930; J.S.D., Yale, 1931; m. Gertrude Clemens Palmer, June 28, 1934; children—Edward C., David L., Dorothy M., (Mrs. Donald Rosenthal). Admitted to Mo. bar 1930; mem. faculty Washingion U. Sch. Law, 1931-35; asso. firm Husch, Eppenberger, Donohue, Elson & Cornfeld, and predecessor, St. Louis, 1932-80, partner, 1936-80. Mem. St. Louis Council Human Relations, 1949; pres. Jewish Community Relations Council St. Louis, 1947-51. Bd. dirs. Jewish Fedn. St. Louis, 1952-55. Sterling fellow Yale Law Sch., 1930; recipient alumni citation Washington U. Mem. Am., Mo. bar assns., Bar Assn. St. Louis, Am. Law Inst., Am. Judicature Soc., Mo. Assn. Social Welfare, NCCJ, St. Louis Com. Fgn. Relations, Phi Beta Kappa, Order of Coif, Order of Artus. Contbr. articles legal jours. Mng. editor St. Louis Law Rev., i930. Home: University City, Mo. Died Sept 4, 1980.

ELTING, VICTOR, JR., advt. exec.; b. Winnetka, Ill., Aug. 12, 1905; s. Victor and Marie (Winston) E.; grad. Hotchkiss Sch., 1924; B.S., Princeton, 1928; m. Helen Stanley, May 7, 1932; children—Helen (Mrs. Walter Love Stratton), Victor III, Sarah (Mrs. Lewis J. Finocchio, Jr.). With Quaker Oats Co., Chgo., 1931-71, mgr. new products, 1942-48, advt. brand mgr., 1948-52, advt. dir., 1952-53, v.p. charge advt., 1953-59, v.p. advt. and merchandising, 1959-63, v.p. advt., 1963-70, v.p. marketing services, 1970-71. Pres. Libertyville Countryside Assn. Trustee Condell Meml. Hosp., Libertyville, Ill., Village of Mettawa. Mem. Am. Advt. Fedn. (nat. chmn. 1970-71). Republican. Episcopalian (jr. warden). Clubs: Winter, Onwentsia (Lake Forest); Merchants and Manufacturers (Chgo.). Home: Libertyville, Ill. Died Dec. 8, 1980.

ELTSE, RALPH R. (ELSE), lawyer, ex-congressman; b. Oskaloosa, Ia., Sept. 13, 1885; s. John J. and Jennie Sarah (West) E.; A.M., Penn Coll., Oskaloosa, Ia., 1909; A.B., Haverford Coll., 1910; grad. student in law, U. of Calif., 1912-14; m. Oma Almona Davis, Aug. 16, 1915 (dec.); m. 2d, Mildred Rule Gilbert, Sept. 23, 1947. Practice of law since 1915; member 73d Congress (1933-35), 7th California District. Director Young Men's Christian Assn., Community Chest; treas. War Ration Board, Calif. Mem. Am. Calif. State and Alameda County bar assns. Presbyterian. Lion. Club: City Commons, Traveler, lecturer. Home: Lafayette, Calif.

EMBRY, LLOYD BOWERS, artist, portrait painter; b. Washington, Nov. 22, 1913; s. Ashton Fox and Harriet Grace (Frost) E.; B.F.A., Yale, 1936; m. Virginia J. Block, Feb. 8, 1941; children—Penelope Lamm (Mrs. Robert J. McGoey), Lloyd Bowers, Dean Frost, Wendy Delahaye. Exhbns. include Audubon Soc., N.Y.C., 1947, Norton Mus., West Palm Beach, Fla., 1948, Corcoran Biennial, 1951, Am. Scandinavian Found., N.Y.C., 1953; portraits and sculptures rep. permanent collections Rice U., Riksbank, Stockholm, Sweden, U.S. Senate Bldg. and Dist. Bldg., State Capitol Bldg., Nashville, Swedish embassy, Washington, Yale Gallery, Dept. Def., U.S. Ho. Reps., Georgetown U. Med. Sch., Phila. Hist. Mus., Grace Luth. Ch., Washington, Western Md. Coll., Westminster, U. Md., Rosewood Sch. Retarded Children, Harvard Club, N.Y.C. (sculpture John F. Kennedy), U.S. Post Office Dept., Washington, Internat. Am. Life Ins. Co., NSF, Washington, Ithaca (N.Y.) Coll., Miami U., Oxford, Ohio, U. South, U. Ky., dirs. CIA, Washington, comptroller U.S. Treasury, Flagship Banks, Inc., Miami Beach, Fla., chief staff USAF Acad. painted arctic landscapes for USAF, 1958. Recipient 1st prize portraiture Soc. Washington Artists, 1946, New Haven Paint and Clay Soc., 1948. Mem. Provincetown (Mass.) Art Assn. (life). Address: Washington, D.C. Died Sept. 20, 1979.

EMENY, BROOKS, lectr., educator; b. Salem, Ohio, July 29, 1901; s. Frederick James and Elizabeth Miller (Brooks) E.; grad. Mercersburg (Pa.) Acad., 1920; A.B., Princeton, 1924; postgrad. Sorbonne, Paris, France, 1924-25, London (Eng.) Sch. Econs., 1925-26, Kohsular Akademie, Vienna, Austria, U. Madrid (Spain), 1926-27; Ph.D., Yale, 1934; m. Winifred Rockefeller, Dec. 15, 1928 (dec. 1951); children—Elizabeth Brooks (dec.), Faith R. (Mrs. Richard S. Conger), Winifred Theodate (dec.), Josephine Brooks (dec.); m. 2d, Barbara Cox, Nov. 27, 1954. Instr. govt. Yale, 1927-31, research govt., 1931-33; research, writing, Washington, 1933-35; asso. prof. internat. relations Cleve. Coll., 1935-47; dir. Fgn. Affairs Council, 1935-42; pres. Cleve. Council World Affairs, 1943-47; bd. dirs. Fgn. Policy Assn., 1947-80, pres., 1947-53; adv. council Internat. Orgn. Research Program, Maxwell Grad. Sch. Citizenship and Pub. Affairs, 1965-69; cons. Dept. State, 1941-59; chmn. fgn. affairs com. White House Conf. People-to-People Program, 1956-59; lectr. USIS, Middle East, 1957, S.E. Asia, 1958, Africa, 1960; U.S. del. Ann. Atlantic Assembly Meetings, 1963-80. Mem. adv. councils Princeton Woodrow Wilson Sch. Pub. and Internat. Affairs 1957-80, dept. Oriental Studies, 1958-69, dept. modern langs. and lits., 1959-69, dept. East Asian studies, 1974-80, Am. U. Sch. Internat. Service, Washington, 1960-65. Bd. dirs. Avon Old Farms Sch., Atlantic Council of U.S. Mem. Am. Acad. Polit. and Social Sci., Am. Geog. Soc., AAAS, Fgn. Policy Assn. (hon.), Council Fgn. Relations, Acad. Polit. Sci., Asia Soc. Clubs: Metropolitan (Washington); Century, Univ. (N.Y.C.); Nassau, Bedens Brook, Prospect (Princeton, N.J.); Bras Coupé Hunting and Fishing (pres. 1964-77) (Que., Can.); Rolling Rock (Ligonier, Pa.); Yeamans Hall (Charleston, S.C.). Author: Mainsprings of World Politics; Strategy of Raw Materials; Great Powers in World Politics; Theodate Pope Riddle and the Founding of Avon Old Farms School; The Founding of the Cleveland Council on World Affairs. Contbr. articles to profl. jours. Home: Princeton, N.J. Died July 12, 1980.

EMERICH, IRA, former newspaper exec.; b. Balt., Apr. 11, 1894; s. David and Adeline (Sulzbacher) E.; m. Cornelia Watts Van Siclen, Oct. 17, 1958. Sales dir. Esquire Features, Inc., 1934-41, Chgo. Sun Syndicate, 1941-42; sales dept. Hall Syndicate, 1946-55, sales dir., 1955-56, exec. v.p., 1956-67, dir., 1958-67; dir. newspaper relations Pubs.-Hall Syndicate, 1967-68. Chief press distbn. sect. OWI, 1942-44; newspaper liaison officer War Finance Program, Treasury Dept. 1944-46. Master ceremonies Washington Stage Door Canteen, 1943-45. Served with F.A., U.S. Army, World War I. Recipient Distinguished Service citation Treasury Dept., 1945. Clubs: Nat. Press (Washington); Forty Plus (dir. 1971-73) (N.Y.C.). Home: New York, N.Y. Died Oct. 22, 1975.

EMERSON, ALFRED EDWARDS, zoologist; b. Ithaca, N.Y., Dec. 31, 1896; s. Alfred and Alice Louisa (Edwards) E.; B.S., Cornell U., 1918, A.M., 1920, Ph.D., 1925; Sc.D., Mich. U., 1961; m. Winifred Jelliffe, May 3, 1920 (dec. 1949); children—Helena Leeming (Mrs. Eugene Wilkening), William Jelliffe; m. 2d, Eleanor Fish, Sept. 3, 1950 (dec. 1972). Asst., Tropical Research Sta., N.Y. Zool. Soc., 1919, asso., 1920, asst. dir., 1924; instr. U. Pitts., 1921-23, asst. prof., 1923-25, asso. prof., 1925-29; asso. prof. U. Chgo., 1929-34, prof., 1934-62, emeritus, 1962-76; asst. Am. Mus. Natural History, 1920, research asso., 1940-76; research asso. Chgo. Natural History Mus., 1942-76. Guggenheim Meml. Found. fellow, 1926-27; Belgian Am. Edn. Found. fellow, 1948; instr. biology lab., Cold Spring Harbor, N.Y., 1922; Distinguished prof. natural sci. Mich. State U., 1960. Fellow N.Y. Zool. Soc.; mem. Ecol. Soc. Am. (sec.-treas. 1931, pres. 1941, Eminent Ecologist citation 1967), Am. Entomol. Soc. (v.p.), Soc. Systematic Zoologists (pres. 1958), Soc. Study Evolution (v.p. 1946, 48, pres. 1960), A.A.A.S. (sect. v.p. 1946), Ill. Acad. Sci. (pres. 1946), Nat. Acad. Sci. Author numerous publs. including: (with W.C. Allee, O. Park, T. Park, K.P. Schmidt) Principles of Animal Ecology, 1949; The Supraorganismic Aspects of the Society, 1952; The Biological Foundations of Ethics and Social Progress, 1952; Biogeography of Termites, 1952; Biological Species, 1954; Social Homeostasis, 1954; Distribution of Termites, 1955; Evolution of Behavior, 1958; Evolution of Adaptation in Population Systems, 1960; Impact of Evolution on Religion, 1960; Vestigial Characters and Processes of Regressive Evolution, 1961; Impact of Darwin on Biology, 1962; Human Cultural Evolution, 1965. Home: Huletts Landing, N.Y. Died Oct. 3, 1976.

EMERSON, CHESTER BURGE, clergyman; b. Haverhill, Mass., July 28, 1882; s. John A. and Abbie Jane E.; A.B., Bowdoin, 1904, D.D., 1919; B.D., Union Theol. Sem., 1909; D.D., Kenyon Coll., 1933; unmarried. Ordained Congl. ministry, 1909; pastor First Parish, Saco, Me., 1909-13, North Woodward Ch., Detroit, 1913-32; canon residentiary Trinity Cathedral (Episcopal), Cleveland, Jan.-Nov., 1933, dean, 1933-51, dean emeritus since 1951; lectr. Gen. Theol. Sem., N.Y.C., 1951-52; locum tenens Calvary Ch., Pitts., 1951-52, St. Peters, Albany, N.Y., 52-53, Ashtabula, O., 1953-54, St. Marks, Toledo, 1955, Christ Ch., Hole Sound, Fla., 1957, St. Michaels in the Valley, Ligonier, Pa., 1959, St. Pauls, Delray, Fla., 1961. Priest-in-charge St. Anne's. Kennebunkport, Me., summers since 1942. Mem. Diocesan Council, deputy, General Convention, October 1940, 1943, September 1946, 1949; member Standing Committee of Diocese. Ohio, 1943-51, diocesan council 1935-41, 42-48. Served under YMCA in France, 1917-18; chaplain Gen. Hosp. No. 36 R.C. Formerly corporate mem. A.B.C.F.M.; mem. exec. Com. State Bd. Congl. Chs.; pres. bd. trustees Mich. Conf., 1919-29; moderator State Conf., 1925; mem. exec. com. Commn. on Missions of Nat. Council Congl. Chs., 1919-28. Overseer Bowdoin Coll.; trustee Hampton Inst.; sometime trustee Olivet Coll., Chgo. Theol. Seminary, Mem. Arts and Crafts Soc., Founders Soc. of Art Museum of Detroit, Detroit Symphony Orchestra (dir., 1920-33), Fine Arts Soc., Alpha Delta Phi. Republican. Mason (32 deg., K.T., Shriner, also 33 deg. from Grand Council of Greece, Athens, also from Northern Jurisdiction U.S. 1932; Grand Prelate of K.T. of the U.S.). Clubs: Union (Cleve.); University (N.Y.C.); Bath & Tennis, Coral Beach. Lectr. in homiletics. Address: Palm Beach, Fla.; Kennebrunkport, Me.

EMERSON, RUPERT, educator; b. Rye, N.Y., Aug. 20, 1899; s. William Key Bond and Maria Holmes (Furman) E.; A.B., Harvard, 1921; Ph.D., London Sch. Econs., 1927; m. Alla Julievna Grosjean, Sept. 14, 1925; children—William Key Bond, Nina Ule, Natasha Maria, Rupert Allan. Reporter N.Y. Sun, 1921-22; instr. Harvard, 1927, prof. internat. relations, 1946-70, prof. govt. emeritus, 1970-79; vis. prof. U. Calif. at Berkeley, 1953-54, 73, at Los Angeles, 1965-71; lectr. Yale, 1937-38, Am. U., Cairo, Egypt, 1972; dir. div. territories and island possessions U.S. Dept. Interior, Washington, 1940-41; apptd. Office of Coordinator of Inter-Am. Affairs, 1941, regional adminstr. for territories and possessions OPA, 1942; asst. adminstr. Lend-Lease, 1943; dir. Liberated Areas Br. FSA, 1944-45. Trustee, Inst. Pacific Relations; pres. Far Eastern Assn., 1952-53. Served as 2d class seaman U.S. Navy, 1917-18. Mem. Am. Acad. Arts and Scis., Am. Polit. Sci. Assn., Assn. for Asian Studies, African Studies Assn. (pres. 1965-66), Council on Fgn. Relations, Inst. of 1770, Spee (Harvard). Author: State and Sovereignty in Modern Germany, 1928; Malaysia, 1937; The Netherlands Indies and the U.S., 1942; Representative Government in Southeast Asia, 1955; From Empire to Nation, 1960; Self-Determination Revisited in the Era of Decolonization, 1964; Africa and United States Policy, 1967. Contbr. articles to profl. jours. Home: Cambridge, Mass. Died Feb. 9, 1979.

EMERY, HARLAN JULIEN, govt. ofc.; b. Bar Harbor, Me., Nov. 16, 1903; s. Julien and Addie (Higgins) E.; B.S. in Agr., U. Me., 1926; M.S. in Agrl. Econs., Ore. State Coll., 1930; student U. Cal. at Berkeley, 1930-33; m. Gwenydd K. Lewis, July 22, 1932; children—Stephen J., Rockwell L., Donald H. With Dept. Agr., 1934—, dir. livestock and dairy policy staff Agrl. Stblzn. and Conservation Service, 1964—. Recipient Superior Service Honor award Dept. Agr., 1959, Certificate of Merit, 1964. Mem. Sigma Nu, Alpha Zeta. Conglist. Home: Falls Church, Va. Died Aug. 13, 1980.

EMGE, LUDWIG AUGUSTUS (EM'GA), emeritus clin. prof. obstetrics and gynecology, Stanford; b. Hanover, Germany, Nov. 12, 1885; s. Alfred Adam and Elizabeth Katherine (D'Aum) E.; student in Germany, France, Italy; B.S., U. of Chicago, 1912; M.D., Rush Med. Sch., 1915; m. Elsa Matthei, Apr. 7, 1915; 1 son, Peter, U.S. Navy Fighter Pilot, killed 1945. Asst. in anatomy, U. Chgo., 1910-12, asst. in pathology, 1913; instr. in obstetrics and gynecology, U. Cal., 1915-17; asst., asso. prof. Stanford Sch. Medicine, 1917-32; clin. prof., chmn. dept. of obstetrics and gynecology, 1932-49, now clin. prof. Emeritus; cons. Letterman Gen. Hosp., Children's Hosp.; chief Med. Officer, Dist. 9, O.C.D., 1943, Med. Dir. Res. Col., USPHS, 1943-49, overseas service, 1944-45, spl. cons. Army Med. Corps, 1951. Diplomate Am. Bd. Obstetrics and Gynecology (dir. 1938-48). Fellow of the American Gynecological Soc. (pres. 1949), Am. Assn. Obstetrics and Gynecol. (hon.), A.C.S., N.Y. Acad. Scis.; mem. A.M.A. (chmn. sect. Obstetrics and Gynecol. 1923), San Francisco Gynecological Society (president 1933-34), Pacific Coast Gynecological and Obstetrics Society (president 1937) California Acad. Medicine, Chgo. Gynecol. Soc., Los Angeles Obstetrics & Gynecol. Soc., Los Angeles Surg. Soc., Washington State Obstetrics Soc., Alaska Med. Assn., Hollywood Academy of Medicine, American College of Obstetrics & Gynecol., Alpha Omega Alpha, Sigma Xi.

EMIL, ALLAN D., lawyer; b. N.Y.C., Mar. 25, 1898 s. Morris and Rose (Dlugasch) E.; student Erasmus Hall High Sch., N.Y.C., 1911-15; student Columbia U. Extension, 1915-16, N.Y. Law Sch., 1916-18; LL.B., Bklyn. Law Sch., 1919; m. Kate Silverman, June 26, 1921; children—Arthur D., Judy Anne. Admitted to N.Y. bar, 1920, practiced in N.Y.C.; partner law firm Roseman, Colin, Kaye, Petschek, Freund & Emil; dir. Square D. Co., Phillips-VanHeuson Co., Walter Reade Orgn., Midland Glass Co., Guardian Mut. Fund. Asso. chmn. Fedn. Jewish Philanthropies, N.Y.C., 1965-66, fund raising campaign chmn., 1966-68. Trustee Albert Einstein Coll. Medicine, Austin Riggs Center, Inc. Bennington Coll.; v.p., dir. Psychoanalytic Found.; exec. v.p. Montefiore Hosp. and Med. Centre: Served with U.S. Navy, 1917-18. Spl. hon. mem. Am. Inst. Aeros. and Astronautics. Dir. George Jr. Republic. Mem. Assn. Bar N.Y.C., N.Y. County Lawyers Assn., Am. Fedn. Arts (trustee). Clubs: Sands Point (L.I.) Golf (hon., trustee); Glen Oaks Golf (Great Neck, N.Y.) (hon., trustee); Harmonie, Grolier. Home: New York, N.Y. Died Feb. 4, 1976.

EMMERT, ARTHUR PHILIP, engineer; born Hamilton, O., Aug. 30, 1884; s. John and Caroline (Geisler) E.; student elec., mech. engring. Internat. Corr. Sch.; m. Maude Golden Post, May 23, 1905; children—Forrest Murrey, Marjorie Bess (wife Rev. Lee Baker Long). Apprentice toolmaker Niles Tool Works, 1898-1903; assembler, foreman, gen. foreman Am. Blower Co., 1903-10; with Northway div. Gen. Motors, 1911-12; gear engr., prodn. mgr., gen. supt. Warner Gear Co., 1912-24; supt. axle div. Hudson Motor Car Co., 1924-32; prodn. supt. Waltham Watch Co., 1932-38; works mgr. exptl. research Warner Gear div. Borg-Warner Corp., 1939-46, pres. Warner Gear div., 1946-52, v.p., mem. operating com., cons. engr. since 1952; pres., div. Warner Gear, Ltd., Can., 1939-52; became v.p. Borg Warner Corp., 1949, cons. engr., 1952, gen. mgr. Detroit Gear Div., 1953-54, ret., 1954. Mem. Soc. Automotive Engrs. Presbyn. Mason. Home: Dunedin, Fla.

EMMONS, GLENN LEONIDAS, banker; b. Atmore, Ala., Aug. 15, 1895; s. John Davidson and Martha Jane (Huggins E.; siudent u. N.Mex., also hon. degree; m. Dorothy Frances Hockaoay, June 11, 1924. Locomotive fireman (when 15 yrs. old), Am. Lumber Co., Zuni Mountains, N.M.; entered banking, Gallup, N.M., 1919; chmn. bd. and pres. First State Bank, Gallup, 1935-64; U.S. conn. Indian Affairs, 1953-61. Mem. nat. adv. bd. Girl Scouts Am.; chmn. Greater U. N.M. Devel. Fund. Bd. mgrs. Sch. Am. Research, Santa Fe, N.M. Served as 1st lt. U.S. Home: m. Banxers Assn. (treas. 1949-51; mem. adminstrv. com.; mem. exec. council; mem. finance com.; mem. pub. relations council, 1946-47), N.M. Bankers Assn. (pres. 1940-41), Newcomen Soc. of England, Pi Kappa Alpha. Republican. Episcopalian. Mason. Club: Albuquerque Country. Home: Albuquerque, NM.

EMPEY, ARTHUR GUY, author, soldier; b. Ogden, Utah, Dec. 11, 1883; s. Robert Arthur and Rose (Dana) E.; ed. pub. schs. and Manual Training High Sch., Brooklyn, N.Y.; unmarried. Traveled around the world to gain practical knowledge before beginning to write. Served in the 47th N.G.N.Y., 4th N.G.N.J. and 71st N.G.N.Y., several yrs.; also in 11th and 12th U.S. Cav. 6 yrs.; pvt. British Army, in France, 18 mos., 1915-16; discharged on account of wounds received in Battle of the Somme, July 1916; served in U.S. Tank Corps, 1917-18; commd. capt. U.S.A.; made recruiting tour of U.S. Episcopalian. Pres. Guy Empey Pictures Corpn., Nat. Motion Picture Instn. of America, Inc. Starred with Rose Stahl and assisted in direction comedy drama, "Pack Up Your Troubles"; starred and supervised direction of 9-reel feature, "Over the Top"; starred, wrote story, and supervised direction 7-reel feature, "The Undercurrent," "A Millionaire for a Day," "The Danger Tide," "Just Orphans," etc. Author: Over the Top, 1917; First Call, 1918; The Coward, 1918; Tales From a Dugout, 1918; The Enemy Within, 1918; The Madonna of the Hills, 1921; Liquid Gold, 1921; The God from Out the Sky; The Phantom Shot; also short stories in mags. Mem. Am. Legion, Vets. of Foreign Wars, Old Guard. Mason, Elk. Clubs: Bergen Beach Gun, Nassau Trapshooting, Lancaster Gun, Robin Hood Gun, Perry Circle Gun, Long Key Fishing. Home: New York.

EMPIE, PAUL CHAUNCEY, clergyman; b. St. Johnsville, N.Y., Feb. 10, 1909; s. Charles Gideon and Grace Louise (Diefendorf) E.; grad. Muhlenberg Coll., 1929, D.D. (hon.), 1944; postgrad Luth. Theol. Sem., Phila., 1929-32; LL.D., Capital U., 1950; L.H.D., Hartwick Coll., 1951; Th.D., U. Goettingen (Germany), 1952; D.D., Gustavus Adolphus Coll., 1960, Augustana Coll., Sioux Falls, S.D., 1962; m. Katharine Goodwin Smith, Dec. 27, 1930; children—Barbara, Charlotte, Susan. Ordained to ministry United Luth. Ch., 1932; established mission church, Phila., organized as Luth. Ch. of Prince of Peace, served as pastor until 1937; supt. Luth. Home for Orphans and Aged, Germantown, Phila., 1937-41; sec. Benevolence of Pa. Ministerium of United Luth. Ch. in Am., 1941-44; asst. exec. dir. Nat. Luth. Council, 1944-48, exec. dir., 1948-66; gen. sec. U.S.A. nat. com. World Luth. Fedn., 1967-72. Dir. Luth. World Action, 1944-72; chmn. Luth. Ch. Prodns., Inc., 1951-65; pres. Luth. Film Assos., 1955-66; chmn. dept. commn. religious liberty Nat. Council Chs. U.S., 1965-67, mem. exec. com. div. overseas ministry, 1966-72; chmn. world service Luth. World Fedn., 1952-70, hon. mem. exec. com., 1973-79; pres. Luth. World Relief, 1968-79; co-chmn. U.S.A. Nat. Luth.-Roman Cath. Theol. Dialogues, 1965-79; periodic visits to Europe, Asia, Africa, S. Am. in interests of relief, reconstrn., service to refugees; alt. del. constituting assembly World Council Chs., Amsterdam, 1948. Trustee Muhlenberg Coll., 1965-79, chmn., 1972-79. Recipient Mannerheim medal; decorated Orders of Finlandia, White Rose and Finland's Lion, 1949; comdr.'s cross Order of Merit (Fed. Republic Germany), 1961; recipient Wichern medal Evang. Ch. in Germany, 1967; Centennial medal for service to truth and humanity St. Olaf Coll., 1972. Author numerous pamphlets. Home: Zionsville, Pa. Died Sept. 1, 1979; interred Zions Evang. Luth. Ch. Cemetery.

EMRICH, DUNCAN BLACK MACDONALD, educator, diplomat, author; b. Mardin, Turkey, Apr. 11, 1908; s. Richard Stanley Merrill and Jeannette (Wallace) E.; student Phillips Andover Acad., 1922-26; A.B., Brown U., 1932; A.M., Columbia, 1933; Doctor en Letras, U. Madrid, 1934; Ph.D., Harvard (Shattuck scholar, Austin fellow), 1937; postgrad. U. Aix en Provence, Sorbonne, U. Cologne, Escuela de Estudios Arabes; grad. Command and Gen. Staff Sch., Ft. Leavenworth, 1943; m. Sally R. Selden, Nov. 20, 1955. Asst. prof. English, U. Denver, 1940-42; chief Archives Am. Folksong, Library Congress, 1945-46, chief folklore sect., 1946-55; cultural relations attache Am. embassy, Greece, 1956-58; consul, cultural affairs officer Am. Consulate Gen. of Calcutta, India, 1959-62; Nr. East analyst USIA, 1962-64; pub. affairs officer Am. embassy, Lome, Togo, 1964-66; desk officer, former French West African colonies USIA, Washington, 1966-69; prof. Am. folklore Am. U., Washington, from 1969. Weekly NBC radio broadcasts on folklore, 1953-55; U.S. rep. Internat. Folk Music Council, London, Internat. Folklore Conf., Paris. Served as maj. AUS, 1942-45. Guggenheim fellow, 1949-50; Fulbright lectr. U. Rome, 1952-53. Fellow Nat. Council Religion Higher Edn.; mem. Parnassos Soc. (hon., Athens, Greece), Hellenic-Am. Union (founder), Indo-Am. Soc. (founder). Author: Who Shot Maggie in the Freckle and other ballads of Virginia City, Nevada, 1940; Casey Jones and other Ballads of the Mining West, 1941; It's an Old Wild West Custom, 1949; Comstock Bonanza, 1950; The Cowboy's Own Brand Book, 1954; The Folklore of Love and Courtship, 1970; The Folklore of Weddings and Marriage, 1970; The Nonsense Book, 1970; The Book of Wishes and Wishmaking, 1971; Folklore on the American Land, 1972; The Hodgepodge Book, 1972; Am. Folk Poetry, 1974; The Whim-Wham Book, 1975. Contbr. articles to profl. jours. Co-editor, The Lucius Beebe Reader, 1967. Home: Washington, D.C., also Virginia City, Nev. Deceased.

ENDICOTT, JAMES LAWRENCE, mech. engr.; b. Phila., Pa., June 1884; s. James Lawrence and Lydia E. (Scull) E.; ed. pub. schs., Phila. and Internat. Corr. Sch.; m. Marie Elizabeth Parkes, June 15, 1914 (died Oct. 23, 1941); m. 2d, Ruth Elizabeth Ennis, Dec. 2, 1944. Apprentice Cramps Ship Yard, 1901-04, exptl. work, 1904; with Hol Tan Co., New York, 1905; gen. mechanic and cons. engring. practice; joined C. F. F. Wearne & Co., engrs., Singapore, Straits Settlements, 1910, as supt. various branches of the co., instructing natives and Chinese in care and operation of machinery; chief engr. and mill supt. Philippine Vegetable Oil Co., Manila, 1913; supt. service station, Hudson Motor Co., San Francisco, 1914-15; service mgr., etc., Chevrolet Motor Co., 1916, until entering army; served with Coconut Products Corp., Baltimore, and as mech. engr. Catalyst Testing Plant and Fixed Nitrogen & Research Laboratory, Washington, D.C.; staff Nat. Bur. Standards (resigned, 1943); with American Steel Company of Cuba to 1946; now in business as consulting engineer. Dir. Standard Credit Union (delegate D.C. Credit Union League), D.C. Credit Union League; pres. Washington Trade School and Washington Aviation Sch., Washington. Served as 1st lt. M.T.C., U.S. Army, World War; organizer and chief tech. instr. M.T.C. Training Sch. for Southern Dept.; liaison officer Engring. Office, M.C.S., Washington. Club: Anchor. Republican. Mason. Author: M.T.C. Motor Manual for War Department, 1918. Co-author: Airline War Training Institute Aircraft Mechanics Training Manual. Home: Arlington, Va.; also Jackson Heights, Long Island, New York.

ENDICOTT, ROBERT RANTOUL, editor, pub. cons.; b. Detroit, Feb. 14, 1905; s. John and Mary Elizabeth (Booth) E.; B.A., Phillips Exeter Acad., 1922; B.A., Harvard U., 1926; m. Harriet Hastings, Mar. 14, 1945; children—John, Eve. Instnl. advt., sales depts. Gen. Motors Corp., 1926-29; advt., publicity dir. Internat. Merc. Marine Co., 1930-31; mng. editor Family Circle mag., 1932-35, editor, 1936-54; editor New Homes Guide and Home Modernizing, 1955-56, Today's Living mag. N.Y. Herald Tribune, 1956-61, Am. Heritage New Illus. History of U.S., 1962-63; pub. cons. Clubs: University, Dutch Treat, Overseas Press, Harvard (N.Y.C.). Home: Washington Depot, Conn. Died Oct. 17, 1977; interred Central Cemetery, Beverly, Mass.

ENGBLOM, ALEXANDER NATANAEL, bus. exec.; b. Södertalje, Sweden, Feb. 17, 1885; s. Eric and Josefina Wilhelmina Helén E.; grad. John Lenning's Weaving Sch., Norrköping, 1906; M.E., Royal Univ. of Tech., Stockholm, Sweden, 1908; m. Elin Kerstin Ragnhild Holmer, June 5, 1919; children—Elsa Thyra Birgitta (wife of Dr. Lars-Erik Floberg), Eric Arvid. Mech. supt. Sidney Blumenthal & Co. Textile Mills, Shelton, Conn., 1910-17; mgr., Litografiska A.B., Norrköping, Sweden, 1917-20; tech. dir. Borås Wäfveri Aktiebolag, Borås, Sweden, since 1920. Pres. bd. Craftschool (Borås); mem. bd. Borås Tech. Sch. and Textile Inst.; pres. bd. Borås Soc. pertaining to history of civilization. Fellow Textile Inst. (Manchester), Am. Soc. M.E.; mem. Royal Swedish Inst. Engring. Research. Decorated Knight of Order of Pole Star, Order Vasa, French Legion of Honor; awarded 3 gold medals. Author of publications on tech., textile, economical and social subjects. Home: Boras, Sweden.

ENGDAHL, JOHN LOUIS, editor; b. Minneapolis, Minn., Nov. 11, 1884; s. Lars J. and Anna Louisa (Anderson) Engdahl; student University of Minnesota, 1903-7; m. Pauline Grace Levitin, of Chicago, Ill., June 27, 1914. Served as city editor and telegraph editor, Minneapolis Daily News, editor Chicago Daily Socialist, mng. editor Chicago Daily World and labor editor and field corr. Milwaukee Leader; editor, The American Socialist (official publ. Socialist Party) since 1914. Del. Internat. Socialist Congress, Copenhagen, Denmark, 1910. Socialist nominee for congressman at-large, Ill., 1916. Author: Saving the Nation's Bread; The Trade Unions and the Social Crisis. Home: Chicago.

ENGEBRETSON, OSCAR EDWIN, clergyman; b. Whalan, Minn., June 3, 1905; s. Halvor and Caroline (Hjelle) E.; student Luther Acad., 1920-23; B.A., Luther Coll., 1927; C.T., B.Th., Luther Sem., 1930; m. Irene Octavia Lembke, July 2, 1930; children—Conrad, Henrik, Mark. Ordained to ministry Evang. Luth. Ch., 1930; pastor Rolette, Overly, N.D., 1930-37, Walcott, N.D., 1937-41, Washington Prairie Luth. Ch. (one of Twelve Great Chs. in Am. 1950), Decorah, Iowa, 1941-52, Trinity Ch., Spring Grove, Minn., 1952-57, Faith Ch., Madison, Minn., 1960-70, Estherville (Iowa) Luth. Ch., 1970-73; evangelist Evang. Luth. Ch., Mpls., 1957-60; mem. commn. research and social action Am. Luth Ch., 1959-74, mem. dept. town and country ch., 1960-64; rural life commn. Evang. Luth. Ch., bd. parish edn., 1944-50; mem. bd. edn., 1950-54; councillor Nat. Luth. Council, 1956-67. Recipient ceriificate of service King Haakon, Norway, 1949; Disting. Service award Luther Coll., 1967; John Schultz Meml. award for promotion and conservation, 1979. Mem. Smyrna Soc. (pres. 1977-78), Norwegian Am. Fedn. Author: Chosen Witnesses, 1952; Faith and Service, 1958; Exile and Restoration, 1967; contbr. articles to religious publs. Home: Decorah, Iowa. Died May 15, 1980; buried Washington Prairie Luth. Ch. Cemetery, Decorah.

ENGEL, IRVING M., lawyer, author, lectr.; b. Birmingham, Ala., Oct. 19, 1891; s. Michael P. and Sophie (Kronenberg) E.; J.D. magna cum laude, Yale U., 1913; D.Litt., Dropsie Coll. Hebrew Learning, 1958; L.H.D., Hebrew Union Coll.-Jewish Inst. Religion, 1958; LL.D., L.I. U., 1964; m. Katharine I. Asher, Jan. 14, 1926 (dec.) 1 dau., Susan E. Levy. Admitted to Ala. bar, 1910, N.Y. bar, 1925; practiced law, Birmingham, 1913-24; N.Y.C., 1924-78, sr. partner Engel & Judge, Title ins. adv. com. Title Guarantee Co. 1948-71; mem. bd. govs. Real Estate Bd. N.Y., 1948-51, arbitration bd. and legislation com.; lectr. real estate, taxation Practicing Law Inst., Am. Bar Assn., N.Y. U. Mem. Nat. Com. on Segregation in Nation's Capital, 1949; pres. Ednl. Found. for Jewish Girls, 1945-50, now hon. chmn. bd.; co-chmn. gov. bd. consultative council Jewish Orgns., 1954-59; mem. Citizens Com. on Displaced Persons, chmn. policy com. 1947-50; mem. Am. Com. for Israel's Tenth Anniversary Celebration, vice chmn. policy com. 1958; pres. Am. Jewish Com., 1954-59, now hon. pres.; mem. Pres.'s Com. on Govt. Contract Compliance, 1951-53; mem. Mayor's Com. on Judiciary, 1962-65; mem. state com. Pub. Employee Security, 1954. Candidate for Congress, Democratic and Liberal parties 17th dist. N.Y., 1950; alternat del. Dem. Nat. Conv., 1952, alternate-at-large, 1956, mem. fgn. policy sub-com. nat. adv. council Nat. Dem. Com., 1959-61; chmn. exec. com. N.Y. Com. for Dem. Voters, 1959-60, chmn., 1961, chmn. adv. council, 1962-63; chmn. civil rights com. Dem. State Adv. Com.; chmn. polit. and planning com. N.Y. Citizens for Kennedy and Johnson, 1960. Del. German-Am. Confs. East-West Tensions, 1959, 61, 62, 67; mem. Pres.' Spl. Mission, inauguration Pres. Ramon, Panama, 1952. Bd. dirs. Nat. Com. against Discrimination in Housing. Served to 1st lt. F.A., U.S. Army, A.E.F., 1917-19. Decorated grand officer Order Micham Iftikhar (Tunisian Legion Honor), 1954; chevalier French Legion of Honor, 1958. First pres. Alabama Jr. C. of C., 1920-21. Mem. Council Fgn. Relations, Yale Law Sch. Assn. (v.p., dir.), Nat. Citizens Com. on Community Relations. Clubs: University, City (N.Y.C.), Yale. Author: Income Taxes and Real Estate. Home: New York City, N.Y. Died Dec. 4, 1978.

ENGEL, LEWIS LIBMAN, biochemist; b. N.Y.C., Sept. 2, 1909; s. Adolph and Esther (Libman) E.; B.S., Harvard, 1930; Ph.D., Columbia U., 1936; LL.D., U. Glasgow, 1969; m. Margaret Fisher Knox, Nov. 21, 1938 (dec. Dec. 1973). Asst. biol. chemistry Columbia U., 1931-33; guest investigator Royal Cancer Hosp., London, 1936-37; instr. biochemistry Mayo Found. Med. Edn. and Research, 1942-43; asso. prof. biol. chemistry Mass. Gen. Hosp. and Harvard U. 1958-66, Am. Cancer Soc. prof. biol. chemistry, 1966-76; acting chmn. bd. tutors biochem. sci. Harvard U., 1957-58, 63-65, chmn. dept. biol. chemistry Harvard Med. Sch., 1976-78; Macfarlane prof. Glasgow (Scotland) U., 1967-68; Fachhoerer Fed. Poly. Inst., Zurich, Switzerland, 1935-36. Bd. dirs. Mass. div. Am. Cancer Soc., 1968-78, med. v.p., 1972-74, pres., 1974-76. Served to capt. San. Corps, AUS, 1943-46. Recipient Bronze medal Am. Cancer Soc., 1967. Mem. Am. Soc. Biol. Chemists, Am. Acad. Arts and Scis., Endocrine Soc. (Eli Lilly award 1970, pres. 1972-73). Editor: (with C.A. Villee) Mechanism of Action of Steriod Hormones, 1961. Physical Properties of Steriod Harmones, 1963. Editorial bd. Endocrinology, 1957-65, Jour. Biol. Chemistry, 1959-64, 65-71. Home: Boston, Mass. Died Sept. 13, 1978.

ENGH, HAROLD V., business exec.; b. Chicago, July 12, 1893; s. Anton A. and Anna (Johnson) E.; ed. Lane Tech. Sch.; m. Helen Whittemore, June 5, 1918; children—Jean, Barbara, Harold, Dorothy Anne. Began with Chicago Insulated Wire Mfg. Co.; when cos. merged to form Inland Wire & Cable Co., became pres.; when latter merged into Anaconda Wire & Cable Co.. Became exec. v.p. and dir.; pres. and dir. Pyle-Nat. Co 1947-55; chmn. Bd. Turner Corp., Sycamore, Ill.; dir. Lyon Metal Products, Inc., Aurora, Ill. Home Sycamore, Ill. Died Nov. 1978.

ENGLAND, BAYARD L(ANNING), business exec., b. Newark, N.J., Nov. 2, 1903; s. Frank C. and Henrietta (Lanning) E.; student Temple U., 1922-23; m. Kathryn Bradley. Chmn. Atlantic City Electric Co.; dir Prudential Ins. Co. Am., Fed. Res. Bank of Phila., VI Corp. Home: Ventnor, N.J. Died Oct. 18, 1980.

ENGLE, JOHN RAYMOND (ENG'GEL), b Palmyra, Pa., Mar. 13, 1885; s. Samuel F. and Agne (Balsbaugh) E.; A.B., Yale, 1906; LL.B., U. of Va., 1908 LL.D., Lebanon Valley Coll., 1925; m. Nelle Moyer Sept. 3, 1908; children—Mary Elizabeth, Eleano Caroline. Began law practice at Huntington, W.Va 1908, Lebanon, Pa., 1910; treas. E. Pa. Conf. of Ch. c United Brethren in Christ, 1916; mem. bd. adminstrn U. B. Ch., 1917; trustee Lebanon Valley Coll., 191 chmn. endowment campaign, 1924; chmn. finance com and pres. bd. trustees, 1929, acting pres., 1932; pre Palmyra Improvement Co.; solicitor and dir. Valle Trust Co. Pres. Palmyra Bd. of Edn., 1929. Truste Bonebrake Theol. Sem., Dayton, O. Mem. Delta Ch

Republican. Mason. Clubs: Pennsylvanians, Pennsylvania German Society. Home: Palmyra, Penn. *

ENGLER, KYLE, agrl. engr., educator; b. Hutchinson, Kan., Oct. 13, 1903; s. Harry and Charlotte Beatrice (Turner) E.; student U. of Cincinnati, 1924-25, Hutchinson Jr. Coll., 1933-34; B.S. in elec. engring., Kan. State Coll., 1930, B.S. in agrl. engineering, 1935; research fellow Iowa State College, 1935-36, M.S. in Agricultural Engineering, 1936; married Thelma Helen Rawlings, June 6, 1931; children—Phillip Vaughn, Robert Kyle, Janet Elizabeth. Student engr. Southwestern Bell Telephone Co., Wichita, Kan., 1930-32; wheat farmer, Hutchinson, 1932-34; instr. agrl. engring. Ia. State Coll., 1936-37; asst. prof. U. of Ark., 1937-42, asso. prof., 1942-45, acting head dept. agrl. engring., 1943-45, prof., head dept. agrl. engring. 1945-71, prof. emeritus, 1971-77; rep. War Surplus Equipment, 1946-48; engr. in charge project ground water resources Ark. Agrl. Expt. Sta., from 1937, project leader mechanization cotton prodn., from 1945; collaborator U.S. Dept. Agr., 1948; chmn. Ark. Irrigation Com. for development Ark.-White-Red River Basin, 1950-53; member of Arkansas Water Resources Conservation and Development Council, from 1952; project leader for Ark. Agr. Expt. Sta. on ground water recharge. Registered profl. engr. Fellow American Society Agriculture Engineers (pres. S.W. sect. 1947-48); mem. American Assn. U. Profs., Am. Geophys. Union, American Society of Engineering Education, Boy Scouts of America (cub-master), Gamma Sigma Delta. Presbyn. Club: Kiwanis. Author articles in profl. jours. Inventor Farm-Size Grain Drier (with E. L. Barger and A. H. Thompson), patent 1946. Home: Fayetteville, Ark. Died Jan. 25, 1977.

ENGLISH, E(UGENE) SCHUYLER, editor, author; b. N.Y.C., Oct. 12, 1899; s. Eugene Montgomery and Clara (Stoiber) E.; grad. Phillips Acad., Andover, Mass., 1918; student Princeton, 1918-20; Litt.D., Wheaton (Ill.) Coll., 1939; m. Eva Linde Schultz, March 2, 1937 (dec. August 1956); m. 2d Ruth Hill Kephart, July 4, 1959; stepchildren—Katharine K. Barnes, Susan K. Simpson. Sec. Sterling Pure Food Co., Phila., 1920-21; asst. purchasing agt. Curtis Pub. Co., 1922-31; pres. Am. Bible Conf. Assn., Inc., 1930-47; mng. editor Revelation mag. 1931-39; mem. faculty Phila. Sch. Bible, 1935-47, pres., 1936-39; asso. editor Our Hope mag., 1939-45, editor, 1946-58; editor The Pilgrim (missionary publ.), 1944-81; radio broadcaster Phila. Stas. on Bible Study themes, 1935-46. Served as pvt. U.S. Army, Sept.-Dec. 1918. Author: Studies in the Gospel According to Matthew, 1935; By Life and By Death, 1938; The Life and Letters of St. Peter, 1941; Studies in the Gospel According to Mark, 1943; Studies in the Epistle to the Colossians, 1944; The Shifting of the Scenes, 1945; H.A. Ironside, Ordained of the Lord, 1946, 2d edit, 1976; Things Surely to Be Believed, 1946; Studies in I and II Thessalonians, 1947; Robert G. Lee, A Chosen Vessel, 1949; Re-Thinking the Rapture, 1951; Studies in the Epistle to the Hebrews, 1954. Editor-in-chief Pilgrim Edition of The Holy Bible, 1948. Chmn. editorial com. New Scofield Reference Bible, 1967. Editor: Revised N.T. Berkley Bible, 1969; A Companion to New Scofield Reference Bible, 1972. Home: Merion, Pa. Died Mar. 16, 1981; buried St. Christopher's Ch., Gladwyne, Pa.

ENGLISH, EARL FORMAN, engring. exec.; b. Jersey City, Dec. 8, 1886; s. Alfred Alexander and Sara Earl (Anderson) E.; M.E., Stevens Inst. Tech., 1906, D.Eng. (hon.), 1953; m. Mercedes Rodrigo, July 9, 1931; children—Elizabeth (Mrs. Richard O'Brien), Earl Rowland. Test dept. Gen. Electric Co., 1906-08; student cadet Pub. Service Electric Gas Co., 1908-10; gen. engr. S. S. Barston Co., 1910-12; power engr. N.Y. Telephone Co., 1912-19; asst. chief engr. J. G. White Management Corp., 1919-21; utilities management and investigation engr. Sanderson Porter, 1921-22; v.p., chief engr. Gen. Engring. Management Corp., 1922-26; pres. U.S. Engring. Corp., 1926-29, Standard Management & Operating Corp., 1929-35; v.p. W. A. Bechtel Co., Bechtel McCone Corp., (now Bechtel Internat. Corp.), 1936—; dir.-v.p. and tech. adviser Thermal Power Co., 1959—; engring. cons. Wells Fargo Bank, San Francisco. Navy Dept. Meritorious Civilian Service Award for work with Pacific Naval Bases, 1944. Mem. A.S.M.E. Clubs: Engineers (San Francisco, N.Y.C.); University, Bankers (N.Y.C.); The Family (San Francisco). Originator of studies and plans for supplying Europe with Middle East natural gas. Home: San Francisco

ENGLISH, JAMES HENRY, prof. of Romance langs.; b. Armagh, Ire., Sept. 10, 1886; s. John and Ellen (Kew) E.; A.B., Dartmouth Coll., 1912; Ph.D., Columbia Univ., 1926; fgn. study, Univ. of Dijon, France, 1911, Madrid, Spain, 1927-28; m. Sarah Conover, July 12, 1922; 1 dau., Elizabeth (dec.). Instr. French, Latin, Lafayette Coll., Easton, Pa., 1912-14, Rutgers Prep Sch., Rutgers Coll., 1914-16, Choate Sch., Wallingford, Conn., 1916-18; instr. French, Columbia Univ., extension teaching, 1918-24; asst. prof. Spanish, N.Y. Univ., 1924-30; prof. Romance lang., Lincoln Memorial Univ., 1930-31; head mod. lang. dept. Grove City (Pa.) Coll. since 1931. Mem. Modern Lang. Assn. Am., Am. Assn. Univ. Profs. Republican. Presbyterian. Author: The Alternation of H and F in Old Spanish, N.Y., 1926; French Reading and Grammar. Home: Grove City, Pa.

ENGLISH, SPOFFORD GRADY, cons. chemist; b. Mt. Pleasant, Tenn., Nov. 16, 1915; s. Spofford G. and Ruby May (Warnock) E.; student U. Chattanooga, 1933-34; B.S., U. Okla., 1938, M.S., 1940; Ph.D., U. Calif. at Berkeley, 1943; m. Muriel K. Frodin, Sept. 18, 1942; children—Susan P., Elizabeth H., Helen W. Chemist, Okla. Geol. Survey, 1936-40; teaching asst. chemistry U. Calif. at Berkeley, 1940-42; group leader Manhattan Project, U. Chgo., 1942-43; sect. chief chemistry div. Clinton Lab., Oak Ridge, 1943-46; asst. prof. chemistry U. Calif. at Berkeley, 1946-47; mem. staff AEC (became ERDA 1975), 1947-76, dep. dir. research, 1960-61, asst. gen. mgr. research and devel., 1961-73, asso. dir. div. phys. research, 1973-76, chmn. plowshare adv. com., 1960-76; chemistry cons., 1977-81; tech. adviser U.S. del. UN Disarmament Conf., London, 1955, U.S. del. Conf. Cessation Nuclear Weapons Test, Geneva, 1959; mem. U.S. del. IAEA, 1956. Mem. Phi Beta Kappa, Sigma Xi. Home: Bethesda, Md. Died Apr. 6, 1981.

ENRIGHT, WILLIAM FAIRLEIGH, banker; b. St. Joseph, Mo., Feb. 23, 1894; s. Charles Frederick and Jennie (Fairleigh) E.; A.B., Harvard, 1916, postgrad. Sch. Bus. Adminstrn., 1916-17; m. Lucie Graham Howell, Feb. 5, 1918 (div. 1933); children—Jane Fairleigh (Mrs. Jane Enright Davis), William Fairleigh; m. 2d, Maurine O'Malley, Aug. 16, 1944. With Empire Trust Co., St. Joseph, 1919-75, bookkeeper, teller, sec., treas. and v.p. to 1935, pres., 1935-60, consol. with Tootle Nat. Bank, 1960, chmn. bd. Tootle-Enright Nat. Bank (consol. with Am. Nat. Bank 1963), St. Joseph, co-chmn. exec. com.; v.p., dir., Mo. Water and Stream Supply Co. Col. on staff of Gov. of Mo., 1937-41, 49-53, 57-65; mem. adv. bd. Mo. State Conservation Commn.; del. from Mo. to 1st Inter-Am. Travel Congress, San Francisco, 1939; del. from Mo. to Nat. Rivers and Harbors Congress, Washington, 1939; chmn. Selective Service Bd. No. 1 Buchanan County, Mo. mem. City Planning Commn. St. Joseph. Bd. dirs. Northwest Mo. Assn. for Blind; mem. bd. edn. Mo. Sch. Dist.; mem. Mo. State Commn. Resources and Devel. Chmn. bd. trustees Employees Retirement Fund St. Joseph Sch. System. Active in Dem. Party in Mo.; organized Dem. Boosters Club, St. Joseph, 1930, pres. 1930-34. Entered 1st O.T.C., Ft. Riley, Kans., May 10, 1917; commd. 2d lt. Coast Arty. Corps, U.S. Army, Fortress Monroe, Va.; served with 75th Arty., 1919. Elk. Clubs: Benton, St. Joseph, St. Joseph Country; Harvard (N.Y.C.); Garden of the Gods, Cheyenne Mountain Country, Broadmoor Golf (Colorado Springs, Colo.) River (Kansas City, Mo.). Home: Saint Joseph, Mo. Died Dec. 22, 1975.

ENSIGN, RAYMOND POWELL, art educator; b. River Falls, Wis., Aug. 4, 1883; s. Frank DeForest and Harriet Newell (Powell) E.; grad. State Normal Sch., River Falls, Wis., 1902; grad. Pratt Inst., Brooklyn, N.Y., 1905; married. Teacher architectural drawing, N.Y. Evening High Sch., 1905-10; teacher drawing and design, Pratt Inst., 1906-12; supervisor Dept. of Design and Interior Decoration, same, 1912-18; head Dept. Decorative Design, Cleveland Sch. of Art, 1918-22; dean of Sch. of Art Institute Chicago, 1922-27. Dir. Berkshire Summer Sch. of Art, and one of its founders in 1915; dir. Newark Sch. of Fine and Industrial Art, 1928-35; exec. sec. Eastern Arts Assn. since 1935. Asso. mem. N.E.A. Home: New York, N.Y.

ENSLEY, FRANCIS GERALD, clergyman; b. Morrow County, O., Aug. 12, 1907; s. Louis Alfred and Nellie Jane (McConnell) E.; A.B., Ohio Wesleyan U., 1927, S.T.B. magna cum laude, Boston U., 1931, Ph.D., 1938; D.D., 1957; postgrad. (Jacob Sleeper fellow) U. Berlin (Germany), 1931-32; D.D., Ohio Wesleyan U., 1946, Westmar Coll., 1963; LL.D., Baker U., 1964, Ia. Wesleyan Coll., 1953; L.H.D., Simpson Coll., 1953, Mount Union Coll., 1969; Litt.D., Morningside Coll., 1960, Am. U., 1961, Rio Grande Coll., 1966; Ecum.D., Ohio No. U., 1965; Pd.D., Baldwin-Wallace Coll., 1966; m. Eunice Irene LeBourveau, July 6, 1935; children—Frederick Louis, Philip Chalfant, Elizabeth (Mrs. Grime), Charlotte (Mrs. Linville). Ordained to ministry Meth. Ch., 1936; asso. minister Islington (Mass.) Community Ch., 1932-33; minister North Hampton (N.H.) Congl. Ch., 1933-35, United Church of Norwood (Mass.), 1935-44; instr. homiletics Boston U. Sch. Theology, 1938-44, prof. systematic theology, 1944; minister North Broadway Met. Ch., Columbus, O., 1944-52; consecrated bishop Meth. Ch., 1952, assigned to Ia. area, 1952-64, Ohio West area, Columbus, 1964-76. Chmn. div. higher edn. Meth. Ch., 1960-64, pres. gen. bd. social concerns, 1960-64, chmn. commn. on ecumenical affairs, 1964-68; pres. Am. sect. World Meth. Council, 1966-76; v.p. Council on World Service and Finance, 1969-73, pres., 1973-76; chmn. com. on evangelism world Meth. Council, 1970-76; Willson lectr., 1966, Loud Meml. lectr., 1949; Mendenhall lectr. DePauw U., 1959; mem. Gen. Conf. Meth. Ch., 1948, 52, Ecumenical Conf., 1951-56, 61-66. Trustee Alaska Meth. U., Mt. Union, Baldwin-Wallace colls., Ohio Wesleyan U., Ohio No. U. Mem. Delta Sigma Rho, Omicron Delta Kappa, Torch, Mason (33 deg.). Contbr. to Ency. Religion, Personalism in Theology, A Symphony of Prayer. Author: John Wesley, Evangelist; Paul's Letters to Local Churches; The Marks of Christian Education; Persons Can Change. Home: Columbus, Ohio. Died Sept. 21, 1976.

ENTREKIN, PAUL BRINTON, steel co. exec.; b. Coatesville, Pa., Oct. 16, 1901; s. Norman R. and Anna S. (Brinton) E.; E.M., Lehigh U., 1925; m. Ruth Terhune, February 14, 1936; one daughter, Ann Brinton Entrekin Von Thaden. Began career with Bethlehem Steel Co., from 1925, gen. mgr. mining division, 1949-57, asst. v.p., dir. 1957-63, vice president and director, from 1963; dir. Mem. iron ore industry adv. com. Office Minerals Mblzn., Dept. of Interior. Mem. Am. Iron and Steel Inst., Am. Inst. Mining, Metall. and Petroleum Engrs., Am. Mining Congress, Am. Iron Ore Assn. (dir.), Sigma Chi. Republican. Mem. Soc. of Friends. Clubs: Mining, University (N.Y.C.); Saucon Valley Country (Bethlehem, Pa.). Home: Sarasota, Fla. Died Dec. 8, 1979.

ENYART, ARTHUR DELANO (EN'YÄRT), coll. dean; b. Dayton, O., May 5, 1882; s. James Homer and Susan Cart (McCarter) E.; A.B., Ohio Wesleyan U., 1906, A.M., 1910; S.T.B., Boston U., 1910, Litt.D., 1914; grad. study Brown U., 1911-12, Harvard, 1913-14; unmarried. Asst. pastor Trinity M.E. Ch., Portsmouth, O., 1910; instr. E. Greenwich (R.I.) Acad., 1910-11; dean Rollins Coll., Winter Park, Fla., 1911-17; dean Burdette Coll., Boston, 1919-29; dean of men, Rollins Coll. since 1930. Served as 2d lt., Y.M.C.A. personnel work, A.E.F., France, 1917-18. Mem. Assn. Deans of Men, Am. Coll. Personnel Assn., Am. Econ. Assn., Chamber of Commerce, Pi Gamma Mu, Sigma Chi Omega, Omicron Delta Kappa. Phi Kappa Psi. Mason. Club: University (Winter Park). Home: Winter Park, Fla.

EPLEY, DEAN GEORGE, educator; b. Carrollton, Ohio, Nov. 9, 1917; s. John and Laura Olga (Kratz) E.; B.S., Kent State U., 1947, M.A., 1950; Ph.D., Mich. State U., 1953; m. Pauline Lawton, May 2, 1941; children—Deanna, Paul, David, Thomas, Bryan, John, Laurabeth. Tchr. pub. schs. Ohio, 1937-50; asst. prof. sociology Memphis State U., 1952-54; prof., chmn. human relations U. Miami at Fla., 1954-61; dir. counseling Concord Coll., W.Va., 1961-64; prof., chmn. sociology Bradley U., Peoria, Ill., 1964-69; prof. chmn. sociology Monmouth (Ill.) Coll., 1970-77. Vis. prof. Mich. State U., 1953, U. Nijmegen, Netherlands, 1957, Oakland U., 1960, Western Ill. U., 1967; cons. U. Penang, U. Malaysia, Office Prime Minister Malaysia, 1969-70. Pres., W.Va. Assn. Mental Health, 1963-64; founder, Suicide Prevention Service, Peoria, 1968-69; Malaysian del. World Fedn. Mental Health, 1970. Sr. Fulbright lectr. MARA Inst. Tech., Malaysia, 1969-70, cons., 1973. Recipient research and travel grants Benjamin Bronston Found., Samuel Blank Family Found., NSF. Fellow Am. Sociol. Assn., Royal Anthrop. Inst. of Gt. Britain and Ireland, Soc. Applied Anthropology; mem. Soc. Study Social Problems, AAUP, Phi Beta Kappa, Kappa Delta Pi, Pi Gamma Mu, Phi Alpha Theta. Methodist. Author: Theory and Practice in Human Relations, 1956; Human Relations in Higher Education, 1960; An Annotated Bibliography of Human Relations, 1962; Exercises and Experiments in the Sociological Tradition, 1965. Editor: The Ill. Sociologist, 1967-69. Home: Monmouth, Ill. Died Jan. 25, 1977.

EPLEY, MALCOLM, newspaperman; b. Broken Bow, Nebr., July 13, 1904; s. Lloyd L. and Mina (Hall) E.; A.B., U. Oreg., 1929; m. Jane Dudley, Jan. 8, 1927; children—Malcolm, John MacNaughton, Alexandra (Mrs. Richard Traver). Reporter, Riverside (Calif.) Enterprise, 1923-25; news editor Eugene (Oreg.) Register, 1928-30; mng. editor Klamath Falls (Oreg.) Herald & News, 1931-49; columnist, polit. editor, editor Long Beach (Calif.) Ind. and Press.-Telegram, 1949-79. Past mem. bds. numerous city, county, state bds. including trustee Long Beach Meml. Hosp. Named Citizen of Year, City of Long Beach, 1971; hon. Ky. col. Mem. Sigma Alpha Epsilon, Alpha Phi Gamma, Sigma Delta Chi. Republican. United Methodist. Clubs: Elks (dist. dep. Oreg. South 1946), Rotary (pres. Klamath Falls 1941-42, Long Beach 1961-62), International City. Author: Highlights and Anecdotes-An Illustrated History of Long Beach. Home: Fort Bidwell, Calif. Died Mar. 4, 1979; buried Ft. Bidwell (Calif.) Cemetery.

EPPINGER, EUGENE, physician; b. Pendleton, Oreg., Sept. 30, 1902; s. Charles A. and Catherine (Vaughan) E.; A.B., Williams Coll., 1926; M.D., Harvard, 1930; m. Catherine Codman, July 13, 1935; children—Catherine Codman, Margaret Vaughan. Successively jr., sr., asso. and physician Peter Bent Brigham Hosp., Boston, from 1937, acting physician-in-chief, 1951-52; asst. in medicine, instr. med. sch. Harvard, 1937-42, asst. dean, 1945-66, asst. clin. prof., 1945-58, asso. clin. prof., 1958-64, clin. prof. medicine, 1964-69, clin. prof. emeritus, 1969; indsl. relations div. Proctor & Gamble Co., Cin., 1936-37; asso. physician Boston Lying In Hosp.; cons. Free Hosp. for Women; cons. in medicine to Surgeon Gen., U.S. Army. Served as col. M.C., AUS, 1942-45. Fellow A.C.P.; mem. Am. Soc. Clin. Investigation, Am. Clin. and Climatol. Assn., Am. Heart Assn., Soc. Med. Consultants World War II, Assn. Am. Physicians. Home: Chestnut Hill, Mass. Deceased.

EPPINGER, JOSUA, JR., ret. editor, pub. relations cons.; b. San Francisco, Oct. 7, 1902; s. Josua and Hilda (Levy) E.; B.S., U. Calif., 1924; m. Helen Kahn, Jan. 8, 1933 (dec. 1956); children—Wendy Claire (Mrs. J.A. Shulman), Josua III, Frederick Dwight; m. 2d, Consuelo B. Hofmann, Aug. 20, 1957; children—Robert, Paul, David, Judith (Mrs. Peter Coy), Michael Hofmann. Reporter San Francisco Examiner, 1924-38, city editor, 1938-46, exec. city editor, 1946, asso. mng. editor, to 1976; pub. relations cons., 1976-79. Bd. dirs. Jr. Achievement, San Francisco Heart Assn. Served as lt. col. AUS, 1941-45. Mem. Alpha Kappa Psi, Delta Sigma Lambda, Sigma Delta Chi. Clubs: Press, Presidio Officers (San Francisco). Home: San Francisco, Calif. Died May 1, 1979.

EPPLEY, GEARY FRANCIS, educator; b. Washington, Dec. 30, 1895; s. Geary Begot and Eva Margretta (Stinzing) E.; B.S., Md. State Coll. Agr., 1920; M.S., U. of Md., 1926; m. Elizabeth Flenner, Sept. 8, 1925; children—Miriam Elizabeth, Danforth, Frances Rita, Geary Wareham. Ednl. training officer Fed. Bd. Vocational Edn. V.A., 1921; asst. prof. agronomy U. of Md., 1922-30, track coach, part time 1926-41, asso. prof. and agronomist Agr. Expt. Sta., 1930-36, dean men since 1936, dir. athletics, 1936-47, dir. student welfare, 1946-58. Director Prince Georges Co. Boys Clubs; pres. So. Conf., 1949-50. Chmn. budget com. Prince Georges County Community Chest; president Atlantic Coast Conference. Served as 2d lt., 2d Cavalry A.E.F., 1918-19; col., exec. officer requirements Sect. Hdqrs. Army Ground Forces, active duty, 1941-46; O.R.C. since 1919. Recipient Legion of Merit, 1945. Past comdr. Am. Legion; mem. Phi Kappa Phi, Sigma Chi, Omicron Delta Kappa, Pi Delta Epsilon, Phi Eta Sigma. Episcopalian. Mason. Home: College Park, Md. Died June 17, 1978.

EPSTEIN, HENRY DAVID, real estate developer; b. Phila., Mar. 4, 1921; s. Solomon A. and Flora K. (Kauffmann) E.; student U. Pa.; m. Dasha Amsterdam, Dec. 10, 1957; children—Robert E. L., Danielle A. Pres., South Village Properties, Inc., 1952-80; chmn., chief exec. officer Gulfstream Land and Devel. Co., Plantation, Fla., 1962-80. Served with USAAF, 1943-45. Home: New York, N.Y. Died July 19, 1980.

EPSTEIN, SAUL LEON, paper co. exec.; b. Bklyn., May 8, 1905; s. Louis and Sarah (Broadman) E.; L.H.D.; Hofstra U., 1970; m. Evelyn Segal, Jan 5, 1930; children—Howard, Raymond. Vice pres. Atlantic Containers Corp., 1934-39; pres. Interstate Container Corp., N.Y.C., dir. Nat. Bank N.Am., N.Y.C. Pres. The Epstein Found. Inc. Trustee Hofstra U.; pres. Jewish Med. Center, N.Y.C., 1950-56, hon. pres., 1956, also trustee Mason (Shriner). Home: New York, N.Y. Deceased.

ERICKSEN, EPHRAIM EDWARD, univ. prof., adminstr.; b. Logan, Utah, Jan. 2, 1882; s. Bendt Jensen and Anna Sophia (Danielsen) E.; A.B., Brigham Young Coll. (Utah), 1908; Ph.D., U. of Chicago, 1918; m. Edna Clark, June 8, 1910; children—Stanford Clark, Sheldon Danielsen, Ephraim Gordon, Edna Margaret (Mrs. Mont Glen Kenney), Howard (dec.). Prin., Murdock Acad., 1911-15; prof. of philosophy, U. of Utah, 1915-48; dean, Sch. of Arts and Sciences, U. of Utah, 1942-48; lecturer, chmn. dept. philosophy, U. of Nev., since 1948; Mem., Citizens' Com., Utah State Employment Service, 1936-41; chmn. Joint Merit System Council since 1941. Mem. Am. Philos. Assn. (pres., Pacific Div., 1941), Phi Kappa Phi, Phi Delta Kappa. Author books. Contbr. articles to jours. Home: Salt Lake City.

ERICKSON, FRANKLIN CARL, educator; b. Worcester, Mass., Dec. 16, 1903; s. Sven August and Hilda (Hendrickson) E.; A.B., Clark U., 1928, A.M., 1930, Ph.D., 1935; Swiss-Am. exchange student, Zurich, 1932-33; m. Albertha May Naas, Sept. 6, 1936; children—Betty Mae, Sally Hilda. Cartographer Macmillan Pub. Co., 1928-29; asso. prof. U.S.C., 1935; prof. geography U. N.C., 1936-43, 44-47; prof. geography Boston U., 1947-72, chmn. dept. 1949-69, asso. dean coll. liberal arts, 1959-69. Chief cartographic sect. Bur. Econ. Warfare, Washington, 1942-44. Mem. Am. Assn. Geographers, Am. Soc. Profl. Geographers, Sigma Xi, Pi Gamma, Mu, Lambda Chi Alpha. Mason. Author articles on land use. Home: Newtonville, Mass. Died Jan. 9, 1981; buried Newton, Mass.

ERICKSON, SIDNEY, army officer (ret.); b. Lakefield, Minn., July 28, 1885; s. Emil and Emily E.; grad. Inf. Sch., 1926, Command and Gen. Staff Sch., 1927, War Coll., 1934; m. Emma Annis Harvey, Sept. 13, 1914; 1 dau., Ursula Mae (Mrs. C. A. Dahlen). Enlisted man, 1907, advanced through grades to brig. gen., 1943; served as prof. military science and tactics, U. of Neb., 1921-25; instr. Command and Gen. Staff Sch., 1929-33; dir. Ground Arms Dept., Air Corps Tactical Sch., 1940; foreign service in P.I. and Alaska: retired with rank of brig. gen., 1946. Club: Army-Navy (Washington, D.C.). Home: San Francisco.

ERLICH, ALVIN LEWIS, food co. exec.; b. N.Y.C., Dec. 27, 1925; s. Benjamin and Bessie (Lewis) E.; student N.Y. U., 1948; m. Patricia Segal, May 17, 1949; children—Betsy, Merry. Advt. mgr. Chunky Corp., N.Y.C., 1950-55, sales mgr., 1955-58, v.p., 1958-67; exec. v.p. Ward Candy Co., N.Y.C., 1967-71, pres., 1971-72, chmn., 1971-77; group pres. Ward Foods, Inc., N.Y.C., 1971-77, pres., 1977-77; pres. Ward-Johnston, 1972-77. Active United Jewish Appeal Greater N.Y., 1965. Chmn. bd. dirs. Nat. Tay-Sachs Assn., N.Y.C., 1957. Mem. Nat. Confectioners Assn., Fgn. Policy Assn., Am. Mgmt. Assn. Clubs: Sky, Advertising (N.Y.C.). Home: New York, N.Y. Died Dec. 26, 1977.

ERNST, FREDERIC, educator, editor; b. Belgium, July 13, 1888; s. Charles and Selma (Milcamps) E.; Licence es Sciences, U. Liege (Belgium), 1909; M.A., U. Wis., 1911; m. Jeanne Romillat, Aug. 4, 1920; 1 son, Maurice. Came to U.S., 1910, naturalized, 1919. Instr., U. Wis., 1910-17, asst. prof., 1919-23; asst. prof. N.Y. U., 1925-27, asso. prof., 1928-30, prof., 1930-76, prof. emeritus, 1976-80, chmn. depts. French, Italian, Russian, 1946-53; dir. Inst. French Edn., Pa. State Coll., 1929-43; gen. editor modern lang. texts Dryden Press, 19.0-53, asso. eoitor Dryden Press, 1953-58; cons. editor Henry Holt & vc Co., N.Y.C., 1950-80. Interpreter in France, U.S. Army, AEF, 1917-19. Decorated Legion of Honor (France). Mem. Modern Lang. Assn., Am. Assn. Tchrs. French, Phi Beta Kappa (hon.). Author: (with Dondo), Principes de Grammaire et de Style 1935; (with Levy) Le Français, 1952; La France et les Français, 1961; Gens de France, 1967. Home: New York, N.Y. Died Sept. 22, 1980; buried Loiret, France.

ERNST, MAX, artist; b. Bruhl, nr. Cologne, Germany, Apr. 2, 1891; s. Phillipp and Louise (Kopp) E.; student U. Bonn; m. Marguerite Guggenheim, Dec. 30, 1941 (div.); m. 2d, Dorothy Tanning; 1 son by previous marriage, Ulrich. Founder Dadaist group, Cologne, after World War I; left Germany for France, 1922, never returned; became a leader of Surrealist movement; took part in Surrealist exhbns.; one-man shows in all parts Europe and U.S., Moderna Museet, Stockholm, 1969; his picture Europe after the Rain exhibited in Artists in Exile show, N.Y.C., 1942; represented in U.S. museums, pvt. collections. Address: Indre-et-Loire, France. Died Apr. 1, 1976.

ERNST, MORRIS LEOPOLD, lawyer; b. Uniontown, Ala., Aug. 23, 1888; s. Carl and Sarah (Bernheim) E.; A.B., Williams Coll., 1909; LL.B., N.Y. Law Sch., 1912; J.D., Nasson Coll., 1963; D.H.L., Lincoln U., 1964; m. Susan Leerburger (dec. 1922); m. 2d, Margaret Samuels, Mar. 1, 1923; children—Constance, Roger, Joan. Mfr. shirts, 1909-11, retail furniture, 1911-15; mem. law firm Greenbaum, Wolff & Ernst, N.Y., 1915-76; spl. counsel Am. Newspaper Guild; served as arbiter for Mayor La Guardia in taxicab strike, 1934; drafted legislation for Gov. Lehman on ins. and banking matters; mem. Pa. Anthracite Coal Commn. Mem. N.Y. State Banking Bd. since inception, by apptmt. Gov. Roosevelt and Gov. Lehman, 1933-45. Counsel Dramatists Guild and Authors League of Am.; spl. asst. atty.-gen. in election fraud matters; counsel to N.Y. State Legislative Commn. for Hard of Hearing; spl. cons. War Prodn. Bd.; personal rep. to Pres. Roosevelt during war on various missions to England; governmental mission, Germany, 1946; mission Virgin Islands, 1935. Apptd. by Pres. Truman to Pres. Truman's Civil Rights Com.; apptd. by Pres. to adv. bd. for the Post Office. mem. chancellor's council U. Tex., 1969. Decorated Order French Legion Honor. Mem. Bar Assn. City N.Y. (Lawyer of Year 1960), N.Y. County Lawyers Assn., P.E.N., Am. Polit. Sci. Assn., Phi Beta Kappa, Phi Gamma Delta, Alpha Kappa Delta (hon.), Gargoyle Soc. Clubs: City (past trustee), Williams, New York U. Faculty (N.Y.); University (Washington); Savile (Eng.). Author: (with William Seagle) To the Pure, 1928; (with Pare Lorentz) Censored, 1930; America's Primer, 1931; Hold Your Tongue (with A Lindey), 1932; (with others) Sex Life of the Unmarried Adult, 1934; Ultimate Power, 1937; (with A Lindey) The Censor Marches On, 1939; Too Big, 1940; The Best Is Yet, 1945; The First Freedom, 1946; So Far So Good, 1948; author with D. Loth: American Sexual Behavior and the Kinsey Report, 1948; The People Know Best, 1949; For Better or Worse, 1952; Report on the American Communist, 1952; Utopia, 1976, (1955); Touch wood (dairy), pub. 1960; Untitled, A Dairy of the 72d year, 1962; (with Alan U. Schwartz) Privacy: The Right to be Let Alone, 1962; (with Alan U. Schwartz) Lawyers and What They Do, 1964, Censorship: The Search for the Obscene, 1964; (with David Loth) How High Is Up, 1964; The Teacher, 1967; (with Judith Posner) Comparative Internat. Almanac, 1968; A Love Affair With The Law, 1968; Triple Crosstricks, 1968; (with Mary Batten) Discovery By Chance, 1968; (with Malcolm A. Hoffmann) Back and Forth, 1969; Training and Technology, 1972; The Great Reversals, 1973. Contbr. to mags. and encys. Lectr. clubs and colls. Home: New York, N.Y. Died May 21, 1976.

ERVINE, ST. JOHN GREER, author; b. Belfast, No. Ireland, Dec. 28, 1883; s. William and Sarah Jane Park (Greer) E.; student Westbourne Nat. Sch., Belfast, 1890-97; LL.D., St. Andrew's U.; Litt.D., Queen's U., Belfast; m. Leonora Mary Davis, July 15, 1911. Clk. ins. office, Belfast, 1897-1900, London, 1900-12; author plays, novels, 1911—; author: (plays) The Magnanimous Lover, Mixed Marriage, Jane Clegg, John Ferguson, Mary, Mary, Quite Contrary, Anthony and Anna, The Lady of Belmont, The First Mrs. Fraser, People of Our Class, Robert's Wife, Boyd's Shop, Esperanza, Friends and Relations, Private Enterprise, My Brother Tom, Charles and Mary, Progress, Old George Comes to Tea, She Was No Lady; (books) Mrs. Martin's Man, 1911, Alice and a Family, Changing Winds, The Wayward Man, The First Mrs. Fraser, Sophia, The Mountain and other Stories, If I were Dictator, Some Impressions of My Elders, A Journey to Jerusalem; The Organized Theatre, How to Write a Play, The Theatre in My Time; (biographies) Parnell, God's Soldier, General William Booth; Craigavon, Ulsterman, Bernard Shaw: His Life, Work and Friends; Oscar Wilde, A Present Time Appraisal; The Wonderful Visit. Served as private later officer Royal Dublin Fusilers, World War I. Mem. Society Authors (Britain, America). Home: Honey Ditches, Seaton, Devon, Eng.

ERWIN, FRANK CRAIG, JR., lawyer, univ. regent; b. Waxahachie, Tex., Jan. 25, 1920; s. Frank Craig and Margaret (Edwards) E.; LL.B., U. Tex., 1948; m. June Carr (dec.); 1 son, Frank Craig. Admitted to Tex. bar, 1948; partner Brown, Erwin, Maroney & Barber, Austin. Mem. bd. regents, chmn. U. Tex.; chmn. Commn. Governing Bds. State-Supported Colls. and Univs. Mem. exec. com., past pres. Austin Symphony Orch. Soc.; bd. dirs., past treas. Tex. Kappa Sigma Ednl. Found.; vice chmn. citizens commn. to draft new city charter for Austin, 1952. Mem. Democratic Nat. Com. for Tex.; vice chmn. Tex. delegation Dem. Nat. Conv., 1964; past chmn., past sec. Tex. Dem. Exec. Com.; chmn. Travis County Dem. Conv., 1962. Served with USNR, 1941-46; PTO. Mem. Am., Travis County (past pres., chmn. bd. dirs.) bar assns., State Bar Tex., Internat. Assn. Ins. Attys., Def. Research Inst., Tex. Assn. Def. Counsel, U. Tex. Ex-Students Assn. (past pres. Travis County; life mem.), T Assn. (hon.), Phi Beta Kappa, Phi Eta Sigma, Phi Sigma Alpha, Phi Delta Phi, Kappa Sigma. Episcopalian. Club: Longhorn (founder). Home: Austin, Tex. Died Oct. 1, 1980.

ERWIN, JOHN D(RAPER), diplomat; b. Meador, Ky., Nov. 14, 1883; s. James and Ella (Moore) E.; student McCallie Preparatory Sch., Chattanooga, 1905-08, Baylor Mil. Sch., 1909; m. Emily Hicklin, Oct. 4, 1917. Reporter Chattanooga News, 1908-13; Washington corr. N.Y. Evening World, 1919-27, Nashville Tennesseean, 1917-37, Memphis Commercial-Appeal, 1927-35; sec. to Senators John K. Shields, of Tenn., Mar.-Aug. 1913, Luke Lea, of Tenn., 1913-17; U.S. minister to Honduras, 1937-43; apptd. ambassador to Honduras, Mar. 1943. Democrat. Clubs: Nat. Press of Washington, D.C. Home: Chattanooga, Tenn.

ESKENAZI, JACOB VICTOR, U.S. atty.; b. Miami, Fla., Sept 10, 1932; s. Victor A. and Marie Eskenazi; B.A., Tulane U., 1955; LL.B., U. Fla., 1960; m. Elaine Nadene Ofsanko, June 29, 1963; children—Victor Joseph, Stacy Marie. Spl. agt. FBI, Phila., 1961-64; asst. State's Atty.'s Office, Miami, 1964-66, U.S. Atty.'s Office, Miami, 1966-71; fed. public defender, Miami, 1971-75; U.S. magistrate, Miami, 1975-77; U.S. atty. So. Dist. Fla., Miami, 1977-80; supervising atty. clin. law program U. Miami, Nova U. Served with USN, 1955-58; capt. USNR. Mem. Am. Bar Assn., Fed. Bar Assn., Fla. Bar, Naval Res. Assn., Audubon Soc., Nat. Wildlife Fedn. Democrat. Unitarian. Club: Masons. Home: Coral Gables, Fla. Died Mar. 2, 1980.

ESKEY, CLIFFORD RUSH (ES'KE), U.S. Pub. Health Service; b. Indianola, Neb., Oct. 5, 1886; s. Franklin Watson and Elma Matilda (Hill) E.; student Kenyon (O.) Mil. Acad., 1903-06; B.S., U. of Chicago, 1910; M.D., Rush Med. Coll., 1912; m. Mae Melinda Bogert, Jan. 1, 1914. Interne Cook County Hosp., Chicago, 1912-13; commd. asst. surgeon U.S. P.H.S., 1916, passed assistant surgeon, 1920, surgeon, 1924, senior surgeon, 1936; med. dir., 1942; apptd. chief quarantine officer, Philippine Islands, 1926; attended interchange health officers in India, 1928; chief quarantine officer, New Orleans, 1929; epidemiologist Pan-Am. Sanitary Bureau to study plague in Ecuador and Peru, 1930-31; investigated bubonic plague Hawaiian Islands, 1932-33; chief quarantine officer, Hawaiian Islands, 1934; in charge investigations of plague among wild rodents in western states, 1935, 47, dir. leprosy investigation station, Honolulu, 1939; chief typhus control activities 1942; in charge Pub. Health Service activities, San Diego, 1946; in charge Plague Lab., San Francisco, 1947-50, ret. Certified Am. Bd. Preventive Medicine and Pub. Health, 1949. Awarde[d] Al Merito, Republic of Ecuador, 1930. Mem. A.M.A., Am. Pub. Health Assn., Alpha Tau Omega, Alph[a] Kappa Kappa. Contbr. sci. articles to jours. Home: Sa[n] Francisco.

ESPINÒS Y BOSCH, MIGUE[L] (AS-PE-NOS'E-BOSK), consul gen. of Spain; b. Barcelona, Spain, Nov. 10, 1886; s. José and Mercede[s] (Bosch) E.; LL.B., Univ. of Barcelona, Spain, 1906; LL.D., Univ. of Madrid, 1907; m. Concepción Pérez, Aug. 15, 1914; children—José, Antonio, Migue[l], Conchita. Attaché of Embassy, 1910, The Hague, Holland, Madrid, Spain; 3d sec. at Tangiers, Morocco, Rio de Janeiro, Brazil; 2d sec. at Rio de Janeiro, Brazi[l]

Tangiers, Morocco, Madrid, Spain; 1st sec. at Havana, Cuba, Madrid, Spain, Tetuán and Tangiers, Morocco; minister plenipotentiary of the 3d class at San José, Costa Rica, Rome, Italy; of the 2d class at Havana, Cuba, Manila, P.I., Salamanca and San Sebastián, Spain, Havana, Cuba, N.Y., U.S.; now consul gen. at New York. Awarded Carlos III and Isabel la Católica by Spain. Club: New York Athletic. Home: New York. *

ESSEX, HARRY, univ. prof. and chemist; b. Meadville, Pa., Nov. 2, 1884; s. Henry and Linda R. (Smith) E.; A.B., Cornell U., 1907; Ph.D., Gottingen U., Germany, 1914; m. Kathryn Buterbaugh, June 15, 1918; 1 dau., Anne Kathryn. Instr. chemistry U. of Ky., 1907-10; research fellow Mellon Inst. Indsl. Research, 1914-18; research chemist Du Pont Co., Wilmington, Del., 1918-20; prof. physical chemistry Syracuse (N.Y.) U. since 1920. Mem. A.A.A.S., Am. Assn. Univ. Profs., Sigma Xi. Democrat. Contbr. articles to sci. jours. on high pressure, chem. kinetics, thermodynamics and radiation chemistry. Obtained patents on synthesis of amyl acetate, glycols and glycerine, motor fuels and temperature control. Home: Syracuse, N.Y.

ESTABROOK, EDWARD LEWIS, petroleum engineer; b. Brandon, S.D., May 10, 1885; s. Lewis Mitchell and Mary Maud (Cornwall) E.; student Wis. Sch. of Mines, Platteville, 1907-08; E.M., U. of Pittsburgh, 1911; Lehigh U., Bethlehem, Pa., 1911-12; m. Florence Anna Mattick, May 15, 1916; children—Mary Abbott, Georgiana Mattick (dec.). Instr. geol. dept., Lehigh U., 1911-13; instr. Wis. Sch. of Mines, 1913-14; geologist Standard Oil Co. of N.Y. (China), 1914-16, Wis. Zinc Co., 1916-17, Johnson & Huntley. (U.S. and S.A.), 1917-18, Midwest Refining Co., 1918-20; petroleum engr. Midwest Refining Co. 1920-25, Pan-Am. Petroleum and Transport Co., 1925-32, Standard Oil Co of New 3Jersey, 1932-48; retired October 31, 1948. Member American Institute of Mining and Metall. Engrs., Am. Assn. of Petroleum Geologists. Club: Orange Lawn Tennis (South Orange, N.J.). Author of articles on engring. subjects. Home: Morristown, N.J.

ESTABROOK, HUBERT ARTHUR, lawyer; b. Dayton, O., Dec. 15, 1890; s. Arthur S. and Willie (Hubert) E.; certificate in law Ohio State U., 1913; m. Gladys Collins, Aug. 18, 1920; 1 son, Hubert Arthur. Admitted to Ohio bar, 1913, since practiced in Dayton; partner Estabrook, Finn & McKee, 1915-79. Dir. emeritus State Fidelity Fed. Savs. and Loan Assn., 1st Nat. Bank of Dayton. Served as 1st lt. Ordnance, AEF, 1917-18. Mem. Am. Ohio, Dayton bar assns., Phi Delta Phi, Sigma Nu. Clubs: Dayton Country; Queen City (Cin.). Home: Dayton, Ohio. Died Dec. 9, 1975.

ESTEP, HARRY ALLISON, ex-congressman; b. Pittsburgh, Pa., Feb. 1, 1884; s. James E. and Isabella S. (Kaye) E.; prep. edn., high sch., Marion, Ind.; student Purdue U., Lafayette, Ind.; LL.B., U. of Pittsburgh, 1913; m. Blanche Alward, of Canton, O., Aug. 10, 1918. Admitted to Pa. bar, 1914, and since practiced at Pittsburgh; served as asst. dist. atty. Allegheny County, Pa., many years, last 5 years as 1st asst.; mem. 70th to 72d Congresses (1927-33), 35th Pa. Dist. Mem. Am., Pa. State and Allegheny Co. bar assns., S.A.R. Republican. Methodist. Mason. Club: Pittsburgh Athletic. Home: Pittsburgh.

ETCHESON, A. THOMAS, banker; b. Webb City, Mo., July 1, 1911; s. Elijah Thomas and Bessie Edith (Holforty) E.; B.S., U. Ill., 1934; m. Genevieve Eileen Mott, June 26, 1937; 1 dau., Patricia Jean. Exec. v.p. Ill. Bankers Assn., 1954-60, dir., 1961-78; exec. v.p. Lake Shore Nat. Bank, Chgo., 1960-61, pres., 1962-78, dir., 1959-78. Pres. Central States Banking Conf., 1959-60; mem. Ill. Banking Adv. Bd., 1958-67; mem. U.S. Treasury Savs. Bond Adv. Com. for Ill., 1955-78. Mem. Hinsdale Health Inst. Trustee Ill. Council on Econ. Edn.; bd. dirs. Lawson YMCA. Served with AUS, 1942-46. Mem. Mil. Order World Wars, Am. Legion, Am. (adv. com. on state legislation 1962-66, state chmn. com. on econ. edn. 1966-67, mem. governing council 1966-69, 71-73, savs. bond coordinator for Ill. 1967-78, contact banker on fed. legislation 1960-78), Ill. (chmn. com. on state legislation 1960-65, 70-71, vice chmn. 1965-70, mem.-at-large 1971-78, mem. council of adminstrn. 1961-68, 70-72, 73-78, treas. 1963-64, hon. life) bankers assns., Asso. Employers Ill. (treas. 1966-78, dir.), Chgo., Ill. chambers commerce, Greater N. Michigan Av. Assn. (dir., treas. 1960-78), 40 and 8, Assn. U.S. Army (dir., pres. Ft. Sheridan-Chgo. chpt. 1972-73), Newcomen Soc., Chgo. Assn. Commerce and Industry, Chgo. Council Fgn. Relations. Rotarian. Clubs: Economic, Bankers, University, Chicago Press, Hundred, Executives (exec. dir. 1947-54, bd. dirs. 1954-58, hon. life (Chgo.); Hinsdale (Ill.) Golf. Home: Hinsdale, Ill. Died Feb. 14, 1978.

ETHERIDGE, WILLIAM CARLYLE (ETH'ER-IJ), prof. field crops; b. Roanoke Island, N.C., June 30, 1885; s. Daniel Warren and Humantla Chauncey (Meekins) E.; B.S., N.C. State Coll. Agr. and Engring., 1906; M.S., Cornell U., 1912, Ph.D., 1915; m. Fannie Elizabeth Cassell, July 15, 1917; children—William Roger, Edward Bruce, David Carroll, Daniel Warren, Fannie Elizabeth. With U. of Mo. since 1916, prof. field crops since Aug. 1, 1916, also chmn. dept. Mem. Am. Soc. Agronomy, Am. Assn. Univ. Profs., Bot. Soc. America. Gamma Sigma Delta, Alpha Zeta, Sigma Xi, Phi Kappa Phi. Author: Field Corps, 1929; Studies in Field Crops, 1946. Home: Columbia, Mo.*

ETHRIDGE, MARK FOSTER, publishing exec.; b. Meridian, Miss., Apr. 22, 1896; s. William Nathaniel and Mary (Howell) E.; student U. Miss., 1914-15, Mercer U., 1916-17; m. Willie Snow, Oct. 12, 1921; children—Mary Snow, Mark Foster, Georgia Cubbedge and William Davidson. Began as reporter for Meridian Star, 1913, later reporter with Columbus (Ga.) Enquirer Sun; city editor Macon (Ga.) Telegraph, 1919-22, mng. editor, 1925-33; with N.Y. Sun and Consol. Press, 1923-24, A.P., 1933; asst. gen. mgr. Washington Post, 1933-34; pres. and pub. Richmond (Va.) Times Dispatch, 1934-36; v.p., gen. mgr. Courier Jour. and Louisville Times, 1936-42, pub., 1942-62, chmn. bd., 1962-63; v.p., editor Newsday, Garden City, L.I., N.Y., 1963-65. Visited Balkans for State Dept., 1945; Am. del. to U.N. Commn. to Study Greek Border Disputes, 1947; chmn. U.S. adv. commn. on information, 1948-50; lectr. journalism U. N.C., 1965-66. Trustee Ford Found., 1954-67. Served from yeoman to ensign USN, 1917-19. Mem. Sigma Alpha Epsilon, Sigma Delta Chi. Democrat. Baptist. Club: Century Assn. Home: Moncure, N.C. Died May 5, 1981.

ETTELSON, LEONARD BERT, lawyer; b. Chgo., Mar. 6, 1905; s. Benjamin J. and Julia (Sanditz) E.; A.B., U. Mich., 1924; J.D., U. Chgo., 1947; LL.D., Ill. Wesleyan U., 1955; m. Luela Bone, Aug. 6, 1934; 1 dau., Leanne. Admitted to Ill. bar, 1927; law clk. Schuyler, Ettelson & Weinfeld, Chgo., 1927; sr. partner firm Ettelson, O'Hagan, Ehrlich & Frankel, Chgo. Chmn. bd. First Drovers Corp.; chmn. exec. com., dir. Allied Structural Steel Co.; dir. Drovers Nat. Bank, Chgo., Lytton's, Henry C. Lytton & Co., Chgo., Jackson Vibrators, Inc., Lansing, Ill. Mem.-at-large Boy Scouts Am. Trustee Barat Coll.; bd. dirs. Henrotin Hosp., Chgo. Mem. Am. Ill., Chgo. bar assns., Chgo., Mich. alumni assns. Clubs: Michigan Union (Ann Arbor); Tower, Saddle and Cycle, Metropolitan, MidAmerica, Tavern (Chgo.); Bankers, Lawyers (N.Y.C.); Racquet (Palm Springs, Cal.); LaQuinta Country (Cal.). Home: Chicago, Ill. Died Dec. 9, 1976.

ETTINGHAUSEN, RICHARD, educator; b. Frankfurt-on-Main, Germany, Feb. 5, 1906; s. Edmund S. and Selma (Stern) E.; Ph.D., U. Frankfurt, 1931; student Munich U., Cambridge U. (Eng.); m. Basia Gruliow, 1934 (dec. 1935); m. 2d, Elizabeth Sgalitzer, Sept. 22, 1945; children—Stephen Edmund, Thomas Andrew David. Came to U.S., 1934, naturalized, 1938. Asst. Islamic dept. Staatliche Museum, Berlin, 1931-33; asst. to editor A Survey of Persian Art, Oxford U. Press, 1933-34; research asso. Am. Inst. Persian Art and Archaelogy, 1934-37; mem. Inst. Advanced Study, Princeton, 1937-38; asso. prof. Islamic art U. Mich., 1938-44, research prof. Islamic art, 1949-79; asso. Near Eastern art Freer Gal. of Art, Smithsonian Instn., 1944-58, curator, 1958-61, head curator, 1961-67; adj. curator Los Angeles County Mus. Art, 1967-69; adj. prof. Inst. Fine Arts, N.Y. U., 1961-67, prof., 1967-79; consultive chmn. Islamic dept. Met. Mus. Art, N.Y.C., 1969-79. Trustee Phillips Gallery, Washington; trustee, exec. com., chmn. accessions com. Textile Mus., Washington. Decorated Pour le Merite (Germany), Iranian Decoration Imperial Crown. Mem. Coll. Art. Assn. Am., Am. Acad. Arts and Scis., Am. Oriental Soc., Asia House, Am. Research Center in Egypt, Am. Research Inst. in Turkey (vice dir.), Internat. Soc. Oriental Research, Medieval Acad. Am., Am. Philos. Soc., Wash. Soc. Archeol. Inst. Am. (pres. 1960-61, 63-64), Institut d'Egypte (asso.), Bavarian Acad., Deutsche Morgenländische Gesellschaft, German Archeol. Inst. (hon.), French Academie des Inscriptions et Belles Lettres (corr.), Brit. Acad. (hon.), Am. Inst. Iranian Studies (hon. trustee). Author: Studies in Muslim Iconography: The Unicorn, 1950; Freer Gallery of Art Occasional Papers, 1950; Paintings of the Sultans and Emperors of India in American Collections, Lalit Kala Akademie, 1961; Persian Paintings in the Bernard Berenson Collection, 1961; Arab Painting, 1962; Turkish Miniatures From the Thirteenth to the Eighteenth Century, 1965; From Byzantium to Sasanian Iran and the Islamic World, 1972; co-author: Turkey-Ancient Miniatures, 1961; 7000 Years of Iranian Art, 1965; Treasures of Turkey, 1966; Pelican History of Islamic Art. Editor: Annotated Bibliography of Books and Articles of the Near and Middle East, 1952; Aus der Welt der Islamichen Kunst, 1959; The Islamic Garden, Dumbarton Oaks Colloqium, 1976; co-author, co-editor: Highlights of Persian Art, 1980. Editor of Ars Islamica, 1938-50; Near Eastern editor Ars Orientalis, 1954-57, mem. editorial bd., 1957-61; editorial bd. Artibus Asiae, 1971—, Art Bull.; co-editor Kunst des Orients, 1968—. Home: Princeton, N.J. Died Apr. 2, 1979.

EUSTERMAN, GEORGE BYSSHE (YOOS'TER-MAN), internist; b. Lewiston, Minn., Feb. 7, 1882; s. Francis Xavier and Therese (Becker) E.; M.D., U. of Minn., 1908; m. Ethel Katherine Huntimer, June 4, 1919; children—Mary Helen (wife of Dr. Charles Demong), George, Dorothy, Therese and Joseph. With Mayo Clinic, Rochester, Minn., since 1908, med. asst., 1910-12, permanent staff mem. since 1912, head of a sect. in medicine, 1920-50, sr. consultant in medicine, 1938-50, emeritus consultant; prof. of medicine, Mayo Found., U. Minn., 1935-50, emeritus prof., 1950—; chief of medicine and dir. med. edn. Sinai Hosp. of Detroit. Served as captain, Med. Reserve Corps, U.S. Army, stationed at base hosps., Camp Jackson and Camp McClellan, during World War I; now major, Medical Reserve Corps. Recipient of the Friedenwald Medal, 1946. Member of City of Rochester Library Bd. Nat. director of the Izaak Walton League. Fellow A.M.A., A.C.P.; mem. Am. Bd. Internal Medicine, International Congress Gastro-Enterology, Minn. Pathol. Soc., Am. Gastro-Enterol. Assn. (pres. 1921-22), A.A.A.S., Minn. Soc. Internists, Central Soc. Clin. Research, Central Interurban Clin. Club, Alumni Assn. of Mayo Foundation, Alpha Tau Omega, Alpha Omega Alpha, Nu Sigma Nu, Sigma Xi. Roman Catholic. Former asso. editor sect. diseases of digestive tract, Year Book of Medicine. Formerly ann. contbr. on alimentary system to Britannica Book of the Year. Home: Rochester, Minn.

EUSTICE, RUSSELL C(LIFFORD), business exec.; b. Wharton, N.J., Mar. 27, 1886; s. John W. and Susannah (Scadden) E.; student New York Prep Sch., 1904-07; m. Ethel M. Hutchison, June 20, 1916; children—John H., Russell C., Ethel Eustice (Mrs. Ralph C. Walter, Jr.). Began career with Union Tank Car Co., Chicago, as office boy, 1902, asst. treas., 1921, treas., 1929, vice pres. and treas., 1944, mem. bd. dirs., since 1922. Republican. Mem. Union Ch. Clubs: Union League (Chicago); Hinsdale (Ill.) Golf. Home: Hinsdale, Ill.

EUWEMA, BEN, ret. educator; b. Chgo., May 3, 1904; s. Ralph and Anna (Helmholt) E.; A.B., Calvin Coll., 1925; A.M., U. Mich., 1926; Ph.D., U. Chgo., 1934; m. Catherine Michmerhuizen, July 4, 1928; children—Robert Noel, Carol Joyce. Instr. English, Westminster (Pa.) Coll., 1928-29, asst. prof., 1929-31, prof., head English dept., 1931-36; asso. prof. English, Kent State U., 1936-37; asst. prof. Mich. State Coll., East Lansing, 1937-39, asso. prof., 1939-42, prof., head dept. lit. and fine arts, 1944-46, prof., head English dept., 1942-46, dir., div. lang. and lit., 1944-46; dean Coll. Liberal Arts Pa. State U., 1946-64, prof. English, 1964-69, emeritus, 1969-76. Mem. Phi Kappa Phi. Author books and articles. Asso. editor Jour. Gen. Edn. Home: State College, Pa., also Sarasota, Fla. Died May 22, 1976

EVANS, ABBIE HUSTON, poet; b 6e, N.H., Dec. 20, 1881; d. Lewis Darenydd and Hester Annette (Huston) Evans; B.A., Radcliffe Coll., 1913, M.A. 1918; LL.D. Bowdoin Coll., 1961. Mem. Adv. Bd. Contemporary Poetry, 1940—; mem. jury Shelley Meml. award, 1940; mem jury 0nited States award (poetry), 1967; staff mem. Settlement Music Sch., Phila., 1923-53, Coll. Settlement Farm-Camp, 1953-57. Recipient Guarantors' prize Poetry Chgo., 1931; Loines award for poetry Nat. Inst. Arts and Letters, 1960; Golden Rose award New Eng. Poetry Club, 1965; citation Me. Commn. on Arts and Humanities, 1970, Pa. Council on Arts and Internat. Poetry Forum, 1970. Mem. Americans for Dem. Action, Civil Liberties Union, Phi Beta Kappa. Author: Outcrop, 1928; The Bright North, 1938; Fact of Crystal 1961; Collected Poems, 1970; also verse in anthologies and collections. Home: West Chester PA. *

EVANS, ALONA ELIZABETH, educator; b. Providence, Feb. 27, 1917; d. Robert R. and Florence (Weatherhead) E.; A.B., Duke, 1940, Ph.D., 1945. Intern personnel adminstrn. War Dept., 1942; jr. divisional asst. State Dept., 1942-43; instr. Duke, 1944-45, Westminster Coll., Pa., 1945; mem. faculty Wellesley Coll., 1945-80, prof. polit. sci., 1958-80, chmn. dept., 1959-70, 72-73, Elizabeth Kimball Kendall prof., 1966-80; vis. prof. internat. law Sch. Law U. Puget Sound, 1973-74. Mem. corp. Woods Hole Oceanographic Instn.; mem. Dept. State Adv. Com. on Hist. Diplomatic Documentation. Fellow Social Sci. Research Council, 1948-49; Fulbright grantee, India, 1961; fellow Harvard Law Sch., 1961-62, 71-72; recipient Harbison Fund award Wellesley Coll., 1954-55; grantee Am. Philos. Soc., 1971-72. Mem. Am. Soc. Internat. Law (chmn. ann. meeting 1975, v.p. 1976-80), Internat. Law Assn. (chmn. Am. br. com. legal problems asylum (1963-72, exec. com. 1971-80, chmn. com. on internat. terrorism 1973-80), Indian Soc. Internat. Law, Am., New Eng. (pres. 1966-67) polit. sci. assns., AAUW (dir. 1963-67, cons. 1968-70, Achievement award 1971), Am. Law Inst. (adv. com.), Assn. Internationale de Droit Penal, AAUP, Phi Beta Kappa, Contbr. articles to legal jours. Editorial bd. Am. Jour. Internat. Law, 1967—; co-editor Legal Aspects of International Terrorism, 1978. Home: Wellesley, Mass. Died Sept. 23, 1980.

EVANS, BERGEN, author, educator; b. Franklin, Ohio, Sept. 19, 1904; s. Rice Kemper and Louise (Cass) E.; A.B., Miami U., Oxford, Ohio, 1924, L.H.D., 1959; A.M., Harvard, 1925, Ph.D., 1932; B.Litt., U. Coll., Oxford, Eng., 1931; D.Litt., Franklin and Marshall

Coll., 1959; m. Jean Whinery, Aug. 5, 1939; children—Derek, Scott. Prof. emeritus English Northwestern U., Evanston, Ill. Author: (with George Mohr) The Psychiatry of Robert Burton, 1944; Natural History of Nonsense, 1946; The Spoor of Spooks, 1954; Comfortable Words, 1962; The Skeptic's Corner dept. Am. Mercury mag., 1946-50. Editor: Fifty Essays, 1936; Essays by Samuel Johnson, 1940; Boswell's Life of Johnson, 1952; The World, The Flesh, and H. Allen Smith, 1954; (with Cornelia Evans) Dictionary of Contemporary American Usage, 1957; Comfortable Words, 1962; Word-A-Day, 1963; Dictionary of Quotations, 1968; Dictionary of Mythology, 1970. Contbr. essays and sketches to Atlantic, New Republic, other nat. mags. Lectr.; master of ceremonies TV Quiz shows Down You Go, The Last Word, English for Americans, Words in the News, Inquiry, Of Many Things. Writer daily syndicated newspaper feature The Last Word. Recipient George Foster Peabody award for excellence in radio and TV broadcasting, 1959. Home: Northfield, Ill. Died Feb. 4, 1978.

EVANS, CHARLES F(LOYD), forester; b. Basswood, Wis., Feb. 26, 1885; s. William T. and Dora (Booher) E.; A.B., U. of Wis., 1909; M.F., Yale, 1912; m. Martha McGilvrey, Mar. 11, 1915; children—Robert Charles, Jean Louise (Mrs. Harry A. Flemister). Forest asst. U.S. Forestry Service, Ida., 1912-18, forest supervisor, 1918-22, asst. chief, div. operations, Ogden, Utah, 1922-27, regional forest insp., New Orleans, 1927-29, Asheville, NC,, 1929-34, asst. regional forester, Atlanta, 1934-50, retired, 1950. Chmn. Ga. State Bd. Registration for Foresters, 1951-54. Awarded plaque for outstanding service, Am. Forestry Assn., 1950. Fellow Soc. Am. Foresters (pres. 1950-51); mem. Am. Forestry Assn. (hon. v.p. 1950), Xi Sigma Pi. Home: Atlanta.

EVANS, CLIFFORD, mus. curator; b. Dallas, June 13, 1920; s. Clifford and Pearl (Weiss) E.; A.A., San Bernardino Jr. Coll., 1939; A.B., U. So. Cal., 1941; Ph.D., Columbia, 1947; m. Betty J. Meggers, Sept. 13, 1946. Asst. archaeology, dept. anthropology Columbia, 1946-48; instr. anthropology U. Va., 1949-51; asso. curator div. archaeology U.S. Nat. Mus., Smithsonian Instn., Washington, 1951-62, curator div. archaeology, 1962-69, chmn. dept. anthropology, 1969-75, curator S. Am. archaeology, 1975-81; archeol. field work, Brazil, Ecuador, Peru, Venezuela, Brit. Guiana, Ponape, Caroline Islands, Dominica in Lesser Antilles. Served to 2d lt. USAAF, 1943-45. Decorated Air medal with cluster; Merit Ofcl. Order (Ecuador); recipient outstanding achievement award in sci. Washington Acad. Scis., 1954; Gold medal 37th Internat. Congress Americanists, 1966. Mem. Am. Anthrop. Assn., Anthrop. Soc. Washington, Assn. Tropical Biology (sec.-treas. 1971-81), Inst. Andean Research (pres. 1960-65), Soc. Am. Archaeology, Phi Beta Kappa, Sigma Xi. Author: (with W.D. Strong) Cultural Stratigraphy in Viru Valley, Northern Peru, 1952; (with B.J. Meggers) Archaeological Investigations at the Mouth of the Amazon, 1957; (with Meggers) Archaeology of British Guiana, South America, 1960; (with Meggers) The Early Formative Culture of Coastal Ecuador, 1965; (with Meggers) Archaeological Investigations on the Rio Napo, Eastern Ecuador, 1968; also articles. Home: Washington, D.C. Died Jan. 19, 1981.

EVANS, EDWARD GORDON, JR., educator; b. Youngstown, Ohio, Nov. 4, 1916; s. Edward Gordon and Helen Marie (Harris) E.; student Youngstown U., 1934-35; Mus.B., Cin. Conservatory Music, 1939; Mus.M., Northwestern U., 1940; Ph.D., Western Res. U., 1950; m. Jeanne Elise Goodman, Mar. 7, 1942 (dec. Jan. 1963); children—Natasha, Vyki, Edward G. III; m. 2d, Helen S. Greene, Oct. 8, 1964. Teaching fellow, instr. Northwestern U., 1939-41; vocational counsellor and psychologist Youngstown VA, 1946-47; asst. prof. Southeastern La. Coll., 1947-48; teaching fellow Western Res. U., 1948-50, asst., then asso. prof., 1950-57, prof. music, 1957-68, chmn. dept., 1957-68, chmn. dept. humanities, 1958-68; prof., chmn. music lit. dept. Eastman Sch. Music, U. Rochester (N.Y.), 1968-70, chmn. musicology and music history dept., 1970-73; head music dept. U. Conn., Storrs, 1973-78; chmn. music history, lit. and musicology Cleve. Inst. Music, 1965-68. Trustee Cleve. Mus. Sch. Settlement. Mus. Arts Assn., Cleve. Chamber Music Soc., Cleve. Friends of Music; adv. bd. Cleve. Philharmonic Orch. Served to maj. USAAF, 1941-46; CBI. Mem. Am. Soc. Aesthetics, Am. Musicol. Soc., AAUP, Author: The Experience of Music, 1972; Munich Ms. 260 and Johannes Martini: Secular Works; also TV syllabus, articles. Adv. bd. Fine Arts mag.; editorial bd. Jour. Aesthetics and Art Criticism. Died Oct. 21, 1978.

EVANS, ELLIOTT WILLARD, lawyer; b. Minden, Nebr., July 28, 1907; s. Willard Vine and Clara (Anderson) E.; J.D., U. Utah, 1930; m. Aline Johnson, Oct. 6, 1933; children—Claudia Ann (Mrs. Richard M. Hunsaker), Susan Jane (Mrs. Leo J. Walz), Elliott W. Admitted to Utah bar, 1930; practice of law, Bingham Canyon, Utah, 1930-47, Salt Lake City, 1947-78; partner Parsons, Behle, Evans & Latimer, 1959-68. Mem. Utah (pres. 1952-53, Am. bar assns., Phi Kappa Phi. Mason (grand master 1953-55). Home: Salt Lake City, Utah. Died Aug. 4, 1978.

EVANS, GEORGE HEBERTON, JR., economist; b. Balt., Jan. 20, 1900; s. George Heberton and Mary Virginia Crawford (Sherlock) E.; A.B., Johns Hopkins U., 1920, Ph.D., 1925, LL.D., 1970; m. Elinor Virdin, Nov. 26, 1924; children—George Heberton III, Richard Virdin, Ellen (dec.). Instr. polit. economy Johns Hopkins U., 1924-27, asso., 1927-35, asso. prof., 1935-42, prof., 1942-70, prof. emeritus, 1970-79, chmn. dept. 1942-60, charge Army's fgn. area and lang. tng. program, 1943-44, dean faculty of philosophy, 1959-66, dean emeritus, 1970-79; seminar asso. Columbia U., 1969-72; corporator Savs. Bank of Balt.; trustee Commn. Govt. Efficiency and Economy, 1943-46, 49-51, 54-56; mem. Md. State Bd. Pub. Accountancy, 1953-67; research asso. Nat. Bur. Econ. Research, 1939-40; chmn. com. on hist. statistics Social Sci. Research Council adv. to U.S. Bur. Census, 1956-60. Trustee Roland Park Country Sch., 1941-53. Served in S.A.T.C., 1918. Ford Found. faculty research fellow, 1956-57. Mem. Am. Econ. Assn., Am. Statis. Assn., AAUP, Econ. Hist. Assn. (past v.p.), Phi Beta Kappa, Beta Theta Pi. Episcopalian. Club: Johns Hopkins (Balt.). Author: British Corporation Finance, 1775-1850: A Study of Preference Shares, 1936; (with George E. Barnett) Principles of Investment, 1940, Spanish edit., 1947; Business Incorporations in the U.S., 1800-1943, 1948; Basic Economics, 1950; Recollections of the Johns Hopkins University, 1916-1970, 1977. Editor: Reprint of Economic Tracts, 1942-70. Contbr. articles to econ. jours. Home: Baltimore, Md. Died Oct. 12, 1979.

EVANS, GORDON GOODWIN, educator; b. Bklyn., Feb. 13, 1921; s. William Fuller and Beatrice Annie (Briley) E.; A.B., Princeton, 1942; Ph.D., Harvard, 1950; m. Doletha Soorn Watt, Oct. 14, 1944; children—Doletha Marian, William Soorn, Jocelyn Briley, Lawrence Watt, Ruth Christina, Charlotte Deirdre. Chemist, E.I. du Pont de Nemours & Co., Inc., Buffalo, 1942-43; instr. chemistry Tufts U., 1949-52, asst. prof., 1952-65, asso. prof., 1965-80, chmn. dept., 1966-68. Served with AUS, 1943-46. Mem. Am. Chem. Soc., A.A.A.S., New Eng. Assn. Chemistry Tchrs. (pres. 1973-75), Am. Assn. U. Profs. Unitarian-Universalist. Home: Bedford, Mass. Died May 19, 1980.

EVANS, GRIFFITH CONRAD, JR., cons.; b. Lynn, Mass., May 17, 1918; s. Griffith Conrad and Isabel (John) E.; A.B. in Anthropology, U. Calif. at Berkeley, 1940; m. Margaret Evelyn Lind; children by previous marriage—Judith, Nancy Lea (dec.), Griffith Conrad, Carol Susan. Clk., State Farm Mut. Automobile Ins. Co., 1940-41; enlisted U.S. Navy, 1941, commd. ensign USNR, 1942, served to lt., 1942-46, returned to active duty, 1950, advanced through grades to capt., 1963; comdr. U.S.S. Everett, 1951-53, U.S.S. Burton Island, 1960-61, U.S.S. Edisto, 1961-62; Thailand rep., comdr. in chief U.S. Pacific Fleet, Bangkok, 1966-67; ret., 1967; chief clk. Matson Nav. Co., 1946-50; exec. sec. Oceanographic Commn. Wash., 1967-73; exec. dir. Oceanographic Inst. Wash., 1968-73, trustee, 1975-78; dir. Sea Use Program, 1968-71; mem. Seattle Aquarium Com., 1968-71. Chmn. steering com. for task force occupational edn. Seattle Sch. Bd., 1968-71; mem. pollution control tech. adv. com. Shoreline Community Coll., 1970-71; bd. dirs. Inst. Applied Physiology and Medicine, 1972-78. Decorated Legion of Merit, Navy Commendation medal; Peninsula in Bellingshausen Sea in Antarctic named for him. Mem. Marine Tech. Soc. Home: Seattle, Wash. Died Sept. 8, 1978; cremated; buried at sea.

EVANS, HAROLD, lawyer; b. Phila., Pa., Oct. 26, 1886; s. Jonathan Evans and Rachel R. (Cope) E.; A.B., Haverford Coll., 1907, LL.D., 1968; LL.B., U. Pa., 1910; LL.D., Wilmington Coll., 1964, Haverford Coll., 1968; m. Sylvia Hathaway, May 1, 1914 (dec.); children—Sylvia (Mrs. Joseph H. Taylor), Margaret (Mrs. John T. Carson, Jr.), Nathaniel H., Faith (Mrs. H. Garth Blakely), Thomas (dec.), Anna (Mrs. Arnold R. Post). Admitted to Pa. bar, 1910; mem. firm MacCoy Evans, Hutchinson & Lewis, Phila., 1911-34, MacCoy, Britain, Evans & Lewis, 1934-49, MacCoy, Evans & Lewis, from 1949. Mcpl. commr. for Jerusalem for UN, 1948. Mem. Pa. Public Service Commn., 1925-26; chmn. Phila. Co. Relief Bd., 1936-37; trustee Community Fund of Phila., 1937-43; chmn. Phila. Emergency Com. on Public Edn., 1938-39; hon. mem. bd. mgrs. Haverford Coll.; trustee Penn Community Services, 1921-61, emeritus, 1969-77; dir. emeritus Am. Friends Service Com., chmn., 1960-63. Mem. Am., Pa., Phila. bar assns., Am. Law Inst., Phi Beta Kappa. Club: Founders Home: Philadelphia, Pa. Died Apr. 27, 1977.

EVANS, HENRY COTHEAL, investment banker; b. Balt., Sept. 17, 1895; A.B., Johns Hopkins U., 1918; m. Eleanor O'Donovan, 1921; 6 children. Chmn. bd., then hon. chmn. Stein Bros. & Boyce, Inc. (now merged into Bache & Co.), mems. N.Y., other stock exchanges, Balt.; past dir. Eutaw Savs. Bank (now merged into Md. Nat. Bank); dir. William E. Hooper & Son Co. Pres. Balt. Stock Exchange, 1939-41. Md. state chmn. U.S.O. Chmn. bd. Enoch Pratt Free Library, Served with Am. Field Service 1917, to capt. F.A., U.S. Army, 1917-19; AEF in France; mem. Md. N.G., 1921-57, advancing to maj. gen.; served from col. to maj. gen., U.S. Army, 1941-57; overseas, 1944-45, ret., 1957. Decorated D.S.C., Silver Star, Legion of Merit, Bronze Star with oak leaf cluster (U.S.); Fourragière, Legion of Honor, Croix de Guerre (France); Croix de Guerre (Belgium, Luxembourg); Knight of St. Gregory (Pope Paul VI); recipient Andrew White medal Loyola Coll., Balt., 1964; Disting. Alumnus award Johns Hopkins U., 1967; Disting. Service medal State of Md., 1970; Silver Beaver award, St. George award Balt. Area council Boy Scouts Am. Mem. Balt. Assn. Commerce (pres. 1962-63). Home: Baltimore, Md. Died Feb. 17, 1976; buried New Cathedral Cemetery, Balt.

EVANS, J. CLAIRE, company exec.; b. Zanesville, O., May 13, 1882; s. David J. and Lydia (Lash) E.; A.B., Ohio U., 1901; m. Bess Wilson, Apr. 18, 1906; children—Dorothy E. (Mrs. K. T. Dreher), Wilson D., Elizabeth E. (Mrs. H. E. Stuard, Jr.), Mildren E. (Mrs. J. L. Bauer). Chemist Clear Creek Mining & Reduction Co., Golden, Colo., 1901-1903, H. E. Wood Ore Testing Co., Denver, 1903-12; dept. mgr. Mine & Smelter Supply Co., 1912 18; v.p. Denver Fire Clay Co., 1918-43, pres., 1943-52, chmn. bd. 1952—; dir. Citizens Savs. Bank, Merchants Fire Insurance Co. Mem. Sci. Apparatus Makers Assn. (pres. 1951-53). Am. Inst. Mining Engrs., Teknik Club, Delta Tau Delta. Presbyn. Mason (Shriner). Clubs: Denver, Denver Country, Mile High, Rotary. Home: Denver.

EVANS, JOHN ELLIS, prof. psychology; b. Brazil, Ind., Jan. 1, 1882; s. William P. and Jennie Mahalia (Barnett) E.; diploma, Ind. State Normal Sch., Terre Haute, Ind., 1907; B.A., Ind. U., 1910. M.A., 1911; studied New York U., 1914; Ph.D., Columbia, 1916; m. Clara Mirian Templer, June 12, 1910; children—Billy Templer, John Templer, Robert Templer (dec.), Rachael Templer (dec.), Jennie Serena. Asst. prof. psychology, Indiana Univ. 1910-14; prof. same, Ohio State U., 1914-20, Ia. State Coll. since 1921, also head of dept. Instr. war aims courses, S.A.T.C., 1917-18; development expert, U.S. Army, 1920-21. Instr. engring. science, and management defense training, and in engring., science, and management war training, 1941-46. Fellow A.A.A.S.; member American Psychological Association, National Society for Study of Edn., Am. Assn. Univ. Profs., Iowa Acad. of Science, Ia. State Mental Hygiene Assn. (v.p.), N.E.A., Phi Kappa Phi, Psi Chi. Republican. Mem. United Brethern Ch. Mason. Author: Influence of Distraction on Reaction Time, and the Transfer of Training, 1916. Contbr. articles on psychology of advertising, and personnel relations. Industrial efficiency consultant. Home: Ames, Ia.

EVANS, LLEWELLYN, elec. engr.; b. near Milbank, S.D., July 16, 1882; s. William Morris and Emma (Geil) E.; B.S., U. of Calif., 1907; m. Clara May Wilt, Aug. 31, 1909; children—Elizabeth Muriel, Ruth Helen. Apprentice electrician, Tacoma, Wash., 1900-03; elec. engr. and contractor with D. T. Dickson, Tacoma, 1908-14; pvt. practice, 1914-16; supt. of light, Dept. of Pub. Utilities, Tacoma, 1916-33; chief elec. engr. Tenn. Valley Authority, Wilson Dam, Ala., 1933-37; chief cons. elec. engr. Tenn. Valley Authority, from 1937; 1942-44 consultant for War Production Board, Washington, D.C.; 1945 consultant for F.E.A., Chinese War Production Board, Chungking; 1946 consultant for Allied Council of Austria, Vienna. Fellow Am. Inst. Elec. Engrs.; mem. Am. Soc. Civil Engrs., Alpha Sigma Phi. Conglist. Elk. Home: Chattanooga, Tenn. Died Sept. 13, 1975.

EVANS, ORRON DRAYTON, ins. exec.; b. Rome, Ga., Sept. 13, 1886; s. Walter McCarthy and Lena A. (Godwin) E.; student Benton Coll., 1908; m. Bessie G. Healey, July 2, 1911 (dec. Nov. 1961); children—Margaret Lee, Jean; m. 2d, Elizabeth W. Robertson, July 1962. Freight car builder So. Car & Foundry, Anniston, Ala., 1902-04, Am. Car & Foundry Co., Memphis, 1904-07; ins. agt. Orron D. Evans Underwriters Agy., Inc., St. Louis, 1908-26, dir., 1926—; chmn. bd. Standard Underwriters, 1957-70. Hon. life mem. St. Louis Ins. Bd. Hon. life trustee Hannibal LaGrange Coll.; hon. trustee Mo. Sch. Religion; life trustee New Orleans Bapt., Central Bapt. theol. sems. Mem. Nat. Assn. Businessman (sec.-treas.), Mo. Archeol. Soc. (chmn. bd.), Rocks and Minerals Assn., State Hist. Soc. (life), Nat. Tax Equality (dir.) Rockwoods Assn. (life), Historic Hermann (hon. life), Baptist (hon. life trustee). Mason (32 deg., Shriner). Clubs: Amateur Archeological. Home: Kirkwood MO also Bonita Springs FL.

EVANS, PERCY GRIFFITH, univ. prof.; b. Saugus, Mass., Nov. 29, 1897; s. Evan and Winniefred (Jones) E.; student Tufts Coll., 1915-16; A.B., Boston U., 1919, A.M., 1924; Ph.D., U. of Illinois, 1929; diploma, Inst. de Estudios Históricos, Madrid, Spain, 1921; student Middlebury French Sch., summer 1937; m. Anna M Jones, June 19, 1926; children—Richard Bates, Rober Wynne. Teacher Spanish, Saugus (Mass.) High Sch. 1919-20, Wellesley (Mass.) High Sch., 1920-21; instr DePauw U., Greencastle, Ind., 1921-26, asst. prof Romance languages, 1926-30, asso. prof., 1930-34, prof from 1934, acting head of dept., 1935-36, head of dept from 1936. Served with U.S. Army, World War I. Mem. Am. Assn. Teachers French, Am. Assn. Teachers Spanish, Am. Legion. Club: Greencastle (Ind.). Author: An Elementary Spanish Reader, 1960. Editor: (with Elena M. Lind) Pata de Zorra (Hugo Wast, pseudonym of Gustavo A. Martínez Zuviría), 1937. Home: Greencastle, Ind. Died June 17, 1980.

EVANS, ROY TRIPP, JR., army officer, can co. exec.; b. Pawtucket, R.I., Feb. 7, 1911; s. Roy Tripp and Lillian (Gradwell) E.; B.S., U.S. Mil. Acad., 1933; grad. Indsl. Coll. Armed Forces, 1948, Advanced Mgmt. Program, Harvard, 1954; m. Virginia Hamilton, Nov. 22, 1934; children—Roy Tripp III, John Gradwell, Alexander Hamilton. Commd. 2d lt. U.S. Army, 1933; advanced through grades to maj. gen., 1959; served in Europe, World War II, in Korea, 1953-54; comdt. Q.M. Sch., 1951-53; dep. chief Army and Air Force Exchange Service, 1957-58; dep. Q.M. gen., 1958-61; with Def. Supply Agy., 1961-63; ret. 1963; gen. mgr. purchases Continental Can Co., Inc., 1963-69, v.p. environmental control, from 1969. Decorated D.S.M., Legion of Merit with 1 oak leaf cluster, Bronze Star; comdr. Order Orange Nassau; Ulchi Distinguished Mil. Service medal with silver star (Republic Korea). Mason. Home: Petersburg, Va. Died Sept. 16, 1976; buried Petersburg.

EVANS, TITUS CARR, educator, radiobiologist; b. Lorena, Tex., Dec. 9, 1907; s. Charles William and Virginia (Whitsett) E.; B.A., Baylor U., 1929; M.S., State U. Ia., 1931, Ph.D., 1934; m. Mertie Ellen Jahnke, June 1, 1935 (dec. Nov. 1968); children—Titus Carr, Susan Ellen, Lucy Virginia; m. 2d, Phyllis Allison, Aug. 9, 1971. Asst. prof. Tex. A&M U., 1936-38; research asst. prof. U. Iowa, Iowa City, 1938-42, research prof. radiology and radiobiology, 1948-75, head Radiation Research Lab., 1948-75; asst. prof. Columbia Coll. Phys. and Surg., 1942-48. Cons., mem. policy adv. bd. Argonne (Ill.) Nat. Lab., 1964-68. Mem. Nat. Council Radiation Protection, Soc. Nuclear Medicine (past pres.), Radiation Research Soc., Biophysics Soc., Am. Physiol. Soc., Am. Roentgen Ray Soc., Radiol. Soc. N. Am., Cancer Research Soc., Soc. for Exptl. Biology and Medicine, Am. Soc. Zoology, Am. Cancer Soc. (pres. Iowa 1965, mem. ho. dels., bd. dirs., 1971-75, award disting. service cancer control 1966), Health Physics Soc., Sigma Xi. Mng. editor Radiation Research, 1952-72; asso. editor Nuclear Medicine, 1960-69. Research, numerous publs. on effects X-ray on cell div. and embryonic devel. in invertebrates, radio-protective effect anoxia in mammals, relative effectiveness fast neutrons, devel. techniques for radiosotopes in biol. and med. research, effects X-rays on ascites tumor cells. Died Apr. 8, 1975.

EVANS, WILLIAM JOHN (BILL), jazz pianist; b. Plainfield, N.J., Aug. 16, 1929; s. Harry L. and Mary (Soroka) E.; B.Music Edn., Southeastern La. Coll., 1950; m. Nenette Zazzara, Aug. 5, 1973; 1 son, Evan. Mem. Herbie Fields Band, 1950-51; flute player at Ft. Sheridan days and pianist in Chgo. jazz clubs nights, 1951-54; pianist with Tony Scott's group, N.Y.C., 1955-56; mem. Miles Davis Sextet, 1959; formed own trio, 1959; albums include: Conversations With Myself (Grammy award for Best Instrumental Jazz Performance by a Soloist), 1963; Alone (Grammy award for Best Jazz Performance by a Soloist), 1970; The Bill Evans Album (Grammy award for Best Jazz Performance by a Group, Grammy award for Best Jazz Soloist), 1972; The Tony Bennett/Bill Evans Album; tchr., lectr. in univ. seminars. Served with U.S. Army, 1951-54. Recipient Down Beat award Internat. Jazz Critics Poll in new star piano div., 1958, 5 other Down Beat awards. Mem. Nat. Assn. Rec. Arts and Scis. Home: Fort Lee, N.J. Died Sept. 15, 1980.

EVANS. JOHN KRYDER, mfr.: b. Elk Lick. Pa.. July 9, 1890; s. John Miles and Ellelia (Bott) E.; Ph.B., Franklin and Marshall Coll., 1911; m. Marion Lloyd Hallowell, Oct. 21, 1916; 1 dau., Janet (Mrs. Alexander McBride 3d). Salesman, asst. sales mgr. Arbuckle Bros., N.Y.C., 1911-18; asst. to pres. Franklin Baker Co., Hoboken, N.J., 1918-27; v.p. Gen. Foods Corp., ret. 1955, gen. mgr. Maxwell House div., Hoboken, 1927-55; cons. exec. com. Pan-Am. Coffee Bur., 1956-65. Trustee, exec. com. Franklin and Marshall Coll., 1940-80; adv. bd. Pace Coll., N.Y.C., 1935-56. Del. 1st World Coffee Conf., Rio de Janeiro, 1958. Recipient Order of So. Cross, Brazil, 1960. Mem. Nat. Coffee Assn. (hon. life; dir. 1939-51, 53-54, exec. com. of bd. 1945-50), Am. Brazilian Soc., Phi Kappa Sigma. Mem. Soc. of Friends. Clubs: Union League (Phila.); Bankers of Am. (N.Y.C.); Granite (Toronto, Ont., Can.). Home: South Orange, NJ. Died Mar. 3, 1980.

EVERETT, FRANK G., periodontist, educator; b. Vienna, Austria, Dec. 28, 1907; s. Otto J. and Frances Antonie (Iltis) E.; came to U.S., 1939, naturalized, 1944; M.D., U. Vienna, 1932, Dental License, 1934; D.M.D., U. Oreg., 1941, M.S., 1948; m. Leonie Schulz, Oct. 18, 1937; children—Suzanne (Mrs. William A. King), Joan (Mrs. Kenneth Knapp), F. Thomas. Instr., Dental Sch. U. Vienna, 1933, guest prof., 1971; instr. U. Oreg. Dental Sch., Portland, 1941-48, asst. prof., 1948-52, asso. prof., 1952-57, prof., 1957-60, clin. prof., 1960-70, chmn. dept. periodontology, 1952-60, prof. emeritus Health Scis. Center, to 1976; pvt. practice periodontics, Portland, 1941-76. Guest prof. U. West Berlin Dental Sch., 1973. Recipient Orban award Loyola U. of Maywood, Ill., 1972. Diplomate Am. Bd. Periodontology. Decorated Austrian Cross of Honor for Sci. and Art 1st class, 1976. Fellow Internat., Am. colls. dentists, Am. Acad. Periodontology, Internat. Coll. Surgeons, A.A.A.S., Portland Acad. Medicine; mem. A.M.A., Austrian (hon.), Am. dental assns., Internat. Assn. Dental Research, Multnomah County Dental Soc. (award for merit and distinction 1972), Alumni Assn. U. Oreg. Dental Sch. (Pres.'s award 1973), Oreg. Soc. Periodontists (hon.), Sigma Xi, Omicron Kappa Upsilon. Rotarian. Club: Multnomah. Author: Periodontics 4th edit. (with C.V. Mosby), 1972. Contbr. articles to profl. jours. Home: Portland, Oreg. Died Apr. 14, 1976.

EVERETT, MONROE GREEN, coll. pres.; born McKenzie, Tenn., July 4, 1885; s. John Edward and Elizabeth (Matheny) E.; B.S. Bethel College, McKenzie, Tenn., 1908; A.B., Whitworth Coll., Spokane, Wash., 1910; grad. McCormick Theol. Sem., Chicago, 1915; grad. work, Ore. State Coll., 1925-27; student U. of Chicago, 1930, U. of Pa., 1940; hon. D.D., Cumberland U., 1932; m. Margaret Myrtle Johnson, Aug. 30, 1911; children—Marjorie Jean, John Rutherford, Margaret Elizabeth. Ordained to ministry of Presbyn. Ch., 1915; pastor First Presbyn. Ch., Camas, Wash., 1917, Fourth Presbyn. Ch., Portland, Ore., 1919-22; dir. of Westminster Foundation for Ore., 1922-31; in charge Presbyn. students' work at Ore. State Coll., 1922-31; dir. of Westminster Foundation for Phila., 1931-42; chmn. com. of social edn. and action, Phila. Presbytery, 1939-41, chmn. com. of Christian edn., 1941-42; pres. Trinity U., San Antonio, Tex., 1942-50, pres. emeritus since 1950. Mason. Club: Rotary. Home: San Antonio, Tex.

EVERETT, NEWTON BENNIE, educator; b. Dundee, Tex., May 12, 1916; s. Henry B. and Lula Mae (Williams) E.; B.S., North Tex. State U., 1937, M.S., 1938; Ph.D. (teaching fellow 1940-42), U. Mich., 1942; m. Naomi Doris Briggs, Sept. 11, 1940; children—Peter Ben, James Briggs. Instr. anatomy U. Mich., 1942-46; asst. prof. U. Wash., 1946-48, asso. prof., 1948-57, adminstrv. officer, 1955-61, prof., 1957-78, chmn. dept. anatomy, prof., chmn. dept. biol. structure, 1961-78. Mem. anat. scis. tng. grant com. NIH, 1963-64, 69-73, chmn., 1971-73, mem. cell biology study sect., 1959-63, chmn., 1965-67; mem. anatomy test com. Nat. Bd. Med. Examiners, 1967-72. Recipient Distinguished Alumnus citation North Tex. State U., 1972. Mem. Am. Assn. Anatomists (pres. 1977-78), Am. Soc. Immunology, Am., Internat. socs. cell biology, Internat., Am. socs. hematology, Royal Soc. Medicine (affiliate), Reticuloendothelial Soc. (councillor 1972-76, pres.-elect 1978), Assn. Anatomy Chmn. (1st pres. 1969-70), Sigma Xi. Asso. editor Anat. Record, 1958-74; adv. editor Internat. Rev. Cytology, Jour. Reticuloendothelial Soc. Home: Seattle, Wash. Died May 23, 1978.

EVERETT, ROBERTS, agrl. writer; b. Merrill, Mich., Mar. 17, 1894; s. John Edward and Helen (Glazier) E.; student Oberlin Coll., 1911-12; B.Litt., Columbia Sch. Journalism, 1915; m. Evelyn Virginia Clay, May 31, 1917 (div. Aug. 1937); 1 dau., Mrs. Helen Everett Seaman; m. 2d, Frieda Wyandt, Apr. 2, 1938. Mem. staff N.Y. Tribune, 1915, N.Y. World, 1915-17; editor Air Travel, 1917; chief staff officer Dairy Industries Supply Assn., 1919-60; mng. dir. Dairy Soc. Internat., 1946-60, writer in agrl. field. Served as flying cadet, 1917-19, commd. 2d lt. Air Service, 1918. Recipient Distinguished Service award Am. Dairy Sci. Assn., 1961. Mem. Nat. Assn. Expn. Mgrs. (hon.). Author indsl. commentaries; contbr. numerous articles to mags. Home: Silver Spring, Md. Died Jan. 28, 1980.

EVERHEART, WILLIAM EDWARD, coll. pres.; b. Pottsboro, Tex., July 7, 1916; s. Joe N. and Mabel (Judd) E.; B.A., Trinity U., 1937, D.D., 1950; Th.M., Princeton, 1940; m. Doris Marlyene Talley, June 3, 1941; children—William Edward, Jo Ann (Mrs. Robert McKnight), Sarah Sandra (Mrs. Leon Greene), Susan M. (Mrs. Dean Alt). Ordained to ministry United Presbyn. Ch., 1940; minister Westminster Presbyn. Ch., Amarillo, Tex., 1951-62; sr. minister First and Calvary Presbyn. Ch., Springfield, Mo., 1962-71; pres. Drury Coll., Springfield, 1971-76. Pres. Springfield chpt. A.R.C., 1964-65, Springfield Area Council Chs., 1965-66. Pres. Springfield Bd. Edn., 1967-71. Trustee Lester E. Cox Med. Center, Springfield. Served with USNR, 1942-45. Mem. Blue Key, Omicron Delta Kappa, Pi Kappa Delta. Presbyn. (chmn. gen. council Synod Mid-Am. 1972-74, chmn. permanent com. on nominations of gen. assembly 1973-74). Home: Springfield, Mo. Died July 5, 1976.

EVERS, JOHN W., utility corporation exec.; born Chicago, Illinois, Oct. 1, 1894; s. John W. and Mary R. (Kelly) E.; educated Chicago pub. schs.; m. Marjorie Crolius, June 3, 1922; 1 son, John W. III. Asst. treas. and asst. sec. Commonwealth Edison Co., 1922-24, sec., 1924-47, v.p., 1943, exec. v.p., 1951, pres., 1953-59; dir. Nat. Blvd. Bank of Chgo., Seaboard Finance Company, Commonwealth Edison Co. Bd. Dirs. A.R.C., Chicago; pres., dir. Rehab. Inst., dir. Hosp. Planning Council Met. Chgo.; trustee Community Fund Joint Appeal Chgo., Graham Found. for Advanced in the Fine Arts. Mem. Met. Fair and Expn. Authority Bd. Mem. Sr. Council Chgo. Assn. Commerce and Industry (pres. 1955-56). Clubs: Commercial, Chicago, Economic, Exmoor, Chicago Athletic Assn. (Chgo.). Home: Boca Raton, Fla. Died Dec. 5, 1980.

EVJUE, WILLIAM THEODORE, newspaper editor; b. Merrill, Wis., Oct. 10, 1882; s. Nils Peter and Mary (Erickson) E.; student U. of Wis., 1902-05; m. Zillah Julia Bagley, May 31, 1913. Began as reporter Milwaukee (Wis.) Sentinel, 1905, night editor, 1908-11; mng. editor Wis. State Journal, Madison, 1911-13, business mgr., 1913-17; founder, 1917, since editor, pres. The Capital Times, Madison; pres. Badger Broadcasting Co., Madison Newspapers, Inc. Mem. Wis. Assembly, 1917-19; mem. Rep. State Central Com., Wis., 1920-24; Rep. presdl. elector, 1924; chmn. of conv. at which new Progressive Party was born, Fond du Lac, Wis., May 1934. Decorated Friedens Cors, 1943, Knight of St. Olav, 1959 (Norway). Mem. Phi Gamma Delta, Sigma Delta Chi (fellow). Clubs: University, Madison. Home: Madison, Wis.

EWING, DRESSEL DEWITT, elec. engr.; b. at Vanlue, O., Oct. 7, 1883; s. Melvin Edward and Elizabeth Ann (Bright) E.; E.E., Ohio Northern U., 1905, M.E 1906, Dr. Engring., 1936; grad. study Purdue U., 1912-13; m. Mary Schantz, Dec. 29, 1906; 1 son, Paul Bruce. Asst. engr. Mo. P. R.R., St. Louis, 1906-07; instr. elec. and mech. engring., Ohio Northern U., 1907-12; asst. prof. elec. engring. Purdue U., 1913-16, asso. prof., 1916-18, prof. since 1918, specializing in electric rys. and power transmission and distribution, head Sch. Elec. Engring. since Apr. 1942; dir. research Am. Electric Ry. Assn., 1925-30, Internat. Steel Tie Co., Cleveland, 1929-32; also cons. engr. Dir. Duncan Electric Mfg. Co. Served as instr. S.A.T.C. Signal Corps, World War I. Trustee, Ohio Northern Univ., 1940-45. Fellow Am. Inst. E.E. (dir.); mem. Soc. for Promotion Engring. Edn., Am. Transit Assn., Ind. Engring. Council, Tau Beta Pi, Eta Kappa Nu, Sigma Xi, Theta Tau. Republican. Presbyterian. Author: (with C. F. Harding) Electric Railway Engineering, 1915; also univ. bulls. Contbr. numerous tech. articles. Contbg. editor Electric Ry. Journal, 1915-21. Home: West Lafayette, Ind.

EWING, EARLY CUNNINGHAM, research dir.; b. Aberdeen, Miss., Apr. 3, 1886; s. Charles Carter and Sally (Cunningham) E.; B.S., Miss. State Coll., 1906; B.S., Cornell U., 1908, M.S., 1909; m. Emma Bell, Jan. 8, 1920; children—Early C., Battle B., Thomas C. Employee bur. plant industry U.S. Dept. Agr., 1909-10; inaugurated and developed cotton breeding research Miss. Agrl. Expt. Sta., 1910-14, (line selections and hybrids since developed into varieties now used in most of central and eastern sect. cotton belt); organized and developed cotton breeding work Delta & Pine Land Co., Scott, Miss., 1915, now director of research; responsible for variety Deltapine, the most extensively planted in U.S., largely grown in Mexico and South Am., with son Early developed improved smooth leaf variety, 1957. Mem. Am. Genetic Assn., Sigma Xi. Contbr. sci. jours. Home: Scott, Miss.

EWING, OSCAR ROSS, lawyer, philanthropist; b. Greensburg, Ind., Mar. 8, 1889; s. George McClellan and Nettie Moore (Ross) E.; A.B., Indiana U., 1910; J.D., Harvard, 1913; LL.D., U. N.C., 1967, Ind. U., 1970; m. Helen E. Dennis, Nov, 4, 1915 (dec. June 1953); children—James Dennis, George McClellan; m. 2d; Mary Whiting MacKay Thomas, Oct. 12, 1955. Instr., U. Ia. Law Sch., 1913-14; mem. Weyl, Jewett & Ewing Indpls., 1915-16; asst. counsel Vandalia R.R. Co., St. Louis, 1916; asst. to gen. counsel Pa. Lines West of Pitts., 1917; mem. Hughes, Schurman & Dwight, N.Y., and predecessor firms 1920-37; mem. firm Hughes, Hubbard & Ewing, 1937-47; spl. asst. to U.S. atty. gen., 1942; Asst. chmn. Democratic Nat. Com. 1940-42, vice chmn. Dem. Nat. Com., 1942-47; Fed. Security Agy. administr., 1947-52. Am. mfrs. del. Conf. for Limitation Mfr. Narcotics, Geneva, 1931. Chmn., Research Triangle Regional Planning Commn., 1963-67. Bd. dirs. Research Triangle Found. Served from 1st lt. to capt. U.S. Army, 1918. Mem. N.Y. County Bar Assn., Assn. Bar City N.Y., Am. Legion, Davison Club of Duke U. Med. Center (charter), Med. Found. U.N.C. Med. Center (charter), Torch Clubs Internat., Beta Theta Pi. Democrat. Episcopalian. Club: University (N.Y.C.).Contbr. legal articles to mags. Home: Chapel Hill, N.C. Died Jan. 8, 1980.

EWING, PARMER LELAND, state edn. ofcl.; b. Casey, Ill., Mar. 12, 1903; s. N.A. and (Frissel) E.; student James Millkin U., 1921-23; B.S., U. Ill., 1930, M.S., 1934; Ed.D., N.Y. U., 1950; m. Lalah Augustus, July 16, 1926; children—Carol Elizabeth (Mrs. John Sutton), Marilyn Louise (Mrs. John Kaneski). Instr. indsl. arts, coach athletics Shelbyville (Ill.) High Sch., 1923-30, prin., 1930-31; supt. schs., Highland, Ill., 1931-42, Alton, Ill., 1942-47, Rockford, Ill., 1947-50, White Plains, N.Y., 1950-53, Buffalo, 1953-57; chmn. dept. adminstrn. and supervision, sch. edn. N.Y. U., 1957-65; prof. ednl. adminstrn., dir. ednl. cons. service So. Ill. U., Carbondale, 1965-68; dir. dept. higher edn. Office Supt. Pub. Instrn. Ill., 1968-81. Active Buffalo

Mus. Sci., Buffalo Philharmonic Soc., Albright Gallery, YMCA, Boy Scouts Am. Recipient Silver Beaver award Boy Scouts Am.; Alumni Merit award Millikin U., 1968; Sch. Edn. Merit award N.Y. U., 1968. Mem. N.E.A. (chem. internat. relation com. of regents com.), Am. Assn. Sch. Administrs. (Disting. Service award 1976), N.Y. State Tchrs. Assn., Buffalo Tchrs. Fedn., N.Y. State Council of Supts., Buffalo Hist. Soc., SAR, Phi Delta Kappa, Alpha Mu Sigma, Sigma Delta Sigma. Methodist. Mason (Shriner). Elk. K.P. Clubs: Rotary, Equality, Buffalo. Home: Springfield, Ill. Died Mar. 5, 1981; buried Bloomington, Ill.

EWINS, EARLE EDLIN, lawyer; b. Cedar Rapids, Ia., Dec. 19, 1893; s. George Madison and Fanny (Edlin) E.; B.A., U. Mich., 1921, J.D., 1922; m. Marie A. Kniest, Mar. 24, 1919; 1 dau., Alice Marie. Admitted to Ill. bar, 1922; partner Musgrave, Ewins, Kalivoda & Anderson, and predecessors, Chgo., from 1922. Mem. Am. Ill. (sr. counselor), Chicago bar assns. Home: Evanston, Ill. Died Dec. 8, 1976.

EXUM, JAMES POWERS, cons. engr.; b. Mobeetie, Tex., Oct. 11, 1900; s. Frank and Nancy Magdeline (Powers) E.; B.S. in C.E., U. Tex., 1922; m. Louise Ramsay, Sept. 6, 1924; 1 son, James Powers. Draftsman, Harrington, Howard & Ash, cons. engrs., Kansas City, Mo., 1922-24, designer bridge div. Tex. Hwy. Dept., 1924-25; designer, chief draftsman Harrington, Howard & Ash, 1925-28; chief draftsman, prin. asst. engr. Ash, Howard, Needles & Tammen, Kansas City, Mo., 1928-32; asst. engr. bridge div. Tex. Hwy. Dept., 1932-38, sr. designing engr., 1938-43, bridge engr., 1943-48; asso. engr., Howard, Needles, Tammen & Bergendoff, N.Y.C., 1948-50, partner, 1950-65, mem. adv. bd.; cons. 1965-77; prin. works: Del. Meml. Bridge, Woodrow Wilson Meml. Bridge, Cooper River Bridge, N.J., Me. and Del. turnpikes, Newark Bay Bridge and Jersey City Expressway, also Route 24 Expressway, NLJ. Recipient Distinguished Engrng. Grad. award U. Tex., 1964. Registered profl. engr., Conn., Del., Maine, N.J., N.Y., S.C., Tex., Va. Mem. Natl., Tex. (pres. 1947) socs. profl. engrs., ASCE (pres. Tex. 1948), Am. Inst. Cons. Engrs. (pres. 1963), Am. Concrete Inst., Tau Beta Pi, Chi Epsilon, Theta Xi. Clubs: Canoe Brook Country (Summit, N.J.); Royal Palm Yacht and Country (Boca Raton, Fla.); Engineers (N.Y.C.). Home: Boca Raton, Fla. Died Dec. 22, 1977.

EYMAN, RALPH LEE (I'MAN), dean; b. Golden, Ill., Aug. 5, 1885; s. Daniel F. and Sarah Emily (Shank) E.; student Western Ill. State Teachers College, Macomb, 1908-10; B.S. in Agr., Univ. of Ill., 1914; Ed.D., U. of Calif., 1928; m. Esther Allen Kern, Aug. 20, 1914; children—David Russell, Ruth Louise (Mrs. William Clyatt), Mary Jeanne (Mrs. L. A. Smith), Robert Lee. Teacher in one room school, 1904-07; principal John Swaney Consolidated School, McNabb, Ill., 1910-12; professor of chemistry and physics, Kent (Ohio), State Teachers Coll., 1914-18; prof. agr., Ill. State Normal U., Normal, Ill., 1918-20; county agrl. agent, Jerseyville, Ill., 1920-26; prof. edn. Florida State University, 1928-37, dean Sch. of Edn., 1937—. Cons. Point IV Program in Thailand, 1951-53. Mem. Alpha Zeta, Kappa Delta Pi, Phi Delta Kappa, Phi Kappa Phi, Zeta Psi. Democrat. Presbyterian. Mason. Home: Tallahassee, Fla.

EYRE, THOMAS TAYLOR, univ. prof.; b. Dolington, Pa., Jan. 8, 1883; s. Barclay and Emma Dutton (Taylor) E.; B.S. in M.E., Purdue, 1905, M.E., 1926; m. Lora Alice Moore, Feb. 23, 1907; 1 dau., Edith K. (wife of Dr. T. Robert White). Instr. Purdue Univ., 1905-13; asst. prof. Case Sch. Applied Science, Cleveland, O., 1913-14; asst. prof. Purdue, 1914-20; dean engring., State Univ. of N.M., 1920-26; prof. mechanical engring., U. of Southern Calif., Los Angeles, 1926-50, ret. Served as capt. engrs., U.S. Army, France, World War I. Mem. Am. Soc. M.E., Am. Soc. E.E., Am. Assn. Univ. Profs., Sigma Xi, Tau Beta Pi, Phi Kappa Phi. Republican. Friend (Quaker). Author: Engines and Boilers, 1922. Home: Los Angeles.

FABER, HAROLD KNIEST, pediatrician; b. Westfield, N.Y., June 19, 1884; s. William Frederic and Dorothea Jeannette (Kniest) F.; A.B., Harvard, 1906; M.D., U. of Mich., 1911; m. Mary Eleanor Kehoe, Feb. 3, 1916. Resident pathologist, Babies Hosp., New York, 1913-14; fellow Rockefeller Inst. for Med. Research, 1914-15; with Stanford U. Sch. of Medicine since 1915, prof. of pediatrics, 1923-49, emeritus; pediatrician-in-chief Stanford U. Hosp., San Francisco, 1919-49, director poliomyelitis research, 1949-59; research grantee of National Foundation for Infantile Paralysis, 1939-53; med. dir. Stanford Convalescent Home, 1923-56. Capt., M.C., A.U.S., 1918-19. Recipient Howland medal; award, Am. Pediatric Soc., 1956. Mem. A.M.A., Am. Pediatric Soc. (pres. 1946-47), Soc. Pediatric Research, Am. Acad. Pediatrics, Soc. Exptl. Biol. and Med., Alpha Omega Alpha, Sigma Xi. Clubs: University, Golf (San Francisco). Author: The Pathogenesis of Poliomyelitis, 1955. Contbr. of med. papers including research work on infantile paralysis. Home: San Francisco.

FABIAN, HAROLD PEGRAM, lawyer; b. Salt Lake City, Apr. 1, 1885; s. Ferdinand John and Minnie (Pegram) F.; student Mercersburg (Pa.) Acad.; A.B., Yale, 1907; LL.B., Harvard, 1910; LL.D., U. Utah, 1969; m. Ruth Chapman, Oct. 19, 1910; children—Ruth P., Ferdinand J. II.; m. 2d, Josephine Cunningham, Feb. 14, 1938. Admitted to Utah bar, 1910, began practice Salt Lake City; mem. firm Dey, Hoppaugh & Fabian, 1910-17, Bagley, Fabian, Clendenin & Judd, 1919-23, later Fabian & Clendenin; pres. Rocky Mountain Packing Corp., 1934-45; exec. v.p., treas., trustee Jackson Hole Preserve, Inc., to 1954, trustee, to 1975; pres., dir. Grand Teton Lodge & Transp. Co., 1946-52, exec. v.p., gen. mgr. dir., 1952-54; treas., trustee Jackson Hole Wild Life Park, 1946-52. Pres., Travelers Aid Soc., Salt Lake City, 1957-58; mem. Utah Pony Express Commn., 1959-60; v.p., trustee Nauvoo Restoration, Inc., 1962-72. Del., Republican Nat. Conv., 1920; mem. Rep. Nat. Com., 1928-32; del.-at-large Rep. Nat. Conv. at Phila., 1940. Vice-pres. Bd. of Edn., Salt Lake City, 1920-26; mem. nat. adv. com. N.Y. World's Fair, 1939; organizer Citizens Def. Corps, Salt Lake City, comdr., 1941-42; mem. Utah Park and Recreation Commn. (pres. 1957-66), hon. life dir., chmn. emeritus. Trustee, St. John's Hosp., Jackson, Wyo., 1963-66; trustee, hon. life mem. Utah Heritage Found. Chmn., Nat. Parks adv. bd., 1962-64; cons., park adv. bd. Sec. Interior; bd. dirs, pres. Sugarhouse Park Authority, Salt Lake City. Served to capt., maj. inf. U.S. Army, World War I. Recipient Forestry Conservation award Utah Foresters, 1958; Outstanding Service award Utah Recreation and Parks Assn., 1958; Pugsley medal Am. Scenic, Historic and Preservation Soc., 1964; Outstanding Conservation Service plaque Gov. Utah, on Harold P. Fabian Day in Utah, 1967; Service award U.S. Dept. Interior, 1969; named hon. life park ranger Nat. Park Service, 1972. Mem. Am. Bar Assn., Utah Bar Assn. (Disting. Citizens award 1972), Wyo. Bar Assn., C. of C. (pres. 1930-31 bd. govs.), SAR (pres. 1947-48), Utah Soc. Mayflower Descs. (gov. 1960-61), Conquistadores del Cielo (hon.), Psi Upsilon. Clubs: Alta, Bonneville (Salt Lake City); Elihu (Yale); Harvard of Utah; Mason (32 deg.). Home: Salt Lake City, Utah. Died Dec. 6, 1975; buried Mt. Olivet Cemetery, Salt Lake City.

FAGOTHEY, AUSTIN JOSEPH, educator, clergyman; b. San Francisco, June 23, 1901; s. Joseph A. and Katherine (McDade) F.; A.B., Gonzaga U., 1923, M.A., 1924; S.T.L., Weston (Mass.) Coll., 1932; Ph.D., Gregorian U., Rome, 1959. Instr. philosophy U. Santa Clara (Cal.), 1932-34, 35-36; instr. theology Alma Coll., Los Gatos, Cal., 1936-38; prof. philosophy U. Santa Clara, 1938-75, chmn. dept., 1938-67, trustee univ., 1943-73. Mem. Am., Am. Cath., Jesuit philos. assns., Metaphys. Soc. Am. Author: Right and Reason, Ethics in Theory and Practice, 5th edit., 1972; Anthology of Right and Reason, 1972. Address: Santa Clara, Calif. Died May 29, 1975; interred Santa Clara Mission Cemetery.

FAHLSTROM, OYVIND, painter; b. Sao Paulo, Brazil, 1928. Came to U.S., 1961. Organizer, dir., participant various intermedia events, including The Ingrid Thulin Story, Ur Mellanöl, Fahlstöms Höona, Moderna Museet, Stockholm, 1964, Kisses Sweeter than Wine, Armory, N.Y.C., 1966; feature film DuGamlaDuFria, Stockholm, 1969-70; exhibited one man shows Galleria Numero, Florence, 1952, Galerie Daniel Cordier, Paris, 1958, 62, Galerie Blanche, Stockholm, 1959, Cordier & Ekstrom, N.Y., 1964, XXXIII Biennale, Venice, 1966, Sidney Janis Gallery, N.Y., 1967, 69, 71, 73, Bucholz, Munich, 1974, Multhipla, Milan, 1974, Ioles, Paris, 1975; exhibited group shows including V Sao Paulo Biennial, 1959, II Bieale de Paris, 1961, Sidney Janis Gallery, 1962, Museo Nacional de Belles Artes, Buenos Aires, 1963, Musee d'Art Moderne de la Ville de Paris, 1964, Musée des Arts Decoratifs, Paris, 1968, L'Aquila, 1965, Guggenheim Mus., N.Y.C., 1966, Galleria Schwarz, Milan, 1967, Chgo. Mus. Contemporary Art, 1967. Recipient Guggenheim Internat. award, 1964. Author: (poems) Bord, 1964, (novel) Den Helige T. Nilsson, 1968 (essays) Om Livskonst, 1970. Address: New York, N.Y. Died Nov. 8, 1976.

FAHR, GEORGE EDMESTON (FÄR), prof. of medicine; b. Meadville, Pa., Jan. 25, 1882; s. Charles and Margaret (Edmeston) F.; B.S., U. of Chicago, 1904; M.D., U. of Wuerzburg, Germany, 1909; m. Alice Hume Pearson, Nov. 3, 1917; children—Samuel Mehard, Charles (dec.), Margaret, George Pearson. Asst., dept. of physiology, U. of Wuerzburg, 1907-10; asst. in physiology, U. of Leyden, 1911-13; instr. in medicine, U. of Wis., 1919-21; asst. prof., asso. prof. and prof. of internal medicine, Univ. of Minn., since 1921; chief medical service, Minneapolis General Hospital and University Heart Clinic, 1926; director Crawford County Dry Goods Co., Citizens Morris Plan Co. Served as 1st lt. Med. Corps, U.S. Army, 1918. Mem. A.M.A., Am. Physiol. Soc., Am. Pharmacol. Assn., Am. Heart Assn., Phi Beta Kappa, Sigma Xi. Republican. Episcopalian. Contbr. numerous articles on med. subjects to tech. jours. Home: Minneapolis. *

FAHS, CHARLES BURTON, educator; b. Bklyn., Sept. 22, 1908; s. Charles Harvey and Sophia Blanche (Lyon) F.; B.S., Northwestern U., 1929, M.A., 1931, Ph.D., 1933; student U. Berlin, 1929-30, Ecole Nationale des Langues Orientales Vivantes, 1933-34, Kyoto Imperial U., 1934-35, Tokyo Imperial U., 1935-36; D.Litt. (hon.), Kokugakuin U., Japan, 1964; L.H.D. (hon.), Miami U., 1979; m. Jamie L. Ross, June 27, 1932; children—James Harvey, Barbara Ruth. Instr. Oriental affairs Pomona Coll., Claremont Coll., 1936-39, asst. prof., 1939-45; vis. prof. Coll. Chinese Studies, Peiping, 1940-41; research analyst Office Coordinator Information, 1941-42, OSS, 1942-45, chief Far East div., 1944-45; acting chief, div. research for Far East, Dept. State, 1945-46; asst. dir. humanities Rockefeller Found., 1946-48, asso. dir., 1949, dir., 1950-62; minister counselor for cultural and pub. affairs Am. embassy, Tokyo, 1962-65, minister for cultural affairs, 1965-67; Harry C. Trexler vis. prof., Muhlenberg Coll., Allentown, Pa., 1967-68; dir. internat. programs, prof. govt. Miami U., Oxford, Ohio, 1968-73; editor-in-chief Japanese Book Knowledge, Grolier, Inc., 1973-75. Decorated U.S. Medal of Freedom; Order of Sacred Treasure (Japan); recipient Japan Found. award, 1979. Mem. Assn. Asian Studies, Japan Soc., The Asia Soc., Chindan Society Korea (hon.), Phi Beta Kappa. Club: Tokyo. Author: Government in Japan, Recent Trends in its Scope and Operation, 1940. Home: Oxford, Ohio. Died Feb. 26, 1980; buried Oxford.

FAHY, CHARLES, judge; b. Rome, Ga., Aug. 17, 1892; s. Thomas and Sarah (Jonas) F.; student U. Notre Dame, 1910-11; LL.B., Georgetown U., 1914, LL.D., 1942; m. Mary Agnes Lane, June 26, 1929; children—Charles (Dom Thomas Fahy, O.S.B.), Anne Marie (Mrs. Rourke Sheehan), Sarah Agnes (Sister Sarah Fahy S.N.D.), Mary Agnes Johnson. Admitted to D.C. bar, 1914, practiced in Washington until 1924; practiced in Santa Fe, 1924-33; city atty. Santa Fe, 1932; apptd. 1st asst. solicitor Dept. Interior, Washington, 1933; apptd. mem. Petroleum Adminstrv. Bd., 1933, chmn., 1934-35; gen. counsel NLRB, 1935-40; asst. solicitor gen. U.S., 1940; mem. Pres.'s Naval and Air Base Commn. to London, 1941; solicitor gen. U.S., 1941-45; legal adviser, dir. Legal Div. Mil. Govt., Germany (U.S.), 1945-46; legal adviser Dept. of State, 1946. Adviser to Am. Del., San Francisco Conf., 1945; U.S. mem. Legal Com., Gen. Assembly UN, N.Y.C., 1946; alt. U.S. rep. to gen. assembly UN, 1947, 1949; chmn. Pres.'s com. on equality of Treatment and Opportunities in Armed Forces, 1948-50; pvt. practice, washington, 1947-49; chmn. personnel security review bd. AEC, 1949; judge U.S. Ct. of Appeals for D.C. Circuit, 1949-67, sr. judge, 1967-79. Served as naval aviator, 1917-19. Decorated Navy Cross, 1920; medal for Merit, 1946; recipient Robert S. Abbott Meml. award (to Pres.'s Com.), 1951; Russwurm award, 1953, John Carroll award Georgetown U. Mem. Am., N.Mex., Fed. (Distinguished Service award) bar assns., D.C. bar (Distinguished Service award 1969). Democrat. Roman Catholic. Home: Washington, D.C. Died Sept. 17, 1979.

FAIR, ETHEL M(ARION), librarian; b. Carlisle, Pa., Nov. 15, 1884; d. Robert Willis and Margaretta (Means) Fair; ed. A.B., Vassar Coll., 1906; Library Sch., New York Public Library (certificate), 1916; student single course, U. of Wis., 1924-25; M.A., U. of Chicago, 1935; unmarried. Teacher in pvt. school for girls, 1906-08; library asst., 1913-17; spl. investigator, cost of living survey, U.S. Bureau of Labor Statistics, 1918; spl. asst., Pa. State Library, 1919-1920; cataloger, Purdue U. Library, 1920-22; instr., U. of Wis. Library Sch., 1922-27; acting librarian, Wilson Coll., Chambersburg, Pa., 1928; acting prin. Carnegie Library Sch., Atlanta, Ga., 1929-30; dir. Library Sch., N.J. Coll. for Women, 1930-50; librarian Am. Univ. at Cairo (Fulbright award), 1950-51. Mem. Asso. Alumnae of Vassar, Am. Assn. Univ. Women, Am. Inst. of Graphic Arts, A.L.A., N.J. Library Assn. (pres. 1945-46), Pa. Library Assn., Spl. Libraries Assn., League of Women Voters. Club: Town Hall (New York); Author: Country-wide Library Service, 1934. Republican. Home: Harrisburg, Pa.

FAIRFIELD, GOLDING, lawyer; b. Battle Creek, Mich., Feb. 28, 1886; s. William Josiah and Nellie (Wheeler) F.; A.B., De Pauw U., 1907; LL.B., cum laude, U. of Denver, 1911; m. Ula Marguerite King, Sept. 30, 1913; children—William, Annie Rachel (dec.) Admitted to Colo. bar, 1912, and practiced since at Denver; prof. real property law, U. of Denver, since 1928; dir. The Title Guaranty Co. Member Colorado House of Representatives, 1918-20; member Colorado State Senate, 1920-32; pres. of Senate 3 times. Mem. Am., Colo., Denver bar assns., Beta Theta Pi, Phi Delta Phi. Republican. Methodist. Mason (Shriner). Clubs: Denver Athletic, Cherry Hills, Rotary. Home: Denver.

FAITH, WILLIAM LAWRENCE, chemical engr.; b. Hancock, Md., May 12, 1907; s. Eugene Francis and Bernadette (Murray) F.; B.S., U. of Md., 1928; M.S., U. of Ill., 1929, Ph.D., 1931; m. Mildred Eunice Dixon, Sept. 2, 1932; children—Michael Dixon, Mary Eunice, Roger Lawrence. Special research assistant, chemical engineering, Engineering Experimental Station, University of Illinois, 1931-33; chemist Nat. Aluminate Corp., Chicago, 1933; asst. prof. chem. engring., Kan. State Coll., Manhattan, Kan., 1933-36, prof. chem. engring., 1936-39, head dept. chem. engring., 1939-42; prof. chem. engring., State U. of Ia., Iowa City, Ia. (on leave), 1942-44; consultant Office Production Research and Development, W.P.B., Washington, D.C., 1942-43, asst. dir., 1944, dep. dir., 1944-45; visiting lecturer chem. engring., Cath. Univ. of Am., Washington, D.C., 1944; dir. development engring., chem. div., Corn Products Refining Co., Argo, Ill., 1945-48, dir. engring., chem. div., 1948-54; chief engr., dep. dir. Air Pollution Found., Los Angeles, 1954-57, mng. dir., 1957-61; cons. chem. engr., San Marino, Cal., from 1961. Bd. trustees Am. San. Engring. Intersoc. Bd. Mem. Air Pollution Control Assn. (dir. 1959-63, pres. 1961-62), Am. Chem. Soc., Am. Inst. Chem. Engrs. (dir. 1954-56), Sigma Xi, Alpha Chi Sigma, Phi Kappa. Catholic. Clubs: Chemists (N.Y.C.). Author: Air Pollution Control, 1959; (with A.A. Atkisson) Air Pollution, 1972. Asso-Author: Industrial Chemicals, 1950. Home: San Marino, Cal. Died July 18, 1979; buried Hancock, Md.

FAJANS, KASIMIR, prof. of chemistry; b. Warsaw, Poland, May 27, 1887; s. Herman and Wanda (Wolberg) F.; student Univ. of Leipzig, 1904-07; Dr. Nat. Phil., Heidelberg, 1909; research work, Zurich, 1909-10, Univ. of Manchester, 1910-11; m. Salomea Kaplan, 1910; children—Edgar W., Stefan S. Asst., Technische Hochschule, Karlsruhe, 1911-17, privat dozent phys. chemistry, 1913-17; asso. prof., U. of Munich, 1917-25; prof., 1925-35; dir. of Inst. for Physical Chemistry, 1932-35; prof. chemistry, U. of Michigan, Ann Arbor, Mich., from 1936. Non-resident lecturer in chemistry, Cornell Univ., 1930; lecturer, Austria, Canada, Denmark, England, Germany, Holland, Norway, Poland, Russia, Spain, Sweden, Switzerland, U.S.A., Belgium; cons. Owens-Ill. Glass Co., Toledo, 1948-55. Establishment Kasimir Fajans award in chemistry, U. Mich., 1956. Recipient Victory Meyer prize, Heidelberg, 1909; medal of U. Liege, 1948. Fellow Am. Phys. Soc.; mem. Faraday Soc., Am. Chem. Soc. (exec. com. div. phys. and inorganic chemistry 1942-44; council 1944), A.A.A.S., Am. Crystallographical Assn., Soc. Freedom in Sci., Leningrad, Munich and Cracow acads. of sci., Polish Inst. Arts and Scis. in Am., Sigma Xi, hon. mem. chem. Soc. Karlsruhe, Soc. Doctors of Madrid, Spanish Soc. for Physics and Chemistry, Royal Institution Great Britain, Phi Lambda Upsilon. Member Council of Deutsche Chem. Gesellschaft, 1921-22, Council of Bunsengesellschaft, 1928-32. Author books including: Refractometry in Physical Methods of Organic Chemistry (with N. Bauer), 1945. Editor various publs.; co-editor: Zeitsch für Kristallographie, 1924-39. Asso. editor: Jour. Physical and Colloid Chemistry 1948-49. Contbr. articles to jours.; sci. material and correspondence donated to Bentley Hist. Library, Ann Arbor. Home: Ann Arbor, Mich. Died May 18, 1975; buried Forest Hill Cemetery, Ann Arbor.

FALBO, ERNEST SALVATORE, educator; b. Spokane, Feb. 14, 1923; s. Pasquale and Lucia (Pittarelli) F.; A.B., Reed Coll., 1949; Ph.D., U. Florence (Italy), 1954; m. Ruth Eilean Lear, July 16, 1956; children—Paula, Carla, Christopher, Francesca. Instr., Portland (Ore.) State Coll., 1955-56; asso. prof. modern langs. Lake Erie Coll., 1956-64; vis. asst. prof. Italian, U. Va., summers 1960, 61; prof. Italian, Gonzaga U., 1964-68, chmn. dept. modern langs., 1965-67; prof. State U. Coll. at Buffalo, 1968-75, chmn. dept. fgn. langs., 1968-75. Dir. Edn. Professions Devel. Act. Inst. in Italian, Florence, summer 1969; dir. Nat. Def. Ednl. Act Inst. Advanced Study Italian, Florence, summers 1967, 68. Served with USAAF, 1943-45. Decorated D.F.C., Air medal with 3 oak leaf clusters; Fulbright fellow, 1949-50. Mem. Pacific Northwest Conf. Fgn. Langs (pres. 1967), Am. Assn. Tchrs. Italian (sec.-treas. 1964-68), Am. Council Teaching Fgn. Langs. (nat. del. 1967-75), Am.-Italian Hist. Assn. (bd. dirs. 1966-75), Soc. for Multi-Ethnic Lit. of U.S. (treas. 1974-75). Editor, translator: (Count Leonetto Cipriani) California and Overland Dairies, 1962; (Charles Olliffe) American Scenes, 1964. Compilor: Dictionary of Am. Assn. Tchrs. Italian, 1965. Founder, co-editor Italian Americana, from 1974. Home: Snyder, N.Y. Died Nov. 18, 1975.

FALKNER, LEONARD, author The President Who Wouldn't Retire, 1967. Home: New York, N.Y. Died Feb. 22, 1977.

FALLERS, LLOYD ASHTON, JR., educator; b. Nebraska City, Neb., Aug. 29, 1925; s. Lloyd A. and Fannie (Lincoln) F.; Ph.B., U. Chgo., 1946, M.A., 1949, Ph.D., 1953; student London (Eng.) Sch. Econs., 1949-50; m. Margaret Elinor Chave, June 18, 1949; children—Winnifred Mary, Beth Laura. Lectr. anthropology Princeton, 1953-54; fellow E. African Inst. Social Research, 1950-52, 54-56, dir. inst., 1956-57; asst., then asso. prof. anthropology U. Calif., Berkeley, 1957-60; mem. faculty U. Chgo., 1960-74, prof. anthropology, 1963-70, prof. anthropology and sociology, 1970-74, Distinguished Service prof. anthropology and sociology, 1973-74. Fellow Center Advanced Study Behavioral Scis., 1958-59. Fellow Am. Acad. Arts and Scis.; mem. Mm. Anthrop. Assn., African Studies Assn., Assn. Social Anthropologists (Great Britain), Internat. African Inst., Royal Anthrop. Inst. (Great Britain). Democrat. Episcopalian. Author: Bantu Bureaucracy, 1956; Law Without Precedent, 1969; Inequality, 1973; Social Anthropology of the Nation-State, 1974. Editor, joint author: The King's Men, 1964. Asso. editor anthropology Internat. Ency. Social Scis., 1962-74. Home: Chicago, Ill. Died July 4, 1974.

FALLON, GEORGE H., congressman; b. Balt., July 24, 1902; s. Lawrence, Sr., and Mary (Dempsey) F.; ed. public schools, Calvert Bus. Coll., Johns Hopkins U.; m. Willa Virginia Thomas, 1929; 1 dau., Mary Joyce. Engaged in advt. sign bus.; partner Lawrence Fallon Co.; elected mem. Dem. State Central Com. Balt., 1938, chmn.; elected to Balt. City Council, 1939, 1943; mem. 79th-91st Congresses 4th District, Md. Democrat. Home: Baltimore, Md. Died Mar. 21, 1980.

FALLS, FREDERICK HOWARD, physician; b. Chicago, Ill., Dec. 14, 1885; s. Samuel Kemp and Florence Mary (Church) F.; prep. edn., Lewis Inst., Chicago, 1900-06; S.B., U. of Chicago, 1909; M.D., Rush Med. Coll., 1910; M.S., U. of Ill., 1916; m. Margaret Haseltine, June 18, 1920; children—Frederick H., Richard H., John L., William H., Hugh C., David C. Private practice, Chicago, 1911-13; research at U. of Ill., teaching and practice, 1913-18; with Chicago Lying-In Hosp., and in private practice, 1919-21; prof. obstetrics and gynecology, U. of Ia., 1921-26; prof. and head dept. of obstetrics and gynecology, University of Illinois College of Medicine, 1926-54, prof. emeritus, 1954—, also in private practice; chief of obstetrical and gynecological staff West Suburban Hosp.; cons. West Lake Hosp., Maywood, Ill., Ill. Dept. Pub. Welfare; consultant, staff Augustana Hosp., Norwegian and Grant Hosp. Diplomate Am. Bd. Obstetrics and Gynecology. Fellow A.C.S., Internat. Coll. Surgeons; mem. A.M.A. (chairman obstetrics and gynecology 1955), Illinois State and Chicago med. socs., Am. Assn. Obstetricians, Gynecologists and Abdominal Surgeons (pres. 1941), Chicago Gynecol. Soc., Am. Gynecol. Soc., Ill. Obstet. and Gynecol. Soc. Episcopalian. Republican. Author: Atlas of Obstetric Complications. Home: River Forest, Ill.

FAMA, SEBASTIAN, govt. ofcl.; b. N.Y.C., Oct. 29, 1918; s. Joseph and Iona (Scarcella) F.; student CCNY, 1935-38; B.C.S., Benjamin Franklin U., 1951, M.C.S., 1952; m. Santa Ann Amatulli, Apr. 3, 1948; children—Joseph T., Rosemary A., James P., Ellen M. With Treasury Dept., Washington, 1952-77, chief deposits br., 1960-62, asst. dep. commr., 1962-65, dep. commr. bur. accounts, 1965-69, dir. govt. fin. ops., 1969-71, dir. cash mgmt., 1971-73, asst. commr. banking and cash mgmt. Bur. Govt. Fin. Ops., 1974-77. Served to warrant officer C.E., U.S. Army, 1941-46; ETO. Home: Washington, D.C. Died Oct. 14, 1977; buried Gate of Heaven Cemetery, Silver Spring, Md.

FARABAUGH, GALLITZEN ALOYSIUS (FÅR'A-BAW), lawyer; b. Loretta, Pa., June 26, 1883; s. Matthias and Elizabeth (Noel) F.; A.B., U. of Notre Dame (Ind.), 1904, LL.B., 1907; post grad. in law, Georgetown U., Washington, D.C.; m. Nano Golley, Oct. 27, 1911; children—Margaret, John, David, William. Admitted to Ind. bar, 1907, and since practiced in South Bend; city judge South Bend, 1910-14; prof. law, U. of Notre Dame, 1907-24; sr. partner Farabaugh, Pettengill & Chapleau. Mem. Am., Ind. State and St. Joseph County bar assns. Democrat. Catholic. Clubs: University, South Bend Country. Home: South Bend, Ind. *

FARAGHER, ARTHUR W., banker; b. Winnipeg, Can., Aug. 2, 1884; s. Thomas and Pauline (Seaborn) F.; student Manitoba Coll., 1901-03; m. Pearl Louise Klenck, June 14, 1910; 1 son, Thomas Robert. Came to U.S., 1903, naturalized, 1912. Constrn. and engring. dept. G.N Ry., 1903-06; asst. treas. Chgo., Milw. & St. Paul Ry., 1906-26; v.p. Marine Central Bank, 1926-30, Central Nat. Bank of Commerce, 1930-33, Nat. Bank of Commerce, Seattle, 1933-46, sr. v.p., 1946-47, v. chmn. bd. since 1948; v.p., dir. Marine Bancorporation, Seattle, 1948; v.p., dir. Marine Nat. Co., King County Bldg. Co., Seattle. Republican. Presbyn. Mason. Clubs: Rainier, Washington Athletic, Broadmoor Golf (Seattle). Home: Seattle.

FARAGO, LADISLAS, author; b. Csurgo, Hungary, Sept. 21, 1906; s. Arthur and Irma (Lang) F.; grad. Acad. Commerce and Consular Affairs, Budapest, Hungary, 1926; m. Liesel Mroz, Mar. 22, 1934; 1 son, John Michael Arthur. Journalist in Hungary; with N.Y. Times-Wide World Bur., Berlin, Germany; spl. corr. A.P., Ethiopia: fgn. editor Sunday Chronicle, London, Eng., 1935; dir. research Com. Nat. Morale, N.Y.C., 1940-42; staff U.S. Office Naval Intelligence, 1942-46; editor Corps Diplomatique, 1946; sr. editor UN World, 1947-50; chief desk X, Radio Free Europe, 1950-52. Author: Abyssinia on the Eve, 1935; Abyssinian Stop Press, 1936; Palestine at the Crossroads, 1937; The Riddle of Arabia, 1937; German Psychological Warfare, 1940; Axis Grand Strategy, 1942; Behind Closed Doors, 1950; War of Wits, 1954; Burn After Reading, 1961: Strictly from Hungary, 1962: The Tenth Fleet, 1962; It's Your Money, 1964; Patton: Ordeal and Triumph, 1964; The Broken Seal, 1967; The Game of the Foxes, 1972; Aftermath, 1974, others; motion pictures include: Patton, Tora, Tora, Tora; radio and TV: Secret Missions, The Man Called X, Behind Closed Doors. Home: Southbury, Conn. Died Oct. 15, 1980.

FARB, PETER, author; b. N.Y.C., July 25, 1929; s. Solomon and Cecelia (Peters) F.; A.B. magna cum laude, Vanderbilt U., 1950; postgrad. Columbia, 1950-51; m. Oriole Horch, Feb. 27, 1953; children—Mark Daniel, Thomas Forest. Feature editor Argosy mag., 1950-52; editor-in-chief Panorama, 1960-61; contbr., cons. to nat. mags., 1953-80; curator Am. Indian Cultures, Riverside Mus., N.Y.C., 1964-71; cons. Smithsonian Instn., 1966-71; vis. lectr. in English, Yale, 1971-72, fellow Calhoun Coll., 1971-78, Judge, Nat. Book Awards Com., 1971. Trustee U. Mass. Libraries, 1976-80. Fellow AAAS, Soc. Am. Historians, Explorers Club; mem. N.Y. Entomol. Soc. (past sec., mem. editorial bd. jour.), Am. Anthrop. Assn., P.E.N. Club, Phi Beta Kappa, Omicron Delta Kappa. Author: Living Earth, 1959; The Story of Butterflies and Other Insects, 1959; The Story of Dams, 1961; The Forest, 1961, 11th edit., 1978; The Story of Life: Plants and Animals through the Ages, 1962; The Insects, 1962, 8th edit., 1977; Ecology, 1963, 9th edit., 1979; Face of North America: The Natural History of a Continent (Book-of-Month Club selection, Outdoor Life Book Club selection, A.L.A. Notable Book selection, President Kennedy Internat. White House Library selection), 1963; The Forest Reader, 1964; Young Reader's Edition of Face of North America, 1964; The Land and Wildlife of North America, 1964, 8th edit., 1978; The Land, Wildlife, and Peoples of the Bible, 1967; Man's Rise to Civilization as Shown by the Indians of North America from Primeval Times to the Coming of the Industrial State (Book-of-Month Club selection, Book Find Club selection, Library of Sci. selection, History Book Club of London selection), 1968, 2d rev. edit. (selection Book-of-Month, Quality Paperback Book and Macmillan Book clubs), 1978; Yankee Doodle, 1970; Word Play: What Happens When People Talk, 1974 (Book Find Club selection, Modern Psychology Book Club selection, Library of Behavioral Scis. selection, others); Humankind, 1978 (selection Book-of-Month, Quality Paperback Book and History Book clubs). Co-author: The Atlantic Shore, 1966; Consuming Passions: The Anthropology of Eating (Lit. Guild alt.). Co-editor: Prose by Professionals, 1961. Address: Amherst, Mass. Died Apr. 8, 1980.

FARBER, BENJAMIN FRANKLIN, clergyman; b. Thorntown, Ind., July 13, 1882; s. John Charles and Ruth Margaret (Sims) F.; A.B., Hanover (Ind.) Coll., 1905; A.M., Princeton U., 1908; grad. Princeton Theol. Sem., 1909; D.D., from Washington and Jefferson Coll. and Grove City Coll., 1921; m. Willie Mitchusson, June 27, 1911 (died Apr. 12, 1924); children—William Edward, Benjamin Franklin (killed in plane crash in Pacific, Feb. 21, 1944); married 2d, Helen Welty, Aug. 1, 1927; one son, Charles Welty. Ordained Presbyn. ministry, 1909; asst. pastor, Germantown, Pa., 1909-10; pastor, Plymouth, Mich., 1910-17; assistant minister of Woodward Avenue Church, Detroit, Mich., 1917-19; pastor Sixth Church, Pittsburgh, Pa., 1919-26, Fourth Ch., N.Y. City, 1926-54; ret. Moderator Presbytery of N.Y., 1938-40; sec. bd. of trustees Princeton Theological Sem. 1944-58. Y.M.C.A. Welfare Service in France, 1918. Mem. Beta Theta Pi. Republican. Mason (32 deg.). Club: Chi Alpha. Home: Cresskill, N.J.

FARBER, LESLIE H., existential psychiatrist, author; M.D., Stanford U., 1938; m. Anne Claque; children—Stephen, Luke, Seth, Phoebe. Faculty chmn. Washington Sch. Psychiatry, 1955-60; tng. and supervisory analyst Washington Psychoanalytic Inst.; dir. therapy Austen Riggs Center, Stockbridge, Mass.; v.p. William Alanson White Psychiat. Found.; pvt. practice, N.Y.C., 1969-81. Mem. Assn. Existential Psychology and Psychiatry (chmn. 1963-77). Author The Ways of the Will; also numerous articles and essays. Home: New York, N.Y. Died Mar. 24, 1981.

FARICY, WILLIAM THOMAS, r.r. exec.; b. St. Paul, Mar. 7, 1893; s. John I. and Thecla (Brown) F.; student Coll. of St. Thomas, St. Paul, 1906-08; LL.B. magna cum laude, St. Paul (now William Mitchell) Coll. Law, 1914; m. Norma Hauser, Apr. 6, 1918; children—Norma H. (Mrs. Ralph W. Condee), Jean (Mrs. John B. Lord) (dec.). Atty. C., St. P. M. & O. Ry. Co., 1914; gen. practice, St. Paul, 1916-17, 1919-20; gen. atty., C., St. P., M. & O. Rd. Co., St. Paul, 1920-24; commerce atty. C. & N.W. Ry. Co., Chgo., 1924-25; v.p. Hauser Securities Co., and asst. to pres. Hauser Constrn. Co., Portland, Oreg., and Long Beach, Calif., 1925-27; Minn. atty. C. & N.W. Ry. Co., St. Paul, 1927-29; gen. solicitor C., St. P. M.&O. Ry. Co., St. Paul, 1929-33; gen. solicitor C. & N.W. Ry. System, Chgo., 1933-42; gen. counsel, C. & N.W. Ry. Co., 1942-44; v.p. and gen. counsel C. St. P. M. & O. Ry. Co., 1942-47, v.p. and gen. counsel C. & N.W. Ry. Co., 1944-47; chmn. Western Conf. of Ry. Counsel, 1944-46; chief counsel, Carriers Conf. Com., rep. Class I Railroads of America, 1945-56

Wage and Rules movement, and 1946 railroad strike; dir. Grant Smith & Co. & McDonnell, Ltd.; adv. dir. Riggs Nat. Bank; chmn. Civilian Components Policy bd. Dept. Def., 1949-50; chmn. U.S. Nat. Commn. Pan-Am. Ry. Congress Assn., 1949-58, mem., 1959-67; pres. Def. Orientation Conf. Assn., 1955-56. Life trustee Northwestern U. Pres. Assn. Am. R.R.'s, 1947-57, chmn. bd., 1957-58. Served as lt., capt. 350th Inf., France, AUS, 1917-19. Decorated officer French Legion of Honor; recipient Nat. Def. Transp. Award for individual def.-supporting achievement, 1958. Fellow Am. Bar Found.; mem. Am., Cal., Ill., Minn. bar assns., Chgo. Bar Assn. (bd. mgrs. 1941-43), Am. Legion (chmn. nat. transp. com. 1950-52). Clubs: Law, Commercial (Chgo.); Bohemian (San Francisco); Metropolitan, Burning Tree, Alfalfa (Washington); Spokane (Wash.). Address: Washington, D.C. Died Apr. 12, 1980; buried Portland, Oreg.

FARKAS, GEORGE, chmn. Alexander's Dept. Stores, Inc. Home: Palm Beach, Fla. Died July 5, 1980.

FARLEY, JAMES A., bus. exec., former postmaster gen.; b. Grassy Point, N.Y., May 30, 1888; s. James and Ellen (Goldrick) F.; grad. Packard Comml. Sch., N.Y.C., 1906; D.C.L., U. of South, 1933, Lincoln Meml. U., 1935, St. Ambrose Coll., 1941, Villanova Coll., 1942; LL.D., Canisius Coll., Manhattan Coll., John Marshall Coll. Law, 1934, Niagara U., 1935, Hendrix Coll., 1939, Oglethorpe U., 1940, Seattle U., 1950, Ithaca Coll., Loras Coll., St. Anselm's Coll., 1951, St. Joseph's Coll., Collegeville, Ind., 1955, L.I. U., 1957, St. Joseph's Coll., Phila., 1960, St. Mary's Coll., San Antonio, 1961, St. Bonaventure U., 1961, Tuskegee Inst., 1963; D.C.S., N.Y. U., 1950, Suffolk U., 1956; Citation, U. Fla., 1950; D.S.S., Duquesne U., 1953; hon. degree Seton Hall U., 1967; m. Elizabeth A. Finnegan, Apr. 28, 1920 (dec. Jan. 1955); children—Elizabeth M. (Mrs. Glenn D. Montgomery), Ann E. (Mrs. Edward J. Hickey III), James A. Began as bookkeeper Merlin Keilholtz Paper Co., N.Y.C., 1906; sales mgr. Universal Gypsum Co., to 1926; organized James A. Farley & Co., 1926, firm merged with five other building material firms, organized as Gen. Builders Supply Corp., 1929, pres., dir., 1929-33, 49-58; chmn. bd. Coca-Cola Export Corp., from 1940, hon. chmn. bd.; chmn. bd. Coca-Cola Interamerican Corp.; pres., dir. Coca-Cola Internat. Corp.; dir. Coca-Cola Co., Coca-Cola Co. Can., Ltd. Trustee Com. Econ. Devel., Cordell Hull Found., Alfred E. Smith Found., Little League Found.; bd. dirs. Nat. Fgn. Trade Council, Boys Clubs Am., Far East-Am. Council Industry and Commerce, Catholic Youth Orgn. N.Y., N.Y. Conv. and Visitors Bur., Freedoms Found. at Valley Forge, Am. Heritage Found., Am.-Australian Assn., Cath. Med. Mission Bd. Town clk. Stony Point, N.Y., 1912-19; supr. Rockland County, 1920-23; port warden Port N.Y., 1918-19; mem. N.Y. State Athletic Commn., 1923-33, chmn., 1925-33; mem. Commn. on Orgn. Exec. Br. Govt., 1953; mem. N.Y. State Banking Bd., 1955-60, N.Y. State Harness Racing Commn., 1959-76. Mem. N.Y. State Assembly, 1923; chmn. Rockland County Democratic Com., 1919-29; sec. N.Y. State Dem. Com., 1928-30, chmn., 1930-44; chmn. Dem. Nat. Com., 1932-40; del. Dem. Nat. Convs., 1924, 28, 32, 36, 40, 44, 48; postmaster gen. U.S., 1933-40; mem. Electoral Coll., 1932, 36, 64, 68. Decorated Order Francisco de Miranda (Venezuela); Cross of Isabel la Catolica (Spain); Order Vasco de Balboa (Panama); recipient Capt. Robert Dollar Meml. award for distinguished contbn. to advancement Am. fgn. trade; Freedoms Found. award, 1956; Living History award Research Inst. Am., 1960; Gold medal Hundred Year Assn. N.Y., 1962; award of Champions, Cath. Youth Orgn. N.Y., 1963; Gold medal Internat. Benjamin Franklin Soc., 1965; John F. Kennedy Meml. award Ancient Order Hibernians, 1966, Laetare medal U. Notre Dame, 1974. Mem. Pan-Am. Soc., Inc., N.Y. State Hist. Assn., Am. Acad. Polit. and Social Sci., Albany Soc. N.Y., N.Y. Bd. Trade (Latin Am. sect.), Mexican C. of C. in U.S., Friendly Sons of St. Patrick, Ancient Order Hibernians, Newcomen Soc. N.Am., Delta Sigma Phi (hon.) Eagle, Elk, Red Man, K.C. (Lantern award 1972). Clubs: Sales Executives, Circumnavigators, Catholic, Economic, N.Y. Athletic, Nat. Democratic of N.Y. (v.p. 1930-76), Lotos (N.Y.C.); Nat. Press (Washington). Author: Behind the Ballots, 1938; Jim Farley's Story, 1948. Home: New York, N.Y. Died June 9, 1976.

FARMER, CLARENCE R., surgeon; b. Elm City, N.C., Oct. 16, 1886; s. John Lawrence and Laura Ann (Brinkley) F.; student Univ. of N.C., 1903-07; M.D., Jefferson Med. Coll., 1909; m. Laura Wohlsen, Jan. 17, 1911; children—John Lawrence, Thomas Wohlsen, Mary Catharine, Clarence Richard. Practiced at Lancaster since 1911; chief of obstet. service, Lancaster Gen. Hosp., 1946-52, ret. active staff, cons. surgeon since 1952; adv. staff, Rossmere Sanatorium. Fellow American College of Surgeons; member A.M.A., Pennsylvania and Lancaster County med. socs. Democrat. Lutheran. Home: Lancaster, Pa.

FARNHAM, WILLARD EDWARD, educator; b. Wichita, Kans., Sept. 29, 1891; s. Edward Willard and Josephine (Reynolds) F.; A.B., U. Wis., 1912, A.M., 1914; Ph.D., Harvard, 1917; LL.D., U. Calif., Berkeley, 1961; m. Corinne Cassard, June 28, 1921 (dec. 1926); 1 dau., Diana Reynolds; m. 2d, Frances Fern Hicks, May 9, 1929; children—Anthony Edward, Nicholas Holt. Instr. English, U. Wis., 1917-18; Sheldon traveling fellow, Harvard, in Eng., France and Italy, 1919-20; asso. prof. English, Washington and Lee U., 1920-23; asso. prof. English, U. Calif. at Berkeley, 1923-35, prof., 1935-59, prof. emeritus, 1959-81; chmn. dept., 1949-50, 52-55; research fellow Henry E. Huntington Library in U.S. and Eng., 1938-39; vis. lectr. Harvard, summer 1947, 1950-51; nat. rep. Woodrow Wilson Nat. Fellowship Found., 1960-61. Served as ensign, Aviation Corps, USNRF, 1918-19. Mem. Modern Lang. Assn. (chmn. Shakespeare group 1946), Philol. Assn. Pacific Coast, Am. Assn. U. Profs., Shakespeare Assn. Am. (adv. bd.), Phi Beta Kappa. Episcopalian. Club: Faculty (Berkeley). Author: the Medieval Heritage of Elizabethan Tragedy, 1936; Shakespeare's Tragic Frontier: The World of His Final Tragedies, 1950; The Shakespearean Grotesque: Its Genesis and Transformations, 1971. Editor: Shakespeare's Hamlet, 1957; Shakespeare's Troilus and Cressida, 1966; Twentieth Century Interpretations of Doctor Faustus, 1969. Contbr. periodicals. Home: CA. Died Feb. 25, 1981.

FARNUM, GEORGE ROSSITER, lawyer; b. Melrose, Mass., May 30, 1885; s. George Peterson and Mary E. (Rossiter) F.; grad. high sch., Melrose, 1904; LL.B., summa cum laude, Boston U., 1907, LL.M., 1908; hon. Litt.D., Calvin Coolidge Coll., liberal arts, 1942; m. Ida Mae Demers, June 19, 1912. Admitted to Mass. bar, 1907, began practice at Boston; asst. U.S. atty., Mass., 1925-26, acting U.S. atty., 1926; asst. U.S. atty. general, 1927-30; former prof. law Suffolk U. Law Sch.; former lectr. on admiralty law, fed. jurisdiction and practice at Boston University Law Sch., former lectr. law Boston College Law School. Special counsel Finance Commission for City of Boston to conduct investigation into municipal adminstrn., 1934-35; special corp. counsel City of Boston in charge continuance said investigation, 1935; special counsel Finance Commn., City of Boston, to conduct further investigations into municipal adminstrn., 1937. Pres. New England Anti-Vivisection Society. Member of the Massachusetts Law Society, also mem. Phi Delta Phi. Republican. Club: Cosmos (Washington). Writer of numerous monographs and articles on legal, philos. and biog. subjects in law jours., periodicals and newspapers. Home: Boston.

FARQUHAR, ALLAN SHANNON, naval officer (ret.); b. Bucyrus, O., Jan. 31, 1884; s. John Yule and Emma (Shannon) F.; B.S., U.S. Naval Acad., 1906; grad. Naval War Coll., 1930; m. Charlotte Monnett, Dec. 26, 1929; children—Charlotte Anne, Jean Monnett, Mary Allan. Commd. ensign, U.S. Navy, Sept. 1906, advanced through grades to rear adm., Nov. 23, 1945; ret. from active duty, 1945. Awarded Navy Cross, Belgian Order of the Crown, Mexican campaign ribbon, World Wars I and II ribbons, 2d Nicaraguan campaign ribbon, Am. Defense ribbon. Presbyterian. Home: Winchester, Mass.

FARR, RICHARD SUMNER, orthopedic surgeon; b. Lodi, N.Y., May 24, 1890; s. Charles Sumner and Sarah (Essom) F.; student Starkey Sem., Lakemont, 1906-09, Cook Acad., 1909-10; M.D., Univ. Vt., 1914; m. Maria Hartong, Sept. 2, 1924; children—Nancy Hartong, Sarah Ann, Jan Richard. Interne St. Johns Riverside Hosp., Yonkers, N.Y., 1914-15; resident N.Y. Orthopedic Hosp., N.Y. City, 1915-18, 1920-23; pvt. practice splty., Syracuse, N.Y., from 1923; instr. orthopedic surgery, Syracuse Univ. Coll. Medicine, 1923-25, asst. prof., 1927-30, asso. professor, 1930-31, prof., 1931-50, professor emeritus 1950-77; sr. attending orthopedic surgeon Meml. Hosp., City Hosp., Psychopathic Hosp., Univ. Hospital, 1931-50; orthopedic consultant USAF, VA Outpatient Clinic, 1968-71; chief med. officer of the VA Regional Office until 1968; v.p. Syracuse Cerebral Palsy and Crippled Children's Assn., 1946-68, hon. bd. dirs., 1968-77. Served as 1st lieutenant in Medical Corps, 1918-19; served with British Army and A.E.F.; lt. col., M.C., U.S. Army, 1942; exec. officer, 52d Gen. Hosp. in England; orthopedic consultant to 12th Hosp. Center, U.S. Army, 1944; Col. Med. Corps Reserve, retired; comdg. officer 814th Hosp. Center Reserve. Awarded Legion of Merit, 1945. Fellow A.C.S.; mem. Soc. Med. Consultants to Armed Forces, AMA, Am. Acad. Orthopedic Surgs., N.Y. Orthopedic Alumni, Assn. of Mil. Surgeons, American Legion, Forty and Eight, Grange, Syracuse Academy of Medicine, Phi Chi, Scabbard and Blade. Republican. Presbyn. Mason (R.A.M., K.T., Council and Commandery, Shriner). Clubs: Gyro; Century. Home: Syracuse, N.Y. Died Jan. 29, 1977; interred Syracuse, N.Y.

FARRAND, CLAIR LORING, engr., mfr.; b. Newark, Oct. 22, 1895; s. Frank L. Brundage and Clara (Wilson) F.; student pub. schs., Phila.; M.E. (hon.) Stevens Inst. Tech., 1949; m. Sara T. McDermott, Jan. 10, 1916; children—John L., Clair L., Robert W., Edward Noel. Design engr. Marconi Wireless Telegraph Co., 1912-19; asst. chief engr. Liberty Electric Corp., 1919-20; chief engr. Wireless Improvement Co., 1921-22; cons. engr. Atwater Kent Mfg. Co., 1922-24; pres. Farrand Mfg. Co., 1924-29, United Research Corp. (subsidiary Warner Bros. Pictures, Inc.), 1930-36; cons. engr. Warner Bros. Pictures, Inc., 1936-37; pres. Independent Research Service Co., Inc., 1937-40, Farrand Optical Co., Inc., N.Y.C., 1940-81. also president of Farrand Controls, New York, Fellow Inst. Radio Engrs., Soc. Motion Picture and TV Engrs.; mem. Am. Phys. Soc., Brit. Kinematograph Soc. Clubs: N.Y. Yacht (N.Y.C.); West Side Tennis, Bronxville Field. Home; Bronxville, N.Y. Died Jan. 27, 1981.

FARRAND, ROBERT KITCHEL, pub. relations; born New Rochelle, N.Y., Aug. 3, 1908; s. Livingston and Margaret K. (Carlton) F.; grad. Deerfield Acad., 1927; student Cornell U., 1928-39; m. Evelyn Sweeney, 1932 (div. 1949); 1 son, Robert K.; m. 2d, Trudy Dye 1958. Asst. circulation mgr. Newsweek mag., 1932-35; advt. staff Good Housekeeping mag., 1944-45, also mgr. retail merchandising; retail merchandising div. mgr. Sat. Eve. Post, Curtis Pub. Co., Phila., 1949-53, merchandising mgr., 1953-55, promotion mgr., 1955-58, marketing mgr. Sat. Eve. Post, 1958-59, v.p., dir. pub. relations Curtis Pub. Co., 1959-62, vice president for corporate adminstration, 1963-65, dir. communications, 1964-65; pres. Farrand, Inc., Phila., 1965-75. Mem. Kappa Alpha. Clubs: Down Town (Phila); New York Yacht, Cornell (N.Y.C.); National Press (Washington). Home: Potomac, Md. Died May 3, 1976.

FARRAR, BENEDICT (FAR'RÄR), architect; b. St. Louis, Mo., Aug. 7, 1885; s. Charles Thruston and Nancy (Gorman) F.; student Washington U., 1904-06; m. Ruth Elisabeth Gregg, Sept. 11, 1917; children—William Gregg, John Thruston, Nancy Gorman. Partner Study & Farrar, 1919-44; asst. chief architect, U.S. War Dept., Feb. 1941, chief architect, to October, 1941; asst. chief architect of Pentagon Bldg. for War Dept. to Dec. 31, 1942, chief materials allocation branch, Transportation Corps, War Dept., Dec. 1942-July 1944; resumed practice of architecture in St. Louis, Mo., with firm Study, Farrar & Majers. Building commr. City of Ladue, since 1938. Director Lafayette Federal Savings & Loan Assn. of St. Louis, 1920—. Dir. A.I.A., 1939-42, pres. St. Louis chapter 1937-39; pres. Mo. Assn. Architects, 1947. Alumnae citation, Washington U., 1956. Mem. Phi Delta Theta. Clubs: Noonday, St. Louis Country (St. Louis). Home: St. Louis.

FARRELL, ALLAN PETER, educator; b. Grand Rapids, Mich., Feb. 14, 1896; s. Peter Daniel and Elfrida May (Allan) F.; student U. Detroit, 1914-16; A.B., St. Louis U., 1922, M.A., 1923; S.T.D., Pontifical Regional Sem. of Campania, Italy, 1930; Ph.D., Nat. U. of Ireland, 1933. Tchr. classical lit. Marquette U., 1923-26; entered Soc. Jesus, 1916; ordained priest Roman Cath. Ch., 1929; tchr. edn. Xavier U., Cin., 1932-34, 40-42, Loyola U., Chgo., 1934-40; prof. edn. U. Detroit, 1948-76, dean Grad. Sch., 1949-62; dir. reorgn. Sophia U., Tokyo, Japan, 1949-50. Dir. higher edn. Chgo. Province S.J., 1934-40. Mem. Jesuit Edn. Assn. U.S. (nat. dir. 1942-44; chmn. commn. grad. schs. 1954-76). Nat. Conf. Christians and Jews (Cath. co-chmn. religious commn. 1943-49; commn. edn. orgns. from 1950), Nat. Cath. Ednl. Assn. (editor publs. on acceleration), Religious Edn. Assn. of U.S. and Can., Midwest Conference of Graduate Deans, Phi Delta Kappa. Author: Jesuit Code of Liberal Education, 1938; Missions and Cultural Life, 1945; The Jesuit Ratio Studiorum of 1599 Translated into English, 1970. Editor: Whither American Education? 1948; Pius XI's Encyclical on Christian Education of Youth, rev. edit. 1954. Editor Jesuit Ednl. Quar., 1938-44; mem. editorial bd. America, 1944-48, contbg. editor, 1948-76. Address: Detroit, Mich. Died Oct. 25, 1976.

FARRELL, FRANCIS WILLIAM, army officer; b. Chgo., May 28, 1900; s. Joseph Denis and Ruth (Mahony) F.; B.S., U.S. Mil. Acad., 1920; grad. Inf. Sch., basic course, 1921. F.A. Sch., battery officers course, 1928, Command and Gen. Staff Sch., 1939. Commd. 2d lt., U.S. Army, 1920, and advanced through grades to maj. gen., A.U.S., 1947, U.S. Army, 1953; became division chief of staff, 11th Airborne Div., 1942; assigned arty. div. comdr., overseas, Mar. 1941. Home: Arlington, Va. Died Dec. 27, 1981.

FARRELL, JAMES AUGUSTINE, JR., shipping exec.; b. Bklyn., Jan. 13, 1901; s. James Augustine and Catherine (McDermott) F.; B.S., Yale, 1924; D.C.S., Duquesne U., 1961; m. Emilie Hill, Jan. 27, 1934. Ship operator and owner, from 1924; chmn. bd. dirs. Farrell Lines, Inc.; dir. Maritime Exchange. Trustee Canterbury Sch. Served to comdr. USNR, 1941-44. Fellow Royal Acad. of Arts (Brit.); mem. Newcomen Soc., Am. Soc. M.E., Soc. Naval Architects, Delta Phi. Clubs: Yale, Leash, India House, Union (N.Y.C.); St. Elmo (New Haven); Edgartown Yacht, N.Y. Yacht, Indian Harbour Yacht, Royal Thames Yacht. Home: Darien, Conn. Died Sept. 15, 1978.

FARRELL, JAMES THOMAS, author; b. Chgo., Feb. 27, 1904; s. James Francis and Mary (Daly) F.; student U. Chgo. 1925-29; hon. degrees Miami U., Oxford, Ohio, Columbia U., Glassboro State Coll., Roosevelt U., Bradley U.; m. Dorothy Patricia Butler, 1931 (div.); m. 2d, Hortense Alden (div. Sept. 1955); children—Kevin, John Stephen; m. 3d, Dorothy Butler, Sept. 1955 (separated 1958). Clk., Am. Ry. Express Co. and cigar store, filling sta. attendant, campus newspaper reporter. Recipient Book of Month Club award for Studs Lonigan, 1937; Messing award St. Louis U. Library Assos., 1973; Emerson-Thoreau medal Am. Acad. Arts and Scis., 1979; Profl. Achievement award U. Chgo., 1979; Guggenheim fellow in creative writing, 1936-37; Nat. Endowment for Arts creative writing fellow, 1978. Mem. Inst. Arts and Letters. Author: Young Lonigan-A Boyhood in Chicago Streets, 1932; Gas House McGinty, 1933; The Young Manhood of Studs Lonigan, 1934; Calico Shoes, and other stories, 1934; Judgment Day, 1935; Guillotine Party and Other Stories, 1935; Studs Lonigan: A Trilogy, 1935; A Note on Literary Criticism, 1936; A World I Never Made, 1936; Can All This Grandeur Perish and Other Stories, 1937; The Short Stories of James T. Farrell, 1937; No Star Is Lost, 1938; Tommy Gallagher's Crusade, 1939; Father and Son, 1940; Ellen Rogers, 1941; $1,000 a Week and Other Stories, 1942; My Days of Anger, 1943; To Whom It May Concern and Other Stories, 1944; The League of Frightened Philistines and Other Papers, 1945; Bernard Clare, 1946; When Boyhood Dreams Come True, 1946; The Life Adventurous and Other Stories, 1947; Literature and Morality, 1947; The Road Between, 1949; A Misunderstanding, 1949; An American Dream Girl, 1950; This Man and This Woman, 1951; The Name Is Fogarty: Private Papers on Public Matters, 1950; Yet Other Waters, 1952; The Face of Time, 1953; Reflections at Fifty and Other Essays, 1954; French Girls are Vicious and Other Stories, 1955; An Omnibus of Short Stories, 1956; A Dangerous Woman and Other Short Stories, 1957; My Baseball Diary, 1957; It Has Come to Pass, 1958; Boarding House Blues, 1961; Side Street & Other Stories, 1961; Sound of a City, 1962; The Silence of History, 1963; What Time Collects, 1964; Selected Essays, 1964; The Collected Poems of James T. Farrell, 1965; Lonely for the Future, 1966; When Time Was Born, 1966; New Year's Eve/1929, 1967; A Brand New Life, 1968; Judith, 1969; Childhood Is Not Forever, 1969, Invisible Swords, 1971; Judith and Other Stories, 1973; The Dunne Family, 1976; Literary Essays, 1954-1974, 1976; Olive and Mary Anne and Other Stories, 1977; Death of Nora Ryan, 1978; (with Jeanette Nolan and Horace Gregory) Poet of the People: An Evaluation of James Whitcomb Riley, 1951; (with others) Dialogue on John Dewey, 1959; contbr. to mags., to Asian press; poet Editor: A Selected Book of Prejudices (H.L. Meneken), 1956; A Dreiser Reader, 1962. Address: New York, N.Y. Died Aug. 22, 1979.

FARRELL, WILLIAM RANDOLPH, bus. exec.; b. Munising, Mich., Aug. 5, 1907; s. Frank G. and Bessie (Penglase) F.; A.B., U. Mich., 1930; m. Jane Cook, Mar. 19, 1934; children—William R., Nancy, John. Account exec. Campbell-Ewald, Detroit, 1930-33; field service rep. A. C. Nielsen Co., N.Y.C., 1933-38, v.p., 1938-43; v.p. Benton & Bowles, 1943-45, Kastor, Farrell, Chesley & Clifford, 1945-47; 1st v.p. Ward Wheelock Co., Phila., 1947-54; mgr. advt. Monsanto Co., St. Louis, 1954-55, dir. advt., 1955-59, dir. marketing services, from 1959. Past chmn. bd. Audit Bur. Circulations. Mem. Better Bus. Bur. Greater St. Louis Inc. (exec. bd.), Assn. Better Bus. Burs. Internat. (gov.), Nat. Better Bus. Bur. Advt. Club. Clubs: Old Warson Country (Ladue, Mo.); Pine Valley Golf (Clementon, N.J.); St. Louis, Stadium; University (N.Y.C.). Home: Ladue, Mo. Died Feb. 4, 1977.

FARRINGTON, HENRY, engr.; b. at Liverpool, Eng., Mar. 27, 1882; s. Robert and Juliana (Hartshorn) F.; Liverpool Coll., 1894-8; B.Sc., Walker Engring. Labs., Univ. Coll. (Victoria U.), Liverpool, 1901, M.Sc., Victoria U., 1904; (hon. B.Eng., Liverpool U., 1904); m. Mary Johnston, Jan. 15, 1910. Importing Am. harvesting machy. and experimenting with early automobiles in Eng., 1899-1900; lecturer in mechanics, Poly. Inst., London, Eng., 1901-4; mech. editor J. B. Lippincott Co., Phila., 1906; mech. specialist and editor on Webster's New Internat. Dictionary, 1906-9; with motor dept. Packard Motor Car Co., Detroit, 1909; asso. editor Electrical Review and Western Electrician, Chicago, 1909-10; tech. editor Shop Notes Quarterly and Popular Mechanics Mag., Nov. 1910-Aug., 1911; editor The Power Wagon, 1911-14; truck sales promotion mgr., Thomas B. Jeffery Co., Kenosha, Wis., 1914-16; truck sales engr., Chicago, for Pierce-Arrow Motor Car Co., 1916-17; editor Agrimotor (tractor trade jour.), and sec. and dir. Halliwell & Patton Pub. Co., Chicago, 1917-21; sales mgr. Antigo (Wis.) Tractor Corpn., Aug. 1921—. Mem. Soc. Automotive Engrs., Instn. Automobile Engrs., Nat. Gas Engine Assn., Am. Tractor Assn. (sec.), Am. Heat Treaters' Assn.; sr. mem. Old Timers' Club; hon. mem. Motor Truck Club America; mem. Royal Societies Club (London). Author of various papers on mech. and engring. topics, before engring. socs. and for press. Queen Victoria's Prizeman in mathematics, 1898. Home: Antigo, Wis.

FARROW, JOSEPH HELMS, surgeon; b. Rocky Mount, Va., June 10, 1904; s. John Montgomery and Maggie (Shumate) F.; B.S., U. Va., 1926, M.D., 1930; m. Florence S. Skinner, Apr. 28, 1939. Intern St. Elizabeth's Hosp., Richmond, Va., 1930-31; resident surgery Watt's Hosp., Durham, N.C., 1931-33; fellow surgery and pathology Presbyn. Hosp., N.Y.C., 1933-34; mem. staff Meml. Hosp., N.Y.C., 1934-77, asso. attending surgeon, 1947-60, attending surgeon, chief breast service, 1960-69, emeritus, 1969-77; asso. vis. surgeon James Ewing Hosp., N.Y.C., 1959-60, vis. surgeon, 1960-69; asst. dir. tumor clinic, attending radiologist St. Agnes Hosp., White Plains, N.Y., 1938-42; cons. surgeon in oncology Nyack (N.Y.) Gen. Hosp., 1939-73, Vassar Bros. Hosp., Poughkeepsie, 1939-73, Harlem Valley State Hosp., Wingdale, N.Y., 1939-42, U.S. Naval Hosp., St. Albans, N.Y., 1946-71, Yonkers (N.Y.) Gen. Hosp., 1953-73, Stamford (Conn.) Hosp., 1963-73, Fitkin Meml. Hosp., Neptune, N.J., 1963-73, Strang Cancer Prevention Clinic, 1953-62; mem. faculty Cornell U. Coll. Medicine, 1950-69, asso. prof. clin. surgery, 1960-69; asso. clinician Sloan-Kettering Inst. Cancer Research, N.Y.C., 1954-60, clinician, 1960-72. Served to comdr., M.C., USNR, 1942-46. Diplomate Am. Bd. Radiology; fellow A.C.S., AMA, N.Y. Acad. Medicine; mem. N.Y. State Med. Soc., N.Y. County Med. Soc., Am. Radium Soc. (treas. 1961-63, pres. 1964-65), N.Y. Surg. Soc., James Ewing Soc. (pres. 1957), N.Y. Cancer Soc. (treas. 1963-64, pres. 1966-67), Pan-Pacific Surg. Assn., Am. Assn. Cancer Research, Am. Coll. Radiology, AAAS; hon. mem. Va. Surg. Soc., Honolulu Gen. Surg. Soc., Peruvian Acad. Surgery. Contbr. to profl. jours. Home: New York, N.Y. Died Mar. 3, 1977 buried Evergreen Cemetery, Roanoke, Va.

FARTHING, PAUL, judge; b. Odin, Ill., Apr. 12, 1887; s. William Dudley and Sarah (Boyd) F.; attended State Sch. for Blind, Jacksonville, Ill., 1901-04; B.S., McKendree Coll., Lebanon, Ill., 1909, LL.D., 1937; J.D., U. of Ill., 1913; m. Harriet Helen Garrigues, June 18, 1914; children—Sarah Mary, Edna Grace, William Dudley, Virginia (dec.). Admitted to Ill. bar, 1913, and practiced at East St. Louis, Ill., until 1930; mem. Farthing and Farthing; county judge, St. Clair County, 1930-33; master in chancery, East St. Louis, 1924-30; judge Supreme Court of Illinois, 1933-42, chief justice, 1937; judge Illinois Court of Claims, from 1952. Dir. Equity Savings Assn., East St. Louis. Mem. Ill. State Bar Assn., Phi Delta Phi, Order of the Coif. Democrat. Presbyterian. Club: Optimist. Co-editor with brother, Philo History. Blind since Sept. 1899, when his eyes were shot out by an older boy. Home: Belleville, Ill. Died Dec. 2, 1976.

FARWELL, CARROLL ANDREW, civil engr.; b. Bolton, Mass., Sept. 13, 1883; s. Joseph W. and Helen E. (Packard) Farwell; S.B., Mass. Inst. of Technology, 1906; married to Alice R. Sargent, 1912 (deceased in 1964); children—Helen Sargent (Mrs. Wm. G. Bartlett), Caroline Lincoln (Mrs. Richard Hosmer), Mary Virginia (Mrs. John C. Waller). With several organizations on design, inspection and supervision of engineering structures, 1906-22; partner of engring. firm Fay, Spofford & Thorndike, design of substructures and supervision of constrn. of heavy structures, 1922-66; now mem. board dirs. and cons. Fay, Spofford & Thorndike, Inc.; supervised constrn. various projects including: Rouses Point Bridge for Lake Champlain Bridge Commn., 1935-37; constrn. of Cape Cod Canal Highway bridges, 1934-35; design of engring. features of Army bases, Newfoundland, Greenland and Northern Can. for U.S. War Dept., 1941-44, various municipal airports in Mass., Vt. and N.H. since 1947; Army bases in Alaska for War Dept. since 1946, and misc. other projects. Member American Institute Consulting Engineers (former president), American Soc. C.E. (past pres. Northeastern Sect.), Boston Soc. Civil Engrs. (past pres.), Soc. Colonial Wars. Home: Sharon, Mass.

FARWELL, STANLEY PRINCE, management engr.; b. Chicago, Sept. 29, 1883; s. Arthur Burrage and Floretta (Woodberry) F.; B.S., U. Ill., 1907, M.S., 1910, Ph.D., 1914; m. Alice Louise Austin, Jan. 1, 1915; children—Myra Jeanette (Mrs. T. J. Campbell, Jr.), Richard Woodbury, Nancy Louise (Mrs. Craig B. Leman). Asst. prof. elec. engring. Centre Coll., Danville, Ky., 1908-10; instr. theoretical and applied mechanics U. Ill., 1910-13; chief service engr. Ill. State Pub. Utilities Commn., 1914-17; v.p. Bus. Research Corp., cons. management engrs., Chicago, 1920-24, president, 1924-25, became chmn. bd., 1955, now retired. Pres. Winnetka (Illinois). Community Chest, 1935-36; chairman Winnetka Zoning Bd. Appeals, 1920-28, adv. bd. Cook Co. (Ill.) Dept. Welfare; chmn. Vocational Schs. Com. State Ill.; trustee Provident Hosp.; dir. Chicago Hospital Council; former Welfare Council Citizens Assn. Chgo. Vice pres., dir., Citizens of Greater Chgo. Adminstr. Village of Northfield, Ill. Mem. Assn. Cons. Management Engrs. (dir.), (past v.p.), Soc. Advancement Management, Sigma Xi, Chi Psi, Tau Beta Pi, Eta Kappa Nu, Gamma Alpha, Phi Kappa Phi. Club: University. Home: Northfield, Ill.

FAULKNER, EDWARD HUBERT, soil developer, vegetable gardener, writer; born Lot, Kentucky, July 31, 1886; son of John Wesley and Rhoanna (Snyder) F.; A.B., Williamsburg Baptist Institute (now Cumberland College), 1909; B.S. in Agriculture, University of Kentucky, 1914; m. Roxy Caddell, June 26, 1913; children—Josephine (Mrs. John Jay McKelvey, Jr.), John Edward; m. 2d, Nettie E. Drummond, Nov. 8, 1926. County agrl. agent, Williamsburg, Whitley County, Ky., 1914-18; Gallipolis, Gallia County, O., 1918-20; teacher high sch. agr. (Smith-Hughes), Harmony Twp. High Sch., Plattsburgh, Clark County, O., 1920-25; conducted soil and crop investigations for Horr-Warner Co., Lodi, O., 1925-26; engaged in business or privately employed, 1926-41; soil studies, field testing theories of soil management, 1939-41; engaged in writing, 1941-43; farm editor, W.T.A.M., Cleveland, Ohio, 1943-45. Mem. Alpha Zeta. Ind. Republican. Conglist. Mason. Author: Plowman's Folly, 1943; Uneasy Money, 1946; A Second Look, 1947. Contbr. articles to various publs. Home: Elyria, Ohio.

FAULKNER, RAFFORD LOCHEAD, cons. engr.; b. Somerville, Mass., Jan. 24, 1909; s. Charles H. and Helen Elizabeth (Taylor) F.; S.B., M.I.T., 1933; m. Concetta Damian, Mar. 31, 1943; children—Carol Ann, Helen Frances. Geologist, Cerro Corp., Peru, 1933-40; engr.-examiner RFC, 1940-49; engr. Export-Import Bank, 1949-50; with div. raw materials AEC, 1950-72, dep. dir., 1957-63, dir., 1963-72; cons. engr. (nuclear fuels). Del. 3d, 4th internat. confs. Peaceful Uses Atomic Energy, 1964, 71, Internat. Nuclear Industries Fair, 1966. Served with USNR, 1943-46. Registered profl. engr., D.C. Mem. Am. Inst. Mining, Metall. and Petroleum Engrs., Am. Nuclear Soc. Home: Bethesda, Md. Died Feb. 22, 1979.

FAULKNER, ROBERT LEE, physician; b. Wattsburg, Pa.; Sept. 18, 1898; s. Lee and Leafy J. (Maynard) F.; B.S., Allegheny Coll., 1919; M.D., Johns Hopkins, 1923; m. Margaret O. Chapin, Aug. 1923; children—Robert Lee, Anne. Gynecology resident Johns Hopkins Hosp., 1924-29; asst. prof. gynecology Western Reserve U. Med. Sch., 1938-51, asso. prof. obstetrics and gynecology 1951-66; asso. gynecologist U. Hosps. 1938-66. Served in U.S. Army as 2d lt., 1918-19. Diplomate Am. Bd. Obstet. and Gynecology. Fellow A.C.S. Mem. S. Atlantic Assn. Obstetricians and Gynecologists, Am. Assn. Obstetricians, Gynecol. and Abdominal Surgeons, Am. Gynecol. Soc. Republican. Methodist Episcopal Ch. Contbr. to med. jours. Home: Eastlake, Ohio. Died Mar. 23, 1973; buried Evergreen Cemetery, Union City, Pa.

FAULKNER, VIRGINIA LOUISE, editor, educator; b. Lincoln, Nebr., Mar. 1, 1913; d. Edwin Jerome and Leah Louise (Meyer) Faulkner; student U. Nebr., 1928-30, Moxley Sch., Rome, 1930-31, Radcliffe Coll., 1932-33. Spl. writer Washington Post, 1933-34; asst. editor Town and Country, 1934-35; scenarist Metro-Goldwin-Mayer, 1935-38; free lance writer, 1938-56; asst. editor U. Nebr. Press., 1956-59, editor-in-chief, 1959-80, asso. prof. English, 1969-71, prof., 1971-80. Bd. govs. Willa Cather Pioneer Meml., 1960-80. Mem. Modern Lang. Assn., Alpha Phi. Republican. Presbyn. Club: Lincoln U. Author: My Heyday, 1940; Friends and Romans, 1934; The Barbarians, 1935; (with Dana Suesse) It Takes Two, 1946; (with Robert Beadell) Out to the Wind, 1979; compiler, editor: Roundup: A Nebraska Reader, 1957; Hostiles and Friendlies; Selected Short Writings of Mari Sandoz, 1959; Willa Cather's Collected Short Fiction, 1892-1912, 1965; Sandhill Sundays and Other Recollections of Mari Sandoz, 1970; Editor: (with Bernice Slote) The Art of Willa Cather, 1974; asso. editor Prairie Schooner, 1962—. Contbr. articles to periodicals and mags. Home: Lincoln, Nebr. Died Sept. 15, 1980; buried Wyuka Cemetery, Lincoln.

FAULKNER, (HERBERT WINTHROP) WALDRON, architect; b. Paris, Jan. 21, 1898 (parents Am. citizens); s. Herbert Waldron and Mary (John) F.; Ph.B., Yale U., 1919, B.F.A., 1924, M.Arch., 1973; m. Elizabeth Coonley, Nov. 18, 1926; children—Avery Coonley, Winthrop Waldron, Celia Ferry (Mrs. Raymond C. Clevenger III). Practice of architecture, N.Y.C., 1927-34, Washington, 1934-79, specializing instnl. bldg.; with A.B. Trowbridge, 1934-39; partner Faulkner, Kingsbury, Washington, 1939-46, sr. partner firm Faulkner, Stenhouse, Fryer & Faulkner and predecessor firms, 1946-68; cons. Faulkner, Fryer & Vanderpool, 1968-79; pres. Inter-Soc. Color Council, 1956-57; mem. Commn. on Ch. Architecture and Allied Arts, 1948-54; maj. commns. include: Coonley Sch., Downers Grove, Ill., 1933; Faulkner Residence, Washington, 1937; Suburban Hosp., Bethesda, Md., 1943-65; Am. U., Washington, 1946-67; George Washington U., Washington, 1936-66; Potomac Sch., McLean, Va., 1951; Providence Hosp., Washington, 1955-65; Brookings Instn. Hdqrs., 1960-63; St. Agnes Hosp., Balt., 1961; Evening Star Newspaper Bldg., Washington, 1961; Am. Chem. Soc. Hdqrs., 1961; Nat. Portrait Gallery, Washington, 1965; Nat. Collection Fine Arts, Washington, 1965. Bd. examiners and registrars architects, D.C., 1946-51. Bd. dirs. Internat. Student House, 1966-79; trustee Gunnery Sch., 1967-71; pres. Queene Ferry Coonley Found., 1970-79; bd. dirs. Lisner-Louise Home, 1954—, Washington Cathedral Chpt., 1961-68. Recipient Tremaine award for alumni achievement Gunnery Sch., 1972. Fellow AIA (pres. Washington 1942-43); mem. Washington Housing Assn. (pres. 1947-51), NAD (asso. mem.), Washington Urban League (pres. 1938-41). Episcopalian (jr. warden 1969-71, sr. warden 1971-77). Clubs: Gibson Island (Md.); Century Assn. (N.Y.C.); Chevy Chase, City Tavern, Cosmos (pres. 1953), Yale (pres. 1943-44) (Washington). Author: Architecture and Color, 1972. Home: Washington, D.C. Died May 11, 1979.

FAUST, ERNEST CARROLL, prof. med. parasitology; b. Carthage, Mo., Sept. 7, 1890; s. John Samuel and Mary Elizabeth Frances (Fenner) F.; A.B., Oberlin Coll., 1912; A.M., U. of Ill., 1914, Ph.D., 1917; student U. of Mich., summers, 1908, 12, and Woods Hole Biol. Lab., summers, 1911, 1913; Doctor of Laws, Tulane University, 1962; m. Lola Ernesta Swift, Aug. 12, 1919; 1 dau., Jean Louise. Research asst. in zoölogy (parasitology), U. of Ill., 1912-14, instr. 1917-19; asso. in parasitology, Peking Union Med. Coll., 1919-23, asso. prof., 1923-28; prof. parasitology, Tulane U. Sch. Medicine, 1928-47, prof. tropical diseases and hygiene, 1947-60, prof. emeritus, 1961; field coordinator Tulane-Colombia Med. Edn. Program, ICA-USOM, Colombia, 1956-61; head division of parasitology, 1928-56, director post-graduate courses in tropical medicine, Tulane U., 1941-47; vis. asso. prof. helminthology, Johns Hopkins, 1923-24; mem. Hutchinson Memorial Clinic; consultant USPHS, from 1936; res. cons. Armed Forces Inst. Pathology, 1949-56; mem. com. revision U.S. Pharmacopeia, 1950-60; mem. expert panel on parasitology, WHO. Honorary prof. several Latin American universities. Recipient of the Walter Reed medal American Society Tropical Medicine and Hygiene, 1963; Cert. of Merit for outstanding service Mayor of New Orleans, 1972. Fellow A.A.A.S., Royal Society Tropical Medicine and Hygiene of London, Am. Acad. Tropical Medicine (pres. 1950), Am. Soc. Tropical Medicine and Hygiene (pres. 1942), Am. Soc. Parasitologists (pres. 1948); mem. numerous profl. socs. and orgns. Democrat. Presbyn. Mason (32 deg.). Clubs: Boston, University, Round Table (New Orleans). Author several books, including Clinical Parasitology, 8th edit., 1970; contbr. to profl. med. books; author more than 300 monographs and papers on parasitology and tropical medicine in Am. and fgn. jours.; member editorial board scientific journals in U.S., Switzerland. Home: New Orleans, La. Died Nov. 2, 1978; buried Garden of Memories Cemetery, Metairie, La.

FAUTEAUX, ELLA LOUISE WARNER (FO-TO'), dean; b. Georgetown, Colo., Dec. 25, 1882; d. Gray and Carrie Lucinda (Griswold) Warner; A.B., Colorado Coll., 1904; M.R.E., Boston U., 1925; m. Louis Dearborn Fauteaux, Aug. 2, 1919 (died 1920). High school teacher, Monte Vista, Colo., Jan.-June 1907, Denver, Colo., 1907-19; dir. of girls' work Washington Park Community Ch., Denver, 1922-23; teacher Boston U. Sch. of Religious Edn., 1925-29, also head Resident Hall, same, 1926-29; dean of women, Colorado Coll., since 1929. Mem. Nat. Assn. Deans of Women, Am. Univ. Women, Phi Beta Kappa. Conglist. Club: Reviewers (Colorado Springs). Address: Colorado Springs, Colo.

FAWCETT, ROGER KNOWLTON, ret. pub. co. exec.; b. St. Paul, Dec. 3, 1909; s. W.H. and Viva Claire (Meyer) F.; student U. Minn., 1928-29; m. Helen Aline Bergquist, Oct. 17, 1934 (dec. Aug. 1971); children—John R., Thomas Knowlton; m. 2d, Helen Healey Lombardo. Editor, Fawcett Publs., Inc., N.Y.C., 1933-35, sec.-treas., 1935-40, v.p., gen. mgr., 1940-69, pres., 1969-77; pres. Fawcett World Library, Crest Books, Gold Medal Books, Premier Books, Fawcett Printing Corp. Mem. Minn. Trapshooting Hall of Fame, Hunting Hall of Fame, Phi Kappa Psi. Republican. Episcopalian. Club: N.Y. Athletic. Home: Darien, Conn. Died Oct. 3, 1979.

FAYER, MISCHA HARRY, ret. educator; b. N.Y.C., June 6, 1902; s. Max and Sara (Feldman) F.; B.A., U. Minn., 1926, M.A., 1928; Ph.D., Columbia, 1945; Litt. D., Middlebury Coll., 1969; widowed, 1964; m. 2d, Florence L. Kleinman, May 18, 1968. Organizer, head Russian dept. Middlebury (Vt.) Coll., 1943-67, Russian Sch., 1945-67, Inst. Soviet Studies, 1958-67; prof., chmn. dept. Slavic and Oriental langs. U. Ky., 1967-72. Mem. Am. Assn. Tchrs. Slavic and Eastern European Langs., MLA, AAUP. Author: Gide, Freedom and Dostoevsky, 1946; Basic Russian I, 1959, 2d edit., 1969; Basic Russian II, 1961; Simplified Russian Grammar, 3d edit., 1975. Home: Lexington, Ky. Died Apr. 14, 1977.

FEARNS, JOHN M. A., bishop; b. N.Y.C., June 25, 1897; s. Robert Joseph and Margaret Ann (McLaughlin) F.; A.B., St. Joseph's Sem. and Coll., 1918; S.T.D., Propaganda U., Rome Italy, 1923; student Gregorian U., Rome, 1924-25; LL.D., Fordham U., 1941, Manhattan Coll., 1951. Ordained priest Roman Cath. Ch., 1922, named domestic prelate, 1941, prothonotary apostolic, 1950; asst. in chs., N.Y.C., New Rochelle, N.Y., 1923; chaplain, instr. catechetics St. Clare's Acad., Hastings, N.Y., 1925-26; asst. Ch. of Resurrection, Rye, N.Y., 1927-30; prof. moral theology and canon law St. Joseph's Sem., Dunwoodie, N.Y., 1930-40; pres. St. Joseph's Coll. and Sem., 1940-56; pastor St. Francis de Sales Ch., N.Y.C., 1956-66, St. Patrick's Ch., Newburgh, N.Y., 1966-72; consecrated aux. bishop of N.Y. and titular bishop of Geras, 1957; Episcopal vicar Orange and Rockland Counties, N.Y., 1966-72. Mem. matrimonial ct. Archdiocese N.Y., 1931-38, judge, 1938-40; censor librorum Archdiocese N.Y., 1942-56, bd. consultors, 1948-77; chmn. Archdiocesan Liturgical Commn. Mem. Orange County Mental Health Bd., 1966-71. Charter mem. Cath. Theol. Soc. Am. (research com. 1945-51, pres. 1953); mem. Nat. Cath. Edn. Assn. (v.p. sem. sect. 1945, exec. bd. 1946, 53-56), Canon Law Soc., Marian Soc., St. Paul's Guild (Am. rep.), Assn. Bishops English Speaking Countries, Conf. Cath. Am. Bishops (mem. priestly formation com. 1965-70, liaison com. for religious 1966-70, doctrine com., commn. human values. Address: Yonkers, N.Y. Died July 4, 1977.

FEARON, GEORGE RANDOLPH, lawyer; b. Oneida, N.Y., Mar. 12, 1883; s. George and Anna Elizabeth L. Nichol (Charlow) F.; LL.B., Syracuse U., 1905; m. Cora L. Nichols, Nov. 17, 1909; children—Helen (Mrs. Louis E. Ginter), Elizabeth (Mrs. Royal L. O'Day); m. 2d, Katherine P. McBride, Aug. 5, 1953. Admitted to N.Y. bar, 1905, since practiced in Syracuse; sr. mem. Costello, Cooney & Fearon, 1920—. Mem. N.Y. State Assembly, 1916-20; N.Y. State Senate, 1921-36, pres. pro tem and majority leader, 1931-32, minority leader, 1933-36; mem. N.Y. State Constl. Conv., 1938. Fellow Am. Coll. Trial Lawyers; mem. Am., N.Y. State (v.p. 1952-56), Onondaga County (past pres.) bar assns. Mason (32, Jester). Clubs: entury, Onondaga (Syracuse); Skytop (Pa.). Home: Syracuse NY 13203.

FEE, GEORGE EDWARD, lawyer, corp. exec.; b. Newport, Ky., July 12, 1904; s. George E. and Josephine (McKernan) F.; student Xavier U., Cin., 1922-25; LL.B., U. Cin., 1927; m. Jean Van Horne, Oct. 21, 1933; 1 son, George E. Admitted to Ohio bar, 1927; asso. Dolle, O'Donnell & Cash, Cin., 1927-37; partner Dolle, O'Donnelle & Cash, Cin., 1937-52; sr. partner Dolle, O'Donnell, Cash, Fee & Hahn, Cin., 1952-71; counsel to Paxton & Seasongood, Cin., 1971-78; prof. law Salmon P. Chase Law Sch., 1935-47; lectr. Coll. Law U. Cin., 1952. Chmn. bd. Lodge & Shipley Co., Cin., 1956-66, dir., 1952-68, gen. counsel, 1952-75. Mem. Am., Ohio, Cin. bar assns., Order of Coif. Home: Bal Harbour, Fla. Died Mar. 13, 1978.

FEENBERG, EUGENE, physicist, educator; b. Ft. Smith, Ark., Oct. 19, 1906; s. Louis and Esther (Siegel) F.; B.A., M.A., U. Tex., 1929; Ph.D., Harvard U., 1933; m. Hilda Rosenberg, May 30, 1940; children—Andrew L., Daniel Richard. Instr. physics Harvard U., 1933-35; lectr. physics U. Wis., 1935-36; fellow Inst. Advanced Study, Princeton, N.J., 1936-38; mem. faculty Washington Sq. Coll., N.Y.U., 1938-46; micro-wave engr. Sperry Gyroscope Co., 1941-45; mem. faculty Washington U., St. Louis, 1946-78, Wayman Crow prof. emeritus. Mem. Am. Phys. Soc., Nat. Acad. Sci. Author: (with G.E. Pake) Notes on the Quantum Theory of Angular Momentum, 1953; Small Theory of the Nucleus, 1955; Theory of Quantum Fluids, 1970. Home: Clayton, Mo. Died Nov. 1978.

FEENEY, LEONARD, author; b. Lynn, Mass., Feb. 15, 1897; s. Thomas Butler and Delia (Leonard) F.; student Woodstock Coll., Md., 1918-21, M.A., 1925-27, Weston Coll., 1927-29. Prof. English, Boston Coll. Grad. School, 1931-36. Entered Jesuit Order, 1914; ordained to priesthood, 1928; literary editor America, the national Catholic weekly, 1936-40; prof. Sacred Eloquence, Weston Coll., 1940-43; dir. St. Benedict Center, Cambridge, Mass., 1943-58, Still River, Mass., 1958-68; founder, superior Slaves of Immaculate Heart of Mary, 1949-68. Pres. Catholic Poetry Soc., 1939-41. Author poetry and books including: The Leonard Feeney Omnibus, 1943; London Is a Place, 1951; Bread of Life, 1952. Superior: The Slaves of the Immaculate Heart of Mary. Home: Still River, Mass. Died Jan. 30, 1968.

FEERICK, ROBERT J., profl. basketball exec.; grad. Santa Clara Coll., 1937-41. Played profl. basketball with Washington Capitols Nat. Basketball Assn. team, 1941-45; coach Santa Clara (Cal.) Coll., 1945-57; gen. mgr. San Francisco Warriors. Address: San Francisco, Calif. Died June 8, 1976.

FEHN, ED J., pub.; b. Feb. 10, 1884, Evansville, Ind.; s. John M. and Eva (Bortzmeier) F.; ed. pub. schs.; m. Flora M. Crider, Jan. 10, 1920. Successively bus. mgr., gen. mgr., v.p., pub. The Evansville (Ind.) Courier, pres., pub. since 1939, chmn. of bd. Evansville Printing Corp., since 1939. Dir. Evansville Printing Corp., Nat. City Bank. Mem. Asso. Press, Am. Newspaper Pubs. Assn. Methodist. Mason. Club: Evansville Country. Home: Evansville, Ind.

FEIBELMAN, JULIAN BECK, rabbi; b. Jackson, Miss., Mar. 23, 1897; s. Abraham and Eva (Beck) F.; A.B., Millsaps Coll., 1918; LL.D., 1946; rabbi, Hebrew Union Coll., 1926, D.D. honoris causa, 1955; M.A., U. Pa., 1929, Ph.D., 1939; m. Mary Anna Fellman, Oct. 20, 1938; 1 son, Julian B., Jr. Rabbi, Temple Keneseth Israel, Phila., 1926-36; rabbi Temple Sinai, New Orleans, 1936-68, rabbi emeritus, 1968-80; lectr. history of religions Tulane U. 1948-50. Am.-Jewish rep. Internat. Conf. Christians and Jews to study European Anti-Semitism, Switzerland, 1947; city chmn. U.N. Appeal for Children, 1948; mem. exec. bd. Central Conf. Am. Rabbis, 1948, chmn. Interfaith Com. Mem. bd. govs. Hebrew Union Coll. since 1951; pres. combined alumni assn. of Hebrew Union Coll., Cin., and Jewish Inst. Religion N.Y. Mem. Prison Interfaith Bd. Ministers for Parolees; v.p. ch. activity br. La. Safety Assn., 1960; bd. Anti-Defamation League, Vols. Am., Parish Prison Chaplains Commn., Jewish Community Center; pres. New Orleans Rabbinical Council, 1963-64. Mem. bd. Kingsley House, 1963-80; hon. life mem. bd. Louise S. Davis School, 1963; mem., 1st vice chmn. lay bd. DePaul Hosp.; bd. dirs. Met. Area Com.; mem. overseers adv. bd. of Hebrew Union Coll. Served U.S. Army, World War I; spl. rep. W.L.B.; chmn. com. home service, field dir., mem. exec. bd., New Orleans Red Cross, World War II. Recipient citation Millsaps Coll., 1967; gold medal St. Mary's Dominican Coll., 1967; Weiss award NCCJ, 1967; Times Picayune Loving Cup, 1968; Greek Orthodox Ch. spl. merit award, 1970; Clergyman of Yr. award Kiwanis Club, 1971; Paul Harris fellow Rotary Club, 1980. Mem. Mayor's Adv. Com. New Orleans, 1946. Mem. La. Soc. Mental Hygiene (past pres.), New Orleans Assn. Social Hygiene (past pres.), NCCJ (Southwestern adviser), New Orleans Urban League (v.p.), Family Service Soc. (pres. 1950), New Orleans Race Relations, Jewish Pub. Soc. Phila. (editorial bd.), New Orleans Fgn. Policy Assn. (exec. bd.), New Orleans Tb Assn., Jewish Statis. Bur., United Jewish Appeal Bd., Am. Jewish Com. Bd., Vet.'s Information Center, Boy Scouts (exec. bd.; awarded Silver Beaver 1951), Hebrew Union Coll. Alumni Assn. (pres. 1952), Ch. and Industry Com. (exec. bd.), New Orleans Assn. Commerce. Clubs: Rotary (pres. 1950-51), Athletic (New Orleans), Lakewood Country. Author: The Making of a Rabbi. Editor: New Orleans Jewish Ledger, 1940-44. Dedicated new chapel Julian B. Feibelman chapel, 1972. Home: New Orleans, La. Died Oct. 10, 1980.

FEIDLER, ERNEST REYNOLD, lawyer; b. Superior, Wis., Apr. 15, 1910; s. Ernest William and Agnes Amelia (Swanson) F.; Ed.B. magna cum laude, Wis. State Coll., Superior, 1930; J.D. cum laude, U. Wis., 1934; Sterling fellow in law, Yale, 1934-35; m. Lydia Keown, July 25, 1936. Admitted to Wis. bar, 1934, D.C. bar, 1946; various capacities Office Gen. Counsel, Treasury Dept., 1935-43, asst. to gen. counsel, 1942-43; sec., gen. counsel The A. W. Mellon Ednl. and Charitable Trust, 1946-51, also sec. Old Dominion Found.; adminstr. Nat. Gallery of Art, Washington, 1954-65, sec., treas., gen. counsel, 1965-70. Mem. USCG Bd. Rev. Mil. Justice, 1951-53. Trustee, Superior State U. Found., Allentown Art Mus., Mus. of African Art, Washington. Served from lt. comdr. to comdr., USCG Res., 1943-46, active, 51-54, rear adm., 1961. Mem. Am., Wis., D.C. bar assns., Chi Phi. Clubs: Army and Navy, Cosmos (Washington); N.Y. Athletic. Contbr. articles legal jours. Home: Arlington, Va. Died Sept. 4, 1976; buried Arlington Nat. Cemetery.

FEIR, JAMES (FAIR), co. exec.; b. Can., Apr. 2, 1884; m. Margaret Christie June 7, 1916; children—Peggy (Mrs. James Crumpacker), Cleone (Mrs. Alfred Stoloff). Came to U.S., 1933, naturalized, 1939. Mgr., Marshall Wells Co., Regina, Saskatchewan, Can., 1920-32, Duluth, Minn., 1933-35, Portland, Ore., 1935-50, exec. v.p., dir. Duluth head office since 1950. Home: Duluth, Minn.

FEIRER, WILLIAM ANTHONY (FIR'ER), physician; b. Roselle Park, N.J., Jan. 18, 1900; s. Frank and Mary Ann (Salzmann) F.; B.S., Rutgers U., 1922; D.Sc., Johns Hopkins, 1925, M.D., 1930; Sc.D., (honorary), Philadelphia College Pharmacy and Sci., 1943, Rutgers University, 1954; married Jeanne Corrington, Feb. 10, 1932; Asso. prof. bacteriology Johns Hopkins U., 1923-30, staff physician Johns Hopkins Hosp., 1932-36; with Sharp & Dohme, Phila., 1930-32, dir. biol. labs., 1936-37, dir. med. div., 1937-40, dir. med. research div., since 1940, vice pres., 1942-47, exec. vice pres., 1947-50; mem. bd. dirs., vice president in charge scientific affairs E. R. Squibb & Sons, 1950-52, v.p., dir. Squibb Inst. Med. Research since 1952. Mem. exec. com., dir. Health Information Found.; trustee Rutgers University. Fellow American Public Health Assn., American College Physicians; member of A.M.A., A.A.A.S., Soc. Am. Bacteriologists; hon. mem. Sigma Xi, Alpha Omega Alpha, Delta Omega. Methodist. Clubs: University (New York and St. Louis). Home: Oklawaha, Fla. Died Nov. 4, 1976.

FEISE, (KARL RICHARD WILHELM) ERNST (FI'ZE), prof. German; b. Braunschweig, Germany, June 8, 1884; s. Johannes and Auguste (Witzell) F.; Gymnasium, Braunschweig, 1893-1902; studied U. of Berlin, 1902-03, U. of München, 1903-05, U. of Leipzig, 1905-08, Dr. Ph.; Litt.D. (honorary), Middlebury Coll., 1949; married Dorothy Flint Findlay, Sept. 6, 1910; children—Richard Ernst, Frederik Findlay, Dorelen. Came to U.S., 1908, naturalized citizen, 1931. Successively instr., asst. prof. and asso. prof. German, U. of Wis., 1908-17; prof. German, Colegio Aleman, Mexico City, 1920-24; insp. English, Mexican pub schs., 1923-24; asst. prof. German, Ohio State U., 1924-27; asso. prof. German, Johns Hopkins, 1927-28, prof., 1928-52, ret. Dir. Middlebury Coll. Sch. of German, Bristol, Vt, 1931-48. Mem. Modern Lang. Assn. Am. (mem. council, 1945-48), Am. Assn. U. Profs., Am. Assn. Tchrs. of German (pres. 1939 and 40), Phi Beta Kappa. Author: Xenion, 1950. Editor and co-editor various books. Contbr. articles and revs. Home: Rolandview Rd., Ruxton 12. Md.

FEIST, IRVING J., exec. Boy Scouts Am.; b. Newark, Jan. 6, 1907; s. Abram and Irene (Sickle) F.; B.S., Newark Acad., 1925, B.S., U. Pa., 1929; LL.D., Monmouth Coll., m. Dorothy Blair, Nov. 30, 1930; children—John Alan, Margaret Louise (Mrs. Claude Foussier). Pres. Feist & Feist, real estate and ins., Newark and N.Y.C., 1931-78. Pres. Boy Scouts Am., 1968-70, hon. v.p. Active fund-raising campaigns, community activities; mem. exec. com., nat. bd. govs. Nat. Conf. Christians and Jews, Inc.; chmn. World Scouting, 1975-77; nat. adv. council Girl Scouts U.S.A.; bd. dirs., v.p. U.S. Found. for Internat. Scouting. Nat. trustee, past state chmn. Ducks Unltd.; chmn. council trustees Freedoms Found., Valley Forge, Pa.; trustee Sport Fishery Found., Springfield Coll.; bd. dirs. Am. League of Anglers. Recipient Silver Beaver, Silver Antelope, Silver Buffalo awards Boy Scouts Am. Golden Pheasant, Boy Scouts Japan; golden medalion Korea; Silver Wolf award Brit. Scout Assn., 1967; Silver Tamarow award Boy Scouts Philippines, 1968; Silver Elephant award Boy Scouts India, 1968; Bronze Wolf, World Scouting's highest award, 1969. Mem. Newark, N.Y. real estate bds., Greater Newark C. of C., World Wildlife Fund (trustee), Wild Fowl Found., Am. Forestry Assn. (trustee), Am. Soc. Real Estate Counselors, Soc. Indsl. Realtors, Internat. Real Estate Fedn. Clubs: Newark Downtown, Essex (Newark); Hollywood Golf (past pres.) (Deal, N.J.); Adventurers; St. Hubert's Soc. (founder, chmn. bd.); Wall Street., Univ., Explorers, Madison Sq. Garden (N.Y.C.); U. Pa., Manasquan Fishing. Home: New York, N.Y. Died Feb. 27, 1978.

FEITEL, DONALD GOTTSCHALK, editor; b. New Orleans, Oct. 8, 1925; s. Nathaniel H. and Bertha (Wolbrette) F.; B.A., U. Chgo., 1943; m. Barbara Scope, Nov. 12, 1950; children—Thomas E., Charles D., Elizabeth L. Salesman Reliable Linen Co., Denver, 1946-48; reporter Met. Sunday Newspapers, N.Y.C., 1949-53, mng. editor, 1954-64, editorial dir., 1965-76. Served with USAAF, 1943-46. Mem. Am. Assn. Sunday, Feature Editors, Overseas Press Club. Author: Guide to Freelancing, 1961. Contbr. articles to popular mags. Home: Pelham Manor, N.Y. Died June 3, 1976.

FELAND, JOHN J., farm coop. exec.; b. Danville, Ky., Nov. 24, 1923; s. Armstead Milner and Elizabeth (Jackson) F.; student U. Ky., 1941-43; m. Joan Stoughton Ridlehouse, Nov. 20, 1947. With So. States Coop., Richmond, Va., 1945-80, chief exec. officer, 1973-80; pres. Farmers Forage Research; vice chmn. Texas City Refining, Inc.; vice chmn. CF Industries, Inc., dir. Overnite Transp. Co., First & Mchts. Nat. Bank, First & Mchts. Corp., Agri-Petro Internat., Inc. Bd. dirs. Richmond Eye and Ear Hosp., Nat. Council Farmer Coops.; mem. adv. bd. Salvation Army. Clubs: Commonwealth, Downtown, Country of Va., Masons. Died Mar. 12, 1980; buried Louisville, Ky.

FELDMAN, MAURICE, public relations counsel; b. Vienna, Austria, July 24, 1914; s. Samuel and Gisela (von Fiderer) F.; Ph.D. in Econs., U. Vienna, student univs. Stockholm (Sweden) and Geneva (Switzerland). Came to U.S., 1939, naturalized, 1943. Financial and bus. editor Der Tag, Vienna, 1933-38; fgn. trade editor Stockholms Tidningen, Sweden, 1938-39; mem. staff King Features Syndicate, N.Y.C., 1939-40; spl. writer Christian Sci. Monitor, U.S. corr. Public Relations Rev.; lectr. U. St. Gallen (Switzerland), Innsbruck, Austria, 1966, 67-73; owner Maurice Feldman Pub. Relations, N.Y.C. Recipient decorations from USAF, Austria; Golden Cross Vienna and Burgenland; named prof. by Fed. Pres. Austria, 1972. Fellow Inst. Directors (London); mem. Pub. Relations Soc. Am., Air Force Assn. Author: Economic Barriers of Europe; History of Public Relations; Public Relations in Modern Economy; also articles. Address: New York, N.Y. Died May 7, 1976.

FELTON, RALPH A., educator, clergyman; b. Arkansas City, Kan., July 26, 1882; s. Marshall A. and Isabelle (Nichols) F.; A.B., Southwestern Coll., 1905; M.A., Columbia, 1912; B.D., Union Theol. Sem., 1913; student U. Pa., 1920-23; Ph.D., Drew Theol. Sem., 1932; m. Blanche Shimer, Aug. 19, 1914; children—Mary (Mrs. Judah Drob), Ralph, Margaret (Mrs. James H. Pyke), Robert. Instr. Am. U., Beirut, Lebanon, 1907-10; asst. in charge rural ch. surveys Presbyn. Dept. Church and Country Life, 1913-19, asst. in charge inservice tng. rural pastors Meth. Rural Church Dept., 1919-23; extension N.Y., 1923-30; prof. rural church Drew Sem., Madison, N.J., 1930-52; vis. tchr. Union Sem., Nanking, China, 1936-37, Korea, 1937-38, Mexico City, Mexico, 1943; field progKorea, 1937-38, Mexico City, Mexico, 1943; field program analyst Agrl. Missions, Inc., N.Y.C, 1952-56, cons., 1957-58. Author: The Rural Church in the Far East, 1938; Man's Use of God's Earth, 1945; Hope Rises from the Land, 1955; Church Bells in Many Tongues, 1958; The Pulpit and the Plow; and also writer of numerous others (also in Spanish, Korean, Japanese langs.). Home: Madison, N.J.

FENGER, FREDERIC(K) ABILDGAARD (FENG'ER), naval architect; b. Chicago, May 1, 1882; s. Christian and Caroline (Abildgaard) F.; M.E., Cornell U., 1907; work, in naval architecture, Mass. Inst. Tech., winter of 1908-09; m. Katharine Lindsay Swift, Sept. 16, 1912; 1 son, Christian. Worked in machine shop, Chicago, later specializing in hull design, and mem. Swazey, Raymond and Page, Inc., Boston, until 1910; since then has devoted entire time to travel and study, contbg. to newspapers and mags. Cruised alone length of Lesser Antilles in the "Yakaboo," a 17 ft. sailing canoe, in 1911; eighteen months' expdn. to Bahamas and throughout West Indies, navigating the 52 ft. schooner "Diablesse," for hist. study and mag. material, 1913-15. Active service in U.S. Navy, Mar. 1917-Jan. 1919; 14 months on U.S.S. Chester in submarine zone; later constrn. officer of U.S.S. Prometheus at Brest. Active service in U.S. Navy, lt. comdr., construction duty, 1942-45. Member Sigma Alpha Epsilon. Republican. Conglist. Clubs: Cruising Club America, Cohasset Yacht, Cornell Club of N.E. Author: Alone in the Caribbean, 1917; The Golden Parrot, 1921; The Cruise of Diablesse, 1926. Originated and was first to describe the "Main Trysail" rig and the "Dhow" hull type which have since been applied in yacht form. Home: Summer St., Norwell, Mass.

FENNELL, EDWARD O'BRIEN, airline exec.; b. Washington, Dec. 6, 1925; s. Anthony B. and Madeleine (O'Brien) F.; student U. Md., 1943-44, 45-47; LL.B., Am. U., 1950; m. Barbara E. Duborg, Apr. 15, 1951; children—Karen Ann, Kevin George, Stephen Edward. Admitted to D.C. bar, 1950, Ill. bar, 1957; trial atty. Justice Dept., 1950-51, asst. U.S. atty., 1951-57; with United Air Lines, Inc., 1957-76, sr. v.p. law, sec., Chgo., 1972-75, sr. v.p., gen. counsel, sec., 1975-76; gen. counsel, sec. UAL, Inc., 1975-76. Mem. Chgo. Crime Commn. Served with USNR, 1944-45. Mem. Am., Ill., Chgo., D.C. bar assns. Clubs: International, Congressional Country (Washington); Knollwood (Lake Forrest, Ill.). Home: Lake Forest, Ill. Died Sept. 9, 1976.

FENNELLY, LEO C., lawyer; b. N.Y.C., 1897; A.B., Manhattan Coll., 1919; LL.B., Fordham U., 1922. Admitted to N.Y. bar, 1922; now mem. Fennelly, Douglas, Eagan, Nager & Voohees; asst. U.S. atty., 1934-39; spl. asst. to atty. gen. U.S. 1939-40. Mem. Assn. Bar City N.Y. (jud. com. 1950-52, exec. com. 1953-79). Died 1979.

FENNER, DARWIN SCHRIEVER, ret. investment banker, broker; b. New Orleans, 1908; s. Charles E. and Virginia (Schriever) F.; student Tulane U., 1925-29; m. Flora Hardie, 1931; children—Darwin Charles, James Hardie, Flora Sanders (Mrs. Ronald J. French). Clerk for firm Fenner & Beane, 1929-34, partner, 1934-41; partner Merrill Lynch, Pierce, Fenner & Beane, 1941-57; v.p., dir. Merrill Lynch, Pierce, Fenner & Smith, Inc., 1957-70, sr. v.p., 1964-70, also dir.; pres. Gulf States Assets Mgmt. Inc., 1971-77; pres. GSA Properties, Inc., 1977-79. Co-founder New Orleans United Way. Bd. adminstrs. Tulane U., 1953-73, chmn., 1964-69, mem. adv. bd., 1973; chmn. Health Edn. Authority La., 1968-71, mem. bd., 1971-79; chmn. original bd. New Orleans Ednl. TV Found., 1953, bd. dirs., 1954-58, hon. chmn., 1959-79; pres. Council for a Better La., 1974-75; original sponsor Met. Leadership Forum of Met. Area Com. and Tulane U. Mem. Kappa Alpha. Served as maj. USAAC, 1942-46. Home: New Orleans, La. Died June 9, 1979.

FENNINGER, CARL W(IKER), banking exec.; b. nr. Lancaster, Pa., June 11, 1884; s. Michael B. and Laura Louisa Fenninger; student evening sch., U. of Pa., 1907; m. Eleanor Simons; children—Carl W., Margaret (Mrs. Griesinger). Chmn. exec. com. and dir. Alan Wood Steel Co., Conshohocken, Pa., since 1941; dir. Cotiga Development Co., Phila., since 1925, became pres., 1930, now chmn. bd., dir.; dir. John T. Dyer Quarry Co., John J. Felin & Co., Inc., Wm. Freihofer Baking Co., P. H. Glatfeler Co., Imperial Foods Co., Inc., Provident Trust Co. of Phila., John Wanamaker, Phila., Inc., John Wanamaker, Wilmington, Inc., York Corp. Pres. John J. Tyler (Painter) Arboretum, Lima, Pa., since 1943, mem. bd. since 1936. Trustee Acad. Natural Scis. Mem. Am. Entomol. Soc., Am. Assn. Botanical Gardens and Arboretums (sec. and treas.). The Gen. Alumni Soc. of Univ. of Pa. (v.p.), Zool. Soc. of Phila., Franklin Inst. (Phila.), N.Y. Botanical Garden. Clubs: Union League, Midday (Phila.), Science and Arts (Germantown). Home: Chestnut Hill, Philadelphia.

FENSTERSTOCK, HOWARD WARREN, former govt. ofcl., lawyer; b. N.Y.C., Aug. 4, 1908; A.B., Coll. City N.Y., 1928; LL.B., Harvard, 1931; m. Elvera Stewart Johnson, June 22, 1946; 1 stepson, John Stewart Johnson. Admitted to N.Y. bar 1932; gen. practice law, N.Y.C., 1932-42, 47-49; asst. counsel-USAF div. Armed Services Renegotiation Bd., 1950-51; atty. Renegotiation Bd., 1951-52, asst. gen. counsel, 1953-56, gen. counsel, 1956-73. Served from 1st lt. to lt. col. CWS, AUS, 1942-46; assigned as chmn. Chem. Warfare Price Adjustment Bd., 1945-46. Mem. Fed., Am. bar assns. Clubs: Nat. Press. Nat. Lawyers, Harvard, Army Navy Country (Washington). Home: Arlington, Va. Died Feb. 22, 1977.

FERGUSON, ALFRED LYNN, chemist; b. Grass Lake, Mich., June 6, 1884; s. George and Addie (Ferguson) F.; Life Certificate, Mich. State Normal Coll., 1903, B.Pd., 1904; A.B., U. of Mich., 1908, A.M., 1909, Ph.D., 1915; m. Oril Chapman, June 19, 1909; 1 son, Allyn Chapman. High sch. prin., Northville, Mich., 1904-07; supt. schs., Lawton, Mich., 1909-10; mem. faculty, U. of Mich. since 1911, prof. of chemistry since 1944; electrochemical consultant since 1935; has served as dir. of research projects for Pa. Salt Mfg. Co., Am. Electroplaters Soc., Federal Mogul Corp., etc.; expert witness in patent cases since 1935. Mem. Am. Chem. Soc., The Electrochem. Soc. (pres., 1949-50), Am. Electroplaters Soc., A.A.A.S., Mich. Coll. Chem. Teachers Assn., Mich. Acad. Sci., Alpha Chi Sigma, Gamma Alpha, Phi Lambda Upsilon, Sigma Xi. Mason (life mem.). Clubs: Michigan Schoolmasters, Research (U. of Mich.). Made extensive study of rural edn. Home: Whitmore Lake, Mich.

FERGUSON, CLARENCE MEADD, educator; b. Parkhill, Ont., Can., June 21, 1899; grad. Ont. Agr. Coll., 1921; student Mich. State Coll., Ohio State U.; m. 1927; 2 children. Instr. Ont. Agr. Coll., 1921; extension work in poultry Mich. State Coll., 1922-23, asst. prof., 1923-28; agr. technician Ministry of Agr., Colombia, 1928; extension service Ohio State U., 1929-48, dir., 1949-53; adminstr. fed. extension service U.S. Dept. Agr., 1953-60; asst. sec. agr., 1960-61; prof. Nat. Agrl. Extension Center for Advanced Study, U. Wis., 1961-64; prof. dept. adult edn. N.C. State U., from 1964. Home: Raleigh, N.C. Died Aug. 11, 1978.

FERGUSON, DONALD NIVISON, author, ret. educator; b. Waupun, Wis., June 30, 1882; s. Drysdale J. and Emily Agnes (Nivison) F.; B.A., U. Wis., 1904; M.A., U. Minn., 1922; music student, London, Eng., 1905-08; postgrad., U. Vienna, 1929-30; m. Arline Calista Folsom, Sept. 4, 1915; children—Donald John, Mary Barbara, David Lee, Griselda Alice (Mrs. Griselda F. White). Mem. faculty music U. Minn., 1913-50, prof., 1928-50; program annotator Mpls. Symphony Orch., 1930-60; condr. Bach Soc., 1934-50; head, dept. music Macalester Coll., St. Paul, 1950-59. Mem. Minn. Music Tchrs. Assn. (pres. 1925-29), Phi Beta Kappa. Author: History of Musical Thought, 1935; Short History of Music, 1940; Piano Music of Six Great Composers, 1948; Masterworks of the Orchestral Repertoire, 1954; Music as Metaphor, 1960, Chamber Music, 1964; The Why of Music, 1969. Address: Minneapolis, MN 55409.

FERGUSON, GEORGE VICTOR, ret. newspaper editor; b. Cupar Fife, Scotland, Apr. 20, 1897; s. James Thompson and Maud Mant (Martin) F.; student U. Alta., 1915-16, 19-21; B.A., Oxford U., 1924; LL.D., U. New Brunswick, 1950, U. Alta., 1960, McGill U., 1967, Queen's U., 1968; m. Mary Simpson Doupe, Dec. 27, 1930; children—David Martin, Stephen Somerville. Deskman, Times of London, 1924; reporter Winnipeg Free Press, 1925-27, editorial writer, 1927-31, news editor, 1931-36, mng. editor, 1936-44, exec. editor, 1944-46; editor Montreal Star, 1946-58, editor-in-chief 1958-68, editor emeritus, from 1968. Fellow Royal Soc. Can. Author: John W. Dafoe, a memoir, 1949. Home: Montreal, Que., Can. Died Jan. 26, 1977.

FERGUSON, JOHN HOWARD, pathologist; b. Elmira Heights, N.Y., Sept. 5, 1902; s. John C. and Ina (Fisher) F.; M.D., Syracuse U., 1926; m. Ruth Cadzow, Sept. 3, 1926; children—John Howard, James Cadzow. Fellow in pathology Upstate Med. Center, SUNY (formerly Syracuse U., Coll. Medicine), 1926-27, instr. in pathology, 1927-29, asst. prof., 1929-32, asso. prof., 1932-42, prof., 1942-69, emeritus, 1969-78; attending pathologist Univ. Hosp., 1934-42; pathologist Syracuse Med. Center Hosps., 1942-63; attending pathologist State U. Hosp., 1963-69, sr. attending pathologist, 1969; county necrotomist, Onondaga County, 1927-50. Mem. adv. council N.Y. State Joint Hosp. Survey and Planning Commn., 1946-61. Recipient Gold Headed Cane award SUNY Coll. Medicine, 1976. Mem. Am. Cancer Soc. (mem. exec. com. N.Y. State div.; chmn. fellowship com. 1946-48, chmn. med. service and adv. com. 1948-53), Am. Assn. Pathologists and Bacteriologists, N.Y. State Assn. Pub. Health Labs. (pres. 1944-46), Tumor Clinic Assn. N.Y. State (sec.-treas. 1947-69), Syracuse Acad. Medicine, Sigma Xi, Alpha Omega Alpha, Nu Sigma Nu, Phi Kappa Psi. Republican. Contbr. to med. periodicals. Home: Syracuse, N.Y. Died Dec. 25, 1978; interred White Chapel Memory Gardens, Dewitt, N.Y.

FERMI, LAURA, author; b. Rome, Italy, June 16, 1907; d. Augusto and Costanza (Romanelli) Capon; student U. Rome, 1926-28; m. Enrico Fermi, July 19, 1928 (dec.); children—Nella (Mrs. Weiner), Giulio. Came to U.S., 1939, naturalized, 1944. Author: Atoms in the Family, 1954; Atoms For the World, 1957; Mussolini, 1961; The Story of Atomic Energy (juvenile), 1961; Illustrious Immigrants, 1968; (with Ginestra Amaldi) Alchimia Del Tempo Nostro, 1936; (with Gilberto Bernardini) Galileo and the Scientific Revolution, 1961. Mem. Chgo. Air Pollution Control Com., 1960-68. Bd. govs. Internat. House Chgo., 1955-66; mem. women's bd. U. Chgo. Guggenheim fellow, 1957. Recipient prize Friends of Lit., 1968.

Mem. League Women Voters Chgo., Authors' Guild. Home: Chicago, Ill. Died Dec. 26, 1977.

FERNANDEZ, ROYES, dancer; b. New Orleans, July 15, 1929; s. Manuel Paul and Francoise (Blanchin) F.; grad. high sch., New Orleans. Debut, Original Ballet Russe, 1946-47; soloist Markova-Dolin Ballet, 1947-48; soloist Ballet Alicia Alonso, 1948-50, premier danseur, 1952-54; premier danseur Australia's Borovanskv Ballet, 1954-56; soloist Am. Ballet Theatre, 1950-53, prin. dancer, 1957-80, premier danseur, 1962-80, also tours sponsored by Dept. State to Europe, 1958, 60, USSR, 1960, 66, Latin Am., 1964; premier danseur London's Festival Ballet, summer 1962; participated Fonteyn World Tour, summer 1963; with Gala Matinee of Ballet, London, Drury Lane Theatre, Royal Acad. Dancing, Dec. 1963; guest artist Australian Nat. Ballet, Sydney and Melbourne, spring 1964, Jacob's Pillow, Lee, Mass., 1961, 62, 63, 64, 66, 70; guest appearances numerous ballet cos., with symphony orchestras and on TV; spl. performance at the White House, 1968; prin. roles include La Sylphide, Nutcracker, Giselle, Sleeping Beauty, La Fille Mal Gardee, Swan Lake, Coppelia, Les Sylphides, also contemporary ballets Etudes, Lilac Garden, Theme and Variations, Lady from the Sea, Aleko, Las Hermanas, Moor's Pavane, The Traitor, Gaite Parisienne. Hon. chmn. La. ballet council La. Council for Music and Performing Arts, 1968-80; recipient 1st Ann. award, 1968. Mem. Am. Guild Mus. Artists. Home: New York, N.Y.; buried Covington, La.

FERREE, JOHN WILLARD, physician; b. Marion, Ind., Aug. 26, 1904; s. John Daniel and Mary A. (Heaston) F.; A.B., U. Pa., 1925; M.D., Ind. U., 1932; M.P.H., Johns Hopkins, 1939; m. Roberta North, June 10, 1930; children—Barbara F. Barden, John Daniel, Rebecca (Mrs. Calvin R. Harvey). Intern Harper Hosp., Detroit, 1932-33; resident Passavant Meml. Hosp., Chgo., 1933-34, Evanston (Ill.) Hosp., 1934-35; dir. local health adminstrn. Ind. State Bd. Health, 1936-40, state health commr., 1940-42; dir. ednl. services Am. Social Hygiene Assn., 1946-47; asso. dir. Nat. Health Council, 1947-49, sec., 1961; dir. community service and edn. Am. Heart Assn., 1949-57, asso. med. dir., 1957-59; exec. dir. Nat. Soc. Prevention Blindness, 1959-69. Sec. for Western Hemisphere, Internat. Assn. Prevention Blindness, 1959-69, sec. gen., 1968-69; mem. nat. adv. eye council NIH, 1968-70. Bd. dirs. Am. Found. Overseas Blind, from 1968, Nat. Accreditation Council for Agys. Serving Blind and Visually Handicapped, from 1967, Illuminating Engring. Research Inst., 1960-72. Dir. 1st Nat. Conf. on Cardiovascular Diseases, 1950. Trustee Mt. Pleasant Library, 1970-75. Served from lt. comdr. to comdr. M.C., USNR, 1942-46. Diplomate Am. Bd. Preventive Medicine And Pub. Health. Fellow Am. Pub. Health Assn., A.C.P., Am. Coll. Preventive Medicine; mem. Assn. State and Territorial Health Officers (sec. 1942), S.A.R., Alpha Omega Alpha, Beta Theta Pi, Nu Sigma Nu. Presbyn. Home: Pleasantville, N.Y. Died Oct. 24, 1975; buried Fairview Cemetery, Bluffton, Ind.

FERRELL, HARRISON HERBERT, educator; b. Chgo., Aug. 28, 1900; s. Harrison Herbert and Susanna (Reed) F.; B.S., Northwestern U., 1924, A.M., 1925, Ph.D., 1928; violin pupil Ludwig Becker, Columbia Sch. Music, Chgo.; L.H.D., Culver Stockton Coll., 1964; LL.D., Marshall U., 1966; H.H.D., W.Va. State Coll., 1971; m. Emily Miriam Grazia Bell, Sept. 15, 1929. Research fellow Germanic philology Northwestern U., 1924-27; prof., head dept. German, W.Va. State Coll., 1928-66, acting dean, 1930-32, asst. dean, 1932-33, acting registrar, 1934-35, registrar, 1935-37, dean, 1937-66; dir. Upward Bound project, prof. German, coordinator instl. studies W.Va. State Coll., 1966-70; adminstrv. asst. Guthrie Center, State W.Va. Dept. Mental Health, 1970-73. Dir. 5th Allegheny Regional Liberal Arts Conf., North Central Assn., W.Va. Wesleyan Coll., 1953. Violinist, founder and condr. Ferrell Symphony Orch. (founded as meml. to Harrison Herbert Ferrell, Sr.); pres. Chgo. Music Assn., 1928. Bd. dirs. W.Va. State College Strings; trustee, mem. exec. com. W.Va. Easter Seal Soc. Crippled Children and Adults, 1963-77, pres., 1971-73, chmn. Kanawha County com.; vice chmn. adv. bd. Bluefield (W.Va.) State Coll., 1970-77. W.Va. Black Cultural Festival dedicated to him, 1979; Adminstrn. Bldg. of W.Va. State Coll. named for him, 1980. Mem. MLA, Am. Tchrs. Assn., Nat. Assn. Negro Musicians (adv. bd. 1928-30), W.Va. Fgn. Lang. Assn. (sec. 1935-45), AAUP, NEA, W.Va. Edn. Assn. (mem. exec. com. 1955-57), W.Va. Assn. Higher Edn. (pres. 1954-55, chmn. program com. 1955-70), W.Va. Assn. Acad. Deans (pres. 1958-59, exec. com. 1959-60), W.Va. Arts and Humanities Council (chmn. 1976-77), Kappa Alpha Psi, Sigma Pi Phi. Lion (pres.). Dunbar 1972-73). Address: Institute, W.Va. Died Nov. 18, 1977; interred Lincoln Cemetery, Chgo.

FERRIS, DEWARD OLMSTED, surgeon, educator; b. Niagara Falls, Ont., Can., Jan. 5, 1907; s. Thomas Elward and Martha (Olmsted) F.; M.D., C.M., Queen's U., Kingston Ont., 1931; M.S. in Surgery, Mayo Found., U. Minn., 1941; m. Edythe Culcheth, Mar. 16, 1938; children—Nancy, William D. Came to U.S., 1937, naturalized, 1943. Intern Kingston Gen. Hosp., 1931, Hamilton Gen. Hosp., 1932; practice gen. medicine, Niagara Falls, Ont., 1933-37; asst. to surg. staff Mayo Clinic, 1937-45, mem. permanent staff, 1945-77, head surg. sect., 1945-77; mem. faculty Mayo Grad. Sch. Medicine, U. Minn., 1947-77, prof. clin. surgery, 1962-77. Diplomate Am. Bd. Surgery. Fellow A.C.S.; mem. Am., Minn. med. assns., Central, Western surg. assns., Internat. Soc. Surgery, Soc. Surgery Alimentary Tract, Minn. Surg. Soc., Zumbro Valley Med. Soc., Sigma Xi. Presbyn. Mason. Contbr. articles in field. Home: Rochester, Minn. Died Apr. 5, 1977.

FERRIS, FRANK HALLIDAY, clergyman, tchr.; b. Bklyn., May 5, 1892; s. Edwin Sherwood and Mary A. (Halliday) F.; grad. Hackensack High Sch., 1910; A.B., Amherst, 1914, A.M., Columbia U., 1917; B.D., Union Theol. Sem., 1917; Ph.D., Drew U., 1931; Dr. Divinity, Roanoke College, 1947; Litt.D., College of Wooster, Ohio, 1957; married Minna Proctor, May 15, 1917; children—Frank Halliday, Jr., Robert Proctor, Dorothy (Mrs. John G. Allen, Jr.), Jean Alden (Mrs. Peter Ruh). Ordained to Congl. ministry, 1917; transferred to Presbyn. ministry, 1920; pastor First Congl. Ch., Pulaski, New York, 1917-20, First Presbyterian Church, East Cleveland, Ohio, 1920-26, South Park Ch., Newark, N.J., 1926-31, Fairmount Presbyterian Church, Cleveland Heights, Ohio, 1931-50 (new edifice erected, 1941), pastor emeritus since 1950; vis. prof. of religion Coll. of Wooster (O.), 1952-56; instr. Chautauqua Instn., 1952-65, interim minister 1st Presbyn. Ch., Niagara Falls, N.Y., 1961-62, First Presbyn. Ch., Jamestown, N.Y., 1962-63, First Presbyn. Ch., Titusville, Pa., 1963-64. Lt. (j.g.) chaplain USN, 1917-19, on U.S.S. Mercy (cruiser and transport), U.S.S. Texas (fleet). Frank Halliday Ferris chair of philosophy established and endowed in his honor at Wooster (Ohio) Coll., 1964. Mem. Phi Beta Kappa, Delta Sigma Rho, Delta Tau Delta. Author: Standing Up to Life, 1953: The Perpetual Miracle, 1959. Contbr. to periodicals and anthologies. Home: Mayville, N.Y. Died Apr. 30, 1974.

FERRIS, WALTER, educator; b. Green Bay, Wis., Apr. 23, 1882; s. Hiram Jaynes and Harriet (Sanborn) F.; B.A., Beloit Coll., 1905; B.D., Yale, 1909; m. Alice J. Cheney, of New Haven, Conn., 1910. Instr. English, Yale, 1911-17; headmaster Roxbury Sch., 1917-24, now director. Mem. Authors' League of America, Dramatists' Guild, Sigma Chi (Beloit), Book and Snake (Yale). Conglist. Clubs: Graduate, Elizabethan, New Haven Country (New Haven, Conn.); Yale (New York); Highland Country (Meriden). Author of "The First Stone," play prod., New York, 1927. Home: Cheshire, Conn.

FESS, GILBERT M(ALCOLM), prof. modern langs., author; b. Alden, N.Y., July 10, 1886; s. Benjamin and Mary Emna (Mapes) F.; Ph.B., Alfred U., 1912; A.M., Syracuse U., 1914; Ph.D., U. of Pa., 1924; student Cornell U., U. of Mich., Université de Genéve, Université de Lausanne, Université de Clermont-Ferrand; m. Anka Doycheff, Dec. 26, 1931. Prof. modern langs. Hillsdale (Mich.) Coll., 1915-21, 1923-26, U. of Tenn., 1926-27, U. of Mo. since 1927. Mem. Modern Lang. Assn. of Mo. (pres.), Modern Lang. Assn. of Am., Am. Assn. Univ. Profs., Mo. Writers Guild, Delta Sigma Phi, Phi Sigma Iota, Phi Beta Kappa. Odd Fellow. Author books including: The American Revolution in Creative French Literature, 1941; also articles fiction, poetry in mags. Home: Columbia, Mo.

FICKEN, FREDERICK ARTHUR, educator; b. Moore's Hill, Ind., Aug. 13, 1910; s. Richard Oscar and Grace (Fagley) F.; A.B., Oberlin Coll., 1931; M.A., Ohio State U., 1932; B.A. (Rhodes scholar), Oxford (Eng.) U., 1934; Ph.D., Princeton, 1938; m. Mary Elizabeth Harman, Sept. 11, 1940; 1 son, William Harman. Instr. math. Cornell U., 1938-42; prof. math. U. Tenn., 1942-59; prof. math. University Heights, N.Y. U., 1959-73, chmn. dept., 1959-67; cons. to Operations Research Group USN, 1944-45; research asso. Inst. Math. Scis., N.Y. U., 1949-51; cons. Union Carbide Nuclear Co., Oak Ridge, 1946-64. Fellow A.A.A.S. (sec. Sect. A math. 1969-74); mem. Math. Assn. Am., Am. Math. Soc., A.A.U.P., Am. Civil Liberties Union, Soc. Indsl. and Applied Math., Phi Beta Kappa, Sigma Xi, Phi Kappa Phi. Author: The Simplex Method of Linear Programming, 1961; Linear Transformations and Matrices, 1967; also articles. Editor Am. Math. Monthly, 1962-66. Home: Pelham, N.Y. Died Dec. 20, 1978; buried Kensico Cemetery, Valhalla, N.Y.

FIDDES, CLYDE WILLIAM, ret. railroad exec.; b. Mpls., Aug. 26, 1907; s. William Gibson and Mathilde Cecile (Westerman) F.; B.A., U. Minn., 1930, J.D., 1932; postgrad. advanced mgmt. program Harvard, 1954; m. Alice Elizabeth Culhane, June 30, 1937. Admitted to Minn. bar, 1932, Tex. bar, 1955, Mo. bar, 1946, also U.S. Supreme Ct.; practice in Mpls., 1932-42; with legal service OPA and Office Def. Transp., Washington, 1942-43; with law dept. St. Louis Southwestern Ry. Co., Tyler, Tex., 1946-72, gen. solicitor, 1954-57, gen. counsel, 1957-72; dir. Memphis Union Sta. Co., 1969-72, St. Louis Southwestern Ry. Co. Tex., 1957-72. Served to capt. AUS, 1943-46. Mem. Assn. ICC Practitioners, Phi Delta Phi, Alpha Tau Omega. Roman Catholic. Clubs: Petroleum, Willow Brook Country (Tyler). Home: Tyler, Tex. Died Oct. 21, 1980; buried Rose Hill Cemetery, Tyler.

FIEDLER, ARTHUR, musical condr.; b. Boston, Dec. 17, 1894; s. Emanuel and Johanna (Bernfeld) F.; student Boston Latin Sch., 1907-10, Royal Acad. of Music, Berlin, 1911-15; M.A. (hon.), Tufts Coll., 1931; Mus.D., Boston U., 1951, Am. Internat. Coll., 1959, Southeastern Mass. Technol. Inst., 1965, Merrimack Coll., 1969, U. Mass., 1970, Tufts U., 1971, New Eng. Conservatory Music, 1971, Springfield Coll., 1971, Bowdoin Coll., 1973, U. Maine at Portland-Gorham, 1974, Our Lady of Lake Coll., 1974; D.F.A., Ripon Coll., 1960; D. Mus., U. Miami, 1963, Music and Arts Inst., San Francisco, 1963, Jacksonville University, 1964; D. Fine Arts, Northeastern U., 1966; D. Humanities, Glassboro State Coll., 1973; hon. degrees Stonehill Coll., 1976, Framingham Coll., 1976, Dartmouth Coll., 1976, Harvard U., 1976; m. Ellen M. Bottomley, Jan. 8, 1942; children—Johanna, Deborah, Peter. Made concert debut at age of 17; organized Boston Sinfonietta, 1924; organized Esplanade Concerts, Boston, 1929, condr., from 1929; condr. Boston Symphony Pops Concerts, from 1930; former condr. Cecelia Soc. Boston, U. Glee Club, Providence, MacDowell Club Orch. of Boston; mem. faculty Boston U.; mus. cons. VA, Boston; guest condr. at San Francisco, N.Y. Philharmonic, Mpls., Chgo., 1923, Montreal, Toronto, Dallas, Seattle N.B.C. Symphony, Portland, Phila., Japan, Korea. S. Africa, Australia, New Zealand, Europe, S.Am., Eng., others; condr. RCA Victor Broadcast. Served in U.S. Army, World War I and World War II. Decorated Croix de l'Officier d'Academie; chevalier Legion of Honor (France), 1954; named number 8 in classical field Top Artists on Campus Poll, 1968; col. on staff Gov. of Ky., 1946; hon. Fire Chief in about 350 cities of world; recipient certificate of appreciation USIA, 1975; medal for multitude of broadcasts Voice of Am., 1975; Humanitarian of Year award March of Dimes, 1975; Boston medal Emmanuel Coll., 1976; Distinguished Pub. Service award USN, 1976; Morality in Media award, 1976; Sword of Loyola, Loyola U., Chgo., 1976; Presdl. Medal of Freedom, Pres. Gerald R. Ford, 1977; certificate of merit for outstanding contbns. in field of music Stereo Rev., 1977; Am. Exemplar medal Freedoms Found. at Valley Forge, 1977. Mem. Harvard Musical Assn. Boston Soc. Recorded Music (pres.). Home: Brookline, Mass. Died July 10, 1979.

FIELD, RICHARD H., lawyer, educator; b. Phillips, Maine, May 29, 1903; s. Daniel F. and Clara E. (Hinckley) F.; grad. Phillips Exeter Acad., 1922; A.B., Harvard, 1926, LL.B. magna cum laude, 1929; m. Carolyn Crosby, June 28, 1930 (dec. Sept. 1966); children—Mary (Mrs. Rienzi B. Parker, Jr.), Margaret (Mrs. David L. Aronson), Daniel; m. 2d, Laura Deane Shaw, Apr. 19, 1968; stepchildren—Robert, Christopher, Elisabeth, Caleb, Arthur, Caroline. Admitted to Mass. bar, 1929, Maine bar, 1973; mem. firm Brown, Field & McCarthy, Boston, 1930-42; asst. counsel spl. comn. on control and conduct pub. utilities Mass. State, 1929-30; regional atty. O.P.A., Boston, 1942-43, chief legal adviser to adminstr. and acting gen. counsel, Washington, 1943-44, gen. counsel, 1944-46; vis. prof. law Harvard Law Sch., 1946-47, prof., 1947-68, Story prof., 1968-73, emeritus, 1973-78; of counsel Murray, Plumb & Murray, Portland, Maine, 1973-78; vis. Am. prof. Inst. Advanced Legal Studies, U. of London, 1970-71. Cons., Econ. Stblzn. Adminstrn., 1950-51, Maine Adv. Commn. on Rules of Evidence, 1973-78. Mem. bd. selectmen Town of Weston (Mass.), 1956-58, town moderator, 1962-68. Pres. bd. trustees Cambridge Sch., 1949-55. Fellow Am. Bar Found.; mem. Am. Law Inst. (chief reporter div. of jurisdiction between state and fed. courts 1960-68), Am., Mass., Maine bar assns. Permanent sec. Harvard Class of 1926, 1926-51. Author: (with Benjamin Kaplan) Materials for a Basic Course in Civil Procedure, 1953, rev. 1968, 73; (with V.L. McKusick) Maine Civil Practice, 1959, (with V.L. McKusick and L.K. Wroth) 2d edit., 1970; (with P.L. Murray) Maine Evidence, 1976. Home: South Freeport, Maine. Died Jan. 26, 1978.

FIELD, WOOSTER BARD, architect, educator; born Columbus O., July 29, 1886; s. Henry Waterman and Emma Jeanette (Thompson) F.; C.E. in Architecture, Ohio State U., 1911; m. Margie Fulkman, June 10, 1912. Began practice architecture, 1912; with Schenck & Wiliams, Dayton, 1912-13, Howell & Thomas, Columbus, O., 1913-14, Richards, McCarty & Bulford, Columbus, 1915-17; teacher drawing Columbus Trades Sch., 1917; instr. engring. drawing, Ohio State U., 1917-21, asst. prof., 1921-30, asso. prof., 1930-36, prof. since 1936. Mem. Am. Inst. Architects, Am. Soc. for Engring. Education, Theta Xi, Tau Sigma Delta. Republican. Baptist. Mason. Club: Faculty. Author: Architectural Drawing, 1922; An Introduction to Architectural Drawing, 1932 (2d edition 1943); Spanish edit., 1946; House Planning, 1940. Home: Columbus, O.

FIELDEN, CLARENCE FRANKLIN, JR., health care adminstr.; b. Knoxville, Tenn., July 25, 1919; s. Clarence Franklin and Bonnie Carter (Dutton) F.; student U. Tenn., 1936-39, Harvard Grad. Sch. BUs., 1943; m. Georgia May Freeman, July 16, 1942; children—C. Franklin, Landis Michaux. Hosp. adminstr. and cons., 1946-70; sr. v.p. Med. Facilities, Inc., Nashville, 1968-70; pres. Med. Mgmt. Systems,

Memphis, 1970-72; pres. N.C. Hosp. Corp., Atlanta, 1972-73; health care cons. Jackson Enterprises, Indpls., 1973-74; pres. Health Care Mgmt. Corp., Atlanta, 1974-76; v.p. Psychiat. Inst. Am., Washington, 1976-79; chief adminstrv. officer St. Albans Hosp., Radford, Va., 1979-80; chmn. hosp. adv. bd. Nat. Data Communications; cons. Colo. Dept. Health. Served to capt. AUS, 1941-46. Research fellow Brit. Ministry Health, 1959. Fellow Royal Soc. Health, Internat. Hosp. Fedn., Inst. Hosp. Adminstrs.; mem. Am. Coll. Hosp. Adminstrs., Am., Ga., Colo., N.C. hosp. assns. Rotarian. Club: Richland Country. Contbr. articles to profl. jours. Home: McLean, Va. Died Dec. 8, 1980, buried Nashville.

FIELDING, JERRY, composer and arranger; b. Pitts., June 17, 1922; student Carnegie Inst. Tech.; m. Camille Williams; 4 daus. Composer scores for films: Advise and Consent, 1962, Crazy World of Laurel and Hardy, 1968, The Wild Bunch (nominee Acad. award), 1969, Johnny Got His Gun, 1971, Straw Dogs, 1971 (nominee Acad. award), The Nightcomers, 1971, Suppose They Gave a War and Nobody Came, 1970, The Mechanic, 1972, Lawman, 1971, Junior Bonner, 1972, Scorpio, 1973, The Super Cops, 1974, The Outfit, 1974, Chato's Land, 1972, Bring Me the Head of Alfredo Garcia, 1974, The Gambler, 1974, The Blackbird, 1975, The Killer Elite, 1975, The Bad News Bears, 1976, The Outlaw Josey Wales (nominee Acad. award), The Enforcer, 1976, Demon Seed, 1977, The Gauntlet, 1977, Gray Lady Down, 1978, The Big Sleep, 1978, Outlaw Josey Wales (Western Heritage award Cowboy Hall of Fame), 1978; TV themes for McMillan and Wife, Bionic Women; composer and arranger TV series Hogan's Heroes; compositions include: City of Brass, Polynesian Peace Chant, Paris Magicque, The Essence of Calculated Calm. Mem. Acad. Motion Picture Arts and Scis. Home: Hollywood, Calif. Died Feb. 17, 1980.

FIELDING, WILLIAM JOHN, author, editor; b. Wharton, N.J., Apr. 10, 1886; s. William and Mary (Mitchell) F., ed. public schools; m. Elizabeth C. Veale, of Newark, N.J., June 20, 1910 (now dec.); children—Elsie (dec.), John Carbis; m. 2d, Margaret L. Cameron, of East Orange, N.J., June 21, 1929. Editor Newark Leader, 1915-18; lit. editor New Jersey Leader, 1919-22; editor Know Thyself, 1923-24; dramatic editor Golden Rule Mag., 1925-27; Sketch Book Magazine since 1927. Mem. A.A. A.S., Am. Social Hygiene Assn., Am. Birth Control League, Soc. for Constructive Birth Control and Racial Progress (London), Freethinkers of America (honorary vice pres.), Author's League of America, Pi Gamma Mu. Author: Pebbles from Parnassus, 1917; Sanity in Sex, 1920 (Japanese ed., 1921); Psychoanalysis—the Key to Human Behavior, 1921; The Puzzle of Personality, 1922; The Caveman Within Us, 1922; Health and Self-Mastery Through Psycho-Analysis and Autosuggestion, 1923; Autosuggestion—How It Works, 1923; Rejuvenation, 1924; Rational Sex Series, 13 vols., 1924-25; Teeth and Mouth Hygiene (collaboration), 1925; Dual and Multiple Personalities, 1925; The Cause and Nature of Genius, 1926; Sex and the Love Life, 1927; Woman—the Eternal Primitive, 1927; Woman—the Criminal, 1928; Woman—the Warrior, 1928; Unconscious Love Elements in Psycho-Analysis, 1929; How the Sun's Rays Give Health, 1930; The Marvels and Oddities of Sunlight, 1930; Boccaccio—Lover and Chronicler of Love, 1930; The Art of Love, 1931; Love and the Sex Emotions, 1932; Sex in Civilization (symposia), 1929; The Shackles of the Supernatural 1938. Poems have appeared in several anthologies). Home: Newark, N.J.

FIELDS, EDWARD, carpet designer, mfr.; b. Bklyn., Dec. 4, 1912; s. Jon Jacob and Jeanette C. (Sewal) F.; student pub. schs.; m. Eleanor Feldstein, Nov. 10, 1935; 1 son, Jon Jacob. Various positions carpet mfg., 1928-35; organizer Edward Fields, Inc., N.Y.C., 1935, pres., 1935-79, also chmn. and chief exec. officer; established custom carpet mill, 1949; partner Calypso Textiles Co., N.Y.C., 1951-79; pres. Internat. Dyeworks, Inc., Flushing, N.Y., 1953-79; v.p. Williams Rug Co., Cedarhurst, N.Y., 1946-79; established 1st Am. tapestry factory, Flushing, N.Y. Served with U.S. Maritime Service, 1944-45. Mem. Am. Inst. Decorators, Nat. Soc. Interior Designers. Wove and donated 1st carpet made in modern times to White House; furnished custom carpeting for Exec. Mansion during adminstrns. of John F. Kennedy and Richard M. Nixon; designed spl. carpet for Air Force One during Lyndon B. Johnson adminstrn.; wove scenic tapestry for Am. Airlines passenger terminal, Dallas-Ft. Worth Internat. Airport. Home: New York, N.Y. Died Apr. 17, 1979; buried Mt. Hebron Cemetery, Flushing, N.Y.

FIELDS, HARVEY GOODWYN, lawyer; b. Marksville, Pa., May 31, 1884; s. Theodore Thomas and Carrie (Goodwyn) F.; student Ruston (La.) Poly. Inst., 1900-01, Bachelor of Industry, 1904; student La. State U., 1901-02, Tulane U., 1904-06; m. Evelyn Sanders, Dec. 31, 1908; 3 children. Teacher, 1902-19; admitted to La. bar, 1906, and in practice at Marksville, La., 1906-08; dist. atty. for Third Dist., La., 1922-25; State senator, La., 1916-20; pub. service commr. of La., 1927-36; U.S. atty. for Western Dist., La., Feb. 1937-June 1941 (apptd. by President). Former law partner of Huey P. Long; pres. La. Huey P. Long Memorial Foundation of Shreveport, La. Chmn. La. Dem. State Central Com., 1926-29. Del. to Dem. Nat. convs., 1924, 28, 32, 36. Mem. La. State Poly. Inst. Alumni (pres. 1930-32), Tau Kappa Nu. Democrat. Presbyterian, Elk, Odd Fellow, Woodmen of World. Writer; speaker. Club: Lions (Farmerville, La.). Address: Farmerville, La. *

FIELDS, TOTIE, comedienne; b. Hartford, Conn., May 7, 1930; student pub. schs., Conn.; m. George Johnston, May 19, 1951; children—Jody, Debbie. Comedienne, TV and night-clubs. Recipient Georgie award for Comedy Star of Year, AGVA, 1977. Home: Los Angeles, Calif. Died Aug. 2, 1978.

FIERMAN, HAROLD LEE, lawyer; b. N.Y.C., Apr. 1, 1898; s. Morris and Anne (Ackerman) F.; LL.B., Fordham U., 1919; m. Ruth Kaplan, Feb. 15, 1922 (dec.); children—Joan (Mrs. Alan Lerrick), Karel (Mrs. Sigmund Wahrsager) m. 2d, Minnie Ganz Sarnoff, Jan. 27, 1963. Admitted to N.Y. State bar, 1920; spl. counsel Kaye, Scholer, Fierman, Hays & Handler, N.Y.C., from 1922, dir., mem. exec. com. J.W. Mays, Inc.; dir. Petrie Stores Corp. Pres. Fierman Found., Inc.; trustee, v.p., mem. exec. com. Beth Israel Med. Center; trustee Mt. Sinai Sch. Medicine, Brandeis U. Mem. Am. Bar Assn. Clubs: Lawyers, Harmonie (N.Y.C.). Home: New York, N.Y. Died Aug. 1978.

FIESER, LOUIS FREDERICK, educator, chemist; b. Columbus, O., Apr. 7, 1899; s. Louis Frederick and Martha Victoria (Kershaw) F.; A.B., Williams Coll., 1920, hon. D.Sc., 1939; Ph.D., Harvard, 1924; postgrad., Frankfort-on-Main, 1924-25, Oxford U., 1925; Dr. honoris causa, U. Paris, 1954; m. Mary A. Peters, June 21, 1932. Asst. and asso. prof. chemistry Bryn Mawr Coll., 1925-30; asst. prof., asso. prof. chemistry Harvard, 1930-37, prof., 1937-39, Sheldon Emery prof. organic chemistry, 1939-68, prof. emeritus, 1968-77; scholar in residence State U. N.Y., 1969; Neilson prof. Smith Coll., spring 1968. Engaged in research relating to cancer and chemotherapeutic studies. Mem. Nat. Def. Research Com., 1940-46, Surgeon Gen.'s Adv. Com. Smoking and Health, 1963; cons. on cortisone synthesis. Mem. Alos Mission, ETO, U.S. Army. Served in O.T.C., 1918. Recipient Katherine Berkan Judd prize for work on cancer-producting hydrocarbons Meml. Hosp., 1941; award for teaching Mfg. Chemists Assn., 1959; Norris award, 1959; Nichols medal Am. Chem. Soc., 1963; Am. Chem. Soc. award in chem. edn., 1967. Fellow Nat. Acad. Sci., 1939. Author: Experiments in Organic Chemistry; (with Mary Fieser) Organic Chemistry, Style Guide for Chemists; Reagents for Organic Synthesis, 9 vols.; also over 300 research papers. Mem. editorial bds. Organic Syntheses, others. Home: Belmont, Mass. Died July 25, 1977.

FIFFER, ROBERT SEYMOUR, lawyer; b. Chgo., Oct. 11, 1926; s. Gene S. and Celia (Harris) F.; A.B., U. Chgo., 1944, J.D., 1947; m. Elaine Rose, Oct. 29, 1947; children—Steven J., James, Thomas. Admitted to Ill. bar, 1948; in law practice with Archie H. and Nathan M. Cohen, 1948-53; partner law firm Fiffer and DeAngelo, Chgo. Chmn. Ill. Employment Security adv. Bd., 1961-72; mem. Ill. Commn. on Human Relations, 1962-68; master in chancery Circuit Ct. of Cook County, 1963-65; sec., gen. counsel Balt. Colts; gen. counsel Chgo. Press Club; mem. Ill. Cemetery Care Adv. Bd. Vice pres. Jewish Community Centers Chgo. Mem. Am., Ill., Chgo. bar assns., Am. Judicature Soc., Decalogue Soc. Lawyers, Phi Sigma Delta. Club: Standard (Chgo.). Home: Glencoe, Ill. Died Feb. 1975.

FILBERT, ROBERT BROBST, JR., research co. exec.; b. Womelsdorf, Pa., Feb. 15, 1921; s. Robert Brobst and Helen R. (Luft) F.; B.S., Pa. State U., 1941, M.S., 1947; m. Joan Marie Brown, July 1, 1950; children—Thomas R., Anne R. Design engr. Hercules Powder Co., Wilmington, Del., 1940-43; research engr., div. chief, mgr. research and devel., corporate mgr. property devel. Battelle Meml. Inst., Columbus, O., from 1947. Resident cons. to govt. Chile, Santiago, 1970-71. Mem., chmn. Municipal Devel. Commn., Worthington, O., from 1963, Citizens Research, Columbus, from 1965, Mid-Ohio Regional Planning Commn., Columbus, from 1972. Mem., pres. City Council, Worthington, 1956-63. Pres., trustee Engrs. Found. Ohio, Columbus. Served to lt. USNR, 1943-46. Named Tech. Man of Year, Columbus Tech. Council, 1957. Registered profl. engr., Ohio. Fellow Am. Inst. Chemists; mem. Ohio Soc. Profl. Engrs. (citation of merit 1967), Am. Inst. Chem. Engrs. (nat. dir. from 1971), Am. Chem. Soc., Chemists Club N.Y., Ohio, Greater Columbus chambers commerce, Phi Eta Sigma, Tau Beta Pi, Pi Mu Epsilon, Phi Lambda Upsilon. Methodist. Editor: Liquid Propellants Handbook, 1958; Process Chemistry in Progress in Nuclear Energy, Series III, Vol. 2, 1958. Contbr. articles profl. jours. Patentee in field. Home: Worthington, Ohio. Deceased.

FILBEY, FRANCIS STUART, labor union ofcl.; b. Wrightsville, Pa., July 4, 1907; s. Harry Stuart and Elizabeth (Lambert) F.; grad. pub. schs.; m. Evelyn Irene Schminke, June 18, 1926; children—Harry Stuart, Elizabeth (Mrs. William Lawrence Smith). Post office clk., Balt., 1926-62; pres. Balt. Fedn. Labor, 1954-58; pres. Balt. Council AFL-CIO Unions, 1959-62; adminstrv. aide United Fedn. Postal Clks., 1962-69, pres., 1969-71; gen. pres. Am. Postal Workers Union, 1971-77. Served with AUS, 1944-45. Moose. Home: Silver Spring, Md. Died May 17, 1977.

FINCH, EDWIN PERKINS, ret. tobacco co. exec.; b. Henderson, N.C., May 9, 1910; s. Edwin G. and Ida (Fox) F.; A.B., Duke, 1932; m. Lucy Marshall Goode, Feb. 3, 1940; 1 dau., Anne Marshall. With Brown & Williamson Tobacco Corp., Louisville, from 1932, exec. v.p., 1962-64, pres., 1964-73, chmn. and chief exec. officer, 1973, also dir.; dir. First Nat. Bank of Louisville; mem. Ky.-Tenn. adv. bd. Liberty Mut. Ins. Co. Mem. Alpha Tau Omega. Clubs: Louisville Country, Pendennis (Louisville). Home: Louisville, Ky. Died July 16, 1976.

FINCH, PETER, actor; b. London Eng., Sept. 28, 1916; ed. Sydney, Australia. Stage debut in While Parents Sleep, Australia, 1935; appeared in motion pictures including The Nun's Story, Operation Amsterdam, Kidnapped, Rachel Cade, Trials of Oscar Wilde, No Love for Johnnie, Breaking Point, In the Cool of the Day, Girl With Green Eyes, The Pumpkin Eater, Judith, The Flight of the Phoenix, 10:30 on a Summer's Evening. Died Jan. 14, 1977.

FINE, SIDNEY HENRY, businessman, fgn. service officer; b. Yonkers, N.Y., Dec. 11, 1906; s. Max and Anna (Steinberg) F.; student Columbia University, 1929-30; asso. degree in pub. adminstrn., Am. U., 1957, B.A. in Polit. Sci., 1963; m. Margery I. Wood, Aug. 2, 1947; children—Barbara A., David E. Reporter, Newark Star-Eagle, 1926-29; rewriteman N.Y. American, 1929, N.Y. Daily Investment News, 1929-32; reporter, rewriteman N.Y.C. News Assn., 1933-41; editor, field corr. FCC, 1941-44; writer OWI, 1944-45; cultural affairs officer Am. embassy. Moscow, 1945-46; information officer Dept. Commerce, 1946-48; press relations officer ECA, Paris, France, 1948-53, U.S. Mission to NATO, Paris, 1953; dir. Office Pub. Information, U.S. Information Agy., 1954-57; assigned Russian Lang. study Georgetown U., 1957-58; pub. relations officer Am. Nat. Exhbn., Moscow, 1959; 1st sec. Am. legation, Sofia, Bulgaria, 1960-62; pub. affairs adviser Bur. African Affairs, Dept. of State, 1962-69; pres. The Map Store, Washington, 1972-81. Mem. Fgn. Service Assn., Pi Sigma Alpha. Club: Nat. Press (Washington). Home: Bethesda, Md. Died Apr. 18, 1981.

FINEGAN, JAMES JOSEPH, ry. ofcl.; b. Nyack, N.Y., Aug. 10, 1904; s. James P. and Jane (Burke) F.; student Drake's Bus. Coll., N.Y.C.; m. Marie Livingston, Aug. 3, 1930; children—James W., William F., Robert J., Ann Therese. With T.&P. Ry., N.Y., 1920-66, successively clk., sec., chief clk. to sec.-treas., asst. sec., asst. treas., sec., asst. to exec. v.p., asst. to pres., 1920-56, v.p., 1956-66; pres., dir. New Orleans Pacific Ry. Co.; v.p., dir., mem. exec. com. Trans-Miss. Terminal Co., Fort Worth Belt Ry. Co., Denison & Pacific Suburban Ry. Co., Texas-New Mexico Railway Co., Tex. Pacific-Mo. Pacific Terminal R.R. of New Orleans, Weatherford, Mineral Wells & Northwestern Ry. Co.; v.p., dir. Abilene & So. Ry. Co., Eagle Ford Land & Indsl. Co., Mchts. Cold Storage Co.; dir., mem. exec. com. Tex. & Pacific Motor Transport Co., Great Southwest R.R., Inc.; dir., mem. finance com. Trailer Train Co.; sec. Tex. M.P.R.R. Co. Clubs: Cipango, Imperial, Downtown, City, Dallas Athletic (Dallas); Serra Internat.; Ft. Worth (Tex.). Home: Dallas, Tex. Died May 6, 1975.

FINEMAN, HAYIM, prof. English lit.; b. Russia, Feb. 12, 1886; s. Morris J. and Bella (Diamond) F.; A.B., U. of Pa., 1907, Ph.D., 1917; m. Simma Abuhove, of Phila., June 4, 1911; 1 son, Daniel A. With Temple U. since 1910, prof. English lit. and head of English dept. since 1911. Sec. of Labor Commn. to investigate conditions in Palestine, 1919-20. Trustee Teachers' Sem. of N.Y. Mem. Modern Lang. Assn. America. Author: John Davidson, a Study of His Ideas and Poetry, 1916; Poale Zionism, 1918; Report of Zionist Labor Commission, 1921. Home: Philadelphia, Pa.

FINERTY, ROY E., banker; b. Jerseyville, Ill., Jan. 2, 1886; s. Frank C. and May C.F.; ed. grade and high schs., Oklahoma City; LL.B., U. of Mich., 1908; m. Alice E. Kirkpatrick, of Oklahoma City, Apr. 7, 1909; 1 dau., Alleyne. Farm mortgage business, Oklahoma City, since 1908; pres. and gen. mgr. Finerty Investment Co. since 1914; chmn. bd. Fidelity Nat. Bank. Republican. Presbyn. Clubs: Oklahoma, Oklahoma Golf and Country. Home: Oklahoma City, Okla.

FINKEL, LEONARD E., mfg. co. exec.; b. N.Y.C., 1906; LL.B., N.Y. U., 1928; m. Helen Kuriloff; children—Donald, Gail Calder, Leslie Gabosh. Admitted to N.Y. State bar, 1930, practiced law until 1940; with Finkel Umbrella Frame Co., N.Y.C., 1939-65, co. acquired by Aberdeen Mfg. Corp., 1965; pres., chmn. bd., chief exec. officer, dir. Aberdeen Mfg. Corp., N.Y.C., 1965-70, chmn. exec. com., 1970-80; former mem. adv. bd. Bronx br. Mfrs. Hanover Trust Co. Clubs: Masons (past master), N.Y. U., Beach Point,

Rotary (past pres. Bronx club). Home: Larchmont, N.Y. Died Jan. 21, 1980.

FINKELSTEIN, HERMAN N., lawyer; b. Syracuse, N.Y., Aug. 31, 1900; s. Simon J. and Hannah (Breger) F.; B.A., Coll. City N.Y., 1921; J.D., Columbia, 1924, S.J.D., 1932; m. Theresa Oakes, Oct. 26, 1926; children—Anne Oakes (Mrs. Stephen Kandel), Michael Oakes. Admitted to N.Y. bar, 1925, since practiced in N.Y.C.; counsel firm Nickerson, Kramer, Lowenstein, Nessen, Kamin & Soll 1973-77. Trustee Eastern Gas and Fuel Assos. Author: Legal Aspects of Commercial Letters of Credit, 1930. Home: New York, N.Y. Died June 24, 1977.

FINKENBINDER, ERWIN OLIVER, psychologist; b. Kent, Ill., Aug. 22, 1884; s. David Oliver and Emma Elizabeth (Werkheiser) F.; grad. State Normal Sch., De Kalb, Ill., 1908; A.B., U. of Ill., 1910; A.M., Clark U., 1911, Ph.D., 1913; m. Lena Althea Walworth, of Urbana, Ill., June 27, 1912. Teacher elementary schs., 1903-05; fellow and research asst. in exptl. psychology, Clark U., 1910-13; instr. psychology and edn., State Normal Sch., Milwaukee, Wis., 1913-20; in charge dept. of research, U.S. Govt. Social Hygiene Sch., Milwaukee, 1918-20; head of dept. and prof. edn., in charge bur. placement of teachers, Cornell Coll., Mt. Vernon, Ia., 1920-21; prof. edn. and in charge Psychol. Lab., Ia. State Teachers Coll. since 1921. Mem. Nat. Soc. for Study of Edn., A.A.A.S., Ia. Acad. Science, Kappa Delta Pi. Lutheran. Mason. Contbr. to psychol. and ednl. mags. Home: Cedar Falls, Ia.

FINLETTER, THOMAS KNIGHT, lawyer, former ambassador; b. Phila., Nov. 11, 1893; s. Thomas Dickson and Helen (Grill) F.; ed. Episcopal Acad., Phila., 1905-10; A.B., U. Pa., 1915, LL.B., 1920, LL.D., 1950; LL.D., U. Rochester, 1950, Syracuse U., 1950, Coll. St. Joseph, 1951, Rutgers U., 1959; m. Gretchen Blaine Damrosch, July 17, 1920 (dec. Dec. 1969); children—Margot (Mrs. John F.B. Mitchell), Lili (Mrs. Lee O'Neill); m. 2d, Eileen Wechsler Geist, Jan. 13, 1973. Admitted to Pa. bar, 1920, N.Y. bar, 1921; lawyer with Cravath & Henderson, 1920-26; partner Coudert Brothers, 1926-41, 44-50, 53-61; lectr. U. Pa. Law Sch., 1931-41; spl. asst. to sec. of state, Washington, 1941-44; cons. to U.S. delegation to UN Conf. on Internat. Orgn., San Francisco, May 1945; chmn. President's Air Policy Commn., 1947-48; minister in charge E.C.A. Mission to U.K., 1948-49; sec. of air force, 1950-53; U.S. ambassador NATO, 1961-65. Capt. F.A., U.S. Army, 1917-19. Mem. Council Fgn. Relations, Bar Assn. City N.Y., Delta Phi. Clubs: Knickerbocker, Century (N.Y.); Metropolitan (Washington); Athenaeum (London). Author: Principles of Corporate Reorganization, 1937; Cases on Corporate Reorganization, 1938; The Law of Bankruptcy Reorganization, 1939; Can Representative Government Do the Job?, 1945; Power and Policy, 1954; Foreign Policy; The Next Phase, 1960; Interim Report, 1968. Address: New York, N.Y. Died Apr. 24, 1980.

FINLEY, DAVID EDWARD, ret. museum ofcl.; b. York, S.C., Sept. 13, 1890; s. David Edward and Elizabeth Lewis (Gist) F.; A.B., U. S.C., 1910, Litt.D., 1950; LL.B., George Washington Law Sch., 1913, LL.D., 1960; Arts D., Yale, 1946; L.H.D., Georgetown U., 1960; m. Margaret Morton Eustis, June 10, 1931. Practiced law, Phila., 1915-17. Served as 2d lt. U.S. Army, 1917-18; asst. counsel War Finance Corp., 1921-22; mem. war loan staff U.S. Treasury, 1922-27; spl. asst. to sec. treasury, 1927-32; adviser Am. delegation London Financial Conf., July 1931; hon. counselor Am. embassy, London, Eng., 1932-33; practiced law, Washington, 1933-37; dir. Nat. Gallery of Art, 1938-56. Pres. Am. Assn. Museums, 1945-49; chmn. U.S. Commn. Fine Arts, 1950-63; chmn. Nat. Trust for Historic Preservation, 1950-62; v.p. Internat. Council of Museums, 1946-49; chmn. U.S. Nat. Com. on Internat. Cooperation among Museums, 1945-49; vice chmn. Am. Commn. for Protection and Salvage of Artistic and Historic Monuments in War Areas, 1943-46, chmn. White House Historical Assn., 1961-77; mem. Nat. Protrait Gallery Commn. and Nat. Collection Fine Arts Commn. of Smithsonian Instn., 1967; mem. Washington Nat. Monument Soc.; trustee emeritus Corcoran Gallery of Art. Mem. Com. The People-to-People Program, 1956-60. Recipient Theodore Roosevelt Distinguished Service medal, 1957; Henry medal Smithsonian Inst., 1967. Hon. fellow Nat. Sculpture Soc.; hon. mem. A.I.A.; mem. Assn. Art Museum Dirs., Sigma Alpha Epsilon, Phi Delta Phi, Phi Beta Kappa. Episcopalian. Mason. Clubs: Metropolitan, Alibi, Chevy Chase (Washington); Century (N.Y.). Home: Washington, D.C. Died Feb. 1, 1977.

FINLEY, ROBERT CORPENING, judge; b. Marion, N.C., Nov. 7, 1905; s. Robert Sylvester and Willie Grace (Corpening) F.; A.B., Duke U., 1930, LL.B., 1934; LL.M., Georgetown U., 1936; m. Werdna Karen Phillips, Dec. 4, 1937; children—Patricia Helen Karen, Robert Andrew, Mary Ellen. Admitted to Wash bar, 1941, D.C. bar, 1935; atty. Fed. Housing Adminstrn., 1934-35; examiner-atty. Alcohol Control Administrn., 1935-37; probation officer U.S. Dist. Ct., Bur. Prisons, Dept. of Justice, Western N.C., 1937-38; alien property custodian and claims div. Dept. Justice, 1938-40; asst. atty. gen. State Wash., 1940-42; dist. enforcement atty. O.P.A., State Wash., 1942-44; dir. food enforcement O.P.A., Washington, 1944-45; pvt. law practice, Seattle and Renton, Wash., 1945-51; judge Supreme Ct., State Wash., 1951-76, chief justice, 1961-62, 67-68. Mem. Am., Washington State, Seattle bar assns. Order of Coif, Pi Kappa Alpha. Club: Iredell Law (Duke U.). Wash. bar assns. Home: Tumwater, Wash. Died Mar. 24, 1976.

FINN, FENTON HARRISON, consultant; b. Ridgway, Pa., June 27, 1904; s. Charles H. and Louise A. (Van Aken) F.; B.S., Carnegie Inst. Tech., 1928, E.M., 1942; m. Jeanette Folmar, July 8, 1930. Field geologist, subsidiaries Columbia Gas & Electric Co., Pitts., also Binghamton, N.Y., 1928-32; geologist, N.Y. State Natural Gas Corp., 1932-39, chief geologist, prodn. engr., 1939-42, v.p., 1951-53, pres. and dir., 1953-60; geologist Peoples Natural Gas Co., Wellsboro, Pa., also Pitts., 1932-39, chief geologist, prodn. engr., Pitts., 1939-42; system chief geologist, dir., mem. exec. com. Consol. Natural Gas Co., Pitts., 1942-60, cons. geologist and engr., from 1960, cons. other cos. Recipient Carnegie Inst. Tech. Alumni merit award, 1960. Registered profl. engr. State of N.Y. Fellow Geol. Soc. Am., A.A.A.S.; mem. Am. Assn. Petroleum Geologists, Am. Gas Assn., Am. Petroleum Inst., Am. Inst. Mining and Metall. Engrs., Tau Beta Pi, Beta Theta Pi. Clubs: University, Duquesne. Contbr. articles profl. publs. Home: Pittsburgh, Pa. Died Oct. 21, 1978.

FINN, SIDNEY BERNARD, dentist; b. Freedom, Pa., Feb. 2, 1908; s. Abel and Rebecca (Gordon) F.; B.A., Ohio State U., 1930; M.S., U. Rochester, 1940; D.M.D., Harvard U., 1934; D. Odontology (hon.), Umea (Sweden) U., 1977; m. Irma Harriet Rubens, May 7, 1938; children—Catherine Ruth Finn Fitzpatrick, Andrew Alan. Practice dentistry, Rochester, 1935-38; asso. research dentist N.Y. State Dept. Health, 1944-50; prof. dentistry, chmn. dept. pedodontics U. Ala., Birmingham, 1951-68, prof. dentistry, chmn. applied research Inst. Dental Research, Med. Center, 1968-74, prof. emeritus, 1974-79; Lister Hill lectr., 1974; cons. in field; mem. dental study sect. NIH, 1964-67; dir. Dental Clinics, Ala. Sch. for Deaf and Blind, Talladega, 1951-73. Carnegie fellow, 1939-40; hon. faculty mem. U. Santo Domingo, from 1957; recipient Fuller award U. Ala. Dental Alumni Assn., 1971; award of excellence Am. Soc. Dentistry for Children, 1968; Distinguished Faculty award U. Ala. Med. Center, 1970, Distinguished Alumni award Harvard Dental Sch., 1975. Fellow Am. Coll. Dentists, Am. Acad. Pedodontics; mem. ADA, U. Ala. Dental Alumni Assn., Internat. Assn. Dental Research. Author: Clinical Pedodontics, 1957-73; editor: The Biology of the Dental Pulp Organ, 1968; co-editor: Year Book of Dentistry, 1967-75. Home: Birmingham, Ala. Died June 6, 1979.

FINNEMANN, WILLIAM, bishop; b. Bueninghausen, Germany, Dec. 18, 1882; s. Bernard and Elizabeth (Nasse) F.; ed. in Germany, Holland and Austria; D.D., ex officio. Missionary priest, R.C. Ch., Province of Abra, Sept. 1912-18; prof. Latin and Greek. St. Mary's Coll., Techny, Ill., 1919-22; procurator for the Soc. of the Divine Word in the P.I., 1923-26; rector Holy Ghost Parish, Manila, 1926-29; consecrated titular bishop of Sora and apptd. auxiliary bishop of Manila, 1929; named first ordinary of Mindoro, Dec. 4, 1936; hon. member Permanent Com. Internat. Eucharist Congresses. K.C. Author of a Grammar of the Ilocano Language and translation of Extracts of the Holy Bible into Ilocano and Tagalog. Address: Calapan, Mindoro, P.I. *

FINNER, PAUL F(REDERICK), psychologist; born Arcadia, Wis., Nov. 19, 1883; s. Fred William and Louise (Garbe) F.; Ph.B., U. of Wis., 1911, Ph.D., 1923; A.M., U. of Chicago, 1915; m. Bertha Pearl Winn, Dec. 28, 1911; children—Winn Frederick, Richard Webster. Prin. elementary sch., Iron Mountain, Mich., 1907-09; prin. Scales Mound (Ill.) High Sch., 1909-10; supt. of school, Cassville, Wis., 1911-15; supt. of schools, Banger, Wis., 1917-18; fellow in psychology U. of Wis., 1916-17; head, dept. edn. and psychology State Teachers Coll., Mayville, N.D., 1918-22; head, dept. psychology and dir. lab. Fla. State Coll. for Women, 1922-47, Fla. State U., 1947-48, prof. psychology since 1948. Fellow A.A.A.A.; mem. Am. Assn. Univ. Profs., Am. Ethical Union, Psychometric Soc., Soc. Advancement Edn., Soc. for Religious Culture, Am. Statis. Assn., Am. Humanist Assn., Southern Soc. Philosophy and Psychology, Fla. Acad. Scis. (chmn. social sci. sect. 1948-49), Am., Fla. (pres. 1947; council 1948-49) psychol. assns., Fla. Edn. Assn. (chmn. sect. on mental hygiene 1938); Kappa Delta Pi, Phi Kappa Phi. Mason. Author: Introduction to Experimental Psychology, 1935. Home: Tallahassee, Fla.

FINNERUD, CLARK WYLIE, dermatologist, syphilologist; b. Watertown, S.D., Apr. 3, 1895; s. Hans Martin and Mary Alice (McIntyre) F.; B.S., U. of Wis., 1916; M.D., Rush Med. Coll., U. of Chicago, 1918; post-grad. student Vienna, Paris and London, 1924-25; married Gertrude Delight Putnam, February 28, 1922; children—Ann (Mrs. C. Bartlett Sprague), Mary (Mrs. John Sherman Ashby, Jr.). Interne Presbyterian Hospital, Chicago, 1918-19; instructor dermatology and syphilology, Rush Medical College, 1919-27, asst. clin. prof., 1927-40; Rush asst. prof. dermatology and syphilology, U. Ill., 1940-43, asso. prof., 1943-61, emeritus, 1961-77; cons. dermatologist Fresh Air Fund Sanitorium Chicago, from 1930, also for C.M.&St.P. R.R., and to Department Public Health, State of Ill., Springfield, Ill., Chicago Eye, Ear, Nose and Throat Hosp., Chicago Tumor Inst.; dermatologist Presbyn. Hosp., 1925-58; cons. dermatologist Presbyn. St. Lukes Hospital, 1958-77; Children's Meml. Hosp., Chgo., 1920-32, Cook County Hosp., 1925-32, Central Free Dispensary, Rush Med. Coll., from 1918. Served Med. Reserve Corps, O.T.C., World War I. Mem. sub-com. on medical food requirements of Nat. Research Council 1943-46. Member of International Dermatological Congress, Budapest, 1935; delegate to International Dermatological Congress, Stockholm, 1957, Washington, 1962. Clark W. Finnerud ann. award established in his honor Am. Dermatology Found. Diplomate American Bd. Dermatology and Syphilology. Corr. mem. Wiener Dermatologische Gesellschaft (Vienna), Swedish (Stockholm), Austrian dermatol. socs., A.M.A. (chairman sci. exhibit com. sect. on dermatology and syphilology, 1935-38; chmn. sect. on dermatology and syphilology, 1942-44), Am. Acad. Dermatology and Syphilology (hon. mem., lecturer and dir. 1938-40; v.p. 1940; chmn. scientific exhibit com. 1940), Am. Dermatol. Assn. (hon. mem., pres. 1957-58), Am. Soc. Investigative Dermatology (v.p. 1941-42), Ill. Med. Soc., Inst. Medicine, Chgo., Chgo. Med. Soc., Chgo. Dermatol. Soc. (pres. 1927), Am. Assn. Ry. Surgeons, Nu Sigma Nu, Chi Psi, Sigma Sigma. Republican. Conglist. Clubs: University (Chicago). Co-author: Cutaneous Diseases of Congenital Origin, 1926; Diseases of the Mouth, 1936; Skin Diseases of Children, 1937; Diseases of the Skin, 1937; Surgical Diseases of the Skin, 1941-42, contbr. to med. books and jours. Home: Minocqua, Wis. Died Oct. 10, 1977; interred Hills of Rest, Sioux Falls, S.D.

FINNEY, HARRY ANSON, author, accountant; born Postville, Ia., Nov. 19, 1886; s. Solon B. and Ellen (Bike) F.; Ph.B., U. of Chicago, 1913; grad. work in accounting, Northwestern U., 1915-16; C.P.A., Ill., 1917; m. Lois Ingram, Nov. 24, 1920; children—Richard Anson, Stephen Ingram, Janet Sue; married second, Hazel M. Hale, February 9, 1946. Member Baumann, Finney & Co., certified public accountants, retired; formerly prof. accounting, Northwestern U. Mem. Am. Inst. Accountants, Ill. Soc. C.P.A. (expres.), Am. Accounting Association, Delta Sigma Pi, Beta Gamma Sigma, Acacia. Methodist. Mason. Author books including: Corporation and Manufacturing Accounting, 1942. Editor students' dept. Jour. of Accountancy, 1920-29. Home: Chgo. *

FINNEY, THOMAS DUNN, JR., lawyer; b. Idabel, Okla., Jan. 20, 1925; s. Thomas Dunn and Bettie (Higgs) F.; A.B., U. Okla., 1945, LL.B., 1948; m. Sally Van Horn, June 25, 1945; children—Susan Finney Ford, Kathleen Finney Jaxtheimer, Deirdre, Thomas Dunn III. Admitted to Okla. bar, 1948, D.C. bar, 1963; partner firm Finney & Finney, Idabel, 1948-51; with U.S. Fgn. Service, Copenhagen, 1952-55; with firm Foliart, Hunt & Shepherd, Oklahoma City, 1955-57; adminstrv. asst. to U.S. Senator A.S. (Mike) Monroney, 1957-63; mem. firm Clifford, Glass, McIlwain & Finney, and predecessor, Washington, 1963-78; dir. Continental Airlines. Trustee Citizens' Research Found.; trustee Green Acres Sch., Bethesda, Md., 1968-72, pres., 1969-71; mem. staff Presdl. Task Force Fgn. Policy, 1960; dep. spl. asst. to President Kennedy for fgn. trade policy, 1962; spl. counsel to credentials com. Democratic Nat. Conv., 1964. Served to lt. (j.g.) USNR, 1943-46. Mem. Am., Okla., D.C., Fed. bar assns., Am. Judicature Soc., Phi Gamma Delta, Phi Delta Phi, Delta Sigma Rho. Unitarian. Clubs: Nat. Lawyers, Federal City (Washington). Home: Bethesda, Md. Died Jan. 30, 1978.

FISCHER, EMIL EISENHARDT, clergyman, educator; b. Philadelphia, Pa., July 14, 1882; s. Christian G. and Emily (Eisenhardt) F.; A.B., Rutgers, 1904, A.M., 1907; grad. Luth. Theol. Sem., Phila., 1907; D.D., Muhlenberg Coll., 1920, LL.D., 1948, L.H.D., 1952; D.D., Rutgers U., 1933; LL.D., Temple U., 1944; m. Anita Emily Lins, June 19, 1912; children—Theodore Lins, Jean (Mrs. L. M. Reese). Ordained Lutheran ministry, 1907; pastor Holy Trinity Church, Brooklyn, 1907-13; instructor in Hebrew, Lutheran Theological Seminary, Philadelphia, 1910-13; pastor Christ Ch., Allentown, Pa., 1913-20; prof. systematic theology, Luth. Theol. Sem., Phila., 1920-43; president Lutheran Ministerium of Pa., 1943-53. Mem. Delta Upsilon. Republican. Author books: contbr. to publs. Home: Phila. *

FISCHER, HARVEY A., lawyer; b. Detroit, 1900; A.B., U. Mich., 1922, LL.B., 1924. Admitted to Mich. bar, 1924; mem. firm Fischer, Franklin & Ford, Detroit Mem. Am., Detroit bar assns., State Bar of Mich.

FISCHER, HERMAN ARTHUR, lawyer; b. Wheaton, Ill., Aug. 25, 1882; s. Herman A. and Julia Waters (Blanchard) F.; A.B., Wheaton Coll., 1903; LL.B., Harvard, 1908. Admitted to Ill. bar, 1908, since practiced in Chgo.; member law firm Fischer, Guy, Jacobson & Parker, and predecessor law firms, 1915—.

Pres. of the Gary-Wheaton Bank, 1931-52, chmn. bd., 1952-66; v.p., dir. Cuneo Press, Inc. Chmn. bd. trustees Wheaton College Member American, Illinois, Chicago, Du-Page Company bar associations, American Legion. Republican. Conglist. Clubs: Union League, Chicago Golf. Home: Wheaton, Ill.

FISCHER, JOHN, editor, writer; b. Texhoma, Okla., Apr. 27, 1910; s. John S. and Georgia (Caperton) F.; student U. Okla., 1928-32; Rhodes scholar Oxford (Eng.) U., 1933-35; LL.D., Kenyon Coll., 1954, Bucknell U., 1954; D.H.L., U. Mass., 1956; m. Elizabeth Wilson, 1936; children—Nicolas, Sarah. Reporter, Daily Oklahoman, Oklahoma City, Amarillo (Tex.) Globe-News, and other newspapers in Okla. and N.Mex., 1928-33; reporter U.P.I., Eng. and Germany, 1933-35, A.P., Washington, 1935-37; with U.S. Dept. Agr., 1937-42; various positions with Bd. Econ. Warfare, Washington, 1942-43; chief rep. Bd. Econ. Warfare and Fgn. Econ. Adminstrn. in India, 1943-44, in charge econ. intelligence and lend-lease; with Fgn. Econ. Adminstrn., Washington, 1944; asso. editor Harper's Mag., 1944-47, editor in chief, 1953-67, contbg. editor, 1967-78; cons./mem. selection com. Inst. Internat. Edn., John Hay Whitney Found., Rhodes Trust, Fund for Adult Edn., Nat. Book Com.; Regents prof. U. Calif.; lectr., U.S. and Europe; vis. fellow Yale. Mem. Presdl. Commn. on Rural Poverty, 1966-78. Trustee Brookings Instn. Recipient award Soc. Mag. Writers. Mem. Am. Polit. Sci. Assn., Phi Beta Kappa. Club: Century Assn. Author: Why They Behave Like Russians, 1947; Master Plan, U.S.A., 1951; The Stupidity Problem, 1964; Six in the Easy Chair, 1973; Vital Signs, U.S.A., 1975; From the High Plains, 1978. Contbr. articles to New Yorker, Harper's Reader's Digest, Life, etc. Home: Guilford, Conn. Died Aug. 18, 1978.

FISCHER, WILLIAM AUGUST, geologist; b. Litchfield, Ill., Jan. 6, 1919; s. August Ernst and Juliette Marie (Niemeyer) F.; B.S., McKendree Coll., Lebanon, Ill., 1940; student U. Ill., 1940-41; m. L. Blanche Youngblood, Sept. 8, 1941; children—Judith Lynn (Mrs. Court Soloff), William Jeffrey. Tchr. chemistry, physics Christopher (Ill.) High Sch., 1941; with U.S. Geol. Survey, 1941-44, 46-66, chief photogeology sect., 1950-60, charge lunar probe photometric analyses, 1960-62, research geologist charge remote sensing project, 1962-66, research coordinator Earth Resources Observation Systems Program, Dept. Interior, 1966-72, sr. scientist, 1972-80; prin. lectr. pilot course aerial surveys for geology UN, Tokyo, Japan, 1961. Rep. Dept. Interior orgn. meeting Orgn. Europeenen d'Edudes Photogrammetriques Experimentales, Brussels, Belgium, 1952; chmn. U.S. delegation UN seminar aerial survey methods, Bangkok, Thailand, 1960; chief U.S. rep. orgn. meeting UNESCO conf. integrated surveys, Paris, France, 1963; chief U.S. delegation Internat. Congress Photogrammetry, 1964; mem. com. remote sensing environment Nat. Acad. Scis., 1964-80. Served as officer USNR, 1944-46. Fellow A.A.A.S. (rep. council 1957-58), Am. Soc. Photogrammetry (pres. 1964-65, also dir., mem. exec. com.), Dept. Interior Recreation Assn. (pres. 1961). Club: Cosmos (Washington). Author numerous papers and maps. Home: Lake of the Woods, Va. Died July 29, 1980; buried Meml. Gardens, Falls Church (Va.) Episcopal Church.

FISCHETTI, JOHN, cartoonist; b. Brooklyn, N.Y., Sept. 27, 1916; s. Pietro and Emanuela (Navarra) F.; student Pratt Inst., 1937-40; D.F.A. (hon.) Colby Coll., 1969; m. Karen Mortenson, Oct. 25, 1948; children—Peter, Michael. Worked on animated films for Walt Disney; drew his 1st editorial cartoons for Chgo. Sun (now Sun-Times); did illustrations for Coronet, Esquire, Sat. Eve. Post, Collier's N.Y. Times; became syndicated cartoonist Newspaper Enterprise Assn., 1950, staff cartoonist N.Y. Herald Tribune, 1962; later cartoonist Publishers' Newspaper Syndicate (now subsidiary Field Enterprises Inc.); chief editorial cartoonist Chgo. Daily News; with Field Newspaper syndicate. Served with Signal Corps, AUS. Recipient Pulitzer Prize, 1969; named Best Editorial Cartoonist, Nat. Cartoonist Soc., 4 times, Sigma Delta Chi award, 1954, 56, Am. Civil Liberties award, 1972, N.Y. Newspaper Guild Front-page award, 1962. Home: Chicago, Ill. Died Nov. 18, 1980.

FISH, CHARLES JOHN, biol. oceanographer; b. Fall River, Mass., May 13, 1899; s. Charles Frederick and Emily Victoria (Teale) F.; Ph.B., Brown U., 1921, Sc.M., 1922, Ph.D., Feb. 10, 1923; Sc.D., U. R.I., 1966; m. Marie Dennis Poland, Feb. 10, 1923; 1 dau., Marilyn Poland (Mrs. J. Barnes Munro Jr.). Sci. asst. U.S. Bur. Fisheries, 1922-24, asso. hydrobiologist, 1924-27; dir. Buffalo Mus. Sci., 1928-34; asst. prof. zoology R.I. State Coll., 1934, asso. prof., 1935-36, prof. zoölogy, 1937, chmn. dept., 1938-48, prof. marine biology, 1948-62, prof. oceanography, 1962-66, prof. emeritus, 1966-78, acting dean grad. sch. of oceanography, 1961-62, dir. Narragansett Marine Lab., 1937-46, 48-66, adv. emeritus dir., 1966-78. Mem. council Yenching U., China, 1934-78; cons. marine biology, 1946-48; asso. in marine biology Woods Hole Oceanographic Inst., 1946-64, hon. staff, 1964-78; mem. fisheries adv. com. N.Y. World's Fair, 1939; mem. Atlantic Fisheries Biologists, 1940-78; mem. Gov.'s adv. council on R.I. Div. of Fish and Game, 1939-52; mem. North Atlantic Fisheries Commn., 1942-43; mem. internat. com. on oceanography Internat. Council of Sci. Unions, 1946-55; mem. U.S. com. on oceanography of Pacific, N.R.C., 1947-55; sci. adviser U.S. State Dept. Delegation Indo-Pacific Fisheries Council, Bangkok, 1954. Mem. econ. adv. com. N.E. Council Econ. Devel. and Regional Cooperation, Bd. dirs. R.I. Wildlife Fedn. Served with USNRF, 1918; from lt. comdr. to capt. USNR, 1942-46. Decorated Legion of Merit; Officer d'Academie (France), 1947; recipient Stamford Mus. award for sci. achievement, 1963; Charles J. Fish Oceanographic Lab. dedicated at U. R.I., 1960. Fellow A.A.A.S.; mem. R.I. Acad. Sci., Audubon Soc. R.I. (v.p. 1937-43), Am. Soc. Limnology and Oceanography, Phi Sigma, Phi Kappa Phi, Phi Beta Kappa, Sigma Xi, Theta Delta Chi. Episcopalian. Club: Kiwanis (hon.). Editor oceanographic sect. Am. Geophys. Union, 1944-47. Address: Kingston, R.I. Died Dec. 21, 1978; interred Oakgrove Cemetery, Fall River, Mass.

FISH, HAROLD DUFUR, educator; b. Tunbridge, Vt., Aug. 13, 1883; s. Edgar John (M.D.) and Eliza Ann (Lyman) F.; A.B., Dartmouth, 1906; student Dartmouth Med. Coll., 1907-08, Kan. State Agrl. Coll., 1912, Columbia, 1927-28; M.S., Harvard, 1915; m. Ethel Miriam Deering, Aug. 9, 1913; children—Edgar John (dec.) William Deering, David Hall. Supt. schs., Woodstock, Vt., 1909; head dept. of biology, Highland Coll., Highland, Kan., 1911-12; Austin teaching fellow in zoölogy, Harvard, 1913-14; asst. in zoölogy, Harvard and Radcliffe 1914-15; head dept. of zoölogy, Dennison U., 1915-19; prof. in charge of heredity, Marine Biol. Lab., Cold Spring Harbor, L.I., N.Y., summers 1919 and 1920; research asso. in genetics, Carnegie Inst., Washington, D.C., 1919-25; head dept. of zoölogy, U. of Pittsburgh, 1920-27; research asso. Pittsburgh Skin and Cancer Foundation, 1923-27; dir. Jungle Lab. of Tropical Biology, Kartabo, British Guiana, S.A., 1924-26; prof. genetics, dept. cancer research, U. of Mich., 1927-29; nat. dir. conservation Izaak Walton League, 1931; teacher gen. science, Nichols Sch., Evanston, 1932-38; prof. microscopic anatomy, Chicago Med. Sch., 1938-41; asst. mng. directory Am. Soc. for the Control of Cancer, 1941-42; dir. school service, 1943-47; coordinator research fellowships and grants Stritch Sch. of Medicine, Loyola University, 1949-50, professor zoology Loyola University, Chicago since 1950. Served as field asst. in increased crop production, United States Department of Agrl., 1918. Chmn. Tropical Research Bd. since 1929; mem. Nat. Research Council. Fellow A.A.A.S.; mem. Am. Soc. of Mammalogists, Ecol. Soc. of America, Eugenics Research Assn., Izaak Walton League, Ornithologists Union, Sigma Nu, Alpha Kappa Kappa, Gamma Alpha, Sigma Xi. Republican. Conglist. Mason. Clubs: Explorers, Harvard, Town Hall (New York); Lake Shore Athletic, Adventurers (Chicago); University (Evanston, Ill.). Lecturer on the tropics and their resources, conservation, education, evolution, heredity, cancer, etc. Home: Evanston, Ill.

FISHBEIN, MORRIS, physician, editor; b. St. Louis, Mo., July 22, 1889; s. Benjamin and Fanny (Gluck) F.; B.S., U. Chgo., 1910; M.D., Rush Med. Coll., 1912; D. Pharmacy (hon.), Rutgers U., 1942; LL.D. (hon.), Fla. So. Coll., 1957; D.Sc. (hon.), Chgo. Med. Sch., 1965; m. Anna Mantel, July 7, 1914; children—Barbara Fishbein Friedell, Morris (dec.), Marjorie Fishbein Clavey, Justin Mantel. Fellow in pathology Rush Med. Coll., 1912; asst. editor to editor Jour. of A.M.A., 1913-49; editor of Hygeia, until 1949; editor Bull. of Soc. of Med. History, Chgo.; contbg. editor Postgrad. Medicine, 1950-70; mem. chief bd. editors Excerpta Medica, 1949-71; editor Med. World News, 1960-75; med. editor Family Health Mag., 1969-76; chmn. sci. adv. bd. Municipal Tb San. and City of Hope; prof. emeritus medicine U. Ill. Coll. Medicine, U. Chgo.; editor med. sect. Britannica Book of Year, 1938-72; contbg. editor McCall's, 1959-67. Decorated knight comdr. Order of Crown of Italy; Nat. Order of Merit of Carlos J. Finlay (Cuba); Certificate of Merit from Pres. Truman, 1948; Comdr. Civil Order Health (Spain), 1952; officer's cross Order Orange-Nassau, Netherlands, 1954; comdr. cross Royal Order of Phoenix (Greece), 1967; recipient Jesse L. Rosenberger medal for achievements in pub. medicine and med. edn. U. Chgo., 1968, Willard Thompson medal Am. Gerontol. Soc., 1972. Mem. several profl., advt. coms. and orgns. Fellow Am. Pub. Health Assn.; mem. A.A.A.S., Phi Delta Epsilon, Alpha Omega Alpha, Sigma Delta Chi. Clubs: Variety, Lotos, Chgo. Literary, Quadrangle, The Tavern, Standard, Arts. Author numerous books, 1925-76, later ones include: Joseph Bolivar DeLee; Crusading Obstetrician (with Sol Theron DeLee), 1949, Handy Home Medical Adviser, 1972. Editor numerous books and reports, later ones include: Modern Family Health Guide, 1967; Heart Care, 1960; Modern Home Medical Adviser, 1969; Morris Fishbein, MD, Autobiography, 1969. Home: Chicago, Ill. Died Sept. 27, 1976.

FISHER, ADRIAN ROBERT, business exec.; b. New Brunswick, N.J., Mar. 27, 1895; s. William F. and Medora (Rose) F.; B.S. in Engring., Rutgers U., 1916; m. Grace Marie Booraem, Dec. 8, 1917; 1 dau., Wanda Elizabeth (Mrs. John J. Ludwig). Supt. roofing dept. Barber Asphalt Co., Perth Amboy, N.J., 1916-17; factory mgr. Stowell Mfg. Co., 1917-23; supt., factory mgr., prodn. mgr. Johns Manville Corp., N.Y. City, 1923-46, became sr. v.p. in charge prodn., 1946, pres., dir., 1951-58, chmn., chief exec. officer, 1957-58; ret., 1958; also pres., dir. Johns-Manville Dutch Brand Products Corp., Johns-Manville Sudamericana, Ltd., Canadian Johns-Manville Asbestos, Ltd., Johns-Manville Corps. of Ga., Oregon, California, Johns-Manville Construction Corporation, Canadian Johns-Manville Company, Limited, Southern Johns-Manville Products Corp., Johns-Manville Products Corp. of Mass., Johns-Manville Products Corp. of Pa., Johns-Manville Sales Corp., Johns-Manville Products Corp. Canadian Johns-Manville Ont., Ltd., Johns-Manville Internat. Corp., Rhodesian Asbestos Ltd.; dir. Asbestos & Danville Ry. Co., Johns-Manville Co., Ltd. Mem. Delta Kappa Epsilon. Republican. Conglist. Clubs: Yale, Union League, Pinnacle. Home: Belleair, Fla. Died Dec. 18, 1976.

FISHER, BOYD, author; b. Council Bluffs, Ia., May 26, 1886; s. Charles Simmons and Carrie Lillian (Patton) F.; A.B., Harvard, 1910; spl. student Cass Tech. High Sch., Detroit, 1914-15; unmarried. Pres. Peoples Recreation Co., N.Y. City, 1913, also mgr. Efficiency Soc.; v.p. Executive Club, Detroit, Mich., 1914; consultant in management, 1919; dir. of personnel. Aluminum Castings Co., Cleveland and Detroit, 1919-20; advisory service mgr. Lockwood, Greene & Co., Boston, 1920-3. Commd. capt. Ordnance Dept., U.S.A., 1917, and assigned duty organizing training of employment mgrs. for depts. of War, Navy, Labor and Shipping Bd.; organized teaching of employment management in many colls. Mem. Am. Soc. M.E., Taylor Soc. Democrat. Unitarian. Mason. Clubs: Harvard (Boston and New York). Author: Industrial Loyalty, 1918; Mental Causes of Accidents, 1922. Home: Staten Island, N.Y.

FISHER, CHARLES HENRY, educator; b. York, Pa., Apr. 25, 1880; s. Henry and Amelia (Carls) F.; A.B., Lebanon Valley Coll., Annville, Pa., 1904; B.D., Union Theol. Sem., 1907; A.M., U. of Pa., 1914; grad. study U. of Pa. and Columbia; m. Mary Light, Aug. 4, 1909; children—Robert, William, Mary, Charles. Sec. Y.M.C.A., N.Y. City, 1907-08; instr. in history, high sch., York, 1908-12; head of history dept., high sch., Trenton, N.J., 1912-15; head of dept. of edn., State Teachers Coll., West Chester, Pa., 1915-19; also acting prof. edn., Swarthmore Coll., 1916-19; asst. dir. Teachers Bur., Pa. State Dept. Pub. Instruction, 1919-20; pres. State Teachers Coll., Bloomsburg, Pa., 1920-23; pres. Western Wash. Coll. of Edn., Bellingham, Wash., 1923-39; lecturer in edn., N.Y. Univ., 1939-41; dean, Huron Coll., Huron, S.D., 1942-43; bus. mgr. State Schs. for the blind, Wash., since 1945. Mem. Phi Delta Kappa. Home: Vancouver, Wash.

FISHER, CLYDE PALMER, coll. dean; b. Blackwell, Okla., Aug. 15, 1920; s. Charles Webster and Sarah Rose (McCrady) F.; A.B., U. Okla., 1942; A.M., U. So. Cal., 1947, Ph.D., 1955; m. Helen Frances Motsenoocker, June 14, 1942; children—Clyde Palmer, Margaret Ellen. Teaching asst. math. U. So. Cal., 1946-47; mem. faculty Cal. Poly. State U., 1947-75, dean coll., 1960-61, dean applied scis., 1961-70, dean sci. and math., 1970-75. Chmn. finance com. Mercy Bowl Football Game, 1961. Pres. bd. Cal. Poly. Student Meml. Fund, 1960-71. Served to capt. AUS, 1942-46; lt. col. Res. Mem. A.A.A.S., Nat. Geog. Soc., Am. Sci. Affiliation. Mem. Church of Nazarene (trustee, Sunday sch. tchr.). Home: San Luis Obispo, Calif.; buried Los Osos (Calif.) Valley Meml. Park.

FISHER, HAROLD HENRY, author; b. Morristown, Vt., Feb. 15, 1890; s. Henry Jonas and Elizabeth Malona (Cole) F.; grad. Peoples Acad., Morrisville, Vt., 1907; A.B., U. Vt., 1911, L.H.D., 1936; m. Helen C. Dwight, May 14, 1917; 1 son, Anthony Henry Dwight. Teacher Black Hall (Conn.) Sch., 1912, Mercersburg (Pa.) Acad., 1912-14, Hill Sch., Pottsdown, Pa., 1914-17; chief of hist. dept., Am. Relief Administrn, 1920-24; lecturer in history, 1924-33; vice chmn. Hoover War Library, 1924-44, chmn. since 1944; dir Russian Rev. Inst., 1930-42, asso. prof. history Stanford, 1933-36, prof., 1936-55; chmn., 1944-55, emeritus, 1955; prof. internat. relations San Francisco State Coll., 1955-60; vis. professor Columbia Univ., 1940, 57, Tokyo U., 1954; vis. prof. polit. sci. U. Calif., Berkeley, 1960-61, Mills Coll., 1961-64. Dir. Civil Affairs Tng. Sch., 1943-45; dir. Civil Communications Intelligence Sch. 1946; dir. School Naval Administration, 1946-48; dir. Belgian-American Edn. Found., 1943-64. Served as 1st lt., capt., F.A., A.E.F., 1917-19; relief work for Am. Relief Adminstrn. in Russia, 1922. Recipient Peabody award. Mem. Am. Hist. Assn., Institute Pacific Relations (chmn. Pacific council 1953-61), Soc. Am. Historians, Am. Polit. Sci. Assn., Delta Psi. Author books including: American and Russia in the World Community, 1946; The Communist Revolution, 1955; Soviet Russia and the West, 1957. Editor publs. including: Life of a Chemist: Memoirs of V. N. Ipatieff, 1946; Am. Research on Russia, 1959; hon. editor Slavic Rev. Home: Palo Alto, Calif. Died 1975.

FISHER, HOPE, educator; b. Marion, O. May 8, 1886; d. Charles Clement and Rose Ida (Scofield) F.; A.B., Vassar Coll., 1908; M.A., Columbia, 1912; Ph.D., U. of Mich., 1922. Secondary sch. teacher, Ind. and Mich., 1908-23; house dir., Erskine Sch., Boston, 1923-24; asso. dir. studies, Cambridge-Haskell Sch., 1924-26; prin. Bancroft Sch., Worcester, Mass., since 1926. Mem. Headmistresses Assn. of the East, Nat. Assn. Prins. Schs. for Girls, Boston Pvt. Sch. Assn., N.E. Assn. Schs. and Colls., Progressive Edn. Assn., Am. Geog. Soc., Acad. of Polit. Science, Sorosis. Republican. Episcopalian. Clubs: Players, College, Tatnuck Country; Vassar (New York). Home: Worcester, Mass.; (summer) Princeton, Mass. *

FISHER, HOWARD T(AYLOR), architect, planner, educator; b. Chgo., Oct. 30, 1903; s. Walter L. and Mabel (Taylor) F.; S.B. magna cum laude, Harvard U., 1926; m. Marion Hall, Feb. 11, 1939; children—Ann Bourne (dec.), Morgan Hall, Alan Hall. Grad. student, tchr. Harvard U., 1926-28; engaged in gen. profl. practice (including research in constrn. methods and materials, low cost housing, drive-in shopping centers), 1928-65; organizer Gen. Houses, Inc., pioneer prefabricating co., 1932; war housing work, Washington, 1940-44; cons. U.S. Govt. vets. housing program, 1946-47, UN, Pan Am. Union, Orgn. Am. States in Inter-Am. Housing and Planning Center, Bogota, 1952-54; conductor spl. tng. courses on integrated bldg. design and constrn. McGill U., Va. Poly. Inst., Lake Forest Coll., 1952-55, on computer cartography Northwestern U., Harvard, from 1964; research cons. Center Urban Studies, U. Chgo., 1965; cons. U.S. Census Bur., Dept. Def., 1966-68; mem. faculty Northwestern U. Inst. Tech., 1957-64; (devel. SYMAP computer mapping program 1963); vis. sr. lectr. Mass. Inst. Tech., 1965-66; mem. faculty Harvard Grad. Sch. Design, 1965-75, founder, 1st dir. Lab. Computer Graphics and Spatial Analysis, 1965-68, prof. city planning, 1966-70, research prof. cartography, 1970-75. Former mem. vis. com. Harvard Grad. Sch. Design; mem. council Harvard Found. Advanced Study and Research; tech. adv. com. on comml. land use Chgo. Plan Commn.; guest of honor, del. for UN, U.S.A. and A.I.A., 8th Congress Pan Am. Architects, Mexico City, 1952; chmn. McGill U. Conf. Constrn. Industry Integration, Montreal, 1953; lectr. State Dept. and Brit. Nat. Computing Center on computer mapping in Spain and Britain, 1969. Fellow A.I.A.; mem. Am. Inst. Planners. Author: (with James M. Carpenter) Color in Art, 1974. Author numerous articles in field. Editor, annotater: (with Mrs. Fisher) Life in Mexico: The Letters of Fanny Calderon de la Barca. Editor, contbr. Harvard papers in theoretical cartography, 1976-79. Home: Newmarket, N.H. Died Jan. 23, 1979.

FISHER, JAMES ROBERT, educator; b. El Paso, Tex., Sept. 18, 1928; s. James Bissel and Louella (Spikes) F.; B.S., Tex. Western Coll., 1950; M.A., U. Tex., 1952, Ph.D., 1954; m. Nanette Gatlin, Nov. 12, 1929; children—Gary, Randy. Research fellow U. Tex., 1954-55; prof. chemistry Fla. State U., 1955-76. Served with AUS, 1946-48. Rosalie Hite postdoctoral fellow, 1954-55; USPHS fellow, Karolinska Inst., Stockholm, Sweden, 1971. Mem. Am. Soc. Biol. Chemists, Soc. Devel. Biology, Am. Soc. Zoologists, Sigma Xi. Contbr. articles profl. jours. Home: Tallahassee, Fla. Died June 3, 1976.

FISHER, R. B., business exec.; b. Grand Rapids, Mich., Mar. 26, 1884; s. Oscar D. and Millie E. Fisher; student Mich. State Coll., East Lansing, 1900-03; m. Constance Chilcott; children—Benson B., Leigh C., Adela C. Began as asst. engineer, Detroit United Ry.; successively engr. William Wharton Co., Phila., Juniata Hydro Elec. Co., Huntington, Pa., chief engr. New York Switch and Crossing Co., 1902-10; engr., Okla. Ry. Co.; assoc. with The Buda Co. since 1910 as engr., chief engr., asst. to pres., gen. sales mgr.: vice pres. and dir., since 1920. Past pres., dir. and sec. Nat. Ry. Appliances Assn. Mem. Am. Ry. Engring. Assn., Western Ry. Maintenance of Way Assn. Club: Olympia Fields Country. Republican. Episcopalian (ch. treas.). Home: Harvey, Ill.

FISHER, ROBERT DEAN, found. exec.; b. Warsaw, N.Y., July 22, 1903; s. Addison Washburn and Pearl (Nettleton) F.; A.B., Oberlin Coll., 1926; J.D., Western Res., 1931; LL.D., Calif. Coll. Medicine, 1954, Whittier Coll., 1969, U. So. Calif., 1974; m. Elizabeth Gould Woodruff, Dec. 23, 1929; children—Martha Joan (Mrs. Donald L. Winston), Rowland Addison, John Woodruff. Practice law, Painesville, Ohio, 1931-34; office counsel Western Res. U., 1934-36, sec., 1936-43, v.p., 1940-43; sec. Cleveland-Cliffs Iron Co., Cliffs Corp. and affiliated cos., 1943-46; financial v.p. U. So. Calif., 1946-58; v.p., dir. Cyprus Mines Corp., 1958-62; fin. cons., 1962-68; chmn. Seeley G. Mudd Fund, 1968-78; dir., v.p. Good Hope Med. Found., 1964-78. Mem. Pres.'s Commn. on Fed. Statistics, 1970-71. Pres. Sch. Bd. Palos Verdes, 1950-52; chmn. Palos Verdes Good Schs. Assn., 1953-54; mem. citizens Com. on Reorgn. Community Chest, Los Angeles, 1950-52; profl. adv. com. on restudy needs of Calif. in Higher Edn., 1953-54; charter mem., sec. Assn. Independent Calif. Colls. and Univs., 1955-58, trustee, 1955-58, 62-78; mem. bd. overseers Hoover Instn. on War, Revolution and Peace, 1971-77. Congregationalist. Club: California (Los Angeles). Home: Rolling Hills, Calif. Died Aug. 30, 1978.

FISHER, WILLIAM JOHN, corp. exec.; b. York, Pa., Feb. 7, 1886; s. Henry F. and Amelia J. (Carls) F.; student Y.M.C.A. Night Sch.; LL.D. (hon.), Lebanon Valley College, 1955; married Mary Decker, Nov. 17, 1909; children—Edward H., Margaret Amelia (Mrs. K. S. Holtman). With A.B. Farquhar Co., York 1902, pres., 1944-52; v.p. Oliver Corp., Chgo., 1952-56, also dir.; dir. Oliver Corp.; chairman of the board York Fed. Savs. & Loan Assn. Past pres. Farm Equipment Inst. President York Hosp.; trustee chmn. finance Lebanon Valley Coll., trustee YMCA. Member A.S.M.E. (life), York Manufacturers Assn. (dir.). Republican. Mason Clubs: York Country, Lafayette. Home: York, Pa.

FISHER, WILLIAM WILSON, educator; b. at Ironton, O., Jan. 11, 1882; s. Joseph and Mary Ellen (Wilson) F.; grad. Howe (Ind.) Sch., 1900; A.B., cum laude, Harvard, 1904; m. Byrd Williams Burgher, of Dallas, Tex., Feb. 25, 1908. With Dallas T.&S. Bank, 1905-8; real estate and loan business, Dallas, 1908-16; headmaster of Howe Sch. since Nov. 17, 1916 (trustee since 1911). Mem. Am. Forestry Assn., A.A.A.S., N. Central Academic Assn., Howe Sch. Alumni Assn. (pres. 1912-14), Alpha Delta Tau (Howe), Pi Eta (Harvard). Episcopalian. Mason (32 deg., Shriner). Clubs: Harvard of Dallas (pres. 1913-15); University (Dallas and Chicago). Home: Howe, Ind.

FISK, MCKEE, educator; b. Alton, Ill., Feb. 4, 1900; s. Elmer McReynolds and Maud Ella (McKee) F.; A.B., Oklahoma City U., 1923; A.M., U. So. Calif., 1926; Ph.D., Yale, 1936; m. Laura R. Best, Nov. 26, 1931; children—Donald M., Karolus A., Patricia Ann. Tchr. Denison (Tex.) High Sch., 1923-25; instr. Santa Ana (Calif.) Coll., 1925-26, dean, 1926-35; instr. Yale, 1935-36; prof. bus. edn. Okla. State U., 1936-40, U. N.C. at Greensboro, 1940-43; chief bus. and sales tng. div. vocational rehab. and edn. Central Office VA, 1943-45; editor bus. edn. McGraw-Hill Book Co., 1945-48; prof. bus. adminstrn., dean sch. bus. Calif. State U., Fresno, 1948-69, dean emeritus, 1969-78, accreditation com. Bus. Sch., 1950-68; prof. bus. adminstrn. Grad. Sch. Bus., U. Santa Clara, 1969-78; AID adviser, cons. to dean bus. adminstrn. faculty and dir. Inst. Bus. Adminstrn., U. Karachi, Pakistan, 1962, 64; prof. U. So. Cal., Bitburg, Germany, 1970; mem. of bus. profl. adv. com. Calif. Dept. Edn., 1952-56; chmn. adv. com. San Joaquin Valley Council on Econ. Edn., 1952-55; mem. bd. Inst. of Antiquity and Christianity. Recipient Distinguished Service awards United Bus. Schs. Assn., 1955, Collegiate Schs. Bus., 1968, Calif. Bus. Edn. Assn., 1969; Am. Vocational Assn. award, 1966; John Robert Gregg award in bus. edn., 1968. Mem. Nat. Bus. Tchrs. Assn. (hon.), Calif. Bus. Edn. Assn. (pres. 1952-53), Nat. Bus. Edn. Assn. (hon.), Blue Key, Phi Chi Theta (hon.), Delta Pi Epsilon (nat. pres. 1939-41), Phi Kappa Phi, Alpha Kappa Psi, Sigma Alpha Epsilon, Beta Gamma Sigma. Conglist. Author: (with W.E. Grimes) Farm Accounting, 1938; (with D.A. Pomeroy) Applied Business Law, 1944, rev., 1950, (with J.C. Snapp), 1955, rev. edit., 1960, 66, (with N.J. Mietus), 1972; Introduction to Business Law, 1957, rev. edit., 1962, 67. Editor: Nat. Bus. Tchrs. Assn. Yearbook 1940, 41, 42, 43. Contbr. to Colliers Ency. Home: Santa Cruz, Calif. Died Apr. 18, 1978.

FISK, SHIRLEY CARTER, physician; b. N.Y.C., June 25, 1910; s. Arthur Lyman and Alice Bowie (Carter) F.; grad. Hill Sch., 1927; B.A., Yale, 1931; M.D., Columbia, 1935; m. Mary Averell Harriman, Apr. 27, 1940; children—Robert Carter, Kathleen Lawrance, Averell Harriman. Intern Presbyn. Hosp., N.Y.C., 1935-37, asso. attending physician, 1958-73; pvt. practice internal medicine, N.Y.C., 1937-63; attending physician VA Hosp., Kingsbridge Rd., N.Y., 1945-63; cons. Tuxedo Meml. Hosp., Tuxedo Park, N.Y., 1951-63; asso. clin. prof. medicine Columbia, 1958-73, asso. dean Coll. Phys. and Sur., 1967-73, asso. prof. clin. medicine, 1967-73, dep. asst. sec. def. for manpower, health and medicine Dept. Def., 1963-67. Mem. Health Resources Adv. Com.; ex-officio mem. Nat. Adv. Health Council, 1963-67. Served to maj. M.C., AUS, 1941-45. Diplomate Am. Bd. Internal Medicine. Mem. Soc. Med. Cons. Armed Forces, A.M.A., A.C.P., N.Y. County Med. Soc., N.Y. Acad. Medicine, Alpha Omega Alpha. Club: Century Assn. (N.Y.C.). Home: New York, N.Y. Died Dec. 25, 1979.

FISKE, CYRUS HARTWELL, biochemist; b. St. Paul, Minn., Sept. 22, 1890; s. Frederick William and Isabella Tiffany (Hartwell) F.; student St. Paul Acad., 1900-06; A.B., U. of Minn., 1910; M.D., Harvard Med. Sch., 1914; m. Josephine K. Bissman, Sept. 22, 1917; children—Catherine (Mrs. James C. Higgins), Robert Hartwell. Assistant biological chemistry, Harvard Medical Sch., 1914-15; asso. in biochemistry, Western Reserve University Med. Sch., 1915-17, asst. prof., 1917-18; asst. prof. biol. chemistry, Harvard Med. Sch., 1918-29, asso. prof. 1929-35, prof. from 1935. Fellow Am. Acad. Arts and Sciences, Am. Inst. of Chemists, A.A.A.S.; mem. Am. Soc. Biol. Chemists (treas. 1931-36), Am. Chem. Soc., Nu Sigma Nu, Sigma Xi, Alpha Omega Alpha. Home: Lexington, Mass. Died Dec. 11, 1978.

FISKE, KENNETH MORTON, lawyer; b. Chgo., June 16, 1894; s. John T. and Jennie (Frazier) F.; LL.B., Chgo.-Kent Coll. Law, 1916, LL.M., 1917, J.D., 1969; m. Eunice Van Dyne, Sept. 29, 1923; children—Kenneth Van Dyne, Mary Virginia Boorom. Admitted to Ill. bar, 1916, practiced in Chgo.; sr. partner Defrees & Fiske, of counsel corp. real estate and probate law; faculty Walton Sch. Commerce, Chgo. Served as ensign Overseas Transport Service, USN, World War I. Mem. Am., Ill., Chgo., McHenry County bar assns., Am. Legion, Phi Alpha Delta. Republican. Methodist. Mason. Clubs: Union League; Chicago Farmer's (past pres.). Home: Crystal Lake, Ill. Died Sept. 2, 1978; interred Oakland Cemetery, Woodstock, Ill.

FISTER, GEORGE MORGAN, phys. and surg.; b. Logan, Utah, May 22, 1892; s. George and Jennie (Morgan) F.; B.S., Utah State Agrl. Coll., 1913; B.S., U. Chgo., 1916; M.D., Rush Med. Coll., 1918; postgrad., London, Vienna, 1936; m. Ruby L. Ostler, Sept. 23, 1914; children—Franklin G., Mary (wife of William K. Martin, USAF). Spl. tng. urology Henry Ford Hosp., 1923-26, Presbyn. Hosp., 1926-28; surg. staff Thomas D. Dee Meml. Hosp., Ogden, Utah, State Tb Sanatorium, St. Benedict's Hosp.; lectr. surgery U. Utah. Health adv. com. Office Civil and Def. Moblzn. Dir. Utah div. Am. Cancer Soc.; trustee Utah State Sch. Deaf and Blind, 1946-48, Utah State U., 1952-54; bd. regents U. Utah. Mem. med. res. USN, 1917-20; capt. med. detachment Utah N.G. 1919-23. Recipient citation for pub. service U. Chgo., 1951; (with Dr. George W. Cochran) first prize for lab. research Am. Urol. Assn., 1955. Diplomate Am. Bd. Urology. Mem. A.M.A. (trustee 1957-61, pres. 1962-63, chmn. council on legislative activities), Am. Geriatric Soc., Pan. Am., Utah (past pres., council), World med. assns., Am. Urol. Assn. (past pres. Western sect.), A.C.S., Am. Soc. for Study Sterility, Am. Med. Writers Assn., Am., Western assns. r.r. surgeons, N.Y. Acad. Scis., Weber County Med. Soc. (past pres.), Ogden Surg. Soc. (past pres.), Ogden C. of C. Republican. Mem. Ch. of Jesus Christ of Latter Day Saints. Clubs: Fort Douglas Country (Salt Lake City); Weber (past pres.) (Ogden). Home: Ogden, Utah. Died May 11, 1976.

FITCH, AUBREY WRAY, naval officer; b. St. Ignace, Mich., June 11,1883; s. Ernest and Emily Louisa (Wray) F.; ed. St. John's Mil. Acad., 1898-1900, U.S. Naval Acad., 1902-06 (B.S.), Naval War Coll., 1937; married Gwyneth Hungerford Conger, June 11, 1912; children—Aubrey Wray, Omar Conger, John Cecil. Commd. ensign, 1908, and advanced to captain 1931; advanced to vice adm., 1942; served aboard various ships until 1914; comd. U.S.S. Yankton, 1915-17, on staff commander in chief, Atlantic Fleet, Gunnery officer Wyoming, 1917-19; inspector of ordnance, Naval Ammunition Depot, at Hingham, Mass., 1919-21; comd. U.S.S. Luce, U.S.S. Mahan, 1921-22; naval mission, Brazil, 1922-27; exec. officer U.S.S. Nevada, Mar.-Nov. 1927; comdg. officer Arctic, 1927-29; fight training Pensacola, 1929-30; comdg. officer Wright, 1930-31, Langley, 1931-32, Naval Air Sta., Norfolk, Va., 1932-35, U.S.S. Lexington, 1936-37; comdt. Naval Air Station, Pensacola, 1938-40; comdr. Patrol Wing Two May, Oct. 1940; comdr. Carrier Division One, Nov. 1940, comdr. various carrier task forces; first comdr. Air Force Pacific Fleet, 1941-42; comdr. aircraft, S. Pacific Force, Sept. 1942-Apr. 1944; in command combined air forces of Army, Navy, Marines, New Zealand Air Force in S. Pacific, 1943; dep. chief, Naval Operations (Air), Ang. 1944-July 1945; superintendent, U.S. Naval Academy, and comdt. Severn River Command, 1945-47; spl. asst. to sec. of navy, Jan.-June 1947; retired with rank of adm., 1947; now vice pres. Gen. Tire & Rubber Export Co., hdqrs. Washington. Decorated D.S.M. (for Coral Sea action), Gold Star in lieu of 2nd Dist. Service Medal (for service as comdr. Aircraft S. Pacific Force, Sept. 21, 1942 to April 15, 1944), Distinguished Flying Cross, Victory medal with Grand Fleet clasp; Mexican Campaign and Cuban expeditionary medals; Legion of Merit; Am. Defense Service Medal, Fleet Clasp; Asiatic-Pacific Area Campaign Medal with 5 combat stars; Knight Comdr. Order of Brit. Empire; Officer Superior Order of Southern Cross of Brazil; Croix de Guerre with Palms, Comdr. French Legion of Honor. Mem. Delta Sigma Nu. Episcopalian. Clubs: New York Yacht (New York); Racquet (Phila.); Chevy Chase, Army-Navy (Washington). Home: Washington.

FITCH, GEORGE ASHMORE, author; b. Soochow, China, Jan. 23, 1883; s. Rev. George Field and Mary (McLellan) F.; (parents Am. citizens); B.S., U. Wooster, 1906, LL.D., 1939; grad. Union Theol. Sem., N.Y.C., 1909; student Columbia, 1906-09; m. Alberta Casterlin Kempton, Aug. 3, 1910; children—Marion Kathleen (Mrs. John Exter), George Kempton, Albert Casterlin, Edith Louise (Mrs. Alex Swapp); m. 2d, Geraldine Townsend, June 30, 1924; children—John Townsend, Robert McLellan. Chaplain, Riverview Mil. Acad., Poughkeepsie, N.Y., 1906-07; asst. pastor 1st Presbyn. Ch., N.Y.C., 1907-09; sec. internat. com. YMCA, N.Y.C., from 1909, Shanghai, China, 1909-36,

Nanking, 1936-38, Chungking, 1938-44, Northwest China, 1944-45, Lanchow, 1945, Korea, 1947-49; adviser War Area Service Corps, Nanking, 1936-37; dir. Nanking Safety Zone during siege and occupation by Japanese, 1937-38; exec. adviser, Chinese Indsl. Coops., 1941-43; dep. dir. UNRRA, Kaifeng, Honan, China, 1946; sec. Nat. Council YMCA of Korea, 1947-49, from 50. Vice-pres. Chinese-Fgn. Famine Relief Commn.; dir. Hwai Valley Conservancy Bd.; trustee Instn. for Chinese Blind; hon. adviser Chinese Mission to Lepers; mem. exec. com. China Nat. Child Welfare Assn.; mem. Labor Welfare Commn. of City Govt. of Greater Shanghai; mem. Nat. Famine Relief Commn.; founder, adviser Nat. Blind Welfare Assn. of China; v.p. Chinese-Am. Inst. Cultural Relations; mem. Fgn. Policy Assn., Royal. Asiatic Soc., Am. Assn. China (past pres.), Pan-Pacific Assn. (dir.); fellow Royal Geog. Soc. (Eng.). Decorated Order of Chia-Ho (3d rank), Order of Precious Jade (with Cravatte), Chiaotung (Communications Medal). Presbyn. Mason; mem. Order Eastern Star. Clubs: Rotary (past pres.), American University, International (Nanking); Shanghai Tiffin of New York (fgn. v.p.). Author: To the Mecca of Inner Mongolia; My Eighty Years in China, 1967, rev. edit., 1974. Contbr. to mags.; corr. for newspapers. Witness at war crimes trial, Tokyo, 1946. Address: Pomona, Calif. Deceased.

FITZGERALD, JOSEPH JOHN, lawyer, lumber co., exec.; b. Maple Park, Ill., Sept. 21, 1904; s. James and Teresa (McGirr) F.; student U. Ill., 1922-24, Northwestern U. Law Sch. 1925-26; m. Dorothy Poss, Dec. 26, 1938; children—Susan (Mrs. Donald Rice, Jr.), Gail (Mrs. Gerald James); Anne (Mrs. Joseph O'Neill). Admitted to Ill. bar, 1929; with Edward Hines Lumber Co., Chgo., 1932-79, gen. atty., 1945-79, exec. v.p., 1963-72, also dir.; pres., dir. So. Mineral Corp. Bd. dirs. St. Vincent de Paul Center. Recipient Citizenship award Lumber Industry, 1965; named hon. alumnus Loyola U., Chgo., 1973. Mem. Am., Ill. bar assns., Nat. Forest Products Assn. (dir.). Home: Wilmette, Ill. Died Aug. 9, 1979.

FITZGERALD, SHEPLER WARD, army officer; b. Burden, Kan., Nov. 11, 1884; s. William T. and Emma Belle (Frye) F.; LL.B., George Washington U., 1907; grad. Army Industrial Coll., 1925, Air Corps Tactical Sch., 1931, Army War Coll., 1932; rated command pilot, combat observer, tech. observer; m. Adeline Kellogg, Dec. 8, 1915; 1 son, Shepler Ward (Army Air Force). Commd. 2d lt., Dec. 20, 1911, and advanced through the grades to brig. gen., Apr. 1942; commdg. gen. Tech. Sch., Army Air Forces, Madison, Wis. Sigma Chi. Mason. Club: Army and Navy (Washington, D.C.). Address: Madison, Wis. *

FITZGIBBON, RUSSELL HUMKE, educator; b. Columbus, Ind., June 29, 1902; s. Thomas Francis and Frances A. (Moore) F.; A.B., Hanover Coll., 1924; LL.D., 1952; A.M., Ind. U., 1928; Ph.D., U. Wis., 1933; m. Irene Cory, July 6, 1929; children—Alan Lee, Katherine Irene (Mrs. David G. Lilly). Research asst. polit. sci. U. Wis., 1931-33; instr., asst. prof., asso. prof., prof. history and polit. sci. Hanover Coll., 1924-36; asst. prof. polit. sci. UCLA, 1936-42, asso. prof., 1942-48, chmn. dept., 1942-43, 1948-50, prof., 1948-64, dir. Center Latin Am. Studies, 1959-62, acad. asst. to pres., 1962-64, 1967-68; prof. polit. sci. U. Calif., Santa Barbara, 1964-72; vis. prof. Ariz. State U., 1972-73, research asso. Latin Am. center, 1973-79, adj. prof., 1974-79; Del Amo Found. fellow, Latin Am., 1943-44, Spain, 1959, Doherty Found.-Social Sci. Research Council fellow, Latin Am., 1951; sr. polit. analyst Office Inter-Am. Affairs, Washington, 1944-45; vis. prof. polit. sci (summers) Ohio State U., 1952, U. Nebr., 1954, U. Ill., 1956, Ind. U., 1960, Georgetown U., 1963, 64. Fulbright research grantee, Italy, 1958-59. Decorated Order of Don Cristóbal Colón (Dominican Republic). Mem. Am. Polit. Sci. Assn. (bd. editors 1946-47), Western Polit. Sci. Assn. (exec. council 1951-53, 57-58, pres. 1956-57), Phi Delta Theta (nat. editor 1931-36), Pi Sigma Alpha (exec. council 1948-50), Pi Gamma Mu, Alpha Phi Gamma. Author: Cuba and the United States, 1935; Outline of Latin American History, 1937; Uruguay; Portrait of a Democracy, 1954; Latin America: A Panorama of Contemporary Politics, 1971, 2d edit., 1981; The Agatha Christie Companion, 1980; co-author: Latin America, Past and Present, 1946. Editor: The Civilization of the Americas, 1938; Forty Years on Main Street (editorials of William Allen White), 1938; Global Politics, 1944; The Constitutions of the Americas, 1948, The Era of Trujillo (with Jesús de Galíndez, 1973. Mem. bd. contbg. editors: Handbook of Latin American Studies, 1941-45; bd. editors Inter-Am. Econ. Affairs 1949-79; internat. adv. bd. Hispanic Am. Report, 1949-62. Contbr. articles profl. publs. Home: Sun City, Ariz. Died Jan. 8, 1979.

FITZPATRICK, FREDERICK LINDER, educator; b. Iowa City, May 6, 1900; s. Thomas J. and Mary (Linder) F.; A.B., Iowa State U., 1919, M.S., 1921, Ph.D., 1924; m. Margaret C. Smith, July 17, 1923; 1 son, Frederick M. Asst. prof. biology, Colo. Coll. Edn., 1923-25; prof. Coe Coll., 1925-31; asso. prof. natural sciences, Teachers Coll., Columbia University, 1931-38, prof. since 1938, head dept., from 1952, dir. Science Manpower Project, from 1956. Director American-Philippine Science Foundation. Served as commander, USNR, officer in charge curriculum section (United States Navy), 1943-45; reports officer Bikini Sciences Resurvey, 1947. Fellow A.A.A.S.; member Nat. Sci. Tchrs. Assn., Acad. Polit. Sci., Assn. Edn. Tchrs. Science, National Association for Research in Science Teaching, Sigma Xi, Phi Kappa Phi, Phi Delta Kappa, Kappa Delta Pi, Beta Theta Pi, Mason, Republican. Presbyterian. Author books including: The Teaching of Biology in Secondary Schools of the United States (with Riddle and others), 1942; The Biology of Flight (with Stiles), 1942, Living Things (with others), 1962; Living Things Workbook, 1962; Policies for Science Education, 1960; Our Animal Resources, 1963; Our Plant Resources, 1964. Contbr. ednl. and sci. jours. Address: New York, N.Y. Died Apr. 21, 1976.

FITZPATRICK, HUGH FRANCIS, surgeon, educator; b. Am. Falls, Idaho, Jan. 20, 1919; s. Hugh Francis and Leone (McDermott) F.; B.S., Creighton U., 1941, M.D., 1943; D.Sc., Columbia U., 1956; m. Lucy A. Jobson, Oct. 10, 1953; children—Tracy E., Amy M., Hugh F., Timothy R. Intern St. Joseph's Hosp., Omaha, 1944; instr. dept. physiology U. Pa., Phila., 1948-49; asst. resident in surgery Presbyn. Hosp., N.Y.C., 1949-53; resident in surgery, 1953-54; resident in cardiovascular surgery St. Francis Hosp. for Cardiac Children, Roslyn, N.Y., 1955; asst. to dir. surgery St. Luke's Hosp. Center, N.Y.C., 1955-69, asst. attending surgeon, 1955-57, asso. attending surgeon, 1958-61, attending surgeon, 1962-80; vis. surgeon St. Francis Hosp. for Cardiac Children, Roslyn, 1955; dir. surgery St. Luke's Hosp. Center, N.Y.C., 1971-80; instr. surgery Columbia U., N.Y.C., 1955-56, asso. in surgery, 1956-57, asst. clin. prof. surgery, 1957-61, asso. clin. prof. surgery, 1961-71, prof. surgery, 1971-76, Clark prof. surgery, 1977-80; clin. cons. surgery and cardiovascular surgery N.Y. Dept. Health and N.Y.C. Dept. Health, 1959-80; cons. in thoracic surgery Elizabeth A. Horton Meml. Hosp., Middletown, N.Y., 1972-80. Served to lt. M.C. USNR, 1943-46; ATO. Diplomate Am. Bd. Surgery, Am. Bd. Thoracic Surgery. Fellow ACS; mem. Am. Med. Assn., Soc. Univ. Surgeons, Am. Surg. Assn., Am. Assn. Thoracic Surgery, Soc. for Vascular Surgery, Internat. Cardiovascular Soc., Halsted Soc., Am. Soc. Artificial Organs, AAAS, Am. Trudeau Soc., Am. Geriatrics Soc., Am. Heart Assn., N.Y. Surg. Soc., N.Y. Soc. Thoracic Surgery (pres. 1970-72), N.Y. Soc. Cardiovascular Surgery, N.Y. Acad. Medicine (trustee 1974-78, council mem. 1974-78), N.Y. Soc. Med. Research, Med. Soc. State of N.Y. (pres. surg. sect. 1972-73), Med. Soc. of County of N.Y., N.Y. Heart Assn., N.Y. Clin. Soc., Hawthorne Surg. Soc., Allen O. Whipple Surg. Soc., Internat. Coll. Angiology, N.Y. Bronchoscopic Club, Soc. of Alumni of St. Luke's Hosp. Center (pres. 1976-77), N.Y. Med. and Surg. Soc., Alpha Omega Alpha, Alpha Sigma Nu. Clubs: Englewood Field, Century Assn. N.Y.C. Contbr. numerous articles in field to med. jours. Home: Tenafly, N.J. Died Aug. 21, 1980.

FITZPATRICK, JOHN JOSEPH, editor; b. Boston, Mass., Sept. 24, 1886; s. Louis Joseph and Margaret (Sullivan) F.; ed. pub. schs.; m. Mary J. Mulroy, Oct. 23, 1909; children—John Joseph, Paul William. Identified with newspaper business since 1907: news editor Boston American, 1922-26; mng. editor Boston Advertiser, 1926-27, Washington Times, 1928-29, Boston American, 1929-30; again mng. editor Washington Times, 1931-37; editor Miami Tribune, 1937; now mng. editor Phila. Inquirer. Club: National Press. Home: Drexel Hill, Pa.; (summer) Harvey Cedars, N.J.

FITZSIMMONS, FRANK E., labor union ofcl.; b. Apr. 7, 1908; hon. doctorate in pub. service St. Joseph's Coll., Rensselaer, Ind.; m. Mary Patricia Fitzsimmons; 4 children. Dockworker, Detroit; then truck driver; bus. agt. Teamster Local 299, Detroit, 1937-40, v.p., from 1940-61; sec.-treas. Mich. Conf. Teamsters; later co-founder Central States Drivers' Council; gen. exec. bd. Internat. Brotherhood Teamsters, from 1961, v.p., 1961-67, gen. v.p., 1967-71, gen. pres., 1971-81, chmn. negotiating com., 1971-81. Mem. or former mem. Nat. Commn. on Productivity, Pres.'s Com. on Employment of Handicapped, Labor Dept. Interdepartmental Workers' Compensation Task Force, White House Conf. on Capital Investment and Employment in Am. Economy, Nat. Petroleum Council, Adv. Com. for Trade Negotiations under Trade Act of 1974, Com. of 100 for Nat. Health Ins., Pres.'s Labor-Mgmt. Adv. Com. to Cost of Living Council; former mem. Labor Mgmt. Collective Bargaining Com. in Constrn.; labor mem. Pay Bd. Active fund raising for Frank E. Fitzsimmons Med. Research Complex, also Little City Found., Palatine, Ill.; mem. nat. vol. service adv. council ACTION; v.p. Muscular Dystrophy Assn. Am.; sponsoring mem. Citizens for Treatment of High Blood Pressure. Recipient Nat. Spirit of Love award, Four Freedoms award, 1972, Silver Anniversary medal State of Israel, 1973. Home: Washington, D.C. Died May 6, 1981.

FIZZELL, ROBERT BRUCE, lawyer; b. Taylorville, Ill., Sept. 20, 1889; s. James Albert and Martha Catherine (Allen) F.; A.B., U. Ill., 1910; LL.B., Harvard, 1913; m. Florence Edith Hoover, Nov. 27, 1916 (dec. 1963); children—Robert Bruce, Dorothy Florence; m. 2d, Vera L. Hagen, July 10, 1965. Admitted to Mo. bar, 1913, since practiced in Kansas City; partner Stinson, Mag, Thomson, McEvers & Fizzell to 1978. Trustee-Kansas City Art Inst., Friends of Art of Kansas City (pres. 1937-39). Chmn. Jackson County Charter Commn., 1948. Mem. Am., Mo., Kansas City bar assns., Lawyers Assn. of Kansas City (pres. 1947), Phi Beta Kappa, Delta Sigma Rho. Democrat. Clubs: University, Kansas City Country. Home: Kansas City, Mo. Died June 22, 1978.

FLAGG, MILDRED BUCHANAN (MRS. FRANCIS JOHN FLAGG), writer, lectr.; b. Moravia, N.Y., May 1, 1886; d. B. Frank and Julia (McCormick) Buchanan; A.B., Syracuse U., 1908; A.M., Boston U., 1927; D.Sc.O. (hon.), Curry Coll., 1958; Litt.D. (hon.), Boston U., 1963; L.H.D. (hon.), Portia Law School, 1965; m. Francis John Flagg, Oct. 7, 1914; children—David Buchanan (dec.), Julia Buchanan (Mrs. Kenneth A. Williams), Nancy Ferard (Mrs. Robert E. Gibney). Head English dept. high sch., Palmyra, N.Y., 1911-13, Watertown, N.Y., 1913-14; in ednl. work and active as lectr. and writer since 1914; dir. Am. Students Abroad, 1929-33; dir. Flagstaff Radio Hour (sta. WCOP), Boston, 1935-37. Dir. United Cerebral Palsy Assn. of Mass., 1947-54, Boston U. Women's Council, 1931-34, Com. on Pub. Health, Newton Council for Better World Order, nat. chmn. Books for Norway, 1947-49; chmn. Celebrity Breakfasts, 1945-62; sponsor Caney Creek Community Center, Pippa Passes, Ky., 1925-62; mem. N.E. com. Anatolia Coll., Greece; vice-comdr. Women's Field Army for Control of Cancer; trustee Flora Koralsky Scholarship Fund, 1955-60; dir. Writers Workshop, Nat. Found. for Study of Aging; trustee Brusch Med. Research Center, Inc.; trustee and mem. corp. Curry Coll., 1963-67. Mem. Mass. State Teachers Fdn. (pub. relations com.), N.E. Women's Press Assn. (pres. 1931-33), Am. Assn. U. Women (state pres. 1930-32, state chmn. TV-radio 1948-52), English-Speaking Union (mem. bd. (Syracuse), The Pres.' Club of Mass. (pres. 1937-38), Boston-Syracuse Alumnae Assn. (pres. 1920-37), Boston U., Grad. Sch. Alumni Assn. (pres. 1935-37), Newton Center Woman's Club (lit. chmn. 1945-48), Women's City Club of Boston, Am. Numismatic Assn., YWCA, Nat. Fedn. Bus. and Profl. Women's Clubs, N.E.A. (hon. life), Authors League (pres. Central N.Y.), Profl. Women's League, English Speaking Union, Boar's Head, Phi Beta Kappa, Theta Sigma Phi, Delta Kappa Gamma. Republican. Conglist. Clubs: Professional Women's (pres., 1931-33), Boston Authors (pres. 1947-49, from 1964, dir. 1950-52); National League American Pen Women (pres. Boston br., nat. lectrs. chmn. 1954-56); Boston Travel; Zonta, Onaway (Syracuse, N.Y.). Author: Community English, 1921; Camera Adventures in Africa, 1935; Plymouth Maid, 1937; Boy of Salem, 1939; Celebrity Chatalogs, 1945; A Lad of Old Nantucket, 1947; Approaching Old Age, 1955; Uncle Sam's Forgotten Children, 1956; Notable Boston Authors, 1965; Boston Authors Now and Then, 1966; Profiles of New York Authors; also articles in various publications. Editor: Study Outlines in Pocket Classics (6 vols.), 1921-33; A Certain Rich Man (William Allen White), 1923, 30. Home: Syracuse, N.Y. Died Jan. 2, 1980.

FLAHERTY, FRANK (JOHN FRANCIS), journalist; b. Caledon, Ont., Can., Dec. 18, 1903; s. James and Anne (Wallace) F.; B.A., U. Toronto, 1925, M.A., 1928; m. Dorothy Eva Rhodes, Aug. 28, 1934; children—Mary Anne, Helen Theresa (Mrs. John Dempster), Roderick John, Kathleen Dorothy. Reporter, Toronto (Ont.) Daily Star, 1925-26; reporter, wire-editor, Parliamentary corr. Canadian Press, 1927-45; Parliamentary corr. Toronto Globe and Mail, 1946-47; Canadian corr. Chgo. Daily News, 1947-70; pub. nat. bus. news report Buchanan's Bull., 1945-69; mgr. Nat. Editorial Bur., 1965—. Organized pub. relations and information services for Marian Congress Ottawa, 1948; 1st Bowater award for journalism, 1956. Mem. Canadian Inst. Internat. Affairs, Canadian C. of C., Parliamentary Press Gallery, Sigma Delta Chi. Club: Nat. Press Canada (past pres.). Home: Ottawa, Ont., Canada. Died May 11, 1980; buried Silver Creek Parish Cemetery, Caledon, Ont.

FLANAGIN, NORRIS CORNELIUS, ins. exec.; b. Chgo., Feb. 7, 1904; s. Cornelius Alfredo and Edna (Elden) F.; Ph.B., U. Chgo., 1924; m. Virginia Riddell, Apr. 25, 1928; children—Neil, Charles R., William E.; m. 2d, Mary Humphrey Cranage, May 10, 1968. Western mgr. Theatre mag., 1925-29; account exec. Matthew G. Pierce, 1930-32, Doremus & Co., 1932-34; emeritus dir. Fidelity Life Assn., Fed. Kemper Life Assurance Co., dir. Kemper Financial Services. Served as lt. USNR, World War II. Mem. Alpha Delta Phi. Clubs: Chicago, Tower (Chgo.); Glen View (Golf, Ill.); Hole-in-the-Wall, Yacht (Naples, Fla.). Home: Wilmette, Ill. Died Dec. 26, 1978.

FLANNER, JANET, writer; b. Indpls., Mar. 13, 1892; d. Frances and Mary-Ellen (Hockett) Flanner; student Tudor Hall, Indpls., U. Chgo.; Litt.D. (hon.), Smith Coll., 1958. Fgn. corr. New Yorker mag., writer Letter from Paris, from 1925. Decorated Legion of Honor. Mem. Nat. Inst. Arts and Letters. Author: (novel) The Cubical City, 1926; (collected New Yorker Profiles)

American in Paris, 1940; (art monographs) Men and Monuments, 1957; Paris Journal I, 1944-65 (Nat. Book award 1966); Paris Journal II, 1965-71; (with Irving Drutman) Paris Was Yesterday, 1972, London Was Yesterday, 1975. Translator: Claudine a L'Ecole and Cheri (by Colette); Ma Vie avec Maeterlinck (by Mme. Georgette Le Blanc). Home: New York, N.Y. Died Nov. 7, 1978.

FLAVIN, JAMES WILLIAM, actor; b. Portland, Me., May 14, 1906; s. James William and Katherine Louise (Rice) F.; B.S., U.S. Mil. Acad., 1926; m. Lucile Browne, Sept. 17, 1933; 1 son, William James. Actor Jefferson Stock Co., Portland, 1927, Broadway stage, 1928-31; under contract Universal Studios, 1931-32; appearances motion pictures and TV, from 1931, including Broadway revival Front Page, 1969-70. Mem. Acad. Motion Picture Arts and Scis. Home: Los Angeles, Calif. Died Apr. 23, 1976.

FLEISHER, MOYER SPRINGER, bacteriologist; b. Phila., Pa., May 13, 1884; s. Alexander and Martha (Springer) F.; B.S., U. of Pa., 1904, M.D., 1907; m. Adele E. Levis, Jan. 1, 1914. Asst. exptl. pathologist, U. of Pa., 1907-10; pathologist Barnard Free Skin and Cancer Hosp., St. Louis, 1910-15; asst. prof. bacteriology, St. Louis U. Sch. of Medicine, 1915-19, prof. bacteriology and hygiene 1919-39, head of dept., 1924-39. Research bacteriologist Jewish Hosp. of St. Louis since 1939. Served as capt. Med. R.C., 1918-19. Fellow A.A.A.S.; mem. Am. Assn. Immunologists, St. Louis Med. Soc. (asso.), Soc. Am. Bacteriologists, Soc. Exptl. Biology and Medicine, Am. Soc. Exptl. Pathology, Am. Pub. Health Assn., Sigma Xi, Alpha Omega Alpha, Pi Gamma Mu. Home: St. Louis.

FLEISHHACKER, MORTIMER, JR., mfg. exec.; b. San Francisco, May 3, 1907; s. Mortimer and Bella (Gerstle) F.; A.B., U. Cal., 1927; m. Janet L. Choynski, May 1, 1929; children—Delia (Mrs. John Ehrlich), Mortimer, David. Vice pres. Anglo Cal. Nat. Bank, San Francisco, 1931-40; pres. Chemicals, Inc., 1940-56; v.p. Lord Baltimore Press of Cal. (formerly Fleishhacker Paper Box Co.). San Francisco, 1953-60; chmn. bd. Precision Instrument Co., 1960-70; v.p., dir. Natomas Co., Ltd. partner Golden Gateway Center; dir. Crocker-Citizens Nat. Bank. Former chmn. Bay Area Edn. TV Assn.; v.p. San Francisco Symphony Assn.; trustee San Francisco Mus. Art, World Affairs Council of No. Cal., Asia Found.; chmn. bd. regents U. San Francisco; v.p., dir. Internat. House, Berkeley; bd. dirs. Cal. Theatre Found. Served as lt. comdr. USNR, World War II. Home: San Francisco, Calif. Died Mar. 14, 1976.

FLEMING, DENNA FRANK, educator; b. Paris, Ill., Mar. 25, 1893; s. Albert and Eleanor (McCormick) F.; grad. Eastern Ill. State Coll., 1912, Pe.D., 1949; A.B., U. Ill., 1916, A.M., 1920, Ph.D., 1928; student Columbia, 1928; m. Doris Sigrid Anundsen, June 29, 1929. Prin. high sch., Hume, Ill., 1912-14, tchr. high sch., Freeport, 1916-17, Walla Walla, Wash., 1917; prin. high sch., Tonica, Ill., 1919-21, and Colfax, 1921-22; asst. prof. social sci. Monmouth Coll., 1922-23, asso. prof., 1923-24, prof., chmn. dept., 1924-27; asst. prof. polit. sci. Vanderbilt U., 1928, asso. prof., 1930, prof., 1938, chmn. dept., 1940, research prof., 1951-61, prof. emeritus, 1961-80; research asso. Stanford U., 1966; vis. prof. U. Ariz., 1964, 66, Calif. State Coll. Los Angeles, 1965, Simon Fraser U., Vancouver, B.C., 1968-69. Instr., Iowa State Tchrs. Coll., summers 1926-27, Middle Tenn. State U., 1970; Penfield traveling scholar, 1932-33, 1938-39; mem. Inst. for Advanced Study, Princeton, 1946, 48, 49; adviser atomic energy sect. State Dept., 1946. Fgn. editor Nashville Evening Tennessean, 1934-37; fgn. commentator WSM, 1939-47; radio commentator Woodrow Wilson Found., 1944-46, dir., 1950-55; Fulbright lectr. Conf. on Am. Studies, Cambridge U., 1954, Sch. Internat. Studies, New Delhi, 1959-60, Bertrand Russell Centennial, Vienna, 1972. Served with AEF, World War I. Recipient Distinguished Alumni award Eastern Ill. U., 1975. Mem. A.A.U.P. (exec. council), Am. Com. in Geneva Staff, 1932, Am. Acad. Polit. and Social Sci., Am. (v.p. 1943), So. (pres. 1941) polit. sci. assns., Phi Beta Kappa Assos., Acacia, Delta Sigma Rho, Kappa Delta Pi, Phi Beta Kappa, Phi Kappa Phi. Democrat. Methodist. Mason. Club: Nashville Round Table (pres. 1937). Author: The Treaty Veto of the American Senate, 1930, 73; The United States and the League of Nations 1918-1920, 1932, 68; The United States and World Organization, 1920-33, 1938, 66; Can We Win the Peace? 1943; While America Slept, 1944; The United States and the World Court, 1945-68; The Cold War and its Origins, 1917-1960, Vols. I and II, 1961, 68; The Origins and Legacies of World War I, 1968, 73; America's Role in Asia, 1969; The Issues of Survival, 1972, 2d edit., 1973. Home: Nashville, Tenn. Died Sept. 3, 1980.

FLEMING, JAMES R., lawyer, pub.; b. Henry Co., Ind., Nov. 8, 1881; s. George R. and Sarah (Cummins) F.; LL.B., U. of Mich., 1904; m. Jennie Adair, Dec. 24, 1906; children—Marian (Mrs. James Abromson), Virginia. Pros. atty. 58th Jud. Circuit, Ind., 1906-10; U.S. dist. atty. for northern Dist. of Ind., 1933-41; resigned to enter private practice, 1941; chmn. bd., pres., pub. Ft Wayne Journal-Gazette. Mem. Ind. Ho. of Reps., 1913-15, Ind. Senate, 1915-19; mem. Dem. State Central Com., 1922-26. Chairman Governor's Commission on the Arts; mem. UN Ednl., Scientific and Cultural Orgn.; mem. Mayor's Youth Council, Ft. Wayne, Ind. Mem. Am., Ind., Allen County bar assns., Ind. Soc. of Chgo., Ind. Hist. Soc., Am. Soc. Newspaper Editors. Presbyterian. Mason. Elk. Clubs: Nat. Press (Washington); Fort Wayne Country, Press (Ft. Wayne, Indiana); Olympia; Columbia (Indpls.); Indianapolis Athletic. Home: Fort Wayne, IN.

FLEMING, SAMUEL WILSON, JR., cons. engr.; b. Harrisburg, Pa., July 7, 1885; s. Samuel Wilson and Mary (deSausser) F.; B.A., Princeton, 1906; M.E., Lehigh U., 1909; m. Sarah Fullerton Hastings, Jan. 8, 1918; children—Barbara (Mrs. George W. Reily III), Frances (Mrs. George B. Barnard), Samuel Wilson III; m. 2d, Nancy Robinson Simmons, Aug. 23, 1948. Engr. Central Hudson Gas & Electric Co., Newburgh, N.Y., 1909-15; partner, treas. Gannett Fleming Corddry & Carpenter, Inc., engrs., Harrisburg, 1915—, now chmn., treas.; pres. Owego Waterworks; dir. Cayuga Rock Salt Co., Nat. Central Bank & Trust Co., Gen. Waterworks Corp. Trustee Temple U. Served as maj. 315th Inf., 79th Div. AEF, World War I; lt. col. 104th Cav., Pa. N.G. Decorated D.S.C., Order Purple Heart, Legion of Honor; Croix de Guerre (France). Mem. Am. Soc. French Legion of Honor, Engrs. Soc. Pa (past pres.), C. of C. (past pres.). Presbyn. (trustee). Home: Harrisburg, Pa.

FLETCHER, ANDREW, business exec.; b. N.Y.C., Feb. 6, 1895; s. Andrew and Jean L. (Drummond) F.; ed. Yale, 1916; E.D. (hon.), U. Mo., 1949, Mont. Sch. Mines, 1964; LL.D., St. Frances Xavier U., 1953, Seton Hall U., 1957; m. E. Dorothea Camp, Oct. 19, 1918. Shipyard mechanic Harlan and Hollingsworth, Wilmington, Del., until 1917; foreman Balt. Dry Dock Co., 1917-18; sec. W. and A. Fletcher Co., Hoboken, N.J., 1918-24; in charge Fletcher shipyard 1924-29, when plant merged with 6 other N.Y. shipyards under title United Dry Docks, Inc.; v.p., treas., dir. St. Joseph Lead Co., 1929-46, exec. v.p., 1946-47, pres., 1947-60, chmn. bd., 1960-67, hon. chmn. bd. trustees, chmn. finance com., 1967-77; past pres. Meramec Mining Co., 953 Fifth Ave. Corp. Mayor, Mendham, N.J., 1964-70. Past pres. United Engring. Trustees; trustee Engring. Found. Bd. (N.Y.). Hon. mem. Am. Mining Congress. Mem. AIME (pres.), Am. Mining Congress (v.p.), Am. Bur. Metal Stats. (dir.), Soc. Naval Architects and Marine Engrs., Lead Industries Assn. (past pres., dir.), Am. Zinc Inst. (dir.), Mining and Metall. Soc., Inst. of Metals (London), Australasian Inst. Mining and Metallurgy (hon.), Yale Engring. Assn. Mason. Clubs: Yale, Mining, University (N.Y.C.). Home: Mendham, N.J. Died Jan. 30, 1977.

FLETCHER, ARTHUR BOYD, business exec.; born Monrovia, Ind., Jan. 24, 1886; s. Rufus A. and Martha (Henley) F.; ed. pub. schs. and high sch.; m. Katherine E. Dennis, Dec. 10, 1910; 1 son, Robert D. Vice pres. and dir. Internat. Shoe Co. Mem. bd. trustees Sch. of Ozarks, Hollister, Mo. Mason (Shriner). Home: St. Louis *

FLETCHER, FRANK JACK, naval officer; b. Marshalltown, Ia., Apr. 29, 1885; s. Thomas Jack and Alice (Glick) F.; B.S., U.S. Naval Acad., 1906; grad. U.S. Naval War Coll., 1930, U.S. Army War Coll., 1931; m. Martha Richards, Feb. 10, 1917. Commd. ensign U.S. Navy, 1908, and advanced through the grades to vice adm., 1942; flag lt. and fleet signal officer, U.S. Atlantic Fleet, 1914-15; comd. U.S.S. Dale, Chauncey, Margaret, Benham, Gridley, Whipple, Sacramento, New Mexico, Cruisers Pacific Fleet; in comd. North Pacific Forces; chmn. Gen. Bd. U.S. Navy; retired as adm., May 1947. Decorated Medal of Honor for distinguished service at Vera Cruz, 1914; Navy Cross for distinguished service in command of U.S.S. Benham in war zone, 1918; D.S.M. for distinguished service in command of Task Forces at battles of Coral Sea and Midway; Army D.S.M. for duty in comd. N. Pacific Forces, U.S. Pacific Fleet. 1943-45; Purple Heart; Companion Order of the Bath (British); Order of the Green Dragon of Amxam (French), Clubs: New York Yacht; Chevy Chase, Army and Navy (Washington, D.C.) Home: "Araby," La Plata, Md.

FLETCHER, HARVEY, coll. dean, physicist; b. Provo, Utah, Sept. 11, 1884; s. Charles E. and Elizabeth (Miller) F.; B.S., Brigham Young U., 1907; Ph.D., U. Chgo., 1911; D.S. (hon.), Columbia, 1935, Kenyon Coll., Stevens Inst., Case Sch., U. Utah, 1944, Brigham Young U.; m. Lorena Chipman, Sept. 9, 1908; children—Phyllis, Stephen Harvey, James Chipman, Robert Chipman, Harvey J., Paul C. Head dept. physics Brigham Young U., 1911-16, dir. research, 1952—, dean Coll. Phys. and Engring. Scis., 1953—, engring. staff research dept. Bell Telephone Labs., 1916-48, dir. phys. research, 1933-49; prof. elec. engring. Columbia, 1949-52. Recipient Louis Edward Levy medal for phys. measurements of audition, 1924, Gold medal Soc. Motion Pictures Engrs., 1949; Gold medal Audio Engring. Soc., 1958; Founders award and medal I.E.E.E., 1967. Fellow Am. Phys. Soc. (pres. 1945), A.A.A.S. (v.p. 1937-38), Am. Inst. E.E.; mem. Am. Soc. Hard of Hearing (pres. 1929-30), Nat., Utah (pres. 1915-16) acads. scis., Acoustical Soc. Am. (pres. 1929-30; Gold medal 1957), Phi Beta Kappa, Sigma Xi; hon. mem. Am. Otological Soc. Author: Speech and Hearing, 1929; Speech and Hearing in Communications, 1952. Contbr. papers in field. Research on audition. Home: Provo, UT. *

FLETCHER, JOHN DUNDAS, business exec.; b. Pasadena, Calif., Apr. 27, 1886; s. Alfred and Charlotte (Dundas) F.; A.B., U. of Calif., 1907, M.A., 1909; m. Jessie Clark, June 1, 1911; children—Margaret, John D. Western traffic mgr. Luckenbach Steamship Co., San Francisco, 1912-17; with Food Adminstrn., Washington, 1918-1919; v.p. P. N. Gray & Co., Inc. export co., N.Y. City, 1919-24; partner Wm. Cavalier & Co., investment banking, San Francisco, 1925-29; export mgr. and v.p. Caterpillar Tractor Co. since 1929. Dir. Nat. Foreign Trade Council; mem. Am. Relief Adminstrn. Commn. for Relief in Belgium. Mem. Rockfeller Center Club. Home: N.Y. *

FLETCHER, MAURICE JOHN, army ofcr.; b. Avoca, Ia., Sept. 21, 1906; s. John and Mary (Schmidt) F.; student Engring. Sch., Ia. State Coll., 1927, 28; m. Norma L. Jory, Nov. 25, 1931; 1 dau., Patricia M. Wheeler. Commnd. cav. res., U.S. Army, 1931, advanced through grades to col., Med. Service Corps; inf. instr. Camp Robinson, then chief hand and shoulder weapons sect., field service, ordnance dept., during World War II; dir. research U.S. Army Prosthetics Research Labs., Walter Reed Army Med. Center, retired 1961; mem. faculty Northwestern U. Sch. Prosthetics, Rehab. Inst. Chgo., periodically from 1961. Chmn., mem. cons. spl. phases prosthetics research and development Prosthetics Research Bd., Nat. Acad. Scis.-NRC. Decorated Army Commendation ribbon, Legion of Merit); recipient Holley medal Am. Soc. M.E., 1959; Golden Plate award Acad. of Achievement, 1961. Mem. Assn. Mil. Surgeons, Internat. Soc. Welfare of Cripples (instr., conferee internat. prosthetics courses braces and artificial limbs). Co-author: Human Limbs and their Substitutes, 1954; Orthopaedic Appliances Atlas, Vol. II. Patentee comml. engring. and mech. devices, weapons, prosthetics. Home: Ely, Minn. Died May 13, 1980.

FLEXNER, HORTENSE (MRS. WYNCIE KING), writer; b. Louisville, Ky., Apr. 12, 1885; d. Jacob A. and Rosa (Maas) F.; prep. edn., Flexner Sch., Louisville, Ky.; student Bryn Mawr, 1903-04; A.B., U. of Mich., 1907, M.A., 1910; m. Wyncie King, of Bryn Mawr, Pa., Apr. 30, 1919. English reader, U. of Mich., 1909-10; newspaper work, Louisville, Ky., 1912-19; free lance writer, 1919-21; mgr. girls' club (promotive writing), Curtis Pub. Co., since 1923. Mem. Poetry Soc. America, Phi Beta Kappa. Author: Clouds and Cobblestones, 1920; (plays) Voices (prod.); The Faun; The Broken God (prod. Little Theatre Soc. of Ind.); The New Queen (prod. U. of Louisville Players). Contbr. verse to mags. Home: Bryn Mawr, Pa.

FLINT, JOHN GARDINER, investment banker; b. Milw., Aug. 17, 1902; s. Wyman K. and Jennie L. (Ray) F.; A.B. cum laude, Harvard U., 1923; m. Eleanor Musgrave, June 6, 1925; children—John Gardiner, Jean Flint Wilson. With Stone & Webster, Inc., 1923-26, Stone & Webster and Blodget, Inc., 1927-31; joined Kidder, Peabody & Co., Inc., Boston, 1931, partner, 1936-64, v.p., 1964-78; trustee Suffolk Franklin Savs. Bank, Boston, 1945-75, hon. trustee, 1975-78. Chmn. Mass. Victory Fund Com., U.S. Treasury, 1942-43; bd. dirs. Better Bus. Bur. Eastern Mass., Inc., 1938-76, chmn., 1968-72; mem. corp. Children's Hosp. Mem. Investment Bankers Assn. Am. (gov. 1943-46). Clubs: Somerset (Boston); Longwood Cricket (Chestnut Hill, Mass.); Myopia Hunt (Hamilton, Mass.); Everglades (Palm Beach, Fla.). Home: Beverly Farms, Mass. Died June 19, 1978.

FLINT, RICHARD FOSTER, geologist; b. Chgo., Mar. 1, 1902; s. Nott William and Edith Burnham (Foster) F.; B.S., U. Chgo., 1922, Ph.D., 1925; A.M. (hon.), Yale, 1945; Sc.D. (hon.), U. Dublin, 1963; Sc.D. (hon.), U. Wroclaw, Poland, 1966; m. Margaret Cecil Haggott, Dec. 29, 1926; 1 dau. Asst. in geology U. Chgo., 1922-25; instr., asst. prof., prof. Yale, 1925-56, Henry Barnard Davis prof., 1957-70, emeritus, 1970-76; dir. grad. studies in geology, 1951-57, chmn. dept., 1957-64; chmn. adv. bd. Yale Geochronometric Lab., 1953-60; exchange prof. U. Paris, lectr. U. Cambridge, Joly lectr. Trinity Coll. (Dubin), 1951; Bownocker lectr. Ohio State U., 1967; temp. geologist U.S. Geol. Survey and other geol. surveys; served as sr. scientist Boyd Arctic expdn., 1937; cons. Research and Devel. Bd., 1946-53, Army Engrs., 1949-63; chmn. compilation com. Glacial Map of N.A., NRC, 1939-45, Glacial Map U.S., 1956-59; mem. com. on Carbon 14 Am. Anthrop. Assn., 1949-51. Pres. 7th Congress Internat. Quaternary Assn., 1965. Maj., intelligence, USAAF, 1943-45; lt. col. CE, USAR, 1949-53. Guggenheim fellow, 1965-66; recipient Albrecht Penck medal German Quaternary Assn., 1966; Prestwich medal Geol. Soc. London, 1972. Fellow A.A.A.S., Geol. Soc.

Am., Arctic Inst. N.Am. (gov. 1945, chmn. 1950), Am. Acad. Arts and Scis.; mem. Am. Geophys. Union, Glaciol. Soc., Phi Beta Kappa, Sigma Xi; hon. mem. Internat. Union Quaternary Research; hon. fgn. mem. geol. socs. Edinburgh, London, Stockholm, Finland, and Argentina. Author: Glacial Geology and the Pleistocene Epoch, 1947; Glacial and Pleistocene Geology, 1955; Glacial and Quaternary Geology, 1971; The Earth and its History, 1973. Co-author: Physical Geology, 1932, 37, 48, 69, 74, 77; Introduction to Physical Geology, 1955, 62. Asso. editor Am. Jour. Sci., Quaternary Research, Zeitschr. f. Geomorphologie, Pacific Geology, Quaternaria; co-editor Radiocarbon. Contbr. articles in field. Home: New Haven, Conn. Died June 6, 1976.

FLOCH, JOSEPH, painter; b. Vienna, Austria, Nov. 5, 1895; s. Samuel and Jeanette (Mauksch) F.; ed. Acad. Fine Arts, Vienna; m. Hermine Frankl, May 12, 1934; children—Jenny Eva, Suzanne Marguerite. Came to U.S., 1941, naturalized, 1952. Represented in permanent collections M.H. De Young Mus., San Francisco, Toledo Mus. Art, Mus. Modern Art, Paris, Jeu de Paume, Paris, Nat. Art Gallery, Wellington, N.Z., William Rockhill Nelson Gallery, Kansas City, Mo., Belvedere Mus., Mus. Vienna, Smithsonian Instn., Washington, Ind. Mus. Art, Indpls., Albertina Mus., Vienna, Mus. Lille (France), Mus. Lyon (France), Mus. City of Paris, Springfield Mus. Fine Arts, Montclair Art Mus., Mus. Mulhouse, France, Mus. Tel Aviv, Met. Mus. Art, N.Y.C., Whitney Mus., N.Y.C., others; exhibited retrospective show Belvedere Mus., Vienna, Austria, 1972; faculty mem. New Sch. Social Research. Recipient Gold medal Paris Internat. Exhbn., 1937; Lippincott prize Pa. Acad. Fine Arts, 1945; award Nat. Inst. Arts and Letters, 1951; Breevoort-Eickemeyer prize Columbia, 1955; Wm. Palmer Meml. prize Nat. Acad., N.Y.C., 1960, gold medal of merit, 1968, Palmer meml., 1969; Chevalier French Order Arts and Letters; Isidor Meml. gold medal Nat. Acad.; Clara Obrig prize Nat. Acad.; Saltus gold medal for merit, 1967; Andrew Carnegie award, 1969. Mem. Salon d'Automne (Paris), Fedn. Modern Painters and Sculptors, Nat. Acad., Salon des Tuileries (Paris); 1st prize Eastern States Art Exhibits Springfield Mus., 1966. Home: New York, N.Y. Died Oct. 25, 1977; interred Mt. Hope Cemetery, Hastings-on-Hudson, N.Y.

FLOERSHEIMER, ALBERT, JR., motion picture communications co. exec.; b. N.Y.C., Apr. 14, 1917; s. Albert and Fannie (Markwell) F.; student N.Y. U., 1934, Columbia, 1935; m. Adriana Musa, Nov. 11, 1956 (dec. 1971); 1 dau., Adrienne; m. 2d Gilda Goodman, June 1, 1973. Reporter Macy-Westchester newspapers, 1934-42; v.p. pub. relations and catering Walter Reade, Inc., 1946-58; dir. pub. relations Theatre Owners of Am., N.Y.C., 1958-62; pres. AMPA, N.Y.C., 1961-62; dir. advt. and publicity Walter Reade Orgn., Inc., Oakhurst, N.J., 1963-64, adminstrv. asst. to pres., sec., asst. treas., from 1966. Mem. Middletown (N.J.) Tercentennial Commn., 1968; chmn., trustee Walter Reade Employees Fund; sec. Walter Reade Found.; sec., trustee Walter Reade Employees Pension Plan. Served to capt. Signal Corps, AUS, 1941-46. Mem. Assn. Motion Picture Advertisers (pres.). Democrat. Jewish. Home: Middletown, N.J. Died June 2, 1980.

FLOM, SAMUEL LOUIS, steel co. exec.; b. Lithuania, June 10, 1901; s. Morris and Sarah (Notes) F.; came to U.S., 1906, naturalized, 1939; C.E., Lehigh U., 1921; m. Julia Mittle, June 1, 1927; children—Joann (Mrs. Harry G. Greenberg), Edward, Mary Sue (Mrs. Frederick M. Rothenberg). Br. mgr. Truscon Steel Co., Tampa, Fla., 1925-37; sec.-treas. Fla. Steel Products, Inc., Tampa, 1937-56; sec.-treas. Fla. Steel Corp., Tampa, 1956-59, pres., 1959-64, chmn., 1964-73, chmn. exec. com., 1973-80. Trustee Univ. Community Hosp., Tampa. Mem. Am. Iron and Steel Inst. Mason, Rotarian. Clubs: Palma Ceia Golf and Country, University, Tampa Yacht and Country, Tower (Tampa). Home: Tampa, Fla. Died Mar. 10, 1980; buried Tampa.

FLORA, A(BRAM) C(LINE), supt. of schools; b. Roanoke, Va., July 2, 1885; A.B., Bridgewater (Va.) Coll., 1912, LL.D., 1943; M.A., U. of S.C., 1916; grad. study, U. of Va., U. of Chicago and George Peabody Coll.; m. Lulu M. Humbert, June 19, 1913; children—Mel Lee (Mrs. Attis E. Crowe), Abram Cline, Jr. Teacher, Danville, Va., 1912-13; prin. Union (S.C.) High Sch., 1913-14, Logan Elementary Sch., Columbia, S.C., 1914-17, Columbia (S.C.) High Sch., 1917-28; supt. of schools, Columbia, since 1928. Pres. S.C. council Boy Scouts America for 10 yrs., mem. nat. council Boy Scouts America since 1940. Mem. S.C. High Sch. League (pres.); S.C. Education Assn. (pres., dept. of superintendence), S.C. Ednl. Commn. (chmn.), N.E.A. (state dir., 1932-42, 1st vice pres., 1941-42, pres., 1942-43, chmn. budget com., 1940, sec. bd. of trustees since 1946, mem. ednl. policies commn. since 1945, chmn. bd. trustees, since spring 1948; Sigma Chi. Baptist. Clubs: Kiwanis, Cosmos.

FLOROVSKY, GEORGES, clergyman, educator; b. Odessa, Russia, Aug. 28, 1893; s. Basil and Claudia (Poprouzhenko) F.; diploma grad. studies U. Odessa, 1916, research fellow, 1916-19; D.D., St. Andrews U. (Scotland), 1937; S.T.D., Boston U., 1950; Th.D., U. Salonica, 1959; LL.D., Notre Dame U., 1966; D.D., St. Vladimir's Sem., Crestwood, N.Y., 1968; Yale, 1973, Princeton, 1974; m. Xenia Simonov, Apr. 27, 1922. Came to U.S., 1948, naturalized, 1954. Lectr. philosophy U. Odessa, 1919-20; lectr. philosophy of law Russian Faculty Law, Prague, 1922-26; prof. patristics Orthodox Theol. Inst., Paris, 1926-48; ordained priest Greek Orthodox Ch., 1932; prof. divinity St. Vladimir's Orthodox Theol. Sem., N.Y.C., 1948-55, dean, 1950-55; adj. prof. history and theology Eastern orthodoxy Union Theol. Sem; adj. prof. religion Columbia, 1950-55; asso. prof. Greek Archdiocese Holy Cross Theol. Sch., Brookline, Mass., 1955-59; prof. Eastern ch. history Harvard Div. Sch., 1956-64, prof. ereritus, 1964-79; sr. vis. fellow council humanities, vis. prof. religion and Slavics, Princeton, 1964-72, vis. lectr. Princeton Theol. Sem., 1972-79, prof. patristic theology and philosophy of religion Holy Cross Theol. Sch., Brookline, Mass., 1963-65; vis. lectr. ch. history Boston U., 1954-55. Mem. acad. council Ecumenical Inst.for Advanced Theol. Studies Jerusalem, 1945-79. Fellow Am. Acad. Arts and Scis.; corr. fellow Brit. Acad.; mem. Royal Acad. of Athens (Greece) (corr. mem.), Am. Soc. Ch. History, World Council Chs. (mem. provisional com. 1938-46; assembly del. 1948, 54, 61, 68; central and exec. coms., del confs., 1937, 52, 63), Nat. Council Chs. Christ U.S.A. (v.p. 1954-57), Am Hist. Assn., Am. Assn. for Advancement Slavic Studies. Home: Princeton, N.J. Died Aug. 11, 1979.

FLORSHEIM, RICHARD ABERLE, artist; b. Chgo., Oct. 25, 1916; s. Leonard S. and Bertha (Aberle) F.; student U. Chgo., 1934-36; pvt. art studies, Europe and Near East, 1936-38; m. Helen Porfirieff, Feb. 14, 1948. Painter, printmaker, Chgo., 1938-42, 46-80, tchr., lectr., 1946-80; one man shows Art Inst. Chgo., Inst. Nacional de Bellas Artes (Mexico), New Sch. Social Research, Milw. Art Inst., pvt. galleries; works represented permanent collections Mus. Modern Art, Met. Mus., Art Inst. Chgo., Cin. Art Mus., Library of Congress, Mus. of Modern Art Paris, Rome, Sao Paolo, Lima, Bibliothèque Nationale (Paris), others U.S. and abroad. U.S. del. Internat. Assn. Plastic Arts, 1963; mem. Ill. Arts Council, 1965-73. Bd. dirs. Fine Arts Work Center, Provincetown. Served as lt. USNR, 1942-46; mem. Res. Asso. Nat. Acad. Design; mem. Artists Equity Assn. (pres. 1954-55, hon. pres. 1955—), Soc. Am. Graphic Artists, Audubon Soc. Artists, Renaissance Soc. U. Chgo., Arts Club Chgo., Provincetown Art Assn. (hon. v.p., trustee). Clubs: Lotos, Century (N.Y.C.); Beachcombers (Provincetown, Mass.). Painting, Night City, reproduced in Eliot's 300 Years of Am. Painting, 1958. Subject of book: Richard Florsheim: The Artist and His Art, 1976. Home: Chicago, Ill. Died Nov. 20, 1979.

FLORY, HARRY RUSSELL, newspaperman; b. Maysville, O., June 11, 1899; s. John and Mary Alice (Hess) F.; B.A., Coll. of Wooster, 1920; B.Litt., Columbia U., 1922; L.H.D., Coll. of Wooster, 1943; m. Florence King Gilman, Jan. 22, 1925; children—Harry R. (dec.), Marjorie Anne, Stewart Gilman. Worked as newsboy, printer's devil, pressman, reporter Wooster Daily News while attending high sch., coll.; reporter Akron Times, summer 1920; acting city editor Wooster Daily Record, summer 1921; staff corr. Internat. News Service, N.Y. City, Kansas City, Indianapolis, Chicago, Paris and London, 1922-26, Paris bureau mgr., 1926-28, London bureau mgr., 1928-31; staff corr. United Press, London, 1931-34, asst. European News mgr., London, 1934-38, European news mgr. 1938-43 (hdqrs. transferred to N.Y. City, Dec. 1940), fgn. news mgr., dir. communications, 1943-52; gen. manager communications, 1952-64; communications cons. to Am. Newspaper Pubs. Assn., N.Y.C., from 1964. Established special communications arrangements between London and Amsterdam bureaus of United Press, Oct. 1939. Observer Internat. Telecommunications Conf., Cairo, 1938. Served as 2d lt. U.S. Army, Sept.-Dec. 1918. Trustee, Coll. of Wooster, 1948-51. Mem. Phi Beta Kappa, Phi Sigma Kappa, Sigma Delta Chi. Club: University (N.Y.C.). Home: New York, N.Y. Died Nov. 9, 1976.

FLOWER, BARDWELL HASTINGS, physician; b. Rupert, Vt., Apr. 27, 1902; s. Albert H. and Mary E. (Roberts) F.; A.B., Wesleyan U., Middletown, Conn., 1923; M.D., Harvard, 1928; D.Sc. (hon.), Assumption Coll., Worcester, Mass., 1970; m. Maveret E. Hughes, Aug. 9, 1927; children—Constance (Mrs. Robert L. Porter), Martha Hughes (Mrs. William J. Stromer), David Albert (dec.), Bardwell Hastings (dec.). Intern, Worcester (Mass.) City Hosp., 1929-30; sr. physician Worcester State Hosp., 1931-34; asst. supt. Grafton State Hosp., North Grafton, Mass., 1934-38; asst. commr. Mass. Dept. Mental Health, 1938-41; supt. Worcester State Hosp., 1941-69; forensic examiner indicted felons Worcester Area, 1941-69; cons. forensic psychiatry Vt. State Hosp., Waterbury, 1970-80. Diplomate Am. Bd. Psychiatry and Neurology. Life fellow Am. Psychiat. Assn.; mem. AMA, Mass. Med. Soc., New Eng. Soc. Psychiatry, Vt. Psychiat. Assn. Rotarian. Address: West Rupert, Vt. Died June 25, 1980.

FLYNN, CLARENCE EDWIN, clergyman, writer; b. Greene County, Ind. May 22, 1886; s. John Wesley and Matilda Caroline (Cullison) F.; A.B., DePauw University, 1911, D.D., 1924; m. Mayme King, October 21, 1911 (died Feb. 15, 1942); 1 daughter, Nancy Caroline (Mrs. Stuart G. Kelsey). Ordained to the ministry of M.E. Ch., 1910; served churches in Ind., Calif., New York and Iowa; also served as publicity sec. Educational Jubilee Movement; supt. Bloomington (Ind.) Dist. of M.E. Church; dir. of the Wesley Foundation of Indiana Univ. Mem. Phi Gamma Delta, Pi Gamma Mu. Author: Windows; also writer of stories, articles and verse appearing in periodicals and anthologies. Home: Berkeley, California.

FLYNN, J. WALTER, editor, pub., artist; b. Bayonne, N.J., Dec. 16, 1910; s. Walter Joseph and Alice Gertrude (Molloy) F.; grad. Cooper Union Coll., 1928; m. Ruth L. Simmons, May 28, 1932; children—Francine Ruth, Maureen Mary. Successively promotion art dir. Conde Nast Publs., art editor Asia mag., exec. art editor Street & Smith Publs., asso. editor, v.p. Triangle Publs., asso. editor Hearst Mags., asso. editor Liberty Mag., editor in chief Everywoman's Mag., N.Y.C., editor N.M. State Mag., Santa Fe, creative printing cons. Precision Press, Inc., Dallas, editor, pub. La. Forests and People mag., editor Arkansas State Mag., Little Rock, editor, pub. Fla. State Mag., Longwood; editor, pub. Carte Blanche mag., Los Angeles, 1971-77; artist, works exhibited Berkshire Gallery, Roerich Mus., Art Students League, Art Dirs. Club, Soc. Illustrators, Met. Mus. Art, N.Y.C., Grand Central Art Galleries. Recipient citation U.S. Treasury Dept., World War II; 1st award for editorial achievement Indsl. Marketing Assn.; award for distinctive merit Nat. Exhbn. Advt. and Editoral Art, Art Dirs. Club N.Y.; certificate of excellence Am. Inst. Graphic Arts; Graphic Arts award Printing Industries Am., 1969; 1st place award best functional typography, also honorable mention best in-depth reporting Fla. Mag. Assn.; 1st place Explore Can. award Travel Industry Assn. Can., 1975. Mem. Soc. Typographic Arts Chgo., Art Dirs. Club N.Y., Soc. Publ. Designers. Clubs: Greater Los Angeles Press; The Lambs (N.Y.C.); Westport Artists, Inc. (Conn.); Cal. Knights of the Vine. Home: Santa Monica, Calif. Died Feb. 4, 1977.

FLYNN, JOHN EDWARD, architect; b. Cin., Jan. 10, 1930; s. John George and Ethel Mary (Brauer) F.; B.Arch., U. Mich., 1953; m. Iris Pumroy, Feb. 1, 1954; children—Sheryl Ann, J. Michael, James P., Shawn Louise. Staff architect Gen. Electric Co., Nela Park, Cleve., 1955-64; prin. John Flynn, Architect and Cons., Cleve., 1964-73; prof. arch. Kent (Ohio) State U., 1967-73; prof. archtl. engring. Pa. State U., 1973-80. Served with U.S. Army, 1953-55. Recipient Arnold Brunner Scholarship award Archtl. League N.Y., 1965; registered profl. architect, Ohio. Fellow Illuminating Engring. Soc. (dir. 1974-80, sr. v.p. 1978, pres. 1979-80), Internat. Assn. Lighting Designers; mem. AIA, Internat. Commn. Illumination (internat. chmn. com.), Inter-Soc. Color Council, Tau Sigma Delta, Alpha Rho Chi. Author: Architectural Lighting Graphics, 1962; Architectural Interior Systems, 1970; contbr. articles to profl. jours. Research on effects of light and color on judgment and behavior. Home: State College, Pa. Died Aug. 25, 1980; buried Graysville (Pa.) Cemetery.

FOCKE, ARTHUR BERNARD, lawyer; b. Dayton, Ohio, Aug. 12, 1911; s. Bernard Matthias and Stella (McFadden) F.; student U. Dayton, 1929-32; LL.B., Georgetown U., 1936; student Cath. U. Am., 1938-40; m. Marianne Kernan, Aug. 24, 1935; children—Michael, Marian. Admitted to D.C. bar, 1935, also U.S. Supreme Ct. bar; claims examiner, atty. GAO, 1935-42; atty. Bur. Budget, Office Mgmt. and Budget, Exec. Office Pres., 1946-51, legal adviser, 1951-58, gen. counsel, 1958-72; dep. dir., counsel state criminal justice action program Nat. Gov.'s Conf., 1972-73; sr. info. analyst Informatics, Inc., Rockville, Md., 1974-75; cons. atty. Mead Data Central, N.Y.C., 1975-76. Served to comdr. USNR, 1942-46. Mem. Am., Fed. bar assns. Clubs: Nat. Press, Nat. Lawyer's. Home: Washington, D.C. Died Apr. 17, 1980; buried Gate of Heaven Cemetery, Wheaton, Md.

FOGARTY, ANNE, designer; b. Pitts., Feb. 2, 1919; d. Robert and Marion (Bosoranoff) Whitney; student Allegheny Coll., 1936-37, Carnegie Tech., 1937-38, E. Hartman Sch. Design, 1939; m. Thomas E. Fogarty, Jr., Aug. 10, 1940; 1 son, 1 dau. Began career in advt., modeling; fashion stylist Dorland Internat., 1947-48; fashion designer Youth Guild, 1948-50, Margot Dresses, Inc., 1950-57; designer for Saks 5th Avenue, 1958-62; designer, pres. Anne Fogarty, Inc., N.Y.C., 1960-80; designer lingerie, costume jewelry, shoes, hats, coats, suits. Recipient merit award Mademoiselle, 1951; fashion award Bonwit Teller, 1951; award Am. Fashion Critics, 1951; fashion award Neiman-Marcus, 1953; 20th Century world of fashion award Phila. Fashion Group, 1953; Internat. Silk Assn. award, 1955; Cotton Fashion award, 1957; Sports Illustrated Magazine Designer of Year award, 1960; Am. Express Annual Fashion award in 1962. Member of Council Fashion Designers of Am. (charter mem.), Fashion Group, Am. Fedn. of Radio Artists. Republican. Roman Catholic.

Author: Wife Dressing, 1959. Contbr. publicity articles popular mags., newspapers, U.S. and Europe. Home: New York, N.Y. Died Jan. 14, 1980.

FOGLE, OSCAR MATHIAS, educator; b. Woodsboro, Md., July 14, 1882; s. Charles Calvin and Martha Ellen (Bowers) F.; A.B., Roanoke Coll., Salem, Va., 1902; A.M., Columbia, 1923; Ed.M., Harvard, 1930; m. Clara Lena Davis, of Hyattstown, Md., Dec. 22, 1907 (died 1919); children—Oscar Mathias, Mary Davis, Richard Springer; m. 2d, Rhoda Mary Hartman, of Cavetown, Md., June 21, 1923; 1 dau., Elizabeth Hartman. High sch. prin. and sch. supt. in Md., 1902-29; prof. and head dept. edn. and psychology, Lincoln Memorial U., Harrogate, Tenn., 1930-31; prin. Pleasant Hill Acad. since 1931. Mem. Am. Assn. Univ. Profs., N.E.A., Progressive Edn. Assn. Democrat. Conglist. Mason. Club: Exchange (Crossville, Tenn.). Home: Pleasant Hill, Tenn.

FOLCH-PI, JORDI, physician; b. Barcelona, Spain, Mar. 25, 1911; s. Rafael Folch Capdevila and Maria Pi Ferrer; B.S., Instituto Balmes, Barcelona U., 1927; M.D., U. Barcelona, 1932; M.S. (hon.), Harvard, 1951; D.Sc., U. Montpellier, 1967; M.D., U. Chile, 1969; m. Willa G. Babcock, June 23, 1945; children—Raphael Charles, Diana Maria, Frederic Albert. Came to U.S., 1936, naturalized, 1947. Student intern dept. gen. surgery Hosp. Clinico, Barcelona, 1930-33, asst. resident physician dept. metabolic disease, 1933-35; Rockefeller Found. fellow, vol. asst. Rockefeller Inst. Hosp., N.Y.C., 1935-37, asst., 1937-42, asso., 1942-44; asst. prof. biol. chemistry Harvard Med. Sch., 1944-51, asso. prof., 1951-55, prof. neurochemistry, from 1956, prof. emeritus, to 1979; dir. sci. research McLean Hosp., Belmont, Mass., 1944-79; hon. prof. faculty medicine, Barcelona, 1975. Chmn. bd. sci. counselors NIMH, from 1960; chmn. sci. rev. com. Kennedy labs. Mass. Gen. Hosp. Boston, 1961-79; mem. Nat. Adv. Council Mental Health, 1972-79. Mem. Nat. Acad. Scis., Am. Soc. Oil Chemistry, A.A.A.S., Am. Soc. Biol. Chemists, Harvey Soc., Soc. Research Mental and Nervous Disorders, Am. Acad. Arts and Scis., Acad. Neurology, Internat. (sec. 1967-79), Am. (sec. 1969-79) socs. neurochemistry, Am. Neurol. Assn. Clubs: Appalachian Mountain, Harvard (Boston). Editor: Jour. of Neurochemistry. Author sci. papers. Home: Boston, Mass. Died Oct. 3, 1979; interred Center Sandwich, N.H.

FOLENDORF, GERTRUDE MARAY, hosp. adminstr.; b. Cadott, Wis., May 8, 1885; d. Ross and Agnes Elizabeth (Worrell) Hardy; grad., U. of Calif. Sch. of Nursing, 1920; m. Charles A. Folendorf, Aug. 26, 1912 (died, 1918). Supervisor med. dept. of U. of Calif. Hosp., asst. dir. of nursing, 1921-23; supt. Shriners Hosp., San Francisco, 1923-35, dir. of nursing Shriners Hosps. for Crippled Children, 1935-38, adminstr. Shriners Hosps. (16 hosps.), since 1938. Mem. Advisory Com. for Crippled Children, U.S. Children's Bureau. Fellow Am. Coll. of Hospital Adminstrs. Mem., former pres., U. of Calif. Sch. of Nursing Alumni Assn., San Francisco County Nurses Assn., Calif. State Nurses Assn., League of Nursing Edn., Am. Hosp. Assn., Am. Red Cross (chmn. San Francisco area during World War II). Republican. Eastern Star. Club: San Francisco Women's City. Contbr. numerous articles to professional mags. Home: San Francisco.

FOLEY, HENRY ELLIOTT, lawyer; b. Boston, Mar. 30, 1902; s. Henry J. and Ella J. (Carroll) F.; A.B., Boston Coll., 1922; LL.B., Harvard U., 1925, S.J.D., 1926; m. Catherline E. Sullivan, Sept. 10, 1931; children—Carol Surkin, Henry Elliott. Admitted to Mass. bar, 1926; practiced in Boston, 1926-79; partner firm Foley, Hoag & Eliot 1938—; corp. counsel City of Boston, 1934-38; chmn. Overseers of Pub. Welfare, 1950-52; prof. Boston Coll. Law Sch., 1930-40, acting dean, 1938-39; clk. corp. Air New Eng., Inc. Trustee, New Eng. Med. Center Hosp., Social Law Library. Fellow Am. Bar Found.; mem. Am. Law Inst., Am., Boston bar assns. Clubs: Knights of Malta, Lyford Cay (Bahamas); Algonquin, Union, St. Botolph, Federal (Boston); Edgartown Yacht, Edgartown Reading Room. Home: Boston, Mass. Died Feb. 1979.

FOLGER, JOHN CLIFFORD, investment banker, ambassador; b. Sheldon, Iowa, May 28, 1896; s. Homer and Emma (Funston) F.; B.S., State Coll. Washington, 1917, M.S., 1918; m. Mary Kathrine Dulin, Nov. 2, 1929; children—John Dulin, Lee Merritt. Chmn. bd. Folger Nolan Fleming Douglas Inc., Piedmont Mortgage Co., Washington; dir. Va. Industries, Inc., Washington Star Communications, Inc.; mem. adv. bd. IBM, Hilton Hotels; Am. ambassador to Belgium, 1957-59. Former mem. bd. govs. New York Stock Exchange. Chmn. Rep. Nat. Finance Com. 1955-57, 60-61. Gen. chmn. Washington Community Chest, 1940; chmn. D.C. chpt. ARC, 1942, hon. chmn.; mem. Washington Cathedral. Pres. Investment Bankers Assn. Am., 1943-45. Mem. Nat. Inst. Social Sci. Republican. Clubs: Alfalfa, The Brook, Chevy Chase, Metropolitan, 1925 F Street (Washington); Down Town Assn. (N.Y.C.); Everglades, Bath and Tennis (Palm Beach). Home: Washington, D.C. Died Mar. 24, 1981.

FOLGER, WILLIAM POLK (FOL'JER), chief nat. bank examiner; b. Dobson, N.C., Oct. 27, 1885; s. Thomas W. and Ada D. (Robertson) F.; ed. The Dobson Acad., N.C.; unmarried. Bank clerk, Mt. Airy, N.C., 1914-18; asst. nat. bank examiner, 1918-20, nat. bank examiner, 1920-25, dist. chief nat. bank examiner, Fifth Fed. Res. Dist., 1925-29; exec. v.p. Norfolk Nat. Bank of Commerce, Va., 1929; chief nat. bank examiner since 1929. Club: Burning Tree (Washington, D.C.). Home: Washington

FOLLIARD, EDWARD THOMAS, newspaperman; b. Washington, May 14, 1899; s. Thomas and Rose (Greene) F.; student George Washington U., 1924-25; m. Helen Liston, June 19, 1933; children—Nancy, Michael. Mem. staff Washington, (D.C.) Herald, 1922, Washington Post and Times Herald (formerly Washington Post), 1923-76, assignments have included nat. polit. campaigns since 1928. Canadian tour of King George and Queen Elizabeth, 1930, Roosevelt-Churchill war confs. at Quebec, 1943-44; U.S. war corr. in France, Belgium, Luxembourg and Germany, 1944-45. Awarded Pulitzer prize for distinguished reporting on nat. affairs in United States May 1947; National Headliners Club Award, 1948; named to Hall of Fame, D.C. chpt. Sigma Delta Chi. Served as seaman, U.S. Navy, 1917-19. Mem. White House Corr. Assn. (pres. 1946), Overseas Writers, Am. Legion. Roman Catholic. Clubs: Nat. Press, Alfalfa, Gridiron (pres. 1955). Home: Washington.

FOLLMER, FREDERICK VORIS, judge; b. Milton, Pa., Dec. 13, 1885; s. Dr. John Samuel and Elizabeth B. (Voris) F.; A.B., Bucknell U., 1906, D.C.L. (hon.), 1956; LL.D. (hon.), Lycoming Coll., 1959; m. Ella Brown, May 30, 1921; 1 dau., Mary Elizabeth (Mrs. Robert E. LaCroix). Admitted to Pa. bar, 1910, practicing in Milton; asst. dist. atty. Northumberland County, 1911-14; U.S. atty. for Middle Dist. Pa., 1935-46; U.S. dist judge, Eastern, Middle and Western dist., Pa., 1946-55; U.S. dist. judge Middle dist. Pa., 1955—. Mem. Phi Beta Kappa. Democrat. Mason (33). Club: Rotary (past pres.) Home: Milton, PA.

FOLSOM, MARION BAYARD, former sec. health, edn. and welfare; b. McRae, Ga., Nov. 23, 1893; s. William B. and Margaret Jane (McRae) F.; A.B., U. Ga., 1912; M.B.A., Harvard, 1914; LL.D., U. Rochester, 1945, Hobart and William Smith Colls., 1951, Syracuse U., Tufts U., 1955, Brown U., 1957, Swarthmore Coll., 1957, Hamilton Coll., 1962; D.C.L. Rollins Coll., 1957; D.C.S., N.Y. U., 1950; D.P.S., Springfield Coll., 1962; D.Sc., Albany Med. Coll., 1966; m. Mary Davenport, Nov. 16, 1918; children—Jane McRae (dec.), Marion Bayard, Frances. With Eastman Kodak Co., 1914, treas., 1935-53, dir., 1947-52, 58-68; pres. Eastman Savs. & Loan Assn., 1947-52; trustee Rochester Savs. Bank, 1931-49, 58-63; dir. Lincoln-Rochester Trust Co., 1929-52, 58-63; under sec. treasury, 1953-55; sec. Dept. Health, Edn. and Welfare, 1955-58. Staff dir. spl. com. postwar econ. policy and planning U.S. Ho. Reps., 78th-79th Congresses. Mem. Pres.'s Adv. Council Econ. Security, 1934-35; pres. Rochester Council Social Agys., 1934-36; U.S. employer del. Internat. Labor Conf., Geneva, 1936; mem. Fed. Adv. Council Social Security, 1937-38; div. exec. Nat. Adv. Def. Commn., 1940-41, vice chmn. Pres.'s Adv. Com. Mcht. Marine, 1947-48; mem. social security adv. council U.S. Senate Finance Com., 1948; mem. Regional War Manpower Commn., 1942-45; mem. N.Y. State Adv. Council Unemployment Ins., 1935-50; mem. Bus. Council 1936; chmn. adv. com. personnel study USPHS, 1961-62; dir. U.S. C. of C., 1942-48; trustee Com. Econ. Devel., 1942, chmn. trustees, 1950-52, vice chmn., 1960-68; chmn. Nat. Commn. Community Health Services, 1962-67; mem. Fed. Hosp. Council, 1965-68, Fed. Adv. Council Social Security, 1963-65, N.Y. State Hosp. Rev. and Planning Council, N.Y. State Adv. Health Planning Council, 1969, Pres.' Commn. Heart Disease, Cancer and Stroke, Fed. Adv. Council Employment Security, 1966-70, Nat. Health Adv. Council, 1970—, Health Council Monroe County, 1961-67; vice chmn. White House Conf. Health, 1967. Bd. dirs. Nat. Bur. Econ. Research, Monroe Community Coll., Brookings Instn., 1958-63, Rochester Community Chest, Genesee Regional Hosp. Council, Rochester Bur. Municipal Research; trustee Rochester C. of C. (past pres.); trustee U. Rochester, 1948-63, chmn. exec. com., 1957-63; bd. overseers Harvard Coll., 1951-57. Served with U.S. Army, 1917-19. Recipient Albert Einstein medal citizenship, 1958; Bronfman prize pub. health achievement, 1963; Edward Mott Moore award Monroe County Med. Soc., 1970. Hon. fellow Am. Coll. Hosp. Adminstrs., Acad. Medicine Rochester; mem. Am. Hosp. Assn. (hon.), N.E.A. (hon. life), Acad. Arts and Scis., Phi Beta Kappa Assos. (former dir.), Phi Beta Kappa, Sigma Nu. Presbyn. Clubs: University, Rochester Country, Pundit (Rochester); Harvard (N.Y.C.). Home: Rochester, N.Y. Died Sept. 28, 1976; buried Arlington (Va.) Nat. Cemetery.

FOLTZ, LEROY (STEWART) (FOLTS), univ. prof.; b. Chandlerville, Ill., Nov. 27, 1884; s. Horace Newton and Effie (Stewart) F.; B.S., U. of Ill., 1911; M.S. (John W. Mackay Fellow), U. of Calif., 1917; m. Emily Louise Proctor, July 1, 1915; children—Elva Lea (Mrs. Howard C. Clark), Ermald Newton, Eldon Leroy, Fay Ola (Mrs. M. M. Ash, Jr.). Draftsman, Electric Wheel Co., Quincy, Ill., and The Maytag Co., Newton, Ia., 1907-09; asso. prof. electrical engring. Mich. State Coll., 1920-24, prof. and acting head elec. engring. dept., 1924-25, prof. and head dept., 1925-47, distinguished prof., 1947-50, distinguished prof. emeritus since 1950; prof. elec. engring. Lawrence Inst. of Tech., Detroit, since 1951. Registered profl. engr., Mich. Fellow Am. Inst. E.E.; mem. Am. Assn. Univ. Profs., Am. Soc. Engring. Edn., Phi Kappa Phi. Mem. Peoples Ch. E. Lansing, Mich.; elder; Sunday Sch. supt., teacher adult Sunday Sch. class). Clubs: Lansing Engineers (organizer and former pres.). Home: East Lansing, Mich.

FOMON, SAMUEL, physician, author; b. Chicago, Ill., Jan. 11, 1886; s. Jacob and Rosie F.; Ph.D., U. of Ill., 1902, M.D., 1906; m. Isabel Sherman, of Appleton, Wis., Oct. 2, 1920. Practiced at Chicago since 1906; asst. prof. medicine, U. of Ill. Coll. of Medicine. Served as maj. M.C., U.S.A., at Ft. Oglethorpe, World War. Pres. Fomon Medical Review Course. Mem. A.M.A., Ill. State Med. Assn., Chicago Med. Soc. Author: Medicine and Allied Sciences, 3 vols., 1920. Home: Chicago.

FOOT, LEROY ALBERT, lawyer; b. Melrose, Minn., Sept. 9, 1882; s. Loren S. and Sarah M. (Trace) F.; LL.B., U. of N. Dak., 1906; m. Clara P. Pitts, Sept. 1, 1910; children—Elizabeth Sarah, Clare Mabel. Admitted to North Dakota bar, 1906; settled at Kalispell, Mont., 1906; admitted to Montana bar, 1907; asst. atty. gen. of Mont., 1921-24; apptd. atty. gen. to fill vacancy, Aug. 31, 1924, and elected to same office for term 1925-28, reëlected, 1928, for term 1929-32 inclusive; admitted to practice in Supreme Court U.S. Atty. for Dept. of Army, Engr. Corps, Sacramento, Calif. In U.S. Army, World War, from Mar. 26, 1917; with A.E.F. in France, 18 mos.; div. machine gun officer and asst. chief of staff G3, 41st Div.; hon. discharged, May 15, 1919; brig. gen. Nat. Guard (retired). Mem. Internat. Assn. Attys. Gen. (sec.-treas. 1928-29), Fed. Bar Assn., Nat. Sojourners, Am. Legion, Society American Military Engineers. Republican. Presbyterian. Mason (K.T., Shriner), Past Grand Master, Mont.). Home: Sacramento, Cal.

FOOTE, ELLSWORTH, congressman; b. North Branford, Conn., Jan. 12, 1898; ed. Yale Bus. Coll., 1916; LL.B., Georgetown Univ., 1923; m. Ruth McGill; children—Robert, Roberta, Richard, Anne Marie. Admitted to bar of Conn. and U.S. Supreme Court; engaged in private practice of law, since 1924; spl. asst. to atty. gen. in war transaction sect., Dept. of Justice, Washington, D.C., 1925-26; judge, probate, N. Branford Dist., corp. counsel, town North Branford, 1924-26; acting judge, probate, New Haven Probate Court, 1944-45. Mem. 80th Congress (1947-49), 3d Conn. Dist. Served in Troop A Cav., Conn. Nat. Guard; capt. Gov's Foot Guard. Mem. Am. Bar Assn., New Haven Co. Bar Assn., Totoket Grange P. of H. Republican. Conglist. Club: New Haven Choral. Home: North Branford, Conn. Died Jan. 18, 1977.

FOOTE, FRANCIS S., civil engr.; b. Brooklyn, N.Y., Mar. 31, 1883; s. Francis Seeley and Addie S. (Jameson) F.; E.M., Sch. of Mines (Columbia), 1905; m. Margaret L. Kingsbury, July 15, 1913; children—Elizabeth Luella (Mrs. William L. Argo), Francis Seeley, John Kingsbury. Engineer for Cumberland Mountain Coal & Timber Company, Dunlap, Tennessee, 1905, railroad location, Springdale Association, Louisville, Ky., 1905-06; asst. engineer, New York Central Railroad Co., 1906-07; asst. in civil engring., Columbia U., 1907-10; instr. ry. civ. engring., U. of Ill., 1910-12; asso. prof. railroad engring, 1912-17, prof. since 1917, dir. Surveying Camp, 1912-41, Univ. of California. Member American Soc. C.E.; mem. Am. Ry. Engring. Assn. Pacific Ry. Club, Delta Tau Delta, Tau Beta Pi, Sigma Xi. Conglist. Club: Faculty. Co-author (with Raymond E. Davis); Surveying Theory and Practice. Home: Berkeley, Calif.

FOOTE, IRVING P(ARRISH), univ. prof.; b. Centerville, La., Aug. 6, 1884; s. Newton John and Cora M. (Parrish) F.; student, La. State Normal Sch., 1902-05, La. State U., summer 1908, U. of Chicago, summers 1914, 15; A.M., Peabody Coll., 1920, Ph.D., 1931; m. Edith Trahan, Dec. 9, 1908; children—Irving P., M. Edith Vick, Cora Ann Jungkind, Teacher, La. Pub. Sch., 1901-12; prof. edn., Southwestern La. Inst., 1912-20, dean coll. edn., 1920-24; prof. edn., La. State Univ. since 1924. Mem. Phi Delta Kappa, Kappa Delta Pi, Phi Kappa Phi (pres. La. State U. Chap. 1947-48). Author: The Story of Our Republic (elementary sch. text), 1932. Presbyterian. Home: Baton Rouge.

FOOTE, WILLIAM JENKINS, ret. editor; b. New Haven, Apr. 27, 1905; s. Harry Ward and Martha (Jenkins) F.; B.S., Yale, 1927; m. Dorothy Hope Bennett, June 4, 1932; children—Christopher, Edward,

William, Mary. Reporter, N.Y. Herald Tribune, 1928-30; editorial writer Hartford (Conn.) Courant, 1930-41, asst. mng. editor 1941-49, mng. editor, 1949-67, editor editorial page, 1967-74. Past pres. Conn. Children's Aid Soc., Hartford Orphan Asylum. Mem. Conn. Circuit Asso. Press (pres.), Am. Soc. Newspaper Editors, A.P. Mng. Editors Assn., Berzelius. Clubs: Elizabethan, University (Hartford). Home: West Hartford, Conn. Died Sept. 6, 1976; interred, Guilford, Conn.

FORBES, GEORGE SHANNON, chemist; b. Boston, Mass., Mar. 17, 1882; s. George Fairfield and Elizabeth Lemmon Prentice (Shannon) F.; A.B., summa cum laude, Harvard, 1902, A.M., 1904, Ph.D., 1905; John Harvard fellow, univs. of Leipzig and Berlin, 1906-07; m. Marie Louise Hersey, June 1, 1918; children—Richard W., Elizabeth S., George F. Asso. in chemistry, Bryn Mawr, 1907-09; instr. chemistry, 1909-13, asst., prof., 1913-20. asso. prof., 1920-26, professor (Harvard), 1926-48, professor emeritus since 1948; professor (part time) Northeastern University, 1948-49. Chairman of Department of Chemistry, 1944-47, Harvard. Member Associates of Radcliffe Coll., 1917-20. Mem. com. on photochemistry Nat. Research Council, 1925-37. Fellow Am. Acad. Arts and Sciences, A.A.A.S.; mem. Am. Chem. Soc. (chmn. northeastern sect., 1920, councilor, 1920-25 and 1931-33; chmn. div. physical and inorganic chemistry, 1926-27), Phi Beta Kappa. Episcopalian. Specializes in photochemistry and electrochemistry. Contbr. Jour. Am. Chem. Soc. Home: Cambridge, Mass.

FORD, BENSON, business exec.; b. Detroit, July 20, 1919; s. Edsel Bryant and Eleanor (Clay) F.; student Princeton U., 1938-40; m. Edith McNaughton, July 9, 1941 (dec. Aug. 1980); children—Benson, Lynn McNaughton. Asst. purchasing agt. Ford Motor Co., 1940-41, asst. supt., 1941-42, dir. parent co. and subs.'s; became v.p. Ford Motor Co., gen. mgr. Lincoln-Mercury div., now v.p., chmn. dealer policy bd. Ford Motor Co.; mem., trustee Edison Inst.; dir. Seaboard Properties Co. Mem., trustee Ford Found., 1947-76; mem., trustee, chmn., chief exec. officer Henry Ford Hosp., Detroit; bd. dirs. Detroit Symphony Orch.; Hwy. Users Fedn. for Safety and Mobility, 1970-76; hon. chmn., bd. dirs., Detroit United Found.; Protestant co-chmn. NCCJ, 1951-55; chmn. Automotive Safety Found., 1964-66, Traffic Safety Assn., Detroit, 1959-66; trustee Dermatology Found., 1966-71, Citizens Conf. on State Legislatures, 1965-68; bd. dirs. United Community Funds and Councils Am., 1962-68, Nat. Safety Council, 1959-67. Served as capt. USAAF, World War II. Republican. Episcopalian. Clubs: Country of Detroit, Detroit, Detroit Athletic, Economic, Grosse Pointe, University, Cap and Gown. Home: Grosse Pointe Shores, Mich. Died July 27, 1978.

FORD, FRANCIS J. W., judge; b. Boston, Mass., Dec. 23, 1882; s. Cornelius J. and Josephine (Murphy) F.; grad. Boston Latin Sch., 1900, Harvard Coll., 1904, Harvard Law Sch., 1906; m. Ann Cresswell, Mar. 6, 1916; 1 dau., Dr. Barbara Ford Carter. Admitted to Mass. bar, 1906, since practiced, Boston; mem. Boston City Council, 1917-22, pres. 1919; apptd. U.S. dist. atty. for Mass., Sept. 22, 1933; apptd. U.S. District Judge for Mass., June 27, 1938. Mem. American and Boston bar assns., Am. Judicature Soc., Jud. Conf. of U.S. Democrat. Catholic. Club: Harvard Varsity, Harvard (Boston). Home: Houston.

FORD, HORACE SAYFORD, corp. exec.; b. Gloucester, Mass., Jan. 9, 1885; s. Frederick Eugene and Marilla Frances (Elwell) F.; Dr. of Laws, Middlebury College, 1953; married Mary Frances Currier, June 4, 1907 (dec. Mar. 1956); children—Horace Sayford, Philip. Bank clk., teller Old Colony Trust Co., Boston, 1902-11, asst. cashier, 1911-14; bursar Mass. Inst. Tech., 1914-34, treas., 1934-50, now life mem. corp., chmn. finance com., mem. bldg. and development coms.; inc., dir., mem. exec. com. Am. Research & Development Corp., Godfrey L. Cabot, Inc., Boston; dir., mem. exec. investment and pension coms. Liberty Mut. Ins. Co. (Boston), Arthur D. Little, Inc. (Cambridge); dir., mem. investment com. Liberty Mut. Fire Insurance Company (Boston); dir. Cleve. Pneumatic Tool Company (Cleveland); trustee George Putnam Fund, Bond Investment Trust of Am. (Boston), Sixty Trust (Providence); adviser Gas Industries Fund (Boston). Trustee, mem. investment and pension coms. Worcester Found. Exptl. Biology, Mus. Sci., Boston; life mem. trustee, mem. investment and development coms. Middlebury (Vt.) Coll., Brooks Hosp., Brookline. Mem. Am. Acad. Arts and Scis. Clubs: Union, Commercial, Merchants, Thursday Evening (Boston); Faculty of MIT (Cambridge). Home: Cambridge, Mass.

FORD, JOHN ANSON, former county ofcl.; b. Waukegan, Ill., Sept. 29, 1883; s. James Tooker and Sarah (Holmes) F.; A.B., Beloit Coll., 1907, LL.D., 1952; H.H.D. (hon.), Los Angeles Conservatory Music and Art, 1950; m. Lois Goldsmith, 1911; 1 son, John Arnold. Newspaper reporter Chgo. Tribune, 1914-15; asst. editor Popular Mechanics, 1915-19; news writer Dept. Agr., Washington, 1919-20; mem. Hogg and Ford, advt. and pub. relations, 1920-27; head John Anson Ford Co., advt. and pub. relations, 1927-34; sr. mem. Ford-Long Co., Los Angeles, 1949-52; dir. pub. information for radio KRHM, 1959. Mem. Los Angeles County Bd. Suprs., 1934-58, chmn. bd., 1952-54, 57; mem. Los Angeles Coliseum Commn., 1945-58; acting chmn. Civic Center Authority, 1952; chmn. Cal. Fair Employment Practices Commn., 1959-63, commr., 1963-68. Mem. El Pueblo State Hist. Monument Commn. Chmn. county central com. Democratic Party, 1936; mem. state central com., 1942-50, nat. Dem. committeeman from Cal., 1952-53; del. nat. convs., 1944, 48, 52, 56. Cal. chmn. Kefauver-for-Pres., 1952. Bd. dirs. Hollywood Bowl, Los Angeles Art Inst., Las Fiestas de las Americas. Recipient Foundacion Internacional Eloy Alfaro medal for Inter-Am. friendship, 1950; judge Hollzer bronze award for inter-racial good-will, 1950; Golden Anniversary award Los Angeles Ch. Fedn., 1960; citation Japan Am. Citizens League, 1965. Mem. Japan Am. Soc. (pres. 1960-61), Death Valley 49ers (pres. emeritus), Los Angeles County Sr. Citizens Affiliated Com., Descanso Garden Guild (trustee), Sigma Chi, Delta Sigma Rho, Pi Sigma Alpha. Conglist. Author: Thirty Explosive Years in Los Angeles County, 1961. Home: Los Angeles, CA.

FORD, NEVIL, investment banker; b. Boston, Apr. 18, 1891; s. Edwin and Anne Paddock (Hopkins) F.; B.S., Harvard U., 1913; m. Louise McAlister, Aug. 6, 1917. Factory worker and salesman, A. H. Davenport Co., Boston, 1914; securities salesman, Jackson & Curtis, 1915-20; with First Boston Corp., 1921-60, mem. exec. com., 1935-56, sr. v.p., 1950-56, dir., 1935-60; pres., dir. Huntington Purchase, Inc., 1945-69; dir. and chmn. bd.; mem. exec. com. Heritage Fed. Savs. & Loan Assn., adv. dir., 1975; dir., treas., mem. exec. com. Fgn. Bondholders Protective Council, Inc.; v.p., dir. 825 Fifth Av. Corp. Trustee, mem. exec. and finance coms., chmn. audit com., N.Y. U.-Bellevue Center; chmn. N.Y. Univ.-Bellevue Med. Fund, 1947-51. Pres., dir. Peoples Symphony Concerts, N.Y. Dir. North Suffolk chpt. A.R.C.; bd. dirs., mem. exec. com. Netherlands-Am. Found. Served as lt. (j.g.), U.S. Naval Flying Corps. 1918-19. Served as state adminstr. for Defense Savings; staff N.Y., U.S. Treas. Dept., 1941. Exec. mgr. War Finance Com., N.Y. U.S. Treas. Dept., 1942-43, chmn., 1944-45. Chmn. and dir. Armed Forces Convalescent Services, Huntington, since 1945. Mayor Village Lloyd Harbor, 1950-58. Dir., chmn. Pub. Health Research Inst. City of N.Y., Inc., L.I. Biol. Assn. (chmn., dir., mem. exec. com.). Dir. Huntington Township YMCA; chmn. trustees com. Univ. Hosp., 1964-66; adv. com. Pub. Health Practice Research Center, N.Y.C. Dept. Health; bd. dirs. Better Bellevue Assn.; overseers vis. com. for biology Harvard Coll., 1964-70, mem. com. Colby Coll. Art Mus. Mem. Med. and Health Research Assn. N.Y.C. (dir. until 1970), N.Y. Panel Arbitrators, N.Y. Stock Exchange (dir.), Nat. Assn. Securities Dealers, Assn. Crippled Children (dir.; exec. com., chmn.), Found. for Child Devel., Am. Shakespeare Festival Theater and Acad. (dir.), Nat. Health Council (dir.), Council on Fgn. Relations, Italy-Am. Soc. (dir.), Pan Am. Soc., Philharmonic Symphony Soc. N.Y. (dir.), Huntington (N.Y.) C. of C., Delta Kappa Epsilon. Clubs: Huntington (N.Y.) Country; Harvard (Boston); Lloyd Neck Bath (Huntington, N.Y.), Harvard (N.Y.C.); Bankers of Am., Bond (former pres.; N.Y. City). Home: New York City, N.Y. Died June 10, 1979; interred Oakwood Cemetery, Troy, N.Y.

FORD, PAUL, actor; b. Balt., Nov. 2, 1901; s. Louis Clarence and Effie (Ford) Weaver; m. Nell Campbell, Dec. 27, 1924; children—Paul, Jean (Mrs. Harold Priest), Katherine (dec.), Lois A. Goehrig, Donald. Broadway appearances include Decision, Another Part of the Forest, Command Decision, Thurber Carnival, Teahouse of the August Moon, Never Too Late, Three Bags Full; motion picture appearances include House on 92d Street, The Matchmaker, Teahouse of the August Moon, Advise and Consent, Music Man, Never Too Late, Big Hand for the Little Lady, The Russians Are Coming, The Russians Are Coming, The Comedians; various television appearances, including The Bilko Show, others; pres. Grandandy Prodns., Inc., N.Y.C., 1964-76. Mem. Actors Equity (past mem. council), Screen Actors Guild, A.F.T.R.A. Club: Players (N.Y.C.). Address: New York, N.Y. Died Apr. 12, 1976.

FOREMAN, CLARK H., assn. exec.; b. Atlanta, Feb. 19, 1902; s. Robert Langdon and Effie Park (Howell) F.; A.B., U. Ga., 1921; Ph.D., Columbia, 1932; student Harvard, London Sch. Econs.; m. Mairi Elizabeth Fiona Fraser, July 26, 1933; children—Shelagh Alexandra (Mrs. Stephen O. Chastain), Joan Fraser (Mrs. Dietrich Klakow), Hugh Quin (dec.). Soc. Ga. Com. for Interracial Coopn.; asst. to dir. Phelps-Stokes Fund; dir. studies Julius Rosenwald Fund; adviser on econ. status of negroes to sec. of interior; spl. counsel to sec. of interior; dir. power div. P.W.A.; dir. defense housing. Fed. Works Adminstrn.; scientist operational research, for U.S. Navy Dept.; asst. prof. Black Mountain Coll.; dir. tng. program Bur. of Applied Social Research, Columbia; pres. Southern Conf. Human Welfare; dir. emeritus Emergency Civil Liberties Com. Democrat. Club: Cosmos (Washington). Author several books. Home: Adjuntas, P.R. Died June 15, 1977.

FORMAN, HARRISON, explorer, author, lectr.; b. Milw., June 15, 1904; student Chgo. Acad. Fine Arts, 1922-23; Layton Sch. Art, Milw., 1923-24; B.A., U. Wis., 1929; m. Selmah Holcombe (Sandra Carlyle Forman, profl. name), Aug. 10, 1934; children—Brenda Lu, John Holcombe. In Mexico, 1929; instr. nav. and meterology United Sch. Aeros., San Francisco, 1930; tech. dir. Columbia Pictures Corp., Hollywood, 1936-37; expdn. across Gobi Desert of Mongolia, 1937; 3d expdn. Tibet (interview and motion pictures of Jamv Japa, 4th in the hierarchy of Living Buddhas of Tibet), 1937; made motion pictures of Chinese Communist Red Army, 1937, of bombardment of Shanghai (released through March of Time), 1937, of Russo-Japanese hostilities at Changkufeng Hill on Siberia-Manchuria-Korea border, 1938, bombardment of Warsaw, 1939; Japanese invasion Indo-China, 1940; China War Theatre, 1941-45; Battle of the Yangtze and Communist capture of Shanghai, 1949; anti-communist wars in Malaya and Indo-China, 1950; Dutch withdrawal from Indonesia, 1950; visited and reported from East and Nr. East countries and S.A., 1950-54; interviewed Dalai Lama of Tibet, 1959; expdns. to N. Philippines, Malaya, Island of Komodo in S. Seas, 1955-56, Afghanistan, Middle East, 1957, Indonesia, Nepal, 1958, Russia, Central Asia, 1959, South East Asia, Celebes, Moluccas, 1960, Siberia and Mongolia, 1964, W. Africa and Central Africa, 1965, Pakistan and Nepal, India, 1969, South Pacific, S. Am., 1969, Thailand, Tanzania, Iran (ruins of Persepolis, capital of Darius the Great), 1967; tech. dir. Lost Horizon (Acad. award); fgn. corr. Far East for N.Y. Times, London Times, and NBC; lectr. internat. relations; ednl. photog. assignments Far East, 1960, Iron Curtain Countries of Europe, Africa, Timbuktu in Sahara Desert, 1961, also Siberia and Outer Mongolia, 1964; pres. Harrison Forman World Photos, N.Y.C. Mem. Explorers Club (life), Am. Soc. Journalists and Authors (founder-mem.). Clubs: Clipper, Overseas Press. Author: Through Forbidden Tibet, 1935; Horizon Hunter, 1940; Report from Red China, 1945, 75; Changing China, 1948; Blunder in Asia, 1950; How to Make Money with your Camera, 1951; The Land and People of Nigeria, 1964; Micronesia and People's Republic of China, 1973; Hunza in the Karakorum Highlands of the Himalayas, 1974. Contbr. to mags. Home: New York, N.Y. Died Feb. 1, 1978.

FORMAN, PHILLIP, judge; b. N.Y.C., Nov. 30, 1895; s. Morris and Tilly (Peters) F.; LL.B., Temple U., 1919; m. Pearl Edith Karlberg, Apr. 12, 1937. Admitted to N.J. bar, 1917; practiced in Trenton; mem. Forman & Levy, 1919-32; asst. U.S. atty., Dist. N.J., 1923-28, U.S. atty., 1928-32; judge, U.S. Dist. Ct., N.J., 1932-59, chief judge, 1951-59; judge U.S. Ct. Appeals, 1959-61, sr. judge, 1961-78. Trustee emeritus Rutgers U. Jewish. Home: Trenton, N.J. Died Aug. 17, 1978.

FORNOF, JOHN RENCHIN, newspaper pub.; b. Streator, Ill., June 23, 1889; s. John W. and Sarah Jane (Seavey) F.; B.A., U. Ill., 1910; m. Helen Honeywell, Sept. 14, 1910 (dec.); children—Elizabeth Jane, John Honeywell. Reporter and mgr. Free Press, Streator, 1910-23, owner and pub., 1923-27; v.p. Times Press Pub. Co., from 1927, also pub. Streator Times-Press; v.p., dir. Union Nat. Bank; dir. Citizens Loan & Investment Co. Past pres., dir. La Salle County Tb Sanitarium; trustee Riverview Cemetery Assn.; past trustee, past pres. bd. trustees U. Ill. Mem. Streator C. of C. (dir., past pres.), Phi Kappa Psi. Republican. Universalist. Mason, Elk, Odd Fellow. Clubs: University (Chgo.); Streator (Streator). Home: Streator, Ill. Died Mar. 1978.

FORREST, EARLE ROBERT, author; b. Washington, Pa., June 29, 1883; s. Joshua Rhodes and Mary Belle (Boyle) F.; B.S., Washington and Jefferson Coll., 1908; grad. student in forestry U. Mich., 1908-09; m. Margaret Bingham, June 29, 1909; 1 dau., Margaret Isobel. Cowboy on ranches in Colo., Ariz.; civil engr., 1910-13; forest ranger Deerlodge Forest, Mont., 1913-14; newspaper feature writer, 1914—. Recipient Hazzard medal in natural history Washington and Jefferson Coll., 1906-08; Award of Merit, D.A.R., 1955. Mem. Cooper Ornithol. Club Cal., Quivira Soc., Westerners, Washington County Hist. Soc. (hon. pres.), Sigma Phi Epsilon. Republican. Mason, Rotarian. Author: History of Washington County, Pa., 1926; Missions and Pueblos of the Old Southwest, 1929; (with J. E. Milnor) California Joe, Noted Scout and Indian Fighter, 1935; Some Pioneer Historical Items, published 1940; (with Edwin B. Hill) Lone War Trail of Apache Kid, published 1947; Arizona's Dark and Bloody Ground, rev., 1950 (pub. Brit. Empire 1953); Covered Bridges of Washington County, Pa., 1952; Covered Bridges of Greene County, Pa., 1953; National Pike in Washington County, Pa., 1955; National Pike in Fayette and Somerset Counties, Pa., 1956; Snake Dance of the Hopi, 1961; The House of Romance, pub. 1964; also contributor of historical articles to Brand Books, 1947—; serials and articles to mags. Ethnographic photographer among Navajo and Hopi Indians, Pueblo tribes of N.M. Home: Washington, Pa.; (winter) San

Macino, Cal.

FORREST, LEONARD JOSEPH, mfg. co. exec.; b. Shelton, Wash., Dec. 8, 1906; s. James and Helen (Carstairs) F.; m. Claribel Raasch, Sept. 16, 1937; children—Judith Ann, William Morgan. Dir. Polson Logging Co., Hoquiam, Wash., 1943-47; with ITT Rayonier, Inc. (name change due to merger 1968), 1947-74, mgr. N.W. timber div., 1958-61, v.p., mgr. div., Hoquiam, 1961-74; chmn. bd., dir. Timbermen's Nat. Bank of Hoquiam; dir. Western Forest Industries, Ltd., Nat. Bank Washington. Pres. Assn. Wash. Industries, 1960-62. Mem. Indsl. Forestry Assn. (pres., dir.). Mason (32 deg., Shriner), Rotarian, Elk. Home: Aberdeen, Wash. Died Sept. 24, 1976; buried Hoquiam, Wash.

FORSBERG, ROBERT LEE, utility exec., fin. cons.; b. Columbus, Ohio, May 20, 1916; s. Frederik and Martha (Vorpe) F.; B.S.C., Miami-Jacobs Bus. Coll., Dayton, O., 1939; m. Janet L. Blakley, Jan. 27, 1942; children—Terry Lee, James Lind. Successively budget dir., comptroller, dir. market research Airtemp div. Chrysler Corp., 1936-58; with G.E. Schumacher, Dayton, 1958-61; with Ariz. Pub. Service Co., Phoenix, 1961-76; treas., 1963-80, asst. sec., 1963-80, fin. v.p., 1967-71, exec. v.p. fin. and corporate affairs, 1971-75, v.p. corp. services, 1975-76, also dir.; fin. cons., 1976-80. Bd. dirs. United Fund, 1963-69, treas., 1966, pres., 1967, 68; treas. Phoenix operation Guide Dogs for Blind, 1964-68; mem. fin. com., adv. bd. Theodore Roosevelt council Boy Scouts Am., 1964-66; fin. com., adv. bd. ARC, 1972-80, chmn. centennial roll call com. Maricopa County chpt. Served with AUS, 1944-46. Mem. Am., Pacific Coast (chmn. exec. com., adminstrv. services sect. 1968) gas assns., Phoenix Soc. Fin. Analysts (pres. 1968-69), Fin. Execs. Inst. (pres. Ariz. chpt. 1975-76), Financial Analysts Fedn., Nat. Assn. Accountants, Pacific Coast Electric Assn., Edison Electric Inst., Newcomen Soc. N. Am., A.I.M. (pres.'s council), Phoenix C. of C., Ariz. Acad., Phi Theta Pi. Home: Phoenix, Ariz. Died Feb. 5, 1980; buried Greenwood Meml. Park, Phoenix.

FORSTER, WILLIAM BLAIR, hosp. cons.; b. Martin's Ferry, Ohio, July 1, 1911; s. Emmett Reed and Pearle (Stewart) F.; A.B., Mt. Union Coll., 1933; m. Christeen Lanning, Mar. 6, 1938. Bookkeeper, Alliance (Ohio) City Hosp., 1929-33; asst. adminstr. Elyria (Ohio) Meml. Hosp., 1933-38; asst. adminstr. St. Luke's Hosp., Cleve., 1938-42, Akron (Ohio) City Hosp., 1942-56; adminstr. Bexar County Hosp. Dist., San Antonio, 1956-67; adminstr. Harris County Hosp. Dist., Houston, 1967-69; adminstrv. cons. Methodist Hosp. Houston, 1969-75. Mem. adv. council on health aspects of civil def. Tex. Dept. Health, from 1964; past pres. Greater Houston Hosp. Council. Recipient Modern Hosp. Gold medal for significant contbn. to hosp. lit., 1942. Fellow Am. Coll. Hosp. Adminstrs. (life); mem. Am., Tex. (past pres.) hosp. assns., Nat. League Nursing (past Tex. bd.). Contbr. articles to profl. jours. Home: Houston, Tex. Died Mar. 28, 1975; buried Memorial Cemetery, Houston.

FORSYTHE, JOHN EVANS, lawyer; b. Media, Pa., Nov. 27, 1905; s. John Evans and Helen Lucretia (MacDonald) F.; B.A., Haverford Coll., 1927; LL.B., Yale, 1930; m. Margaret Pancoast Longaker, Sept. 30, 1933; children—Felicia, Alice Mary. Admitted to Pa. bar, 1930, practiced in Phila., 1930-74; partner MacCoy, Evans & Lewis, 1943-74; of counsel Montgomery, McCracken, Walker and Rhoads, Phila., 1976-77. Twp. solicitor Lower Merion Twp., Montgomery County, 1943-72, solicitor Lower Merion Twp., Bd. Health, 1943-72; Treas., trustee, dir. Bryn Mawr Coll., from 1953; treas. Haverford Friends Sch., 1947-75. Mem. Phila. Bar Assn., Phi Beta Kappa, Phi Delta Phi. Mem. Soc. of Friends. Clubs: Merion Cricket (Haverford); Vespers (Phila.). Home: Wynnewood, Pa. Died June 25, 1977.

FORSYTHE, WARREN ELLSWORTH, physician; born Joseph, Ore., Nov. 8, 1885; s. Elmer Johnson and Amy Edna (Templeton) F.; B.S., Ore. State Agrl. Coll., 1907, hon. Sc.D., 1937; Ph.C., U. of Mich., 1908, M.D., 1913; Dr. P.H. Johns Hopkins Univ., 1925; m. De Etta Brodie, June 19, 1915; 1 son, George Elmer. Began as interne and coll. health service physician, U. of Mich.; health service dir. Pa. State Coll., 1915; jr. field dir. Internat. Health Bd., 1917; prof. hygiene and pub. health, dir. univ. health service U. Mich., 1917-55, now emeritus. Fellow Am. Pub. Health Assn.; mem. Am. Med. Assn., Am. Student Health Assn. (pres.), Phi Delta Kappa, Phi Lambda Upsilon, Delta Phi, Phi Chi, Phi Kappa Phi. Democrat. Presbyn. Rotarian. Author: Health Service in American Colleges and Universities, 1926. Contbr. on health topics. Address: Eugene, Ore.

FORTE, FELIX, judge; b. Boston, Mass., June 30, 1895; s. Peter and Francesca (Santamaria) F.; LL.B. cum laude, Boston U. Sch. of Law, 1916, LL.M., 1919, A.M., 1928; S.J.D., Harvard U. Law Sch., 1932; LL.D., Boston U., 1941; Doctor of Art of Oratory, Staley College of the Spoken Word, 1943; J.D., Calvin Coolidge College, 1957; married Alma Locatelli, June 28, 1922; children—John Peter, Virginia F., Felix, Jr. Admitted to Mass. bar, 1916; bar U.S. Dist. Court, 1917; admitted to practice before Supreme Court of U.S., 1929; engaged in gen. practice of law at Boston, Mass., 1916-39; asso. prof. law, Boston Univ. Sch. of Law, 1922-29; prof., 1929-39; became spl. justice Dist. Ct. of Somerville, 1930; professor emeritus, Boston Univ. School of Law, 1946. Commdr. Order of Merit, Republic of Italy. Appointed asso. justice, Superior Court of Massachusetts, 1939; served, 1939-72. Served as vice chmn. Rep. State Conv., 1920; mem. Rep. State Com. (mem. exec. com. 1929-33, treas. 1933-36), Rep. City Com. (Somerville, Mass.). Rep. candidate for atty. gen. of Mass., 1936. Mem. Boston U. Law. Sch. Alumni Assn. (sec. 1929-33, treas. 1933-35, v.p. 1935-36, pres. 1937). President Home for Italian Children, Inc. Mem. Am., Mass., Boston and Somerville bar assns., Am. Justinian Soc. Jurists (pres. 1971), Lambda Chi Alpha, Phi Delta Phi. Decorated with Cross of Chevalier of Crown (Italy), 1930. Awarded Medal for Distinguished Service, by Regular Vets. Assn., 1946. Republican. Roman Catholic. K.C. Grand Venerable, Mass. Grand Lodge, 1925, 1933-35, Supreme Venerable of Supreme Lodge, Order of Sons of Italy in Am., 1940-47; Knight of Malta. Home: Somerville, Mass. Died Aug. 26, 1975.

FORTSON, BENJAMIN WYNN, JR., Ga. sec. state; b. Tignall, Ga., Dec. 19, 1904; s. Benjamin Wynn and Lillie (Welborn) F.; student Emory U., 1919-20, Starkes U., 1920-23, Ga. Inst. Tech., 1923-24; LL.D., John Marshall Law Sch., 1949; m. Mary Cade, May 15, 1926 (dec.); 1 dau. Ann McNeill (Mrs. George Mandus). With Citizens Nat. Bank, Washington, Ga., 1924-25, Atlanta and Lowry Nat. Bank, 1925-26; asst. cashier Washington Loan and Banking Co., 1927-29; sec. state State of Ga., Atlanta, from 1946; asso. in humanities Reinhardt Coll., 1973. Sec., treas. Wilkes County chpt. A.R.C., pres. Ga. Soc. for Crippled Children, 1954-56. Mem. Ga. Senate, 1939-40, 41-42; mem. Ga. Ho. of Reps., 1943-46. Trustee, Mary Willis Library Recipient Great Georgian award; Gold medal S.A.R., 1973. Mem. Nat. Assn. Secs. of State (pres. 1954). Alpha Kappa Psi (hon.), Pi Sigma Alpha (hon.), Demonsthenian Lit. Soc. U. Ga. (hon. life). Democrat. Methodist. Mason. Home: Washington, Ga. Died May 19, 1979.

FORWARD, CHARLES HAMILTON, lawyer; b. Pitts., Mar. 19, 1886; s. John F. and Ella F. (Dillon) F.; student U. Cal., 1904-05, 10-11, U.S. Coast Guard Acad., 1906-09; m. Zella E. Saint, June 24, 1914; 1 son, Charles H. Admitted to Cal. bar, 1911, since practiced in San Diego; partner Luce, Forward, Hamilton & Scripps. Captain of port, San Diego, Cal. Served as lt. Comdr., USCGR, 1943-46. Mason. Clubs: Cuyamaca, University. Home: San Diego, CA. *

FOSBURGH, JAMES WHITNEY, artist; b. N.Y.C., Aug. 1, 1910; s. James B. A. and Leila (Whitney) F.; A.B., Yale, 1933, M.A., 1935; student Royal U., Rome, 1933-34; m. Mary Cushing, 1953. Lectr., Frick Collection, N.Y.C., 1935-54; tchr. painting Parsons Sch. exhibited group shows, pvt. collections, galleries; exhibited one-man show Durlacher Bros., 1952, 55, 57, San Francisco Palace Legion of Honor, 1955, Los Angeles County Mus., 1955, Kennedy Galleries, 1968; lectr. Nat. Gallery Art, Yale, Met. Mus. Art, 1950-60; represented in collections Yale, Harvard, Joseph E. Hirschhorn Mus., Washington, Met. Mus. Art, Boston Mus. Fine Arts, Pa. Acad. Fine Arts, Toledo Mus. Fine Arts, pvt. collections. Design, 1952; paintings chmn. com. for Paintings for White House, 1961-63; mem, Landmarks Preservation Commn., N.Y.C., 1962-78, Com. for Preservation White House, 1964-78. Served in USAAF, 1942-46. Contbr. to profl. publs. Home: New York, N.Y. Died Apr. 23, 1978.

FOSCO, PETER, union exec.; b. Russia, May 13, 1892; s. Vincent and Antonia Fosco; student U. Ill.; m. Carmela Santucci, Dec. 3, 1916; children—Angelo, James. Financial exec. sec. Local Union #2 Laborers' Internat. Union of North Am., Chgo., 1916-20, pres., 1920-38, mgr. Chgo. regional office, 1936-68, gen. sec.-treas., 1950-68, gen. pres., Washington, 1968-75; v.p. AFL-CIO, 1st v.p. Bldg. & Constrn. Trades Dept. Democratic ward committeeman, Chgo., Dem. commr. Cook County, 1938-46. Named Man of the Year, Amerita Soc., 1972. Mem. Italian Soc., K. of C. Democratic. Roman Catholic. Club: Dem. Home: Chicago, Ill. Died Oct. 26, 1975.

FOSS, CARL LUDVIGSEN, clergyman, educator; b. Eau Claire, Wis., Jan., 1886; s. Rev. Ludvig Colbjornsen and Ida Pauline (Hanson) F.; student Pacific Luth. Acad., Parkland, Wash., 1903-07; A.B., Luther Coll., Decorah, Ia., 1912; theol. candidate, Luther Theol. Sem., St. Paul, Minn., 1915; m. Ella Caroline Tvete, of Seattle, Wash., July 10, 1917. Ordained ministry Luth. Ch., 1915; pastor Grace Luth. Ch., San Francisco, Calif., 1915-18, Our Saviour's Luth. Ch., Bremerton, Wash., 1920-21, Trinity Luth. Ch., Parkland, Wash., 1921-23, also teacher of Bible and French, Pacific Luth. Coll., 1921-23; teaching fellow, U. of Wash., 1923-24; pastor Phinney Ridge Luth. Ch., Seattle, 1924-27; pres. Spokane (Wash.) Coll. since 1927. Grad. Training Sch. for Chaplain Candidates, Camp Zachary Taylor, Louisville, Ky., summer, 1918. Served as 1st lt. chaplain U.S. Expeditionary Forces in France, Sept. 1918-July, 1919, World War. Republican. Home: Spokane, Wash.

FOSS, FLORENCE WINSLOW, coll. prof. (emeritus); b. Dover, N.H., Aug. 29, 1882; d. Frederick Hill and Emma Susan (Spurling) F.; A.B., Mount Holyoke College, 1905; A.M., Wellesley College, 1913; grad. study, U. of Chicago, (summer) 1915, 17, Radcliffe Coll., 1929-30, Harvard U. (summer sch.), 1931; unmarried. Prof. dept. art and archaeology, Mount Holyoke Coll., 1926-48, chmn. dept., 1939-48; sculpture exhibited: Pa. Acad. Annuals 1935, 36, 37, 38, Soc. Washington Artists (D.C.), 1936, 37, Nat. Acad., N.Y., 1937, Chicago Art Inst. Annuals 1936, 40, Conn. Acad., 1937-49 (mem. since 1943), Springfield Art League, 1937-47, Tricker Galleries, N.Y., 1936, 37, Addison Gallery, Andover, Mass., 1942, New Haven Paint and Clay Club, 1940, 44, Smith Museum, Springfield, Mass., 1946, New Haven Pub. Library, 1947, Friends of Art Exhibitions, Mt. Holyoke Coll., 1936-48; in permanent collections; Dwight Art Bldg., Mt. Holyoke Coll. Awards: Society of Washington Artists (Corcoran Gallery, Washington, D.C.) hon. mention, 1936: Springfield Art League (Mass.) Sculpture Prize, 1940, 43. Mem. Am. Assn. Univ. Profs., Conn. Acad. (Hartford, Conn.), Springfield Art League (Springfield, Mass.), Phi Beta Kappa. Episcopalian. Republican. Home: Brockway Rd., South Hadley Center, Mass.

FOSS, HAROLD LEIGHTON, surgeon; b. Malden, Mass., Feb. 14, 1883; s. Eliphalet J. and Louise W. (Sanborn) F.; M.D., Jefferson Med. Coll., Phila., Pa., 1909; hon. Sc.D., Bucknell University, Lewisburg, Pennsylvania, 1933; graduate study, University of Pa., 1912-13; student Berlin, Vienna, 1914; m. Isabel Grier Polk, June 22, 1917; children—Mrs. Elizabeth F. Foster, Mrs. Barbara Foss Markle. Resident physician Phila. Gen. Hosp., 1909-10; surgeon in chief Fairhaven Hosp., Candle, Alaska, 1911-12; asst. surgeon Mayo Clinic, Rochester, Minn., 1913-15; surgeon in chief and chief of staff Geisinger Memorial Hosp., Danville, Pa., since 1915; cons. surgeon Pa. State Hospital for Insane. Mem. Founders Group, American Board of Surgery. Regent and fellow American Coll. Surgeons (pres. 1952-53); mem. A.M.A., Pan-Pacific, Am., So. surg. assns., Detroit Academy Surgery, Pennsylvania Med. Soc., Am. Hosp. Assn., Am. Assn. Ry. Surgeons, Am. Assn. for Study of Goiter, Assn. Ex-Resident Physicians of Mayo Clinic (pres. 1917-19), Soc. Int. de Chirg., Nu Sigma Nu, Alpha Omega Alpha. Capt. Civil Air Patrol. Republican. Presbyterian. Mason (33 deg.). Clubs: Edgartown Yacht, North American Yacht Racing Union. Home: Danville, Pa.

FOSTER, ALLEN EVARTS, lawyer; b. New Haven, Feb. 18, 1885; s. John P. C. and Josephine Theresa (Bicknell) F.; A.B., Yale, 1906; LL.B., Harvard, 1909. Admitted to N.Y. bar, 1910, since practiced in N.Y.C.; clk. Lord, Day & Lord, 1909-19, partner since 1919. Trustee Sheltering Arms Children's Service, 1917-59, Kips Bay Boys Club (N.Y.C.); pres. Art Commn. City N.Y., 1953-57; mem. Landmarks Preservation Commn. City N.Y.; hon. trustee Berea Coll. Served from 1st lt. to capt., machine gun bns. U.S. Army, World War I. Fellow of Branford Coll. Yale. Fellow Am. Bar Found., N.Y. Hist. Society, Morgan Library; member Am., N.Y.C. bar assns., Am. Law Inst., Psi Upsilon. Clubs: Elihu, Elizabethan (Yale); Anglers, Yale, University, Church, Grolier, Century (N.Y.C.). Author: A Check List of Illustrations by Winslow Homer. Home: Guilford, Conn.

FOSTER, DOROTHY, coll. prof.; b. Salem, Mass., July 21, 1883; d. James Measury and Genevieve (Stimson) Foster; A.B., Bryn Mawr Coll., 1904; A.M., Radcliffe Coll., 1908, grad. student, 1913-14; grad. student Harvard, 1939. Research work abroad, British Museum and Public Record Office, London; Bodleian, Oxford; Regensburg, Germany. Successively reader, instr., asso. prof., prof., and emeritus prof. English, Mt. Holyoke Coll., since 1904; a dir. Geneva (Switzerland) Women's Coll., 1935-37. Mem. Modern Lang. Assn. Am., Am. Assn. Univ. Profs., Am. Assn. Univ. Women, Nat. Geog. Soc. Unitarian. Contbr. to lit. reviews. Home: South Hadley, Mass.

FOSTER, ELIZABETH ANDROS, educator; b. Taunton, Mass., Sept. 20, 1885; d. Charles and Elizabeth (Andros) Foster; grad. Wheaton Sem. (now Wheaton Coll.), 1903; student Gilman Sch. Girls, 1903-04; B.A., Bryn Mawr Coll., 1908, M.A., 1909; Ph.D., Smith Coll., 1920. Instr. French and Spanish Wells Coll., 1911-15; insdr. to prof. Spanish Smith Coll., 1916; ret. 1953. Chief observer Northampton Observation Post, Ground Observers Corps, U.S. Air Def. Command since June 1953. Corr. mem. Acad. Am. Franciscan History. Author: The Elements of Spanish Grammar, 1936, Spanish Composition, 2d edit., 1939. Translator, ed.: Motolinia's History of the Indians of New Spain, 1950. Home: Northampton, Mass.

FOSTER, J. T., investment banker; b. Ashland, Pa., June 1, 1885; s. Rufus D. and June (Taylor) F.; grad. The Hill Sch., 1904; Yale, 1908; m. Jeannette Schlager, Oct 8, 1908; children—E. James 2d, J. Taylor, Jr., Sarah P. (Mrs. A. Oram Fulton, Jr.). Vice pres. and dir. Lee

Higginson Corp., N.Y. City; dir. The Duriron Co., The Kerite Co., P. R. Mallory & Co., Inc., River Brand Rice Mills, Inc., Verona Chem. Co., Williams & Co., Inc. Clubs: The Links, City Midday, Yale (N.Y.); Round Hill (Greenwich, Conn.); The Hartford (Conn.); Graduates, Lawn (New Haven, Conn.); The Duquesne (Pittsburgh). Home: Greenwich, Conn. *

FOSTER, JEANNE ROBERT (MRS. MATLACK FOSTER), author, editor; b. Johnsburgh, Warren Co., N.Y., Mar. 10, 1884; d. Francis and Lucia (Newell) Oliver; ed. Rochester (N.Y.) Athenaeum and Mechanics' Inst., Boston U., and Harvard Extension (spl. courses); grad. Stanhope-Wheatcroft Dramatic Sch., New York; m. Matlack Foster, of N.Y. City, 1901. Began writing for newspapers in childhood; teacher common schs., Adirondack Mountains; writer for Boston newspapers 3 yrs.; lit. editor Review of Reviews, 1910-22; Am. editor Transatlantic Rev. Studied housing and city planning in Europe. Mem. Authors' League America, Poetry Soc. America, Woman's Trade Union League, Acad. Polit. Science, Nat. Civic Fed., English-Speaking Union, League Am. Penwomen. Catholic. Clubs: National Arts, Pen and Brush (New York); Woman's City (Boston); Woman's (Schenectady, N.Y.); Am. Women's (London). Author: Wild Apples (poems), 1916; Neighbors of Yesterday (narrative poems of the Adirondacks), 1916; Rock-Flower (poems), 1922. Contbr. articles and poems to periodicals. Edited John Quinn Letters (2 vols.), 1925. Address: New York, N.Y. *

FOSTER, LEE BYRON, corp. exec.; b. Titusville, Pa., July 4, 1882; s. Aaron and Lena (Sable) F.; student Iron City Bus. Coll.; m. Pauline L. Livingston, June 10, 1909; children—Adrienne (Mrs. Milton Porter), Jay L. Sr. partner L. B. Foster Co., Pitts., 1903-18, pres., 1918-52, chmn. 1953, now vice chmn. bd., chmn. finance com. and dir.; hon. chmn. bd., dir. Copperweld Steel Co., Pitts.; v.p. Foster Export Co., N.Y.C., Foster Internat. Co. Chmn. Montifiore Hosp. Research Inst.; dir. Montefiore Hosp.; mem. bd. Pitts. YM and YWHA. Clubs: Concordia, Westmoreland Country (mem. bd.), One Hundred (Pitts.); Harmonie (N.Y.C.); Montauk (N.Y.) Yacht. Home: Pittsburgh, PA.

FOSTER, MINARD IRWIN, govt. ofcl.; b. Miami, Fla., Dec. 8, 1915; s. Irwin Bell and Mary (Johnstone) F.; B.B.A., U. Miami, 1950, M.A., 1951; Ph.D., U. Fla., 1953; m. Margaret Freeman, Mar. 30, 1946; children—Mary (Mrs. William J.P. Marshburn), Michael Bruce, Robert Freeman. Asst. prof. econ. U. Miami, 1953-54; with TVA, 1954-79, economist, supr. borrowing, and investment, 1958-62, chief navigation resources br., 1962-67, dir. navigation devel. and regional studies, Knoxville, Tenn., 1967-79. Lectr., U. Chattanooga, 1954-63. Mem. U.S., internat. commns. Permanent Internat. Assn. Nav. Congresses. Served with USAAF, 1943-45. Mem. Am., So. econ. assns., Order of Artus, Phi Beta Kappa, Alpha Kappa Psi. Home: Knoxville, Tenn. Died Oct. 8, 1979.

FOSTER, NORMAN, writer, dir., actor, producer; b. Richmond, Ind., Dec. 13, 1903; s. Charles Foster and Blanche M. (Cummings) Hoeffer; m. Sally Blane; children—Gretchen, Robert. Actor, N.Y.C., London, Hollywood, Calif.; dir., writer, producer documentaries. Recipient Christopher award for Davy Crockett, Disney Prodns. Address: Los Angeles, Calif. Died July 7, 1976; interred Holy Cross Cemetery, Los Angeles.

FOSTER, WARREN DUNHAM, patent attorney, inventor, editor; b. Geneseo, Ill., Nov. 13, 1886; s. William Horton and Edith (Dunham) F.; educated public schools, Geneseo, Illinois; University School, Chicago, and University of Chicago; m. Willie Curtis, August 31, 1908 (div. Nov. 1, 1944); children—Elizabeth (Mrs. De Witt Clinton II), William; m. 2d, Sigrid Morsbach, April 26, 1947. Member, editorial staff Chicago Daily Journal, 1905-06; reader in English, U. of Chicago, 1907; instr. in English, Ia. State Coll., 1908-09; with The Youth's Companion, 1909-16, dept. editor, 1912-16; pres. Community Motion Picture Service and chmn. Community Service, Ltd., of Great Britain, furnishing practically all pictures used in army and navy camps of Am. and allied armies and navies, in America and throughout the world, through Y.M.C.A., K. of C., and other welfare and governmental agencies, 1917-21; pres. Kinatome Patents Corp., Camera Patents Corp., and related cos.; chmn. Kinema Patents, Ltd. (London). Mem. Mass. Homestead Commn., 1910-20. Director Nat. Com. on Prisons and Prison Labor. Member Delta Upsilon; fellow Royal Geog. Soc., Soc. Motion Picture Engineers. Methodist. Clubs: Lotos, City (New York); Cosmos (Washington). Author: (with Elmer C. Adams) Heroines of Modern Progress, 1912. Editor: Heroines of Modern Religion; Heroines of the Modern Stage; Debating for Boys; etc.; inventor (over 65 patents including 2700 claims) of photographic and projection apparatus, including (with C. L. Oswald), "ultra-violet" system sound recording now used by majority of film producers. Home: Eustis, Fla., and "Seven Chimneys." Washington Twp. Bergen County (post office Ridgewood), N.J.

FOWLE, JAMES LUTHER, clergyman; b. Washington, N.C., Oct. 14, 1897; s. Samuel Richardson and Mary (Payne) F.; student Randolph Macon Acad., Bedford City, Va., 1913-14; A.B., Davidson Coll., 1918; student Johns Hopkins, 1918; B.D., Union Theol. Sem., 1921 (Hoge fellow 1921-22); S.T.M., Princeton Theol. Sem., 1923; D.D., Westminster Coll., Fulton, Mo., 1928, Davidson Coll., 1928; LL.D., U. Chattanooga, 1942; Litt.D., King Coll., 1949; m. Katharine Ferguson, Jan. 26, 1925 (dec. May 1950); 1 dau., Mary Payne. Ordained Presbyn. ministry, 1923; pastor Central Presbyn. Ch., St. Louis, 1923-29, First Presbyn. Ch., Chattanooga, 1929-67; active in adminstrn. of Prebyteries, from 1927, commr. gen. assemblies, mem. councils of ch.; joint moderator Gen. Assembly Presbyn. Church U.S., 1951, mem. bd. ch. extension, 1948-56, mem. bd. annuities and relief, 1956-62, 66-72, vice chmn. 1966, chmn. permanent nominating com., v.p.; mem. gen. assembly Presbyn. Ch. U.S.; spl. tchr. U. Chattanooga, 1948-68. Chaplain, City of Chattanooga, from 1944; chaplain Girls Prep Sch., Half Century Club, Huegenots Tenn.; internat. chaplain Civitan Clubs, 1970-71. Pres. Chattanooga Community Chest, 1936-46, mem. exec. com. 1946-56, mem. bd., from 1956; active in exec. adminstrn. community civic activites such as clinics, hosps., Boy Scouts, YMCA, YWCA, USO, Traveler's Aid, others; v.p. Tenn. div. Am. Cancer Soc., 1953-56, pres. Tenn. div., 1956-57; mem. bd. Girls Clubs, Opportunity Home for Girls, Greater Chattanooga United Fund. Past pres. of Chattanooga Bible Inst., Chattanooga Tumor Clinic; trustee King Coll., Bristol, Tenn., Calsted Home (chmn. bd. 1970-71), Girls Prep. Sch., Chattanooga, Bachman Home, Colored Orphans Home, U. Chattanooga, U. T.C. Endowment Fund; trustee Montreat Assn., 1934-56; exec. com. Asso. Services for Armed Forces. Recipient Kiwanis social service award, 1947. Mem. Chattanooga Pastors Assn., Kappa Alpha, Omicron Delta Kappa, Alpha Phi Omega. Clubs: Civitan (chaplain), Kiwanis (hon.), Rotary (hon.), Chattanooga Golf and Country. Author: So Many People, 1943; Planned Services for Church Groups, 1946. Home: Chattanooga, Tenn. Died Nov. 13, 1978; buried Forest Hills Cemetery, Chattanooga.

FOWLE, LUTHER RICHARDSON, treas. Am. Bd. Missions; b. of Am. parents at Talas, Turkey, July 30, 1886; s. James Luther and Carrie Palmer (Farnsworth) F.; prep. edn., Lawrenceville (N.J.) Sch., 1900-03; B.A., Williams, 1908; student Union Theol. Sem., N.Y. City, 1909-11; m. Helen Curtis, Sept. 10, 1912; children—Curtis, Wilson Farnsworth, James Warren, Helen Joy, Richardson. Treas. Am. Mission, Aintab, Turkey, 1912-14; asst. treas. Am. Bd. Missions in Turkey, 1914-23; treas. Am. Bd. Missions in Near East since 1923. Am. attaché at Swedish Legation, Constantinople, charged with protection of Am. interests in Turkey, 1917-19. Asst. treas. and treas. Am. relief activities in Turkey, 1915-19. Mem. bd. mgrs. Constantinople Am. Hosp.; dir. Am. Chamber Commerce for the Levant, Constantinople Y.M.C.A. Conglist. Home: Rumeli Hissar, Istanbul. *

FOWLER, CODY, lawyer; b. Arlington, Tenn., Dec. 8, 1892; s. Orin Scott and Maud (Cody) F.; student U. Mo., 1911-12; LL.B., Cumberland U., 1913, LL.D.; LL.D., U. Miami; H.H.D., U. Tampa; m. Maude Stewart, Apr. 28, 1915 (dec.); children—Betty Fowler Campbell (dec.), Maude Fowler Pallardy, Cody Fowler Davis; m. Eva C. Florez, Jan. 30, 1977. Admitted to Tenn. bar, 1913, Fla. bar, 1914, Okla. bar, 1916; practiced in Jacksonville, Fla., 1914-16, Oklahoma City, 1919-24; with Macfarlane, Pettingill, Macfarlane & Fowler, Tampa, Fla., 1924-35; practiced in Tampa and Miami, Fla., 1935-43; with Fowler, White, Burnett, Hurley, Banick & Knight, Miami, also Fowler, White, Gillen, Boggs, Villareal & Banker, and predecessors, Tampa, St. Petersburg, Clearwater, Lakeland, after 1943; chmn. bd., dir. Freedom Fed. Savs. & Loan Assn., Tampa. Served with F.A., U.S. Army, 1917-19. Recipient Human Relations award Fla. Anti-Defamation League of B'nai-B'rith, 1961; Distinguished Service award Stetson U.; Hall of Fame award Com. of 100, Greater Tampa C. of C., 1976. Mem. Am. Bar Assn. (ho. of dels., life mem., bd. govs. 1946-52, pres. 1950-51) Am. Coll. Trial Lawyers (past pres.), Fla., Hillsborough County, Dade County, Inter-Am. (past pres.), Internat. bar assns., Am. Law Inst., Am. Judicature Soc., Maritime Law Assn., Am. Law Library of Middle Temple (hon.), U.S., Tampa chambers commerce, Am. Legion, Order of Coif, Phi Delta Theta. Democrat. Episcopalian. Clubs: Elks, Masons, Shriners, K.T., Rotary, Propeller, Gasparilla Krewe, Yacht and Country, Univ. (Tampa); Lawyers of Dade County (Fla.); Miami; Wall St. (N.Y.C.). Home: Tampa, Fla. Died Sept. 8, 1978.

FOWLER, GEORGE STARKWEATHER, b. New Haven, Conn., Aug. 20, 1884; s. Charles Holt and Kate Carpenter (Starkweather) F.; B.A., Yale, 1906; m. Marguerite L. Woodruff, of Mt. Carmel, Conn., Apr. 6, 1910. With Yale Pub. Assn., 1906-9, also business mgr. Yale Weekly; adv. dir. Colgate & Co., New York, since 1909; business mgr. Christmas membership campaign of Am. Nat. Red Cross, 1917, and exec. sec. at nat. hdqrs., Washington, D.C., for 2d Red Cross war fund campaign, 1918. Mem. Zeta Psi. Republican. Clubs: Yale Assn. Nat. Advertisers, Inc. (pres. 1921-2), Glen Ridge Country (N.J.). Home: Glen Ridge, N.J.

FOWLER, HAROLD LEES, ret. coll. dean; b. Boston, Sept. 11, 1907; s. Herbert Lees and Sybil Gertrude (Major) F.; A.B., Dartmouth, 1928; M.A., Harvard, 1930, Ph.D., 1934; m. Theodosia Jeannette Marshall, Dec. 2, 1934. Instr., West Nottingham Acad., Colora, Md., 1928-29; asst. in history Harvard, 1930-34; faculty Coll. William and Mary, Williamsburg, Va., 1934-74, prof. history, 1946-74, head dept., 1959-64, dean faculty, 1964-74, dir. Am. studies Program, 1960. Vis. prof. U. N.C., summers 1951-52, Cal. Inst. Tech., 1956-57. Served as lt. USNR, 1943-46. Mem. Inst. Early Am. History and Culture (council 1960-63), Am. So. hist. assns., A.A.U.P., Cum Laude Soc., Flat Hat Club Soc., Phi Beta Kappa, Lambda Chi Alpha, Omicron Delta Kappa, Kappa Phi Kappa, Tau Kappa Alpha. Episcopalian (sr. warden). Home: Williamsburg, Va. Died Mar. 11, 1977.

FOWLER, JAMES RANDLETT, govt. ofcl.; b. Boulder, Colo., Dec. 11, 1920; s. Samuel Ross and Louise White (Randlett) F.; B.A. magna cum laude (Kiwanis scholar), U. Colo., 1943; B.A. (Rhodes scholar), Oxford U., 1949; m. Margaret Williamson, Apr. 19, 1947; children—Pamela Leighton (Mrs. Timothy Pishon Gardner), Deborah Randlett, Michael Ross. Instr. English, U. Colo., 1946-47; with Bur. for UN, Office Dependent Area Affairs, Dept. State, 1950-53; with internat. div. Bur. Budget, 1953-56; with Office Dep. Dir. Planning, ICA, 1956-58, with Office Far East Affairs, 1960-61, with Office Dep. Coordinator for Mut. Security, Dept. State, 1958-60; dep. asst. adminstr. for Far East, AID, 1961-63, mission dir., Bogota, Colombia, 1964-67; dep. U.S. coordinator Alliance for Progress, Dept. State, Washington, 1967-70, spl. asst. to adminstr. AID, 1970, detailed to Sr. Sem. in Fgn. Policy, Dept. State, 1970-71, spl. asst. to adminstr. AID, exec. dir. Com. on Environment and Devel. AID, 1971-74. Mem. U.S. Com. for Man and Biosphere, U.S. Nat. Commn. for UNESCO, 1973-75. Served to 1st lt., inf. AUS, 1943-46. Mem. Am. Acad. Polit. and Social Scis., Am. Assn. Rhodes Scholars, Am. Fgn. Service Assn. Democrat. Episcopalian. Club: Gibson Island (Md.). Home: Chevy Chase, Md. Died Dec. 11, 1977.

FOWLER, RICHARD BROSING, newspaper editor; b. Sedalia, Mo., Aug. 15, 1902; s. Richard Dillon and Mathilda Geyer (Brosing) F.; student Westminster Coll., Fulton, Mo., 1919-21, U. Mo., 1926-27; B.S. in Commerce, Washington U., St. Louis, 1923; m. Elinor Carr Montgomery, Feb. 9, 1924; children—Richard Brosing, Lee Montgomery, Giles Merrill. Mem. staff Kansas City (Mo.) Star, from 1930, editor editorial page, 1954-60, dir., from 1958, editor, 1960-67, pres., roving corr., from 1968. Recipient Distinguished Service Alumnus award Westminster Coll., 1968, Kansas City Alumnus of Year award, 1956; Fellow award for history Kansas City Mus., 1971. Trustee Childrens Mercy Hosp., U. Kansas City; bd. dirs. Midwest Research Inst. Mem. State Hist. Soc. Mo. (trustee from 1968), Sigma Delta Chi, Beta Theta Pi. Author: Leaders in Our Town, 1952. Co-author: City of the Future, 1950. Home: Kansas City, Mo. Deceased.

FOX, ABIJAH UPSON, investment exec.; b. Bklyn., Jan. 20, 1905; s. Abijah Charles and Helen Manlove (Shawhan) F.; Litt.B. cum laude, Rutgers U., 1926; m. Isabel Place Sullivan, Nov. 26, 1935; children—Abijah Shawhan, Jarvis Powell, Suzanne Angevine. Accountant and pro-mgr. Nat. City Bank, Tokyo, 1926-34; partner Swan, Culbertson & Fritz, investment bankers and brokers, Shanghai, Hongkong and Manila, 1934-41; dep. dir. fgn. funds control U.S. Treasury Dept., Washington, 1941-44; dir. Office of Surplus Property, 1945, dep. dir. fin. div. Mil. Govt., Germany, 1945-46; chmn., dir. Mathison Chem. Corp. N.Y.C., 1946-48; treas. Am. Thread Co., 1948-59; dir., 1949-59; v.p., 1950-59; gen. partner investment firm Hayden, Stone & Co., 1959-62; v.p. Hayden, Stone, Inc., 1962-72, Riter, Pyne, Kendall & Hollister, 1972-73, Smith, Barney, Harris, Upham & Co., Norwalk, Conn., 1973-79, Shearson Hayden Stone, Inc., Greenwich, Conn., 1979-80. Mem. Conn. Gov.'s Adv. Council on Aging, 1971-76, State Bond Commn., 1978, Juvenile Justice Commn., 1976-78; vice-chmn. Fiscal Reform Commn., 1977-78; state rep. 152d dist. Conn. Gen. Assembly, 1968-72, 149th dist., 1973-78. Episcopalian. Clubs: Indian Harbor Yacht, Belle Haven (Greenwich, Conn). Home: Greenwich, Conn. Died Sept. 8, 1980.

FOX, DAVID, retail co. exec.; b. N.Y.C., 1885; m. Estella Goldstone; children—Mrs. Arthur Ochs Sulzberger, Barbara. Pres., treas., dir. Jay Thorpe, Inc., N.Y.C. until 1962. Home: New York, N.Y. Died Apr. 21, 1976.

FOX, EUGENE JACKSON, coll. dean; b. Drumright, Okla., July 14, 1914; s. Jacob Harold and Gertrude (Jackson) F.; B.S., Central State Coll., Okla., 1938; M.A., Okla. U., 1944; Litt.D., U. Nacional de Mex., 1951; m. Margaret Halley Dec. 24, 1942; 1 son, Steven H. Tchr.-coach Tryon (Okla.) High Sch., 1938-41; instr. Spanish, Okla. Mil. Acad., Claremore, 1944-48; asst. prof. Spanish, N.Mex. Mil. Inst., 1948-59; faculty

Eastern N.Mex. U., Portales, 1959-80, prof. modern langs., 1964-80, dean gen. coll., 1967-80, now emeritus; cons. in field, 1938-80. Mem. N.G., 1936-38; served with USAAF, 1942-44. Recipient Fulbright award, 1958; Pres.'s Faculty award Eastern N.Mex. U., 1965. Mem. Modern Lang. Assn., Rocky Mountain Lang. Assn. (co-chmn. standards com. 1964, exec. bd. 1974), NEA, Phi Delta Kappa, Phi Kappa Phi. Author: Guide for College Students, 1968; Roadside Wildflowers of New Mexico, 1979; also poems, articles, fiction. Home: Portales, N. Mex. Died Sept. 23, 1980.

FOX, JOHN GASTON, physicist, educator; b. Biggar, Saskatchewan, Can., Mar. 5, 1916; s. Jacques Gaston and Lulu Margaret (Connell) F.; B.Sc., U. Saskatchewan, 1935, M.Sc., 1937; Ph.D., Princeton, 1941; m. Constance Mary Sullivan, July 15, 1947; children—Wendy Elizabeth, Grant Sullivan, Paul John. Came to U.S., 1940, naturalized 1955. Physicist Hercules Powder Co., 1941-45, Los Alamos Sci. Lab., U. Calif., 1945-46, asst. prof. physics Carnegie Inst. Tech., 1946-49, asso. prof.. 1949-56, asst. head dept., 1950-56, prof., 1956-80, head dept., 1956-61; vis. prof. Indian Inst. Tech., Kanpur, India, 1967-69, program leader, 1971-72. Physicist, Laboratoire Joliot-Curie de Physique Nucleaire, Orsay, France, 1962-63. Fellow Am. Phys. Soc.; mem. AAUP, Am. Assn. Physicists in Medicine, Am. Assn. Physics Tchrs., Soc. Nuclear Medicine, Sigma Xi, Phi Kappa Phi. Contbr. numerous articles. Home: Oakmont, Pa. Died July 24, 1980.

FOX, THOMAS G., JR., research chemist; b. Union Deposit, Pa., Feb. 19, 1921; s. Thomas G. and Kathryn (Fasnacht) F.; B.S. in Chemistry, Physics and Math., Lebanon Valley Coll., 1940, D.Sc. (hon.), 1967; Ph.D. in Phys. Chemistry, Columbia, 1943; m. 2d, Mary Jo MacCallum, Dec. 27, 1972; children—(by previous marriage) Joyce Melinda, Margaret Leigh, Mary Louise. Asst. in chemistry Columbia, 1940-43, instr., 1943-44; Allied Chem. & Dye Co. fellow, 1942-43; research chemist Goodyear Tire & Rubber Co., 1946-48; research asso. Cornell U., 1948-50; head Polymer Lab., Rohm & Haas Co., 1950-57; asst. dir. research Mellon Inst., Pitts., 1957-61, dir. research, 1961-62, staff fellow, mem. adv. bd., 1962-77; prof. chemistry, polymer sci. Carnegie-Mellon U., Pitts., 1967-77, also spl. asst. to pres.; spl. research phys. chemistry polymers, intrinsic viscosities and thermodynamics of polymer solutions, molecular weights of polymers, melt viscosities and 2d order transitions polymers, crystallization in polymers, kinetics of polymerization, polymer structures. Science adviser to gov. Pa., 1965-77. Chmn. Pa. Sci. and Engring. Found.; mem. Pa. Planning Bd., 1969-77, vice chmn., 1970-77; mem. Nat. Gov.'s Council on Sci. and Tech., 1970-77, vice chmn., 1970-71, chmn., 1971-72; mem. Commerce Tech. Adv. Bd., Washington; mem. Gov.'s Energy Council, 1974-77; chmn. adv. bd. Carnegie-Mellon Inst. Research, 1975-77. Fellow Am. Phys. Soc.; mem. Am. Chem. Soc., Soc. Rheology, Sigma Xi, Phi Lambda Upsilon. Editor: Jour. Polymer Sci., 1965-77. Home: Pittsburgh, Pa. Died Nov. 28, 1977.

FOX, VIRGIL (KEEL), organist; b. Princeton, Ill., May 3, 1912; s. Miles S. and Birdie E. (Nichols) F.; Artist's Diploma, Peabody Conservatory Music, 1932; Mus.D. (hon.), Bucknell U., 1963; student of Wilhelm Middelschulte, 1928-29, Marcel Dupre, 1932-33. Profl. debut, Cin., 1926; debut in London, Eng., 1933, N.Y.C., 1933; head organ dept. Peabody Conservatory Music, 1938-42; performed Library of Congress, 1946; organist Riverside Ch., N.Y.C., 1946-65; 1st organ soloist Lincoln Center, N.Y.C., 1963; dir. organ series Gallery Mod. Art, N.Y.C., 1965-66; concert tours throughout U.S., Can. and Europe, 1933-80; rep. U.S. 1st Internat. Conf. Sacred Music, Bern, Switzerland, 1952; soloist with N.Y. Philharmonic, Phila., Boston, Balt., Rochester, Detroit, Dallas, Grand Rapids, CBS Symphony, Los Angeles Festival orchs.; rec. artist for Kapp, Columbia, RCA Victor, Capitol, Command, Decca, Crystal Clear, Helden Records. Served with USAAF, 1942-46. Winner Nat. Fedn. Music Clubs biennial contest. 1929; named most popular organist Choral and Organ Guide mag., 1952, Contemporary keyboard, 1977, 78, 79; named to Contemporary Keyboard Hall of Fame, 1980; recipient Disting. Alumni award Peabody Conservatory Alumni Assn., 1964. Mem. Am. Guild Organists, Phi Mu Sinfonia. Died Oct. 25, 1980.

FOX-MARTIN, MILTON, marketing cons.; b. Kansas City, Mo., May 14, 1913; s. Asa Earl and Anna Elizabeth (Fox) M.; diploma Haverford Sch., 1931; B.A., Yale, 1935; m. Mary Warner, June 25, 1938 (div. Aug. 1950); children—Elizabeth Fay (Mrs. Peter C. Funk), Ludlow; m. 2d, Isabel Fountain Brackett, Aug. 26, 1950 (div. June 1960); 1 child, Belle (Mrs. B. Fox-Martin-Kirk); m. 3d, Ferle Hoffman, July 22, 1960 (div. Dec. 1967); m. 4th, Nancy Verkuil, Jan. 13, 1968; 1 child, Shana. Sales exec. U.S. Indsl. Chems., Inc., Transfilm Inc., McArthur Advt. Corp., Martin Sales Devel. Corp., N.Y. Herald Tribune, 1935-51; mgr. mut. fund dept. Kidder, Peabody & Co., 1951-54; mgr. dealer relations Wellington Co., 1954-58; pres. Broad St. Sales Corp., 1958-60; v.p. sales Hugh W. Long & Co., Inc., 1961-62, pres., 1962-64; pres. underwriting div., v.p. Anchor Corp., 1964-68; internat. marketing cons., after 1969. Republican. Presbyn. (elder). Author: (with Lawrence Madison) Life With Baby, Trout Lore, 1942; Sales Bulletins series, Positive Attitude Posters series. Home: Amsterdam, Holland. Died June 21, 1977.

FOY, EDWARD JAMES, naval officer; b. Little Rock, Ark., Sept. 7, 1886; s. Patrick John and Ellen (Mullin) F.; B.S., U.S. Naval Acad., 1908; grad. U.S. Naval War Coll., 1930, Army War Coll., 1932; m. Elise Dandridge, June 6, 1916. Commd. ensign, U.S. Navy, 1910, advancing through the grades to rear adm., 1945; served on staff Adm. Henry T. Mayo, comdr. in chief U.S. Fleet, World War I; comd. U.S.S. Little and U.S.S. Selfridge (destroyers) and U.S.S. Raleigh (light cruiser), Mediterranean Sea, during Spanish Civil War, 1936-37, U.S.S. Oklahoma (battleship), 1940-41 (detached shortly before loss at Pearl Harbor; naval instr. Army War Coll., 1937-40; dep. comdt. Army and Navy Staff Coll.; trustee and treas. Naval Historical Foundation. Decorated D.S.M., Victory Medal with silver star, 2d Nicaraguan Medal, U.S. Defense Medal with star, Asiatic Pacific Medal with star. Clubs: Army and Navy (Washington); Chevy Chase (Md.); New York Yacht. Home: Washington, D.C.

FOYE, ARTHUR BEVINS, accountant; b. Bklyn., June 20, 1893; s. Frank Melvin and Sarah (Bevins) F.; B.C.A. magna cum laude, N.Y. U., 1914; m. Emma Graham, Oct. 7, 1914; 1 dau., Barbara Bricknell (Mrs. Wiley Washington Merryman, Jr.). Instr. accounting N.Y.U., 1915-17; joined Haskins & Sells, 1923, sr. partner, 1945-56; dir. Haskins and Sells Found. Mem. overseas econ. ops. task force Hoover Commn. C.P.A., N.Y., N.J., La. Mem. Far East-Am. Council of Commerce and Industry (past pres.), Am. Inst. C.P.A.'s (past pres.), Accountants Club Am. (past pres.), Pilgrims U.S. Saint George Soc., Acad. Polit. Sci., Internat. C. of C. (trustee U.S. council), Am. Accounting Assn., Nat. Assn. Accountants, state socs. C.P.A.'s N.Y. (past pres.), N.J., La. Episcopalian. Clubs: Arcola Country, Downtown Athletic, Paris Am., Skytop, Union League, N.Y.U., Opera, Harbor View (N.Y.C.). Home: Ridgewood, N.J. Died June 18, 1976.

FRAMPTON, JAMES VILLARD, lawyer; b. Clarion County, Pa., July 24, 1883; s. B. H. and Nellie (Mohney) F.; Ph.B., Bucknell U., 1903; m. Lavinia Magee, 1910; 1 son, William. Admitted to Pa. bar, 1907; mem. firm Frampton & Courtney, Oil City, Pa., 1907—. Vice pres. Charles N. Hough Mfg. Co.; treas. Humphrey-Stone-McColl Corp.; dir. Oil City Nat. Bank, Pennland Tankers, Inc., Clare M. Marshall, Inc., Henry I. Beers Corp., Rayland Corp. Exec. com. Pa. Assn. for Blind; pres. Venango County Assn. for the Blind; pres. bd. trustees Polk State Sch. Mem. Am., Pa. (bd. govs., v.p. 1957—) bar assns., Pa. Soc. of N.Y., Sigma Chi. Republican. Presbyn. Mason (32 deg., Shriner, K.T.). Home: Oil City, Pa.

FRANCIS, EDWIN AUGUSTUS, journalist; b. Salem, Mass., Dec. 2, 1919; s. Edwin Fisk Allen and Ethel (Bradeen) F.; ed. U. Wis., Marquette U., Layton Sch. Art, Mass. Coll. Art; m. Dorothy Loraine Mantyh, Aug. 28, 1946; children—Thomas, John. Editor publs. Allis-Chalmers Mfg. Co., 1947-56; editor Pub. Relations Mgmt. Newsletter, 1950-51; real estate editor, bus. writer Milw. Sentinel, 1951-62; bus.-financial editor Boston Record Am. and Sunday Advertiser, from 1962; former bus. editor Boston Herald Am. and Boston Herald Advertiser. Dir. seminar urban affairs Marquette U., 1959-60. Served with USCGR, 1940-46. Recipient Harry Apple award Milw. Press Club, honor award Nat. Assn. Editors. Mem. Sigma Delta Chi. Author articles on met. problems. Home: Marblehead, Mass. Died Dec. 1977.

FRANCIS, MAY E., state supt. schs.; b. Blue Earth Co., Minn., Nov. 2, 1884; d. Henry and Adda (Van Tuyl) F.; student State U. of Ia., 1908; B.A., Ia. State Normal Sch., 1910; M.A., Teachers' Coll. (Columbia), 1922. Began as teacher pub. schs.; supt. schs., Denver, Ia., 1913-15; county supt. schs., Bremer Co., 1915-19; insp. rural schs., Ia., 1919-21; state supt. pub. instrn., Ia., term, 1923-27. Mem. Daughters of Vets., O.E.S. Republican. Methodist. Club: Women's Rotary.

FRANCKE, DONALD EUGENE, pharmacist, editor; b. Athens, Pa., Aug. 28, 1910; s. Edward Owen and Margaret Carmalita (Kinney) F.; B.S., U. Mich., 1936, M.S., 1948; D.Sc. (hon.), Purdue U., 1951, U. Mich., 1967; m. Maxine Hafey, Aug. 18, 1937; children—Markay, Stephanie, David, Michel, Jon; m. 2d, Gloria Niemeyer, Apr. 15, 1956. Dir. pharmacy service U. Mich. Hosp., 1944-63; dir. sci. services Am. Soc. Hosp. Pharmacists, 1963-66; cons. hosp. pharmacy Surg. Gen. Army, VA; lectr. hosp. pharmacy U. Mich. Coll. Pharmacy, 1948-51, asst. prof. pharmacy, 1951-62, asso. prof. pharmacy, 1962-63; pharmacy adviser WHO; prof., chmn. dept. hosp. pharmacy Coll. Pharmacy, U. Cin., 1967-71, dir. Inst. Studies Hosp. Pharmacy, 1967-71; dir. pharmacy service Cin. Gen. Hosp., 1967-71, VA Central Office, 1971-72; dir. Aud-Pharm. Service in Hosp., USPHS grant, 1956-59, dir. hosp. pharmacy technician study, 1970-73; pres. Drug Intelligence Publs., from 1971; prof. clin. pharmacy Howard U., from 1975. Mem. Am. Pharm. Assn. Mission to Japan, Supreme Command Allied Powers, 1949; mem. Mich. Bd. Pharmacy, 1950-52; mem. revision com. U.S. Pharmacopeia, 1950-60. Lt. comdr. USPHS Res., 1949; pharmacist dir. Res., 1954. Recipient J. Leon Lascoff Meml. Found. award for contbns. pharmacy, 1947, J. Leon Lascoff Meml. award, 1948, H.A.K. Whitney lecture award, 1953, Remington Hon. medal, 1970, Donald E. Francke medal, 1973; Distinguished Alumnus award U. Mich., 1976. Fellow A.A.A.S., Am. Coll. Clin. Pharmacology, mem. Am. Chem. Soc., Am. Hosp. Assn., Am. Pharm. Assn. (dir. div. hosp. pharmacy 1949-56, council, 1948-56, chmn. com. on publs., 1951-56, pres. 51-52), Am. Soc. Hosp. Pharmacists (pres. 1943-46, editor jour. 1944-66), Am. Assn. U. Profs., Am. Acad. Polit. and Social Sci., Internat. Pharm. Fedn. (mem. council, v.p. 1958-66, pres. sect. press and documentation), N.Y. Acad. Scis., Am. Med. Writers Assn., Sociedada de Farmacia e Quimica de Sao Paulo, Brazil (hon.), Associacion Farmaceutica y Bioquimica Argentina (hon.), Japanese Pharm. Assn. (hon.), Pharm. Soc. Gt. Britain (hon.), Pharm. Soc. Greece (hon.), Drug Information Assn. (pres. 1969), Am. Inst. History Pharmacy, Rho Chi, Phi Delta Chi. Club: Cosmos (Washington). Author: Hospital Formulary of Selected Drugs; (co-author) Art of Compounding, Remington's Practice of Pharmacy; Report of Audit of Pharmaceutical Services in Hospitals; sr. author Mirror to Hospital Pharmacy, 1964. Editor: Formulary U. of Mich. Hosp.; co-editor: Perspectives in Clinical Pharmacy, 1971; asso. editor: U. Mich. Med. Bull., 1950-58; editor Internat. Pharm. Abstracts, 1964-66, Drug Intelligence and Clin. Pharmacy, 1967-78, Drug Information Bull., 1967-71. Contbr. articles to pharmacy and hosp. jours. Home: Washington, D.C. Died Nov. 6, 1978.

FRANDSEN, JULIUS, JR., press cons.; b. Moscow, Ida., July 12, 1907; s. Julius Herman and Mattie (Madsen) F.; A.B., U. Neb., Lincoln, 1927; m. Eleanor Cameron, Sept. 1, 1931 (dec. 1953); m. 2d, Ruth Gmeiner, Aug. 8, 1954; 1 son, Jon Christian. Editorial work Springfield (Mass.) Republican, 1927-29; with United Press (now U.P.I.) in reportorial and managerial capacities, N.Y.C. and Washington, 1929-73, news editor Washington Bur., 1939-60, Washington mgr., 1961-65, v.p., Washington mgr., 1966-73; cons., 1973-76. Chmn., Sigma Delta Chi Found. of Washington, 1965-72, Thomas L. Stokes Award Com., 1966-71. Mem. Delta Upsilon, Sigma Delta Chi (chmn. nat. freedom information com. 1964-65). Clubs: Gridiron (pres. 1962, sec. 1965-71), Nat. Press (Washington). Home: Washington, D.C. Died Nov. 14, 1976.

FRANK, GRACE (MRS. TENNEY FRANK), educator; b. New Haven, June 28, 1886; d. Murray Charles and Frances (Ullman) Mayor; A.B., U. Chgo., 1907; grad. student Bryn Mawr Coll., 1908-10, 13-16, U. Goettingen and Berlin, 1911; research, France, Italy, Eng.; m. Tenney Frank, May 28, 1907; (dec. Apr. 1939). Faculty Bryn Mawr Coll., 1926—, successively lectr., asso. prof., prof., 1926-52, prof. emeritus, 1952—; vis. prof. Johns Hopkins, 1934-36. Fellow Mediaeval Acad. Am. (v.p. 1949-52); mem. Modern Lang. Assn. (v.p. 1957), Phi Beta Kappa. Clubs: Johns Hopkins, Hamilton Street. Author: Palatine Passion, 1922; Míracle de Théophile, 2d edit., 1949; Livre de la Passion, 1930; Passion d'Autun, 1934; Proverbes en Rimes, 1937; Medieval French Drama, 1954, 67; French Literature in the Fourteenth Century, 1961. Adv. editor Modern Language Notes, 1934-54. Contbr. Cabeen, Critical Bibliog. French Lit., Ency. dello Spettacolo, artices jours. Home: Balt.

FRANK, PHILIPP, physicist; b. Vienna, Austria, Mar. 20, 1884; s. Ignaz and Jenny (Feilendorf) F.; Ph.D., U. of Vienna, 1906; m. Hania Gerson, Nov. 16, 1920. Privatdozent of physics, U. of Vienna, 1910-12; prof. theoretical physics, U. of Prague, Czechoslovakia, 1912-38; came to United States, 1938; lecturer on physics and mathematics and research associate in physics and philosophy, Harvard, since 1939. Founding member Conference on Religion, Philosophy and Science. Fellow American Academy Arts and Sciences, Boston. Club: Faculty of Harvard (Cambridge, Mass.). Author: Das Kausalgesetz und seine Grenzen, 1932; Das Ende der mechanistischen Physik, 1935; Le Loi de Causalité et ses Limites, 1936; La Fin de la Physique Mècaniste, 1936; Rozvrat mechanisticke fysiky, 1938; Interpretations and Misinterpretations of Modern Physics, 1938; Between Physics and Philosophy, 1941; Foundations of Physics, 1945; Einstein, His Life and Times, 1947. Co-author and editor: (with R. V. Mises) Differentialgleichungen der Mechanik und Physik, 1925; associate editor of the Journal of Philosophy of Science; co-editor: International Encyclopedia of Unified Science, 1938; also author articles on scientific subjects. Home: Cambridge, Mass. *

FRANK, WALTER, lawyer; b. N.Y. City, Feb. 10, 1882; s. Philip and Josephine (Louis) F.; prep. edn., Horace Mann; A.B., Columbia, 1903; LL.B., New York Law Sch., 1905; m. Eva F. Auerbach, Nov. 28, 1915 (died 1932); m. 2d, Adelaide Schulkind, April 22, 1944. Admitted to N.Y. bar, 1905, and since practiced N.Y.C.; mem. Kurzman & Frank. Vice chmn. exec. com. Citizens Union. Mem. Am. Civil Liberties Union,

Nat. Consumers League (v. chmn.), Citizens League Indsl. Democracy, 1956; citation for exceptional civic service Citizens Union, 1966. Mem. N.Y., N.Y. County, N.Y. State bar assns., Bar Assn. City N.Y., Phi Beta Kappa, Pi Gamma Mu. Home: N.Y.C.

FRANK, WALTER HALE, business exec.; b. Humphrey, N.Y., Apr. 23, 1886; s. Albert and Agnes (House) F.; B.A., U.S. Mil. Acad., 1910; grad. Air Corps Engring. Sch., 1920, Air Corps Tactical Sch., 1925, Command and Gen. Staff Sch., 1926, Army War Coll., 1931; m. Hazel M. Smith, June 25, 1913; 1 dau., Helen Smith (wife of Brooke Empie Allen, U.S.A.F.). Commd. 2d lit., June 15, 1910; promoted through grades to maj. general, 1941; detailed to Aviation Sect. Signal Corps, 1917; comdg. officer Ellington Field, 1918; comdg. gen. 3d Air Force, Tampa, Fla., 1941-42; comdg. gen. 8th Air Force Service Command, London, Eng., June 23, 1942-Nov. 15, 1942; comdg. gen. Army Air Forces Air Service Command, Patterson Field, Fairfield, O., Nov. 1942-July 1944; mem. Army Pearl Harbor Bd., 1944; spl. asst. comdg. gen. Army Air Forces, Nov. 1944-Sept. 1945; retired, Dec. 31, 1945. Asst. to pres., Sears Western Hemisphere Trading Corp. since 1945; pres., Sears, Roebuck, S.A. Comercio e Industria (a Brazilian corp.), Rio de Janeiro, 1946-50; president Sears Roebuck S.A. Comercio e Indsl. (Argentine Corp.) Buenos Aires, 1946—; dir. foreign expansion Sears Roebuck & Company, 1950-55, Washington representative, 1954—. Episcopalian. Mason. Clubs: Army and Navy, Army and Navy Country, Nat. Press (Washington); International (Rio de Janeiro, Brazil). Home: Washington.

FRANKEL, CHARLES, educator, author; b. N.Y.C., Dec. 13, 1917; s. Abraham Philip and Estelle Edith (Cohen) F.; A.B. with honors in English and Philosophy, Columbia, 1937, Ph.D., 1946; student Cornell U., 1937-38; LL.D., Mercer U., 1968; D.Litt., Duke U., 1978; m. Helen Beatrice Lehman, Aug. 17, 1941; children—Susan, Carl. Mem. faculty Columbia U., from 1939, prof. philosophy, 1956-70, Old Dominion prof. philosophy and pub. affairs, from 1970; pres., dir. Nat. Humanities Center, from 1977; asst. U.S. sec. state ednl. and cultural affairs, 1965-67; cons. Orgn. for Econ. Cooperation and Devel.; vis. scholar Russell Sage Found., 1971-72. Co-chmn. Nat. Assembly for Teaching Prins. Bill of Rights, 1962-65. Chmn. U.S. delegation UNESCO Gen. Conf., 1966; mem. N.Y. State Commn. on Quality, Cost and Financing Edn., 1969-72. Pres. bd. trustees Rockland Country Day Sch., Congers, N.Y., 1959-64; bd. dirs. N.Y. State Civil Liberties Union, 1960-65; chmn. Internat. Council on Future Univ., from 1973; chmn. bd. trustees Nat. Humanities Center, 1976-77. Guggenheim fellow, 1953-54; Fulbright prof. U. Paris (France), 1953-54; Carnegie Corp. reflective year fellow, 1959-60. Served to lt. USNR, 1942-46. Fellow Am. Acad. Arts and Scis.; mem. Am. Philos. Assn., AAUP (chmn. com. profl. ethics 1956-59), Authors Guild (council), P.E.N., Council Fgn. Relations, Phi Beta Kappa. Club: Century Assn. (N.Y.C.). Author: The Faith of Reason, 1948; The Bear and the Beaver, 1951; The Case for Modern Man, 1956; The Democratic Propect, 1962; The Love of Anxiety and Other Essays, 1965; The Neglected Aspect of Foreign Affairs, 1966; Education and the Barricades, 1968; High on Foggy Bottom, 1969; The Pleasures of Philosophy, 1972; A Stubborn Case, 1972; prin. author The Power of the Democratic Idea, 1960. Gen. editor: Introduction to Contemporary Civilization in the West, 1941; editor (Rousseau) Social Contract, 1947; The Uses of Philosophy, 1955; Issues in University Education, 1959; The Golden Age of American Philosophy, 1960; Controversies and Decisions, 1976. Contbr. articles to profl. publs. Home: Bedford Hills, N.Y. Died May 10, 1979.

FRANKLIN, DWIGHT, artist; b. N.Y. City, Jan. 28, 1888; s. Joseph Frederick and Jeannie Whittemore (Dwight) F.; ed. pvt. schs., N.Y. City; m. Mary C. McCall, Jr., January 16, 1928 (divorced 1943); children—Sheila McCall, Alan McCall, Gerald McCall; married 2d, Elizabeth Darling, February 20, 1947. Artist with American Museum of Natural History, New York City, 1906-14; staff artist, William Beebe's Arcturus Expedition, 1925; art director, Douglas Fairbanks, 1925; became mem. staff Museum City of New York, 1929; now designer of motion pictures. Mem. Ship Model Soc., Calif. Hist. Soc., Soc. Am. Sword Collectors, E'Clampus Vitus. Clubs: Players, Armor and Arms (New York); Westerners (Los Angeles). Contbr. papers to American Association Museums. Originator of miniature group type now in use in many museums. Address: Rustic Canyon, Santa Monica, Calif.

FRANKLIN, EDGAR WILLIAM, investment co. exec; b. Muskogee, Okla., Mar. 18, 1916; s. Edward James and Mildred Elizabeth (Borum) F.; student U. Tulsa, 1933-34; B.S. in Bus. Administrn., U. Mo., 1938; m. Joanne Quentel Weber, Jan. 24, 1945; 1 dau., Lynne Diane. Salesman Walter O'Bannon Co., Tulsa, 1939-41; salesman Dittmer & Co., Dallas, 1946-49, br. mgr., v.p., 1950-68, dir., 1967-68; sr. v.p., sec., treas., dir. Schneider, Bernet & Hickman, Inc., Dallas, 1968-76. Dir. Municipal Adv. Council Tex., 1965-66. Served as pvt. AUS, 1941, maj. USAAF, 1942-46. Mem. Tex. Group Investment Bankers Assn. (chmn. 1969), Investment Bankers Assn. Am. (gov. 1970-71). Beta Theta Pi. Episcopalian. Clubs: Dallas Municipal Bond (pres. 1964), City, Chaparral, Northwood Country (Dallas). Home: Dallas, Tex. Died Dec. 15, 1976.

FRANKLIN, JOSEPH AMOS, univ. adminstr.; b. Madison County, Ind., July 5, 1904; s. Pierce and Emma (Zetta) F.; B.S., Ind. U., 1927; m. Beatrice Long, June 9, 1926; children—Richard Paul, Zetta Ann Franklin Anderson, Janet Franklin Carrell, Joseph Arnold. Accountant, auditor Ind. U., 1927-34, chief accountant, 1934-37, asst. comptroller, 1937-42, asst. treas., 1942-46, treas., 1946-48, v.p., treas., 1948-71, fiscal counsel to pres., 1971-75. Chmn. bd. Monroe Devel. Corp.; hon. trustee Lions Cancer Control Fund of Indiana, Inc.; past mem. Ind. Med. Edn. Found., Beck Chapel Com.; past treas. Ind. U. Annuitants' Assn.; chmn. Ind. Outdoor Folklore Mus. Com.; bd. dirs., treas. Ind. U. Retirement Community, Inc.; mem. Riley Patient Care Com.; Riley Lockerbie Home Com., Riley Investment Com.; chmn. Riley Bradford Camp Com.; mem. Historic Preservation Com.; mem. Fame Laundry Bd., Found. Econ. Bus. Studies; bd. dirs. Brown County Playhouse. Recipient Distinguished Alumni Service award Ind. U., E. Ross Bartley award; Gov.'s Sagamore of Wabash award, Gov.'s award Ind. Lions Cancer provision equipment Med. Center Radiology Clinic. Mem. Nat., Central assns. of coll. and univ. business officers, James Whitcomb Riley Meml. Assn. (life gov.,) C. of C., Hoosier Salon Patrons Assn., Assn. Univs. for Research in Astronomy, Ind. U. Alumni Assn. (life), Smithsonian Assos., Nat. Trust Historic Preservation, Hoosier Realty Bd., Beta Gamma Sigma, Acacia. Mem. Ch. of Christ. Clubs: Lions, Columbia, Bloomington Country. Contbr. articles on bus. adminstrn. Home: Unionville, Ind. Died July 19, 1980; buried on Nat. Rd. 36, Mechanicsburg, Ind.

FRANTZ, RALPH JULES, journalist; b. Springfield, O., Nov. 1, 1902; s. George F. and Lillian R. (Schaefer) F.; student Wittenberg Acad., Springfield, 1917-18; Wittenberg Coll., 1919-20; m. Loulette Isabelle Desrumaux, Mar. 6, 1926 (dec. Jan. 28, 1967); m. 2d, Maxine Coulson, June 15, 1968. Reporter, later sports editor, Springfield (O.) Sun, 1919-22; with Cleveland Times in various capacities including day city editor, state editor and Sunday editor, 1922-25; joined Paris edition, Chicago Tribune, Dec. 1, 1925, night editor, 1927, mng. editor, 1929 until merger of paper with Paris Herald, 1934; with New York Herald Tribune from 1935, asst. to night editor 1950-51, telegraph editor, 1951-65, suburban editor, 1965-71. Trustee, sec. Corrs. Fund. Head psychol. warfare br. Allied Force Headquarters in Morocco, April-August 1943, in Algiers, September-December 1943, in Sicily, Jan. 1944-Mar. 1945; established U.S. information service for State Dept. in Palermo, Sicily, Mar.-Nov. 1945. European tour, 1925. Clubs: Overseas Press of America (a founder, 1939, treas. 1940-43, 46-50; v.p., 1950-51; trustee Corrs. Fund), Silurians. Home: Fair Lawn, N.J. Died Nov. 2, 1979.

FRARY, FRANCIS COWLES (FRA'RI), chemist; b. Minneapolis, Minn., July 9, 1884; s. Francis Lee and Jeanette (Cowles) F.; A.C., U. of Minn., 1905; M.S., 1906, Ph.D., 1912; studied U. of Berlin 1 yr.; m. Alice Hall Wingate, June 12, 1908; children—Faith Margaret, John Loveland. Instr. in chemistry, U. of Minn., 1905-11, asst. prof., 1911-15; research chemist, Oldbury Electrochem. Co., Niagara Falls, N.Y., 1915-18; capt. Ordnance O.R.C. and maj. Chem. Warfare Service, U.S. Army, 1918 (Edgewood Arsenal); dir. of research, Aluminum Co. of America, New Kensington, Pa., since Dec. 15, 1918. Received Pittsburgh Award, Acheson Medal, Perkin Medal, Gold Medal of the Am. Soc. for Metals. Member Am. Chem. Soc., The Electrochem. Soc. (past pres.), Am. Inst. Mining and Metall. Engrs., Am. Inst. Chem. Engrs. (past pres.), Inst. of Metals, Alpha Chi Sigma. Republican. Presbyterian. Author: Laboratory Manual of Glassblowing, 1914; (with J. D. Edwards and Zay Jeffries) The Aluminum Industry (2 vols.). Home: Oakmont, Pa.

FRASCA, JOHN ANTHONY, newspaperman; b. Lynn, Mass., May 25, 1916; s. Michele A. and Mary (Jordan) F.; B.A., Miss. Coll., 1940; m. Louise Cummings, Dec. 20, 1948; children—Charlotte (Mrs. Gene Krupa), Sydney (Mrs. Vincent Giovenco), Karen, Michele (Mrs. John Krentzman), John Anthony. Free-lance polit. analyst, cons. weekly newspapers, also radio commentator, 1958-64; mem. staff Tampa (Fla.) Tribune, 1964-69. Recipient award for best feature of year in Tex., A.P., 1954; Pa. Mental Health Bell award, 1956; Phila. Good Citizenship award, 1956; Pa. Optimist Club award, 1957; Best Writing of Year award Phila. Press Assn., 1956; 2d prize campaign series, My Ten Days in a Mental Hosp., Pa. Newspaper Pubs. Assn., 1956, best campaign series Children Who Walk Alone, 1957, best feature award Inside Israel, 1957, 2d award ct. coverage Injustice for Our Kids, 1957, hon. mention spot news White Woman Unknown, 1957; Pultizer prize, also Heywood Broun award for Robert Lamar Watson series, 1966. Author: The Mulberry Tree (spl. Edgar Allen Poe award Mystery Writers Am. 1968), 1967; Con Man or Saint?, 1969; A Sharecropper's Best Stories, 1970; The Unstoppable Glenn Turner, 1971; Motivational Genius, 1972; The Sun Rose Late, 1973. Home: Tampa, Fla. Died Dec. 3, 1979.

FRASCH, JOSEPH FREDERICK, univ. pres.; b. Logan, Ohio, Aug. 30, 1911; s. Lewis G. and Minnie (Kleinschmidt) F.; B.S., Capital U., 1933; M.A., Ohio State U., 1939, Ph.D., 1962; m. Esther Lucille Morehart, Feb. 1, 1941; children—Joseph F., Lewis G. Prin., Darby Twp. (Ohio) High Sch., 1933-35; sci. tchr. Hilliards (Ohio) High Sch., 1935-41; insp. Army Ordnance, Wolf Creek Ordnance Plant, Milan, Tenn., 1941-43; tng. specialist VA, Columbus, Ohio, 1946-51; pres. Franklin U., Columbus, 1951-77. Served to lt. USNR, 1943-46. Named One of Ten Outstanding Citizens of Columbus, Citizen Jour., 1971. Mem. Am. Assn. Higher Edn., Phi Delta Kappa. Lutheran (pres. ch. council 1972). Clubs: Sertoma, Torch. Home: Columbus, Ohio. Died July 29, 1977; buried Logan, Ohio.

FRASER, ALBERT SCOTT, banker; b. Nova Scotia, Can., Feb. 10, 1886; s. Robert Patterson and Anna Grant (Fraser) F.; m. Elizabeth Coll, Oct. 17, 1927; children—A. Scott, Elizabeth (Mrs. E. S. MacLatchy), Joan (Mrs. Neil B. Ivory). With Bank of Nova Scotia, Halifax, Can., 1902-17, now dir., Toronto; with Equitable Trust Co., Balt., 1917-18, Nat. City Bank of N.Y., 1919-28; chmn., dir. Eastern Trust Co., Halifax; pres., mng. dir. Investment Foundation, Ltd. Montreal; dir. Sun Life Assurance Co. of Can., Montreal. Gov., Dalhousie U., United Theol. Coll., Montreal, Can., Montreal Children's Hosp., Montreal Gen. Hosp. Home: Westmount, P.Q., Can.

FRASER, ALISTAIR, ex-govt. ofcl. Can.; b. New Glasgow, Nova Scotia, Mar. 15, 1886; s. Hon. D. C. and Bessie (Graham) F.; B.A., Dalhousie U., 1906, LL.B., 1908, LL.D., 1952, D.C.L.; m. Jane Graeme Ross, Sept. 18, 1919; children—Alistair G., Ian R., Duncan C. Called to bar of Nova Scotia, 1911; read law with Hector McInnes, K.C.; created King's Counsel, 1921, practiced law, Moose Jaw, Saskatchewan, Can., 1912-14; apptd. gen. solicitor, Canadian Nat. Railways, 1919, commn. counsel, 1923, asst. gen. counsel, 1929, became v.p. in charge of traffic, 1932; lt. gov. N.S. until 1957. Commd. lt., 17th Bn., Canadian Army, 1914; joined Princess Pats in France, 1915, and later joined 15th Canadian Bn.; promoted capt. and adjt., Apr. 1916, major comdg. company, July 1916; wounded Vimy Ridge, 1917; a.d.c. to Canadian Corps Comdr., 1918-19. Decorated Mil. Cross. Clubs: St. James's (Montreal); Rideau (Ottawa); Halifax. Address: Guysborough, N.S.

FRASER, OLIVER B(RANIFF) J(OSEPH), metall. engr.; b. Brockville, Ont., Can., Dec. 22, 1895; s. Oliver Kelly and Margaret Aloysius (Braniff) F.; B.S., Queens U., 1916; m. Evelyn Josephine LeFebvre, Sept. 11, 1923; 1 son, Malcolm James. Came to U.S., 1922, naturalized, 1936. Joined The Internat. Nickel Co., Inc., Bayonne, N.J., 1917, asst. manager of development and research division, 1947-61; ind. tech. cons., after 1961. Fellow Chem. Inst. of Canada, A.A.A.S., Am. Inst. Chemists; member Society Chemical Industry, N.Y. Acad. Scis., Nat. Geog. Soc., Am. Inst. Mining and Metall. Engrs. (v.p. 1952-55), Am. Welding Soc. (pres. 1949-50, Miller Medal, 1951, hon. mem. 1956), Armed Forces Chem. Assn., Canadian Soc. N.Y., St. Andrew's Soc. State N.Y., Mining and Metall. Soc. Am., Canadian Inst. Mining and Metall., Inst. Metals (Gt. Britain), Am. Soc. for Metals, ASTM, Am. Chem. Soc., Electrochem. Society, American Institute of Chem. Engrs., ASME, Societe de Chimie Industrielle (pres. U.S. sect. 1959-60, Honor Scroll 1965), Comml. Chem. Development Assn., Chem. Market Research Association, N.J. Mineral. Soc., Fgn. Policy Association, Acad. Polit. Sci., Société des Ingeneurs Civils de France, American Ordnance Association, American Petroleum Institute, American Gas Association, Canadian Geographic Society, Soc. Hist. of Tech. K.C. Clubs: Mining, Chemists, Engineers (pres. 1961-62), India House (N.Y.C.). Author tech. papers. Home: Westfield, N.J. Died Nov. 25, 1978.

FRAZER, ALBERT DANNER, banker; b. Mobile, Feb. 28, 1917; s. Mell Alexander and Mary Virginia (Danner) F.; grad. Stonier Grad. Sch. Banking, 1950; m. Clara Hughes Little, Sept. 14, 1938; children—Anne Hughes, Albert Danner, Kathleen Ross. With Am. Nat. Bank & Trust Co., Mobile, 1934-41; with First Nat. Bank, Mobile, 1941-42, 48-57; v.p., 1954-57; asst. treas. U.S. Steel Corp., Birmingham, Ala., 1957-62; pres. Salisbury Nat. Bank (Md.), 1962-64; sr. v.p. First Nat. Bank Md., Balt., 1964-66; pres., chmn. Am. Nat. Bank & Trust Co., Mobile, 1966-77, also dir.; vice chmn., dir. Ala. Bank Corp.; dir. Mobile Gas Service Corp., Mobile Paint Mfg. Co. Del. Inc., Mobile Paint Mdg. Co. P.R., Inc., Keywall Covering Inc., B.L.P. Mobile Paint Indsl. Sales Corp.; bd. dirs. Mobile C. of C., 1967-69, 71-73, Mobile Indsl. Devel. Bd., 1967-74. Bd. regents Springhill Coll., Mobile. Served with AUS, USAAF, 1942-47. Decorated D.F.C., Air medal with 7 oak leaf clusters, Purple Heart; hon. fellow Mobile Coll.; recipient President's award Springhill Coll., 1975. Mem. Am., Ala. bankers assns., Robert Morris Assos. Presbyn. Clubs: Mobile Country, Lakewood Golf (Point Clear, Ala.); Downtown, Birmingham Athelstan,

Mobile. Home: Mobile, Ala. Died Oct. 13, 1977; interred Magnolia Cemetery, Mobile.

FRAZER, JOHN WILLIAM, clergyman; b. Evergreen, Ala., Feb. 11, 1885; s. John Stanley and Mary Ella (Chapman) F.; A.B., Southern U., Ala., 1905; B.D., Vanderbilt, 1909; grad. work, U. of Chicago, Litt.D., Birmingham Southern Coll., 1922; m. Sarah Knickerbocker, June 14, 1911 (died July 1, 1915); 1 dau., Vivian; m. 2d, Lncy Bomar, Mar. 1922; children—Frank Betts, Nancy Bomar. Ordained to the ministry of Methodist Episcopal Church, South; pastor Av. Ch., Montgomery, Ala., 1909-10, Marion, Ala., 1911-13, Auburn, 1914-15; presiding elder Mobile Dist., 1915; pastor Dexter Av. Ch., Montgomery, 1915-16, Central Ch., Spartanburg, S.C., 1917-21, later 1st Ch., Pensacola, Fla., Court Street Methodist Ch., Montgomery, Ala., and Church Street M.E. Church, Selma, Ala.; presiding elder Montgomery District, 1935-37, Mobile Dist. since 1937. Chaplain 214th Engineers, 14th Div., U.S. Army, World War; chaplain Spartanburg Post and S.C. Div., Am. Legion. Mem. Phi Beta Kappa, Alpha Tau Omega. Omicron Delta Kappa. Democrat. Mason. Club: Kiwanis. Author: The Untried Civilization, 1921. Contbr. to ch. periodicals. Pastor of the Dexter Avenue Methodist Church, Montgomery, Alabama; now pastor Church St. Methodist Ch., Selma, Ala. Home: Selma, Ala.

FRAZIER, JAMES TAYLOR, machinery distbr.; b. Pocahontas, Va., Mar. 10, 1905; s. Charles s. Charles C. and C. and Bertha E. (Wood) F.; B.S. in Bus. Adminstrn., U. Richmond, 1926; m. Dorothy M. Connally, June 21, 1928; children—Betty C. (Mrs. Frank M. Winterholler), James Taylor, Reva M. (Mrs. B.F. Parrott, Jr.). Pres. Bluefield Supply Co. (W.Va.), 1956-67, chmn. bd., pres., after 1967; pres. Monte Vista Park Cemetery, Bluefield from 1950; pres. Rish Equipment Co., Bluefield, 1960-67, chmn. bd., pres., from 1967; pres. Skyland, Inc., Bluefield, Skyland Hosp. Supply, Bluefield; chmn. bd., pres. Dixie Appliance Co.; dir. Flat Top Nat. Bank, S & S Machinery Co., Inc., Richlands, Va. Past bd. dirs. local ARC, Boy Scouts Am., Salvation Army, Community Chest; bd. dirs. Bluefield Area Devel. Corp.; adv. panel W.Va. Found. for Ind. Colls., 1972-73. Mem. Am. Automobile Assn. (past nat. dir.), Bluefield (past pres.; dir.), U.S. chambers commerce, Bluefield Assn. Credit Men (past pres.), Bluefield Auto Club (past pres.; dir.), Pi Kappa Alpha. Methodist. Home: Bluefield, W.Va. Died Jan. 1977.

FRAZIER, ROBERT HAINES, lawyer; b. Greensboro, N.C., Jan. 8, 1899; s. Cyrus Pickett and Lucetta (Churchill) F.; student Guilford Coll., 1917-18; A.B., U. N.C., Chapel Hill, 1922; student Columbia Grad. Sch., 1929; LL.D., N.C. Agrl. and Tech. State U., 1970; m. Florence Hyde. Admitted to N.C. bar, 1922, D.C. bar, 1947; practiced in Greensboro, 1922-25; partner firm Frazier & Frazier, 1925-74, Frazier, Frazier, Mahler & Walker, from 1974; sr. atty. OPA, 1943, chief counsel Office Export-Import, 1944-47. With Am. fgn. service, 1918-20, Oslo, Norway, Murmansk, Russia, and Havre, France; vice consul, Oslo, 1920. Dir. in orgn. N.C. Broadcasting Co., 1929. Mem. Am. Friends Service Com., chmn. Southeastern region, 1948-54; mem. Guilford County Bd. Health, 1951-55; mem. permanent bd. N.C. Yearly Meeting of Friends, 1940-64, Friends World Com., 1953-69, rep. Friends World Conf., Swarthmore, Pa., 1934, Oxford, Eng., 1952, Gilford, N.C., 1967; chmn. John Motley Morehead Meml. State Commn., 1959-72; mem. Regional Export Expansion Council, 1972-75. Councilman, Mayor pro-tem. City of Greensboro, 1949-51, mayor, 1951-55 (rep. U.S. Conf. Mayors at Internat. Conf. Mayors, Rome, Italy, 1955). Chmn. bd. Greensboro Pub. Library, 1941-49; pres. Greensboro Community Chest, 1950; dir. Greensboro YMCA, 1952-55; trustee Guilford Coll., 1932-74, chmn., 1950-69, trustee emeritus, from 1974; trustee N.C. Agrl. and Tech. State Univ., chmn., 1957-70; trustee Oak Ridge Acad. Found., 1965—; trustee Wooglin Found., chmn., 1932. Recipient Charles A. Cannon Hist. award, 1955. Fellow Am. Bar Found., Am. Coll. Probate Counsel (regent 1967-74); mem. N.C. Soc. Preservation Antiquities (dir., v.p. 1954-69), Greensboro Travelers Aid Soc. (pres. 1937-43), Fed., Internat. (presented paper London Conf. 1950), Am. (chmn. sect. on real property, probate and trust law 1961-62, mem. ho. dels. 1962-64), N.C. (chmn. exec. com. and v.p. 1953-54), Greensboro (pres. 1950-51) bar assns., S.A.R. (pres. Gen. Green chpt. 1949), Nat. Conf. Christians and Jews (pres. Greensboro chpt. 1949), Am. Judicature Soc. (dir. 1966-69), Am. Soc. Internat. Law, Am. Law Inst., Beta Theta Pi (nat. trustee, v.p. 1936-42), Phi Delta Phi. Mem. Soc. of Friends (Quakers). Kiwanian. Clubs: Greensboro Barristers (pres. 1928), Greensboro Merchants and Manufacturers (pres. 1929, 33), Greensboro Country; University (Washington). Author: A Christmas City—Christiana, Norway, 1926; Nantucket and North Carolina, 1936 (monographs); Coltrane and Frazier Genealogy, 1961; various legal briefs. Editor U. N.C. Law Rev., 1922. Home: Greensboro, N.C. Died Aug. 21, 1978.

FRAZIER, WALTER STEPHEN, architect; b. Aurora, Ill., Oct. 29, 1895; s. Walter S. and Clara (Pfrangel) F.; student U. Ill., 1913-15; B.S. in Architecture M.I.T., 1919; student Ecole des Beaux Arts, Paris, 1919-20. With Holabird & Root, Chgo., 1920-24; pvt. practice, from 1924; partner Frazier, Orr, Fairbank & Quam, Inc., architects, Geneva, Ill., 1945-76. Served to 2d lt., Air Corps, U.S. Army, 1917-19; to lt. col. USAAF, 1943-46. Fellow A.I.A. Clubs: Tavern, Arts (Chgo.). Home: Geneva, Ill. Died Apr. 30, 1976; buried Spring Lake Meml. Garden, Aurora.

FRED, EDWIN BROUN, educator; b. Middleburg, Va., Mar. 22, 1887; s. Samuel Rogers and Catherine Conway (Broun) F.; prep. edn., Randolph Macon Acad., Front Royal, Va., 1902-03; B.S., Va. Poly. Inst., 1907, M.S., 1908; Ph.D., U. of Göttingen, Germany, 1911, recipient Golden Diploma, 1961; LL.D., Lawrence Coll., 1945, Northwestern U., 1947, Mich. State Coll., 1955; D.Sc., Marquette U., 1945, Beloit Coll., U. N.C., Northland Coll., Ashland, Wis., 1946, U. Wis., 1958; m. Rosa Helen Parrott, June 21, 1913; children—Ann Conway, Rosalie Broun (Mrs. Thomas Moffatt). Asst. bacteriology Va. Poly. Inst., 1907-08, asst. prof. bacteriology, 1912-13; asst. prof. U. Wis., 1913-14, asso. prof., 1914-18, prof., 1918-58, dean Grad. Sch., 1934-43, dean Coll. of Agr. and dir. Agr. Expt. Sta., 1943-45, pres. U. Wis., 1945-58, pres. emeritus, prof. emeritus, from 1958. Mem. Nat. Adv. Health Council, 1945-50; trustee Nutrition Found., 1945-50, Carnegie bd. trustees, 1946-58; mem. U.S. Adv. Commn. on Ednl. Exchange 1949-54; NSF Bd., 1950-56; mem. nat. adv. and infectious diseases council NIH, 1956-57; adv. com. for biology and medicine AEC, 1956-57; Am. Council on Edn. Commn. on Edn. and Internat. Affairs, 1958-61; Pres.'s Internat. Devel. adv. bd., 1959. Trustee Vilas Trust, from 1961; mem. U. Wis. Found., from 1961. Apptd. as 1st lt. Chem. Warfare Service, U.S. Army, 1918. Decorated Medal for Merit for services during World War II; recipient meritorius service citation Va. Poly. Inst. Chem. Adv. Com. Biol. Warfare of Nat. Acad. of Scis., 1941-43, Acad. citation Wis. Acad. Sci., Arts and Letters, 1974. Fellow A.A.A.S.; mem. Nat. Acad. Sci., Am. Philos. Soc., Soc. Am. Bacteriologists (pres. 1932), Sigma Xi, Phi Beta Kappa, Alpha Sigma Epsilon, Gamma Alpha, Phi Sigma, Epsilon Sigma Phi, Phi Kappa Phi. Democrat. Co-author: Textbook of Agricultural Bacteriology (with F Löhnis), 1923; Laboratory Manual of Microbiology (with S. A. Waksman), 1928; Root Nodule Bacteria and Leguminous Plants (with Baldwin and McCoy), 1932. Home: Madison, Wis. Deceased.

FREDENDALL, LLOYD R., army officer; b. Cheyenne, Wyo., Dec. 28, 1883; student U.S. Mil. Acad., June 1901-Jan. 1902, Aug. 1902-Jan. 1903; grad. Army Signal Sch., Field Officers Course, 1922, Command and Gen. Staff Sch., 1923, Army War Coll., 1925. Commd. 2d lt., Feb. 13, 1907; promoted through grades to brig gen., Dec. 1939, major gen., Oct. 1940, lt. gen., June 1943; on gen. staff, 1927-31; comd. 11th Army Corps directing landing of U.S. forces in N. Africa, Nov. 1942; comd. 2d Corps, U.S. Army, N. Africa, 1943; comd. 2d Army.

FREDERICK, CHRISTINE MCGAFFEY, writer, lecturer; b. Boston, Feb. 6, 1883; d. Wyatt and Mimi (Scott) McGaffey; Northwest Div. High Sch., Chicago; B.S., Northwestern U., 1906 (Phi Beta Kappa); spl. work Lewis Inst. and U. of Chicago; m. J. George Frederick, of New York, June 29, 1907. Pioneer in teaching application of business systems to management of home; established Applecroft Experiment Sta., L.I. Consulting household editor Ladies' Home Journal. Author: The New Housekeeping, 1913; Housekeepers' Food Chart; moving picture film, Efficiency in the Home, 1917; Household Engineering, 1918. Address: Greenlawn, L.I., New York.

FREDRIKS, GERRITT JAMES, lawyer; b. Cincinnati, May 24, 1882; s. Gerritt Jacobis and Sophia Emily (Oehlmann) F.; student U. Cin., Solomen P. Chase Coll.; m. Texanna Peacock, Jan. 1, 1908; children—Ruth Arkana (Mrs. Arwood Liggett), Ella Emily (Mrs. Robert D. Williamson). Admitted to Ohio bar, 1907, since practiced in Cin.; with Thorndyke, Frederiks & Cappelle, 1907-12, Fredriks & Huffman, 1912-16; pvt. law practice since 1916; now sr. mem. firm Fredricks & Liggett, Cin.; title officer Title Guaranty & Trust Co., 1908-09; gen. mgr. Bankers Surety Co., 1907-17. Pres. Federated Civic Assns. Hamilton Co.; chmn. bd. Food and Home Show. Lt. Inf., U.S. Army, World War I. Mem. Am. (past mem. house of dels.), Ohio State (pres. 1939-40) Cin. bar assns., Zool. Soc. Cin. (trustee, past pres.). Republican (past sec. Blaine club and past pres. Federation Republican clubs. Hamilton Co.). Mason (Shriner; past monarch, past thrice potent master; hon. mem. Sovereign Grand Insps. Gen. of 33 deg.). Club: Hyde Park Businessmen's (past pres.). Home: Cincinnati, OH. *

FREEDMAN, LEO, educator; b. Hungary, Jan. 15, 1884; s. Mor and Dorothea (Edelman) F.; brought to U.S. 1899; ed. in New York and abroad; student Columbia Univ., 1904-05, 1906-08 (Earl scholarship, 1907-08), B.S. and B.Ed., 1908, postgrad. work, lit. and philology, 1920-24; student New York U., 1905-06; m. Carolina Berger, of Hungary, Sept. 25, 1908; children—Edna Grace, Hortense Josefa. Teacher schools, N.Y. City, 1906-08; instr. in pedagogy, Porto Rico, 1908-09; founder, 1910, pres. and headmaster until 1924, Rhodes Prep. Sch., N.Y. City; founder, 1926, and pres. since, Beverly School for Boys, Los Angeles, Calif. Fellow Am. Geog. Soc.; mem. A.A.A.S., Metropolitan Mus. Art, Am. Mus. Natural History, Modern Language Assn. America, Los Angeles Chamber Commerce, Pi Gamma Mu. Republican. Club: City. Author of numerous monographs under various pseudonyms on edn. of boys. Home: Los Angeles, Calif.

FREEMAN, HARRY, journalist; b. N.Y.C., Mar. 2, 1906; s. Isaac and Stella (Lvovitch) F.; A.B., Cornell, 1926; student Columbia, 1928; m. Vera Shapiro, Oct. 7, 1927. Reporter, various N.Y.C. newspapers, 1926-39; corr. for Tass agy., 1929-30, asst. mgr., mng. editor Am. Bur., Tass agy., 1930-80. Mem. standing com. UN Corrs., 1946-48. Mem. Fgn. Press Assn. (v.p. 1946-48), UN Corrs. Assn., Acad. Polit. Sci., Phi Beta Kappa, Phi Kappa Phi. Club: Nat. Press (Washington). Contbr. to New Times, Life Abroad, Internat. Affairs, other fgn. publs. Home: New York, N.Y. Died Jan. 14, 1978.

FREEMAN, HARRY BOIT, banker; b. Newton, Mass., Oct. 17, 1896; s. Franklin W. and Helen (Boit) F.; grad. Cheshire Acad.; student U. Wash., 1915-16, Yale, 1919; m. Theodora Hollander, Oct. 10, 1925; children—Harry B., Willard C., Peter B. With Harris Forbes & Co., 1920-33; resident partner Whiting, Weeks & Knowles, 1933-42; trust officer Providence Nat. Bank, 1942-45, v.p., 1945-47; pres. Phenix Nat. Bank, 1947-52; dir., exec. v.p. Rhode Island Hosp. Trust Co., 1953-57; pres., 1958-63, chmn. bd., 1963-69; chmn. bd. Providence Jour. Co.; dir. Providence Gas Co., Providence Mutual Ins. Co., Fields PT Manufacturing Co. Chairman Community Fund, 1952; v.p. United Fund, 1954-56, pres., 1959-61. Served with Air Corps, U.S. Army, World War I. Home: Providence, R.I. Died Apr. 27, 1976.

FREEMAN, JOHN HENRY, lawyer; b. San Antonio, Oct. 23, 1886; s. James D. and Rose (Phelps) F.; student U. Chgo., 1908-10; LL.D., Baylor U., 1950; m. Edna Stewart, Dec. 5, 1912; children—Winifred (Mrs. R. L. Davis, Jr.), John Henry. Admitted to Tex. bar, 1913, Supreme Ct. U.S., 1928, since practiced in Houston; partner, Campbell, Myer & Freeman, 1916-23; mem. Fulbright, Crooker & Freeman, 1923-42, Fulbright, Crooker, Freeman, Bates & Jaworski, 1942—; city atty. Houston, 1928-29; bd. dirs., chmn. trust com. First City Nat. Bank, Houston. Trustee M. D. Anderson Found., Houston, 1936—, pres., 1940—; trustee Tex. Med. Center, Shrine Crippled Children's Hosp. Mem. Am., Tex. State, Houston, City N.Y. bar assns. Clubs: Ramada, River Oaks Country (Houston). Home: Houston, TX. *

FREEMAN, JULIAN, business exec., architect; b. Bklyn., Oct. 17, 1897; s. Abraham Louis and Rae (Waldman) F.; student Crane Coll., 1914-16, Art Inst. Chgo., 1914-16; m. Esther Freeman, August, 9, 1924 (dec. June 1958); 1 dau., Janet (Mrs. Maurice Cooper); m. 2d, Belle Kline Dobrowitz, Aug. 14, 1960. Tchr. manual tng. Chgo. Pub. Schs. 1916-17; architect from 1919; pres. Freeman Store Equipment Co., Inc., 1933-63; gen. mgr. Freeman Building Corp., from 1952. Pres. Council Jewish Fedns. and Welfare Funds, 1950-55, past nat. chmn. com. for achieving stable and unified nat. fund raising, chmn. commn. to study Jewish Cultural Agys. U.S.; bd. dirs. Community Chests and Councils Am., also mem. nat. budget com.; past pres. Indpls. Jewish Welfare Fedn., East Central States Region Council Jewish Fedns. and Welfare Funds; bd. dirs., past v.p. Indpls. Jewish Community Center Assn.; past mem. bd., exec. com. Indpls. Community Fund; chmn. com. on middle east Nat. Community Relations Adv. Council, also vice chmn. council. Chmn. bd. Nat. Found. Jewish Culture; former overseer Jewish Theol. Sem. Served as 1st lt. F.A., AUS, 1917-19. Mem. United Synagogue Am. (dir., past v.p., past chmn. nat. com. philosophy and program conservative movement), United Service for New Americans (dir.), Am. Jewish Congress (v.p., chmn. com. internat. affairs), Joint Distbn. Com., Am. Jewish Com., Am. Legion. Jewish religion (past pres. temple, now hon. pres.). Mason B'nai B'rith. Home: Indianapolis, Ind. Died Nov. 29 1980.

FREEMAN, MARGARET B., museum curator; b West Orange, N.J.; d. Orville E. and Sarah Adelaide (Sigler) Freeman; B.A., Wellesley Coll., 1923; M.A. Columbia, 1924. Staff Newark Mus., 1924-25, Dan Hall Sch., 1925-27, Wellesley Coll. Art Mus., 1927-28 staff Met. Museum of Art, 1928-1980; was curator o The Cloisters, medieval br. of mus. Mem. Am Museums Association, Museum Council, Mediaeval Academy of America, Phi Beta Kappa. Club: Medieval of Metropolitan Area. Author: Herbs for the Mediaeval Household, 1945; The Story of the Three Kings, 1955 the Unicorn Tapestries, 1976. Home: New York, N.Y. Died May 24, 1980.

FREEMAN, NELSON WRIGHT, corp. exec.; b Charleston, Ill., Aug. 6, 1908; s. Ernest and Mabel (Wright F.; student U. Ill.; m. Norma Greenlese, Sep

11, 1928; children—Nancy (Mrs. Henry Hughes), Jody (Mrs. Spann Greenwood). Br. mgr. Universal Credit Corp., Detroit, 1929-34; pres., gen. mgr. Freeman & Riesen Motor Co., Milw., 1934-38; mgr. Assos. Investment Co., Houston, 1938-42; personnel and safety dir. Lummus Co., 1942-43; mgr. personnel dept. Tenn. Gas Transmission Co. (now Tenneco Inc.), 1943-47, asst. to pres., 1947-50, v.p., 1950-54, sr. v.p., 1954-59, pres., 1966-72, chief exec. officer, 1968-74, chmn. bd., 1971-75, dir. until 1978; pres. Midwestern Gas Transmission Co., 1954-61, dir.; natural gas cons., 1962-64; pres., dir. Houston Nat. Bank, 1964-66; dir., chmn. exec. com., 1966; chmn. bd. Tenneco Corp., Tenneco Internat., Inc.; dir. East Tenn. Natural Gas Co., Tenneco Oil Co., Tenn. Gas Transmission Co., Packaging Corp. Am., J.I. Case Co., Newport News Shipbldg. & Dry Dock Co., Heggblade-Marguleas-Tenneco, Inc., Tenneco West, Inc., Tenneco Realty, Inc.; chmn. bd., dir. Houston Nat. Co.; dir. Petro-Tex Chem. Corp., Phila. Life Ins. Co., Tenn. Life Ins. Co., Am. Gen. Ins. Co., Albright & Wilson Ltd.; asso. dir. Republic of Tex. Corp.; adv. dir. Farmers Nat. Bank, Brenham, Tex.; Bayshore Nat. Bank, LaPorte, Tex. Bd. dirs. Hwy. Users Fedn. for Safety and Mobility; trustee Nat. Safety Council; nat. adv. council Nat. Cystic Fibrosis Research Council. Mem. Houston C. of C. (dir.), Internat. C. of C. (trustee U.S. council), UN Assn. (dir.). Clubs: River Oaks, Ramada (Houston): Links, Recess, Board Room (N.Y.C.); Chicago: Burning Tree (Washington). Home: Houston, Tex. Died June 4, 1980.

FREEMAN, WILLIAM RAYMOND, lighting equipment mfr.; b. Lewisburg, W.Va., Dec. 4, 1905; s. Charles Minot and Suzanne (Goheen) F.; student Fla. So. Coll., 1922-25; m. Dorothy R. Ade, Jan. 18, 1925; children—William R., Robert M., Joan (Mrs. J. J. McKew), Barbara (Mrs. Richard Forrest), Nancy (Mrs. William E. Russell, Jr.). Editor, Montclair (N.J.) Times, 1925-32; v.p., gen. mgr. Ladnew Corp., Jersey City, 1932-36; v.p., sales mgr. Birdseye Electric Co., Gloucester, Mass., 1936-39; sales and advt. mgr. Manning Bowman Co., Meriden, Conn., 1939-41; v.p. sales Wabash Corp., Bklyn., 1941-47; v.p. Lustra Corp. Am. and affiliate Amplex Corp., 1947-59, exec. v.p., 1959-65; pres. Amplex Corp., 1965-67; pres. Amplex div., exec. v.p. Lustra div., chmn. bd. Internat. Tel. & Tel. Illumination Corp., 1967-69, sr. adv. cons. ITT Illumination div., from 1969. Mem. Illuminating Engring. Soc., Nat. Fed. Sales Exec., Am. Mgmt. Assn., Nat. Elec. Photographic Mfrs. and Distbrs. Assn. (v.p.), Nat. Assn. Photographic Mfrs., Am. Hotel Assn., N.Y. Sales Execs. Club, Elec. Asso. Club: Hempstead Country (past pres.). Home: Fort Lauderdale, Fla. Deceased.

FREIBERG, ALBERT DANIEL, customer researcher; b. Stanton, Nebr., Feb. 9, 1904; s. Albert Fred and Frieda Hoffmeyer F.; A.B., North Central Coll., 1926; Ph.D., Cornell U., 1936; m. Harriet Winthrop Hall, Jan. 1, 1937; children—Susan Lane (Mrs. Thomas R. Coolidge), Ann Hall (Mrs. Allan M. Benton). Instr., Mich. State Coll., 1929-33; staff Psychol. Corp., N.Y.C., 1935-58, sec., 1940-44, v.p., 1944-47, dir. market research, 1944-58, dir., 1946-60, 1st v.p., 1947-58; pres. Profl. Research Assn., Inc., Profl. Mktg. Assos., from 1958. Mem. Market, Copy Research councils, Am. Eastern, N.Y. State psychol. assns., AAAS, Am. Mktg. Assn., Am. Assn. Pub. Opinion Research, Sigma Xi. Clubs: Cornell, Greenwich Country. Home: Greenwich, Conn. Died Dec. 18, 1977.

FRENCH, FRANK JOHN, chem. co. exec.; b. N.Y.C., Nov. 27, 1906; s. Chester Odlin and Christine (Grab) F.; B.S. in Chem. Engring., Lehigh U., 1932; m. Bettina Plummer, June 30, 1934; children—Bettina (Mrs. Pinkney C. Smith), William Plummer. With Allied Chem. Corp., N.Y.C., 1932-68, pres., gen. chemical division, 1960-63, president of fibers division, 1963-68; exec. v.p., dir. Jim Robbins Seat Belt Co., Royal Oak, Mich., from 1966; sr. exec. v.p., dir. Heplon Industries, Inc., West Conshohocken, Pa., from 1966; dir. Allied Chem. (Australia) Pty. Ltd., Sherkat Sahami Aliaf, Tehran, Iran. Mem. Man Made Fibers Assn., Broadway Assn. (dir.). Home: Pine Plains, N.Y. Died Mar. 21, 1976.

FRENCH, JOHN CALVIN, educator; b. Monmouth, Ill., Jan. 21, 1875; s. Jonathan and Elizabeth Lydia (Sprout) F.; A.B., Johns Hopkins, 1899, Ph.D., 1905; studied Harvard, 1899-1900; m. Jennie E. Beck, Apr. 8, 1901 (died 1911); children—Ruth, Helen A.; m. 2d, Anna S. Sievers, Apr. 4, 1917. With Johns Hopkins U. since 1900, instr. in English, 1904-09, associate, 1909-14, asso. prof., 1914-25, prof., 1925-27, librarian, 1927-43, emeritus since 1943. Member American Library Association, American Assn. University Profs., Phi Beta Kappa, Omicron Delta Kappa, Phi Gamma Delta. Founder and 1st pres. Edgar Allan Poe Soc. of Baltimore. Clubs: Johns Hopkins, Tudor and Stuart. Author: The Problem of the Prologs to Chaucer's Legend, 1905; The Speech for Special Occasions (with others), 1911; Writing, 1924; English in Business (with others), 1925; College Writing (with others), 1932; Practice Work in College English (with others), 1934; A History of the University Founded by Johns Hopkins, 1946. Home: Baltimore.

FRENCH, SIDNEY JAMES, coll. dean, author; b. Superior, Wis., Mar. 1, 1894; s. James Buchanan and Fannie Ramsey (Coffin) F.; B.S., U. of Chicago, 1922; M.S., U. of Wis., 1927, Ph.D., 1928; m. Florence B. Felten, Aug. 17, 1929; 1 dau., Roni Lou (Mrs. P. Malcolm Smith, Junior). Teacher of the Superior High Sch., 1916-17 and 1919-22, asst. prin., 1919-21; teacher Superior Teachers Coll., 1922-25; asst. and grad. student, U. of Wis., 1925-28; prof. chemistry, Franklin Coll., 1928-32; asst. prof. chemistry, Colgate U., 1932-38, prof. 1938-54, dean faculty 1945-54; dean Rollins College, Winter Park, Fla., 1954-58; dean Coll. Basic Studies, then acad. dean U. S.Fla., Tampa, 1958-62, dean of acad. affairs, 1962-64, emeritus, from 1964, part-time prof. edn., 1964-71, dir. grad. seminar on coll. tng., 1964-70; cons. Fla. Inst. for Continuing University Study; lectr. in field. Served with 312th Inf., A.E.F., 1917-19, served to 1st lt. 78th div., World War I; cons. on Jap. U. gen. edn. U.S. Army Occupation, Japan, 1950-51. Member of American Chemical Society, mem. Alpha Chi Sigma, Sigma Xi, Phi Lambda Upsilon (pres. Colgate U. chpt.), Phi Beta Kappa, Acacia (pres. U. Wis., Madison chpt.). Author several books, latest: Accent on Teaching (with others), 1954; also chpts. ednl. publs.; contbr. articles to profl. jours. including Mil. Jour., Jour. Chem. Edn.; research on alloy of rare metals; developed low-melting alloy with indium. Home: North Redington Beach, Fla. Died May 20, 1979.

FRENCH, WILLIAM CULLEN, univ. prof.; b. Weston, Tex., Mar. 18, 1883; s. John Wesley and Eliza (Webb) F.; student Grayson Coll., Whiteright, Tex., 1898-1902; A.B., U. of Okla., 1907; A.M., U. of Chicago, 1923; Ph.D., New York U., 1929; m. Susie Lawrence, June 1907; children—John Lawrence, William Culler, Helen (Mrs. C. J. Walsh); m. 2d, Marline Ray, May 1920; 1 son, Robert Bruce. Teacher country sch., 1902-03; supt. schs., Wynnewood, Okla., 1904-06, 1907-10; same, Wagoner, Okla., 1910-13; prof. edn., Central State Teachers Coll., Edmond, Okla., 1913-14; supt. schs., Lawton, Okla., 1914-17, Drumright, Okla., 1917-22, 1924-27; instr. in edn., New York U., 1927-29; prof. edn., George Washington U., since 1929. Mem. N.E.A. Awarded Gen. Edn. Bd. fellowship, 1923. Democrat. Presbyterian. Author: Breed-French Speller (with F. S. Breed), 1927; Child Story Readers (with F. N. Freeman, Grace Storm and Eleanor M. Johnson), 1927. Editor: Self Directing Series of Workbooks, 1925-32. Home: Gaithersburg, Md.

FREUD, BENJAMIN BALL, chemist, educator; b. Chicago, Ill., Feb. 12, 1884; s. Adolph B. and Annette (Ball) F.; B.S., Univ. of Chicago, 1904, Ph.D., 1927; Chem. E., Armour Inst. Technology, 1915; m. Henrietta Zollman. With Ill. Inst. Tech. since 1904, was prof. chemistry and former chmn. dept. chem. now prof. emeritus; vis. prof. phys. sci. U. of Ill. undergrad. div. Col. Hon. Res. Home: Chicago.

FREUDENTHAL, ALFRED MARTIN, educator, engr.; b. Stryj, Poland, Feb. 12, 1906; s. Simon and Gustafa (Mueller) F.; Civil Engr., Technische Hochschule, Prague, Czechoslavakia, 1929, D.Sc. in Engring., 1930; M.Sc. in Theoretical Physics, Charles U., Prague, 1930; m. Mary Ann Silberstein, Feb. 9, 1939, remarried, 1972; m. 2d, Maria Ronay, Aug. 24, 1962; 1 son, Pierre Simon. Came to U.S., 1947, naturalized, 1953. Design engr. reinforced concrete and steel, Prague, 1930-34; cons. eng., Warsaw, Poland, 1934-35; from structural engr. to resident engr. Port of Tel Aviv, Palestine, 1935-45; cons. to chief engr. Brit. Army, Palestine, and Transjordan, 1941-44; cons. engr. Tel Aviv, 1945-47; lectr., later prof. civil engring. Hebrew Inst. Tech., Haifa, Palestine, 1937-49; vis. prof. theoretical and applied mechanics U. Ill., 1947-48; lectr. and research cons. Columbia, 1948-49, U. Ill., 1948-57; prof. civil engring. Columbia, 1949-69, dir. Inst. Fatigue and Structural Reliability, 1962-69; prof. civil and materials engring. and dir. Inst. Materials Engring. and Structural Reliability George Washington U., 1969-76, prof. emeritus from 1976, chmn. dept. civil, mech. and environmental engring., 1970-74; vis. prof. Fed. Inst. Tech., Zurich, Switzerland, 1970, 71; vis. prof. U. Hamburg (Germany), 1975-76; sr. scientist award German Fed. Govt., 1975; cons. engr. Recipient Norman medal Am. Soc. C.E., 1948, 57, medal Royal Swedish Aero. Soc., 1956, von Karman medal ASCE, 1971. Fellow ASCE (Freudenthal medal established 1976); mem. Soc. Rheology, Internat. Assn. Bridge and Structural Engrs., Internat. Assn. Navigation Congresses, Sigma Xi, Tau Beta Pi. Author: Verbundstuetzen f. Hohe Lasten (Berlin), 1933; Inelastic Behavior of Engineering Materials and Structures, 1950; Introduction to Mechanics of Solids, 1966. Editor: Fatigue in Flight Structures, 1956; Elevated Temperature Design, 1964; Structural Reliability, 1972. Contbr.: Handbook of Physics, 1958; also tech. and science papers civil engring., applied mech., reliability and materials. Home: Chevy Chase, Md. Died Sept. 27, 1977.

FREUND, MAX (FRIEDRICH ERNST), educator; b. Hainichen, Saxony, Germany, Feb. 27, 1879; s. Friedrich Wilhelm and Augusta Laura (Heidel) F.; ed. Realschule, Realgymnasium and U. of Leipzig, Germany, The Sorbonne, Paris, France; M.A., Ph.D., U. of Leipzig, Germany, 1902; m. Anna Regine Keck, July 28, 1927; children—Helene Hasel Heidi, Margarete Anna Regina. Asst. lecturer in German, Univ. Coll., Liverpool, England, 1903; prof. modern langs., Queen's Coll., Belfast, 1903-09; prof. German and Teutonic philology, Queen's U., Belfast, 1909-14; lecturer in modern English language and literature, universities of Giessen and Marburg, 1915-25; professor German, Rice Inst., Houston, Texas, 1925-47; prof. emeritus from Sept. 1947. Author: Die moralischen Erzäblungen Marmontels, 1904; Die Universitätslektorate für Neuere Fremdsprachen, 1922. Editor: Beaumarchais' Le Barbier de Seville, 1910; Die Freundsche Chronik von Lucka, 1933. Translator: (with Clara Barth) Die Wildgans (George Moore), 1922. Editor and translator: Houston Journal (Gustav Dresel), 1954. Home: Houston, Tex. Died June 16, 1980.

FREY, BRICE A., JR., ins. co. exec.; b. N.Y.C., Mar. 31, 1915; A.B., Harvard. Asst. mgr. N.Y.C. office indemnity Ins. Co. N. Am., 1939-54; v.p. Gen. Reins. Corp., N.Y.C., 1954-68, sr. v.p., 1968; pres., dir. Herbert Clough Inc., 1970. Former trustee Tuxedo Park Library, Tuxedo Park Sch. Served to capt. USAAF, 1942-45. Decorated D.F.C., Air Medal. Mem. Newcomen Soc. N. Am., Casualty and Surety Club, Mayflower Soc., Smithsonian Assos., Am. Mgmt. Assn. Clubs: Corsicana Country; Union, City Midday, Tuxedo (N.Y.C.). Home: Corsicana, Tex. Died May 26, 1976.

FREY, MICHAEL J., newspaper pub.; b. Wallhalla, N.D., Aug. 28, 1898; s. John and Leopoldina (Schuster) F.; m. Adelaide Wilson, June 20, 1922 (dec.); children—J. Richard, Marilyn S; m. 2d, Rosemary Dwyer, Nov. 19, 1949. With The Oregonian, from 1915, country circulation : mgr., 1923-32, circulation promotion mgr., 1932-34, circulation mgr., 1934-39, bus. mgr. 1939-46, gen. mgr., 1946-53, pub., 1953-68, chmn. bd. Oregonian Publishing Co. Former dir. Better Bus. Bur.; pres. Pacific Northwest Newspaper Assn. Mem. Oreg. Newspaper Pubs. (past pres.), Am. Newspaper Pubs. Assn. (dir.), Portland C. of C., Sigma Delta Chi, Alpha Delta Sigma. Republican. Presbyn. Clubs: Waverly Country, Arlington, Multnomah Athletic; Eldorado Country (Indian Wells, Calif.). Home: Portland, Oreg. Died May 18, 1978.

FREY, NOAH J., life ins.; b. Sterling, Ill., Feb. 20, 1883; s. Henry B. and Elizabeth (Kreider) F.; grad. Carroll Coll. Acad., Waukesha, Wis., 1906; matriculated U. of Wis.; m. Cynthia P. Probert, June 30, 1909; children—Margaret E., Robert H. (dec.). With C&N.W. Ry., in Ia., 1901-1903, Waukesha (Wis.) Canning Co., 1903-07; asst. actuary, State Insurance Dept., Wis., 1907-11; sec. and mgr. Wisconsin Life Insurance Co., 1911-22, pres., 1922-45, chmn. bd. dirs., 1945—. Republican. Presbyn. Mason (33 deg.). Author: Cost of Insurance, 1915; Co-insurance and Reinsurance of Excess Risks. Home: Madison, Wis.

FREYGANG, GUSTAV GEORGE, educator; b. N.Y. City, Apr. 15, 1886; s. George and Theresa (Wenz) F.; M.E., Stevens Inst. Tech., 1909; A.M., Columbia, 1913; m. Doretta Suhrbier, Apr. 25, 1911 (dec. 1942); children—Gustav George, Dorothea Augusta; m. 2d Charlotte W. Behnken, June 24, 1944. With engring. dept. Nat. Electric Lamp Assn., 1909-10; Gen. Electric Co., 1910-11; faculty mem. Stevens Inst. Tech., Hoboken, N.J., since 1911, prof. mechanics since 1939; partner Fezandie, Freygang & Moser, Inc., cons. engrs., since 1947. Mem. Tau Beta Pi, Pi Delta Epsilon. Home: Weehawken, N.J.

FRICK, FORD CHRISTOPHER, newspaperman, nat. commr. baseball; b. Wawaka, Ind., Dec. 19, 1894; s. Jacob and Emma (Prickett) F.; B.A., De Pauw U., 1915, L.H.D., 1955; LL.D., Fla. So. Coll., 1952, Colo. Coll., 1958; m. Eleanor Cowing, Sept. 15, 1916; 1 son, Frederick Cowing. Asst. prof. English, Colo. Coll., Colorado Springs, 1915-17; surp. tng. Vets. Bur., Denver, 1918-19; mem. staff Colorado Springs Telegraph, 1919-21, N.Y. Jour., 1921-34; radio news commentator, 1930-34; pres. Nat. League of Profl. Baseball Clubs, 1934-51, nat. commr. baseball, 1951-65; manpower cons. Econ. Devel. Council of N.Y.C. Trustee Babe Ruth Found.; chmn. bd. Nat. Baseball Hall of Fame. Received Thomas Jefferson award for advancement of democracy (pub. relations div.), 1948; named to Nat. Baseball Hall of Fame, 1970. Civilian lectr. in orientation course U.S. Army. Trustee De Pauw U. Mem. Advt. Club Am., Am. Legion, Sigma Delta Chi, Phi Kappa Psi. Episcopalian. Clubs: St. Andrews Golf (Hastings); Siwanoy Golf (Bronxville). Home: Bronxville, N.Y. Died Apr. 8, 1978; inurned Christchurch Columbarium, Bronxville.

FRIEDEL, SAMUEL NATHANIEL, congressman; b. Washington, Apr. 18, 1898; s. Philip and Rose (Franklin) R.; student pub. schs., Balt.; m. Regina B. Johnson, Mar. 8, 1939. Mem. 83d-91st Congresses, 7th Dist. Md., chmn. house adminstrn. com., chmn. transp. and aeronautics subcom, vice chmn. joint com. on printing, vice chmn. joint com. on library. Mem. Md. Ho. Dels., 1934-38; mem. Balt. City Council, 1939, 43, 51. Mem. Mt. Washington Improvement Assn., Balt. Democrat. Elk. Home: Baltimore, Md. Died Mar. 14, 1979.

FRIEDELL, W(ILHELM) L(EE), naval officer (ret.); b. Texarkana, Ark., Aug. 22, 1883; s. Emile Frederick and Jessie (Deupree) F.; B.S., U.S. Naval Acad., 1905; m. Lucie Matthews, Sept. 1, 1913; 1 dau., Lucie (Mrs. H.G.G. Ogilvie). Commd. ensign U.S. Navy, 1905, advanced through grades to rear adm., 1938; ret. from active service, 1946. Awarded Navy Cross for submarine duty, World War I; Legion of Merit with gold star, World War II. Republican. Mason (Shriner). Home: Coronado, Calif.

FRIEDMAN, ARTHUR, educator; b. Maroa, Ill., Dec. 13, 1906; s. Samuel Arthur and Catherine (Edmunds) F.; A.B., U. Calif. at Los Angeles, 1928; Ph.D., U. Chgo., 1938; m. Natalie Pannes, 1936 (div. 1941); m. 2d, Marchia Meeker, 1943 (div. 1953); children—Arthur Meeker, Margaret Lois; m. 3d, Ann B. Heekin, 1957. Mem. faculty U. Chgo., 1932-81, successively research asst. English, instr. humanities, instr. English, asst. prof., asso. prof., 1932-52, prof. English, 1952-71, distinguished service prof. English, 1971-75, prof. emeritus, 1975-81, chmn. dept. English, 1960-63. Guggenheim fellow, 1957-58. Mem. Modern Lang. Assn., Internat. Assn. U. Profs. English. Clubs: Quadrangle (Chgo); Les Cheneaux Yacht (Cedarville, Mich.). Author: (with others) English Literature. 1660-1800: A Bibliography of Modern Studies (3 vols.). 1950, 52, 62. Editor: Collected Works of Oliver Goldsmith (5 vols.), 1966; She Stoops to Conquer (Goldsmith), 1968; The Vicar of Wakefield (Goldsmith), 1974; The Plays of William Wycherley, 1979. Editor: Modern Philology, 1967-73. Contbr. articles learned jours. Home: Lakeside, Mich. Died Apr. 24, 1981.

FRIEDMAN, EDMUND, civil engr., cons.; b. Nashville, Nov. 10, 1897; s. Bernard and Lottie (Whitelaw) F.; B. Engring. summa cum laude, Vanderbilt U., 1918. Asst city engr., Jackson, Miss., 1925; city engr., Coral Gables, Fla., 1925-29, city mgr, 1929-31; county engr., Dade County, Fla., 1932-42; chmn. bd. Connell Assos., Inc., cons. engr., also partner Connell, Pierce, Garland & Friedman, architects-engrs., Miami, Fla. Served to maj. C.E., AUS, 1942-45. Recipient Distinguished Service to Engring. Profession award, Fla. Engring. Soc. award, 1963, Engr. of Year award, 1964, Registered profl. engr., 8 states. Fellow ASCE (nat. pres. 1962-63), Fla. Engring. Soc. (Engr. of Year, Miami sect. 1964); mem. Soc. Am. Mil. Engrs., Fla. Bd. Engr. Examiners (pres, 1936-40), Am. Road Builders Assn. (v.p. So. Dist. County Hwy Ofcls. div. 1942), Am. Inst. Cons. Engrs., Nat. Soc. Profl. Engrs., Inst. Traffic Engrs., Tau Beta Pi. Home: Coral Gables, Fla. Died Jan. 19, 1977.

FRIEDMAN, IGNACE, pianist, composer; b. Cracow, Poland, Feb. 14, 1882; ed. U. of Leipzig, Vienna, Gymnasium at Cracow; studied composition with Hugo Riemann, piano with Leschetizky; m. Marie de Schidlowsky, of St. Petersburg, 1909. Concertized extensively in Europe, S. America and Australia; came to U.S., 1920, and appeared with great acceptance throughout the country. Composer: Concerto for piano and orch.; chamber music; compositions for piano; songs, etc. Editor works of Chopin, Liszt, Bach, Mendelssohn, Schumann. *

FRIEDMAN, JOSEPH, industrialist; b. Phila., June 28, 1906; s. William and Etta (Middleman) F.; student Benton Coll. Law, St. Louis, 1925-27; m. Lily Mae Brody, Nov. 15, 1926; children—Carol Ellen (Mrs. Irvin Goldfarb), Stephanie Joan, William Hersh. Sales exec. E.A. Friedman Co., Madison, Ill., 1924-33, v.p., dir., from 1930; sales mgr. Chgo. dist. Band Box Corp., St. Louis, 1933-36, v.p. gen. mgr., 1936-39; individual dry cleaning unit sales mgr. U.S. Hoffman Machinery Corp., 1939-44, gen. export, lend lease sales dir., 1944-46, v.p. merchandising mgr., 1946-53, 1st. v.p., 1953-55, exec. v.p., 1955-57; pres. Chromalloy-Am. Corp., 1958-59, chmn. bd., chief exec. officer, from 1959; pres. Investment Exchange, Inc., St. Louis, from 1958; chmn. bd. Cardionics Corp., Belgium; dir. Valley Lines Co., Chromalloy Europa, Amsterdam. Decorated Order of Merit Republic Italy. Mem. NCCJ. Zionist Orgn. Mem. B'nai B'rith. Club: Friars (N.Y.C.); Mo. Athletic; Wings. Home: St. Louis, Mo. Died Dec. 20, 1977.

FRIEDMAN, LEOPOLD, lawyer, business exec.; b. Saalfeld, Germany, June 10, 1887; s. Abraham and Rosalie (Lederman) F.; brought to U.S., 1892, naturalized, 1910; LL.B., N.Y. Law Sch., 1908; m. Ruth Holzman, October 1939. Admitted to the New York bar, 1911; dir. of the Loew's Theatres, Inc. Trustee of the Central Synagogue, New York City; trustee, vice president Hospital for Joint Diseases. Served in U.S.N., World War I. Member Association Bar City N.Y., N.Y. Co. Lawyers Assn. Club: Quaker Ridge Golf and Country (Scarsdale, N.Y.). Home: New York, N.Y. Died Dec. 18, 1978.

FRIEDMAN, SAMUEL JOHN, research co. exec.; b. Cleve., Jan. 25, 1918; s. Adolph Jacob and Margaret Helen (Smith) F.; B.S., Case Western Res. U., 1939, M.S., 1941; m. Saralee Long, Oct. 21, 1950; children—Alden James, Brion David. Chem. engr. E.I. duPont de Nemours & Co., Inc., Wilmington, Del., 1941-47, indsl. engr., Parlin, N.J., 1947-48, chem. engr., Wilmington, 1948-50, sr. engr., Camden, S.C., 1950-52, group leader, 1952-53, research supr., Waynesboro, Va., 1953-57, sr. tech. supr., 1957-62, research mgr., Wilmington, 1962-63, tech. supt., 1963-69, lab. dir., Old Hickory, Tenn., 1969-78, research mgr., Wilmington, 1978-79. Mem. AAAS, Am. Inst. Chem. Engrs., Am. Chem. Soc., ASME, Phi Kappa Tau, Gamma Phi, Tau Beta Pi, Sigma Xi. Club: DuPont Country (Wilmington). Patentee in field. Contbr. articles to profl. jours. Home: Wilmington, Del. Died Nov. 18, 1979.

FRIESS, HORACE LELAND, educator; b. N.Y.C., Mar. 4, 1900; s. Louis G. and Louise S. (Jagle) F.; A.B., Columbia, 1918, Ph.D., 1926: Cutting Travelling fellow, Heidelberg U., 1924-25; m. Ruth Adler, June 25, 1923; 1 dau., Anne. Instr. philosophy Columbia, 1921-26, asst. prof., 1926-36, asso. prof. 1936-46, prof. philosophy, 1946-75, Joseph L. Buttenwieser prof. emeritus human relations exec. officer, dept. religion, Barnard Coll., 1940-47; chmn. dept. religion Columbia, 1962-65. Guggenheim fellow, 1942-43. Bd. leaders N.Y. Soc. Ethical Culture, 1950-75. Mem. Am. Philos. Assn., Am. Ethical Union, Phi Beta Kappa. Ethical Culture religion. Author books including: (with H.W. Schneider) Religion in Various Cultures, 1932; Our part in this world (edited selections from Felix Adler), 1946; Felix Adler and Ethical Culture: Memories and Studies, 1981. Editor The Review of Religion, 1942-58. Contbr. articles. Home: New York, N.Y. Died Oct. 12, 1975.

FRINGS, KETTI, author; b. Columbus, Ohio, d. Guy H. and Pauline (Sparks) Hartley; student Principia Coll.; m. Kurt Frings, Mar. 18, 1938 (div.); children—Kathie, Peter. Author: (novels) Hold Back the Dawn, 1942, God's Front Porch, 1945; (plays) Mr. Sycamore, 1943, Look Homeward, Angel, 1957; The Long Dream, 1960; (screen plays) Come Back Little Sheba, 1952, About Mr. Leslie 1954, Fox Fire, The Shrike, 1955. Recipient Pulitzer prize for best play, Look Homeward, Angel, N.Y. Drama Critics Circle award, 1957. Address: Los Angeles, Calif. Died Feb. 11, 1981.

FRINK, JAMES LUKE, ret. army officer; b. Ida Grove, Ia., Mar. 10, 1885; s. James and Ruth (Ingman) F.; student Drury Coll., Springfield, Mo., 1904-05; grad. Army Industrial Coll., 1925, Army War Coll., 1926, Command and Gen. Staff Sch., 1929; m. Irma Eldridge McKelden, Sept. 14, 1908; children—Marjorie McKelden (wife of James T. Darrah, U.S. Army), James Luke (dec.), Alice McIntosh (wife of Charles Bainbridge Westover, USAF), Irma McKelden (wife James B. Bunnell Jr., U.S. Army), Barbara Lee (wife Lew Allen, Jr., USAF). Pvt., Co. G, 2d Btln., U.S. Engrs., 1906; commd. 2d lt. Inf., 1908, advanced through grades to maj. gen., 1943; Q.M. Fourth Corps Area, 1940-42; dep. Q.M. gen. Oct. 1942-July 1943; commanding gen., U.S. Services of Supply, Southwest Pacific Area, Aug. 1943-June 1945; commanding gen. U.S. Army Services of Supply Japan, June-Nov. 1945, retired from military service, Aug. 1946; city mgr., Greensboro, N.C., 1946-47; vice pres. Burlington Mills Corp., 1949-52; mem. bd. trustees Burlington Mills Found., 1952—. Participated in Somme defensive, Meuse Argonne, W W I, 1918, campaigns in New Guinea and Philippines 1943-45 and initial occupation of Japan, Aug. 1945. Awarded Distinguished Service Medal, 1918, Oak Leaf Cluster, 1946, Air Medal, Legion of Merit. Episcopalian. Mason. Clubs: Army and Navy (Washington, D.C.); Rotarian; Greensboro Country. Home: Greensboro, N.C.

FRISHMUTH, HARRIET WHITNEY, sculptor; b. Phila., Sept. 17, 1880; d. Frank B. and Louise Otto (Berens) Frishmuth; studied art in Paris under Rodin and Injalbert, in Berlin under Prof. Cuno Von Enchtritz, Art Students League, N.Y., under Borglum and McNeil, and was awarded the St. Gaudens 1st prize. Exhibited at N.A.D., Archtl. League, Nat. Assn. Womem Painters and Sculptors, Acad. Fine Arts, Phila., San Francisco Expn., Salon, Paris; all writings, drawings, plaster casts in permanent collection Syracuse (N.Y.) U. Awarded Helen Foster Barnet prize; Nat. Arts Club prize, 1921; Watrous gold medal Nat. Acad., 1922, Julia A. Shaw meml. prize, 1923; Joan of Arc silver medal Nat. Assn. Women Painters and Sculptors, 1924, sketch exhbn. for speed; hon. mention San Francisco Expn.; Gold medal Catherine Lorillard Wolfe Art Club; 1st recipient award Council Am. Artists Soc. Prin. works: Joy of the Waters, fountain Mus. Fine Arts, Dayton, O.; meml. sundial, Englewood, N.J.; Slavonic Dance, Met. Mus. New York; Vine, Met. Mus.; Play Days, Dallas Mus.; Morton meml., Windsorville, Conn.; marble portrait bust Woodrow Wilson, Capitol, Richmond, Va., Crest of the Wave, fountain, Bot. Gardens, St. Paul. Fellow, academician N.A.D.; fellow Nat. Sculpture Soc.; mem. Nat. Assn. Women Painters and Sculptors, Allied Artists Am., League Am. Artists, Art Alliance Am. Republican. Episcopalian. Club: National Arts (N.Y.). Home Southbury, Conn. Died Jan. 4, 1980.

FRIZZELLE, JESSE PAUL, judge; b. Snow Hill, N.C., Sept. 2, 1882; s. Jesse T. and Love Cornelia (Brooks) F.; B.A., Trinity Coll.; m. Nina Warner, Dec. 26, 1906; children—Cornelia Elizabeth (Mrs. E. D. Callahan), Nina (Mrs. Edwards), Jesse Paul, Barbara Warner (Mrs. O. P. Miller), Sophia Grey (Mrs. T. J. Edmondson), Mary Mordecai. Admitted N.C. bar, 1906; pvt. practice, 1906-30; judge N.C. Superior Ct., 1931—. Trustee Duke. Mem. N.C. Bar Assn., State Bar, Inc., Order of the Coif, Omicron Delta Kappa. Address: Snow Hill, N.C.

FROELICH, WILLIAM JOSEPH, lawyer; b. Stromsburg, Neb., Mar. 1, 1901; s. William and Nellie (Morgan) F.; attended U. of Neb., 1920-21, Georgetown U., 1922-26; m. Irma Frances Stout, July 21, 1926; children—William J., Nancy Catherine, Mary Ellen, James, Charles. Asst. U.S. atty., Omaha, 1926-29; spl. asst. to U.S. atty. gen. hdqrs. in Chgo., 1929-34; engaged in practice of law 1934-74; dir. C., M., St. P. & P R.R. and various cos. Mem. Ill., Chgo. bar assns., Kappa Sigma. Roman Catholic. Home: O'Neill, Nebr. Died Feb. 5, 1980.

FROHMAN, CHARLES EUGENE, banker, mfr.; b. Sandusky, Ohio, Aug. 9, 1901; s. Daniel and Helen (Wagner) F.; B.S., in Econs., U. Pa., 1923; J.D., Yale, 1926; D. in Bus. Adminstrn., Bowling Green U., 1958; m. Ruth Elisabeth Dunsmore, June 10, 1933; children—David James, Daniel Charles. Asso. mem. law firm, King Ramsey & Flynn, Sandusky, 1926-32, King Flynn & Frohman, 1932-36, Flynn, Frohman, Buckingham, Py and Kruse, 1936-46; gen. counsel Hinde & Dauch Paper Co., Sandusky, 1932-48, v.p., dir., 1941-49, pres., dir., mem. exec. com., 1949-58; vice chmn., dir. Hinde & Dauch Paper Co. Can., Ltd., 1940-59; dir. 3d Nat. Bank, from 1938, v.p., from 1953; dir., v.p. O.P. Craft Co., 1935-70. Trustee R.B. Hayes Found. Mem. Ohio, Sandusky chambers commerce, Ohio Hist. Soc. (trustee pres. 1961-63), Philomathean, Am. Bar Assn., Acacia, Theta Alpha Phi, Beta Gamma Sigma, Delta Theta Phi. Episcopalian. Mason (32, K.T.). Elk. Clubs: Yale (N.Y.); Rotary, Rockwell Trout. Author: History of Sandusky, 1965; Rebels on Lake Erie, 1965; Sandusky's Yesterdays, 1968; Cedar Point Yesterdays, 1968; Put-in-Bay, 1971; Sandusky's Third Dimensions, 1971; Sandusky's Editor, 1972; Sandusky Miscellany, 1973; Sandusky Potpourri, 1974. Bd. editors Yale Law Jour., 1925-26. Home: Sandusky, Ohio. Died Sept. 10, 1976.

FROMBERG, GERALD, artist, educator; b. Bklyn., July 19, 1925; s. Charles and Anna (Feldman) F.; B.A., Bklyn. Coll., 1946; M.F.A., U. N.Mex., 1951; postgrad. Bklyn. Mus. Sch. Art, 1949, New Sch. Social Research, 1947; m. LaVerne Ray, Sept. 13, 1952; children—Paul, Robert Matthew, Steven. Instr. art U. Wash., 1952-53, Dillard U., 1953-55; instr. art Bradley U., 1955-58, asst. prof. Sch. Art, 1958-64, asso. prof., 1964-71, prof., 1971-77, acting dir., 1972-73; tchr.-mem. Peoria (Ill.) Art Center; comml. artist Metro Asso Services, 1946-47, Fromberg and Charles, 1947-49, Marwell Advt., 1949, Advt. Aides, 1951; filmmaker Burdon Advt., Peoria, Ill., 1969-77; group exhbns.: Momentum Midcontinental, Chgo., 1954, Northwest Ann., Seattle, 1952, Contemporary Arts Gallery, N.Y.C., 1952, 53, New Orleans Art Assn. Ann., 1954, 55, Audubon Artists Ann., 1956, 57, Denver Ann. Western Artists, 1958, 62, Butler Inst., 1958, New Horizons in Sculpture, Chgo., 1967, N. Mississippi Valley Artists Invitational, 1968, 69, Ill. Arts Council Traveling Exhibit, 1969-70, Artists Who Teach Exhibit, Springfield, Ill., 1969, Md. Film Festival, Balt., 1969, Athens (Ohio) Film Festival, 1976; one man shows N.Mex. Mus., 1951, U. N.Mex., 1951, Henry Gallery, Seattle, 1953, Bradley U., 1962, 64, Smolin Gallery, N.Y., 1964, Lakeview Center, Peoria, Ill., 1966, Bradley U., 1967, Ill. Wesleyan U., 1969, Springfield (Mo.) Art Mus., 1969; 2 man shows (with wife) Dillard U., 1954, 55, 331 Gallery, New Orleans, 1955, Contemporary Artists Gallery, Peoria, 1956, 60, Barone Gallery, N.Y.C., 1957, Bradley U., 1961, Contemporary Gallery, Dallas, 1968, Fulton Gallery, N.Y.C., 1969, S.E. Ark. Arts & Sci. Center, Pine Bluff, 1969, Bibo Gallery, Peoria, 1971. Mem. Visual Arts Panel Ill. Arts Council, 1971-74. Recipient 1st prize oil painting Pacific Northwest Arts Fair, 1952, 53, 54; medal of honor Audubon Artists Exhbn., 1957; 2d prize Peoria Art Center mems. show, 1957; 2d prize abstract painting Heart of Ill. Fair, 1958, 62; 2d prize water color Ill. State Fair, 1962; 2d prize Nat. Exhbn. Small Paintings, 1962; 1st prize Peoria Art Center mems. Show, 1963, Central Ill. Exhbn. Painting, 1963; 1st prize and Purchase award Lakeview Center Ann. Area Show, Peoria, 1965; Putnam award for excellence in teaching Bradley U., 1968. Mem. Artists Equity (dir. Seattle 1953), Coll. Art Assn., Univ. Film Assn., Delta Phi Delta, Phi Kappa Phi. Home: Peoria, Ill. Died Nov. 27, 1977.

FROMM, ERICH, psychoanalyst; b. Frankfurt, Germany, Mar. 23, 1900; s. Naphtali and Rosa (Krause) F.; Ph.D., U. Heidelberg, 1922; postgrad. U. Munich, 1922-26; student Psychoanalytic Inst., Berlin; m. Frieda Reichmann, June 16, 1926 (div.); m. 2d, Henny Gurland, July 24, 1944 (dec. 1952); m. 3d, Annis Freeman, Dec. 18, 1953. Lectr., Psychoanalytic Inst., Frankfurt, also Inst. Social Research, U. Frankfurt, 1929-32, Internat. Inst. Social Research, N.Y.C.,

1934-39; guest lectr. Columbia U., 1940-41; lectr. Am. Inst. Psycholanalysis, 1941-42; Terry lectr. Yale U., 1949; faculty Bennington (Vt.) Coll., 1941-50; fellow faculty William Alanson White Inst. Psychiatry, N.Y.C.; prof. Nat. U. Mex., 1951-65; Mich. State U., 1957-61; adj. prof. N.Y. U., 1962-68. Diplomate in clin. psychology Am. Psychol. Assn. Fellow N.Y. Acad. Sci., AAAS; mem. Washington Psychoanalytic Soc., Mexican Nat. Acad. Medicine (hon.). Author numerous books including: Escape from Freedom, 1941; Man for Himself, 1947; Psychoanalysis and Religion, 1950; The Forgotten Language, 1951; The Sane Society, 1955; The Art of Loving, 1956; Sigmund Freud's Mission, 1959; Zen Buddhism and Psychoanalysis, 1960; May Man Prevail?, 1961; Marx's Concept of Man, 1961; Beyond the Chains of Illusion, 1962; The Dogma of Christ and Other Essays on Religion, Psychology and Culture, 1963; The Heart of Man, 1964; You Shall Be As Gods, 1966; Revolution of Hope, 1968; The Crisis of Psychoanalysis, 1970; (with Michael Maccoby) Social Character in a Mexican Village, 1970; The Anatomy of Human Destructiveness, 1973; To Have or To Be?, 1976; Greatness and Limitations of Freud's Thought, 1980. Contbr. articles to profl. jours. Home: Muralto, Switzerland. Died Mar. 18, 1980.

FROMME, FRED DENTON (FROM'E), prof. botany; b. St. Paris, O., Apr. 2, 1886; s. Frank Wilder and Stella (Riker) F.; student Ohio State U., 1903-05, Winona Tech. Inst., Indianapolis, Ind., 1906-07; B.S., S.D. State Coll., 1911; Ph.D., Columbia, 1914; m. Bess May Fridley, 1913; children—Jean Louise, Anne, Barbara. Began teaching at Columbia, 1911; prof. botany and plant pathology, Va. Poly. Inst., also botanist and plant pathologist, Va. Agrl. Expt. Sta., 1915-28; dean of Coll. Agr., W.Va. U., and dir. W.Va. Agrl. Expt. Sta., 1928-38, dir. agrl. extension, 1933-38; principal experiment station adminstr. U.S. Dept. Agriculture, 1938-48, research coordinator since July 1, 1948. Member S.D. National Guard 2 years. Fellow A.A.A.S.; mem. Bot. Soc. America, Am. Phytopathol. Soc. (pres. 1924), Nat. Research Council (div. biology and agr.), W.Va. Acad. Science, Sigma Xi, Phi Kappa Phi; mem. bd. dirs. Crop Protection Inst., 1921-24. Author of about 30 tech. papers. Home: Falls Church, Va.

FROMMEYER, WALTER BENEDICT, JR., educator, physician; b. Cin., Nov. 23, 1916; s. Walter Benedict and Alma (Donahue) F.; A.B., U. Cin., 1939, M.D. (Peter T. Kilgour award 1942), 1942; m. Elizabeth Ann Lee, Jan. 8, 1944; children—Elizabeth Lee, Virginia (Benners). Intern Cin. Gen. Hosp., 1942-43, jr. asst. resident, sr. asst. resident, 1946-48; research fellow medicine Thorndike Meml. Lab., also asst. medicine Harvard Med. Sch., 1948-49; dir. Tumor Clinic, U. Hosp. and Hillman Clinic, chief med. service Birmingham VA Hosp., 1953-54; mem. faculty U. Ala. Sch. Medicine, 1949-79, asso. dean, 1954-57, prof. medicine, 1957-79, Distinguished prof. U. Ala. System, 1968-79, distinguished faculty lectr., 1971, chmn. dept. medicine, 1957-68, dir. physicians' asst. program, 1972-76, dir. student health service, 1973-76, editor-in-chief Ala. Jour. Med. Scis., 1973-79, chmn. instnl. rev. bd. for human use, 1972-77; physician-in-chief Univ. Hosp., 1957-68, chief staff, 1963-64, 65-66; chmn. dean's com. Birmingham VA Hosp., 1954-59. Mem. exec. com. Jefferson County Coordinating Council Health Services, 1955. Served from 1st lt. to maj. M.C., AUS, 1943-46. Decorated Bronze Star medal with oak leaf cluster, Purple Heart; recipient Gold Heart award Am. Heart Assn., 1971; Distinguished Internist of Year award Am. Soc. Internal Medicine, 1977; named to Ala. Acad. Honor, 1977. Diplomate Pan Am. Med. Assn., Am. Bd. Internal Medicine (dir. 1962-68, vice chmn. 1967-68; emeritus mem. 1968-79). Fellow A.C.P. (master, bd. govs. 1960-66, bd. regents 1967-75, v.p. 1969-70, exec. com. bd. regents 1968-75, chmn. annual sci. session com. 1967-70, chmn. com. ednl. activities 1970, chmn. com. postgrad. courses; pres. 1973-74, Alfred Stengel award 1977), Am. Coll. Cardiology; mem. So. Med. Assn. (past sec. sect. medicine), So. Soc. Clin. Investigation, Vis. Nurses Assn. (past mem. exec. com., trustee), Am. (pres. 1968-69, dir., dir. at large, chmn. com. med. edn.; hon. fellow council cardiology), Ala. (trustee, past pres., chmn. bd.; Distinguished Service award) heart assns., Assn. Am. Physicians, AAAS, AMA, Med. Assn. Ala., Am. Fedn. Clin. Research, Council Med. Specialty Socs. (pres. 1975-76), Sigma Xi, Nutrition Today Soc. (pres. 1973-76, chmn. bd. 1975-76), Alpha Omega Alpha, Omicron Delta Kappa, Pi Kappa Epsilon. Clubs: Mountain Brook; Ponte Vedra (Fla.). Mem. editorial adv. bd. Nutrition Today; mem. editorial adv. bd. Jour. Family Practice, 1974-79. Contbr. articles to med. jours. Home: Birmingham, Ala. Died Jan. 8, 1979; interred Elmwood Cemetery, Birmingham.

FROST, ARTHUR CHESTER, consul gen.; b. Arlington, Mass., Feb. 4, 1886; s. J. Peabody and M. A. (Tarr) F.; A.B. cum laude, Harvard U., 1909; student of Grad. Sch. of Business Adminstrn., Harvard, 1908-09; Law Sch. of George Washington Univ., 1911-12; m. Clara M. Barse, Apr. 12, 1913. Sec. to members of Congress, 1910-15; consul at Genoa, Italy, 1915-17; consul at Algiers, Algeria, 1917-20, at Barrauquilla, Colombia, 1920-21, at Guatemala City, Guatemala, 1921-23, at Habana, Cuba, 1923-26; promoted to consul gen. June 5, 1924; consul gen. at Tampico, Mexico, 1926-27, at Prague, Czechoslovakia, 1927-31, Calcutta, India, 1931-34, at Zürich, Switzerland, 1934-40, also to Liechtenstein, 1938, at Barcelona, Spain, 1940-43, on assignment to Division of Foreign Service Personnel, Department of State, 1943-44, assigned as consul gen., Toronto, Canada, Oct. 12, 1944; retired Dec. 31, 1947. Pres. Am. Fgn. Service Protective Assn., 1944. Made foreign service officer of Class I, Oct. 1, 1935, sec. diplomatic service, 1936. Observer for U.S. Govt., 16th Plenary Assembly of Internat. Parliamentary Conf. of Commerce, Prague, 1931. Clubs: University (San Francisco); Commonwealth of Calif. Address: San Francisco.

FRUIT, FRED T(HOMAS), lawyer; b. Sharon, Pa., May 22, 1886; s. James S. and Caroline E. (Semple) F.; A.B., Princeton, 1908; LL.B., U. Pa., 1911; LL.D. (hon.), Grove City (Pa.) Coll. Admitted to Pa. bar, 1911, since practiced in Sharon; partner Fruit, Dill and Goodwin, 1962—; dir. Shenango Valley Water Co. (Sharon), Sharon Steel Corporation, Merchants & Mfrs. Nat. Bank of Sharon, Valley Savings & Loan Assn. (Sharon), Inland Investors (Cleve.). Home: Sharon, Penn.

FRY, WILFRED EYLES, ophthalmologist; b. DeLand, Fla., Aug. 18, 1899; s. William Wilson and Melvina Caralyn (Eyles) F.; M.D., U. Pa., 1924, D.Sc. in Medicine, 1930; m. Irene Fort, July 5, 1930; children—Edward Fort, Margaret Eyles. Practice ophthalmology, Phila., from 1930; prof. ophthalmology Grad. Sch. U. Pa., from 1944; asso. prof. ophthalmology U. Pa. Med. Sch., from 1951; attending surgeon Wills Eye Hosp., Phila.; ophthalmologist Overbrook Sch. for Blind, Phila. Mem. Phila. Com. Prevention of Blindness. Mem. bd. Pennsylvania Working Home for the Blind. Mem. AMA, Am. Ophthal. Soc. (pres.), Am. Acad. Ophthalmology and Otolaryngology, Coll. Physicians Phila., Pan-Am. Ophthal. Soc. Clubs: Phila. Country, Merion Cricket (Phila.). Editor Transactions of Am. Ophthalmological Soc., 1944-51. Home: Ardmore, Pa. Died Apr. 1976.

FUCILLA, JOSEPH GUERIN, educator; b. Chgo., Dec. 14, 1897; s. John and Marie Frances (De Marco) F.; B.A., U. Wis., 1921, M.A., 1922; Ph.D., U. Chgo., 1927; m. Reba Ann South, May 9, 1925; children—Jasper South, Van South. Instr. Romance langs. Ia. State Coll., 1921-23; asst. prof. Butler U., 1923-28; vis. asst. prof. U. Chgo., spring 1927, summer 1929, prof., summers 1949, 50; asst. prof. Romance lang. Northwestern U., 1928-32, asso. prof., 1932-36, prof., 1936-66, emeritus, 1966-81; vis. prof. U. Wis., 1966-67, U. Colo., 1967, U. Cal. at Santa Barbara, 1967-69. Fulbright grantee, Italy, 1952-53. Recipient Nat. Fgn. Lang. Achievement award Nat. Fedn. Modern Lang. Tchrs. Assns.; Distinguished Achievement medal, Dante Soc. Am. Mem. Modern Lang. Assn., Am. Assn. U. Profs., Am. Assn. Tchrs. Italian (hon. pres.), Am. Assn. Tchrs. Spanish, Dante Soc., Renaissance Soc., Am. Name Soc., Phi Beta Kappa, Phi Kappa Phi; fgn. mem. Arcadian Acad. (Rome, Italy); hon. mem. Accademia Cosentina; corr. mem. Hispanic Soc. Am., Real Academia Sevillana de Buenas Letras. Commendatore al merito della Repubblica Italiana. Author: Forgotten Danteiana, 1939; Universal Author Repertoire of Italian Essay Literature, 1941; The Follett Spanish Dictionary, 1943; Our Italian Surnames, 1949; Studies and Notes (Literary and Historical), 1953; Relaciones Hispanoitalianas, 1953: Saggistica Letteraria Italiana: 1938-1953, 1956; Estudios sobre el Petrarquismo en España, 1960; Superbi colli e altri saggi, 1963; The Teaching of Italian in the United States, 1967. Co-author: Bibliografia Analitica Tassiana, 1935; D'Annunzio Abroad (two volumes), 1935, 1937; Italian Criticism of Russian Literature, 1937; A Bibliographical Guide to the Romance Languages and Literatures, 8th edit., 1971. Editor: Grazia Deledda, Il Vecchio della Montagna, 1932; Carlo Goldoni, La Locandiera (with E. Hocking), 1939; Pedro Antonio de Alarcón; Novelas Cortas, 1952; Cuentos Hispano-americanos de Ayer y de Hoy (with F. D. Maurino), 1956; García de la Huerta, Raquel, 1965. Editor of Italica, 1943-68; adv. bd. Philol. Quar., Forum Italicum. Translator and annotator of Count Ciano's manuscript diary in draft form for Chicago Daily News (with A. Borselli and A. B. Fallico). Translator Metastasio, Pietro: Dido Forsaken, 1952. Contbr. articles to various lit., philol. and linguistic publs. Home: Evanston, Ill. Died Mar. 22, 1981.

FULBRIGHT, FREEMAN, pub. relations counsel; b. Atlanta, Apr. 26, 1925; s. Ernest Alexander and Lessie (Freeman) F.; student Ohio State U., N.Y. U.; m. Jane Meese, Aug. 4, 1947; children—Carolyn Frances, Charles Cary Freeman. Reporter, Durham (N.C.) Morning Herald, 1941-43, Cin. Post, 1943-45; legis. corr. I.N.S., Columbus, Ohio, 1945-46, news editor, Chgo., 1947-50, Washington corr., 1951-52; night-mng. editor, N.Y.C., 1952-55; v.p., gen. mgr. Walker & Crenshaw, Inc., pub. relations, 1955-57; gen. editor Newsweek, 1957-61; exec. editor N.Y. Herald Tribune, 1961-62; exec. v.p. Selvage & Lee, Inc., 1962-68; sr. v.p. Hill and Knowlton, Inc., 1969-73, exec. v.p., from 1973; mng. dir. Hill and Knowlton Can. Ltd., from 1976; cons. in field. Mem. Sigma Delta Chi. Presbyterian (elder). Clubs: N.Y. Plaza, Wings (N.Y.C.); Nat. Press (Washington). Home: New York, N.Y. Died June 6, 1978; buried New Philadelphia, Ohio.

FULBRIGHT, G(EORGE) S(MITH), coll. prof.; b. Brownsville, Tenn., Aug. 27, 1885; s. Thomas L. and Adelia (Smith) F.; A.B., Baylor U., 1906, grad. student, 1908; gen. culture diploma, (Curry) Sch. of Expression, 1914, teachers diploma, 1923; student Columbia Sch. of Oratory, summer 1922; grad. student Northwestern U., 1932. Began as high sch. teacher, 1906-13; student instr. (Curry) Sch. of Expression, 1913-14, 1915, and several summer sessions; instr. speech Columbia Theol. Sem., 1916-20; prof. rhetoric and public speaking Shurtleff Coll., Alton, Ill., 1920-22; asst. prof. public speaking Washington and Lee U., 1922-25; prof. public speaking Washburn Coll. (now Washburn Municipal U.) since 1926; instr. speech Belhaven Coll., Jackson, Miss., summer 1931, Central Theol. Sem., 1940-43. Y.M.C.A. sec. during World War I. Democrat. Baptist. Mem. Pi Kappa Delta, Sagamore. Home: Topeka, Kan.

FULCHER, GORDON S(COTT) (FOOL'SHER), physicist and economist; b. Evanston, Ill., Mar. 21, 1884; s. Edwin M. and Eliza (Scott) F.; B.S., Northwestern Univ., Evanston, Ill., 1905, M.A., 1906; Ph.D., Clark U., 1910; m. Louise Morgan, Sept. 16, 1913 (divorced 1923); children—Anne Elizabeth, John; m. 2d, Hilda Burton Melville, June 24, 1931. Instr. in physics, Amherst, 1908-09; instr. and asst. prof., U. of Wis., 1909-18; engr. Div. Science and Research Bur. Aircraft Production, World War, Feb. 1918-Jan. 1919; scientific asso. Nat. Research Council, 1919-20; research physicist Corning Glass Works, 1920-31; in charge physics exhibits, "World's Century of Progress Exposition, Chicago, 1933," 1931-33; dir. of research for Corbart Refractories Co., Louisville, Ky., 1934-38; writer on saving and other economic subjects since 1938; consultant to Div. 1 of the Nat. Defense Research Com., 1942-44, with Div. 7, 1944-45. Mng. editor of Physical Review, 1923-25; consultant Legislative Reference Service, Library of Congress since 1949; lectr. logic and sci. method Am. U., 1950-51. Fellow Am. Phys. Soc., A.A.A.S., American Ceramic Society; member American Econ. Association, Beta Theta Pi, Phi Beta Kappa, Sigma Xi, Gamma Alpha. Assisted in developing leak-proof gasoline tank for airplanes. Inventor of electrocast refractory blocks and process of making them (patented). Author: Better Thinking for Better Living, 1948. Home: Washington, D.C.

FULKERSON, JIMMY KENNETH, ins. co. exec.; b. Ft. Worth, Mar. 14, 1941; s. Richard Glen and Jessie (Lee) F.; B.B.A. in Accounting, Tex. Christian U., 1968, B.B.A. in Data Processing, 1969; m. Nancy F. Hannan, July 1, 1960; 1 dau., Janet Lynn. Vice-pres, data processing World Service Life Ins. Co., Ft. Worth, 1969-71, 1st v.p., sec., 1971-74, sr. v.p., asst. to pres., 1974-77. Fellow Life Office Mgmt. Inst. Address: Fort Worth, Tex. Died Feb. 1977.

FULLER, CLEMENT, painter, writer; b. London, Feb. 8, 1907; s. Arthur William and Florence Margaret (Montgomery) F.; came to U.S., 1943; student Stonyhurst Coll., 1918-24, also in Europe; student Gray's Inn, London, 1925-29. Reporter, writer, editor newspapers in London, 1929-42; commentator, chief sub-editor central news BBC, London, 1942-43, N.Am. corr., N.Y.C., 1943-45; mem. staff N.Y. Post, 1945-46; writer, painter, 1946-47; writer, producer NBC, 1947-52; co-owner TV package house Custom Video, N.Y.C., 1952-56; mem. promotion and fund raising staff internat. Rescue Com., 1956-61, tchr. Searing Prep. Sch., N.Y.C., 1961-66; owner Campion Records, 1966-68; editor-in-chief, communications analyst, dept. community medicine Mt. Sinai Sch. Medicine, N.Y.C., 1969-73; paintings rep. in pvt. collections; writer, painter, rec. artist Talking Book program Library of Congress, 1973-75. Author 8 plays, musical comedy, musico-drama, novella, TV and radio scripts, films, articles. Home: New York, N.Y. Died Oct. 1975.

FULLER, FRANCES LEONORE (MRS. WORTHINGTON C. MINER), actress; b. Charleston, S.C., Oct. 4, 1907; d. Wallace Watt and Leonore (Byrnes) Fuller; student Manhattanville Coll., 1927-28; L.H.D., Pace U., 1974; m. Worthington C. Miner, Mar. 30, 1929; children—Peter, Margaret (Mrs. Hugh Rawson), Mary Elizabeth. Actress appearing in Broadway plays The Front Page, 1929, Animal Kingdom, 1932, Stage Door, 1937, Home is the Hero, 1952, Lady of the Camellias, 1966; actress appearing in films One Sunday Afternoon, 1933, Girl in the Red Velvet Swing, 1962, They Might be Giants, 1969, Homebodies, 1973; TV actress series Love of Life, 1963-68; tchr. Am. Acad. Dramatic Arts, N.Y.C., 1948-50, 54-74, dir., pres., 1954-64, dir., 1964-74, chmn. bd., 1974-80. Mem. Actors Equity Assn., A.F.T.R.A., Screen Actors Guild, Author's League, Broadcast Music Inc. Home: New York, N.Y. Died Dec. 18, 1980; buried Woodland.

FULLER, GEORGE GREGG, foreign service officer; b. Rochester, N.Y., Oct. 29, 1886; s. George R. and Helen (Gregg) F.; A.B., Yale, 1910; A.M., Queen's Univ., 1934; grad. study U. Berlin; m. Therese Alston

Williams, Feb. 27, 1926. Officer various telephone cos., 1910-13; successively v.p. Standard Automotic Machinery Co., Lindsay-Fuller, Inc., and dir. Bjornsen & Co., Oslo and Berlin. Served in Mexican border campaign with New York cav.; maj. on Gen. Staff, Washington, during World War; maj. M.I. Res. Vice consul Oslo and Trondhjem, Norway, 1920, Malmo, Sweden, 1921, Reval, Esthonia, 1922; vice consul and judge of Consular Court, Jerusalem, 1923, Bushire and Teheran, Persia, 1924-25; successively consul Berlin. Niagara Falls, Kingston, Winnipeg, St. John (N.B.); consul gen., Antwero, Antwerp, Tunisia, Malta and Tripolitania; Dept of State, 1922-23; asst. chief, Div. Polit. and Econ. Info., Sec., Interdept. Econ. Liaison Com.; western Europe, 1927, trade cons., 1934-37; prof. internat. econs. Georgetown U., Am. U., lectr. Mem. President's Com. for Reciprocity Information Mem. Fgn. Service Assn., Res. Officers Assn., Diplomatic and Consular Officers Ret. (hon. gov., chmn. Welfare com.), S.A.R., Tunis Am. C. of C. (hon. pres.), Psi Upsilon. Clubs: Met., Washington Figure Skating, National Press (Washington); Yale (New York); Winter (Winnipeg). Contbr. articles on internat. economics, trade, European recovery, and fgn. investments. Home: Washington, D.C. Died Mar. 12, 1973.

FULLER, GILBERT EDMUND, travel tours; b. Springfield, Mass., Dec. 13, 1882; s. William Albert and Harriet Eliza (Fuller) F.; A.B., Harvard, 1905; m. Sidney Michaelis, Apr. 5, 1911; children—Harriet Sidney (Mrs. Keon Eldred Hughes), Gilbert Edmund. With U.S. Mortgage and Trust Co., N.Y., 1905; with publicity concern of Michaelis and Ellsworth, 1906-07; financial dept. Am. Express Co., 1908-10; became v.p. Raymond & Whitcomb Co., Boston, Nov. 1910, mng. dir., 1920, chmn. bd., 1928; pres. Raymond-Whitcomb, Inc., since 1931. Hearings officer Nat. War Labor Board (Wash.), 1943-47. Decorated Knight (1st class) Order of St. Olav (Norway); Chevalier, Legion of Honor (France). Visitor Dept. Asiatic Art, Boston Museum Fine Arts. Mem. Ancient Order of the Noble Buffalo. Clubs: St. Botolph (Boston); Harvard (N.Y.C.); Mermaid (life mem., Rye, Eng.). Home: Boston.

FULLER, HORACE H., army officer; b. South Dakota, Aug. 10, 1886; B.S., U.S. Mil. Acad., 1909; distinguished grad. Command and Gen. Staff Sch., 1923; grad. Army War Coll., 1928, Chem. Warfare Sch., 1935. Commd 2d lt., U.S. Army, 1909, and advanced through the grades to col., 1938, brig. gen. (temp.), Oct. 1940, maj. gen. (temp.), Dec. 1941. Served as lt. col., World War I; on Gen. Staff Corps, 1929-33; apptd. comdr. 41st Inf.Div., Dec. 1941.*

FULLER, HOYT WILLIAM, editor, author; b. Atlanta, Sept. 10, 1926; s. Thomas and Lillie Beatrice Ellafair (Thomas) F.; B.A., Wayne State U., 1948, later postgrad. Reporter, Detroit Tribune; feature editor Mich. Chronicle, Detroit; asso. editor Ebony mag., Chgo.; W. African corr. Haagse Post, Amsterdam, Holland; asst. editor Collier's Ency., N.Y.C.; formerly exec. editor Black World (formerly Negro Digest), Chgo.; exec. editor First World mag. First World Found., Atlanta, 1976-81; tchr. fiction-writing seminar Columbia Coll., Chgo., Afro-Am. lit. Northwestern U., Ind. U., Wayne State U.; vice chmn. N. Am. zone 2d World Black and African Festival of Arts and Culture, Lagos, Nigeria, 1976. Served with AUS. John Hay Whitney Opportunity fellow, 1965-66. Author: Journey to Africa; contbg. author: Black Expression: Essays in the Creative Arts By and About Black Americans; American Negro Short Stories; The Black Aesthetic; Black Literature in America; Points of Departure; Beyond the Angry Black; Collier's Ency. Yearbook; The Black American Writer; Afro-American Writing; contbr. articles to mags. and jours. including The New Yorker, The Nation, The New Leader, N.Am. Rev., Chgo. Jewish Forum, African Forum, N.Y. Times Book Rev., Arts in Soc., Jour. Negro History. Home: Atlanta, Ga. Died May 11, 1981; buried College Park Memorial Cemetery.

FULLER, LON LUVOIS, educator; b. Hereford, Tex., June 15, 1902; s. Francis Bartow and Mary Salome (Moore) F.; student U. Calif., 1919-20; A.B., Stanford, 1924, J.D., 1926; m. Florence Gail Thompson, Aug. 11, 1926 (dec. 1960); children—Francis Brock, Cornelia; m. 2d, Marjorie D. Chapple, Nov. 5, 1960. Instr. law U. Oreg. Law Sch., 1926-28, U. Ill. Coll. Law, 1928-31; prof. law Duke U., 1931-40; vis. prof. law Harvard U., 1939-40, prof. law, 1940-48, Carter prof. jurisprudence, from 1948, emeritus, to 1978. Mem. Mass. bar; asso. firm Ropes, Gray, Best, Coolidge & Rugg, Boston, 1942-45; lectr. summer schs. U. Chgo., 1930-33, U. Wash., 1931, U. N.C., 1934, U. So. Calif., 1937. Received Phillips award Am. Philos. Soc., 1935. Mem. Am. Acad. Arts and Scis., Delta Chi, Phi Delta Phi, Phi Beta Kappa, Order of Coif. Democrat. Author: The Law in Quest of Itself, 1940; The Morality of Law, 1964; Legal Fictions, 1967; Anatomy of the Law, 1968. Home: Cambridge, Mass. Died Apr. 8, 1978.

FULLER, MORRIS GREENLEAF, ins. exec.; b. Gallipolis, Ohio, Feb. 24, 1892; s. William Burtt and Ada (Morris) F.; student Kenyon Mil. Acad.; m. Octavia Carr, June 19, 1917 (dec. 1960); children—Myra (Mrs. Charles A. Harper), Douglas G.; m. 2d, Alice Warren, Feb. 24, 1961. Actuarial clk., statistician Am. Central Life, 1912-17; agt., agy. mgr., agy. supt., various ins. firms, 1919-29; with State Farm Life, Bloomington, Ill., 1929-80, successively v.p., exec. v.p., pres., 1952-61, vice chmn. bd. dirs., 1961-80; dir. State Farm Mut. Auto, 1953-80. Served as 1st lt. 143d Inf., N.G. U.S., World War I; capt. 92d Engrs., AUS, World War II. Home: Fort Myers, Fla. Died Apr. 14, 1980.

FULLER, RICHARD EUGENE, museum pres., dir.; b. N.Y.C., June 1, 1897; s. Eugene and Margaret Elizabeth (Mactavish) F.; Ph.B., Yale 1918; B.S., U. Wash., 1924, M.S., 1925, Ph.D., 1930; LL.D., Wash. State Coll., 1944; m. Mrs. Elizabeth Morrison Emory, Oct. 9, 1951 (dec. 1975); 1 dau., Elizabeth (Mrs. E.H. Friday). Asst. prof. U. Wash., 1930-34, research appointment, asso. prof., 1934-40, research prof., from 1940; dir. Barkon Tube Lighting Corp., 1933-35, chmn., 1935-37, pres., 1937-39; dir. Cornucopia Gold Mines, Seattle, 1935-36, v.p., treas., 1935-38, pres., 1938-41; dir. Northwestern Glass Co., 1940-48, chmn., 1948-68. Served with Am. Field Service, France, 1917; lt. 42d C.A.C., A.E.F., 1918-19; maj. Army Specialist Corps, 1942-43. Pres. Art Inst. Seattle, 1930-33; pres. Western Assn. Mus. Dirs., 1935-37; pres., dir. Seattle Art Mus. (donor with his mother), 1933-73, emeritus, from 1973. Pres. Seattle Found., 1946-50; chmn. Pacific Northwest div. Inst. Pacific Relations, 1950-51. Co-chmn. Northwest regional audition bd. Met. Opera, 1957-61, regional chmn. nat. council, 1962. Incorporator Pacific Sci. Ct. Found., 1962-67. Treas. trustee Seattle C. of C. (chmn. arts and edn. com. 1946-48). Recipient award Seattle Real Estate Bd. for outstanding civic service, 1940, King's medal (Gt. Britain) for service in the cause of freedom, 1946; Raymond W. Huff award Seattle World Affairs Council, 1960; asso. officer Am. Soc. Order of Hosp. St. John of Jerusalem (Brit.), 1964, asso. commr., 1969. Dir. Seattle War Chest, 1942-44, Brit.-Am. War Relief, 1941-44, Russian War Relief, 1941-45; chmn. Seattle Com., 1943-45; chmn. U.S. Com. for Study Particutin (Mexican volcano), div. geology NRC, 1944-50. Fellow Geol. Soc. Am., Mineral. Soc. Am., A.A.A.S.; mem. Am. Geophys. Union (pres. volcanology sect. 1944-47), Am. Assn. Museums (council 1954-64), Internat. Council Museums (mem. U.S. nat. com. 1958-62), Japan Soc. Seattle (pres. 1957-58), A.I.D. (hon.), Assn. Art Mus. Dirs. (pres. 1962-63), A.I.A. (hon.), Phi Beta Kappa, Sigma Xi. Clubs: Rainier, University, Rotary (Seattle); Yale, Century (N.Y.C.). Contbr. articles on geology to sci. jours. Home: Seattle, Wash. Died Dec. 10, 1976.

FULLERTON, JAMES DAVIS, corp. exec.; b. St. Louis, Jan. 17, 1917; s. Robert and Ora (Davis) F.; A.B., Stanford, 1939; M.B.A., Harvard, 1941; m. Harriet Anson Price, Feb. 19, 1943; children—Katherine Alexa, James Price, Victoria Chandler. Security analyst Lester & Co. (later Lester, Ryons & Co.), Los Angeles, 1941-42; free lance journalist, 1946-49; ins. broker Ingham, Coates & Payne, Pasadena, Calif., 1950-57; sr. v.p., dir. Capital Research & Mgmt. Co., Los Angeles; v.p. Am. Mut. Fund, Inc., Los Angeles, 1962-68, sr. v.p., 1968-75, vice chmn., from 1975; v.p. Internat. Resources Fund, Los Angeles, 1962-65, also dir.; pres. AMCAP Fund, Inc., Los Angeles, 1966-68, chmn. bd., chief exec. officer, after 1968; sr. v.p., dir. Capital Group, Inc., Los Angeles, 1968-72, chmn. bd., from 1972; sr. v.p. Investment Co. Am., from 1968; v.p. Investment Co. Am., Los Angeles, from 1962; v.p., dir. Greenwich Mgmt. Co. (Conn.), 1970-74; dir. Capital Guardian Trust Co., Los Angeles, Capital Mgmt. Services, Los Angeles. Gov., chmn. pub. information com., mem. exec. com. Investment Co. Insts., chmn. bd. govs., 1974-75. Bd. dirs. Family Service Pasadena, 1955-57; vice chmn. Pasadena Citizens Com. for Good Govt., 1955; trustee Poly. Sch., Pasadena, 1955-65. Served to maj. AUS, 1942-46. Decorated Bronze Star. Mem. Beta Theta Pi. Republican. Episcopalian. Clubs: Annandale Golf, Valley Hunt (Pasadena); California (Los Angeles); Valley of Montecito. Home: Pasadena, Calif. Died Oct. 1976.

FULTON, FRASER FOWLER, elec. mfg. co. exec.; b. Saint John, N.B., Can., June 28, 1905; s. Robert Gilpin and Josephine (Fraser) F.; student Mt. Allison U., 1923-26; B.Sc., McGill U., 1928; D.C.L., Bishop's U., 1966; D.Sc. (hon.), Sir George Williams U., 1972; LL.D. (hon.), Mt. Allison U., 1970; m. Iris Allo Nichols, July 24, 1930; children—Robert J., Josephine (Mrs. Malcom B. Fraser). With No. Electric Co. Ltd., Montreal, Can., 1927-77, gen. mgr. telephone contract div., 1957-61, v.p., adminstrn., 1961-77. Bd. govs. Montreal Tech. Inst., 1962-77; mem. exec. bd. Met. YMCA, 1962-77, chmn. bd. govs., 1962-77; chancellor Sir George Williams U., 1965-77; v.p. Queen Elizabeth Hosp., 1964-77. Served to brig. Canadian Army, 1939-45. Decorated Order British Empire; comdr. Order St. John. Mem. Engring. Inst. Can., Assn. Higher Edn. Club: St. James's (Montreal). Home: South Lancaster, Ont., Can. Died Feb. 4, 1977.

FULTON, MARSHALL NAIRNE, physician; b. Keokuk, Iowa, Mar. 10, 1899; s. William and Jessie Macqueen (Fisher) F.; Ph.B., Brown U., 1920, Sc.D., 1960; B.A. with honors in physiology (Rhodes Scholar), Oxford U., Eng., 1923; M.D., Johns Hopkins, 1925; m. Mary Howe De Wolf, June 22, 1940; children—Edith H. Weeks, Harriet M. Fisher, Winthrop DeW., Frank T. II, Mary Jewett McClure, Nancy P. Bragard, Katherine H. Sparrow, Holly M. Intern, asst. resident Peter Bent Brigham Hosp., Boston, 1926-29, resident, 1929-31, vis. physician on staff, 1931-46; asst. Harvard Med. Sch., 1929-32, instr., 1932-36, asso. in medicine, 1936-46; practice internal medicine, 1946-77; physician in chief R.I. Hosp., 1948-63; prof. medicine emeritus Brown U. at R.I. Hosp.; former cons. physician Providence Lying-In, Westerly, Roger Williams, Pawtucket Meml., Miriam hosps. Served with rank of major in charge dept. cardiovascular disease, and asst. chief of med. service, Walter Reed Hosp., Washington, 1942; chief med. service, with rank of lt. col., Valley Forge Gen. Hosp., 1942-45; chief med. serv. Ashford Gen. Hosp., White Sulphur Springs, 1945-46; promoted col., 1945. Decorated Legion of Merit. Mem. Joint Commn. Accreditation of Hosps., 1963-72. Fellow A.M.A., A.C.P. (gov. R.I., chmn. bd. govs., 1959-62, 1st v.p. 1962-63, regent 1963-69, Alfred Stengel medal 1971); mem. Am. Soc. Clin. Investigation, Assn. Am. Physicians, Providence Med. Assn., R.I. Med. Soc., Am., N.E. (v.p. 1948-49), R.I. (pres. 1956) heart assns., Am. Clin. and Climatol. Assn. (sec. treas. 1950-58; pres. 1959-60), Alpha Delta Phi, Phi Beta Kappa, Sigma Xi, Alpha Omega Alpha. Republican. Episcopalian. Clubs: Hope, Agawam Hunt (Providence). Address: Bristol, R.I. Died May 16, 1977; buried Bristol.

FULTON, WILLIAM JOHN, JR., newspaper corr.; b. Sycamore, Ill., Feb. 12, 1907; s. William John and Laura (Busey) F.; grad. Exeter (N.H.) Acad., 1925; A.B., U. Ill., 1939; m. Joan Eileen Twelftree; children—Jill Mary, Sally Ann, Elizabeth, William Scott. Newspaper reporter Aurora (Ill.) Beacon-News, 1928, Rockford Republic, 1929-30, Chgo. Am., 1930; with Chgo. Tribune, 1931-74, chief London bur., 1946-49, Eastern corr. 1949-72, UN corr., news columnist, 1954-74; covered peace conf. Paris, France, 1946; fgn. ministers confs., London, Moscow, N.Y.C. Recipient Chgo. Tribune ann. Bech award, 1954. Served with USAAF, 1944-45. Mem. UN Corrs. Assn., Phi Delta Theta. Republican. Conglist. Club: Overseas Press (N.Y.C.). Home: Cos Cob, Conn. Died Mar. 16, 1977.

FULTON, WILLIAM YOST, investment banker; b. Chgo., Mar. 7, 1903; s. William H. and Mary Brank (Yost) F.; A.B., Wabash Coll., 1923, LL.D., 1974; m. Elizabeth Jackson; children—Edward, James, Marylou. Employed as salesman, Maynard H. Murch & Co., Cleve., 1924, partner, 1943-50, partner successor firm Fulton, Reid & Co., 1950-56; pres., dir. Fulton Reid & Co., Inc., 1956-63, chmn. bd., dir., 1963-67; chmn. bd., dir. Fulton, Reid & Staples, Inc., 1967-71; pres., dir. The Clariden Corp.; dir. Roadway Express, Inc., TopRoc Precast Corp., Chardon Rubber Co., R-Land Corp., Quality Service Co. Treas. Cleve. Humane Soc.; life trustee Children's Services. Mem. Phi Gamma Delta. Presbyn. Clubs: Rockwell Springs Trout; Union (Cleve.); Capitol Hill (Washington); Union League (Chgo.). Home: Cleveland Heights, Ohio. Died Feb. 16, 1980.

FUNKE, ERICH (ALFRED), Germanist; b. Rogaetz-Elbe, Germany, Dec. 11, 1891; s. Wilhelm and Anna (Boeis) F.; student Real-gymnasium Magdeburg, Abitur, 1903-12; student U. Leipzig, 1912-14, U. Munich 1914, U. Zurich, 1918-1919 Ph.D., U. Halle, 1921; m. Lydia Gunzenhauser, June 12, 1937; children—Thomas, Elizabeth, Barbara. Came to U.S., 1931, naturalized, 1937. Tchr. langs. German high schs. Bitterfeld, 1924-26, Halle-Saale, 1927-31; asst. abt f. Sprechkunde U. Halle, 1928-31; guest lectr in phonetics, State U. Iowa, summer 1931; asst. prof. German, U. Iowa, 1931-32; asso. prof. German, State U. Iowa, 1932-37, prof. and head dept. German, 1937-60, prof. emeritus, 1960-74, in charge fgn. langs. phonetics lab., 1942-60. Mem. MLA, Am. Assn. Tchrs. German (exec. council 1946-48), A.A.U.P., Delta Phi Alpha (nat. v.p. 1947-52). Club: Triangle (pres. 1945). Author books including: Die Umgangssprache, 1945. Coauthor: Kriegsdeutsch, 1942; Gesprochenes Deutsch, 1953; Translingua Script, 1957. Co-editor: The Philol. Quar., 1932-74. Phonetic and artistic speech records. Contbr articles to profl. jours. Home: Iowa City, Iowa. Died Nov. 5, 1974.

FUOSS, ROBERT, dept. store exec.; b. Saline, Mich., Dec. 16, 1912; s. Martin and Edith Eliza (Mattison) F.; A.B., U. Mich., 1933; m. Mary Holton Leckner, Aug. 30, 1936; 1 dau., Mary Marshall (Mrs. Kenneth E. Claus, Jr.). Mng. editor Saturday Evening Post, 1942-45, exec. editor, 1956-61, editor-in-chief, 1961-62; v.p. pub. relations Federated Dept. Stores, Inc., 1962-64, exec. v.p., 1965—; sr. editor Reader's Digest, 1964-65; Bd. dirs. Presbyn. Life trustee Dickinson Coll. Recipient Distinguished Service award Overseas Press Club, 1961. Mem. Theta Chi, Sigma Delta Chi. Home: Cincinnati, Ohio. Died Jan. 27, 1980.

FURBER, PERCIVAL ELVERTON, bus. exec.; b. Paris, May 16, 1906; s. Percy Norman and Cornelia Chamberlain (Chapman) F.; student Princeton, 1927; m. Dorothy Adele McMillan, Feb. 26, 1931; 1 dau., Audrey Furber (Mrs. Donohue). Student Equitable Trust Co., brokerage firm, 18 mos.; joined Trans-Lux Corp., rental projection equipment and operation theatres, 1931, chmn. bd. chmn. subsidiaries, chmn.

emeritus; dir. Fedders Corp., Fedders Financial Corp., Tampax, Inc. Episcopalian. Clubs: Racquet and Tennis; Wee Burn (Darien, Conn.). Home: Darien, Conn. Died Aug. 16, 1979.

FURLONG, CLAIR WILLITS, banker; b. Weaver, W.Va., Oct. 31, 1905; s. John C. and Emma (Willits) F.; LL.B., Chgo-Kent Coll. Law., 1926; m. Elizabeth Angela Tamblyn, Oct. 12, 1927 (dec.); 1 dau., Jean Ann (Mrs. Robert Russell Foster); m. 2d, Janet Callender Buffington, Aug. 27, 1971; 1 stepdau., Janet C. Gohres, Admitted to Ill. bar, 1927; practiced in Chgo., 1927-28; with Continental Ill. Bank & Trust Co., Chgo., 1929-70, asst. sec., 1937-41, trust officer, 1941-44, 2d v.p., 1944-47, v.p., 1947-65, sr. v.p., 1965-70; mem. pension com. Weil-McLain Co., 1970-73; dir. Blackfoot Coal & Land Corp. Treas., trustee Chgo. Bar Assn. Found., 1959-66; adv. bd. Ill. Masonic Hosp.; exec. com. estate planning program Loyola U., 1963-70, Beloit Coll., 1962-71; trustee, v.p., Ill. Childrens Home and Aid Soc., 1962-73; v.p., trustee Chgo-Kent Coll. Law, chmn. adv. bd., 1969-70; bd. dirs. United Charities Chgo., 1969-72; trustee Wm. M. Scholl Found.; mem. Northwestern U. Assos.; mem. citizens bd. U. Chgo.; sec., treas. A.C. Buehler Found. Mem. Am. (chmn. com. on banking instns. and regulated investment cos. of taxation sect. 1957-59), Ill., Chgo. (treas.ex-officio mem. bd. mgrs. 1957-59) bar assns., Corp. Fiduciaries Assn. Chgo. (pres. 1957-58), Ill. Bankers Assn. (pres. exec. com. trust div. 1961-62), Assn. Rehab. Inst. Chgo., Newcomen Soc., Chgo. Council Fgn. Relations. Chgo. Assn. Commerce and Industry. Clubs: Law, Legal, Bankers, Union League, Economic; Commercial, Tavern Chicago (Chgo.); Exmoor Country (Highland Park, Ill.) Home: Wilmette, Ill. Died Mar. 6, 1979.

FURLONG, THOMAS RAPHAEL, journalist, trust adminstr.; b. Sault Ste. Marie, Mich., Dec. 27, 1905; s. Patrick Manning and Anna (McCann) F.; student U. Mich., 1924-26; m. Winifred Castle, Apr. 3, 1934; children—James Castle, Robert McCann, Thomas Castle. Reporter, City News Bur. Chgo., 1926-28; gen. news and bus. news reporter, Chgo. Tribune, 1928-32, asst. financial editor, 1932-39, financial editor, 1939-52; mng. editor Times-Herald, Washington, 1952-54; city editor Chgo. Tribune, 1954-61, asst. mng. editor, 1961-67, mng. editor features, 1967-69, exec. editor, 1969-70; exec. dir. Robert R. McCormick Charitable Trust; v.p., dir. Postrib Corp. until 1970, Chgo. Tribune Press Service, Inc.; dir. Chgo. Tribune-New York News Syndicate, Inc., Chgo. Am. Pub. Co. Clubs: Press, Tavern (Chgo.); Westmoreland Country (Wilmette, Ill.). Author pamphlets; Taxes That Destroy, 1945; Who Owns U.S. Wealth, 1946. Home: Evanston, Ill. Died Mar. 11, 1977; buried St. Ignace, Mich.

FURLONG, WILLIAM REA, naval officer; b. Washington County, Pa., 1881; s. William Allen and Ethel A. (Grant) F.; Ed.M.E., Tchrs. Coll., California, Pa., 1898; B.S., U.S. Naval Acad., 1905; M.A., Columbia, 1914; Naval War Coll., 1933; m. Cora Glover, 1910; 1 son, William Rea Jr.; m. 2d, Lula McKie Stephens, Nov. 26, 1969. Ensign U.S. Navy, 1907, and advanced through grades to rear adm., 1937; on staff of Adm. Fletcher after landing at Vera Cruz, 1914; gunnery officer U.S.S. South Carolina, 1916, and U.S.S. Nevada, 1917; attached to Brit. battleship Ramailles, 1918; during World War I served as gunnery officer Atlantic Fleet and as gunnery observer in Grand Fleet of Brit. Navy in North Sea, at Scapa Flow and Firth of Forth; also on staff of Adm. Sims at London hdqrs.; in charge design and procurement navy fire control, 1919-20; sent to Germany to investigate German ordnance materials and methods; introduced into U.S. Navy, Synchronous fire control system and remote control of guns by power; fleet gunnery officer U.S. Pacific Fleet, 1921-23; in charge of Island Govts. under the Navy, 1923-26; comdg. officer of Chicago (cruiser), Nechez (oil tanker), div. destroyers; comd. Marblehead, 1932-33, Naval Proving Ground, 1934-35; captain West Virginia (flagship), 1936; on staff comdr.-in-chief U.S. Fleet, Adm. Hepburn, 1937; rear adm. and chief Bur. of Ordnance, Washington, Aug. 1937-Feb. 1941; comdr. Minecraft Battle Force, Apr. 1941; engaged in def. of Pearl Harbor, Dec. 7, 1941, when his flagship, U.S.S. Oglala, was sunk by Japanese torpedo; comdt. Navy Yard and Pearl Harbor Operating Base, Dec. 1941-45, in charge salvage operations on ships sunk during Japanese attack, also of repairs on ships of Pacific Fleet engaged in North and South Pacific actions. Decorated Legion of Merit and gold star; recipient Freedoms Found. award, 1950. Mem. Am. Legion, V.F.W., S.A.R., Mil. Order of World Wars (nat. comdr. 1949). Clubs: Army and Navy, Chevy Chase. Author articles on history and origin of U.S. Flag, also book (funded by Ford Found.) pub. jointly by U.S. Naval Alumni Assn. and Smithsonian Instn., 1981. Home: Washington, D.C. Died June 2, 1976, buried Arlington (Va.) Nat. Cemetery.

FURNISS, JOHN NEILSON, M.D., surgeon; b. Selma, Ala., Nov. 2, 1879; s. John Perkins (M.D.) and Elizabeth Mathews (Dawson) F.; student U. of Ala., 1895-96, U. of the South, 1896-97; M.D., U. of Va., 1900, New York U., 1901; m. May Hooper, of Selma, Ala., Nov. 6, 1906; children—Elizabeth Dawson, John Perkins, Caroline McKee, Jane Hooper. Began practice at Selma, 1903; surgeon Ala. Bapt. Hosp. (chmn. of staff), Good Samaritan Hosp.; dir. Selma Nat. Bank, Selma Trust & Savings Bank. Mem. Vol. Med. Corps, Dallas County Med. Advisory Bd. Trustee Dallas Acad. (Selma), Selma Pub. Schs. Fellow A.M.A., Am. Coll. Surgeons; mem. Ala. State Med. Assn., Southern Surg. Assn., Southern Med. Assn., Phi Delta Theta. Democrat. Episcopalian. Mason (32 deg., K.T., Shriner). Clubs: St. Paul's Men's, Selma Town and Country. Home: 602 Lauderdale St.

FURTH, JACOB, physician; b. Miskolc, Hungary, Sept. 20, 1896; s. Jonas and Henrietta (Sussman) F.; M.D., German U., Prague, 1921; D.Sc. (hon.), U. Pa., 1968, Columbia U., 1976; m. Olga Berthauer, Aug. 1, 1924; children—John J. and Eugene D. (twins). Came to U.S., 1924, naturalized, 1930. Asst. bacteriology and hygiene German U., Prague, 1921-22; clin. asst. 2 med. Clinic Charity Hosp., Berlin, Germany, 1923; asst., then asso. Henry Phipps Inst., U. Pa., 1924-26, 28-32; asst. Rockefeller Inst., 1926-28; asst. pathologist N.Y. Hosp.; instr. to prof. pathology Cornell U., 1923-47; chief pathologist VA, Dallas, 1947-49; sect. chief biology Oak Ridge Nat. Lab., 1949-53; asso. dir. Children's Cancer Research Found., Boston, 1954-59; clin. prof. pathology Harvard, 1958-59; head exptl. pathology dept. Roswell Meml. Research Inst., Buffalo, 1959-61; prof. exptl. pathology, 1959-61; prof. pathology Columbia U., N.Y.C., 1961-66, emeritus prof. pathology, spl. lectr., 1966-79, acting dir. Inst. Cancer Research, 1968-69, dir. labs. F. Delafield Hosp. div., 1961-67. Mem. vis. com. Asso. U.; mem. Surgeon Gen's Adv. Com. Smoking and Health. Diplomate in pathologic anatomy Am. Bd. Pathology. Fellow AAAS, Nat. Acad. Scis., Am. Acad. Pathology; mem. Am. Assn. Cancer Research (hon. mem.; pres. 1957-58), Am. Assn. Pathologists and Bacteriologists, Am. Soc. Exptl. Pathology (pres. 1956-60), Soc. Exptl. Biology and Medicine, Am. Acad. Arts and Scis., Endocrine Soc., N.Y. Acad. Scis. (hon. life), Endocrinology Soc. Chile (hon. life), Cancer Soc. Peru (hon. life), N.Y. Pathol. Soc. (pres. 1947), Harvey Soc., A.C.P., Soc. Pharm. and Environ. Pathologists (hon. life), Sigma Xi. Home: New York, N.Y. Died July 22, 1979; buried Surry, Maine.

GABIN, JEAN (ALEXIS JEAN MONTCORGEL), motion picture actor; b. Paris, France, May 17, 1904; ed. in Paris; m. 3d, Dominique Fournier, 1949; 1 son, 2 daus. Formerly mason, unskilled laborer, shopkeeper; extra at Folies-Bere)res; singer, 1923-30; film actor since advent of talkies; sometimes stage actor. Decorated Medaillie Militaire, Croix de Guerre, officer, Legion of Honor; recipient Venice prizes, 1951, 54, Prix Populiste, 1956. Motion pictures include Pépé le Moko; Bandera; Belle Equipe; Bete Humaine; Bas Fonds; Grande Illusion; French Can-can; Port of Shadows; Jour se léve; Gueule d'amour Remorques; marie du port; Au dela des prilles; Minute de Verite; Touchez pas au Grisbi; La Nuit est mon royaume; Crime and Punishment; Chnouf; En cas de Malheur; The Case of Doctor Laurent; Maigret Tond Un Piege; La Clochard; UN Singe en Hiver; co-producer L'Age Ingrat, 1964. Address: Paris, France. Died Nov. 15, 1976.

GABO, NAUM, sculptor; b. Briansk, Russia, Aug. 5, 1890; s. Boris and Fannie (Osersky) Pevsner; student Munich U., 1910-14; hon. doctorate Royal Coll. Art, London, 1967; m. Miriam Israels, Oct. 13, 1936; 1 dau., Nina Serafima. Came to U.S., 1946, naturalized, 1952. Exhibited, Oslo, 1916, Moscow, 1920, Germany, 1922, Paris, 1925; chief designer ballet La Chatte, for Diaghileff, 1926; first Am. exhbn., 1926, Chgo., 1933, London, 1937, Mus. Modern Art, N.Y.C., 1948; works represented European Museums, Mus. Modern Art, Mus. Non-Objective Art, N.Y.C., Providence Mus., Wadsworth Atheneum, Phillips Coll., Washington, Yale U., also pvt. colls.; 80 ft. sculpture unveiled in Rotterdam, Netherlands, 1957. Decorated comdr. Order Brit. Empire. Mem. Nat. Acad. Arts and Letters, Acad. Arts and Scis., Royal Acad. of Sweden (fgn. mem.). Author: Gabo, 1957; of Divers Arts, 1962. Editor: Circle (London, Eng.), 1937. Home: Middlebury, Conn. Died Aug. 23, 1977.

GABRIELSON, GUY GEORGE, lawyer; b. Sioux Rapids, Ia., May 22, 1891; s. Frank August and Ida (Jansen) G.; B.A., U. Ia., 1914; J.D., Harvard, 1917; LL.D. (hon.), Upsala Coll., 1932, Colby Coll., 1953; m. Cora M. Speer, Feb. 5, 1918; children—Guy George, Nancy G. Owens. Admitted to N.J. bar, 1919, in private practice, N.J.; also practice in N.Y.C., from 1931; chmn., dir. Nichold Co.; dir. First Nat. State Bancorp., Newark. Trustee Drew U., Madison, N.J. Mem. N.J. Ho. of Assembly, 1926-30, majority leader, 1928, speaker, 1929; Republican nat. committeeman for N.J.; chmn. Rep. Nat. Com., 1949-52. Served as 2d lt. Air Service, Aircraft Prodn., World War I. Mem. N.J. Bar Assn. N.Y. County Lawyers Assn., Am. Legion, S.A.R. Republican. Methodist. Mason. Clubs: Union League, Downtown Assn. (N.Y.C.); Essex (Newark); Nat. Press (Washington); Roxiticus Country; Spring Lake Golf and Country; Ocean Reef (Fla.). Home: Mantoloking, N.J. Died May 1, 1976.

GABRIELSON, IRA NOEL, biologist; b. Sioux Rapids, Ia., Sept. 27, 1889; s. Frank August and Ida (Jansen) G.; B.A., Morningside Coll., 1912, LL.D., 1941; postgrad. Lakeside Lab. of State U. Ia., Lake Okoboji, 1911, 13, D.Sc., Ore. State Coll., 1936; D.Sc. (hon.), Middlebury Coll., 1959, Colby Coll., 1969; m. Clara Speer, Aug. 7, 1912; children—Clara June (dec.), Iris V. (dec.), Dorothy Jean, Grace Gail. Tchr. biology Marshaltown (Ia.) High Sch., 1912-15; with Bur. Biol. Survey, USDA, 1915-46, asst. in econ. ornithology, 1915; food habits research, 1918, rodent control in N.D., S.D., Ia. and Ore., 1918-30, Pacific Coast regional supr. rodent and predatory control, 1930-34, game mgmt. dir., 1934-35, asst. chief div. wild life research, 1935, chief bur., 1935-40, dir. U.S. Fish and Wildlife Service (formed by consolidation of Bur. Biol. Survey and Bur. Fisheries), 1940-46; pres. Wildlife Mgmt. Inst., Washington, 1946-70. Pres. World Wildlife Fund., 1961-72; chmn., No. Va. Regional Park Authority; vice chmn. Va. Commn. on Outdoor Recreation. Recipient Audubon Conservation award; Dept. of Interior distinguished service award; Leopold medal The Wildlife Soc.; Hugh Bennett award; Distinguished Service award Am. Forestry Assn., 1962; decorated comdr. Golden Ark (Netherlands). Mem. Soc. Systematic Zoology, Am. Ornithologists Union, Wilson Ornithologist Club, Cooper Ornithol. Club, Pacific N.W. Bird and Mammal Club, Ecol. Soc. Am., Wash. Biologists Field Club. Ore. Audubon Soc., Izaak Walton League, Washington Acad. Sci. Methodist. Club: Cosmos. Author: Western American Alpines, 1932; Birds of Oregon (with S.G. Jewett), 1940; Wildlife Conservation, 1941; Wildlife Refugees, 1943; Wildlife Management, 1951; The Birds of Alaska (with F.C. Lincoln), 1958; also many articles on birds, mammals and plants. Editor: The Fisherman's Encyclopedia, 1950. Home: Oakton, Va. Died Sept. 7, 1977.

GABRO, JAROSLAV, bishop; b. Chgo., July 31, 1919; s. John and Katherine (Tymusz) G.; student St. Procopius Coll., Lisle, Ill., 1937-39, St. Charles Coll., Catonsville, Md., 1939-40; student St. Basil's Coll., Stamford, Conn., 1940-42, B.A., Cath. U., 1945. Ordained priest Ukrainian Catholic Ch., 1945; bishop St. Nicholas Ukrainian Cath. Diocese, Chgo., 1961-80. Home: Oak Park, Ill. Died Mar. 28, 1980.

GADSDEN, HENRY WHITE, chem. co. exec.; b. N.Y.C., Apr. 16, 1911; s. Philip Henry and Estelle (White) G., B.S., Yale, 1933; m. Patricia Parker, July 31, 1943; children—Christopher H., Thomas P., William F., Robert W. With Banker Trust Co., N.Y.C., 1933-34; sales engr. R.A. Lasley, Inc., N.Y.C., 1934-37; asst. to exec. v.p. Sharp and Dohme, Inc., Phila., 1937-42; dir. prodn., engring., 1946-49, v.p., 1949-55, dir., 1952-53; exec. v.p., dir. Merck & Co., Inc., Rahway, N.J., 1955-65, pres., chief exec. officer, 1965-71, chmn., chief exec. officer, 1971-76, also dir. dir. C.R. Bard Inc., Ford Motor Co., Campbell Soup Co. Trustee Seeing Eye. Served from 1st lt. to lt. col. AUS, 1942-46; dist. chief Phila. Ordnance Dist., U.S. Army, 1948-55. Mem. Bus. Council. Clubs: Baltusrol Golf, Short Hills; Yale (N.Y.C.); Mountain Lake (Lake Wales, Fla.). Home: Short Hills, N.J. Died Dec. 15, 1980.

GAFFORD, BURNS NEWMAN, educator; b. Roger, Tex., Dec. 9, 1900; s. Benjamin Ford and Elizabeth (Payne) G.; B.S. in Elec. Engring., U. Tex., 1923, M.S., 1928; m. Thelma Barker, Aug. 23, 1942. Instr. elec. engring. U. Tex., 1923-28, asst. prof., 1928-30, asso. prof., 1939-44, prof., 1944-65; thereafter cons. to various elec. cos. Chmn. Power Distbn. Conf. from 1948. Registered profl. engr., Tex. Fellow AIEE; mem. Am. Soc. Engring. Edn., Nat. Soc. Profl. Engrs., Sigma Xi, Tau Beta Pi, Eta Kappa Nu. Author articles tech. jours. Home: Austin, Tex. Died Apr. 2, 1976.

GAGE, CHARLES ELLSWORTH, agrl. cons.; b. Dorchester, Neb., Oct. 12, 1882; s. Arunah and Sarah Fidelia (Sanford) G.; ed. High Sch., Bus. Coll., spl. studies at various schs. and colls.; m. Kathleen Maude Riley, Dec. 21, 1908. Stenographer ry. and bus. offices, St. Louis, Mo., 1903-05; stenographer Dept. of Agr., Washington, D.C., 1906-17, chief clerk Bur. Crop Estimates, 1917-19, officer in charge of field records, 1920, crop and livestock reports, 1921-26, mem. crop reporting bd., 1922-29, in charge newly created tobacco sect., Bur. Agrl. Econ., 1929, dir. Tobacco Br., Prodn. and Marketing Adminstrn. (formerly Agr. Marketing Adminstrn.), 1942-48; agricultural cons. Am. Tobacco Co. since 1948. Served as chairman and U.S. mem. tobacco com. of Combined Food Bd., World War II; U.S. del to World Tobacco Congress, Amsterdam, Holland, Sept., 1951; mem. tobacco advisory committee to the Secretary of Agriculture, 1951-62. President of Falls Ch. Temple Corp., 1934-44. Mem. Falls Ch. (Va.) Town Council, 1929-38, mem. planning commn., 1938-42; mem. Falls Church Historic Development Commn. Recipient citation Am. Marketing Assn., 1963. Mem. Am. Farm Econ. Assn., Agrl. History Soc., Mo. Hist. Soc., Mo. Archeol. Soc. Democrat. Mason (32 deg., Shriner). Club: Cosmos (Washington). Author: American Tobacco Types, Uses, and Markets (U.S. Dept. Agr. Circular 249), 1933 (revised 1942); The Tobacco Industry in Puerto Rico (U.S. Dept. Agr. Circular 519), 1939. Contbr. articles on tobacco. Initiated monthly crop reports on tobacco by types. Address: Falls Church, Va.

GAGE, H(ENRY) PHELPS, physicist; b. Ithaca, N.Y., Oct. 4, 1886; s. Simon Henry and Susanna Stewart (Phelps) G.; A.B., Cornell U., 1908, Ph.D. from same,

1911; m. Luella Cowan, June 30, 1914; children—William Whitney, Priscilla Van Tassel. In charge of optical laboratory, Corning Glass Works 1911-47; retired since 1947; assisted in development of railway signal lenses and of signal apparatus, colored glass for railway and for scientific uses, "Conaphore" front glasses for automobile headlamps, and a new type of condenser for motion picture projection, also "Daylite" glass for color identification and reading lamps. With J. C. Mock (M.C. R.R.) and Dr. K. S. Gibson (Nat. Bureau Standards) prepared revised specification for colored signal glass for Assn. Am. R.Rs. Fellow Illuminating Engring. Soc. (v.p., 1926-30), Soc. Motion Picture Engrs.; member Optical Soc. of America, Franklin Institute, Sigma Xi. Club: Rotary International. Author: (with Prof. Simon Henry Gage) Optic Protection, 1914. Home: Corning, N.Y.

GAGE, WALTER HENRY, univ. pres.; b. Vancouver, B.C., Can., Mar. 5, 1905; B.A., U. B.C., 1925, M.A., 1926, LL.D., 1958. Pres. U. B.C., Vancouver. Mem. Am. Math. Soc., Math. Assn. Am. Home: Vancouver, B.C., Canada. Died Oct. 3, 1978.

GAHMAN, FLOYD, artist; b. Elida, Ohio, Oct. 14, 1894; s. William Henry and Nancy (Brenneman) G.; tchrs. certificate Valparaiso U., 1916; B.S., Columbia U., 1924, M.A., 1939; studied art with Hobart Nichols, Henry Varnum Poor, Dong Kingman; m. Ruth Louise Leyse; 1 dau., Phyllis. Asst. prof. art Pa. State U., 1948-60. Landscape painter: exhibited nationally; represented in permanent collections Pa. State U., Ind. U. Served as 2d lt., combat pilot, U.S. Army Air Forces, World War I, in U.S. and France; 1st lt., Res U.S. Army, 1919-24; capt. USAAF, 1943-46. Recipient prizes, Scarsdale (N.Y.) Art Assn., 1936-37, Salmagundi Club, 1938, 39, 42, 61, Allied Artists Am., 1943, Kirk prize Ogunquit Art Center; Gold medal Am. Artists Profl. League, 1962; landscape prize Acad. Artists, 1966, Salmagundi Club, 1970, 73, 74, 75, Allied Artists Am., 1970, Hudson Valley Art Assn., 1970, Knickerbocker Artists, 1974. Mem. NAD, Allied Artist Am., Audubon Artists, Ind. Art Assn., Phi Delta Kappa. Club: Salmagundi. Home: New York City, N.Y. Died Nov. 1, 1979.

GAINES, TILFORD CRAIG, banker; b. Spokane, Wash., Oct. 12, 1920; s. Grover and Lillian (Allen) G.; A.B., M.A., Washington U., St. Louis, 1946; Ph.D., Columbia, 1959; m. Ruth Burkhalter, Dec. 27, 1940 (div. Oct. 1964); 1 dau., Pamela Dolores; m. 2d, Regina Oddone, Dec. 12, 1964; 1 dau., Carla E. Instr., Fla. State U., 1950-51; economist Fed. Res. Bank N.Y., 1951-60; v.p. charge govt. bond operations First Nat. Bank Chgo., 1961-67; v.p., economist Hanover Trust Co., 1967-80. Served with USAAF, 1944-46. Mem. Am. Econ. Assn., Am. Finance Assn., Am. Statis. Assn., Chgo. Assn. Commerce and Industry, Internat. C. of C. (chmn. monetary relations com.), Nat. Assn. Bus. Economists. Clubs: University, Economics (Chgo.). Home: Lake Forest, Ill. Died Apr. 14, 1980.

GAINEY, DANIEL CHARLES, bus. exec.; b. Winona County, Minn., Nov. 28, 1897; s. Daniel and Ella (Leach) G.; A.B., Hamline U., St. Paul, 1921, D.B.A., 1948; D.Litt., Coll. St. Thomas, 1974; m. Harriette Swearingen, July 17, 1924; 1 son, Daniel James; m. 2d, Elaine L. Frock, 1962. Coll. sports writer Mpls. and St. Paul papers; athletic coach, Hancock, Minn., 1921-22, with Josten's Owatonna, Minn., 1922-79, pres., 1933-59, chmn. bd., chief exec. officer, 1933-68, chmn. bd. emeritus, 1968-79; pres. Charles Rochester Co., Am. Yearbook Co., Owatonna, 1950-59; pres. Arabian Horse Club Registry Am., 1958-72, dir., 1948-73, pres. and dir. emeritus, 1973-79; v.p. Danco Fund, Inc.; past dir. First Trust Co. of St. Paul; rancher, Scottsdale, Ariz. and Santa Ynez, Calif. Trustee Hamline U.; trustee emeritus Am. Grad. Sch. Internat. Mgmt., Phoenix; mem. Mayo sponsors Mayo Found., Rochester, Minn.; officer Gainey Found.; bd. regents U. Minn., 1939-73; past bd. trustees Minn. Community Research Council, Inc. Del. Rep. Nat. Conv., 1948, 52, 56, 60, 64; Stassen Floor leader Rep. Conv., 1952; past nat. treas. Republican Party; mem. nat. com. Citizens for Eisenhower, 1956; nat. finance chmn. Goldwater campaign, 1964; mem. Rep. Nat. Fin. Com. Mem. Ednl. Jewelry Mfrs. Assn. (past pres. and dir.), NAM, State Employers Assn. (dir.), C. of C., Delta Sigma Phi. Republican. Clubs: Minneapolis, Minikahda (Mpls.); Paradise Valley Country (Scottsdale Ariz.). Home: Owatonna, Minn. Died Apr. 7, 1979.

GAINSBRUGH, MARTIN REUBEN, economist; b. Rochester, N.Y., Jan. 29, 1907; s. Jocob and Rachel (Isaacs) G.; A.B., U. Rochester, 1928; postgrad. Columbia, 1929-32; LL.D., Grove City Coll.; m. Elizabeth J. Augsbury, July 4, 1935; children—Susan Rachel (Mrs. James Buchanan), Jonathan Jo, Glenn Martin. Econ. analyst Trade-Ways, Inc., 1933-38; chief economist Nat. Indsl. Conf. Bd., 1939-72, v.p., 1962-65, sr. v.p., 1966-72; cons. panel Comptroller-Gen. U.S., from 1967; lectr. econs., N.Y. U., 1944-48, adj. asso. prof. econs., 1949-50, adj. prof. econs., 1951-72; econ. cons. Nat. Dividend Plan, 1973-75. Chmn. Bus. Research Adv. Council Bur. Labor Statistics, 1955-57; mem. bus. adv. com. Council Econ. Advisers, 1947-57; cons. Council for Advancement Secondary Edn., 1955-57; bd. advisers Indsl. Coll. Armed Forces, 1958-66; mem. econ. adv. com. Council for Econ. Growth and Security, Inc., from 1960; mem. Pres.'s Com. to Appraise Employment and Unemployment Statistics, 1961-62; mem. Adv. Group on Research Program of Social Security Adminstrn., 1961-64; chmn. nat. quota com. Nat. Budget and Consultation Com., 1963-71; adv. com. on mgmt. automatic data processing Exec. Office Pres., 1963-64; mem. pvt. sector task force Nat. Adv. Com. on Civil Disorders, 1967. Recipient merit award Citizens Com. for Hoover Report, 1952, citation Freedom Found., 1953, certificate of award U.S. Dept. of Labor, 1957. Fellow A.A.A.S., Am. Statis. Assn. (council, chmn. program com. 1955, v.p. 1956-58, pres. 1961); mem. Royal Statis. Soc., Met. Econ. Assn. Conf. Bus. Economists (chmn. 1955), Soc. Bus. Adv. Professions (pres. 1957), Am. Econ. Assn., Am. Finance Assn., Phi Beta Kappa. Contbr., author, editor publs. and books. Home: Plessis, N.Y. Died Apr. 25, 1977.

GALAMIAN, IVAN ALEXANDER, musician, educator; b. Tabriz, Persia, Jan. 23, 1903; s. Alexander J. and Sarah (Khounoutz) G.; grad. Philharmonic Sch., Moscow, USSR, 1923; Mus.D., Curtis Inst., 1954, Cleve. Inst. Music, 1968; hon. degree Oberlin Coll., 1966; m. Judith Johnson, Nov. 22, 1941. Came to U.S., 1937, naturalized, 1944. Mem. violin faculty Russian Conservatory, Paris, France, 1925-39, Ecole Normale de Masique, Paris, 1936-39, Curtis Inst. Music, from 1944, Julliard Sch. Music, N.Y.C., from 1946; dir. Meadowmount Sch. Music, Westport, N.Y., from 1952. Pres. Soc. for Strings, Inc., 1952. Hon. mem. Royal Acad. Music. Author: Principles of Violin Playing and Teaching, 1962. Home: New York, N.Y. Died Apr. 14, 1981.

GALANTIERE, LEWIS, writer, cons. internat. relations; b. Chgo., Oct. 10, 1895; m. Nancy N. Davis, 1938. With Internat. C. of C., Paris, 1920-27, Fed. Res. Bank of N.Y., 1928-40; dir. French operations OWI, U.S., London and Paris, 1942-45; counsellor Free Europe Com., 1952-64. Organizer, mem. Am. Round Table of Advt. Council, 1951-52; mem. Fulbright Selection Com. for France, 1951-53; subcom. books abroad Nat. Book Com., 1953-55; mem. study groups Democratic leadership, Germany, U.S. and European Capitalism, France, East Europe, of Council Fgn. Relations, 1957-65; pres. P.E.N. Am. Center, 1965-67. Pres. 34th Internat. P.E.N. Congress, N.Y.C., 1966. Bd. dirs. Am. Civil Liberties Union, 1951-66, mem. editing com. report on Am. Democracy, Rockefeller Bros. Fund, 1959. Decorated officier Ordre des Arts et des Lettres (France). Guggenheim fellow, 1941. Mem. Acad. Polit. Sci., Mediaeval Soc. Am., Authors League Am. (council 1966-69), Am. Translators Assn. (dir. 1962-65, recipient Gode medal). Clubs: Century Assn., Coffee House (N.Y.C.). Publs: France Is Full of Frenchmen; America Today; America and the Mind of Europe; (plays) And Be My Love, Lamachus, adaptation 1946, constant performance, Anouith's Antigone; Goncourt Journals 1851-70; Portable Maupassant; (with G. de Poncins) Kabloona. Translator numerous works; contbr. polit. and lit. mags. Address: New York, N.Y. Died Feb. 20, 1977.

GALBRAITH, WILLIAM JAMES, JR., lawyer; b. Harford, Pa., Feb. 21, 1883; s. William James and Alice E. (Nugent) G.; Belmont (Calif.) Mil. Sch.; A.B., Stanford U., 1906; J.D., U. of Chicago, 1908; m. Lucy Souther, of Springfield, Ill., Nov. 26, 1907; children—Nancy Alice, Elizabeth Souther, Lucy Latham. Began practice at Phoenix, Ariz., 1909; asst. atty. gen. of Ariz., 1909-12; city atty., Glendale, 1916-19; mem. Ariz. Ho. of Rep., 1919-21; atty. gen. of Ariz., 1921-23. Formerly instr. law, U. of Ariz.; mem. commn. on Uniform Legislation. Mem. Delta Tau Delta, Phi Delta Phi. Republican. Christian Scientist. Home: Phoenix, Ariz.

GALE, GEORGE GORDON, pub. utilities; b. Quebec, Can., Oct. 9, 1882; s. George Goldsworthy and Eliza E. (Piddington) G.; B.S. in Electricity and Mining, McGill U., 1903; M.S., 1905; m. Marian Masson, April 5, 1911; children—Marian Gordon (Charleson), Charles Gordon. Asst. chief engr. Canadian Rubber Co., Montreal, 1904-06; v.p. and gen. mgr. The Hull Electric Co., Hull, Que., 1907-26, pres. and dir. since 1926; gen. mgr. Gatineau Power Co., Ottawa, Can., 1926, v.p. 1927-34, pres. since 1934, dir. since 1927; pres. The E. B. Eddy Co., Hull, Can., 1940-48; pres. Ottawa Valley Trust Co.; pres., dir. Gatineu Bus Co., Ltd., Gatineau Electric Light Co., Ltd., Gatineau Transmission Co., Saint John River Storage Co.; v.p., dir. Internat. Hydro-Electric System. Past pres. Canadian Street Ry. Assn., Ottawa Valley Grads. Soc. of McGill U.; mem. bd. govs. McGill University, 1943-46; mem. Engring. Inst. of Canada, Professional Engrs. of Quebec. Clubs: Rideau, Country, Royal Ottawa Golf (Ottawa); St. James, University (Montreal). Home: Ottawa, Can.

GALE, WALTER JOHN, ednl. adminstr.; b. Phila., July 14, 1914; s. Walter E. and Kathryn Gertrude (Ryan) G.; B.S., N.J. State Coll., Glassboro, 1936; M.Ed., Duke, 1946, Ph.D., 1950; m. Mary E. De Mauro, Oct. 27, 1944 (div.); children—Geraldine M., Cynthia K., Gregory W., Karen L.; m. 2d, Barbara Ann Ransel, Oct. 25, 1969. Instr. ednl. psychology Duke, 1946-48; prin Broughton High Sch., Raleigh, N.C., 1948-52; prof. ednl. psychology Woman's Coll. of U. N.C., 1952-55; vis. lectr. U. N.C., 1955-56; pres. Pembroke (N.C.) State Coll., 1956-63; dean West Chester (Pa.) State Coll., 1963-65; dir. Nat. Def. Student Loan Program, U.S. Office of Edn., Washington, 1965-72, dir. vets. programs unit, 1972-75. Served with USNR, 1941-45. Mem. Am. Sociol. Soc., N.E.A., Am. Soc. Curriculum Devel. Home: Brandywine, Md. Died Sept. 9, 1976.

GALL, EDWARD ALFRED, educator, physician; b. N.Y.C., June 10, 1906; s. Julius and Eva (Fleischl) G.; student Coll. City N.Y., 1923-27; M.D., Tulane U., 1931; m. Phyllis H. Rivard, Sept. 17, 1933; children—Eric Papineau, Thomas Monroe. Intern Sydenham Hosp., N.Y.C., 1931-33; dist. physician Boston Dispensary, 1933-35; resident, asst. pathologist Mass. Gen. Hosp., 1935-40; dir. labs. Bethesda Hosp., Cin., 1941-48, Cin. Gen. Hosp., 1948-71; asst. medicine, instr. pathology Tufts Med. Sch., 1933-40; instr. pathology Harvard Med. Sch., 1940-41; asst. and asso. prof. pathology U. Cin., 1941-48, Mary M. Emery prof. pathology, 1948-71, prof. emeritus, 1976-79, v.p., dir. Med. Center, 1970-74, v.p., dir. emeritus, 1976-79, distinguished service prof. pathology, 1974-79. Cons. Armed Forces Inst. Pathology, VA, Daniel Drake, Dunham, Children's hosps. Decorated grand officer Order Daniel Carrion (Peru); recipient Isadore Dyer medal Tulane U., 1931; Townsend Harris medal Coll. City N.Y., 1968; E.T. Bell Meml. medal U. Minn., 1975; fellow U. Cin., 1970. Mem. Am. Assn. Pathologists and Bacteriologists (pres. 1963-64), Sociedad Peruana de Anatomiá Patalógica (hon.), Internat. Acad. Pathology (exec. council 1962-65, pres. 1969-70), Am. Soc. Exptl. Pathology, Soc. Exptl. Biology and Medicine, Am. Soc. Clin. Pathologists (dir. 1962-68, Ward Burdick medal 1976), Central Soc. Clin. Research, Japanese Am. Soc. Pathologists Tokyo (hon.), Arthur Purdy Stout Soc. Surg. Pathologists (hon. 1978), Am. Assn. for Cancer Edn. (pres. 1971-72), Am. Fedn. Clin. Oncologic Socs. (pres. 1973-74), Pan-Am. Med. Assn. (pres. sect. on gen. pathology), Nat. Bd. Med. Examiners, Council Fgn. Med. Grads., Sigma Xi, Alpha Omega Alpha. Asso. editor Am. Jour. Clin. Pathology, 1949-57; editor-in-chief Am. Jour. Pathology, 1957-66. Home: Cincinnati, Ohio. Died Jan. 31, 1979.

GALLAGHER, BUELL GORDON, educator; b. Rankin, Ill., Feb. 4, 1904; s. Elmer David and Elma Maryel (Poole) G.; B.A., Carleton Coll., 1925, LL.D., 1959; B.D., Union Theol. Sem., 1929; student London Sch. Econs., 1929-30; Ph.D., Columbia, 1939, LL.D., 1954; D.D., Oberlin Coll., 1943, Pacific Sch. Religion, 1970; LL.D., Doane Coll., 1953, Lincoln U., 1954, Brandeis U., 1954, Hebrew Union U., 1961, Tuskegee Inst., 1963; Litt.D., U. Cin., 1957; L.H.D., Wagner Coll. 1954, Moravian Coll., 1958, Adelphi Coll., 1966, Alfred U., 1967, Iona Coll., 1967, Akron U., 1970, City Coll. N.Y., 1972, Talladega Coll., 1973; m. June Lucille Sampson, Sept. 1, 1927; children—Helen Maryel (Mrs. Sidney S. Herman), Barbara Lucille (Mrs. F. Tomasson Jannuzi). Instr., Doane Coll., 1925-26; ordained to ministry Congl. Ch., 1929; sec. Intersem. Movement, 1930-31; pastor, Passaic, N.J., 1931-33; pres. Talladega Coll., 1933-43; prof. Christian ethics Pacific Sch. Religion, 1944-49; cons. Fed. Security Adminstrn., 1949; asst. commnr. U.S. Office Edn., 1950-52; pres. Coll. City N.Y., 1952-61, 62-69; chancellor Calif. State Colls., 1961-62. Chmn. U.S. gen. com. World Univ. Service, 1953-66, chmn. internat. assembly, 1962-66; mem. Permanent Panel Ednl. and Corp. Relations, 1956-78; commn. religion and race Nat. Council Chs., 1962-78. Bd. dirs. N.A.A.C.P., 1934-76, vice chmn., 1971-76; bd. dirs. Manhattanville Community Centers, Herman Muehlstein Found. Democratic nominee for U.S. Congress, 1948. Decorated chevalier Legion of Honor; recipient Outstanding Civilian Service medal U.S. Army, 1961; medal City N.Y., 1961; John H. Finley medal City Coll. N.Y. Alumni Assn., 1962; gold medal San Francisco Chronicle, 1961, also recipient Amistad medal, 1968. Mem. Phi Beta Kappa, Delta Sigma Rho. Author: American Caste and the Negro College, 1939; Color and Conscience, 1946; Portrait of a Pilgrim, 1946; Campus in Crisis, 1974. Editor, co-author: College and the Black Student, 1972. Home: Granite Springs, N.Y. Died Aug. 30, 1978.

GALLAGHER, JAMES JOSEPH, JR., educator, lawyer; b. Bryn Mawr, Pa., Nov. 6, 1926; s. James Joseph and Grace (McCarthy) G.; B.A., Albright Coll., Reading, Pa., 1950; LL.B., U. Pa., 1953; m. Mary Diane Bechtel, Feb. 14, 1953; children—Kevin, Sean, Kerry. Admitted to Pa. bar, 1954; asst. prof. Wharton Sch. Finance and Commerce, U. Pa., 1952-62; asst. to dir., joint com. continuing legal edn. Am. Law Inst. and Am. Bar Assn., 1962-63; v.p. Pub. Fidelity Life Ins. Co., 1963-65; prof., head law dept. Drexel U., Phila., 1965-79; cons. in field. Mem. Lynnewood Park Civic Assn. Served with AUS, 1945-46. Recipient Distinguished Tchr. award U. Pa., 1959; scroll of appreciation Am. Coll. Life Underwriters, 1965; Outstanding Edn. award Beta Nu, Drexel U., 1966-67; Pedagogue award Commerce and Engring. Sch., Drexel U., 1968; Outstanding Achievement award Sr. Class, Drexel U., 1968; Pre-Jr. Class Appreciation award

Drexel U., 1969, Lindback award. Mem. Am Contract Bridge League (life master), Sigma Tau Delta, Pi Gamma Mu. Democrat. Clubs: Lawyers (Phila.); Drexelbrook (Drexelhill, Pa.). Home: Havertown, Pa. Died Mar. 6, 1979.

GALLAGHER, LOUIS JOSEPH, clergyman, educator; b. Boston, Mass., July 22, 1885; s. James and Sarah (Dempsey) G.; A.B., Woodstock (Md.) Coll., 1911, A.M., 1912; studied theology, same college, 1917-21; LL.D., Georgetown Univ., 1933. Joined The Society of Jesus (Jesuits), 1905; ordained priest R.C. Ch., 1920; prof. classical langs., Fordham U., 1912-17; headmaster Xavier High Sch., N.Y. City, 1921-22; asst. dir. Papal Relief Mission to Russia, 1922-23, also mem. Am. Relief Administration in Russia and supervisor Orenburg div. of Papal Relief; dean Coll. of Arts and Sciences, Georgetown Coll., 1924-26, also mem. bd. dirs., regent and sec.; dir. general of studies of the N.E. Jesuit Province, 1926-31; pres. Boston Coll., 1932-37; asst. dir. Inst. of Social Order since Nov. 1940. Diplomatic courier to transport relics of Andrew Bobola, Polish Jesuit martyr, from Moscow to Rome; mem. State Adv. Com. on U. Extension (Mass.), 1933-36. Author: The China That Was; Episode on Beacon Hill, others. Address: Pomfret Center, Conn.

GALLAGHER, WILLIAM HENRY, lawyer; b. Alabaster, Mich., Oct. 28, 1884; s. William Henry and Clementine Marion (De Brabander) G.; A.B., U. of Detroit, 1903, A.M., 1906; LL.B., Detroit Coll. Law, 1906; m. Esther Mary Masurette, July 18, 1921; children—Mary Esther (dec.), Joan Eileen, Madeline Sophia (dec.), James P. Admitted to Mich. bar, 1906, and began practice at Detroit. Mem. Am., Mich. State and Detroit bar assns., Delta Theta Phi Fraternity. Mem. Knights of Columbus. Clubs: Detroit Athletic, Detroit Golf. Home: Rochester, Mich.; and Detroit.

GALLEGOS FREIRE, RÓMULO (GAL-YA'GOS), Venezuelan educator and writer; b. Caracas, Venezuela, 1884; s. Rómulo Gallegos Oslo and Rita Freire Guruceaga; ed. Colegio Sucre, U. of Venezuela; m. Teotiste Arocha Egui. Dir. of Colegio Federal of Barcelona, Venezuela, 1912; asst. dir. of the Liceo de Caracas, 1912-18; and of the Normal School for Men, 1918-20; dir. of Liceo Andrés Bello, 1922-30, where he was prof. philosophy and history of philosophy; lived in voluntary exile, 1931-36, for political reasons; minister of public instruction, 1936; deputy for Federal Dist., 1937; elected mem. of Council of Parish of Naiguatá. Awarded prize of the Asociación del Major libro del mes of Madrid for his novel Doña Barbara, 1929 (English transl., N.Y., 1931); author of other novels and dramas. Address: Venezuela. *

GALLICO, PAUL WILLIAM, writer; b. N.Y.C., July 26, 1897; s. Paolo and Hortense (Erlich) G.; B.S., Columbia, 1921; m. Alva Thoits Taylor, Sept. 5, 1921 (div. 1934); children—William Taylor, Robert Leston; m. 2d, Elaine St. Johns, Apr. 12, 1935 (div. 1936); m. 3d, Baroness Pauline Gariboldi, 1939 (div.); m. 4th, Baroness von Falz-Fein, July 19, 1963. Movie critic N.Y. Daily News, 1922-23, sports writer, 1923-24, sports editor, columnist, 1924-36; free lance fiction writer, 1936-76; war corr. Cosmopolitan mag., 1944. Served as seaman gunner R.F., USN, 1918. Clubs: Fencer's, Quiet Birdman (N.Y.C.); Bucks, EPEE' (London). Author: Farewell to Sport, 1938; Adventures of Hiram Holliday, 1939 (London, 1939); The Secret Front, 1940; The Snow Goose, 1941; Lou Gehrig, Pride of the Yankees, 1942; Golf Is a Friendly Game, 1942; Confessions of a Story Writer, 1946; The Lonely (London), 1947, N.Y.C., 1949; The Abandoned, 1950; Jennie (London), 1950; Trial by Terror, 1952; The Small Miracle, 1952; The Foolish Immortals, 1953; Snowflake, 1953; Love of Seven Dolls, 1954; Thomasina, 1957; The Steadfast Man, 1958; Mrs. 'Arris Goes to Paris, 1958; Ludmila, 1959; Too Many Ghosts, 1959; The Hurricane Story, 1960; Mrs. Arris Goes to New York, 1960; Further Confessions of a Story Writer, 1961; Coronation, 1962; Scruffy, 1962; Love, Let Me Not Hunger, 1963; The Hand of Mary Constable, 1964; The Silent Miaow, 1964; The Day the Guinea-Pig Talked, 1964; Mrs. 'Arris Goes to Parliament, 1965; The Golden People, 1965; The Day Jean-Pierre was Pignapped, 1965; The Man Who Was Magic, 1966; The Day Jean-Pierre Went Round the World, 1966; The Story of Silent Night, 1967; The Revealing Eye, 1967; Manxmouse, 1968; The Poseidon Adventure, 1969; The Day Jean-Pierre Joined the Circus, 1969; Matilda, 1970; The Zoo Gang, 1971; Honorable Cat, 1972; The Boy Who Invented the Bubble Gun, 1974; Mrs. 'Arris Goes to Moscow, 1975; Miracle in the Wilderness, 1975; Beyond the Poseidon Adventure, 1978; The House That Wouldn't Go Away, 1980. Contbr. fiction to Sat. Eve. Post, Good Housekeeping, Esquire. Home: Antibes, France. Died July 15, 1976.

GALLMAN, WALDEMAR JOHN, fgn. service officer; b. Wellsville, N.Y., Apr. 27, 1899; s. John and Henrietta (Engelder) G.; A.B., Cornell U., 1917-21; student Georgetown Law Sch., 1923-24; m. Marjorie Gerry, July 29, 1925; children—John Gerry, Philip Gerry. Instr. English, Cornell U., Ithaca, N.Y., 1921-22; became sec. Am. embassy, 1922; assigned to Habana, State Dept., 1923, Am. legation, San Jose, Costa Rica, 1925, Quito, Ecuador, 1926, Riga, Latvia, 1930, Am. embassy, Warsaw, Poland, 1934; apptd. consul Free City of Danzig, 1934; asst. chief div. European affairs State Dept., 1941; 1st sec., London, Eng., 1942; counselor, London, 1944; minister, London, 1945; became ambassador to Poland, 1948; dep. for Fgn. Affairs, Nat. War Coll., 1950-51; ambassador Union South Africa, 1951, Iraq, 1954; dir. gen. Fgn. Service, 1959-61; mem. faculty grad. sch. George Washington U., 1961-80; adviser Fgn. Service Tng. Inst., Korean Ministry Fgn. Affairs, Seoul, 1963-65, Fgn. Service Tng. Center South Viet Nam Ministry Fgn. Affairs, 1966-70. Mem. S.A.T.C.; Cornell, 1918. Author: Iraz Under General Nuri-My: Recollections of Nuri-Al-Said, 1954-58. Address: Washington, D.C. Died June 28, 1980.

GALLOWAY, BLANCHE, librarian; b. Liscomb, Ia., Jan. 28, 1884; d. John and Lydia Rue (Haas) G.; grad. high sch., Marshalltown, Ia., 1903; library course, State U. of Ia., 1903; Drake U., Des Moines, 1904-6. With Marshalltown Pub. Library, 1902-3; asst., 1906-8, librarian, 1908-10, Drake U. Library; br. librarian, Queensborough Pub. Library, N.Y. City, 1910-18; camp librarian (1st woman to be apptd.), Pelham Bay Naval Training Sta., N.Y., Apr. 1918-Feb. 1919; overseas service, A.L.A., Brest, France, Mar.-May 1919, Gievres, France, June-Aug. 1919; hospital librarian with Army of Occupation, Coblenz, Germany, Sept. 1919-May 1920; head of sch. dept. Kern County Free Library, Bakersfield, Calif., Sept. 1921-June 1923; now county librarian, Madera County Free Library. Mem. A.L.A. Home: Madera, Calif.

GALLOWAY, GERALD EDWARD, army officer; b. N.Y.C., Dec. 4, 1902; B.S., U.S. Mil. Acad., 1925; C.E., Cornell U., 1927; grad. Engr. Sch., Ft. Belvoir, Va., 1928. Indsl. Coll. Armed Forces, 1949; married; 1 son. Gerald Edward (U.S. Army). Commd. 2d lt. C.E., U.S. Army, 1925, advanced through grades to maj. gen., 1956; company officer 1st Engrs., Ft. DePont, Del., 1925-26; instr. chemistry and electricity U.S. Mil. Acad., 28-32; assigned 11th Engr. Regt., Corozal, Canal Zone, 1932-35; asst. to dist. engr., Mobile, Ala., 1935-39; asst. to chief operations and tng. div. Office Chief of Engrs., Washington, 1939-40; asst. to dist. engr., Puerto Rico, 1940, also exec. to dist. engr.; dir. tng. Engr. Amphibian Command, Camp Edwards, Mass., 1942; comdr. 543d Engr. Amphibian Regt., 3d Engr. Spl. Brigade, 1942, later regt. comdr., birgade exec., brigade comdr., New Guinea, New Britain, P.I., Japan, Camp Stoneman, Cal.; dist. engr. Little Rock Engr. District, Ark., 1946-48; chief constrn. and operations div. Mil. Constrn., Office Chief of Engrs., Washington, 1949-51; engineer IX U.S. Corps, Korea, 1951-53; asst. comdt. Engr. Sch., Ft. Belvoir, Va., 1953-56; Missouri River div. engr., C.E., Omaha, Neb., 1956-58; comdg. gen. Engr. Center and Fort Belvoir; comdt. U.S. Army Engr. Sch. and comdg. gen. U.S. Army Engr. Research and Development Lab., 1958-60; Pacific Ocean div. engr. C.E., Honolulu, from 1960. Mem. Bd. Engrs. for Rivers and Harbors, 1956-58; mem. Miss. River Commn., U.S. on Large Dams Decorated Legion of Merit with cluster. Bronze Star medal with cluster. Air medal. Fellow Am. Soc. C E.; mem. Nat. Water Resources Inst., Soc. Am. Mil. Engrs., Newcomen Soc., Permanent Internat. Assn. Navigation Congresses (reporter gen. 19th congress London 1957, sec. gen. 20th Balt. 1961). Home: Annandale, Va. Died Apr. 28, 1980.

GALLOWAY, THOMAS (CYRUS), physician; b. Boise, Ida., Mar. 17, 1886; s. Thomas Cyrus and Mary (Flournoy) G.; B.S., U. Ida., 1907; S.M., U. Chgo., 1910; M.D. Rush Med. Coll., 1912; grad. study U. Vienna, 1923; D.Sc. (hon.), University of Idaho, 1957; married Grace Beckler, 1929; 1 daughter, Mera G. Ferrin. Intern Cook County Hospital, Chgo., 1912-14, resident, 1921, attending laryngologist, 1926-47; practicing physician, Evanston, Ill., 1921—; prof. emeritus otolaryngology Northwestern U. Recipient Newcomb award Am. Laryngol. Assn. Diplomate Am. Bd. Otolaryngology. Mem. A.M.A., Ill., Chgo. med. socs., Chgo. Laryngol. and Otol. Soc., Am. Acad. Ophthalmology and Otolaryngology, Am. Laryngol. Assn., Am. Laryngol. Rhinol. and Otol. Soc., Am. Otol. Soc. Author monograph; Respiratory Emergencies; also articles on laryngology. Home: Evanston, Ill.

GALTSOFF, PAUL SIMON, biologist; b. Moscow, Russia, Mar. 28, 1887; s. Simon Peter and Sophia (Poletaev) G.; grad. Classical Sch., Moscow, 1905; Diploma First Degree, Imperial Moscow U., 1910; Ph.D., Columbia, 1924; m. Eugenia Troussoff, Nov. 5, 1911. Came to U.S., 1921, naturalized, 1927. Research fellow dept. zoology and instr. invertebrate zoology, Moscow U., 1910-13; senior biologist in charge marine lab, at Sebastopol, Crimea, Russian Acad. of Science, 1914-20; extensive study of effect of dam construction in life of Mississippi River, 1921-22; naturalist of U.S.S. Albatross, U.S. Bur. of Fisheries, 1922-25; in charge of section of shellfishery investigation, U.S. Fish and Wildlife Service; research biologist with Service, 1948; student process regeneration in sponges, Marine Biological Laboratory, Woods Hole, Mass; leader govt. expedition to explore pearl oyster resources of Hawaiian Islands, 1938-39; at request of British Govt. studied sponge disease in West Indies; at request of Panamanian govt. studied pearl fishery and biology of pearl oyster in Gulf of Panama, 1948; made biol. exploration nr. Margarita Island, Venezuela, 1948. Sci. observer Bikini atom bomb tests, 1946; dir. U.S. Shellfishery Lab., Woods Hole, Mass., until 1964; advisor Marine Lab., University of Miami. Trustee International Oceanographic Foundation. In Russian Army, 1914-19. Member internat. secretariat, United Nations Conf. trustee Marine Biol. Lab., Woods Hole and Bermuda Biol. Lab.; former pres. Nat. Shellfisheries Assn.; mem. grad. council, George Washington U. Awarded Moscow U. gold medal for research, 1910; Bogandov Prize of Moscow Soc. of Friends of Natural History, 1914; Gold medal for outstanding service Dept. of Interior. Fellow A.A.A.S. Mem. Wash. Acad. Sciences, American Society of Zoologists, American Naturalists, Society General Physiologists, American Society of Limnology and Oceanography, Washington Biological Society, Sigma Xi. Club: Cosmos (Washington). Author: Limnological Observations in the Upper Mississippi River, 1924; Regeneration After Dissociation, 1925; Pearl and Hermer Reef, Hawaii, 1933; Culture Methods for Invertebrate, 1937; Red Tide, 1948; The Pearl Oyster Resources of Panama, 1950; The Pearl Fishery of Venezuela, 1950; The Story of the Fish, 1962; The American Oyster (Dept. of Interior prize), 1964. Author and editor: Gulf of Mexico, Its Origin, Waters and Marine Life, 1954. Home: Woods Hole, Mass. Died Aug. 23, 1979.

GAMMON, LANDON HAYNES, lawyer; b. Saltville, Va., Sept. 28, 1896; s. Landon Haynes and Rosa Cabell (Miller) G.; A.B., U. Va., 1918; LL.B., Harvard, 1922; m. Katherine C. Conn, June 30, 1926. Admitted to Tenn. bar, 1922, since practiced law, Chattanooga; mem. Goins, Gammon, Baker & Robinson and predecessor firms, 1925-75; spl. judge Ct. Appeals, Tenn., 1959-60. Trustee Chattanooga Pub. Library. Served in U.S. Army, World War I; mem. Selective Service Bd., World War II. Mem. Am., Tenn., Chattanooga bar assns., Selden Soc., Am. Legion. Democrat. Presbyn. Contbr. articles law jour. Home: Chattanooga, Tenn. Died Apr. 1975.

GAMON, JOHN ARTHUR, ex-consul gen.; b. Wheaton, Ill., Feb. 9, 1882; s. B. H. and Jennie T. (Daniels) G.; A.B., University of Mich., 1905; m. Minnie Moulton, of Glen Ellyn, Ill., Oct. 1, 1907; children—Virginia, John Arthur, David Louis. In ticket auditor's office, C.,M.&St.P.Ry., Chicago, 1899-1900; ry. survey work, Mexico, 1902-03; salesman, Jones & Laughlin Steel Co., Chicago, 1905-14; consul at Puerto Cortes, Honduras, 1914-15, Corinto, Nicaragua, 1915-16, Acapulco, Mexico, 1917-21; assigned to Cobh (Queenstown), Ireland, 1921, consul gen. same, 1924-25, London, 1925-28, Marseilles, France, 1928-35, retired. Home: Berkeley, Calif.

GANNER, THOMAS ALAN, cons. accountant; b. N.Y.C., Mar. 9, 1921; s. Russon Giddings and Claire M. (Whelan) G.; student N.Y. U., 1938-41; B.S. summa cum laude, Ohio State U., 1947; m. Donna Marie Daron, May 26, 1950; children—Thomas Alan, William Russon. With Price Waterhouse & Co., C.P.A.'s, N.Y.C., 1947-79; gen. partner, 1958-76, mem. policy com., 1965-76, vice chmn., 1972-76, cons., 1976-79. Served to 1st lt. AUS, 1941-45. C.P.A., N.Y. Mem. Am. Inst. C.P.A.'s, Beta Gamma Sigma, Beta Alpha Psi. Clubs: Union League (N.Y.C.); Canoe Brook Country (Summit). Home: Summit, N.J. Died Mar. 31, 1979.

GANTT, FRED, JR., educator; b. Foreman, Ark., Nov. 12, 1922; s. Fred and Bettie (Taaffe) G.; A.A., So. State Coll. of Ark., 1941; B.A., So. Meth. U., 1943, M.A., 1948; Ph.D., U. Tex., 1962. Instr. polit. sci. So. Meth. U., 1947-51; adminstrv. asst. to personnel dir. Lone Star Ordnance Plant, Texarkana, Tex., 1952-55; instr. social scis. Texarkana Coll., 1955-58; teaching fellow U. Tex., 1959-61, vis. prof. govt., 1968, 74; instr. polit. sci. Tex. A. and M. Coll., 1961-62; asst. prof. polit. sci. North Tex. State U., Denton, 1962-64, asso. prof., 1964-66, prof., 1966-75, chmn. dept., 1969-75; cons. Nat. Gov.'s Conf., 1968, Tex. Constnl. Revision Commn., 1967-68; cons. to Commrs. Ct., Dallas County; vis. prof. Lyndon B. Johnson Sch. Pub. Affairs, U. Tex., Austin, 1973. Del. Democratic State Conv., 1964. Served with AUS, 1944-46. Named outstanding prof. North Tex. State U., 1970. Mem. Am. So., Midwest, Western Southwestern (pres. 1970-71) polit. sci. assns., Am. Soc. Pub. Adminstrn., Pi Sigma Alpha, Phi Theta Kappa, Psi Chi. Methodist. Author: The Chief Executive in Texas: a Study in Gubernational Leadership, 1964, The Texas Constitution, Its Impact on the Executive, 1973; co-author: The Use of Land Resources in Dallas County, Texas. . ., 1972. Editor: (with others) Governing Texas: Readings and Documents, 3d edit., 1974. Contbr. articles to profl. jours. Home: Denton, Tex. Died Nov. 26, 1975.

GANTT, PAUL HAWKINS, lawyer, ret. govt. ofcl.; b. Vienna, Austria, Mar. 26, 1907; s. Henry and Olga (Otte) Gans; J.U.D., U. Vienna, 1931; J.D., Coll. William and Mary, 1942; m. Hilda E. Delaney, June 26,

1948. Admitted to Va. bar, 1942, D.C. bar, 1950; practiced law in Vienna, Austria, 1935-38; atty. Arthur T. Vanderbilt, Newark, 1943-44, Nat. Housing Agy., 1944-45, U.S. Bur. Mines, 1945-46; trial atty., chief counsel War Crimes, Nuernberg, Germany, 1946-49, dir. spl. projects div., 1947-49; atty. Bur. Reclamation, Denver, 1950-52; atty.-adviser office solicitor Dept. Interior, 1952-58, procurement counsel, 1958-59, chmn. bd. contract appeals, 1959-64; chmn. bd. contract appeals AEC, Washington, 1964-74; individual practice, Washington, 1974-76. Mem. D.C. Civil War Centennial Commn., 1962-65. Served with inf. AUS, 1942-43. Mem. Am., Fed. (past pres.), Va. bar assns., United League Lawyers (pres. U.S. sect.), Nat. Lawyers Club (past dir.), Am. Legion (past post comdr.), D.C. Lincoln Group (past pres.), The Westerners (past sheriff). Author: The Case of Alfred Packer, the Man-Eater, 1952; (with Irvin M. Gottlieb) Uncle Sam as a Landlord Under the Federal Tort Act, 1967; Decisions Relating to Condominiums, 1976. Home: Towson, Md. Died June 7, 1979; interred New Cathedral Cemetery, Balt.

GANTT, W(ILLIAM) HORSLEY, physician; b. Wingina, Va., Oct. 24, 1892; s. Thomas Perkins and Ann Maria Perkins (Horsley) G.; B.S., U. of North Carolina, 1917; M.D., U. of Virginia, 1920; student U. of London, 1924; m. Mary G. Richardson, June 23, 1934 (dec. 1964); children—William Andrew Horsley, Emily Perkins (Mrs. Leo Kahn); m. 2d, Rebecca Esler, Aug. 8, 1965. Interned in Balt., 1920-22; medical chief, Petrograd unit Am. Relief Administration, Russia, 1922-23; conducted research on physiology of brain in laboratories of Prof. Pavlov, Petrograd, Russia, 1925-29; established, and since connected with, Pavlovian Lab., for study neurophysiology and neurotic behavior in animals and human beings, dept. of medicine, Johns Hopkins U., 1929; asso. prof., psychiatry, 1945-58, emeritus; chief Psychophysiol. Labs., VA, from 1958; cons. psychiatrist Veterans' Adminstrn., from 1949; prof. pharmacology, U. Puerto Rico, 1954-55; prof. clin. psychiatry U. Md., 1973-80; adj. prof. U. Louisville, 1976-80. Vice chairman Russian War Relief, Baltimore, Md. Mem. Fgn. Policy Assn. (sec. 1935-44; chmn. 1944-46; exec. bd. since 1945), Baltimore Med. Soc. (chmn. neuropsychiatric sect.; past sec.), Am. Psychopath. Assn. (pres. 1961), Psychosomatic Soc., A.M.A., A.A.A.S., Am. Physiol Soc., Am. Neurol. Assn., Am. Psychiatric Assn., Soc. Biol. Psychiatrists (vice president 1958, president, 1959), Society Pharmacology and Experimental Therapeutics, Pavlovian Society for Research (president 1955-66, mem. exec. com. 1966-80), Internat. Brain Research Orgn., Collegium Internationale Neuro-Psychopharmacologicum, Collegium Internationale Activitatis Nervosae Superioris (pres. 1966-80), Am. Acad. Neurology, Royal Society Medicine, Purkinje Acad. Medicine (hon. mem.), Sigma Xi. Club: 14 W. Hamilton St. Translator, co-author several works, including Conditioned Reflexes and Psychiatry, 1941. Editor: Cortex and Internal Organs, 1947, American Lectures in Objective Psychiatry, 1955. Author: Experimental Basis Neurotic Behavior, 1944; Russian Physiology in the Atomic Age; Adaption and Preventive Psychiatry, 1955; Physiological Psychiatry, 1958; also many research articles. Lasker Award for research in nervous diseases, 1946; Am. Heart Assn. award for research on causes of high blood pressure, 1955. Mem. adv. bd. Medico. Editor-in-chief Pavlovian Jour. of Biol. Psychiatry. Home: Baltimore, Md. Died Feb. 26, 1980; buried Rock Cliff, Nelson County, Va.

GANZI, RICHARD LOUIS, cons. mgmt. engr.; b. N.Y.C., Jan. 24, 1923; s. Louis and Mary (Genarro) G.; B.B.A., Manhattan Coll., 1948; M.B.A., N.Y. U., 1950; m. Kathleen; children—Alicia Ganzi Reich, Denise Irene. Mgr., indsl. engr. Alexander Smith, Inc., Yonkers, N.Y., 1948-53; sr. cons. Paul B. Mulligan & Co., Inc., Scarsdale, N.Y., 1953-57, pres., 1958-78, also dir.; dir. Venetian Constrn. Co., Inc., N.Y.C. Served with USMCR, 1942-45; PTO. Mem. Assn. Cons. Mgmt. Engrs., Nat. Assn. Cost Accountants, Office Execs. Assn., Am. Inst. Indsl. Engrs., Am. Mgmt. Assn., Nat. Office Mgmt. Assn. Author: How to Gain and Maintain Control of Office Costs, 1963. Home: Rye, N.Y. Died Nov. 18, 1978.

GARBER, JOHN ADAM, clergyman, educator; b. nr. Mt. Sidney, Va., May 1, 1884; s. Jacob William and Susan (Ham) G.; B.A., Ashland (O.) Coll., 1908, B.D., 1915; student Bonebrake Theol. Sem., Dayton, O., 1911-15, Sch. of Religious Edn., Northwestern U., summer 1920, Hartford Theol. Sem., 1921-22, 1924, 25; m. Iva Leslie, of Ashland, Sept. 22, 1909; children—Paul Leslie, Joseph Allen (dec.). Ordained ministry Brethren Ch., 1905; pastor successively at Elkhart, Ind., Johnstown, Pa., W. Alexandria, O., until 1915; teacher, Ashland (O.) Coll., 1915-27; became head dept. of religious edn., Lane Theol. Sem., Cincinnati, 1928; became dir. Christian edn. Presbytery of Cincinnati, 1928; prof. of sociology, Presbyn. Sem. of Chicago, since 1931; moderator Gen. Conf. Brethren Ch., also of Ohio Conf. same ch.; pres. Christian Endeavor Union, Brethren Ch.; gen. sec. and edn. supt. Nat. Sunday Sch. Assn., Brethren Ch.; mem. exec. com. Internat. Council of Religious Edn.; gen. sec. Ashland County Council of Religious Edn. Mem. Nat. Religious Edn. Assn., Presbytery of Cincinnati, Pi Gamma Mu. Democrat. Club: Internat. Rotary (Ashland). Author: (booklets) Teacher Training Up-to-Date, 1920; Studies in the Way of Life, 1924. Contbr. to Westminster Leader. Address: Chicago, Ill.

GARBERG, PETER B., lawyer; b. Revillo, S.D., Dec. 25, 1882; s. Gunder Paulson and Gunhild (Paulson) G.; prep. edn., Red Wing (Minn.) Sem.; student U. of Minn., 1905-09; m. Sophia Borgen, June 11, 1910. Admitted to Minn. bar, 1909, and began practice at Minneapolis; state's atty., Adams County, N.D., 1914-20; mem. N.D. State Senate, 1920-23; asst. U.S. dist. atty., N.D. Dist., 1923-29, U.S. dist. atty., 1929-33; returned to pvt. practice as mem. firm Garberg & Johnson. Republican. Lutheran. Mem. Elks, Sons of Norway. Home: Fargo, N.D.

GARBNER, ALFRED RAYMOND, banker; b. Prairie Creek, Ore., Jan. 31, 1884; s. James Perry and Martha Jane (Shaver) G.; grad. Whitman Acad., Walla Walla, Wash., 1905; student Whitman Coll., 1905-06; m. Mabel Kirkland, May 24, 1908; 1 dau., Jean (Mrs. James R. Ritchay). Reporter and news editor Walla Walla (Wash.) Daily Union, 1906-09; editor and co-pub. Kennewick (Wash.) Reporter and Courier-Reporter, 1909-24; sec. to gov., State of Wash., 1925-27; dir. of efficiency State of Wash. (supervising state banks and savings and loan assns.), 1928-30; exec. sec. Wash. Savings & Loan League, 1931; pres. Fed. Home Loan Bank of Chicago since 1932; chmn. bd. trustees Retirement Fund of Fed. Home Loan Bank System. Mem. Sigma Delta Chi. Republican. Clubs: Union League, Executives (Chgo.). Home: Evanston, Ill.

GARCEAU, GEORGE JOSEPH, physician; b. Anoka County, Minn., May 24, 1896; M.D., Northwestern U., 1925; m. Julia Davidson, June 2, 1927; children—Mary Dolores (Mrs. Charles Pickerell), Diana Ruth (Mrs. W.W. Scamman). Intern, Meth. Episcopal Hosp., 1924-25, St. Francis Hosp., Miami Beach, Fla., 1925-26; resident Shriners' Hosp. for Crippled Children, Chgo., 1926-27; mem. attending staff Meth. Episcopal, St. Francis and St. Vincent's hosps.; chief orthopaedic surgeon Ind. Hosps.; chief orthopaedic surgeon and chief resident James Whitcomb Riley Hosp. for Children, 1928-33. Distinguished Service prof. emeritus dept. orthopedic surgery Ind. U. Med. Center. Fellow AMA, Internat. Coll. Surgeons, Internat. Soc. Orthopedic Surgery and Traumatology; mem. Am. Acad. Orthopaedic Surgeons, Clin. Orthopaedic Soc., Am. Orthopaedic Assn. Home: Indianapolis, Ind. Died Dec. 7, 1977.

GARDINER, RAYNOR MONTEITH, lawyer; b. Colorado Springs, Colo., Sept. 19, 1885; s. Charles F. and Daisy (Monteith) G.; B.S., Harvard, 1909, LL.B., 1913; married Alice Cushing Underwood, November 9, 1911 (dec. 1959); 1 daughter, Anne (Mrs. Warren S. Archibald; m. 2d, Mary Howbert, Oct. 22, 1961. Admitted to the Massachusetts bar, 1913; staff Boston Legal Aid Society, 1913-17, general counsel, 1924-64, general counsel emeritus, 1965—; member of staff War Trade Bd., Washington, 1917-19, dir. War Trade Intelligence, 1918-19; practice of law, Boston, 1919-24; mem. board directors William Underwood Co., Watertown, Mass.; president Franklin Company, Lewiston, Me. Member exec. com. Mass. Defenders Com., 1960—; dir. National Legal Aid and Def. Assn., 1948-60. Mem. Am. (treasurer commn. on legal aid 1947-50), Mass., Boston bar associations, Massachusetts (president 1926-27), New England (secretary-treas. 1928-48) golf associations. Clubs: Country (Brookline, Mass.); Yeamans Hall (Charleston, S.C.); Harvard (N.Y.C., Boston); Royal and Ancient Golf (St. Andrews, Scotland); Nantucket Yacht Sankaty Head Golf (Nantucket). Home: Boston.

GARDNER, AUSTIN THAYER, elec. utility exec.; b. Chgo., Oct. 7, 1908; s. George Albert and Charlotte May (Thayer) G.; Ph.B., U. Chgo., 1930; m. Mary N. Miller, Sept. 2d, 1933; children—Diane G. (Mrs. Padgett), George T. With Utilities Power & Light Corp., Chgo., 1930-37, Asso. Electric Co., N.Y., 1937-43; with Delmarva Power & Light Co., Wilmington, Del., 1943-78, pres., dir., 1960-67, pres., chief exec. officer, 1967-69, chmn. bd., pres., chief exec. officer, 1969-73, chmn. bd., 1973-76, dir., 1976-78. Past pres. Health Planning Council. Bd. dirs., past pres. Greater Wilmington Devel. Council; hon. bd. mem., past treas. Del. chpt. A.R.C. Mem. Soc. Gas Lighting, Sigma Alpha Epsilon. Club: Wilmington Country. Home: Wilmington, Del. Died Dec. 22, 1978; buried Silverbrook Cemetery, Wilmington.

GARDNER, FULTON QUINTUS CINCINNATUS, army officer; b. LaFayette Springs, Miss., Nov. 8, 1882; s. Dr. Daniel Matthew and Anetta Ellen (Goolsby) G.; B.S., U.S. Mil. Acad., 1904; student Mass. Inst. Tech., 1910-11; honor grad. Coast Arty. Sch., reg. course, 1910, advanced course, 1911, 1927; grad. Mounted Service Sch., 1907, Army War Coll., 1922, Command and Gen. Staff Sch., 1928; m. Eleanor Haight, Apr. 14, 1917; 1 dau., Shirley (Mrs. Perry H. Eubank). Commd. 2d lt. Arty. Corps, U.S. Army 1904, and advanced through the grades to brig. gen., May 1938 and maj. gen., Oct. 1940; served with F. A. Corps, 1904-07, Coast Arty. Corps, 1907-38; asst. to chief of Coast Arty., 1911-12; in charge Submarine Mine Depot before World War and engaged in installation of submarine nets in U.S. harbors after declaration of war; mem. War Dept. Gen. Staff, 1917-21; with Coast Arty., Panama, 1922-25; mem. Gen. Staff, 8th Corps Area, Ft. Sam Houston, Texas, 1928-32; with Coast Arty., Ft. Kamehamela, 1932-33; chief of staff, Hawaiian Separate Coast Arty. Brig., 1934-35; asst. comdt. Coast Arty. Sch., Ft. Monroe, Va., 1935-37; comdr. Ft. Hancock, N.J., 1937-38; comdr. Provisional Coast Arty. Brig. (anti-aircraft), Ft. Bragg, N.C., 1938 (in charge of establishing civilian observers); command Hawaiian Separate Coast Arty. Brig., 1938-41; command A.A.T.C., Camp Haan, Calif., 1941; comdg. 4th A.A. Command Jan. 1942-May 1944; comdg. Northeastern Sector, E.D.C., May 1944-May 1945; comdg. Hdqrs. and Hdqrs. Detachment, 2d Army, Ft. Jackson, S.C. 1945-46. Retired Nov. 30, 1946. Decorated D.S.M. for service, World War I and World War II. Club: Army and Navy (Washington, D.C.). Address: Summerville, S.C.

GARDNER, GEORGE MILTON, retired, radio and TV mfr.; b. Balt., Mar. 24, 1885; s. Frank Everett and Florence May (Allan) G.; student pub. schs.; m. Viola Johanson, Mar. 24, 1914; children—Grant, Karen (Mrs. Frank S. Righeimer, Jr.), Allan. Sales mgr. Globe Electric Co., Milw., 1918-24; with Wells-Gardner & Co, Chgo., 1924—, v.p. sales, 1924-37, pres., 1937-46, chmn., 1946-59; retired, 1959. Clubs: The Tavern, Boys (Chgo.); Outrigger, Pacific (Honolulu, T.H.). Home: Honolulu.

GARDNER, GEORGE PEABODY, found. exec.; b. Boston, Jan. 28, 1888; s. George Peabody and Esther (Burnett) G.; grad. St. Mark's Sch., Southboro, Mass., 1906; A.B. cum laude, Harvard, 1910; m. Rose Phinney Grosvenor, Jan. 28, 1913; children—Katharine Peabody (Mrs. James V. Coleman), Isabella Stewart (Mrs. Tate), George Peabody, John Lowell, Rose Phinney (Mrs. Philip Cutler), Robert Grosvenor. Sec. Harvard Corp., 1911-14; dir. emeritus Gen. Electric Co.; ret. dir. Am. Tel. & Tel. Co. Trustee Humane Soc. Commonwealth Mass., Mus. Fine Arts, Boston; pres. Isabella Stewart Gardner Mus. Commd. capt. O.R.C., 1917, q.m. USNR, 1918, ensign Naval Aux. Res., 1918. Mem. Phi Beta Kappa. Republican. Episcopalian. Clubs: Somerset, Tavern, Harvard (Boston); Harvard (N.Y.C.). Author: Chiefly the Orient, 1912; Ready About, 1959; Turkish Delight, 1964. Home: Brookline Mass. Died Sept. 17, 1976; interred Burial Park, Southboro, Mass.

GARDNER, JULIA, geologist; b. Chamberlain, S.D., Jan. 26, 1882; d. Charles Henry and Julia (Brackett) G.; A.B., Bryn Mawr (Pa.) Coll., 1905; Ph.D., Johns Hopkins, 1911; unmarried. Asst. in paleontology, Johns Hopkins, 1911-15; paleontologist, U.S. Geol. Survey, 1920-24, asst. geologist, 1924-28, geologist since 1928. Served with Am. Red Cross, France, 1917-19. Mem. A.A.A.S., Washington Acad. Science, Paleontol. Soc., Am. Assn. Petroleum Geologists, Geol. Soc. America, Am. Assn. Univ. Women, Phi Beta Kappa. Episcopalian. Club: Arts. Home: Washington.

GARDNER, MAX WILLIAM, plant pathologist; b. Lansing, Mich., May 11, 1890; s. Frank L. and Frances Eliza (Murray) G.; B.S., Mich. State Coll., 1912; M.S., U. of Wis., 1915, Ph.D., 1918; D.Sc. (hon.), Michigan State College, 1950; married Margaret Briggs, Sept. 6, 1922; children—Mary Frances, Murray Briggs. Research asst. Pa. Chestnut Blight Commn. and U.S. Dept. Agr., 1912-14; instr., U. of Mich., 1917; asst. pathologist U.S. Dept. Agr., 1918-19; asso. botanist, Purdue U. Agr. Expt. Sta., 1919-29, botanist, 1930-32; prof. of plant pathology and plant pathologist of Expt. Sta., U. of Calif., 1932-57. Mem. Nat. Research Council (div. of biology and agr.), A.A.A.S. (council Pacific div.) Am. Phytopathol. Soc., Bot. Soc. Am., Am. Soc. Naturalists, Ind. Acad. Science, Mich. Acad. Science, Sigma Xi. Republican. Club: Faculty (U. of Calif.). Author of experiment station bulletins; contributor to scientific journals. Home: Berkeley, Calif. Died Oct. 31, 1979.

GARDNER, MURRAY FRANK, educator; b. Lansing, Mich., Dec. 17, 1897; s. Frank L. and Frances Eliza (Murray) G.; student Mich. Agrl. Coll., 1916-17; B.S. in E.E., U. of Mich., 1920; M.S., in Elec. Engring., Mass. Inst. Tech., 1924; m. Helen F. Newman, July 6, 1932; 1 dau., Susanne Shepherd. Research asst. Mass. Tech., 1920-21; elec. engr., cable works, Am. Steel & Wire Co., Worcester, Mass., 1921-22; asst. and instr. Mass. Inst. Tech., 1922-29, asst. prof. elec. engring., 1929-37, asso. prof. 1937-44, prof. from 1944. Recipient First Paper Prize, Am. Inst. E.E., 1925. Fellow A.A.A.S., American Inst. E.E.; member Tau Beta Pi, Sigma Xi, Alpha Delta Phi. Author: (with John L. Barnes) Transients in Linear Systems, Vol. 1, 1942. Home: Belmont, Mass. Died Aug. 4, 1979; buried Elgin, Ill.

GARDNER, STEPHEN SYMMES, govt. ofcl.; b. Wakefield, Mass., Dec. 26, 1921; s. George F. and Mildred (Edmands) G.; student Harvard Coll., 1946-47; M.B.A., Harvard, 1949; m. Consuelo Andonegui, May 15, 1943; children—Susan C. (Mrs. Lanfranco Reitlinger), Seth T., Hilary S., Pierce S., S. Symmes.

With Girard Bank, Phila., 1949-74, pres., 1966-71, chmn. bd., 1971-74; dep. sec. Dept. Treasury, Washington, 1974-78; vice chmn. bd. govs. Fed. Res. System; dir. INA Corp., Amstar Corp., Budd Co., Narco Sci. Industries, Millville Mfg. Co. Chmn., Greater Phila. Movement, 1973-74; mem. Mayor's Adv. Com., 1973-74. Bd. dirs. United Fund, Phila. Orch. Assn., Phila. Coll. Art, Phila. Devel. Corp., Penn's Landing Corp., Fairmount Park Art Assn. Served with AUS, 1942-45. Decorated Bronze Star. Mem. Greater Phila. C. of C. (dir.). Clubs: Philadelphia, Harvard of Phila., Rittenhouse, Union League. Home: Wawa, Pa. Died Nov. 1978.

GARMON, WILLIAM F., mfg. co. exec.; b. Kansas City, Mo., May 15, 1922; s. Lee F. and Hope Y. G.; B.S. in Elec. Engring., Kans. State U., 1951; cert. UCLA Grad. Sch. Bus., 1966; m. Marjorie, June 6, 1948; children—Peggy, Ann, Robert. Vice pres. Ditmco, 1954-60; pres. Univ. Sound Co., 1960-70; sr. v.p. ops. ALTEC Corp., Richardson, Tex., 1970-77, pres., Anaheim, Calif., 1977-78, also dir. Served with USCG, 1942-46; ETO. Mem. IEEE, Eta Kappa Nu. Republican. Lutheran. Home: Corona Del Mar, Calif. Died Jan. 21, 1978.

GARNER, CLEMENT LEINSTER, hydrographic and geodetic engr.; b. Bogue, N.C., Sept. 22, 1884; s. Lemuel Allen and Alice Adeline (Bell) G.; B.S. in civil engring., N.C. State Coll., 1907, Eng. Dr., 1940; m. Mary Clark, June 25, 1913; children—Mary Frances, Alice Elizabeth. With U.S. Coast and Geodetic Survey since 1907, chief of survey party, 1913-23, comdr. ship "Discoverer," 1923-27, inspector in charge N.Y. Field Station, 1927-29, asst. chief Div. of Geodesy, 1929-36, chief, 1937-45; spl. assignment on cooperative projects, 1946. Chairman Federal Bd. of Surveys and Maps, 1938-40. U.S. delegate Pan-American Consultations, Caracas, Venezuela, 1946, Buenos Aires, Argentina, 1948. Mem. Wash. Acad. Sciences (president 1944), Am. Geophys. Union, Am. Soc. C.E., Philos. Soc. of Wash., Wash. Soc. Engrs. (pres. 1945), Soc. Am. Mil. Engrs., Am. Soc. Photogrammetry, A.A.A.S., Heroes of '76, Sojourners. Mason (32 deg., Shriner). Club: Cosmos (Washington). Author: Precise Triangulation in Texas, Rio Grande Arc. (Spl. Pub. No. 78), 1922. Geodetic Operations in U.S., 1936-38.*

GARNER, ERROLL (LOUIS), composer, jazz pianist; b. Pitts., June 15, 1923; s. Ernest and Estella Garner; ed. pub. schs. Profl. piano debut, 1930; with radio program ensemble Candy Kids, KDKA, Pitts.; accompanist dance orch., Pitts.; appeared Strand Theatre, N.Y.C., 1946; jazz recs. Columbia Records; now rec. for Octave Record Co., London Records; jazz musician Festival in Paris, 1949; solo recital jazz Music Hall in Cleve., 1950, concert Town Hall, N.Y.C., 1950, Cleve. Symphony, 1957; on tour U.S., 1958-59; Carnegie Hall Concert debut, 1959; tours, soloist maj. symphony orchs.; composer for motion pictures; composer numerous compositions including Misty (title song film Play Misty for Me), Dreamy, Solitaire, Dreamstreet, That's My Kick, Up In Erroll's Room, Gaslight, Mood Island, Feeling Is Believing (best jazz piano album 1970 Internat. Critics Poll of JAZZ and POP mag.), Gemini, Something Happens; main themes for film A New Kind of Love, 1963. Recipient French Prix du Disque for jazz rec., Paris, 1957; award album Concert by the Sea (Brazil), 1957; chosen best pianist Internat. Jazz Critics Poll, Downbeat mag., 1957; Man of Year award Variety Club, Pitts., 1966; album That's My Kick chosen as best piano album Internat. Critics Poll, Jazz and Pop Mag., 1967; key to numerous cities U.S.; others. Mem. A.S.C.A.P. Roman Catholic. Died Jan. 2, 1977.

GARNETT, EDWARD BERNARD, author, editor; b. at Kansas City, Mo., Aug. 8, 1885; son of Edward Prescott and Anna (Garnett) G.; educated public schools; married Esther Clark, October 24, 1921; 1 son, Richard Gordon. Associate editor Lumber Review, Kansas City, 1907; joined staff Kansas City Star, 1907, telegraph editor, 1909-17; traveled in Europe, 1914, 38, 55, 62; contbr. articles, short stories to mags.; dramatic critic Kansas City Star, 1917-24, Sunday editor, 1919-60, advisory editor, 1960—. Past president Native Sons of Kansas City; trustee of Kansas City Museum, Kansas City Art Institute, Starlight Theatre Association, Kansas City. Mem. Sigma Delta Chi. Club: Kansas City Country, Kansas City Press. Author: Life on the Star, 1964. Home: Shawnee Mission, Kan.

GARNSEY, LEON LESLIE, metal products co. exec.; b. Brewster, N.Y., Feb. 16, 1924; s. Leon and Anna M. (O'Hara) G.; student U. So. Calif., 1955; m. Margaret Bradbury, Jan. 17, 1942; 1 dau., Lesley (Mrs. Frederick R. McCarty). With Heat-X, Inc., Brester, N.Y., 1947-53; gen. mgr. Dunham-Bush, Inc., Riverside, Calif., 1953-57, asst. treas., West Hartford, Conn., 1957-64, treas., 1964-77, v.p., 1969-77, sec., dir., 1968-77; dir. Durham-Bush of Can., Ltd., 1968-77. Served with USAAF, 1943-45. Home: Avon, Conn. Died Apr. 16, 1978.

GARRETT, CLYDE L., congressman; b. Gorman, Tex., Dec. 16, 1885; s. William Virgil and Sallie G.; student Rankin's Normal Coll., Gorman, Tex.; m. Sallie Day, of Eastland, Tex., Dec. 19, 1912; children—Carl, Clyde, Mary Katheryne, Virginia Nell, Sarah Elizabeth. Began as sch. teacher, 1907; deputy in offices of tax collector, county clk., and sheriff, 1910-12; county clk., Eastland Co., Tex., 1912-18; county judge Eastland Co., 1928-34; mem. 75th and 76th Congresses (1937-41), 17th Tex. Dist. Mem. West Texas County Judges and Commrs. (pres. 1935); Texas County Judges and Commrs. (pres. 1936). Democrat. Baptist. Mason (32 deg., Shriner). Address: Eastland, Tex.

GARRETT, JOHNSON, former govt. service officer; b. Balt., Oct. 26, 1912; s. Robert and Katharine Barker (Johnson) G.; student Princeton U., 1931-35; m. Margaret Dodge, Aug. 5, 1936. With Safe Deposit & Trust Co., Balt., 1935-41; sta. mgr. Pan Am. World Airways, Damascus, Syria, 1946-48; with Nat. City Bank of N.Y., 1949-60, mgr. Paris br., 1952-60; asst. sec.-gen. for prodn., logistics and infrastructure NATO, Paris, 1960-65; indsl. devel. attaché Am. embassy, Paris, 1966-74; dir. Standing Conf. Atlantic Orgns., 1974-79. Sr. warden Am. Cathedral, Paris. Served from 1st lt. to lt. col. AUS, 1941-45. Clubs: Cercle de l'Union Interalliée, Am. (pres. 1957-59) (Paris); Met. (Washington); Princeton of N.Y. Home: Washington, D.C. Died Jan. 15, 1979.

GARRETT, RAY, JR., lawyer; b. Chgo., Aug. 11, 1920; s. Ray and Mabel May G.; B.A., Yale U., 1941; LL.B., Harvard U., 1949; m. Virginia Hale; children—Nancy Worcester, Susan Dunn, Anne Burfield, Richard H. Teaching fellow Harvard Law Sch., 1949-50; asst. prof. N.Y. U. Sch. Law, 1950-52; admitted to Ill. bar, 1952, U.S. Supreme Ct. bar, 1957; asso. firm Gardner, Carton & Douglas, Chgo., 1952-54, mem. firm, 1958-73, 75-80; dir. div. corporate regulation and other staff positions SEC, Washington, 1954-58, chmn. commn., 1973-75; dir. Lincoln Nat. Corp., Chgo. Title and Trust Co.; vis. lectr. Northwestern Sch. Law, 1961-65; lectr. legal seminars; chmn. adv. com. Corporate Debt Financing Project, Am. Law Inst., 1965-70, cons. Fed. Securities Code Project, 1969-80; vice chmn. public oversight bd. SEC practice sect. Am. Inst. C.P.A.'s, 1978-80. Served to capt. U.S. Army, 1942-46; ETO. Decorated Bronze Star. Mem. Am. Bar Assn. (chmn. sect. corp., banking and bus. law 1965-66), Nat. Assn. Securities Dealers (pub. gov. 1976-79). Clubs: Univ. (Chgo.); Skokie Country (Glencoe, Ill.); Met. (Washington). Home: Winnetka, Ill. Died Feb. 3, 1980; buried Meml. Park, Evanston, Ill.

GARRETT, RUBY DWIGHT, lawyer; b. Alamance County, N.C., July 22, 1882; s. Rev. John Newton and Mary Ellen (Phillips) G.; student Yadkin Coll., 1898-1902; LL.B., Kansas City U., 1908; m. Alma Marie Ahlfeldt, Feb. 9, 1909; children—Ruby, Rachel (Mrs. C. Weber Jr.), Bonnie. Admitted to Mo. bar, 1908, and since practiced in K.C.; mem. Garrett & Rurak, 1925-52, now senior member of Garrett and Weed; assistant prosecuting attorney Kansas City, 1910-11; gen. counsel Kansas City C. of C., 10 yrs., Nat. Aviation Assn., 3 yrs.; mem. at large Kansas City Council, 1931-40. Mem. Council of Boy Scouts of Am.; adv. bd. Salvation Army (chmn. 3 yrs.); past v.p., dir. Kansas City Chamber of Commerce pres. K.C. Social Hygiene Soc., 3 yrs. Trustee Liberty Memorial Association. Served with C.A., and Signal Corps, U.S. Army, 1902-05; capt. signal troops Mo. Nat. Guard, 1909-16, including service on Mexican border; chief signal officer (col.) Rainbow Div., A.E.F., 1917-19; participated Luneville, Baccart and Esperance-Souain sectors, also Champagne; in Champagne-Marne and Aisne-Marne defensives, St. Mihiel, Essey, Pannes and Meuse-Argonne and Sedan offensives; with Army of Occupation, Germany, Nov. 1918-Apr. 1919. Decorated Croix de Guerre with palm (France), Purple Heart (U.S.); Exceptional Civilian Service award, Army, 1959. Member Am. Legion (active as organizer and an incorporator), U.S. Signal Corps Assn., Reserve Officers Assn., Disabled Am. Vets., Vets. Fgn. Wars, Rainbow Div. Vets. Assn., Mo. and American Bar Associations, Phi Delta Phi. Democrat. Unitarian. Mason (32 deg., Shriner). Clubs: Athletic (pres. 2 yrs.), Triangle, Kansas City (Kansas City). Home: Kansas City.

GARRISON, GEORGE NELVIN, educator; b. Walhonding, Ohio, Sept. 11, 1905; s. Frank Orlin and Gladys Adeline (Young) G.; B.S., Denison U., 1927; M.A., Ohio State U., 1929; Ph.D. in Math., Princeton, 1939; m. Mildred Louise Koch, Aug. 25, 1934; 1 dau., Helen Marguerite. Instr. math. Case Inst. Tech., 1929-31; tchr. DeWitt Clinton High Sch., N.Y.C., 1934-47; mem. faculty CCNY, 1937-46, 48-64, prof. math., 1957-64, chmn. dept., 1952-64, prof. emeritus, 1964-79; asso. dir. grad. summer sch., lectr. math. Wesleyan U., Middletown, Conn., 1964-71, lectr. math. emeritus, 1971-79; asst. prof., then asso. prof. math. Lehigh U., 1946-48. Memo Am. Math. Soc., Math. Assn. Am., Phi Beta Kappa, Sigma Xi. Home: Middletown, Conn. Died July 22, 1979.

GARRISON, JOHN DORSEY, lawyer; b. N.Y.C., Aug. 12, 1909; s. Elsiha Ely and Helen (Hotchkiss) G.; grad. Taft Sch., 1927; B.A., Yale, 1931, LL.B., 1934; m. Edith Hooe, Apr. 2, 1932; children—Jean (Mrs. Charles O. Thompson), John Dorsey. Admitted to N.Y. bar, 1936; with firm Lord, Day & Lord, N.Y.C., 1934-80, mem., 1943-80. Dir. Crane Co., 1961-80, Research Corp., 1962-80, Simmons Co., 1975-80. Served to lt. USMCR, 1944-45. Mem. Am., N.Y. bar assns., Assn. Bar City N.Y., Maritime Law Assn., Marine Corps Res. Officers Assn., Wolfshead Soc. Clubs: Anglers of N.Y., Yale, Links (N.Y.C.); Round Hill (Greenwich, Conn.). Home: New York, N.Y. Died Mar. 27, 1980; buried Grove St. Cemetery, New Haven, Conn.

GARRITY, DEVIN ADAIR, editor, publisher; b. S.I., N.Y., Nov. 26, 1905; s. Henry and Cecil (Engleheart) G.; B.S., Princeton, 1928; m. Joan Tucker Holt, Sept. 26, 1936; children—Page, Sheila, Adair, Norah, Devin Adair, Joan. With Farmers Loan & Trust Co., N.Y.C., 1928-31, R.H. Macy Co., N.Y.C., 1931-34; with Devin Adair Co., N.Y.C., 1935-81, v.p., 1937, pres., 1939-81. Bd. govs. Nature Conservancy, Washington, 1955-66, Natural Food Assos. of Tex.; panelist Answers for Ams., Sta. WOR-radio-TV, 1953-56; v.p. Ind. Citizens Research Found., Ardsley, N.Y. Mem. 101st Cav., N.Y. N.G., 1930-42. Mem. Linaean Soc. N.Y. Clubs: Ex-Mems. Squadron A, Dutch Treat, University, Explorers (N.Y.C.); Am. Yacht (Rye). Editor: New Irish Poets, 1948; 44 Irish Short Stories, 1955; The Irish Genius, 1958; Mentor Book of Irish Poetry, 1965; Ecol. Book Club and Veritas Book Club, 1972-81. Home: Rye, N.Y. Died Jan. 6, 1981; buried Albany Rural Cemetery.

GARROU, ALBERT FRANCIS, textile co. exec.; b. Praly, Italy, July 22, 1893; s. John and Marie (Pons) G.; student pub. schs.; m. Louise Victoria Holloway, June 22, 1918 (dec. Nov. 1955); children—Alba Louise (Mrs. J.G. Johnson), Leith Holloway, Jane Gardner (Mrs. Eddie Lane), Mary Frances (Mrs. Parks Sherrill), Louis William, Albert Francis; m. 2d, Hilda Yoder, Nov. 3, 1956. Mgr., Waldensian Hosiery Mills, Valdese, N.C., 1928-48; chmn. bd. dirs. Alba-Waldensian, Inc., 1962-74, dir. emeritus; chmn. bd. dirs. Valdese Mfg. Co., 1956-78; dir. Morganton br. Wachovia Bank & Trust Co., N.A., Colonial Theaters, Valdese Savs. & Loan Co. Trustee Grace Hosp., Morganton, Valdese Gen. Hosp. Served with U.S. Army, 1917-19. Mem. Platform Assn., Newcomen Soc. Presbyn. Mason (Shriner, Jester). Address: Valdese, N.C. Died Nov. 3, 1978; interred Waldensian Presbyn. Cemetery, Valdese.

GARTNER, ARTHUR EDWARD, utility exec.; b. Jersey City, May 10, 1910; s. Edward George and Edith (Tayler) G.; B.C.S. cum laude, N.Y. U., 1935, postgrad. Sch. Bus. Adminstrn., 1940; m. Elise Catherine Behrer, June 15, 1940; children—Arthur Edward, Richard, James, Lynn Ann. Accountant, Standard Oil Co. (N.J.), 1927-43; with Consol. Natural Gas Co., N.Y.C., 1943-75, asst. treas., 1951-56, controller, 1956-72, v.p., 1972-75. Mem. Am. Gas Assn. Club: Economic (N.Y.). Home: Garden City, N.Y. Died Apr. 16, 1978.

GARVEY, DAN E., ex-governor; b. Vicksburg, Miss., June 19, 1886; s. Andrew F. and Johanna (Horrigan) G.; student St. Aloysius Coll., Vicksburg, Miss., 1901; m. Thirza Jeannette Vail, Feb. 20, 1912; children—Dan E., Dorothy (Mrs. C. I. Smith Jr.). Accountant, I.C.R.R., Vicksburg and Greenville, Miss., 1903-09, Ariz. Eastern R.R., Tucson, Globe, Phoenix; S.P. R.R. of Mexico, Tucson, Ariz., 1909-27; accountant, Guadalajara, Mexico, 1927. Councilman City of Tucson, 1930-31, county treas. Pima Co., Ariz., 1935, 36, 37, 38; treas. City of Tucson, 1938, asst. sec. of State, 1939-42, sec. of state, 1942-48, acting gov. May 1948-Jan. 1949, governor State of Ariz., 1948-51; now mgr. Phoenix br. R.F.C. Democrat. Catholic. Elk, W.O.W. K.C. Home: Phoenix.

GARVIN, LUCIUS, ednl. adminstr.; b. Cumberland, R.I., Feb. 2, 1908; s. Lucius Fayette Clark and Sarah Emma (Tomlinson) G.; A.B., Brown U., 1928, A.M., 1929, Ph.D., 1933; m. Evelyn Eaton Walmsley, June 8, 1933; 1 son, Eliot Wayne. Instr. philosophy Ind., U., 1933-35, Oberlin Coll., 1935-38, asst. prof., 1939-46, asso. prof., 1946-48, prof., 1948-52; prof. and head dept. philosophy U. Md., 1952-61; dean Macalester Coll., St. Paul, 1961-65, v.p. acad. affairs, 1965-66, exec. v.p., provost, 1966-71; ret., 1971. Mem. Am. Philos. Assn., Am. Soc. Aesthetics, Phi Beta Kappa, Sigma Phi Sigma. Author: A Modern Introduction to Ethics, 1953; The Free Man in a Free Society, 1959. Contbr. articles to Jour. Philosophy, Analysis, Philosophy and Phenomenological Research, Philos. Rev., Ethics, also contbr. discussions and revs. Home: San Diego, Calif. Died Apr. 10, 1977.

GARWOOD, HARRY CRAWFORD, educator; b. Champaign, Ill., Oct. 8, 1884; s. James Edward and Eva (Ross) G.; A.B., John B. Stetson Univ., 1913, Th.M., Southern Baptist Theol. Sem., 1917; student Peabody Coll., 1924-29-30; Ph.D., Yale, 1934; m. Grace Leona Smith, Sept. 10, 1914. Teacher in public schs., 1903-05; deputy clerk Circuit Court, 1905-06; pastor, Carlyle Av. Baptist Ch., Louisville, Ky., 1915-17, Stanton Memorial Ch., Miami, Fla., 1917-21; prof. religion, John B. Stetson U., since 1921, dean since 1941, acting pres., 1947-48, dean coll. lib. arts, 1950-52, now dean emeritus. Served Chaplains Tng. Sch., Camp Taylor, Louisville, 1918. Mem. Am. Acad. Polit. and Social Scis., So. Bapt. Hist. Society, Assn. So. Bapt. Tchrs. Bible and Religious Edn., Fla. Assn. Colls. Clubs:

Athenian (DeLand, Fla.). Rotary. Home: DeLand, Fla.

GARY, HOWLAND R., rep. govt. contractors; born Washington, D.C., Sept. 1, 1886; s. William Thomas and Lucy (Walker) G.; student George Washington U., 1905-08; married Isabel Scott, Nov. 17, 1915; children—Janet (Mrs. F. Preston), Barbara (Mrs. K. K. Davis), Thomas Scott, Robert Morville. Machinist apprentice, Washington Navy Yard, 1903-07; draftsman, Bur. of Steam Engring., U.S. Navy Dept., 1808-09; engring. asst., Naval Trail Bd., 1909-10; inventor of marine instruments, 1910; owner and mgr. Cummings Ship Instrument Works, Boston, 1911-25, branch mgr., asst. salesmgr., asst. to pres. and vice pres., Autocar Sales & Service Co., 1925-41. Served as lt. comdr., comdr., capt., commodore, U.S. N.R., 1941-46; in charge of ship repair and conversion contracts. Chairman Joint Army-Navy-WSA. Master Repair Contract Board, 1942-46. Awarded Legion of Merit. Formerly member and chairman board selectmen, Town of Wellesley, Mass. Mason. Club: Wellesley (Wellesley Hills, Mass.) Country (past pres.). Home: Wellesley Hills, Mass.

GARY, ROMAIN, author, French diplomat; b. Nice, France, May 21, 1914; student U. Aix-en-Province; Degree in Law, U. Paris; diploma Slavic langs., U. Warsaw; m. Lesley Blanch. Sec., French Embassy, Sofia, 1945-49, Bern, Switzerland, 1949-52; 1st sec., spokesman French delegation to UN, N.Y.C., 1952-55; sec. French Embassy, London, 1955; consul gen. of France, Los Angeles, from 1956. Pilot French Air Force, 1937-40; capt. R.A.F., 1940-46; mem. Lorraine Bombing Squadron of Free French, Abyssinia, Libya, Syria, 1940-43. Decorated Croix de la Liberation, Croix de Guerre, Chevalier Legion of Honor (France). Author: Education Européenne, 1945; Company of Men, 1951; Colors of the Day, 1952; The Roots of Heaven, 1956. Address: Paris, France. Died Dec. 2, 1980.

GASPARD, LEON (GAS'PARD), painter; b. Vitebsk, Russia, 1882; s. Maximov G.; studied art at Nat. Acad. of Russia, Moscow, and Académie Julien, Paris, France; m. Evlyn Adelé, of Paris. Came to U.S., 1916; exhibited in cities of Belgium, Salon d'Artistes Française, Salon d'Autumn, Paris, also in New York, Phila., Chicago, New Orleans; Museum du Luxembourg, Paris, France; Nat. Museum, Toronto, Can., etc. Awarded gold medal, Nat. Acad., Russia; hon. mention, Salon Française. Works on exhbn. Art Inst., Chicago, Rockford (Ill.) Mus., etc. Naturalized citizen of U.S. Club: Salmagundi

GASSAWAY, FRANKLIN DRENNAN, physician; b. San Francisco, Sept. 5, 1918; s. Franklin Eugene and Ruth (Richardson) G.; B.S., U. Md., 1941, M.D., 1944; M.S. in Surgery, U. Pa., 1949; m. Kathleen Goggin, Aug. 4, 1972; children (by previous marriage)—Michael, Jean. Intern S. Balt. Gen. Hosp., 1944-45, resident 1945-46; resident U. Pa. Grad. Sch., 1948-49, Western Pa. Hosp., 1949-52; v.p. Gulf Oil Corp., also pvt. practice surgery, Pitts., 1952-79; sr. surgeon Western Pa. Hosp., 1958-79, mem. med. bd.; clin. asso. prof. U. Pitts. Med. Sch., 1962-79; mem. teaching staff U. Tex. Med. Sch., 1953; spl. research lymphosarcoma intestinal tract; bd. dirs. several corps. Adviser ILO Meeting 1973, Geneva. Trustee Internat. Found.; bd. dirs. Indsl. Health Found. Am., St. Joseph's House, Nat. Royal Aging. Served to lt. USNR, 1946-48; col. Res., 1961. Recipient award of merit Community Chest Allegheny Co., 1954; Certificate Appreciation Physicians Volunteering for Surgery in S. Vietnam. Diplomate Am. Bd. Surgery, Interant. Coll. Surgeons. Fellow Am., Internat. colls. surgeons, Indsl. Med. Assn., Am. Coll. Chest Physicians; mem. Pa., Allegheny Co. med. socs., AMA. Pitts. Surg. Soc., Pitts Acad. Medicine, Acad. Occupational Medicine, World Med. Assn., N.Y. Acad. Scis., Am. Inst. Ultrasound, Am. Coll. Indsl. Medicine, Am. Acad. Indsl. Medicine, Internat. Assn. Overseas Physicians, Royal Soc. Health, Planned Parenthood Assn., Royal Soc. Tropical Medicine (London), Am. Wind Symphony, Phi Delta Chi, Nu Sigma Nu. Clubs: Duquesne, Rolling Rock; Petroleum (Houston); Royal Naval Volunteer Res. (London). Author articles in field. Address: Pittsburgh, Pa. Died Jan. 24, 1979; buried Rector, Pa.

GASSER, WILLIAM DANIEL, educator; b. Rochester, N.Y., Aug. 13, 1913; s. Alfred and Anna (Schmitt) G.; student St. Michael's Coll., Toronto, Ont., Can. 1932-33; B.B.A. cum laude, Niagara U., 1937; m. Catherine Mowie, Sept. 2, 1939; children—William D., Marilyn Ann. Various positions Miller, Franklin, McLeod & Co., C.P.A.'s (merged with Haskins & Sells, Rochester, 1958), Rochester, 1937-47, gen. partner, 1947-57, sr. partner, 1957-58, gen. partner, 1958-60, partner charge Rochester office, 1960-67; asso. prof. Sch. Bus., asst. dir. Extended Service div. Rochester Inst. Tech., 1967-71, prof. accounting, 1971-77; dir. Heany Industries, Scottsville. Bd. examiners Am. Inst. C.P.A.'s, 1965; mem. N.Y. State Bd. C.P.A. Examiners; adv. council Rochester Inst. Tech. Bd. dirs. Monroe County unit Am. Cancer Soc. Recipient Golden Key award Acad. Sacred Heart, 1962; Distinguished Teaching award Rochester Inst. Tech., 1971; named Outstanding Kiwanian of Year, 1962; Boss of Year, Flower City chpt. Nat. Secs. Assn., 1965; William D. Gasser Distinguished Lectureship series established in his honor at Rochester Inst. Tech., 1977, William D. Gasser Library Fund established, 1977. Mem. Am. Inst. C.P.A.'s (council 1955-58), A.I.M. (pres.'s council), Assn. C.P.A. Examiners (treas. 1961-65, v.p. 1965-77), N.Y. (v.p. 1957-58, past dir.), Calif. socs. C.P.A.'s, Am. Accounting Assn., Accountants Club Am., Nat. Assn. Accountants, Niagara U. Alumni Assn., Rochester C. of C., Am. Assn. Hosp. Accountants, Niagara U. Alumni Assn., Rochester C. of C., Am. Assn. Hosp. Accountants, Rochester Soc. Investment Analysts, Delta Mu Delta, Beta Alpha Psi. K.C. (4 deg., Knight of Year, Pope Pious XII Council 1977). Clubs: Kiwanis, University, City (Rochester). Author: Routine Auditing Procedures for Interdepartmental Auditors, Model City, U.S.A. Home: Rochester, N.Y. Died Aug. 21, 1977.

GATELY, JAMES HAYES, mcht.; b. Chgo., Nov. 12, 1882; s. William and Alice (Hayes) G.; student pub. schs., Orr Bus. Coll.; m. Gertrude A. Crane, June 11, 1912; children—John, Dorothy Squyres, Alice Ryan, Rita Kelly. Pres. Peoples Store, Chicago, Ill., 1917-55, chairman, since 1955—, also treasurer. Chairman of the Board of Zoning Appeals, Chgo., 1935-45; pres. Chgo. Park Dist., 1945—. Clubs: South Shore Country, Chicago Athletic (Chgo.). Home: Chicago

GATES, ARTEMUS L., consultant; b. Cedar Rapids, Nov. 3, 1895; s. Marvin J. and Emma (Lamb) G.; A.B., Yale, 1918, M.A., 1942; m. Alice T. Davison, Jan. 3, 1922. Vice pres., later pres. New York Trust Co.; dir. Time, Inc., U.P. R.R. Company, also The Boeing Company, also dir. Safeway Stores, Inc., Middle S. Utilities, Inc.; trustee Mut. Life Ins. Co. Served as asst. sec. of navy for air, 1941, under-sec. of navy, July-Dec. 1945. Trustee, Presbyn. Hosp. Home: Locust Valley, N.Y. Died June 14, 1976; buried Locust Valley.

GATES, EDWARD PERCY, travel adviser; b. Fulton, Kan., June 21, 1886; s. Charles Joseph and Ella (Wickersham) G.; grad. Central High Sch., Washington, D.C., 1904; A.B., George Washington U., 1908, LL.B., 1910; m. Estella Jorgensen, of Chicago, Ill., Jan. 10, 1914; 1 son, Charles Edward. Field sec. Ill. Christian Endeavor Union, 1911-20; gen. sec. Internat. Soc. Christian Endeavor, 1920-31; also sec. World's Christian Endeavor Union; adviser in Am. and foreign travel since Jan. 1, 1931. Chmn. Belmont Sch. Com. Mem. bar of D.C., Delta Sigma Rho, Sigma Phi Epsilon. Baptist. Mason. Home: Belmont, Mass.

GATES, JAMES EDWARD, educator, economist; b. Louisville, Nov. 21, 1908; s. George Demorrier and Ellen Theresa (Bullock) G.; B.S., U. Ky., 1929; postgrad. U. Chgo., 1930-31; Ph.D., U. Va., 1935; m. Mary Ann Chester; children (by previous marriage)—Patricia Lee, Jeffrey Reed. Price investigator NRA, 1933-35; utility rate investigator Fed. Power Commn., 1935-37; prof. econs. and govt. Clemson Agrl. Coll., S.C., 1937-40; asst. prof. marketing Ind. U., 1940-41; economist and materials officer WPB, 1941-45; economist Container Corp. Am., 1945-47; economist Bur. Pub. Adminstrn., U. Va., 1947; prof. econs., dean Coll. Bus. Adminstrn., U. Ga., 1948-62, prof. mgmt., 1962-76, also dir. exec. devel. program; econ. cons. to paperboard and paperboard container fields, 1947-76. Chmn., chief exec. officer Lee House, 1969-76. Mem. creative leadership council Creative Edn. Found. Fellow A.I.M.; mem. Am., So. econ. assns., Acad. Mgmt., So. Inst. Mgmt. (ednl. counselor), Alpha Phi Omega, Beta Gamma Sigma, Omicron Delta Kappa, Delta Sigma Pi, Pi Sigma Alpha, Pi Sigma Epsilon. Democrat. Methodist. Mason, Elk. Clubs: Athens Country, Gridiron. Author: (with R.A. Egger) Municipal Ownership of Electric Undertakings in Virginia, 1937; (with Harold Miller) Personal Adjustment to Business, 1958. Home: Athens, Ga. Died Aug. 4, 1976.

GATES, JAY RAYMOND, coll. pres.; b. Steubenville, Ohio, Feb. 23, 1892; s. James M. and Katherine Elizabeth (Koontz) G.; A.B., Washington and Jefferson Coll., 1913; J.D., Case Western Res. U., 1922; m. Gertrude Slater, June 10, 1914; children—Jayne (Mrs. Homer A. Forsythe), Kathryn (Mrs. William H. Kavanaugh); m. 2d, Gertrude Hollmer, Nov. 20, 1931; 1 son, Jay Hollmer. Admitted to Ohio bar, 1922: practiced in Cleve. until 1937; pres. Dyke Coll. (formerly Dyke and Spencerian Coll.), Cleve., 1935-77. Mem. Nat. Bus. Tchrs. Assn. (past pres.), Ohio Bus. Schs. Assn. (past pres.), Bus. Edn. Research Assos. (trustee), Cleve. C. of C., Cleve. Advt. Club, Order of Coif, Delta Tau Delta, Phi Delta Phi. Rotarian, Mason (32 deg., Shriner). Club: Cleveland Executives. Author: Gates' Ohio Corporation Law, 2d edit., 1932. Asso. editor: Throckmorton's Ohio Code, 1924; Baldwin's Ohio Code Service, 1926; Bates' Ohio Digest, 1926. Home: Lakewood, Ohio. Died Sept. 3, 1977.

GATESON, DANIEL WILMOT (GAT'SON), clergyman; b. Brooklyn, N.Y., July 14, 1884; s. Daniel Thompson and Augusta Virginia (Smith) G.; B.A., Trinity Coll., Conn., 1906; grad. Gen. Theol. Sem., N.Y., 1909; studied Columbia, 1918-20; M.A., Lehigh, 1925; D.D., Hahnemann Med. Coll. and Hospital, 1936; m. Marian Anne Blackstone, July 1, 1912; children—Marianne Augusta (Mrs. James Evans Riely), Constance Blackstone (Mrs. T. E. Murray), Elizabeth Wilmot (Mrs. G. H. Friend, Jr.), Gloria (Mrs. R. S. Neely). Deacon and priest, Protestant Episcopal Ch., 1909; rector St. Paul's Ch., Georgetown, Del., 1909-12; vicar St. Thomas Chapel, N.Y. City, 1912-17; rector Trinity Ch., Williamsport, Pa., 1917-22; dean Pro-Cathedral of the Nativity, Bethlehem, Pa., 1922-31, also chaplain Lehigh U.; rector Church of the Saviour, Philadelphia, since 1931. Member Delta Kappa Epsilon. Club: Union League. Author: The Rector's Brief Case (annually, 1939-53). Atonement as Harmonious Unity, The Life of Devotion, The Seven Godly Virtues (privately printed). Home: Phila.

GATESON, MARJORIE, actress; b. Bklyn., Jan. 17, 1900; d. Daniel T. and Augusta V. (Smith) Gateson; student Packer Collegiate Inst., Bklyn. Conservatory Music. Debut in chorus The Dove of Peace, Damrosch operatta; appeared in The Little Cafe, Her Soldier Boy, Fancy Free, Little Miss Charity, The Rose Girl, Lady Butterfly, The Love Letter, For Goodness Sake, Strange Bedfellows, As Good As New, Sweethearts, Parthy Ann in Showboat; played Mother Barbour in One Man's Family (TV), 1949-52; played Grace Tyrell in Secret Storm (TV); featured in about 100 films. Starred in Kiss and Tell, U.S.O., Italy, 1944-45. Mem. Actors Equity Assn. (council 10 yrs.). Died Apr. 17, 1977.

GATHINGS, EZEKIEL CANDLER, congressman; b. Prairie, Miss., Nov. 10, 1903; s. Melville W. and Virgie Eva (Garner) G.; student U. of Ala., 1923-26; LL.B., U. of Ark., 1929; m. Tolise Kirkpatrick, Apr. 6, 1939; children—Tolise Kirkpatrick, Joseph Royston, II. Admitted to Ark. bar, 1929, and began practice in Helena, Ark.; 76th to 90th congresses from 1st Ark. District. Mem. Ark. Senate, 1934-39. Mem. Phi Alpha Delta, Pi Kappa Alpha, Blue Key. Baptist. Mason (Shriner). Hon. mem. West Memphis Rotary Club. Home: West Memphis, Ark. Died May 2, 1979.

GATHINGS, JAMES ANDERSON, educator; b. Peachland, N.C., Sept. 10, 1900; s. William Daniel and Nora (Rivers) G.; A.B., Furman U., 1925; A.M., Duke, 1930; fellow polit. scis., U. Chgo., 1930-31; Ph.D., N.Y. U., 1937; m. Elizabeth Daniel, Aug. 6, 1931 (dec. Mar. 1962); 1 dau., Elizabeth Jane (Mrs. David S. Snook). Prin. Simpsonville (S.C.) High Sch., 1925-27, supt. schs., 1927-29; asst. prof. polit. sci. Tex. Christian U., 1931-32; faculty Bucknell U., 1932-76, prof. polit. sci., 1946-71, emeritus, 1971-76, chmn. dept. 1947-69; tech. adviser Pa. Unemployment Compensation Bd. Rev., 1938. Recipient Lindbach award inspirational teaching Bucknell U., 1962, Burma-Bucknell Bowl for contbn. to internat. understanding, Bucknell U., 1968. Mem. Am. Polit. Sci. Assn., Am. Soc. Internat. Law, Pa. Polit. Sci. and Pub. Adminstrn. Assn. (pres. 1948-50), Pi Sigma Alpha, Omicron Delta Kappa. Author: International Law and American Treatment of Alien Enemy Property, 1940; A Survey of Governments, 1950. Editor: Politics and The American Businessman, 1960. Home: Lewisburg, Pa. Died Mar. 4, 1976.

GAUD, WILLIAM STEEN, assn. exec.; b. N.Y.C., Aug. 9, 1907; s. William S. and Isabel Cleland (Williams) G.; B.A., Yale, 1929, LL.B., 1931; m. Eleanor Mason Smith, June 1, 1935; 1 dau., Anne Timothy. Instr. Yale Law Sch., 1931-33; practiced law, N.Y.C., 1933-35; asst. corp. counsel, N.Y.C., 1935-41; spl. asst. to sec. war, 1945-46; mem. law firm Carter, Ledyard & Milburn, 1946-61; asst. adminstr. Bur. for Nr. East and S. Asia, AID, Dept. State, 1961-64, dep. adminstr. AID, 1964-66, adminstr., 1966-69; exec. v.p. Internat. Finance Corp., Washington, 1969-74; cons. World Bank Group, 1974-76; nat. chmn. Population Crisis Com., 1976-77. Served from capt. to col. AUS, 1942-45; CBI. Decorated Legion of Merit with oak leaf cluster; Order Brit. Empire. Home: Washington, D.C. Died Dec. 4, 1977; interred, Charleston, S.C.

GAUMNITZ, WALTER HERBERT, rural edn. specialist; b. Rice, Minn., Oct. 10, 1891; s. Frederick Oscar and Louise (Meisner) G.; B.S., U. Minn., 1921, M.A., 1924; Ph.D., George Washington U., 1935; spl. diploma, Columbia, 1924-25; m. Agnes M. Cooper, Apr. 4, 1920; children—Gordon Arthur, Jean (Mrs. Robert H. Gruber), Walter Glen. Tchr., prin. Ottertail County, Minn., 1914-16; supt. schs., Lake Wilson, Minn., 1916-18; instr. U. Minn., 1920-22, high sch. Mpls., 1922-24; head social sci. dept., State Tchrs. Coll. Madison, S.D., 1925-27; specialist, rural high schs., U.S. Office Edn., 1927-31, sr. specialist, rural edn. problems, 1931-45, prin. specialist rural and small high schs. 1945-55; prin. specialist rural school research and statistics, 1956-62, chief edn. research and statistics local schs., 1960-62; lectr. summer schs.; mem. survey staffs and ednl. confs. Served as sgt., U.S. Army, A.E.F. 1918-19. Awarded Purple Heart, Distinguished Service Award U. Minn., 1963. Chief U.S. rep., Internat. Conf on Edn., Geneva, 1939; study guest of German Fed Republic, 1952. Fellow A.A.A.S.; mem. N.E.A., Am Schoolmen's Club, Nat. Com. Coordination in Secondary Edn., D.A.V., Internat. Platform Assn. P Gamma Mu, Phi Delta Kappa. Conglist. Mason. Autho numerous books and ofcl. reports, latest being: Surve of Education in 1200 Rural Counties, 1959; also articles ednl. jours. Home: Washington, D.C. Died Aug. 5, 1979.

GAVAN, PAUL A., army officer; b. Smithfield, Mo., July 18, 1903; B.S., U.S. Mil. Acad., 1928; grad. Arty. Sch., 1934, Army Command and Gen. Staff Coll., 1941, Canadian War Coll., 1949, Nat. War Coll., 1952, also Arty. and Guided Missiles Sch. Command. 2d lt. U.S. Army, 1928, advanced through grades to maj. gen., 1957; battery officer arty. regts., 1928-33; assigned 82d F.A., Ft. Bliss, Tex., then 77th F.A.; asst. to div. chief of staff Am. Div. Solomon Islands Campaign, 1942-44; head Am. team Nationalist 54th Army, 1944-45, Nanking Hdqrs. Command, 1945-46; staff Intelligence Div. G-2, Dept. Army, Washington, 1946-48; head maneuver br. G-3, U.S. Army, Europe, 1949-51; arty. career mgmt. br. Office Mil. Assistance, Dept. Def., 1952-54; sr. adviser V ROK Corps, Korea, 1954-55; arty. comdr. I Corps, U.S. Army Forces Far East, 1955; arty. comdr. 1st Inf. Div., Ft. Riley Kan., 1955-56; asst. chief staff G-1, U.S. Army Europe, 1958-59; comdr. So. Area Command, Europe, 1959-62; comdg. gen. Mil. Dist. Washington, from 1962. Decorated Silver Star, Legion of Merit with 2 oak leaf clusters, Bronze Star medal with oak leaf cluster, Presdl. citation (U.S.); Spl. Breast Order of Yun Hui with ribbon (China); Ulchi medal, Taeguk medal (Korea). Home: Alexandria, Va. Died Feb. 1, 1979.

GAY, LESLIE NEWTON, physician; b. Shamokin, Pa., Nov. 7, 1891; s. Harry Scott and Sarah Jane (Batdorf) G.; Ph.B., Lafayette College, Easton, Pa., 1913, Sc.D. (hon.) 1948; M.D., Johns Hopkins, 1917; married Julia Adele Griffith, June 4, 1919; 1 son, Leslie Newton. Engaged to practice as physician, Balt., from 1917; asso. in medicine, Johns Hopkins University, 1932-45, asst. prof., 1945-48; asso. prof., 1948-58, asso. professor of medicine emeritus, 1958-78; physician to Johns Hopkins Hospital, founder, director asthma and hay fever clinic, 1921; cons. Walter Reed Hosp., Washington, USPHS. Served as 1st. lt. Med. Corps, U.S. Army, World War I. Diplomate A.C.P. Fellow A.C.P.; mem. AMA, AIAS, Am. Soc. Immunology, Am. Acad. Allergy (mem. advisory com.; pres. predecessor orgn. Soc. for Study of Asthma and Allied Diseases, 1930), So. Med. Soc., Delta Kappa Epsilon, Nu Sigma Nu, Phi Beta Kappa. Clubs: Maryland, Elkridge (Balt.); Gibson Island (Md.). Author: The Diagnosis and Treatment of Brochail Asthma, 1946. Developed dramamine, universal motion sickness medicine. Home: Roland Park, Md. Died May 1, 1978; buried Balt.

GAY, THOMAS BENJAMIN, lawyer; b. Richmond, Va., May 22, 1885; s. Thomas Bolling and Mary Radcliffe (Ellett) G.; law student U. Va., 1904-06; m. Lenore Temple Skeen, June 10, 1916; 1 son, Thomas Benjamin; m. 2d, Mary Stuart Pattison, Nov. 25, 1921. Admitted to Va. bar, 1906, began practice in Richmond; mem. Hunton, Williams, Gay & Gibson, 1916—; former counsel So. Ry., State Planters Bank; counsel Scott Protective Com. of Stockholders of C. & O. Ry. which defeated Van Sweringen plan of uniting C. & O. with Nickel Plate, 1924-25; rep. N.Y. Stock Exchange before Congl. coms. which drafted Nat. Securities Exchange Act, 1934. Vice pres. U. Va. Law Sch. Found. Bd. visitors U. Va., 1946-54. Recipient Fellows Am. Bar Found. Fifty-Year award, 1966. Mem. Bar Assn. D.C., Am. (chmn. ho. of dels. 1939-41), Va. (pres. 1946-47), Richmond (pres. 1936-37) bar assns., Assn. Bar City N.Y., Assn. Life Ins. Counsel, U. Va. Law Sch. Assn. (pres. 1944-45), Am. Law Inst., Am. Judicature Soc., Phi Beta Kappa, Raven Soc. Episcopalian. Clubs: Cosmos (Washington); Commonwealth, Country of Va., Deep Run Hunt, Masters of Foxhounds Assn. of America; Farmington Country. Home: Richmond, VA. *

GAYLORD, BRADLEY, investment banker; b. Vienna, Austria, Sept. 19, 1895 (parents U.S. citizens); s. Harvey Russell and Bessie May (Ketcham) G.; grad. William Coll., 1917; m. Katharine Witherbee Francis, Oct. 15, 1925; children—Bradley, Barbara. Vice pres. Vietor Common & Co., Buffalo, 1920-33; partner Laurence M. Marks & Co., N.Y.C., 1933-41; v.p. Madison Fund, Inc., Wilmington, Del., 1945-53, pres., dir., 1953-59, chmn. bd., 1957-59; dir. Atlantic Coast R. R. Co., Canton Co., Balt., Gen. Pub. Utilities Corporation, Houston Oil Co. Served as combat pilot, United States Army, World War I, col. U.S.A.A.F., 1941-45; participated submarine mission to bring Gen. Giraud out of France, 1942; brig. gen. U.S.A.F.R., 1941-53. Decorated D.S.C., Legion Merit with oak leaf cluster; Legion of Honor, Croix de Guerre (France); Comdr. Oussam Alloute (Morocco); Comdr. Isham Ifticar (Tunisia). Home: Niantic, Conn. Died Mar. 17, 1981.

GAYLORD, ROBERT MARCH, corp. exec.; b. Mpls., Oct. 11, 1888; s. Edson Starr and Louise (March) G.; B.A., U. Minn., 1911; m. Mildred Ingersoll, Oct. 30, 1915 (dec.); children—Robert March, Clayton Russell, Edson Ingersoll, Helen (Mrs. David G. Townsend); m. 2d, Elma Morlan Birch, May 18, 1949 (dec.). With Mpls. Steel & Machinery Co., 1911-12, Emerson Brantingham Co., Rockford, 1912-14; v.p. Gray tractor Co., Mpls., 1914-17; v.p. Ingersoll Milling Machine Co., Rockford, 1917-28, pres., 1928-58, chmn. bd., 1958-68, chmn. exec. com., from 1968. Trustee Ducks Unltd. Found., N. Am. Wildlife Found. Mem. Machinery and Allied Products Inst. (v.p. 1937-44), Ill. Mfrs. Assn. (pres. 1941), NAM (pres. 1944), Nat. Machine Tool Builders Assn. (pres. 1932), Ducks Unltd. (pres. 1953-54), Rancheros Visitadores, Chi Psi, Republican. Episcopalian. Clubs: Country, Mid-Day (Rockford); Tavern, Univ. (Chgo.): Oglethorpe (Savannah, Ga.). Home: Rockford, Ill. Died Aug. 19, 1980.

GEE, CLARENCE STAFFORD (GE), clergyman; b. Ashtabula, O., Aug. 22, 1884; s. Frank E. and Ida May (Stafford) G.; A.B., Coll. of Wooster (O.), 1910; B.D., Auburn (N.Y.) Theol. Seminary, 1914; D.D., Coll. of Wooster, 1939; m. Kathryn Sebring Anderson, Aug. 3, 1916; 1 son, Thomas Stafford. Editor Hershey (Pa.) Press, 1910-11; ordained minister Presbyn. Ch. in U.S.A., 1914; pastor South Ch., Cleveland, O., 1914-18; asso. pastor Miles Park Ch., Cleveland, 1919-21; teacher of Bible, Western Reserve Acad., and pastor First Congregational Church, Hudson, O., 1921-26; pastor First Presbyterian Church, Delaware, O., 1926-37; pastor First Presbyterian Church, Granville, Ohio, since November 1944; general presbyter Columbus and Marion Presbyteries, Synod of Ohio, and chairman and treasurer General Presbyter Service staff, Synod of Ohio, 1937-47; mem. administrative council, Board of National Missions, N.Y. (1938). Instr. in church organization and adminstrn., summer school, Union Theol. Sem. and Columbia U., 1942. Member Ohio Presbyterian Historical Society (librarian), Society of Mayflower Descendants, (national elder gen., 1940-45; mem. bd. of assts.; dep. gov. gen. Nat. Soc., 1945; governor Ohio Society, 1945, 1946; Elder, Ohio Society since 1947), the American Revolution. Pi Gamma Mu, Alpha Tau Omega. Republican. K.P. Contbr. of articles on hist. research to jours. Home: Granville, O.

GEER, WILL, actor; b. Frankfort, Ind., Mar. 9, 1902; Ph.B., U. Chgo., 1924; student Columbia U., 1924; m. Herta Ware (dec.); children—Ellen, Kate, Tad, Raleigh. Stage debut with Sothern-Marlowe Shakespearean Repertory Co., 1920; appeared with numerous repertory cos.; made Broadway debut in the Merry Wives of Windsor, 1928; stage appearances include Bury the Dead, Waiting for Lefty, Sing Out the News, Tobacco Road, An Evening's Frost, Horseman Pass By, Scratch, Will Geer's Americana; movie appearances include The Misleading Lady, 1932, Deep Waters, 1948, Broken Arrow, 1950, Winchester '73, 1950, Tall Target, 1951, Salt of the Earth, 1953, Advise and Consent, 1961, Seconds, 1966, In Cold Blood, 1967, Brandol, 1968, The Reivers, 1969, Brother John, 1970, Napoleon and Samantha, 1972, Jeremiah Johnson, 1972, The Blue Bird, 1976. Moving Violation, 1976; TV series The Young Rebels, 1970-71, The Waltons; TV movies include The Brotherhood of the Bell, Who Killed the Mysterious Mr. Foster, 1971, Hurricane, 1974, The Night that Panicked/Law and Order, 1976; numerous guest appearances TV series Love, American Style, The Bold Ones, Hawaii Five-O, Cade's Country, Gunsmoke, Bonanza, Mission: Impossible, Name of the Game. Co-recipient Lola D'Annunzio award, 1966; recipient Emmy award as best supporting actor in drama series for the Waltons, 1975. Mem. Actors Equity Assn., AFTRA, Screen Actors Guild. Narrator record Woody's Story, 1973. Died Apr. 22, 1978.

GEER, WILLIAM DRENNAN, publisher; b. Galion, O., Oct. 8, 1905; s. William John and Edith Kathryn (Drennan) G.; A.B., Yale University 1929; married Mary Geraldine Sidnell, July 3, 1930; children—Ann, William Drennan, Jill, Jeremy Jane, Thomas Sidnell. Editorial writer, Time, 1929-30; with circulation promotion dept., 1930-32; circulation promotion mgr., 1932-34; editor, March of Time, radio program, 1934-36, mng. editor, March of Time, monthly movie, 1937; promotion mgr., Time, Incorporated, 1939-41; assistant to president, 1939-42; gen. mgr., Fortune, 1942; asst. v.p., Time, Inc., from 1942; pub. Fortune, 1943-48; asso. pub. Life since 1949. Presbyn. Club: University (New York). Home: New York, N.Y. Died Aug. 20, 1976.

GEFFEN, MAXWELL MYLES, editor, publisher; b. Bklyn., May 31, 1896; s. Abraham D. and Anna (Levit) G.; Litt.B., Columbia, 1916; m. Pauline Felix, 1916; children—Roger, Joan; m. 2d, Helen Catherine Dowling, 1936; 1 dau., Melinda; m. 3d, Florence Kallander, 1951; 1 son, Peter. Reporter, N.Y. American, 1916; pres. Select Printing Co., 1919-42; pub. N.Y. Med. Week, 1922-41, This Week in N.Y., 1930-40, Med. World News, 1960-68; pub. Family Media, including Family Health Mag., 1001 Decorating Ideas, 1969-80, now chmn. bd.; pub., editor Omnibook, Book-Mag., 1938-57; chmn. bd. Arrow Press, Inc., 1957-63; chmn. bd. David McKay Pub. Co., Morgan-Grampian, Inc., N.Y., 1970-78, Travel Illustrated, 1979-80. Clubs: Sky, Hemisphere. Deepdale Golf (Manhasset, N.Y.); Mayacoo Lakes Country (West Palm Beach, Fla.). Editor: Treasury of Modern Best Sellers (with Victor W. Knauth), 1944. Died Oct. 11, 1980.

GEHLE, FREDERICK W. (GA'LE), public relations; b. London, Apr. 9, 1886; s. Henry D. and Anna Sabina (Bauer) G.; unmarried; student New York U., 1905-06. Reporter N.Y. Evening Post, 1906-12, asst. financial editor, 1912-16; publicity dir. and author monthly econ. review, Mechanics and Metals Nat. Bank, N.Y. City, 1916-22, v.p., 1922-26; vice pres. Chase Nat. Bank, N.Y. City, 1926-50; dir. Union Labor Life Insurance Company. Executive Co. Exec. director Greater New York Fund, 1949-52. Past v.p. Allied War Relief, 1940; nat. v. chmn. commerce and industry div., chmn. labor div. of Brit. War Relief Soc., Incorporated, 1941-43. Executive director and state chairman N.Y. War Finance Com, 1944-45 (heading campaigns that yielded 26 billion dollars in war bond sales). Dir. Greek War Relief Assn.; treas. Friends of Luxembourg, Austrian Relief, Belgium War Relief Soc. Awarded U.S. Treasury citation, Award of Merit, Veterans Foreign Wars, 1951. Decorated Officer The Crown (Belgium), Comdr. The Crown (Luxembourg). Comdr. Order White Rose (Finland), Comdr. Order of British Empire. Clubs: Metropolitan, Economic, Silurians, Pilgrims, N.Y. Athletic, Nat. Republican. (New York). Episcopalian. Author: Steps to Victory, 1917; The World's War Debt, 1918; The World Tomorrow, 1919; Our Dubbledam Journey, 1941. Home: N.Y.C.

GEHRES, LESLIE E., naval officer; b. Newark, N.Y., Sept. 23, 1898; s. Charles Peter and Phebe Ann (Thomas) G.; student U.S. Naval Acad., 1918; naval aviator, Naval Aviation Sch., Pensacola, Fla., 1927; m. Rhoda Elizabeth Cooley, June 16, 1923; 1 dau., Leslie Virginia. Commd. ensign U.S. Navy, 1918, and advanced through grades to commodore, July 1943; re-appointed, capt. 1944; comdr. Fleet Air Wing Four in Aleutians and North Pacific operations, 1941-44; comdr. U.S.S. Franklin which was nearly destroyed by Japanese, 1945, comdg. officer, U.S. Naval Air Station, San Diego, Calif., 1945-49; retired as rear adm., 1949; dir. pub. and community relations, San Diego (Calif.) Employers Assn., from May 2, 1949; v.p. indsl. relations Westgate-Calif. Corp., San Diego, from 1971. Pres., Calif. Assn. Republican County Chmn. 1967-71; presdl. appointee Am. Battle Monuments Commn., from 1969; chmn. San Diego County Rep. Central Com. and mem. exec. com. Calif. State Rep. Central Com., from 1971; trustee Calif. Maritime Acad., from 1971. Awarded Navy Cross, Legion of Merit (twice), Distinguished Flying Cross, Purple Heart, Victory Medal, Am. Defense Medal with bronze star, Pacific-Asiatic Theatre Medal with 3 bronze stars, North Am. Theatre Medal. Clubs: San Diego, San Diego Country, Princess Anne (Hunt, Va.). Home: 8001 Vista Dr., La Mesa, Calif. San Diego Employers Assn., San Diego, Calif. Home: La Mesa, Calif. Deceased.

GEHRKENS, KARL WILSON (GAR'KENS), music educator, lexicographer; b. Kelleys Island, O., Apr. 19, 1882; s. Henry F. and Elizabeth (Ricker) G.; A.B., Oberlin Coll., 1905, A.M., 1912, also student Oberlin Conservatory of Music; post-grad. work Columbia, winter and spring 1917; Mus.D., Ill. Wesleyan U. and Capital U., 1939; m. Ruth Grey Bedford, Aug. 16, 1905; children—Virginia E., Adeline B. With Oberlin Coll., 1907—, prof. emeritus, 1942—; vis. prof. U. Cal. at Los Angeles, 1944-45. Adviser music curriculum Pepperdine Coll. (Los Angeles), also Roosevelt U. (Chgo.), 1948-51; vis. prof., summers, numerous colls. and univs., 1917-45. Music Edn. Library, Oberlin Coll., renamed Gehrkens Music Edn. Library, 1952. Mem. Music Educators Nat. Conf. (past pres.), Music Tchrs. Nat. Assn. (past pres.). Author: Music Notation and Terminology, 1914; Essentials in Conducting, 1919; An Introduction to School Music Teaching, 1919; Fundamentals of Music, 1924; Handbook of Musical Terms, 1927; Twenty Lessons in Conducting, 1930; Universal Series (14 books for tchrs. and pupils) (with Walter Damrosch and George Gartlan), 1923-36; Music in the Grade Schools, 1934; Music in the Junior High School, 1936; The Teaching and Administration of Music in the High School (with P. W. Dykema), 1941. Editor: School Music, 1928-34; editor mus. terms Webster's New Internat. Dictionary, 2d edit., 1936, Proc. of Music Tchrs. Nat. Assn., 1937-39; editorial asso. Etude—The Music Mag., 1934-55, Music Educators Jour., 1923-56; editorial writer Ednl. Music Mag., 1942-54. Contbr. ednl. publs. Address: Elk Rapids, Mich.

GEIER, ERNEST CONRAD, corp. exec.; b. Ramsen, Schaffhusen, Switzerland, Apr. 26, 1888; s. Arnold and Barbara (Kuebler) G.; student Weaving Sch., Zurich, Switzerland, 1904-06; m. Anna Lee Stapleton, Dec. 23, 1932 (dec.). Came to U.S., 1909. With the Duplan Corp., N.Y. City, from 1909, dir., from 1918, pres., 1937-50, chmn. bd., from 1950. Hon. mem. Am. Assn. Textile Technologists. Mason. Club: Union League. Home: Stamford, Conn. Died Mar. 30, 1976.

GEIGER, JACOB CASSON, pub. health; b. Alexandria, La., Nov. 18, 1885; s. Jacob Valentine and Celine (Hernandez) G.; A.M., Tulane U., 1905, M.D., 1912, D.P.H. (hon.), 1919, D.Sc. (hon.), 1919, 1944, La. State U., 1935; LL.D., Santa Clara U., 1938; A.M., (hon.), Hahnemann Med. Coll., 1939; Litt.D., (hon.), Nat. Acad. Panama, 1943; LL.D. (honorary), University of California, 1963; m. Florence Clay Gourrier, January 19, 1913 (dec. 1918); m. 2d Anne Elsie Morse, 1921; children—James, John, Anita. Asst. dir., later dir. labs. Calif. State Bd. Health, and acting dir. Bur. Communicable Diseases, 1913-16; asst. prof.

dept. hygiene U. Calif., 1913-18; asst. epidemiologist and edpdemiologist U.S.P.H.S., 1916-24, surgeon (res.), 1916-24, sr. surgeon (res.), 1924-36; research fellow medicine Hooper Found. for Med. Research, U. Calif., 1919-22; asso. prof. epidemiology U. Chicago, 1922-27, professorial lectr., 1927-28; asst. commr. health, Chgo., 1924-28, exec. officer, 1927-28; asso. prof. epidemiology Hooper Found. for Med. Research U. Cal., 1928-30, prof., 1930-32; clin. prof. epidemiology med. sch., U. Cal., 1932-39; prof. clin. epidemiology, curricula pub. health U. Cal., 1938-39; clin. prof. pub. health, preventive medicine Stanford, 1940-52; prof. pub. health, preventive medicine College Physicians and Surgeons, San Francisco, 1943-52; clin. professor epidemiology dept. microbiology U. Cal. Med. Sch., San Francisco, 1952—; lectr. pub. health, preventive medicine U. So. Cal., 1940-50; cons. pub. health several corps.; public health cons. Oakland, California, 1955-57; pvt. practice consultant in public health, San Francisco, 1956—. Chief examiner public health for Nat. Bd. Med. Examiners, 1930-52. Lt. col., U.S. Army M.C. Res., 1939-42; dir. Evacuation Hosp. No. 59, A.U.S., San Francisco. Recipient 38 honors and awards from foreign govts. for pub. health work done in or for their countries. Fellow Am. Pub. Health Assn., A.C.P., Pan-American Medical Society (president 1941-44), American International Academy (hon.), Cal. Acad. Scis.; mem. A.M.A. and fgn. state and local med. assns. and sci. socs. including A.A.A.S., Sigma Xi, Delta Omega, Tau Kappa Omega (hon.). Episcopalian. Mason. Club: Faculty (U. Cal.). Author: several handbooks; editor yearbooks; contbr. pub. health jours. Home: San Francisco.

GEIGER-TOREL, HERMAN BERTHOLD, opera dir.; b. Frankfurt am Main, Germany, July 13, 1907; s. Rudolf Emil and Rosy Auguste (Kullmann) G.; student Goethe U., Frankfurt am Main, 1926, Dr. Hoch's Conservatory Music, Frankfurt am Main, 1926; LL.D. (hon.), Prince of Wales Coll., Charlottetown, P.E.I., Can., 1967; m. G. Eleonore Zander, May 11, 1950. Opera in Europe. S. and N. Am., from 1928; gen. dir. Canadian Opera Co., Toronto, from 1959; asso. prof. opera U. Toronto, from 1948; stage dir. TV operas prod. in Toronto, from 1953; guest dir. Stratford, Montreal, Vancouver and Guelph festivals. Bd. govs. Central Hsop., Toronto, Elliot Lake Centre Continuing Edn. Recipient Centennial medal Can., 1967; Nat. Music award U. Alta., 1970; decorated officer Order Can., 1969. Home: Toronto, Ont., Canada. Died Oct. 6, 1976.

GEISMAR, MAXWELL DAVID, writer; b. N.Y.C., Aug. 1, 1909; s. Leon and Mary (Feinberg) G.; B.A., Columbia, 1931, M.A. (Moncrief Proudfit fellow letters), 1932; teaching fellow, Harvard, 1932-33; m. Anne Rosenberg, Sept. 11, 1931; children—Katherine (Mrs. Lovis Seiden), Peter, Elizabeth. Mem. dept. lit. Sarah Lawrence Coll., 1933-47; free-lance writer, historian, critic, lectr., 1945—; contbg. editor The Nation, 1945-50. Guggenheim fellow 1943-44; fellow Boston U. Libraries, 1966-79; recipient award lit. work Nat. Acad. Arts and Letters, 1952. Author: Writers in Crisis, 1942; The Last of the Provincials, 1947; Rebels and Ancestors, 1952; American Moderns, 1958; Henry James and the Jacobites, 1963; Mark Twain: an American Prophet, 1970; Ring Lardner and the Portrait of Folly, 1972. Editor: Thomas Wolfe Portable, 1944; Walt Whitman Reader, 1955; Short Stories of Sherwood Anderson, 1962; Ring Lardner Reader, 1963; Mark Twain and the Three R's, 1973; The Higher Animals: A Mark Twain Bestiary, 1976. Sr. editor Ramparts mag.; founding editor Scanlan's Monthly; adv. editor Chgo. Rev., 1973-79. Contbr. to N.Y. Times Book Rev., Herald Tribune Books, Am. Scholar, Sat. Rev., Yale Rev., Va. Quar., Ency. Brit., Compton's Ency. Address: Harrison, N.Y. Died July 24, 1979.

GEISSMAN, THEODORE ALBERT, educator; b. Chgo., June 17, 1908; s. Theodore Kenneth and Lina (Herold) G.; B.S., U. Wis., 1930; Ph.D., U. Minn., 1937; m. Loraine Skinner, Dec. 31, 1936; children—James Roger, Anne Elizabeth. With Standard Oil Co. (Ind.), 1930-34; postdoctoral research asso. U. Ill., 1937-39; instr. UCLA, 1939-48, prof. chemistry, from 1948; cons. USPHS adv. panels, Walter Reed Army Research Inst. Fulbright research scholar, 1957-58, Guggenheim fellow, 1949-50, 64-65. Mem. Am., Mexican (hon.) chem. socs., Chem. Soc. (London), Phytochem. Soc. N. Am., Soc. Econ. Botany. Author: Principles of Organic Chemistry, 1968; (with D.H.G. Crout) Organic Chemistry of Secondary Plant Metabolism, 1970. Editor: Chemistry of Flavonoid Compounds, 1962. Contbr. articles profl. jours. Patentee in field. Home: Santa Monica, Calif. Died Nov. 13, 1978.

GELLER, BRUCE, writer, producer, dir.; b. N.Y.C., Oct. 13, 1930; s. Abraham N. and Dorothy (Friedlander) G.; B.A., Yale U., 1952; m. Jeannette Marx, Sept. 7, 1953; children—Catherine, Lisa. Author: Man on a White Horse for Kaiser Aluminum Hour, 1956; author books and lyrics for musical Livin' the Life, N.Y.C., 1957, musical comedy All in Love, N.Y.C., 1961-62, London, 1964; author, dir. duPont Show, Shirley Temple Show, Dr. Kildare, Zane Grey Theatre, The Westerner, 1959-62; author screenplay Sail a Crooked Ship, 1962; author, producer Dick Powell Show, 1963, Rawhide, 1964; created TV series, author, producer Mission Impossible, 1965, exec. producer, 1966-73; developer series, author, producer Mannix, 1966, exec. producer, 1967-78; producer film Corky 1972; producer, dir. film Harry In Your Pocket, 1973, Supercops, 1974; exec. producer, developer TV series Bronk, 1975-78; producer, dir. film The Savage Bees, 1976. Recipient Silver Gavel award Am. Bar Assn., 1963, Western Heritage awards (2), 1964 Emmy awards (2), 1966, Golden Globe awards, 1967-71, Image award NAACP, 1967. Died May 21, 1978.

GEMMELL, GEORGE ALBERT (GEM'MEL), educator; b. McCune, Kan., July 29, 1882; s. Archibald James Cochran and Cora Idella (Clay) G.; B.S., Kan. State Teachers Coll., 1917; B.S.A., Kan. State Coll. of Agr. and Applied Sci., 1920, M.S., 1922; Ph.D., Univ. of Mo. (fellowship student), 1930; m. Mary Virginia Smith, June 28, 1905; children—A. Lee, Nena Virginia (Mrs. Robert A. Anderson). Supt. of schs., Crawford Co., Kan., 1907-11; supt. city schs., Arcadia, Kan., 1911-12; sci. teacher, Crawford Co. High Sch., 1912-15, prin., 1915-18; asso. prof. of agr. (home study dept.), Kan. State Coll. of Agr. and Applied Sci., 1918-22, prof. of extension edn. and head, home study dept., since 1922; program dir. and announcer, coll. radio sta., KSAC, 1926-27. Mem. Epsilon Sigma Phi, Phi Delta Kappa, Alpha Pi Zeta, Alpha Kappa Delta, Phi Kappa Phi, Gamma Sigma Delta, Alpha Zeta, Kappa Delta Pi, Tau Kappa Epsilon. Republican. Methodist. Mason. Clubs: Kan. Educator's (pres., 1932-33), Kan. Author's, Am. Quill. Author: County Public Welfare Work in Missouri, 1930. Contbr. numerous articles as lectures on coll. radio sta. Engaged in research for Kan. Acad. of Sci. on the relation of the awn to yield in Kan. wheat, 1933. Home: Manhattan, Kan.

GEPPERT, WILLIAM L., editor and pub.; b. Cincinnati, O., September 18, 1882; s. William and Nettie (Kilmartin) Geppert; student W.Va. U., 1907-10; m. Ruth Henking, of San Diego, Calif., Apr. 5, 1911; children—William Henking, Ruth Dionis. Began as reporter Gallipolis (O.) Daily Journal, 1898; editor in chief Clarksburg (W.Va.) Daily Telegram, 1901-34; now editor and gen. mgr. Cumberland (Md.) News. Admitted to W.Va. bar, 1911. Mem. W.Va. State Council Journalism. Republican. Episcopalian. Clubs: Rotary, Cumberland Country. Contbr. to various newspapers and mags. Home: Cumberland, Md.

GERHARDT, CHARLES H., army officer; b. Lebanon, Tenn., June 6, 1895; s. Charles and Kate (Watkins) G.; B.S., U.S. Mil. Acad., 1917; grad. Cav. Sch., 1922, Advanced Course, Cav. Sch., 1923, Command and Gen. Staff Sch., 1933; m. Nina McCleskey, June 14, 1922; children—Nina, Charles H. Commd. 2d lt., U.S. Army, 1917 and advanced through the grades to maj. gen., June 26, 1942. Decorated Order of Leopold (Belgium); World War medal, St. Mihiel and Meuse-Argonne medals; Silver Star Medal, Bronze Star Medal, American Defense Ribbon, Legion D'Honneur au grade d'officier (France), Croix de Guerre with Palm (France), European Theater of Operations (with 3 campaign stars), Army of Occupation (World War I), Legion of Merit, Victory Medals both World Wars Croix de Guerre with palm (Belgium), Ordem de Merito Militar (Brazil), D.S.M., Grand Officer of Order of Orange Nassau (Netherlands), Ordre de la Couronne with palm (Belgium), battle participation stars for: Normandy, Northern France (D Day Bronze Arrowhead), Rhineland, Central Germany. Died Oct. 9, 1976.

GERHARDT, HARRISON ALAN, corp. exec.; b. Bklyn., Jan. 9, 1909; s. Jacob Herman and Rose (Schneider) G.; B.S., U.S. Mil. Acad., 1932; M.A., Columbia, 1942; grad. Command and Gen. Staff Sch., 1943, Armed Forces Staff Coll., 1947, Nat. War Coll., 1952; m. Eleanor Mason, June 21, 1949. Commd. 2d lt., C.A.C., U.S. Army, 1932, advanced through grades to maj. gen., 1961; assigned C.A. Sch., 1938-39, U.S. Mil. Acad., 1939-43, War Dept. Gen. Staff, 1943; exec. officer Office Asst. Sec. War, 1943-45; U.S. sec. Allied Control Council, Berlin, 1945-48; assigned Dept. Army Gen. Staff, 1948-49; spl. asst. to U.S. High Commr., Germany, 1949-51; div. dir. Dept. Def., 1952-54; comdg. officer 19th ARAD Group, 1954-55; faculty Nat. War Coll., 1955-56; comdg. gen. 31st Arty. Brigade, Tacoma, 1957-58; chief staff I Corps, Korea, 1958-59; dep. chief legislative liaison Dept. Army, 1959-61, chief, 1961-62; comdg. gen. So. European Task Force, Italy, 1962-64, 1st ARAD COM Region, 1964-67; project dir. UN Assn., N.Y.C., 1967-69; pres. Norala, Inc. Mil. adviser Council of Fgn. Ministers, 1947, 49, 50, 54, 3d Gen. Assembly UN, 1948, NATO Ministerial Council, 1952, 53, 54. Decorated D.S.M. with cluster, Order White Lion, Distinguished Mil. Medal Merit (Czechoslovakia); Order Ulchi (Korea); Knight Officer (Italy); hon. citizen Wash. State. Mem. Smithsonian Instn., Royal Arcanum, Am. Acad. Polit. Sci. Assn. U.S. Army, West Point Soc., Council Fgn. Relations, Washington Inst. Fgn. Affairs, UN Assn. U.S.A. (dir.). Club: Army and Navy (Washington). Home: Westgate, Md. Died Feb. 18, 1980.

GERHART, JOHN K., army officer; b. Saginaw, Mich., Nov. 27, 1907; s. Percy M. and Alice (Koehler) G.; Ph.B., U. Chgo., 1928; grad. (pilot) Air Corps Flying Sch., 1929, Air Corps Tech. Sch., 1931, Air Corps Tactical Sch., 1940, Fighter Comd. Sch., 1943, Harvard Advanced Mgmt., 1948; m. Helen O'Brien, May 20, 1932. Comd. 2d lt., Air Corps, U.S. Army, 1930, and advanced through grades to gen.; served in E.T.O. as group comdr. 95th Bombardment Group (H), operations officer, 3d Bombardment Div., comdg. gen. 93d Combat Wing; Maj. Gen. USAF, spl. asst. Joint chiefs of staff; comdr. of the 12th Air Force, Germany; Lieutenant Gen., USAF, deputy chief of staff, 1957-62; comdr.-in-chief N. Am. Air Def. Command, 1962-81. Decorated Air Medal with 3 clusters, D.F.C., Silver Star with 2 clusters, Legion of Merit, D.S.M., Bronze Star; French Croix de Guerre with palm; Belgian Croix de Guerre with palm. Mem. Alpha Delta Phi. Clubs: Cheyenne Mountain Country, Columbia Country. Home: Colorado Springs, Colo. Died Jan. 9, 1981.

GERIG, BENJAMIN, b. Smithville, Ohio, Jan. 18, 1894; s. Rev. Jacob S. and Mary (Smucker) G.; A.B., Goshen (Ind.) Coll., 1917; A.M., U. of Ill., 1922; D.Sc., U. of Geneva, 1929; m. Mary Blosser, June 14, 1922; children—Carolyn Janet, John Sebastian. Instr. polit. economy, U. of Ill., 1921-23; prof. economics, Simmons Coll., Boston, 1923-28; fellow Post-grad. Inst. Internat. Studies, Geneva, 1928, 29; mem. information sect. League of Nations Secretariat, 1930-40, also attached to League Mandates Section; commissioner general, League of Nations, at N.Y. World's Fair, 1939-40; associate prof. of government. Haverford College, 1940-42; dir. office Dependent Area Affairs, Dept. of State. Deputy rep. U.S. in Trusteeship Council of United Nations. Mem. Am. Polit. Science Assn. Mem. Soc. of Friends. Author: The Open Door and the Mandates System, 1930. Home: Chevy Chase, Md. Died Feb. 26, 1976.

GERLOUGH, DANIEL LAUDER, educator; b. San Diego, May 31, 1916; s. Ludwig Sherman and Margaret E. (Lauder) G.; B.S. in Engring., Calif. Inst. Tech., 1937; M.S. in Elec. Engring., U. Calif., Berkeley, 1948; Ph.D. in Engring., UCLA, 1955; m. Jean Claire Shearer, Aug. 3, 1939; 1 dau., Constance Claire (Mrs. David H. Boyd); 1 foster dau., Liv Johnsen (Mrs. Willard R. Stevens, Jr.). Chief geophys. field party Mott-Smith Corp., Houston, 1937-40; research analyst, methods analyst N.Am. Aviation, Inc., Los Angeles, 1940-42; research engr., quality control engr. Plomb Tool Co., Los Angeles, 1942-44; quality control engr. Pettit Engring. Co., Los Angeles, 1944-45; research engr. Menasco Mfg. Co., Burbank, Calif., 1945-47; mem. faculty UCLA, 1948-59, asso. prof. engring., asso. research engr. Inst. Transp. and Traffic Engring., 1956-59; head traffic systems sect. Thompson Ramo Wooldridge Inc., R-W Div., Canoga Park, Calif., 1959-63; mgr. traffic systems sect. Planning Research Corp., Los Angeles, 1963-67; prof. transp. engring. U. Minn., 1967-77; cons. in field, 1956-77. Mem. Inst. Traffic Engrs., IEEE, Ops. Research Soc. Am., Am. Soc. Engring. Edn., Sigma Xi. Contbr. articles to profl. jours. Patentee in field. Home: St Paul, Minn.; buried Napa, Calif.

GERMANI, GINO, sociologist, educator; b. Rome, Itay, Feb. 4, 1911; s. Louis and Lina (Catalini) G.; student faculty econ. scis., U. Rome, 1930-34; Licenciado in Philosophy, U. Buenos Aires (Argentina), 1943; M.A. (hon.), Harvard, 1965; m. Celia Carpi, Nov. 12, 1954; children—Louis, Anna. Came to U.S., 1966. Research asso. Inst. Sociology, U. Buenos Aires, 1941-45; prof. sociology Colegio Libre de Estudios Superiores, Buenos Aires and Rosario, Argentina, 1946-55; prof. sociology U. Buenos Aires, 1955-65; dir. research Inst. sociology, 1955-65; prof. sociology Harvard, 1966-79; vis. prof. U. Chgo., 1959, U. Cal. at Berkeley, 1961-62, Columbia, 1964-65, U. Montevideo (Uruguay), 1958, 59, 63. Mem. Internat. Social Sci. Council, 1962-67; pres. Asociacion Sociologica Argentina, 1962-66. Mem. Internat. Sociol. Assn. (v.p. 1962-66), Conselo Latino Americano de Censias Sociales (exec. com. 1967-79); fgn. hon. mem. Am. Acad. Arts and Scis., Consiglio Italiano per le Scienze Sociali, 1974-79. Author: Estructura Social de la Argentina, 1955; La Sociologia Cientifica, 1956; Politica y Sociedad, 1962 (Portuguese transl. 1973); Politica e Massa, 1960; La Sociologia en America Latina, 1964; Estudios de Sociologia y Psicologia Social, 1966; Sociologia de la modernizacion, 1969 (Portuguese transl. 1974); Politique et Societe, 1972; Urbanization, Modernization and the Urban Crisis, 1973 (Italian transl. 1974); Autoritarismo, fascismo e classi sociali, 1975. Co-editor: Argentina Sociedad de Masas, 1965; also articles. Home: Rome, Italy. Died 1979.

GERNERT, ROBERT EUGENE, advt. exec.; b. Lancaster, Pa., Sept. 16, 1930; s. Eugene Byron and Fannie Elizabeth (Snyder) G.; B.A., Swarthmore Coll., 1952; M.B.A., Harvard, 1957; m. Joyce Carolyn Powell, June 19, 1954; children—Douglas Powell, Catherine Joy. Account exec. McCann-Erickson, N.Y.C., 1957-62; v.p. Foote, Cone & Belding, 1962-69; sr. v.p. Nat. Student Mktg. Corp., 1969-72; pres. Campus Pac Corp., 1970-72; exec. v.p. Grey Advt., Inc., N.Y.C., 1972-80. Served to lt. (j.g.) USNR, 1952-55. Mem. Pubs. Advt. Club, Am. Soc. Travel Agts., Delta Upsilon. Republican. Presbyterian. Clubs: Harvard Bus. Sch., Univ., Harvard (N.Y.C.); Whippoorwill (Armonk, N.Y.); Sleepy Hollow Country (Scarborough, N.Y.); Wings. Home: Chappaqua, N.Y. Died July 21, 1980.

GEROW, RICHARD OLIVER, bishop; b. Mobile, Ala., May 3, 1885; s. Warren Rosencranz and Annie A. (Skehan) G.; prep. edn., McGill Inst., Mobile; A.B., Mt. St. Mary's Coll., Emmitsburg, Md., 1904, A.M., 1906, LL.D., 1957; S.T.D., North Am. Coll., Rome, 1909. Ordained priest R.C. Ch., 1909; asst. Cathedral, Mobile, vice chancellor and chancellor, 1909-20, rector, 1920-24; bishop of Natchez, 1924-57; bishop of Natchez-Jackson, 1957-66. Home: Jackson, MS.

GERRITY, JOE WARREN, business exec.; b. Prospect, Me., Dec. 14, 1886; s. James F. and Nancy (Killman) G.; A.B., U. Me., 1909; m. Margaret McKee, Jan. 1914; children—Joe Warren, J. Francis II. Dir. Gerrity Co., Orono Corp., Gerrity Co., Inc., Warfran Corp., Workingmen's Co-op. Bank of Boston, Prospect Trust, Commonwealth Land & Trading Co., Marriner & Co.; dir., adv. com. State St. Bank & Trust Co. Dir., trustee Roscoe B. Jackson Meml. Lab., Bar Harbor, Me.; trustee Historic Landmarks, York, Me., Gerrity Found. Clubs: Second, Appalachian Mountain (Boston); Braeburn Country (West Newton, Mass.). Home: Newton, Mass.

GERSCHENKRON, ALEXANDER, economist, educator; b. Russia, Oct. 1, 1904; s. Paul and Sophie (Kardow) G.; Dr. Rerum Politicarum, U. Vienna, 1928; D.Litt. (hon.), Oxford (Eng.) U., 1974; m. Erica Matschnigg, 1928 (dec. 1980); children—Helga-Susanna, Maria-Renate. Came to U.S., 1938, naturalized, 1945. Research asso. Austrian Inst. for Bus. Cycle Research, 1937-38, dept. econs. U. Cal., 1938-42, lectr., 1942-44; staff mem. Bd. Govs. Fed. Res. System, 1944-48, chief fgn. areas sect., from 1946; asso. prof. econs. Harvard, 1948-51, prof., 1951-55, Walter S. Barker prof. econs., from 1955, Frank W. Taussig research prof. econs., 1961-62, dir. econ. history workshop, from 1959. Dir. econ. projects Russian Research Center, 1949-56; Ford research prof. U. Calif., Berkeley, 1958; vis. fellow St. Catherine's Coll., Oxford, Eng., Guggenheim fellow, 1954-55; vis. fellow Inst. for Advanced Study, Princeton, N.J., 1968-69, 71-72. Corr. fellow Brit. Acad.; mem. Royal Swedish Acad. Scis., Am. Statis. Assn., Am. Hist. Assn., Am. Philos. Soc., Am. Econ. Assn. (Distinguished fellow), Econ. History Assn. (pres. 1966-68), Econ. History Soc., Phi Beta Kappa (hon.). Author: Bread and Democracy in Germany, 1943; Economic Relations with the U.S.S.R., 1945; A Dollar Index of Soviet Machinery Output, 1951; Economic Backwardness in Historical Perspective, 1962; Continuity in History and Other Essays, 1968; Europe in the Russian Mirror, 1970; Mercator Gloriosus, 1973; An Economic Spurt that Failed, 1977. Contbr. articles to profl. jours. Home: Cambridge, Mass. Died Oct. 26, 1978.

GERSHAW, FREDERICK WILLIAM, Canadian senator; b. Emerson, Manitoba, Apr. 11, 1883; s. Theodore and Margaret (Clark) G.; M.D. C.M., Manitoba U., 1908; m. Harriet Robinson, June 17, 1912. Elected as Federal mem. for Medicine Hat constituency, 1925, 26, 35, 40; called to Senate of Canada, 1945. Fellow Am. Coll. of Surgeons; mem. Royal College Surgeons, Canadian Med. Assn. Mem. United Church of Can. Mem. Liberal party. Home: Medicine Hat, Alberta, Can. *

GERSHENFELD, LOUIS, bacteriologist; b. Phila., Dec. 25, 1895; s. George and Jennie (Stupe) G.; P.D., Phila. Coll. Pharmacy and Sci., 1915, B.Sc., 1917, Ph.M., 1920, D.Sc., 1940; postgrad. U. Pa., 1919; spl. student Jefferson Med. Coll., U. Pa; m. Bertha Miller, Nov. 17, 1918; children—George, Marvin A. With Phila. Coll. Pharmacy and Sci., from 1917; dir. Gershenfeld Lab., 1919-70, prof. emeritus, dir. emeritus dept. bacteriology, 1968-79, also hon. chmn. faculty council; chemist, bacteriologist Upper Darby Twp. Dept. Health, 1930-66; sci. cons., past sec., mem. bd. govs. Dropsie U.; mem. sterile adv. bd. U.S. Pharmacopoeia XII, XIII, XIV; chmn. bacteriol. and serological com. Pharm. Syllabus; exec. fin. com., v.p. Nat. Biol. Stain Com.; chmn. com. clin. lab. preparations Nat. Formulary VII; mem. com. antisepticity tests, com. ingredients bacteriol. media; biol. products and diagnostic tests com., past chmn. com. bacteriology and immunology Nat. Council Pharm. Research; past chmn. pub. com. Am. Jour. Pharmacy; chmn. pub. com. Biol. Stains. Fellow AAAS, Am. Pub. Health Assn.; mem. Am. Pharm. Assn., Am. Soc. Microbiologists, Am. Acad. Polit. and Social Sci., N.Y. Acad. Sci. Author: Bacteriology and Sanitary Science; Biological Products; The Jew in Science; Urine and Urinalysis; author handbooks, monographs, articles; asso. editor U.S. Dispensatory, XXII, XXIII, Remington's Practice of Pharmacy (9th, 10th edit.); collaborator: Ficarra's Emergency Surgery, Reddish's Antiseptics and Disinfectants; Disinfection, Sterilization and Perservation (Lawrence, Block), others. Home: Philadelphia, Pa. Died Apr. 6, 1979.

GERTH, HANS HEINRICH, educator; b. Kassel, Germany, Apr. 24, 1908; s. Karl Jonas and Anna (Schmidt) G.; Ph.D., U. Frankfurt am Main (Germany), 1933; m. 2d, Nobuko Yabuno, June 27, 1957; children—Anne K. (Mrs. Thomas H. Logan), Julia C., Richard J. Research asst. Kiel (Germany) U., 1932-33; journalist, Berlin, Germany, 1934-37; vis. asst. prof. U. Mich., 1938-39, U. Ill., 1939-40; asst. prof. U. Wis., Madison, 1940-47, professor sociology; vis. prof. U. Frankfurt am Main, U. Tokyo (Japan). Author: (with C. Wright Mills) Character and Social Structure, 1953; (translation with C. Wright Mills) From Max Weber, Essays in Sociology, 2d edit., 1958. Home: Madison, Wis. Died Jan. 4, 1979.

GESCHWIND, IRVING I., scientist, educator; b. N.Y.C., Dec. 20, 1923; s. Morris and Hannah Ruth (Blau) G.; B.S., CCNY, 1945; Ph.D., U. Calif., Berkeley, 1949; m. Maizie Stanley, Aug. 3, 1948; children—Julie Ann, Laurie Jill. Research endocrinologist U. Calif., Berkeley, 1949-60, lectr. anatomy, 1950-54; mem. faculty U. Calif., Davis, 1960-78, prof. animal sci., from 1966, prof. human physiology, 1973-78. Mem. endocrinology study sect. NIH, 1960-64, 67-69, chmn., 1969-71; bd. dirs. Laurentian Hormone Conf., 1972-78. NSF sr. postdoctoral fellow, Copenhagen, 1958-59; Guggenheim fellow, London, 1971-72. Fellow AAAS; mem. Am. Soc. Zoologists, (exec. com.), Endocrine Soc., Soc. Endocrinology (Eng.), Am. Soc. Biol. Chemistry, Biochem. Soc. (Eng.), AAUP (nat. council 1972-75). Editor-in-chief Endocrinology, 1973-78; editorial bd. Gen. and Comparative Endocrinology, Jour. Clin Endocrinology and Metabolism, Biology of Reprodn. Home: Davis, Calif. Died July 11, 1978.

GESSLER, A(LBERT) E(DWARD), chemist; b. Metzingen, Wurtt, Germany, May 8, 1885; s. Edward Albert and Marie Louise (Leuze) G.; B.S., U. of Stuttgart, 1905; Ph.D., U. of Berlin, 1907; m. Mildred B. Murray, Feb. 2, 1915; children—Isolde (Mrs. Craig P. Smith), Albert; married 2d, Helen Yarnall, Mar. 31, 1932; 1 daughter Sally (Mrs. F. G. Appleton). Came to United States, 1908, became naturalized, 1922. Chemist, G. Siegle Co., Rosebank, N.Y., 1908, vice pres. and mem. bd., 1914-18; partner and vice pres. Ultro Chem. Corp., 1918, firm consol. with Zinsser & Co., 1926; chief chemist, mem. bd. and exec. com. Zinsser & Co., 1926-34; dir. research Interchem. Corp., N.Y. City, 1934-44, vice pres. and dir. research, 1944-52, director emeritus of research since 1952; now engaged in private practice as chemical cons. Recipient certificate awarded for effective research in connection with atomic bomb, 1945; certificate awarded for effective service in work on camouflage organized through Nat. Defense Research Council, Mar. 1, 1945; recipient grant for cancer research from Lillia Babbitt Hyde Found., 1944-53; Ault Award, National Assn. Printing Ink Makers. Fellow N.Y. Acad. Sci.; mem. Am. Chem. Soc. (councilor), Am. Assn. Cancer Research, A.A.A.S., Electron Microscope Society, Assn. Research Dirs. Rep. Luth. Club: University (Winter Park, Florida). Contributor of papers to chemical and to medical publications. Holder chemical patents. Full family name—Gessler von Braunegg with hereditary rank of Knight decreed by Emperor Charles VI of Austria, 1726. Address: Sarasota, Fla.

GESTER, GEORGE CLARK (JES'TER), geologist; b. Buffalo, N.Y., June 16, 1884; s. William Burr and Kate Darling (Howell) G.; B.S. in Mining and Geology, U. of Calif., 1909; m. Lillian McCauley, Apr. 24, 1913 (died 1926); children—Thomas Clark (dec.), George Clark, James William; m. 2d, Helen Hill, Apr. 16, 1929. Instr. in mineralogy and Geology, U. of Calif., 1908-09; geologist, S.P. Co., 1909-14; geologist in charge Standard Oil Co. of N.Y. Expdn. to Peru, 1914-16; pvt. geologist engaged in oil and mine examinations, western United States, 1916-17; chief geologist Standard Oil Co. of California, 1917-44, consulting geologist, 1944-49, ret., 1949; present occupation consulting geologist. Fellow A.A.A.S.; mem. Am. Petroleum Inst., Am. Assn. Petroleum Geologists (v.p. 1921; pres. 1927), Geol. Soc. Am., Am. Inst. Mining and Metall. Engrs., Calif. Acad. Science, Sigma Xi, Theta Tau. Republican. Unitarian. Contbr. tech. articles. Address: Berkeley, Calif.

GETTY, JEAN PAUL, business exec.; b. Mpls., Dec. 15, 1892; s. George Franklin and Sarah McPherson (Risher) G.; student U. Cal. at Los Angeles, U. Cal. at Berkeley; grad. in econs. and polit. sci. Oxford (Eng.) U.; LL.D., Ohio No. U., 1966; m. Jeannette Dumont, 1923 (div.); 1 son, George Franklin II (dec.); m. 2d, Allene Ashby, 1926 (div.); m. 3d, Fini Helmie, 1928 (div.); 1 son, Jean Ronald; m. 4th, Ann Rork, 1932 (div.); children—Jean Paul, Gordon Peter; m. 5th, Louise Dudley Lynch, Nov. 14, 1939 (div.); 1 son, Timothy Christopher (dec.). Ind. oil producer, from 1914; pres., gen. mgr. George F. Getty, Inc., 1930-33; dir. Petroleum Corp., 1932-34; dir. Tidewater Asso. Oil Co., 1932-36; pres., gen. mgr. Minnehoma Financial Corp. (formerly Spartan Aircraft Co.), 1942-61, prin. owner, 1942-76; pres. Mission Devel. Co., 1948-67, Mission Corp.; pres., prin. owner Getty Oil Co., 1956-76. Founder, trustee J. Paul Getty Mus., 1953-76. Mem. N.Y., Cal. chambers commerce. Clubs: Explorers (N.Y.); Beach (Santa Monica, Cal.); Los Angeles Athletic; Nouveau Cercle (Paris). Author: History of the Oil Business of George Franklin and J. Paul Getty, 1903-39, 1941; Europe in the 18th Century, 1947; Collector's Choice (with Ethel LeVane), 1956; My Life and Fortunes, 1963; The Joys of Collecting, 1965; How To be Rich, 1966; The Golden Age, 1968; How to be a Successful Executive, 1971. Home: Malibu, Calif. Died June 6, 1976.

GETZ, DONALD ANDREW, broadcasting exec.; b. Chgo., Aug. 16, 1918; s. Andrew James and Claire Anne (Raiser) G.; student North Park Coll., Chgo., 1936-37, Ripon (Wis.) Coll., 1937-40; B.A., Northwestern U., 1940; m. Elaine Wahlstrom, Oct. 24, 1942; children—Carolyn Elaine Getz Tribble, Lawrence Donald. With A.C. Nielsen, 1946-47; research mgr. WGN, Inc., Chgo., 1947-49, sales promotion mgr., 1949-54, sales account exec., 1954-60, Western div. sales mgr., 1960-65, asst. sales mgr., 1965-70, gen. sales mgr., 1970-71; v.p. WGN Continental Broadcasting Co., 1971-80; v.p. WGN Continental Broadcasting Sales Co., 1978-80, also dir. Served to capt. USAAF, 1942-46. Mem. Broadcast Pioneers, Broadcast Advt. Club, Ripon Coll. Alumni Assn. (nat. pres.). Methodist. Clubs: Elks; International; Mid-America; Univ. (Park Ridge). Home: Park Ridge, Ill. Died Feb. 12, 1980; buried Graceland Cemetery, Chgo.

GEWIN, WALTER PETTUS, judge; b. Nanafalia, Ala., Dec. 9, 1908; s. John Walker and Julia (Crenshaw) G.; A.B. cum laude, Birmingham So. Coll., 1930, LL.D., 1973; B.A. in Library Sci., Emory U., 1932; LL.B., U. Ala., 1935, LL.D., 1976; m. Anna Fidelia Sledge, Dec. 5, 1936; children—Walter Pettus, James William, Margaret Juliette. Admitted to Ala. bar, 1935, practiced in Birmingham, 1935, Greensboro, 1936-51, Tuscaloosa, 1951-61; judge U.S. Ct. Appeals, 5th circuit, 1961-77, sr. circuit judge, 1976-81; state pros. Hale County, Ala., 1943-51; mem. Temporary Emergency Ct. of Appeals of U.S., 1977-81. Mem. Code Com. of Ala., 1940. Mem. Ala. Ho. of Reps., 1939-43; mem. Ala. Democratic Exec. Com., 1943-47. Bd. dirs. Ala. Law Sch. Found.; trustee Birmingham-So. Coll. Served with judge adv. gen. dept. AUS, 1944-45. Recipient Dean's award for outstanding service U. Ala. Law Sch., 1972. Mem. Am., Ala. (pres.), Tuscaloosa bar assns., Am. Coll. Trial Lawyers, Am. Law Inst. Presbyn. (elder). Mason (Shriner). Home: Tuscaloosa, Ala. Died May 15, 1981; buried Tuscaloosa.

GEYELIN, PHILIP LAUSSAT, journalist; b. Devon, Pa., Feb. 27, 1923; s. Emile Camille and Cecily (Barnes) G.; grad. Episcopal Acad., Overbrook, Pa., 1940; B.A., Yale, 1944; m. Cecilia Sherman Parker, Jan. 28, 1950; children—Mary Sherman, Emile Camille, Philip Laussat, Cecily Parker. With Washington bur. A.P., 1946-47; mem. staff Wall St. Jour., 1947-66, diplomatic corr., 1960-67; mem. editorial staff Washington Post, 1967-79, editor editorial page, 1968-79. Bd. dirs. Alliance Francaise, Washington, 1964-79; pres. bd. trustees Georgetown Day Sch., 1971-74. Served to 1st lt. USMCR, 1943-46. Fellow Inst. Politics, Harvard Sch. Govt., 1967; recipient Pultizer prize for editorial writing, 1969. Clubs: Gridiron, Metropolitan, Overseas Writers, Federal City (Washington). Author: Lyndon B. Johnson and the World, 1966. Home: Washington, D.C. Died Mar. 23, 1979.

GEYER, BENJAMIN FRANKLIN, pump mfg.; b. Plymouth, Ind., May 7, 1882; s. Ferdinand F. and Augusta (Wollenhaupt) G.; grad. high school; m. Blanche M. Miller, Aug. 24, 1909. Served as asst. advt. mgr. S. F. Bowser & Co., 1907-12; advt. mgr. Wayne Co., 1912-14, sales mgr., 1914-19, gen. mgr., 1919-28, pres. and dir., 1928-48, chairman board 1948-54; dir. Lincoln National Bank and Trust Company; director First Fed. Savings & Loan Assn., Ft. Wayne. Pres. Ft. Wayne Sch. Bd. Mem. Ind. State bd. of commerce. Club: Quest. Home: Ft. Wayne, Ind.

GIANERA, W(ILLIAM) C(HARLES), clergyman; b. Stillwater, Minn., Feb. 12, 1890; s. William and Rachel (Miramonte) G.; student Santa-Clara Coll., 1905-07; A.B., Gonzaga U., Spokane, Wash., 1919, A.M., 1920; theol. studies, Oña, Spain, 1920-24. Entered Society of Jesus, 1907; ordained priest Roman Cath. Ch., 1922; Instr., Gonzaga U., 1925-26; vice pres. U. of Santa Clara, 1926-28, dean of faculties, 1928-45. pres., 1945-51; dean coll. of arts and scis. Loyola U., Los Angeles, from 1951. Died July 3, 1976.

GIBB, JOHN MCGREGOR, JR., prof. chemistry; b. Phila., Feb. 5, 1882; s. John McGregor and Leonora Baker (Walton) G.; B.A., Wesleyan U., Conn., 1904; m. Katherine Candlin, of Tientsin, China, Dec. 27, 1905. Prof. chemistry, Peking U., China, since October 28, 1904. Treas. N. China Tract Soc. Methodist. Mem. Delta Tau Delta. Club: Peking.

GIBBONS, HELEN DAVENPORT (MRS. HERBERT ADAMS GIBBONS), author; b. Phila., Pa., Dec. 2, 1882; d. Clement M. and Emily Eckert (Myers) Brown; Bryn Mawr Coll., 1902-05; Simmons Coll., 1906-07; m. New York, Rev. Herbert Adams Gibbons, June 3, 1908; children—Christine Este, Lloyd Irving, Mimi, Hope Delarue. Mem. bd. mgrs. Student Hostel, Paris; extensive traveler. Founder of French relief orgn., "Sauvons les Bébés." Y.M.C.A. lecturer with A.E.F., 1917-18; corr. Century Mag., Peace Conf., 1919; lecturer Chautauqua Summer Assembly, 1920; in Middle West and Calif. for Near East colleges, 1925; Albert Kahn around the world traveling fellow,

1929-30. Mem. Am. Legion Auxiliary, St. Nazaire Assn.; del. Paris Conv. same, 1927. Hostess, Byrd transoceanic flight crew, in France, 1927. Presbyn. Clubs: Present Day (Princeton); Bryn Mawr, Town Hall (New York); American Women's, Autour du Monde (Paris). Author: The Red Rugs of Tarsus, 1917; Les Turcs ont Passés Là! 1918; A Little Gray Home in France, 1919; Paris Vistas, 1919; Four Little Pilgrims, 1926. Translator: Donnay's Lysistrata, 1919; Chauvelot's Parvati, 1920; Séché's Radiant Story of Jesus, 1927. Contbr. to Century, Harper's, Pictorial Rev., Cosmopolitan, and other mags. Home: Princeton, N.J.

GIBBONS, MYLES F., lawyer; b. Scranton, Pa., Nov. 27, 1910; s. Patrick Francis and Mary Christine (Madden) G.; A.B., Georgetown U., 1932; LL.B. Harvard, 1935; m. Margaret Mack Chandler, Sept. 5, 1942; children—Patrick Chandler, James Henry, Helen. Admitted to N.Y. bar, 1936, Pa. bar, 1939, Ill. bar, 1956; with Root, Clark, Buckner & Ballantine, N.Y.C., 1935-37, Donovan Leisure, Newton & Lumbard, N.Y.C., 1937-38, Comml. Credit Co., N.Y.C., 1938; atty. R.R. Retirement Bd., 1939-42, gen. counsel, 1944-74. Served as lt. USNR, 1942-44. Home: Wilmette, Ill. Died Aug. 2, 1980; buried Calvary Cemetery, Evanston, Ill.

GIBSON, DANIEL PARKE, business cons., author, lectr., pub.; b. Seattle, Oct. 8, 1930; s. Everett Brooks and Emma (Parker) G.; student Coll. City N.Y., 1955. Partner Laws-Gibson Assos., Inc., Phila., 1952-54; advt. rep. Interstate United Newspapers, N.Y.C., 1954-56; advt. rep. Ebony Mag., 1956-57; promotion mgr., 1957-59; promotion dir. Chgo. Daily Defender, 1959; pres. Gibson Assos., N.Y.C., 1960-79; dir. Intramerica Life Ins. Co.; sr. cons. D. Parke Gibson Assos., Inc. Bd. dirs. Interracial Council Bus. Opportunity, 1970-72, United Service Orgns., 1970-72. Served with USAF, 1948-52. Mem. Pub. Relations Soc. Am. Author: The Billion Dollar Negro, 1969; $70 Billion in the Black, America's Black Consumers, 1978; pub.: The Gibson Report, 1960; Race Relations and Industry, 1966. Home: New York, N.Y. Died May 12, 1979.

GIBSON, (WILLIAM) HAMILTON, educator; b. Brooklyn, N.Y., Apr. 1883; s. William Hamilton and Emma Ludlow (Blanchard) G.; prep. edn., Gunnery and Ridge schs.; A.B., Harvard, 1906; m. Brooke van Dyke, of Princeton, N.J., June 1908; children—William Hamilton, Ellen van Dyke, Henry van Dyke, Roger Dana, Edward Brooke. Began teaching at Berkshire Sch., 1907; headmaster Gunnery Sch., Washington, Conn., 1922-37. Mem. Headmasters Assn. Clubs: Century, Harvard (New York). Home: Washington, Conn.

GIBSON, ISAAC HOWARD, realtor and insuror; b. Hendersonville, Tenn., Aug. 19, 1882; s. Andrew J. and Sarah Frances (Coppage) G.; B.A., U. of Nashville, Tenn., 1910; B.S., George Peabody Coll. for Teachers, Nashville, Tenn., 1920; m. Mary J. Bates, Dec. 21, 1910; children—Julia Frances, Andrew Bates, Howard Lea. Principal high schs., 1902-05; teacher mathematics and German, Montgomery Bell Acad., Nashville, Tenn., 1905-16; bus. mgr., Buford Coll. for Girls, Nashville, 1916-17; asst. mgr., Camp Sherman Laundry, Chillicothe, O., 1917-20; realtor and insuror, Nashville, Tenn., since 1920. Dir. Nashville (Tenn.) Real Estate Bd.; pres. Civitan Internat., Birmingham, Ala.; mem. bd. of edn., Nashville, Tenn., 1932-37; pres. Nashville Civitan Club, 1936-37; dist. gov. Tenn. Dist. of Civitan, 1937; chmn. bd. elders, Russell St. Ch. of Christ, Nashville, 1935-41. Mason (32 deg.), Shriner.

GIBSON, JAMES J., psychologist, educator; b. McConnelsville, Ohio, Jan. 27, 1904; s. Thomas Benton and Mary Gertrude (Stanbery) G.; B.S., Princeton, 1925, A.M., 1926, Ph.D., 1928; D.Sc., Edinburgh U. (Scotland), 1973; D.Phil. h.c., Uppsala (Sweden) U., 1976; m. Eleanor Grier Jack, Sept. 17, 1932; children—James Jerome, Jean Grier. Instr. to asso. prof. psychology Smith Coll., 1928-49; research asso. Yale, 1935-36; prof. psychology, Cornell U., Ithaca, N.Y., 1949-72, chmn. dept., 1961-64; vis. prof. U. Calif., Berkeley, 1954-55, M.I.T., 1973, U. Calif., Davis, 1978; vis. scientist Salk Inst., La Jolla, Calif., 1979; sr. Fulbright research scholar U. Oxford, 1955-56; mem. Inst. Advanced Study, 1958-59; fellow Center for Advanced Study in Behavioral Scis., Stanford, Calif., 1963-64; dir. research unit AAF Aviation Psychology Program, 1942-46. Served from capt. to lt. col. USAAF, 1942-46. Recipient Howard Crosby Warren medal, 1952; NIH Career Devel. award, 1964-72. Fellow Am. Psychol. Assn. (Sci. Contbn. award 1961, pres. div. III 1954-55, pres. div. X 1958-59); mem. Soc. Exptl. Psychologists, Soc. for Psychol. Study Social Issues, AAUP, Nat. Acad. Scis., Eastern Psychol. Assn. (pres. 1959-60), Am. Acad. Arts and Scis., Sigma Xi. Author: The Perception of the Visual World, 1950; The Senses Considered as Perceptual Systems, 1966; The Ecological Approach to Visual Perception, 1979. Editor-author: Motion Picture Testing and Research (Aviation Psychology Research Report 7), 1947. Contbr. articles, revs. to profl. jours. Home: Ithaca, N.Y. Died Dec. 11, 1979.

GIBSON, JOHN W., chmn. Displaced Persons Commn.; b. Harrisburg, Ill., Aug. 23, 1910; s. John Joseph and Nellie (Guard) G.; student Wayne U., Detroit, Mich., 1936-37, U. of Mich., 1941-42; m. Jennie Pacotti, May 12, 1934; children—Jennie Lee, John Eugene. Coal miner, 1925-26 and 1928-33; auto worker, 1926-28 and 1933-34; milkman, 1934-37; sec. United Dairy Workers No. 83, sec. Labor's Non-Partisan League, vice pres. Mich. CIO Council, and asst. dir. of CIO for State of Mich., 1937-39; sec. Mich. CIO Council, 1939-41; chmn. dept. labor and industry, State of Mich., also guest instr. U. of Mich., Mich. State Coll. and Wayne U., 1941-43; pres. Mich. CIO Council, 1943-45; special assistant to secretary of labor, 1945-46; assistant secretary of labor, 1946-50; apptd. chmn. Displaced Persons Commission, 1950. Member adv. committee for W.P.B., O.P.A. War Manpower Commn. and Office Civilian Defense, 1943-45; mem. Govt. Tax Study Com., 1943-45; mem. Mich. State Planning Com., 1943-45; mem. Govt. Com. on Adult Workers Edn., 1943-45. Mem. Soc. Professional Safety Engrs., Am. Indsl. Hygiene Soc. Author: Handbook on Workmen's Compensation, 1943; Industrial Safety, 1943. Home: Alexandria, Va. Died Oct. 22, 1976.

GIBSON, JOSEPH VINCENT, lawyer; b. Tunnelton, W.Va., Aug. 25, 1882; s. Milford Cramer and Mary Anna (Jackson) G.; student W.Va. Wesleyan Coll., 1901-04; LL.B., W.Va. Univ., 1912; m. Ethel, LaRue, Feb. 12, 1912; children—Milford LaRue, Nancy Jackson (Mrs. Bradford Price), Margaret Jane (Mrs. Thornton S. McIntire), Joseph Vincent. Admitted to W.Va. bar, 1912, and since practiced at Kingwood; asst. U.S. atty., 1934-38; U.S. atty. for Northern Dist., W.Va., since Feb. 1938. Mem. Am. Bar Assn., Preston Co. Bar Assn., W.Va. Bar Assn., Am. Judicature Soc., U.S. Dist. Atty.'s Assn. (pres. southeastern dist., 1939-40), W.Va. State Bd. of Co. Edn. Soc. (pres. 1936-38), Phi Kappa Psi; hon. mem. Phi Delta Phi. Democrat. Methodist. Mason, Elk. Club: Preston County Country. Address: Kingwood, W.Va.

GIBSON, KASSON STANFORD, assn. exec.; b. Afton, N.Y., Jan. 7, 1890; s. Stanford Jay and Gertrude (Sage) G.; A.B., Cornell U., 1912, Ph.D., 1916; m. Mildred Lovett Brown, July 12, 1917; 1 son, Gilbert Lewis. Instr. physics Cornell U., 1912-16; physicist Nat. Bur. Standards, 1916-55, chief colorimetry and spectrophotometry sect., 1933-41, chief photometry and colorimetry sect., 1941-55; ret. 1955; sec. Optical Soc. Am., Washington, from 1957. Chmn. awards com. Nat. Bur. Standards, 1949-55. Mem. Optical Soc. Am. (pres. 1939-41). Home: Chevy Chase, Md. Died Jan. 5, 1979; interred Norwich, N.Y.

GIBSON, ROBERT MCKENZIE, lawyer; b. Montclair, N.J., Mar. 11, 1916; s. Samuel and Ida (Hornsby) G.; grad. Phillips Acad., 1934; B.A., Yale U., 1938; J.D., Harvard U., 1941; m. Ruth-Elizabeth Hall, July 22, 1950; children—Diana Hall, Samuel Hornsby. Admitted to N.Y. State bar, 1942; pvt. practice law, N.Y.C., 1941-42, Hartford, Conn., 1946-47; atty. United Shoe Machinery Corp., Boston, 1947-53; pvt. law practice Portland, Ore., 1953-55; counsel Sayford Corp., Bklyn. and Litchfield, Conn., 1955-64; atty. Am. Overseas Petroleum Ltd., N.Y.C., 1964-69, Gen. Foods Corp., White Plains, N.Y., 1969-70; v.p., counsel Burger Chef Systems, Inc., Indpls., 1970-72, White Plains, N.Y., 1972-75; corporate counsel Gen. Foods Corp., White Plains, 1975-78. Served to maj. AUS, World War II. Mem. Am. Bar Assn., Assn. Bar City N.Y. Club: Yale (N.Y.C.). Home: Ridgefield, Conn. Died Jan. 26, 1978.

GIBSON, TRUMAN KELLA, life ins. exec.; b. Macon, Ga., Aug. 5, 1882; A.B., Atlanta U.; A.B., Harvard D.Bus. Adminstrn. (hon.), Central State Coll.; L.H.D., Atlanta U.; m. Alberta Dickerson (dec.); children—Truman Kella, Harry H.C., Alberta Marshall. Organizer Fireside Mut. of Ohio, Supreme Life & Casualty of Ohio; now hon. chmn. bd. Supreme Life Ins. Co. Am., Chgo.; ins. cons. Pres. Moton Meml. Found., Gloucester, Va. Recipient Harmon award. Mem. Chgo. Assn. Commerce and Industry, Sigma Pi Phi, Alpha Phi Alpha. Club: City of Chicago. Home: Chgo.

GIDLEY, WILLIAM FRANCIS, coll. prof.; b. Holly, Mich., Nov. 5, 1882; s. Benjamin Franklin and Anna Bailey (Reynolds) G.; Ph.C., U. of Mich., 1908, B.S., 1908; student U. of Mich., 1908-09, summers 1909-11, U. of Chicago, summers, 1912-15, 1917; m. Mamie Winifred Belford, Sept. 7, 1910; children—Anna Dell (Mrs. Wayne Francis Bales), William Francis (deceased), Lois Mildred (Mrs. Gordon Fisher), Willa May (Mrs. William Brydson). Began as drug store clerk, 1900; tutor, U. of Michigan, 1908-09; dean, Mercer University College of Pharmacy, 1909-12; bacteriologist and chemist, City of Macon, Ga., 1910-12; prof. of materia medica, Purdue U., 1912-17; prof. of pharmacy, 1918-24; asst. chief of med. staff E. R. Squibb, New York, 1917-18; dean Coll. Pharmacy, U. of Tex., 1924-47, now prof. Mem. Am. Pharm. Assn., Am. Chem. Soc., A.A.A.S., Tex. Acad. Sci., Kappa Sigma, Phi Delta Chi, Sigma Xi. Awarded Schlotterbeck award, American Pharm. Assn., 1908. Methodist. Mason (Shriner). Club: Kiwanis (Austin, Tex.). Home: Austin, Tex.

GIESECKE, ALBERT ANTHONY (GE'SEK-KE), educator; b. Phila., Nov. 30, 1883; s. Albert and Catherine Elizabeth G.; B.S. in Economics, Central High Sch., Phila., 1902, U. Pa., 1904, LL.D., 1951; Univs. Berlin, Paris and Lausanne, 1905, 1906; Ph.D., Cornell U., 1908; hon. Prof. of Law, U. of Cuzco, 1938; m. Esther Matto, Jan. 19, 1914; children—Esther Catherine, Albert Anthony. Instr. political sci. Cornell U., 1906-08, U. of Pa., 1908-09; prof. commercial geography and economics, Central High Sch., Phila., 1908-09; apptd. spl. expert in commercial edn. for govt. of Peru, 1909; pres. U. of Cuzco, Peru, Feb. 1910-23; dir. gen. of pub. edn., Peru, 1924-30; tech. adviser to minister of education, 1930—; apptd. by President of Peru mem. Peruvian delegation of Plebiscitary Commn. of Tacna-Arica, 1925; collaborated with Kemmerer Financial Commn. to Peru, Jan.-Apr. 1931; spl. asst. to American ambassador to Peru, 1954—. Recipient Distinguished Service Award of Department of State, 1951, award of the America's Foundation, 1964. Mem. staff or of dels. to several inter-Am. confs., 1924—. Supvr. of conservation of ancient ruins at Pachacamac and Cajamarquilla, Peru, 1938. Pres. com. for erection statue of first Inca Emperor Manco Capacc. Mem. profl. assns. and socs., U.S. and S.A.; hon. mem. or corr. mem. several profl. or sci. socs. Latin Am. Discovered remains of prehistoric animals and archaeological remains in Dept. of Cuzco. Clubs: Nacional, Terrazas (both of Lima). Author: Municipal Civics: The Commercial Policy of the U.S. before 1789; also numerous articles. Mem. editorial staff Annals of Am. Acad. Polt. and Social Sciences; editor Guía General del Sur del Peru, also Boletin Comite Proteccion Naturaleza. Address: Lima, Peru.

GIFFEN, ROBERT CARLISLE, naval officer; b. West Chester, Pa., June 29, 1886; s. Major R. E. Giffen and Mary (Musser) G.; grad. U.S. Naval Acad., 1907; m. Elsie Hodgman, March 27, 1909; children—Mary (wife of Comdr. S. S. Miller, U.S. Navy), Lt. Comdr. R. C. Giffen, Jr., U.S. Navy. Entered Navy, June 26, 1903; commissioned Ensign, U.S. Navy, Feb. 1907; advanced through grades to Rear Admiral, 1941. Vice Admiral, 1944; comd. Atlantic Neutrality Patrol, April 1941 to Dec. 7, 1941; comd. Task Force operating with British Home Fleet engaged in covering convoys to Russia; comd. Task Force in U.S. occupation N. Africa, Nov. 1942; comd. Task Force in Pacific participating in actions resulting in occupation of Guadalcanal, Kiska. Attu. Gilbert and Marshall Islands; commandant Tenth Naval District and commander Caribbean Sea Frontier, 1944-45; apptd. comdr. Service Force in Atlantic, July 1945. Twice awarded D.S.M., also holds Navy Cross, Legion of Merit, Order of Suvorov (Russian). Club: New York Yacht Club. Home: Mas Que Farm. Spa Road, Annapolis, Maryland.

GIFFORD, FANNIE STEARNS DAVIS (MRS. AUGUSTUS MCKINSTRY GIFFORD), author; b. Cleveland, O., Mar. 6, 1884; d. William Vail Wilson and Rebecca Frances (Stearns) Davis; A.B., Smith Coll., 1904; m. Augustus McKinstry Gifford, of Pittsfield, Mass., Jan. 24, 1914; 1 dau., Rebecca. Teacher of English, Kemper Sch., Kenosha, Wis., 1906-07. Mem. Poetry Soc. America, N.E. Poetry Club. Author: Myself and I, 1913; Crack o' Dawn, 1915; The Ancient Beautiful Things (verse), 1923. Contbr. prose and poetry to Harper's, Century, Atlantic and other mags. Home: Pittsfield, Mass.

GILBERT, ELIZABETH ANN DINWIDDIE, coll. librarian; b. nr. Berea, Ky., Apr. 15, 1907; d. Joseph C. and Laminia Walker (Armstrong) Gilbert; B.A., Berea Coll., 1930; B.S., Western Res. U., 1938; postgrad. Columbia, Western Res. U. Library supr. circulation Berea Coll., 1930-44, librarian, chmn. dept. library sci., 1944-73, prof. library sci., 1965-73, prof., librarian emeritus, 1973-78. Mem. Ky. Librarian's Certification Bd., 1957-73. Named Outstanding Coll. Librarian, 1966, Ky. col., 1973. Mem. ALA (Ky. rep. coll. and reference libraries div.), Southeastern (Ky. rep. 1966-70), Ky. (pres. 1945-46) library assns., AAUP, AAUW, D.A.R., Kappa Delta Pi, Phi Kappa Phi. Club: Progress. Contbr. to Libraries in the Southeast, 1949; Kentucky, A Pictorial History, 1971. Home: Berea, Ky. Died Oct. 17, 1978.

GILBERT, GUSTAVE MARK, psychologist, educator; b. N.Y.C., Sept. 30, 1911; s. Mark and Ethel (Nierenberg) G.; B.A., Coll. City N.Y., 1932; M.A., Columbia, 1936, Ph.D., 1939; m. Matilda Safran, June 15, 1941; children—Robert, John, Charles. Instr., Conn. Coll. for Women, 1939-40, Bard Coll., 1940-42; prison psychologist Internat. Mil. Tribunal, Nuremberg, Germany, 1945-46; asso. prof. Princeton, 1947-50; chief psychologist VA Hosp., Northport, L.I., 1950-51; asso. prof. Mich. State U., 1951-59; prof. psychology, chmn. dept. L.I. U., Bklyn., 1959-77, pres. univ. faculty senate, 1967-68. Cons. VA, Mich. Dept. Correction, 1952-58; cons., witness Eichmann trial, Jerusalem, 1961; cons. Peace Corps, 1963-70, N.Y.C. Dept. Correction, from 1972. Served with AUS, 1942-45. Mem. Am., Eastern N.Y. State psychol. assns., Inter-Am. Soc. Psychology (pres. 1959-61), Sigma Xi. Author: Nuremberg Dairy

1947; The Psychology of Dictatorship (Bernays award 1950), 1950; personality Dynamics: a Biosocial Approach, 1970. Home: Great Neck, N.Y. Died Feb. 6, 1977.

GILBERT, HENRY BOAS, stock broker; b. Harrisburg, Pa., Jan. 3, 1909; s. Henderson and Sarah Wister (Boas) G.; B.S., Haverford Coll., 1933; certificate in bus. adminstrn. U. Pa. Wharton Extension Sch., 1936; m. Jean Lidgerwood, Apr. 14, 1939 (div. Apr. 13, 1966); children—Lyman D., Irene D.; m. 2d, Elizabeth Leiby, Dec. 26, 1969. With Dauphin Deposit Trust Co., Harrisburg, 1933-74, asst. sec., 1946-54, sec., 1954-74; rep. W.H. Newbold's Son and Co., Harrisburg, from 1974; dir., asst. sec. Penn Harris Hotel Co., to 1975. Treas. Pa. Heart Assn., 1970-72; v.p., dir. Harrisburg chpt. ARC, 1968-73. Served with USNR, 1943-45. Mem. Pa. C. of C. (past treas.), Navy League (treas. Harrisburg council 1966-77), Beta Rho Sigma. Presbyterian (treas. 1970-77). Clubs: Rotary; West Shore Country (Camp Hill, Pa.); Farmington Country (Charlottesville, Va.). Home: Bowmansdale, Pa. Died Dec. 19, 1977.

GILBERT, JACOB H., congressman; b. Bronx, N.Y., June 17, 1920; s. Isidore and Rose (Miller) G.; LL.B., St. John's U., 1943; m. Irma Steuer, June 7, 1949; children—Miriam Sharon, Sandra, Samuel Stephen. Admitted to N.Y. bar, 1944, practiced in N.Y.C.; asst corp. counsel N.Y.C., 1949-50; mem. N.Y. State Assembly, 1951-54, N.Y. State Senate, 1955-60; mem. 86th- 91st congresses 22d Dist. N.Y. State, mem. ways and means com. Mem. South Bronx Community Council; adv. bd. community center Pub. Sch. 65. Mem. Bronx County Bar Assn., Fed. Bar Assn. N.Y., N.J., Conn., Plaintiffs Trial Law Assn., Bronx Bd. Trade, Am. Jewish Congress, A.F.L.-C.I.O., Bronx C. of C. Democrat. Lion, Elk; mem. B'nai B'rith. Home: New York, N.Y. Died Feb. 27, 1981.

GILBERT, LOU, actor; b. Sycamore, Ill., Aug. 1, 1909; s. Morris and Rose (Chosid) Gitlitz; ed. pub. schs., Cleve.; m. Martha Lou Hawkins, May 5, 1951; children—Nicholas David, Frances E. Appeared with Cleve. Play House, 1925, Chgo. Repertory Group, 1933, Arena Theatre, Washington, D.C., 1967-68; Broadway appearances have included Beggars Are Coming to Town, 1944, Dream Girl, 1946, Detective Story, 1948-49, Enemy of the People, 1951, Diary of Ann Frank, 1957-58, The Great White Hope, 1968, The Egg, 1961, In the Counting House, 1962, Frogs of Spring, 1963, Good Woman Setzuwan (at Lincoln Center), 1970; Time of Your Life (on tour), 1971-72, The Price (on Tour), 1973, Community of Two (on tour), 1974; Creation of the World, 1972; appeared off-Broadway in Nourish the Beast, 1973; played in Joe Papp's Shakespearean Festival in The Tempest and King Lear, 1962, Much Ado about Nothing, 1972, As You Like It, 1973; appearances in various motion pictures included Viva Zapata, 1950, Juliet of the Spirits, 1965, Goldstein, 1964, Across the River, 1959, Requiem for a Heavyweight, 1963, Middle of the Night, 1959, The Great White Hope, Petulia, Marathon Man, 1976, Raid on Entebbe, 1976. Recipient Derwent award Actors Equity, 1949, Yale U. Drama award, 1965. Mem. Actors Studio. Died Nov. 6, 1978.

GILBERT, NATHAN, educator; b. N.Y.C., Sept. 27, 1913; s. Solomon Isaac and Goldie (Rabinowitz) G.; B.S. in Chemistry, U. Cal. at Berkeley, 1936; Ph.D. in Phys. Chemistry, U. Wis., 1942; m. Hilda Kessler, June 30, 1940; children—Miriam Anne, David Mark. Lab. asst. Shell Devel. Co., Emeryville, Cal., 1935-39; asso. chemist, project leader TVA, Muscle Shoals, Ala., 1942-53; asso. prof. U. Cin., 1953-59, prof. chem. engring., 1959-77; vis. lectr. NSF Conf., on Systems Engring., 1960; vis. prof. Okla. State U., 1969; cons. Hilton-Davis Chem. Co., Cin., 1959-77, Richardson-Merrell Nat. Labs., 1974-77. OEO Coop. Sr. Vis. fellow Manchester (Eng.) Coll. Sci. and Tech., 1961-62. Mem. Am. Soc. E.E., Am. Inst. Chem. Engrs. (chmn. local sect. 1951-52), Phi Beta Kappa, Sigma Xi, Phi Lambda Upsilon, Alpha Chi Sigma. Mem. B'nai B'rith. Research on oxides of nitrogen, air pollution problems, control theory, optimization; developed Wis. process for nitrogen fixation, 1939-42. Home: Cincinnati, Ohio. Died Jan. 21, 1977; buried Rest Haven Cemetery, Montgomery, Ohio.

GILBERT, WILLIAM PAUL, physicist, educator; b. Centerburg, O., Sept. 18, 1904; s. Frank David and Elbertine Hawkins (Pickering) G.; A.B., Oberlin Coll., 1929; Ph.D., Cornell U., 1935; M.A. (honorary), Lawrence University, 1966; m. Margaret Mary Shea, June 22, 1932; children—Joan Paula, Judith Louise, Margaret Mary. Asst. physics Cornell U., 1929-30, 33-35, research asst. spectroscopy, 1930-33; instr. physics Oberlin Coll., 1935-37; asst. prof. Lawrence Coll., 1937-41, asso. prof., 1941-43, prof. physics, 1943-66, past Sawyer prof. physics; prof. physics Hawaii Loa College, 1966-67; research asst. spectroscopy Inst. Paper Chemistry, Appleton, summers 1941, 46. Ford Found. fellow Harvard, 1952-53; NSF sci. faculty fellow Stanford, 1962-63. Mem. A.A.A.S., Am. Assn. Coll. Physics Tchrs., Wis. Acad. Arts and Scis., Phi Beta Kappa, Sigma Xi, Phi Kappa Phi, Phi Kappa Tau. Home: Forest Grove, Ore. Died May 30, 1978.

GILCHRIST, RALPH TOWNS (GIL'KRIST), physician; b. Oskaloosa, Ia., Mar. 19, 1882; s. William Hamilton and Mary Melinda (Towns) G.; B.S., Penn Coll., Oskaloosa, 1906; M.D., U. Chicago, 1910; m. Anna Elizabeth Eggert, Sept. 19, 1913; children—Jean Mary (Mrs. Frederick Hobe), Ralph Edward. Intern, resident Milwaukee Co. Hosp., 2 1/2 yrs.; indsl. Milwaukee, 5 yrs.; pvt. practice, 1920-24; asst. med. dir. Northwestern Mut. Life Ins. Co., Milw., 1924-52; former attending physician Vets. Bur. Served as maj. M.C., U.S. Army, overseas, World War I; lt. to lt. col. A.U.S. Med. Res. Corps. Diplomate Bd. Life Ins. Medicine. Mem. A.M.A., A.A.A.S., Milw. Acad. Medicine, Med. Soc. Milw. Co., Am. Life Conv. (mem. med. sect.), Alpha Mu Pi Omega. Mason (32 deg.). Address: Milw.

GILCREEST, EDGAR LORRINGTON (GIL'KREST), surgeon; b. Gainesville, Tex., Nov. 29, 1882; s. Jacob Edward and Emma (Looney) G.; A.B., Univ. of Tex., 1906; studied U. of Heidelberg, 1908; M.D., Johns Hopkins Univ., 1910. Served as interne Lakeside Hosp., Cleveland, 2 yrs., under Dr. George Crile, and later surg. service in hosps. at Gratz (Austria), Rome and Bordeaux; with surg. dept., U. of Calif. Med. School, 1920-44. Surgeon with Serbian Red Cross, Turko-Balkan War, 1913; with Am. Red Cross, World War, 1915; surgeon maj. Med. Corps, U.S. Army, with A.E.F., June 1917-July 1919. Mem. Am. Bd. of Surgery (founders group); fellow Am. Coll. Surgeons; past pres. Am. Assn. for Surgery of Trauma (founders group); fellow Am. Med. Assn.; mem. Am. Assn. for History of Medicine, Pacific Coast Surg. Assn. (founders group), Pan-Pacific Surg. Assn. (founders group), Southern Surg. Assn., Western Surg. Assn., Calif. Acad. Medicine, Calif. Med. Association, California Safety Council (dir.), San Francisco Medical Society, Texas Society of California (past pres.), Beta Theta Pi, Phi Chi. Mem. advisory bd. Am. Assn. Occupational Therapy, The Living Age. Democrat. Clubs: Bohemian, Commonwealth of Calif., Olympic. Author of various monographs and biog. studies, also many scientific articles in surg. jours. Contbg. editor Medical Times; mem. editorial bd. Western Journal of Surgery, Obstetrics and Gynecology. Home: San Francisco.

GILES, WARREN CRANDALL, baseball exec.; b. Tiskilwa, Ill., May 28, 1896; s. William Francis and Isabelle (Slattery) G.; student Jubilee Coll., Oak Hill, Ill., 1912-13, Staunton (Va.) Mil. Acad., 1914-16; m. Mabel Jane Skinner, Oct. 29, 1932 (dec. July 1943); 1 son, William Yale. Pres., Rochester (N.Y.) Baseball Club, 1928-36; v.p. Cin. Baseball Club, 1937-47, pres., 1948-77. Pres. Internat. League, 1936; pres. Nat. League Profl. Baseball Clubs, 1951-70, pres. emeritus, 1971-79; mem. Maj. League Exec. Council, 1948-69. Chmn. bd. dirs. Nat. Baseball Hall of Fame, 1971-79. Mem. Am. Legion, D.A.V., Ohio Philos. and Hist. Soc. Republican. Episcopalian. Elk. Clubs: Variety, Cuvier Press, Queen City (Cin.). Home: Cincinnati, Ohio. Died Feb. 7, 1979.

GILKEY, CHARLES WHITNEY (GIL'KE), clergyman; b. Watertown, Mass., July 3, 1882; s. James Henry and Mary Lottie (Johnson) G.; A.B., Harvard, 1903, A.M., 1904; student sec., Internat. Com. Y.M.C.A., 1903-05; B.D., Union Theol. Sem., 1908; univs. of Berlin and Marburg, 1908-09; United Free Ch. Coll., Glasgow, New College, Edinburg, and Oxford University, 1909-10; D.D. from Williams College, 1925, Hillsdale College, 1925, Yale, 1927, Brown, 1928, Harvard, 1929, Colby College, 1930, Oberlin, 1946; L.H.D., Beloit Coll., 1944; m. Geraldine Gunsaulus Brown, July 26, 1915; children—Mary Jane, Langdon Brown. Ordained Bapt. ministry 1910; pastor Hyde Park Ch., Chicago, 1910-28; prof. preaching U. of Chicago Div. Sch., 1926-47; dean of the chapel, Univ. of Chicago, 1928-47; associate dean, Univ. of Chicago Div. School, 1938-47. Lecturer on homiletics, Andover Newton Theol. Sch., since 1948. Univ. preacher at Harvard, Yale, Princeton, Cornell, Chicago, Toronto, Wellesley, Stanford, Purdue, Etc.; interim minister Central Union Ch., Honolulu, 1951-52. Apptd. by U. Chgo. Barrows lectr. to university centres of India, 1924-25. Trustee U. of Chicago, 1919-29, George Williams Coll., since 1929; Union Theol. Sem., since 1945; Harvard Bd. Overseers, 1946-48. Mem. Phi Beta Kappa. Author books. Home: South Yarmouth, Mass.

GILKEY, HERBERT JAMES, educator, engr.; b. Montesano, Wash., Jan. 2, 1890; s. Herbert Luville and Mary Olive (Karr) G.; ed. pub. schs., Medford and Grants Pass, Ore.; B.S., Ore. State U., 1911; S.B., Mass. Inst. Tech., 1916; B.S., Harvard, 1916; M.S., U. Ill., 1923; Sc.D. (hon.), Buena Vista Coll., 1939; m. Mildred Virginia Talbot, Aug. 18, 1923 (dec. Dec. 1969); children—Herbert Talbot, Arthur Karr (dec.). Civil engr. various pub. constrn. projects, 1911-14, pvt. projects, 1916-21; mem. faculty U. Ill., 1921-23, U. Colo., 1923-31; prof., head dept. theoretical and applied mechanics Ia. State U., 1931-55, prof., 1955-76. Mem. various research and adv. coms. concrete constrn.; cons. Hoover Dam, 1931-33. With Am. Relief Adminstrn., Paris, 1919. Served from 1st lt. to capt. Engr. Res., U.S. Army, 1917-19; AEF. Recipient Wason medal, 1939, Am. Concrete Inst., Henry C. Turner gold medal, 1958; Distinguished Service plaque Ia. Engring. Soc., 1960. Fellow A.A.A.S.; mem. Am. Soc. C.E., Am. Soc. Testing Materials (hon.), Am. Concrete Inst. (pres. 1949; hon. mem.), Soc. Am. Mil. Engrs. (charter), Western Soc. Engrs., Am. Soc. Engring. Edn. (v.p. 1943), Sigma Xi, Tau Beta Pi, Phi Kappa Phi, Chi Epsilon. Club: Osborn Research. Author or co-author books, hand-books and portions of publs. Home: Ames, Iowa. Died Aug. 13, 1976.

GILL, ATTICUS JAMES, physician, educator; b. Okmulgee, Okla., June 8, 1914; s. X.R. and Martha (Trotter) G.; M.D., Duke, 1938; m. Lucille Hodge, Nov. 8, 1941; children—Frank Harrison, Mary, James Hodge. Intern, residency tng. pathology Duke Hosp. and St. Pauls Hosp., Dallas, 1938-41; instr. pathology U. Tenn., 1941-42, asst. prof., 1942-43; asst. prof. pathology Southwestern Med. Sch., 1943-46, asso. prof., 1947-49, prof., 1950-77, prof. emeritus, 1977—, asso. dean, 1950-51, asst. dean, 1952-55, dean, 1955-67; staff Parkland Meml. Hosp.; cons. staff Baylor Hosp., Presbyn. Hosp., St. Paul's Hosp., Dallas. Diplomate Am. Bd. Pathology. Fellow Am. Soc. Clin. Pathologists, Coll. Am. Pathologists, A.C.P.; mem. AMA, So., Tex. (v.p. 1977-78; Disting. Service award 1968), med. assns., Tex. Soc. Pathologists, Dallas So. Clin. Soc. (Marchman award 1966), Dallas County Med. Soc. (dir. 1956-58), Sigma Xi, Alpha Omega Alpha, Sigma Phi Epsilon, Phi Chi. Home: Dallas, Tex. Died Aug. 18, 1979; buried Oakwood Cemetery, Corsicana, Texas.

GILL, CHARLES A., transportation exec.; b. Buffalo, N.Y., Jan. 19, 1884; s. Zachery Taylor and Mary (Hurley) G.; ed. pub. schs. of Baltimore; m. Magdalene Lauer. Call boy, Riverside Shops, B. & O., R.R., 1897; successively machinist and special duty man on Northern Central R.R. (Pa. R.R.), foreman on C.B. & Q. R.R., Sheridan, Wyo., and foreman N.P. Ry., Livingston and Missoula, Mont., and Wallace, Ida., 1901-09; became enginehouse foreman B.&O. R.R., Washington, Ind., 1909; later master mechanic on C.H. & D., Dayton & Union (both now B. & O.) and Cincinnati & Indianapolis Western; gen. master mechanic B. & O. R.R., Md. Dist., 1913-17, supt. motive power, eastern lines, 1917-31; loaned to Russian Govt. to serve on Russian railroads, 1931-32; asst. chief of motive power, B.&O. R.R., and special rep. to operating v.p. of Reading Co., 1932; with Reading Co. and Central R.R. Co. of N.J. as supt. of motive power, 1932-36, gen. mgr., 1936-41, v.p. in charge of operation and maintenance, 1941-43; v.p. operation and maintenance, Reading Co., 1943-44; asso. No. Metals Co., Tacony, Pa. 1944-46; consultant dir. transport, Mil. Gov. U.S., German r.r., 1946-47; mem. staff J. G. White Engring. Corp., since 1948, in Far East, China, Formosa, 1948-50, Indonesia 1950-54. Mem. Am. Soc. M.E., Newcomen Society. Clubs: New York Railroads, New York Railroad Machinery; Union League (Phila). Home: Balt. Retired.

GILL, JOHN KERMODE, JR., shipping co. exec.; b. Cleve., July 22, 1930; s. John Kermode and Elizabeth (McIntyre) G.; grad. Episcopal High Sch., Alexandria, Va., 1950; B.S., Va. Poly. Inst., 1957; part-time student Case Western Res. U., 1968; m. Barbara T. Houchins, Aug. 21, 1951; children—John M., Jane T., James P. With Clevite Corp., Cleve., 1957-69, sec., 1968-69, treas., 1969; sec., Gould Inc., 1969-72; treas. Ogle Bay Norton Co., 1972-74; dir. Body Bros. Inc. Trustee, exec. com., treas. Community Dialysis Center; treas. Christ Ch. Found. Mem. Am. Soc. Corp. Secs., Ohio Soc. C.P.A.'s, Tax Execs. Inst., Tax Club Cleve. Episcopalian (treas.). Clubs: Mayfield Country, Cleveland Treasurers, Union (Cleve.). Home: Shaker Heights, Ohio. Died July 10, 1978; buried Lakeview Cemetery, Cleve.

GILL, JOHN PAUL, educator; b. Warrior-Run, Pa., Jan. 7, 1910; s. John and Hedwig (Ryto) G.; student Pa. State Coll., 1929-31; A.B., U. Ala., 1932, M.A., 1934; Ph.D., U. Tex., 1950; m. Bernice Victoria Alman, May 24, 1932; 1 son, John Paul. Asst. instr. Sch. Bus. Adminstrn., U. Ala., 1932-34, instr. comml. math., 1934-42, instr. bus. statistics, statistician Bur. Bus. Research, 1942-43, asst. prof., 1945-46; head math. dept. John E. Brown Coll., summers 1934-35; research statistician dept. research Fed. Res. Bank, Dallas, 1943-45; chief research and progress analysis div. Houston regional office War Assets Adminstrn., 1946-47; instr. U. Tex., 1947-49; asst. prof. Fla. State U., 1949-51; prof. econ. statistics, dir. div. research, also editor Atlanta Econ. Rev., Sch. Bus. Adminstrn., Atlanta div. U. Ga., 1951-54, prof. econs., dir. Bur. Bus. Research, coordinator grad. studies, also editor Ga. Bus., U. Ga. Coll. Bus. Adminstrn., 1954-60; prof., head dept. bus. statistics Sch. Commerce and Bus. Adminstrn., U. Ala., 1960-72, prof. statistics, 1972-75, prof. statistics emeritus, 1975-78. Mem. Am. Statis. Assn. (past chpt. pres.), Pi Mu Epsilon, Alpha Kappa Psi, Beta Gamma Sigma (nat. exec. com. 1958-61). Author booklet on indexes of retail sales, also chpt. 1953-54 Credit Mgmt. Year-Book; numerous articles in field. Editor: Southeastern Resources Handbook, vols. I, II, III. Home: Northport, Ala. Died June 11, 1978; interred Tuscaloosa (Ala.) Meml. Park.

GILL, LOUIS JOHN (GIL), architect; b. Syracuse, N.Y., May 9, 1885; s. John David and Harriet Mary (Thompson) G.; B.Arch., Syracuse U., 1911, D.F.A., 1938; m. Mildred Elizabeth Stillman, Oct. 2, 1915; children—John Stillman, Donald Seamans, Louis Dodge. Architect with Irving J. Gill, 1911-19; practiced under own name, 1919—. Mem., past pres. Cal. Bd. Archtl. Examiners, 1929-49; mem., Nat. Bd. Accrediting Archtl. Schs., 1947-54; mem., past pres., Nat. Council Archtl. Registration Bds., 1936-49; mem. co-operating com., Sch. Architecture, Syracuse U., 1937-58; mem. Architects Bur. Cal., 1933-46. Mem. San Diego Civic Center Com.; dir. San Diego Fine Arts Gallery, acquisition com., San Diego Fine Arts Gallery. Fellow A.I.A. (past pres. San Diego). Club: University (San Diego). Address: San Diego, Cal. *

GILL, MCCUNE (MC-CUNE GILL), title ins. exec.; b. Mexico, Mo., Mar. 20, 1883; s. George Murray and Olive (McCune) G.; LL.B., Washington U., St. Louis, 1904; m. Peggy Shannon, June 6, 1912. Admitted to Mo. bar, 1904; with Title Ins. Corp. (purchased Title Guaranty Trust Co.), since 1927, asst. sec., 1910-19, dir. since 1927, v.p., 1919-50, pres. 1950, now chmn.; faculty dept. law Washington U. 1945—. Mem. St. Louis Mortgage Bankers Assn. (pres.), Mortgage Bankers Assn. Am. (dir.), Am. (pres.), Mo. (pres. title assns., Mo. Hist. Soc. (trustee), Phi Delta Phi, Order of Coif. Author: Gill on Missouri Titles, 1921; Gill's Missouri Real Estate Forms, 1924; Treatise on Real Property, 1950; The St. Louis Story, 1952. Author articles on hist. subjects. Home: St. Louis. *

GILLEN, JOHN STEWART, ret. newspaper editor; b. Bklyn., Jan. 29, 1914; s. Edward T. and Sara (O'Donnell) G.; m. Mary Kathryn Crouser, Jan. 22, 1937; 1 dau., Patricia. With Phila. Inquirer, 1937-72, mng. editor, 1954-72. Home: Wynnewood, Pa. Died Aug. 17, 1977; buried Calvary Cemetery, West Conshohoken, Pa.

GILLEN, STANLEY JAMES, automotive exec.; b. Toledo, Aug. 10, 1911; s. Bernard J. and Johanna P. (Spillane) G.; B.Sc., U. Detroit, 1933; m. Mary Elizabeth Marks, Aug. 10, 1935; children—Elizabeth C. (Mrs. William R. Doyle), Mary M. O'Kieffe, Catherine A. (Mrs. Michael D.M. Ann). Financial analyst Fisher Body div. Gen. Motors Corp., 1933-47; contract adminstr. dep. products Ford Motor Co., 1947-48, controller steel div., 1948-55, controller tractor and implement div., 1955-56; asst. gen. mgr. steel div. Ford Motor Co., 1956-60, gen. mgr., 1960-61, gen. mgr. parts div., 1961-65; chmn. Autolite Products, Ltd., of Eng., 1962-65; dir. Ford Motor Credit Co., Ltd., London, 1965-67; mng. dir., chief exec. officer Ford of Britain, 1965-67; v.p. mfg. Ford of Europe, Inc., Eng., 1967-69, chmn., chief exec. officer, 1969-71; v.p. Ford Motor Co. U.S.A., 1967-71; dir. Ford of Europe, Inc., 1967-71, Ford of Britain, 1965-71, Ford Werke A/G (Koln, Germany), 1970-71, Sangamo Weston Ltd., Enfield, Eng., 1972-78, Sangamo Electric U.S.A., 1973-75, Ambac Industries Inc., U.S., 1976-78, Fabrica Espanola Magnetos S.A. (FEMSA), Castenedolo Mfg. Co. S.p.A., Brescia, Italy, Ambac B.V. Terheijdenseweg, Breda Holland, Brown Bros. Ltd., Harlow, Essex, Eng.; mem. nat. adv. council Motor Mfg. Industry London, 1966-67; mem. Brit. mfrs. exec. com. Soc. Motor Mfrs. and Traders, Ltd., 1965-67. Recipient Lord Wakefield Gold Medal, 1971. Mem. Am. C. of C. (U.K.) (dir. 1967-78). Clubs: American (dir. London); Sunningdale Golf (Bucks, Eng.); White Lake (Mich.) Golf, White Lake Yacht. Home: London, England. Died July 15, 1978.

GILLENTINE, EZRA CHAMBLY (GIL'LEN-TIN), clergyman; b. Dorsey, Miss., Feb. 27, 1886; s. John Chambly and Mary Etta (Kitchen) G.; student Jacksonville Baptist Coll., Jacksonville, Tex., 1916-17; grad. Central Sch. of Music, Little Rock, Ark., Feb. 1914; m. Verda May Voyles, June 10, 1913; children—Bogard (dec.), John Roy, R. B. (dec.). Music teacher, 1907-16; ordained Bapt. minister, June 10, 1916; missionary McCurtain Bapt. Association, 1917-20; pastor Okla., 1920-25; editor and business mgr. Okla. Baptist, 1923-25; also missionary Okla. State Baptist Assn., Miss., 1926-27; pastor chs. Ala., 1928-31, Miss., 1932-38, Liberty Baptist Ch., Okla., 1938-41; editor-in-chief Sunday Sch. and Baptist training course lit. of Am. Baptist Assn. 1941-42; served as pres. or moderator Yellow Creek Baptist and State Assns., Ala. and Miss. State Assn. of Baptist Chs., Okla. State Baptist Gen. Assembly, Liberty Baptist Assn., Am. Baptist Assn. Writer of various religious pamphlets. Home: Texarkana, Ark.-Tex. *

GILLESPIE, GUY TILLMAN, minister, educator; b. Arkabutla, Tate County, Miss., Feb. 10, 1885; s. George Yancey (M.D.) and Lillie Davis (Barry) G.; A.B., U. of Miss., 1905; Union Theol. Sem. in Va., 1908-11; D.D., Southwestern University, Memphis, Tenn., 1928; m. Lula Tyler, December 30, 1913; children—Sarah Barry (wife of Dr. David B. Wilson), Elizabeth, George Edward, Guy Tillman, Virginia. Ordained Presbyn. ministry, 1911; pastor Emporia, Va., 1908-11, Cordell, Okla., 1911-13, Lexington, Miss., 1913-21, also Durant, Miss., 1913-23; pres. Belhaven Coll., Jackson, Miss., since 1921. Chmn. State Adjustment Bd. for Miss., NRA; pres. Southern Assn. of Colls. for Women, 1934; mem. Nat. Council Boy Scouts of America; pres. Jackson Area Council of Boy Scouts of America, 1934; special rep. U.S. Dept. of Labor; supervisor of merit examinations, Miss. Employment Service, 1937; chmn. advisory com. on personnel, Miss. Unemployment Compensation Commn., 1938-39; moderator Synod of Miss. Presbyn. Ch. in U.S., 1939; baccalaureate preacher, Univ. of Miss., 1939; mem. Permanent Com. on Cooperation and Union, Gen Assembly of Presbyn. Ch. in U.S., 1947-53; dir. Jackson Chamber Com., 1947; fraternal del. from Presbyn. Ch. in U.S. to United Presbyn. Ch., 1947. Mem. Delta Psi. Club: Kiwanis (pres.). Address: Jackson, Miss. *

GILLETTE, CLAUDE SEXTON, naval officer; b. Cherokee, Ia., Feb. 1, 1886; s. Mark Daniel and Mary (Hull) G.; grad. U.S. Naval Acad., 1909, B.S., 1916; M.S., Columbia U., 1917; m. Lydia Baxter, Sept. 7, 1937. Commd. ensign, U.S. Navy, 1909, advancing through the grades to rear adm., 1942; served in various capacities in ships and stations throughout the world, with specialization in industrial and ship maintenance activities; industrial mgr. U.S. Navy Yard, Pearl Harbor, T.H., Apr. 1939-June 1942; directly in charge of salvage and rehabilitation of vessels damaged and sunk in the catastrophe of Dec. 7, 1941, and indsl. reconstruction and preparation of that great base for the Pacific war. Manager, Puget Sound navy yard, 1942-45. Decorated Silver Star (World War I), overseas campaign medals for World War I and World War II. Mem. U.S. Naval Engineers Naval Architects and Marine Engrs. Home: Bath, Me. *

GILLETTE, JAMES ROBERT, organist, composer and conductor; b. Roseboom, N.Y., May 30, 1886; s. Willard and Carrie (Hess) G.; B.M., Syracuse U., 1913; m. Mildred Bennett, June 9, 1914; children—Ruth Sprague, James Robert. Début as concert organist, at Syracuse, 1913; guest organist, Chautauqua Summer Sch., N.Y., 1916, 19, 24; soloist Nat. Assn. Organists' Conv., Springfield, Mass., 1916, Philadelphia, 1922; soloist Minneapolis Symphony Orchestra, 1917, and of Sesquicentennial Expn., Phila., 1926; recitals throughout U.S.; prof. organ and college organist, Carleton Coll., 1923-37; founder, 1923, and condr., 1923-38, Carleton Symphony Band; organist and choirmaster, First Presbyn. Ch., Lake Forest, Ill., since 1939. Mem. Am. Soc. Composers, Authors and Publishers, Kappa Sigma, Phi Mu Alpha. Republican. Episcopalian. Author: The Organist's Handbook, 1926. Composer of 2 cantatas, 3 symphonies for modern band and over 70 compositions for band, orchestra, ensembles, and organ. Home: Lake Forest, Ill. *

GILLIAM, FRANK J(OHNSON), coll. dean; b. Lynchburg, Va., Apr. 22, 1895; s. James Richard and Jessie Belfield (Johnson) G.; A.B., Washington and Lee, 1917; A.M., Columbia, 1928; m. Louise Fontaine Johnson, June 18, 1924; children—Fontaine Johnson, Louise Hopkins. Instr., Augusta (Va.) Mil. Acad., 1919-20; dir. of edn., Southern Presbyn. Mission, Belgian Congo, Africa, 1920-26; asst. prof. English, Washington and Lee Univ., 1926-28, asso. prof. English, from 1928, dean of students, from 1931, dir. of admissions, from 1944. Vice pres., Peoples National Bank. Member executive board Diocese of S.W. Virginia. Trustee Woodrow Wilson Birthplace Foundation, Virginia Espicopal Theological Seminary. Served as first lieutenant, A.E.F., U.S. Army, 1917-19; major, A.U.S., 1943. Mem. Va. Hist. Soc., Soc. of the Cincinnati in State of Va.; Sigma Alpha Epsilon, Omicron Delta Kappa, Phi Eta Sigma, Sigma Upsilon, Phi Kappa Phi. Democrat. Author transl. and sch. texts in Buluba dialect, Central Africa, 1921-26. Died Mar. 9, 1976.

GILLIS, JOHN LAMB, chem. co. exec.; b. Fargo, N.D., May 23, 1911; s. John Daniel and Mary (Lamb) G.; B.S., Washington U., 1933; m. Carol Randolph, June 18, 1938; children—John Lamb, Carol Gillis Manning, Ann Carter, Mary Gillis Menousek. Asst. export mgr. Monsanto Co., St. Louis, 1933-38, export mgr., 1938-41, asst. dir. fgn. dept., 1941-44, dir. fgn. dept., 1946-49, gen. mgr. Merrimac Div., Boston, 1949-51, gen. mgr. organic chems. div., also v.p. Monsanto Co., 1950-54, v.p. marketing, 1954-68, sr. v.p., 1968-76, also dir.; dir. Am. Investment Co., Boatmen's Nat. Bank St. Louis. Pres., president's council St. John's Mercy Med. Center; pres.'s council St. Louis U. Trustee, Govt. Research Inst., St. Louis; dir., v.p. Central Inst. for Deaf; bd. dirs., mem. exec. com. St. Louis Symphony Soc. Mem. Mo. Hist. Soc. (pres.), Am. Soc. Corporate Execs. Clubs: Links (N.Y.C.); St. Louis Country (Clayton, Mo.); Racquet, Bogey (St. Louis); Bohemian (San Francisco). Home: Creve Coeur, Mo. Died Mar. 19, 1976.

GILLULY, JAMES, geologist; b. Seattle, Wash., June 24, 1896; s. Charles Elijah and Louisa Elizabeth (Briegel) G.; B.S., Univ. of Wash., 1920; Ph.D., Yale, 1926; student Innsbruck Univ., Tirol, Austria (winter, 1932); Sc.D., Princeton University, 1959; married to Enid Adelaide Frazier, June 30, 1925; children—Molly Frazier, Sara Frazier. Jr. geologist, Nat. Refining Co., Lewistown, Mont., 1921; geologic aide, U.S. Geol. Survey, 1921-23, asst. geologist, 1923-25, asso. 1925-29, geologist, 1929-36, sr. geologist, 1936-42, prin. geologist, 1943-50, research geologist, 1950-59, chief gen. geology br., 1954-57, chief, fuels br., 1957-59, staff scientist, from 1959; prof. geology U. Cal., Los Angeles, 1938-50, chmn. dept. geology, 1945-47; Bownocker lectr. Ohio State University, 1951; consulting geologist Office Chief Engineer, South West Pacific Areas, 1944; William Smith lectr., Geol. Soc. London, 1962. Chmn. division of earth scis. NRC, 1961-63. Served as ensign, USNRF, 1917-19. Recipient Penrose medal Geol. Soc. Am., 1958; Distinguished Service medal, U.S. Dept. Interior, 1959; John Simon Guggenheim Foundation fellow, 1960. Fellow Mineral. Soc. Am., Am. Acad. Arts and Scis.; mem. Nat. Academy Scis., Geological Society London, Am. Geophy. Union (sec. sect. volcanology 1938-40), Geol. Soc. of Am. (chmn. Cordilleran sect. 1940, councillor 1943-45, v.p. 1947, pres. 1948, past pres. 1949), Soc. of Econ. Geologists (councilor 1938-40), A.A.A.S. (Centennial Com. 1948), American Assn. Petroleum Geologists; Soc. Econ. Paleontologists and Mineralogists; Seismol. Soc. of Am., Geol. Soc. of Washington, Washington Acad. Scis., Sigma Xi. Dem. Unitarian. Club: Cosmos (Washington, D.C.). Editorial board Copper Resources of the World, 18th Internat. Geological Congress, Washington, 1933. Author: Principles of Geology (with A. C. Waters and A. O. Woodford, 1951, 59. Contbr. articles in various geol. pubs. Home: Lakewood, Colo. Died Dec. 30, 1980.

GILMAN, JAMES HENRY, banker; b. New Hartford, Conn., June 26, 1883; s. Henry P. and Katherine (Crowe) G.; ed. pub. schs., New Hartford; m. Gladys Moore, of Brookline, Mass., Apr. 11, 1916; children—James H., Gloria Moore, George Claflin. Began as office boy and clk., Bank of Bay Biscayne, Miami, Fla., 1902, now pres. City commr., Miami, 1921-27. Republican. Conglist. Mason, Elk. Clubs: Bath, Country. Home: Miami, Fla. *

GILMER, HOWARD CECIL, JR., lawyer; b. Pulaski, Va., Dec. 27, 1906; s. Howard Cecil and Lila (Saul) G.; A.B., Hampden-Sydney Coll., 1928; French studies, U. Poitiers (France), 1925; LL.B., U. Va., 1931; m. Mary Berkeley Cosby, July 28, 1931; children—Berkeley (Mrs. R.W. MacAdoo), Sally Lou (Mrs. C.C. Hundley), Betsy (Mrs. David Brown), Page Va. Senate, 1919; admitted to Va. bar, 1930, U.S. Supreme Ct. bar; practiced in Pulaski, 1930-75, mem. firm Gilmer, Sadler, Ingram, Sutherland & Hutton; asst. U.S. atty. for Western Dist. Va., 1934-46, acting U.S. atty., 1946-48, U.S. atty., 1948-53; dir. and counsel Va. Nat. Bank, First Fed. Savs. & Loan Assn., Va. Maid Hosiery Mills. Mem. jud. conf. U.S. Fourth Circuit Vice chmn. Va. Council Higher Edn., 1956-66. Fellow Am. Coll. Trial Lawyers; mem. Am., Va. (pres. 1944-46), W.Va. (hon.), Pulaski County bar assns., Phi Beta Kappa, Pi Kappa Alpha, Omicron Delta Kappa. Democrat. Methodist. Elk (exalted ruler, dist. dep. grand exalted ruler), Mason. Home: Pulaski, Va. Died Nov. 1, 1975; buried Oakwood Cemetery, Pulaski.

GILMORE, DONALD SHERWOOD, dept. store exec.; b. Kalamazoo, Mar. 7, 1895; s. James F. and Carrie M. (Sherwood) G.; grad. Lawrenceville Sch., 1916; student Yale, 1916; LL.D., Kalamazoo Coll. 1956; m. Genevieve Upjohn, Dec. 16, 1916; children—Carol (Mrs. Robert M. Boudeman), Jane (Mrs. Harold J. Maloney), Martha (Mrs. Raymond T. Parfet, Jr.). Various exec. positions Gilmore Bros. Dept. Store, Kalamazoo, 1916-30, v.p., 1930—, also dir.; dir. Upjohn Co., mfrs. pharm. products, Kalamazoo, 1929-79, v.p., 1930, v.p., gen. mgr., 1936, pres., gen. mgr., 1944-52, chmn. bd., mng. dir., 1953-61, vice chmn. bd., 1962-69, ret., 1963, then dir. Trustee, Kalamazoo Found, 1928-79, pres., 1934-75; bd. dirs. W. W. Upjohn Inst. Employment Research, 1932—. Served with USNR, 1918. Mem. Am. Drug Mfrs. Assn. (pres. 1952-54). Home: Kalamazoo, Mich. Died Dec. 21, 1979.

GILMORE, GEORGE NORMAN, lawyer; b. Detroit, Apr. 13, 1904; s. William George and Gertrude Anne (Williams) G.; student Highland Park Jr. Coll., 1921-23; LL.B., U. Mich., 1926; m. Romaine Salmans, July 26, 1960; children—William D., Thomas C., John F., Judith A.; 1 stepdau., Janie. Admitted to Mich. bar, 1927; asst. treas. Gilmore & Chavenelle Corp., Detroit, 1926-29; atty. Home Owners Loan Corp., Detroit, 1934-40; mem. legal staff Detroit Ordnance Dist., U.S. Army, 1942-45; pvt. practice, Detroit, 1929-78; partner firm Reid & Gilmore, 1953-77; of counsel McClintock Donovan Carson and Roach, Detroit, 1977-78; adj. prof. Wayne State U. Law Sch., 1973-74; lectr. Inst. Continuing Legal Edn., 1975-77. Mem. Am., Detroit bar assns., Am. Judicature Soc., State Bar Mich. (chmn. real property law com. 1970-71, chmn. real property law sect. 1973-75), Sigma Pi. Republican. Presbyterian. Clubs: Bayview Yacht (past commodore), Commodores, Detroit River Yachting Assn., Detroit Power Squadron. Contbr. articles to legal jours. Home: Grosse Pointe Woods, Mich. Died July 5, 1978.

GILMORE, MYRON PIPER, educator, historian; b. Walpole, Mass., July 4, 1910; s. Charles Austin and Eunice Ethel (Piper) G.; A.B., Amherst Coll., 1932, L.H.D., 1962; A.M., Harvard, 1933, Ph.D., 1937; L.H.D., Washington U., St. Louis, 1967; Litt.D., U. Florence, 1976; m. Sheila Dehn, Apr. 2, 1938; children—Janet (Mrs. Christopher Greene), Diana Piper (Mrs. Lawrence Fane), Thomas North, John Allen Dehn. Instr. history Harvard, 1937-42, asso. prof., 1942-54, prof., 1954-74, Gurney prof. history and polit. sci., 1975-78; dir. Villa I Tatti, Center Italian Renaissance Studies, Florence, Italy, 1964-73. Served from lt. (j.g.) to lt. comdr., USNR, 1942-45. Honored by Italian Govt. for restoration of art treasures damaged by flood of Florence. Mem. Am. Acad. Arts and Scis., Am. Hist. Assn., Medieval Acad. Am., Renaissance Soc. Am., Am. Soc. Reformation Research, Colonial Soc. Mass., Mass. Hist. Soc., Am. Philos. Soc., Accademia Degli Intronati (Siena), Century Assn. Author: Argument from Roman Law in Political Thought 1200-1600, 1941; The World of Humanism, 1952; Humanists and Jurists: Six Studies in the Renaissance, 1963. Home: Cambridge, Mass. Died Oct. 27, 1978.

GILMORE, RALPH J(OHN), prof. biology; b. Williamsport, Pa., Dec. 18, 1885; s. John W(illets) and Mary Anna (Lehman) G.; A.B., Lehigh U., 1907, A.M., 1910; Ph.D., Cornell U., 1914; m. Ruth Adelaide Carson, of Bedford, Ia., May 27, 1916; children—Mary Ella, Ruth Carson, Ralph John (dec.). Acting prof. biology, Adelbert Coll. (Western Reserve U.), 1912-13; prof. biology, Huron (S.D.) Coll., 1914-19; prof. same, Colo. Coll., 1949—. Mem. A.A.A.S., Sigma Xi, Gamma Alpha, Phi Gamma Delta. Democrat. Presbyn. Mason. Club: Lions (dist. gov. Colo., 1927). Has specialized in comparative anatomy of vertebrates. Home: Colorado Springs, Colo.*

GILMORE, WILLIAM STEELE, editor; b. Princeton, Ind., June 22, 1884; s. Dr. Steele Francis and Henrietta (Blair) G.; student Ind. U., 1903-05; m. Hazel Nirdlinger, June 23, 1917; 1 dau., Mary Jane (Mrs. Philip A. Baer). Began as reporter Princeton (Ind.) Clarion News, 1905; then with Terre Haute Tribune, Terre Haute Star, Indianapolis Star; with Detroit News since 1909, telegraph editor, asst. city editor, and news editor, 1909-27, mng. editor, 1927-33, editor-in-chief, 1933-53, now cons. editor. Mem. Am. Soc. Newspaper Editors (pres. 1942-43), Indiana Soc. of Chicago, Phi Kappa Psi, Sigma Delta Chi. Republican. United Presbyterian. Address: La Jolla, Cal. *

GILMOUR, LLOYD STRAUBE, investment banker; b. Fresno, Cal., Feb. 12, 1892; s. William E. and Laura (McGee) G.; A.B., U. Cal., 1915; m. Margery Blyth, Dec. 11, 1926; children—Lloyd S., Blyth. Vice pres. Blyth, Witter & Co., investment bankers, San Francisco, 1915-20; v.p., dir. Blyth & Co., Inc., N.Y.C., 1920-34; formed group to acquire firm of Eastman Dillon & Co., 1935 (merged with Union Securities Corp. 1956, name changed to Eastman Dillon, United Securities & Co., merged with Blyth & Co. 1972, name changed to Blyth Eastman Dillon & Co. Inc.), sr. partner, chief exec. officer until 1967, ltd. partner, from 1967; hon. dir. Suburban Propane Gas Corp., 1967-79; dir. West Coast Transmission; former dir. numerous other corps. Chmn. of Upper Brookville, L.I., Planning Bd., 1946-52; trustee Village of Matinecock, Oyster Bay, N.Y., 1964-68. Trustee Zeta Psi Frat. of N.Am., 1930-33, Zeta Psi Ednl. Found., 1947; vice chmn. bd. trustees N.Y. U., 1958-69, trustee emeritus, 1969-79; pres. Blythmour Corp., 1950-79. Mem. Investment Bankers Assn. (gov. 1941-44, indsl. securities com. 1942, fed. legislation com. 1943). Clubs: Union, Brook (N.Y.C.); Piping Rock, Creek (Locust Valley, N.Y.); Pacific-Union (San Francisco); Ekwanok Country (Manchester, Vt.); Everglades, Beach, Bath and Tennis (Palm Beach, Fla.); Gulf Stream (Fla.) Golf. Home: Locust Valley, N.Y. Died Dec. 23, 1979.

GILREATH, ESMARCH SENN, educator; b. North Wilkesboro, N.C., Sept. 21, 1904; s. Frank Hackett and Mamie (Williams) G.; A.B., U. N.C., 1926, M.A., 1927, Ph.D., 1945; m. Sara Taylor, Oct. 17, 1936. Instr. chemistry Ga. Tech., 1927-29; high sch. chemistry tchr., 1933-42; instr. chemistry U. N.C., 1942-44, vis. prof. chemistry, summer 1949; research chemist Am. Enka Corp., 1945-46; asst. prof. chemistry Washington and Lee U., Lexington, Va., 1946-52, asso. prof., 1952-54, prof., 1954-75, head dept. chemistry, 1954-70, prof. emeritus, 1975-76; vis. prof. chemistry summers U. Oreg., 1957, U. B.C., 1959, Ore. State U., 1961. Mem. Am. Chem. Soc., Phi Beta Kappa, Sigma Xi, Alpha Chi Sigma, Alpha Epsilon Delta. Author: Qualitative Analysis, 1954; Inorganic Chemistry, Experimental Procedures in Elementary Analysis, 1968; Quantitative Chemistry, 1969. Home: Lexington, Va. Died Mar. 3, 1976.

GILSON, ETIENNE H., philosopher and historian of thought, educator, author; D.Litt. U. Paris, Sorbonne, 1913; hon degrees, univs. Oxford, Montreal, Aberdeen, St. Andrews, Glasgow, Harvard, Columbia, Milan Angelico, Rome, Laval U., others; m. Thérèse Ravise, 1908; Founder Pontifical Inst. Mediaeval Studies St. Michael's Coll., Toronto, Ont., Can., 1929, dir. studies, 1928-78; Gifford lectr. U. Aberdeen, Scotland, 1930-31, William James lectr. Harvard, Cambridge, Mass., 1936; Mellon lectr., Washington, 1955. Pres. Scientifique Institut Franco-Canadien, Montreal, Que., Can. Decorated officer Legion of Honor (France); War Cross; Orden pour le Merite; recipient Christian Culture medal Assumption Coll., Windsor, Ont., 1949; Cardinal Spellman Thomas Aquinas medal, 1952. Fellow Royal Soc. Can., French Acad., Polish Acad., Brit. Acad. (Serena medal for Italian studies 1952), Royal Acad. Denmark, Royal Acad. Holland, Acad. Moral Scis., Am. Acad. Arts and Scis. Author: Thomism, 6 edits., from 1921; The Spirit of Mediaeval Philosophy, 1936; Mediaeval Universalism and Its Present Value, 1937; The Unity of Philosophical Experience, 1937; The Philosophy of St. Bonaventure, 1925; Faith and Reason in the Middle Ages, 1938; Being and Some Philosophers, 1948; Jean Duns Scot, 1952; History of Christian Philosophy in the Middle Ages, 1955; Elements of Christian Philosophy, 1959; The Spirit of Thomism, 1964; The Arts of the Beautiful, 1965; (with A. Meurer and T. Langan) History of Philosophy, 4 vols.; Linguistique et Philosophie, 1969; D'Aristote á Darwin et Retour, 1971, others. Died Auxerre, France, Sept. 19, 1978; interred North Cemetery, Melun, France.

GILTINAN, CAROLINE (MRS. LEO P. HARLOW) (GIL-TE'NAN), author; b. Philadelphia, Pa., Apr. 19, 1884; d. David and Helen (McCaffrey) Giltinan; ed. Convent of the Sacred Heart, pub. schs. of Philadelphia and U. of Pa.; m. Leo P. Harlow (lawyer), Aug. 14, 1920; 1 dau., Faith. Formerly with Paris and New York headquarters, Associated Press; served with Herbert Hoover's Am. Relief Assn.; founder and editor The Carillon (quarterly verse), 1929-34. Served with A.E.F. in France as sec. U.S. Base Hosp. No. 38, and "sick and wounded div." of med. headquarters, World War. Mem. Poetry Soc. America, Poetry Soc. Va., Catholic Poetry Soc. America (acad. mem.; v.p.), Women's Overseas Service League. Catholic. Author: (verse) The Divine Image, 1917; The Veiled Door, 1929; Testimony, 1931. Contbr. verse to mags. Home: Alexandria, Va. *

GIMBEL, BRUCE A., dept. store exec.; b. N.Y.C., July 28, 1913; s. Bernard Feustmann and Alva (Bernheimer) G.; student Choate Sch., 1931; B.A., Yale, 1935; m. Barbara Poulson, Nov. 10, 1945; children—Robert Bruce, Judith Caton (Mrs. Benjamin Mendelsund), Bernard Bacon. With Gimbel Bros., Inc., 1935-76, joined Saks Fifth Ave., 1936, v.p. Saks, 1946-53, pres. Gimbel Bros., Inc., 1953-73, chmn. bd., chief exec. officer, 1973-75, also dir., 1946-76; dir. Crane Co., Nat. Aviation Co. Mem. Met. Transp. Authority, 1965-70. Mem. bd., v.p. Greater N.Y. council Boy Scouts Am., Boys' Clubs Am.; mem. bd. Mus. City N.Y. Mem. Nat. Retail Mchts. Assn. (dir.), Am. Retail Fedn. (chmn. 1970). Home: Greenwich, Conn. Died Oct. 7, 1980.

GINGERY, DON, ex-congressman; b. Woodland, Pa., Feb. 19, 1884; s. Dorsey J. and Ada Mary (Albert) G.; student Ohio and Northern U., 1900-01; m. Anna Leavy, Clearfield, Pa., 1912; children—Donald E., Sarah L., Mary Louise, Hugh Albert. Began as civil engr., 1903; in hardware and mine supplies business, 1902-34; with Logan-Gregg Hardware Co., Pittsburgh; mem. Pa. legislature, 1915-16; mem. 74th and 75th Congresses (1935-39), 23d Pa. Dist. Was Clearfield Co. chmn. Dem. Com. and mem. Dem. State Com. and State Exec. Com. Formerly capt. Pa. N.G. Democrat. Methodist. Mem. Eagles, Moose. Home: Clearfield, Pa.*

GINGRICH, ARNOLD, editor, author; b. Grand Rapids, Mich., Dec. 5, 1903; s. John Hembling and Clara Alice (Speare) G.; A.B., U. Mich., 1925; m. Helen Mary Rowe, Oct. 24, 1924 (dec. 1955); children—Rowe W., John A., Michael G.; m. 2d, Jane Kendall Abeli, Nov. 13, 1955. Advt. copy writer, 1925; editor Apparel Arts, Chgo., 1931-45, editor Esquire, 1933-45, Coronet, 1936-45; v.p. Esquire, Inc., 1933-45, pub., sr. v.p., 1952-74; sr. v.p., editor-in-chief Esquire, Gentleman's Quar. mag., 1974-76; European editor Esquire and Coronet, 1945-49; v.p. Cowles Mag., Inc., also gen. mgr. Flair, 1949-51. Mem. Phi Beta Kappa, Phi Sigma Kappa. Clubs: Overseas Press (N.Y.C.); Fario (Paris); Joe Jefferson (Saddle River). Author: Cast Down the Laurel, 1935; The Well-Tempered Angler, 1965; Toys of a Lifetime, 1966; Business and the Arts, 1969; A Thousand Mornings of Music, 1970; Nothing But People: The Early Days at Esquire, 1971; The Joys of Trout, 1973; The Fishing in Print, 1974. Home: Ridgewood, N.J. Died July 9, 1976.

GINSBERG, LOUIS, poet, educator; b. Newark, Oct. 1, 1895; s. Peter and Rebecca G.; B.A., Rutgers U., 1918; M.A., Columbia, 1924; m. Naomi Lewy (dec.); children—Eugene, Allen; m. 2d, Edith Cohen, Mar. 24, 1950. Tchr. English, Central High Sch., 1921-61; mem. faculty Rutgers U., 1948-76, adj. asso. prof. Mem. Poetry Soc. Am. (exec. bd.). Author: The Attic of the Past, 1920; The Everlasting Minute, 1937; Morning in Spring, 1970; poems pub. in numerous anthologies including Modern American and British Poetry (Untermeyer); Poetry: Its Appreciation and Enjoyment; Discovery I; also in Atlantic Monthly, Am. Scholar, New Yorker, Saturday Rev., Sat. Eve. Post, other mags. Home: Paterson, N.J. Died July 8, 1976.

GINSBERG, STEWART THEODORE, physician, psychiatrist; b. St. Paul, Apr. 18, 1906; s. Jacob and Mollie (Balkind) G.; B.S., M.B., U. Minn., 1932, M.D., 1933; m. Ada Leah Leach, Aug. 31, 1930; children—Barbara Cecil (Mrs. Samuel Tisherman), Janet Mary (Mrs. Alvin Klein), Mark Bruce. Intern, St. Mary's Hosp., Duluth, Minn., 1932-33; practice medicine specializing in psychiatry VA hosps., St. Cloud, Minn., Augusta, Ga., Marion, Ind., 1936-53; mgr. VA Hosp., Pitts., 1953-55; chief psychiatry div., psychiatry and neurology service VA Central Office, Washington, 1955-57; Ind. commr. mental health, 1957-66; dir. VA Hosp., Lyons, N.J., 1966-71; supt. Ga. Mental Health Inst., Atlanta, 1971-73; faculty psychiatry Ind. U. Sch. Medicine, 1948-53, asso. prof., 1957-61, prof., 1961-66; asso. clin. prof. psychiatry Georgetown U. Med. Sch., 1956-57; clin. prof. psychiatry Emory U., 1971-79; asst. examiner Am. Bd. Psychiatry and Neurology, 1950-79. Cons. community services br. Nat. Inst. Mental Health, 1959-62, in-service tng. mental health tng. com., 1963-65; chmn. subcom. treatment, care and rehab. Conf. on Vol. Services to Psychiat. Patients, 1958; mem. exec. med. adv. com. Indpls. Hosp. Devel. Assn., 1964-66; mem. council legislation and pub. policy Nat. Assn. Mental Health, 1967-70; mem. profl. adv. com. Met. Atlanta Mental Health Assn. cons. Task Force to Revise Standards Psychiat. Hosps. and Clinics, 1968-70; Mem. accreditation council for psychiat. facilities Joint Commn. on Accreditation Hosps., 1970-77, chmn., 1972-74. Pres., bd. dirs. Grant County (Ind). Council Social Agys.; v.p., bd. dirs. Family Service Soc., Marion; bd. dirs. Jewish Social Service, Indpls., Community Services Council Met. Indpls., Community Friendship, Atlanta, 1972-79, Jewish Family and Childrens Bur., Atlanta, 1972-79, Health Planning and Devel. Center, Atlanta, 1977-79. Served from maj. to lt. col. M.C., AUS, 1944-46. Recipient Distinguished Service award Ind. Pub. Health Assn., 1964, award of merit Tri-State Hosp. Assembly, Chgo., 1964. Diplomate Am. Bd. Psychiatry. Hon. fellow Internat. Coll. Dentists; fellow Am. Psychiat. Assn. (past mem. council), Am. Coll. Psychiatrists, Am. Pub. Health Assn.; mem. Grant County Med. Soc. (past pres.), Ind. Rehab. Assn. (past pres.), Assn. Med. Supts. Mental Hosps. (council), N.J. Neuropsychiat. Assn. (mem. council), Am. Assn. Vol. Service Co-ordinators (adv. com. 1962-79), AMA, Assn. Med. Rehab Dirs. and Co-ordinators (hon.). Editorial bd. Hosp. and Community Psychiatry, 1967-73, chmn., 1972-73. Contbr. articles to profl. jours. Address: Decatur, Ga. Died Dec. 3, 1979.

GIVEN, SAMUEL, corp. exec.; b. Chgo., 1885. Chmn. Waste King Corp., Los Angeles; pres., dir. Given Machine Co. Home: West Los Angeles, Cal.

GIVENS, MEREDITH BRUNER, economist; b. Des Moines, Jan. 11, 1899; s. D. Findley and Celeste (Bruner) G.; A.B., Drake U., 1920; postgrad. U. Chgo., 1920-21; fellow econs. U. Wis., 1921-22, Ph.D., 1929; m. Ruth Wheelock Ayres, Oct. 6, 1929; 1 son, Richard Ayres. Teaching asst. U. Wis., 1922-24, research asst. labor, 1924-25; staff Nat. Bur. Econ. Research, 1925-26, 28-30; labor cons. Am. Radiator Co., 1926-27; spl. agt. U.S. Bur. Labor Statistics, 1927-28; sec. for industry and trade Social Sci. Research Council, 1929-63; lectr. Wharton Sch. Finance and Commerce, U. Pa., 1930-32; mem. adv. com. Sec. of Labor, 1933-35; mem. tech. bd. occupational research U.S. Employment Service, 1933-46; mem. Central Statis. Bd., Washington, 1933-36; exec. sec. com. on Govt. Statistics and Information Services, Washington, 1933-36; cons. Pres.'s Com. on Econ. Security, 1934, Social Security Bd., 1935; dir. indsl. studies Research and Planning Bd., N.R.A., 1935; dir. research and statistics Employment div. Dept. Labor, N.Y., 1936-59; cons. statis. standards U.S. Bur. Budget, 1943-53; mem. adv. com. econ. statistics Bur. Census, 1948-52; chmn. manpower panel, com. human resources Research and Development Bd., Dept. Def., 1949-53; vis. expert U.S. Mil. Govt. Germany, 1949; cons. manpower NSRB, 1950-53; exec. dir. N.Y. State Interdept. Com. on Low Incomes, 1956-59; mem. com. on statis. programs, N.Y.C., 1955-59; Smith-Mundt tech. cons. Philippine Govt., 1951-52; prof. statistics U. Philippines, 1954-55; prin. UN adviser Statis. Center, Manila, 1954-55; adviser human resources Planning Commn., Govt. of Pakistan, 1959-61; sr. staff Inst. Pub. Adminstrn., N.Y.C., 1961; expert manpower ILO, Pakistan, 1962; dir. Office Research in Econs. and Sci., Dept. State, Washington, 1963-66; chief manpower and human resources planning Office Tech. Coop. and Research, AID, 1966-67; Ford Found. adviser manpower Govt. of Ghana, 1968-70; econ. cons., 1971-76; chmn. Franconia (N.H.) Am. Revolution Bicentennial Com.; adviser North County Council (N.H.); mem. Econ. Devel. Com., 1975-76. Recipient Certificate of Merit, Philippine Govt., 1952; Alumni Distinguished Service award Drake U., 1957. Fellow Am. Statis. Assn. (pres. N.Y. chpt. 1953-55), A.A.A.S.; mem. Philippine Statis. Assn. (founding), Am. Econ. Assn., Soc. for Internat. Devel. (pres. D.C. chpt. 1965-67), Indsl. Relations Research Assn., Assn. Amateur Chamber Mus. Players, Phi Beta Kappa, Phi Delta Theta, Phi Mu Alpha, Lambda Alpha. Club: Cosmos. Author monographs, tech. articles. Home: Franconia, N.H. Died Feb. 22, 1976; interred Elmwood Cemetery, Franconia.

GIVENS, RAYMOND LUELLING, lawyer; b. Salem, Ore., Feb. 9, 1884; s. John Weeks and Ellen Elizabeth (Luelling) G.; student Gordon Acad., Salt Lake City, Utah, 1899-1902, Colo. Coll., 1902-06; LL.B., U. of Denver, 1909; LL.D. (honorary), University of Idaho, 1954; married Margaret A. O'Donnell, March 6, 1916; children—Raymond David, James William, John Wallace. Admitted to Ida. bar, 1909, and began practice at Boise; pros. atty. Ada County, Ida., 1911-17; mem. Ida. Ho. of Rep., 1919; asst. atty. gen. of Ida., 1919-20; dist. judge 3d Ida. Dist., 1920-24; justice Supreme Court of Ida., 1925-54. Mem. Mountain View Council Boy Scouts Am. Mem. Sigma Chi, Phi Delta Phi. Republican. Mason, Elk. Home: Boise, Ida. *

GIVENS, WILLARD EARL, association executive; born in Anderson, Indiana, Dec. 10, 1886; son John Luther and Amanda Elizabeth (Hersberger) G.; student Butler Coll., Indianapolis, 1908-09; A.B., Indiana Univ., 1913, LL.D., 1938; A.M., Columbia U., 1915; diploma Union Theol. Sem., 1916; grad. student in sociology, Columbia, 1915-17; grad. student (part-time) in edn., U. of California, 1925-33; Ed.D., Miami University, Oxford, O., 1941; fellow, Educational Inst. of Scotland, 1947; H.H.D., Coll. Ida., 1950, U. of Pacific, 1951; married Neva Lillian Galbreath, December 10, 1917; children—Willard Earl, Stuart Ray. Rural and high school teacher, elementary and secondary sch. prin., in Indiana, T.H., and California, 1906-23; supt. pub. instrn., T.H., 1923-25; asst. supt. schs., Oakland, Calif., 1925-27; supt. schs., San Diego, Calif., 1927-28; supt. schs., Oakland, Calif., 1928-35; exec. sec. Nat. Edn. Assn., 1935-52. Vis. prof. of education Brigham Young University, two terms, Claremont Graduate School, two terms. Chmn. bd. of trustees, Sr. Citizens of Am., 1954—; ednl. cons. for U.S. to Philippines, 1953; chmn. U.S. Nat. Commn. for UNESCO, 1956; ednl. adv. to U.S. del. to World UNESCO Conf. in New Delhi, 1956. Instructor Naval Officers' Training School, Mare Is., World War I. Campaign chmn. Oakland Community Chest, 1930-32. Pres. Calif. Teachers Assn., 1932-35; mem. Am. Youth Commn. of Am. Council on Edn. Life mem. N.E.A. (state dir. for Calif. 2 yrs., Hawaii 2 yrs.); mem. Ednl. Policies Commn., Am. Acad. Political and Social Science, A.A.A.S. Conglist. Mason (Shriner, 33 deg.; dir. of education The Supreme Council 33 deg. Scottish Rite Mason, So. Jurisdiction 1958-69. Author numerous articles in ednl. and lay mags. Mem. U.S. Education Mission to Japan, 1946. Mem. Bd. visitors Air Univ., 1946-50; member com. Armed Forces Edn. Program, 1949-53; chmn. National Conf. for Mobilization of Edn., 1950; educational rep. World Town Hall Seminar, 1949; chmn. 2d U.S. Education Mission to Japan, 1950. Author: People to People, 1949; The Association of Nations, 1954; co-author Our Public Schools, The Road to Freedom, Our U.S.A., Communism Menaces Freedom, Private Enterprise. Address: Washington. Retired 1969. *

GLADDERS, GLENN WARREN, transp. co. exec.; b. Coal City, Ill., Aug. 1, 1914; s. Luke and Emily (Nicholson) G.; student U. Mich., 1934-35, 39, So. Ill. U., 1936-38; A.B., U. Ill., 1938; m. Jean Martin, Oct. 7, 1939; children—Thomas Luke, Emily Jean, Warren. Asst. sec.-treas. Martin Oil Co., St. Louis, 1939-47, sec.-treas., 1947-71, pres., 1950-71; pres. Gladders Towing Co., Inc., 1950-73, chmn., 1973-80; chmn. Am. Waterways Operators, Inc., 1968-69; dir. Security Bank, St. Louis, 1952-59, Merc. Trust Co., St. Louis, 1959-71, Nat. Bank Carbondale, 1947-71. Pres., Marine Transp. Council, 1972-73. Mem. exec. com. So. Ill. U. Found., 1956-65, pres., 1950, 56-57; pres. Carbondale (Ill.) Sch. Bd., 1947-50. Served as lt. (j.g.) USNR, 1944-45; PTO. Mem. Nat. Def. Transp. Assn., Oil Men's Club (past pres.), Mid Am. Gasoline Marketers (past pres.), World Bus. Council, So. Ill. U. Alumni Assn. (past pres.). Clubs: Mo. Athletic (past pres. St. Louis); Old Warson Country. Clayton. Home: Saint Louis, Mo. Died Apr. 3, 1980.

GLADWIN, HAROLD STERLING, author; b. N.Y.C., Dec. 21, 1883; s. James Lamoreaux and Sarah (Terry) G.; student Wellington Coll., Berkshire, Eng., 1901; m. Winifred Jones, Mar. 23, 1933; 1 son, Harold Sterling. With Huhn Edey & Co., 1904-08, N.Y. Stock Exchange, 1908-22; ret., 1922; co-founder, dir. Gila Pueblo, 1927-50. Bd. dirs. Gila Pueblo Archaeol. Found., Alexander-Bee Found., Santa Barbara, Cal. Fellow A.A.A.S.; mem. Am. Anthrop. Assn., Epigraphic Soc. Author: series Medallion Papers, 1929-47; Men Out of Asia, 1947; A History of the Ancient Southwest, 1958; Men Out of the Past, 1975. Contbr. articles on archaeology and anthropology to profl. publs. Address: Santa Barbara CA. *

GLANDER, CHARLES EMORY, lawyer; b. W. Alexandria, Ohio, Mar. 5, 1903; s. Charles Dietrich and Carrie Alice (Brower) G.; B.A., Ohio State U., 1925, J.D., 1930; student U. Mich., summers 1926-28; m. Frances Fay Chandler, Apr. 15, 1931; children—Charles Franklin, David Gordon. Debate coach Purdue U., 1925-27, Ohio State U., 1927-43; admitted to Ohio bar, 1930; practice law, 1930-40, 51-79; partner firm Wright, Harlor, Morris, Arnold & Glander, Columbus, Ohio, 1953-71, Glander, Brant, Ledman & Newman, Columbus, 1971-79; atty. Ohio Div. Securities, 1940; exec. sec. Gov. Ohio, 1941-45; tax commr. Ohio, 1945-51; lectr. Ohio State U. Coll. Law, 1948-64, adj. prof., 1965-74. Pres. Council Social Agencies, Columbus and Franklin County, 1955-57, Ohio Citizens Council Health and Welfare, 1959-61; trustee, chmn. bd., pres. Citizens Research Inc.; trustee, moderator, pres. Columbus Town Meeting, weekly TV and radio forum. Mem. Nat. Assn. Tax Adminstrs. (pres. 1948-50), Ohio State U. Assn. (nat. pres. 1957-59), Ohio State U. Law Alumni Assn. (pres. 1952-53), Nat. Tax. Assn. (pres. 1962-63), Am., Ohio (chmn. taxation com. 1960-63), Columbus bar assns., Columbus Area C. of C. (chmn. pub. finance com.), Kappa Sigma, Delta Sigma Rho, Phi Delta Phi. Conglist. Clubs: Kiwanis (pres. 1951), Kit-Kat, University (Columbus); Faculty (Ohio State U.). Contbr. articles law jour. Home: Columbus, Ohio. Died Jan. 26, 1979; buried Columbus.

GLASER, JOHN FREDERIC, educator; b. Hamilton, O., Oct. 27, 1920; s. Carl Edward and Verna (Thoma) G.; A.B., Washington and Jefferson Coll., 1941; A.M., Harvard, 1942, Ph.D., 1949. Instr. history Washington Sq. Coll., N.Y. U., 1948-52, 53-54; asst. prof., asso. prof. history Ripon (Wis.) Coll., 1954-63, prof., 1963-79, chmn. dept. history, 1962-69, 75-76. Served to 1st lt. AUS, 1942-46. Am. Council Learned Socs. scholar, 1952-53. Mem. Am. Hist. Assn., Midwest Conf. Brit. Studies (pres. 1972-74), Phi Beta Kappa, Phi Alpha Theta. Conglist. Home: Ripon, Wis. Died Sept. 30, 1979.

GLASGOW, SAMUEL MCPHEETERS, clergyman; b. Fincastle, Va., Mar. 18, 1883; s. Frank Thomas and Grace Woodson (McPheeters) G.; grad. Ann Smith Acad., Lexington, Va., 1899; A.B., Washington and Lee Univ., 1903, D.D., 1921; B.D., Union Theol. Sem., Richmond, Va., 1908, Hogue fellow, same, 1908-09; m. Mary Finley McIlwaine, Oct. 28, 1909. Ordained ministry Presbyn. Ch. in U.S., 1909; missionary on Tex. border, at Mercedes, Tex., 1909-13, 1914-16; prof. Greek and homiletics, Austin (Tex.) Theol. Sem., 1913-14; pastor Bream Memorial Ch., Charleston, W.Va., 1916-20, First Ch., Knoxville, Tenn., 1920-31, Independent Presbyn. Ch., Savannah, Ga., 1931-44; supply preacher First Presbyn. Ch., Charlotte, N.C., since 1945. Mem. Phi Gamma Delta. Author: Border Trails, 1912; (brochure) The Frontier, 1912; Brief Book Studies in the General Epistles, 1929; My Tomorrow's Self, 1931; Daily Communion, 1933; The Splendor of Grace, 1937, Chapels—Today's Evangelistic Frontier, 1939. Part author: Needed Counsel for New Christians, 1922. Author of Gospel hymns. Home: Charlotte, N.C.

GLASS, ROBERT RIGBY, mgmt. cons.; b. Me., Aug. 18, 1914; ed. Mil. Acad. Me.; B.S., U.S. Mil. Acad., 1935; grad. Command and Gen. Staff Sch., 1946, Armed Forces Staff Coll., 1950, Army War Coll., 1954; m. Phyllis Clarke Thompson; 5 children. Commd. 2d lt. U.S. Army, 1935; advanced through grades to maj. gen., 1965, ret., 1969; mgmt. cons. Planning Research Corp., McLean, Va., from 1969. Decorated Legion of Merit with 2 oak leaf clusters, D.S.M., Bronze Star, Air medal. Co-author: Intelligence Is for Commanders. Home: Arlington, Va. Died Aug. 28, 1979.

GLASSCOCK, RALPH, vending co. exec.; b. Clinton, Mo., Feb. 5, 1928; s. Ralph Smith and May (Woods) G.; student Kansas City Coll. Commerce, 1948-49; m. Thelma Maye Rainer, June 10, 1951; children—Vicki Lee, Timothy Ray, Barry Alan. Sales rep. Fitts Dry Goods Co., Kansas City, Mo., 1949-50; partner G & G Furniture Co., Clinton, Mo., 1950-51; owner Clinton Distbrs., 1951-62; owner, pres. Golden Valley Vendors, Clinton, 1962-77; pres. Glasscock Enterprises Inc., Clinton, 1972-77; exec. com. Modern Security Life Ins. Co., Springfield, Mo. Pres. Optimist Internat. Found., St. Louis, 1974-75. Bd. dirs. Kansas City Area council Boy Scouts Am. Served with USNR, 1945-48. Mem. Clinton C. of C. (pres. 1965), V.F.W., Am. Legion. Home: Clinton, Mo. Died Jan. 12, 1977; buried Englewood Cemetery, Clinton.

GLASSFORD, PELHAM DAVIS, army officer (ret.), artist; Las Vegas, N.M., Aug. 8, 1883; s. William A. and Allie Seymour (Davis) G.; B.S., U.S. Mil. Acad., 1904; grad. Mounted Service Sch., 1907, Sch. of the Line, 1922, Gen. Staff Sch., 1923, Army War Coll., 1924; m. Cora Arthur Carleton, Dec. 25, 1907 (divorced); children—Guy Carleton, Elizabeth (Mrs. Lee W. Parke), Pelham D., Dorothy Seymour (Mrs. William Graham); m. 2d, Lucille K. Painter, Sept. 5, 1934. Commd. 2d lt., arty., U.S. Army, 1904, and advanced through grades to lt. col., 1928; retired with rank of brig. gen., 1931. Dir. internal security Office of Provost Marshal Gen., World War II. Decorated D.S.M., Purple Heart, Silver Star citation, World War I; Legion of Merit, World War II. Awarded 3d prize, mural painting, State House, Boston, 1926. Artist mem. Laguna Beach Art Assn. Episcopalian. Clubs: Army and Navy Country, Army-Navy (Washington). Co-author of several textbooks of U.S. Mil. Acad. and Command and Gen. Staff Sch. Contbr. articles to Scripps-Howard, Universal Service and other news publ. services. Home Laguna Beach, Calif. *

GLASSMAN, HARRY PAUL, justice Maine Supreme Ct.; b. N.Y.C., Feb. 21, 1928; s. Max and Lottie (Silverstein) G.; student U. So. Calif., 1944-46, 47-48; B.A., U. Calif., Berkeley, 1949, LL.B., 1951; LL.M., U. Va., 1962; m. Caroline Duby, May 22, 1953; 1 son, Max Avon. Admitted to Calif. bar, 1952, U.S. Supreme Ct. bar, 1958; gen. practice law, San Francisco, 1952-61; instr. U. Va. Law Sch., 1961-62; asso. prof. law U. Maine, 1962-64, prof. law, 1964-71; justice Superior Ct. of Maine, Portland, 1971-81, regional presiding justice Region I, 1975-79; justice Maine Supreme Jud. Ct., 1979-81; reporter to criminal rules adv. com. and cons. Maine Supreme Jud. Ct., 1963-71; chmn. Maine Gov.'s Planning Com. on Criminal Law Adminstrn., 1966-68; mem. Maine Law Enforcement Plan and Assistance Agy., 1968-72, chmn., 1971-72. Served with U.S. Army, 1946-47. Mem. Am. Law Inst. Democrat. Jewish. Author: Maine Practice, Rule of Criminal Procedure with Commentary, 1967. Home: Portland, Maine. Died May 15, 1981.

GLAVIS, LOUIS RUSSELL (GLA'VIS), lawyer; b. Eastern Shore, Md., June 10, 1883; s. George Oscar and Loucette Estelle (Smith) G.; student Lawrenceville (N.Y.) Sch., 1897-99. Began as spl. agent Gen. Land Office, Dept. Interior, 1904; admitted to Calif. Bar, 1914, and practiced, San Francisco and Washington, D.C.; formerly atty. and spl. investigator for U.S. Senate Com. on Indian Affairs; dir. investigations Dept. Interior, 1933-36; chief investigator Senate Campaign Expenditures Com., July 1936-Jan. 1937; returned to private law practice. Mason. Clubs: Yarmouth (Nova Scotia) Golf; Arctic (Seattle); Columbia Country (Washington, D.C.); Gibson Island Yacht (Gibson Island, Md.); Missouri Athletic (St. Louis, Mo.). Contbr. series of articles to mags. on Tea Pot Dome oil scandal, Ku Klux Klan, prohibition law, etc. Home: Yarmouth, Nova Scotia. Address: Washington, D.C. *

GLEED, THOMAS F., bus. exec.; b. Glenwood, Wis., Sept. 5, 1900; student U. Wash., 1918-22; m. Mary Elizabeth Balmer, Sept. 29, 1923; children—Betty Delanne, Thomas B. Service sta. salesman Standard Oil Cal., 1922-25; bond salesman Carstens & Earles, Inc., 1925-27; mgr. bond dept. Met. Nat. Bank, 1927; v.p. First Nat. Co. Seattle, 1929-46, dir., 1934, pres., 1946; became asst. v.p. Seattle-First Nat. Bank, 1934-37, v.p., 1937-45, dir., pres., 1945-51; pres. Simpson Timber Co., 1951-62, chmn. finance com., 1962-65; pres. Gleed & Co.; chmn. bd. Crows Nest Industries, Ltd.; dir. emeritus UAL, Inc.; presiding dir. Seattle Times; dir. Eddy Investment Co., Port Blakely Mill Co.; bd. advisers Puget Sound Nat. Bank. Bd. advisers U. Puget Sound Law Sch. Bd. dirs. Arboretum Found. Wash. Mem. Newcomen Soc., Chevaliers du Tastevin, Internat. Order St. Hubert, Sigma Chi. Clubs: Vancouver (B.C., Can.); Twenty Nine, Tuft and Field, Raffles (N.Y.C.); Bohemian, Pacific Union (San Francisco); University, Rainier, Seattle Golf, Tennis, Yacht, 380, 487 (Seattle); Le Mirador Country (Switzerland); Tacoma; Balboa (Mazatlan). Home: Seattle, Wash. Died Sept. 3, 1977.

GLEESON, WILLIAM F., lawyer; b. Bklyn., Nov. 15, 1883; student N.Y. Law Sch., Fordham U. With Lehigh Valley R.R. Co. since 1908, gen. counsel, N.Y.C., since 1948.

GLENN, CHARLES LESLIE, clergyman; b. N.Y.C., Mar. 17, 1900; s. Charles and Elizabeth Jane (McComb) G.; M.E., Stevens Inst. Tech., 1921, D.E., 1973; B.D., Va. Sem., 1926; D.D., 1938; S.T.D., Dickinson Coll., 1948; children by previous marriage—Georgiana Sibley (Mrs. William B. Rodiger), Margaret Harper (Mrs. John S. Estey), Charles Leslie; m. 2d, Amelia Neville Johnson Barry, July 15, 1956. Ordained to ministry Episcopal Ch., 1926; nat. sec. for coll. work Episcopal Ch., 1927-30; rector Christ Ch., Cambridge, Mass., 1930-40, St. John's Ch., Washington, 1940-56; mental health researcher U. Mich. Med. Sch., 1956-60; sub-dean Washington cathedral, 1968-76. Active Boy Scouts Am., YMCA, More Men for Ministry Found., Ch. Soc. for Coll. Work. Bd. dirs. Berea (Ky.) Coll., Ross Found., Camp Dudley. Served with USNRF, World War I; to capt., chaplain, USNR, World War II. Mem. Friendly Sons of St. Patrick, Tau Beta Pi. Mason. Clubs: Alfalfa, Metropolitan, Chevy Chase, F Street, Rotary, Nat. Press. (Washington); Century (N.Y.C.). Author: A Scornful Wonder, 1976. Home: Washington, D.C. Died Nov. 8, 1976.

GLESMANN, LOUIS GEORGE, mfg. exec.; b. Rome, N.Y., Aug. 21, 1893; s. Louis and Amelia Elizabeth (Hammann) G.; Chem.E., Lehigh U., 1915; m. Eleanor Bradford Brainerd, Oct. 2, 1916; children—Louis George, John Brainerd, Mary Carolyn. Metallurgist Rome Brass & Copper Co., 1915-35; supervisor of methods Rome Div., Revere Copper and Brass, Inc., 1935-37, asst. works mgr., 1937-48, works mgr. 1948-53; v.p. charge mfg. Revere Copper and Brass, Inc., 1953-58, cons., 1958-61, dir.; dir. Kent Co., Rome Farmers' Nat. Bank and Marine Midland Bank, Rome Mem. Rome C. of C. (past pres.), Delta Tau Delta

Mason. Presbyn. Home: Rome, N.Y. Died May 28, 1980; buried Rome.

GLOVER, CHARLES CARROLL, JR., banker; b. Washington, Jan. 1, 1888; s. Charles Carroll and Annie C. (Poor) G.; B.A., Yale, 1910, M.A., 1915; LL.B., George Washington U., 1912, LL.D., 1952; m. Marion Everett Wise, May 10, 1913; children—Marion Everett (dec.), Charles Carroll, Nancy Everett (Mrs. A. Lloyd Symington). Former partner Glover & Flather; pres. Washington Stock Exchange, 1927-28; now hon. chmn. bd. Riggs Nat. Bank. Enlisted in navy, res. officers' course, Annapolis, 1918; asst. supply officer on U.S. transport Antigone; lt. comdr. USNRF, ret. State del. to Republican conv., 1940. Hon. trustee George Washington U.; hon. trustee, past pres. Corcoran Gallery Art; D.C. rep. on Unemployment Relief Commn., 1931-32; mem. Bd. Pub. Welfare, D.C., 1929-32; past chmn. Asso. Charities; past vice chmn. Yale Alumni Adv. Bd.; hon. mem. Washington Nat. Monument Soc.; past vice chmn., trustee D.C. Community Chest; mem. Com. of 100 on Fed. City; hon. trustee Washington Cathedral, Netherlands-Am. Found. (Washington chpt.). Deocrated Order Orange-Nassau by Netherlands govt.; recipient 1968 bowl Washington Yale Club. Mem. Soc. Colonial Wars. S.A.R., Columbia Hist. Soc., Elihu, Alpha Delta Phi, Phi Delta Phi, Omicron Delta Kappa. Clubs: Metropolitan (pres. 1939); Yale (pres. 1921); Chevy Chase, Alibi, Cosmos, Alfalfa (Washington); Brook (N.Y.C.). Home: Washington, D.C. Died Nov. 13, 1976.

GLOVER, JOHN DESMOND, educator, cons.; b. Australia, Feb. 15, 1915; Ph.B., Brown U., 1936; M.B.A., Harvard U., 1939, A.M., 1942, Ph.D., 1947; m. Ruth Eleanor Adams, Sept. 12, 1938; children—Elizabeth Trias, Katherine, Margaret. Mem. staff U.S. C. of C., 1936-37; instr. and tutor econs. dept. Harvard U., 1939-42, faculty Grad. Sch. Bus. Adminstrn., 1942-76, successively instr., asst. prof., asso. prof., 1949-54, prof. bus. adminstrn., 1954-76, Learned-Lovett prof., 1970-76, mem. faculty Law Sch., 1974-76; chmn. bd. dirs. Cambridge Research Inst.; spl. cons. USAF, 1943-52; secretariat U.S. Strategic Bombing Survey, 1945, civilian rank of col.; chmn. internat. seminars corp. and govt. policy, Rotterdam, Barcelona, Bizerte; dir. Allied Chem. Corp.; cons. Hon. fellow U. Tel Aviv, 1970—. Author: Public Loans to Private Business, 1948, 79; The Attack on Big Business, 1954; (with R.M. Hower and Renato Tagiuri) The Administrator, Cases on Human Relations in Business, 5th edit., 1973; (with Gerald A. Simon) Chief Executives Handbook, 1975; The Revolutionary Corporations, 1980. Clubs: Harvard (N.Y.C. and Boston); Cosmos (Washington). Home: Cambridge, Mass. Died Feb. 16, 1981.

GLUECK, BERNARD (GLIK), psychiatrist; b. Poland, Dec. 10, 1884; M.D., Georgetown U., 1909; studied univs. of Munich and Berlin, 1911. Mem. staff Govt. Hosp. for Insane, 1909-16; mental examiner of immigrants, Port of New York, 1913; dir. psychiatric clinic, Sing Sing Prison, 1915-18; dir. of mental hygiene dept., N.Y. Sch. of Social Work, and Bur. of Child Guidance, 1918-23. Capt. Medical Corps, U.S. Army, 1918; chief of staff Stony Lodge Foundation, Ossining-on-Hudson. Mem. A.M.A., Am. Psychiatric Assn., Am. Psychopathol. Assn., Am. Psychoanalytic Assn., N.Y. Soc. Psychopathology and Psychotherapy (ex-pres.). Author: Studies in Forensic Psychiatry, 1916. Translator: (with John E. Lind) Neurotic Constitution (by Alfred Adler), 1917; Introduction to a Psychoanalytic Psychiatry (by Paul Schilder), 1927; (with Bertram D. Lewin) Psychoanalysis of the Total Personality (by Franz Alexander), 1930. Lecturer New School for Social Research. Address: New York, N.Y.; and Ossining, N.Y. *

GLUECK, SHELDON, criminologist; b. Warsaw, Poland, Aug. 15, 1896; s. Charles and Anna (Steinhardt) G.; brought to U.S., 1903, naturalized, 1920; student Georgetown U. Law Sch., 1914, 15; A.B., George Washington U., 1920, S.S.D., 1963; LL.B., LL.M., Nat. U. Law Sch., 1920; student Harvard Law Sch., 1926; A.M., Harvard U., 1922, Ph.D., 1924, Sc.D., 1958; LL.D., U. Thessaloniki (Greece), 1948; m. Eleaor Touroff, Apr. 16, 1922 (dec.); 1 dau., Anitra Joyce Rosberg (Dec.). Instr. criminology and penology, dept. social ethics Harvard U., 1925-29, asst. prof. criminology Law Sch., 1929-31, prof., 1931-50; Lowell lectr., 1935, Roscoe Pound prof. law, 1950-63, emeritus, 1963-80, dir. basic researches into causes, mgmt. and prevention of juvenile delinquency, 1925-80; bd. advisers Psychiatry and the Law Found.; ofcl. del. U.S. govt. to Internat. Prison Congress, Prague, 1930, Paris, 1950; mem. Adv. Com. on Rules of Criminal Proc., U.S. Supreme Ct., Am. Law Inst. for Youth Correction Authority and the Model Penal Code; adviser to Justice Robert H. Jackson on law governing War Crime Criminals. Bd. overseers Brandeis U. Center Study of Violence. Served with A.E.F., World War I. Recipient Isaac Ray award Am. Psychiat. Assn., 1961; (with wife) August Vollmer award Am. Soc. Criminology, 1961; Gold medal Inst. Criminal Anthropology, U. Rome, 1964; Beccaria Gold medal German Soc. Criminology, 1964. Fellow Am. Acad. Arts and Sci., AAAS, Am. Psychiat. Assn. (hon.), Internat. Acad. Law and Sci.; mem. Am. Soc. Criminology (past v.p.), Am. Bar Assn. (juvenile delinquency com.), N.Y. State Bar. Club: Harvard Faculty. Author numerous books, including: Mental Disorder and the Criminal Law, 1925; Crime and Justice, 1936; The Nuremberg Trial and Aggressive War, 1946; Crime and Correction: Selected Papers, 1952; Law and Psychiatry: Cold War or Entente Cordiale?, 1962; Roscoe Pound and Criminal Justice, 1965; Continental Police Practice, 1973; (with Eleanor T. Glueck) books including: One Thousand juvenile Delinquents, 1934, After-conduct of Discharged Offenders, 1944, Unraveling Juvenile Delinquency, 1950, Delinquents in the Making, 1952, Physique and Delinquency, 1956, Predicting Delinquency and Crime, 1959, Family Environment and Delinquency, 1962, Ventures in Criminology, 1964; Delinquents and Non-Delinquents in Perspective, 1968, Toward Typology of Juvenile Offenders: Implications for Therapy and Prevention, 1970; Lives of Labor-Lives of Love; editor publs. including: The Welfare State and the National Welfare, 1952; The Problem of Delinquency, 1958; (with Eleanor Glueck) Identification of Predelinquents, 1972; cons. editor Community Mental Health jour.; contbr. articles to profl. jours. Died Mar. 10, 1980.

GLUECKSMAN, J(OE) D(AVE), lawyer; b. Berlin, Germany, Apr. 21, 1924; s. Egon and Hanna Joan (Wiernik) G.; came to U.S., 1941, naturalized, 1943; student Syracuse U., 1946-49; A.B., Cornell U., 1949, J.D., 1952; m. Lila Paul, Jan. 2, 1949; children—Karen, Arielle, Lorene Michelle. Admitted to Cal. bar, 1953; practiced in Los Angeles, 1953-76; partner firm Irwin & Gluecksman, Los Angeles, 1967-76. Arrangements chmn. State Bar Conf., 1975. Mem. Mayor's Adv. Com., Los Angeles, 1964-66. Served with AUS, 1943-46; ETO. Mem. Los Angeles County (trustee 1973-75), Beverly Hills (gov. 1962-65), Century City (trustee 1969-75) bar assns., Counsel Affiliated Bar Pres. (chmn. 1973-75), Phi Delta Phi. Address: Sherman Oaks, Calif. Died Dec. 20, 1976.

GOAD, LOUIS CLIFFORD, motor vehicle mfg. exec.; b. Petersburg, Ind., Feb. 9, 1901; s. William and Katherine (French) G.; M.E., U. Ill., 1923; m. Frances Creek, Aug. 1926; children—Thomas C., David L. Engr., Delco Remy Co., Anderson, Ind., 1923-28, mgr., Muncie, Ind., 1928-33; gen. mgr., AC spark plug div., Gen. Motors Corp., Flint, Mich., 1933-40, asst. to v.p., Detroit, 1940-42, gen. mgr. Eastern aircraft div., Linden, N.J., 1942-45; v.p. Gen. Motors Corp. 1943-51, dir., 1946-66, Gen. Motors group exec., 1945-46, 1948-51, exec. v.p., 1951-66, gen. mgr. Fisher Body Division, 1946-48. Mem. Soc. Auto. Engrs. Clubs: Detroit Athletic, Recess (Detroit); Bloomfield Hills Country (Bloomfield Hills, Mich.); University (N.Y.). Home: Bloomfield Hills, Mich. Died Nov. 14, 1979; buried Woodlawn Cemetery, Detroit.

GOAR, EVERETT L., physician; b. in Clinton Co., Ind., Nov. 13, 1886; s. Eli J. and Orpha L. (King) G.; A.B., Ind. U., 1907; M.D., Rush Med. Coll., 1909; student N.Y. Eye and Ear Infirmary, 1920; Dr. Ophthalmology, University of Colorado, 1922; married Italia West, 1917; 1 son, Everett L.; married 2d, Eleise Hailey, 1930; children—Robert J., Ann Catherine. Intern at the Cook County Hospital Chicago, 1909-10; pvt. practice ophthalmology, Houston, since 1921; head dept., ophthalmology Baylor U. Coll. Medicine since 1943, U.S. Vets. Hosp., 1949. Served as maj. U.S.M.C., World War I. Diplomate Am. Bd. Ophthalmology. Fellow A.C.S.; mem. Am. Ophthal. Soc. (pres. 1954-55), Nat. Soc. Prevention Blindness (director, 1952—, chairman professional committee and Texas committee), Am. Acad. Ophthalmology and Otolaryngology, So. Med. Assn., A.M.A., Alpha Tau Omega, Phi Rho Sigma. Presbyn. Mason. (32 deg.). Author: Handbook of Ophthalmology, 1948; Manual of Slit Lamp Microscqpy (with Thorpe, Masters and Kronfeld), 1948. Home: Houston. *

GODDARD, JAMES (H.), operatic basso; b. at Maryville, Tenn., May 15, 1884; s. James A. and Mary C. (Bowles) G.; ed. Maryville Coll.; unmarried. Went west at 18, and sang in 1st M.E. Ch., Tacoma, Wash., 2 yrs.; removed to Chicago and studied with William Clare Hall, and 2 yrs. with Jean De Reszke, in Paris, France; début in Covent Garden, London, Oct. 19, 1911; sang King Mark, in "Tristan and Isolde," Landgraf Hermann, in "Tannhauser," and other leading rôles; has appeared in prin. cities of Germany, England, U.S. and Can.; with Chicago Grand Opera Co., 1915. Song leader U.S.A., Sept. 1, 1918-Jan. 1, 1919; concert and oratorio appearances since 1919. Home: New York, N.Y. *

GÖDEL, KURT, logician, educator; b. Bruenn, Czechoslovakia, Apr. 28, 1906; came to U.S., 1940, naturalized, 1948; s. Rudolf and Marianne (Handschuh) G.; Ph.D., U. Vienna, 1930; Litt.D., Yale, 1951; Sc.D., Harvard, 1952, Amherst U., 1967, Rockefeller U., 1972; m. Adele Porkert, Sept. 20, 1938 (dec. Feb. 4, 1981). Privatdozant U. Vienna, 1933-38; mem. Inst. Advanced Study, Princeton, 1933, 35, 38-52, prof., 1953-77, research in math. and philosophy. Co-recipient Einstein award Lewis and Rosa Strauss Meml. Fund, 1951; Nat. medal of Sci., 1975. Mem. Nat. Acad. Scis., Am. Acad. of Arts and Scis., Am. Philos. Soc., London Math. Soc. (hon.), Assn. for Symbolic Logic, Royal Soc. of London (U.K.); corr. mem. Ac Sci mor pol., Paris, Brit. Acad., London. Author: Ueber formal unentscheidbare Saetze, 1931; The Consistency of the Continuum Hypothesis, 1940; Rotating Universes in General Relativity Theory, 1950. Home: Princeton, N.J. Died Jan. 14, 1977; buried Princeton.

GODSOE, JOSEPH GERALD, textile co. exec.; b. Halifax, N.S., Can., Mar. 16, 1908; s. Walter M. and Nan G. Godsoe; student Collegiate Inst., Halifax; A.B., Dalhousie U., 1926, LL.B., 1928, LL.D., 1955; m. Margaret Graham Cowperthwaite, Aug. 6, 1932; children—Valerie, Peter, Gerald, Jane. Read law with Hon. J.A. Walker; called to bar N.S., 1928, Ont., 1936; asso. Burchell, Smith, Parker & Fogo, Halifax, 1928-30; pvt. sec. Cyrus S. Eaton, industrialist and financier, Cleve., 1930-31; joined Confederation Life Assn., Toronto, 1931, formed legal dept., 1931, asst. solicitor, 1934-36; exec. asst. and solicitor, 1936-39, asst. gen. mgr., 1939-45; v.p., dir. Brit. Am. Oil Co., Ltd., 1945-55, exec. v.p., 1955-58; chmn. exec. com. Great Western Garment Co., Great Western Garment Co. (Eastern) Ltd.; chmn., dir. Dana Securities Ltd.; chmn. Newconex Holdings Ltd.; chmn. exec. com. Great Western Garment Co. (Man., Can.) Ltd.; dir. Copperfields Mining Corp., Ltd., Canatogs, Ltd., RCA Victor, Crown Life Ins. Co., Dominion & Anglo Investment Corp., Internat. Paints (Can.), Ltd., Canadian Alpha Lessors, Ltd., Citizens Research Inst. Can., Rocky Mountain Equipment Ltd., Vancouver Equipment Rentals Ltd., Vancouver Equipment Corp. Ltd., Newconex Indsl. Securities (Western) Ltd., Indsl. Sales (1972) Ltd., Union Tractor Ltd. Mem. ct. referees under Dominion Unemployment Ins. Act; internat. adv. com. Boston Conf. on Diston.; mem. Nat. Agy. Rev. Com. Bd. dirs. Toronto Gen. Hosp.; past pres. Toronto Bd. Trade; v.p., dir. Ont. Safety League; bd. dirs. Community Chest Greater Toronto, Canadian Nat. Exhibition; mem. bd. Canadian Council Christians and Jews, Right Honourable C.D. Howe Found., Boys' Village; bd. govs. Dalhousie U. Decorated comdr. Order British Empire. Mem. Canadian C. of C. (v.p.), Canadian Mfrs. Assn. (vice chmn. edn. com.), Assn. Canadian Clubs (exec. com.), Canadian Inst. Internat. Affairs (exec. com. and co-opted mem. nat. council). Clubs: Canadian, Toronto (hon. sec. 1940-42, pres. 1942-43), National, York (Toronto); Rideau (Ottawa). Home: Toronto, Ont., Can. Died Jan. 12, 1977.

GOEBEL, MAX THEODORE, former chemist; b. Compton, Ill., Oct. 28, 1906; s. August and Louise (Brueckner) G.; A.B., U. Ill., 1928, Ph.D. in Organic Chemistry, 1934; m. Marguerite Kuehn, Feb. 6, 1932; children—Margaret, Richard. Research chemist Comml. Solvents Corp., Ind., 1928-30; asst. chemist U. Ill., 1930-32; research chemist exptl. sta. E. I. du Pont de Nemours & Co., Wilmington, Del., 1934-38, research group leader, 1938-41, asst. dir. exptl. lab., Cleve., 1941-44, dir., 1944-48, asst. dir. research div. indsl. and biochems. dept., Wilmington, 1948-50, research dir., 1950-70. Vice pres. Agrl. Research Inst., NRC, 1958, chmn. budget and finance com., mem. governing bd., 1959. Home: Chadds Ford, Pa. Died Dec. 21, 1979.

GOETHALS, GEORGE RODMAN, construction engr.; b. West Point, N.Y., Mar. 4, 1886; s. Gen. George W. and Effie (Rodman) G.; grad. Central High Sch., Washington, 1904; grad. U.S. Mil. Acad., 1908; grad. U.S. Engr. Sch., Washington, 1910; m. Priscilla Jewett Howes, of Watertown, N.Y., Oct. 11, 1910; 1 son, George W. II. Duty with Isthmian Canal Commn. most of time, 1908-14, as asst. engr. in charge constrn. Panama Canal defenses; instr. Dept. Civ. and Mil. Engring. and prof. practical mil. engring., U.S. Mil. Acad., 1914-18; v.p. George W. Goethals and Co., cons. engrs., and industrial mgrs., New York, 1919-23; with Dwight P. Robinson & Co. since 1923, now asst. to constrn. mgr. Commd. 2d lt. Engrs., U.S.A., Feb. 1908; promoted through grades to col. Aug. 1918; lt. col. retired Aug. 4, 1919. Served as engr. officer Hdqrs. Army Arty., First Army, A.E.F.; later comdr. 316th Engrs. and div. engr. 91st Div.; mem. A.E.F. bd. to report on systems of sea coast defenses of the Allies, Austria and Turkey. Mem. Am. Soc. C.E., Soc. Am. Mil. Engrs., Permanent Internat. Assn. Navigation Congresses, New York Soc. of Panama Canal. Awarded Roosevelt Panama Medal, Victory Medal (3 clasps). Republican. Episcopalian. Clubs: University (New York); Army and Navy (Washington and Chicago); Adventurers (Chicago). Home: Mass.

GOETTELMANN, PAUL AUGUSTE, architect, educator; b. Bellevue, Ky., May 5, 1907; s. Fernand Camille and Germaine Helene (Schirr) G.; B.S. in Arch., Cath. U. Am., 1929, M.A. in Arch., 1930, Arch.D., 1933; diploma Beaux Arts Inst. Design, 1930; m. Emma Helene Laufenberg, June 20, 1933; children—Michael, Paula, Christine (Mrs. Franklin Calkins). Partner Locraft & Asso., 1954-64, Goettelmann & Xepapas, 1964-76 (both Washington); instr. Cath. U. Am., Washington, 1935-40, asst. prof., 1940-49, asso. prof., 1949-59, prof., 1959-76, chmn. dept. arch., 1959-65, asso. dean, chmn. dept. arch., 1965-70, asso. dean, chmn. dept. arch. and planning,

1970-76. Chmn. Urban Renewal Panel, Alexandria, Va., 1963-66; mem. archtl. cons. panel D.C. Hwy. Commn., 1964-66; pres. Bd. Registrars and Examiners for Architects, Washington, 1962-67; mem. Commn. Sacred Art, Archdiocese Washington, 1966-76, D.C. Bldg. Code Adv. Com., 1970-76. Trustee Fontainbleau (France) Sch. Fine Arts. Served to lt., USNR, World War II. Recipient Bene Merenti medal Pope Paul VI, 1964; Excellence in Design award Washington Bd. Trade, 1965, 66; award Cath. U. Am. Alumni Assn., 1966; Senator's Alumni award Cath. U. Am., 1967; Meritorious Pub. Service award D.C., 1967. Fellow A.I.A. (past pres. Washington Met. chpt.); mem. Soc. Archtl. Historians, Assn. Collegiate Schs. Architecture, Nat. Council Arch. Registration Bds. Kiwanian. Clubs: Cosmos (Washington). Prin. works include Our Lady Good Counsel Ch., Vienna, Va., 1971; Holy Spirit Ch., Forestville, Md., 1970; St. Catherine Greek Orthodox Ch., Northern, Va., 1969; Our Lady Sorrows, Takoma Park, Md., 1964; Chapel, Marine Corps, Quantico, Va., 1941, St. Anthony's Ch., 1940, St. Luke's Ch., 1960, Cath. U. Am. Hartke Theatre Social Center, 1970, Washington Permanent Bldg. and Loan Assn., 1960, Enterprise Fed. Bldg. and Loan Sch. of Linguistics, Georgetown U., 1958, Ambassador McClintock residence, 1968 (all Washington). Home: Silver Spring, Md. Died Sept. 16, 1976.

GOLDBERG, MORRELL, hosp. adminstr.; b. Lawrence, Mass., Oct. 12, 1910; s. Samuel and Jennie (Hartman) G.; B.A., Dartmouth, 1933; postgrad. Columbia, 1937-39; m. Ruth Lazar, Feb. 22, 1941; children—Susan, Daniel, Jane. Asst. adminstr. Beth-El Hosp., Bklyn., 1937-41; adminstr. Jewish Hosp. Chronic Diseases, 1941-42; exec. v.p. Brookdale Hosp. Med. Center, Bklyn., 1946-77; lectr. pub. health Columbia, 1961-77. Pres. Hosp. Credit Exchange. Bd. dirs. Mayor N.Y.C.'s Comprehensive Health Planning Agy.; mem. coms. Blue Cross, N.Y. State Dept. Health; trustee Health and Hosp. Planning Council So. N.Y., N.Y. State Urban Devel. Corp. Served to capt. AUS, 1942-46. Fellow Am. Coll. Hosp. Adminstrs., Royal Soc. Health; mem. Greater N.Y. Hosp. Assn. (pres. 1974-75), Hosp. Assn. N.Y. State. Club: Dartmouth (N.Y.C.). Home: New York, N.Y. Died Dec. 5, 1977.

GOLDBERG, REUBEN LUCIUS (RUBE), sculptor; b. San Francisco, July 4, 1883; s. Max and Hannah G.; B.S., U. of Cal., 1904; m. Irma Seeman, Oct. 17, 1916; children—Thomas Reuben, George Warren. Cartoonist on San Francisco Chronicle, 1904-05, Bulletin, 1905-07, N.Y. Evening Mail, 1907-21; cartoons syndicated 1921-64; sculptor, 1964—. Dir. cartoon course Farmous Artists Sch. Winner 1948 Pulitzer Prize, best editorial cartoon; Reuben Nat. Cartoonists Soc. Award of Yr., 1968. Mem. Soc. Illustrators, Nat. Cartoonists Society (hon. pres.), Clubs: Coffee House, Dutch Treat, also Artists and Writers Golf Association. Author books including: Soup to Nuts (motion picture), 1930; Rube Goldberg's Guide to Europe, 1954; How to Remove Cotton from Bottle of Aspirin; I Made My Bed; Rube Goldberg vs. The Machine Age, 1968. Creator of Boob McNutt, Mike and Ike, Lucifer Butts, A. K. polit. cartoons. Home: N.Y.C. *

GOLDFARB, JACOB A., clothing mfg. exec.; b. Warsaw, Russia, June 15, 1895; s. Aaron and Sarah (Fisher) G.; student CCNY 1909-10; fellow Brandeis U., 1953, L.H.D.; m. Bertha Leventhal, Sept. 14, 1930; children—Betty (Mrs. Robert Watson, Jr.), Miriam (Mrs. Landon K. Thorne, Jr.), Ruth Elaine (Mrs. William Lese), Robert Jack. Founder, chmn. Union Underwear Co., Inc., until 1973; chmn. bd. CFC Corp., Fruit of Loom, Inc., until 1972; dir. Empire State Bank, Kansas City, Mo., Sterling Nat. Bank & Trust Co., N.Y.C.; mem. adv. bd. Phila & Reading Corp., until 1972; pres. Goldfarb Investing Corp. Trustee Grand St. Boys Found., 1954-78; trustee, treas. Brandeis U.; v.p., trustee N.Y.U. Jewish Culture Found.; v.p., chmn. nat. finance com. Inst. Human Relations. Served with U.S. Army, World War I. Mem. Fedn. Jewish Charities (trustee-at-large), Marketing Policy Inst. (dir., treas. 1951), Nat. Knitwear Assn. (exec. com. 1943). Mason; mem. B'nai B'rith. Clubs: Harmonie, Metropolis Contry (N.Y.C.). Home: New York, N.Y. Died May 28, 1978.

GOLDFINE, WILLIAM, banker; b. Warsaw, Poland, Oct. 28, 1898; s. Morris and Helen (Hochzeit) G.; ed. high sch.; m. Pauline Berger, Dec. 8, 1929; children—Joyce L. (Mrs. Richard A. Walzer), Carol A. (Mrs. Bernard I. Fain). Treas., mgr. Bronx Credit Union, 1919-32, Underwriters Trust Co., 1932-34; asst. v.p. Nat. Safety Bank, 1934-44; v.p. Nat. Bronx Bank, 1944-49, Mfrs. Trust Co., 1949-51; exec. v.p. Royal Nat. Bank of N.Y., 1951-61, pres., chief exec. officer, 1961-76, former chmn. bd., also dir.; vice chmn. Security Nat. Bank; dir. Dritch Crystal Dairies, Inc., Zion Kosher Products Corp., Security Mutual Ins. Co.; past chmn. bd. Royal Bus. Funds, Inc. Hon. chmn. Greater N.Y. Israel Bond Orgn. Pres. William Golfine found., Inc.; treas. Hebrew Home for Aged, New Bldg. Found. Fund; hon. pres. Hebrew Home for Aged at Riverdale; v.p. Bronx YM and YWCA, pres. of Pythian Camp. Mem. Am. Bankers Assn., Bronx Bd. Trade Bronx C. of C., Bronx Real Estate Bd., Bldg. Industry League. K.P. (past grand chancellor N.Y.), Mason (past lodge master), mem. B'nai B'rith (past lodge pres.). Home: New York, N.Y. Died Dec. 25, 1976.

GOLDFINGER, NATHANIEL, economist; b. N.Y.C., Aug. 20, 1916; s. Leo and Lena (Francis) G.; B.S., Coll. City N.Y., 1938; postgrad. New Sch. Social Research, 1941-42, Am. U., 1949-50; m. Elizabeth Claire Gordon, Mar. 5, 1954; children—Judith Susan, Ruth Irene. Dir. edn., research United Paperworkers Am., 1944-50; sec. CIO Com. Econ. Policy, 1950-53; asso. dir. research CIO, 1950-55; economist dept. research AFL-CIO, Washington, 1955-58, asst. dir. dept. research, 1958-60, dir., 1963-76. Bd. dirs. Nat. Bur. Econ. Research; exec. com. Joint Council Econ. Edn., mem. adv. com. Export-Import Bank, 1964-69. Mem. Am. Econ. Assn., Indsl. Relations Research Assn. (pres. 1974). Home: Silver Spring, Md. Died July 22, 1976.

GOLDMAN, RICHARD FRANKO, educator, condr., composer, author; b. N.Y.C., Dec. 7, 1910; s. Edwin Franko and Adelaide (Maibrunn) G.; A.B. with honors, Columbia, 1930; D.H.L., Lehigh U., 1964; D.F.A. (hon.), U. Md., 1971; D.Mus. (hon.), Mannes Coll. Music, 1972; m. Alexandra Rienzi, June 8, 1934; 1 son, Daniel Franko. Fellow fine arts and archaeology Columbia, 1931; composer, author, music critic, 1931-80; asso. condr. Goldman Band, 1937-56, condr., 1956-80; faculty Juilliard Sch. Music, 1947-60, chmn., dept. lit. and materials of music, 1953-60; faculty Princeton U., 1952-56, Columbia U., 1961, N.Y. U., 1963; Guggenheim fellow, 1962; prin. N.Y. critic Musical Quar., 1948-68; editor Juilliard Rev., 1953-58, dir. Peabody Conservatory Music, 1968-80; pres. Peabody Inst., Balt., 1969-77, pres. emeritus, 1977-80; pres., treas. Goldman Band Concerts, Inc.; lectr., guest condr. univs., communities U.S.; recs. with Goldman Band for Decca, Columbia, New World Recs., Capitol. Chmn. Assn. Ind. Colls. Music, 1970-73; adviser Elizabeth Sprague Coolidge Found., Library of Congress. Sec.-treas. Md. Ind. Coll. and U. Assn., 1971-73. Recipient commn. Nat. Fedn. Music Clubs, 1948, Nat. Band Assn., 1962; Juilliard Mus. Found. award, 1955, Little Orchestra Soc. award for opera libretto, 1960; Alice M. Ditson Conductor's award, 1961; Key to City of New Orleans, 1963, Distinguished Service in Music award Kappa Kappa Psi, 1971, Hall of Honor award Balt. Arts Council, 1971, Deems Taylor-ASCAP award for critical writing, 1975, Andrew White medal Loyola Coll., 1976. Served with OSS, AUS, 1942-45. Mem. ASCAP, Am. Bandmasters Assn., League Composers (past exec. dir.). Phi Beta Kappa, Delta Omicron (nat. patron), Phi Mu Alpha (hon.), Phi Beta Mu, Kappa Kappa Psi, Kappa Delta Psi, Tau Beta Sigma. Composer numerous works for band, orch., chamber groups. Author: The Band's Music, 1938; The Concert Band, 1946; The Wind Band, 1961; Harmony in Western Music, 1965. Translator: The Mandarin and other stories (Eca de Queiroz), 1965. Contbr. to New Oxford History of Music, Musik in Geschichte und Gegenwart, Grove's Dictionary, others. Contbr. articles and fiction to numerous musical, scholarly and gen. publs. Address: Baltimore, Md. Died Jan. 19, 1980.

GOLDMAN, ROBERT PHILIP, lawyer; b. Cin., May 17, 1890; s. Louis J. and Rose (Frohman) G.; A.B., Yale, 1911; LL.B., Harvard, 1914; student Université de Paris, Faculté de Droit, 1919; m. Therese Wolfstein, Oct. 16, 1921; children—David Wolfstein, Agnes Edna, Barbara Therese (Mrs. J.L. Cohen). Admitted to Ohio bar, 1914; asso. firm Paxton, Warrington & Seasongood, Cin., 1914-23, mem. firm, 1923-27; mem. Paxton & Seasongood, 1927-70; of counsel, 1971-76. Former pres. Proportional Representation League. Trustee, Salinger, A.B. Dolly and Ralph Cohen founds.; past trustee, hon. trustee Hebrew Union Coll.-Jewish Inst. of Religion, chmn. bd., 1958-62; hon. trustee City Charter Com., chmn. bd., 1955-58; trustee, then hon. trustee Union Am. Hebrew Congregations, pres., 1937-43; chmn. Charter Revision Com., Cin., 1949; pres. Isaac M. Wise Temple, 1928-30, Cin. Jewish Community Council, 1944-47; co-chmn. Cin. chpt. Nat. Conf. Christians and Jews, 1958-62, hon. award, 1963. Served with 309th Supply Train, 84th Div., and with Sorbonne Detachment, U.S. Army, with A.E.F., 1918-19. Recipient Distinguished Service medal Ohio Bar Assn., 1966, Ohio Bar Found., 1973. Mem. Ohio Archaeol. and Hist. Soc. (trustee 1932-38), Am., Ohio (com. bnkg. and comml. law 1949-61, chmn.), Cin. (pres. 1954-55) bar assns., Am. Law Inst., Phi Beta Kappa. Clubs: Cin. Lawyers, University, Losantiville Country (Cin.); Yale (N.Y.C.). Author: (with Clyde M. Abbott) Anderson's Ohio Corporation Desk Book, 1951, 56, 66, supplements, 1968-74. Contbr. law revs. profl. jours. Home: Cincinnati, Ohio. Died Apr. 10, 1976; buried Cin.

GOLDMARK, PETER CARL, radio, TV exec.; b. Budapest, Hungary, Dec. 2, 1906; s. Alexander and Emmy G.; student U. Vienna, 1925-31, B.S., Ph.D.; D.Sc., Fairfield U., 1967, Poly. Inst. Bklyn., 1968; D.H.L., Dartmouth Coll., 1974, Adelphi Coll., 1976; children—Peter Carl, Frances C., Christopher W., Andrew G., Jonathan, Susan. Came to U.S., 1933, naturalized, 1937, TV engr. in charge dept. Pye Radio, Ltd., Cambridge, Eng., 1931-33; cons. engr. N.Y.C., 1934-35; chief engr. TV dept. CBS, N.Y.C., 1936-44, dir. engring. research and devel., 1944-50, v.p. engring. research and devel. dept., 1950-72, pres. CBS Labs. div. CBS, 1972; pres. Goldmark Communications Corp., from 1972. War research part time Radio Research Lab. Harvard U.; vis. prof. med. electronics U. Pa. Med. Sch.; vis. prof. communications Fairfield (Conn.) U. Mem. Smithsonian Council; mem. Gov.'s Commn. on Conn.'s Future. Recipient Morris Liebman Meml. prize for electronic research, 1946; Vladimir K. Zworykin award for devel. and utilization electronic TV, 1961; George Washington award for contbns. to sci., 1967; Nat. Urban Service award for efforts war on poverty, 1967, Sarnoff Gold Medal award for pioneering contbrns. to communications, 1969; Elliott Cresson medal for devel. of LP record, color television broadcast system and electronic recording, 1969. Soc. Motion Picture and Television Engring. Soc. Progress medal, 1970, Indsl. Research Medal, 1972, Carnegie Mellon award, 1972; Golden Omega award, 1973; Nat. Govs. Council award, 1973; Harold Pender award U. Pa., 1974; Trustee award Nat. Acad. Television Arts and Scis., 1975; Nat. Human Relations award NCCJ, 1975. Poynter fellow Yale. Fellow Am. Inst. Elec. Engrs., Inst. Radio Engrs., Soc. Motion Picture Engrs., Franklin Inst., TV Soc. (London); mem. Nat. Acad. Scis., Nat. Acad. Engring. Author: Autobiography, 1973. Contbr. to profl. Jours. Patentee in field TV, radio. Deceased.

GOLDRING, WILLIAM, physician, educator; b. Anniston, Ala., May 8, 1898; s. Paul and Rebecca (Rosenfeld) G.; student St. John's Coll., Fordham U., 1916-18; B.S. in Medicine, N.Y. U., 1920, M.D., 1922; m. Helen Heffner, Sept. 4, 1928; 1 dau., Roberta (Mrs. Robert Coles). Intern Bellevue Hosp., N.Y.C., 1922-24, resident 1924-26, mem. staff, 1926-81, vis. physician, 1945-81; mem. faculty N.Y. U. Sch. Medicine, 1926-81, prof. medicine, 1960-81; cons. physician Goldwater Meml. Hosp., Beth Israel Hosp., Manhattan VA Hosp.; attending physician N.Y. U. Hosp., 1949-81, mem. exec. com. med. bd., 1950-53. Mem. Macy Found. Confs. Hypertension, 1949-53; med. adv. bd. Ruth Papier Nephrosis Found., 1950-81; cons. cardiovascular diseases WHO, 1951-53. Recipient Alumni Sci. award N.Y. U. Sch. Medicine, 1961, Med. Sch. Alumni medallion, 1965. Diplomate Am. Bd. Internal Medicine (cardiovascular disease). Fellow ACP, N.Y. Acad. Medicine; mem. Harvey Soc., Am. Physiol. Soc., Soc. Exptl. Biology and Medicine, Am. (council high blood pressure research 1939-61, chmn. program com. peripheral vascular sect. 1939-40, exec. com. sci. council 1956-57, bd. dirs. 1956-57, mem. central com. 1957-58, chmn. council circulation 1957-59), N.Y. (chmn. com. vocational guidance cardiacs 1928-35, mem. exec. com. 1943-81, bd. dirs. 1945-81, chmn. adv. council research 1946-47, 61-63, pres., 1959-61, mem. med. adv. com. 1963-81) heart assns., Sigma Xi, Alpha Omega Alpha. Contbr. numerous articles profl. jours. Home: New York, N.Y. Died Feb. 13, 1981.

GOLDSTEIN, DAVID HENRY, physician; b. New Orleans, Sept. 20, 1908; s. Gustav and Eva (Small) G.; B.A., Cornell U., 1928; M.D., N.Y.U., 1933, Med Sci. D., 1940; m. Joyce N. Benoit, Nov. 23, 1966; children-Paul, Janet. Prof. environmental medicine N.Y.U. Med Center, from 1951, prof. emeritus., to 1978. Mem. exec. com. med. adv. bd. Hotel Trades, 1959-78. Served to maj., M.C., AUS, World War II. Recipient N.Y. U. Meritorious Alumni Service medallion , 1969. Diplomate Am. Bd. Internal Medicine, Am. Bd. Preventive Medicine (Occupational Medicine). Fellow N.Y. Acad. Medicine, Am. Acad. Occupational Medicine, Indsl. Med. Assoc. (pres. 1968-69); mem. AMA (editorial bd. Archives Environmental Health 1963-71), N.Y. U Sch. Medicine Alumni Assn. (pres. 1966-67), N.Y. U. Alumni Fedn. (v.p. 1967-70). Contbr. profl. jours. Home: New York, N.Y. Died Aug. 6, 1978.

GOLDSTEIN, MARK E., psychologist; b. Jamaica, N.Y., May 7, 1931; s. Samuel Avon and Betty (Krakow) G.; B.A., Adelphi U., 1953; M.A., N.Y. U., 1954; M.S., Ph.D., Yeshiva U., 1958. Lectr. mental hygiene Hebrew Edn. Soc., Bklyn., 1958-59; co-founder, cons. Gamblers Anonymous, Bklyn., 1960-62; supervising psychologist Cumberland Hosp., Bklyn., 1960-61; group psychotherapist L.I. Cons. Center, Forest Hills, N.Y., 1959-62; psychologist Trouble Shooting Clinic, Elmhurst Gen. (N.Y.) Hosp., 1959-62; practice psychology, Jamaica, 1961-79; faculty New Sch. for Social Research, 1970-72; cons. Marriage Conciliation Bur. N.Y. State Supreme Ct., 1967-71, Great Neck (N.Y.) Pub. Sch. System, 1969-71; psychotherapist Community Guidance Service, N.Y.C., 1979. Mem. Am. Soc. Clin. Hypnosis, Am. Psychol. Assn. (divs. clin. psychology and psychopharmacology), Internat. Soc. Hypnosis, Am. Group Psychotherapy Assn., Am. Acad. Psychotherapists, Acad. Psychologists in Marital and Family Therapy, Am. Soc. Group Psychotherapy and Psychodrama, N.Y. Inst. Gestalt Therapy, Queens-Nassau Psychologists in Pvt. Practice. Producer documentary film on marathon encounter therapy Nat. Ednl. TV, 1971. Address: Jamaica, N.Y. Died Nov. 3, 1979; buried Montefiore Cemetery, St. Albans, N.Y.

GOLDSTEIN, MAX FULLMORE, lawyer; b. Birmingham, Ala., July 17, 1886; s. David and Sarah (Fullmore) G.; B.L., U. Ga., 1906; LL.B. cum laude, Yale, 1909; m. Sarah Ray London, Dec. 29, 1914; children—Elliott, Grace (Mrs. Burton Goldstein). Admitted to Ga. bar, 1906; mem. Powell, Goldstein, Frazer & Murphy, Atlanta, and predecessor, Little,

Powell, Smith, Goldstein, 1913-39; pres. Nat. Albany Corp.; asst. sec. Sterling Pulp & Paper Co.; dir. Wellhouse Co. Mem. Am., Ga., Atlanta bar assns., Order of Coif. Jewish religion. Mason. Contbr. articles to various ins. and legal publs. Home: Atlanta GA. *

GOLDSTEIN, MOISE HERBERT (GOLD'STEN), architect; b. New Orleans, La., Sept. 17, 1882; s. Julius and Julie (Schwartz) G.; B.E., Tulane U., 1902; M.S., Mass. Inst. of Technology, 1905; student American Acad. in Rome, 1906-07; m. Lois Goetter, Aug. 27, 1924; children—Louis Allan, Moise Herbert, Jr., Nathalie (wife of Dr. Aaron Stern). Practiced as architect with the firm of Moise H. Goldstein & Assos., 1914-47; Goldstein, Parham & Labouisse, 1947-63, Moise H. Goldstein & Louis A. Goldstein, 1963—; prin. archtl. works include Civic Center, New Orleans, 1956-58, Moisant Internat. Airport, New Orleans, 1957-59, Dillard U., 1933-63. Member National Architectural Accrediting Bd., 1941-44. Fellow A.I.A. (bd. dirs. 1936-39). Home: New Orleans. *

GOLDSTEIN, NATHANIEL LAWRENCE, lawyer, former atty. gen. N.Y. State; b. N.Y.C., June 9, 1896; s. Max and Mollie (Marayna) G.; B.C.S., N.Y. U., 1915; J.D., N.Y. Law Sch., 1918, LL.D., 1957; LL.D., Syracuse U., 1949, Yeshiva U., 1952, Hobart and William Smith Colls., 1950, Hebrew U., 1968; D.C.L., Pace Coll., 1969; m. Etta May Brown, 1931; children—Lois Elaine (Mrs. Jerome Lowenstein), Stephen Martin. Admitted to N.Y. bar, 1918; C.P.A., 1919; pub. mem. Interboro Rapid Transit Depreciation Fund Bd., 1938-40; elected atty. gen. State of N.Y., 1942, 46, 50, ret. 1954; mem. firm Goldstein, Shames & Hyde. Vis. prof. forensic medicine Einstein Coll. Medicine. Asst. chief counsel Dir. Selective Service, N.Y., 1940-42; v.p., dir. Willkie Meml. of Freedom House; dir. Park Av. Synagogue; trustee Pace U., N.Y.C., N.Y. Law Sch.; chmn. emeritus bd. overseers Albert Einstein Coll. Medicine; bd. overseers Fletcher Sch. Law and Diplomacy; dep. chmn. bd. dirs. Hebrew U.; vice chmn. Gallatin Assos., N.Y. U.; chmn. bd. overseers Harry S. Truman Research Center, Mt. Scopus, Israel. Mem. U.S. delegation to UN Narcotic Drug Control Commn. Mem. Am., Bklyn. bar assns., Am. Legion (past post comdr.), Sigma Omega Psi (nat. pres.), Alpha Epsilon Pi. Mason. Clubs: Harmonie (N.Y.C.); Capitol Hill (Washington). Contbr. to legal publs. Home: New York, N.Y. Died Mar. 24, 1981.

GOLDTHWAITE, RALPH HARVARD (GOLD'THWAT), army officer, (ret.); b. Holbrook, Mass., Sept. 17, 1882; s. Charles Henry and Ellen White (Vinin) G.; A.B., Harvard, 1903, M.D., 1906; grad. U.S. Army Med. Sch., 1909, advance course, Field Med. Sch., 1934; m. Agnes Pruyn, Oct. 20, 1914; 1 dau., Isabel Janet; m. 2d Helen Adams Butler, Dec. 20, 1934. Commd. col. (temp.) World War I and advanced through the grades to brig. gen. (temp.), 1943; with A.E.F. in France, 1917-19; specialist in eye, ear, nose, and throat administrative duties since 1937. Fellow Am. Coll. Surgeons, Acad. Ophthalmology and Otolaryngology; mem. Assn. Military Surgeons, Am. Coll. Surgeons, A.M.A. Club: Army-Navy (Washington, D.C.). Address: Santa Barbara, Calif. *

GOLDWATER, ROBERT, educator; b. N.Y.C., Nov. 23, 1907; s. S.S. and Clara (Aub) G.; B.A., Columbia, 1929; M.A., Harvard, 1931; Ph.D., N.Y. U., 1937; m. Louise Bourgeois, Sept. 12, 1938; children—Michel, Jean-Louis, Alain. Instr. fine arts N.Y. U., 1934-39; from asst. prof. art to prof. Queens Coll., 1939-57; prof. fine arts N.Y. U. Grad. Sch., 1957-74; dir. Mus. Primitive Art, N.Y.C., 1957-63, chmn. adminstrv. com., 1963-73; editor Mag. of Art, 1947-53, Carnegie fellow, 1930-31; Guggenheim fellow, 1944-45; Fulbright scholar, 1950-51. Mem. Coll. Art Assn. (dir. 1956-59), Soc. Aesthetics, Internat. Assn. Art Critics. Author: Primitivism in Modern Painting, 1938; Rufino Tamayo, 1947; Modern Art in Your Life, 1949; Jacques Lipchitz, 1954; Gauguin, 1957; The Sculpture of the Bambara, 1960; Senufo Sculpture, 1964; Primitivism in Modern Art, 1967; Space and Dream, 1967; What is Modern Sculpture, 1970; also articles. Home: New York, N.Y. Died Mar. 26, 1973.

GOLDWYN, SAMUEL (GOLD'WIN), (SURNAME ADOPTED), motion picture producer; b. Warsaw, Poland, 1882; s. Abraham and Hannah Goldfish; came to U.S., 1896, naturalized citizen, 1902; educated night sch.; married. Organized Jesse Lasky Feature Photoplay Co., 1913, Goldwyn Pictures Corp., 1916, Eminent Authors Pictures, Inc., 1919, also Samuel Goldwyn, Inc., Famous Players-Lasky Corp.; dir. United Artists Corp. until 1940; chmn. bd. Samuel Goldwyn Prodn., Inc. A pioneer in inducing eminent authors to work actively in writing for motion pictures; introduced Vilma Banky, Eddie Cantor, Gary Cooper, Dana Andrews and Danny Kaye to the screen. Recipient Motion Picture Acad. award for prodn., The Best Years of Our Lives, 1947; Irving Tholberg Award for consistent high quality. Home: Beverly Hills, Calif. *

GOLINKIN, JOSEPH WEBSTER, painter, lithographer, ret. naval officer; b. Chgo., Sept. 10, 1896; s. Mathieu DeVos and Ellen (Webster) G.; student Art Inst. Chgo., Art Students League N.Y., navy schs.; m. Lucile Hunnewell, 1931; m. 2d, Ruth Forman Fowler, Dec. 16, 1949; 1 son, Webster Fowler. Has exhibited at Carnegie Internat., Chgo. Art Inst., Nat. Acad., Pa. Acad., Pan-Am. (S.A.), Am. Exhibit (Paris, 1924) Los Angeles, Buffalo, Corcoran Museums, Am. Water Colo Soc., Spectrum Fine Art Gallery, N.Y.C., N.Y. Water Color Club; one-man shows; Mus. City of N.Y. (group of pictures of N.Y.), MacBeth, Sporting Gallery, Ferargil Galleries, Gumps, San Francisco, Art Assn. of Newport, Van der Straeten Gallery Contemporary Artists, N.Y.C., Raymond & Raymond Galleries, Beverly Hills, Calif.; his work has appeared in N.Y. Times, Vanity Fair, Fortune, Coronet, Country Life and other mags. Am. Artists group series, Raymond & Raymond reprodns.; work included in anthologies of Am. art, such as Water Color Painting of Today (Adrian Bury), Eyes on America (Hall-Studio pub.), Incredible New York (Lloyd Morris), Life in America (Met. Museum, Davidson), 200 Years of Sport in America (Wells Twombly), 1976; artist, co-author: New York Is Like This (text by H.I. Brock), 1929; The American Sporting Scene (text by John Kieran), 1941; Twelve Meter Challenges for the America's Cup (text by Norris Hoyt), 1977. Served in U.S. Navy, World Wars I, II; USNR and N.Y. Naval Militia, 1919-58, ret. with rank of rear adm. USN, 1958; rear adm. N.Y. Naval Militia. Awarded Bronze Star, Naval Res. medal with two stars, Victory medal with clasp, Haitian medal, Am. Def. with star, Am. Area, European-African Area with two stars, Asiatic-Pacific Area with six stars, World War II Victory, Japan Occupation medal, Philippine Liberation medal with star, N.Y. Conspicuous Service, N.Y. Long Service; recipient 1st Gold Medal Internat. Exhbn. of Art in relation to sport 1932 Olympiad; medal 1936 Olympiad. Fellow Internat. Inst. Arts and Letters. Clubs: Century Assn., Seawanhaka-Corinthian Yacht, Corinthian Yacht (Phila.). Address: Oyster Bay, N.Y. Died Sept. 12, 1977; buried Arlington Nat. Cemetery.

GOMORY, ANDREW LOUIS, business exec.; b. Szeged, Hungary, Nov. 12, 1891; s. Lajos and Vilma (Bischof) G.; grad. Berlin (Germany) U. Sch. of Commerce, 1912; m. Marian Schellenberg, Sept. 8, 1924 (died 1947); children—Paul Lewis, Ralph Edward; married 2d, Elisabeth M. de Zario, Aug. 20, 1950. Indsl. dept. Hungarian Gen. Credit Bank, Budapest, 1912-13; asst. to pres. Transatlantic Trust Co., N.Y. City, 1914-19, foreign rep. 1920-21; asst. mgr. foreign dept. Mfrs. Trust Co., N.Y.C., 1922-28, asst. v.p., 1928-35, v.p., 1935-55, sr. v.p., from 1955. Mem. fgn. exchange New York Money Market. Chmn. Am. Com. for Short-Term Creditors of Germany and Hungary; mem. Pan Am. Soc.; mem. bd. govs. Brooklyn Heights Assn.; bd. regents Long Island Coll. Hosp.; dir. South Brooklyn Neighborhood Houses. Decorated Grand Cross of Merit (Republic of Austria), Officer in Order of Merito (Italy). Mem. Netherlands C. of C. (dir.), Bankers Assn. for Fgn. Trade, Brooklyn Institute of Arts and Sciences (trustee), Far East.-Am. Council Commerce and Industry (bd. dirs.), Internat. C. of C. (trustee Am. council). Clubs: Old Inlet (Bellport, N.Y.); Bankers, Wall Street (N.Y.C.); Heights Casino (Bklyn.). Home: Brooklyn Heights, N.Y. Died Sept. 24, 1979.

GONNERMAN, HARRISON FREDERICK, cons. engr.; b. Dixon, Ill., Aug. 24, 1885; s. Conrad and Catherine (Fernau) G.; B.S. in C.E., Univ of Ill., 1908, M.S., 1913; m. Gertrude Jamison, Dec. 23, 1911; children—Harrison Frederick, Alice Michal. Asst. engring. expt. sta., Univ. of Ill., 1908-10, instr. in theoretical and applied mechanics, 1910-14, 1st asst., engring. expt. sta., 1914-17, research asso., 1917-18, research assistant prof., 1918-20, in private business, Los Angeles, Calif., 1920-22; asso. engr. structural materials research lab. Lewis Inst., and research lab., Portland Cement Assn., Chicago, Ill., 1922-27, mgr. research lab., Portland Cement Assn., 1927-46, dir. of research, 1947-48, asst. to v.p. for research, development, 1948-52. Recipient Wason medal Am. Concrete Inst., 1929, 44; San- ford E. Thompson award Am. Society for Testing Materials, 1952, Award of Merit, 1956; Turner medal, Am. Concrete Inst., 1960. Mem. Am. Concrete Inst. (dir. 1943-49, pres. 1946, hon. mem. 1951), Am. Soc. C.E., Western Soc. Engineers, American Soc. Testing Materials (director 1936-39, 1949-52), Illinois Academy of Science, A.A.A.S., Tau Beta Pi, Sigma Xi, Psi Upsilon, Triangle. Contbr. numerous papers, discussions and bulls. on cement, concrete materials, reinforced concrete and methods of testing to tech. jours. Address: Oak Park, Ill.

GOOCH, WILBY T., prof. of chemistry; b. Waco, Tex., Dec. 22, 1885; s. Joseph Withers and Emma (Wells) G.; B.S., Baylor U., 1906, M.S., 1908; Ph.D., U. of Chicago, 1918; m. Artie Burton Muse, Dec. 29, 1908; children—Wilby T., Lucy Frances (Mrs. Cary D. Canon). Teacher of science Grandview, (Tex.) High Sch., 1906-07; instr. in chemistry, Baylor University, 1908-09, professor of chemistry since 1909, head dept. chemistry, 1909-49; dean grad. sch., 1947-56, emeritus dean grad. school 1956—, interim pres., 1948, adminstr. v.p., 1948—; chemist Waco City Water Department, 1918-52. Fellow A.A.A.S., Tex. Acad. Sci. (v.p. 1935-36, pres. 1938-39; hon. life mem.); mem. Am. Chem. Soc. (sec. Central Tex. Soc. 1932-36, Councillor 1937), Am. Assn. Univ. Profs., Am., Tex. (hon. life mem.; pres. 1924) Water Works Assns.; chmn. bd. Tex. Water and Sanitation Research Found.; chmn., Adv. Licensing Com., Texas Waterworks Short School; Sigma Xi, Alpha Epsilon Delta. Democrat. Baptist. Author of Typical Calculations in Elementary Chemistry, 1919. Home: Waco, Tex. *

GOOD, ALBERT IRWIN, missionary; b. of Am. parents, Libreville, French Congo, Apr. 12, 1884; s. Adolphus Clemens and Lydia Belle (Walker) G.; came to U.S., 1894; B.A., College of Wooster, 1906, D.D., 1926; B.D., Western Theol. Sem., Pittsburgh, Pa., 1909; m. Mary R. Middlemiss, Jan. 10, 1918; children—Philip Clemens, Elizabeth Louise, Edwin Marshall. Presbyterian missionary since 1909; member of West Africa Mission and elected its field secretary, 1942; collector scientific material (insects, mammals, etc.) for Carnegie Museum, Pittsburgh, since 1909; collector birds for Cleveland Museum Natural History since 1930; vice moderator Gen. Assembly Presbyn. Ch., 1935; head of Mission Language Sch., condr. spl. language sch. for new missionaries since 1952. Fellow Royal Geog. Soc.; mem. Am. Ornithol. Union, Phi Beta Kappa. Republican. Author: Book of Forms for Ministers in Bulu, 1934; Bulu Handbook Supplement, 1934. Translator greater part of Old Testament in Bulu language. Editor: Hymns in Bulu (with music), 1928; Banok Hymns, 1936; Mabea Hymns, 1938; Birds of Cameroon, Vol. I, 1952. Contributor of an article "Drum Talk is the African's Wireless" to Natural History mag., 1942. Stamp collector specializing in Cameroun. Retired 1950. Home: Wooster, O. *

GOOD, GROVER CHARLES, educator; b. Cleveland, O., Oct. 17, 1884; s. James Richard and Bertha (Erdmann) G.; grad. Howe (Ind.) Sch., 1904; A.B., Harvard, 1909; grad. study in edn., St. John Baptist Coll., Oxford, Eng., 1910; m. Nora Clements, Grand Rapids Mich., June 12, 1915. Registrar, 1908-10, headmaster, Nov., 1911—, Howe Sch., also trustee. Republican. Episcopalian. Mem. Am. Soc. Psychical Research, A.A.A.S., Nat. Econ. League, Am. Geog. Soc., North Academic Assn. (sec.), Phi Beta Kappa. Mason (32 deg.). Club: University (Chicago). Address: Howe, Ind.*

GOODALE, FRANCIS GREENLEAF, lawyer; b. Saco, Me., Sept. 14, 1883; s. George Lincoln and Henrietta Juell (Hobson) G.; A.B., Harvard, 1905, LL.B., 1907; m. Margaret Penhallow Davis, Sept. 9, 1908; children—Caroline Juell (Mrs. Lyman S. Hayes), Charles Folsom (dec.), Anne Penhallow (Mrs. R. Boland Brooks), Walter (dec.). Admitted to Mass. bar, 1906; with H.D. Tudor, Esquire, 1907-12; partner Goodale & Nash, 1912-16, Hill, Barlow & Homans, 1919-35, Hill, Barlow, Goodale & Wiswall, 1935-56, Hill, Barlow, Goodale and Adams, 1956—, partner firm of Hill and Barlow, since 1965— (all Boston); spl. asst. U.S. atty. Dist. of Mass., 1916-19; spl. asst. to U.S. Atty. Gen., 1919-21; U.S. commr. Dist. of Mass., 1928-32; mem. Mass. Spl. Commn. Pardon and Parole, 1939-41; also various commns., arbitration bds.; dir. Aeolian-Skinner Organ Co., Inc. Chmn. War Price and Rationing Bd. (Weston, Mass.), 1942-45. Town Moderator, 1949-58. Fellow American Bar Foundation; member of American Massachusetts State, Boston bar assns. Clubs: Union (Boston); Harvard (N.Y.C.). Home: Weston, Mass. *

GOODALL, HERBERT WHITTAKER, banker; b. Philadelphia, Pa., Jan. 1, 1884; s. Frank B. and Elizabeth (Hartley) G.; ed. pub. schs.; m. Ruth Ferguson Dorr, June 5, 1909; children—Herbert Whittaker, Robert Dorr, Patricia. Began as broker's clk., Isaac Starr, Jr., & Co., 1898; with The Pennsylvania Co., 1903-11, asst. treas., 1909-11; partner Evan Randolph & Co., 1911-14; mem. Goodall, Wistar & Co., 1914-18; v.p. Guarantee Trust & Safe Deposit Co., 1918-26, pres., 1926-28; pres. Tradesmen's Nat. Bank & Trust Co. 1928-47, v. chmn., 1947-48; dir. Bd. of City Trusts (Phila.), Pennroad Corp., Commonwealth Land Title Ins. Co., Pittsburgh & W.Va. Ry. Co. Roman Catholic. Mason. Clubs: Racquet, Rittenhouse, Cricket (Phila.). Home: Philadelphia.

GOODBODY, MARCUS, stockbroker; b. Dublin, Ireland, Nov. 20, 1876; s. Robert and Isabel (Pim) G.; Ph.B., Sheffield Sci. Sch., 1897; m. H. Augusta Hudson, Oct. 12, 1902; 1 son, Robert. Clk. G.N. Ry., 1897-98; with Robert Goodbody & Co. since 1898, partner, 1902— (firm name changed to Goodbody & Company); mem. New York Stock Exchange, 1911-23. Dir. N.Y. Osteopathic Clinic of N.Y. since 1918. Home: Stamford, Conn. *

GOODCHILD, CHAUNCEY GEORGE, educator; b. New Castle, Pa., June 18, 1912; s. James Dean and Jane Ellen (McKnight) G.; B.S., Westminster (Pa.) Coll., 1933, LL.D., 1961; Ph.D., N.Y. U., 1941; m. Hazel Gertrude Fisher, Dec. 6, 1934; children—David George, James Fisher, Susan Jane. Teaching asst.

biology Westminster Coll., 1930-33, research asst. phys. chemistry, 1933-34, instr. biology, 1934-36, acting chmn. dept., 1935- 36; grad. teaching asst. N.Y. U., 1936-40, Sandham fellow biology, 1940-41; instr. biology Coll. City N.Y., 1940-41; asso. prof. biology S.W. Mo. State Coll., Springfield, 1941-45, prof., 1945-52; instr. invertebrate biology Marine Biol. Lab., Woods Hole, Mass., 1943-52; asso. prof. biology Emory U., Atlanta, 1952-55, prof., 1955-60, Charles Howard Chandler prof., from 1960, chmn. dept., 1957-64, mem. NSF coop. fellowship com. at univ., 1958-61. Summer research Marine Biol. Lab., Woods Hole, 1943-52; mem. tng. grant com. NIH, 1957-60, mem. com. internat. center med. research and tng., 1960-63. Chmn. publicity Easter Seal Drive, Springfield, Mo., 1949-52; bd. dirs. Greene County Soc. Crippled Children and Adults, 1949-52; pres. Springfield Civic Music Assn., 1951-52. Fellow A.A.A.S.; mem. Am. Soc. Zoologists, Am. Soc. Parasitologists, Am. Micros. Soc., Assn. S.E. Biologists, Corp. Marine Biol. Lab., Am. Soc. Tropical Medicine and Hygiene, Soc. Systematic Zoology (exec. com. 1957-60), Am. Assn. U. Profs. (exec. com. Emory U. 1959-63), Sigma Xi. Kiwanian (dir. Springfield 1951-52). Author: Laboratory Manual of General Zoology, 1958; also research papers. Asst. editor Jour. Parasitology, 1956—, Emory U. Quar., 1959-69. Contbr. to Ency. Brit., Ency. Sci. and Tech. Home: Atlanta, Ga. Died Nov. 10, 1980.

GOODEN, ROBERT BURTON, clergyman, educator; b. Bolton, Eng., Sept. 18, 1874; s. James and Hannah (Burton) G.; came to U.S., 1888; B.A., Trinity Coll., Conn., 1902, M.A., 1904, D.D., 1922; B.D., Berkeley Div. Sch., 1904, D.D., 1931; Dr. Canon Law, Ch. Div. Sch. Pacific, 1966; m. Alice Leonard Moore, Nov. 7, 1904; children—Alice Mary, Carolyn Frances, Robert Burton, Reginald Heber, Muriel Margaret. Ordained deacon P.E. Ch., 1904, priest, 1905; rector St. Paul's Ch., Ventura, Cal., 1904-06, Trinity Ch., Escondido, 1906-07, St. Luke's Ch., Long Beach, 1907-12; headmaster Harvard Sch., 1912, v.p. bd. trustees, 1937-49; pres. Province of Pacific, 1946-50; v.p. bd. trustees Bishop's Sch., LaJolla, Cal.; suffragan bishop of Los Angeles, 1930-47, acting bishop, 1947-48. Sec. standing com Diocese of Los Angeles, 1910-29, pres. standing com., 1929-30, exam. chaplain, 1907-30, pres., 1929-30, bd. dirs. Christian Edn., Diocese Los Angeles; bd. dirs. Episcopal Home for Aged. Elected pres. bd. trustees, hon. life mem. Ch. Div. Sch. of Pacific, Berkeley, 1941; hon. life trustee Bishop's Sch., La Jolla, Cal.; trustee Bishop Gooden Home Alcoholic Men, Pasadena, Cal. Mem. Phi Beta Kappa, Alpha Chi Rho. Democrat. Contbr. P.E. Ch. Congress papers, 1927, P.E. Church press, from 1928. Home: Glendale, Calif. Died Aug. 24, 1976.

GOODHART, ARTHUR LEHMAN, educator; b. N.Y.C., Mar. 1, 1891; s. Philip J. and Hattie (Lehman) G.; B.A., Yale, 1912, M.A., 1914, LL.D., 1948; B.A., LL.B., Cambridge (Eng.) U., 1914, M.A., 1918, LL.M., 1926, LL.D., 1931, D.Litt., 1969; D.C.L., Oxford (Eng.) U., 1931, N.Y.U., 1955; LL.D., Wesleyan U., 1940, U. Edinburgh, 1946, U. Calif., 1952, Queen's U., 1953, Columbia, 1954, London U., 1954, Princeton, 1956, Williams, 1956, Harvard, 1957, Dartmouth, 1957, Dalhousie U., Can., 1958, U. Pa., 1958, Melbourne U., 1959, Tulane, 1960; L.H.D., Cin. U., 1964; m. Cecily Carter, July 2, 1924; 3 sons. Admitted to bar, 1915; asst. corp. counsel, N.Y.C., 1915-17; counsel to Am. Mission to Poland, 1919; barrister at Law, Inner Temple, Eng., 1919; Hon. Bencher, Lincoln's Inn, 1938, King's Counsel, 1943; fellow and lectr. Corpus Christi Coll., Cambridge U., 1919-31, also sec. to vice chancellor of univ., 1921; vis. prof. Yale, 1929, Harvard Law Sch., 1964, U. Va. Law Sch., 1965, McGill U. Law Sch., 1966; prof. jurisprudence and fellow Univ. Coll., Oxford U., 1931-53, master, 1951-63; asso. fellow Jonathan Edwards Coll., Yale, 1933; del. Oxford U. Press, 1942; fellow Nuffield Coll., Oxford, 1944, Brit. Acad., 1952; curator Bodleian Library, 1947, hon. fellow Corpus Christi Coll. Cambridge, 1942, Trinity Coll., 1955, Trinity Hall, 1960; scholar-in-residence N.Y.C. Bar Assn., 1966-67. Decorated knight comdr. Order Brit. Empire, 1948. Chmn. So. Region Price Regulation Com., 1940-48; mem. Monopolies Commn., 1954-57; mem. Royal Commn. on the Police, 1960; chmn. Internat. Law Assn.; v.p. Société Internat. de Philosophie du Droit; pres. Internat. Assn. U. Profs., 1948; mem. Soc. Public Tchrs. Law (pres. 1950), Pedestrians Assn. (pres. 1950), Am. Law Inst., Phi Beta Kappa, Alpha Delta Phi. Officier d'Academie of France, 1920. Mem. Lord Chancellor's Law Revision Comm., 1937; mem. Co. Law Revision Com., 1944; Alternative Remedies Com., 1945, Supreme Ct. Com., 1947; mem. Scottish Constn. Com., 1969. Clubs: Yale, City (New York); Athenaeum, Oxford and Cambridge, Queen's, Savile (London); University, Century (N.Y.C.). Author: Poland and the Minority Races, 1920; The General Strike, 1927; Essays in Jurisprudence and the Common Law 1931; Precedent in English and Continental Law, 1934; What Acts of War are Justifiable, 1941; English Contributions to the Philosophy of Law, 1949; Five Jewish Lawyers of the Common Law, 1950; English Law and the Moral Law, 1954. Editor of Cambridge Law Jour., 1921, Law Quarterly Rev., 1926-75. Address: Oxford, England. Died Nov. 10, 1978.

GOODMAN, E(DWARD) URNER, orgn. exec.; b. Phila., May 15, 1891; s. George R. and Ella Dora (Jacobs) G.; grad. Phila. Sch. Pedagogy, 1913; student Temple U., 1913-14, U. Pa., 1914; Dr. of Humanics, Mo. Valley Coll., 1951; m. Louise W. Waygood, June 18, 1920; children—Theodore Wynkoop, Goerge Walter, Lydia Ann. Boys' work sec. Men and Religion Movement, Phila., 1911; tchr. Phila. schs., 1913-15; field scout exec. Boy Scouts Am., Phila., 1915-17 (founded Order of the Arrow, 1915), scout exec., Phila., 1917-27, Chgo., 1927-31, nat. program dir., 1931-51, then nat. field scout commr., mem. nat. council, exec. com. New Eng. Region; gen. dir. United Ch. Men Am., 1951-55, dir. emeritus, from 1955. Secretary Nat. Education Recreation Council, 1944-47, vice chmn., 1947-48, chmn., 1949; Boy Scout Am. del. 11th Internat. Scout Conf., France, 1947; presiding officer first convocation Gold Star Fathers and Mothers World War II, 1945; vice chmn. Gold Stars United. Mem. bd. overseers Mo. Valley Coll. from 1952. Served with inf. U.S. Army, World War I. Awarded Silver Buffalo, Boy Scouts Am., 1954; Green Lily, Boy Scout Assn. Norway. Mem. S.A.R., Nat. Com. Religion in Am. Life, Hymn Soc. Am., Grange, Alpha Phi Omega. Methodist (lay speaker). Mason. Author: Leaders Handbooks for the Boy Scouts of America, 1932; No Broken Pillar, 1946; Churchmen's Manuals, 1951; Hymn for the Rural Home, 1956; Hymns for Christian Edn., 1959; Stewardship, 1960. Editor: The Pastor Talks to the Pastor, 1955. Contbg. editor to Youth Leaders Digest, 1944-52. One of founders Eastern Conservatory Music and Arts, 1945, chmn. bd. 1949. Home: Bondville, Vt. Died Mar. 13, 1980; buried Penney Farms (Fla.) Cemetery.

GOODMAN, HOWARD, business executive; b. Chicago, Ill., Feb. 17, 1898; s. Herbert Edward and Jean (Strawbridge) G.; B.A., Williams Coll., 1919; M.B.A., Harvard Grad. Sch. of Business Adminstrn., 1923; m. Anna Frances Paton, June 8, 1921; children—Jean (Stumpf), Thomas (dec.), Margaret (Backes). With Goodman Mfg. Co. (now Mangood Corp.), mfrs. coal mining machinery, from 1923, dir., from 1931, pres., 1958-63, from 1966, chmn., chief exec. officer, from 1958; dir. Superior Steel & Mallcable Castings Co. (Benton Harbor, Mich.). Dir. Southeast Chgo. Commission. Trustee Univ. of Chgo. Baptist Theol. Union, Y.M.C.A. of Chgo., Hull House Assn. Republican. Clubs: University, Quadrangle, Commercial (Chgo.); Williams (N.Y.C.), Chikaming Country (Lakeside, Mich.). Home: Chicago, Ill. Died Feb. 2, 1977.

GOODRICH, EDWARD THAYER, lawyer; b. Detroit, July 5, 1902; s. Clarence Edward and Virginia (Thayer) G.; student Assumption Coll., Windsor, Ont., Can., 1917-19, U. Detroit, 1919-24; LL.B., U. Detroit, 1924; m. Margaret Elizabeth Grix, Jan. 20, 1934. Admitted to Mich. bar, 1925, since practiced in Detroit; partner firm Hill, Lewis, Adams, Goodrich & Tait, and predecessors, 1952-76. Dir. Palmer Shile Co., Detroit, 1960-76, sec., 1964-76. Mem. Delta Theta Phi. Republican. Roman Catholic. Clubs: Detroit; Grosse Pointe (Mich.) Yacht; Lawyers (N.Y.C.). Home: Grosse Pointe Farms, Mich. Died Mar. 26, 1976.

GOODWIN, HOWARD, insurance exec.; b. Hartford, Conn., Feb. 12, 1884; s. Lester Henry and Esther (Campbell) G.; A.B., Yale, 1906; m. Charlotte Alton, June 9, 1909 (died 1936); children—Margaret (Mrs. Emmet N. O'Brien), Charlotte (Mrs. W. Bradford Craig), James A.; m. 2d, Mrs. Ruth E. Hine, Mar. 29, 1944. Entered employ of Phoneix Mutual Life Ins. Co. Mar., 1907; asst. sec., 1917-29, sec., 1929-30; 2d vice pres., 1930-34, vice pres. in charge of underwriting since 1934. Dir. Inst. of Living (past sec.), (honorary) Open Hearth Association. Former treasurer Hartford Junior College. Member Home Office Life Underwriters Association (pres. 1936-37, mem. exec. council, 1932-42), Alpha Delta Phi, Scroll and Key. Republican. Conglist. Clubs: Hartford, Hartford Golf, Twentieth Century (ex-pres.), Yale (N.Y.), Graduate of New Haven, Dauntless (Essex, Conn.). Home: Hartford. *

GOODWIN, WILLIAM N., judge; b. McKenna, Wash., Aug. 17, 1909; B.A., Wash. State Coll., 1931; LL.B., U. Ore., 1934. Admitted to Ore. bar, 1934, Wash. bar, 1937; practiced law, Tacoma; mem. firm Gordon, Goodwin, Sager & Thomas, Tacoma; U.S. Atty. for Western Dist. Wash., from 1964; then judge U.S. Dist. Ct. for Eastern and Western Wash., Tacoma. Bd. regents Wash. State U., from 1957. Fellow Am. Coll. Trial Lawyers; mem. Am., Wash., Tacoma bar assns. Home: Tacoma, Wash. Died Dec. 31, 1975; buried Mt. View Cemetery, Tacoma Pierce County, Wash.

GOODY, MARVIN EDWARD, architect; b. N.Y.C., Jan. 6, 1929; s. Charles and Pauline Evelyn (Wolfe) G.; B.A. in Architecture, U. Pa., 1950; M.A. in Architecture, Mass. Inst. Tech., 1951; Master City Planning, Yale, 1953; m. Joan Bernice Edelman, Dec. 18, 1960. Asso. prof., then prof. architecture Mass. Inst. Tech., 1953-64; partner Hamilton & Goody, 1955-59; pres. Marvin E. Goody, John M. Clancy & Assos., Inc., 1959-80; Fulbright lectr., Denmark, 1963, Chile, 1965. Vice pres. Boston Archtl. Center, 1966-68; sec. Mass. Bd. Registration of Architects, 1971-80; mem. Mayor's Art Commn., Boston, 1966-80. Bd. dirs. Friends of Boston Pub. Gardens. Served to 1st lt. USAF, 1951. Fellow A.I.A. Club: Mass. Inst. Tech. Faculty. Author: Staggered Truss System, 1967; Construction Technology and Its Application UDC Housing, 1970. Designer Monsanto House of the Future, Anaheim, Cal., 1957. Home: Boston, Mass. Died May 18, 1980.

GOODYEAR, BRADLEY, lawyer; b. at Buffalo, N.Y., Oct. 18, 1885; s. Charles W. and Ella Portia (Conger) G.; A.B., Yale, 1907, LL.B., 1910; m. Isabelle Jeanette Bissell, of Buffalo, June 23, 1910. Practiced at Buffalo since 1910; partner firm Donovan & Goodyear. Commd. 1st lt. 65th Regt., N.Y.N.G., Feb. 8, 1916; promoted capt., Aug. 1916, and served on Tex. border with 3d N.G.F.A., until Mar. 1917; capt. 106th F.A., Aug. 5, 1917; arrived in France, May 1918; participated in Meuse-Argonne offensive; hon. discharged as maj., Mar. 31, 1919. Clubs: Buffalo, Saturn. Home: Buffalo, N.Y. *

GOOLD, HERBERT STEWART, foreign service officer; b. San Francisco, Calif., Aug. 10, 1886; s. Edmond Louis and Louise Keating (Stewart) G.; B.A., Stanford, 1909; m. Cora Butterworth Smith, May 3, 1920; children—Cora Butterworth (dec.), Louise Stewart, Mary Frances. Office boy, clk., Parrott & Co., shipping, commn. and ins. agts., San Francisco, 1909-11; admitted to Calif. bar, 1909; in law office of H. M. Anthony, 1911-15; legal asst. to sec. Spring Valley Water Co. of San Francisco, 1915-16; service with U.S. Dept. of State since 1916, sec. of legation or embassy at Vienna, 1917, Santo Domingo, 1917-18, La Paz, 1918-20, Guatemala City, 1920-21, Bogota, 1921, Managua, 1921-22, London, 1922-24, Athens, 1924-29, San José de Costa Rica, 1929-31; consul gen., Beirut, Syria, 1931-34; 1st sec. and consul gen., Helsingfors, 1934-36; counselor of Legation, Apr.-Sept. 1936; consul gen., Toronto, 1936-37; became consul gen., Casablanca, 1937; now on special detail. *

GORDON, CAROLINE (MRS. GORDON TATE), author; b. Todd County, Ky., Oct. 6, 1895; d. James Morris and Nancy Minor (Meriwether) Gordon; A.B., Bethany Coll., 1916; Litt.D., 1946; Litt.D., St. Mary's Coll., Notre Dame, Inc., 1964; m. Allen Tate, Nov. 2, 1924 (div.); 1 dau., Mrs. Percy H. Wood, Jr. Reporter, staff Chattanooga News, 1920-24; Guggenheim fellow, 1932; writer in residence Woman's Coll., U. N.C., 1938-39; lectr. creative writing Sch. Gen. Studies, Columbia, from 1946; vis. writer in residence U. Wash., 1953, U. Kans., 1956; writer in residence U. Calif. at Davis, 1962-63; lectr. creative writing New Sch. Social Research. Recipient $10,000 grant Nat. Council on Arts, 1966. Roman Catholic. Author novels including: Aleck Maury, 1934; None Shall Look Back, 1937; Green Centuries, 1941; The House of Fiction (with Allen Tate), 1950; The Strange Children, 1951; The Malefactors, 1956; How to Read a Novel (criticism), 1957; (short stories) The Forest of the South, 1945; Old Red and Other Stories, 1963; The Glory of Hera, 1971. Contbr. to publs., rep. in anthologies. Home: San Cristobal de las Casas, Mex. Died Apr. 11, 1981.

GORDON, EDGAR STILLWELL, educator, physician; b. Chgo., Nov. 6, 1906; s. Edgar Bernard and Edna (Stillwell) G.; B.S., U. Wis., 1927, M.A., 1929; M.D., Harvard, 1932; m. Lola A. Gray, June 27, 1936; children—Joan Elizabeth (Mrs. Arthur W. Owens), Stuart Gray, Robert Bruce. Intern, Billings Meml. Hosp., Chgo., 1932-34; resident medicine Mass. Gen. Hosp., Boston, 1935, U. Wis. Hosps., 1936; practice medicine specializing in endocrinology and metabolism, Madison, Wis., 1938-75; faculty U. Wis. Med. Sch., 1938-75, prof. medicine, 1952-75, chief staff Univ. Hosp., 1970-75. Cons. AEC, Oak Ridge Inst. Nuclear Studies, NASA; mem. program project com. Inst. Arthritis and Metabolic Diseases, NIH; hon. mem. Midwest Dental Seminar, 1969; pres. Interstate Postgrad. Med. Assembly, 1973. Pres. bd. dirs. Wis. Idea Theater Found. Diplomate Am. Bd. Internal Medicine, Am. Bd. Nutrition. Fellow N.Y. Acad. Sci.; mem. Assn. Am. Physicians, A.C.P., Am. Soc. Clin. Investigation, Central Soc. Clin. Research, Endocrine Soc., Am. Inst. Nutrition, Am. Diabetes Assn., Am. Clin. and Climatol. Assn., Am. Soc. Clin. Nutrition, Sigma Xi. Author: Nutritional and Vitamin Therapy, 1942. Editor: Steroid Hormones. Contbr. articles to profl. jours. Home: Madison, Wis. Died Apr. 4, 1975.

GORDON, EDWARD S., educator; b. Chgo., May 2, 1919; s. Hyman and Hannah (Schulman) G.; M.B.A., U. Chgo., 1940; m. Frances Fogel, Aug. 31, 1941; children—Barbara, Kenneth, Joseph. Service specialist Spiegel, Inc., 1940-41; tchr. Austin Jr. Coll., 1941-42; chmn., prof. marketing Roosevelt U., Chgo., 1945-76, asso. dean Walter E. Heller Coll. of Bus. Adminstrn., 1965-70, acting dean, 1970; owner Am. Research Assos., 1947, Readers Xposure Reports, 1971-76; analyst Firestone Tire cons. research dir. Haywood Pub. Co., 1955-63; marketing cons. Arthur Retlaw & Assos., 1969-76. Mem. sch. bd., Skokie, Ill., 1956-62; adv. com. Tri-County div. Ill. Sch. Bd. Assn., 1959-62. Trustee Roosevelt U., 1962-66. Served with USAF, 1942-45. Ford Found. research fellow, 1962. Mem. Am.

Marketing Assn. (v.p. Chgo. chpt. 1968-69), Nat. Retail Mchts. Assn. (careers com. 1963), Am. Assn. U. Profs., Sales and Marketing Execs. Assn., Assn. Indsl. Advertisers. Author: Home Improvement Course for Professional Plumbing and Heating Salesmen; Principles of Marketing; Your Efforts; A Demographic Study of the Optometric Profession; A Statistical Study of Osteopathic Physicians. Home: Skokie, Ill. Died Aug. 18, 1976.

GORDON, ELLIOTT MORTON, business exec.; b. Connersville, Ind., Apr. 14, 1909; s. Charles Taylor and Anna (Morton) G.; student U. Calif., 1928-29; B.S., Purdue U., 1932, hon. E.D., 1950; Sloan fellow Mass. Inst. Tech., 1938-39; m. Mary Hutchinson, Sept. 7, 1935; children—John Elliott, David William, Mary Gillette, James Peter. Chief engr., asst. supt. Moore Corp., Joliet, Ill., 1932-34; asst. personnel dir. Fleetwood Body Corp., Gen. Motors Corp., Detroit, 1934-35; indsl. engr. mgmt. div. Ernst & Ernst, Chgo., 1935-37; asst. to v.p. and prodn. engr. Griggs, Cooper & Co., St. Paul, 1937-40; dir., v.p., gen. mgr. Gorham Mfg. Co., Gorham Co., Alvin Corp.; v.p., dir. Mt. Vernon Silver Co.; dir. Black, Starr & Gorham, Inc., until 1956; pres., past chmn., gen. mgr., dir. Towle Mfg. Co.; dir. Millipore Filter Corp., Liberty Mut. Ins. Co. Former trustee Gov. Dummer Acad. Mem. Am. Soc. M.E., Am. Mgmt. Assn., Tau Beta Pi, Sigma Chi, Sigma Delta Chi. Club: Newcomen (N.Y.C.). Home: Wolfeboro, N.H. Died Nov. 26, 1979.

GORDON, GEORGE LONGAN, JR., lawyer; b. Kansas City, Mo., Feb. 10, 1901; s. George L. and Ernestine (Snead) G.; student U. Kans., 1936, Oxford U., 1937; J.D., U. Mo., 1924; m. Jane T. Hemingway, Sept. 2, 1930 (dec.); children—George Hemingway, Jean Arabell, Elizabeth Ernestine; m. 2d, Alice P. Scarritt, Sept. 14, 1966. Admitted to Mo. bar, 1924, U.S. Supreme Ct. bar, 1935; partner Gordon & Gilmore, 1934, Lathrop, Righter, Gordon & Parker, 1956-70; counsel White Eagle div. Socony Mobil Oil Co., 1947-55; gen. atty. Mo. & Iowa, Atchison, Topeka & Santa Fe Ry., 1956-71; gen. counsel, dir. Bus. Men's Assurance Co. Am., 1945-72, Black, Sivalls & Bryson, Inc., 1946-69; sec.-treas., dir. Westport Television, Inc., 1964-72. Mem. exec. com. Mo. Pub. Expenditure Survey. Chmn. bd. trustees Children's Mercy Hosp.; trustee Linda Hall Library Sci. and Tech., U. Kansas City, 1953-65. Mem. Am., Mo. (chmn. trusts and real estate law com. 1947-51), Kansas City bar assns., C. of C., Assn. Life Ins. Counsel (exec. com. 1958-61), Am. Life Conv. (state v.p. 1953-54), Lawyers Assn. Kansas City. Clubs: Kansas City Country, Kansas City; Monterey Peninsula Country, River. Home: Kansas City, Mo. Died Mar. 30, 1980.

GORDON, HERBERT FORD, govt. official, retired; b. Kingsborough, P.E. Island, June 10, 1882; son Rev. John Alexander and Margaret Ann (Ford) G.; grad. McGill Univ., 1903; m. Alice May Brock, Sept. 5, 1922; children—Hugh John, Adele Sybil (Mrs. Cecil Hyndman). Supt. Soldier Settlement Bd., Ottawa, 1920-35; director Farmers Creditors Arrangement Act, 1935-39; adminstr. Municipal Improvements Assistance Act, 1937-39; adminstrn. officer Dept. Nat. Defence, 1939-40; asst. dep. minister Nat. Defence for Air, 1940-44; dep. minister, 1944-47. Mem. Nat. War Labour Bd., Insp. Bd. of United Kingdom and Can., Inventions Bd. of Can.; vice pres. supervisory bd. of British Commonwealth Air Training Plan. Served with Can. Field Arty. in France, 1916-19. Decorated Companion of the Order of St. Michael and St. George, Czechoslovakian Air Force Wings. Clubs: Royal Ottawa Golf, Rideau. Home: Ottawa, Can. *

GORDON, JOHN, museum curator; b. Bklyn., Jan. 20, 1912; s. Charles A. and Margaret M. (Dunne) G.; A.B., Dartmouth Coll., 1934. Adminstrv. asst. dept. circulating exhbns. Mus. Modern Art, 1944-45; sec. Bklyn. Mus., 1945-52, curator paintings and sculpture, 1952-59; curator Whitney Mus. Am. Art, 1959-69; dir. Soc. Four Arts, Palm Beach, Fla., 1969-78; mem. adv. bd. The Drawing Soc. Author: (exhibition catalogs) Face of America, Bklyn. Mus., 1959, Biennial Internat. Watercolor Exhbns., Bklyn. Mus., 1955, 57, 59, (with Una E. Johnson) 14 Painter-Printmakers exhbn., Bklyn. Mus., 1955; Karl Schrag, 1960; José de Rivera, 1961; Geometric Abstraction in America, 1962; Richard Pousette-Dart, 1963; A Selection of American Prints from the New York Hilton at Rockefeller Center, 1963; New York, New York, 1965; Louise Nevelson, 1967; Isamu Noguchi, 1967; Franz Kline, 1968; Jim Dine, 1970. Clubs: Everglades, Bath and Tennis (Palm Beach). Address: Palm Beach, Fla. Died Sept. 12, 1978.

GORDON, KERMIT, instn. exec., economist; b. Phila., July 3, 1916; s. H. B. and Ida E. (Robinson) G.; B.A. with highest honors in Econs., Swarthmore Coll., 1938, LL.D., 1963; postgrad. (Rhodes scholar), U. Coll. Oxford (Eng.) U., 1938-39; LL.D., Colgate U., 1966, Williams Coll., 1974; m. Mary King Grinnell, Dec. 26, 1941; children—Katherine (Mrs. Thomas J. Kline) Emily (Mrs. George A. Sher), Andrew. Research asso. econs. Swarthmore Coll., 1939-40; adminstrn. fellow Harvard, 1940-41, tchr. econs., 1950, 54; with OPA, 1941-43; spl. asst. Office Asst. Sec. Econ. Affairs, Dept. State, 1945-46, cons., 1946-53; faculty Williams Coll., 1946-62, prof. econs., 1955-62, David A. Wells prof. polit. economy, 1961-62; mem. Council of Econ. Advisers, 1961-62; dir. Bur. of Budget, 1962-65; v.p., Brookings Instn., Washington, 1965-67, pres., 1967-76. Dir. Gen. Reins. Corp. Asso. to adminstr. Merrill Found. for Advancement Financial Knowledge, 1947-56; cons. White House, 1950, OPS, 1951; exec. asso. Ford Found., 1956-57, dir. program econ. devel. and adminstrn., 1960-61, trustee, 1967-75; mem. Council Fgn. Relations, from 1967; chmn. Health Ins. Benefits Adv. Council, 1965-67; mem. Social Security Adv. Council, 1969-71; mem. Gen. Adv. Com. on Arms Control and Disarmament, 1969-73, Fed. Pay Bd., 1971-72; trustee Com. Econ. Devel.; bd. mgrs. Swarthmore Coll., 1965-72. Served to 2d lt. AUS, 1943-45. Fellow Am. Acad. Arts and Scis.; mem. Am. Philos. Soc., Am. Econ. Assn., Am. Assn. Rhodes Scholars, Phi Beta Kappa. Club: Cosmos (Washington). Editor: Agenda for the Nation, 1968. Bd. editors Am. Econ. Rev., 1958-60. Home: Washington, D.C. Died June 21, 1976.

GORDON, MAX, theatrical producer; b. N.Y.C., 1892. Began career in vaudeville. Produced (with Albert Lewis) The Family Upstairs; The Jazz Singer; Easy Come, Easy Go; (alone) Three's a Crowd, 1930; The Band Wagon, 1931; The Cat and the Fiddle, 1931; Flying Colors, 1932; Design for Living, 1933; Roberta, 1933; The Shining Hour, Dodsworth, The Great Waltz, Spring Song, The Farmer Takes a Wife, 1934; Jubliee (with Sam H. Harris), Pride and Prejudice, 1935; Ethan Frome, The Women, St. Helena, 1936; Othello, 1937; Sing Out the News, 1938; Missouri Legend (with Guthrie McClintic), 1938; The American Way (with Sam H. Harris), 1939; My Sister Eileen, 1941; Junior Miss, 1942; The Doughgirls, 1942; Over Twenty-One, 1944; The Late George Apley, 1944; Born Yesterday, Park Avenue, Years Ago, 1946; The Solid Gold Cadillac, 1953. Film producer; became dir. TV prodn., NBC, 1939. Author: (with Lewis Funke) Max Gordon Presents, 1963. Home: New York, N.Y. Died Dec, 15, 1978.

GORDON, ROBERT AARON, economist, educator; b. Wash., July 26, 1908; s. Harry Goldstein and Lena (Walpert) G.; A.B., Johns Hopkins, 1928; A.M., Harvard, 1931, Ph.D., 1934; m. Margaret Shaughnessy, Aug. 15, 1936; children—Robert James, David Michael. Instr., Harvard, 1931-38; asst. prof. U. Calif. at Berkeley, 1938-40, asso. prof., 1940-47, prof., 1947-76, prof. emeritus, 1976-78, chmn. dept. econs., 1959-63; dir. Ford Found. Study Bus. Edn., 1956-58; Guggenheim fellow, 1956-57; bd. dirs. Nat. Bur. Econ. Research, 1961-76; chmn. Pres.'s Commn. on Employment and Unemployment Statistics, 1961-62. Officer, Combined Raw Materials Bd., 1942-45. Mem. research adv. bd. Com. for Econ. Devel., 1954-58, 60-63; mem. Nat. Task Force Econ. Edn., 1960-61. Fellow Am. Acad. Arts and Scis.; mem. Royal Econ. Soc., Am. Econ. Assn. (exec. com. 1950-52, v.p. 1960, distinguished fellow 1972, pres. 1975), Phi Beta Kappa, Beta Gamma Sigma. Author: Business Leadership in the Large Corporation, 1945; Business Fluctuations, 1952, rev. edit., 1961; The Goal of Full Employment, 1967; Economic Instability and Growth: The American Record, 1974; Disaggregating the Goal of Full Employment, 1978; also articles in econ. jours.; co-author: Higher Education for Business, 1959; Measuring Employment and Unemployment, 1962; Institutional Economics, 1963; Editor: Toward a Manpower Policy, 1967; co-editor: Readings in Business Cycles, 1965; Prosperity and Unemployment, 1966. Home: Berkeley, Calif. Died Apr. 7, 1978.

GORDON, ROBERT CHARLES, ret. mag. exec.; b. Hingham, Mont., Oct. 23, 1915; s. Clarence Eugene and Delia Sophia (Lybeck) G.; m. Margaret Ruth Noble, Nov. 14, 1948; children—Dee Scott, Robert Charles. With E.M. Hale Pub. Co., 1945-46; sales mgr. Tran-Film, Inc., 1946-50; with Time Inc., 1950-70, asst. pub., 1960-61, advt. sales dir., 1961-68, corporate v.p., 1968-70; cons. Trade adviser Dept. Commerce, 1958. Mem. Sales Execs. Club. Clubs: Misquamicut, Watch Hill Yacht. Home: Watch Hill RI also New York died Mar. 1, 1976.

GORDON, ROBERT LASHBROOK, financial cons.; b. Stirling, Alta., Can., Mar. 19, 1904; s. Robert John and Fannie Vernon (Schutt) G.; student U. Utah, 1921-23, U. Calif., Los Angeles, 1923-25; grad. Advanced Mgmt. Program, Harvard U., 1955; m. Helen Moore Hicks, Aug. 9, 1973; children by previous marriage—Robert Lashbrook, Charles N., Susan Jane. With Bank Am. N.T.&S.A., 1928-69, exec. v.p., 1964-69; chmn. bd. Beverly Enterprises, Pasadena, Calif., 1974-76, dir., 1974-78; chmn. exec. com. Ralph M. Parsons Co., Pasadena, 1975-77, dir., 1969-78; dir. Transcon Lines, 1969-74, Los Angeles Dodgers Profl. Baseball Team, 1969-78, Hargrom Services Corp., 1969-78; cons. Am. Protection Industries. Chmn. Los Angeles Better Bus. Bur., 1967; pres. Los Angeles Central City Assn., 1966; pres. Los Angeles Area C. of C., 1968, chmn., 1969. Republican. Mormon. Clubs: Calif. (Los Angeles); Marrakesh Country (Palm Desert, Calif.). Author mag. articles. Home: Palm Desert, Calif. Died Apr. 13, 1978.

GORDON, ROBERT S., multi-indsl. corp. exec.; b. Atlanta, Oct. 30, 1923; s. Nathan Morton and Dora G.; student U. So. Calif.; 1940-42; m. Jacqueline Gordon, May 11, 1953; children. Sales mgr. Community Rental Services, Los Angeles, 1947-53, exec. v.p., 1953-60; gen. partner Nathan M. Gordon Co., Beverly Hills, Calif., 1960-67; pres. Environmentals, Inc., Beverly Hills, 1967-72; corp. v.p. Angelica Corp., St. Louis, 1969-72, sr. v.p., 1972-78, pres., chief operating officer, 1978, pres., chief exec. officer, 1979-80, also dir. Served to lt. AC, U.S. Army, 1942-45. Republican. Died Oct. 10, 1980.

GORDON, THURLOW MARSHALL, lawyer; b. Methuen, Mass., Nov. 20, 1884; s. Albert Brigham and Elizabeth Jane (Hamlet) G.; A.B. summa cum laude, Dartmouth, 1906; LL.B. cum laude, Harvard, 1911; m. Pauline Sawyer, Nov. 12, 1912; children—Thurlow M., Frances. Admitted to Mass. bar, 1911, U.S. Supreme Ct. bar, 1914, N.Y. Bar, 1918; spl. asst. Atty.-Gen. U.S., 1912-16; atty. FTC, 1916-17; asso. Spooner & Cotton, N.Y., 1917; partner McAdoo, Cotton & Franklin, now Cahill, Gordon, Sonnett, Reindel & Ohl. Trustee Mt. Desert Island Hosp. Mem. Am., N.Y. State, N.Y. City bar assns., Soc. Bus. Adv. Professions, Soc. Colonial Wars, English Speaking Union, Pilgrims, Acad. Polit. Sci. Republican. Episcopalian. Clubs: Century, University, Harvard, Down Town, Economic (N.Y.C.); Cosmos (Washington); Harbor (Seal Harbor, Me.); Bar Harbor, Pot and Kettle (Bar Harbor, Me.). Author various articles and speeches relating to fed. anti-trust laws. Home: Methuen MA. *

GORDON, WALTER ARTHUR, judge; b. Atlanta, Oct. 10, 1894; s. Henry B. and Georgia (Bryant) G.; A.B., U. Cal. at Berkeley, 1918, J.D., 1922, LL.D., 1958; m. Elizabeth Fisher, July 22, 1920; children—Walter, Edwin, Betty. Policeman, Berkeley, Cal., 1919-30; asst. football coach U. Cal. at Berkeley, 1919-43; admitted to Cal. bar, 1923; practiced, 1923-44; atty. Golden State Ins. Co., Cal., 1935-44, adminstrv. adviser, 1944-76; gov. V.I., 1955-58; judge Dist. Ct. of V.I., 1958-76. Chmn. Adult Authority, State of Cal., 1945-55. Mem. bd., YMCA. Mem. Am. Prison Assn., Nat., Cal. parole and probation assns., Alpha Phi Alpha. Elk. Club: Commonwealth (San Francisco). Died Apr. 1, 1976.

GORHAM, SIDNEY SMITH, JR., lawyer; b. LaGrange, Ill., Dec. 23, 1906; s. Sidney Smith and Myrtle (Willett) G.; grad. Phillips Exeter Acad., 1924; student Princeton, 1924-27; Ph.B., U. Chgo., 1928, J.D., 1930; m. Corinne McVoy, Sept. 22, 1928; children—Sidney Smith, III, E. Timothy, Jeffrey H. Admitted to Ill. bar, 1930, practiced in Chgo.; partner Miller, Gorham, Wescott & Adams (later Gorham, Adams, White & DeYoung), Chgo., 1932-75, Gorham, Metge & Bowman, 1976-78. Mem. Am., Ill., Chgo. (treas. 1952-54) bar assns. Club: Law, Legal, Tavern, Mid-day, Saddle and Cycle (Chgo.). Home: Chicago, Ill. Died Aug. 18, 1978.

GORINI, LUIGI, bacteriologist; b. Milan, Italy; grad. U. Pavia, 1925. Sci. researchist U. Milan, 1928; research fellow U. Paris, 1947; vis. investigator N.Y. U., 1955; mem. med. faculty Harvard, 1957-76, Am. Cancer Soc. prof. microbiology and molecular genetics. Recipient Ledlie prize for work on streptomycin Harvard, 1966. Mem. Nat. Acad. Scis., Am. Acad. Arts Scis. Home: Brookline, Mass. Died Aug. 13, 1976; buried Pavia, Italy.

GORMAN, JOHN JEROME, congressman; b. Minneapolis, Minn., June 2, 1883; student Loyola U.; m. Mary E. Hanrahan, of Chicago. Admitted to Ill. bar; mem. Constl. Conv. of Ill., 1920; mem. 67th and 69th Congresses (1921-23 and 1925-27), 6th Ill. Dist. Republican. Club: Hamilton. Home: Chicago, Ill. *

GORMAN, PATRICK EMMET, labor union exec.; b. Louisville, Nov. 27, 1892; s. Maurice and Ellen (Dwyer) G.; LL.B., U. Louisville, 1917; D.Social Sci., 1974; m. Harriet Lee Dove, June 1, 1914 (dec. July 1971); m. 2d, Dorothy Montague, May 16, 1973. Admitted to Ky. bar, 1917; joined Amalgamated Meat Cutters and Butcher Workmen of N.Am., 1911, bus. agt. Local 227, 1912-20, spl. organizer internat. union, 1917-20, gen. v.p., 1920-23, pres., 1923-42, sec.-treas., 1942-76, chmn. bd., 1976-80. Fraternal del. AFL to Brit. Trade Union Congress, 1948; exec. bd. Internat. Food and Drink Workers Assn., 1951-80. Active numerous civic causes, 1920-80. Mem. bd. Religion and Labor Council Am.; trustee Roosevelt U.; adv. com. trade union com. Harvard; pres. Eugene V. Debs. Found. Named St. Jude Man of Year, 1963; recipient Coronet award St. Edward's U., Austin, Tex., 1963, Clarance Darrow award, 1963, St. Joseph the Worker award, Buffalo, 1963, Good Am. award Chgo., 1963, Brotherhood award Chgo., 1963, Humanitarian award N.Y. Fur Industry, 1964, Pontifical medal of honor, 1973, Humanitarian service award Abraham Lincoln Center, 1975, Israel Prime Minister's medal, 1976. Home: Chicago, Ill. Died Sept. 3, 1980; buried Calvary Cemetery, Louisville, Ky.

GORMAN, WILLIAM JOSEPH, business exec.; b. Frankfort, Ky., Sept. 6, 1917; s. William J. and Genevieve (Weitzel) G.; B.C.S., U. Ky., 1939; m. Mary Jane Smith, Sept. 16, 1940; children—Mary Ann, Martha Lyn, Sarah, Susan, Elizabeth. Sales dept. B. F. Goodrich Rubber Co., Cin., 1939-40; asso. oil tax staff Leslie E. Martlew, Evansville, 1941-44, 46-48; gen. mgr. Ryan Oil Co., Evansville, 1949-76; chmn. bd. So. Cal. Aircraft Corp., Ontario, Calif.; v.p., dir. Devel., Inc., indsl. consultants, Louisville; chmn. bd. Desert Bermuda Devel. Co., Palm Springs, Calif.; dir. Mahoe Developers, Ltd. Pres. bd. trustees Redevel. Commn., Evansville. Served as lt. USNR, 1944-46. Mem. Ind. Oil Producers Assn. Tri-State (pres.), A.I.M. Home: Evansville, Ind. Died July 23, 1976.

GOSS, HAROLD ISAAC, sec. of state; b. Kennebunk, Me., Nov. 12, 1882; s. Isaac W. and Elizabeth May (Wentworth) G.; LL.B., Univ. of Me., 1909; m. Esther F. Lowell, Aug. 7, 1934. Admitted to Me. bar and practiced Maine, 1909-21; salesman, Caffin & Burr, Inc., 1921-31; law practice Maine, 1931-37; dep. sec. of state, Me., 1937-42, acting sec. of state, 1942-43, sec. of state, Me., since 1943. Mem. Me., Kennebec County (past pres.) bar assns., Am. Assn. Motor Vehicle Adminstrs. (past pres. region 1, internat.). Republican. Mem. Universalist Ch. Mason, K.P., Odd Fellow. Clubs: Rotary. Home: Gardiner, Me. *

GOSS, HOWARD ARCHIBALD, clergyman; b. Cuba, Mo., Mar. 6, 1883; s. William Clinton and Margaret J. (Gillette) G.; student Apostolic Bible Sch., Houston, 1905, Pentecostal Bible Conf., 1908-09; m. Ethel Elizabeth Wright, Sept. 1, 1911; children—Joseph Allon, David Alvohn, Daniel Leonard, Evangeline Esther (Mrs. William Love), Bethel Ruth, Rebecca (Mrs. Freeborn Corey). Ordained to ministry Pentecostal Ch., 1906; field dir. Apostolic Faith Movement, Tex., 1907-08; pastor, Hot Springs, Ark., 1911-18; helped promote orgn. Assemblies of God, Hot Springs, 1913-14, gen. presbyter, 1914-17; helped promote re-orgn. Pentecostal Assemblies of the World, 1920-25, gen. presbyter, 1920-24; organizer Pentecostal Assembly of Can., 1918-20; pastor, founder Bethel Pentecostal Ch., Inc., Toronto, Can., 1932-39; gen. supt. Pentecostal Ch., Inc., Houston (now St. Louis), 1925-32, 39-45; helped negotiate merger Pentecostal Ch., Inc. and Pentecostal Assemblies of Jesus Christ (United Pentecostal Ch.), 1944-45, gen. supt., 1945-52, hon. gen. presbyter; specialized Bible teaching evangelism since 1952. Home: Picton Ont., Can.

GOSSICK, BEN ROGER, educator; b. Fairfield, Iowa, May 6, 1914; s. Harlan and Floss (Rogers) G.; B.A., Pomona Coll., 1939; M.A. (Mosenthal fellow, Barker scholar), Columbia, 1941; M.S., Purdue U., 1954, Ph.D., 1954; m. Jean Koehler, Aug. 22, 1941; children—Elizabeth (Mrs. James Lauer), Mary (Mrs. Harold Symms), Katherine (Mrs. K.D. Petrey), Vicky. Prof. physics Ariz. State U., Tempe, 1957-63; prof. State U. N.Y. at Binghamton, 1963-66, chmn. dept., 1965-66; prof. physics and astronomy U. Ky., Lexington, 1966-77, chmn. dept., 1969-73. Cons. Oak Ridge Nat. Labs., 1950-56, 57-62, Sandia Corp., Albuquerque, 1957-60; mem. adv. bd. Nininger Meteorite Collection, Tempe, 1961-63. Bd. dirs. Blue Grass Sch., Lexington, 1967-69. Fellow Am. Phys. Soc., AAAS; mem. IEEE, Sigma Xi, Phi Beta Kappa, Phi Kappa Phi, Sigma Pi Sigma, Phi Mu Alpha. Author: Potential Barriers in Semiconductors, 1964; Hamilton's Principle and Physical Systems, 1967. Editorial bd. Nat. Electronics Conf., 1953-54. Contbr. profl. jours. Home: Lexington, Ky. Died Nov. 12, 1977; interred Lakewood Cemetery, Mpls.

GOTAAS, HAROLD BENEDICT, engr., educator; b. Mellette, S.D., Sept. 3, 1906; s. Halfdan C. and Emma E. (Cady) G.; B.S., U. S.D., 1928, Sc.D. (hon.), 1955; M.S., Ia. State Coll., 1930; S.M., Harvard, 1937, Sc.D., 1942; D.Eng., Rose Poly. Inst., 1969; m. Alice McLaughlin, Apr. 10, 1931; 1 son, Richard McLaughlin. With Am. Bridge Co., Ambridge, Pa., 1930-31, Ia. Hwy Commn., Ames, 1931, Clinton (Ia.) Bridge Works, 1931-32; asst. prof. civil engring. U. S.D., also city engr., 1932-36; asst. prof., later prof. san. engring. U. N.C., 1937-42; also cons. engr., 1937-42; entered U.S. Army, 1942; assigned as chief engr. and asst. dir., div. of health and sanitation, Inst. Inter-Am. Affairs, 1942-44, dir. div. health and sanitation and exec. v.p., 1944-45, pres. inst., 1945-46; prof. san. engring. U. Cal., 1940-57, dir. San Engring. Labs., 1949-57, chmn. div. civil engring., 1948-54; dean Technol. Inst., Northwestern U., Evanston, Ill., 1957-70, prof. civil engring., 1957-67, Walter P. Murphy prof., from 1967. Spl. cons., environ. health study sect. USPHS, 1948-54; cons. WHO, from 1954; mem. nat. health adv. council HEW, 1956-60; mem. com. on bio-astronautics NRC, 1959-60; mem. engring. panel NSF, 1960-63; chmn. adv. com. on mil. environ. research NRC; mem. Gt. Lakes Commn., chmn. pollution control com., 1961-73; chmn. water resources com. N.E. Ill. Planning Commn., from 1962; chmn. solid waste com., from 1971; mem. Ill. Water Pollution and Water Resources Commn., 1966-69; mem. Rockefeller Mission to Latin Am., 1969. Served from capt. to col. San. Corps, U.S. Army, 1942-46. Decorated Legion of Merit; Cross of Boyaca (Colombia); Order of Honor and Merit (Haiti); Order of Merit (Chile), Order of Condor of Andes (Bolivia); recipient awards including James Croes and Rudolph Hering medals, Harrison P. Eddy and Gordon M. Fairand medals, Kenneth Allen award, Wisdom award Honor; Engr. of Year award Ill. Soc. Profl. Engrs., 1962; Marston medal Ia. State U., 1975. Mem. Nat. Acad. Engring. (hon.), Western Soc. Engrs. (hon.), Am. Soc. C.E. (chmn. research com. 1959-60, named Chgo. Engr. of Year 1974), Am. Soc. Engring. Edn., Am. Pub. Health Assn., Inter-Am. Assn. San. Engrs. (pres. U.S. sect. 1959), Am. Water Works Assn., Water Pollution Control Assn. (pres. Cal. sect. 1951-52), Engring. Coll. Research Counci (dir. 1959-62), Am. Acad. Environ. Engring. Inter-soc. Bd. (dir., v.p.), Triangle (nat. hon. mem.), Sigma Xi, Phi Kappa Phi, Tau Beta Pi, Delta Omega, Chi Epsilon, Kappa Sigma, Sigma Phi Delta. Clubs: Economic (Chgo.). Author books. Contbr. articles to profl. jours. Home: Evanston, Ill. Deceased.

GOTTLIEB, LEWIS, banker; b. Baton Rouge, Aug. 11, 1894; s. Joe and Rebecca (Hahn) G.; A.B., La. State U., 1913, LL.B. with honors, 1916. Admitted to La. bar, 1916; v.p. City Nat. Bank of Baton Rouge, 1934-46, pres., 1946-57, chmn. bd., 1957-72, chmn. bd. emeritus, 1972-75; sec., dir. Lottie Land & Devel. Co., Inc.; pres., dir. Baton Rouge Realty Co., Ltd., Standard Motors, Inc., Bistineau-Webster Oil Co.; v.p., dir. Louis Levy Grocery Co.; dir. Pan-Am. Life Ins. Co., New Orleans br. Fed. Res. Bank, 1961-64, Atlanta, Gen. Equipment Inc. Past pres. United Givers Fund of Greater Baton Rouge; mem. nat. budget com. United Community Funds and Councils Am., Nat. Social Welfare Assembly, 1954-75. Mem. bd. suprs. La. State U. A. and M. Coll., Baton Rouge, 1939-40, 50-58, chmn., 1954-56; trustee Delgado Mus. Art, New Orleans, 1960-61. Recipient Brandeis award, 1960, Golden Deeds award, 1960, Brotherhood award Nat. Conf. Christians and Jews, 1963. Mem. La. Bankers Assn. (pres. 1955-56), Baton Rouge C. of C. (pres. 1932-34), La. State U. Alumni Fedn. (pres. 1931-35), Tau Kappa Alpha, Phi Kappa Phi, Omicron Delta Kappa, Zeta Beta Tau (Man of Year award 1963). Home: Baton Rouge, La. Died May 31, 1975.

GOTTSCHALK, HANS W., educator; b. Berlin, Germany, Dec. 31, 1914; s. Richard and Margaret (Dittmann) G.; came to U.S., 1923, naturalized, 1936; B.A., N.Y. U., 1941, M.A., 1943; Ph.D., U. Iowa, 1949; m. Anna Elizabeth Schmelzle, Nov. 20, 1941. Asst. head sales order dept. Am. Bemberg Corp. and N. Am. Raye Corp., N.Y.C., 1936-43; Eastern office mgr. Ill. Zinc Co., N.Y.C., 1943-45; instr. English dept. Ohio State U., 1947-50; asst. prof. Wis. State Coll., Eau Claire, 1950-53; sr. tchr. New Lincoln Sch., N.Y.C., 1954; asst. prof. Duquesne U., 1954-55; asso. prof., prof. English, chmn. dept. SUNY, Geneseo, 1955-76, prof. emeritus, 1976-78; cons. English linguistics project U.S. Office Edn., State U. N.Y., Buffalo, 1963-65; dir. NDEA Insts. in English, 1966, 68, evaluator proposals Instns. in English, 1966-67; cons. to English to numerous N.Y. State sch. systems; Distinguished Service prof. State U. N.Y., 1975. Fellow N.Y. State English Council. Democrat. Roman Catholic. Contbr. articles to profl. jours. Home: Geneseo, N.Y. Died July 22, 1978; interred St. Mary's Cemetery, Geneseo.

GOUDSMIT, SAMUEL ABRAHAM, physicist, editor; b. The Hague, Netherlands, July 11, 1902; s. Isaac and Marianne (Gompers) G.; student U. Amsterdam; Ph.D., U. Leiden (Netherlands), 1927; D.Sc. (hon.), Case Inst. Tech., 1958, U. Chgo., 1972, Utah State U., 1972, Northwestern U., 1975; m. Jaantje Logher, Jan. 19, 1927 (div. 1960); 1 dau., Esther Marianne; m. 2d, Irene Bejach, July 8, 1960. Came to U.S., 1927. Faculty U. Mich., 1927, prof. physics, 1932-46; Rockefeller fellow, 1926, Guggenheim fellow, 1938; vis. prof. Harvard U., 1941; prof. physics Northwestern U., 1946-48; vis. prof. Rockefeller U., 1955-74; Disting. vis. prof. dept. physics U. Nev., Reno, 1975-78; on leave to Radiation (Radar) Lab. Mass. Inst. Tech. and Eng., 1942-46; sr. scientist Brookhaven Nat. Lab., 1948-70; editor-in-chief Am. Phys. Soc., 1951-74; Morris Loeb lectr. Harvard, 1975. Detailed to War Dept. as chief sci. intelligence mission in Europe, 1944-45. Decorated Medal of Freedom, officer Order of Brit. Empire, Comdr. Order of Orange-Nassau (Netherlands); recipient Research Corp. Sci. award, 1954; Max Planck medal German Phys. Soc., 1965, Karl T. Compton medal Am. Inst. Physics, 1974, Nat. Medal of Sci., 1976. Fellow Am. Phy. Soc., Netherlands Phys. Soc., Nat. Acad. Scis., Am. Nuclear Soc.; mem. Am. Philos. Soc.; corr. Netherlands Royal Acad. Scis. Author books including: Alsos, 1947. Founder Phys. Rev. Letters. Contbr. sci. articles to profl. jours. Discoverer (with G.E. Uhlenbeck) of spin of electron, 1925. Home: Reno, Nev. Died Dec. 4, 1978.

GOULART, JOAO BELCHLOR MARQUES, pres. of Brazil; b. nr. Sao Borja, Rio Grande do Sul, Mar. 1, 1918; student law Porto Alegre U. Cattle rancher; charge labor movement, then labor minister Brazil during presidency Getulio Vargas; constl. v.p. Brazil during presidency Juscelino Kubitchek; head trade mission to Red China; pres. of Brazil, 1961-64. Died Dec. 6, 1976.

GOULD, ALBERT J., lawyer; b. Denver, Jan. 1, 1897; s. Albert James and Grace (Glascoe) G.; student U. of Colo., 1915-17; LL.B., cum laude, U. of Denver, 1921; m. Eleanor W. Whitford, Nov. 21, 1923; children—Edith, Elaine; m. 2d, Ellen Browne Loeber, Feb. 18, 1950. Admitted Colo. bar, 1921, practiced Denver; pub. adminstr. city and county of Denver, 1933-37; dir. sec., attorney for Fox Theatres, Rocky Mt. Div. Served with heavy arty., U.S. Army, Ft. Monroe, Va., 1917-18. Mem. Denver Bar Assn. (sec. 1924-32, pres. 1932-33), Phi Beta Kappa. Sigma Chi, Phi Delta Phi. Mason (32 deg., Shriner). Clubs: Denver, Denver Country, Denver Athletic. Home: Denver, Colo. Died Mar. 9, 1976.

GOULD, CLARENCE PEMBROKE, university prof., author; b. Church Hill, Md., Nov. 1, 1884; s. William Dunbar and Josephine Trenchard (Faithful) G.; Baltimore City Coll., 1904; A.B., Johns Hopkins, 1907, Ph.D., 1911; unmarried. Instr. history, 1911-12, Michael O. Fisher prof. history, 1912-18, Coll. of Wooster; ensign, 1918, lt. (j.g.), 1919, U.S.N.R.F.; pres. Washington Coll., Chestertown, Md., 1919-23; asst. prof. history, 1924-25, asso. prof. and asst. dean, since 1925, Adelbert Coll., Western Reserve U. Episcopalian. Mem. Am. Hist. Assn., Md. Hist. Soc., Hist. Soc. of Eastern States and Md., Phi Beta Kappa (Johns Hopkins). Author: Land System in Maryland, 1720-1765, 1913; Money and Transportation in Maryland, 1720-1765, 1915. Home: Cleveland, Ohio. *

GOULD, GORDON THOMAS, JR., air force officer; b. Mobile, Ala., Jan. 7, 1916; s. Gordon Thomas and Minnie (Gaston) G.; B.S., U.S. Mil. Acad., 1941; M.S., Mass. Inst. Tech., 1950; grad. Air War Coll., 1954; m. Lois Sameth, June 12, 1941; children—Gordon Thomas III, Beverly L., Darcy A. Commd. 2d lt. USAAF, 1941, advanced through grades to lt. gen., 1971; served as signal and communications officer, China, 1944-46; chief communications-electronics div. Hdqrs. SAC, Offutt AFB, Neb., 1960-64; dep. comdr. Hdqrs. Air Force communications service Scott AFB, Ill., 1964-65; dir. command control and communications Hdqrs. USAF, Washington, 1965-71; dir. Def. Communications Agy., 1971-74. Decorated D.S.M. with 2 oak leaf clusters, Legion of Merit with 2 oak leaf clusters; Spl. Vest Order Yun Hui (China). Fellow I.E.E.E., A.A.A.S.; mem. Armed Forces Communications and Electronics Assn. (v.p.), Sigma Xi. Home: Fairfax, Va. Died Aug. 7, 1979; buried Arlington (Va.) Nat. Cemetery.

GOULD, LESLIE, financial cons.; b. Phila., Feb. 8, 1902; s. Alexander and Rosa Montgomery (Jenks) G.; student Bellefonte (Pa.) Acad. 1920-21; grad. Elmira Free Acad. 1921; m. Althea Mundorff O'Hanlon, June 14, 1957. Reporter, Advertiser, Telegram and Herald, Elmira, 1918-20; police reporter Rochester Democrat-Chronicle, N.Y., 1921-22; copyreader Syracuse Herald, 1922-23; telegraph editor Atlantic City Press 1923-25; rewrite, Los Angeles Times, 1925; copyreader and editor st. sale edits. Oakland (Cal.) Tribune 1925-28; financial reporter Asso. Press, N.Y.C., 1928-29; financial reporter N.Y. Post, 1929-30; financial editor N.Y. Jour. American, 1930-66, N.Y., World Jour. Tribune, 1966-68; condr. daily column Behind the News in Business, syndicated by King Features Service, 1948-68. Trustee Beekman-Downtown Hosp., N.Y.C.; hon. mem. bd. N.Y. Assn. for Blind. Recipient Americanism award Wall St. Post, Am. Legion, 1949; Valley Forge award Freedom Found., 1949, 50, 51; Loeb newspaper award U. Conn., 1958-64; Bus. News award Newspaper Reporters Assn. of N.Y.C., 1965; James Wright Brown award Deadline Club, 1965. Clubs: Dutch Treat (gov.), Coffee House, Metropolitan, Amateur Comedy, Recess; Royal Poinciana (Naples, Fla.). Home: Naples, Fla. Died Sept. 23, 1977; buried Naples.

GOULD, LYMAN JAY, educator; b. N.Y.C., May 5, 1925; s. David and Yvette (Pearlman) G.; A.B. cum laude, Colby Coll., 1948; M.A., U. Mich., 1949, Ph.D., 1958; m. Ann Rodney, Aug. 30, 1950; children—Ellen Yvette, Michael Rodney. Teaching fellow U. Mich., 1952; instr. U. Vt., 1953-57, asst. prof., 1957-61, asso. prof., 1961-66, dir. program of Latin Am. studies, 1962-65, prof., 1966-76, chmn. dept. polit. sci., 1966-72, chmn. Center for Area Studies, 1965-69; moderator Center for Research on Vt., 1974-75. Mem. Burlington City Charter commn., 1958-60, Burlington Com. on community relations, 1957-62, Jud. Council of Vt., 1967-69. Served with AUS, 1943-46, U. Vt. summer faculty research grantee, 1960, 65, U. Vt. Ford Found. travel grantee, 1963. Mem. Am. Polit. Sci. Assn., Latin Am. Studies Assn., Phi Beta Kappa, Pi Gamma Mu. Author: People, Power and Politics, 1961; La Ley Foraker, 1969, 2d edit., 1975. Contbr. essays to periodicals. Home: South Burlington, Vt. Died Oct. 3, 1976.

GOULDNER, ALVIN WARD, educator, sociologist; b. N.Y.C., July 29, 1920; s. Louis and Estelle (Fetbrandt) G.; B.B.A., Bernard Baruch Coll., 1941; M.A., Columbia, 1945, Ph.D., 1953; m. Janet Lee Walker, Feb. 5, 1966; children—Richard Lee, Alan Jeremy, Andrew Ward, Alessandra Walker. Asst. prof. sociology U. Buffalo, 1947-51; asso. prof. Antioch Coll.,

Yellow Springs, Ohio, 1952-54; asso. prof. U. Ill. at Urbana, 1954-57, prof., 1957-59; chmn. dept. sociology Washington U., St. Louis, 1959-64, prof., 1959-67, Max Weber Research prof., 1967-80; lectr. Free U. Berlin, 1965, Stockholm Sch. Econ., 1965, 77, Hebrew U. Jerusalem, 1966, Warsaw (Poland) U., 1966, Goldsmith's Coll., London, 1977, U. Copenhagen, 1977, U. Zagreb, 1977; prof. U. Amsterdam, 1972-76; founder, editor-in-chief Trans-Action mag., 1963-66; co-founder, editor-in-chief Theory and Society, Amsterdam, 1974-80; editor-in-chief New Critics Press, St. Louis, 1969-80; editor Bobbs-Merrill Reprint Series, 1960-80; cons. editor Penguin Books, London, 1969-74; fellow Center Advanced Study Behavioral Scis., 1961-62. Mem. Am. Sociol. Assn., Soc. Psychol. Study of Social Issues, Soc. Study of Social Problems (pres. 1962), Sociol. Research Assn. Author: Patterns of Industrial Bureaucracy, 1954; Wildcat Strike, 1954; (with R. A. Peterson) Notes on Technology and the Moral Order, 1962; Enter Plato, 1965; Coming Crisis of Western Sociology, 1970; For Sociology, 1973; Dialectic of Ideology and Technology, 1976; Future of Intellectuals and Rise of New Class, 1979; The Two Marxisms: Contradictions and Anomalies in the Development of Theory, 1979; editor: Studies in Leadership: Leadership and Democratic Action, 1950; Emile Durkheim's Socialism and Saint-Simon, 1958; (with H.P. Gouldner) Modern Sociology, 1963; (with S.M. Miller) Applied Sociology, 1965. Home: Saint Louis, Mo. Died Dec. 15, 1980.

GOURLEY, WALLACE S., judge; b. Wellsville, O., Aug. 4, 1904; s. Harry A. and Mary Margaret (Barclay) G.; LL.B., Ohio State U., 1929, LL.D.; m. Mildred R. Plunkett, Mar. 30, 1934. Admitted to Ohio bar, 1929, Pa. bar, 1931; 1st asst. dist. atty. Washington County, Pa., 1936-44; mem. Pa. Senate, 1941-45; judge U.S. Dist. Ct. for Western Dist. Pa., 1945-51, chief judge Western Dist. Pa., 1951-76. Rep. to 3d Jud. circuit Jud. Conf. U.S. Mem. Nat. adv. Com. on Intercircuit Assignments, Nat. Com. on Trial Practice and Technique. Mem. Am., Pa., Washington County, Allegheny County bar assns., Am. Judicature Soc., Delta Theta Phi, Alpha Sigma Phi. Author: Gourley Instant Research Index Service, 6 vols. Home: Pittsburgh, Pa. Died Sept. 23, 1976; buried Homewood Cemetery, Pitts.

GOUWENS, TEUNIS EARL (GOU'ENZ), clergyman; b. South Holland, Ill., July 13, 1886; s. Rollin Arie and Annie (Paarlberg) G.; A.B., Hope Coll., Michigan, 1909, M.A., 1912; student Princeton Theol. Sem., 1909-10, New Brunswick Theol. Sem., 1910-13, Union Theol. Sem., New York, 1913-15; B.D., Rutgers Coll., 1912; D.D., Centre Coll., Ky., 1924; m. Alma Fannie Staelin, Sept. 29, 1914; 1 son, Teunis Earl. Ordained ministry Ref. Ch. in America, 1913; asso. pastor and pastor Fort Washington Ref. Ch., N.Y. City, 1913-15; pastor Mountain Lakes, N.J., 1915-21, 2d Presbyn. Ch. Louisville Ky., 1921-48, ret., Exchange pastor in England, summer 1938. Asso. del. Oxford Conf. on Ch., Community and State, 1937. Instr. in Homiletics, Louisville Presbyn. Seminary, 1940, 1941. Mem. board Lees Junior College, Jackson, Ky.; member board Louisville Presbyterian Theological Sem., Louisville, Ky. Club: Pendennis. Author: The Rock Taht Is Higher, 1922; Why I Believe, 1930; The Stirred Nest, 1933; Can We Repeat the Creed?, 1936; He Opened the Book, 1940; The Far Horizons of Scripture, 1942; Keep Your Faith, 1943. Contbr. to religious jours. Home: Sarasota, Fla.

GOW, PAUL A., mining engr.; b. Fontanelle, Ia., June 6, 1883; s. George L. and Laura Belle (Purviance) G.; E.M., Colo. Sch. of Mines, 1907; m. Gertrude Nelson, Apr. 15, 1905; children—Elizabeth Purviance (Mrs. H. Hartwell Bass, Jr.), George Loudon. Engring. dept., Anaconda Copper Mining Co., 1907-11; city engr., Butte, Mont., 1911-13, commr. pub. works, 1913; supt. Pilot Butte Mining Co., 1913-16; general manager Tuolumne Copper Co., 1916-26; general manager N. Butte Mining Co., 1926-28, pres. since 1928; pres. Unity Gold Corporation; dir., secretary and treasurer Community Gasoline Company. Trustee School District No. 1, Butte, 1916-19; pres. Butte Chamber of Commerce, 1919-23. Mem. Sigma Nu, Tau Beta Pi. Republican. Mason (32 deg., Shriner) Elk. Home: Butte, Mont. *

GOWIN, ENOCH BURTON, educator; b. Benson, Minn., Feb. 28, 1883; s. James Madison and Eliza (Burton) G.; M.Di., Ia. State Teachers' Coll., 1906; Ph.B., U. of Wis., 1909, Ph.M., 1910; Ph.D., Columbia; m. Lucy Ada Case, of Milwaukee, Wis., Sept. 8, 1911. Retail merchant; investigator for Com. on Safety for N.Y. City and for the State Factory Commn. of N.Y. State; asst. prof., Sch. of Commerce, New York U.; director of course, Am. Inst. of Finance; sec. Executives Club of N.Y. Member Am. Economic Assn., Economic Club (New York). Republican. Congregationalist. Author: The Executive and His Control of Men, 1915; The Selection and Training of the Business Executive, 1918; Developing Executive Ability, 1919. Co-Author: Vocational Guidance, 1915.

GRACE, JOHN JOSEPH, social welfare adminstr.; b. Jersey City, May 26, 1902; s. Joseph J. and Elizabeth (Mitchell) G.; grad. Salvation Army Sch. Officers Tng., N.Y.C., 1922; m. Alice Owen, Apr. 18, 1930. Commd. officer Salvation Army, 1922, various field adminstrn. appointments, 1922-45; territorial pub. relations dir., N.Y.C., 1945-47; divisional comdr., Buffalo, 1947-50, Phila., 1950-61; nat. chief sec., adminstrv. asst. to nat. comdr., N.Y.C., 1961-70; dir. Salvation Army team under contract to AID, Vietnam, 1969-71. Home: Philadelphia, Pa. Died July 23, 1972.

GRAEBNER, WALTER, business cons.; b. Prairie Twp., O., Dec. 16, 1909; s. John R. and Hedwig (Sievers) G.; student U. Wis., 1928-31; m. Jean Fairchild Bellis, Nov. 10, 1933 (div.); children—Gretchen (Mrs. Morgan), John; m. 2d, Constance Grange Lailey, Oct. 2, 1948. Employed by Time, Inc., 1931-53, as corr. in Chgo., London and Moscow, chmn., mgr. dir. Erwin Wasey, Ruthrauff & Ryan, Ltd., 1953-63; advt. pub. relations cons. Interpublic, Ltd., Lonodn, Eng., 1963-65. Mem. Alpha Delta Phi. Lutheran. Author: Round Trip to Russia, 1943; Conservation in London (with Stephen Laird), 1942; My Dear Mr. Chruchill, 1965. Editor: (with Allan A. Michiel Their Finest Hour, 1941; Lights of Freedom, 1942. Home: London, England. Died Nov. 9, 1976.

GRAFE, PAUL, constrn. engr., contractor; b. Clay City, Ind., Apr. 19, 1895; s. John Henry and Margaret (Edmonds) G.; grad. Rose Poly. Inst., 1920, D.Eng. (hon.), 1950; spl. study U. Glasgow (Scotland); m. Helen Louise Thickstun, Dec. 11, 1917; children—Helen, Louise, Paula. Engr. Pa. R.R., 1919; timekeeper, supt. C.R. Cummins Co., constructing belt line for Pa. R.R. in Detroit, also substructure for Marysville Power Plant for Detroit Edison Co.; with Grafe-Callahan Constrn. Co., Los Angeles and Dallas, from 1922, in charge constrn. work, v.p., pres., later chmn. bd.; supervised Ill. River levee work, River De Pere's sewer project in St. Louis, Marseilles (Ill.) Canal, Mississippi River levees in Ark. and Mo., Bagnell Dam found. on Osage River, Mo., Madden Dam, C.Z., All-Am. Canal, Calif., dam and tunnels on Casper Alcova project, Wyo., shafts, tunnels on Delaware Aqueduct for Bd. of Water Supply, City of N.Y.; work on Shasta Dam, Central Valley Project, Redding, Calif., Prado Dam, Orange County Flood Control, Calif., Caddoa (Colo.) Dam, pipe and tunnel sects. of San Diego Aqueduct, Granby Dam and pumping plant, Horsetooth Dam, Soldiers Canyon Dam on Colo. Big Thompson project, Hungry Horse Dam, Mont., Davis Dam, Ariz., Duchesne Tunnel, Utah, tunnels for City of Chgo., constrn. NASA Hdqrs., Colorado Springs, Titan Missile Base, Mountain Home, Idaho; exec. dir. on secret war work in Pacific, NW Can. and Brit. Isles; constructing water tunnels Bd. Water Supply, N.Y. Served in engring. dept. Motor Transport Corps in France and Scotland, 1917-19. Breeder thoroughbred and quarter horses, Aberdeen Angus cattle. Regent Loyola U., Los Angeles; bd. dirs. Carrie Estell Doheny Found.; bd. mgrs. Rose Poly. Inst., Terre Haute, Ind. Decorated knight Equestrian Order of Holy Sepulchre of Jerusalem; recipient Golden Beaver award for mgmt., 1973. Mem. Acad. Polit. Sci., Los Angeles World Affairs Council. Republican. Roman Catholic. Clubs: California, Los Angeles Country, Greater Los Angeles Press (Los Angeles); Valley Country (Montecito, Calif.); Union (Panama); City, Petroleum (Dallas); Tyee (B.C.); Rancheros Visitadores (Santa Barbara). Home: Santa Paula, Calif. Died Sept. 6, 1980.

GRAFLY, DOROTHY, writer; b. Paris, France, July 29, 1896 (parents Am. citizens); d. Charles and Frances (Sekeles) Grafly; brought to U.S. in infancy; B.A., Wellesley, 1918; grad. work under Prof. George P. Baker of Harvard, 1918-19; m. Charles Hawkins Drummond, Aug. 9, 1946. Art critic, Phila. North American, 1920-25, art editor and editorial and feature writer, 1925; art editor Public Ledger, Phila., 1925-34; art critic Evening Publ. Ledger, 1934; art editor Phila. Record, 1934-42; spl. corr. Christian Sci. Monitor, 1920-63; Phila. corr. Am. Mag. of Art to 1928; curator of collections Drexel Inst., 1934-45; dir. mag. publicity Phila. Art Alliance, 1944-48; dir. research and art Philip Ragan Assos., 1942-48, contbg. editor American Artist, 1946-56; contbg. critic Art Digest (under name Dorothy Drummond), to 1953; art editor Tempos Mag., Phila., 1955-59, The Evening and Sunday Bull., 1956-70; lectr. art Temple U., 1938-39, Drexel Inst., 1940-42. Recipient citation for civic and cultural contbns. City of Phila., 1972. Fellow in perpetuity Pa. Acad. Fine Arts, 1957. Elected Distinguished Dau. Pa., 1960. Mem. Phila. Art Alliance, Alumnae Assn. Wellesley Coll., Nat. Geog., Am. Assn. Museums, Phila. Mus. Art, Am. Fedn. Arts, Pa. Acad. Fine Arts, Pi Gamma Mu. Clubs: New Century Guild (Phila.), Phila. Altrusa (charter mem.; pres. 1930-32), Phila. Water Color Club (hon.). Club: Nat. Travel. Wrote and produced Masque of Night, Masque of Life, The Phoenix, Metamorphosis, Images (all produced Gloucester, Mass.), 1914-20; winner prize for one-act play, Plays and Players' Club, Phila., 1921. Author: History of the Philadelphia Print Club, 1929; series of American art biographies under title Parade of American Art, 1936-37; series of articles dealing with living European sculptors, nat. What Sells series, Am. Artist, 1948-49. Contbr. Dictionary Am. Biography, Ency. Brit. and to mags. Editor-pub. Art in Focus. Lectr. on art. One of six American critics invited by Chgo. Art Inst. to broadcast over nat. hook-up at opening of 1934 Century of Progress Expn. Art Exhbn. Home: Philadelphia, Pa. Died Nov. 13, 1980; buried Arlington Cemetery, Drexel Hill, Pa.

GRAH, RUDOLF FERDINAND, forester, educator; b. San Diego, Calif., Aug. 21, 1915; s. Rudolf and Elin (Anderson) G.; B.S., Oreg. State U., 1939; M.S., U. Calif., Berkeley, 1941; Ph.D., (Shoen-Rine fellow), U. Mich., 1957; m. Mary Edna Beahrs, Aug. 24, 1941; children—Nancy, Mary Ellen, Katherine, Charles, Oliver, David. Forester, Rubber Devel. Corp., Brazil, 1942-46; extension forester cooperative extension U. Calif., Berkeley, prof. forestry, 1954-78, chmn. dept. forestry, 1974-78. Sr. research fellow Forest Research Inst., New Zealand. Mem. Soc. Am. Foresters, Sigma Xi. Republican. Congregationalist. Contbr. articles to profl. jours. Home: Orinda, Calif. Died May 25, 1978.

GRAHAM, BENJAMIN, security analyst; b. London, Eng., May 9, 1894; s. Isaac Grossbaum and Dorothy (Gasundhelt) G.; B.S., Columbia Coll., 1914; m. Estelle Messing, Mar. 12, 1943. Came to U.S., 1895, naturalized, 1921. With Newburger, Henderson & Loeb (mem. N.Y. Stock Exchange), 1914-23, jr. partner, 1921-23; mgr. investment funds, 1923-56; chmn., later vice chmn., Govt. Employees Ins. Cos., 1950-64. Governor of N.Y. Inst. Finance; professor Finance, U. Cal. at Los Angeles, 1956-76; regent Security Analysts Seminar, 1957-61. Mem. Am. Econ. Assn., N.Y. Soc. Security Analysts., Am. Finance Assn. (past v.p.), Phi Beta Kappa. Author: Interpretation of Financial Statements (with McGolrick), 1964; Storage and Stability, 1937; World Commodities and World Currency, 1944; The Intelligent Investor, 1964; Security Analysis (with Dodd, Tatham), 1961. Home: Beverly Hills, Calif. Died Sept. 21, 1976.

GRAHAM, DAVID, corp. ofcl.; b. No. Ireland, Mar. 11, 1905; s. William J. and Agnes J. (Clark) G.; came to U.S. as Commonwealth Fellow, 1927, naturalized, 1942; grad. Queens U., 1926; grad. Mass. Inst. Tech., 1929, Harvard Sch. Bus., 1931; m. Clover E. Henry, Sept. 1933; children—Rae H. (dec.), David (dec.), Philip; m. 2d, Florence Ruth Comer, Oct. 1948. Asso. with J. P. Morgan & Co., N.Y.C., 1931-32; dir. J. Walter Thompson Co., London, 1932-37, L. Rose & Co., Ltd., London, 1934-43; treas. W. Va. Pulp and Paper Co., N.Y.C., 1945-48; financial v.p. Weyerhaeuser Timber Co., Tacoma, Wash., 1948-52; financial v.p., dir. Standard Oil Co. (Ind.), 1952-62; chmn. corporate finance dept., gen. partner Hornblower & Weeks-Hemphill, Noyes, N.Y.C., 1962-69; dir. Gen. Fireproffing Co., Del. Labs., Inc., Olinkraft, Inc. Pres. Weyerhaeuser Timber Found., 1948-51. Chief pulp sect. Pulp and Paper Br. WPB, 1942; dir. Office of Pulp Allocation, Forest Products Bur., 1943. Mem. bd. govs., bd. dirs. Chgo. chpt. A.R.C.; dir., past pres. Community Fund, Chgo. Trustee Northwestern U., Woodrow Wilson Nat. Fellowship Found. Mem. Harvard Bus. Sch. Alumni Assn., Am. Inst. E.E., N.A.M. (dir. 1949-51, 57-62), Chgo. Planetarium Soc. (trustee). Presbyn. Clubs: Links, India House, Wall Street, Harvard, Union League (N.Y.C.); Chicago, Commercial (Chgo.); Ocean, Country of Fla. (Delray Beach). Home: Delray Beach, Fla. Died Jan. 24, 1976.

GRAHAM, DONALD, univ. dean; b. Lansing, Kan., Dec. 13, 1917; s. Frank L. and Bertha (Carrington) G.; B.S., Kan. State Coll., Pittsburg, 1939, M.S. 1940; Ph.D. in History, State U. Ia., 1953; m. Ailene Louise Boyer, Oct. 21, 1943. Mem. faculty Buena Vista Coll., Storm Lake, Ia., 1946-55; mem. faculty Wis. State U.-Whitewater, 1955-76, dean Sch. Grad. Studies, from 1965, chmn. dept. history, from 1972; cons. U.S. Office Edn. Served with USAAF, 1941-45. Home: Whitewater, Wis. Died June 29, 1976; buried Whitewater.

GRAHAM, JOHN STEPHENS, business and financial consultant; b. Reading, Mass., Aug. 4, 1905; s. Joseph L. and Margaret (Nowell) G.; S.B. in Commerce, U. N.C., 1927; student law, Harvard, 1931-32; student U. Va., 1932-34; m. Elizabeth Breckinridge, June 22, 1935; children—Louise (Mrs. Charles W. Hayes, III), Margaret (Mrs. Joseph H. Coreth), Katherine, Susan. With Brown and Williamson Tobacco Company, Winston-Salem, North Carolina, also Louisville, 1928-31; admitted to North Carolina bar, 1935, practiced in Winston-Salem, 1936-42, jr. partner Vaughn & Graham, specializing tax law; exec. asst. to under-sec. of treasury, 1946-48; asst. sec. from 1962; commr., AEC, 1957-62; director of Zeigler Coal & Coke Company. Served from lieutenant to comdr. USNR, 1942-46. Democrat. Episcopalian. Home: Washington, D.C. Died Oct. 20, 1976.

GRAHAM, SHIRLEY LOLA (MRS. W. E. B. DUBOIS), author, composer; b. Indpls., Nov. 11, 1906; d. David Andrew and Etta (Bell) Graham; B.A., Oberlin Coll., 1934, M.A., 1935; postgrad. (Julius Rosenwald fellow 1938-40), Yale U. Drama Sch., 1939-41, N.Y. U., 1944-46, Guggenheim fellow, Sorbonne U., Paris, France, 1946-47; m. Shadrach T. McCants (div. 1928); 1 son, David Graham; m. W.E. Burghardt DuBois, Feb. 14, 1951 (dec. 1963). Composer words and music;

music drama Tome-Tom, prod. 1932; opera for children Little Black Sambo (dir. 1st prodn.), 1938. Author: (with George Lipscombe) Dr. George Washington Carver, Scientist, 1944; Paul Robeson, Citizen of the World, 1946; The Story of Phillis Wheatley, 1949; There was Once a Slave, 1947; Your Most Humble Servant, 1949, Jean Baptiste Pointe de Sable. Founder of Chicago, 1953; The Story of Pocahantas, 1954; Booker T. Washington, Educator, 1955. Trustee Library of Intercultural Studies, from 1955. Recipient Julian Messner award, 1947, Anisfield-Wolf award, 1950, Nat. Acad. Arts and Letters award, 1950. Mem. Kappa Delta Pi, Sigma Delta Theta. Club: P.E.N. Died Mar. 27, 1977.

GRAHAM, THOMAS WESLEY, clergyman, educator; b. Carlsbad, Ont., Can., Oct. 12, 1882; s. John and Margaret Marion (Snyder) G.; grad. Ottawa Collegiate Inst., 1899; A.B., U. of Toronto, 1903; student McCormick Theol. Sem., 1904-07; Free Ch. Coll., Glasgow, Scotland, 1907-08; D.D., Macalester Coll., 1920; m. Kate Fullerton, June 16, 1910 (dec. Jan. 1958); m. 2d, Beatrice B. Smith, Oct. 1, 1959. Came to U.S., 1904, naturalized citizen, 1920. Sec. Univ. Y.M.C.A., Toronto, 1903-04, Univ. Y.M.C.A., U. of Minn., 1909-12; ordained Presbyn. ministry, 1908; pastor Andrew Ch., Minneapolis, 1912-20; prof. homiletics, Oberlin Grad. Sch., 1920-48, dean Grad. Sch. of Theology, 1923-48; counsellor on religious work YMCA, N.Y.C., 1948-59; asst. minister First Presbyn. Ch., Greenwich, Conn., 1959-68, minister emeritus 1st Presbyn. Ch., since 1968—. Represented The Bd. for Christian Colleges in China, Taipei, Formosa, 1953-54. College preacher at many colleges and universities; lecturer at many student confs. in U.S. and Can., also for World's Student Christian Fed. Awarded Alumni Medal for distinguished service to Oberlin Coll., 1949. Mem. Nat. Bd. YMCA chmn. Centennial Com. Nat. Council YMCA; counsellor on religion, Y.M.C.A. of New York City, mem. Nat. Com. Student Y.M.C.A.; mem. Internat. Com. Y.M.C.A. Army Y.M.C.A. sec., Ft. Snelling, Minn., and Paris, France, 1917-19; bd. dirs. Greenwich (Connecticut) Community Chest, Mem. Fgn. Policy Association. Clubs: Quill, Shanghai Tiffin, Canadican Soc. (N.Y.C.); The Belle Haven (Greenwich, Conn.). Editor: The Story of Jesus, 1925. Author religious articles. Home: Greenwich, Conn. *

GRAHAM, WILLIAM DONALD, physician, army officer; b. Birmingham, Eng., Oct. 5, 1905; s. John and Lilian (Abels) G.; came to U.S., 1915, naturalized, 1922; B.Sc., U. Minn., 1930, M.D., 1931; M.P.H., U. Cal. at Berkeley, 1949; m. Dorothy Margaret Quinlen, Apr. 7, 1934 (dec. Jan. 1970); 1 dau., Ann (Mrs. Gerald E. Bouchoux); m. 2d, Jacqueline Campbell VanGieson, May 31, 1971. Pvt. practice medicine and surgery, Hanska, Minn., 1931-34; commd. in M.C., U.S. Army, 1934, advanced through grades to maj. gen.; exec. dir. Dependents Medicare Program, 1960-62; comdg. gen. Tripler Army Med. Center, Honolulu, also chief surgeon U.S. Army, Pacific, 1962-65; dep. dir. Hawaii Regional Med. Program, U. Hawaii, 1966-68. Decorated D.S.M., Legion of Merit. Fellow A.C.P., Am. Coll. Hosp. Adminstrs., Assn. U.S. Army, Assn. Mil. Surgeons, Phi Rho Sigma. Episcopalian. Rotarian, Mason (Shriner). Home: Honolulu, Hawaii. Died July 30, 1976.

GRAHL, CHARLES HARRY HANS, govt. ofcl.; b. Council Bluffs, Ia., Sept. 23, 1894; s. Harry Hans and Louisa Ludawika (Bock) G.; ed. pub. schs. of Ia.; hon degree Ames Agrl. Coll.; m. Mary Magdaline Phillips, June 12, 1923; children—Charles Phillips, Robert Louis. Advt. dept. Des Moines Register and Tribune, 1913-10; mgr., dir. advt., Des Moines Capital, 1920-21; asst. cashier Comml. Savings Bank, Des Moines, 1919-24, Ia. Des Moines National Bank, 1924-27; asst. adj. gen. of Ia., 1927-32, adj. gen. of Ia., 1932-50; with SSS, 1940-60, state dir. Ia., 1940-50; became regional dir. Region III, 1950, regional field officer Phila., 1950-54, asst. chief planning officer, Nat. Hdqrs., 1954-56, assistant to dir. Lt. Gen. Lewis B. Hershey, 1956-60. Enlisted Co. B, 3d inf. Ia. N.G. 1924; overseas with 168th; commissioned major general, Ia. Nat. Guard, 1955. Secretary Ia. Aeronautics Commn., 1934-43. Awarded D.S.M., Army Commendation ribbon. Member Adj. Gen. Assn. of U.S. (sec. 1938, president, 1939-40, army area vice pres., 1946-47), N.G. Assn. of U.S. (mem. legislative com.), Nat. Sojourners, Argonne Post Am. Legion, Rainbow Div. Vets., Reserve Officers Assn., Theta Xi. Republican. Episcopalian. Mason (32 deg.), Elk. Clubs: Rotary, Service Men's, Prairie, Hyperion Field. Methodist Men (Narbeth, Pa., Bethesda); Beth Meth Drama; Canoe (Phila.). Home: Bethesda, Md. Died Feb. 16, 1981; buried Arlington Nat. Cemetery.

GRAMATKY, HARDIE, artist, author; b. Dallas, Apr. 12, 1907; s. Bernhard and Blanche (Gunner) G.; student Stanford U., 1926-28, Chouinard Art Sch., 1928-30; m. Dorothea Cooke, Aug. 20, 1932; 1 dau., Linda Anne (Mrs. Kendall Borden Smith). Head animator Walt Disney Studios, Hollywood, 1930-36; artist-reporter Fortune mag., 1937-39; illustrator True, Today's Woman, Collier's, Cosmopolitan, etc., from 1940; supr. prodn. tng. films for Army Air Force, 1942-45. Commd. artist-of-war in Vietnam, Air Force, 1966. Represented permanent collections Bklyn. Mus., Chgo. Art Inst., Toledo Art Mus., Mus. Fine Arts, Springfield, Mass., Marietta (Ohio) Coll., 1972, Frye Mus., Seattle; children's book illustrations in Kerlan collection U. Minn., U. Oreg., U. So. Miss. Numerous watercolor prizes including Chgo. Internat. 1939, Am. Watercc• r Soc., 1941, 52, 73, 79, Audubon Artists, 1945, 52, Salmagundi award, 1952, Conn. Watercolor Soc., 1969, Soc. of Illustrators, 1970, Main Streams '72 award Marietta, 1972. Mem. Am. Watercolor Soc. (bd. control from 1953), Soc. Illustrators (dir. 1940-41), Cal. Watercolor Soc. (dir. 1935-36), N.A.D. Conglist. Author, illustrator: (children's books) Little Toot, 1939 (Lewis Carroll Shelf award U. Wis. 1969); Hercules, 1940; Loopy, 1941; Creepers Jeep, 1948; Sparky, 1952; Homer and The Circus Train, 1957; Bolivar, 1961; Nikos and the Sea God, 1963; Little Toot on the Thames, 1964; Little Toot on the Grand Canal, 1968; Happy's Christmas, 1970; Little Toot on the Mississippi, 1973; Little Toot Through The Golden Gate, 1975. Home: Westport, Conn. Died Apr. 29, 1979; buried Green's Farms (Conn.) Ch. Cemetery.

GRANAHAN, KATHRYN E., sec. US. Treasury; b. Easton, Pa.; d. James R. and Julia (Reilly) O'Hay; grad. Mt. St. Joseph Coll., Phila.; m. William Thomas Granahan, Nov. 20, 1948 (dec. May 25, 1956). Began pub. career as supr. pub. assistance Auditor Gen.'s Dept., also liaison officer between the dept. and Dept. Pub. Assistance, Pa.; elected, 1956, mem. 84th Congress, 2d Pa. Dist., to fill vacancy caused by death of husband; elected mem. 85th-87th Congresses, 2d Pa. Dist.; treasurer of U.S., 1962-1966. Democrat. Home: Philadelphia, Pa. Died July 20, 1979.

GRANDIN, THOMAS B., writer, bus. analyst, radio sales exec., photographer; b. Cleve., July 19, 1907; s. George Wilbert and Mabel Gordon (Burnham) G.; grad. Kent (Conn.) Sch.,1926; B.A., Yale U., 1930; postgrad. Ecole des Sciences Politiques, Paris (France), 1931, U. Berlin (Germany), 1932; m. Natalia Parligras, Feb. 8, 1940 (dec.); children—Thomas, George, Natalia; m. 2d, Beulah Thompson Paul, Mar. 21, 1970. Research analysis and writing, 1933-38, on railroad and truck transp. for Internat. C. of C., on internat. finance for Council on Fgn. Relations, on polit. use of radio and techniques of persuasion for Rockefeller Found.'s Geneva Research Centre; spl. corr. in France for CBS, 1938, covering Munich crisis; bus. rep. and chief corr. CBS, France, 1939-40; chief editor Fgn. Broadcast Intelligence Service, FCC, 1942-43, dir. ops. in U.S. and abroad, confidential govt. mission to Algeria, Tunisia, Italy, Egypt, Turkey, India and Eng.; war corr. ABC, 1944, officially qualified U.S. Army parachutist, broadcast all U.S. networks first eyewitness radio report Normandy landings, Omaha beachhead; apptd. spl. asst. to dir. of news ABC, 1945; account exec. D'Arcy Advt. Co., 1946; bus. analyst Soc. Savs., Cleve., 1947-48; nat. fleet sales mgr. Hull-Dobbs, Inc., 1949-50; rancher in Ariz., 1953-70; now engaged in writing and freelance photography. Clubs: Nat. Press (Washington); Phoenix Executives. Author: The Political Use of Radio, 1939, also mag. articles and lectrs. Address: Phoenix, Ariz. Died Oct. 19, 1977.

GRANDY, CYRUS WILEY, banker; b. Norfolk, Va., Mar. 22, 1920; s. Cyrus Wiley and Mary Carter (Randolph) G.; student U. Va., 1939-41; m. Ann Sterrett, Nov. 13, 1943; children—Carter Randolph Scott, Cyrus Wiley V., Hatch Dent Sterrett. With Nat. Bank Commerce, Norfolk, 1941-42; with Office Coordinator Information and successor, OSS, 1942-45; with Investment Corp. Norfolk (co. name changed to United Va. Mortgage Corp.), 1945-80, v.p., 1956-64, pres., 1964-72, chmn., 1972-80; v.p. Investment Corp. Va., 1960-64, pres., 1964-68; vice chmn. Mut. Assurance Soc. Va. (Richmond); dir. Charters Devel. Corp., United Va. Bank, Seaboard Nat., Property Mgmt. Corp., Wythe Corp., Williamsburg Va. Trustee, treas. Norfolk Acad.; trustee Norfolk Gen. Hosp. (pres. 1968-70); v.p. Hermitage Found., Norfolk Historic Found.; pres., trustee Mary F. Ballentine Home Aged, Norfolk; v.p. Howard Assn., Norfolk; bd. dirs. United Communities Fund Children's Art Center, Norfolk, Navy YMCA, Norfolk, Order Cape Henry 1607, Hampton Roads chpt. Navy League U.S. Mem. Newcomen Soc. N. Am. Episcopalian (past sr. warden). Clubs: Norfolk Yacht and Country, Virginia (pres. 1962-64), Harbor (pres. 1980), Mallory Country (Norfolk); Princess Anne Country (Virginia Beach). Home: Norfolk, Va. Died Nov. 14, 1980.

GRANGER, CHRISTOPHER MABLEY, forester; b. Detroit, Mich., Nov. 25, 1885; s. George Frederick and Helena May (Mabley) G.; B.S., Michigan State Coll., 1907, Dr. Forestry, 1932; m. Louise Ireland, Sept. 20, 1928; children—Stephen Ireland, David Ireland, Paula, Christopher Ireland. With U.S. Forest Service since 1907, tech. asst., 1907-11, forest supervisor, 1911-13, asst. regional forester, Denver, Colo., 1913-24, regional forester for Ore. and Wash., Portland, Ore., 1925-30, dir. forest survey of U.S., Washington, D.C., 1930-33, in charge Civilian Conservation Corps activities of Forest Service, 1933-35, asst. chief, U.S. Forest Service in charge nat. forest adminstrn., since 1935. Served as capt., later promoted major, Engrs., forestry, A.E.F., 1917-19. Mem. Soc. Am. Foresters, Alpha Zeta. Clubs: Cosmos (Washington); Chevy Chase (Md.). Home: Bethesda, Md. *

GRANT, DAVID ALEXANDER, psychologist; b. Des Moines, May 17, 1916; s. Alexander Haswell and Charlotte Elizabeth (David) G.; student Kan. City Jr. Coll., 1934-36; B.A., State U. Ia., 1938; M.A., U. Wis., 1939; Ph.D., Stanford, 1941; m. Mary Lucille Brodie, July 22, 1938; children—Marjorie E. Skuldt, Douglas Henry, Edward Alexander. Prof. psychology U. Wis., 1948-77, Clark L. Hull research prof. psychology, 1967-77, chmn. dept., 1950-54, from 1970; vis. prof. psychology U. Cal. at Berkeley, 1959-60; lectr. Northwestern U., 1948, Stanford, 1949, Columbia, 1953, U. Cal. at Los Angeles, U. So. Cal., 1955. Mem. sect. psychology-anthropology, NRC, 1957-59; study sect. exptl. psychology NIH, from 1960. Social psychologist War Dept., 1944. Fellow Am. Psychol. Assn. (pres. exptl. psychology div. 1961); mem. Am. Statis. Assn., Psychometric Soc., Inst. Math. Statistics, Soc. Exptl. Psychologists, Midwestern (sec.-treas. 1949-52, pres. 1953), Wis. (exec. com.) psychol. assns., Psychonomic Soc. (governing bd. 1960-66, chmn. governing bd. 1965). Clubs: Sierra; Am. Alpine. Author articles psychol. jours. Asso. editor Jour. Exptl. Psychology, 1957-62, editor, from 1962. Cons. editor Psychol. Rev. and Jour. Gen. Psychology. Home: Madison, Wis. Died Dec. 28, 1977.

GRANT, EVVA H., editor, educator; b. Rock Island, Ill.; d. Morris and Ida (Learner) Handelman; A.B., Augustana Coll., 1934; A.M., State U. Ia., 1937; m. Herman Grant, June 5, 1934; 1 son, David. Tchr. pre-sch. and parent edn. St. Louis, 1936-37; editor P.T.A. Mag., editor-in-chief Nat. Congress Parents-Tchrs., 1940-72; asso. Boutwell, Crane, Moseley Assos., ednl. and pub. consultants, 1972-77; interpreter on Baxters radio program sponsored by P.T.A. and NBC. Vis. Lectr. Northwestern U., summers 1945, 46, cons. pub. adv. bd. FOA, 1954; gen. council U.S., nat. com. Internat. Union Family Orgns.; mem. bd. consultants Mental Health Materials Center; mem. adv. bd. Am. Child Guidance Found., Singer Learning Center for Early Childhood Edn. Mem. Ednl. Press Assn. Am. (pres. 1941-43, exec. com. 1943-45), Nat. Congress Parents and Tchrs. (hon. life), Nat. Assn. Nursery Edn. (adv. bd. 1945-47), N.E.A., Delta Kappa Gamma, Sigma Xi. (asso.). Author: Parents and Teachers as Partners, 1971. Cons. editor; Community Life in a Democracy (Nat. PTA), 1942; editor: Guiding Children as They Grow, 1959; PTA Guide to What's Happening in Education, 1965. Contbr. to ednl. jours. Home: Chicago, Ill. Died Oct. 3, 1977.

GRANT, THIRZA EUNICE, educator; b. Holland Patent, N.Y., Nov. 13, 1886; d. Martin Ellis and Dessie (Ellis) Grant; student Oberlin Coll., 1903-05, Olivet Coll., 1905-06; A.B., Oberlin Coll., 1907; Diploma, Sch. of Library Sci., Western Reserve U., 1908; B.L.S., N.Y. State Library Sch., 1915. Asst., Cleveland Pub. Library, 1908; instr. Sch. of Library Science, Western Reserve U., 1909-13; asst. in charge of reference div. Mich. State Normal College, Ypsilanti, 1913; reference librarian Oberlin Coll., 1915-16; instr. Sch. of Library Science, Western Reserve U., 1916-17, asst. prof., 1917-25, prof. since 1925, acting dean, 1943-44, dean since 1944. Mem. Am. Library Assn., Ohio Library Assn., Nat. Vocational Guidance Assn. Modern Lang. Assn., Cleveland Museum of Art. Club: Library of Cleveland (pres. 1947-48). Home: Cleveland. *

GRAPER, ELMER DIEDRICH (GRA'PER), univ. prof.; b. Princeton, Ind., June 24, 1885; s. August Diedrich and Alvina (Luhring) G.; A.B., North Central Coll., Naperville, Ill., 1911; Ph.D., Columbia, 1921; m. Ada Leffler, Sept. 2, 1913; (dec.); children—Marian Louise, Nancy Loanne (Mrs. Ronald Voelker). Instructor in history and government, Bradley Polytechnic Institute, Peoria, Illinois, 1911-16; instr. in govt., Columbia, 1919-23; asst. prof. polit. science, U. of Pittsburgh, 1923-24, asso. prof. 1924-25, prof. 1925—, prof. and head dept. polit. science, 1930-55, prof. emeritus 1955. Sec. U. Senate, 1945-54. Chmn. Police Research Commn., City of Pittsburgh, 1934-36; mem. Allegheny County Bd. for Assessment and Revision of Taxes, 1936-37; mem. Governor's Com. on Constitutional Revision, 1935. Dir. Inst. of Local Govt., U. of Pitts., 1945-55; chairman Pa. Civil Service Commn., 1956-63. Mem. Pa. Polit. Sci. Assn. (pres. 1943-46), Am. Assn. U. Profs., Phi Beta Kappa. Author: American Police Administration, 1921. Contbr. articles on govt. to Jours. Home: Pitts. *

GRAS, NORMAN SCOTT BRIEN (GRAS), college prof.; b. Toronto, Ont., Can., July 18, 1884; s. Meredith and Isabella (Brien) G.; B.A., Western U., London, Ont., 1906, M.A., 1906; M.A., Harvard, 1909; Harvard traveling fellow in Europe, 1910-12, Ph.D., 1912; hon. LL.D., U. of Western Ontario, 1924; m. Ethel G. Culbert, June 18, 1915; children—Edwin Culbert, Ranulf Worcester, Alfred Edward, Jane London (dec.). Naturalized citizen of U.S., Mar. 18, 1920. Asst. prof. history, Clark Coll., 1912-17; asso. prof. history, Clark U., 1917-18; lecturer in econ. history, Harvard, 1915, 16, 18; prof. econ. history, U. of Minn., 1918-27; prof. business history, Harvard, 1927-50. Research asst. War

Trade Bd., June-Aug. 1918. Pres. Bus. History Found., 1947-52. Fellow Mediaeval Acad. Am.; mem. Am. Hist. Assn., Am. Econ. Assn., Bus. Hist. Soc. Author books including: Shifts in Public Relations, 1945; Are You Writing a Business History?, 1947. Editor: Harvard Studies in Business History. *

GRASSO, ELLA T. (MRS. THOMAS A. GRASSO), gov. Conn.; b. Windsor Locks, Conn., May 10, 1919; d. James and Maria (Oliva) Tambussi; student pvt. schs.; B.A. magna cum laude, Mt. Holyoke Coll., 1940, M.A., 1942; m. Thomas A. Grasso, Aug. 31, 1942; children—Susane, James. Asst. in dept. econs. and sociology Mt. Holyoke Coll., 1942; apptd. asst. state dir. research War Manpower Commn., 1943-46. Mem. Conn. Legislature, 1953, 55, floor leader, 1955; state sec. State of Conn., 1958-70; mem. 92d-93d congresses from 6th Dist. Conn.; gov. State of Conn., 1975-80; founding mem. Coalition of Northeastern Govs., 1977, vice-chmn., 1978; chmn. New Eng. Govs. Conf., 1977; vice-chmn. Dem. Govs. Assn., 1978; chmn. platform com. Conn. Democratic Com., 1956-68; mem. nat. platform com. Nat. Dem. Com., 1960, co-chmn. resolutions com. Dem. Nat. Conv., 1964, 68; del. Dem. floor leader Constl. Conv., 1965. Mem. Bd. Fgn. Scholarships, 1960-66. Hon. dir. Urban League Greater Hartford; mem. adv. bd. Hartford, Am. Com. Italian Migration. Recipient Amita award as outstanding women of Italian parentage, 1959, Am. Heritage award, 1961, Americanism award Conn. Valley council B'nai B'rith, 1963, Italian-Am. Gold medal Conn. lodge Order Sons of Italy in Am., 1963; named Woman of Year, Hartford Bus. and Profl. Women's Club, 1964, Ladies Aux. Conn. dept. V.F.W., 1971, Greater Hartford chpt. Am. Com. Italian Migration, 1972; recipient Silver Apple award Conn. Edn. Assn., Most Distinguished Service citation Am. Legion, Knight in Order Merit Republic Italy, 1968; Merit award Conn. dept. Italian Am. War Vets. U.S., 1972; Outstanding Service award Conn. Cystic Fibrosis Assn.; Marconi award Sons Italy in Am. and Can.; 1st Humanitarian award Knights of Khorassan; Thomas Jefferson award Tex. Tech U., Tex. Daily Newspaper Assn., Tex. Assn. Broadcasters, Tex. Press Assn. Mem. AAUW, Conn. Council Catholic Women (dir.), Order of Sons of Italy (citation for work on Cooley's anemia), Conn. Assn. for Children with Perceptual Learning Disabilities, League Women Voters, Kappa Delta Pi (citation Central Conn. State Coll. chpt. 1960), Alpha Delta Kappa. Club: Mt. Holyoke (Hartford). Home: Windsor Locks. Died Feb. 5, 1981; buried St. Mary's Cemetery, Windsor Locks.

GRATTAN, CLINTON HARTLEY, author; b. Wakefield, Mass., Oct. 19, 1902; s. Leonard and Laura (Campbell) G.; A.B., Clark Coll., Worcester, Mass., 1923; D. Litt., Clark U., 1953; LL.D. (hon.), Australian Nat. U., 1977; m. Beatrice Kay, Oct. 22, 1926 (div. 1934); m. 2d, Marjorie Sinclair Campbell, June 3, 1939; children—Rosalind Campbell (Mrs. Arthur von Au), Jennifer Hartley (Mrs. Alan Corner), Jacqueline Allison (Mrs. Conrad Smeeth), John Hartley. Head dept. English, Urbana (Ohio) Jr. Coll., 1923-25; freelance writer, N.Y.C., 1926-64; vis. fellow Australian Nat. U., 1960, 71, 75; curator Grattan Collection of Southwest Pacificana, univ. prof. history U. Tex., Austin, 1964-74, emeritus prof., 1974-80. Author books including: Way We Fought, 1929, 66; Bitter Bierce: A Mystery of American Letters, 1929, 66; The Three Jameses: A Family of Minds, 1932, 62; (with Paxton Hibben) The Peerless Leader: William Jennings Bryan, 1929, 67; Introducing Australia, 1942, rev. edit., 1947; Australia (U.N. Series), 1947: In Quest of Knowledge, 1955; The United States and The Southwest Pacific, 1961; The Southwest Pacific: A Modern History, 2 vols., 1963. Editor publs. including: Such is Life, by Tom Collins, 1948; American Ideas about Adult Education 1710-1951, 1959, also others. Contbr. to Harpers, Am. Mercury, Scribners and other nat. mags., 1924—; writer on S.W. Pacific history and current affairs, 1927— Home: Austin, Tex. Died June 25, 1980; cremated.

GRAUER, BEN, radio, TV reporter; b. N.Y.C., June 2, 1908; s. Adolph and Ida Kunstler (Goldberg) G.; B.S.S., Coll. City N.Y., 1930; m. Melanie Kahane, Sept. 25, 1954. Played in motion pictures and theatre, 1915-25; with NBC 1930-73, covering every type of spl. event and news broadcast including Olympic games, 1932, presdl. inaugurations, from 1937, Democratic and Republican convs, from 1944; UN Conf., 1945; Paris Conf., 1946; Israel-Arab War, 1948; Gen. Assembly, Paris, 1948; Berkshire Music Festival, 1949; Brit. Coronation, 1953; UN Security Council, 1960, NBC Symphony under Toscanini, 1940-54; Spanish commentator on Telstar, 1962; master ceremonies NBC's Atlantic Spotlight (with BBC). Moderator TV panel show, It's a Problem, Producer-narrator, Señor Ben and His PanAm. Hwy. of Melody; narrator TV documentary March of Medicine; editor-host TV program Big Story; host-commentator radio program Toscanini—The Man Behind the Legend; reporter Daily Bus. Trends; moderator TV panel program Newslight; communicator Monitor program; host weekly short wave program New York, New York, on Voice of Am.; co-producer of Shaw's Mrs. Warren's Profession. Recipient George Sandham prize Coll. City N.Y., 1930; Nat. winner, H.P. Davis announcers award, 1944; Alumnae Service medal, 1949; Civilian Service citation U.S. Army, 1951; Crusade for Freedom citation, 1953; recipient Man of Year Award Nat. Fedn. Temple Brotherhood, 1955; Peabody award for conv.-election coverage, 1972; Townsend Harris medal, 1973; Ben Graver scholarship established in his honor Grad. Sch. Journalism, Columbia U.; decorated chevalier Legion of Honor. Mem. Bibliog. Soc. Am., Nat. Music League (pres.), Acad. TV Arts and Scis. (nat. sec.), OPC Corr. Fund (pres.), Tau Delta Phi, Sigma Delta Chi. Clubs: Overseas Press (trustee), Grolier. Author: March on Pharoah, 1932; Bernal Diaz Reborn, 1956. Editor: NBC News Picture Book of the Year, 1967, 68, 69. Home: New York, N.Y. Died May 31, 1977; buried Westchester Hills Cemetery, Hastings, N.Y.

GRAUL, DONALD PHILIP, air force officer; b. Lehighton, Pa., Feb. 24, 1906; s. Philip Melanchton and Mary Zernah (Fenstermacher) G.; student Pa. State U., 1923-25; B.S., U.S. Mil. Acad., 1929; M.S. in Meteorology, Cal. Inst. Tech., 1937; m. Margaret Honeycutt, June 19, 1936; children—Margaret, Philip Harmon. Commd. 2d lt. U.S. Army, 1929, advanced through grades to maj. gen. USAF, 1960; assigned various mil. establishments, 1929-41; staff officer A-4, Hdqrs. USAAF, 1941-42; dir. communications VIII Fighter Command, Eng., 1942-44, 8th Air Force, Eng., 1944-45; comdr. Watson Labs., USAF, Red Bank, N.J., 1945-48; student Indsl. Coll. Armed Forces, 1948-49; chief electronics div. directorate research and devel. Hdqrs. USAF, 1949-52; comdr. 1808th Airways and Air Communications Service Wing, Tokyo, Japan, 1953-57, Rome Air Devel. Center, Air Research and Devel. Command, Griffies AFB, N.Y., 1957-61; dep. comdr. Air Force Communications Service. Scott AFB, Ill., from 1961. Decorated Legion of Merit with cluster, Bronze Star with cluster; Croix de Guerre with palm (France and Belgium). Sr. mem. Inst. Radio Engrs.; mem. Air Force Communications Electronics Assn., Tau Kappa Epsilon. Lutheran. Died Apr. 3, 1979.

GRAVES, BENJAMIN CLIFFORD, business exec.; b. N.Y. City, Jan. 26, 1886; s. Edmund Johnston and Marian Horner (Oughton) G.; ed. Flushing (N.Y.) pub. schs.; m. Edna Martin, Nov. 19, 1912; children—Donald Clifford, Roger Edward. With Union Tank Car Co., since 1903, dir., 1922, v. pres., 1925, mem. exec. com., 1926, exec. v.p., 1944, pres. 1946. chmn. board, chief exec. officer, and dir., 1955—. member board directors Products Tank Line; consultant to Office of Defense Transportation, Washington, D.C., mem. Joint Tank Car subcom., petroleum administration for war, Chicago, etc.; member National Petroleum Council, Petroleum Adv. Council, Transportation Council, Washington. Former president, member board Family Service of Evanston, Illinois; trustee Union League Boys Club Found. Member American Petroleum Inst. (director), National Petroleum Assn., Western Refiners Assn., Association Tank Car Lessors. Republican. Presbyn. Mason. Clubs: Executives (exec. com.), Union League, Chicago, Glen View Golf, Traffic (Chicago), Crystal Downs Country (Frankfort, Mich.); Capitol Hill (Washington). Home: Evanston, Ill. *

GRAVES, C(HARLES) EDWARD, conservationist; b. Hatfield, Mass., Feb. 22, 1885; s. Charles and Susan Hannah (Wing) G.; A.B., Wesleyan U., Conn., 1908; traveled and studied in Europe, 1908-09; student N.Y. State Library Sch., Albany, 1911-13; m. Emily B. Melcher, Sept. 2, 1915; 1 son, Edward Melcher. Clk. 1st Nat. Bank, Northampton, Mass., 1901-04; instr. Romance langs., Wesleyan U., 1909-11; with U. of Ill. Library, 1914-17; librarian Minn. Hist. Soc., St. Paul, 1917-20; organizer and sec. Ore. Nature Lovers' Club (later Wiyeast Club), Hood River, Ore., 1922-24; librarian Humboldt State Coll., Arcata, Calif., 1924-45; western representative Nat. Parks Assn., 1956—. Member A.L.A., Calif. Library Assn., Mazamas, Kappa Rho Sigma, Phi Beta Kappa. Club: Sierra. Producer, Colorful America, a series of 2x2 color slides of outstanding American scenery, lecturer on Appreciation of Nature, 1945—; western rep. Nat. Parks Assn., 1953—. Home: Carmel, Cal. *

GRAVES, DIXIE BIBB, ex-senator; b. Montgomery Co., Ala., July 26, 1882; d. Peyton and Isabel (Tharp) Bibb; ed. Girls High Sch., Montgomery, Ala.; Litt.D., Ala. Coll., Montevallo; LL.D., Bob Jones Coll., Cleveland, Tenn.; m. Bibb Graves, of Montgomery, Oct. 10, 1900. Apptd. U.S. senator to fill vacancy caused by resignation of Senator Hugo L. Black, 1937. Trustee Ala. Boys Industrial Sch.; mem. bd. Y.W.C.A., Montgomery. Mem. Daughters of Confederacy (formerly pres. Ala. Div.), Gen. Fed. Women's Clubs (ex-chmn. illiteracy com.), Ala. Fed. Women's Clubs (ex-v.p.), Am. Legion Auxiliary of Montgomery (ex-pres.). Democrat. Mem. Christian Ch. Clubs: No Name Club, Ionian (Montgomery). Home: Montgomery, Ala. *

GRAVES, LOUIS, editor; b. Chapel Hill, N.C., Aug. 6, 1883; s. Ralph Henry and Julia Charlotte (Hooper) G.; A.B., University of North Carolina, 1902, LL.D., from same university, 1941; m. Mildred Moses, June 1921. On staff New York Times, 1903-06; with city govt. New York, 1913-16; mem. Mayor's Com. on Nat. Defense, 1916, 17; prof. journalism, Univ. of N.C., 1921-24; editor and propr. Chapel Hill Weekly 1923-54, contributing editor, 1954—. Commissioned captain in the infantry, United States Army, May 26, 1917; served in France, 1918-19, Army of Occupation, Coblenz, Germany. Mem. Zeta Psi, Phi Beta Kappa. Author: Leaves from a Coblenz Diary, serially in Atlantic Monthly, 1919; An American in Asia, serially in Asia Mag., 1920-21; stories, articles and essays in Sat. Eve. Post, Harpers, and other leading mags.; occasional essayist Balt. Sun. Club: West Side Tennis (N.Y.C. life mem.). Home: Chapel Hill, N.C. Died Jan. 25, 1965.*

GRAY, ARTHUR, banker; b. Canton, Ohio, Sept. 11, 1891; s. Simon and Sarah (Stone) G.; student pub. schs., Can.; m. Beatriz Lerner, Jan. 13, 1920; children—Joan (Mrs. Samuel Untermyer), Arthur. Sr. partner Arthur Gray & Co., N.Y.C., 1937-80; pres. Arthur Gray Corp., 1939-80. Chmn. bd. Lerner Maine Lab., Am. Mus. Natural History; gov. Internat. Game Fish Assn.; bd. dirs. Nat. Hosp. for Speech Disorders. Mem. Am. Arbitration Assn. (founder 1922, dir.). Home: New York, N.Y. Died Mar. 2, 1980.

GRAY, FRANCIS CALLEY, banker; b. Chestnut Hill, Mass., Jan. 22, 1890; s. Morris and Flora (Grant) G.; A.B., Harvard, 1912, LL.B., 1915, D.C.S., Suffolk U., 1952; L.H.D., Tufts Coll., 1954; m. Helen Rotch Bullard, Sept. 16, 1916; children—Morris, Francis Calley, John Bullard. Practiced law with Ropes, Gray, Boyden & Perkins, 1915-22; partner Shattuck & Gray, 1922-28; v.p., later pres., Lee, Higginson Trust Co., 1928-32; v.p. Fiduciary Trust Co., 1932-44, dir., 1932-66, pres., 1944-57, chmn. bd., 1957-61; dir. Colonial Fund, Inc., State St. Investment Corp.; hon. trustee Chase Fund of Boston, Shareholders Trust of Boston, Income and Capital Shares of Boston; trustee, mem. investment bd. Provident Inst. Savs., 1925-65. Sec., Mass. Gen. Hosp., 1920-30, trustee, from 1935, chmn. bd. trustees, 1946-64, pres., from 1964; treas., trustee Radcliffe Coll., 1930-70, Rotch Traveling Scholarship; bd. mgrs. Greater Boston Charitable Trust; trustee Boston U., 1940-65, hon. trustee, 1965-76; trustee Humane Soc. Commonwealth Mass.; bd. dirs. Hosp. Planning for Greater Boston, Inc. Mem. Boston Sch. Com., 1926-32, chmn. 1928-30; mem. Council Boston Bar Assn., 1928-30; gen. chmn. Greater Boston 1940 Community Fund campaign; mem. Mass. Emergency Pub. Works Commn., 1933-34, Boston Sch. Ho. Commn., 1943-45; mem. exec. com. Greater Boston Community Survey, 1947-49; dir. N.E. Conf. Christians and Jews, Del., Mass. Republican Pre-Primary Conv., 1936; alternate del Rep. Nat. Conv., 1944; mem. Mass. Eisenhower Sponsoring Com. Served as 1st lt. 303d F.A., 1917-19, World War I; maj. to col. Mass. State Guard, World War II. Fellow Am. Acad. Arts and Scis. Clubs: Somerset (Boston); Tavern. Home: Boston, Mass. Died July 11, 1976.

GRAY, FRANK, JR., U.S. judge; b. Franklin, Tenn., Feb. 25, 1908; s. Frank and Mary Hall (Philips) G.; LL.B., Cumberland U., 1928; m. Faye Anders, Feb. 14, 1941 (dec. 1975); m. 2d, Norma W. Eubank, Jan. 29, 1977. Admitted to Tenn. bar, 1928; practice in Franklin, 1928-61; U.S. judge Middle Dist. Tenn., 1961-78, chief judge, 1970-77, sr. judge, 1977-78. Mayor of Franklin, 1947-61. Mem. Am., Tenn. (bd. govs. 1956-58) bar assns., Am. Judicature Soc., Order of Coif. Democrat. Presbyterian. Home: Franklin, Tenn. Died Sept. 6, 1978; interred Mt. Hope Cemetery, Franklin.

GRAY, NORMAN BRIGGS, ret. justice; b. Bloomfield, Neb., Oct. 24, 1902; s. George and Caroline Alice (Leigh) G.; LL.B., U. Neb., 1928; m. Alma May Sanders, Nov. 26, 1938; children—Norma Lee, Susan Ann. Sec. Pub. Service Commn., Wyo., 1932-38; trial examiner, FPC, 1938-42; pvt. practice, Cheyenne, 1942-47, 51-60; atty. gen. Wyo., 1947-50, 60-63; justice Wyo. Supreme Ct. Justice, 1963-72, chief justice, 1969-70. Mem. Sigma Alpha Epsilon, Phi Delta Phi. Democrat. Home: Cheyenne, Wyo. Died June 22, 1976; interred Lakeview Cemetery, Cheyenne, Wyo.

GRAY, R(OBERT) A., former sec. of state, Fla.; b. Cairo, Ga., Aug. 2, 1882; s. William J. and Mary (Howren) G.; student So. Fla. Mil. Inst. and Georgetown Univ. Law Sch.; LL.D., Florida Southern College; married Grace Mullins, Dec. 23, 1903, Asst. state auditor Fla., 1913-14, state auditor, 1914, pvt. sec. to gov., 1915-16; mem. staff, Office State Comptroller, 1919-29, asst. state comptroller, 1928-29, sec. of state, 1930-61; pvt. sec., U.S. Senator Park Trammell, 1917. Served as mem. Fla. State Legislative, 1911. Capt. U.S. Army, 1918-19. Past hon. chancellor Fla. Southern Coll.; past. dept. comdr. Am. Legion; past pres. Nat. Assn. Secs. State; mem. Theta Chi. Democrat. Methodist. Mason (K.T., Shriner), Woodman of World; past grand patron O.E.S. Club: Rotary. Author: Gray's Civil Government of Florida, 1924. Home: Tallahassee, Fla.

GRAY, ROBERT DAVIS, economist, educator; b. Warren, Pa., Oct. 14, 1909; s. Robert Elmer and Clara Florence (Davis) G.; B.S. in Econ., U. Pa., 1930, postgrad. Grad. Sch., 1930-36; m. Mary V. Adams, Dec. 23, 1942; 1 dau., Mary Belinda. Research asst. and asso.

indsl. research dept. U. Pa., Phila., 1927-39, instr. in industry, 1934-37; asst. prof. econs. U. Conn., 1937-40; spl. research asst. Life Office Mgmt. Assn., 1939-40; asso. prof. econs. and indsl. relations Cal. Inst. Tech., 1940-42, dir. Indsl. Relations Center, 1941-79, prof. econs. and indsl. relations, 1942-79. Mem. Cal. Personnel Bd., 1944-63, v.p., 1946-47, pres., 1947-49, 1958-60; bd. adminstrs. Cal. State Employees Retirement System, 1956-63; dir. Family Service Pasadena (Cal.), 1946-49, pres., 1947-48; mem. adv. council Cal. Dept. Employment, 1967-69. Trustee Assn. Ind. Cal. Colls. and Univs. Fellow Acad. Mgmt.; mem. Personnel and Indsl. Relations Assn. (life), Tournament of Roses Assn., Pasadena C. of C., CIvic Assn. of Pasadena (dir. 1950-56, pres. 1953-54), Am. Soc. Personnel Adminstrs., Am. Soc. Tng. Dirs., Am. Assn. U. Profs. Roman Catholic. Clubs: Athenaeum, Twilight. Author books, 1929-79, latest pubs. include: A Guide to Systematic Wage and Salary Administration, 1959; The Roles of Benefit Plans in Protection, Compensation, and Cost, 1960; Supervision of Engineers, 1964; Evaluating the Personnel Department, 1965; Conducting an Employee Opinion Poll, 1966; Supervisor of the 70s, 1970. Editor: Frontiers of Industrial Relations, 1959. Home: Altadena, Calif. Died July 4, 1979.

GRAY, WELLINGTON BURBANK, educator; b. Albany, N.Y., Apr. 25, 1919; s. Wellington and Lilla Maude (Burbank) G.; B.S., Kutztown (Pa.) State Coll., 1947; M.A., N.Y. U., 1948, Ed.D., 1954; student Pa. State U., U. Philippines; m. Norma Laree Wallace, Dec. 26, 1942; children—Bruce Wellington, Brian Erwin. Art supr. pub. schs., Connellsville, Pa., 1947-49; art dir. Highland Park (Ill.) High Sch., 1949-54; dean Art Sch., Edinboro (Pa.) State Coll., 1954-56; dean Sch. Art, East Carolina U., Greenville, N.C., 1956-77; lectr. fine arts Alliance Coll., 1955-56; instr. N.Y. U., summers 1950, 51; hon. faculty Q.M. Sch., Ft. Lee, Va. Partner Gray Assoc., design cons., Greenville, 1960-77; paintings in permanent collections Atlanta, Akron, O., Albany, N.Y., Highland Park Mobile, Greenville; exhibited Carnegie Inst. Tech., Art Inst. Chgo., Albany Inst. History and Art; one man shows Highland Park, Greenville, Erie, Pa., Goldsboro, N.C., Mt. Olive, N.C., Kinston, N.C. Former sec. Pitt County Republican Com. Mem. N.C. Awards Commn., 1973. Served to lt. col. AUS, World War II; PTO. Mem. Internat. Assn. Deans of Fine Arts, Am. Assn. U. Profs., Nat. Art Edn. Assn., Southeastern Arts Assn., Am. Soc. Interior Designers, Phi Delta Kappa, Kappa Delta Pi, Delta Phi Delta. Episcopalian. Author: Student Teaching in Art, 1960; also articles. Adv. bd. Colorcast and Design Quar. Home: Greenville, N.C. Died Nov. 29, 1977.

GRAY, WILLIAM LAFAYETTE, JR., lawyer; b. Laurens, S.C., Nov. 10, 1902; s. William L. and Mary (Dunklin) G.; A.B., Wofford Coll., 1923; postgrad. U. S.C., 1923-24; law student Harvard, 1925-26; J.D., U. Fla., 1927; LL.D. (hon.), Wofford Coll., 1965; m. Jean Hancock, June 10, 1931; 1 son, William Lafayette III. Admitted to Fla. bar, 1927; partner Huber, Clements & Blackwell, Miami, 1927-30; asst. county solicitor Dade County, Fla., 1931-32; 1st asst. gen. counsel Fla. Power & Light Co., Miami, 1933-41; partner Blackwell, Walker, Gray, Powers, Flick & Hoehl, and predecessor, Miami, 1941-76; mem. Wofford Assos., 1966-76; mem. spl. com. on drafting rules of civil procedure Fla. Indsl. Commn., 1947. Chmn. large donations Coral Gables chpt. A.R.C., 1945; pres. Dade County unit Am. Cancer Soc., 1963; dir. Coral Gables Youth Center; troop com. Boy Scouts Am. Chmn. inst. on continuing legal edn. U. Miami, 1960-76; mem. council U. Fla. Law Center, 1972-76; bd. dirs., treas. World Center for Liturgical Studies, 1965-68; mem. Fla. Bd. Bar Examiners, 1960-65, chmn., 1975-76; bd. dirs. Crime Commn. Greater Miami, 1966-76. Fellow Am. Coll. Probate Counsel; mem. Am. Soc. Internat. Law, Am., Dade County (dir. 1960-62, 63-66, pres. 1941) bar assns., Fla. Bar (bd. govs. 1966-67), C. of C., Junior C. of C., S.A.R., Kappa Sigma, Phi Alpha Delta. Methodist (steward, chmn. bd. trustees). Clubs: Century (bd. govs. 1965-76), Kiwanis (Coral Gables); Miami (founder mem.); Beale Law (Harvard); Riviera Country (bd. govs., sec.); Committee of 100 (bd. govs. 1975-76) (Miami Beach, Fla.); Two Hundred of Greater Miami (pres. 1973, bd. govs. 1970-76). Home: Coral Gables, Fla. Died Sept. 15, 1976; buried Woodlawn Park Cemetery, Miami.

GREBANIER, BERNARD, author; b. N.Y.C., Mar. 8, 1903; s. Benjamin and Ottillie (von Storenberg) G.; A.B., Coll. City N.Y., 1926; M.A., N.Y. U., 1930, Ph.D., 1935; m. Frances Winwar, Sept. 22, 1925 (div. Dec. 1942). Instr., Coll. City N.Y., 1926-30; faculty Bklyn. Coll., 1930-77, prof. English, 1957-63, prof. emeritus, 1963-77; lectr. Pace Coll., 1958-63; lectr. adult edn. Hofstra Coll., 1971, YM and YWCA, 1974-77; lectr. poetry workshop Delbrook Coll., Riverton, Va., 1971, 72; dir. plays Off-Broadway including Phaedra, Othello, Merchant of Venice, King Lear, Oedipus the King, The Importance of Being Ernest. Recipient Samuel French award for best teaching in playwriting, 1957, 58. Mem. Eleanor Gay Lee Found. (charter), Poetry Soc. Am. (lectr. 1971), P.E.N., Author's Guild, Burr Artists (charter), Composers, Authors and Artists Am. (pres. N.Y. chpt. 1972-77, nat. 1st v.p. 1973-77). Club: Players. Author: (with S. Thompson) English Literature and its Backgrounds, 2 vols., 1939-40; (with H. Hintz) Modern American Vistas, 1941; Fauns, Satyrs and a Few Sages, 1945; Mirrors of the Fire, 1946; Essentials of English Literature, 2 vols., 1948-49; (with V. Hopper) Essentials of European Literature, 2 vols., 1950-51; Bibliography of European Literature in English Translation (with V. Hopper), 1953; The Other Love, 1957; Racine's Phaedra, an English Acting Version in Verse, 1958; College Writing and Reading, 1958; Moliere's The Misanthrope, an English Acting Version, 1959; An Introduction to Imaginative Literature, 1960; The Heart of Hamlet, 1960; Playwriting, 1961; Chaucer, 1962; Milton, 1962; The Truth about Shylock, 1962; Moliere, 1963; Rousseau, 1963; Thornton Wilder, 1963; Shakespeare's Henry IV, Part I, 1964; The Great Shakespeare Forgery, 1965; Armenian Miniatures, 1967; The Uninhibited Byron, 1970; Edwin Arlington Robinson, 1971; The Angel in the Rock, 1971; Pegasus in the Seventies, 1972; Then Came Each Actor, 1975; The Enjoyment of Literature, 1975; also contbr. to encys., mags. Editor: Living Shakespeare Recordings, 1965-67. Home: New York, N.Y. Died Mar. 17, 1977.

GREEFF, THEODORE, home furnishings co. exec.; b. Bonn., Germany, Nov. 26, 1909; parents Am. citizens; s. Enno and Anna (Kind-deBavier) G.; A.B., Princeton U., 1931; m. Catherine Stevens, July 23, 1943; children—Diana Greeff MacVeagh, Stevens Greeff deVargas-Machuca. Pres., Greeff Fabrics, Inc., N.Y.C., 1933-72, chmn. bd., 1972-78; chmn. bd. Simmons Co., Atlanta and N.Y.C., 1978-80, also dir.; dir. Warner & Sons, Ltd., London. Served to lt. comdr. USNR, 1942-45. Mem. Am. Soc. Interior Decorators (hon.), Decorative Fabrics Assn. Presbyterian. Clubs: Union (N.Y.C.); Round Hill (Greenwich, Conn.); Sunningdale (Eng.); Travellers (Paris); Royal and Ancient (St. Andrews, Scotland). Died July 23, 1980; buried Greenwich, Conn.

GREEN, CHARLES, corp. exec.; b. N.Y.C., 1908; m., 2 sons, 1 dau. Chmn. bd. United Whelan Corp.; dir. N.Y.,N.H.&H. R.R. Co., Consol. Laundries, Inc.; chmn. Green Sales Co.; partner Chalgren Assos. Club: Elmwood Country (Elmsford, N.Y.). Home: Harrison, N.Y. Died Jan. 27, 1980.

GREEN, CHARLES EDWARD, lawyer; b. Woodstock, Ill., Jan. 4, 1894; s. Thomas Patrick and Mary (Dacy) G.; LL.B., Chgo.-Kent Coll. Law, 1915; post-grad., Sorbonne U., 1919; m. Lucile C. Black, Sept. 5, 1920; children—Donna (Mrs. Robert V. Nystrom), Elaine (Mrs. John R. Coath). Admitted to the Illinois state bar, 1915, practiced in Chgo.; gen. counsel, Motorola, Inc. Served with inf. U.S. Army, AEF, 1918. Mem. Am., Ill., Chgo. bar assns., Chgo. Law Inst., Soc. Trial Lawyers. Clubs: Mid-Day, Butterfield Country (Hinsdale, Ill.). Home: River Forest, Ill. Died Jan. 6, 1981.

GREEN, DANIEL CRANDALL, chmn. Central Service Corpn.; b. nr. Patriot, Indiana, Nov. 16, 1884; s. William Martin and Sadie (Crandall) G.; B.S., Purdue Univ., 1908; m. Frances Elizabeth Sexton, of Rushville, Ind., Jan. 28, 1910; 1 son, John Sexton. First managed various utility cos. connected with H. M. Byllesby & Co. of Chicago and later managed utility companies in the Electric Bond & Share group; v.p. Electric Bond and Share Co., New York, 1930-33; trustee Middle West Utilities Co. and pres. Middle West Corporation, Chicago, 1933-37; pres. Central Service Corpn., 1937-39, chmn. since 1939. Clubs: Chicago, Casino, Saddle and Cycle, Mid-Day, Old Elm. Home: Chicago.

GREEN, EDWARD HENRY, lawyer; b. New York, N.Y., Aug. 2, 1886; s. Morris and Lena J. Green; A.B., Columbia Coll., 1905; LL.B., Harvard, 1908; m. A. Margaret Morgenstern, June 10, 1913; 1 son, William Morris. Admitted to N.Y. bar, 1908, and became law clerk Sullivan & Cromwell, partner, 1920—. Dir. emeritus Campbell Soup Co., Cluett, Peabody & Company, Inc., Merck and Company, Inc.; director Orinoka Mills. Mem. Am., N.Y. State, N.Y. County bar assns., Assn. Bar City of N.Y., Phi Beta Kappa. Republican. Trustee of Riverside Church. Clubs: Columbia University, Wall Street, City Midday, City (New York City); Westchester Country (Rye, N.Y.) Home: N.Y.C.

GREEN, EDWARD MELVIN, banker; b. Milledgeville, Ga., Nov. 22, 1904; s. Edward Melvin and Ann (Craig) G.; student Center Coll. of Ky., 1920-21; B.S., Princeton, 1925. Mem. North China dept. Standard Oil Co. of N.Y., N.Y.C., 1925-28; with Bell Telephone Co. of Pa., 1929; with Dauphin Deposit Trust Co., Harrisburg, Pa., 1929-73, pres., 1966-70, chmn. bd., 1969-73; exec. v.p. L. B. Smith Founds., Inc., Camp Hill, Pa.; dir. AMP, Inc., Harrisburg. Mem. finance com. Pa. Council Chs., 1957-76, pres., 1962-64; commnr. Pa. Human Relations Commn., 1964-68; mem. Pa. Pub. Welfare Adv. Com., 1965-67. Pres. bd. mgrs. Harrisburg Hosp.; adv. bd. Harrisburg State Hosp., 1961-71; trustee Wilson Coll., United Presbyn. Found., Harrisburg Acad., Wormleysburg, Pa.; bd. dirs. Pa. Mental Health, Inc., Phila., 1956-76, chmn., 1964-65; bd. dirs., treas. Harrisburg Symphony Assn., 1952-63. Served with USNR, 1942-46. Mem. Sigma Chi. Democrat. Presbyn. Clubs: Princeton (N.Y.C.); Nassau (Princeton, N.J.), Harrisburg Country Club. Home: Camp Hill, Pa. Died Apr. 23, 1976; buried Harrisburg Cemetery.

GREEN, EDWIN GEORGE, college pres.; b. Yorkshire, N.Y., Mar. 24, 1884; s. Rev. Thomas Styan and Mary Elizabeth (Ensminger) G.; A.B., U. of Denver, 1906; post-grad. work, U. of Denver and U. of Chicago; unmarried. Prin. high sch., Central City, Colo., 1906-10; prof. Latin, Ft. Worth (Tex.) U., 1910-11; prof. Latin, 1911-18, registrar, 1913-19, acting chancellor, 1918-19, Meth. U. of Okla., Guthrie, Okla.; pres. Okla. City Coll. since Apr. 1919. Mem. Sigma Alpha Epsilon. Methodist. Rotarian. Address: Oklahoma City, Okla. *

GREEN, FLETCHER MELVIN, educator; b. Gainesville, Ga., July 12, 1895; s. Robert Chambers and Mary Mahalia (Haynes) G.; Ph.B., Emory U., 1920, Litt.D., 1957; A.M., U.N.C., 1922, Ph.D., 1927; U. Chgo., 1925; Litt.D., Washington and Lee U., 1960; m. Mary Frances Black, Aug. 16, 1930; children—Fletcher Melvin II, Mary Carolyn, Robert Ramsey, Elizabeth Haynes. Tchr. history Lindsey-Wilson Prep. Sch., 1920-21; fellow in history U. N.C., 1921-22, instr. 1922-23: prof. history Sparks Coll., 1923-24; asst. prof. history Vanderbilt U., 1924-25; fellow Inst. Research in Social Sci., U. N.C., 1925-27; asst. prof. history U. N.C., 1927-30, asso., 1930-33, prof., 1936-46, Kenan prof. 1946-78, chmn. dept. history, 1953-60; prof. history Emory U., 1933-36; lectr. summer schs. Coll. William and Mary, U. Tenn., Duke, U. Mo., Columbia, 49, 50; vis. prof. history Harvard, 1944-45, Stanford, summer 1956, Northwestern U., summer 1957; Lamar lectr. Mercer U., 1968; Harmsworth prof. Am. history Oxford U., 1968-69. Mem. exec. bd. N.C. Dept. Archives and History, 1955-78, research fellow Huntington Library, 1967. Served in M.C., U.S. Army, with A.E.F., 1918-19. Mem. Am., Miss. Valley (Exec. council 1946-49, bd. editors rev. 1955-56, pres. 1960-61), So. (pres. 1945), Ga. hist. assns., Agrl., N.C. (pres. 1953) hist. socs., N.C. Lit. and Hist. Assn. (pres. 1955), Alpha Tau Omega, Phi Beta Kappa. Democrat. Methodist Club: Chapel Hill Country. Author: Essays in Southern History, 1949; The Lides Go South and West, 1952; The Ferry Hill Plantation Journal Jan. 4, 1938-Jan. 15, 1939, 1961; The Role of the Yankee in the Old South, 1972. co-author: Travels in the New South, Vol. I., The Postwar South, 1865-1900. Editor: The Civil War and Reconstruction in Florida (William Watson Davis), 1964; Memorials of a Southern Planter (Susan Dabney Smedes), 1965; Southern Wealth and Northern Profits (Thomas Prentice Kettell), 1965; editor, contbr. hist. jours.; bd. editors Jour. So. History, 1935-36, 41-46. Home: Chapel Hill, N.C. Died Feb. 27, 1978.

GREEN, JOSEPH COY, fgn. service officer; b. Cin., O., Apr. 12, 1887; s. James Albert and Louise Washburn (Coy) G.; A.B., Princeton, 1908, A.M., 1909; grad. work U. of Grenoble, 1909, U. of Paris, 1909-10, 1913-14, Princeton, 1908-09, 1914-15; m. Harriet Stearns, June 15, 1912 (died 1912); m. 2d, Helen Kinsey, July 5, 1920 (died 1923); children—Suzanne, Helen; m. 3d, Gertrude Henshaw Norris, Feb. 22, 1927; 1 son, Joseph Norris. Fellow in history, Princeton, 1908-09, 1914-15; instr. History, Bordentown Mil. Inst. 1910-11, Columbia U., 1911-13; asst. prof. History, Politics, Princeton, 1920-24, associate professor History, 1924-30; member of staff of United States Department of State 1930-52, as assistant in Division of Western European Affairs, 1930-35, special rep. of U.S. at Internat. Inst. of Agr., Rome, 1931-32, special asst. to Am. Minister at Bern, 1931-32; chairman Com. to Revise Foreign Service Exams. 1931-46; chief Office of Arms and Munitions Control, 1935-39; chief Division of Controls, 1939-41; exec. sec. Nat. Munitions Control Board, 1935-46, chief, spl. div., 1941-43; special asst. to Sec. of State, 1941-44; adviser on Arms and Munitions Control, 1944-46; mem. exec. dir. Bd. of Examiners, Fgn. Service, 1946-52, with rank of minister 1947; chmn. of the Advisory Committee on Foreign Service Examinations, 1946-52; member Mission to observe Greek Elections, with rank of minister, 1946; minister E.E. and M.P. to Hashemite Kingdom of Jordan, 1952; ambassador to Jordan, 1952-53; foreign service reserve officer, Class I, 1953. Member Served as interpreter, lieutenant, captain to major, United States Army, 1917-19; major in Mil. Intelligence Res., 1936-42. Awarded A.E.F. Campaign medal with four clasps; chevalier Legion of Honor; Chevalier Order Crown of Belgium; Comdr. Order Star of Rumania; medaille de la Reconnaissance Française; medaille Commemorative du Comite National (Belgium); Grand Cordon of the Star of Jordan, 1st. degree. Mem. bd. trustees Palestine Archaeological Museum; dir. Belgian Am. Ednl. Foundation. Fellow A.A.A.S.; member Council on Foreign Relations, Am. Hist. Soc., Acad. of Polit. Science, Am. Assn. of Univ. Profs., Am. Ethnol. Soc., American Anthropological Assn., Washington Lit. Soc. Club: Metropolitan. Editor of American Indian terms, Webster's Internat. Dictionary, 1929-35. Contbr. to reviews. Home: Chevy Chase, Md. Died Aug. 2, 1978; buried Rock Creek Cemetery, Washington.

GREEN, LEON, educator; b. Oakland, La., Mar. 31, 1888; s. William Morris and Emily Frances (McCormick) G.; A.B., Ouachita Coll., 1908; LL.B., U.

Tex., 1915; student U. Mich., summer 1921; M.A. (hon.), Yale, 1928; LL.D., La. State U., 1938, Northwestern U., 1971; m. Notra Anderson, Dec. 22, 1909; children—Notra Nevin, Leon. Indsl. and land devel., Jones County, Tex., 1908-11; admitted to Tex. bar, 1912, began practice in Austin; mem. firm Rector & Green, 1912-15; adj. prof. law U. Tex., 1915-18; with Locke & Locke, Dallas, 1918; mem. firm Wynne, Johnson, Green & Morgan, Fort Worth, 1919-20; prof. law U. Tex., 1921-26, prof. law, 1947-58, prof. law, 1960-79; prof. law, dean Sch. Law, U. N.C., 1926-27; vis. prof. law Yale, 1927, asso. prof. law, 1927-28, prof., 1928-29; prof. law, dean Sch. Law Northwestern U., 1929-47; prof. law U. Cal. Hastings Coll. Law, 1958-59. Adv. editorial council Jour. Criminal Law and Criminology. Mem. Tex., Conn., Ill., Chgo. bars, Philos. Soc. Tex., Order of Coif (nat. sec.-treas. 1963-70), Phi Delta Phi. Democrat. Unitarian. Author; Rationale of Proximate Cause, 1927; Judge and Jury, 1930; The Judical Process in Tort Cases, 1931, 2d edit., 1939; Injuries to Relations, 1940; My Philosophy of Law, 1941; Traffic Victims: Tort Law and Insurance, 1958; The Litigation Process in Tort Law, Adminstrs. Co-author: Cases on The Law of Torts, 1957, 68; Injuries to Relations, 1968. Contbr. articles to legal periodicals. Home: Austin, Tex. Died June 16, 1979.

GREEN, MARCUS HERBERT, biologist, educator; b. Harrisburg, Pa., July 31, 1905; s. Herbert Ritchie and Katherine (Grosz) G.; B.S. in Biology, Albright Coll., 1929; M.S., U. Pitts., 1935; Sc.D., Lebanon Valley Coll., 1964; m. Leona Gladys Christopher, Apr. 26, 1930; children—Thomas Francis, John Foster. High sch. instr., 1929-30; mem. faculty Albright Coll., Reading, Pa., 1930-76, prof. biology, 1962-66, Henry Pfeiffer prof. biology, 1966-71, prof. emeritus, 1971-76, dir. devel. program scis. for non-sci. majors; cons. in field. Mem. steering com. Friends of Reading Pub. Mus., 1966. Recipient award for service to mankind Del. dist. Sertoma Club, 1956; Christian R. and Mary F. Lindbeck Found. award for distinguished teaching, 1963. Mem. A.A.A.S., Am. Assn. Profl. Biologists, Fedn. Am. Soc. Exptl. Biology, Mengal Natural History Soc. (past pres.), Pa. Acad. Sci. (past v.p.), Sigma Xi, Pi Gamma Mu. Mem. United Ch. Christ (past elder). Mason. Research and articles on vascular system, interactions of brain and skull, dental hypertrophy in rodent. Home: Reading, Pa. Died Dec. 5, 1976.

GREEN, MELVILLE SAUL, educator, physicist; b. Jamaica, N.Y., June 9, 1922; s. Maurice S. and Ella (Prichep) G.; B.A., Columbia, 1944; M.A., Princeton, 1947, Ph.D., 1952; m. Vivian Grossman, Feb. 12, 1950; children—Aliza, Joel. Mem. faculty, U. Chgo., 1947-51; research asso. Inst. Fluid Dynamics and Applied Math., U. Md., 1951-54; chief statis. physics sect. Nat. Bur. Standards, Washington, 1954-68; prof. physics Temple U., Phila., 1968-79. Vis. lectr. Weitzmann Inst. Sci., Rehovoth, Israel, 1958; with Office of Asst. Sec. Commerce for Sci. and Tech., Washington, 1963; OAS lectr. in statis. mechanics Inst. Polytechnico Nacional de Mexico, 1964, dir. course critical phenomena Enrico Fermi Summer Sch. Physics, Varenna, Italy, 1970; vis. prof. Hebrew U., Jerusalem, 1973-74. Recipient Gold medal for Distinguished Achievement in Fed. Service, U.S. Dept. Commerce, 1965. Fulbright grantee, 1957, Guggenheim fellow, 1957, 73. Fellow Am. Phys. Soc. Editor: (with J.V. Sengers) Critical Phenomena: The Report of a Conference, 1965; bd. editors Phys. Rev., 1944-79, Jour. Math. Physics, 1953-65, 71-74, Jour. Physics of Fluids, 1966-72, Jour. Statis. Physics; co-editor Phase Transitions and Critical Phenomena, Vols. I-II, 1972, Vol. III, 1974, Vols. IV, V, VI, 1976. Research in statis. mechanics, especially theory of irreversible processes, theory of dense systems, kinetic theory of gases, critical phenomena. Home: Philadelphia, Pa. Died Mar. 27, 1979; interred Har Yehuda Cemetery, Upper Darby, Pa.

GREEN, PAUL ELIOT, author, tchr.; b. Lillington, N.C., Mar. 17, 1894; s. William Archibald and Betty Lorine (Byrd) G.; grad. Buies Creek (N.C.) Acad., 1914; A.B., U. N.C., 1921, postgrad., 1921-22; postgrad. Cornell U., 1922-23; Litt.D. (hon.), Davidson Coll., Western Res. U., U. N.C., U. Louisville, Berea Coll., Campbell Coll., N.C. Sch. Arts, Moravian Coll., Duke U.; m. Elizabeth Atkinson Lay, July 6, 1922; children—Paul Eliot, Nancy Byrd, Betsy McAllister, Janet McNeill. Prof. philosophy U. N.C., 1923-39, prof. dramatic art, 1939-44. Editor, The Reviewer, 1925. Mem. exec. com. U.S. Nat. Commn. for UNESCO, 1950-52; del. UNESCO conf. at Paris, 1951. Guggenheim fellow, 1928-30. Mem. Nat. Inst. Arts and Letters, 1941; founder Inst. Outdoor Drama, 1963. Author plays, motion pictures and various works, 1925— including The Lost Colony (play), 1937; The Laughing Pioneer (novel), 1932; This Body the Earth (novel), 1935; Johnny Johnson (play), 1937; Out of the South (15 plays), 1939; The Highland Call (play), 1941; The Hawthorn Tree (essays), 1943; Salvation on a String (stories), 1946; The Common Glory (play), 1948; Dog on the Sun (short stories), 1949; Faith of Our Fathers (play), 1950; Peer Gynt (modern adaptation Ibsen's play), 1951; Dramatic Heritage (essays), 1953; Wilderness Road (play), 1955; The Founders (play), 1956; The Confederacy (play), 1958; Drama and the Weather (essays), 1959; Wings for to Fly (3 plays), 1959; The Stephen Foster Story (play), 1959; Plough and Furrow (essays), 1963; Five Plays of the South, 1963; Cross and Sword (play), 1965; The Sheltering Plaid (play), 1965; Texas (play), 1966; Texas Songbook, 1967; Words and Ways (stories), 1968; Sing All a Green Willow (play), 1969; Home to My Valley (stories), 1969; Trumpet in the Land (play), 1970; The Honeycomb (play), 1972; Drumbeats in Georgia (play), 1973; Louisiana Cavalier (play), 1975; Land of Nod and Other Stories (stories), 1976; We the People (play), 1976; The Lone Star (play), 1977; Palo Duro (sound and light drama), 1978. In Abraham's Bosom awarded Pulitzer prize for best American play, 1927; recipient ATA award for disting. service to theatre, 1978; named N.C. Dramatist Laureate, 1979. Home: Chapel Hill, N.C. Died May 4, 1981.

GREEN, THOMAS SAMUEL, bus. exec.; b. Worcester, Mass., Feb. 9, 1886; s. James and Mary Angeline (Messinger) G.; A.B., Harvard, 1909; m. Maud Caroline Gutterson, July 18, 1913; children—Thomas S., Jr., Maud (Mrs. Richard Park), Priscilla Phelps, James Wilder. Salesman E.A. Shaw & Co., cotton buyers, Boston and New Bedford, Mass., 1909-15; sales div. Norton Co., Worcester, 1915-20; mgr. Norton Co. French plant, Cie des Meules Norton, Paris, France, 1920-31; treas., Behr-Manning Corp., Troy, N.Y., 1931-50; gen. mgr., treas., and pres., Norton Pike Co., Littleton, N.H., since 1939; dir. Norton Co., Behr-Manning Corp., Cie des Meules Norton, Norton Pike Co., State Bank of Albany, N.Y. Home: Green Pastures, Center Berlin. *

GREEN, WILLIAM JOHN, paper co., exec.; b. Muncie, Ind., July 25, 1915; s. George Wyatt and Blanche (Young) G.; student Ball State U., 1933-34, Ind. U., 1938-39; m. Judith Heiman, May 24, 1964; children—Stephen John, Philip Wyatt, Douglas Hanson, Christina Fields, Nicholas William. Sales mgr. Ball Bros. Co., Muncie, 1939-44; pres. Stone & Co., Louisville, 1944-52; pres. Thatcher Glass Mfg. Co., N.Y.C., 1952-62; chmn. bd. Clevepak Corp., N.Y.C., 1962-79; dir. Seagram Co. Ltd. Home: Mount Kisco, N.Y. Died Jan. 22, 1979.

GREENBERG, SAM U., chem. mfg. co. exec.; b. Stamford, Conn., Sept. 20, 1907; s. Isaac and Mary (Wittenberg) G.; B.S., U. Calif., 1929; m. Edith Wilson, Mar. 18, 1932; children—Sydne (Mrs. K. Howard), Robert David. Tech. dir. Calif. Ink Co., 1940-42; tech. mgr. Dorward & Sons Co., 1943-46; mgr. resin dept. Pacific Paint & Varnish Co. subs. Sears, Roebuck & Co., 1947-50, gen. mgr., 1951-53, Sears, Roebuck Paint & Wallpaper Factories, 1953-56; pres., dir. DeSoto Chem. Coatings, Inc. (name changed to DeSoto, Inc.), 1956-67, chmn. bd., chief exec. officer, 1967-68, chmn. exec. com., 1969-71, also dir. Mem. Am. Chem. Soc., Sigma Xi, Sigma Alpha Mu. Deceased.

GREENBURG, SAMUEL, graphic artist, painter; b. Uman, Western Ukraine, Europe, June 23, 1905; came to U.S., 1911, naturalized 1920; s. Isaac Samuel and Nadia (Antonow) G.; grad. Bezalel Art Sch., Jerusalem, 1927; student Académie André Lhote, Paris, 1927-28; A.B., Univ. of Chicago, 1944, A.M., 1946; m. Leah Rozalsky, July 3, 1928; children—Daniel, Naomi. Exhibited: Chicago Art Inst. Internat. Watercolor Shows, 1935, 36, and others, including Pa. Acad., Phila. Print Club, Library of Congress, N.Y. World Fair, 1939, Corcoran Gallery, Washington, D.C., 1942; San Francisco Museum, 1942, Ill. State Mus., Carnegie Inst., Pitts., Bklyn. Art Mus., Cleve. Art Mus., Seattle Art Mus., others; One-man show, Creative gallery N.Y.C., 1951, 53; room Chgo. Art, Art Inst. of Chicago, 1947; Hillel Foundation at Northwestern U., 1960; executed murals for Chocolate Products Company, Chicago, 1937; represented in collections: Art Inst. Chgo., Bezalel Art Museum, Jerusalem, Library of Congress (print), Washington, art museums of Jerusalem, Tel Aviv, Ein Harod, Lochamei Hagettaot Mus., Calif. Coll. of Arts and Crafts, Oakland, Judah L. Maynes Mus., Berkeley, Calif., Bd. Jewish Edn., Chgo., others. art instructor, Tuley High School, 1934-62; supr, art dist. 8 Chgo. Bd. of Edn., 1962-70; supervisor of art Board of Jewish Education, Chicago, 1949-51. Awarded first prize for war poster, Chicago Art Institute, 1942, 2d prize (oil painting) Ill. State Fair, 1956; purchase prize Union League Club, 1972. Member of Renaissance Soc., Chgo. Soc. Artists (dir.; print prize 1960, 61, 73, 79), Coalition of Chgo. Artists, Chgo. Tchrs. Union, Chicago Art Educators Assn., Phi Beta Kappa. Club: American Jewish Arts (6 painting awards 1954-79). Author and illustrator: Making Linoleum Cuts, 1947; author: Arts and Crafts in the Jewish School (with Maurice Yochim), 1952; contbr. articles to Life mag., Cath. Digest, N.Y. Times. Home: Chicago, Ill. Died Feb. 23, 1980; buried Meml. Park Cemetery, Skokie, Ill.

GREENE, CHARLES EMMETT, univ. ofcl.; b. Lucerne, Mo., Aug. 23, 1886; s. John Samuel and Martha Ellen (Williams) G.; A.B., U. of Denver, 1910, A.M., 1911, LL.D., 1942; A.M., Columbia, 1919; m. Nora Lorena Wathen, Dec. 26, 1912; children—Dorothea Ruth (Mrs. Stuart Dunlop), Georgia Muriel (Mrs. Donald McNassor, dec.), Lorena Helen (Mrs. James Wing), Joan Margaret; married 2d. Ruth Bicking Morison, September 23, 1949. Teacher, Caldwell, Ida., 1910, principal of high school, 1911-13; principal, Guthrie, Okla., 1913-15; superintendent of schools, Silverton, Colo., 1915-18, Idaho Springs, 1918-20; dir. teacher training, State Teachers Coll., Neb., 1920-23; dir. measurements, Denver Pub. Schs., 1923-28, dir. research, 1928-33, asst. supt., 1933-39, supt. schs. 1939-47; dean, Denver Junior College, 1947-49; secondary coordinator pub. schools, Stockton, Calif., since 1949. Formerly trustee U. of Denver. Mem. Nat. Soc. for Study of Edn., Phi Delta Kappa. Mason (Scottish Rite). Home: Stockton, Calif. *

GREENE, ERNEST W(OODRUFF), sugar exec.; born N.Y. City, Mar. 23, 1885; s. David S. and Alice Neal (Hubbell) G.; grad. Pratt Inst., Brooklyn, 1907; m. Ethel Jane Townsend, Apr. 30, 1910; 1 dau., Barbara (Mrs. William C. Bentley). With Henry R. Worthington Co., 1907-10, Alberger Pump & Condenser Co., 1910-14, Cotton Neill & Co., Honolulu, 1914-20; asst. mgr. Oahu Sugar Co., Waipahu, Hawaii, 1920-23, mgr., 1923-37; v.p. Hawaiian Sugar Planters Assn., resident in Washington, 1937-56, cons. 1956—; dir. Nat. Savs. & Trust Co., Anson Mills Found. Pres. Sugar Research Foundation, N.Y.C., 1946-48, 60-64, now dir. Mem. The Sugar Assn. N.Y.C. (pres. 1952-64). Episcopalian. Clubs: Chevy Chase. Metropolitan (Washington); Oahu Country, Pacific (Honolulu). Home: Washington. *

GREENE, ESTHER, librarian; b. Greene, Ia., Sept. 15, 1901; d. Walter Vernon and Alma Maud (Lyford) Greene; A.B., Grinnell Coll., 1923; B.S., Simmons Coll., 1928; grad. student Western Res. U. Childrens librarian Cleve. Pub. Library, 1928-31; librarian Park Sch., Cleve., 1931-35. Lewis Carroll Room of Cleve. Pub. Library, 1935-36; head childrens dept. New Rochelle (N.Y.) Pub. Library, 1936-43; asst. dir. program and membership Bus. and Profl. Womens Clubs, N.Y.C., 1943-44; librarian Barnard Coll., 1944-67. Mem. A.L.A., Assn. Coll. and Reference Librarians, P.E.O., Phi Beta Kappa. Co-author: Library Orientation Test for College Freshmen, 1955. Contbr. articles profl. jours. Home: East Orleans, Mass. Died Dec. 26, 1977; buried Greene, Iowa.

GREENE, JAMES ETHERIDGE, univ. dean; b. Columbus, Ga., Feb. 22, 1911; s. Robert C. and Eleanor (Jenkins) G.; D.V.M., Auburn U., 1933, M.S., 1939; m. Mary Lynton McGehee, Oct. 22, 1934; children—James Etheridge II (dec.), Bruce McGehee, Edward Chesley, Mary Katherine. Gen. practice vet. medicine, 1933-34; jr. vet. U.S. Bur. Animal Industry, 1935; grad. asst. anatomy Ala. Poly. Inst., Auburn, 1937-38, asso. prof. small animal surgery and medicine, 1938-42, head depts. large and small animal surgery, 1946-58, dean Sch. Vet. Medicine, 1958-77. Nat. cons. USAF, 1965-66; cons. div. physician manpower, gen. research support sci. adv. and rev. com. USPHS; mem. commn. on edn. for health professions Nat. Assn. State Univs. and Land Grant Colls. Councilman, Auburn City, Ala., 1955-56. Served to maj. USAAF, 1942-46. Mem. Am. Vet. Med. Assn. (chmn. exec. bd. 1965-66; award 1975), Ala. Vet. Medicine Assn. (pres. 1957), Sigma Xi, Omicron Delta Kappa, Phi Eta Sigma, Phi Zeta. Rotarian. Clubs: Auburn Country, Auburn Faculty. Author: (with J.V. LaCroix) Questions and Answers, 1951; (with W.S. Bailey) Metazoan Infections, Canine Medicine, 1953. Contbr. chpt. on Infectious Diseases, Yearbook of Agriculture, 1956. Contbr. articles to profl. jours. Home: Auburn, Ala. Died Sept. 20, 1977.

GREENE, JOHN JAMES, Canadian govt. ofcl.; b. Toronto, Ont., Can., June 24, 1920; s. Peter and Andree (Champagnol) G.; B.A., U. Toronto, 1948; grad. cum laude Osgoode Hall, 1950; m. Corinne Bedore, Sept. 2, 1948; children—Glenn, Peter, Jocelyn, Stephanie, Virginia. Called to Canadian bar, 1950; practice in Arnprior, Ont., 1950-65; mem. Ho. of Commons, 1963-78; co-chmn. spl. joint com. Senate and Ho. of Commons on Consumer Credit; minister of agr. of Can., 1965-68; minister energy, mines and resources, 1968-72; apptd. Queen's Counsel, 1972; mem. Canadian Senate, 1972-78. Canadian del. 54th Inter-Parliamentary Union Conf., Dublin, Ireland, 1965; chmn. UN/FAO World Food Program Pledging Conf., 1966; vice chmn. meeting ministers agr. to OECD, Paris, France, 1966. Served to flight lt. RCAF, 1941-45. Decorated D.F.C. Mem. Canadian Legion. Mem. Liberal Party. Mem. Anglican Ch. Clubs: Rideau, Royal Ottawa Golf; University (Toronto); Niagara Falls (Canada). Home: Arnprior, Ont., Can. Died 1978.

GREENE, LAURENZ, horticulturist; b. Lincoln, Kan., May 13, 1883; s. Ogden Norman and Mary (George) G.; student Kansas Christian Coll., Lincoln, 1899-1900; B.S., Kan. State Coll., 1906; M.S. in Agr., Ia. State Coll., 1909; Ph.D., U. of Calif., 1932; m. Gertrude Mereness, Dec. 27, 1911 (died Apr. 3, 1941). Asst. horticulturist Fort Hays branch expt. sta., Hays City, Kan., 1906; asst. in horticulture New Mexico A. and M. Coll., 1906-07, Ia. State Coll., 1907-09; experimentalist Ia. Agrl. Expt. Sta., 1909-17; head dept. horticulture and chief in horticulture, Purdue Agrl. Expt. Sta., 1917-50; field service consultant Office of Foreign Agrl. Relation, U.S. Dept. of Agr. since 1950; head dept. horticulture Centro Nacional de Agronomia, El Salvador, C.A., 1947-48, since 1950; field consultant in horticulture Office of Fgn. Agrl. Relations of U.S. Dept. Agr. in Ecuador S.A. and Central Am. on cacao research, 1949. Dir. Purdue State Bank. Mem. A.A.A.S., Am. Soc. Hort. Sci. (pres. 1933), Am. Soc. Plant Physiologists, Am. Soc. Agronomy, Soil Sci. Soc., Inst. Food Technologists, Ind. Hist. Soc., Ind. Hort. Soc., Sigma Xi, Alpha Zeta, Acacia. Republican. Presbyterian. Attended International Conf. on cacao at Turrialba, Costa Rica, 1947 and 1949. Home: West Lafayette, Ind. *

GREENE, PEYTON W(ILLIAM), business exec.; b. Staunton, Va., Dec. 14, 1884; s. William Hastings and Cornelia Bernard (Peyton) G.; ed. pub. and pvt. schs., Staunton; m. Vera A. Jones, Aug. 31, 1940. Clerk Norfolk & Western Ry. Co., Roanoke, Va., 1903-04; clerk, accounting dept., Southern Bell Telephone & Telegraph Co., Atlanta, 1904-05, cashier, Augusta, Ga., 1905-06, Jacksonville, Fla., 1906-09, asst. sec. and asst. treas., 1925-37, sec.-asst. treas., 1937-50, ret. Asso. mem. Nat. Fire Protection Assn., C. of C. of U.S. Republican. Episcopalian. Club: Atlanta Athletic. Home: Atlanta. *

GREENE, STEPHEN, pub. cons.; b. Boston, Dec. 18, 1914; s. Edwin Farnham and Charlotte (Nichols) G.; A.B., Harvard, 1937; m. Janet Churchill Gould, June 29, 1944; children—Jennifer, Stephanie Nichols Fitch Greene. With Japan Advertisgr, Tokyo, 1937-78, New York Herald Tribune, Paris and London, 1939-41, Fgn. Broadcast Intelligence Service, Portland, Ore., Washington and abroad, 1941-45; farmer, free lance writer, Dover, Vt., 1945-54; owner Book Cellar, Brattleboro, Vt., 1954-72; pres. Stephen Greene Press, Brattleboro, 1957-78, Greenemont Books, Inc., 1978-79. Mem. Dover Sch. Bd., 1949-55, Vt. Ednl. TV Com., 1953-55; chmn. Forest Festival Com., 1955-59; mem. Vt. Scenic Preservation Council, 1966-67; mem., chmn. Gov's Rev. Panel of Woodlands and Woodlands Industry, 1963-64. Mem. Vt. Ho. of Reps., 1953-56. Bd. dirs., pres. Marlboro Guild Theater, 1975-79; bd. dirs. Windham County Humane Soc., 1974-78, pres. 1975-76. Mem. Assn. Am. Pubs. (mem. exec. council gen. pub. div. 1974-78). Episcopalian. Author: (Hegen Petersen) Kissing Bridges, 1965. Editor: Treasury of Vermont Life, 1958; Green Mountain Treasury, 1961. A sr. editor: Vt. Life mag., 1954-77. Home: West Dover, Vt. Died May 25, 1979; buried Mountain View Cemetery, West Dover.

GREENE, WILLIAM BERTRAM, mfr.; b. Lisle, Ill., Sept. 4, 1886; s. William Spencer and Jessie (Hibbard) G.; B.S., University Ill., 1908; H.H.D. (honorary), Aurora College, 1962; m. Eva Jane Smith, Dec. 27, 1910; children—Maxson Hibbard (dec.), Sarah (Mrs. Benton D. Mathews), William Alexander, Anthony Storm. Co-founder Barber-Greene Co., 1916, v.p., treas., 1917-45, pres., 1945-54, chairman, 1954—; member board directors Growth Industry Shares, Inc. Dir. Aurora Found.; dir. Aurora Coll.; mem. U. Ill. Found. Clubs: Union League (Chgo.); Union League, Aurora, Kiwanis, Aurora Country (Aurora, Ill.). Home: Aurora, Ill. *

GREENHILL, J. P., gynecologist, obstetrician; b. N.Y.C., Feb. 28, 1895; s. Charles and Fanny (Pearl) G.; B.S., Coll. City N.Y., 1915; M.D., Johns Hopkins, 1919; m. Olga B. Hess, Mar. 16, 1929. Resident house officer Johns Hopkins Hosp., 1919-20; asst. resident Sinai Hosp., Balt., 1920-21; first resident Chgo. Lying-in-Hosp., 1921-23, later sr. attending obstetrician; sr. attending obstetrician, gynecologist Michael Reese Hosp., Chgo., 1931-75; attending gynecologist Cook County Hosp., Chgo., 1925-75, chmn. dept., 1941-47; prof. gynecology Cook County Grad. Sch. Medicine, 1936-75; asso. obstetrician Northwestern U., 1922-32; prof. obstetrics, gynecology, vice chmn. dept. Loyola U., Chgo., 1933-47; hon. prof. Nat. U., Peru. Mem. White House Conf. Com., 1930. Decorated chevalier Legion of Honor, 1957, conseiller d'Honneur, Inst. Endocrinologie, Haiti, 1960; recipient Fulbright Travel award, 1962. Diplomate Am. Bd. Obstetrics and Gynecology (charter). Fellow A.C.S. (life), Am. Coll. Obstetrics and Gynecology (charter), Am. Acad. Psychomatic Medicine, Chgo. Inst. Medicine; hon. fellow Internat. Coll. Surgeons (treas., trustee), Internat. Fertility Soc. (charter, v.p.); mem. Am. Med. Writers Assn., A.M.A. (chmn. com. female genital system for standard nomenclature diseases and operations), Ill., Chgo. med. socs., Am. Pub. Health Assn., Central Assn. Obstetrics and Gynecology (charter), Am. Geriatric Soc., Chgo. Gynecol. Soc. (pres. 1954-55), A.A.A.S., Am. Assn. Anatomists, Venereal Disease Assn., Johns Hopkins Med. and Surg. Assn., Ill., N.Y. acads. scis., Am. Assn. Study Internal Secretions, Am. Soc. Cancer Control, Soc. Sci. Study Sex (charter), Am. Soc. Abdominal Surgeons, Pan-Pacific Surg. Assn.; hon. mem. obstet. and gynecol. socs. S. Africa, Dominican Republic, Chile, Argentine, Panama, Brazil, Uruguay, Venzuela, Portugal, Algeria Turkey, Guatemala, Hawaii, Philippines, Cuba, W.Va.; gynecol. socs. France, Germany, Brazil, S.W., Med. Assn. Maternity Hosp. Lima, Peruvian Acad. Surgeons, Hollywood Acad. Medicine, fertility socs. Brazil, Argentina, Portugal. Author: Obstetrics for the General Practitioner, 1935; Office Gynecology, 9th edit., 1965; Obstetrics in General Practice, 4th edit., 1948; Obstetrics, 13th edit., 1965; Surgical Gynecology, 4th edit., 1969; Analgesia and Anesthesia in Obstetrics, 2d edit., 1962 (trans. Japanese, Spanish, Portuguese, Italian, Serbian); The Miracle of Life, 1971. Editor: (with J.B. DeLee) Year Books of Obstetrics, 1923-31; Year Book of Gynecology, 1931-42; Year Book of Obstetrics and Gynecology, from 1942; book rev. editor Fertility and Sterlity, 1949-67. Book reviewer, mem. editorial bd. numerous med. jours. U.S., Europe, S.Am. Editor: Hosp. Publs., Inc., 1964. Home: Chicago, Ill. Died Dec. 22, 1975.

GREENHILL, MAURICE H., psychiatrist, educator; b. Terre Haute, Ind., Aug. 16, 1909; s. Louis Lester and Estelle (Herzberger) G.; A.B., U. Rochester, 1931; M.D., U. Chgo., 1936; m. Estelle Markin, Sept. 6, 1936; children—Laurence, William, Andrew, Barry. Postgrad. study psychiatry Worcester (Mass.) State Hosp., 1937-39, Mass. Gen. Hosp., Boston, 1939-40, Boston City Hosp., 1940-41; mem. faculty Harvard Med. Sch., 1939-41; asso. prof. Duke U. Sch. Medicine, 1943-52; prof. psychiatry U. Md., 1952-55; prof. psychiatry, chmn. dept., dir. Psychiat. Inst., U. Miami (Fla.), 1955-57; dir. Community Mental Health Bd., N.Y.C., 1957-58; clin. prof. psychiatry Albert Einstein Coll. Medicine, N.Y.C., 1957-65, prof. clin. psychiatry, 1966-67, prof. psychiatry, 1968-81, dir. psychiatry hosp., 1966-81; cons. High Point Psychiat. Hosp., Port Chester, N.Y., 1958-81, also chmn. bd. govs.; pvt. practice psychiatry, 1958-81; research and ednl. cons. to numerous med., govt., social agys.; cons. NIMH: spl. cons. surgeon-gen. U.S. Army, UPSHS. mem. nat. adv. council Mended Hearts, Inc., 1976-81. Bd. dirs. Highland Hosp., Ashville, N.C.; chmn. bd. Richmond Fellowship of Am.; trustee Gralnick Found., N.Y.C. Rockefeller Found. fellow, 1940-41. Diplomate Am. Bd. Psychiatry and Neurology. Fellow Am. Psychiat. Assn. (life), Am. Coll. Psychiatrists, A.A.A.S.; mem. Group Advancement Psychiatry (chmn. com. on med. edn.), Am. Psychosomatic Soc., Assn. Research Nervous and Mental Diseases, Phi Beta Kappa, Sigma Xi, Alpha Delta Phi. Author: Evaluation in Mental Health, 1955. Mem. editorial bd. Communications in Psychology, Psychiatry and Behavior, 1975-81. Contbr. articles to profl. jours. Home: Rye, N.Y. Died Jan. 20, 1981.

GREENLEAF, ELIZABETH ADELE, educator; b. Winthrop, Mass., Nov. 4, 1919; d. Herrick E. H. and L. Blanche (Bryant) Greenleaf; A.B., DePauw U., 1941; M.A., U. Wis., 1947; Ed.D., Ind. U., 1952. Tchr., counselor pub. schs. Ind., 1941-50; dir. activities center, asst. prof. guidance So. Ill. U., Carbondale, 1952-57; asso. dean students, dean women San Jose (Calif.) State U., 1957-59; asst. dean students, dir. residence hall counseling Ind. U., Bloomington, 1959-69, asst. prof. edn., 1959-63, asso. prof., 1963-67, prof., 1967-79, chmn. dept. student personnel adminstrn., 1970-79. Mem. AAUW (br. pres. 1966-68), Am. Coll. Personnel Assn. (past nat. pres.), Am. Personnel and Guidance Assn. (bd. dirs. 1967-68, mem. senate, 1964-67, 69-72), Nat. Assn. Women Deans (nat. pres. 1971-72), Delta Kappa Gamma (Ind. pres. 1969-71). Contbr. articles to profl. jours. Home: Bloomington, Ind. Died May 28, 1979; buried Forest Hills Cemetery, Greencastle, Ind.

GREENMAN, JUDD, business exec.; b. Kansas City, Kan., 1885. Pres., dir. Oregon-American Lumber Corp., Venonia, Ore.*

GREENOUGH, ALLEN JACKSON, railroad exec.; b. San Francisco, Sept. 20, 1905; s. Earnest Allen and Nellie (Jackson) G.; B.S. in Civil Engring., Union Coll., Schenectady, 1928, Dr. Engring. (hon.), 1960; m. Jean Lytel, Apr. 8, 1933; children—Allen Lytel, Norman Jackson; m. 2d, Julie McCormack Waterman, Oct. 29, 1966. With Pa. R.R., 1928-68, engring. dept., 1928-45, operating dept., 1945-53, v.p., 1953-59, pres., 1959-68, ret., 1968; dir. Lehigh Valley R.R. Co., Merchants Warehouse Co., Raymond Internat., Inc.; trustee Penn Mut. Life Ins. Co. Trustee Union Coll. Mem. Soc. Colonial Wars, Chi Psi, Sigma Xi. Clubs: Round Hill (Greenwich); Pine Valley Golf. Home: North Salem, N.Y. Died Sept. 21, 1974.

GREENSLADE, RUSH MOLLAND, business exec.; b. Lima, O., June 24, 1885; s. James Molland and Margaret (Taggert) G.; A.B. Ohio State U., 1906; student Western Reserve Law Sch., 1907; m. Jessie Varley, Aug. 1, 1912; children—Sara Jane (Mrs. Walter V. LaSelle), Rush Varley. Admitted to bar of Ohio, 1908, Okla., 1909; practiced law Muskogee, Okla., 1908-14; lawyer Gypsy Oil Co., 1914-23, asst. to vice pres., 1923-26; vice pres. (now Gulf Oil Corp.), Gulf Pipe Line Co. of Okla. (now Gulf Refining Co.) since 1926, Canadian Gulf Oil Co., ret. 1950. Mem. bd. of dir. Tulsa Community Chest, Philbrook Art Mus.; trustee U. of Tulsa. Mem. Am. Petroleum Inst., Mid-Continent Oil & Gas Assn., Am. Bar Assn., Okla. Bar Assn., S.A.R., Newcomen Soc., Tulsa Bibliophiles. Episcopalian. Clubs: Tulsa, Southern Hills Country. Author: chapter VI, "Elements of the Petroleum Industry," 1941. Home: Tulsa, Okla. *

GREENSON, RALPH ROMEO, physician; b. Bklyn., Sept. 20, 1911; s. Joel O. and Katherine (Goldberg) G.; student Columbia U., 1928-30; M.D., U. Berne (Switzerland), 1934; m. Hildegard Troesch, July 14, 1935; children—Daniel, Joan (Mrs. Andreas Aebi). Intern, Cedars of Lebanon Hosp., Los Angeles, 1934-35; resident U. Vienna, Austria, 1935-36; practice medicine specializing in psychiatry, Beverly Hills, Calif., 1936-42, 46-79; tng. analyst Los Angeles Psychoanalytic Inst., Beverly Hills, 1947-79; clin. prof. psychiatry UCLA Med. Sch., 1951-79. Chmn. sci. adv. bd. Found. for Research in Psychoanalysis, 1964-79. Served to maj. M.C., AUS, 1942-46. Mem. Am. Psychoanalytic Assn., Los Angeles Psychoanalytic Soc. (pres. 1951-53). Author: The Technique and Practice of Psychoanalysis, vol. I, 1967; Explorations in Psychoanalysis, 1978. Contbr. articles to profl. jours. Home: Santa Monica, Calif. Died Nov. 24, 1979.

GREENWOOD, GEORGE HERBERT, banker; b. La Crosse, Wis., May 8, 1884; s. Marcellus Bixby and Clara Eliza (Bradish) G.; A.B., University of Mont., 1904; M.C.S., Dartmouth, 1905; LL.D. (hon.). University of Montana, 1944; m. Victoria Whitaker, Sept. 21, 1908; children—Bixby Aldridge (dec.), William Whitaker, James Frederick (adopted). Clk., Daly Bank & Trust Co., Anaconda, Mont., 1905-07, Old Nat. Bank, Spokane, Wash., 1907-14, asst. cashier, 1914-21, cashier, 1921-25, v.p. and dir., 1925-28, pres. Pacific Nat. Bank, Seattle, 1928-44; chmn. bd., 1945; retired July 1, 1947. Home: Del Mar, Calif.*

GREER, ROBERT EVANS, aerospace co. exec.; b. Orange, Cal., Aug. 7, 1915; s. Jack and Agnes (Burbank) G.; B.S., U.S. Mil. Acad., 1939; postgrad. Columbia, 1946-47; m. Geraldine Roberts, Dec. 15, 1939; children—Virginia (Mrs. Charles H. Bonesteel IV), Robert E., James, Gery (Mrs. Robert C. Ruddick). Commd. 2d lt. USAAF, 1939, advanced through grades to maj. gen. USAF, 1962; successively pilot trainee, flying instr., pilot, 1939-49; assigned The Pentagon, 1949-52; with 3d Air Force, SHAPE, 1954-57, Missiles and Air Force Space Program, 1959-65; ret., 1965; with Rockwell Internat. Corp., 1965-76, exec. v.p. Los Angeles div., 1970-72, pres. B-1 Div., 1972-76. Trustee Long Beach Community Hosp.; mem. adv. group Chapman Seven Seas Coll. Decorated D.S.M., Legion of Merit; recipient Distinguished Pub. Service medal NASA, also Pub. Service award; Nat. Service award Air Force Assn. Mem. Am. Astronautical Soc. Republican. Episcopalian. Home: Marina Del Rey, Calif. Died Feb. 14, 1976.

GREGG, ROBERT, corp. exec.; b. Atlanta, Ga., Apr. 14, 1885; s. William A. and Lizzie L. (Jones) G.; B.S., Ga. Sch. of Tech., 1905; M.E., Cornell U., 1906; LL.D. (hon.) Tusculum Coll., 1942, Howard Coll.; m. Elizabeth Adair, Jan. 22, 1913; 1 dau., Betty (Mrs. Crawford Johnson V. Rainwater). With Atlanta (later Atlantic) Steel Co., 1906-12, beginning as clerk in office of general supt., sec., 1912-15; sec. and treas. Atlantic Steel Co., 1915-20, v.p. and treas., 1920-22, pres., 1922-32; v.p. and gen. mgr. of sales Tenn. Coal, Iron & R.R. Co., Birmingham, Ala., 1932-33, pres., 1933-35, and since 1938; v.p. in charge of sales U.S. Steel Corp., New York, 1935-38; pres. and dir. Universal Exploration Co. Lectr. U. Fla. Mem. bd. dirs. Birmingham Community Chest (gen. chmn. annual appeal 1938-39). Member Gainesville C. of C., Fla. Engring. Soc., American Institute Mining and Metallurgy Engineers, American Iron and Steel Institute, Newcomen Society, Kappa Sigma. Methodist. Mason. (Shriner). Clubs: Rotary (president Atlanta Club 1925-26), Mountain Brook; University (New York); Piedmont Driving Capital City (Atlanta); Rotary, Gainesville (Fla.) Golf and Country. Home: Gainesville, Fla. Ret. Jan. 1951. *

GREGG, RUSSELL TAAFFE, ret. educator; b. Fairfield, Ill., July 24, 1903; s. John Lewis and Bertha Lee (Taaffe) G.; B.S., U. Ill., 1928, M.A., 1929, Ph.D., 1934; m. Genevieve Catherine Owen, June 7, 1930; children—Jane Gregg (Mrs. Hockett), Richard Owen. Rural sch. tchr., Wayne County, Ill., 1923-24; elementary sch. tchr., Fairfield, 1924-25; asst. in edn. U. Ill., 1928-33; instr. edn., asst. prin. U. Ill. High Sch., 1933-36, supr. visual aids library, 1933-36; asst. prof. edn. Syracuse U., 1936-39, asso. prof. edn., 1939-42, dir. curriculum workshops, 1939-42, supr. ednl. film library, 1938-42; asso. prof. edn. U. Wis., Madison, 1945-48, prof. ednl. adminstrn., 1948-72, emeritus, 1973, chmn. dept. ednl. adminstrn., 1967-70, dir. Fellowship Program in Urban Sch. Adminstrn., 1968-72, dir. Research Tng. Program for State Dept. Edn. Personnel, 1967; vis. prof. U. So. Calif., 1950, U. Calif., Berkeley, 1955, UCLA, 1960. Cons. Pa. Gov.'s Com. on Edn., 1960; participant Wilton Park (Eng.) Internat. Conf., 1971; cons. Nat. Project Staff Devel. in State Ednl. Agencies, 1971-72. Pres. Shorewood Hills (Wis.) Bd. Edn., 1952-58. Trustee Univ. Council for Ednl. Adminstrn., 1958-61. Served to lt. comdr. USNR, 1942-45. Decorated Navy Commendation medal. Mem. Am. Assn. Sch. Adminstrs. (Distinguished Service award 1973), Internat. Com. Ednl. Adminstrn., Am. Ednl. Research Assn., Am. Friends of Wilton Park, Nat. Conf. Profs. Ednl. Adminstrn. (dir. 1946-49, pres. 1948-49), Nat. Soc. for Study Edn., Acacia, Phi Kappa Phi, Phi Eta Sigma, Phi Delta Kappa, Kappa Delta Pi.

Conglist. Rotarian. Clubs: University (Madison), Blackhawk Country (Shorewood Hills, Wis.). Co-editor, author: Administrative Behavior in Education, 1957. Author: (with others) A Functional Program of Teacher Education, 1941, Schools in Our Democratic Society, 1951, Personal Expenditures for High School Education, 1951, The County Superintendency in Wisconsin, 1957, Instructional Change and Its Relationship to Decision Making in School Systems, 1966, The School Board as an Agency for Resolving Conflicts, 1967, Wisconsin Educational Assessment Study, 1969; Staff Development in State Education Agencies, 1973. Mem. editorial adv. bd. Sch. Exec. mag., 1955-60. Home: Madison, Wis. Died Sept. 13, 1973.

GREGG, WILLIAM LEE, M.D.; b. Brooklyn, N.Y., Jan. 18, 1884; s. Robert and Jennie (Van Schaick) G.; pub. schs., Chicago; student Harvey Med. Coll., 1903-05; M.D., Dearborn Med. Coll., Chicago, 1907; M.D., U. of Ill., 1911; m. Ida Amelia Ditchburne, 1907 (died 1929); 1 dau., Ruth Evelyn (Mrs. August R. Ortlepp); m. 2d, Faye Burney, 1932. Practiced in Chicago since 1911; trustee and med. dir. Washington and Jane Smith Home (for care of aged); mem. attending staff and trustee Englewood Hosp. (chmn. program com.). Mem. Draft Bd., World War. A founder Oakhaven Old Peoples Home, Chicago. Fellow Am. Med. Assn.; mem. Ill. State Med. Soc., Chicago Med. Soc., Am. Social Hygiene Assn., Am. Unitarian Soc., Theta Kappa Psi. Republican. Mason (K.T., Shriner). Club: Medinah. Home: Chicago. *

GREGORY, EDWARD WADSWORTH, JR., educator; b. Chase City, Va., Sept. 29, 1903; s. Edward Wadsworth and Kate Winn (Cleveland) G.; A.B., U. Va., 1925, M.A., 1926, Ph.D., 1931; m. Margaret Louise Jeffreys, Aug. 28, 1934; 1 son, Allen Wadsworth. Instr. sociology, U. Va., 1925-28; asst, prof. sociology, U. Ala., 1928-29, asso. prof., 1929-35, prof., 1935-45; prof. sociol. U. Md., 1946; prof. sociol. U. Richmond (Va.) 1946-72, prof. emeritus, 1972—. Chmn. Tuscaloosa Co. (Ala.) Bd. Pub. Welfare, 1940-43; pres. Ala. Conf. Social Work, 1941-42; pres. Va. Council Social Welfare, 1950-51; mem. Commn. on Aging, Virginia, 1962-68; chmn. Welfare and Instns. Va., 1964-71; chmn. adv. bd. Pub. Welfare, Richmond, 1953-55. Pres. Richmond Area Community Council, 1951-53; mem. War Price and Rationing Bd. of Tuscaloosa Co., 1942-43; mem. commn. on Reorgn. State Govt., Va., 1947. Served to lt. comdr. USNR, 1943-46. Mem. Am. Sociol. Soc., So. Sociol. Soc. (pres. 1939), Nat. Council on Family Relations (nat. adv. council, 1939-42), AAUP, Va. Social Sci. Assn. (pres. 1951-52), Family and Children's Service Richmond (dir.), Delta Sigma Phi, Delta Sigma Rho, Phi Beta Kappa, Phi Delta Kappa, Alpha Kappa Delta, Raven. Methodist. Clubs: Country of Va.; Torch. Author: Introductory Sociology (with Lee Bidgood), 1939; co-author: Social Control, rev. edit., 1956; contbr. articles to profl. jours. Home: Richmond, Va. Died Feb. 23, 1981; buried Woodland Cemetery, Chase City, Va.

GREGORY, EUFEMIA GIANNINI, educator, musician; b. Phila., Nov. 8, 1895; d. Ferrucio A. and Antoninetta (Briglia) Giannini; early mus. tng. from parents; voice student, Milan, Italy; m. Edward B. Gregory, May 15, 1924. Debut as Mimi in Boheme, Turin, Italy, 1916; singer leading soprano roles, Europe 1916-18, U.S., 1918-24; tchr. vocal diction Curtis Inst. Music, Phila., 1927-37, mem. voice faculty, 1937-79; pupils include Anna Moffo, Ian Frank Guarrera, Ellen Faull, Judy Blegen, others. Mem. Phila. Art Alliance, Phila. Acad. Arts. Home: Philadelphia, Pa. Died Jan. 15, 1979.

GREGORY, HOLLINGSWORTH FRANKLIN, business exec., air force officer; b. Rockwall, Tex., Jan. 13, 1906; s. Louis Franklin and Glennie (Hollingsworth) G.; A.B., Miss. Coll., 1926; m. Sarah Elizabeth Kohr, June 24, 1944; children—Glennie Elizabeth, Hollingsworth Franklin. Commd. 2d lt. Air Corps U.S. Army, 1929, advanced through grades to brig. gen. U.S. Air Force, 1954; flying cadet at Brooks and Kelly Fields, Tex., 1928-29; squadron officer Maxwell Field, Ala., 1929-31; student Army Air Corps Tech. Sch., Chanute Field, Ill., 1931-32; engring. officer Post Field, Ft. Sill, Okla., 1932-36; officer in charge autogiro tests, 1936-37; project officer for autogiros Wright Field, Dayton, Ohio, 1937-38; asst. comdt. Army Air Corps Autogiro Sch., Patterson Field, 1938; project officer rotary wing aircraft Wright Field, 1938-39, chief miscellaneous aircraft projects, tech. staff engring. div., 1939-44; asst. chief of staff, intelligence, also materiel, and operations, 7th AF, 1944-46; with Research and Devel. Bd., Office Sec. Def., 1948-49; air attaché, France, 1952-56; comdr. Air Force Office Sci. Research, 1956-58; v.p., dir. Midwestern Instruments, Inc., 1960-62, asst. to chmn. bd. 1962-78;•chmn. bd. Guaranty Nat. Bank, Tulsa; asst. to chmn. bd. Telex Corp., Tulsa; dir. City Nat. Bank, Tulsa; chmn. bd., pres. World Resources Corp., Tulsa. Mem. adv. bd. Salvation Army, Tulsa. Decorated Legion of Merit with bronze star, Air Medal Commendation Medal, Chevalier Legion d'Honneur (France), Medaille Aeronautique (France). Recipient Thurman H. Bane award for contribution to military and comml. development of helicopter, 1944. Asso. fellow Inst. Aero Scis.; hon. fellow Am. Helicopter Soc.; mem. Air Force Assn., Am. Def. Preparedness Assn., A.A.A.S., Nat. Rifle Assn., Am. Radio Relay League, Quarter Century Wirless Assn. Air Force Acad. Athletic Assn., Order Daedalians. Baptist (mem. brotherhood deacons). Rotarian, Mason (32 deg., Shriner). Clubs: National Aviation; Travelers, Automobile of France (Paris). Author: Anything a Horse Can Do—The Story of the Helicopter, 1944, The Helicopter, 1975. Contbr. to aero. publs., popular mags. Pioneered development autogiros and helicopters. Home: Tulsa, Okla. Died Nov. 11, 1978.

GREMSE, ALBERT RUDOLPH, constrn. co. exec.; b. Bklyn., Sept. 14, 1907; s. Ferdinand R. and Elise (Detrich) G.; student N.J. Law Sch., 1926-27; B.C.S., N.Y. U., 1933; m. Jean Elizabeth Faust, Mar. 26, 1941; children—Joan (Mrs. Douglas Peterson), Kathleen (Mrs. Max Myers), Helen (Mrs. Allan Childers, Jr.), Martha (Mrs. James Norris, Jr.), David. Chief accountant Fidelity Union Title & Mortgage Guarantee Co., Newark, 1925-37; sr. accountant Haskins & Sells, Newark, 1937-39; chief accountant Sperry Products, Inc., Hoboken, N.J., 1939-43; tax supr., controller Va. Bridge Co., Roanoke, 1943-52; asst. controller Am. Bridge div. U.S. Steel Corp., Pitts., 1952-55; sec., controller, dir. Blount Bros. Corp., Montgomery, Ala., 1955-71, v.p., treas., 1965-71, then dir.; v.p., sec., treas. Blount, Inc., 1971-73, sec., 1971-77; sec., dir. B.F. Shaw Co., J.P. Burroughs & Son, Inc., Young Am. Homes, Inc., Global Erectors Inc., Jupiter Constrn. Corp., Scotchcraft Windows, Inc., Paramount Equipment Rental & Sales, Indon Industries, Inc., Mercury Constrn. Corp. Mem. Montgomery County Pensions and Security Bd., from 1969, vice chmn., from 1970. Mem. council com. Boy Scouts Am., from 1955; mem. del. assembly Montgomery Area United Appeal, from 1970. Treas., exec. com. Montgomery County Republican Party, from 1955. Bd. dirs. St. James Sch., Tumbling Waters Mus. Flags; v.p., trustee Am. Youth Found. N.H. Recipient Silver Beaver award Boy Scouts Am., 1964; Liberty Bell award Montgomery Bar Assn., 1974. Mem. Fin. Execs. Inst. (dir., past pres. Birmingham chpt.), Am. Mgmt. Assn., Newcomen Soc. N. Am., Sigma Sigma Sigma. Methodist. Club: Optimist (past lt. gov., pres.) Montgomery). Home: Montgomery, Ala. Died Sept. 28, 1977; buried Montgomery.

GRENDON, FELIX, writer; b. London, England, Nov. 23, 1882; s. Carl H. and Emma (Henry) G.; came to U.S., 1895; B.S., Coll. City of New York, 1900; Ph.D., Columbia, 1909; m. Lucille Warner, of Brooklyn, N.Y., 1909. Book critic, Internat. Mag., 1909-11; dramatic critic New Review, 1913-15; asst. prof. English lit., Coll. City of New York, 1915-26. Mem. Authors' League America, Fabian Soc. (London, Eng.). Author: The Anglo-Saxon Charms, 1910; Will He Come Back? (play), 1916; Nixola of Wall Street, 1919; Love Chase, 1922. Contbr. to London New Leader, London Observer, New York Nation, etc., on social and lit. matters. Address: London, Eng. *

GRENFELL, ELTON WATTERS, naval officer; b. Fall River, Mass., Nov. 6, 1903; s. John Henry and Emma (Watters) G.; B.S., U.S. Naval Acad., 1926; M.S., U. Cal., 1936; grad. Indsl. Coll. of Armed Forces, 1952; m. Martha Fronk Lindsey, Mar. 15, 1944; children—Eugene Elbert Lindsey, Marv Grenfell (Mrs. Colby), (foster children), Elizabeth Anne, Stephen John Fronk, Jane Douglass. Commd. ensign USN, 1926, advanced through grades to vice adm., 1960; assigned U.S.S. Florida, Lexington, Childs, 1926-28, submarine R.

GRETSCH, FRED, JR., banker; b. Bklyn., Mar. 10, 1905; s. Frederick and Charlotte (Sommer) G.; B.A., Cornell U., 1926; m. Helen A. Mooney, May 24, 1952 (dec. Jan. 1977); 1 dau., Helen Marie; m. 2d, Dorothy Digiorgio Antolini, Mar. 17, 1979. Chmn. bd. trustees The Lincoln Savs. Banks, chief exec. officer, 1971-75; chmn. exec. com., 1975-78; dir. emeritus Baldwin-United, Inc.; dir. Interboro Ins. Co. Trustee Indsl. Home for Blind. Served with USNR, 1942-46. Mem. Bklyn. C. of C. (dir. 1952-80). Clubs: North Hempstead Country; Manhasset Bay Yacht; Cornell, Union League (N.Y.C.); Brooklyn. Home: Manhasset, N.Y. Died May 26, 1980.

GREVE, WILLIAM MARCUS, b. New York, N.Y., June 26, 1884; s. William Marcus and Rebecca (Westfall) G.; student Poly. Prep. Sch., Brooklyn, N.Y., Stevens Inst. of Tech., Hoboken, N.J.; m. Clara Louise Furgueson, of Brooklyn, N.Y., Oct. 31, 1907; 1 dau., Lillian Elizabeth (Mrs. T. Grant Caldwell). With Realty Associates (name became N.Y. Investors, Inc., 1929), 1901-33; dir. and mem. exec. com. M.K.&T. Ry., Madison Sq. Garden Corpn.; dir. and mem. finance com. Thompson-Starrett Co.; dir. N.Y. Rapid Transit Co., Manhattan Fire and Marine Ins. Co., Brooklyn-Manhattan Transit Corpn., Jamaica Buses, Inc., Jamaica Central Rys. Episcopalian. Clubs: Metropolitan, Cloud, City Midday, Crescent Athletic-Hamilton, Montauk, Seminole, Madison Square Gardens, N.Y. Yacht, Deepdale Golf, United Hunts Racing Assn., Crockford's. Home: New York, N.Y. *

GREWEN, ROBERT FRANCIS, coll. pres.; b. Johnstown, N.Y., Aug. 19, 1906; s. John A. and Mary F. (Meagher) G.; student Holy Cross Coll., 1923-24, St. Andrew-on-Hudson, Poughkeepsie, N.Y., 1924-28; M.A., Weston Coll., 1931; S.T.L., Woodstock Coll., 1938, Ph.D., 1938. Entered Soc. of Jesus, 1924, ordained priest, 1936; tchr. classics Bklyn. Prep. Sch., 1931-33; prof. philosophy St. Peter's Coll., 1938-39; dir. retreats Loyola House of Retreats, Morristown, N.J., 1939-44; dir. Christ the King Retreat House, Diocese of Syracuse, N.Y., 1944-51; organized retreat house for laymen and priests, Syracuse, 1945; purchases site of Le Moyne Coll., 1946; prof. theology Canisius Coll., 1951-54, organized Sch. of Adult Edn. in Theology, 1954; pres. Le Moyne Coll., 1954-79. Author: His Father's Business, 1942; Know Your King, 1944. Address: Syracuse, N.Y. Died Jan. 28, 1979.

GREY, FRANK HERBERT, musical condr., composer; b. Phila., Pa., Nov. 15, 1883; s. Elmer Herbert and Bertha Alice (Dann) G.; student Harvard, 4 yrs. (non-grad.); while at Harvard U. studied harmony, counterpoint, canon and fugue with Prof. W. Spaulding, orchestration with Prof. J. K. Paine, and free composition with Frederick Converse; studied piano with Charles Dennee at N.E. Conservatory; m. Retta M. Spelley, Feb. 24, 1909. Conductor light opera since 1909; musical conductor for Joe Weber's "Honey Dew" Co., New York, also for Shubert production, "Blossom Time"; pres. New Dawn Music Corp., music publishers. Mem. Authors' League Am., Am. Soc. Composers, Authors and Pubs., Song Writers Protective Assn., Society Mayflower Descendants of Calif., S.A.R. (Calif.) (mem. com. to bring Am. opera to Calif.), Pi Eta (Harvard). Episcopalian. Clubs: Pleiades (pres. 1928-29), Harvard (New York) (So. Calif.); Verdi (hon.). Composer: Sunny Sicily; (violin and piano number) Dream of Summer; (songs) Cesoir, Cesoir, Cherie; Last Night, Love Is Mine, To Romany and You, Forever, Mother of My Heart, Think Love of Me, In the Dusk, Kappa Sigma Waltz, and numerous other songs; musical comedies, Sue, Dear, 1922, The Matinee Girl, 1926, Happy, prod. 1927, contributions to The Little Show, 1930, etc., and more than 400 instrumental orchestral pieces and over 200 songs. Completed Concerto in G Major for Piano and Orchestra dedicated to Jose Iturbi. Recently made hon. mem. Pleiades Club of Calif. *

GRIBBLE, WILLIAM CHARLES, JR., army officer, cons. engr.; b. Ironwood, Mich., May 24, 1917; s. William Charles and Maud (Slade) G.; student Mich. Technol. U., 1934-37, D. Engring. (hon.), 1969; B.S., U.S. Mil. Acad., 1941; M.S., U. Chgo., 1948; postgrad. Nat. War Coll., 1960-61; m. Martha Jane Watson, June 21, 1941; children—William Charles III, Nancy Jane, Donald James, Judith Ann. Commd. 2d Lt. U.S. Army, 1941, advanced through grades to lt. gen., 1971; staff mem. Los Alamos Sci. Lab., 1948-52; staff AEC, Washington, 1953-56; with Alaska Engr. Dist., 1956-60; with Office Chief Army Engrs., 1961-63; div. engr. North Central Engrs. Div., 1963; dir. research and devel. Army Material Command, 1963-66; dep. asst. chief of staff Dept. Army Gen. Staff, 1966-69; comdg. gen. U.S. Army Engr. Center, 1969-70; chief research and devel. Dept. Army, 1971-73; chief engrs. U.S. Army, 1973-76; cons. engr., 1977-79. Decorated D.S.M., Legion of Merit medal with oak leaf clusters. Registered profl. engr., D.C. Mem. Am. Ordnance Assn., Soc. Am. Mil. Engrs., Assn. U.S. Army, Tau Beta Pi, Theta Tau. Home: Alexandria, Va. Died June 2, 1979; buried Arlington Nat. Cemetery, Arlington, Va.

GRICE, HOMER LAMAR, clergyman; b. Citra, Fla., Apr. 12, 1883; s. Albert Gallatin and Sarah Lee (Bennett) G.; A.B., Mercer U., Macon, Ga., 1912, D.D., 1921; A.M., George Peabody Coll. for Teachers, 1929; grad. study Boston Univ. Sch. of Religious Edn. and Social Service, and Vanderbilt Univ. Sch. of Religion; m. Ethel Harrison, Aug. 21, 1912. Teacher pub. schs., Ala., 1899-1901; in ry. mail service, U.S. Govt., 1902-09; prof. English, Ouachita Coll., Arkadelphia, Ark., 1913-15; ordained Bapt. ministry, 1913; pastor First Ch., Washington, Ga., 1915-24; sec. in charge Vacation Bible Sch. Dept., editor Vacation Bible Sch. text books of Baptist Sunday Sch. Bd., since 1924, also editor New Graded Intermediate S.S. Lessons and lesson writer for 14-year and 15-year pupils, 1930-33. Mem. Phi Delta Kappa. Author: The Vacation Bible School Guide, 1926; V.B.S. Intermediate—Book Three—Studies in Acts, 1927; Intermediate—Book One—Studies in Mark, 1928; the Vacation Bible School Joint Service Book, Vols. 1-12, 1938-49; joint author of 3 Vacation Bible School Intermediate text books, The First Book About Jesus (Mark), 1942; The First Book About Missions (Acts), 1940; The First Missionary Letters (Paul's), 1945; regular contbr. to religious periodicals. Home: Nashville, Tenn. *

GRIFFIN, CHARLES CARROLL, historian; b. Tokyo, Japan, May 24, 1902; s. Charles Sumner and Mary Avery (Greene) G.; A.B., Harvard, 1922; A.M., Columbia, 1933, Ph.D., 1937; m. Jessica Frances Jones, Aug. 27, 1934; children—Thomas Carroll, Nancy Evarts. With fgn. dept. First Nat. Bank of Boston,

1922-23; Cia. Argentina de Cemento Portland, 1923-25, Cia. Uruguaya de Cemento Portland, 1925-30; rep. in Spain of European Mission, Library of Congress, 1931-32; faculty Vassar Coll., Poughkeepsie, N.Y., 1934-67, prof. history, 1944-67, chmn. dept. history, 1944-46, 50-52, 60-64, dean faculty, 1965-67; dir. Asso. Colls. Mid-Hudson area, 1968-69. Exchange prof., Venezuela, 1940-41; div. Am. reps. State Dept., 1943-44; vis. prof. U. Wis., 1949-50, U. de Chile, Santiago, 1954, Harvard, 1959-60, Columbia, 1966, Princeton, 1968; Fulbright lectr., Chile, 1966. Trustee Marist Coll., Poughkeepsie, 1967-74, Southeast N.Y. Library Resources Council, 1968-70, 72-76. Recipient Distinguished Service award Conf. on Latin Am. History, 1970. Author: United States and the Disruption of the Spanish Empire 1810-1822, 1937; The National Period in the History of the New World, 1961; Los temas sociales y economicos en la epoca de la independencia, 1962; Ensayos Sobre historia de America, 1969. Editor Concerning Latin American Culture, 1940; Latin America-A Guide to the Historical Literature, 1971; contbg. editor Handbook of Latin American Studies, 1940-43, 55-58, chmn. adv. bd., 1960-65; mng. editor Hispanic Am. Hist. Rev., 1950-53. Home: Hyde Park, N.Y. Died June 13, 1976.

GRIFFIN, CLARE ELMER, educator; b. Allegan, Mich., Mar. 22, 1892; s. Frank and Ethel May (Lewis) G.; B.A., Albion (Mich.) Coll., 1914; M.A., U. Ill., 1915, Ph.D., 1918; m. Florence Lovina Parsons, Dec. 27, 1917; children—Frances Ethel (Mrs. Edward S. Bres., Jr.), Nancy Letitia (Mrs. Francis DuBois). Instr. econs. Dartmouth, 1916-17; instr. transp. Johns Hopkins, 1917-18; expert U.S. Shipping Bd. and Central Bur. of Planning and Statistics, Washington, 1919; asso. prof. mktg. U. Mich. 1919-27, prof. mktg., 1925-43, dean Sch. Bus. Adminstrn. and dir. Bur. Bus. Research, 1927-43, Fred. M. Taylor prof. of bus. econs., 1943-61. Ednl. dir. Detroit chpt. Am. Inst. Banking, 1923-25; Econ. cons. to Cement Inst., Am. Meat Inst. and other orgns.; research staff Com. for Econ. Devel., 1943-46. Pres. Am. Assn. Collegiate Schs. of Bus., 1942-43. Mem. Nat. Adv. Com. on War Tng. U.S. Office of Edn., 1941-44. Served as 1st lt., U.S. Army, 1918-19. Mem. Am. Econ. Assn., Am. Mktg. Assn., Research Club (U. Mich.), Mont Pelerin Soc., Phi Beta Kappa, Delta Sigma Rho, Phi Kappa Phi. Club: University. Author: Principles of Foreign Trade, 1924; Life History of Automobiles, 1926; Enterprise in a Free Society, 1949; Britain, a Case Study for Americans, 1950; An Economic Approach to Antitrust Problems, 1951; The Free Society, 1965. Contbr. articles in various profl. jours. Home: Ann Arbor, Mich. Died Nov. 30, 1979.

GRIFFIN, DAVID BURTON, business exec.; b. Liverpool, La., Sept. 11, 1885; s. William W. and Temperance (Renfro) G.; student U. of South, Sewanee, Tenn., 1914; U. of Cincinnati, 1920-21; m. Florence Boyle, Aug. 25, 1915; children—David Burton, Beverly Milnor. Stenographer, bookkeeper, 1913; accountant, Mansfield Hardwood Lumber Company, 1915-18; prodn. expert, War Dept. Bur. Aircraft Prodn., 1918-19; staff mem. Shannon, Reynolds & Bone, pub. accountants, 1919-20; sec. and auditor E. Sondheimer Co., 1920-24; partner Maceo & Griffin, 1924-25; partner D. B. Griffin & Co., 1925-27; staff mem. Haskins and Sells, 1927-28; land bank examiner, Fed. Farm Loan Bur., 1928-30; asst. treas. and comptroller, Fed. Land Bank of Louisville, 1930-32; sr. asst. treas. Reconstrn. Finance Corp., since 1932; asst. treas. Disaster Loan Corp., 1936-45; asst. treas. Export-Import Bank of Washington, D.C., 1934-44; treas. Export-Import Bank of Washington, D.C., 1944-46; former asst. treas. Defense Homes Corp.; asst. treas. Federal National Mortgage Association, 1948-49. Certified pub. accountant Tex., Ky., and Tenn. Mem. Kappa Sigma. Democrat. Baptist. Mason (Shriner). Club: Columbia Country. Home: Washington. *

GRIFFIN, FRANK H., corporation official; b. Chester, Pa., July 16, 1886; s. John and Nancy Hastings (Mills) G.; student Drexel Institute Technology, 1903-06; Dr. Engring. (hon.) Drexel Institute, 1947; B. S. Swarthmore Coll. 1910; M. S., Columbia 1916; m. Priscilla Cooper Goodwyn, Apr. 9, 1913; children—Adele (wife of James A. Sands), Frank Hastings, John Tyler, Priscilla Tyler. Instructor in chemistry, Drexel Institute Technology and Hahnemann Medical College, 1909-18; with American Viscose Corporation, Philadelphia, since 1918, as chemist, chief chemist, gen. mgr., dir. of the corp., vice-pres. and technical director since 1936; dir. Delaware County Nat. Bank Am. Insulator Corp. Dir. Del. County (Pa.) C. of C., Mfrs. Assn. of Del. County. Member board trustees, Drexel Institute Technology, Member Army-Navy Munitions Bd. Mem. Am. Chemical Soc., Franklin Institute, Sigma Xi, Kappa Sigma. Vestryman, Christ Church, Media, Pa. Clubs: Rose Tree Fox Hunting, Racquet, Rittenhouse. As a pioneer in manufacture of rayon, formulated and perfected many procedures now in use. Home: Wawa, Pa. *

GRIFFIN, JOHN HOWARD, author, photographer; b. Dallas, June 16, 1920; s. Jack W. and Lena Mae (Young) G.; certificate of studies, Conservatoire de Fontainebleau, 1946; certificates from Benedictines and Dominicans in France; LL.D., Bellarmine U.; Litt.D., Marycrest Coll., 1972; m. Elizabeth Ann Holland, June 2, 1953; children—Susan Michele, John Howard, Gregory Parker, Amanda Claire Dominique. Author syndicated columns for the Internat. News Service and also King features, 1957-60; student primitive cultures, intergroup and intercultural relationships; lectr., from 1950. Recipient award Nat. Assn. Negro Women; Christian Culture award, 1966; co-recipient Pope John XXIII Pacem in Terris, Peace and Freedom Award, 1964. Mem. Am. Soc. of Mag. Photographers. Author: (novels) Devil Rides Outside, 1952, Nuni, 1956; (history) Land of the High Sky, 1959; (non-fiction) Black Like Me (Anisfield Wolf award Sat. Rev. 1961), 1961; (non-fiction) The Church and The Black Man, 1968; A Hidden Wholeness: The Visual World of Thomas Merton, 1970; Twelve Photographic Portraits, 1973; Jacques Maritain: Homage in Words and Pictures, 1974; A Time To Be Human, 1977; also articles, short stories, photo-journalistic studies. Address: Fort Worth, Tex. Died Sept. 9, 1980.

GRIFFING, ROBERT PERKINS, JR., museum cons.; b. Riverhead, N.Y., Mar. 27, 1914; s. Robert Perkins and Ethel Counselman (Sharp) G.; grad. Phillips Andover Acad., 1931; B.A., Yale, 1935; M.F.A., Princeton, 1940; postgrad. U. Paris (France), 1939; D.F.A., U. Hawaii, 1959; m. Marjorie Cophine Lewis, Apr. 23, 1948 (dec.); children—Peter Allerton (dec.), Alison Leilani. Instr. art and archeology Princeton, 1938-39; instr. Johns Hopkins, 1940-41; dir. edn. Honolulu Acad. Arts, 1946-47, dir., 1947-63, cons., 1963-71, hon. cons., 1971-73. Hon. cons. Bernice P. Bishop Mus., Honolulu; mem. Advisory Council E. Asian Art Columbia U.; dir. UNESCO-Japanese Govt. Seminar on Asian Museums, Tokyo, 1960, UNESCO-Indian Govt. Seminar on Asian Museums, New Delhi, 1966. Mem. Gov.'s Com. for State Capitol, 1958, Com. for Internat. Center Auditorium, 1952-54, 60-63. Past bd. dirs. Honolulu Symphony, Honolulu Community Fund Found., Pacific and Asian Affairs Council; trustee Hanahauoli Sch., Adult Ednl. Council, Honolulu. Served to lt. USNR, 1941-46; PTO. Recipient medal for ednl. and cultural service Govt. Republic of Korea, 1959. Mem. Royal Asiatic Soc. (Korea br.), Internat. Council Museums, Southeast Asian Ceramic Soc. (Singapore). Clubs: Pacific (Honolulu); Elizabethan (New Haven); Princeton (N.Y.C.). Author: Barbara Hutton Collection of Chinese Porcelain, 1958; The Museum as a Cultural Centre in the Development of the Community, 1966; The Art of the Korean Potter, 1968. Contbr. articles to profl. jours. Address: Honolulu, Hawaii. Died Aug. 10, 1979.

GRIFFITH, DUDLEY DAVID, coll. prof.; b. Evanston, Ill., Apr. 16, 1882; s. Amos Elza and Mary Alice (Dudley) G.; A.B., Simpson Coll., 1903; fellow in English U. of Chicago, 1915-16, Ph.D., 1916; m. Anna Hewitt Moran, May 30, 1929. Prof. Greek, Mo. Wesleyan Coll., 1903-05; acting prof. Greek, Simpson Coll., 1905-06; instr. in Greek, Park College, Parkville, Mo., 1906-10; prof. English, Simpson Coll., 1910-13; asst. in English, U. of Chicago, 1913-16; prof. English, Grinnell (Ia.) Coll., 1916-23; prof. English, U. of Wash., since 1924, dean of Coll. of Liberal Arts, 1930-34, executive officer, dept. of English, 1926-47; prof. English since 1926. Mem. Modern Lang. Assn. Am., Phi Beta Kappa, Alpha Tau Omega, Sigma Delta Chi. Methodist. Mason. Clubs: Men's Faculty, Univ. Golf, Rainier. Author two books. Editor: Modern Language Quarterly. Contbr. articles and reviews. Home: Seattle. *

GRIFFITH, F(RANKLIN) WEBB, surgeon; b. Upper Marlboro, Md., Feb. 28, 1885; A.B., Western Md. Coll., 1902, A.M., 1905; M.D., Johns Hopkins, 1906; m. Grace H. Lemmon, Dec. 26, 1912. Mem. resident staff, Johns Hopkins Hosp., 1906-11; in practice surgery and gynecology, Asheville, N.C., since 1911; cons. surgeon, State Hosp., Morgantown, N.C.; surgeon, Asheville (N.C.) Mission Hosp.; former mem. Bd. of Med. Examiners of N.C. Mem. Founders Group of Am. Bd. of Surgery. Fellow Am. Coll. Surgeons; mem. Am. and Buncombe County med. assns., N.C. State Med. Soc. (pres.), Southern Surg. Assn. Contbr. to Kelly's Medical Gynecology. Retired. Home: Asheville, N.C. *

GRIFFITH, HUGH, actor; b. Anglesey, Wales, May 30, 1912; s. William and Mary (Williams) G.; ed. (Gold medal), Royal Acad. Dramatic Art, London; D.Litt. (hon.), U. of Wales; m. Adelqunde M.B. von Dechend, Oct. 27, 1947. Appeared on Broadway in Look Homeward Angel, Andora; motion pictures include, Ben Hur (recipient of the Academy award for role of Sheik), 1960, Exodus, 1961, The Counterfeit Traitor, Mutiny on the Bounty, Tom Jones, How to Steal a Million, 1965, The Chastity Belt, Oh Dad, Poor Dad . . ., The Fixer, Oliver, also appeared in Two Times Two; TV appearances include The Waltz of the Toreadors, Treasure Island, The Citadel, The Inn of the Flying Dragon, Dare I Weep, Dare I Mourn. Served as officer Royal Welch Fusiliers, British Army, 1940-46. Hon. Druid of Welsh Gorsedd of Bards. Club: Garrick (Ldn). Home: London, England. Died May 14, 1980.

GRIFFITH, JOHN KELLER, congressman; b. Port Hudson, La., Oct. 16, 1882; s. William Phipps and Henrietta (Williams) G.; student La. State U., 1897-1901. M.D., Tulane U., 1907; m. Vivian Comfort, of Slidell, La., Dec. 21, 1912; children—John Keller, Carolyn Vivian. Resident phys. East La. State Hospital, Jackson, 1909-10; practicing physician, Slidell, La., 1910-37; mem. 75th and 76th Congresses (1937-41), 6th La. Dist. Dir. Bank of Slidell, Slidell, La. Commd. 1st lt., med. corps, U.S.A., 1918-19. Mem. A.M.A., La. State Med. Soc., 6th Dist. Med. Soc., St. Tammany Parish Med. Soc., Kappa Sigma, Phi Chi. Received Silver Beaver Award, Boy Scouts of America. Democrat. Mason. Home: Slidell, La.*

GRIFFITH, LYNN B., judge; b. West Farmington, Ohio, Oct. 30, 1886; s. Herbert F. and Lovira (Snyder) G.; A.B., Oberlin Coll., 1910; LL.B., Western Res. U., 1914; m. Stata Norton Miller, Sept. 9, 1916; children—David Miller, Patricia Ann, Lynn B. City solicitor, Warren, Ohio, 1925-26; county pros. atty., 1927-28; common pleas judge, Trumbull County, Ohio, 1931-50; judge Ct. of Appeals, 7th Dist. Ohio, 1950-62; judge Supreme Ct. of Ohio, 1962-78; mem. Letson, Letson & Griffith, Warren, O., 1965-78; dir. First Nat. Bank, Girard, Ohio, Girard Fed. Savs. & Loan Assn. Pres. Warren Pub. Library, Oakwood Cemetery Assn.; chmn. adv. bd. YWCA. Home: Warren, Ohio. Died July 8, 1978.

GRIFFITHS, GEORGE FINDLEY, business exec.; b. Chgo., Feb. 18, 1906; s. George Harold and Mabel May (Green) G.; student U.S. Mil. Acad., 1925-27; B.A., Amherst Coll., 1929; m. Marion E. Winterrowd, Feb. 15, 1941; children—Jean Winterrowd, William Harold, Judith Holland, Robert Pennell. Salesman, United Screw & Bolt Corp., 1929-31, U.S. Steel Corp., 1931-38; salesman Sharon Steel Corp. (Pa.), 1938-40, dist. mgr. sales, 1940-46, gen. mgr. sales, 1946-47, v.p., gen. mgr. sales, 1947-49; asst. to exec. v.p. Acme Steel Co., Chgo., 1950-51, asst. to pres., 1952, v.p., 1953-58, exec. v.p. sales, 1958-60, pres., chief exec. officer, chmn. exec. com., 1961-64, dir., 1954-64; chmn. bd., chief exec. officer Interlake Steel Corp. (merger Acme Steel Co. and Interlake Iron Corp. 1964), 1964-69, chmn. bd., 1969-71, also dir., mem. exec. com. Mem. Am. Iron and Steel Inst. (past dir.), Ill. C. of C. (past dir.), Psi Upsilon. Republican. Christian Scientist. Clubs: Executives (past dir.), University (past dir.), Chicago (Chgo.); Hinsdale (Ill.) Golf; Commercial; Hole-in-the Wall Golf (Naples, Fla.). Home: Hinsdale, Ill. Died Apr. 1, 1980; buried Montclair, N.J.

GRIGGS, DAVID TRESSEL, geophysicist, educator; b. Columbus, O., Oct. 6, 1911; s. Robert F. and Laura (Tressel) G.; A.B., Ohio State U., 1932, A.M., 1933; postgrad. (jr. fellow), Harvard, 1934-41; m. Helen Avery, May 4, 1946; children—Nicola F. (Mrs. J. Andron), Stephen F. Research asso. radiation lab. Mass. Inst. Tech., 1941-42; chief nuclear energy sect. Project RAND, 1946-48, cons., 1948-74; prof. geophysics Inst. Geophysics and Planetary Physics, U. Cal. at Los Angeles, 1948-74; chief scientist USAF, 1951-52, sci. adv. bd. 1952-72; chmn. ballistic systems div. adv. group USAF, 1963-65; cons. Armed Forces Spl. Weapons Project, 1951-56; cons. various govtl. agys., also AEC; mem. Nat. Geog. Soc. Expdn. to Valley 10,000 Smokes, 1930; lectr. Lowell Inst., 1938; dir. FMA, Inc., Inglewood, 1960-67. Expert cons. Office Sec. of War, 1942-46; chief sci. adv. group Far East Air Forces, 1945; sci. adv. group U.S. Strategic Air Force, 1944-45; mem. Def. Sci. Bd., 1964-72, Army Sci. Adv. Panel, 1965-73, OST Panel for Earthquake Prediction, 1965-66; asso. sci. adviser COMUSMAC, Vietnam, 1968; sci. adv. com. Def. Intelligence Agy., 1974. Decorated Purple Heart, 1944, President's Medal for Merit, 1946; USAF award for exceptional civilian service, 1953; Bucher medal Am. Geophys. Union, 1970; Centennial Achievement award Ohio State U., 1970; Day medal Geol. Soc. Am., 1973. Fellow Geol. Soc. Am., Am. Phys. Soc.; mem. Nat. Acad. Sci., Am. Geophys. Union (pres. sect. tectonophysics 1964-68), Am. Acad. Arts and Scis., Phi Beta Kappa, Sigma Xi. Clubs: Cosmos (Washington); Riviera Country (Los Angeles). Author: Rock Deformation, 1960. Home: Los Angeles, Calif. Died Dec. 31, 1974.

GRIGGS, RICHARD LESLIE, banker; b. Barclay, Pa., Dec. 8, 1886; s. Eli Zelotes and Anna (Kinney) G.; A.B., U. Minn., 1907; m. Neva Warner, Sept. 20, 1911; children—Leslie Elizabeth, Richard Clemson, Harold Warner. Began with Bank of Virginia (Minn.), 1899, treas. Virginia Electric Power & Water Co., 1910-14; engaged in real estate, ins. and automobile business, Duluth, Minn., 1914-17; sec. Northern Nat. Bank, Duluth, 1917-21, vice pres., 1921-29, pres., 1929-46, chmn. bd. 1946-50, ret. 1950; pres., dir. Kinney Corp., W.Va.; v.p. and dir. Sterling Motor Co.; dir., mem. exec. com. Minn. Power & Light Co.; trustee Whitney Materials Co.; dir. Greyhound Corp., 1st Nat. Bank (Hibbing), 1st Nat. Bank (Va.) (all Minn.), Andresen Ryan Coffee Co. Bd. dirs. Duluth chpt. Infantile Paralysis Found. Am.; bd. regents U. Minn., 1939-63, regent emeritus, 1963—. Served as pvt. F.A., United States Army, Camp Taylor, 1918. Recipient

Outstanding Achievement award U. Minn., also Regents award, Regents award of merit; Hall of Fame award City of Duluth; Faculty and Staff Honor award U. Minn. at Duluth, also Alumni Distinguished Service award, Student Commn. Recognition award; Public Service citation Joint Session Senate and House Minn. State Legislature, 1963; Public Service citation 8th Dist. Legislators Minn.; Pres.'s award Kappa Sigma. Citations Duluth Community Chest, Minn. Arrowhead Assn.; Klineburger Trophy award as sr. big game hunter of World Game Conservation Internat., 1973. Mem. Newcomen Soc., Am. Legion. Republican. Episcopalian. Mason (32 deg.), Elk. Clubs: Kitchi Gammi, Northland Country, Duluth Athletic. Home: Duluth, MN. *

GRIMES, JOHN WESLEY, newspaperman; b. Crothersville, Ind., Oct. 5, 1894; s. Rev. Walter Bruce and Ada (Lenover) G.; Ph.B., U. Chgo., 1917; L.H.D. (honorary), Rockford College, 1962; m. Mollie Neumann, 1918. News and mng. ed. Rockford Daily Republic, 1919-30; mng. editor Rockford Morning Star, 1930-51; exec. editor Rockford Morning Star and Register-Republic, 1951-59, editor 1959-61. Served with U.S. Army, 1917-19. Mem. Am. Legion. Republican. Home: Rockford, Ill. Died May 29, 1980.

GRIMES, SAMUEL, bishop; b. B.W.I., Jan. 3, 1884; s. Samuel and Loretta Grimes; student Shelton Coll., 1917; m. May 17, 1917. Dir. Pentecostal Assemblies of World. Home: N.Y.C. *

GRIMES, WILLIAM ALEXANDER, lawyer; b. St. Louis, June 7, 1904; s. William Hearne and Isabelle (Seguenot) G.; A.B. magna cum laude, Harvard, 1925, LL.B., 1928; m. Adela Lawrance Ax, Feb. 13, 1934 (dec. July 1973) m. 2d, Earline H. Selby, Aug. 8, 1974. Admitted to Md. bar, 1929, practiced in Balt.; mem. firm Ober, Grimes and Shriver, and predecessors, 1931-77; asst. gen. counsel Fed. Alcohol Adminstrn., 1934; mem. adv. com. admiralty rules U.S. Supreme Ct., 1960-72. Dir. Fingles Co., 1955-77, Lanman & Kemp-Barclay & Co., Inc., 1971-77; asst. sec. F. and M. Schaefer Brewing Co., 1963-77. Served to maj. AUS, 1942-45. Recipient 1st prize for thesis Chgo. Trust Co., 1925. Mem. Am., Md. (chmn. com. fed. jud. appointments 1964-65, 67-68, bd. govs. 1968-69), Balt. bar assns., Md. Bar Found. (pres. 1974-77), Maritime Law Assn. (exec. com. 1960-63), Phi Beta Kappa. Clubs: Rule Day, Round Table, Harvard, Baltimore Country, Elkridge, Center (Balt.). Author: Financing Automobile Sales on the Time Payment Plan, 1926; also sects. in books. Home: Baltimore, Md. Died May 17, 1977; interred Greenmount Cemetery, Balt.

GRIMM, PETER, hotel corp. exec.; b. Savanyukut, Hungary, May 30, 1905; s. Julius John and Josepha Veronica (Herczog) G.; grad. Gymnasium, Budapest, Hungary, 1923, Master Diploma in Hotel Mgmt., 1932; student U. Hamburg, Germany; m. Susan Fulop, June 25, 1932; 1 son, Peter Gabriel; m. 2d, Gertrude Joy, Dec. 5, 1942. Came to U.S., 1939, naturalized, 1944. Purchasing agt. Gen. Motors Peninsular in Spain, 1926-30; mgr. Hotel Pension Grimm, Budapest, Hungary, 1930-38; mgr. Schmidt Bros. Printing Ink Factory, Budapest, 1938-39; fgn. trade adviser Chgo. Assn. Commerce, 1939-40; field sales mgr. Kemper Thomas Co., Cin., 1940-41; exec. Hotel New Yorker, N.Y.C., 1941-42, Hotel Willard, Washington, 1942-44; gen. mgr. Drake Hotel, Phila., 1944-45, The Town House, N.Y.C., 1945-48; with Intercontinental Hotels Corp., N.Y.C., 1948-60, operations mgr., then asst. to pres., gen. mgr. hotel operations, v.p. hotel operations, pres., 1957-60; gen. mgr. Hotel Div. Schine Enterprises, Inc., N.Y.C., 1960-62; pres. Transmar Hotels Corp., 1960-62; co-founder, pres., dir., chief exec. officer Transmar-Downtowner Corp., 1969-72; cons. Internat. Bank for Reconstruction and Fin. (World Bank), from 1973. Mem. Village Green Community Council, Sarasota, from 1974. Mem. N.Y.C., Inter-American (v.p.) hotel assns., Am. Arbitration Assn. (nat. panel of arbitrators), S.G.V.G. Condominium Assn. (pres. sect. 7). Home: Sarasota, Fla. Died Sept. 23, 1978.

GRIMM, PETER, real estate exec.; b. N.Y.C., Jan. 12, 1886; s. Adam and Josephine (Henry) G.; B.S., Columbia, 1911; m. Harriet Lawrence, Feb. 11, 1922; children—Peter, Laurie. Real estate broker Stephen H. Tyng and Co., N.Y.C., 1911-20; owner real estate bus., 1920-29; pres., dir. William A. White and Sons, 1929-44, dir., chmn. bd., 1944; dir. various cos.; spl. asst. to sec. Treasury Dept.; 1935-36; 1st minister, operation chief Am. Embassy, Rome, 1965-67. Pres., dir. Grand Central Art Galleries; pres. Sailors Snug Harbor, 1951, 52. Founder, 1st chmn. Citizen's Budget Com.; chmn. Mayor's Com. on Taxation, 1932-54; mem. N.Y.C. Plan Commn., 1934; mem. real estate adv. bd. War Dept., 1941; mem. race and housing commn. Fund for Republic, 1963-64; mem. Mayor's Fiscal Commn., 1963-64; chmn. Mayor's Com. for constrn. wing to Gracie Mansion, 1969. Exec. com. Nat. Inst. Social Scis., 1960-75; pres. N.Y.C. Baseball Fedn., 1963-65; chmn. Columbia Coll. Council, Netherland Am. Found.; dir., mem. exec. com. United Cerebral Palsy Assn.; trustee, chmn. real estate com. Columbia-Presbyn. Hosp.; trustee N.Y. Zool. Soc.; bd. dirs. Nat. Book Com. Served from capt. to maj., A.S., U.S. Army, 1917-18. Decorated grand officer Order Cristobal Colon (Dominican Republic); comdr. Order Orange-Nassau (Netherlands); grand officer Order Merit Republic of Italy; Benjamin Franklin fellow of Order of St. John of Jerusalem (Great Britain); recipient Columbia U. medal for social service, 1934, Alumni medal, 1954, Alexander Hamilton medal, 1965; Plaque for Distinguished Service, Municipal Art Soc. N.Y.C., 1965; citation for distinguished service Explorer's Club, 1965; Man of Year award Realty Found., 1965; Bi-annual award Fifth Ave. Assn. N.Y., 1967; Medal of City N.Y., 1968; named to Hall of Fame Com. of Gt. Ams. Fellow Royal Soc. Arts, Royal Soc. Fine Arts London; mem. N.Y. State C. of C. (pres. 1946-48), Am.-Italy Soc. (Pres. 1958-65). Clubs: Rockefeller Center, University, Columbia University, Century, Pinnacle, Grolier, Explorers' (N.Y.C.); Piping Rock (L.I.); Bohemian (San Francisco). Home: New York, N.Y. Died Feb. 16, 1980.

GRIMM, RANDOLPH MACON, U.S. Pub. Health Service; b. Warren County, Va., Sept. 13, 1882; s. Edgar Randolph and Fannie Belle (Barnes) G.; A.B., Randolph-Macon Coll., 1902, A.M., 1903; M.D., Johns Hopkins, 1908; m. Heloise Percifull, Nov. 5, 1913; 1 son, Randolph Percifull. Commd. asst. surgeon U.S. Pub. Health Service, 1908, passed asst. surgeon, 1912, surgeon, 1921, sr. surgeon, 1930, med. dir., 1934; med. officer in charge U.S. Marine Hosp., Seattle, Wash., 1936-42; med. officer in charge, U.S.P.H.S. Relief and Quarantine Sta., San Diego, Calif., 1942-46. Retired, 1946. Mem. A.M.A., Assn. of Mil. Surgeons of U.S., Phi Beta Kappa. Mason (K.T. Shriner). Address: Bethesda, Md. *

GRIMMETT, ELMER JESSE, food co. exec.; b. Calhoun County, Ark., July 11, 1902; s. Joseph H. and Minnie (Groves) G.; B.S. in Mich. Engring., Miss. State Coll., 1923; m. Mildred Argust, Apr. 2, 1929; children—Gordon G., Janice L. Design, cons. work Empire Co., Bartlesville, Okla., also Miss. Power and Light Co., Tupela and Baldwin, Miss., 1923-25; gen. design, supervisory work Proctor & Gamble Co., Ivorydale, Ohio, 1925-28, plant engr., St. Louis, 1928-29, charge expansion program Port Ivory (S.I.) plant, 1929, supr. expansion and modernization, St. Louis, 1929-30, supr. maintenance inedible div., S.I., 1930; ' with Gen. Foods Corp., from 1930, beginning in Post products plant, successively asst. plant engr. charge design major constrn., supr. design and constrn. new factories at Kankakee, Ill. and Hoboken, N.J., chief engr. adv. supervision all engring., div. mfg. mgr., dir. mfg. and engring, 1930-57, v.p., 1957-66; cons. manufacturing and engring., from 1966; dir. Firemen's Mut. Insurance Co., Providence. Bd. dirs. Westchester County United Fund. Registered engr., N.Y., N.J. Mem. ASME, Nat. Soc. Profl. Engrs., Pi Tau Sigma. Presbyterian. Clubs: Winged Foot Golf (Mamaroneck, N.Y.). Home: Scarsdale, N.Y. Died Sept. 6, 1978.

GRIMSON, GUDMUNDUR, jurist; b. Iceland, Nov. 20, 1878; s. Steingrimur and Gudrun (Jonsdotter) G.; brought to U.S., 1882, naturalized, 1894; A.B., U. N.D., 1904, A.M., 1905, LL.B., 1906, LL.D., 1939; Fellowship U. Chicago, 1905-06; LL.D., U. Iceland, 1930; m. Ina Sanford, Sept. 5, 1906; children—Keith S. and Lynn G. Admitted to N.D. bar, 1906; trustee Village of Munich, 1908-10; states atty. Cavalier Co., 1911-24; spl. asst. atty. gen., 1923-25; prosecutor Martin Tabert-whipping boss investigation in Florida, 1923; judge of the District Court, Second Judicial District, North Dakota, 1926-49; judge Supreme Court of North Dakota, 1949—, chief justice, 1957—. Mem. N.D. State Bd. Pardons, 1957—. Mem. awards jury, Freedoms Found., Valley Forge, 1956—. Chairman com. to revise rules and practice for Revised Code of N.D., 1943. N.D. rep. Millenial Celebration Icelandic Athling, 1930; awarded Order of Falcon by Icelandic Govt., 1939; recipient distinguished service citation University N.D. Alumni Association, 1956, citation for 50 years of legal service N.D. Bar Association. Member American, N.D. bar assns., N.D. Hist. Soc. (pres. 1956—), N.D. Conf. Social Welfare (pres. 1945), Order of Coif, Phi Beta Kappa, Phi Delta Theta. Lutheran. *

GROENINGER, JOSEPH GEORGE (GRON'ING-ER), foreign service; b. Baltimore, Md., Nov. 22, 1884; s. John J. and Anne (Jennings) G.; ed. pub. schs., Baltimore; m. Ella M. Ibsen, Mar. 19, 1921 (died May 3, 1927). With Standard Oil Co., Pub. Athletic League, and Children's Playground Assn., all of Baltimore; apptd. clk. Am. Legation, Copenhagen, Dec. 7, 1911; vice consul at Copenhagen, 1919-20; assigned to Am. Commn., Berlin, and consulate gen., Berlin, 1920-25; consul at Tallinn, Esthonia, 1925-26, Rotterdam, Holland, 1926-27, Batavia, 1927-31, Karachi, India, 1931-35, Auckland, New Zealand, 1936-41; Bradford, Eng., since 1942. Catholic. Club: Army and Navy (Washington). Home: Baltimore, Md. *

GROLLMAN, ARTHUR, research physician; b. Balt., Oct. 20, 1901; s. Simon and Bessie Flora (Karu) G.; A.B., Johns Hopkins, 1920, Ph.D., 1923, M.D., 1930; student U. Chgo., 1924-25, U. Mich., 1926; m. Anna Louise Costello, Mar. 1926; children—Arthur Patrick, Catherine Anne, Evelyn Frances. Instr. chemistry Grad. Sch. Johns Hopkins, 1923-24, asso. prof. physiology Med. Sch., 1930-32, asso. prof. pharmacology and therapeutics, 1932-41; Guggenheim Meml. fellow U. London, Med. Acad. Dusseldorf, U. Berlin, U. Heidelberg, 1930- 31; research prof. medicine Bowman Gray Sch. Medicine, Winston-Salem, N.C., 1941-44; prof. medicine and chmn. dept. exptl. medicine Southwestern Med. Sch. U. Tex., Dallas, 1944-70, prof. exptl. medicine dept. pathology, 1970-76, prof. emeritus, 1976-80, acting prof. pharmacology and chmn. dept. physiology and pharmacology, 1946-50; cons. internal medicine Baylor U.; cons. VA Hosp., USAAF Hosp., Wilford Hall, Lackland AFB; nat. civilian cons. to Surg. Gen. USAF, Surgeon (R) USPHS, 1945-50; hon. prof. medicine Guadalajara, Mexico; Gorgas lectr., 1946; Long lectr., 1952, Boynton lectr., 1958, Duluth lectr., 1956; vis. prof. pharmacology U. S.D., 1976; vis. prof. medicine U. Ala., 1976-78; vis. prof. med. sci. U. Ill., 1978-79. Mem. advisory bd. U. Dallas. Recipient Guggenheim Meml. award, 1930, Marchman award, 1950; Oscar B. Hunter award Am. Therapeutic Soc., 1968. Fellow A.C.P., N.Y. Acad. Scis.; mem. Am. Physiol. Soc., AMA, Am. Soc. Pharmacology and Therapeutics, Fed. Soc. Biology, Phi Beta Kappa, Sigma Xi; hon. mem. Portugese Endocrinol. Soc., Korean Med. Soc. Author: Cardiac Output of Man, 1932; The Adrenals, 1936; Pharmacology and Experimental Therapeutics, 1965, 8th edit., 1974; Acute Renal Failure: Pathogenesis and Treatment, 1954; Clinical Endocrinology, 1964, 3d edit., 1972; editor: The Functional Pathology of Disease, 1963, 2d edit., 1973; research on peritoneal lavage, adrenals, endocrinology, circulation and hypertension. Contbr. chpts., articles to profl. publs. Mem. revision com. U.S. Pharmacopoea 1960-70. Home: Dallas, Tex. Died Jan. 31. 1980.

GRONER, POWELL CAMPBELL, lawyer, corp. exec.; b. Norfolk, Va., Feb. 13, 1892; s. John Archibald Campbell and Elizabeth Stith (Powell) G.; ed. U. Va.; m. Marjorie Hayes Wolcott, July 18, 1917; children—Powell Campbell, William Wolcott. Admitted to bar Va., 1913, N.Y., 1915, Ill., 1918, Mo., 1925, Kan., 1928, U.S. Supreme Ct., 1928; asso. with William H. Page, Chgo. and N.Y.C., 1913-22; rep. Newman, Saunders & Co., investment bankers N.Y.C. and New Orleans, 1922-27; counsel, reorgn. com. Kansas City Rys. Co., 1924-27; pres. and dir. Kansas City Pub. Service Co. and Wyandotte Rys. Co., 1927-57; pres., dir. Kansas City Pub. Service Motor Transport Co., 1935-57; dir. Pierce Industries and subs., 1958-61; mem. law firm Watson, Ess, Groner, Barnett & Whittaker, Kansas City, Mo., 1926-50, Rice, Groner, Nugent and Baska, Kansas City, Kan., 1958-66; pvt. practice, from 1966; dir. Westgate State Bank, Kansas City, Kan.; sec., dir. Sherold Crystals, Inc. and subsidiaries, 1964-70. Gen. chmn. Kansas City Allied Charities Campaign, 1938; gen. chmn. Red Cross War Fund Campaign, Jackson County, 1943, dir., 1943-50. Dir. C. of C. Kansas City, Mo., 1932-34, 38-40; mem. exec. com. Am. Transit Assn., 1932-34, v.p., 1941-42, pres., 1942-43. Nat. councillor of U.S. C. of C., 1932-40, dir., 1943-54, v.p., 1947-49, 51-54, mem. exec. com., 1944-45, 47-49, 51-53. Chmn. Transp. and Communications Com., 1943-47, Labor Relations Com., 1952-53, Nat. Def. Com., 1953-54; mem. Pres.'s labor-mgmt. conf., Washington, 1945; mem. Kansas City Charities Com., 1939-49. Trustee Kansas City Art Inst.; chmn. Trustee Kansas City Philharmonic Orch., 1933-41; chmn. exec. com. Conservatory of Music, Kansas City, 1934-53, pres. 1944-46, chmn., 1954; mem. Jud. Council Mo., 1934-35; bd. dirs. Boys Clubs of Am., 1951-62. Mem. Am., Mo. bar assns., Lawyers Assn. (Kansas City, Mo.), Wyandotte County Bar (Kansas City, Kan.), Phi Sigma Kappa, Delta Sigma Chi. Episcopalian. Clubs: Kansas City, Kansas City Country, Press (Kansas City); River. Home: Kansas City, Mo. Deceased.

GRONINGER, HOMER M., army officer; b. Port Royal, Pa., July 24, 1884; s. R. Elliott and Mary (McLaughlin) G.; student Airyview Acad., Port Royal, Pa., 1901-02, Pa. State Coll., 1903-04; B.S., U.S. Mil. Acad., 1908; student Sch. of Musketry, Monterey, Calif., 1912, Command and Gen. Staff Sch., 1918-21 (distinguished grad. 1923), Cavalry Sch., 1922, Army War Coll., 1926; m. Gertrude Pomeroy, Sept. 19, 1913. Commd. 2d lt., 1908; promoted through grades to major gen., Aug. 2, 1942; served in Punitive Expdn., Mexico, 1916-17, 2d and 3d Div., Meuse Argonne, 1918, in Germany, 1918-19; comdr. New York Port of Embarkation, Brooklyn, Ft. Hamilton, N.Y., Fort Slocum, N.Y., Camp Kilmer, N.J., Fort Dix, N.J., Camp Shanks, N.Y. Awarded Punitive Expdn. medal and victory medal, World War. Home:Ft. Hamilton, N.Y.*

GROPPER, WILLIAM, artist; b. N.Y.C., Dec. 3, 1897; s. Harry and Jennie (Nidel) G.; student N.A.D., 1913-14, N.Y. Sch. Fine and Applied Art, 1915-18; m. Sophie Frankle, Oct. 10, 1924; children—Gene, Lee. Began as artist N.Y. Tribune, 1919; Ford Found. award artist in residence under Am. Fedn. Art, 1965; artist in residence Tamarind Lithographic Workshop, Los Angeles, 1967. Prin. murals U.S. Post Office, Freeport, L.I.; New Interior Bldg., Washington; Wayne State U., Detroit; Schenley Corp., N.Y.; stain glass windows

Temple Har Zion, River Forest, Ill.; represented Met. Mus. Art. Mus. Modern Art, Whitney Mus. Am. Art (all N.Y.C.), Mus. Western Art, Moscow, USSR, Hartford (Conn.) Mus., Art Inst. Chgo., Phillips Art Mus., Washington, Dr. Paul Sachs Coll., Fogg Art Mus., Mus. U. N.Y., Bklyn. Mus., Cambridge, Mass., St. Louis Art Mus., Newark Mus., Walker Art Center, Mpls., U. Ariz., Pa. Acad. Art, Phila. Mus. Art, Library of Congress, Ency. Brit. collection, Abbott collection, U. Me., Los Angeles County Mus., John Herron Art Inst. Recipient Collier prize for illustration, 1920; Harmon prize, 1930; Young Israel prize, 1931, 3d prize Carnegie Inst., 1946, Gimbel collection, 1946, Artists for Victory lithograph prize, 1944, John Herron Art Inst. prize for lithography, 1944; Los Angeles County Mus. purchase award, 1945, Thomas B. Clark prize Nat. Acad. Design, 1973, purchase award Albrecht Gallery, St. Joseph, Mo., 1973. John Simon Guggenheim fellow, 1937. Mem. Inst. Arts and Letters, Soc. Am. Graphic Artists, Artists Equity Assn. Author: Portfolio of Caucasian Studies, 1950; American Folklore Lithographs, 1953; The Little Tailor, 1954; The Lost Conscience, 1955; (lithographs) Capricios, 1957; Portfolio of Twelve Etchings; (portfolio lithographs) The Shtetl, 1970. Illustrator numerous books, most recent being: The Crime of Imprisonment (George Bernard Shaw), 1945; Here Comes Daddy (Gale T. Parks), 1951; Hound Dog Moses and the Promised Land (W.D. Edwards), 1954. Contbr. to mags. Home: Great Neck Estates, N.Y. Died Jan. 6, 1977.

GROSS, BEN S., radio-TV editor, critic, author, lectr.; b. Birmingham, Ala., Nov. 24, 1891; s. Adolph and Sarah (Kaufman) G.; student Tulane U., 1911-12; LL.B., U. Ala., 1914; m. Kathleen Cotter, Dec. 31, 1921 (dec.). Reporter, feature writer Birmingham News, 1911-14; admitted to Ala. bar, 1915; practiced in Birmingham, 1915-17; mem. firm Banks, Deedmeyer & Birch; reporter Bronx (N.Y.) Home News, 1919; editor World Traveler mag., N.Y.C., 1919-20; reporter, columnist N.Y. Morning Telegraph, 1922-23; reporter, feature writer N.Y. Morning Telegraph, 1922-23, N.Y. Am., 1923; reporter-rewriteman AP, N.Y.C., 1924; reporter, labor editor, radio-TV editor and critic, N.Y. Daily News, 1925-71; news, polit. commentator Radio Sta. WMCA, N.Y.C., 1940-41; spl. commentator polit. convs., NBC, 1944; commentator Sta. WPIX-TV, N.Y.C., 1948. Served with 348th Inf., 87th Div., AEF, U.S. Army, 1918-19; France. Mem. Radio Pioneers, U. Ala. Alumni Assn., Nat. Press Club, Overseas Press Club. Author: I Looked and I Listened, 1955, 70; (with M.H. Aylesworth) Mem. Mikes and Money; (comedy) Husbands, 1927; (comedy) (with Charles Zerner) What This Town Needs, 1937; contbr. articles to popular mags., newspapers. Home: New York, N.Y. Died Aug. 13, 1979.

GROSS, JOHN H. (GROS), b. Mount Pleasant, Pa., June 7, 1884; s. William H. and Samantha E. (Hickernell) G.; Mus.B., Findlay (O.) Coll., 1903, A.B., 1906, A.M., 1912; A.B., U. of Pittsburgh, 1912; student Western Theol. Sem., Pittsburgh, 1909-11; grad. Princeton Theological Seminary, 1912, Babson Inst., Wellesley Hills, Mass., 1921; D.D., College of Emporia (Kan.), 1924; LL.D., Lincoln Univ., 1947; m. Kathryn Nichols Davis, Feb. 26, 1908; children—Virginia Tallman, John William (dec.). Teacher of history, Ft. Scott, Kan., 1907-09; ordained Presbyn. ministry, 1912; pastor Covington, O., 1912-16, Marietta, 1916-20, Ft. Scott, Kan., 1922-25; treas. and investment officer Bd. of Pensions of Presbyn. Ch. in U.S.A., 1925-36; investment counsel since 1936; pres. and dir. Geo. P. Robinson & Co., Inc., Counsellors on Investments, N.Y. City; propr., John H. Cross & Co., Investment Counselors, Phila. Overseas with Y.M.C.A., 1918-19. Trustee Lincoln Univ. (Pa.), Princeton Theol. Sem. (N.J.), Presbyterian Hosp. (Phila.), College of the Ozarks (Ark.), Blind Relief Fund of Philadelphia, Inc. Club: University (Phila.). Home: Lansdowne, Pa.

GROSS, MASON WELCH, educator, found. adminstr.; b. Hartford, Conn., June 1, 1911; s. Charles Welles and Hilda Frances (Welch) G.; student Taft Sch., 1925-29, U. Aberdeen, 1929-30; B.A., Cambridge U., 1934, M.A., 1937; Ph.D., Harvard, 1938; LL.D., Princeton, 1959, Lafayette Coll., 1960, Washington Coll., 1961, Muhlenberg Coll., 1962, Rider Coll., 1964, Seton Hall U., 1966, St. Peter's Coll., 1967, U. Fla., 1970, Rutgers U., 1971; D.Sc., Stevens Inst. Tech., 1963; L.H.D., Waynesburg Coll., 1964; m. Julia Kernan, Sept. 6, 1940; children—Ellen Clarissa (Mrs. Francis A. Miles), Katharine Wood (Mrs. Clayton H. Farnham), Charles Welles, Thomas Welch. Asst. in philosophy Harvard, 1937-38; instr. philosophy Columbia, 1938-42; asst. prof. philosophy, asst. to dean Coll. Arts and Scis., Rutgers U., 1946-47, asso. prof. philosophy, asst. dean, 1947-49, prof. philosophy, 1949-71, emeritus, 1971-77; pres. Harry Frank Guggenheim Found., 1972-77, provost, 1949-59, pres., 1959-71, emeritus, U., 1971; bd. mgrs. Howard Savs. Instn., Newark. Chmn. Nat. Book Com., 1968-71; dir. Am. Council Edn., 1966-70; N.J. chmn. United Negro Coll. Fund, 1965-74. Trustee, past pres. Middlesex Gen. Hosp.; trustee Solomon R. Guggenheim Found., Vassar Coll., N.J. Symphony Orch., Inst. Internat. Edn.; bd. regents St. Peters Coll., Jersey City. Raritan Area adminstr. N.J. Dept. Civil Def., 1950-54; Served with USAAF, 1942-45. Decorated Bronze Star. Mem. Am. Philos. Assn., Regional Plan Assn. (dir.), N.J. Council On Arts, Phi Beta Kappa. Clubs: Harvard, University, Century Assn. (N.Y.C.). Editor: (with F.S.C. Northrop) Alfred North Whitehead: An Anthology, 1953. Home: Rumson, N.J. Died Oct. 11, 1977.

GROTHAUS, JULIA (GROT'HOUS), librarian; b. San Antonio, Tex., Feb. 12, 1886; d. Fred and Caroline (Schorre) Grothaus; grad. Southwest Tex. State Tchrs. Coll., 1913; student Ill. Library Sch., 1916-17. Army library service, 1919-21; mem. staff San Antonio Public Library since 1922, asst. librarian, 1922-32, chief librarian since 1932. Mem. A.L.A., Southwestern (sec.) and Tex. (sec., pres.) library assns. Club: Bexar Library (pres.). Contbr. articles to profl. jours. Home: San Antonio, Tex. *

GROVE, ROBERT BRAGONIER, public utilities; b. Sharpsburg, Md., Apr. 9, 1886; s. Robert White and Nannie (Bragonier) G.; ed. pub. schs., Sharpsburg, and private tutors; m. Helen Olivia Ten Eyck, July 21, 1932. Teacher and asst. prin. in Md. schools, 1904-07; with the United Electric Light & Power Co., New York, 1907-35, as draftsman, 1907-14, engineering asst., 1914-19, asst. to elec. engr., 1919-20, asst. to v.p. and gen. mgr., 1920-25, asst. sec. and asst. to v.p. and gen. mgr., 1925-28, sec., 1928-31, v.p. and dir., 1931-35, exec. v.p., 1935; v.p. and dir. N.Y. Edison Co., 1932-35, exec. v.p., 1935; exec. v.p. N.Y. Edison Co., Inc., 1935-36; v.p. Consol. Edison Co. of N.Y., Inc., since 1936; v.p. Brooklyn Edison Co., Inc., and N.Y. & Queens Electric Light & Power Co., 1937-45, when merged with Consol. Edison Co. of New York, Inc.; mem. exec. com., Westchester Lighting Co. since 1935; v.p., dir. Green Mountain Lake Farms, Inc., 1936-47; dir. Westchester Lighting Co., N.Y. Steam Corp.; Consol. Telegraph & Elec. Subway Co., Yonkers Electric Light & Power Co., Edison Savings and Loan Assn. Member exec. com. Fed. Grand Jury Assn. Mem. Elec. and Gas Assn. of New York, Commerce and Industry Assn. of N.Y., Grand Jury Assn. of N.Y. County, New York Southern Soc., Museum of Natural History. Democrat. Episcopalian (vestryman). Club: Manhattan. Home: Briarcliff Manor, N.Y. *

GROVE, ROBERT ECCLES, advt. exec.; b. Pitts., Apr. 23, 1891; s. John Williamson and Eliza (Eccles) G.; B.S. in Econs., U. Pitts., 1914; m. Louise Wolfe, Dec. 17, 1925. Began as salesman, 1914; asst. to pres. Tenn. Iron & Chem. Co., Pitts., 1919-23; in advt. from 1923; chmn. bd., dir. Ketchum, MacLeod & Grove, Inc. Trustee Presbyn.-U. Hosp., Pitts. Served as 2d lt. AS, U.S. Army, 1917-18. Mem. Am. Assn. Advt. Ags. (sec., treas. 1954-55), Pitts. Advt. Club (past pres.), Sigma Alpha Epsilon, Omicron Delta Kappa. Republican. Presbyn. (elder). Clubs: Duquesne, Fox Chapel Golf (Pitts.); Rolling Rock (Ligonier, Pa.). Home: Pittsburgh, Pa. Died Mar. 31, 1976.

GROVEN, LOUIS JEAN, Belgian diplomat; b. Kerniel, Belgium, Feb. 18, 1910; s. Henri Jean and Antoinette Josephine (Notelaers) G.; M.S., U. Brussels, 1934, Ph.D., 1947; m Simone Gabrielle Radart, Dec. 13, 1937; children—Annie (Mrs. Douglas Long), Claude-Michel, Jean-Pierre. Mem. faculty U. Brussels, 1934-55, asso. prof. physics, 1954-55; sci. counselor, Washington, 1955-81. Decorated Order Crown, laureate Concours Bourses de Voyage, Belgium, 1946; UNESCO fellow, 1952. Mem. Societe Francaise de Physique, Am. Phys. Inst., Am. Nuclear Soc. Author: Emission de Rayons Pares Gaz Rarefies, 1939. Home: Chevy Chase, Md. Died Jan. 18, 1981.

GROVES, GLADYS HOAGLAND, author; b. Boston, Mass., Apr. 3, 1894; d. Rev. Napoleon Stage and Julia Ann (Comley) Hoagland; B.A., U. of N.H., 1918, L.H.D., 1953; m. Ernest R. Groves, Feb. 25, 1919; children—Ruth E., Lois M. Resident Pillsbury Settlement House, Mpls. 1918-19; associate editor monthly dept. marriage, Am. Family Mag., 1942-49. Editor, Marriage and Family Living, 1950-53; asso. editor (U.S.). Marriage Hygiene, The International Journal of Sex and Sex Problems, 1947-48. Executive director Marriage and Family Council, Inc., Chapel Hill, N.C., since 1940; Dir. Groves Conf. Marriage and the Family, since 1941. Mem. Nat. Conf. on Family Life, 1947-48. Mem. Am. Com., Internat. Cong. on Population and World Resources in Relation to the Family, from 1948. Fellow American Orthopsychiat. Assn., Am. Sociol. Soc., Am. Assn. Marriage Counselors; mem. Nat. Council on Family Relations (pres. 1955), Am. Assn. U. Women, N.C. Mental Hygiene Society, N.C. Family Life Council (exec. com., 1949-55). Planned Parenthood Fedn. Am. Inc. Author: several books latest are (with E. R. Groves and Catherine Groves) Sex Fulfillment in Marriage, 1942. Author: Marriage and Family Living, 1942. Co-author (with E. R. Groves) The Contemporary Am. Family, 1947. Home: Chapel Hill, N.C. Died July 11, 1980.

GROVES, JAMES KIRK, state justice; b. Grand Junction, Colo., Aug. 29, 1910; s. John W. and Olive Jean (Mann) G.; A.B., U. Colo., 1932, LL.B., 1935; LL.D. (hon.), William Mitchell Coll. Law, 1977; m. Verna Mable Collins, Dec. 29, 1935; children—Judith Ann (Mrs. Richard C. Woodbury), John Willis, James Richard. Admitted to Colo. bar, 1935; practiced in Grand Junction, 1935-68; dep. dist. atty., Grand Junction, 1940-44, asst. dist. atty., 1948, city atty., 1952-56; justice Colo. Supreme Ct., 1968-80. Dir. First Nat. Bank Grand Junction, 1960-65. Trustee Rocky Mountain Law Found., 1955-68, pres., 1963-64. Trustee Iliff Sch., Theology, 1965-80. Served with USNR, 1944-46. Recipient Distinguished Alumnus award Mesa Coll., 1969; William L. Knous award U. Colo., 1969. Fellow Am. Coll. Trial Lawyers; mem. Am. (ho. dels 1958-80, chmn. 1972-74), Colo. (pres. 1949-50; award merit 1959) bar assns., Grand Junction C. of C. (pres. 1940-41), Order of Coif, Sigma Nu, Phi Delta Phi. Methodist. Mason, Rotarian. Club: University (Denver). Editor-in-chief Rocky Mountain Law Rev., 1934-35; co-editor Am. Law Mining, 1960. Home: Littleton, Colo. Died Apr. 6, 1980; buried Grand Junction, Colo.

GROVES, JOHN HURST, lawyer; b. East Chicago, Ind., Oct. 4, 1908; s. Hurst Kohler and Edith S. (Johnson) G.; A.B., U. Mich., 1930, LL.B., 1933; student accounting Northwestern U. Sch. Commerce, 1934-36; m. Mary E. Sisco, Feb. 2, 1935; 1 son, Hurst Kohler II. Admitted to Ind. bar, 1932, Ill. bar, 1933; with firm Cooke, Sullivan & Ricks, Chgo., 1933-34; partner firm Lawyer & Garrett, Chgo., 1934-38, Evans & Hebel, Indpls., 1938-42, Barnes, Hickam, Pantzer & Boyd, Indpls., 1942-77. Gen. counsel Ind. Gas Co., Inc., 1948-72; counsel Indpls. Power & Light Co., 1942-74. Bd. dirs. Central Newspapers Found., Inc. Served with USNR, 1944-46. Mem. Am., Ind. (chmn. corp. law com. 1946-48), Indpls., 7th Circuit bar assns., Indpls. Com. Fgn. Relations, Ind. Soc. Chgo., Art Assn. Indpls., Sigma Phi Epsilon. Republican. Presbyn. Clubs: Columbia, Lawyers (past pres.), Woodstock Country, Traders Point Hunt (Indpls); Lawyers (Ann Arbor, Mich.). Home: Indianapolis, Ind. Died Mar. 7, 1977.

GRUBB, H. DALE, aerospace cons.; b. Henryetta, Okla., Apr. 23, 1925; s. Hiram D. and Buena Vista (Troth) G.; B.A. in Journalism, U. Okla., 1951; m. Martha Ann Ports, July 8, 1967. With U.S. Secret Service, 1951, NASA, 1959-60, Avco Corp., 1960-68; spl. asst. to Pres. Nixon, 1969-70; asst. adminstr. legislative affairs NASA Hdqrs., Washington, 1970-73; cons. Rockwell Internat., 1974; asst. dep. adminstr. VA, Washington, 1975-77; cons. to aerospace industry, 1977-81; pres. Cherokee Co. Served as pilot USAAF, World War II. Mem. U. Okla. Alumni Assn. (pres. Washington chpt. 1962), Delta Tau Delta. Clubs: Nat. Space (pres. 1965-66) (Washington); Burning Tree (Bethesda, Md.). Home: Arlington, Va. Died Apr. 6, 1981; buried Arlington Nat. Cemetery.

GRUBERT, CARL, cartoonist; b. Chgo., Sept. 10, 1911; s. Karl and Christine (Schwartz) G.; B.S., U. Wis., 1934; student Chgo. Acad. Fine Arts, 1929-30; m. Gloria Alexander, Feb. 27, 1937; children—Carleen, Carl; m. 2d, Lorraine Whitney, July 13, 1946; children—Jon, Jan, James, Jean. Creator, cartoonist The Berrys, internationally syndicated cartoon, 1942; exhibitions at the Nat. Cartoonists Soc. Exhibit, 1950, 51, Met. Mus. Art, 1951, Library of Congress, 1941. Staff artist Great Lakes Bull., Pub. Information 9th Naval Dist., 1944-45. Recipient U.S. Treasury award of Merit, 1950, Freedom's Found. Medal, 1950. Mem. Nat. Cartoonists Soc. Lion, Elk. Home: Des Plaines, Ill. Died Sept. 26, 1979; buried All Saints Cemetery.

GRUEN, VICTOR, architect; b. Vienna, Austria, July 18, 1903; s. Adolph and Elizabeth Lea (Levy) Gruenbaum; student Tech. Inst. and Acad. Fine Arts, Vienna; m. Lazette Van Houten, Sept. 28, 1951 (dec.); children (by former marriage) Michael Stephen, Margaret; m. Kemija Salihefendic, February 28, 1963. Came to U.S., 1938, naturalized 1943. Bldg. supervisor Edmund Melcher, and engr. Steiner, Vienna, 1923-32; own practice architecture, designed important residential and commercial projects, Austria, Germany, Czechoslovakia, with office at Vienna, 1932-38; archtl. practice, N.Y.C., later additional offices at Los Angeles, and Chgo., Europe; pres. Victor Gruen Planning and Architecture, Inc., Switzerland; planning and archtl. cons. to state and city govts. and pvt. orgns. in France, Belgium, Vienna, Austria, Scandinavian countries; projects for J.L. Hudson Co., (Northland, Eastland regional shopping centers; shown Nat. Gallery, Washington, as a part of A.I.A. centennial exhibit), Westland Regional Shopping Center, Dayton Company, Minneapolis (Southdale regional shopping center); city planning projects Ft. Worth, Kalamazoo, Mich., Boston; planning redevel. city Core Fresno, Cal., Paterson, N.J., Rockville Center, N.Y. Lectr. before profl. orgns., also in European countries. Formed Victor Gruen Found. for Environmental Planning, Los Angeles. Awarded So. Cal. A.I.A. award for Archtl. Merit, 1949, honor award, 1951; Av. of the Americas Assn. plaque, 1952; award of merit (Northland Shopping Center), A.I.A., 1954, planning citation, Downtown Redevel. for Greater Fort Worth, Tex. Progressive Architecture's 4th ann. design award program, 1957. Exhibited, 1952, 53 Gold Medal exhibits, Archtl. League of N.Y., VIII Pan Am Congress of Architects, Mexico City, 1952, Sokolnik Park, Moscow, 1959, Internat. Congress Foo

Distribution, Lausanne, Switzerland, 1959. Dir. Citizens' Housing and Planning Council N.Y., Inc. Registered architect in Cal., D.C., Va., Tex., N.Y., N.J., Nev., Md. Fellow A.I.A.; mem. Am. Arbitration Assn., Am. Inst. Planners, Nat. Assn. Housing and Redevel. Ofcls., Yale Arts Assn. (charter mem., exec. com.), Mich. Soc. Architects, Urban Land Inst. Clubs: Economic (Detroit); Archtl. League of N.Y. Author: How to Live with Your Architect, 1950; (with Larry Smith) Shopping Towns, U.S.A.; The Heart of Our Cities, 1964. Home: Los Angeles, Calif. Died Feb. 14, 1980.

GRUENBERG, FREDERICK PAUL, civic worker; b. Minneapolis, Minn., Nov. 19, 1884; s. John and Charlotte (Mayberg) G.; bro. Benj. C. Gruenberg; student Coll. City of N.Y., 1898-99, DeWitt Clinton High Sch., 1899-1902; B.C.S., New York U., 1911; post-grad. study U. Pa., 1916-18; m. Bertha Sanford, Dec. 29, 1909; children—Edith (Mrs. Stephen M. Harris), John, 2d. Began as bookkeeper, 1902; engaged in financial and accounting work, Wall Street, 8 yrs.; dept. head Brown Bros. & Co., Philadelphia, 3 yrs.; with Philadelphia Bur. of Municipal Research, 10 yrs. (dir. 8 yrs.); mem. Phila. Charter Revision Com., 1917-19 (sec. 1917); treas. Bankers Bond & Mortgage Co. and Bankers Securities Corp. (both Phila.), 7 yrs.; apptd. pub. service commr. of Pa. by Gov. Pinchot, 1931, for term expiring 1940 (commn. abolished by Legislature, Mar. 31, 1937); directed nation-wide study of governmental research for Social Sci. Research Council, June 1937-38; exec. sec. City Charter Com. of Phila., 1938-40; area rent dir. Phila. Defense Rental Area, Office of Price Adminstrn., 1942-44; exec. dir., treas. Samuel S. Fels Fund, 1944-59, cons.; volunteer settlement resident, Southwark House and Coll. Settlement, 1911-14; spl. lectr., Hobart Coll., Geneva, N.Y., 1917-18; mem. faculty Pa. Sch. for Social Work, 1917-24. Asst. in office of chmn. U.S. Shipping Bd., Washington, latter part of World War I. Former trustee Nat. Farm School, Doylestown, Pa. Dir. Phila. Housing Assn., Crime Prevention Assn. of Phila.; past dir. Pa. Public Edn. Assn.; past mem. adv. bd. Inst. Local and State Govt., U. Pa. Recipient Samuel S. Fels award for civic and social service, 1966. Mem. Am. Polit. Sci. Assn. (mem. council 1921-24), Am. Acad. Polit. and Social Sci., Nat. Municipal League, Governmental Research Assn. (chmn. 2 terms, pres. 1921-24, established Frederick P. Gruenberg award 1975). Mem. Am. Soc. for Pub. Adminstrn.; mem. Pa. Polit. Sci. and Pub. Adminstrn. Assn., Philadelphia Com. on Pub. Affairs, Lambda Sigma Phi, Phi Alpha Sigma. Ind. Republican. Mem. Ethical Soc. Clubs: Constitutional (Phila.), The Franklin Inn. Home: Philadelphia, Pa. Died Feb. 16, 1976. Cremated.

GRUENE, HANS FRIEDRICH, research engr.; b. Braunschweig, Germany, May 24, 1910; s. Eduard Hugo Hans and Anna Alwine (Bertram) G.; Dipl. Ing., Tech. Hochschule Braunschweig, 1935; Dr.-Ing., 1941; m. Edith Geier, Dec. 23, 1937; children—Karin, Peter. Came to U.S., 1945, naturalized, 1954. Research engr. AEG and Siemens Schuckertwerke A.G., 1935-43, Rocket Research Center, Peenemünde, 1943-45; rocket research engr. for U.S. Army, Ft. Bliss, Tex., Huntsville, Ala., 1945-61; engaged in launch vehicle devel. NASA 1961-63; dir. launch vehicle operations Marshall Space Flight Center, Launch Operations Center, Cape Kennedy, Fla., 1963-64; dir. launch vehicle operations John F. Kennedy Space Center, Cocoa Beach, Fla., 1964-74. Asso. fellow Am. Inst. Aeros. and Astronautics. Contbr. to Handbook of Astronautical Engineering. Home: Cocoa Beach, Fla. Died Oct. 22, 1979.

GRUENTHER, HOMER H., travel agy. exec., govt. ofcl.; b. Platte Center, Nebr., May 23, 1900; s. Christian M. and Mamie (Shea) G.; student Christian Bros. Sch., St. Joseph, Mo., St. Thomas Coll., St. Paul, Creighton U., Omaha, 1919-21; m. Elizabeth Mahoney, Aug. 14, 1926 (dec.). Entered newspaper work as sports editor Omaha Daily News; sec. Nebr. State Seante, 1933; became sec. to Congressman (later Senator) Edward R. Burke, Washington, 1933; adminstrv. asst. to Sec. of Commerce, 1941; sec. to Senator Kenneth Wherry, 1946-51, then to successor Senator Fred Seaton, 1951-52; spl. aide to Gen. Eisenhower, 1952; spl. asst. to Presidents Eisenhower, Kennedy and Johnson, 1953-65; pres. Gruenther Travel Agy., Washington, from 1966. Co-author Burke-Wadsworth Bill for creation SSS, 1940; writer Wherry Bill for creation SSS, 1940; writer Wherry Mil. Housing Bill authorizing pvt. constrn. multiple housing projects on Army bases, St. Lawrence Seaway and Colorado River projects. Home: Washington, D.C. Deceased.

GRUSSING, BON DIRCK, advt. exec.; b. Chippewa County, Minn., Jan. 27, 1904; s. Dirck and Jennie (Bontjes) G.; A.B., Carleton Coll., 1927; postgrad. Mpls. Coll. Law, 1930-32, U. Minn., 1963-66; m. Phyllis Larson, Apr. 16, 1932 (dec. 1934); 1 child, Bon Dirck; m. Evelyn Florence Pearson, July 18, 1936; children—Theodore, Bruce Douglas; 1 son by previous marriage, Bon Dirck. Sales mgr. Northfield (Minn.) Iron Co., 1928; real estate loan appraiser, 1928-29; publicity mgr. Redpath Chautauqua Soc., 1929; salesman Procter & Gamble Co., Mpls., 1929-30, Shaw-Walker, Chgo., also Mpls., 1931-35; copywriter, dir. pub. relations, advt. and sales promotion mgr. Minneapolos-Moline Co., Mpls., 1935-56, dir. merchandising, 1956; v.p., dir. merchandising Brown & Bigelow, 1956-57; v.p., dir. sales Louis F. Dow Co., 1957-67; nat. account exec. Osborne-Kemper-Thomas, 1967-68; dist. mgr. Shaw-Barton, 1968-69; dir. Grussing & Assos., Inc., Costa Mesa, Calif., 1968-77. Rep. candidate 7th Congl. Dist. Minn., 1928. Bd. dirs. Villa Pacific Community Assn. Recipient George Washington Medal of Honor, Freedoms Found; Izak Walton League award. Mem. Soil Conservation Soc. Am., Advt. Fedn. Am., Army Ordnance Assn. Republican. Lutheran. Mason (32, Shriner). Clubs: Athletic (Mpls.). Author: From Adam to Atom, 1947. Contbr. articles to trade papers. Writer, producer, dir. many travelogs, conservation and ecology movies. Home: Huntington Beach, Calif. Died Apr. 18, 1977.

GRYZMISH, REUBEN BERTRAM, hotel exec.; b. Boston, 1885; grad. Harvard Coll., 1906. Chmn., pres., treas. Alles & Fisher, Inc., Boston; vice chmn. Hotel Corp. of Am.; pres., dir. Hubb Amusement Co.; treas., dir. Hotel Somerset, Boston, Hotel Puritan, Boston, Hotel Samoset, Rockland, Me., Edgewater Beach Hotel, Chgo., Whitehall Beach Hotel, Palm Beach, Fla.; dir. Biscayne Fronton Co. Trustee Beth Israel Hosp., Brandeis U. Home: Brookline, Mass. *

GUBBELS, JACOBUS LEONARDUS, landscape architect; b. Groningen, Holland, July 31, 1896; s. Johanes Jacobus and Fenna (Grosman) G.; ed. Sch. of Botany and Art, Groningen, Holland, 1912-14, Kunst and Gewerbe Schule, Bielfeld, Germany, 1914-16; m. Margarete Neumann, June 16, 1923. Came to U.S., 1923, naturalized, 1934. Horticultural adviser, Sumatra, Dutch East Indies, 1917-22; designer of City of Bielfeld, Germany, 1922-23; with S. R. DeBoer, landscape architect, Denver, Colo., 1923-27; cons. landscape architect, Houston and Austin, Tex., 1927-33; dir. roadside development for Tex. Highway Dept., 1933-47; pvt. practice from 1947, planner Padre Island in Gulf of Mexico. Dir. urban planning, Texas Highway Dept. from Jan. 1, 1943; prin. Jac. L. Gubbels & Assos., Cons., Austin, from 1952. Pres. Bus. Property Analysis Service; agt. for imports of Dutch bldg. materials from Netherlands. Mem. Environ. Resources Bd., City of Austin, 1972-75; adv. Inst. Advanced Environ. Studies. Mem. Am. Soc. Planning Ofcls., Tex. (central chpt.) Soc. Architects. Club: Rotary (Austin, Tex.). Author: American Highways and Roadsides, 1938; Illustrated Studies Controlled Access Highways, 1946; School Sites for Austin—a 20-year Plan, 1947; and other books, also a series of booklets on roadside development, and articles. Home: Austin, Tex. Died Oct. 14, 1976.

GUBOW, LAWRENCE, U.S. dist. judge; b. Detroit, Jan. 10, 1919; s. Jacob and Dora (Rubin) G.; A.B., U. Mich., 1940, LL.B., 1950, hon. certificate real estate, 1958, hon. certificate in building; m. Estelle Schmalberg, June 27, 1948; children—David Mark, Mona Joy, Janey Ann. Admitted to Mich. bar, 1951; practicing atty., 1951-53; dir. investigations Mich. Corp. and Securities, 1953, dep. commr., 1953-56, commr., 1956-61; U.S. atty. Eastern Dist. Mich., 1961-68; U.S. dist. judge Eastern Dist. Mich., from 1968. Chmn. investment companies com. N. Am. Securities Adminstrn., 1958-61; mem. Gov. Mich. Com. Study Housing Law for State, 1959-60, Gov. Mich. Com. Study Tax Procedures for State, 1959-60, Gov. Mich. Task Force Studying Govt. Reorgn. Field Vets. Affairs, 1959-60, Gov. Mich. Task Force Studying Govt. Reorgn. Field Tax Procedures and Collections, 1959-60. Pres. Jewish War Vets. Meml. Home Assn., 1960-62; gen. chmn. Jewish War Vets. Nat. Conv., 1962; judge advocate Allied Vets. Council Wayne County, 1956-58, legal adviser, 1962-78, chmn. legislative council, 1956-59; treas. Jewish Community Council Met. Detroit, 1959-62, v.p., 1962-68, pres., 1968-71; bd. govs., mem. exec. com. Jewish Welfare Fedn., 1968-78, chmn. community relations div., 1972-78; mem. exec. com. Nat. Community Relations Adv. Council, 1969-76; chmn. 17th Dist. Young Democratic Club, 1953-55, Dem. Housing Com. Mich., 1958-61. Bd. dirs. Jewish Nat. Fund, Detroit Service Group. Served to capt., Inf., AUS, 1941-48. Named Wayne County Vet. of Year, 1958, Mich. Vet. of Year, 1959; recipient Civic award Eastern Mich. Realty Assn., 1959, Distinguished Service award Detroit Real Estate Brokers Assn., 1961; Outstanding Federal Adminstrator award, 1967; Man of the Year award Jewish War Veterans, 1967; Distinguished Service award Yeshiva Univ., 1969; Bicentennial Man-of-Yr. award Men's Club, Congregation Shaarey Dedek, 1976. Mem. Am., Fed., Mich., Detroit bar assns., Am. Judicature Soc., Nat. Assn. Licensed Law Ofcls., Jewish War Vets. U.S.A. (bronze medal award 1960, 69; comdr. Mich. 1956-57, nat. exec. com. 1956-76, gold medal of merit 1976), Am. Legion (judge Univ. Mich. 1960-61), 106th Inf. Div. Assn. (pres. 1956-57), AMVETS, V.F.W., D.A.V., Disabled Officers Assn., Ret. Officers Assn., Real Estate Alumni Mich. (hon.), Fed. Bus. Assn. (treas.), Fed. Exec. Assn. (v.p. 1966-67), U. Mich. Alumni Assn. Detroit (bd. govs. from 1969). Home: Bloomfield Hills, Mich. Died Mar. 26, 1978.

GUENTHER, CARL FREDERIC, architect; b. Cleve., Apr. 8, 1909; s. Herman Richard and Marie Sophia (Brandt) G.; B.Arch., Western Res. U., 1930; diploma architecture Fontainebleau (France) Sch. Fine Arts, 1930; certificate Beaux Arts Inst. Design, N.Y.C., 1931; spl. student (24th Paris prize in architecture), Ecole des Beaux Arts, Paris, 1931-34; m. Marie Anne Davis, June 29, 1936 (div. Feb. 1952); children—Ann Christine (Mrs. Michael R. Stadler), Florence Anne (Mrs. Thomas J. Connole); m. 2d, Laverne Jane Bell, Oct. 10, 1952. Designer, Walter R. MacCornack, Architect, Cleve., 1934-35; chief design, asso. architect, Great Lakes Exposition, 1935-37; pvt. practice, Cleve., 1937-39; partner Miller & Guenther, Cleve. 1939-42; sr. project planner region V, Fed. Pub. Housing Authority, 1942-44; asso. and chief designer Maier-Outcalt-Dickerson & Assos., Cleve., 1944-45; partner firm Outcalt, Guenther and Assos., Cleve., 1945-60, Outcalt, Guenther and Van Buren, architects, Cleve. 1960-62, Outcalt-Guenther Partners, Cleve., 1962-68, ret.; critic, lectr. archtl. design Western Res. U., 1934-41. Author programs, mem. juries Beaux Arts Inst. Design, 1934-78; mem. Architects Educators Conf., 1953, 54. Adv. com. to reorganize Sch. Architecture, Western Res. U., 1950-51, trustee univ., 1951-56, gov., 1957-68; mem. Collier County (Fla.) Sch. Bd., 1976-78. Bd. dirs. Naples Civic Assn., 1972-76. Recipient two individual awards U.S. Post Office competition, 1938; first award for suburban location of office bldg., 1956; Flat Glass award Pitts. Plate Glass Co., 1957. Fellow AIA (com. nat. honor awards 1956-57; past pres. Cleve.); mem. Fla. Assn. AIA, Nat. Inst. Archtl. Edn., Fontainebleau Alumni Assn. Clubs: Pontiac Game (Sheenboro, Que., Can.); Royal Poinciana Golf (Naples, Fla.). Author articles. Home: Naples, Fla. Died July 3, 1978.

GUERRA, EMILIO LOUIS, educator; b. Hoboken, N.J., Aug. 27, 1909; s. Francesco and Maria (Parano) G.; A.B., Coll. City N.Y., 1931, M.S. in Edn., 1933; Ph.D., N.Y. U., 1942; m. Alice Hendler, Dec. 12, 1931; 1 son, Robert. Tchr. Spanish, Italian and French, N.Y.C. high schs., 1932-39, community coordinator Benjamin Franklin High Sch., N.Y.C., 1939-43; chmn. dept. fgn. langs., 1943-57; supr. teaching English as a 2d lang. high sch. div. N.Y.C. pub. schs., 1957-63, acting . dir. fgn. lang., 1963-65; prof., head div. fgn. langs. and internat. edn. N.Y. U., 1965-74, prof. emeritus, 1974-80; instr. gen. lang. Adelphi U., 1955-59; adj. asso. prof. Romance langs. N.Y. U., 1957-65; Smith-Mundt lectr. U. Central del Ecuador, 1956, 57, U. de Guayaquil (Ecuador), 1957; Fulbright lectr. U. Nat. de Buenos Aires, 1958; lectr. applied linguistics NDEA Inst., Ohio State U., 1962; lectr. Inst. Guatemalteco Americano, 1956, 57. Named cavaliere dell' ordine Al Merito Della Repubblica Italiana, 1967. Mem. Am. Assn. Tchrs. Spanish and Portuguese (pres. N.Y. chpt. 1938), AAUP, Am. Assn. Tchrs. French, Am. Assn. Tchrs. Italian, N.E.A., Internat. Linguistic Assn., Am. Assn. Sch. Adminstrs., Modern Lang. Assn., N.Y. State Fedn. Fgn. Lang. Tchrs., Am-Council Tchrs. Fgn. Lang., Assn. Supervision and Curriculum Devel., Am. Soc. Italian Legion of Merit, Phi Delta Kappa, Sigma Delta Pi. Author: Getting to Know Spain and Latin America, 1957; A First Course in Spanish, 1961; A Second Course in Spanish, 1965. Home: Richmond Hill, N.Y. Died Mar. 18, 1980.

GUERRE, LOUIS FRANCIS, army officer; b. La., July 29, 1884. Enlisted as private, La. Nat. Guard, Sept. 1907, and advanced to capt., 1913; commd. major on induction into Fed. service for Mexican border troubles, 1916; served as major, Inf., World War I; again major, La. Nat. Guard, 1919, and advanced to brig. gen., 1929; comd. 31st Div. La. Nat. Guard, 1936-40; active duty U.S. Army since 1940; became provost marshal, 8th Corps Area, Jan. 1942. Assigned commanding general A.S.F.T.C. Camp Claiborne, La. Aug. 1944. Address: Camp Claiborne, La.*

GUGGENHEIM, PEGGY, art collector and patron; b. N.Y.C., Aug. 26, 1898; d. Benjamin and Florette (Seligman) Guggenheim; m. Laurence Vail, Mar. 15, 1923; children—Sindbad, Pegeen (Mrs. Rumney); m. 2d, Max Ernst, Dec. 30, 1941. Directed, financed gallery Guggenheim Jeune, London, Eng., 1938-39, Art of This Century, N.Y.C., 1943-47, Mus. Palazzo Venier dei Leoni, Venice, Italy, 1951-79; exhbns. of pvt. collection throughout Europe, 1951-79. Named hon. citizen of Venice, 1962. Author: Out of This Century, 1946, 68, 79, 80; Una Collezionista Ricorda, 1956; Confessions of An Art Addict, 1960; also articles, introductions. Address: Venice, Italy. Died Dec. 23, 1979; buried Garden of Palazzo Venier dei Leoni, Venice.

GUICE, HARVEY HUNTER, educator; b. Campbell, Tex., Mar. 24, 1885; s. James Beriah and Elizabeth Canzada (Marshall) G.; B.A., East Tex. State Teachers Coll., 1903; Ph.B., U. of Chicago, 1916, J.D., 1918; m. Edna Hamilton, Sept. 5, 1922; children—Harvey Hamilton, Edward Farr. Teacher in rural schs., Tex., 1903-04; prin. ward sch., Ennis, Tex., 1905-08; teacher of English, high sch., Wichita Falls, Tex., 1907-10; prin. high sch., Anson, 1910-11, Stamford, 1911-14; supt. schs., Stamford, 1914-16; practiced law, Dallas, 1919-24; teacher Bryan St. High Sch., Dallas, 1919-21; asst. prof. business law, Southern Methodist U.,

1921-24, asso. prof. polit. science, 1924-25, dir. Arnold Sch. of Govt., 1925-33, prof. economics, 1933-34, pub. adminstrn. since 1934. Attended F.A. Training Camp, Camp Zachary Taylor, 1918. Mem. Am. Polit. Science Assn., Southwestern Social Science Assn., Delta Chi, Pi Sigma Alpha. Democrat. Methodist. Mason. Home: Dallas, Tex. *

GUIJARRO, LUIS G., economist, Spanish diplomat; b. Valencia, Spain, Sept. 9, 1883; s. Luis G. and Josefa Guijarro Andreu; M.A., Univ. of Valencia, 1902; M.L., Univ. of Madrid, 1904; Ph.D., J.D., Sorbonne, Paris, 1907; student Ecole des Sciences Politiques, Paris, 1907-08, Yale, 1909-10; m. Anita Ramos, Sept. 30, 1946. Asso. prof. arts, Univ. Central, Madrid, 1908-16; lecturer, U. of Toulouse (France), 1911-12; entered Spanish diplomatic service, 1916; vice consul, Hamburg (Germany), 1916-17; consul, Newcastle on Tyne, Eng., 1920-23; fgn. office, Madrid, 1924-28; minister plenipotentiary, Prague, 1935-36; minister, Commercial counselor, Spanish Embassy, Washington, since 1943. Rep. from Valencia to Spanish Parliament, 1916-23, 1932-36; mem. Spanish Nat. Assembly, 1928-30; commr. of customs, 1930-31. Mem. Acad. Fine Arts San Carlos, Valencia, 1925; hon. mem. Centrol Cultura Valenciana; mem. of C.E.D.A. (Confederation of Spanish Right Parties). Roman Catholic. Author: El Socialismo Catholico, 1909, Origen de la Sociedad Humana, 1909, Las Fuerzas Sociales de America, 1913, Notas Americanas, 1913, Agustin Sales, Estudio bio-bibliografico, 1910, El Guerrillero Romeu, 1908, El Sentido de la Historia en Roma, 1915, Bases del Derecho Inmobiliario en Legislacion Comparada, 1916, La Valoracion de Mercancias en el Comercio Exterior, 1924, La Agricultura de Exportacion Expañola y su importancia en el Comercio Exterior, 1925, Informe para las negociaciones de un Tratado de Comercio con Cuba, 1926, Efectos de las bajas temperaturas en las Plantas y Frutos de Agrios, 1927, Problema Arrecero en España, 1927, Relaciones comerciales Hispano-Britanicas, 1927, Relaciones comerciales Hispano-Alemanas, 1929. Contbr. to Yale Review, 1909, Am. Review of Reviews, 1909. Home: (U.S.) Washington, D.C.; (Spain), Valencia, Spain. *

GUILD, HENRY RICE, lawyer; b. Boston, Feb. 14, 1896; s. Samuel Eliot and Jessie (Motley) G.; student Noble and Greenough Sch., Dedham, Mass., 1902-13; A.B., Harvard, 1917, LL.B., 1922; m. Martha Pintard Bayard, Oct. 1, 1927 (dec. Dec. 1970); children—Henry R., Sheila, Bayard. Partner law firm Herrick, Smith, Donald, Farley & Ketchum (now Herrick & Smith), Boston, 1928-75; of counsel, 1975-80; mem. exec. com., dir. Boston Edison Co., 1942-73; trustee Pub. Reservations, Century Shares trust; dir. Tampa Electric Co.; dir., mem. exec. com. Fiduciary Trust Co., 1940-73. Served as ensign and lt. (j.g.), chief g.m., USN, World War I. Vice pres., trustee Mass. Gen. Hosp.; gen. chmn. Greater Boston Community Fund Campaign, 1941, chmn. exec. com., 1944-46; pres. Greater Boston Community Council Social Agys., 1942-44; chmn. adv. council Mass. Dept. Pub. Welfare, 1945-46. Mem. Boston Bar Assn. (council), Mass. Bar Assn. Republican. Unitarian. Clubs: Boston Harvard; Longwood Cricket (pres. 1932-35); New England Lawn Tennis Assn. (pres. 1936-37); Commercial of Boston; Tavern; Dedham Country and Polo; Country (Brookline, Mass.). Home: Needham, Mass. Died May 3, 1980.

GUILDS, JOHN CALDWELL (GILDS), coll. pres.; b. Cordesville, S.C., Mar. 12, 1886; s. John Calhoun and Ada (Anderson) G.; B.A., Wofford Coll., Spartanburg, S.C., 1906, Litt.D., 1922; M.A., Vanderbilt U., 1910; m. Lucille Folk, Dec. 28, 1910; children—Mildred Anderson (Mrs. Vernon Peele), John Caldwell. Instr. Carlisle Sch., Bamburg, 1906-09, head master, 1910-20; pres. Columbia Coll. since 1920. Chmn. Council of Defense, Bamberg County, S.C., World War, also in loan drives and war savings work. Trustee Carlisle Sch. Mem. Southern Assn. Colleges for Women (pres. 1932-33), Pi Kappa Alpha. Democrat. Mem. Meth. Church; mem. Gen. Conf., 1930, 34, 40; mem. Gen. Bd. of Lay Activities, Meth. Ch. (sec. since 1942); Mem. Fed. Council of Chs. of Christ in America. Past Grand Chancellor Grand Domain of S.C. of K.P. Kiwanian. Home: Columbia,S.C.*

GUILER, WALTER SCRIBNER (GIL'ER), prof. education; b. Seven Mile, O., Sept. 10, 1882; s. George and Mary (Fisher) G.; B.A., Miami U., 1909; M.A., Columbia, 1912; Ph.D., U. of Chicago, 1923; m. Lorena Marco Thetford, Nov. 2, 1922; children—Miriam, Ruth, Dickinson. Supervising prin. pub. schs., Covington, Ky., 1909-14; dist. supervisor, Butler County, O., 1914-16; asso. prof. edn., Sch. of Edn., Miami Univ., 1916-18, prof., 1918-26, prof. edn. and dir. of remedial instrn. since 1926. Member American Educational Research Assn., Nat. Conf. on Research in Elementary School English, Ohio State Teachers' Assn., Southwestern Ohio Teachers' Assn., Western Ohio Supts'. Round Table, Delta Kappa Pi, Phi Beta Kappa. Author textbooks, 1924-39. Co author since 1931, latest: Getting the Meaning, 1939; Selected References on Spelling, 1942-53; Reading for Meaning, 1945; also series of Diagnostic Tests and Individualized Remedial Workbooks in Computational Arithmetic. Contbr. articles in ednl. journals. Home: Oxford, O. *

GUINN, DICK HENRY, cons., univ. adminstr. and naval officer; b. Palestine, Tex., Mar. 27, 1918; s. Jack Simpson and Ruby Aurelia (Johnson) G.; student U. Tex. at El Paso, 1934-36; B.S., U.S. Naval Acad., 1941; postgrad. Nat. War Coll., 1959-60; m. Muriel Parker, July 25, 1942; children—Daryl Hale Guinn Wilson, Charisa Jaqueline Claire Guinn Shay. Commd. ensign USN, 1941, advanced through grades to vice adm., 1970; comdg. officer Fighter Squadron Two Able, 1947-48; staff operations officer, exec. officer Field Command, Armed Forces spl. weapons project, 1949-52; exec., comdg. officer Night Fighter Squadron 3, 1952-54; operational requirements officer Office Chief Naval Operations, 1954-56; comdg. officer Carrier Air Group Six, 1956-57; weapons readiness officer staff comdr. Naval Air Force, Atlantic Fleet, 1957-58; officer detailer Bur. Naval Personnel, 1958-59; operations officer 7th Fleet Staff, 1960-61; comdg. officer U.S.S. Rigel, 1962-63, U.S.S. Forrestal, 1963-64; aviation capts. detailer Bur. Naval Personnel, 1964; program appraisal Office Sec. Navy, 1964-65; comdr. Carrier Div. Four, 1965-67; chief Naval Air Basic Tng., Naval Air Sta., Pensacola, Fla., 1967-69; dep. chief Naval Personnel, Washington, 1969-70, chief Naval Personnel, 1970-72; dep. Cinclant/Cinclant Fleet, Norfolk, Va., 1972-73; ret.; v.p. for univ. relations U. West Fla., Pensacola, 1973-75. Bd. dirs. Council for Aging, Pensacola Heritage Found. Decorated Navy Cross, D.S.M., Legion of Merit, Air medal with gold star. Mem. Order of Daedalians. Home: Pensacola, Fla. Died Aug. 26, 1980.

GUION, CONNIE M. (GION), physician; b. Lincolnton, N.C., Aug. 29, 1882; d. Benajmin Simmons and Catherine (Caldwell) Guion; student Kate Ship Sch., Lincolnton, Northfield (Mass.) Sem.; A.B., Wellesley Coll., 1906, D.Sc. (hon.), 1950; A.M., Cornell, 1913, M.D., 1917, D.Sc. (hon.), Women's Medical Coll. of Pa., 1953; D.Sc. (honorary), Queen's College, Charlotte, N.C., 1957; Doctor of Laws, Univ. of North Carolina, 1965. Successively instr. of chemistry, Vassar Coll., prof. of chemistry and head dept., Sweet Briar (Va.) Coll., asst. attdg. physician, Bellevue Hosp., Cornell U. div. and N.Y. Infirmary for Women and Children; chief med. clinic, Cornell U. Med. Coll., 1929-32; clinic became part of New York Hosp., 1932, and since served as chief med. clinic; asst. prof. medicine, Cornell U. Med. Coll., 1929-36, asso. prof., 1936-46, prof. of clinical medicine, 1946-52, professor of clinical medicine emeritus, 1952—; asst. attending physician, N.Y. Hosp., 1932-42, asso. attending physician, 1942-43, attending physician, 1943-50, now cons.; pvt. practice med., N.Y.C. specialist in internal medicine. Recipient Elizabeth Blackwell citation, N.Y. Infirmary for Women and Children, Jan. 1949. Mem. bd. dir., 1956, Sweet Briar Coll. Served as mem. indsl. council, Dept. of Labor of State of N.Y. Formerly chmn. Med. Appeals Unit. Mem. adv. com., Nat. Health and Safety Council of Girl Scouts. Recipient, Award of Distinction, Cornell U. Medical College, 1951, Northfield Award for distinguished service, 1951, Jane Addams medal for distinguished service Rockford Coll., 1963. Diplomate American Bd. Internal Medicine. Member New York Academy of Medicine, New York State Medical Assn., Med. Women's Assn., Shakespeare Soc., Phi Beta Kappa, Sigma Xi, Alpha Omega Alpha. Club: Wellesley (N.Y. City), Cosmopolitan. Contbr. numerous papers on med. subjects. *

GUISE, CARL CONRAD, dean junior coll.; b. Minersville, O., Apr. 30, 1884; s. Charles and Sarah Saphronia (Gilmore) G.; A.B., Campbell Coll., Holton, Kan., 1911; A.M., U. of Kan., 1914; grad. study, U. of Chicago, 1916, 18, 29, 30; m. Frances Dighton Rowland, of Savannah, Ga., Dec. 21, 1918; children—Katherine, Edna Frances. Supt. schs. Havensville, Kan., 1911-13; asst. prof. philosophy, Park Coll., Parkville, Mo., 1914-16; prof. philosophy and edn., Piedmont Coll., Demorest, Ga., 1916-19; pres. State Bank of Oneida (Kan.), 1919-20; prof. edn., Tarkio (Mo.) Coll., 1920-21; prof. philosophy, Parsons Coll., Fairfield, Ia., 1921-32, dean, 1923-32; dean Itasca Junior Coll. since 1932. Mem. Phi Kappa Phi. Democrat. Presbyn. Home: Coleraine, Minn.*

GULICK, ADDISON, biochemist; b. Osaka, Japan, Apr. 2, 1882; s. John Thomas and Frances Amelia (Stevens) G.; came to U.S., 1898, derivative citizenship; A.B., Oberlin (O) Coll., 1904; A.M., Harvard, 1905; student Strassburg (Alsace) Univ., 1906-08; Ph.D. summa cum laude, Wuerzburg (Germany) U., 1910; m. Margaret Buckingham, Mar. 29, 1916; children—Mary Buckingham, Anne Darracott. Fellow in biochemistry, Toronto U., 1910-11; instr. physiology, U. of Minn., 1911-12, U. of Mo., 1912-13, asst. prof., 1913-18, asso. prof., 1918-21, prof. physiol. chem. Univ. Mo. Med. Sch. since 1921, chmn. biochem. dept. since 1931. Mem. A.A.A.S., Mo. Acad. Sci., Am. Chem. Soc. Am. Zoölogists, Am. Physiol. Soc., Soc. Study Internal Secretions, Am. Soc. Naturalists, Am. Inst. Nutrition, Sigma Xi. Club: Appalachian Mountain. Author: Biography of John Thomas Gulick, 1932. Contbr. articles on biochemistry of cell nuclei, carbohydrate luxus consumption, basal metabolism and temperature regulation, chem. genetics, aspects of biol. evolution, paleontol. of Bermuda, in numerous professional jours. Home: Columbia, Mo. *

GULICK, J(OHN) HALSEY, camp dir.; b. Springfield, Mass., Dec. 27, 1899; s. Luther Halsey and Charlotte (Vetter) G.; ed. Phillips Exeter Acad., 1916-18, Princeton, 1919-22; L.H.D., Springfield (Mass.) College, 1952; married Dorothy Merrill, June 21, 1931; children—Katherine Merrill, Charlotte Vetter, Louise. Director Camp Timanous since 1923; director Luther Gulick Camps since 1928; asstant in physical education, Lehigh University, 1924-27, Princeton University, 1927-28; organizer Curtiss-Wright Flying Camp for coll. under-grads. at Scarboro, Me., 1928-29; teacher The Fessenden Sch., West Newton, Mass., 1931-33; teacher The Mary C. Wheeler School, Providence, R.I., 1933-34; headmaster Proctor Acad., Andover, N.H., 1935-52. Served as private inf., U.S. Army, 1918. Trustee, Stoneleigh-Prospect. Sch., Greenfield, Mass., Waynflete Sch., Portland, Maine; trustee, past pres. The Nathaniel Hawthorne Assn., South Casco. Mem. Newcomen Soc., N.E. Assn. of Camp Dirs. (past pres.), Mason. Club: Princeton (N.Y.C.). Home: South Casco, Maine. Died Sept. 16, 1980.

GULICK, MERLE AMERSON, life ins. exec., cons.; b. Jackson, Mich., 1906; s. Frank M. and Maud Mae (Dickes) G.; grad. Hobart Coll., 1930; LL.D., Hobart and William Smith Colls., 1966; m. Edna Zeller, Apr. 28, 1934 (dec. April 1960); 1 son, Peter L.; m. 2d, Helen Manzo Hindmarsh, Nov. 1, 1962. Asso. with Equitable Life Assurance Soc., N.Y.C., from 1930, successively service supr. group dept., mgr. Phila. group office, mgr. N.Y. Group dept., exec. asst. to pres., gen. mgr. group dept., 2d v.p., 1930-52, v.p., 1952-60, v.p. pub. relations-personnel, 1960-68, v.p. corporate affairs, after 1968, later cons. Exec. vice chmn. Greater N.Y. Fund, 1939; chmn. greater N.Y. men's com. United Negro Coll. Fund, Inc., 1953, mem. steering com., 1953-55; chmn. greater N.Y.C. com. Nat. Fund Med. Edn.; mem. exec. com. Com. on Alcoholism, Community Council Greater N.Y., mem. Manhattan Council on Alcoholism; co-chmn. labor mgmt. com. on alcoholism, 1967-70. Trustee Hobart and William Smith Coll. 1950-68, chmn. bd., 1957-68, now hon. trustee; bd. dirs. N.Y.C. Cancer Com.; chmn. exec. com. N.Y.C. div. Am. Cancer Soc.; bd. dirs. Nat. Football Found. and Hall of Fame Inc., Nat. Assn. Prevention Blindness, West Side Assn. Commerce; trustee Morehouse Coll.; bd. advisers Internat. U. Communications mem. council execs. on co. contbns. Nat. Indsl. Conf. Bd. Served with USCGR, 1942-46; chief port security div.; capt. Res. Decorated Legion of Merit; recipient Marts and Lundy medal, 1965; named to Football Hall of Fame, 1965. Mem. Ins. Soc. N.Y., N.Y. C. of C. (chmn. ins. com., mem. exec. com., 1966-68), Nat. Council Alcoholism (pres. 1963-65), Pub. Relations Soc. Am., Newcomen Soc. N.Am., Coast Guard League (founder), Holland Soc. N.Y. S.A.R., Kappa Alpha (nat. pres. 1951). Clubs: Overseas Press; Hobart (N.Y.C.). Home: New York, N.Y. Died Aug. 30, 1976.

GULLIVER, WILLIAM HENRY, lawyer; b. Portland, Me., Feb. 9, 1904; s. William Henry and Agnes Margaret (Gilroy) G.; A.B., Bowdoin Coll., 1925; LL.B., Harvard, 1928; m. Catherine P. McGahan, Sept. 3, 1939 (dec. Jan. 1964); children—William, Ann Derby (Mrs. David G. Hanes), Catherine James; m. 2d, Elin A. Tulloch, Dec. 29, 1965. Admitted to Mass. bar, 1928, thereafter practiced in Boston; partner firm Powers and Hall and predecessor firms, 1950-76. Dir. Reece Corp., Torrington Mfg. Co., Workingsmens Coop. Bank, Raymond Engring., Inc., Marriner & Co., Inc., Dolan Steel Co., Inc. Chmn. Wellesley (Mass.) Adv. Com., 1947-50; chmn. Port of Boston Commn., 1953-57. Treas., dir. Frances E. Willard Homes, Boston, 1945-70, pres., 1965-70; bd. overseers Bowdoin Coll., 1965-76. Mem. Am., Mass., Boston bar assns., Clubs: Harvard, Algonquin (Boston). Home: Boston, Mass. Died Mar. 20, 1976; buried Wellesley, Mass.

GULLIXSON, THADDEUS FRANK (GUL'LIKS-SUN), ch. official; b. Bode, Ia., Sept. 4, 1882; s. Andrew and Anna (Rossing) G.; prep. edn., Brufiat Acad., Portland N.D., and Luther Acad., Albert Lea, Minn.; A.B., Luther Coll., Decorah, Ia., 1903; grad. Luther Sem., St. Paul, Minn., 1906; student Johns Hopkins, 1906-07; m. Bessie A. Fries, Oct. 21, 1908; children—Lillian Cecelia, Solveig Magdalene, Thomas Fredrick (dec.), Bessie Frieda, Mary Frances. Ordained ministry Luth. Ch., 1907; pastor, Pierre, S.D., 1907-11, Minot, N.D., 1911-30; pres. and prof. practical theology, Luther Theol. Sem., St. Paul, 1930-55. Vice pres. The Evangelical Lutheran Church, 1925-48; mem. Bd. Foreign Missions, 1920-30; pres. Am. Luth. Conf., 1934-38; councillor Nat. Luth. Council, 1943-55; del. Luth. World Conv., Sweden, 1947, Germany, 1952. Chmn. Minn. Commn. on Resettlement of Displaced Persons, 1949-53; mem. President's Commn. on Immigration and Naturalization, 1952. Home: St. Paul.

GUMMERE, RICHARD MOTT (GUM'ER-E), curator; b. Burlington, N.J., Aug. 3, 1883; s. Francis Barton and Amelia Smith (Mott) G.; prep. edn.

Haverford (Pa.) Sch., Marlburia Sch., Switzerland; A.B., Haverford Coll., 1902; A.M., Harvard, 1904; Ph.D., from same, 1907; hon. M.A., Univ. of Pa., 1923; L.H.D., Haverford College, 1952; married Christine Robinson, June 30, 1908 (deceased April 1964); children—Eleanor (deceased), Richard M. Engaged as instructor Latin, 1907-12, asst. prof., 1912-18, asst. to the pres., 1915-18, Haverford Coll., trustee, 1920-40; headmaster William Penn Charter School, Philadelphia, 1918-35; chmn. com. on admission, lecturer Latin, Harvard, 1935-52; curator Lowell Inst., Boston, 1952-66. Fellow Am. Acad. Arts and Scis.; mem. Pa. Hist. Soc., Am. Philol. Assn., Headmasters' Assn. (pres. 1934-35), Country Day Sch. Headmasters' Assn., Coll. Entrance Examination Bd. (chmn. 1936-39), Shakespeare Soc. of Phila., Colonial Soc. of Mass. (pres. 1957-61), Mass. Hist. Soc., Am. Antiquarian Society, also member of Phi Beta Kappa. Mem. Soc. Friends. Clubs: Tavern (Boston); Harvard (N.Y., Phila.). Author: The American Colonial Mind and the Classical Tradition, 1963; author and translator philos. books. Home: Cambridge, Mass. Retired. *

GUNDERSEN, GUNNAR, physician; b. LaCrosse, Wis., Apr. 6, 1897; s. Adolf and Helga (Isaksaetre) G.; B.S., U. Wis., 1917; M.D., Columbia, 1920; m. Mary Baldwin, June 23, 1923; children—Gunnar A., Mary (Mrs. F. M. Bugge), Cameron B. Intern, LaCrosse Luth. Hosp., 1920-22; practicing physician, LaCrosse, Wis., since 1920; mem., co-founder Gundersen Clinic, LaCrosse, 1927; mem. bd. dirs. LaCrosse Community Trust, from 1942; chairman distribution committee, from 1959. Pres. Wis. State Board Health, 1943-49. Regent U. Wis., 1931-37. Diplomate Am. Bd. Surgery. Fellow A.C.S., Internat. Coll. Surgeons; mem. A.M.A. (bd. trustees, from 1948, chmn., 1955-58, pres. 1958-59), World Med. Assn. (mem. council, from 1953), Wis. State Med. Soc. (pres. 1940-41). Home: LaCrosse, Wis. Died May 22, 1979.

GUNDY, CHARLES LAKE, investment exec.; b. Toronto, Ont., Can., Feb. 6, 1905; s. James Henry and Serena Lake (Clarke) G.; student Appleby Coll., Oakville, Ont., 1913-23, U. Toronto, 1923-26; LL.D., U. Toronto, 1969; m. Virginia Diana Antoinette Ritchi, June 2, 1939. With Wood Gundy Ltd., Toronto, 1926-78, sales mgr., 1939-41, v.p., 1945-48, pres., 1948-67, chmn., 1967-78, also dir.; partner Wood, Gundy & Co.; dir. Abitibi Paper Co., Ltd., Can. Cement Lafarge Ltd., Massey-Ferguson Ltd., Simpsons, Ltd., Simpsons-Sears, Ltd., United Corps., Ltd. Chmn. bd. trustees Hosp. for Sick Children, 1960-72. Served to maj. with Canadian Army, 1941-45. Mem. Canadian Soc. Clin. Investigation (hon.), Canadian Assn. for Advancement Health Scis. (founding), Investment Dealers Assn. Can. (hon. pres. 1961, chmn. sr. adv. com. 1969), Bd. Trade, Zeta Psi. Mem. United Ch. Can. Clubs: Toronto, Golf, York (Toronto); Can. (London, Eng.); Mount Royal, St. James (Montreal); Vancouver (B.C.); Leaver Winter, Hunt; Griffith Island; Toronto and North York Hunt; Glenmajor Angling. Home: Toronto, Ont., Canada. Died Sept. 15, 1978.

GUNG'L, JOHN C. (GUN'G'L), lawyer; b. Camp Supply Indian Ty., Sept. 19, 1882; s. Carl S. and Annie (Gung'l) G.; student U. of Ariz., 1901-02; LL.B., U. of Mich., 1909; m. Esther Lowdermilk, Sept. 13, 1913. Admitted to Ariz. bar, 1909, Mich. bar, 1909, Calif. bar, 1924, and began practice at Willcox, Ariz.; city atty., Willcox, 1915-26; U.S. dist. atty., Ariz. Dist., Mar. 1, 1929-May 11, 1933. Colonel Judge Adv. Gen. Dept., U.S. Army Reserve. Pres. Bd. of Edn., Willcox Dist., 1920-28. Mem. Am., Ariz., California and Michigan bar assns.; president Cochise County Bar Association, 1929-33; Pima County (Ariz.) Bar Assn., 1939. Republican. Mason (32 deg., Shriner). Home: Tucson, Ariz. *

GUNNER, MATTHEW J., army officer; b. Texas, Mar. 31, 1886; C.E., U. of Texas, 1909; grad. Tank Sch., 1921, Inf. Sch., advanced course, 1923, Command and Gen. Staff Sch., 1924, Army War Coll., 1930. Commd. 2d lt., U.S. Army, 1912, and advanced through the grades to brig. gen., 1944. Home: Washington, D.C. *

GUNTER, CHARLES WESLEY, banking and investments; b. Lagrange, Miss., Feb. 6, 1884; s. Andrew Jackson and Sarah Elizabeth (Givens) G.; ed. public schools and Bennett Acad., Mathiston, Miss.; m. Louise Jane Currie, Nov. 20, 1907; children—Louise Currie, Charles W., Jane Elizabeth. Began in the insurance business, Jackson, Miss., 1901; state agt. Penn-Mutual Life Ins. Co. of Philadelphia, Oklahoma City, Okla., 1909-18; vice-pres. and chmn. bd. Guaranty Bank, Oklahoma City, 1912-18; one of organizers, 1918, pres., 1922-25, Liberty Nat. Bank; vice-pres. Security Nat. Bank, 1925-27, pres. until bank was merged, 1929, with Am. First Nat. Bank, under name of First Nat. Bank and Trust Co. of which was vice-chmn. bd. and chmn. exec. com. until Dec. 31, 1936. Chmn. Selective Draft Exemption Bd., Oklahoma City, and United War Work campaign; also mem. all Liberty Loan campaigns, World War. Former pres. bd. dirs., Y.M.C.A., Oklahoma City. Democrat. Mason (32 deg., Shriner). Home: Los Angeles.

GUNTER, HERMAN, geologist, state ofcl.; b. Brooklyn, July 2, 1885; s. Herman and Anna (Palm) G.; B.S., U. Fla., 1907, Sc.D. (hon.), 1944; m. Bertha Jones, 1910 (dec. 1933); 1 son, Herman; m. 2d Eva Pennington, 1943. Geologic aide to asso. geologist Fla. Geol. Survey, 1907-19, state geologist, dir. since 1919. Fellow Geol. Soc. Am.; mem. A.A.A.S., Assn. Petroleum Geologists, Geophys. Union, Water Works Assn., Soc. Vertebrate Paleontology, Am. Inst. Mining and Metall. Engrs., Southeastern Geol. Soc. (pres. 1944), Fla. Engring. Soc., Soil Sci. Soc. Fla. (pres. 1947), Assn. Am. State Geologists (president, 1953), Kappa Alpha. Author sci. articles. Home: Tallahassee. *

GURFEIN, MURRAY IRWIN, judge; b. N.Y.C., Nov. 17, 1907; s. Louis and Rose (Feld) G.; A.B., Columbia, 1926; LL.B. magna cum laude, Harvard, 1930; LL.D., Bard Coll., 1972; m. Eva Hadas, Aug. 6, 1931; children—Abigail (Mrs. Robert Hellwarth), Susan Hadas (Mrs. Arthur Rosett). Admitted to N.Y. bar; law clk. to U.S. Circuit Judge Julian W. Mack, 1930-31; asst. U.S. atty. So. Dist. N.Y., 1931-33; pvt. practice law, N.Y.C., 1933-35; chief asst. investigation organized crime to Hon. Thomas E. Dewey, 1935-38; asst. dist. atty., N.Y. County, 1938-42; partner Judd and Gurfein, N.Y.C., 1946-54, Goldstein, Judd and Gurfein, 1955-68, Goldstein, Gurfein, Shames & Hyde, 1968-71; judge U.S. Dist. Ct., So. Dist., N.Y., 1971-74, U.S. Ct. Appeals 2nd Circuit, 1974-79. Mem. N.Y. State Temporary Commn. Cts., 1953-58. Former pres. United Hias Service, Internat. Council Jewish Social and Service Orgns. Served as lt. col., chief intelligence Psychol. Warfare Div., Supreme Hdqrs. Allied Expeditionary Force, OSS and AUS, 1942-45; asst. to Hon. Robert H. Jackson, U.S. Chief Counsel in Nuremberg Trials, 1945. Decorated Legion of Merit; hon. officer Order of Brit. Empire; Croix de Guerre (France). Fellow Am. Coll. Trial Lawyers, Am. Bar Found.; mem. Am., N.Y. State bar assns., Assn. Bar City N.Y., Harvard Law Sch. Assn. N.Y. (pres. 1977-78), Council Fgn. Relations, Phi Beta Kappa. Club: Harmonie (N.Y.C.). Home: New York, N.Y. Died Dec. 16, 1979.

GURLEY, FRED G., ry. exec.; b. Sedalia, Mo., Feb. 20, 1889; s. Horatio Nelson and Mary E. (Glasse) G.; student grade and high sch., Kansas City and Warrensburg, Mo.; m. Margaret Smith, Apr. 12, 1913 (dec.); 1 d., Margaret (Mrs. Harry A. Dow, Jr.); m. 2d, Ruth Brown, Sept. 16, 1920; 1 son, Robert Hayes. Began as clk., Burling R.R., Sheridan, Wyo., summer 1906, div. supt., 1920-25, gen. supt., 1925-32, asst. v.p., 1932-39; v.p. A.,T.&S.F. Ry. Co., 1939-44, pres., chmn. exec. com., 1944-57, chmn. bd., 1957-59, also director. Member bd. trustees Midwest Research Institute; honorary trustee Museum of Science and Industry; associate Northwestern University; member of Citizen's Board, University Chicago; member business advisory council United States Department Commerce. Member Assn. Western Rys. (director), Transportation Assn. America (dir.), Chgo. Crime Commn., Soc. Colonial Wars, S.A.R., (Ill., mem. bd. mgrs.), Newcomen Soc. N.A. Republican. Episcopalian. Mason. Clubs: Chicago, Commercial, Traffic, Economic, Executives, also mem. Western Railway, Chicago Sunday Evening (Chgo.); Capitol Hill (Washington); Bohemian (San Francisco); Glenview (Golf, Ill.), California (Los Angeles), Saddle and Sirloin (Kansas City, Mo.). Home: Chicago, Ill. Died July 4, 1976.

GURLEY, SAM, JR., steel co. exec.; b. Metropolis, Ill., Aug. 19, 1917; s. Sam and Susan (Snyder) G.; B.S. in Chem. Engring., U. Mo., 1939; m. Norma Thomasine Williams, July 12, 1941; children—Phillip S., Susan E. Vice pres. sales Reichhold Chems., Inc., 1948-52, H.K. Porter, Inc., 1952-55, Olin Mathieson Chem. Corp., 1955-57; pres., chief exec. officer Tubesales, 1957-76. Served to lt. comdr. USNR, 1939-44. Mason. Home: Newport Beach, Calif. Died Nov. 5, 1976.

GUSTAD, JOHN WILBERT, educator; b. St. Pual, Oct. 28, 1922; s. John and Mary Elizabeth (Stringer) G.; A.B. cum laude, Macalester Coll., 1943; M.A., U. Minn., 1948, Ph.D., 1949; children—Ann Kathryn, Charles K.; m. Dorris Adams Burdick. Teaching asst. dept. psychology U. Minn., 1946, instr., 1947-49; asst. prof. psychology, dir. counseling service Vanderbilt U., 1949-52; vis. asst. prof. George Peabody Coll., summer 1950; mem. seminar improvement undergrad. instrn. psychology Cornell U., summer 1951; operations analyst research Dept. Army, Korea, 1952; asso. prof. psychology, dir. counseling service U. Md., 1952-56; cons. USN Sch. Hosp. Adminstrn., Bethesda, Md., 1952; cons. VA Vocational Counseling Service, Washington, 1953-59; mem. seminar on occupational choice theory Ohio State U., summer 1954; prof. psychology, dir. counseling center U. Md., 1956-60; cons. sci. teaching improvement program A.A.A.S., 1957-58; project dir. Coll. Teaching Career Research Project, 1957-58; cons. Yale U. Sch. Math. Study Group, 1958-60; vis. prof. Harvard, summer 1959; dir. coll. tchr. program New Eng. Bd. Higher Edn., 1959-60; dean Coll. Liberal Arts, Alfred U., 1960-63, acting dean Grad. Sch., 1962-63; provost and dean coll. New Coll., 1963-66; vis. prof. higher edn. and psychology Ohio State U., 1965-66, asso. dean Coll. Arts and Scis., 1966-68; coordinator Nebr. State Colls., 1968-69; pres. Ft. Hays (Kans.) State Coll., 1969-75, prof. psychology and edn., 1975-78; dir. 1st Nat. Bank of Hays. Bd. dirs. Hadley Reigonal Med. Center. Served to lt. (s.g.), USNR, 1943-46. Fellow Am. Psychol. Assn. (council reps. 1954-57, bd. profl. affairs 1957-60), A.A.A.S.; mem. AAUP, Am. Council Edn. (commn. on acad. affairs), Am. Assn. Higher Edn. (chmn. com. on teaching), Am. Assn. State Colls. and Univs. (mem. com. policies and purposes), Kans. C. of C., Sigma Xi, Phi Delta Kappa, Pi Phi Epsilon. Presbyn. Rotarian. Club: Smoky Hill Country. Author: Improving Undergraduate Instruction in Psychology; Graduate Education in Psychology: How to Interview; The Choice of a Career in College Teaching; numerous articles in psychol. jours. Home: Hays, Kans. Died Dec. 16, 1978.

GUSTAV VI ADOLF, King of Sweden; b. Stockholm, Sweden, Nov. 11, 1882; s. King Gustaf V and Victoria, Princess of Baden; ed. pvt. tutors; student U. Uppsala, 1902-03, U. Oslo, 1903-04; hon. degrees: U. Lund, 1918, Princeton, Yale, and Clark univs., 1926, Cambridge U., 1929, Dorpat U., 1932, Harvard, 1938, Stockholm University, 1944, Helsingfors U., 1952; Oxford, 1955; m. Margaret, Princess of Great Britain and Ireland, June 15, 1905 (deceased 1920); children—Gustaf Adolf, Duke of Vasterbotten (deceased 1947); Sigvard; Ingrid, Queen of Denmark; Bertil, Duke of Halland, Carl Johan; m. 2d, Lady Louise Mountbatten, former Princess of Battenberg, Nov. 3, 1923 (dec. 1965). Crown Prince, 1907-50, King of Sweden, 1950—. Commd. to Army, 1902, advanced through grades to gen., 1932. Promoter humanistic research in general in Sweden; an organizer Swedish humanistic scholarship; a founder and pres. Swedish Archaeol. Inst. in Rome, 1925, in Athens, 1948; pres. Humanistic Research Fund, 1928-50, Royal Acad. Hist. and Antiquities, 1945-40, Swedish-Chinese Research Com. from its foundation 1922; of Swedish Cyprus Com. since 1926. Active part in archaeol. excavations in Sweden, Greece, Cyprus and China. Pres. Swedish Olympics com., 1912. Mem. Swedish Sports Fedn. (pres. 1903-33), Central Assn. Promotion Athletics (pres. 1907-33), Nat. League Against Tuberculosis (hon. pres.), Swedish Export Assn. (hon. pres.); fgn. mem. Académie des Inseriptions et Belles Lettres; mem. numerous other Swedish, fgn. socs., Archeol. Inst. d.deutschen Reiches. British Acad. clubs. Interested in archaeology and art, particularly ancient Chinese art. Address: Stockholm, Sweden. *

GUSTIN, HARLEY WEMPLE, lawyer; b. Salt Lake City, Apr. 22, 1902; s Frank Jasper and Dora (Harley) Gustin; LL.B., U. Utah, 1924; m. Margaret Strunk, Dec. 7, 1945; children—(by previous marriage) Violet Eugenia (Mrs. John C. McKay), Beverly Jane (Mrs. K.F. Campbell), Frank Johannesen. Admitted to Utah bar, 1924, and since practiced in Salt Lake City; mem. firm Gustin & Gustin; asst. dist. atty. Third Jud. Dist. of Utah, 1933-34. Mem. Salt Lake City Bd. Edn., 1933-39. Fellow Am. Coll. Trial Lawyers; mem. Utah State (commr. 1948), Am., Salt Lake County (pres. 1951) bar assns., S.A.R., Sigma Chi, Delta Theta Phi. Episcopalian. Mason (Shriner), Elk. Club: University. Home: Salt Lake City, Utah. Died Oct. 24, 1977.

GUSTON, PHILIP, painter; b. Montreal, Que., Can., June 27, 1913; D.F.A. (hon.), Boston U., 1970. One-man shows Sidney Janis Gallery, N.Y.C., 1956, 58, 60, 61, Santa Barbara Mus. Art, 1966, Jewish Mus., N.Y.C., 1966, Brandeis U., Waltham, Mass., 1966, Boston U., 1970, Marlborough Gallery, N.Y.C., 1971, Met. Mus. Art, N.Y.C., 1973, David McKee Gallery, N.Y.C., 1974-75, 76-78, others; exhibited retrospectives V Bienal, Sao Paolo, Brazil, 1959, XXX Biennale, Venice, 1960, Solomon R. Guggenheim Mus., N.Y.C., 1962, San Francisco Mus. Art, 1980, later exhibited at Stedelijk Mus., Amsterdam, Musee des Beaux-Arts, Brussels, Whitechapel Gallery, London, Los Angeles County Mus. Art; represented in pub. collections Tate Gallery, London, Solomon R. Guggenheim Mus., Mus. Modern Art, N.Y.C., Phillips Collection, Washington, Met. Mus. Art, N.Y.C., Whitney Mus. Am. Art, Albright-Knox Art Gallery, Buffalo, Cleve. Mus. Art, Art Inst. Chgo., Los Angeles County Mus., City Art Mus. St. Louis, Worcester (Mass.) Art Mus., Va. Mus. Fine Arts, Richmond. Trustee Am. Acad., Rome, 1970—. Recipient 1st prize for outdoor mural N.Y. World's Fair, 1939, 1st prize Carnegie Inst., 1945, Prix de Rome, 1948; subject film Philip Guston, 1972; subject of book Yes But, A Critical Study of Philip Guston (Dore Ashton), 1976. Guggenheim fellow, 1947, 68. Mem. Nat. Inst. Arts and Letters, Am. Acad. Arts and Scis. Address: Woodstock, N.Y. Died June 7, 1980.

GUTE, HERBERT JACOB, artist, educator; b. Jeffersonville, N.Y., Aug. 10, 1907; s. Rudolph Herman and Martha (Mueller) G.; B.F.A., Yale, 1933; m. Catherine M. Schaefer, Oct. 18, 1936; children—Herbert Schaefer, David Mueller. Staff artist Dure-Europos Expdn., 1933-35; tchr. U. Va., 1937; mem. faculty Yale, 1938-73, asst. prof. drawing and painting, 1936-73, fellow Calhoun Coll., 1955-73; exhbns. include Am. Water Color Soc., from 1949, Silvermine Guild, from 1956, Boston Art Festival, 1938, Watercolor U.S.A., 1961, 200 Years of Am. Watercolor,

Met. Museum of Art, 1965; represented permanent collections O'Hara Coll., Sweetbriar Coll., Yale Art Gallery, Dept. Interior, Louvre, Dura, Paris, France, Jewish Mus., Dura, IBM collection, Antheneum, Hartford, Conn., Walker Art Mus., others; chmn. from Am. Battle Monuments Commn. for mural U.S. Mil. Cemetery, Cambridge, Eng., 1953-54. Adviser on art therapy for mentally ill Conn. Mental Hosp., 1949-53. Recipient Muriel Alvord prize Yale, 1935, 1st prize Conn. Contemporary Painting, Springfield, Mass., 1951, 2d Internat. Hallmark award, 1954. A.N.A.; mem. Audubon Soc., Phila. Water Color Club, Silvermine Guild, Am. Water Color Soc. Club: Yale (New Haven). Illustrator; (M. Rostovtzeff) Dura Europos, 1936; (J. Geise) Man in the Western World, 1940. Rep. Ten Best Books of the Year, 1941-48. Home: New Haven, Conn. Died July 9, 1977.

GUTHMANN, HARRY GEORGE (GUTH'MÄN), finance; b. East Syracuse, N.Y., Dec. 16, 1896; s. Martin and Margaret D. (Storer) G.; A.B., Syracuse U., 1917; M.B.A., New York U., 1921; Ph.D., U. of Chicago, 1929; m. Bernice Jones Montgomery, 1930. Certified pub. accountant; instr., later asst. prof., Syracuse U., 1917-22; asso. prof., U. of Tex., 1922-25; with Northwestern Univ. from 1927, prof. finance from 1935, Morrison prof. from 1949. Trustee, Teachers Ins. and Annuity Assn., 1947-51. Mem. Am. Econ. Assn., Am. Finance Assn. (pres. 1946), Am. Assn. U. Profs., Phi Beta Kappa, Beta Alpha Psi, Beta Gamma Sigma, Alpha Kappa Psi. Clubs: University (Evanston), Investment Analysts. Author books, latest: Corporate Financial Policy (with H. E. Dougall), 1962; Investment Principles and Practices (with R.E. Badger and H.W. Torgerson), 1961. Contbr. to financial publs. Cons. on finance and investments. Home: Evanston, Ill. Died Mar. 15, 1981.

GUTHMANN, WALTER S., educator, chemist; b. Chgo., Apr. 3, 1907; s. William B. and Ida (Seligmann) G.; B.S., Yale, 1928, Ph.D., U. Chgo., 1932; m. Edith Greenbaum, Oct. 16, 1940; children—Babette (Mrs. David Steinbrecher), William Alan. Co-founder Edwal Labs., Chgo., 1933, v.p., 1933-41, pres., 1947-53; pres. Ringwood Chem. Co., 1953-58, Morton Chem. 1965-74; 1958-61; mem. faculty Roosevelt U., Chgo., 1961-74, prof. chemistry, 1965-74, chmn. dept., 1966-73, trustee, 1972-74. Cons. in field, 1935-76; dir. Ventron Corp. Mem. Bd. Edn. dist. 111, Highland Park, Ill., 1953-59; chmn. jr. coll. com. Highland Park-Deerfield, 1962-67; Cons. examiner Commn. on Inst. Higher Edn. North Central Assn. Colls. Served to maj., C.W.S., AUS, 1941-45. Mem. Am. Chem. Soc. (chmn. Chgo. sect. 1972-76, nat. councilor 1965-76), Mfg. Chemists Assn. (chmn. edn. activities com. 1963-65), Soc. Chem. Industry, Sigma Xi. Clubs: Chemists (Chgo.). Contbr. articles to jours. Research in organo-metallic reactions. Home: Huntersville, N.C. Died Mar. 2, 1976.

GUTIÉRREZ CORTINES, MANUEL, utilities exec.; b. Santander, Spain, Feb. 15, 1901; s. Juan Gutérrez and Dolores Cortines; student Deusto U., Bilbao, 1917-18, Superior Tech. Sch. Indsl. Engrs. Madrid, 1919-24; Ph.D., Madrid, 1925; m. María Corral Pérez, Aug. 19, 1931; children—Juan, Manuel, Maria (Mrs. Julio Calero), Mercedes (Mrs. Francisco Gorriti), Cristina (Mrs. Jose Egea), Dolores (Mrs. Martín Silvan), Antonio, Teresa (Mrs. Jorge Gracia). Mgr, Cable Factory, Standard Electrica Santander, 1927-30; mng. dir. Standard Electrica, Madrid, 1931-41, Electra de Viesgo, Spain, 1941—80; chmn. bd. Compañia de Contadores, Barcelona, Spain, 1973—80; pres. Nuclenor. FORATOM (Forum Atomique Europeen), 1976—80; dir. Fenosa, Compañia Electrica de Langero, Empresa Nacional del Uranio. Trustee Patronato Montañes de Enseñanza, Institution Cultural Cantabria; chmn. bd. trustees U. Santander, 1974-75. Decorated officer French Legion of Honor; Knight Great Cross Order Civil Merit Spain. Mem. Nat. Coll. Indsl. Engrs. Spain (pres. 1962-70), Atomic Forum of Spain (chmn 1968—80), Atomic Indsl. Forum U.S. (mem Western European sect. adv. council 1973—80, bd. dirs. 1974—80), Am. Nuclear Soc. Contbr. articles on atomic energy and nuclear plants. Home: Santander, Spain. Died Aug. 16, 1980.

GUTTENTAG, MARCIA, social psychologist, educator; b. N.Y.C., Nov. 9, 1932; d. Morris and Flora (Kaufman) Blumberg; B.A. with honors, U. Mich., 1953; Fulbright scholar U. Freiburg (W.Ger.), 1953-54; Ph.D., Adelphi U., Garden City, N.Y., 1960; m. Paul Frank Secord, Sept. 21, 1972; children—Lisa Andra, Michael Daniel. Asst. prof. Queens Coll., 1965-69; mem. faculty Grad. Sch., City U. N.Y., 1970-74, prof. psychology, 1970-74, dir. Harlem Research Center, 1970-72; Richard Clarke Cabot vis. prof. social ethics Harvard U., 1972-73, dir. social devel. project Grad. Sch. Edn., 1973-77; prof. psychology U. Mass., Boston; trustee Research for Social Change; mem. ethics com. HEW. Named Distinguished Woman in Sci., U. Mich., 1973; Distinguished Alumna, Adelphi U., 1975; recipient Distinguished Sci. Contbn. award N.Y. State Psychol. Assn., 1970. Mem. Soc. Psychol. Study Social Issues (past pres.), Am. Psychol. Assn. (past div. pres., founder pub. interest coalition 1974), Evaluation Research Soc. (founder, pres. 1976-77), Emily Dickinson House Com. Jewish. Club: Harvard (N.Y.C.). Author: The Evaluation of Mental Health Training, 1974; Undoing Sex Sterotypes, 1976; co-author: Local Control of Education, 1972; Principles and Practices of Community Mental Health Center Evaluation, 1976; Public Policies for Women, 1977; Families Abandoned: Mental Health in Today's Society, 1977. Co-editor: Handbook of Evaluation Research, 1975. Home: Cambridge, Mass. Died Nov. 4, 1977.

GUTTING, FERD J., brewery exec.; b. St. Louis, 1910; ed. La Salle Extension U.; married. Sec., treas., dir. Griesedieck Bros. Brewery Co., until 1958; with Falstaff Brewing Corp., St. Louis, 1958—, asst. treas., 1964-67, v.p. planning, 1967-68, v.p., controller, 1968-72, pres., chmn. bd., from 1973. Home: Ladue, Mo. Died Dec. 10, 1980.

GUY, CHARLES WALKER, gas co. exec.; b. Mansfield, La., Jan. 20, 1914; s. J. Walker and Frances (Parsons) G.; student La. State U., 1936, B.S., 1970; m. Ana Guess, Apr. 21, 1973; children—Sibyl J. (Mrs. T. Neil Carmena), Charles W., Frances J. Engaged as field auditor with La. Dept. Revenue, 1936-38; from auditor to exec. v.p. Gen. Gas Corp., Baton Rouge, 1939-54; v.p., treas., dir. Tex. Natural Gasoline Corp., Tulsa, 1954-58; retired, 1958; exec. v.p., dir. Gen. Gas Corp., 1958-60, Delta Tank Mfg. Co., Inc., Baton Rouge, 1958-60; now propr. Guy Gas and Chem. Co., Houston. C.P.A., La. Mem. La. Soc. C.P.A.'s, Nat. Liquified Petroleum Gas Assn. (past chmn. transp. com.), Butane-Propane Inst. La. (past pres.), Order Ancient Gassers, Am. Inst. C.P.A.'s, Pi Kappa Alpha. Clubs: Sugar Creek Country, Houston. Home: Sugar Land, Tex. Died Aug. 16, 1980.

GUY, CHESTER CHAPPELL, surgeon; b. Danville, Ill., Oct. 2, 1899; s. John Milton and Nannie (Kelly) G.; B.S., U. Chgo., 1921; M.D., Rush Med. Coll., Chgo., 1923; m. Helen Smith, Apr. 11, 1928; children—Chester Chappell, Suzanne (Mrs. Henry Behr). Intern Cook County Hosp., 1923-25, resident pathologist, 1925-27; asso., then attending surgeon Cook County Hosp. and Ill. Central Hosp., 1927-42; pathologist St. Bernard Hosp., Chgo., 1927-42, cons. surgeon, 1946-76; pvt. practice, Chgo., 1927-76; chief surgery Ill. Central Hosp., 1948-66, coordinator profl. services and med. edn., 1966-76; clin. prof. surgery U. Ill. Coll. Medicine, 1964-76. Trustee Hektoen Inst., Chicago, 1957-76. Served to col., M.C., AUS, 1942-46. Mem. American (past pres. Chicago), International (v.p. U.S.) colls. surgeons, Am. Med. Association, Western Surg. Assn., Am. Assn. Surgery Tranma, Indsl. Med. Assn., Am. Assn. R.R. Surgeons (past pres., chmn. exec. com.), Ill. Surg. Soc. (pres. 1963-64), Alpha Omega Alpha. Author articles in field. Editor: Pathological Conferences, 1940; Indsl. Medicine and Survey, from 1967. Home: Chicago, Ill. Died Aug. 24, 1976.

GUY, ROBERT JEFFERSON, hosp. adminstr.; b. Summitville, Ind., Aug. 22, 1912; s. Daniel Jefferson and Bertha (Dobson) G.; student La. State U., 1936-37; B.A., Emory U., 1940; m. Martha Elizabeth Jackson, Aug. 30, 1940; children—Robert Leland, Carol Lynn, Elizabeth Elaine. Asst. to adminstr. Ga. Bapt. Hosp., Atlanta, 1940-43; gen. mgr. Ridgecrest Bapt. Assembly, 1946-50; adminstr. Baton Rouge Gen. Hosp., 1950-62; adminstr. Mo. Bapt. Hosp., St. Louis, 1962-72, exec. dirs., from 1972. Trustee YMCA, Baton Rouge, 1955-61, pres., 1957-58. Served from 2d lt. to capt. AUS, 1943-46. Fellow Am. Coll. Hosp. Adminstrs. (regent 1967-74); mem. Am. (del. 1970-72, chmn. com. hosp. chaplains 1972-74), Am. Protestant (pres. 1963; chmn. com. on accreditation chaplains 1969-72; del. 1972-73), Bapt., Mo. (pres. 1969, trustee) hosp. assns., Hosp. Assn. Met. St. Louis (treas. 1967-69, pres. 1970-71), Sigma Chi. Democrat. So. Baptist. Rotarian (Paul Harris fellow). Home: St. Louis, Mo. Deceased.

GUYANT, CLAUDE E., consular service; b. Decatur, Ill., Feb. 17, 1886; ed. pub. schs. Clk. and stenographer to the Isthmian Canal Commission, 1906-08; deputy consul general, Panama City, 1908-09, vice and deputy consul gen., 1909-10; v. and dep. consul gen., Mexico City, 1910-12; consul at Salina Cruz, Mar.-Nov. 1912; v. consul in charge of consulate, Ensenada, 1912-13; v. and dep. consul, Ensenada, 1913-15; consul, Feb.-Oct. 1915; consul Progreso, Yucatan, Oct. 1915-July 1916; consul at Barranquilla, Colombia, 1916-20, San José, Costa Rica, 1920-21, Lima, Peru, 1921-25, Nottingham, England, since 1925. Address: Nottingham, Eng. *

GUYTON, BILLY SYLVERTER (GI'TUN), oculist, aurist; b. Blue Mountain, Miss., Jan. 11, 1884; s. John Franklin and Mary Lettie (Thornton) G.; student Miss. Coll., 1901-02 and 1905-08, B.S., 1908; B.S., U. of Miss., 1910, M.A., 1911; M.D., U. of Va., 1913; Oph.D., U. of Colo., 1919; studied U. of Vienna, summer 1928; m. Kate Smallwood, Dec. 23, 1913; children—Jack Smallwood, William Franklin, Arthur Clifton, Ruth Elizabeth. Intern Martha-Jefferson Sanatorium, Charlottesville, Va., 1912-13, Orange (N.J.) Memorial Hosp., 1913-14; prof. pathology and bacteriology, U. of Miss., 1915-20, asso. prof., (part time) 1920-26, instr. in physical diagnosis and minor surgery, (part time) 1926-30, instr. minor surgery, (part time) 1930-35, dean Sch. of Medicine, 1935-44, now dean emeritus, prof. surgery since 1936; specialized in treatment of eye, ear, nose and throat, Oxford, Miss. since 1916. Diplomate Am. Bd. of Otolaryngology since 1927. Fellow Am. Acad. Opthalmology and Otolaryngology, Am. Coll. Surgeons, International College of Surgeons, A.M.A.; mem. La.-Miss. Ophthalmol. and Otolaryngol. Soc. (pres. 1941), Miss. Eye Ear Nose and Throat Soc. (pres. 1952-53), Mississippi State Medical Association (president 1950-51), Sigma Chi, Phi Beta Kappa. Democrat. Methodist. Club: Rotary (Oxford). Home: Oxford, Miss. *

GYGAX, FELIX XERXES (GI'GAX), naval officer; b. Twin Creek, Osborne County, Kan., Mar. 30, 1884; s. Rudolph and Regina (Zimmerman) G.; B.S., U.S. Naval Acad., 1906; student U.S. Naval War Coll., 1920-21; m. Estelle Ise, Nov. 14, 1911; children—Felix X., Rex. Commd. ensign, U.S. Navy, 1908, and advanced through grades to rear admiral, 1940; served in U.S.S. Kearsarge on round-the-world cruise of Battle Fleet, 1907-09; transferred to U.S.S. Minnesota, 1909; spl. duty with Diesel engines, also naval attaché, Switzerland, 1911; duty with submarines, 1913-20 (pioneered as officer in charge of Submarine Sch., New London, Conn., and established submarine base at Pearl Harbor, T.H.); navigator U.S.S. Mississippi, 1921; in charge engring. sect. Fleet training Div., U.S. Navy Dept., 1924-25; aide and flag sec. of comdr. Battle Force, and comdr. in chief of U.S. Fleet, 1926-27; sec. War Plans Div., Office Chief of Naval Operations, 1927-28; aide to chief of naval operations, 1928-30; exec. officer U.S.S. Colorado, 1930-32; prof. of naval science and tactics and in charge of Naval R.O.T.C., U. of Calif., 1932-35; comdg. officer U.S.S. Augusta, flagship U.S. Asiatic Fleet, 1935-37; dir. Naval Reserve, Navy Dept., 1937-40; comdr. Cruiser Div. 3, U.S. Pacific Fleet, 1940-41; comdt. Norfolk Navy Yard, Aug. 1, 1941-44; comdt. First Naval Dist. and U.S. Navy Yard, Boston, 1944-46, retired, 1946. Decorated Victory medal with submarine clasp World War I, Am. Defense Service medal with bronze star, Legion of Merit (U.S.), Comdr. Order Brit. Empire; designated First Citizen of Portsmouth, Va., 1943. Mem. Nat. Geog. Soc., U.S. Naval Inst., Mil. Order of Caraboa; hon. mem. Scabbard and Blade. Mason. Clubs: Army and Navy (Manila, R.I.); Army and Navy Country (Washington). Address: Rancho Santa Fe, Calif. *

GYORGY, PAUL, physician, educator; b. Nagy Varad, Hungary, Apr. 7, 1893 (came U.S., 1935, naturalized, 1941); M.D., U. Budapest, 1915; M.D. (hon.), Heidelberg U., 1958; m. Margaret A. John, Oct. 23, 1920. Prof. pediatrics Heidelberg U., 1920-33; research fellow U. Cambridge (Eng.), 1933-35; vis. research prof. Western Res. U., 1935-44; prof. pediatrics U. Pa., Phila., 1944-58, emeritus, 1958-76. Chmn. organizing com. 5th Internat. Congress on Nutrition, Washington, 1960; chmn. protein adv. group WHO, FAO, UNICEF, 1958-61. Recipient Borden award Am. Inst. Nutrition and Acad. Pediatrics; Mendel award Am. Inst. Nutrition; Goldberger award A.M.A.; Markle fellow U. Toronto; Howland award Am. Pediatric Soc., 1968. Fellow Royal Soc. Medicine. Pioneer in discovery riboflavin, vitamin B6, biotin, growth factors in human milk, exptl. dietary liver injury. Home: Rosemont, Pa.

HAAGEN-SMIT, ARIE JAN, educator, bio-organic chemist; b. Utrecht, Holland, Dec. 22, 1900; B.A., M.A., Ph.D., Rijks U., Utrecht. Head asst. dept. organic chemistry U. Utrecht, 1929-34; lectr. organic chemistry Harvard, 1936-37; mem. faculty Calif. Inst. Tech., 1937-77, prof. bio-organic chemistry, 1940-71, prof. emeritus, 1971-77, also dir. Plant Environmental Labs. Mem. Air Sanitation Com. Cal.; mem. Sci. Com. Los Angeles County; biochem. adv. com. AEC; cons. Los Angeles County Air Pollution Control Dist., abatement br. HEW, Nat. Center Air Pollution; chmn. Air Resources Bd. Calif., President's Task Force on Air Pollution. Trustee Arboretum Found. Los Angeles County. Decorated knight Order Orange Nassau, 1947 recipient Chambers award Air Pollution Assn. Am. Community Service award D.A.R.; Hodgkins meda Smithsonian Instn., Washington; B.Y. Morrison Lecture award Dept. Agr., 1970. Fellow N.Y. Acad Scis.; mem. Am. (Fritzsche award 1950, Tolman awarc Calif. sect. 1962, award for pollution control 1972) Swiss, Dutch chem. socs., Nat. Acad. Scis. (Cottrel award 1972); corr. mem. Royal Acad. Sc (Netherlands). Author articles in field. Spl. researcl isolation and synthesis plant hormones. Home Pasadena, Calif. Died Mar. 18, 1977.

HAAS, FRANCIS BUCHMAN, educator; b. Phila Pa., June 6, 1884; s. Frederick and Emma (Roberts) H A.B., Central High Sch., Phila., 1904; Collegiat Certificate, Phila. Sch. of Pedagogy, 1906; B.S., Temp Univ., 1913, Pd.D., 1925; M.A., U. of Pa., 1922; ho degrees, Temple U., Juniata Coll., Bucknell U Waynesburg Coll., Univ. of Pittsburgh; m. Miria Rider, June 27, 1916; children—Jean, Mary, Francis B Jr. Teacher pub. schs., Y.M.C.A. evening sch., Girar Coll. Summer Sch., Phila., later demonstration teache Sch. of Pedagogy, and teacher of mathematics, Phil Evening High Sch.; apptd. mem. faculty, Sch. Pedagogy, and supervisor recreation center, Phila 1915; supervising prin. Breck Sch., Keyser-Meeha

Sch., Benson Sch., 1916-20; asst. dir. teacher bur. of State Dept. Pub. Instrn., Pa., 1920; dir. administration bur. of same, 1922; commd. deputy supt. of pub. instn., 1925, supt., 1925-27; pres. State Teachers College, Bloomsburg, Pa., 1927-39; Supt. of Public Instn. State of Pa. 1939-56, ret.; member federal, state and local adv. coms. on a variety of civic activities and others relating to edn. Mem. bd. trustees, Temple U., Pa. State Univ. Music Festival Assn. Central Pa., gov.'s adv. committee on Higher Edn. Facilities, citziens com., Russell H. Conwell Foundation; dir. Josiah W. and Bessie H. Kline Foundation, Incorporated; board directors American Cancer Soc. (Pa. div.), sponsoring com. Gimbel Pa. Art Collection. Distinguished service medal, Pa. State Edn. Assn., 1928; Laymen's Honor award, Pennsylvania State Assn. for Health, Physical Education and Recreation. Mem. profl. socs., ednl. assns., also Knights of the Red Cross of Constantine, Patriotic Order Sons of Am., Lambda Sigma, Phi Delta Kappa, Kappa Delta Pi, Phi Sigma Pi, Kappa Phi Kappa. Republican. Methodist. Mason (33 deg., Shriner). Clubs: Schoolmen's (Phila.); Craftsman (Bloomsburg). Home: Harrisburg, Pa. *

HAAS, FRITZ, biologist; b. Frankfort-on-Main, Germany, Jan. 4, 1886; s. Benjamin and Clara (Gruenebaum) H.; Doctor's degree, U. Heidelberg, Germany, 1910; m. Helene Ganz, Mar. 30, 1922; children—Ernst Bernhard, Edith Pauline Clara (Mrs. Melvin Cornfield). Came to U.S., 1938, naturalized, 1944. Asst. keeper lower invertebrates Naturmuseum Senckenberg, Frankfort-on-Main, 1911-21, Keeper, 1922-36; curator lower invertebrates Chgo. Natural History Mus., 1938-59. Mem. Am. Malacogical Union, Malacological Soc. Gt. Britain and Ireland, Deutsche Malakozoologische Gesellschaft, Real Academia de Cienc. Artes (Barcelona), Inst. Catalana de Historia Natural, Acad. Natural Sci. Phila. Home: Chgo. *

HAAS, GEORGE CHRISTIAN OTTO, Orientalist; b. New York, N.Y., Mar. 28, 1883; s. George Christian Frederick and Anna Sophia (Hansen) H.; A.B., Columbia, 1902, A.M., 1903, Ph.D., 1909; m. Beulah F. Thompson, of Binghamton, N.Y., 1930. Fellow in Indo-Iranian langs., Columbia, 1905-06; tutor Coll. City of New York, 1904-11; instr. in German, 1911-16; translator Dept. of Justice, Washington, D.C., 1917; censor same, at Ellis Island, 1917-20; tech. translator for patent attys., 1921-35; director, Institute of Hyperphysical Research, New York, since 1933. Ordained to ministry Universal Spiritual Church, 1927. American collaborator Orientaische Bibliographie, Berlin, 1907-14; joint editor Journal American Oriental Soc., 1916-18. Was organist and choirmaster St. Mark's Evang. Luth. Ch., New York, 1906-08. Mem. Am. Oriental Soc. (rec. sec. 1911-18), Advisory Council Simplified Spelling Bd., Phi Beta Kappa. Mason. Author: The Dasarupa, a Treatise on Hindu Dramaturgy, by Dhanamjaya, 1912. Contbr. on Oriental subjects. Home: Bayside, N.Y. *

HAAS, WALTER A., business exec.; b. San Francisco, 1889; s. Abraham and Fannie (Koshland) H.; B.L., U. Calif., 1910; LL.D., U. Calif. at Berkeley, 1958, Mills Coll., 1968, U. San Francisco, 1974; m. Elise Stern, Oct. 18, 1914; children—Walter A., Peter, Rhoda (Mrs. R. N. Goldman). Pres., dir. Levi Strauss & Co., San Francisco, 1928-56, chmn., dir., 1956-70, hon. chmn. bd., dir., 1970-79; pres. Iris Securities Co., from 1927; pres. Frontier Investment Co.; dir. Pacific Gas & Electric Co., Pacific Intermountain Express Co., Crocker Citizens Nat. Bank, San Francisco Bank, Haas, Baruch & Co., Calif. Pacific Title Co., Nat. Ice & Cold Storage Co., Tidewater Associated Oil Co. Former mem. adv. council U. Calif. Sch. Bus. Adminstrn. Former pres. San Francisco C. of C., San Francisco War Chest; former dir., mem. exec. com. World Affairs Council, San Francisco Federated Fund; former v.p. Mt. Zion Hosp.; former trustee Mills Coll.; past pres. Jewish Welfare Fedn.; past pres. Recreation and Park Commn., City and County of San Francisco; mem. Blyth-Zellerbach Com.; bd. dirs. Save-the-Redwoods League. Served as 2d lt. F.A., World War I. Republican. Jewish. Clubs: Family, Stock Exchange, Concordia-Argonaut (San Francisco); Faculty (Stanford, Calif.). Home: San Francisco, Calif. Died Dec. 7, 1979; interred Home of Peace, Colma, Calif.

HABER, PHILMORE JOSEPH, lawyer; b. Cleve., May 24, 1895; s. Marcus and Rickie (Lorber) H.; A.B., Western Res, U., 1915; LL.B., Cleve. Law Sch., 1917; m. Constance Mayer, Mar. 14, 1918; children—Richard, James. Admitted to Ohio bar; formerly sr. partner, now of counsel firm Burke, Haber & Berick. Past vice chmn. Cuyahoga County Mental Health Commn. Past Trustee Mt. Sinai Hosp. Cleve. Mem. Cleve. C. of C., Citizens League, Nat. Conf. Christians and Jews (past co-chmn.). Clubs: Oakwood Country (past trustee), City. Home: Cleveland, Ohio. Died Apr. 26, 1977; buried Mayfield Cemetery, Cleve.

HABERLY, LOYD, writer, educator; b. Ellsworth, Ia., Dec. 9, 1896; s. Lewis Benote and Nora (Galligan) H.; student Reed Coll., 1915-18; A.B., Harvard, 1921; M.A. (Rhodes Scholar), Oxford U., 1924; LL.D., Fairleigh Dickinson Univ., 1954; m. Virginia Dean, 1942; 1 son, David Tristram. Organizer, operator Seven Acres Press, Eng., 1925-34; dir. Gregynog Pres., Wales, 1934-36; excavator Notley Abbey, Buckshire, 1933; lectr. Harvard, 1938; staff U. N.H. Writer's Conf., from 1940; asst. prof. Washington U., 1942-45; asso. prof. vets. coll. U. Mass., 1945-48; prof., chmn. dept. English, Fairleigh Dickinson University, 1948-59, dean of arts and sciences, 1959-66, academic head Wroxton Coll., Banbury, Eng., 1965-68; Distinguished professor of humanities, 1968-75. Served with 13th Inf., U.S. Army, World War I; member Mo. Nat. Guard, World War II. Mem. Poetry Society Am. (pres. 1963-68). Author: Collected Poems, 1931; Medieval English Pavingtiles, 1937; Silent Fame, 1945; Pursuit of the Horizon, a Biography of George Catlin, 1948; Highlights, a Book of Verse, 1960. Writer, illustrator, printer, binder of numerous hand-press books, from 1926. Editor: Pliny's Natural History, compacted edit. 1956. Home: Rutherford, N.J. Died Mar. 26, 1981.

HACKER, VICTOR N., coal and coke producer; b. Greenville, Tenn., July 21, 1884; s. Joseph E., and Jessie B. H.; prep. edn., high sch., Greenville; B.A., U. of Tenn., 1906; m. Lois Caldwell, of Knoxville, Tenn., Mar. 25, 1916; children—Martha, Lois. Pres. Pruden Coal & Coke Co.; dir. various cos.; executor and trustee Estate of Thomas Pruden since 1916. Mem. Southern Appalachian Coal Assn. (pres. since 1919), Nat. Coal Assn. (dir.), Am. Mining Congress, Chamber Commerce of U.S., Phi Gamma Delta. Republican. Baptist. Clubs: Old Colony, Cherokee Country (pres. 2 terms). Home: Knoxville. *

HACKETT, BOBBY, cornetist; b. Providence, Jan. 31, 1915; s. William F. and Rose (Mulvaney) H.; ed. public schs., Providence; m. Edna L. Lee, July 26, 1937; children—Barbara, Ernie. Trumpeter with Horace Heidt Band, 1939, Glenn Miller Band, 1941-42, NBC staff orch., 1943, Glen Gray Band, 1944-45, Paul Whiteman Band and ABC staff orch., from 1947; rec. artist for Capitol, Columbia, Epic Records, also Benny Goodman Concert Group; frequent TV concerts. Named to R.I. Hall of Fame, 1972, Newport Jazz Co. Hall of Fame, Nat. Acad. Rec. Arts and Scis. Hall of Fame. Mason. Home: Chatham, Mass. Died June 7, 1976.

HADDEN, JOHN ALEXANDER, lawyer; b. Cleve., July 11, 1886; s. Alexander and Frances (Hawthorne) H.; A.B., Harvard, 1908, LL.B., 1910; m. Marianne Elisabeth Millikin, Jan. 7, 1922; children—John Alexander, Alexander Hawthorne, Elisabeth Severance Alexander. Admitted Ohio bar, 1910; now mem. firm Arter, Hadden, Wykoff & Van Duzer; asst. dist. atty. No. dist. Ohio, 1912-13; dir., mem. exec. com. Youngstown Steel Door Co., Erie R.R. Co.; dir. Union Bank of Commerce, Enos Coal Mining Co., Enoco Collieries, Inc. Dep. regional dir. WPB, 1942-43. Trustee Elizabeth Severance Prestiss Found.; trustee, mem. exec. com. U. Hosp.; Ohio chmn. Harvard Law Sch. Fund, 1944. Mem. Ohio Legislature, 1925-31. Served as sgt. Troop A, 1st Squadron, Ohio N.G. on Mexican border, 1916-17; capt. 135th F.A., U.S. Army, 1917-19; with A.E.F., 1918-19. Mem. Am. Bar Assn., Ohio, Cleve., bar assns., Sigma Alpha Epsilon. Republican. Clubs: Union, Tavern, Kirtland, 50 (Cleveland); Ottawa, Shooting (Fremont, O.). Home: Cleveland OH. *

HADER, BERTA HOERNER (MRS. ELMER STANLEY HADER), writer, illustrator; b. San Pedro, Coahuila, Mexico; d. Albert and Adelaide (Jennings) Hoerner; student, U. Wash., 1909-12; Calif. Sch. Design, San Francisco, 1915-18; m. Elmer Stanley Hader, July 14, 1919. Began as fashion designer, 1914; newspaper artist, San Francisco Bulletin, 1916-18; miniature portrait painter, 1916-37; illustrator and writer of children's books 1919-77. Author and co-author numerous books including: Little Stone House, 1944; Rainbow's End, 1945; The Skyrocket, 1946; Little Chip, 1958; Reindeer Trail, 1959; Mr. Billy's Gun, 1960; Quack-Quack, 1961; Little Antelope, 1962. Illustrator with Elmer Stanley Hader: Adventures of Theodore Roosevelt, Humpy, Stripey; The Big Snow, 1948 (awarded Caldecott Medal). Author illustrator (with husband): Little Appaloosa, 1949; Squirrely of Willow Hill, 1950; Lost in the Zoo, 1951; Little Whitefoot, 1952; The Friendly Phoebe, 1953; Wish on the Moon, 1954; Home on the Range, 1955; The Runaways, 1956; Ding Dong Bell, 1957; Snow in the City, 1963; Two is Company, Three's a Crowd, 1965. Contbr. stories and drawings to mags. Home: Grand View-on-Hudson, N.Y. Died Feb. 5, 1977.

HADER, ELMER STANLEY, illustrator, writer; b. Pajaro, Calif., Sept. 7, 1889; s. Henry and Lena (Nyberg) H.; student Calif. Sch. Design, San Francisco, 1907-10; Julian Acad., Paris, France, 1912-14; m. Berta Hoerner, July 14, 1919. Began as landscape artist and portrait painter, 1914; illustrator and writer of children's books 1919-75. Zoning adminstr. Village of Grand View-on-Hudson, N.Y., 1925-75; mem. adv. bd. dirs. Hudson River Conservation Soc. Served camoufluer, engrs., U.S. Army in World War, 1918-19. Author and co-author numerous books including: The Little Stone House, 1944; Rainbow's End, 1945; The Skyrocket, 1946; Little Chip, 1958; Reindeer Trail, 1959; Mr. Billy's Gun, 1960; Quack-Quack, 1961; Little Antelope, 1962. Illustrator (with Berta Hoerner Hader): Bingo Is My Name, Here, Bingo, Humpy, Stripey, The Big Snow, 1948 (awarded Caldecott Medal). Author, illustrator (with wife): Little Appaloosa, 1949; Squirrely of Willow Hill, 1950; Lost in the Zoo, 1951; Little White Foot, 1952; The Friendly Phoebe, 1953; Wish on the Moon, 1954; Home on the Range, 1955; The Runaways, 1956; Ding Dong Bell, 1957; Snow in the City, 1963; Two is Company, Three's a Crowd, 1965. Contbr. stories and drawings to mags. Home: Grand View-on-Hudson, N.Y. Died Sept. 7, 1975.

HADLEY, HAMILTON, lawyer; b. New Haven, Jan. 13, 1896; s. Arthur Twining and Helen Harrison (Morris) H.; B.A., Yale, 1919, LL.B. cum laude, 1923; m. Emily Hammond Morris, July 13, 1929; 1 dau., Anne (Mrs. John Keith Howat). Partner, law firm Winthrop, Stimson, Putnam and Roberts, N.Y.C., 1929-40; trustee U.S. Trust Co., N.Y.C., 1936-68, hon. trustee, 1968-75; v.p., dir. Am. Superpower Corp., 1929-40; in period of orgn. and original financing v.p. Niagara Hudson Power Corp., Commonwealth and So. Corp.; dir. Research Corp., 1930-57. Dir. and trustee The Brearley Sch., 1930-54; asso. fellow Branford Coll., Yale, 1939-75; councillor Am. Geog. Soc.; gov. N.Y. Hosp., 1947-65, hon. gov., 1966-75, pres., 1953-57. Served as capt. A.E.F., U.S. Air Service, World War I. Life mem. Am. Mus. Natural History, Acad. Polit. Sci., Am. Geog. Soc.; mem. Assn. Bar City N.Y., Am., N.Y. State bar assns. Clubs: Century Assn., Down Town Assn., Yale (N.Y.); New Haven Lawn, Graduates, Elizabethan (New Haven). Author: A Free Order, 1963. Address: Armonk, N.Y. Died 1975.

HADLEY, MORRIS, lawyer; b. New Haven, Mar. 21, 1894; s. Arthur Twining and Helen Harrison (Morris) H.; B.A., Yale, 1916, LL.D., 1963; LL.B., Harvard, 1921; m. Katherine Cumnock Blodgett, July 12, 1919 (dec. Aug. 1980); children—Arthur Twining II, Katherine Morris Michel (dec.), John W.B. Barbara (Mrs. Dixon L. Stanton). Admitted to N.Y. bar, 1922, practiced in N.Y.C.; partner firm Milbank, Tweed, Hadley and McCloy and predecessor firms, 1924-79. Served in Conn. N.G., 1915-16; commd. maj. 302d Field Arty., U.S. Army, 1917; served with A.E.F. in Meuse-Argonne campaign, 1918; mem. staff, Army of Occupation, 1919. Fellow corp. Yale U., 1940-62; trustee Carnegie Corp., 1947-67, chmn., 1955-66; trustee N.Y. Pub. Library, pres., 1943-58; trustee Pierpont Morgan Library. Mem. Am., N.Y. State, N.Y. County bar assns., Assn. Bar City of N.Y. Republican. Conglist. Clubs: Century, Down Town (N.Y.C.). Author: The Citizen and the Law, 1941; Arthur Twining Hadley, 1948. Home: New York, N.Y. Died Jan. 17, 1979; interred New Haven.

HADLOCK, WENDELL STANWOOD, museum adv. dir.; b. Islesford, Maine, May 12, 1911; s. George R. and Edna (Campbell) H.; A.B., U. Maine, 1936; M.A., U. Pa., 1946; m. Susan Sadler, July 3, 1936; 1 dau., Jean Campbell. Curator hist. collection, Islesford, summers 1929-35; curator Robert Abbe Mus. of Stone Age Antiquities, Bar Harbor, Maine, 1936-50; mus. asst. Peabody Mus., Salem, Mass., 1948-49, adminstrv. asst., 1949-50; dir. William A. Farnsworth Library and Art Mus., Rockland, Maine, 1951-76, adv. dir., 1976-78; archeol. explorations, Maine, New Brunswick, Conn.; cons. Maine Hwy. Commn.; historian, archeologist Acadia Nat. Park. Mem. Am. Acad. Arts and Sciences, Sigma Xi. Contbr. articles to archeol., hist. jours. Home: Rockland, Maine. Died Dec. 19, 1978; interred Woodbine Cemetery, Ellsworth, Maine.

HAFFNER, CHARLES CHRISTIAN, JR., printing co. exec.; b. Bloomville, Ohio, Mar. 15, 1895; s. Charles Christian and Minnie (Zahner) H.; ed. St George's Sch., Newport, R.I., 1911-14; A.B., Yale U., 1919; m. Clarissa Donnelley, Oct. 10, 1925; children—Clarissa Haffner Chandler, Charles Christian III, Frances Ann Haffner Colburn, Phoebe Haffner Andrew; m. 2d, Mary Cotton. Exec. v.p. City Nat. Bank & Trust Co., 1933-34; treas., v.p., pres. R. R. Donnelley and Sons, 1934-52, chief exec. officer, chmn. bd., 1952-64, chmn. fin. com., 1964-77; chmn. bd. dirs. Lakeside Bank, 1965-70. Served to capt. F.A., U.S. Army, 1918; served as maj. gen. AUS, 1942. Mem. NAM (nat. v.p. 1953-55), Ill. Mfrs. Assn. (pres. 1954), U.S. C. of C. (past dir.), Chicago Assn. Commerce and Industry (past dir.). Clubs: Chicago, Commercial (Chgo.); Ontwentsia (Lake Forest). Home: Lake Forest, Ill. Died Feb. 13, 1979.

HAGEN, OSCAR CARL, investments; b. Upsala, Sweden, Aug. 11, 1883; s. Carl Augustus and Permelia (Anderson) H.; came with parents to U.S., 1890; ed. pub. schs.; LL.D., College of the Ozarks, Clarksville, Ark.; m. Daise Hoffman, of Canton, Illinois, 1902 (dec.); 1 dau., Dorothy; m. 2d, Emma Julia Ernst, of Chicago, Ill., Feb. 13, 1926; children (adopted)—Virginia, James. Began in investment business, Chicago, 1909. Trustee Olivet Inst., College of Wooster, College of the Ozarks, Beaver College, Millikin University; dir. Presbyn. Theol. Sem., Church Extension Bd., McKinley Memorial Foundation of U. of Ill. Republican. Mason (32 deg.). Clubs: Medinah Athletic, Bob O'Link Golf, South Shore Country,

Olympia Country (Chicago); Bel-Air (Calif.) Country; Barrington Hills Country. Home: Chicago. *

HAGGERTY, PATRICK EUGENE, electronics mfg. co. exec.; b. Harvey, N.D., Mar. 17, 1914; s. Michael Eugene and Lillian (Evenson) H.; B.S. in Elec. Engring., Marquette U., 1936, LL.D., 1960; LL.D. (hon.), St. Mary's U., San Antonio, 1959, U. Dallas, 1964, Cath. U., 1971; D.Eng., Poly. Inst. Bklyn., 1962, Rensselaer Poly. Inst., 1972, U. Notre Dame, 1974; Sc.D. (hon.), N.D. State U., 1967; m. Beatrice E. Menne, Feb. 26, 1938; children—Sheila Margaret, Kathleen Mary, Patrick Eugene, Teresa Ann, Michael Gamble. Asst. gen. mgr. Badger Carton Co., Milw., 1935-42; gen. mgr. lab. and mfg. div. Texas Instruments, Inc. (and predecessors), Dallas, 1945-50, exec. v.p., dir., 1951-58, pres., dir., 1958-66, chmn., chief exec. officer, 1967-69, chmn., chief corp. officer, 1969-76, gen. dir., hon. chmn., 1976; ret., 1976; dir. A.H. Belo Corp.; chmn. Nat. Council on Ednl. Research, 1973-74; mem. Pres.'s Commn. Accident at Three Mile Island, 1979. Chmn. bd. trustees, mem. exec. com. Rockefeller U.; trustee, mem. exec. com. U. Dallas. Served as lt. USNR, 1942-45. Recipient Medal of Honor, Electronics Industry Assn., 1967, Founders award IEEE, 1968; medal Industrial Research Institute, 1969, Wema Medal of Achievement 1972; named Alumnus of Year, Marquette U., 1972. Fellow IEEE (John Fritz medal 1971), Tex. Acad. Sci.; mem. Nat. Acad. Engring., AAAS, Bus. Council, Sigma Phi Delta, Tau Beta Pi, Eta Kappa Nu, Alpha Sigma Nu. Home: Dallas, Tex. Died Oct. 1, 1980.

HAGOPIAN, PETER B., psychiatrist, hosp. adminstr.; b. Adana, Turkey, Dec. 25, 1908; s. Sarkis and Maritsa (Kachadoorian) H.; brought to U.S., 1921, naturalized, 1931; B.S., Tufts U., 1935, M.D., 1935; m. Teriz Malootian, Dec. 23, 1951; children—Debby, Peter B., Paul G. Intern, Boston City, Carney hosps., Boston, 1935-37; resident in psychiatry Danvers State Hosp., Hathorne, Mass., 1937-41, chief staff, 1946-49, supt., med. dir., from 1953; instr. psychiatry Med. Sch. Tufts U., 1947-49; asst. psychiatry Harvard Med. Sch., from 1965; 1st asst. commr. Mass. Dept. Mental Health, Boston, 1949-53, acting commr., 1950-51, chmn. civil def. com., from 1958; asso. dir. psychology Mass. Gen. Hosp., from 1964; cons. staff Salem Hosp., from 1973; chief psychiatry service VA Hosp., Brockton, Mass., from 1974. Served with AUS, 1941-46. Diplomate Am. Bd. Psychiatry and Neurology. Fellow Am. Psychiat. Assn. (pres. No. New Eng. dist. br. 1959-60); mem. AMA, Mass., Essex South Dist. med. socs., New Eng. Soc. Psychiatry (past pres.). Club: Rotary. Contbr. articles to profl. jours. Address: Danvers, Mass. Died Nov. 11, 1977.

HAHN, EDGAR A., lawyer; b. Cleve., Nov. 25, 1882; s. Aaron and Therese (Kalb) H.; LL.B., Western Res. U., 1903; spl. course Columbia, 1903-04; D.H.L., Case Inst. Tech., 1965; LL.D., Western Res. U., 1967, John Carroll U., 1967; D.H.L., Wilberforce U., 1969; m. Irene Moss, Jan. 10, 1910 (dec. 1939); children—Alice (Mrs. Stanley J. Goodman), Katherine (Mrs. B.S. Bercovici). Admitted to Ohio bar, 1904, since practiced in Cleve.; now sr. partner Hahn, Loeser, Freedheim, Dean & Wellman; dir. several business firms. Mem. 1st charter commn. of Cleve., 1912. Trustee Musical Arts Assn., Cleve. Mus. Art; trustee, pres. Louis D. Beaumont Found. Recipient Fletcher Reed Andrews award Western Res. U., 1964; medal pub. service Cleve. C. of C., 1965; Ursula Lauras medal Ursuline Coll., 1966. Mem. Am., Ohio, Cleve. bar assns., Cleve. C. of C., Soc. Benchers (charter). Clubs: Oakwood, Mid-Day, Rowfant. Home: Bratenahl, OH 44108. *

HAIEN, JOHN, dir. air craft training; b. Esens, Ostfreesland, Germany, Jan. 16, 1885; s. Heye Janssen and Magdalene (Hoffrath) H.; came to U.S., 1892, naturalized, 1905; student Ia. Wesleyan Acad., 1905-08, Boston U., 1909-10, Harvard U., 1910-11; independent study in Boston and Cambridge, Mass., 1911-14; m. Ella Pugh Keith, 1914; children—Keith Addison, Jean Magdalene, Jack, Jeannette. Began as factory sweeper, 1899, factory foreman, 1904; lecturer on statistics and economics, Babson Statis. Orgn., 1914-16; now dir. youth training and aircraft training, Chrysler Corp., Detroit; formerly dir. manual and mech. training, National Youth Adminstrn. Member Society Automotive Engineers, Beta Theta Pi. Episcopalian. Mason. Founded numerous tool libraries for boys. Home: Ann Arbor, Mich. *

HAIG-BROWN, RODERICK LANGMERE, author; b. Lancing, Sussex, Eng., Feb. 21, 1908; s. Alan Roderick and Violet (Pope) H-B.; student Charterhouse Sch., 1921-25; LL.D., U. B.C., 1952; m. Ann Elmore, Jan. 20, 1934; children—Valerie Joan, Mary Charlotte (Mrs. F. O. Bowker), Alan Roderick, Evelyn Celia (Mrs. Ted Vayro). Author: Silver, 1931; Pool & Rapid, 1932; Panther, 1934; The Western Angler, 1939; Return to the River, 1944; Timber, 1942; Starbuck Valley Winter, 1943; A River Never Sleeps, 1946; Saltwater Summer, 1948; Measure of the Year, 1950; On the Highest Hill, 1949; Mounted Police Patrol, 1954; Fisherman's Spring, 1951; Fisherman's Winter, 1954; Captain of the Discovery, 1956; Fisherman's Summer, 1959; The Farthest Shores, 1960; The Living Land, 1961; Fur and Gold, 1962; The Whale People, 1962; A Primer of Fly Fishing, 1964; Fisherman's Fall, 1964; The Salmon, 1974; Bright Waters, Bright Fish, 1980; The World of Roderick Haig-Brown (edited by Valerie Haig-Brown), 3 vols., 1980-81; contbg. author Canadian Lit., The New Yorker, The Atlantic Monthly, The CBC, Sports Illus., Life mag., American Sportsman, other periodicals; asst. to Nat. Film Bd. in producing films; Country Magistrate, Fisherman's Fall; magistrate, judge Provincial Ct. B.C., 1941-75. Adviser B.C. Wildlife Fedn., Fedn. Fly Fishermen; mem. Fed. Saltwater Sports Fishing Adv. Com., Fed. Fisheries Devel. Council, Fed. Electoral Boundaries Commn., 1964-65, 72-73, 75, Internat. Pacific Salmon Commn., 1970-76. Chancellor U. Victoria, 1969-72; bd. dirs. Nat. 2d Century Fund. Trustee Nature Conservance Can.; nat. dir. Trout Unlimited (U.S.). Served with Canadian Army, World War II. Recipient Can. Library Assn. medal, 1946, 63; Gov.-Gen.'s Citation, 1948; U. Alta. Nat. award in Letters, 1956; Burien Guild (Seattle) Library award, 1964; Crandall Conservation award, 1955; Harkin award Nat. Parks Assn. Can. Home: Campbell River, B.C., Can. Died Oct. 9, 1976.

HAIGH, FRANK COYAL (HAG), prof. chemistry; b. Green Lake, Wis., Nov. 25, 1885; s. Willis Sanford and Fanny Minnie (Dike) H.; A.B., Ripon (Wis.) Coll., 1908; Ph.D., Yale, 1912; m. Mabel Frost, Aug. 23, 1913; children—John Willis, Helen Lucy. Instr. in chemistry, Sheffield Sci. Sch., Yale U., 1912-15; prof. of chemistry and head of chemistry dept., Whitman Coll., Walla Walla, Wash., since 1916, dean of the faculty since 1948. Mem. American Chem. Soc., Sigma Xi. Mem. First Congl. Ch., Walla Walla, Wash. Mason (32 deg.). Home: Walla Walla, Wash. *

HAINES, CHARLES GROVE, educator; b. Abbottstown, Pa., Dec. 10, 1906; s. Wilbur Emory and Helen Estella (Wolf) H.; A.B., Ursinus Coll., 1927; A.M., Clark U., 1928, Ph.D., 1933; postgrad. U. Rome (Italy), 1930-31; m. Frances Elizabeth Marble, June 28, 1928; 1 dau., Frances M. Asst. econs. and govt. Worcester Poly. Inst., 1928-30; mem. faculty Syracuse U., 1931-45, prof. history, 1943-45; dir. area and lang. program, 1943-44; vis. prof. history Columbia, spring 1945; prof. diplomatic history Sch. Advanced Internat. Studies, Johns Hopkins, 1945-55, founder, dir. Bologna Center, Johns Hopkins U., (Italy), 1955-74. Mem. Fgn. Service Res., research attaché to Milan, Italy and Trieste, 1948-49; cons. Dept. State, 1950-54. Am. Exchange Fellow to Italy, 1930-31. Mem. bd. govs. Middle East Inst., 1946-48. Decorated officer Order of Merit (Italy); Order of the Silver Eagle (Austria); recipient Medal of Honor for service in field of internate. relations, Fed. Republic Germany, 1975. Mem. Am. Hist. Assn., The Burke Soc., AAUP, Fgn. Policy Assn., Phi Beta Kappa, Tau Kappa Alpha, Phi Kappa Phi. Democrat. Unitarian. Clubs: Syracuse University (N.Y.); Cosmos. Author: (with W. B. Walsh), The Development of Western Civilization 1941; The Origins and Background of the Second World War (with R. J. S. Hoffman), 1943, 46; Fgn. Policy Assn. Reports on Italian Questions, 1943-46. Editor: The Threat of Soviet Imperialism; Africa Today, 1955; European Intergration, 1957. Editorial bd Jour. of Modern Hist., 1948-49; editor headline series Fgn. Policy Assn., 1944-45; mem. editorial bd. The Middle East Jour., 1946-76; dir. The American Review. Contr. articles to jours. Radio broadcaster; public lectr. Home: Sienna, Italy. Died May 25, 1976.

HAINES, CHARLES JAMES, bus. exec.; b. Thomas, Okla., Oct. 6, 1896; s. James and Mary Frances (Spotts) H.; B.S. in Engring., U. Mo., 1917; m. Marguerite Fralick, Jan. 18, 1936; 1 dau., Heather (Mrs. W. E. Richmond, Jr.). Supt. Am. Cotton Oil Co., Chgo., 1917-20; supt. Electrox Co., Peoria, Ill., 1920-23; exec. Nat. Cylinder Gas Co. (name changed to Chemetron Corp., 1958), Chgo., 1923-72, dir., 1934-72; pres., 1937-60, chmn. bd., chief exec. officer, 1960-67, chmn, bd. dirs., 1967-70, hon. chmn. bd., 1970-72. Fellow Am. Inst. Scientists; mem. Am. Inst. Chem Engrs., Am. Chem. Soc., Tau Beta Pi, Alpha Chi Sigma, Phi Kappa Psi. Clubs: Chicago, University (Chgo.); ExmoorCountry (Highland Park, Ill.) Home: Chicago, Ill. Died Feb. 17, 1979.

HAINES, RALPH EDWARD (HANZ), army officer; b. Vinton, Ia., Aug. 4, 1883; s. Alfred and Flora M. (Conklin) H.; student Pomona Coll., Claremont, Calif., 1902-04; B.S., U. of Calif., 1907; hon. grad. Coast Arty. Sch., 1916; grad. advance course, same, 1923; distinguished grad. Command and Gen. Staff Sch., 1924; grad. Army War Coll., 1927; m. Ethel Lyman Smith, Oct. 9, 1912; children—Ralph E., John L. Commd. 2d lt., Coast Arty. Corps, June 20, 1910; promoted through grades to brig. gen. U.S. Army, Jan. 29, 1941; commanded successively harbor defenses of Narragansett Bay, New York-Philadelphia sector, harbor defenses of San Francisco, Northern California Sector, Western Defense Command (present command). Awarded Victory medal. Mem. Scabbard and Blade. Home: San Diego, Calif.*

HAINES, RICHARD CARLETON, archaeol. architect; b. Tabernacle, N.J., Dec. 22, 1904; s. Carleton and Annie (Templeton) H.; B.Arch., Carnegie Inst. Tech., 1928; m. Irene Garwood, June 29, 1940; children—Alice Elizabeth, Richard Carleton. Draftsman in archtl. offices, 1928-30, 45-49; field architect Oriental Inst., U. Chgo., 1930-42, 49-72; archaeol. excavations in Turkey, Syria, Iran, Israel, Iraq, 1930-40, 49-65; field dir. Nippur Expdn., 1956-64; mem. faculty U. Chgo., 1959-71, asst. prof., 1963-71, emeritus, 1971-77. Author: Excavations in the Plain of Antioch II, 1971; co-author Soundings at Tell Fakhariyah, 1958; A Byzantine Church at Khirbat al-Karak, 1960; Nippur I, 1968. Home: Cape May Court House, N. J. Died Feb. 15, 1977.

HALAS, GEORGE STANLEY, JR., profl. football exec.; b. Chgo., Sept. 4, 1925; s. George Stanley and Minnie (Bushing) H.; B.S. in Commerce, Loyola U. Chgo., 1950; m. Patricia Navilio, Aug. 27, 1978; children by previous marriage—Christine, Stephen. Treas., Chgo. Bears Football Club, 1953-63, pres., gen. mgr., 1963-74, pres., 1974-79. Bd. dirs. Chgo. Assn. Retarded Children, United Cerebral Palsy. Served with USNR, 1944-46. Fellow St. Joseph's Coll., Rensselaer, Ind., 1964. Roman Catholic. Clubs: Chgo. Athletic Assn., Ridgemoor Country (Chgo). Home: Chicago, Ill. Died Dec. 16, 1979.

HALBERSTAM, MICHAEL JOSEPH, physician; b. Bronx, N.Y., Aug. 9, 1932; s. Charles Abraham and Blanche (Levy) H.; A.B., Harvard U., 1953; M.D., Boston U., 1957; m. Elliott Anna Jones, Dec. 11, 1975; children by previous marriage—Charles, Eben. Intern, Montefiore Hosp., N.Y.C., 1957-58; resident Mary Fletcher Hosp., Burlington, Vt., 1960-62; cardiology fellow George Washington Hosp., Washington, 1962-64; pvt. practice medicine specializing in cardiology and internal medicine, Washington, 1964-80; asst. clin. prof. medicine George Washington U. Med. Sch., 1972-80. Bd. dirs. Coalition for a Democratic Majority, 1975-77. Served with USPHS, 1958-60. Diplomate Am. Bd. Internal Medicine. Mem. Inst. Medicine, Cogswell Soc. Democrat. Jewish. Clubs: Federal City, Potomac Boat. Author: The Pills in Your Life, 1972; A Coronary Event, 1976; The Wanting of Levine, 1978; sr. med. editor Modern Medicine, 1975-76, editor, 1977-80; contbr. articles to med. jours. Home: Washington, D.C. Died Dec. 5, 1980.

HALDEMAN, WILLIAM S(TRUBHAR), educator; born Pine Grove, Pa., Apr. 25, 1881; s. John and Sarah (Strubhar) H.; Diploma Pa. State Normal School, 1904; B.S., U. of Pa., 1914; A.M., Harvard, 1920; student U. of Ill., summer sessions, 1920, 22, 23, 24; married Ruth Bishop, March 21, 1958. Began as county school teacher near Pine Grove, Pa., 1901-02; high sch. teacher, Aldenville, Pa., 1904-09; instr. Keystone State Normal Sch., Kutztown, Pa., 1909-13, 1914-15; student grad. sch., Harvard, 1915-16; instr. Friends Coll., Wichita, Kan., 1916-18; prof., head chemistry dept. Monmouth (Ill.) Coll., 1918-58, now prof. chemistry, emeritus. Recipient the 1950 Gold medal Midwest award from St. Louis sect. Am. Chem. Soc. for meritorious contribution to chemistry. Fellow A.A.A.S.; mem. American Chem. Soc. (councilor Ill.-Ia. sect., mem. standing com., chem. edn. 1953-55, 56-58), Ill. Acad. Scis., Alpha Chi Sigma. Republican. Rotarian (hon.).

HALE, BEATRICE FORBES-ROBERTSON, lecturer, author; b. N.Y. City, Sept. 11, 1883; d. Ian and Gertrude F. (Knight) Forbes-Robertson; ed. St. Leonard's Sch., St. Andrews, Scotland; Bedford Coll., U. of London; m. Swinburne Hale, lawyer, of N.Y. City, June 30, 1910; children—Sanchia, Rosemary and Clemency (twins). Début on stage at 17, in Manchester, Eng., under Sir Henry Irving in his revival of "Robespierre"; came to U.S. with Ellen Terry, 1907, and returned, 1908, 1909, under direction of Charles Frohman; with the New Theatre Co., New York, during its first season, 1910; has devoted her attention largely to lecturing on the drama and the woman's movement, since 1910; has spoken for woman suffrage in over 30 states; lectured for Progressive Party, 1912; lectures for League of Nations Union, Great Britain and France. Mem. U.S. Food Administration, Washington, 1918. Clubs: Woman's City (New York); Sesame (London). Author: What Women Want, 1914; The Nest-Builder, 1916; Little Allies, 1918; What's Wrong with Our Girls? 1923.

HALE, FRANK CONNELL, lawyer, former govt. ofcl.; b. Madisonville, Tex., Feb. 14, 1906; s. William N. and Florence (Harrison) H.; student John Brown U., 1924-25, U. Tex., 1925-26; LL.B., George Washington U., 1933; m. Sue M. Smith, May 31, 1946; children—Susan Harrison (Mrs. John C. Whitten), Jane Alison (Mrs. Joseph F. Murphy). Admitted to Tex. bar, 1935, D.C. bar, 1961; with FTC, 1928-63, 1965-70, dir. bur. deceptive practices, 1968-70, spl. dep. atty. gen. Hawaii, 1963-65. Commr., Arlington County Consumer Protection Commn., from 1971. Served as spl. agt., officer CIC, AUS, 1942-45; PTO. Recipient Distinguished Service award FTC, 1963. Mem. State Bar Tex., D.C., Fed. (chmn. antitrust com. 1962-63) bar assns., Sigma Alpha Epsilon. Methodist. Mason. Clubs:

Belle Haven Country (Alexandria, Va.); Pinehurst (N.C.) Country. Home: Arlington, Va. Died Sept. 21, 1976.

HALE, MARICE RUTLEDGE (MRS. GARDNER HALE), author (pen name Marice Rutledge); b. N.Y. City, Nov. 24, 1886; d. George Rutledge and Laura (Belden) Gibson; ed. Miss Spence's Sch., New York, and in Paris, France; m. Morgan Goetchius, of New York; m. 2d, Edmond van Saanen Algi, of Roumania; m. 3d, at Paris, Gardner Hale (artist), of Chicago, Sept. 22, 1916. Author: Anne of Tréboul, 1910; The Blind Who See, 1912; Wild Grapes, 1914; Children of Fate, 1917; also The Thing They Loved, repub. from Century, in book of Prize Stories (O. Henry Memorial Soc.), 1920; Sad Adventures, 1924. Contbr. Century, Harper's, Atlantic Monthly, Smart Set, Saturday Evening Post, etc. Address: New York, N.Y., and Paris, France. *

HALE, MARK PENDLETON, social worker; b. Salisbury, Mo., Feb. 13, 1912; s. Holly Morgan and Dora Blanche (Pendleton) H.; A.B., Hiram (O.) Coll., 1932; M.A., U. of Mo., 1933; student Sch. of Social Service Adminstrn., U. Chgo., 1941-42, Ph.D., 1956; m. Allean Lemmon, Dec. 31, 1936; children—Susanna Lemmon, Mark Pendleton. Supr. Mo. Nat. Youth Adminstrn., St. Joseph, 1935; social analyst Mo. State Children's Bur., Jefferson City, 1935-37, Mo. State Social Security Commn., 1937-41; research asst. and instr. Sch. Social Service Adminstrn., U. Chgo., 1942, summer,1943, 45; asso. prof. research Nashville Sch. of Social Work, 1942-43, Tulane Sch. of Social Work, 1943-46, prof. social economy, 1946-47; prof., chmn., dept. social work U. Mo., 1947-55; prof., dir. sch. of social work State U. Ia., 1954-62; dir. Jane Addams Grad. Sch. Social Work, U. Ill., 1962-75. Mem. accrediting commn., Nat. Council Social Work Edn., 1952; pres. central dist., Mo. Assn. Social Welfare; mem. Social Work Research Group; cons. Tenn. Personnel div., 1943. Recipient Fulbright sr. research scholarship, 1957-58. Mem. Am. Assn. Schs. Social Work (chmn. subcom. on tchg. materials in research from 1947), Am. Assn. Social Workers, Nat. Research Commn. (chpt. chmn. New Orleans 1946), Nat. Conf. Social Work, Am. Assn. U. Profs., La. Conf. Social Welfare (1st v.p. 1946), Mo. Assn. Social Welfare (sec. 1948), Council on Social Work Edn. (chmn. grad. sch. div., chmn. commn. on schs. and depts. 1956, chmn. accreditation commn. 1963-68), Ia. Welfare Assn. (pres. 1961), Nat. Conf. Social Welfare (nat. bd. 1961-62), Am. Pub. Welfare Assn. (nat. bd. 1961-63, 1st v.p. 1966-68). Mem. Ch. Disciples of Christ. Home: Urbana, Ill. Died Nov. 4, 1977; buried Columbia, Mo.

HALE, RICHARD WALDEN, JR., archivist; b. Boston, Aug. 5, 1909; s. Richard Walden and Mary (Patterson) H.; A.B., Harvard U., 1930, Ph.D., 1937; B.A. with honors in History (Fiske scholar), Cambridge (Eng.) U., 1932; m. Elisabeth Fairbanks, Aug. 9, 1940; children—Peter, Thomas, Frances (Mrs. Douglas Vigneron), Martha (Mrs. Robert Abshear). Instr., Antioch Coll., 1932-33, Princeton, 1935-40; mem. staff Newberry Library, Chgo., 1941-43; head history dept. Roxbury Latin Sch., Boston, 1943-47; lectr. edn. Wellesley Coll., 1948-52; curator Canadian history Harvard Coll. Library, 1953-57; editor Guide to Photocopied Hist. Materials, 1957-60; archivist Commonwealth of Mass., from 1961; acting chmn. Mass. Hist. Commn., 1964-72; pres., Nat. Conf. State Historic Preservation Officers, 1969-72. Fellow Soc. Am. Archivists, Pilgrim Soc. Plymouth; mem. Am. Antiquarian Soc., Colonial Soc. Mass., Am. Records Mgmt. Assn., Mass. Hist. Soc., Am., Canadian hist. assns., Brit. Records Assn., Phi Beta Kappa. Clubs: Union (Boston); Century (N.Y.C.); Chgo. Literary; Savile (London). Author: Democratic France, 1870-1940, 1941; Tercentenary History of Roxbury Latin School, 1946; Story of Bar Harbor, 1949; Britain, Her Peoples and the Commonwealth (with Robert Eckles), 1954. Editor: Guide to Photocopied Historical Materials, 1960. Home: Chestnut Hill, Mass. Died Feb. 25, 1976.

HALE, ROBERT, congressman; b. Portland, Maine, Nov. 29, 1889; s. Clarence and Margaret (Rollins) H.; A.B., Bowdoin, 1910, LL.D., 1947; Rhodes scholar, Oxford, 1910-13, B.A., 1912, M.A., 1921; Harvard U. Law Sch., 1913-14; M.A., U. Maine, 1931; married Agnes Burke, Apr. 20, 1922; 1 dau., Patricia (Mrs. Cornelius John Tyson). With Choate, Hall & Stewart. Boston, 1914-16; with Verrill, Hale, Booth & Ives, Portland, Maine, 1917-20, except when in mil. service; partner same firm and its successor, Verrill, Hale, Dana & Walker, 1920-42. Enlisted U.S. Army, November 27, 1917; commd. 2d lt. inf., Mar. 1918; with A.E.F. in France, 1917-19; mem. staff of mission sent by U.S. Peace Commn. to Finland, Estonia, Latvia and Lithuania, 1919; hon. disch., Sept., 1919; mem. Maine Ho. of Reps. 1923-30, speaker of House, 1929-30; mem. 78th to 84th Congresses 1st Maine Dist. apptd. by Pres. Eisenhower to commn. to conciliate differences between U.S. and Switzerland. Bd. overseers Bowdoin Coll.; active Maine State Soc. Mem. Am. Bar Assn., Psi Upsilon, Phi Beta Kappa. Republican. Conglist. Club: Met. Home: Washington, D.C. Died Nov. 30, 1976.

HALEY, JACK, actor, real estate exec.; b. Boston, 1899; s. John Joseph and Ellen (Curley) H.; LL.D. (hon.), Stonehill Coll., 1957; m. Florence MacFadden, Feb. 25, 1921; children—Gloria (Mrs. Milan Radovich), Jack. Appeared in numerous motion pictures including Good News, 1928, Follow Through, 1929, Alexander's Ragtime Band, Wake Up and Live, Pigskin Parade, Wizard of Oz; pres. Madera Ranchos, Inc. Served with USO, World War II. Decorated knight of Malta. Mem. Am. Guild Variety Artists (pres.), K.C. (4). Clubs: New York Athletic; Bel-Air Country (Beverly Hills). Home: Beverly Hills, Calif. Died June 6, 1979.

HALFORD, RALPH STANLEY, ret. educator; b. Vallejo, Calif., Apr. 21, 1914; s. John Jefferson and Kathleen (Loftus) H.; B.S., U. Calif., 1935, Ph.D., 1938; m. Marion Kee Glover, Mar. 3, 1939. Instr. chemistry U. Calif., 1938-40; NRC fellow Harvard, 1940-41, instr. chemistry, 1941-43, lectr., 1943-46; asso. prof. Columbia, N.Y.C., 1946-51, prof. chemistry, 1952-77, vice-provost projects and grants, 1959-67, dean grad. faculties, 1961-67, asst. to pres., 1967, v.p. spl. projects, 1968-77, prof. and dean emeritus, 1977-78; vis. com. chemistry dept. Brookhaven Nat. Lab., 1954-56. Staff OSRD, 1944; NRC adv. com. Office Ordnance Research, 1951-52; nat. selection com. on Fulbright awards to U.K., 1954-56. Trustee Asso. Univs., Inc., 1959-74. Guggenheim fellow, 1952-53. Fellow Am. Phys. Society; mem. Am. Chem. Soc., N.Y. Acad. Scis., Sigma Xi, Alpha Chi Sigma. Asso. editor Jour. Chem. Physics, 1950-52. Home: New York, N.Y. Died Dec. 7, 1978.

HALL, ALBERT RICHARDSON, ex-congressman; b. West Baden, Ind., Aug. 27, 1884; s. Joseph A. and Mary Frances (Apple) H.; prep. edn., high sch.; student Indiana University, 1911; A.B., Earlham Coll., Richmond, Ind., 1912; m. Evelyn Wood, 1913 (dec.); children—James Gibson, Albert Morris, Martha Frances. Elected county supt. schs., Grant Co., Ind., 1921; mem. 69th to 71st Congresses (1925-31), 11th Ind. Dist.; now pres. Hall Printing Co., Inc. Republican. Presbyn. Mason. Rotarian. Home: Marion, Ind.*

HALL, ALONZO CLEVELAND, univ. prof.; b. Burlington, N.C., Dec. 15, 1886; s. Robert Jehu and Susan (Sellars) H.; ed. Fonville's Acad., 1900-02, Burlington (N.C.) High Sch., 1902-06; student Oxford (Eng.) Univ., summer 1908; A.B., Elon Coll., 1910; student Harvard, 1911-12, U. of Va., 1918; A.M., Columbia, 1913; m. Mary Virginia Farmer, June 24, 1913; children—Alonzo C. (dec.), Mary Sue (Mrs. Robert D. Schapiro). Head English dept. Calhoun (Ga.) High Sch., 1910-11, Columbus High Sch., 1913-16; asst. prof. English dept., Woman's Coll., U. of N.C., 1916-23, chmn. sophomore English, since 1916, prof. of English and Am. lit. since 1923. Chmn. Greensboro Housing Authority, since 1940. Mem. Nat. Council English Tchrs. (v.p.), N.C. Council of English Teachers (pres.), Modern Lang. Assn. (southern br.). Democrat. Presbyterian (treas. and bus. mgr. since 1936; deacon 1931-43; ruling elder since 1943). Club: Kiwanis (past pres.). Author: Outlines of American Literature, 1925; Outlines of English Literature, 1930, Grave Humor, 1949. Editor: Alumnae Miscellany (50th anniversary vol.), 1942. Contbr. articles to various publs. Home: Greensboro, N.C. *

HALL, ARTHUR BENEDICT, real estate exec.; b. Mt. Vernon, O., Mar. 27, 1881; s. Russell T. and Mary (Tyler) H.; A.B., Yale, 1902; m. Elsie Springer, Oct. 18, 1910; children—Russell Edward, Barbara. Entered joint office of Bryan Lathrop and Thomas A. Hall & Co. in 1902; became mem. of firm of Thomas A. Hall & Co., 1909; with partner William Marshall Ellis succeeded to the business of Bryan Lathrop and Thomas A. Hall & Co., 1916, adopting Hall & Ellis as the new firm name; dir. Chicago Dock & Canal Co.; pres. and director of Graceland Cemetery Company. Trustee Univ. of Chicago, Carroll Coll., Orchestral Association, Chicago YMCA; member board of directors of La Salle Extension University. Member Chicago Real Estate Bd., Art Inst. Chicago (life). Republican. Presbyterian. Clubs: University, Yale, City; La Grange Country; Phi Gamma Delta, Phi Beta Kappa. Home: La Grange, Ill. Died Jan. 5, 1972.

HALL, FRANK WILLIAM, advt. exec.; b. N.Y.C., July 2, 1920; s. Frank Lownes and Evelyn (Batchelor) H.; B.A., Dartmouth, 1941; m. Suzanne Louise Riley, Oct. 3, 1943; children—Frank William, Suzanne Louise (Mrs. Brian E. Chafin), Mary Evelyn. Asst. dir. athletic publicity Dartmouth, 1941-42; with Albert Frank-Guenther Law, Inc., N.Y.C., 1946-76, v.p., 1953-70, chmn. exec. com., 1966-76, pres., 1970-76, also dir. Served with AUS, 1942-45; ETO. Decorated Bronze Star. Mem. N.Y. Financial Advertisers Marketing Assn. (pres. 1965), Bank Marketing Assn. Clubs: Cherry Valley (Garden City); Wall St., Bankers (N.Y.C.). Home: Garden City, N.Y. Died Dec. 6, 1976; buried Holy Rood Cemetery, Westbury, N.Y.

HALL, GILBERT PHELPS, architect; b. Brooklyn, N.Y., Oct. 15, 1884; s. William A. and Abigail K. (Underhill) H.; ed. Rutgers Prep. Sch., New Brunswick, N.J., 1900-04; Bach. of Arch., Cornell, 1909; diplome École National des Beaux Arts, Paris, 1914; m. Virginia Foley, June 9, 1917; 1 dau., Ann Elizabeth (Mrs. Lewis C. Davis); m. 2d, Mary H. Mack, October 14, 1932. Began practice of architecture, 1914; designer in firm of Holabird & Root, Chicago, since 1914, junior partner since 1928; worked on designs of many bldgs. in Chicago (Daily News Bldg., Palmolive Bldg., Board of Trade Bldg., Stevens Hotel, etc.) and throughout the U.S.; apptd. to Federal Housing Branch Number 2, of Public Works Administration, Washington, D.C., Dec. 2, 1935; commissioned to go to London for 3 mos., Aug. 1935, to design Earl's Court, Exhbn. Bldg., covering about 12 1/2 acres. Commd. 1st lt. 119th F.A., 32d Div., 40th Engrs. Camouflage, France 1 year; 6 mos. at the front in St. Mihiel. Mem. Beaux Arts Soc. Clubs: Saddle and Cycle, Arts, Tavern (Chicago). Home: Chicago. *

HALL, HESSEL DUNCAN, specialist internat. affairs; b. Glen Innes, New South Wales, Mar. 8, 1891; s. William Hessel and Jeannie (Duncan) H.; A.B., Sydney U., 1912, A.M., 1915; B. Litt., Balliol Coll., Oxford, Eng., 1920; m. Jenny Waelder, Sept. 10, 1943; one son, three daus. by previous marriage. Australian corr. Manchester Guardian, 1921-25; mem. League of Nations Secretariat, Geneva, Switzerland, 1927-39; vis. prof. internat. affairs, Harvard, 1940; Brit. Raw Materials Mission, Washington, 1942-45; dir. Brit. Ofcl. War Histories (civil), 1945-47; hist. adv., Brit. Embassy, Washington, 1947-56; Guggenheim fellow for history of Brit. Commonwealth, 1955. Observer at Brit. Commonwealth Parliamentary confs., London, 1948, Ottawa, 1952, Africa, 1954, Jamaica, 1956, Australia, 1959. Duncan Hall Collection established Australian Nat. Library. Author; British Commonwealth of Nations, 1920; Mandates, Dependencies and Trusteeship (Carnegie Endowment for International Peace), Washington and London, 1948; North American Supply, 1955, Studies of Overseas Supply in Brit. Ofcl. World War II History Series, 1956; Commonwealth: A History of the British Commonwealth of Nations, 1971. Joint editor and contbr. The British Commonwealth at War, 1943. Home: Bethesda, Md. Died July 8, 1976.

HALL, IVAN CLIFFORD, bacteriologist; b. Bellaire, Mich., Aug. 7, 1885; s. John G. and Lorene Redmond (Munkirs) H.; B.Pd., Colo. State Normal Sch., 1906; B.A., Colo. Coll., Colo. Springs, 1908; M.S., U. of Calif., 1911; Ph.D., U. of Chicago, 1921; m. Elizabeth Perry Hall, July 5, 1909; children—Will Chambers, Thomas Redmond, Flora Lorene Hammerberg. Research bacteriologist Cutter Biol. Labs., Berkeley, Calif., 1911-15; asst. prof. bacteriology, U. of Calif., 1915-18, asso. prof., 1918-24; prof. bacteriology, Cornell U., 1924-25; prof. and head dept. bacteriology and public health, U. of Colo. Med. Sch., 1925-42; dir. central lab. contaminated wound project, sub-com. on surgical infections, Nat. Research Council, Columbia-Presbyn. Med. Center, N.Y. City, 1942-44; prof. and chmn. dept. bacteriology, N.Y. Med. Coll., 1944-45; bacteriologist McIntire Research Unit for Rheumatic Fever, U.S. Naval Hosp., Dublin, Ga., 1947-50; cons. bacteriology Crawford W. Long Memorial Hospital. Member of the Society of American Bacteriologists (dir. local br. 1922-26; councilor 1923-25 and 1932-34), Soc. Exptl. Biology and Medicine, Internat. Soc. Microbiology, Sigma Xi; fellow A.A.A.S. Author: Laboratory Manual of General Bacteriology, 1916; contbr. to Jour. of Infectious Diseases, Jour. Am. Med. Assn., Jour. of Bacteriology. Address: Atlanta. *

HALL, JOSEPH B., business exec.; b. Harvey, Ill., July 13, 1899; s. Joseph B. and Harriet Holzman (Kurtz) H.; Ph.B., U. of Chicago, 1921; D.C.S. (hon.), University of Cincinnati, 1959; m. Mildred Eastburn Wessel, Oct. 20, 1924; children—Joseph Parker, Janice Gail, Wayne. Began as bookkeeper, Morris & Co., 1921; with Gordon Strong & Co., real estate management, 1923-28; became pres. Hamilton Bond and Mortgage Co., later exec. sec. Chicago Mortgage Bankers Assn.; then asst. mgr. real estate dept. Continental Illinois Bank and Trust Co.; with The Kroger Co. from 1931, beginning as mgr. real estate dept., transferred to retail div. as mgr. of St. Louis branch, later becoming eastern div. mgr., Cleveland, became vice pres. in charge of mfg. and dir. of co., 1942, treas., 1943, exec. v.p., 1944, pres., 1946-62, chmn. bd. 1962-64; dir. Armco Steel Corporation, Champion Papers, Incorporated, Tenneco, also Goodyear Tire & Rubber Company, Cincinnati & Suburban Bell Telephone Co., Little Miami R.R. Co., Transit Casualty Co.; chmn. bd. Fed. Reserve Bank Cleve. Hon. mem. exec. bd. Cin. Area council Boy Scouts Am.; charter mem., past pres. Am. Inst. Real Estate Appraisers; pres. Cin. Redevelopment Corp.; trustee of Christ Hosp., Cin. Institute Fine Arts, Ohio U.; past chmn. trustees Cin. Symphony Orch. Mem. Bus. Council, Phi Beta Kappa Assos. Presbyn. Mason. Clubs: Cincinnati Country, Camargo, Queen City, Biltmore Forest Country, Commonwealth, Commercial, Optimists. Home: Cincinnati, Ohio. Died June 1978.

HALL, LEONARD WOOD, lawyer, chmn. Republican Nat. Com.; b. Oyster Bay, N.Y., Oct. 2, 1900; s. Franklyn H. and Mary A. Hall; LL.B., Georgetown U., Washington, 1920; Doctorate (hon.), C. W. Post Coll.; m. Gladys Dowsey, May 10, 1934.

Admitted to N.Y. bar, 1923; practiced in N.Y.C., 1921-27; mem. N.Y. Assembly, 1927-28, 34-38; sheriff Nassau County, N.Y., 1929-31; former chmn. Rep. Com. Town of Oyster Bay; mem. 76th to 82d congresses from 2d N.Y. Dist.; chmn. Rep. Nat. Com., 1953-57; thereafter sr. partner Hall, Dickler, Lawler, Kent & Howley. Dir. Servo Corp. Am., Madison Sq. Garden Corp., Beneficial Nat. Life Ins. Co. Founder L.I. United Fund. Mem. N.Y. State, Nassau County bar assns. Episcopalian. Mason, Elk. Clubs: Internat., Metropolitan (Washington). Home: Locust Valley, N.Y. Died June 2, 1979.

HALL, PAUL, labor union ofcl.; b. Ala., Aug. 21, 1914; m. Rose Hall; 2 children. Mem. Seafarers Internat. Union N. Am., from 1938, sec.-treas. Atlantic, Gulf, Great Lakes and In Land Waters dists., from 1948, 1st v.p., 1948-57, pres., from 1957; pres. maritime trades dept. AFL-CIO, from 1957, nat. v.p., mem. exec. com., from 1962. Mem. Nat. Com. Immigration, Citizens Com. Free China; former mem. Nat. Commn. for Indsl. Peace; former mem. Pres.'s labor mgmt. adv. com. Cost of Living Council; mem. Labor Mgmt. Adv. Com. on Econ. Matters. Bd. dirs. Am. Immigration and Citizenship Conf.; a founder, mem. nat. council Eleanor Roosevelt Found.; trustee George Meany Found.; sponsor, trustee Coordinating Council Edn. to Disadvantaged; v.p. Civic Center Clinic, N.Y.C. Recipient Humanitarian award Civic Center Clinic; citation of honor Nat. Com. Rural Schs. Address: Brooklyn, N.Y. Died June 22, 1980.

HALL, PEIRSON MITCHELL, judge; b. Armour, S.D., July 31, 1894; s. Robert A. and Mary M. (Cripps) H.; student U. So. Cal. Law Sch. 1912-16; m. Kathryn Kyle Black, Nov. 23, 1956; children by previous marriage—Mary Ellen, Suzanne. Admitted to Cal. bar, 1916; pvt. law practice in Los Angeles until apptd. to bench, 1939; mem. City Council, Los Angeles, 1925-29; U.S. dist. atty. So. Dist. Cal., 1933-37, judge, 1942-79; judge Superior Ct. of Los Angeles County, 1939-42. Mason. Died Dec. 8, 1979.

HALL, RAYMOND WILLIAMS, lawyer; b. Weston, Mo., Aug. 15, 1891; s. Charles D. and Laura B. (Williams) H.; A.B., U. Mo., 1913, LL.B., 1915; m. Anne Woodroof, June 6, 1924 (dec. Jan, 1981); 1 son, Douglas Jackson. Admitted to Mo. bar, 1915, mem. Hall & Hall, Kansas City, 1915-26; trust officer First Nat. Bank of Kansas City, Mo., 1926-28, v.p., 1928-42; v.p., gen. counsel Fed. Res. Bank of Kansas City, 1950-52, chmn. bd., 1952-62; v.p. Hallmark Cards, Inc., Kansas City, 1945-59; counsel firm Hillix, Brewer, Hoffhaus, Grier & Whittaker, Kansas City, Mo., from 1969; dir. E.R.C. Corp., Employers Reins. Corp. Bd. govs. Am. Royal Assn.; vestryman and warden St. Andrew's Episcopal Ch. Recipient Silver Beaver award Boy Scouts Am. Mem. Phi Gamma Delta. Rotarian. Clubs: Forty Yr., Kansas City Country. Home: Kansas City, Mo. Died Nov. 8, 1976; interred Forest Hill Cemetery Chapel, Kansas City, Mo.

HALL, THEODORE PARSONS, engr., corp. exec.; b. Wallingford, Conn., Dec. 18, 1898; s. Charles Storrs and Flora (Fordham) H.; E.E., Syracuse U., 1927; M.S., Mass. Inst. Tech., 1928; m. Marion E. Parsons, April 6, 1929; children—Marguerite Parsons (Mrs. John R. Stitt), Janet C. Hall Backer), Theodora P. (Mrs. Robert E. Burton). With Gen. Electric Co., N.Y.C., 1919-22; engr. Thomas-Morse Aircraft Corp., Ithaca, N.Y.; research engr. Cunningham-Hall Aircraft Corp., Rochester, N.Y., 1929-31; chief devel. engr. Consol. Aircraft Corp. (now div. Gen. Dynamics, Inc.), 1931-48; pres., chief engr. T.P. Hall Engring. Corp., San Diego, 1949-74; developed Hall Flying Automobile, mil. airplanes. Served with U.S. Army, AEF, overseas, 1917-19. Decorated for bravery. Mem. Soc. Automotive Engrs., Inst. Aero. Sci., Acacia, Theta Tau. Mason. Patentee. Home: San Diego, Calif. Died Mar. 18, 1978; interred El Camino Meml. Park, San Diego.

HALL, WILLIAM O., cons., ret. diplomat; b. Roswell, N.Mex., May 2, 1914; s. William O. and Margaret (Barnard) H.; A.B., U. Oreg., 1936; postgrad. U. Minn., 1938-39; m. Jayne Bowerman, Sept. 6, 1939; children—Sarah Booth Hall Stenglauz, William Jay, Robert Barnard. Research asst., field cons., adviser, asst. dir. in charge city hall office, acting dir. and acting exec. sec. Bur. Municipal Research and League of Oreg. Cities, 1936-38, 1939-40; budget examiner, adminstrv. analyst U.S. Bur. Budget, 1940-44, 46; supr. Bur. Adminstrv. Mgmt. and Budget, UN, 1946; dir. Office Budget and Planning, also budget officer U.S. State Dept., 1947-50, dir. Office Internat. Confs. and Adminstrn. 1950-52; dep. rep. interim com. gen. assembly UN, finance and adminstr. U.S. mission to UN, 1952-56; counselor Am. embassy, London, 1956-58; dep. asst. sec. state, 1958-59; minister counselor, dep. chief of mission Am. embassy, Karachi, Pakistan, 1959-63; asst. adminstr. AID, 1963-67; U.S. ambassador to Ethiopia, 1967-71; dir. gen. U.S. Fgn. Service, 1971-73; cons. State Dept./AID, 1973-77; prof. internat. affairs Lewis and Clark Coll., Portland, Oreg., 1975-77. Staff mem. U.S. del. preparatory commn. UN, 1945-46; asst. exec. sec. for adminstrn., preparatory commn. Internat. Refugee Orgn., 1947; spl. adviser on adminstrv., budgetary and organizational aspects, U.S. participation in UN and specialized internat. orgns., State Dept., 1946-47; mem. UN Gen. Assembly adv. com. on adminstrv. and budget questions, 1948-56; del. Geneva Conf. on Peaceful Uses of Atomic Energy, 1955. Served with USNR, 1944-46. Mem. City Mgrs. Assn., Pub. Adminstrn. Soc., Am. Fgn. Service Assn., Phi Beta Kappa. Club: Cosmos (Washington). Home: Portland, Oreg. Died Nov. 8, 1977.

HALLADAY, DANIEL WHITNEY, univ. chancellor; b. Santa Ana, Calif., Oct. 13, 1920; s. Harlow Monroe and Marion (Winans) H.; B.A., Pomona Coll., 1942; M.A., Claremont Grad. Sch., 1947; postgrad. U. So. Calif., 1949; Ed.D., Columbia, 1955; m. Elaine Owings, Aug. 21, 1941 (dec.); children—Whitney Sue (Mrs. Ernest Whitelaw), Steven Owings, m. 2d, Cherie Longeway, May 19, 1972. Athletic coach Pomona Coll., Claremont, Calif., 1946-47; asso. prof. phys. edn. and health U. Fla., Gainesville, 1947-51; lectr. health edn. Columbia, N.Y.C., 1953-54, asst. provost Tchrs. Coll., 1954-55; prof. of edn., dean of students U. Ark., Fayetteville, 1955-66; pres. East Tex. State U., Commerce, 1966-72; pres. Tex. A. and I. U. at Corpus Christi, 1972-76; acting chancellor, pres. Tex. A. and I. U. System, 1976-77; chancellor Univ. System of South Tex., 1977-80; pres. Council of Presidents State Sr. Colls., 1967-68; mem. adv. com. on formulas for sr. colls. and univs., coordinating bd. Tex. Coll. and Univ. System; mem. spl. adv. com. to commr. higher edn. State of Tex. Bd. visitors U.S. Mil. Acad., 1970-73. Served to capt. AUS, 1942-46, to maj., 1951-53, now lt. col. Res. Decorated Silver Star, Bronze Star with two clusters, Purple Heart with cluster. Mem. U.S. (edn. and manpower devel. coms.), South Tex. (dir.) chambers of commerce, Am. Assn. State Colls. and Univs. (dir.), Tex. Assn. Colls. and Univs. (chmn. commn. on ednl. policy), Corpus Christi Area Conv. and Tourist Bur., Center for Econ. Studies (chmn. bd.), Kappa Delta Pi, Phi Delta Kappa. Methodist. Kiwanian. Home: Corpus Christi, Texas. Died July 12, 1980.

HALLDEN, KARL WILLIAM, mfg. exec.; b. Halmstad, Sweden, Feb. 12, 1884; s. Alec Julius and Kristina (Svenson) H.; brought to U.S., 1893; B.S., Trinity College, 1909, M.S. (honorary), 1948, Sc.D. (honorary), 1954; married Margaret Justine Maligan, July 5, 1931. Assistant mechanical engineer Plume & Atwood Mfg. Co., Thomaston, Conn., 1909-14; mech. engr. Seymour (Conn.) Mfg. Co., 1914-16; founder, pres., treas. Hallden Machine Co., Thomaston since 1917; asso. with W.H.A. Robertson Co., Ltd., Bedford, Eng., Hallden-Okura Co., Tokyo, Japan, Hallden-Robertson Co., Dusseldorf, Germany. Trustee Trinity Coll.; incorporator Waterbury (Conn.) Hosp., Morton Plant Hosp., Clearwater, Fla. Decorated Knight Santa Lucia Soc. Stockholm, Sweden, 1963. Recipient Eigenbrodt Trophy, Trinity College, 1954; Silver medal Technical Museet, Stockholm, Sweden, 1963. Mem. Pi Kappa Alpha, Pi Tau Sigma, Tau Alpha. Episcopalian. Mason. Clubs: Rotary, University, Country City (Waterbury); University (Litchfield Co.); Rod and Gun (Thomaston); University (Hartford); Carlouel (Clearwater, Fla.). Inventor Hallden Flying Shear; patentee. Donor Hallden Engring. Lab., Trinity Coll., 1946. Home: Thomaston, Conn. also Belleair Estates, Clearwater, Fla. *

HALLENBERG, HERBERT, banker; b. Fargo, N.D., Feb. 26, 1884; s. Carl A. and Charlotte (Johanson) H.; LL.B., Univ. of Mich., 1906; m. Marjory Marsh, Nov. 19, 1910; children—Phoebe (Mrs. Robert E. Hansen), Mary (Mrs. Russell S. Maetzold), Herbert, John D. Admitted to the N.D. bar, 1907; atty. Fargo, N.D., 1907-09; sec. senate judiciary com., N.D. Legislature, 1907; bank exec. Carson, N.D., 1910-20; bank examiner Federal Reserve Bank, Minneapolis, Minn., 1920-28; nat. bank examiner Second Federal Reserve dist., New York, N.Y., 1928-29; chief examiner Northwest Bancorporation, Minneapolis, Minn., 1929-45, vice pres. and treasurer, 1945-50, Dir. Union Investment Co., Northwestern Mortgage Co., Minneapolis. Mem. Robert Morris Associates, Phi Kappa Sigma. Republican. Episcopalian. Mason. Clubs: Minneapolis Golf, Minneapolis. Home: Minneapolis, Minn. *

HALLER, ELLIS METCALF, editor; b. Carthage, N.Y., Mar. 20, 1915; s. Willis Andrew and Maude E. (Metcalf) H.; A.B., Syracuse U., 1937; m. Dorothy G. Rourke, Nov. 24, 1938; children—Mark Metcalf, Elizabeth Hewitt. Upstate N.Y. corr. Watertown (N.Y.) Daily Times, 1933-37; with Wall Street Jour., N.Y.C. and Chgo., 1937-44, chief Chgo. bur., 1943-44, chief Washington bur., 1948-52, indsl. editor, hdqrs. N.Y.C., 1952-56; asso. editor U.S. News & World Report, Washington, 1956-61, asso. editor and exec. asst. to editor, 1961-63, spl. editor bus. and finance, 1963-65, gen. editor, nat. staff, 1965-70, asso. exec. editor, 1971-76, asst. mng. editor, 1976-81; instr. typography Syracuse (N.Y.) U., 1937; asso. in journalism Columbia, N.Y.C., 1954-56; guest lectr. Am. Press Inst., 1954-56. Mem. dept. info. services Episcopal Diocese of Washington. Vice chmn. Sigma Delta Chi Found. of Washington, 1973-76, chmn., 1976-81. Recipient Free Enterprise Newswriter award Nat. Mgmt. Assn., 1955. Mem. White House Corrs. Assn., English Speaking Union, Phi Beta Kappa, Phi Kappa Phi, Sigma Delta Chi. Club: Nat. Press (Washington). Home: Washington, D.C. Died Apr. 7, 1981; buried Beaver Falls, N.Y.

HALLERBERG, ARTHUR EDWARD, educator; b. Farmington, Mo., June 9, 1918; s. Herman A. and Laura (Luken) H.; A.B., Ill. Coll., 1940, D.H.L. (hon. post obitum), 1979; A.M., U. Ill., 1941; postgrad. U. Chgo., summers 1946-47; Ed.D. in Math., U. Mich., 1957; m. Katherine W. Rausch, June 16, 1947; 1 dau., Gretchen Anne. Tchr., Bushnell (Ill.) High Sch., 1941-42; instr. Ill. Coll., 1942-44, from asst. prof. to prof., 1946-60, chmn. dept. math., 1957-60; mem. faculty Valparaiso (Ind.) U., 1960-79, prof., chmn. dept. math., 1965-70, dir., instr. NSF summer insts. math., 1961-66, 68-70; vis. lectr. U. Mich., summers 1960, 67; vis. prof. Mich. State U., 1970-71. Served with USNR, 1944-46; recipient Disting. Alumnus Citation Ill. Coll., 1977. Mem. Math. Assn. Am., Nat. Council Tchrs. Math. (editor Hist. Topics Yearbook), Historia Mathematica, Sch. Sci. and Math. Assn., Ind. Acad. Sci., Luth. Acad. for Scholarship, Phi Beta Kappa, Sigma Xi, Pi Mu Epsilon. Democrat. Lutheran. Author: Logic in Mathematics, 1974; Mathematical Proof, 1974. Home: Valparaiso, Ind. Died Nov. 23, 1978; buried Graceland Cemetery, Valparaiso.

HALLOWELL, CHARLOTTE RUDYARD (CHARLOTTE RUDYARD), editor, critic, writer; b. New York, N.Y., Nov. 14, 1883; d. William Clarence and Martha J. (des Jeroux-Wheeler) Rudyard; ed. prep. sch. dept. of Pratt Inst., Brooklyn; A.B., Vassar Coll., 1904; m. Apr. 11, 1916, Robert Hallowell (div., Paris, 1926; he died 1939). Editorial staff Brooklyn Daily Eagle, 1904-05; lit. editor Harper & Bros. pubs., 1907-10; asst. editor Harper's Mag., 1910-13; asso. editor on original staff The New Republic, 1914-16; editor and reader for various publishers, also dramatic and music critic under pseudonym. Contbr. of verse and lit. criticism to Harper's Magazine, Harper's Weekly, Independent, North Am. Review, Times Review of Books, Saturday Review of Literature, Nation, etc. Mem. Foreign Policy Assn., English-Speaking Union. Clubs: Cosmopolitan, Town Hall. Address: New York, N.Y. *

HALLOWELL, MADELEINE A., M.D.; b. at Conshohocken, Pa., March 21, 1885; d. of Horace Gates Jones and Annie M. (O'Brien) H.; M.D., Woman's Medical Coll. of Pa., 1906; special work in orthopedic surgery and neurology, same, 1905-08; unmarried. Resident phys. Phila. Maternity Hospital, 1907; asst. phys. N.J. State Village for Epileptics, at Skillman, N.J., 16 mos., 1908-09; med. dir. and supt. N.J. State Institution for Feeble Minded Women, May 1909—. Mem. com. of five apptd. by gov. to study and plan for care and provision of the feeble minded and epileptics of N.J.; mem. Nat. Assn. for Study of Feeble Minded, N.J. State Assn. Charities and Corrections, N.J. State Charities Aid and Prison Reform Assn., Nat. Conf. Social Work, Nat. and Phila. neurol. and psychiatric socs. Home: Atlantic City, N.J. *

HALNON, WILLIAM, educator; b. at Londonderry, Ireland, Nov. 7, 1886; s. Edward and Mary (Lambert) H.; Dublin U., 1904-8; Trinity Coll., Dublin, 1908, M.A.; Plattville (Wis.) State Normal Sch., 1909-11; m. Myrtle Kinch, of Chicago, June 30, 1910. Began teaching at Londonderry; came to U.S., 1909; pres. Vincennes (Ind.) U. since Sept. 1914. Mem. N.E.A. Episcopalian. Mason. Rotarian. Home: Vincennes, Ind.*

HALOFTIS, TIMOTHY, clergyman; b. Megara, Greece, Sept. 10, 1917; s. George P. and Constantina (Panou) H.; Degree of Theology, U. Athens, 1939; postgrad. (French Govt. scholar), Inst. Catholique of Paris, 1949-51. Ordained deacon and archmandrite Greek Orthodox Ch., 1936; father superior Monastery of Transfiguration of Savior, Karystia, Greece, 1938-40; preacher of Karystia, 1940-41; chancellor Metropolis of Argolis, 1942-47; mil. chaplain during Italian invasion of Greece, 1940; mil. chaplain of Evelpis, Athens, 1947-49; dir. High Mil. Adminstrn. of Attica and the Islands, 1947-49; presbyter priest Ch. of St. George of Kypseli, Athens, 1947-56; dir. Apostolic Mission of Ch. of Greece, 1951-56; dir. Advance Seminars for Priests of Archdiocese of Athens, 1951-56; prof. advanced seminars Ryzareion Theol. Sem., 1955-56; presbyter priest, Winnipeg, Man., Can., 1956-57; priest Ch. of St. Eleftherios, N.Y.C., 1957-60; chancellor Greek Archdiocese, 1960-62; mem. faculty Holy Cross Orthodox Theol. Sch., Brookline, Mass., 1960; titular bishop of Rodostolon, 1962-77, bishop 10th (S.Am.) Diocese, Buenos Aires, Argentina, 1962-63, 9th (Canadian) Diocese, Toronto, Ont., 1963-68, 2d (Midwestern States) Diocese, Chgo., 1968-77. Pres., Council Priests 1st Archdiocesan Dist., 1960-62; pres. Inst. for Aged of Greek Archdiocese, Yonkers, N.Y., 1959-62. Decorated Cross of Holy Sepulchre by Patriarch of Jerusalem; Gold Medal of Byzas, City of Megara. Author: Consultations for Confession, 1953; The Confession of Children, 1954; also numerous articles in Greek and English newspapers and mags. Office: Chicago, Ill. Died Dec. 21, 1977; buried Megara, Attica, Greece.

HALPRIN, ROSE L., Zionist leader U.S.; b. N.Y.C.; d. Philip and Rebecca (Isaacson) Luria; ed. Columbia Tchrs. Coll.; D. Jewish Lit. (hon.), Jewish Tchrs. Sem. and People's U., 1977; m. Samuel Halprin, Apr. 26, 1914; children—Larry, Ruth. Nat. pres. Hadassah, 1932-34, 47-52, rep. to Actions Com., 1939-46, 68-73, chmn., Palestine, 1939-41, polit. chmn., 1941-47, rep. to Am. Zionist Emergency Council, from 1942, mem. Jewish Agy. Exec., 1946-68; vice chmn. Am. Zionist Council, 1953; liaison officer Nat. Bd. Hadassah, Women's Zionist Orgn. of Am. and Hadassah Med. Orgn. in Palestine, 1934-39; mem. legis. council for Zionist affairs between Zionist congresses, 1938; treas. Am. Zionist Emergency Council, 1942, vice chmn., 1945-47; mem. Am. Com. of 8 of World Zionist Orgn., 1946; mem. secretariat for orgn. Am. Jewish Conf., 1946, becoming mem. interim com., exec. com. and chmn. Palestine com.; del. Paris Conf. Jewish Agy. Execs.; hon. life pres. World Confedn. Gen. Zionists; chmn. Am. sect. Jewish Agy. for Israel, 1960-68; hon. chmn. Am. sect. World Jewish Congress, 1968-71; nat. chmn. Hadassa for Israel Bonds, 1972-78. Recipient Bublick award Hebrew U., Jerusalem, 1976. Home: New York, N.Y. Died Jan. 8, 1978.

HALSEY, JAMES H., educator; b. Hammond, Ind., May 11, 1906; s. Hilary and Gertrude (Herron) H.; A.B., Wabash Coll., 1927, LL.D., 1958; M.A., Columbia, 1939; postgrad. Yale; L.H.D., U. Bridgeport, 1971; m. Julia McElhiney Walker, June 18, 1930; children—James Herron, John Easton, George Rogers. Teaching and adminstrv. positions, MacJannet Sch., Paris, France, 1927-30, Hammond (Ind.) High Sch., 1930-33, Morgan Park Mil. Acad., Chgo., 1935-37, Irving Sch., Tarrytown, N.Y., 1937-38; with Jr. Coll. of Conn. (later U. Bridgeport), 1938-78, pres. U. Bridgeport, 1946-62, chancellor, 1962-71, chancellor emeritus, also cons. to pres. internat. affairs, 1971-72, dir. internat. grad.student program, 1972-78, dir. internat. grad. scholarship program later named in his honor. Prof. Honorario Universidad Argentina John F. Kennedy; hon. fellow Inst. for Am. Univs., Aix-en-Provence, France. Dir. Value Line Funds, N.Y.C. State chmn. UN Day, 1954-62; New Eng. regional chmn. UN Day, 1962-65. Sec.-treas. MacJannet Found., Bridgeport, 1968-78. Bd. dirs. New Eng. Bd. Higher Edn. Past sec. com. on instns. of higher edn. N.E. Assn. of Colls. Conn. Conf. of Jr. Colls. (past pres.), New Eng. Jr. Coll. Council (past pres.). Decorated comdr. Order Acad. Palms (France); knight Order of Merit (Italy). Mem. UN Assn. U.S.A. (state pres. 1965-69, hon. pres. 1969). United Conglist. Clubs: Rotary, Brooklawn Country. Contbr. articles to ednl. periodicals. Died Mar. 31, 1978; cremated. Home: Bridgeport, Conn.

HALSMAN, PHILIPPE, photographer, author; b. Riga, Latvia, May 2, 1906; s. Max and Ita (Grintouch) H.; B.A., Vidus Skola, Riga, 1924; student Sch. Engring., Dresden, Germany, 1924-28; m. Yvonne Moser, Apr. 1, 1937; children—Irene Aline, Jane Ellen. Came to U.S., 1940, naturalized, 1949. Photographer for Vogue, Vu and Voila mags., Paris, France, 1931-40; contbg. photographer to Life, Sat. Eve. Post, Look, other mags., 1941-79; portrait photographer Winston Chruchill, Dwight Eisenhower, John F. Kennedy, Robert F. Kennedy, Edward M. Kennedy, Lyndon B. Johnson, Richard Nixon, Harold Macmillan, Mrs. Eleanor Roosevelt, Albert Einstein, Andre Gide, Gen. Marshall, others; exhbns. in Paris, N.Y.C., Tokyo; represented in permanent collections Met. Mus. Art, Smithsonian Instn., Bibliothèque Nationale, Paris, Mus. Modern Art, Library of Congress, Mus. Sci. and Industry, Chgo.; retrospective exhbn. Mus. Internat. Center of Photography, 1979; dir. motion picture For a Livable America, 1968; faculty mem. Famous Photographers Sch., Westport, Conn., 1969-79, New Sch., 1971-79. Named one of 10 greatest photographers in internat. poll Popular Photography mag., 1958; recipient of Newhouse award, 1963; Golden Plate award Am. Acad. of Achievement, 1967; photographs of Adlai Stevenson, Albert Einstein and John Steinbeck used on U.S. postage stamps; photograph of André Gide used on French postage stamp. Mem. Am. Soc. Mag. Photographers (1st pres., Life Achievement award 1975). Clubs: Dutch Treat, Overseas Press (N.Y.C.). Photographer: (books) The Frenchman, 1949, Piccoli, 1953, Dali's Mustache, 1954, Philippe Halsman's Jumpbook, 1959; Halsman on the Creation of Photographic Ideas, 1961; Sight and Insight, 1972; catalogue of Halsman Exhbt., 1979. Address: New York City, N.Y. Died June 25, 1979.

HALSTEAD, GEORGE CHAPPELL, shipping co. exec.; b. Bklyn., May 12, 1917; s. Kenneth Burt and Marjory (Chappell) H.; B.S., M.I.T., 1940; postgrad. N.Y. U., 1947-51; m. Maude Hooper, Sept. 27, 1944; children—Peter Chappell, Timothy Hooper, Christopher Van Duzer, John Prescott, Alexander Brooks. With Sun Shipbldg. and Drydock Co., Chester, Pa., 1940-41; with Alcoa Steamship Co., N.Y.C., 1945-78, pres., 1963-78; dir. Nat. Cargo Bur., Am. Mcht. Marine Inst., Am. Steamship Owners Mut. Protection, Indemnity Assn., Microdot, Inc. Mem. bd. mgrs. Am. Bur. Shipping; chmn. Am. com. Lloyd's Register of Shipping; mem. vis. com. M.I.T. Served to lt. comdr. USN, 1941-45. Mem. Soc. Naval Architects and Marine Engrs., Phi Kappa Sigma. Republican. Episcopalian. Clubs: Whitehall Lunch, Westhampton Country, Westhampton Yacht Squadron, Aspatuck Yacht, Quantuck Beach; Duquesne (Pitts). Home: Manhasset, N.Y. Died Apr. 11, 1978.

HALVORSON, HALVOR ORIN, educator; b. River Falls, Wis., Mar. 26, 1897; s. Hallie and Elizabeth (Heyerdahl) H.; B.S., U. Minn., 1921, Chem. E., 1922, Ph.D., 1928; D.Sc. (hon.), St. Olaf Coll., 1948; m. Selma C. Halvorson, Aug. 1922; children—Betty Jean (Mrs. Theodore Caspar), Harlyn, Loren, Gayle Adair (Mrs. John Mosand). Teaching fellow U. Minn., 1922-23, instr., 1923-28, asst. prof., 1928-30, asso. prof., 1930-40, prof., 1940-49; dir. Hormel Inst., 1943-49; prof., head dept. bacteriology U. Ill., 1949-60, dir. Sch. Life Scis., 1959-65; research prof. dept. biochemistry U. Minn., St. Paul, 1965-71. Cons. san. engring. and food tech., from 1928. Civilian with Office Sci. Research and Devel., 1943-45, panel mem. Office Naval Research, 1947-51, NIH, 1949-54, mem. council Inst. of Allergy and Infectious Diseases, 1954-58; mem. subcom. food stability NRC, 1955-57. Served as 1st lt. C.A.C., U.S. Army, 1917-19. Named Outstanding Am. Investigator, Am. Mfrs. Assn., 1940; recipient Pasteur award, 1960. Mem. Soc. Am. Bacteriologists (past pres.), Am. Acad. Microbiology (chmn. bd. govs. 1956-57), Sigma Xi, Phi Kappa Phi, Phi Lambda Upsilon, Alpha Chi Sigma, Gamma Alpha. Author: Quantitative Bacteriology, 1933; contbg. author: The Chemistry and Technology of Food and Food; contbr. articles to sci. jours. Home: Minneapolis, Minn. Deceased.

HAM, JOHN WILEY, evangelist; b. Jackson, Ga., Apr. 29, 1882; s. Thomas Wilkinson and Elizabeth Elmina (Higgins) H.; student Moody Bible Inst., Chicago, 1904-05, Mercer U., Macon, Ga., 1907, U. of Chicago, winter terms 1916, 17; m. Sara Jean Ousley, of Middendorf, S.C., June 23, 1908. Ordained ministry Missionary Bapt. Ch., 1905; pastor Bapt. Tabernacle, New Bern, N.C., 1907-09; asst. pastor Bapt. Tabernacle, Atlanta, 1910-12; evangelist, 1913-15; pastor Tabernacle Ch., Atlanta, 1917-24 (membership increased to 3,250 and S.S. to 2,500); pres. Atlanta Bible Conf., 1918-24; in evangelistic work on nation-wide basis since 1924; also widely known as speaker on nat. and internat. questions. Democrat. Mason. Author: Present Tense Salvation, 1927; Scarlet to White, 1928; Honey in the Rock, 1928. Address: Atlanta, Ga. *

HAMBRO, EDVARD ISAK, diplomat of Norway; b. Oslo, Norway, Aug. 22, 1911; s. Carl Joachim and Gudrun (Grieg) H.; LL.B., Oslo U., 1934; Dr. es Scis. Politiques, U. Geneva (Switzerland), 1936; m. Elisabeth Jacqueline Raverat, June 8, 1940; children—Anne Nicoline (Mrs. Egil Alnaes), Carl Joachim, John Christian George, Linda Margaret. Collaborator secretariat League of Nations, 1933; leader internat. relations dept. Christian Michelsens Inst., Bergen. Norway, 1938-40; guest lectr. Northwestern U., 1941; sec. Norwegian Ministry Fgn. Affairs, London, Eng., 1943-45; chief legal sect. UN, 1945-46; registrar Internat. Ct. Justice, the Hague, 1943-53; lectr., later prof. law Norwegian Sch. Econs. and Bus. Adminstrn., Bergen. 1953-66; vis. lectr. U. Cambridge (Eng.), 1953-54, U. Calif., Berkeley, 1958; mem. Norwegian Parliament, 1961-66; lectr. Hague Acad. Internat. Law, 1950, 60, also others univs., U.S. and Europe; ambassador, permanent rep. Norway to UN, 1966—71, pres. 25th Gen. Assembly, 1970; lectr. internat. law U. Oslo, 1972. Dir. first sessions Dag Hammarskjold Sem., The Hague, 1963, 64; head commn. study Chinese refugees in Hong Kong, 1954; mem. appeals bd. Orgn. Econ. Coop. and Devel.; chmn. adminstrv. tribunal Council of Europe, 1966; mem. Permanent Ct. Arbitration, 1965; pres. Permanent Conciliation Commn. Germany and Netherlands, 1965; mem. Franco-German arbitral bd. for Saar; mem. permanent conciliation com. between Finland and U.S., between Norway and Spain, between Portugal and Switzerland. Vice pres. Norwegian Red Cross, 1960-66. Decorated knight Order of St. Olav (Norway). Mem. Inst. du Droit Internat. Author: L'Exécution des Sentences Internationales, 1936; Norway and The League of Nations, 1938; The Law of Aliens, 1950; (with L. Goodrich) The Charter of the United Nations, 2d edit., 1949; The Case Law of the International Court, Vol. I, 2d edit., 1958, Vol. II, 1960, Vol. III, 1963, Vol. IV, 1965, Vol. V. 1968; Peaceful Settlement of Disputes, 1956; Choice of Law and Choice of Jurisdiction in Norwegian International Contract Law. 1957; also articles. Home: New York, N.Y. Died Feb. 1, 1977.

HAMILTON, ANN RUTH FRANCES, magazine editor; b. Phila., Aug. 7, 1948; d. Daniel David and Florence Barbara (Moses) Barrow; B.A. in Sociology, Barnard Coll., 1970; m. Alan Stephen Hamilton, Aug. 2, 1970. Editor, Lover Girl mag., asst. editor Silhouette Slimming and Health mag. and Tomorrow's Woman, Williams Pub. Ltd., London, 1971-72; editor Internat. Mag. Features, asst. editor Provincial Press Features, Features Internat. Ltd., London, 1972-73; free-lance editor Romance mag. Williams Pub. and Impassen Prodns., London, 1973; editor Truly Yours mag., also editor My Confession mag., Mag. Mgmt Corp., N.Y.C., 1974-75; editor Movie Stars mag., also Screen and TV Album mag., Ideal Pub. Corp., N.Y.C., 1975-77, creative developer Teen Beat mag., 1976; sr. editor Penthouse Forum mag., Penthouse Internat. Ltd., N.Y.C, 1977-78. Mem. Phi Beta Kappa. Author: David Cassidy Annual, 1975; also mag. articles. Home: New York, N.Y. Died Apr. 11, 1978; buried Har Nebo Cemetery, Phila.

HAMILTON, CHARLES EDGAR, ret. mfr.; born Richmond, Ind., Apr. 8, 1886; s. Charles M. and Julia (McMeans) H.; student Wilmers Prep. Sch., Annapolis, Md., Earlham Coll., Richmond, Ind., 1905-06; m. Ruth E. Mashmeyer, Dec. 27, 1911; 1 dau., Margaret Ann (Mrs. Robert C. Jacobs). Pres. Automotive Gear Works, Inc., now div. Eaton Mfg. Co. Richmond, 1922-57; v.p. Richmond American Realty Co., 1955—; director Central Broadcasting Co.; dir. Eaton Mfg. Co., Cleve. Mem. automotive adv. com. WPB, OPM. Trustee Earlham Coll., Estelle Peabody Meml. Home, North Manchester, Ind. Mem. N.A.M. (past v.p., dir., regional v.p.), Ind. Mfrs. Assn. (past dir.). Clubs: Rotary; Fort Lauderdale Yacht; Little Harbor (Harbor Springs, Mich.); Richmond Country; Union (Cleve.). Home: Richmond, Ind. *

HAMILTON, CHARLES HORACE, educator, sociologist; b. McLennan County, Tex., June 10, 1901; s. William Clark and Amy Jane (Whittenberg) H.; A.B., So. Meth. U., 1923; M.S., Tex. A. and M. Coll., 1925; Ph. D., U. N.C., 1932; student U. Chgo., 1925, Harvard, 1930-31; m. Maurine Phifer, Sept. 9, 1928; children—Charles Edward (dec.), Elizabeth Ayers (Mrs. Charles W. Darden), Mary Bellamy (Mrs. Douglas E. Hosler). Prof. edn. Lon Morris Coll., Jacksonville, Tex., 1925-26; asst. rural sociologist Va. Agrl. Expt. Sta., 1927-31; asst. and asso. prof. rural sociology N.C. State Coll., 1931-36; economist in rural life Tex. Agrl. Expt. Sta., 1936-39; sr. social scientist, bur. agrl. econs. U.S. Dept. Agr., Washington, 1939-40; head dept. rural sociology N.C. State Coll., 1940-60, William Neal Reynolds prof. rural sociology, 1960—77; vis. prof. U. Wis., 1959-60; vis. prof. sociology and biostatistics, asso. dir. Carolina Population Center, U. N.C., Chapel Hill, 1967-71; on leave as dir. sociol. research Commn. on Hosp. Care, Chgo., 1945-46; mng. editor Rural Sociology, Jour. of Rural sociol. Soc., 1940-50; cons. research grants div. NIH, USPHS, 1946-49. Pres. N.C. Conf. for Social Service, 1961-62; sec. rural sub-com. Gov's Commn. on Hosp. and Medical Care, also chmn. statistics and publs. sub-com.; mem. adv. com. on population 1950 U.S. Census. Recipient Oliver Max Gardner award, 1958; Social Science Research Council fellow, 1930-31. Fellow Am. Statis. Assn.; mem. Am. Rural Sociol. Soc. (pres. 1949-50), Am. Assn. U. Profs., So. Sociol. Soc. (pres. 1957-58), Population Assn. Am. (pres. 1960-61), Internat. Population Union. Author bulls., contbr. to profl. jours. Home: Raleigh, N.C. Died Aug. 1, 1977.

HAMILTON, CLARENCE HERBERT, teacher, author; b. Des Moines, Ia., Jan. 8, 1886; s. George Lee and Carrie Eva (Wood) H.; A.B., Univ. of Chicago, 1910, Ph.D., 1914; student Union Theol. Sem., 1920-21; m. Lulu Snyder, Apr. 18, 1916; children—Ruth (Mrs. Donald H. Edwards), Miriam (Mrs. Arthur K. Berliner), Harry Edward, Robert Lee. Prof. and head dept. of philosophy and psychology, Univ. of Nanking, China, 1914-27; vis. lecturer on Oriental religions, Columbia, winter session, 1927; vis. prof. of philosophy, Univ. of Chicago, spring quarter, 1928; prof. of Eastern philosophy, Coll. of Missions, Hartford Sem. Foundation, 1928-31; prof. of missions Oberlin Grad. Sch. of Theology, Oberlin (O.) Coll., 1931-32; prof. of philosophy of religion and Christian missions, Oberlin Grad. Sch. since 1932; teacher of Far Eastern philosophy summer seminar on Far Eastern Studies, Univ. of Calif. (under auspices Am. Council of Learned Socs.), June 25-Aug. 3, 1934. Mem. Am. Council of Learned Socs. (com. on Far East studies (chmn.), com. on research and teaching personnel in the humanities), Am. Oriental Soc., Am. Assn. Univ. Professors, The Far Eastern Society, The National Geographic Society. Member of Disciples of Christ. Clubs: Oberlin Cosmos, Social Science, Rotary International. Author: A Psychological Interpretation of Mysticism, 1916; Buddhism in India, Ceylon, China and Japan, 1931; Wei Shih Er Shih Lun, or The Treatise in Twenty Stanzas on Representation-Only—a translation from the Chinese version by Hsüan Tsang (T'ang Dynasty) of a Buddhist philos. work by Vasubandhu, 1938; chapter on Buddhism in the China vol. of the United Nations Series, 1946; (article) Indian Thought and Its Metaphysical Goal, 1948. Home: Oberlin OH. *

HAMILTON, EDWARD PARMELEE, publisher; b. East Orange, N.J., Oct. 3, 1883; s. Edward P. and Alice (Wiley) H.; student Hill Sch., Pottstown, Pa., 1899-1903, C.E., Rensselaer Poly. Inst., Troy, N.Y., 1907, E.D., 1957. Civil engring. work 1907; with Cuban Engring. & Contracting Co., building sewer in Havana, 2 years; with Snare & Triest Co., constrn. of Catskill aqueduct, 1 1/2 years; with New Eng. Power Co., design and constrn. of water power plants in Mass., 2 years; with John Wiley & Sons, pubs. of science and technical books, N.Y.C., 1914—, secretary, 1916-25, vice pres., treas., 1925-41, president, 1941-56, chairman, 1956-66, honorary chairman, 1966—. Served with Troop D, Squad A, N.Y. Nat. Guard (6 months on Mexican border), 1914-17; commd. 2d lt., Field Arty.,

U.S. Army, 1917, 1st lt., 1918; with A.E.F. in France at Oise-Aisne and Meuse-Argonne; capt. F.A. Res., several years. Past chmn. bd. trustees Kips Bay Boys Club, N.Y.C. Hon. trustee Rensselaer Polytech. Institute. Mem. American Institute Mining and Metall. Engrs., Soc. for Promotion Engrng. Edn., A.A.A.S., Theta Xi (past pres.), Sigma Xi; associate mem. Am. Soc. C.E. Clubs: University, Engineers, The Players (N.Y. City); Bedford (N.Y.) Golf and Tennis. Home: Katonah, N.Y. *

HAMILTON, HOLMAN, historian; b. Ft. Wayne, Ind., May 30, 1910; s. Allen and Helen (Knight) H.; A.B., Williams Coll., 1932; Ph.D., U. Ky., 1954, Litt.D. (hon.), 1977; L.H.D. (hon.), Franklin (Ind.) Coll., 1966; LL.D. (hon.), Lincoln Meml. U., Harrogate, Tenn., 1973, Ind. U., 1976; m. Suzanne W. Bowerfind, Oct. 7, 1939; 1 dau., Susan C. Reporter, Ft. Wayne Jour. Gazette, 1932-34, editorial writer, 1935-42, 46, 47-50; mem. faculty U. Ky., Lexington, 1954-75, prof. history, 1965-75, Hallam prof., 1969-71; Fulbright prof. U. Chile, Santiago, 1966. Trustee Lincoln Meml. U., 1957-63. Served to maj. AUS, 1942-46. Recipient Pelzer prize Miss. Valley Hist. Assn., 1954; faculty research award U. Ky., 1965, Gt. Tchr. award, 1968, 75, Disting. Prof. award Coll. Arts and Scis., 1971; Guggenheim fellow, 1946. Mem. Am. Hist. Assn., Orgn. Am. Historians, Soc. Am. Historians, So. Hist. Assn. (nat. pres. 1978-79), Ind. Hist. Soc., Ky. Hist. Soc. Clubs: Nat. Press (Washington); Idle Hour (Lexington); Williams (N.Y.C.). Author: Zachary Taylor: Soldier of the Republic, 1941; Zachary Taylor: Soldier in The White House, 1951; White House Images and Realities, 1958; Prologue to Conflict, 1964; The Three Kentucky President's, 1978; co-author: The Democratic Experience, rev. edit., 1977; editor: Three American Frontiers, 1968; co-editor: Indianapolis in the Gay Nineties, 1964; contbr. to various dictionaries, encys. Address: Lexington, Ky. Died June 7, 1980; buried Lexington, Ky.

HAMILTON, ROGER STANTON, educator; b. Thurman, N.Y., Aug. 9, 1904; s. Frederick Lewis and Edna (Crandall) H.; student Cornell U., 1923-25; A.B., U. of Pittsburgh, 1929; A.M., Tufts Coll., 1931; Ph.D., Harvard, 1940; m. Doris Allcott Goodwill, Aug. 27, 1932; children—Stanley Roger, Peter Goodwill. Braker teaching fellow, Tufts Coll., 1929-31; instr. in economics Northeastern U., Boston, 1931-33, asst. prof., 1933-38, asso. prof., 1938-40, prof. econs., head dept., 1940-66, dean Coll. Bus. Adminstrn., 1944-65; prof. econs. New Eng. Coll., Henniker, N.H., from 1965. Member bd. of trustees Wildey Savings Bank. Member of national panel of Am. Arbitration Assn. Mem. Am. Econ. Soc., Am. Mgmt. Assn., Delta Sigma Rho. Home: Henniker, N.H. Died Jan 11, 1977.

HAMILTON, THOMAS HALE, estate and edn. adviser; b. Marion, Ind., Aug. 4, 1914; s. Burr and Etta (Hale) Hamilton; A.B., DePauw U., 1936, LL.D., 1961; A.M., U. Chgo., 1940, Ph.D., 1947; L.H.D., Alfred U., 1960; LL.D., Rollins Coll., Colgate U., 1961, U. So. Calif., 1967; H.D., Oakland U., 1967; Sc.D., Temple U., 1968; m. Virginia Prindiville, June 1, 1940; children—Thomas P., Ann Hale. Fellow dept. polit. sci. U. Chgo., 1939-40, asst. dean univ. coll., 1946-48; instr. Lawrence Coll., 1940-42, asst. prof. govt., 1942-43, asst. dean, 1941-43; v.p., prof. polit. sci. Chatham Coll., 1948-53; asst. to dean basic coll. Mich. State U., 1954-56, v.p. acad. affairs, 1956-59; pres. State U. of N.Y., 1959-62; pres. U. Hawaii, 1963-68; spl. columnist Honolulu Sunday Star Bull. and Advertiser; adviser to Bishop Estate, 1971-79, also Kamehameha Schs. Dir. Hawaiian Telephone Co., Am. Security Bank, Kapalua Land Co. Pres. Hawaii Visitors Bur., 1968-71; mem. staff Commn. on Implications of Armed Services Edn. Programs, 1946-47; cons. to Exploratory Com. on Financing Higher Edn. and Research, 1948; cons. Council for Study Higher Edn. Fla., 1955; commn. instrn. and evaluation Am. Council Edn., 1957-59; adv. bd. coll. presidents Nat. Scholarship Service and Fund Negro Students, 1959-68; mem. exec. com. Gov.'s Adv. Council Indsl. Research and Devel., 1960-63; cons. U. Philippines, 1958-59; chmn. bd. govs. Kamehameha Schs., 1969-71; trustee Hawaii Pacific Coll.; chmn. Honolulu Media Council, Gov.'s Visitor Industry Council. Served from ensign to lt., USNR, 1943-46. Recipient Am. Acad. Achievement award in edn., 1965; Paul Bachman award for promotion of understanding in the Pacific and Asia, 1969. Mem. Fgn. Policy Assn. (sec. bd. dirs. Pitts. 1950-53), World Affairs Forum (dir. Pitts. 1951-52), Hawaiian Hist. Soc., Am. Council Edn. (dir., past chmn. com. higher edn. and civil def.). Clubs: Waialai, Pacific. Author: The Armed Services and Adult Education (with Houle, Yale and Burr), 1948; The Teaching Profession Comes of Age (with others), 1954; The Basic College of Michigan State (with others), 1955; The Government Study of the University of the Philippines (with others), 1958; The Democracy of Excellence, 1964; Hawaii 2000 (with others), 1973. Home: Honolulu, Hawaii. Died Dec. 25, 1979.

HAMILTON, WESLEY D., steel exec.; b. Reading, Pa., Dec. 25, 1911; s. George Victor and Margaret (Dunbar) H.; student Hamilton Coll., 1931-32; B.S. in Econs., U. Pa., 1934; m. Evaline Igleheart, June 15, 1939; children—Lynn (Mrs. Albert Meyer, Jr.), Wesley, Joan. Mgr. br. store Saks Fifth Av., 1934-40; v.p. Internat. Steel Co., Evansville, Ind., 1940-56, pres., 1956-59, chmn. bd., dir., 1959-60; with ICA, Dept. State, 1960; dir. Poduct Acceptance and Research, Evansville, Ind., from 1960; pres., dir. Project Mgmt., Inc., Fort Lauderdale, from 1963; dir. Mur-Mil. Inc., Louisville, Italcambio C.A., Milan, Italy; pres. Ry. Equipment Leasing Corp., Inc.; v.p., dir. Protyl Press, Inc. Exec. com. Evansville chpt. A.R.C. Mem. C. of C. (dir.) Knights of Malta. Clubs: Country of Evansville (past pres.), Evansville Petroleum; Chicago, Racquet, Cat Cay, Country of Fla., Gulf Stream Golf, Lost Tree Golf, Coral Beach (Palm Beach, Fla.); Manalapan, Manalapan Yacht (Point Manalapan, Fla.); Home: Manalapan, Fla. Died Mar. 30, 1977.

HAMLETT, BARKSDALE, army officer, univ. pres.; b. Hopkinsville, Ky., Dec. 30 1908; student Lindsey Wilson Jr. Coll.; B.S., U.S. Mil, Acad., 1930; grad. Ecole de Guerre, France, 1946, Nat. War Coll., Washington, 1949; m. Frances Underwood, 1931; one dau., Otilia Crume. Commd. 2d lt. F.A., 1930, advanced through the grades to general, 1962; assigned 12th F.A., Ft. Sam Houston, Tex., 1930-32, 11th F.A., Schofield Barracks, T.H., 1932-35, 18th F.A., Ft. Sill, Okla., 1934, 15th F.A., Ft. Sam Houston, 1939; asst. arty. officer II Corps, 1942-43; asst. G-3 Army Ground Forces, Washington, 1943-44; arty. comdr. 16th Armored Div., 1944-45; comdr. 190th F.A. Group Europe, 1945, asst. arty. officer Arty. Theatre Gen. Bd., 1945; gunnery instr. Arty. Sch., Ft. Sill, 1946, dir. dept. gunnery, 1947, dir. tng., 1947-48; exec. officer G-4 Sect. Far East Command, 1949-51, chief plans and operations div., 1951, arty comdr. 24th Inf. Div., Korea, 1951-52; asst. for planning coordination Office Dep. Chief Staff for Plans, Army Hdqrs., 1952-55; arty. comdr. VII Corps, U.S. Army Europe, Heidelberg, Germany, 1955-56; comdg. gen. 10th Inf. Div., 1956-57, U.S. comdr., Berlin, 1957-59; asst. dep. chief of staff for mil. operations Dept. Army, 1959-61, dep. chief of staff, 1961-62, vice chief of staff, 1962-64, ret.; pres. Norwich U., Northfield, Vt., 1965-72. Decorated Bronze Star medal, Silver Star, Legion of Merit with 2 clusters, D.S.M. Mem. Ret. Officers Assn. (pres. 1973-75). Home: Hilton Head Island, S.C. Died Aug. 26, 1979.

HAMLIN, FRANK THOMPSON, engineer, lawyer; b. Anderson, S.C., Mar. 19, 1882; s. Jabal Calhoun and Sue Adger (Thompson) H.; prep. edn., Patrick Mil. Inst., Anderson; B.S., Clemson (S.C.) Coll., 1904; unmarried. Served with Isthmian Canal Commn., 1904-07, with Panama Canal, 1907-27; admitted to Canal Zone bar, 1924. Del. to Dem. Nat. Conv., 1924; mem. Dem. Nat. Com. for Canal Zone, 1924-28; organizer Panama Democratic Club, 1917, sec.-treas., 1917-28. Presbyn. Mason (K.T., Shriner), Odd Fellow, Elk, K.P. Clubs: Union, Century, Panama Golf (Panama City). Home: Ancon, Canal Zone.*

HAMMETT, FREDERICK SIMONDS, biologist; b. Chelsea, Mass., Nov. 18, 1885; s. Charles Freeman and Nellie Alice (Hunt) H.; A.B., Tufts, 1908; M.S., R.I. State Coll. of Agr. and Mechanic Arts, 1911; A.M., Harvard, 1914, Ph.D., 1915; m. 3d, Dorothy Wall Smith, Mar. 27, 1931; children—Frederick Simonds, Richard Lewis. Asst. in chemistry, Tufts, 1907-08; asst. chemist, R.I. Agrl. Expt. Sta., 1909-12; teaching fellow in biochemistry, Harvard Med. Sch., 1913-15, asst. comparative anatomy, 1914-15; prof. biochemistry and physiology, U. of Southern Calif., 1915-17; instr. histology, Harvard Med. Sch., 1917-18; secretary Harvard Grad. Sch. of Medicine, 1918-19; fellow in biochem., Wistar Inst., Anatomy, Phila., 1919-22, asst. prof., 1922-27; scientific dir., Research Inst. of Lankenau Hospital, Phila., Pa., 1927-47. Mem. Assn. of Harvard Chemists. Fellow A.A.A.S.; mem. Am. Soc. Zoölogists, Am. Soc. Biochemists, Am. Physiol. Soc., Am. Genetics Assn., N.Y. Acad. Sci., Phila. Co. Med. Soc. (hon.), Boston Soc. Natural History, Order Founders and Patriots America, Soc. Colonial Wars, S.A.R., Fortean Soc. (hon. founder), Soc. for Study of Growth and Development (honorary member), Phi Beta Kappa and Sigma Xi. Episcopalian. Club: Beachcombers (Provincetown). Member advisory council Yenching Univ., Peiping, China. Author: "The Nature of Growth" and several scientific papers. Founder and editor of Growth. Address: 493 Provincetown, Mass. *

HAMMITT, JOSEPH OTIS, civic reformer; b. at Kingston, N.Y., Aug. 6, 1883; s. Joseph and Mary Lucina (Craig) H.; grad. Brooklyn Boys' High Sch., 1900; New York Law Sch., 1907-8; unmarried. Newspaper work, 1900-7, Washington corr., polit. corr. and spl. traveling corr., principally for Brooklyn Times, also traveling political corr., New York Evening Post; visited Martinique and St. Vincent to write descriptions of volcanic eruptions of Mont Pelée and Mont Soufriere, 1902. Active in primary and election reforms during administrations of Gov. Hughes, 1907-10; legislative agt., 1908-9, sec., 1909-13, Citizens Union, New York; one of organizers of Legislative Voters' Assn., etc.; mgr. Municipal Govt. Assn. N.Y. State, 1912; chief of Bur. of Fire Prevention of the New York Fire Dept., 1914-17; head of community dept. of Air Nitrates Corpn., building and operating explosives plants for U.S. Govt., 1918; labor relations, Am. Cyanamid Co., 1919—. Episcopalian. Mem. Nat. Municipal League, Nat. Inst. Social Sciences. Clubs: City, Transportation. Home: Brooklyn. *

HAMMOND, CHARLES HERRICK, architect; b. Crown Point, N.Y., Aug. 8, 1882; s. Charles Lyman and Mary Electa (Stevens) H.; ed. pub. schs.; grad. Chicago Manual Training Sch.; B.S. in Architecture, Armour Inst. Tech., 1904; winner Traveling Scholarship, Chicago Architectural Club; studied in Paris; m. Marion Eugenia Rogers, Oct. 4, 1911 (died Apr. 2, 1933); 1 dau., Marion Rogers; m. 2d, Mrs. L. K. Stout, February 22, 1934; 1 stepson, Richard H. Stout, U.S.N.R. Practiced at Chicago since 1907; member Chatten & Hammond, 1907-27, Perkins, Chatten & Hammond, 1927-33, Burnham & Hammond since Oct. 28, 1933. Supervising architect. State of Illinois, since 1929. Served as maj. res. mil. aviator, Air Service, World War I, Chief Architect 6th Corps Area U.S. Army World War II. Former trustee Foundation for Architecture and Landscape Architecture; former vice-pres. Chicago Assn. Commerce; U.S. del. Internat. Congress Architects, 1937. Fellow A.I.A. (pres. 1928-30; past pres. Chicago chpt.); mem. Ill. Soc. Architects (past pres.); corr. mem. Royal Inst. of British Architects; U.S. del. Pan-Am. Congress Architects (Havana, Cuba), 1950. Mem. Congl. Ch. Clubs: University, Indian Hill, Country, Arts, Chicago Curling. Home: Winnetka, Ill. *

HAMMOND, PAUL LYMAN, indsl. banker, yachtsman; b. Egypt, Mass., Dec. 16, 1882; s. William L. and Adelaide (Nowell) H.; grad. Thayer Acad., 1902; student Harvard, 1906; m. Susan R. Sedgewick, Mar. 30, 1929. Sr. partner, Hammond, Kennedy & Co., Inc., and predecessors, pvt. indsl. bankers, N.Y.C., 1906-65, chairman bd. dirs., 1965-71; dir. Perkin-Elmer Corp., Wall St. Investing Corp.; treas., dir. Sutton Pl. South Corp.; financial cons. hdqrs. financing UN. Adv. com., past treas. U.S. Com. for UN. Assn.; hon. trustee, mem. corp. com., mem. devel. com. Woods Hole Oceanographic Instn.; mem. overseers com. to visit dept. astronomy Harvard; trustee, dir. Whaling Museum Soc., Cold Spring Harbor, L.I. Served as lt. comdr. USN, 1917-18; as capt. USNR, 1940-46. Decorated Bronze Star with citation for devel. anti-U boat weapons and rockets, U.S. Navy; Order Brit. Empire; also the Al Merito (Ecuador). Clubs: Seawanhaka Corinthian Yacht (Oyster Bay, Long Island); River, Yacht, The Sky, Harvard (N.Y.C.); Harvard Faculty (Cambridge, Mass.); Pilgrims; Royal Yacht Squadron, Royal Naval Sailing Assn., Royal Ocean Racing (Gt. Brit.); Real Club de Regatas de Sanander (Spain). Comdr. yacht, the Niña, winner Queen of Spain's Cup in trans-Atlantic race, 1928. Home: New York, N.Y. Died May 5, 1976.

HAMMOND, THOMAS GUY, ins. exec.; b. Wellsville, O., Dec. 19, 1885; s. Thomas Greenwood and Mary Elizabeth (Henderson) H.; student Ohio State U., 1903-04; A.B., Harvard, 1907; student U. Washington Law Sch., 1909-12; m. Francys Gildart Brotherton, Aug. 27, 1913; children—Elizabeth, Thomas Guy, Jr. Admitted to Wash. bar, 1912; claims atty., U.S. Fidelity & Guaranty Co., Seattle, 1919-22; asso. mgr. Nat. Surety Co., San Francisco, 1922-24; Northwest Surety supt. for Hartford Accident and Indemnity Co., 1924-26; partner Allen, Connor & Hammond, Inc., 1926-28; v.p., N.Y. Indemnity Co., San Francisco, 1928-29; exec. v.p. and dir. United Pacific Ins. Co., Seattle, since 1929. Mem. city council, Wellsville, 1907-09. Mem. Seattle Park Bd., 1928-29. Mem. Phi Delta Phi, Sigma Alpha Epsilon. Methodist. Mason. Club: Young Mens Republican (pres. 1921), Rotary, Rainier, Washington Athletic. Home: Seattle. *

HAMMONS, WALTER SCOTT, banker; b. Boston, Mass., July 25, 1886; s. Harry Clifford and Susie Louise (Smith) H.; ed. pub. schs. and Chandler Normal Shorthand Sch., Boston; m. Margaret Prince Cox, Sept. 17, 1915; children—Margaret Elizabeth, Barbara. Formerly chmn. bd. Hammons & Co., and dir. of many corpns. and pub. utility cos. Served as lt., later capt., Q.M.C., U.S.A, Aug.-Dec., 1918. Mem. Cumberland Co. Agrl. and Hort. Soc., Mass. Hort. Soc., Me. Hist. Soc., Mil. Order World War, Am. Legion, Portland Chamber Commerce, Miami Beach Chamber Commerce. Episcopalian. Mason (32 deg., K.T, Shriner). Clubs: Portland Country, Portland Yacht; Congressional Country (Washington); Recess, Bankers, New York Yacht (New York); Surf Club, Indian Creek (Miami Beach). *

HAMPTON, AMBROSE GONZALES, newspaper exec.; b. Columbia, S.C., May 17, 1900; s. Frank and Gertrude (Gonzales) H.; B.S., The Citadel, 1921, C.E., 1928, LL.D., 1965; postgrad. N.C. State U., 1939, 51; L.H.D. (hon.), U. S.C., 1978; m. Henriette duBose Dargan, Oct. 10, 1923; children—Henriette Dargan (Mrs. Ben Rankin Morris), Ambrose Gonzales. Resident engr. bridge constrn. S.C. Hwy. Dept., 1921-32; dist. engr. Forest Service Eastern S.C., 1932-36; dist. engr. hwy. and bridge constrn. U.S. Bur. Public Rds. in N.C., Raleigh, 1936-42, dist. engr. access rds. to mil. posts, 1942-45, dist. engr. charge design,

1945-55; asst. to pres. State-Record Co., Columbia, 1955-63, pres., 1963-71, chmn. exec. com. 1972-80; chmn. bd. State-Record Pub. Co. (now Columbia Newspapers, Inc.), 1966-71, Bestway Express, State Printing Co., Gulf Pub. Co., 1968-71; pub. The State, The Columbia Rec., from 1963, Daily Herald, Gulfport-Biloxi, Miss., from 1971; dir. S.C. Nat. Bank, 1963-71, dir. emeritus, 1973; Commr., Richland County Historic Preservation Commn.; former pres., bd. dirs. United Community Services; v.p., trustee Historic Columbia Found.; bd. dirs. S.C. Bus. Devel. Corp., 1968-78; bd. dirs. Citadel Devel. Found., 1969-76, v.p., 1973-76. Served with U.S. Army, 1918. Mem. ASCE, Columbia C. of C. (past dir.), Sigma Delta Chi. Episcopalian (vestryman, sr. warden). Clubs: Cosmos, Forest Lake, Palmetto, Springdale Hall, St. Cecilia, Cotillion, Quadrille, Flamenco. Home: Columbia, S.C. Died Feb. 26, 1980.

HAMPTON, JOHN PEYTON, lawyer; b. Canton, Mo., Nov. 11, 1895; s. William DeKalb and Pattie Jane (Smith) H.; J.D., U. Mich., 1920; m. Edith Helen Eilrich, Sept. 1, 1939. Admitted to Ill. bar, 1920, thereafter practiced in Chgo.; asst. state's atty., Cook County, Ill., 1928-32; partner firm Dent, Hampton & McNeela. Served with U.S. Army, 1918. Home: Oak Park, Ill. Died Jan. 25, 1976.

HANCOCK, STEWART FREEMAN, lawyer; b. Syracuse, N.Y., Apr. 4, 1883; s. Theodore E. and Martha B. (Connelly) H.; A.B., Wesleyan U., 1905; LL.B., Syracuse U. Law Sch., 1907; m. Marion McLennan, June 8, 1912; children—Theodore McLennan, Helen (Mrs. Henry L. McClintock), Marion (Mrs. James L. McConaughy, Jr.), Martha Christina (Mrs. David Northrup), Stewart Freeman, Constance. Admitted to the New York bar, 1907; member of the law firm of Hancock, Dorr, Ryan & Shove (successors to Hancock, Hogan & Hancock) since 1908; asst. corp. counsel, Syracuse, 1908-14, corp. counsel, 1917-20; pres. City Bank & Trust Co., 1921-23. Dir. First Trust & Deposit Co., First Fed. Savings & Loan Co., Lipe-Rollway Corp., Iroquois China Co., Wilson & Greene Lumber Co.; Easy Washing Machine Corp., Rollway Bearing Co., Porter Cable Machine Co.; dir. Nat. War Fund, Nat. War Prisoners' Aid Com. Pres. N.Y. State United War Fund, 1943-45; pres. Syracuse Community Chest, 1942. Trustee Wesleyan U. since 1928. Mem. Alpha Delta Phi, Phi Beta Kappa, Phi Delta Phi. Republican. Unitarian. Mason. Clubs: Century, Onondaga Country (Syracuse). Home: Syracuse, N.Y. *

HAND, WILLIAM HENRY, chem. co. exec.; b. South Nyack, N.Y., Sept. 21, 1900; s. Walter S. and Kate Adelma (Storms) H.; B.S., Haverford Coll., 1924. Asso. with Thomas A. Edison as personal research asst., 1924-30; tchr. E.S. Harkness Found., Commonwealth Fund, 1931-41; founder, dir. research and devel. Hand Lab. Electrochem. Research & Devel., South Nyack, 1930-78. Life mem. Am. Ordnance Assn., Nat. Trust Historic Preservation, Naval Hist. Found., N.Y., Nat. hist. socs. Franklin Inst., Phila., Constn. Island Assn., West Point. Club: Industrial Management (treas.) (Rockland County, N.Y.). Pioneer devel. synthetic organic plastics catalytically controlled. Home: South Nyack, N.Y. Died 1978.

HANDLEY, WILLIAM J., govt. ofcl., educator; b. Netherlands Guiana, Dec. 17, 1918 (parents Am. citizens); student U. London, 1935-37; B.A., U. Md., 1942, Am. U., 1943-44. Announcer, program writer for broadcasting sta., 1936-39; mgr. import co., Brit. Guiana, 1937-39; priority specialist WPB, 1942-44; analyst Fgn. Econ. Adminstrn., 1944; econ. analyst U.S. Fgn. Service aux., 1944; attache, Cairo, 1945, Addis Ababa, Baghdad, Beirut, Damascus, Jerusalem, Jidda and Teheran, 1947; U.S. observer 1st ILO meeting for Near East govts., 1947; assigned State Dept., 1948-49, labor adviser Bur. Near East, South Asian and African Affairs, 1949-51, Office Asst. Sec. State, 1951; pub. affairs officer, attache, New Delhi, 1951-52, planning officer, attache, 1952-53; joined USIA in New Delhi, 1953, dep. chief pub. affairs officer, attache, New Delhi, 1954-55; assigned USIA, Washington, 1955-61, chief Near East policy staff, 1955-56, dep. asst. dir. Near East, South Asia and Africa, 1956-57, asst. dir., 1957-61; U.S. ambassador to Mali, 1961-64; dep. asst. sec. for Near Eastern affairs Dept. State, 1964-69; U.S. ambassador to Turkey, 1969-73; sr. adviser to sec. state, coordinator internat. narcotics matters, also exec. dir. Cabinet com. on internat. narcotics control Dept. State, 1973-74; ret., 1974; vis. prof. internat. relations Coll. of Charleston (S.C.), also The Citadel, Charleston, from 1975; vis. prof. internat. relations, ambassador-in-residence Lewis and Clark Coll., Portland, Oreg. Recipient Superior Service USIA, 1956. Address: Portland, Oreg. Died Nov. 5, 1979.

HANES, JAMES GORDON, mfr. hosiery; b. Winston-Salem, N.C., June 12, 1886; s. John Wesley and Anna (Hodgin) H.; A.B., U. of N.C., 1909; m. Emmie Drewry, Nov. 12, 1911 (dec. 1916); 1 son, James Gordon; m. 2d, Molly Ruffin, Apr. 1, 1924 (dec. 1957) In hosiery business, 1909—; chmn. bd. Hanes Hosiery Mills Co., 1938-54, now dir.; dir. Wachovia Bank & Trust Co., Winston-Salem Southbound Ry. Co., other corps. Mayor of Winston-Salem, 1921-25; chmn. bd. County Commrs. of Forsyth County, N.C., 1927-50. Methodist. Club: Twin City, Forsyth Country. Home: Winston-Salem, N.C. *

HANEY, JILES WILLIAM, prof. of mech. engring.; b. Guin, Ala., Nov. 17, 1886; s. Willis Jiles and Emma Francis (McDonald) H.; B.S. in mech. engring., U. of Mo., 1913, M.S. in mech. engring., 1914, A.M., 1915; m. Mary Aileene Martin, June 11, 1916; 1 dau., Mary Maxine (Mrs. Charles F. Long). Chief Engineer Commerce Power Co., Kansas City, Mo., 1915-16; instructor mechanical engring., Penna. State College, 1916-18; with Univ. of Nebraska since 1918, successively asst. prof., asso. prof. and prof. mech. engring., 1918-26, prof. mech. engring. and chmn. dept. 1926-47, now prof. emeritus. Asst. dir. civil aeros. program for Neb. and dir. civilian pilot training program, U. of Neb., beginning World War II. Served as instr. in auto mechanic and truck driving schs., U.S. Army, 1918; capt. Q.M.C., U.S. Reserve, Feb. 1, 1924; commissioned maj., Apr. 2, 1930; called to active duty, Jan. 20, 1942; assigned to Hdqrs. of Quartermaster Replacement Training Center as asst. dir. Motor Maintenance Sch., June 2, 1942; lt. col., Oct. 10, 1942; asst. dir. Motor Maintenance Training Branch, Feb. 1943; chief of Instr. Guidance Branch, Mar. 1943; on overseas service, July 1943-Feb. 1945. Mem. Am. Inter-professional Inst., American Society Mech. Engrs., Soc. for Promotion Engring. Edn., Neb. Engineering Soc., Heroes of '76, Sojourners (past pres. Fort Francis E. Warren chapter), Sigma Xi, Sigma Tau, Pi Tau Sigma, Theta Chi. Democrat. Presbyterian. Mason (Shriner). Clubs: Engineers', Open Forum, Hiram (Lincoln); Am. Inter-Professional Inst. Author of booklets and bulletins published by U. of Neb. and U. of Mo. Engring. Expt. Stations. Co-author of a research bulletin published by Mo. Univ. Engring. Expt. Station; contbr. tech. articles to jours. Home: Lincoln, Neb. *

HANGER, WILLIAM ARNOLD, exec. engr., farmer; b. Richmond, Ky., Feb. 5, 1896; s. Harry Baylor and Elizabeth (Arnold) H.; grad. Lawrenceville (N.J.) Sch., 1916; wartime certificate Wharton Sch. Finance, U. Pa., 1921; LL.D. (hon.), 1958; m. Hope Yandell, 1931 (div.); m. 2d, Joanne Glassell, 1942 (div.). Became pres. Silas Mason Co., 1949, Mason & Hanger Co., 1954, following merger of cos., pres. Mason & Hanger-Silas Mason Co., Inc., heavy constrn., engring., plant constrn., design and operation in fields of explosives and chem. engring.; spl. field testing work for AEC; mng. dir. Arlington Farm, Richmond, Ky., from 1925, Hartland Farm, Versailles, Ky., from 1936, Arlington Ranch, Kenansville, Fla., from 1939; pres. Tri-State Utilities, Richmond, from 1927; dir. Lafayette Hotel Co., Lexington, Ky., Churchill Downs. Trustee, U. Miami, Coral Gables, Fla., also mem. athletic com., constrn. com.; chmn. bd. Lowe Gallery, U. Miami dir., trustee Keeneland Racing Assn., Lexington, Ky.; mem. finance com. N.Y. Infirmary; mem. Ky. Med. Found., U. Ky. Served from ensign to lt. (j.g.) USN, 1917-19. Mem. Engrs. Club, Am. Ordnance Assn. (Gold medal), United Hunts Racing and Steeplechase Assn., V.F.W., Am., Brit. (hon.) legions, U.S. Naval Inst. Am. Democrat. Clubs: Jockey, Brook (N.Y.C.); St. Elmo (U. Pa.); Idle Hour Country, Iriquois Hunt (Lexington, Ky.); Meadowbrook Country (L.I.); La Gorce Country, Indian Creek Country, Surf, Bath, Gun (Miami Beach, Fla.); Phildelphia Gun. Mason, Elk. Home: Richmond, Ky. Died May 31, 1976.

HANIG, MARTIN, educator; b. Bklyn., Jan. 6, 1913; s. George and Renee H.; B.A., N.Y. U., 1937; postgrad. U. Minn., 1946; m. Mary Margaret Devore, June 28, 1947; 1 son, David Martin. Asst. prof. U. Mich., 1947-51; asst. prof. U. Pitts., 1951, prof., 1966-75, prof. biophysics emeritus, 1975. Served with AUS, 1946. USPHS grantee, 1951-66. Mem. Am. Chem. Soc., Soc. Biol. Chemists. Biophys. Soc., A.A.A.S., AAUP, Sigma Xi. Home: Pittsburgh, Pa. Died June 1975.

HANLEY, DEXTER L., clergyman, educator; b. Ft. Worth, June 26, 1919; s. Thomas James, Jr. and Cecelia (Meilleur) H.; A.B., Georgetown U., 1940, LL.B., 1956; Ph.L., Woodstock Coll., 1945, S.T.L., 1952; LL.M., Harvard, 1958. Joined Soc. Jesus, Md. Province, 1940; ordained priest Roman Catholic Ch., 1952; dean Summer Schs., Georgetown U., 1952-53, prof. law, from 1959, dir. Inst. Law, Human Rights and Social Values, from 1965; pres. U. Scranton, Pa., 1970-75. U.S. del. Econ. and Social Council of UN, 1967. Mem. Am. (sec. labor law sect. 1967, 70), Fed. (nat. council 1968-77) bar assns., Phi Beta Kappa, Delta Mu Delta, Omicron Delta Epsilon, Phi Delta Phi, Phi Delta Kappa. K.C. (4 deg.). Home: Scranton, Pa. Died May 19, 1977.

HANLON, BYRON HALL, naval officer; b. Rocklin, Calif., Sept. 27, 1900; s. Peter and Susan Jane (Hall) H.; student U. Calif., 1916; B.S., U.S. Naval Acad., 1920; postgrad., 1925-26; M.S., Lehigh U., 1928; m. Lady Jane Brown, June 7, 1922; children—Peter, Kevin. Commd. ensign, U.S. Navy, 1920, advanced through grades to admiral, 1958; comdg. officer U.S.S. Lamson, 1938-39; staff comdr. battle force, Pearl Harbor, 1939-41; dep. chief staff Task Force I, 1941-42; planning officer U.S. Naval Gun Factory, Washington, 1943-44; comdr. underwater demolition teams Amphibious Forces, P.T.O., 1944-45; comdg. officer U.S.S. North Carolina, Pacific area, 1945-46; comdg. officer U.S. Naval Powder Factory, Indian Head, Md., 1946-48; comdr. mine force U.S. Atlantic Fleet, 1948-50; comdr. U.S. Naval Ordnance Lab., White Oak, Md., Mar.-July 1950; supt. Naval Gun Factory July, 1950-52; dep. chief of staff for comdr.-in-chief Far East, 1952-54; comdr. several task forces, 1954-58; ret., 1958; then exec. with Magnavox Co. Decorated Navy Cross, Legion of Merit with gold star. Bronze Star with combat V, Presdl. unit citation, Commendation ribbon with gold star, Purple Heart, Army disting. service medal, Navy disting. service medal, Legion of Honor (Brazil), Order of White Elephant (Thailand), Mil. Order of Taguk with gold star (Korea). Mem. Am. Ordnance Assn., Nat. Security Indsl. Assn. Home: Charleston, S.C. Died Jan. 9, 1977.

HANN, ROBERT HENRY, steel co. exec., lawyer; b. Hornell, N.Y., June 19, 1907; s. Charles William and Gertrude (Ingalls) H.; J.D., Rutgers U., 1940; grad. Indsl. Coll. Armed Forces, 1959; m. Pauline E. Pierce, May 3, 1930. Admitted to N.J. bar, 1941, Ohio bar, 1942, U.S. Supreme Ct. bar, 1974; pvt. sec. to judge Circuit Ct. N.J., 1938-41; atty. Erie R.R. Co., 1942-44, asst. gen. atty., 1944-46, gen. atty., 1946-52, corporate sec., 1952-72, sec.-treas., 1964-66 (co. now Erie-Lackawanna R.R. Co.), also dir. several subs.'s; sec. Wean Industries, Youngstown, Ohio, 1966-72, Wean Engring. Co. Can. Ltd., Hamilton, 1967-72; asst. sec. Wean United, Inc., Pitts., 1968; mem. fin. com. Trailer Train, Inc.; treas. Buffalo Creek R.R. Chmn., R.R. Community Com., Cleve., 1961; chief warden Civil Def., 1949-52; pres. West Hill Colony, Inc. Mem. U.S., Ohio, Youngstown chambers commerce, Am. Soc. Corporate Secs. (past pres.), Rutgers U. Alumni Assn., Delta Theta Phi (past dean, mem. emeritus). Episcopalian (past jr. and sr. warden). Clubs: Masons, Rotary, Tryon (N.C.) Country. Home: Columbus, N.C. Died June 24, 1977.

HANNA, ALFRED JACKSON, historian, educator; b. Tampa, Fla., May 5, 1893; s. Josiah Calvin and Sarah Emily (Jackson) H.; A.B., Rollins Coll., 1917, L.H.D., 1945; grad. study U. Madrid (Spain), 1931, U. Mex., 1934; m. Kathryn T. Abbey, July 5, 1941 (dec. Apr. 1967). Successively adminstrv. officer, instr., asst. prof., asso. prof. and prof. history Rollins Coll., 1917-70, also dir. Inter-Am. studies, 1942-65, Weddell prof. history, 1946-70, v.p., 1951-70, trustee, 1969-78. Served with USNRF, 1918-19. Decorated officer d'Academie, Palmes Universitaires (France), 1935; Confederate Cross Mil. Service, 1974, recipient Award of Merit, Am. Assn. State and Local History, 1977; Social Sci. Research Council-Am. Philos. Soc. research grantee, France, 1952. Mem. Hispanic Inst. Fla. (pres. 1933-40), Fla. Acad. Scis., Fla. Audubon Soc. (past pres.), Kappa Alpha. Episcopalian. Republican. Clubs: Cosmos (Washington); University (Winter Park). Author: Fort Maitland, 1935; Founding of Rollins College, 1936; Flight Into Oblivion, 1938; (with Branch Cabell) The St. Johns River (in Rivers of Am. series), 1943; A Prince in Their Midst, 1946; (with Kathryn Abbey Hanna) Lake Okeechobee (Am. Lake series), 1948, Florida's Golden Sands, 1950, Confederate Exiles in Venezuela (Confederate Centennial series), 1960, Napoleon III and Mexico: American Triumph over Monarchy, 1971, Spanish edit., 1973. Editor: Rollins Alumni Record, 1925-32; Recommended Readings for the Florida Centennial, 1945. Contbr. hist. articles mags., also Dictionary Am. Biography, Dictionary Am. History, Ency. Americana, Ency. Britannica. Home: Winter Park, Fla. Died Mar. 13, 1978.

HANNAN, JAMES MACCLYMONT, automotive supply co. exec.; b. Lincoln, Neb., Dec. 1, 1908; s. William Everett and Janet (MacClymont) H.; A.B., Yale, 1933; m. Mary Luther, June 24, 1950; 1 dau., Mary Elizabeth (Mrs. George H. Glover, Jr.). Dept. mgr. R.H. Macy & Co., N.Y.C., 1933-40; sales exec. J.S. Blank & Co., N.Y.C., 1940, 46-47; gen. sales mgr. Standard Products Co., Cleve., 1948-57; exec. v.p. Automotive Materials Corp., Detroit, 1957-62, pres., 1962-66; dir. Am. Safety Equipment Corp., N.Y.C., 1964-77, v.p., 1965-68, exec. v.p., 1968-71, sr. v.p., 1971-77; pres., treas. Am. Safety Equipment Corp. Mich., 1965-68. Chmn. U.S. Naval Sea Cadet Corps, 1966-67. Pres. Bloomfield Village Assn., 1969; bd. mgrs. St. Joseph Mercy Hosp., Pontiac, Mich., pres. lay adv. bd., 1969; mem. bd. African Art Gallery com. Detroit Inst. Arts, 1974-77. Served to comdr. USNR, 1941-46; PTO. Decorated Bronze Star with Combat V; recipient Disting. Public Service award Sec. Navy, 1966-71; Disting. Service award Dept. Transp.-Comdt. USCG, 1971. Mem. Cum Laude Soc., Navy League of U.S. (nat. pres. 1969, 70, nat. dir. 1964-77, chmn. nat. adv. council 1971-73), Ret. Officers Assn. (1st v.p. 1975-77), Mil. Order of Carabao, Beta Theta Pi. Democrat. Episcopalian. Clubs: Orchard Lake (Mich.) Country; Recess, Detroit, one hundred (Detroit); Huron River Hunting and Fishing (Farmington, Mich.); Yale (N.Y.C.); Army-Navy Country (Arlington, Va); Army and Navy (Washington); Chevy Chase (Md.). Home: West Bloomfield, Mich. Died May 22, 1977.

HANNER, GUY M., hosp. adminstr.; b. Sumner, Ia., May 3, 1885; s. Joseph and Ellen (Bullock) H.; student Cornell, 1906-09; m. Grace Wilbanks, May 29, 1911.

Supt. Beth-El Hosp., Colorado Springs, Colo., 1921-41; adminstr. Desert Sanatorium, Tucson, 1941-43, Hilo Meml. Hosp., Hawaii, 1943-45, Good Samaritan Hosp., Phoenix, since 1945. Fellow Am. Coll. Hosp. Adminstrs.; mem. Am. Hosp. Assn. (life mem.), Ariz. Hosp. Assn. (sec.-treas.). Club: Arizona. Home: Phoenix. *

HANNETT, ARTHUR THOMAS, ex-gov.; b. Lyons, N.Y., Feb. 17, 1884; s. William and Mary Emily (McCarthy) H.; student Coll. of Liberal Arts (Syracuse U.), 1 yr.; student U. of Buffalo Coll. of Law, 1 yr.; LL.B., Syracuse U., 1910; honorary LL.D. from Syracuse Univ., 1926; m. Louise Estella Westfall, Aug. 13, 1913; 1 son, William. Began practice at Gallup, N.M., 1911; city atty., Gallup, 1914-16; del. Nat. Conv., Baltimore, 1912, San Francisco, 1920; mayor of Gallup, 1918-22; chmn. N.M. State Highway Commn., 1923-25; gov. of N.M., term 1925-27. Food Administrator McKinley County, N.M., World War. Mem. bd. visitors Syracuse (N.Y.) U. Coll. of Law. Mem. Dem. Nat. Com., 1936-44. Mem. Am., N.M., and Bernalillo County bar assns. Democrat. Episcopalian. Mason (32 deg.), Elk. Home: Albuquerque, N.M.*

HANNON, THOMAS EUGENE, govt. ofcl.; b. Lowell, Mass., Apr. 7, 1921; s. Thomas J. and Ellen (Hunt) H.; B.B.A. cum laude, Northeastern U., 1956. Regional personnel officer GSA, Boston, 1949-62, dep. regional adminstr., Boston, 1962-63, regional adminstr., San Francisco, 1963-78. Mem. San Francisco Fed. Exec. Bd., 1963-80. Served with USNR, 1942-45. Recipient Disting. Service medal GSA, 1963. Home: Castro Valley, Calif. Died May 25, 1978; buried in Lowell, Mass.

HANNY, WILLIAM F., cartoonist; b. Burlington, Ia., Nov. 21, 1882; s. Gustave and Minnie (Hackman) H.; ed. grammar sch., and Art Students' League, New York; m. Alida Wikoff, Sept. 23, 1915. With St. Joseph (Mo.) News Press, 1912-22, except 1 yr. at Art Students' League; with Pioneer Press, St. Paul, 1922-24, Philadelphia Inquirer, 1924-34, Chicago Herald and Examiner, 1934, New York American, 1935-36, Chicago Herald and Examiner, 1937-39. Address: Swarthmore, Pa. *

HANSEN, EJNAR NIELS, artist; b. Copenhagen, Denmark, Jan. 9, 1884; s. Yens Jorgen and Laura (Rydstrom) H.; student Tech. Sch. of Copenhagen, Royal Acad. Fine Arts, Copenhagen, 1904-07; m. Helga Kristensen, Aug. 1921; 1 son, Jorgen. Came to U.S., 1914, naturalized, 1925. Tchr. Los Angeles County Art Inst., 1940—, Pasadena City Coll., 1947—, Pasadena Sch. Fine Arts, 1950—; exhibited, Copenhagen, 1906-12, Chgo. Art Inst., 1916-23, N.Y. World's Fair, 1939, San Francisco World's Fair, 1939-40, also numerous museums and galleries Am., including Met. Mu(s., Concoran Gallery; one man shows Los Angeles Mus., San Diego Fine Arts Gallery, Pasadena Art Mus.; represented in collections N.Y. Pub. Library, Sacramento State Fair, Los Angeles County Fair, Nat. Orange Show, King Frederik IX of Denmark. Recipient 1st Municipal Art League award Chgo. Art Inst., 1923, 1st award Los Angeles County Mus., 1928, Cal. State Fair, 1937, San Diego Fine Arts Gallery, 1941, Pasadena Soc. Artists, 1942, Sacramento State Fair, 1948, 56, Spaulding Meml. award Pasadena Art Mus., 1955, Laguna Beach Art Festival, 1957, Scandinavian-Am. Art Soc., 1958, 1st award, Pasadena Society of Artists, 1960. Member of Am. Watercolor Soc., Cal. Watercolor Society, Pasadena Soc. Artists, Laguna Beach Art Assn. (hon.), Scandinavian-Am. Art Soc. (hon.). Address: Pasadena, Cal. *

HANSEN, HARRY, editor; b. Davenport, Iowa, Dec. 26, 1884; s. Hans and Christine (Jochims) H.; Ph.B., U. Chgo., 1909; m. Ruth McLernon, Apr. 29, 1914; children—Ruth Eleanor, Marian Hope Hansen Stankard. Alumni sec., 1909-11; war corr. Chgo. Daily News with German, Belgian, French and Austrian armies and in Baltic zone, 1914-16, corr. at Paris Peace Conf., 1919, lit. editor, 1920-26, N.Y. World, 1926-31, N.Y. World-Telegram, 1931-48; reviewer for Harper's Mag., 1923-39, Redbook, 1940-50, for Survey, 1940-52; lectr. on reviewing Columbia, 1928-33, on biography, etc., 1939-41, U. Colo., 1940; v.p. Hastings House, Pubs., Inc., N.Y.C. from 1965. Mem. editorial bd. Armed Services Editions; book bd. East and West Assn.; judge MGM and Nat. Book (novel) award. Mem. Ill. Hist. Soc., Hist. Soc. Iowa, Sigma Alpha Epsilon. Clubs: Dutch Treat, Coffee House, Overseas Press (N.Y.C.); Tavern (Chgo.). Author: The Adventures of the Fourteen Points, 1919; Midwest Portraits, 1923; Carl Sandburg, the Man and His Poetry, 1924; Your Life Lies Before You, 1935; The Chicago (Rivers of America), 1942; North of Manhattan, 1950; Scarsdale: From Colonial Manor to Modern Community, 1954; The Fighting Constitution, 1955; The Story of Illinois, 1956; The Civil War, 1961; The Boston Massacre, 1969; Longfellow's New England, 1972; co-author: Writing Up the News, 1940; Journalism in Wartime, 1943; The Aspirin Age, 1949; also essays, magazine articles. Translator: A Peace Congress of Intrigue (by F. Freksa), 1918; Faber (by Jacob Wassermann), 1925. Editor: O. Henry Prize Stories, 1933-40, World Almanac, 1949-65; The Stories of O. Henry, 1968; California, 1967; New England Legends and Folklore, 1967; Texas, 1969, All Quiet on the Western Front, 1969; Colorado, 1970; Louisiana, 1971; Illinois, 1974; Alabama, 1975; New Jersey, 1977. Contbr. to Ency. Britannica, Universal Jewish Ency. Home: Mt. Vernon, N.Y. Died Jan. 2, 1977.

HANSON, EARL PARKER, engr., geographer; b. Berlin, Germany (parents U.S. citizens), Mar. 16, 1899; s. Albert Parker and Lida (Siboni) H.; B.S., U. Wis., 1922; postgrad. U. Chgo., 1933; m. Dorothy Lane, Feb. 4, 1933; 1 son, John Parker; m. 2d, Charlotte Leeper, Oct. 1, 1938; children—David Parker, Nancy Leeper (dec.). Engr., Chuquicamata, Chile, 1922-25; editor tech. publs., N.Y.C., 1926; ind. exploratory research in Iceland, 1927; editor in N.Y.C., 1928-29; exploratory research in subarctic Can., 1929; writer on geog. subjects, 1929-31, exec. sec. Explorers' Club, 1931; expdn. to Amazon and Orinoco basins for Carnegie Instn. of Wash., to study fluctuations of earth's magnetic field, 1931-33; research technician for Nat. Resources Com., Washington, 1934-35; planning cons., mem. exec. bd. P.R. Reconstrn. Adminstrn., San Juan, 1935-36; cons. O.Q.-M.G., U.S. Army, on clothing and equipment for jungle warfare, 1942-44; adviser, mem. U.S. Army Engineers' expdn. to Rio Orinoco and Rio Negro, 1943; cons. USAAF, 1944; spl. rep. of F.E.A. in Liberia, spl. asst. to U.S. Minister in Liberia, and spl. agt. of U.S. Comml Co., 1944-46; cons. com. on geophysics and geography Nat. Research and Devel. Bd., 1949-51; vis. lectr. geography U. Md., spring 1948; prof. geography, chmn. dept. geography and geology U. Del., 1949-56; organized areas study course in P.R., 1952; conducted course in geography U.S. Navy War Coll., Newport, R.I., 1952; cons. econ. devel., Monagas, Venezuela, 1955; cons. Dept. of State, Commonwealth of P.R., 1956-69, Commonwealth of P.R. Planning Bd., 1958; weekly columnist on world affairs, Island Times, San Juan, 1955-64; survey econ. devel. Peruvian Amazon, 1965; lectr. sci. subjects. Decorated knight ofcl. Liberian Humane Order of African Redemption 1946; knight order Icelandic Falcon, 1953. Fellow Am. Geog. Soc. Club: Explorers (N.Y.C.). Author: Journey to Manaos, 1938; Highroad to Adventure, 1941; Chile, Land of Progress, 1941; Stefansson, Prophet of the North, 1941; New Worlds Emerging, 1949; Transformation, The Story of Modern Puerto Rico, 1955; The Amazon, A New Frontier, 1944; Puerto Rico, 1956; Chile, 1957; Bolivia, 1959; Puerto Rico, Land of Wonders, 1960; Puerto Rico, Ally for Progress, 1962; South from the Spanish Main, 1967. Editor: New World Guides to Latin America; Index to Millionth Map of Hispanic America, 1942-43. Contbr. mags. Home: Santurce, P.R. Died July 19, 1978.

HANSON, HOWARD, composer, condr., educator; b. Wahoo, Nebr., Oct. 28, 1896; s. Hans and Hilma (Eckstrom) H.; student Luther Coll., Wahoo, U. Nebr. Sch. of Music, Inst. Musical Art, N.Y. City; Mus. B., Northwestern U., 1916; Mus.D. honoris causa, Northwestern U., Syracuse U., Horner Inst., Augustana Coll. and Theol. Sem., U. Nebr., Am. Conservatory Mus., Columbia, Capital U., Shurtleff Coll., Hartt Coll., of Music, New Eng. Conservatory, Temple U., Newcomb Coll. of Tulane U., U. Mich., Mus. Fund Soc. Phila., N.Y. State Bd. Regents, U. Ariz., Gustavus Adolphus Coll., Boston U.; LL.D., U. Ky., Ill. Wesleyan U., Coll. of the Pacific, Ball State Tchrs. Coll., St. John Fisher Coll.; Litt.D., Keuka Coll., Wooster Coll.; L.H.D., Drury Coll., Valparaiso U., Ohio State U., Midland Luth. Coll., Denison U., D.F.A., Drake U., 1966, U. Portland, 1968; D.Sacred Music, Kenyon Coll., Youngstown U.; m. Margaret Elizabeth Nelson, July 24, 1946. Mem. staff theory dept. Coll. of the Pacific, San Jose, Calif., 1916, dean Conservatory Fine Arts, 1919-21, dir. Eastman Sch. Mus., U., Rochester, 1924-64, dir. Inst. of Am. Music, 1964—; Phi Beta Kappa visiting scholar, 1964-65. Cons. U.S. Dept. of State; adv. com. arts Nat. Cultural Center, Washington; mem. exec. com. of UN-ESCO. Served as guest condr. major cities both U.S. and fgn.; works have been performed by major fgn. and U.S. orchs. and bands. Winner several awards 1921—, including Pulitzer Prize, 1944, George Foster Peabody Award, 1946, Huntington Hartford Found. award, 1959, and several others. Fellow Am. Acad. Rome, 1921-24, Royal Acad. Music in Sweden, 1938; mem. N.Y. State Council Arts (concert adv. panel), Am. Acad. Arts and Scis., Am. Acad. and Inst. Arts and Letters, Am. Philos. Soc., Newcomen Soc., Phi Beta Kappa. Lutheran. Composer wide variety musical compositions, including 7 symphonies, symphonic poems, symphonie operas, mixed choruses, male choruses, instrumental selections for particular instruments, including among many others: Dies Natalis, Laude, Two Yule-tide Pieces, Opus 19; Concerto in G Major, Opus 36 for piano and orchestra; "Vermeland" from Scandinavia Suite, Opus 13, for organ; Chorale and Alleluia for symphonic band; oratorio New Land, New Convenant; Concerto for organ, strings and harp, Opus 22; Sea Symphony for chorus and orch.; opera Merry Mount; also Harmonic Materials of Modern Music. Clubs: Country of Rochester; Century Assn., Bohemians (N.Y.C.); Cosmos (Washington). Home: Rochester, N.Y. Died Feb. 26, 1981.

HANWAY, WILLIAM AUGUSTUS, paper co. exec.; b. Bklyn., Jan. 26, 1897; s. John and Alice (King) H.; student Hill Sch.; A.B., Yale, 1919; m. Ruth Salisbury Shriver, Apr. 1922; m. 2d, Caroline S. Hulse, 1930; children—David William, Jane Van Brunt. With Am. Fgn. Banking Corp., 1920, Harris Forbes & Co., 1920-29; v.p. Internat. Paper & Power Securities, Inc., 1929-35; pres. Paper & Power, Inc., 1935-41; sec. Internat. Paper Co. 1941-68. Pres., Internat. Paper Co. Ednl. Found. Mem. Am. Soc. Corp. Secs., Squadron A Ex-Mems. Assn. (bd. govs.), Am. Legion. Home: New York, N.Y. Died Feb. 21, 1979.

HARA, JAMES ELLSWORTH, oil co. exec.; b. Cleve., June 19, 1918; s. Arch and Elizabeth (Cowan) H.; B.B.A. with honors (scholar, award Am. Bankers Assn. 1940), Miami U., 1940; LL.B., U. Tex., 1947; m. Margaret Sue Parker, June 12, 1943 (dec. Oct. 1974); children—James Paul (dec.), Susan Margaret; m. 2d, Katherine Ewing Smith, June 28, 1975. Admitted to Tex. bar, 1947, Okla. bar, 1948; asso. atty. firm Critz & Kuykendall, Austin, Tex., 1947-48; with Skelly Oil Co., Tulsa, 1948-77, v.p., asst. to pres., 1960-63, exec. v.p., 1963-75, pres., 1975-77, also dir.; exec. v.p., dir. Skelly Oil Co., Iran; pres., dir. Skelly Mozambique Oil Co., Skelly Oil of Great Britain, Ltd., Skelly Internat. Oil Co.; dir. Skelly Oil Co. Libya, Skelly Pipe Line Co., Hawkeye Chem. Co., Nuclear Fuel Services, Inc., Skelly Leasing Co., Skelly Oil Can. Ltd., Boulder Bank & Trust Co., 1st Nat. Bank and Trust Co., Skelly Mining Co., Skelly Oil Exploration (U.K.) Ltd., Skelly Oil Norway, Ltd.; mem. policy com. Chemplex Co. Bd. dirs. Tulsa Community Chest; adv. bd. Tulsa Salvation Army; trustee Children's Med. Center, U. Tulsa, Tulsa Charity Horse Show, Hillcrest Med. Center; adv. bd. Indian Nat. Council Boy Scouts Am. Served as aviator USNR, 1941-45; PTO. Decorated D.F.C. with gold star, Navy Air medal with 3 gold stars. Mem. Am., Okla., Tex. bar assns., Am. Petroleum Inst. (dir.), Ind. Petroleum Assn. Am. (dir.), Mid-Continent Oil and Gas Assn. (dir.), Nat. Petroleum Refiners Assn. (v.p., dir.), Internat. Petroleum Expn. (pres., dir.), Tulsa C. of C. (dir.), Phi Beta Kappa, Phi Delta Phi, Delta Sigma Pi. Clubs: Summit (dir.), Southern Hills Country, Tulsa. Home: Tulsa, Okla. Died June 20, 1977.

HARBAGE, ALFRED BENNETT, author, educator; b. Phila., July 18, 1901; s. John and Elizabeth (Young) H.; A.B., U. Pa., 1924, A.M., 1926, Ph.D., 1929, Litt.D., 1954; m. Eliza Price Finnesey, Sept. 7, 1926; children—Diana (Mrs. Alan Baker), Klara (Mrs. David Manzella), Alfred, John. From instr. to asso. prof. English, U. Pa., 1924-42, prof. and grad. chmn., 1942-47; prof. English and comparative lit. Columbia, 1947-52; prof. Harvard, 1952-60, Cabot prof. English lit., 1960-70, emeritus, 1970-76. Guggenheim fellow, 1953-54, 65-66. Del. Shakespeare Conf. Eng., 1947; Alexander lectr. U. Toronto, 1954-55; Brit. Acad. Shakespeare lectr., 1969. Mem. Shakespeare Assn., MLA, Am. Acad. Arts and Scis., Am. Philos. Soc. (Jayne lectr. 1974), Elizabethan Club, Phi Beta Kappa. Author: Shakespeare's Audience, 1941; As They Liked It; on Shakespeare and Morality, 1947; Shakespeare and the Rival Traditions, 1952; Theatre for Shakespeare, 1955; William Shakespeare: A Reader's Guide, 1963; Conceptions of Shakespeare, 1966; Shakespeare's Songs, 1970; Shakespeare Without Words, 1972; A Kind of Power: the Shakespeare-Dickens Analogy, 1975. Gen. editor Pelican edit. Shakespeare. Contbr. jours. Home: Cherry Hill, N.J. Died May 2, 1976.

HARBESON, JOHN WESLEY, public school adminstrn.; b. Farmington, Ia., Sept. 10, 1884; s. Wesley A. and Eximena F. (Luther) H.; A.B., U. of Kansas, 1911; A.M., Columbia, 1916; Ph.D., U. of Southern Calif., 1931; student U. of Chicago, 1919-20; m. Lilla M. Hay, Sept. 15, 1915. Prin. of public school, Perry, Kan., 1911-13, Rosedale (Kan.) High Sch., 1913-14; supt. pub. schs., Tonganoxie, Kan., 1916-19; teacher social science, Pasadena (Calif.) High Sch., 1920-21; dir. child welfare, Pasadena City Schs., 1921-24; dean, Pasadena Jr. Coll., 1924-27, prin. 1927-50. Served with After-Care Red Cross Service, World War I. Mem. N.E.A. (mem. implementation com. Department Secondary Sch. Prins.), American Assn. Jr. Colls. (pres. 1942); Am. Assn. Sch. Adminstrs., Phi Beta Kappa, Phi Kappa Phi, Delta Sigma Rho, Acacia, Mason, Rotarian. Author: Classifying Jr. College Students, 1931; The New American College (with John A. Sexson), 1945. Home: Pasadena. *

HARBIN, ELVIN OSCAR (HAR'BIN), author, educator; b. Pleasantville, Ind., April 4, 1885; s. David Melvin and Sara Eliza (Newkirk) H.; grad. Louisville (Ky.) High School; A.B., U. Louisville; grad. Ky. Theol. Sem.; student Columbia; m. Mable Atchison Stallard, Sept. 18, 1906; children—Tommy, Mary Elizabeth. Post office clerk; mem. staff, General Bd. Edn., Meth. Ch., specializing in youth work and recreation, since 1919. Served with Y.M.C.A., World War I. Mem. Am. Assn. of Leisure Time Educators. Author: several books including Youth and Recreation, 1949; Gay Parties for All Occasions, 1950; Games for Boys and Girls, 1951; The Recreation Leader, 1952. Contbr. to religious jours. Home: Nashville, Tenn.

HARBISON, FREDERICK HARRIS, labor economist, educator; b. Sewickley, Pa., Dec. 18, 1912; s. Ralph Warner and Helen (Harris) H.; A.B., Princeton, 1934, Ph.D., 1940; m. Josephine Koppelman, Jan. 17, 1941; children—Ralph W., William A., Henry H. Research asst. indsl. relations sect. Princeton, 1938-40; instr. econs. U. Chgo., 1940-41; labor, manpower cons. WPB, War Labor Bd., ASF, Petroleum Adminstrn. for War, 1941-45; prof. econs., exec. officer indsl. relations sect. U. Chgo., 1945-55; prof. econs., dir. indsl. relations sect. Princeton U., 1955-67, Roger W. Straus prof. social scis., prof. econs., 1967-76; cons. U.S. Dept. Labor, AID, ILO, UNESCO. Trustee Am. U. Cairo. Mem. Am. Econ. Assn., Nat. Acad. Arbitrators, Indsl. Relations Research Assn., Am. Philos. Soc., Nat. Acad. of Edn. Author: Seniority Policies and Procedures as Developed Through Collective Bargaining, 1941; (with Robert Dublin) Patterns of Union-Management Relations, 1947; (with John Coleman) Goals and Strategy in Collective Bargaining, 1951; Human Resources for Egyptian Enterprise, 1959; Management in Industrial Society (with Charles A. Myers), 1959; Education, Manpower and Economic Growth, 1963; Human Resources as the Wealth of Nations, 1973. Author articles on collective bargaining, mgmt., edn., unions. Home: Princeton, N.J. Died Apr. 5, 1976.

HARBISON, MCCLARTY, investment exec.; b. Shelbyville, Ky., Oct. 7, 1895; s. Howard and Anna Pennebaker (McClarty) H.; A.B., U. Ky., 1917; m. Frances Dudley Geisel, Nov. 19, 1919; children—Edward McClarty, Frances Dudley. Real estate bus., Lexington, Ky., 1919-21; partner Dunk Harbison & Co., Los Angeles, 1923-43, Harbison & Gregory, 1943-48, Harbison & Henderson, 1948-64; pres. Los Angeles Stock Exchange, 1932-45, chmn., 1946-78; former vice chmn., bd. govs. Pacific Coast Stock Exchange; v.p. McDonnell & Co., Inc., mems. N.Y. Stock Exchange, 1964-69. Mem. city council, San Marino, 1954-64. Past chmn. San Marino Public Library. Served as 1st lt. U.S. Army, 1917-19; AEF. Mem. U.S., Calif., Los Angeles chambers commerce. Clubs: Amnandale Golf (Pasadena, Calif.); Los Angeles Stock Exchange, Los Angeles Bond. Home: San Marino, Calif. Died Mar. 30, 1978.

HARBISON, SAMUEL POLLOCK, II, surgeon; b. Sewickley, Pa., Mar. 15, 1909; s. Ralph Warner and Helen (Harris) H.; A.B., Princeton, 1931; M.D., Cornell, 1936; m. Mary Jane Bierman, July 13, 1949; 1 son, Samuel Pollock III. Intern Barnes Hosp., St. Louis, 1937, resident surgeon, 1940-41, instr. surgery, 1941-46; prof. surgery Sch. Medicine, U. Pitts., from 1950, chmn. dept. surgery, 1950-63, asso. dean, from 1963. Served to lt. col. M.C., AUS, 1942-46. Decorated Legion of Merit. Diplomate Am. Bd. Surgery. Fellow A.C.S. (sec. 1962-68, 1st v.p. 1971); mem. Excelsior Surg. Soc., Am., Central Surg. assns., Soc. U. Surgeons. Home: Pittsburgh, Pa. Died July 19, 1976.

HARBURG, EDGAR Y., lyricist, librettist, author; b. N.Y.C., Apr. 8, 1896; s. Lewis and Mary (Ricing) H.; B.S., CCNY, 1918, D.Arts (hon.), 1979; Litt.D. (hon.), U. Vt., 1971; D.F.A., Columbia Coll., Chgo., 1978; m. Alice Richmond, Feb. 23, 1923; children—Marjorie, Ernest; m. 2d, Edelaine Roden, Jan. 16, 1943. Propr. elec. appliance co., 1921-29; contbr. light verse newspapers, mags., 1916-29; lyricist theatrical prodns. Earl Carroll's Sketchbook, 1929; The Garrick Gaieties, 3d edit., 1930; Earl Carroll's Vanities, 8th edit., 1930; Shoot the Works, 1931; Ballyhoo of 1932, 1932; Americana, 3d edit., 1932; Walk a Little Faster, 1932; Ziegfield Follies, 1934; Life Begins at 8:40, 1934; Hooray for What, 1937; Hold on to Your Hats, 1940; Bloomer Girl, 1944; lyricist, co-librettist theatrical prodns. Finian's Rainbow, 1947; Flahooley, 1951; Jamaica, 1957; The Happiest Girl in the World, 1961, Darling of the Day, 1968; numerous lyrics for films, 1930-81, including Wizard of Oz, 1938, Day at the Circus, 1939, Cabin in the Sky, 1940, Kismet, 1944, Can't Help Singing, 1944; Centennial Summer, 1946, Stage Struck, 1946, California, 1946, Gay Purree, 1961. Recipient Oscar award for Over the Rainbow, Acad. Motion Picture Arts and Scis., 1938, also citations for Brother Can You Spare a Dime?, Happiness is a Thing Called Joe, Cabin in the Sky, More and More; Townsend Harris award outstanding alumni Coll. City N.Y., 1950, James K. Hackett award, 1972; Henderson award for best mus. comedy Finian's Rainbow, 1947-48; Humanity in Arts award Wayne State U., 1979; Horatio Alger award, 1979. Mem. A.S.C.A.P., Dramatists Guild, Am. Guild Authors and Composers, Authors League Am, Screen Writers Guild, Acad. Motion Picture Arts and Scis. Author: Rhymes for the Irreverent, 1965; At This Point in Rhyme, 1976. Home: New York, N.Y. Died Mar. 5, 1981.

HARDENBERGH, WESLEY, assn. exec.; b. Youngsville, N.Y., July 14, 1894; s. Spencer and Elizabeth (Fetz) H.; B.Litt., Columbia U., 1918; m. Mary Jean Slater, Oct. 22, 1925; children—William Spencer, James Slater, Mary Jean (Mrs. James K. Norman), Margaret (Mrs. James L. Talbot). Editor, Liberty (New York) Register, 1919; member staff public relations dept. Am. Meat Inst. (formerly Inst. of Am. Meat Packers), 1920-28, v.p., 1928-39, pres. 1939-57, vice chmn., from 1957; pres. Am. Meat Inst. Found. Chicago U. 1944-58. Vice pres. Am. Trade Assn. Execs., 1942-43, pres., 1944-45; pres. Trade Assn. Execs. Forum of Chgo., 1943. Mem. adv. bd. Countryside Assn. Retarded Children, from 1958. Mem. adv. bd. Lake County Forest Preserve Dist., from 1959. Mem. Holland Soc. N.Y., Ill. Soc. SAR, Delta Upsilon. Republican. Methodist. Club: Lake Zurich Golf. Home: Lake Zurich, Ill. Died Jan. 1979.

HARDENBROOK, DONALD JOHNSON, investment banker; b. Jamaica, N.Y., Feb 10, 1896; the son of David Langdon and Laurestine (Johnson) Hardenbrook; student Jamaica Normal Sch., 1902-11; Polytech. Prep. Sch., Brooklyn, 1911-15; m. Helen Vinson, Dec. 20, 1946; children (by previous marriage)—Marilyn A., Hope (Mrs. Whitley Y. Dresser). With Atlas Portland Cement Co., N.Y. City, 1915-17; ship broker, 1919-20; pres. Am. Internat. Shipping Co., First Nat. Bank N.Y., 1920-21, investment banker, mgr. Taylor Ewart & Co., N.Y. office, and partner Harrison, Smith & Co., 1921-29; pres. Am. Internat. Securities Corp., 1929-32; mem. New York Stock Exchange, 1933-43; asst. to pres. Union Bag-Camp Paper Corp., N.Y. C., 1942-45, v.p., 1945-62; chmn. Am. Creosoting Corp., 1961-62; investment banker; a founder, chmn. Inst. Applied Econometrics. Member of President's Com. on Youth Employment. Pres., Keep Am. Beautiful, Inc.; nat. pres. Junior Achievement, Inc.; dir. N.Y.C. div. American Cancer Soc.; dir. Research Found. N.Y. Acad. Osteopathy; pres., dir. Osteo. Hosp. and Clinic N.Y. Served as ensign USNRF, 1917-19. Mem. N.A.M. (pres. 1962, chmn. bd. 1963, chmn. exec. com. 1964), N.Y. C. of C. (exec. com.). Club: Merchants (N.Y.C.). Home: Nantucket, Mass. Died July 5, 1976.

HARDER, ERWIN EMIL, musician; b. Beaver Dam, Wis., Jan. 21, 1883; s. Henry Karl and Pauline (Krueger) H.; student Ziegfeld Musical Coll., Chicago, 1906-12; Chicago Musical Coll., 1916-17; pupil Joseph Schreurs, 1904-08; unmarried. Began in Beaver Dam, Wis., with Harder's Mil. Band, 1898-1900; professional musician, clarinetist, composer, teacher, since 1901; appeared with well-known bands and symphony orchestras throughout the U.S., including Colo. Midland Band, Denver Municipal Band, St. Louis, Chicago, Detroit, New Orleans and Southern symphony orchestras and orchestra of Chicago City Opera Co.; organized and directed Progressive symphony Orchestra, 1924; formerly mem. faculty Sherwood Music Sch., Chicago; played with Sherwood Music Sch. Orchestra many years, and De Paul U., Orchestra, 1923-25; lecturer on "The Family of Clarinets" and similar subjects. Author: The First Clarinet; Jokes, Episodes and Poems (Nos. 1 and 2) 1 Reminiscences of Hot Springs. Composer: From Distant Worlds, and Fish Stories; Grand Piscatorial Phantasmagoria, Vol. 2; Tropical Episodes, Fairy Dances and Characteristic Pieces for Piano; Harder Studies; Wood-wind Trios; Concerto for B flat Clarinet; several symphonies. Home: Chicago. *

HARDIE, HARRY, textile patents exec.; b. New Orleans, Nov. 30, 1886; s. Thomas Gary and Louise Cutter (Carter) H.; A.B., Tulane U., 1907; m. Agnes Thornton George, Nov. 16, 1915; 1 son, Thomas Cary II. Trust officer Comml. Trust & Savs. Bank of New Orleans, 1915-18; v.p. New Orleans Can Co., 1918-22, pres., 1922-26; treas. Newman Saunders & Co., New Orleans, 1919-26; pres. Faultless Mfg. Co., Balt., 1926-33, Nobelt, Inc., 1933-47; Hugo Strues Corp., 1940-42, Nobelt Co., Balt., 1947-56; dir. Standard Shares, Inc., N.Y.C. (formerly Standard Power & Light Co.), 1949—. Dep. dir. Balt. area War Manpower Commn., 1942-45. Mem. Sigma Chi. Presbyn. (elder). Clubs: Boston (New Orleans); Merchants (Balt.). Home: Balt. *

HARDIN, FRANK HAMMOND, mechanical engr.; b. Gainesville, Ga., June 14, 1886; s. Francis Marion and Mary Jane (Hammond) H.; B.S. in M.E., Ga. Sch. of Tech., Atlanta, Ga., 1908; studied Columbia, 1908-09; m. Jessie Frances Mason, Sept. 14, 1915. With N.Y.C.R.R., 1909-36, as spl. apprentice, 1909-11, terminal foreman, 1911-14, spl. engr. president's staff, 1914-17, master mechanic, 1917-18, asst. to federal mgr., 1918-20, chief engr. motive power and rolling stock, 1920-26, asst. to the president, 1926-36; pres. Assn. of Mfrs. of Chilled Car Wheels since 1936. Mem. Am. Soc. Mech. Engrs., Phi Kappa Sigma, Phi Kappa Phi. Methodist. Clubs: Cloud, (New York); Chicago; Siwanoy Country. Home: Bronxville, N.Y. *

HARDIN, LOUIS SAMUEL, lawyer; b. Charleston, Ill., Feb. 28, 1895; s. A.L. and Mary Jane (Wyeth) H.; A.B., Yale, 1917; J.D., U. Chgo., 1921; m. Mary Anthony Drake, June 28, 1930 (div. 1948); children—Edith Drake (Mrs. Charles Seymour), Carol Hardin Henderson; m. 2d, Shirley Garnett, August 19, 1950. Admitted to Ill. State Bar, 1921, practiced in Chicago since 1921; asso. with Cutting, Moore & Sidley, 1921-24, with Wilson & McIlvaine, 1924-28; asso. with Pam, Hurd & Reichmann, 1928-33, partner, from 1933; firm reorganized as Schiff, Hardin, Waite, Dorschel & Britton. Director Bliss & Laughlin, Inc., Community Pub. Service Co. Dir. Ill. Inst. Tech., Armour Research Found. Mem. Am., Ill., Chgo. bar assns., Chgo. Law Club. Legal Club. Clubs: Rqcquet, Chicago (Chgo.). Home: Chicago, Ill. Died Feb. 14, 1979.

HARDING, CHARLES BARNEY, broker, investment banker; b. Phila., Pa., Sept. 11, 1899; s. James Horace and Dorothea Elizabeth Allen (Barney) H.; grad. Groton Sch., 1918; B.S., U.S. Mil. Acad., 1920; grad. Field Arty. Sch., 1921; m. Marion Choate, December 3, 1924; children—Joan (Mrs. Thomas J. King), Robert Shaw Oliver. Served as second lieutenant, then 1st lt., F.A., United States Army, 1920-22; 1st lt. F.A. Reserve, 1922-26, capt., 1926-31; lt., U.S. Naval Reserve, Nov. 1940: on active duty 1941; capt., Mar. 1945; disch. Oct., 1945. Began with Chas. D. Barney & Co., brokers and investment bankers, 1922, became partner, 1925, partner Smith Barney & Co., from 1938, sr. partner from 1944; dir. Scott Paper Co. Gov. N.Y. Stock Exchange, 1937-40, vice chmn. bd., 1938-40, chmn. bd. May 1940-May 1941; dir. Cerro Corp. until 1975, dir. Midland Ross Corp., Motor Terminals, Inc., Union Tex. Natural Gas Corp. Mem. com. of three which redrafted the Constn. of the Exchange, 1938. Recipient Legion of Merit, 1946. Chmn. bd. mgrs. N.Y. Bot. Gardens. Trustee, Frick Collection, Am. Acad. in Rome, Hampton Inst., Presbyn. Hosp., Eisenhower Exchange Fellowships, Inc. Mem. indsl. adv. com. Advt. Council; mem. Nat. Council, Boy Scouts Am. Councilman, Rumson, N.J. Mem. Electoral Coll. N.J., 1948. Mem. N.Y. State C. of C. Republican. Episcopalian. Clubs: Rumson (N.J.) Country; Army and Navy, Chevy Chase (Washington, D.C.); Links, Recess, Century (N.Y.C.). Home: Rumson, N.J. Died Oct. 25, 1979.

HARDING, DOROTHY STURGIS (MRS. LESTER W. HARDING), artist; b. Boston, Mass., July 28, 1891; daughter of Richard Clipston Sturgis and Esther Mary (Ogden) Sturgis; student Winsor School, Boston, 1901-09, Boston Museum of Fine Arts, 1910; married Lester William Harding, June 1, 1912; children—Margaret Helen (Mrs. Robert Dudley), Lester William, Clipston Sturgis. Black and white artist, specialty book plates; has designed plates for Mrs. Franklin Delano Roosevelt, Charles A. Coolidge, Augustus Peabody Loring, Vance and Gertrude McCormick, Robert Lincoln O'Brien, Fred Bates Lund, Mrs. Alvan T. Fuller, Sir Wilfred T. Grenfell, William Roscoe Thayer, Norman Rockwell, and others. Representative groups in the print depts. of Metropolitan Museum, N.Y., and British Museum. Junior engineering draftsman, Portsmouth Navy Yard, from Oct. 1942. Episcopalian. Home: Portsmouth, N.H. Died Jan. 1978.

HARDING, GEORGE L(ABAN), business exec.; b. Indianapolis, Sept. 27, 1893; s. Henry Laban and Alma (Duzan) H.; A.B., Ind. Univ., 1915; M.B.A., Harvard, 1917; m. Georgia Lena Cole, Apr. 19, 1917 (died June 24, 1923); 1 son, Henry Laban; m. 2d, Signe Christine Berg, July 3, 1924; married 3d, Dorothy Harriet Huggins, Jan. 4, 1961. Asst. comptroller Todd Dry Dock & Constrn. Corp., Tacoma, 1919-23; acct. Pacific Tel. and Tel. Co., 1928-40, gen. accountant, 1940-44, asst. comptroller, 1944-46, sec. and treas., 1946-58; treas., sec. Bell Tel. Co. of Nev., 1946-58. Served as lt. (j.g.) Supply Corps, USNR, 1917-19. Recipient from Boy Scouts of Am., Silver Beaver, 1946, Silver Antelope, 1951; member exec. com. Stanford area council, 1940-60, pres., 1942-46, treas., 1947-48, mem. regional exec. com. Region XII Los Angeles, from 1947, chmn., 1953-56, mem. exec. com. San Francisco area council, pres., from 1960. Mem. Cal. Hist. Soc. (pres. 1958-59, trustee from 1945), Book Club Cal. (dir. 1944-53, pres. 1949-51, 59), Am. Soc. Corporate Secs. (hon.; dir. 1948-58, pres. 1955-56), Am. Antiquarian Soc., Phi Gamma Delta. Clubs: Commercial, Roxburghe (San Francisco); California, Zamorano (Los Angeles); Grolier, Harvard (New York City). Republican. Member Protestant Episcopal Church. Author several books including: Don Agustin V. Zamorano, Statesman, Soldier, Craftsman, and California's First Printer, 1934; The Tahitian Imprints of the London Missionary Society, 1810-1834 (with B. Kroepelien), 1950; A Census of California Spanish Imprints, 1833-1845, 1933. Contbr. bibliog. and hist. periodicals. Donor extensive library on history of Am. printing and publishing to library of Calif. Hist. Soc., San Francisco. Home: Berkeley, Calif. Died Aug. 30, 1976; ashes interred Crown Hill Cemetery, Indpls.

HARDING, MARGARET SNODGRASS, editor; b. Chicago, Ill., Jan. 6, 1885; d. James Hathorn and Florence (Bearce) Snodgrass; A.B., Ind. U., 1904, A.M., 1911; grad. student U. of Minn., 1921-22; m. Prof. Samuel B. Harding, May 2, 1918 (died 1927); children—John, Margaret, Mary Katherine. Teacher high schs., Bloomington, Ind., Indianapolis, and Chicago, 1904-18; exec. sec. Dept. Women in Industry, Women's Com. of the Nat. Council of Defense, 1918; 1st nat. sec. Am. Fed. of Teachers, 1916-18; instr. history, Macalester Coll., St. Paul, Minn., 1924-26; editor, mng. editor and dir. Univ. of Minn. Press since 1927. Appointed to National Commission on Children and Youth of the United States Children's Bureau, 1946. Mem. Zonta, Nat. Women's Trade Union League, Am. Assn. of Univ. Women, Minn. Hist. Soc., League of Women Voters, Kappa Alpha Theta. Democrat. Author: Story of Europe (with S. B. Harding), 1912;

New Medieval and Modern History (with S. B. Harding), 1913; Old World Background to American History (with S. B. Harding), 1919. Home: Minneapolis. *

HARDING, RUTH GUTHRIE (MRS. RICHARD BURTON), writer; b. Tunkhannock, Pa., Aug. 20, 1882; d. Frank Hastings Hamilton and Jennie (Leighton) Thomson; student Wyoming Seminary, Kingston, Pa., 1896-98; special student Bucknell Univ., 1899-1900; studied harmony and composition, 1900; married John W. Harding, Oct. 24, 1901 (died 1926); 1 daughter, Mrs. Jean Harding Birely; married 2d, Richard Burton, Aug. 24, 1931 (died 1940). Writer, especially poetry; lecturer on poetry, Experiential Coll. Groups, New York City, 1932; lectures on literature; teacher of prosody. Awarded first prize by National League American Pen Women, 1943. Member Pen & Brush (New York City), American Association Univ. Women, Soc. Fine Arts of Central Fla.; hon. mem. Soc. of the Libra (Rollins Coll.), Cum Laude Soc. (Wyoming Sem.). Clubs: Town Hall (N.Y. City); Woman's (Paterson, N.J.); Woman's (Winter Park, Fla.). Author: A Lark Went Singing (poems) 1916; Mr. Boythorne-Bierce, 1925; Three Parts Scotch, 1946. Contbr. essays and poems to mags. and anthologies. Home: Ridgewood, N.J. *

HARDMAN, LAMARTINE GRIFFIN, JR., textile mfr., banker; b. Commerce, Ga., July 5, 1908; s. Lamartine Griffin and Emma (Griffin) H.; student Ga. Mil. Acad.; B.S., U. Ga., 1930; m. Dorothy Shell, Oct. 16, 1934; children—Lamartine Griffin III, John, Shell (Mrs. Wyck A. Knox, Jr.). Chmn. bd. dirs., pres. First Nat. Bank, Commerce; chmn., chief exec. officer, treas. Harmony Grove Mills, Inc., Commerce; dir. Ga. Power Co., Bibb Mfg. Co., Macon, Ga. Past trustee Mercer U., Macon, Truett-McConnell Jr. Coll., Cleveland, Ga. Mem. Cotton Mfg. Assn. Ga. (past pres.), Am. Cotton Mfg. Inst. (past pres.), Phi Delta Theta. Democrat. Baptist. Clubs: Kiwanis, Capital City, Piedmont Driving (Atlanta). Home: Commerce, Ga. Died July 12, 1978; buried Commerce.

HARDWICK, GORDON ALWARD, business exec.; b. Postville, Ia., Apr. 15, 1893; s. Charles A. and Ella L. (Alward) H; B.S., U. Pa., 1916; m. Anita Marjory Taylor, June 16, 1920 (dec. March 26, 1954); children—Gordon A. (dec.), Anita M. (Mrs. F. X. Lawson; deceased), Taylor, Charles Arthur; married 2d, Hannah Green Wood, May 12, 1956. With Gen. Chemical Co., 1916-17; with Tubize Art Silk Co., 1919-30, sec.-treas., 1920-30, v.p., dir., 1924-30; comptroller Penn Mutual Life Ins. Co., 1931-44, v.p., 1934-44; chmn. Letholite Research Found., 1944-46; partner Montgomery, Scott & Co., 1946-50; corporator, dir., mem. finance com. Presbyn. Ministers' Fund for Life Ins.; dir. Tubize Chatillon Corp., Girard Fire & Marine Ins. Co. Former chmn. Philadelphia Co. Bd. Pub. Assistance, Phila. Com. Pa. Economy League; mem. Phila. Council Def., 1941-45. Chmn. spl. gifts com. A.R.C., 1934; trustee University Pennsylvania; board manager Graduate Hospital; past director Philadelphia Hospital Council; dir. Eastern Pa. Psychiatric Inst.; founder, pres. Coll. Placement Council Inc.; trustee Episcopal Ch. Farm Sch Served as lt. (j.g.) USNR, 1917-19; mem. 1st troop Phila. City Cav.; capt, Cav. Pa. N.G., ret. Former trustee Hosp. Assn. Pa.; pres. Gen. Alumni Soc. U. Pa., 1941-43, recipient award of merit, 1944, permanent pres. Class of 1916. Dir. Pa. Plan for Devel of Research Scientists in Medicine, Fairmount Park Art Assn, Mem. Life Office Mgmt. Assn. (past pres. and dir.). Clubs: Sunday Breakfast, Union League, Penn, Peale (Phila.). Home: Bryn Mawr, Pa. Died Mar. 20, 1979.

HARDY, ARTHUR C., physicist; b. Worcester, Mass., Dec. 2, 1895; s. Charles Clough and Helen Estelle (Cobb) H.; A.B., U. Calif., 1917, A.M., 1919, LL.D. (hon.), Sc.D. (hon.), St. Lawrence U., 1938; m. Charlotte Lansing, 1920 (dec. 1954); 1 son, Robert Lansing (dec.); m. 2d, Elizabeth Osgood Beaman Hardy, 1975. Asst. in physics M.I.T., 1917, instr. physics, 1919; with Kodak Research Labs., 1920-22; asst. prof. optics and photography M.I.T., 1922-28, asso. prof., 1928-33, prof., 1933-61, prof. emeritus, 1961-77. Served as comdg. officer 23d Photog. Sect., U.S. Army, with AEF, 1918; lt. comdr. USNR, 1936-40; NDRC sect. chief, World War II. Recipient Longstreth medal Franklin Inst., 1939; Presdl. Cert. of Merit, 1948; Modern Pioneer award, 1940; Frederic Ives medal Optical Soc. Am., 1957; Progress Medal award Soc. Motion Picture and TV Engrs., 1963. Fellow Photog. Soc. Am., Am. Acad. Arts and Scis., Soc. Motion Picture Engrs., Disting. Service Found. of Optometry; mem. Optical Soc. Am. (pres. 1935-37, sec. 1940-57), Am. Assn. Physics Tchrs., Sigma Xi. Inventor rec. spectrophotometer. Author books and sci. papers on light and color. Home: Wellesley, Mass. Died Oct. 31, 1977.

HARDY, DAVID ROSS, lawyer; b. Versailles, Mo., Aug. 4, 1917; s. David Crockett and Jana Ross (Witten) H.; student Westminster Coll., Fulton, Mo., 1934-36; LL.B., U. Mo., 1939; m. Eleanor Louise Kincaid, June 8, 1940; children—David Kincaid, Sarah Elizabeth. Admitted to Mo. bar, 1939; asso. firm Sebree, Sebree & Shook, Kansas City, 1939-42; partner firm Shook, Hardy & Bacon and predecessors, 1942-76. Lawyer-mem. 16th Circuit Jud. Selection Com., 1956-61; chmn. 16th Circuit Bar Disciplinary Com., 1956-60, mem., 1960-72. Dir. Fidelity Security Life Ins. Co., Myron Green Cafeterias, Myron Green Bldg. Co., United Mo. Bank South. Chmn., Mayor's Commn. on Civil Disorders, 1969. Trustee, pres. U. Mo. Law Sch. Found., 1959-60; trustee Mo. Sch. Religion, 1958-61. Served to capt., Corps Mil. Police, AUS, 1942-46. Mem. Am., Mo., Kansas City (pres. 1959-60) bar assns., Lawyers Assn. Kansas City, Kansas City (Mo.) Claims Assn. (pres. 1958), Am. Coll. Trial Lawyers, Internat. Acad. Trial Lawyers, Internat. Soc. Barristers, Nat. Assn. Railroad Trial Lawyers, Internat. Assn. Ins. Counsel, Fedn. Ins. Counsel, Order of Coif, Kappa Alpha, Phi Delta Phi. Democrat. Mem. Christian Ch. (trustee Ch.). Mason. Clubs: University, Mission Hills Country (Kansas City, Mo.). Home: Kansas City, Mo. Died Sept. 28, 1976.

HARDY, JOHN FORSTER, ret. oil co. exec.; b. Carnegie, Pa., Dec. 31, 1895; s. George and Lillian (Forster) H.; M.E., Lehigh U., 1919; m. Grace Lucille Borgerding, June 17, 1955. With sales dept. Cadillac Motor Co., 1919-20; engr. Jones & Laughlin Steel Co., Pitts., 1920-23; mgr. New Eng. office Pitts. Water Heater Co., Boston, 1923-26; asst. to pres. Benedum-Trees Oil, Pitts., 1926-54; dir., gen. mgr. Central Leduc Oils, Ltd., also Del Rio Producers, 1954, following their merger became v.p., dir., gen. mgr. Central-Del Rio Oils Ltd., later pres. and chmn.; pres., gen. mgr., dir. Central-Del Rio Oils, Inc., U.S.; v.p., dir. Minerals Ltd. Served to 2d lt. as pilot USAC, World War I; col. USAAF, 1942-44. Mem. Can. Petroleum Assn. (former gov., dir. exec. com. Alta. div.), Order Daedalians, Alpha Iota Epsilon, Delta Tau Delta. Republican. Episcopalian. Mason (32 deg., Shriner). Clubs: Aero, Chartiers Country (Pitts.); Calgary Golf and Country, Ranchmen's, Calgary Petroleum (Calgary). Home: Calgary, Alta., Can. Died July 31, 1977.

HARKNESS, ALBERT, architect; b. Hamilton, N.Y., Nov. 8, 1886; s. Albert G. and Katherine M. (Beebee) H.; A.B., Brown U., 1909; B.S., Mass. Inst. Tech., 1912; m. Sara Arden Cheesman, Aug. 29, 1914; children—Albert, John Cheesman, Livingston Arden (dec.); m. 2d, Mrs. Thomas Ives Hare Powel, Sept. 2, 1954. Employed in archtl. offices Delano & Aldrich; H. Van Buren Magonigle; McKim, Mead & White, 1912-18; in pvt. practice, Providence, 1919-73. Dir. Providence Athenaeum, 1930-32, 38-46; mem. R.I. Bd. Exam. and Registration Architects, 1936, 40-54, 59-64. Ofcl. in mfr. munitions Gorham Mfg. Co., 1943-44; AIA rep. to U.S. Com. for UNESCO, 1947-48. Mem. Providence Redevel. Agy., 1947-66, vice chmn. 1947-54. Fellow AIA (dir. 1937-39, pres. R.I. chpt. 1933-34, 45-46); asso. NAD; mem. Alpha Delta Phi. Republican. Baptist. Clubs: Century Assn. (N.Y.C.); Hope, Art (Providence). Home: Providence RI. *

HARKNESS, RICHARD LONG, radio and television news commentator, journalist, govt, ofcl.; b. Artesian, S.D., Sept. 29, 1907; s. Rev. Samuel Dacke and Anne Marie (Long) H.; A.B., U. Kans., 1928; Litt.D. (hon.), Keuka Coll., 1946; m. Gladys Estelle Suiter, Feb. 6, 1934; children—Richard Long, Peter Anthony, Christopher Rollin; m. 2d, Mrs. Franklin Watkins. White House corr. United Press Assns., 1936-37; Washington Bur. Phila. Inquirer, 1937-42, Congressional corr., covering Am. fgn. policy debate in U.S. Senate; Washington corr. NBC, 1943-72, covering Roosevelt-Churchill war confs., Que., United Nat. Orgn. sessions, San Francisco, Security Council meetings, N.Y.C. and Paris, NATO meeting, Rome, E.T.O., assigned nat. polit. convs. and campaigns, 1936-68; originated N.B.C.'s 1st network TV news program from Washington, Story of the Week. Cons. on narcotics U.S. Dept. of State, 1971; exec. dir. public info. White House Narcotics Control Program. Mem. Delta Chi, Sigma Delta Chi. Clubs: Overseas Writers, Gridiron (Washington). Home: Washington, D.C. Died Feb. 16, 1977.

HARKRADER, CHARLES JOHNSTON, ret. editor, banking exec.; b. Blountville, Tenn., Sept. 13, 1885; s. Fletcher Lloyd and Susan M. (White) Harkrader; ed. pub. schs.; studied law, 1904-05; m. Louise Moorman, Nov. 27, 1908 (dec. June 1973); children—Harriett (Mrs. R.P. London, Jr.), Charles Johnson Carlton Allen, Elva (Mrs. W. E. Latture). Newspaper reporter until 1913; pub. Bristol Herald Courier, 1919-50, established Johnson City (Tenn.) Press (daily newspaper), 1934, which in Jan. 1935 absorbed its two rival newspapers; pres. Robert Porterfield's Barter Theatre of Va., Inc.; dir. First Nat. Bank of Sullivan County, H.p. King Co. Chmn. Va. A.P. membership, 1930; mem. Va. War Bond Com.; covered San Francisco UN Conf., 1945; regional dir. civilian def. for 14 counties in western Va., also set up rationing and selective service bds. in these counties, 1941. Chmn., Bristol chpt. A.R.C. Mem. Va. Senate, 1936-40, mem. roads and gen. laws com., active for enlarged hwy. program; del. Dem. Nat. Conv., 1932, 36, 40. Mem. Va. Press Assn., Soc. Am. Newspaper Editors, Asso. Press., Am., So. (editorial com.) newspaper pubs. assns. Methodist. Mason (Shriner). Clubs: Rotary (hon.), Bristol Country. Covered as a reporter every Dem. Nat. Conv., 1920—. Author: Witness to an Epoch, 1965. Home: Bristol VA. *

HARLEY, ALVIN E., architect; b. Portage La Prairie, Manitoba, Can., Mar. 10, 1884; s. Frank and Jane (McLeod) H.; matriculated, London Collegiate Inst., London, Ont., 1901; study in private schs., Detroit, Mich., 1903-07; m. Mary A. Slyfield, Sept. 7, 1909; 1 dau., Jean Katherine (Mrs. Garrett H. Voorhees). Draftsman and designer, Albert Kahn, George D. Mason, 1903-08; private practice, Harley & Atcheson, 1908-12; pvt. practice under name of Alvin E. Harley, 1912-33; partner Harley and Ellington, architects and engrs., Detroit, Mich., 1933-43; now mem. firm Harley, Ellington, Cowin, & Stirton, Inc.; engaged in general practice of architecture and engring. in residential, ednl., memorial, indsl. and institutional work, including: Temple of Memories, White Chapel Cemetery, Horace H. Rackham Ednl., Memorial, War Vets. Memorial Bldg., Civic Center, Holy Sepulchre Community Mausoleum, Student Activities Bldg. and Dormitory for U. Detroit (all Detroit), Beverage plants for Anheuser-Busch, Inc., Newark, N.J., Jos. Schlitz Brewing Co., Los Angeles, Queen of Heaven Community Mausoleum for Cath. Diocese of Chicago, Dept. of State Office Building, Washington. Fellow American Inst. Architects (past pres. Detroit chapter); member Mich. Soc. Architects (past pres.), Engring. Society Detroit, Am. Cemetery Assn., Detroit Execs. Assn., Newcomen Soc., Nat. Cemetery Assn. Mason (K.T., Shriner). Republican. Presbyterian. Clubs: Key, Athletic (Detroit). Boat. Home: Detroit. *

HARLOW, JAMES GINDLING, SR., found. exec., univ. pres., pub.; b. Oklahoma City, June 11, 1912; s. Victor Emmanuel and Gertrude (Gindling) H.; student Oklahoma City U., 1926-28; A.B., U. Okla., 1931. M.S., 1933; Ph.D., U. Chgo., 1954; H.H.D., Waynesburg Coll., 1967; D.Sc., Alderson Broddus Coll., 1974; D. Humanistic Studies, Marshall U., 1976; m. Adalene Agnes Rae, Aug. 15, 1932; children—James Gindling, Dan Rae, Mary Adalene. Tchr. high sch., Hobart, Okla., 1932-33, Seminole, Okla., 1933-34, Classen High, Oklahoma City, 1934-37; sci. tchr., head dept. Northeast High, Oklahoma City, 1937-41; editor Harlow Pub. Corp., Oklahoma City, 1934-41, 46-48, then chmn. bd. dirs., pres.; dir. high sch. sci. service, instr. physics U. Okla., 1948-51, asso. dean Univ. Coll., asst. prof. physics, 1951-53, dean coll. Arts and Sci., 1952-53, prof., dean Coll. Edn., 1958-67; pres. W. Va. U., 1967-77, pres. emeritus, 1977-78; research asso. U. Chgo., 1953-54, asso. prof. edn., 1954-57. Dir. Fed. Res. Bank Richmond, Balt., 1973-77, chmn, 1975-77; dir. Consol. Natural Gas Co. Pitts., Pub. Broadcasting System, Mut. Fed. Savs. and Loan, Oklahoma City Exec. v.p. Frontiers of Sci. Found. of Okla. 1957-67; trustee Claude W. Benedum Found., Pitts., 1967-78, pres., 1977-78; mem. Nat. Adv. Council Career Edn., 1977-78. Served from lt. (j.g.) to lt. comdr., USNR, 1942-46; comdr. ret. Named W.Va. Man of Yr., Charleston Gazette-Mail, 1975; named to Okla. Hall of Fame, 1976. Fellow Okla. Acad. Sci. (editor proc. 1949-53); mem. AAAS, Am. Assn. Sch. Adminstrs., Phi Beta Kappa, Sigma Pi Sigma, Kappa Delta Pi, Phi Delta Kappa. Clubs: Duquesne (Pitts.); Ft. Henry (Wheeling, W.Va.); University (Washington). Contbr. numerous articles to profl. jours. and encys. Home: Norman, Okla. Died Mar. 10, 1978.

HARLOW, S. RALPH, educator; b. Boston, Mass., July 20, 1885; s. Rev. Samuel A. and Caroline (Usher) H.; A.B., Harvard, 1908; grad. Union Theol. Sem., New York, 1912; A.M., Columbia, 1919; Ph.D., Hartford (Conn.) Theol. Sem., 1929; m. Marion Stafford, Feb. 1, 1912; children—John Stafford, Ruth Carol, Elizabeth. Ordained ministry Congl. Ch., 1912; asst. minister Spring St. Presbyn. Ch., N.Y. City, 1909-11; chaplain and head of dept. sociology, Internat. Coll., Smyrna, 1912-22; prof. religion and social ethics, Smith Coll., Northampton, Mass., since 1923. Dir. Student's Internat. Union, Geneva, 1931; prof. Y.M.C.A. Summer Sch., Blue Ridge, N.C.; mem. Nat. Com. of Peaceways, Inc.; dir. Nat. Assn. for Advancement of Colored People; dir. Postwar World Council; mem. executive council Am. Palestine Com.; mem. Academic Council Yiddish Scientific Institute. Mem. Cum Laude Society; trustee Alice Freeman Palmer School, Sedalia, N.C.; interchange minister to Great Britain, 1939. Mem. U.N.R.R. A. Mission Greece, 1945-46; visiting prof. Pierce Coll., Athens, 1945-46; mem. Academic Council Nat. Fedn. Constl. Liberties; dir. Friends Am. Studies, Greece; mem. Nat. Council, League for Ind. Democracy; trustee, Marthas Vineyard Assn.; pres. Harlow Family Assn., 1946-47. Mem. Nat. Assn. Biblical Instructors (pres. 1936), Am. Assn. Univ. Profs., Am. Fedn. of Teachers, Pi Gamma Mu, Harvard Club of Conn. Valley, Harvard Club of Marthas Vineyard. Author, works include: Honest Answers to Honest Questions, 1941; Prayers for Times Like These, 1942. Contbr. to religious publs. Home: Northampton, Mass. *

HARMAN, JOHN, govt. ofcl.; b. Braceville, Ill., Dec. 25, 1884; s. Martin and Louisa (Larson) H.; student pub. schs.; am. Alma Jennie Swanson, June 27, 1908;

children—Clifford M., Leonard G., Lester J., William G. Clk. Sears, Roebuck & Co., 1906-10; clk. Chgo. Post Office, 1910-32, supervisor, 1932-51; dir. regional accounting office, bur. accounts Post Office Dept. since 1951. Mem. Mission Covenant Ch. (vice chmn. bd. trustees). Mason. Home: Chgo. *

HARMON, ERNEST N., univ. pres., army officer; b. Lowell, Mass., Feb. 26, 1894; s. Ernest Josiah and Junietta (Spaulding) H.; student Norwich U., 1912-13, S.M. (hon.) 1931, D.Eng. (hon.), 1965; B.S., U.S. Mil. Acad., 1917; student Command and Gen. Staff Coll., 1931-33, Army War Coll., 1934; LL.D. (hon.), Middlebury Coll., 1952, St. Michael's, 1955, U. Vt., 1966; m. Leona Tuxbury, Aug. 15, 1917; children—Barbara Ruth (Mrs. Sylvester Roll), Halsey W., Robert S., Ernest N., Jeane L. (Mrs. Oliver). Commd. 2d lt. U.S. Army, 1917, advanced through grades to maj. gen., 1942; served in France, 1918-19; assigned to 2d cav., Ft. Riley, Kan., 1919-20, Cav. Sch., 1920-21; instr. U.S. Mil. Acad., 1921-25; with 6th cav., Ft. Oglethorpe, Ga., 1925-27; prof. mil. sci. and tactics, Norwich U., 1927-31; comdr. squadron 8th cav., Ft. Bliss, Tex., 1934-35; served on War Dept. Gen. Staff, Washington, 1935-39; asst. chief of staff for supply armored forces, later chief of staff of armored Force, Ft. Knox, Ky., 1939-41; comdg. gen. 2d armored div., 1942; on loan as dep. corps comdr., battle of Kasserine Pass, Feb. 1943; comdr. 1st armored div., Tunisian campaign, Cassino and Anzio, Italy, 1943-44; comdg. gen. 2d armored div., Belgium, Battle of Bulge, 1944-45; comdr. XXII Army Corps, France, 1945; 1st mil. gov. of Rhine province, 1945 and comdr. U.S. Army of occupation, Czechoslovakia, 1945; comdr. U.S. Constabulary, Germany, 1946-47; dep. comdr. ground forces, U.S., 1947; ret. from active duty, Mar. 1, 1948; pres. Norwich U., 1950-65. Decorated D.S.C., D.S.M. (3), Legion of Merit (3), Silver Star, Bronze Star, Air medal, Purple Heart, comdt. Legion of Honor and Croix de Guerre (France), Order of Bath (Gt. Britain), Star of Ouissam (Morocco), grand officer, Order of Orange Nassau with swords (Netherlands), Order of Red Banner (Russia), Order of St. Maurice and Lazarus and Silver Star (Italy), Comdr., Order of Leopold I (Belgium), Order of White Lion 2d class and War Cross (Czechoslovakia), Croix de Guerre and Fouragier (Belgium). Author: Combat Commander, 1970. Home: Sarasota, Fla. Died Nov. 13, 1979.

HARMON, FRANCIS STUART, editor, lawyer; b. Paulding, Miss., Jan. 3, 1895; s. Rev. Gus Shaw and Jessie Bruce (Banks) H.; B.A., U. Va., 1916, M.A., 1917; LL.B., Harvard Univ., 1922; LL.D., Millsaps Coll., Jackson, Miss., 1936; m. Lucile Waverley Harwood, Apr. 16, 1927; children—Virginia Blackwell (Mrs. John F. Jameson II), Francis Stuart. Began practice of law with Wells, Stevens & Jones, Jackson, Miss., 1922; asst. atty. gen., Miss., 1924, 25; candidate for Dem. nomination for Congress, 1926; editor, pub. Hattiesburg (Miss.) American, 1926-33, pres., 1928-60. Pres. Nat. Council Y.M.C.A.'s of U.S., 1929-31; gen. sec. Internat. Com. Y.M.C.A.'s of U.S. and Can., 1932-37; dir. N.Y.C. Y.M.C.A. Mem. exec. staff Motion Picture Producers and Distributors of Am., Inc., 1937-41, v.p., 1945-51; v.p. Motion Picture Export Assn., Inc., 1945-51; exec. vice chmn. and industry coordination, war activities com., Motion Picture Industry, 1942-45. Trustee State U. and Colls. of Miss., 1926-29; v.p., Nat. Council Chs. of Christ in U.S.A., 1958-60; v.p., trustee The Interchurch Center, N.Y.C., 1957-77; trustee Mohonk Trust, 1963-77. Served as 2d lt. F.A., AUS, World War I; in action at St. Mihiel and Meuse-Argonne, France. Mem. Am. Bar Assn., Kappa Sigma, Phi Beta Kappa. Author: The Command Is Forward, 1944; A Good Inheritance, 1960; Adam's Eves, 1965; Religious Freedom in America: A Study Guide, 1973. Home: New York, N.Y. Died Apr. 27, 1977.

HARMSWORTH, HARRY CLAYTON, educator; b. Aurora, Mo., May 4, 1902; s. Charles William and Mary Lavina (Clayton) H.; A.B., Colo. State Coll. Edn., 1928, M.A., 1932; Ph.D., U. So. Calif., 1943; m. Ruth Viola Lane, June 1, 1927; children—Clayton Lane, Donald Kemp. Tchr. Colo. pub. schs., 1925-35; asst. prof. sociology and econs. Southwestern State Tchrs. Coll., Weatherford, Okla., 1935-39; asst. prof. sociology Tex. Western Coll., 1941-44; asso. prof. sociology U. Idaho, 1944-54, prof., chmn. dept., 1954-67, prof. emeritus, 1967-77; prof. sociology Winona (Minn.) State Coll. Pres. Pacific Northwest Conf. Family Relations, 1960-61; mem. Gov.'s Conf. on Problems of Older Citizens, 1956. Fellow Inst. Social Gerontology, Am. Sociol. Assn.; mem. Pacific Sociol. Soc., Nat. Council Family Relations, Population Assn. Am., Alpha Kappa Delta, Phi Delta Kappa, Pi Gamma Mu, Alpha Psi Omega. Author: Sixty Years of population Growth in Idaho, 1890-1950, 1952; A Survey of the Alcohol and Narcotics Problem in Idaho, 1954; Population Trends in Idaho, 1950-60, 1965; Vital Statistics and Population Projections for Idaho, 1960-1980, 1967. Editorial bd. N.W. Science, 1950-56. Contbr. articles on sociology to revs. Home: Lacey, Wash. Died May 26, 1977.

HARNED, MALCOLM STUART, aircraft co. exec.; b. Wichita, Kans., June 11, 1921; s. Frank Simpson and Ada (Sleeth) H.; B.S., U. Kans., 1943; M.S., Calif. Inst. Tech., 1948; m. Jo Ann Glatt, Mar. 16, 1953; children—Douglas Stuart, Holly Ann. Instr. math U. Kans., 1943; structures engr., project engr. N.Am. Aviation, Los Angeles, 1943-50; chief tech. engr., asst. chief engr. Marquardt Corp., Van Nuys, Calif., 1950-55; project mgr. Aircraft Nuclear Propulsion Dept., Gen. Electric Co., Cin., 1955-59; v.p. engring aircraft div. Hughes Tool Co., Culver City Calif., 1959-64, v.p. operations, 1964-67; exec. v.p., gen. mgr. Aircraft div. Lear Jet Industries, Wichita, 1967-70; group v.p. Cessna Aircraft Co., Wichita, 1970-73, sr. v.p. aviation operations, 1973-74, exec. v.p., 1974-75, pres., 1975-80; dir. Kans. State Bank & Trust Co. Fellow Am. Inst. Aeros. and Astronautics (asso.); mem. Wichita C. of C., Soc. Automotive Engrs., Tau Beta Pi, Sigma Tau, Theta Tau. Club: Wichita Country. Home: Wichita, Kans. Died Oct. 21, 1980.

HARNED, ROBEY WENTWORTH (HAR'NED), entomologist; b. near Bryantown, Charles County, Md., July 16, 1884; s. Edward Nathan and Helen Marion (Robey) H.; student Franklin Coll., New Athens, O., 1901-02; B.S. in Agr., Ohio State U., 1906; student Cornell U. summers 1908, 14, U. of Chicago, summer 1926; m. Edna Johnson, Oct. 24, 1911; children—Hilda (Mrs. Laurence C. Newcomb), Helen (deceased), Edward Johnson, Margaret (Mrs. Walter C. Wright, Jr.). Asst. biologist, Miss. Agrl. and Mech. Coll. and Miss. Agricultural Expt. Sta., 1906-08, acting professor zoology and entomology and acting entomologist, 1908-10, prof., and entomologist, 1910-31; prin. entomologist in charge Div. of Cotton Insects, Bur. of Entomology and Plant Quarantine, U.S. Dept. of Agr. since 1931; entomologist, sec. and exec. officer, State Plant Bd. of Miss., 1918-31; chmn. Southern Plant Bd., 1926-28; mem. Nat. Plant Bd., 1928-31. Trustee, Sidwell Friends Sch., Washington, D.C. Mem. Society of Friends. Fellow A.A.A.S., Entomol. Soc. America; mem. Am. Assn. of Economic Entomologists 2d v.p., 1922; 4th v.p., 1924; pres. 1927), Am. Genetic Assn., Entomological Soc. of Washington (pres. 1943), Biol. Soc. of Washington, Texas Entomological Soc., Sigma Xi. Club: Cosmos (Washington). Home: Washington. *

HARNISH, WILLIAM MAX, bus. exec., ret. naval officer; b. Bradford, Ill., Nov. 1, 1919; s. Wilber E. and Bess (Davidson) H.; student U. Ill., 1937-39; B.S., U.S. Naval Acad., 1942, U.S. Navy Postgrad. Sch., 1950; M.S. in Aero. Engring., M.I.T., 1951; grad. Naval War Coll., 1958; m. June Markert, July 22, 1944; children—Karen E., Leslie S. Commd. ensign U.S. Navy, 1942, advanced through grades to rear adm., 1968; assigned battleship South Pacific, 1942-44; naval aviator, 1945; fighter and attack squadron duties, grad. edn. and tech. duties in aircraft weapons and Polaris devel., 1946-59; navigator, exec. officer, comdg. officer various aircraft carriers, 1959-66; nuclear propulsion tng. AEC, 1960; dep. dir. systems analysis div. Office Chief Naval Ops., 1966-67; dir. Office Program Appraisal for sec. navy, 1967-69; comdr. Carrier Div. 6, 1969-70, dep. comptroller of navy, 1970-72; comdr. Pacific Missile Range, Point Mugu, Calif., 1972-74; with Bechtel Inc., San Francisco, 1974-79. Decorated Legion of Merit (3), D.F.C., Air medal (3), Navy Commendation medal (2). Mem. Phi Gamma Delta. Home: Lafayette, Calif. Died Sept. 19, 1979; interred Arlington Nat. Cemetery.

HARPER, HEBER (REECE), educator, pub. official; b. Manchester, Eng., Feb. 27, 1885; s. Henry and Mary (Reece) H.; came to U.S., 1890; B.A., Allegheny Coll., 1910; S.T.B., Boston U., 1913; Jacob Sleeper fellow, Halle and Leipzig, 1913-14; student Harvard, 1914-15, U. of Chicago, summer 1916; D.D., Allegheny, 1922, De Pauw, 1922; LL.D., Colo. Coll., 1924; Ph.D., Columbia Univ., 1931; m. Rachel Harris Rathbun, 1925; children—Philip Rathbun, David Harris, Richard Reece (dec.). Ordained M.E. ministry, 1907; pastor Meth. and Congl. chs. until 1913; mem. faculty Boston U. Sch. of Theology, 1914-21 (with leave of absence); exec. sec. Boston U., 1921-22; chancellor U. of Denver, 1922-27; Laura Spelman Rockefeller Memorial fellowship for research in Europe in comparative education, 1927-30; prof. education Teachers College, Columbia, 1931-36; regional dir. Social Security Bd., 1936-48; regional dir. Office Community War Services, 1941-46, regional dir. Fed. Security Agency, since July 1948. Overseas service, British and American Y.M.C.A., 1917; lecturer United War Work Campaign, Pacific Coast and Hawaiian Islands, 1918; with Army Ednl. Corps, A.E.F., in France and Germany, Feb.-July 1919; ednl. specialist with U.S. Navy to assist in creating a new educational system, 1920-21. Consultant, United Nations Relief and Rehabilitation Administration, Washington, D.C., 1943-44. Chief, European Section, Division of Cultural Cooperation, Department of State, 1944. Awarded Denver Civic Service honor medal, 1925. Mem. Phi Beta Kappa, Phi Delta Theta, Delta Sigma Rho, Phi Delta Kappa. Clubs: Denver Country, Rotary Internat., Mile High. Author: What European and American Students Think on International Problems, 1931. Home: Denver, Colo. *

HARPER, HOWARD VINCENT, clergyman, author; b. Kenton, Ohio, June 1, 1904; s. Earl Vincent and Grace (Howard) H.; Ph.B., Kenyon Coll., 1927, D.D. (hon.), 1953; B.D. cum laude, Bexley Hall, Gambier, Ohio, 1930; m. Elizabeth Lane, Dec. 2, 1935 (dec. May 1968); m. 2d, Josephine Montgomery Williams, June 7, 1969. Ordained to ministry Episcopal Ch., 1931; served as pastor in Cleve., 1931-33, Hudson, Ohio, 1933-35, Waycross, Ga., 1935-40, The Plains, Va., 1940-42, Jackson, Mich., 1942-53; asst. to bishop of Mich., 1952-53; nat. dir. laymen's work Episcopal Ch., 1953-67; hon. canon St. Paul's Cathedral, Detroit, 1952-78; founder, 1st pres. Nat. Diocesan Press, 1938. Mem. religious adv. com. Nat. Safety Council, 1961. Bd. dirs. North Conway Inst. Alcoholics and Alcoholism, Boston, 1960-67. Mem. Psi Upsilon. Author: Days and Customs of All Faiths, 1957; Customs and Holidays Around the World, 1963; The Vestryman's Manual, 1964; Profiles of Protestant Saints, 1967; The Episcopalian's Dictionary, 1974; also numerous articles, tracts and syndicated column Days and Customs of All Faiths, 1952-78. Asso. editor So. Churchman. Address: Marco Island, Fla. Died Aug. 30, 1978; inurned St. Mark's Ch. Columbarium, Marco Island, Fla.

HARPER, ROBERT HENRY, clergyman, writer; b. Columbia, La., Sept. 20, 1882; s. Rev. Jacob Dick and Virginia (Fox) H.; A.B., Centenary Coll. La., 1904, D.D., 1923; graduate student Louisiana State Univ., 1933; m. Edna Skipwith, March 29, 1905; children—Henry Skipwith (dec.), Robert Earl. Ordained ministry M.E. Ch., S., 1907; pastor Parker Memorial Ch., New Orleans, La., 4 yrs., 1st Ch., New Orleans, 7 yrs.; presiding elder New Orleans dist., 1926-28; editor New Orleans Christian Advocate, 1929-30; pastor First M.E. Ch., Lake Charles, La., 1931, First M.E. Ch., Baton Rouge, 1932-33, First M.E. Ch., Lafayette, La., 1934-36; district supt. Alexandria District, 1937-42; pastor Napoleon Av. Meth. Church, New Orleans, 1943-44; pastor First Meth. Ch., Mansfield, La., 1944-45, Parker Memorial Ch., New Orleans, 1945-46; church at Opelousas (Louisiana) since 1946. Sec. La. Conf., 1920-47; editor, Louisiana Conference Annual, 1921-47; delegate General Conference, 1926; member committee of 12 elders investigating case of Bishop Cannon, Feb. 1931; former member General Hospital Bd.; mem. com. on entertainment and first alternate del. Gen. Conf., 1934 (all M.E. Ch., S.); del. Gen. Conf. Methodist Church, Atlantic City, and del. and asst. sec. South Central Jurisdicational Conf., 1940; mem. com. on location and entertainment Gen. Conf., 1944. Mem. Kappa Alpha. Democrat. Mason; Grand Prelate K.T. of U.S., 1922; Past Grand Chaplain F. and A.M. of Louisiana, Past Grand Prelate K.T. in La. Club: Rotary. Author: Land of New Acadie; Louisiana Methodism. Home: Opelousas, La. *

HARPER, SINCLAIR OLLASON, engr.; b. Pacific Grove, Calif., June 6, 1883; s. Thomas and Mary (Ollason) H.; B.S. in C.E., U. of Calif., 1907; Sc.D., University of Colorado, 1940; m. Mabel Esta Roberts, June 20, 1911 (deceased February 1951); children—Robert Donald, Thomas Sinclair, John Cline; m. 2d, Genevieve Josephine Short, June 27, 1953. With U.S. Bureau of Reclamation, 1907-44; jr. engr., asst. engineer, const. engineer, 1907-17; project manager Grand Valley project, Colorado, 1917-25; general supt. of construction and assistant chief engr. Bur. of Reclamation, Denver, Colo., 1925-40, chief engr., 1940-44, in charge of investigation, design constrn. and operation of govt. reclamation and power projects in 17 western states, including Hoover Dam and Power Plant, All-American Canal, Shasta Dam, Central Valley project, Calif., and Grand Coulee Dam and Power Plant. Rep. of U.S. and chmn. commn. negotiating compact between Colo., N.M. and Tex., for division of waters of Rio Grande, 1934-39; cons. engr., pvt. practice, since 1945; staff cons. Kaiser Engrs., Oakland, Cal.; mem. bds. cons. engrs. on Mo. River dams for U.S. Army Engrs.; mem. Internat. Commn. reporting to govt. of Egypt on power development at Aswan dam; cons. engr. Damodar Valley Corp., India, and other projects in India, Afghanistan, Iraq and Lebanon. Member American Society Civil Engineers, Colorado Society of Engineers, Phi Kappa Sigma. Hon. life mem. Nat. Reclamation Assn., Reclamation Tech. Club, Chi Epsilon. Methodist. Mason. Clubs: Cosmos (Washington); Commonwealth, Engineers (San Francisco). Address: Oakland, Cal. *

HARRAH, WILLIAM FISK, hotel and casino exec.; b. S. Pasadena, Calif., Sept. 2, 1911; s. John and Amanda (Fisk) H.; student Chapman Coll., 1931, UCLA, 1932; m. Verna Rae Harrison, June 15, 1974; children—John Adam, Tony Lee. Operator circle game, Venice, Calif., 1932-37; founder Harrah's Casino, Reno, 1937, Harrah's Tahoe Casino, 1955, Harrah's Automobile Collection, Sparks, Nev., 1962; chmn. bd. Harrah's Hotels and Casinos. Named Disting. Nevadan, U. Nev., 1972; Civic Leader, Greater Reno C. of C., 1975. Mem. Soc. Automotive Engrs. Republican. Home: Reno, Nev. Died June 30, 1978.

HARRELSON, WILLIAM LOUIS, state ofcl.; b. Mullins, S.C., July 25, 1913; s. Maxey Clarence and Dora (Page) H.; student The Citadel, 1931-32; LL.B., U. S.C., 1937, J.D.; m. Grace Hough, Mar. 29, 1956; children—Cynthia Page, William Louis. Admitted to

S.C. bar; farmer, Mullins, 1932-76; dir. Davis Nat. Bank, Mullins and Marion Broadcasting Co.; mem. S.C. Ho. of Reps., 1941-42, State Senate, 1953-55; commr. agr. State of S.C., 1956-76. Chmn., S.C. Marketing Commn. Past pres. So. Assn. State Depts. Agr.; bd. dirs. Nat. Assn. State Depts. Agr., rep. So. region, 1971. Served with USCGR, 1942. Mem. S.C. Crop Improvement Assn., Farm Bur., Blue Key, Phi Delta Phi, Gamma Sigma Delta. Democrat. Presbyn. (elder). Mason. Clubs: Mullins Cotillion; Pineland Country. Home: Mullins, S.C. Died Oct. 9, 1976; buried Millers Cemetery, Mullins.

HARRIMAN, E. ROLAND, banker; b. N.Y.C., Dec. 24, 1895; s. Edward Henry and Mary W. (Averell) H.; A.B., Yale, 1917, LL.D., 1960; LL.D., Columbia U., 1955; m. Gladys C.C. Fries, Apr. 12, 1917; children—Elizabeth (dec.), Phyllis. Banking bus. N.Y.C., 1922-78, partner Brown Brothers Harriman & Co.; chmn. bd. U.P.R.R., 1946-69, hon. chmn., 1969-78; hon. chmn. Union Pacific Corp. Chmn. Boys Club of N.Y.; hon. trustee Am. Mus. Natural History; corp. mem. Presbyn. Hosp., N.Y. Served as lt. Ordnance Dept., World War I. Republican. Episcopalian. Clubs: Yale, University, Racquet and Tennis, Links, Tuxedo.

HARRINGTON, MILDRED P(RISCILLA), prof. library science; b. Buffalo, Nov. 18, 1886; d. James Bishop and Sarah Jane (Smith) Harrington; A.B., Western Reserve U., 1926; student Carnegie Library Sch., Pittsburgh, 1913; M.A., U. of Chicago, 1931. Children's librarian Cleveland Pub. Library, 1913-15; elementary sch. librarian, 1918-21; jr. high sch. librarian, 1921-23, and 1925-27; Young People's librarian, 1917-18; parents and teacher's room librarian, 1916-17; branch librarian, Minneapolis, 1923-25; high sch. librarian, Parker Dist., Greenville, S.C., 1927-29; prof. library sci., Library Sch., La. State U. since 1931. Fellowship U. of Chicago Grad. Library Sch., 1930-31. Instr. Univ. Coll., U. of Chicago, 1930-31, summer sch. U. of Tenn., 1929, U. of Ky., 1930, 1931. Mem. Am. Library Assn. (chmn. sch. libraries sect. 1933), Southwestern Library Assn. Compiler: Ring-A-Round, 1931; co-compiler: Our Holidays in Poetry, 1930. Contbr. articles to Library Jour., Libraries, Elementary English and other periodicals. Home: Faculty Club, Louisiana State University Campus, Baton Rouge, La.

HARRIS, ALEXANDRINA ROBERTSON, artist; b. Aberdeen, Scotland, July 11, 1886; d. Gordon Hunt and Elizabeth (Lawson) Robertson; brought to U.S., 1900, naturalized, 1904; student Adelphi Coll., 1910-12, Art Students League, 1914, Am. Sch. Miniature Painting, 1918, Fontainebleau Sch. Fine Arts, 1926; m. George W. Harris, Aug. 24, 1904. Exhibited at Royal Soc. Miniature Painters, London, Eng., Corcoran Gallery, Pa. Acad. Fine Arts, Met., Bklyn., Los Angeles, Balt. museums, Century of Progress Exhbn., N.Y. World's Fair Exhbn., High Mus., Atlanta; miniatures represented Pa. Mus., Corcoran Gallery, Hermitage Found., Norfolk, Va., Dept. Archives (State Capitol Ala.). Awarded Charlotte Ritchie Smith Meml. prize, miniature, Water Color Club, Balt., 1922; Nat. Assn. Women Painters and Sculptors, 1935; 2d sustaining prize, Cal. Soc. Miniature Painters, 1941, 1st award, 1947; Nat. Assn. Women Artists medal, 1944, 51, Pa. Soc. Miniature Painters medal of honor, 1950. Mem. Am. Soc. Miniature Painters and Sculptors (pres. 1933-35), Bklyn. Soc. Miniature Painters (pres. 1929-40), Bklyn. Soc. Artists, Grand Central Art Galleries, Pa. Soc. Miniature Painters, Portraits, Inc., Am. Water Color Club (asso.); hon. mem. Royal Soc. Miniature Painters (London). Home: Hollis, L.I., N.Y. *

HARRIS, C. ADDISON, JR., banker; b. Phila., Pa., July 11, 1882; s. Charles Addison and Frances Spooner (Kimball) H.; grandmother was flower girl at reception to Lafayette upon his visit to U.S. in 1825; ed. pub. schs. Clk. in father's wholesale shoe business, 1902-04; with Franklin Trust Co. since 1904, pres. since Feb. 1920, also pres. Franklin Building Corpn.; dir. Thomas E. Coale Lumber Co., A. Wilt & Sons Co., Am. Manganese Bronze Co., Keystone Mut. Fire Ins. Co., Manton Mut. Fire Ins. Co., Atlantic Mut. Fire Ins. Co. Active in Liberty Loan drives, World War. Republican. Presbyn. Clubs: Union League, Penn Athletic, Merion Cricket, Racquet. Home: Ardmore, Pa.*

HARRIS, CARLETON, state supreme ct. justice; b. Pine Bluff, Ark., Dec. 31, 1909; s. Frank A. and Ada (Rodgers) H.; student Union U., Jackson, Tenn., 1929-31; LL.B., Cumberland U., 1932; LL.D., Quachita Baptist Coll., 1960; m. Marjorie Wilson, Apr. 20, 1934; 1 son, Eugene Starke. Admitted to Ark. bar, 1932; practiced in Pine Bluff, 1932-48; pros. atty. 11th Judicial Dist., 1947-48; judge 4th Chancery Dist. Ark., 1949-57; justice Ark. Supreme Ct., 1957-80. Pres. Ark. Jud. Council, 1955. Mem. Ark. Ho. of Reps., 1933-38. Disaster relief chmn. Jefferson County A.R.C., 1943-80; past v.p. Jefferson County Men of Chs. Recipient Distinguished Alumni citation Cumberland Sch. Law, 1974, Outstanding Lawyer award Ark. Bar Assn.-Ark. Bar Found., 1974. Mem. Am., Ark., Jefferson County (pres. 1942) bar assns., Conf. Chief Justices (nat. chmn. 1966-67), Central States Shrine Assn. (past pres.). Democrat. Baptist (exec. com. So. Bapt. Conv. 1967-75). Mason (Shriner), Lion (pres. Pine Bluff 1936). Home: Pine Bluff, Ark. Died Dec. 21, 1980; buried Graceland Cemetery, Pine Bluff.

HARRIS, CHESTER R. R., wire and cable mfr.; b. Randolph Co., Ind., Jan. 14, 1882; s. D. Thomas and Mary B. (Borkin) H.; student Pratt Inst.; m. F. MaBelle Skeele, Apr. 20, 1912; 1 son, Franklin S. Insp. material engring. dept. Western Electric Co., 1905-19; with engring. dept. Western Union Telegraph Co., 1910-17; asst. to pres. Kerite Co., N.Y.C., 1917-26, v.p., 1926-43, pres., 1943, now chmn., dir. Mem. Am. Inst. E.E. (life). Clubs: Rail Road Machinery (gov.; N.Y.C.); Montclair Country (gov.); New Haven Lawn. Home: Montclair, N.J. *

HARRIS, COLLAS G., govt. cons.; b. Staunton, Va., Oct. 20, 1906; s. Louis Van Meter and Sallie Crimora (Ballard) H.; grad. Augusta Mil. Acad., 1928; student Washington and Lee U., 1928-31, Georgetown, U., 1934, Civil Affairs Tng. Sch., July-Aug. 1945; grad. A.A.F. Officers Tng. Sch., 1942, A.A.F. Intelligence Sch., 1943, Mil. Govt. Sch., 1945; m. Ann McSwain, Apr. 25, 1943; children—Collas G., James Louis. Exec. officer Nat. Archives, Washington, 1934-42, def. coordinator, 1942, dir. adminstrv. services, 1948-49; adminstrv. officer Nat. Archives and Records Service, Gen. Services Adminstrn., 1949-52; sr. cons. U.S. Govt., 1952-57; asst. U.S. Air Attache, Am. Embassy, Melbourne, Australia, 1957-59; ret. from CIA and U.S. Air Force Res., 1968. Exec. sec., chmn. exec. com., committee conservation cultural resources Nat. Resources Planning Bd., 1941-42; mem. Interdepartmental Com. Air Raid Protection, 1942. Served as 1st lt. to maj. A.A.F., 1942-46; intelligence officer, 1943-45; mem. Oversea Planning Bd., Civil Affairs Staging Area, Monterey, Cal., Aug.-Oct. 1945; dep. chief analysis and research div., civil information and edn. sect., GIIQ, SCAP, Tokyo, Japan, 1945-47. Decorated Bronze Star medal (6), Army Commendation, Asiatic-Pacific Theatre, Philippines Liberation, Am. Def., Occupation, Victory ribbons, Mem. Soc. Am. Archivists (chmn. com. emergency transfer and storage archives, 1941, com. protection archives against war hazards, 1942), Am. Hist. Assn., Acad. Polit. Sci., Res. Officers Assn. U.S., Nat. Geog. Soc., Sigma Alpha Epsilon. Epis. (vestryman). Author, ed. articles and papers profl. jours. Home: Great Falls, Va. Died May 14, 1981.

HARRIS, EDWARD ARNOLD, writer, newspaperman; b. St. Louis, Oct. 20, 1910; s. Nathan and Rose (Goldman) H.; A.B., Washington U., St. Louis, 1933; M.S. in Journalism, UCLA, 1958; m. Miriam Sima Levy, Oct. 5, 1938; children—Linda Gail, Mark Geoffrey, Robert Nathaniel. Campus corr. Washington U. for St. Louis Star-Times, 1931-33; columnist, gen. reporter Star-Times, 1933-40; city hall reporter St. Louis Post-Dispatch, 1940, reporter, local polit. writer, 1940-43, Washington corr., 1943-54, chief West Coast bur., 1954-58; St. Louis corr. Fortune, Life and Time, 1936-43; syndicated columnist, 1960-63; pres. Edward A. Harris & Assos., 1963-76. Recipient Pulitzer prize for distinguished nat. correspondence, 1946; journalism award in behalf of Post-Dispatch Washington bur. Fontbonne Coll., St. Louis, 1947; co-recipient Heywood Broun runner-up award, 1951; Alumni citation Washington U., 1957; award of distinciton UCLA Dept. Journalism, 1958; Agrl. writers award, 1961. Mem. Nat. Press Club, Sigma Delta Chi. Author: (with J.T. Salter, editor) Public Men, In and Out of Office, 1946; Love Thy Neighbor, 1958. Contbr. articles on nat. affairs to mags. Home: Huntly, Va. Died Mar. 14, 1976; interred Jordan River Farm, Huntly.

HARRIS, GEORGE GORDON, lawyer; b. Smithton, Mo., Feb. 13, 1883; s. John Vaughn and Margaret (Summerville) H.; LL.B., U. Mo., 1908; m. Laurine Shireman, Sept. 7, 1930. Admitted to Mo. bar, 1908, Cal. bar, 1908, Wash. bar, 1908, Mont. bar, 1912; mem. firm Church, Harris, Johnson & Williams, Great Falls, Monts., 1941—. Dir. Great Falls Fed. Savs. & Loan Assn. Chmn. State Bd. Pub. Welfare, Helena, 1940-44. Served with U.S. Army, World War I. Mem. Great Falls C. of C. (dir.), Am. Legion, Phi Delta Phi. Mason. Clubs: Pivitan, Meadow Lark Country (dir.) (Great Falls). Home: Great Falls MT. *

HARRIS, HENRY ELLIS, profl. philatelist; b. Atlanta, Jan. 21, 1902; s. Stephen Coates and Harriet Isabel (Fitch) H.; grad. Balt. City Coll., 1919; m. Gertrude L. Mulvey, Aug. 15, 1922 (div. Sept. 1942); children—Betty L. (Mrs. Munyan), Henry Ellis, Robert Stephen; m. 2d, Laura G. Costello, Oct. 4, 1974 (dec. 1975); children—Georgia Ellice, Janet Elaine. Founder H.E. Harris & Co., philatelic dealer, Balt., 1916-19, Boston, 1919-73, became ind. subs. Gen. Mills Inc. under guidance of Parker Bros. Inc., Salem, Mass., remained as cons., 1973-77. Mem. Am. Philatelic Soc., Am. Topical Assn., Am. Stamp Dealers Assn., Boston Philatelic Soc., Soc. Philatelic Americans, Am. Airmail Soc., Collectors Club N.Y., Cardinal Spellman Philatelic Mus. (founder group). Mason. H.E. Harris & Co. recognized as world's largest stamp concern. Home: Wellesley Hills, Mass. Died Dec. 29, 1977.

HARRIS, HUGH PATE, army officer; b. Anderson, Ala., June 15, 1909; s. Leo C. and Maude Ethel (Alsup) H.; B.S., U.S. Mil. Acad., 1931; student Inf. Sch., 1938, Armed Forces Staff Coll., 1946, Command and Staff Coll., 1948, Nat. War Coll., 1950; m. Jane Boyd, Aug. 24, 1934 (dec. 1958); 1 dau., Beverly Boyd; m. 2d, Kathleen Burns, 1961; 1 adopted dau., Betsy. Commd. 2d lt. U.S. Army, 1931, advanced through grades to gen.; unit comdr. 22d Inf., 1931-34, Hawaiian Div., 1934-37, 5th Inf. Div., 1940-41; assigned airborne units, Ft. Benning, Ga. and Ft. Bragg, N.C., 1942-46; instr. Army Staff Coll., 1948; chief staff U.S. 13th Airborne Div., 1944-46, 18th Airborne Corps, 1951-52, 2d Army, 1953-55; liason with Canadian Army, Joint Chiefs Staff, 1948; regt. comdr. 224th Inf., 40th Div., Korea, 1952; dep. chief staff for operations 8th Army, Korean War, 1953; comdg. gen., Berlin, 1955; div. comdr. 11th Airborne Div., Germany, 1956; dep. chief of staff for operations, plans and tng. G3, U.S. Continental Army Command, Fort Monroe, Va., 1958-60; comdt. U.S. Army Inf. School and comdg. gen. U.S. Army Inf. Center, Ft. Benning, 1960; comdg. gen. I Corps (Group), Korea, 1961, 7th Army, 1962, Continental Army Command, 1964; comdr.-in-chief Army Strike Forces, 1964; pres. The Citadel, Charleston, S.C., 1965-70. Mem. S.C. Wildlife Commn., S.C. Atomic Energy Commn., So. Interstate Nuclear Bd., S.C. Commn. Higher Edn. Bd. dirs. S.C. Wildlife Fedn. Decorated D.S.M. with oak leaf cluster, Silver Star, Legion Merit with clusters (U.S.); D.S.M. with cluster (Korea). Mem. Airborne Assn. (past nat. pres.). Mason, Optimist, Hibernian. Assisted preparation airborne lit. for U.S. Army tng. system. Home: Bonneau, S.C. Died Nov. 3, 1979; interred Arlington Nat. Cemetery (Va.).

HARRIS, JED, theatrical producer; b. Vienna, Austria, Feb. 25, 1900; s. Meyer W. and Esther (Schurtz) Howowitz; brought to U.S., 1901; student Yale, 1917-20; m. Anita Green (div. 1928); m. 2d, Louise Platt (div. 1944); 1 dau., Abigail; m. 3d, Bebe Allan, Apr. 1, 1957 (div. 1962). Theatrical reporter with The Clipper, 1921; editor, press agt., co. mgr., 1921-26; producer, 1926-79; producer plays Broadway, 1926, Coquette, 1927, The Front Page, 1926, The Royal Family, 1928, Uncle Vanya, 1930, The Green Bay Tree, 1933, Our Town, 1938, One-Man Show, 1945, The Heiress, 1945, Red Gloves, 1949, Child of Fortune, 1956. Co-author: Operation Mad Ball. Died Nov. 15, 1979.

HARRIS, LOUIS CARL, newspaper editor; b. Montgomery, Ala., Feb. 20, 1912; s. Augustus J. and Florence (Hirsch) H.; student public schs.; m. Margaret M. Brown, Aug. 9, 1944; children—Jeffrey Peden, Louis Carl, William McCollough. Carrier, Montgomery Advertiser, 1931-32; asst. circulation mgr. Augusta (Ga.) Chronicle, 1932-34, reporter, telegraph editor, 1934-38; reporter Pontiac (Mich.) Daily Press, 1938-40, telegraph editor, 1946-47; news editor Columbus (Ga.) Ledger, 1947-74; news editor Augusta Chronicle and Herald, 1947-78, editor, 1959-74, v.p., exec. editor, 1974-78; v.p. Southeastern Newspapers Corp., 1966-78. Dir. Richmond Assos., Inc. Bd. dirs. Augusta United Fund, 1952-58. Served to capt. USAAF, 1940-45. Decorated Bronze Star. Nieman travel fellow, Japan, 1956. Mem. Ga. Associated Press News Council (pres. 1950, 52), Am. Soc. Newspaper Editors, Augusta C. of C. (v.p.), Ga. Press Assn. (pres. 1967-68). Presbyterian (deacon). Club: Kiwanis (dir. Augusta 1950). Home: Augusta, Ga. Died June 23, 1978.

HARRIS, LYNN H(AROLD), educator; b. at Milton, Pa., Nov. 26, 1885; s. James Lynn and Mary Annie (Polsgrove) H.; B.A., Dickinson Coll., 1906; M.A. in Philosophy, Boston U., 1909; M.A. in English, Yale, 1910, Ph.D., 1914; m. Rhoda Edna Reeser, Aug. 27, 1941; 1 dau., Elizabeth Reeser (Mrs. W. Mark Noble). Instructor English, Northwestern University, 1912-13; pres. Beaver Coll. for Women, 1923-27; coll. acquired Beechwood, Inc., in 1925, and moved from Beaver to Jenkintown, Pa.; pres. Howard Seminary and Jr. Coll., West Bridgewater, Mass., 1927-37; pres. Blue Ridge Coll., New Windsor, Md., 1937-39; dean Nat. Park Coll., Forest Glen, Md., 1939-42, when college was taken over by U.S. Army as hospital; mem. English staff, Stephens College, Columbia, Mo., 1942-45; asso. prof. English, Southeast Mo. State Coll., Cape Girardeau, 1945-47, prof. since 1947. Mem. Modern Lang. Assn. Am., Am. Assn. Univ. Profs., Tenn. Philol. Assn., Nat. Council Teachers of Eng., Am. Poetry Assn. (v.p. 1930-33), S.A.R., Phi Beta Kappa, Alpha Chi Rho, Pi Kappa Delta, Theta Alpha Phi, Sigma Tau Delta. Mason. Editor: Ben Jonson's Catiline (critical edition), 1916. Contbr. of religious and ednl. subjects. Home: Cape Girardeau, Mo. *

HARRIS, MARGUERITE, publisher, poet; b. Bklyn., July 5, 1899; d. Vincent and Addelaide Elizabeth (LeFurge) Schmous; privately educated; m. Moses Harris, Apr. 14, 1943; children—Jane E. Ross, Margaret Ross Diederich, Hannah. Publisher Cymric Press, N.Y.C., 1974-78; founder, dir. Woodstock (N.Y.) Poetry Festival, 1964; dir. Dr. Generost's Poetry Series, N.Y.C., 1970-78; condr. poetry workshops, 1965-78. Recipient Edward Markham award Poetry Soc. Am., 1968. Author: (poems) Reconciling of Rivers, 1964, The Cymric Spell, 1968, Time of the Playback, 1976. Editor: Emily Dickinson: Letters from the World, 1968; Loves, etc., 1973; A Tumult for John Berryman, 1976. Manuscript transcriber James Boswell dairies and corr., 1928. Address: New York, N.Y. Died Jan. 1, 1978.

HARRIS, ROBERT EDWARD GEORGE, educator, writer; b. Bloomington, Ind., Apr. 3, 1903; s. C. Edward and Frances (Whiteley) H.; A.B., Ind. U., 1925, M.A., 1926; postgrad. Yale, 1926-27; m. Edna Welton, Aug. 8, 1925 (dec.); 1 dau., Nancy W. (Mrs. Robert R. Kirsch). Instr. English, Bucknell U., 1925-26; asso. editor Hollywood Mag., 1927-29; instr. journalism and public affairs Los Angeles City and State colls., 1929-42; chief editorial writer Los Angeles Daily News, 1945-49; editorial columnist Los Angeles Times, 1949-52; prof. journalism dept. UCLA, 1950-70, chmn. dept., 1955-60, prof. emeritus, 1970-77. Cons. to Pres. Truman, 1952; guest prof. Institut fûr Publizistik U. Vienna, 1970-71; lectr. Kyoto U. (Japan), Waseda U. (Japan), 1968; editor-in-chief Capricorn TV Enterprises, 1962. Exec. com. Calif. Congressional Reorgn. Plan, from 1956; mem. gov. planning com. Mental Health in Calif., 1949. Served as lt. USNR, 1942-44. Am. specialist grantee, Dept. State, Turkey and Iran, 1959; Del Amo fellow, Spain Mem. AAUP, Sigma Delta Chi. Democrat. Methodist. Author: The Press in an Authoritarian State, 1964; Spain's Mass Cultural Communications Media, 1966; Spain's Move Toward Freedom of the Press, 1966; The Spanish Press in Transition, 1967; What Vienna's Editors Think, 1969. Editor: Poster Propaganda of the Spanish Civil War, 1970; Anthology of Spanish Civil War in Pictures, 1972; (anthology) Spain's Generation of 98, 1973; The Many Faces of Spain, 1974; The Monuments of Spain, 1975. Home: Los Angeles, Calif. Died Mar. 9, 1977.

HARRIS, ROY ELLSWORTH, composer; b. Lincoln County, Okla., Feb. 12, 1898; s. Elmer Ellsworth and Laura (Broddle) H.; student U. Calif., 1919-20; Mus.D. (hon.), Rutgers U., 1941, U. Rochester, 1946; student of music under mother, Arthur Farwell and Nadia Boulanger; m. Beula Duffey, Oct. 10, 1936; 3 children; m. 2d, Johana Harris; 2 children. Composer from 1926; composed 6 symphonies, music for schools, bands, orchestras, choruses; 3 string quartets, string and piano quintets, choral compositions and piano solos. Guggenheim fellow, 1928-30; creative fellowship Pasadena Music and Art Assn., 1930-33. Composer in residence Cornell U., 1941-42, Colo. Coll., Colorado Springs, 1942-48, Utah State Agrl. Coll., 1948-67, UCLA, from 1967. Served with U.S. Army, 1918; mus. dir. with Office of War Information, 1945. Awarded 1st honors for most important score (Folk Song Symphony), Committee for Appreciation of Am. Music, 1940; Nat. Assn. for Composers and Conductors, 1940; Coolidge medal for eminent contbn. to chamber music Library of Congress, 1942. Fellow Nat. Inst. Arts and Letters; mem. ASCAP, Am. Composers Assn., Nat. Assn. Composers and Conductors, Nat. Composers Congress (dir. 1944-45), Fellowship Am. Composers (pres. 1946-50), Sinfonia; hon. life mem. Pitts. Musicians Club, Phi Mu Gamma, Phi Mu Alpha. Clubs: Clef (Cornell); Lotos (N.Y.C.); El Paso (Colorado Springs). Editor: Singing Through the Ages, 2 vols., 1940. Contbr. articles to Scribner's N.Y. Times, Twice a Year, Mus. Quar., Modern Music, Music News, etc. Folk Song Symphony (No. 4 and 5) recorded by U.S. Govt. for distribution in allied camps. Sixth (Lincoln) Symphony premiere, Boston Symphony, 1944. Home: Pacific Palisades, Calif. Died Oct. 1, 1979.

HARRIS, SAM, lawyer; b. New Kensington, Pa., July 17, 1912; s. Harry and Milly (Miller) H.; B.A. with highest honors, U. Calif., Los Angeles, 1933; LL.B. cum laude, Yale, 1936; m. Madelyn J. Brown, May 3, 1944; children—Jack Brown, Steven Brown. Admitted to Calif. bar, 1936, N.Y. bar, 1947, D.C. bar, 1971; supervising atty. charge opinion sect. SEC, Washington, 1939-40; counsel trustees Asso. Gas Electric Corp., N.Y.C., 1940-42; chief econ. sect. Nuremberg Trial against Goering et al, 1945-46; mem. firm Fried, Frank, Harris, Shriver & Jacobson, N.Y.C., 1946-80, sr. partner; acting chmn. Communications Satellite Corp., Washington, 1962; dir. Rio Tinto-Zinc Corp. Ltd., London, Eng., Rio Algom Ltd., Toronto, Energy Fund, N.Y.C., Callahan Mining Corp., Darien, Conn., U.S. Borax & Chem. Corp., Los Angeles, GAF Corp., N.Y.C. Treas., Stevenson for Pres. Com., N.Y., 1956; co-chmn. Citizens for Kennedy and Johnson, N.Y., 1960, Citizens for Johnson and Humphrey, N.Y., 1964. Trustee Ednl. Alliance, 1950-56. Served to capt. J.A.G. Dept., AUS, 1942-46. Decorated Bronze Star. Mem. Am. Bar Assn. (chmn. com. on fed. regulation of securities 1962-66, chmn. com. devels. in bus. financing 1972-73), N.Y. State Bar Assn., Bar Assn. City New York, Am. Bar Found., N.Y. County Lawyers Assn., Am. Judicature Soc., Order of Coif, Phi Beta Kappa Assos., Phi Beta Kappa, Pi Gamma Mu, Pi Kappa Delta, Pi Sigma Alpha. Clubs: Yale, Century Country. Contbr. articles to profl. jours. Home: New York, N.Y. Died Nov. 13, 1980.

HARRIS, THOMAS P., ins. co. exec.; b. Columbus, Miss., Dec. 16, 1898; B.A., Fisk U., 1922; J.D., U. Chgo., 1929. Engaged in ins., Ark., 1922-24; asst. mgr. Little Rock dist., 1924-26; admitted to Ill. bar, 1929; formerly asst. atty. for receivership Binga State Bank, then asso. mém. firm Edward H. Morris and James B. Cashin, Chgo.; legal adviser Chgo. Met. Mut. Assurance Co., 1932-34, v.p., gen. counsel, 1934-56, pres., 1956-61, chmn. bd. dirs. 1961—78, also chmn. exec. com., dir.; dir. Drexel Nat. Bank. Mem. Nat. Ins. Assn. (pres. 1959, chmn. bd. 1960-61), Am., Nat., Cook County bar assns., A.I.M. (asso.), Chgo. C. of C., Nat. Assn. Real Estate Brokers, Cosmopolitan C. of C., Royal Coterie Snakes, Chgo. Urban League, Chgo. Assembly, Frontiers of Am., Dearborn Real Estate Bd., N.A.A.C.P., Alpha Phi Alpha. Address: Chicago, Ill. Died Aug. 13, 1979.

HARRIS, THOMAS RUSSELL, mgmt. cons. firm exec.; b. Buffalo, N.Y., July 18, 1907; s. Sherwin B. and Maude N. (Negley) H.; B.S., U. Buffalo, 1928; postgrad. in Indsl. Mgmt. U. Pitts., 1932-33, Pa. State Coll., 1933-34; m. Ruth L. Mayer, June 29, 1929; children—Thomas Russell, Craig M., Elaine R. (Mrs. Robert Gomperts). Gen. mgr. Dejur Amsco Corp., L.I. City, N.Y., 1954-58; exec. v.p. Holly Corp., N.Y.C., 1958-62; pres. Exec. Service Co., N.Y.C., 1962-70; pres. Robert Heller Assos. Inc., Greenwich, Conn., 1970-76; pres. Fed. Cement Tile Co., Hammond, Ind., 1960-62; ret., 1976. Home: Vero Beach, Fla. Died Aug. 7, 1979.

HARRISON, BAYA M., JR., lawyer; b. Tampa, Fla., Sept. 14, 1912; LL.B., U. Fla., 1935. Admitted to Fla. bar, 1935; practice in St. Petersburg; mem. Harrison, Greene, Mann, Davenport, Rowe & Stanton and predecessor firm; lectr. law trial and appeal practice John B. Stetson U. Fellow Am. Coll. Trial Lawyers; mem. Am., St. Petersburg, Tampa, Hillsborough County bar assns., Fla. Bar (pres. 1957-58), Fed. Communications Bar Assn., Internat. Assn. Ins. Counsel, Phi Delta Phi. Address: St. Petersburg, Fla. Died Feb. 19, 1975.

HARRISON, MISS FANNEAL, educator; b. Decatur, Ga., June 12, 1882; d. Zadoc Daniel and Laura (Hendree) Harrison; ed. Washington Sem., Atlanta, Ga., 1888-98; student Sch. of Osteopathy, Kirksville, Mo., 2 yrs., U. of Mich., 2 yrs., and Radcliffe Coll. and Boston U., 1 yr. each. With Associated Charities, Atlanta, Phila. and El Paso until 1908; dir. orthopedic clinic, Atlanta, 1910-12; with Am. Jr. Red Cross, Czechoslovakia, Austria, Poland and France, 1914-21, Hoover relief, Belgium, 1921-23; with Out-of-Door Sch., Sarasota, Fla., since 1924, dir. and owner since 1924. Democrat. Episcopalian. Address: Sarasota, Fla.

HARRISON, FLORENCE, home economist; b. Lafayette, Ind., Aug. 31, 1884; d. Charles and Rosanna (Roberts) Harrison; B.S. in Agr., U. of Ill., 1908; M.A. in Edn., Columbia University, 1918; Sc.D. (hon.), Kansas State Coll., 1947. Teacher high sch., Centralia, Ill., 1908-09, Champaign, Ill., 1909-10; with U. of Ill., 1910-19, successively extension worker, head of home economics extension, critic teacher of home econ. edn., and Smith-Hughes supervisor; dean of home economics, State Coll. of Wash., 1919-38; chmn. dept. of home economics, U. of Mo., 1938-48; chmn. home economics dept., Berea Coll. since 1949. Mem. Am. Home Economics Assn., Mo. Ednl. Assn., Mo. State Home Econ. Assn. (pres.), League of Women Voters, Phi Kappa Phi, Omicron Nu, Pi Lambda Theta, Phi Upsilon Omicron, Delta Kappa Gamma, Gamma Sigma Delta. Episcopalian. Club: Altrusa. Home: Berea, Ky. *

HARRISON, GEORGE RUSSELL, univ. dean, physicist; b. San Diego, July 14, 1898; s. Ernest and Magda (Lincke-Tiesel) H.; A.B., Stanford U., 1919, A.M., 1920, Ph.D., 1922; Sc.D. (hon.), Northeastern U., 1943, St. Lawrence University, 1952; LL.D. (hon.), Middlebury College, 1955; Doctor of Engring. (hon.), Drexel Institute, 1956; m. Florence Kent, December 25, 1922 (dec. 1955); children—Mary Lou, Nancy Kent, David Kent; m. 2d. Elizabeth Headley, Mar. 9, 1957. Instr. Stanford U., 1919-23; National Research fellow, Harvard U., 1923-25; asst. prof. physics, Stanford U., 1925-27, asso. prof., 1927-30; prof. physics and dir. research lab. of exptl. physics M.I.T., 1930-42, dean Sch. of Sci., 1942-64, prof. emeritus until 1979. Awarded Rumford medal, 1939; Ives Medal, 1949; Cresson Medal, 1953; Pitts. Spectroscopy Award, 1957. Mem. Am. Physical Soc., Am. Philos. Soc., A.A.A.S. (v.p. 1953), Optical Soc. Am. (pres. 1946-48), Am. Acad. Arts and Scis. (v.p. 1944-46), Am. Astron. Soc., Am. Inst. Physics (mem. bd. govs. 1940), chmn. bd., 1947-54). Chief, optics div. Nat. Def. Research Com., 1942-46, chief physics div., 1945-46; asst. chief, Office Field Service, Office of Sci. Research and Devel., 1944; chief, research sect., Gen. MacArthur's hdqrs., 1944. Awarded Medal of Freedom, Presdl. Medal for Merit, 1946. Author books including: Practical Spectroscopy (with Lord and Loufbourow), 1948; What Man May Be, 1956; Atoms in Action 1939-59. Editor Jour. of Optical Soc. Am., 1940-50. Home: Concord, Mass. Died July 27, 1979.

HARRISON, GREGORY ALEXANDER, lawyer; b. San Francisco, Sept. 9, 1896; s. Edward Charles and Mary Gertrude (Bodkin) H.; B.S., U. Calif., 1917; LL.B., Hastings Coll. of Law, 1921; m. Christine Finnell Wheeler, October 29, 1966; children—Gregory Alexander, Patricia H. (Mrs. J.W. Brown, Jr.), Michael B., Elizabeth R., Barbara Ann. Admitted to Calif. bar, 1920, since practiced in San Francisco; partner firm Brobeck, Phleger & Harrison, 1931-79. Dir. emeritus Pacific Power & Light Co. Trustee War Meml. of San Francisco, pres. bd. trustees San Francisco Law Library. Mem. Am. Coll. Trial Lawyers. Home: San Francisco, Calif. Died Jan. 31, 1979.

HARRISON, HENRY STUART, iron ore co. exec.; b. Cleve., Nov. 25, 1909; s. Henry Thomas and Regina (Troler) H.; B.A., Yale U., 1932; LL.D. (hon.), Mich. Technol. U., 1964, No. Mich. U., 1967; m. Suzanne Brookhart, Oct. 30, 1943; children—Mary S. Harrison Lansing, Henry Stuart, Virginia Foster Harrison Knight. With Corrigan McKinney Steel Co., 1932-33, Central Hanover Bank & Trust Co., 1932-36, Lionel D. Edie & Co., Investment Counsel, 1936-37; with Cleve.-Cliffs Iron Co., 1937-80, asst. treas., 1940-45, treas., 1945-52, v.p., treas., 1952-53, v.p. fin., 1954-58, dir., 1957-80, exec. v.p., 1958-60, pres., 1960-77, chief exec. officer, 1961-77, chmn., chief exec. officer, 1974-76, chmn. bd., 1976-77, chmn. exec. com., 1977-80; trustee Northwestern Mut. Life Ins. Co., also dir.; dir. Republic Steel Corp., Cleve. Trust Co., Midland-Ross Corp. Trustee, chmn. fin. com. Cleve. Inst. Art; vice chmn., mem. exec. com. Univ. Hosps.; past chmn. distbn. com. Cleve. Found.; v.p., trustee United Way Services, Inc., Gt. Lakes Shakespeare Festival, Fedn. Community Planning, Cleve.; chmn. Univ. Circle, Inc. Mem. Greater Cleve. Growth Assn., Am. Iron Ore Assn., Am. Iron and Steel Inst. (past dir., mem. exec. com.), Am. Mining Congress (past mem. exec. com., vice chmn.), Phi Beta Kappa. Republican. Presbyterian. Clubs: Union, Chagrin Valley Hunt, Tavern, Kirtland (Cleve.); Ottawa, Pepper Pike, Pa.). Home: Cleveland, Ohio. Died July 21, 1980.

HARRISON, JOSEPH, judge; b. Shreveport, La., June 10, 1904; s. Leon and Charlotte (Rosenberg) H.; B.S., Tufts Coll., 1926; LL.B., Harvard, 1929; m. Amy Harvey, Aug. 13, 1938 (dec. 1961); children—Joseph Leon, George Harvey; m. 2d, Frances Boehm Ginsberg, 1967. Admitted to N.J. bar, 1930, since practiced in Newark; state dep. atty. gen., assigned Bd. Public Utility Commrs., 1947-52, spl. counsel, public utility, railroad rate matters; partner firm Harrison and Jacobs, 1960-70; judge Essex County Ct., 1970-74. Dep. state rationing adminst. for OPA, 1941-42, state rationing atty., 1942-44; sec. N.J. Com. for Constl. Revision, 1944-47; mem. Montclair Civil Rights Commn., 1952-65; mem. N.J. Supreme Ct. adv. com. profl. ethics; co-chmn. N.J. Com. Fair Representation; mem. Gov.'s Com. Legal Services Poor; chmn. N.J. Law Enforcement Council, 1957, counsel Gov.'s Transition Com., 1969-70; chmn, N.J. Election Law Revision Com., 1970; commr. from N.J., Nat. Conf. Commrs. Uniform State Laws, 1954-56; lectr. Rutgers Law Sch., 1956-59; mem. adv. com. profl. ethics N.J. Supreme Ct.; mem. Commn. Correctional Facilities and Services, 1974-76. Recipient World Federalist award for contbns. to world peace through world law, 1965; Joseph Harrison fellowship established in his honor Flectcher Sch. of Law and Diplomacy, Tufts U., 1976. Mem. Am. (chmn. standing com. Bill of Rights 1958-59, exec. com. world peace through law 1962-63, council sect. individual rights and responsibilities 1966-70), N.J., Essex County, bar assns., Am. Assn. UN (N.J. pres. 1960-62), Am. Judicature Soc. (bd. dirs.), Phi Beta Kappa. Republican. Mem. B'nai B'rith. Editor N.J. Law Jour., 1937-42, 51-70. Contbr. articles legal jours. Home: Livingston, N.J. Died Jan. 28, 1976.

HARRISON, LELAND, diplomat; b. New York City, Apr. 25, 1883; s. W. Henry and Helen (Skidmore) H.; B.A., Harvard, 1907; m. Anne C. Coleman, June 27, 1925. Pvt. sec. to ambassador to Japan, 1907-08; apptd. 3d sec. of Embassy, Tokyo, 1908; 2d sec. of Legation, Peking, 1909; 2d sec. Embassy, London, 1910; sec. Legation, Bogota, Colombia, 1912; assigned duty Dept. of State, 1915; dip. sec. Am. Commn. to Negotiate Peace, rank of counselor, Nov. 30, 1918; counselor Am. Embassy, Paris, May 1920; spl. duty Dept. of State, 1921; expert asst. to Am. Commrs., Conf. on Limitation of Armament, 1921-22; became asst. sec. of state, Mar. 31, 1922; apptd. E.E. and M.P. to Sweden, 1927; chmn. Am. delegation to Internat. Telegraph Conf., Brussels, 1928; E.E. and M.P. to Uruguay, 1929-30; chief of internat. relations div. U.S. Tariff Commn. Nov. 1930-Nov. 1931; Am. mem. Internat. Conciliation Commn. under 1929 Treaty with Estonia, 1934-35; E.E. and M.P. to Rumania, 1935-37, to Switzerland since 1937. Clubs: Union, The Brook (New York); Philadelphia (Phila.); Metropolitan, Burning Tree, Chevy Chase, Alibi (Washington, D.C.). Address: Berne, Switzerland. *

HARRISON, PRESTON ERSHELL, physician; b. Bryans Mill, Tex., Aug. 26, 1911; s. Alonzo Louis and Ola (Henson) H.; B.S., East Tex. State Coll., 1932; M.A., U. Tex., 1936; M.D., Baylor U., 1941; Ph.D. (Mary Strong Sheldon fellow), U. Chgo., 1946; m. Elizabeth Badgett, Jan. 17, 1970; children—Preston Ershell, Robert. Instr., Baylor U., Houston, 1941-43, asst. prof., 1943-46, asso. prof., 1946-48, prof., 1948-49; intern Baylor U. Hosp., 1942-43; resident Menninger Found., 1957-58; gen. practice medicine, Maud, Tex., 1949-53; clin. dir. Big Spring (Tex.) State Hosp., 1953-57, acting supr., 1957-58, supt., 1958-75; research asso., instr. U. Chgo., 1945-46; clin. asso. prof psychiatry Baylor Coll. Medicine, Houston, Tex. Tech.

Med. Coll., Lubbock. Fellow A.A.A.S., Am. Psychiat. Assn. (mem. achievement awards com., pres. West Tex. chpt.); mem. A.M.A., Am. Hosp. Assn., Am. Soc. Clin. Hypnosis, Soc. Clin. and Exptl. Hypnosis, SIgma Xi, Alpha Omega Alpha Rotarian. Home: Big Spring, Tex. Died Aug. 8, 1975.

HARRISON, W. EARL, banker; b. Ellis County, Tex.; s. Robert E. and Lucretia (Vestal) H.; law degree under pvt. tutorship, 1936; grad. Rutgers U. Sch. Banking, 1939; m. Minnie Louise Howell, June 1, 1926; 1 son, William Earl. Admitted to Tex. bar, 1935; with First Nat. Bank Waco, Tex., 1926-79, pres., 1965-79, vice chmn., 1970-73, chmn., 1973-77, chmn. emeritus, 1977-79, also dir.; dir. Waco Hardware Co., Baylor Bear Club. Bd. dirs. Tex. Good Roads Assn; trustee Council for Instl. Devel.; trustee McLennan Community Coll.; past pres., dir. Waco YMCA, Waco Library. Served to lt. USNR, World War II. Mason (Shriner), Lion (past pres., bd. dirs. Waco). Club: Ridgewood Country (Waco). Home: Waco, Tex. Died Oct. 24, 1979.

HARRISON, WALTER TROUSDALE, physician; b. Stilwell, Kan., Feb. 1, 1886; s. Thomas Trousdale and Mary Samantha (Taylor) H.; grad. Emporia (Kan.) State Normal Sch., 1907; M.D., Univ. Med. Coll., Kansas City, Mo., 1911; m. Lillian Grace Lamon, May 27, 1912. Resident physician St. Mary's Hosp., Kansas City, Mo., 1911-12; instr. anatomy N.Y. U., 1912-13; pathologist Napa (Calif.) State Hosp., 1914-16; commd. asst. surgeon, U.S.P.H.S., 1916, passed asst. surgeon, 1920, surgeon, 1924, sr. surgeon, 1936, med. dir., 1942; U.S. Quarantine and Immigration Service, San Francisco, Calif., in plague suppressive measures; at Nat. Inst. of Health, 1922-40; assigned Ninth Corps Area Hdqrs. U.S. Army, Presidio of San Francisco, 1940; dir. Dist. No. 5, U.S.P.H.S., 1942. Mem. A.M.A., Am. Pub. Health Assn. Mason. Clubs: Bohemian, Commonwealth (San Francisco). Address: San Francisco. *

HARSHMAN, JOHN BURNETT, lawyer; b. nr. Dayton, O., Nov. 20, 1882; s. John Fremont and Alethea Ann (LaFong) H.; student Shauck's English Classical Tng. Sch., Dayton, 1899-1900; A.B., Ohio State U., 1904, LL.B., 1907; grad. O.T.S., 1918; m. Mary Louise Longbrake, July 28, 1914 (dec. 1954); children—Mary Anne (Mrs. Louis L. Haas), John Burnett, Rebecca Jane (Mrs. Charles H. Stowe, Jr.). Admitted to Ohio bar, 1907; asso. O. F. Davisson, Dayton, 1907-14; clk. Dayton (O.) Commn. (including sec. to mayor) under Commn. Mgr. Charter, 1914-18, asst. city atty., 1919-21, city atty., 1921-31; pvt. practice, 1932—; partner in law firm of Harshman & Young, and successor firm of Harshman, Young, Colvin & Alexander, 1940—; solicitor, Village of West Carrollton, 1912-47, City of Miamisburg, 1943-46. Served with U.S. Army, 1918-19, maj. Res., 1927-39. Mem. Am., Ohio, Dayton (pres. 1946-47) bar assns., Am., Dayton rose socs., Federated Ins. Council (v.p. 1949), varsity "O" Assn., Delta Chi (nat. treas. 1913-29; nat. pres. 1929-35; executive board 1913-52, trustee of the educational foundation). Presbyterian. Mason (grand high priest Ohio, 1938-39; treas. chapt. of Research, RAM of Ohio; pres. Ohio council Annointed High Priests since 1939; 33 deg., K.T., Shriner), York Cross of Honor, Red Cross Constantine (sovereign 1950), Royal Order Jesters, Royal Order Scotland. Clubs: Kiwanis (pres. 1940). Compiled: Health Laws of Ohio and Dayton, 1909; Code of General Ordinances, 1927. Contbr. articles legal, Masonic publs. Home: Dayton. *

HARSTAD, OSCAR NORRIS, ry. official; b. Sioux City, Ia., Dec. 25, 1886; s. Ole O. and Lena H.; ed. high sch.; m. Hazel B. Straub, of Sioux City, Dec. 15, 1909. With C.M. & St.P. Ry. since Jan. 11, 1904, successively chief clk. to div. supt. until 1911, chief clk. to gen. supt., 1911-17, trainmaster, 1917-18, div. supt. at Aberdeen, S.D., 1918-23, gen. supt., 1923-24, asst. gen. mgr., 1924-25, gen. mgr. operating dept., Eastern Lines, at Chicago, since Nov. 25, 1925. Republican. Club: Evanston Golf. Home: Evanston, Ill. *

HART, (JULIAN) DERYL, educator; b. Buena Vista, Ga., Aug. 27, 1894; s. John Deryl and Fannie Walter (Mathews) H.; A.B., Emory U., 1916, A.M., 1917; M.D., Johns Hopkins, 1921; LL.D., University of North Carolina, 1962, and Duke University, 1964; m. Mary Elizabeth Johnson, June 16, 1932; children—Elizabeth (Mrs. Edward King), Julia (Mrs. Charles Warner), Julian Deryl, John Martin Hicks, William Johnson, Margaret Louise (Mrs. Russell Harrison). Instr. surgery, Johns Hopkins Hosp., 1921-22, asst. resident in surg. and surgical pathology, 1923-27, resident surgeon, 1927-29, asso. surgeon, 1929-30; asst. in pathology, Johns Hopkins U., 1922-23; instructor in surgery, 1923-29; asso. in surgery, 1929-30; prof. of surgery Duke University Sch. of Medicine, 1929-64, chmn. dept. and chief of surgery, 1929-60, consultant to dept. of surgery, from 1964, pres. univ., 1960-63, pres. emeritus, from 1963. Dir. Cen. Carolina Bank & Trust Co. Mem. Govs.' Commn. Edn. Beyond High Sch. Served in Med. Reserve Corps, 1917-18, S.A.T.C., Sept.-Dec. 1918. Fellow A.C.S., (gov.; exec. com. of board of governors), A.M.A.; mem. American Assn. Thoracic Surgery, So. Soc. Clin. Surgeons (v.p. 1956-57, pres. 1957-58), Internat. Surg. Soc., So. Surg. Assn. (pres. 1956-57), Am. Surg. Assn., Johns Hopkins U. Soc. of Scholars, Nu Sigma Nu, Phi Beta Kappa, Alpha Omega Alpha. Democrat. Methodist. Rotarian. Contbr. numerous articles to profl. jours. Home: Durham, N.C. Died June 1, 1980.

HART, ERNEST, mfg. exec.; b. Rochester, N.Y., July 18, 1891; s. Ernest and Martha (Dannals) H.; B.S., Mich. State Coll., 1914, M. Hort., 1920, Doctor of Agriculture (hon.), 1953; m. Myra K. Timmerman, Feb. 14, 1942; 1 son, Bernard E. Technical horticulturist, Niagara Sprayer Co., Middleport, N.Y., 1914-21, v.p. and sales mgr., 1921-28; v.p. and sales mgr. Niagara Sprayer & Chem. Co., Inc., 1928-47, Niagara Chem. div., Food Machinery & Chem. Corp., July-Sept. 1947, pres. since Sept. 1947; v.p., Food Machinery & Chem. Corp., San Jose, Calif., 1947-56, pres., 1956-60, dir., 1949-66, mem. exec. com. until 1966, exec. v.p. chem divs., Food Machinery and Chem. Corp., N.Y.C, 1952-56, pres., 1956-60, dir. and mem. exec. com. until 1966. Mem. Mfg. Chemists (dir. from 1956), Nat. Agrl. Chems. Assn. (pres., dir.). Clubs: Park Country (Buffalo), Elks (Medina, N.Y.). Home: Medina, N.Y. Died Mar. 17, 1976.

HART, HENRY MAYER, banker; b. San Antonio, Jan. 28, 1884; s. Nathan and Betty (Hollis) H.; grad. Am. Inst. Banking; m. Ethel L. Levvis, Apr. 19, 1906; 1 son, William Lewis. With Nat. Bank of Commerce, San Antonio, 1900—, formerly v.p., then exec. v.p., vice chmn. exec. com. and dirs. San Antonio Symphony Soc. Mem. Am. Inst. Banking (past pres. San Antonio), Am. (past exec. council), Tex. (past treas.), bankers assns., Assn. Res. City Bankers, Investment Bankers Assn. Am. (fed. financing com.), San Antonio Clearing House Assn. (past pres.). Presbyn. (elder). Mason. Clubs: San Antonio Country, San Antonio, St. Anthony. Home: San Antonio, Tex. *

HART, PHILIP A., U.S. senator; b. Bryn Mawr, Pa., Dec. 10, 1912; s. Philip A. and Ann (Clyde) H.; A.B., Georgetown U., 1934; J.D., U. Mich., 1937; m. Jane Briggs, June 19, 1943; children—Ann Clyde, Jane Cameron, Walter Briggs, James Cox, Michael Patrick, Clyde William, Mary Catherine, Laura Elizabeth. Admitted to Mich. bar, 1938, practiced in Detroit until entering public office. Mich. Corp. and Securities commr., 1949-51; dir. Mich. OPS, 1951-52; U.S. atty. Eastern Dist. of Mich., 1952-53; lt. gov. of Mich., 1955-59; U.S. senator from Mich., 1959-76; instrumental in shaping civil rights, consumer and antitrust legislation. Legal adviser to Gov. G. Mennen Williams, 1953-54. Served to lt. col., 4th Inf. Div. AUS until 1946. Decorated Bronze Star, Purple Heart (U.S.); Croix de Guerre (France). Democrat. Home: Mackinac Island, Mich. Died Dec. 26, 1976.

HART, RALPH ALBERT, oil co. exec.; b. Cleve., Feb. 20, 1913; s. Albert Ernst and Adeline (Quere) H.; A.B., Ohio U., 1934; LL.B., Cleve. Marshall Law Sch., 1939; J.D., Cleve. State U., 1968; m. Lorna Kydd, Sept. 3, 1938; children—James, Charles, Valerie. Admitted to Ohio bar, 1939; with Standard Oil Co. (Ohio), 1934-76, asst. to pres., 1957-62, v.p., 1962-64, adminstrv. v.p., 1964-66, sr. vice pres., dir., 1966-76; dir. Sohio Petroleum Co., Boron Oil Co., Vistron Crop., Old Ben Coal Corp., BP Oil Corp. Bd. dirs. Goodwill Industries, Better Bus. Bur., Ohio Public Expenditures Council, Govtl. Research Inst. Mem. Am. Bar Assn., Am. Mgmt. Assn., Fgn. Affairs Council. Home: Lakewood, Ohio. Died July 1976.

HARTE, ROBERT ADOLPH, biochemist, info. scientist; b. N.Y.C., July 28, 1911; s. Edward A. and Sadie (Martin) H.; B.S. CCNY, 1931; m. Florence Rhea Powell, Sept. 2, 1934; 1 dau., Janet (Mrs. Robert C. Abbe) (dec.). Asst., Rockefeller Inst., N.Y.C., 1932-42; chief research chemist Arlington Chem. Co., Yonkers, N.Y., 1942-49; research adminstr. Sharp & Dohme, Inc., Glendolden and West Point, Pa., 1949-53; coordinator sci. info. Merck & Co., Inc., West Point, 1953-61; exec. officer Am. Soc. Biol. Chemists, also mgr. Jour. Biol. Chemistry, Bethesda, 1962-77; cons. to dir. Nat. Library Medicine. Exec. sec. 6th Internat. Congress Biochemistry, 1964; chmn, 31st Internat. Congress Fedn. Internat. Documentation, 1965; mem. U.S. Nat. com. Internat. Union Biochemistry, Nat. Acad. Scis.-NRC, 1957-60; mem. exec. com. Office Biochem. Nomenclature, NRC, 1963-77, chmn., 1976-77; mem. U.S. nat. com. Internat. Fedn. Documentation, 1961-69, chmn., 1968-69, councillor, 1967-72, v.p., 1973-76; dir. Phila Sci. Council, 1955-61; chmn. Gordon Research Conf. on Food and Nutrition, 1956, Gordon Research Conf. Sci. Info. Problems in Research, 1961, 69; mem. adv. com. sci. publs. USPHS, 1962-65. Mem. Am. Soc. Biol. Chemists, Am. Inst. Nutrition, Council Biology Editors (chmn. 1970), Am. Chem. Soc., Sigma Xi. Club: Cosmos. Contbr. articles to profl. jours. Home: Derwood, Md. Died Oct. 1, 1977.

HARTER, DONALD ROBERT, lawyer; b. Moravia, N.Y., Nov. 17, 1917; s. Ralph Amenzo and Mabel B. (Hull) H.; B.A. magna cum laude, Hobart Coll., 1939, LL.D., 1976; J.D. with distinction, Cornell U., 1942; m. Ruth Marion Ashdown, Sept. 6, 1941; children—Ralph M., Peter, Geoffrey, J., Laurie Susan. Admitted to N.Y. bar, 1942; asso. firm Wiser, Shaw, Freeman, Ickes & Williams and predecessor, Rochester, 1942-50, mem. firm, 1950-65; sr. partner Wiser, Shaw, Freeman, VanGraafeiland, Harter & Secrest, 1965-75; sr. partner Harter, Secrest and Emery, 1975-80. Dir. H. L. Baughman, Inc., H. L. Baughman Equipment Corp., Inc., H. L. Baughman Transit-Mix Corp., Inc., Rochester. Commr., N.Y. Commn. to Revise Laws of Estates. 1963-64. Pres. Penfield High Sch. P.T.A., 1963-64; bd. dirs. Otetiana council Boy Scouts Am., 1963-70, Dr. Ebsary Charitable Found., F.G. Ebsary Inc.; pres., bd. dirs. Estate Planning Council Rochester, 1966. Mem. finance com. Monroe County Republican Party, 1950—. Bd. dirs. Rochester Maternal and Adoption Service, 1958-65, Rochester Orthoptic Center; vice chmn. bd. trustees Hobart and William Smith Colls., 1971-79, hon. trustee, 1979-80; trustee Clifton Springs Hosp., 1968-69; pres. bd. trustees Margaret Woodbury Strong Mus.; sec. bd. dirs. Ch. Home Rochester, 1959-79; pres. alumni adv. council Cornell U. Law Sch., 1974-79; mem. corp. Rochester Community Chest; chancellor Episcopal Diocese Rochester, 1960-80; bd. govs. Genessee Hosp. Served to 1st lt. AUS, 1943-46. Fellow Am. Coll. Probate Counsel; mem. Am., N.Y., Monroe County bar assns., Am. Bar Found., Am. Judicature Soc., Hobart Coll. Alumni Assn. (pres.), Order of Coif, Phi Phi Delta Alumni Assn., Phi Beta Kappa. Episcopalian. Clubs: Kent, Oak Hill Country, Webhanet Country, Genesee Valley (pres. 1972-73) (Rochester). Mng. editor Cornell Law Quar., 1941-42; editor-in-chief Echo of the Seneca, 1939. Home: Penfield, N.Y. Died Jan. 14, 1980; buried Kennebunkport, Maine.

HARTER, DOW W(ATTERS), ex-congressman; b. Akron, O., Jan. 2, 1885; s. Josiah J. and Anna Lillian (Watters) H.; LL.B., U. of Mich., 1907; m. Winifred Marie Cole, 1911; children—Harry Allan, John David. Began law practice at Akron, O., later practiced at Washington, D.C.; member 73d to 77th Congresses (1933-43), 14th Ohio Dist. Mem. Ohio State Bar Assn., Am. Bar Assn., D.C. Bar Assn. Democrat. Episcopalian. Mason. Clubs: Akron City, Univ., National Press, The Metropolitan (Washington), Portage Country. Home: Washington. *

HARTFORD, ELLIS FORD, educator; b. Fordsville, Ky., Mar. 13, 1905; s. Ellis Casnor and Attella (Ford) H.; A.B., U. Ky., 1930, A.M., 1934; Ed.D., Harvard (Rosenwald fellow, Univ. scholar), 1942; LL.D.(hon.), Georgetown U., 1978; m. Alma Jane Barker, Dec. 23, 1939; children—Jane Barker, Ellis Ford. Prin., Williamstown (Ky.) High Sch., 1930-33; supt. Williamstown Public Schs., 1933-35; chmn. social studies dept. duPont Manual High Sch., Louisville Public Schs., 1935-39; specialist in instructional materials TVA, 1939-42; dir. Univ. schs., prof. edn., chmn. div. found U. Ky., 1946-64, on leave, head Bur. Instrn. Ky. Dept. Edn., Jan. to Sept. 1956; exec. sec. Ky. Council on Public Higher Edn., 1962-64; dean Community Coll. system, U. Ky., 1964-70, v.p. com. colls., 1970, prof. edn., 1970-74, prof. emeritus, 1974-80. Vis. prof. N.Mex. Western Coll., summers 1955-58, U. Maine, summers 1953, 57, 61, Georgetown Coll., 1974-76; cons. Ky. Dept. Edn., 1956-58; pres. Ky. Council Social Studies, 1936-38; coordinating agt. Com. Curricular Problems and Research, So. Assn. Colls. and Secondary Schs., 1946-49; pres. Ky. Assn. Colls., Secondary and Elem. Sch., 1959-60. Trustee Lincoln Found., 1959-78; mem. Ky. Adv. Council for Vocat. Edn., 1968-78. Served from lt. to lt. comdr. USNR, 1943-46; vis. expert Civil Information and Edn., G.H.Q., SCAP, Tokyo, Feb.-May, 1949. Named Adm. of Ky. Waters, 1975, Hon. Ky. col., 1977; recipient Sullivan medallion U. Ky., 1979. Mem. Am. Assn. Ret. Persons, John Dewey Soc., History Edn. Soc., Nat. Council for Social Studies, N.E.A., Kappa Delta Pi, Phi Delta Kappa (State Service award 1974). Author: Our Common Mooring, 1941; Emphasizing Moral and Spiritual Values in a Kentucky High School, 1952; Moral Values in Public Education, 1958; Planning A Teaching Career, 1958; A Plan Book for Future Teachers, 1961; Education in These United States, 1964; The Little White Schoolhouse, 1977; (with others) Citizenship Problems for Young Americans, 1938; Emphasizing Values in Five Kentucky Schools, 1954. Editor: The Public Schools, Religion, and Values, 1956. Home: Lexington, Ky. Died Jan. 30, 1980.

HARTIG, ROBERT LEE, lawyer; b. Marysville, Kans., Oct. 3, 1928; s. Henry William and Berniece May (Coffey) H.; B.S. in Geology, Kans. State U., 1953, M.S. in Geology, 1955; J.D., Duquesne U., 1963; m. Alice Rae Davis, Aug. 6, 1950; children—Alan Robert, Lawrence Lee, Glenn Stuart. Admitted to Alaska bar; geologist Mobil Oil Corp., 1954-67; asst. atty. gen., chief civil div. and natural resources sect. State of Alaska, 1967-71; practiced in Anchorage, 1971-80; partner firm Cole, Hartig, Rhodes & Norman; mem. Alaska Ho. of Reps., 1973-75. Chmn. profl. div. Community Chest, 1972; v.p. City View Little League, 1972-73, pres., 1971-72; del. Alaska Republican Conv., 1972, 76; mem. Greater Anchorage Area Borough Sch. Bd., 1974-76; bd. dirs. YMCA. Served with USNR, 1946-48, 51-52. Mem. Anchorage C. of C. (dir. 1972-78, pres. 1976-77), Am., Alaska, Wyo., D.C. bar assns., Am. Assn. Petroleum Geologists, Am. Assn.

Petroleum Landmen. Clubs: Elks, Petroleum (Anchorage). Home: Anchorage, Alaska. Died Aug. 24, 1980; cremated.

HARTIGAN, JOSEPH JOHN, bank holding co. exec.; b. N.Y.C., Nov. 30, 1915; s. Joseph and Florence (Martin) H.; B.S., St. John's U., N.Y.C., 1950; m. Mary C. Bolger, Nov. 26, 1947 (dec.); children—Mark, Bryan. Mortgage analyst East River Savs. Bank, N.Y.C., 1934-51; with Midlantic Mortgage Corp., Newark, 1951-75, sr. v.p., to 1975; v.p., corp. sec., risk and ins. mgr. Midlantic Banks Inc., West Orange, N.J., 1975-80. Served to capt., inf. U.S. Army, 1942-46. Decorated Silver Star. Mem. Am. Soc. Corp. Secs., Risk and Ins. Mgmt. Soc. Home: Livingston, N.J. Died Mar. 25, 1980.

HARTMAN, CHARLES DUDLEY, army officer; b. Brookhaven, Miss., Aug. 22, 1886; s. Frank Hiram and Mary (Eitel) H.; B.S., U.S. Mil. Acad., 1908; M.B.A., Harvard, 1929; m. Marjorie Tripp, Jan. 22, 1913; children—Charles Dudley, Joseph Wentworth. Commd. 2d lt., Inf., U.S. Army, 1908, and advanced through the grades to brig. gen., Aug. 1, 1940; with 3d Inf., Spokane, Wash., 1908; active service, Moro insurrection, P.I.; returned to U.S., 1912; assigned to Madison Barracks, N.Y.; served during Tex. border trouble; O.T.C., Madison Barracks, 1917; maj. Q.M. Corps, Washington, D.C., in charge Repair and Operation Div. constructing housing for all troops in World War, 1917-19 (awarded D.S.M.); Graves Registration, 1919-20; asst. dir., later dir., sales of surplus war materials, 1920-24; duty Fort Myer, Va., 1924-26; exec. officer constrn., Office Q.M. Gen., 1934-35; Gen. Staff, War Dept., 1935-38; exec. officer constrn., 1938-39; supt. Army Transport Service, San Francisco, 8 months; chief constrn., Office Q.M. Gen., 1940-41; comd. Q.M. Replacement Training Center, May 1941-June 1943; retired from active duty April 1943, as brig. general. Home: Washington, D.C. *

HARTMANN, ARTHUR (MARTINUS), violinist; b. Hungary, July 23, 1882; s. Sigmond and Peppi (Schweiger) H.; began study of music under father, at 3 1/2 yrs. of age; m. Claire Marie Tucker, of Paris, France, Dec. 21, 1909; children—Gregory Kemènyi, Helen Elizabeth. Has toured in every country of Europe and throughout U.S.; appeared as soloist with the leading orchestras, and in recitals, in Paris, with Claude Debussy; leader Hartmann String Quartet. Decorated Order of Bene Merenti, 1st class; Comdr. St. Sava (Servia). Theosophist. Club: Bohemian (New York). Wrote essay on the Chaconne of Bach, which has been translated into 14 langs.Composer violin pieces, songs, choruses, piano pieces, etc.*

HARTSON, LOUIS D(UNTON), educator; born Anamosa, Ia., Nov. 24, 1885; s. Dewitt Wellington and Mary Eleanor (Dunton) H.; Ph.B., Grinnell (Ia.) Coll., 1908; Pd.M., N.Y. Univ., 1909; Ph.D., Clark Univ., 1911; student Columbia, 1909-10, summers 1913, 1918, Univ. Lyon, 1919, Univ. Vienna, 1933-34; m. Mary Reed, June 24, 1914; children—Dorothy Helen, Robert, Mary Elizabeth (Mrs. Robert Anthony Ryan). Instr. psychology and edn., Grinnell Coll., 1911-13, asst. prof., 1913-17, asso. prof., 1917-23; asst. prof. psychology, Oberlin Coll., 1923-25, asso. prof., 1925-27, prof., 1927-52, prof. emeritus since 1952, head dept., 1939-51; lecturer on psychology Ohio State University, 1952-53; associate professor education, Univ. Mont., summers 1922, 1923; asso. prof. psychology, Ohio State University, summer 1932. Fellow Am. Psychol. Assn.; member Ohio Acad. Sci. (vice pres. 1932, 42), Psychometric Soc.; Phi Beta Kappa, Sigma Xi. Independent. Conglist. Home: Columbus. *

HARTSON, NELSON THOMAS, lawyer; b. Spokane, Wash., Nov. 26, 1887; s. Millard T. and Margaret S. (Roberson) H.; LL.B., U. Wash., 1912; m. Vera C. Bobbitt, Mar. 5, 1925 (dec. Nov. 1960); m. 2d, Elizabeth Robinson de Sibour, July 9, 1963. Practice law, Seattle, 1912; asst. corp. counsel City Seattle, 1919-22; apptd. asst. solicitor IRS, Washington, 1922, solicitor, 1923-25; sr. partner Hogan & Hartson, 1925-73; gen. counsel, dir. Riggs Nat. Bank, 1944-68; adv. dir. Woodward and Lothrop; gen. counsel D.C. Bankers Assn., 1944-59; counsel Washington, D.C. Clearing House Assn., 1944-59; prof. taxation Georgetown U. Law Sch., 1934-36. Pres. U. Washington Alumni Assn., 1920-21. Gov., Menninger Found., Topeka; mem. exec. com., chmn., dir. D.C. chpt. ARC, chmn, Washington regional blood program, 1960-61. Trustee, v.p. D.C. Public Library, 1947-66, Washington Hosp. Center (hon.); hon. mem. chpt. Protestant Episcopal Cathedral Found., Washington. Entered first O.T.C. at the Presidio, San Francisco, May 12, 1917; commd. 2d lt. and assigned to machine gun co. 363d Inf., 91st Div.; served with A.E.F. in France; advanced to capt. and adj. 316th Ammunition Train; hon. discharged, May 26, 1919. Fellow Am. Bar Found.; mem. Am., D.C. bar assns. Washington Inst. Fgn. Affairs, SAR, Columbia Hist. Soc., Phi Delta Phi, Sigma Delta Chi, Phi Delta Theta. Republican. Episcopalian. Clubs: Metropolitan (president 1960-62). Alibi, Alfalfa (pres. 1957-58), National Press, Lawyers (pres. 1958-59). Rotary (Washington); Bohemian (San Francisco). Home: Washington, D.C. Died Nov. 8, 1976.

HARTWELL, OLIVER WHITCOMB, hydraulic engr.; b. Somerville, Mass., July 5, 1886; s. Haywood and Mary Reed (Whitcomb) H.; A.B. magna cum laude, Harvard, 1908; m. Gladys E. Wood, Feb. 12, 1912; children—Mary Louise, James Haywood, Oliver Whitcomb, Carolyn W. Asst. Mass. Bd. Health, 1908-09; with water resources div. U.S. Geol. Survey, 1909-56, dist. engr., Harrisburg, Pa., 1919-21, Trenton, N.J., 1921-56; cons. on water resources problems, 1956—. Member Am. Society C.E. (national dir. 1953-56), Harvard Engring. Soc. Methodist (chmn. finance com.; financial sec.). Home: Trenton, N.J. *

HARVEY, CHARLES DAGGETT, restaurant exec.; b. Chgo., Nov. 24, 1906: s. Byron Schermerhorn and Helen (Daggett) H.; grad. St. Mark's Sch., A.B., Yale, 1928; J.D., Northwestern U., 1933: m. Jean Wilhelm, June 22, 1935 (dec. Apr. 1969); children—Jean (Mrs. Alfred G. Vanderbilt), Daggett, Melissa; m. 2d, Jane W. Wood, Aug. 18, 1972. Admitted to Ill. bar, 1933; asso. Sidley, McPherson, Austin & Burgess, Chgo., 1933-42; v.p. Fred Harvey, Inc., Chgo., 1946-55, vice chmn., 1955-65, chmn., 1965-71; dir. Amfac, Inc., Baxter Labs. Mem. Chgo. Crime Commn., Ill. Arts Council, Chgo. Commn. on Human Relations; bd. govs. Urban Gateways. Chmn., dir. Chgo. Maternity Center; bd. dirs. Gt. Books Found., Prentice Women's Hosp. and Maternity Center of Chgo., Inst. for Philos. Research, Lincoln Park Zool. Soc., Chgo. Acad. Sci., Norwestern Meml. Hosp; vice-chmn., dir. Adlai E. Stevenson Inst. Internat. Affairs; chmn, exec. com., bd. dirs. Lyric Opera Chgo.; trustee Northwestern U., Chgo. Orchestral Assn., Lake Forest Coll., Shedd Aquarium; nat. bd. dirs. Santa Fe Opera Co. Served as lt. comdr. USNR, 1942-45. Decorated chevalier French Legion of Honor. Mem. Chgo. Council Fgn. Relations, Art Inst. Chgo., Chgo. Bar Assn. Episcopalian. Clubs: Confrerie des Chevaliers du Tastevin, Commonwealth, Law, Commercial, Wayfarers, Chicago, Caxton, Mid-Am., Tavern, Saddle and Cycle (Chgo.). Home: Chicago, Ill. Died Nov. 10, 1976.

HARVEY, JASPER ELLIOTT, govt. ofcl., educator; b. Sweetwater, Tex., July 15, 1924; s. Wiley James and Julia Mae (Nolen) H.; B.A., U. Tex., 1950, M.Ed., 1952, Ph.D., 1960; m. Kathryn McDaniel, Nov. 27, 1947; children—Laurel, Leigh. Dir. spl. edn., Texas City, Tex., 1952-53; spl. edn. tchr. disturbed and retarded, Austin, Tex., 1953-54; dir. Variety Sch. Exceptional Children, Las Vegas, 1954-57, lectr. spl. edn. U. Tex., summer 1954, advanced grad. student, research asso. ednl. psychology, 1957-59, lectr. ednl. psychology, summers 1958, 59; chmn. dept. spl. edn. U. Ala., 1959-69, prof., 1963-69; chmn. dept. spl. edn. U. Tex. Coll. Edn., 1969-73, prof., 1969-76; dir. div. personnel preparation Bur. of Edn. for the Handicapped, U.S. Office Edn., HEW, 1976-79, Dept. Edn., 1979-80; cons. in field, 1963-80. Mem. adv. bd. handicapped children project So. Regional Edn. Bd., 1964-68; Ala. rep. Am. Assn. Mental Deficiency, 1966-69; field reader U.S. Office Edn., 1966-76; mem. exec. com. Ala. Gov.'s Com. Statewide Plan Vocational Rehab., 1966-69; gov. bd. Council Exceptional Children, Reston, Va., 1967-69, 72-74, chmn. govt. relations com., 1972-74, 1st v.p., 1974-75, pres. elect, 1975-76, pres., 1976; program chmn. 54th Ann. Internat. Council Exceptional Children Conv., Chgo., 1976; interim com. Reorgn. Ala. Dept. Edn., 1967-69; chmn. med. profl. adv. and evaluation bd. United Cerebral Palsy Ala., 1966-69; adv. bd. mental retardation Ala. Bd. Mental Health, 1967-69; rep. White House Conf. Mental Retardation, 1963; spl. edn. communications systems task force Bur. Edn. for Handicapped; adv. bd. Nat. Center Law and Handicapped, 1972-76; chmn. staff devel. com. of profl. services program com. United Cerebral Palsy Assns., N.Y.C., 1975-76; mem. nat. adv. com. on hyperkinesis Nutrition Found. N.Y., 1974-76. Served with AUS, 1944-46. Decorated Combat Med. badge. Mem. Council Exceptional Children, Am. Assn. Mental Deficiency, Am. Psychol. Assn., Am. Speech and Hearing Assn., Am. Acad. for Cerebral Palsy and Developmental Medicine, Phi Kappa Phi. Episcopalian. Author reports, chpts. and articles in field. Home: Washington, D.C. Died Nov. 26, 1980.

HARVEY, M. J., pipe mfg. co. exec.; b. Center, Tex., 1898; married. With Tyler Pipe Industries, Inc., Tyler, Tex., from 1935, pres., chmn. bd., 1937-65, chmn. bd., from 1965, also dir.; dir. Tyler Bank & Trust Co., Tyler Corp. Home: Tyler, Tex. Died Nov. 24, 1977.

HARWI, FRANK EDWIN, wholesale hardware; b. Atchison, Kan., Oct. 11, 1884; s. Alfred Jonathan and Elizabeth (Whitehead) H.; prep. edn. Atchison High Sch., Midland Coll. and Phillips Acad., Andover, Mass.; student Yale, 1 yr., U. of Kan., 1 yr.; m. 3d, Jessie Burnette, of Wichita, May 1, 1934; children (by former marriage)—Alfred J. (dec.), Lucy E., Frank E., Robert C. In hardware business since 1910; pres. The A. J. Harwi Hardware Co., Atchison, Kan.; chmn. bd. Exchange Nat. Bank. Mem. Phi Gamma Delta, Chamber of Commerce (dir.). Republican. Episcopalian. Rotarian. Address: Atchison, Kan.*

HARWOOD, ALBERT LESLIE, JR., lawyer; b. Newton, Mass., Aug. 7, 1884; s. Albert L. and Jennie C. (Davis) H.; A.B., Harvard, 1905, LL.B., 1908; m. Hattie Kistler, Dec. 2, 1908; children—Henry, Hugh. Admitted to Mass. bar, 1907; practice of law, Boston, 1908—; partner Harwood & Gray; hon. chmn., dir. Drexel Furniture Co.; pres. Tanner Trading Co., 1947—, Am. Tanners, Ltd., 1948—; mem. of bd. directors Morganton Hosiery Co. Former pres. Newton Community Chest, Norumbega council Boy Scouts Am. Trustee Newton UMCA. Recipient Silver Beaver award Boy Scouts of America. Member American Judicature Society, American, Mass., Boston bar assns. Club: Harvard (Boston). Home: Newton Centre, Mass. *

HASBROOK, CHARLES PHILLIPS, b. Kansas City, Mo., Oct. 28, 1884; s. Charles Electus and Delia (Ekins) H.; ed. U. of Minn.; m. 2d, Marcia Beamer, Nov. 27, 1937. Pres. and pub. The Burlington Daily News and Broadcasting Sta. WCAX, Burlington, Vt. Home: Jericho, Vt. *

HASBROUCK, LOUISE SEYMOUR, writer, editor; b. Ogdensburg, N.Y., May 8, 1883; d. Louis and Emmeline E. (Knap) H.; Wellesley Coll., 1900-02; m. Bruno Louis Zimm, sculptor, Oct. 28, 1919; 1 son, Bruno Hasbrouck Zimm. Asst. editor Good Housekeeping, 1911-12. Professional genealogist; contbg. mem. N.Y. Geneal. and Biog. Soc.; trustee Ulster Co. (N.Y.) Hist. Soc.; ex-pres. Woodstock Historical Society. Member Long Island Historical Soc., N.Y. State Historical Assn., Descendants New Platz Patentees. Author: LaSalle, 1916; Israel Putnam, 1916; Chokecherry Island, 1917; Hall with Doors, 1920; Mexico From Cortez to Carranza, 1918; Those Careless Kincaids, 1928; At the Sign of the Wild Horse, 1929; Hoodooed Inn (serial). Compiler: Boy's Parkman, 1912; Rivals for America (from Parkman), 1915; Insect Adventures (from J. H. Fabre), 1917. Contbr. to historical periodicals. Home: Woodstock, N.Y.*

HASELTON, NORRIS SWIFT, fgn. service officer; b. Cleveland, Oct. 27, 1902; s. Hyatt S. and Almena (Doolittle) H.; grad. Lawrenceville Sch., 1921; A.B., Princeton, 1925; m. Elizabeth Garrett, Mar. 11, 1933; 1 son, Norris S. Fgn. service officer since 1935; consular and diplomatic officer in Mexico, Eng., India, Chile, Brazil, New Zealand; also duty in Dept. of State and as adviser Naval War Coll., Newport, R.I.; inspector gen. Fgn. Service, 1962-64. Clubs: Capital Yacht, Metropolitan (Washington). Home: Washington, D.C. Died Apr. 10, 1981.

HASKELL, DOUGLAS, editor; b. Monastir, Turkey, June 27, 1899 (parents Am. citizens); s. Edward Bell and Martha (Miller) H.; A.B., Oberlin Coll., 1923, D.F.A. (hon.), 1961; m. Helen Lacey, Aug. 22, 1924. Asst. editor Creative Art mag., 1928; asst. editor, contbr., sr. asso. editor Archtl. Record, 1929-49; archtl. editor Archtl. Forum, 1949-51, editorial chmn., 1952-54, editor, 1955-64; lectr. Pratt Inst., 1950-51; adj. prof. Columbia Sch. Architecture, 1960-63; mem. Pres.'s Council on Pennsylvania Ave., 1962-64; vis. lectr., critic at archtl. schs. various univs. and colls.; vice chmn. archtl. adv. com. Pub. Housing Adminstrn., 1949-50. Hon. bd. dirs. Am. Farm Sch., Thessaloniki, Greece, 1978-79. Fellow AIA (spl. citation N.Y. chpt. 1978, medal for contbrs. to archtl. practice 1979); mem. Soc. Archtl. Historians, N.Y. Archtl. League, Assn. Collegiate Schs. Architecture, Mcpl. Art Soc. N.Y., Nat. Council Chs. (archtl. adv. com.), Citizens Union N.Y. Clubs: Nat. Arts, Univ. Editor: Rehousing Urban America (Henry Wright), 1935; Building U.S.A., 1957; contbr. articles to archtl. publs., popular mags. Address: New York, N.Y. Died Aug. 11, 1979.

HASKINS, JOHN CHRISTOPHER, music critic; b. St. Joseph, Mo., Sept. 2, 1918; s. Aaron Benjamin and Margaret (Feld) H.; B.Mus., Cath. U. Am., 1950, M.A., 1952; m. Margaret Varda, Sept. 20, 1945; 1 dau., Maria Caterina. Music critic Washington Times-Herald, 1952-54; contbg. music critic Washington Post, 1954-59; program specialist Pan Am. Union, 1955; music dir. radio sta. WGMS, Washington, 1956-57; contract script writer Voice of Am. USIA, 1957-59, 61-65; cultural attache U.S. embassy, Ottawa, Ont., Can., 1959-61; contbg. music critic Washington Evening Star, 1961-65; instr. music dept. George Washington U., 1964-65; music editor Kansas City (Mo.) Star, 1965-77; lectr. Conservatory Music, U. Mo. at Kansas City, 1965-71. Served with USNR, 1942-46; PTO. Recipient resolution Mo. Ho. of Reps., 1977. Mem. Music Critics Assn. (sec.), Nat. Press Club, Inter-Am. Assn. Music Critic (a founder 1976). Contbr. articles to profl. publs. Home: Kansas City, Mo. Died Sept. 16, 1977; interred Nat. Cemetery, Fort Leavenworth, Kans.

HASLER, FREDERICK EDWARD, banker; b. Wethersfield, Essex, Eng., Feb. 27, 1882; s. Thomas and Jane Chatterson (Banyard) H.; ed. pvt. schs. England; M.A. (hon.), Bowdoin Coll., 1943; LL.D., Columbia, 1955, Trinity College, Conn., 1957; married Marguerite Isabel Messent, Sept. 5, 1912; children—Audrey, Shirley, Marjory. Came to U.S., 1901, naturalized, 1919. Began as clk., London, 1899; chartering clk. J. H. Winchester & Co., New York, 1903-06; mgr. Am.

Smelters S.S. Co., 1906-08; asst. to pres. Chesapeake & Ohio Coal & Coke Co., 1908-09; sr. partner Hasler Bros., 1909-23; v.p. Bank of America, 1923-26; pres. Internat. Trust Co., 1929-31; became chmn. exec. com. Continental Bank & Trust Company, 1931, chmn. bd., 1941-48; chmn. U.S. bd. N. Brit. & Merc. Ins. Co. Ltd. and subsidiaries, 1946-61; cons., mem. adv. com. of bd., mem. Lower Manhattan adv. bd. Chem. Bank N.Y. Trust Co.; chmn. Haytian Am. Sugar Co., S.A., 1938-67, now dir.; chmn., dir. Signet Fund (Bermuda) Ltd., 1957-68; chmn., dir. Hermes Enterprises, Ltd. (Bermuda); dir. La Plantation Dauphin, S.A., Haiti West Indies Co., ECL Industries, Ltd., Haitian Am. Devel. Corp., S.A.; incorporator Litchfield Savs. Soc. Trustee Sch. Indsl. Relations, Cornell U., 1943-45, Leake and Watts Children's Home, St. Margaret's Sch. and others; hon. dir. Americas Found.; dir. Inter-Am. Literacy Found. and others; pres. C. of C. State of New York, 1942-44, now hon. life mem. Pan Am. Soc. U.S., 1940-46, now hon. pres., dir.; Decorated Honneur et Merite (Haiti); Orden del Merito Comercial (Cuba); Orden del Libertador Bolivar (Venezuela); Orden Nacional do Cruzeiro do Sul (Brazil); Sul Orden Mexicana del Aguila Azteca (Mexico); Orden al Merito (Ecuador), Orden Nacional del Merito de Carlos Manuel de Cespedes (Cuba), Orden del Condor de los Andes (Bolivia); Orden de Cristobal Colon, Orden del Merito Juan Pablo Duarte (Dominican Republic), Orden de Vasco Nunez de Balboa (Panama); Orden de Ruben Dario (Nicaragua), others. Episcopalian. Clubs: Pilgrims, University (N.Y.C. Home: Washington Depot, Conn.; also, N.Y.C. *

HASSRICK, ROMAIN CALVIN, lawyer; b. Shumans, Pa., June 28, 1885; s. John Frederick and Mary (Brown) H.; A.B., Bucknell U., 1906; student U. of Pa., 1914; m. Ethel Mildred Royal, Oct. 20, 1914; children—Royal Brown, Kenneth R., Diana (Mrs. William A. Goff, Jr.); m. 2d, Blanche Hoffman Scott, Sept. 21, 1937. Newspaper reporter, Williamsport (Pa.) News, 1906-08, North American, Phila., Pa., 1908-12; polit. editor, Pub. Ledger, Phila., Pa., 1912-16; admitted to Pa. bar, 1914; asst. city solicitor, Phila., Pa., 1921; chief and organizer Municipal Bur. of Legal Aid, Dept. Pub. Welfare, Phila., Pa., 1922-28; chmn. Registration Commn. of Phila., 1931-35; counsel Pa. Sabbath Sch. Assn., Inc.; dir. and counsel Baptist Orphanage of Phila.; counsel and dir. Lord's Day Alliance of Pa. Capt., Ordnance Dept., U.S. Army, 1917-18. Pres. Bucknell Alumni Club of Phila., Phila. Alumni chapter Sigma Chi. Mem. Art Alliance, Pennsylvania, Philadelphia bar associations, National Association of Legal Aid Organization (exec. com.), Sigma Chi Found. (pres.). Clubs: Kiwanis (pres. 1959—), Constitutional, Union League (Phila.). Home: Bryn Mawr, Pa. *

HASTIE, WILLIAM HENRY, judge; b. Knoxville, Tenn., Nov. 17, 1904; s. William Henry and Roberta (Child) H.; A.B., Amherst Coll., 1925, A.M. (hon.), 1940, LL.D. (hon.), 1960; LL.B., Harvard U., 1930, S.J.D., 1933; LL.D. (hon.) Hampton Inst., 1946, Va. State Coll., 1947, Lincoln U., 1950, Ohio Wesleyan, 1951, Knoxville Coll., 1952, Rutgers U., 1953, Howard U., 1955, Yale U., 1957, Central State Coll., 1959, Temple U., 1961, U. Pa., Atlanta U., 1964; m. Beryl Lockhart, Dec. 25, 1943; children—Karen Roberta, William Henry. Admitted to bar, 1930; practiced law, 1930-33; asst. solicitor Dept. of Interior, 1933-37; judge Dist. Ct. V.I., 1937-39; dean Howard U. Sch. of Law, 1939-46; civilian adie to the sec. of war, 1940-42; gov. of V.I., 1946-49; judge 3d U.S. Circuit Ct. of Appeals, 1949-71. Mem. Caribbean Commn., 1947-51. Trustee Amherst Coll. Fellow Am. Acad. Arts and Scis; mem. Phi Beta Kappa, Omega Psi Phi. Mason. Home: Philadelphia, Pa. Died Apr. 14, 1976.

HASTINGS, EDWIN KILPATRICK, hotel exec.; b. Bklyn., Feb. 13, 1903; s. Thomas G. and Florence (Kilpatrick) H.; student Richmond Hill (N.Y.) Bus. Coll.; m. Nancy W. Stahlman, June 1, 1942. Cruise dir. Hamburg-Am. Line, 1926-34; cruise dir., Western mgr. Raymond-Whitcomb, 1934-40; mgr., v.p. The Waldorf-Astoria Hotel; N.Y.C., 1940-55; v.p. hotels Matson Nav. Co., Honolulu, 1955-60; gen. mgr. The Barkley and Park Lane Hotels, N.Y.C., 1960; v.p. Pacific, Hilton Hotels Internat., v.p., gen. mgr. Hilton Hawaiian Village, Honolulu, 1961-77; exec. v.p. Hilton-Burns Hotel Co., Inc., 1965-77; sr. v.p. Hawaiian div. Hilton Hotels Corp., 1966-77. Mem. Nat. Tourism Resources Rev. Commn., 1971-73. Bd. dirs. Hawaii Visitor's Bur. Served from 1st lt. to lt. col. USAAF, 1942-46; CBI; col. Res. Mem. Am. Soc. Travel Agts. (chmn. Am. hotel com.), Am. Hotel Assn., Mil. Order World Wars, Am. Legion, Hawaii Hotel Assn. (pres. 1959, dir.). Clubs: Skal, Waialae Country, Pacific. Home: Honolulu, Hawaii. Died Feb. 1977.

HASTINGS, JOHN SIMPSON, judge; b. Washington, Ind., June 30, 1898; s. Elmer Ellsworth and Bertha Jane (Garten) H.; B.S., U.S. Mil. Acad., West Point, 1920; LL.B., Ind. U., 1924, LL.D., 1959; LL.D., Northwestern U., 1961; m. Mary Esther Smiley, June 2, 1925; children—William Elmer and James Roland (twins). Admitted to Ind. bar, 1924, practiced in Washington, Ind.; mem. Hastings, Allen & Hastings, 1924-57; judge U.S. Ct. of Appeals, 7th Circuit, Chgo., 1957-77, chief judge, 1959-68, sr. judge, 1969-77, temp. emergency Ct. Appeals U.S., 1972-77. Hon. dir. Ind. U. Found., v.p., 1951; trustee Ind. U., 1936-59, pres. bd., 1950-59; mem. Ind. State Bd. Law Examiners, 1949-54, pres., 1951. Gov. Riley Hosp. Crippled Children, Indpls. Recipient Ill. Lincoln medal, 1967. Mem. Am., Ill., Ind. (past gov.), Chgo., 7th Circuit bar assns., Chicago Law Club, Ind. U. Alumni Assn. (past pres.), Am. Legion, Am. Law Inst., Am. Judicature Soc., Chgo. West Point Soc., Order of the Coif, Phi Beta Kappa, Phi Delta Phi, Sigma Delta Chi, Phi Gamma Delta. Republican. Presbyn. Mason, Rotarian (hon.). Clubs: Union League, Legal, Standard. Home: Chicago, Ill. Died Feb. 7, 1977; interred Oak Grove Cemetery, Washington, Ind.

HATCH, CHESTER ELBERT, cotton mfr.; b. Salem, Mass., Feb. 21, 1882; s. Elbert J. and Marion (Trull) H.; student Furman U., Greenville, S.C., 1900-01; m. Maybelle Sunderland, Sept. 20, 1905; 1 son, Chester Elbert. Cotton mill operative Pelham, S.C., 1897-98; shipping clerk Pelham, S.C., 1898-1904; shipping clerk Brandon Corp., cotton mfrs., Greenville, S.C., 1904-08, sec., 1908-14, gen. mgr., 1914-28, vice president and assistant treasurer, 1928-35; president and treasurer, 1935-47, chmn. bd. since 1947; director Peoples Nat. Bank, Piedmont and Northern Ry. Co., Camperdown Co., Piedmont Plush Mills, Textile Hall Corp. Clubs: Poinsett, Country (Greenville, S.C.) Home: Greenville, S.C. *

HATCH, WILLIAM HENRY PAINE, theologian; b. Camden, N.J., Aug. 2, 1875; s. Adolphus D. and Rose M. (Powell) H.; A.B., Harvard, 1898, A.M., 1899, Ph.D., 1904, S.T.B., 1906; B.D., Episcopal Theol. Sch., Cambridge, Mass., 1902; D.D., in course, Union Theol. Sem., New York, 1915, D. Theol., Strasbourg, 1925; m. Marion Louise Townsend, Sept. 5, 1906; 1 son, Rt. Rev. Robert McConnell. Ordained, P.E. Ch., 1902; asst. St. Philip's Ch., Cambridge, Mass., 1902-03; rector St. James's Ch., Lake George, N.Y., 1904-05, Ch. of Our Redeemer, Lexington, Mass., 1905-08; instr. in lit. and interpretation of N.T., 1908-09, adj. prof., 1909-13, prof. lang. and lit. of N.T., 1913-17, Gen. Theol. Sem., N.Y.; prof. lit. and interpretation of N.T., Episcopal Theol. Sch., 1917-46; vicar Christ Church, Boston, Mass., 1941-46. Annual professor American School of Oriental Research, Jerusalem, 1922-23, lecturer, 1928-29. Visiting prof. of divinity, University of Toronto, 1944. Candidate for N.Y. legislature in 1903. Fellow Am. Academy of Arts and Sciences; member American Oriental Society, Society Biblical Literature and Exegesis (president 1938), Mediaeval Academy of America, Phi Beta Kappa. Democrat. Clubs: Faculty, Twenty Club, Ministers' Club (Boston); Randolph Mountain Club (Randolph, N.H.). Author: The Pauline Idea of Faith, 1917; The Gospel Manuscripts of the General Theological Seminary (with C. C. Edmunds), 1918; The Idea of Faith in Christian Literature from the Death of Saint Paul to the Close of the Second Century, 1925; Greek and Syrian Miniatures in Jerusalem, 1931; The Greek Manuscripts of the New Testament at Mount Sinai, 1932; The Greek Manuscripts of the New Testament in Jerusalem, 1934; The "Western" Text of the Gospels, 1937; The Principal Uncial Manuscripts of the New Testament, 1939; An Album of Dated Syriac Manuscripts, 1946; Facsimiles and Descriptions of Minuscule Manuscripts of the New Testament (in press); also numerous articles, monographs and revs. Home: Randolph, N.H. Died Nov. 11, 1972; buried Randolph.

HATCH, WINSLOW ROPER, coll. dean; b. Lexington, Mass., Mar. 1, 1908; s. Roy Winthrop and Bertha May (Roper) H.; A.B., Dartmouth, 1930; Ph.D., Johns Hopkins, 1934; m. Dita Alvarado Keith, June 30, 1937; children—Robert Winslow, John Keith, Rosita Alvarado. Instr. botany Johns Hopkins, 1934-35; instr., dir. Ross Garey Biol. Field Sta., Johns Hopkins, summer 1935; Nat. Research fellow in botany Harvard, 1935-36; instr. botany Dartmouth, 1936-39; asst. prof., head dept. botany State Coll. Wash., 1939, asso prof., 1941, prof., 1945, chmn. div. of biol. scis., 1949, asso. dean Coll. of Scis. and Art, 1953-55; dean Coll. Gen. Edn., Boston U., 1955-57; dir. clearing house of studies on higher edn. Office Edn., Dept. Health, Edn., Welfare, Washington, author, editor New Dimensions in Higher Edn.; collector Johns Hopkins Expdn. to Am. Tropics, 1932-34. Mem. Am. Mycol. Soc., Bot. Soc. Am., A.A.A.S., Sigma Xi, Phi Kappa Phi, Phi Gamma Delta, Phi Beta Kappa. Editor: Northwest Sci., 1944-55; nat. editorial adv. bd. Improving College and Univ. Teaching. Author: Inquiry (series 7 articles improving coll. and univ. teaching); contbr. articles to sci. publs. Home: McLean, Va. Died May 18, 1980; buried Princeton, Mass.

HATCHETT, STEPHEN PINCKNEY, govt. ofcl.; b. Mogollon, N.Mex., June 30, 1915; s. Samuel Pinckney and Annie Margaret (Huther) H.; A.B., Am. U., 1937; A.M., U. Mich., 1938, Ph.D., 1943; m. Dorothy Belle Chandler, July 16, 1945; children—Stephen Pinckney, Anne Elizabeth (Mrs. Mark W. Owen). Prof. biology Presbyn. Coll., S.C., 1946-47; asst. prof. biology Am. U., 1947-48, asso. prof., 1948-50, prof., 1950-55, chmn. dept. biology, 1947-55, chmn. div. natural sci., 1948-53; asst. chief career devel. rev. br. NIH Div. Research Grants, Bethesda, Md., 1955-58, chief, 1958-63, dep. dir. div. research grants, 1963-69, dir. div. research grants, 1969-76. Fellow A.A.A.S.; mem. Soc. Systemic Zoology, Am. Soc. Limnology and Oceanography, Nat. Assn. Biology Tchrs., Am. Micros. Soc., Sigma Xi, Beta Beta Beta, Phi Kappa Phi, Phi Sigma, Alpha Sigma Phi. Home: Bethesda, Md. Died Aug. 22, 1976.

HATFIELD, W. WILBUR, editor and teacher; b. Pittsfield, Ill., Apr. 1, 1882; s. Walter R. and Margaret (Hunter) H.; A.B., Illinois Coll., 1902; Litt.D., (hon.), Chgo. Tchrs. Coll., 1939; student (intermittently) U. Chgo., 1905-12, Columbia U., 1919-20; m. Grace Harriet Chamberlain, Aug. 22, 1907; children—Jean Carleton (Mrs. Wendell F. Barclay), Ruth Harriet (Mrs. Merlin F. Starkweather). Instr., Fairmount Coll., 1906, Parker High Sch., Chgo., 1912-15; instr. Chgo. Tchrs. Coll., 1915-21, head English dept. 1921-47; asso. editor, The English Journal, 1917-21, editor from 1922; editor College English from 1939. Member National Council Teachers of English (sec.-treas. 1920-53), MLA, Nat. Conf. on Research in English, Conf. on College Composition and Communication. Editor: Experience Curriculum in Eng., 1935. Author books; coauthor books including: A Grammar of Living English, 1939. Home: Chicago, Ill. Died Apr. 27, 1976.

HATHAWAY, ALTON HASTINGS, wholesale baking; b. Cambridge, Mass., May 4, 1882; s. Charles Francis and Carrie Trull (Hastings) H.; ed. pub. schs.; student Harvard, 1899-1900; m. Bertha Louise Hannah, May 26, 1906; children—Frederick Hannah (dec.), Alton Hastings, Persis, Anne, Jane. In baking business, 1911-35; president, Hathaway & Son, Inc.; president of Hathaway Baking Company since 1926; president Hathaway Bakeries, Inc. Served as state chairman of Bakers' Service Com., U.S. Food Adminstrn., World War. Mem. Nuttall Ornithol. Club. Unitarian. Elk. Home: Bedford, Mass. *

HATHAWAY, EDWARD STURTEVANT, prof. zoology; b. Maryville, Tenn., Oct. 17, 1886; s. William Evans and Martha Taylor (Ashley) H.; A.B., U. of Cincinnati, 1909; A.M., U. of Wis., 1921, Ph.D., 1925; m. Martha Emma Gahagan, June 9, 1919; children—Edward Gahagan (dec.), Marcia Carolyn. Prof. biology, Tusculum Coll., 1911-22; instr. zoölogy, U. of Wis., 1923-25; asso. prof. zoölogy, Tulane U., 1925-27, prof. since 1927, dir. division of biological sciences, since 1945. Served as 2d lieut., later 1st lieut. and capt., U.S. Army, World War. Mem. Soc. for Exptl. Biology and Medicine, Ecol. Soc. America, Am. Soc. Ichthyologists and Herpetologists, Am. Soc. Parasitologists, Entomol. Soc. America, Nat. Malaria Soc., Wildlife Soc., Sigma Xi, Gamma Alpha, Phi Sigma. Contbr. repts. of researches on fishes and ecology of marsh lands. Home: New Orleans, La. *

HATHAWAY, GAIL ABNER, civil engr.; b. Menomonie, Wis., Oct. 11, 1895; s. Lewis and Myrtle Estelle (Crossman) H.; B.S.C.E., Oreg. State Coll., 1922; D.Eng. (hon.), Drexel Inst. Tech., 1951; m. Mary R. Peterson, Sept. 21, 1917; children—(twins) Norman Edward, Neal Leroy, Geraldine. Constrn. engr. various pvt. constrn. cos., 1919-22, public bodies, 1922-28; with Corps of Engrs., U.S. Army, 1928-57, field assignments, 1928-37, chief reservoir regulation, and hydrology sect., Office Chief of Engrs., Washington, 1937-45; spl. asst. to chief of engrs., Dept. Army on flood control, river and harbor project planning and constrn. programs Office Chief Engrs., Washington, 1945-57; engring. cons. Internat. Bank Reconstrn., Devel., 1957-63; engaged in practice as consulting engineer, from 1963. With USNG, 65th regt. Army Arty. Corps in France, World War I; chmn. U.S. Commn. on Large Dams, 1948-52, pres. Internat. Commn. on Large Dams, 1952-58; chmn. U.S. nat. com. World Power Conf., 1952-58, vice chmn. internat. exec. council, World Power Conf., 1952-58; U.S. mem. Internat. Lake Ontario Bd. Engrs., Internat. Joint Commn., 1953-59; chmn. U.S. sect. Internat. St. Lawrence River Bd. Control Internat. Joint Commn., 1954-57, Mem. ASCE (pres. 1951), Soc. Am. Mil. Engrs., Am. Geophys. Union, Am. Meteorol. Soc., Engineers Joint Council, Sigma Tau, Tau Beta Pi. Clubs: Columbia Country, Cosmos (Washington, D.C.). Mason (K.T.). Contbr. to prof. jours. Home: Hyattsville, Md. Died Oct. 1, 1979.

HATZFELD, HELMUT ANTHONY, educator; b. Bad Duerkheim, Germany, Nov. 4, 1892; came to U.S., 1940, naturalized, 1945; s. Conrad and Hortense (Maas) H.; B.A., Gymnasium Neustadt, 1911; Ph.D., U. Munich, 1915; Dr.h.c., U. Grenoble, 1959; L.H.D. (hon.), Assumption Coll., 1959, Lasalle Coll., 1960 Cath. U. Am., 1964, U. Notre Dame, 1966, Marquette U., 1967, George Washington U., 1968; m. Herta Scheitel, Aug. 6, 1924. Privatdozent U. Frankfurt, 1922, extraordinary prof., 1923-32; substitute for ordinary prof. U. Königsberg (Germany), 1928-29; prof. Romance langs. U. Heidelberg (Germany), 1932-35; vis. prof. Louvain U., 1939-40; vis. prof. Cath. U. Am., Washington 1940-42, prof. Romance langs., 1942-68; cons. comparative lit., 1949-70, Revue de Littérature Comparée, from 1958. Recipient awards Institut d' Estudis Catalans, 1925, Academie Francaise, 1961,

Institut des Inscriptions et Belles Lettres, 1962; Oxford award MLA, 1949. Mem. Am. Assn. Tchrs. French, Am. Assn. Tchrs. Italian, Am. Assn. Tchrs. Spanish and Portuguese, Hispanic Soc. Am. (corr.), Bavarian Acad. Scis. (corr.). Author: Der Don Quijote als Wortkunstwerk, 1927; Literature through Art, 1952; Trends and Styles in Twentieth Century French Literature, 1957; Bibliographie Critique de la Nouvelle Stylistique, 1961; Saggi di Stilistica Romanza, vol. I, 1967, vol. II, 1971; Estudios Sobre el Barroco, 1968; Santa Teresa, 1969; Rococo Eroticism, Elegance and Wit in European Literature, 1972; Explicación de Textos Literarios, 1973; Estudios de Estibístied, 1975. Editor: Romanistische Stilforschung, 1975. Home: Washington, D.C. Died May 18, 1979.

HAUBER, ULRICH ALBERT (HOU'BER), prof. biol.; b. Bavaria, June 28, 1885; s. Joseph and Cacilia (Knauer) H.; brought by parents to U.S., 1890; A.B., St. Ambrose Coll., Davenport, Ia., 1905; ordained, St. Francis (Wis.) Sem., 1908; A.M., Catholic U., Washington, D.C., 1918; Ph.D., State U. of Ia., 1924. Teacher of biology, St. Ambrose Coll., 1908-15, prof. biology since 1915, pres. of coll., 1926-30. Appointed Domestic Prelate by Pope Pius XI, 1937. Fellow A.A.A.S.; mem. Am. Soc. Zoölogy, Am. Genetic Assn., Ia. Acad. Science, Am. Bot. Soc., Sigma Xi. Author: Evolution Controversy, 1925; Inheritance of Mental Defect, 1930; Biology, Textbook for Colleges, 1937; God's World, 1941; Research on Tendipedidae of Iowa, 1945-48; Essentials of Zoology: Textbook for Colleges, 1949. Address: Davenport, Ia. *

HAUBIEL, CHARLES, composer-pianist; b. Delta, Ohio, Jan. 30, 1892; s. Edward Marion Pratt and Mary Matilda (Haubiel) Pratt; student Berlin, 1909-13, Paris, 1919; grad. David Mannes Coll. of Music, 1919-24; pupil of Rudolph Ganz, Josef and Rosina Lhevinne in piano, Rosario Scalero in composition; Mus. D., Southwestern Convervatory of Fine Arts, Dallas; m. Mary Rice Storke, 1954. Concert pianist; tchr. piano Kingfisher Coll., 1913-15, Musical Art Inst., Oklahoma City, 1915-17, Inst. of Musical Art of Juilliard Found., 1922-30; prof. composition N.Y.U., 1923-47; pres. The Composers Press, 1935-67. Composer Berta (Mexican Folk opera), 1950; recorded compositions include: New Music for the Piano Teacher, Portraits (for symphony orch.); In the French Manner (trio flute, cello, piano); Sonata for Cello and Piano; Gothic Variations and Nuances for Violin and Orch., Solari for Orch. Metamorphoses (piano solo); Miniatures for String Orch.; Minuet for Orch.; Pioneers for Orch. Prize works include: Karma (Of Human Destiny) (Schubert Centennial award 1928); Ritratti, Swift Symphonic contest, 1935; The Plane Beyond, N.Y. Philharmonic Symphony Soc. contest, 1938; Disting. Service to Music award, Internat. Piano Tchrs. Assn., 1953; Martha Kinney Cooper citation Ohioana Library Assn., 1953, Pegasus award, outstanding cultural contbns., 1967; Double Three Star award of merit Nat. Fedn. Music Clubs, 1963, Special Two Star award of merit, 1965. Served as 2d lt., bandmaster, U.S. Army, 1917-19. Recipient Johann award Viennese Culture Soc., 1977. Mem. ASCAP, Nat. Assn. Composers U.S.A. Republican. Episcopalian. Clubs: Bohemians, Musicians (N.Y.C.). Home: Los Angeles, Calif. Died Aug. 26, 1978.

HAUCK, HERMAN JOHN, ednl. adminstr., clergyman; b. Cliffside, N.J., Dec. 11, 1911; s. Charles and Frances (Greubel) H.; A.B., Gonzaga U., 1935, M.A., 1936; S.T.L., Alma Coll., 1942; M.A., Yale U., 1951. Joined Soc. of Jesus, 1929; instr. English, Santa Clara (Calif.) U., 1936-38, asst. prof. theology, 1942-43, pres., 1951-58; regional dir. studies Calif. Jesuit Univs., 1958-73; asso. pastor Blessed Sacrament Ch., Hollywood, Calif., 1973-78; asso. prof. English, U. San Francisco, 1949-51. Superior summer sch. Loyola U., 1949; rector Mission Santa Clara, 1951-58; sec.-treas. Conf. Reglious Dirs. Edn., 1968-72; chmn. Jesuit Assn. Personnel Edn., 1970-71; commr. State of Calif. Scholarship Program, 1955-67, vice chmn., 1959-61, chmn., 1962-67, Bd. dirs. Calif. Citizens for Ednl. Freedom, 1972-73. Mem. Jesuit Edn. Assn. (mem. exec. com. 1958-64), Am. Council Edn. (mem. Pacific Coast Com. 1956-58), Nat. Cath. Edn. Assn. (chmn. S.W. region, coll. div. 1954-55, vice chmn. 1964-66, chmn. 1966-67), Western Coll. Assn. (v.p. 1954-55, pres. 1955-56), Calif. Ind. Found. (v.p. 1956-57), Western Assn. Schs. and Colls. (sr. commn. 1965-70). Contbr. articles to profl. jours.; lectr. in field. Home: Hollywood, Calif. Died June 13, 1978.

HAUGEN, BERNHART, business exec.; b. Rice Lake, Wis., Apr. 6, 1899; s. Nels A. and Ida (Wahl) H.; grad. Rice Lake (Wis.) High Sch., 1920; unmarried. Pub. accountant Ernst & Ernst, Chicago, 1924-29; asst. comptroller The Oliver Corp., Chicago, 1929-31, comptroller 1931-41, comptroller and treas., 1941-44, v.p., treas., from 1944, also dir., chmn. finance com., 1958-60, v.p. finance, 1960-62. C.P.A., Wis., Ill. Mem. Controllers Institute, Am. Legion. Republican. Home: Honolulu, Hawaii. Died May 22, 1977; buried Nora Cemetery, Rice Lake.

HAUGHT, DAVID L., college president; b. Uniontown, W.Va., Dec. 6, 1882; s. George W. and Elizabeth A. (LeMunyon) H.; diploma West Liberty Normal, 1912; A.B., Salem (W.Va.) Coll., 1918; A.M., U. of Mich., 1921; Ed.D., Pittsburgh U., 1934; m. Pearl Anderson, May 19, 1907; 1 dau., Viva Elizabeth (Mrs. William D. Herring). Rural teacher, 1900-06; prin. elementary sch., 1906-10; dist. supervisor and county supt., Wetzel County, 1913-18; supervising prin., Wheeling, 1918-22; prin. Moundsville High Sch., 1922-26; dean and prof. edn. West Liberty State Coll., 1926-33, Concord Coll., 1933-42; pres., Glenville State Coll., since 1942. Mem. Phi Delta Kappa, N.E.A., W.Va. State Edn. Assn., Kappa Delta Pi. Methodist. Democrat. Mason. Club: Rotary. Home: Glenville, W.Va.*

HAVENS, GEORGE REMINGTON, educator; b. Shelter Island Heights, N.Y., Aug. 25, 1890; s. George R. and Elizabeth (Jennings) H.; B.A., Amherst, 1913; Ph.D., Johns Hopkins, 1917; European travel and study periodically; Guggenheim fellow, 1929-30; L.H.D., U. Mich., 1959, Ohio State U., 1964; m. Louise Curtiss, July 18, 1917. Tchr. Riverview Mil. Acad., Poughkeepsie, N.Y., 1913-14, Mt. Vernon Collegiate Inst., Balt., 1914-16; instr. in French, Ind. U., 1917-18; asst. prof. French, Ohio State U., 1919-21, prof., 1921-61, emeritus; tchr. summers, Johns Hopkins, U. Chgo., U. Calif., U. Pa., Columbia. Mem. MLA, Phi Beta Kappa, Delta Tau Delta. Author: The Abbé Prévost and English Literature, 1921; The Age of Ideas, 1955, rev. 1962; Frederick J. Waugh, American Marine Painter, 1969; Rousseau, 1977. Editor lit. works: Selections from Voltaire, 1925, rev., 1969; (with Olin H. Moore) Selected Stories from Guy de Maupassant, 1928; Voltaire's Marginalia on Rousseau, 1933; Voltaire's Candide, 1934, rev., 1969; J.J. Rousseau, Discours sur les Sciences et les Arts. 1946; A Critical Bibliography of French Literature, Vol. IV, The 18th Century (with Cabeen and Bond, others), 1951; (with Norman L. Torrey) Voltaire's Catalogue of His Library at Ferney, 1959; critical edit. Voltaire's Discours en vers sur l'Homme. Contbr. to learned and profl. jours. Home: Columbus, Ohio. Died Sept. 27, 1977.

HAWKES, NATHAN WILLIAM, railroad official; b. Appleton, Me., July 21, 1882, s. Alonzo J. and Annie M. (Evans) H.; grad. Cambridge (Mass.) High and Latin Sch., 1899; m. Bertha L. Adams, of Cambridge, June 6, 1906; children—Nathan William, Barbara. With G.T. Ry., Boston, Mass., 1900-15; gen. freight agt., Central Vt. Ry., St. Albans, Vt., 1915-20; chmn. N.E. Freight and Passenger Assn., Boston, 1920-24; N.E. traffic mgr., Canadian Nat. and Central Vt. rys., Boston, 1924-26; system freight traffic mgr., Canadian Nat. Rys., Montreal, Que., Can., 1926-27; v.p. Boston & Me. R.R., 1927-31; mem. Official Classification Com., 1931-33; Trunk Line Association since 1933. Methodist. Mason (K.T., Shriner). Club: Oakley Country (Watertown, Mass.). Home: Belmont, Mass. *

HAWKINS, EDLER GARNETT, clergyman; b. N.Y.C., June 13, 1908; s. Albert and Annie (Lee) H.; B.A., Bloomfield, Coll., 1935, D.D., 1960; B.D., Union Theol. Sem., N.Y.C., 1938; m. Thelma Burnett, Jan. 30, 1944; children—Renee, Ellen. Ordained to ministry Presbyn. Ch., 1938; pastor St. Augustine Presbyn. Ch., Bronx, N.Y., 1938-70; moderator Presbytery N.Y., 1958-60; vice moderator Gen. Assembly United Presbyn. Ch. U.S.A., 1960-61, moderator, 1964-65; prof. practical theology Princeton. Mem. central com. World Council Chs.; chmn. Presbyn. Econ. Devel. Corp. Home: Princeton, N.J. Died Dec. 18, 1977.

HAWKINS, FRANK LEE, judge; b. Waxahachie, Tex., Nov. 18, 1866; s. Benjamin Franklin and Mary (Pinnell) H.; student Marvin Coll., Waxahachie, 1885-86, Southwestern U., Georgetown, Tex., 1887; B.L., U. of Tex., 1889; children—Mary Modena, Eddy Clifton, Christine. Admitted to Tex. bar, 1889, and practiced in Waxahachie; asst. atty. Ellis County, 1894-96, county atty., 1896-1900, county judge, 1902-06; judge 40th judicial dist., 1906-21; judge of Ct. of Criminal Appeals Appeals since 1921. Mem. Tex. Bar Assn., Sigma Alpha Epsilon. Democrat. Methodist. Mason. Home: Austin, Tex. *

HAWKINS, GEORGE ANDREW, engr., educator; b. Denver, Dec. 11, 1907; s. George Herbert and Pauline Katherine (Erbshauser) H.; B.S. in Mech. Engring., Purdue U., 1930, M.S. in Mech. Engring., 1932, Ph.D., 1935; m. Alma Mae Williams, Aug. 15, 1931; 1 son, James Edward. Asst. applied mechanics Purdue U., 1930-32, instr., 1932-36, asst. prof. mech. engring., 1936-38, asso. prof., 1938-42, prof. 1942-43, prof. thermodynamics, 1943-78, research asst. Engring. Exptl. Sta., 1932-36, research asso., 1936-44, Westinghouse research prof. heat transfer, 1944-53, 71-78, asst. dean Grad. Sch., 1947-50, acting dean, 1948-49. Research dir. small arms div. U.S. Army Ordnance Exptl. Stat., 1941-51; vis. prof. engring. U. Calif., 1949-50; asso. dir. Engring Expt. Sta. Purdue U., 1950-53, dir., 1953-61, dean engring. Purdue U., 1953-67, v.p. acad. affairs, 1967-71, v.p. emeritus acad. affairs, 1971-78, acting provost, 1974. Recipient certificate appreciation War Dept., 1945, gold medal Pi Tau Sigma, 1940; Lamme Gold medal award Am. Soc. Engring. Edn., 1974. Fellow Am. Inst. Chem. Engrs.; mem. Nat. Soc. Profl. Engrs., ASME (hon. mem.), Am. Phys. Soc., Am. Soc. Engring. Edn. (pres. 1970-71), Nat. Acad. Engring. Math., Army Ordnance Assn., Scabbard and Blade, Sigma Xi, Phi Kappa Phi, Tau Beta Pi, Pi Tau Sigma, Sigma Pi Sigma, Phi Eta Sigma. Mason, Elk. Author and co-author books including: Thermodynamics, 1950; Elements of Heat Transfer, 1957; Engineering Thermodynamics, 1960; Multilinear Analysis for Students in Engineering and Science, 1963; Editor: Student's Engineering Manual, 1968. Home: West Lafayette, Ind. Died Apr. 6, 1978; interred Tippecanoe Meml. Gardens, West Lafayette, Ind.

HAWKINS, JOSEPH ELMER, educator; b. Mt. Calm, Tex., Dec. 6, 1883; s. Martin Eugene and Sophronia Elizabeth (Davis) H.; B.S., Baylor U., 1907; grad. student U. Munich, 1912-13; Ph.D., U. Wis., 1922; m. Maude Burke Schlenker, Dec. 30, 1908; children—Joseph Elmer, Richard Cosier, Maude Ellen. Prof., chmn. German dept. Baylor U., 1916—; condr. ednl. tours to Europe. Mayor City of Waco, Tex., 1948-49. Mem. Modern Lang. Assn., Tex. Archeol. Soc. Home: Waco, Tex. *

HAWKINS, ROBERT BRUCE, lawyer; b. Phila., Dec. 12, 1928; s. Harry Linton and Jessica Loretta (Cutlip) H.; B.A., Amherst Coll., 1951; postgrad. Harvard, 1953-54, U. Pa. Grad. Sch. Econs., 1954-56; J.D., U. Minn., 1960; m. Nancy Jane Perry, Aug. 30, 1954; children—Philip, Mike, Martha. Asst. personnel mgr. Esterbrook Pen Co., 1954-56; advt. rep. Phila. Bull., 1956-57; admitted to Minn. bar, 1960; asso. firm Oppenheimer, Wolff, Foster, Shepard & Donnelly, Mpls., 1960-63, partner, 1964-74; v.p., gen. counsel, sec. Control Data Corp., 1974-80. Atty., Village of North Oaks, 1963-76. Mem. Am., Minn. bar assns., Order of Coif, Alpha Delta Phi, Phi Delta Phi. Clubs: Mpls., North Oaks Golf, Decathlon, St. Croix Yacht. Home: Saint Paul, Minn. Died Jan. 27, 1980; buried Sunset Meml. Park; Mpls.

HAWKINS, THOMAS FRANCIS, univ. adminstr.; b. Chgo., June 12, 1914; s. Thomas Francis and Hazel Josephine (Barry) H.; diploma in commerce Northwestern U., 1944; student Loyola U., Chgo., 1944, U. Omaha, 1951-53; m. Irene Ellen Murphy, May 6, 1939; children—Kathleen (Mrs. Dimitris N. Triantafillou), Thomas Francis, John Joseph, Joan (Mrs. John A. Pionke), Robert Michael. With Arthur Young & Co., C.P.A.'s, Chgo., 1932-36; asst. sec., asst. treas. H.A. Brassert & Co., N.Y.C., Chgo. and Pitts., 1936-41; asst. controller Esquire, Inc., Chgo., 1941-45; treas., controller Nachman Corp., Chgo., 1945-51; bus. mgr. Loyola U., Chgo., 1951-76, v.p., 1956-68, v.p. finance, 1968-76; dir. Chgo. Fed. Savs. and Loan Assn. Mem. adv. bd. grad. edn. Ill. Commn. Higher Edn., 1957-76; mem. U.S. Found. for Internat. Scouting; mem. nat. council, nat. coms. Boy Scouts Am., 1954-76, mem. nat. exec. bd., 1971-76; mem. vice chmn. Nat. Cath. Com. Scouting, 1961-70, chmn., 1970-76; Bd. dirs. Am. Hearing Research Found.; trustee Am. Humanics Found. Recipient Silver Beaver award, Silver Antelope award, Distinguished Eagle Scout award, Boy Scouts Am.; St. George award Cath. com. scouting Boy Scouts Am.; Knight of Malta. C.P.A., Ill. Mem. Am. Inst. C.P.A.'s, Ill. Soc. C.P.A.'s, Am. Accounting Assn., Financial Execs. Inst., Nat. Assn. Accountants, Am. Mgmt. Assn., Nat. Assn. Coll. and Univ. Bus. Officers, Chgo. Council on Fgn. Relations, Blue Key, Delta Sigma Pi, Pi Gamma Mu, Beta Alpha Psi. Clubs: Union League, Economic (Chgo.). Home: Oak Brook, Ill. Died Aug. 20, 1976.

HAWKS, HOWARD WINCHESTER, film dir.; b. Goshen, Ind., May 30, 1896; student Phillips Exeter Acad., Cornell U.; m. Nancy Roe Gross (div.); m. 2d, Dee Hartford (div.). Began career as profl. racing car driver; from prop boy to story editor Paramount pictures; producer, film industry, from 1922, directed first film Road to Glory, 1926; other films include Dawn Patrol, Scarface, Ceiling Zero, Bringing Up Baby, Only Angels Have Wings, Sergeant York, Red River, Rio Lobo, I Was A Male War Bride, O. Henry's Full House, Gentlemen Prefer Blondes, Rio Bravo, Hatari!, Red Line 5000, El Dorado. Served as 2d lt. AAC, World War I. Subject of retrospective Mus. Modern Art; N.Y.C., 1962; recipient spl. Academy Award for contbns. to film industry, 1975. Address: Beverly Hills, Calif. Died Dec. 26, 1977.

HAWLEY, GRAHAM, author; b. at Plainfield, N.J., Dec. 6, 1885; s. Frederick Barnard and Fannie Walworth (Jenkins) H.; grad. Washington Irving High Sch., Tarrytown, N.Y., 1902; student Columbia U. Sch. of Architecture; unmarried. Practiced architecture until 1912. Republican. Mem. Presbyn. Ch. Author: A Freshman Scout at College, 1914, The Doings of Troop Five, 1914; Troop Five at Camp, 1914; The Jackal Patrol of Troop Five, 1915; The Norfolk Boy Scouts, 1916. Home: Arrocliar, Staten Island, N.Y. *

HAWLEY, JESS BRADFORD, lawyer; b. Quartzburg, Ida., June 18, 1882; s. James Henry and Mary Elizabeth (Bullock) H.; LL.B., Columbian (now George Washington) U., 1903; m. Jennie Frances Smith, June 29, 1912; children—Genevieve, Jesse B., Mary E., James, John, Pauline, Eileen. Admitted to Ida. bar, 1903, and began practice at Boise; mem. Hawley &

Hawley. Mem. Bd. Ida. State Legal Advisers and chmn. Ada County Council-Defense, 1917-18; chmn. Ida. State Rep. Conv., 1928; chmn. Ida. Corp. Code Commn., 1928-29. Chmn. Idaho State Counsel of Defense since 1942. Mem. Am. Bar Assn., Ida. State Bar Assn. (Western commr. 1927-30; pres. 1929-30; mem. judicial council), Ada County Bar Assn., Lincoln Day Assn. (pres. 1916-24), Kappa Sigma. Elk, K.C. (organizer Ida K.C., 1904). Clubs: Rotary, Arid. *

HAWLEY, JOHN BLACKSTOCK, JR., corp. exec.; b. Ft. Worth, July 11, 1899; s. John Blackstock and Sue Anna (Terrell) H.; student Tex. Christian U., Colo. Coll., U. Tex.; C.E., Cornell U., 1920; D. Sc., Colo. Coll., 1970, Tex. Christian U., 1972; m. Helen Winston Thurston, 1925; children—Terrell Thurston, John Blackstock III; m. 2d, Anne McGill, May 30, 1937; children—McGill Joseph, Michael Augustine; m. 3d, Rosita Hofmeister, Mar. 30, 1946; children—MacDonald S., James, Lisa, Lane H. Gen. mgr. Anaconda Gravel Co., Ft. Worth, 1921-22; cons. engr. John B. Hawley, Ft. Worth, as chief designer on work covering water supply and san. engring., 1922-23; inventor mech. devices, specializing in perfection of oil well pumping devices; became constrn. engr. and v.p. No. Pump Co., 1928, owner, pres. Recipient Navy Distinguished Pub. Service award. Mem. ASCE (life mem.). Delta Kappa Epsilon. Clubs: Woodhill Country (Lake Minnetonka); Wayzata (Minn.) Country; Indian Creek Country, Bal Harbour (Miami Beach, Fla.). Patentee in field. Home: Wayzata, Minn. Died June 29, 1980.

HAWORTH, LELAND JOHN, sci. adminstr.; b. Flint, Mich.; July 11, 1904; s. Paul Leland and Martha (Ackerman) H.; A.B., Ind. U., 1925, A.M., 1926, D.Sc., 1961; Ph.D., U. Wis., 1931, D.Sc., 1962; D.Sc., Bucknell U., 1961; Engring.D., Stevens Inst. Tech., 1961; D.C.L., Union Coll., 1964; D.Sc., Columbia, 1965, U. Ill., 1965; LL.D., Rider Coll., 1964, Del. State Coll., 1965, L.I. U., 1965; m. Barbara Mottier, July 2, 1927 (dec. 1961); children—Barbara Jane (Mrs. Charles Beck), John; m. 2d, Irene Benik, May 15, 1963. High sch. tchr., Indpls., 1926-28; instr. physics U. Wis., 1930-37; Lalor fellow phys. chemistry M.I.T., 1937-38; asso. physics U. Ill., 1938-39, asst. prof. physics, 1939-44, prof. physics, 1944-47, staff mem. Radiation Lab., 1941-46, group leader, 1942-43, div. head, 1943-46; asst. dir. projects Brookhaven Nat. Lab., 1947-48, dir. 1948-61; v.p. Asso. Univs., Inc., 1951-60, pres. 1960-61; mem. U.S. AEC, 1961-63, dir. NSF, Washington, 1963-69; spl. asst. to pres. Asso. Univs., Inc., Upton, N.Y., 1969-79. Former chmn. exec. com. Nat. Sci. Bd.; past chmn. com. on acad. sci. and engring. Fed. Council Sci. and Tech.; mem. or officer other govt. adv. groups. Bd. dirs. Oak Ridge Asso. Univs., 1959-61, 70-79. Recipient certificate of merit from Pres. U.S. Fellow Am. Nuclear Soc. (dir. 1955-60, pres. 1957-58), Am. Phys. Soc., AAAS; mem. Nat. Acad. Scis., Am. Philos. Soc., Am. Acad. Arts and Scis., Phi Beta Kappa, Sigma Xi, Gamma Alpha, Lambda Chi Alpha. Club: Cosmos. Author numerous articles for profl. sci. jours., also several chpts. Radiation Lab. Tech. Series. Home: Port Jefferson, N.Y. Died Mar. 5, 1979; interred West Newton, Ind.

HAY, ISAAC KLINE, lawyer, former govt. ofcl.; b. Covington, Ga., Feb. 26, 1905; s. Samuel Martin and Medora (Peek) H.; J.D., U. Ga., 1928; m. Florice Caldwell, Sept. 6, 1935; 1 son, Isaac Kline. Admitted to Ga. bar, 1928; partner firm King & Hay, Covington, 1928-31; sec. Exec. Dept. Ga., 1931-33; asso. state counsel HOLC, 1933-34; 1st asst. U.S. dist. atty., Atlanta, 1934-39; with ICC, 1939-68, asso. gen. counsel, 1951-63, dep. gen. counsel 1963-68; now transp. cons. Pres. Atlanta Fed. Bus. Assn., 1936-38; bd. dirs. Atlanta Jr. C. of C., 1935-39. Sec. Ga. Bd. Electors, 1931-33. Served to lt. col. AUS, 1942-46. Mem. Am., Fed. bar assns., Am. Judicature Soc., Judge Adv. Assn., Sigma Delta Kappa (pres. Atlanta 1935-36; nat. v.p. 1937). Baptist. Mason. Clubs: Kiwanis, Atlanta Lawyers, Commerce (Atlanta); Sphinx, Blue Key, Gridiron Honor (U. Ga.); Kenwood Country (Washington); Tower (Ft. Lauderdale). Author, dir. radio series, Uncle Sam at Work, 1936-37. Jaycees Highway Safety Campaign, 1935. Home: Covington, Ga. Died May 13, 1978; buried Lawnwood Meml. Park, Covington.

HAYDEN, PAUL VINCENT, utility exec.; b. Pawtucket, R.I., 1903; s. Frank and Myra (Baldwin) H.; B.S. in Elec. Engring., Brown U., 1925; m. Margaret Carter Hindle, June 4, 1927; children—Robert, Paul Vincent, Lane. With Westinghouse Electric Co., 1925-29; with Conn. Light & Power Co., 1929-76, v.p., 1953-62, exec. v.p., 1962-64, pres. 1964-76, also dir.; advisor U.S. Dept. State; dir. Waterbury Nat. Bank, Island Light & Power Co., Millstone Point Co., Research Park, Inc., N.E. Utilities Service Co; founder, pres., dir. Life Ins. Co. Conn., New Haven; trustee N.E. Utilities. Chmn, bd. trustees Conn. Pub. Expenditure Council; bd. dirs. New England Council, Gaylord Hosp.; mem. Internat. Exec. Service Corps.; mem. Conn. Legislature, 1969-71. Mem. Electric Council New Eng., New Eng. Gas Assn. (dir.), Edison Electric Inst., Nat. Indsl. Conf. Bd., Conn. C. of C. (dir.). Republican. Home: Cheshire, Conn. Died Nov. 13, 1976.

HAYDEN, ROBERT EARL, poet, educator; b. Detroit, Aug. 4, 1913; s. Asa and Gladys Ruth (Finn) Sheffey; B.A., Wayne State U., 1942; M.A., U. Mich., 1944; D. Litt. (hon.), Grand Valley State Coll., 1975, Brown U., 1976, Fisk U., 1976; m. Erma I. Morris, June 15, 1940; 1 dau., Maia. Successively asst. prof., asso. prof., prof. English, Fisk U., 1946-69; prof. U. Mich., 1969-80; author books: Selected Poems, 1966; Night-Blooming Cereus, 1972; Angle of Ascent, 1975; American Journal, 1978; vis. prof. U. Louisville, 1969; vis. poet U. Wash., summer 1969, Conn. Coll., 1974; cons. in poetry Library of Congress, 1976-78; mem. Mich. Arts Council, 1975-76. Recipient Hopwood award for poetry U. Mich., 1942; Rosenwald fellow in creative writing, 1947; Ford Found. grantee, 1954. Mem. Acad. Am. Poets, PEN, Am. Poetry Soc., Authors Guild, Phi Kappa Phi. Baha'i. Address: Ann Arbor, Mich. Died Feb. 25, 1980.

HAYES, CHARLES WILLARD, JR., lawyer; b. Washington, Sept. 11, 1902; s. Charles Willard and Rosa (Paige) H.; Ph.B., Brown U., 1925; LL.B., Georgetown U., 1929; m. Annie Graham Hume, June 11, 1929; children—Sally Cox (Mrs. Carl Sydney Dorn), Charles Willard III. Admitted to D.C. bar, 1928; with Cushman, Bryant & Darby, patent law, Washington, 1927-29, partner, then sr. partner successor firm Cushamn, Darby & Cushman, 1942-71, counsel, 1971-78. Mem. Am. (ho. of dels. 1959-61), D.C. bar assns., Am. Patent Law Assn. (chmn. laws and rules com. 1952-54, pres. 1957-58), Nat. Council Patent Law Assns. (chmn. legislative com. 1955-56, chmn. council 1958-59), Psi Upsilon. Clubs: University (Washington); Chevy Chase. Home: Chevy Chase, Md. Died Feb. 21, 1978; buried Rock Creek Cemetery, Washington.

HAYES, CLARA EDNA, physician; b. at Bement, Ill., Aug. 23, 1884; d. Abram and Nancy Ellen (Wilkin) Hayes; M.D., Coll. Phys. and Surg. (U. of Ill.), 1912. Med. staff Peoria (Ill.) State Hosp., 1912-17; supt. state Training Sch. for Girls, Geneva, Ill., 1917-21; dir. Div. of Child Hygiene, State of S.Dak., 1922-27; in charge sch. health study for Western states, Am. Child Health Assn., 1927-28. Former chmn. pub. health S.Dak. Fedn. Women's Clubs; former dir. dept. health S.Dak. Parent-Teacher Assn.; spl. agt. of U.S. Children's Bur. for S.Dak., 1922-27; ex-chmn. Child Welfare Com. of S.Dak. State Medical Assn.; in charge of work for indigent crippled children of S.Dak., 1924-27; dir. of medical service, Am. Child Health Assn., 1934-35; senior medical officer U.S. Children's Bureau; retired since Feb. 22, 1947. Fellow Am. Public Health Assn.; mem. Am. Acad. of Pediatrics, Nu Sigma Phi. Republican. Presbyterian. Address: West Plains, Mo. *

HAYES, EDWARD WILLIAM, physician and surgeon; b. Millville, Minn., July 4, 1883; s. James Hayes and Elizabeth Joanna (Doran) H.; B.S., Carleton Coll., Northfield, Minn., 1909; M.D., U. of Minn. Med. Sch., 1913; m. Villa Mary Harris, Oct. 15, 1913; children—George Harris, Mary Catherine (Mrs. Darrell Joice Holman), Edward William, Frank James (dec.), Elizabeth Joan. Gen. practice, Brown Valley, Minn., 1913-18; postgrad. work in tuberculosis, Saranac Lake, N.Y., 1918-19; specializing in diseases of chest, Tucson, Ariz., 1919-21; Banning, Calif., 1921-22; Monrovia, Calif., since 1922; mem. attending staff, Los Angeles Gen. Hosp. since 1922; chief div. diseases of chest, Orange County Hosp. since 1926, San Bernardino County Hosp., 1937-38; med. dir. Maryknoll Sanatorium, Monrovia, since 1922; asso. prof. Coll. of Med. Evangelists, Los Angeles; controller of tuberculosis, Imperial County, Calif. Mem. draft bd. Traverse County, Minn., World War. Pres. Monrovia Democratic Club, 1930; past pres. Monrovia Chamber of Commerce and Business and Professional Assn. Fellow Am. Coll. of Physicians; mem. Am. Coll. Chest Physicians (pres. 1936-37); mem. bd. regents, chmn. Council on Undergrad. Edn. in Am. med. schs., Los Angeles County Med. Soc., Calif. State Med. Soc., A.M.A., Nat. Tuberculosis Assn.; mem. Am. Bd. Internal Medicine, Calif. Heart Assn., Am. Trudeau Soc., Delta Sigma Rho, Phi Beta Pi, K. of C. Club: Kiwanis (past pres.). Home: Morovia, Cal. *

HAYES, FRANK J., labor leader; b. What Cheer, Ia., May 4, 1882; s. Michael L. and Mary E. (Breslyn) H.; ed. Mt. Vernon (Ill.) High Sch.; unmarried. Identified with labor movement since 1903; pres. United Mine Workers of America, 1917-20 (resigned). Apptd. mem. U.S. War Labor Bd., Mar. 29, 1918; assisted in negotiating wage agreements for war period with coal operators, and adjusting many labor disputes. Mem. K. of P. Club: Independent Athletic (Indianapolis). Home: Collinsville, Ill.*

HAYES, JOHN CORNELIUS, judge; b. Chgo., Sept. 5, 1909; s. John Christopher and Mary Catherine (Ryan) H.; A.B. magna cum laude, Georgetown U., 1931; J.D., Loyola U., Chgo., 1937; Litt. D., Aquinas Coll., Grand Rapids, 1961; LL.D., St. John's U., 1963, Loras Coll., 1964. Admitted to Ill. bar, 1938; instr. Loyola Acad., Chgo., 1931-39; lectr. history Loyola U., Chgo., 1935-37, asst. prof. law 1938-42, prof., 1942-77, on leave, 1972-77, dean law, 1959-67; atty. Office Alien Property Custodian, Washington, 1946; justice Appellate Ct. Ill. 1st Dist., Cook County, 1972-77. Cons., Ill. Legislative Nonpub. Elementary and Secondary Schs. Study Commn., 1970-71; lectr. Nat. Trust Sch., Am. Bankers Assn., 1960-77; bd. dirs. Better Govt. Assn., 1965-71. Bd. dirs. Nat. Council Cath. Laity, 1971-73. Served to capt., USAAF, 1942-46. Mem. Am., Ill., Chgo. bar assns., Nat. Council Cath. Men (pres. 1959-61, dir. 1952-71), Pi Gamma Mu, Phi Alpha Delta. Home: Wilmette, Ill. Died Feb. 24, 1977.

HAYES, RALPH LEO, clergyman; b. Pittsburgh, Pa., Sept. 21, 1884; s. Patrick N. and Mary (O'Donnell) H.; A.B., Holy Ghost Coll., Pittsburgh, Pa., 1905; D.D., U. of the Propaganda, Rome, Italy, 1910; student Catholic U., Washington, D.C., 1912-13. Asst. pastor, Holy Rosary Parish, Pittsburgh, 1910-12; with Diocesan Mission Band, Diocese of Pittsburgh, 1913-17, supt. of parish schools, 1917-25, pastor, St. Catherine's Ch., 1925-33; bishop, Diocese of Mont., 1933-35; rector, North American Coll., Rome, Italy, 1935-44; bishop of Davenport, Ia., 1945. Home: Davenport, Ia. *

HAYES, ROLAND, tenor; b. Curryville, Ga., June 3, 1887; s. William and Fanny H.; student Fisk U.; extension course, Harvard; pupil W. Arthur Calhoun 2 yrs., Jennie A. Robinson, Fisk U., 4 yrs., Arthur J. Hubbard, 2 yrs.; also studied in Europe, 1920, under Ira Aldridge, Victor Beigel, Sir George Henschel, Dr. Theo Leierbammer; Mus. D., Fisk U., 1932, Ohio Wesleyan U., 1939, Boston U., 1948, Howard U., 1950, Temple U., 1956, New Eng. Conservatory Music, 1961; H.H.D., W.Va. State Coll., 1944; LL.D., Morehouse Coll.; L.H.D., Va. Union U., 1951; m. Helen A. Mann; 1 dau. Africa Fanzada. Conducted own concert tour U.S., 1916-76; studying and conducting concert tours, Europe, 1921; command performances before George V of Eng., 1920, Queen Mother Maria Christina of Spain, 1925; sung with Orch. Collonne, Paris, Orch. Mengelberg, Amsterdam, Vienna and Berlin, other mus. centers of Europe; toured U.S., singing with Boston, Phila., Detroit and N.Y. symphony orchs. Recognized for interpretation of classics and traditional Negro melodies. Recipient Spingarn medal for most outstanding achievement among colored people, 1925; Purple Ribbon award for services to French music (France), 1949 Fellow Am. Acad, Arts and Scis. Address: Brookline, Mass. Died Dec. 31, 1976.

HAYNES, (NATHAN GALLUP) WILLIAMS, chemical economist, author, publisher; b. Detroit, Mich., July 29, 1886; s. David Oliphant and Helen Dunham (Williams) H.; special student in economics, chemistry and biology, Johns Hopkins U., 1908-11; m. Elizabeth Bowen Batchelor, June , 1911; 1 dau., Elizabeth Williams (Mrs. R. W. Simons); m. 2d, Dorothy Farrand, June 5, 1926; children—Rhoda Farrand, Helen (Mrs. Geo. G. Keith). Editor Field and Fancy, 1906-07; spl. corr. Can., Europe, 1911-16; editor Northampton (Mass.) Herald, 1914-15; sec. and editorial dir. D. O. Haynes & Co., 1916-20; pub. Chem. Industries, 1920-39; pres. Pequot Press 1945—. Trustee, Pequot-Sepos Wildlife Sanctuary, League Conn. Hist. Socs. Awarded Pugsby Medal, 1952; Dexter award, American Chemical Society, 1956. Mem. Am. Chem. Soc. (council, 1922-23), Society Chemical Industry (London) American Economic Association, Newcomen Soc., Conn. Hist. Soc., New London Hist. Soc., Mayflower Descendants, S.R., Econ. Hist. Assn., Soc. Am. Historians, Am. Scenic and Historic Preservation Soc. (trustee), Soc. Colonial Wars. Delta Phi. fellow Royal Econ. Soc. Clubs: Chemists', Lawn (New Haven); Phila. Chem. (hon.). Author: Scottish and Irish Terriers, 1912; The Fox Terrier, 1914; Practical Dog Breeding, 1915; Casco Ray Yarns, 1916; Sandhills Sketches, 1916; Chemical Economics, 1933; Men, Money and Molecules, 1935; Chemistry's Contrbns., 1936; Chem. Pioneers, 1939; The Stone That Burns, 1942; Rationed Rubber (with Ernst Hauser), 1942; This Chem. Age, 1942. 2d edition, 1943; Spanish translation, 1943; Swedish translation, 1943; Portuguese, 1945; French translation, 1947; England edit., 1945; The Chem. Front, 1943; Spanish transl. 1945; American Chemical Industry, a History, 6 vols., 1945-52; Southern Horizons, 1946; Stonington Chronology, 1949; Chemical Trade Names and Commercial Synonyms, 1950; Cellulose, the Chemical that Grows, 1952; Brimstone, 1959. Home: Mystic, Conn. *

HAYS, PAUL R., judge; b. Des Moines, Apr. 2, 1903; s. Everett Hollingsworth and Fae Susan (Hatch) H.; A.B., Columbia, 1925, M.A., 1927, LL.B., 1933; m. Eleanor K. Williams, Feb. 1, 1924 (div. Dec. 1943); 1 son, Rhys Williams (dec.); m. 2d, Elinor Rice, Nov. 19, 1949. Instr. Greek and Latin, Columbia, 1926-32; associated with law firm, Cravath, de Gersdorff, Swaine & Wood, N.Y.C., 1933-34, 1935-36; counsel Nat. Recovery Adminstrn., Resettlement Adminstrn., Washington, 1934-35; asst. prof. law, Columbia, 1936-38, asso. prof. law, 1938-43, prof. law, 1943-57, Nash prof. law, 1957-61, prof. law, 1961-71, emeritus, 1971-80; U.S. Circuit judge, second circuit, 1961-80. Mem. N.Y. State Bd. Mediation, 1940-44, U.S. Bd. Legal Examiners, 1941-44; legal cons. N.Y. State

Banking Dept., 1936-37, N.Y. State Law Revision Com., 1937, 45, U.S. Dept. Justice, 1944, 45, labor arbitrator and impartial chmn. many industries, 1940-61; mem. N.Y.C. Bd. Health, 1954-60. Chmn. gov.'s com. on welfare funds, 1957-60. Chmn. Liberal Party, 1960-61; presidential elector, 1960. Mem. Am. (sec. sect. on labor relations law 1959-60), N.Y. State bar assns., Assn. of Bar of City of N.Y., Phi Beta Kappa. Club: Century. Author: The Judicial Function in Federal Administrative Agencies (with Jos. P. Chamberlain and Noel T. Dowling), 1942, 2d edit., 1970; Cases and Materials on Civil Procedure, 1947; Cases on Labor Law (with Milton Handler), 1950, rev. edit., 1963; Labor Arbitration: A Dissenting View, 1966; also articles in periodicals. Home: New York, N.Y. Died Feb. 13, 1980; buried Ferncliff Cemetery, Hartsdale, N.Y.

HAYWARD, WILMER, shipping co. exec.; b. New Orleans, Nov. 28, 1883; s. James B. and Mary E. (Moore) H.; m. Mary B. Vaught, Nov. 12, 1906; children—Mary W. (Mrs. John Thornton Kilpatrick), Elizabeth B. (Mrs. Julian J. Fertitta). Engaged in lumber export, Liverpool, Eng., Rotterdam, Holland, Hamburg and Dusseldorf, Germany, 1903-05; mgr. W. A. Powell Co., Ltd., Pensacola, Fla., 1905; asst. mgr. Florida-Alabama Lumber Co., Pensacola, 1905-08; organized W. Hayward Export Co., 1908 (merged with Pensacola Lumber Co., 1910); pres. Pensacola Lumber Co., 1910-33, New Orleans, 1933-35 (merged with Standard Export Lumber Co., New Orleans, 1935); v.p., dir. Standard Export Lumber Co., New Orleans, 1935—; organnized Pensacola Builders Supply Co., 1927, pres., 1927-43, gen. partner, 1943—; pres., dir. Empresas Nolen, Nicaragua, 1951—; member board of directors Mississippi Shipping Co., 1937—, chmn., 1956—. Clubs: Boston, Internat. House (a founder), Propeller (New Orleans). Home: New Orleans.

HAYWOOD, JOHN WILFRED, clergyman; b. Madry County, Tenn., July 4, 1883; s. Charles and Jennie (Kennedy) H.; A.B., Lincoln Univ., Pa., 1903, A.M., S.T.B., 1911, S.T.D., 1925, LL.D. (hon.), 1940; D.D. (hon.) Gammon Theol. Sem., Atlanta, Ga., 1926; m. Lottie J. Burnett, Aug. 4, 1904; children—John Wilfred, Rendall Burnett, Violet G. (Mrs. Violet H. Bate). Ordained to ministry of Meth. Ch., 1910; pastor Brooklyn, N.Y., 1911-12, Marshall, Tex., 1912-17; dean Wiley Coll., Marshall, Tex., 1917-19; prof. edn., Morgan Coll., Baltimore, Md., 1920-24, dean 1924-36; pres. Morristown Jr. Coll., Morristown, Tenn., 1936-4. *

HAYWOOD, RICHARD MANSFIELD, educator; b. Lynn, Mass., June 12, 1905; s. Charles Edward and Annie (Moulton) H.; A.B., Dartmouth Coll., 1926; Ph.D., Johns Hopkins, 1932; m. Margaret Rider Mowbray, Sept. 6, 1930; children—Richard Mowbray, Anne Mowbray, Mary Coale (Mrs. Donald L. Metz). Tchr., Johns Hopkins, 1932-44, Hotchkiss Sch., 1944-50; mem. faculty N.Y. U., 1950-73, prof. Classics, 1960-73. Guggenheim fellow, 1939-40; Fulbright research fellow Italy, 1960-61. Mem. Phi Beta Kappa. Author: Studies on Scipio Africanus, 1933; Roman Africa, 1938; The Myth of Rome's Fall, 1958; Ancient Greece and the Near East, 1964; Ancient Rome, 1967; The Ancient World, 1971. Home: Charlottesville, Va. Died Mar. 31, 1977.

HAZARD, LELAND, lawyer, corp. exec., educator; b. Kansas City, Mo., July 7, 1893; s. Henry E. and Lucinda (Holderbaum) H.; A.B., U. Mo., 1916; student Law Sch., Harvard, 1919-20, U. Chgo., 1926; LL.D., Carnegie Mellon U., 1970; m. Mary Chorn, Dec. 22, 1923. Admitted to Mo. bar, 1920, Pa. bar, 1940; practiced law Kansas City, Mo., 1920-38; gen. counsel, v.p., dir. PPG Industries, Inc., 1940-58, dir.-cons., 1959-65, cons., 1965-68; prof. indsl. adminstrn. and law Carnegie-Mellon U., 1959-61, prof. emeritus, lectr., 1961-80; hon. chmn. Met. Pitts. Ednl. TV Sta. (WQED). Hon. bd. dirs. Pitts. Symphony Soc.; trustee Archeol. Inst. Am.; pres. Community Chest, Pitts., 1949-50; bd. mem. Pitts. Regional Indsl. Devel. Corp., Allegheny County Port Authority; cons. Ford Found. Mgmt. Program, India, 1963-65; chmn. Gov.'s Com. Transp., Pa., 1966-70; bd. dirs. Pitts. Urban Transit Council. Served First O.T.C., U.S. Army; maj., Adj. Gen.'s Dept.; with 89th Div., A.E.F., in France and Germany during World War I. Mem. Nat. Planning Assn. (trustee, mem. steering com., 1959-67), Am., Pa., Mo., Allegheny County bar assns., Am. Legion, Sigma Nu, Phi Alpha Delta, Omicron Delta Kappa. Clubs: Century Association (N.Y.C.); Duquesne, University (Pitts.); Rolling Rock (Ligonier, Pa.); River (Kansas City, Mo.). Author: Law and the Changing Environment; Empire Revisted; Leland Hazard on Transportation; Attorney for the Situation, 1975. Home: Pittsburgh, Pa. Died Aug. 17, 1980.

HAZELTINE, LOUIS ALAN, research engr.; b. Morristown, N.J., Aug. 7, 1886; s. Louis Rawson and Henrietta Maud (Ahern) H.; M.E., Stevens Inst. Tech., 1906; m. Philipine H. Miller, of Hoboken, N.J., June 16, 1910; m. 2d, Elizabeth Barrett, Jan. 16, 1931; 1 son, Barrett. With elec. engring. department of Stevens Inst. Tech., all grades, 1907-25, prof. elec. engring., 1917-25. Cons. engr. in radio, Washington Navy Yard, 1918-19; cons. engr. for Albert F. Ganz, Inc., specializing in electrolysis investigations, 1917-23. Mem. first 3 radio confs. called by Secretary Hoover; mem. Am. Com. on Electrolysis, 1918-20; chmn. Am. Gas Assn. Com. on Electrolysis, 1920. Fellow Am. Inst. E.E., Inst. Radio Engrs. (mgr. 1923-27), Am. Physical Soc.; mem. Soc. for Promotion Engring. Edn., Am. Math. Soc., A.A.A.S., Tau Beta Pi. Author: Electrical Engineering, 1924; also scientific papers, especially on oscillating audion circuits (Proc. I.R.E., 1918). Inventor of neutrodyne radio receiver. Home: Paris, France. *

HAZEN, ALLEN TRACY, educator; b. Portland, Conn., Nov. 4, 1904; s. Rev. Carleton and Julia (Trask) H.; A.B., Yale, 1927, Ph.D., 1935; A.M., Harvard, 1932; m. Edith Patterson; 1 son. Tutor Am. Coll., Tarsus, Turkey, 1927-30; master, Romford Sch., Washington, Conn., 1930-31; instr. in English, Yale, 1935-40; bibliographer and cataloguer, Yale Library, 1940-42; instr. in English, Hunter Coll., N.Y.C., 1942-45; cons. in bibliography, Library of Congress, summer, 1942; asso. prof. of English and bibliographer U. Library Chgo., 1945-47, prof. English and dir. U. Library, 1947-48; prof. English, Columbia, 1948-71, prof. emeritus, 1971-77; Guggenheim fellow, 1952-53. Mem. Modern Lang. Assn., Bibliog. Soc. (London), Am. Library Assn., Bibliog. Soc. Am., Phi Beta Kappa. Selden fellow in English Yale, 1933-34. Presbyterian. Author: Samuel Johnson's Prefaces and Dedications, 1937; (with R.W. Chapman) Johnsonian Bibliography, a supplement to Courtney, 1939; Bibliography of the Strawberry Hill Press, 1942; Bibliography of Horace Walpole, 1948; Catalogue of Walpole's Library, 3 volumes, 1969. Compiler: (with E.L. McAdam) Catalogue of Exhibition of books by Johnson in Yale Library, 1935. Asst. in ann. bibliography, English lit., 1660-1800, Philological Quarterly, 1939-41. Contbr. of short articles on literary and bibliog. problems to various publs. Gen. editor Yale edition of Samuel Johnson's Works, 1958-66. Home: New York, N.Y. Died Dec. 23, 1977.

HAZEN, ARLON GIBERSON, coll. dean; b. Stillwater, Okla., Feb. 25, 1920; s. Leslie Eugene and Ella V. (Brooks) H.; B.S. in Agrl. Engring., Okla. State U., 1940; M.S., Iowa State U., 1941; m. Betty Mae Sewell, June 3, 1940; children—Leslie Ray, Gale Arlon. Instr. agrl. engring. U. Ark., 1941-42; supt. Williston (N.D.) Br. Expt. Sta., 1946-51; asst. to dir. Agrl. Expt. Sta. N.D. State U., 1951-56, dean Coll. Agr., also dir. Agrl. Expt. Sta., 1956-79. Served to lt. col., C.E., AUS, 1942-46; ETO. Mem. Am. Soc. Agrl. Engrs., Alpha Zeta. Home: Fargo, N.D. Died Jan. 28, 1979; interred Fairlawn Cemetery, Stillwater, Okla.

HAZEN, HAROLD LOCKE, educator; b. Philo, Ill., Aug. 1, 1901; s. Wirt Mandeville and Elta Belle (Brewer) H.; S.B., Mass. Inst. Tech., 1924, S.M., 1929, Sc.D., 1931; m. Katherine Pharis Salisbury, Sept. 5, 1928; children—Stanley Seamans, Martha Locke (Mrs. William Liller), Nathan Lord, Anne Webb (Mrs. John G. Bowen). With Mass. Inst. Tech., 1925—, research asst. in elec. engring., 1925-26, instr., 1926-31, asst. prof., 1931-35, asso. prof., 1935-38, prof., head dept. elec. engring., 1938-52, dean Grad. Sch., 1952-67, fgn. study adviser, 1967-72; mem. adv. council dept. elec. engring. Princeton, 1948-56; chief div. 7, Nat. Def. Research Comm., 1942-46, exchange prof. elec. engring. Ohio State U., 1934-35; cons. on engring. edn. Robert Coll. Istanbul, 1955, interim pres., 1961; cons. engring. edn. Am. U. Beirut, 1957, Ministry of Edn., Iceland, 1958. Mem. U.S. Naval Weapons Lab. adv. council, 1953-65; chmn. edn. com. Engrs. Council for Profl. Devel., 1954-56, exec. com., 1954-58; chmn. Engring Edn. Mission to Japan, 1951, cons. engring, edn. UN Mission to U. Brasilia, 1962. Trustee Robert Coll. Bebek, Istanbul, Turkey, 1956-72, Coll. of Petroleum and Minerals, Dhahran, Saudi-Arabia, 1965-72; bd. visitors U.S. Air U., 1956-59. Recipient Levy medal of Franklin Inst., 1935; Lamme Gold medal Am. Soc. Engring. Edn., 1962; Presdl. Certificate of Merit, 1948; L.E. Grinter award Engrs. Council Profl. Devel., 1975, Rufus Oldenburger medal ASME, 1977. Served as 2d lt. Air Service, 1924-29; lt. comdr. USNR, 1936-49. Fellow I.E.E.E. (life), Am. Acad. Arts and Scis. (council), Franklin Inst. (life); mem. Am. Soc. Engring. Edn. (life mem.; chmn. com. devel. engring. faculties), Inst. Elec. Engrs. Japan (hon.), Sigma Xi, Tau Beta Pi, Eta Kappa Nu. Contbr. articles on instrumental calculation, automatic control devices, engring. edn., accreditation. Home: Belmont, Mass. Died Feb. 21, 1980.

HAZLETT, THEODORE LYLE, physician; b. North Washington, Pa., Apr. 19, 1885; s. William J. and Margaret (Lyle) H.; M.D., U. Pitts.; 1912; post grad. student N.Y. Polyclinic Med. Sch. and Hosp., 1917; m. Clara Barndollar, Nov. 21, 1917; children—Theodore Lyle, Robert Dunlap. Gen. practice as physician, 1913-14; med. dir. Mount Alto State Tb Hosp., Westinghouse Electric Corp. 1920-50, ret. 1950; cons. USPHS, 1954; prof. and head dept. indsl. medicine, U. Pitts., 1937-56, emeritus prof.; mem. staff Braddock Gen. Hosp., Presbyn. Hosp. Diagnostic Clinic Westinghouse Order of Merit, 1942. Served as surgeon with A.R.C., Russia, 1914-16; served from maj. to lt. col., M.C., A.U.S., 1917-19. Fellow A.C.P.; mem. C. of C, A.M.A., Pa. State and Allegheny County med. socs., Am. Assn. Indsl. Physicians and Surgeons, Am. Trudeau Soc., Am. Soc. Heating and Ventilating Engrs., Am. Pub. Health Assn., Am. Indsl. Hygiene Assn., Alpha Omega Alpha. Club: University (Pittsburgh). Editor: Introduction to Industrial Medicine, 1944. Author: (pamphlets) Tuberculosis Prevention Work in a Large Plant, 1925; Practical Results of Physical Examinations in Industry, 1928; The Physician-Administrator, 1930; Medical-Engineering Control of Industrial Health Hazards, 1936; Safeguarding Worker Health, 1942; Industrial Medical Problems in War Production, 1944. Co-author: Evolution of Industrial Medicine in Western Pennsylvania, 1850-1950. Home: Coral Gables, Fla. *

HEAD, ALBERT JOSEPH, fiber co. exec.; b. Potowattamie County, Okla., Nov. 7, 1914; s. Francis Marion and Adele Agnes H., B.C.E., U. Okla., 1937; m. Adeial Bongman, Sept. 4, 1965; children—Jo Ellen Head Rice, Judith Ann Head Powell. With Phillips Petroleum Co., 1937-57, 63-66, Phillips Chem. Co., 1957-63; pres., chmn, bd. Phillips Fivers Corp., Greensville, S.C., from 1966; chief exec. officer Revonah Spinning Mills, from 1968; dir. S.C. Nat. Bank; adj. prof. Clemson/Furman univs. grad. program bus. administrn.; mem. joint legis. com. Gov. S.C. Com. to Study Textile Industry; dir. Textile Hall Corp., Greenville; adv. bd. Furman U. Mem. Health Systems Agy. Bds. S.C., from 1975; bd. dirs. exec. com. S.C. Appalachian Health Council, from 1973; mem. Blue Ridge council Boy Scouts Am., from 1972. Mem. Am. Textile Mfrs. Inst., S.C. Textile Mfrs. Assn. (dir. from 1974, chmn. edn. and personnel com. 1976-77), Man-Made Fibers Producers Assn. (dir., exec. com. from 1970), S.C. C. of C. (dir. exec. com., v.p. Western sect. from 1976. Methodist. Clubs: Rotary, Green Valley Country, Poinsett (Greenville). Home: Greenville, S.C. Deceased.

HEADLEY, LOUIS SHERMAN, lawyer, banker; b. Fairmont, Minn., Sept. 19, 1885; s. Charles W. and Sara (Sherman) H.; B.S., Carleton Coll., 1907; LL. B., Harvard, 1912; m. Sylvia Knight, Sept. 18, 1915; children—Sara (Mrs. Roger B. Page), William K., Sherman K., Russell K. Admitted to N.Y. bar, 1913, Minn. bar, 1914; asso. Rounds, Hatch, Dillingham & Debevoise, N.Y.C., 1912-13; staff atty. gen. Minn., 1914-16; pvt. practice, St. Paul, 1916-18; officer First Trust Co. of St. Paul (formerly Northwestern Trust Co.), 1918-51; retired as pres., 1951; spl. asso. firm Morgan, Raudenbush, Morgan, Oehler & Davis, St. Paul, 1951—; faculty Grad. Sch. Banking, Rutgers U., 1942-54; instr. St. Paul Coll. Law, 1928-31. Dir. First Trust Co., Minn. Tribune, Canmore Mines, Ltd., Rundle Mountain Trading Co. Chmn. Nat. Com. on Community Found., St. Paul Community Chest, 1939-40. Pres. St. Paul YMCA, 1927-31, Children's Hosp., 1947-49, St. Paul Rehabilitation Center, 1951-56; chmn. bd. trustees Carleton Coll., 1955—; dir. St. Paul Found., Tozer Found., Gilfillan Found. Mem. Am. (pres. trust div. 1942-43), Minn. bar assns., St. Paul YMCA (past pres.), Phi Beta Kappa. Republican. Unitarian. Clubs: Minnesota, Athletic, Rotary (pres. 1935-36), Informal (sec.) (St. Paul). Home: South St. Paul, Minn. *

HEALD, HENRY TOWNLEY, consultant; b. Lincoln, Nebr., Nov. 8, 1904; s. Frederick De Forest and Nellie (Townley) H.; B.S., State Coll., Wash., 1923; M.S., U. Ill., 1925; D.Eng. (hon.), Rose Poly. Inst., 1942, Clarkson Coll. Tech., 1948; LL.D. (hon.), Northwestern U., 1942, Rutgers U., 1952, Columbia U., 1954, Hofstra Coll., 1955, Fairleigh Dickinson Coll., 1955, Princeton U., U. Pitts., 1956, N.Y. U., 1962, U. Ill., 1963, Ill. Inst. Tech., 1966; D.C.L. (hon.), N.Y. U., 1956, Case Western Res. U., 1968; L.H.D. (hon.), Rollins Coll., 1953, Pacific Luth. U., 1966, Brandeis U., 1966, Coll. Wooster, 1966; D.Sc. (hon.) Pratt Inst., 1954, Newark Coll. Engring., 1954, Union Coll., 1956; D.H.L. (hon.), Cornell Coll., 1967; m. Muriel Starcher, Aug. 4, 1928. Asst. prof. to pres. Armour Inst. Tech., 1927-40; pres. Ill. Inst. Tech., Armour Research Found., Inst. Gas Tech., 1940-52; chancellor N.Y. U., 1952-56; pres., trustee The Ford Found., N.Y.C., 1956-65; partner Heald, Hobson & Assocs., N.Y.C., 1965-67; chmn. Heald, Hobson & Assos., Inc., 1967-71; Bd. trustees Rollins Coll., Winter Park, Fla. Recipient distinguished service awards Chgo. Jr. Assn. Commerce, 1940, Ill. Jr. C. of C., 1940; Navy award for distinguished civilian service, 1945; Washington award, 1952; Nat. Inst. Social Sci. medal, 1956; Hoover medal 1959; Distinguished Alumni Award Wash. State U., 1962; Alumni Honor award Coll. Engring. U. Ill., 1966; Albert Gallatin award N.Y. U., 1969. Chmn. Mayor's Com. (to reform) Chgo. Bd. Edn., 1946; trustee John Crerar Library, 1945-52; commr., vice chmn. Chgo. Land Clearance Commn., 1947-52; chmn. South Side Planning Bd., Chgo., 1946-52; trustee Town Hall, Inc., 1952-56; vice chmn. Mayor's Com. for Better Housing, N.Y.C., 1954-56; commr. Nat. Commn. on Accrediting, 1950-56; chmn. N.Y. State Com. on Higher Edn., 1960. Mem. Am. Soc. Engring. Edn. (pres. 1942-43), A.A.A.S. (v.p. 1946-47), Am. Pub. Works Assn., ASCE, ASME, Western Soc. Engrs. (pres. 1945-46), Nat.

Acad. Engring., Tau Beta Pi, Sigma Tau, Phi Kappa Phi, Chi Epsilon, Theta Xi; also several hon. affiliations. Rotarian. Clubs: University (N.Y.C. and Winter Park); Commercial. Home: Winter Park, Fla. Died Nov. 23, 1975.

HEALEY, GEORGE, lawyer; b. Lincoln, Nebr., July 7, 1905; s. Thomas Martin and Wilhemina (Simon) H.; LL.B., U. Nebr., 1929; m. Rose M. Gerhold, Feb. 5, 1930; children—Patrick W., Janet (Mrs. David P. Weber), Susan Rose (Mrs. Edward Fitzgerald, Jr.). Admitted to Nebr. bar, 1929, practiced in Lincoln; mem. law firm Healey, Healey, Brown & Wieland. Mem. bd. examiners Nebr. Bar Commn., 1942-72. Mem. Am. Coll. of Trial Lawyers, Am. Bar Assn., Nebr. Bar Assn. (pres. 1962-63; mem. ho. of dels. 1954-55, jud. council 1954-57), Lincoln Bar Assn. (pres. 1946-47), Nat. Conf. Bar Examiners (sec. 1952-53), Internat. Assn. Ins. Counsel, Assn. Ins. Attys., Phi Delta Phi, Delta Sigma Rho. Republican. Roman Catholic. Home: Lincoln, Nebr. Died Apr. 14, 1979; interred Lincoln Meml. Park.

HEALY, ARTHUR KELLY DAVID, artist, author, educator, architect; b. N.Y.C., Oct. 15, 1902; s. Thomas and Elizabeth (Kelly) H.; A.B., Princeton, 1924, M.F.A., 1926; student Fontainebleau (France) Summer Sch. Fine Arts, 1925; fellow Am. art, U. Pa., 1945; m. Troy Tapp, Sept. 2, 1944; children—Sophia Warner, Arthur Kelly David. Practice architecture, N.Y.C. and Rutland, Vt., 1957; supr. PWA, 1938-40; archtl. engr. Portsmouth (Vt.) Navy Yard, 1941-43; mem. faculty Middlebury (Vt.) Coll., 1943-78, prof. dept. fine arts, 1958-68, prof. emeritus, 1968; numerous exhbns. paintings through Italy, Eng., U.S.; 10 one man exhbns., Boston, N.Y.C.; works rep. Harvard, Canajoharie (N.Y.), Mus., New Britain (Conn.) Mus., Kansas City (Mo.) Mus., Boston Mus. Fine Arts, Fleming Mus., Burlington, Vt., Portland (Me.) Mus., Addison Gallery Am. Art, Andover, Mass., Bennington (Vt.) Mus., Middlebury Coll. (Vt.), Norwich U., Northfield, Vt., also pvt. collections; illustrator comml. jours. Pres. Motion Picture Operation Symphony Theatre, Inc., N.Y.C., from 1944. Former Democratic candidate for Vt. senator, also town rep. Middlebury. Chmn. planning com., trustee Yaddo Corp., Saratoga Springs, N.Y., 1956-78; chmn. bd. Sheldon Mus., Middlebury; mem. Vt. Bd. Historic Sites, 1967; chmn. Champlain Celebration, 1960; mem. bd. Mt. Independence Assos. Recipient prizes for water color painting Am. Water Color Soc., Audubon Artists, Boston Soc. Ind. Artists, Boston Soc. Water Color Painters, No., Mid. and So. Vt. Artists, Springfield (Mass.) Art Assn., Stockbridge (Mass.) Art Assn. Vt. Profl. Artists, Exhbn. Vt. Artists Norwich U., 1968, 69, 70, others. Mem. N.Y.C., Washington water color clubs, Am., Phila. water color socs., Audubon Artists, Springfield Art Assn., Boston Festival Fine Arts, College de Pataphysique (Paris), Club di Rigalio (Rome, Italy), Irish Georgian Soc. Author: (with Alfred Frankenstein) Two Journeymen Painters; also numerous articles. Home: Middlebury, Vt. Died Oct. 9, 1978.

HEALY, GEORGE WILLIAM, JR., editor, mus. ofcl., author; b. Natchez, Miss., Sept. 22, 1905; s. George William and Rosa Lee (Longmire) H.; A.B., U. Miss., 1926; m. Margaret Hoy Alford, Sept. 22, 1927; children—George William III, Floyd Alford (dec.). Began as corr. for A.P., and several newspapers while at coll.; reporter Knoxville (Tenn.) Sentinel, 1926; with The Times-Picayune, New Orleans, 1926-72, reporter, then city editor, 1931, mng. editor, 1936, editor, 1952-72; exec. editor The Times-Picayune-New Orleans States- Item, 1964-69; treas. Times-Picayune Pub. Corp., 1939, v.p., 1942-80, dir., 1948-80; dir. A.P., 1957-66, v.p., 1965-66; lectr. (part time), Tulane U., 1946-52; dir. domestic branch, O.W.I. on leave from the Times-Picayune, 1944; cons. on domestic problems O.W.I., 1945. Trustee Jefferson Mil. Coll. 1950-62; bd. dirs. The Adv. Council, Inc., 1954-60; pres. Gallier House, New Orleans, 1973-74. Decorated Caballero de Order de Cristobal Colon (Domincan Republic) 1946; Order Leopold II (Belgium), 1956; Star of Solidarity (Italy), 1958. Chmn. New Orleans chpt. A.R.C., 1956-58. Mem. A.P. Mng. Editors Assn. (chmn. 1943-46), Am. Soc. Newspaper Editors (pres. 1958-59), Inter Am. Pres Assn. (dir. 1950-58), S.A.R. (pres. La. 1951), Sigma Nu, Sigma Delta Chi (pres. 1946), Omicron Delta Kappa. Democrat. Methodist. Mason. Clubs: Recess (pres. 1947-48), Boston, Louisiana, Internat. House (v.p. 1964-67) (New Orleans); Circumnavigators (N.Y.C.); National Press (Washington); Mount Kenya Safari (East Africa). Author: A Lifetime on Deadline, 1976. Home: New Orleans, La. Died Nov. 2, 1980.

HEANEY, ROBERT CECIL CURTIS, lawyer; b. Big Rapids, Mich., Jan. 22, 1906; s. Herbert Melville and Harriet Irene (Emmons) H.; student Grand Rapids Jr. Coll., 1924-26; A.B., J.D., U. Mich., 1930; m. Barbara Helen Patton, Feb. 14, 1931; children—Robert Daniel (dec.), Brian Richard, Marilyn Jean Heaney Sainsot. Admitted to Mich. bar, 1930, Ariz. bar, 1971; practiced Grand Rapids, 1930-73, Tucson, from 1972. Treas. Mich. Republican State Central Com., 1949-57. Bd. dirs. YMCA, Grand Rapids, 1935-73, dir. emeritus, 1973—; bd. dirs. Arthritis Found., past pres. Mich. chpt., past pres. dir. So. Ariz. chpt. Mem. Am. Judicature Soc., Am., Mich., Ariz., Grand Rapids, Pima County bar assns., Tucson C. of C., Phi Sigma Kappa, Phi Alpha Delta. Presbyterian. Clubs: University Mich. Alumni (past pres.), U. Mich. Pres.'s; Rotary (Tucson), Tucson Nat. Golf; Garden of the Gods (Colorado Springs). Home: Tempe, Ariz. Died Apr. 10, 1981.

HEARD, JACK WHITEHEAD, army officer; b. N.Y.C., Mar. 6, 1887; s. Gen. John Wilkinson and Mildren Jewell (Townsend) H.; B.S., U.S. Mil. Acad., 1910; attended numerous other military schs., 1915-37; m. Ella Agnes McCarthy, June 11, 1917; children—John Wilkinson (lt. col. U.S. Army), Elizabeth Fitzgerald (wife of John Russell Dean, Jr., col., U.S. Army), Ralph Varnell, Richard Townsend (maj. U.S. Army). Served in Cav., AUS, 1910-15, in Aviation Sect. Signal Corps and Air Corps, 1915-19, Motor Transport Corps, 1919-20, Cav., 1920-32, at U.S. Bureau of Budget, 1932-33, Cavalry, 1933-40; armored Force, 1940-43; War Dept., Manpower Bd., 1943-46; maj. gen. U.S. Army, 1941. Mem. S.A.R., Soc. Cin., Newcomen Soc., Soc. Mil. and Naval Officers of World War, Early Birds. Mason (32 degree). Clubs: Ft. Sam Houston Officers; Army-Navy (Washington). Home: Silver Lake, N.H.; also San Antonio, Tex.

HEATH, JANET FIELD (MRS. S. ROY HEATH), author; b. Trenton, N.J., Jan. 5, 1885; d. Charles Prentice and Janet Hunter (Rhodes) Curtis; grad. State Model Sch., Trenton, 1902; and State Normal Sch., 1904; m. (Samuel) Roy Heath, of Trenton, Feb. 1910; children—Curtis Franklin, Mary Elizabeth, Dartha, Samuel Roy. Democrat. Unitarian. Club: Contemporary. Author: The Twins, 1897; Ann's Family, 1925; The Hygienic Pig, 1925; Ann at Starr House (and Far Away From It), 1927; The Built Upon House, 1928; also verse, children's stories and children's plays, in mags. Home: Trenton, N.J. *

HEBBARD, WILLIAM LAWRENCE, internat. fin. ofcl.; b. Ishpeming, Mich., Mar. 18, 1912; s. William J. and Louise (Hicks) H.; B.S., No. Mich. U., 1934; M.A. in Econs., U. Mich., 1935, postgrad., 1935-38, 39-40; postgrad. Grad. Inst. Internat. Studies, Geneva, 1938-39; m. Ethel Frances Mikulich, May 3, 1945; children—Barbara L., Patricia J., Bruce L. Asst. to chmn. Geneva Research Centre, 1938-39; with Office Internat. Finance, Treasury Dept., 1940-54, U.S. Treasury rep., London, 1948-50, asst. dir., 1950-54; with exchange restrictions dept. Internat. Monetary Fund, Washington, 1954-64, dep. sec., 1964-67, sec., 1967-77. Recipient Distinguished Alumnus award No. Mich. U., 1968. Traveling fellow Social Sci. Research Council, 1938-39. Unitarian. Home: Kensington, Md. Died Mar. 20, 1978.

HEBBEL, ROBERT, medical educator; b. Windom, Minn., Sept. 23, 1906; s. Henry and Christine (Mensen) H.; B.S., U. Minn., M.B., 1932, M.D., 1933, M.S., 1939, Ph.D., 1942; m. Beulah Agre, Mar. 13, 1942; children—Robert Peter, Elizabeth Agre. Intern Mpls. Gen. Hosp., 1933; resident pathology U. Minn. Hosp., 1937-41; instr. pathology U. Minn. Med. Sch., Mpls., 1941-45, asst. prof., 1945-47, asso. prof., 1947-51, prof. pathology, 1951-77. Served with M.C., AUS, 1942-45. Decorated Bronze Star. Mem. Hennepin County Med. Soc., Minn. Med. Assn., Am. Assn. Pathologists and Bacteriologists, A.M.A., Am. Soc. Clin. Pathologists, Coll. Am. Pathologists, Am. Assn. Cancer Research, Internat. Acad. Pathology, Alpha Omega Alpha, Phi Delta Theta, Nu Sigma Nu. Office: Jackson Hall U Minn Minneapolis MN 55455 Home: St. Paul, Minn. Died Jan. 30, 1977; inurned Sunset Meml. Park, St. Anthony Village, Minn.

HEBERT, F. EDWARD, editor, congressman; b. New Orleans, Oct. 12, 1901; s. Felix Joseph and Lea (Naquin) H.; student Tulane U., 1920-24; LL.D. (hon.), Loyola U. of South; m. Gladys Bofill, Aug. 1, 1934; 1 dau., Dawn Marie (Mrs. John Malcolm Duhe, Jr.). Sports reporter The New Orleans Times-Picayune, 1919-20, asst. sports editor, 1920-25; asst. sports editor New Orleans States, 1925-26, polit. editor and columnist, 1929-37, city editor, 1937-40, when paper broke "Louisiana Scandals," 1939, resulting in overthrow of Huey Long polit. machine (paper subsequently awarded Delta Sigma Chi plaque for "courage in journalism"); publicity Loyola U., New Orleans, 1926-29; dir. Central Homestead Assn.; mem. 77th-94th Congresses, 1st La. Dist., ret., 1976; chmn. house armed services com., 1971-74, chmn. armed services investigating subcom.; mem. house ethics com. Pres. Young Men's Bus. Club New Orleans, 1932. Recipient Internat. Merit of Honor, City of New Orleans; Distinguished Service medal Dept. Army; Distinguished Civilian Service medal Dept. Navy; Distinguished Civilian medal USAF; Outstanding Patriotism award Congl. Medal of Honor Soc.; Distinguished Service medals U.S. Selective Service, Am. Legion, Order of World Wars; Congl. award VFW; Man of Year award Ret. Officers Assn. Mem. Blue Key Soc., Delta Sigma Phi (nat. v.p. 1937-49). Democrat. Roman Catholic. Author: I Went, I Saw, I Heard; Last of the Titans: The Life and Times of F. Edward Hebert. Home: New Orleans, La. Died Dec. 29, 1979.

HEBERT, PAUL MACARIUS, univ. dean; b. Baton Rouge, Nov. 1, 1907; s. Paul Armand and Annie (Byrne) H.; A.B., La. State U., 1929, LL.B., 1929; J.S.D., Yale, 1930; LL.D., Loyola U., New Orleans, 1968; m. Estelle Le Jeune, May 18, 1926; children—Barbara Clare, Mary Sunshine, Paul Macarius. Admitted to La. bar, 1929; prof. law Loyola U., New Orleans, 1930-31, prof., dean Law Sch., 1932-36; asst. prof. law La. State U., 1931-32, prof. law, dean adminstrn., 1936-37, dean Law Sch., prof. law, 1937-39, acting pres., 1939-41, dean law, 1941-49, dean univ., prof. law, 1949-51, dean law, 1952-57, 59-76; mem. firm Breazeale, Sachse, Wilson & Hebert, 1951-52, 57-59; spl. asst. atty. gen. La. for La. Coast Line Litigation, 1965-67. Atty., La. Legislative Bur., 1932, 34, 36, 38; sec., mem. council La. State Law Inst., 1938-76; mem. La. Ednl. Survey Commn., 1940-42; mem. gen. com. to draft new constn. State of La., 1946-76; civilian judge U.S. Mil. Tribunals, Nurnberg, Germany, 1947-48; mem. panel Fed. Mediation and Conciliation Service; mem. loyalty rev. bd. U.S. Civil Service Commn., 1948-53; chmn. La. Labor Mediation Bd., 1953-67; mem. La. Labor-Mgmt. Commn. Inquiry, 1967-76. Served from capt. to lt. col., AUS, 1942-45. Decorated Legion of Merit; recipient Hutton W. Sumners award Southwestern Legal Found., 1976. Mem. Am. Arbitration Assn. (panel), Nat. Acad. Arbitrators (panel), Am., La. (bd. govs. 1946-47, 53), Assn. Am. Law Schs. (chmn. com. inter-Am. coop. 1945-47, exec. com. 1946-47), Order Coif, Delta Kappa Epsilon, Phi Delta Phi, Phi Kappa Phi, Omicron Delta Kappa. Democrat. Roman Catholic. K.C. Home: Baton Rouge, La. Died Feb. 3, 1976.

HECHT, FRANK ABNER, (HEKT), investments; b. Chicago, Ill., July 29, 1888; s. Frank Abner and Clara (Kaestner) H.; B.A., U. Wis.; m. Margaret Elizabeth Lipps, April 28, 1917; 1 dau., Margaret Elizabeth (Mrs. Wm. K. Wimsatt Jr.); m. 2d Mrs. Leroy Gregory Peed, June 1, 1953. Pres., gen. mgr. Kaestner & Hecht Co., electric elevator builders, until 1926 (co. acquired by Westinghouse Electric Corp.); private investments, from 1926. Dep. adminstr. N.R.A., 1934-35; div. chief Chicago Ordnance Dist., 1942-43. Formerly pres. Barrington Countryside Assn., West Central Assn., v.p., dir. Chgo. Assn. of Commerce; trustee Ill. Inst. of Technology, Armour Research Found. Mt. Vernon Sem. (Washington); dir. Employers Assn. Chgo., Pilgrims, Newcomen, Alliance Francaise Honolulu (pres.). Awarded Navy's Dist. Pub. Service Award, 1951. Mem. Navy League U.S. (pres., dir.), English Speaking Union (dir.), Delta Tau Delta, Republican. Mason. Clubs: Metropolitan, 1925 F St. (Washington); University, Tavern (Chgo.). Home: Chicago, Ill. Died Apr. 10, 1976.

HECHT, GEORGE JOSEPH, publisher; b. N.Y.C., Nov. 1, 1895; s. Meyer and Gella (Stern) H.; ed. Ethical Culture Sch., N.Y.C., 1902-13; A.B., Cornell U., 1917; L.H.D., Temple U., 1956; m. Freda Epstein, Jan. 6, 1930; children—Susan (Mrs. Feer), George M. Founder, Better Times Mag., 1919, N.Y.C., editor until 1931; founder, sec., dir. Welfare Council N.Y.C. (now Community Council N.Y.C.), 1926-45; a founder Greater N.Y. Fund, Inc., sec., 1938-44; founder, pub. Parents' Mag., 1926-78, pub. Expecting, Baby Care, Children's Digest, Young Miss, Humpty Dumpty's Mag.; pres. Parents' Mag. Enterprises, Inc., 1926-78; past chmn. F.A.O. Schwarz; pres. Internat. Fedn. Periodical Press, 1963-65. Chmn. Am. Parents Com., Inc. Pres., Hecht-Parents Mag. Found. for Child Welfare, Inc. Chmn. Child Welfare League Am., 1918-19. Head U.S. Govt. Bur. Cartoons, U.S. Com. Pub. Information, World War I. Served in statis. div. Gen. Staff, U.S. Army, World War I. Decorated Palmes Academique (France). Mem. Ethical Culture Soc. Club: Sunningdale Country. Editor and compiler: Above Cayuga's Waters, 1916; The War in Cartoons, 1921. Chmn. Nat. Com. Observance Mother's Day. Home: New York, N.Y. Died Apr. 23, 1980

HECHT, SAMUEL M., merchant; b. Balt., Jan. 28, 1908; s. Moses S. and Blanch (Hartman) H.; B.S., Johns Hopkins, 1928; m. Ruth Samler, Dec. 28, 1951. Controller's office Hecht Co., 1928-29, controller, 1929-42, asst. treas., 1936-42, v.p., treas., asst. to chmn. bd., 1945-47, pres., dir., 1947-55, chmn. bd., 1955-60, dir., to 1970; dir. Terryphone Corp., May Co. Chmn. Balt. County Citizens Adv. Com., Balt. Wholesale Produce Market; chmn. exec. com. Provident Hosp., Md.; bd. dirs. Loyola Coll., Associated Jewish Charities. Served as capt. USAAF, 1942-45. Home: Owings Mills, Md. Died Nov. 30, 1979; buried Balt. Hebrew Cemetery, Reisterstown, Md.

HECK, ARCH OLIVER, educator; b. Bardolph, Ill., Sept. 30, 1887; s. David Stout and Matilda Angeline (Davis) H.; B.S., Hedding Coll., 1913; M.S., U. Ill., 1914; student, Columbia U., 1919-20; Ph.D., Ohio State U., 1924; m. Frances Margaret Agnew, June 9, 1922; children—David Stout, Walter Webb, James Baker, Martha Elizabeth. Rural sch. teacher, Prairie City, Ill., 1905-06; village sch. teacher and prin. New Philadelphia, Ill., 1909-11; prin. Hedding Acad., Abingdon, Ill., 1914-17; head physics dept. Richmond (Ind.) High Sch., 1918-19; dir. research Akron (O.) Pub. Schs., 1920-23; asst. prof. sch. adminstrn., Ohio State U., 1924-28, asso. prof., 1928-33, prof. edn., 1933-58, emeritus, 1958-76; mem. ednl. commn. of fifteen to train School Superintendents, Japan, 1948-49, and 1949-50. Coordinator ednl. program conf., Ohio State U. by U.S. Dept. State and Office Edn., 1956, 57, 58, 59, 61. Served as 1st class pvt. U.S. Army, May-Aug. 1918, 2d lt. Field Arty., August-December 1918. Mem. S.A.R., N.E.A., A.A.S.A., Am. Ednl. Research Assn., Phi Delta Kappa. Sigma Xi. Republican. Methodist. Author: A Study of Child Accounting Records, 1925; Adminstration of Pupil Personnel, 1929; A Study of the Ohio Compulsory Attendance and Child Labor Laws, 1930; Handbook of Compulsory Education (with L. H. Munzenmayer), 1931 The Education of Exceptional Children, 1940 (published in Japanese, 1951), revised edition, 1953; Introduction to Pupil Personnel, 1956. Editor and writer: Pupil Personnel, Guidance and Couseling, 1933, 2d edit., 1936. Contbr. to Nations Sch., Schoolboard Jour., Review of Ednl. Research, Ency. of Ednl. Research, Ency. of Modern Edn., Dictionary of Edn. Mem. editorial bd. Nation's Schs. Home: Columbus, Ohio. Died Mar. 17, 1976.

HECKER, WILLIAM FRANTZ, lawyer; b. Detroit, Aug. 19, 1900; s. Albert Hopkins and Eleanor (McDermott) H.; A.B., Western Res. U., 1922, LL.B., 1924; m. Hannah Elizabeth Kagy, Oct. 10, 1925. Admitted to Ohio bar, 1924, since practiced law in Cleve. Pres. Cleve. Crime Commn., 1949-51, Euclid (Ohio) Bd. Edn., 1941-42, Euclid Pub. Library Bd., 1960-67; area chmn. United Appeal Greater Cleve. Met. div., 1958-62; mem. Euclid Charter Commn., 1950-51, chmn., 1962-63. Trustee Euclid Gen. Hosp. Served to maj. AC, AUS, 1942-45; ETO. Mem. Am., Ohio, Cleve. (pres. 1961-62) bar assns., Am. Judicature Soc., Greater Cleve. Growth Assn., Delta Tau Delta, Phi Delta Phi. Club: Mayfield Country (South Euclid). Home: Euclid, Ohio. Died Apr. 24, 1975.

HECKSCHER, ROBERT VALANTINE, author; b. Phila., Nov. 19, 1883; s. John Austin Stevens and Celeste Du Lompré (Massey) H.; A.B., cum laude in 1905, Harvard, class of 1906; m. Sophie Elizabeth Ernst, of Nova Scotia, Can., 1909. First pub. work appeared in Atlantic Monthly, Sept., 1907. Episcopalian. Mem. Inst. of 1770, Alpha Delta Phi. Author: Through Dust to Light, Poems from an Apprenticeship, 1911; Rose Windows (lyrical poems), 1912. Address: Kensington, London, Eng. *

HEDDENS, BARRET SPENCER, JR., banker; b. Kansas City, Mo., Dec. 5, 1924; s. Barret Spencer and Hattie Lee (Barton) H.; B.S., Mo. Valley Coll., 1949; m. Kathryn Sue Rogers, Oct. 15, 1949; children—Barret Spencer, Helen Lee. Asst. cashier Johnson County Bank & Trust Co., Prairie Village, Kans., 1949-52; with 1st Nat. Bank, Kansas City, 1952-77, pres., dir., 1961-71, chmn. bd., 1971-77; chmn., chief exec. officer 1st Nat. Charter Corp.; dir. Cook Paint and Varnish Co., Unitog Co., Skaggs Cos., Inc., Russell Stover Candies, Inc., ERC Corp., Employers Reins. Corp., Ward Paper Box Co. Bd. dirs. Kansas City Crime Commn., 1962-77; bd. dirs., treas. Kansas City Assn. Trusts and Founds., 1961-77, bd. dirs., v.p. 1st Nat. Found., 1962-77, E.F. Swinney Found., 1962-77; bd. dirs. Jacob L. and Ella C. Loose Found., 1961-77, pres., 1973-76; trustee Midwest Research Inst., U. Kansas City, 1964-77; individual co-trustee Mason L. Dean Charitable Trusts, 1962-77. Named Boss of Year Jr. C. of C., 1965. Served with USNR, 1943-46. Mem. Am. Bankers Assn., Assn. Bank Holding Cos., Assn. Res. City Bankers, Robert Morris Assos., Newcomen Soc., Am. Royal Assn., Inc. (dir., v.p.), Sigma Nu (Man of Year 1971). Home: Kansas City, Mo. Died June 23, 1977.

HEDLUND, GLENN WILBER, agrl. economist; b. Raymond, Nebr., June 11, 1909; s. Claus Oscar and Huldah (Lundquist) H.; B.S., U. Nebr., 1930, Ph.D., Cornell, 1936; m. Helen Howard, July 5, 1939; children—James Howard, Jean Helen, Mary Beth. Asst. Cornell, 1930-33, instr., 1933-36, asst. prof., 1937-41, prof. agrl. economics, 1946-74, prof. emeritus, 1974-76, acting head dept., 1952-54, head dept., 1954-68; prof. U. Nanking, China, 1936-37; prof., head dept. agrl. econs. Pa. State U., 1941-46; vis. prof. U. Philippines, 1956-57; cons. Govt. Bermuda, 1939, Farm Credit Adminstrn., 1944-46, Ford Found., India, 1964, Agrl. Devel. Fund, Iran, 1972, Govt. Bangladesh, 1975. Mem. Am. Agrl. Econs. Assn., Internat. Assn. Agrl. Economists, Sigma Xi, Alpha Zeta, Gamma Sigma Delta, Phi Kappa Phi. Home: Ithaca, N.Y. Died Ithaca, N.Y., June 24, 1976.

HEERMANCE, RADCLIFFE, dean; born in Rhinebeck, New York, April 18, 1882; son of Martin and Nina (Radcliffe) H.; A.B., Williams, 1904, A.M., 1906; A.M., Harvard, 1908, Princeton, 1909; m. Elizabeth Platt Adams, Dec. 18, 1912 (died Oct. 27, 1919); m. 2d, Beatrice Weatherbee Donnelly, Feb. 11, 1945. Instr. Lawrenceville (N.J.) Sch., 1904-06, 1907-08; Scribner fellow in English, 1908, instr. English, 1909, asst. prof., 1912-21, supervisor of freshmen since 1921, prof. and director of admission since 1922, dean of freshmen, 1925-42, Princeton, acting dean of the college, 1943-44. Chairman College Entrance Examination Bd., 1933-36. Commd. capt. inf. U.S.R., Nov. 27, 1917; maj. U.S. Army, Aug. 20, 1918; comdg. U.S. Training Detachment, Atlanta, Ga., 1918; prof. mil. sci. and tactics, Harvard, and comdg. S.A.T.C., 1918; lt. col. O.R.C., 1923. Mem. Soc. War of 1812, Alpha Delta Phi, Holland Soc. of New York, Dutchess County Soc. of New York. Mem. Dutch Ref. Ch. Clubs: Nassau (Princeton); University, Williams Club, Ends of the Earth (New York City); Army and Navy (Washington). Home: Princeton, N.J. *

HEEZEN, BRUCE CHARLES, oceanographer, geologist; b. Vinton, Iowa, Apr. 11, 1924; s. Charles Christian and Esther (Schirding) H.; B.A., State U. Iowa, 1948; M.A., Columbia, 1952, Ph.D., 1957. Geologist Woods Hole (Mass.) Oceanographic Inst., 1947-48; fellow in geology Columbia, 1948-51, asst. in geology, 1951-53, lectr., 1953-55, research asso., 1955-57; sr. research scientist Lamont Geol. Obs., Palisades, N.Y., 1957-60, mem. academic staff, 1960-77; asst. prof. geology Columbia, 1960-64, asso. prof., 1964-77; cons. U.S. Naval Oceanographic Office, 1968-77; mem. guiding com. for gen. bathymetric chart of the oceans; pres. commn. marine geology Internat. Union Geol. Scis.; pres. commn. marine geophysics Internat. Assn. Phys. Scis. of the Ocean; coordinator IUGS Atlantic, Indian and Pacific Oceans of Geol. World Atlas. Recipient Henry Bryant Biglow medal, prize in oceanography for contbn. to marine sci.; Cullum Geog. medal; Shepard medal for excellence in marine geology. Fellow A.A.A.S., Am. Geog. Soc., Geol. Soc. Am., Iowa Acad. Sci., Marine Biol. Assn. of U.K., Royal Astron. Soc.; mem. Am. Assn. Petroleum Geologists, Am. Geophys. Union, Am. Soc. Limnology and Oceanography, Geochem. Soc., N.Y. Acad. Scis., Seismol. Soc. Am., Soc. Exploration Geophysicists, Socitea Limnologae Internalis, Sigma Xi, Sigma Chi. Unitarian. Author: The Floors of the Oceans: The Face of the Deep. Contbr. over 300 articles to profl. jours. Home: Piermont, N.Y. Died June 21, 1977; interred Greenwood Cemetery, Muscatine, Iowa.

HEFFERLINE, RALPH FRANKLIN, psychologist; b. Muncie, Ind., Feb. 15, 1910; s. Samuel Thomas and Blanche (Cecil) H.; B.S., Columbia, 1941, M.A., 1942, Ph.D., 1947; m. Dorothy Halliday, Aug. 25, 1939. Faculty, Columbia, N.Y.C., 1948-74, prof., 1967-74, pre-med. adviser, 1949-54, chmn. dept. psychology, 1965-68. Fellow Am. Psychol. Assn., A.A.A.S., N.Y. Acad. Scis.; mem. Psychonomic Soc., Eastern Psychol. Assn., Soc. for Gen. Systems Research, Soc. Psychophysiol., Bio-Feedback Soc., Soc. Neuroscis.; affiliate mem. Royal Soc. Medicine (London). Research. Author: (with F.S. Perls and P. Goodman) Gestalt Therapy, 1950. Research on significance of patterns of muscular tension for psychoneurosis and anxiety, electromyographic study of very small responses as behavioral counterpart of mental processes. Home: New York, N.Y. Died Mar. 16, 1974.

HEFFNER, EDWARD HOCH, prof. Latin; b. Dryville, Pa., Sept. 15, 1886; s. Henry and Amelia Diener (Hoch) H.; A.B., Franklin and Marshall Coll., 1911; A.M., Columbia, 1914; Ph.D., U. of Pa., 1916; Harrison fellow, 1915-16; m. Emma Wilhelmina Merkle, Sept. 17, 1925. Head of dept. Latin, Franklin and Marshall Acad., 1911-14; instr. in Latin, Univ. of Pennsylvania, 1914-20, assistant professor, 1920-26, professor since 26, assistant to dean of Graduate School, 1926-28. Member American Philol. Assn., Archaeol. Inst. America (sec. for South Atlantic States), Am. Classical League, Classical Assn. Atlantic States, Phila. Classical Soc., Phila. Soc. for Promotion of Liberal Studies (ex-pres.), Phi Beta Kappa. Club: Phila. Classical (ex-pres.). Asso. editor Am. Jour. Archaeology, 1925-32. Editor: The Classical Weekly, 1945-49, chmn. dept. classical studies since 1950. Contbr. to classical periodicals. Home: Phila. *

HEFLEBOWER, ROY CLEVELAND, army officer (ret.); b. Washington, Oct. 25, 1884; s. George Washington and Annie Maria (Clark) H.; M.D., George Washington U., 1906; hon. grad. U.S. Army Med. Sch., 1910; distinguished grad. Army Sch. of the Line, 1922; grad. Gen. Staff Sch., 1923, Army War Coll., 1924, Army Indsl. Coll., 1927; m. Mrs. Mayre Lawson Noelke, Mar. 25, 1935; children—(by 1st marriage) Dorothy Margaret (Mrs. John Bischoff) and Col. Roy Cleveland; (adopted) Helen Mildred (Mrs. Charles Stegman). Began practice of med., 1906; served as intern Emergency Hosp., Washington; commd. 1st lt., Med. Res. Corps, 1909; promoted through grades to brig. gen. (temp.), U.S.A., Dec. 15, 1941. Ret. as brig. gen., 1946; now asst. dir. M.D. Anderson Hosp. for Cancer Research. Awarded gold medal and $500 for prize essay on "Prisoners of War—The Causes of Their Sufferings in the Past and the Best Way to Prevent Them". U.S. Army Legion of Merit 1945, U.S.A. Commendation Ribbon, 1946. Fellow A.M.A.; mem. Assn. of Mil. Surgeons, Phi Chi, Nat. Sojourners. Episcopalian. Mason (Scottish Rite 32 deg.), Mystic Shrine. Clubs: Army and Navy Country (Washington). Home: Houston. *

HEHRE, FREDERICK WILLIAM, physician; b. Harrison, N.J., Dec. 19, 1923; s. Frederick William and Florence Francis (Feickert) H.; B.A., Columbia Coll., 1944; M.D., Columbia U., 1947; m. Josephine Frances Carvill, Oct. 18, 1947; children—Frederick William III, Carol Jean Hehre Slocum, Richard C. Intern, St. Clares Hosp., N.Y.C., 1947-48; resident anesthesiology Presbyn. Hosp., N.Y.C., 1948-50, asst., asso., asst. attending anesthesiologist, 1950-56; practice medicine, specializing in anesthesiology, N.Y.C., 1950-56, New Haven, 1956-75, Boston, 1975-80; asso. dir. anesthesiology Yale New Haven Hosp., 1956-75; chmn. dept. anesthesiology Boston U. Med. Center, 1975-80; instr., asso. anesthesiologist Columbia U., 1950-56; asst. prof., asso. prof. anesthesiology Yale U., 1956-75; prof. anesthesiology Boston U. Sch. Medicine, 1975-80. Served with AUS, 1941-46; to capt., M.C., U.S. Army, 1953-55. Diplomate Am. Bd. Anesthesiology. Fellow Am. Coll. Anesthesiology; mem. Am. Soc. Anesthesiology, Mass. Soc. Anesthesiology, Assn. U. Anesthesiologists, AMA, Mass. Med. Soc., Suffolk County Med. Soc., Internat. Anesthesiol. Research Soc., N.E. Soc. Anesthesiology, Sigma Xi. Republican. Episcopalian. Contbr. sci. articles to med. jours. Home: Boston, Mass. Died Apr. 11, 1980; buried West Tisbury Cemetery, Martha's Vineyard, Mass.

HEIM, RAYMOND WALTER (HIM), vocational education officer, State of Del.; b. Williamsport, Pa., Oct. 13, 1886; s. David Jacob and Hulda (Schaeffer) H.; B.S., Pa. State Coll., 1913; A.M., Columbia U., 1921; student Cornell U., summer 1918, Rutgers U., summer 1934; LL.D., U. Del., 1952; m. Bess Fye, Aug. 5, 1913. Supervisor agr., Waterford (Pa.) Acad., 1913-15; state dir. for vocational edn. State Dept. Pub. Instrn., Del, 1919-52; prof. vocational edn., University of Del., 1919-52; state adminstr. for World War Orphans' Edn. since 1929; state dir. for War Prdn. Training Programs, 1940-45; exec. officer for state bd. for Vocational Edn., rehabilitation div., since 1943. Member Indsl. Club of Del., Consumers League of Del., Newark (Del.) Chamber of Commerce, Del. Rehabilitation Council. Member Delegate State Educational Association, N.E.A., Del. and Am. vocational associations, Phi Kappa Phi, Phi Delta Kappa, Alpha Zeta (asso. at large). Mason (32 deg., Shriner). Clubs: Torch, Rotary, Faculty (University Del.). Author several books, latest: 30 Years Vocational Education in Delaware, 1949. Home: Newark, Del. *

HEIM, SCHUYLER F(RANKLIN) (HIM), naval officer (ret.); b. Plymouth, Ind., Jan. 14, 1884; s. Peter and Henrietta (Wade) H.; grad. U.S. Naval Acad., 1907, Naval War Coll., 1929, Army Indsl. Coll., 1934; m. Ramona McCudden, June 24, 1914. Commd. ensign, U.S. Navy, 1909, and advanced through grades to commodore, 1944; sea duty in battleships, cruisers, repair ships and destroyers; shore duty, Mare Island Navy Yard, 1913-15, U.S. Naval Acad., 1918-20, 23-26; Atlantic convoy and transport duty, U.S.S. Charleston, 1916-18; with Navy Dept., Washington, 1934-36; comd. U.S.S. Richmond, 1935-37, destroyer squadron of Neutrality Patrol, 1939-40; duty at Naval Operating base, Terminal Island, Calif., 1940-45, also comdt. naval activities in Los Angeles-Long Beach area; ret. from active duty, 1946. Awarded Legion of Merit, World War II. Clubs: Army-Navy, Army and Navy Country (Washington), Propreller of America; Pacific Coast (Long Beach). Home: Long Beach, Calif. *

HEINDEL, RICHARD HEATHCOTE, educator; b. Hanover, Pa., Aug. 24, 1912; s. Franklin E. and Lelia I. (Heathcote) H.; A.B., Harvard U., 1933; M.A., U. Pa., 1934, Ph.D. (Penfield fellow), 1938; student Gettysburg Coll., 1929-31; Litt.D., Wagner Coll., 1957; m. Elizabeth Calvert, June 30, 1934 (dec. June 1962); children—Heath, Thomas, Bridget; m. 2d, Dorothy Pushaw, June 1963 (div. 1969); m. 3d, Ruth V. Noble, 1969. Tchr. Drexel Inst., 1934-36; Field fellow Social Sci. Research Council, 1936-37, exec. asso., 1949-50; instr., later asst. prof. modern European history U. Pa., 1938-46; dir. Am. Library, Am. Embassy, London, Eng., 1942-45; chief div. libraries and insts. State Dept., 1946-47; profl. staff asso. Senate Fgn. Relations Com., 1947-49; staff asso. Pub. Library Inquiry, 1947; consultant U.S. Nat. Commn. UNESCO, 1949-50, dep. dir. UNESCO relations staff State Dept. 1950-54; cons.-lectr., inst. world affairs Pa. State College, summer 1952, 53, 54; prof. history and govt. U. Buffalo, 1954-58, dean Coll. Arts and Sci., 1954-56, vice chancellor, 1956-58; pres. Wagner Coll., S.I., N.Y., 1958-61; pres. Pratt Inst., Bklyn., 1961-67; prof. internat. relations Capitol Campus, Pa. State U., Middletown, 1967-79, dean faculty, 1967-77. Mem. U.S. nat. commn. for UNESCO, 1958-62; cons. Nat. Resources Planning Bd., 1942; dir., organizer War Documentation Service, 1939-42; field dir. Fgn. Policy Assn., 1939-40; regional dir. Survey Fed. Archives, 1936; dir. Phila. Survey Hist. Manuscripts, 1936; member U.S. delegation Gen. Conf., UNESCO, Paris, France, 1951; Am. observer Books and Periodicals Commn., Conf. Allied Ministers Edn., London, 1943-45; secretary Com. Interchange Persons, Conf. Bd. Asso. Research Councils, 1949-50, 54; exec. sec. Nat. Commn. Conservation Cultural Resources, 1941; overseas corr. sec. Am. Council Learned Socs., 1943-45; mem. com. on lang. devel. U.S. Office Edn., 1958-63; mem. commn. internat. edn. Am. Council Edn. Hon. fellow Library Congress, 1941-55; adv. bd. Internat. Soc. Ednl., Am. Studies Assn., Cultural and Sci.

Exchanges. Mem. Am. Hist. Assn., Am. Polit. Sci. Assn., Soc. Advancement Edn. (trustee), Soc. Historians Am. Fgn. Relations, Internat. Studies Assn., Fgn. Policy Assn. (pres. Harrisburg 1977-78), Phi Sigma Kappa, Phi Beta Kappa. Author: The American Impact on Great Britain, 1940; War Check List, 1941; Integration of Federal and Non-Federal Research, 1942; The Present Position of Foreign Area Studies in the U.S., 1950; also numerous articles, reviews, govt. reports. Editor book revs. Social Studies, 1939-42; American Influence Abroad, 1950; editorial cons. Doubleday & Co., 1950; editor Internat. Affairs sect. Intellct, 1974-78. Address: Harrisburg, Pa. Died July 31, 1979; buried Hanover, Pa.

HEINEMANN, GUSTAV W., pres. West Germany; b. Schwelm/Westfalen, July 23, 1899; s. Otto and Johanna (Walter) H.; D. Polit. Sci., U. Marburg (Germany), 1921; D.Law, U. Münster (Germany), 1929; Th.D. (hon.), U. Bonn, 1967; m. Hilda Ordemann, Oct. 28, 1926; children—Uta Ranke-Heineman (Mrs. Edmund Ranke), Christa (Mrs. Eduard Delius), Barbara (Mrs. Manfred Wichelhaus), Peter. Aux. judge, Lunen/Westfalen; atty, Essen, Germany, 1926; lawyer, also legal counsel and confidental clk. Rheinische Stahlwerke, 1928-39; bd. mem. Rheinische Stahlwerke, Essen, 1936-39; lectr. mining, 1933-39, also econ. law U. Cologne; mayor of Essen, 1946-49; provincial del. in Düsseldorf, 1947; minister of justice Nordrhein-Westfalen, 1947-48; fed. minister of interior, 1949-50; lawyer, notary Essen, 1951; resigned from Christian Dem. Union, 1952; co-founder Gesamtdeutsche Volkspartei, 1952; dissolution of Gesamtdeutsche Volkspartei, 1957; joined SPD, 1957; mem. German Parliament, 1957; mem. party bd. SPD, 1955-76; fed. minister justice W. Germany, 1966; fed. pres. W. Germany, 1969-74. Active Bekennenden Kirche, 1933-76; chmn. CVJM, Essen, 1936; mem. council EKD, Treysa, 1945-67, wrote Stuttgart Declaration, 1945; mem. direction Evangel. Ch., Rheinland, 1945-62; mem. Commn. Internat. Affairs World Council Chs., 1948-61; pres. Constl. Ch. Assembly in Eisenach, 1948; pres. synod EKD, 1949-55; participant constl. found. German Evangel. Ch. Council, 1949. Home: Essen, West Germany Died July 7, 1976.

HEINER, ROBERT GRAHAM, lawyer; b. West Point, N.Y., Aug. 19, 1900; s. Gordon Graham and Elizabeth Cloyd (Kent) H.; A.B., Johns Hopkins, 1921; B.A. in Jurisprudence, Oxford (Eng.) U., 1923; m. Frances Eliot Cassidy, July 31, 1926 (dec. July 1958); children—Clinton Graham, Frances Eliot; m. 2d, Nina King Colgate, Jan. 22, 1967. Admitted to N.Y. bar, 1929; asso., then partner firm Cotton & Franklin, N.Y.C., 1924-42; asst. gen. counsel office Lend-Lease Adminstrn., 1943; partner Cahill, Gordon, Reindel & Ohl, and predecessor, N.Y.C., 1943-61. Bd. dirs. Planned Parenthood of N.Y.C. (pres. 1972-74), Planned Parenthood Fedn. Am., 1963-68; trustee Knickerbocker Hosp., N.Y.C., 1961-72. Home: New York, N.Y. Deceased.

HEINISCH, DON, truck mfg. co. exec.; b. Chgo., Aug. 23, 1923; s. Gustav O. and Marie (Hausdorf) H.; B.S., Washington U., St. Louis, 1942; C.P.A., LaSalle Extension U., Chgo., 1948; m. Alyce N. Lovell, Jan. 23, 1946; 1 son, Kelby G. Gen. mgr. Darling Co., 1946-50; sec.-treas. Crescent Industries div. Sears-Roebuck, 1950-56; treas. AMI div. Automatic Canteen Corp., 1956-57; pres. Recordio Corp., 1957-63; pres. Diamond-Reo div. White Motors Corp., 1963-68; pres. FWD Corp., Clintonville, Wis., 1968-74. Bd. dirs. Clintonville Community Hosp.; mem. exec. com. Valley council Boy Scouts Am Served with USAAF 1943-46; CBI. Mason. Rotarian. Home: Clintonville, Wis. Died 1974.

HEINL, ROBERT DEBS, JR., marine corps officer, writer; b. N.Y.C., Aug. 12, 1916; s. Robert Debs and Helen Margaret (Corbin) H.; B.A. with orations (cum laude), Yale Coll., 1937; m. Nancy Gordon Wright, Sept. 23, 1939; children—Pamela Gordon (Mrs. John R. Burdick), Michael Charles. Commd. 2nd lt. USMC, 1937, advanced through grades to col.; service Pearl Harbor, Dec. 7, 1941; assigned relief expdn. Wake Is., 1941, S. Pacific, 1942, Guam, 1944, Iwo Jima, 1945, Japan, 1945, N. China, 1946; dir. Marine Corps history, 1946-49; with 1st Marine Div., also comdr. E. Coast Islands, Korea, 1952-53; comdr. U.S. Mil. Group and U.S. Naval Mission, Port-au-Prince, Haiti, 1958-63; ret. 1963; mil. corr. Detroit News, 1967-78; def. corr. N. Am. Newspaper Alliance, 1978-79. Cons. long-range gun systems Navy Dept., 1967-68; guest lectr. Yale, Brown U., Nat., Naval, and Air War Coll., Fgn. Service Inst., InterAm. Def. Coll., U. Peking. Decorated Legion of Merit with combat V, Bronze Star with combat V; recipient award of merit U.S. Naval Inst., 1968. Fellow Pierson Coll. Yale, 1975-79. Mem. Inst. Strategic Studies, Am. Mil. Inst., Naval Inst., White House Corr. Assn., Sigma Delta Chi, Chi Delta Theta. Episcopalian. Clubs: Army and Navy, Nat. Press (Washington); N.Y. Yacht, Yale (N.Y.C.); American (London, Eng.); Carabao; Mory's. Author: The Defense of Wake, 1947; Marines at Midway, 1948; The Marshalls: Increasing the Tempo, 1954; The Marine Officer's Guide, 4th edit., 1977; Soldiers of the Sea, 1962; Dictionary of Military and Naval Quotations, 1966; Victory at High Tide (Alfred Thayer Mahan award U.S. Navy League), 1968; Handbook for Marine NCOs, 2d edit., 1979; (with Nancy G. Heinl) Written in Blood, 1978. Contbr. to Ency. Brit., Dictionary Am. Biography, Dictionary Am. History; also articles. Home: Washington, D.C. Died May 5, 1979.

HEINRICH, HELMUT GUSTAV, aerodynamicist, educator; b. Berlin, Germany, Aug. 5, 1910; s. Karl Herman and Anna (Groth) H.; B.E. Mech., State Engineering Sch., Stettin, Germany, 1931; B.E. Aero., Technische Hochschule, Stuttgart, Germany, 1936, M.E. Aero., 1938, D.Eng., 1943; m. Luise Wilhelmine Giller, Dec. 10, 1938; children—Hildegard, Eva, Klaus. Came to U.S., 1946, naturalized, 1954. Asst. prof. applied mechanics Inst. Tech., Stuttgart, Germany, 1938-40; head dept. aerodynamics Research Inst., Graf Zennelin, Stuttgart, 1940-46; tech. adviser Wright Air Development Center Wright Field, O., 1946-56; lectr. U. Dayton, 1950-56; prof. aero. engring. U. Minn., from 1956, project sci. Aerodynamic Retardation. Armed Forces Steering Com., U. Minn.; cons. NASA Marshall Space Flight Center, Honeywell, Litton Industries, and Schieldahl Company. Decorated The Kriegs-Verdienst-Kreuz (Germany); recipient Thurman H. Bane award Inst. Aero. Scis., 1954; Aeronaut Leo Stevens Meml. medal Leo Stevens Meml. Com., 1956. Fellow AIAA (Aerodynamic Deceleration Systems award 1979), Royal Aero. Soc. Gt. Brit.; asso. fellow Inst. Aero. Scis.; mem. Wissenschaftliche Gesellschaft fuer Luft fahrt Forschung, Sigma Gamma Tau. Author sci. articles. Inventor guide surface parachute: holder numerous U.S., fgn. patents. Home: Minneapolis, Minn. Died Mar. 7, 1979.

HEINRICH, RUDOLF, stage designer; b. Halle, Germany, Feb. 10, 1926; s. Otto and Theresa (Foerster) H.; m. Joan Carroll, Oct. 5, 1960 (div. June 1966). Designer for Leipzig Opera, 1948-50, Halle Opera, 1950-54, Komische Opera, Berlin, Germany, 1954-61; prof. stage design and costumes Akademie der Bildenden Künste, Munich, Germany, 1964-75; guest designer La Scala, Milan, Italy, Theatre de Nation, Paris, France, Stanislawsky Theatre, Moscow, USSR, Göteborg (Sweden) Theatre, Hamburgische (Germany) Staatsoper, Frankfurt (Germany) Opera, Cologne (Germany) Opera, Munich Opera, Residenz Theater, Munich, Kammerspiele, Munich, Vienna (Austria) Staatsoper, Burg Theater, Vienna, Zurich (Switzerland) Opera, Santa Fe Opera, Boston Opera, Met. Opera, Royal Nat. Theater, London, Eng., also Salzburg Festival, 1966. Died Nov. 30, 1975.

HEIZER, ROBERT FLEMING, anthropologist; b. Denver, July 13, 1915; s. Ott Fleming and Martha (Madden) H.; A.B., U. Calif., 1936, Ph.D., 1941; D.Sc., U. Nev., 1965; m. Nancy Elizabeth Heizer, July 31, 1940 (div.); children—Stephen Rodney, Michael Madden, Sydney Alison. Instr., U. Oreg., 1940-41; instr. U. Calif. at Los Angeles, 1945-46, asst. prof. at Berkeley, 1946-48, asso. prof., 1949-52, prof., 1952-76, emeritus, 1976-79, dir. U. Calif. Archeol. Survey, Berkeley, 1948-60, dir. Archeol. Research Facility, dept. anthropology, 1960-76, curator N. Am. Archeology Lowie Mus. Anthropology, 1950-79. Grantee Am. Philos. Soc., 1945-49, Wenner Gren Found. Anthrop., 1955-60, Nat. Geog. Soc., 1955, 57, 65, 68, 71, 72, NSF, 1958-60, 63-64, 68-71; Guggenheim fellow, 1963, 72. Fellow AAAS; mem. Soc. Am. Archeology (v.p. 1959-60), Am. Anthrop. Assn., Societé des Americanistes de Paris, Nat. Acad. Scis., Assos. Tropical Biogeography, Inst. Andean Research. Author: Francis Drake and the California Indians, 1947; (with John E. Mills) The Four Ages of Tsurai, 1952; A Guide to Archeological Field Methods, rev. edit., 1958; The Archeologist at Work, 1959; (with M.A. Baumhoff) Prehistoric Rock Art of Nevada and Eastern California, 1962; Man's Discovery of His Past, 1962; The California Indians, rev. edit., 1971; (with F. Hole) An Introduction to Prehistoric Archeology, 1965, 2d rev. edit., 1973; (with T. Kroeber) Almost Ancestors, 1968; (with A. Almquist) The Other Californians, 1971; (with C. Clewlow) Prehistoric Rock Art of California, 1973; They Were Only Diggers, 1973; The Destruction of California Indians, 1974; Elizabethan California, 1975; (with F. Hole) Prehistoric Archeology, a Short Introduction, 1977; numerous articles in field. Home: El Cerrito, Calif. Died July 17, 1979.

HEKMAN, EDWARD JOHN, cons.; b. Grand Rapids, Mich., July 5, 1914; s. John and Cornelia (Haan) H.; A.B., Calvin Coll., 1935; m. Florence Stuart, Sept. 25, 1937; children—Marilyn (Mrs. John Clark), Judy (Mrs. DuBois S. Thompson), John, Susan. With Hekman Biscuit Co., div. of United Biscuit Co. Am., 1935-60, v.p., 1946-50, pres., gen. mgr., 1951-60; dir. United Biscuit Co. Am. (co. name changed to Keebler Co. 1965), 1950-68, v.p., 1954-59, pres., 1960-67, vice chmn. bd. dirs., 1967-68; v.p. Valparaiso (Ind.) U., 1968-69; adminstr. Food and Nutrition Service U.S. Dept. Agr., 1969-76; cons., 1977-80. Trustee Pine Rest Hosp., Grand Rapids, Nutrition Found. Served from ensign to lt. (j.g.) USNR, 1943-46. Lutheran. Clubs: Sea Pines (Hilton Head, S.C.); Kenwood Country (Washington). Address: Washington, D.C. Died Mar. 18, 1980.

HELD, ADOLPH, orgn. exec., editor; b. Poland, May 16, 1885; s. Jacob and Yetta (Taube) H.; came to U.S., 1894, naturalized; B.S., Coll. City N.Y., 1906; m. Lillian Michaels, Sept. 22, 1913. City editor Jewish Daily Forward, N.Y.C., 1906-12, bus. mgr., 1912-17; alderman, N.Y.C., 1917-19; dir. immigration work Hebrew Immigrant Aid Soc., N.Y.C., 1921-25; pres. Amalgamated Bank, 1925-45; dir. welfare and health benefits Internat. Ladies Garment Workers' Union; pres. Forward Assn. (pub. Jewish Daily Forward), Radio Sta. WEVD, N.Y.C. Chmn. Jewish Labor Com.; dir. joint distbn. com. Hebrew Immigrant Aid Soc. Mem. Jewish Edn. Soc. (nat. refugee com.). Liberal Party. Home: N.Y.C. *

HELLER, PHILIP ALTER, assn. exec.; b. Austria, Aug. 6, 1911; s. Abram and Dina (Salat) H.; student Bklyn. Coll., 1930-34; B.A., N.Y. U., 1959; m. Evelyn Elkin, Sept. 27, 1941. Chief records and statistics employment div. City of N.Y., 1933-37; ednl. dir. Knitgoods Workers Union, N.Y.C., 1937-49; information officer ECA Mission to Austria and U.S. High Commn. to Germany, 1949-53; asst. to pres. Internat. Upholsterers Union, 1954-55; polit. officer Am. embassy, Conakry, Guinea, 1960-63; chief polit. sect., 1st sec. Am. embassy, Nairobi, Kenya, 1964-66; charge d'affairs, Bujumbuna, Burundi, 1966, State Dept., 1966; supervising polit. officer, Frankfurt, Germany, 1967-69; dir. internat. affairs Am. Fed. State, County and Municipal Employees, 1969-75; tchr. Georgetown U., Fed. City Coll., 1975-76, CSC. Dir. Internat. Solidarity Com., 1945-49. Recipient Meritorious Service award Dept. State, 1963, Superior honor, 1967; Econs. Honor award, Founders Day Honor award N.Y. U. Mem. Am. Acad. Polit. and Social Sci., Acad. Polit. Sci. Home: Washington, D.C. Died Dec. 6, 1976.

HELLIWELL, PAUL LIONEL EDWARD, lawyer, banker; b. Bklyn., Sept. 17, 1913; s. L.H. and Nola C. (Harless) H.; A.B., U. Fla., 1937, J.D., 1939; m. Marjorie Mueller, Aug. 8, 1942; 1 dau., Anne Elizabeth. Admitted to Fla. bar, 1939, since practice in Miami; sr. partner firm Helliwell, Melrose, De Wolf; sec., gen. counsel Am. Bankers Life Assurance Co. of Fla., from 1952; chmn. bd. Bank of Perrine, from 1962, Bank of Cutler Ridge, Miami, from 1964, Fla. Shares, Inc., from 1973; dir. First Nat. Bank Homestead, Palm Beach Mall Bank, others. Chmn. Fla. Citizens for Eisenhower, 1952, 56; del. Republic Nat. Conv., 1952, 56. Served as col. M.I. and OSS, U.S. Army, 1941-46. Decorated Legion of Merit with oak leaf cluster, Army Commendation medal with oak leaf cluster; Order Cloud and Banner (China); comdr. Order White Elephant (Thailand). Mem. Am., Fla., Dade County, Orange County bar assns., Bar Assn. City N.Y., Fedn. Ins. Counsel, Fla. Council of 100, Chi Phi, Phi Alpha Delta. Clubs: Miami Bankers; River (Jacksonville, Fla.): Kings Bay Yacht; Univ. (Orlando, Fla.); Ocean Reef (Key Largo). Home: Coral Gables, Fla. Deceased.

HELLMAN, GEOFFREY THEODORE, writer; b. N.Y.C., Feb. 13, 1907; s. George S. and Hilda Emily (Josephthal) H.; A.B. (columnist Yale Daily News 1927-28), Yale, 1928; m. 2d, Katherine Henry, Aug. 18, 1960 (dec. Nov. 30, 1980); children—Daisy (by previous marriage), Katharine. Reporter, asso. editor New Yorker mag., 1929-31; asso. editor Fortune mag., 1931-32; staff writer New Yorker mag., 1932-36; asso. editor Life mag., 1936-38; staff writer New Yorker mag., 1938-77; on leave of absence as staff writer Office Coordinator Inter-Am. Affairs, 1942-44; spl. cons. Hdqrs. USAAF, 1944; mem. history sect. OSS, 1944-45. Mem. Chi Delta Theta. Clubs: Grolier, Coffee House, Century, Dutch Treat, (N.Y.C.); Graduates, Elizabethan (bd. govs. 1926-27) (New Haven); Cosmos (Washington). Author: How to Disappear for an Hour, 1947; Mrs. DePeyster's Parties, 1963; The Smithsonian, 1967; Bankers, Bones and Beetles: The First Century of the American Museum of Natural History, 1968. New Yorker Profiles and satirical articles have appeared in several anthologies.

HELLMAN, MORTON J., mathematician, educator; b. N.Y.C., Jan. 28, 1918; s. Jacob and Bess (Frank) H.; B.S., Coll. City N.Y., 1938, M.S., 1942; Ph.D., N.Y. U., 1954; m. Martha Dorothea Kaufman, Dec. 31, 1942; children—Paul Victor, Charles David, George Edward. Mem. faculty Newark Coll. Arts and Scis., Rutgers State U., 1946-66, asso. prof., 1958-65, prof., 1965-66; prof. math. L.I. U., Bklyn., 1966-80, chmn. dept., 1966-79, dir. NSF coop. coll-sch. sci. program grant, 1972-73, dir. NSF pre-coll. tchr. devel. in sci. project grant, 1978-79. Served to lt. USNR, 1943-46. Recipient Outstanding Tchr. award Newark Rutgers U., 1966; NSF grantee, 1979-80, 80-81. Mem. AAUP, Am. Math. Soc., Math. Assn. Am. (vice chmn. met. N.Y. sect. 1969-71, chmn. 1971-73), Nat. Council Tchrs. Math., Phi Beta Kappa, Sigma Xi. Author: College Algebra 1956, rev. edit., 1963. Contbr. articles to profl. jours Home: New York, N.Y. Died Oct. 15, 1980.

HELLMAN, SAM, writer; b. San Francisco, Calif., July 4, 1885; s. Benjamin and Leah (Stelmach) H.; A.B., U of Calif., 1906; m. Selma Schwartz, of St. Louis, Mo. June 22, 1913; children—Emmy Lou, Verna Ruth

Newspaper reporter and editor, 1906-20; mag. writing and motion picture scenarios exclusively since 1920. Mem. Authors' League of America. Clubs: Friars (New York); Lakeville Golf and Country. Author: Low Bridge, 1926; Toll Bridge, 1930. Contbr. to Saturday Evening Post, Red Book, etc. Address: Beverly Hills, Calif. *

HELMKE, WALTER EDWARD, lawyer; b. Ft. Wayne, Ind., Dec. 17, 1901; s. Herman and Mary (Engel) H.; LL.B., Ind. U., 1925, LL.D., 1973; m. Wilma L. Wehrenberg, June 3, 1926; children—Walter Paul, Mary Ann (Mrs. Charles R. Scheele), Carolyn (Mrs. Charles K. Stoltz). Admitted to Ind. bar, 1925, practiced in Ft. Wayne; sr. mem. Helmke, Beams, Boyer & Wagner; pros. atty. Allen County, Ind., 1930-31; city atty. Ft. Wayne, 1935-47; v.p., dir. Jefferson Nat. Life Ins. Co., Indpls.; dir. Jefferson Corp. Indpls. Republican candidate for 74th U.S. Congress, 4th Congl. Dist. Ind., 1934, for gov. Ind., 1948; Rep. County chmn. Allen County, 1940-50; ind. del. Rep. Nat. Conv., Phila., 1948. Trustee Ind. U., 1954-56; bd. dirs. Foellinger Found., Ft. Wayne; bd. govs. James Whitcomb Riley Meml. Hosp., Indpls., 1970-76; former mem. adv. bd. Valparaiso U.; adv. bd. Ind. U., Ft. Wayne, 1972-76. Mem. Allen County (past pres.). Am., Ind. bar assns., Tau Kappa Alpha, Phi Delta Phi, Phi Kappa Psi. Lutheran (pres. Internat. Walther League 1933-39). Home: Fort Wayne, Ind. Died Feb. 4, 1976.

HELMS, E. ALLEN, educator; b. Veedersburg, Ind., Sept. 24, 1897; s. Allen Walker and Mary (Purdue) H.; A.B., U. Ill., 1922, M.A., 1923, Ph.D., 1927; m. Lois Light, July 26, 1924; 1 dau., Louise Marie (Mrs. Robert S. Smith). Mem. faculty Ohio State U., 1925-79, prof. polit. sci., 1937-67, prof. emeritus, 1967-79, chmn. dept., 1959-62; vis. prof. George Peabody Coll., summer 1927-37, U. Ill., 1941, Mich. State U., 1946, U. Oxford (Eng.), 1950-51, U.Wis., 1952. Mem. Am. Polit. Sci. Assn., Midwest Conference Polit. Scientists (pres. 1962-63, exec. council 1963-64. Author: Eighteenth Amendment, 1928. Co-author: Democracy in Transition, 1938: American Politics, 2d edit., 1947; The Presidency in Transition, 1949; Goals for Political Science, 1951; Nomination Politi, 1952. Home: Columbus, Ohio. Died Jan. 23, 1979.

HELPERN, MILTON, physician, forensic pathologist; b. N.Y.C., Apr. 17, 1902; s. Moses and Bertha (Toplon) H.; B.S., CCNY, 1922, LL.D. (hon.) 1972; M.D., Cornell U., 1926; LL.D. (hon.), Ghent U., 1970, N.Y. Law Sch., 1976; m. Ruth Vyner, July 10, 1927 (dec. Jan. 1953); children—Nancy (Mrs. Edward Moldover), Susan (Mrs. Paul Nettler), Alice (Mrs. Elliot M. Gross); m. 2d, Beatrice L. Nightingale, Jan. 1, 1955; stepchildren—William and Stuart Nightingale. Intern 2d Med. Div., Bellevue Hosp., N.Y.C., 1927-29, resident pathologist, 1929-31, pathologist 2d Surg. Div., 1929-31; asst. med. examiner Office Chief Med. Examiner, City N.Y., 1931-43, dep. chief med. examiner, 1943-54, chief med. examiner, 1954-74; asst. prof. forensic medicine N.Y. U. Schs. Medicine, 1935-49, asso. prof., 1949-54, prof., chmn. dept. forensic medicine, 1954-74, prof. emeritus, 1974-77, adj. prof. Sch. Law, 1963-77; asst. prof. clin. medicine, lectr. pathology Cornell U., 1940-66, vis. prof. pathology, 1966-75, emeritus prof., 1975-77; dir. labs. Hosp. Spl. Surgery, 1941-58, cons. pathologist, 1958-68, chief pathology emeritus, 1968-74, hon. chief pathology, 1974-77; Distinguished vis. prof. pathology Center Biomed. Edn., CCNY, 1974-77; mem. med. adv. bd. N.Y. State Athletic Commn., 1965-74; cons. pathologist Knickerbocker Hosp., Englewood Hosp., Bellevue Hosp., FAA, 1960-71; cons. U.S. Bur. Medicine, USPHS Hosp., S.I.; cons. Armed Forces Inst. Pathology, 1958-70, hon. cons., 1972-77; vis. prof. pathology S.C. Med. Coll., 1969-77; spl. cons. War Dept., 1943-46. Decorated officer Order Leopold II (Belgium); recipient gold medal and citation Law Sci. Inst. and Found., U. Tex. Law Sch., 1958; Townsend Harris medal Alumni Assn. CCNY, 1958; Distinguished Alumnus award Cornell U. Med. Coll. Alumni Assn., 1964; Municipal Assn. for Mgmt. and Adminstrn. award City N.Y., 1972; distinguished and exceptional service award City N.Y., 1972; Virchow gold medal and award, 1972; presdl. citation N.Y. U., 1972; Chaim Yassky award Hadassah; Milton Helpern Library Legal Medicine and Milton Helpern Internat. Center Forensic Scis. of Kans. U., Wichita, and Milton Helpern Inst. Forensic Medicine of N.Y. U. named in his honor; Milton Helpern Internat. Exchange Fellowship in Forensic Scis. established at Milton Helpern Internat. Center, Wichita, 1977; Meml. resolution City Council N.Y., 1977; Meml. plaque Andrew Menchell Infant Survival Found., 1977; Gold medal Am. Acad. Forensic Scis., 1978; Milton Helpern Ann. Lectureship established Nat. Assn. Med. Examiners, 1978, Cornell U. Med. Coll., 1978, N.Y.C. affiliate Nat. Council Alcoholism, 1978; Meml. ceremony Internat. Acad. Legal Medicine and Social Medicine, Lyon, France, 1979, World Meeting on Med. Law, Ghent, Belgium, 1979. Fellow N.Y. Acad. Scis., Am. Soc. Clin. Pathologists (Ward Burdick award 1972), Coll. Am. Pathologists (award outstanding leadership in forensic pathology 1972), Am. Acad. Compensation Medicine (pres.), N.Y. Acad. Med., Internat. Coll. Surgeons (hon.); mem. Internat. Acad. Legal Medicine (past v.p.); hon. mem. fgn. med. socs.; mem. A.A.A.S., Soc. Med. Jurisprudence (trustee, (past pres.), Nat. Assn. Med. Examiners (founder, past pres., award 1971), Med. Soc. State N.Y. (del., trustee), N.Y. County Med. Soc. (past pres.), A.M.A. (del., distinguished physicians service award 1972), Internat. Acad. Traffic and Accident Medicine (past pres.), Internat. Meetings in Forensic Scis. (past pres.), Am. Acad. Forensic Scis. (founding mem., past pres., distinguished service award 1972), Am. Assn. Pathologists and Bacteriologists, N.Y. Path. Soc. (past pres., sec.), Soc. Alumni Bellevue Hosp. (past pres.), Cornell U. Med. Coll. Alumni (past pres.), Phi Beta Kappa (hon. and alumni Gamma chpt.; v.p. 1976, pres. 1977), Alpha Omega Alpha; hon. mem. 22 fgn. med. and legal socs. Jewish religion. Author: (with T.A. Gonzales, M. Vance, C.J. Umberger) Legal Medicine, Pathology and Toxicology, 2d edit., 1954; (with Bernard Knight) Autopsy: Memoirs of Dr. Milton Helpern, the World's Greatest Medical Detective, 1977, paperback edit., 1979; also articles in field. Editor Internat. Microform Jour. Legal Medicine; editorial bd. Zeitschrift fur Rechtsmedizin, Bulletin de Medecine Legale et de Toxicologie Medicale; asso. editorial bd. N.Y. State Jour. Medicine (Redway Gold medal). Address: New York, N.Y. Died Apr. 22, 1977; interred Kensico Cemetery, Valhalla, N.Y.

HELSON, HARRY, pyschologist; b. Chelsea, Mass., Nov. 9, 1898; s. William and Ida H.; A.B., Bowdoin Coll., 1921; A.M., Harvard, 1922, Ph.D., 1924; m. Lida Georgette Anderson, Sept. 3, 1926; children—Henry Berge, Martha Alice. Instr. in psychology Cornell U., 1924-25, U. Ill., 1925-26; asst. prof. psychology U. Kans., 1926-28; asso. prof psychology dir. lab., Bryn Mawr Coll., 1928-33, prof. 1933-49; prof. psychology, chmn. dept. Bklyn. Coll., 1949-51; prof. psychology U. Tex., 1951-61; John C. Peterson distinguished prof. Kans. State U., 1961-67; distinguished prof. psychology York U., 1967-68; prof. psychology U. Mass., 1968-71; acting prof., Thomas Welton Stanford fellow, Stanford, 1948-49; vis. prof. (summers) Cornell U., 1928, U. So. Calif., 1933, 47, Harvard, 1948, UCLA, 1950, U. Calif., Berkeley 1959, U. Colo., 1961, Lawrence U., 1974; co-dir., anti-aircraft fire-control labs. Foxboro Co. (Mass.), 1942-44; dir. Radiobiol. Lab., U. Texas and USAF, 1952-54. Hogg Found. Research scholar, 1956-57. Recipient Howard Crosby Warren medal Soc. Exptl. Psychologists, 1959; Distinguished Sci. Contbn. award Am. Psychol. Assn., 1962; I.H. Godlove award Inter-Soc. Color Council, 1969. Fellow A.A.A.S. (council, 1941-42, 50-51), Am. Psychol. Assn. (pres. div. 1, 1959, div. 10, 1954); mem. Soc. Exptl. Psychologists, Eastern Psychol. Assn. (sec.-treas. 1939-41, sec. 1941-42), Phi Beta Kappa, Sigma Xi, Sigma Nu. Author: The Psychology of Cestalt, 1926; Adaptation-Level Theory, 1964. Contbr. articles profl. jours. Editor: Theoretical Foundations of Psychology, 1951; co-operating editor Am. Jour. Psychology, 1940-70; cons. editor Jour. Exptl. Psychology, 1947-50; editor Psychol. Bull., 1959-64; co-editor Contemporary Aproaches to Psychology, 1967. Home: Berkeley, Calif. Died Oct. 13, 1977.

HELTON, ROY ADDISON, author; b. Washington, D.C., Apr. 3, 1886; s. Addison Smith and Marian Virginia (Hazard) H.; grad. Eastern High Sch., Washington, D.C., 1904; B.S., U. of Pa., 1908; m. Anne Watson, of Phila., Pa., June 28, 1909; children—Frank Addison, Robert. Teacher of lit., Central Manual Training Sch., Phila., 1909, W. Phila. Boys High Sch., 1911-23, William Penn Charity Sch., 1923-30; research supervisor Pa. State Planning Bd. since 1938. Lecturer on modern poetry, people of the southern mountains, etc. Mem. Sigma Phi Epsilon. Clubs: Contemporary, Franklin Inn. Author: Youth's Pilgrimage (verse), 1914; Outcasts in Beulah Land (verse), 1918; Jimmy Sharswood, 1924; The Early Adventures of Peacham Grew, 1925; Lonesome Water (Kentucky mountain verse), 1930; Nitchey Tilley (novel), 1934; Sold Out to the Future, 1935. Winner of "Nation" poetry prize, 1921, and of "Contemporary Verse" poetry prize, 1923. Home: Upper Darby, Pa. *

HEMENWAY, CHARLES FRANCIS, investment banker; b. Auburn, N.Y., Apr. 10, 1890; s. Charles C. and Ida E. (Shackelford) H.; A.B., Hamilton Coll., 1910; m. Eleanor Lord, Apr. 17, 1922; children—Anne (Mrs. Merle E. Dowd), Charles C. Clk., salesman Patterson Sargent Co., Kansas City, Mo., 1910-12; salesman, mgr. Chgo. officer Smith & Hemenway Co., tool mfrs., 1912-26; mgr. Chgo. office Utica Drop Forge & Tool Co., 1926-28; salesman Ill. Mchts. Bank & Trust Co. (merger Continental Ill. Co.), Chgo., 1928-33; an organizer, v.p. Ill. Co., Inc., Chgo., 1933-62, chmn. bd., 1962-72, chmn. emeritus, 1972-76. Alderman 1st ward, Evanston, Ill., 1943-55. Bd. dirs., pres. Scholarship Fund Found., 1952-66, chmn. bd., 1966-72, chmn. emeritus, 1972-76; life trustee Hamilton Coll.; trustee Evanston Schs., 1956-76. Served to ensign USNR, 1917-19. Mem. Psi Upsilon. Republican. Presbyn. Clubs: Union League, Univ., Bond, Municipal Bond (pres. 1949) (Chgo.); Westmoreland Country (Wilmette, Ill.). Home: Evanston, Ill. Died May 4, 1976.

HEMINGWAY, LOUIS LEE, banker; b. New Haven, Conn., Apr. 25, 1886; s. Samuel and Minerva Lee (Hart) H.; grad. Hopkins Grammar Sch., New Haven, 1904; A.B., Yale, 1908; m. Ruth Alicia Porter, June 3, 1913; children—Kate H. Keefe, Louis Lee. Began as runner, Second Nat. Bank of New Haven, 1908, chmn. bd. dirs.; dir. New Haven Water Co., Malleable Iron Fittings Co., Branford, Conn., Security Ins. Co. of New Haven, Conn. Indemnity Co.; Security-New Haven Life Ins. Co., Second Nat. Bank of New Haven. Asso. fellow Berkeley Coll., Yale. Trustee Permanent Fund of New Haven Orphan Asylum; dir. Grace-New Haven Hosp.; a propr. Common and Undivided Grounds, known as Proprietors Com.; pres. trustees, Yale Alumni Assn. of New Haven, Inc., Torch Honor Soc., Mory's Assn., Newcomen Soc. Eng., Alpha Delta Phi, Wolf's Head. Rep. Clubs: New Haven Lawn, Faculty, Graduate. Home: New Haven, Conn. *

HEMPHILL, JAMES C., investment banker; b. Lancaster, Ky.; s. James C. and Sallie (Currey) H.; Ph.B., U. Chgo. Comml. paper bus. Hathaway & Co., Chgo., until 1932; with Goldman Sachs and Co., investment bankers, Chgo., 1932-76, gen. partner, 1942-76. Trustee, Chgo. Symphony; exec. v.p., bd. dirs. Lyric Opera of Chgo.; bd. dirs. Chgo. Boys Clubs, Rehab. Inst. Chgo.; bd. dirs. Met. Opera, N.Y.C., sec., mem. exec. com. Mem. Delta Kappa Epsilon. Clubs: Mid-America, Attic, Saddle and Cycle, Metropolitan, Casino (Chgo.); Knollwood (Lake Forest, Ill.). Home: Chicago, Ill. Died Nov. 22, 1976.

HENDERSHOT, CLARENCE, educator; b. Bad Axe, Mich., Aug. 24, 1901; s. Horatio P. and Emma Jane (McGregor) H.; B.A., Alma Coll., 1923; M.A., U. Chgo., 1928, Ph.D., 1936; m. Elva O. Jenkins, 1928; children—Gladys Elaine (Mrs. John Christian Munson), James Brooks. Tchr. high sch., Midland, Mich., 1923-24; prin. Cushing High Sch., Rangoon, Burma, 1924-27; tchr., prin. Branch High Sch., Escondido, Cal., 1928-29; asso. prof. edn. and history U. Ala., 1929-31; prof. history Judson Coll., Rangoon, 1932-35; lectr. Central YMCA Coll., Chgo., 1935-36; dir. Warren br. of Hiram Coll., 1936-37; asst. prof. Hiram Coll., 1937-38; asso. prof. history U. Redlands, Calif., 1938-44, dean of men, 1942-44; specialist S.E. Asia, OWI, Washington, 1944-45; pub. affairs officer USIS, Rangoon, 1945-46; chief S.E. Asia br., pub. affairs area Dept. of State, 1946-48, mem. planning staff Office Public Affairs, 1949-52, UN affairs officer USIA, 1952-54; chief Far East-South Asia br., edn. div. ICA, Washington, 1954-57; chief edn. div. U.S. Ops. Mission to Korea, 1957-61, to Iran, 1961-65; asst. dean internat. services div., lectr. S.E. Asia history So. Ill. U., 1965-71. Mem. adv. com. to dir. pub. instrn. in Burma, 1925-27; mem. U.S. del. conv. Internat. Red Cross, Toronto, 1952; mem. U.S. del. UN, 1953, to UNESCO World Lit. Conf., Teheran, 1965. Past mem. gen. council Am. Bapt. Conv.; past v.p. nat. council Am. Bapt. Men; past mem. brotherhood commn. So. Bapt. Conv. Mem. Nat. Assn. Fgn. Student Affairs, Assn. for Asian Studies, Phi Delta Kappa. Baptist. Contbr. articles, book reviews to profl. publs. Home: Silver Spring, Md. Died May 3, 1979.

HENDERSON, JOHN WILLIAM, JR., mgmt. cons.; b. Culver, Ind., Dec. 30, 1924; s. John William and Norma (Wilson) H.; B.S. in Math., Denison U., 1949; M.B.A., Northwestern U., 1950; Ph.D. in Econs., U. Wis., 1960; m. Mary Josephine Works, Sept. 12, 1953; children—Harriet Anne, John William III, David Wilson, Mary Josephine. With Oscar Mayer & Co., 1950-52; sec., mfg. supt. Wooster (Ohio) div. Borg-Warner Corp., 1953-55; mgr. aircraft div. Bellanca Corp., 1955-56; asso. McKinsey & Co., mgmt. cons., 1957-62; exec. v.p. Buckeye Steel Castings Co., Columbus, Ohio, 1963-64, pres., gen. mgr., dir., 1964-79; pres., chief exec. officer, dir. Buckeye Internat., Inc., 1967-70; pres. Henderson & Assos., 1970-79. Home: Columbus, Ohio. Died Apr. 26, 1979.

HENDERSON, LESTER DALE, educator; b. Lenox, Ia., Apr. 13, 1886; s. James Leander and Elizabeth (Hamilton) H.; A.B., Tarkio (Mo.) Coll., 1911; post-grad. work, U. of Calif. and Columbia U.; A.M., Stanford U., 1930, Ed.D., 1935; m. Blanche Rae Mashin, Dec. 10, 1920; children—Joyce Lee, Charlotte. Teacher dist. schs., Ia., 1906; teacher science and athletics, high sch., Emmett, Ida., 1911-, Coeur d'Alene, 1912-14; supt. schs., Juneau, Alaska, 1914-17; apptd. first commr. of edn., Alaska, 1917-29; supt. of schs., Burlingame, Calif., since 1930. Mem. N.E.A., Nat. Assn. for Constl. Govt., Phi Delta Kappa. Elk. Republican. Presbyn. Mason (32 deg., Shriner). Home: Burlingame, Calif.*

HENDERSON, PAUL, b. Lyndon, Kan., Mar. 13, 1884; s. Clark E. and Flora A. (Waddel) H.; ed. high sch., Chicago; m. Mabel B. Madden, of Chicago, 1910; children—Paul, Martin M., Clark Lee, Josephine and Floranne (twins). With Western Stone Co., Chicago, 1907-16, advancing to pres.; sec. Guthrie (Okla.) Gas Co. since 1908; treas. Andrews Engring. Co., Chicago; 2d asst. postmaster gen. in charge of postal transportation, 1922-25; pres. Nat. Air Transport, 1930; v.p. and dir. United Aircraft and Transport, 1931, United Air Lines, 1931. Served with A.E.F. in France as capt. and maj., Feb. 1918-19; col. R.C., U.S.A. Republican. Presbyn. Clubs: Union League (Chicago);

Engineers' (New York). Home: Washington, D.C. *

HENDRICKS, WALTER, coll. pres., pub.; b. Chgo., July 24, 1892; s. Otto and Hilda (Johannesen) H.; student Northwestern U.; 1912-14; B.A., Amherst, 1917; postgrad. U. Grenoble, France, 1927; M.A., U. Chgo., 1930; Ph.D., Northwestern U.; L.H.D. (hon.), Windham Coll., 1977; m. Flora Bishop, Mar. 27, 1926; children—Hildamarie, Cynthia, Geoffrey, Nathaniel, Jon Sothern. Instr. English Armour Inst. Tech., Chgo., 1922-23, asst. prof., 1923-26, asso. prof., 1926-32, prof., 1932-34, prof., chmn. dept., 1934-40; prof., chmn. dept. Ill. Inst. Tech., 1940-47; on leave as head dept. English, Biarritz Am. U., Biarritz, France, 1945-46; founder and pres. Marlboro (Vt.) Coll., 1946-51; founder and pres. Windham Coll., Putney, Vt., 1951-64, Mark Hopkins Coll., Brattleboro, Vt., 1964-72; v.p., gen. editor Hendricks House-Farrar Straus, N.Y.; pres. Hendricks House, Inc., N.Y.; gen. editor Univ. Classics. Served as lt. Aviation Corps, U.S. Army, 1917; instr. in flying, 1918-19; col. U.S. Army, Info. and Edn. Div., 1945-46. Mem. So. Vt. Assn. (past pres.), Greater Vt. Assn. (past dir.), N.E. Assn. Colls., Phi Delta Theta, Phi Beta Kappa. Mem. Soc. of Friends. Clubs: Amherst, Lions. Author: Double Dealer, 1931; Flames and Fireflies, 1926; Spires and Spears, 1928; Early Poems, 1967. Home: Putney, Vt. Died Sept. 29, 1979; buried Putney, Vt.

HENDRIX, BYRON M., univ. prof.; b. Gratis Twp., Preble County, O., May 16, 1886; s. Edwin Washington and Martha (Jordon) H.; B.Sc., Ohio State U., 1909; Ph.D., Yale, 1915; m. Roberta Cowgill, Sept. 9, 1915; children—Robert Cowgill, Jean Cowgill. Asst. chemist, Bureau of Chemistry, U.S. Dept. of Agr., 1910-13; instr. in physiol. chemistry, U. of Pa., 1915-20, asst. prof., 1920-22; prof. biol. chemistry, U. of Tex., since 1922, acting dean of med. branch (at intervals), 1935-39. Trade expert, War Trade Bd., 1918. Mem. Am. Chem. Society, A.A.A.S., Am. Soc. Biol. Chemists, Soc. for Exptl. Biology and Medicine, Am. Assn. Univ. Profs. Conducts research on denaturation of proteins.

HENDRYSON, IRVIN EDWARD, orthopedic surgeon; b. Denver, June 20, 1912; s. Harry Edward and Zora (Beckwith) H.; B.A., U. Denver 1932; M.S., M.D., U Colo., 1936; m. Mary Short, July 17, 1942; children—Susan Jay, Robert Michael, John Galt, Jane Lacy, Mary Ann; m. 2d, Elizabeth Stayer Margulis, Sept. 25, 1965. Intern U. Colo. Med. Sch. and Hosps., 1936-37; resident U. Pa., 1939-40; pvt. practice orthopedic surgery, Denver, 1941-67; asso. clin. prof. surgery U. Coll. Sch. Medicine, 1949-67; asso. prof. surgery U. N. Mex. Sch. Medicine, 1967—77, asst. dean Sch. Medicine, 1967-69, dir. Emergency Med. Services project, 1969—77, commr. Navajo Health Authority, Window Rock, Ariz., also dir. div. manpower, dir. Allied Health Edn. Center; med. adviser Nat. Ski Patrol System, 1948-64; asst. med. dir V111 Winter Olympics, 1960. Cons. med. devices FDA, Health Services Adminstrn. Sol. Research soft tissue injury, disease of knee, elbow and foot; adv. com. Nat. Inst. Alcohol and Alcohol Abuse; trustee Nat. Council Alcoholism, 1960—77, pres., 1971—77, pres., chmn. bd. Denver Med. Soc., 1957-62; adv. bd. Nat. Library Medicine. Trustee Denver United Fund, 1958-60, Denver Good Will Industries, 1958-66, Denver chpt. A.R.C., 1966, Colo. chpt. Am. Cancer Soc., 1960, Colo. chpt. Soc. Crippled Children and Adults; bd. dirs., founder Nat. Registry Emergency Technicians. Served to lt. col., M.C., AUS, 1942-46. Decorated Purple Heart, Bronze Star; recipient Presdl. citation Nat. Found. Infantile Paralysis, 1960; award of merit Denver United Fund, 1958; named outstanding Ski Patrolman, Asociacion Sky Y Andinismo, 1958-59; Silberne Ehrenabzeichen, Osterreichischer Skiverband, 1950; Silver Key, Nat. Council on Alcoholism; Bronze award Am. Physchiat. Assn.; award from Gov. of N.M. Diplomate Am. Bd. Orthopaedic Surgery, Mem. A.M.A. (trustee 1965-70, chmn, commn. on emergency med. services 1967-72, certificate of Merit, Billings medal 1973), Am Trauma Soc. (dir. 1968—77). A.A.A.S. (mem. council 1967-70), Am. Acad. Orthopaedic Surgery, A.C.S. Ednl. Council Fgn. Med. Grads. (bd.); hon. mem. Colo. Med. Soc. (chmn. bd. 1954-56; del. 1957-65; award merit 1968). Author numerous articles in field. Home:, Albuquerque N. Mex. Died Apr. 11, 1977.

HENDY, PHILIP, mus. dir., art historian; b. Carlisle, Cumberland, Eng., Sept. 27, 1900; s. Frederick James Roberts and Caroline (Potts) H.; student Westminster Sch., 1914-19; M.A., Christ Ch., Oxford, 1919-22. Asst. keeper Wallace Collection, London, 1922-27; curator of paintings Mus. Fine Arts, Boston, 1930-33; dir. Nat. Gallery, London, Eng., 1946-67; adviser Israel Mus., Jerusalem, 1968-71. Specialist in Italian medieval and Renaissance painting particularly Venetian Renaissance. Created Knight. Mem. Internat. Council Museums (pres. Found.). Author: Piero della Francesca and the Early Italian Renaissance, 1968; Catalogue of the Exhibited Paintings, Isabella Stewart Gardner Mus., 2d edit., 1973. Home: Oxford, England. Died Sept. 6, 1980.

HENKE, ROBERT HENRY, metals co. exec.; b. West View, Pa., Dec. 9, 1920; s. Henry J. and Edna (Janke) H.; B.S. in Metallurgy, Pa. State U., 1942; m. Frances Kurtz, June 24, 1945. With Am. Manganese steel div. Am. Brake Shoe Co., Chgo., 1943-44, U.S. Steel Corp., 1944-45; process metallurgist A.M. Byers Co., Ambridge, Pa., 1945-46; chief metallurgist Allegheny Ludlum Steel Co., Brackenridge, Pa., 1946-59; asst. dist. mgr., then dist. mgr. Republic Steel Corp., Massillon, Ohio, 1959-64; v.p. Reynolds Metals Co., 1964-69; v.p. operations planning and enengring. Allegheny Ludlum Industries, Inc., Pitts., 1969-77, also pres. subsidiaries Internat. Powder Metallurgy Co., King Electronics, 1969-77; pres. Hattree, Inc., 1972-77. Mem. Am. Iron and Steel Inst., Am. Soc. Metals, Am. Inst. Mining and Metall. Engrs., Am. Inst. Steel Engrs. Home: Pittsburgh, Pa. Died Mar. 15, 1978; buried Allegheny County Meml. Park, Pittsburgh.

HENN, MARY J., physician, educator; b. Fargo, N.D., Jan. 4, 1919, d. Joseph L. and Myrtle (Davenport) H.; A.B., U. Nebr., 1940, M.D., 1950; M.S., U. Minn., 1944. Intern, Research and Ednl. Hosps., U. Ill., 1950-51; fellow Mayo Clinic, Rochester, Minn., 1951-54; asso. prof. internal medicine U. Nebr., 1954-69, prof., from 1969, asst. dean student affairs; mem. health council United Community Services, 1958-59. Mem. Nebr. Gov.'s Commn. Status of Women; bd. dirs. Nebr. Arthritis and Rheumatism Found.; trustee Nebr. Multiple Sclerosis Soc. Diplomate Am. Bd. Internal Medicine. Fellow A.C.P.; mem. Am. Fedn. Clin. Research, Pan Am. Med. Assn., Am., Nebr. (dir.) diabetes assns., Assn. Am. Med. Colls., Sigma Xi, Delta Delta Delta, Alpha Omega Alpha. Republican. Roman Catholic. Club: Altrussa. Home: Omaha, Nebr. Deceased.

HENNEY, CHARLES WILLIAM F., M.D., ex-congressman; b. Dunlap, Ia., Feb. 2, 1884; s. George Elbridge and Sarah Jane (Hanigan) H.; Ph.G., Fremont (Neb.) Normal Sch., 1907; M.D., Northwestern U., 10; grad. study, Europe, 1927; m. Margaret Tierney, Oct. 28, 1915; children—John Joseph, Thomas Edward. Intern Cook County (Ill.) Hosp., 1910-12; in practice at Royal, Ia., June-Oct. 1912; asst. to Dr. F.D. Bentley, surgeon, Portage, Wis., 1912-16; div. surgeon, C.M. St.P.&P. Ry., 1913-42; cons. surgeon, 1942-45; attending surgeon, St. Saviors Gen. Hosp., Portage, Wis., 1916-45, chief of staff, 1940-45; cons. surgeon, St. Marys Hosp., Columbus, Wis., 1930-45; chief examiner Columbia County Selective Service System, 1941-45. Pres. Park Bd., Portage, Wis., 1926-45. Mem. 73d Congress (1933-35), 2d. Wis. District. Fellow Am. Coll. Surgeons; mem. A.M.A., Wis. State Med. Soc., Internat. Post. Grad. Med. Soc., Phi Alpha Sigma. Democrat. Knight of Columbus (state dep. 1944-46), Elk, Moose. Home: Portage, Wis. *

HENNEY, RICHARD BERNARD, found. exec.; b. Upper Montclair, N.J., June 21, 1918; s. David Simonds and Stella Caroline (Bruggeman) H.; B.A., U. Va., 1950; M.B.A., Hofstra Coll., 1957. With First Nat. City Bank N.Y., 1937-41, 50-53, ofcl. asst., 1950-53; with Duke Endowment, 1953-79, treas., 1961-66, sec., 1966-73, exec. dir., 1971-79; treas. Doris Duke Trust, 1961-66, sec. 1966-73, exec. dir., 1971-79; sec. Angier B. Duke Meml., Inc., 1966-73, v.p., 1970-79; asst. treas. Duke Power Co., 1961-67, chmn. finance, 1967-74, also dir.; mem. adv. bd. Rockefeller Center office Chem. Bank, 1973-79. Served to capt. AUS, 1941-47; PTO. Mem. Newcomen Soc. N.Am., Assn. Ex-Mems. Squadron A, Am. Legion, Phi Beta Kappa, Phi Eta Sigma, Phi Kappa Psi, Alpha Kappa Psi. Elk. Clubs: Hemisphere, Rockefeller Center Luncheon (N.Y.C.). Home: Merrick, New York. Died May 30, 1979.

HENRICH, JOHN B., lawyer, bus. exec.; b. N.Y.C., June 14, 1912; s. John B. and Mary Agnes (Roxbury) H.; A.B. summa cum laude, Fordham U., 1933, LL.B., 1936; spl. studies in patent law, Columbia, 1939-40; m. Marion E. Coleman, Jan. 28, 1938. Instr. Latin and philosophy Fordham U., 1933-35; admitted to N.Y. bar, 1937, practiced in N.Y.C.; asst. sec. Nat. Lead Co., 1943-48, sec. and counsel, 1948-67, exec. v.p., gen. counsel, 1967-68, pres., 1968-74, dir.; former officer, dir. Baker Castor Oil Co., Canadian Titanium Pigments, Ltd., Nat. Lead Co. Ohio, Morris P. Kirk & Son, Inc.; dir. Titanium Metals Corp. Am. Mem. bar U.S. Supreme Ct., Fed. Bar; registered patent atty. in U.S., 1939, in Can., 1942. Mem. Am., N.Y. State, City N.Y. bar assns., Fordham U. Alumni Assn., Newcomen Soc. N. Am. Clubs: Lawyers (N.Y.C.); Wee Burn Country (Darien). Home: Darien, Conn. Died Jan. 21, 1977.

HENRICI, MAX (HEN-REE-SEE), editor; b. Economy, Pa., June 8, 1884; s. Jacob and Viola (Irons) H.; student U. Pa., 1901-02; D.Sc., Washington and Jefferson Coll., 1955; married Hilda Gundelfinger, Mar. 5, 1928. Schooltchr., Barranquitas, P.R., 1903; reporter Pitts. Press, 1904-08, N.Y. Herald, 1908-10; city editor, news editor Spartanburg (S.C.) Herald, 1910-14; financial editor Pitts. Sun, 1915-17; editorial writer Pitts. Sun and Pitts. Post, 1919-27, Pitts. Sun-Telegraph since 1928, author signed Nature column since 1943. Served as 2d lt. A.S., U.S. Army, attached to Bur. Aircraft Prodn., 1918. Mem. S.A.R., Soc. War 1812. Republican. Presbyn. Author: Cy and Max Abroad, 1923. Home: Coraopolis, Pa. *

HENRY, FRANK ANDERSON, foreign service officer; b. Garden City, N.Y., Dec. 10, 1883; s. James Buchanan and Louisa (Anderson) H.; Chem.E., Lehigh U., 1906; m. Gladys Martin, Jan. 29, 1921; 1 dau., Pamela Joan. Consul Guadeloupe, French West Indies, 1912-13, Puerto Cabello, Venezuela, 1917-19, Teneriffe, Canary Islands, 1919-23, Barcelona, Spain, 1923-31, Valparaiso, Chile, 1931-35, Nassau, Bahamas, 1935-36, Melbourne, Australia, 1936-38, Valletta, Malta, 1938-42, Port Elizabeth, Union of South Africa, since 1942. Awarded Chilean Order Al Merito. Mem. Fgn. Service Assn., English-Speaking Union, Kappa Alpha. Episcopalian. Club: Port Elizabeth. Address: Union of South Africa. *

HENRY, J(OHN) PORTER, lawyer; b. Jefferson City, Mo., Mar. 28, 1884; s. Jesse W. and Kate (Davison) H.; LL.B., Washington U., St. Louis, 1909; m. Imogen Adams, Jan. 5, 1911; s. J. Porter, Jr., Kilbourne A.; m. 2d, Mrs. Clara Ann Bent, Sept. 22, 1959. Admitted to Mo. bar, 1909, sr. partner Green, Hennings, Henry & Arnold; dir. J.H. Miller Co. Mem. Am. Bar Assn., Sigma Chi, Phi Delta Phi. Club: Algonquin Golf. Home: Webster Groves, Mo. *

HENRY, JOSEPH WARD, lawyer, asso. justice Tenn. Supreme Ct.; b. Lynnville, Tenn., Sept. 20, 1916; s. Joseph Walter and Annie Louise (Ward) H.; student Middle Tenn. State U., 1935-37; LL.B., Cumberland U., 1938; postgrad. Washington Coll. Law, 1939-40; m. Marjorie Royster Clark, June 28, 1943; children—Joseph Ward, Robert Clark. Admitted to Tenn. bar, 1940; individual practice law, Pulaski, Tenn., 1941-74; asso. justice Tenn. Supreme Ct., 1974-80; city atty. City of Pulaski, 1947-53; mem. Tenn. Ho. of Reps., 1949; adj. gen. State of Tenn., 1953-59. Chmn. Democratic Exec. Com. Giles County (Tenn.), 1967-71; bd. dirs. Cumberland Heights Found., Nashville. Served with AUS, 1941-46. Decorated Bronze Star. Fellow Am. Bar Found.; mem. Tenn. (pres. 1970-71), Am. (ho. dels.) bar assns., Tenn. Trial Lawyers Assn. (pres. 1964-66), Am. Judicature Soc. (dir. 1971-80), Am. Legion. Methodist. Home: Pulaski, Tenn. Died June 9, 1980.

HENRY, ROBERT LLEWELLYN, JR., judge; b. Chicago, Ill., Nov. 4, 1882; s. Robert Llewellyn and Ada Camille (Badger) H.; Ph.B., U. of Chicago, 1902, J.D., 1907; Rhodes scholar at Worcester Coll., Oxford, Eng., 1904-07, B.C.L., Oxford, 1907, D.C.L., 1926; m. Elaine Goodale Read, of Baton Rouge, La., June 30, 1908; children—Robert L., Alvan Read, McClelland. Prof. law, La. State U., 1907-11; asst. prof. law, U. of Ill., 1911-12; prof. law and dean Coll. of Law, U. of N.D., 1912-14; prof. law, U. of Calif., summer, 1914; prof. law, State U. of Ia., 1914-16. Capt. inf., O.R.O., Nov. 13, 1916; maj., Mar. 8, 1919; instr. officers training camps and schs., Ft. Sheridan, Ill., Camp Grant, Ill., Camp Lee, Va., May 1, 1917-Mar. 8, 1919; mem. constrn. de-mobilization com., Gen. Staff, Washington, D.C., Mar. 8-Aug. 1, 1919; mem. War Dept. Bd. Contract adjustment, Washington, D.C., 1919-20; lecturer at Oxford U., 1921-22; now judge Mixed Court, Alexandria, Egypt. Democrat. Mem. Chi Psi, Phi Delta Phi. Author: Liens and Pledges, 1913; Consideration in Contracts, 601 A.D. to 1520 A.D. (article), 1917; Anglo-Saxon Contracts (article), 1917; Contracts in the Local Courts of Medieval England, 1926. Address: Alexandria, Egypt. *

HENSHAW, FRANCIS HAROLD, library cons.; b. New Castle, Ind., Feb. 8, 1903; s. Logan and Mary Knorr (Allen) H.; A.B., Occidental Coll., 1927; certificate Library Sch., Los Angeles Pub. Library, 1929; M.S., Columbia, 1932; m. Marie Hermine Molnar, May 27, 1932 (dec.); children—Hermine, William, Logan, Kenneth (dec.). Asst. Los Angeles Pub. Library, 1929-31; asst. to dir. Queensborough (N.Y.) Pub. Library, 1932-34; librarian Berkshire Athenaeum, Pittsfield, Mass., 1934-46; state librarian Tex. State Library, Austin, 1946-50; instr. sch. library service Columbia, 1945-46, 47; asst. chief card div. Library of Congress, 1950-51, adminstrv. officer, processing dept. 1951, then chief, catalog maintenance div., chief, order div., 1953-71; cons. library adminstrn., 1971-79. Chmn. Ex-officio Tex. Bd. Library Examiners. Carnegie fellow 1931. Mem. com. Littlefield Fund for So. History. Mem. ALA, Mass. (pres. 1940-42), Tex. library assns., Tex. Hist. Assn. (exec. com.), Phi Beta Kappa. Contbr. profl. publs. Home: Hollywood, Md. Died Dec. 10, 1979; buried Cedar Hill Cemetery, Suitland, Md.

HENSHAW, HARRY PRESTON, ry. official; b. Bunker Hill, W.Va., Dec. 21, 1886; s. Edwin Smith and Mary Elliot (Campbell) H.; ed. Shepherd Coll., 1903-04, Shenandoah Valley Mil. Acad., 1904-07, W.Va. U., 1907-08; m. Mabel Virginia Bowen, Apr. 29, 1914; 1 son, Harry Preston, Jr. Began as farmer and still owns and operates a farm; with Swift & Co., Baltimore, Md., 5 years; W.Va. highway commr., 1931-33; sec. W.Va. R.R. Assn., 1933-36; asst. to v.p. C.&O. Ry. Co. 1936-37; asst. v.p. Western Pocahontas Corp. and Western Pocahontas Fuel Co., 1937; asst. v.p. C.&O. Ry. Co. and Pere Marquette Ry. Co., 1937-39; v.p

C.&O. Ry. Co. since Mar. 14, 1939; asst. vice pres. Western Pocahontas Corp.; director First Huntington Nat. Bank. Mem. W.Va. House of Reps., 1917-18, Senate, 1921-31. Mem. Beta Theta Pi. Presbyterian. Address: Huntington, W.Va. *

HENSKE, JOSEPH ALOYSIUS, physician; b. St. Louis, Apr. 2, 1886, s. Andrew A. and Theresa (Klaren) H.; student St. Louis (Mo.) U., 1897-98, St. Francis Solan's Coll., Quincy, Ill., 1898-1900; M.D., Barnes U., St. Louis, 1907; m. Kathryn G. McClanahan, Nov. 3, 1915; children—Kathryn (Mrs. Walsh), Joseph Aloysius, Jr., John McClanahan. Clinic attendant Berlin and Leipsig, Germany, and Vienna, Austria, 1906; in practice of pediatrics, Omaha, Neb.; prof., chmn. dept. of pediatrics U. Neb. Med. Coll., Omaha, 1941-49, prof. pediatrics since 1949; former chmn. med. staff Methodist Episcopal Hosp., Omaha; past pres. staff Children's Memorial Hosp., Omaha; former chairman pediatric staff University Hospital, Omaha; clinical service for crippled children Rheumatic Fever Program, State of Neb., 1944. Served as capt., M.C., U.S. Army, 1917-19. Diplomate Am. Bd. Pediatrics. Fellow Am. Acad. Pediatrics, Am. Coll. Physicians; mem. Neb. Pediatric Soc., A.M.A., Neb. State Med. Soc., Omaha-Douglas County Med. Soc., City Hosp. Alumni (St. Louis). Home: Omaha, Neb. *

HEPBURN, JOSEPH SAMUEL, chemist; b. Phila., Pa., Aug. 25, 1885; s. Samuel Martin and Mary Minor Waite (Danenhower) H.; A.B., Central High Sch. of Phila., 1903, A.M., 1908; B.S. (Chem.), U. of Pa., 1907, M.S., 1907; Ph.D., Columbia, 1913; M.D., Hahnemann Med. Coll. and Hosp., Phila., 1934, Chem.D., 1946. Sci. asst. Food Research Lab., Bur. Chem., U.S. Dept. of Agr., 1907-08, asst. chemist, 1908-12, 1913-20; fellow in biol. chemistry Columbia, 1912-13; instr. chemistry, Hahnemann Med. Coll. and Hosp. of Phila., 1920-22, lecturer, 1922-25, asso. prof., 1925-39, prof., 1939-50, research asso. gastroenterology, 1937-50, registrar, 1943-50. emeritus incumbent in previous positions, 1950—; archives researcher Franklin Inst., 1954—. Secretary, dir. Eberhard Foundation, 1951—. Consulting biological chemist Broad Street Hospital; consulting physiologist, Women's Homeopathic Hosp.; sec., treas., mgr. Hahnemann Research Foundation; historian Associated Alumni of Central High Sch., Philadelphia. Received Longstreth Medal, 1911, Certificate of Merit, 1921, Franklin Inst. Recipient Special Alumni award. Central High Sch., 1956; Certificate of Appreciation, Atwater Kent Mus., 1958. Diplomate Am. Bd. Clin. Chemistry. Fellow American College Gastroenterology (life); mem. Am. Inst. Homeopathy (hon. asso.), Am. Chem. Soc. (councilor, 1925; abstractor for jour. since 1915). Am. Soc. Biological Chemists, Pa. Chemical Soc. (gov. since 1938), Academy Natural Sciences of Phila., Physiol. Soc. of Phila., Franklin Inst. (sec., section physics and chemistry, 1909-23; mem. com. on sci. and the arts in charge of medal awards, since 1919; mgr., 1943-44, 48-50, 52-56), American Assn. U. Profs., American Association for the History of Medicine, City Hist. Soc. of Phila. (pres., dir.), Phi Beta Pi, Sigma Xi, Pi Upsilon Rho. Republican. Episcopalian. Co-author: (with William A. Pearson) Physiological and Clinical Chemistry, 1925-38. Contbr. to many profl. jours. Home: Phila. *

HERBERG, WILL, educator; b. N.Y.C., Aug. 4, 1909; s. Hyman Lewis and Sarah (Wolkov) H.; B.A., Columbia, 1928, M.A., 1930, Ph.D., 1932; L.H.D., Park Coll., 1956; Litt.D., Franklin and Marshall Coll., 1960; LL.D., Ohio Wesleyan U., 1963; widower. Research analyst. ednl. dir. Internat. Ladies Garment Workers Union, 1935-48; lectr., writer, 1948-55; grad. prof. Judaic studies and social philosophy Drew U., 1955-63, grad. prof. philosophy and culture, 1963-77. Mem. Am. Philos. Assn., Am. Hist. Assn., Metaphys. Soc. Am., Am. Sociol. Assn., Am. Studies Assn., Medieval Acad. Am., Am., Am. Theol. Soc., Am. Judicature Soc., Assn. Ch. History, Philosophy of Edn. Soc. Conservative. Jewish. Author: Judaism and Modern Man, 1951; Protestant-Catholic-Jew, 2d edit., 1960; The Writings of Martin Buber, 1956; Four Existentialist Theologians, 1958; Community, State and Church, 1960. Home: Madison, N.J. Died Mar. 27, 1977.

HERBERICK, BERNARD FELIX, assn. exec.; b. Marlborough-on-Hudson, N.Y., Jan. 1, 1910; s. Bernhardt and Crescentia (von Brücksteine) Zimmermann; A.B., Fordham U., 1931; postgrad. Sch. Fgn. Service, Georgetown U., 1932, N.Y. U. Sch. Commerce, 1934; m. Lucy Augusta Rosser, June 18, 1938; 1 son, James Bernard. Book rev. editor Prentice-Hall, Inc., N.Y.C., 1937-38, asso. editor, dir. pub. relations, 1938-42; with Nat. Indsl. Conf. Bd., N.Y.C., 1946-71, asst. v.p., 1963-65, exec. dir. operations services, 1965-71; dir. spl. projects Council Better Bus. Burs., Inc., 1971-73; v.p. research Consumers United for Progress, 1973-79; instr. pub. relations Baruch Sch. Bus. Adminstrn., Coll. City N.Y., 1948-57; lectr. Escuela de Periodismo, U. Chile, Santiago, Escuela de Caribineros, Santiago, U. Católica, Valparaiso, 1957, Soc. Fomento Fabril, Santiago, Inst. Chileno de Administracion Rationale de Empresas, Santiago, U. Costa Rica, San Jose, 1963. U.S. Govt. assignments to Chile, 1957, Costa Rica, 1963. Pres. Cedar Gate Assn., 1954-55. Served with OSS, 1942-46; CBI. Decorated Purple Heart. Mem. Shanghai Tiffin, Vets. OSS, Newcomen Soc., Tokeneke Assn., MENSA, Inst. Chileno de Relaciones Publicas (hon.), Corps Arminia (U. Jena). Author: Bitter Laughter, 1951; Management Guide for Competitive Marketing, 1954; (with Angel Sanhueza) Relacions Publicas: Una Introducion, 1958. Home: Darien, Conn. Died Oct. 22, 1979.

HERBERT, HUGH, motion picture actor; b. Binghamton, N.Y., Aug. 10, 1885; s. John and Mary (Gallagher) H.; m. Rose Epstein, Aug. 13, 1925. Actor, comedian, playwright; has written numerous playlets and vaudeville sketches produced by Sam Harris and A. H. Woods; joined Fox Movietone to write and play "Mind Your Business," 1927; wrote "Lights of New York," pioneer all-talking picture; actor with Warner Bros., appearing in 40 pictures, 1933-38; played in "The Great Waltz," "The Lady's from Kentucky," "The Family Next Door," "Eternally Yours," 1939; "Little Accident", "LaConga Nights," "Slightly Tempted," "Little Bit of Heaven," 1940; "Hit Parade of 1941," "Meet the Chump," "The Black Cat," "Hello Sucker," "Bad Lands of Dakota," 1941, "Hellzapoppin'," "Mrs. Wiggs of the Cabbage Patch," "Kismet," "Music for Millions," "Men in her Diary," "One Way to Love," "A Miracle Can Happen," starred in stage play "Oh, Brother"; and was on radio program series entitled "That's My Pop." Mem. Screen Actors Guild (bd. of dirs.), Masquers Club (Hollywood). Home: North Hollywood, Calif. *

HERBST, WILLIAM PARKER, genito-urinary surgeon; b. Washington, Nov. 15, 1893; s. William Parker and Louise (Willige) H.; M.D., Georgetown U., 1915; M.S. in Surgery, U. Minn., 1923; m. Catherine Meredith Arnold, June 12, 1920; children—Catherine, Patricia (wife of Dr. William L. Howell), William Parker III, Robert van Cortlandt. Intern Georgetown U. Hosp., 1915-16; staff Central Dispensary and Emergency Hosp., Columbia Hosp. for Women, Lying-In Asylum, Doctor's Hosp., Garfield Meml. Hosp., Georgetown U. Hosp.; prof. urology Georgetown U., 1945-47, prof. clin. urology, 1957-65, emeritus prof. clin. urology, 1965-79. Cons. Walter Reed Army Med. Center, U.S. Naval Med. Center, Bethesda, NIH Clin. Research Center, Bethesda. Served as lt., M.C., USN, 1917-19. Diplomate Am. Bd. Urology (pres.). Fellow A.C.S.; mem. Am. Assn. Genito-Urinary Surgeons, Am. Urol. Assn. (chmn. research com.), A.M.A., So. Med. Assn. Home: Castle Gregory, Ireland. Died Dec. 30, 1979.

HERBUT, PETER ANDREW, pathologist, univ. pres.; b. Edson, Alta., Can., July 6, 1912; s. Andrew and Ahafia (Smetana) H.; student U. Alta., 1930-35; M.D., McGill U., 1937; m. Margaret Fetsko, Feb. 16, 1940; children—Linda, Paula. Came to U.S., 1937, naturalized, 1942. Intern Childrens Meml. Hosp., Montreal, 1936-37, Gen. Hosp. Wilkes-Barre, Pa., 1937-38; resident pathologist Med. Coll. Va., 1938; faculty and staff Jefferson Med. Coll. and Thomas Jefferson Univ. Hosp., Phila., 1939-76, prof. pathology, head dept., 1948-66, dir. clin. labs., 1952-66, pres. Thomas Jefferson U., 1966-76; pathologist Meth. Hosp., Phila., 1952-76, attending pathologist Thomas Jefferson U. Hosp. Recipient McCrae award Jefferson Med. Coll., 1947, Ward Burdick award Am. Soc. Clin. Pathologists, 1950. Fellow Coll. Am. Pathologists, A.C.P.; mem. Am. Soc. Exptl. Pathology, Am. Assn. Cancer Research, Am. Soc. Pathologists and Bacteriologists, Am. Soc. Clin. Pathologists, Soc. Am. Bacteriologists, Phila. Path. Soc., Coll. Physicians Phila., A.M.A., A.A.A.S., Am. Med. Writers Assn., Phila. County Med. Soc., Med. Soc. Pa., Jefferson Soc. Clin. Investigation, Pa. Assn. Clin. Pathologists, Pa. Trudeau Soc., World Med. Assn., Conf. State and Provincial Pub. Health Lab. Dirs., Internat. Acad. Pathology, Nat. Geog. Soc., Med. Club. Phila. Republican. Mem. Am. Orthodox Ch. Clubs: Union League (Phila.); Aronomink Golf (Newtown Square, Pa.). Author: Surgical Pathology, 2d edit., 1954; Urological Pathology, vol. 1 and 11, 1952, Spanish edit., 1959; Gynecological and Obstetrical Pathology, 1953; Pathology 2d edit., 1959; also numerous articles. Home: Rosemont, Pa. Died Mar. 31, 1976.

HEROD, WILLIAM ROGERS, bus cons.; b. Indpls., Feb. 13, 1898; s. William P. and Mary Beaty (Applegate) H.; Ph.B. in Mech. Engring. magna cum laude, Sheffield Sci. Sch., Yale, 1918; m. Caroline K. Fries., Aug. 10, 1949. Student engr., test course Gen. Electric Co., Schenectady, 1919, spl. asst. constrn. engring. dept., 1919-29; asst. to pres. Internat. Gen. Electric Co., N.Y.C., 1929-34; asst. to mng. dir Asso. Elec. Industries, Ltd., London, 1934-37, dir., 1945-51; v.p. Internat. Gen. Electric Co., 1937-42, exec. v.p., July-Sept. 1945, pres., 1945-60, ret, 1960, dir., 1945-52; v.p. Gen. Electric Co., 1952-60, ret., 1960; dir. numerous fgn. companies, 1945-60; cons. on internat. bus., 1960-74; dir. Transatlantic Fund, Inc., 580 Park Av., Inc., others. Apptd. coordinator def. prodn. NATO, 1951, with personal rank of minister. Mem. City Planning Commn., Schennetady, 1923; mem. Mayor's Com. Golden Jubilee, N.Y.C., 1948. Served as pvt. 10th Regt., Conn. N.G., 1916; mem. R.O.T.C., Yale, 1917-18; from pvt. to 1st lt. U.S. Army, 1918; 1st lt. F.A., O.R.C., 1919-24; commd. lt. col. USAAF, 1942, col., 1943; inactive status, 1945. Mem. univ. council Yale and chmn. com. div. engring., 1948-51; ex-offico mem. Yale Alumni Bd., 1952-74; asso. fellow Pierson Coll., Yale, 1948-51. Mem. Latin-Am. Subcom. Bus. Adv. Council, Washington, 1948-51, 56-58, chmn., 1950; dir. emeritus Internat. House, N.Y.C.; dir. Spanish Inst., Inc. Profl. engr., N.Y. Decorated Commenda dell'Ordine al Merito della Republica Italiana; Order of Sacred Treasure, 3d Class (Japan), 1957; oficial Ordem Nacional do Cruzeiro do Sul (Brazil), 1958; caballero Gran Cruz de la Orden del Merita Civil (Spain), 1958; Capt. Robert Dollar Meml. Award for distinguished contbn. to advancement fgn. trade Nat. Fgn. Trade Council, 1958. Mem. Council Fgn. Relations; dir. Nat. fgn. Trade Council, 1946-67, Philharmonic-Symphony Soc. N.Y.; mem. China Med. Bd., 1947-68. Mem. I.E.E.E. (life), Am. Soc. M.E. (life), Inst. Internat. Edn. (hon. trustee), Atlantic Council U.S. (dir.), Nat. Inst. Social Scis., Acad. Polit. Sci., Internat. C. of C. (U.S. council), Archaeol. Inst. Am., Assn. Yale Alumni (assembly 1972—), Japan Soc., Asia Soc., Council on Fgn. Relations, Sigma Xi. Republican. Clubs: Explorers, Pilgrims, University, Union, Yale, Metropolitan Opera (N.Y.C.); Graduates, Lawn (New Haven); American (London); Mohawk (Schenectady). Patentee elec. discharge due change humidity atmosphere. Home: New York, N.Y. Died July 19, 1974.

HEROLD, AMOS LEE, prof. English; b. Mill Gap, Va., Aug. 8, 1885; s. Wise and Kate Elizabeth (Ruckman) H.; B.A., Washington and Lee U., 1909, M.A., 1912; Ph.D., Columbia, 1926, spl. study, summer 1931; m. Virginia L. Smith, 1917. Instr. McGuire's U. Sch., Richmond, 1909-11; headmaster, Horner Mil. Sch., N.C., 1913-15; instr. in English, U. of Cincinnati, 1916-19; prof. English lit., Bucknell U., 1920-23; prof. and head.of English dept., U. of Tulsa, 1923-34; asso. prof. of English, Tex. State Coll. for Women since 1935. Lt. and personnel adj. U.S.A., in charge official papers and pay rolls for 1600 men, World War. Pres. Okla. Council Teachers of English, 1933-34. Mem. Tex. State Teachers Assn., Am. Assn. of Univ. Profs., Modern Lang. Assn., Alpha Chi Rho, Pi Kappa Delta, Sigma Tau Delta, Pi Gamma Mu. Winner of essayist's medal and 2 scholarships in coll. Author: James Kirke Paulding, Versatile American, 1926. Contbr. to Dictionary of Am. Biography and magazines. Traveled in 8 European countries in 1926. Address: Denton, Tex. *

HERRICK, GEORGE Q., electronics exec.; b. Newburgh, N.Y., May 14, 1915; s. Henry F. and Clara B. (Quinette) H.; student N.Y. U., 1932-34; m. Lillian A. Campbell, July 22, 1938; children—Christopher, Gavin (dec.), George, Kathleen. Chief engr. Hearst Radio, Inc., 1935; now cons. engr. and design engr. UN, MBS and Capital Rec. Co.; became chief engr. OWI, 1942; designer radio master control and rec. system, 1943; rehab. Munich Short Wave installations, 1946; designer IBd-Clipper amplifiers, 1948; chief of facilities br. Internat. Broadcast Div., Dept. State, 1948, responsibilities including design, constrn., installation, ops. and maintenance of all radio broadcast facilities of the dept., both overseas and domestic; dir. U.S. anti-jam operations Dept. of State, 1949-53; asst. to v.p. engring. products Gen. Precision Lab. Inc., 1953-57; v.p., gen. mgr. research and devel. Prodn. Research Corp., Thornwood, N.Y., 1957-60; v.p., gen. mgr. research and devel. div. Radio Condenser Co., Camden, N.J., 1960-63; electronics product mgr. Singer Metrics div. The Singer Co., Bridgeport, Conn. 1963-67; dir. ops. Radio Liberty, Munich, Germany, 1967-73, dir. network div., 1973-77. Recipient Superior Service medal Dept. State (2). Democrat. Home: Bronxville, N.Y. Died Jan. 27, 1977.

HERRICK, H. T., labor arbitrator; b. N.Y.C., Apr. 24, 1920; s. Horace Terhune and Elinore (Morehouse) H.; B.S., Hamilton Coll., 1942; LL.B., Cornell U., 1948; m. Virginia Boardman Leigh, Oct. 6, 1945 (dec. 1964); children—Christine Terhune, David Morse; m. 2d, Allison Butler, May 1, 1965. Admitted to N.Y. bar, 1949; asso. firm Paul, Weiss, Wharton & Garrison, N.Y.C., 1948-50; atty. NLRB, 1950-57; labor atty. Westinghouse Electric Corp., 1957-61; asst. to asst. sec. labor, 1961-63; gen. counsel Fed. Mediation and Conciliation Service, 1963-65; dir. div. of labor relations ERDA, AEC, Dept. Energy, 1966-78; labor arbitrator, 1978-80; adj. prof. Georgetown U. Sch. Law, 1965. Served with USAAF, 1942-45. Mem. Am., Fed. bar assns. Unitarian. Home: Washington, D.C. Died Feb. 1980.

HERRICK, HOWARD U., business exec.; b. Syracuse, N.Y., 1886. Chmn. bd. E. W. Bliss Co., Canton, O.; chmn. bd. Cleveland Instrument Co.; dir. Harter Bank & Trust Co. Home: Ft. Lauderdale, Fla. *

HERRICK, MRS. MARGARET BUCK, librarian; b. Spokane, Sept. 27; d. Nathan Kimball and Adaline (Morie) Buck: A.B., U. Wash., 1927, B.S. in L.S., 1928. Children's librarian Yakima (Wash.) Pub. Library, 1928-29, city librarian, 1929-31; librarian Acad. of

Motion Picture Arts and Scis., Hollywood, Calif., 1931-43, exec. dir., 1943-70, dir. emeritus, from 1971. Mem. AAUW, ALA. Republican. Episcopalian. Home: Laguna Hills, Calif. Deceased.

HERRING, CLYDE EDSEL, lawyer; b. Des Moines, Mar. 24, 1915; s. Clyde L. and E. Pearl (Spinney) H.; A.B., State U. Iowa, 1937; LL.B., Drake U., 1940, J.D., 1968; m. Mary Lou Becker, Aug. 7, 1945; children—Victoria Louise, Mary Jane. Admitted to Iowa bar, 1940, D.C. bar, 1965; mem. firm Davis, Huebner, Johnson, Herring & Burt, Des Moines, 1955-60; asst. county atty., Polk County, Ia., 1947-48; county atty., 1951-52, 53-54; dist. dir. Bur. Census, 1949-50; commr. ICC, Washington, 1959-64; practice law, Washington, 1964-76. Democratic candidate for gov. Iowa, 1954. Served to capt. U.S. Army; POW. Home: Washington, D.C. Died Sept. 24, 1976.

HERRINGTON, HUNLEY W(HATLEY), univ. prof.; b. Evergreen, Ala., Sept. 15, 1885; s. William Hampton and Nannie (Martin) H.; A.B., Washington Univ., 1910; M.A., Harvard, 1911, Ph.D., 1916; m. Lydia Wilkinson Sumner, June 27, 1916; children—Anne (Mrs. R. C. Haskett), Barbara Sumner (Mrs. Nelson Goodyear). Entered business, St. Louis, 1903-07; asst. in English, Harvard, 1913-16; asst. prof. English, Washington U., 1916-19; asso. prof. English, Syracuse U., 1919-20, prof., since 1920, acting chmn. dept. of English, 1944-47; vis. prof. Harvard summer sessions, 1929, 1931. Mem. Am. Assn. Univ. Profs., Modern Lang. Assn., College English Assn., N.Y. State Folklore Soc., Phi Beta Kappa, Phi Kappa Phi. Episcopalian. Clubs: Faculty, Liederkranz. Editor (with notes and introduction): English Masterpieces, 2 vols., 1931, rev. edit., 1937; contbr. B. Wendell memorial vol., Harvard, 1926; also various articles and reviews to jours. Specialist in folklore, history of language, Elizabethan period. Home: Syracuse, N.Y. *

HERSEY, MAYO DYER, mech. engr.; b. Pawtuxet, R.I., Aug. 30, 1886; s. George Milbank and Alice Stafford (Budlong) H.; A.B., Colo. Coll., 1907; A.M., Olivet (Mich.) Coll., 1910; S.B., Mass. Inst. Tech., 1910; fellow in physics, Harvard, 1915-16; m. Frances Lester Warner, June 24, 1922. Asst. in physics, Mass. Inst. Tech., 1909-10, asso. professor, 1920-22, research asso. in mech. engring., 1942-56; physicist Nat. Bur. Standards, 1910-20, 26-31, U.S. Bureau Mines, 1922-26; research asso. engring. Brown U., 1934-40, also visiting professor of engineering, 1957—; lecturer Harvard, 1936-40, 42-43; engineer Kingsbury Machine Works, Inc., Phila., 1936-39; research director Morgan Constrn. Co., Worcester, Mass., 1939-41. Special mission to England, France and Italy, to coöperate in aeronautic instrument problems, 1918. Cons. National Research Council, 1941; war research div. Columbia Univ., 1943-45; Navy Dept., 1946-48; tech. cons. USN Engineering Expt. Sta., Annapolis, 1948-57, acting head developments br., internal combustion engine lab., 1954-55. Fellow Am. Phys. Soc., A.S.M.E. (chmn. research com. 1942-43); mem. Am. Soc. Lubrication Engrs. (hon. life), Am. Soc. Naval Engrs., Philos. Soc. Washington, Franklin Inst. (Levy medalist 1936), Soc. Rheology (v.p. 1935-37), Washington Acad. Scis., Mil. Order of Loyal Legion, S.A.R., Am. Soc. for Engring. Edn. Sigma Xi, Tau Beta Pi. Republican. Congregationalist. Clubs: Cosmos, Harvard, Faculty. Author, co-author tech. publs., latest: Viscosity of Lubricants Under Pressure (with R. F. Hopkins), 1954; Fundamentals of Hydrodynamic Lubrication, 1954; Experiments on Imperfect Lubrication (with C. W. Staples). 1958. Home: Providence, R.I.; also Monument Beach, Mass. *

HERSHEY, LEWIS BLAINE, army officer; b. Steuben County, Ind., Sept. 12, 1893; s. Latta Freleigh and Rosetta (Richardson) H.; B.S., Tri-State Coll., Angola, Ind., 1912, B.Pd., A.B., 1914; student Ind. U., 1917; attended Field Arty. Sch., Fort Sill, Okla., 1922-23, Command and Gen. Staff Sch., 1931-33, Army War Coll. 1933-34, U. Hawaii, 1935-36; LL.D. (hon.). Tri-State Coll., Ohio State U., Oglethorpe U., Norwich U., Albright Coll., Lafayette Coll., Columbia U., Ind. U.; m. Ellen Dygert, Nov. 29, 1917; children—Kathryn Elizabeth (Mrs. A. Alvis Layne, Jr.), Gilbert Richardson, George Frederick, Ellen Margaret (Mrs. Sam L. Barth). Began as country sch. tchr. Jamestown Township Sch., Steuben, Ind., 1910; high sch. prin., Flint, Ind., 1914-16; successively pvt., cpl., sgt., 2d lt., 1st lt. Ind. Nat. Guard, 1911-16; commd. 1st lt. U.S. Army, 1916, and advanced through grades to gen., 1969; asst. prof. mil. sci. and tactics Ohio State U., 1923-27; asst. G-4 Hawaiian Dept., 1934-36; mem. Gen. Staff War Dept., 1936-40; sec. and exec. officer Joint Army and Navy Selective Service Com., 1936-40; promoted to brig. gen. Oct. 1940, in recognition of work in preparing plans for Selective Service System; appointed dep. dir. Selective Service System, Dec. 19, 1940, apptd. dir., July 31, 1941; promoted to maj. gen. U.S. Army, 1942; apptd. dir. Office of Selective Service Records, Mar. 1947; apptd. dir. Selective Service by Pres. Truman, 1948; promoted to lt. gen., 1956, to gen., 1969; spl. adviser to Pres. on manpower moblzn., 1970-73; ret., 1973. Chmn. Montgomery County chpt. A.R.C, 1952-68; past pres. Nat. Capital Area council Boy Scouts Am. Trustee Tri-State Coll., Angola, Ind. Recipient D.S.M. from Army, Navy, and Dept. Def.; D.S.M. of Am. Legion, 1946, also N.G. Assn. U.S., 1954; Disting. Service award Mil. Champlains Assn. U.S., 1957; George Washington medal Freedoms Found., 1958; Bernard Baruch award V.F.W., 1966; Silver Beaver award Boy Scouts, 1961, Silver Antelope award, 1963, Silver Buffalo award, 1966. Republican. Mason. Author: Selective Service in Peacetime; Selective Service in Wartime; Selective Service as the Tide of War Turns; Selective Service in Victory; also mag. articles. Home: Bethesda, Md. Died May 20, 1977.

HERTZBERG, HALFDAN FENTON HARBO, b., Toronto, Ont., Sept. 3, 1884; s. Anton Lund H.; student Upper Canada Coll., St. Andrew's Coll., U. of Toronto, all Toronto, Can.; m. Dorothy Hope Judah, Mar. 19, 1919; children—Peder Harbo Anderdon, Dagmar Hope Elinor, Dorothea Helen Ann. Civil engr. railway location and constrn., 1903-10; chief engr. trussed concrete steel, reinforced concrete design, 1911-14. Comd. 2d Field Co., Can. Engrs., 1905, served in Belgium, France, with Can. Engrs. 1st and 3d Can. Divs., C.E.F., World War I; lt. Royal Can. Engrs., 1915, capt. 1917, maj. and brevet col., 1918, col. and temp. brigadier, 1934, maj. gen., 1938; q.m. gen., 1938-40, adjt. gen., Apr.-July 1940, commandant, Royal Mil. Coll. of Can., 1940-44; retired Sept. 1944. Decorated Companion of Bath, Companion St. Michael and St. George, D.S.O., Mil. Cross; mentioned in dispatches 4 times. Mem. Ch. of England.*

HERTZLER, JOHN ROWE, bus. exec.; b. Lancaster, Pa., Oct. 2, 1905; s. Oliver Henry and Bessie Viola (Rowe) H.; M.E., Lehigh U., 1927; M.A. in Edn., U. Conn., 1962; m. Priscilla Bennett, May 6, 1944; children—Bennett, Timothy, Samuel, Daniel. Trainee York Corp., 1927-30; air conditioning sales engring., met. N.Y. Dist. office York Corp., 1930-35, work at hdqrs., Pa., 1935-42, mgr. air conditioning dept., 1935-37, gen. rep., 1937-40, gen. sales mgr., 1940-42, v.p., gen. sales mgr., 1945-54, dir., 1951-54; pres. Hertzler Enterprises, Inc., from 1954. Propr. Mt. Hope Rabbitry, Mansfield Center, from 1959. Dep. sec. of commerce of Pa., 1955. Chmn. utilities subcom. Mansfield (Conn.) Community Devel. Action Plan, 1969-70. Trustee Windham Community Meml. Hosp., Willimantic, Conn., from 1967. Served as liaison officer USNR active duty WPB, Washington, specializing gen. indsl. equipment, World War II. Mem. Am. Soc. Heating, Refrigerating and Air Conditioning Engrs., Lambda Chi Alpha, Tau Beta Pi, Pi Tau Sigma. Clubs: Engineers (N.Y.C.); Rotary (pres.) (Willamantic). Conglist. Author, editor: Hotel Guest Room Air Conditioning, 1940. Contbr. tech papers to engring. jours. Home: Mansfield Center, Conn. Died Apr. 4, 1980.

HERVEY, JOHN GAINES, lawyer; born at Hillsboro, Texas, February 26, 1900; son of William Edwin and Mollie (Revier) H.; B.A., U. of Okal., 1923, LL.B., 1925; Ph.D., U. Pa., 1928; LL.D. (hon.), U. Tulsa, 1956; L.H.D. (hon.), U. Miami, 1956; Litt.D. (hon.), John Marshall Law Sch., Chgo., 1956; LL.D. (hon.), Bklyn. Law Sch., Cleveland Marshall Law Sch., 1957, U. of San Diego, Seton Hall U., 1962, Howard Coll., 1964; D.C.L. (hon.), Oklahoma City U., 1969; m. Hallie Holloway, Aug. 24, 1925; children—Janis, John Douglas. Admitted Okla. bar, 1925; asst. prof. internat. law, U. of Pa., 1928-30; asso. dean and prof. law, Temple U. Law Sch., Phila., 1930-38, dean, 1939-41; dean Sch. Law, U. Okla., 1941-46; dean Oklahoma City U. School of Law, from 1956, then dean emeritus; also law clk. U.S. Dist. Ct., Western Dist. Okla. Exec. sec., Okla. Bar Assn., 1946-47; adviser legal edn. and admission to bar, Am. Bar Assn.; chief justice Phi Delta Phi, Court of Appeals, 1957-59. Served as private, U.S. Army, Sept.-Dec. 1918. Legislative adviser Pa. Senate Com. Revision of Pub. Service Co. Laws, 1932-33; utility consultant, Gov. of Pa., 1935-36; spl. atty. U.S. Dept. of Justice, 1940-41. Mem. bar of U.S. Supreme Ct., Pa. Supreme Ct., and of Okla., Okla. State Bar Mem. Judicial Coun. of Okla. Acacia (nat. judge advocate from 1935-38), Coif, Lambda Sigma Kappa, Alpha Kappa Psi, Phi Delta Phi (internat. pres. 1955-57), Phi Beta Kappa, Delta Sigma Rho. Democrat. Methodist. Mason (33 deg.). Author, co-author several pubs., latest: co-author: Business and Government, 6th edit. 1953. Editor Okla. Bar Assn. Jour., 1948-75; Annual Review Legal Education, 1947-75. Home: Norman, Okla. Died May 11, 1975; interred Marlow, Okla.

HERZBERG, DONALD GABRIEL, educator, govt. ofcl., author; b. Orange, N.J., May 6, 1925; s. Max John and Edna (Newman) H.; B.A., Wesleyan U., 1946; postgrad. Maxwell Sch., Syracuse U., 1946-48; m. Marlene Grey, July 1, 1953 (div. Nov. 1967); children—John Max, Joan; m. 2d, Barbara Smith Schelling; stepchildren—Andrew Schelling, Melissa Schelling, Timothy Norton Schelling. Asst. to dean Maxwell Sch., Syracuse, N.Y., 1947-48; instr. govt. Wesleyan U., Middletown, Conn., 1948-49; spl. asst. to comptroller State of Conn., 1949-50; legis. asst. to Sen. William Benton, Conn., 1950-53; asst. to pres. Chatham Coll., Pitts., 1953-55; dep. dir. budget div. State of N.Y., 1955-56; dir. Eagleton Inst. Politics, Rutgers U., New Brunswick, N.J., 1956-73, also prof. polit. sci., chmn. polit. sci. sect., 1963-65; dean Grad. Sch., prof. govt. Georgetown (D.C.) U., 1973-80, v.p. for grad. studies and research, 1979-80; cons. elections and politics NBC News, 1962-64, ABC News, 1966—, pub. affairs dept. Ford Found., 1962-65; chief research cons. to pres. pro tem N.Y. Senate, 1965, minority leader N.Y. Assembly, 1969-80, mem. bd. Ops. and Policy Research, Washington, 1967-80; chmn. Nat. Corp. for Policy Research and Ops., N.Y.C., 1968-75, Election Law Revision Commn., N.J., 1966-80; staff dir. Joint Legislative Commn. on Higher Edn., 1965, Pres.'s Commn. on Registration and Voter Participation, 1963-64, Select Commn. on Western Hemisphere Immigration, 1967-68; adviser Prime Minister Guyana, 1965-66. Bd. dirs. United Fund New Brunswick; bd. mgrs. Trenton State Hosp.; trustee Inst. for Am. Univs., Aix-en-Provence, France, Mt. Vernon Coll., Washington, Freedoms Found. at Valley Forge, 1978-80. Mem. Am. Polit. Sci. Assn., AAAS, AFTRA. Democrat. Author: (with Jack Peltason) A Student Guide to Campaign Politics, 1970; (with Jess Unruh) Essays on the Legislative Process, 1970; (with Gerald Pomper) American Party Politics, Essays and Readings, 1966; (with William Baumer) Politics is Your Business, 1960; (with Paul Tillett) The Politics of the Budget of New York, 1959; Political Parties in an Age of Scarcity, 1978; several chpts. in other vols. Home: Washington, D.C. Died Aug. 11, 1980; buried Princeton, N.J.

HERZBERG, JOSEPH GABRIEL, former editor-writer; b. N.Y.C., Jan. 1, 1907; s. Theodore and Sarah (Rosenthal) H.; student Townsend Harris Hall, Coll. City N.Y., 1921-25; m. Marion Burton Warendorff, Aug. 28, 1939; 1 son, Paul Burton. Joined N.Y. Herald Tribune as copy boy, 1925; successively reporter, rewrite man, asst. night city editor, night city editor, city editor 1946-52, Sunday editor, 1952-56; joined N.Y. Times, 1956, asst. city editor, dir. cultural news, 1962-67, spl. writer on edn1., cultural subjects, 1967-70; instr. journalism N.Y. U., 1944-47, 56-57; adj. asst. adj. asst. prof. L.I. U., 1956-57; lectr. Grad. Inst. Book Pubs., 1960-62. Bd. dirs. James Gordon Bennett Found., 1960-70. Poynter fellow Yale, 1968. Editor: Late City Edition, 1947; editorial bd. Information Please Almanac, 1964-67. Home: New Canaan, Conn. Died Feb. 12, 1976.

HERZFELD, KARL FERDINAND, physicist; b. Vienna, Austria, Feb. 24, 1892; s. Charles August (M.D.) and Camilla (Herzog) H.; student Schotten Gymnasium, Vienna, 1902-10, U. Vienna, 1910-12, U. Zurich, 1912-13, U. Göttingen, 1913-14; Ph.D., U. Vienna, 1914; D.Sc. honoris causa, Loyola Coll., Balt., 1932, Marquette U., 1933; D.Sc., U. Md., 1956, Manhattan Coll., 1959; hon. degrees Fordham U., 1960, Inst. Tech. Stuttgart, 1962, Cath. U. Am., 1963, U. Notre Dame, 1965, Providence Coll., 1965; m. Regina Flannery, 1938. Privat-docent Univ. Munich, 1920, a.o. prof., 1923; Speyer guest prof., Johns Hopkins, 1926, prof. physics, 1926-36; head dept. physics Cath. U. Am., 1936-61, prof., 1936-68, prof. emeritus, 1968-78. Served as 1st lt. Austrian Army, 1914-18. Recipient Mendel medal, 1931; Secchi medal Georgetown U., 1938; Certificate of Exceptional Service to Navy Ordnance Devel., 1946; Cardinal Gibbons medal, 1960; USN Meritorious Pub. Service award, 1964; Papal Bene Merenti medal, 1965. Fellow Am. Phys. Soc., A.A.A.S., Acoustical Soc. Am.; mem. Washington Acad. Sci., Washington Philos. Soc., German Phys. Soc., Am. Acad. Arts and Scis., Nat. Acad. Scis., Phi Beta Kappa, Sigma Xi, Gamma Alpha. K.C. Author: Kinetische Theorie der Waerme, 1925; Absorption and Dispersion of Ultrasonic Waves (with T.A. Litovitz), 1959. Home: Washington, D.C. Died June 3, 1978; interred Mt. Olivet Cemetery.

HESKIN, OSCAR E., govt. ofcl., economist; b. Portland, N.D., Dec. 19, 1899; s. Ole N. and Eli (Medalen) H.; A.B., Luther Coll., 1922; student U. of Wis., 1924-25, Thayer grad. scholar in economics, Harvard, 1927-28; A.M., U. of Minn., 1928, Ph. D., 1937; m. Lillien Wick, Sept. 10, 1930. Asst. in economics U. of Minn., 1925-27, instr., 1928-38; asst. prof. U. of Fla., 1938-41, asso. prof., 1941-46, prof., 1946—, head economics dept., 1949—; chief Research and Analysis sect., O.P.A., Fla., 1943; chief Manufactured Food Sect., Bur. of Census, Washington, 1944; sr. economist, Alien Property Custodian, Washington, 1944; attaché, U.S. Embassy, Oslo Norway, 1945-46; consul, Am. Consulate Gen. Shanghai, China, 1948; chief requirements officer American Embassy, Karachi, Pakistan, 1952-55; sr economist US OM, Egypt, Am. Embassy, Cairo 1955-56; chief econ. analyst USOM, Am. Embassy Tripoli, Libya, 1956-57; econ. adviser U.S. Oversea Mission, Am. Embassy, Amman, Jordan, 1957— Member of American. Southern economic associations Am. Assn. U. Profs., Athenaeum Soc., Am. Legion Delta Sigma Pi. Contbr. profl. jours. Home: Gainesville Fla. *

HESLER, LEXEMUEL RAY, coll. dean; b. Veedersburg, Ind., Feb. 20, 1888; s. Clinton F. an Laura Iris (Youngblood) H.; A.B., Wabash Coll., 191 Ph.D., Cornell University, 1914; LL.D. (honorary Wabash College, 1953; married Esther Lillian Collin July 2, 1914. Fellow in plant pathology, Cornell U 1911-12, instr., 1912-14, asst. prof., 1914-19; prof. botany, U. of Tenn., 1919-58 dean Coll. of Liberal Ar

1934-58, prof. and dean emeritus, 1958-77; temp. appointments Agr. Expt. Stations at Wooster, O., and Puerto Rico. NSF grantee, research on mushrooms of N. Am., 1958-77. Fellow A.A.A.S., mem. Bot. Soc. America, Am. Phytopathol. Soc., Mycol. Soc. America, Southern Appalachian Bot. Soc., Tenn. Acad. Science, Sigma Xi, Phi Kappa Phi, Alpha Zeta, Kappa Sigma. Presbyn. Author textbooks; contbr. sci. jours. Home: Knoxville, Tenn. Died Nov. 20, 1977.

HESS, (J.) GEORGE, prof. art; b. Syracuse, N.Y., July 22, 1886; s. Gottlob and Anna Maria (Eppler) H.; B.P., (Hiram Gee fellow), Coll. of Fine Arts, Syracuse U., 1909; Academie de la Grande Chaumiere, Academie Colarossi, Paris, 1909-12; m. Mariam Viola Clark, July 12, 1922; 1 dau., Emily Mariam. Study and travel, Europe, 1909-12; instr., art, Coll. of Fine Arts, Syracuse U., 1912-23, prof. art and research painting since 1923, dir., summer session, art, 1925-45, dir. extension sch., art, 1923-43; exhibitions, carnival designs, portraits, window displays, commercial art. Mem. Syracuse Alumni Assn., Syracuse Turn Verein, Y.M.C.A., Associated Artists (Syracuse), Iroquois Art Assn., Eastern Arts Assn., Graduate Painters Assn. Presbyterian. Clubs: Sketch, Faculty, Citizens. Home: Syracuse, N.Y. *

HESS, JEROME SAYLES, lawyer; b. N.Y.C., June 17, 1882; s. Charles A. and Ida (Doctor) H.; A.B., Yale, 1903; Columbia Law Sch., 1906; married Harriette Orline Peloubet, June 20, 1947. Admitted to N.Y. State, 1906, and practiced, N.Y. City, 1966—; counsel to Hardin, Hess, Eder & Rashap, N.Y.C.; atty. for govt. Mex. in formulating agreements relating to its pub. debt, rep. govt. Italy in consular matters. Decorated Aztec Eagle (Mexico); Order of Crown of Italy (Italy). President American Fgn. Law Assn., 1944-47, former mem. com. on internat. law, com. on courts higher jurisdiction, (former mem. com. on admissions); mem. Assn. Bar City of N.Y.; sec. and mem. com. on judiciary N.Y. County Lawyers Assn.; mem. N.Y. State, Am. bar assns., Internat. Law Assn. (Am. br.), Am. Soc. Internat. Law, Council on Fgn. Relations, Fgn. Policy Assn., Phi Beta Kappa, Zeta Psi. Clubs: Yale University (N.Y.C.), Saratoga Golf (gov.), Turf and Field. Home: N.Y.C. *

HESS, JOHN AMBROSE, univ. prof.; b. Perry, Ill., Aug. 23, 1885; s. August Benjamin and Annie Judson (Short) H.; A.B., U. of Kan., 1908, A.M., 1910; Ph.D., Ind. U., 1928; also student U. of Berlin, U. of Marburg, and Alliance Française (Paris); m. Mary Whitcomb, Aug. 22, 1918; children—Harry Alvah, John Reginald, Mary Carolina. Instr. in German, U. of Kan., 1909-10, instr. in French, 1918-20, asst. prof. of Romance languages, 1920-27; instr. in German, Ind. U., 1910-15, asst. prof., 1915-18; prof. of German Ohio U. since 1927, head dept., 1927-51; lectr. German, Johns Hopkins, summer 1931. Mem. Am. Assn. Tchrs. German, Nat. Fedn. Modern Lang. Tchrs., Phi Beta Kappa. Methodist. Author books, pamphlets, articles. Review editor, German Quarterly, 1945-52. Home: Athens, Ohio. *

HESS, THOMAS B., writer, editor; b. Rye, N.Y., July 14, 1920; s. Gabriel Lorié and Helen (Baer) H.; B.A., Yale, 1942; m. Audrey Stern, June 29, 1944 (dec.); children—William, Helen, Philip. With Art News mag., N.Y.C, 1946-72, exec. editor, 1949-65, editor, 1965-72; art critic Le Monde, Paris, 1970-74 New York mag., from 1972; consultative chmn. dept. twentieth century art Met. Mus. Art, N.Y.C. Mem. of juries and award panels. Pres. Longview Found., 1958-75. Served as pilot USAAF, 1942-45. Mem. Phi Beta Kappa. Author: Abstract Painting, Background and American Phase, 1951; William de Kooning, 1959, 68, 69; Barnett Newman, 1969, 71; De Kooning Drawings, 1972; Reinhardt Satires, 1974; Siskind, 1976. Home: New York, N.Y. Died July 13, 1978.

HESSER, ERNEST GEORGE, educator; born Crestline, O., Feb. 25, 1883; s. George Gaylord and Mary Ellen (Garberich) H.; student Ohio Wesleyan U.; A.B., Winona (Ind.) Coll., 1905; grad. New Sch. of Methods, Chicago, 1908; studied voice with William Miles (Fort Wayne, Ind.), Dr. Carl Dufft (New York), William Shakespeare, Sir Frederick Bridge (London), etc.; Bach. of Music, Metropolitan School of Music (affiliate Butler U.); M.Pd., Cincinnati Conservatory of Music (Univ. of Cincinnati), 1924; Dr. Pd., 1927; M.Sc. in Edn., U. of Cincinnati, 1935; m. Ethel Martin, Oct. 7, 1907; children—James Martin, Ernest Grant. Tchr., supvr. music in pub. schs., Ind., N.Y., Cal., 1906-30 Cin., 1930-36; dir. music Bowling Green (O.) State Normal Coll. 1914-20; head of pub. sch. music dept., Arthur Jordan Conservatory of Music (Butler U.); prof. of methods, Univ. of Cincinnati 1930-36; dir. of music, Coll. of Edn., N.Y. U. 1936-42; dir. music, Baltimore Public Schools, and prof. of methods, Peabody Conservatory, 1942-46; dir. choir and music festivals; lectr. summer schs., condr. community choruses, baritone soloist; conductor Pa. Male Chorus (Crestline); dir. Crestline Mus.; pres. Crestline Hist. Soc.; curator Crestline Shunk Mus.; mem. Crestline Pub. Library Bd. Mem. Govs. Commn. for 1953 Ohio Sesqui-Centennial. Mem. many profl. assns. and orgns., past officer of several. Republican. Presbyterian. Mason. Clubs: Schoolmasters, Portfolio, Burns, Columbia, Rotary, The Bohemians, Beethoven Association. Author song books 1917-22; co-editor song books, 1923-33. Received Nat. Music War Council award for distinguished service, 1944. Contbr. articles on music to mags. and papers; daily hist. column for newspapers. Address: Crestline, O. *

HESTER, E. ELIZABETH, educator; b. Cookeville, Tenn., Dec. 6, 1918; d. John S. and Ellen (Dunn) Hester; B.S., Memphis State U., 1939; M.S., Cornell U., 1947, Ph.D., 1952. Pub. sch. tchr., Memphis, 1939-42; instr., then asst. prof. food and nutrition N.Y. State Coll. Home Econs., 1947-50; asso. prof. food and nutrition Pa. State U., 1952-59; mem. faculty Cornell U., 1959-79, prof. food and nutrition, 1963-69; prof. human nutrition and food N.Y. State Coll. Human Ecology, 1969-79, chmn. dept., 1969-73, prof. nutritional scis., 1974-79. Served to lt. (j.g.) USNR, 1943-45. Fellow AAAS; mem. Am. Assn. Cereal Chemists, Inst. Food Tech., Am. Home Econs. Assn., Sigma Xi (chpt. pres. 1968-69), Phi Kappa Phi, Omicron Nu, Iota Sigma Pi, Sigma Delta Epsilon. Contbr. profl. jours. Home: Ithaca, N.Y. Died July 3, 1979.

HESTER, JOHN HUTCHISON, army officer; b. Albany, Ga., Sept. 11, 1886; s. John Temple and Lily Dale (Hutchison) H.; student U. of Ga., 1903-04; B.S., U.S. Mil. Acad., 1904-08; attended Field Officers Course, Fort Benning, Ga., 1920-21, Command and Gen. Staff Sch., 1921-23, Army War Coll., 1926-27; m. Leila Richardson, Mar. 30, 1910; children—Henry Richardson, John Hutchison. Commd. 2d lt., U.S. Army, 1908, and rose through grades to brig. gen., 1940, major gen., Feb. 1942; exec. for reserve affairs to chief of staff, Washington, D.C., 1940-41; comdg. gen., Camp Wheeler, Ga., 1941; comdg. 43d Inf. Div., 1941-43; comdg. gen. Tank Destroyer Center, Camp Hood, Tex., 1943-44, Camp Croft, S.C. since 1944. Mem. Alpha Tau Omega. Episcopalian. Address: Camp Croft, S.C.*

HESTON, JOSEPH CARTER, psychologist; b. Pataskala, Ohio, Jan. 17, 1909; s. Joseph Z. and Luvadelle (Carter) H.; A.B., Muskingum Coll., 1931; M.A., Ohio State U., 1938, Ph.D., 1941; m. Martha Jane Allen, Aug. 25, 1934; children—Joseph Allen, Julie Lou. Tchr. high sch., West Jefferson, Ohio, 1932-39; asst. psychology Ohio State U., 1939-41; prof. psychology DePauw U., 1941-52; guidance dir. Fresno (Calif.) State Coll., 1952-55; prof. psychology Albion (Mich.) Coll., 1955-78, chmn. dept., 1961-63, dir. instl. research and counseling, 1963-78, prof. emeritus, 1974-78; vis. prof. Nat. Def. Act Guidance Inst., Ohio U., 1960-62; vis. prof. U. Ill., U. N.Mex., U. Nebr., N.Y. U., Iliff Sch. Theology, Bay View Summer Coll. Cons. FSA, 1941-42, Nat. Bd. Edn. Meth. Ch., 1946-52, Ministerial Tng. Bd. Mich. Conf. Meth. Ch., 1961-78; mem. guidance com. Mich. Dept. Pub. Instrn., 1959-78; vocational cons. Social Security Adminstrn., 1962-78. Fulbright grant sr. lectr. psychology Australian Nat. U., Canberra, 1965. Diplomate guidance Am. Bd. Examiners Profl. Psychology (cons.). Fellow Am. Psychol. Assn.; mem. Am. Personnel and Guidance Assn., Mich. Psychol. Assn., AAUP, Assn. Instl. Research (charter), Nat. Council Measurement Edn., Sigma Xi, Phi Delta Kappa, Phi Mu Alpha. Club: Alban (Muskingum Coll.). Author: Heston Personal Adjustment Inventory, 1949; How to Take a Test, 1953; Learning About Tests, 1955; Personal Traits Analysis, 1966; Counseling for the Liberal Arts Campus, 1968; About Tests, 1969; also articles. Home: Brunswick, Ga. Died Aug. 5, 1978; interred at Concord, N.H.

HETRICK, JACOB ADAM WERNER, coll. pres., otolaryngologist; b. Asbury Park, N.J., Apr. 22, 1895; s. Jacob Adam Werner and Linnie S. (Evans) H.; M.D., N.Y. Med. Coll., 1918, D.Sc. (hon.); postgrad. in Vienna, Austria, 1927; m. Lilliam Morgan, Nov. 21, 1918; 1 dau. Lillian Janet. Interne Flower Hosp., N.Y.C., 1918-20; prof. otolaryngology N.Y. Med. Coll., Flower and Fifth Ave. Hosps., 1927, registrar, 1925-27, asst. dean, 1927-39, asso. dean, 1939-40, dean, 1940, pres., 1942-58. Fellow A.C.S., Acad. Opthalmology, N.Y. Acad. Medicine; mem. A.M.A., N.Y. State Homeo. Soc. (pres. 1933-34), Acad. Path. Sci. (pres. 1928), Harvey Soc., N.Y. Com. Internships and Residencies, Nat. Inst. Social Scis., Acad. Polit. Sci., Alpha Sigma, Alpha Kappa Kappa, Alpha Omega Alpha. Mason. Clubs: Wheelman (Asbury Park, N.J.); Deal (N.J.) Golf and Country. Contbr. articles to med. jours. Home: Brielle, N.J. Died Nov. 24, 1979; interred Old Tennet Cemetery, Tennet, N.J.

HEUCHLING, FRED G., banker; b. at Chicago, Ill., Mar. 1, 1886; s. Theodore W. (M.D.) and Margaret (Moller) H.; B.S., Armour Institute Tech., Ch.E., 1910; m. Mabel A. Koch (A.B., Smith Coll.), of Chicago, June 29, 1912. Instr. industrial engring., Armour Inst., 1907-9; structural and railroad engr., C.,M.&St.P.Ry., 1909-10; efficiency engr., City of Chicago, 1910-11; supt. employment, West Chicago Park Commn., 1911-19; mem. staff of Arthur Young & Co., pub. accountants, Chicago, 1912 and 1919-20; mem. staff U.S. Congressional Commn. on Reclassification of Federal Employes, 1919; v.p. Northwestern Trust & Savings Bank, Chicago, since 1920; pres. Financial Advertisements Corpn. since 1923. Mem. Tau Beta Pi. Clubs: City, Union League. Home: Chicago. *

HEWATT, WILLIS GILLILAND, educator; b. Hood, Tex., July 10, 1904; s. John Walter and Susie Irma (Gilliland) H.; B.S., Tex. Christian U., 1927, M.S., 1929; Ph.D., Stanford, 1934; m. Elizabeth Georgine Harris, Dec. 19, 1931; children—Elizabeth (Mrs. R.L. Sifford), Joan (Mrs. Johnny Ray Swaim). Mem. faculty Tex. Christian U., 1933-74, prof. biology, 1942-74, prof. emeritus, 1974-80, chmn. depts. biology, 1952-69, geology, 1952-64; vis. prof. Woods Hole Marine Biol. Lab., summer 1942, La. State U., 1944-45, U. P.R., 1945-46; marine biology cons. Tex. A. and M. Research Found., 1947-51; research cons. Socony Mobil Oil Co., Inc., 1954-61; marine biology cons. Va. Inst. Marine Sci., 1950-80. Bd. dirs. Council Sci. Socs. Ft. Worth-Dallas (chmn. bd. 1966), Ft. Worth Regional Sci. Fair, 1952-71, Ft. Worth Mus. Sci. and History (pres. bd. dirs. 1969). Recipient Distinguished Alumnus award Tex. Christian U., 1961; Piper award as prof. of 1968. Mem. A.A.A.S., Ecol. Soc. Am., Nat. Shellfish Soc., Soc. Am. Limnologists and Oceanographers, Am. Soc. Systemmatists, Phi Beta Kappa (founding mem. Delta Chpt. 1971). Mem. Christian Ch. Contbr. articles to profl. jours. Home: Fort Worth, Tex. Died Feb. 5, 1980.

HEWINS, KENNETH F., journalist, educator; b. Evansville, Ind., Nov. 16, 1902; s. Dan and Etta (Gardner) H.; B.A., Ind. U., 1925, M.A., 1926; postgrad. U. Miss., 1952; m. Lillian Louise Loge, July 3, 1927 (dec.); children—Marilyn June Hewins Duncan, Eleanor Joyce Hewins Robinson; m. 2d, Ila Pesnell Henderson, Apr. 27, 1973. Reporter, Evansville Press, summer 1922; editor-in-chief Ind. U. Daily Student, 1924; city editor Bloomington (Ind.) Star, 1924; asst. editor Ind. U. Alumnus, 1924-26; alumni editor, mgr. Press Bur. U. Ark., 1926-29; asst. prof. to prof., head journalism dept., dir. publicity La. Tech. U., Ruston, 1929-68; cons. in journalistic field, 1968-77; columnist The Morning Paper, Ruston, 1979-81. Mem. Ind. U. Emeritus Club, Acacia, Sigma Delta Chi, Sigma Tau Delta. Democrat. Methodist. Club: Masons. Author: Mississippi Press Laws, 1952. Home: Ruston, La. Died Jan. 29, 1981; buried Forest Lawn Cemetery, Ruston.

HEWITT, ROY RENO, lawyer, educator and writer; b. Yamhill County, Ore., August 5, 1883; s. James Andrew and Mary Jane (Rose) H.; Ph.B., LL.B., Willamette Univ., Salem, Ore., 1909; A.M., Clark U., 1920; grad. study, U. of Southern Calif.; m. Lena Mae Heise, of Salem, Ore., Sept. 20, 1908; 1 son, Ronald Roy. Admitted to Ore. bar, 1909; teacher in high schs., Ore., 1909-12; mem. law firm Langs Hewitt and Nott, McMinnville, Ore., 1912-17; fellow Clark U., and lecturer on jurisprudence, 1919; asst. prof. polit. science, Ore. State Coll., 1920-26, asso. prof., 1926-27; dean Coll. of Law, Willamette University, 1927-32; in practice of law at Salem since 1932. Served as sergt. inf., U.S.A., Mexican border, 1917; welfare work with U.S. forces overseas, 1918. Mem. Pi Gamma Mu, Phi Kappa Tau and Delta Theta Phi frats. Mem. Methodist Ch. Author: Oregon supplement to state adopted text on government, 1924. Co-Author: Outline of Oregon Government, 1922. Writer of numerous articles on social, economic and polit. subjects. Traveled in Asia and South America, 1929-31. Home: Salem, Ore. *

HEWITT, SAM PARKER, plant physiologist; b. Bethel, Mo., Sept. 2, 1908; s. Clarence Elmer and Edith Ellen (Cheuvront) H.; B.S. in Edn., N.E. Mo. State U., 1932; M.Ed., U. Mo., 1936; Ph.D., Cornell U., 1947; m. Mary Jo Busbee, Sept. 21, 1940. Tchr. high schs., Mo., 1932-39; grad. asst., then instr. Cornell U., 1940-47; prof. biology Central Mo. State U., Warrenburg, 1947-69, chmn. div. sci. and math., 1969-72, dean Sch. Arts and Scis., 1972-75, dean emeritus, 1975; dir. NSF summer instrs., 1961-64; research plant physiologist, 1947-75. Hon. trustee bd. assos. Research Hosp., Kansas City, Mo. Served with AUS, 1943-45. Mem. Bot. Soc. Am., Am. Inst. Biol. Scis., A.A.A.S., Sigma Xi, Sigma Tau Gamma (O.F. Grubb award 1974), Phi Kappa Phi, Phi Delta Kappa. Baptist (trustee). Rotarian (sec. Warrensburg 1955-57). Home: Warrensburg, Mo. Died Nov. 8, 1975; interred Warrensburg Meml. Gardens.

HEYLIGER, WILLIAM, author, editor; b. Hoboken, N.J., Mar. 22, 1884; s. Daniel and Ellen (Sullivan) H.; pub. schs. and Sacred Heart Acad., Hoboken; m. Catherine C. McDermott, June 12, 1906; children—Ellen, Cecilia, Margaret, William, Jr., Elizabeth, Robert, Catherine, Donald; m. 2d, Fluer C. Banekov, February 27, 1949. In mercantile business and newspaper work until 1912; editor lit. for youth-fiction dept. Westminster Press, Phila. Roman Catholic. Author since 1911, latest publs.: Son of the Apple Valley, 1940; You're on the Air, 1941; Gasoline Jockey, 1942; SOS Radio Patrol, 1942; Top Lineman, 1943; Home Is a One-Way Street, 1945. Home: Drexel Hill, Pa. *

HEYWORTH, JOHN RUSHTON, clergyman; b. Bacup, Lancashire, Eng., June 20, 1882; s. John Edward and Susannah (Rushton) H.; ed. pub. and continuation schs., tech. sch., Bacup; grad. in theology (gold medalist in pub. speaking), Victoria U., Toronto, Ont., Can.; post-grad. work Chicago Theol. Sem.; m. Isabel Marky Georgine Burger, Apr. 3, 1912; children—Helen Willet, Eileen Rushton. Came to U.S. 1914, naturalized citizen, 1923. Ordained Congl. ministry, 1912; asso. pastor Calvary Ch., Montreal, 1911-12; pastor Paris, Ont., Can., 1912-14, Lombard, Ill., 1914-18, Park Manor, Chicago, 1918-24, New England Congl. Ch., Chicago, 1925-30, Unity Ch., Chicago, since 1931. Organizer and sponsor Chicago Young Men's Ch.; chaplain Forty Club. Was state rep. for Ill. for Chicago Theol. Sem., 1924. Pres. of Lake View Council on Religious Action since 1941. Republican. Club: Lake View Kiwanis. Home: Chicago Ill. *

HIBBARD, CLAUDE WILLIAM, educator, paleontologist; b. Toronto, Kan., Mar. 21, 1905; s. Charles E. and Evie (Johnson) H.; B.A., U. Kan., 1933, M.A., 1934; Ph.D., U. Mich., 1941; m. Faye Louise Ganfield, Sept. 8, 1934; 1 dau., Katherine (Mrs. John P. Mull). Wildlife technician Nat. Park Service, 1934-35; mem. faculty U. Kan., 1935, 37, 38-46, curator, asst. prof., 1941-46; mem. faculty U. Mich., Ann Arbor, 1946-73, prof. geology, 1953-73, curator fossil vertebrates, 1953-73. Fellow Geol. Soc. Am.; mem. Kan. (past pres.), Mich. (past pres.) acads. sci., Mich. Geol. Soc. (past pres.), Soc. Vertebrate Paleontology (past pres.), Soc. Mammalogists, Soc. Ichthyologists and Herpetologists, Am. Assn. Petroleum Geologists, Paleontol. Soc. Discoverer of nearly complete Late Cenzoic faunal sequence. Home: Ann Arbor, Mich.; buried Toronto Cemetery, Toronto, Kans. Died Oct. 9, 1973.

HIBBARD, MELVILLE LOUIS, pub. utilities; b. Farnham, Quebec, Can., Feb. 21, 1883; s. William Louis and Nancy Elizabeth (Buck) H.; Sc.B., McGill U., Montreal, Can., 1906; m. Adele Gloria LaSalle, Oct. 20, 1910; 1 son, William Daniel. Came to U.S., 1908, naturalized, 1921. Test engr. Gen. Electric Co., Pittsfield, Mass., 1906-07; shopman Montreal St. Ry. Co., 1907-08; supt. elec. dept. Union Light, Heat & Power Co., Fargo, N.D., 1908-09; chief engr. San Antonio (Tex.) Gas & Electric Co. and San Antonio Traction Co., 1910-11; gen. mgr. Union Light, Heat & Power Co., Fargo, 1911-23; v.p. and gen. mgr. Fargo and Moorhead St. Ry. Co., Fargo, 1914-23; asst. v.p. in charge operations Northern States Power Co., Minneapolis, 1923-27; asst. gen. mgr. Ida. Power Co., Boise, 1928, v.p. and gen. mgr., 1929-30, pres. and gen. mgr., 1931-33; pres. and gen. mgr. Minn. Power and Light Co., Duluth, 1933-54. chmn. bd., 1954-62, cons., 1962—, director, 1933—; chmn. Superior (Wis.) Water, Light and Power Co., 1945-59. Pres. No. League Profl. Baseball Clubs, 1916-17; dir. Duluth Community Fund, 1933-60, also Minn. Arrowhead Assn., Duluth; v. chmn. adv. bd. St. Mary's Hosp. Recipient Legion of Honor of DeMolay, 1958. Mem. N. Central Electric Assn. (exec. com.), Duluth Engrs. Club, Phi Delta Theta. Republican. Episcopalian. Mason (32 deg., Shriner), Elk. Clubs: Kitchi Gammi (pres. 1946-48), Duluth Athletic Automobile Engineers, Rotary (Duluth); Minneapolis Golf, Minneapolis Athletic (Minneapolis). Home: Duluth, Minn. *

HICKAM, HUBERT, lawyer; b. Spencer, Ind., Apr. 19, 1892; s. Willis and Sallie (Meek) H.; LL.B., Indiana U., 1913; m. Ruth Moffett, Oct. 28, 1915 (dec. Jan. 22, 1935); 1 dau., Barbara (Mrs. Audley Wasson); m. 2d, Mary Elizabeth Randolph Woods, Sept. 9, 1939; children—James P. Woods, Mrs. Elizabeth W. Adams. Associated with law firm Hickam & Hickam, Spencer, Ind., 1913-19; removed to Indianapolis, 1919; mem. firm Noel, Hickam & Boyd, 1923-26, Noel, Hickam, Boyd & Armstrong, 1926-40, Barnes, Hickam, Pantzer & Boyd, from 1940. Mem. Ind. General Assembly, 1915. Member alumni board of visitors of School of law, at Indiana U., from 1964, recipient Distinguished Alumni award, 1967. Served as 1st lt. QMC, U.S. Army, 1918-19. Chairman Alien Enemy Hearing Bd., Southern Dist. of Ind., 1941; selective service appeal agent, World War II. Fellow Am. Coll. of Trial Lawyers; mem. Am. Law Inst. (joint com. on continuing edn. legal edn.), Am. chmn. antitrust section 1958-59, joint com. on continuing edn. legal edn.), Fed., 7th Fed. Circuit, Ind., Indpls. (ex-pres.) bar assns., and also mem. National Assn. R.R. Trial Lawyers, Mil. Order Loyal Legion, Phi Kappa Psi. Presbyn. Mason. Clubs: Woodstock, University, Athletic Traders Point Hunt, Contemporary (past pres.), Lawyers (past pres.) (Indpls.); Tavern (Chgo.). Author: A Civil Action: From Pleadings to Trial; co-author Preparation for Trial. Home: Indianapolis, Ind. Died May 30, 1978; interred Crown Hill cemetery, Indpls.

HICKCOX, ARTHUR PERCY, mfg. exec.; b. Watertown, Con., Feb. 29, 1884; s. Howard M. and Amelia (Atwood) H.; ed. Taft Sch., Wesleyan U.; m. Florence Atwood, Jan. 23, 1909; 1 dau., Jean. Clerk Waterbury Clock Co., 1907-10; in purchasing dept. Scovill Mfg. Co., Waterbury, since 1910, v.p. and dir. of purchases since 1940. Dir. Scovill Mfg. Co. Trustee The Taft School. Republican. Methodist (trustee Watertown Ch.). Club: Waterbury. Home: Watertown, Conn. *

HICKERSON, THOMAS FELIX, univ. prof.; b. Ronda, N.C., Apr. 30, 1882; s. Dr. James and Annie Eliza (Weaver) H.; A.B., U. of N.C., 1904, A.M., 1907; S.B. in C.E., Mass. Inst. Tech., 1909; grad. student, Columbia, 1911; unmarried. Teacher Bingham Mil. Sch., Asheville, N.C., 1904-05; at U. of N.C. since 1905, instr. math. and grad. student until 1908, asso. prof. civil engring., 1910-20, prof. civil engring., 1920-38, prof. applied mathematics since 1938, Kenan professor applied mathematics since 1945. Member N.C. State Highway Commn., 1915-19. Served as engr. in various parts of N.C.; highway engr. N.C. Geol. Survey, 1912-14; chief engr. N.C. State Highway Commn. on highway locations, Surry and Orange counties; etc. Mem. Plattsburg Army Trai0ing Camp, 1918. Mem. Am. Soc. C.E. (pres. N.C. Sect. 1942), Math. Assn. Am. Sigma Xi, Tau Beta Pi, Phi Delta Theta, Order of Gimghouls. Democrat. Episcopalian. Author: Culverts and Bridges for North Carolina Highways (with C. R. Thomas), 1910; Use of The Abney Hand Level, 1914; Notes on Military Map Reading, 1918; Highway Curves and Earthwork, 1926; Continuous Beams and Frames, 1932; The Strength of Materials, 1933; Structural Frameworks, 1934; Highway Surveying and Planning, 1935; Statically Indeterminate Structures, 1937; Happy Valley (history and genealogy), 1940, Navigational Handbook with Tables, 1944; Latitude, Longitude and Azimuth by the Sun or Stars, 1946. Asso. editor of General Engineering, 1939. Home: Chapel Hill, N.C. *

HICKEY, MAURICE JOHN, ret. dentist, physician; b. Solvay, N.Y., Aug. 27, 1907; s. Daniel Coveny and Eleanor (Cole) H.; student Syracuse Univ., 1926-28; D.M.D., Harvard, 1932; M.D., Columbia, 1937; m. Doris Harrison, July 3, 1933; children—Jean Karen, Dean Harrison. Interne surgery Strong Meml. Hosp., Rochester, N.Y., 1937-38; fellow Nat. Cancer Inst., Presbyn. Hosp., N.Y., 1938-41; instr. surgery Columbia, 1940-45, prof. oral surgery, 1945, faculty of medicine, 1946-56, exec. officer dept. dentistry, 1949-56; asso. dean, faculty medicine Columbia Sch. Dental and Oral Surgery, 1949-56; head, div. oral surgery, 1945-56; asst. attending surgeon Presbyn. Hosp., 1945-56; dean sch. dentistry U. Wash., 1956-73; cons. oral surgery, Kingsbridge Vets. Hosp. Entered Dental Corp., U.S. Army, 1942, command. maj., 1942, advanced to lt. col., 1943. Diplomate Am. Bd. Oral Surgery, 1947, N.Y. State Bd. Oral Surgery, 1947 (dir. 1947-76). Fellow N.Y. Acad. Dentistry; mem. A.M.A., ADA, Am. Soc. Plastic and Reconstrn. Surgery, Am. Soc. Maxillo-Facial Surgeons, N.Y. State and County Med. Soc., N.Y. State Dental Soc., First Dist. Dental Soc., Omicron Kappa Upsilon. Republican. Home: Seattle, Wash. Died Oct. 1, 1976.

HICKEY, ROBERT FERDINAND, naval officer; b. Red Bluff, Calif., Dec. 28, 1897; s. Thomas and Augusta (Young) H.; student U. of Calif., 1915-17; grad. U.S. Naval Acad., 1921; m. Virginia Burnham, June 30, 1928; children—Patricia Ann, Robert Ashley. Comdg. officer Naval Air Sta., Bermuda, 1941-42, U.S.S. Hancock, 1944-45; U.S. Naval attache for air, asst. Naval attache, London, Eng., 1945-47; comdr. Fleet Air Wings, Atlantic, 1948-50; chief information Navy Dept., Washington, 1950; rear adm. comdg. Carrier Div. Five, Korean waters; chief of staff comdr. Naval Forces Far East, 1954-55; comdr. Fleet Air, Naval Air Sta., Alameda, Cal., 1955-58; comdr. Fleet Air, Pearl Harbor, Hawaii, from 1958. Clubs: Army and Navy, Nat. Press (Washington). Home: LaJolla, Calif. Died Sept. 18, 1980.

HICKLIN, WAYNE, cosmetic co. exec.; b. Missouri City, Mo., Dec. 29, 1911; s. James Benton and Clara Belle (Munkres) H.; student Central Bus. Coll., Kansas City, Mo., 1931-32, Kansas City (Mo.) Bus. Coll., 1933-35; m. Hallie Bernice Hulsey, Mar. 18, 1933; 1 dau., Linda (Mrs. Edwin H. Morgens). With Avon Products, Inc., 1928-74, sr. v.p., 1960-62, exec. v.p., 1962, pres., 1962-67, chmn. bd., 1968-74, chief exec. officer, 1968-72, also dir.; dir. Irving Trust Co., Prudential Ins. Co. Am. Mem. Cosmetic, Toiletry and Fragrance Assn. (v.p., dir. 1969-71, chmn. 1971-80). Mason. Clubs: Wee Burn Country (Darien); Norwalk (Conn.) Yacht; Union League (N.Y.C.). Home: Darien, Conn. Died May 11, 1980.

HICKMAN, FRANKLIN SIMPSON, educator; b. Ft. Wayne, Ind., Sept. 14, 1886; s. John Wesley and Emma Jane (Tessier) H.; A.B., De Pauw, 1917; S.T.B., Boston U. Sch. of Theology, 1920; A.M., Northwestern, 1922, Ph.D., 1923; m. Veva Castell, 1913; 1 daughter, Anna Jeannette (dec.). In employ Pennsylvania R.R. 1903-11; licensed Methodist Episcopal ministry, 1911, ordained, 1913; pastor successively Fremont, Fillmore and Harmony, Ind., Nahant, Mass., Albion, Ind., Epworth Memorial Ch., South Bend, Ind., until 1921; instr. in New Testament, Chicago Training Sch., 1921-24; instr. in religious edn., Hamline U., 1924-25; pastor First M.E. Ch. and director Wesley Foundation, Minneapolis, Minn., 1925-27; professor of psychology of religion, Duke Univ. since 1927, preacher to the university since 1932, prof. of preaching, 1938-44, and dean of the Chapel, 1938-48. Mem. Phi Beta Kappa, Delta Sigma Rho, Omicron Delta Kappa, Phi Delta Kappa, Theta Phi. Author: Introduction to the Psychology of Religion, 1926; Education and Religion (joint author), 1929; Christian Vocation, 1930; The Possible Self, 1933; Signs of Promise, 1943. Home: Durham, N.C. *

HICKMAN, ROGER WAYNE, educator, administr.; b. Wooster, Ohio, July 5, 1900; s. John Fremont and Bertha E. (Wildman) H.; A.B., Whittier Coll., 1922; A.M., U. Calif., 1925; A.M., Harvard, 1926, Ph.D., 1932; m. Priscilla Crosby, 1932; children—Nancy Carol (Mrs. Robert A. Lufburrow), William Crosby. Served as acting professor of physics, Earlham Coll., 1928-29; instr. and tutor, dept. physics, Harvard, 1932-38, lecturer, tutor and asst. dir. physical labs., 1938-45. lecturer and asso. dir., 1945-47, lecturer and dir., Jefferson Phys. Lab. since 1947, co.-dir. Lyman Lab. of Physics, 1947-53, dir., 1953-66, asst. to provost, 1948-53, asst. to dean faculty, 1953-66. Fellow Inst. Radio Engrs., Am. Phys. Soc., Am. Acad. Arts and Scis., A.A.A.S.; mem. Sigma Xi, Gamma Alpha. Mem. Soc. of Friends. Author articles on sci. research. Home: Ojai, Calif. Died Dec. 1975.

HICKOK, JAMES PARKER, banker; b. Farmington, Mo., Sept. 28, 1902; s. Chauncery Chaucery E. and Margaret (Parker) H.; A.B., U. Mo., 1926; m. Florence Brooks, Apr. 26, 1938; two children. Nat. bank examiner, 1928-30; cashier Clayton (Mo.) Nat. Bank, 1930-33; exec. v.p. Manchester Bank, St. Louis, 1933-35, pres., 1935-43; pres. Mfrs. Bank & Trust Co., St. Louis, 1943-50; with First Nat. Bank St. Louis, 1950-71, chmn. bd., 1962-71, chmn. exec. com., 1970-71, also dir.; dir. St. Louis Union Trust Co., I.C. R.R., St. Louis Nat. Baseball Clubs, Inc. Trustee Westminster Coll.; bd. dirs. YMCA, United Fund, Municipal Theatre Assn. Clubs: Racquet, Noonday, Bogey, Mo. Athletic, Old Warson County (St. Louis). Home: St. Louis, Mo. Died Apr. 30, 1977; interred Oak Grove Mausoleum, St. Louis.

HICKS, BEATRICE ALICE, mgmt. cons.; b. Orange, N.J., Jan. 2, 1919; d. William Lux and Florence Benedict (Neben) Hicks; B.S. in Chem. Engring., N.J. Inst. Tech., 1939; M.S. in Physics, Stevens Inst. Tech., 1949; grad. study Columbia; Sc.D., Hobart and William Smith Colls., 1958; D.Eng., Rensselaer Poly. Inst., 1965, Stevens Inst. Tech., 1978, Worcester Poly. Inst., 1978; m. Rodney D. Chipp, Aug. 12, 1948 (dec. Dec. 1966). Research asst. Newark Coll. Engring., 1939-42; research, design, mfg. quartz crystal oscillators Western Electric Co., Kearny, N.J., 1942-45; chief engr. Newark Controls Co., Bloomfield, N.J., 1945-46, v.p., chief engr., 1946-55, pres., 1955-67; lectr., writer cons. U.S. del. Internat. Mgmt. Congress, Sao Paulo, Brazil, 1954, Paris, 1957, Australia, 1960, N.Y., 1963, Netherlands, 1966, Japan, 1969, Munich, 1972, Caracas, 1975. Mem. Def. Adv. Com. on Women in Services, from 1960-63; vis. com. Margaret Morrison Carnegie Coll., 1963-79; dir. 1st Internat. Conf. on Women Engrs. And Scientists, N.Y.C., 1964. Trustee Newark Coll. Engring. Alumni Assn., pres., 1958-59. Recipient Newark Coll. Engring. Alumna award, 1961. Registered profl. engr., Pa., D.C., N.J., N.Y. Fellow Internat. Acad. Law and Sci.; mem. Nat. Acad. Engring., Soc. Women Engrs. (pres. 1950-52, trustee scholarship fund also hdqrs. fund), IEEE, ASME, Nat. Soc. Profl. Engrs., Women's Engring. Soc. Gt. Britain, Eta Kappa Nu. Address: Randolph, N.J. Died Oct. 21, 1979.

HICKS, CLIFFORD MILTON, educator; b. Lincoln, Nebr., Feb. 8, 1903; s. Charles Edwin and Gertrude Ethel (Wheeler) H.; A.B., U. Nebr., 1924, J.D., 1925, M.A., 1927; m. Clarice Greene, June 12, 1928; children—Miriam Jane (Mrs. Robert Kinder), Marolyn Grace (Mrs. Lloyd Reed). Instr. Coll. Bus. Administrn., U. Nebr., Lincoln, 1925-30, asst. prof., 1930-38, asso. prof., 1938-50, prof., chmn. dept. bus. orgn. and mgmt., 1950-79. Cons. custom pension designs and investment programs, 1968-79. Mem. nat. budget com. United Community Funds and Councils. Chmn. finance com. Camp Fire Girls, 1946-56, chmn. nat. bd. dirs., 1956-60; bd. dirs. Family Welfare Assn., Lincoln; trustee Lincoln Symphony Orch. Found., 1959-79. Recipient distinguished teaching award Bd. Regents U. Nebr., 1955. Mem. Am. Interprofl. Inst. (pres. Lincoln chpt. 1949), Lincoln C. of C. (dir. 1939), Nat. Assembly for Social Policy and Devel., Am., Midwest econ. assns., Am. Finance Assn., Omaha-Lincoln Financial Analysts, Nebr. Bar Assn., Phi Beta Kappa (sec. Nebr. chpt, 1927-57), Beta Gamma Sigma, Alpha Kappa Psi, Phi Alpha Delta. Presbyn. (deacon, trustee, elder). Clubs: Lincoln Country, Lincoln University (dir. 1956-59, 65-68, treas. 1966). Author: Introduction to Business, latest rev. edit., 1960; Corporation Finance, 4th rev. edit., 1964; Business Law, 1958, 3d rev. edit., 1968. Home: Lincoln, Nebr. Died Aug. 21, 1979.

HICKS, PHILIP MARSHALL, educator; b. West Chester, Pa., Apr. 27, 1885; s. John Henry and Rachel Lapp (Price) H.; student London Grove Friends Sch., 1894-1900, Martin Acad., 1900-01, Woodbrooke, Selly Oak, Eng., 1908-09, U. Chili, summer 1941; A.B., Swarthmore Coll., 1905, M.A., 1913; Ph.D., U. Pa., 1923. Instr. pub. speaking Swarthmore (Pa.) Coll., 1913-19, asst. prof., 1919-24, asso. prof. English lit., 1924-30, professor, 1930-53 (now emeritus), chairman of department of English literature, 1946-53, director Studies for Chinese Naval Unit, 1943-44. Served as ensign, United States Naval Aviation, 1918-19. Mem.

Modern Lang. Assn., Am. Assn. U. Profs., Phi Beta Kappa, Phi Kappa Psi. Mem. Religious Soc. of Friends. Author: Extemporaneous Speaking (with Paul M. Pearson), 1913. Home: Woodview Farm, Avondale. *

HICKS, T. ROSS, clergyman; b. Butternut Ridge, N.B., Can., Oct. 25, 1883; s. James Melbourne and Adelaide Selina (Seely) H.; grad. Worcester (Mass.) Acad., 1905; A.B., Boston U., 1909; S.T.B., Boston U. Sch. of Theology, 1911; Th.M., Xenia Theol. Sem., St. Louis, Mo., 1927; student U. of N.D., 1937-39; D.D., Central Wesleyan Coll., 1934; m. Mabel Louise Kinnecome, June 23, 1909; children—Harold Edwin, Irving Ross, Philip Stanley. Ordained ministry of Meth. Church, April, 1910; pastor, Arlington Street Meth. Ch., Nashua, N.H., 1909-11; First Meth. Ch., Claremont, N.H., 1911-15; Lincoln, N.H., 1915; dist. supt. Dover Dist., N.H. Conf. Meth. Ch., 1915-20; dist. supt, Southern Dist, 1920-23; dir. Adult Work, Bd. of Edn., Meth. Ch., 1923-26; pastor, First Meth. Ch., Webster Groves, Mo., 1926-33; First Meth. Ch., Sedalia, Mo., 1933-36; First Meth. Ch., Grand Forks, N.D., 1936-40; pres. Wesley Coll., Grand Forks, N.D., 1940-46, pastor 1st Meth. Ch., Northampton, Mass., 1946-50, ret. Mem. New England Conf., Theta Delta Chi. Methodist. Mason. Club: Kiwanis. Home: Florence, Mass. *

HIDY, RALPH WILLARD, historian, educator; b. Portland, Ind., Apr. 21, 1905; s. Urban Wilson and Helen Varella (Willard) H.; A.B., Miami U., 1926; M.A., Clark U., 1928; Ph.D., Harvard, 1935; m. Muriel Emmie Wagenhauser, June 12, 1928; 1 dau., Ann Helen. Tchr. history, high sch., Portsmouth, Ohio, 1926-27; instr. Norwich U., 1928-30, Wheaton Coll., 1932-36, asst. prof., 1936-41, asso. prof., 1941-46, prof., 1946-47; prof. history Grad. Sch. Arts and Sci., N.Y. U., 1950-57; Isidor Straus prof. bus. history Grad. Sch. Bus. Adminstrn., Harvard, 1957-71. Served as comdr. USNR, 1941-46. Mem. Econ. History Assn. (sec. 1950-62, pres. 1970-71), Am. Hist. Assn., Orgn. Am. Historians, Econ. History Soc. (Eng.), Phi Beta Kappa. Author: The House of Baring in American Trade and Finance, 1949; (with Muriel E. Hidy) Pioneering in Big Business, 1882-1911, 1955; (with Edward C. Bursk, Donald T. Clark) The World of Business, 1962; (with F.E. Hill and Allan Nevins) Timber and Men, The Weyerhaeuser Story, 1963; also articles in profl. jours. Editor: Harvard Studies in Bus. History, 1962-71; editor-in-chief Bus. History Review, 1962-65. Home: Belmont, Mass. Died Dec. 5, 1977.

HIEBERT, JOHN MARK, drug co. exec.; b. Hillsboro, Kans., Feb. 21, 1904; s. J. K. and Sarah (Eitzen) H.; B.A., Tabor Coll., Hillsboro, Kans.; postgrad. U. Kans.; M.D., Boston U., 1932; Pharm.D. (hon.); m. Dorothy Prior, Sept. 22, 1933; 1 son, John Mark. Asst. in pharmacology Sch. Medicine, Boston U., 1929-31; med. house officer Mass. Meml. Hosp., 1931-33, Mass. Gen. Hosp., 1933-34; pres. Sterling Drug, Inc., 1955-63, chmn. bd., 1960-74, chief exec. officer, 1963-74, dir., 1949-76, adv. dir., 1976-78; adv. dir. Irving Trust Co. Trustee Tabor Coll. Recipient Gold medal N.Y. Bd. Trade, 1961. Mem. A.M.A., Internat. C. of C. (trustee U.S. council), A.M.A., N.Y. State, New York County med. socs., N.Y. Acad. Scis., N.Y. C. of C. and Industry Inc. (past pres., dir.), Newcomen Soc. N. Am., Phi Chi. Baptist. Mason. Clubs: Kansas, Union League (N.Y.C.); Delray Dunes Golf and Country, Ocean of Fla.; Garden of Gods (Colorado Springs, Colo.). Home: Ocean Ridge, Fla. Died Sept. 16, 1978; interred West Palm Beach, Fla.

HIGGINS, AILEEN CLEVELAND (MRS. JOHN ARCHIBALD SINCLAIR), author; b. Perry, Ill., Dec. 7, 1882; d. James Redding and Mary Louise (Cleveland) H.; A.B., Stanford, 1920; m. John Archibald Sinclair, of Duluth, Minn., June 14, 1911; 1 son, Kent. Episcopalian. Mem Gamma Phi Beta. Club: Lyceum (London, Eng.). Author: Dream Blocks, 1908; The Little Princess Series, 5 vols.; Psychology of Nursing, 1921. Contbr. to mags. Garden Architect. Home: San Mateo, Calif. *

HIGGINS, EDGAR TURLEY, finance co. exec.; b. Richmond, Ky., Apr. 3, 1906; s. Charles Faris and Elizabeth (Turley) H.; A.B., U. Ky., 1927; LL.B., Harvard, 1930; m. Allene Ruthven McKay, Oct. 7, 1933; children—Edgar Turley, Harriet Caldwell. Reporter, Richmond Daily Register, 1920-25, Lexington (Ky.) Daily Herald, 1925-27; admitted to N.Y. bar, 1933, N.J. bar, 1943, atty. Nat. Electric Power Co., N.Y.C., 1930-31, Nat. Dairy Products Corp., N.Y.C., 1931-33; atty. Beneficial Mgmt. Corp., Morristown, N.J., 1933-76, gen. counsel, 1965-76, chmn. bd., 1965-71; vice chmn. bd. Beneficial Corp., Wilmington, Del., 1969-71, chmn. bd., chief exec. officer, 1971-76, also mem. exec. com.; dir. Spiegel, Inc., Chgo. Mem. Summit (N.J.) Common Council, 1956-58, Nat. Bus. Council for Consumer Affairs, 1971-73; trustee Nat. Found. Consumer Credit. Chmn. bd. trustees Hodson Trust; chmn. N.J. Coll. Fund Assn., 1974-76. Recipient Outstanding Chief Exec. Officer award Fin. World mag., 1975. Mem. Am. Bar Assn., Sigma Alpha Epsilon. Republican. Methodist. Clubs: Baltusrol Golf (Springfield, N.J.); Canoe Brook Country (Summit). Home: Summit, N.J. Died Aug 10, 1976.

HIGGINS, HOWARD DAVID, bishop; b. N.Y.C., Aug. 23, 1903; s. Peter David and Emma (Howard) H.: A.B., Columbia, 1927, A.M., 1938; B.D., Ref. Episcopal Theol. Sem. Phila., 1924, D.D., 1939; Th.M., Princeton Theol. Sem., 1928; m. Ethel Louise Scott, Sept. 23, 1944. Ordained presbyter of Ref. Episcopal Ch., 1925; rector First Ref. Episcopal Ch., New York, 1928-54; became asst. bishop, N.Y. and Phila. Synod, 1937, bishop co-adjutor, Oct. 1939; bishop Synod, 1942-72; lectr. theology, Ref. Episcopal Theol. Sem., 1930-37, lectr. practical theology, 1933-37, prof. church hist. and apologetics, 1937-72; presiding bishop Reformed Episcopal Church, 1957-75. Trustee Ref. Episcopal Theol. Sem.; Bd. Fgn. Missions (v.p.), N.Y. and Phila. Synod (pres.), Bd. Home Missions, Lord's Day Alliance U.S. (dir.), Gen. Council R.E. Ch. (gen. com.). Editor: "Episcopal Recorder". Home: Pipersville, Pa. Died Apr. 6, 1980; buried West Laurel Hill Cemetery, Bala-Cynwyd, Pa.

HIGGINS, RUTH LOVING, educator; b. Columbus, Ohio, June 21, 1895; d. Charles and Jessie Hoover (Schatzman) Higgins; B.A., B.S. in Edn., Ohio State U., 1917, M.A. (scholarship), 1921, Ph.D. (2 fellowships), 1926; postgrad. U. Wis., summer 1922, Cambridge (Eng.) U., summer 1929; LL.D. (hon.), Beaver Coll., 1953. Tchr. history, civics Ohio high schs., 1917-20, 22-23, instr. history, polit. sci. Elmira (N.Y.) Coll., 1924-25; asst. prof. Earlham Coll., Richmond, Ind., 1925-26; prof., head dept. Huntingdon Coll. (formerly Woman's Coll. of Ala.), Montgomery, 1926-34; mem. history faculty U. Ala., summers 1930-31; dean coll., prof. history Beaver Coll., Glenside, Pa., 1934-60, chmn. dept. history and govt., 1949-60, emeritus, 1960-79. Trustee Cheltenham (Pa.) Adult Sch., 1940-48, pres., 1943-45. Mem. Am. Conf. Acad. Deans (hon. life; sec., treas. 1945-47, editor 1946-48), Japan Internat. Christian U. Found. (mem. women's com.), Am. Acad. Polit. and Social Sci., Am. Hist. Assn., Orgn. Am. Historians (exec. com. 1936-39), Nat. (editorial com. 1935-37), Pa. (chmn. publs. 1938-41) assns. women deans, administrs. and counselors, Assn. Higher Edn., Ohio State U. Alumni Assn., A.A.U.W., Ohioana Library Assn., Ohio Hist. Soc., D.A.R., Delta Kappa Gamma (state founder Ala. and Pa.). Presbyn. Author: Expansion in New York with Especial Reference to Eighteenth Century, 1931; American Conference of Academic Deans-Developments and Abstracts, 1945-69, 1969; also articles, hist. revs. Home: Columbus, Ohio. Died Dec. 27, 1979.

HIGHET, GILBERT, educator; b. Glasgow, Scotland, June 22, 1906; s. Gilbert and Elizabeth Gertrude (Boyle) H.; ed. Hillhead High Sch., Glasgow, 1912-24; M.A., Glasgow U., 1929, D. Litt., M.A. (Craven scholar and Chancellor's prizeman), Oxford U., 1936, D. Litt., 1956; L.H.D., Case Inst. Tech., 1952, U. Mass., 1973; D.Litt., Syracuse U., 1960, Columbia U., 1977; L.H.D., Adelphi U., 1964; m. Helen Clark McInnes, Sept. 22, 1932; 1 son, Gilbert Keith MacInnes. Came to U.S., 1937, naturalized, 1951. Fellow and tutor in classics St. John's Coll., Oxford, Eng., 1932-38; vis. asso. in classics Columbia, 1937-38, prof. Greek and Latin, 1938-50, Anthon prof. Latin lang. and lit., 1950-72, emeritus, 1972. Guggenheim fellow, 1951. Served Brit. mission, U.S. and Can., 1941-43; Brit. Army, 1943-46; lt. col. mil. govt. Germany, 1945-46. Recipient Wallace award Am.-Scottish Found., 1973. Fellow Royal Soc. Lit.; hon. mem. Phi Beta Kappa. Clubs: Maidstone (East Hampton); Century (N.Y.C.). Author: The Classical Tradition, 1949; The Art of Teaching, 1950; People, Places and Books, 1953; Man's Unconquerable Mind, 1954; The Migration of Ideas, 1954; A Clerk of Oxenford, 1954; Juvenal the Satirist, 1954; Poets in a Landscape, 1957; Talents and Geniuses, 1957; The Powers of Poetry, 1960; The Anatomy of Satire, 1962 (award of merit Am. Philol. Assn. 1963); Explorations, 1971; The Speeches in Vergil's Aeneid, 1972; The Immortal Profession, 1976. Translated Werner Jaeger's Paideia, 1939-44; poems in The Oxford Book of Greek Verse. Mem. bd. judges Book of the Month Club. Home: East Hampton, N.Y. Died Jan. 20, 1978.

HIGHSMITH, EDWIN MCKOY, educator; b. Sampson County, N.C., Jan. 27, 1886; s. Noah Franklin and Ann Julia (Lewis) H.; prep. edn., Buiés Creek Acad., N.C., 1901-03; Ph.B., U. of N.C., 1907, A.M., 1914, Ph.D., 1923; studied summers, Teachers Coll. (Columbia), 1910, 13; A.M., Peabody Coll., 1915, fellow, 1914-15, summer 1936; m. Winifred Brandon, Aug. 1916 (died July 1917); 1 dau., Winifred; m. 2d, Annette Paris, Dec. 25, 1920; children—Anne, Nancy, Edwin McKoy. Prin. high schs.; N.C. and Fla. 7 yrs. until 1914; later prof. edn. and summer school dir., Furman U., 1930-36; research and writing, Peabody Coll., 1936-37; prof. edn. and chmn. Div. of Edn., Mercer U., 1937-56, now emeritus; tchr., summers, Peabody Coll., Ill. State Normal, U. of Okla., U. of N.C., Duke Univ., Ind. Univ. Served as army Y.M.C.A. dir. Kelly Field No. 2, San Antonio, Tex., also with Ednl. Corps, A.E.F. overseas. Mem. Am. advisory bd. Yenching Univ., Peiping, China. Clerk, Macon Baptist Association (Georgia). Mem. N.E.A., Phi Delta Kappa, Tau Kappa Alpha, Pi Gamma Mu, Alpha Chi Omega. Democrat. Baptist. Mason (32 deg.). Clubs: Lions, Kiwanis, Rotary. Author: The Outlook for Christian Education; Educational Objectives of a Liberal College. Home: Macon, Ga. *

HIGINBOTHAM, NOE, educator; b. Sullivan County, Ind., Sept. 6, 1913; s. Charles Francis and Cora (Tarrh) H.; A.B., Butler U., 1935; student Johns Hopkins, 1935-37; Ph.D., Columbia, 1940; m. Betty Louise Wilson, Apr. 3, 1937. Instr. algae Chesapeake Biol. Lab., 1941; Theresa Seessel research fellow Yale, 1941-42; plant physiologist Tex. Agrl. Expt. Sta., Beaumont, 1942-45; asst. prof. U. Notre Dame, 1945-47; sr. scientist Argonne Nat. Lab., 1947-48; asso. prof. Wash. State U., 1948-53; chmn. botany dept., 1949-55, prof., 1953-80; guest prof. Botanische Inst. Technische Hochschule Darmstadt, West Germany, 1975; U.S. Sr. Scientist Humboldt award, Darmstadt, W. Ger., 1977-78. Fulbright research scholar, Australia, 1963. Fellow A.A.A.S.; mem. Biophys. Soc., Bot. Soc. Am., Am. Soc. Plant Physiologists (chmn. Western sect. 1957-58), Am. Bryological Soc., Am. Assn. U. Profs., N.W. Sci. Assn. (councillor 1952-55), Sigma Xi. Mem. editorial bd. Plant Physiology, 1967-70, 72-74, editor, 1974-80. Home: Pullman, Wash. Died Feb. 6, 1980.

HIGLEY, HARVEY DOUGLAS, army officer; b. Cedar Rapids, Ia., July 16, 1882; s. Elmer A. and Helen (Olds) H.; B.S., U.S. Mil. Acad., 1908; attended Gen. Service Sch., 1924-25, Army War Coll., 1929-30; m. Margaret Hoyle, Sept. 7, 1910; children—Harvey Douglas, Madeleine deBessiere. Began as clerk in head office of Burlington, Cedar Rapids & Northern Ry., 1901; commd. 2d lt., 6th F.A., U.S. Army, 1908, 1st lt., 1911; capt., 2d F.A., 1916, maj., 1920; lt. col., 17th, F.A., 1931; col., 76th F.A., 1936; brig. gen., U.S. Army, since 1940; became chief of staff, 3d Army, San Antonio, Tex., 1940; retired for physical disability, Apr. 30, 1941. Address: Carmel, Calif.*

HILDEBRAND, JOEL HENRY, ret. chemist; b. Camden, N.J., Nov. 16, 1881; s. Howard Ovid and Sarah Regina (Swartz) H.; B.S., U. Pa., 1903, Ph.D., 1906, D.Sc. (hon.), 1939; student U. Berlin, 1906-07; LL.D., U. Cal., 1954; Sc.D., Eastern Mich. U., 1972; m. Emily J. Alexander, Dec. 17, 1908; children—Louise, Alexander, Milton, Roger Henry. Instr. chemistry U. Pa., 1907; asst. prof. chemistry, 1913, asso. prof., 1917, prof., 1918-52, prof. emeritus, 1952, dean of men, 1923-26, faculty research lectr., 1936, dean Coll. Letters and Sci., 1939-43, chmn. dept. chemistry U. Cal., 1941-43, dean Coll. Chemistry, 1949-51. Cons. chemist U.S. Bur. Mines, 1924-26; liaison for OSRD, Am. embassy, London, 1943-44. Mem. citizen's adv. commn. to Joint Com. on Edn. of Cal. Legislature, 1958-60; mem. adv. com. to Cal. Bd. Edn., 1966. Commd. capt. O.R.C., 1917; maj. Chem. Warfare Service, 1918; lt. col., 1919; dir. C.W.S. lab. nr. Paris, later comdt. Hanlon Field, nr. Chaumont, which included exptl. field and A.E.F. Gas Def. Sch. Mem. chem. referee bd. War Prodn. Bd., 1942-43; expert cons. mil. planning div. Q.M.C., 1942-45. Decorated D.S.M. (World War I); King's Medal (Brit.), 1948; Citation by Army and Navy for OSRD service, World War II; Nichols medal, 1939; Guthrie lectr. Phys. Soc., London, 1944; Walker Meml. lectr., 1944, Romanes lectr., 1953 (both U. Edinburgh); Remsen Meml. lecture and award, 1949; Am. Chem. Soc. award in chemistry edn., 1952, Priestley medal, 1962, James Norris Flack award New Eng. sect., 1961, S.C. Lind Lectr. Eastern Tenn. sect., 1974; Spiers Meml. lectr. Faraday Soc., 1953; Bampton lectr. Columbia U., 1956; Willard Gibbs medal Chgo. sect. Am. Chem. Soc., 1953; William Proctor prize Sci. Research Soc. Am., 1962. Fellow A.A.A.S. (v.p. Pacific div. 1924-27, pres. 1933-34; mem. exec. com. 1929-35), Am. Phys. Soc.; hon. fellow Royal Soc. Edinburgh, Cal. Acad. Sci.; mem. Am. Philos. Soc., Am. Chem. Soc. (pres. 1955), Nat. Acad. Scis., Faraday Soc. (hon. life), Am. Inst. Chemists (hon.), Phi Beta Kappa, Sigma Xi. Clubs: Faculty, Sierra (pres. 1937-40). Author: Principles of Chemistry, 1918, 7th edit., 1964; (with R.L. Scott) Solubility of Non-electrolytes, 1924, 36, 1951; Reference Book of Inorganic Chemistry (with W. M. Latimer), 1929, 40; Camp Catering (with Louise Hildebrand), 1938, 41; Science in the Making, 1956; An Introduction to Molecular Kinetic Theory, 1963; Is Intelligence Important?, 1963; Regular and Related Solutions (with J.M. Prausnitz and R.L. Scott), 1970; also numerous papers on chemistry, edn., skiing. Mgr. U.S. Olympic Ski Team, 1936; Joel Henry Hildebrand Hall dedicated by U. Cal., 1966. Home: Berkeley CA. Only the teacher who himself takes pleasure in pursuing knowledge can be expected to assist a student to find pleasure in that pursuit. If a researcher is a poor teacher it is not the fault of his research but of snobbery or natural dullness, and dullness is hereditary, not voluntary. In research, there is a great advantage in working mainly for fun instead of a prize; you can have the satisfaction of discovery almost any day, whereas prizes come rarely, if at all. One who spends his life in envying his superiors will always be unhappy, because there will always be superiors to envy. He will be wiser and happier if he just competes with himself. *

HILDEBRAND, KENNETH NORMAN, clergyman; b. Los Angeles, Oct. 29, 1906; s. John Augustine 3d and Grace Wadleigh (Clemons) H.; B.A., Coll. of Emporia, 1930, D.D., 1945; diploma, McCormick Theol. Sem., 1933, M.A., 1938; postgrad. Northwestern U., 1948-50; m. Nell Benson, Aug. 10, 1926; children—Grace (Mrs. Bernard E. Welch), Ruth (Mrs. Vernon L. Welge, Jr.). Ordained to ministry Presbyn. Ch. U.S.A., 1933; pastor

Brighton Park Ch., Chgo., 1933-36, Chgo. Lawn Ch., 1936-42; asso. pastor 4th Ch., Chgo., 1942-48; pastor Central Ch. of Chgo. (nondenominational), 1948-73, pastor emeritus, 1973-79. Radio and TV personality appearing on various Chgo. programs, WGN-TV; cruise chaplain Gripsholm, S.S. Independence, S.S. Constitution. Bd. dirs. Nat. Safety Council, Wabash YMCA Hotel; past bd. dirs. McCormick Theol. Sem.; mem. citizens adv. com. U. Ill. invocator Nat. Democratic Conv., 1968. Named 1 of 100 Outstanding Chgo. Citizens, 1971. Mem. Broadcast Pioneers, Nat. Acad. Religion and Mental Health, Newcomen Soc. N.Am. (Chgo. Com.), Chgo. Bible Soc. (dir.). Clubs: Saddle and Cycle (Chgo.); Ill. Athletic. Author: Achieving Real Happiness, 1955; contbr. Success Unlimited Mag. Home: Chicago, Ill. Died Mar. 14, 1979.

HILDING, ANDERSON CORNELIUS, physician; b. Tacoma, June 29, 1892; s. Gustav Adolph and Anna Lavinia (Tilderquist) Anderson; student U. Wash., 1910-13; B.S., U. Minn., 1915, M.B., 1918, M.D., 1919, M.A., 1922, Ph.D., 1929; postgrad U. Vienna, 1925-26, Mayo Clinic, 1930-32, Eye Clinic of Sir Henry Holland, India, 1934; Sc.D. (hon.), Gustavus Adolphus Coll., 1957; m. Inez Marie Melander, Jan. 1, 1929; children—David, Cecile, Wendell, Stephen, Jean. Intern, Mpls. Gen. Hosp., 1917-19, practice medicine, specializing in ophthalmology and otorhinolaryngology, Duluth, 1921-54; cons. and surg. practice in fields of ophthalmology and otology, 1954-64; research St. Luke's Hosp., Duluth, 1954-77; clin. prof. otolaryngology U. Minn., 1944-60, emeritus, 1960-77; vis. prof. research otolaryngology Columbia Coll. Physicians and Surgeons, N.Y.C., 1951-52; Recipient Research award Minn. Soc. Internal Medicine, 1929; cert. of merit for devoted service Regents and Pres., U. Minn., 1960; Harold S. Diehl award for disting. service Alumni Assn. U. Minn. Med. Sch., 1968; diplomate Am. Bd. Otolaryngology, Am. Bd. Ophthalmology. Fellow A.C.S.; mem. AMA, Am. Acad. Ophthalmology and Otolaryngology (certs. of merit 1940, 42, Honor Key 1951, Wherry Meml. lectr. 1960, citation of honor 1960), Am. Broncho-Esophagol. Assn. (Chevalier Jackson award 1970), Minn. (cert. of appreciation 1944), St. Louis County med. socs., Minn. Acad. Ophthalmology and Otolaryngol., Am. Triological Soc. (emeritus), Collegium Oto-Rhino-Larynologicum (Shambaugh prize 1963, mem. jury 1968-71), Am. Otol. Soc. (award of merit 1965), Royal Physiograph. Soc. Lund, Alumni Assn. Mayo Found. for Med. Edn. and Research, A.A.A.S., N.Y. Acad. Sci., Am. Laryngol. Assn. (Casselberry award 1934, pres. 1963-64, chmn. DeRoaldes award, Casselberry award coms. 1969-70, chmn. research com. 1970-73, hon. mem. 1975, de Roaldes award 1976), Assn. Research in Otolaryngology, Sigma Xi. Lutheran. Contbr. articles in field. Research in kidney disease, hypertension, retinitis, cataract surgery, exptl. nasal and sinus surgery, anatomy of bronchial tree, common cold; studies in anatomy and physiology of internal ear, theory of hearing, anatomy and physiology of eye, epithelial transplants in the eye; physiology and anatomy of respiratory tract. Home: Duluth, Minn. Died Dec. 5, 1977; buried Forest Hill Cemetery, Duluth.

HILL, DANIEL GRAFTON, JR., univ. dean; b. Annapolis, Md., May 26, 1896; s. Daniel Grayton and Margaret Phoebe (Peck) H.; B.A., Lincoln U., 1917; B.D., Iliff Sch. Theology, 1928, Th.D., 1946; M.A., U. Oreg., 1932; S.T.M., Pacific Sch. Theology, 1935; m. May Louise Edwards, Apr. 20, 1918; children—Jeanne Marie, Daniel Grayton III, Margaret Theresa, Doris May. Ordained to ministry Methodist Ch., 1921; pastor in Mo., Colo., Oreg., Calif., 1922-45; mem. faculty Howard U., 1945-79, prof. practical theology, 1957-79, dean chapel, 1946-57, dean School of Religion, 1957-64, dean emeritus, 1964-79. Supr. Calif. Pub. Relief Adminstrn., Oakland, 1937-39; mem. Mayor Oakland and Berkeley Def. and Recreation Com., 1939-41; chmn. race relations council Denver Council Chs., 1941-42; chmn. Denver Fair Employment Practices Com., 1942-43; chmn. Inst. Religion, Washington, 1957-79. Bd. dirs. Howard U., United Givers Fund, 1958-59. Served to 2d lt., inf., U.S. Army, World War I. Mem. Am. Acad. Polit. and Social Sci., Nat. Assn. Coll. and Univ. Chaplains (treas.), Fellowship of Reconciliation, NAACP, Urban League, Am. Soc. African Culture, Nat. Council Prevention War (exec. bd.), Internat. Platform Assn., Alpha Phi Alpha. Editor: Well-Springs of Life, 1956. Contbr.: Best Sermons, 1947-48; also encys. Home. Washington, D.C. Died Oct. 21, 1979.

HILL, DUDLEY TOLL, newspaper editor; b. Albany, N.Y., Dec. 11, 1883; s. Erastus Dudley and Mary Grace (Toll) H.; B.S., Union Coll., 1907; LL.B., Albany (N.Y.) Law Sch., 1909; m. Anne W. Scheurer, Dec. 11, 1912; children—Anita Elizabeth, Philip Toll II, Albert Karel. Began as reporter, Schenectady Gazette, 1910, mng. editor, 1911-49. Auditor Schenectady County, 1922-23; mem. Bd. Supervisors, Schenectady County, 1924-25; apptd. mem. State Census Commn., 1929. Vice-chmn. Schenectady Co. War Council. Pres. Schenectady Co. Bar Assn (1943); mem. N.Y. State Bar Assn. Mem. Alpha Delta Phi, Phi Delta Phi. Democrat. Presbyn. Mason (K.T., Shriner), Odd Fellow. Rotarian (pres. 1945). Author: Toll Family Genealogy, 1941. Home: Schnectady Country, N.Y. *

HILL, EVERETT WENTWORTH, writer; b. Russell, Kan., Jan. 10, 1884; s. John Harris and Frances Emily (Wentworth) H.; student Cascadilla Prep. Sch., Ithaca, N.Y., 1903; B.S. in Econs., Wharton Sch. Finance and Commerce, U. Pa., 1907; m. Ethel Laing, June 3, 1908 (dec.); 1 dau., Ethel Frances; m. 2d, Cleo Shaffer Riley. With Standard Oil Co., 1907-08; settled at Shawnee, Okla., in ice mfg. and cold storage 1908; settled at Oklahoma City, 1922; moved to Indian Bluff Farm, located on James River in Ozarks, nr. Springfield, Mo., 1941; moved to Lakeshore Gardens, nr. Polson, Mont., 1945; moved to Springfield, Mo., 1963, Oklahoma City, 1969; owner extensive farm lands. Mem. internat. bd. dirs. Waterton-Glacier Internat. Peace Park. Mem. Nat. Boys and Girls Week com. Mem. Kansas Ind. Oil and Gas Assn., Am. Acad. Polit. and Social Sci., Nat. Econ. League, Phi Kappa Sigma, Rotary Internat. (1st v.p. 1923-24; pres. 1924-25). Democrat. Episcopalian. Mason (32 deg., Shriner). Clubs: Rotary, Oklahoma City; Polson (hon. mem.). Author: Toward the Sun; Light Across the Valley; He Who Seeks Gold; also writer of verse, essays, philosophy, articles and short stories. Mem. Sunshine Magazine Adv. Staff. Speaker before Rotary clubs in N. Am., other countries. Address: Oklahoma City OK. *

HILL, JAMES LEVAN, educator; b. Altoona, Pa., May 29, 1907; s. James H. and Lillie (Mullin) H.; B.S., State Tchrs. Coll., California, Pa., 1943; M.Ed., Pa. State U., 1945, D.Ed., 1953; m. Marion V. Truax, Jan. 23, 1942. Apprentice, journeyman, machinist Pa. R.R., McLanahan & Stone Machine Co., Hollidaysburg, Pa., also Westinghouse Mfg. Co. Lester, Pa., 1923-39; faculty State Tchrs. Coll., California, Pa., 1941-43; tchr. pub. schs., Progress, Pa., also Altoona, Pa., 1943-48; vis. instr. Pa. State U., summers 1947-52; prof., chmn. dept. indsl. arts and engring. drawing Bowling Green State U., 1954-66, prof. indsl. edn., 1966-75, prof. emeritus, 1975-76; Exhibited works at Exhbn. Craftsmen Central States Mus. Contemporary Crafts, N.Y.C., Herron Mus. Art, Indpls.; one man show of silver at Toledo Mus. Art, also Massillon Mus., 1965. Recipient art ambassadors popularity award Toledo Area Artists Exhbn. at Toledo Mus. Art, 1957, 1st award, 1963, 64, 65; purchase award, 1964; best in show prize Ohio Artists' and Craftsmen's Show, Massilon Mus., 1966. Mem. Nat. Assn. Indsl. Tchr. Educators, Ohio Indsl. Arts Assn., Am. Vocational Assn., Epsilon Pi Tau, Iota Lambda Sigma, Phi Delta Kappa. Methodist. Mason (Shriner). Home: Bowling Green, Ohio. Died Oct. 21, 1976.

HILL, JAMES TOMILSON, JR., lawyer, bus. exec.; b. Salt Lake City, Mar. 2, 1916; s. James T. and Clara Frances (Quirk) H.; A.B. with great distinction, Stanford, 1937; LL.B., cum laude, Harvard, 1940; m. Dorothy Helen Kutcher, July 6, 1941; children—Susan, James Tomilson III. Admitted to Wyo. bar, 1940, N.Y. bar, 1941, U.S. Supreme Ct., 1945; law clk., pvt. practice law, N.Y.C., 1940-42, 47-50; spl. asst. to Under Sec. of Navy, 1942-43; counsel Bur. Aeros., Navy Dept., also asst. gen. counsel, gen. counsel Navy Dept., 1946-47; gen. counsel, later asst. sec. Dept. Air Force, 1950-53; gen. partner Wm. A.M. Burden & Co., pvt. capital investments, N.Y.C., 1954-65; exec. v.p. Inmont Corp., 1965, pres., 1966-69, chief exec. officer, 1969, dir., mem. exec. com., 1961-69; pres., dir. Contractors Mut. Assn., 1971-73; dir. Alcan Aluminium, Ltd., ITEK Corp., Turner Constrn. Co., Vanguard Group Investment Cos. Trustee Wellesley Coll., Com. Econ. Devel., Riverside Research Inst.; former trustee, mem. exec. comm. Nightingale-Bamford Sch. Served from ensign to lt. comdr. USNR, 1943-46. Mem. Am. Bar Assn., Am. Arbitration Assn., Council Fgn. Relations, Stanford Assos., Pilgrims of U.S., Phi Beta Kappa, Phi Beta Kappa Assos. Clubs: Century Assn., Harvard, Knickerbocker (N.Y.C.); Metropolitan (Washington); Wianno (Mass.) (gov.; mem. exec. com.); Meadow Brook (Jericho, N.Y.); Country of Fla., Ocean of Fla. (Delray Beach). Home: New York, N.Y. Died Mar. 21, 1978.

HILL, MERTON EARLE, educator; b. Garden Grove, Calif., Feb. 18, 1882; s. John Wright and Mariette (Bradley) H.; grad. Los Angeles State Normal Sch., 1902; B.S., Pomona Coll., 1908, A.M., 1912; Ed.D., U. of Calif., 1928; m. Carrie Reed, Aug. 11, 1903; children—Dr. Lowell Reed, Mrs. Mary Louise Hill Bean, Mrs. Dorothy Caroline Hill Bean, Dr. Walter Bradley, Dr. Merton Earle, Jr., Margaret (Riutcil), Edith (Orr). Began as principal of Lugo School, Los Angeles County, 1902-03, Garden Grove (California) School, 1903-06; prin. schools, Upland, Calif., 1908-11; prin. Chaffey Union High Sch. and Jr. Coll. Ontario, Calif., 1911-31; prof. of edn., U. of Calif. at Berkeley, Los Angeles, 1931-49, ret., also dir. admissions, 1931-46; also supt. schs., Beverly Hills, 1939-43; on leave as expert ednl. consultant to dir. army specialized training, 9th Service Command, hdqrs. Ft. Douglass, Salt Lake City from Apr. 1, 1943 to Apr. 10, 1944; curriculum consultant Upland Coll., 1949, Calif. Coll. Arts and Crafts since 1950; historian and jr. coll. consultant Orange County Supt. of Schs. Dept., 1950. President California Fed. Jr. Colls., 1931; mem. Calif. Curriculum Commn., 1928-31. Mem. Calif. High Sch. Teachers Assn. (pres. 1916), Calif. High Sch. Prins. Assn. (mem. affiliation com. 1919-45, Calif. Teachers' Assn. (pres. southern sect. 1922), Western Assn. of Secondary Schs. and Colleges (v.p. 1933-36; pres. 1937-39), Phi Beta Kappa. Mem. Junior Coll. Conf. Com., 1934-40. Republican. Methodist. Past pres. Upland Rotary Club. Author: Patriotic Writings for American Students, 1924; American Patriotism, 1926; The Development of an Americanization Program, 1928; A Study of the Junior College Movement, 1933; The Functioning of the California Junior Colleges, 1939. Editor Reports of Western Assn. of Secondary Schools and Colleges, 1934, 37, 38. Contbr. articles: A Study in Admissions, 1933; A Procedure to Determine the Comparative Merits of Different Methods of Admission to the University, 1935; Counseling Students for Admission to the University, 1937; Education for Work vs. Education for Leisure, 1942; The Present and Future of the Junior College, 1943; The Army Specialized Training Program, 1944; Building a Community High School and Junior College, 1946; History of the Junior College Movement, 1949; One Hundred Years of Public Education in Orange County, 1951. Home: Laguna Beach, Calif. *

HILL, NORMAN LLEWELLYN, educator, author; b. Afton, N.Y., Dec. 17, 1895; s. Henry Thomas and Virginia (Taylor) H.; A.B., Oberlin Coll., 1917, A.M., 1920; student, Sorbonne, Paris, 1919; Ph.D., U. of Wis., 1924; m. Mary Thompson Sherwood, Aug. 30, 1922; children—Elizabeth Sherwood, Virginia Louise. Instr. polit. science, O. Wesleyan U., 1920-21; instr. polit. sci., Denison U., 1921-22; instr. polit. science, Western Res. U., 1924-26; asst. prof. internat. relations, U. of Neb., 1926-27, asso. prof., 1927-35, prof., from 1935; mem. faculty, summer sch. University of Rochester, 1935; visiting professor U. Wash., 1954; Fulbright Exchange prof. internat. relations U. Wales, 1958-59; vis. prof. internat. politics U. Tenn., 1963-64, 66. Served as sergt., Q.M.C., U.S. Army, 1918-19. Fellow in Internat. Law, Carnegie Endowment, 1921-22. Mem. Am. Political Science Association (member council, 1955-58), American Society of International Law (exec. council, 1946-49). Am. Teachers of Internat. Law (exec. com., 1937-40), Am. Assn. of Univ. Profs. Presbyterian. Author: text books; Claims to Territory in International Law and Relations, 1945; Readings and Documents International Relations 1950; International Organization, 1952; Contemporary World Politics, 1954; If the Churches Want World Peace, 1958; International Politics, 1963; Mr. Secretary of State, 1963; The New Democracy in Foreign Policy Making, 1970. Home: Berea, Ky. Died Nov. 27, 1976.

HILL, ROBERT C., bus. dir., diplomat; b. Littleton, N.H., Sept. 30, 1917; s. Allen and Catherine Lyle (Morse) H.; grad. Taft Sch., Watertown, Conn., 1938, Dartmouth, 1942; LL.D., New Eng. Coll., Henniker, N.H., 1957, St. Mary's U., 1960, Dartmouth, 1960; L.H.D., U. Dallas, 1960; hon. degree Mexican Acad. Internat. Law; m. Cecelia Gordon Bowdoin, Dec. 1, 1945; children—W. Graham Bowdoin, James Bowdoin. Vice consul Fgn. Service Am., 1944-46; clk. Senate Com. on Banking and Currency, 1947; asst. v.p. W.R. Grace & Co., N.Y.C., 1949-53; ambassador to Costa Rica, 1953-54, to El Salvador, 1954-55; spl. asst. to under sec. of state for Mut. Security Affairs, 1955-56; asst. sec. of state for congl. relations, 1956-57; ambassador to Mexico, 1957-61; mem. N.H. Ho. of Reps., 1961-62; ambassador to Spain, 1969-72; asst. sec. for internat. security affairs Dept. Def., 1973-74; ambassador to Argentina, 1974-77; dir. E.T. Barwick Co., Atlanta, Todd Shipyards Corp., N.Y.C. Spl. Ambassador to inauguration, El Salvador, 1956, Costa Rica, 1958-61, Mexico, 1958, Mexico's 150th Anniversary Independence Ceremonies, 1960. Chmn., Republican Nat. Com. Fgn. Policy Task Force, 1965-68; mem. Rep. Coordinating Com. Task Force on Nat. Security, 1967-68. Decorated Defensores de la Republica Mexicana y Sus Descendientes, Aztec Eagle, La Orden Mexicana del Derecho y La Cultura (Mexico); Grand Cross of Merit (Peru); Gran Cruz de la Orden de Isabela la Catholica (Spain); Gran Orden de Merito (Argentina); recipient Distinguished Service award USAF; recipient 1st ann. frats. award Mexico City Coll., Mexico; Am. award Rollins Coll., Winter Park, Fla. Mem. Pan Am. Soc. New Eng., Pan Am. Soc. U.S., N.H. Hist. Soc., Mayflower Soc. N.H., World Affairs Council Boston, Alpha Delta Phi. Republican. Conglist. Clubs: Metropolitan, Chevy Chase (Md.); University (Washington); Elkridge (Balt.); Metropolitan (N.Y.C.). Contbr. Orbis, Readers Digest, Washington Report. Home: Littleton, N.H. Died Nov. 28, 1978; buried Wheeler Hill Cemetery, Littleton, N.H.

HILL, ROSS D., pres., treas. Union Dime Savs. Bank, N.Y.C., to 1974; chmn. bd., chief exec. officer Chase Realty Trust, to 1975. Pres., Ave. of Americas Assn.; trustee Hamilton Investment Trust, Savs. Bank Life Ins. Fund. Address: New York, N.Y. Died Feb. 29, 1976.

HILL, THOMAS RUSSELL, bus. exec., lectr., writer; b. Williamstown, Ky., Dec. 15, 1894; s. George William and Mary Elizabeth (Hayden) H.; A.B., Georgetown Coll., 1915, LL.D., 1940; H.H.D., Lincoln Meml. U. 1949; m. Iris Francis, Nov. 19, 1921 (dec.). Coach football, high sch. prin. and supt. schs., 1915-18; lectr Redpath Chautauqua, summers 1915-18; pres

Hill-Lawson Co., Corbin, Harlan and Middlesboro, Ky., 1920-29; with RKO Lyceum Bur., 1927-31; state mgr. advancing to v.p. and dir. Air-Way Electric Appliance Corp., Toledo, 1929-35; chmn. Rexair, Inc., Detroit; former pres. Martin-Parry Corp., Martin-Parry, Ltd., Ward Industries Corp., Ward Industries, Ltd. Trustee, Lincoln Meml. U., Harrogate, Tenn., Kalamazoo Coll. Past pres. Middleboro (Ky.) C. of C.; nat. councillor U.S. C. of C. Mem. Kappa Alpha. Baptist (chmn. trustees). Mason (Shriner), Rotarian (hon.), Elk, Kiwanian (past pres.). Author: Press On; Out Front; How Big; Producers; Gimme; 16 to 1; Dig, Ships, Bata. Home: Detroit, Mich. Died Mar. 4, 1975.

HILL, WILLIAM CALVIN, gas co. exec.; b. Fairfax, Ala., Oct. 3, 1924; s. Walter Calvin and Fannie Alma (Sanders) H.; B.S., Auburn U., 1947; J.D., U. Va., 1949; m. Rosemary Irene Dennery, Feb. 20, 1946; children—William Dennery, Michael Sanders, John Walter, Charles Paul. Admitted to Va. bar, 1948, D.C. bar, 1949; partner firm Steptoe & Johnson, Washington, 1949-65; chmn. bd. Pargas, Inc., Waldorf, Md., 1965-79; dir. Bank of So. Md., Preston Trucking Co. Served with F.A., AUS, World War II. Mem. Nat. Liquefied Petroleum Gas Assn. (dir.). Home: LaPlata, Md. Died Dec. 9, 1979.

HILLE, (CARL) EINAR, research mathematician; b. N.Y.C., June 28, 1894; s. Carl August and Edla Johanna (Ekman-Hille) Heuman; student U. Stockholm, 1911-16, 17-18, doctor's degree; student Harvard U., 1920-21, U. Copenhagen, U. Göttingen, 1926-27; hon. A.M., Yale U., 1933; m. Kirsti Ore, Aug. 10, 1937; children—Harald, Bertil. Instr., Stockholm U., 1915-16, 1920; with Swedish Civil Service, 1918-21; instr. math. Harvard U., 1921-22; instr. Princeton U., 1922-23, asst. prof. math., 1923-30, asso. prof., 1930-33; prof. math Yale, 1933-62, dir. grad. studies in math., 1938-62; Fulbright lectr. U. Nancy, France, 1952, Sorbonne, 1953, U. Mainz, Germany, 1956; vis. prof. U. Stockholm, U. Uppsala, 1949, U. Mainz, 1956, Tata Inst. Bombay, India, 1963, 64, Australian Nat. U., 1965-67, U. Calif., Irvine, 1965-66, U. Oreg., 1967-68, U. N.Mex., 1968-72, Technion, Haifa, 1970, U. La Laguna, 1971, San Diego State U., 1972-73; research mathematician U. Calif., San Diego, 1973-80. Fellow Am. Acad. Arts and Scis.; mem. Nat. Acad. Scis., Am. Math. Soc. (pres. 1947-48), Conn. Acad. Arts and Scis., Royal Physiog. Soc. Lund, Royal Swedish Acad. Sci., Royal Soc. Scis. and Arts of Gothenburg. Author: Functional Analysis and SemiGroups, 1948, 2d edition (with R.S. Phillips, 1957); Selecta, 1975; Lectures on Ordinary Differential Equations, 1969; Ordinary Differential Equations in the Complex Domain, 1976; and others. Editor: Annals of Mathematics, 1929-33. Asso. editor Transactions Am. Math. Soc., 1923-37, editor, 1937-43. Contbr. articles to profl. jours. Home: La Jolla, Calif. Died Feb. 12, 1980.

HILLER, ERNEST THEODORE, sociologist; b. Cisne, Ill., Dec. 9, 1883; s. Michael and Caroline (Feller) H.; student Southern Ill. Normal U., Carbondale, Ill., 1902-07, Lewis Inst., Chicago, 1910-11; A.B., Northwestern U., 1912, A.M., 1913; Ph.D., U. of Chicago, 1924; m. Eunice Gertrude Wattenbarger, Aug. 25, 1920. Sec. Y.M.C.A., Peoria and Chicago, 1907-14; dir. welfare work internment camp, Prisoners of War, 1917-19; social research, Interchurch World Movement, 1919-20; instr. sociology, U. of Tex., 1920, Washington State Coll., 1921-23; instr. in sociology, U. of Ill., 1923-26, asso., 1926-28, asst. prof., 1928-31, asso. prof., 1931-34, prof. 1934-49, emeritus, acting head dept., 1928-37. Mem. Am. Sociol. Society, Am. Statis. Assn., Am. Assn. Univ. Profs., Alpha Kappa Delta. Methodist. Club: University (Urbana). Author: The Strike—a Study in Collective Action, 1928; Rural Community Types (with Faye Corner and Wendell East), 1930; Principles of Sociology, 1933; Outline Guide for Study of Sociology, 1934; Houseboat and River-Bottoms People, 1939; Social Relations and Structures, 1947.*

HILLES, FREDERICK WHILEY, educator; b. Lancaster, O., June 1, 1900; s. Charles Dewey and Sarah Bell (Whiley) H.; student in Cambridge, Eng., 1922-23; A.B., Yale, 1922, Ph.D., 1926; L.H.D., St. Lawrence U., 1959; m. Susan Toy Morse, June 14, 1930; children—Susan E. (Mrs. Geoffrey Bush), Frederick W. Instr. English, Yale, 1926-30, asst. prof., 1931-40, asso. prof., 1940-48, prof., 1948-65, Bodman prof., 1952-65, dir. humanities, 1956-59, bd. govs. Yale Press, 1958-74. Served from capt. to lt. col. AUS, 1942-46. Decorated Order Brit. Empire; Legion of Merit (U.S.). Mem. Modern Lang. Assn. (N.Y.C.), Alpha Delta Phi. Republican. Episcopalian. Clubs: Century Assn., Grolier (N.Y.C.); Somerset (Boston). Author: Literary Career of Sir Joshua Reynolds, 1936. Editor: Portraits by Sir Joshua Reynolds, 1952; The Age of Johnson, 1949; New Light on Dr. Johnson, 1959; mem. editorial bd. Yale edits. Samuel Johnson's Works, Private Papers of James Boswell; co-editor From Sensibility to Romanticism, 1965. Home: Hamden, Conn. Died Dec. 10, 1975.

HILLIS, WILLIAM H., ry. official; b. Colona, Ill., Mar. 31, 1886; s. John and Mary Harper (Wallace) H.; ed. high sch.; m. Madalin Alicia Doran, Oct. 27, 1917; children—Robert William, Wiliam H., Jr. Entered railroad service as rodman for Chicago, Burlington & Quincy Ry., Beardstown, Ill., serving until 1911 in engring. dept., roadmaster various divs., 1911-16, trainmaster Aurora Div., 1916-25, dist. engr. maintenance, Ill. Dist., Galesburg, 1925-27, asst. supt. LaCrosse Div., 1927-30, asst. supt. Galesburg Div., 1930-31, supt. constrn. in charge constrn. of 110-mile line in Tex., 1931, asst. supt. LaCrosse Div., 1931-36; engr. C.R.I. & P. Ry. (Rock Island Lines), 1936-39, asst. chief operations officer, 1939-42, operating officer, 1942-48, vice pres. in charge operations, Chicago, since 1948; dir. Belt Ry., Chicago, Denver Union Terminal Ry. Co., Denver; pres. Joliet Union Depot Co.*

HILLMAN, HERMAN DAVID, lawyer, educator; b. N.Y.C., Aug. 8, 1911; s. Max and Rae (Brown) H.; A.B., CCNY, 1932; J.D., N.Y. U., 1936; m. Edith N. Geilich, April 2, 1939; children—Richard, Robert, Alan. Admitted to N.Y. bar, 1936; asst. mgr. Bur. Legal Research, N.Y. U. Sch. Law, 1936-38, mem. grad. faculty Grad. Sch. Pub. Adminstrn., also faculty law, 1946-77, adj. prof. pub. adminstrn., 1962-77, adj. prof. law, 1963-77; atty. U.S. Housing Authority, 1939-42, Fed. Pub. Housing Adminstrn., 1942-43; atty. PHA, 1946-49, regional atty., 1949-53, acting dir. N.Y. regional office, 1953-54, dir., 1954-66, adminstr. housing assistance N.Y. regional office HUD, 1966-70; v.p., asso. gen. counsel Stirling Homex Corp., 1970-72; spl. prof. law Hofstra Law Sch., Hempstead, N.Y., 1972-74, prof. law, 1974-77; adj. prof. housing N.Y. U., 1957. Mem. nat. council Boy Scouts Am., 1967-77. Bd. dirs. Nat. Housing Conf., Washington, 1974-76, Citizens Housing and Planning Council N.Y., Housing Devel. Corp., Council Chs., N.Y. Served lt. USNR, 1943-46. Recipient Distinguished Service award HHFA, 1956, Service citation N.Y. U., 1971. Mem. Am. Bar Assn. (com. on land use, planning and zoning sect. local govt. law), Nat. Assn. Housing and Redevel. Ofcls., Lambda Alpha. Jewish. Contbr. articles to legal periodicals. Home: Rockville Centre, N.Y. Died Mar. 17, 1977.

HILLMAN, JAMES NOAH, college pres.; b. Coeburn, Wise County, Va., Nov. 6, 1883; s. Benjamin Franklin and Nancy Susanna (Greear) H.; A.B., William and Mary Coll., 1903, A.M., 1909, LL.D., 1931; LL.D., Hampden-Sydney, 1926; student Harvard, summer 1919; m. Ethel Lee Powell, June 28, 1906. Prin. high sch., Williamsburg, 1905-09; instr. Latin, William and Mary Coll., 1905-08; supt. schs., Wise County, Va., 1909-17; sec. State Bd. of Edn., Va., 1917-22; pres. Emory and Henry Coll., 1922-41; exec. sec. Holston Conf. Board of Education, Methodist Church, 1941-44, grand sec. Grand Lodge A.F. and A.M. of Va. since 1944. Mem. Phi Beta Kappa, Kappa Phi Kappa, Pi Gamma Mu, Tau Kappa Alpha. Mason (past grand master of Va.). Democrat. Methodist. Home: Richmond, Va.*

HILLS, GEORGE STROUGH, lawyer; b. Winter Park, Fla., Nov. 1, 1900; s. Elijah Clarence and Metta V. (Strough) H.; A.B., Ind. U., 1922; LL.B., Harvard U., 1925; m. Alice G. Shaw, Sept. 14, 1926; children—Joan Lee (Mrs. Walter T. Faulkner), Alice Ann (Mrs. W. Hubert Plummer). Admitted to N.Y. bar, 1926, U.S. Supreme Ct., 1936; partner firm Menken, Ferguson & Hills, N.Y.C., 1930-37, Rogers Hoge & Hills, 1939-80; gen. counsel AMF Inc., 1941-65, dir., 1941-71, dir. emeritus, 1971-80; sec. Bacardi Corp., San Juan, P.R., 1944-74, dir., gen. counsel, 1944-76; dir., gen. counsel Life Savers Corp.; N.Y.C., 1950-56; dir., gen. counsel Sterling Drug Inc., N.Y.C., 1940-73, adv. dir., 1973-75, sec., 1946-73, vice-chmn., 1960-70; dir. Am. Viscose Corp., N.Y.C., 1946-69, gen. counsel, 1960-69; mem. adv. com. Accounting Principles Bd., 1957. Bd. govs. New Rochelle (N.Y.) Hosp. Med. Center, 1959-80, sec., 1960-74, pres., 1975-77; mem. New Rochelle Bd. Edn., 1967-70. Mem. Assn. Bar City N.Y., Am. Bar Assn., Westchester Bar Assn., Am. Law Inst., Beta Theta Pi. Clubs: Union League, Sky (N.Y.C.); Larchmont (N.Y.) Yacht; University (Washington). Author: The Law of Accounting and Financial Statements, 1957; Managing Corporate Meetings-A Legal and Procedural Guide, 1976. Contbr. numerous articles to legal jours. Home: New Rochelle, N.Y. Died Sept. 2, 1980.

HILLS, RALPH GORMAN, physician; b. Washington, Jan. 19, 1902; s. Ralph Warren and Mary Edna (Gorman) H.; grad. Hill Sch., Pottstown, Pa., 1921; B.S. (Pyre prize), Princeton, 1925; M.D., Johns Hopkins, 1929; m. Mary Joe Dixon, Aug. 11, 1928; children—Joseph Dixon, Ralph Warren. Intern, asst. resident Union Meml. Hosp., Balt., 1929-31, vis. physician, 1936-77; asst. resident, resident pvt. wards Johns Hopkins Hosp., 1931-33; practice medicine specializing in internal medicine, Balt., 1933-77; vis. physician Greater Balt. Med. Center, 1936; asst. vis. physician Ch. Home and Infirmary, Balt.; courtesy staff Sinai Hosp.; asst. prof. internal medicine Johns Hopkins, 1950. Alumni trustee Princeton, 1956-60. Served to lt. col. AUS, 1942-45. Diplomate Am. Bd. Internal Medicine. Mem. Md. Med. Assn. (councilor 1955-59, v.p. 1959), A.C.P., Am. Clin. and Climatol. Assn., Soc. Med. Cons. to Armed Forces U.S. Clubs: Bachelors Cotillion, Elkridge (Balt.); Ivy (Princeton, N.J.). Contbr. articles, monographs on internal medicine. Mem. U.S. Olympic Track and Field Team, 1920, 24 (winner medal for shot put). Home: Baltimore, Md. Died Sept. 20, 1977.

HILTON, CONRAD N., hotel exec.; b. San Antonio, N.Mex., Dec. 25, 1887; s. August H. and Mary (Laufersweiler) H.; ed. St. Michael's Coll., Santa Fe., N. Mex., 1901-02, N.Mex. Sch. Mines, Socorro, 1907-09; LL.D., U. Detroit, 1953, Adelphi Coll., 1957, N.Mex. Coll. Archtl. and Mech. Arts, 1957, U. Albuquerque, 1975; Litt.D., DePaul U., 1954, Sophia U., Tokyo, 1963; L.H.D., Barat Coll. Sacred Heart, 1955; m. Mary Barron, 1925; children—Conrad Nicholson (dec.), William Barron, Eric Michael; m. 2d, Sari Gabor. Partner of father in mercantile bus.; organizer, cashier, later pres., 1922, N.Mex. State Bank, San Antonio; rep. in 1st State Legislature, N.Mex., 1912-13; built Hilton Hotel, Dallas, 1925, and Hilton Hotels in Waco, Longview, Plainview, Lubbock, El Paso and Marlin, Tex., 1926-31; chmn. Hilton Hotels Corp.; chmn. Hilton Internat. Co.; chmn. bd. Hilton-Burns Hotels Co., Inc., 1965-79; chmn. Hotel Waldorf Astoria Corp., owners, operators hotels major U.S. and fgn. cities. Served with R.O.T.C., Presidio, Calif., 1917; served with A.E.F. as lt. Q.M. Corps. Recipient Brotherhood award NCCJ; decorated chevalier de la Legion d'Honneur (France); Order Ruben Dario (Nicaragua), knight comdr. Order of Merit (Italy); knight Sovereign Mil. Order of Malta; grand knight Order St. Birgitta. Elk. Author: Be My Guest, 1957; Inspirations of an Innkeeper, 1963. Home: Beverly Hills, Calif. Died Jan. 3, 1979; buried Dallas, Tex.

HILTON, JAMES CARROLL, retired corp. exec.; b. Baltimore, Md., Sept. 6, 1883; s. James Anthony and Florida Virginia (Livesay) H.; student City Coll., 1898-1903, U. of Md.; m. Harriet Pendleton Williams, Dec. 3, 1910; 1 son, James Garrett. Commd. ensign Supply Corps, U.S. Navy, 1905, resigning rank comdr., 1921; in charge Logistics and Fuel, Navy Bur., Supplies and Accounts and special asst. to sec. of navy, during World War, requisition of vessels and procurement, storage and delivery fuel supplies for support of Fleet and Troop Transport Service; liaison between Fuel Administration, Petroleum War Service Com. and War Agencies created for mobilization and maintenance essential industries; Navy's rep. with leading interests to determine Am. Tank Tonnage position and participation in production, refining and transportation of fuel; served with Shipping Bd. in matters of compensation for vessels requisitioned; with Dept. of Justice, in litigation growing out of War Emergency Legislation, War Plans Div., Naval Operations; member Naval Fuel Oil Bd., and commn. which in 1919 reported on facilities for upkeep and operation reorganized Pacific Fleet; asst. purchasing agent Standard Oil Co. of New Jersey, 1921-27, purchasing agent, 1927-30, dir. in charge of purchases, 1930-31, dir. and v.p., 1936-40; pres. Standard Oil Co. of La., New Orleans, 1931-36. Dir. Nat. Assn. of Mfrs., 1937-39. Awarded Navy Cross and special letter commendation for Services during World War. Baptist. Clubs: Army and Navy, University (Washington, D.C.); India House (N.Y. City); Manursing Island (Rye, N.Y.). Home: New York, N.Y. *

HINCKLEY, JULIAN, author; b. Lawrence, L.I., N.Y., Feb. 6, 1884; s. Samuel Parker and Rosalie (Neilson) H.; A.B., Harvard, 1906 (class poet); unmarried. Episcopalian. Author: "E" (novel), 1914; The Family Tradition (novel), 1918. Contbr. Saturday Evening Post and other mags. Home: Cedarhurst, L.I., N.Y.*

HINES, CHARLES ANDERSON, lawyer; b. Guilford County, N.C., Feb. 14, 1886; s. E. DeVault and Belle (Wright) H.; ed. Jefferson Acad., McLeansville, N.C., 1900-02, Elon (N.C.) Coll., 1902-04, U. N.C. Law Sch., 1907-08; m. Ida Edwards Winstead, Nov. 12, 1912, (dec.); children—Dorothy Byrd, Charles Anderson, Winstead (dec.); m. 2d, Annie McNairy. Tchr. in Guilford County, 1903-04; reporter Greensboro Telegram, 1904-05; editor Lumberton Robesonian, 1905-06; city editor Greensboro Daily News, 1906-07; admitted to N.C. bar, 1908, practiced in Greensboro; admitted to U.S. Supreme Ct., 1928; city atty. Greensboro, 1917-22; spl. judge Superior Ct., 1925; chmn. emeritus Gate City Bldg. and Loan Assn.; hon. chmn. bd. Woodmen of World Life Ins. Soc., Omaha; hon. chmn. bd. E.F. Craven Co., Greensboro. Served as N.C. state senator, 1927-29; chmn. State Bd. of Elections, 1928-30. Past mem. bd. trustees Moses H. Cone Meml. Hosp.; also former N.C. Fraternal Congress. Awarded 1929 Civitan Citizenship Trophy for unselfish vol. civic service to city of Greensboro. Mem. Am., N.C., Greensboro bar assns. Democrat Methodist (mem. ofcl. bd., chmn.). Mason, Woodman of World Club: Civitan. Home: Greensboro, N.C. Died Jan. 28, 1976.

HINES, HERBERT WALDO, educator; b. Boston, Aug. 14, 1887; s. John Henry and Jennie Henderson (Gwinn) H.; A.B., Harvard U., 1909, A.M., 1910; B.D., U. Chgo., 1911, Ph.D., 1922; studied U. Berlin, Germany, 1912-13, Marburg, 1913-14; LL.D. (hon.), Westminster Coll., 1954; m. Helen Gartside, June 21, 1910; children—Herbert Waldo, Bedell, Paul Henry, Harold Cheney, Wallis Gartside, Marion Louise, Mildred Elizabeth, Marshall, Burton Abbott, Donald

Alan. Ordained Bapt. ministry, 1912; pastor, El Paso, Ill., 1915-21, 1st Ch., Kankakee, 1921-25, Central Ch., Springfield, 1925-35; sabbatical year of travel and writing, 1935-36; dir. Inst. of Internat. Understanding and developer Found. Student fellowships for advanced study abroad for Rotary Internat., 1936-51; pres. Rocky Mountain Coll., 1951-58, now emeritus; prof. Russian lang. Morningside Coll., 1958-63, Hope Coll., Holland, Mich., 1963-65. Young People's Com. Bapt. World Alliance, 1928-33; mem. and sec. exec. com. Ill. Bapt. State Conv., 1931-34; moderator Bloomington (Ill.) Bapt. Assn., 1919-21; moderator Springfield (Ill.) Bapt. Assn., 1926-27; recording sec. Bapt. Young People's Union of Am., 1921-22, mem. exec. com., 1923-25; spl. lectr. in humanities Chgo. Jr. Colls., 1938-51. Rotary Found. fellow, 1974. Mem. MLA, Republican. Mason (32 deg., Shriner). Clubs: Harvard (Chgo.), Rotary (mem. of dist. conf. com., gov. of Rotary Dist. 167 1953-54). Author: Missionary Education in the Local Church, 1925; Clough, Kingdom Builder in South India, 1929. Contbr. numerous articles on young people's problems, fgn. travel and internat. relations; made several cultural and research trips to Europe, 4 to Latin Am. countries, and one around-the-world tour. Home: Lansing MI. Died Dec. 26, 1979.

HINES, HUGH TIM, assn. exec.; b. Burlington, Ia., July 24, 1931; s. William G. and Irma (Bershee) H.; B.A. in Journalism, Polit. sci. and Sociology, U. Ia., 1958; grad. U.S. Chamber Inst. Orgn. Mgmt. and Acad., 1970; m. Mary Ann Knoll, Dec. 26, 1951; children—Kevin, Rebecca, Martha Lee, Sarah, Jennifer. Mgr. Grinnell (Ia.) C. of C., 1958-59; asst. mgr. Ft. Dodge (Ia.) C. of C., 1959-60; dir. civic affairs div. Met. Evansville C. of C., 1961-64, dir. tax research div., 1964-65, exec. v.p., 1965-79. Vice pres., dir. Ind. Assn. Retarded Children, 1966-67; pres. Evansville Assn. Retarded children, 1964-65, dir., 1961-66. Served with USN, 1951-55. Mem. Am. C. of C. Execs. Assn. (mem. mgmt. standards com. 1968-73), U.S. C. of C., Inst. Bd. Regents., Ind. Commerce Execs. Assn. (pres. 1969-70). Roman Catholic. Clubs: Press, Petroleum (Evansville); Columbia (Indpls.). Home: Evansville, Ind. Died Jan. 21, 1979.

HINMAN, CHARLTON JOSEPH KADIO, educator; b. Ft. Collins, Colo., Feb. 10, 1911; s. Claude Harrison and Ethel (Charlton) H.; B.A., Cornell U., 1933; B.A. (Rhodes scholar 1933-36), Oxford (Eng.) U., 1936, M.A., 1939; Ph.D. (Du Pont Research fellow), U. Va., 1941; m. Jane van Meter, Nov. 8, 1936 (div. Sept. 1966); 1 dau., Barbara; m. 2d, Myra Mahlow, Feb. 22, 1968. Instr. U. Mo., 1937-39; research fellow Folger Shakespeare Library, Washington, 1941-42, hon. fellow, 1952-58; asst. prof. Johns Hopkins, 1946-50; prof. English, U. Kans., 1960-63, Univ. Distinguished prof., 1963-77. Guggenheim fellow, 1954-55; Bollingen Research fellow, 1956-58; fellow Folger Shakespeare Library. Served to comdr. USNR, 1942-46, 50-52. Mem. Bibliog. Soc. London, Malone Soc. Oxford, MLA, Shakespeare Assn. Am., Phi Beta Kappa. Author: The Printing and Proof-reading of the First Folio of Shakespeare, 2 vols., 1963; also articles. Editor: Shakespeare Quarto Facsimiles, 1960-77; The Norton Facsimile of the First Folio of Shakespeare, 1968. Inventor Hinman collating machine. Home: Lawrence, Kans. Died Mar. 16, 1977.

HINMAN, JOHN HOLMES, paper co. exec.; b. North Stratford, N.H.; grad. Dartmouth Coll., 1908. Joined Internat. Paper Co., 1913, pres., 1943-63, chief exec. officer, 1948-63, chmn. bd., 1954-63, chmn. bd. emeritus, dir., 1963-81. Home: Pelham, N.Y. Died May 20, 1981.

HINSEY, JOSEPH CLARENCE, med. educator; b. Ottumwa, Iowa, Apr. 29, 1901; s. Joseph Edgar and Sarah Belle (Majors) H.; student Iowa Wesleyan Coll., 1918-20; B.S., Northwestern U., 1922, M.S., 1923, D.Sc., 1951; Ph.D., Washington U. Sch. Medicine, St. Louis, 1927; D.Sc. (hon.), Union Coll., 1955, Iowa Wesleyan Coll., 1958, Boston U., 1969; D.H.L., N.J. Coll. Medicine, 1965; m. Sarah Lillian Callen, June 18, 1926; children—Elaine (Mrs. Donald P. Reynolds), Joseph. Asst. in zoology Northwestern U., 1921-23; instr. biology Western Res. U., 1923-24; asst. in neuroanatomy Washington U., 1924-27, asst. prof., 1927-28; asst. prof. in neuroanatomy Northwestern U. Med. Sch., 1928-29, asso. prof., 1929-30; prof. anatomy Stanford, 1930-36; prof. physiology, head dept. Cornell U. Med. Sch., N.Y., 1936-39, prof. anatomy, head dept., 1939-53, dean, 1942-53; dir. N.Y. Hosp.-Cornell Med. Center, 1953-66, cons., 1966-69; prof. neuroanatomy Cornell U. Med. Coll., 1956-67, prof. anatomy emeritus, 1967-81. Chmn. China Med. Bd. N.Y., 1956-70. Mem. Pres.'s Commn. on Med. Needs of Nation, 1952. Mem. bd. mgrs. Meml. Hosp. N.Y.C., 1942-70; trustee Sloan-Kettering Inst., 1947-70, mem. advisory bd., 1970-81; trustee China Med. Bd., 1943-71; chmn. NRC commn. acad. radiology, 1966-68. Faculty rep., bd. trustees Cornell U., 1942-53; co-founder Ams. Found., 1941, Nat. Found. Med. Edn., 1947, Assn. Academic Health Centers, 1956. Recipient Merit award Nu Sigma Nu, 1956; Abraham Flexner award for service to med. edn. Assn. Am. Med. Colls., 1958; Medal award N.Y. Med. Coll., 1960; distinguished service award N.C. Coll. Medicine, 1964, Alumni Merit award Northwestern U., Washington U., Iowa Wesleyan Coll. Fellow A.A.A.S. (v.p. 1950), N.Y. Acad. Scis. (v.p. 1949), Assn. Am. Med. Colls. (pres. 1949; chmn. exec. council 1946-54), Calif. Acad. Sci., Am. Neurol. Soc. (hon.); mem. Am. Assn. Anatomists, Am. Physiol. Soc., Soc. Exptl. Biology and Medicine, Harvey Soc., N.Y. Acad. Medicine, Calif. Acad. Medicine, S.A.R., Pilgrims U.S., Newcomen Soc., St. Andrews Soc., Phi Beta Kappa, Sigma Xi, Phi Delta Theta, Nu Sigma Nu, Alpha Omega Alpha. Republican. Presbyn. Mason (K.T., Shriner). Club: Cornell (N.Y.C.). Contbr. to med. jours. Home: Scarsdale, N.Y. Died Mar. 25, 1981; buried Ottumwa.

HINTON, RALPH C., mfg. co. exec.; b. Wichita, Kans., Sept. 28, 1936; s. Joseph Robert and Besse M. (Carnahan) H.; B.S. in Bus. Adminstrn., Wichita State U., 1959; m. Elizabeth Moody, Dec. 15, 1956; children—Denise, Diane, Laura. Systems rep. Service Bur. Corp. subs. IBM, Houston, 1957-63; group v.p. fin. Gulf and Western Industries, N.Y.C., 1963-74, also dir. subsidiaries; exec. v.p. Nat. Homes Corp., Lafayette, Ind., 1974-80. Republican. Baptist. Home: Lafayette, Ind. Died Nov. 5, 1980; buried Rest Haven Meml. Park, Lafayette.

HINTON, WILLIAM MILLER, psychologist, educator; b. Paris, Ky., Mar. 19, 1907; s. William Miller and Eddie Chiles (Spears) H.; A.B., Washington and Lee U., 1929, M.A., 1930; Ph.D., Ohio State U., 1937; m. Mary Moore Harper, Dec. 22, 1934; 1 son, William Miller. Instr. Washington and Lee U., 1931-36, asst. prof., 1937-42, asso. prof., 1946-51, prof., 1951-77, emeritus, 1977-79, head dept. psychology, 1959-72; dir. Washington and Lee U. Counseling Service, 1946-52; personnel cons. U.S. Army, 1942-44, chief counseling br. Separation Center, Ft. Meade, Md., 1944-46; vis. prof. U. Va., 1947-73; field psychologist George Fry & Assos., 1953-79; cons. counseling psychology VA Central Office, 1955-79. Served from 1st lt. to maj. AUS, 1942-46; lt. col. Res., 1950-79. Fellow Am. Psychol. Assn., A.A.A.S.; mem. Va. Acad. Sci. (pres. 1959-60), Va. Psychol. Assn. (pres. 1956-57), So. Soc. Philosophy and Psychology (council 1957-60; pres. 1961-62). Democrat. Episcopalian. Home: Lexington, Va. Died Jan. 1, 1979.

HINTZ, AUGUST MCCURDY, clergyman; b. Syracuse, Mo., Apr. 14, 1914; s. Fredrick Jacob and Alice (McCurdy) H.; B.A., William Jewell Coll., 1936, D.D., 1948; B.D., Colgate Rochester Div. Sch., 1939; D.H.L. (hon.) Sioux Empire Coll., 1966; postgrad. Am. Bapt. Sem., 1969; D.D., Linfield Coll.; m. Dorothy Storm, June 22, 1939; children—John McCurdy, Judith Leigh Cox, Robert August and William August (twins). Ordained to ministry Baptist Ch., 1939; pastor, Buckner, Mo., 1934-36, Pittsford, N.Y., 1937-39; asso. pastor, Dayton, O., 1939-41; pastor, Sioux Falls, S.D., 1941-53, North Shore Bapt. Ch., Chgo., 1953-63; minister First Bapt. Ch. Seattle, to 1976; lectr. Redpath Bur., Asso. Clubs: condr. radio counseling series The Pastor's Study, WGN, Chgo., 1956-58, devotional programs Power for Living, WMAQ, 1958-59, Outline for Living, 1962; speaker The Layman's Hour, radio program, 1965-66, Good Things Happening series KIRO Radio, 1971-72; program planning com. ABC. Bd. mgrs. Am. Bapt. Fgn. Mission Soc., 1946-56, pres., 1956-57; bd. dirs. Ch. Council Greater Seattle, Wholeperson; mem. program com. Am. Bapt. Conv., 1968-69. Bd. dirs. Alcohol Problem Assn. Mem. Newcomen Soc. Eng. Mason (32 deg., Shriner). Clubs: Wash. Athletic, Swedish of Seattle. Co-author: One Blood. Contbr. to Ministers' Ency. Address: Seattle, Wash. Died Feb. 25, 1976.

HINTZE, WILLIAM ROBERT, coll. pres.; b. El Paso, July 10, 1925; s. Otto Charles and Pearl Evelyn (Greene) H.; B.S., U. Tex. at El Paso, 1947; M.Div., Southwestern Theol. Sem., 1958, Th.D., 1968; m. Barbara Laughman, Sept. 12, 1952; children—Robin Ruth (Mrs. David William Kreutzberg), Fred, Richard, Willie. Prof., dir. Ecuadorian Bapt. Theol. Inst., Guayaquil, 1961-65; asst. prof. religion, dir. religious activities Grand Canyon Coll., 1969-71, asso. prof. religion, 1971-72, v.p. acad. affairs, prof. religion, 1972-73, v.p. acad. affairs, interim pres., prof. religion, 1973, pres., prof. religion, 1973-78; pastor chs., Mo., Okla., Tex., Ariz., 1957-72; chmn. Ariz. Commn. Post-Secondary Edn., 1976. Active Boy Scouts Am., mem. exec. bd., 1974, v.p., 1976-78. Served with USNR, 1943-45. Recipient Silver Beaver award Boy Scouts Am., 1953. Mem. Ariz. Coll. Assn., Soc. Bibl. Lit., Am. Acad. Religion, Ariz. Acad., Am. Assn. Higher Edn., Ariz. Hist. Soc. Rotarian. Home: Phoenix, Ariz. Died Nov. 17, 1978; cremated.

HIRSCH, ARTHUR HENRY, educator, research specialist, writer; b. LeMars, Iowa; s. John Leonard and Louise (Kluckhohn) H.; A.B., Cornell Coll., Mt. Vernon, Iowa, 1901, A.M., 1907; Ph.D. (Ohio Hist. Commn. fellow, stipend scholar), U. Chgo., 1915. Asst. prof. history and polit. sci. Earlham Coll., 1911-13; prof. history and polit. sci. Ursinus Coll., 1913-16; prof. history Morningside Coll., 1916-19; prof. Am. history on James S. Britton Found., head dept. Ohio Wesleyan U., 1919-33; vis. prof. Am. history U. Mich., 1928-30, Roosevelt Coll., 1946-47; editor publs. United Educators, Inc., 1942-44; picture editor publs. Amalgamated Book Prodn. Syndicate, Inc., 1946-76. Lectr., Am. history Duke, summers 1924-27; prof. Am. history U. Colo., summer 1925; research Library of Congress, summer 1922-23, 25, New Eng. libraries, 1927; investigator Ill. Commn. Occupational Diseases, 1912; nation wide research projects; exec. dir. Human Relations Research Found. Mem. Netherlands-Walloon-Huguenot Commn., 1924, White House Conf. on Marriage and Family. Fellow Royal Hist. Soc. (Britain), Soc. for Sci. Study Sex.; mem. Am. Hist. Assn., Huguenot Soc. S.C. (life), Am. Assn. U. Profs., Ohio Acad. Social Scis., Nat. Council for Social Studies, Mississippi Valley, Ohio (pres. 1919-20) hist. socs., Authors League Am., Phi Beta Kappa. Methodist. Mason, Kiwanian. Club: University (Ann Arbor, Del., Ohio). Author: The Huguenots of Colonial South Carolina, 1925; Sexual Misbehavior of the Upper Cultured in the U.S., 1930, 1955; The Love Elite. Contbr. numerous articles to ednl. and profl. publs. including Dictionary Am. Biography. Address: Sebring, Fla. Died Mar. 10, 1976.

HIRSCH, EDWIN FREDERICK, physician; b. Milw., Aug. 18, 1886; s. John Fred and Maria Louise (Weiland) H.; A.B., Northwestern U., 1910; A.M. in Zoology, U. Ill., 1911; Ph.D. in Pathology, U. Chgo., 1914, M.D., 1916; Sc.D. (hon.), Morningside Coll., 1955; m. Marion Sharp Lane, Aug. 3, 1918 (dec. Aug. 1945); children—Catharine Louise (Mrs. Alex Ayala), Helen Sharp (Mrs. William P. Kent), Jean Lane (Mrs. Robert E. Priest); m. 2d, Helen Kotas, Mar. 19, 1949. Intern Presbyn. Hosp., Chgo., 1916-17; from fellow to asso. prof. pathology U. Chgo., 1912-51, asso. prof. emeritus, 1951—; dir. Henry Baird Favill Lab., St. Luke's Hosp., Chgo., 1919-59; emeritus pathologist Presbyn.-St. Luke's Hosp., Chgo., 1959—; dir. labs. Columbus, Cuneo and St. Francis Cabrini hosps., Chgo., 1963—. Served to capt., M.C., U.S. Army, 1917-19. Mem. Phi Beta Kappa, Sigma Xi, Gamma Alpha, Alpha Omega Alpha. Home: Chgo. *

HIRSCH, LEO HENRY, JR., lawyer; b. N.Y.C., Mar. 21, 1911; s. Leo Henry and Gertrude (Joseph) H.; A.B., Princeton, 1931; LL.B., Columbia, 1934, J.D., 1969; m. Geraldine Schwabe, July 30, 1937; children—Leo Henry III, William Joseph. Admitted to N.Y. bar, 1934; U.S. Supreme Ct. bar; practiced in N.Y.C., 1934-80. Sec., dir. Am. Plan Corp., Am. Fidelity Fire Ins. Co., Am. Consumer Ins. Co., J.M.L. Trading Corp.; sec. Morey Machinery, Inc. Treas., Scarsdale Democratic Town Com., 1955-62, Scarsdale Com. for Kennedy-Johnson, 1960. Sec., trustee Lexington Sch. for Deaf. Served with Coast Arty., AUS, 1943-46. Mem. Assn. Bar City N.Y., N.Y. State Bar Assn. Mem. B'nai B'rith. Club: Mamaroneck Beach Yacht and Cabana. Author: (with Samuel R. Feller) Insurance and the Anti-Trust Laws, 1941. Home: White Plains, N.Y. Died Jan. 24, 1980.

HITCHCOCK, ALFRED JOSEPH, motion picture dir.; b. Eng., Aug. 13, 1899; s. William and Emma H.; student St. Ignatius Coll., London; D.F.A. (hon.), U. Calif. at Santa Cruz, 1968; D.H.L., Columbia, 1972; m. Alma Reville; 1 dau. Began as jr. technician Famous Players Lasky Brit, Studios, 1920; scenario writer, prodn. mgr., art dir. Gainsborough Studios, Islington, Eng., 1923; became motion picture dir., 1925; dir. motion pictures including The Lodger; Downhill; Easy Virtue; The Farmer's Wife; The Ring; Blackmail; Pleasure Garden, 1925; Juno and the Paycock, 1932; Murder; The Skin Game, 1932; Waltzes from Vienna, 1933; The Man Who Knew Too Much, 1934; The 39 Steps, 1935; Secret Agent, 1937; Sabotage; A Woman Alone, 1937; The Girl Was Young, 1937; The Lady Vanishes, 1938; Young and Innocent; Jamaica Inn, 1939; Rebecca, 1940; Foreign Correspondent, 1940; Mr. and Mrs. Smith, 1941; Suspicion, 1941; Saboteur, 1942; Shadow of a Doubt, 1942; Lifeboat, 1943; Spellbound, 1944; Notorious, 1945; The Paradine Case, 1947; Rope, 1948; Under Capricorn, 1949; Stage Fright, 1950; Strangers on a Train, 1951; I Confess; Dial M for Murder; Rear Window; To Catch a Thief; The Trouble with Harry; The Man Who Knew Too Much; The Wrong Man; Vertigo; North by Northwest; Psycho; The Birds; Marnie; Torn Curtain; Topaz; Frenzy; Family Plot; presented television series Alfred Hitchcock Presents, 1955-61; Alfred Hitchcock Hour, 1961-65. Bd. visitors Coll. Five, U. Calif. at Santa Cruz. Decorated chevalier French Nat. Order Legion of Honor; created knight Brit. Empire; recipient Irving G. Thalberg Meml. award Acad. Motion Picture Arts and Scis., 1968. Editor: My Favorite in Suspense, 1959; Alfred Hitchcock's Ghostly Gallery, 1962; Stories My Mother Never Told Me, 1963, others. Address: Universal City, Calif. Died Apr. 29, 1980.

HITCHCOCK, PHILIP STANLEY, coll. ofcl.; b. Pomeroy, Wash., Sept. 28, 1904; s. Cecil Glenn and Ethel (Gammon) H.; A.B., Wash. State U., 1926; postgrad. U. Oreg., 1954-55; LL.D., Whitworth Coll., Spokane, 1962, Storm Lake (Iowa) Coll., 1966; m. Sally Wyatt, July 22, 1939; children—Martha, Philip Stephen. Owner, Hitchcock Delivery Service, Lewiston, Idaho, 1930-34; partner Hitchcock & Crawford Lumber Co., Sisters, Oreg., 1934-43; pres. W. Hitchcock Corp., Klamath Falls, Oreg., 1943-54; dir. ch. and pub. relations Lewis and Clark Coll., Portland,

Oreg., 1954-58; v.p., logging supt. White Swan Lumber Co., White Swan, Oreg., 1958-64; pres. United Presbyn. Men, 1961, exec. dir., 1964-70; asst. to pres. Lewis & Clark Coll., 1970-72; chmn. Oreg. Bd. Parole and Probation, 1972-74; asst. to pres. Central Oreg. Community Coll., 1974-77. Moderator Presbyn. Synod Oreg., 1948; pres. Oreg. Council Chs., 1948-49; mem. gen. council United Presbyn. Ch. U.S.A., 1962-64; commr. to 4th World Conf. Faith and Order, Montreal, 1963; mem. Oreg. Senate, 1948-54; Republican primary candidate U.S. Senate, 1956. Bd. dirs. Whitworth Coll., Tarkio (Mo.) Coll. Recipient Brotherhood citation Oreg. chpt. NCCJ, 1955. Kiwanian (gov. Pacific N.W. div. 1943). Address: Sisters, Oreg. Died Oct. 12, 1977.

HITCHENS, WILLIAM FRANK, prof. architecture; b. Delmar, Del., Nov. 12, 1885; s. William Smith and Fannie Catherine (Parker) H.; B.S. in Architecture, U. of Pa., 1909. With Carnegie Inst. Tech. since 1913, prof. architecture since 1925. Registered architect of Pa. Served as 2d lt. F.A., U.S. Army, 1918. Mem. Sigma Xi. Home: Pitts. *

HITTI, PHILIP KHURL, Orientalist; b. Shimlan, Lebanon, June 24, 1886; s. Iskandar and Sa'da (Newfal) H.; B.A. with first honors, Am. U. Beirut, 1908, L.H.D., 1969; Ph.D., Columbia, 1915; Litt.D. (hon.), Princeton, 1966; m. Mary George, May 1918; 1 dau., Viola. Came to U.S., 1913, naturalized, 1920. Tchr., Am. High Sch., Lebanon, 1903-06, Am. U. Beirut, 1908-13; lectr. Oriental dept. Columbia, 1915-19; prof. history Am. U. Beirut, 1919-26; mem. faculty Princeton, 1926-54, ret. as prof. Semitic lit. and chmn. dept. Oriental langs., 1954. Founder, pres. Syrian Edn. Soc. 1916; trustee Ecole Nationale, Beirut, 1921-24; asso. mem. Corp. Am. Schs. Oriental Research 1934-54 hon. prof., 1946; mem. cultural com. East and West Assn., 1942-54, v.p. 1954; trustee of donations for edn. in Near East 1952-54; bd. trustees Am. U. Beirut, 1945-78; hon. trustee Lebanon Coll., Su al-Gharb, 1947-78; active promotion of internat. cultural orgns.; del. various internat. confs. Decorated Lebanese Republic La Médaille d'Honneur du Mérite Libanais en Vermeil; officer de l'Ordre du Cèdre 1946 and several others, including Order of Merit, First Degree, Syrian Govt., 1953, comdt. de l'ordre National du Cèdre, Lebanon, 1956. Hon. fellow Indo-Arab Cultural Assn. of Bombay, 1947-78. Mem., past officer several profl. assns. Author many works on Oriental subjects, 1916-78; later ones include: Lebanon in History, 1957; Ta'rikh Suriyah wa-Lubnan wa-Falastin, 1958; Syria: A Short History, 1959; Lubnan fi al-Ta'rikh, 1959; The Near East in History, 1961; A Short History of Lebanon, 1965; Short History of the Near East, 1966; History of the Arabs, 1967; A Short History of the Near East, 1966; Makers of Arab History, 1968; Islam: A Way of Life, 1970; Capital Cities of Arab Islam, 1973. Gen. editor of Princeton Oriental Texts (now Studies), 15 vol., 1930-54; contbg. editor to numerous works including both Ency. Americana, Ency. Brit. Home: Princeton, N.J. Died Dec. 24, 1978.

HOAG, ARTHUR EDMUND, surgeon; b. Millerton N.Y., June 17, 1885; s. Arthur Francis and Jessie L. (Wheeler) H.; M.D., Cornell Med. Coll., 1908; m. Araminta Ruth Hawkins, Mar. 4, 1913; 1 son, Arthur Edmund. Intern Bellevue Hosp., N.Y. City, 1908-10; instr. surgery Cornell U. Med. Coll., 1911-20; pvt. practice surgery, N.Y. City, since 1911; med. dir. Socony-Vacuum Oil Co., Inc., since 1912, United Cigar-Whelan Stores Corp. since 1937; dir. surgery Community Hosp., N.Y. City, 1926-47; consultant surgery Luth. Hosp. since 1940. Mem. med. adv. council The N.Y. Hotel Trades Council and Hotel Assn. Health Center, Inc. Fellow A.C.S.; member A.M.A., Am. Petroleum Inst. (mem. med. adv. com., chmn. 1949), Am. Pub. Health Assn., A.A.A.S., N.Y. State Pharm. Assn., N.Y. State Occupational Cancer Com., William H. Luckett Med. Assn., Med. Soc. County of N.Y. (chmn. spl. com. on indsl. med., 1949-50), Phi Alpha Sigma. Mason. Author: Treatment of Colles' Fractures, 1914; Myositis Crepitaris, 1914; Preserve Your Health, 1918, 2d edit., 1950. Contbr. med. articles The Socony-Vacuum News and The Flying Red Horse since 1945. Home: N.Y. *

HOBART, DOUGLAS ROSEBERRY, mech. engr.; b. New York, Jan. 8, 1882; s. Nathaniel Potts and Anne (Roseberry) H.; Hill Sch., Pottsville, Pa., Stevens Prep. Sch., Hoboken, N.J., 1900, Stevens Inst.; M.E., Columbia, 1905; m. Mary Williams Gordon, of Baltimore, Dec. 15, 1908. Engring. staff N.Y. & N.J. Telephone Co., Newark, N.J., 1905, Am. Locomotive Motor Car Co., 1906, Autocar Co., Ardmore, Pa., 1907; asso. editor Horseless Age, 1907-9; asso. and tech. editor University Cyclopaedia, 1909-10; tech. consultation and contbns. on commercial automobiles, motorcycles, etc., 1910—. Episcopalian. Jr. member Am. Soc. Mech. Engrs.; tech. rep. Federation of Am. Motorcyclists; member Phi Sigma Kappa. Clubs: New York, Columbia. Home: New York. *

HOBBES, ALAN BUXTON, optical corp. exec., lawyer; b. N.Y.C., June 30, 1917; s. Stephen Bertram and Laural Albertine (Buxton) H.; A.B., Washington and Lee U., 1939; J.D., George Washington U., 1947, LL.M., 1950; m. Ann Marie Katalinich, June 6, 1946; children—Thomas Buxton, Laurence Parsons, Martha Felicity Ann, Elizabeth Marie. Admitted to D.C., Mass. bars, also U.S. Supreme Ct.; with accessions div. Library of Congress, Washington, 1939-42; dean Marine Corps Inst., Washington, 1946-48; atty. FTC, Washington, 1948-55, legal asst. to Fed. Trade Commr. W.C. Kern, 1955-59, asst. gen. counsel, FTC, 1959-61; asst. to gen. counsel Am. Optical Corp., Southbridge, Mass., 1961-67, gen. counsel, 1967-69, sec., gen. counsel, 1969-77; dir. Todd-AO Corp. Mem. finance com., Sturbridge, Mass., 1969-71. Served to capt. USMCR, 1942-46. Decorated Purple Heart. Mem. Mensa, Dickens Fellowship, Friends of York Minster, Buxton Family Assn. (past pres.), Am., Boston bar assns., S.A.R. (pres. D.C. Soc. 1957-58, nat trustee, 1958-59) Democrat. Episcopalian (warden 1971-74). Contbr. articles to law jours., Everyman's Ency. Home: Sturbridge, Mass. Died Sept. 23, 1977.

HOBLIT, HARRIS KEYS, banker; b. Springfield, Ill., Aug. 10, 1882; s. Alvin Bailey and Annie (Keys) H.; ed. pub. and high schs., Bloomington, Ill.; m. Florence Herrick, Apr. 7, 1905; children—Barbara Herrick, Harris K. Began with State Nat. Bank, Bloomington, 1899, cashier, 1915-20; pres. State Bank of Bloomington, 1920-21; v.p. First Nat. Bank, 1921-29; pres. First Nat. Bank & Trust Co. since 1930. Chmn. Liberty Loan drives, McLean Co., Ill., World War. Dir. and treas. Withers Pub. Library; pres. Bloomington Assn. Commerce, 1929-30. Republican. Mason. Clubs: Bloomington, Bloomington Country. Home: Bloomington, Ill. *

HOCHSCHILD, HAROLD K., mining co. exec.; b. N.Y.C., May 20, 1892; s. Berthold and Mathilde (Blumenthal) H.; student Yale, 1908-12, M.A. (hon.), 1962; LL.D., St. Lawrence U., 1963; L.H.D., Hamilton Coll., 1968; Litt.D., Princeton, 1968; m. Mary Marquand, Nov. 1941; 1 son, Adam. With Am. Metal Co., Ltd., N.Y.C., from 1913, chmn., 1947-57, hon. chmn., from 1957. Chmn., N.Y. State Commn. on Mus. Resources, 1959-62. N.Y. State Adirondack Study Commn., 1969-71. Hon. chmn. bd. African-Am. Inst.; trustee African-Am. Inst., Valeria Home, Correctional Assn. N.Y., Inst. Advanced Study, Princeton. Served to lt. col. AUS, World War II. Mem. Adirondack (pres.), N.Y. (trustee, mem. bd.) hist. assns. Clubs: Yale, Century (N.Y.C.). Author: Township 34. Home: New York, N.Y. Died Jan. 23, 1981.

HODES, BARNET, lawyer; b. La Salle, Ill., May 13, 1900; s. Simon and Ruth (Mansfield) H.; J.D., Northwestern U., 1921; m. Eleanor Cramer, Apr. 23, 1936; children—Scott, Kay Lynn. Began legal practice in Chgo., 1921; asst. corp. counsel City Chgo., 1923-37; pvt. practice, 1927-33; alderman 7th Ward, 1931-33; mem. Ill. Tax Commn., 1933-35; corp. counsel of Chgo., 1935-47. Pres. Nat. Inst. Municipal Law Officers, 1944; chmn. Chgo.'s Redevel. Commn., 1942-45; vice chmn. Chgo. Archtl. Landmarks Comm.; mem. U.S. Civilian Def. Vol. Participation Com.; sec.-treas. Triopian Found., Cassandra Found.; pres. Patriotic Found. Chgo.; impartial arbitrator Ladies Dress Industry. Active participant in numerous Chgo. city activities such as memls., fund drives, Christmas benefits, civilian def., planning commns.; also at state level on interfaith coms., and other civic activities Mem. bd. govs. Louis A. Weiss Meml. Hosp., Mus. Contemporary Art, Chgo. Served to lt. comdr. USNR, 1944-47. Decorated cross chevalier Legion of Honor (France); recipient Civic Merit award Jr. Assn. Commerce, Chgo., 1934; Chgo. Civil Liberties Com. award for distinguished service in def. of democracy, 1939; Decalogue Soc. of Lawyers award of merit for distinguished services, 1941. Mem. Am., Ill., Chgo. bar assns., Delta Sigma Rho, Nu Beta Epsilon (founder), and other assns. and orgns. Democrat. Mason, Elk. Clubs: Standard, Quadrangle, Arts (Chgo.). Author three books. Home: Chicago, Ill. Died Dec. 25, 1980.

HODGDON, ALBION REED, educator, botanist; b. Boothbay, Me., Nov. 1, 1909; s. Lewis Percival and Laura (Hodgdon) H.; B.S., U. N.H., 1930, M.S., 1932; Ph.D., Harvard, 1936; m. Audrey MacKown, Aug. 11, 1940; children—Alan Lewis, Anthony Jason, Ariel Josephine. Plant collecting trips for Harvard, Cuba, Va., Fla., Ky., 1936-40, ind. collecting, Mexico, 1938; head bot. dept. N.H. Agrl. Expt. Sta., 1941-67; curator U. N.H. Herbarium, 1941-76; head bot. dept. U. N.H., 1941-67, asso. prof., 1941-49, prof., 1949-76; ecol. work for Boston U. in N. Alaska, 1952. Fellow A.A.A.S.; mem. N.H. Acad. Sci. (sec. 1942-46, pres. 1952-53), New Eng. Bot. Club, Soc. Plant taxonomists, Soc. Study Evolution, Nature Conservancy (v.p. N.H. chpt. 1971-76), Sigma Xi. Author: Taxonomic Study of the Genus Lechea, 1938; Woody Plants of New Hampshire, 1958, Rubus Subgenus Eubatus (blackberries) in New England, 1966, Trees and Shrubs of Northern New England, 1968; (with R. Pike) Flora of Wolf Islands, N.B., 1963, Flora of Bird Islands on the Gulf of Maine, 1969. Editor: Taxonomic Jour. Rhodora, 1962-76. Home: Barrington, N.H. Died Dec. 31, 1976.

HODGDON, DANIEL RUSSELL, educator, lawyer; b. Winthrop, Me., Apr. 13, 1885; s. Daniel Russell and Mary Ann (Sawyer) H.; A.B., Bates, Lewiston, Me., 1908; B.A., U. of Me., 19; post-grad. work, Columbia, 1910-12, 1925-26, Teachers Coll., 1911-12; studied New York U., 1917, J.D., 1926, Ph.D., 1931; LL.D., Valporaiso U., 1920; LL.B., N.Y. Law Sch., 1925. Principal Corinna (Me.) Union Academy, 1906-08; v. prin. Me. State Normal Sch., 1908-10; head science dept. Rutgers Coll. Prep Sch., 1910-11, Passaic High Sch., 1911-13, N.J. State Normal Sch., 1913-18, State Summer Sch. for Teachers, N.J., 1913-18; dir. Newark Tech. Sch., and founder, and pres. Coll. of Engring., 1918-20; pres. Hahnemann Med. Coll. and Hosp., Chicago, 1920-22, Columbus Sch., New Rochelle, N.Y., since 1922. Lecturer New York U. Inst. Arts and Sciences, 1917-19, 1925-26; radio lecturer over Sta. WABC, 1927-29, Sta. WEAF, 1928-29; instr. in Sch. of Edn., N.Y. Univ., 1931-33; asst. prof. edn., Brooklyn Coll., 1934-40; lecturer St. Elizabeth Coll., 1935-36, also New York U., 1937-41; prof. of education, Seton Hall Coll. since 1937, dir. School of Edn., Urban Div., since 1940, dean of School of Education since 1945; assistant professor of edn., Hofstra Coll., Hempstead, N.Y., since 1940. Director of work for rehabilitation of wounded soldiers, Newark, 1919-20. Member New York State Teachers' Association, N.J. State Teachers' Assn., N.J. Chem. Soc., N.Y. State Bar Assn., Phi Delta Kappa, Pi Upsilon Rho, Pi Gamma Mu. Clubs: Kiwanis, Internat. Lions. Author: Hodgdon's General Science, 1918; Everyman's Science, 1918; Living and Dead Teaching, 1919; Hodgdon's Junior Science, 1920; Creative Science (6 vols.), 1939; Parties to Mortgages; Corpus Juris, 1925; also legal Aspects in the Control and Administration of School Property; Some Nutritional Factors in the Conservation of Child Life. Contributing editor Newark Star Eagle, Washington Post, Brooklyn Standard Union, Boston Post, Camden Courier, Philadelphia Record, New Haven Register. Contbr. to mags. Retired. Home: Santa Barbara, Calif. *

HODGES, J(AMES) ALLISON, neurologist; b. 1858; M.D., U. of Va., 1883. Practiced at Richmond, Va., since 1893; prof. clin. nervous and mental diseases, Med. Coll. of Va. Fellow A.M.A.; mem. Am. Coll. Physicians, Am. Psychiatric Assn., Med. Soc. of Va. *

HODGES, JOHN IREL HALL, librarian; b. Paducah, Ky., Aug. 2, 1911; s. William Herman and Nell Fuller (Hall) H.; B.A., U. Ky., 1931; M.A., Vanderbilt U., 1932; B.S. in L.S. (fellow Gen. Edn. Bd. 1934-35), U. Ill., 1935; m. Elizabeth Ann Johnson, June 28, 1941. Mem. library staff U. of South, Sewanee, Tenn., from 1933, asst. librarian, 1935-41, librarian, 1941-62, associate librarian, 1962-66, librarian emeritus, 1966-74; librarian Sewanee Mil. Acad., 1967-72. Served to lt. (s.g.) USNR, 1943-46. Fellow Gen. Edn. Bd., 1939-40. Mem. Southeastern, Tenn. library assns., Blue Key, Omicron Delta Kappa, Delta Tau Delta, Sigma Upsilon. Episcopalian. Democrat. Home: Sewanee, Tenn. Died May 6, 1974; buried University Cemetery, Sewanee.

HOENIG, SIDNEY B., educator; b. N.Y.C., Apr. 6, 1907; s. Joseph and Lena (Goldfarb) H.; B.S.S., Coll. City N.Y., 1927; rabbi, Yeshiva U., 1931, D.L.H., 1975; Ph.D., Dropsie Coll., 1934; m. Ann Whitehorn, Mar. 28, 1939; children—Hava, Joseph (dec.), Herschel, Fredda, Jacob. Ednl. dir. Young Israel Movement, 1939-41; prin. Hebrew Tchrs, Tng. Sch. Girls, 1941-45; Jewish chaplain Bklyn. House Detention, 1947-75; dir. adult edn. Yeshiva U., 1955-71, prof. Jewish history, 1934-76, dean Bernard Revel Grad. Sch., 1971-75, prof. emeritus, 1975-79; adj. prof. Talmudic Studies Dropsie U., 1977. Pres. Jewish book council Jewish Welfare Bd. Nat. Endowment Humanities fellow, 1975-76. Author: Passover Haggadah, 1949; The Great Sanhedrin, 1953; A Guide to the Prophets, 1957; Jewish Identity, 1965; Dr. Revel: Rabbinics and Research, 1968; Solomon Zeitlin Bibliography, 1971; Dr. Belkin: Jewish Law and Lore; also articles. Contbr. Ency. Brit., Jewish Quar. Rev., Interpreters Dictionary of the Bible, Ency. Judaica. Home: Rockaway Park, N.Y. Died Dec. 7, 1979.

HOEVEN, CHARLES BERNARD (HOO'VEN), congressman; b. Hospers, Ia., March 30, 1895; s. Gerrit and Lena (Weiland) H.; A.B., Ia. State U., 1920, LL.B., Coll. of Law, 1922; LL.D., Westmar Coll., 1956; m. Velma Ruth Pike, May 19, 1928; children—Pauline Ruth Marshall, Charles Pike. Admitted to Ia. bar, 1922; practiced in Alton; county atty., Sioux County, 1925-37. Mem. of Iowa State Senate, 1937-41, pres. pro tem, 1939-41; mem. 78th-87th Congresses, 8th Dist. Ia., member 88th Congress 6th District Iowa; dep. Rep. whip House of Representatives, from 1953; chmn. Rep. Conf. Ho. of Reps., 1957-63. Permanent chmn. Iowa Rep. State Conv., 1940; temp. and permanent chmn. Iowa Rep. State Judicial Conv., 1942. Served as sergt. Co. D., 350th Inf., 88th Div., and with Intelligence Sect., 1st Batt., A.E.F., World War I. Decorated Victory medal, with Defensive Sector and Meuse-Argonne bars. Past pres., Bd. of Edn., Alton Pub. Sch. Certificate of Accomplishment from State U. of Ia. Dir. Alton Savings Bank. Member Sioux County, 21st Jud., and Ia. State bar assns., Phi Alpha Delta. Mason. Presbyn. Club: Rotary of Alton (hon.). Home: Alton, Ia. Address: Washington, D.C. Died Nov. 9, 1980.

HOFFA, J. MILTON, banker; b. Hatfield, Pa., Dec. 18, 1908; s. David and Bertha (Mertin) H.; m. Nellie E. Wink, Oct. 2, 1935. With Columbia Av. Trust Co., 1926-29, Integrity Trust Co., 1929-40; with Girard Trust Bank, Phila., 1940-70, asst. v.p., 1950-51, comptroller, 1952-70; past v.p., treas. Girard Internat. Investment Corp., Girard Internat. Bank, The Girard Co.; past treas., dir. Finance Bldg. Corp., Girard Financial Corp.; past treas. Studley, Shupert & Co., Inc., Phila. Mem. Financial Execs. Inst., Bank Adminstrn. Inst., Am. Inst. Banking, Acad. Natural Scis. Lutheran. Home: Sarasota, Fla. Died Sept. 26, 1975; interred Sarasota (Fla.) Meml. Park.

HOFFER, JOE RALPH, social worker; b. N.Y.C., Mar. 22, 1907; s. Andrew and Mary Lottie (Hoffer) H.; B.S., Ohio State U., 1932, Ph.D., 1942; m. Mary B. Rusnak, Nov. 28, 1936. Activities dir. (Xenia) Ohio Soldiers and Sailors Orphan Home, 1933-35; dir. community orgn., N.Y.A. in Ohio, 1935-37; sec. community div. Council Social Agencies Phila., 1937-42; exec. officer U.S. Joint Com. on Evacuation, Washington, 1942-43; dir. capitol liaison office UNRRA, Nanking, China, 1945-46; exec. dir. Social Work Vocational Bur., N.Y.C., also cons. Am. Assn. Social Workers, 1946-48; exec. sec. Nat. Conf. Social Welfare, 1948-72; sec. gen. Internat. Conf. Social Work, 1948-66; vis. prof. Sch. Social Work, Ohio State U., 1972-73; dir. div. planning research and staff devel. Ohio Dept. Pub. Welfare, 1973-75, chief div. med. assistance, 1975-77. Served as seaman first class USN, 1943-45. Distinguished Centennial awardee Sch. Adminstrv. Sci. Ohio State U.; 1970; Distinguished Centennial awardee Ohio State U., 1970. Fellow Am. Sociol. Assn.; mem. Nat. Internat. confs. social work; Nat. Assn. Social Workers, Acad. Social Work (treas. 1969-71), Am. Pub. Welfare Assn., Am. Soc. Info. Sci. (chmn. Central Ohio chpt.), Delta Tau Delta, Sphinx, Bucket and Dipper, Varsity O Assn. Author: An Activity Analysis of the Duties of Recreation and Informal Education Leaders and Supervisors, 1942; Outline for Agency Self-Evaluation of Personnel Practices, 1947; A Community Plan for Youth, 1947. Mng. editor Social Welfare Forum, ann., 1948-71; Social Work Practice ann., 1962-71; A Manual for a Hand-Sort Punch Card System for Indexing Social Welfare Publs. Home: Columbus, Ohio. Died Sept. 28, 1977.

HOFFMAN, ELMER J., congressman; b. DuPage County, Ill., July 7, 1899; s. Joseph and Susan (Yackley) H.; student pub. schs., Wheaton, Ill.; m. Frances Elick, June 8, 1921; 1 dau., Joan Ann. Sheriff, DuPage Country, 1938-42, 46-50; pres. 2d Appellate Ct. Dist. Ill., 1950-52; treas. State of Ill., 1953-58; mem. 86th-87th Congresses, 14th Dist. Ill., mem. Rules Com. Pres., First Little League, 1951—. Chmn. DuPage County Republican Central Com., 1948-70; county treas., 1966-70; mem. DuPage County Bd., 1970-72. Served with C.A.C., U.S. Army, 1917-18; AEF in France. Mem. Ill. Sheriffs Assn. (past sec.-treas.), Ill. County Chmns. Assn. (v.p. 1950-52), Farm Bur. Ill., Nat. Assn. State Auditors, Comptrollers and Treasurers, Am. Legion, 40 and 8, VFW, Mystic Workers Moose, Elk, K.C. (4 deg.). Editor Ill. Sheriffs News, 1944-75. Home: Wheaton, Ill. Died June 25, 1976; interred St. Michael's Cemetery, Wheaton.

HOFFMAN, FRANCIS BURRALL, architect; b. New Orleans, Mar. 6, 1882; s. Francis Burall and Lucy (Shattuck) H.; A.B., Harvard, 1903; diploma Ecole Beaux Arts, Paris, 1907; m. Mary Virginia Kimball, May 19, 1927. Draftsman, Carrers & Hastings, N.Y.C., 1903-08; pvt. practice, N.Y., N.J., Mass., Washington, Ky., Cal., Fla., France, 1909—; asso. Harry Ingals, 1910-18; prin. works include Deering residence, Miami, Fla., 1912-17, Little Theatre, N.Y.C., 1910, apt. house, N.Y.C., 1928, World Bank, Paris, 1958. Recipient Gold medal San Francisco World's Fair. Mem. Archtl. League, Soc. Architects de Govt. Republican. Catholic. Club: Knickerbocker (N.Y.C.). Home: Hobe Sound, Fla. Died Nov. 27, 1980; buried St. Ann's Cemetery, Lenox, Mass.

HOFFMAN, LESLIE ARTHUR, banker; b. Phila., Dec. 7, 1909; s. William Albert and Mary Ellen (McKenna) H.; B.S.C., Temple U., 1931; hon. grad. Am. Inst. Banking, 1940, Stonier Grad. Sch. Banking, Rutgers U., 1945; m. Ruth Kathryn Cruikshank, June 7, 1933; 1 dau., Carolyn A. (Mrs. Carroll B. Ripley, Jr.). With Girard Trust Bank, Phila., 1931-79, v.p., 1955-79, sec., 1963-79; v.p., sec. Girard Internat. Bank; sec. The Girard Co., 1969-79, Girard Financial Corp., 1970-79; sec. Studely, Shupert Co., 1970-79, dir., 1973-79; sec. Girard Trust Bank Found. Past pres., trustee Westminster Found., 1968; past pres. Presbyn. Social Union Phila., 1970; vice chmn. Phila. Commn. for United Ministries in Higher Edn., 1968-79; past chmn. ann. fund, mem. exec. com. devel. council Temple U., 1965. Mem. Am. Soc. Corp. Secs. (v.p., adv. com. middle Atlantic group), Am. Inst. Banking (past pres. Phila.), Temple U. Sch. Bus. Adminstrn. Alumni Assn. (mgr., past pres.), Stonier Grad. Sch. Banking at Rutgers U. Alumni Assn. (past pres. Delaware Valley), Gen. Alumni Assn. Temple U. mem. bd.), U. Pa. Banking Club (past pres.), Phila. Bank Officers Club, Delta Sigma Pi. Clubs: Temple U. Downtown (past pres.); Wyncote Men's (past pres.). Home: Wyncote, Pa. Died Feb. 28, 1979.

HOFFMANN, J(OHN) WESLEY, educator; b. Maplegrove, Minn., Aug. 26, 1895; s. Jacob John and Katie Dorothy (Bitzer) H.; A.B., U. of Minn., 1918; A.M., U. of Chicago, 1922, Ph.D., 1937; student Univs. of Berlin and Bonn, 1926-27; m. Gertrude J. Glesen, June 25, 1927; children—Charles Wesley, Lois Kathryn. Instr. of history, John Fletcher College, Oskaloosa, Ia., 1919-20; asst. prof., Morningside Coll., Sioux City, Ia., 1922-24; instr., State U. of Iowa, 1925-26; instr. U. of Chicago, 1927-28; prof. and head, Morningside Coll., 1928-34; asst. prof., Mont. State Coll., Bozeman, 1934-35, 1936-37; asst. supervisor of rural research for Mont., Bozeman, 1935-36; prof. of history, U. of Tenn., 1937-65, head dept. of history, 1944-65; professor of history Maryville College, from 1965. Seaman, U.S. Navy, 1918. Conductor European tours. Member Am. Association Univ. Profs., Am. Hist. Assn., So. Hist. Assn. Methodist. Club: Civitan (Knoxville). Author: The Montana Citizen (with Rolland R. Renne), 1937. Contbr. articles in history publs. Home: Knoxville 17, Tenn. Deceased.

HOFLING, CHARLES KREIMER, psychiatrist, educator; b. Cin., Apr. 22, 1920; s. Charles A. and Edith (Kreimer) H.; student Ohio U., 1937-39; B.A., U. Cin., 1942, M.D., 1946; m. Madelyn Gibson Laymon, Dec. 24, 1945; children—Deborah Gayle, Charles Andrew, Karen Clark, Mark Laymon. Resident in psychiatry Cin. Gen. Hosp., 1947-48, 49-50, Menninger Clinic, 1948-49; fellow May Inst. Med. Research, 1947-48; instr. psychiatry Coll. Medicine U. Cin., 1950-55, asst. prof., 1955-64, asso. prof., 1964-68, vis. prof., 1968-80; lectr. Grad. Sch. Arts and Scis., 1957-68; prof. psychiatry, mem. grad. sch. faculty St. Louis U., 1968-80; cons. med. dept. Procter & Gamble Corp., 1967-69. Mem. bd. rev. Episcopal Chaplaincy, U. Cin., 1963-68; trustee Menninger Found., 1974-80. Served as capt. USAF, 1952-54. Fellow Am. Coll. Psychiatrists, Am. Coll. Psychoanalysts; mem. AMA, Am. Psychosomatic Soc., AAAS, Pan-Am. Med. Assn., Am. Psychiat. Assn., Assn. Applied Psychoanalysis, Internat. Shakespeare Assn., Soc. Sci. Study Religion, St. Louis Psychoanalytic Soc. (hon.), Phi Beta Kappa, Sigma Xi, Alpha Omega Alpha. Episcopalian. Clubs: Univ. (Cin. and St. Louis); Cin. Tennis; Cosmos (Washington); Playing Card Soc. (London). Author: (with Madeleine Leininger) Basic Psychiatric Concepts, 1961, 4th edit., 1979, Japanese edit., 1968, 78, Spanish edit., 1970, 77, French edit., 1976; Textbook of Psychiatry for Medical Practice, 1963, 3d edit., 1975, Spanish edit., 1965, 74; (with Paul Ornstein) Memos to Maury, 1968; (with Gene Usdin) Aging: the Process and the People, 1978; (with Jerry Lewis) The Family: Evaluation and Treatment, 1979; contbr. articles to profl. jours. Home: Saint Louis, Mo. Died May 17, 1980; buried Oak Hill Cemetery, St. Louis.

HOGAN, MICHAEL JOHN, ophthalmologist, educator; b. Kemmerer, Wyo., Aug. 26, 1907; s. Arthur John and Vilate (Douglas) H.; A.B., U. Utah, 1930; M.D., Cornell U., 1932; m. Vera Merrill, 1937; children—Judith Ann, Michael Timothy, Shelley. Intern Paterson (N.J.) Gen. Hosp., 1932-33; resident surgeon Bellevue Hosp., N.Y.C., 1933-35; pvt. practice medicine, San Diego, 1935-38; resident ophthalmology U. Calif., San Francisco, 1938-40, instr. dept. ophthalmology, 1941-43, asst. clin. prof., 1946-48, asso. clin. prof., 1948-51, clin. prof., 1951-57, prof., from 1957, prof. emeritus, to 1976, vice chmn. dept., 1951-59, chmn. dept. ophthalmology, from 1959. Bd. dirs. U. Calif. Eye Bank; dir. Francis I. Proctor Found., 1947-59; trustee Nat. Med. Found. for Eye Care, Nat. Com. Research in Ophthalmology and Blindness, Joint Com. on Eye Banks; mem. sci. adv. com. Nat. Council to Combat Blindness; v.p. Nat. Soc. Prevention of Blindness; pres. No. Calif. Soc. Prevention of Blindness; v.p. Internat. Council Ophthalmology, 1970; mem. grants adv. com. Seeing Eye, Inc., N.J., 1973. Diplomate, asso. examiner Am. Bd. Ophthalmology. Fellow A.C.S.; mem. Calif. Med. Assn., A.M.A., Assn. U. Profs. Ophthalmology, Am. Ophthalmol. Soc., Assn. Research Ophthalmology, Pacific Coast Oto-Ophthalmology Soc., Nat. Soc. Prevention Blindness, Am. Acad. Ophthalmology. Home: Mill Valley, Calif. Died Nov. 6, 1976.

HOGAN, SAMUEL J., pres. Nat. Marine Engrs. Beneficial Assn.; b. New Orleans, La., Mar. 27, 1883; s. Samuel P. and Isabel M. (Dugan) H.; ed. parochial schs., New Orleans; m. Lydia G. Tompson; m. 2d, Laura E. Wolters, June 9, 1924; children—Samuel J., Charles D., Robert L. Pres. Nat. Marine Engrs. Beneficial Assn. Mem. Joint Railway Labor Executives Com. on War Effort. Home: Washington. *

HOGBEN, LANCELOT, author, educator; b. Southsea, Hampshire, Eng., Dec. 9, 1895; s. Thomas and Margaret (Prescott) H.; ed. Trinity Coll. (Senior Scholar, Frank Smart prizeman); M.A., Cambridge U., Eng., D.Sc., London Univ.; LL.D. (hon.), Birmingham U.; fellow Royal Society; m. Enid Charles, 1918 (div. 1957); children—Ennyd Sylvia, Charles Adrian Michael, Clare Estelle, David Julian Lancelot; m. 2d. Sarah Jane Evans, 1957. Prof. emeritus medical statistics U. Birmingham, hon. sr. fellow linguistics, 1961; vice chancellor U. Guiyana, from 1963. Awarded Keith prize and gold medal Royal Soc. Edinburgh, 1936. Croonian Lecture, Royal Society, 1943. Author: Comparative Physiology of Internal Secretions, 1927; Genetic Principles in Medicine, 1931; Nature and Nurture, 1933; Mathematics for the Million, 1936; Science for the Citizen, 1938; From Cave Painting to Comic Strip, 1950; Chance and Choice, 1950; Statistical Theory, 1957; Mathematics in the Making, 1960; The Mother Tongue, 1964; also sci. articles in Proc. Royal Soc. Jour. Genetics, others. Address: Tregeriog, Llangollen, North Wales. Died Aug, 1975.

HOGE, JOHN HAMPTON, lawyer; b. Washington, Sept. 24, 1889; s. Emory Eaton and Georgie (Rust) H.; student U. Va., 1909, Balt. Law Sch., 1912; m. Mary Estelle McIntosh, Dec. 10, 1910; 1 son, J. Hampton. Admitted to Md. bar, 1914, Calif. bar, 1919, Supreme Ct. U.S., 1924; practice in Md., 1914-19, San Francisco, 1919-51; mem. firm Hoge, Fenton, Jones & Appel, San Jose, Monterey and San Luis Obispo, Calif., 1951-77. Mem. Am. Coll. Trial Lawyers, Delta Phi, Phi Alpha Delta. Episcopalian (past vestry mem. bldg. com). Club: Pebble Beach. Home: Monterey, Calif. Died Aug. 27, 1977.

HOGE, WILLIAM MORRIS (HOG), army ofcr.; b. Boonville, Mo., Jan. 13, 1894; s. William McGuffey and Annette (Fiery) H.; student Wentworth Mil. Acad., 1906-11; B.S., U.S. Mil. Acad., 1916; B.S. in Civil Engrng., Mass. Inst. Tech., 1922; grad. Command and Gen. Staff Sch., 1928; m. Nettie Fredendall, May 1, 1917; children—William Morris (U.S. Army), George F. (U.S. Army). Commd. 2d lt. Corps of Engrs., U.S. Army, 1916, and advanced through the grades to general, 1953; with first and seventh Engrs. in U.S., France and Luxembourg, 1916-19; Commanding general charge construction of Alaskan-Canadian Mil. Highway, 1942; commander Armored Force, 1942-43; comdg. general 5th and 6th Engr. Spl. Brigade, Nov. 1943-July 1944; comdg. gen. 16th Port, July-Oct. 1944; assigned 9th Armored Div., Oct. 1944-Mar. 1945; comdg. 4th Armored Div. Mar, 1945. Commanding gen. Ft. Belvoir, Va., 1946-48, Trieste, 1948-51, IX Corps, Korea, 1951, Fourth Army, Ft. Sam Houston, Tex., 1952-53, Seventh Army, 1953; comdr. in chief U.S. Army in Europe, 1953-55, retired; chmn. bd. dirs. Interlake Iron Corp., from 1957. Awarded Distinguished Service Cross and Silver Star, World War I; awarded oak leaf cluster to Silver Star, D.S.M. with two oak leaf clusters, Legion of Merit, Purple Heart, Bronze Star, Air Medal (U.S.); Chevalier Legion of Honor, Croix de Guerre with Palme (France); Companion of the Bath, D.S.O. (Brit.) War Cross (Czechoslovakia); l'Order de la Couronne (Belgium); Order of Fatherland, 1st Class (Russia). Mem. Am. Soc. Civil Engrs., Soc. Am. Mil. Engrs. Presbyn. Club: Army and Navy (Washington). Contbr. to Mil. Engr. Home: Cleveland, Ohio. Died Nov. 1, 1979.

HOGG, DAVID, ex-congressman; b. Jackson Co., Ind., Aug. 21, 1886; s. Nelson T. and Nancy E. (Waters) H.; A.B., Ind. U., 1909, LL.B., 1912; m. Mildred Sellers, of Angola, Ind., May 20, 1925. Admitted to Ind. bar, 1913, and began practice at Ft. Wayne; chmn. Rep. County Com., Allen Co., 1922-24; mem. firm of Hogg & Leonard (Judge George H. Leonard) since 1924; mem. 69th to 72d Congresses 1925-33), 12th. Ind. Dist. Baptist; teacher Bible class. Mason, Odd Fellow, K.P. Lecturer on Life as a Masterpiece; The Measure of a Man; Who Wrote the Bible. Home: Ft. Wayne, Ind. *

HOGREFE, PEARL, educator; b. Holt County, Mo., Sept. 17; d. John Henry and Rosanna (Van Gundy) Hogrefe; B.A., Southwestern Coll., Winfield, Kans., 1910; M.A., U. Kans., 1913; Ph.D., U. Chgo., 1927. Instr. English, Iowa State Tchrs. Coll., Cedar Falls, 1921-25, prof. 1925-28; prof., head dept. English, La. Poly. Inst., 1928-31; asso. prof. English, Iowa State U., 1931-44, prof., 1944-77. Fellow Folger Shakespeare Library, Washington, 1951, 61. Mem. Renaissance Soc. Am., MLA, Shakespeare Assn., AAUP, AAUW (Founders fellow 1952-53; chmn. fellowship Iowa 1941-46, pres. Iowa 1946-48, mem. nat. com. higher edn. 1954-60), Phi Kappa Phi, Delta Kappa Gamma. Author: (poems) Renewal, 1940; The Process of Creative Writing, rev. edit., 1963; The Sir Thomas More Circle, 1959; The Life and Times of Sir Thomas Elyot, Englishman, 1967; Tudor Women: Commoners and Queens, 1975; Women of Action in Tudor England, 1975; also articles. Co-editor: Interpreting Experience, 1935. Home: Ames, Iowa. Died Mar. 21, 1977.

HOHLEN, KARL SIEGFRIED JOHN (HO'LEN), surgeon; b. Germany, Apr. 24, 1886; s. John and Gesima (Bunting) H.; brought to United States, 1887; Northwestern U. Sch. of Pharmacy, 1901; M.D., Chicago Coll. Medicine and Surgery (Loyola U.), 1908; post-grad. work Neurol. Inst., Vienna, 1929; m. Mina E. Kauf, July 15, 1910 (dec. 1943); 1 son, Karl Siegfried; m. 2d, Lydia S. Hirschfeldt, Oct. 17, 1949. Externe Augustana Hosp., Chgo., 1906-08; interne Francis Willard Hospital, Chgo., 1908; practiced at Hastings 1909-12; moved to Lincoln, Neb., 1912; attending surgeon Bryan Memorial, Lincoln Gen. hosps., now emeritus; hon. mem. surg. staff St. Elizabeth Hosp.; member of staff Lincoln State Hospital. Medical examiner of Selective Draft Board, 1917-1940-45. Fellow American College Surgeons, International College of Surgeons; member Am. Med. Assn., Neb. State Med. Assn. (ex-pres.), Lancaster County Med. Soc. (ex-pres.), Phi Chi. Republican. Lutheran. Mason (Shriner). Clubs: University. Address: Lincoln, Neb. *

HOHMAN, ELMO PAUL, economist; b. Salem, Ill., Jan. 27, 1894; s. John Albert and Emma Pauline (Steffen) H.; student, Elmhurst (Ill.) Coll., 1911-12; A.B., U. of Ill., 1916, A.M., 1917; A.M., Harvard, 1920, Ph.D., 1925; m. Helen Vastine Fisher, Aug. 19, 1919; 1 dau., Elinor. Asst. and tutor, dept. econs., Harvard, 1920-23; instr. econs., Northwestern U., 1923-25, asst. prof., 1925-31, asso. prof., 1931-38, prof. since 1938; spl. referee, div. of unemployment compensation, Ill. Dept. of Labor, 1939-42; regional price exec., OPA, Chgo., 1942, dist. price exec. Chgo. Met. office, 1942-44; vice chmn., shipbldg. commn. Nat. War Labor Bd., 1944, war shipping panel, 1945; chmn. adv. com., Yale Fund for Seamen's Studies since 1946; observer, vis. scholar, Internat. Labor Office, 1928-29, 1936-37, 1946, 1958-59; nat. panel arbitrators Fed. Mediation and Conciliation Service; member maritime division ILO, Geneva. Student, 3d R.O.T.C., Camp Grant, Ill., 1918; commander 2d lt. infantry, 1918; asso. field dir., A.R.C. transport service, 1919. Member Am. Econ. Assn., Soc. of Midland Authors, Am. Assn. Univ. Profs., Industrial Relations Research Assn., Phi Beta Kappa, Alpha Pi Zeta, Delta Sigma Pi, Delta Phi. Winner of conf. medal for athletics and scholarship, U. of Ill., 1916. Club: Univ. (Evanston), City (Chicago, mem. bd. of arbitrators). Author: The Am. Whaleman, 1928; Seaman Ashore, 1952; History of American Merchant Seamen, 1956. Numerous articles, reports, decisions. Home: Evanston, Ill. Died Jan. 1, 1977.

HOIJER, HARRY, anthropologist; b. Chgo., Sept. 6, 1904; s. John Oscar and Agnes Sophia (Peterson) H.; A.B., U. Chgo., 1927, A.M., 1929, Ph.D., 1931; m. Dorothy Jared, June 7, 1927; children—Charlotte, Peter, Susan. Instr. anthropology U. Chgo., 1931-40; mem. faculty UCLA, 1940-70, prof. anthropology, 1940-70, prof. emeritus, 1970-76, chmn. dept. anthropology and sociology, 1948-51. Fellow Center Advanced Study in Behavioral Scis., 1959-60. Mem. Am. Anthrop. Assn. (v.p. 1949, Memoirs editor 1948-52, pres. Western states br. 1950, nat. pres. 1958), Linguistic Soc. Am. (pres. 1959), Sigma Xi. Author: Studies in the Athapaskan Languages, vol. 29, 1963; (with Ralph Beals) Introduction to Anthropology, 1965; (with Edward Sapir) the Phonology and Morphology of the Navaho Language, 1967. Editor: (with Leonard Bloomfield) Language History; Conference on the Interrelation of Language and Other Aspects of Culture, 1954; A Navajo Lexicon, 1974. Contbr. monographs, articles. Home: Los Angeles, Calif. Died Mar. 4, 1976.

HOISINGTON, ROBERT MORRIS, govt. ofcl.; b. Claflin, Kan., July 10, 1907; s. Morris Earl and Bess (Henderson) H.; B.A. in Bus., U. Colo., 1931; M.S. in Pub. Adminstrn., Syracuse U., 1931; m. Hazel Harriet Carton, Aug. 28, 1937; 1 dau., Donna Lee. Exec. sec. Cin. Regional Crime Commn., 1931-35; property mgr. TVA, 1936-44; mgmt. adviser FPHA, 1944-45; city mgr., Ashtabula, O., 1945-49, Springfield, O., 1950-54, Sioux City, Ia., 1954-58, Huntington, W.Va., 1958-63; pub. adminstrn. adviser AID, Vietnam, 1964-73. Address: Sun City, Ariz. Died May 16, 1977; interred Sun City, Ariz.

HOKE, ROY EDWARD, cons. psychologist; b. York, Pa., July 3, 1896; s. Edward John and Mary Margaret (Rhodes) H.; A.B., Franklin and Marshall Coll., 1916, A.M., 1917; student Theol. Sem., Lancaster, Pa., 1917-18; Ph.D., Johns Hopkins, 1922; m. Erma Ethel Ramsburg, Dec. 22, 1921; children—Elizabeth Ramsburg, Margaret Ann. Minister Presbyn. Ch., U.S., 1919-21; prof. psychology and edn., Birmingham Southern Coll., 1921-28, dean Sch. of Edn., also organizer, 1922, and dir. Summer Sch.; prof. psychology and religious edn., Emory and Henry Coll., 1928-44; prof. edn. and psychology Davidson Coll., professor psychology, 1946-48; professor psychology, dir. guidance King's Business Coll., from 1948. Served as sgt. in Medical Dept., U.S. Army, World War I; asst. to chaplain, Ft. Oglethorpe, Ga., served as chaplain, World War II. Mem. Am. Psychol. Assn., Am. Assn. Advancement Sci., Am. Philos. Assn., Phi Beta Kappa, Omicron Delta Kappa, Kappa Phi Kappa. Presbyterian. Mason, Rotarian. Author: The Improvement of Speed and Accuracy in Typewriting, 1922; (booklet) How You Can Have Success Unlimited, 1956. Lecturer on ednl., psychol., religious problems. Contbr. to various national periodicals. Writer of weekly newspaper column on psychology; condr. weekly program Psychology Today, Sta. WBTV. Founder of Psychological Service Center in Charlotte, N.C., 1946. Home: Charlotte, N.C. Died Nov. 3, 1975; buried Evergreen Cemetery, Charlotte.

HOLBROOK, CHRISTINE, editor; b. Dublin, Ireland, July 12, 1886; d. Peter and Anne (Mayne) White; student convents, Brussels, Belgium and Davenport, Ia.; m. Dr. Francis R. Holbrook, Apr. 12, 1917; children—Carmel, John, Patricia (Mrs. Frederic G. Burk, Jr.). Came to U.S., 1895, naturalized, 1903. Asso. editor home furnishings dept. Better Homes and Gardens mag., 1930-51; editor-in-chief Better Living Mag. since 1951. Worked with Am. Fund for French Wounded, Paris, France, World War I. Recipient Dorothy Dawe Am. Furniture Mart award for distinguished original reporting of home furnishings for 1948. Mem. Am. Inst. Design (asso.), Home Fashions League, Des Moines Art Center. Roman Catholic. Home: N.Y.C. *

HOLBROOK, LUTHER GARDNER, bus. exec.; b. Walpole, Mass., Aug. 25, 1912; s. Henry G. and Marian S. (Higgins) H.; B.S., Bowdoin Coll., 1934; M.B.A., Harvard, 1936; m. Ruth Price, Dec. 5, 1936; children—Deborah (Mrs. John Winthrop), Penelope (Mrs. Watson D. Reid), Sarah (Mrs. Abbot Cutler), Henry G. II. Employed comml. banking dept. Worcester County Trust Co. (Mass.), 1936-40; asst. dean Harvard Bus. Sch., 1940-48, asst. prof., 1944-48; asst. v.p. T. Mellon & Sons, Pitts., 1949-56, v.p. and gov., 1957-58, v.p., treas., gov., 1958-70; v.p. Richard K. Mellon & Sons, Pitts., 1971-79; dir. First Boston Corp., Gen. Reins. Corp., Gen. Reassurance Corp., Herbert Clough, Inc., Greenwich, Conn., Gen. Reins. Life Corp., North Star Reins. Corp. N.Y., Reins. Co. Australasia Ltd., Sydney, Australia. Trustee Richard King Mellon Found., Richard King Mellon Charitable Trusts, Pitts., Brookings Instrn., Washington, Wheaton Coll., Norton, Mass., Blue Hill (Maine) Meml. Hosp., Inc., Blue Hill Pub. Library, Eisenhower Exchange Fellowships. Clubs: Duquesne (Pitts.); Allegheny Country, (Sewickley, Pa.); Rolling Rock (Ligonier, Pa.); Links, Harvard (N.Y.C.); Kollegewidgwok Yacht, Blue Hill Country (Blue Hill). Home: Sewickley, Pa. Died Sept. 5, 1979.

HOLCOMB, STUART, baseball club exec.; b. Lincoln, Nebr., Sept. 11, 1910; s. Howard and Effie (Houghton) H.; B.A., Ohio State U., 1932, M.A., 1936; m. Mary Elizabeth Dority, Nov. 29, 1934; children—Stuart, Judith (Mrs. Ailbe Burke), Douglas, Bryan. Coach all sports Findlay (Ohio) Coll., 1932-36; coach, athletic dir. Muskingum Coll., New Concord, Ohio, 1936-41; football and track coach Washington and Jefferson U., Washington, Pa., 1942; end coach and basketball coach U.S. Mil. Acad., West Point, N.Y., 1944-46; football coach U. Miami, Oxfors, Ohio, 1942-43, Purdue U., 1946-55; athletic dir. Northwestern U., 1956-66; v.p., dir. pub. relations, also gen. mgr. Chgo. White Sox, 1966-75, ret., 1975. Served with AUS, 1944-45. Elected to Pa. Sports Hall of Fame, 1966. Presbyn. Mason (Shriner). Address: Laurel, Fla. Died Jan. 10, 1977.

HOLCOMBE, ARTHUR NORMAN, ret. educator; b. Winchester, Mass., Nov. 3, 1884; s. Franklin Gibbons and Inez Norman (Maynard) H.; A.B., Harvard, 1906, Ph.D., 1909; postgrad. U. Berlin, 1907-08, London Sch. Econs., 1909; L.H.D., Columbia, 1954; m. Carolyn Hawley Crossett, 1910 (dec. 1956); children—Waldo Hawley, Mary, Robert Crossett, Jane (Mrs. Richard Maynard); m. 2d, Hadassah Moore Leeds Parrot, 1964. Faculty, Harvard, 1909-55; chmn. Commn. to Study Orgn. of Peace, 1955-64. With U.S. Bur. Efficiency, 1917-18, U.S. Tel.&Tel. Adminstrn., 1919; chmn. appeals bd. WPB, 1942-45. Trustee Estate of Edwin Ginn (World Peace Found.), 1917—. Home: North Chatham MA. *

HOLDEN, PAUL EUGENE, educator; b. Indpls., Sept. 17, 1893; s. Charles Lorenzo and Laura Jane (Williams) H.: B.S. in M.E., Purdue U., 1915; m. Laura Ann Ohnstrand, Dec. 28, 1921; 1 dau., Sarah Ann. Spl. apprentice E. C. Atkins & Co., Indpls., 1915-17, production mgr. Canadian plant, Hamilton, Ont., 1919-20; asst. production mgr. Remington Typewriter Co., Ilion, N.Y., 1920-21; mgmt. engr. Library-Bureau Co., Ilion, 1921-22; asst. mgr. Dept. of Mfr., U.S. C. of C., Washington, 1922-26; prof. industrial management Grad. Sch. Bus. Stanford U., 1926-64, emeritus, 1964-76, founding dir. exec. program and Stanford-Sloan program; indsl. and econ. advisor Priorities Div., OPM, 1941; consultant Priorities Field Service, War Production Bd., 1942-43; asso. Booz, Allen & Hamilton, cons. mgmt. engrs., 1947-64; now senior mgmt. cons. Stanford Research Inst. Awarded Gantt Memorial gold medal, 1941. Mem. bd. of dirs. Stanford Convalescent Home. Trustee Castilleja (girls' boarding) Sch. Paul Eugene Holden chair established Stanford Grad. Sch. Bus. Mem. ASME, Acad. Mgmt., Soc. Advancement Mgmt., Tau Beta Pi, Alpha Tau Omega. Republican. Episcopalian. Clubs: Bohemian (San Francisco); Menlo Country (Red Wood City). Co-author: Top-Management Orgn. and Control, 1941; Indsl. Management, 1953. Contbr. and cons. editor various pubs. Home: Menlo Park, Calif. Died Apr. 9, 1976.

HOLLAND, GEORGE FRANKLIN, mfg. exec.; born Athol, Mass., Oct. 3, 1886; s. Charles J. and Charlotte E. (Heath) H.; student pub. schs. Athol; m. A. Mildred Hoyt, Sept. 10, 1907; children—Stanley L., Norman H., Francis E., Marion E., Mildred A., Milton A., Lois E. Apprentice Union Twist Drill Co., Athol, 1905-08, foreman, 1908-17, asst. supt., 1917-21, gen. mgr. Butterfield Div. Derby Line Vt. & Rock Island Que., Can., 1921-47, pres. of co., 1947-56, chairman bd., from 1956. Mem. Metal Cutting Tool Inst. Mason (32 deg., Shriner). Club: Bradenton (Fla.) Country. Home: Athol, Mass. Died Apr. 30, 1977.

HOLLAND, KENNETH G., ednl. adminstr.; b. Los Angeles, May 10, 1907; s. Charles Alfred and Cora Effie (Spring) H.; A.B., Occidental Coll., 1929, LL.D., 1946; M.A., Princeton, 1930; postgrad. U. Grenoble, summer 1931; Am. Field Service fellow U. Paris, 1931-32; LL.D., Middlebury Coll., 1951, Notre Dame U., 1960, Fairleigh Dickinson Coll., 1961, Brandeis U., 1968, U. S.C., 1972, N.Y. U., 1973; D.H.L., Dickinson Coll., 1958; m. Mary Frances Kimball, July 11, 1936; children—Kenneth Kimball, Susan Sawyer, Marcia Spring, Wendell Allen. Sec., Internat. Student Service, 1932-33; dir. edn. Civilian Conservation Corps, New Eng. area, 1933-35; asso. dir. Am. Youth Commn. Am. Council Edn., Washington, 1935-41; chief edn. sect. Office Inter-Am. Affairs, Washington, 1941-42, dir. div. edn., 1942-45; pres. Inter-Am. Edn. Found., Washington, 1945-46; asst. dir. Office Internat. Information and Cultural Affairs, Dept. State, Washington, 1946-48, dir. office ednl. exchange, 1949; pres. Inst. Internat. Edn., N.Y.C., 1950-73; pres. La Napoule Art Fedn., 1973-77. Tech. cons. U.S. del. UNESCO Conf., London, 1945, mem. del., Paris, 1946, 49, Mexico, 1947, Beirut, 1948, Florence, 1950; permanent U.S. rep. UNESCO, Paris, 1948-50; mem. Pres. Eisenhower's Com. on Latin Am. Affairs; mem. task force Pan Am. Union for Alliance for Progress; mem. Gov. Rockefeller mission to Latin Am. for Pres. Nixon, 1970; pres. Council Higher Edn. in Am. Republics, 1958-73. Chmn., Fedn. French Alliances in U.S. Bd. dirs. Swiss-Am Assn., French Inst., Germanistic Soc., Corning Glass Mus. Decorated officer French Legion of Honor; Brazilian Nat. Order Cruzeiro de Sul; comdr. Order San Carlos (Colombia); comdr. Order of Merit, Fed. Republic Germany; recipient Carnegie Corp. plaque, 1958, Georgetown U. Medal of Honor, 1964, Thomas F. Cunningham Inter-Am. award, 1968, U. Paris award, 1970. Mem. Council Fgn. Relations, Century Assn., (dir.), Germanistic Soc. (v.p.), French Inst. (chmn.), Fedn. French Alliances, Phi Beta Kappa. Clubs: Cosmos (Washington); Bronxville Field, Century. Author: Youth in European Labor Camps, 1938; Youth in the CCC, 1940. Contbr. articles to profl. jours., chpts. to books. Address: Bronxville, N.Y. Died Dec. 9, 1977.

HOLLAND, MAURICE, research adviser; b. Wickford, R.I., Apr. 4, 1891; s. John F. and Elizabeth E. H.; ed. Lowell Inst. of Mass. Inst. Tech., class 1916; special study Harvard, U. of Pa., Tufts Coll., Columbia; m. Marion Ryan; 1 son, Maurice. General engring. asst. constrn. G.T. R.R., 1912-13; asst. to chief engr. Boston Transit Commn., 1913-14; asst. to chief of installation div., Edison Electric Illuminating Co., Boston, 1914-17; cons. aeronautical mech. engr., Engring. Div. Air Service, U.S. Army, 1918-21; organizer and supervisor of indsl. engring. br., Engring. Div. Air Service, 1921-23; dir. div. of engring. and industrial research, National Research Council, 1923-42; consultant on research mgmt. to indsl. companies, research foundations, universities and fgn. govts. Dir. Orgn. European Econ Co-operation, Mission 82, U.S. and Can., mem. 84, Germany, France, Italy, Mut. Security Agy., 1951-52. Served as lt. pilot Air Service, U.S. Army (detached service with Imperial Royal Flying Corps, 1917-18), 1917-20. Mem. com. on comml. aviation, Am. Engring. Council, 1925-26; mem. adv. com. Daniel Guggenheim Sch. Aeros., N.Y. U.; mem. gen. com. Nat. Bd. of Review of Motion Pictures; asst. sec. bd. trustees, Nat. Research Endowment, 1925-27; organizer and exec. sec. Am. Com. World Engring. Congress, Tokyo, Japan, 1929; dir. science advisory com., Chicago Century of Progress Exposition, 1933; liaison officer Science Advisory Board, with Dept. of Commerce, 1933-35; asso. producer and tech. adviser Nobel Science Motion Pictures; organizer and executive officer, Industrial Research Inst., 1938; organizer and lecturer graduate course in Research Laboratory Management, N.Y. Univ.; mem. science advisory com., New York World's Fair, 1939; organizer and dir. Nat. Research Council, Tour of Industrial Exploration of South America, including Colombia, Peru, Chile, Argentina and Brazil, 1941; mem. research adv. group Nat. Assn. Mfrs. Del. 1st World Power Conference, London, 1924; 8d Conf., Washington, 1936. Prague Internat. Management Congress, 1924; 3d Pan-Pacific Science Congress, Tokyo, 1926, Fellow A.A.A.S., N.Y. Acad. Scis., Inst. Aero. Scis. (asso.); mem. Am. Inst. Cons. Engrs., Masaryk Acad. (Praha), Am. Inst. E.E. Exec. dir., Scandinavian Research and Industry Tour Norway, Denmark, Sweden, 1946. Recipient silver medal Royal Acad. Engring. Scis., Stockholm, 1946; hon. fellow Industrial Research Institute, 1946, recipient founders award 1955. Clubs: Engineers (New York); Pelham Country. Author: Industrial Transition of Japan, 1927; Industrial Explorers (with H. F. Pringle), 1929; Profitable Practice in Industrial Research (with others), 1932; Architects of Aviation, 1951; Managements Role in Research, 1956. Contributor to magazines and radio broadcasts. Home: Pelham, N.Y. Died Mar. 22, 1981.

HOLLAND, RAY(MOND) P(RUNTY), editor; b. Atchison, Kan., Aug. 20, 1884; s. Daniel Joseph and Mary Elizabeth (Prunty) H.; ed. pub. schs., Atchison; m. Ruth Mary Perkins, Oct. 16, 1907; children—Robert

Perkins, Raymond Prunty, Daniel John. Began writing for sportsmen's mags., 1903, and has since contributed hundreds of stories and articles; wrote shooting stories under name of "Bob White"; joined staff of U.S. Bureau of Biol. Survey, 1914, active in promotion of federal legislation for protection of migratory birds and in case of State of Mo. vs. Ray P. Holland, v.p. Am. Game Protective Assn., 1919, now pres., edited publs. of the assn.; editor Field and Stream, Mar. 1924-Nov. 1941. Sec.-treas. Internat. Assn. of Game, Fish and Conservation Commrs., 1921-46. Republican. Conglist. Mason. Club: Camp Fire of America. Author several books later ones: The Master, 1946; But Listen, Warden!, 1946; Bird Dogs, 1947; Scattergunning, 1951; Seven Grand Gun Dogs, 1961. Home: Quechee, Vt.*

HOLLAND, YALE CHENOWETH, lawyer; b. New Haven, July 6, 1885; s. Clifton Earl and Sarah Lovina (Chenoweth) H.; B.Sc., LL.B., U. Neb., 1911; m. Gertrude Capser, May 20, 1920. Admitted to Neb. bar, 1911; gen. practice law with Kennedy, Holland, Delacy & Svoboda, Omaha, 1911-56; gen. counsel Cudahy Packing Co.; div. counsel Safeway Stores, Inc. Served as 1st lt. F.A., U.S. Army, 1918. Mem. Am., Omaha (pres. 1940) bar assns., Order of Coif, Sigma Chi, Phi Delta Phi. Club: Omaha Country (pres. 1946-48). Home: Omaha, Neb. *

HOLLEY, J(AMES) ANDREW, coll. dean; b. Clay, Miss., Dec. 29, 1898; s. Andrew and Pamella (Hale) H.; A.B., U. Colo., 1923; M.A., Columbia, 1928, Ed.D., 1947; m. Moreta Burnett, June 14, 1924 (died Mar. 2, 1936); children—William Andrew, Wanda Jean (Mrs. Roy Fish), Helen Jane (Mrs. Tom LeBar); married second to Edith Johnson, June 5, 1937. Tchr. rural schs., Okla., 1916-17, prin. village schs., 1919-21; supt. schs., Luther, Okla., 1923-26; asst. high sch. insp., Okla., 1926-29; chief high sch. insp. Okla. State Dept. Edn., 1929-32, 33-36, dir. curriculum, 1936-39; spl. summer lectr. and instr. Central State Coll., Edmond, Okla., 1926, Okla. A. and M. Coll., 1930, U. Okla., 1931-32, 34-36; dep. adminstr. Nat. Youth Adminstrn., 1939-40; prof., head dept. bus. edn. Okla. State U., 1940-51, dean of College of Education, dir. summer sessions, 1951-64, prof., dean emeritus, 1964; associate in educational adminstrn. (Columbia), 1946-47. Formerly chmn. child edn. sect. Nat. Safety Congress; active N. Central Assn. Colls. and Secondary Schs. since 1929, chmn. Okla. com., 1929-32, 33-39, chmn. com. on secondary schs., 1936-38; chmn. Okla. Com. Tchr. Edn. and Certification, 1953-55; mem. Nat. Commn. Accrediting Bus. Schs., 1952-64; asso. dir. Nat. Council Accreditation Teacher Education, from 1964-70; ednl. cons., 1970-76. Served with United States Navy, 1917-18; ret. commander in Res. Named hon. mem. N. Central Assn. of Colls. and Secondary Schs., 1963; recipient service award Okla. State U., 1964, recognition award, 1967, cert. of internat. service, 1969. Fellow A.A.A.S.; mem. Nat. Assn. Secondary Sch. Prins., Nat. Edn. Assn., Okla. Edn. Assn., Delta Sigma Rho, Phi Delta Kappa, Phi Kappa Phi, Delta Pi Epsilon, Sigma Alpha Epsilon, Tawse. Democrat. Baptist. Rotarian. Author articles; co-author books and surveys. Home: Stillwater, Okla. Died Sept. 3, 1976; buried Fairlawn Cemetery, Stillwater.

HOLLIFIELD, GUY FOSTER, physician, educator; b. Courtland, Va., June 15, 1922; s. June Foster and Nell (Graham) H.; B.S., Va. Mil. Inst., 1943; M.D., U. Va., 1950; m. Katherine Crompton Elmer, Dec. 28, 1946 (div.); children—Guy Foster, William Hart, James Evans. Fellow in medicine U. Minn., 1951-53; B. Armistead Shepherd Meml. fellow med. research U. Va. Med. Sch., 1953-54, instr. medicine, 1954-58, asst. prof. medicine, 1958-60, asso. prof. medicine, 1960-66; prof. medicine Northwestern U. Med. Sch., 1966-75; chmn. dept. medicine Chgo. Wesley Meml. Hosp., Northwestern U. Med. Center, 1966-73, sr. attending physician, 1966-75; dir. medicine Appalachian Regional Hosp., Beckley, W.Va., 1973-79; prof. medicine Marshall U. Sch. Medicine, Huntington, W.Va., also asso. dean for clin. affairs Beckley campus. Served with USAAF, 1943-45. Recipient John Horsley Meml. prize for research, 1962. Fellow A.C.P., Am. Pub. Health Assn.; mem. Am., So. socs. clin. investigation, Central Soc. Clin. Research, Inst. Medicine Chgo., Am. Fedn. Clin. Research, Endocrine Soc., Sigma Xi. Contbr. publs. in endocrinology and metabolic disorders. Died July 14, 1979.

HOLLINGSHEAD, AUGUST DE BELMONT, educator; b. Lyman, Wyo., Apr. 15, 1907; s. William Thomas and Daisy E. (Rollins) H.; A.B., U. Calif., 1931, M.A., 1933; Ph.D., U. Nebr., 1935; m. Carol E. Dempsey, Nov. 4, 1931; children—Anne Marie, Ellen May. Instr. sociology U. Iowa, 1935, U. Ala., 1935-36; instr. sociology Ind. U., 1936-39, asst. prof., 1939-41, asso. prof., 1946-47; Social Sci. Research Council postdoctoral fellow U. Chgo., 1941-42, vis. prof., 1948; vis. prof. U. So. Calif., 1946, 51; asso. prof. sociology Yale, 1947-52, prof., 1952-75, chmn. dept. sociology, 1959-65, William Graham Summer prof., 1963-75, emeritus, 1975-80; vis. prof. Psychiat. Inst., U. London, 1957-58; sr. Fulbright scholar U.K., 1957-58; cons. surgeon gen. USPHS, 1960-69; temporary adviser WHO, Geneva, Switzerland, 1968; mental health cons. U. P.R., 1956-64; research cons. Planned Parenthood, 1956; tech. cons. Nat. Assn. Mental Health, 1969-80. Mem. bd. Nat. Assn. Retarded Children; mem. Midwestern region Nat. Resources Planning Bd., 1937-41. Served to 1st lt. USAAF, 1943-45. Mem. Am. Assn. U. Profs. (pres. Yale 1955-57), Am. (chmn. publs. com. 1953-55, mem. exec. council 1963-66, v.p. 1957), Eastern (exec. com. 1952-55, v.p. 1957, pres. 1961) sociol. socs., Internat. Inst. Sociology, Am. Psychopathol. Assn., Sigma Xi, Alpha Kappa Delta (pres. 1947-50). Republican. Episcopalian. Author: Principles of Human Ecology, 1938; Elmtown's Youth, 1949; sr. author: Social Class and Mental Illness, 1958; Principles of Sociology, 1969; co-author: Trapped: Families and Schizophrenia, 1965; Sickness and Society, 1968; Elmtown's Youth and Elmtown Revisited, 1975. Contbr. sci. jours. Home: Woodbridge, Conn. Died Oct. 28, 1980; buried Christ Episcopal Ch. Cemetery, Bethany, Conn.

HOLLIS, R(OSSIE) THOMPSON (MRS. JAMES G. HOLLIS), church official; b. Elbert Co., Ga., Feb. 10, 1886; d. Columbus T. and Mathilda (Wall) Thompson; B.A., Paine Coll., 1910; m. J. G. Hollis, Dec. 21, 1920. Teacher Paine Coll., 1910-20, Langston U., 1920-22, pub. schs., Nashville, 1922-35; dean women, Texas Coll., 1940-42; pres. Woman's Missionary Council, Colored Methodist Episcopal Ch., Jackson, Tenn. since 1939; elected one of 3 vice presidents, Gen. Dept. of Church Women, Nat. Council Chs. of Christ U.S.A. Mem. Y.W.C.A. Mem. Mothers of the World, Nat. Assn. Advancement of Colored People. Club: Eastside Culture (Spencer). Author articles ch. newspapers. Home: Spencer, Okla. *

HOLLISTER, JOHN BAKER, former congressman, lawyer; b. Cin., Nov. 7, 1890; s. Howard Clark and Alice (Keys) H.; A.B., Yale, 1911; studies U. Munich, 1911-12; LL.B., Harvard, 1915; LL.D., U. Cin., 1960; m. Ellen West Rollins, Aug. 15, 1917 (dec. Mar. 1960); children—Anne (Mrs. Anne H. Stevenson), Alice (Mrs. Daniel Scott), John Baker; m. 2d, Florence B. Wigglesworth. Partner Taft, Stettinius & Hollister, 1925-55, 57-67, sr. partner, 1941-67, counsel, 1967-79; dir. several corps.; mem. U.S. Congress, 1931-36; exec. dir. Hoover Commn., 1953; cons. Secretary State 1954-55; dir. ICA, 1955-57; gov. nat. ARC, 1947-51; chmn. Mission to Netherlands, UNNRA, 1945. Del. to Rep. Nat. Conv., 1940, 44, 48, 52. Served as capt. 46th Arty., C.A.C., 1917-19; with Am. Relief in Poland, 1919, and in charge relief in Lithuania. Mem. Cin. Bd. Edn., 1921-29; trustee Cin. Art Mus. Mem. Am., Ohio, Cin. bar assns., Psi Upsilon. Republican. Presbyterian. Clubs: Queen City, Cin. Country (Cin.); Metropolitan (Washington). Home: Cincinnati, Ohio. Died Jan. 4, 1979.

HOLLOWAY, ASHER EARL, utilities exec.; b. Colfax, Ind., Oct. 19, 1886; s. Jefferson Park and Mary Elizabeth (Dukes) H.; E.E., Purdue, 1909; m. Violet Jessop, Sept. 25, 1912; children—Joseph Parker, Margaret. Apprentice Westinghouse Electric & Mfg. Co., Pitts., 1909-10; salesman, meter tester San Diego (Cal.) Gas & Electric Co., 1910-12, new bus. dept., 1912-15, supt. new bus., 1915-30, v.p., 1930-49, pres., 1949-52, dir. since 1912. Mem. So. Cal. Econ. Council, Pacific Coast Elec. Assn., Pacific Coast Gas Assn. (past pres.), San Diego C. of C. (past pres.), Kappa Sigma. Republican. Mason. Club: Rotary (San Diego, Cal.). Home: Coronado. *

HOLLOWAY, EMORY (HOL'LO-WA), prof. English; b. Marshall, Mo., Mar. 16, 1885; s. Rufus Austin and Ella (Dent) H.; A.B., Hendrix Coll., 1906, LL.D., 1935; A.M., U. of Tex., 1912; studied Columbia U.; m. Ella Brooks Harris, Sept. 7, 1915; children—Robert Howard B., Rita (Tybout). Teacher high sch., Amity, Ark., 1906-08; prof. English, Scarritt-Morrisville Coll., Morrisville, Mo., 1910-11; instr. English, U. of Tex., 1912-13; instr. English, 1914-16, asst. prof., 1916-18, prof., 1919-37, Adelphi Coll., Garden City, N.Y.; asso. prof. English, Queens Coll., 1937-39, prof. since 1939, chmn. of English dept., 1937-41. Transport sec. Y.M.C.A., to France, 1918; ednl. and hut work, and mem. faculty (Army Educational Corps) A.E.F. Univ., Beaune, France, 1918-19. Armed Services rep., Queens College, 1943-44; director Army Spl. Training Program Unit, Queens Coll., 1943-44. Chmn. Walt Whitman Memorial Com., 1925; lecturer Workers' U., 1925-26. Mem. Modern Lang. Assn., Soc. of Am. Historians (founder); hon. mem. Scholarship Society of South. Author: Whitman—An Interpretation in Narrative, 1926 (received Pulitzer prize for biography); Janice in Tomorrow-Land (a child's Utopia), 1936. Contbr. encyclopedias; editor several compilations including: Leaves of Grass (Everyman edit.), 1947. Associate editor Am. Literature, 1940-43, member advisory board, 1943-48. Home: Brooklyn, N.Y.; (summer) Meddybemps, Me. *

HOLLOWAY, WILLIAM WARFIELD, chmn. bd. Wheeling Steel Corp.; b. Wheeling, W.Va., June 22, 1886; s. Jacob James and Mary Patterson (Du Bois) H.; student St. Paul's Sch., Concord, N.H., 1898-1904, Sheffield Scientific Sch. (Yale), 1904-07; m. Margaret Louise Glass, Apr. 26, 1911; children—William Warfield, James Alexander, Sallie Glass. Successively with La Belle Iron Works, Wheeling Corrugating Co. and Whitaker Glessner Co., 1908-20; with Wheeling Steel Corp. since 1920, becoming pres., 1930; now chmn. bd.; chmn. Bridgeport Nat. Bank; dir. Fostoria Glass Co., Wheeling Dollar Savs. & Trust Co. Served as 1st lt., later capt. Ordnance Dept., U.S. Army, World War I. Dir. Am. Iron and Steel Institute. Mem. Ohio Soc. of N.Y. City, Newcomen Soc. (England), Book and Snake Society, (Yale). Republican. Episcopalian. Clubs: Ft. Henry (Wheeling); Yale, Ohio Soc., Banker's, Nat. Republican (New York); Duquesne (Pittsburgh); Wheeling Country; Pike Run (Jones Mills, Pa.); Rolling Rock (Ligonier, Pa.). Home: Bethany Pike. Wheeling. *

HOLLOWOOD, ALBERT BERNARD, journalist; b. Staffordshire, Eng., June 3, 1910; s. Albert and Sarah Elizabeth (Robinson) H.; diploma edn., St. Paul's Coll., Cheltenham, 1931; B.Sc. in Econs., London, U., 1935, M.Sc. in Econs., 1940; M.A. (hon.), Keel, 1968; m. Marjorie Duncan Lawrie, July 22, 1938; children—Jane (Mrs. Jeremy Barlow), Susan (Mrs. Angus Swanson), Duncan. Lectr. econs. Sch. Commerce, Stoke on Trent, also Loughborough Coll., 1932-43; lectr. to His Majesty's forces, 1939-44; mem. staff The Economist, 1944-45; research officer Council Indsl. Design, 1946-47; editor Pottery and Glass, 1944-50; pocket cartoonist Sunday Times, 1957-60, Sunday Telegraph, 1961-68, Times, from 1970; mem. Punch Table, from 1945; editor Punch, 1957-68, broadcaster, from 1939. Mem. ct. govs. London Sch. Econs. Author: Direct Economics, 1943; Money is No Expense, 1946; An Innocent at Large, 1947; Britain Inside Out, 1948; Scowle and Other Papers, 1948; Poor Little Rich World, 1948; Pottery and Glass, 1949; The Hawksmoor Scandals, 1949: Cornish Engineers, 1951; The Story of Morro Velho, 1954; Tory Story, 1964; Pont, 1969; Cricket on the Brain, 1970; Tales of Tommy Barr, 1970. Author numerous papers on econs. Home: Surrey, England. Died Mar. 28, 1981.

HOLM, WILTON ROBERT, former assn. exec.; b. Rock Island, Ill., July 7, 1914; s. Robert Axel and Daisy Ellen (Anderson) H.; B.S., St. Ambrose Coll., 1942; postgrad. U. Iowa, 1942-43; m. Helen Louise Richtman, Apr. 25, 1942; children—Victoria Helen, Cynthia Louise. Instr. physics U. Iowa, 1942-43; dir. research Cinecolor Corp., Burbank, Calif., 1946-52; motion picture specialist, tech. adminstr. E.I. duPont de Nemours & Co., Parlin, N.J., and Los Angeles, 1952-68; exec. dir. Motion Picture and TV Research Center, Los Angeles, 1968-77; v.p. Assn. Motion Picture and TV Producers, Inc., Los Angeles, 1970-77; lectr. U. Wis., U. Calif. at Los Angeles, U. So. Calif., N.Y.U., others. Served with USNR, Recipient Commendation medal for sci. achievements U.S. Navy, 1946. Fellow Brit. Kinematograph, Sound and TV Soc. (hon.), Soc. Motion Picture and TV Engrs. (pres. 1971-72, Gold Medal award 1973); mem. Acad. Motion Picture Arts and Scis., Acad. TV Arts and Scis., Am. Soc. Cinematographers, Soc. Photog. Scientists and Engrs., Optical Soc. Am., Am. Phys. Soc., Soc. Photo-Optical Instrumentation Engrs. Contbr. articles to profl. jours. Home: Rock Island, Ill. Died Oct. 18, 1979.

HOLMAN, CURRIER J., meat processing exec.; b. Sioux City, Iowa, 1911; ed. U. Notre Dame. Chmn., Iowa Beef Processors, Inc., Dakota City, Nebr. Home: Sioux City, Iowa. Died Feb. 16, 1977.

HOLMAN, EMILE FREDERIC, surgeon; b. Moberly, Mo., Aug. 12, 1890; s. Rev. Frank Henry and Caroline (Fieth) H.; A.B., Stanford, 1911; Rhodes scholar from Cal. at Oxford U., 1914-17, B.A., 1916, M.A., 1919; M.D., Johns Hopkins, 1918; m. Ann Peril Purdy (M.D.), Sept, 17, 1921; children—Halsted Reid, Shaun Purdy, David Purdy. Instr. in surgery, Johns Hopkins, 1920-23; teaching fellow, Harvard, 1923-24; asst. prof. surgery, Western Reserve, 1924-25; prof. surgery, Stanford, 1926-55; emeritus, 1955-77; exec. head dept. surgery, Lane and Stanford hosps., 1926-56, emeritus, 1956-77; cons. surgery several orgns.; named lectr. in surgery many universities, U.S. and fgn., 1927-77; sometime visiting prof. surgery several schs. Mem. Med. Corps., U.S. Naval Res., 1941-45. Awarded Medaille de Rol Albert, 1918; Samuel D. Gross prize, Phila. Acad. Surg., 1930, for original research in aneurisms; Yandell Medal in surgery, 1953; Matas Medal in vascular surgery, 1954; Perpetual Student, St. Bartholomews Hosp., London, 1951. Diplomate Am. Bd. Surgery, Am. Bd. Thoracic Surgery. Fellow A.C.S. (v.p. 1937); mem. sometime officer nat., state and local profl. socs., sci. orgns. Sigma Xi, Phi Beta Kappa, Alpha Omega Alpha, Phi Delta Kappa, Nu Sigma Nu. Methodist, Author: Arteriorenous Aneurysm, 1937; New Concepts in Surgery of the Vascular System, 1955. Contbr. numerous papers on blood vessels, lungs, and stomach. Home: San Francisco, Cal. Died Mar. 1977.

HOLMAN, FRANK E., lawyer; b. Sandy City, Utah Jan. 7, 1886; s. Jonathan E. and Abba (Rumel) H.; A.B., U. of Utah, 1908; Rhodes scholar, Oxford U., Eng. 1908-11, B.A., in Jurisprudence 1910, M.A., 1914 LL.D., U. Utah, 1958; S.J.D. (hon.), Suffork U., Boston Mass., 1965; m. Carrol E. Edwards, Dec. 27, 1913 (deceased, May 20th, 1956); children—Francis E. Colin B., William M., James A.; m. 2d, Mrs. Susan

Pitcher Johnson, June 16, 1962. Admitted Wash. bar, 1911, practicing at Seattle; admitted to the Utah bar, 1912; instructer in law, University of Utah, 1912-13, dean of law, 1913-15; practiced at Salt Lake City, 1915-24, at Seattle since 1924; admitted to practice in U.S. courts and in courts of various Western States, United States Supreme Court, 1921; counsel for law firm Holman, Marion, Perkins, Coie & Stone. Chairman of Utah State Board of Bar Examiners, Com. Revision of Washington Corporation Laws. Chairman of Alien Enemy Hearing board for Western Dist of Washington; member national panel for Alien Enemy Examiners; member Seattle Armed Forces Adv. Com.; director Pacific National Bank of Seattle; member adv. bd. Seattle Childrens Orthopedic Hospital; trustee Sch. Pub. Law, Washington. Recipient Vets. Fgn. Wars Certificate of Merit, 1950, Gold Medal, 1953; Chevalier Legion of Honor (France); Am. Freedom Award, 1951, 52; Am. Bar Assn. Gold Medal Award, 1953; Seattle Bar Assn. Distinguished Service Citation, 1953; William Volker Distinguished Service Award, 1954; Lawyer's medal Independent Bar Assn. N.Y., 1965; named Seattle's 1st citizen, 1953. Fellow Am. Bar Found.; mem. Bar of Paris, France (hon.), Am. Bar Assn. (pres. 1948-49; mem. ho. dels. 1942—; mem. adv. bd. A.B.A. Jour.; mem. Am. Bar Com. for Peace and Law, through the United Nations, 1946-47), Wash. State Bar Assn. (president 1945; member committee on revision of Washington corporation laws), Utah Bar Assn. (v.p. 1923), Seattle Bar Assn. (pres. 1941), D.C. Bar Assn. (hon.), Canadian Bar Assn., Order of the Coif, Am. Acad. Pub. Affairs, Am. Soc. Internat. Law, Federal Bar Association, Phi Delta Theta, Phi Delta Phi. Conglist. Clubs: Nat. Lawyers (hon. mem.) (Washington); Monday, Rainier (Seattle); life mem. Oxford Union (Eng.). Author: Story of the Bricker Amendment, 1954; The Problems of The World Court and the Connally Reservation, 1960; Life and Career of a Western Lawyer, 1963; Selected Speeches and Articles, 1964; also articles and pamphlets. Frank E. Holman Law Student Grant established at U. Wash. Law Sch., 1961. Home: Seattle. *

HOLMAN, ROBERT WILLIAM, ret. steel co. exec.; b. Chgo., July 24, 1911; s. William G. and Olga (Kalies) H.; B.S., Purdue U., 1935; m. R. Janice Harlan, Oct. 30, 1938; children—Linda (Mrs. Phillip K. Hargesheimer), Gerald R. With U.S. Steel Corp., 1929-76, asst. gen. mgr. engring. services, 1966-67, asst. gen. mgr. design and engring. services, Pitts., 1967-69, gen. mgr. design and engring. services, 1969-76. Instl. officer Explorer Post 944 Boy Scouts Am., 1970-75. Registered profl. engr., Ind., Ala. Mem. Assn. Iron and Steel Engrs. (pres. 1970), Am. Iron and Steel Inst., I.E.E.E., S.R. Presbyn. (elder). Mason (Shriner). Club: University (Pitts.). Patentee in field. Home: Pittsburgh, Pa. Died Sept. 22, 1976; interred Mt. Lebanon Cemetery, Pittsburgh.

HOLMES, ALLAN, newspaper pub.; b. Georgetown, Ont., Sept. 20, 1882; s. Allan and Jane (Crawford) H.; student U. Toronto, 1900-01; m. Lillian Saunders. Feb. 21, 1914. Publisher Galt Evening Reporter since 1922; pres., dir. Western Publs. Ltd., publishing Moose Jaw (Sask.) Times Herald and Prince Albert (Sask.) Daily Herald; dir. The Thomson Newspapers Ltd. Past pres. Canadian Daily Newspapers Assn. Home: Gaet Ont. Can. *

HOLMES, EUGENE CLAY, educator; b. Paterson, N.J., Oct. 12, 1905; s. Samuel Eugene and Arabelle (Clay) H.; A.B., N.Y. U., 1931; M.A., Columbia 1936, Ph.D., 1942; m. Margaret Cardozo, Jan. 2, 1939. Mem. faculty Howard U., Washington, 1932-70, prof. philosophy, 1961-70, head dept., from 1952; vis. prof. City Coll. N.Y., 1946. Mem. Washington Philos. Soc. (pres. 1962- 63), Am. Philos. Assn., Washington Philosophy Club, Humanist Soc., Peirce Soc., John Dewey Soc., Santayana Soc., A.A.A.S., Am. Assn. Sci. Workers, Alpha Phi Alpha. Author: The Social Philosophy and the Social Mind, A Study of the Genetic Methods of J.M. Baldwin, G. H. Mead and J.E. Boodin, 1942; also articles. Editor: Dictionary of Philosophy, 1940. Home: Washington, D.C. Died July 7, 1980.

HOLMES, FENWICKE LINDSAY, author lecturer; b. Lincoln, Me., Feb. 6, 1883; s. William and Anna C. (Heath) H.; A.B., Colby Coll., 19—, Hartford Theol. Sem., 1908-10; m. Katherine Eggleston Junkermann, of N.Y. City, June 6, 1919; 1 son, Louis A. (adopted). Prof. Latin, Attleboro (Mass.) High Sch., 1907-08; minister Rincon (Calif.) Congl. Ch., 1911-12, Congl. Ch., Venice, Calif., 1912-17; a founder Metaphysical Inst., Long Beach, Calif., 1917, Southern Calif. Metaphysical Inst., Los Angeles, 1917. Lecturer on psychology and metaphysics, 1917-26; pastor First Ch. Divine Science, New York, 1926—. Mem. Phi Beta Kappa, Alpha Tau Omega. Author: The Law of Mind in Action, 1919; How to Develop Faith That Heals, 1919; Being and Becoming, 1920; Practical Healing, 1921; What Is Mental Science? 1921; Songs of the Silence, 1921; The Science of Mind—Psychology and Metaphysics, 1924; The Twenty Secrets of Success, 1926; Visualization and Concentration—How to Choose a Career, 1926; also newspaper and mag. articles. Home: New York, N.Y. *

HOLMES, FREDERICK WILLIAM, educator; b. Framingham, Mass., Mar. 12, 1897; s. William Burgess and Alice Bethia (Ellms) H.; A.B. cum laude, Harvard, 1919; A.M., Boston Univ., 1931; m. Stella Fields, Oct. 16, 1920; 1 dau., Ruth Elizabeth. Reporter and asst. financial editor Boston Evening Record, 1920; instr. and asst. editor Div. of Univ. Extension, Mass. Dept. Edn., 1920-24; instr. in English, Northeastern Univ., 1925-26, asst. prof., 1926-30, asso. prof., 1930-42, chmn. dept. English, 1942-60, prof., 1942-62, prof. emeritus, 1962—; host TV show, Plain English, WGBH, Boston, 1957-58. Served as 2d lt., 34th Machine Gun Bn., U.S. Army, 1918-19. Former mem. Dedham (Mass.) Sch. Com.; mem. bd. dirs. General Theological Library, 1948-60. Recipient Americanism Citation, Mayflower Lodge of B'nai B'rith, 1955; Holmes Hall, Northeastern U., dedicated in his honor, 1980. Mem. Ch. Home Soc. of Boston, College English Assn., Modern Lang. Assn. Republican. Episcopalian (pres. men's div. of Ch. Service League, Diocese of Mass., 1942-47; mem. Diocesan Council, 1948-49; Author: (with Birk, Melvin, Vaughan) Basic Principles of Writing, 1937, 1943. Home: Dedham, Mass.; inurned Forest Hills Crematory, Dedham. Died 1976.

HOLMES, JAMES GARROTT, judge; b. Sidon, Miss., Aug. 3, 1883; s. Charles E. and Katie (Bell) H.; student U. of South, Sewanee, Tenn.; B.S., U. Miss., 1907, LL.B., 1907; post grad. student Columbia, 1910; m. Elsie R. Elliott, June 5, 1917; children—Elsie (Mrs. James Hobson), Mary Ann (Mrs. E.G. Cortright, Jr.). Admitted to Mississippi bar, 1907; practiced law, Yazoo City, and in courts throughout state, 1907-50; city atty., corp. counsel municipality, Yazoo City, Miss., 1915-50; justice Supreme Ct. Miss., 1950-61. Past pres. bd. trustees, pub. schs., Yazoo City; chmn. Four Minute Men, Yazoo Co., World War I, chmn. U.S.O. World War II. Mem. S.A.R., Miss. State Bar Assn., Delta Tau Delta. Address: Jackson, Miss. *

HOLMES, ROBERT DENISON, gov. of Ore.; b. Canisteo, N.Y., May 11, 1909; s. George H. and Amy C. (Crary) H.; student U. Ore., 1928-32; m. Marie Hoy, May 1, 1934; children—Robert Denison, John H. Mem. advt. staff Ore. Jour., Portland, 1926-28, Oregonian, Portland, 1930; mgr. radio sta. KAST, Astoria, Ore., 1943-57; Ore. senator Clatsop County, 1948-56; gov. of Ore., 1956-58; bus. and public relations cons., from 1958. Chmn. Gearhart Sch. Bd., 1942-48, Clatsop Rural Sch. Bd., 1947-48; vice chmn. dist. council Boy Scouts Am., 1948-49; chmn. Astoria Community Chest, 1940. Named Ore. Man of the Year in Edn., 1953. Mem. Ore. Broadcasters Assn. (v.p.), Delta Tau Delta, Alpha Delta Sigma. Democrat (del. conv. 1956). Rotarian (pres. Astoria club 1947-48). Home: Gearhart, Ore. Died June 6, 1976.

HOLT, EARLE PENDLETON, educator; b. Oak Ridge, N.C., May 7, 1883; s. John Allen and Sallie Josephine (Knight) H.; grad. Oak Ridge Mil. Inst., 1899; Ph.B., U. of N.C., 1903; m. Mary Eugenia Harris, May 28, 1912; children—John Allen, Thomas Michael, Earle Pendleton. Instr. and athletic dir., St. Alban's Sch., Radford, Va., 1903-04; instr. and dir. div. of athletics, Oak Ridge Mil. Inst., 1904-14, v.p., 1914-29, pres., 1929-47; retired June 1947. Became col. N.C. Res., 1925. Mem. Zeta Psi. Democrat. Methodist. Mason. Address: Oak Ridge, N.C.*

HOLT, MARMADUKE BURRELL, JR., lawyer; b. Silverton, Colo., Sept. 21, 1905; s. Marmaduke Burrell and Mabel (Brown) H.; A.B., Williams Coll., 1927; LL.B. cum laude, U. Denver, 1931; m. Jessica Matlock, Feb. 7, 1931 (dec. 1940); children—Marmaduke Burrell III, Robert W., Alan M.; m. 2d, Mary S. Barkalow, Oct. 3, 1942; children—John S., Peter B., Katherine B. Admitted to Colo. bar, 1931, practiced in Denver; mem. firm Martin and Holt, 1943-64. Gen. atty. Gt. Western Sugar Co., 1944-55, gen. counsel, 1955-70. Recipient Mayor Denver award pub. service, 1965. Mem. Am., Colo. (v.p. 1952-53, bd. govs. 1961-67), Denver (pres. 1964-65) bar assns., Colo. Bar Found. (chmn.), Order St. Ives, Phi Delta Phi, Delta Psi. Episcopalian (clk., vestryman, sr. warden). Clubs: Law, University, Cactus, Mile High (Denver). Home: Denver, Colo. Died Sept. 14, 1976.

HOLTOM, DANIEL CLARENCE, writer, educator; b. Jackson, Mich., July 7, 1884; s. John and Florence (Conklin) H.; A.B., Kalamazoo (Mich.) Coll., 1907, D.D., 1926; A.B., U. of Chicago, 1908. Ph.D., 1919; B.D., Newton Theol. Instn., 1910; D.D., Brown U., 1933; m. Mary Grace Price, July 21, 1910; children—Harold Thomas, Gordon Francis (dec.), Gerald Price (dec.), Daniel Clarence (dec.), John Howard. Ordained Bapt. ministry, 1910, and sent as educational missionary to Japan. Professor of modern languages, Tokyo, (Japan) Gakuin, 1914-15; professor church history, Japanese Baptist Theological Seminary, Tokyo, 1915-25; visiting professor church history, University of Chicago, 1925-26; professor history of religions and church history, Kwanto Gakuin, Yokohama, 1926-36; dean theol. dept., Kanto Gakuin, 1935-36; prof. theology dept., Aoyama Gakuin, Tokyo, 1936-40; Haskell lecturer, Univ. of Chicago, 1940; Rauschenbusch lecturer, Colgate-Rochester Div. Sch., 1942; instr. Japanese language, U. of Redlands, 1944; traveled eastern Asia, 1938, 1940. Trustee, Kwanto Gakuin, Yokohama. Fellow A.A.A.S.; mem. Anthrop. Assn., Asiatic Society Japan (vice president 1941), Institute Pacific Relations (American council), Am.-Japan Society. Baptist. Republican. Author: Political Philosophy of Modern Shinto, 1922; The Japanese Enthronement Ceremonies, 1928; The National Faith of Japan, 1937; The Meaning of Kami, 1941; Modern Japan and Shinto Nationalism, 1943 (revised, 1947), translated into the Japanese language, 1950; chapters and articles in various books, including: Shintoism, in Great Religions of the Modern World (edited by E. J. Jurji), 1946; Shinto, in Ency. Brit., 1946, 1952. Editor of Christain Movement in Japan, 1922-24, and Trans. of Asiatic Soc. of Japan, 1923-25, 1926-28. Contbr. to various publs. Home: San Gabriel, Calif. *

HOLTZOFF, ALEXANDER, judge; b. Nov. 7, 1886; s. Lazarus and Mary (Holtzoff) H.; A.B., Columbia, 1908, M.A., 1909, LL.B., 1911; m. Louise Cowan (dec. 1966). Admitted to N.Y. state bar, 1911, practiced law, 1911-24; spl. asst. to atty. gen. of U.S., Washington, D.C., 1924-45, exec. asst., 1945; U.S. district judge for Dist. of Columbia since 1945. Sec. to adv. com. Supreme Ct. on Fed. rules of criminal procedure; mem., sec. War Dept. adv. com. on mil. justice, 1946; lectr. Washington Coll. Law, also Sch. of Law, Cath. U. Served as pvt. A.U.S. 1918. Received Navy Distinguished Pub. Service Award, 1948. Mem. Am. (chmn. sect. jud. adminstrn. 1955-56), Fed. bar assns., Bar Association of D.C., Association Bar of City of N.Y., American Legion (past comdr. dept. justice post; past parliamentarian dept. D.C.), Phi Delta Phi (hon.), Phi Beta Kappa. Clubs: Columbia University (New York City); National Press. Author: New Federal Procedure and the Courts, 1941; (with Allen R. Cozier) Federal Procedural Forms, 1941; (with William W. Barron) Federal Practice and Procedure. Contributor of articles in legal periodicals. Home: Washington. *

HOLZ, LEFFERT, lawyer; b. Austria, Aug. 28, 1896; s. Jacob L. and Rose (Manne) H.; student N.Y. U. Law Sch.; m. Alice Englander, Nov. 8, 1921; 1 dau., Ruth (Mrs. Raphal Dubrowin). Admitted to N.Y. bar, 1921; asst. corp. counsel, N.Y.C., 1923-25; supt. ins. State N.Y., 1955-58; now counsel law firm Carb, Luria, Glassner & Cook, N.Y.C.; lectr. Practicing Law Inst. pres., chmn. bd. Mortgage Facilities Corp., 1956-66. Chmn. local bd. N.Y. Selective Service; chmn. com. state and regional orgn. Bur. War Records, Nat. Jewish Welfare Bd., World War II; past trustee Union of Am. Hebrew Congregations, also past chmn. rabbinical pension fund. Served with U.S. Army, World War I. Mem. Real Estate Bd. N.Y. (past v.p., gov.), Assn. Bar City N.Y., N.Y. County Lawyers Assn., Am. Bar Assn., Am. Legion, N.Y. U. Law Alumni Assn., Pi Lambda Phi. Mason. Home: West Palm Beach, Fla. Died 1978.

HOMPE, ROBERT WILBUR, pharm. and chem. mfg. co. exec.; b. Auburn, N.Y., Sept. 10, 1898; s. Henry A. and Isabelle (Downing) H.; student Western Res. U., 1917-21; m. Beatrice Pfanner, Jan. 10, 1928; children—Patricia (Mrs. Jacob A. Gibson, Jr.), Robert Downing. With Strong Cobb & Co., Inc., Cleve., 1922-38, v.p., 1933-38, dir., 1935-38; with Smith, Kline & French Labs., Phila., 1938-62, dir., 1944-63, v.p., 1945-63. Mem. planning commn. Radnor Twp., 1953-58. Bd. visitors, govs. Washington Coll., Chestertown, Md. Served with USMC, 1918. Mem. Delta Tau Delta. Presbyn. Clubs: Merion Cricket, Union League (Phila.); Union (Cleve.); Merion Country. Home: Villanova, Pa. Died Oct. 13, 1975.

HONAMAN, R(ICHARD) KARL, bus. cons.; b. Lancaster, Pa., Sept. 17, 1895; s. Walter H. and Ada R. (Miller) H.; B.S., Franklin and Marshall Coll., 1916, M.S., 1917; m. Alice M. Garman, Dec. 1, 1917; children—Richard Karl (dec.), Ruth Dorothy (Mrs. John T. Burgess). Devel. studies aeros. program, 1917-19; asst. prof. elec. engring. George Washington U., 1918-19; with AT&T, Bell Telephone Labs., N.Y.C., 1919-60, dir. sch. for war tng., 1942-45, dir. publ., 1945-60, ret., 1960; on leave for govt. service, 1954-55; bus. cons., 1960-77; chmn. bd. Visual Internat., Inc., N.Y.C.; cons. to sec. commerce, dir. Office Strategic Info., 1954-55; dep. asst. sec. def. for pub. affairs, Washington, 1955; cons. U.S. Army Mgmt. Engring. Tng. Agy., Rock Island, Ill., Found. Econ. Edn. Clergy, Joint Commn. N.J. Legislature Water Mgmt. Policy, 1968-70. Mem. nat. council, nat. personnel com. Boy Scouts Am., 1942-77. Mayor, Borough of Glen Ridge, N.J., 1948-52; mem. Glen Ridge Municipal Planning Bd. Bd. dirs. N.J. Council Econ. Edn., Burgess Adv. Reports; trustee Mountainside (N.J.) Hosp., 1952-58, v.p., 1954. Recipient Alumni citation Franklin and Marshall Coll., 1956; Seton Hall U. Centennial medal, 1958; Silver Antelope award Boy Scouts Am., 1972. Registered profl. engr., N.Y. Fellow IEEE, AAAS (reviewer for Sci. Books); mem. Am. Mgmt. Assn., N.Y. Elec. Soc. (pres. 1952-54), Soc. for Advancement Mgmt., Nat. Acad. Sci. (exec. com., nat. com. fedn. internationale de documentation 1961-65), Engrs. Joint Council (chmn. com. engring. info. 1956-63), N.Y. Pub. Relations Soc. Republican. Episcopalian. Club: Univ. (N.Y.C.). Address: Glen Ridge, N.J. Died Nov. 16,

1977; interred Restland Meml. Cemetery, Hanover, N.J.

HONCE, CHARLES (ELLSWORTH), newspaperman; b. Keokuk, Ia., Nov. 18, 1895; s. William Henry and Alice (Clark) H.; grad. Keokuk (Ia.) High Sch., 1913; m. Emmanuella Flood, Nov. 16, 1916. Sports editor and city editor Constitution Dem., Keokuk, 1913-15, Keokuk Gate City, 1915-17; city editor Gazette, Burlington, Ia., 1917-18; reporter Capital, Des Moines, 1919; with Asso. Press, Chicago, 1919, central div. news editor, 1927-30, eastern div. news editor, 1930, successively exec. news editor, exec. Sunday editor, gen. news editor, 1937-44, asst. general manager in charge of news-features, Wide World Photos 1944-53, retired, 1953. Member Newspaper Council of Medill School of Journalism, Northwestern University, Illinois, 1929-30. Served in France with battery C, 337th field arty., 88th div., World War I. Mem. Bibliog. Soc. of Am., Mark Twain Research Foundn., Baker Street Irregulars, Ky. Colonels Association, Chicago Press Veterans Association, American Association of Feature and Sunday Editors, Sigma Delta Chi. Club: Dutch Treat. Author: Songs of the Seasons, 1918; Sunlight, 1926; A Sherlock Holmes Birthday, 1938; A Julian Hawthorne Collection, 1939; Authors in Falseface, 1939; Ballade for a Bibliomaniac's Birthday, 1940; Mark Twain's Associated Press Speech, 1940; A Vincent Starrett Library, 1941; News Gathering in War Times, 1941; A Day at Abbey Dawn (with Wallace Havelock Robb), 1941; The Public Papers of a Bibliomaniac, 1942; Sherlock Holmes Still is in the News, 1944; For Loving a Book, 1945; Books and Ghosts, 1948; Notes from a Bookman's Cuff, 1949; To Talk of Many Things, 1950; Murder on Beekman Place, 1951; Tales From a Beekman Hill Library, 1952. Editor: The Uplands of Dream (by Edgar Saltus), 1925; The Adventures of Thomas Jefferson Snodgrass by Mark Twain, 1928; The APME Red Book for 1948, 49, 50, 51, 52; Emmanuella (by Esther Longfellow), 1955; Souvenir Thirty Beekman Place (music by Ferde Grofé), 1956. Contbr. to professional jours. Composer: The Midnight Waltz, Springtime, It's Lovely Tonight, etc. Home: New York, N.Y. Died Aug. 29, 1975; buried Sleepy Hollow Cemetery, Tarrytown, N.Y.

HONEA, BERT N., newspaper co. exec.; b. Longview, Tex., 1886. Formerly chmn., sec., dir. Carter Pubis. Inc., Fort Worth, now cons.; chmn. bds. dirs. WBAP Broadcasting Co., Fort Worth Star-Telegram; dir. Southland Paper Mills. Mason (Shriner). *

HONIGMANN, JOHN JOSEPH, educator; b. N.Y.C., June 7, 1914; s. John Joseph and Agnes (Lobe) H.; B.A., Bklyn. Coll., 1942; M.A., Yale, 1943, Ph.D., 1947; m. Irma Grabel, Oct. 2, 1937; children—David John, Karen Jane Honigmann McHaney. Asst. prof. sociology and anthropology State Coll. Wash., Pullman, 1946-47; research anthropologist Nat. Com. for Community Health Studies, Toronto and Attawapiskat, Ont., Can., 1947-48; asst. prof. anthropology N.Y. U., 1948-51; asso. prof. anthropology U. N.C., Chapel Hill, 1951-55, prof., 1955-77, Kenan prof., 1977; cons. in field. Fulbright grantee, 1957-58; Wenner-Gren Found. grantee, 1949, 50, 55, 60, 64, 67; NSF grantee, 1965-70; NIMH grantee, 1960-61, 65-72; others. Fellow Am. Anthrop. Assn., Soc. for Applied Anthropology; mem. Am. Ethnol. Soc., Internat. African Inst., So. Anthrop. Soc., Sigma Xi. Author: Culture and Ethos of Kaska Society, 1949; The World of Man, 1959; Foodways in a Muskeg Community, 1962; Personality in Culture, 1967; The Development of Anthropological Ideas, 1976. Contbr. articles to profl. jours. Home: Chapel Hill, N.C. Died Aug. 4, 1977.

HONORA, SISTER MARY, coll. pres.; b. Kansas City, Mo.; A.B., Marygrove Coll., Monroe, Mich., 1922; A.M., U. of Notre Dame, 1925; Ph.D., Fordham U., 1928; D.Sc. Ed. (honorary), Wayne University, 1952. Teacher, St. Thomas High School, Ann Arbor, Mich., 1916-24, prin., 1924-26; prof. of English, Marygrove Coll., Detroit, 1928-31, dean, 1930-37, pres., from 1937. Mem. N. Central Assn. Commn. Higher Edn., 1957-61, Mich. State Commn. Teacher Education, from 1959. Mem. Sisters, Servants of the Immaculate Heart of Mary, Adult Edn. Assn. Am., Am. Assn. Sch. Adminstrs. Contbr. to ednl. jours. Roman Catholic. Home: Monroe, Mich. Died July 1974.

HOOD, BEN BENIGHT, mech. engr.; b. Manhattan, Kan., Nov. 1, 1886; s. Ozni Porter and Gertrude (Benight) H.; grad. high sch., Houghton, Mich., 1905; E.M., Mich. Coll. of Mines, 1908; m. Mary Josephine Allen, of Dollar Bay, Mich., July 14, 1910; children—Allen Benight, Evelyn Melissa, Jean, John Merrill. Chief engr. Winona (Mich.) Copper Co., 1909-13; engr. British Am. Nickel Corpn., Sudbury, Ont., Can., 1913-14; supt. in charge concentrating plant, Moose Mountain Co., Ltd., Sellwood, Ont., 1914; with U.S. Metals Refining Co., Carteret, N.J., as engr., boiler room supt., asst. to plant supt. and plant asst. supt., 1914-23; plant engr. Western Electric Co., Kearney Works, 1923-24; chief engr. Am. Chain Co. and subsidiary cos. (13 plants), Bridgeport, Conn., 1924-30; asst. to gen. supt. Procter & Gamble Co. since 1930. Mem. Am. Inst. Mining and Metall. Engrs., Am. Soc. M.E., Tau Beta Pi. Republican. Conglist. Club: Engineers (Cincinnati). Home: Cincinnati, O. *

HOOD, CLIFFORD F(IROVED), steel co. executive; born Monmouth, Ill., Feb. 8, 1894; s. Edward Everett and Ida Florence (Firoved) H.; B.S., U. of Ill., 1915; LL.D., Thiel Coll., 1952, Monmouth Coll., 1954; E.D., Case Inst of Technology, 1953, Northeastern U., 1954; Youngstown University, 1958; H.H.D., Bethany College, 1958; m. Emilie R. Tener, Dec. 8, 1917 (deceased); children—Randall F., Richard.; married 2d, Mary Ellen Tolerton, May 6, 1943. Began as technical apprentice with Packard Elec. Co., 1915; sales engr. Packard Elec. Co., Warren, O., 1915-17; with Am. Steel & Wire Co., 1917-49 (except during military service, World War I), as clerk, May-June 1917, foreman, 1919-25, asst. supt. South Works, 1925-27, supt., 1927-28, asst. mgr., later mgr. Worcester Dist., 1928-35, v.p. in charge operations, 1935-37, exec. v.p., Jan.-Dec. 1937, pres., 1938-40; pres. Carnegie-Ill. Steel Corp., 1950; executive vice pres. U.S. Steel Co., 1951-52; pres. U.S. Steel Corp., 1953-59, now mem. exec. com., dir. Served as 1st lt. with coast arty., A.U.S., with A.E.F., 1917-19. Mem. Am. Iron and Steel Inst., Chi Phi. Republican. Baptist. Mason. Clubs: Duquesne (Pitts.); The Links (N.Y.C.). Home: Pittsburgh, PA. Deceased.

HOOD, HARVEY PERLEY, dairy exec.; Somerville, Mass., Apr. 12, 1897; s. Charles Harvey and Katherine Wyman (Eastman) H.; B.S., Dartmouth, 1918, LL.D. (hon.); postgrad. Harvard, 1919-20; m. Barbara Ellen Churchill, Apr. 18, 1928; children—Charles Harvey, II, Helen Olivia, Barbara Ellen Churchill, Olivia Churchill. Treas. H.P. Hood & Sons, dairy experts, Boston, 1922-39, pres., 1936-62, chmn. bd., chief exec. officer, 1962-66, chmn. bd., 1966-69, dir., 1922-78; dir. Fed. Res. Bank Boston, 1951-58, dep. chmn., 1958; mem. exec. com., adv. bd. State St. Bank & Trust Co. Life trustee, chmn. exec. com. Dartmouth Coll., 1951-67; trustee Children's Hosp.; mem. corp., bd. dirs. Boston Mus. Sci.; bd. overseers Boys' Club of Boston; mem. corp. Northeastern U., Cardigan Mountain Sch., Canaan, N.H., Mass. Gen. Hosp. Clubs: Harvard, Union, University (Boston); Brookline (Mass.) Country; Essex Country; Manchester Yacht; Yale (N.Y.C.). Home: Manchester, Mass. Died Mar. 3, 1978; interred Mt. Auburn Cemetery, Cambridge, Mass.

HOOL, GEORGE ALBERT, structural engr.; b. Lawrence, Mass., Nov. 28, 1883; s. John and Euphemia (McNab) H.; grad. high sch., Lawrence, 1901; S.B., Mass. Inst. Tech., 1905; m. Emma Helen Eber, of Framingham, Mass., Oct. 3, 1906; children—Eleanor Louise, Sherman Eber, Alan Emerson. Formerly engr. N.Y.C. Railroad; prof. civ. engring., Univ. of Okla., 1907-09; prof. structural engring., University of Wis., 1909-29; consulting engineer since 1909. Mem. of American Concrete Institute. Conglist. Clubs: Madison, University, Maple Bluff Golf, Black Hawk Country (1st pres.). Author: Reinforced Concrete Construction (3 vols.), 1912-15; Concrete Engineers' Handbook (Hool and Johnson), 1918; Concrete Designers' Manual (Hool and Whitney), 1921. Editor in chief, (Hool and Johnson) Handbook of Building Construction (2 vols.), 1920; (Hool and Kinne) Structural Engineers' Handbook Library (6 vols.), 1923, 24; Concrete Practice (Hool and Pulver), 1926.*

HOOPER, JOHN JULIAN, newspaper publisher; b. Colorado, Mitchell County, Tex., Mar. 16, 1883; s. John Randolph and Julia Emma (Felker) H.; B.S., Agrl. and Mech. Coll., Tex., 1901; M.S. in Agr., Ia. State Coll., 1907; unmarried. In employ live stock dept. Biltmore Estate, Asheville, N.C., 1904; asst. prof. agr., 1906-09, State Coll. of Ky.; prof. animal husbandry and dairying, 1909-27, U. of Ky., and dairy husbandman of Ky. Expt. Sta., 1912-27; pub. The Review, Hayward, Calif., 1931-44. Investigated live stock conditions in Europe, 1912; dir. Breeding Bur. Ky. State Racing Commn., 1914-19, and official at State and Blue-grass fairs in Ky., 1912-27. Judge at live stock shows; official judge Am. Holstein-Friesian Assn.; lecturer at farmers' insts. Fellow A.A.A.S. Mem. Am. Genetics Assn., Am. Soc. Animal Production, Am. Dairy Science Assn. (chmn. dairy husbandry sect., 1923), Am. Poultry Assn., Grange. Mem. Alpha Gamma Rho. Club: Rotary.*

HOOPER, LESLIE JAMES, hydraulic engr.; b. Essex, Mass., Feb. 15, 1903; s. William John and Ethel (Cruze) H.; B.S., Worcester Poly. Inst., 1924, M.E., 1928; m. Edith Carolyn Stockwell, May 24, 1930; children—Donald Leslie, William Robert, Lee Monroe, Neal Cruze. Hydraulic test engr. Canadian Gen. Finance Co., Brazil, 1924-27; asst. to Prof. Allen, Alden Hydraulic Lab., Worcester Poly Inst., 1928-32, asst., part time tchr., 1932-38, asst. prof., 1938-45, prof. hydraulic engring., dir. lab., 1950-68, prof. emeritus, cons. lab., 1968-77; pvt. cons. practice on flow measurements. Past internat. pres. tech. com. 4 Internat. Electrotech. Commn. Mem. Holden Sch. Com., 1940-49, several coms. on sch. bldg. and water supply, 1947-53. Recipient John R. Freeman scholarship, 1934-36, Charles T. Main, Jr. award, 1937. Fellow Am. Soc. M.E., Am. Soc. C.E.; mem. A.A.A.S., Am. Soc. Engring. Edn., Boston Soc. Civil Engrs. (past pres.), Sigma Xi, Tau Beta Pi. Contbr. articles to profl. jours. Home: Holden, Mass. Died Apr. 9, 1977.

HOOPER, WILLIAM EVERETT, editor; b. Denver, Colo., Mar. 16, 1883; s. Horace Everett and Mary Alice (Woodbury) H.; student Harvard, 1902-06; m. Edith L. Field, of New York, Aug. 12, 1912. Became asso. editor Railroad Gazette, 1908; asst. mng. editor and financial editor Railway Age Gazette, since 1912; financial editorial writer, New York Tribune, 1920-21; railroad expert, Dillon, Read & Co. since 1921. Club: Harvard. Author: Railroad Accounting, 1915. Contbr. articles on railways and allied subjects for new Internat. Ency. Home: New York. *

HOOS, SIDNEY SAMUELS, economist, educator; b. Buffalo, May 20, 1911; s. Jacob and Rose (Gerrish) H.; student U. Maine, 1929-31; A.B., U. Mich., 1934, A.M., 1935; Ph.D., Stanford U., 1939; fellow First Inst. Freedom and Competitive Enterprise, Claremont Coll., 1954; m. Ida Russakoff, June 13, 1942; children—Phyllis Ellen Hoos DeLeon, Judith Marjorie Hoos Fox. Research fellow Food Research Inst., Stanford, 1936-38; instr. U. Calif. at Berkeley, 1938-41, asso. prof. agrl. econs., asso. economist expt. sta., asso. economist Giannini Found. Agrl. Econs. 1946-49, prof. agrl. econs., also prof. econs. and bus. adminstrn., economist expt. sta., Giannini Found. Agrl. Econs., 1950-79, univ. dean acad. personnel U. Calif. System Statewide, 1964-67; sr. economist, asst to pres. CCC, Dept. Agr., 1941-42; chief economist, dep. chief requirements br. Office Q.M. Gen., War Dept., 1942-45; cons. Falk Project Econ. Research, Israel, 1960-61, Agrl. Settlement Dept., Jewish Agy., Israel, 1960-61; econ. cons. various agrl. products, agencies fed. and state govts. Recipient Commendation for Meritorious Service, War Dept., Citation of Merit for research Am. Mktg. Assn.; named to Hall of Fame Canners League Calif. Fellow Am. Agrl. Econs. Assn.; mem. Am., Pacific Coast econ. assns., Am. Statis. Assn., Econometric Soc., Am. (exec. com. 1951, editorial council 1954-57, exec. com. v.p. 1962-63), Western (exec. com. 1950-52, pres., award for research 1951) farm econs. assns., Inst. Mgmt. Scis., Internat. Soc. Hort. Scis. Author monographs and articles on prices, prodn., agrl. marketing and agrl. policy; editor: Agricultural Marketing Boards—An International Perspective, 1979. Home: Berkeley, Calif. Died Sept. 20, 1979.

HOOVEN, MORRIS DANIEL, cons. engr., assn. exec.; b. Weatherly, Pa., May 30, 1897; s. Morris Davis and Laura Emma (Rouse) H.; student Carnegie Inst. Tech., 1914-15; Sc.B. magna cum laude, Bucknell University, 1920, Doctor of Science, 1958; D.Sc., Newark Coll. of Engineering, 1957; married Florence Mary Bleecker, Oct. 14, 1927 (dec. 1955); children—Barbara Bleecker (Mrs. James Clark Fullmer), Daniel Bleecker, Elizabeth Bleecker (Mrs. Edgar M. Morsman III). Chemist Carnegie Steel Corp., 1914-16; engr. Westinghouse Electric Corp., 1920; radio engr. Robbins Electric Co., 1921; engr. transmission, asst. transmission and sub-sta. engr., elec. engr. Pub. Service Electric & Gas Co., Newark, from 1922, cons. engr.; distinguished lectr. Medallion, U. Louisville, 1958. Mem. Engring. Manpower Commn., 1952-55, Nat. Power Policy Commn., 1939-40, Nat. Def. Power Com., 1938-39, Radio Adv. Com., 1929-37, N.J. Adv. Com. Sci. and Engring. Personnel, 1954-55. Served as pfc, Signal Corps, U.S. Army, 1918. Mem. Am. Inst. E.E. (pres. 1955-56, recipient Founders medal 1970), Engineers Council Professional Development (president 1956-58), Engineers Joint Council, (director 1953-58), Montclair Soc. Engrs. (pres. 1942-43), Inst. Radio Engrs., Am. Soc. M.E., Nat. Society Profl. Engrs., Am. Soc. Engring. Edn., Water Resources Assn. of Delaware River Basin (dir. emeritus 1973), Eta Kappa Nu, Phi Kappa Psi, Tau Beta Pi. Presbyn. Mason. Club: Engineers (N.Y.C.). Author tech. papers in field. Home: Montclair, N.J. Died Oct. 18, 1976.

HOOVER, RICHARD ANDREW, performing arts adminstr.; b. Indpls., July 4, 1914; s. Andrew and Mary Jane (Falk) H.; m. Barbara Ruth Henderson, Mar. 1, 1952; children—Meredith (Mrs. Armin E. Wille), Margery (Mrs. Charles H. Stull), Richard E., Michael A., Deborah M. Actor, stage mgr., asst. dir. Civic Theatre Indpls., 1931-38, dir., 1940-42; pres. agt. Pitts. Playhouse, 1938-40, gen. mgr., 1945-67; mng. dir. Milw. Performing Arts Center, 1967-73; co-owner South Shore Players, Cohasset, Mass., 1938-48; sr. lectr. Carnegie Inst. Tech., 1950-67; lectr. theatre mgmt. U. Wis., summers 1960-68. Served with inf. AUS, 1942-45. Decorated Bronze Star with cluster. Mem. ANTA (v.p. 1953-60). Home: Milwaukee, Wis. Died Sept. 4, 1973.

HOPKINS, DAVID LUKE, former banker; b. Balt., Dec. 29, 1898; s. Robert Dixon and Isabel (Luke) H.; A.B., Princeton, 1921; LL.D., Goucher Coll., 1952; m. Katherine Disston Porter, Feb. 12, 1927; children—David Luke, Charles A.P., Florence D. (Mrs Charles A. Borda III), Katherine P. (Mrs. Charles H. Mellon III). With Drovers & Mechanics Nat. Bank, Balt., 1921-30, v.p., 1925-30; exec. v.p., dir. Mercantile-Safe Deposit & Trust Co., 1946-54; v.p., dir. Md. Trust Co., Balt., 1930-45; chmn., dir. Md. Nat. Bank, Balt., 1955-74; dir., exec. com. Chespeake & Potomac Tel. Co. Md., 1938-71, Fidelity & Deposit Co Md., 1951-74, Savs. Bank Balt., 1945-73; dir. Balt Equitable Soc., Westvaco (N.Y.), 1936-69, Canton Co.

1941-56, Canton R.R. Co., 1941-56. Chmn. Balt. Emergency Relief Commn., 1933-35, Balt. Civil Works Adminstrn., 1933; authorized rep. Applied Physics Lab., Johns Hopkins, 1942-46; mem. security survey panel AEC, 1950-52; past commr. Md. Port Authority; asst. sec. gen. NATO, 1952-53. Former mem. bd. mgrs. Family Welfare Assn., Balt. Council Social Agys., Henry Watson Children's Aid Soc., pres. (1930-34); vestryman Ch. of Redeemer, Balt., 1951-56; trustee emeritus Johns Hopkins U., Johns Hopkins Hosp.; chmn. Johns Hopkins Fund, 1958-61; pres. Evergreen House Found., 1963-64; chmn. bd. trustees Walters Art Gallery, 1944-72; trustee Chpt. of Protestant Episcopal Found. D.C. (Washington Cathedral), Greater Balt. Med. Center; bd. mgrs. Harriet Lane Home for Invalid Children; bd. dirs. Loudon Park and Druid Ridge Cemeteries, 1931-70. Served with USN, World War I. Recipient Medal of Merit, 1946. Mem. Permanent Internat. Assn. Nav. Congresses (U.S. nat. commn. 1959-64), Council Fgn. Relations. Episcopalian. Clubs: Maryland; Elkridge; Metropolitan (Washington); Brook (N.Y.C.). Home: Baltimore, Md. Died May 16, 1976; interred Forest Hill Cemetery, Northeast Harbor, Maine.

HOPKINS, FREDERICK DAN, assn. exec.; b. Weedsport, N.Y., Apr. 10, 1886; s. Lazelle R. and Nancy L. (Kent) H.; Ph.B., Syracuse (N.Y.) U., 1908; m. Katherine G. Hinchman, July 21, 1913; children—Mrs. Margaret H. Armstrong, Katherine (Mrs. Albert G. Zimmerman). Reporter, Ithaca (N.Y.) Jour., 1908-09, Syracuse Post Standard, 1909; in advt. dept. Franklin Automobile Co., Syracuse, N.Y., 1910; insp. N.Y. State Bd. Charities, 1910-15; field sec. Nat. Tuberculosis Assn., N.Y. City; 1915-19, supervisor field service, 1920, adminstrv. sec., 1921-27, exec. secretary, 1927-51, retired, consultant since 1951; appointed by State Department to represent U.S. at Conf. of Internat. Union against Tuberculosis, Warsaw, 1934, Lisbon, 1937; del. Nat. Tuberculosis Assn. to meetings council of Internat. Union, Paris, 1947 and 1948; ofcl. rep. Union at meetings of UN in N.Y.C. Recipient Will Ross medal, Nat. Tb. Assn., 1955. Mem. National Assn. Social Workers, Am. Pub. Health Assn., Delta Upsilon. Home: Glen Rock, N.J. *

HOPKINS, FREDERICK MERCER, JR., air force officer; b. N.Y.C., June 8, 1895; s. Frederick Mercer and Cora Belle (Collins) H.; student Columbia U., 1914-17; B.S., N.Y. U., 1926; grad. Air Corps Engring. Sch., 1932, Air Corps Tactical Sch., 1937, Command and Gen. Staff Sch., 1938; m. Henrietta Marsh, Sept. 9, 1920; children—Henrietta Marsh Hopkins Jernigan, Frederick Mercer. Commnd. 2d lt., C.A. Res., 1918, advanced through grades to maj. gen. USAF, 1947; command pilot, combat observer, aircraft observer; dir. observation flying AC Advanced Flying Sch., 1924-25; asst. prof. mil. sci. and tactics N.Y. U., 1926-30; comdt. AC Engring. Sch., 1932-36; instr. AC Tactical Sch., Maxwell Field, Ala., 1938-40; chief, resources div., material and service Hdgrs. U.S. Army Air Corps, 1940-45; comdg. gen. Army and Navy Forces, Iwo Jima, 1945-46, 20th Air Force, Guam, 1946, Pacific Air Service Command and Far East Air Materiel Command, Manila and Fuchu, Japan, 1946-47; dep. comdg. gen. ops. Air Materiel Command, Dayton, Ohio, 1947-51; ret., 1951. Gen. campaign chmn., v.p. Cleve. chpt. Arthritis and Rheumatism Found., 1954-55, pres., gen. campaign chmn., 1956; vice chmn. commerce and industry div. Cleve. Community Chest, 1953-56; mem. Mayor's Traffic Safety Com., aviation sub-com. Cleve. Dept. Port Control, cadet selection bd. CAP. Decorated D.S.M., Legion of Merit with oak leaf cluster. Fellow Inst. Aero. Scis. (vice chmn. Cleve.-Akron sect. 1954-55), Ohio C. of C. (dir.), Scabbard and Blade, Arnold Air Soc., Tau Beta Pi, Iota Alpha, Sigma Nu. Clubs: Mid-Day, Union (Cleve.); Quiet Birdmen; Shaker Heights Country. Home: Shaker Heights, Ohio. Died Jan. 22, 1978.

HOPPE, ALFRED BASTRUP, business exec.; b. Randers, Denmark, Nov. 19, 1886; s. Janus Bastrup and Marie (Hjorth) H.; ed. pub. schs., Denmark and San Francisco; m. Sidonia Sauvlet, June 28, 1913; 1 son, Alfred B. Successively asst. auditor, asst. treas., dept. sales mgr., asst. gen. sales mgr. Liggett Drug Co., N.Y., 1910-36; vice pres. and dir. Passion Fruit Plantation, Los Angeles, 1940-42; exec. v.p. and dir. Loft, Inc., N.Y., 1936-40; v.p. and gen. sales mgr. Pepsi-Cola Co., N.Y., since 1942. Mason. Club: Sales Executives (New York). Home: New York City. *

HOPSON, HOWARD COLWELL, lawyer, accountant, pub. utility consultant; b. Ft. Atkinson, Wis., May 8, 1882; s. Edgar Delos and Mary (Colwell) H.; student U. of Wis.; A.B., George Washington U., 1908, A.M., 1910. Admitted to D.C. bar, 1908; authorized to practice before U.S. Supreme Court, 1913; with Interstate Commerce Commn., 1907-08; head of Division Capitalization, Pub. Service Commn. State of N.Y., 1908-15; practiced as lawyer and pub. utility and tax consultant since 1915. Certified pub. accountant, states of N.Y. and Wis. Mem. Am. Inst. Accountants, Com. of 100 (Miami Beach, Fla.), Phi Delta Phi; asso. mem. Bar Assn. of D.C. Clubs: Lotos, Mid-Day, New York Athletic, Wall Street, Scarsdale Golf, Washington Irving Country, Westchester Country, Fort Orange (Albany); Surf (Miami Beach).*

HORD, PARKER (HORD), playwright, author; b. Mason County, Ky., Dec. 28, 1883; s. Abner and Ellen (Saunders) H.; student U. of Ky., 1900-02; spl. student George Washington U., 1906-07; unmarried. Mem. Sigma Alpha Epsilon. Democrat. Club: Quill. Author: A Mix-Up (3-act farce), 1914; Suite 16 (musical comedy), 1916; Tyndale (play; pub. as book), 1925; A Youth Goes Forth (novel), 1928; also 1-act plays for little theatre groups. Home: Atlanta, Ga. *

HORN, CHARLES LILLEY, explosives mfg. co. exec.; b. Mt. Vernon, Iowa, Mar. 5, 1888; s. George Lilley Horn and Anna May (Cooper) H.; B.L. U. Minn., 1912; Sc.D., Clemson Agrl. Coll., 1953, Cornell Coll., Mt. Vernon, Iowa, 1954, Worcester Poly. Inst., 1960; LL.D., Bucknell U., 1955, U. So. Calif., 1962, Drake U., 1975; Litt.D., Lafayette U., 1956; Sc.D. (hon.), Colo. Coll., 1962; LL.D., Macalester Coll., 1964, Case Inst. Tech., 1966, Colgate U., 1970; L.H.D., Whitman Coll., 1972, Roanoke Coll.; m. Louise Brace, Nov. 20, 1924 (dec.); children—Charles Lilley, William Brace; m. 2d, Alice Robertson, May 1, 1951. Pres. Fed. Cartridge Corp., Mpls., 1921-75, chmn. bd., 1975-78; operated Twin Cities Ordnance Plant, 1941-46, Twin Cities Arsenal, 1950; pres. Hoffman Engring. Corp., Olin Found., Inc. Chmn. commrs. Mpls. Housing and Redevel. Authority, 1960-73. Recipient citation medal for conservation edn. and outstanding leadership Dept. Agr., 1956; Distinguished Grad. award Law Alumni Assn. U. Minn., 1961. Mem. Pilgrims of U.S., Phi Delta Phi, Sigma Alpha Epsilon. Mason. Clubs: Minneapolis, Minikahda (Mpls.). Home: Minneapolis, Minn. Died June 27, 1978; buried Lakewood Cemetery, Mpls.

HORN, CLINTON MORRIS, lawyer; b. Medina, O., Nov. 14, 1885; s. Henry Adam and Ida (Pulsifer) H.; A.B., Western Res. U., 1908, LL.B., 1911; m. Mabel North Reed, Oct. 16, 1912; children—Miriam (Mrs. John A. Greene), Margaret (Mrs. James H. Foster, Jr.), Virginia (Mrs. John T. White), Martha (Mrs. William C. Bradford). Admitted to Ohio bar, 1911, since practiced in Cleve.; partner firm Arter, Hadden, Wykoff & Van Duzer, and predecessors, 1920—. Dir., sec. Ferro Corp., 1919—; legal counsel Holstein Friedian Assn. Am., 1919-60. Mem. Cleve. C. of C., Benchers (Western Res. U. Law Alumni Assn.). Presbyn. (ruling elder). Club: Union (Cleve.). Home: Shaker Heights, O. *

HORN, ERNEST, b. Mercer County, Mo., July 17, 1882; s. Asa and Lillie Mariah (Canady) H.; B.S., U. of Mo., 1907, A.M., 1908; Ph.D., Columbia, 1914; m. Madeline Daggett Darrough, June 4, 1914; children—William Darrough, Thomas Darrough. Teacher, Mercer County, Mo., 1900-05; prin. Univ. Elementary Sch., U. of Mo., 1906-08, asst. in edn., 1908-09; prof. seminary work and dir. playground, Colo. State Teachers' Coll., 1909-12; scholar in edn., Columbia, 1912-13; lecturer, Brooklyn Inst. Arts and Sciences, 1912-14; prin. Speyer Sch., Columbia, 1913-15; actg. prof. edn., summer session, Ind. U., 1913; prof. edn., State U. of Ia., since 1915, also dir. Univ. Elementary Sch.; dir. Scarborough (N.Y.) Sch., 1917-18. Mem. N.E.A., Nat. Soc. for Study of Edn., Coll. Teachers of Edn., A.A.A.S., American Educational Research Assn. (pres. 1946), Phi Delta Kappa, etc. Republican. Unitarian. Author: A Basic Writing Vocabulary, 1927; Methods of Instruction in the Social Studies, 1937; also (with others) Learn to Study Readers; Lippincott's Horn-Ashbaugh Speller; Horn-Ashbaugh Spelling Workbooks; Progress in Reading; The Basic Vocabulary of Business Letters; Spelling You Need; etc. Wrote (thesis) on distribution of opportunity for participation among the various pupils in class room recitations. Home: Iowa City, Ia. *

HORN, ROBERT CHISHOLM, JR., pathologist; b. Allentown, Pa., July 7, 1913; s. Robert Chisholm and Zelie (Soleliac) H.; B.S., Muhlenberg Coll., 1933; M.D., Yale, 1937; m. Dorothy Louise App, Jan. 1, 1940; children—Robert Chisholm III, Thomas Landes, Ethel Marion. Intern Geisinger Mem. Hosp., Danville, Pa., 1937-38; spl. tng. pathology and surg. pathology Columbia-Presbyn. Med. Center, N.Y.C., 1938-42; from asso. to prof. surg. pathology U. Pa. Sch. Medicine, also surg. pathologist and dir. tumor clinic U. Pa. Hosp., 1942-55; chmn. dept. pathology Henry Ford Hosp., Detroit, 1955-76; cons. Armed Forces Inst. Pathology, 1948-76, Phila. VA Hosp., 1948-55, Phila. Naval Hosp., 1944-55. Mem. adv. com. to surgeon gen., 1960-64; mem. pathology study sect. NIH, 1966-70; trustee, exec. com. Mich. Cancer Found., 1965-76, vice chmn., 1972-74, chmn., 1974-76; bd. dirs. Phila. div. Am. Cancer Soc., 1948-55, Southeastern Mich. div., 1956-65; chmn. Nat. Com. Careers in Med. Tech., 1961-66; mem. sci. adv. bd. Armed Forces Inst. Pathology, 1974—. Recipient Distinguished Alumnus awards Muhlenberg Coll., 1965, Geisinger Meml. Hosp., 1965. Mem. A.M.A. (sect. chmn. 1962), Coll. Am. Pathologists (speaker assembly 1964-68, bd. govs. 1968-71, sec.-treas. 1970-71, v.p. 1971-72, pres. 1973-75), Mich., Wayne County med. socs., Internat. Acad. Pathologists (council 1965-68), Mich. Soc. Pathologists (pres. 1965), Am. Soc. Clin. Pathologists (chmn. council anatomic pathology 1968-70), Am. Assn. Pathologists and Bacteriologists, Halstead Soc., Arthur Purdy Stout Soc. (pres. 1970-72), Minn. Soc. Clin. Pathologists (hon.), Sigma Xi, Alpha Omega Alpha. Author articles in field, chpts. in books. Home: Grosse Point, Mich. Died Oct. 4, 1976.

HORNBLOW, ARTHUR, JR., motion picture producer; b. N.Y.C., March 15, 1893; s. Arthur and Natalie (Lambert) H.; student Dartmouth, D.H.L.; student N.Y. Law Sch.; m. Leonora Schinasi, Nov. 4, 1945; 1 son, Michael; one son by previous marriage, John Terry. Admitted to N.Y. bar, 1917; wrote and produced plays in N.Y.C., 1920-27; writer for Samuel Goldwyn, Hollywood, 1927; chief prodn. exec., 1923-33; film producer, Paramount, 1933-42; producer Metr-Goldwyn-Mayer, 1942-52; pictures produced: Ruggles of Red Gap, 1939; Gaslight, 1947; The Hucksters, 1947; Cass Timberlane, 1948; The Asphalt Jungle, 1950; produced film Oklahoma! for Rodgers and Hammerstein; pres. Arthur Hornblow Prodns.; producer Witness for the Prosecution; The War Lover; translator plays from French for Broadway, among them, Pasteur by Sacha Guitry, 1925, The Captive by Edouard Bourdet, 1926. Chmn. theatre adv. board Dartmouth Coll. Served as 1st. lt. U.S. Army attched to counter-espionage section of Intelligence Corps, 1918-19. Decorated: Etoile Noire de la Legion d'Honneur (France); U.S. Presdl. Citation. Clubs: Dartmouth (N.Y.C.); Bucks (London). Author juvenile books: (with Leonora Hornblow) Animals Do the Strangest Things, Insects Are the Strangest Things, Birds Do the Strangest Things, Fish To The Strangest Things, Reptiles Do the Strangest Things, Pre-Historic Monsters Did The Strangest Things. Home: New York, N.Y. Died July 17, 1976.

HORNBY, LESTER GEORGE, etcher, author; b. at Lowell, Mass., Mar. 27, 1882; s. George Henry and Ella May (Given) H.; pub. schs.; R.I. Sch. of Design, Providence, 1890-92; Pape Sch. of Art, Boston, 1894-95; lectures, Brown U., and Art Students' League, New York: art schs., Paris, 1906-07-08, under Jean Paul Laurens and other masters; m. Cambridge, Mass., Margaret Boyd, of Seattle, Wash., Feb. 24, 1911. Represented in Art Inst. of Chicago, Mus. of Arts, Detroit, New York Pub. Library, Boston Pub. Library, Library of Congress, Washington, Fine Art Soc., London, Victoria and Albert Mus., S. Kensington, Galerie Ernst Arnold, Dresden, Salon des Artistes Français, Paris, Mus. Fine Arts, Boston. Exhibited in prin. art centres of America and Europe; Pape silver medal, Chicago Soc. Etchers, 1910. Dir. Am. Art Assn. of Paris, 1907-08. Illustrator of many works. Address: Boston, Mass. *

HORNE, MARK DANIEL, ret. educator; b. Montreal, Can., Sept. 27, 1910 (parents U.S. citizens); s. John Rodbard and May (Hynes) H.; Ph.B., Loyola U., New Orleans, 1934; M.A., La. State U., 1935, Ph.D., 1939; m. Isabel Bouny, Dec. 20, 1937; children—May Alicia (Mrs. James R. Fister), John H., Mark Daniel, Joan (Sister Danielle), Margaret (Mrs. Terry Scafidi), Mary Anne, Michael. Instr., Fortier High Sch., New Orleans, 1935-36; teaching fellow La. State U., 1936-38; mem. faculty Loyola U., New Orleans, 1938-75, prof. English, 1949-75, chmn. dept. journalism, 1964-66; vis. prof. Armstrong State Coll., Savannah. Ga., summer 1966, La. State U., New Orleans, 1968-69. Served to lt. comdr. USNR, 1942-45. Mem. AAUP, MLA, S. Central MLA, Holy Name Soc. Catholic. Contbr. profl. jours. Home: Bay St. Louis, Miss. Died Oct. 15, 1975.

HORNER, GEORGE NORMAN, real estate developer exec.; b. N.Y.C., July 19, 1918; s. J. Milton and Edna (Townsend) H.; B.S., N.Y. U., 1961; m. Betty Huston, Nov. 9, 1946; children—John Huston, Peter Townsend. Pub. accountant Hurdman & Cranstoun, N.Y.C., 1941-48; with Handy & Harman, N.Y.C., 1948-71, controller, 1966-71; sec., treas. Electric Thermometers, Inc., Norwalk, Conn., 1965-71; controller, sec. Thermo-Kinetic Corp., Tucson, 1971-74, Horizon Corp., Tucson, 1974-79; treas., sec. Nat. Housing Consultants, Inc., Gene Lowry Builders Inc. Treas. Edgemont Recreation Com., 1962-63. Treas., v.p., pres. Greenville Republican Club, 1960-63. Served with AUS, 1942-46; ETO. Mem. Fin. Execs. Inst., Nat. Assn. Accountants. Clubs: Knollwood Country (past sec., bd. govs., chmn. youth activities) (White Plains, N.Y.); Tucson Country. Home: Tucson, Ariz. Died Oct. 4, 1979; interred South Lawn, Tucson.

HORNSLETH, POUL, publisher; b. Kingston, Jamaica, Sept. 6, 1918; s. Christian Rasmus and Johanna (Poulsen) H.; A.B., U. Pa., 1940; m. Helen Bennett, Apr. 14, 1941 (div.); children—JoAnn (Mrs. Finn Kai Neilsen), Poul, Helen Faith, Christian Rasmus II. With IBM Corp., Newark, 1940-44; with Forge Mills, Inc., 1945-55; v.p. sales and mgmt. Conde Nast Publs., Inc., N.Y.C., from 1955. Mem. Friar Honor Soc., Delta Kappa Epsilon. Episcopalian. Clubs: Deke (N.Y.C.); Brooklawn Country (Bridgeport, Conn.). Home: Weston, Conn. Died Apr. 7, 1978.

HORSFIELD, BASIL, bus. exec.; b. Cambridge, N.Y., Mar. 2, 1895; s. Frederick Henry Townsend and Marianne (Moneypenny) H.; student U. N.C., 1913-17; m. Chloe Holt Freeland, Aug. 22, 1917; children—Basil, Alice Holt (Mrs. E.S. Williams), Mary Edith (Mrs. M.E. Hogan), Francis, Christopher. Chief chemist Tenn. Chem. Co., Nashville, 1917; tech. process engr., Aluminum Co. Am., Badin, N.C., 1918-22, resident mgr. southern br. aluminum research, Badin, 1922-36; mgr. Orefraction Co., Pittsburgh, 1936-40; v.p. Reynolds Metals Co., to 1959; dir. Reynolds Mining Corp., Reynolds Research Institute, Reynold Jamaica. Trustee So. Research Inst. Mem. Ala. State C. of C.(v.p.), Air Pollution Control Assn. (dir.). Democrat. Episcopalian. Club: Florence Country. Home: Florence, Ala. Died Dec. 1978.

HORTON, ARTHUR J., railway exec.; b. Lenox, Ia., Sept. 10, 1885; s. Ira T. and Agnes (Harper) H.; ed. in pub. schs.; m. Dorothy Carlysle, Nov. 3, 1917. Connected with railroad work since 1900; with C.B. & Q. R.R., 1900-47, advancing from messenger boy to gen. supt. central dist., Burlington, Ia.; v.p. Colo. & Southern Ry., Denter, since 1917. Home: Denver, Colo. *

HORTON, BAYARD TAYLOR, physician; b. Gate City, Va., Dec. 6, 1895; s. Thomas Flurnoy and Ellen Ann (Watkins) H.; B.S., U. Va., 1921, M.D., 1922; M.S., U. Minn. (Mayo Found.), 1928; m. Jane Heyl, June 14, 1922; children—Bayard Taylor, Nancy Ellen (Mrs. Paul E. Bragdon), Thomas Nelson. In practice at Emory, Va., 1923-25; prof. biology Emory and Henry Coll., Emory, Va., 1923-25; entered Mayo Found., Rochester, Minn., as fellow in medicine, 1925, instr. in medicine, 1929-34, asst. prof., 1934-37, asso. prof., 1937-58, cons. in medicine Mayo Clinic, 1930-58, head sect. clin. investigation, 1940. Dir. med. research Boswell Meml. Hosp., Sun City, Ariz., 1972, editor in chief hosp. Proc., 1975. Served as seaman USN, World War I. Recipient John Horsley prize for research work on Pyloric Block, U. Va., 1929; Distinguished Clinician award Am. Assn. for Study Headache, 1974. Diplomate Am. Bd. Internal Medicine. Fellow A.C.P., Am. Geriatrics Soc., Am. Coll. Allergists; mem. AMA, Minn. Soc. Internal Medicine (pres. 1943-44), Am. Soc. for Clin. Investigation, Central Soc. for Clin. Research, N.Y. Acad. Scis., Am. Assn. Study Headache (pres. 1961-63), Phi Beta Kappa, Sigma Xi, Phi Chi, Alpha Omega Alpha. Democrat. Baptist. Author of numerous med. articles, including description of two new disease entities, namely, temporal arteritis (Horton's disease) (with G.E. Brown and T.B. Magath) and histaminic cephalgia (with A.R. Maclean and W. McK. Craig) (Horton's syndrome). Home: Sun City, Ariz. Died July 6, 1980; buried Riverview Cemetery, Charlottesville, Va.

HORTON, OZY ROSCOE, teacher; b. Lowndesville, S.C., Mar. 26, 1886; s. Ozy Roscoe and Dispatch, 1899-1905, San Francisco Chronicle 1905-6; editor-in-chief and pub. San Francisco Call, July 1, 1906—. Active in civic and polit affairs in San Francisco. Republican; twice declined tendered nomination of mayor of St. Paul. Episcopalian. Dir. Am. Newspaper Pubs. Assn., 1900—; pres. San Francisco Newspaper Pubs. Assn., 1908; dir. Panama-Pacific Expn. W*

HORTON, RAY HERBERT, oil co. exec.; b. Denison, Tex., Nov. 19, 1907; s. Harley B. and Stella (Mayhew) H.; B.S. in Geology, U. Okla., 1930; student Advanced Management Program, Harvard University, 1948; m. Elizabeth E. Schenk, July 15, 1938; children—Judith E. (Mrs. Roger Chapman), Susann R. (Mrs. William Rittenhouse), Elizabeth J. (Mrs. Curtis Bean). Humble Oil & Refining Co., 1930, beginning with various prodn. field jobs, successively regional employee relations mgr., employee relations mgr., 1930-55, co. dir., 1955-59, pres. Humble div., 1959-61, v.p. new consol. Humble Oil & Refining Co., in charge S.W. region, 1961-66. Chmn. Tex. Indsl. Commn. Chmn. manpower subcom. prodn. com. dist. 3 Petroleum Adminstrn. War, World War II. Owner, Attoyac Farms, San Augustine, Tex. Pres., Sam Houston area council Boy Scouts Am., 1954-55, mem. nat. council, exec. bd., recipient Silver Beaver, Silver Antelope awards. Bd. dirs., past chmn. Tex. Research League. Mem. Am. Petroleum Inst., Tex. Mid-Continent Oil and Gas Assn. (past dir., exec. com.), E. Tex. C. of C. (pres. 1966), Tex. C. of C. (vice chmn.), U. Okla. Assn., Internat. Good Neighbor Council, Am. Assn. Petroleum Geologists, Alpha Tau Omega, Sigma Gamma Epsilon. Episcopalian. Mason. Clubs: Ramada, Petroleum, Houston Country. Home: Houston, Tex. Died Dec. 1972.

HORTON, ROBERT V., educator; born at Rochester, N.Y., January 2, 1905; s. L. La Verne and Lena Parker (Boyd) H.; student Culver Military Acad., 1920-22; A.B., Cornell U., 1926; M.B.A., Harvard, 1928; M.S. in Economics, Purdue University, 1964; m. Helen Cameron, November 27, 1930; children—Robert Cameron, Barbara Boyd. Investment banker; with Goldman Sachs & Co., 1927-78, gen. partner, 1941-62, ltd. partner, 1963-78; dir. Endicott Johnson Corp., Pillsbury Co., Whirlpool Co., DeSoto Inc., Kilwood Co., Munsingwear Inc.; asso. prof. econs. Purdue U., 1964-74, prof. emeritus econs. edn., 1974-78. Dir. Andrew Freeman Home. Mem. Kappa Sigma. Clubs: Lafayette (Ind.) Country; University (N.Y.C.). Home: Lafayette, Ind. Died Dec. 19, 1978; interred Rochester, N.Y.

HOSE, ROBERT HAVEN, indsl. design cons.; b. Sleepy Eye, Minn., Jan. 12, 1915; s. Robert and Grace (Irish) H.; B.Arch., U. Minn., 1937; M.Arch., M.I.T., 1940; m. Anne Runkle, Aug. 26, 1939; children—John Robert, Judith, Barbara Clair. Mem. tech. staff Bell Telephone Labs., N.Y.C., 1939-46; asso., partner Henry Dreyfuss, N.Y.C., 1946-61; owner Robert Hose Assos., Mountainside, N.J., 1961-77. Registered architect, N.J. Fellow Indsl. Designers Soc. Am. (past pres.); mem. ASME, Acacia. Republican. Home: Mountainside, N.J. Died Mar. 30, 1977.

HOSFORD, HESTER ELOISE, author, lecturer; b. Carthage, N.Y., Apr. 10, 1883; d. Clark Bailey and Edith (Stevens) H.; A.B., U. of Mich., A.M., 1910. Served as head of English dept., High Sch., Orange, N.J.; polit. writer Independent Weekly Mag., New York, 1912-15. Campaign speaker for Dem. Nat. Com. in Calif., 1912; speaker for Rep. Nat. Com., 1916, 20; has spoken in 23 states; lectured to A.E.F. in France and Germany, 1918, 19. Unitarian. Mem. D.A.R., etc. Author: Woodrow Wilson and New Jersey Made Over, 1912; Woodrow Wilson, His Career, His Statesmanship and His Public Policies, 1912; Teaching of the Mother Tongue in France, 1915; Teaching of the Mother Tongue in Germany, 1915; A Warning to Wives; The Constitution and God in Our Government; also a series of pamphlets on Americanism. Contbr. newspapers. Address: Seattle, Wash. *

HOSIER, HARRY M(ENZO), bus. exec.; b. Corning, N.Y., May 21, 1886; s. Menzo and Ann Eliza (Adsit) H.; ed. pub. schs., Corning; m. Alice May Price, Jan. 1, 1906; 1 son, Harry Marvin. Machinist and die maker Corning Glass Works, 1905-, development engr., 1910-20, prodn. supt., 1920-28 factory mgr., 1928-38, prodn. mgr., 1938-42, asst. to pres., 1942-43, v.p. and dir. indsl. relations, 1943-54, hon. vice pres. and advisor to indsl. relations, 1954—; mem. adv. bd. Lincoln Rochester Trust Co., Corning Bank (Corning Trust Co.). Fire commr., 1937—; pres. bd. edn., Dist. 13, 1937-43; board Community Chest, A.R.C., Girl Scouts. Mem. area War Manpower Commn., 1942-45. Mem. Nat. Assn. Mfrs. (active in com. work to 1947), U.S. C. of C., Corning C. of C. Republican. Episcopalian (vestryman). Mason (32 deg., Shriner). Club: Corning Country. Home: Corning, N.Y. *

HOSTETTER, JOHN CLYDE, glass technologist; b. Williamsport, Pa., Feb. 18, 1886; s. John Gardner and Catharine (Clouser) H.; Sc.B. (in absentia), Bucknell U., 1908, Sc.M., 1909, Ch.E., 1930, Sc.D., 1936; Sc.D., Alfred U., Alfred, N.Y., 1937; student U. of Chicago, 1908; m. Ida May Fisher, Aug. 7, 1909; 1 son, John Robert. Instr. chemistry, Bucknell U., 1908-10; asst. chemist, Bur. of Standards, Washington, D.C., 1910-12; asst. physicist and phys. chem., Geophysical Lab., Carnegie Inst., Washington, D.C., 1912-19; War Industries Board, 1918, development of optical glass; asst. mgr. Steuben div., Corning Glass Works, Corning, N.Y., 1919-21, asst. to v.p. in charge mfg., 1921-24, mgr. R.I. Div., Central Falls, R.I., 1924-28, mgr. bulb and tubing div., Corning, N.Y., 1928-30, dir. research and development, 1930-37; v.p. and dir. research and development, Hartford-Empire Co., Hartford, Conn., 1937-43; pres. Mississippi Glass Co., St. Louis, and chmn. bd. Walsh Refractories Co. since 1944. Awarded Howard N. Potts medal from the Franklin Inst., for his part in producing the 200-inch mirror of the world's largest telescope, Calif. Inst. of Tech. Observatory; The Nation's (mag.) Roll of Honor, 1934; Significant Sig medal, 1937. Am. rep. on internat. commn. of glass tech. and attended Internat. Congress on Glass, Italy, 1933, England, 1936, also one of Am. counselors Internat. Chem. Union Luzerne, Switzerland, 1936. Trustee Bucknell U., 1939-44; mem. bd. mgrs., N.Y. State Coll. of Ceramics, Alfred, N.Y. Registered professional engr., N.Y. State. Fellow Am. Ceramic Soc. (pres. 1933-34), Am. Inst. Chemists, Am. Assn. Advancement Sci.; mem. Ceramic Assn. of N.Y. (pres. 1938), Am. Chem. Soc., Am. Inst. of Chem. Engrs., Franklin Inst., Eng. Soc. West. Pa.; Soc. Heat. and Vent. Engrs.; Illuminating Engr. Soc.; Am. Soc. Test. Materials; Washington Acad. Sciences, N.Y. Acad. Sciences, Am. Soc. Mil Engrs., Deutsche Glastechischen Gesellschaft, fellow English Soc. Glass Tech., Keramos, Sigma Chi. Clubs: Cosmos (Washington, D.C.); Chemists (N.Y. City); University, Noonday, Engineers', Missouri Athletic, Racquet (St. Louis). Author of scientific and tech. publications. Now retired. Home: Winter Park, Fla. *

HOTT, LOUIS RANDELL, psychiatrist, psychoanalyst; b. N.Y.C., Feb. 29, 1912; s. Morris Joseph and Anna (Karig) H.; student L.I. U., 1929-32; M.D., U. Bern, Switzerland, 1937; postgrad. N.Y. U., 1947; m. Jacqueline Rose, Dec. 27, 1947; children—Timothy, Lawrence, Sue Merle, Rachel. Intern, Richmond Meml. Hosp., S.I., 1937-38; resident Sea View Hosp., S.I., 1938-39; resident neuropsychiatry VA Hosp., Bklyn., 1947-48; resident, staff psychiatrist Bellevue Hosp., N.Y.C., 1948-53, attending, then sr. psychiatrist, 1948-80; pvt. practice medicine, specializing in psychoanalysis and sex therapy, N.Y.C., 1960-80; med. dir., chmn. med. bd. Karen Horney Psychoanalytic Clinic, 1960-79, med. dir. emeritus, 1979-80; asst. clin. prof. psychiatry N.Y. U. Med. Center, 1952-80; clin. prof. Advanced Inst. Psychol. Studies, Adelphia U., Garden City, N.Y., 1978-80; asst. dean, trustee, mem. faculty council Am. Inst. for Psychoanalysis, 1960-80; psychiat. cons. Supreme Ct. N.Y., N.Y.C. Police Dept., Univ. and Bellevue hosps. Served to lt. col., M.C., AUS, 1941-46. Certified psychoanalyst N.Y. State; certified sex therapist Am. Assn. Sex Educators, Counselors and Therapists. Diplomate Am. Bd. Psychiatry and Neurology. Fellow Am. Psychiat. Assn., AMA, Acad. Psychoanalysis; mem. Assn. for Advancement Psychoanalysis. Club: New York University. Contbr. articles to med. jours. Home: Great Neck, N.Y. Died Mar. 18, 1980.

HOTZ, H(ENRY) G(USTAVE) (HOTS), coll. dean emeritus; b. Scandinavia, Wis., Apr. 13, 1880; s. Herman and Emma (Hartman) H.; grad. Oshkosh State Normal Coll., 1906; Ph.B., U. Wis., 1913, A.M., 1915; Ph.D., Columbia, 1918; m. Stella Palmer, Dec. 22, 1924; children—Henry Palmer, Oscar Hartman. Supt. schs., Spooner, Wis., 1908-11, Hayward, Wis., 1911-12; prof. edn. Coll. of William and Mary, 1918-19; prof. secondary edn. U. Ark., 1919-23, 25-34, dean coll. edn., 1934-35, dir. summer sessions, 1934-45, dean emeritus since 1945, research specialist vocational tchr. edn. since 1948. chmn. univ. com. postwar edn., 1943-45; state high sch. supervisor, Ark., 1923-25. Sec. commn. secondary schs. North Central Assn. Colls. and Secondary Schs., 1930-36. Mem. adv. com. Ark. Program to Improve Instrn. Mem. N.E.A. (life), Ark. Edn. Assn., Phi Beta Kappa Democrat.*

HOUSEL, WILLIAM STUART (HOU'ZEL), civil engr., educator; b. Boulder, Colo., Feb. 16, 1901; s. Edgar Stuart and Clara (Ewing) H.; B.S., U. of Mich., 1923, M.S., 1931; m. Marjorie Jane McKechnie, Feb. 26, 1925; 1 dau., Joanne Florence (Mrs. John A. Taylor). Instr. civil engring. U. of Mich., 1924-29, asst. prof., 1929-36, asso. prof., 1936-46, prof. since 1950, supervisor research in soil mechanics from 1927; research consultant from 1934; cons. airport constrn. U.S. Navy, 1941-42, U.S. Engring. Corps, 1941-42, Pan Am. Airways, S.A. Bases, 1941, Mich. Bd. Aeronautics, 1946-48; cons. founds. V.A. Hosps., U.S. Engring. Corps, V.A. from 1946; cons. steel mill constrn. Armco Steel from 1941, Inland Steel from 1942, J. & L. Steel, 1950; cons. founds. and soil investigation oil fields development Gulf Oil Co., 1947-48, Sun Oil Co., 1948-49, Creole Petroleum Corp., Venezuela, 1950-54; vis. lectr. Post Grad. Sch. U. Chile, Santiago, summer 1960; vis. prof. civil engring. University Hawaii, Honolulu, January-June 1965. Served as lt. commander and comdr. Civil Engr. Corps, U.S.N.R., active duty 1942-46, P.T.O., Am. Theatre Operations, Mem. Am. Soc. C.E. (outstanding civil engr. Southeastern Mich. br. 1965), Am. Soc. Testing Materials (award merit 1966), Highway Research Bd. (Roy W. Crum award 1965), Am. Soc. Engring. Edn. Assn. Asphalt Paving Technologists, Mich., Detroit engring. socs., Sigma Xi, Lambda Chi Alpha. Author: books and soil mechanics articles profl. jours. Home: Ann Arbor, Mich. Died 1978.

HOUSEWRIGHT, JAMES TALBERTT, labor union ofcl.; b. Wesco, Mo., Nov. 23, 1921; s. Thomas Austin and Nora (Asher) H.; grad. pub. schs.; m. Jane M. Wallace, Mar. 20, 1975; children—Lana (Mrs. Charles Joseph Lowthers), Linda (Mrs. Daniel Nostheide), Kathryn (Mrs. Charles James Lowthers), James Talbertt. Sec.-treas. Local 725 Retail Clks. Union, Indpls., 1947-53; organizing dir. Retail Clks. Internat. Assn., Washington, 1953-65, internat. dir. orgn., 1965-66, exec. asst. to pres., 1966-68, internat. pres., 1968-77; v.p. Am. Fedn. Labor and Congress Indsl. Orgns., 1972-77. Mem. exec. com. Internat. Fedn. Comml., Clerical and Tech. Employees; mem. exec. bd. Maritime Trades Dept.; mem. exec. bd. Council AFL-CIO Unions for Profl. Employees. Mem. The Pres.'s Com. on Employment of the Handicapped, 1968-77; mem. Leadership Conf. on Civil Rights, 1970-77; corp. mem. Muscular Dystrophy Assn. Inc. Served with USAAF, 1942-45. Mem. A. Philip Randolph Inst. (exec. bd. 1972-77). Home: Arlington, Va. Died Sept. 19, 1977.

HOUSTON, CLYDE EARL, public utilities; b. May 27, 1882; m. Georgia Berry, Mar. 8, 1916; 1 dau., Helen (Mrs. Boileau). Started with Southern Edison Co., Los Angeles, in 1904, now v.p. Mem. Chamber of Commerce (former pres.), Elec. Organizations, Rotary pres. Los Angeles County Fair Assn. Republican Christian Scientist. Mason. Elk. Home: San Marino Calif. *

HOUSTON, FRANK KITTRELL, banker; b. Woodbury, Tenn., July 4, 1882; s. William Cannon and Lura (Kittrell) H.; B.S., Vanderbilt University, 1904 married Mrs. Silas Sinton, July 24, 1954. Asst. cashier First Nat. Bank, Nashville, Tenn., 1907 14; asst. cashier Third Nat. Bank and v.p. First Nat. Bank, St. Louis Mo., 1914-20; v.p. Chemical Nat. Bank, New York

1920-27; 1st v.p. Chem. Nat. Bank & Trust Company, 1927-35, president, 1935-47; hon. chairman, member adv. committee Chem. Bank New York Trust Company; director Hotel Waldorf-Astoria Corporation. Trustee Vanderbilt University; hon. chairman Cordell Hull Found.; chmn. bd. Thomas Jefferson Meml. Found. Mem. Council Fgn. Relations, Inc., Sigma Alpha Epsilon. Methodist. Clubs: University, Piping, Rock, Racquet and Tennis, Turf and Field, Farmington Country. Home: N.Y.C. *

HOUSTON, JAMES GARFIELD, lawyer; b. Pitts., Sept. 22, 1881; s. James Wilson and Sarah (McCutcheon) H.; A.B., U. Pitts., 1903, LL.B., 1906, M.L., 1918, L.L.D., 1956; m. Grace Preston, June 30, 1926. Admitted to Pa. bar, 1906; pvt. practice law, Pitts., 1906—; partner Blaxter, O'Neill & Houston, 1937—. Asso. prof. law U. Pitts., 1912-38. Served as maj., asst. adj. 18th Inf. Div., U.S. Army, 1917-18. Mem. Allegheny County (pres. 1950-51), Am., Pa. bar assns., Phi Delta Theta, Phi Delta Phi. Presbyn. (trustee). Club: Duquesne. Home: Pittsburgh PA. *

HOWARD, DELTON THOMAS, philosopher; b. South Bend, Ind., Mar. 23, 1883; s. Edward M. and Morie (Snell) H.; A.B., Lawrence Coll., Appleton, Wis., 1910; A.M., U. of Ill., 1912; Ph.D., Cornell U., 1916; Dr. Humane Letters, Grinnell Coll., 1944; married Gertrude Baker, 1916; 1 son, John Baker. Instr. in philosophy, Northwestern U., 1916-18, instr. in psychology, 1918-25, asso. prof., 1925-30, prof., 1930-35, prof. and chmn. dept. philosophy, 1935-47, John Evans professor moral and intellectual philosophy, 1947-48; visiting prof. philos., University Miami, Fla., since 1948; director university personnel, 1926-34. Member American Assn. Univ. Profs., Phi Beta Kappa, Sigma Xi. Methodist. Club: University. Author: John Dewey's Logical Theory, 1918; An Outline of General Psychology (with Robert H. Gault), 1924; Analytical Syllogistics, 1946. Home: Miami, Fla. *

HOWARD, ELSTON GENE, profl. baseball coach; b. St. Louis, Feb. 23, 1929; s. Wayman Hill and Emmaline (Webb) H.; m. Arlene Henley, Dec. 14, 1954; children—Elston Jr., Cheryl, Karen. Player minor league baseball teams, 1950-54; outfielder, then catcher, 1st baseman N.Y. Yankees, 1955-67, 1st base coach, 1969—; catcher Boston Red Sox, 1967-68; mem. All-Star teams, 1957-75. Named Most Valuable Player Internat. League, 1954, Am. League, 1963; named catcher Sporting News Am. League All-Star team, 1961, 63-64, Sporting News All-Star fielding team, 1963-64. Address: Bronx, N.Y. Died Dec. 14, 80.

HOWARD, FINDLEY BURTCH, foreign service officer; b. Papillion, Neb., Oct. 8, 1885; s. Edgar and Elizabeth (Burtch) H.; LL.B., U. of Neb., 1907; m. Edna Healey, Oct. 8, 1919 (dec.); children—Findley Burtch, Martita. Admitted to Neb. bar, 1907, and began practice at Columbus; with Customs Service, Panama Canal Zone; successively asst. fiscal rep., Republic of El Salvador, customs adviser Republic of Chile and Republic of Guatemala; formerly E.E. and M.P. to Paraguay. Mem. Alpha Tau Omega. Democrat. Episcopalian. Mason (K.T.), Elk, Woodman. Home: Columbus, Oh. *

HOWARD, HARRY STANLEY, business exec.; b. Anamosa, Ia., 1891; s. Charles R. and Josephine (Holt) H.; B.S., U. Cal. 1915; m. Blanche Munn, Dec. 4, 1915; 1 son, Harry Stanley. Pres., dir. Wyeth Labs. div. American Home Products Corporation, Philadelphia, 1943-56, chairman board, 1956-74; president and director Collyrium, Inc., from 1940; v.p., John Wyeth Labs., S.A., from 1944; dir. Am. Home Products Corp., N.Y.C., Wyeth Internat., Ltd., Wyeth Mexicana, S.A. Mem. Theta Delta Chi. Republican. Clubs: Union League (Phila.); Merion Golf (Ardmore, Pa.); Seaview Country (Absecon, N.J.); Seigniory (P.Q., Can). Home: Villanova, Pa. Died Mar. 17, 1976.

HOWARD, HERBERT SEYMOUR, naval officer; b. Buffalo, Aug. 5, 1884; s. Clarence Orville and Lucretia Stanley (Barnes) H.; student U.S. Naval Acad., 1900-04, M.I.T., 1906-09, U.S. Naval War Coll., 1927-28; m. Mary Morris McCauley, Nov. 3, 1914; children—Herbert Seymour, Macauley, Mary Chase. Became midshipman, 1904; promoted through grades to rear adm., Jan. 2, 1941; asst. naval attaché, London, 1932-35; head Design Div., Bur. Ships, Navy Dept., 1941-42; dir. David Taylor Model Basin, U.S. Navy, 1942-46; ret., 1946; tech. cons. Stevens Inst. Tech., from 1946. Awarded Cuban Pacification medal, Victory medal (World War I), Jubilee medal (British), Defense Medal, World War II Medal, Legion of Merit, Sec. of Navy's Commendation Ribbon; comdr. Order of British Empire. Mem. Soc. Naval Architects and Marine Engrs., Am. Soc. Naval Engrs., Naval Institute, Institution of Naval Architects (London), Chi Phi. Episcopalian. Clubs: Met. (Washington); New York Yacht, (N.Y. City); Chevy Chase (Chevy Chase, Md.); Merion Cricket (Haverford, Pa.). Address: Washington, D.C. Died Jan. 12, 1977.

HOWARD, HUBERT ELMER, business exec.; b. Fairfield, Iowa, June 19, 1889; s. Elmer A. and Mary (Lamson) H.; Ph.B., Parsons Coll., 1909, LL.D., 1942; LL.B. Harvard, 1912; m. Edith Sacket, Mar. 22, 1918; children—Hubert Elmer, John Addison, Charles Nevin; m. 2d, Helen M. Bishop, 1938. Mem. firm Haase, Hanley & Howard, lawyers, Chgo., 1912-23; pres. Shasta Coal Corp.; pres., chmn. bd. Binkley Coal Co. Chmn., Munitions Board, Dept. Def., 1949-50. Served as Capt. 31st F.A., A.E.F., World War I; fed. prohibition dir. Ill., 1919-21. Mason, Clubs: University, Bob-O-Link, Glenview, Balmoral Jockey, Inc. (pres.). Donor to Parsons Coll. Home: Chicago, Ill. Died Oct. 20, 1976.

HOWARD, NATHANIEL RICHARDSON, newspaper editor; b. Arlington, Columbus, O., Apr. 23, 1898; s. Carlos Newton and Anne McKennan (Richardson) H.; student Oberlin Coll., 1915-18; m. Marjorie Norton, Sept. 13, 1918 (dec. Dec. 1928); children—Mary Anne, Marjorie Norton; m. 2d, Edith E. Moriarty, July 17, 1930. Reporter, Cleve. News, 1917, editor, 1937-60; with Cleve. Plain Dealer, 1918-37, mng. editor, 1930-37, contbg. editor, 1960-63; dir. A.P., 1952-60. Asst. dir. press U.S. Office Censorship, Washington, 1942-43. Mem. Am. Soc. Newspaper Editors (pres. 1947-48). Republican. Conglist. Clubs: Advertising, Union (Cleve.); Cosmos (Washington). Author: Trust for All Time, 1963; The George M. Humphrey Basic Papers, 1965; The First Hundred Years, 1972. Home: Cleveland Heights, Ohio. Died Dec. 24, 1980.

HOWARD, RHEA, newspaper pub.; b. Wichita Falls, Tex., July 25, 1892; s. Ed and Jettie Lee (Maloney) H.; student Trinity U., Waxahachie, Tex., 1910-11, Eastman Coll., Poughkeepsie, N.Y., 1912; m. Kathleen Benson, Oct. 22, 1913; 1 dau., Anna Katherine (Mrs. James B. Barnett). With Times Pub. Co. (Wichita Daily Times, Wichita Falls Record News), from 1913, pres., from 1948; dir. Burlington No. Ry. Bd. dirs. Wichita Falls United Fund, Tex. Law Enforcement Found., Red River Valley Assn., Midwestern U. Found., Wichita Falls Bd. Commerce and Industry, Wichita Falls Art Mus., N. Tex. Rehab. Center, A.R.C., Wichita County Child Welfare and Devel. Found. (chmn.), Wichita Falls Symphony, Tex. Council for Higher Edn., Woman's Forum. Del. Democratic Nat. Conv., 1952, 56, 60, 64. Named Pub. of Year, Headliners Club, 1960; Salesman of Year, Wichita Falls, 1970. Mem. Nat. Press Club, Am. Soc. Newspaper Editors, Tex. Daily Newspaper Assn., N. Tex. Oil and Gas Assn. (dir.), Am., So. (dir.) newspaper pubs. assns., C. of C., Airline Passengers Assn. (mem. nat. adv. council), Sigma Delta Chi. Democrat. Presbyn. Mason (K.T., Shriner, 33 degree). Clubs: President's, Wichita, Wichita Falls Country. Home: Wichita Falls, Tex. Deceased.

HOWARD, WILLIAM EDWARDS, banker; b. Salisbury, Md., June 27, 1904; s. William Edwards and Eunice (Morgan) H.; A.B., U. Del., 1924; m. Evelyn Sale, Mar. 17, 1934; children—Macon Lee, Julia Morgan, Evelyn Sale. Asst. cashier Mchts. Nat. Bank, Hampton, Va., 1924-28; nat. bank examiner, 1928-30; asst. cashier McDowell County Nat. Bank, Welch, W.Va., 1930-32; pres., dir. Braddock Nat. Bank (Pa.), 1932-47; v.p., dir. Wilkinsburg Bank (Pa.), 1938-47; v.p. Mellon Nat. Bank & Trust Co., Pitts., 1947-63, sr. v.p., 1963-69; pres. Columbia Corp., Pitts.; trustee Dollar Savs. Bank of Pitts.; dir. Kennametal, Inc., Latrobe, Pa., O. Hommel Co., Union Title Guaranty Co., H.H. Robertson Co., Pitts., Latrobe Steel Co. (Pa.), Ry. Maintenance Corp., Pitts. Bd. dirs., treas. Western Pa. Conservancy; trustee, treas. Valley Sch. Ligonier (Pa.), Community Coll. Allegheny County. Vice chmn. finance com., treas. United Fund Allegheny County; treas., mem. exec. com. Pitts. Urban Transit Council, Nat. Transp. Center, Pitts.; bd. govs. Nature Conservancy. Episcopalian. Mason (Shriner). Home: Pittsburgh, Pa. Died Mar. 30, 1977.

HOWE, HAROLD, educator, banker; b. Chapman, Kans., Feb. 24, 1901; s. Michael Maurice and Margaret Ann (Kiley) H.; B.S. in Agr., Kans. State Coll., 1922; M.S., U. Md., 1923; Ph.D., U. Wis., 1937; LL.D., St. Benedicts Coll., 1950; m. Ruth Riordan, June 23, 1930; children—Philip, Barbara (Mrs. John W. Stang). Asst. in soils Md. Agrl. Exptl. Sta., 1922-23; asst. in agrl. econs. Wis. Agrl. Exptl. Sta., 1924-25; instr. agrl. econs. Kans. State U., Manhattan, 1925-27, asst. prof., 1927-30, asso. prof., 1930-34, prof., 1934-64, dean Grad. Sch., 1945-64; dir. grad. fellowship br. U.S. Office Edn., Washington, 1961-62; dean Grad. Sch., St. Louis U., 1964-67; project mgr. UN Devel. Program 80, Turrialba, Costa Rica, 1968-70; sr. v.p., dir. Kans. State Bank, Manhattan, 1970-80. Cons. Nat. Resources Planning Bd., 1938-43. City commr. Manhattan, 1951-55, mayor, 1953-54. Mem. exec. com., council on grad. work Assn. Land Grant Colls. and Univs., 1948-52, chmn. council on grad. work, 1950-51. Bd. dirs. Kan. Soc. for Crippled Children, 1945-64; trustee Nat. Soc. Crippled Children and Adults, 1957-60. Mem. Phi Kappa Phi, Alpha Zeta, Gamma Sigma Delta, Pi Kappa Delta, Phi Kappa Theta. Democrat. Catholic. Author numerous bulls. and papers on Pub. finance, land econs. Home: Manhattan, Kans. Died Dec. 16, 1980; buried Sunrise Cemetery, Manhattan.

HOWE, JAMES WONG, cinematographer; b. Kwangtung, China, Aug. 28, 1899; s. Wong How and Dang Shee; brought to U.S., 1904; ed. high sch., Pasco, Wash.; m. Sanora Babb, Sept. 16, 1949. Asst. camerman Lasky Studios, Hollywood, Calif., 1917-22, dir. photography, 1922-76; first film, Drums of Fate, others include Body and Soul (Look award 1947), Rose Tatoo (Acad. award 1955, Look award 1955), Picnic (Look award 1955), Song Without End, Hud (Academy award 1963), The Outrage, Hombre, Seconds, 1967, The Heart is a Lonely Hunter, 1968, The Molly, Maquires, 1969, Funny Lady, 1974. Recipient Medal of Honor, George Eastman Festival Film Artists, 1957; 16 Oscar nominations. Mem. Acad. Motion Picture Arts and Scis., Internat. Photographers Am., Am. Soc. Cinematographers, Dirs. Guild Am., Chinese Hist. Soc., Delta Kappa Alpha. Home: Hollywood, Calif. Died July 12, 1976; interred Westwood Village Meml. Park, West Los Angeles, Calif.

HOWE, JEROME WILLARD, coll. dean; b. Worcester, Mass., Oct. 12, 1886; s. Edward Francis and Ettie Louisa (Cole) H.; B.S., Worcester (Mass.) Poly. Inst., 1909; m. Helen Marion Cole, Sept. 1, 1918; children—Jerome Willard, Beverly. Teacher civil engring., Pa. Mil. Coll., 1909-11; draftsman Phoenix Bridge Co., 1911-13; editor Wireless Age, 1923-24; prof. civil engring., Worcester Poly. Inst., 1924-34, head of dept., 1933-37, dean of admissions and of students since 1937. Second lieut., 10th Cav., U.S. Army, 1913, 1st lt., 1916, capt., 1917, maj., 1917; retired for phys. disability, 1924. Awarded two Silver Star Citations, U.S. War Dept. Mem. Am. Soc. C.E., Am. Soc. Engring. Edn. Worcester Soc. Civil Engrs., Newcomen Soc. Am., Sigma Phi Epsilon, Sigma Xi. Republican. Conglist. Clubs: Bohemians, Dickens Fellowship. Editor. Home: Worcester, Mass. *

HOWE, QUINCY, journalist; b. Boston, Aug. 17, 1900; s. Mark Antony DeWolfe and Fanny Huntington (Quincy) H.; A.B., Harvard, 1921; postgrad. Christ's Coll., Cambridge, Eng., 1921-22; m. Mary L. Post, May 14, 1932; children—Quincy, Mabel Davis. With Atlantic Monthly Co., 1922-28; editor of Living Age, 1929-35; with Simon & Schuster, Inc., pubs., 1935-42; news analyst CBS, 1942-49, in TV, 1949-50; asso. prof. U. Ill., Sch. Journalism, news analyst Sta. WILL, 1950-54; news analyst ABC, 1954-63, Radio N.Y. World Wide, 1966-70, WTFM, 1973-74. Editor Atlas, mag. World Press, 1961-65, contbg. editor Atlas World Press Rev., 1974-77. Pres., Nat. Bd. Rev. Motion Pictures. Recipient George Foster Peabody award for radio-TV news analysis, 1955; Overseas Press Club award for radio-TV news analysis, 1959; Columbia-Catherwood award for responsible internat. journalism, 1962. Mem. Assn. Radio-TV News Analysts, Sigma Delta Chi. Club: Century. Author: World Diary (1929-34), 1934; England Expects Every American to Do His Duty, 1937; Blood Is Cheaper Than Water, 1939; The News and How to Understand It, 1940; A World History of Our Own Times, vol. I The World We Lost: From the Turn of the Century to 1918, Armistice, 1949; vol. II The World Between the Wars, From the 1918 Armistice to the Munich Agreement, 1953; Ashes of Victory: World War II and Its Aftermath, 1972. Home: New York, N.Y. Died Feb. 17, 1977; interred Wollaston Cemetery, Quincy, Mass.

HOWELL, ALBERT CHARLES, life ins. co. exec.; b. N.J., June 10, 1919; s. Albert and Mary Petrinella (Bergquist) H.; S.B., Harvard U., 1941, M.A., 1947; postgrad. Mass. Inst. Tech.; children—Charles Lawrence, Peter Alan. With John Hancock Mut. Life Ins. Co., Boston, 1947-75, 2d v.p., 1968-69, v.p., 1969-75. Chmn. health adv. commn. City of Newton Centre (Mass.), mem. council of health. Served to capt. USAAF, 1942-47. Fellow Soc. Actuaries; mem. Am. Acad. Actuaries, Internat. Assn. Actuaries Club Boston. Republican. Clubs: Harvard, Lognwood Cricket, Harvard Musical. Home: Newton Centre, Mass. Died Jan. 21, 1978; buried Newton Centre.

HOWELL, BENJAMIN FRANKLIN, educator; b. Troy Hills, N.J., Sept. 30, 1890; s. Benjamin Franklin and Caroline Smith (Quinby) H.; B.S., Princeton U., 1913, A.M., 1915, Ph.D., 1920; m. Claire Homan Mead, June 24, 1915; 1 son, Benjamin Franklin. Mem. faculty Princeton, 1915-59, prof. geology, paleontology 1947-59, also curator of invertebrate paleontology from 1924; asso. curator, geology and paleontology, Acad. Natural Scis., Phila., 1936-37, curator, 1937-47, research fellow from 1947; prof. geology and paleontology, Wagner Free Inst. Sci., 1928-47. Fellow A.A.A.S.; mem. Geol. Soc. Am.; Paleontol. Soc.; Fgn. Mem. Geol. Soc. London. Author: 200 papers on paleontology. Home: Princeton, N.J. Died May 28, 1976.

HOWELL, BENJAMIN RANDOLPH, lawyer; b. Roswell, N.M., Sept. 20, 1900; s. Mark and Leona (Randolph) H.; LL.B., U. Tex., 1925; m. Romaine Safford, Apr. 30, 1931; children—Margaret Safford (Mrs. James M. Langford), Mark Franklin. Admitted to Tex. bar, 1925, since practiced in El Paso; former mem. Jones, Hardie, Grambling and Howell. Former v.p., dir. El Paso Natural Gas Company. Mem. Tex. Bd. Edn., 1957-75, chmn., 1969-75. Served as col. AUS, 1940-45. Decorated Legion of Merit. Mem. Am., Tex. (dir.

1946-48), El Paso (pres. 1952) bar assns., Nat. Assn. State Bds. Edn. (area v.p. 1970-71), Tex. Research League (dir.), Pi Kappa Alpha, Phi Delta Phi. Episcopalian. Club: El Paso. Home: El Paso, Tex. Died Dec. 17, 1975.

HOWELL, (GEORGE) EVAN, congressman, lawyer; b. Marion, Ill., Sept. 21, 1905; s. Ernest Truman and Jo Ella (Rainey) H.; B.S., U. Ill., 1927, LL.B., 1930; m. Kathryn Sellers, May 1, 1937; children—Marilyn Lee, Joella Florence, William Evan, John Ernest, Kathryn. Tchr. Harvard (Ill.) Community High Sch., 1927-28; gen. work Pub. Service Co. of No. Ill., Chicago, 1928; instr. Coll. Commerce, U. Ill., 1928-30; admitted to Ill. bar, 1930; asso. Cornelius J. Doyle, Springfield, Ill., 1930-35; engaged in private practice law, Springfield, 1936-47; judge U.S. Ct. Claims, 1947-53; engaged private practice law, 1953-79; dir. Bradner Central Co., Fearn Internat., Inc.; referee in bankruptcy, U.S. Dist. Ct. So. Dist. Mem. 77th to 80th Congresses (1941-49), 21st Ill. Dist. Bd. dirs. Wilmette Family Service Center. Mem. Tau Kappa Epsilon, Phi Delta Phi, Beta Gamma Sigma. Republican. Mason (33 deg., Shriner), Elk, Eagle. Clubs: Sangamo, American Business (Springfield); Burning Tree, Met., Chevy Chase (Washington). Home: Washington, D.C. Died Sept. 18, 1979.

HOWIE, DAVID HEATH, trustee; b. Lynn, Mass., Apr. 28, 1886; s. David and Margaret Ann (Remick) H.; A.B., Harvard, 1907, student Grad. Sch., 1907-09; m. Harriet Neal Baum, June 6, 1911 (dec.); m. 2d, Edith Elliott Craig, Sept. 28, 1946. With Lee, Higginson & Co., 1910-30; sr. v.p. Lee Higginson Trust Co., 1931-32; v.p. Fiduciary Trust Co., Boston, 1932-52, director, 1932-62; director of State Street Investment Corp., Frostimber Company; trustee Rolfe Coal Lands; trustee, member bd. investment Boston Five Cents Savs. Bank. Exec. sec. New Eng. Governors R.R. Com., 1930-31; mem. Boston Port Authority, 1935-45; treas. New Eng. Council, 1936-39. Member of the board of trustees Tufts Coll.; trustee New Eng. Conservatory of Music. Mem. Corporate Fiduciaries Assn. (pres. 1940-41), Mass. Bankers Assn. (treas. 1942-43), Wine and Food Society Boston (pres. 1948-50). Democrat. Unitarian (treas. trustees and proprietors). Clubs: St. Botolph, Union, Algonquin (Boston); Down Town. Home: Boston. *

HOWLAND, ALICE GULIELMA, educator; b. Wilmington, Del., Feb. 14, 1883; d. Charles S. and Mary (Shipley) H.; student Bryn Mawr Coll., 1901-02; grad. Carnegie Training Sch. of Children's Librarians, Pittsburgh, Pa., 1904; unmarried; adopted two girls. Asst. to prin., Miss Shipley's Sch., Bryn Mawr, 1905-06; state student sec. for N.Y. and N.J. for Nat. Bd. Y.W.C.A., 1906-08; prin. Utica (N.Y.) Female Acad., 1908-11; prin. and part owner, Shipley Sch., Bryn Mawr, since 1911. Mem. bd. of dirs. New Mexico Assn. on Indian Affairs; trustee Lab. of Anthropology, Santa Fe, N.M.; dir. Bur. of Household Economics (Phila.); mem. Nat. Assn. of Prins. of Schs. for Girls (pres. 1936-38). Chmn. Am. Wom-Activities Div. Santa Fe County Salvage Bd., Santa Fe Youth Center, Santa Fe, N.M. Quaker. Club: Cosmopolitan (New York). Address: Santa Fe, N.M. *

HOWSE, W. L., JR., religious educator; b. Fayetteville, Tenn., Feb. 26, 1905; s. William Lewis and Emma (Paulk) H.; A.B., Union U., 1926, M.A. magna cum laude, Baylor U., 1932; M.R.E., Southwestern Bapt. Theol. Sem., 1934, D.R.E. cum laude, 1937; L.H.D., Hardin-Simmons U., 1948; LL.D., Union U., Jackson, Tenn., 1958; m. Genevieve Morgan, Oct. 28, 1930; 1 son, William Lewis III. Ednl. dir. Broadway Bapt. Ch., Ft. Worth, 1927-30, minister religious edn., 1935-45; from instr. to prof. Southwestern Bapt. Theol. Sem., Ft. Worth, 1932-54; dir. edn. div. Sunday Sch. Bd. So. Bapt. Conv., Nashville, 1954-71, programming cons. East Asia area Fgn. Mission Bd., 1971-74, Middle Am. and Caribbean area, 1974-76, cons. Mission Support div., 1977; adj. prof. Midwestern Bapt. Sem., Kansas City, Mo., 1977. Mem. Childrens Hosp. Bd., Ft. Worth, 1948-51; pres. Tex. Bapt. Sunday Sch. Conv., 1947-51; pres. Tex. Bapt. Tng. Union, 1929-30, pres. exec. bd., 1937-38; pres. Southwestern Bapt. Religious Edn. Assn., 1941, Inter-Agy. Council So. Bapt. Conv., 1957-58. Bd. dirs. Ft. Worth Community Chest. Mem. Nashville C. of C., Sigma Alpha Epsilon, Kappa Delta Pi. Author several books, pamphlets. Home: Richmond, Va. Died Dec. 27, 1977.

HOWSON, CARL R(OBERT), physician; b. Hornby, Ont., Can., Apr. 25, 1885; s. John Atkinson and Orpha (Hall) H.; M.D., Coll. Phys. and Surg., U. of Southern Calif., 1913; m. Luella Reeves, May 17, 1919. Came to U.S., 1910, naturalized citizen, 1919. In practice at Highland, Calif., 1913-17, Redlands, 1917-18, Los Angeles, specializing in diseases of the chest, since 1918; asso. prof. medicine, Coll. of Med. Evangelists, 1920-33, prof. diseases of chest since 1933; chief attending physician, tuberculosis dept., Los Angeles County Hosp. since 1933; med. dir. La Vina (Calif.) Sanatorium, 1938-44. Chmn. Tuberculosis Consulting Bd. Los Angeles City Schs., 1933-42. Diplomate Am. Bd. Internal Medicine. Fellow Am. Coll. Physicians, Am. Coll. Chest Physicians; mem. Am., Calif. and Los Angeles Trudeau socs., A.M.A., Calif. Health and Tuberculosis Assn. (past president), Calif. Medical Assn., Los Angeles County Med. Assn. (ex-pres.), Nat. Tuberculosis Assn. v.p., 1947-48, Los Angeles Tuberculosis and Health Assn. (dir. 1935-45, v.p. 1947-48), So. Calif. Med. Assn. (ex-pres.), Los Angeles Acad. Medicine. Republican. Mason. Club: University. Home: San Marino, Calif. *

HOYLE, RENE EDWARD DERUSSY (HOIL), army officer; b. West Point, N.Y., Sept. 16, 1883; s. Gen. Eli DuBose and Fanny Cornick (DeRussy) H.; B.S., U.S. Mil. Acad., 1906 grad. Mounted Service Sch., 1910, Command and Gen. Staff Sch., 1924, Army War Coll., 1927; m. Christine Spencer Biddle Guilfoyle, Dec. 21, 1909; children—Rene Edward DeRussy, Susie Lane (wife of Capt. DeV. P. Armstrong, U.S. Army), John Guilfoyle. Commd. 1st lt., 6th F.A., 1907-16; promoted through grades to brig. gen. (temporary), 1940, major general (temporary), February 14, 1942; served on Mexican Border duty, 1914-16, with First F.A., Schofield Barracks, T.H., 1916-17; asst. commandant Sch. of Fire for Field Arty., 1918-19; with A.E.F., France and Germany, 1919; prof. mil. sciences and tactics, Yale U., 1919-23; dir. Dept. of Tactics, Field Arty. Sch., 1930-35; personnel officer and exec. officer Chief of Field Arty., 1935-39; comdr. Ft. Hoyle (named after father), 6th Field Arty. Regt., 1939-40; comdr. 9th Inf. Div., 1940-42; comd. officer 9th Infantry Division since Feb. 1942. Awarded D.S.M., Cuban Pacification medal, Mexican Service medal, Victory medal, World War medal. Mem. Conn. Acad. Arts and Sciences, Soc. of First Div. A.E.F., Assn. of Grads. of U.S. Mil. Acad., New York Soc. Mil. and Naval Officers. Episcopalian. Clubs: Graduate (New Haven); Army and Navy Country (Washington). Address: Camp Roberts, Calif.*

HOYT, AUSTIN, fed. judge; b. Beacon, N.Y., Apr. 26, 1915; s. Ferdinand Augustus and Beatrice (Watson) H.; student U. Ala., 1933-34, St. John's U., 1934-35; LL.B., U. Va., 1938; m. Margaret Llewellyn Carter, Nov. 11, 1939; children—John Carter, Julia Vail, Dale Llewellyn. Admitted to D.C. bar, 1939, N.Y. bar, 1940, Colo. bar, 1949; atty. REA, 1938-40; pvt. practice, Beacon, 1940-42; spl. asst. U.S. atty. gen., 1942-49; asst. chief compromise sect., tax div. Dept. Justice, 1946-49; mem. firm Ziegler & Hoyt, Colorado Springs, Colo., 1949-54, Hoyt & Gallagher, 1954-59; judge dist. ct. 4th Jud. Dist. Colo., 1959-61; judge U.S. Tax Ct., from 1962. Pres. Colorado Springs Symphony Assn., 1958-60, Colorado Springs Sch. for Girls, 1961-62. Served to lt. (s.g.) USNR, 1943-46. Mem. U. Va. Law School Alumni Assn. (mem. council 1965-68, pres. Washington area chpt. 1966-67), Am., Fed., Colo. bar assns., Am. Judicature Soc., Soc. Mayflower Descendants, Order of Coif, Phi Delta Theta, Phi Alpha Delta. Mem. editorial bd. Va. Law Rev., 1937-38. Home:Alexandria, Va. Died June 21, 1976.

HOYT, HARRISON VAL, educator, indsl. engr.; b. Nephi, Utah, Feb. 14, 1885; s. Henry Harrison and Alice (Jenkins) H.; B.S., Purdue U., 1913; M.B.A., Harvard, 1917; Ph.D., Stanford U., 1929; m. Helen Grace, Sept. 9, 1915. Asst. engr., Idaho Power & Light Co., Boise, 1913-15; cons. and indsl. engr., N.Y. City, 1918-20; production mgr., J. G. McDonald Chocolate Co., Salt Lake City, 1920-21; dean school of commerce, Brigham Young U., 1921-31, head dept. accounting and bus., 1938-52; dean, School of Commerce, Ore. State Coll., 1931-32, dean and dir. school of commerce, Ore. State Coll., and School of Bus., U. of Ore., 1932-36; production mgr. J. S. Ivins, Phila., 1936-38. Charter mem. Civil Service Commn., Provo City, since 1938. Served with U.S. Navy, World War I. Mem. National Association of Cost Accountants, Tellunde Assn. (mem. and one time director of its endowment), Beta Gamma Sigma, Alpha Kappa Psi, Alpha Delta Sigma, Beta Alpha Psi. Mem. Church of Latter-Day Saints (mem. bishopric, 1929-31). Clubs: Provo Kiwanis (pres.); Rotary, Eugene. Traveled extensively in maj. countries of world; 7 summers in Middle Am. as hobbist checking for evidence of old Mayan civilization. Home: Provo, Utah. *

HUARD, FRANCES WILSON (BARONESS HUARD), author; b. N.Y. City, Oct. 2, 1885; d. Francis and Mira (Barrie) Wilson; ed. under pvt. tutors in Paris; m. Charles Huard, painter and illustrator, of Paris, France, Nov. 30, 1905. Life mem. Assn. des Dames Francaises, Paris. Canadian Red Cross. Author: My Home in the Field of Honor, 1916; My Home in the Field of Mercy, 1917; Lilies, White and Red; With Those Who Wait, 1918; American Footprints in Paris (with Francois Boucher), 1921. Co-Author: French Rustic Furniture, 1927. Translations: The Flying Poilu, by NadMud, 1916; Military Servitude and Grandeur, by Alfred de Vigny, 1917; Colette Baudoche, by Maurice Barrès, 1918; The Golden Goat, by Paul Arène, 1919; The Chosen People, by Jérôme and Jean Tharaud, 1928. Address: Versailles, France. *

HUBBARD, FRANK WILLIAM, educator; b. San Bernardino, Calif., June 7, 1900; s. Walter and Jessie Lee (Douglass) H.; A.B., U. of Calif., 1922, M.A., 1926; Ph.D., Columbia, 1931; m. Genevieve Gregg, June 20, 1928; children—Jean Louise, Carolyn Lee. Principal, elementary school, Fresno, Calif., 1923-26; dir. of research, Fresno City Schs., 1926; asst. dir. research, NEA, 1926-31, asso. dir., 1931-40, dir., 1940-56, asst, exec. sec. for information services, 1956-65. Mem. Am. Edn. Research Assn., Nat. Edn. Assn. (life), Elem. Sch. Prins. Assn. (research dir. 1965-73), Am. Assn. Sch. Administrs., Phi Delta Kappa. Conglist. Author: Teacher Demand and Supply in the United States, 1931; Co-author: The Elementary School Principalship, 1928; The Principal Studies His Job, 1928; The Principal as a Supervisor, 1929; Population Trends and Their Educational Implications, 1938. Editor yearbooks, Dept. Elementary Sch. Prins., 1928-34. Am. Assn. Sch. Adminstrs., 1933-56. Home: Washington, D.C. Died Aug. 7, 1979; interred Rock Creek Cemetery, Washington.

HUBBARD, LOUIS HERMAN, coll. pres.; b. Feb. 10, 1882; s. Gorham Eustis and Louise (Monsanto) H.; B.S., U. of Tex., 1903, M.A., 1918, Ph.D., 1930, spl. student U. of Tex. and U. of Chicago; LL.D., Austin Coll., 1929; m. Bertha Altizer, July 31, 1912; children—Martha Louise, John Randolph, George Underwood. Prin. ward sch., Sulphur Springs, Tex., 1902; teacher English, Belton, Tex., 1903-04; prin. Belton High Sch., 1904-08; instr. in English, summers, Southwestern U., 1907, 08, 09; prin. high sch., San Angelo, 1908-09; supt. schs., Belton, 1910-24; instr. English, summers, Baylor, 1921-23; lecturer in con. and English, U. of Tex., 1924-26, also dean of students, 1924-26; pres. Texas State Coll. for Women since 1926. Mem. National Education Assn., Tex. Teachers' Assn., Philos. Soc. of Tex. (pres. 1946), Tex. Acad. of Sci., Tex. Assn. State Colleges (pres.), Southern Assn. Colleges and Secondary Schs. (chmn. commn. on instns. of higher edn.), Phi Delta Kappa. Vice pres. Southern Assn. Colleges for Women, 1930; pres. Assn. Texas Colleges, 1930; pres. Southern Assn. Colleges for Women, 1932. Episcopalian. Rotarian. Author: Handbook for English Teachers (with H. W. Morelock), 1914; The Improvement of College Teaching (monograph), 1927; The Private Endowment of Public Education (monograph), 1928; and articles in Texas Outlook and other ednl. jours. Home: Denton, Tex.*

HUBBELL, ALLAN HILDRETH (HUB'B'L), editor; b. Brooklyn, N.Y., July 16, 1885; s. Clarence Eugene and Luella Isadora (Keyes) H.; A.B., Coll. City of New York, 1904; E.M., Sch. of Mines (Columbia), 1908; m. Lillian Forbes, Oct. 23, 1912; children—Allan Forbes, Marion. Editorial staff, Engineering and Mining Journal, 1917-22, mng. editor, 1922-27, asso. editor since 1927. Mem. Am. Inst. Mining and Metall. Engrs., Lake Superior Mining Inst.*

HUBBELL, JAY BROADUS, prof. Am. lit.; b. Smyth County, Va., May 8, 1885; s. Rev. David Shelton and Ruth (Eller) H.; student Windsor (Va.) Acad., 1901-02; A.B., University of Richmond, 1905, Litt. D. (hon.), 1956; A.M., Harvard University, 1908; Ph.D., Columbia, 1922; Litt.D., So. Meth. U., 1951, Clemson College, 1961; married Lucinda Smith, June 1, 1918; children—Jay Broadus, David Smith. Instr. in Latin and Greek, Bethel (Ky.) Coll., 1905-06; instr. in English, U. of N.C., 1908-09; asso. prof. English, Wake Forest (N.C.) Coll., 1911-14; asst. prof. English, Southern Meth. U., Dallas, Tex., 1915-16, asso. prof., 1916-19, E. A. Lilly prof. and head dept., 1921-27; prof. Am. lit., Duke U., 1927-54, emeritus, 1954, dir. grad. studies in English, 1943-48; expert to sec. U.S. Army and vis. prof. Am. lit. U. Vienna, 1949, 50. Fulbright prof. Am. lit. U. of Athens, Greece, 1953; vis. prof. Am. literature U. of Va., 1954-55, Columbia University, 1957-58; vis. prof. English, Tex. Technol. Coll., 1960, U. Ky., 1961. Editor S.W. Rev., 1924-27; chmn. bd. editors Am. Lit. 1928-54. Mem. Field Artillery O.T.C., 1918; 1st lt., O.R.C., 1918-23. Recipient N.C. Mayflower award for the book The South in American Literature, 1955. Mem. Modern Lang. Assn. Am. (chmn. Am. lit. group, 1924-27, 1939; mem. program com., 1936-41, com. on research activities, 1944-47, exec. council, 1946-49 v.p. 1951), Am. Assn. Univ. Profs. Democrat. Clubs: Faculty (Duke University), Erasmus (pres. 1948-49). Author, editor, contbr. numerous lit. publs. Home: Durham, N.C. *

HUBBS, CARL LEAVITT, biologist; b. Williams, Ariz., Oct. 18, 1894; s. Charles Leavitt and Elizabeth (Goss) H.; A.B., Stanford U., 1916, A.M., 1917; Ph.D., U. Mich., 1927; m. Laura Cornelia Clark, June 15, 1918; children—Frances Voorhees, Clark, Earl Leavitt. Asst. curator fishes, amphibians and reptiles Field Mus. Natural History, Chgo., 1917-20; curator fishes, mem. faculty U. Mich., 1920-44; field rep. of sec. Dept Interior, 1939-40; prof. biology Scripps Instn Oceanography, U. Calif., La Jolla, 1944-79; 1st dir. Inst Fisheries Research, Mich. Dept. Conservation 1930-35; bd. dirs. and/or trustee San Diego Zool. Soc. San Diego Natural History Mus., Sea World, Hubbs-Sea World Research Inst., San Diego Maritime Hist. Soc 1944-79; mem. Internat. Commn. Zool. Nomenclature 1963-67. Guggenheim fellow, 1952-53; named Man of Year, Am. Cetacean Soc., 1974; Scientist of Year, San Diego Soc. Natural History, 1974; Headliner of Year San Diego Press Club, 1974; recipient Merit award Am Fisheries Soc., 1973; Leidy award Phila. Soc. Natural History, 1964; Mem. ichthyol. socs. Japan, France (hon.), Nat. Acad. Sci. Clubs: Scholia, Summer (San Diego), Explorers (hon.). Author: Fishes of the Great Lakes Region; Memoir on Hydrographic History and Relict Fishes of the North-Central Great Basin; also numerous articles. Home: La Jolla, Calif. Died June 30, 1979.

HUBER, EDWARD FREDERICK, lawyer; b. Paterson, N.J., Apr. 1, 1906; s. William and Barbara (Zucker) H.; A.B., Fordham U., 1926, LL.B., 1929; m. Mary Elizabeth Fallon, July 26, 1951; children—Barbara, Anne Marie, Catherine, Edward, Mary Liz, William, George, John, Mary Louise, Mary Theresa; m. 2d, Maureen McHugh Brady, Aug. 19, 1973. Admitted to N.Y. bar, 1929; asso. firm Travis, Brownback & Paxson, N.Y.C., 1929-37, partner, 1937-43; partner firm Dean, Magill & Huber, N.Y.C., 1946-54, Holland, Huber & Banigan, Chgo., 1949-54, Naylon, Aronson, Huber & Magill, N.Y.C., 1954-67, Huber, Magill, Lawrence & Farrell, N.Y.C., 1967-77. Served to capt. U.S. Army, 1944-47. Mem. Am., N.Y. bar assns., Judge Advs. Assn. Catholic Lawyer's Guild. Home: Larchmont, N.Y. Died Aug. 31, 1977.

HUBERT, WARREN GENGEMBRE, educator; b. N.Y. City, Sept. 13, 1886; s. Charles Colomb Gengembre and Alice Jane (Evans) H.; B.S., N.Y. City Coll., 1907; M.S., N.Y. U., 1909, Sc.D., 1917; m. Florence Cherril Newhall, June 28, 1911; 1 son, Douglas Gengembre. Tchr. pub. schs., N.Y. City, 1907-10; tchr. math. Stuyvesant High Sch., N.Y. City, 1910-12; faculty mem. N.Y. City Coll. since 1912, chmn. dept. math. since 1947; lectr. actuarial math. Met. Life Ins. Co., N.Y. City, 1918-34. Fellow A.A.A.S.; mem. Am. Math. Soc., Math. Assn. of Am., Delta Kappa Epsilon, Theta Nu Epsilon. Baptist. Club: Adirondack Mountain. Home: Yonkers, N.Y. *

HUBSHMAN, HENRY M., JR., bank exec.; b. N.Y.C., Nov. 21, 1925; s. Henry M. and Sylvia (Cohen) H.; grad. Phillips Acad., Andover, Mass, 1942; B.A., Yale, 1945; m. Barbara Chalk, June 12, 1953; children—Kathryn (Mrs. M.Y. Meganck), Peter, James. Sr. v.p. 1st Nat. City Bank, N.Y.C., 1965-72; chmn. bd. Progress Capital Co., N.Y.C., 1972-75; exec. v.p. Crocker Nat. Bank, San Francisco, 1975-77. Vice chmn. bd. dirs. N.Y. Heart Assn.; bd. dirs. Vis. Nurse Service N.Y.C.; trustee Phillips Acad., Andover. Served with USNR, 1943-46; PTO. Home: Goleta, Calif. Died Nov. 30, 1977.

HUDDLESTON, JACKSON NOYES, lawyer; b. Creston, Wash., Nov. 18, 1908; s. Samuel L. and Agnes (Noyes) H.; A.B., U. Ill., 1930; J.D., Harvard, 1933; m. Rita E. Bussell, Nov. 3, 1934; children—Jackson Noyes, Rita Ellen. Admitted to W.Va. bar, 1933, since practiced Huntington; asso. partner, of counsel Huddleston, Bolen, Beatty, Porter & Copen and predecessor firms, 1933-77; past pres., dir. Huntington Indsl. Corp.; dir. First Huntington Nat. Bank, Multi-State Build-Lease Co., Guyan Eagle Investment Co., Kelly-Hatfield Land Co.; sec., dir. Modern Health Care, Inc.; pres., dir. Law Firm Bldg., Inc. Mem. adv. council St. Mary's Sch. Nursing; charter mem. Huntington Galleries. Fellow Am. Bar Found. (chmn. W.Va.), Am. Coll. Probate Counsel (chmn. W.Va.); mem. Am. Law Inst., Jud. Council of 4th Circuit, Am. (past chmn. W.Va. membership com. jr. bar conf.), W.Va., Inter-Am., Cabell County bar assns., W.Va. State Bar (pres. 1957-58), Nat. Probation and Parole Assn. (local chmn. 1952-53), Newcomen Soc., C. of C., S.A.R. Methodist. Club: Guyan Golf and Country. Home: Huntington, W.Va. Died Apr. 5, 1977.

HUDSON, HINTON GARDNER, lawyer; b. Smithfield, N.C., Nov. 1, 1896; s. James Buchanan and Sarah Agnes (Woodall) H.; A.B., U. N.C., 1916; LL.B., Harvard, 1919; m. Margaret Baggs, Aug. 6, 1927; children—Margaret (Mrs. John M. Blades), Hinton Gardner, Gordon Lamar. Admitted to N.C. bar, 1919, since practiced in Winston-Salem; sr. partner firm Hudson, Petree, Stockton, Stockton & Robinson; lectr. law Wake Forest Coll., 1963. Mem. N.C. Gen. Statutes Commn., 1960-70, chmn., 1967-70. Rep. Gen. Assembly N.C., 1943. Trustee Lees-McRae Coll., 1966-70. Served with USN, 1918. Recipient spl. resolutions of commendation for 10 years service on N.C. Gen. Statutes Commn. (including rewriting of Rules Civil Procedure 1st time since 1868), from N.C. Gen. Assembly, N.C. State Bar and N.C. Bar Assn., 1970. Mem. Am., N.C., Forsyth County (past pres.), Forsyth County Jr. (a founder, past pres.) bar assns., N.C. State Bar (councillor 1959-68), Phi Beta Kappa. Democrat. Methodist. Clubs: Forsyth Country (pres. 1957), Winston-Salem Torch, Twin City. Home: Winston-Salem, N.C. Died July 6, 1979; buried Salem Cemetery.

HUDSON, LILLIAN A., prof. nursing edn.; b. Manitoba, Can., 1886; d. Joseph and Jean (Thompson) Hudson; student Model Sch., 1903, Queens U., Can., 1907-11, Johns Hopkins, 1913-16; B.S., Columbia, 1917, A.M., 1918; unmarried. Teacher elementary schs. Ontario, Saskatchewan, Alberta, Can., 1904-11; mem. nursing staff and child welfare Harriet Lane Home, Johns Hopkins Hosp., 1916; ednl. dir. Henry St. Visiting Nurse Service, N.Y. City, 1918-20; asst. nursing edn., Teachers Coll., Columbia, 1917-18, instr., 1918-23, asst. prof., 1923-28, asso. prof., 1928-35, prof. since 1935. Mem. Child Welfare Survey Inst., St. Johns, Newfoundland, 1917; mem. spl. commn. on child welfare, Russia, 1924; survey pub. health nursing, U. of P.I., 1931; survey pub. health nursing edn., P.R., 1941. Mem. bd. Visiting Nurse Service, N.Y. City, since 1947; also mem. ednl. com. since 1947. Fellow American Public Health Assn.; mem. Am. Red Cross Nursing Service, Nat. Nursing Council (frontier nursngservice com.), Maternity Center Assn. (mem. exec. com. midwifery sch.), Milbank Memorial Fund (mem. advisory council, 1922-35; chmn. nursing advisory com., 1927-35), Nat. Orgn. for Pub. Health Nursing (mem. edn. com., 1920-37; accreditation com. since 1942), Assn. Collegiate Schs. of Nursing (mem. com. on standards, 1933-41). Home: New York, N.Y. *

HUDSON, PAUL HAROLD, banker; b. Suspension Bridge, N.Y., Feb. 26, 1884; s. Rev. Henry B. and Hattie May (Smith) H.; student Cooper Union, 1900-03; B.C.S., N.Y. U., 1906, C.P.A., 19; LL. D., McMaster University, Hamilton, Ont., 1951; L. H.D. (honorary), Rollins College, 1957; married Jennie Edwards, Jan. 26, 1911; children—Ruth Louise (Mrs. Basil Goldsmith), Edward Warren, Margaret Alice (Mrs. James Tuohig), John Henry. Clerk Knickerbocker Trust Co. and successor co., 1901-08, auditor, 1908-13; with Empire Trust Co., N.Y. City, since 1913, asst. sec., 1913-23, asst. v.p., 1923-25, v.p., 1925-45, dir. since 1941, exec. v.p., 1945-51; v.p., trustee Davella Mills Found., 1935-44, pres., 1944-56. Trustee Law Center Found., 1948—; trustee New York University, 1947—. Member N.Y. U. Men in Finance Club past pres.), Gold Medalist, Alpha Kappa Psi. Member Beta Gamma Sigma, Medallion Soc. N.Y. U. (past pres.). Baptist. Mason. Clubs: Cosmopolitan, N.Y. U. Faculty (N.Y.C.); U. (Winter Park, Fla.). Author various math. tables. Home: Montclair, N.J. *

HUEPER, REMI PAUL (HU'PER), army officer; b. Louisville, Ky., Nov. 19, 1886; s. Louis and Annie Rosalie (Jeunesse) H.; ed. Spencerian Bus. Sch., Louisville, Ky.; grad. Command and Gen. Staff Sch., 1932, Army War Coll., 1936; m. Alice May Rideout, Aug. 21, 1912; children—Louis Rideout, Edith Jeunesse (Mrs. Robert C. Houston), Marjorie Soule (Mrs. Joe Hill Hall). Enlisted in U.S. Navy, April, 1902-03; commd. capt., Q.M. Dept., U.S. Army, June 21, 1917, Finance Dept., 1920, and advanced through the grades to brig. gen., Sept. 10, 1942; asst. chief of finance, U.S. Army, Nov. 1941-Aug. 1946; dep. fiscal dir., Army Service Forces; retired Aug. 31, 1946. Awarded Distinguished Service Medal, Commendation Ribbon. Presbyterian. Mason. Elk, Civitan. Home: Macon, Ga. *

HUEPER, WILHELM C(ARL) HEINRICH (HÜPER), physician; b. Schwerin, Germany, Nov. 4, 1894; s. Wilhelm and Caroline (Dornemann) H.; student Univs. Marburg, Rostock; M.D., U. Kiel, 1920; m. Martha Sennhenn, Aug. 24, 1924; 1 son, Klaus Wilhelm. Asst. pathologist Auguste Viktoria Krankenhaus, Berlin, 1921-23; dir. lab. Mercy Hosp., also asst. prof. pathology Loyola U., Chgo., 1924-30; chief pathologist Cancer Research Lab., U. Pa., 1930-33; asst. dir. Haskell Lab. Indsl. Toxicology, Wilmington, Del., 1934-38, Warner Inst. for Therapeutic. Research, N.Y.C., 1938-48; chief environmental cancer sect. Nat. Cancer Inst., Bethesda, Md., 1948-64; cons. on environmental cancer, Dept. of Labor; mem. occupational cancer committee of the New York Department of Labor. Recipient of A.A.A.S. Fraenkel-Rosenthal award for cancer research, 1959; United Nations Cancer Research award, 1962. Diplomate pub. health, aviation medicine and occupational medicine Am. Bd. Preventive Medicine, in pathologic anatomy Am. Bd. Pathology. Member A.M.A., Am. Assn. Pathology and Bacteriology, Am. Assn. Cancer Research, Am. Soc. Exptl. Pathology, Am. Heart Assn., Am. Soc. Study Arteriosclreosis (pres. 1946), Am. Indsl. Hygiene Assn., A.A.A.S., Am. Gerontol. Soc., Internat. Union Against Cancer (chmn. com. cancer prevention). Author: Occupational Cancer and Allied Diseases, 1942; also contbr. chpts. to several books. Home: Bethesda, Md. Died Dec. 27, 1979.

HUERTER, CHARLES JOSEPH (HER'TER), composer, director; b. Brooklyn, N.Y., Jan. 10, 1885; s. Hubert and Catherine (Presler) H.; student Syracuse U., 1904-07, 1910-13, Royal Acad., Berlin, 1913-14; first lessons in piano under father; studied piano and harmony with Prof. Joseph C. Seiter, counterpoint and composition with William Berwald and Paul Juon, piano with Adolph Frey; m. Elizabeth E. Montges, Sept. 6, 1916. Began at 17 as ch. organist at Pompey, N.Y., later organist and choirmaster, St. Joseph's Ch., Syracuse; organist and choir dir. Ch. of the Most Holy Rosary, Syracuse, 1917-22. Took up study of composition, 1912; and has produced upwards of 700 pub. works, including anthems, sacred and secular songs, violin, cello and piano pieces. Mem. Am. Soc. Composers, Authors and Publishers, Phi Mu Alpha. Catholic. Home: Syracuse, N.Y. *

HUFF, CLARENCE ELMER, b. Oronoque, Kan., Nov. 10, 1882; s. Nathan and Lelia Isadora (Heath) H.; ed. Kan. Christian Coll., Lincoln; m. Myrtle Ella Sherman, Sept. 2, 1908; children—Mrs. Ruth Eleanor Marsh, Mrs. Faith Sherman Smith, Paul Emlyn, Mrs. Hope Alice Laney. Manager and dir. coop. business enterprisgs, 1914-27; pres. Kan. Farmers Union, 1927-29, Nat. Farmers Union, 1928-30, Farmers Nat. Grain Corporation, Apr. 1930-June 1937; general manager insurance companies and other business units sponsored by Farmers Union, 1937-55; gen. cons. to pres. Nat. Farmers Union, 1956. Mem. bd. assos. Chgo. Theol. Sem., 1957; mem. gen. com. dept. Church and Economic Life, Nat. Council Chs., 1957. Home: Denver, Colo. *

HUFFHINES, CLARENCE LESTER, clergyman; b. Richardson, Tex., July 20, 1886; s. Wintield Scott and Fannie (Harris) H.; grad. in bookkeeping, Dallas Business U., 1903; student at Southern Bapt. Theol. Sem., 1906-7, Tex. Bapt. U., 1908; m. Mabel Allen, of Richardson, May 5, 1909. Ordained ministry of Missionary Bapt. Ch., 1906; pastor 1st Ch., Garland, Tex., 1907-10; supply, 1907-8; pastor 1st Ch., Ennis, Tex., Apr., 1910—. Recording sec. Bapt. Missionary Assn. of Tex. and of exec. bd. of missions, same; pres. Pastors' Assn., Ennis. Democrat. Address: Ennis, Tex.*

HUFFMAN, JASPER ABRAHAM, clergyman, educator, author; b. Elkhart County, Ind., Feb. 28, 1880; s. John W. and Martha (Howenstine) H.; grad. Bonebrake Theol. Sem., 1909; A.B., Bluffton (O.) Coll., 1915; B.D., McCormick Theol. Sem., 1919;D.D., Taylor U., 1920; m. Elizabeth D. Lambert, May 5, 1901 (dec. 1949); children—David Paul, Martha Emma (dec.), S. Lambert, John Abram; m. Olive May Sando, Jan. 1, 1951 (dec. 1969). Ordained to ministry, United Missionary Ch., 1904; dean Taylor U. Sch. Religion, 1936-45. Mem. extension faculty Ind. State Normal Sch., 1925; dean Winona Lake Sch. Theology (summer sch.), 1926-39, pres., 1939-54, emeritus, 1954; dean dept. Bible, Bethel Coll., 1954—; ednl. cons. May K. Houck Found., Sarasota, Fla., 1960—. Mem. staff of joint expn. for Palestinian excavation of Xenia Theol. Sem. and Am. Sch. for Oriental Research, 1930. First pres. World-Wide Bible Readers' Fellowship, 1946. Editor: Gospel Banner, 1913-25, Bethel series of Sunday Sch. lit. 1911-51; critical editor of Higley Sunday Sch. Lesson Commentary, 1937—, editor-in-chief, 1960—; editor-in-chief Living Bible Series and Study, Six Year Cycle, Covering Entire Bible, 1963—. Author numerous books, 1904-45; later publs. include: The Stone Cry Out, 1946; Golden Treasures from the Greek New Testament for English Readers, 1951; The Meanings of Things Believed by Christians, 1953; The Revised Standard Version; An Appraisal, 1953; Our Lord's Unique Person, 1955; An Untold Miracle Story Concerning The Revised Standard Version; The Biography of A Soul-Judas, 1957; A Comprehensive System of Christian Doctrine, 1959; Straight Through the Bible in Two Years, 8 vols., 1963; Seventy Years with Pen, Pointer and Pulpit, 1968; Profile of a Modern Penticostal Movement, 1968. Kiwanian. Home: Berne IN. *

HUGHES, ALBERT WILLIAM, business exec.; b. Skaneateles, N.Y., Jan. 21, 1891; s. Charles John and Lillian (Foote) H.; B.A., Colgate U., 1911, LL.D., 1951; m. Gertrude Whitaker, July 6, 1920; children—John, George, Sam. Teacher, 1911-19; with J.C. Penney Co., dept. store chain, Wilmington, Del., since 1920, as salesman and store mgr., 1920-25, personnel dept., 1925-29, asst. to pres., 1929-37, v.p. and director, 1937-46, pres., 1946-58, chmn. bd., 1958-64, dir., to 1979. Mem. Phi Beta Kappa, Delta Upsilon. Methodist. Clubs: Wykagyl Country; Union League (N.Y.). Home: Larchmont, N.Y. Died Mar. 22, 1979.

HUGHES, ALFRED FRANKLIN, college pres.; b. Somerford, O., Mar. 18, 1882; s. George Henry and Sarah Catherine (Prose) H.; A.B., Ohio Wesleyan U., 1907 (Phi Beta Kappa), A.M., 1909, D.D., 1918; S.T.B., Boston U., 1909; m. Bertha Blanche Bowdle, of Delaware, O., Sept. 12, 1907; children—Alfred Elroy (dec.), Borden Edward, Charlotte (dec.), Josephine. Ordained ministry M.E. Ch., 1909; pastor Holbrook, Mass., 1908-09, Shawnee, O., 1909-10, Portsmouth, O., 1910-13, 3d Av. Ch., Columbus, O., 1913-15; pres. Evansville (formerly Moores Hill) Coll., 1916-27 (raised fund of $1,000,000 to relocate the college); pres. Hamline U. since July 1927. Mason. Address: St. Paul, Minn. *

HUGHES, ARTHUR LLEWELYN (HUZ), prof. physics; b. Liverpool, Eng., Dec. 18, 1883; s. John and Elizabeth (Parry) H.; B.Sc., Liverpool U., 1906, M.Sc., 1908, D.Sc., 1912; A.B., Cambridge U., 1910; research and post grad. work, Cavendish Lab., Cambridge U., 1908-12; m. Jessie Alice Paterson Smyth, July 15, 1919; children—David Ferrar, Ann Elizabeth, John Peter. Came to U.S., 1913. Asst. prof. physics, Rice Inst., Houston, Tex., 1913-19; research prof. physics, Queen's U., Kingston, Ont., Can., 1919-23; prof. physics, Washington U., since 1923; asst. dir. Manhattan. Project, N.M., 1943-44, In anti-submarine div., British Admiralty, 1917-18. Mem. Am. Physical Soc., A.A.A.S. (pres. sect. B, 1941). Episcopalian. Author several books, articles profl. publs. Joint author: Photoelectric Phenomena, 1932. Home: St. Louis. *

HUGHES, EDWARD CHARLES, obstetrician, gynecologist; b. Syracuse, N.Y., Feb. 13, 1901; s. Arthur G. and Marie M. (Hiendorf) H.; B.S., Syracuse U., 1922; M.D., 1924; m. E. Marion Peters, June 16, 1927; children—Jeanne (Mrs. Russell Greenhalgh), Edward. Interen Bklyn. Hosp., 1924-25, resident, 1925-27; pracitice medicine specializing in obstetrics and gynecology, 1930-76; instr. obstetrics and gynecology SUNY Coll. Medicine (now Upstate Med. Center), 1928-33, asst. prof., 1933-38, asso. prof., 1938-40, clin. prof., 1940-44, prof., 1944-67, prof. emeritus, 1967-76; chmn. dept. obstetrics, 1944-61. cons. Syracuse Gen. Crouse Irving, Syracuse psychopathic hosps., Univ. Hosp. of Good Shepherd; attending obstetrician City Hosp.; dir. maternal health and hygiene, City of Syracuse after 1944; vis. prof., Honolulu, Bombay, India; cons. in field. Diplomate Am. Bd. Obstetrics and Gynecology. Fellow A.C.S.; mem. Am. Coll. Obstetricians and Gynecologists (pres.), Am. Assn. Obstetricians and Gynecologists, Am. Gynecologic Soc., N.Y. State Med. Soc. (del. council), Maternal Welfare Committee, N.Y., N.Y. Acad. of Scis., Internat. Fedn. Gynecology and Obstetrics (del.), Internat. Coll. Surgeons (pres. obstetric and gynecologic sect. 1959-62), A.M.A., Am. Fertility Soc., Am. Fedn. Clin. Research, Onondaga County Med. Soc., Central N.Y. Assn. Obstetricians and Gynecologists, Alpha Omega Alpha, Psi Upsilon, Nu Sigma Nu, Sigma Xi, numerous hon. soc. Clubs: University (Syracuse) Onondaga Golf and Country, Century (Syracuse). Contbr. articles to profl. jours. Home: Jamesville, N.Y. Died Nov. 6, 1976.

HUGHES, HAROLD DEMOTT, college prof.; b. Antioch, Ill., Jan. 16, 1882; s. Hugh David and Jessie Ann (Yule) H.; B.S., Univ. of Ill., 1907; M.S., Univ. of Mo., 1908; m. Lulu MacIntosh Lego, Oct. 14, 1908; children—John Nelson, Daniel Edison, Alice Miriam (Mrs. W. Hugh Missildine). Instr. in agromony U. of Mo., 1907-10; prof. farm crops Ia. State Coll. since 1910, chief farm crops research Ia. Agrl. Expt. Sta., 1910-48. Perfected seed scarifying machine, 1913, pneumatic seed sampler, 1916; developed and introduced Hubam clover, 1919. Del. to Internat. Grassland Congress, Great Britain, 1937. Fellow Am. Soc. Agronomy; mem. Assn. Official Seed Analysts (pres. 1917), Am. Soc. of Agronomy (pres. 1946), A.A.A.S., Am. Assn. Univ. Prof., Sigma Xi, Alpha Zeta, Gamma Sigma Delta. Republican. Mem. Ch. of Christ (elder). Author: Crop Production (with Edwin R. Henson), 1930; Forages (with Maurice Heath and Darrel Metcalfe), 1951. Home: Ames, Ia. *

HUGHES, RICHARD ARTHUR WARREN, author; b. Weybridge, Eng., Apr. 19, 1900; s. Arthur and Louisa Grace (Warren) H.; student Charterhouse Sch., 1913-18; B.A., Oriel Coll., Oxford (Eng.) U., 1922; D.Litt. (hon.), U. Wales; m. Frances Catharine Ruth Bazley, Jan. 8, 1932; children—Robert Elistan-Glodryd, Penelope, Lleky Susannah, Catharine Phyllida, Owain Gardner Collingwood. Author: (plays) The Sisters' Tragedy, produced London, 1922, A Comedy of Good and Evil, produced London, 1924 (revived and produced in N.Y.C. as Minnie and Mr. Williams, 1948); co-founder Portmadoc Players, Welsh theatrical co., 1923; 1st vice chmn. Welsh Nat. Theatre Co.: for 3 years Gresham prof. of rhetoric, London; author of radio plays, 1924—, including Danger, 1st radio play in world, 1924, also sundry film scripts. Served in Brit. Admiralty, 1940-45. Decorated Order Brit. Empire; recipient Feminia Vie Heureuse prize, 1931. Fellow Royal Soc. Letters hon. mem. Am. Acad. Arts and Letters, Nat. Inst. Arts and Letters. Author: Gipsy Night and Other Poems, 1922; The Sisters' Tragedy and Other Plays, 1922; A Moment of Time (collected stories), 1926; Confessio Juvenis (poems), 1926; Plays, 1928; A High Wind in Jamaica (The Innocent Voyage), 1929; The Spider's Palace (children's stories), 1931; In Hazard, 1938; Don't Blame Me (children's stories), 1940; vol. in ofcl. history of the war (civil series) The Administration of War Production (with J.D. Scott), 1956; The Fox in the Attic, Vol. 1 of the Human Predicament, 1961, The Wooden Shepherdess, Vol. II, 1973, first 12 chpts. of Vol. III, 1981; Gertrude's Child (children's story), 1966; Plays, 1966; The Wonder Dog, 1977; In the Lap of Atlas, 1979. Home: Merioneth, Wales. Died Apr. 28, 1976; buried Llanfinangel-y-Traethau Churchyard, Gynedd, Wales.

HUGON, PAUL D., writer, linguist; b. Bordeaux, France, June 26, 1882; s. Ernest and Isabelle (Garat) Desdemaines-Hugon; ed. in English and French private schools; m. Lena Standing, 1908; children—Wendy Klein, Dani Ferguson. Prof., City of London Coll., 1906-08; mem. Internat. Language Commn., Paris, 1907; foreign editor London Evening News, 1909-12; dir. Pathe films, London, 1912-14; editor Pathe News, New York, 1915-16; supervising editor Universal Pictures, Hollywood, 1922-24; prof. of journalism, Woodbury Coll., Los Angeles, 1925-27; edn. counselor United Parcel Service, 1928-40. Author: The Modern Word Finder, 1926; Our Minds and Our Motives, 1929. Home: La Cañada, Calif. *

HUISKING, CHARLES LOUIS, chem. mfr.; b. Bklyn., Feb. 2, 1885; s. Paul Henry and Bertha (Quabach) H.; D.C.S., St. John's U., 1959; m. Catherine Frances Perridge, Aug. 29, 1911; children—Frank R. (dec.), Charles Louis, William W., Edward P., Richard V., Evelyn (Mrs. Robert P. Daly), Jean (Mrs. Richard Steinschneider, Jr.), Claire (Mrs. Taylor W. Hanavan). With Charles L. Huisking & Co., Inc., and affiliates, N.Y.C., 1910—, chmn., 1958—, also dir.; dir. Warner Lambert Pharm. Company; chairman and director Glyco Chemicals, Incorporated President Huntington (New York) Hosp., 1934-35; adv. bd. St. Clare's Hosp., N.Y.C., 1945—, also mem. research com., hon. mem. med. staff Inst. Research; member of advisory board Notre Dame University, 1952. Named knight first class Order St. Olav (Norway), 1935; knight of Malta, 1946, knight of Holy Sepulchre, 1948 (Pope Pius). Hon. mem. Drug and Chem. Club N.Y.C. Club: Union League (N.Y.C.). Author: Herbs to Hormones The Evolution in Drugs and Chemicals that Revolutionized Medicine, 1968. Home: N.Y.C. *

HULBERT, JAMES ROOT, univ. prof.; b. Eldora, Ia., Mar. 8, 1884; s. James C. and Adda Louise (Root) H.; A.B., U. of Chicago, 1907, Ph.D., 1912; post-grad. study, U. of London, 1911, Harvard U., 1916-17; m. Viola Blackburn, June 15, 1922 (deceased, Sept. 13, 1944). Began as assistant instructor in English, University of Chicago, 1907, advancing to prof. English, specializing on Old and Middle English, history of the English language and medieval literature, ret. 1949; vis. prof. of Eng., U. of Ark., since 1949. Served as civilian volunteer War Dept., Washington, D.C., 1918; capt. Officers' Reserve Corps, U.S. Army, 1919. Mem. Modern Lang. Assn. America, Phi Beta Kappa. Congregationalist. Contbr. articles on medieval English lang. and lit. to philol. jours. and to books. Author: Chaucer's Official Life, 1912; (with V. B. Hulbert) Effective English, 1929. Co-editor: Dictionary of American English. Home: Fayetteville, Ark.; (summer) Georgetown, Me. *

HULBERT, LUCIUS GAYLORD, lawyer; b. Detroit, Sept. 6, 1895; s. Prescott Metcalf and Elizabeth Augusta (Gaylord) H.; B.S. in Engring., U. Mich., 1917; J.D., Detroit Coll. Law, 1938; m. Gertrude Sheehan, Nov. 30, 1922 (dec.); 1 son, Lucius Gaylord; m. 2d, Helen Pendlebury King, July 2, 1945 (dec.); m. Laura Roberts Montee, Oct. 24, 1964. Metallurgist Packard Motor Car Co., Detroit, 1917-19, Mercer Motors Co., Trenton, N.J., 1920, Locomobile Co., Bridgeport, Conn., 1921; admitted to Mich. bar, 1938, U.S. Supreme Ct. bar, 1960; patent atty., mem. firm Whittemore Hulbert & Belknap, Detroit, 1921-80. Served to 2d lt. Aviation Sect., Signal Corps, AUS, 1918. Mem. Soc. Automotive Engrs., Am. Chem. Soc., Am. Soc. Metals, Am., Detroit, Mich. bar assns., Internat. Patent and Trademark Assn., Am. Mich. patent law assns., Hermitage Fraternity, Phi Lambda Upsilon. Republican. Presbyterian. Club: Detroit Athletic. Home: Grosse Pointe Shores, Mich. Died June 24, 1980; buried Northview Cemetery, Dearborn, Mich.

HULBURD, DEFOREST, b. Chicago, Ill., Dec. 22, 1886; s. Charles Henry and Anna Richmond (Belknap) H.; B.A., Yale, 1908; m. Marie Hessert, Jan. 29, 1916; children—Charles Henry, II, Marie Louise. Lumber business, Idaho, 1908-10; with Elgin Watch Co., 1910-31, asst. to pres., 1911-14, v.p., 1918-24; pres., 1924-31, now dir.; sr. partner, Hulburd, Warren & Chandler, stock brokers, since 1931. Served in U.S. Navy, World War I; ensign U.S.N.R.F.; in U.S. Navy as lt. comdr. in World War II, 1942-45; now on inactive duty. Mem. advisory bd. The Salvation Army; trustee, Jas. C. King Home, Graceland Cemetery. Mem. Zeta Psi. Republican. Conglist. Clubs: University, Chicago Commonwealth, Chicago Athletic Assn., Commercial. Shoreacres. Home: Lake Forest, Ill.*

HULL, BLAKE D., engr.; b. Galesburg, Mich., Sept. 12, 1882; s. Porter C. and Fannie J. (Blake) H.; B.S. in Elec. Engring., U. of Kan., 1905; m. May Woodward, Nov. 7, 1906; children—Sidney Blake, Barbara Mary. Engr., Southwestern Bell Telephone Co., 1905-47, chief engr., 1936-47, retired, 1947; dir. State Bank of Delphos, Kan. Dollar-a-year consultant for govt., 1940-42. Fellow Am. Inst. E.E. (vice pres. 1928-30; dir. 1931-35; pres. 1947-48). Presbyterian. Mason. Clubs: Engineering of St. Louis (past dir.), Dallas Electric (past pres.). Contbr. articles to elec. engring. jours. Home: Dallas. *

HULL, DOSSIE CLEVELAND, lawyer; b. Plant City, Fla., Dec. 25, 1884; s. Millard Fillmore and Henrietta (Hood) H.; grad. Plant City High Sch., 1905; LL.B., John B. Stetson U., 1909, B.S., 1910, LL.D., 1945; m. Marian Wright, Jan. 15, 1919. Admitted to Fla. bar, 1909, since practiced in DeLand; partner Landis, Fish & Hull until 1926, Hull, Landis & Whitehair, 1926-42, Hull, Landis, Graham & French since 1942; firm counsel for A.C.L. R.R., Florida East Coast Railway Co., etc.; instructor in law John B. Stetson U., 1911-12. DeLand city atty., 1926-35. Mem. Am. and Fla. State bar assns., Delta Sigma Phi, Phi Alpha Delta. Democrat. Home: De Land, Fla. *

HULL, HEROD B., investment banker; b. Aurora, Ill., Feb. 24, 1884; s. Joseph M. and Alice (O'Briant) H.; ed. pub. schs., and Jennings Sem., Aurora; m. Margaret Caas, of Aurora, May 17, 1910. Pres. Ill. Mortgage Corpn., Improvement Finance Corpn.; dir., Aurora Refining Co., H. B. Hull & Co. Mason, Elk, Moose. Clubs: Union League, Aurora Country, Fox Valley Country. Home: Aurora, Ill.*

HULLEY, ELKANAH BUNCE, b. Chester, Pa., Apr. 17, 1884; s. William Currie and Theresa (Bunce) H.; grad. Keystone Acad., Factoryville, Pa., 1903; B.S., Bucknell U., 1907; D.Eng., Stetson U., 1929; m. Mabel B. Moore, Dec. 22, 1908. Builder of houses (about 2000), Pittsburgh, Pa., since 1912; president Liberty Housing Corp. Mgr. Pittsburgh War Farms Commn., 1916-18; student O.T.C., Camp Taylor, Ky., 1918. Trustee John B. Stetson U. Mem. Phi Gamma Delta (editor in chief nat. jour., 1911-17). Republican. Baptist. Mason. Home: Pitts. *

HUME, SAMUEL JAMES, theatre dir. and producer; b. San Francisco, Calif., June 14, 1885; s. James Bunyan and Lida (Munson) H.; student of Calif., 1903-8; A.B., Harvard, 1913, A.M., 1914; m. Maude Crawford Izett Dick, of Edinburgh, Scotland, Sept. 11, 1912. Visited European theatres, 1909-12; associated with Edward Gordon Craig; organized 1st exhbn. of stagecraft in U.S., 1914, and exhibited in Boston, New York, Chicago, Detroit and Cleveland; dir. pageants, masques and spl. productions, Newark, N.J., Boston, St. Louis, St. Paul, Detroit, etc.; dir. Arts and Crafts Theatre, Detroit, 1916, 17, 18; asst. prof. dramatic lit. and art, U. of Calif., since Oct. 1, 1918, also dir. Greek Theatre; dir. Detroit Symphony Soc. repertory, drama season, 1921. Hon. pres. Drama Teachers' Assn. of Calif.; sec.-treas. Western Assn. Art Museum Directors. Lectured at U. of Minn., Harvard, Wellesley, Radcliffe, Smith Coll., etc. Mem. Am. Pageant Assn. (dir.). Clubs: Bohemian (San Francisco), Players (Detroit), Alpha Delta Phi. Home: Berkeley, Calif.*

HUMMEL, EDWARD AARON, govt. ofcl.; b. Gackle, N.D., Mar. 26, 1909; s. John and Emma (Odenbach) H.; B.A., N.D. State Tchrs. Coll., Valley City, 1930; M.A., U. Colo., 1931; postgrad. U. Minn., 1932-35; m. Vibekke Kjelland, Aug. 30, 1932; children—John Olaf, Kathrine Marie (Mrs. Felix Fegette). Tchr. pub. schs., N.D., 1928-30; historian, regional office Nat. Park Service, Omaha, 1935-42, regional dir., San Francisco, 1963-66, asst. dir. Nat. Park Service, 1966-68, asso. dir., 1968-71; supt. Fredericksburg and Spotsylvania Nat. Mil. Park, 1942-43, 46, Colonial Nat. Hist. Park, Yorktown, Va., 1946-52, Great Smoky Mountain Nat. Park, 1952-58, Glacier Nat. Park, 1958-62. Served from lt. (j.g.) to lt. USNR, 1943-46. Home: Springfield, Va. Died June 9, 1976.

HUMMER, WAYNE, company exec.; b. LaSalle, Ill., Aug. 24, 1884; s. William B. and Tillie (Nafziger) H.; student Princeton, 1907; m. Anne McNally; children—Wayne, Barbara Anne Johnson, William B., Philip Wayne. Sr. partner Wayne Hummer & Co., Chgo., since 1931. Pres. Ill. Bankers Assn., 1924-25, Ill. C. of C., 1930-31. Republican. Episcopalian. Clubs: Union League (Chgo.); Deer Park Fishing (LaSalle, Ill.). Home: LaSalle, Ill. *

HUMPHREY, GEORGE NORWOOD, musician; b. Bellaire, O., Aug. 25, 1904; s. George Latham and Mable May (Long) H.; grad. New Eng. Conservatory Music, 1929; student Curtis Inst. Music, 1930-31; m. Mildred Martha Weber, Oct. 2, 1929; children—George Lee, John Robert, Eric Richard. With Mpls. Symphony Orch., 1929-30; with Boston Symphony Orch., 1934-80; mem. research group Mass. Inst. Tech., 1961-64; mem. missions State Dept., Iceland, 1955, 56, 57, 58, 59; Am. rep. Japan Philharmonic Orch., 1968; one man photog. shows, Boston, N.Y.C., Phila., Washington, also libraries in New Eng. Patentee musical accessory. Home: Arlington, Mass. Died Apr. 23, 1980.

HUMPHREY, GILBERT WATTS, business exec.; b. Saginaw, Mich., July 4, 1916; s. George Magoffin and Pamela (Stark) H.; A.B., Yale U., 1939, LL.B., 1942; m Louise Ireland, Dec. 27, 1939; children—George Magoffin II, Margaret, Gilbert Watts. Admitted to Ohio bar, 1946; asso. firm Jones, Day, Cockley & Reavis, 1946-47; joined M.A. Hanna Co., 1948, pres., 1960-61 chmn. bd., 1961-65; dir., chmn. bd., chief exec. officer mem. exec. com. Hanna Mining Co., also dir. affiliated cos.; dir., chmn. exec. com. Nat. Steel Corp.; dir. Su Life Assurance Co. Can., Scott Paper Co., Hamilto Bros. Petroleum Corp., Nat. City Bank Cleve. Massey-Ferguson, Ltd., Gen. Reins. Corp. Bd. mgrs Elizabeth Severance Found., Cleve.; trustee Ta Found., Inc.; mem. council Rockefeller U., N.Y.C. trustee, vice chmn. exec. com. Univ. Hosps. of Cleve Mem. Bus. Council, Bus. Roundtable (policy com.) Clubs: Union, Tavern, Chagrin Valley Hunt, Peppe Pike Country, Clevelander (Cleve.); Pacific Union (Sa

Francisco); Links (N.Y.C.); Augusta (Ga.) Nat. Golf; Cypress Point (Pebble Beach, Calif.). Home: Chagrin Falls, Ohio. Died June 17, 1979.

HUMPHREY, GRACE, author; b. Springfield, Ill., Sept. 3, 1882; d. J Otis (U.S. judge) and Mary Ellen (Scott) Humphrey; B.A., Wellesley, 1905; studied U. of Chicago, 1907. Republican. Baptist. Clubs: Pen and Brush, Wellesley (both of N.Y. City). Author: Illinois—the Story of the Prairie State, 1917; Women in American History, 1919; Heroes of Liberty, 1921; Stories of the World's Holidays, 1923; The Story of the Marys, 1923; The Story of the Elizabeths, 1924; The Story of the Johns, 1925; Under These Trees, 1925; Stories of Our Great Inventions, 1925; The Story of the Williams, 1926; The Story of the Catherines, 1927; Father Takes Us to New York, 1927; Father Takes Us to Boston, 1928; The Story of the Janes, 1928; Father Takes Us to Philadelphia, 1929; Flags, 1929; Poland the Unexplored, 1931; Father Takes Us to Washington, 1931; Come With Me Through Budapest, 1933; Come With Me Through Krakow, 1934; Come With Me Through Warsaw, 1934; Poland Today, 1935; Hungary, Land of Contrasts, 1936; Pilsudski, Builder of Poland, 1936; The Story of the Annes, 1937. Decorated Polish Gold Cross of Merit, 1937. Home: Springfield, Ill. *

HUMPHREY, HUBERT HORATIO, JR., U.S. senator, former vice pres. U.S.; b. Wallace, S.D., May 27, 1911; s. Hubert Horatio and Christine (Sannes) H.; student Denver Coll. Pharmacy, 1932-33; B.A., U. Minn., 1939; M.A., La. State U., 1940; postgrad. U. Minn., 1940-41; recipient numerous hon. degrees; m. Muriel Fay Buck, Sept. 3, 1936; children—Nancy Faye (Mrs. C. Bruce Solomonson), Hubert Horatio III, Robert Andrew, Douglas Sannes. Pharmacist with Humphrey Drug Co., Huron, S.D., 1933-37; asst. instr. polit. sci. La. State U., 1939-40, U. Minn., 1940-41; mem. adminstrv. staff WPA, later head state div.; asst. state supr. adult edn., chief war services sect., dir. tng. re-employment div., 1941-43; asst. regional dir. War Manpower Commn., 1943; vis. prof. polit. sci. Macalester Coll., St. Paul, 1943-44, prof., 1969-70; state compaign mgr. Roosevelt-Truman Com., 1944; mayor City of Mpls., 1945-48; U.S. senator from Minn., 1948-64, 71-78, elected senate majority whip, 1961; vice pres. U.S., 1965-69; prof. social sci. U. Minn., 1969-70; dir., chmn. bd. cons. Ency. Brit., Ency. Brit. Ednl. Corp. U.S. del. UN, 1956-58; del. UNESCO Conf., Paris, 1958. Hon. chmn. Pres.'s Council on Equal Opportunity, Pres.' Com. on Equal Employment Opportunity, Nat. Aeros. and Space Council, Peace Corps Adv. Council; mem. Nat. Security Council. Democratic nominee President U.S., 1968. Bd. regents Smithsonian Instn. Recipient Jr. Assn. of Commerce award for Outstanding Minneapolitan, 1945; named Outstanding Young Man in State, Minn. Jr. Assn. of Commerce, 1945. Mem. Am. Polit. Sci. Assn., Pub. Adminstrn. Soc., Am. Acad. Arts and Scis., Phi Beta Kappa, Delta Sigma Rho. Author: America and the Now Generation; Cause is Mankind: A Liberal Program for Modern America; Political Philosophy of the New Deal; Young America in the Now World; School Desegregation: Documents and Commentaries. Home: Washington, D.C. Died Jan. 13, 1978.

HUMPHREY, ROBERT LEE, business exec.; b. Muskogee, Okla., Mar. 9, 1907; s. Walter Glenn and Pearl Rosamond (Hedges) H.; student U. Colo., 1925-26, U. Okla., 1927-28; m. Irene Elizabeth Utley, Jan. 25, 1930; children—Robert Lee, Gary Knight. Sales promotion dir. Dallas News, 1930-35; nat. advt. mgr. Ft. Worth Press, 1935-37; dir. sports and entertainment Pan Am. Expo, Dallas, 1937; sales promotion dir. Houston Chronicle, 1937-39; v.p., gen. mgr. Asso. Pubs., Inc., Dallas, 1939-45; mgr. sales personnel oilwell supply div. U.S. Steel, New Orleans, Houston, Dallas, 1946-51; nat. dir. pub. affairs N.A.M., Washington, N.Y.C., 1951-63; founder, pres. Bus.-Industry Polit. Action Com., Washington, 1963-75, bd. dirs., cons., 1976; legislative, govt. relations cons. Mem. Am. Olympic Com., 1935-37; organizer, dir. first Pan Am. Games, 1937; pres. S.W. AAU; dir., mem. exec. com. Nat. AAU. Served from lt. to lt. col. USAAF, 1942-46. Clubs: Dallas Athletic; New Orleans Country, Petroleum (New Orleans); Cornell, Knollwood Country, Rockefeller Center (N.Y.C.); Washington Golf and Country (Va.); International, Army and Navy (Washington); Millbrook Country (Greenwich, Conn.). Home: Falls Church, Va. Died Jan. 1976.

HUMPHREYS, RICHARD DUANE, glass co. exec.; b. Bergen Point, N.J., 1882; Harvard, 1905; Chmn. bd., dir. Mississippi Glass Co., N.Y.C. Home: Mt. Kisco, N.Y. *

HUNDLEY, JAMES MANSON, physician; b. Summitville, Ind., Apr. 17, 1915; s. Frank Martin and Mabelle Moselene (Johnson) H.; B.S., Ind. U., 1937, M.D. (McLanden research fellow), 1940; m. Grethel Ann Hendricks, Apr. 19, 1940; children—Phyllis, Marjorie, June, Joyce, Frank. Intern, Marine Hosp., N.Y.C., 1940-41; officer USPHS, 1941-66; dist. health officer Ind. Bd. Health, 1941-42; bubonic plague control, San Francisco, Tacoma, Western states, 1942-43; nutrition research NIH, 1944; med. officer USCG and PTO, 1944-45; with NIH, 1945-56, chief nutrition sect., 1948-50, chief lab. biochemistry and nutrition, 1951-56, chief lab. research Nat. Inst. Arthritis and Metabolic Diseases, Bethesda, Md., 1953-56; cons. nutrition NSRB, 1950-51, FCDA, 1951-56; FAO nutrition adviser to UNICEF, 1956-58; spl. asst. internat. affairs NIH, 1958-59; asst. Surgeon Gen. USPHS, 1960-66; exec. dir. Inst. Med. Scis., Presbyn. Med. Center, San Francisco, 1966-68; exec. dir. Am. Heart Assn., N.Y.C., 1968-72. Recipient Fleming award Washington C. of C., 1954. Fellow Am. Public Health Assn.; mem. Am. Assn. Public Health Physicians, Am. Dietetic Assn., Am. Inst. Nutrition, Am. Soc. Clin. Nutrition, Am. Bd. Nutrition, AAAS, Washington Acad. Scis., N.Y. Acad. Scis., Sigma Xi, Alpha Omega Alpha. Asso. editor Nutrition Rev., 1948-50. Contbr. articles to profl. jours. Home: San Rafael, Calif. Died Dec. 17, 1975.

HUNGERFORD, HERBERT BARKER, entomologist; b. Mahaska, Kan., Aug. 30, 1885; s. Artemus Manwarring and Bertha Estelle (Barker) H.; prep. edn. Kan. State Normal Sch., Emporia, Kan.; B.A., U. of Kan., 1911, M.A., 1913; Ph.D., Cornell U., 1918; m. Mary Frances Kenney, Aug. 30, 1905; 1 dau., Helen Estelle (Mrs. Andrew B. Hamilton). Prin. schs., Haddam, Kan., 1904-06; supt. schs., Enterprise, Kan., 1906-09; with U. of Kan. since 1911, successively as instr. entomology until 1913, asst. prof., 1913-17, asso. prof., 1917-20, prof. entomology, 1920-24, head dept. entomology, 1924-49; state entomologist, also mem. Kansas Entomological Commn., 1924-49; research professor of entomology, 1949; Biological Surveys: Western Kans., Colo., Wyo., Mont., Minn.; member staff U. of Minn., summer 1921; mem. staff, Biol. Sta., U. of Mich., since 1923. Fellow A.A.A.S.; mem. Entomol. Soc. Am (pres 1936), Am Assn. Econ. Entomologists, Society Systematic Zoology (pres. 1953), Kan. Acad. Science, Kan. Hort. Soc., Kan. Entomol. Soc. (pres. 1929-30, 1942-43), Limn. Soc. Amer., Sigma Xi (pres. 1938-40), Phi Beta Kappa. (pres. 1948-50). Baptist. Mason. Club: Rotary (pres. 1924-25). Author several sci. publs., tech. papers. Home: Lawrence, Kan. *

HUNNICUTT, BENJAMIN HARRIS, coll. pres.; b. Turin, Ga., Sept. 25, 1886; s. James Benjamin and Emily (Page) H.; B.S. in Agr., Mississippi Agrl. and Mech. Coll., 1905; M.S. in Agr., U. of Georgia, 1913; m. Gladys Allyn, 1909; 1 son, Horace Allyn; m. 2d, Nannie Hall Kolb, Nov. 26, 1915; children—Benjamin Harris, Wilbur Kolb, John Edward, George Frederick, James Page, Charles Robert (dec.). Dir. Lavras Agrl. Sch. (college), Lavras, Minas, Gerais, Brazil, 1908-26, professor, 1927-30; exec. sec. World's Sunday School Convention, Rio de Janeiro, 1931-32; pres. Gammon Inst., Lavras, 1933; pres. Mackenzie Coll., São Paulo, Brazil, since 1934. Dir. Ebenezer Free Med. Clinic (São Paulo). Pres. Instituto Cultura Religioso. Decorated Comdr. of Order of Southern Cross of Brazil, Life mem. Brazilian Rural Soc. Vice pres. São Paulo Rotary Club, 1941, Brazil-U.S. Cultural Union, 1941-42 (hon. mem. since 1943). Presbyterian (elder). Author: O Milho, 1917, rev. edits., 1924, 1932; Algo dão Cultura e Commercio, 1937; The Story of Agricultural Missions. (with William W. Reid), 1928; Brazil Looks Forward, 1945; Brazil World Frontier, 1949. Contbr. articles to numerous publs. in Brazil and U.S. Lecturer in U.S. on Brazilian affairs, 1908, 1912, 1919, 1927, 1934, 1938 and 1945. Home: São Paulo, Brazil. *

HUNNICUTT, CLARENCE WILLIAM, educator; b. Whittier, Calif., Aug. 19, 1907; s. Jesse Faulkner and May (Williams) H.; B.S., U. Ariz., 1930, M.A., 1931; Ed.D., Stanford U., 1942; m. Lillie McAlister, June 1, 1932 (dec. Sept. 1954); children—Alice Lucile (Mrs. Richard L. Entin), William McAlister, Charles Gilbert, Karl Sands; m. 2d, Ardelle Whitman, Oct. 25, 1958. Sch. prin., Scottsdale, Ariz., 1930-38; curriculum coordinator, Santa Barbara County, Calif., 1939-40; head elementary edn. Syracuse U., 1940-67, asst. prof., 1940-44, asso. prof., 1944-47, prof., 1947-67; mem. faculty U. South Fla., Tampa, 1967-77, acting dean Coll. Edn., 1971-72; mem. summer staff U. N.C., 1939, Drake U., 1940, U. Ill., 1950, U. So. Calif., 1960; vis. prof. Stanford U., 1952-53, U. Philippines, 1953-54; pub. sch. ednl. cons., N.Y.C., 1940-41, Caddo Parish, La., 1948, Dade County, Fla., 1951, Corpus Christi, Tex., 1951, Manteca, Calif., 1953, Tulsa, 1956, Oklahoma City, 1957-58, 60, Los Angeles County, Calif., 1961, 63; cons. Coronet Films, Handwriting Found.; cons. AID-ROCAP textbook project Central Am., 1965-70. Mem. NEA, N.Y. State Assn. Supervision and Curriculum Devel. (past pres.), Nat. Council Social Studies, Assn. Higher Edn., Am. Edn. Research Assn. Author: Answering Children's Questions, 2d edit., 1954; sr. author: Singer Social Studies Series, 30 titles, 1957-67; co-author: What Does Research Say About Arithmetic, 2d edit., 1958; Research in the Three R's, 1958, also editor 6 books. Home: Longboat Key, Fla. Died Aug. 12, 1980.

HUNSAKER, JEROME CLARKE, ret. aero. engr.; b. Creston Ia., Aug. 26, 1886; s. Walter J. and Alma (Clarke) H.; grad. U.S. Naval Acad., 1908; M.S., Mass. Inst. Tech., 1912, D.Sc., 1916; D.Sc., Williams Coll., 1943, Adelphi Coll., 1955; D.Eng., Northeastern U., 1945; m. Alice Porter Avery, June 26, 1911 (dec. 1966); children—Mrs. Sarah P. Swope, Jerome Clarke, James (dec.), Mrs. T.A. Bird. Officer, later advancing to comdr. Constrn. Corps, USN, 1909-26; instr. aero. engring. Mass. Inst. Tech., 1912-16; in charge aircraft design Navy Dept., Washington, designed airship Shenandoah, and flying boat NC4 (1st to fly Atlantic), 1916-23; asst. naval attach, Paris, Berlin, Rome, 1923-26; asst v.p. Bell Telephone Labs. (wire and radio services for airways), 1926-28; v.p. Goodyear Zeppelin Corp., 1928-33; head depts. aero. engring. and mech. engring. Mass. Inst. Tech., 1933-51, now prof. emeritus. Mem. Guggenheim Medal Bd., Sperry Medal Bd.; chmn. Nat. Adv. Com. Aeros., 1941-56. Decorated Navy Cross, Medal for Merit (U.S.); Legion of Honor (France); recipient Daniel Guggenheim medal; Franklin medal; Wright Brothers medal; Godfrey L. Cabot trophy, 1950; Langley medal, 1955; gold medal Royal Aero. Soc. (Gt. Britain), 1957; Navy awqrd for distinguished public service, 1958; Stratton award Swiss Soc., 1969. Fellow Am. Phys. Soc., Am. Acad. Arts and Scis., Inst. Aero. Scis. (hon.), Royal Aero. Soc. Britain (hon.) Imperial Coll. Sci. (London) (hon.); hon. mem. Am. Soc. M.E., Instn. Mech. Engrs. (London); mem. Am. Soc. Naval Architects and Marine Engrs., Am. Soc. Automotive Engrs., Nat. Acad. Scis., Am. Philos. Soc., Sigma Xi, Delta Kappa Epsilon. Clubs: Century (N.Y.C.); Army and Navy (Washington); St. Botolph (Boston). Contbr. articles to profl. jours. Home: Boston MA. *

HUNSCHER, HELEN ALVINA (MRS. H. P. WILKINSON), educator emeritus, nutritionist; b. Gates Mills, Ohio, Aug. 5, 1904; d. Ernest Henry and Cora Annis (Knapp) Hunscher; A.B., Ohio State U., 1925; postgrad. (fellow in nutrition research), Merrill-Palmer Sch., Detroit, 1926-27, Laura Spelman Rockefeller fellow, 1927-28; Ph.D. (NRC fellow), U. Chgo., 1932; m. Howard Paul Wilkinson, Dec. 23, 1939; children—Jeanne (Mrs. Mark E. Goebel), James H. Asst in nutrition research Merrill-Palmer Sch. and Children's Hosp. Mich., 1928-29; instr. home econs. U. Chgo., 1930-31; asso. in research Children's Fund Mich., Detroit, 1931-37; profl. lectr. in nutrition Wayne U., Detroit, 1931-37; prof., chmn. home econs. Case Western Res. U., Cleve., 1937-63, chmn. nutrition, 1963-74, prof. emeritus, cons., 1974-78. Mem. spl. med. adv. group VA, 1948-54. Mem. Am. Bd. Nutrition, Am. Dietetic Assn. (Copher award 1958, pres. 1947-48), Am. Home Econs. Assn. (chmn. food and nutrition div. 1945-46), Am. Inst. Nutrition, Am. Chem. Soc., Pub. Health Assn., Soc. for Exptl. Biology and Medicine, Soc. for Research in Child Devel., A.A.A.S., Phi Beta Kappa, Sigma Xi, Sigma Kappa, Phi Upsilon Omicron, Omicron Nu, Iota Sigma Pi. Episcopalian. Contbr. articles to profl. jours. Author: Gates Mills and a History of Its Village Church. Home: Gates Mills, Ohio. Died Nov. 11, 1978.

HUNT, ALBERT FREDERICK, meat packing; b. Boston, Mass., Feb. 17, 1886; s. Albert John and Lydia Bunker (Hinckley) H.; student pub. schs. of Boston, Mass.; m. Eunice Blance Quimby, Feb. 8, 1911; children—Blanche Endicott, Albert Frank. Began as messenger, 1902, and advanced successively as salesman, mgr., div. mgr.; v.p. Swift & Co., 1936-49, retired 1949; dir., 1941; vice-pres. A.C. Lawrence Leather Co., 1930-33, pres., 1933-36, dir. since 1930. Republican. Episcopalian. Mason. Home: Rancho Santa Fe, Calif. *

HUNT, GEORGE HALSEY, physician; b. Newton, Mass., May 31, 1903; s. Rolla Elijah and Nellie (Tillinghast) H.; A.B., Brown U., 1924; M.D., Columbia U., 1928; m. Mildred L. Gertzen, Jan. 22, 1932 (dec. July 1976); 1 dau., Barbara T. (Mrs. Herbert S. Ketay); m. 2d, Helen DeLury McGuire, July 16, 1977. Intern, jr. fellow in surgery Presbyn. Hosp., N.Y.C., 1928-32; pvt. practice medicine, Red Bank, N.J., 1932-36; entered regular corps, USPHS, 1936; commd. p.a. surgeon (capt.), 1936, advanced through grades to med. dir. (col.), 1949; asst. chief, chief surg. services, marine hosps, USPHS, 1936-45, asst. chief, div. hosps., 1947-49, chief div. hosps., 1949-52, asst. surgeon gen., asso. chief Bur. Med. Services, 1952-56; dir. Center for Aging Research, 1956-58; chief div. Gen. Med. Scis., 1958-62; asso. dir. Ednl. Council for Fgn. Med. Graduates, Phila., 1962, exec. dir., 1963-73. Bd. trustees Med. Service of D.C., Inc., 1948-57, 59-62. Diplomate Am. Bd. Surgery. Fellow A.C.S. (gov. 1948-57), Am. Pub. Health Assn.; mem. AAAS, Phi Beta Kappa, Alpha Omega Alpha. Home: San Diego, Calif. Died Feb. 2, 1980.

HUNT, HARRY COLE, business exec.; b. San Francisco, Apr. 24, 1884; s. Henry Brown and Emma Lake (Cole) H.; student St. Mary's Coll., 1897-1901; grad. U. of Calif., 1906; m. Jane Elana Selby, Feb. 23, 1923; 1 son, Harry Selby. Pres. Jesse Moor Hunt Co., 1910-18; v.p. and dir. Dabney Oil Co., 1920-25, Delaney Oil Co., 1925-33, Hogan Petroleum Co., 1934-49; pres. and dir. Hunt Properties, Inc.; dir. Tide Water Asso. Oil Co. Mem. Phi Gamma Delta. Republican. Roman Catholic..Clubs: Pacific Union (San Francisco); Burlingame (Calif.) Country; Cypress Point (v.p. and dir.; Pebble Beach, Calif.). Home: Pebble Beach, Calif. *

HUNT, HEROLD CHRISTIAN, educator; b. Northville, Mich., Feb. 9, 1902; s. George E. and Katherine E. (Herold) H.; A.B., U. Mich., 1923, M.A., 1927; Ed.D., Tchrs. Coll., Columbia, 1940; M.A., Harvard, 1953; LL.D., Park Coll., Parkville, Mo., 1947, Western Mich. Coll. Edn., Kalamazoo, 1947, Wis. U., 1951, St. Louis U., 1955; L.H.D., Mo. Valley Coll., 1966; m. Isabel Lucile Wright, Aug. 24, 1927; 1 son, Douglas Wright. Tchr. social studies Hastings (Mich.) Pub. Sch., 1923-27; prin. St. Johns (Mich.) High Sch., 1927-28, 29-31; asst. cashier and trust officer St. Johns Nat. Bank, 1928-29; supt. schs., St. Johns, 1931-34, Kalamazoo, 1934-37, New Rochelle, N.Y., 1937-40, Kansas City, Mo., 1940-47; gen. supt. city schs., Chgo., 1947-53; prof. edn. Grad. Sch. Edn., Harvard, 1953-70, Charles William Eliot prof. edn. emeritus, 1970-76; under sec. HEW, Washington, 1955-57; instr. summer session Columbia, 1938, U. Chgo., 1944; lectr. summer session U. Colo., 1942, 45, U. Kansas City, 1943-44, 46, 47, Northwestern U., 1944, U. Denver, 1945, U. Wis., 1946, 48, Okla. A. and M. Coll., 1946. Pres. Am. Assn. Sch. Adminstrs., 1947-48, 1st v.p., 1948-49; 2d v.p. Nat Congress Parents and Tchrs., 1948-51; chmn. Am. Council Edn., 1948-49; chmn. bd. trustees Ednl. Testing Service, 1949-50; chmn. accrediting commn. Nat. Home Study Council; mem. 1943 yearbook commn., chmn. 1948 yearbook commn. Am. Assn. Sch. Adminstrs.; mem. 1943 yearbook commn. Sch. Pub. Relations Assn., 1946 yearbook commn. Nat. Soc. for Study Edn.; mem. Am. Council on Edn.'s commn. to Study implications of Armed Services Ednl. Program, Commn. Internat. Edn. and Cultural Relations; commn. edn. orgns. NCCJ; bd. dirs. Nat. Safety Council; v.p., mem. adv. council Nat. council Boy Scouts Am.; trustee Am. Sch., Chgo. Recipient Am. Edn. award, 1958; Silver Beaver, Antelope, Buffalo awards Boy Scouts Am. Mem. Soc. Mayflower Descs., Soc. Colonial Wars, N.E.A (life), Horace Mann League Am., S.R., Phi Delta Kappa, Pi Delta Epsilon. Republican. Episcopalian. Mason. Clubs: Rotary (pres. Kansas 1946-47); University, Rotary (Chgo.); Faculty (Harvard). Author: (with Paul R. Pierce) The Practice of School Administration, 1958; (with R. Oliver Gibson) The School Personnel Administrator, 1965. Cons. to World Book Ency.; editorial adviser Houghton Mifflin Co.; also ednl. articles. Home: Lexington, Mass. Died Oct. 17, 1976.

HUNT, REED OLIVER, former mfg. co. exec.; b. Wollochet Bay, Wash., Oct. 12, 1904; s. Arda Roy and Edna Elisabeth (Oliver) H.; student Smith Sch. Nav., Seattle, 1923-24, Harvard Advanced Mgmt. Program, 1951; m. Sarah Elizabeth Trombley, Mar. 23, 1926; children—Reed Oliver, Patricia (Mrs. Jack Gordon Nevin). Deck hand, purser, mate, master Puget Sound and deep sea vessels, various cos., 1916-27; clk., accountant, asst. office mgr. Pulp & Paper Mills, Crown Zellerbach Corp., 1927-35, office mgr., 1935-43, asst. to v.p. in charge mfg. hdqrs. parent co., San Francisco, 1943-46, asst. gen. mgr. mfg., 1946-51, v.p. mfg., 1952-54, v.p. ops., 1954-56, dir., exec. v.p., 1956-70, pres., chief exec. officer, 1959-63, chmn. bd., chief exec. officer, 1963-69, chmn. exec. com., 1969, then dir. emeritus; dir. emeritus Canadian Imperial Bank of Commerce, Toronto, Union Oil Co., Singer Co., N.Y.; dir. Peninsula State Bank, Gig Harbor, Wash. Chmn., President's Commn. Financial Structure and Regulation. Vice pres., bd. dirs. Crown Zellerbach Found.; trustee U. Puget Sound, Tacoma, Wash. Republican. Episcopalian. Clubs: Commonwealth, Pacific Union (San Francisco); Ranier (Seattle). Home: Gig Harbor, Wash. Died Nov. 26, 1977; interred Artondale Cemetery, Gig Harbor.

HUNT, WALTER FREDERICK, prof. petrology; b. Cincinnati, Sept. 6, 1882; s. Henry William and Ida (Balser) H.; A.B., U. of Mich., 1904, A.M., 1905, Ph.D., 1915; m. Stella T. Edwards, June 3, 1909; children—Marjorie Louise, Frederick William; m. 2d, Janice A. Goodall, June 30, 1950. With U. of Mich. since 1906, successively instr., asso. prof., 1918-22, prof. petrology since 1922, also chmn. Dept. of Mineralogy and dir. Mineral. Lab. since 1933. Fellow Geol. Soc. America, Mineral. Soc. America, A.A.A.S.; mem. Am. Assn. of Univ. Profs., Sigma Xi, Gamma Alpha fraternities. Republican. Conglist. Author: Tables for Determination of Minerals (with E. H. Kraus), 1911, 1930; Mineralogy—An Introduction to the Study of Minerals and Crystals (with E. H. Kraus and L. S. Ramsdell), 1920, 28, 36. Editor of The American Mineralogist since 1922. Home: Ann Arbor, Mich. *

HUNTER, CHARLES W., engineer; born Baltimore, Md., Feb. 13, 1882; s. James Welsh and Mary Loretta (Devereux) H.; student Baltimore City Coll.; M.E., Cornell U., 1905; m. Georgena Morrill, Feb. 18, 1918; children—Anne, Georgena Devereux. Constrn. engr., Astoria Light & Power Co., 1905-07. Retort Coke Oven Co., Cleveland, O., 1907-08, Peoples Gas Light & Coke Co., Chicago, 1908-10; gas engr., Stone & Webster, Boston, 1910-22; became v.p. Davis & Farnum Mfg. Co., Waltham, Mass., 1922; v.p. U.G.I. Contracting Co., Philadelphia, 1925-28; v.p. United Engrs. & Constructors, Inc., Phila., since 1928; dir. Dwight P. Robinson & Co., Day & Zimmermann Engring. & Constrn. Co., The U.G.I. Contracting Co. Organizer of Toluol div., Ordnance Dept., U.S. Army, World War. Mem. Am. Gas Assn., Delta Tau Delta. Republican. Catholic. Club: Midday. Home: Ardmore, Pa. *

HUNTER, CLARENCE E., ret. govt. ofcl.; b. Wellsburg, N.Y., Sept. 2, 1884; s. Wilmot and Clara (Emerick) H.; grad. Schissler Coll. Bus., Norristown, Pa., 1901; night courses in engring. Drexel Inst., Phila.; m. Sara Jane Landis, Jan. 10, 1905. With Hale and Kilburn Mfg. Co., Phila., 1901-19, Liberty Nat. Bank, N.Y.C., 1919-21; credit mgr. N.Y. Trust Co., 1921, asst. treas., 1922, asst. v.p., 1926, v.p. charge fgn. bus., 28-49; ret., 1949; dir. Walter Kidde and Co., Inc., Belleville, N.J., 1943-53; chief ECA spl. mission to Netherlands, 1949-51, Mut. Security Adminstrn. spl. mission for econ. cooperation, Netherlands, 1952-53; U.S. Treasury rep. U.S. mission to NATO, OECD, 1953-61. Dir. Council on Fgn. Relations, N.Y.C., 1942-53; life councillor Nat. Indsl. Conf. Bd. Decorated comdr. Order of Lion (Finland); grand cross Order of Orange Nassau (Netherlands). Republican. Episcopalian. Mason (32 deg.). Metropolitan (N.Y.C. and Washington); St. Cloud Golf (Garches, France); Union Interalliee (Paris). Address: Philadelphia, PA 19103. *

HUNTER, DONALD FLEMING, publisher; b. Toronto, Ont., Can., Jan. 22, 1911; s. Horace T. and Christine (Fleming) H.; student U. Toronto, 1930; m. Mary Holton, May 29, 1937; children—Donald Holton, Mary Margaret. With Maclean-Hunter, Ltd., Toronto, from 1945, mng. dir., 1952-64, pres., 1964-69, chmn. bd., from 1969; chmn. Greatlakes Broadcasting System Ltd.; dir. Shoreacres Broadcasting Co. Ltd., CFCN-TV Ltd., Voice of Prairies, Ltd., Maclean-Hunter Cable TV Ltd., Toronto Dominion Bank, Co-op Book Centre of Can. Ltd., Data Bus. Forms Ltd., M-H Communications Ltd., CFCN Communications Ltd., I.D.C. Pub. Co. Ltd., Metro Toronto News Co. Ltd. Served to maj. Canadian Army, 1940-45. Home: Toronto, Ont., Canada. Died Oct. 18, 1976.

HUNTER, EDWARD, editor, author; b. N.Y.C., July 2, 1902; s. Edward and Rose (Weiss) H.; self educated; m. Tatiana Pestrikoff, June 30, 1932 (div. May 1961); children—Robert, Tate Ann. Reporter, news editor of various newspapers, including Newark Ledger, New Orleans Item, N.Y. Post, N.Y. American; reporter Paris edit. Chgo. Tribune, 1924-25; news editor Japan Advertiser, Tokyo, 1927; editor Hankow (China) Herald, 1928-29, Peking Leader, 1929-30; covered Japanese conquest of Manchuria, Spanish Civil War, Italian conquest of Ethiopia, Internat. News Service, 1931-36; chmn. Anti-Communist Liaison, Inc., 1962-78; publisher-editor of monthly TACTICS (also bound in ann. vols.), 1964-78. Cons. psychol. warfare USAF, 1953-54. Served as propaganda warfare specialist AUS, with morale operations sect. OSS, Asia, World Warr II. Recipient various Freedom awards including Order of Lafayette. Clubs; Overseas Press, Silurians. Author: Guide to Peking, 1930; Brain-Washing in Red China, rev. edit., 1971; Brainwashing; The Story of Men Who Defied It, 1956, rev. as Brainwashing: From Pavlov to Powers, 1971; The Story of Mary Liu, 1957; The Black Book on Red China, 1958; The Past Present: A Year in Afghanistan, 1959; In Many Voices: Our Fabulous Foreign-Language Press, 1960; Attack by Mail, 1963. Contbr. articles on psychol. warfare, polit. extremism to numerous periodicals. Address: Arlington, Va. Died June 24, 1978.

HUNTER, GRAHAM CHAMBERS, clergyman; b. Toronto, Can., Dec. 5, 1882; s. William Armstrong and Eliza (Chambers) H.; A.B., Princeton Univ., 1904; B.D., Union Theol. Sem., 1909; A.M., Columbia, 1909; D.D., Occidental Coll., 1925; m. Louise Holden. Oct. 19, 1911 (died 1942); adopted children—Irene, Stuart (killed in South Pacific, Jan. 18, 1944); m. 2d, Marcia Kerr (Wellesley, 1913) 1944. Instructor, Mid-Pacific Institute, Honolulu, H.T., 1904-06, Presbyn. minister, Laramie, Wyo., 1909-11, Hunts Point, N.Y., 1911-14, Ch. of the Covenant, New York, 1914-24, Fullerton, Calif., since 1924; lecturer Occidental Coll., 1927-30. Mem. Am. Red Cross, Palestine Unit, 1918-19; asso. sec. Universal Christian Conf. on Life and Work, Stockholm, 1925; mem. Commn. to Rumania on Rights of Religious Minorities, 1927. Author: Luke, First Century Christian, 1937; John Muir, Mystic, 1938. Contbr. to religious mags. Co-Author: Rumania Ten Years After, 1928. Home: Cathedral City, Calif. *

HUNTER, MILTON REED, ch. ofcl.; b. Holden, Utah, Oct. 25, 1902; s. John E. and Margaret (Teeples) H.; B.S., Brigham Young U., 1929, M.S., 1931; Ph.D., U. Calif., Berkeley, 1935; m. Ferne Gardner, July 30, 1931; children—Milton Reed, Margaret, Lois A., Linda, Alison, Michael H. Sch. prin., St. Thomas, Nev., Leamington and Lake View, Utah, 1924-28; prin. sems., Lyman, Wyo., Ferron, Utah, 1928-34; tchr. Ch. of Jesus Christ of Latter-day Saints Sem., Provo, Utah, 1935-36; asst. dir. Latter-day Saints Inst. Religion, Utah State U., 1936-45; mem. First Council of Seventy, Latter-day Saints, 1945-75. Pres., John A. Widtsoe Meml. Found., 1952-62; v.p. New World Archaeol. Found., 1952-75. Mem. Sons Utah Pioneers, Delta Phi (nat. hon. pres.). Author: Utah in Her Western Setting, 1943; also numerous other books, articles. Home: Salt Lake City, Utah. Died June 25, 1975; interred Salt Lake City Cemetery.

HUNTER, ROBERT EDWARD, banker; b. Chgo., Nov. 20, 1886; s. Edward S. and Elizabeth (Mallers) H.; student Throop Poly. Sch., Pasadena, Cal., 1903-07, Sheffield Sci. Sch., Yale, 1911; m. Gwendolyn Mitchell, Sept. 27, 1913; children—Helen (Mrs. Wolfe), Louise, Robert Edward. Pres. Hunter Dubin & Co., investment bankers, Los Angeles, 1921—; adv. council, exec. com. Bank Am. Nat. Trust & Savs. Assn. Served to capt., F.A., U.S. Army, 1917-18; AEF in France. Mem. Psi Upsilon, Book and Snake. Home: Santa Barbara, Cal. *

HUNTER, WILLIAM CARROLL, govt. ofcl., lawyer; b. White Hall, Md., Aug. 12, 1886; s. Charles C and Mary R. (Slade) H.; LL.B., U. Md., 1910. Sec. to dean Md. U. Law Sch., 1910-13; admitted to Md. bar, 1911; asso. firm Haman, Cook, Chestnut and Markell, Balt., 1913-15; pvt. practice, Balt., 1916-33; atty. U.S. Dept. Agr., Washington, 1933-53, solicitor (gen. counsel), 1946-53. Served as 2d lt. F.A., U.S. Army, World War I. Democrat. Presbyn. Clubs: Loudoun (Va.) Hunt; Fairfax (Va.) Hunt. Home: Purcellville, Va. Died Jan. 6, 1978.

HUNTINGTON, JOHN WILLARD, architect; b. Hartford, Conn., Oct. 19, 1910; s. Robert Watkinson and Constance (Willard) H.; B.A., Yale, 1932; B.Arch., Columbia, 1936; m. Patricia Hannah Shaffer, June 20, 1936; children—John W., Sara (Mrs. Nicholas Ohly), Derek U. Designer, firm Harrison & Fouilhoux, N.Y.C., 1936-41; asso. architect for Pentagon Bldg., Washington, 1941-43; chief engr. facilities div. War Dept., Washington, 1943-45; partner firm Huntington & Darbee, Hartford, 1954-76. Instr. art history Hartford Coll. Women, 1956. Panelist What in the World TV series. Mem. West Hartford Town Council, 1961-71, mayor, 1967-69; pres. Environ. Center; regent U. Hartford; v.p. Conn. Arts Commn.; chmn. bd. dirs. Hartford State Co.; trustee Wadsworth Atheneum (pres. 1972-74), Noah Webster House Found., Horace Bushnell Meml., Hartford Art Sch. Fellow A.I.A. (recipient Bronze medal 1955). Democrat. Episcopalian. Clubs: Hartford, Hartford Golf, Hartford Canoe; Century Association (N.Y.C.). Home: Hartford, Conn. Died Dec. 23, 1976.

HUNTLEY, MICHEL CARTER, educator; born at Lumberton, Miss., Apr. 19, 1898; s. William Henry and Josie (Warren) H.; A.B., Millsaps Coll., Jackson, Miss., 1920, LL.D., 1939; A.M., Emory U., Atlanta, Ga., 1925; grad. student Johns Hopkins, 1929; U. of Chicago, summer 1933; Litt.D., University of Miami, 1957; married Sue Lillard Lee, August 31, 1930; one dau., Sue Lee (dec.). Instr., Millsaps Acad., Jackson, Miss., 1920-22; city editor Jackson (Miss.) Daily Clarion-Ledger. 1923; Memphis (Tenn.) Commercial Appeal, 1924; asso. prof. of English Birmingham So. Coll., 1925-29; executive sec. Southern Assn. of Colls. and Secondary Schs., 1930-49; dean of faculties Auburn University, from 1949; chmn. Commission on Colleges and Univs., 1953-56; dean of adminstrn., U. of Alabama, 1942-45. Served with 140th F.A., U.S. Army, 1917-19. Mem. Pi Kappa Alpha, Omicron Delta Kappa, Phi Beta Kappa. Democrat. Methodist. Home: Auburn, Ala. Died 1979.

HUNTLY, PHILIP CONRAD, prof. civil. engring.; b. Camden, Ark., Sept. 27, 1885; s. James E. and Susan (Grissom) H.; B.C.E., U. of Ark., 1910; m. Jean Elwood, June 3, 1922 (dec.); 1 dau., Phyllis Jean. Designer, Kansas City, Mo., 1910-11; asst. prof. U. of Ark., 1908-13; designer Morey & Newgard, Chicago, Ill., 1913-14; designer C.M.St.P.&P. Ry., summer, 1912; C.B.&Q. Ry. Co., summer, 1916; instr., later asst. prof., asso. prof., prof. mech. engring. Armour Inst., 1914-39; prof. civil engring. Ill. Inst. Tech., 1939-48. Past president Village of Riverside. Mem. Am. Soc. M.E., Am. Soc. for Metals, Soc. for Promotion of Engring. Edn., A.C.I., Triangle, Sigma Chi, Tau Beta Pi, Chi Epsilon, Pi Tau Sigma, Tau Omega. Mason (Shriner). Club: Brookwood Country. Home: Harlingen, Tex. *

HUNTON, (EDWARD) DEANE, coll. dean; b. Madison, Va., July 4, 1885; s. Thomas and Mora (Evans) H.; S.B. (engring.), U. of Wyo., 1911; B.A.M., Harvard Grad. Sch. of Bus. Adminstrn., 1916; diplomas, 4 yrs. commercial training, 1902-11; m. Einna D., Oct. 2, 1912; 1 dau. Head, teacher, bus. div. of commerce U. of Wyo., 1912-47, dean, 1947-48, dean emeritus, since 1948; gen. adviser commerce students; asst. prof., mil. sci., U.S. Shipping Bd., 1918; teacher, coll. of commerce, U. of Calif., 1919, so. branch, 1925. Dir., Laramie Newspapers, Inc.; chmn. student loan com., U. of Wyo., mem. pres. adv. bd., curriculum com., bd. of athletic control, mgr. athletics, faculty mgr. student finances, Mem. Chamber of Commerce, Army Adv. Com. for 5th U.S. Army, Laramie, Wyo., Alpha Kappa Psi, Sigma Alpha Epsilon. Democrat. Presbyterian.

Mason. Contbd. to journs. Home: 211-11th St., Laramie, Wyo. *

HUNTON, EPPA, IV, lawyer; b. Richmond, Va., July 31, 1904; s. Eppa, Jr., and Virginia Semmes (Payne) H.; B.A., U. Va., 1925, LL.B., 1927; LL.D., Va. Commonwealth U., 1976; m. Caroline Homassel Marye, Sept. 28, 1936 (dec. July 15, 1962); children—Caroline (Mrs. John H. High), Virginia (Mrs. Randolph F. Totten), Eppa. Admitted to Va. bar, 1926, D.C. bar, 1966; asso. firm Hunton, Williams, Anderson & Gay, 1927-34; partner firm Hunton & Williams, and predecessors, Richmond, 1934-76; dir. First & Mchts. Nat. Bank & Corp. Bd. visitors Med. Coll. Va., 1932-51, 54-58, 59-63, 64-68, chmn. exec. com., 1954-58, 65-68, chmn. bd., 1960-63; bd. visitors Va. Commonwealth U., 1968-70, vice rector, 1968-69, rector, 1969-70; trustee Richmond Eye Hosp., 1953-76; pres. Med. Coll. Va. Found., 1972-76; alumni bd. trustees Va. Mus. Fine Arts, 1934-37, U. Va. Endowment Fund, 1974-76. Served from 1st lt. to maj. AUS, 1942-46. Decorated Bronze Star. Mem. Am., Va., Richmond bar assns., Soc. Cincinnati in Va. (v.p. 1970-73), Va. Hist. Soc. (exec. com. 1946-76, pres. 1966-69), Delta Kappa Epsilon, Phi Delta Phi. Democrat. Episcopalian. Clubs: Downtown, Commonwealth, Country of Va., German (pres. 1968-70). Home: Richmond, Va. Died Nov. 23, 1976.

HUPP, JAMES LLOYD, historian, archivist; b. Hemlock, Ohio, Jan. 5, 1891; s. James Linley and Linnie (Powell) H.; B.S., Ohio U., 1916; A.M., Columbia, 1919; Ph.D., Ohio State U., 1931; m. Luella E. Sherwood, June 8, 1918; children—Virginia (Mrs. Grant W. Speer), James Sherwood, Robert William. Asso. prof. edn. W.Va. Wesleyan Coll., 1942-43, prof. edn. and psychology, dean students, 1943-55, prof. edn., 1955-61, chmn. div. applied arts and scis., chmn. dept. edn., 1959-61, dir. dept. archives and history 1961-76. Historian, archivist W.Va., 1961-76; sec.-treas. W.Va. Hist. Commn., 1961-67, W.Va. Antiquities Commn., from 1965; exec. sec. W.Va. Hist. Soc., 1961-76, dir. dept. archives and history, 1961-76. Dir. adult work Bd. Edn. W.Va. Conf. Meth. Ch., 1943-53, adv. council adult edn., bd. edn. Gen. Conf. Meth. Ch.; editor adult edn. dept. Christian Edn. Bull. Mem. N.E.A., Soc. for Advancement Edn., Nat. Soc. for Study Edn., Am. Assn. State and Local History, A.A.A.S., Soc. Archtl. Historians, Am. Acad. Polit. and Social Sci., AAUP, So. Conf. Ednl. Fund (sec. bd. dirs.), Am. Assn. UN, Internat. Council Religious Edn., W.Va. Soc. S.R. (past pres.), W.Va. Philos. Soc. (past pres.), Nat. Trust Historic Preservation, Nat. Geneal. Soc., W.Va. Archeol. Soc., Phi Delta Kappa. Mason (K.T.), Rotarian. Author: (with C.P. Smith) Items Found on Report Forms in Use in Schools in the U.S., 1929; Administrative Problems in the Field of History Teaching, 1932; William Torrey Harris: Teacher, Administrator, Philosopher and Writer, 1933; (with C.H. Roberts, R.G. Wood) The Ohio Survey of the Social Sciences, 1934; Eliminating Discrimination, 1950; What Influences Students to Prepare to Teach on the Secondary Level?, 1951; James Rumsey's Memorial in London, 1957; The Movement for West Virginia Statehood, 1962; The West Virginia Flag: It's Development and Meaning, 1962; Storehouse of Treasurers, 1964; The Movement for the Formation of the West Virginia Department of Archives and History, 1966. Contbr. articles for profl. jours., bulls. Home: Buckhannon, W.Va. Died Mar. 7, 1976.

HUPPELER, LAMBERT MATHIAS, ins. exec.; b. Wahpeton, N.D., Apr. 19, 1908; s. William M. and Gertrude (Kraker) H.; B.S., U. N.D., 1932; m. Ruth E. Tallmadge, Aug. 4, 1936; children—Carol Marie, James Lambert. Supt. agencies Mass. Mut. Life Ins. Co., 1947; gen. agt. N.E. Mut. Life Ins. Company, Boston, from 1948, vice president, 1953-60, president L. M. Huppeler Company, chmn. bd., from 1960. Former mem. pension and profit sharing conferences Purdue U. C.L.U. Mem. Life Mgmt. Assn. (v.p., dir. 1953), Life Underwriters Assn. N.Y. (dir. 1949-52, from 1962), Nat. Assn. Life Underwriters, Million Dollar Round Table (life mem.), Life Ins. Agy. Mgmt. Assn. (dir. 1958-60), Research Agys. Group, N.Y. N.D. Alumni Assn., Alpha Tau Omega. Clubs: Union League (N.Y.C.); Canadian (Boston); Bonnie Briar Country (Larchmont, N.Y.); Westchester Country (Rye, N.Y.). Author papers. Home: Greenwich, Conn. Died May 12, 1978.

HURLBURT, WILLIAM BLAIR, lawyer; b. Mt. Vernon, Iowa, Apr. 19, 1892; s. Rollo Franklin and Mary Halsey (Blair) H.; A.B., U. Ia., 1914, LL.B., 1915; m. Alice Fay Willard, Apr. 6, 1918 (dec.); 1 son, Willard Blair. Admitted to Iowa bar, 1915 and since practiced in Des Moines; mem. firm Hurlburt, Blanchard, Cless & Porter and predecessor firm; spl. asst. U.S. attorney and gen. hearing officer, conscientious objector cases for So. Dist. Iowa, 1944-56. Served as 1st lt. inf., 85th div. U.S. Army, World War I. Mem. Am., Iowa (gov. 1950-51), Polk County (pres. 1949-50) bar assns., Sigma Alpha Epsilon (pres. 1914, province sec. 1916-17), Phi Delta Phi, Sigma Delta Chi. Clubs: Des Moines, Hyperion Field (past pres.). Home: Des Moines, Iowa. Died Dec. 24, 1976.

HURLEIGH, ROBERT FRANCIS, broadcasting co. exec.; b. Fairmont, Md., July 28, 1912; s. Robert Francis and Elizabeth Nancy (Lankford) H.; grad. McDonogh Mil. Sch.; m. Marjorie Marie Peterson, Oct. 7, 1939; children—Maryland Beth, Robert Blake, Robin Marie, Steven Lankford, Jan Theresa. News editor Sta. WOL, Washington, 1934-35, Sta. WCAO, Balt., 1935-36, Sta. WFBR, 1936-41; central div. mgr. Asso. Press Radio, 1941-43; news analyst CBS, Chgo., 1943-45; dir. news Sta. WGN and midwest bur. chief MBS, 1945-53, dir. Washington operations, 1953-57, v.p., 1957-59, pres., 1959-66; pres. Master Communications, Inc., 1966-72, Am. Labor-Mgmt. Communications, Inc., N.Y.C., from 1972; pres. Nat. News Service, communications cons. firm, Washington, until 1980. Mem. Sigma Delta Chi. Clubs: Nat. Press (Washington); Kenwood Country; Chicago Press; N.Y. Athletic. Home: Bethesda, Md. Died Aug. 10, 1980.

HURLEY, DONALD JOSEPH, lawyer; b. Gardner, Mass., May 4, 1907; s. Cornelius Joseph and Rose (O'Loughlin) H.; A.B. magna cum laude, Harvard, 1928, LL.B., 1931; m. Miriam Greene, Aug. 28, 1937; children—Cornelia Greene, Donald, Jr., Stephen Nash, Rosamond Page. Admitted to Mass. bar, 1931; with Goodwin, Procter & Hoar, Boston, 1931-78, partner, 1939-78; asso. counsel Mass. Pardon and Parole Commn., 1938-40; spl. counsel gov. Mass. in preparation of charter Mass. Bus. Devel. Corp., 1953; chmn., dir. Merrimac Paper Co., Inc., Aquamac Corp., Northkraft Industries, Inc.; pres., dir. Arcade Malleable Iron Co.; dir., clk., Sec. Stop & Shop Cos., Inc.; dir., clk. Cambridge Grant Farm, Inc., Domino Airways, Inc., Wallace Industries, Inc.; pres., dir. Mass. Bus. Devel. Corp.; trustee, mem. bd. investment Charlestown Savs. Bank; dir., mem. exec. com. Boston Safe Deposit and Trust Co., Boston Co., Inc., Boston Old Colony Ins. Co.; sec. Fed. Street Capital Corp.; dir. Equitable Fire Ins. Co., J.L. Hammett Co., Lilly Chem. Products, Inc., Putnam Duofund. Inc., Putnam Equities Fund, Inc., Putnam Vista Fund, Inc., Putnam Investors, Inc., Putnam Income Fund, Putnam Convertible Fund, Inc., Chasaba Corp., Continental Corp., Continental Ins. Co., Fidelity and Casualty Ins. Co. N.Y., Niagara Fire Ins. Co., Putnam Mariner Fund, Putnam Voyager Fund, Seaboard Fire & Marine Ins. Co., Texstar Corp., Comml. Ins. Co., Newark, Firemen's Ins. Co., Newark, Glen Falls Inc. Co., Kansas City Fire and Marine Ins. Co., Pacific Ins. Co. Trustee Civic Found. Boston, Boston Urban Found., George Putnam Fund Boston, Putnam Growth Fund, New Eng. Aquarium; hon. trustee Concord Acad.; mem. corp. Mass. Gen. Hosp., Mus. Sci.; former dir. Harvard Alumni Assn. Chmn. Boston Mid-Century Jubilee, 1960-78; gen. chmn. 25th reunion Harvard Class of 1928, 1953; former chmn. Mayor's Com. of 100 for Civic Progress in Boston; former trustee Boston U.; pres., dir. Com. of Permanent Charity Fund of Boston, Inc.; past dir. Internat. Center of New Eng., Inc., overseer Boy's Clubs Boston, Inc.; trustee Lowell Tech. Inst., 1955-58, Plimoth Planation; mem. bus. and profl. friends com. Nat. Center for State Cts. Served from lt. to lt. comdr. USNR, 1943-46. Mem. Greater Boston C. of C. (pres. 1954-56, chmn. exec. com. 1957, dir. 1949-66), Am. Law Inst., Am., Boston bar assns. Clubs: Union (Boston); Harvard (N.Y.C.); Weston (Mass.) Golf; Edgartown Reading Room (Martha's Vineyard, Mass.). Home: Weston, Mass. Died Nov. 29, 1978.

HURLEY, JULIEN A., lawyer; b. La Fayette, Yamhill Co., Ore., Apr. 1, 1885; s. Andrew M. and Mary Almiras (Smith) H.; ed. Ore. State NonoW Sch. and U. of Ore.; studied law in office of Col. R. G. Wheeler, of Vale; m. Fay Clark, of Vale, Ore., Feb. 9, 1919. Admitted to Ore. bar, 1908, began practice at Vale, later mem. firm Wheeler & Hurley; mem. Ore. Senate, sessions 1917-19; apptd. asst. U.S. atty. Anchorage, Alaska, Jan. 1, 1922. U.S. atty., 4th Div. of Alaska, July 26, 1924-1933. Completed course at O.T.C., Eugene, Ore., Oct. 1918. Mem. Pi Gamma Mu. Republican. Conglist. Grand Chancellor K.P., Domain of Ore., 1920; Mason, Elk. Home: Fairbanks, Alaska.*

HURLEY, RUBY, former assn. exec.; b. Washington; d. Edward and Alice (Patterson) Ruffin; student Miner Tchrs. Coll., Terrell Law Ch. Nat. youth sec. NAACP, 1943-51, regional coordinator, 1951-52, Southeast regional dir., Atlanta, from 1952. Active YWCA; mem. research and planning com. North Ga. Conf., United Methodist Ch., also Christian social involvement mission coordinator; past pres. United Meth. Women of Warren Meml. United Meth. Ch. Recipient Citizen of Year award Birmingham chpt. Omega Psi Phi, 1953; award for spl. distinction civil and human rights Friends of Nat. Council Negro Women, 1957; First Medgar Evers award Capital Press Club, Washington; Freedom award West Coast region NAACP, Berkeley, Calif.; Distinguished Service award Savannah State Coll. chpt. NAACP; award for outstanding contbns. in fight for freedom, Region V NAACP and Fla. conf. Quarter of Century Service to NAACP award, numerous others; named Woman of Year, Utility Club, N.Y.C., 1968; mem. Chgo. Defender Honor Roll of Democracy; named Bronze Woman of Year in human relations Delta chpt. Iota Phi Lambda, 1972; Wilberforce U. award. Mem. So. Interagy. Conf. Home: Atlanta, Ga. Died Aug. 9, 1981.

HURST, M. L., ins. co. exec.; b. Ft. Scott, Kan., 1892; ed. U. Tenn., 1911. Ret. treas. Western Casualty & Surety Co., Ft. Scott, Western Fire Ins. Co.; dir. Western Ins. Securities Co. Home: Fort Scott, Kans. Deceased.

HURT, JOHN TOM, ret. educator; b. Waco, Tex., Mar. 12, 1908; s. Solon Osomus and Vivian (Eikel) H.; B.A., Rice U., 1931, M.A., 1932, Ph.D. (fellow), 1935; m. Ches Lee Pursley, Jan. 31, 1939; 1 dau., Maxine Hurt Fisher. Mem. faculty Tex. A. and M. U., College Station, 1936-79, prof. math., 1948-74, emeritus, 1974-79; cons. Western Electric Co., 1926-27, S.W. Bell Telephone Co., 1928, Gulf Oil Corp., 1929, Geophys. Service, 1934-37, Texaco Corp., 1935-36, San Jacinto Ordinance Depot, 1941, Westinghouse Research Labs., 1945, Rocketdyne div. N.Am. Aviation, 1957-58. Mem. Am. Math. Soc., AAAS, Phi Beta Kappa, Pi Mu Epsilon. Club: Masons (32 deg.). Home: Bryan, Tex. Deceased.

HUSBAND, ALEXANDER CHAPMAN, cons. engr.; b. Troy, N.Y., Mar. 27, 1914; s. James A. and Ann (Anderson) H.; B.N.S., U.S. Naval Acad., 1935; M.C.E., Rensselaer Poly. Inst., 1940; grad. Advanced Mgmt. Program, Harvard Bus. Sch., 1961; D.Eng., Rensselaer Poly. Inst., 1967; m. Mary Hodges Bacon, July 26, 1941. Commd. ensign, U.S. Navy, 1935, advanced through grades to rear adm., 1963-78, staff civil engr. Comdr. Amphibious Force, Pacific Fleet, 1946-47, officer charge constrn. Aleutians, 1950, comdg. officer constrn. battalion center, Davisville, R.I., 1955, dist. pub. works officer First Naval Dist., 1958; dir. European-Mid East div. Bur. Yards and Docks, 1962-64; dep. chief civil engrs. Navy Dept., 1964-65, comdr. Naval Facilities Engring. Command and chief Civil Engrs., 1965-69; v.p. constrn. Consol. Edison Co., N.Y.C., 1969-71; cons. engr., 1971-78. Decorated D.S.M., Legion of Merit, Bronze Star medal with Combat V. Registered profl. engr., R.I., N.Y., Conn. Fellow ASCE; mem. Soc. Am. Mil. Engrs. (past nat. pres.), Nat. Soc. Profl. Engrs., Am. Inst. Cons. Engrs., Am. Arbitration Assn., Sigma Xi, Newcomen Soc. Club: Essex, N.Y. Yacht. Home: Old Saybrook, Conn. Died Jan. 23, 1978; interred Arlington Nat. Cemetery (Va.).

HUSSEY, ALLEN SANBORN, educator; b. Concord, N.H., Jan. 27, 1918; s. Percy Brookes and Helen (Greene) H.; B.S., U. N.H., 1939, M.S., 1941; Ph.D., Ohio State U., 1946; m. Charlotte Louise Bronson, Sept. 2, 1941; children—Frederick Bronson, Eileen Jacklyn, Stephen Robert, Margaret Ellen, Christopher Allen. Research chemist Armstrong Cork Co., Lancaster, Pa., 1941-42; research engr. Battelle Meml. Inst., Columbus, Ohio, 1945; successively instr., asst. prof., asso. prof. Northwestern U., 1945-62, prof. 1962-76, asst. dean Coll. Arts and Scis., 1963-68. Mem. Am. Chem. Soc., A.A.A.S., Catalysis Soc. Am., Sigma Xi, Phi Kappa Phi, Phi Lambda Upsilon. Club: Catalysis (past pres.) (Chgo.). Contbr. articles profl. jours. Home: Evanston, Ill. Died Dec. 26, 1977.

HUSTON, LUTHER ALLISON, author, journalist; b. Paulina, Ia., Nov. 18, 1888; s. Luther Allen and Alice (Noble) H.; student U. So. Calif., 1908-11; m. Dora Lee Carey, Feb. 15, 1929; 1 dau., Ann Noble. Reporter, Bellingham (Wash.) Herald, 1912-14, Seattle Times, 1914-17; reporter, bur. mgr., fgn. corr., news editor, sales mgr. Internat. News Service, 1917-34; city editor Washington Post, 1934-35; bur. mgr., staff corr. Washington bur. N.Y. Times, 1935-57; dir. pub. info. Dept. Justice, Washington, 1957-61; asst. to dir. Am. Bar Assn., Washington, 1961-63; with Ernest Wittenberg Assos., pub. relations, 1964-65; Washington corr., editor and pub., 1966-75. Recipient George Polk Meml. award, 1954. Fellow Sigma Delta Chi (Wells key 1949, nat. pres. 1947-48). Episcopalian. Club: Nat. Press (gov. 1952-57, chmn. 1957). Author: Pathway to Judgment, A Study of Earl Warren, 1966; The Department of Justice, 1967. Home: Franklin, N.C. Died Nov. 26, 1975; interred St. John's Episcopal Ch., Franklin.

HUSTVEDT, SIGURD BERNHARD (HUST'VET), prof. English; b. Northwood, Ia., Mar. 28, 1882; s. Rev. Halvor Bjorn and Anne Marie (Reque) H.; B.A., Luther Coll., Decorah, Ia., 1902; grad. Luther Theol. Sem., St. Paul, 1905; M.A., U. of Calif., 1912; M.A., Harvard, 1914; Ph.D., 1915; m. Janet Hale Freeze, June 21, 1924; children—Eric Stephens (dec.), Joan Karin, Hugh Robert. Pastor St. Paul's Luth. Ch., Oakland, Calif., 1905-11; teaching fellow in English, U. of Calif., 1911-12; instr. English, U. of Illinois, 1915-17; instr. and asst. prof. rhetoric and English, U. of Minn., 1918-21, asst. prof., later asso. prof. English, U. of Calif. at L.A., 1921-31, prof., 1931-49, now emeritus. Capt. inf., N.A., Camp Grant, Ill., 1917-18. Member Modern Lang. Assn. of America, Am. Assn. Univ. Profs., Soc. for Advancement Scandinavian Study, Am. Scandinavian Foundation, Am. Musicological Soc., Norwegian-Am. Hist. Assn., Norsk Folkeminnelag, Calif. Folklore Soc., Am. Folklore Soc. (1st v.p.), Parker traveling fellow (Harvard) in Eng. and Scandinavia, 1914-15; fellow Am.-Scandinavian Foundation in Norway, 1922-23. Author: Ballad Criticism in Scandinavia and Great Britain, 1916; Ballad Books and Ballad Men, 1930; Melodic Index of Child's Ballad Tunes, 1936. Translator: Muneh's Norse Mythology, 1926. Editor (with F. J. Klingberg), The Warning Drum, 1944. Co-editor: Western Folklore (formerly Calif.

Folklore Quar.). Address: 405 Hilgard Av., Los Angeles 24, Calif. *

HUTAFF, G. HARRY, banker; b. San Francisco, Sept. 24, 1918; s. J. Harry and Mabel (Troppmann) H.; m. Mildred Ada Mowll, Aug. 31, 1940; children—Douglas Wayne, Mark Charles, Debra Joan. Asst. cashier Bank of Am., 1936-48; operations analyst Bank of Hawaii, 1948-51; v.p., cashier Bank of Calif., N.A., 1951-64; sr. v.p., controller First Hawaiian Bank, Honolulu, 1964-73, exec. v.p., chmn. control group, dir., 1973-78; v.p., treas. First Hawaiian, Inc.; pres. Olomana Farm. Mem. Am. Mgmt. Assn., Am. Soc. Personnel Adminstrn., Nat. Assn. Accountants, Financial Execs. Inst. (adv. council). Clubs: Oahu Country (Honolulu); Mid Pacific Country. Home: Kailua, Hawaii, Died July 10, 1978.

HUTCHIN, CLAIRE ELWOOD, JR., army officer, state ofcl.; b. Decatur, Ill., Jan. 9, 1916; s. Claire Elwood and Helen Josephine (Francis) H.; B.S., U.S. Mil. Acad., 1938; grad. Army War Coll., 1953; m. Katharine Porter Steel, June 15, 1938; children—Katharine Keen (Mrs. Ronald J. Menhennet), Claire Elwood III, William Ellis, Marion Belt. Commd. 2d lt. U.S. Army, 1938, advanced through grades to lt. gen., 1967; asst. to Gen. of Army Marshall on Presdl. mission to China, 1946; exec. officer Gen. Wedemeyer on mission to China/Korea, 1947; comdg. officer 1st Bn., 23d Inf., Korea, 1950-51; asst. to Adm. Radford, chmn. Joint Chiefs Staff, 1953-57; comdg. officer 12th Inf., 1957-58; chief staff VII Corps, Europe, 1960; dir. plans and policy Dept. Army, 1960-63; comdg. gen. 4th Inf. Div., Ft. Lewis, Wash., 1963-65; dep. chief staff Pacific Command, 1965-67, chief of staff Pacific Command, 1967-69; comdg. gen. V U.S. Corps, Europe, 1969-71, 1st U.S. Army, Fort George Meade, Md., 1971-73; ret., 1973; exec. dir. Md. Bicentennial Commn., 1973-77. Mem. exec. bd. Mt. Rainier council Boy Scouts Am., 1963-65, Aloha council, 1965-69, Balt. Council, 1971-80, mem. Nat. bd., 1970-80, v.p. North Atlantic Council, North Trans-Atlantic Council, 1969-71, chmn. Silver Beaver awards com., 1970-71, v.p. SE area region one, 1972-74; chmn. Md. Combined Fed. Fund Campaign, 1971-73; state chmn. Md. Cancer Crusade, 1974, 75, vice chmn. bd. dirs. Md. div. Am. Cancer Soc., 1976-77, chmn., 1977-78; del. Bicentennial Council Thirteen Original States, 1974-76. Decorated D.S.C. with oak leaf cluster, D.S.M. with oak leaf cluster, Silver Star, Legion of Merit with 5 oak leaf clusters, Legion of Valor, Bronze Star, Purple Heart with oak leaf cluster; Pa. Distinguished Service award; various fgn., unit and service awards; recipient Silver Beaver award Boy Scouts Am. Mem. Assn. Grad. U.S. Mil. Acad., Assn. U.S. Army, Ret. Officers Assn., Assn. U.S. Army War Coll. Home: Severna Park, Md. Died June 22, 1980; buried Arlington Nat. Cemetery.

HUTCHINGS, PAUL RAYMOND, trade union exec.; b. Milw., July 4, 1909; s. Raymond Hallock and Clara Marie (Ebert) H.; student U. Wis., 1928-31; B.E., Milw. State Tchrs. Coll., 1933; grad. study George Washington U., 1938-39; m. Lorna Backey, Aug. 27, 1940; children—Lynn, Paul. Code labor adviser, labor adv. bd. N.R.A., 1934-36; organized Officer Workers Union, A.F. of L., Milw., 1936; asst. research dir. Internat. Assn. Machinists, A.F. of L., 1937-41, research dir., 1941-43; pres. Office Employes Union, A.F. of L., Washington, 1938-42, sec-treas. internat. council, 1942-45; pres., chmn. exec. bd. Office Employes Internat. Union, A.F. of L. 1945-53, research dir. metal trades dept., 1954-74; cons. labor affairs Fgn. Operations Adminstrn., 1954. Mem. Tau Kappa Epsilon. Author: Handbook on the National Labor Relations Board, 1937; International Association Machinists, The Wagner Act After Ten Years, 1945, Bureau National Affairs (contbr. chpt. Effect on the Trade Union). Editor, Office Worker, 1943-53. Home: Arlington, Va. Died Oct. 14, 1974.

HUTCHINGS, WILLIAM LAWRENCE, educator; b. Lehi, Utah, Oct. 2, 1903; s. William Ely and Alice (Naylor) H.; student U. Chgo., 1924-26; A.B., U. Calif., Ph.D., 1935; m. Phyllis Hayford, May 27, 1934 (dec. 1965); 1 dau., Lucy. Teaching asst. U. Calif. at Berkeley, 1932-34; from instr. to asso. prof. math, Rollins Coll., 1935-43; mem. faculty Whitman Coll., 1943-78, Alexander I. Anderson prof. math., 1947-75, prof. emeritus, 1975—78, chmn. dept., 1947-69. Home: Walla Walla, Wash. Died Aug. 16, 1978.

HUTCHINS, LEE MILO, plant pathologist; b. Fennville, Mich., Apr. 21, 1888; s. Henry Hudson and Harriet C. (Robertson) H.; B.S., Mich. State Coll., 1913; student U. Montpelier, 1919; Ph.D., Johns Hopkins, 1924; student Wageningen and Paris, 1930. Asst. pathologist, bur. plant industry, soils and agrl. engring U.S. Dept. Agr., 1914-17, through grades to sr. pathologist, 1919-41, in charge field labs. fruit disease investigation, 1921-41, head pathologist in charge div. forest pathology, 1941-53, chief, div. forest disease research Forest Service, 1945-55, collaborator in U.S. Dept. Agr., pathologist with FAO of UN in Yugoslavia, 1956, with Wis. Alumni Research Found., 1957; investigator diseases of cacao Am. Cocoa Research Inst. and Interam. Inst. of Agrl. Scis., Turrialba, Costa Rica, 1958-76; engaged in research, Costa Rica, 1976-78; collaborator U.S. Dept. Agr. Served as lt. San. Corps, U.S. Army, 1917-19. Received Superior Service award from U.S. Dept. Agr., 1955; Alumni award for Meritorious Service from Mich. State Coll., 1955. Fellow Am. Phytopath. Soc. (pres. 1942); mem. Bot. Soc., Bot. Soc. Wash. (pres. 1952), Soc. Foresters, Plant Physiologists, Soc. Hort. Sci., Soc. of Comp. Pathology (France), French Botanical Soc., Hort. Soc. France (hon.), Wash. Acad. Sci., Sigma Xi. Club: Cosmos (Washington). Author tech. papers on virus disease of fruit trees, oxygen-supplying power of soil, gall diseases of cacao. Address: San José, Costa Rica. Died Apr. 13, 1978; buried San Pedro de Montes de Oca, San Jose, Costa Rica.

HUTCHINS, ROBERT MAYNARD, fund exec.; b. Bklyn., Jan. 17, 1899; s. William James and Anna Laura (Murch) H.; student Oberlin Coll., 1915-17; A.B., Yale, 1921, A.M. (hon.), 1922, LL.B., 1925; LL.D., W.Va. U., Lafayette Coll., Oberlin Coll., 1929, Williams Coll., 1930, Berea Coll., 1931, Harvard, 1936, Tulane U., 1938; hon. doctoral degrees U. Copenhagen, 1946, U. Ill., 1947; LL.D., U. Frankfurt, 1948, U. Stockholm, 1949, Rollins Coll., 1950. U. Chgo., 1951, Colby Coll., 1956, U. Rochester, 1958, Lewis and Clark Coll., 1967; D.Litt., Georgetown U., 1964, Hebrew Union Coll., 1964; m. Maude Phelps McVeigh (div.); children—Frances Ratcliffe, Joanna Blessing, Clarissa Phelps; m. 2d, Mrs. Vesta Sutton Orlick. Master English, history Lake Placid (N.Y.) Sch., 1921-23; sec. Yale, 1923-27; lectr. Yale Law Sch., 1925-27, acting dean, 1927-28, dean, 1928-29, prof. law, 1927-29; pres. U. Chgo., 1929-45, chancellor, 1945-51; asso. dir. Ford Found., 1951-54; chief exec. officer Fund for Republic, 1954-74; chief exec. officer Center for Study Democratic Instns., 1954-74, life fellow, 1974, pres., 1975-77; pres. Fund for the Republic, 1975-77; dir. Ency. Brit., Inc., 1947-74, Ency. Brit. Films, Inc., 1947-74. Served in ambulance service U.S. Army, 1917-19; Italian Army, 1918-19. Decorated Croce di Guerra (Italian), 1918; officer Legion, 1969, Honor, 1938; recipient Goethe medal, 1948; Aspen Founders award, 1960. Mem. Chgo. Bar Assn., Order of Coif, Phi Beta Kappa. Clubs: University, Tavern (hon.) (Chgo.). Author: No Friendly Voice, 1936; The Higher Learning in America, 1936; Education for Freedom, 1943; St. Thomas and the World State, 1949; Morals, Religion and Higher Education, 1950; The Democratic Dilemma, Some Questions about Education in North America, The Great Conversation, 1951; The Conflict in Education, 1953; The University of Utopia, 1953; Freedom, Education and the Fund, 1956; Some Observations on American Education, 1956; The Learning Society, 1968; Dr. Zuckerkandl, 1968. Bd. editors Ency. Brit., 1946-74. Address. Santa Barbara, Calif. Died May 14, 1977.

HUTCHINSON, E(LIZABETH) B(ARTOL) DEWING, author; b. New York, Nov. 26, 1885, d. Thomas Wilmer and Maria Richards (Oakey) Dewing (both q.v.); ed. Brearley Sch., New York, 1899-1903; m. Frederick Porter Hutchinson, of New York, Oct. 16, 1911. Mem. Ethical Culture Soc. Author: Other People's Houses, 1909; A Big Horse to Ride, 1911. Address: Wamscott, L.I., N.Y.*

HUTCHINSON, HOWARD, ins. co. exec.; b. St. Clairsville, Ohio, May 4, 1913; s. Joseph and Florence (Woodcock) H.; student pub. schs.; m. Selma Grace Henderson, June 14, 1933; children—Shirley Jean (Mrs. Richard C. Laudick), Howard Hayes; m. 2d, Mabel E. Crawford, Dec. 20, 1969. With Nationwide Ins. Cos. (formerly Farm Bur. Ins. Cos.), Columbus, Ohio, 1932-68, dir. agys., 1948-51, v.p. sales, 1951, v.p. operations, 1951-54, v.p. ins. operations, 1954-62, sr. v.p., 1962-68; exec. v.p., dir. Nationwide Corp., Columbus, 1968-72; pres., dir. Nat. Services, Inc., 1969-72; pres., dir. Gates, McDonald & Co., 1969-72; chief exec. officer, chmn. bd. Allied Fidelity Corp., 1976-78, Allied Fidelity Ins. Co., 1976-78. Mem. econ. life com. Nat. Council Chs.; mem. gen. bd. Columbus YMCA. Mem. Health Ins. Assn. Am. (membership and ethical standards com.), Inst. Life Ins. (environmental information system steering com.), Columbus Maennerchor. Republican. Methodist. Mason (32 deg., Shriner). Clubs: Athletic, Scioto Country (Columbus); P.G.A. Country. Home: Riviera Beach, Fla. Died Aug. 15, 1978.

HUTCHINSON, WILLIAM THOMAS, historian, former educator; b. Freehold, N.J., Mar. 9, 1895; s. Thomas Combs and Anne (Thomas) H.; A.B., Rutgers U., 1916, Litt.D., 1941; A.M., Columbia, 1917; Ph.D., U. Chgo., 1927; m. Frances Runyon, Nov. 23, 1921 (dec.); children—Anne (Mrs. Walter Sharp), Judith (Mrs. John K. Powell). Supercargo, U.S. Shipping Bd., 1919-21; instr. history Rutgers U. 1921-24; mem. faculty U. Chgo., 1924-70, acting chmn. dept. history, 1942-43, chmn., 1943-50, Preston and Sterling Morton prof. Am. history, 1955-62, Preston and Sterling Morton prof. emeritus, 1962-76; sec. Charles R. Walgreen Found. 1938-45 (publs., 15 volumes "Walgreen Studies in Democratic Institutions". Mem. War Dept. com. history of war, 1946-56; mem. James Madison Meml. Commn., 1960-76. Served from pvt. to 1st lt., 5th Regt., 2d Div., USMC, AEF, 1917-19. Decorated Croix de Guerre with two citations, Purple Heart. Mem. Am., Miss. Valley (pres. 1958-59, bd. editors rev. 1946-49) hist. assns., Phi Beta Kappa. Baptist. Club: Quadrangle (Chgo.). Author: Biographies of Cyrus H. McCormick and Frank O. Lowden. Editor: (with W.M.E. Rachal, others) Papers of James Madison, 7 vols., 1962-71. Home: Chicago, Ill. Died Nov. 23, 1976.

HUTCHISON, CLAUDE BURTON, mayor, Berkeley, Cal.; b. Chillicothe, Mo., Apr. 9, 1885; s. William Moses and Adriana B. (Smith) H.; B.S. in Agr., U. Mo., 1908, LL.D., 1937; M.S. in Agr., Cornell U., 1913; M.S., Harvard, 1917; hon. D.Agr., U. Sophia, Bulgaria, 1939; LL.D., U. Cal., 1953; m. Roxie Ruth Prichard, Dec. 23, 1908; children—Helen, Ruth, Betty, Lucille; m. 2d, Mabel B. Bull, Oct. 3, 1931; 1 son, Claude Burton, Jr. With U. of Mo., advancing to prof. agronomy, 1908-13, prof. farm crops, 1913-16; prof. plant breeding, Cornell U., 1916-22; prof. same, U. of Calif., also dir. branch of the Coll. of Agr., 1922-24; asso. dir. agrl. edn. for Europe, Internat. Edn. Bd., 1924-26, dir., 1926-28; prof. agr. and dir. Giannini Foundation of Agr. Economics, U. of Calif., 1928-31, prof. agr., dean of Coll. of Agriculture, also director of Agricultural Experiment Sta., 1930-49, v.p. univ., 1945-52, ret.; dean agr. U. Nev., 1952-54; mayor, City of Berkeley, Cal., from 1955. Chairman China-United States Joint Agricultural Mission to China, 1946. Chairman California State Soil Conservation Commission, 1940-48; president Assn. Land Grant Colls. and Univs., 1943-44. Member Calif. Bd. Agriculture, 1944-52; Agrl. Bd. Nat. Research Council, 1944-48. Trustee China Foundation for Promotion Edn. and Culture, since 1947. Fellow A.A.A.S.; mem. Bot. Soc. America, Am. Soc. Agronomy, Am. Genetics Assn., Am. Soc. of Naturalists, Genetics Soc. of America, Sigma Xi, Alpha Zeta (nat. pres. 1914-23), Gamma Alpha; corr. mem. Czechoslovakian Acad. Agr. Decorated Order of White Lion (Czechoslovakia); Agrl. Decoration of 1st Class (Belgium); Officier du Merite Agricole (France). Presbyn. Mason. Home: Berkeley, Calif. Died Aug. 25, 1980; interred Chapel of the Chimes, Oakland, Calif.

HUTT, ROBERT BINES WOODWARD, indstl. psychologist; b. Glen Mills, Pa., Nov. 13, 1886; s. William Henry (M.D.) and Josephine Borden (Smith) H.; B.S., U. of Pa., 1909, M.A., 1911, Ph.D., 1924; grad. student Gen. Theol. Sem., N.Y. City, 1914; m. Florence Duncan Spruance, Apr. 12, 1915; 1 dau., Donna. Ordained ministry P.E. Ch., 1914; rector St. Mark's Ch., Casper, Wyo., 1914-18, St. John's Ch., Phila., 1920-22, Ch. of Our Saviour, Jenkintown, Pa., 1924-27; instr. in psychology, U. of Pa., 1920-23; psychologist Montgomery Sch., Wynnwood, Pa., 1923-24; asst. prof. psychology Trinity Coll., 1927-30, prof., 1930-43; psychol. examiner Hartford Police, 1942-43, for State Vocational Rehabilitation of Physically Handicapped, 1942-43; psychol. consultant Ensign-Bickford Company, Simsbury, Conn., 1943, manager of training, 1943-47. SerVed as chaplain, United States Army, World War. Capt. 1st Co. (Conn.), Governor's Foot Guard Secretary Officers Association, 1st Governor's Foot Guard, 1942. President Hartford Club, University of Pennsylvania Alumni, 1936; member U. of Pa. Hartford Bicentennial Com. Fellow A.A. A.S.; mem. Eastern Assn. Psychologists, Mil. Order Loyal Legion, Theta Delta Chi. Republican. Episcopalian. Mason (32 deg.). Author: Job Aptitude, 1943; Training in Industry: A Bibliography, 1943; Selection for Training, 1947. Co-inventor of the Hutt-Abild ergograph; inventor Hutt Confusion Recorder, Hutt Tachistoscope, Hutt-Allen Formboard. Home: Moylan, Pa.*

HUTTON, BARBARA, socialite; b. N.Y.C., Nov. 14, 1912; d. Franklyn Laws and Edna (Woolworth) H.; m. Prince Alexis Mdivani (div.); m. 2d, Count Haugwitz Hardenberg Reventlow (div. 1941); 1 son, Lance (dec. July 1972); m. 3d, Cary Grant, 1941 (div.); m. 4th, Prince Igor Troubetzkoy, 1947 (div.); m. 5th, Portfirio Rubirosa, 1954 (div.); m. 6th, Baron Gottfried von Kramm, 1961 (div.). Address: Cuernavaca, Murelos, Mexico. Died May 11, 1979.

HUTTON, HUGH MCMILLEN, editorial cartoonist; b. Lincoln, Nebr., Dec. 11, 1897; s. Elmer S. and Eugenia (McMillen) H.; student U. Minn., 1919-21; m. Dorothy Wackerman, May 24, 1924; children—Elizabeth Jean, Robert Wackerman. With St. Paul Pioneer Press, 1925, United Features, N.Y.C., 1929, Phila. Pub. Ledger, 1933, Phila. Inquirer from 1934; exhibitor etchings, lithographs, cartoons. Mem. Nat. Cartoonists Soc., Am. Assn. Editorial Cartoonists. Republican. Presbyn. Club: Phila. Sketch. Contbr. cartoons to various publs. Home: Philadelphia, Pa. Died Jan. 2, 1976; interred Long Wood Cemetery, Kennett Square, Pa.

HUTTON, JAMES, educator; b. Airth, Stirlingshire, Scotland, Nov. 30, 1902; s. John and Elizabeth (Arthur) H.; A.B., Cornell U., 1924, A.M., 1925, Ph.D., 1927. Instr. Greek and Latin, Columbia, 1926-27; instr. classics Cornell U. 1927-29, asst. prof., 1929-38, prof., 1938-61, Kappa Alpha prof., 1961-73, Kappa Alpha prof. emeritus, 1973-80, chmn. dept., 1946-52. Mem. com. Renaissance studies Am. Council Learned Socs., 1944-50. Guggenheim fellow, 1958-59. Fellow Soc. for Humanities (hon.); mem. Am. Philol. Assn., Modern Lang. Assn. of Am., Phi Beta Kappa, Phi Kappa Phi. Author: The Greek Anthology in Italy, 1935; The

Greek Anthology in France and in Latin Writers of The Netherlands, 2d edit., 1967; also articles. Joint editor: Cornell Studies in Classical Philology. Home: Ithaca, N.Y. Died Oct. 29, 1980.

HUTTON, SIDNEY BUCHANAN, horticulturist; b. Brookeville, Md., Jan. 26, 1889; s. Ulric and Mary Brooke (Janney) H.; B.S., Earlham Coll., 1908; m. Laura Doan, Sept. 6, 1911 (dec. Jan. 1970); children—Sidney Buchanan, Robert D., Richard J. Drainage engr. U.S. Dept. Agr., 1908-09; dep. county surveyor, Chariton County, Mo., 1909; drainage engr., sec. Morgan Engring. Co., Memphis, 1910-16; accountant War Dept., Washington, 1916-19; devel., cultivation blueberries Jos. J. White, Inc., Whitesbog, N.J., 1919-26; cultivation blueberries, mgr. Blueberry Coop. Assn., New Lisbon, N.J., 1927-30; with Conard-Pyle Co., Star Rose Growers, West Grove, Pa., 1930-76, v.p., 1937-51, pres., 1951-64, chmn. bd., 1964-76; pres. All-Am. Rose Selections, Inc., 1953-55; dir. Nat. Bank & Trust Co., Kennett Sq. Pres. Avon-Grove Community Chest, West Grove, 1946-70; mem. bd. assistance, Chester County, Pa., 1948-56, chmn., 1955-56. Recipient Man of Year award Southeastern Chester County C. of C., 1971; Hall of Fame award Am. Assn. Nurserymen, 1971. Mem. Am. Rose Soc., Nat. Rose Soc. Eng., Royal Hort. Soc. Eng. Home: Kennett Square, Pa. Died Aug. 11, 1976.

HUTZLER, JOEL GUTMAN DAVID, ret. dept. store exec.; b. Balt., Dec. 23, 1892; s. David and Ella (Gutman) H.; A.B., Johns Hopkins, 1915; m. Carolyn H. Fuld, Oct. 22, 1929; children—Katherine A. (Mrs. Arthur L. Troutner), Betty Rose (Mrs. William Ives), Joel Gutman David, David A. With Hutzler Bros. Co., Balt., 1916-74, sr. v.p., 1951-54, vice chmn. bd., 1954-65, chmn. be., 1965-73, chmn. emeritus, 1973-74. Dir. Asso. Jewish Charities, 1931-49, 1st v.p., 1943-45; past dir. YM and YWHA, treas., 1934-36. Bd. dirs. A.R.C., Balt., 1948-53; trustee Commn. on Govtl. Efficiency and Economy, Inc., Balt., 1944-47, Hutzler Fund, Inc., 1944-74, Balt. Opera Co., 1973-77. Served as ensign USNRF, 1918-19. Mem. Retail Mchts. Assn. Balt. (dir. 1925-46, pres. 1936-38), Howard Street Assn. (past v.p., dir.). Jewish. Clubs: Center, Johns Hopkins (Balt.). Home: Pikesville, Md. Died Jan. 12, 1977; interred Har Sinai Cemetery.

HUXTABLE, RICHARD SCOTT, corp. ofcl.; b. Cleve., Sept. 20, 1913; s. Harold Stafford and Mary Frances (Scott) H.; student U. Pa., 1931-33, Gen. Motors Inst., 1934-36; B.S. in Mech. Engring., Cleve. State U., 1940; m. Martha June Mix, Sept. 1, 1950; children—Richard C., Scott C. Asst. to gen. mgr. Cleve. diesel engine div. Gen. Motors Corp., 1934-47; exec. v.p., dir., gen. mgr. Fawick Airflex Co., Inc., 1947-52; pres. Fawick Corp., Cleve., 1952-54; v.p., dir. Fawick Flex-Grip Co., 1948-54; chmn. Clamco Corp., 1954-76; pres. Ray-Dor Mfg. Co., 1955-63, Ray-Dor Sales Corp., 1957-59, Howes Iron Works, 1957-59, Richfield Hills Corp., 1954-76; exec. v.p. Nat. Mgmt., Inc., 1958-64. Mem. Newcomen Soc., Soc. Naval Engrs., Navy League U.S. (past pres. Cleve. council), Am. Ordanance Assn., Better Bus. Bur. (past dir.), C. of C. (Man of Year award 1948), Sigma Alpha Epsilon. Republican. Mason (32 deg., Shriner, Jester). Clubs: Westwood Country; Athletic (Cleve.). Home: Richfield, Ohio. Died Oct. 27, 1976.

HYDE, MELVIN WATSON, coll. pres.; b. Hazel, S.D., Mar. 17, 1905; s. Orlow Miner and Anna Lucinda (Watson) H.; B.S., Dakota Wesleyan U., 1926; A.M., Columbia, 1930, Ph.D., 1932; LL.D., U. Evansville, 1968; m. Claudia Marie Bray, Aug. 28, 1929; children—James Stewart, Joanne Marie. Instr., Parker (S.D.) High Sch., then Sioux Falls (S.D.) High Sch., 1926-29; head dept. edn. Dakota Wesleyan U., 1931-32, dean, 1932-36; dean, head dept. edn. Mt. Union Coll., Alliance, Ohio, 1936-49; asst. pres. Drake U., Des Moines, 1949-55; pres. U. Evansville (Ind.), 1955-67, pres. emeritus, 1967-79; ednl. cons., 1967-79. Mem. N.E.A., Phi Delta Kappa, Phi Kappa Phi, Pi Kappa Delta, Pi Gamma Mu, Sigma Tau Delta. Republican. Methodist. Rotarian. Home: Estes Park, Colo. Died Dec. 2, 1979; interred Loveland, Colo.

HYMAN, ELIOT, motion picture producer. A pioneer in recognizing profit potential in distbn. feature motion pictures to TV; founder Asso. Arts Prodn., Inc. (now United Artists Asso.), 1947; then pres. Seven Arts Prodn. Ltd.; became chmn. bd. Warner Bros.-Seven Arts, Ltd., 1967; co-producer, financier motion pictures including Lost Boundaries, Moulin Rouge, Moby Dick, The Misfits, By Love Possessed, Lolita, Whatever Happened to Baby Jane, Gigot. Home: Westport, Conn. Died July 23, 1980.

ICELY, LAWRENCE BLAINE, business exec.; b. Leaf River, Ill., Nov. 2, 1884; s. Elias and Emma Rebecca (Harrison) I.; student pub. schs.; m. Kathryn Flynn, Aug. 3, 1907. With Wright & Ditson Co., 1905-17, first as asst. mgr. Chicago Div., 1905-09, mgr. Pacific Coast Div., 1909-15, and Western sales mgr. at Chicago, 1916-17; joined Wright & Ditson-Victor Co. as gen. sales mgr. and sec. at New York, 1917-18; pres. Wilson Sporting Goods Co. (formerly Thomas E. Wilson & Co.), Chicago, since 1918. Mem. Athletic Goods Mfrs. Assn., Golf Club Mfrs. Assn., Golf Ball Mfrs. Assn. Elk. Clubs: Rotary Number One of Chicago, Chicago Athletic Assn., Evanston Golf. Home: Evanston, Ill. *

IDDLES, HAROLD AUGUSTUS, chemist; b. South Haven, Mich., May 20, 1896; s. Thompson Andrew and Alice (Lilly) I.; B.S., Mich State Coll., 1918; M.S., State U. Iowa, 1922; Ph.D., Columbia, 1925; student Univ. of Graz, Austria, 1926, Manchester (England) Univ., 1927, Univ. of Munich, Germany, 1928; D.Sc. (hon.), U. N.H., 1965. Instr. in chemistry, Mich. State Coll., 1918-20; asst. in chemistry, State U. Iowa, 1920-22; instr. in chemistry, Columbia, 1925-29; prof. chemistry, U. N.H., 1929-76, chmn. dept.; vis. prof. chemistry, Harvard, summers 1947, 48, also M.I.T.; dir. elem. and coll. programs NSF; pres. Durham (N.H.) Trust Co., 1947-62. Cutting traveling fellow, Columbia, 1927-28. Mem. Am. Chem. Soc. (chmn. Northeastern sect., 1943-44, 1944-45), Sigma Xi, Alpha Chi Sigma, Phi Lambda Upsilon, Alpha Zeta, Phi Kappa Phi. Conglist. Home: Durham, N.H. Died Aug. 15, 1976; interred South Haven, Mich.

IGNATIEFF, GEORGE, univ. provost; b. St. Petersburg (now Leningrad), Russia, Dec. 16, 1913; s. Paul and Natalie (Mestchersky) I.; B.A., U. Toronto, 1936; B.A. (Rhodes scholar), Oxford U., 1938, M.A., 1960; LL.D., U. Toronto, 1968, U. Guelph, 1970, Brock U., 1967, U. Sask., 1973, York U., 1975; D.C.L., Bishop's Coll., 1973; hon. fellow St. John's Coll., 1973; m. Alison Grant, Nov. 17, 1945; children—Michael Grant, Andrew Grant. Permanent rep. Can. to NATO, 1963-65; Canadian ambassador Disarmament Com., Geneva, 1968-71; pres. UN Security Council, 1967, 68; permanent rep. of Can. to European Office of UN, Geneva, 1971-72; provost Trinity Coll., U. Toronto, from 1972. Chmn. bd. trustees Nat. Museums of Can., 1973. Decorated companion Order of Can. Home: Toronto, Ont., Canada. Deceased.

IJAMS, ELVIN H. (I'AMZ), coll. pres.; b. Florence, Ala., May 30, 1886; s. Joseph Henson and Frances Elizabeth (Oakley) I.; grad. State Normal Sch., Florence, 1906; B.S., Peabody Coll. for Teachers, Nashville, Tenn., 1918, M.A., 1927; post grad. work, U. of Southern Calif., 1931-32; m. Una Constance Hartley, 1915; children—Joe Hartley, Reba Catherine, Elva Malinda. Teacher and prin., rural schs., Ala., 1906-12; prin. Striplin Sch., Gadsden, Ala., 1912-16, Martin Sch., Birmingham, 1917-19; prin. city and county schs., Savannah, Ga., 1920-23; prof. of edn., David Lipscomb Coll., Nashville, 1923-27; religious ednl. and survey work, Los Angeles, 1928-32; dean, David Lipscomb Coll., 1932-34, pres., 1934-44; dir. radio and religious edn., Central Ch. of Christ, since 1944. Mem. A.A.A.S., Phi Delta Kappa. Mem. Ch. of Christ. Club: Civitan. Home: Nashville, Tenn. *

IKENBERRY, OLIVER SAMUEL, educator; b. Roanoke, Va., Jan. 6, 1908; s. Jacob and Edith (Stauffer) I.; A.B., McPherson Coll., 1929; A.M., Colo. State Coll. Edn., 1932, Ed.D., 1941; postgrad. Columbia U., 1935-36; m. Margaret Moulton, June 11, 1933; children—Stanley, Betty, Jane. Supt. schs., Haswell, Colo., 1930-33; prin. Union High Sch., Lamar, Colo., 1933-37; prin. schs., Delta, Colo., 1937-41; extension instr. Colo. State Coll. Edn., 1933-36, Western State Coll. Colo., 1937-41; dean coll., prof. edn. Salem (W.Va.) Coll., 1941-47; prof. edn. W.Va. U., summers, 1946, 47; pres. Shepherd State Coll., Shepherdstown, W.Va., 1947-68, pres. emeritus, 1968-78; with Inst. Edn., Oxford U., 1968-69; prof. edn. emeritus George Peabody Coll., Nashville,1969-75; adv. dir. Potomac Edison Co. of W.Va., 1952-68. Coordinator Civil Aeros. Adminstrn. War Service for Salem Coll. and Armed Services rep., 1941-44; pres. W.Va. council State Coll. and Univ. Pres.'s, 1954-56, Colo. Assn. Classroom Leaders Western Div., 1938. Colo. Assn. Secondary Sch. Prins., 1939-40, Coop. Research Assn., Colo. State Coll., 1941, Assn. Higher Edn. W.Va., 1946; rep. Am. Assn. Colls. for Teacher Edn. to Am. Council Edn., 1956-59; mem. W.Va. White House Conf. on Edn., 1956-59, 66-69; mem. Gov.'s Adv. Com. on Mental Health, 1964-68; higher edn. cons. U.S. Office Edn., 1966-70; rep to World Conf. on Orgns. Teaching Profession, Kingston, Jamaica, 1971. Recipient citation of merit for distinguished service McPherson Coll., 1969; named Ky. col., 1967. Mem. Am. Assn. Higher Edn., NEA, Tenn. Edn. Assn., W.Va. Council State Coll. and Univ. Pres.'s (pres. 1954), Am. Assn. State Colls. and Univs. (state rep. 1966-68), W.Va. Acad. Sci., W.Va. Assn. Coll. Pres.'s (sec.), W.Va. Intercoll. Athletic Assn. (sec.-treas. 1952-55), C. of C., Friends of Nashville Pub. Library (pres. 1975-77), UN of Nashville (dir. 1973-78), Phi Delta Kappa (v.p. 1971, faculty sponsor 1972-75), Kappa Delta Pi. Presbyterian (elder 1977). Clubs: Rotary (pres. 1951); Univ. (Nashville); Freolac Discussion (Nashville). Author: Comparative Inequalities in Educational Finance, 1932; Economic Factors Affecting Education in an Agricultural Community, 1939; Leisure Activities in a Community, 1941; Health, Government, Education and Religion in a Community, 1941; (textbook) American Education Foundations: An Introduction, 1974; also articles ednl. jours.; editor The Colorado Clearing House Bull., 1938-40. Home: Nashville, Tenn. Died Apr. 2, 1978.

ILIFF, SIR WILLIAM (ANGUS BOYD), bank dir.; b. N. Ireland, Oct. 2, 1898; m. Jacqueline Reepmaker-d'Orville. Served in various capacities including financial counsellor, Embassy, Tehran, Iran, financial adviser to gov. of Burma, Brit. treasury rep. in Middle East, Brit. Civil Service, 1922-47; loan dir. Internat. Bank for Reconstruction and Development, 1948-51, asst. to the president, 1951-56, vice president, 1956-72. Served as commd. officer, Brit. Army, Mesopotamia, N. Persia, Russia, 1916-22, France, Dunkirk, 1939-40. Created Knight Bachelor, 1961. Decorated Companion of Most Distinguished Order of St. Michael and St. George; Order of Brit. Empire. Home: London. Died Dec. 29, 1972.

ILLICK, JOSEPH S(IMON) (IL'IK), forester; born Easton, Pa., Sept. 16, 1884; s. John and Anna Louise (Unangst) I.; A.B., Lafayette Coll., 1907, Sc.D., 1927; B.F., Biltmore Forest Sch., 1911, F.E., 1913; grad. study, U. of Munich, 1910-11; M.S., Juniata Coll., 1925; LL.D. (honorary), Syracuse University, 1952; married Della May Brotzman; children—Dorothy Emelyn, Joseph Francis, Anna May, Ira Ellwood, Helen Josephine. Instr. in forestry, Pa. State Forest Sch., 1907-10, prof. forestry, 1911-18, acting dir., 1918-19; chief of silviculture and research, Pa. State Dept. Forestry, 1919-27; state forester, Pa., 1927-31; head of dept. forest management, N.Y. State Coll. of Forestry. 1931-43, acting dean, 1943-45, dean, 1945-52, dean emeritus since 1952. Chief cons. N.Y. State Joint Legislative Com. Natural Resources. Fellow Soc. Am. Foresters, A.A.A.S.; mem. Am. Forestry Assn., Am. Soc. Pub. Adminstrn., ex-officio mem. N.Y. State Forest Practice Bd. Republican. Lutheran. Mason, Shriner. Clubs: Univ.; Rotary. Author books. Contbr. bulls. and articles. Home: Syracuse, N.Y. *

IMHOFF, WERNER, newspaperman. Washington corr. Neve Zurcher Zeitung, maj. Swiss newspaper, for 27 yrs. Recipient Fgn. Press award, 1967; Julius Adams Stratton prize for cultural achievement Friends of Switzerland, 1971. Address: Washington, D.C. Died Jan. 17, 1977.

INGE, FREDERICK DOUGLASS, educator; b. Charlottesville, Va., May 30, 1896; s. George Pinkney and Kate Virginia (Ferguson) I.; B.S., U. Minn., 1924; M.S., Ia. State Coll., 1937, Ph.D., 1940; m. Lucille Elliott, Sept. 3, 1953. Asso. prof. biology So. U., 1929-36; prof. biology Fla. A. and M. Coll., 1937-44; prof. biology Bennett Coll., 1944-45, chmn. dept. natural scis., 1944-45; prof. biology Hampton Inst., 1945-71, chmn. dept. natural scis., 1957-61, prof. emeritus, 1971-78. Served as bn. supply sgt. 809th Inf., U.S. Army, World War I. Fellow A.A.A.S.; mem. N.Y. Acad. Sci., Am. Soc. Plant Physiologists, Bot. Soc. Am., Torrey Botany Club, Sigma Xi, Beta Kappa Chi. Contbr. articles to profl. publs. Address: Hampton, Va. Died Jan. 26, 1978.

INGELFINGER, FRANZ JOSEPH, physician, educator; b. Dresden, Germany, Aug. 20, 1910; s. Joseph and Eleanor (Holden) I.; brought to U.S., 1922, naturalized, 1931; A.B., Yale, 1932; M.D., Harvard, 1936; D.Sc. (hon.), Marquette Sch. Medicine, 1970, Boston U., 1973, Mass. Coll. Pharmacy, 1975, Rochester U. Sch. Medicine, 1976, Coll. Medicine and Dentistry N.J., 1977, Yale U., 1979, Mt. Sinai Sch. Medicine, 1979; LL.D. (hon.), George Washington U., 1978; m. Sarah Shurcliff, Aug. 23, 1941; children—Joseph Abbott, Alice. Intern Boston City Hosp., 1937; fellow Thorndike Meml. Lab., resident Boston City Hosp., asst. medicine, Harvard, 1938; fellow gastroenterology, asst. medicine U. Pa. Hosp., 1939; instr. medicine Boston U., 1940-42, asst. prof., 1942-45, asso. prof., 1945-58, prof. medicine, 1958-67, 1st Conrad Wesselhoeft prof. medicine, 1961-67, clin. prof. medicine, 1967-80; dir. V and VI med. services Boston City Hosp., 1961-67; mem. staff R. D. Evans Meml. Hosp., Boston, 1944-80; vis. physician, chief gastrointestinal clinic U. Hosp., 1943-67, mem. cons. staff, 1967-80; dir. Med. Found. Inc., 1960-64; asso. staff gastroenterology New Eng. Center Hosp., 1957-71; cons. gastroenterology Robert B. Brigham Hosp., 1960-71, Boston VA Hosp., 1952-73, Lemuel Shattuck Hosp., 1955-71; Disting. physician VA, 1979; fellow Inst. Society, Ethics and Life Scis., Hastings Center, Hastings-on-Hudson, N.Y., 1974-80; mem. adv. com. on medicine Med. Research and Devel. Command, U.S. Army, 1963-67; nat. adv. council Nat. Inst. Arthritis and Metabolic Diseases, 1961-65; mem. commn. on enteric infections Armed Forces Epidemiological Bd., 1966-72; spl. cons. NIH, 1966-69; nat. cons. to surgeon gen. USAF, 1967-70; cons. Medlars com. Nat. Library Medicine, 1967-73; med. and sci. com. Mass. chpt. Arthritis Found., 1967-70, chmn. research com., 1968-80, mem. exec. bd., 1969-70, trustee, 1969-80; mem. biomed. communications study sect. Pub. Health Service, 1968-72, chmn., 1970-72; cons. adv. panel system Bur. Drugs FDA, 1970-75; mem. corp. vis. com. Mass. Inst. Tech. Dept. Medicine, 1976-80. Trustee Tufts Med. Center Assn. Found., 1977-80, Univ. Hosp., Boston, 1977-80. Recipient Friedenwald medal Am. Gastroent. Assn., 1969; Disting. Service to Med. Edn. award Am. Assn. Med. Colls., 1976; others; diplomate in gastroenterology Am. Bd. Internal Medicine (mem.

subspecialty bd. gastroenterology 1966-68). Fellow Royal Coll. Physicians, Inst. Social, Ethics and Life Scis.; master A.C.P. (Disting. Tchr. award 1975); mem. AMA (mem. adv. com. med. sci. 1970-76, chmn. 1974-75), Am. Soc. Clin. Investigation, AAAS, Am. Gastroent. Assn. (v.p. 1959-61, pres. 1961-62), Assn. Am. Physicians (Kober medal 1979), Am. Assn. for Study of Liver Diseases, Interurban Clinical Club, Am. Acad. of Arts and Sci. (councilor 1960-64, mem. Amory prize com. 1963-69), Phi Beta Kappa, Alpha Omega Alpha, Beta Theta Pi, Nu Sigma Nu. Clubs: St. Botolph, Aesculapian (Boston). Editor: Gastroenterology sect., Year Book of Medicine, 1953-69. Contbr. articles, chpts. med. publs. Mem. editorial bd. New Eng. Jour. Medicine, 1961-67, editor, 1967-77; mem. editorial bd. Disease-a-Month; chmn. editorial bd. Gastroenterology, 1964-68. Home: Cambridge, Mass. Died Mar. 26, 1980.

INGERSOLL, ROYAL EASON, naval officer; b. Washington, June 20, 1883; s. Rear Adm. Royal Rodney and Cynthia (Eason) I.; grad. U.S. Naval Acad., 1905; m. Louise Van Harlingen, June 29, 1910; children—Royal Rodney (lt. U.S. Navy, killed in action, Battle of Midway, June 4, 1942), Alice Jean. Apptd. midshipman U.S. Navy, 1901; promoted through grades to admiral, 1942; communication officer Navy Dept., 1916-18, Paris Peace Conf., 1918-19; Comd, U.S.S Nokomis, 1924-26; Naval War Coll., 1926-28; asst. chief of staff Battle Fleet, 1928, U.S. Fleet, 1929; chief of staff U.S. Fleet, 1930; comd. U.S.S. Augusta, 1933, U.S.S. San Francisco, 1934-35; tech. asst. U.S delegation London Naval Conf., 1935; dir. War Plans Div. Operations, 1936-38; comdr. Cruiser Division Six, U.S. Fleet, 1938-40; asst. chief naval operations, 1940-41, commander-in-chief U.S. Atlantic Fleet, 1942-44; comdr. Western Seas Frontier, 1944-45; retired Aug. 1946. Recipient Navy Cross, D.S.M., Victory Medal (U.S.), Hon. Knight Comdr. Order British Empire (Gt. Britain), Grand Officer Order Orange Nassau (Netherlands) Grand Cross Naval Order of Merit (Brazil), Comdr. Legion of Honor (France). Club: New York Yacht (New York). Home: La Porte, Ind. Died May 20, 1976.

INGLE, DWIGHT JOYCE, educator, physiologist; b. Kendrick, Idaho, Sept. 4, 1907; s. David J. and Mattie (Self) I.; B.S., U. Idaho, 1929, M.S., 1931, D.Sc. (hon.), 1962; Ph.D., U. Minn., 1941; m. Geneva McGarvey, Oct. 25, 1930; children—David, Ann, Jane. Mayo Found. fellow, 1934-38; George S. Cox med. research fellow U. Pa., 1938-41; Upjohn fellow Upjohn Co. research div., 1941-43, sr. research sci. company, 1943-53; prof. physiology Ben May Lab., U. Chgo., 1953-73, prof. emeritus, 1973-78, chmn. dept. physiology, 1959-68; vis. prof. chemistry U. Idaho, 1973-74, 75-76. Recipient Roche-Organon award Laurentian Hormone Conf., W.E. Upjohn prize; Outstanding Achievement award U. Minn., 1964; Modern Medicine Distinguished Achievement award, 1967. Fellow Am. Acad. Arts and Scis., N.Y. Diabetes Assn., AAAS; mem. Am. Physiol. Soc., Soc. Exptl. Biology and Medicine (pres. 1965-67), Endocrine Soc. (pres. 1959-60; Koch award 1963), Nat. Acad. Scis., Phi Beta Kappa, Sigma Xi (pres. Chgo., 1959-60), Alpha Omega Alpha. Clubs: Chgo. Literary (v.p. 1971-72); Wabigama (pres. 1970-71). Author: Physiological and Therapeutic Effects of Corticotropin (ACTH) and Cortisone, 1953; Principle of Research in Biology and Medicine, 1958; I Went to See the Elephant, 1962; Who Should Have Children?, 1973; Is It Really So?, 1976; also sci. papers. Founder, editor Perspectives in Biology and Medicine (Honor award of AMWA, 1964, 68, 70, advisory editor 1973-78). Home: Rapid City, Mich. Died July 28, 1978.

INGLE, LESTER, educator; b. Howard, Kans., July 30, 1908; s. Jess Newton and Martha Ellen (Gadberry) I.; B.S., Kans. State Coll., 1932; M.S., Brown U., 1934, Ph.D., 1936; m. Edith Jaeger, Sept. 7, 1935; children—Linda I. Rain, Paul Edward. NRC fellow U. Chgo., 1936-37; instr. U. Ill. at Urbana, 1937-41, asst. prof., 1942-46, asso. prof., 1946-52, prof., 1952-73, emeritus, 1973-80; cons. toxicology of pesticides to industry. Recipient Excellence of Teaching award U. Ill., 1967. NIH grantee on toxicology of pesticides. Mem. AAAS, Am. Inst. Biology, Am. Soc. Entomology. Author (with Zim): Seashores, 1955; Animal Biology, 9th edit., 1971. Editor: Resources in Sci.-Biology, 1966. Home: Urbana, Ill. Died Feb. 25, 1980.

INGLES, HARRY CLYDE, army officer; b. Pleasant Hill, Nebr., Mar. 12, 1888; s. William and Martha (Turner) I.; student U. Nebr., 1906-09; B.S., U.S. Mil. Acad., 1914; d. Eng., U. Nebr., 1945; graduate Army Signal School, Ft. Monmouth, N.J., 1920, Command and General Staff Sch., Ft. Leavenworth, 1928, Army War Coll., Washington, D.C., 1931; D. Eng., Brooklyn Polytechnic Inst., 1946; m. Grace Murray Salisbury Dec. 26, 1914; children—Martha Salisbury, Mary Osborne, John Stephen. Commd. 2d lt., Inf., U.S. Army, 1914, advanced through the grades to brig. gen., Apr. 25, 1941, major gen., Dec. 2, 1942; served as capt. and major Inf. and Signal Corps, World War I; chief of staff, Caribbean Defense Command, Mar.-Dec. 1942; Panama Mobile Forces, Dec. 16, 1942-Feb. 23, 1943; deputy comdr. ETO, Mar. 1, 1943-May 25, 1943; Chief Signal Officer U.S. Army, July 1, 1943-March 31, 1947, Received Distinguished Service Medal (U.S.); Officer Legion of Honor (Fr.); Comdr. Order British Empire (Eng.); Comdr. Orden de Boyaca (Columbia); Comdr. Orden de Liberatador (Venezuela). Now cons., dir. RCA; dir. RCA Communications, Inc., N.B.C. Fellow Am. Inst. Elec. Engrs.; sr. mem. Inst. Radio Engrs.; mem. Beta Theta Pi. Mason. Clubs: Army and Navy (Washington); University (N.Y.). Home: Washington, D.C. Died Aug. 15, 1976.

INGOLD, ERNEST, business exec.; b. Chicago, Ill., Mar. 26, 1885; s. Arthur Johnson and Maggie (Thompson) I.; grad. Lawrence Acad., Appleton, Wis., 1904; Lawrence College, 1904-06; B.S. in Mech. Engring., University of Illinois, 1909; married Gene Cox, November 21, 1911 (deceased June 1958); 1 son, Ernest II, m. 2d, Mrs. D. LaMar Christy, April 21, 1961. Pres. Ernest Ingold, Inc. (holding co.); pres. Ernest Ingold Co., automobile dealer, San Francisco, 1933-57; v.p. Ernest Ingold Investment Co., 1955-61; adv. com. Crocker-Anglo Cal. Nat. Bank; director World Trade Center; Mayor of Hillsborough, California, 1943-60. Director of Boys Clubs Am.; chairman and director San Francisco Boys club; trustee U. of Ill. Found., Ernest Ingold Charitable Trust, San Francisco Boys Club Endowment, Rotary Found. San Francisco. Decorated Order of the Crown of Oak (Luxembourg); recipient Silver Keystone award Boys Clubs Am. Mem. San Francisco C. of C. (pres. 1943), U.S. C. of C. (dir. 1945), California Bar Association; member Better Business Bureau (president 1942), Phi Delta Theta, Mason (Shriner), Rotarian. Clubs: Electric, Bohemian (San Francisco). Author: Tales of a Peddler, 1942; The House in Mallorca, 1952. Home: Hillsborough, Cal. *

INGRAM, WALTER ROBINSON, educator; b. Liverpool, Eng., Feb. 12, 1905; s. Walter and Elizabeth (Robinson) I.; came to U.S., 1909, naturalized, 1936; A.B., Grinnell Coll., 1926; M.S., U. Iowa, 1928, Ph.D., 1929; m. Lydia Margaret Bowen, Sept. 3, 1929; children—Walter Bowen, William Edmund. Instr. zoology Syracuse U., 1929-30; instr. neurology Med. Sch., Northwestern U., 1930-31, asso., 1931-32, asst. prof., 1932-36; asst. prof. anatomy Coll. Medicine, U. Iowa, Iowa City, 1936-37, asso. prof., 1937-40, prof., 1940-73, prof. emeritus, 1973-78, head dept., 1940-66, exec. com. Coll. Medicine, 1949-53. Commonwealth Fund fellow, 1958-59. Fellow Am. Electroencephalographic Soc. (hon.); mem. Royal Soc. Medicine (affiliate), Anat. Soc. Gt. Britain and Ireland, AAAS, Am. Neurol. Assn., Am. Acad. Neurology, Am. Assn. Anatomists, Am. Physiol. Soc., Soc. Exptl. Biology and Medicine, Soc. for Neurosci., Phi Beta Kappa, Sigma Xi, Alpha Omega Alpha, Phi Beta Pi. Author: A Student's Introduction to Neurology, 1964; A Synopsis of Neuroanatomy; (with Fisher and Ranson) Diabetes Insipidus: Anatomical Neurology, 1976; A Review of Anatomical Neurology, 1976; also papers neuroanatomy and neurophysiology. Home: Iowa City, Iowa. Died Dec. 26, 1978; interred Oakland Cemetery, Iowa City.

INLOW, HARVEY EDGAR, educator; b. Eagle Point, Ore., Dec. 17, 1886; s. Franklin Berkeley and Sarepta Ellen (Winters) I.; A.B., Pacific U., Forest Grove, Ore., 1915; LL.B., U. of Ore., 1914; M.A., Stanford U., 1933; m. Eva Lou Skaggs, of Pleasant Hill, Ore., May 23, 1907; children—Eva Hope, Alice Alexandra, Edgar Burke, Jean Laray. Began as teacher and prin. rural and elementary schs., 1905; supt. schs. Cottage Grove, Forest Grove and Pendleton, Ore., 1909-29; dir. Eastern Ore. summer session, Ore. Normal Sch. (Pendleton, Ore.), 1920-26; pres. Eastern Ore. Normal Sch. (La Grande, Ore.), 1929-37; dir. Dept. In-Service Extension Edn. for Ore. since 1937. Admitted to Ore. bar, 1916; mem. Pendleton Planting Commn., 1924-29. Mem. N.E.A. (life), Ore. State Teachers Assn. (past pres.), Phi Delta Kappa. Conglist. Mason. Club: University (Portland). Home: Monmouth, Ore.*

INNERFIELD, IRVING, educator, research physician; b. Bklyn., June 15, 1912; s. Maurice and Frances (Schmetterling) I.; B.S., L.I. U., 1932; M.D., N.Y. Med. Coll., 1936; m. H. Jean Pozefsky, Dec. 17, 1944; children—Ronald, Billie, Carla, Michael. Intern Queens Gen. Hosp., 1936-39; resident Columbia Coll. Phys. and Surg., 1939-42; practice medicine specializing in internal medicine, Nyack, N.Y., 1945-50, N.Y.C., 1950-55; asst. prof. physiology N.Y. Med. Coll., 1949-53; research asso. medicine Mt. Sinai Hosp., N.Y.C., 1953-56; research prof. biology L.I. U., 1956-60; asst. pathologist Harlem Hosp., N.Y.C., 1959-60; mem. faculty Fairleigh Dickinson U., 1960-76, prof. biochemistry, 1960-72, chmn. dept., 1962-71; research prof. medicine N.Y. Med. Coll., N.Y.C., 1971-76; attending physician Met. Hosp., N.Y.C.; attending physician Bird S. Coler Hosp., N.Y.C., also dir. Coagulation lab. Trustee L.I. U. Served with USNR, World War II. Named Alumnus of Year, L.I. U., 1957. Fellow N.Y. Acad. Scis.; mem. Am. Fedn. Clin. Research, A.A.A.S., Am. Assn. U. Profs., A.M.A., Bergen County Med. Soc., Soc. Exptl. Biology and Medicine. Author: Enzymes in Clinical Medicine, 1960. Discoverer anti-inflammatory effect proteolytic enzymes, 1951; inventor intra-muscle and oral forms of proteolytic enzymes. Home: Tenafly, N.J. Died Dec. 4, 1976.

INÖNÜ, ISMET (ENO-NOO), president of Turkey; b. Izmir, Asia Minor, Sept. 24, 1884; s. Reshid and Djevriye; student military High School and mil. arty. coll., Istanbul (grad. 1906); m. Emine Mevhibe, Apr. 13, 1916; children— Ömer, Erdal, Özden. Commd. capt., 1906, advanced through the grades to general, 1926; brig. gen., 1922; retired since 1927. Captain with 2d Army, 1906; member General Staff, 4th Army Edirne, Asia Minor; member expeditionary force against Arabian revolutionists, 1910; chief of Gen. Staff of Army of Yemen, Arabia, 1912; dir. 1st Sect. Great Gen. Staff, Istanbul, later mil. adviser to delegations to negotiate peace with Bulgaria at end of Balkan War, 1913; chief of Gen. Staff, 2d Army, Eastern Thrace, 1915; comdr. 4th Army Corps against Russians on Eastern Front, World War, 1916; comdr. 20th Army Corps, later 3d Army Corps, Syria, 1917; undersec. Ministry of War, Istanbul, 1918; comdr. Western Front, 1920-22 (won Battle of Inönü over Greece and given surname of Inönü by Kemal Atatürk); deputy from Edirne, Great Nat. Assembly; chief Great General Staff, 1920; minister of Foreign Affairs, 1922; signed Treaty of Lausanne, July 24, 1923; served as Premier of Turkey, 1923-24, 1925-37, president since 1938. Hon. prof. polit. sci., Ankara, faculty of law, Higher Inst. Agr.; hon. pres. Turkish Ednl. Soc. Formerly v.p. Rep. Peoples Party, leader of party since 1939. Moslem. Awarded Medal of Independence, after War of Independence, 1920-22. Author of numerous published speeches. Address: Cumhurbaskani, Ankara, Turkey. *

INZER, WILLIAM HENRY, judge; b. Pontotoc, Miss., Jan. 5, 1906; s. James William and Lou Delia (Caldwell) I.; grad. U. Miss., LL.B., 1931; m. Charline Lawrence, Mar. 18, 1938 (dec.); 1 son, William Henry. Admitted to Miss. bar, 1931, practiced in Miss., 1931-36; Pontotoc County atty., 1936-40; circuit judge, 1940-43; chancellor, 1943-65; asso. justice Miss. Supreme Ct., Jackson, 1965-78. Mem. bd. bar examiners, 1938-40. Chief Miss. delegation Democratic Nat. Conv., 1964. Served to maj. AUS, 1943-46; NATOUSA. Mem. Phi Alpha Delta. Home: Jackson, Miss. Died Mar. 1, 1978; buried Calhoun City, Miss.

IRELAND, E. WARD, educator; b. Unadilla, N.Y., Jan. 8, 1884; s. Orville L. and Celestia E. (Ward) I.; diploma Oneonta (N.Y.) Normal Sch., 1906; B.S., Teachers Coll., Columbia, 1908, A.M., 1912; Ph.D., Yale, 1937; m. Adelaide Sweet, June 8, 1919. Teacher, Sidney, N.Y., 1903-06; head dept. of history Hackensack (N.J.) Pub. Schs., 1908-12; supervisor of rural schs., Conn. Dept. of Edn., Hartford, 1912-14; dir. Norwalk (Conn.) Jr. High Schs., 1914-16; regional dir. rural schs., Conn. Dept. of Edn., 1916-25; supt. Stratford (Conn.) Schs., 1925-40; state dir. adult edn., Conn. Dept. Edn., 1940-42; pres. New Haven State Teachers Coll., 1943-46, ret. 1946. Life mem. N.E.A. (mem. dept. supts.). Mem. Conn. Supts Assn. (mem. exec. com. of Oct. Conf. for exchange of ednl. opinion, pres. 1932-33), Conn. State Teachers' Assn. (chmn. tenure com., 1936-37), Conn. Mental Hygiene Soc., Conn. Civil Service Assn., Conn. Social Welfare Soc., U.N. Assn. of Conn. Episcopalian (vestryman). Clubs: Graduates (New Haven); University (Hartford). Home: West Haven, Conn. *

IRELAND, EDWARD JOSEPH, pharmacologist, educator; b. Victor, Colo., Mar. 27, 1904; s. George Victor and Eleanor (Harrington) I.; A.B., U. Wis., 1926, B.S., 1929, M.S., 1930, Ph.D., 1935; m. Elve Louise Newman, Jan. 23, 1945; children—Edward Joseph, Thomas Newman, Elma Leonce. Instr. pharmacognosy and pharmacology U. Fla., Gainesville, 1935-39; prof. pharmacology Loyola U. of South, New Orleans, from 1930, dean Coll. Pharmacy, 1958-65, prof. pharmacology Sch. Dentistry, 1939-62, 1965-69; chief of narcotics and drug control State of La., 1971-72. Toxicologist, City of New Orleans, 1950-52, chmn. hist. pharmacy commn., dir. Hist. Pharmacy Mus., from 1957. Mem. Am. Inst. History Pharmacy (pres. 1964-65), Blue Key, Sigma Xi, Rho Chi (nat. pres. 1944-47), Phi Sigma, Kappa Psi, Phi Kappa. Home: New Orleans, La. Died Dec. 4, 1972.

IRELAND, GLEN, business exec.; b. Independence, Ia., Sept. 4, 1895; s. Frank Brunner and Lula (Smale) I.; B.Engr., Univ. Ia., 1917; m. Edith Stone Bancroft, 1926; 1 dau., Elizabeth Bancroft (Mrs. John H. Burnett). Mem. engring. dept. Northwestern Bell Tel. Co., Des Moines, 1919-23; American Telephone & Telegraph Company, New York City, 1923-46; vice president Pacific Tel. and Tel. Company regulatory matters, San Francisco, Jan. 1947-July 1949; vice pres. and gen. mgr. No. Calif. and Nev. area, Pacific Co., July 1, 1949-June 1951, on leave as asst. to adminstr. and dep. adminstr., Nat. Prod. Auth. Washington, Oct. 1950-April 1951; vice pres. personnel, Pacific Co., San Francisco, California, 1951-57, vice president of operations, 1957—. Served as lt., F.A., 1917-19. Fellow Am. Inst. E.E.; mem. Tau Beta Pi, Sigma Xi, Theta Xi. Rep. Presbyn. Clubs: Commonwealth, Stock Exchange, Transportation (San Francisco). Home: San Mateo, Calif. *

IRELAND, STEPHEN, insurance executive; b. Somerville, Mass., Nov. 5, 1883; s. Rasselas W. and Adeline (Perkins) I.; ed. Winchester High Sch.; Comers Commercial Coll., Boston; m. 2d, Ruth Jaynes, Nov. 29, 1939. With State Mut. Life Assurance Co., as cashier Boston office, 1903-08, in various depts. home office, Worcester, Mass., 1908-16, inspector of agencies, 1916-18. supt. of agencies, 1918-29, vice pres. and supt. of agencies 1929-43, vice pres. since 1929, dir., 1930-43. Trustee and auditor Worcester Five Cents Savings Bank. Clubs: Worcester, Rotary, Players, Worcester Country, Worcester Economic. Home: Worcester, Mass. *

IRENEY, METROPOLITAN (JOHN BEKISH), bishop; b. S.W. Russia, Oct. 2, 1892; s. Dimitry and Agnia (Saltrukovich) Bekish; grad. Theol. Sem., Kholm, Russia, 1914. Came to U.S., 1952, naturalized 1957. Ordained priest Russian Orthodox Ch., 1916; asst. rector Cathedral of Lublin, Poland, 1916-19; mem. Polish consisitory Diocese of Pinsk, 1935-47, also chmn. missionary com.; dean Counties of Sarna, Kamen-Kashursk and Pinsk, 1938-44; displaced person, Germany, 1944-47; rector Russian Orthodox Ch., Charleroi, Belgium, 1947-52, Holy Trinity Ch., McAdoo, Pa., 1952-53; bishop of Tokyo and Japan, 1953-60; archbishop of Boston and New Eng., 1960-65; archbishop of N.Y., Met. all Am. and Can., 1965-70; primate Orthodox Ch. Am., 1970-77; Home: Syosett, N.Y. Died Mar. 18, 1981; buried St. Tikhon's Cemetery, South Canaan, Pa.

IRISH, JAMES M., naval officer; b. Utica, N.Y., July 25, 1885; s. Charles G. and Louise C. (Standin) I; student Hobart Coll., 1903-04; B.S., U.S. Naval Acad., 1908; M.S., Columbia, 1915; D.Sc., Hobart. 1943; m. Frederica Lyman Savage. Nov. 4, 1916 (div. 1945); children—James M., Jerry S.; m. 2d, Alice Swift Child, 1947. Commd. ensign U.S. Navy, 1908, and advanced through the grades to rear adm., 1942; asst. chief bur. of engring., 1938-41; supervisor of shipbldg., 1941-43; inventory control officer and asst. chief naval operations, Washington, 1943-45; chmn. bd. Tampa Shipbldg. Co., 1946-48; on Navy retired list, 1946. Awarded Legion of Merit. Mem. Am. Soc. of Naval Engrs., Kappa Alpha. Clubs: Army Navy (Washington); New York Yacht. Home: Pebble Beach, Cal. *

IRONS, ROBERT BRUCE, JR., mktg. exec.; b. Rapid City, S.D., Dec. 17, 1914; s. Robert Bruce and Frances (Lambert) I.; ed. public schs.; m. Mary Corning Winslow, Dec. 23, 1938; children—Emily (Mrs. Robert W. Rogers, Jr.), Robert Bruce III, Victoria. With Standard Oil Co., Ind., 1940-57, asst. div. mgr., Grand Rapids, Mich., 1953-57; advt. exec. Standard Oil Co., Ind., Am. Oil Co., Chgo., 1957-62; dir. marketing Am. Internat Oil Co. and overseas affiliates, 1962-64; pres. Fletcher Richard Co. Inc., and affiliates of Interpublic Group Cos., Inc., 1964-68, chmn. Communications Counselors Network, Inc., 1968-71; chmn. exec. com., dir. Ken Snyder Enterprises, 1971-76; dir., mem. exec. com. Haniel-AMOCO, A.G., Basel, Switzerland, 1962-64; dir. AMOCO-Fina, S.A., Brussels, Belgium, 1962-65. Chmn. finance com. Off The Street Boys Club, Chgo., 1960-62; pub. relations counselor, bd. edn. Wilmette (Ill.) Community Fund, 1958-59. Recipient Advt. award Freedom Found., 1960. Mem. Am. Assn. Advt. Agys. Republican Episcopalian. Clubs: Players (N.Y.C.); Tryon Riding and Hunt, Tryon Country (N.C.). Home: Tryon, N.C. Died Oct. 19, 1979.

IRVING, JULES, theater dir.; b. Bronx, Apr. 13, 1925; s. Jacob and Ida (Emanuel) Israel; B.A. in English Lit., N.Y.U., 1947; M.A. in Theater and Drama, Stanford, 1949; m. Priscilla Pointer, Dec. 28, 1947; children—David, Katie, Amy. Co-founder, mem. Actor's Workshop, San Francisco, 1952-65; dir. The Repertory Theater of Lincoln Center, N.Y.C., 1965-73; prof. drama San Francisco State Coll., 1949-62; chief instr. Fordham U., 1970-71. Served with inf. AUS, 1943-46; ETO. Mem. Theatre Communications Group (exec. com. from 1960), Orgn. Legitimate Theatres (pres.), Soc. Stage Dirs. and Choreographers (past mem. exec. bd.). Home: New York, N.Y. Died July 28, 1979.

IRVING, LAURENCE, biologist; b. Boston, May 3, 1895; s. Wm. Nathaniel and Esther (Messenger) I.; prep. edn., Roxbury Latin School; A.B., Bowdoin Coll., 1916, Charles Carroll Everett grad. scholar, 1916-17, Sc.D. (hon.), 1959; A.M., Harvard, 1917; Ph.D., Stanford, 1924; M.D. (hon.), U. Oslo, 1956; D.Sc. (hon.), U. Alaska, 1968; m. Florence A. Binsley; children—Susan, William Nathaniel, Laurence, Alan. Instr. Wm. Warren Sch., Menlo, Calif., 1921-23, Stanford, 1924-27; NRC fellow U. Frankfurt-am-Main (Germany), 1925-27; asso. prof. physiology U. Toronto, 1927-31, prof. exptl. biology, 1931-37; prof. biology Swarthmore Coll., 1937-49, chmn. dept. zoology, dir. Edward Martin Biol. Lab., 1937-49; lectr. physiology U. Pa., 1937-49; chief physiology sect. Arctic Health Research Center, USPHS, Anchorage, 1949-62; prof. zoophysiology Lab. of Zoophysiology, U. Alaska, 1962-75, emeritus prof., 1975-79, dir. Inst. Arctic Biology, 1962-66, adv. sci. dir., 1966-79; George Cyril Graves lectr. in physiology, U. Ind., 1948-49; hon. research asso. Woods Hole Oceanographic Inst., 1956-68, Smithsonian Instn., 1958-69. Chmn. 2d, 3d, and 22d Alaskan Science Conf. Mem. corp. Marine Biol. Lab. Served as lt., 165th Inf., U.S. Army, with A.E.F. and Army of Occupation, 1917-19; commd. maj., then lt. col., USAAF, 1943; chief physiol. test sect. Army Air Force Proving Ground Command, Eglin Field, Fla., 1943-45; chief physiol. br. Aero Med. Lab., Wright Field, 1945-46; sci. dir. Arctic Research Lab., Pt. Barrow, Alaska, 1948. Fellow Arctic Inst. N. Am. (gov. 1964-70, Fellows award 1974), AAAS (pres. Alaska div.), Can. (hon.) physiol. socs., Am. Soc. Zoologists, Am. Soc. Naturalists, Phila. Physiol. Soc. (v.p. 1940-42, pres. 1942); mem. Norwegian Acad. Sci. and Letters, Phi Beta Kappa, Sigma Xi, Delta Kappa Epsilon. Chmn. panel Expeditionary Physiology, Joint Research and Devel. Bd., 1947; leader expdn. for physiol. research Office of Naval Research and Swarthmore Coll., Point Barrow, Alaska, 1947-49. Unitarian. Author articles. Clubs: Explorers (N.Y.C.); Cosmos, (Washington). Research physiology. Home: College, Alaska. Died Nov. 20, 1979.

IRVING, ROBERT SHIPPEN, mortgage banker; b. Phila., June 15, 1909; s. Robert Archibald and Bertha (Shippen); grad. Phillips Exeter Acad., 1926; A.B., Williams Coll., 1930; m. Ruth Winchester, May 27, 1933; children—Robert Winchester, Kathleen Winslow (Mrs. Paul B. Repetto), Nancy Shippen. Underwriting supr. FHA, Washington, 1934-40; exec. v.p. W.A. Clarke Mortgage Co., Phila., 1940-61; sr. v.p. 1st Pa. Banking & Trust Co., Phila., 1961-68, sr. v.p., 1968-70; on loan as sr. v.p. finance, treas. Nat. Corp. for Housing Partnerships, Washington, 1970-73; trustee Realty Growth Investors, Balt. Mem. Am. Bankers Assn. (mem. mortgage finance com. 1969-70, mem. housing task force 1970), Phila. Mortgage Bankers Assn. (pres. 1961-62), Beta Theta Pi. Episcopalian. Clubs: Exchange (1st pres.), Corinthian Yacht (Phila.); Merion Golf (Ardmore, Pa.); University (Washington); Poplar Islands Yacht, Talbot Country (Easton, Md.). Home: Bozman, Md. Died Nov. 13, 1980.

IRWIN, FORREST ATLEE, educator; b. Eldorado, Ohio, July 13, 1888; s. Robert L. and Emma Annetta (Foust) I.; student DePauw Univ., 1909-11; B.S., Northwestern, 1915; A.M., Columbia, 1926, part time grad. work, 1926-31; LL.D. (honorary) Fairleigh Dickinson U., 1956; m. Loa Leone Tolbert, July 21, 1915; children—Forrest A., Ilda (Mrs. Gerhard V. Kellner), Helen (Mrs. Carl N. Shuster, Jr.). Teacher rural schs., Huntington County, Ind., 1906-09; prin. Decker (Ind.) High Sch., 1911-12, supt, schs., 1912-13; prin. George Rogers Clark Jr. High Sch., Vincennes, Ind., 1915-18; prin. Lab. Jr. High Sch. and dir. training of Jr. high sch. teachers, Bloomsburg (Pa.) State Teachers Coll., 1921-24; prin. Nishuane Elementary and Jr. High Sch., Montclair, N.J., 1924-31; vice pres. and head dept. of edn., New Jersey State Teachers Coll., Trenton, N.J., 1931-46; pres. N.J. State Teachers Coll., 1946-54, pres. emeritus; prof., dean Sch. Edn., Fairleigh Dickinson U., from 1954; vis. prof. Western Wash. Teachers Coll., summers 1924 and 26, Rutgers Univ., 1927-32. Mem. Eastern State Association of Preparatory Schools for Teachers (past president), N.J. Council on Edn., N.E.A., New Jersey Edn. Association, Kappa Delta Pi, Phi Delta Kappa, Presbyterian. Club: New Jersey Schoolmasters' (past president). Author: (with Alice C. Smithick) The Demonstration School of Trenton Teachers College (studies in edn. Number 4), 1939; (with Gladys E. Poole) Student Leadership in Community Clubs (studies in edn. Number 5), 1941. Contbr. to Proc. Eastern States Assn. of Profl. Schs. for Tchrs., other ednl. jours. Home: Westfield, N.J. Died Jan. 8, 1977.

ISAAC, CHARLES MARTIN, realtor; b. Phila., Jan. 11, 1896; s. M.J. and Violet (Francis) Behr; legally adopted son of William J. and Mary (Griffiths) I.; A.B., George Washington U., m. Gula Louise Welsh, Mar. 1, 1920; 1 dau., Marijean. Engaged in retail bus., 1922-34; pres., exec. mgr. Canton (Ohio) Retail Mchts. Bd., 1934-42; exec. asst. to pres. Am. Retail Fedn., Washington, 1942-44; mgr. domestic distbn. dept. C. of C. U.S., 1944-51; exec. v.p. Retail Jewelers of Am., N.Y.C., 1951-60; pres. Behr Enterprises, Inc. 1960-69; asso. Joseph T. Roy Realty, Inc., Ft. Lauderdale, Fla., 1969-70, Louis M. Jenkins, from 1970; lectr. distbn. Northwestern U., 1943, Yale, 1946, U. Pa., 1946, N.Y.U., 1958. Mem. Nat Distbn. Council, 1944-52. Chmn. advancement com. McKinley chpt. Boy Scouts Am., (canton). Bd. dirs. C. of C., ARC, Travelers Aid Soc., Community Fund. Served as mem. staff insp. gen. SOS, U.S. Army, World War I; AEF. Decorated Purple Heart; recipient certificate of Merit; John N. van der Vries award Northwestern U.; award Am. Trade Assn. Execs. Mem. Artus, Sigma Chi, Alpha Kappa Psi. Republican. Presbyn. (ruling elder). Rotarian, Mason (32 deg.). Clubs: University (Washington and N.Y.C.). Contbr. trade jours. Home: Fort Lauderdale, Fla. Deceased.

ISAACS, JOHN DOVE, III, oceanographer; b. Spokane, Wash., Mar. 28, 1913; s. John Dove and Constance Ashley (DeSpain) I.; student Oreg. State U., 1930-41; B.S., U. Calif., Berkeley, 1944; postgrad. Scripps Inst. Oceanography, U. Calif., San Diego, 1950; m. Mary Carol Zander, Nov. 11, 1938; children—Ann Katherine, Jon Berkeley, Caroline Marie, Kenneth Zander. Project engr. Seaplane Base Constrn., Austin Co., Astoria, Oreg., 1941-43; field and project engr. waves investigation U. Calif., Berkeley, 1944-48; asso. oceanographer Scripps Inst. Oceanography, La Jolla, Calif., 1948-55, asst. to dir., asso. oceanographer, 1951-55, asst. to dir., asso. prof. oceanography, 1955-58, dir. marine life research, prof., 1961-80, dir. Inst. Marine Resources, 1971-80, program dir. N. Pacific Study, 1968-73; cons. to White House, 1962-67. Fellow World Acad. Arts and Scis., Am. Acad. Arts and Scis., AAAS (pres. Western div. 1972-73), Am. Geophys. Union; mem. Nat. Acad. Engring., Nat. Acad. Sci., Sigma Xi, Pi Mu Epsilon, Chi Epsilon. Contbr. articles in field to profl. jours. Home: Rancho Santa Fe, Calif. Died June 6, 1980; interred Pendleton, Oreg.

ISAACS, RUFUS PHILIP, mathematician, educator; b. N.Y.C., June 11, 1914; s. Philip Simon and Alice (Cohn) I.; B.S. in Gen. Engring., Mass. Inst. Tech., 1936; M.A. in Math., Columbia U., 1940, Ph.D., 1942; m. Rose Bicov, Jan. 25, 1942; children—Ellen Sara, Frances Carol. Engr., Carrier Corp., 1936-38; sr. analytical engr. Hamilton Standard Propellers Co., 1941-45; asst. prof. U. Notre Dame, 1945-47; research engr. N. Am. Aviation Co., 1947; mathematician Rand Corp., 1947-55; sr. scientist Lockheed Aircraft Co., 1955-56; research mathematician Hughes Aircraft Co., 1955-58; mathematician Inst. Def. Analyses, 1958-62, Center Naval Analyses, 1962-67; prof. applied math. Johns Hopkins, 1967-77, prof. emeritus, 1978-81; professorial lectr. George Washington U., from 1961. Mem. Am. Math. Soc., Am. Math. Assn., Ops. Research Soc. Am. (Lanchester prize 1965), Soc. Indsl. and Applied Math. (lectr. 1961-63), Sigma Xi. Club: Johns Hopkins. Author: Differential Games, 1965; also articles on monodiffric functions, aerodynamics, elasticity, fractional order iteration; game, graph and number theories. Originator differential games. Home: Baltimore, Md. Died Jan. 18, 1981.

ISAACS, WALTER F., art teacher; b. Gillespie, Ill., July 15, 1886; s. Abram and Nancy Emily (Fruit) I.; B.S., James Millikin U., Decatur, Ill., 1909; student Art Students League, 1910, Art Inst. Chicago, 1913-14, Columbia U. Teachers Coll., 1919; pupil of Charles Guerin and Othon Friesz, Paris, 1920-23; m. Mildred Julian, July 25, 1927. Head of dept. of art, Colo. State Teachers Coll., 1914-19; head of Sch. of Art, U. of Wash., Seattle, since 1923. Exhibited in Paris Salon, 1922, 23. Served in arty. officers training camp, Louisville, Ky., 1918. Mem. Am. Assn. of Univ. Profs., Am. Soc. for Aesthetics, Sigma Alpha Epsilon. Home: Bellevue, Wash.*

ISE, JOHN, prof. economics; b. Downs, Kan., June 5, 1885; s. Henry C. and Rosa C. (Haag) I.; Mus. B., U. of Kan., 1908, A.B., 1910, LL.B., 1911; A.M., Harvard, 1912, Ph.D., 1914; m. Lillie Bernhard, of Lawrence, Kan., 1921; children—John, Charles Henry. Asst. prof. economics, Ia. State Coll., 1914-15, asso. prof., 1915-16; with U. of Kan. since 1916, prof. economics since 1920. Mem. Am. Economic Assn., Am. Geog. Soc., Am. Forestry Assn., Phi Beta Kappa, Phi Delta Phi, Phi Mu Alpha, Delta Sigma Pi. Unitarian. Author: United States Forest Policy; United States Oil Policy. Asso. editor Am. Economic Review. Home: Lawrence, Kan.*

ISELIN, PHILIP H., football and racing club exec.; L.H.D., Monmouth Coll., 1969. Pres., chief exec. officer N.Y. Jets football team; pres., chmn. bd. Monmouth Park Jackey Club. Home: Oceanport NJ Home: New York, N.Y. Died Dec. 1976.

ISERMAN, MAURICE, corp. exec., lawyer; b. N.Y.C., May 25, 1900; s. Samuel and Dorothy (Cahn) I.; B.S., CCNY, 1920; LL.B., Columbia, 1923; m. Helyn Barley, July 11, 1931; children—Jane, Robert. Fellow Sch. Edn., CCNY, 1920-23, instr. govt., summer 1922; admitted to N.Y. bar, 1924, since practiced in N.Y.C.; formerly lectr. Practicing Law Inst., N.Y.C.; with Webb & Knapp, Inc., N.Y.C., 1938-65, dir., gen. counsel, 1949-65, v.p., 1951-65, trustee Employees Profit Sharing Plan, 1949-75; gen. counsel, dir. Roosevelt Field, Inc.; dir. Gulf States Land & Industries, Inc.; dir., sec., gen. counsel Am. Encaustic Tiling Co., Inc., Lansdale, Pa., 1936-58; dir., counsel, v.p. Horizon Corp., Tucson, 1967-75. Trustee Irving Geist Found.; mem. adv. council, com. on bequests, legacies and deferred gifts to Mt. Sinai Med. Center. Mem. Am., N.Y. State bar assns., Assn. Bar City N.Y., County Lawyers Assn., Phi Beta Kappa. Club: Columbia (N.Y.C.). Bd. editors: Columbia Law Rev., 1922-23. Home: New Rochelle, N.Y. Died Dec. 30, 1975; interred Ferncliff, Hartsdale, N.Y.

ISGRIG, FREDERICK ARTHUR (IZ'GRIG), lawyer; b. Dixie, Ark., Oct. 5, 1884; s. William Alonzo and Nancy Jane (Noah) I.; student Hendrix Coll., Conway, Ark.; LL.B., U. of Ark., 1910; m. Mittie Jane Jones, Nov. 10, 1908; 1 dau., Nancy Jane. Began as salesman, 1906; sec. to mayor of Little Rock, Ark., 1909; admitted to Ark. bar, 1910; judge Municipal Court, Little Rock, 1913-15; now practicing alone; alderman Little Rock, 1917-23; U.S. atty. Eastern Dist. of Ark., 1934-39. V.p. and mem. bd. Pulaski Nat. Farm Loan Assn. Mem. Ark. State and Little Rock bar assns. Democrat. Methodist. Home: Little Rock, Ark. *

ISRAELS, SYDNEY, physician; b. Regina, Sask., Can., Dec. 31, 1915; s. Simon and Sarah (Girtle) I.; B.Sc., U. Sask., 1936; M.D., U. Man., 1939; m. Rita Aronoff, Sept. 21, 1941; children—Carla (Mrs. Ben Levinson), Sherri Anne. Resident pediatrics U. Man., 1939-40; fellow Harvard, 1944-45; asso. prof. U. Man., 1945-64; prof., head dept. pediatrics U. B.C., 1964-77; chief pediatrics staff Children's Hosp., Vancouver; pediatrician-in-chief Vancouver Gen. Hosp., 1964-77. Served with RCAF, 1941-45. Fellow Royal Coll. Physicians, A.C.P., Am. Acad. Pediatrics. Home: Vancouver, B.C., Canada. Died July 17, 1978.

ITURBI, JOSÉ, pianist, orch. condr., composer; b. Valencia, Spain, Nov. 28, 1895; s. Ricardo and Teresa (Baguena) I.; educated at Escuela de Musica de Maria Jordan, Valencia, 1900-05, Conservatorio de Musica, Valencia (with Jose Bellver), 1903-05; grad. Conservatoire de Musique, Paris, France, 1913; m. Maria Giner, June 8, 1916 (dec.); 1 dau., Maria (dec.). Gave piano concerts in all prin. cities of Europe, N. and S. America, Asia, Russia, Africa and East Indies, U.S. debut Oct. 1929; conducted N.Y. Philharmonic-Symphony and symphony orchs. of Phila., Los Angeles, San Francisco, Detroit, Chgo., Detroit, St. Louis, Cin., Concertgebouw (Holland), London, Madrid, Buenos Aires, Mexico City, Paris, La Scala, Milan, Israel, etc.; also BBC Orch.; condr. Ford Sunday Evening Hour Orch. on radio; musical dir. Rochester (N.Y.) Philharmonic Orch., 1935-44; musical and artistic dir. Valencia (Spain) Symphony Orchs., from 1956; mus. dir., condr. Bridgeport Symphony Orch., 1967-72. Composer Fantasy for piano and orch., Soliloquy and Seguidilla both for orch., Spanish Dance, Cradle Song, for piano. Decorated commandeur Legion d'Honneur (France); grand cross Isabel La Catolica (Spain); Alphonso el Sabio, Spain, St. Georges (Greece); recipient Gold Medal of Labor (Spain), 1968; Quevedo prize (Spanish Nobel prize) for the arts, 1972. Maj. and Nat. Music Dir., Civil Air Patrol. Mem. Read Academia de Bellas Artes de San Fernando (Madrid), Real Academia de Bellas Artes de San Carlos (Valencia, Spain). Home: Beverly Hills, Calif. Died June 28, 1980; interred Holy Cross Cemetery Mausoleum.

IVANISSEVICH, OSCAR, diplomat; b. Buenos Aires, Argentina, Aug. 5, 1893; s. Antonio and Elena (Defilipi) I.; M.D., Univ. of Buenos Aires, 1918; Doctor Honoris Causa Univ. of Sao Paulo, 1945; m. Maria Esther Lopez Cabanillas, Sept. 8, 1921; children—Mary (Mrs. Luis Camino Dibos), Elena, Guillermo Oscar, Jr. Practitioner Nat. Hosp., Buenos Aires, 1913-16, sr. practitioner, 1917-18; chief surgeon Inst.. of Surg. Clinic, Nat. Hosp. Sch. of Medicine, 1918-30, asst. prof. surgery, 1932-42; head prof., 1942-45; nat. interventor Univ. of Buenos Aires, 1946; ambassador of Argentina to U.S. from 1946; later, minister of edn. Argentine Govt., resigned; 1975. Hon. prof., Univ. of San Simon, 1946. Hon. mem. Faculty of Medicine, Mexico City, Peruvian Acad. of Surgery, Lima, Colegio Brasileiro de Cirurgioes, Brazil, Faculty of Medicine, Costa Rica; School of Medicine, Univ. of San Marcos, La Paz, Bolivia. Roman Catholic. Author: 100 Experiences of Drainage in Abdominal Surgery; Hydatid Disease of the Bones; History of the First Chair of Surgical Clinic. Contbr. more than 200 scientific articles to med. jours. Home: Buenos Aires, Argentina. Died June 6, 1976.

IVERSON, MARVIN ALVIN, psychologist; b. Waseca, Minn., Feb. 26, 1924; s. Ole T. and Frieda (Ristau) I.; B.S. with high distinction, U. Minn., 1944, A.M., 1947; M.A., U. Pa., 1950, Ph.D., 1953; m. Mary E. Reuder, July 11, 1953; children—Carol, Kent. Research psychologist Am. Insts. for Research, Washington, 1952-54; asst. prof. psychology Adelphi U., Garden City, N.Y., 1954-59, asso. prof. 1959-65, prof., 1965-79, chmn. dept. 1966-72, dean Grad. Sch. Arts and Scis., 1972-79; mem. N.Y. State Psychology Adv. Council, 1968-71; mem. doctoral council N.Y. State Edn. Dept., 1974-79. Fellow Am. Psychol. Assn. (conv. bd. 1969-70), AAAS (council reps. 1964-72), N.Y. Acad. Scis. (chmn. sect. psychology, 1968-70), Sigma Xi; mem. Eastern Psychol. Assn. (exec. sec. 1961-67, historian 1968-79), N.Y. State Psychol. Assn. (pres. div. social psychology 1968, 73, council of reps. 1967-69, 72-74, recipient Kurt Lewin award in social psychology 1979), AAUP, Am. Statis. Assn., Biometric Soc., Psychonomic Soc. Author: (monograph with M.E. Reuder) Ego Involvement as an Experimental Variable, 1956; contbr. articles to profl. jours. Home: East Williston, N.Y. Died Dec. 11, 1979; interred St. Ann's Cemetery, Shohola, Pa.

IVEY, ZIDA CASWELL, museum dir., historian, artist; b. Fort Atkinson Wis., July 8, 1884; d. Lucien Beal and Eliza Moak (Pearce) Caswell; student U. of Wis., 1902-03; grad. Minn. Sch. of Business, 1922; pvt. art lessons, Fort Atkinson and Madison, Wis., 1934-37, 1939-40; student Federal Art Schs., Minneapolis, 1938-39; m. Dr. William R. Ivey, May 8, 1912; 1 son, William Lucien; m. 2d, J. E. Brough, Jan. 6, 1930. Began as bank clerk, 1905; now writing feature articles and poems, painting, and engaged in historical research; director of the Dwight Foster Historical Museum, Fort Atkinson, Wis., since 1933. Manager hdqrs. office for local and county war work, served on health and recreation coms., and recruiting officer for nurse reserve, Jefferson Co., World War I; jury commr., Jefferson Co., since 1936. Mem. advisory council Camp Fire Girls, Pythian Sisters and Am. Red Cross. Organizer and sec. Fort Atkinson Hist. Soc.; mem. Lake Mills Hist. Soc., Wis. Soc. of Ornithology, mem. State Archeol. Soc. (mem. adv. com. and pub. collections com.), State Hist. Soc., Watertown Hist. Soc., Ft. Atkinson Tuesday Club, Wis. Allied Arts Club, Ft. Atkinson Sketch Club, World Fellowship Council, Gleaners Auxiliary, D.A.R., City, Jefferson County and State Fedn. of Women's Clubs. Republican. Conglist. Author articles and occasional verse in local papers, Am. Poetry Mag., etc.; poems and anthologies. Contbr. to mags. Dir. Badger State Folk Lore Soc. Home: Ft. Atkinson, Wis. *

IVISON, MAYNARD C., broker; b. Cleve., Sept. 21, 1895; s. William Crane and Celia Mae (Cady) I.; A.B., Yale, 1918; m. Alice R. Thayer, Dec. 4, 1919; children—Audrey (Mrs. Audrey Pattinson), Maynard Thayer. With Anglo-Am. Comml. Corp., 1919-20, Fgn. Commerce Corp. Am., 1920-21, G.M.P. Murphy & Co., 1921-23; with Mechanics & Metals Nat. Bank, 1923-26, mgr. bond dept., 1925-26; with Chisholm & Chapman (mem. N.Y. Stock Exchange), 1926-27, Chase Nat. Bank, 1927-29; partner Abbott, Hoppin & Co. (mem. N.Y. Stock Exchange), 1929-34, Abbott, Proctor & Paine 1934-70; subordinated lender Paine Webber Jackson & Curtis, Inc., N.Y.C., 1970-79. Mem. bd. govs. N.Y. Stock Exchange, 1954-57. Served as 1st lt. 303d F.A., U.S. Army, 1917-19, Mem. Assn. Stock Exchange Firms (bd. govs. 1947-53, v.p. 1950-52). Clubs: Union (N.Y.C.); Rockaway Hunting (Cedarburst, L.I., bd. govs. 1950-53); Lawrence Beach (Atlantic Beach, L.I., bd. govs. 1927-56, pres. 1930-33). Home: New York, N.Y. Died Apr. 3, 1979.

IVY, ANDREW CONWAY, physiologist; b. Farmington, Mo., Feb. 25, 1893; s. Henry McPherson and Cynthia (Smith) I.; A.B., B.Pd., State Normal Sch., Cape Girardeau. Mo., 1913; B.S., U. Chgo., 1916, M.S., 1917, Ph.D., 1918; M.D., Rush Med. Coll., 1922; D.Sc. (hon.) U. Neb., 1947, Grinell (Iowa) Coll., 1947, Boston U., 1948; LL. D. (hon.). Loyola U., 1950; D.Sc., Hastings (Nebr.) Coll., 1951, Cole Coll., Iowa; a 1957; m. Emma Kohman, Dec. 24, 1919; children—John Henry, William Harvey, Andrew Conway, Horace Kohman, Robert Emerson. Instr. in physiology, U. Chgo., 1917, asso. prof., 1922-25; asso. prof. physiology Loyola, 1919-22; intern Mercy and Augustana hosps., Chgo., 1920-22; head div. physiology and pharmacology, Northwestern U. Med. Sch., 1925-46; v.p. charge Chgo. Profl. Colls., U. Ill., 1946-53; distinguished prof. physiol., head dept. clin. sci., 1946-61, distinguished prof. emeritus, 1961-78; prof. emeritus biochemistry, dir. lab. med. research Roosevelt U., Chgo., 1962-78; sci. dir. Naval Med. Research Inst., 1942-43; cons. Q.M. AUS, 1943-44; mem. Nat Adv. Cancer Council, 1944-51, exec. dir., 1947-51. Dep. dir. Chgo. Med. Civil Defense from 1950. Mem. Com. Aviation Med. N.R. Council, 1941; co-founder Space Med. Soc., 1945; cons. Sec. War on War Crimes, 1946-47; mem. Internat. and Nat. Commn. Prevent Alcoholism; pres. Partal House, Rehab. Alcoholics, 1951. Dir. Ivy Cancer Research Found. Served as 2d lt., M.N.G., 1912-13; student officer, M.O.T.C., AUS, 1917-18: Mem. bd. mgrs. YMCA from 1955. Recipient Pope Leo XIII award, Hoover award. Fellow A.C.P., Gorgas Med. Soc. (hon.); mem. A.M.A. (chmn. sect. physiology and pathology 1931), Ill. Chgo. med. socs., Soc. Internal Medicine (pres. 1941-42), Am. Assn. U. Profs. (council 1929-31), Am. Gastro-Enterol. Assn. (pres. 1940-41; D.S.M.; mem. editorial bd.), Harvey Soc. (hon.), Am. Physiol. Soc. (sec. 1935-39; pres. 1939-41; editorial bd.), Soc. Exptl. Biology (editorial bd.), Des Moines Acad. Med. (hon.), Chgo. Inst. Med. (pres. 1943), Am. Inst. Nutrition, Ill. Acad. Sci., Assn. Study Internal Secretions, Comm. Chronic Illness (exec. com.), Alpha Omega Alpha, Phi Beta Kappa (hon.), Sigma Xi, Alpha Kappa Kappa, A.A.A.S. Methodist. Mason. Clubs: Commercial, Executive (Chgo.). Author: Nuremburg Code; Peptic Ulcer; Observations on Krebiozen in Management of Cancer Patients, 1956, 1550 sci. articles. Co-founder, mng. editor Gastroenterology 1942-52. Home: Oak Park, Ill. Died Feb. 7, 1978.

IVY, HORACE MACAULAY, educator; b. Sedalia, Mo., Jan. 19, 1884; s. Henry McPherson and Cynthia (Smith) I.; student State Normal, Cape Girardeau, Mo., 1896-1900; A.B., Central Coll., Fayette, Mo., 1903, A.M., 1904; student Univ. of Mo., 1904-05, Univ. of Chicago, 1906; Ph.D., George Peabody Coll. for Teachers, 1922; m. Beryl Smith, June 5, 1907; children—Horace M., Henry Berry, Beryl (Mrs. Franklin Mayo). Athletic coach, high sch. teacher, Yazoo City, Miss., 1905-08; prin. Flora, Miss., 1908-10, Yazoo City, Miss., 1910-12, supt. schs., Canton, Miss., 1912-18; supt. Yazoo City, Miss., 1918-19; state supervisor secondary schs., Jackson, Miss., 1920-23; supt. schs., Meridian, Miss., 1923-53; ednl. cons., 1953—; dir. Asso. Cons. Edn. vis. instr. education, summer sessions: State Teachers Coll., Cape Girardeau, Mo., 1919; George Peabody Coll. for Teachers, 1928; Univ. of Va., 1926-35; Univ. of Ga. 1937-38. Trustee Millsaps Coll., 1932-44, George Peabody Coll. for Teachers since 1939; mem. state bd. of trustees Inst. of Higher Learning in Miss., 1944-56, pres. 1953-56; elector Hall of Fame, New York U., 1954—. Director YMCA, C. of C., Boy Scouts of Am. Co-chmn. Community Chest Campaign. Recipient citation from U. Miss. with 1st Fed. Found. award for service to State of Miss., 1964. Life mem. N.E.A. (core. com. legislative commn., chmn. 1940-48, exec. com., 1948-50). Mem. Nat. Soc. Study of Edn., Am. Assn. Sch. Adminstrs. (mem. 1940 Yearbook commn.), Southern Assn. Colleges and Secondary Schs. (mem. secondary commn., higher edn. commn., pres. 1928, chmn. com. on approval Negro schs. and colls., 1928-50), Miss. Edn. Assn. (pres. 1926, mem. legislative and exec. coms.), Phi Delta Kappa. Democrat. Methodist. Mason, K.P. Club: Rotary (past pres.). Author: Relation of Certain Factors to the Pay of Teachers, 1922; Workbook Old World Background, 1927; (with Lanie Holland) Geography Workbooks, 1931. Contbr. to ednl. jours. Address: Meridian, Miss. *

IVY, ROBERT HENRY, physician; b. Southport, Eng., May 21, 1881; s. Robert Sutcliffe and Annie Edith (Cryer) I.; D.D.S., University of Pennsylvania, 1902; M.D., 1907; D.Sc. (honorary), 1954; married Norma C. Crossland, June 19, 1912; children—Cynthia Thompson, Robert Henry, Eleanor Anne, Peter Cryer. Practiced in Phila., 1907-15, Milwaukee, Wis., 1915-17. Capt., Med. R.C., 1917, and on duty Office of Surgeon Gen., U.S. Army, Washington, until Aug. 1918; maj. Feb. 1918, lt. col., Aug. 1919; A.E.F., France, Sept. 1918-Feb. 1919; on duty Surgeon Gen.'s Office and Walter Reed Gen. Hosp., Feb.-Oct. 1919; col. M.R.C. Member committee on surgery and chairman subcommittee on plastic and maxillo-facial surgery of National Research Council, 1940-46. Civilian consultant plastic surgery, office Surgeon Gen., U.S. Army. Mem. bd. hon. consultants, Army Med. Library, Washington, D.C. Prof. maxillo-facial surgery, U. of Pa., from 1919, prof. plastic surgery, 1944-51, emeritus from 1951; chief cleft palate section Pa. State Health Department; formerly trustee of University. Received certificate of appreciation, War Dept., 1946, U. Pa. Alumni Award of Merit, 1946. Fellow Am. Coll. Surgeons; mem. Am. Soc. Plastic and Reconstructive Surgery, Am., Pennsylvania State and Philadelphia County medical socs., Am. Surg. Assn., Coll. Physicians of Phila., Phila. Pathol. Soc., Phila. Acad. Surgery, Am. and Pa. State dental socs., Academy Stomatology of Philadelphia, American Association Plastic Surgeons, Loyal Legion. Republican. Clubs: University, Philadelphia Country (Philadelphia); Army and Navy (Washington). Author: Applied Anatomy and Oral Surgery, 1911; Applied Immunology (with B.A. Thomas), 1916; Essentials of Oral Surgery (with V. P. Blair), 1923; Fractures of the Jaws (with L. Curtis), 1931. Editor in-chief Plastic and Reconstructive Surgery. Home: Lansdowne, Pa. Died June 23, 1974.

JACKSON, ANDREW, govt. ofcl.; b. Littleton, N.H., Jan. 8, 1882; s. James Robert and Lydia Ann (Drew) J.; A.B., Dartmouth Coll., 1903; LL.B., Boston U., 1912; student Univ. of Caen, 1919; unmarried. Admitted to Mass. bar, 1912, N.H. bar, 1913; practiced law in Boston and Rochester and Lisbon, N.H., 1912-33; atty. Federal Trade Commn., 1933-34, Securities and Exchange Commn., 1934-42, asso. dir. Division of Corporation Finance, Washington, since 1942. Served as enlisted man with 103d Inf., U.S. Army, France, 1917-19. Home: Littleton, N.H. *

JACKSON, ARCHER L., business exec.; b. Winchester, Ind., July 23, 1886; s. Benjamin S. and Celina Florence (Harris) J.; B.S. in C.E., Purdue Univ., 1908; m. Verna Marqus, Nov. 10, 1924; 1 son, Archer L. Div. engr., C.B.&Q. R.R., 1908-11; engr. Marshall and Fox, Chicago, 1911-16; partner Robert S. De Golyer, architect and engr., 1919-22; with Collins, Murphy and Jackson, builders, 1922-28; pres. A. L. Jackson Co., contractors engrs., since 1928; dir. Chicago Fed. Savings and Loan Assn. since 1936. Served with U.S. Army as capt. engr. corps, 1917-19. Mem. Western Soc. of Engrs., Asso. Gen. Contractors, Builder Assn., Boy Scout Council (Evanston), Phi Kappa Sigma (mem. nat. bd. since 1923, pres., 1933-39). Clubs: Builders, Illinois Athletic, Sunset Ridge Country. Home: Evanston, Ill. *

JACKSON, C(ICERO) FLOYD, univ. prof., ret.; b. White Co., Ind., Sept. 30, 1882; s. Wm. Franklin and Yensi Evangeline (Thomas) J.; A.B., DePauw U., Greencastle, Ind., 1905; M.A., Ohio State U., 1907; m. Alma Irene Drayer, June 20, 1905 (deceased); 1 son, Herbert William m. 2d, Erma L. Andrews, 1946. Asst. in biology, DePauw University, 1903-05; fellow in zoölogy, Ohio State Univ., 1905-07; instr. in zoölogy, Ohio State Univ., 1907-08; with Univ. of N.H. since 1908, prof., 1910-52, prof. emeritus since 1952, dean coll. of liberal arts, 1930-39, dir. Isles of Shoals Marine Lab., 1928-41, dir. Biol. Inst. 1939-48; tech. adv. to Atlantic States Marine Fisheries Commn., since 1946; Marine biologist and tech. adviser N.H. Fish and Game Dept., 1951. Fellow A.A.A.S.; member N.E. Association of Colleges and Schools, Am. Entomol. Society, Ecol. Soc. America, Am. Genetic Assn., Am. Soc. Mammalogists, N.H. Acad. Science, Boston Soc. Natural History, Phi Kappa Phi, Sigma Xi, Phi Sigma,

Kappa Alpha. Republican. Congregationalist. Club: Appalachian Mountain. Writer of many articles, reviews, etc. Home: Durham, N.H. *

JACKSON CLARENCE A., ins. exec.,; b. Columbus, O., June 29, 1891; s. Charles and Isa (Frampton) J.; student Wabash Coll., 1915, LL.D., 1965; m. Edith Gronendyke, Oct. 28, 1916; children—Ann, Robert Gronendyke. Sales mgr. Hoosier Mfg Co., 1928-32; partner Smith-Jackson Co., wholesalers, 1918-33; organizer, dir. Ind. State Gross Income Tax Div., 1933-39, Ind State Employment Security Div., 1936-39; spl. asst. adminstr. Fed. Security Agy., 1939-40; exec. v.p. Ind. C. of C., 1939-52; pres. Am. United Life Ins. Co., Indpls., 1952-62, chmn. bd. from 1957. Vice chmn. Ind. Com. Econ. Devel., 1943-48; chmn Ind. Bd Tax Commrs. 1968-69; vice chmn. Ind War History Commn. Chmn. devel. bd. Wabash Coll., 1960-64. Mem. Nat. Fedn. Tax Adminstrs. (founder), Am. Legion (state comdr. 1926, pres. res. finance com. Ind.). Council State C. of C. (past pres.). Sigma Chi, Beta Gamma Sigma. Methodist. Mason, Elk. Clubs: Athletic, Columbia, Pres (Indpls.). Home: Indianapolis. Ind. Died Nov. 22, 1976.

JACKSON, EDITH BANFIELD, physician; b. Colorado Springs, Colo., Jan. 2, 1895; d. William and Helen Fiske (Banfield) Jackson; A.B., Vassar, 1916; M.D., Johns Hopkins, 1921; grad. student Inst. Psychoanalysis, Vienna, 1930-36. Interne U. Ia Hosp., 1921-22; intern pediatrics Bellevue Hosp., N.Y.C., 1922-23; asst. physician U.S. Childrens Bur., New Haven, 1923-28; asst. physician St. Elizabeth Hosp., Washington, 1928-29, asst. in pediatrics Yale Sch. Medicine, 1924-25, instr., 1925-27, clin. instr., 1927-29, clin. instr. psychiatry and mental hygiene, 1936-39, asst. clin. prof., 1939-41, asst. clin. prof. pediatrics (psychiatry), 1941-45, asso. clin. prof., 1945-49, clin. prof. pediatrics and psychiatry, 1949-59, emeritus 1959; vis. prof. pediatrics and psychiatry U. Colo., from 1960; attending pediatrician (psychiatric cons.) Grace-New Haven Community Hosp. (unit service). 1936-59, dir. rooming-in project, 1946-53; dir. Sigmund Freud Archives, Inc. Fellow Am. Psychiat. Assn. (Agnes McGavin award preventive psychiatry 1964). Am. Acad. Child Psychiatry; mem. Denver Psychoanalytic Soc., Am. Acad. Pediatrics (hon. asso.; C. Anderson Aldrioh award child devel. 1968). Am. Com. Maternal Welfare, Am. Orthopsychiat Assn., World Fedn. Mental Health (asso.), Am. Psychoanalytic Assn., Am. Psychosomatic Soc., Am. Pediatric Soc. Editor (with Genevieve Trainham); Family Centered Maternity and Infant Care, supplement to Problems of Infancy and Childhood Trans., 4th Conf., 1950, of Josiah Macy, Jr., Found. Contbr. articles to profl. jours. Home: Denver, Colo. Died June 5, 1977.

JACKSON, FRED, author; b. Pittsburgh, Sept. 21, 1886; s. Henry and Elizabeth (Levy) J.; ed. Washington and Jefferson Acad., Pa., and Columbia U.; unmarried. Contbr. to mags. since 1904; dramatized Robert W. Chambers "The Firing Line," 1910. Author: The Hidden Princess, 1910. Address: New York, N.Y. *

JACKSON, HEZEKIAH, coll. dean; b. Greensburg, La., Feb. 8, 1917; s. Harvey and Dicy (Lewis) J.; B.S., So. U., 1941; M.S., Mich. State U., 1947, Ph.D., 1952; m. Adele Martin, May 26, 1949; children—Reginald Jerome, Raymond Eugene, Ronald Keith. Prof. horticulture, head dept. So. U., Baton Rouge, 1947-56, dir. div. agr., 1956-58, dir. internat. program, dean Coll. Agr., 1958-79, also coordinator Coop. State Research Service programs; mem. nat. adv. com. Hort. Crops Research; mem. La. State adv. com. Agrl. Stblzn. Conservation Service. Mem. La. Small Bus. Adv. Council; vice chmn. African-Am. Scholars Council; mem. com. policy, program and role State Univs. and Land Grand Colls.; active local YMCA, United Givers Fund, Blundon Orphange. Served to capt., inf. AUS, 1941-45. Mem. Am. Soc. Hort. Sci., Am. Soc. Plant Physiologists, Bot. Soc. Am., Phi Beta Sigma. Republican. Methodist (chmn. fin. commn.). Club: Masons (32 deg.). Home: Baton Rouge, La. Died Aug. 16, 1979; interred So. Meml. Gardens, Baton Rouge.

JACKSON, RICHARD, lawyer; b. Medford, Mass., Dec. 28, 1910; s. Henry Clinton, Jr. and Clara Wild (Goodwin) J.; grad. Phillips Andover Acad., 1929; A.B., Dartmouth, 1933; LL.B., Columbia, 1938; m. Helen Pfeiffer, Sept. 16, 1939; children—Deborah, Faith. Instr. Latin, Phillips Acad., Andover, Mass., 1933-35; admitted to N.Y. bar, 1938, Mass. bar, 1946, R.I. bar, 1963; asso. law firm Simpson, Thacher & Bartlett, N.Y.C., 1938-43; law staff B & M. R.R., Boston, 1946-57, gen. counsel, 1954-57; asst. sec. personnel and res. forces Navy Dept., 1957-61; v.p., gen. counsel Fram Corp., East Providence, 1961-66; v.p. law Eric-Lackawanna R.R., Cleve., 1966—76. Served as lt. comdr. USNR. 1943-46. Mem. Am. Bar Assn., U.S. (nat. def. com.). Greater Providence (chmn. nat. legislation com.) chambers commerce. Home: Cleveland, Ohio. Died Oct. 19, 1976.

JACKSON, RICHARD SEYMOUR, editor; b. New Haven, Aug. 30, 1910; s. John Day and Rose Marie (Herrick) J.; grad. Taft Sch., 1929; B.A., Yale, 1934; m. Helene Danforth Coler, Oct. 10, 1942 (div. Mar. 1954); children—Helene Danforth, Rosemary Herrick; m. 2d, Jean W. Washburn, Nov. 15, 1956. Reporter, legislative corr. New Haven Register, 1934-37, asst. to pub., 1937-52, asst. pub., 1953-60, asso. ed., 1958-60, editor, co-pub., 1960-72; pres. Asso. Dailies of Conn. 1942-45; pub. New Haven Jour. Courier, 1951-52; dir. Carrington Pub Co., New Haven, 1947-64; v.p., sec. dir. Register Pub. Co., 1956-60, sr. v.p., 1960, pres., dir., 1960-73, trustee, dir., 1973-74. Mem Mayor's Human Rights Com., 1963-64, gov's Clean Air Task Force, 1966, gov's Clean Water Task Force, 1968, Environmental Policy Com., 1970; v.p., mem. bd. dirs. New Haven Preservation Trust, 1961-73. Trustee Hosp. St. Raphael, New Haven; bd. dirs. Gaylord Hosp., Wallingford, Conn. Fellow Pierson Coll., Yale; recipient David Russell Lyman Gold medal Gaylor Hosp., 1974. Fellow Am. Geog. Soc.; mem. Am. Soc. Newspaper Editiors, Soc. Colonial Wars, Internat. Press Inst., Soc. Cin., Inter Am. Press Assn., Newcomen Soc., Sigma Delta Chi, Chi Psi. Episcopalian. Clubs: Laurel; Devon Yacht (bd. govs.); Maidstone (East Hampton, N.Y.); Yale (N.Y. C.); Graduates, Mory's, New Haven Lawn, Faculty (New Haven). Home: Hamden, Conn. Died Dec. 12, 1974.

JACKSON, ROBERT ARNOLD, baking co. exec.; b. Chgo., Nov. 27, 1896; s. William J. and Eliza J. (Preston) J.; B.A., Dartmouth, 1919; m. Mildred E. Morrissey, July 30, 1949; 1 son, William John II. With Ward Baking Co., N.Y.C., from 1919, beginning as baker, successively shop supt., salesman, asst. mgr., mgr., regional mgr.; gen. sales mgr., v.p. sales and marketing, 1919-57, dir., mem. exec. com., pres., 1957-61, chmn. bd., mem. exec. com., from 1961. Mem. Delta Kappa Epsilon. Clubs: Kittansett Golf (Marion, Mass.); Ponte Vedra. Home: Ponte Vedra Beach, Fla. Died 1979.

JACKSON, ROBERT CHARLES, JR., aero. co. exec.; b. Racine, Wis., Feb. 26, 1908; s. Robert Charles, and Gertrude (Carson) J.; A.B. in Econs., Stanford, 1929, M.B.A., 1931, C.P.A., 1934; m. Elizabeth Jane Burdell, Nov. 24, 1937; children—Bruce B., Robert D., Mark B. With Lybrand, Ross Bros. & Montgomery, 1931-34, security dept. First Nat. Bank Los Angeles, 1934-36; v.p. West Shore Co., 1936-60; dir. Ryan Aero. Co., 1957-69, Teledyne Ryan Aero., exec. com., 1958-69, exec. v.p., vice chmn., 1959-61, pres., 1961-69, chmn., 1969-79, chief exec. officer, 1969-75, dir. Teledyne, Inc., 1969-79, also group chmn., 1969-73; chmn. bd. Continental Motors Corp., 1965-70; pres., dir. Jackson Investment Co., 1946-79, Emtor, Inc., 1953-69, Wis. Motors, 1967-69; gen. partner Carter Investment Co., Carter Co., 1946-79; dir. Security Pacific Nat. Bank, Los Angeles. Bd. dirs. San Diego Mgmt. Council for Merit Employment, 1967-68; mem. steering com. Urban Coalition, San Diego, 1968-70. Trustee U. Redlands, 1968-74. Served to 2d lt. U.S. Army, 1929-37, capt. to lt. col. AUS, 1942-46; ETO. Decorated Bronze Star medal. Mem. Def. Orientation Conf. Assn., Air Force Assn., Army Aviation Assn., Nat. Mgmt. Assn., Navy League U.S., Aerospace Industries Assn. Am., San Diego C. of C. (dir. 1965-69). Clubs: California, Los Angeles Country, San Diego Country, Cuyamaca, San Diego Yacht, San Diego Country (dir. 1970-73), Burning Tree (Bethesda, Md.). Home: San Diego, Calif. Died Feb. 20, 1979.

JACOB, CARY FRANKLIN, educator; b. Richmond, Virginia, Sept. 14, 1885; s. John Franklin and Nettie Moore (Sneed) J.; prep. edn., high sch., Richmond, Va., and Peabody Inst., Baltimore, Md.; B.S., U. of Va., 1912, M.S., 1916, Ph.D., 1917; unmarried. Prof. English lit., summer session U. of Va., 1918; same, Coll. William and Mary, 1919-25; asso. prof. of Spoken English, Smith Coll., since 1927. Lecturer on Shakespeare, Nat. U. of Mexico, summer 1925. Mem. Modern Lang. Assn. America, Am. Linguistic Soc., Authors' League America, Dramatists' Guild, Am. Shakespeare Assn., A.A.A.S., Nat. Assn. of Teachers of Speech, Delta Phi, Phi Beta Kappa, Pi Gamma Mu, Theta Alpha Phi, Phi Delta Gamma, Phi Kappa Phi, University of Va. Club (New York), Farmington Country Club. Democrat. Author: Driftwood and Foam (poems), 1914; The -Foundations and Nature of Verse, 1918; also plays and novels under pen name. Home: Northampton, Mass. *

JACOB, PEYTON, coll. pres.; b. Learned, Miss., Nov. 4, 1883; s. Simeon Sebastian and Lorena Jerome (Peyton) J.; A.B., Mississippi Coll., Clinton, 1905, A.M., 1908; U. of Chicago, 1911, 16-17; studied Peabody Coll. for Teachers, 1922-23; m. Maggie Agnes Burkley, June 4, 1907; children—Marjorie, Doris, Joseph Simeon, Peyton. Prin. and supt. pub. schs., Miss., 1905-11; prof. philosophy and edn., Baylor Coll., Belton, Tex., 1911-18; prof. edn., Mercer U., 1918-33, dean Sch. of Edn., 1920-33, dean Coll. of Liberal Arts, 1926-28; chmn. div. of edn., 1933; pres. Ga. Southwstern Coll., Americus, Jan. 1, 1934-June 30, 1948, pres. emeritus, since July 1948. Member Miss. Text Book Commission, 1910. Pres. Southern Association Junior Colleges, 1942. Member Southern Soc. for Philosophy and Psychology, Phi Delta Kappa, Kappa Phi Kappa. Democrat. Baptist. Home: Decatur, Ga. *

JACOBS, JAMES ALBERT, educator; b. Sioux City, Iowa, Apr. 10, 1913; s. James Ernest and Grace (Gillespie) J.; A.B., State U. Iowa, 1937, M.S., 1940, Ph.D., 1941; m. Phyllis Margaret Moorcroft. Asst. prof. physics, dir. electronics State U. Iowa, Iowa City, 1942-45, then prof. physics; prof physics Va. Poly. Inst., 1960-78, head dept. physics, 1960-73. Mem. Am. Phys. Soc., AAUP, Am. Assn. Physics Tchrs., Iowa Acad. Scis., Phi Beta Kappa, Sigma Xi. Home: Blacksburg, Va. Died May 29, 1980; buried Blacksburg.

JACOBS, LAWRENCE PIERCE, assn. exec.; b. Houston, Mar. 31, 1912; s. Joseph and Helen Crosby (Pierce) J.; B.S., Ga. Sch. Tech., 1935; grad. Army Command and Gen. Staff Sch., 1946, Armed Forces Staff Coll., 1952, Nat. War Coll., 1958, advanced mgmt. program Harvard, 1960; m. Cogee Pauline Comer, June 18, 1938; 1 dau., Barbara A. Hobbs. Asst. chief engr. Bibb Mfg. Co., Macon, Ga., 1935-41; commd. 1st lt., U.S. Army, 1941, advanced through grades to brig. gen., 1962; ret., 1966; exec. dir. Am. Soc. Photogrammetry, Falls Church, Va., 1966-77. Decorated Distinguished Service Medal, Legion of Merit with oak leaf cluster, Army Commendation medal. Mem. Armed Forces Communications Electronics Assn., Nat. Assn. Uniform Services, Ga. Tech., Harvard alumni assns., Delta Sigma Phi. Methodist (adminstrv. bd.). Club: Harvard Business School (Washington) Home: Arlington, Va. Died Jan. 20, 1977.

JACOBS, PAUL, author; b. N.Y.C. Aug. 24, 1918; s. Julius and Tecia (Schmidt) J.; student Coll. City NY., U. Minn.; m. Ruth Rosenfield, Jan. 1, 1939 (dec. Nov. 1977) Organizer, Internat. Ladies Garment Workers Union, 1941-43; race relations specialist Am. Jewish Com., 1946-48; internat. rep. Oil Workers Internat. Union, 1948-51; mem. staff Center Study Democratic Instns., Santa Barbara, Calif., 1956-69; research staff Center Study Law and Soc., U. Calif., Berkeley, 1964-72; asso. fellow Inst. for Policy Studies Washington, from 1970. Editor, newspaper columnist, filmmaker, TV commentator. Served with USAAF, 1943-46. Recipient award for pub. service to journalism Sigma Delta Chi, 1958. Mem. Soc. Mag. Writers. Author: (with F. Pinner, P. Seiznick) Old Age and Political Behavior, 1959; (with M. Harrington) Labor in a Free Society, 1959; The State of the Unions, 1963; Is Curly Jewish, 1965; (with S. Landau) The New Radicals, 1966; Prelude to Riot, 1968; Between the Rock and the Hard Place, 1970; (with Saul Landau, Eve Pell) To Serve the Devil. 1970; The Black and Brown Experience in America, 1971. Contbr. articles to profl. jours. Home: San Francisco, Calif. Died Jan. 13, 1978.

JACOBSEN, CHRISTIAN F., banker, assn. exec.; b. Washington, Nov. 30, 1884; s. Charles and Mary C. (Sippel) J.; student Emerson Inst., Washington, 1901; m. M. C. Dierken, June 20, 1906 (died 1933); children—Charles J., Mary Jeanne, John S.; m. 2d Edna Parker, June 20, 1940. Employed as messenger The Nat. Met. Bank of Washington, 1903, cashier, 1917, exec. v.p., 1938, pres., 1939-58; treas. and dir. J. Frank Kelly, Inc.; dir., vice chmn. board American Security and Trust Company, 1958—, director Potomac Ins. Co., Fidelity Storage Co. Treasurer National Assn. Motor Bus. Operators, Am. Planning and Civic Assn., Woodlawn Pub. Found., Incorporated, National Trust for Historic Preservations; treasurer Fine Arts Committee; advisory committee D.A.R. Mem. D.C. Bankers Assn., Washington Bd. Trade, Better Business Bur. Newcomen Soc. N.A., Association Oldest Inhabitants, Columbia Hist. Soc., Boys Club Washington. Lutheran. Mason (Jester), Elk. Club: Early Birds Breakfast. Home: Bethesda, Md. *

JACOBSEN, LYDIK SLEGUMFELDT, prof. mech. engring.; b. Nyborg Denmark, June 17, 1897; s. Hans Christian and Ellen Marie Elisabeth da Cour (Siegumfeldt) J.; came to U.S., 1917, naturalized, 1927; A.B., Stanford Univ., 1921, Ph.D., 1927; m. Doris Isabelle Wetzel, June 29, 1928; children—Erland Lydik, Ian Christian, Ellen Andrea. Research engr. Westinghouse Electric & Mfg. Co., East Pittsburgh, Pa., 1921-24; instr., Stanford Univ., 1924-26, asst. prof., 1926-30, asso. prof., 1930-36, prof., 1936, head mech. engring. dept., 1940-43, and from 1946; Guggenheim fellow 1931-32 doing research in applied mechanics at various European insts.; Fulbright lect. Tech. U. Denmark, 1953-54. Director Earthquake Research Lab., Stanford, 1926-43, and from 1946; consultant: U.S.C.&G. survey in seismology from 1928, U.S. Army Engrs. from 1940, City of San Francisco dept. pub. works, Sandia Corp., Aubuquerque, Armed Forces Spl. Weapons Project. Served as comdr. U.S.N.R. in charge of noise reduction and vibration problems, Navy Yard, Mare Island and other Pacific Coast Yards, 1943-46. Awarded commendation citation of U.S. Navy. Mem Am. Soc. Mech. Engrs., Am. Seismological Soc. Am. (pres.), Structural Engr. Assn. of Northern Calif., Soc. for Theoretical and Applied Mechanics, Soc. Promotion of Engineer Edn., Tau Beta Pl, Sigma Xi. Author: Engineering Vibrations, 1958. Contributor of numerous technical research papers to prof. jours. Home: Woodside, Calif. Died Dec. 21, 1976.

JACOBSON, IRVING, actor, producer; b. Cin., 1905; s. Joseph and Betty J,; ed. pub. schs., N.Y.C.; m. Mae Schoenfeld, 1929 (dec. 1977); 1 son, Joel. With Yiddish Theater, N.Y.C., from 1920; Nightclub performer, London, Eng., 1951-52; actor in plays including Abi Gezunt, 1949, It's a Funny World, 1956, Man of La Mancha, 1965-68 (all N.Y.C.); actor and producer Mazeltov, Molly, 1950, Don't Worry, 1951. Girl of My Dreams (also co-dir), 1952, Wish Me Luck, 1954, Go Fight City Hall, 1961 (all N.Y.C.). Mem. Actors' Euity Assn., Hebrew Actors' Union, Screen Actors Guild. New York, N.Y. Died Dec. 17, 1978.

JACOBSON, SAMUEL DAVID, hosp. adminstr,; b. Detroit, 1913; M.D., Wayne U., 1937, M.Sc. in Internal Medicine, 1941. Intern, Wayne County Gen. Hosp., Eloise, Mich., 1937-38, resident internal medicine, 1938-40, research fellow medicine, 1940-44, jr. attending medicine, physician in chief Wayne County Gen. Hosp. and Infirmary; asso. prof. Wayne U.; jr. attending med. staff Detroit Receiving Hosp. Diplomate Am. Bd. Internal Medicine, 1946. Fellow A.C.P.; mem. A.M.A., Central Soc. Clin. Research, Am Fedn. Clin. Research. Home: Eloise, Mich. Deceased.

JACOBY, NEIL HERMAN, economist; b. Dundurn, Sask., Can., Sept. 19, 1909; s. Herman Reynold and Christina (MacMillan) J.; came to U.S., 1930, naturalized, 1937; B.A., U. Sask., 1930, LL.D., 1950; Ph.D., U. Chgo., 1938; m. Clair Gruhn, Dec. 23, 1933; children—Neil Herman, Christina. Supr. legal and research divs. State Dept. Finance, 1933-36; chmn. Sask. Taxation Commn., 1936; mgr. research dept. Lawrence Stern & Co., Chgo., 1937; asst. prof. fin. U. Chgo., 1938-40, asso. prof., 1940-42, prof., sec., 1942-48, v.p., 1945-48; prof, bus and econ. policy dean U. Calif. Grad. Sch. Bus. Adminstrn., Los Angeles, 1948-68, Armand Hammer prof. bus. econs, and policy, 1968-79. cons. Rand Corp., 1951-61; chmn. Ill. Emergency Relief Commn., 1940-41; mem. research adv. bd. Com. for Econ. Devel., 1942-48, mem. research staff Nat. Bur. Econ. Research, 1940-45; mem. Pres's Council Econ. Advisors, 1953-55; U.S. rep. Econ. and Social Council UN, from 1957. dir. Occidental Petroleum Corp., 1959-79. chmn., mem. exec. com. 2nd audit com.; 1972-79; head U.S. Aid Evaluation Mission to Taiwan, 1965; chmn. Pres.'s Task Force on Econ. Growth, 1969; pub. mem. The Pay Bd., 1971-73. Mem. Am. Econ. Assn., Royal Econ. Soc., Nat. Tax Assn., Beta Gamma Sigma, Pi Gamma Mu. Clubs; Cosmos (Washington); Internat., U. Calif. Los Angeles Faculty. Author books including: (with R.J. Saulnier) Business Finance and Banking, 1946; Can Prosperity Be Sustained, 1956; U.S. Aid to Taiwan, 1966; European Economics: East and West, 1967; Corporate Power and Social Responsibility, 1973; Multitudinal Oil, 1974; Bribery and Extortion in World Business, 1977. Home: Los Angeles, Calif. Died May 31, 1979.

JAHN, THEODORE LOUIS, educator; b. New Orleans, Dec. 17, 1905; s. Edward Charles and Aline (Blair) J.; A.B. with distinction, Rice Inst., 1927; M.S., N.Y. U., 1929, Ph.D., 1931; m. Frances Floed, July 18, 1931. Nat. Research fellow in zoology Yale U., 1931-33, instr., 1933-34; research asso. State U. Iowa, 1934-36, asso. zoology, 1936-37, asst. prof., 1937-41, asso. prof., 1941-48; prof. zoology UCLA, 1948-73, chmn. dept., 1949-58, prof. biology emeritus, 1973-79. Mem. adv. panel gen. biology Am. Inst. Biol. Scis., Office of Naval Research, 1950-52; panel mem. NIH, 1960-64, NSF, 1961-64; mem. com. internat. exchange persons Conf. Bd. Asso. Research Councils, 1960-63; adv. panel behavioral biology Am. Inst. Biol. Scis.-NASA, 1965-67; bd. dirs. council on biol. scis. information Nat. Acad. Scis., 1969-79, pres., 1970-79; bd. dirs. Com. on Advanced Sci. Tng., Los Angeles, 1968-70, v.p. bd. dirs., 1969-70; mem. Council Biol. Editors. Recipient Distinguished Alumni award N.Y. U., 1968; Award of Merit, Com. on Advanced Sci. Tng., 1967; named to Wisdom Soc. Hall of Fame; Theodore Louis Jahn Fund established by Soc. Protozoologists, 1978. Mem. AAAS (exec. com. Pacific div. 1961-66, pres. Pacific div. 1969-70, mem. nat. council 1969), Am. Micros. Soc. (hon. mem., pres. 1954-55), Am. Soc. Cell Biology, Soc. Gen. Physiologists, Soc. Protozoologists (hon. mem., sec. 1947-49, v.p. 1949-50, pres. 1952-53, mem. exec. com. 1953, 56), Soc. Systematic Zoologists, Iowa Acad. Sci., Western Soc. Naturalists (pres. 1974-75), N.Y. Acad. Sci., Am. Soc. Zoologists (treas. 1953-56, chmn. div. comparative physiology 1964-65), Biophys. Soc., Am. Soc. Microbiology, Internat. Soc. Biorheology, Am. Physiol. Soc., NRC, Soc. Exptl. Biology and Medicine, Phycological Soc., Internat. Assn. Microbiol. Socs. (documentation com. sect. on cultural collections), Am. Soc. Naturalists, Optical Soc. Am., Sigma Xi. Author: How to Know the Protozoa (with Frances Jahn), 1949, rev. edit. (with E.C. Bovee and F. Jahn), 1978; contbr. articles to sci. jours.; editorial com. Ann. Rev. Microbiology, 1958-63; contbg. author: Protozoa in Biological Research, 1941; Comparative Animal Physiology, 1950; Research in Protozoology, 1967; Primitive Motle Systems in Cell Biology, 1964; Infectious Blood Diseases in Man and Animals, 1968; The Biology of Euglena, 1968; editorial bd. Jour. Protozoology, 1960-63, Am. Midland Naturalist; trustee Biol. Abstracts, 1963-68, pres. bd. trustees, 1966-67. Home: Los Angeles, Calif. Died May 1, 1979.

JAMES, ARTHUR HORACE, ex-gov., Pa.; b. Plymouth, Pa., July 14, 1883; s. James D. and Rachel (Edwards) J.; LL.B., Dickinson Sch. of Law, 1904; LL.D. (hon.), Susquehanna U., 1927, Dickinson Coll., 1938, Temple U., Jefferson Med. Coll., Muhlenberg Coll., Pa., Mil. Coll., Franklin and Marshall Coll., Washington and Jefferson Coll., 1939, U. of Pa., 1940, Moravian Coll., 1941, Lafayette Coll., 1941, Grove City Coll., 1942, Bucknell U., 1942; Gettysburg College, 1942; hon. D.C.L., Hahnemann Med. Coll. and Hospital, 1939; married Ada Morris, October 23, 1912 (died 1935); children—Dorothy Rachel, Arthur Horace (deceased); m. 2d, Emily R. Case, October 1, 1941. Began as a breaker boy, Nottingham Breaker, Plymouth, Pa., 1896; admitted to Cumberland County (Pa.) bar, 1904, Luzerne County bar, 1905; in practice law, Plymouth and Wilkes-Barre, Pa., 1905-19; dist. atty., Luzerne County, Pa., 1919-26; lt. gov., Pa., 1927-31; judge Pa. Superior Court, 1932-39; gov. Commonwealth of Pa., 1939-43. Mem. bd. of incorporators Dickinson Law Sch. Mem. Pa. Bar Assn. Republican. Methodist (mem. bd. trustee Plymouth PA *

JAMES, DANIEL, JR., air force officer; b. Pensacola, Fla., Feb. 11, 1920; s. Daniel and Lillie Anna (Brown) J.; B.S. in Phys. Edn., Tuskegee Inst., 1942; grad. Air Command and Staff Coll., 1957; LL.D., U. W. Fla., 1971, U. Akron, 1973, Va. State U., 1974, Del. State Coll., 1975, U. St. Louis, 1976, Fisk U., 1977; m. Dorothy Agusta Watkins, Nov. 3, 1942; children—Danice (Mrs. Frank Berry, Jr.), Daniel III, Claude A. Commd. USAAF, 1943, advanced through grades to gen. USAF; flight leader 12th Fighter Bomber Squadron, Philippines, 1949; pilot, Korea, 1950, Otis AFB, Mass., 1951-55; comdr. 60th Fighter Interceptor Squadron, 1955-56; staff officer Office Dep. Chief Staff Ops. Air Def. Div., 1956-60; asst. dir. Ops. 81st Fighter Wing RAF, Bentwaters, Eng., then dep. wing. comdr., 1960-64; dir. operational tng., dep. comdr. ops. Davis-Monthan AFB, Ariz., 1964-66; dep. comdr. ops. Ubon Royal Thai Air Base, Thailand, 1966; vice comdr. 8th Tactical Fighter Wing. 1967; vice comdr. 33d Tactical Fighter Wing, Eglin AFB, Fla., 1967-69; comdr. 7272d Flying Tng. Wing, Wheelus Air Base, Libya, 1969; dep. asst. sec. def. for pub. affairs, Pentagon, Washington, 1970-73; prin. dep. asst. sec. pub. affairs, 1973-74; vice comdr. Mil. Airlift Command, Scott AFB, Ill., 1974-75; comdr. in chief N. Am. Air Def. Command/Aerospace Def. Command. 1975-78; spl. asst. Chief of Staff, Hdqrs. U.S. Air Force, Washington, 1978. Decorated Legion of Merit with oak leaf cluster, D.F.C. with two oak leaf clusters, D.S.M. with oak leaf cluster; Air Medal with 13 oak leaf clusters, numerous others; named Young Man of Year Mass., 1954, Fla. Jr. C. of C. Young Man of Year, 1969; recipient George Washington Freedom Found medal, 1967, 68, Phoenix Urban League award, 1970; Nat. Comdr.'s Pub. Relations award Am. Legion, 1971; V.F.W. Gold medal, 1971; Par Excellence award Black Book Minority Bus. and Reference Guide, 1976; Silver Helmet award Amvets, 1976; Americanism award V.F.W., 1976; Gen. Jimmy H. Doolittle chpt. Air Force Assn. Man of Year award, 1976; Outstanding Citizen award Am. Youth Hostel Assn., 1976, Distinguished Am. award, 1977; U.S.O. Liberty Bell award. 1976; Distinguished Service award United Negro Coll. Fund, 1976; Horatio Alger award, 1976; Kitty Hawk Mil. award, 1976, 1st ann. medal Tuskegee Airmen, 1976; Robert L.F. Sikes award Fla. State Soc. Washington, 1976, 77; Pres.'s Cabinet award U. Detroit, 1977; Armed Services and Vets. Meritorious Service award NAACP, 1977; numerous others. Home: South Arlington, Va. Died Feb. 25, 1978.

JAMES, ERNEST KELLY, lawyer; b. Maple Hill, N.C., June 29, 1895; s. Gibson and Annabelle (Murray) J.; A.B., Maryville (Tenn.) Coll., 1920; J.D., U. Chgo., 1923; m. Mary Summers, July 6, 1929. Admitted to WVa bar, 1923; practice of law, specializing public utility law and taxation, from 1923; mem. firm James, Wise, Robinson & Magnuson and predecessor firm. Mem. W. Va. Legislature, 1934-36; state tax commr. W. Va., 1937-41. Served as lt. A.S., U.S. Army, 1917-19. Mem. W.Va Ry. Assn. (chmn. exec. com.), W.Va. C. of C. (pres. 1947-52, dir.), Am., W.Va (pres. 1952-53), Charleston bar assns., Am Judicature Soc., Phi Alpha Delta. Democrat. Presbyn. Mason. Clubs; Edgewood Country. Home: Charleston, W.Va. Died Nov. 13, 1977.

JAMES, JAMES CHARLES, lawyer; b. Aurora, Ill., Feb. 21, 1882; s. George Albert and Mary (Rooney) J.; A.B., U. of Wis., 1904; student George Washington U. Law Sch.; m. Julia Brady Haring, July 11, 1910; children—Marion, Martha, James Charles, Jr. Admitted to Illinois bar, 1905, Supreme Court U.S., 1926; practiced law at Aurora, Ill., 1905-17; assistant state's attorney Kane County, Illinois, 1907-10; member firm of Alschuler, Putnam & James, Aurora, 1910-17; local atty. C.,B.& Q. R.R. Co., 1914-17; asst. to Ill. dist. atty., same road, Chicago, 1917-19, gen. atty., 1919-24, gen. solicitor, 1924-38, gen. counsel, 1938-49, v.-pres. and director, 1939-49, mem. exec. com., 1941, exec. vice president, gen. counsel 1949-52, ret., 1952, dir. mem. exec. com., 1962—. Dir. Aurora Found. Mem. adv. bd. St. Joseph Mercy Hosp. Mem. Phi Kappa Psi. Republican. Club: Chicago. Home: Aurora, Ill. *

JAMES, JULES, naval officer (ret.); b. Va., Feb. 14, 1885; s. John and Anne Maria (Jones) J.; Danville (Va.) Mil. Inst., Va. Mil. Inst., 1906; A. B., U.S. Naval Acad., 1908, A.M., Columbia, 1916; grad Naval War Coll., 1936; m. Eleanor Standish Gamble, Oct. 30, 1928; children—Eleanor, Anne, Mabel. Commd. ensign U.S. Navy, 1910, and advanced through grades to vice adm., 1946; served in battleships, cruisers, destroyers, European and Asiatic fleets; White House aide to Pres. Wilson, 1912-13; asst. Naval attache, France, Spain, Portugal, 1923-26; comdr., U.S.S. Edsall, 1928, U.S.S. Philadelphia, 1936-38, destroyer squadron, 1938; dir., Naval Intelligence, 1940-41; comdt., U.S. Naval base, Bermuda, also combined U.S. and Brit. forces, Bermuda, 1941-43; comdt. 6th Naval Dist. and Navy Yard, Charleston, S.C., 1943-45; comdt. So. Group Atlantic Sea frontier, 1943-45; comdr., U.S. Naval Forces, Mediterranean, 1945-46; ret. from active duty, 1946; spl. rep. of Nat. Lead Co. in Europe, since Feb. 1948. Decorated Grand Officer, Order of Honor and Merit (Haiti); Chevalier, Legion of Honor (France); Grand Officer, Order of Merit (Santo Domingo); Royal Order of Phoenix with swords (Greece); Grand Cross of Order of Crown (Italy); Comdr., Order of Brit. Empire; awarded Legion of Merit with star, Mexico, Yangtze, Atlantic campaign medals, Victory medal (World War II), various other campaign, area, battle medals, ribbons and stars, Episcopalian. Clubs: Army Navy (Washington and Manila), Chevy Chase (Md.), N.Y. Yacht, St. Nicholas (N.Y. City), Royal Yacht (Bermuda). Holds patent on gun sight, 1938. Home: Baltimore, Md. *

JAMES, PHILLIP, composer, conductor; b. Jersey City, May 17, 1890; s. Philip William and Ernestine (Wildhagen) J.; A.B., CCNY, 1910; Mus.D., N.Y. Coll. Music, 1946; m. Millicent Eady, Sept. 7, 1916 (dec. July 1945); m. 2d, Helga Boyer, Feb. 3, 1952; children—Vivien, Philip. Mus. dir. operettas for Victor Herbert and prodns. Winthrop Ames, N.Y.C., 1911-16; condr. N.J. Symphony Orch., 1922-29, Bklyn. Orchestral Soc., 1928-29; prof. music, head music dept., N.Y. U., prof. emeritus; instr. music Columbia U.; v.p. Llangollen Internat. Mus. Eisteddfod, North Wales; condr. Bamberger Symphony Orch., Radio Sta. WOR; guest condr. Nat. Symphony Orch., Washington, N.Y. Orch., NBC Orch., Phila. Orch., CBS, N.Y. Philharmonic-Symphony Orch., Bronx Symphony Orch. Served as 2d lt., inf., U.S. Army, later bandmaster and comdg. officer A.E.F. Hdgrs. Band, World War I. Recipient 1st prize ($5000) NBC for suite for orch.; hon. mention for overture Bret Harte Philharmonic Symphony Soc. N.Y., 1936; Juilliard Found. Publ. award, 1937; 1st prize Women's Symphony Orch. N.Y., 1938; Award of Merit for outstanding service to Am. music Nat. Assn. Am. Composers and Conductors, 1970. Hon. fellow Trinity Coll., London, Eng., 1938. Mem. Nat. Inst. of Arts and Letters, Soc. Publ. Am. Music (chmn. bd.), Am. Musicol. Soc., MacDowell Allied Mems. (pres. 1953), Edw. MacDowell Assn. (v.p.), A.S.C.A.P., Phi Beta Kappa, Mu Sigma. Episcopalian. Club: Century Assn. (N.Y.C.). Composer two symphonies, five suites, seven concert overtures, choral works, chamber music and songs. Home: Southampton, N.Y. Died Nov. 1, 1975.

JAMESON, JAY PAUL, consular service; b. at Washington, D.C., Nov. 3, 1883; s. Albion B. and Lavilla (Hendershott) J.; Ph.B., Dickinson Coll., Carlisle, Pa., 1907, A.M., 1916. Apptd. student interpreter in China, Aug. 27, 1907; dep. consul gen. and interpreter, Shanghai, 1909-10; v. and dep. consul gen., 1910-11; designated to exercise judicial authority in civil and criminal cases, 1911; v. and dep. consul gen. and interpreter, Hankow, 1911-14; consul at Antung, Manchuria, 1914-15, Nanking, China, 1915-19. Sent to Russia and Siberia, 1918, on spl. duty for Dept. of State; apptd. consul at Riga, Russia, 1919; assigned to Dept. of State, Div. of Far Eastern Affairs, Apr. 15, 1920, and to Div. of Russian Affairs, Aug. 12, 1920. Tech. del. to Conf. on Limitation of Armament and Far Eastern Questions, at Washington, D.C., 1921; apptd. officer Dept. of State, and assigned to Div. of Far Eastern Affairs, Mar. 15, 1923. Mem. Mil. Order of Loyal Legion. Clubs: Cosmos, Sigma Alpha Epsilon, Congressional Country. Home: Bloomsburg, Columbia Co., Pa. Address: Washington, D.C. *

JANEWAY, CHARLES ALDERSON, physician, ret. educator; b. N.Y.C., May 26, 1909; s. Theodore C. and Eleanor C. (Alderson) J.; A.B., Yale, 1930; postgrad. Cornell U. Med. Coll., 1931-32; M.D., Johns Hopkins, 1934; M.A. (hon.), Harvard, 1946; M.D. (hon.), U. Uppsala (Sweden), 1964; Dr. honoris causa, U. Reims (France), 1969; m. Elizabeth Bradley, July 9, 1932; children—Anne Alderson, Elizabeth (Mrs. Ronald Gold), Charles A., Barbara Bradley. Hosp. tng. Boston City Hosp. and Johns Hopkins Hosp., 1934-37; mem. dept. bacteriology and immunology Harvard Med. School, 1938-39, dept. medicine, 1940-42, dept. pediatrics, 1943-78, Thomas Morgan Rotch prof. pediatrics, 1946-74, prof. pediatrics, 1975-78; physician-in-chief Children's Hosp. Med. Center, 1946-74, emeritus, 1975-81; chmn. com. on blood and blood derivatives NRC, 1948-51; chmn. com. on blood and blood derivatives, vice chmn. exec. com., adv. bd. on health services A.R.C., 1946-50; mem. med. adv. council Iran Found., 1955-64, pres., 1958-65, chmn. med. adv. council 1965-76; pres. Protein Found., 1955-60, sci. dir., 1960-68, bd. dirs., 1955-72, v.p. Center for Blood Research, 1972-81; chmn. med. adv. bd. Nat. Found. Muscular Dystrophy, 1954-60; chmn. med. adv. bd. Nat. Found. Neuromuscular Disease, 1960-68, hon. chmn., 1968-69; mem. exec. bd. Internat. Pediatric Assn., 1956-62, chmn. exec. com., 1963-68; mem. adminstrv. bd. Internat. Children's Center, Paris, 1967-81; hon. chmn. med. adv. bd. Nat. Genetics Found., 1969-81; mem. Nat. Adv. Allergy and Infectious Diseases Council, NIH, 1970-73; mem. Johns Hopkins Soc. Scholars, 1969-81. Recipient Peter Bent Brigham medal, 1963; Rosen von Rosenheim medal Swedish Paediatric Assn., 1964; Child Health award Charles H. Hood Found., 1971; Samuel Z. Levine award Found. Internat. Child Health, 1973, medal Internat. Pediatric Assn., 1974. Alan Gregg travel fellow China Med. Bd., N.Y., 1965-66; Merriman lectr. U. N.C. Med. Sch., 1976. Mem. Brit. Paediatric Assn. (hon.), Soc. de Pediatrie de France (corr.), Finnish Paediatric Assn. (hon.), Korean Acad. Pediatrics (hon.), Assn. de Professores de Pediatria de Mexico (hon.), Can. Pediatric Assn. (hon.), Mass. Med. Soc., New Eng. Pediatric Soc., Am. Acad. Pediatrics, Am. Acad. Arts and Scis., Am. Soc. for Clin. Investigation (v.p. 1953), Soc. for Pediatric Research (pres. 1955), Am. Pediatric Soc. (pres. 1971, Howland award 1978), Assn. Am. Physicians, Philippine Pediatric Soc. (hon.), Czechoslovak Pediatric Soc. (hon.), Interurban Clin. Club, Irish and Am. Paediatric Soc. Contbr. sci. articles to jours. Editorial bd. Pediatrics, 1954-60. Home: Weston, Mass. Died May 28, 1981.

JANSSEN, DAVID, actor, songwriter; b. Naponee, Nebr., Mar. 27, 1931; s. Harold Meyer and Berniece Graf; ed. U. Calif. at Los Angeles; m. Dani Crayne. Began acting career at age 9; under contract Universal Pictures, 1951-56; recent movies include Hell to Eternity, My Six Loves, The Green Berets, Shoes of the Fisherman, Where It's At, Marooned, Generation, Macho Callahan, Two Minute Warning, Once is Not Enough, The Swiss Conspiracy, 1979; guest star various TV shows; role Richard Diamond, TV series, 1957-60; title role The Fugitive, ABC-TV series, 1963-67, Ohara U.S. Treasury, CBS-TV series, 1972, Harry-O, ABC-TV series, 1974-76; also movie of the week A Sensitive Passionate Man, also writer title song and 7 other songs; TV movies: Stalk the Wild Child, 1976, Mayday at 40,000 Feet, 1976, Nowhere to Run, 1978, Golden Gate Murders, 1979. Actor United Way film Little Boy Lost. Served with AUS, 1952-54. Recipient TV Guide award, TV-Radio Mirror award, 1964; selected Man of Year on TV, Radio-TV, Daily, 1964; Emmy nomination Nat. Acad. TV Arts and Scis., 1964, 66; Spl. Editor's award Photoplay Mag., 1965; recipient Golden Globe, Hollywood Fgn. Press. Assn., 1965; Gold Camera award as most popular star in S. Am., Ecran mag., Santiago, Chile, 1966, Western Heritage Wrangler award. Mem. AFTRA, Acad. Motion Picture Arts and Scis., Acad. Television Arts and Scis., ASCAP, AGVA, Screen Actors Guild, Artists Equity Assn. Clubs: Friars; Canyon Country (Palm Springs, Calif.); Beverly Hills (Calif.) Tennis. Home: Malibu, Calif. Died Feb. 13, 1980; buried Hillside Meml. Cemetery, Los Angeles.

JAQUA, ERNEST JAMES (JA'KWA), educator; born Reinbeck, Ia., Oct. 24, 1882; s. Albert and Mary Jane (Watson) J.; A.B., Grinnell (Ia.) Coll., 1907, LL.D., 1927; studied Columbia, 1909-12, M.A., 1910; B.D., Union Theol. Sem., 1912; Ph.D., Harvard, 1919; m. Julia Gwendolen Evans, Sept. 4, 1912; children—Mary Alice, Eleanor Stark, William Ernest, John Evans, Ernest Lyman. College sec., State Y.M.C.A. of Ind., 1907-09; dean of men and asst. to pres., Grinnell Coll., 1912-17; dean of men and prof. edn., Colorado Coll., Colorado Springs, 1922-23; dean of faculty and prof. edn., Pomona Coll., 1923-27; pres. Scripps Coll., Claremont, Calif., 1927-42; head employment specialist, Bur. of Training, War Manpower Commn., 1943; ednl. dir. Baruch Com. on Physical Medicine, 1944. Mem. N.E.A., Phi Beta Kappa, Phi Delta Kappa. Republican. Conglist. Club: Harvard (New York). Retired. Address: Cottage Grove, Ore. *

JARMAN, WALTON MAXEY, apparel co. exec.; b. Nashville, May 10, 1904; s. J.F. and Eugenia (Maxey) J.; ed. Mass. Inst. Tech.; LL.D., Stetson U., Georgetown Coll.; m. Sarah Anderson, Oct. 10, 1928; children—Franklin, Anne, Eugenia. Sec.-treas. Jarman Shoe Co., 1925-32, pres., 1932-33; pres. Gen. Shoe. Corp. (became GENESCO, Inc. 1959), 1933-47, chmn., 1947-69, chmn. exec. and finance com., 1969-73; dir. Nashville City Bank & Trust Co., Fin. Fedn.; trustee Mut. Life Ins. Co. N.Y., Genesco Retirement Fund. Mem. Tenn. Tax Commn., 1949; chmn. Gov's Study on Cost Control, 1971. Trustee Moody Bible Inst.; v.p. So. Bapt. Conv., 1950. Mem. Christian Bible Soc. (trustee), Pi Delta Epsilon, Theta Delta Chi, Theta Tau, Eta Mu Pi, Beta Gamma Sigma. Republican. Baptist. Clubs: Bellemeade Country; Everglades, Bath and Tennis (Palm Beach, Fla.). Author: A Businessman Looks at the Bible; O Taste and See. Home: Nashville, Tenn. Died Sept. 8, 1980.

JARMAN, WILLIAM JACKSON, clergyman; b. Kansas City, Jan. 18, 1916; s. Eugene Oswald and Alpha Ellen (Bratten) J.; A.B. with distinction in English, U. Mo., 1937, postgrad., 1940-41; B.D., Union Theol. Sem., N.Y.C., 1940; D.D., Culver-Stockton Coll., 1959; m. Mary Mona Love, May, 1, 1946; children—William Jackson, Mona, Mary. Ordained to ministry Christian Ch. (Disciples of Christ), 1933; pastor, Paris, Mo., 1941-42, Mexico, Mo., 1946-48, Univ. Pl. Ch. Champaign, Ill., 1948-65, Park Ave. Christian Ch., N.Y.C., 1965-77; lectr. Union Theol. Sem., N.Y., 1966-77. Pres. bd Ill. Disciples Found., Champaign, 1948-66, Council Christian Unity, 1957-64; mem. gen. bd. Nat. Council Chs., 1957-72; bd. higher edn. Disciples of Christ, 1948-65, commn. ministry Ill. Disciples, 1948-65, mem. exec. com. Consultation on Ch. Union, 1966-74; mem. exec. com. Champaign County Mental Health Clinic, 1956-65. Pres. bd. trustees Disciples Div. House of U. Chgo., 1960-66; trustee Christian Theol. Sem., Indpls., 1966-72; chmn. Unity Commn of Christian Chs. Served to lt. comdr. as chaplain USNR, 1942-46. Mem. Religion in Am. Life (program com. 1966-77. Author: Manual for Burial of the Dead at Sea, 1942; Looking Toward Marriage, 1960. Home: Teaneck, N.J. Died Dec. 23, 1977.

JARRELL, JAMES HOYT, life ins. exec.; b. Milltown, Ala., Nov. 26, 1902; s. James Robert and Cora (Northen) J.; A.B., Samford U., 1924. Pres., Old Republic Life Ins. Co., Chgo., 1943-68, chmn. bd., 1968-76; chmn. bd. Old Republic Ins. Co., Greensberg, Pa., 1955, Old Republic Internat. Corp., Chgo., 1969, Motorists Beneficial Ins. Co., Chgo., Old Republic Life Ins. Co. of N.Y., Home Owners Life Ins. Co., 1971-76; mem. adv. com., underwriter Old Republic Lloyds of Tex., 1976-77. Served with USNR, 1941-44; lt. comdr. res. Mem. Sigma Nu. Home: Chicago, Ill. Died July 11, 1976.

JARRELL, JOHN WILLIAMS, newspaper corr.; b. Holton, Kans., July 13, 1908; s. John Frank and Myra (Williams) J.; student, Washburn Coll., Topeka, Kans., 1926-30; m. Lois Stephens, Sept. 12, 1940; 1 stepson, Andrew. Reporter, Topeka Daily Captial, 1930, Topeka State Jour., 1931-35, rejoined 1938, city editor, 1940-41; reporter, Shanghai (China) Evening Post-Mercury, 1935, Kansas City Star, Salt Lake Telegram, 1938; spl. rep. Santa Fe R.R. pub. relations dept., Chgo., 1936-37; Internat. News Service Staff, N.Y., 1941; war corr. Africa, Asia, Europe, 1942-44; joined Omaha World-Herald, 1944, chief Washington Bur., 1946-71. Recipient medal of Freedom, USAF; medal of France's Liberation Paris, 1949. Mem. White House Corrs. Assn., Overseas Writers, Sigma Delta Chi, Phi Delta Theta. Clubs: National Press; Gridiron. Home: Washington, D.C. Died Dec. 8, 1978.

JAVITS, BENJAMIN ABRAHAM, lawyer, author, economist; b. N.Y.C., Oct. 21, 1894; s. Morris and Ida (Littman) J; student CCNY, 1909-11; LL.B., Fordham U., 1918; m. Lily Birnbaum, Feb. 12, 1926; children—Joan Ellen, Eric M. Various positions selling, mgmt, indsl. reorgn., bus counseling, 1911-22; admitted to N.Y. bar, 1922, practiced in N.Y.C. and Washington, 1922-69; counsel, mem. Javits & Javits, N.Y.C. and Washington, ret., 1969. Sponsored movement to amend anti-trust laws, 1926; organized nat. conf. for nat. econ. planning, Washington, 1929; filed petition in bankruptcy for Am. creditors of Kreuger and Toll affairs, 1932; assisted drafting Nat. Indsl. Recovery Act, 1933; pres., founder United Shareowners Am., Inc., 1950; co-founder Investors League, Inc. Pres. bd. Shareowners Ednl. Found., Inc., Fair Return League, Inc. Republican. Mason. Clubs: Palm Beach Country; Noyak Golf, Overseas Press, City Athletic. Author: Make Everybody RichIndustry's New Goal, 1929; Business and the Public Interest-Trade Associations. The Anti-Trust Laws and industrial Planning, 1932; The Commonwealth of Industry, The Separation of Industry and the State, 1936; Peace by Investment, 1950; How the Republicans Can Win in 1952, 1952; The Manifesto of Freedom for Mankind, 1962; Ownerism; A Better World for All Through Democratic Ownership, 1969; also pamphlets, articles. Fordham U. Sch. Law known as Benjamin A. Javits Halls of Law. Home: Palm Beach, Fla. Died May 18, 1973.

JAYNES, LAWRENCE C., corp. exec.; b. Coalton, Ohio, Aug 10, 1891; s. William M. and Mary Margaret (McMonigle) J.; grad. Inf. Sch., 1928, Command and Gen. Staff Sch., 1935, Army War Coll., 1939; m. Georgia Rose Joyner, July 19, 1926 (dec.); 1 dau., Margaret Gail; m. 2d, Frances Lacy Adams, Jan. 15, 1966. Commd. 1st lt. Ordnance, O.R.C. 1918. active duty. 1918; pvt. sgt. comdg. 2d lt Tank Corps, 1918; commd. 1st lt. inf. U.S. Army, 1920, advanced through grades to brig. gen., 1942, maj. gen., 1943; comdg. gen., combat command A 13th Armored Div., 1942-44, comdg. gen. replacement and tng. command, MTO, 1944-45; theater insp. gen., 1945, dep. theater comdr., 1945-47, chief of staff. 1946-47; dep. chief of staff Allied Force Hdgrs., 1946-47, chief of staff, 1947; comdg. gen. MTO, 1947; comdg. gen., N.Y.-N.J.-Del. Mil. Dist., 1947-1950; spl. asst. to chief of staff U.S.A. for civilian component affairs, 1950-53, ret; pres Nat. Trailways Bus System & Trailways Travel Bur. Corp., from 1954. chmn. bd., from 1955. Mem. Travel Adv. Com. Dept Commerce. Decorated D.S.M., Legion of Merit with oak leaf cluster, Bronze Star, Victory Cross; Occupation medal (Italy); companion Most Honorable Order Bath (Gt. Britain); officer Legion of Honor, Croix de Guerre, Legionaire, first class hon. (France); Medal of War (Brazil); Cross of Grand Officers Order of St. Maurice and St. Lazarus, Cross of Grand Officers Order Crown of Italy, Order Crown of Italy, comdr's Degree, Cross of War (Italy). Life mem. Nat. Def. Transp. Assn., Res. Officers Assn. U.S., Assn. U.S. Army, Nat. Assn. Travel Orgns., Am. Soc. Travel Agts., U.S. C. of C. Washington Bd. Trade. Methodist. Mason (32 deg.), Rotarian. Home: Washington, D.C. Died June 20, 1977.

JEFFERS, DWIGHT SMITHSON, univ. prof.; b. DeLand, Ill., May 21, 1883; s. Elijah Marion and Florence (Smithson) J.; A.B., Illinois Wesleyan Univ., 1906; M. F., Yale U. Sch. of Forestry, 1911, Ph.D., Grad. Sch., 1931; m. Helen Anette Nelson, Dec. 1914; children—Dwight Nelson, Betty Jo. With U.S. Forest Service, 1911-21, begining as forest asst., later becoming forest supervisor; asso. prof. forestry, Ia. State Coll., 1921-31; prof. of forestry U. of Wash. Coll. of Forestry, 1931-35; dean and prof. forestry, U. of Ida., since Sept. 1935. Fellow Soc. Am. Foresters; mem. Sigma Xi, Alpha Zeta, Xi Sigma Pi, Phi Kappa Phi, Tau Kappa Epsilon. Mason. Methodist. Club: Moscow Kiwanis. Contbr. articles to periodicals. Home: Moscow, Ida. *

JEFFERS, JOHN LEROY, lawyer; b. Ferris, Tex., Oct. 15, 1909; s. Theodore Franklin and Cynthia (Ewing) J.; LL.B. with highest honors, U. Tex., 1932; m. Nell Elise Walker, Feb. 8, 1935; children—John Leroy, Mary Nell (Mrs. H. Malcolm Lovett, Jr.). Admitted to Tex. bar, 1932; practice in San Antonio, 1932-42; asst. criminal dist. atty., San Antonio, 1935-39; mem. firm Vinson, & Elkins, Houston, 1942-79; past mem. faculty St. Mary's U. Sch. Law, San Antonio, South Tex. Sch. Law, Houston; lectr. Southwestern Legal Found, 1966-79. Mem. Tex. Constl. Revision Commn., 1973-74; chmn. Gov.'s Conf. on Criminal Justice Standards and Goals, 1974. Del.-at-large Democratic Nat. Conv. 1952. Bd. regents U. Tex., 1953-59, chmn., 1957-59; chmn. bd. trustees Houston Legal Found., South Tex. Sch. Law, Tex. Bill of Rights Found., Univ. Cancer Found., U. Tex. Law Sch. Found., Episcopal Theol. Sem. Southwest. Recipient Outstanding Alumnus award U. Tex. Law Sch., 1969; Distinguished Alumnus award U. Tex., 1974. Fellow Am. Coll. Trial Lawyers, Am. Bar Found.; mem. Am. (ho. dels. 1966-67, 72-79, chmn. anti-trust sect. 1970-71), Houston (pres. 1968-69) bar assns., State Bar Tex. (pres. 1973-74), Order of Coif, Delta Theta Phi. Home: Houston, Tex. Died July 4, 1979.

JEFFERY, EDWIN T., business exec.; b. Cleve., 1908; grad. Fenn Coll. Chmn. bd. W.S. Tyler, Inc., Cleve,; dir. Soc. Nat. Bank Cleve., Soc. Corp., Combustion Engring., Inc., Liberty Reed Co., Tyler Wayne Research Co., Tylinter, Inc. Trustee St. Vincent Charity Hosp., John Carrol U., Am. Cancer Soc. Home: Shaker Heights, Ohio. Died Dec. 31, 1977.

JEFFERY, WARREN CRAIG, metall. engr.; b. Birmingham, Ala., Apr. 7, 1920; s. Craig and Sadie (Swanson) J.; student Ga. Inst. Tech., 1937-39; B.S. in Metall. Engring., U. Ala., 1947, M.S. in Metall. Engring., 1951; m. Katherine Minna Langner, Feb. 9, 1940; 1 dau., Wanda Kay. Chemist, Sloss Sheffield Steel & Iron Co., Birmingham, 1939-41; metallurgist Jackson Industries, Inc., Birmingham, 1948-50; asso. prof. metall. engring. U. Ala., 1950-60; product devel. mgr. McWane Cast Iron Pipe Co., Birmingham, from 1960; gen. mgr. Empire Coke Co., Birmingham, 1962-65; cons. to metalcasting industry, 1950-60; spl. research ductile cast iron. Served to officer AUS, 1941-46. Named Outstanding Tchr., U. Alabama, 1959. Registered profl. engr., Ala. Hon. life mem. Am. Foundrymen's Soc. (chmn. ductile iron research com. 1964, nat. bd. dirs. 1962, regional v.p. 1962, internat. v.p. 1964-65, internat. pres. 1965-66, trustee Tng. and Research Inst. 1963-67), Am. Inst. Mining and Metall. Engrs., Am. Soc. Metals, Soc. Applied Spectroscopy, Sigma Xi, Tau Beta Pi. Baptist. Co-designer spl. liningless hot blast cupola, 1960, analytical method for trace elements, 1965; inventory spl. ductile iron pipe joints, 1965-66. Home: Birmingham, Ala. Died Oct. 6, 1975.

JEFFREY, A(RTHUR) A(LLAN), editor and writer; born LaCrew, Ia., July 9, 1882; s. Asael Hiram and Mary Delia (Hampton) J.; A.B., Simpson Coll., Indianola, Ia., 1905; m. Edna Lisle, June 27, 1906; children—Eleanor (Mrs. John P. McKay), Frances, Allan Hampton, Lisle. Local editor Clarinda (Ia.) Herald, 1905-12; staff corr., Capper Farm Papers, Topeka, Kan., 1915-20; asso. editor Missouri Ruralist, Topeka, 1916-20; agrl. editor U. of Mo. since 1921. Official observer of bird migration U.S. Bird Survey, 1900-06. Local nature indstructor Boys Scouts and Campfire Girls. Recipient National Certificate of Recognition from Epsilon Sigma Pi, 1937, Silver Beaver award, Boy Scouts Am., 1939. Mem. Mo. Writers Guild, Central Mo. Area Boy Scout Council (mem. at large); mem. exec. com. Columbia bd. sponsoring local work Salvation Army. Mem. Gamma Sigma Delta, Epsilon Sigma Phi. Ind. Democrat. Methodist. Club: Kiwanis (hon. life mem.). Contbr. to gen. farm and religious jours.; also fiction in young peoples ch. papers. Home: Columbia, Mo. *

JELLIFFE, WALTER SCRIBNER, bank exec.; b. Mansfield, O., June 18, 1886; s. Charles W. and Margaret (Ward) J.; B.A., Oberlin (O.) Coll., 1908; m. Jean Cameron Brownlie, Sept. 20, 1916; children—Dorothy Cameron (Mrs. Jelliffe von Feilitzen), Mary Brownlie (Mrs. Mary Jelliffe Miller), Walter Scribner. Engaged in lumber ins. business, N.Y. City and Portland, Ore., 1908-18; with Nat. Park Bank, N.Y. City, 1918-29, vice-pres., 1927-29, vice-pres. Chase Nat. Bank, N.Y. City, since 1929. Republican. Presbyterian. Clubs: St. Andrew's Golf; Yacht (Riverdale-on-Hudson, N.Y.). Home: N.Y. *

JENCKES, VIRGINIA ELLIS, ex-congresswoman; b. Terre Haute, Ind., Nov. 6, 1882; d. James Ellis and Mary (Oliver) Somes; edited pub. schs.; m. Ray Greene Jenckes, February 22, 1912 (died 1921); 1 dau., Virginia Ray (deceased). Engaged in farming since 1912. Mem. 73d to 75th Congresses (1933-39), 6th Ind. Dist. Head of woman's work, Ind. Equality for Agriculture, 1928 Presidential Campaign. U.S. del. Inter-Parliamentary Union, Paris, 1937. Democrat. Episcopalian. Clubs: Ind. Woman's Democratic, Ind. Federated Woman's. Home: Terre Haute, Ind. *

JENKINS, AB, ex-mayor; b. Spanish Fork, Utah, Jan. 25, 1883; s. David Abbott and Elizabeth (Hurlow) J.; student Salt Lake City (Utah) pub. schs.; m. Evelyn Thorstenberg, Dec. 1, 1915; children—Edna, Ruth, Marvin Edward. Began as apprentice in coach dept. Denver & Rio Grande R.R. Co. shops, Salt Lake City, 1897-1904; bldg. contractor, 1905-26; automobile test driver and engr., 1926-40, in which capacity established all world speed records above ten miles to 48 hours time and 10,000 kilometers distance; awarded nat. "Champion of Champion" trophy, 1940; Salt Lake City "First Citizen" award, 1935; mayor Salt Lake City until Jan. 1, 1944. Member Rotary International, Lions, Footprinters, Internat. Soc. of Automotive Engrs. Republican. Mormon. Author: Salt of the Earth, 1939. Home: East Salt Lake City, Utah. *

JENKINS, GLENN LLEWELLYN, pharm. chemist; b. Sparta, Wis., Mar. 25, 1898; s. Thomas and Laura Elizabeth (Rathbun) J.; Ph.G., U. of Wis., 1921, B.S., 1922, M.S., 1923, Ph.D., 1926; m. Serena Elizabeth Forberg, June 29, 1926; children—Serena Elizabeth, Thomas Nelson, Glenn Llewellyn, Carol Ruth. Asst. instr. in pharmacy, U. of Wis., 1924-26, instr., 1926-27; prof. and head dept. of pharm. chemistry, U. of Md., 1927-36, U. of Minn, 1936-41; dean Sch. of Pharmacy, Purdue U., from 1941. Served as private U.S. Army, September-November 1918. Awarded Ebert medal by Am. Pharm. Assn, for pharm. research, 1936 award for stimulation of research, 1962; Remington medal for advancement in pharmacy, 1963. Fellow A.A.A.S. (member council) chmn. sub-section on pharmacy 1939-54, v.p. 1955); mem. Am. Pharm. Assn. (vice chmn. exec. council, vice pres. 1938; chairman, 1939-41, 53-55; chairman Ho. Dels, 1944, pres. 1949) Am. Assn. Colls. Pharmacy (mem. exec. com.; pres. 1944), Am. Chem. Soc. (chmn. Purdue Sect, 1945), Am. Council Pharmaceutical Edn., Indiana Academy Science, Indiana Pharm. Assn., Indiana Interprof. Health Council (chairman 1941-54), Indiana Board of Health (chairman of the board 1957-59), American Institute Hist. Pharm., Sigma Xi, Gamma Alpha, Rho Chi (nat. pres., 1928-32), Theta Chi, Kappa Psi, Phi Delta Chi, Phi Lambda Upsilon frats., Am. Legion. Congregationalist. Clubs: Lafayette Rotary (president 1945), Purdue University (president 1946). Author books including: The Chemistry of Organic Medicinal Products (with W. H. Hartung), 1957; The Art of Compounding, 1957; Quantitative Pharmaceutical Analysis, 1957. Asso. editor Pharm. Archives; contbr. to profl. jours.: mem. rev. com. of U.S. Pharmacopoeia (chmn. sub-com. on reagents); mem. Pharm. Syllabus Committee (pub. 1942). Home: West Lafayette, Ind. Died Jan. 14, 1979.

JENKINS, JOSEPH ALTON, lawyer; b. Salt Lake City, Jan. 30, 1919; s. Joseph and Bessie (Iverson) J.; B.A. in Econs., U. Utah, 1939; J.D., Georgetown U., 1944; m. Betty Everett, Jan. 3, 1940 (div. Mar. 1948); 1 dau., Josephine M.; m. 2d, Antoinette DHooge, Sept. 28, 1948. Export, import broker on articles moving from U.S. to Belgium; admitted to N.Y. bar, 1947, Tex. bar, 1952, D.C. bar, 1957, N.Mex. bar, 1963; atty. NLRB, Ft. Worth, 1948-51; chief enforcement and litigation br., region 10, Nat. Wage Stblzn. Bd., 1951-53; partner Rawlings, Savers Scurlock & Edison, Ft. Worth, 1953-57; mem. NLRB, Washington, 1957-61, dir. regional office, Albuquerque, 1961-63; pvt. practice law as Jenkins & Watkins, Inc., P.C., and predecessor firms, Dallas, from 1963. Mem. panel arbitrators Fed. Mediation and Counciliation Service and Am. Arbitration Assn.; chmn. Irving Civil Service Comm., 1971-73. Served from ensign to lt. comdr. USNR, 1942-46. Cited by City of Antwerp, Belgium. Mem. Internat. Platform Assn., Am., Fed., Tex., Dallas, N.Mex. bar assns., Bar Assn. D.C., Nat., Tex., Dallas criminal def. lawyers assns., Am. Judicature Soc., Res. Officers of Naval Res., Fort Worth-Tarrant County Res. Officers Assn. (pres. 1955), VFW, Nat. Lawyers Club, S.W. Legal Found., Indsl. Relations Research Assn., Phi Beta Kappa, Phi Kappa Phi, Tau Kappa Alpha, Delta Theta Phi. Club: Cosmos. Author: Treatise on Labor Law (4 vols.), 1968; also articles profl. publs. Died Mar. 8, 1975. Home: Irving, Tex. Deceased; interred Salt Lake City.

JENKINS, MARTIN DAVID, ednl. adminstr.; b. Terre Haute, Ind., Sept. 11, 1904; s. David and Josephine (Miller) J.; B.S., Howard U., 1925; A.B., Indiana State Coll., 1930; M.S., Northwestern U., 1933, Ph.D., 1935; m. P. Elizabeth Lacy, Sept. 6, 1927. Inst. Va. State Coll. 1930-32; prof. edn. and registrar Agrl. and Tech. Coll. of N.C., Greensboro, N.C., 1935-37; dean instrn. Cheyney State Tchrs. Coll. Pa., 1937-38; prof. edn. Howard U., 1938-48; sr. specialist higher edn. U.S. Office Edn., 1940-42; pres. Morgan State Coll., Balt., 1948-79; dir. office urban affairs Am. Council on Edn., Washington, 1970-74. cons. on coll. orgn. and adminstrn. Staff mem. U.S. Office of Edn. Nat. Survey Higher Edn. of Negros, 1940-42, Survey Delaware Pub. Schs., 1946, Survey Higher Edn. in Md., 1946. Trustee Nat. Urban League, Inst. for Services to Edn. Dept. Housing and Urban Devel.; adv. bd. Urban Studies Fellowship. Awarded Selective Service Medal. Diplomate Am. Bd. Examiners in Profl. Psychology (counseling and guidance). Mem. N.E.A., Kappa Alpha Psi. Baptist. Author: National Survey Higher Education of Negroes (co-author Vols, II and III); co-author; Black and White of Rejections for Military Service, 1944; The Morgan State College Program—An Adventure in Higher Education, 1964; numerous articles in ednl. and psychol, jours. on superior Negro children and adults, higher edn. of Negroes, and on urban affairs. Address: Washington, D.C. Died June 11, 1978.

JENKINS, RAY HOWARD, lawyer; b. Unaka, N.C., Mar. 18, 1897; s. Columbus Sheridan and Amanda (Nicholson) J.; LL.B., U. Tenn., 1920; m. Evalyn Lavinia Nash, Nov. 20, 1926 (deceased); 1 dau., Eva Lois (Mrs. Alexander Marion Cuningham, Jr.); m. Eva Crouch Tedder, Dec. 15, 1963. Admitted to Tenn. bar, 1919; practice in Knoxville, 1920-80; spl. counsel Senate Permanent Sub-com. on Investigations in Army-McCarthy Hearings, 1954. Rep. presidl. campaign mgr., 1940. Mem. Tenn. Bar Assn., Tenn. Soc. S.R., Am. Legion, Order of Coif, Am. Coll. of Trial Lawyers, Phi Kappa Phi, Phi Delta Phi, Tau Kappa Alpha. Episcopalian. Clubs: Cherokee Country, City (Knoxville). Home: Knoxville, Tenn. Died Dec. 26, 1980.

JENKS, FRANK WILLIAM, business exec.; b. Richmond, Va., Aug. 7, 1897; s. Frank W. and Ella Nora (Beeton) J.; ed. public schools and John Marshall High Sch., Richmond, Va.; m. Thelma Sneed Bagby, Feb. 3, 1921; 1 dau., Shirley Emerson. With International Harvester Co., Chicago, Ill., since 1914, in office, 1914-25, asst. branch mgr., 1925-28, branch mgr., 1928-30, asst. dist. sales mgr., 1930-33, credit mgr., 1933-41, credit and collection mgr., 1941-44, vice pres., 1944-56, exec. v.p., 1956-57, pres., 1957-62, chief executive officer, 1958-62, director, mem. executive com.; dir. Continental Ill. Nat. Bank and Trust Co., Chicago. Trustee Illinois Inst. of Technology. Past pres. past dir. Ill. C. of C. Advisor Future Farmers Am. Found.; v.p. Farm Equip. Inst., mem. exec. com.; citizens bd. U. Chgo.; citizens bd. U. of Illinois; trustee Farm Found., Farm Film Found. Served with U.S. Army during World War I. Episcopalian. Mason (Shriner). Clubs: Skokie Country (Glencoe); Commercial (Chgo.). Home: Evanston, Ill. Died Dec. 27, 1976.

JENNEWEIN, CARL PAUL, sculptor; b. Stuttgart, Germany, Dec. 2, 1890; s. Louis and Emilie (Weber) J.; art edn. Art Students League, N.Y.C.; Prix de Rome scholar Am. Acad. in Rome, 1912-21; m. Gina Pirra, Jan. 27, 1918; children—Paul Romano, Emilia Pirra, Alessandro Louis, James Joseph, Peter Gino. Came to U.S., 1907, naturalized, 1915. Prin. works; Sculpture for Phila. Mus. Art, many public bldgs. and memorials, portraits and medals, including work for House Office Bldg., Washington; statue and frieze Washington Meml. Valley Forge Tower; two panels for White House, Washington; also executed many bronzes including, four pylons, N.Y. World's Fair, and several others, bronzes on permanent exhbn. at Met. Mus. Art, N.Y.C., Balt. Mus Art, Corcoran Art Galleries, Washington, Cin. Mus. Art, Detroit Mus. Art; most recent work includes Sancho Panza in aluminum for Brookgreen Gardens, 1970, tablet for U. Rochester, 1971, John F. Kennedy medal for dedication Kennedy Center Performing Arts, 1971; represented in Bklyn Mus. Art. Newark Mus. Art, Houston Mus. of Art, Hartford Mus. of Art, Pa. Acad, Fine Arts, Brookgreen Gardens, Georgeton, S.C., others. Awarded several medals and prizes including Saltus medal NAD 1942 Elizabeth N. Watrous Gold medal, 1960, 150th Anniversary Gold medal, 1975; Sanford Saltus award. 1949; Golden Plate award Am. Acad. Achievement, 1966; Medal of Honor, Nat. Sculpture Soc., 1967; Benjamin West Clinedinst Meml. medal, 1967; 50th Anniversary medal Am. Legion; Hall of Fame medal James Monroe, Outstanding Aerospace Rescue, Recovering award Albert P. Loening trophy, 1968; Gold medal Am. Artists Profl. League. 1968: Gold medal 75th Ann. Exhbn. Nat. Sculpture Soc., 1968. A.N.A. Numis. Art award. 1970; Daniel Chester French medal NAD, 1972. Mem N.G., N.Y., 1915-16; served with ARC, Italy, World War. A.N.A. 1930, N.A., 1933. Fellow Am. Acad. in Rome, Nat. Sculpture Soc. (pres. 1960-63, now hon. pres.), Am. Numis. Soc.; mem, NAD (past v.p.), Beaux Arts Inst. Architects, AIA, Nat. Inst. Arts and Letters Alumni Assn., Brookgreen Gardens (pres. 1963-76, pres. emeritus 1976-78). Club: Century Assn. (N.Y.). Home: Bronx, N.Y. Died Feb. 22, 1978.

JENNEY, MELVIN RICHARD, lawyer; b. Boston, Aug. 23, 1900; s. Frederic H. and Mabel (Tukey) J.; S.B., Mass. Inst. Tech., 1921; postgrad. Suffolk Law Sch., Boston; m. Anne D'Orsay, Sept. 16, 1927; children—Richard F., Robert M., Louise (Mrs. James Rouvalis). Admitted to Mass. bar, 1926, practiced in Boston; mem. firm Keaway & Jenney, 1947-80. Mem. Melrose (Mass.) Bd. Appeal, 1947-74. Served with USNRF, 1918. Mem. Am., Mass., Boston bar assns., Boston Patent Law Assn. (pres. 1952-53). Republican. Methodist. Mason. Home: Melrose, Mass. Died Sept. 26, 1980.

JENNISON, MARSHALL WALKER, bacteriologist; b. Portland, Maine, May 27, 1905; s. William Walker and Harriet (Marshall) J.; B.S., Mass. Inst. Tech., 1927, Ph.D., 1932; m. Cynthia M. Lamb, Aug. 15, 1929 (dec.); children—Cynthia M., Margaret W.; m. 2d, Margaret Kerfoot, Jan. 3, 1952. Asst. in biology Mass. Inst. Tech., 1927-30, instr., 1930-35, asst. prof. san. biology, 1935-41, asso. prof. bacteriology, 1941-46; prof. bacteriology Syracuse U., 1946-71, chmn. dept. bacteriology and botany, 1956-69; vis. lectr. Harvard Sch. Pub. Health, 1945. Fellow Am. Pub. Health Assn., AAAS, Am. Acad. Microbiology; mem. Am. Inst. Biol. Scis., Am. Soc. Microbiology (chmn. com. bacteriological technic 1948-53), Mycol. Soc. Am., Soc. Indsl. Microbiology, Signa Xi, Kappa Sigma. Editorial bd. Jour. Bacteriology, 1931-51. Contbr. to sci. jours. in field. Home: Boulder, Colo. Died Sept. 17, 1979; buried Syracuse, N.Y.

JENNISON, RALPH DRURY, public utility executive; b. Chicago, Ill., Aug. 12, 1885; s. Nahum E. and Mabel (Drury) J.; B.S., U. of Mich., 1908; m. Lucile Ballard, July 1918; children—Sally (Mrs. Henry Riter), David, Philip. Engaged in public utility business since 1909; vice pres. W. S. Barstow Management Assn., 1920-29; v.p. Utilities Management Corp., 1929-36, pres., 1936-40; became pres. N.Y. State Electric & Gas Corp., 1941, now chmn. bd., dir.; dir. Del., Lackawanna & Western R.R. Co., Utilities Mutual Ins. Co., Maine Midland Trust Co. Dir. Edison Electric Inst., 1944-47. Mem. Sigma Xi, Delta Kappa Epsilon. Home: Binghamton, N.Y. *

JENSEN, ALFRED JULIUS, artist; b. Guatemala City, Guatemala, Dec. 11, 1903; s. Peter and Anna (Shipke) J.; studied at Horsholn, Denmark, 1910-19, with Hans Hofmann, 1927-28; student Ecole Scandinave, Paris, 1929-34, Fine Arts Mus., San Diego, 1925-26; m. Regina Bogat, Nov. 12, 1963; children—Anna Bogat, Peter Bogat. Came to U.S., 1934. One-man shows: Tanager Gallery, 1955, Bertha Schaefer Gallery, 1957, Martha Jackson Gallery, 1959, 61, Guggenheim Mus., 1961, Graham Gallery, 1962, 64, 65, Fairleigh-Dickinson U., 1963, Kornfeld and Klipstein, Berne, Switzerland, 1963, 75, Kunsthalle, Basel, Switzerland, 1964, 75, Rolf Nelson Gallery, Los Angeles, 1964, Stedelijk Mus., Amsterdam, 1964, Royal Marks Gallery, 1966, Galerie Ziegler, Zurich, Switzerland, 1966, Cordier and Ekstrom, 1967, 69, Pace Gallery, 1972, 73, Kestner-Gesellschaft, Hannover, Germany, 1973, Mus. Louisiana, Humbleback, Denmark, 1973, Kunsthalle, Baden Baden, Germany, 1973, Kunsthalle, Dusseldorf, Germany, 1973, Kunsthalle, Bern, 1973, Kunsthalle, Basel, 1975, Galerie Kornfeld, Zurich, 1977, Albright Knox Art Gallery, Buffalo, 1978, New Mus., N.Y.C., 1978; exhibited numerous group shows, 1954-81, including Inst. Contemporary Art, Boston, 1960, St. Louis City Art Mus., 1960, Art Inst. Chgo., 1961, Guggenheim Mus., 1961, Corcoran Gallery Art, Washington, 1962, Whitney Mus. Am. Art, 1962, 63, 66, 71, San Francisco Mus. Art, 1963, Nat. Gallery Art, Washington, 1963, Los Angeles County Mus., 1964, Venice Biennale, 1964, 78, Brown U., 1965, Sao Paulo (Brazil) Biennial, 1977; represented in permanent collections: Mus. Modern Art, N.Y.C., Rose Art Mus., Brandeis, Dayton Art Mus., Whitney Mus. Am. Art, N.Y.C., Chase Manhattan Bank, N.Y.C., Time, Inc., N.Y.C., Am. Rep. Ins. Co., Des Moines, Galerie Beyeler, Basel, Hayes Galleries, N.Y.C., also numerous pvt. collections. Ford Found. grantee, summer 1965. Home: Glen Ridge, N.J. Died Apr. 4, 1981.

JENSEN, CECIL LEON, cartoonist; b. Ogden, Utah, Jan. 17, 1902; s. Arthur Lorenzo and Lucy Mary (Rose) J.; ed. high sch., Ogden; student Chgo. Acad. Fine Arts; m. Margaret Buchmiller, May 3, 1924; children—Patricia (Mrs. Frank Benson), Barbara (Mrs. Norman Nuckolis); m. 2d, Mary Lou Allegretti, Oct. 10, 1969. Circulation dist. mgr. Ogden Standard-Examiner, 1919; comic artist Bell Syndicate, 1921; cartoonist Salt Lake Telegram, 1922; editorial cartoonist Los Angeles Daily News, 1924-28; cartoonist

Chgo. Daily News, 1928-76, also editor. Creator comic strip Little Debbie, also Syncopating Sue and Elmo. Recipient Sigma Delta Chi award for editorial cartooning, 1952. Address: Fayetteville, Ark. Died May 16, 1976; interred in Ogden, Utah.

JENSEN, JENS, mining exec.; b. Espe, Denmark, Jan. 9, 1882; s. Hans Peder and Louise (Kristiansen) J.; grad. Danish Sch. Commerce, Odense, Dgnmark, 1901; m. Bertha Brown, Nov. 30, 1957. Came to U.S., 1902, naturalized, 1911. Dir., officer Metaline Falls Light & Water Co., 1910-29; dir., officer Pend Oreille Mines & Metals Co., 1929—, pres., 1955—; dir., officer Reeves MacDonald Mines, Ltd., 1929—, pres., 1955—;— pres., dir. Burgoyne Farms, Ltd. Mem. Am. Inst. Mining Metal and Petroleum Engrs., Am. Zinc Inst., Lead Industries Assn., Northwest Mining Assn., Mining Assn. Brit. Columbia. Mason (K.T., Shriner). Clubs: Spokane City; Vancouver. Home: Spokane. *

JENSEN, MERRILL MONROE, educator, historian; b. Elkhorn, Iowa, July 16, 1905; s. John Martin and Julia (Seymour) J.; B.A., U. Wash., 1929, M.A., 1931; Ph.D., U. Wis., 1934; m. Genevieve Margaret Privet, Dec. 24, 1929; 1 dau., Julanne (Mrs. David G. Pease). From instr. to asso. prof. history U. Wash., 1935-44; mem. faculty U. Wis., 1944-76, prof. history, 1946-76, prof. emeritus, 1976-80, Vilas Research prof. of history, from 1964, chmn. dept., 1961-64; Harmsworth prof. history U. Oxford (Eng.), 1949-50; vis. prof. U. Tokyo (Japan), 1955, U. Ghent (Belgium), 1960; prof. Am. studies summer seminar Kyoto (Japan) U., 1971; Anson G. Phelps lectr. N.Y. U., 1973; commemorative speaker 200th ann. 1st Continental Congress, U.S. Ho. of Reps., 1974; historian USAAF, 1944. Mem. Orgn. Am. Historians (pres. 1969-70), Mass. Hist. Soc. (corr.), Am. Antiquarian Soc., Colonial Soc. Mass. Author: The Articles of Confederation, 3d edit., 1959; The New Nation: A History of the U.S. During the Confederation, 1950; American Colonial Documents to 1776, 1955; The Making of the American Constitution, 1964; Tracts of the American Revolution, 1967; The Founding of a Nation; A History of the American Revolution 1763-1776, 1968; The American Revolution within America, 1974; The Documentary History of the Ratification of the Constitution, vols. I and II, 1976, vol. III, 1978; The Documentary History of the First Federal Elections, vol. I, 1976. Editor: Regionalism in America, 1951; Documentary History of the Ratification of the Constitution, 1970-80. Editor Pacific Northwest Quar., 1935-42. Home: Middleton, Wis. Died Jan. 30, 1980.

JENSEN, MORONI LUNDBY, state senator; b. Ogden, Utah, Jan. 10, 1912; s. Hans Simon and Christine (Jensen) J.; grad. Snow Jr. Coll., 1932; B.S., Brigham Young U., 1946; M.A., Columbia U., 1950; m. Vivian Nelson, Mar. 8, 1934; children—M. Leon Jerold Tchr. elementary Sch. Sevier (Utah) Sch. Dist., 1932-35, teaching prin., 1935-45; field dir. ARC Overseas PTO, 1945-46; supervising prin. Salina (Utah) Elementary Sch., 1946-49; prin. Richfield (Utah) Jr. High Sch., 1951-52, Valley Jr. High Sch., Salt Lake City, 1953-59, Cyprus High Sch., Magna, Utah, 1959-65, 70-72, Granger (Utah) High Sch., 1965-68; dir. continuing edn., prin. adult evening high sch. Granite Sch. Dist., Salt Lake City, 1968-70, dir. secondary edn., from 1973; mem. Edn. Commn. of States, 1977-79; mem. Utah Ho. of Reps., 1965-71; mem. Utah Senate, from 1971; pres., 1977-79. Active Boy Scouts Am.; mem. Utah Art Curriculum Com., from 1956; pres., founder David Gourley Scholarship Fund Granite Sch. Dist.; councilman City of Salina, 1941-43, mayor, 1943-45; mem. Utah Central Republican Com., 1949-51. Recipient Distinguished Service award Salina Jr. C. of C., 1941. Mem. So. Utah (pres. 1938), Sevier (pres. 1937) tchrs. assns., Utah Elementary Prins. Assn. (pres. 1943), Utah Edn. Assn. (pres. 1961-63, pres. dept. adminstrs. and suprs. from 1974), Nat. Council State Assn. Pres.'s (pres. 1962-63), NEA (dir. Utah chpt. 1965-69), Utah Secondary Prins. Assn. (pres. 1959-60). Mormon. Clubs: Rotary, Lions. Home: Salt Lake City, Utah. Deceased.

JERGER, EDWARD REMINGTON, newspaper pub.; b. Thomasville, Ga., Feb. 3, 1884; s. Louis Henry and Mary Sheldon (Remington) J.; A.B., U. of Ga., 1903; m. Emily Neilson Hatch, of Asheville, N.C., Jan. 29, 1916; children—Maragret McRee (dec.), Emily Remington. Editor and pub. Thomasville Times-Enterprise since 1908; pres. Three Toms Tavern, Inc. Chmn. Thomasville Planning Bd.; pres. Thomasville Bd. of Edn., Thomasville League, Thomasville Chapter Am. Red Cross; trustee and sec. John D. Archbold Memorial Hosp., Thomasville Pub. Library. Capt. and adj. Ga. N.G., 1910. Mem. Thomasville Chamber Commerce (ex-pres.), Kappa Alpha. Mem. Dem. State Exec. Com., Ga.; mem. governor's staff. Mem. bd. of advisers, Inst. of Pub. Affairs (U. of Ga.). Episcopalian. Mason (Shriner). Clubs: Rotary, Glen Arven Country. Home: Thomasville, Ga. *

JESSEL, GEORGE, actor; b. N.Y. City, Apr. 3, 1898; s. Joseph Aaron and Charlotte (Schwartz) J.; m. Florence Courtney; m. 2d, Norma Talmadge; m. 3d, Lois Andrews; 1 dau., Jerilynn; m. 4th, Paula Jacobson, 1960. Began career as nickelodean singer and bat boy for N.Y. Giants; 1st singing partner of Walter Winchell; teamed with Eddie Cantor in Gus Edward's Vaudeville Acts, 1910; 1st Broadway appearance in Shubert Gaieties of 1918; appeared in dramas The Jazz Singer, Joseph and His Brethren, The War Song; co-author with Fannie Brice in musical Sweet and Low; again teamed with Eddie Cantor for 2-year tour beginning at N.Y. Palace theatre; wrote and appeared in musical plays High Kickers, Show Time; joined 20th Century Fox as producer and author, 1943-63; produced several well known stage prodns.; chmn. bd. Israel Hotel Co., Inc.; toured in That Wonderful World of Vaudeville, 1975. Active City of Hope, Govt. of Israel, numerous other orgns. Mem. Nat. Vaudeville Artists (pres.). Clubs: Friars of Cal. (abbot); Jewish Theatrical of Am. (v.p.). Author: So Help Me (autobiography), 1943, Hello Momma, 1946; Elegy in Manhattan, 1961; This Way, Miss; Jessel Anyone; You Too Can Make A Speech; The Toastmaster General's Guide to Successful Public Speaking, 1969; The Toastmaster General's Favorite Jokes, 1973; (with John Austin) The World I Lived In, 1975. Address: Los Angeles, Calif. Died May 24, 1981.

JESSEN, CARL ARTHUR, sch. organization executive; b. Larimore, N.D., Apr. 15, 1887; A.B., Luther Coll., 1909; A.M., Northwestern U., 1922; student of Chicago, 1912-13, of Montpelier (France), 1919, Stanford, summer 1927; Sc.D. in edn. (hon.), Boston Univ., 1954; married Ethel Gage, July 28, 1921. Prin. of high schs., Granite Falls, Minn., Kalispell, Mont., Grand Rapids, and Red Wing, Minn., 1910-21; state supervisor of high schs., Mont., 1921-27; specialist in secondary education, United States Office of Edn., 1927-45; chief secondary sch. orgn. and supervision, 1945-50; chief of secondary schs., 1951-52; exec. sec. Cooperative Study Secondary Sch. Standards, 1952-60; mem. finance com. Nat. Assn. Secondary Sch. Prins., from 1960. Served as engr. AUS, with A.E.F., 1918-19. Sec. Nat. Com. Coordination in Secondary Edn., 1927-47; coordinator Nat. Survey of Secondary Edn., 1929-32; sec. Cooperative Study of Secondary Sch. Standards 1933-51. Recipient of Centennial Award for the Advancement of Secondary Education, Shattuck School, 1958. Mem. N.E.A., Nat. Soc. for Study of Edn., Am. Ednl. Research Assn., National Assn. Secondary School Principals, American Legion. Author: Mignonette and Other Poems, 1952. Author of high school courses of study for Montana, 1923-27; bulletins of Office of Edn.; contbr. to ednl. mags. Participant in sch. surveys. Home: Washington, D.C. Died June 19, 1978.

JESSUP, ANDREW SIMES, supt. schools; b. Madison, Ind., Dec. 30, 1885; s. Asa William and Hannah Ann (Welch) J.; B.S., Central Normal Coll., Danville, Ind., 1907; A.B., Ind. U., 1911; A.M., U. of Colo., 1926; m. Florence Ruby Schmidlap, of Madison, Ind., Sept. 2, 1907; 1 dau., Florence Genevieve. Teacher and prin. pub. schs., 1904-15; supt. pub. schs., Central City, Colo., 1915-17; prin. high sch., Cheyenne, Wyo., 1917-18, supt. schs. since 1918. Mem. N.E.A. (dept. of superintendents), Wyo. State Teachers Assn. (ex-pres.), Wyo. Tuberculosis Assn. (mem. exec. com.), Phi Delta Kappa. Baptist. Mason (32 deg.), Rotarian (pres. Cheyenne Club 1933-34). Home: Cheyenne, Wyo. *

JESSUP, ELON, author; b. N.Y. City, Dec. 11, 1885; s. John Colgate and Carrie (Huntington) J.; student U. of Rochester, N.Y., 1903-05; forestry course Utah Agrl. Coll., Logan, Utah, 1907-08; m. Mary Alden Hopkins, of Brookfield, Conn., Apr. 22, 1920. With U.S. Forest Service, in Utah, 1908; mem. Com. of Mercy Relief Expdn., and newspaper corr., Serbia, 1915; corr. Ford Peace Expdn., 1915-16; asst. editor "Adventure," 1916-17; asso. editor "Outing," 1917-21; free lance writer. Mem. Alpha Delta Phi. Clubs: Town Hall, Dutch Treat (New York). Author: Intimate Golf Talks (with J. D. Dunn), 1921; The Motor Camping Book, 1922; Roughing It Smoothly, 1923; Snow and Ice Sports, 1923; Camp Grub, 1924; The Boy's Book of Canoeing, 1926.*

JESSUP, JOHN KNOX, editor; b. Rochester, N.Y., Mar. 5, 1907; s. John Colgate and Louise (Foote) J.; A.B., Yale, 1928; m. Margaret Tarbox, Sept. 23, 1932; 1 son, John Knox; m. 2d, Eunice Clark Rodman, Sept. 11, 1937; children—Nathaniel Foote, Amos Huntington, Rebecca Phelps, Maria Forward. Asst. in English, Yale, 1928-29; asst. editor Yale Alumni Weekly, 1928-30; with J. Walter Thompson, advt., 1930-35; with Time, Inc., 1935-69, chief editorial writer Life mag., 1951-69; editorial broadcaster CBS Radio, 1971-76. Mem. Council Fgn. Relations, Sigma Delta Chi. Clubs: Yale, Century Assn. (N.Y.C.). Editor: The Ideas of Henry Luce, 1969; author: (collected works) The Third Estate, 1980. Home: Wilton, Conn. Died Oct. 26, 1979; buried Hillside Cemetery, Wilton.

JETT, DANIEL BOONE, prof. engring.; b. nr. Rewey, Lafayette County, Wis., July 4, 1886; s. Abraham and Jessie Ellen (Westrope) J.; student Mo. Sch. of Mines, 1907-08, Ohio Northern U., 1911; B.S. in C.E., Mo. Sch. of Mines, 1926; m. Louise Johannah Trauernicht, Aug. 18, 1921; children—Marie Louise, Daniel Boone, Dorothy Ellen. Chainman, rodman, insp. sewer constrn., San Benito (Tex.) Land & Water Co., Internat. Boundary Commn., M.K.&T. Ry., Kansas City Southern Ry., Northern La. Traction Company; rodman, instrumentman and chief of party M.P. R.R., Oct. 1913-May 1917 and Aug. 1919-July 1921; teacher mathematics and student Mo. Sch. of Mines, 1921-26; instr. civil engring., New Mex. State Coll., 1926-27, asst. prof., 1927-29, asso. prof., 1929-32, prof. since 1932, dean of engring., 1938-47, professor civil engring. since 1947; chairman New Mexico board registration for professional engineers and land surveyors. Served as private and private, 1st class, 12th Engrs. (light ry.), U.S. Army, May 1917-July 1919. Mem. Am. Soc. Civil Engrs., Soc. Promotion Engring. Edn., Tau Beta Pi, Lambda Chi Alpha. Methodist. Mason (K.T.). Rotarian. Home: Las Cruces, N.M. *

JEWETT, CHARLES WEBSTER, lawyer; b. Franklin, Ind., Jan. 7, 1884; s. Edward Parker and Mary Alma (Aten) J.; A.B., DePauw U., 1907; Harvard, 1910; m. Elizabeth Dougherty, Oct. 25, 1911. Practiced at Indianapolis since 1910; member firm Weyl & Jewett; former dir. Fletcher Trust Co. Rep. candidate for Congress, 1938. Chmn. Marion Co. (Ind.) Rep. Central Committee, 1914, 15, 16; Mayor of Indianapolis, 1918-22. Trustee DePauw U., Greencastle, Ind. Mem. Am., Ind. and Indianapolis bar assns., Phi Delta Theta (pres. Epsilon Province). Methodist. Mason (32 deg., Shriner), K.P., Elk. Home: Indianapolis. *

JOECKEL, CARLETON BRUNS (JOK'EL), librarian; b. Lake Mills, Wis., Jan. 2, 1886; s. John and Emma Wilhelmina (Bruns) J.; B.A., U. of Wis., 1908; B.L.S., N.Y. State Library Sch., Albany, 1910; M.A., Univ. of Mich., 1928; Ph.D., the University of Chicago, 1934; m. Emma H. Kelly, 1911 (div.); married 2d, Gladys E. Hatch, Nov. 27, 1929. Libr. sec. St. Louis Pub. Library, 1910-11; asst. reference librarian and supt. of circulation, U. of Calif. Library, 1911-14; librarian Berkeley Pub. Library, 1914-17, 1919-27; asso. prof. library science, U. of Mich., 1927-30, prof., 1930-35; prof. of library science, U. of Chicago, 1935-45, dean, Grad. Library Sch., U. of Chicago, 1942-45; prof. Sch. of Librarianship, U. of Calif., 1945-50; chairman Librarian's Committee, Library of Congress, for survey of processing departments, 1940. Served as 2d lieut., 1st lieut. and capt. 363d Inf., 91st Div. U.S. Army, 1917-19. Mem. Am. and Calif. library assns. Democrat. Clubs: Faculty. Author: The Pub. Libr. under the City-Manager Form of Government, 1931; The Government of the American Public Library, 1935. Library Service, 1938; (with Leon Carnovsky) A Metropolitan Library in Action: A Survey of the Chicago Public Library, 1940; A National Plan for Public Library Service (with Amy Winslow), 1948. Editor: Current Issues in Library Administration, 1939; Post-War Standards for Public Libraries, 1943; Library Extension: Problems and Solutions, 1946; Reaching Readers: Techniques of Extending Library Services, 1949. Contbr. library govt. and adminstrn. Home: Berkeley, Calif. Retired 1950. *

JOFFE, J(ACOB) S(AMUEL), prof. and pedologist; b. Russia, Sept. 1886; s. Israel and Tona (Zhiv) J.; student Baron-de-Hirsch Agrl. Sch., 1909-10; B.S., Rutgers U., 1918, Ph.D., 1922; m. Anna Hoffman, Dec. 24, 1917 (dec. Dec. 13, 1939); m. 2d, Esther Gitla Maimon, Aug. 3, 1940. Came to U.S., 1907, naturalized, 1915. Asst. soil microbiologist N.J. Agrl. Expt. Sta., 1919-23, chemist in soil research, 1923-25, research specialist in soils since 1945; asso. reearch in microbiology N.Y. Agrl. Expt. Sta., Geneva, N.Y., 1923; lecturer natural sci. Jewish Teachers Sem., N.Y., 1930-36; prof. pedology Rutgers U. since 1937. Mem. nat. com. for labor Israel; chmn. N.J. state com. for Histradut in Israel. Served as pvt. U.S. Army, 1918-19. Fellow A.A.A.S.; mem. Yiddish Sci. Inst. of N.Y. (bd. dirs. since 1940), Am. Soc. Agronomy, Soil Sci. Soc. of Am., Am. Geographic Soc., Sigma Xi, Phi Lambda Upsilon, Workmen's Circle Frat. Jewish religion. Author: several texts also sci. papers in English, Russian and Hebrew. Home: New Brunswick, N.J. *

JOHN, OTTO MARION, coll. dean; b. of Am. parents, Great Grimsby, Eng., Aug. 23, 1883; s. Adelbert Allen and Elsie Christina (Hansen) J.; A.B., Union Coll., College View, Neb., 1908; studied Ohio State U., 1909; M.S., George Washington U., 1916; grad. work, same univ., 1917-20; m. Deborah S. Secor, of Mt. Vernon, O., Aug. 9, 1911; children—Edward Allen, Donald Lee, Marian Jennilee. Head of science dept., Mt. Vernon (O.) Coll., 1908-14, Washington Missionary Coll., Takoma Park, D.C., 1914-18; asst. sec. edn. dept. Gen. Conf. Seventh Day Adventists, 1918-22; pres. Union Coll., 1922-25; dean Emmanuel Missionary Coll., since 1925. Home: Berrien Springs, Mich. *

JOHNS, DALE MARTIN, journalist; b. Iowa Falls, Iowa, Dec. 1, 1913; s. Lincoln Eugene and Veva (Martin) J.; B.A., U. Nebr., 1939; m. Ruth Dobson, June 6, 1939; children—Stephen, Michael, Martha. Reporter, bur. mgr. United Press, 1939-43; with U.P.I., 1946-76, Northeastern div. mgr., 1954-62, central div. mgr., Chgo., 1962-70, N. Am. bus. mgr., 1970-72, dir. personnel relations, 1972-76. Served to lt. (j.g.) USNR, 1943-46. Mem. Am. Soc. Journalists, Chgo. Press Vets.

Assn., Sigma Delta Chi (pres. New Eng. chpt. 1957-58). Episcopalian (vestry 1952-54). Clubs: Deadline of N.Y., Chgo. Press. Home: Riverside, Conn. Died Feb. 19, 1977; interred St. Paul's Episcopal Ch., Riverside.

JOHNS, JAY WINSTON, bus. exec.; b. Uniontown, Pa., July 14, 1888. Former pres., Atlas Fuel Corp., Pittsburgh, Pa.; dir. Va. Electric & Power Co., Charlottesville, Va. Pres., dir. Stonewall Jackson Meml., Lexington, Va.; bd. visitors Va. Mil. Inst.; trustee Va. Mus. Fine Arts, Richmond; pres. Va. Trust Historic Preservation. Clubs: Metropolitan (N.Y.C.); Collonnade; Commonwealth (Richmond). Home: Charlottesville, Va. Died Dec. 23, 1974.

JOHNS, RALPH STANLEY, certified pub. accountant; b. Oak Park, Ill., July 8, 1904; s. Albert Frederick and Gertrude Martha (Bartusch) J.; B.S. with high honors, U. Ill., 1925, M.S., 1926; m. Elizabeth Louise Florin, Sept. 2, 1933; children—Gordon Malcolm, Barbara Marilyn. Asso., Haskins & Sells, C.P.A.'s N.Y.C., 1926-78, partner, 1943-78, sr. resident partner, Chgo., 1951-69; pres. Assn. C.P.A. Examiners, 1958-59. Mem. Haskins and Sells Found.; trustee Village of Wilmette (Ill.). Mem. Am. Inst. Accountants, Am. Accounting Assn., Ill., N.J., N.Y. State socs. C.P.A.'s, U. Ill. Alumni Assn. (pres. 1969-71). Baptist. Clubs: Union League (Chicago); Royal Palm Yacht and Country (Boca Raton, Fla.). Author: Auditing (with Bell), 1952; Accountants' Working Papers (with Palmer and Bell), 1950; Written Contributions of Selected Accounting Practitioners, 1977. Home: Pompano Beach, Fla. Died Sept. 5, 1978.

JOHNSON, ALBIN IVER, univ. dean; b. Woburn, Mass., Jan. 27, 1924; s. Carl Albin and Ida (Bengson) J.; B.Sc., U. Toronto (Ont., Can.), 1946, Ph.D., 1950; M.Ch.E., Bklyn. Poly. Inst., 1948; m. Edith E. Cottrell, Dec. 27, 1950; children—Carl A., Elizabeth J., David R., June K. Research chem. engr. Woburn Chem. Corp., Harrison, N.J., 1946-48; asst. prof. Johns Hopkins, 1950-52; asst. prof. U. Toronto, 1952-55, asso. prof., 1955-61; asso. prof. McMaster U., 1961-62, prof., 1962-71, chmn., 1962-65; prof., dean engring. sci. U. Western Ont., London, 1971-77; pres. ENGSYS Ltd. Mem. Assn. Profl. Engrs. Ont. (councillor 1968-70), NRC (chmn. asso. com. automatic control 1971-76). Author (with others): Chemical Plant Simulation, 1971. Contbr. numerous articles to tech. jours. Home: London, Ont., Canada. Died Oct. 8, 1977.

JOHNSON, ARTHUR B., railroad exec.; b. 1886, West Pittston, Pa.; grad. Dickenson Coll., Carlisle, Pa., 1909. Vice pres. Erie R.R.; v.p. and dir. Erie Land & Improvement Co. of Pa., Indsl. Center Land Co.; dir. Chicago & Erie R.R. Co., N.Y., Susquehanna & Western R.R., Northern R.R. of N.J., Caldwell Ry.; gen. land and tax agent and dir. Buffalo Properties, Inc., New Jersey & New York R. R., Paterson & Hudson River R.R. Trustee Huron Rd. Hosp. Home: Shaker Heights. *

JOHNSON, B. ELEANOR, educator; b. Zumbrota, Minn., Nov. 16, 1886; d. Charles Emil and Bertha (Field) Johnson; B.S., U. of Pittsburgh, 1921; A.M., Columbia, 1923; Ph.D., U. of Chgo, 1931; unmarried. High sch. home economics teacher, Pittsburgh, 1917-20, Detroit, 1921-23; chmn. dept. textiles and clothing, Stout Inst., 1923-27; asst. prof. home economics, Kan. State Teachers Coll., Pittsburg, 1928-29; prof. home economics and dir. sch. of home economics, University of Arizona since 1933. Research assistant, committee on household management, Pres. Conf. on Home Bldg. and Home Ownership, 31. Mem. Am. Home Economics Assn. (regional councilor, com. chmn.), Am. Assn. Univ. Profs., Ariz. Home Economics Assn. (pres., councilor, com. chmn.), Pi Lambda Theta. Club: Altrusa (past pres.). Author: Household Employment in Chicago, Bull. of Women's Bur., U.S. Dept. of Labor, 1933. Contbr., occasional mag. articles. Home: Tucson, Ariz. *

JOHNSON, BRIARD POLAND, army officer; b. Lynn, Mass., Feb. 7, 1905; s. Justin Brown and Bertha (Poland) J.; B.S. in Civil Engring., Norwich U., 1927, LL.D., 1963; grad. Army Command and Gen. Staff Coll., 1947, Air War Coll., 1950; m. Helen Sigrid Nelson, June 15, 1929; children—Eleanor June (Mrs. John Merritt Archibald), Barbara Phyllis (Mrs. Charles F. Muckenbirn), Helen Sigrid (Mrs. Bernard Roy Johnson). Civil engr., 1927-33; commd. 2d lt. (Res.) cav., U.S. Army, 1927, advanced through grades to maj. gen., 1958; served in Morocco, Sicily, Normandy, No. France, Ardennes, Rhineland, Central Europe, World War II; comdr. 67th Armored Regt., 2d Armored Div., 1945-46; assigned Office Sec. Def. for Research and Devel., 1949; comdr. Combat Command B. 2d Armored Div., 1951-53; assigned U.S. Army Gen. Staff, research and devel. 1954; chief Mich. Mil. Dist., also comdr. Ft. Wayne, Mich., 1955; chief Army Maneuver Test and Evaluation Group, 1955-56; comdr. 8th U.S. Army Support Command, Korea, 1956-57, comdr. U.S. Mil. Assistance Group to Thailand, 1959-62; asst. chief of staff U.S. Continental Army Command, Ft. Monroe, Va., 1962-63, chief of staff, 1963. Trustee Norwich U., 1964-69. Decorated D.S.M., Silver Star, Legion of Merit, Bronze Star with 2 oak leaf clusters, D.S.M., numerous service medals; Legion of Honor, Croix de Guerre with palm (France); Order of Fatherland 1st class (USSR). Mem. Assn. U.S. Army, U.S. Armor Assn. Home: Williamsburg, Va. Died Mar. 23, 1980; buried Arlington Nat. Cemetery.

JOHNSON, CARLTON MYLES, editor; b. nr. Monroeville, Ala., Sept. 11, 1925; s. Henry Riley and Martha Izola (Wilson) J.; student U. Ga., Athens, 1947, at Columbus, 1948; m. Constance Pilkinton, Sept. 18, 1954. With Ledger, Columbus, Ga., 1946-77, editor Ledger and Sunday Ledger-Enquirer, 1962-68, exec. editor Ledger-Enquirer Newspapers, 1968-77. Mem. Citizens' Conf. Ga.'s Jud. System, 1966-77. Bd. dirs. Salvation Army, 1968-77. Served with USNR, 1943-46. Nieman fellow Harvard, 1954. Mem. Ga. Press Assn., Am. Soc. Newspaper Editors Presbyn. (elder). Kiwanian. Club: Big Eddy. Home: Columbus, Ga. Died Aug. 22, 1977.

JOHNSON, DOUGLAS VALENTINE, army officer, government official; born at Dansville, Virginia, September 27, 1900; s. Edgar T. and Edna L. (Oliver) J.; B.S. in C.E., Va. Mil. Inst., 1922; m. Helen J., Ingold, Dec. 28, 1938; children—Douglas Valentine, Jeanne L. Pvt. Va. N.G., 1922-23; commnd. 2d lt., F.A., U.S. Army, 1923, advanced through grades to maj. gen., 1955; various assignments, U.S., Philippines, 1923-42; operations div. War Dept. Gen. Staff, Washington, 1942-44; asst. G-3, VII Corps, U.K. and France, 1944; comdg. officer 223d F.A. Group, Pacific, 1944-46; chief of staff Western Pacific Base Command, also commndg. officer Army Ground Forces, Saipan, 1946-47; asst. G-3 1st Army, Governor's Island, 1947; staff Nat. Security Council, also asst. chief and chief plans div., G-3, Dept. of Army Gen. Staff, 1947-51; comdg. gen. 43 Inf. Div. Arty., Augsburg, Germany, 1952-53; asst. chief of staff G-3, also dep. chief of staff operations USAREUR, Heidelberg, Germany, 1953-55; dep. chief umpire Exercise Sage Brush, Langley Field, Va., 1955; dep. comdg. gen., also chief of staff 3d Army, Ft. McPherson, Ga., 1956-57; dir. plans and policy Office Joint Chiefs of Staff, 1958-60, ret. 1960; dir. policy review Office Asst. Sec. Def., 1960-64; cons. Research Analysis Corp., McLean, Va., 1965-77. Decorated Legion of Merit, D.S.M., Bronze Star Medal, Army Commendation Ribbon. Home: Alexandria, Va. Died Apr. 24, 1977.

JOHNSON, GEORGE D., hotel co. exec.; b. Manassas, Va., July 15, 1906; s. R. E. Lee and Emma C. (Dawson) J.; student pub. schs.; m. Lula M. Hixson, Oct. 8, 1932; 1 dau., Nancy Kathryn (Mrs. Frank J. Stanley III). Vice pres., gen. mgr. Washington Properties, Inc., 1931-63; sr. v.p., dir. Sheraton Corp. Am., Boston, 1963-73, dir. all Sheraton subsidiaries. Home: Boston, Mass. Died May 11, 1976.

JOHNSON, GEORGE TEWKSBURY, mfr.; b. Portsmouth, O., July 23, 1885; s. Albert Tracy and Margaret Fulton (Tewksbury) J.; grad. Univ. Sch., Cleveland, O., 1902; M.E., Sibley Coll., Cornell, 1906; m. Esther D. Sharp, Oct. 20, 1909 (died 1930), Children—George T., Albert T., Jane (Mrs. R. D. Webster); m. 2d, Florence Rodgers Jeffrey, Jan. 31, 1942. Entire career with The Buckeye Steel Castings Co., Columbus, O.; in foundry, openhearth and test depts., 1906-08, chief insp., 1908-12, prodn. engr., 1912-14, chief engr. production, 1914-28, 3d v.p., 1928-30, 2d v.p., 1930-36, 1st vice pres. in charge of sales and engring., 1936-45, pres. and gen. mgr., 1945-48. Dir. Buckeye Steel Castings Co., Huntington Nat. Bank, Columbus, O. Mem. Am. Soc. M.E., Transportation Assn. of Am., Ry. Bus. Assn., Army Ordnance Assn., Alpha Delta Phi. Republican. Clubs: Cloud (New York); Columbus, Rocky Fork Hunt and Country (Columbus). Home: Columbus. *

JOHNSON, GERALD WHITE, journalist; b. Riverton, N.C., Aug. 6, 1890; s. Archibald and Flora Caroline (McNeill) J.; A.B., Wake Forest Coll., 1911; Litt.D., 1928; studies U. of Toulouse, France; LL.D., Coll. of Charleston, S.C., 1935; LL.D., U. N.C., 1937; D.C.L., U. South, 1942; LL.D., U. N.C. at Greensboro, 1966; Litt.D., Goucher Coll., 1969; m. Kathryn Hayward, Apr. 22, 1922; 2 daughters. Established Thomasville (N.C.) Davidsonian, 1910; with Lexington (N.C.) Dispatch, 1911-13; with Greensboro (N.C.) Daily News, 1913-24; prof. journalism U. N.C., 1924-26; editorial writer Balt. Evening Sun, 1926-39, The Sun, 1939-43, free-lance, 1943-80; news commentator on station WAAM-TV, 1952-54; contbg. editor The New Republic, 1954-80; author mystery novels under name Charles North. Served with 321st Infantry, 81st Div., U.S. Army, 1917-19; with A.E.F. France 1 yr. Recipient DuPont Commentators' award, 1953; Sidney Hillman Found. award, 1954; George Foster Peabody award, 1954; Gold medal State of N.C., 1964; Andrew White medal Loyola Coll., Balt., 1969. Mem. Phi Beta Kappa. Democrat. Author: The Story of Man's Work (with W.R. Hayward), 1925; The Undefeated, 1926; What Is News? 1926; Andrew Jackson-An Epic in Homespun, 1927; Randolph of Roanoke—A Political Fantastic, 1929; By Reason of Strength, 1930; Number Thirty Six, 1933; The Secession of the Southern States, 1933; The Sunpapers of Baltimore (with Frank R. Kent, H.L. Mencken and Hamilton Owens), 1937; A Little Night Music, 1937; The Wasted Land, 1937; America's Silver Age, 1939; Roosevelt: Dictator or Democrat?, 1941; American Heroes and Hero-Worship, 1943; Woodrow Wilson, 1944; An Honorable Titan, 1946; The First Captain, 1947; Liberal's Progress, 1948; Our English Heritage, 1949; Incredible Tale, 1950; This American People, 1951; Pattern for Liberty, 1952; Lunatic Fringe, 1957; Peril and Promise, 1958; The Lines Are Drawn, 1958; America: A History for Peter (3 vols.), 1959-60; The Man Who Feels Left Behind, 1960; Hod-Carrier, 1964; Communism; An American's View; Franklin D. Roosevelt, 1967; The Imperial Republic, 1972; America-Watching, 1976. Clubs: West Hamilton Street; Century (N.Y.C.). Home: Baltimore, Md. Died Mar. 22, 1980; inurned Green Mount Cemetery, Baltimore.

JOHNSON, GUY DIBBLE, corp. exec.; b. New Orleans, Oct. 8, 1885; s. Homer Alonso and Mary (Dibble) J.; ed. pub. schs. New Orleans; m. Helen Perez. Railroad work in Central Am., 1902-05; with Nat. Paper & Type Co., N.Y.C., 1907, v.p., gen. mgr. Buenos Aires br., 1930-45, pres., 1945-53; pres. Guy D. Johnson, Inc., 1953—. Clubs: Metropolitan (N.Y.C.). Home: New York City NY. *

JOHNSON, HAROLD LESTER, astronomer, educator; b. Denver, Apr. 17, 1921; s. Averill C. and Marie (Sallach) J.; B.S., U. Denver, 1942; Ph.D., U. Calif., Berkeley, 1948; Dr. honoris causa, U. Mex., 1978; m. Mary Elizabeth Jones, July 1, 1954; children—August Harold, Selma Marie. Asst. prof. astronomy U. Chgo., 1950-52; astronomer Lowell Obs., Flagstaff, Ariz., 1952-59; prof. astronomy U. Tex., 1959-61, chmn. dept., 1961; research prof. lunar and planetary lab. U. Ariz., 1962-69, asso. dir. lab., 1967-69, astronomer Steward Obs., research prof. Optical Scis. Center, 1969-74; investigator titular Instituto de Astronomia, Universidad Nacional Autonomo de Mexico, Mexico, D.F., 1968-80; dir. Dept. de Física Aplicada, Centro de Investigación Científica y Educación Superior de Ensenada, Baja California, Mexico, 1973-74; research prof., astronomer Steward Obs., U. Ariz., Tucson, 1974-79. Mem. Am. Astron. Soc. (Helen B. Warner prize 1956), Optical Soc. Am., Instrument Soc. Am., Astron. Soc. Pacific, N.Y. Acad. Scis., Internat. Astron. Union, Nat. Acad. Scis. Address: Mexico City. Died Apr. 2, 1980.

JOHNSON, HARRY GORDON, economist; b. Toronto, Ont., Can., May 26, 1923; s. Henry Herbert and Frances (Muat) J.; B.A., U. Toronto, 1943, M.A., 1947; B.A., U. Cambridge (Eng.), 1946, M.A., 1951; A.M., Harvard, 1948, Ph.D., 1958; M.A., Manchester (Eng.) U., 1960; LL.D., St. Francis Xavier U., N.S., Can., 1965, U. Windsor, Ont. Canada, 1966, Queen's U., Can., 1967, U. Sheffield, 1969, Carleton U. (Canada), 1970, U. Manchester, 1972, U. Western Ont., 1973; m. Elizabeth Scott Serson, May 28, 1948; children—Steven Ragnar, Karen Eve. Came to U.S., 1959. Lectr., Cambridge U., also fellow King's Coll., 1949-56; prof. econ. theory U. Manchester, 1956-59; prof. econs. U. Chgo., 1959-74; prof. London (Eng.) Sch. Econs. and Polit. Sci., 1966-74; Charles F. Grey Distinguished Service prof. U. Chgo., 1974-77. Wicksell lect., 1968; Johnsson lectr., 1970, de Vries lectr., 1971; Irving Fisher vis. rof. econs. Yale, 1972-73; Skelton Clark vis. prof. Queen's U., Kingston, Ont., Can., 1975; Commonwealth Prestige fellow, New Zealand, 1975. Mem U.S. Rev. Com Balance of Payments Statistics, 1963-65. Served with inf. Royal Canadian Army, 1944-46. Fellow Brit. Acad., Econometric Soc.; mem. Canadian Polit. Sci. Assn. (pres. 1965-66). Am. Assn. (exec. com. 1964-66), Am. Acad. of Arts and Scis., Royal Econ. Soc., Eastern Econ. Assn. (pres-elect 1975-76). Author: International Trade and Economic Growth, 1958; Money, Trade and Economic Growth, 1962; The Canadian Quandary, 1963; The World Economy at the Crossroads, 1965; Economic Policies Toward Less Developed Countries, 1967; Essays in Monetary Economics, 1967; Comparative Cost and Commercial Policy Theory for a Developing World Economy, 1968; The Theory of Tariffs, 1971; The Two-Sector Model of General Equilibrium, 1971; Macroeconomics and Monetary Theory, 1972; Inflation and the Monetarist Controversy, 1972; Further Essays in Monetary Economics, 1973; The Theory of Income Distribution, 1973. General Equilibrium Analysis, 1974; Of Economics and Society, 1975. Home: Chicago, Ill. Died May 8, 1977.

JOHNSON, HAYDEN BRIGGS, city planner; b. Cleve., Apr. 24, 1917; s. Roger Arthur and Elizabeth (Briggs) J.; B.A. Amherst Coll., 1937; B. Arch., Columbia, 1941, M.S. in Planning and Housing, 1942; m. Jean Ruth Noland, Oct. 15, 1945; children—Courtney Hayden and Hardy Elizabeth (twins). Community planner TVA, 1942-44; exec. dir. Tenn. Planning Commn., 1944-48, Poughkeepsie (N.Y.) Area Devel. Assn., 1948-51; city mgr., Poughkeepsie, 1952-55; chief planning div. Port Authority of N.Y. and N.J., 1955-61, dep. dir. port devel., 1961-66, dep. dir. planning and devel., 1966-76. Bd. dirs. Am. Soc. Planning Ofcls., 1953-57, pres., 1962-63; bd. dirs. Citizens Housing and Planning Council N.Y.; U.S. mem. bur. Internat. Fedn. Housing and Planning, 1967-74. Mem. Am. Inst. Planners (pres.

N.Y. Met. chpt. 1963-65). Internat. City Mgrs. Assn., Am. Soc. Public Adminstrn. Episcopalian. Club: Poughkeepsie Tennis. Home: Port Washington, N.Y. Died May 4, 1976.

JOHNSON, HERBERT FISK, business exec.; born Racine, Wis., Nov. 15, 1899; s. Herbert F. and Helen (Converse) J.; A.B., Cornell, 1922; LL.D., Northland Coll., 1958, U. Wis., 1963; L.H.D., Carthage Coll., 1963; m. Irene Purcell, 1941; children—Karen Andrea (Mrs. W. H. Keland), Samuel Curtis. Chmn. S. C. Johnson & Son, Inc., Racine; chmn. bd., dir. S. C. Johnson & Son, Ltd., Brantford, Ont., Can., S. C. Johnson & Son, Ltd., Frimley Green, Eng.; bd. directors Johnson's Wax Nederland N.V., S. C. Johnson & Son Italian, Milan, Italy, S. C. Johnson & Son Pty. Ltd., Rosebery, N.S.W. Australia; dir.-partner La Johnson Francaise, St. Denis, Seine, France; member. Midwest adv. board Lumbermens Mut. Cas. Co., Chgo.; dir. Am. Motorists Ins. Co. (Chgo.). Hon. mem. exec. com. region 7 Boy Scouts Am.; hon. dir. Racine Community Chest; hon. trustee Council of Profit Sharing Industries; trustee Profit Sharing Research Found. Trustee James S. Kemper Found., Cornell U., Northland Coll., Asheville (N.C.) Sch.; dir. U. Wis. Found. Decorated Chevalier Nat. Order of So. Cross (Brazil), 1957. Mem. Nat. Indsl. Conf. Bd., U.S. Com. Refugees, Royal Society of Arts London, International Chamber of Commerce (exec. com. U.S. council). Clubs: Am. (London), Racine Country; University (Milw.); University (Chgo.); Metropolitan (N.Y.C.); Bohemian (San Francisco). Home: Racine, Wis. Died Dec. 13, 1978.

JOHNSON, HERBERT MARTIN, lawyer; b. Woodhull, Ill., May 11, 1904; s. Otto A. and Emma A. (Samuelson) J.; A.B., Augustana Coll., 1926; postgrad. U. Chgo., 1927-28; J.D., Northwestern U., 1932; m. Shirley Elizabeth Oliver, Feb. 6, 1932 (dec. Aug. 1956); children—Judith E. (Mrs. Steve R. Brown), James; m. 2d, Gladys P. Murray, May 17, 1958; 1 dau., Marilyn R. (Mrs. Richard Fredrichsen). Instr. English, Harvard Sch. for Boys 1927-28; admitted to Ill. bar, 1933; Schuyler, Wienfeld & Hennessy, Chgo., 1929-37; atty. Chgo. Rapid Transit Co., 1937-47; gen. atty. Chgo. N. Shore & Milw. Ry. Co., Chgo., 1947-49; former sr. mem. firm Johnson, Zahler, Campbell, Boughner & Stitt, Chgo.; sr. v.p., gen. counsel, sec. Ill. Mid-Continent Life Ins. Co., 1957-64, pres., 1964; pres. Combination Investments, Inc., 1963-65; then sr. mem. law firm Johnson, Snow, Holmgren and Burden; free-lance writer. Mem. Ill. Senate from 19th Dist., 1956-58, Chmn. bd. dirs. Beverly YMCA, 1951-52; pres. bd. trustees Garrett Theol. Sem., 1952-71; pres Ridge Civic Council, 1948-50. Recipient Outstanding Meth. Churchman award, 1952; Outstanding Citizen citation Augustana Coll., 1956; voted outstanding senator Ill. News All-Alumni, Ill. newspapers and Ind. Voters Ill., 1956. Mem. Am. Ill., Chgo. bar assns., Am. Judicature Soc., Chgo. Art Inst. (life), Chgo. Natural History Mus., Nordic Law Club Newcomen Soc. Republican. Methodist (lay leader, 1946-52). Clubs: University, Executives (Chgo.). Home: Lakeland, Fla. Died Mar. 3, 1976.

JOHNSON, HUGH ALBERT, stock broker; b. Cleve., Aug. 9, 1907; s. Charles Edward and Anna Elizabeth (Edwards) J.; A.B., Dartmouth, 1930; m. Alyce Elizabeth Murther, July 8, 1931; children—Lynn (Mrs. William Kopman), Anne (Mrs. Michael Kenefick), Hugh Albert, Stuart R. With Harris, Forbes & Co., N.Y.C. 1930-33, George D.B. Bonbright & Co., 1933-50; chmn. Hugh Johnson & Co., Inc. Buffalo, 1950-70; pres. Johnson's Charts, Inc. Your Tomorrow, Inc. Club: Dartmouth (N.Y.C.). Author: Trustee Investor and Making Money with Mutual Funds, 1955; 25 edits. Johnson's Charts, from 1949. Home: Buffalo, N.Y. Died Nov. 23, 1977.

JOHNSON, IVER MAGNI, clergyman; b. Fagerhult, Sweden, Feb. 27, 1885; s. John Magnus and Caroline (Gustafson) J.; student Knox Coll., 1907-10; B.A., Northwestern U., 1912; B.D., Garrett Bibl. Inst., Evanston, Ill., 1914; student U. of Jena (Germany), 1914-15; student U. of Chicago, 1915-16; hon. D.D., Ill. Wesleyan U., 1928; m. Naomi Nyman, June 23, 1914; children—Bruce Willard, Marjorie Eleanor. Ordained Meth. Minister, 1916; pastor, Bradley, Ill., 1916-18, Varna, 1918-20, Milford, 1920-24, Farmington, 1924-25, Pekin, 1925-27, Springfield, 1928-31; pastor Grace Ch., Decatur, 1932-41, Chicago Temple, 1941-43, Calvary Methodist Church, 1943-50, Julia Gay Memorial Ch. since 1950. Mem. Phi Beta Kappa. Republican. Address: Chicago. *

JOHNSON, JACK VERNON, economist, educator; b. Ennis, Tex., Feb. 3, 1884; s. William Scott and Sallie (Webb) J.; A.B., U. of Tex., 1921, A.M., 1924, Ph.D., 1931; m. Nancy Belle Turner, July 8, 1907; 1 dau., Rita Pauline (Mrs. Robert Eden Adams). Supt. of schs., Palmer, Tex., 1908-17; admitted to Tex. bar, 1921; teacher of social studies, Oak Cliff High Sch., Dallas, Tex., 1922-25; prof. economics, North Tex. State Coll., Denton, 1925-33, dir. dept. of economics and sociology since 1933, dean, Grad. Sch. since 1943; adminstrv. consultant to Fed. Relief Adminstrn. in Tex., 1935-36; lecture courses for the Radio Forum of Dallas Civic Fedn., 1938. Mem. Texas Legislature, 1917-21, chmn. edn. com. of House, 1919-21. Served as public mem. W.L.B. Panel, 8th Region, 1942-45. Made economic survey of the Southwest for the Aviation Enterprise in its application to the Civil Aeronautics Bd. for a certificate of convenience and necessity, known as The Texas-Oklahoma Case, 1944. Mem. Am. Economics Assn., Am. Assn. U. Profs., Southwestern Social Sci. Assn. (chmn. Economics sect. 1936), Tex. Bar Assn., Tex. State Teachers Assn., Texas Coll. Classroom Teachers Assn. Home: Denton, Tex. *

JOHNSON, JAMES, librarian; b. Roswell, N.Mex., June 28, 1917; s. Leonard J. and Blanche (Davenport) J.; B.A., Eastern N.Mex. Coll., 1941; B.S. in L.S., U. Denver, 1947; m. Leah Johnson, June 2, 1939; children—Timothy, Robert, Judith. Tchr., N.Mex. pub. schs., 1936-47; asst. librarian N.W. Mo. State Coll., Maryville, 1948-49, librarian, 1949-72, chmn. dept. library sci., 1949-79. Danforth asso., 1956-80. Mem. Mo. Library Assn. Kiwanian (pres. 1967). Home: Spotsylvania, Va. Died May 15, 1980.

JOHNSON, KENNETH LEROY, physiologist, educator; b. Wausa, Nebr., May 24, 1914; s. Victor August and Mathilda (Anderson) J.; B.S., Bethany (Kans.) Coll., 1934; M.S., U. So Calif., 1940, Ph.D., 1950; m. Katherine Louise Watts, June 5, 1938. Instr. sci and speech Canton (Kans.) High Sch., 1934-37; asst. prof. biol. sci., dean men Bethany Coll., 1937-43; instr. Navy V-5 Program, U. Kans. 1943-44; instr. physiology Iowa State Coll., 1944-45; instr. biol. sci., dean men Reedley (Calif) Jr. Coll., 1945-46; asst. prof. physiology San Jose (Calif.) State Coll., 1947-51; mem. faculty Long Beach (Calif.) State U., 1951-76, prof. physiology, 1952-76, chmn. div. natural sci., 1952-67; mem. Calif. State Colls. State Acad. Senate, 1968-71; spl. research hypothermia-metabolism relationships. Mem. A.A.A.S. Calif., So. Calif. acads. scis., Sigma Xi, Pi Delta Kappa, Phi Kappa Phi. Home: Long Beach, Calif. Died Sept. 5, 1976.

JOHNSON, LEE SALTONSTALL, aircraft co. exec.; b. Montville, Conn., Sept. 12, 1903; s. Frederick Allen and Grace (Lee) J.; B.A., Yale, 1926; m. Jean Mulligan, Sept. 12, 1933; children—Kathleen (Mrs. F. Donald Brigham, Jr.), Susanne, Edwin L. Various prodn. assignments Pratt & Whitney Aircraft div. East Hartford, Conn., 1929-41, asst. to factory mgr., 1941-44, exec. asst. to gen. mgr., 1944-55; sr. asst. gen. mgr. Sikorsky Aircraft div. United Aircraft Corp., 1955-56, div. pres., 1957-68; v.p. United Aircraft Corp., East Hartford, 1957-68; dir. Bullard Co., Conn. Nat. Bank of Bridgeport, Bridgeport Hydraulic Co.; trustee People's Savs. Bank, Bridgeport. Bd. dirs. Bridgeport Hosp., Bridgeport Engrng. Inst., YMCA; trustee Mus. of Art, Sci. and Industry; adv. com. Coll. Bus. Adminstrn., U. Bridgeport. Mem. Mfrs. Assn. (exec. bd.). Home: Fairfield, Conn. Died Apr. 23, 1978.

JOHNSON, MAURICE O., educator; b. Rosemont, Nebr., July 18, 1913; s. Oscar Theodore and Alice Welthia (Cook) J.; A.B., U. Nebr., 1935, A.M., 1936; Ph.D., Columbia, 1949; m. Nancy Coe Dilworth, Oct. 21, 1945; children—Laurie (Mrs. Robert Lopatin), Kate, Scott Dilworth, Amy. Instr. English lit. and lang. U. Nebr., 1936-38, Carnegie Inst. Tech., 1939-42; asst. prof. Syracuse U., 1948-50; mem. faculty U. Pa., 1950-78, prof. English, 1962-78, chmn. grad. English dept., 1962-65; vis. lectr. Columbia, summer 1956. Served with AUS, 1942-46. Mem. Modern Lang. Assn., Delta Upsilon, Sigma Upsilon. Author: Walt Whitman as a Critic of Literature, 1938; The Sin of Wit: Jonathan Swift as a Poet, 1950; Fielding's Art of Fiction, 1961; (with Kitagaki and Williams) Gulliver's Travels and Travelers to Japan, 1976; also articles; contbr. to English Writers of the Eighteenth Century, 1971; editor The History of Nourjahad (Frances Sheridan), 1977. Asso. editor Prairie Schooner, 1933-38; adv. editor Satire Newsletter, 1964-73. Home: Swarthmore, Pa. Died Nov. 14, 1978.

JOHNSON, MORDECAI WYATT, univ. pres.; b. Paris, Tenn., Jan. 12, 1890; s. Rev. Wyatt and Carolyn (Freeman) J.; prep. edn., Acad. of Roger Williams U., Nashville, Tenn. and Howe Inst., Memphis, A.B., Morehouse Coll. (colored). Atlanta, Ga., 1911, LL.D., 1935; A.B., U. of Chicago, 1913; B.D., Rochester Theol. Sem. 1921; S.T.M., Harvard Univ., 1922; D.D., Howard Univ., Washington, 1923, Gammon Theol. Sem., Atlanta, 1928; LL.D., Delaware State Coll. 1948. Colby Coll., 1950, Mich. State Coll., 1955, Atlanta University, 1960, Virginia State University; D.H.L., Temple University, 1954; D.C.L., University Liberia, 1956; married Anna Ethelyn Gardner, Dec. 25, 1916; children—Carolyn Elizabeth, Mordecai Wyatt, Archer Clement, William Howard, Anna Faith. Prof. English, later prof. economics and history, Morehouse Coll. 1911-13; student pastor Second Bapt. Ch., Mumford. N.Y., 1913-16; student sec. Internat. Com. Y.M.C.A., 1916-17; ordained Bapt. ministry, 1916; pastor First Ch., Charleston, W.Va, 1917-26; pres. Howard U., 1926-60, thereafter emeritus, Dir., del. Atlantic Congress, NATO Parliamentaries Conference, London, 1959. Member advisory council for the Virgin Islands; adv. council, Nat. Youth Adminstrn.: nat. adv. council on edn., Am. Youth Commn.; dir., nat council United Negro Coll. Fund; gen. exec. bd. Nat. Religion and Labor Found; vice chmn. Nat. Council Prevention of War; dir. Nat. Council Christians and Jews Decorated Order of Varco Minez de Balboa. Panama: Order of Star of Honor with Grand Cordon, Ethiopia, Home: Washington, D.C.

JOHNSON, NUNNALLY, writer; b. Columbus, Ga., Dec. 5, 1897; s. James Nunnally and Pearl (Patrick) J.; educated grade and high schs., Columbus; m. Dorris Bowdon, Feb. 4, 1940; children—Christie, Roxanna, Scott Bowdon; children by previous marriages—Marjorie, Nora. Newspaperman, 1916; reporter on Columbus Enquirer Sun, Savannah (Ga.) Press, N.Y. Tribune, Bklyn. Daily Eagle, N.Y. Herald Tribune; columnist Bklyn. Daily Eagle, N.Y. Evening Post and PM; writer stories and articles for Saturday Evening Post and other mags.; writer, producer of films, from 1932, writer screenplays. The House of Rothschild; The Country Doctor; Jesse James; Grapes of Wrath; Holy Matrimony; The Gunfighter; The Mudlark; The Desert Fox; How to Marry a Millionaire. Wrote, produced and directed Night People; Black Widow; Oh, Men, Oh. Women; The Three Faces of Eve. Wrote and directed: The Man in the Gray Flannel Suit; writer screenplay The World of Henry Orient, (with Lukas Heller) The Dirty Dozen, 1967. Served in the U.S. Army, 1916-18. Author: There Ought to Be a Law (short stories), 1930. Home: Hollywood, Calif. Died Mar. 25, 1977.

JOHNSON, ROBERT DAVIS, ex-congressman; b. nr. Slater, Mo., Aug. 12, 1883; s. Wm. Harvey and Sarah Jane (Davis) J.; ed. high sch., Portland, Ind., 1898-1901; m. Frances F. Speck, Jan. 18, 1905; children—J. D. (dec.), Thelma F. (Mrs. Morrison D. Fenner), Inez L. (Mrs. Joe Price Frerking), Robert E. Lee, Ella Mary. Deputy clk. Circuit Court, Saline Co., Mo., 1907-15, clk., 1915-23; admitted to Mo. bar, 1917; pros. atty. Saline Co., 1924-28; mem. 72d Congress (1931-33), 7th Mo. Dist.; mem. firm Johnson and Bacon. Mem. Mo. Bar Assn. Democrat. Mem. Disciples of Christ Ch. Mason. (Shriner), K.P., Modern Woodman. Club: Marshall Country. Home: Marshall, Mo. *

JOHNSON, ROBERT EDWARD, gas co. exec.; b. Ottumwa, Iowa, July 5, 1921; s. Carl William and Beulah Margaret (Boyles) J.; B.A., George Washington U., 1950; m. Alice Charline Chandler, July 14, 1946; children—Robert Carl, Deborah Lea. Financial analyst SEC, Washington, 1941-57; asst. treas. Mich.-Wis. Pipe Line Co., Washington, 1958-62; v.p., controller Wis. Gas Co., Milw., 1963-76. Served with USCGR, 1942-46. Episcopalian. Clubs: Univ., Milw. Yacht (Milw.). Home: Milwaukee, Wis. Died Apr. 15, 1976.

JOHNSON, ROBERT EMERSON LAMB, ret. mcht.; b. Phila., Aug. 24, 1905; s. Howard Cooper and Edith (Lamb) J.; A.B., Swarthmore Coll., 1927; postgrad. Harvard Bus. Sch., 1929; m. Mary Livingston Marshall, Sept. 14, 1929; children—Anne Livingston (Mrs. Clark), Robert Emerson Lamb. Service mgr., asst. buyer, br. store mgr. Strawbridge & Clothier, Phila., 1929-42; exec. v.p. Good House Stores, Inc., Phila., 1946-48; successively asst. v.p., v.p., exec. v.p. and dir. Woodward & Lothrop, Inc., Washington, 1948-73, later chmn. bd., chief exec. officer, dir.; dir., chmn. exec. com. Frederick Atkins, Inc., N.Y.C., 1955-56, pres., 1957, chmn. bd., 1958-59; dir., mem. exec. com. Fed. Res. Bank Richmond, 1960-67. Bd. dirs. Maine Coast Meml. Hosp.; pres. Gibson Island Corp., 1969, also dir. Served to lt. comdr. USNR, 1942-46. Mem. Met. Washington Bd. Trade (dir. 1962-65), Dixie Dist. Lightning Class Assn. (commodore 1953), Central Soup Soc. (past v.p., dir.), Pa. Soc., Newcomen Soc., Gibson Island Yacht Squadron, Eta Mu Pi, Delta Upsilon. Mem. Soc. Friends. Clubs: Northeast Harbor Fleet (Maine); Causeway, (pres. 1970-72, dir.) (Southwest Harbor, Maine); Met. (Washington); Alfalfa; Gibson Island (dir., sec. 1967-69); Southwest Harbor Fleet (commodore 1963-65). Home: Gibson Island, Md. Died Mar. 12, 1977.

JOHNSON, ROY EVERARD, writer; b. Buffalo, July 10, 1899; s. Edwin Henry and Mayme Belle (Armstrong) J.; student Alexander Hamilton Bus. Inst., 1919-21, Millard Fillmore Coll., 1922, Canisius Coll., 1935-36; m. Catherine Koenig, Jan. 1, 1918; children—Theodore Roy, David Ivan. Asst. supt. King Iron Works, Buffalo, 1920; various sales positions, 1922-32; entered veterans service work with Am. Legion, 1932; joined nat. staff Am. Red Cross, 1935; established nat. training sch. for Red Cross war workers, 1942; inspected overseas operations, South Pacific and North Africa, 1943; supervised expansion of Red Cross Services to veterans, 1944-45; assistant dir. pub. relations Nat. Hdqrs. A.R.C., past director of Office Pub. Information; free-lance writer; member of the President's com. on nat. "employe the physically handicapped" week. Mem. Vets. Adminstrn. nat. adv. com. on voluntary services. Mem. nat. public relations adv. council United Community Funds and Councils of Am. Served with North Sea Mine Force, United States Navy, World War I; retired as ensign, S.C., USNR, 1931. Mem. Nat. Pub. Relations Council (bd. dirs.), Pub. Relations Soc. Am., American Legion, Disabled American Veterans, Veterans Fgn. Wars, Vets. World War I. Odd Fellow. Clubs: National Press, Toastmasters (past area governor), Post Mortem (Washington); Old

Dominion Boat (Alexandria, Va.). Author: (booklet) Public Relations Roles for Everyone. Home: Tavares, Fla. Died Aug. 25, 1980.

JOHNSON, SHERMAN ELLSWORTH, econ. cons.; b. Scandia, Minn., July 31, 1896; s. Emil and Eva (Johnson) J.; B.S., U. Minn., 1924, M.S., 1926; Ph.D., Harvard, 1938; m. Evelyn Hedin, June 27, 1925; children—Lenore (Mrs. W.W. Cowan), Paul, Katherine (Mrs. R.R. Nelson). Instr. agrl. econs. U. Minn., 1924-25; asst. economist La. State U., 1925; asst., asso. prof. Mont. State Coll., 1926-29; head, dept. agrl. econs. S.D. State Coll., 1930-33; wheat specialist Brookings Instn., 1933-34; regional dir. land utilization program U.S. Dept. Agr., 1934-36; prin. agrl. economist Bur. Agrl. Econs., 1936-37, head. div. farm mgmt. and costs, 1937-46, asst. chief Bur. Agrl. Econs., 1946-53, dir. farm and land mgmt. research Agrl. Research Service, 1954-56, chief economist, 1957-60; dep. adminstr. Econ. Research Service 1961-65, collaborator, 1965-73; econ. cons., from 1965. Dir., Food Prodn. Br., War Food Adminstrn., World War II. Recipient Outstanding Achievement award U. Minn., 1956; Distinguished Service award Dept. Agr., 1958; Pres.'s award Distinguished Civilian Service, 1963. Fellow Am. Farm Econs. Assn. (pres. 1943); mem. Internat. Assn. Agrl. Economists (hon. life mem.; pres. 1956-61), Am. Econ. Assn., Agrl. History Soc., Alpha Zeta, Gamma Sigma Delta. Presbyn. Sr. author: Managing a Farm; Getting Started in Farming; author From the St. Croix to the Potomac—Reflections of a Bureaucrat; also agrl. and tech. bulls. Contr. articles to profl. jours. Home: Strasburg, Va. Died Apr. 28, 1978.

JOHNSON, THOMAS E., educator; b. Thetford, Ont., Can., Mar. 10, 1883; s. Herbert J. and Rebecca (Howard) J.; U. of Mich., 1901-03, 1910-11; A.B., Alma (Mich.) Coll., 1916; post-grad. work, U. of Mich., 1919, 20; LL.D., Lincoln Memorial U., 1920, Olivet, 1923, Alma, 1923; M.Ed., Mich. State Normal Coll., 1922; m. Mildred M. Milks, of Saginaw, Mich., Aug. 7, 1907; children—Stanley Howard, Patricia Hope. In U.S. since 1889; teacher and head of schs. until 1910; supt. city schs., Onaway, Mich., 1910-14, Coldwater, 1914-19; supt. pub. instrn., Mich., 1919-27; pres. Mich. Commercial Corporation since 1927. President Florida Tourist Schools, Lansing Home Sites Corporation; v.p. Mich. Surety Co.; dir. Peoples State Bank (Plymouth), Mich. Employers Casualty Co., Wolverine Ins. Co., Raab Realty Co. V.p. Mich. State Bd. of Edn., 1917-19. Mem. N.E.A., Nat. Council of Edn. Republican. Episcopalian. Mason. Author of sch. code of Mich., and of work on School Finance. Speaker, and writer of short articles on ednl. topics. Address: Lansing, Mich. *

JOHNSON, VICTOR LONG, sugar co. exec.; b. Norfolk, Va., Aug. 24, 1914; s. Lindsay Franklin and Flora (Long) J.; B.S., Columbia, 1936, Chem.E., 1937; m. Erica E. Ehrentraut, Feb. 21, 1942; children—Linda Ann, Erica Ellen, David Lindsay. With Amstar Corp., 1937-76, v.p., 1949-71, sr. v.p., 1971-76, also dir.; chmn. Internat. Sugar Research Found., 1968-70, dir., 1970-73; com. mem. Nutrition Found., mem. industry liaison panel Food and Nutrition Bd., Nat. Acad. Scis. Mem. Am. Inst. Chem. Engrs., Am. Chem. Soc., Inst. Food. Technologists. Home: Sparta, N.J. Died Oct. 21, 1976.

JOHNSON, WALTER SAMUEL, lumber co. exec., philantropist; b. East Saginaw, Mich., Nov. 10, 1884; s. Alfred A. and Mary (Calkins) J.; LL.B., U. Calif., 1914; m. Mabel Brady, Nov. 18, 1914; m. 2d, Pauline Cook, May 11, 1938 (div. 1964); m. 3d, Margherita Dan, Apr. 3, 1965. Circulation mgr. San Francisco Bull.; pres., mgr. Johnson's Inc., book stores, 1906-11; admitted to Calif. bar, 1914, practiced in San Francisco, 1914-17; organized Am. Box Corp., now Am. Forest Products Corp., pres. 1928-56, chmn. bd., 1956-70; pres. Friden, Inc., 1945-63, chmn. bd., 1963-65. Served to capt. Signal Corps U.S. Army, 1917-19. Mason (32, Shriner). Clubs: Bohemian, Castlewood Country, Commonwealth. Donated series of gifts, eventually totalling $4 million, for restoration of Palace of Fine Arts, San Francisco. Home: Pleasanton, Calif. Died 1978.

JOHNSTON, ARCHIBALD ANDERSON, college pres.; b. New Galilee, Pa., Aug. 18, 1882; s. William Pollock and Clara (Anderson) J.; B. A., Geneva Coll., Beaver Falls, Pa., 1903; postgrad. student of U. of Edinburgh, Scotland, 1905; student Ref. Presbyn. Sem., Pittsburgh, Pa., 1905-8; M.A., Princeton, 1910; D.D., Westminster Coll., 1922. Ordained Ref. Presbyn. ministry, 1910; pastor, Walton, N.Y., 1910-16; prof. economics, Geneva Coll., 1916-20, pres. since 1920. With Army Ednl. Corps, Beaune, France, 1919. Clubs: Rotary, Beaver Valley Country. Home: Beaver Falls, Pa. *

JOHNSTON, CLEMENT DIXON, bus. exec.; b. Crestwood, Ky., Nov. 7, 1895; s. Clement B. and Lula G. (Johnston) J.; B.S., Centre Coll., Danville, Ky., 1916, LL.D., 1951; student Harvard Med. Sch., 1916; L.H.D., William Jewell Coll., 1954; m. Lutie Walcott Douthat, July 21, 1950. Sales mgr. Johnston Bros. Co., Inc., Louisville, 1919-26; founder Roanoke Pub. Warehouse (Va.), 1926, pres.; Bristol Grocery Co. (Va.) 1937-79, Williamson Grocery Co. (W.Va.), 1935-79; v.p. Abingdon Grocery Co. (Va.), Huff, Andrews & Thomas, Bluefield, W.Va.; mgr. Morris Plan Bank Va.; dir. Mullens Grocery Co., (W.Va.), F.B. Thomas & Co., Roanoke, So. Investment Co., Roanoke, Sublette Feed & Supply Co., Bluefield, W.Va., Walker Machine & Foundry Corp., Roanoke, Moore of Bedfore Inc. (Va.). Mem. Tabor Com. (investigative staff Ho. Reps. appropriations com.), 1953; nat. chmn. Project Adequate Roads, 1953-79; cons. warehousing Office Def. Transp., RFC; chmn. warehouse industry adv. com. OPA; dept. dir. Office Civil Def. Planning Washington, 1948; chmn. study group U.S. Commn. Intergovtl. Relations, 1954-55; nat. council, exec. com. region III Boy Scouts Am., 1934-79; vice chmn. United Community Campaigns Am.; spl. rep. U.S. Senate fgn. relations com. for aid program in S.E. Asia, 1956-57; pub. mem. 12th selection bd. Dept. State. Bd. regents James Monroe Meml.; trustee Community Hosp. Roanoke Valley. Served to capt., 33d Inf., U.S. Army, World War I; lt. col. ordnance dept., control div. services of supply, Washington, also ordnance supply officer East China, World War II. Decorated Legion of Merit. Mem. Internat. (mem. Am. com., U.S.) (past pres., chmn. 1955-79), Va. (pres.) chambers commerce, Conf. Nat. Orgns. (nat. chmn.), Am. Warehousemen's Assn. (pres.), Am. Chain Warehouses (pres.), Omicron Delta Kappa, Beta Theta Pi, Alpha Kappa Psi. Methodist. Rotarian (dist. gov.). Clubs: Pendennis (Louisville); Shenandoah, Roanoke Country (Roanoke); Metropolitan (Washington). Address: Roanoke, Va. Died Oct. 17, 1979.

JOHNSTON, DON P(ORTER), forester, exec.; b. Hopewell, O., Mar. 2, 1884; s. Samuel and Luetta (Porter) J.; student Ohio No. U., Ohio State U., 1902-06; m. Petrona Powell, Oct. 12, 1915; 1 son, Don P. Engr. United Verde Copper Co., 1907; supervisor Gila, Santa Fe, Coronado nat. forests, chief of operation, Albuquerque, N.M., Madison, Wis., San Francisco, mem. inter-dept. com. on boundaries of Nat. Forests, Nat. Monuments, Nat. Parks, Indian Reservations, 1908-20; sec.-mgr. W. C. Powell Land Co., mgr. Johnston-McNeill Co. (naval stores), exec. v.p. Peoples Bank, Okeechobee, Fla., 1921-28; pres. Royal Cotton Mills, Wake Forest, N.C., 1929-45; advisor to employer del. Internat. Tri-partite Textile Labor Conf., 1937; dir. Cotton Textile Inst., chmn. carded yarn group, 1938-40; dir. N.C. Freezer Locker Assn., 1946-48; pres. N.C. Forestry Assn., 1948-51; pres. Am. Forestry Assn., 1952—. Chmn. 4th Am. Forest Congress, Washington, 1953; chmn. 79th annual conv., Portland, Ore., 1954. Member of the National Council Boy Scouts of Am. Mem. Soc. Am. Foresters, Am. Assn. Engrs., Am. Acad. Polit. and Social Sci., Forest Research Found., Delta Tau Delta. Episcopalian. Mason (32 deg., K.T., Shriner). Clubs: Western University (N.Y.); Cosmos (Washington), Rotary (pres. 1960-61) (Wake Forest, N.C.). Home: Wake Forest, N.C. *

JOHNSTON, EDWARD R., lawyer; b. Ida Grove, Ia., Apr. 13, 1882; s. Richard and Amanda L. (Thompson) J.; Ph.B., State U. Ia., 1904; LL.B., Harvard, 1907; m. Caroline M. Rogers, Apr. 25, 1910; 1 son, Alan R. Admitted to Ill. bar, 1907, partner Gregory, Poppenhusen & McNab. Chicago, 1911-14, Newman, Poppenhusen, Stern & Johnston since 1914 (present firm Johnston, Thompson, Raymond & Mayer), specialized in anti-trust cases since 1924. Mem. bd. dirs. Western Light & Telephone Co., 1935-44. Trustee Village of Glencoe, Ill., 1920-25, Counsel War Savings Com., Washington, 1917-19. Mem. Am., Ill., Chicago bar assns., Phi Beta Kappa. Republican. Presbyn. Clubs: Skokie Country (pres., 1931-33, Glencoe, Ill.); Law (pres., 1936-37), University, The Chicago, Mid-Day (Chicago). Home: Lake Forest, Ill. *

JOHNSTON, ELLIS MURRAY, textile mfr.; b. Lebanon, Ky., Dec. 21, 1883; s. William and Sarah B. (Oliver) J.; ed. U. of Ky.; m. Juliet Tarkington; 1 son, James S. Branch mgr. Am. Rolling Mill Co., Middletown, O., 1915-23; pres. Am. Tube & Stamping Co., Bridgeport, Conn., 1923-27; pres. Woodside Cotton Mills Co., Greenville, S.C., 1930-36; now chmn. of bd. Woodside Cotton Mills Co., Easley Cotton Mills. Served as 1st lt. U.S.A., 1918. Mem. New York Southern Soc., Sigma Nu. Club: Greenville Country. Home: Greenville, S.C. *

JOHNSTON, GARVIN HOWELL, ret. state ofcl.; b. Jefferson Davis County, Miss., Nov. 17, 1909; grad. Pearl River Jr. Coll.; B.S., Ed.D., U. So. Miss.; M.A., U. Ala.; m. Willene Bullock; 1 dau., Elizabeth Johnston Walley. Tchr., prin. and supt. elementary and high sch., supr. high sch. Miss. Dept. Edn.; pres. Pearl River Jr. Coll., Poplarville, Miss., 1953-68; supt. edn. State of Miss., Jackson, 1968-76. Chmn., Miss. Bd. Edn., Miss. Jr. Coll. Commn.; mem. Council Chief State Sch. Officers, 1968-76, also rep. other bds.; mem. state adv. com. for vocat. and tech. edn. Bd. dirs. Miss. Econ. Council, former mem. edn. com. Served with AUS, World War II. Named Citizen of Year, Poplarville, 1967, Miss. Ednl. Adminstr. of Yr., 1973; recipient Gov.'s Outstanding Mississippian award, 1975, Service to Humanity award Miss. Coll., 1976, numerous other awards and citations for leadership and service; Dr. Garvin H. Johnson Ave. of Magnolias meml. hwy. named in his honor. Mem. Am. Legion, Am. Acad. Polit. and Social Sci., Miss. Edn. Assn. (past pres.), Miss. Jr. Coll. Assn. (past pres.), Miss. Assn. Colls. (past pres.), Miss. Hist. Soc., Miss. Art Assn., Miss. Assn. Mental Health. Baptist (deacon). Clubs: Poplarville Rotary (past pres.), Masons. Home: Jackson, Miss. Died Jan. 27, 1978; interred Hollywood Cemetery, McComb, Miss.

JOHNSTON, JAMES AMBLER, archtl. engr.; b. Rockbridge County, Va., May 18, 1885; s. Nathaniel Burwell and Mary Sayre (Macon) J.; B.S., Virginia Polytechnical Institute, 1904, M.E., 1905; M.E., Cornell, 1906; m. Lucy Newton Christian, Jan. 5, 1910 (dec. 1955); children—Walter C. (dec.), Jacquelin A. (Mrs. John Spencer Gilmore), Page Burwell (Mrs. John S. Karling). Archtl. engr., Richmond, 1908; mem. Carneal & Johnston, architects for Va. Mil. Inst., Va. Poly. Inst., U. of Richmond, Wash. and Lee U., Law Bldg., Chapel and Library at Fork Union (Va.) Military Academy, Va. Highway Dept.; asso. Virginia State Library, Richmond Housing Authority, U.S. Army Richmond Gen. Depot, Richmond Gen. Hosp., Q.M. Depot, Va. Penal System, Richmond Sch. Bd., Marine Forwarding Depot, Virginia Electric & Power Co., Life Ins. Co. Va., Albemarle Paper Co., Va. Employment Commn. Bldg., Home Beneficial Life Ins. Co.; practice largely institutional, commercial and industrial. Mem. adv. bd. State Planters Bank & Commerce & Trusts, Adv. bd. Nat. Civil War Centennial Commn.; hon. life member Civil War Round Tables of Richmond, Chicago, New York City and Louisville. Fellow Am. Soc. M.E.; mem. A.I.A., Va. Inst. for Sci. Research (dir., mem. exec. com.), Am. Soc. Heating and Ventilating Engrs., Am. Soc. Refrigerating Engrs., S.R., Va. Poly. Inst. Alumni Assn. (pres. 1938-40), Va. Hist. Soc. (exec. com.), Assn. for Preservation Va. Antiquities. (adv. com.), Omicron Delta Kappa, Tau Beta Pi, Phi Kappa Phi. Democrat. Episcopalian. Clubs: Torch, Commonwealth, Newcomen Society of England; Rotary. Home: Richmond, Va. *

JOHNSTONE, BURTON KENNETH, architect; b. Chgo., Jan. 20, 1907; s. Burton Clermont and Margaret (Wulff) J.; B.S. in Architecture, U. Ill., 1928; B.F.A., Yale, 1929; fellow Am. Acad. in Rome (Italy), 1929-32; student Lake Forest (Ill.) Found. for Architecture and Landscape Architecture, summer 1928; m. Helene Estelle Hetzel, Aug. 27, 1938; children—Dorn Kenneth, Robert Philip. Draftsman, Granger and Bollenbacher, Chgo., 1924; teaching asst. U. Ill., 1928, Yale, 1929; mem. faculty Pa. State Coll., 1933-79, successively asst. prof. architecture, asso. prof., prof. and head dept. architecture, 1938-45; dean Coll. Fine Arts, Carnegie Inst. Tech., 1945-52. Recipient Rome prize in Architecture, 1929, Scarab gold medal, 1941. Fellow AIA; mem. Pa. Soc. Architects, Assn. Collegiate Schs. Architecture (past pres.), Tau Beta Pi, Sigma Tau, Phi Eta Sigma, Pi Kappa Alpha, Scarab (past nat. pres.). Author: (with others) Building or Buying a House, 1945. Contbr. to profl. jours. Home: Pittsburgh, Pa. Died Jan. 1, 1979.

JONAS, H(ARRY) A(LFRED), business exec.; b. San Francisco, Feb. 8, 1885; s. Alfred and Adelaide (Golden) J.; ed. in pub. schs., San Francisco; m. Hermanie Baer, Mar. 6, 1924; children—Harriet Little, Carl Little. Connected with General Cigar Co. since 1902; vice pres. since 1945, dir. since 1942. Clubs: Lake Merced Golf and Country (past pres.), Concordia-Argonaut, Commonwealth (San Francisco). Home: Sausalito, Calif. *

JONES, ARCHIE NEFF, ret. univ. dean; b. Atlantic, Iowa, Sept. 20, 1900; s. Archie Israel and Edith Lorraine (Neff) J.; diploma U. Nebr., 1925; B.S., U. Minn., 1929, M.A., 1931; Mus. D. (hon.), MacPhall Coll., 1940; m. Gladys Miller Allen, Aug. 30, 1969; children—(by previous marriage) Catherine (Mrs. John Longenecker), Elizabeth (Mrs. Allen R. Moers), Archie Alan. Supr. music, Marshall, Minn., 1924-27; dir. music State tchrs. Coll., La Crosse, Wis., 1927-28; chmn. music edn. dept. U. Minn., 1928-35; dir. music U. Idaho, 1935-40; prof. music edn. U. Tex., 1940-59; dean Conservatory Music, U. Mo. at Kansas City, 1959-70; guest prof. U. So. Calif., U. Mont., U. Wyo., U. S.D., Okla. U., U. Denver., Brigham Young U., Mich. State U., Colo. Coll. Mem. Nat. council U.S.O., 1961-71, chmn. nat music council-Dept. Def. overseas tours com., 1961-71. Pres. Sinfonia Found., 1960-64. Recipient Distinguished Service award Mu Phi Epsilon, 1964; Distinguished Service award U.S.O. Bd. Govs., 1971; Distinguished Service citation Nat. Fedn. Music Clubs, 1971; certificate of esteem Dept. Def., 1972. Mem. Am. Choral Dirs. Assn. (pres. 1958-60), Internat. Assn. Concert Mgrs. (pres 1958-61), Music Tchrs. Nat. Assn., Music Educators Nat. Conf. (life; past pres. Southwest div.), Phi Mu Alpha (pres. 1950-60, recipient Man of Music award 1964), Omicron Delta Kappa, Sigma Nu, Phi Delta Kappa, Pi Kappa Lambda, Kappa Delta Pi. Mason (Shriner), Rotarian. Author: Introduction to Musical Knowledge, 1935; Pronouncing Guide to French, German, Italian and Spanish, 1948; Techniques in Choral Conducting, 1949; First Steps to Choral Music, 1957; Music Education in Action, 1960. Contbr.

articles to profl. jours. Compositions for mixed chorus. Home: Austin, Tex. Died Nov. 18, 1979.

JONES, ARNOLD ROOSEVELT, educator; b. Haddam, Kans., May 30, 1904; s. John H. and Miriam G. (Jones) J.; B.S. in Bus., U. Kans., 1927; postgrad. Kans. State Coll., 1930-31, U. Denver, summer 1931, U. Kans., summer 1932, U. Colo., 1953-54; m. Ruth D. Cress, Nov. 6, 1927; children—A. Richard, Virginia L. Accountant, Peat, Marwick, Mitchell & Co., Kansas City, Mo., also Ozark Oil Co., Joplin, Mo., 1928; C.P.A. practice as Stewart & Jones, A.R. Jones & Co. and Breisford, Gifford & Jones, Manhattan and Topeka, Kans., 1929-42; instr., asst. prof. accounting Kans. State Coll., 1928-33; asst. budget dir. and state accountant, Kans., 1933-37; lectr. accounting Washburn U., 1935-39, treas., bus. mgr., 1937-39; mem. Kans. Corp. Commn., 1939-42; dir. div. adminstrn. Office Gov. Kans., 1951-53; dean financial adminstrn., chief financial officer Kans. State Coll., 1945-58, prof. accounting, 1945-58; dep. dir. U.S. Bur. Budget, 1956-57; Distinguished lectr. in accounting U. South Fla., Tampa, 1966-67. Mem. Def. Mblzn. Bd.; adv. bd. Econ. Growth and Stability; alternate budget dir. N.S.C. and Pres.'s Cabinet; chmn. Interdeptl. Com. on User Charges; vice chmn. bd. dirs. TVA, 1957-66; mem. Kan. Bd. Edn., 1969; vol. Internat. Exec. Service Corps, 1970—. Mem. Kans. Bd. C.P.A. Examiners, 1941-44. Trustee, sec.-treas. Kan. State U. Endowment Assn., 1947-56. Served from 1st lt. to capt. AUS, 1942-45. C.P.A., Kans. Mem. Am. Inst. C.P.A.'s, Am. Accounting Assn., Kan. C. of C., Kan. Soc. C.P.A.'s (exec. dir. 1968-69), Phi Kappa Phi, Phi Sigma Kappa (nat. financial v.p.), Alpha Kappa Psi; hon. mem. Tenn. Soc. C.P.A.'s. Home: Bradenton, Fla. Died May 30, 1975; interred, Cedar Point, Kans.

JONES, BENJAMIN ROWLANDS, lawyer; b. Wilkes-Barre, Pa., May 29, 1906; s. Benjamin Rowlands and Margaret Hannah (Williams) J.; student Wyoming Sem., Kington, Pa., 1923; A.B., Princeton U., 1927; LL.B, U. Pa., 1930; m. Dorothy Richards, 1935 (dec.); children—Benjamin Rowlands, Morgan R.; m. 2d, Jane Randall Griffith, 1956; 1 stepson, Edward Griffith. Admitted to Pa. bar, 1930; partner Bedford, Waller, Jones & Darling, Wilkes-Barre, 1930-51; pres. judge Orphans' Ct. of Luzerne County, 1952-57; justice Pa. Supreme Ct., 1957-72, chief justice, 1972-77; of counsel Dilworth, Paxson, Kalish & Levy, Phila., 1977-80. Trustee Wyoming Sem. Served with USNR, 1944-45. Mem. Am., Pa. bar assns., Wilkes-Barre Law and Library Assn (past pres). Home: Benton, Pa. Died July 27, 1980.

JONES, CHARLES AUBREY, business and civic executive; b. Deer Park, Md., Feb. 25, 1885; s. Wilbur Clark and Olive F(orman) J.; student W.Va. Conf. Sem., 1900-04; A.B. cum laude, Ohio Wesleyan University, 1907; LL.D. (honorary), West Virginia Wesleyan Coll., 1949; m. Ireta Eleanore Lowe, Aug. 20, 1907; children—Robert Gordon, Elizabeth Eleanore (Mrs. Herbert Lea Jones), Virginia Lee (Mrs. Raymond B. Ziesler). Newspaper writer, 1907-15; sec. Ohio Tax Commn., 1915-17; newspaper writer, 1917; publicity dir. or other official, Ohio Rep. campaigns, 1914-28; publicity rep. Meth. Ch., China, Japan, Korea, 1919-20; pvt. sec. U.S. Senator Frank B. Willis, 1921-28; clk. U.S. Senate Com. on Territories and Insular Possessions, 1923-28; receiver Fed. Bank, 1928; pvt. sec. Gov. Myers Y. Cooper of Ohio, 1929-30; receiver Fed. Banks, 1931-33; exec. sec. Community Fund, Columbus and Franklin County, and Council Social Agencies, 1934-39; asst. treas. Am. Edn. Press, Inc., 1939-49, v.p., 1949-50. Mem. Columbus Bd. Health, 1954—, pres., 1957—; finance dir. Columbus (O.) Hospital Federation. Trustee and treas. White Cross Hosp. since 1936; dir. Godman Guild Settlement House since 1939 (treas. since 1944); former trustee Lakeside Assn., trustee Ohio Wesleyan U.; dir. and treas. United Service Orgns., Columbus, O., 1940-44; pres. U.S.O. (Columbus) 1945-46; pres. Central Ohio Council Boy Scouts, 1941-44 (mem. nat. council since 1943); hon. life mem. Ohio Hist. Soc.; director, past pres. Franklin Co. Hist. Soc.; mem. Ill. Hist. Soc., Sigma Chi. Secretary Ohio Lincoln Sesquicentennial Committee. Publicity dir. Meth. Centenary, 1919; del. Gen. Conf. M.E. Ch., 1936; del. Meth. Uniting Conf., 1939; lay leader delegation from Ohio conf. to Gen. Conf. Meth. Ch., 1940, del. Gen. Conf., 1944 (sec. Com. Twenty-One recommending $25,000,000 postwar ch. work, member of Com. Two Hundred, executive com. directing Crusade for Christ program; vice chmn. com. successfully contgnding for revision ch. declaration on war); mem. (mem. exec. com.) Commn. on World Service and Finance, Meth. Ch., 1936-52. (sec. 1948-52); mem. Meth. Gen. Conf., 1948; mem. Meth. N. Central Jurisdictional Confs., 1940, 44, 48, 56, 60. Dir. Citizens Research Inc. Awarded Silvgr Beaver, Silver Antelope Boy Scouts Am. Mem. Internat. Assn. Torch Clubs, Inc. (dir.; pres. 1958-59), S.A.R. (nat. exec. com. 1953-54, 55-56, 58-59, 60-61, secretary general 1956-58, president general 1959-60, secretary, treasurer Ohio Society, Benjamin Franklin chpt.). Mason (32 deg.). Clubs: Torch (pres. 1942-43), Kiwanis, Crichton (Columbus). Owner collection Lincolniana. Home: Columbus. *

JONES, CHARLES SHERMAN, aviator; b. Castleton, Vt., Jan. 11, 1894; s. John and Helen (Sherman) J.; student Middlebury (Vt.) Coll., Harvard Sch. Phy. Edn.; m. Marguerite Williams, Oct. 31, 1917 (dec. July 1967); children—Charles Sherman, Deborah Harrison; m. 2d Hulda Cole, Nov. 26, 1967. With Curtiss Wright Corp., airplane mfrs., 1919-33; founder, pres. Casey Jones Sch. Aeros., Newark, 1932-56, Acad. Aeros., La Guardia Field, N.Y., 1940-63, chmn bd., from 1964; pres. J.V.W. Corp., 1933-41, partner, 1942-64. Mem V.I. Port Authority, from 1968. Served with AC, U.S. Army, 1917-18. Recipient John J. McGraw award, 1956. Fellow Am. Inst. Aeros. and Astronautics; mem. Am. Soc. Engring. Edn., Phi Beta Kappa, Chi Psi. Club: Wings (past pres.) (N.Y.C.). Winner 2d pl. N.Y.-Toronto race, 1919, Am. Derby, Kansas City, Mo., 1921, winner 2 1st pl. and 2d pl. Nat. Air Races Omaha, 1921, 2d pl. On to Detroit race, 1922, On to St. Louis race, 1923, On to Dayton race, 1924, Central Union Speed race, 1924; won 2 events Nat. Air Races, Mitchel Field, 1925, 1st and 2d pl., Phila., 1928; winner of race for cabin ships. Chgo 1930 Home: St Thomas, V.I. Died Feb. 12, 1976.

JONES, CLIFFORD BARTLETT, banker; b. Rico, Colo., Apr. 9, 1885; s. Charles Adam and Virginia (Bartlett) J.; grad. high sch.; LL.D., McMurray Coll., Abilene, Tex., 1939; LL.D., Southwestern U., Georgetown, Tex., 1941; LL.D., Tex. Technol. U., Lubbock, 1941; m. Alice Louise Palmer, June 24, 1908 (dec. May 1919); m. 2d, Audrey Lynn Barber, Sept. 27, 1922 (dec. May 1969). Purchasing agt. Kansas City Bag Mfg. Co. (Mo.), 1904-07; v.p., treas. Jacques Steel Co., Kansas City, 1907-10; asst. ranch mgr. S.M. Swenson & Sons of N.Y.C., Spur, Tex., 1911-13, ranch mgr., 1913-38; pres. Tex. Technol. U., 1938-44; pres. Spur Nat. Bank, 1936-55, chmn. bd., 1955-62; pres. Spur Cattle Loan Co., 1914-19; pres. Dickens County Agrl. Credit Corp.; dir., chmn. bd. Lubbock Nat. Bank, 1944—; dir. Ft. Worth & Denver R.R. Co., Merc. Nat. Bank, Dallas, Southwestern Pub. Service Co., Merc. Security Life Ins. Co., Dallas, Fed. Regional Agrl. Credit Corp., Ft. Worth. Organizer, pres. Ft. Worth-Roswell Hwy. Assn., 1914; v.p. Tex. Hwy. Assn., Austin; pres. Tex. Transcontinental Trail, Ft. Worth. Mem. Tex. Centennial Commn., 1936—; chmn. Dickens County Draft Bd., World War I; mem. Dist. Appellate Draft Bd., No. Judicial Dist. Tex., World War I; regional adviser PWA for Tex., La. and N.M., 1934. Mayor, Spur, 19—. Pres., bd. dirs. Tex. Tech. Found.; bd. dirs. Tex. Safety Council, Tax Conservation Council Tex., Scottish Rite Found. Tex., Lubbock Symphony, W. Tex. Mus.; trustee Tex. Technol. U. Sch. Law. Recipient Good Citizenship award Tex. Soc. S.A.R., 1959, MacArthur award S.A.R., 1965. Named spl. Tex. Ranger. Fellow Tex. Acad. Sci.; mem. Tex. Cowboy Reunion Assn. (life), Lubbock C. of C., Philos. Soc. Tex., Am. Inst. Banking, A.A.A.S., Acad. Polit. Sci., Tex., W. Tex. hist. assns., N.E.A., Tex. Soc. S.A.R. (pres., life mem.), Sons Republic Tex., Knights of San Jacinto, Phi Delta Theta. Episcopalian. Mason (33, K.T., Shriner), Rotarian. Clubs: Ft. Worth, Lubbock, Block and Bridle Tex. Technol. U. (Lubbock). Home: Lubbock TX. *

JONES, DAVID JOHN, oil co. exec.; b. Chgo., July 12, 1920; s. Robert Thomas and Florence (Phillips) J.; student London Sch. Econs., 1937-40, Columbia Grad. Sch., 1946; M.B.A., Harvard, 1947. Asst. treas. Esso Export Corp., London, Eng., 1950-52; financial mgr. Esso Standard Societe Anonyme Francaise, Paris, 1953-57; with Exxon Corp., 1947-80, mgr. coordination and planning dept., 1963-65, treas., 1965-70, v.p. finance, 1970-80. Bd. dirs. Salzburg Seminar in Am. Studies; trustee Tax Found. Served to 1st lt. AUS, 1942-45. Decorated Legion of Merit; Croix de Guerre, (France); Valore Militare (Italy). Mem. Am. Petroleum Inst., Am. Econ. Assn., Council Fgn. Relations, Am. Acad. Polit. Sci. Home: New York, N.Y. Died Mar. 22, 1980.

JONES, E(LI) STANLEY, missionary; b. Baltimore, Md., Jan. 3, 1884; s. Albin Davis and Sarah Alice (Peddicord) J.; A.B., Asbury Coll., Wilmore, Ky., 1906, A.M., 1912; D.D., Duke University, 1928; S.T.D., Syracuse University, 1928; married Mabel Lossing, February 11, 1911; 1 daughter, Eunice Treffry (Mrs. J. K. Mathews). Evangelist to high castes of India since 1907. Elected bishop of M.E. Ch., 1928, but resigned to continue missionary work. Founder of two Christian Ashrams at Sat Tal and Lucknow, India. Author: The Way, 1946; Mahatma Gandhi: An Interpretation, 1948; The Way to Power and Poise, 1950; How to be a Transformed Person, 1951, and many others 1925-46. Contbr. to Christian Herald, Christian Advocate.

JONES, EDMUND LYDDANE, lawyer; b. Rockville, Md., Feb. 6, 1894; s. Charles Benedict and Lavinia (Lyddane) J.; LL.B., Georgetown U., 1916; m. Bettina Evans Prescott, Nov. 17, 1917 (dec. Oct. 1967); children—Bettina (Mrs. John Curtis), Edith Kellogg (Mrs. Edward Picken), Edmund Lyddane; m. 2d, Bessie Lewis, Sept. 14, 1968. Admitted to D.C. bar, 1916; practice law, Washington from 1916; mem. firm Hogan & Hartson, 1938-74. Served from 2d lt. to 1st lt. U.S. Army, 1917-18; AEF. Fellow Am. Coll. Trial Lawyers; mem. Am. Bar Assn., Bar Assn. D.C., Delta Theta Phi. Clubs: Lawyers, Metropolitan, Barristers, Burning Tree, Chevy Chase (Washington). Home: Washington, D.C. Died Dec. 11, 1980.

JONES, EDWARD BRANT, osteopathic surgeon, urologist; b. Canton, O., Oct. 30, 1885; s. Paul Dick and Margaret (Stubenvoll) J., D.O. Coll. of Osteopathic Physicians and Surgeons, Los Angeles, 1910; post grad. work, Vienna, Austria, 1924; m. Adele Young, Apr. 10, 1910; children—Dr. Jean Lorenz, Philip Curtis, Barbara Evelyn. Began as asst. to adv. mgr. of Am. Radiator Co., Jersey City, N.J., 1904; in practice as osteopathic surgeon and urologist in Calif. since 1910; prof. Urological Surgery Coll. of Osteopathic Physicians and Surgeons, Los Angeles, 1914-30; mem. staff, Los Angeles County Osteopathic Hosp., 1930-40, mem. med. bd., 1938-39, pres. med. bd., 1939; pres. Am. Coll. Osteopathic Surgeons (hon.) since 1940. Pres. and mem. Bd. of Osteopathic Examiners, State of Calif., 1934-40. Mem. Iota Tau Sigma, Sigma Sigma Phi (hon.). Republican. Methodist. Mason (Blue Lodge, Scottish Rite, Jesters, Shriner). Clubs: Bel Air (Calif.) Country; Calif. Yacht (Wilmington, Calif.); Los Angeles Optimist (pres. 1935). Contbr. articles to med. jours. Home: Los Angeles. *

JONES, EDWARD VASON, architect; b. Albany, Ga., Aug. 3, 1909; s. Piamus Walter and Nella Cutliff (Vason) J.; student Vanderbilt U., 1927-29, Northwestern U., 1929-33; m. Maria Isabel Martin, Nov. 28, 1937; children—Jeanette Jones Balling, Nella Vason. Pvt. practice architecture, Albany, Ga.; architect for diplomatic reception rooms U.S. Dept. State; cons. architect for Fine Arts Commn. for Preservation of White House; architect for period rooms 19th Century Am. exhibit Met. Mus. Art, 1970; cons. architect, furnishings cons. Tryon Palace Commn., New Bern, N.C.; cons. architect, furnishings cons. Gov.'s Mansion, State of Miss. Trustee Phoebe Putney Meml. Hosp., Albany, Ga.; life fellow Met. Mus. Art. Mem. Appraisers Assn. Am. Episcopalian. Clubs: Oglethorpe, Chatham (Savannah, Ga.). Home: Albany, Ga. Died Oct. 1, 1980.

JONES, ERNEST VICTOR, chemist; b. Bronaugh, Mo., Jan. 7, 1882; s. Alfred Persia and Maria Irene (Jones) J.; A.B., Morrisville (Mo.) Coll., 1905; A.M., Vanderbilt U., 1909, Ph.D., 1912; student U. of Chicago, 1909, 10, 36, U. of Mo., summers 1907, 08, Columbia, 1921, U. of Calif., 1927-28; m. Eunice Beth Vaughan, Aug. 9, 1908. Prof. of chemistry Southern U., Greensboro, Ala., 1912-13; head depts. of chemistry and physics Soochow (China) U., 1913-22; prof. phys. and inorganic chemistry U. of Nanking, China, 1922-27; head dept. of chemistry Birmingham-Southern Coll., 1928-46; prof. inorganic chemistry U. of Ala. 1947-52; cons. Carbide & Carbon Chem. Co., Oak Ridge. Secretary East China Assn. of Colls. and Univs., 1921-22; sec. China Assn. of Christian Higher Edn., 1922; pres. East China Athletic Assn., 1922-25. Fellow A.A.A.S.; mem. Am. Chem. Soc. (chmn. Ala. sect., 1933), Ala. Acad. Sci. (hon.), So. Assn. of Sci. and Industry, Ala. Acad. Sci. (pres. 1943-44)), Phi Beta Kappa, Omicron Delta Kappa, Phi Tau Phi. Theta Chi Delta (nat. pres. 1933-35, 1942-46). Methodist. Club: Civitan. Editor: Journal of Ala. Acad. Sci., 1930-42. *

JONES, EUGENE KINCKLE, social work; b. Richmond, Va., July 30, 1885; s. Joseph Endom and Rosa Daniel (Kinckle) J.; grad. Wayland Acad., Richmond, 1902; A.B., Va. Union U., Richmond, 1906, LL.D., 1924; A.M., Cornell U., 1908; m. Blanche Ruby Watson, Mar. 11, 1909; children—Eugene Kinckle, Adele Rosa. Instr. in social sciences, State U., Louisville, Ky., 1908-09; teacher, Central High Sch., Louisville, 1909-11; exec. sec. Nat. Urban League, 1911-41, gen. sec. 1941-50, cons. exec. bd. since 1950. Adv. on Negro affairs to United States Dept. of Commerce, 1933-37. Mem. N.Y. State Planning Bd., 1934-35. Chmn. Associates in Negro Folk Edn.; chmn. Negro advisory com., Tex. Centennial Expn., 1936-37. Mem. exec. bd. Nat. Conf. of Social Work, 1923-30, v.p., 1932-33; mem. bd. of dirs. New York Adult Edn. Council, 1933-35; chmn. Flushing Edn. Com., 1920-35; pres. Alumni Assn. of Va. Union U., 1932-34; trustee Va. Union U.; mem. advisory com. on welfare, New York World's Fair 1939, Unemployment Insurance State Advisory Council (New York), 1938-45; mem. Fair Employment Bd. of U.S. Civil Service Commn., Washington, since 1948. Mem. Am. Assn. Social Workers, Alpha Phi Alpha. Baptist. Home: Flushing, L.I., N.Y. *

JONES, EVERT LEON, coll. pres.; b. Wharton, O., Dec. 1, 1883; s. Elias and Rozilla J.; prep. edn., high sch., Terre Haute, Ind.; A.B., Albany (Ore.) Coll., 1909; LL.B., Portland Law Sch., 1911; studied U. of Chicago, 1917-18, Columbia, 1923; D.D., Buena Vista Coll., 1925; m. Phelura Gilham, of Glendale, Ore., Dec. 7, 1909; children—Gwendolyn Elaine, Margaret Elizabeth. Admitted to Ore. bar, 1911, and began practice at Portland; dep. dist. atty. Multnomah Co., Ore., 1912-14; studied theology, San Francisco Theol. Sem.; ordained Presbyn. ministry, 1917; pastor at Chicago, Spokane and Phila., Pa.; pres. Buena Vista Coll., Storm Lake, Ia., since May 1, 1924. Mem. Bd. Ednl. Examiners, Ia. Winner at state oratorical contest of Intercollegiate Oratorical Assn. of Ore., 1906, and state prohibition oratorical contest of Ore., 1907; won interstate oratorical contest, Wash., Ore., and Calif., 1907; rep. of Pacific coast in nat. prohibition oratorical contest, Columbus, O., 1908. Republican. Club: Rotarian. Home: Storm Lake, Ia. *

JONES, FRANK PIERCE, educator; b. Appleton, Wis., Apr. 10, 1905; s. George W. and Maud F. (Sackett) J.; student Lawrence Coll., 1922-23, U. Wis., 1923-24; B.A., Stanford, 1926, M.A., 1928; postgrad. U. Chgo., 1929-30; Ph.D., U. Wis., 1937; studied kinesthetic perception with F.M. and A.R. Alexander, 1938-45; m. Helen Bartlett Rumsey, Aug. 10, 1931; children—Thomas R., Emlen V. (Mrs. Michael A. O'Keeffe), John Evan. Asst. in gen. lit. Reed Coll., 1927-29; instr. Greek, Latin classics Brown U., 1937-41, asst. prof., 1941-44; asst. prof. English, Pa. Mil. Coll., 1944-45; pvt. teaching, research in kinesthetic perception, Boston, N.Y.C., 1945-54; research asso. Inst. for Psychol. Research, Tufts U., 1954-68, lectr. classics, 1955-64, prof. classics, 1964-70, lectr. psychology, 1968-70, prof. emeritus classics, 1970-75, prof. psychology, summer 1972-74, faculty mentor Coll. Within, 1972-73. Carnegie grantee, 1954-56; USPHS grantee, 1956-64, 66-67. Mem. Am. Philol. Assn., Am., New Eng. psychol. assns., A.A.A.S., Phi Beta Kappa, Sigma Xi. Author: Body Awareness in Action, 1976. Contbr. articles on classical subjects, kinesthetic perception of postural reflex patterns to profl. jours. Home: Cambridge, Mass. Died Oct. 15, 1975; interred Mt. Auburn Cemetery, Cambridge.

JONES, GALEN, edn. council exec.; b. Grundy Center, Ia., July 12, 1896; s. Jesse Edwin and Etta Maria (Strickler) J.; A.B., McPherson (Kan.) Coll., 1918; A.M., Tchrs. Coll., Columbia U., 1921, Ph.D., 1935; LL.D., Upsala Coll., 1946; m. Grace Everts, Aug. 14, 1922; children—Royce Emerson (dec.), Galen Everts, Thomas Hugh. Tchr., prin., supt. pub. schs., 1919-33; prin. Plainfield (N.J.) High Sch., 1934-42, E. Orange High Sch., 1942-45; tchr. grad. div. U. Mo., Columbia, summers 1927-28; Ohio State U., Columbus, 1930-32; Pa. State Coll., State College, Pa., 1936-37, Alfred (N.Y.) U., 1938; U. Pa., Phila., 1939, 40, 41; Harvard, 1942, Tchrs. Coll., Columbia, Saturdays, 1942-43, 1943-44; Lehigh U., Bethlehem, Pa., Saturdays, 1944-45; U. N.H., Durham, summers 1944-45: dir. div. secondary edn. U.S. Office Edn., 1945-51, dir. orgn., instrn. and services br., 1951-54; dir. Council for Advancement of Secondary Edn., until 1971; cons. ednl. relations Field Enterprises Ednl. Corp., 1965-67. Served with F.A. Central Officers Tng. Sch., Camp Taylor, Louisville, Ky., 1918. Chmn. U.S. del. 10th, 11th, 14th, Internat. Conf. Pub. Edn., Geneva, 1947, 48, 51; del. I.L.O. adv. com. on salaried employees and profl. workers, Geneva, 1954; mem. U.S. nat. com. UNESCO, 1954-59. Mem. Middle States Assn. Colls. and Secondary Schs. (pres. 1947-48; v.p. 1946-47), N.E.A., Nat. Assn. Secondary Sch. Prins. (pres. 1947-48), Headmasters Assn. (hon.), Phi Delta Kappa, Kappa Delta Pi. Mason. Author books on edn. Home: Southern Pines, N.C. Died Dec. 2, 1974.

JONES, GILBERT HAVEN, educator; b. Ft. Mott, S.C., Aug. 23, 1883; s. Joshua H. and Lizzie (Martin) J.; student Ohio State U.; A.B., Wilberforce U., 1902, B.S., 1903; Ph.B., Dickinson Coll., Carlisle, Pa., 1906, A.M., 1907; studied univs. of Göttingen and Jena, Ph.D. from latter, 1909; LL.D., Howard U., 1925; m. Rachel Gladys Coverdale, June 10, 1910; children—Gladys Havena, Gilbert Haven, Ruth Inez, Donald Coverdale. Principal Lincoln High Sch., Carlisle, Pa., 2 yrs.; prof. philosophy and edn., St. Augustine Collegiate Inst., Raleigh, N.C., 1909-10; prof. ancient langs., Agrl. and Normal U., Okla., 1910-14; dean Coll. Liberal Arts and v.p. Wilberforce U., 1914-24; pres. Wilberforce U., 1924-32, prof. politics and govt. Wilberforce U., 1932-36, v.p. and dean Coll. of Edn. since 1937. Mem. Am. Acad. Social and Polit. Sciences, Ohio Archaeological Historic Soc., Sen Mer Rekh Honor Soc., Kappa Alpha Psi, Pi Gamma Mu, Zeta Sigma Pi, Kappa Alpha Mu (nat. honor soc.). Methodist. Author: Education in Theory and Practice. Home: Wilberforce, Ohio. *

JONES, HARRY LEE, II, army officer; b. Kansas City, Mo., Oct. 27, 1918; s. Harry Lee and Hazel (Hixon) J.; student Washington U., St. Louis, 1937-40; A.B., George Washington U., 1950, M.A., 1963; M.B.A., Harvard, 1953; grad. Army War Coll., 1963; m. Gloria Carolyn Raeder, Mar. 26, 1947; children—Patricia (Mrs. Chris Sullivan), Harry Lee. Joined U.S. Army, 1940, commd. 2d lt., 1943, advanced through grades to maj. gen., 1970; finance officer 24th Inf. Div., 1942-46; mem. Gen. Staff, 1958-62; adv. to dir. finance and audit Ministry Def., Vietnam, 1963-65; chief finance and accounting Office Comptroller Army, 1967-70; asst. comptroller for information systems, Washington, 1969-70; chief Army Audit Agy., Washington, 1970-72; instr. U. Md., Heidelberg, Germany, 1953-56. Bd. dirs. Army Mut. Aid Assn., Fort Myer, Arlington, Va., 1967-75. Decorated D.S.M., Legion Merit with 2 oak leaf clusters, Bronze Star, Army Commendation medal with oak leaf cluster; Medal Honor 1st class (Republic Vietnam). Mem. Assn. U.S. Army, Army Finance Assn. (nat. pres., 1967-70), Am. Soc. Mil. Comptrollers (nat. v.p.). Home: El Paso, Tex. Died Jan. 2, 1980; buried Ft. Bliss Nat. Cemetery, El Paso, Tex.

JONES, HARRY R., lawyer; b. Hubbard, Tex., Nov. 16, 1902; s. James R. and Ida (Walton) J.; A.B., Baylor U., 1923, LL.B., 1926; m. Hazel Tanner, Aug. 7, 1929; children—Mary Owen (Mrs. Charles M. Sloan), Janet (Mrs. Thomas Garth), Harry R., Steven E. Admitted to Tex. bar, 1926, since practiced in Waco and Houston; partner firm Andrews, Kurth, Campbell & Jones, 1936-80; gen. counsel dir., mem. exec. com. Southwest Forest Industries, Inc. Mem. Am., Tex. Houston (pres. 1952) bar assns., Am. Law Inst., Am. Bar Found., Am. Coll. Trial Lawyers. Kiwanian (pres. Houston 1949). Home: Houston, Tex. Died June 24, 1980; buried Forest Park Cemetery, Houston.

JONES, HOWARD MUMFORD, author; b. Saginaw, Mich., Apr. 16 1892; s. Frank Alexander and Josephine Whitman (Miles) J.; student State Normal Sch., La Crosse, Wis., 1910-12; B.A., U. Wis., 1914; M.A., U. Chgo., 1915; Litt.D., Harvard, 1936; L.H.D., Tulane U., 1938, Ohio State U., Hebrew Union Coll., 1962, Northwestern U., 1966, Clarkson Coll. Tech., 1968; Litt.D., U. Colo., 1938, Western Res. U., U. Wis., 1948, Clark U., 1952, N.Y. U., 1969, U. Pa., 1976; LL.D., Colby Coll., 1962, U. Utah, 1966, U. Windsor, 1969; m. Clara Edgar McLure, July 13, 1918; 1 dau., Eleanor McLure; m. 2d, Bessie Judith Zaban, June 11, 1927. Adj. prof. English and gen. lit. U. Tex., 1916-19, asso. prof. comparative lit., 1919-25; asso. prof. English, U. N.C., 1925-27, prof. English lit., 1927-30, prof. English, U. Mich., 1930-36; prof. English, Harvard, 1936-60, Lawrence Lowell prof. humanities, 1960-62, prof. emeritus, 1962-80, editor, Harvard Library Bull., 1966-68, dean Grad. Sch. Arts and Scis., 1943-44, ednl. cons. Provost Marshal Gen's Office, 1945, Chmn. Am. Council Learned Socs., 1955-59; chmn. Weil Inst., 1959-60; Paley vis. prof. Hebrew U., Jerusalem, 1964; Gov. Winthrop Rockfeller Distinguished lectr. U. Ark., 1975. Guggenheim fellow, 1933, 36; fellow Center Advanced Studies, Stanford U., 1959, 64-65. Mem. Mass. Hist. Soc., Modern Lang. Assn. Am., Colonial Soc. Mass., Tex. Philos. Soc., Am. Acad. Arts and Scis. (pres. 1944-51), Am. Philos. Soc., Phi Belta Kappa (prize and medal for humanities 1973), Sigma Delta Chi, Delta Sigma Rho. Author: A Little Book of Local Verse, 1915; Gargoyles (poems), 1918; (play) The Shadow (in Wisconsin Plays) 1917; (brochure) The King in Hamlet, 1921; (with R.H. Griffith) A Bibliography of Works and Mss. of Byron, 1924; America and French Culture (1750-1848), 1927; The Romanesque Lyric (with P.S. Allen), 1928; The life of Moses Coit Tyler, 1933; They Say the Forties, 1937; The Harp That Once, 1937; Ideas in America, 1944; Education and World Tragedy, 1946; The Theory of American Literature, 1948; The Frontier in American Fiction, 1956. Translated Heine's poem The North Sea, 1918, The Bright Medusa, 1952; The Pursuit of Happiness, 1953; American Humanism, 1957; Reflections on Learning, 1958; One Great Society, 1959; Emerson on Education, 1966, History and the Contemporary, 1964; O Strange New World, 1964 (Pulitzer prize for gen. nonfiction 1964; Emerson prize Phi Beta Kappa); Jeffersonianism and the American Novel, 1966; Belief and Disbelief in American Literature, 1967; The Literature of Virginia in the Seventeenth Century, 1968; The Age of Energy, 1971; Revolution and Romanticism, 1974; (with Bessie Zaban Jones) The Many Voices of Boston, 1976; Autobiography, 1979. Editor: The Poems of Edgar Allan Poe, 1929; Plays of Restoration and Eighteenth Century (with D. MacMillan), 1930; Major American Writers (with E.E. Leisy), 1935; The College Reader (with R.M. Lovett), 1936; Oliver Wendell Holmes (with S.I. Hayakawa), 1939; Primer Intellectual Liberty, 1949; Modern Minds(with Richard Ludwig and Marvin Perry), 1949; Letters of Sherwood Anderson (with Walter B. Rideout), 1953; Guide to American Literature and Its Backgrounds Since 1890, 1959, rev. (with Richard M. Ludwig), 1964, 72; A Treasury of Scientific Prose (with I. Bernard Cohen) 1963; contbr. to periodicals. Address: Cambridge, Mass. Died May 11, 1980.

JONES, JAMES, author; b. Robinson, Ill., Nov. 6, 1921; s. Ramon and Ada (Blessing) J.; student U. Hawaii, 1942, N.Y.U., 1945; M. Gloria Mosolino, 1957; children—Kaylie, Jamie. Served with U.S. Army, 1939-44. Decorated Purple Heart, D.S.M. Author: From Here to Eternity (Nat. Book award), 1951; Some Came Running, 1957; The Pistol, 1959; The Thin Red Line, 1962; Go to the Widow-Maker, 1967; The Ice-Cream Headache, 1968; The Merry Month of May, 1971; A Touch of Danger, 1973; Viet Journal, 1974. Home: Sagaponack, L.I., N.Y. Died May 9, 1977.

JONES, JOHN KENYON NETHERTON, educator; b. Birmingham, Eng., Jan. 28, 1912; s. George Edward and Florence (Goodchild) N.; B.Sc. with 1st class with honors, Birmingham U., 1933, Ph.D., 1936, D.Sc., 1947; m. Marjorie Ingles Noon, July 29, 1937; children—Stephanie (Mrs. William Buckeridge), Stephen Howard, Jonathan Ingles. Mem. faculty U. Bristol (Eng.), 1936-45, 45-48, U. Manchester (Eng.), 1945-48; Chown Research prof. Queen's U., Kingston, Ont., Can., 1953-77. Bd. dirs. Ont. Research Found. Fellow Royal Soc., Royal Soc. Can., Chem. Inst. Can.; asso. Royal Inst. Chemists. Research and numerous publs. on chemistry of sugars, biol. origin and function in man and plants. Home: Kingston, Ont., Can. Died 1977.

JONES, JOSEPH L., newspaperman; b. Moody, Mo., June 18, 1897; s. Charles Warren and Cora (Powell) J.; A.B., Drury Coll., Springfield, Mo. 1921, LL.D. (hon.), 1957; B.Litt., Columbia, 1922; m. Helen Sullivan, Sept. 24, 1924 (dec. 1971); children—Peter Taylor, Elizabeth Townsend (Mrs. Graham H. Jeffries), Constance Hamilton. Office boy West Plains (Mo.) Jour., 1914; with U.P.I., 1921—, fgn. editor, 1924, assigned to London, 1925-26, to Lima, Santiago, Buenos Aires and Caracas, 1928-29, gen. fgn. mgr., from 1937, v.p. 1942-64, cons. to internat. dept., 1965-80; asso. in journalism Columbia, 1932-55. Presbyn. Club: University. Home: Pelham, N.Y. Died Dec. 7, 1980.

JONES, LEMUEL THEOPHILUS, candy mfr. and retailer, civic and religious leader; b. Ebensburg, Pa., Jan. 23, 1896; s. Thomas Daniel and Mary Ann (Hughes) J.; A.B., U. Ia., 1921; LL.D., Parsons Coll., 1950; L.H.D., Tarkio Coll., 1950; m. Jessie E. Stover, Dec. 22, 1921; children—Lemuel Theophilus, Russel Stover, Thomas Daniel (dec.), Sally Jacquelyn, Mary Ann, John Paul. High sch., coll. instr., 1921-28; partner Russell Stover Candies, Kansas City, Mo., 1928-60; pres. Russell Stover Candies, Inc., 1960-61; pres. Russell Corp.; v.p., dir. Empire State Bank, Kansas City, Mo., dir. Millcon Corp., Lincoln Redevel. Corp., sr. v.p. Logistics Research, Inc., Aviation Research, Inc. Industry World Alliance Cocoa Producers, Chocolate Mfrs. and Confectioners, London, 1957; industry adviser Am. delegation FAO Cocoa Study Group, Nigeria, 1957, Ghana, 1961. Mem. Kansas City Crime Commn., from 1951, Commn. Charitable Solicitations, 1953-63; adv. com. Regional Health and Welfare Council; bd. Nat. Council Community Chests Am.; pres. Helping Hand Inst., United Funds Kansas City, Kansas City Community Chest (past pres); Urban League of Kansas City exec. bd., chmn. career fair; nat. dir. Nat. Conf. Christians and Jews, 1953-56; a founder, dir. Kansas City Conf. Christians and Jews; mem. nat. council United Negro Coll. Fund, 1949-54; bd. govs. Am. Royal; nat. dir. YMCA, 1952-55, pres. West Central area, 1946-50, pres. Kansas City, 1946-50, former v.p., nat. council; co-chmn. Billy Graham Heart of Am. Crusade, 1967. Chmn., Mo. Republican Finance Com., 1960-62, Mo. State Rep. Central Com., 1961-62, mem. Rep. Nat. Finance Com. Pres. bd. trustees U. Ia. Found., Mo. Valley Coll.; trustee Mo. Bible Coll., Bapt. Meml. Hosp., 1947-67, Kansas City Conservatory of Music, from 1951; bd. dirs., exec. com. Martin Luther King, Jr. Meml. Hosp.; bd. dirs. Am. Humanics Found., YMCA Rockies Starlight Theater, Presbyn. Lay Com., Inc. Served as ensign, USN, 1917-19. Recipient Silver Beaver award Boy Scouts. Mem. Mo. C. of C. (dir.), C. of C. U.S., Kansas City C. of C., N.A.M., Nat. Assn. Confectioners, Nat. Council Chs. Christ in Am. (pres. United Ch. Men 1950-54, gen. bd. mem, Nat. Council Presby. Men pres. 1950-52, exec. com., nominating com.), Religion in Am. Life (Laymen's com.), Am. Bible Soc. (chmn. Kansas City 1943-50), Mo. (past v.p.), Kansas City (exec. com. mem. at large) councils of chs., Sunday Sch. Union (hon. v.p.). Presbyn. (elder). Mason, K.P. Home: Kansas City, Mo. Deceased.

JONES, MARVIN, judge; b. nr. Valley View, Tex.; s. H.K. and Dosia J.; A.B., Southwestern U., 1905; LL.B., U. Tex., 1907; LL.D., Tex A. and M. Coll. Admitted to Tex. bar, 1907; practiced at Amarillo; appted. chmn. bd. legal examiners 7th Supreme Jud. Dist. Tex., 1913; mem. 65th to 76th Congresses, 18th Tex. Dist., chmn. House Com. on Agr.; 1931-40; judge U.S. Ct. Claims, 1940-45, on leave 1943-45; chief justice. U.S. Ct. Claims, Washington, 1947-64, sr. judge, from 1964. Asst. to Hon. James F. Byrnes 1943; pres. UN Conf. on Food and Agr., 1943; mem. War Moblzn. Com., U.S. food adminstr., 1943-45. Mem. Am. Legion, Order of Coif (hon.). Democrat. Methodist. Mason, Woodman, Elk. Author: How War Food Saved American Lives; Should Uncle Sam PayWhen and Why? Home: Amarillo, Tex. Died Mar. 4, 1976.

JONES, MERLE SILAS, TV exec.; b. Omaha, Aug. 14, 1905; s. Alan W. and Ida (O'Donnell) J.; LL.B., U. Nebr., 1929; m. Frances Evelyn Green, Mar. 21, 1932. Admitted to Neb. bar, 1929, practiced law, 1929-32; mem. sales dept. Radio Sta. WAAW, Omaha, 1932-34; nat. sales mgr., Radio Sta. KMBC, Kansas City, Mo., 1934-36; asst. mgr. Radio Sta. KMOX, St. Louis, 1936-37, gen. mgr., 1937-44; v.p., gen. mgr. Cowles Broadcasting Co., Washington, 1944-47; gen. mgr. Radio Sta. WCCO, Mpls., 1947-49; gen. mgr. Radio Sta. KNX and Columbia Pacific Network and TV Sta. KTSL, Los Angeles, 1949-July 1951; v.p. chare co. owned stas. and gen. services CBS TV, N.Y.C., 1951-56, exec. v.p., 1956, pres., 1956-58; pres. CBS Films, Inc., also pres. Terrytoons div., 1958-69, CBS Japan, Inc., 1964-69; chmn. bd. CBS Ltd., London, 1958-69, CBS (Europe) S.A., Zug, Switzerland, 1959-69. Dir. Bus. Council for Internat. Understanding. Mem. TV Bur.

Advt. (dir.), Nat. Assn. Radio and TV Broadcasters (dir.), Radio Pioneers (dir.), Broadcast Pioneers (pres. 1960), TV Program Export Assn. (dir.), Alpha Tau Omega, Phi Delta Phi. Home: Rancho Mirage, Calif. Died Mar. 24, 1976.

JONES, PAUL C(ARUTHERS), journalist, congressman; b. Kennett, Mo., Mar. 12, 1901; s. Will A. and Wirtie (Caruthers) J.; B.J., U. of Mo., 1923; m. Ethel Rockholt, Aug. 2, 1923; children—Betty Anne (Mrs. Joe D. Cash), Paul Caruthers, Jr., Nell (Mrs. Tom B. Mobley). Newspaper pub., Kennett, Mo., 1923-53; general manager radio station KBOA, 1947-66; mem. city council of Kennett, 1931-33. Mayor, 1933-34; mem. Mo. Ho. of Reps., 1935-36, Mo. Senate, 1937-44 (chmn. appropriations com. 1943-44; chmn. Mo. State Highway Commn., 1945-48); elected to 80th Congress, Nov. 1948, to serve for unexpired term; mem. 81st to 90th Congresses, 10th Mo. Dist. Mem. bd. edn., Kennett, 1937-48; pres. Miss. Valley Flood Control Assn., 1959-60. Directed orgn. 6th Mo. Inf. of State Guard, comdg. officer, 1940-46. Mem. Scabbard and Blade, Alpha Delta Sigma, Kappa Tau Alpha, Pi Kappa Alpha. Democrat. Mason. Club: Lions (past dist. gov. of Lions Internat.). Home: Kennett, Mo. Died Feb. 10, 1981.

JONES, PAUL VAN BRUNT, prof. history; b. Ann Arbor, Mich., Aug. 26, 1882; s. Samuel Arthur and Maria Jane (Van Brunt) J.; A.B., U. of Mich., 1906, A.M., 1908; Harrison fellow in history, U. of Pa., 1910-12, Ph.D., 1912, Harrison research fellow, 1912-13; m. Irma Frida Haller, Sept. 1, 1914; 1 son, Paul Haller. Instr. in history, U. of Mich., 1906-10; asso. in history, Bryn Mawr, 1913; at U. of Ill. since 1914, asst. prof. history, 1920, asso. prof., 1921-30, prof., 1930-50; retired 1950; professor Modern European history at Trinity University, San Antonio, Texas, since 1951; sumer sessions at U. Mich. and Northwestern. Mem. Am. Hist. Assn., Am. Assn. Univ. Profs., Phi Beta Kappa, Phi Eta. Conglist. Club: University. Author: The Household of a Tudor Nobleman, 1917; Analytical Survey of Modern European History, 1930, revised enlarged edit., 1937. Translator: Calvin, Educateur des Consciences (Eugène Choisy), 1930. Contbr. to The World Book Encyclopedia; articles and reviews to mags. Home: Urbana, Ill.; (summer) Empire, Mich. *

JONES, PRESTON ST. VRAIN, playwright, actor; b. Albuquerque, Apr. 7, 1936; s. James Brooks and Maud Gwinn (St. Vrain) J.; B.A., U. N.Mex., 1960; M.A., Trinity U., San Antonio, 1966; m. Mary Sue Birkhead, Sept. 7, 1963. Asst. dir., mgr. Dallas Theatre Centre, 1963-79; author: (3 plays) A Texas Triology, 1975; A Place on the Magdalena Flats, 1976; Santa Fe Sunshine, 1977; Remember. Recipient Frank Nick award Dallas Theatre Centre, 1971; Golden Apple award Cue mag., 1976; Drama Desk award, 1977; Outer Critics award, 1977; grantee Rockefeller Found., 1975. Mem. Tex. Inst. Arts and Letters, Tex. Commn. Arts and Humanities, Am. Playwrights Theatre (gov.), Kappa Alpha. Democrat. Roman Catholic. Home: Dallas, Tex. Died Sept. 19, 1979.

JONES, RALPH TATTON, newspaper editor; b. Liverpool, Eng., July 19, 1885; s. Robert and Hannah (Tatton) J.; ed. Bickerton Sch., Birkdale, Eng., 1895-1902; m. Bessie May Lipscomb, Jan. 14, 1913; children—Elizabeth Tatton (Mrs. Clyde M. Wiley), Hannah Tatton (Mrs. Felix Reid, Jr.), Ralph Tatton, Christine Lipscomb Tatton. Naturalized, 1939. On news staff Toronto (Can.) Globe, 1905; on news and editorial staffs of various papers in Ont., N.Y., N.C., S.C., etc. to 1912; on staff Atlanta (Ga.) Constitution since 1912, asso. editor since 1937. Democrat. Presbyterian. Writer of daily column in Atlanta Constitution; public speaker. Home: Decatur, Ga. *

JONES, RICHARD EARLE, lawyer; b. Jones Mill, Ala., Apr. 5, 1894; s. James Wiley and Mary Frances (Hughes) J.; A.B., U. Ala., 1914, M.A., 1915, LL.B., 1919; m. Lucille Foster, June 10, 1922; children—Richard Earle, Sara Frances. Admitted to Ala. bar, 1919; partner firm Knox, Jones, Woolf & Merrill, Anniston; dir. First Nat. Bank of Anniston, Classe Ribbon Co. Inc. Mem. Ala. State Democratic Exec. Com., 1924-40, elected pres. and v.p., 3 terms. Mem. City Bd. Edn., Anniston, 1935-46; chmn. merit system council County Depts. Pub. Welfare, 1947-51. Capt. F.A., AUS, World War I. Mem. Anniston C. of C., Am. Calhoun County bar assns., Ala. State Bar, Phi Beta Kappa, Baptist. Kiwanian. Home: Anniston, Ala. Died May 31, 1977.

JONES, ROBERT COPELAND, investment banker; b. Washington, Aug. 23, 1898; s. Wentworth C. and Elizabeth (Tolson) J.; student schs., Washington, also Md.; m. Virginia C. Lewis, Mar. 26, 1921 (dec. 1959); children—Robert Copeland, Kenneth Page, Virginia Aline; m. 2d, Jille Romney, 1959. With John L. Edwards & Co., investment securities, Washington; co-mgr. at Washington for N.Y. Stock Exchange Ho. of G.M.P. Murphy & Co., 1927-30; established investment banking house of Robert C. Jones & Co., 1939, became sr. partner; sr. partner Jones, Kreeger & Hewitt, mem. N.Y. Stock Exchange, from 1952; partner Jones, Kreeger & Co., Washington, 1959-65. Served from 2d lt. to capt., U.S. Army, World War I; AEF; from lt. col. to col., USAAF, World War II. Decorated Legion of Merit. Mem. Washington Bd. Trade, N.Y. and Washington Stock Exchange, Soc. Colonial Cavaliers, Soc. Colonial Wars, Soc. War of 1912, Soc. of Cincinnati, S.A.R. Clubs: Army and Navy, Army-Navy Country, University (Washington). Home: Rockville, Md. Died May 30, 1980.

JONES, RUSSELL, reporter; b. Mpls., Jan. 5, 1918; s. Lewis Russell and Elizabeth (McLeod) J.; student pub. schs., Mpl. and Stillwater, Minn.; m. Martha 'Sennyey von Kissenye, July 29, 1955; step children—Jozsef Karolyi van Nagykaroly, Erzsebet Karoli von Nagykaroly. Reporter, radio columnist St. Paul Dispatch 1938-41; co-founder, combat reporter The Stars and Stripes, 1942-45, civilian reporter, 1947-48; co-owner, editor for or Germany, Weekend mag., Paris, 1948-49; with U. P., 1949-58, London, Prague, Vienna, Frankfurt, chief Eastern European corr., 1956-58; Middle Eastern corr. CBS News, from 1958; later with ABC News, bur. chief in Beirut, Tel Aviv and Moscow; ret.; 1977. Recipient Pulitzer, Sigma Delta Chi prizes for fgn. corr., George Polk Meml. award for reporting under hazardous conditions (coverage Hungarian Revolution Oct. 1956). Author:(with others) This is Germany, 1950. Home: Vienna, Austria. Died June 9, 1979.

JONES, THEODORE FRANCIS, prof. European history; b. Dover, Mass., Dec. 5, 1885; s. Theodore and Helen M. (Dunn) J.; A.B., Harvard, 1906; Ph.D., 1910; studied Ecole libre des sciences politiques, Paris, 1906-07; unmarried. Asst. in history, Harvard, 1908-10; instr., New York U., 1910-12, asst. prof. European history, 1912-20, asso. prof., 1920-24, prof. since 1924, also dir. University Heights Library. Served as lt. U.S.N.R.F., 1917-21; asst. naval attaché, Madrid, 1918. Mem. Am. Hist. Assn. Club: Harvard. Home: New York, N.Y. *

JONES, THOMAS NORMAN, business exec.; b. Richmond, July 15, 1882; s. Thomas Norman and Kate Gifford (Skelton) J.; student U. of Va., 1903-04; m. Elizabeth Landon Wellford, Oct. 18, 1911; children—Katharine Skelton, Robert Carter Wellford. Mem. engring. corps in charge constrn. of Potomac R.R. yards porth of Alexandria, Va., 1904-06; entered elec. dept. of elec. and transportation properties, Richmond, Va., 1906; foreman car barns, transportation dept., 1906; supt. Richmond and Chesapeake Bay Ry. Co., between Richmond and Ashland, Va., supt. Va. Light & Power Co., Ashland, Va., 1907; chief engr. railways Va. Ry. & Power Co., 1911; asst. gen. mgr. Norfolk & Portsmouth div. of Va. Ry. & Power Co., 1917, gen. mgr. Norfolk & Portsmouth div., 1920; v.p. Va. Elec. & Power Co. (name changed from Va. Ry. & Power Co., 1925); 1928-50, vice president personnel, 1952-53; in charge of Virginia Electric and Power Company public transportation operations, 1934-45. Mem. bd. trustees Funds of the Protestant Epis. Ch., Diocese of Va.; pres. Richmond Community Fund, 1937-39; v.p. Va. Hosp. Service Assn., 1935-47. Mem. Richmond C. of C. (former dir.), Va. C. of C., Newcomen Soc. of Eng., S.A.R., Delta Psi. Home: Richmond. *

JONES, VERNON, univ. prof.; b. Portsmouth, Va., Oct. 13, 1897; s. Frank A. and Pattie A. (McLemore) J.; A.B. and A.M., U. Va., 1920; A.M., Columbia, 1925, Ph.D., 1926; m. Harriet Clement Marble, Nov. 2, 1929; children—Patricia (Mrs. Hugh Lovell), Nancy Clement (Mrs. Roy Pearson, Jr.). Began as tchr. and asst. prin. Appalachia (Va.) High Sch., 1917; prin. East Stone Gap (Va.) High Sch., 1918-19, Ashland (Va.) High Sch., 1920, Richmond (Va.) Sch. System, 1921-23; dir. research Richmond Pub. Schs., 1924; asso. in edn. Teachers Coll., Columbia, 1925-26; asso. prof. ednl. psychology Clark U., 1926-37, prof., from 1938, chmn. dept. psychology and edn., 1937-49, chmn. dept. edn., 1949-66. Mem. planning com. Nat. Citizenship Conf., from 1962. Fellow Am. Psychol. Assn.; mem. N.E.A., Nat. Soc. Study Edn., A.A.A.S., Am. Edn. Research Assn. (award for research 1940), Raven Soc., Phi Beta Kappa. Baptist. Author: Character and Citizenship Education, 1950; Youth Decides, 1952; The Effect of Age and Experience on Tests of Intelligence, 1926; others. Contbr. to Ency. of Ednl. Research; Manual of Child Psychology, Colliers Ency. Home: Worcester, Mass. Died Mar. 4, 1980.

JONES, WALTER CLYDE, JR., lawyer; b. Chgo., Dec. 7, 1902; s. Walter Clyde and Emma (Boyd) J.; B.A., Yale, 1925; J.D., Northwestern U., 1928; m. Emily Watt, June 12, 1929; children—Mary Helen (Mrs. Stuart A. McKeldin), Emily Hubbard (Mrs. John G. Meeker), Walter Clyde III, William Watt. Admitted to Ill. bar, 1928; asso. firm Jones, Addington, Ames & Seibold, Chgo., 1928-31, Cutting, Moore & Sidney, now Sidley and Austin, Chgo., 1931-36; asst. gen. atty. Ill. Bell Telephone Co., Chgo., 1936-40, gen. atty. 1940-51, gen. solicitor, 1951-67. Mem. Am., Ill., Chgo. bar assns., Beta Theta Pi, Phi Delta Phi, Order of Coif. Club: Skokie Country (Glencoe). Home: Glencoe, Ill. Died July 4, 1979.

JONES, WILLIAM ALFRED, mgmt. cons.; b. N.Y.C., Feb. 5, 1905; s. William John and Anna Elizabeth (Valentine) J.; ed. pub. schs.; m. Dorothy Bray Buck, July 21, 1928; 1 dau., Barbara (Mrs. Edward Stanley Savage). With Bridgeport Brass Co. (Conn.), 1923-71, v.p., controller, 1961-71, mgmt. cons., 1971-76; v.p., dir. Bridgeport Engravers Copper, H.B. Egan Co. Can., Piedmont Mfg. Co. Mem. Bridgeport Bd. Apportionment and Taxation, 1966-76; chmn. Community Health and Welfare Agy. Survey, 1968-69; mem. steering com. St. Vincent's Hosp., 1971-76; mem. bd. assos. U. Bridgeport, 1969, mem. adv. bd., 1969-76; mem. planning bd. United Community Services, 1969-76; mem. exec. bd. Pomperaug council Boy Scouts Am. Bd. dirs. Barnum Festival Soc.; trustee Conn. Pub. Expenditures Council. Mem. Greater Bridgeport C. of C. (pres. 1970), Newcomen Soc. N. Am., So. Conn. Financial Execs. Inst. (pres.), Conn. Mfg. Assn. Mason (32 deg.), Rotarian. Address: Bridgeport, Conn. Died Mar. 30, 1976; interred Mt. Grove Cemetery, Bridgeport, Conn.

JONES, WILLIAM BLAKELY, U.S. Judge; b. Cedar Rapids, Iowa, Mar. 20, 1907; s. James Patrick and Isabel Cecilia (Blakely) J.; A.B., U. Notre Dame, 1928, LL.B., 1931; m. Alice Danicich, Nov. 17, 1937; 1 dau., Barbara. Admitted to Mont. bar, 1931, D.C. bar, 1945, Md. bar, 1954; spl. asst. atty. gen. Mont., 1935-37; individual practice, Helena, Mont., 1931-37; atty. Dept. Justice, 1937-43, OPA, 1943; exec. asst. to Am. chmn. Joint Brit.-Am. Patent Interchange Com., 1943-46; individual practice, Washington, 1946-62; judge U.S. Dist. Ct. for D.C., 1962-79, chief judge, 1975-77, sr. judge, 1977-79. Fellow Am. Coll. Trial Lawyers, Am. Bar Found.; mem. Am., D.C. bar assns. Clubs: Lawyers, Nat. Lawyers, Metropolitan (Washington); Columbia Country (Chevy Chase). Home: Chevy Chase, Md. Died July 31, 1979.

JONES, WILLIAM CLINTON, III, retail supermarket exec.; b. Minersville, Pa., Oct. 14, 1928; s. William C. and Helen (Siroka) J.; B.A., Rutgers U., 1953; m. Margaret Helen Helm, Sept. 25, 1954; children—Barbara Helen, William C. With Link Belt Co., Phila., 1953-54; with Penn Fruit Co., Phila., 1954-70, chief accountant, 1960-64, controller, 1964-70; asst. controller Day & Zimmerman, Phila., 1970-73; asst. controller Foodarama Shop-Rite Supermarkets, Freehold, N.J., 1973-74, controller, 1974-77, instr. supermarket mgmt. Brookdale Community Coll., Lincroft, N.J., 1975-77. Home: Oreland, Pa. Died Oct. 23, 1977.

JOOST, NICHOLAS TEYNAC, educator; b. Jacksonville, Fla., May 28, 1969; s. Nicholas Teynac and Margaret (Wrigley) J.; B.S.S., Georgetown U., 1938; M.A., U. N.C., 1939, Ph.D., 1947; m. Laura Reed, May 25, 1943; children—Anna, Mary Elizabeth, Nicholas. Teaching fellow U. N.C., 1940-47; instr. Northwestern U., 1947-49; asst. prof. Loyola U., Chgo., 1949-54; mem. editorial staff Poetry mag., 1951-54, acting editor, asso. editor, 1953-54; asso. prof. Assumption Coll., 1954-58; mem. faculty So. Ill. U., Edwardsville, 1958-78, prof. English, 1960-78, head humanities div., 1960-63; Fulbright lectr. U. Nijmegen (Netherlands), 1963-64; editorial cons. Bollingen Found., 1954-60. Bd. commrs. Hayner Dist. Library, 1969-73; bd. dirs. Lewis and Clark Library System, 1971-73, pres., 1973. Served with USAAF, 1942-45. Recipient French Acad. award Georgetown U., 1938; Bollingen Found. grantee Worcester (Mass.) Art Mus., 1957-58; recipient Faculty Service award So. Ill. U., 1960, award for excellence in scholarship, 1972; Chapelbrook Found. grantee, 1970-71. Mem. William Clark So., Cath. Renaissance Soc., Midcontinent Am. Studies Assn. (pres.), Delta Epsilon Sigma (nat. pres. 1957-58, editor bull. 1957-63), The Westerners. Author: Was All for Naught? Robert Penn Warren and New Directions in the Novel: Fifty Years of the American Novel, 1951; The Authorship of the Free Thinker: Studies in the Early English Periodical, 1957; Moore's The Jerboa, 1962; Scofield Thayer and The Dial (Top Honor award Chgo. Book Clinic), 1964; Years of Transition: The Dial, 1912-1920; Studies in the Art and Age of Geoffrey Chaucer, 1967; Ernest Hemingway and the Little Magazines, 1968; D.H. Lawrence and The Dial, 1970; Reveille in the West: Travelers on the Western Frontier, 1970; The Dial, Two Author Indexes, 1971; Toward the Modern, 1972; Sherwood Anderson and the Dial: Proceedings of the Sherwood Anderson Centenary Conference, 1977; Richard Smith Elliott and the Mexican War: Proc. of the Conference on Literature of Travel and Exploration. Editor. Papers Lang. and Lit., 1964-74, cons., 1974-80, editor Bicentennial Issue, 1976. Contbr. articles to profl. jours. Home: Jacksonville, Fla. Died Mar. 23, 1980; buried Oaklawn Cemetery, Jacksonville.

JORDAN, HARRY EDWARD, assn. executive; born Coulterville, Illinois, November 15, 1882; s. Walter Scott and Susan (Woodworth) J.; B.S., Franklin (Indiana) College, 1903, D.Sc., 1938; married Ruth Low, Sept. 12, 1907; children—Celeste (Mrs. Blodgett E. Brennan), Lois (Mrs. Edward G. Schulze). Chemical engineer, Indianapolis Water Co., 1903-36; president American Water Works Association, 1934-35, exec. sec. since 1936, editor of Journal of same since 1936. Captain, later major, Construction Div., Gen. Staff, U.S.

Army, World War I, 1918-19. Hon. member American Water Works Assn., New England Water Works Assn. Mem. Am. Soc. C.E., Am. Public Health Assn., American Chem. Soc., Sigma Alpha Epsilon. Republican. Mason. Clubs: Service, Literary (Indpls.); Chemists (N.Y.C.). Home: Port Washington, N.Y. *

JORDAN, HOWARD SHELDON, educator; b. Mpls., Dec. 19, 1906; s. William Henry and Frances (Sheldon) J.; B.A., U. Minn., 1929, M.A., 1930, Ph.D., 1936; m. Sarah Kathleen Burrell, July 6, 1946; children—James Burrell, William Sheldon. Teaching fellow French, U. Min., 1929-30, instr. French, 1930-39; asst. prof. French, Brown U., 1939-44; prof. French, head dept. modern fgn. langs. Salem Coll., 1944-49; prof. French, head dept. modern fgn. langs. U. Ga., 1949-62, prof. French, 1962-74, emeritus prof. French, 1974-79; NDEA lectr.-evaluator, 1962, dir. Lang. Insts., 1959, 60. Decorated Croix de chevalier dans L'Ordre des Palmes Academiques, 1958. Lutheran. Home: Athens, Ga. Died May 31, 1979; buried Athens, Ga.

JORDAN, PAUL H., nat. guard officer; b. Chattanoga, Aug. 14, 1904; s. Calvin H. and Sarah (McCollister) J.; student U. Tenn., 1924-25; grad. Command and Gen. Staff Sch., 1943; m. Ada Frances Graham, July 1, 1926; children—Robert H., James Perry, Patricia Jane, Jordan Aytes. Owner Northside Lumber & Supply Company, Chattanooga; minister Meth. Ch. Enlisted Tenn. N.G., 1923; advanced through grades to maj. gen.; with U.S. Army, 1941-45. Ordained to ministry Baptist Ch. Decorated Bronze Star medal with V and oak leaf cluster; ETO ribbon with 3 battle stars; Am. Def., Am. Theatre, Army Occupation, Victory ribbons (U.S.); Distinguished Service, Commendation ribbons (Tenn.). Mem. C. of C., Am. Legion (past post comdr.). Mason (33 deg.; past potentate; Shriner). Home: Hixson, Tenn. Died Apr. 27, 1976; interred Hamilton Meml. Gardens, Chattanooga.

JORDAN, WAYNE, editor, writer; b. Lower Salem, Ohio, June 1, 1902; s. Elmer Webber and Blanche (Lewis) J.; A.B., Marietta Coll., 1924; A.M., Columbia, 1939; m. Harriet H. Kuenzel, Dec. 25, 1927 (dec. 1968); m. 2d, Agnes A. Jackson, Apr. 12, 1969. Prin. Washington, Township-Graysville (Ohio) High Sch., 1922-23; teacher Marietta (Ohio) High Sch., 1924-25; with Marietta Register, 1925; teaching asst. Am. history U. Cin., 1925-26; reporter Toledo Times, 1926-27; copyreader Detroit Free Press, 1927-28, Philadelpha Public Ledger, 1928-30; night city editor, then news editor, Toledo Times, 1930-31; news editor and asso. editor Detroit Free Press, 1931-36; mng. editor. Philadelphia Inquirer, 1936-38; mem. N.Y. staff Business Week, 1939-42, 1945-46; editor the Bangor (Maine) Comml., 1953-54; with Buffalo Evening News, 1954-55, spl. writer, 1960-70; editor The Lorain (Ohio) Jour., 1955-59; newspaper columnist, author Sgt. Dalzell's Civil War Album. Prof. journalism U. Maine, 1946-52. In Germany on missions for Stars and Stripes, 1947, mil. govt., 1948; state dept., 1952-53; with Internat. Air Edition N.Y. Times, summers 1950, 51, 52. On active duty as lt. and capt., U.S.M.C.R., 1942-45, adj., MCAS Ewa, Oahu, T.H., 1944; lt. col. Res. Home: Buffalo, N.Y. Died Mar. 16, 1979; interred Pataskala, Ohio.

JORDAN, WILBUR K., educator, historian; b. Lynnville, Ind., Jan. 15, 1902; s. William and Emma (Shepard) J.; B.A., Oakland City Coll., 1923, D.Litt. (hon.), 1960; M.A., Harvard, 1926, Ph.D. 1931; L.H.D., Bates Coll., 1944; LL.D., U. Vt., 1962; Dartmouth Coll., 1965, Reed Coll., Portland, Oreg., 1967; Litt.D., Oxford Univ., 1964; m. Frances Ruml, Apr. 13, 1929. Instr. history U. Mo., 1924-25; instr. history and tutor history, govt. and econs., Harvard, 1931-37; prof. history, Scripps Coll., Claremont, Calif., 1937-40, Claremont Colls., 1937-40; asso. prof. and prof., Eng. History and gen. editor, Univ. Press, U. Chgo., 1940-43; prof. history, Harvard, 1946-65, LeRoy B. Williams prof. history and polit. sci., 1965-72, prof. emeritus, 1972-80; pres. Radcliffe Coll., 1943-60; Sterling traveling fellow, Harvard, 1929-30; Guggenheim fellow, 1943. Fellow Royal Hist. Soc., Brit. Acad. (corr.); mem. Am. Acad. Arts and Scis., Am. Hist. Assn., Mass., Cambridge, Vt. hist. socs. Author: The Development of Religious Toleration in England (4 vol.), 1932-40; Men of Substance, 1942; Philanthropy in England, 1480-1660, 1959; The Charities of London, 1480-1660, 1960; The Charities of Rural England, 1961; Social Institutions in Kent, 1961; The Social Institutions of Lancashire, 1962; The Chronicle and Political Papers of King Edward VI, 1966; Edward VI: the Young King, 1968; Edward VI: The Threshold of Power, 1970; with M.R. Gleason) The Saying of Northumberland—1553, 1975. Home: Cambridge, Mass. Died June 3, 1980.

JORGENSEN, EUGENE CLIFFORD, coll. dean; b. Hayward, Calif., Oct. 22, 1923; s. Soren Christian and Edith Mae (Peck) J.; B.S., U. Calif. at Berkeley, 1947, M.S., 1949, Ph.D., at Los Angeles, 1954; D.Sc. (hon.), Sorbonne, 1980; m. Patsy Ann Smith, Jan. 28, 1951; children—Lynn Dale, William Howard. Research chemist U. Calif. Radiation Labs., Berkeley, 1949-50; mem. faculty Sch. Pharmacy, U. Calif. at San Francisco, 1953-81, prof. chemistry and pharm. chemistry, 1963-81, asso. dean, 1972-79, acting dean, 1979-81. Guest prof. Inst. Molecular Biology and Biophysics Swiss Fed. U., Zurich, 1970-71; mem. medicinal chemistry study sect USPHS, 1963-67, pharmacology and toxicology tng. grant com., 1967-71. Served with 75th Inf. Div., AUS, 1943-46. Decorated Combat Infantryman's badge; recipient Research Achievement award in medicinal chemistry Am. Pharm. Assn.-Acad. Pharm. Scis., 1978; Ernest H. Volwiler award Am. Assn. Colls. of Pharmacy, awarded posthumously, 1981. USPHS grantee, 1959-81; Gustavus Pfeiffer fellow Tech. U., Munich, Germany, 1960-61. Mem. Am. Chem. Soc., Am. Pharm. Assn., Acad. Pharm. Sci. (chmn. medicinal chemistry sect. 1970-71, Achievement award in medicinal chemistry 1978), Am. Thyroid Assn. Research on relationships between chem. structure and biol. activity of thyroid hormones and polypeptide hormones; author more than 150 research publs. and abstracts. Home: San Anselmo, Calif. Died Feb. 13, 1981.

JOSEPH, RICHARD, writer, travel commentator; b. N.Y.C., Apr. 24, 1910; s. Isaac and Harriet Maurine (Isaacson) J.; B.S., Ohio State U., 1932; postgrad. Alliance Francaise, Paris, France, 1937-38; m. Morgan Howard, Sept. 5, 1954; children—Jamieson Anne, Richard Matthew, Reporter, Columbus (Ohio) Citizen, 1932, N.Y. Evening Journ., 1933-37, N.Y. Post, 1939-40; dir. Walt Disney-Mickey Mouse, S.A., Paris, 1937-39; engaged in pub. relations, 1940-42; asso. editor Esquire mag., 1946-47, travel editor, 1947-76, travel columnist N.Y. Post, Chgo. Tribune-N.Y. News Syndicate, 1959-76; travel commentator NBC TV, 1956-59, CBS Radio Network, 1961-65, Westinghouse Broadcasting Co., 1974. Served AUS, 1942-46; ETO. Decorated Croix de Guerre (France); Star of Solidarity (Italy); recipient Travel Journalism award Am. Soc. Travel Agts., 1950, 51, 56; Pacific Area Travel Assn., 1961, 62, 65, 67, Ethioplan Airlines, 1964, Trans World Airlines, 1952-62, 64-72; Strebig Dobben award, 1963; George Hedman Meml. award, 1966; officer Ordre de Merite Touristique (France), 1962. Mem. Soc. Am. Travel Writers (bd. govs. 1960-63), N.Y. Travel Writers Assn. (pres. 1949-51). Clubs: Silurians, Overseas Press (N.Y.C.). Author: Your Trip Abroad, 1950; Your Trip to Britain, 1951; Richard Joseph's World Wide Travel Guide, 1952; A Letter to the Man Who Killed My Dog, 1956; Richard Joseph's Comprehensive Guide to Europe, 1956; Esquire's Europe in Style Contbr. numerous articles to various publs. Home: New York, N.Y. Died Sept. 30, 1976.

JOSEPHS, DEVEREUX COLT, bus. exec.; b. Newport, R.I., Oct. 16, 1893; s. Lyman Colt and Alice Vernon (Wilson) J.; grad. Groton (Mass.) School, 1911; A.B., Harvard, 1915, LL.D., 1957; m. Margaret Thayer Graham, June 26, 1922; children—Margaret G. (Mrs. Peter B. Nalle). Devereux Colt. In investment banking, 1915-39; with Tchrs. Inc. and Annuity Assn., 1939-45; pres. Carnegie Corp. of N.Y., 1946-48; retired as chmn. bd. N.Y. Life Ins, Co. 1959; bd. Ednl. Broadcasting Corp. (channel 13). Dir. Met. Mus. Art, N.Y. Pub. Library. Republican Episcopalian. Clubs: Century Assn., Harvard (N.Y.C.). Home: New York, N.Y. Died Jan. 4, 1977.

JOSEPHSON, MATTHEW, author; b. Bklyn., Feb. 15, 1899; s. Julius and Sarah (Kasindorf) J.; A.B., Columbia, 1920; m. Hannah Geffen (dec. 1976); May 6, 1920; children—Eric Jonathan, Carl Philip Emmanuel. Editor, Broom, 1922-24; account rep. N.Y. Stock Exchange firms, 1924-26; Am. editor Transition, 1928-29; asst. editor New Republic, 1931-32; spl. lectr. U. Calif., Irvine, 1968-69. Elected mem. Nat. Inst. Arts and Letters 1948. Author: Galimathias, 1923; Zola and His Time, 1928; Portrait of the Artist as American, 1930; Jean-Jacques Rousseau, 1932; The Robber Barons, 1934; The Politicos, 1938; The President Makers, 1940; Victor Hugo, 1942; Empire of the Air, 1944; Stendhal: or the Pursuit of Happiness, 1946: Sidney Hillman: Statesman of American Labor, 1952; Union House, Union Bar, 1956; Edison: A Biography (Francis Parkman prize Soc. Am. Historians 1960), 1959; Life Among the Surrealists: a Memoir, 1962: Infidel in the Temple: A Memoir of the 1930's, 1967; (with Hannah Josephson) Al Smith: Hero of the Cities (Van Wyck Brooks prize for biography and history), 1969; The Money Lords: The Great Finance Capitalists, 1925-1950, 1972. Contbr. to mags. Guggenheim traveling fellow for creative lit., 1933-34. Address: Sherman, Conn. Died Mar. 13, 1978; interred Sherman, Conn.

JOSSELYN, PAUL REITLER, foreign service officer; b. Cedar Rapids, Ia., Dec. 18, 1885; s. Henry S. and May (Reitler) J.; A.B., Beloit (Wis.) Coll., 1909; m. Jean Dudley, Dec. 30, 1919; children—Marion, Paul, Marjorie. Began as student interpreter at Am. Legation, Peiping, China, 1910; vice consul at Tientsin, 1912-14, Canton, 1914-17, Tientsin, 1917-18; consul at Chungking, 1918-21; sec. at Am. Legation, Peking, 1921-27; on duty in State Dept., Washington, D.C., 1927-30; consul at Shanghai, 1930-34; consul gen. at Hankow, 1934-39, at Vancouver, B.C., Canada, May 1939-Jan. 1944; on duty, Dept. of State, 1944-45; consul gen., Shanghai, Aug. 1945; Singapore, Apr. 1946; retired 1948. *

JOY, ALFRED HARRISON, astronomer; b. Greenville, Ill., Sept. 23, 1882; s. Frank Pierce and Louise Alfreda (Maynard) Joy; Ph.B., Greenville College, Greenville, Ill., 1903, honorary, D.Sc., 1945; A.M., Oberlin (O.) College, 1904; graduate study, Princeton, 1910-11; m. Margherita O. Burns, July 23, 1919; children—Richard Pierce, Edith Woodbury. Instr. astronomy, Am. U. of Beirut, Syria, 1904-10, prof. astronomy and dir. obs., 1910-16; instr. Yerkes Obs., U. of Chicago, 1914-15; astronomer Mount Wilson Obs. (Carnegie Instn., Washington, D.C.), Pasadena, Calif., 1915-48, sec., 1920-48, research asso. 1950-52, Cal. Inst. Tech. 1949-52. Member Nat. Acad. Sciences, A.A.A.S. (chmn., Sec.D., 1948-49), Am. Astron. Soc. (pres., 1949-52). Astron. Society of Pacific (pres. 1931, 39), Royal Astron. Soc. of Can., Internat. Astron. Union, Royal Astron. Soc. (London). Presbyn. Clubs: University, Athenaeum. Home: Pasadena, Cal. *

JOY, CHARLES RHIND, editor and writer; born Boston, Dec. 5, 1885; son Robert S. and Arabella S. (Parke) J.; A.B., with distinction in English, Harvard, 1908, S.T.B., cum laude, 1911; S.T.B., Andover Theol. Sem., 1911; S.T.D., Pacific Unitarian Sch. for Ministry, 1933; m. Lucy Alice Wanzer, June 29, 1911; children—Alice Parke, Lucy Parke, Robert Arthur, Nancy. Minister Unitarian ch. numerous cities in U.S. 1911-40; European commr. Unitarian Service Com., 1940-42, acting exec. dir., 1942-44; exec. dir., 1944-46; asso. exec. dir., European dir. Save The Children Fedn., 1947-50; nat., internat. field representative CARE, 1950-52, chief of CARE in Korea, 1952-54, executive cons. for African affairs CARE, 1954-55. Active internat. social work projects of ch. and U.S. Mem. Phi Beta Kappa. Decorated Médaille Commémorative de la Grande Guerre (France), Cruz Vermelha de Dedicacao, Cruz Vermelha de Merito, Cruz Vermelha de Benemerencia (all Portugal); Palme Academique (France); Officer of French Acad. Unitarian. Editor, compiler, translator several works. Author several books, latest being: Harper's Topical Concordance, 1962; Emerging Africa, 1964; others. Editor, consultant several church mags. Contbr. various periodicals. Address: Albany, N.Y. *

JOYNES, EDITH B., educator; b. Union Mills, Ind., Mar. 24, 1884; dau. Charles M. and Ella C. (Evans) Dowd; A.B., Ind. Univ., 1909; student Mich. Univ., 1905-06, William and Mary Coll., 1919, summer student Mich. U., Calif., Colo., Wis., Pittsburgh, Syracuse, Harvard, New York Univs.; m. Thomas E. Joynes, Apr. 14, 1919. Prin. West Lebanon (Ind.) elementary and high school, 1909; elementary prin. Norfolk County, Va., 1916-18; teacher Tarentum (Pa.) high school, 1918-Mar. 1919, Norfolk (Va.) City Sch. System high school, 1919-29, elementary prin. Washington Gatewood Sch., 1929-45, James Monroe Sch. since 1945. Mem. citizens park planning com. of Norfolk 3 yrs. Recipient Business and Professional Womans Club citation as outstanding woman citizen of Norfolk 1943-44. Mem. N.E.A. (life mem., pres. 1943-44, vice pres. and mem. exec. bd. dept. elementary prins., 1937-41, pres. dept. classroom teachers, 1928-29, dir. for Va., 1931-43), World Fedn. of Edn. Assn. (del. to Switzerland, 1929, Denver, Colo., 1931), Va. Edn. Assn. (pres. dept. classroom teachers, orgn. dept. 1925), Delta Gamma, Delta Kappa Gamma (past pres.), Kappa Delta Pi. Clubs: Business and Professional Women's (mem. exec. bd., chmn. edn. com.), Quota (mem. state and nat. com. edn.). Author articles in Year Book of N.E.A., placed in Congressional Library, Washington, D.C., 1928. Compiler Year Book of Classroom Dept., 1929, Year Book of N.E.A., 1943-44. Home: Norfolk. *

JUDD, NEIL MORTON, archaeologist; b. Cedar Rapids, Nebr., Oct. 27, 1887; s. Lucius P. and Phoebe (Cummings) J.; A.B., U. Utah, 1911; A.M., George Washington U., 1913; m. Anne S. MacKay, Oct. 29, 1938. Settled in Salt Lake City, 1901; pub. school teacher, 1907-08; expdns., 1907-14; aid in ethnology, U.S. Nat. Museum, 1911-17, asst. curator anthropology, 1918, curator Am. archeology, 1919-29, curator archeology, 1930-49, hon. asso. in anthropology, Jan. 1950. Field dir. various archeol. expdns. for Smithsonian Instn., dir. Nat. Geog. Soc.'s exploration of Chaco Canyon, N. Mex., 1920, of its Pueblo Bonito expdn., 1921-27, of its San Juan expdn., 1923, etc. Cadet flyer and observer, aviation sect., Signal Corps, U.S. Army, Jan 21, 1918-Dec. 18, 1918. Mem. ofcl. del., rep. Smithsonian Instn. to Seventh Am. Sci. Congress, Mexico City, 1935; rep. Smithsonian Instn. to 2d Assembly Pan-Am. Inst. Geography and History, Washington 1935; mem. advisory bd. Lab. of Anthropology, Santa Fe, 1927-47. Fellow A.A.A.S. (v.p. and chmn. of Sect. H, 1939), Soc. Am. Archaeology (pres. 1939); mem. Washington Acad. Sciences, Am. Anthrop. Assn. (treas. 1916-18; pres. 1945), Anthrop. Soc., Washington, D.C. (v.p. 1920-23, pres. 1925-27), Nat. Geog. Soc. (life mem. hon.). Rep of Am. Anthrop. Assn. on NRC, 1925-28, 1931-32 and 1937-39. Club: Cosmos (Washington, D.C.). Contbr. on archeol. topics. Address: Washington, D.C. Died Dec. 19, 1976.

JUDD, ORRIN GRIMMELL, judge; b. Bklyn., Sept. 6, 1906; s. Orrin Reynolds and Bertha Rebecca (Grimmell) J.; A.B., Colgate U., 1926, LL.D., 1964; student Sorbonne, Paris, France, 1926-27; LL.B. summa cum laude, Harvard, 1930; m. Persis Mae Dolloff, Apr. 25, 1936; children—Persis Ruth, Orrin D., Betsy Ann, John M. Law clk. to Circuit Judge Learned Hand, 1930; engaged in practice of law with firm Davies, Auerbach, Cornell & Hardy, N.Y.C., 1931-43, mem. firm, 1934-43; solicitor gen. N.Y. State, 1943-46; mem. firm Goldstein, Judd & Gurfein, 1946-64, 65-68; judge Surrogate Court of Kings County, N.Y., 1964; U.S. dist. judge Eastern Dist. N.Y., 1968-76; spl. counsel to Gov. Dewey matters relating to UN, 1946. Hearing officer conscientious objector cases, 1953-58. Pres. Bklyn. Citizens League, 1937-40; mem. exec. com. Citizens Union, N.Y.C., 1937-43; pres. Assn. for Chinese Blind, Inc., 1940-48; mem. bd. of higher edn. City of N.Y., 1942-43. Bd. dirs. Am. Bapt. Fgn. Mission Soc.; v.p. Protestant Council, N.Y.C.; trustee Colgate U.; chmn. bd. dirs. Brotherhood-in-Action, 1971-75. Recipient Alumni award Colgate U., 1962; Churchman award United Ch. of Christ, 1969. Mem. N.Y. State Bar Assn., Am. Soc. Internat. Law, Phi Beta Kappa, Delta Rho (nat. treas. 1936-45). Republican. Baptist. Clubs: Down Town, Century, Quill (N.Y.); Rembrandt (Bklyn.). Author: A Century of Change, 1939. Contbr. articles to legal periodicals. Home: Woburn, Mass. Died July 7, 1976; interred Colgate U. Cemetery, Hamilton, N.Y.

JUDSON, SYLVIA SHAW (MRS. SIDNEY HASKINS), sculptor; b. Chgo., June 30, 1897; d. Howard and Frances (Wells) Shaw; student Sch. Art Inst. Chgo., 1916-20; studies in Paris, 1920-21; Dr. Sculpture (hon.), Lake Forest Coll., 1952; m. Clay Judson, Sept. 3, 1921 (dec. Nov. 1960); children—Alice Clay (Mrs. Edward L. Ryerson, Jr.), Clay; m. 2d, Sidney Gatter Haskins, Dec. 1, 1963, Exhibiting sculptor, from 1922; one man shows Art Inst. Chgo., 1938 (tour of 5 other middle western museums 1938), Arden Gallery, N.Y.C., 1940, Ill. State Mus., Springfield, 1948, Chgo. Pub. Library, 1955, Sculpture Center N.Y., 1957; exhibited Phila. Mus. Art, Whitney Mus. Art, Mus. Modern Art, Met. Mus., Century of Progress Exhbns. at Chgo. Art Inst., N.Y., San Francisco world's fairs; mus. collections Chgo. Art Inst., White House, Phila., Dayton, Ohio, Springfield, Ill., Davenport, Iowa. Recipient Logan prize, 1929, hon. mention, 1925, 35, 45, Clyde Carr prize, 1947; Art Inst. Chgo.; hon. award in fine arts Chgo. chpt. A.I.A., Chgo. Assn. Commerce and Industry, 1956; Municipal Art League prize Chgo. No. Jury Show, 1957; Speyer prize Am. Acad. Design, 1957; medal Garden Club of Am., 1957. Fellow Nat. Sculpture Soc.; mem. N.A.D. Mem. Soc. of Friends. Author: The Quiet Eye, 1954; For Gardens and Other Places, 1968. Home: Lake Forest, Ill. Died 1978.

JUNG, CHARLES CHESTER, bus. exec.; b. Delavan, Wis., Sept. 11, 1903; s. Charles Eugene and Hattie (Seston) J.; A.B., U. Mich., 1926; m. Gwen Drew, Dec. 16, 1927; children—Nancy Ellen, Constance Drew, Charles Chester; m. 2d, Margaret Elizabeth Norse, 1951. Asso. Halsey, Stuart & Co., Chgo., 1926-28, A. G. Becker & Co., 1928-34; exec. v.p., gen. mgr., dir. Sheridan, Farwell & Morrison, Chgo., 1940-49; pres., dir. Scudder, Stevens & Clark, Inc., Chgo., 1949-53, dir., 1953-60; v.p. Calumet & Hecla, Inc., Chgo., 1953-62, chmn. bd., 1962-68, chief exec. officer, 1965-68, also dir.; chmn. bd. Calif. Cold Storage & Distbg. Co., Long Beach, Hayward Marum, Inc.; dir. State Nat. Bank, Evanston, Gen. Finance Corp., Evanston, Universal Oil Products Co., Des Plaines, Ill. Past pres., dir. Glencoe Community Chest; past pres. Glencoe Park Bd.; dir. YMCA Hotel, Chgo. Mem. Navy League, Beta Phi Theta, Acacia. Mason (K.T.). Clubs: Skokie Country (Glencoe); University (Chgo., Evanston and Milw.); Swedish, Executives (Chgo.); Lauderdale Yacht, Tower (Ft. Lauderdale). Home: Evanston, Ill. Died Aug. 19, 1978; interred Spring Grove Cemetery, Delavan, Wis.

JUNGEBLUT, CLAUS WASHINGTON, bacteriologist; b. St. Paul, June 12, 1897; s. Nicholas and Gertrude (Kypke) J.; student Kaiser Friedrich Gymnasium, Berlin, 1903-15; M.D., U. Bern (Switzerland), 1921; m. Dora Blom, Mar. 5, 1923 (div.); 1 son, Roland; m. 2d, June Magor Beckwith, Dec. 14, 1951. Vol. asst. Robert Koch Inst., Berlin, 1921-22, Inst. Exptl. Therapy, Berlin-Dahlem, 1922-23; bacteriologist N.Y. State Dept. Health, 1923-27; fellow in medicine NRC, 1927; asso. prof. bacteriology and exptl. pathology Stanford, 1927-29; asso. prof. bacteriology Columbia, 1929-36, prof. bacteriology, 1936-62; research cons. microbiology Lenox Hill Hosp., N.Y.C., 1962-76. Engaged in study infectious diseases, infantile paralysis, exptl. tumors; Fulbright vis. lectr. Cairo U., 1960-61; vis. prof. microbiology Postgrad. Med. Center, Karachi, Pakistan, 1962-63. Fulbright award for research in Netherlands, 1951. Mem. N.Y. State Bd. Med. Examiners, 1946-55. Mem. A.M.A., N.Y. Acad. Sci., Am. Soc. Exptl. Pathology, Soc. Exptl. Biology and Medicine. Lutheran. Contbr. articles to med. jours. Home: Westport, Conn. Died Feb. 1, 1976.

JUSTIS, GUY R., pub. welfare adminstr.; b. Topeka, Dec. 27, 1911; s. Guy Tracy and Amy (Reynolds) J.; M.A., U. Denver, 1953; student U. Chgo., 1936; m. Ardis Caroline Larson, July 20, 1936; children—Joan Roslyn (Mrs. Brent Shaw), Richard Alan, Robert Tracy. Research cons. Colo. Emergency Relief Adminstrn., 1934-35; dist. supr. Colo. Dept. Pub. Welfare, 1935-42, supr. field services, 1942-43, dir. dept., 1954-64; adminstv. cons. Am. Pub. Welfare Assn., 1947-52, pres., 1963-64, dir., 1964-73; state relations officer Chgo. regional office HEW, Social Security Adminstrn., Bur. Supplemental Income, 1974-79; mgr. welfare Denver Dept. Welfare, 1952-54; cons. on aging to sec. health, edn. and welfare, 1963-66, mem adv. council on pub. welfare, 1964-66. Served with USNR, 1943-45; PTO. Home: Park Forest, Ill. Died Feb. 12, 1980; buried Crown Hill Cemetery, Denver.

KADAR, JAN, motion picture director; b. Budapest, Hungary, Apr. 1, 1918; s. Rudolf and Luisa (Tyroler) K.; student Charles U., Prague, Czechoslovakia; m. Judith Sacher, Mar. 12, 1958. Engaged in documentary film business since World War II; script writer, asst. dir. Barrandov Feature Film Studio, from 1947; filmmaker-in-residence Center for Advanced Film Studies, Am. Film Inst., Los Angeles, 1975-79; co-dir. with Elmer Klos: Kidnapped, 1952, Death is Called Engelchen (1st gold medal Moscow Film Festival), 1963, The Accused, 1964, The Defendent (grand prize Karlovy Vary Internat. Film Festival), 1964, Shop on Main Street (Acad. award for best fgn. lang. picture), 1965. Decorated State prize Czechoslovakia, 1964, 66; named Artist of Merit, 1965. Address: Prague, Czechoslovakia. Died June 1, 1979.

KAHN, ALBERT M., bus. exec.; b. Lithuania, Nov. 5, 1897; s. Maurice and Sarah (Cole) K.; brought to U.S., 1907, naturalized, 1920; student Rensselaer Poly. Inst., 1915-17, C.E. (hon.), 1954; m. Mildred Gilman, June 20, 1920; children—Shirley (Mrs. William Ross), Marilyn (Mrs. G. de Turenne); m. 2d, Lillian Feldman, Apr. 25, 1955. Various positions Consol. Products Co., Inc., 1919-25, pres., 1925-51; rehab. Spreckles Sugar Refinery, Yonkers, N.Y., 1935-39, Franklin Foundry & Machine Co., Providence, Farr-Alpaca, Holyoke, Mass., 1939-42; treas. Winter & Co., 1942-45, dir., 1945-58; rehab. High Rock Knitting Co., Philmore, N.Y., 1943-45; pres. Acme Hamilton Mfg. Co., from 1945, also chmn. bd.; pres. Spear & Co., 1951; chmn. bd. Ludwig Baumann-Spear's, 1952-53; Pioneer in orgn. United Jewish Appeal; active in fund drives Union Am. Hebrew Congregations, Union Coll. Jewish Inst. Religion. Trustee Jewish Hosp., Bklyn. Mem. Alumni adv. council, gen. devel. council Rensselaer Poly. Inst.; founder Albert Einstein Coll. Medicine; bd. dirs. Weizmann Inst. Sci., Am. Friends of Hebrew U., Albert Einstein Coll. Medicine Hosp. Mem. Am. Legion, Phi Epsilon Pi Mason. Home: Thousand Oaks, Calif. Died Nov. 15, 1976.

KAHN, ALFRED GANS, banking; b. Little Rock, Ark., June 9, 1886; s. Herman and Marion (Cohn) K.; grad. Phillips Acad., Andover, Mass., 1903; A.B., Harvard, 1907; m. Bess Hirsh, June 4, 1914; children—Alfred, Marion May, Jane. With Union Trust Co. (now Union Nat. Bank), since 1907, pres. since 1928, now chmn. bd.; president Union Securities Co., Rose City Cotton Oil Mill. Member Interstate Cottonseed Crushers Assn. (pres. 1922), Ark. Cottonseed Crushers Assn. (pres. 1918), Little Rock Chamber Commerce (pres. 1927). Democrat. Jewish religion. Mason, Elk. Clubs: Rotary (ex-pres.), Concordia, City. Home: Little Rock, Ark. *

KAHN, JOSEPH, steamship co. exec.; b. Berezino, Russia, May 25, 1916; s. Isaac and Anya (Nisnevich) K.; came to U.S., 1930, naturalized, 1942; student pvt. schs.; m. Susan Cohen, Sept. 15, 1946. Vice pres. Kahn Bros. & Pinto, fur mfrs., N.Y.C., 1938-50; pres. Tak Shipping Corp., N.Y.C., 1951-59; pres. Transeastern Assos., Inc., N.Y.C., 1957-79; chmn. Seatrain Lines, Inc., N.Y.C., 1965-79; mem. Manhattan adv. com. Chase Manhattan Bank, 1969-79. Mem. Bus./Labor Working Group, N.Y.C., 1976-79; trustee Webb Inst. Naval Architecture, 1970-79; chmn. bd. trustees Transp. Inst., Washington, 1975-79; bd. mgrs. Am. Bur. Shipping, 1971-79. Served to 1st lt. AUS, 1941-46. Mem. Am. Maritime Assn. (exec. dir. 1962-79, pres. 1975-79). Home: New York City, N.Y. Died Dec. 3, 1979.

KAHOE, WALTER, publishing co. exec.; b. Yellow Springs, Ohio, Nov. 21, 1905; s. Lawrence Harry and Maude Emma (Garvin) K.; A.B., Antioch Coll., 1928; A.M. (Austin Tchrs. scholar), Harvard, 1931; Ph.D., U. Pa., 1949; m. Mildred May Hawxhurst, July 26, 1935; children—Eleanor Elizabeth (Mrs. Joseph Emery III), Margaret Anne (Mrs. Dennis Fowler). Instr. to asso. prof. philosophy Antioch Coll., 1928-35; adminstrv. asst. to chmn. bd. TVA, 1936-39; dir. med. publs. J.B. Lippincott Co., Phila., 1946-73, sr. v.p., sec., dir., mem. exec. com., 1944-73; ret., 1973; dir. J.B. Lippincott Co. of Can. Ltd. Mem. Bus. Exec. Move for Peace, 1968-78; bd. mgrs., mem. exec. com. Pendle Hill. Rockefeller Found. research fellow in pub. adminstrn. Harvard, 1937-38. Fellow Am. Med. Writers Assn. (Swanberg award for service to med. writing 1963), Athenaeum of Phila. (life). Democrat. Mem. Soc. Friends. Club: Downtown (Phila.). Author: Clarence Pickett, A Memoir, 1966; Arthur Morgan: A Biography and Memoir, 1977. Home: Moylan, Pa. Died Mar. 28, 1978; interred Providence Meeting Cemetery, Media, Pa.

KAISER, ROBERT LOUIS, steel co. exec.; b. Elyria, O., Apr. 2, 1914; s. L.P. and Elsie (Hahn) K.; A.B. cum laude, Miami U., Oxford, O., 1935; J.D., summa cum laude, Cleve. Law Sch., 1940; m. Ruth Gill, Aug. 19, 1939; children—Tom, Sally, Mary Elizabeth. From auditor to asst. sec. Nat. Refining Co., 1935-43; admitted to Ohio bar, 1940; with Otis & Co., Cleve., from 1946, v.p., from 1950, sec., from 1947, also dir., v.p. of finance; with Portsmouth Steel Corp., Cleve., 1950-60, v.p., 1959-60, sec., 1950-60, also dir.; co. acquired by Detroit Steel Co., 1960, v.p. finance, also dir.; v.p. Cleve. Indians Inc., 1962-66; dir. Iron Ores Ltd., Steep Rock Iron Mines, Limited, from 1968. Served to Lt. (j.g.) USNR, 1943-46. Mem. Am. Iron and Steel Inst., Am. Ordnance Assn., Ohio Bar Assn., Econ. Club Detroit, Phi Beta Kappa. Home: Grosse Pointe Farms, Mich. Died Apr. 6, 1979; interred Elyria, Ohio.

KAJECKAS, JOSEPH, diplomat; b. Shenandoah, Pa., June 17, 1897; s. Peter and Ona (Malakauskas) K.; diploma U. Montpellier (France), 1929, also Ecole Libre des Scis. Politiques, Paris; m. Ona Viburis, Feb. 16, 1931; 1 son, Gabriel. With Lithuanian Ministry Fgn. Affairs, 1929-76; 1st sec. Lithuanian legation, London, 1930-35; with Lithuanian Fgn. Ministry, 1935-39; counselor Lithuanian Legation, Berlin, 1939-40, Washington, from 1940, charge d'affaires of Lithuania, 1957-76. Sec. gen. Lithuanian Red Cross Soc., 1935-39. Home: Washington, D.C. Died July 2, 1978.

KALIJARVI, THORSTEN VALENTINE, diplomat educator; b. Gardner, Mass.; s. Gustaf and Ida Christina (Kuniholm) K.; A.B., Clark U., 1920, A.M., 1923; Carnegie Endowment fellow, Harvard, 1920-22; LL.B., LaSalle; Ph.D., U. Berlin, 1935, also A.L.M.; student Hague Acad. Internat. Law, Geneva Sch. Internat. Studies, 1929; m. Dorothy Corbett Knight, Sept. 4, 1926; 1 dau., June. Head dept. polit. sci. U. N.H., 1927, prof. govt., 1939-45; exec. dir. N.H. Planning and Devel. Commn., mem. nat., state, regional commns., 1942-47; prin. analyst European affairs Legislative Reference Service, Library Congress, 1947; research counsel internat. relations, 1947-50, sr. specialist fgn. affairs, 1950-52; staff asso., cons. Senate Fgn. Relations Com., 1947-53, dep. asst. sec. state for econ. affairs, 1953-57, asst. sec. state for econ. affairs, 1957; acting under-sec. state for econ. affairs, 1956-57; U.S. ambassador to El Salvador, 1957-61; cons. Dept. of State, 1961; Distinguished prof. internat. and pub. affairs Pa. State U., 1962-64; dean faculty Cape Cod Com. Coll., 1964-68, prof. emeritus, 1968-80; lectr. history and govt. Am. U., 1947-53, dir. Insts. on Communism and Am. Constitutionalism, 1963, adj. prof., 1964-66; lectr. Johns Hopkins 1952-53; lectr., cons. internat. affairs. Pub. panel mem. War Labor Bd., Region I; arbitrator labor disputes; cons. Planning Research Corp., 1968-70; dir. Manchester Pub. Forum, 1937. Served in S.A.T.C., 1918. Fellow Am. Acad. Scis.; Am. Legion, Phi Kappa Phi, Pi Gamma Mu. Clubs: Dacor, Cosmos (Washington). Author: Recent American Foreign Policy, 1952; Modern World Politics, 1953; Soviet Power and Policy, 1954; Central America, Land of Lords and Lizards, 1962. Editor: Congress and Foreign Relations, 1953, Fascism in Action, 1948. Contbr. articles jours. Address: Washington, D.C. Died June 5, 1980.

KALKUS, JULIUS WILBUR (KAL'KUS), pathologist; b. Atkinson, Neb., Sept. 14, 1886; s. Julius Louis and Josie (Drasky) K.; D.V.S., Kansas City Vet. Coll., 1909; m. Louise Ann McGavick, July 11, 1916; children—Julius Hugh, Patricia Louise. Asst. state veterinarian of Neb., 1909; instr. pathology and histology, 1909-11, asst. veterinarian, Expt. Sta. staff, 1909-15, head of div. vet. science, Expt. Sta. since 1915, asst. prof. pathology and histology, 1911-15, prof., 1916-23, all vet. dept. State Coll. of Wash.; veterinarian Western Wash. Expt. Station, 1923, supt. since 1926; vice-director State College Exptl. Stations, 1943. Mem. bd. trustees Wash. Co-Op. Farmers Assn. since 1928; mem., v. chmn. Filbert Nut Control Bd. since 1949. Mem. Am. Vet. Med. Assn., Wash. State Vet. Med. Assn. (pres. 1914), Alpha Psi. Republican. Elk. Wrote chapter on Immunity in 2d edit. Kinsley's Vet. Pathology, also many tech. bulletins. Demonstrated by research in domestic animals that congenital goitre can be prevented by use of iodine. Home: Puyallup, Wash. *

KALODNER, HARRY ELLIS, U.S. judge; b. Phila., Mar. 28, 1896; s. David and Ida (Miller) K.; LL.B., U. Pa., 1917; L.H.D., Yeshiva U., 1950; m. Tillie Poliner, Dec. 20, 1925; children—Philip Poliner, Howard Isaiah. Admitted to Pa. bar, 1917; practice in Phila.; mem. staff Phila. N. Am., 1919-25; financial and polit. editor Phila. Record, 1928-34; sec. revenue Commonwealth Pa., 1935; judge Ct. Common Pleas, No. 2, Philadelphia County, 1936-37, U.S. Dist. Ct. Eastern Dist. Pa., 1938-46, U.S. Ct. Appeals, 3d Circuit, from 1946. Bd. dirs. Independence Hall Assn., Phila. Psychiat. Hosp., Fedn. Jewish Agys. Greater Phila.; trustee Yeshiva U.; chmn. bd. govs. Cancer Inst., Hahnemann Med. Coll. and Hosp., Phila.; mem. nat. council Am. Jewish Joint Distbn. Com. Served with J.A.G. Dept., U.S. Army, France and Germany, World War. Recipient hon.

mention Pulitzer prize for journalism, 1931, 32. Mem. Phila., Pa., Am. bar assns., Lawyers Club Phila., Am. Legion, Brandeis Lawyers' Soc. Democrat. Club: Socialegal. Home: Philadelphia, Pa. Died Mar. 15, 1977.

KAMINSTEIN, ABRAHAM LOUIS, govt. ofcl., lawyer; b. N.Y.C., May 13, 1912; s. Max and Sarah (Shulman) K.; B.S. in Social Sci., Coll. City N.Y., 1932; LL.B., Harvard, 1935; LL.M., 1936; m. Barbara Glesin, Apr. 28, 1941; 1 son, Dana Seth. Research fellow Harvard Law Sch., 1936-37; admitted to N.Y. bar, 1935; chief examining div. U.S. Copyright Office, 1947-60, dep. register, 1959-60, acting register, 1960, register copyrights, 1960-71, hon. cons. in domestic and internat. copy. Adviser U.S. delegation at meeting preliminary draft Universal Copyright Conv. prepared 1951; chmn. panel cons. gen. revision U.S. Copyright Law, 1960-71; chmn. U.S. Delegation Neighboring Rights Diplomatic Conf., 1961; co-chmn. U.S. Del. Universal Copy, Conv. Diplomatic Conf. Paris, 1971. Recipient Richard Strauss medal GEMA, 1971; Jefferson medal, 1972. Mem. Am. Fed. bar assns. Copyright Soc. U.S. Author: Divisibility of Copyrights, 1957. Home: Washington, D.C. Died Sept. 10, 1977.

KAMM, MINNIE WATSON, author; b. Fostoria, Mich., Dec. 8, 1886; d. Samuel J. and Annie (Galliver) Watson; A.B., Olivet (Mich.) Coll., 1909; M.S., U. of Ill., 1913, Ph.D., 1915; m. Oliver Kamm (Ph.D.), of Detroit, Mich., Aug. 30, 1916; children—Robert Luscombe, George Nelson. Mem. Am. Microscopic Soc., Am. Soc. Parasitologists, Am. Fern Soc., Mich. Acad. Arts and Sciences, Sigma Xi. Episcopalian. Author: Studies on Gregarines, 1916, 22; The Pre-School Age, 1925. Home: Detroit, Mich. *

KAMMER, ALFRED CHARLES, lawyer; b. New Orleans, Dec. 28, 1884; s. Philip J. and Catherine (Meyer) K.; student pub. schs. New Orleans; legal edn. pvt. study; m. Kate Jane McCulloch, June 30, 1909 (dec. July 13, 1940); children—Katherine McCulloch (Mrs. Eugene J. Bergeret), Nolan Charles; m. 2d Mary Wilmuth Warren, Nov. 15, 1944. Admitted to La. bar, 1912; mem. Rosen, Kammer, Hopkins, Burke & Lapeyre, and predecessors, New Orleans, since 1919; lectr. sch. law Loyola U., 1925-29. Mem. New Orleans (pres. 1948-49), Am., La. State bar assns., Internat. Assn. Ins. Counsel, New Orleans C. of C. Roman Catholic. Clubs: Boston, Country (New Orleans). Home: New Orleans. *

KAMPMANN, VIGGO, mem. parliament Denmark; b. Frederiksberg, Denmark, July 21, 1910, s. Conrad and Ellen (Fischer) K.; cand. polit., U. Copenhagen, 1934; m. Eva Brinch, May 2, 1942. Engaged in statis. and econ. work Danish Sate's Service, 1934-50; minister of finance, 1950, 53-60; mem. Danish Parliament, 1953; prime minister, 1960-62, ret., 1962. Chmn. Social-Democrat party. Home: Kbenhavn S., Denmark. Died June 3, 1976.

KANDEL, PHOEBE MILLER, nurse and teacher; b. Greentown, O., Aug. 20, 1882; dau. Daniel and Susan (Miller) Kandel; Diploma, Canton Actual Bus. Coll., 1902; grad. Lakeside Hosp. Training Sch. for Nurses (now Frances Payne Bolton Sch. of Nursing, Western Reserve Univ.), 1908; B.S., Teachers Coll., Columbia, 1923, A.M., 1934; unmarried. Secretarial work, Canton, O., 1902-05; instr. Jewish Hosp. Sch. of Nursing, Cincinnati, O., 1916-18; supt. City Hosp., Springfield, O., 1918-18; instr. of nursing Univ. of Cincinnati, 1919-24, dir. and asso. prof. of nursing, 1924-26; state dir. of nursing edn. Neb., 1928-30; prof. and dir. of nursing edn. Colo. State Coll. Edn., Greeley, Colo., 1930-41; prof. and dir. of nursing edn. Univ. of Utah, 1942-43, Univ. of Ga., Athens, 1944-49; nurse edn. cons. Miss. State Bd. Nurses' Examiners and Registration, Jackson, since Sept. 1949. Mem. Athens Citizens Council; chairman nursing Council Cincinnati Health Com., 1924-26. Mem. Internat. Council of Nurses, Am. Pub. Health Assn., Am. Nurses Assn., Nat. Pub. Health Nursing Orgn., Nat. League of Nursing Edn. (vice pres., 1941-47), Colo. State League of Nursing Edn. (pres. 1937-38), Ga. State League of Nursing Edn., Ga. State Nurses Assn., Kandel Club, Alpha Alpha Pi, Delta Kappa Gamma. Democrat. Episcopalian. Author: From Mud to Crystal, 1923; Hospital Economics for Nurses, 1930. Address: Canton, O. *

KANE, WILBUR PRICE, govt. ofcl.; b. Altoona, Pa., Feb. 5, 1916; s. Charles Ray and Grace Irene (Price) K.; student Johns Hopkins, 1943-45, Am. U., 1947-48; LL.B., Nat. U., 1942; m. Lois Irene Humphries, June 3, 1944; children—Sean, Christiana, Cort, Kerry. With PWA, 1938-40; with Dept. Interior, from 1940, asst. commr. Bur. Reclamation, from 1963. Admitted to D.C. bar, 1942. Chmn. bd. Oakview Recreation Corp. Served with USCGR, 1942-45. Named citizen of the year Oakview, Md., 1964; recipient Distinguished Service award Dept. of Interior, 1973. Methodist. Mason. Home: Silver Spring, Md. Died May 23, 1976; interred Roseland Cemetery, Reedville, Va.

KANE, WILLIAM, fgn. service officer; b. Czechoslovakia, Oct. 29, 1906 (parents U.S. citizens); s. Frank and Anna (Linhart) K.; B.A., Prague (Czechoslovakia) Bus. Coll., 1928; m. Dagmar Odehnal, Nov. 14, 1936; children—William J., Loretta A., Eva D. Joined U.S. Fgn. Service, 1930; assigned Prague, 1930-40, Vienna, Austria, 1940-41, State Dept. and OSS, 1941-44, London, Eng., 1944-45, Prague, 1945-48, Piedras Negras, Mexico, 1948-51, Caracas, Venezuela, 1951, Bogota, Colombia, 1951-54, State Dept., 1954-57, Seoul, Korea, 1957-59; consul Montreal, Can., 1959-62; as signed State Dept., 1963-66. Recipient Commendable Service award State Dept., 1962. Home: McLean, Va. Died Nov. 20, 1979.

KANN, GUSTAVE HERMAN, steel abrasive mfr.; b. Pittsburgh, Pa., Dec. 22, 1886; s. Myer Milton and Bertha (Friedlander) K.; student Carnegie Inst. Tech., 1905-08; m. Mary A. Popovec, June 10, 1943. Began as mgr., 1908; with Carnegie Steel Co., 1908-10; with Pittsburgh Crushed Steel Co. since 1910, pres. since 1915; pres. Globe Steel Abrasive Co., Am. Steel Abrasives Co., Steel Shot & Grit Co., Ambassador Apts., Inc.; v.p. Hopkan Rivet Co., Acme Protection Equipment Co. of Pittsburgh; pres. Latham Machine Co., Coated Products Corp.; dir Globe Varnish Co., Duquesne Smelting Co. Pres. United Jewish Fund of Pittsburgh; v.p. Young Men and Women's Hebrew Assn. (Pittsburgh); dir. Walter P. Steffen Memorial Fund (Pittsburgh). Served in U.S. Navy, 1917-18. Republican. Jewish religion. Mason. Clubs: Concordia, Hundred (Pittsburgh); Westmoreland Country. Home: Morewood Gardens, Pa. *

KANNER, LEO, med. educator; b. Klekotow, Austria, June 13, 1894; s. Abraham and Klara (Reisfeld) K.; grad. Sophiengymnasium, Berlin, 1913; M.D., U. Berlin, 1921; m. June Lewin, Feb. 11, 1921; children—Anita (Mrs. Theodore Gilbert), Albert Victor. Came to U.S., 1924, naturalized, 1930. Vol. asst. Charity Hosp., Berlin, Germany, 1920-23; pvt. practice medicine, Berlin, 1921-23; sr. asst. physician Yankton (S.D.) State Hosp., 1924-28; Commonwealth Fund fellow psychiatry Johns Hopkins, 1928-30, Josiah Macy Jr. Found. research fellow child psychiatry, 1930-32, asso. psychiatry, 1932-33, asso. prof. psychiatry, 1948-81, prof. child psychiatry, 1957-59, prof. emeritus child psychiatry, 1959-81; dispensary psychiatrist Johns Hopkins Hosp., 1928-30, psychiatrist charge children's psychiat. service, 1930-59, hon. cons., 1959-81, asst. psychiatrist, 1933-42, asso. psychiatrist, 1942-47, psychiatrist, 1947-81, pediatrician, 1948-81; cons. psychiatrist Juvenile Ct. Balt., 1930-41; vis. lectr. Dalhousie U., 1937, U. Mich., 1945, U. Minn., 1946, Goucher Coll., 1948-51, U. Tex., 1951, Mt. Sinai Hosp., N.Y.C., 1956; Kemper Knapp distinguished vis. prof. U. Wis., 1956. Dir. Child Study Center Md., 1937-44, League Emotionally Disturbed Children; exec. com. Children's Guild Balt.; adv. bd. Woods Schs., Langhorne, Pa., Devereux Schs., Devon, Pa., Cove Sch., Racine, Wis. Recipient award outstanding contbn. field medicine Assn. Help Retarded Children, 1954; 1st ann. award. Nat. Orgn. Mentally Ill Children, 1960; Gutheil Meml. medal Am. Assn. Advancement Psychotherapy, 1962; Stanley R. Dean award 1965. Fellow Am. Psychiat. Assn. (chmn. sect. child psychiatry 1942-43), Am. Assn. Mental Deficiency, Am. Acad. Child Psychiatry, Am. Orthopsychiat. Assn.; mem. Nat. Assn. Retarded Children (research adv. com.), Md. Psychiat. Soc. (pres. 1957-58), Assn. History Medicine, A.A.A.S., Internat. League Against Epilepsy, Md. Soc. Med. Research, Balt. City Med. Soc., Am. Assn. U. Profs., Johns Hopkins Med. Soc. Author: Folklore of the Teeth, 1928; In Defense of Mothers, 1941; Miniature Textbook of Feeblemindedness, 1949; Child Psychiatry, rev. edit., 1957; A Word to Parents About Mental Hygiene, 1957; History of the Care and Study of Mentally Retarded, 1964. Contbr. articles profl. jours. Editor Jour. Autism and Childhood Schizophrenia. Home: Baltimore, Md. Died Apr. 3, 1981.

KANTOR, HARRY SIMKHA, govt. ofcl.; b. Russia, Nov. 3, 1903; s. David and Freda Susan (Grabois) K.; brought to U.S., 1904; B.A., Columbia, 1924, M.A., 1925, grad. study, 1927, 29, 31; m. Anne Golden, Oct. 17, 1936; children—Paul, Fred, Freda Susan. Mem. staff Dept. Agr., other govt. agencies, 1926-38; with Dept. Labor, 1938-69, successively price analyst, economist, statistician, 1938-55, asst. adminstr. wage and hour and pub. contracts div., 1955-58, analyst Office Research and Devel., Office Sec. Labor, 1958-64, analyst with Office of Policy Planning, 1964-69, ret., 1969, cons. Office Sec., 1969-72. Mem. U.S. del. to negotiate current trade agreement Republic of Philippines, 1954; mem. Nat. Inventor's Council, 1963-65, cons., 1972-80. Recipient Distinguished Service award Dept. Labor for work in enactment first minimum wage law in P.I., 1951. Mem. Am. Econ. Assn., Am. Statis. Assn., Phi Beta Kappa. Home: Silver Spring, Md. Died June 18, 1980; buried King David Meml. Park, Falls Church, Va.

KANTOR, MACKINLAY, novelist; b. Webster City, Iowa, Feb. 4, 1904; s. John Martin and Effie Rachel (McKinlay) K.; grad. Webster City High Sch., 1923; student high schs., Des Moines and Chgo.; D.Litt., Grinnell Coll., 1957, Drake U., 1958, Lincoln (Ill.) Coll., 1959, Ripon Coll., 1961; LL.D., Iowa Wesleyan Coll., 1961; m. Florence Irene Layne, July 2, 1926; children—Carol Layne, Tim MacKinlay. Reporter, Webster City Daily News, 1921-24; worked as advt., claim corr., Chgo., 1925-26; reporter Cedar Rapids (Iowa) Republican, also free lance writer, 1927; columnist Des Moines Tribune, 1930-31; scenario writer Paramount Prodns., Metro-Goldwyn-Mayer, 20th Century Fox, Samuel Goldwyn; worked with uniformed div. N.Y.C. Police Dept., 1948-50. Mem. Nat. Council Boy Scouts Am. Trustee Lincoln Coll., 1960-68, hon. trustee, 1968—; hon. cons. Am. letters Library of Congress, 1967-73. War corr. ETO with Brit. and U.S. Air Forces, 1943, 45; war corr. Korean war, 1950; tech. cons. USAF, 1951-53; studied personnel, equipment, tng., operations at Mediterranean bases Italian and Royal Hellenic (Greece) air forces, 1963. Recipient Medal of Freedom. Fellow Soc. Am. Historians, Am. Soc. Psychical Research; mem. Nat. Assn. Civil War Musicians, Sons Union Vets., Mil. Order Loyal Legion (hereditary companion). Author: Diversey, 1928; El Goes South, 1930; The Jaybird, 1932; Long Remember, 1934; Turkey in the Straw (verse), 1935; The Voice of Bugle Ann, 1935; Arouse and Beware, 1936; The Romance of Rosy Ridge, 1937; The Noise of Their Wings, 1938; Here Lies Holly Springs, 1938; Valedictory, 1939; Cuba Libre, 1940; Gentle Annie, 1942; Angleworms on Toast (juvenile), 1942; Happy Land, 1943; Author's Choice, 1944; Glory for Me, 1945; But Look, The Morn, 1947; Midnight Lace, 1948; Wicked Water, 1949; The Good Family, 1949; Signal Thirty-two, 1950; Lee and Grant at Appomattox (juvenile), 1950; Don't Touch Me, 1951; Warwhoop, 1952; Gettysburg (juvenile), 1952; The Daughter of Bugle Ann, 1953; God and My Country, 1954; Andersonville (Pulitzer prize 1956) 1955; Lobo, 1957; The Work of St. Francis, 1958; If the South had won The Civil War, 1961; Spirit Lake, 1961; (with Gen. Curtis LeMay) Mission With LeMay: My Story, 1965; Story Teller, 1967; Beauty Beast, 1968; The Day I Met A Lion, 1968; Missouri Bittersweet, 1969; (with Tim Kantor) Hamilton County, 1970; I Love You, Irene, 1972; The Children Sing, 1973; Valley Forge, 1975. Contbr. to Sat. Eve. Post, Atlantic Monthly, other mags. Home: Sarasota, Fla. Died Oct. 11, 1977; buried Webster City, Iowa.

KAPLAN, ABBOTT, coll. pres.; b. N.Y.C., Jan. 12, 1912; s. Nahum and Leah (Beilowitz) K.; B.S., Columbia, 1933, M.A., 1934, Ph.D., 1942; B.J.P., Jewish Theol. Sem. Am., 1933; L.H.D., Hebrew Union Coll., 1976; m. Beatrice Dresher, Nov. 1, 1936. Tchr., 1933-37; asst. prin. Chestnut St. Jr. High Sch., Springfield, Mass., 1937-38; prin. High Sch. Commerce, Springfield, 1938-39; dir. adult edn., guidance and placement pub. schs., Springfield, 1939-43; dir. for France, Am. Joint Distbn. Com., 1945-46; head extension services Inst. Indsl. Relations, U. Calif. at Los Angeles, 1946-49, asst. dir. Inst., 1950-52, asso. dir. Inst., asst. dir. univ. extension, 1952-57, asso. prof., 1955-64, prof. edn., 1964-66, dir. univ. extension South area, 1960-66, asso. dean (statewide), 1960, prof. theater arts, asso. dean Coll. Fine Arts, 1966; pres. State U. N.Y. Coll. at Purchase, N.Y., 1967-77, also prof. theatre arts and inter-disciplinary studies. Founder, chmn. bd. Theatre Group Los Angeles, 1959-67; chmn. Calif. Arts Commn., 1964-66; vice chmn. Cal. Commn. Compensatory Edn., 1965-66. U.S. rep. UNESCO internat. meeting of experts, France, 1953; mem. panel Rockefeller Bros. Fund Study of Performing Arts Am., 1963; mem. State Cal. Commn. on Cultural Arts. Served as lt. comdr. USNR, 1943-45. Fulbright fellow, 1949-50. Mem. Nat. Acad. Arbitrators. Club: Century (N.Y.C.). Author: Adventures in Growing Up, 1941; Socio-Economic Circumstances and Adult Participation in Educational Activities, 1943; Study Discussion in the Liberal Arts, 1960. Editor: The Cultural Arts in California, 1964. Home: Brentwood, Calif. Died July 13, 1980.

KAPLAN, JOSEPH, artist; b. Minsk, Russia, Oct. 3, 1900; s. Samuel and Mary (Cohen) K.; student Nat. Acad. Design, N.Y.C.; m. Virginia Haber, Nov. 1928. Exhibited one-man shows major cities, U.S.; exhibited group shows major cities U.S.; represented collections Newark Museum, U. Ky., Butler Inst. Am. Art, Decatur Art Center; represented numerous pvt. collections. Recipient Adolph and Clara Obrig prize, 1967; Proctor prize, 1970. Mem. Audubon Artists, Artists Equity (dir. N.Y. chpt. 1960-63), Provincetown Art Assn. (trustee 1959-61, 69-71). Jewish. Address: Provincetown, Mass. Died Feb. 28, 1980.

KAPLAN, MORRIS AARON, physician, educator; b. Bklyn., Apr. 5, 1907; s. David and Eva (Erenberg) K.; student Crane Jr. Coll. and Lewis Inst., 1924-27; B.S., U. Ill., 1929, M.S. (Sigma Xi prize for undergrad. research), 1931, M.D., 1932, grad. study, 1931-41, Nat. Naval Med. Sch., 1943-44; m. Celia S. Furlett, Dec. 27, 1931. Intern, Cook County Hosp., 1931-33; pvt. practice, specialist in allergy, Chgo., 1933-77; instr. physiol. chemistry coll. medicine U. Ill., 1929-31, asst. medicine, 1933-37, instr., 1937-41, asso., 1941-46, clin. asso., 1946-50, lectr. allergy, dept. physiol. chemistry, 1933-50, cons. allergy, dept. pediatrics, 1946-50, instr. post-grad. clin. allergy, 1946-50, attending physician allergy clinics Research and Ednl. Hosp., 1933-50, chief allergy clinics, 1946-50; asst. attending physician Michael Reese Hosp., 1946-52, attending physician allergy Mandel Clinic, 1946-52, lectr. allergy Nurses Tng. Sch., 1946-52; instr. allergy postgrad. instrn. course Am. Coll. Allergists, 1948, 51, 53-58; dir. allergy research unit Chgo. Med. Sch. and Mt. Sinai Research Found., 1954-73, also clin. prof. medicine, 1971-77; research asso. prof. div. enzymology and exptl. hypersensitivity Chgo. Med. Sch., clin. prof. biochemistry, 1969-77; clin. prof. biochemistry Grad. Sch., Chgo. Med. Sch., U. Health Scis., 1969-77; attending physician Mount Sinai Hosp., 1953-73, Weiss Meml. Hosp., 1955-77, St. Joseph Hosp., 1975; allergy cons. Chgo. Bd. Edn.; regional cons. allergy Nat. Jewish Home for Asthmatic Children, Denver, 1951-77; mem. staff Franklin Blvd. Hosp., 1946-77, Roosevelt Meml. Hosp., 1966-77. Cons. Asthmatic Children's Found. Pres., Ill. Found. for Asthma. Dir. Peterson Bank, Chgo. Bd. Dirs. Ill. Found. Asthma; bd. dirs. Chgo. chpt. Am. Found. for Allergic Diseases; mem. med. adv. bd. Asthmatic Children's Aid; bd. dirs. Allergy Found. Am. Served from lt. to lt. comdr. M.C., USNR, World War II; lt. comdr. M.C., Vol. Med. Unit 9-20, 1946-77. Fellow Am. Coll. Allergists (past pres.; chmn. bd. dirs.), Am. Acad. Allergy, Internat. Assn. Allergy, Am. Med. Writers Assn., Am. Coll. Chest Physicians, Chgo. Inst. Medicine; mem. Am. Assn. Immunology, Assn. Am. Med. Coll., A.M.A., Soc. Exptl. Biology and Medicine, Am. Fedn. Clin. Research, Assn. Allergists Mycological Investigation, Chgo. Soc. Allergy (sec.-treas. 1947, pres. 1949, exec. com. 1949-77), Ill. State (chmn. sect. allergy), Chgo. med. socs., A.A.A.S., N.Y. Acad. Sci., Internat. Corr. Soc. Allergy, Ill. Acad. Sci., Asthma and Allergy Fedn. Greater Chgo. (dir.), American, Chgo. assns. immunologists, Royal Soc. Medicine (London, Eng.), Sigma Xi, Phi Delta Epsilon. Jewish. Mem. B'nai B'rith; Mason. Editorial bd. Annals of AllergV, 1948. Contbr. med. publs. Home: Chicago, Ill. Died Jan. 6, 1977; interred Rosehill Mausoleum, Chgo.

KAPLAN, WALTER L., cosmetics co. exec.; b. N.Y.C., 1914; B.A., Coll. City N.Y., 1934; m. 2d, Nancy Braasch, Dec. 6, 1964; 1 dau., Susan. With M. Abrams Co., 1935-36, Gibbs & Co., 1936-38; salesman M. Waho & Son, 1938-39; salesman Helene Curtis Industries, Inc., Chgo., 1939-46, sr. v.p.-adminstrn. and v.p.-adminstrn. profl. salon div., 1946-72, pres., mem. exec. com., 1972-79, vice chmn., 1979, also dir. Home: Chicago, Ill. Died Sept. 16, 1979; buried Rosehill Cemetery, Chgo.

KARINSKA, BARBARA, costume designer; b. Kharkov, Russia, Oct. 1886; d. Andrei Zhmoudsky; m. 2d, Karinsky. Editor socialist paper, H Kharkov; owner embroidery and dress show, Moscow; exhibited paintings in group shows, Moscow; costume maker, Paris, 1932, U.S., 1938; costume designer Bourée Fantasque, N.Y. City Ballet Co., 1949, The Nutcracker, 1954, Liebeslider Walzer, 1960, Valses et Variations, 1961, Midsummer Night's Dream, 1962, Western Symphony, 1968; also made costumes for prodns. Met. Opera Co.; costumer for films Lady in the Dark, 1944, Gaslight, 1944, Frenchman's Creek, 1944, Kismet, 1944, Kitty, 1945. Recipient (with Dorothy Jeakins) Oscar for costumes Joan of Arc, Acad. Motion Picture Arts and Scis., 1948. Address: New York City NY. *

KARNOSH, LOUIS JOSEPH, physician, educator; b. Bellaire, O., Mar. 30, 1892; s. John Joseph and Katherine (Stock) K.; B.S., Berea Coll., 1913, Sc.D., 1926; M.D., Western Res. U., 1920; m. Eva Pauline Milton, Dec. 28, 1923; children—Patricia (Mrs. Albert Charles Lammert), Joan Louise, Katherine (Mrs. Yngyar Lovat Fraser Hvistendahl, Jr.). Intern Cleve. City Hosp., 1920-21, dir. neuropsychiatry, 1928-46; dir. neuropsychiatry Cleve. Clinic, 1946-58; clin. prof. neurology Western Res. U. Med. Sch., 1946-63, emeritus clin. prof. neurology, 1963-77. Cons. SSS, 1942-45; mem. council Ohio Dept. Mental Hygiene, 1957-77. Trustee Berea (Ky.) Coll. Diplomate Am. Bd. Psychiatry and Neurology (dir. 1947-51). Fellow Am. Psychiat. Assn.; mem. Am. Neurol. Assn., Soc. Biol. Psychiatry (v.p.), Central Neuropsychiat. Assn. (pres. 1941), Am. Acad. Neurology, Alpha Omega Alpha. Author: Handbook of Psychiatry, 1944; Psychiatry for Nurses, rev. edit., 1958. Home: Shaker Heights, Ohio. Died Aug. 16, 1977.

KARNS, RUSSELL DALE, petroleum corp. exec.; b. Oswego, Kans., Oct. 6, 1909; s. James Henry and Rutha E. (Tower) K.; grad. Advanced Mgmt. Program, Harvard U., 1951; m. J. Anita Spivey, Feb. 1, 1930; 1 dau., Ina Kay (Mrs. Donald E. Loeffler). With Phillips Petroleum Co., 1928-34; with Amoco Prodn. Corp., 1934-72, asst treas., 1959-63, treas., 1963-72; cons. Sooner Pipe & Supply Corp., Tulsa, 1972-76. Hon. mem. staff gov. Okla., 1955. Bd. dirs. Asso. Industries Okla. Mem. Tulsa C. of C., Am. Petroleum Inst. Presbyn. Clubs: Oaks Country, Petroleum (Tulsa). Home: Westlake Village, Calif. Died Jan. 18, 1978.

KARRER, MAX RAYMOND, rubber co. exec.; b. nr. York, Nebr., June 21, 1907; s. Frederick William and Zena M. (Pyle) K.; B.S., U. Nebr., 1928; m. Nedra E. King, June 19, 1929; 1 son, Max C. Research and devel. B.F. Goodrich Co., Akron, Ohio, 1929-39; chmn. bd., pres., chief exec. officer Electric Hose & Rubber Co., Wilmington, Del., from 1939; dir. Bank of Del., Continental Investment Co., Retirement Living; mem. Del. adv. bd. Liberty Mut. Ins. Co. Vice pres., bd. dirs. Del. Safety Council; trustee Brandywine Coll. Recipient Distinguished Service award U. Nebr. Alumni Assn., 1970. Mem. Del. C. of C. (dir., past pres.), Rubber Mfrs. Assn. (dir.), Soc. Plastics Industry, ASTM, Am. Chem. Soc. Home: Chadds Ford, Pa. Died Jan. 3, 1980; interred Lower Brandy Cemetery, Wilmington, Del.

KARSNER, HOWARD THOMAS (KARZ'NER), pathologist; b. Phila., Pa., Jan. 6, 1879; s. Charles W. (M.D.) and Martha M. (Wright) K.; B.S., Central High Sch., Phila., 1897; Phila. Sch. of Pedagogy, 1899; M.D., Univ. of Pa., 1903; LL.D., Western Reserve University, Cleveland, 1949; m. Audrey W. Stanwood, Dec. 11, 1912 (died 1944); m. 2d Daisy Stanley-Brown, Mar. 12, 1946 (died 1949); married 3d Jessie Spencer Beach, July 5, 1950. Demonstrator pathology, Univ. of Pennsylvania, 1908-11; asst. prof. pathology, Harvard Med. Sch., 1911-14; prof. pathology, Western Reserve U., 1914-49; med. research adviser to Bur. Medicine and Surgry, U.S. Navy, since 1949; dir. Inst. Pathology, 1929-49; dir. Pathology, University Hosps.; div. chief of labs., City Hosp., 1914-49; cons. to Surg. Gen., U.S.A. Mem. sci. adv. bd. Armed Forces Inst. Pathology, adv. med. bd. Leonard Wood Meml. for Eradication Leprosy. Served as capt., Med. R.C., with A.E.F. in France, 1917-Feb. 11, 1918. Awarded W. W. Gerhard Medal, Phila. Path. Soc., Centennial Award, Northwestern U., 1951; Capt. Robert Dexter Conrad award, U.S. Navy, 1961. Fellow Aero. Med. Assn. (hon.), N.Y. Acad. Scis.; mem. Nat. Bd. Med. Examiners (pres. 1951-54), A.M.A., Assn. American Physicians, Am. Coll. Physicians, Am. Soc. Exptl. Pathol., Internat. Soc. Geog. Path. (vice president, Assn. Pathologists and Bacteriologists Society Exptl. Biology and Med., A.A.A.S. (v.p. Sect. N, 1931), Sigma Xi, Alpha Omega Alpha; corr. mem. various orgns. Rep. Club: Army and Navy. Author: Human Pathology, 1926, 55. Editor Year Book of Pathology, 1941-53. Contbr. tech. jours. Chmn. div. med. sciences, Nat. Research Council, 1927-28, chmn. com. on Pathology 1948-58; consultant in pathology, Army Air Forces, Army Med. Mus. and Office Scientific Research and Development, 1943-46; spl. cons. Secretary of War, 1946. Home: Washington. *

KASAK, MICHAEL, physician; b. Nereta, Latvia, May 13, 1884; s. Andrew and Maria (Klavin) K.; B.Sc., U. of Wis., 1915; M.S., Washington U. Sch. of Medicine, 1917; student Harvard Med. Sch., 1919, Univ. of Berlin, 1923; m. Lauma Betin, Oct. 17, 1926; 1 dau., Nenia. Asst. in medicine, Washington University, St. Louis, 1917-19; clinical director Milwaukee County Hospital for Mental Diseases, Wauwatosa, Wis., 1925-39, acting supt., 1939-40, med. dir., 1940-56, ret.; acting supt. Milw. County Asylum for Chronic Insane, Wauwatosa, 1939-40; special lecturer, Milwaukee-Downer Coll. and Mount Mary Coll., Milwaukee, since 1927; asso. clin. prof. of psychiatry, Marquette U. Sch. of Medicine, 1931-46, dir. and clin. prof. of psychiatry, 1946-54. Diplomate, Am. Bd. of Psychiatry and Neurology; fellow, A.M.A., Am. Psychiat. Assn.; mem. Am. Inter-Professional Inst., A.A.A.S., Am Genetic Assn., Central Neuro-Psychiat. Assn. Home: Milw. *

KASZNAR, KURT SEWISCHER, actor; b. Vienna, Austria, Aug. 12, 1913; s. Nathan and Leopoldine (Schweiger) Serwischer; grad. Schuttel Gymnasium, Vienna, 1930, Max Rheinhard Sem., 1932; m. Cornelia Woolley, 1938 (dec. 1947); m. 2d, Leora Sheppherd Dana, June 29, 1952 (div.). Actor starring motion pictures, Broadway shows, TV; theatrical credits include Don Juan in Hell, Joy to the World, Montserrat, The Happy Time, Seventh Heaven, Six Characters in Search of an Author, Waiting for Godot, Look After Lulu, The Sound of Music, Barefoot in the Park, My Three Angels, Once More with Feeling, The Little Hut, Arms and the Man; films include The Happy Time, Valley of the King, Lonely to Look At, Glory Alley, Talk About a Stranger, Anything Can Happen, All the Brothers Were Valiant, Kiss Me Kate, Give a Girl a Break, Sombrero, Ride Vaquero, Lili, The Last Time I Saw Paris, Jump Into Hell, Flame of the Islands, My Sister Eileen, Anything Goes, The Light Touch, Legend of the Lost, A Farewell to Arms, For the First Time, The Journey, 55 Days at Peking, Casino Royale, The King's Pirate; TV role in Land of the Giants. Served with Signal Corps, U.S. Army, World War II. Died Aug. 6, 1979.

KATH, TERRY ALAN, guitarist; b. Chgo., Jan. 31, 1946; s. Raymond Elmer and Evelyn (Haugan) K.; grad. high sch.; m. Camelia; 1 son. Lead singer and guitarist with musical group Chicago, 1967-78. Composer music and lyrics for 30 compositions, including introduction, Alma Mater, Till We Meet Again; winner 11 platinum records. Home: Los Angeles, Calif. Died Jan. 22, 1978.

KAUFFMAN, DRAPER LAURENCE, naval officer; b. San Diego, Aug. 4, 1911; s. James Laurence and Elizabeth Kelsey (Draper) K.; grad. Kent Sch., 1929; B.S., U.S. Naval Acad., 1933; student Naval War Coll. 1950-51; m. Margaret Cary Tuckerman, May 1, 1943; children—Margaret Cary, Draper Laurence, Edith Kelsey. Commd. lt. USNR, 1941, transferred to U.S. Navy as comdr., 1946, advanced through grades to rear adm., 1961; organizer, 1st comdg. officer Navy Bomb Disposal Sch., 1942; organizer Navy Underwater Demolition Teams, 1943; comdr. underwater demolition teams on Saipan, Tinian, Iwo Jima and Okinawa, World War II; comdr. U.S.S. Gearing, 1948-50, U.S.S. Bexar, 1957-58, U.S.S. Helena, 1960-61, Destroyer Div. 122, 1953-54, Cruiser Destroyer Flotilla 3, 1961-62; aide, exec. asst. to sec. navy Gates, 1955-57; chief strategy plans and policy div. Joint Staff, Joint Chiefs Staff, 1962-63; dir Office Program Appraisal on staff sec. navy Nitze, 1963-65; supt. U.S. Naval Acad., 1965-68; comdt. 9th Naval Dist., Great Lakes, Ill., until 1973; pres. Marion Mil. Inst.; Ala.; 1974-76. Decorated Navy Cross with gold star, Legion of Merit, Commendation ribbon with 2 bronze stars; Croix de Guerre with star (France); Oak Leaf and Def. medal (England). Mem. U.S. Naval Inst. (v.p. from 1965). Home: Annapolis, Md. Died Aug. 18, 1979.

KAUFFMAN, GEORGE WHITTEN, wholesale drug exec.; b. Columbus, Ohio, May 28, 1915; s. George H. and Marguerite (Fair) K.; A.B. cum laude, Harvard, 1937; m. Jean Leckie, June 20, 1941; children—Sally Point, Nancy Whitten, Jean Stuart. With Kauffman-Lattimer Co., Columbus, 1937-77, pres., 1949-77; dir. Druggists Service Council, N.Y.C., 1957-63, Banochio Corp., Columbus. Bd. dirs. United Appeals Franklin County, 1955-65, pres., 1961; trustee Children's Hosp., from 1951, pres., 1962-64. Served to capt. U.S. Army, 1942-46. Mem. Nat. Wholesale Druggists Assn. (bd. dirs. 1951-54, pres. 1953), Nat. Assn. Wholesalers (pres. 1956-57), Columbus C. of C. (bd. dirs. 1963-66), Columbus Better Bus. Bur. (bd. dirs. 1949-51). Clubs: Columbus, Country (Columbus), Rocky Fork, Golf. Home: Columbus, Ohio. Died Aug. 26, 1977.

KAUFMAN, BEN, orgn. dir.; b. Buffalo, Mar. 10, 1894; s. Peter and Anna K.; A.B., Syracuse U., 1915; m. Dorothy Finkle; 1 dau., Rita (Mrs. Leonard Devries). Gen. sales mgr., Siegel Brothers, Trenton, N.J., 1916-21; mgr., U.S. Employment Service, Trenton, 1937-45; supervisor of the bus excise tax, Dept. of Motor Vehicles, Dept. of N.J., 1933-37; proprietor of B. Kaufman, wholesale luggage, Phila., 1945-47; field service dir., Jewish War Veterans, N.Y. City, 1947-48, exec. dir. since June 1948. Mayor of distinguished guest com., Trenton, 1922-39. Chmn. lay adv. bd., Trenton, N.J. Dept. of Public Assistance, 1937-44; chmn., Mercer County, N.J. State Commn. Against Discrimination, 1944-47. Served with U.S. Army, 1917-19. Decorated Congressional Medal of Honor, 1918. Awarded Medaille Militaire, Croix de Guerre with palms, France; Italian War cross, Medal of Honor from Montenegro. Mem. Jewish War Vets. of U.S. (past nat. comdr.), Am. Legion, Vets. Fgn. Wars, Disabled Am. Vets., Order of the Purple Heart, Zionist Organization of Am. Jewish religion. Elk. Mason. Home: Trenton, N.J. Died Feb. 5, 1981.

KAUFMAN, ELKIN, tobacco co. and advt. exec.; b. Louisville, May 23, 1905; s. Edwin and Adele (Straus) K.; student Harvard, 1927; m. Gertrude Winkler, Nov. 24, 1934; 1 son, Eli Winkler. Sales promotion mgr. Esquire mag., 1934-40; co-founder exec. v.p., dir. William H. Weintraub & Co., Inc., 1941-55, name changed to Norman, Craig and Kummell Inc., pres. 1955-57; sr. v.p. Lennen & Newell, Inc., 1957-66; mgr. spl. projects Philip Morris, Inc., N.Y.C. 1966-70; ret., 1970. Bd. dirs. Grand St. Settlement, Altro Health and Rehab. Services (Tb rehab.), George Jr. Republic. Clubs: Harvard, Dutch Treat (N.Y.C.). Home: New York, N.Y. Died Nov. 27, 1977.

KAUFMAN, JOSEPH W., lawyer, judge; b. N.Y.C., Mar. 27, 1899; s. Samuel and Adelaide (Brenner) K.; A.B., Columbia, 1920, LL.B., 1923, J.D., 1969. Former law sec. Judge John C. Knox; practice law, N.Y.C., Washington; mem. Col. William J. Donovan's legal staff in bankruptcy investigation, 1932; spl. trial examiner N.Y. Labor Relations Bd., 1939-41; gen. counsel Smaller War Plants Corp., Dept. Commerce, World War II; dep. chief counsel Nuremberg War Crime Trials, chief pros. Krupp case, 1947 part, counsel on rev.; chief counsel Ho. Reps. Small Bus. Com., 1949-50; referee appeals council Social Security Adminstrn., 1956-61; adminstrv. law judge FTC, 1961-69; spl. master U.S. Ct. Appeals. Recipient Distinguished Service award and citation, 1969. Mem. nat. and labor panel arbitrators Am. Arbitration Assn.; mem. panel Nat. Mediation Bd.; lectr. law schs. Served with U.S. Army, World War I. Mem. Am., Fed. bar assns., Assn. Bar City N.Y., Fed. Adminstrv. Law Judges Conf. Club: Columbia U. Contbr. articles to profl. jours. Home: Washington, D.C. Died Feb. 14, 1981; buried Wellwood Cemetery, Farmingdale, N.Y.

KAUFMAN, SUE (MRS. JEREMIAH A. BARONDESS), author; b. L.I., N.Y., Aug. 7, 1926; d. Marcus and Anna (Low) Kaufman; A.B., Vassar Coll., 1947; m. Jeremiah A. Barondess, 1953; 1 son, James. Asst. to fiction editor Mademoiselle mag., N.Y.C., 1947-49; free-lance writer, 1949-77. Recipient hon. mentions Martha Foley collections short stories.

Author: The Happy Summer Days, 1957; Green Holly, 1962; Diary of a Mad Housewife, 1967; Headshrinker's Test, 1969; Falling Bodies, 1974. Contbr. numerous short stories to mags. Address: New York, N.Y. Died June 25, 1977.

KAUFMANN, BERWIND PETERSEN, biologist; b. Phila., Apr. 23, 1897; s. Rudolph and Ida (Petersen) K.; B.S., U. Pa., 1918; A.M., 1920, Ph.D., 1925; m. Jessie Thomson McCulloch, Apr. 12, 1924; children—Berwind Norman, Carl Bowman, Anders Joseph. Asst. dept. biology U. Pa., 1916-24; tchr. biology Northeast High Sch., Phila. 1919-25; prof. biology Southwestern U., Memphis, 1926-28; prof., head dept. botany U. Ala., 1928-36; NRC fellow in biol. sci. Calif. Inst. Tech., 1932-33; guest investigator dept. genetics Carnegie Instn., 1936, 37, resident investigator, 1937-62, acting dir., 1960-61, dir., 1961-62; prof. zoology and botany, sr. research scientist U. Mich., Ann Arbor, 1962-67, prof. emeritus, 1967-75; co-prin. investigator sci. research program USPHS; guest investigator Brookhaven Nat. Lab., 1955-63; dir. grad. program devel. Adelphi Coll., 1962-64. Mem. Biology Council; mem. exec. com. NRC; mem. Marine Biol. Corp., Woods Hole, Mass.; mem. Biol. Stain Commn. Fellow A.A.A.S.; mem. L.I. Biol. Assn. (asst. sec., dir.), Am. Soc. Cell Biology, Am. Soc. Naturalists (v.p. 1951), Bot. Soc. Am., Am. Soc. Zoologists, Genetics Soc. Am. (sec.-treas. 1941-43, v.p. 1944, pres. 1961), Soc. Cell Biology, Nat. Acad. Scis., Soc. for Study Evolution, Radiation Research Soc., Soc. for Study Devel. and Growth, Phi Beta Kappa, Sigma Xi, Omicron Delta Kappa, Alpha Epsilon Delta, Lambda Chi Alpha. Author: (with M. Demerec) Dorsophila Guide, 8th edit., 3d printing. Editor, gen. animal, human cytology and cytochemistry sect. Biol. Abstracts; asso. editor Jour. Morphology, The Nucleus, Internat. Jour. Radiation Biology. Author articles on plant and animal cytology and cytology and cytogenetics. Home: Myrtle Beach, S.C. Died Sept. 12, 1975.

KAUFMANN, CECIL DAVID, jeweler; b. Detroit, Sept. 18, 1904; s. Saul and Cora (Samter) K.; student U. Pa., 1922-23; m. Isabelle Gotta Dec. 14, 1923; children—Jean Carol, Edmund I., Cora Lee (Mrs. Max S. Gross). With Hadley Furniture Co., Springfield, Mass., 1924-25, Hecht Co., Washington, 1925-26; buyer furniture Kaufmann Furniture Co., Washington, 1926-29; pres. Franc Jewelry Co., Washington 1929-34; supr. Midwestern stores Kay Jewelry Stores, Inc., Washington, 1934-35; chmn. bd., 1935-46, pres., 1946-73, chmn. emeritus Kay Corp., 1973-76; pres. Ad-Masters Advt. Agy., Washington, 1936-46, Fairfax Distbg. Co., Inc., Washington, from 1953. Bd. dirs. Laurel Harness Racing Assn., Ky. Harness Racing Assn., Federal City Council. Co-founder, past pres. Jewelry Industry Council, Nat. Found. Consumer Credit. Pres. Cora and Saul Kaufmann Meml. Found., Jewish Fund for Med. Research, Kay Asso. Stores Charitable Found.; founder, hon. pres. Kaufmann Camp for Washington Boys and Girls; hon. life mem. bd. dirs. Jewish Community Center, Washington; bd. dirs. Washington chpt. A.R.C., Washington Heart Assn., Washington council Boy Scouts Am.; mem. Washington Businessmens' Assn. (past pres.). Balt-Washington Mfg. Assn. (past pres.), Advt. Club Washington, Washington Bd. Trade, Zeta Beta Tau. Mason. Clubs: Variety (Washington); African Safari (Washington and Fla.); Woodmont Country. Home: Washington, D.C. Died May 18, 1976.

KAUFMANN, HENRY HANS, grain research mgr., author; b. Hanau, Germany, June 5, 1919; s. Arthur and Lilly (Weil) K.; came to U.S., 1939, naturalized, 1943; B.S. in Food Tech., U. Minn., 1953; m. R. Marianne Rosenstock, Dec. 20, 1949; children—Wendy E., Kenneth M., Ronald S., Daniel G. Mgr. grain research lab. Cargill, Inc., Mpls., 1953-79, tech. dir., 1971-80. Served with AUS, 1942-46. Decorated Bronze Star. Mem. Am. Assn. Cereal Chemists, Am. Soc. Agrl. Engrs., Grain Elevator and Processing Soc. (chmn.); Nat. Grain and Feed Assn., Minn. Engring. Soc. Author: (with C.M. Christensen) Grain Storage, 1969 (recipient McKnight award U. Minn. Press, 1970). Contbr. articles to mags. Patentee in fields grain handling, storage. Home: Minneapolis, Minn. Died Jan. 21, 1980.

KAUFMANN, WALTER (ARNOLD), educator, author; b. Freiburg, Germany, July 1, 1921; s. Bruno and Edith (Seligsohn) K.; came to U.S., 1939, naturalized, 1944; B.A., Williams Coll., 1941; M.A., Harvard, 1942, Ph.D., 1947; m. Hazel Dennis, July 12, 1942; children—Dinah, David. Mem. faculty Princeton, 1947-80, prof. philosophy, 1962-80, Stuart prof. philosophy, 1979-80; vis. prof. Cornell U., 1952, Columbia, 1955, U. Wash., 1958, U. Mich., 1959, Purdue U., 1966; Fulbright research prof. Heidelberg U., 1955-56; Fulbright prof. Hebrew U., Jerusalem, 1962-63; Phi Beta Kappa vis. scholar, 1971-72; vis. fellow History of Ideas unit Research Sch. Social Scis., Australian Nat. U., Canberra, 1974; vis. prof. Inst. Philosophy, Hebrew U., 1975; resident scholar Villa Serbelloni, fall 1970, spring 1975; mem. faculty Alpbach European Forum (Austria), 1966, 68, 76; one-man shows of color photographs at Internat. Center Photography, N.Y.C., 1978, Boston Public Library, 1979, Princeton U., 1979, Linfield (Oreg.) Coll., 1979. Mem. adv. screening com. philosophy and religion Com. Internat. Exchange of Persons, 1957-61, chmn., 1959-61; co-founder, chmn. bd. InterFuture (student exchange program), 1970-71; acting dir. Gauss Seminars in Criticism, 1967-68, 72, 75-76. Served with M.I., AUS, 1944-46. Recipient Internat. Leo Baeck prize, 1961. Mem. Phi Beta Kappa. Author: Nietzsche, 1950, rev., enlarged 4th edit., 1974; Critique of Religion and Philosophy, 1958; From Shakespeare to Existentialism, 1959, rev., enlarged edit., 1960; The Faith of a Heretic, 1961; Cain and Other Poems, 1962, 3d enlarged edit., 1975; Hegel, 1965; Tragedy and Philosophy, 1968; without Guilt and Justice, 1973; Existentialism, Religion, and Death, 1976; Religions in Four Dimensions, 1976; The Future of the Humanities, 1977; Man's Lot: A Trilogy, Photographs and Text (Life at the Limits, Time is an Artist, What is Man), 1978; Discovering the Mind (Triology), Vol. I, Goethe, Kant and Hegel, 1980, Vol. II, Nietzsche, Heiddegger and Buber, Vol. III, Freud versus Adler and Jung, 1981. translator: Leo Baeck's Judaism and Christianity, 1958; Goethe's Faust, 1961; Twenty German Poets, 1962, expanded edit. Twenty-five German Poets, 1975; Nietzsche's Zarathustra and three other works in the Portable Nietzsche, 1954; Nietzsche's The Will to Power, 1967; Beyond Good and Evil and four other works in Basic writings of Nietzsche, 1968; Martin Buber's I and Thou, 1970; Nietzsche's The Gay Science, 1974. Editor: Existentialism from Dostoevsky to Sartre, 1956, enlarged edit., 1975; Hegel's Political Philosophy, 1970; also series of intellectual biographies, 1973—. Contbr. to encys., anthologies. Address: Princeton, N.J. Died Sept. 4, 1980.

KAUP, ELIZABETH BARTOL DEWING (KOUP), writer; b. N.Y. City, Nov. 26, 1885; d. Thomas Wilmer and Maria Richard (Oakey) Dewing; ed. Brearley Sch., 1898-1903; m. Carl Bender, Nov. 25, 1923 (dec.); children—Elizabeth Ann, Mary Bartol; m. 2d, William C. Kaup, Sept. 13, 1930 (div.). Assistant chief, State Military Census, mem. Women's Military Reserves and capt., Women's Navy League, World War I, British War Relief, Office Civilian Defense, World War II, Army Service Forces, 1944. Author: Other People's Houses, 1909; A Big Horse to Ride, 1911; My Son John, 1926; Eagles Fly High, 1929; So Refined (play), 1937; Not for the Meek, 1941, Seed of the Puritan, 1944; Repeat with Laughter, 1948. Also author many short stories. Address: N.Y. *

KAVANAGH, THOMAS CHRISTIAN, cons. engr., urban planner, educator; b. N.Y.C. Aug 17, 1912; s. Patrick F. and Anna C. (Unger) K.; student Tech. U., Berlin, Germany, 1930-31; B.S., Coll. City N.Y., 1932. M.S. in Civil Engring., 1933; M.B.A., N.Y.U., 1942, Sc.D. in Engring., 1948; Eng.D. (hon.), Lehigh U., 1974; m. Kerstin E. Berglund, Sept. 18, 1937; children—Patricia Frances, Kenneth Thomas, Susan Karin. Tech. asst. to research dir. Johns-Manville Corp., 1935-37; structural engr., designer, squad and sect. leader Devenco, Inc., Frederick R. Harris, Inc., M.W. Kellogg Inc., Fairchild Aircraft, Office Chief Engr. City N.Y., 1933-45; asst. prof. civil engring. N.Y.U., 1945-48, chmn. dept. civil engring., prof. structural engring., 1952-54, adj. prof., 1954-55; adj. prof. civil engring. Columbia, 1956-65; prof. civil engring. Pa. State U., 1948-52; partner Praeger-Kavanagh-Waterbury, cons. engrs. architects, 1953-69, v.p., from 1969; v.p. Madigan-Hyland, Inc., from 1969; sr. v.p. Madigan-Praeger, Inc., 1969-75; v.p. Louis Berger Internat. Inc., East Orange, N.J., 1975-78; cons. atomic blast protection U.S. govt. Recipient awards profl. bridge design Lincoln Arc Welding Found., 1949, 50-52; Gold Medal award engring. Archtl. League N.Y., 1954; N.Y.U. Centennial citation; Lincoln Progress award, 1956; Steinman award N.Y. Acad. Scis., 1957; Ernest E. Howard award ASCE, 1969; David B. Steinman medal Coll., U. City N.Y., 1969, also citation, 1973; named Engr. of Year for Westchester, Nat. Soc. Profl. Engrs., 1973; N.Y. U. Distinguished Engring. Alumnus, 1973; Distinguished Alumnus, Poly. Inst. N.Y., 1975. Fellow N.Y. Acad. Scis. (hon. life; v.p., gov.), ASCE, Cons. Engrs. Council; mem. Nat. Soc. Profl. Engrs., Am. Concrete Inst., AAAS, Am. Soc. Engring. Edn., Internat. Assn. Bridge and Structural Engring., Am. Welding Soc., Column Research Council Engring. Found., Nat. Acad. Engring. (founding mem., 1st treas.), ASTM, Marine Tech. Soc., Internat. Assn. Shell Structures, N.Y. Assn. Cons. Engrs., Engrs. Joint Council (v.p.), Offshore Tech. Conf., (past chmn.), Bldg. Research Adv. Bd., N.Y. Bldg. Congress, Soc. Am. Value Engrs., Internat. Soc. Soil Mechanics, Fedn. Engring., Phi Beta Kappa, Sigma Xi, Tau Beta Pi, Chi Epsilon. Co-author: (text) Design of Foundations for Buildings; author sects. in various engring, handbooks. Contbr. numerous papers profl. lit. Home: Hastings-on-Hudson, N.Y. Died May 1978.

KAVINOKY, EDWARD H., lawyer; b. Buffalo, May 29, 1903; s. Samuel and Caroline (Cohn) K.; B.A., Harvard, 1923, LL.B., 1926; L.H.D., Canisius Coll.; LL.D., D'Youville Coll.; m. Irene Rose, July 1, 1926; children—Katherine (Mrs. Henry Goldman), Andrew. Admitted to N.Y. bar, 1926, practiced Buffalo; pres. Kleinhans Hall Mgmt., Inc.; sr. partner Kavinoky, Cook, Hepp, Sandler, Gardner & Wisbaum. Dir. Gomco Surg. Mfg. Corp., 1st Mark Corp., Internat. Life Ins. Corp., Welcome Radio, Inc. Pres. Council Social Agys., Buffalo, 1944, nat. bd. Community Chests and Councils, 1946; pres. Jewish Fedn. Buffalo, 1948, Jewish Welfare Soc., 1935-41; chmn. Buffalo chpt. A.R.C., 1950-53, adv. com. Atlantic Area, 1951-53; mem. Buffalo Regional State Commn. Against Discrimination in Employment, 1941-68; hon. chmn. Brotherhood Week, 1951; mem. White House Conf. on Aging, 1961; chmn. Commn. Human Relations City Buffalo, 1966-74. Bd. dirs. Community Chest, Buffalo Studio Theatre; bd. dirs. Buffalo Philharmonic Orch. Soc., pres., 1954; trustee 8th Jud. Dist. Law Library; chmn. bd. dirs. D'Youville Coll., Buffalo; trustee, chmn. Buffalo and Erie County Library. Fellow Brandeis U. Mem. Am., N.Y. State, Erie County (past trustee, pres.) bar assns., Buffalo Lawyers Club, Buffalo Roundtable Christians and Jews (co-chmn. 1953-55, nat. award 1960), Council World Affairs (chmn. Buffalo chpt.), Am. Law Inst. Clubs: Harvard (N.Y.C.); Buffalo, Marshall, Harvard (pres. 1950, Man of Year 1970) (Buffalo). Home: Buffalo, N.Y. Died Jan. 22, 1977.

KAYDEN, EUGENE MARK (KA'DEN), educator; b. Russia, Nov. 19, 1886; s. Mark and Dora (Maunewich) K.; A.B., U. of Colo., 1912; fellow in economics, Harvard, 1912-13, A.M., 1913; fellow in economics, Princeton, 1913-14; grad. study, Columbia, 1916-17; unmarried. Came to U.S., 1903, naturalized citizen, 1912. Instr. in economics, U. of Colo., 1914-15, Pa. State Coll., 1915-16; economist and trade expert, U.S. War Trade Bd., 1917-19, U.S. Dept. State, 1919-20; instr. in economics, Yale, 1920-22; cons. economist U.S. Dept. Agr., 1922-24; prof. economics, U. of the South, since 1924. Mem. Am. Econ. Assn., Am. Assn. for Labor Legislatibn, Am. Sociol. Soc., Foreign Policy Assn., Phi Beta Kappa, Pi Gamma Mu; fellow Royal Econ. Soc. (England). Fellow Social Science Research Council, 1932-33. Democrat. Episcopalian. Author books; translator publs. including: Selected Poems of M. Lermontov (transls. from Russian), 1951. Contbr. articles. Asso. editor Sewanee Review, 1925-27. Home: Sewanee, Tenn. *

KAYE, SYDNEY MILTON, lawyer; b. N.Y.C., Feb. 3, 1900; s. Ludwig and Elvira (Metz) K.; student Townsend Harris Hall, 1914-17; A.B., Columbia, 1921, LL.B., 1923; m. Muriel Gray, Aug. 21, 1941. Admitted to N.Y. bar, 1924; mem. firm Rosenman, Colin, Kaye, Petschek, Freund and Emil, N.Y.C., 1961-75; counsel Rosenman Colin Freund Lewis & Cohen, 1975-79. Chmn. bd. emeritus Broadcast Music, Inc. Mem. U.S. delegation Conf. Copyright Experts Am. Republics, Washington, 1952, Inter-Govtl. Copyright Conf., Geneva, Switzerland, 1952, Diplomatic Conf. Protection Performer's Rights, Rome, 1962, Intellectual Property Conf., Stockholm, 1967, Inter-Govtl. Conf. Revision Copyright Treaties, Paris, 1971; mem. panel cons. Gen. Revision Copyright Law and Neighboring Rights Panel, U.S. Copyright Office; mem. internat. copyright panel Dept. State. Hon. trustee Cancer Research Inst., Inc. Recipient Broadcast Pioneers award, 1960, Richard Strauss medal, 1971. Mem. Am., N.Y. State, Fed. Communications bar assns., Copyright Soc. U.S.A., Assn. Bar City N.Y., N.Y. County Lawyers Assn., Broadcast Pioneers (dir.). Club: Lotos (N.Y.C.). Home: New York, N.Y. Died Aug. 27, 1979.

KEARNEY, BERNARD W., congressman; b. Ithaca, N.Y., May 23, 1889; s. Patrick B. and Josephine (Oster) K.; LL.B., Union U., 1914; m. Lillian Dean, March 31, 1917; children—Eileen (dec.), Marion (Mrs. George V. Lynch), Joan (Mrs. Robert Wade), Patricia (dec.), Patricia (Mrs. W. Dexter Bryant). Admitted to the New York bar in 1914; became recorder City of Gloversville, N.Y., 1920-24; asst. dist. atty., Hamilton Co., 1925-28. Fulton County, 1928-31, dist. atty., 1932-42; elected mem. 78th Congress, 30th N.Y. Dist., 1943, 79th to 82d Congresses, 31st New York Dist., 84th and 85th Congresses, 32d New York District. Served as captain, infantry, A.E.F., France, 1918; capt. to maj. gen. N.Y.N.G., 1920-40. Decorated Croix de Guerre, Legion of Honor (France), Comdr. Legion of Honor, P.I. Mem. N.Y. State Bar Assn., Delta Chi. Elk, Eagle. Home: Lake Pleasant, N.Y. Died June 3, 1976.

KEARNEY, JAMES EDWARD, Bishop; b. Red Oak, Iowa, Oct. 28, 1884; s. William Patrick and Rosina (O'Doherty) K.; student N.Y. Tchrs. Coll., N.Y.C., 1901-03, St. Josephs Sem., Dunwoodie, Yonkers, N.Y., 1903-08; S.T.B., Catholic U. Am., 1909, J.C.L., 1909. Ordained priest Roman Cath. Ch., 1908; asst. rector St. Cecilia's Ch., N.Y.C., 1909-28; founder, 1928, pastor, 1928-32, Ch. of St. Francis Xavier, N.Y.C.; prof. apologetics Good Counsel Coll., N.Y.C., 1928-32; bishop of Salt Lake, 1932-37, of Rochester, N.Y., 1937-66; retired, 1966. Home: Rochester, N.Y. Died Jan. 12, 1977.

KEARNS, AMOS RAGAN, hosiery mfr.; b. High Point, N.C., July 22, 1905; s. Gurney Harriss and Katherine (Ragan) K.; A.B., Duke, 1927; m. Louise Copeland, Nov. 25, 1933; children—Amos Ragan, Jane (Mrs. James Marlowe). Sec.-treas., dir. Crown Hosiery Mills, Inc., High Point, 1927-62, pres., treas., 1962-74 chmn. bd., treas., 1974-79; pres. Asso. Industries, Inc., 1946-48; v.p., treas. G.A.C. Corp., real estate, 1935-62 v.p., sec., 1962-79; dir. High Point Bank & Trust Co. vice chmn., dir. Tom Haggai & Assos. Chmn. finance com. High Point City Council, 1939-48, mayor

1951-53; dir. Bd. Conservation and Devel. N.C., 1953-61, past chmn. state parks div.; mem. of Electoral Coll., 1949, del. Democratic Nat. Conv., 1956. Trustee Duke Endowment; bd. dirs., mem. exec. com. N.C. Citizens Assn.; past regional dir. Com. Econ. Devel.; past dir. Research Triangle Found., N.C.; trustee, mem. exec. com. Duke U., chmn. bd. visitors Med. Center, 1963-67; bd. visitors Guilford Coll.; mem. adv. council Maryfield Nursing Home; hon. trustee emeritus for life High Point Meml. Hosp.; mem. adv. bd. Westchester Acad.; trustee Angier B. Duke Meml. Mem. High Point C. of C. (past pres.), Duke Alumni Assn. (past pres.), Newcomen Soc., Alpha Tau Omega. Methodist (bd. stewards). Rotarian. Clubs: Emerywood Country (past pres.); Union League (N.Y.C.); String and Splinter (past pres.). Home: High Point, N.C. Died July 28, 1979; buried Oakwood Cemetery, High Point.

KEARNS, CARROLL D., ex-congressman, metalcraft co. exec.; b. Youngstown, Ohio, May 7, 1900; s. Patrick Henry and Ida May (Carroll) K.; Mus.B., Chgo. Mus. Coll., 1921, D.Mus., 1948; B.S., Westminster Coll., Pa., 1933; M.Ed., U. Pitts., 1938; m. Nora Lynch, Aug. 30, 1933. Asst. dir. spl. schs., Chgo., 1922-25; supr. music, Greenville, Pa., 1931-38; head dept. music Slippery Rock (Pa.) State Tchrs. Coll., 1938-41; supt. Farrell (Pa.) Schs., 1941-46; mem. 80th to 82d congresses 28th Pa. Dist., 83d-87th congresses 24th Pa. Dist.; dir. Shenango Metalcraft Co. Recipient Farrell C. of C. award, 1946; Am. Legion Distinguished Service award, 1946; Benjamin Rush medal, 1950; 1st Alumni Achievement award Westminster Coll., 1955. Mem. Northwestern Pa. Sportsmen's Assn. (hon.), Phi Mu Alpha (life). Republican. Lutheran. Elk, Mason (Shriner). Clubs: Congressional Country (Washington); Iroquois, Conneaut Lake (Pa.). Home: Conneaut Lake, Pa. Died June 11, 1976; interred Lakeview Cemetery, Conneaut Lake.

KEARNS, WILLIAM MICHAEL, ins. exec.; b. Gardiner, Me., May 1, 1899; s. Peter and Mary (Barron) K.; B.A., U. Me., 1923; LL.B., N.J. Law Sch., 1934; m. Doris Mae Hodgkinson, Aug. 19, 1933; children—William Michael, Joan. Br. mgr. Liberty Mut. Ins. Co., Newark, 1923-33, Am. Lumbermans Mut. Ins. Co., N.Y.C., 1934-35; asst. sec. Sun Indemnity Co. N.Y., 1936, soc., 1938, v.p., dir., 1948, pres. 1950-55 (merged with Patriotic Ins. Co. Am., Sun Underwriters Ins. Co. N.Y.), pres. Sun Ins. Co. of N.Y., 1955-57, chmn. bd., 1957-64; U.S. gen. atty. Sun. Ins. Office Ltd., 1957-64; past financial sec., dir. Albany Ins. Co., Provident Ins. Co.; past financial sec. Atlas Assurance Co., Ltd., Royal Assurance Co., Ltd. Past mem. U.S. adv. com. Brit. Marine Trust Fund; past mem. exec. com. Nat. Bd. Fire Underwriters. Mem. Beta Theta Pi, Kappa Phi Kappa. Club: University. Home: , N.J. Died Nov. 28, 1972.

KEATOR, BEN C(HAPMAN) (KATOR), business exec.; b. Moline, Ill., June 22, 1885; s. Benjamin C. and Grace Deere (Webber) K.; student Choate Sch., 1903, Hill Sch., 1905; B.A., Yale, 1908; m. Priscilla Rand, Dec. 14, 1924; children—Suzanne (Mrs. A. F. Bovet), Priscilla (Mrs. Edmund P. Pillsbury). Vice pres., gen. mgr. John Deere Plow Co., Portland, Ore., 1925-36, San Francisco, 1936-50, West Coast br. house supervisor since 1950; dir. Deere & Co. since 1949. Served as 1st lt., 337th F.A., U.S. Army, 1917-19. Mem. Chi Phi. Clubs: Burlingame (Cal.) Country; Pacific Union (San Francisco). Home: Burlingame, Cal. *

KECK, GEORGE FRED, architect; b. Watertown, Wis., May 17, 1895; s. Fred George and Amalie (Henze) K.; student U. Wis., 1914-15; B.S., U. Ill., 1920; D.F.A., Lawrence U., 1950; m. Lucile Liebermann, Nov. 26, 1921. Designer various archtl. offices, Chgo., 1920-26; instr. design U. Ill., 1923-24; individual practice architecture, Chgo., 1926-80; partner William Keck, 1937-80; head dept. architecture Inst. Design, 1938-44; several one-man shows. Mem. Hyde Park-Kenwood Community Conf., Am. Civil Liberties Union. Bd. dirs. S.E. Chgo. Commn. Served to 2d lt. U.S. Coast Arty., 1917-19. Mem. Arts Club Chgo., Renaissance Soc. Contbr. articles to profl. jours. Painter watercolors. Important works include House of Tomorrow, Crystal House Chgo. Worlds Fair 1933-34, pub. housing projects Chgo. Housing Authority, Chgo. Child Care Soc. Bldg. Home: Chicago, Ill. Died Nov. 21, 1980.

KEEFER, RICHARD EDWARD, r.r. assn. ofcl.; b. Washington, Feb. 23, 1910; s. Edward Albert and Gertrude (Dooley) K.; B.C.S., Benjamin Franklin U.; m. Winifred Ann Jones, May 14, 1938; children—Richard Edward, Sheila M. (Mrs. Rolf Ungert), Patricia A. (Mrs. Dennis Russell), J. Stephen, Michael C., Thomas D. Stenographer, Ry. Accounting Officers Assn., 1928-32; sec. to v.p. R.R. Credit Corp., 1932-36, asst. comptroller, asst. sec., 1937-43, comptroller, asst. sec., 1943-47; sec. joint com. traffic execs. and accounting officers Assn. Am. R.R.'s, 1934-36, asst. to sec. finance, accounting, taxation and valuation dept., 1936-37, asst. to sec. then office mgr., 1947-52, sec. dept., also accounting and treasury divs., 1952-57, asst. sec.-treas. assn., Washington, 1957-58, sec.-treas., 1958-64, sec.-treas., administrv. asst. to pres., 1964-66, exec. asst. to pres. sec.-treas., 1966-75. Served with AUS, 1944-46. Mem. Def. Transp. Assn. Am. (life). Roman Catholic Club: Kenwood Golf and Country. Home: Bethesda, Md. Died Apr. 5, 1977.

KEELER, CHARLES ADDISON, lawyer; b. Binghamton, N.Y., Apr. 11, 1897; s. Charles and Aldruda (Addyman) K.; A.B., Hamilton Coll., 1920; m. Esther Montgomery, Aug. 8, 1929; children—Charles Addison, Emily Ann (Mrs. James M. Ludwig, Jr.), John Montgomery. Admitted to N.Y. bar, 1924; mem. firm Lewis & Keeler, Binghamton, 1925-26, Hinman, Howard & Kattell, Binghamton, 1926-79. Chmn., Broome County (N.Y.) Council Commn. Against Discrimination, 1945-55; pres. N.Y. State Assn. YMCA's, 1958-65, past pres., Binghamton, mem. nat. council, bd. and exec. com., 1956-65; past pres. bd. visitors Binghamton State Hosp.; pres. Binghamton Community Chest, 1931, Broome County United Fund, 1956. Former chmn. trustees Link Found. Served with U.S. Army, 1918-19; with AEF in France. Fellow Am. Coll. Trial Lawyers; mem. Am., N.Y. State (past pres., past chmn. exec. com., pres. Found. 1960), Broome County (past pres.) bar assns., Binghamton (past pres.), Empire State (past dir.) chambers commerce, Am. Legion (past post and county comdr.). Presbyn. (trustee, former chmn. bd. trustees Presbytery Susquehanna Valley). Club: Binghamton (past pres.). Home: Binghamton, N.Y. Died June 25, 1979.

KEELER, CLINTON CLARENCE, educator; b. Lamont, Okla., Nov. 14, 1919; s. Elon Theodore and Margaret Bell (Meeker) K.; B.A., Okla. State U., 1940; postgrad. Johns Hopkins, 1941-42; Ph.D., U. Minn., 1953; m. Lorene Adda Wulz, Dec. 27, 1941; children—Theodore E., Gregory C. Jr. instr. English, Johns Hopkins, 1941-42; instr. U. Minn., 1947-52; prof. English, State U. N.Y. at Cortland, 1952-56; prof. Okla. State U., 1956-79, head dept. English, 1968-75; poet, works published in U.S. and fgn. periodicals. Served as lt. USNR, 1942-46; PTO. Named a tchr. of year Okla. State U., 1964. Mem. World Poetry Soc., Modern Poetry Assn., Am. Studies Assn., Modern Lang. Assn., Nat. Council Tchrs. English, Am. Studies Assn. Midcontinent (exec. council). Editor: Cimarron Review, 1968-79. Home: Stillwater, Okla. Died Feb. 17, 1979; buried Meml. Park Cemetery, Enid, Okla.

KEELER, DONALD GRAY, newspaper exec.; b. Chicago, Ill., Dec. 27, 1884; s. Bronson C. and Maud (Gray) K.; m. Myra Keller, Dec. 31, 1909. With St. Louis (Mo.) Chronicle, 1903-05; in advt. dept. Los Angeles Evening Express, 1905-07, advt. mgr., 1907-09, bus. mgr., 1909-13; bus. mgr. Los Angeles Evening Herald, which became Los Angeles Herald and Express, 1931, 1913-44, gen. mgr., 1944-49. Home: Los Angeles. *

KEENAN, JOSEPH HENRY, educator, engr.; b. Wilkes-Barre, Pa., Aug. 24, 1900; s. Joseph Henry and Wilhelmina (Maurer) K.; B.S., M.I.T., 1922; LL.D., U. Glasgow, 1966; m. Isabel Morrison, Jan. 30, 1924; children—Esther Marie (Mrs. John W. Carr III), Matthew Arnold. Steam turbine engr. Gen. Electric Co., Schenectady, 1922-28; asst. prof. mech. engring. Stevens Inst. Tech., 1928-34; asso. prof. M.I.T., 1934-39, prof., 1939-66, prof. emeritus, sr. lectr., 1966-71, head dept. mech. engring., 1958-61; Fulbright lectr. Cambridge U., Imperial Coll. Sci. and Tech., 1951; John Orr lectr. South African Instn. Mech. Engrs., 1968. Dir. Thermo Electron Corp. Del. Internat. Confs. on Properties of Steam, 1929-74. Served to lt. comdr. USNRF, 1940-53. Fellow Am. Acad. Arts and Scis., ASME (hon.; Worcester Reed Warner medal 1954); mem. Inst. Aero. Scis., Am. Assn. Physics Tchrs. (hon.), Am. Soc. Engring. Edn., AAUP, Tau Beta Pi, Sigma Xi. Clubs: Siasconset (Mass.) Casino; Belmont Hill (Mass.); Harvard Musical Assn.; Nantucket (Mass.) Yacht. Author: Steam Tables and Mollier Diagram, 1930; (with F.G. Keyes) Thermodynamic Properties of Steam, 1936; Thermodynamics, 1941; (with J. Kaye) Gas Tables, 1948; (with G.N. Hatsopoulos) General Thermodynamics, 1965; (with F.G. Keyes, P.G. Hill and J.G. Moore) Steam Tables, 1969. Contbr. Ency. Brit., 15th edit., also papers to profl. lit. Patented equipment for processing coffee, cocoa; devices for separating dust from gas streams. Home: Belmont, Mass. Died July 17, 1977.

KEENEY, BARNABY CONRAD, ednl. adminstr.; b. Halfway, Oreg., Oct. 17, 1914; s. Robert Mayro and Maud Barnaby (Conrad) K.; A.B., U. N.C., 1936; A.M., Harvard, 1937; Ph.D., 1939; Guggenheim Post Service fellow, 1945-46; LL.D., Tufts Coll., 1955, U. N.C., 1956, Princeton, 1956, Franklin and Marshall Coll., 1957, U. R.I., 1958, Boston Coll., 1958, Northwestern U., 1958, Columbia, 1959, Lafayette Coll., 1958, Brown U., 1967, Providence Coll., 1959, Yeshiva U., 1961; Ed.D., R.I. Coll. Edn., 1959; J.D., Portia Law Sch., 1959; L.H.D., Ohio U., 1962, L.H.D., Brandeis U., 1966; D.Sc., Bryant Coll., 1962; Litt.D., Clark U., 1964; m. Mary E. Critchfield, June 27, 1941; children—Barbara Alice (Mrs. Michael Clark), Thomas, Elizabeth. Tutor, instr. history Harvard, 1939-42; asst. prof. history Brown U., 1946-49, asso. prof., 1949-51, prof., 1951, asso. dean Grad. Sch., 1948, dean, 1949-53, dean of coll., 1953-55, pres. univ., 1955-66; chmn. Nat. Endowment for Humanities, Washington, 1966-70; chief exec. officer Consortium of Univs., Washington, 1970-71; pres. Claremont Grad. Sch., 1971-76. Served to capt. AUS, 1942-45; hdqrs., 35th Inf. Div. Decorated Purple Heart, Bronze Star, Silver Star; recipient Jaffe medal for service to humanities, 1970. Fellow Am. Acad. Arts and Scis.; mem. R.I., Mass. hist. socs., Mediaeval Acad. Am., Am. Philos. Soc., Phi Beta Kappa. Club: Hope (Providence). Author: Judgement by Peers, 1949; also articles and revs. profl. jours. Asst. editor Speculum, 1947-50, adv. bd., 1950-61. Home: Little Compton, R.I. Died June 18, 1980.

KEETON, WILLIAM D., justice; b. Armour, Ter. Dakota, Dec. 2, 1884; s. John Facon and Henrietta (Cather) K.; LL.B., U. of Mich., 1908; m. Flora Ruth Bennett, Jan. 17, 1918; children—Katherine H. Parkison, Virginia R. Gale, Billie B. Turner, Joyce Walker. Admitted to Ida. bar, 1910, practiced in St. Maries, 1912-49; pros. atty., Benewah County, Ida., 14 yrs.; justice Supreme Ct. of Ida., 1949—, chief justice 1957-58. Mem. Ida. Legislature, 1923. Home: Boise, Ida. *

KEETON, WILLIAM TINSLEY, educator, zoologist; b. Roanoke, Va., Feb. 3, 1933; s. William Ivie and Doris (Tinsley) K.; A.B., U. Chgo., 1952, S.B., 1954; M.S., Va. Poly. Inst., 1956; Ph.D., Cornell U., 1958; D.Sc. (hon.), Coe Coll., 1980; m. Barbara Sue Orcutt, Aug. 9, 1958; children—Lynn Sue, Nancy Lee, William Scott. Instr., Radford (Va.) Coll., 1956; Schuyler Gage fellow Cornell U., Ithaca, N.Y., 1956-58, mem. faculty, 1958-80, prof. biology, 1969-77, Liberty Hyde Bailey prof. biology, 1977-80, chmn. dept. neurobiology and behavior, 1970-76. Cons. N.Y. State Dept. Edn., 1961-66; guest prof. Max-Planck Inst. Verhaltensphysiologie, Germany, 1972-73, U. Konstanz (Germany), 1978-79; guest lectr. numerous colls. and univs. U.S., Can., Europe. Pres., Periculum Corp., Ithaca. Bd. dirs. Cornell Lab. Ornithology, 1971-77. Fellow AAAS (council 1963-73), Animal Behavior Soc., Am. Ornithol. Union; mem. Am. Inst. Biol. Sci., Soc. Study Evolution, Soc. Systematic Biology, Am. Entomol. Soc., Am. Soc. Zoologists, Brit. Ornithol. Soc., N.Y. Acad. Scis., Sigma Xi, Phi Kappa Phi, Gamma Alpha (recorder 1960-76), Alpha Zeta (hon.), Phi Gamma Delta. Author: Biological Science, 3d edit., 1980; Elements of Biological Science, 2d edit., 1973; also articles. Research in animal behavior, especially avian orientation and navigation. Home: Ithaca, N.Y. Died Aug. 17, 1980.

KEGAN, ELIZABETH HAMER (MRS. LAWRENCE R. KEGAN), librarian; b. Copperhill, Tenn., Jan. 4, 1912; d. John Earl and Fanny Elizabeth (Wallace) Edwards; B.A., U. Tenn., 1933, postgrad. (fellow history), 1933-34; postgrad. history and polit. sci. U. Chgo., Am. U.; m. Philip May Hamer, May 10, 1940 (dec. Apr. 1971); m. 2d, Lawrence R. Kegan, Jan. 4, 1973. With Survey of Fed. Archives in the States, 1936-40; various editorial and pub. relations positions Nat. Archives and Records Service, 1942-47, exhibits and info. officer, 1947-50, chief exhibits and publs. sect., 1950-51; info. and publ. officer Library Congress, Washington, 1951-60, asst. librarian pub. affairs, 1960-63, asst. librarian of Congress, 1963-76, asst. librarian of Congress for Am. and library studies, 1976-78. Library of Congress rep. Nat. Hist. Publs. and Records Com., 1968-78, Am. Revolution Bicentennial Commn., 1972-73, Fed. Agy. Bicentennial Task Force, 1974-76; alternate for librarian of Congress, Lincoln Sesquicentennial Commn., 1958-60; mem. Fed. Council on Arts and Humanities, Comm. on New Tech. Uses Copyrighted Works, Nat. Study Commn. on Records and Documents Fed. Ofcls., Woodrow Wilson Internat. Center for Scholars; del. White House Conf. Internat. Cooperation, 1965, Internat. Congress on Archives, Florence, Italy, 1956, Brussels, 1964, Washington, 1966, Madrid, 1968, Moscow, 1972, Washington, 1976, Internat. Fedn. Library Assns., The Hague, 1966, Copenhagen, 1969, Washington, 1974; mem. 3d World Congress program com. Agrl. Librarians and Documentalists, 1965; mem. Govt. Liaison Group on Staffing Internat. Orgns., from 1964; mem. pres.'s council Grad. Sch. Arts and Scis., N.Y.U. 1968-75; adv. com. on archives Rockefeller Found., 1973-76; mem. U.S. com. for Am. Library in Paris, from 1970; ofcl. observer UN World Population Conf., Bucharest, 1974; del. Oxford Conf. on Exploding Cities, 1974; mem. tribune UN Internat. Women's Year, Mexico City, 1975. Trustee Greater Washington Ednl. TV Assn. 1960-65, hon. trustee, 1966-78. Fellow Library Mass. Hist. Soc.; hon. fellow Harry S. Truman Library; mem. Soc. Am. Archivists (a founder; hon. fellow 1960, council 1969-73, chmn. or mem. com. archives-library relations 1969-73, v.p. 1974-75, pres. 1975-76, chmn. profl. standards com. 1976-77), ALA (program com. 1969-74, chmn. com. conf. format 1970-71, chmn. joint com. library-archives relationships 1971-74), Am. So. hist. assns., Orgn. Am. Historians, Manuscript Soc., Mass., S.C. hist. socs., Internat. Council Archives, Am. Assn. State and Local History, Nat. Trust for Historic Preservation, Phi Kappa Phi. Author govt. brochures. Contbr. articles profl. jours. Home: Alexandria, Va. Died Mar. 9, 1979.

KEIGHTON, WALTER BARKER, JR., educator, chemist; b. Swarthmore, Pa., June 17, 1901; s. Walter Barker and Jennie Hunter (Johnston) K.; B.A.,

Swarthmore Coll., 1923; Ph.D. (John Lockwood fellow), Princeton, 1933; m. Eleanor Mary Paxson, Aug. 21, 1926; children—Charles Earl, Robert Laurie, June (Mrs. Jerome K. Furlow), James Douglas, Walter Leslie. Chemist, E.I. duPont de Nemours & Co., Inc., 1923-25, Sharples Splty. Co., 1925-29; mem. faculty Swarthmore Coll., 1931—, prof., 1952-71, Edmund Allen prof. chemistry, 1961-71, chmn. dept., 1958-71, prof. emeritus, 1971—; chemist Sinclair Oil Co., summers 1938-40; tchr. Pa. State Coll., summer 1941; cons. Pa. Salt Co., 1948, Frankford Arsenal, 1951, Bartol Research Found., 1946-59; chemist U.S. Geol. Survey, 1951-72; vis. scientist Am. Chem. Soc., 1960-67, mem. evaluation team, 1954-69. Mem. Am. Chem. Soc., Am. Assn. U. Profs., Delaware Valley Ornithol. Club, Phi Beta Kappa, Sigma Xi, Sigma Tau. Mem. Soc. of Friends. Author: The Investigation of Chemical Quality of Water in Tidal Rivers, 1954; (with C.N. Durfor) Chemical Characteristics of Delaware River Water, 1954; (with Garald Parker, Allen Hely, Franklin Olmsted) Water Resources of the Delaware River Basin, 1960; Quality of Delaware River Water at Trenton, N.J., 1964; Water Quality in the Delaware Estuary for Two Years of Drought, 1969; other publs. dealing with quality natural waters, chem. hydrology. Contbr. articles tech. jours. Home: PA. Died May 3, 1979.

KEITH, CHARLES ALEXANDER, educator; b. Hot Springs, Ark., Feb. 28, 1883; s. Henry P. and Melinda (Jones) K.; student U. of Ark., 1905-07, U. of Tex., 1909-10; Rhodes scholar from Ark., 1907; B.A., Exeter Coll., Oxford U., Eng., 1911, M.A., Oxon., 1920; grad. student in history, Indiana U., 1925-26; m. Anna Dickson Roe, 1912; children—Theodore Henry Roe, Eugene Dickson. Instr. history and civics, high sch., Little Rock, Ark., 1911-12; head of dept. history and social science, Eastern Kentucky State Coll., 1912, dean of men since 1921. State dir. for Kentucky of U.S. School Garden Army. Lecturer State Council of Defense, World War I; mem. State Commission on War Bonds; chairman County Ration Board, World War II. Redpath lecturer on Americanization, 1920; president Ky. Ednl. Assn., 1924-25; condr. of teachers' insts. Past mem. Selection Com. of Rhodes Scholars from Ky. Mem. Am. Hist. Assn., Nat. Hist. Soc. (life), Am. Polit. Science Assn., Miss. Valley Hist. Assn., Sigma Nu, Southern Hist. Assn. Democrat. Presbyterian. Mason (K.T., K.C.C.H.), Past Grand Master of Grand Lodge of Ky.; Grand High Priest, Grand chpt. R.A.M. 1951. Writer on hist., govt. and ednl. topics. Home: Richmond, Ky. *

KEITH, NORMAN MACDONNELL, physician; b. Toronto, Ont., Can., June 8, 1885; s. George and Agnes (Dow) K.; B.A., U. of Toronto, 1908; M.D., Johns Hopkins, 1911; m. Edna I. Alexander, Aug. 31, 1920; children—Helen Mary, Janet Isobel, Alexander Macdonald. Came to U.S., 1920, naturalized, 1938. Interne New York Hosp., 1912-14; instr. in medicine, Johns Hopkins Med. Sch., 1914-16; staff mem. Bloomingdale Hosp., White Plains, N.Y., 1919; clinician U. of Toronto, med. dept., 1919-20; asst. in medicine, Mayo Clinic, Rochester, Minn., 1920-21; asso. prof. of medicine, Mayo Foundation, Grad. Sch., U. of Minn., 1921-36, prof. of medicine since 1936; cons. physician Mayo Clinic, Rochester, Minn., now emeritus. Served as capt. Med. Corps, Brit. Army, with B.E.F., 1916-19. Mem. A.M.A., Am. Soc. Clin. Investigations, Assn. American Physicians and others. Home: Rochester, Minn. *

KELEHER, TIMOTHY JEROME, naval officer (ret.); b. Perth Amboy, N.J., Feb. 17, 1885, s. Timothy C. and Mary (Thees) K.; B.S., U.S. Naval Acad., 1908; M.S., Columbia, 1917; m. Eugenia Whitford FitzSimons, Feb. 16, 1911. Commd. ensign, U.S. Navy, 1908, advanced through grades to rear adm., 1942; ret. July 1943. Served in World Wars I and II. Awarded Navy Cross, 1919. Mem. Am. Soc. of Naval Architects and Marine Engrs. Clubs: Univ. (N.Y. City) India House (N.Y. City) Army-Navy (Washington). Contbr. half chapter to Shipbuilding Bus. in the U.S.A., 1948. Home: Annapolis, Md. *

KELLER, ARTHUR R(IPONT), exec. secretary; born Buffalo, N.Y., July 28, 1882; s. William Martin and Louisa S. (Ripont) K.; C.E., Cornell, 1903; LL.B., Nat. U., 1907; M.S. in C.E., Harvard, 1916; M.S., Mass. Inst. Tech., 1916; hon. D.Sc., U. of Hawaii, 1942; m. Lora T. Keegan, Oct. 20, 1908. Asst. engr. C.,C.,C. & St.L. Ry., 1903; jr. engr. U.S., 1904-07; asst. mgr. Ala. Marble Co., 1907-09; with Coll. of Hawaii (now U. of Hawaii), 1909-46; executive sec. Ter. Retirement & Pension Commn., 1946-49; prof. engring., dean Coll. Applied Sci., 1921-46, v.p. since 1934, acting pres., 1941-42; licensed engr. Hawaii. Capt. Engrs., World War, Maj. Engr. Reserves. Mem. City Planning Commn., Honolulu, 1927-36, territorial bd. health 1911-15, 1943-47 (term), Hawaii Housing Authority, 1935-41 (sec., 1938-41); engr. Pub. Utilities Commn. Hawaii, 1928-32, dir. Queen's Hosp., Honolulu. Mem. A.A.A.S., Soc. Promotion Engring. Edn., Am. Soc. C.E. (asso. mem.), local engring. socs., Sigma Nu. Unitarian. Republican. Club. Pacific. Home: Honolulu. *

KELLER, GRETA, singer; b. Vienna, Austria, Feb. 8, 1909. Singer in night clubs, musicals, radio, TV, records; profl. debut at age twelve; appeared in play "Broadway," Vienna, 1928; 800 single recs., twelve albums recorded for Stanyan Records, Fiesta Records, Monitor Records and others; albums include: (with Rod McKuen) An Evening in Vienna; I Remember Vienna; Kinder Lieder; Love is A Daydream; Great Songs of the Thirties. Home: New York, N.Y. Died Nov. 4, 1977.

KELLER, JACK (JOHN A. C. KELLER), newspaperman; b. Columbus, Ohio, Oct. 23, 1911; s. Edwin Louis and Mildred Elizabeth (Riedel) K.; B.Sc., Ohio State U., 1933; m. Claire Elizabeth Schrader, June 10, 1931; children—John Jay, Patricia Mae. With Columbus Citizen-Jour., 1933-77, as reporter, asst. sports editor, asst. city editor, news editor, 1933-54, mng. editor, 1954-77, asso. editor, 1977; ret., 1977. Mem. Olympian. Mem. 1932 Olympic Track Team, high hurdles, world record holder 220 yd. low hurdles; elected posthumously to Varsity O Hall of Fame, Ohio State U., 1980. Home: Columbus, Ohio. Died June 3, 1978; buried Greenlawn Cemetery, Columbus.

KELLER, JAMES G., clergyman; b. Oakland, Calif., June 27, 1900; s. James and Margaret (Selby) K.; student St. Patrick's Coll., 1920-24; M.A., Cath. U., 1925; LL.D., Mt. Mary Coll., 1949, Canisius Coll., 1949. Ordained priest, Roman Cath. Ch. 1925; founder, dir. The Christophers, Inc., N.Y. City, 1945. Author: The Priest and A World Vision, 1946; You Can Change The World, 1948; Three Minutes a Day, 1949; Careers That Change Your World, 1950; One Moment Please, 1950; Government is Your Business, 1951; Just for Today, 1952; All God's Children, 1953; Stop, Look and Live, 1954; Give Us This Day, 1956; It's Your Day, 1957; A Day At a Time, 1958. Home: New York, N.Y. Died Feb. 7, 1977.

KELLER, RAYMOND NEVOY, educator, chemist; b. Wolcott, Ind., Apr. 21, 1909; s. Benjamin and Priscilla (Blume) K.; A.B., Ind. U., M.A., 1937; Ph.D., U. Ill., 1940; m. Mollie Goodrich, Dec. 19, 1936; children—Roger Raymond, Mark Douglas, Janet Mollie. Teaching asst. dept. chemistry Ind. U., 1936; teaching asst. dept. chemistry U. Ill., Urbana, 1937-39, fellow, 1939-40; instr. chemistry U. Wis., 1940-42; instr. U. Mich., 1942-45, asst. prof., 1945-51; research chemist Argonne Nat. Lab., Chgo., 1950-51; asst. prof. chemistry U. Colo., 1951-52, asso. prof., 1952-60, prof., 1960-76. Mem. Am. Chem. Soc., Chem. Soc. London, Colo.-Wyo. Acad. Sci., Sigma Xi, Phi Beta Kappa, Phi Kappa Phi, Phi Lambda Upsilon. Republican. Presbyn. Contbr. articles profl. jours. Research in inorganic chemistry, especially pseudohalide complexes and boroxines. Home: Boulder, Colo. Died Sept. 21, 1976.

KELLER, ROBERT FRANKLIN, govt. ofcl.; b. Washington, Aug. 22, 1913; s. Paul D. and Edna S. (Wells) K.; student George Washington U., 1931-32; LL.B., Washington Coll. Law, 1937; B.C.S., Benjamin Franklin U., 1952; m. Mary Benton Robinson, Nov. 11, 1939; children—Elizabeth Wright (Mrs. Edward L. Koepenick) Katherine Wells (Mrs. Robert A. Graves). Admitted to D.C. bar, 1936; with GAO, 1935-42, 46-80, gen. counsel, 1958-69, dep. controller gen. U.S., 1969-80; legislative atty. Office Comptroller Gen. U.S., 1946-50, asst. to comptroller gen., 1950-53, prin. asst., 1953-58. Served from ensign to lt., USNR, 1942-45; asst. to officer charge Navy Purchasing Office, San Francisco, also gen. counsel. Recipient Alumni Achievement award Benjamin Franklin U., 1972; commendation sec. navy; Rockefeller Pub. Service award, 1965; Career Service award Nat. Civil Service League, 1976. Mem. Fed., Am. bar assns., Nat. Contract Mgmt. Assn., Sigma Nu Phi. Lion. Club: Kenwood Golf and Country (Bethesda, Md.). Home: Chevy Chase, Md. Died Aug. 28, 1980; buried Romney, W.Va.

KELLEY, ROBERT FRANCIS, U.S. foreign service; b. Somerville, Mass., Feb. 13, 1894; s. John Henry and Caroline Bertha (Miller) K.; A.B., magna cum laude, Harvard, 1915, A.M., 1917; post grad. work, U. of Paris, France, 1915-16; unmarried. Asst. mil. attaché, Denmark, Finland and mil. observer, Baltic States, 1920-22; vice consul Calcutta, India, 1923; asst. chief, div. Eastern European Affairs, U.S. Dept. of State, Washington, D.C., 1925-26, chief, 1926-37; counselor American Embassy, Turkey, 1937-45; trustee Export-Import and Second Export-Import Bank of Washington, D.C., 1934-37. Served in U.S. Army as 2d lt., Oct. 1917-Mar. 1918, 1st lt., Mar. 1918-Apr. 1921; apptd. capt., Apr. 28, 1921; resigned Dec. 15, 1922. Mem. Am. Hist. Assn., Am. Soc. Internat. Law, Phi Beta Kappa. Catholic. Club: Metropolitan. Home: Washington, D.C. Died June 2, 1976.

KELLOGG, CHARLES EDWIN, soil scientist; b. Ionia County, Mich., Aug. 2, 1902; s. Herbert Francis and Eunice Irene (Stocken) K.; B.S., Mich. State Coll., 1925, Ph.D., 1929; D.Sc., U. Gembloux (Belgium), 1960, U. Ghent (Belgium), 1963, N.D. State U., 1962; m. Lucille Jeanette Reasoner, Dec. 25, 1925; children—Robert Leland, Mary Alice. Fellow in soils Mich. State Coll., 1926-28; soil scientist Wis. Geol. Natural History Survey, 1928-30; asst. prof., then prof. soils N.D. Agrl. Coll., Fargo, 1930-34; chief soil survey U.S. Dept. Agr., 1934-71, asst. adminstr., soil conservation service, 1953-63, dep. adminstr., 1963-71; now free lance writer, cons. Del. 3d Internat. Congress Soil Sci., Oxford, Eng., 1935, gen. assembly Internat. Inst. Agr., Rome, 1938, 2d Inter-Am. Conf. Agr., Mexico City, 1942, 7th Pacific Sci. Congress, New Zealand, 1949; head U.S. delegation 4th Internat. Congress Sci., Amsterdam, 1950, 5th Internat. Congress Soil Sci., Leopoldville, 1954, 6th Internat. Congress Soil Sci., Paris, 1956; chmn. U.S. Mission on Soil Sci. USSR, 1958; guest scientist India, 1958, 59, S. Viet Nam, 1959; Messenger lectr. Cornell U., 1945; Sigma Xi lectr., 1947; guest Acad. Scis. USSR for Jubilee Anniversay Sessions, Moscow and Leningrad, 1945; guest scientist, France, 1947, Belgian Congo, 1947, Britain, 1948, Ireland, Portugal and Iceland, 1950, Israel, 1952, Gold Coast, 1954. Recipient Distinguished Service award, gold medal U.S. Dept. Agr., 1950; Distinguished service citation Mich. State U., 1955. Fellow A.A.A.S., Am. Soc. Agronomy; mem. Assn. Am. Geographers, Profl. Soil Classifiers Assn. N.D. (hon.), Internat. Soc. Soil Sci. (hon.) Soil Sci. Soc. Am. (pres. 1941, hon. recognition 1974), Royal Soc. New Zealand (hon.), Indian Soc. Soil Sci. (hon.), Sigma Xi, Phi Kappa Tau, Alpha Zeta. Mason. Club: Cosmos (Washington). Author: The Soils that Support Us, 1941; Soil Survey Manual; Our Garden Soils, 1952; (with D.C. Knapp) The College of Agriculture-Science in the Public Service, 1966; Agricultural Development: Soil, Food, People, Work, 1975. Contbr. numerous bulls. and papers to profl. lit. Home: Hyattsville, Md. Died Mar. 9, 1980; buried Palo, Mich.

KELLOGG, CHARLOTTE HOFFMAN (MRS. VERNON KELLOGG), d. Mrs. Regula Hoffman; Ph.B., U. of Calif., 1900; m. Prof. Vernon Kellogg, Apr. 27, 1908; 1 dau., Charlotte Jean. Head dept. English, Miss Head's Sch., Berkeley, Calif., 1903-07. Worked in occupied Belgium, 1916, as mem. of Commn. for Relief in Belgium, and in Belgium and France, 1918-19; speaker for U.S. Food Adminstrn., 1917-18; Mem. Am. Assn. U. Women, Poetry Soc. Am., Nat. Inst. Social Sciences; mem. Belgian-Am. Ednl. Federation; mem. Kosciusko Found., Gamma Phi Beta. Decorated Chevalier de l'Ordre de la Couronne, Médaille de la Reine Elizabeth, Médaille Commémorative du Comité National (Belgium); Reconnaissance Francaise (France); Polonia Restituta (Poland). Author: Women of Belgium, 1917; Bobbins of Belgium, 1920; Mercier, the Fighting Cardinal, 1920; Jadwiga—Queen of Poland, 1936; The Girl Who Ruled a Kingdom, 1938; Pacific Light (poems), 1939. Contbr. prose and poetry to mags. Translator: Pierre Curie (from Ms. of Marie Curie), 1923. Home: Carmel, Calif. *

KELLOGG, GEORGE EDGAR, railroad ofcl.; b. Galva, Iowa, Oct. 1, 1922; s. Lloyd Leslie and Bessie Bernice (Whitsitt) K.; student Coll. Advanced Traffic, Chgo., 1946; m. LaVonne Gertrude Stanley, Mar. 5, 1946 (dec. Feb. 10, 1975); children—Georgia Kay, Peggy Louise, Robert Wesley, Rodney Leslie; m. 2d, Joanne Lippold Vater, Apr. 23, 1976; stepchildren—Dennis, Douglas, Deborah (Mrs. B. Edstrom), Susan, Stephen, Kevin, Daniel Vater. With C.G.W. R.R., 1946-65, sec., comptroller, 1961-62, v.p., sec., comptroller, 1962-65; v.p., sec. Kansas City So. Industries, Inc., and subsidiaries, 1967-76, sr. v.p., sec., 1976-79, controller, 1967-70; v.p., sec., controller K.C.S. Ry. and subsidiaries, 1967-70, La. & Ark. Ry. Co., 1967-79; v.p., sec., dir. Kansas City So. Ry. Co., 1970-76, sr. v.p., sec., 1976-79; v.p., sec. La. & Ark. Ry. Co., 1970-76, sr. v.p., sec., 1976-79. Served with AUS, 1942-45. Mem. Tax Execs. Inst., Assn. Am. Railroads, Stock Transfer Assn., Corporate Transfer Agts. Assn., Am. Soc. Corporate Secs., Nat. Investor Relations Inst. Methodist. Clubs: Union League (Chgo.); Kansas City. Home: Leawood, Kans. Died Sept. 6, 1979; buried Mt. Moriah, Kansas City, Mo.

KELLOGG, HAMILTON HYDE, bishop; b. Skaneateles, N.Y., Sept. 6, 1899; s. Walter Hamilton and Jennie Louise (Kellogg) K.; student Syracuse U., 1917-18, LL.D., 1956; A.B., Williams Coll., 1921, D.D., 1944; grad. Gen. Theol. Sem., N.Y.C., 1924, S.T.D., 1946; M.A., Columbia, 1924; D.D. U. of South, 1946, Hamilton Coll., 1954, Seabury-Western Theol. Sem., 1957; m. Mildred Sarah Haley, June 10, 1929. Ordained deacon and priest P.E. Ch., 1924; priest-in-charge St. Alban's Ch., Syracuse, N.Y., also St. Mark's Ch., Jamesville, N.Y., 1924-25; curate Christ Ch., Greenwich Conn., 1925-29; rector St. James' Ch., Danbury, Conn., 1929-41, Christ Ch., Houston, 1946-49; 1st dean Christ Ch. Cathedral, Houston, 1949-52; consecrated bishop coadjutor Diocese of Minn., 1952; bishop of Minn., 1956-70. Dir. Ministers Life & Casualty Union, 1957-72. Past mem. bd. dirs. of United Fund, Mpls.; past pres. bd. trustees Breck Sch., Mpls., St. James Sch., St. Mary's Hall, Shattuck Sch.; dir. Bishop-Seabury Mission, Faribault, Minn.; hon. chmn. bd. trustees Seabury-Western Theol. Sem., Evanston, Ill., 1952-58, chmn. 1958, 67-69; trustee Carleton Coll., 1956-70, St. Barnabas Hosp., Mpls., St. Luke's Hosp., St. Paul, 1956-70; past trustee Gen. Theol. Sem., N.Y.C., St. Stephen's Sch. and Sem. of S.W., Austin, Tex. Served as sgt. USMC, World War I; 1st lt. Chaplain's Corps, U.S. Army, 1928-29; capt. Conn. N.G., 1929-41; col. AUS, World War II. Decorated Bronze Star (U.S.); Croix de Guerre with palm (Belgium). Mem. Mil. Order World Wars, Delta Kappa Epsilon, Mason. Clubs: Minneapolis, Minikahda (Mpls.); Town and Country, University (St. Paul); Wayzata (Minn.) Country. Home: Minneapolis, Minn. Died July 5, 1977.

KELLY, ALFRED HINSEY, educator, historian; b. Pekin, Ill., June 23, 1907; s. Raymond Ransom and Bessie Mae (Case) K.; Ph.B., U. Chgo., 1931. A.M., 1934, Ph.D., 1938; m. Emily May Peterson, Sept. 22, 1935; children—Elizabeth Marie (Mrs. Donald Breneau), Virginia Jayne, Alfred Herbert. Mem. faculty Wayne State U., Detroit, 1935-76, prof. history, chmn. dept., from 1952. Tech. adviser preparation Supreme Ct. brief Brown vs. Board, N.A.A.C.P., 1953; apptd. to Oliver Wendell Holmes Devise, 1970. Mich. co-chmn. Vols. for Stevenson, 1952, Detroit chmn., 1956. Served to lt. USNR, 1944-46. Mem. Am. So. hist. assns., Orgn. Am. Historians. Club: Orpheus (Detroit). Author: (with W. A. Harbison) The American Constitution; Its Origins and Development, 4th edit., 1970. Editor, author: American Foreign Policy and American Democracy, 1954; Foundations of Freedom, 1958. Contbr. articles profl. jours. Home: Grosse Pointe Park, Mich. Died Dec. 14, 1976.

KELLY, CLARENCE FRANCIS, govt. ofcl.; b. Lawton, N.D., Oct. 18, 1906; s. Alfred Ernest and Christine (Vobayda) K.; B.S., N.D. State U., 1931; M.S., 1933, D.Sc. (hon.), 1963; m. Elizabeth Jamison, Nov. 4, 1937; 1 son, Robert Ernest. Engr. Ill. Dept. Conservation, 1933-35; with Bur. Agrl. Engring., U.S. Dept. Agr., 1936-50; agrl. engr. Coop. State Research Service, 1972-73; lectr., asso. agrl. engr. U. Calif., 1950-58, prof. agrl. engr., 1950-72, dir. Calif. Agrl. Expt. Sta., 1965-72. Served with USNR, 1942-45. Recipient Cyrus Hall McCormick medal Am. Soc. Agrl. Engrs., 1963. Fellow Am. Soc. Agrl. Engrs. (pres. 1972-73); mem. Internat. Soc. Biometeorology, A.A.A.S., Nat. Acad. Engring. Club: Commonwealth (San Francisco). Research on grain storage, farm structures, effects of environment on livestock in hot climates. Home: Kensington, Calif. Died May 5, 1976.

KELLY, EMMETT LEO, pantomine clown; b. Sedan, Kan., Dec. 9, 1898; s. Thomas and Mollie (Schimick) K.; ed. pub. schs.; m. Eva Moore, July 23, 1923; children—Emmett, Thomas Patrick; m. 2d Elvira Gebhardt, Apr. 20, 1954; children—Stasia, Monika. Cartoonist, Ad. Film Co., Kansas City, Mo., 1920-21; created Wearie Willie pen and ink cartoon, 1920; joined circus as clown, 1921, trapeze artist, 1924-31, clown, 1931-79; pictures include The Fat Man, Greatest Show on Earth, Wind Across the Everglades, and TV film The Captain from Keopenick; TV appearances include Ed Sullivan Show, Gary Moore Show, What's My Line, Jackie Gleason Show, Dave Garroway Show, Person to Person, Bob Crosby Show, Captain Kangaroo, Jack Linkletter on the Go, replacement Perry Como Show; filmed TV series The Emmett Kelly Show for 7 Arts Corp. Author: Clown My Life in Tatters and Smiles, 1954. Home: Sarasota, Fla. Died Mar. 28, 1979.

KELLY, ERNEST BYRON, JR., investment banker; b. Chgo., Oct. 27, 1915; s. Ernest Byron and Clara (Johnson) K.; A.B. U. Ill., 1937; LL.D. (hon.), Nat. U., San Diego, 1977; m. Kathryn Sumner Canfield, Mar. 7, 1942; children—Ernest Byron III, Michael W. Sales trainee Halsey, Stuart & Co. Inc., Chgo., 1937-39, salesman, Detroit, 1940-41, mgr. Detroit 1946-65, pres., chief exec. officer Chgo., 1968-70, chmn., chief exec. officer, 1970-76; v.p. Blyth & Co., Inc., 1965-67; dir., exec. com. Bache & Co., 1973-76, vice chmn. bd., 1974-76; dir. Bache Group, Inc., 1974-78; vice chmn. Bache Halsey Stuart Shields Inc., 1977-78. Chpt. chmn. United Found. Torch Dr., Detroit, 1961-64; mem. Wayne County Bd. Suprs., 1964-67, City Council Grosse Pointe, Mich., 1963-67. Bd. govs. Chgo. Assn. Stock Exchange Firms, 1970-75, chmn. bd., 1973; trustee Municipal Adv. Council Mich., 1958-67, chmn., 1967; trustee, exec. com. Loyola U., Chgo., 1972-76, chmn. investment com., 1974-76; mem. adv. com. Coll. Commerce, U. Ill., 1968-78; bd. dirs. U. Ill. Found., 1973-78, chmn. investment com., 1974-78, mem. Pres.'s club, 1969-78. Served with USNR, 1941-45; lt. comdr. Res. (ret.). Mem. Securities Industry Assn. (chmn. municipal com. Central States chpt. 1976—), Mil. Order World Wars, U. Ill. Alumni, Midwest, Am. (asso.), N.Y. (allied) stock exchanges, Chgo. Assn. Commerce and Industry, Art Inst. Chgo., Nat. Wildlife Assn., Audubon Soc., Delta Kappa Epsilon. Republican. Presbyn. Clubs: Bond (pres. 1952-53) (Detroit); Mid Am., Little LaSalle Street (dir.), Chicago, Bond, Executives, Commercial, Metropolitan, Attic (Chgo.); Wall Street (N.Y.C.); Onwentsia (Lake Forest, Ill.). Home: Lake Bluff, Ill. Died June 24, 1978.

KELLY, HARRY CHARLES, univ. adminstr.; b. Wilkes Barre, Pa., Sept. 3, 1908; s. Thomas A. and Josephine Magdalene (Reilly) K.; B.S., Lehigh U., 1931, M.S., 1933; Ph.D., M.I.T., 1936; LL.D., U. Hokkaido (Japan); m. Irene E. Andes, Dec. 14, 1940; children—Henry C., William T. Teaching fellow Lehigh U., 1931-33; teaching fellow Mass. Inst. Tech., 1933-36, research asso. radiation lab., 1942-45; research engr. Am. Thermos Co., Conn., 1936-37; asst. prof., then asso. prof. physics Mont. State Coll., 1937-41; dir. labs. St. John's Coll., Md., 1941-42; chief sci. and tech. div., spl. projects unit U.S. Army Occupation, Japan, 1945-50; head sci. sect. Office Naval Research, Chgo., 1950-51; asst. dir., head div. sci. personnel and edn. NSF, 1951-59, asso. dir., ednl. and internat. activities, 1959-62; dean faculty N.C. State U., Raleigh, 1962-67, provost, 1967-74, vice chancellor, 1971-74, emeritus, 1974-76. Co-chmn. U.S.-Japan Com. Sci. Coop., 1961-69. Recipient commendation for meritorious civilian service U.S. Occupation Forces, 1949; Order Sacred Treasure, Japan, 1969; certificate of merit State Dept., 1969. Fellow Am. Acad. Arts and Scis., A.A.A.S.; mem. Phys. Soc. Japan (hon.), Phi Beta Kappa. Author sci. and ednl. articles. Home: Raleigh, N.C. Died Feb. 2, 1976.

KELLY, HENRY HAGANS, govt. cons.; b. Bloomfield, Ohio, Aug. 27, 1897; s. William Brandon and Mary (Clark) K.; student U. Pittsburgh, 1914-15; m. Edna Milson, Dec. 19, 1929; 1 son, John Hagans. Sec. and editor Daily News Pub. Co., Braddock, Pa., 1915-23; asst. chief, automotive div. U.S. Dept. of Commerce, Washington, 1923-25, U.S. automotive trade commr. to Europe, Paris, France, 1925-28; spl. rep. Hudson Motor Car Co., Asiatic terr., Detroit, 1928-30; sec. 6th Internat. Road Congress, Washington 1930; highway transport splist. U.S. Bur. Pub. Roads 1931-35; chief, sect. motor carrier safety Interstate Commerce Commn., 1935-41; chief allocations sect. Office Defense Transportation, 1941-42, dir. materials and equipment div., 1942-45; N.Am. regional dir. European Central Inland Transport Orgn., 1945-47 asst. dir. and inland transport adviser of Office of Transport and Communications Policy, U.S. Dept. State, 1947-55; dir. Internat. Travel Office: Dept. Commerce, 1955-59; cons. UN, US ICA, other agencies, 1959-79. U.S. del. to numerous international confs.; chmn. U.S. delegation to U.N. Conf. on Road and Motor Transport, Geneva, 1949; UN Conf. Customs Facilities Tourists, 1954; Sixth Inter-Am. Travel Congress, San Jose, Costa Rica, 1956. Served with A.U.S., overseas, 1918-19. Mem. Soc. Automotive Engrs., Am. Soc. Travel Writers. Mason. Club: Cosmos. Author: Tourist Facilities on the Inter-American Highway, 1960. Editor: Proceedings of 6th International Road Congress, 1931. Contbr. numerous mag. articles on transportation and travel. Home: Washington, D.C. Died Nov. 28, 1979.

KELLY, JOHN JOSEPH, coll. pres.; b. Worcester, Mass., July 24, 1883; s. Henry Joseph and Annastasia Maria (Murphy) K.; grad. Fitchburg (Mass.) Normal Sch.; B.S. in Edn., Boston U.; Ed. M., Boston College; LL.D., Providence (R.I.) College, 1945; Ed.D. Rhode Island College of Education, 1946; m. Kathryn A. Gaffney, Aug. 4, 1920; 1 son, John Joseph Jr. Instr. and supervisor, grades and high school North Easton, Mass., 1914-17; instr. grade school, Springfield, Mass., 1917-18, Bridgewater (Mass.) Normal Sch., 1918-22; dean of men and asst. to prin., Bridgewater Normal School, 1922-31; dean of men, supervisor and asst. to pres. State Teachers Coll., Bridgewater, Mass., 1931-37, pres. since 1937. Mem. Eastern States Assn. Professional Schs. for Teachers, New England Teacher Preparation Assn., Mass. Schoolmasters Club, Plymouth County Teachers Assn. (past pres.), New England Sch. Supts. Assn., Irish Charitable Assn., St. Vincent de Paul Soc., Kappa Delta Pi. Knight of Columbus. Home: Bridgewater, Mass. *

KELLY, JOHN MARTIN, petroleum cons.; b. Chelsea, Mass., Oct. 1, 1914; s. James B.A. and Elizabeth B.A. (Ford) K.; B.S., N.M. Sch. Mines, 1936, Petroleum Engr., 1939; D.Sc., N.M. Inst. Mining and Tech., 1963; m. Esther E. Ladenburg, Dec. 29, 1938; children—Joseph J., Patricia E., Mary Ann, J. Michael. Mining engr. Rosedale Gold Mines, 1936; mine chemist Am. Metal Co., 1936-37; petroleum engr. Lea County Operators Com., 1937-41; state geologist N.M., 1941-45; exec. sec. mem., dir. N.M. Oil Conservation Commn., dir. N.M. Bur. Mines and Mineral Resources, coordinator mines in N.M. for WPB, 1941-45; cons. mining, petroleum engr., geologist, mineral adviser N.M. State Land Commr., 1945-61; pres. Elk Oil Co., 1945-61; dir. Yucca Water Co.; asst. sec. for mineral resources Dept. Interior, Washington, 1961-65; petroleum cons., Washington, 1965-77. Regent, N.M. Inst. Mining and Tech., 1975-77. Decorated knight St. Gregory, knight Holy Sepulchre; recipient Distinguished Service Honor award Dept. Interior, 1966. Registered profl. engr., N.M. Mem. Am. Inst. Mining Engrs., Am. Assn. Petroleum Geologists, Am. Assn. Petroleum Landmen, Am. Inst. Profl. Engrs., Am. Petroleum Inst., Ind. Petroleum Assn. Am., Mining Club N.Y.C., N.M. Oil and Gas Assn., N.M. Mining Assn., N.M. Landmens Assn., N.M., Roswell geol. socs., Rocky Mountain Coal Mining Inst., A.A.A.S., Geol. Soc. Am., Mining and Metall. Soc. Am. Home: Roswell, N.Mex. Died Sept. 19, 1977.

KELLY, MILTON, editor; b. St. Louis, Nov. 2, 1927; s. Herbert and Lillian (Rodgers) K.; student U. Miami; m. Montyna Montayne, Oct. 6, 1946; 1 dau., Karen Lynn (Mrs. James Doak). Reporter Miami (Fla.) News, 1942-47, asso. mag. editor, 1947-54; with Ft. Lauderdale (Fla.) News, 1954-80, exec. editor, 1968-71, v.p., mem. exec. bd., 1971-80. Am. columnist London (Eng.) Daily Mirror, 1958-60; freelance mag. writer. Recipient numerous nat. newspaper awards. Mem. A.P. Assn. Fla. (pres. 1964-65), Fla., Am. socs. newspaper editors, Ft. Lauderdale C. of C. Contbr. articles to mags. Address: Ft. Lauderdale, Fla. Died June 25, 1980; buried Evergreen Cemetery, Fort Lauderdale, Fla.

KELLY, STEPHEN EUGENE, assn. exec.; b. Bklyn., May 13, 1919; a Stephen Peter Paul and Lillian Catherine (Walters) K.; B.A. in English Lit., Hamilton Coll., 1940; m. Harriet Southard, Dec. 30, 1942; children—Stephen, Jeffrey, Peter. Pres. Mag. Pubs. Assn., N.Y.C., 1969-78; formerly pub. The Saturday Evening Post, Holiday mag., McCalls. Sec., bd. dirs. Madison Sq. Boys' Club, N.Y.C.; bd. dirs. Advt. Council. Served with USNR, 1941-45. Recipient highest award for citizenship and contbn. to coll. Hamilton Coll., 1940, Henry Johnson Fisher award, 1976. Mem. Theta Delta Chi (chmn. honor ct.). Clubs: University; Madison Square Garden; Nat. Golf Links Am. (Southampton); Fed. City (Washington). Home: New York, N.Y. Died Apr. 6, 1978.

KELLY, WILLIAM ROBERT, lawyer; b. Mound City, Mo., Feb. 22, 1883; s. David and Christian (Kennish) K., B.A., U. Colo., 1905, LL.B., 1907; m. Caroline Ettella Smith, June 29, 1911; 1 son, David Potter. Admitted to Colo. bar, 1908; practiced at Ft. Collins, 1908, Greeley 1908—; referee in water adjudication, Dists. 1 and 2, under Denver and Weld county courts, 1911-25; city atty., Greeley, 1916-21, county atty., Weld County, 1921-28; spl. counsel U.S. Supreme Ct. Wyo. vs. Colo., Neb. vs. Colo., 1930-38; atty. No. Colo. Water Conservancy Dist., 1935-56; partner Kelly & Snyder, 1941-48, Kelly and Clayton, 1949-56. Mem. Greeley Pub. Library Bd., 1912-38; chmn. bar com. Supreme Ct., Bd., of Law Examiners, 1920-37. Mem. 2d O.T.C., Aug. 1918; chmn. bd. Instrn. Registered Men, 1918; mem. Local Draft Bd. No. 14, 1940-41. Pres. Greeley C. of C., 1916; mem. Weld County Hosp. Bd., 1944-54; dir. Colo. Bar. Assn. Found., 1941-70. Recipient award 4 States Irrigation Council, 1967. Fellow Am. Bar Found., Newcomen Soc.; mem. Am., Colo. (pres. 1940), Weld County bar assns., Order of Coif, Phi Delta Phi, Alpha Tau Omega. Episcopalian (vestryman 29 yrs.). Republican. Clubs: Greeley Rotary (pres. 1932), Westerners. Author: Navigation and Irrigation in the Mountain States, 1945; also articles in revs. and jours. Home: Greeley CO. *

KELSEY, WILLIAM KLINE, newspaper writer; b. Toledo, O., July 28, 1885; s. Harrison Mitchell and Ella Louise (Kline) K.; A.B., University of Michigan, 1907; m. Gladys L. Hatt, 1917; children—Barbara Frances (Mrs. Paul Madison), Harry Mitchell, Jane (Mrs. Jacob F. Fahrner, Jr.). Became a reporter for Detroit News, 1907, Corr. at Washington, 1918, London, 1919-22, Paris, 1923, editorial writer, 1924-36; news commentator since 1936. Home: Birmingham, Mich. *

KELSO, ALBERT DONALD, corp. exec.; b. Middletown, N.Y., June 9, 1898; s. Henry G. and Emma (Sears) K.; A.B., Harvard, 1919; m. Florence L. Merwin, Sept. 29, 1923; children—Albert Donald, Florence M. (Mrs. Harold Bierman), John Glover. With Am. Glue Co., 1921-23, H. H. Barton & Son Co., 1923-27, U.S. Sandpaper Co., 1927-29, Durex Corp., 1930-51; pres., dir. Norton Internat. Inc. (formerly Norton Behr-Manning Overseas Inc.), Worcester, Mass., from 1951; dir. Norton Co., Worcester, Behr-Manning Corp., Troy, N.Y., also several fgn. affiliates of above cos. Dir. Nat. Fgn. Trade Council, Inc.; a founder, cons. Internat. Exec. Service Corps, 1965-80. Served as col., ordnance dept., AUS, 1943-45. Recipient Legion of Merit, Legion of Honor. Mem. Sigma Alpha Epsilon. Home: Shrewsbury, Mass. Died July 17, 1980; interred Mountain View Cemetery, Shrewsbury.

KELSO, ALEXANDER PEEBLES (KEL'SO), prof. philosophy; b. of Am. parents in Saharanpur, U.P., India, Dec. 10, 1886; s. Alexander Peebles and Louisa Mary (Bolton) K.; A.B., Washington and Jefferson Coll., 1906. D D, 1931; S.T.M., Western Theol. Sem., Pittsburgh, 1910; student U. of Leipzig, 1910-12; B.A., Oxford U., Eng., 1912, B.Sc., 1913, M.A., 1927; m. Clarice Ridley Wharam, Oct. 17, 1914; children—Edith Louise, Janet Beatrice. Pastor Mt. Pleasant (Pa.) Presbyn. Ch., 1914-18; prof. Bibl. history and lit., James Millikin U., Decatur, Ill., 1918-25; prof. philosophy, Southwestern Coll., since 1925. Mem. Soc. Bibl. Lit. and Exegesis. Presbyterian. Club: Egyptians (Memphis). Wrote: Matthew Arnold on Continental Life and Literature, 1914. Contbr. to religious and secular press. Home: Memphis, Tenn. *

KELSO, JAMES LEON, archaeologist, author; b. Duluth, Minn., Oct. 21, 1892; s. Evan E. and Bertha (Walle) K.; A.B., Monmouth (Ill.) Coll., 1916, D.D., 1926, LL.D., 1951; Th.M., Xenia Theol. Sem., St. Louis, 1918, Th.D., 1927; A.M., Ind. U., 1921; m. Adolphina Pearson, Jan. 28, 1920. Ordained to ministry U.P. Ch., 1918; pastor Bloomington, Ind., 1918-23; prof. O.T., Xenia Theol. Sem., 1923-30, Pitts.-Xenia Theol. Sem., 1930-59; prof. O.T. history and bibl. archaeology Pitts. Theol. Sem., 1960-63, prof. emeritus, 1963-78; staff archaeol. excavations Tell Beit Mirsim, Palestine, 1926, 30, 32; pres. staff Bethel Archaeol. expdn., 1934; dir.

excavations Tulul Abu el Alayiq and Nitla, Jordan, 1950; dir. Bethel Archaeol. Expdn., 1954, 57, 60; pres. asst. dir. staff Tell el Ful excavations, 1964. Moderator, U.P. Ch., 1952. Dir. Am. Sch. Oriental Research, Jersualem, 1949-50; pres. bd. trustees Palestine Archaeol. Mus., Jerusalem, 1949-51. Mem. Am. Oriental Soc., Archaeol. Inst. Am., Soc. Bibl. Lit. Republican. Author: The Ceramic Vocabulary of the Old Testament; The Excavation of New Testament Jericho, 1955; Archaeology and Our Old Testament Contemporaries, 1966; The Excavations of Bethel, 1934-60; Archaeology and the Ancient Testament, 1968; An Archaeologist Looks at the Gospels, 1969; An Archaeologist Follows the Apostle Paul, 1970. Contbr. numerous archael. articles to various tech. jours. Archeol editor S.S. Times, 1934-43. Home: Lebanon, Pa. Died July 28, 1978; buried Pittsburgh, Pa.

KEMP, EDWIN C., consular service; b. East Douglas, Mass., Aug. 24, 1884; s. Charles Edwin and Harriet Elizabeth (Moulton) K.; ed. pub. schs., Atlanta, Ga.; m. Bernette Zoe Chase, Sept. 12, 1909 (died Oct. 28, 1918); 1 dau., Marjorie; m. 2d, Anna Durkee Smith, Nov. 26, 1919; children—Charles Ernest, Janet. Am. consul at St. Pierre-Miquelon, 1914-15, Marseilles, France, 1915-16, Tunis, 1916-19, Bucharest, 1919-21, Budapest, 1921-23, Danzig, 1923-29, Havre, France, 1929-33, Moncton, N.B., Canada, 1933-35; consul gen. Winnipeg, Man., 1935-37, Bremen, Germany, 1937-41, Halifax, N.S., 1941-45, Kingston, Jamaica, B.W.I., 1946-47; retired. Episcopalian. Mason. Address: Melrose, Mass. *

KEMPE, RUDOLF, orch. conductor; b. Dresden, Germany, June 14, 1910; student State Orchestra Sch., Dresden. Prin. oboist and repetitor, Gewandhaus, Leipzig, 1929-36; conductor, Leipzig, 1936; dir. music State Orchestra, Dresden, 1949, State Opera of Munich (Germany), 1952; conductor Salzburg, Edinburgh, Bayreuth festivals; sometime condr. Met. Opera N.Y.C., Opera Covent Garden; conductor numerous orchestras and appeared various opera houses, also conductor for broadcasts and recs; artistic dir. Royal Philharmonic Orch., London, from 1963, Tonhalle Orch., Zürich, 1965-76; gen. music dir. Münchemer Philharmoniker, München, from 1967. Address: Zurich, Switzerland. Died May 11, 1976.

KEMPER, CLARENCE WORTHINGTON, clergyman; b. Freemansburg, W.Va., June 30, 1883; s. William Scott and Martha (Gibson) K.; grad. Broaddus Inst., Clarksburg, W.Va., 1905; A.B., Denison U., Granville, Ohio, 1909, D.D., 1930; A.M., U. of Chicago, 1911, B.D., 1912; LL.D., Alderson-Broaddus Coll., Philippi, 1952; m. Mary Edna McDaniel, June 30, 1910; children—Martha Edna (Mrs. C. D. Deeds), Mary Elizabeth (Mrs. Albert S. Davis, Jr.), Clarence McDaniel. Ordained to the ministry of the Baptist Church, 1910; pastor of Windsor Park Ch., Chicago, 1910-12, Wyoming Ch., Cincinnati, 1912-14, Temple Ch., Minneapolis, 1914-19, 1st Ch., Lansing, Mich., 1919-22, Bapt. Temple, Charleston, W.Va., 1923-34, First Ch., Denver, 1934-45, First Bapt. Ch., Boulder, Colo., 1945-50; lectr. Berkeley Bapt. Divinity Sch. 1950; minister emeritus First Bapt. Ch., Denver, since 1945; interim pastor several different chs., 1950—; has been active in all phases of Bapt. Ch. orgn., serving as mem. or chmn. numerous coms. and on bd. mgrs. various subsidiary orgns. and of convs. Served as leader both state and local councils of chs.; acted as pres. or other officer state Bapt. conv. Trustee Colorado Women's Coll.; mem. bd. of mgrs. Davis Child Shelter; served as interim president Alderson Broaddus Coll., 1951. Mem. Federal Council Chs. of Christ in America; rep. Northern Bapt. Conv. before Internat. Conv. of Disciples, Denver, 1938; staff lecturer, Illiff Sch. of Theology, Denver (summer), 1948; member faculty Boulder School of Missions (interdenom.), 1937; v.p. Denver Council Chs., 1941—; dir. Colo. branch Am. Civil Lbierties Union, 1938—. Vice pres. Boulder Unity Council, 1947; member exec. com. Boulder Council of Social Action, 1947; mem. board dirs. Colo. Town Meeting, Inc., 1947. Democrat. Mason (32 deg.). Clubs: Kiwanis (dir.); Kanawha Country. Author several books; contbr. to compilations of religions materials. Editor Rocky Mt. Churchman, 1936—, editor-in-chief, 1950; contbg. editor; staff corr. Christian Century, 1939—. Religious news broadcaster, KBOL, Boulder, Colo., 1947—. Home: Boulder, Colo. *

KEMPER, JAMES SCOTT, ins. co. exec.; b. Van Wert, O., Nov. 18, 1886; s. Hathaway and Mary Jane (Scott) K.; ed. pub. and high schs., Van Wert; LL.D., Miami U., Oxford, O., Ripon (Wis.) Coll., Wittenberg Coll., Middlebury Coll., Northwestern U., 1963, Ill. Inst. Tech., 1964; m. Mildred Estelle Hooper, Apr. 5, 1913 (dec. Nov. 27, 1927); children—James Scott, Rosemary, Mildred Jean; m. 2d, Mrs. Gertrude Ziesing Stout, Jan. 17, 1931. Spl. agt. in Ind. and Western Ohio, Central Mfrs., 1907-11; mgr. western dept., Chicago, same orgn., also mgr. Asso. Lumber Mutuals and Lumbermens & Mfrs. Ins. Agy., 1911; v.p., gen. mgr. Lumbermens Mutual Casualty Co., Chgo., 1912-19, pres., 1919-45, chmn., 1946-57, chmn. bd., 1958—; chmn. bd., pres. Am. Motorists Ins. Co., Fed. Kemper Life Assurance Co.; chmn. bd. Am. Mfrs. Mut. Ins. Co. (N.Y.), James S. Kemper & Co. (Chgo.), Sequoia Ins. Co., Menlo Park, Cal., Fed. Kemper Ins. Co., Chgo., Lumbermens & Mfrs. Mut. of Ill.; officer or dir. several ins. orgns.; dir. S.C. Johnson & Son, Inc. U.S. ambassador to Brazil, 1953-55. U.S. sec. Inter-Am. Council Commerce and Prodn., past pres. Trustee Ill. Inst. Tech., Chgo. Wesley Meml. Hosp.; chmn. James S. Kemper Found.; bd. dirs. Inst. Am. Strategy; mem. adv. bd. Greater Chgo. Safety Council; dir. Boys Clubs of Am. Chmn. Republican Nat. Finance Com., 1944-46; treas. Rep. Nat. Com., 1946-48; del. nat. convs., 1936, 40, 44, 48, 52, 64; Rep. Nat. Committeeman, Ill., 1960—. Decorated grand cross Order So. Cross (Brazil); comdr. Order of Merit (Ecuador); recipient Thomas F. Cunningham award for outstanding service in Inter-Am. Relations, 1948; Internat. Chicagoan of Year award, 1962, Chgo. medal of merit, 1962; named Businessman of Americas, U.S. sect. Inter-Am. C. of C. and Prodn., 1963. Mem. Nat. Indsl. Conf. Bd. (res. fund com.), YMCA (life mem. Rio de Janeiro), Internat. Assn. Chiefs Police (distinguished life), U.S. C. of C. (bd. dirs. 1920-28, v.p., 1937-40, pres., 1940-41; mem. sr. council), Internat. C. of C. (trustee), Ins. Forum San Francisco (hon.), Am. C. of C. for Brazil (hon. pres.), Am. Inst. Property and Liability Underwriters (trustee), Alpha Kappa Psi, Iota Nu Sigma. Clubs: Casino, Chicago, Glen View, Racquet, Saddle and Cycle, Tower, Executives, Post and Paddock (Chgo.); California (Los Angeles); Racquet, Thunderbird, Com. of Twenty-five, El Dorado (Palm Springs); Bohemian (San Francisco); Bath and Tennis, Everglades (Palm Beach); Metropolitan, Downtown Assn. (N.Y.C.); Chevy Chase, Metropolitan, Capitol Hill (Washington). Home: Barrington IL. *

KEMPTON, RUDOLF THEODORE, educator; b. Haverhill, Mass., May 30, 1902; s. Eugene Judson and Laura Emma (Sanborn) K.; B.S., Bates Coll., 1924; M.A., Columbia, 1925; Ph.D., N.Y. U., 1932; m. Elizabeth Thomas Leader, Dec. 25, 1926; 1 dau., Laura Estelle. Student asst. Bates Coll., 1922; asst. in biology N.Y. U., 1924-26, instr. 1926-32; research asso. pharmacology U. Pa., 1932-35; asst. prof. biology Princeton, 1935-37; prof. zoology and curator Natural History Museum, Vassar Coll., 1937-67, chmn. dept. zoology, 1940-62, prof. emeritus biology, 1967-75; teaching staff in physiology Marine Biol. Lab., 1941-47; tchr. physiology Army U. Center, Shrivenham, Eng., 1945-46; researcher Marineland of Fla., 1964-65. Trustee Marine Biol. Lab., Woods Hole, Mass., 1948. Mem. Am. Soc. Zoologists (sec. 1954-58), Physiol. Soc. Phila., Soc. Gen. Physiol., Phi Beta Kappa, Sigma Xi. Methodist. Club: University (Poughkeepsie, N.Y.). Author: (with M.E. Little) Laboratory Manual for Comparative Anatomy, 1926; (with Fred Brown) Sex Questions and Answers, 1948. Home: St Augustine, Fla. Died June 9, 1975.

KENDALL, DAVID WALBRIDGE, lawyer; b. Indpls., Feb. 11, 1903; s. Calvin Noyes and Alla Perkins (Field) K.; student Phillips Acad., 1918-20; A.B., Princeton, 1924; LL.B., U. Mich., 1931; LL.D., Ind. Central Coll., 1964; m. Elizabeth Way, Dec. 17, 1934; 1 son, David Walbridge. Newspaper reporter, editorial writer, 1925-28; admitted to Mich. bar. 1931, since practiced in Jackson; mem. firm McKone, Badley, Kendall & Domke; gen. counsel U.S. Treasury, 1954-55; asst. sec. of Treasury, 1955-57; mem. firm Cummings, Sellers, Reeves, Conner & Kendall, 1957-58, Cummings & Sellers, 1961-62; v.p. legal affairs Chrysler Corp., 1962-68; then of counsel Butzel, Eaman, Long, Gust & Kennedy; chmn. bd. incorporators Nat. R.R. Passenger Corp., 1971; spl. counsel to Pres. of U.S. 1958-61; dir. Acacia Mut. Life Ins. Co., Washington. Mem. Lawyers Com. for Civil Rights Under Law. Trustee Fed. City Council, from 1961; chmn. Jackson Housing Authority; past pres. bd. edn. Union Sch. Distr., Jackson. Past v.p. United Givers Fund, Washington, pres. Grosse Pointe War Meml.; mem. nat. council, gen. div. laymen's work P.E. Ch.; trustee Episcopal Diocese of Mich. Mem. Republican Nat. Com., 1952-56. Mem. adv. com. U.S. Coast Guard Acad.; trustee Kenyon Coll., Gambler Ohio, mem. bd. Hutzel Hosp., Med. Center Devel. Corp., Detroit. Served as combat intelligence officer, USAAF, 1942-45. Mem. Am. Fed. bar assns., Am. Judicature Soc., Am. Law Inst., Newcomen Soc., Mil. Order World Wars, Am. Legion, V.F.W., Res. Officers Assn. (judge advocate Mich. dept.), Assn. Gen. Counsel, Bar Assn., N.Y. (congl. ethics com.), Alumni Council Phillips Acad. (v.p.) Phi Delta Phi, Episcopalian (vestryman 1961-62). Mason, Elk. Clubs: Metropolitan, Chevy Chase (Washington); Detroit, Detroit Athletic, Yondotega (Detroit); Town (Jackson); Princeton, University (N.Y.C.). Contbr. articles to mil. publs. Home: Grosse Pointe Farms, Mich. Died Dec. 27, 1976.

KENDALL, HARRY TAYLOR, lumberman; b. Clay Center, Kan., May 26, 1882; s. David Alden and Eliza Mendal (Taylor) K.; student pub. schs. of Wis. and Mo.; m. Helen Lucille Pendleton, Nov. 30, 1910 (died Sept. 3, 1924); children—Harry Taylor, George P., Robert A., Suzanne (dec.); m. 2d Rubey Williams Reeds, Jan. 29, 1927; 1 step dau., Marjorie Reeds (Mrs. Donald G. McNeely). Gen. sales mgr. Kirby Lumber Co., Houston, 1913-26; asst. gen. mgr. and gen. sales mgr. Central Coal & Coke Co., Kansas City, 1926-32; gen. mgr. and dir. Wyerhaeuser Sales Co., St. Paul, 1934-51, chmn. bd. since 1950; pres. and dir. Globe Box Co., Houston; dir. Allied Bldg. Credits, Inc. Spl. consultant to Munitions Bd., 1950; chmn. lumber mfg. industries Nat. Industry Adv. Com., Dept. of Commerce and Nat. Prodn. Authority, 1950; dir. C. of C. of U.S. Trustee The Am. Heritage Found.; dir. St. Luke's Hosp. Mem. Nat. Lumber Mfrs. Assn. (dir.). Presbyn. (trustee). Mason. Clubs: Minnesota (past pres.), Somerset Country (past pres.) (St. Paul); Tacoma, Tacoma Country and Golf (Tacoma). Home: St. Paul. *

KENDALL, VALERIUS HORATIO, business exec.; b. Fairbury, Neb., Mar. 26, 1886; s. Wallace Warren and Lillian Genevieve (Bradshaw) K.; B.Sc., U. Neb., 1907; m. Genevieve Ward Brown, June 27, 1911 (dec.); 1 son, Warren Frederic. Sales exec., gen. mgr. Kawnfer Co., Niles, Mich., 1907-15; product sales mgr. Motor Products Corp., 1916-19; v.p., gen. mgr. H. Jay Hayes Industry, Lansing, Mich., 1929-32; pres. Detroit Moulding Corp., 1933-42; dep. chief mfg. br. U.S. Army Ordnance Tank Automotive Center, Detroit, 1942-43; v.p., gen. mgr. N. A. Woodworth Co., 1943-44; with Universal Products Co. since 1950, now pres. Clubs: Athletic, Golf (Detroit); Recess. Home: Detroit. *

KENDRICK, BAYNARD HARDWICK, author; b. Phila., Apr. 8, 1894; s. John Ryland and Julia (Lawton) K.; ed. Tome School, Port Deposit, Md. and Episcopal Acad., Phila.; m. Edythe Stevens, 1919 (dec.); children—Baynard, Edythe, Julia; m. 2d, Jean Morris. Sec. Selden Cypress Door Co., Palatka, Fla., 1921-27; pres. Trades Pub. Co. Phila., 1928; gen. mgr. Peter Clark, Inc., N.Y.C., 1929; gen. mgr. Bing & Bing's Hotels, N.Y.C., 1930-31; free lance writer, 1932-77. Enlisted in Can. Army within one hour after Can. declared war, Aug. 1914; served in C.E.F., 1914-18. Awarded 1914-15 Star, Canadian War medal, Brit. War medal; Robert Meltzer award, 1951, Spearhead medal from 3d Armored Div. Club, 1951. Cons. to staff, Old Farms Convalescent Hosp. for Blinded Veterans, U.S. Army, Avon, Conn., during World War II; sighted adviser and hon. life mem. Blinded Vets. Assn. Recipient plaque from Gen. Omar N. Bradley for service to blinded veterans of World War II. Mem. Authors League, Mystery Writers Am., Inc. (1st pres.; grand master 1967), Washington Sq. Assn., Florida Hist. Soc. (dir., regional v.p.), Democrat, Episcopalian. Mason. Clubs: Carolina Yacht (Charleston, S.C.); Marshall Chess (N.Y. City). Author: Blood on Lake Louisa, 1934; The Iron Spiders, 1936; The Eleven of Diamonds, 1936; The Last Express, 1937; The Whistling Hangman, 1937; Death Beyond the Go-thru, 1938; The Odor of Violets, 1941; Blind Man's Bluff, 1943; Death Knell, 1945; Out of Control, 1945; Lights Out, 1945; Flames of Time, (Lit. Guild selection), 1948; The Tunnell, 1949; You Die Today, 1952; They Never Talk Back (with Heinrich Trefflich), 1953; Blind Allies, 1954; Reservations for Death, 1957; Clear and Present Danger, 1958; Hot Red Money, 1959; The Aluminum Turtle, 1960; Frankincense and Murder, 1961; Florida Trails to Turnpikes, 1915-65; Flight From A Firing Wall, 1966; motion pictures include; The Last Express, 1938; Eyes in the Night (starring Edward Arnold and Ann Harding), 1942; The Hidden Eye (Edward Arnold), 1945; Bright Victory (starring Arthur Kennedy and Peggy Dow). Contbr. to mags. Books have been transcribed into Braille. Home: Leesburg, Fla. Died Mar. 23, 1977.

KENISON, FRANK ROWE, judge; b. Conway, N.H., Nov. 1, 1907; s. Arthur Edson and Isadore Gertrude (Rowe) K.; A.B., Dartmouth, 1929, LL.D., 1954; LL.B., Boston U., 1932, LL.D., 1955; Dr.Juristic Sci., Suffolk U., 1959; LL.D., U. N.H., 1966, Franklin Pierce Coll., 1966; m. Loretta M. Landry, Apr. 8, 1939; children—Thomas, Mary Ann, Frank. Admitted to N.H. bar, 1932; Carroll County solicitor, 1935-37; asst. atty. gen., 1937-40, atty. gen., 1940-42, 45-46; asso. justice N.H. Supreme Ct., Concord, 1946-52, chief justice, 1952-77. Served with USNR, 1942-45. Mem. Am., N.H. bar assns., Am. Judicature Soc., Am. Law Inst., State-Fed., N.H. jud. councils. Home: Concord, N.H. Died Dec. 14, 1980.

KENISTON, (RALPH) HAYWARD, college prof.; b. Somerville, Mass., July 5, 1883; s. Charles Edgar and Sarah Elvina (Hayward) K.; A.B., Harvard, 1904, A.M., 1910, Ph.D., 1911; studied in Europe, 1911-13; m. Florence M. Robinson, May 20, 1911; children—Florence, Martha, Allen; m. 2d, Roberta Cannell, June 16, 1928; children—Kenneth, Marjorie. Instr. in Latin, Colby Coll., 1904-05; master Hotchkiss Sch., 1905-07; instr. Romance langs., Harvard, 1908-10; asst. librarian, Hispanic Soc. of America, 1910-11; instr. Romance langs., Harvard, 1913-14; asst. prof. Romance langs., 1914-19, prof., 1919-25, and dean Grad. Sch., 1923-25, Cornell; prof. Spanish lang., University of Chicago, 1925-40; prof. Romance langs., Univ. of Michigan, 1940-53, dean, Coll. of Literature, Science and the Arts, 1945-51; vis. lecturer at Duke University, 1952-53; cultural relations attaché American Embassy, Buenos Aires, 1942-44; Y.M.C.A. secretary, La Valbonne, France, and Florence, Italy, 1918; speaker for Italian Ministry of Propaganda, in Central Italy, 1918; assistant in office of Military Attaché, Am. Embassy, Rome, 1918. Mem. Am. Acad. Arts and Sciences, American Philos. Society, Modern Lang. Assn. America, Phi Beta Kappa, Hispanic Soc. America; Linguistic Society of America (president, 1948). Author: Las Treinta of Juan Boscán, 1911; The Dante Tradition in the Fourteenth and Fifteenth Centuries, 1915; List of Works for the Study of Hispanic-American History, 1920; Garcilaso de la Vega (a critical study of his life and works), 1922; Spanish Idiom List, 1929; The Syntax of Castilian Prose, 1937. Editor: La Barraca por V. Blasco Ibáñez, 1910; Maria por Jorge Isaacs, 1918; Fuero de Guadalajara, 1924; Works of Garcilaso de la Vega, 1925. Contbr. to reviews. Home: Ann Arbor, Mich. *

KENNALLY, VINCENT IGNATIUS, bishop; b. Boston, June 11, 1895; s. Willam J. and Mary Ann (Murphy) K.; A.B., Woodstock (Md.) Coll., 1921, M.A., 1922. Joined Soc. of Jesus, 1915, ordained priest Roman Cath. Ch., 1928; tchr. Atenco de Manila, 1922-25; asst. editor Jesuit Missions, 1930-31; prof. philosophy Boston Coll., 1929-30; superior Mission Cagayan de Oro, Philippines, 1933-39; rector, master novicces, Novaliches, Philippines, 1940-45; adminstr. apostolic and religious superior Caroline and Marshall Islands, 1946-51; vice provincial Jesuit Vice Province of Philippines, 1952-56; bishop of Caroline and Marshall Islands, also aux. chaplain, 1957-77. Mem. U.S. Cath. Conf., Nat. Conf. Cath. Bishops Conferentia Episcopal Pacific. Address: Truk, Caroline Islands. Died Apr. 12, 1977; buried Novaliches, Philippines.

KENNARD, EARLE HESSE (KEN-NÄRD'), physicist; b. Columbus, O., Aug. 2, 1885; s. Edwin Orson and Flora (Hesse) K.; A.B., Pomona Coll., 1907; Rhodes scholar from Calif., Oxford U., 1908-11, B.S., 1911; Ph.D., Cornell, 1913; m. Margaret.Dance Jarman, Dec. 23, 1919; children—Jarman George, Anne Dance, Paul Hesse. Asst. in physics, Cornell U., 1912-13, instr., 1913-14, 1916-17; instr., U. of Minn., 1914-16; asst. prof. physics, Cornell U., 1919-27, prof. 1927-46; physicist, David Taylor Model Basin, Navy Dept., Washington, D.C., since 1946, in charge of structural mechanics lab., 1950-56. Fellow Am. Physical Soc., A.A.A.S.; mem. Phi Beta Kappa, Gamma Alpha. Contbr. to Physical Rev., etc. Home: La Verne, Cal. *

KENNEDY, CHARLES WILLIAM, coll. prof.; b. Port Richmond, S.I., N.Y., Jan. 13, 1882; s. T. Livingstone and Marie Alice (Bush) K.; grad. Phillips Acad., Exeter, N.H., 1899; A.B., Columbia, 1902; New York Law Sch., 1903-04; M.A., Princeton, 1905; Charles Scribner fellowship, 1905-06; Ph.D., Princeton University, 1906; married Lucy Baldwin Walradt, June 3, 1911; 1 daughter, Barbara Cary; married 2d, Elizabeth Deane, March 25, 1940. Instructor in English, 1906-07, Princeton University, Porter Ogden Jacobus fellowship, 1907-08, instructor English, 1908-10, assistant professor, Robert Stockton Pyne Preceptor in English, 1910-19, associate prof., 1919-21, prof. English, 1921-38, Murray prof. of English literature, 1938-44, Murray professor, emeritus, since 1944; visiting prof., Colorado Coll., summer session, 1936, 37, 38; College of Chestnut Hill, spring term, 1938. Commd. 1st lt. Ordnance Res. Corps, May 28, 1917; capt., Ordnance Department, N.A., Jan. 22, 1918; on active duty, July 12, 1917-Jan. 10, 1919; service with A.E.F., Sept.-Dec. 1918. Chmn. Princeton Board Athletic Control, 1923-32; pres. Nat. Collegiate Athletic Assn., 1930-32, hon. pres., 1932—; v.p. Am. Olympic Com., 1928-32. Mem. Modern Lang. Assn. of Am., Huguenot Soc. of Am., Sons of the Am. Revolution, Phi Beta Kappa. Episcopalian. Clubs: Tiger Inn, Key and Seal, Princeton (N.Y.C.). Author The Legend of Juliana, 1906; The Poems of Cynewulf, 1910; The Caedmon Poems, 1916; The Walls of Hamelin, 1922; College Athletics, 1925; Sport and Sportsmanship, 1931; Old English Elegies, 1936; Beowulf, 1940; The Earliest English Poetry, 1943; Early English Christian Poetry. 1952; An Anthology of Old English Poetry, 1960; Early English Christian Poetry. 1963. Home: LaJolla, Cal. Died July 13, 1969. *

KENNEDY, CLEMENT, investment co. exec.; b. Fall River, Mass., Aug. 16, 1893; s. William Francis and Clementine (McAllister) K.; A.B., Harvard, 1916; D.S. in Bus. Administrn., Bryant Coll., 1949, LL.D., 1954; D.Art and Oratory, Staley Coll., 1950; m. Katherine Devine, Oct. 16, 1920 (dec.). Newspaper corr. Boston Jour., A.P., 1914-16; clerical positions New Ocean House, Swampscott, Mass., Hotel Tichfield, Jamaica, B.W.I., 1916-17; v.p. New Ocean House, 1922-29, pres. gen. mgr., 1929-59; mng. dir. Vinoy Park Hotel, St. Petersburg, Fla., 1928-41; dir. Hotel Service Inc., Boston, from 1955; trustee, sr. cons. Endicott Jr. Coll., Beverly, Mass., from 1958, pres. treas. Mayflower Holding Corp., Swampscott, from 1959. Lectr. in hotel mgmt. Boston U., 1924-47, Cornell Sch. Hotel Administrn., 1949, U. N.H., 1952; dir. First Fed. Savs. & Loan Assn., Boston, Dorchester Mut. Fire Ins. Co., Boston. Mem., Assay Commn., U.S. Mint, 1951; civilian aide to U.S. sec. army, 1958-62; mem. adv. council Suffolk U.; dist. rep. U.S. Mil. Acad. Trustee Peter Bent Brigham Hosp., Boston; trustee Bryant Coll., Worcester Acad., Lynn Hosp., Hillside Sch.; mem. Harvard Crimson Grad. Bd. Served to 1st lt. U.S. Army, 1917-19; AEF; to col. AUS, 1941-46. Decorated Legion of Merit; Legion of Honor (France); Sovereign Mil. Order of Malta, Equestrian Order of Holy Sepulchre; recipient Outstanding Civilian Service medal Dept. Def., 1962. Mem. Mass. Soc. Mayflower Descs. (past pres.), Nat. Soc. Old Plymouth Colony Descs., Order First Families Va., West Point Soc. (hon.), Soc. Colonial Wars, S.A.R., Am. Legion, V.F.W., Mil. Order World Wars, Order of Lafayette, Pilgrim Soc. Clubs: Harvard, Union (Boston); Faculty (Harvard), Eastern Yacht (Marblehead, Mass.); Beach, Tedesco Country (Swampscott) Home: Swampscott, Mass. Died Nov. 7, 1977.

KENNEDY, GEORGE CLAYTON, geologist, educator; b. Dillon, Mont., Sept. 22, 1919; s. Clayton Tierney and Maude (Coley) K.; B.A., Harvard U., 1940, M.A., 1941, Ph.D., 1947; m. Sally Slocum, Oct. 1, 1951; children—Clayton S., Deborah E., Jennifer A.; m. 2d, Ruth Porter, May 11, 1968. Mem. faculty Harvard U., 1946-52; mem. faculty U. Calif. at Los Angeles, 1952-80, prof. geology, 1953-80. Vice pres. Los Angeles County Museum Alliance, 1955-80; chmn. Los Angeles Ethnic Arts Council, 1970. Recipient award Minerol. Soc. Am., 1956. Fellow Am. Acad. Arts and Scis. Contbr. profl. jours. Club: Explorers (vice chmn. 1967-68) (Los Angeles). Home: Los Angeles, Calif. Died Mar. 18, 1980.

KENNEDY, GERALD HAMILTON, bishop; b. Benzonia, Mich., Aug. 30, 1907; s. Herbert Grant and Marian (Phelps) K.; A.B., Coll. of Pacific, 1929, D.S.T., 1952; A.M., Pacific Sch. Religion, 1931, B.D., 1932; D.D., 1952; S.T.M., Hartford Theol. Sem., 1933, Ph.D., 1934; LL.D., Coll. of Puget Sound, 1949; Litt.D., Nebr. Wesleyan U., 1950; L.H.D., Beliot Coll., 1952; LL.D., Ohio Wesleyan U., 1952; D.D., Redlands U., 1954, Bucknell U., 1959; H.H.D., Bradley U., 1956; L.H.D., Calif. Western U., 1967; m. Mary Grace Leeper, June 2, 1928. Ordained ministry Methodist Ch., 1932; pastor First Congregational Church, Collinsville, Conn., 1932-36, Calvary Meth. Ch., San Jose, Calif., 1936-40, First Meth. Ch., Palo Alto, Calif., 1940-42; acting prof. homiletics Pacific Sch. Religion, 1938-42; pastor St. Paul Meth. Ch., Lincoln, Nebr., 1942-48; bishop of Methodist Ch., Portland area, 1948; bishop Meth. Ch., Los Angeles area, 1952; dir. Wesley Found., Stanford U., 1940-42; lectr. in religion Nebr. Wesleyan U., 1942; radio preacher, KFAB and KFOR, Lincoln, Nebr., Sundays, 1945-48; book program, KEX, Portland, Oreg., Tuesday, 1949; Pilgrimage in World of Books, ABC, 1954; Earl lectr. Pacific Sch. Religion, 1946; Peyton lectr. So. Meth. U., 1949; Slover lectr. Southwestern U., 1950; Quillian lectr. Emory U., 1951; Mendenhall lectr. Depauw U., 1954; Beecher lectr. Yale, 1954; Ayer lectr. Colgate-Rochester, 1955; Grey lectr. Duke, 1957; Auburn lectr. Union Theol. Sem., 1957; Willson lectr. Southwestern Coll., 1964; sr. minister First Meth. Ch., Pasadena, Calif., 1969-73; Denman lectr. Perkins Sch. Theology, Dallas; Voigt lectr. McKendree Coll., 1968. Mem. exec. co. Community Chest, Lincoln, Nebr., 1945-48; pres. Council Social Agys., Lincoln, 1946-48; pres. Council of Bishops of Meth. Ch., 1960-61; mem. bd. trustees Pacific Sch. Religion, So. Calif. Sch. Theology; pres. Gen. Bd. Evangelism, Methodist Church, 1964-68; executive bd. Nat. Council Churches. Mem. Calif. State Bd. Edn. Clubs: University, Pasadena. Author: His Word Through Preaching, 1947; Have This Mind, 1948; The Best of John Henry Jowett (edited), 1948; The Lion and the Lamb, 1950; With Singleness of Heart, 1951; Go Inquire of the Lord, 1952; A Reader's Notebook, 1953; Who Speaks for God?, 1954; God's Good News, 1955; The Christian and His America, 1956; The Methodist Way of Life, 1958; I Believe, 1958; Readers Notebook, 2, 1959; The Parables, 1960; While I'm On My Feet, 1963; For Preachers and Other Sinners, 1964; Fresh Every Morning, 1966; Seven Worlds of the Minister, 1968; For Laymen and Other Martyrs, 1969; My Third Reader's Notebook, 1974. Home: Laguna Hills, Calif. Died Feb. 17, 1980; buried Forest Lawn Meml. Park, Hollywood Hills, Calif.

KENNEDY, GERALD S., mfg. exec.; b. St. Paul, Oct. 29, 1894; s. Patrick J. and Mary E. (Lynskey) K.; student St. Thomas Coll., 1908-14; m. Mary Hubbard, June 7, 1921; children—John Paul, Thomas Patrick, Kathleen Mary. Began career with Washburn Crosby Co., 1914-28; grain and prodn. mgr. Gen. Mills, Inc., Buffalo, 1928-39, operations mgr. from 1939, adminstr. flour and feed div. from 1953, dir., from 1948, mem. exec. com., from 1955, exec. v.p., 1958, chmn. bd., from 1959. Trustee Cath. Boys Home, Mpls. Served as pvt. U.S. Army, 1918. Mem. Am. Legion, Flour Millers Export Assn. (past pres.), Millers Nat. Fedn. (pres., chmn. exec. com. 1957-58, dir.). Clubs: Minikahda, Minneapolis (Mpls.). Author: Minutes and Moments in the Life of General Mills, 1971; Stepping Stones and Stumbling Blocks, 1972. Home: Minneapolis, Minn. Deceased.

KENNEDY, HOWARD ERNEST, ret. banker; b. Wilkes-Barre, Pa., May 22, 1910; s. Howard William and Lillian (Vivian) K.; A.B., Dickinson Coll., 1932, J.D., 1935; m. Marian Carol Jones, Nov. 12, 1938; children—David Robert, John Howard. Admitted to Pa. bar, 1937; practiced in Wilkes-Barre, 1937-40; solicitor City of Wilkes-Barre, 1940-41, 46-55; with United Penn Bank, Wilkes-Barre, 1955-77, sr. v.p., 1962-75, trust officer, 1955-75, ret., 1975, cons. trust dept., 1975-77, also past dir. and sec. United Penn Corp.; lectr. Pa. Bankers Trust Sch. Mem. Wyoming Valley Indsl. Devel. Com., 1955-73. Bd. dirs. Vis. Nurses Assn.; bd. dirs. Wyoming Valley Tb Soc. Served as lt. comdr. USNR, 1942-46. Mason (Shriner). Home: Stuart, Fla. Died May 3, 1979; buried Wilkes-Barre.

KENNEDY, JAMES WALTER, profl. sports orgn. exec.; b. Stamford, Conn., June 8, 1912; s. Michael James and Lottie (Hofman) K.; B.A. in Edn. and Journalism, U. Notre Dame, 1934; m. Marion McRedmond, Nov. 28, 1940; children—David Michael, Robert Francis, Kathleen Marie. Social worker Cath. Charities, Stamford, 1934-37; athletic coach St. Basil's Prep. Sch., Stamford, 1937-39; head Cath. textbook dept. Macmillan Pub. Co., 1939-41, Loyola U. Press, Chgo., 1941-43; dir. pub. relations U. Notre Dame, 1943-46; propr. pub. relations firm, N.Y.C., Stamford, 1946-59; mayor Stamford, 1959-63; commr. Nat. Basketball Assn., 1963-75; ret. chmn. bd. 1st Stamford Bank and Trust Co.; pres. Robustelli Travel Services, Inc. Mem. Stamford Bd. Edn., 1948-51, Stamford Park Commn., 1955-59; mem. Conn. Commn. Higher Edn., 1966-67, Conn. Devel. Commn. Campaign mgr. for U.S. Senator Ribicoff, 1962. Chmn. trustees State Colls. Conn., 1966-67; chmn. bd. Spl. Olympics for Mentally Retarded, Washington; pres. Naismith Basketball Hall of Fame, Springfield, Mass. Named knight of St. Gregory, 1966. Democrat. Home: Stamford, Conn. Died June 26, 1977.

KENNEDY, JOHN J., engr.; b. St. Paul, Minn., Oct. 20, 1885; s. Jerimiah Cashmere and Mary Jane (Milner) K.; E.M., U. Minn., 1908; m. Irene Murphy, 1928. Vice pres., dir. trade relations, Ingersoll-Rand Co. Mem. Am. Soc. Mining and Metall. Engrs., Washington Soc. Engrs., Psi Upsilon, Theta Tau. Clubs: University, Columbia Country, Congressional. Home: Chevy Chase, Md. *

KENNEDY, SELDEN BROWN, officer Marine Corps; b. Kenton, Tenn., Aug. 30, 1886; s. John Franklin and Olivia Ada (Canada) K.; A.B., U. of Tenn., 1908; graduate Marine Officers' Sch., 1910; Command and General Staff Sch., 1931; Marine Corps Schs. (senior course), 1936; m. Jessie V. McConaha, Dec. 7, 1912; children—Virginia Frances (wife of Lt. Robert R. Sampson, U.S. Navy), Alice Elizabeth (wife of Capt. August Larson, U.S.M.C.) and Selden Brown, Jr. Commissioned 2d Lt., U.S. Marine Corps, Aug. 11, 1909, and advanced through grades to colonel, May 1, 1938. Served at various posts in United States, Philippines, Haiti and China; at sea in the U.S.S. Denver, the U.S.S. Virginia and the U.S.S. Arkansas; director of Personnel, Headquarters Marine Corps, Washington, D.C., since June 1938. Awarded (service medals) Mexico; Marine Corps Expeditionary; Victory; also Distinguished Service Medal by the Republic of Haiti. Mem. Phi Kappa Phi. *

KENNEDY, WALTER WALLACE, banker; b. Birmingham, Dec. 20, 1898; s. Hughes Benjamin and Katherine (Hausman) K.; LL.B., U. Ala., 1921; student Grad. Sch. Banking, Rutgers U., 1945-47; m. Myra Belle Pope, Sept. 28, 1926; children—Walter, Ann Carter, Carol Pope. Admitted to Ala. bar, 1921; practiced in Birmingham, 1921-26; asst. to pres. Birmingham Electric Co., 1926-29; asst. trust officer First Nat. Bank Birmingham, 1929-35; trust officer First Ala. Bank of Montgomery N.A., 1935-43, exec. v.p., 1943-48, pres., 1948-64, chmn. bd., 1964-69, hon. chmn. bd., 1969-78, also dir.; v.p. 1st Ala. Bancshares, Inc., 1970-78. Chmn. bd. regents Grad. Sch. Banking, Rutgers U., 1963-67. Treas., Community Chest Montgomery, 1947-49, v.p., 1953; Montgomery Tb Sanitorium, 1948-49; pres. Montgomery Area council Boy Scouts Am., 1937-40; dir. Montgomery County A.R.C., v.p., 1952-53. Served lt., inf. U.S. Army, 1918-19; lt. col. USAAF, 1942-45; col. USAF Res. (ret.). Mem. Am. Amateur Artists Assn., U. Ala. Alumni Assn. (pres. 1949), Am. Bar Assn., Ala. (past pres.), Am. (pres. trust div. 1957-58) bankers assns., Omicron Delta Kappa, Phi Delta Phi, Phi Gamma Delta. Episcopalian. Rotarian. Clubs: Montgomery Country; Redstone (Birmingham). Author textbooks. Contbr. articles to legal, banking jours. Home: Montgomery, Ala. Died Jan. 2, 1978; buried Greenwood Cemetery, Montgomery.

KENNEDY, WILLIAM DEMPSEY, chem. co. exec.; b. Chgo., Dec. 10, 1914; s. Clarence Clyde and Jessie (Waggy) K.; B.A., Stanford U., 1936, Ph.D., 1940; m. Jean Eleanor Young, Aug. 19, 1941 (dec.); children—Richard Carl, Martha Jane Kennedy Ross, Barbara Anne; m. 2d, Jessie Mae Cover Wright, May 5, 1973. Research asst., then research asso. Harvard U., 1940-43; research supr. Woods Hole (Mass.) Oceanographic Instn., 1943-46; with Tenn. Eastman Co., Kingsport, Tenn., 1946-79, gen. supt. ops., 1970-72, asst. works mgr., 1972-73, v.p., dir. research labs., 1973-79; mem. Kingsport Sci. Seminar. Bd. dirs. Kingsport Girls Club; mem. planetarium com. Bays

Mountain Com. Recipient Presdl. certificate of merit, 1948. Mem. Am. Chem. Soc., Tenn., N.Y. acads. scis., AAAS, Assn. Harvard Chemists, Am. Def. Preparedness Assn., Kingsport C. of C., Phi Beta Kappa, Sigma Xi, Phi Lambda Upsilon, Alpha Chi Sigma, Gamma Alpha. Club: Ridgefields Country. Author, patentee in field. Home: Kingsport, Tenn. Died Jan. 16, 1979.

KENNEDY, WILLIAM THOMSON, gynecologist; born Agincourt, Ont., Can., Mar. 13, 1884; s. John and Agnes Hamilton (Thomson) K.; A.B., U. Toronto, 1908, A.M., 1909, M.B., 1915; m. Janet Gordon Camp, Aug. 7, 1918; children—Martha Clark (Mrs. Lee Cooper), Agnes Hamilton (Mrs. DeF. T. Whipple), Janet Gordon (Mrs. James D. Benedict). Intern, Hosp. for Sick Children, Toronto, 1915, Manhattan Maternity Hospital, N.Y. City, 1916, Women's Hosp., 1916-17; practice gynecology, obstetrics, N.Y. City, since 1919; with Womans Hosp., 1919-47, consultant surgeon, 1947—; with Booth Meml. Hosp., 1919-49, cons. surgeon, 1949—; dir. Cuban Am. Sugar Co., N.Y. City, 1925—. Licentiate Med. Council Can., 1916. Diplomate Am. Bd. Obstetrics and Gynecology. Mem. N.Y. Co. Med. Soc., N.Y. Obstet. Soc. (past pres.), A.M.A., Acad. Medicine N.Y., St. Andrew's Soc. Canadian Soc., Med. Com. Planned Parenthood (past pres.), Oratorio Soc. N.Y. (chmn.), N.Y. Gynec. Soc. (1st pres.). Presbyn. Clubs: University Waccabuc Country. Author: Mechanism of the Female Urethra; articles on physics and gynecol. subjects in profl. jours. Home: Ridgefield, Conn. *

KENNY, NICHOLAS NAPOLEON, (NICK KENNY), newspaper columnist; b. Astoria, L.I. City, N.Y., Feb. 3, 1895; s. Richard Joseph and Josephine (Duval) K.; student short story and scenario writing Columbia, 1922; m. Kathryn Judge, Oct. 2, 1927; children—Patricia Patricia (Mrs. Pat Goebel), Joy (Mrs. Tom Kelly). Sports writer, writer column Getting an Earful, and rewrite man Bayonne (N.J.) Times, 1920-23; sports editor, rewriteman Boston Am., 1923-24; rewrite man N.Y. Jour., 1924-27, N.Y. Daily News, 1927-30; radio columnist N.Y. Daily Mirror, 1930-63; writer syndicated column Nick Kenny Speaking (poetry, news about radio TV, stage and screen personalities), 1930-63, pres. Goldmine Music, Inc., music pubs., from 1946; columnist Sarasota (Fla.) Herald Tribune, from 1963. Served with USN, 1911-18; Mcht. Marine, 1918-20. Decorated by Cardinal Spellman for canteen work, entertaining servicemen, World War II; received awards from Army and Navy Depts. for similar work. Mem. Songwriters Protective Assn., Newspaper Guild, Am. Fedn. Radio Artists, Am. Guild Variety Artists, Profl. Music Men's Contact Assn., Am. Soc. Composers, Authors and Pubs. Roman Catholic. Elk. Club: Winged Foot Golf. Writer lyrics of songs including: There's a Gold-mine in the Sky, Love Letters in the Sand, Carelessly, In My Cabin of Dreams, Little Old Cathedral in the Pines, Makebelieve Island, While a Cigarette Was Burning, Beyond the Purple Hills, Scattered Toys, Gone Fishin', It's Funny But It's True, Undertow. Author: Collected Poems of Nick Kenny; Poems To Inspire; others. Lectr. newspaper bus. poetry. Home: Sarasota, Fla. Died Dec. 1, 1975.

KENNY, ROBERT WALKER, judge; b. Los Angeles, Aug. 21, 1901; s. Robert Wolfenden and Minnie (Carleton) K.; A.B., Stanford, 1921; m. Sara McCann, Oct. 14, 1922 (dec. 1968). Corr., United Press Assn., San Francisco, London (Eng.), Los Angeles, 1920-23; on staff Chgo. Tribune, Paris, France, 1923, Los Angeles Eve. Herald, 1924-27; admitted to Cal. bar, 1926, since practiced in Los Angeles; municipal judge Los Angeles County, 1931-32, superior judge, 1932-38; mem. Cal. Senate from Los Angeles County, 1939-42; atty. gen. Cal., 1943-47; superior ct. judge, 1966-75. Mem. Lawyers Guild (nat. pres. 1940-48), Phi Gamma Delta. Democrat. Clubs: California, Los Angeles Athletic (Los Angeles); Press (San Francisco). Home: Los Angeles, Calif. Died July 20, 1976.

KENOYER, LESLIE ALVA (KEN-OI'ER), botanist; b. Dover, Ill., Apr. 14, 1883; s. Frederic Lawrence and Eva (Hammer) K.; A.B., Campbell Coll., Holton, Kan., 1906; M.A., U. of Kan., 1908; Ph.D., U. of Chicago, 1916, Ia. State Coll., 1916; m. Aletha Kelly, June 16, 1915; 1 dau., Elizabeth Jane. Instr. in science, high sch., Salina, Kan., 1908-09; prof. biology, Leander Clark Coll., Toledo, Ia., 1910-15, Ewing Christian Coll., Allahabad, India, 1916-22; asst. prof. botany, Mich. State Coll., 1922-23; chmn. dept. biology, Western Mich. Coll. of Edn., Kalamazoo, Mich., since 1923. Fellow A.A.A.S.; mem. Bot. Soc. America, Ecol. Soc. America, Mich. Acad. (pres. 1941), Sigma Xi. Club: Torch. Author: General Biology (with N.H. Goddard); laboratory Manual for General Biology (with F. J. Hinds); Flora of Mexican Highways; books and papers on tropical botany (India, Panama, Mexico), and on plant ecology. Home: Kalamazoo, Mich. *

KENT, AMOS EUGENE, mech. engr.; b. Mt. Ivy, N.Y., May 16, 1908; s. Maurice E. and Kathryn M. (Kelly) K.; student Ga. Sch. Tech., 1928-31; B.S. in Engring., U. R.I., 1934; m. Dorothy C. Carr, July 2, 1938; 1 son, Clayton E. Engr., Blackstone Valley Gas & Electric Co., Pawtucket, R.I., 1934-37, E. Pulver Cook, Inc., Providence, 1937-42; with Buerkel & Co., Inc., Boston, 1945-74, pres., 1967-74, also dir.; v.p. Charles T. Main, Inc., Boston, 1972-74, staff cons., 1974-78; instr. Franklin Tech. Inst., 1946-51. Active Newton council Boy Scouts Am., from 1945, mem. exec. bd. Norumbega council, from 1955; sr. warden Trinity Ch., Newton Center, Mass., 1958-78. Served with USAAF, 1942-45. Registered profl. engr., Mass., R.I., Conn., N.H., Vt., Maine, N.Y., Pa., Minn., N.J., Ind., Ohio, Wis. Fellow Am. Soc. Heating, Refrigeration and Air Conditioning Engrs. (life); Cons. Engrs. Council New Eng. (pres. 1973-74), Nat. Council Engring. Examiners (pres.-elect 1977), Mass. Profl. Engrs. and Land Surveyors (bd. registration 1967-78, chmn. bd. 1971-78), Nat. Soc. Profl. Engrs., May Homer Soc. Home: Needham, Mass. Died July 9, 1978; buried Riverbend Cemetery, Westerly, R.I.

KENTON, STANLEY NEWCOMB, musician; b. Wichita, Kans., Feb. 19, 1912; s. Thomas Floyd and Stella E. (Newcomb) K.; grad. high sch.; m. Violet R. Peters, July 31, 1935 (div. Feb. 1950); 1 dau., Leslie B.; m. 2d, Margaret Ann Richards, Oct. 18, 1955 (div.); children—Dana Lynn, Lance N. Organized band Artistry in Rhythm, 1941; leader Stan Kenton Orch., from 1941; worldwide concert appearances, billed as artistry in rhythm, progessive jazz, innovations in modern music; condr. Los Angeles Neophonic Orch.; organizer Stan Kenton Clinics Teenage Musicians, 1965. Recipient popularity poll recognition and awards U.S. and abroad. Home: Los Angeles, Calif. Died Aug. 25, 1979.

KENYON, ALLAN TITSWORTH, physician; b. Rochelle, Ill., Dec. 13, 1900; s. Allan Clark and Edna (Titsworth) K.; Ph.B., Univ. of Chicago, 1922; M.D., Rush Med. Sch., U. of Chicago, 1926; M.S., Northwestern U., 1929; m. Lois Gardner, Aug. 16, 1929; children—Barbara (Mrs. C. A. Whitmore), Judith (Mrs. J. P. Kirscht), Richard, Thomas. Worked under a fellowship in medicine at Northwestern U., 1926-29; asst., instr., asst. prof., and asso. prof. in medicine, U. of Chicago, 1929-46, prof. of medicine since 1947. Mem. com. on growth, Nat. Research Council, 1947-50. Recipient Gold Key award U. Chgo. Med. Alumni Assn., 1971. Mem. Am. Soc. Clin. Investigations, Assn. Am. Physicians, Endocrine Soc. (pres. 1955), Am. Soc. Human Genetics, Fed. Soc. Exptl. Biol. (pharmacology), Laurentian Hormone Conf., A.M.A., Ill., Chgo. med. assns., A.A.A.S. Author sci. papers on hormones and growth. Home: Chicago, Ill. Died May 26, 1978.

KENYON, HELEN, public welfare service; b. Brooklyn, N.Y., June 19, 1884; d. Clarence and Emma Josephine (Kelsey) Kenyon; A.B., Vassar Coll., 1905; unmarried. Began career as mem. bd. Willoughby House Settlement, Brooklyn, N.Y., 1905; chmn. pub. health com., Poughkeepsie, N.Y., 1915-17; recorder for co., N.Y. Census, Dutchess Co., 1947; pres. Asso. Alumnae, Vassar Coll., 1918-21, treas. salary endowment fund, 1921-23, alumnae trustee, 1923-28, chmn. bd. trustees, 1929-39; mem. bd. of home missions, Congl. Christian Chs., 1938-48; chmn. Missions Council, 1944-46; asst. moderator, Gen. Council Congl. Christian Chs., 1946-48, moderator, 1948-49; mem. bd. dirs., United Council Ch. Women, 1940-43; campaign chmn., Greater Poughkeepsie War Chest, 1943. Home: Cornwall, Conn. *

KEPLINGER, JOHN CARPER, business exec.; b. Canton, O., Dec. 15, 1891; s. Charles William and Fannie (Barr) K.; student Tome Sch. for Boys, Port Deposit, Md., 1906-10; B.S., Cornell, 1914; m. Mildred Laiblin, May 10, 1917; children—John Carper, William Laibin; m. 2d, Virginia Waltner, June 15, 1946. With Hercules Motors Corp., Canton, from 1926, sales mgr., dir. of sales, v.p. of sales, executive vice president, 1948-53, and president, from, also director; director of Canton Nat. Bank, 1964-69; trustee Aultman Hosp., Canton. Mem. basic tools subcom., internal combustion engine industry adv. com. Def. Supply Mgmt. Agy. Munitions Bd. Mem. Am. Ordnance Assn., Farm Equipment Inst., Soc. Automotive Engrs., Internal Combustion Engine Inst., Nat. Security Indsl. Assn., Armed Forces Communications Assn., Navy League, Am. Soc. Automotive Engrs., Canton Area adv. council of Naval Affairs. Clubs: Canton; Union (Cleve.). Home: Canton, Ohio. Died May 6, 1978.

KER, CHARLES H., mfg. exec.; b. Chgo., July 28, 1903; s. Charles H. and Ethelyn L. (Hoskins) K.; A.B., Wabash Coll., 1924; m. Jessie M. Anglin, Sept. 2, 1933; 1 son, Charles A. With Endicott Industries, Inc., Warsaw, 1927-76, cost clk., supt., gen. supt., v.p., 1927-52, pres., 1952-59, chmn. bd., 1959-68, hon. chmn., 1968-76; dir. Lake City Bank, Warsaw. Mem. Ind. Mfrs. Assn., Gray Iron Founders Soc. (pres. 1955). Presbyn. Mason. Club: Union League (Chgo.). Home: Warsaw, Ind. Died Aug. 30, 1976; interred Warsaw Cemetery.

KERCHER, JOHN WESLEY, JR., accountant; b. Columbus, Ohio, Jan. 26, 1915; s. John Wesley and Gudrun C. (Carston) K.; student U. Cin., 1932-34, Antioch Coll., 1934-36; m. Flora Elziabeth Blakeslee, Mar. 26, 1938; children—John Wesley III, William Henry. With Ernst & Ernst, C.P.A.'s, 1942-76, partner charge South Central dist., Atlanta, 1957-76. Bd. sponsors Atlanta Symphony Orch.; bd. dirs. Central Atlanta Progress; bd. advisers Ga. State U. C.P.A. in 10 states. Mem. Am. Inst. C.P.A.'s, Nat. Assn. Accountants, Ga. Soc. C.P.A.'s. Club: Capital City, Cherokee Town and Country (Atlanta). Home: Atlanta, Ga. Died Jan. 30, 1976.

KERNAN, WALTER AVERY, lawyer; b. Utica, N.Y., Dec. 1, 1913; s. Francis K. and Mary (Spratt) K.; grad. Milton Acad., 1932; A.B., Harvard, 1936, LL.B., 1939; m. Leslie Hadden, May 10, 1942; children—Anita (Mrs. Denis Halton), Mary (Mrs. Winthrop Rutherford, Jr.), Emily (Mrs. John P. Rafferty), Nancy, Beatrice, Charles. Admitted to N.Y. bar, 1940, since practice in N.Y.C.; asso. firm Carter, Ledyard & Milburn, 1939-41, 46-51, mem. firm, 1951-75. Trustee Helen Huntington Hull Fund; hon. trustee Fordham U.; v.p., bd. govs. N.Y. Hosp.; bd. dirs. Fresh Air Fund. Served from pvt. to capt., AUS, 1941-46, PTO. Mem. Am., N.Y. State bar assns., Assn. Bar City N.Y. Clubs: Piping Rock (L.I., N.Y.); Links, Harvard, Down Town (N.Y.C.). Home: New York, N.Y. Died Oct. 21, 1975; buried Utica, N.Y.

KERNAN, WARNICK J., lawyer; b. Utica, N.Y., July 24, 1880; s. William and Frances (Warnick) K.; A.B., Georgetown U., 1901; special course Cornell Law Sch., 1902-04; LL.D., Hamilton Coll., 1934; unmarried. Admitted to N.Y. bar, 1904, and since practiced in Utica; mem. Kernan and Kernan; spl. dist. atty., Oneida Co., 1915-16; trustee Savs. Bank of Utica, 1916-55. Mem. Bd. Sch. Commrs., Utica, 1907-14; mem. Law Revision Commn. of State of N.Y., 1934-47, chmn., 1940-47; referee in railroad reorganization proceedings by appointment of U.S. Circuit Court of Appeals, 2d Circuit, 1935; chmn. Alien Enemy Hearing Bd. Northern Dist. of N.Y., 1941-45, by appointment U.S. atty. general. Chmn. Spl. Com. of N.Y. State Bar Assn. to investigate jud. conditions in Albany Co., 1944-45. Counsel to Temp. Commn. on Need for a State U., 1947-48. Pres. bd. of trustees Utica Pub. Library, 1929-62. Temporary chmn. Dem. State Conv., 1927. Pres. N.Y. State Bar Assn., 1940. Charter mem. Am. Law Inst.; mem. Am. Judicature Soc., Am., N.Y. and Oneida County bar assns. Roman Catholic. Clubs: University (N.Y. City): Fort Schuyler, Sadaquada Golf (Utica). Home: Utica NY. *

KERNER, OTTO, judge; b. Chgo., Aug. 15, 1908; s. Otto and Rose Barbara (Chmelik) K.; A.B. Brown, U., 1930; postgrad. Trinity Coll., Cambridge U., Eng., 1930-31; J.D., Northwestern U., 1934; hon. degrees Brown U., Northwestern U., St. Procopius Coll., Lincoln Coll., Quincy Coll., McKendree Coll., Culver-Stockton Coll., So. Ill. U., Ill. Inst. Tech., Bradley U., Chgo.-Kent Coll. Law, Mundelein Coll., Drake U., Ill. State Coll.; m. Helena I. Cermak, Oct. 20, 1934 (dec. 1973); children—Anton J.C., Helena C. Admitted to Ill. bar, 1934; asso. with Cooke, Sullivan, & Ricks, 1934; became partner Kerner, Jaros & Title, law firm, 1935; U.S. dist. atty. No. Dist. Ill., 1947-54; county judge Cook County, 1954-61; gov. Ill., 1961-68; judge U.S. Ct. Appeals, Chgo., 1968-74. Vice pres. Chgo. council, mem. 7th regional exec. council Boy Scouts Am., hon. commr. Chgo. council; dir. Bohemian Charitable Assn., Glenview United Fund, Cancer and Red Cross funds; mem. Chgo. Crime Prevention Council, 1950-53; chmn. Pres.'s Commn. on Civil Disorders, 1968. Trustee Brown U. Mem. Ill. N.G., 106th Cav., 1934-36; trans. to F.A., 1936, advancing from pvt. to capt., 1941, served to maj. gen., inf., 1941-46; PTO. Decorated Soldiers' medal, Bronze Star. Recipient Silver Beaver, Silver Antelope, Silver Buffalo awards Boy Scouts Am. Mem. Am. (alternate del. 1948), Fed., Ill., Chgo., West Suburban bar assns., Bohemian Lawyers, Am. Judicature Soc., Mil. Order World Wars (1st vice comdr. 1946-47), Alpha Delta Phi, Phi Delta Phi, Democrat. Mason (33 deg.), Nat. Soujourner, Red Cross of Constantine, Moose, Odd Fellow, Royal Arcanum. Clubs: Commonwealth, Brown, Wayfarers, Legal, Law, Economic, Commercial, (Chgo.). Home: Chicago, Ill. Died May 9, 1976.

KERR, E. S. WELLS, educator; b. San Francisco, Aug. 4, 1885; s. Alexander J. and Jennie (Wells) K.; A.B., Princeton, 1909. Instr. English and history Asheville (N.C.) Sch., 1921; instr. English, Phillips Exeter (N.H.) Acad., 1921, dean, 1926-53, dean emeritus 1953—; prof. English, Robert College, 1953-54; instr. English, St. Paul's Sch., 1955-58, Colorado Rocky Mountain School, Carbondale, 1960—. Mem. board of Colorado Outward Bound School, Princeton University, Wooster Sch. Clubs: Century Association, Princeton (N.Y. City); Tavern, Appalachian Mountain (Boston). Home: Exeter, N.H. *

KERR, ELMORE COE, JR., art dealer; b. N.Y.C., Sept. 3, 1914; s. E. Coe and Marian (Smyth) K.; grad. St. Paul's Sch., 1933; B.A., Yale, 1937; student Command and Gen. Staff Coll., 1944; m. Sarah Nichols, Sept. 27, 1947 (dec. 1965); 1 son, E. Coe III; m. 2d, Anne Wright Baxter, Aug. 19, 1966. With Knoedler & Co., N.Y.C., from 1937, beginning as asst. print dept., dir., 1948, pres., 1957-69; pres. Coe Kerr Gallery Inc., art dealers, from 1969. Bd. dirs. Fedn. des Alliances

Francaise. Served from pvt. to lt. col. AUS, 1941-46. Decorated Bronze Star with cluster; Croix de Guerre (France). Home: East Hampton, N.Y. Deceased.

KERR, HARRISON, composer; b. Cleve., Oct. 13, 1897; s. Harrison and Elizabeth (Rettig) K.; grad. Cleve. high schs., 1916; student Conservatoirie Americain de Fontainebleau, France, 1921; m. Jeanne McHugh, Aug. 30, 1928; Dir. music Greenbrier Coll., Lewisburg, W.Va., 1927-28, Chase Sch., Bklyn., 1928-35; editor Trend, illus. bi-monthly of arts, 1932-35; sec. Am. Composers Alliance, 1937-78; exec. sec. Am. Music Center, 1940-47; chief Music, Art and Exhibit Sect., Reorientation Br., Civil Affairs Div., Dept. of Army, 1946-49; dean Coll. Fine Arts, U. Okla., 1949-64, prof., composer in residence, 1960-68, emeritus, 1968-78. Mem. exec. bd. Nat. Music Council; mem. bd. dirs. Am. Music Center; mem. music adv. com. UNESCO; formerly sec., mem. bd. dirs. Nat. Music League; recent performances of larger compositions in Austria, Hungary, Germany, Japan, Korea, Thailand, various South Am. Countries and U.S. Compositions include 3 symphonies, other orchestral works, chamber music and many shorter pieces. Home: Norman, Okla. Died Aug. 15, 1978.

KERR, PAUL FRANCIS, univ. prof.; b. Hemet, Calif., Jan. 12, 1897; s. Joseph and Emma (Fowler) K.; B.S., Occidental Coll., 1919, D.Sc., 1960; Ph.D., Stanford U., 1923; m. Helen Richardson Squire, Sept. 2, 1924; children—Paul Squire, Ruth (Mrs. William Jakoby), Nancy (Mrs. Peter Del Grande.) Instr. mineralogy and geology, Stanford, 1923-24, acting asst. prof., summer sessions, 1924-31; instr. Columbia, 1924-26, asst. prof., 1926-32, asso. prof., 1932-40, prof. mineralogy, 1940-65, Newberry prof., 1952-65, prof. emeritus, 1965-81, acting exec. officer dept. of geology, spring 1942, exec. officer, 1944-50, research coordinator, from 1950; vis. Carnegie prof. S.A., 1941; guest prof. U. Oslo (Norway), 1960; cons. Manhattan Project, 1944; panel on geology, Research Devel. Bd., 1947-49; Clay Mineral Standards Project, Am. Petroleum Inst., 1948-50. Served in U.S. Army, 1918. Tech. cons. Army-Navy Munitions Bd., 1942-43. Chmn. com. on Internat. Inspection Radioactive Minerals, Carnegie Endowment for Internat. peace, 1946; UN cons. to review uranium occurrences at Geneva Conf. on Peaceful Uses of Atomic Energy, 1955. Recipient K.C. Li award outstanding work field of tungsten, 1957. Fellow Geol. Soc. Am. (v.p. 1947), Am. Geog. Soc., Mineral. Soc. Am. (sec. 1933-43, pres. 1946); mem. Soc. Econ. Geology, Am. Inst. Mining Engrs., N.Y. Acad. Science, A.A.A.S. (chmn. geol. and geog. div. 1956) Clay Minerals Soc. (distinguished mem.), Mineral Soc. Great Britain, Geol. Soc. Belgium (corr.), Bavarian Acad. Sci., Sigma Xi, Phi Beta Kappa. Methodist. Mason. Club: Men's Faculty (Columbia U.); N.Y. Minerallogical (pres. 1926-27). Author: Thin Section Mineralogy, 1933; Optical Mineralogy, 1941; Tungsten Mineralization in U.S., 1946; Natural Occurrence of Uranium and Thorium, 1955; Uranium Alteration and Mineralization, Marysvale, Utah, 1957. Co-author: Mineral Recognition, 1967. Contbr. articles to tech. jours. and publs. Cons. on applications of geology and mineralogy; Orton Lectr. Am. Ceramic Soc., 1938. Study of Uranium-bearing veins AEC. Home: New York, N.Y. Died Feb. 27, 1981.

KERR, THOMAS STONER, educator; b. Randolph, Kan., Mar. 14, 1885; s. Edward and Anna (Stoner) K.; grad. Pa. State Normal Sch., 1903; A.B., Ind. U., 1913; LL.B., U. of Mich., 1918; m. Josephine Hamm, Apr. 11, 1906; 1 dau., Helen. Teacher in pub. schs. of Pa., later of N.D., 1903-06; supt. schs. Kingman, Ariz., 1909-12, Stanford, Mont., 1914-16, Bonners Ferry, Ida., 1918-24; asso. prof. polit. science and business law, U. of Idaho, 1924-28, prof., 1928-31, became dean of Univ. Jr. Coll., 1931, actg. dean, Letters and Science Coll., 1933, dean, 1938-55; dir. summer session, 1933, acting pres., 1937; instr. Lewiston (Ida.) State Normal Sch., summer 1922, U. of Idaho, summer 1923; guest Carnegie Foundation, Sch. of Internat. Law, summer 1923; dir. Chautauqua Circuit, summer 1920; field sec. Wash. Retailer's Assn., summer 1921. Mem. Ida. State Textbook Commn., 1924. Mem. Idaho State Bd. of Pub. Welfare (pres. 1940); mem. Defense Savings Com. for State of Ida.; mem. exec. com. N.W. Association of Secondary and Higher Schools, 1942-54 (executive coordinator for the Higher Commission, 1955-64). President of the Pacific Coast Intercollegiate Athletic Conf., 1953-55. Member Idaho State Teachers Assn. (treas. 1921), N. Ida. Teachers Assn. (pres. 1924), N.W. Scientific Assn., Am. Polit. Science Assn., Am. Business Law Assn. (pres. 1939), Idaho Bar Assn., Rotary Internat. Author: Business Law, Principles and Cases, 1934, revised edit., 1939; Commercial Law, 1939. Home: Moscow, Ida. *

KERSHAW, ANDREW, advt. agy. exec.; b. Oct. 31, 1921; B.Commerce with honors, U. London; m. Mary Healey; children—Annabel, Juliet. Dep. dir. gen. Brit. Travel Assn., London, Ont., Can., 1946-56; dir. client service MacLaren Advt. Co., Ltd., Toronto, 1956-60; pres. mng. dir. Ogilvy & Mather (Can.) Ltd., Toronto, from 1960; chmn. Ogilvy and Mather, Inc., N.Y.C. until 1978; dir. Am. Express Co. Can. Bd. dirs. Met. Opera. Served as capt. Brit. Army. Mem. Inst. Can. Advt. Home: New York, NY. Died Oct. 1978.

KERWIN, EDWARD MICHAEL, candy mfr.; b. Chgo., June 4, 1884; A.B., U. Chgo., 1905; A.B., DePaul U., 1918, A.M., 1919; m. Marie E. LeTourneux, 1922; children—Michael William, Mary Elizabeth (Mrs. White), Katherine (Mrs. Ryan), Edward Michael, John Francis, Thomas Joseph, Joseph Peter (USN), Paul Charles (USMC). With Maguire Cummings Mfg. Co., Chgo., 1905-07; salesman Sprague Electric div. Gen. Electric Co., 1907-11; sec.-treas. Sellers Mfg. Co., Chgo., 1911-17; with Am. Manganese Steel Co., 1919-21; controller Hayes Pump & Planter Co., Galva, Ill., 1921-22; with E.J. Brach & Sons, 1922—, v.p., 1932-54, sr. v.p., 1954—. Dir. Catholic Charities, Archdiocese of Chgo., 1919—, sec., 1953-57. Served from capt. to maj., ordnance dept., U.S. Army, 1917-18. Decorated knight St. Gregory, 1957. Mem. Ill. Mfrs. Assn. Club: Oak Park (Ill.) Country. Home: River Forest, Ill. *

KERWIN, JEROME GREGORY, educator, polit. scientist; b. Albany, N.Y., Feb. 25, 1896; s. Timothy Edward and Alice (McCarthy) K.; A.B., Dartmouth, 1919; A.M., Columbia, 1921, Ph.D., 1926; LL.D., Holy Cross Coll., Worcester, Mass., 1947; Litt.D., U. Notre Dame, 1953. Instr. polit. sci. Dartmouth, 1921-23; instr. U. Chgo., 1921-26, asst. prof. polit. sci., 1926-29, asso. prof., 1929-41, dean students social sci. div., 1935-41, 57-61, prof. polit. sci., 1941-61, emeritus prof.; dir. honors div. and prof. polit. sci. U. Santa Clara, Calif., 1961-66. Vis. prof. Stanford, 1960, chmn. Walgreen Found., 1945-56; Fenwick lectr. Holy Cross Coll., 1947. Chmn. Chgo. Inst. Social and Religious Studies, 1944-53; v.p. Cath. Assn., Internat. Peace, from 1958. Bd. lay advisers Rosary Coll.; bd. dirs. Inst. European Studies, Chgo. Cath. Interracial Council; exec. com. Stanford-Santa Clara Colloquium on Ecumenism. Mem. Religious Edn. Assn. U.S. and Can. (pres. 1957-62), Am. Acad. Polit. Sci., Am. Polit. Sci. Assn., Am. Acad. Polit. and Social Sci., Serra Internat., Nat. Conf. Christians and Jews, Fedn. Religious Action in Social and Civil Order (adv. council), Thomas More Assn. (dir.), Phi Beta Kappa. Democrat. Roman Catholic. Clubs: Quadrangle, University (Chgo.). Author: Federal Water Power Legislation, 1926; Schools and City Government, 1938; The Great Tradition, 1947; Catholic Viewpoint on Church and State, 1960; Government, Politics and Catholics, 1961. Editor: Civil-Military Relations, 1946; polit. sci. contbr. Cath. Ency.; contbr. Ency. Brit. Commonweal America, also polit. sci. revs. Home: Santa Clara, Calif. Died Aug. 19, 1977.

KERWIN, RICHARD EKMAN, banker; b. Worcester, Mass., Sept. 24, 1926; s. Charles Carlin and Lillian Maria (Ekman) K.; A.B., Dartmouth, 1950; m. Mary Luhman, Sept. 8, 1950; children—John, Peter Kimberly Dee. Self-employed food broker, 1950-53; with United Calif. Bank, Los Angeles, 1953-71, 72-76, asst. v.p., 1960, v.p., 1961-70, sr. v.p., 1970-71, 72-76; exec. v.p. Western Bancorp., Los Angeles, 1971-72. Area vice chmn. United Crusade, 1970-76. Served with USNR, 1944-46. Republican. Mason. Home: Oxnard, Calif. Died Aug. 24, 1976.

KESSEL, JOHN FLENNIKEN, educator; b. Medicine Lodge, Kan., Feb. 28, 1894; s. George Grant and Harriet Levon (Flenniken) K.; ed. Natal Govt. Tchrs. Coll., South Africa, 1913-14; A.B., Greenville (Ill.) Coll., 1919; A.M., U. Cal., 1921, Ph.D., 1923; m. Ruth Elizabeth Brodhead, June 19, 1918; children—Margaret Lucene (Mikkelsen), John Delbert. Teaching fellow U. Cal., 1919 22, Univ. fellow, 1922-25; asso. in parasitology Peking (China) Union Med. Coll., 1923-27; asso. prof. parasitology U. Cal. at Los Angeles, 1927-29; prof. tropical diseases Coll. Medical Evangelists, 1928-31; prof. bacteriology and parasitology Sch. of Medicine, U. So. Cal., 1931-51; prof. infectious diseases (parasitology and tropic diseases), head div., med. sch. U. Cal., Los Angeles, 1951-63; prof. infectious and tropical diseases Sch. Pub. Health, U. Cal. at Los Angeles, 1963-70; chief microbiologist Los Angeles County Hosp., 1928-50. Chmn. Filariasis Found., U. So. Cal., 1947-51; asso. Institut de Recherches Medicales de la Polynesie Francaise; mem. typing com. Nat. Found. Infantile Paralysis, 1948-51; dir. Tropic Diseases Project, U. Cal. at Los Angeles, 1951-71; cons. Cal. Health Dept., 1940-52, USPHS, 1943-61; cons. microbiology Los Angeles County Hosp., 1950-70, Filariasis South Pacific Commn., 1951-65; cons. parasitology WHO, 1951-72, Pacific Science Bd., NRA, 1953-66, Estelle Doheny Eve Found., 1956-64. Diplomate Am. Bd. Microbiology. Fellow A.A.A.S., Am. Pub. Health Assn., Cal. Acad. Scis., Royal Soc. Tropical Medicine and Hygiene, Am. Acad. Microbiology; mem. Internat. Filariasis Assn. (pres. 1963-70), Am. Soc. Tropical Medicine (councillor 1942-47; editorial bd. 1946-52), Soc. Parasitologists (councillor 1938-41; editorial bd. 1941-43), Soc. Exptl. Biology and Medicine (councillor 1934; pres. So. Cal. Br. 1931), Soc. Am. Bacteriologists, Am. Acad. Tropical Medicine (councilor 1951), Western Soc. of Naturalists (pres. 1937), Nat. Malaria Soc., Sigma Xi, Phi Sigma, Phi Kappa Phi. Decorated chevalier de la Legion d'Honneur. Research includes tropical diseases, especially intestional bacteria and protozoa of man and lab. animals; fungus infections of man, including coccidioidomycosis and cryptococcosis; virus infections, including poliomyelitis and infectious myxomatosis, helminth infections, including filariasis and hookworm. Address: Los Angeles, Calif. Died May 1, 1981.

KESSLER, SAMUEL J., architect; b. N.Y.C., Aug. 10, 1886; B.S. in Engring., Cooper Union, 1910; LL.B., N.Y. Law Sch., 1932. Previously propr. firm S. J. Kessler, now S. J. Kessler & Sons. Mem. A.I.A. (pres. Bronx chpt. 1945-47). Address: New York City NY. *

KETCHUM, PHILLIPS, lawyer; b. Portland, Me., Dec. 16, 1884; s. Charles John and Rebekah Kimball (Phillips) K.; A.B., Harvard, 1906, LL.B., 1908; m. Margery S. Amory, May 22, 1928 (dec. Oct. 1948); children—Phillips, Jonathan, Rebekah; m. 2d, Amey P. Amory, Apr. 18, 1953. Partner firm Herrick, Smith, Donald, Farley & Ketchum, Boston; dir. Wyman Gordon Co., Samuel Cabot, Inc. Home: Glen St Natick MA. *

KETCHUM, WILLIAM M., congressman; b. Los Angeles, Sept. 2, 1921; student Colo. Sch. Mines, U. So. Calif., m. Lola Heegaard; children—Robert, Kathy (Mrs. Charles Cole). Formerly engaged in cattle raising and farming; pres. San Luis Obispo County Farm Bur.; mem. Calif. Assembly from 29th Dist., 1966-72; mem. 93d-95th congresses from 18th Dist. Calif. Served with inf. AUS, World War II, with CIC, 1950-53. Republican. Episcopalian. Home: Bakersfield, Calif. Died June 24, 1978.

KETTANEH, FRANCIS ANTHONY BERNARD, bus. exec.; b. Beirut, Lebanon, Nov. 7, 1897; s. Anthony and Ellen (Salameh) K.; student Kaiserswerther Disconissen Schule, Coll. Francais du Sacre Coeur; B.S., Am. U. Beirut, 1914, C.E., 1916; m. Mary Shoucair, Apr. 23, 1934; children—Joyce, Anthony, Lorna, Edward. Came to U.S., 1941, naturalized, 1946. Founded, Eastern Transport Co., Ltd. (now merged with Nairn Transport Co.), 1924; partner Kettaneh Freres, distbrs. in Near East products of Gen. Electric, Siemens, Am. Laundry Machinery Industries, Taylor Instruments, Allied Chem. Internat., Curtis div. Tramsaores, Inc., Nat. Presto Industries, Inc., United Aircraft Internat., A.J. Alsdorf Corp., Volkswagen, Michelin, Barber-Colman Co., Tappan Internat., Regina Co. Made 1st cross-desert trip by car from Beirut to Baghdad, Apr. 1923. Decorated officer Order Cedars (Republic Lebanon); Legion Honor (France). Mem. Soc. Automotive Engrs., Auto Importers Assn. for Lebanon and Syria (hon. life pres.), Council Fgn. Relations, Acad. Polit. Sci., Econ. Council N.Y., Am. Acad. Polit. and Social Sci., Alumni Assn., Am. U. Beirut. Clubs: Grolier, Metropolitan (N.Y.C.). Home: New York, N.Y. Died Mar. 30, 1976.

KEWLEY, JOSEPH EDWARD (KU'LE), corp. official; b. Toledo, O., May 26, 1883; s. Thomas and Eleanor (Oates) K.; LL.B., Ohio State U., 1906; m. Florence Hutchinson, Oct. 7, 1911; children—Ruth Eleanor (Mrs. Henry F. Donahower), Thomas H., Norman E. Admitted to O. bar, 1906, engaging in pvt. practice, Toledo, 1906-10; law dept. Nat. Electric Lamp Assn., Cleveland, 1910-20; asst. mgr. Nat. Lamp Works of Gen. Electric Co., 1920-25, gen. sales mgr., 1925-30; acting mgr., incandescent lamp dept. of Gen. Electric Co., 1930-31, mgr., 1931-34, v.p., 1934-44. Mem. Delta Chi, Sigma Alpha Epsilon. Republican. Presbyterian. Club: Shaker Heights Country (Shaker Heights, O.). Home: Chagrin Falls, Ohio. *

KEYES, FREDERICK GEORGE, physical chemist; b. Kingston, Can., June 24, 1885; s. John George and Margaret (Williams) K.; B.S., R.I. Coll., 1906; M.S., Brown Univ., 1907, Ph.D., 1909; D.Sc., Yale, 1934, D.Sc., R.I. Coll, 1942, Brown U., 1963; m. Gabrielle Alice Bowers, Dec. 27, 1923. Asst. in chemistry, Brown U., 1906-07, instr., 1908-09, G.A.R. research fellow, 1909; research asso. in physical chemistry, Mass. Inst. tech., 1910- 13; chief engr. Cooper-Hewitt Electric Co., 1913-16; asso. prof. phys. chemistry research, 1916-19, prof., 1920-50, dir. research lab. phys. chemistry, 1920-1945, in charge dept. chemistry, 1922-1945, prof. emeritus and lecturer, from 1950, all at Mass. Inst. Tech.; pres., gen. mgr. Keyes Sci. Corp., Cambridge, Mass. Chmn. U.S. commn. Internat. Stean Porperties Com. Commd. capt. U.S. Army, Dec. 1917, major, Sept., 1918; dir. Sci. and Control Lab., A.E.F., at Puteaux, France, 1918-19; citation by comdr.-in-chief A.E.F., June 1919; lt. col. Chem Warfare R.C. Recipient Theodore William Richards Medal Award, 1942; American Society Mech. Engrs. Am. Soc. Mech. Engrs. Award, 1948. Fellow Am. Acad. Arts and Sci. Am. Physical Soc., A.A.A.S.; mem. Am. Chem. Soc., Nat. Acad. Sci., An. Soc. Refrigerating Engrs. (hon.), Phi Sigma Kappa, Sigma Xi. Author: The Thermodynamic Properties of Ammonia, 1916; Thermodynamic Properties of Steam (with J.H. Keepan), 1936. contbr. numerous papers on investigations of the thermodynamic properties of matter, kinetic theory of matter and applications of thermodynamics to chemical equilibria problems, etc. Home: Cambridge, Mass. Died Apr. 14, 1976.

KEYES, JOHN BROOKS, business exec.; b. Baltimore, Md., 1883. Chmn. bd. Central Aguirre Sugar Co.; pres., dir. Aguirre Corp.; dir. Ponce & Guayama R.R. Co., Central Machete Co., S. Shore Nat. Bank, Quincy. Mason. Home: Quincy, Mass. *

KEYSER, RALPH STOVER, officer U.S. Marine Corps; b. Virginia, May 10, 1883; s. Charles Eugene and Mary (Stover) K.; served as pvt., corpl., and sergt., U.S. Army, Apr. 1, 1901-Apr. 29, 1904. Apptd. 2d lt., U.S. Marine Corps, Mar. 29, 1905; m. Charlotte Palmer Capers. Shooting member, coach and capt., Marine Corps Nat. Rifle Team, 1911, 1916 and 1922. Qualified in Japanese language. Served in France, World War I; battalion comdr., inf. div., and mem. A.E.F. gen. staff, World War II. Retired as maj. gen., while serving as asst. comdt., September 26, 1942. Decorated Navy Cross; Distinguished Service Medal; Silver Star, 2 citations; Purple Heart; Legion of Honor, Croix de Guerre (France), 3 citations; Order of the Crown (Belgium). Home: Washington. *

KIBBEE, B. E., steel exec.; b. Bristolville, O., Oct. 9, 1885; s. John E. and Phoebe A. (Barbe) K.; student pub. schs.; m. Idah M. Thompson, June 30, 1908. Exec. v.p. Sharon (Pa.) Steel Corp.; dir. Mullins Mfg. Co., P.& W.Va. R.R. Mem. steel recovery com. WPB, 1942. Clubs: Union (Cleve), Duquesne (Pitts.), Athletic (Detroit). Home: Sharon, Pa. *

KIECKHEFER, ALFRED JOHN (KEK'HE-FER), mfr.; b. Milwaukee, Wis., July 20, 1885; s. Ferdinand August William and Wilhelmine (Kuetemeyer) K.; student U. of Wis., 1905-08; m. Allison More, Oct. 9, 1909; children—James Ferdinand, Elizabeth (dec.), Alfred John (dec.). Began as asst. to supt. Nat. Enameling & Stamping Co., Inc., Milwaukee, 1908; successively asst. supt., factory mgr., asst. mfg. supervisor and asst. to pres., pres. and dir. since 1925-49, now v. chmn. bd.; dir. Granite City Steel Co. Mem. Sigma Chi. Republican. Episcopalian. Clubs: University, Country, Milwaukee. *

KIEFER, CHARLES FREDERICK, mgmt. cons.; b. Hamilton, N.Y., July 1, 1911; s. Charles F. and Belle (Palmer) K.; student U. Pitts., 1932-34; A.B., George Washington U., 1940; M.P.A., Harvard U., 1941; m. Helen Maxine Enlow, Dec. 21, 1941; 1 son, Charles Frederick. With Dept. Agr., 1934-66, dir. Office Mgmt. Appraisal and Systems Devel., 1965, 66; exec. dir. CAB, 1966-70; cons. Schnittker Assos., Washington, Ford Found., World Bank. Served to capt. USAAF, 1942-46. Littauer fellow, 1941-42; recipient Certificate of Merit, Dept. Agr. Mem. Am. Soc. Pub. Adminstrn., Omicron Delta Kappa. Democrat. Conglist. Clubs: Harvard (Washington); International. Home: Arlington, Va. Died May 24, 1979.

KIEFER, PAUL JAMES (KE'FER), educator; born at Camden, Indiana, Nov. 26, 1886; s. Rev. Cornelius Joseph and Ellinoire Loretta (Cainan) K.; A.B., Wittenberg Coll., Springfield, O., 1908; B.S., Case Sch. Applied Science, Cleveland, O., 1911, M.E., 1930; grad. student U. of Pa., 1916-18; m. Lucille Brubaker, June 12, 1913; children—Marjorie Brubaker (dec.), Paul James. Machinist, draftsman, surveyor, 1906-11; power plant designing and construn., U.S. and Can., for Internat. Harvester Co., 1911-13; instr. mech. engring., U. of Pa., 1913-18; asst. prof. mech. engring., U. of Ill., 1919-20; asso. prof. Mech. engring., U.S. Navy Postgrad. Sch., 1920-25, prof., 1925-45, sr. prof. since 1945, chmn. dept. since 1925, acting dean, 1948-49. Served as ensign, lt. (j.-g.), U.S. Navy, 1918-19. Chmn. Annapolis City Planning Commn., 1935-37. Mem. Am. Soc. Mechanical Engrs., Am. Soc. Naval Engrs., Am. Soc. Engring. Edn., Am. Assn. Univ. Profs., Phi Kappa Psi. Presbyn. Mason. Clubs: Rotary, Naval Academy Officers (Annapolis); Army and Navy (Washington, D.C.). Author: Principles of Engring. Thermodynamics (with M. C. Stuart), 1929; (with G. F. Kinney and M. C. Stuart) 1953. Contbr. articles to tech. jours. Home: Annapolis, Md. *

KIEFFER, JOHN SPANGLER, coll. dean; b. Hagerstown, Md., Aug. 6, 1904; s. John Brainerd and Alice Venable Bourne (Hays) K.; A.B., Harvard, 1926, A.M., 1929; Ph.D., Johns Hopkins, 1962; m. Roxana Byrd White, Nov. 26, 1929. Master in French and English, Litchfield (Conn.) Sch., 1927-28; instr. classical langs. St. John's Coll. Annapolis, Md., 1929-34, asst. prof., 1934-39, tutor, 1939-75, mem. bd. visitors and govs., 1943-51, pres., 1947-49, dir. adult edn., 1951-57, dean, 1962-69. Mem. Am. Philol. Assn., Classical Assn. Atlantic States. Democrat. Episcopalian. Clubs: Harvard Club of Maryland; 14 W. Hamilton St. (Balt.). Author: Galen's introduction to Logic: translation and commentary, 1964. Home: Annapolis, Md. Died Mar. 29, 1975.

KIENBUSCH, WILLIAM, artist; b. N.Y.C., Apr. 13, 1914; s. Carl Otto and Mildred (Pressinger) von K.; grad. Hotchkiss Prep. Sch., 1932; B.A., Princeton, 1936; student Art Students League, 1936-37, Colorado Springs Fine Arts Center, Colarossi's, Paris, France, also with Anton Refregier and Stuart Davis, N.Y.C. Exhbns. include Bklyn. Mus., Albright Art Gallery, Buffalo, Chgo. Art Inst., Des Moines Art Center, Walker Art Center, Mpls., Carnegie Art Inst., Pitts., Va. Mus. Arts, Richmond; former instr. Bklyn. Mus. Art Sch.; works represented permanent collections Mus. of Art U. Mich., Toledo Mus. Art, Munson-Williams-Proctor Inst., Utica, N.Y., W.R. Nelson Gallery Art, Kansas City, Mo., Ft. Worth Art Mus., U. Nebr., Met. Mus. Art, Mus. Modern Art, Whitney Mus. Am. Art (N.Y.C.), Newark Mus., Albright Art Gallery, Buffalo, Toronto Art Gallery, Phila. Mus. Art, Pa. Acad. Art, Detroit Mus. Art, Boston Mus. Art, others; purchase Ford Found.; representative exhbn. Am. Art, Brussels World Fair, 1958. Served as sgt. AUS, 1942-45; instr. camouflage 93th Engrs.; constrn. target charts B-29 bombing raids, 949th Engrs. Recipient 1st prize for drawing Bklyn. Artists Biennial, 1952; prize for drawing Met. Mus., N.Y.C., 1952; Guggenheim fellow, 1958; Nat. Inst. Arts and Letters grantee, 1976. Mem. Phi Beta Kappa. Home: New York, N.Y. Died Mar. 23, 1980.

KIENDL, THEODORE, lawyer; b. N.Y.C., May 5, 1890; s. Theodore and Louisa B. (Hearn) K.; A.B., Columbia, 1910, LL.B., 1913; m. Frances G. Vaughan, June 17, 1916; children—Helen (Mrs. Alvin F. Lindsay), Theodore, Jr., Philip Randolph. Admitted to N.Y. bar, 1913, thereafter practiced in N.Y.C.; mem. firm Davis Polk & Wardwell, and predecessor firms, 1921-65, of counsel, from 1965. Spl. trial examiner Bd. Edn. City N.Y.; spl. asst. atty. gen. N.Y., 1952-53. Mem. Am., N.Y. State, N.Y. Co., N.Y.C. bar assns. Home: Bronxville, N.Y. Died July 26, 1976.

KIERNAN, WALTER, news commentator; b. New Haven, Jan. 24, 1902; s. Daniel Harry and Alice M. (Rowen) K.; ed. New Haven High Sch.; m. Helen Hastings, Sept. 3, 1924; children—David, Richard, Jerome. Reporter and feature writer New Haven Union, 1924-26; writer and editor New Haven Register, 1926-28; mem. A.P. staff, 1928-29; dir. publicity and editor K.C. News, New Haven, 1929-31; pub. and editor West Haven Town Crier, 1930-37; Conn. state mgr. Internat. News Service, Hartford, 1937; feature writer, columnist and roving corr., N.Y.C., 1937-43; radio commentator ABC network, N.Y.C., 1943-52; commentator NBC, 1952-60, WOR, 1961-69, One Man's Opinion, WOR-TV, 1964-69. Mem. Acad. TV Arts and Scis., Cath. Actors Guild (past pres.). Roman Catholic. Clubs: The Lambs; Circus Saints and Sinners (N.Y.C. and Washington). Author: One Man's Opinion. Home: Daytona Beach, Fla. Died Jan. 8, 1978.

KIEWIT, PETER, contractor; b. Omaha, Sept. 12, 1900; s. Peter and Anna (Schleicker) K.; student Dartmouth, LL.D., 1960; LL.D., U. Omaha, 1958, Hastings Coll., 1964, U. Nebr., 1964, Creighton U., 1968; m. Mary Drake, Jan. 22, 1922; 1 son, Peter; m. 2d, Evelyn Stotts Newton, July 2, 1952. Apprentice mason, foreman and supt. bldg. constrn. Peter Kiewit Sons' Co., 1920-31, pres. Peter Kiewit Sons' Inc., from 1931, chmn. bd., chief exec. officer; dir. World Herald Co., Omaha. Trustee Hastings Coll., Eisenhower Med. Center, U. Nebr. Found.; bd. dirs. Jr. Achievement Omaha, Eugene C. Eppley Found.; pres. Bishop Clarkson Meml. Hosp. Recipient Moles non-mem. award, 1953. Clubs: Omaha, Omaha Country, Plaza (Omaha); Thunderbird Country (Palm Springs, Calif.); Eldorado Country (Palm Desert, Calif.). Presbyterian (trustee). Home: Omaha, Nebr. Died Nov. 2, 1979.

KILDEE, HENRY HERBERT, agrl. educator; born Osage, Ia., Mar. 1, 1884; s. Michael and Lucy Ann (Stone) K.; grad. Cedar Valley Sem., Osage, 1903; B.S.A., Ia. State Coll., 1908, M.S., 1917, Doctor of Science, 1958; Doctor of Agr., North Dakota State Coll., 1940; m. Ruth E. Sweney, Feb. 16, 1910 (died Nov. 1958); children—Regina (Mrs. Walter B. Adams), Kathleen (Mrs. Frederick N. Minard). Instr. in animal husbandry, Ia. State Coll., 1909, experimentalist, 1909-10, asso. prof. in charge diary prodn., 1910-15, prof. animal husbandry and chief of dairy husbandry, 1915-16; chief of div. dairy husbandry, U. of Minn., 1916-18; head of dept. animal husbandryand chief of sect., Expt. Sta., Ia. State Coll., 1918-35, v. dean div. of agr., 1923-33, dean div. of agr., 1933-49, now dean emeritus; dir. of extension service, 1946-49. Dir. Agr. Experimental Sta., 1948-49; dir., mem. exec. com., Internat. Livestock Expn., 1947—, pres., 1957-65, chmn., 1965—. Has been judge for several livestock expositions since receiving gold medal for inter-collegiate judging, International Exposition, 1908. Has served on tech. coms. several spl. breeds assns., on classes, records, judging and other tech. items. Has served on several different planning groups. Cons. on Livestock Production Problems to Chile, Colombia, Costa Rica, Cuba and Ecuador, others. Gov. Am. Royal Live Stock Show; bd. dir., exec. com. Livestock Conservation, Inc., 1951-56; mem. Nat. Brucellosis com., 1951-55. Awarded Gold medal by Am. Farm Bur. Fedn., 1950; Distinguished Service award, American Agricultural Editors Association, 1955; Gold Medal and Citation, honor society Agrl., Gamma Sigma Delta; Iowa State College Alumni Gold Medal, 1955; citation and gold Medallas Del Merito Pardo Suizo, Asociation Colombiana de Criader de Ganado Pardo Suizo in Bogata, Columbia, 1960. Fellow of Animal Soc. Animal Production (pres. 1934-35); member A.A.A.S., American Dairy Scientific Association, Purebred Dairy Cattle Association (chairman committee to revise criteria), Sigma Xi, Alpha Zeta, Phi Kappa Phi, Gamma Sigma Delta (national pres., 1944—), Delta Upsilon, Acacia. Rep. U.S. as official judge in internat. judging contest, England, 1926. Republican. Conglist. Mason. Club: Saddle and Sirloin (Chicago). Writer of bulls. on feeding, breeding and management of livestock, also land use planning. Established Kildee scholarship of Dairy Shrine Club; animal, dairy and poultry sci. bldg. named Herbert Kildee Hall at Ia. State U. Home: Ames, Ia. *

KILE, OVILLE MERTON (KIL), agrl. economist; born New Vienna, O., Feb. 17, 1886; s. Morris and Morrie (Zinn) K.; B.S., in Agr., Ohio State U., 1912; grad. study same; m. Ruth Flora Clinton, Aug. 18, 1925. Agrl. extension lecturer, Ohio State U., 1912-13; with W.Va. U. as editor publs. and lecturer, 1913-16; mgr. ednl. bureau Nat. Assn. Fertilizer Mfrs., 1916-19; asst. Washington rep. Am. Farm Bureau Fed., 1920-21; mem. bd. dirs. Nat. Press Building Corp. Active in orgn. of farm bloc in Congress. Chairman Farm Hands Club since 1935; Washington rep. Sears Roebuck & Co., 1933-48; now retired. Mem. Nat. Grange, Am. Farm Econ. Assn. Methodist. Club: Nat. Press. Author: The Farm Bureau Movement, 1921; The New Agriculture, 1932; The Farm Bureau Through Three Decades, 1948. Contbr. agrl. and polit. articles to mags. and newspapers. Home: Mohican Hills, Md. *

KILLAM, LLOYD R(ANDOLPH), sec. (retired); born Winfield, Mo., Aug. 25, 1885; s. David Thomas and Cathrine (Magruder) K.; A.B., William Jewell Coll., Liberty, Mo., 1908; student U. of Mo., 1909-10; A.M., Brown University, 1911, Columbia, 1927; married Sadie Lucile Craig, August 20, 1912; children—Robert Craig, Douglas Lloyd, Eleanor Margaret (Mrs. Hartley H. Aram). Direstor religious work, Y.M.C.A., Providence, Rhode Island, 1908; student secretary, U. of Mo., 1909; asso. gen. sec. Y.M.C.A., Honolulu, 1912-25, territorial sec. Hawaiian Islands, 1925-30; dean Hawaii Sch. of Religion, U. of Hawaii, 1930-35; extension sec. Territory of Hawaii Y.M.C.A., 1936-37; exec. sec. Pioneer Fields Com. Nat. Council Y.M.C.A., 1937-38, exec. sec. Southern Area, 1939-45; executive vice president Pacific Laundry Co., Ltd., since 1945; pres. Pacific Properties, Limited. Traveled in China, Japan, Korea, 1922, organized Pacific Y.M.C.A. Conference, which developed into Inst. Pacific Relations, 1925; specialized in work among racial groups. Founder Hawaii Univ. Exchange Plan; exec. bd., Hawaii International House Association, Hawaii Employer's Council. Better Business Bureau. Mem. Southern Regional Inter-racial Council, Am. and Hawaii Councils, Inst. Pacific Relations, Fgn. Policy Assn.; chmn. Hawaii Com. for Relief Japan and Korea; social action com. Honolulu Council of Chs.; mem. bd. Kaimuki Y.M.C.A., mem. Honolulu Chamber Commerce Retail Bd., Hawaii Mental Hygiene Assn., U.N. Assn. (Hawaiian br.), Sigma Nu. Democrat. Conglist. Club: Rotary. Home: Honolulu, Hawaii. *

KILLGORE, ALBERT RUSSELL, Christian Science practitioner, former title and trust official; b. Peru, Kan., Dec. 10, 1882; s. Joseph Allen and Kate (Cooper) K.; A.B., U. of Kansas, 1904; studied law, U. of Southern Calif., 1911-12; m. Elma French, Oct. 8, 1908; children—Nancy Burns, Dorothy French, Allen Russell, Neil Arthur. Began with N. A. Brewster Abstract Co., Sedan, Kan., 1904; began with Title Guarantee & Trust Co., Los Angeles, Calif., 1905, trust officer, 1911-20, sec., 1920-33, exec. v.p., 1925-33; now engaged in the practice of Christian Science; admitted to Calif. bar, 1912. Mem. bd. trustees The Principia (school), St. Louis. Mem. Sigma Alpha Epsilon, Phi Delta Phi. Republican. Christian Scientist. Club: University. Home: Glendale, Calif. *

KILLORAN, CLAIR JOHN, lawyer; b. Weiser, Idaho, Apr. 12, 1905; s. Charles J. and Ada (Percifield) K.; A.B., U. Idaho, 1928; J.D., Georgetown U., 1932; m. Anne Regina Biggs, Nov. 30, 1935; 1 dau., Claire Joanne. Admitted to D.C. bar, 1933, Del. bar, 1934; mem. firm Borton, Melson & Killoran, Wilmington, Del., 1934, Melson & Killoran, 1935-41, Clair John Killoran, 1941-45, Killoran and Van Brunt, from 1946; dep. atty.-gen. State of Del., 1937-39, chief dep. atty.-gen. 1940-43; atty.-gen., 1943-47; gen. counsel Del. Mut. Life Ins. Co., Ernest Di Sobatino & Sons, Inc., Cantera Constrn. Co., Carpenters Motor Freight, Inc.; dir. Rollins Internat., Inc., Wilmington, Del., Registrar & Transfer Co., N.Y.C. Mem. Del. State Bd. Accountants 1947-51. Keynoter Rep. State Conv., 1944-46; Rep. state chmn., 1950-56; chmn. Del. delegation Nat. Rep. Conv., 1952, del., 1956. Fellow Am. Coll. Trial Lawyers; mem. Am. Del. (pres. 1959-61) bar assns., Georgetown U. Alumni Assn. (gov., mem. senate), Kappa Sigma. Elk. Clubs: Wilmington, Biderman Golf, Wilmington Country (dir. from 1959) (Wilmington); Lambs (N.Y.C.); Seaview Country (Absecon, N.J.). Home: Wilmington, Del. Died Oct. 29, 1975.

KIMBALL, ALLEN RUSSELL, army officer; b. Oneida, N.Y., June 20, 1886; s. Myron Henry and Flora Adelaide (Moon) K.; B.S., U.S. Mil. Acad., 1911; grad. Command and Gen. Staff Sch., 1928, Army Indsl. Coll., 1933, Army War Coll., 1934; m. Edna Louise Heath, Sept. 5, 1911; 1 son, Allen Heath (dec.). Commd. 2d lt., U.S. Army, 1911, and advanced through the grades to brig. gen., 1942; served as comdr. camp of U.S. troops, Norfolk, Va., 1917; with Tank Corps, 1918, motor transport officer, 1918; asst. sec. of war, mem. War Dept. Budget Adv. Com., and mem. Joint Economy Bd., Sept. 1, 1938, to June 1, 1940; Q.M. at U.S.M.A., West Point, N.Y., June 1, 1940-Feb. 2, 1942; mem. gen. staff, Hdqrs. Eastern Theater of Operations, Feb. 2, 1942-Apr. 28, 1942; comdg. gen., Jeffersonville Q.M. Depot, Jeffersonville, Ind., May 30, 1942-Mar. 2, 1944; dep. chief Q.M., European theater operations, Mar. 14, 1944-July 31, 1944; hdqrs. comdt., hdqrs. European theater operations since Aug. 25, 1944. Mem. The Q.M. Assn. Clubs: Army and Navy, Army and Navy Country (Washington, D.C.); Louisville Country (Ky.); Pendennis (Louisville, Ky.); Columbia Country (Chevy Chase, Md.). Contbr. to Q.M. Review. Home: Amsterdam, N.Y. *

KIMBALL, YEFFE, painter, sculptor, illustrator, writer; b. Mountain Park, Okla., 1914; d. Other Star Good Man and Martha Clementine Smith; studied at Art Students League of N.Y., 1935-39; studied in France, Italy, 1936-39; studied under Leger in Paris, France, N.Y.C.; m. Harvey L. Slatin. Worked in France, Italy, 1936-39; exhibited in numerous one-man, group shows including at Nat. Gallery Art, 1970, Smithsonian Inst., Washington, 1970, Princeton U., 1970, No. Va. Fine Arts, Alexandria, 1971, Trinity Coll., Hartford, Conn., 1971. Expertised and catalogued 6000 art objects of Pacific N.W. Coast Indians Portland (Oreg.) Art Museum, 1949; arranged collection Am. Indian Exhbn. Mattuck Mus., Waterbury, Conn., 1950; asst. N.W. Indian Art Exhb. Bklyn. Mus., 1951; tech. advisor Americana Found., N.Y., 1951-56; selected Am. Indian art objects for U.S. Dept. State Exhbn. Tour abroad, 1953; exhbn. asst. Am. Indian Exhbn. Isaac Delgado Mus., New Orleans, 1964; dir., juror Brotherhood childrens ann. exhbn. art N.Y.C., Brklyn. high sch., 1950-60; juror Fiber, Clay metal Nat. Exhbn. St. Paul Art Gallery, 1950, Mus. of N.Mex. ann. exhbn. painting, ceramics, sculpture, Nat. Am. Indian Exhbn., Scottsdale, Ariz., 1970, Center for Arts of Indian Am. Exhbn., Dept. Interior, Washington, D.C., 1970, Philbrook Art Center Nat. Exhbn. Am. Indian Art, 1975; tchr. Am. Forum Internat. Study, spl. Am. Indian program Inst. Am. Indian Arts, Santa Fe, 1970; mem. panel Convocation Am. Indian Scholars, Princeton U., 1970; cons., advisor to mus's., pubs., U.S. govt. on Indian history, art. Recipient First Hon. Mention Nat. Exhbn. Am. Indian Painting Philbrook Art Center, 1947, 51, First prize Nat. Indian Exhbn., 1959. Mem. Nat. Congress Am. Indian, Artists Equity Assn. N.Y., Nat. Acad. Design, Audubon Artists, Native No. Am. Artists. Co-author, illustrator: The Art of American Indian Cooking, 1965. Illustrator: Story of the Totem Pole, 1951, The Story of The Pueblo Indians, Caedmon Records, 1955; Some People Are Indians, 1965, The World of Manaboze, 1965; The American Indian and the United States, 1975. Address: New York, N.Y. Died Apr. 10, 1978.

KIMBERG, DANIEL VICTOR, physician, educator; b. N.Y.C., May 31, 1933; s. Morris and Anne (Hoffman) K.; B.A., Washington and Jefferson Coll., 1953; M.D., Columbia, 1957; m. Allison Deane Glatzer, Jan. 21, 1960; children—Leigh Suzanne, Deborah Lynn. Intern, resident medicine Presbyn. Hosp., N.Y.C., 1957-60, chief resident, 1962-63; asst. prof. medicine Columbia, 1964-69; asst. prof. medicine Harvard Med. Sch., 1969-70, asso. prof., 1970-74; Dewey prof., chmn. dept. medicine U. Rochester Sch. Medicine and Dentistry, 1974-76; chmn. dept. medicine Columbia, 1976-78; dir. med. service Presbyn. Hosp., 1976-78; physician-in-chief Strong Meml. Hosp., Rochester, N.Y., 1974-76. Clin. asso. USPHS, NIH, 1960-62. Mem. Am. Soc. for Clin. Investigation, Am. Gastroent. Assn., Endocrine Soc., Am. Physiol. Soc., N.Y. Acad. Scis., Phi Beta Kappa, Alpha Omega Alpha. Contbr. articles to profl. jours. Home: Scarsdale, N.Y. Died Nov. 26, 1978.

KIMPTON, LAWRENCE A., oil co. exec.; b. Kansas City, Mo., Oct. 7, 1910; s. Carl Edward and Lynn (Kennedy) K.; A.B., Stanford, 1931, M.A., 1932; Ph.D., Cornell U., 1935; D.Sc., Beloit Coll., 1952; LL.D., Lake Forest Coll., 1955, Know Coll., 1956, Northwestern U., 1958, U. Mo., 1960, U. Ill. 1961, U. Alaska, 1966; L.H.D., U. Chgo., 1961; m. Marcia Drennon, Oct. 2, 1943 (dec. Mar. 1963). Tchr. Deep Springs (Cal.) Coll., 1935, dean, dir., 1936-41; operator, part owner cattle ranch in Nev., 1941-42; prof. math. and philosophy, dean Coll. Liberal Arts, U. Kansas City, 1942-43; chief adminstrv., officer metall. lab., atomic bomb project, U. Chgo., 1943-44, dean students, sec. faculties, prof. philosophy, and edn., 1944-46, v.p., dean faculties, prof. philosophy and edn., 1946-47; dean students, prof. philosophy Stanford, 1947-50; v.p. devel. U. Chgo., 1950-51, chancellor, prof. philosophy, 1951-60; gen. mgr. planning Standard Oil Ind., 1960-63, v.p., 1963-68, asst. to chmn. bd., 1968-71, also dir.; B & O Chessie System, C. & O. Ry. Chmn., Am. Council Edn., 1957-58; pres. Am. Assn. Univs., 1958. Hon. trustee Mus. Sci. and Industry, Chgo., Newberry Library, Chgo., Robert A. Taft Inst. Govt.; bd. visitors Tulane U. Decorated officer de la Legion d'Honneur (France). Stanford fellow, 1959. Mem. Phi Beta Kappa, Phi Kappa Phi, Delta Sigma Rho. Clubs: Tavern, Chicago, Commercial, Chicago Yacht, Wayfarers (Chgo.); Bohemian (San Francisco). Home: Lakeside, Mich. Died Oct. 31, 1977.

KINDERVATER, GUS GEORGE, business exec.; b. Mpls., Nov. 17, 1885; s. Alvin Ernest and Anna (Brosius) K.; student Toensfeldt Inst., 1894-1904; m. Mayme Van Rice, Aug. 23, 1908. Joined Anheuser-Busch, St. Louis, as bookkeeper, 1904, mgr. Belleville (Ill.) br., 1910, audited records of co.'s ice and cold storage plants upon the advent of prohibition, 1918, mgr. Bronx, N.Y. Ice & Cold Storage plant, 1920, guided entrance of Anheuser-Busch into ice cream market, 1924; gen. mgr. ice cream div. Borden Co., 1930; gen. mgr. brewery brs. Anheuser-Busch, 1935, v.p. in charge refrigeration div., 1947, v.p. charge sales, brewery div., 1950-51; exec. v.p. Condor Films, Inc., ret. 1951. Mem. Met. Ice Cream Mfrs. Assn. (helped organize 1925, pres. 1925-26), N.Y. State Ice Cream Mfrs. Assn. (dir. 1927-28), Internat. Ice Cream Mfrs. Assn. (pres. 1933-34). Rotarian (pres. Bronx, 1926-27, hon. mem. since 1936. Home: Clayton, Mo. Retired. *

KING, BARRY GRIFFITH, physiologist; b. Pitts., Dec. 19, 1904; s. Samuel Victor and Annie M. (Jones) K.; A.B., U. Calif. at Berkeley, 1924, M.A., 1925; postgrad. Pasteur Inst., 1926, Cambridge Inst., 1927; Ph.D., Columbia, 1935; m. Estelle Marie Jochumsen, July 6, 1926; children—Aloysia Fahnestock (Mrs. Edward W. Hard, Jr.), Barry Griffith. Asst. instr. physiology U. Calif. at Berkeley Med. Sch., 1924-26; instr. physiology, then asst. prof. Coll. Phy. & Surg., Columbia, 1927-43; cons. physiol. med. sci. div. Office Naval Research, 1947; chief aeromed. design, div. med. service CAA, 1947-52, research exec., 1952-57; v.p. life sci. Operations Research Inc., Silver Spring, Md., 1958-61; chief research br. injury control USPHS, HEW, 1961-64, sci. adviser, 1965-80; sci. adviser USPHS, 1967-73. Mem. Pres.'s Conf. Indsl. Safety, 1948; dep. dir. com. accidental traumas Armed Forces Epidemiol. Bd., 1951-60; adv. panel Hwy. Traffic Safety Research, Nat. Acad. Scis.-NRC. 1965-80; also mem. spl. com. long range planning Hwy. Research Bd.; adv. panel Nat. Coop. Hwy. Research Program, 1965-80; research rev. bd. Am. Soc. Safety Engrs., 1964-80. Mem. vehicle spltys. com. Govt. Services Adminstrn., 1964-80; cons. surgeon gen. Dept. Army, 1956-60. Served to capt. USNR, 1943-47. Recipient Flight Safety award, 1955; Gold medal Dept. Commerce, 1955; Silver medal HEW, 1973. Fellow Aerospace Med. Assn.; AAAS, Am. Physiol. Soc., Harvey Soc., Soc. Exptl. Biology and Medicine, Indsl. Hygiene Assn. Contbr. numerous texts, articles. Spl. research environmental and aviation physiology, exptl. surgery, stress, effect elec. shock on heart action, accidental injury research. Home: Del Mar, Calif. Died Dec. 18, 1980.

KING, CARLETON JAMES, former congressman; b. Saratoga Springs, N.Y., June 15, 1904; s. James H. and Anna L. (Rose) K.; LL.B., Union U., Albany, N.Y., 1926; m. Constance M. Roddy, Aug. 16, 1933; children—Carleton James, Constance M. (Mrs. James A. Murphy). Admitted to N.Y. bar, 1926, thereafter practiced in Saratoga Springs; mem. firm King, Duval & Murphy; acting city judge, Saratoga Springs, 1934-40; asst. dist. atty. Saratoga County, 1940-50, dist. atty., 1950-61; mem. 87th Congress 31st Dist. N.Y.; mem. 88th-93d Congresses, 29 Dist. N.Y.; then partner firm King, Murphy and Fitzsimmons. Pres. N.Y. State Dist. Attys. Assn., 1955. Republican. Elk (past exalted ruler Saratoga). Clubs: Army-Navy, Touchdown (Washington). Home: Saratoga Springs, N.Y. Died Nov. 19, 1977.

KING, CLINTON, artist; b. Ft. Worth, Oct. 3, 1901; s. John Porter and Lorena (Blair) K.; student Princeton, 1924, Nat. Acad. Design Grand Central Sch. Art, Broadmoor Art Acad., 1924-25; studied engraving with Hayter, Paris, 1969-70, 72-73; m. Duff Stirling Twysden, Aug. 1928 (dec.); m. 2d, Narcissa Swift, Apr. 12, 1941. Numerous one-man shows U.S. and fgn. countries, from 1932, latest being Ohana Gallery, London, Eng., 1959, Galleries Marigny, Paris, France, 1959, 61, Galleries Jeanne Castel, Paris, 1963, William Findlay Gallery, Chgo., 1964, 65, Univ. Club, Chgo., 1965, Brinken Galleries, Stockholm, Sweden, 1966, Gallerie Transposition, Paris, 1966, Lakeview Center Arts and Scis., Peoria, Ill., 1968, Four Winds Gallery, Kalamazoo, Mich., 1974, Galerie Transposition, Paris, 1976; exhibited group shows large cities U.S. and fgn. countries, including Carnegie Inst., Chgo. Art Inst. (Clyde M. Carr prize 1944), Phila. Annual, Nat. Acad. Design, Toledo Mus. Art, Phila. Watercolor Soc., Corcoran Biennial, St. Louis Art Mus., Salon D'Automne, Paris, France, Santa Fe Art Mus., Museum of Bayeux (France); rep. permanent collections City of Paris, Ft. Worth Art Assn., Santa Fe Art Mus., Bibliotheque Nationale, Paris, Balt. Mus. Art, Bowdoin Coll. Mus. Art, Calif. State Coll., Smith Coll., Rockford Coll., Cal. Palace Legion of Honor, Mulvane Art Center, Topeka, Indpls. Mus. Art, Library of Congress, N.Y. Pub. Library, Phila. Mus. Art, Smithsonian Instn., univs. Iowa, Maine, Nebr., N.C., Utah, No. Ill., So. Ill., Mich. State, Ga., Ringling Mus. Art, Sarasota, Fla., Victoria and Albert Mus., London, Mus. Fine Arts, Springfield, Mass., Ind. State U., Dayton Art Inst., Nasson Coll., Kalamazoo Inst. Art, Drury Coll., Wittenberg U., Beloit Coll., numerous others. Club: Chicago Arts. Home: Lakeside, Mich. Died Feb. 23, 1979; buried Lake Forest, Ill.

KING, CLYDE NELSON, govt. ofcl.; b. Springfield, Mo., Mar. 29, 1886; s. David Nelson and Lucinda (Weldon) K.; student pub. schs. of Springfield; m. Mary Blanche Murphy, Apr. 10, 1910; 1 son, Jack Weldon. Enlisted U.S. Navy, 1903, served in European and Asiatic stas., ret., 1908; engaged in farm livestock bus. near Springfield, Mo., 1908-11; with Internat. Harvester Co., 1912-48; v.p. and dir. Internat. Harvester Export Co., 1927-48; chief E.C.A. Spl. Mission to Austria since 1948; econ. advisor to U.S. High Commr. and Mil. Comdr., Vienna. Dir. Anderson Meyer & Co., Shanghai, China. Clubs: Adventuers (N.Y. City and Chicago); Circumnavigators (N.Y. City). Home: Springfield, Mo. *

KING, EARL LESLIE, missionary; b. Chatfield, Minn., Nov. 13, 1886; s. William Leslie and Sara Jane (Ilockenhull) K. (both missionaries to India); A.B., Ripon (Wis.) Coll., 1908, A.M., 1909; studied Kennedy Sch. of Missions, Hartford, Conn., 1917-18, U. of Chicago, 1925-26, 36; m. Edith Broadbooks, Oct. 18, 1913; children—Jean Louise, William Asbury, Robert Leslie, Theodore Wesley. Student pastor, Princeton, Wis., 1907-08; v.prin. and prin. Beynon-Smith High Sch., Belgaum, India, 1909-16; prin. Hardwicke Christian High Sch., Narsingupur, 1918-22; sec. Epworth League in India and Burma, 1922-38; ednl. sec., Meth. Ch., Southern Asia, 1938-48; editor Charterhouse Program materials; editor Christian Education; vis. prof. religious edn., Leonard Theol. Coll., 1912-49; rep. in Southern Asia, Joint Com. on Religious Education in Foreign Fields, Methodist Church, 1949-50. Author: (with E. B. King) Community Middle School Curriculum, 1924; Charterhouse Program of Religious Education, 1924, 29, 31; Handbook of Epworth League, 1924, 30; A Project-Life of Christ, 1927; Pioneers of Life, 1929; Test Exercises in Religious Education, 1929; Youth's Pattern, 1931; Into All the World (with H. E. Fehr), 1933; The Worldchanger, 1934; The New Light (with W. M. Ryburn), 1936; An Introduction to Religious Education, 1941; also many ednl. booklets. Address: Altadena, Calif. *

KING, EDGAR IRWIN, educator, coll. dean, lawyer; b. Logan, Kans., Nov. 18, 1913; s. Edgar Irwin and Frances Emmaline (Brown) K.; student Hays State Coll., 1930-32; A.B., U. Kans., 1934, J.D., 1937; LL.D., Temple U., 1959; m. Anna Grace Vander Velde, Aug. 19, 1937. Admitted to Kans. bar, 1937, Ohio, 1947; practice of law, Logan, Kans., 1937; asst. prof. law U. Kansas City, 1937-41; asso. prof. law U. Louisville, 1941-46; asso. prof. law Western Res. U., 1946-50, prof., 1950-62, asst. dean, 1951-58, dir. grad. law program, 1953-58, dean, 1958-62; prof. law Dickinson Sch. Law, Carlisle, Pa., from 1962, asst. dean, 1967-74, John Edward Fowler Distinguished prof., from 1973, dean, from 1974; vis. prof. Hastings Coll. Law, U. Calif., 1971-72. Chmn. regional enforcement commn. WSB, 1952-53. Served as comdr. USNR, 1943-46. Mem. Am., Pa. bar assns., Am. Law Inst., Order of Coif, Phi Alpha Delta. Co-author: Notes and Annotations to Kentucky Revised Statues, 1944; also articles legal periodicals. Editor: Juvenile Court Handbook. Home: Carlisle, Pa. Deceased.

KING, EDWARD CALDWELL, lawyer; b. Delta, Colo., Aug. 14, 1896; s. Alfred Rufus and Annie Rachel (Caldwell) K.; ed. Warren Acad., Denver; A.B., U. Denver, 1919, LL.B., 1922, LL.D., 1952; LL.D., U. Colo., 1965; m. Mary Jess Hedrick, Aug. 15, 1925; children—Nancy Jane, Neil Caldwell. Admitted to Colo. bar 1922; in gen. practice, Denver, 1922-29; mem. Twitchell, Clark, Burkhardt and King, 1923-27, Gould and King, 1927-29; trust officer Internat. Trust Co., 1929-38, exec. v.p., 1939-40; prof., dean Sch. of Law, U. Colo., 1940-63; counsel law firm Hollenbeck, King, French & Mills, Boulder, Colo., from 1965. Vice chmn. War Labor Bd., 9th Region, 1943; publ. mem. Regional WSB, 1951. Co-dir. Legal research Inst. N.Y.U., Ankara, Turkey, 1957-58. Served as 2d lt., F.A., World War I; commd. maj., Special Res. AUS, May 13, 1943; lt. col. Jan. 1945; served Africa and Italy, Sept. 1943-Oct. 1945; chief, property control div., Allied Com. for Italy. Decorated Legion of Merit; knight officer Order of Crown of Italy. Mem. Colo. Ho. of Reps., 1927-30, Denver Planning Commn., 1938-40, Civic League of Denver, 1930-40; Fellow Am. Coll. Probate Counsel; mem. Am. (chmn. real property, probate and trust law sect., 1956-57), Boulder County, Colo. (pres. 1963-64) bar assns., Law Club, Sigma Alpha Epsilon, Phi Delta Phi, Sigma Delta Chi, Order of Coif. Club; University (Denver). Author: Future Interests in Colorado; Colorado Practice Methods, 2 vols., 1956, 2d edit. 3 vols., 1970. Home: Boulder, Colo. Died Dec. 2, 1975.

KING, EDWARD WARD, transp. co. exec.; b. Surgoinsville, Tenn., Jan. 12, 1896; s. John Rutledge and Margaret (Collup) K.; grad. high sch.; m. Myrtle Charlton, Mar. 27, 1922; children—E. William, John R., Margaret (Mrs. Edwin O. Norris). Founder, King Motor Co., Kingsport, Tenn., 1925-32; founder, pres. Mason & Dixon Lines, Inc., Kingsport, 1932-57, chmn. bd. 1957-74, hon. chmn., dir., 1974-77; chmn. bd. Mason & Dixon Tank Lines, Inc., Kingsport, Crown Enterprises, Inc., Kingsport; past chmn. bd. Kingsport Nat. Bank. Dist. chmn. Am. Cancer Soc., 1962-63; gen. chmn. Appalachia Heart Assn., 1961-62; mem. President's Club, U. Tenn., 1968-77; mem. Tenn. Tax Study Commn., 1967, Tenn. Council on Econ. Edn. Past bd. dirs. Community Chest; trustee Holston Conf. Colls. Served with U.S. Army, World War I; France, Germany. Recipient Legion of Honor award Kiwanis Kingsport, 1937, also Appreciation certificate Am. Cancer Soc., Pioneer Future award Tenn. Jr. C. of C., Appreciation certificate Am. Heart Assn. Mem. Transp. Ins. Co. (dir.), Tenn. Motor Transp. Assn. (past pres.), Am. Trucking Assn. (dir., past v.p.), So. Motor Carriers Rate Conf. (founder, past gov.), Am. Soc. Traffic and Transp. (founder), N.A.M., Transp. Assn. Am., A.I.M., U.S., Kingsport (past dir.) chambers commerce, Am. Legion. Methodist. Democrat. Kiwanian, Moose, Rotarian (hon.). Club: Ridgefields Country. Home: Kingsport, Tenn. Died Mar. 19, 1977.

KING, JOHN HAMILTON, judge; b. Willimantic, Conn., Apr. 21, 1900; s. William Albert and Jennie Stella (Cady) K.; A.B., Yale, 1923, LL.B., 1925. Admitted to Conn. bar, 1925; gen. practice law, Willimantic, 1925-40; law clk. com. on judiciary Conn. Gen. Assembly, 1927-37; sec. law clk. Commn. to Revise Gen. Statutes of Conn., 1927-30; mem. examining bd. Conn. State Bar, 1928-42; asst. atty. gen. Conn., 1929-31; mem. Jud. Council of Conn. 1931-47 county health officer, Windham County, 1934-39; mem. Spl. Commn. to Study Pauper Laws of Conn., 1935-37; judge Superior Ct., 1940-57; justice Conn. Supreme Ct., 1957-63, chief justice, 1963-70; ret.; state referee, 1970-77. Fellow Am. Bar Found.; mem. Windham County Law Library Assn., Am. Judicature Soc., Conn. Windham County bar assns., S.A.R., Am. Legion, Alpha Chi Rho, Republican. Conglist. Clubs: Graduate, Mary's (New Haven); University (Hartford). Home: Willimantic, Conn. Died Aug. 22, 1977.

KING, LAWRENCE SCHMIDT, lawyer; b. Preston, Ia., Sept. 9, 1903; s. Fred S. and Augusta (Schmidt) K.; student Grinnell Coll., 1923-25; LL.B., U. Mich., 1927; m. Elizabeth McDowell, Oct. 1, 1927; children—Lawrence Albert, Roger William, Ruth Ann (Mrs. Jeffry D. Ballard). Admitted to Mich. bar, 1927, practiced in Detroit; with firm Miller, Canfield, Paddock & Stone, 1927-80, mem., 1936-40, sr. mem., 1940-75, counsel, 1975-80. Commr., City Pleasant Ridge, 1944-50. Trustee, past pres. John Scudder Found. for Old People, Luella Hannan Meml. Home; sec., trustee David M. Whitney Fund; a founder, hon. trustee William Beaumont Hosp., Mich. Cancer Found. Mem. Am., Mich., Detroit bar assns., Am. Judicature Soc., Delta Theta Phi. Republican. Presbyn. Clubs: Detroit; Pine Lake Country (Orchard Lake, Mich.); Lighthouse Point, Yacht, Racquet. Home: Boca Raton, Fla. Died June 25, 1980; interrment White Chapel Meml. Cemetery, Troy, Mich.

KING, RICHARD, banking, ranching; b. Nueces County, Tex., Dec. 17, 1884; s. Richard and Elizabeth Pearl (Ashbrook) K.; ed. San Antonio (Tex.) Acad., 1898-1903, U. of Mo., 1904-06; m. Minerva Pierpont Heaney, Oct. 12, 1907; children—Richard, Alfred Ashbrook. Engaged in ranching on large scale since 1906; trustee Estate of R. King, investments in land and cattle; dir. Corpus Christi Nat. Bank since 1913, v.p., 1923-28, pres., chmn. bd.; dir. Nat. Finance Credit Corp., Ft. Worth, Tex.; dir. Regional Agrl. Credit Corp., Houston, Tex. Chmn. Nueces County Navigation Commn. Mem. Sigma Alpha Epsilon Democrat. Episcopalian. Elk. Mason. Home: Corpus Christi, Tex. *

KING, ROBERT SNYDER, mfr.; b. Dayton, O., July 21, 1888; s. Robert N. and Harriet E. (Snyder) K.; ed. Yale U.; m. Helen K. Slack, Oct. 5, 1910; children—Robert S., Helen S., Louis S. Engaged in oil production, 1909-15; pres. State Oil Co., Lincoln, Neb., 1915-23; pres. Refiners Oil Co., 1915-31; v.p. Gen. Petroleum Corp., Los Angeles, Calif., 1931-35; pres. The Pennzoil Co., 1936-40; pres. Philip Carey Manufacturing Company, 1940-48, Chmn. of the board, 1948-67; director King Drilling Company Diamond Match Co., Maryland Casualty Co. Clubs: Miami Valley Hunt and Polo, Buz Fuz (Dayton, O.); Camargo (Cin.); Twenty-Nine (N.Y.C.); Racquet (Chgo.). Home: Cincinnati, Ohio. Died Mar. 1978.

KING, ROBERT WALDO, physicist; b. Sioux Falls, S.D., May 13, 1890; s. William Leonard and Harriet (Lucas) K.; A.B., Cornell, 1912, Ph.D., 1915; m. Dorothy Muriel Babcock, Dec. 28, 1922; children—Robert Waldo, Jerome Babcock. Instr. physics Cornell U., 1913-17; physicist Western Electric Co., 1917-20; engr. AT&T, 1920-27; asst. dir. publ. Bell Telephone Labs., 1927-29; asst. tech. rep. in Europe, AT&T, 1929-35; asst. to pres. Bell Telephone Labs., 1935-40; asst. v.p. AT&T, 1940-44; asst. to pres. Bell Telephone Labs., 1944-49. Fellow Am. Phys. Soc., AAAS; mem. IEEE, N.Y. Elec. Soc. (past pres.), Acad. Polit. Sci., Sigma Xi. Editor Bell System Tech. Jour., 1922-28, 1935-79. Contbr. papers on tech. subjects. Home: Hartland Four Corners, Vt. Died June 12, 1979.

KING, SPENCER BIDWELL, JR., educator; b. Birmingham, Ala., Feb. 19, 1904; s. Spencer Bidwell and Lizzie Emma (Dodson) K.; A.B., Mercer U., 1929; M.A., Peabody Coll., 1936; Ph.D., U. N.C., 1950; student Vanderbilt U., U. Mich.; m. Caroline Janet Paul, Dec. 26, 1934; children—Spencer Bidwell III, Janet Paul (Mrs. Donald Lowell Wayman), Margaret Caroline (Mrs. Robert J. Edenfield). Prin. Fruitland Inst., Hendersonville, N.C., 1930-33; instr. history Mars Hill Coll., 1933-46, asst. dean, 1942-46; vis. prof. Furman U., summers 1940, 43, 44; asso. prof. history Mercer U., 1946-48, prof., 1948-73, emeritus, 1973-77, chmn. dept., 1946-70; vis. prof. history Emory U., summer 1960, U. Ga., summer 1963; columnist Macon Telegraph, 1960-65. Research asst. Inst. Research Social Sci. U. N.C., 1945; chmn. bd. editors Ardivan Press, Macon, 1960-62; trustee Macon Youth Mus., 1956-65. Mem. hist. commn. So. Baptist Conv., 1966-73. Recipient Carnegie grant for hist. research, 1950-51. Named An Outstanding Educator of America, 1971; recipient Daus. Colonial Wars Tchr. award, 1973. Mem. So. Hist. Assn., Ga. Soc. Hist. Research (pres. 1953), So. Bapt. Hist. Soc. (pres. 1970), Middle Ga. Hist. Soc. (pres. 1976), Kappa Phi Kappa, Pi Gamma Mu. Baptist. Club: Palaver. Author: Selective Service in North Carolina in World War II, 1949; (with Coulter and Saye) History of Georgia, 1954; Ebb Tide as Seen Through the Diary of Josephine Clay Habersham, 1863, 1958; Georgia Voices: a documentary history to 1872, 1966; Darien—The Death and Rebirth of a Southern Town, 1981. Editor: J.C. Butler's Historical Record of Macon and Central Georgia, 1958, 69, Eliza Frances Andrews' Wartime Journal of a Georgia Girl, 1960, 3d edit., 1981; Rebel Lawyer: Letters of Theodorick W. Montfort, 1861-1862, 1965. Ga. editor: Ency. of So. Baptists, 3 vols., Ency. Brit., Collier's Ency.; contbr. articles and book reviews in hist., lit. jours. Home: Macon, Ga. Died Dec. 14, 1977; interred Oak Grove Cemetery, Americus, Ga.

KING, WARREN THOMAS, editorial cartoonist; b. Queens, L.I., N.Y., Jan. 3, 1916; s. Thomas Joseph and Rose (Beck) K.; B.S. Fordham U., 1938; student Grand Central Art. 1938, Phoenix Art Inst., 1938-41; m. Nadine Sensabaugh, Mar. 11, 1950; children—Dennis, Patricia, Suzanne. Free lance illustrator for books, advt., mags., movies, N.Y.C., 1940-61; editorial cartoonist Nat. Assn. Mfrs., N.Y.C., 1940-61; editorial cartoonist Nat. Assn. Mfrs., N.Y.C., from 1951, Daily News, N.Y.C., 1955-77. Paintings permanently represented at The Pentagon, Air Force Acad., Colorado Springs, Colo.; paintings exhibited internationally. Recipient Freedom Found. medals of honor, 1953, 59, certificate merit, 1960, Newspaper Guild award, 1959, 61, Soc. Silurians award, 1960, 61, 64, George Washington Honor medal Freedoms Found., 1963, Brotherhood award Nat. Conf. Christians and Jews, 1963, Freedoms Found. Medal of Honor, 1965, Soc. Silurians Honorable Mention, 1965,, Page One award, 1967, Nat. Headliners Club award, 1968, Nat. Art Dirs. Club award, 1968. Overseas Press Club citation, 1968, 73. Mem. Soc. Illustrators, Nat. Cartoonist Soc., Soc. Silurians, Am. Assn. Editorial Cartoonists. Club: Dutch Treat. Home: Wilton, Conn. Died Feb. 9, 1978.

KING, WILFRED STRICKLAND, advt. exec.; b. N.Y.C., Nov. 3, 1907; s. John Strickland and Gertrude Ellen (Williams) K.; student Columbia, 1926-28; m. Bette Ribble, Dec. 2, 1961; children—Joan R. (Mrs. William Dunne), Susan J. With J.M. Mathes, Inc., N.Y.C., 1933-70, exec. v.p., 1959-70, also dir.; dir. Pemberton, Freeman, Mathes & Milne, Toronto, Can., Ribberfin Corp., N.Y.C., Hetland & Stevens, N.Y.C. Clubs: Union League (N.Y.C.); St. Andrews Golf (Ardsley, N.Y.); Royal Bermuda Yacht. Home: Winter Park, Fla. *

KING, WILLARD LEROY, lawyer; b. Batavia, Ill., Dec. 9, 1893; s. Willard E. and Ellen (White) K.; student Knox Coll., 1912-14; Ph.B., Chicago U., 1916, J.D., 1917; D.C.L. (hon.), Bowdoin Coll. 1951; LL.D., Knox Coll., 1954; m. Margaret A. Erickson, Dec. 15, 1930 (dec. Apr. 1971); 1 dau., Margaret (Mrs. Thomas R. Moore). Admitted to Ill. bar, 1917; began practice in Peoria; draftsman Com. on Phraseology and Style, Ill. Constl. Conv., 1919-20; began Chgo. practice with Rosenthal, Hamill & Wormser, 1921, became mem. 1926; now King, Robin, Gale & Pillinger. Mem. Loyalty Rev. Bd., Civil Service Commission, 1951-53. Served as 2d lt. Inf., 1918. Trustee Mus. Sci. and Industry, Menninger Found. Mem. Am., Ill., Chgo. (bd. mgrs. 1929-38) bar assns., Chgo. Law Inst. (pres. 1938), Ill. State, Chgo. (trustee) hist. socs., Delta Sigma Rho, Phi Gamma Delta, Order of Coif. Clubs: University, Chicago Literary (pres. 1941-42), Caxton (pres. 1954-55), Law (pres. 1953-54); Attic, Quadrangle, Grolier (N.Y.). Co-author: Law of Opinion Evidence in Illinois, 1942; author Melville Weston Fuller, 1950; Lincoln's Manager David Davis, 1960. Contbr. articles to Brittannica and Am. encys. and legal mags. Home: Chicago, Ill. Died Mar. 5, 1981; interred Geneva, Ill.

KING, WILLIAM HAVEN, lawyer; b. Huntington, W.Va., Oct. 15, 1911; s. James Edward and Princess (Turner) K.; A.B., Dartmouth, 1933; LL.B., U. Richmond, 1936; m. Suzanne Davis, Aug. 30, 1935; children—Susan (Mrs. W. Hammond Hunt), William Haven. Admitted to Va. bar, 1935, thereafter practiced in Richmond Virginia; partner firm McGuire, Woods and Battle, 1941-78. Mem. Va. Bd. Law Examiners, 1951-78. Vice pres., gen. counsel Citizens Home Ins. Co.; gen. counsel Blue Cross Va., Blue Shield Va. (pres. 1963-66). Chmn. parking bd. City Richmond, 1958-64. Pres. Richmond chpt. A.R.C., 1956-58, bd. dirs. 1949-72; bd. dirs. Richmond YMCA, 1957-65, Westbrook Sanatorium, Inc., 1957-70; pres. Va. League Planned Parenthood, Inc., 1965-66. Mem. bd. mgrs. Nat. Conf. Bar Examiners, 1962-68, chmn. 1966-67. Served to lt. (s.g.) USNR, World War II; PTO. Fellow Am. Bar Found. (state chmn.), Am. Coll. Trial Lawyers; mem. Am. (ho. dels. 1967-68), Richmond (pres. 1957-58) bar assns., Va State Bar (pres. 1960-61, chmn. com. legal ethics (1958-60), Va. Bar Assn. (exec. com. 1946-49), Am. Judicature Soc., Va. Soc. S.R. (pres. 1968-70), Newcomen Soc. Omicron Delta Kappa, Psi Upsilon, Casque and Gauntlet, Clubs: Country of Va., Bull and Bear. Home: Richmond, Va. Died Nov. 1, 1978.

KING, WILLIS JEFFERSON, ret. bishop; b. Rose Hill, Tex., Oct. 1, 1886; s. Anderson William and Emma (Blackshear) K.; A.B. at Wiley College, Marshall, Tex., 1910; S.T.B., Boston U. Sch. of Theol. 1913, Ph.D., 1921; hon. D.D., Boston U., 1933; student Harvard Divinity Sch.; m. Permella J. Kelly, June 4, 1913 (dec. Feb. 1943); children—Velma Norine, Eloise Aurora, Grace Evangeline; m. 2d, Emma Clarissa Arnold, June 28, 1944. Entered ministry M.E. Ch., 1908; pastor Greenville, Tex., 1908-10; asso. pastor St. Mark's Ch., N.Y.C., 1911; pastor Fourth Ch., Boston, St. Paul Ch., Galveston, Tex., Trinity Ch., Houston, until 1918; prof. O.T. and Christian sociology Gammon Theol. Sem. Atlanta, 1918-30, pres., 1932-48, lectr, 1952; elected bishop, 1944, assigned to Liberia, W. Africa; reassigned, 1948; assigned to La., Miss. and Upper Miss. Confs., 1953; resident bishop New Orleans area, central jurisdiction The Methodist Church, 1956-60. Pres., Samuel Houston Coll., 1930-32. Fellow Julius Rosenwald Fund for research in Oxford U. and Palestine, under auspices Am. Sch. of Oriental Research (on leave of absence from Gammon Theol. Sem., 1929-30. Represented Negro students at World's Student Christian Federation, Peking, China, 1922. Recipient Great Band of Humane Order of African Redemption. Liberia, 1956; knight comdr. Order of African Pioneers. Mem. General Conf., M.E. Ch., 1924, 28, 32, 40, 44; del. to Conf. on Life and Work, Oxford, Eng., 1937; del. to World Council Meth. Ch., Oxford, 4951; rep. Bishop's council to Africa Central Conf., Belgian Congo, 1952; mem. Nat. Preaching Mission Staff, 1936-37; mem. Commn. of Unification of Meth. Chs. in Am.; mem. Atlanta Sch. of Social Work; mem. Commn. on Interracial Cooperation, 1940—. Mem. Am. Oriental Soc., Southern Sociol. Soc., Am. Acad. Polit. and Social Science, Am. Schs. Oriental Research. Nat. Geographic Soc., Omega Psi Phi, Democrat. Author: The Negro in American Life, 1926. Collaborator: Personalism in Theology and Christian Bases of World Order, 1943. Contbr. to Ency. of Methodism, 1974; numerous mag. articles. Home: New Orleans LA. *

KING, WYNCIE, illustrator, caricaturist; b. Covington, Ga., Sept. 21, 1884; s. George Whitfield and Susie Davis (Brown) K.; ed. pub. schs.; m. Hortense Flexner, Apr. 30, 1919. Cartoonist with Nashville Banner and Nashville Daily News, 1905; with Louisville Courier Jour., Chicago Record Herald and New York Evening World, 1905-10; cartoons, caricatures and feature drawing with Louisville Herald, 1911-21; made caricatures for editorial page, Public Ledger, Phila., 1921-22; worked for Public Ledger, Life, Judge and N.Y. Times; illustrator Saturday Evening Post, 1925. Water color caricatures exhibited at Louisville Art Assn., Art Inst. Chicago, Pa. Acad. Fine Arts, etc. Mem. Artists Guild. Clubs: Franklin Inn. Philobiblon, Print Club of Phila. Home: Bronxville, N.Y. *

KINGSLAND, LAWRENCE C(HAPPELL), patent lawyer; born in St. Louis, April 11, 1884; s. George and Martha (Chappell) K.; LL.B., Washington U., St. Louis, 1908; m. Ethel Chenault, March 11, 1908; children—Ethel Chenault (Mrs. Christian Baird Peper), Lawrence Chappell, Robert Chenault. Practice of Law, specializing in patent and trade mark, St. Louis, 1908-1935; sr. member of firm of Kingsland, Rogers & Ezell, St. Louis, 1935-47; commr. of patents 1947-49; sr. mem. Kingsland, Rogers, Ezell, Eilers & Robbins; legal advisor Philippine govt. in drafting patent and trade mark statutes, Jan.-April 1947, Manila; chmn. Am. delegation for preliminary discussions on treatment of German trade marks, Nov.-Dec. 1947; mem. patent compensation bd. AEC, 1957—. Commissioned through grades to colonel comdg. 138th inf., Nat. Guard of Mo., 1919-41. Mem. St. Louis Bar Assn., Mo. Bar Assn., Am. Bar Assn., Am. Patent Law Assn., Sigma Chi, Phi Delta Phi. Dem. Presbyn. Club: Engineers, Missouri Athletic, Newcomen Society (New York), Tavern (Chicago). Home: Chesterfield, Mo. *

KINGSLEY, JOHN DONALD, orgn. exec.; b. Cambridge, N.Y., Mar. 25, 1908; s. John Henry and Carolyn (Donaldson) K.; A.B., Syracuse U., 1929, M.A., Maxwell Grad. Sch. of Pub. Affairs, 1930, Ph.D. 1933; grad. work London Sch. of Economics, U. London, 1936-38; LL.D., U. Louisville, 1950; m. Alice W. Boyd, June 1930 (div.); 1 dau. Jennifer Anne; m. 2d, Ruth Caplan, June 1946; children—Peter, Christine. Began career as instr. of government Antioch Coll., 1933-35, post doctoral European fellow Social Science Research Council, 1936-38; prof. govt. Antioch Coll., 1938-42; dir. Middle East and Africa. The Ford Found., 1963-72, spl. rep. for Middle East Affairs, 1968-72. Asst. regional dir. War Manpower Commn., 1942-44, dep. exec. dir., 1944-45; dep. dir. Office of War Mobilization, 1945-46; program coordinator The White House Office, 1946-47; exec. sec. President's Sci. Research Bd., 1946-47; White House liaison President's Commn. on Higher Edn., 1946-47; prin. chief of sections Internat. Labor Office, Geneva, Switzerland, 1947-48; chief of mission to Greece, 1947; asst. Fed. Security Adminstr., 1948-49, dir. gen. Internat. Refugee Orgn., 1949-51; U.N. agt. gen. Korean reconstruction, 1951-53; adminstr., trustee Paris Refugee Reparations Fund 1949-57; exec. dir. Community Council of Greater N.Y., 1953-59. Mem. U.S. delegation to U. N. Econ. and Social Council, 1948. Mem. Nat. Conf. Christians and Jews (dir.), Nat. Health and Welfare Retirement Assn., Tolstoy Found. dir.), Brit. Inst. Pub. Administrn., American Polit. Science Assn., Phi Beta Kappa. Democrat. Author: (with W.E. Mosher) Public Personnel Administration, 1936, 2d edit., 1940; Representative Bureaucracy, 1942. Home: Greenwich, Conn. Died June 1, 1972.

KINNANE, RAPHAEL IGNATIUS, clergyman; b. Lima, O., June 7, 1881; s. John and Dusabelle (Rinehart) K.; grad. cum summa laude, St. Charles Coll., Ellicott City, Md., 1902; student, St. Mary's Sem., Cleve., 1905; S.T.D., Propaganda U., Rome (Italy), 1908. Ordained priest Roman Cath. Ch., 1908; chancellor Diocese of Toledo, 1911-12, vicar gen., 1941—; pastor, Port Clinton, O., 1912-27, Maumee, O., 1927-40, St. Mary's Ch., Tiffin, O., 1940—; domestic prelate, 1925, protonotary apostolic, 1946. Mem. Toledo Rationing Bd., World War II. Served as chaplain U.S. Army, World War II. Address: Tiffin, O. *

KINNEAR, JOHN CHARLES, bus. exec. and engr.; b. Carnoustie, Scotland, Feb. 14, 1885 (parents U.S. citizens); s. James and Mary (Lowson) K.; S.B., Mass. Inst. Tech., 1907; m. Bertha Clark, June 20, 1907; 1 son, John Charles, Jr. With Goldfield (Nev.) Consol. Mines. 1907, Diamondfield Daisy Mining Co., 1908; operator Cochrane Lease, Diamondfield, Nev., 1909-10; engr. Bingham (Utah) and Garfield R.R., 1910; successively metallurgist, smelter operator, engr., asst. supt., supt., gen. supt., asst. to gen. mgr., asst. gen. mgr., gen. mgr. Kennecutt Copper Corp., Nev. (McGill) Mines Div., 1910-45; v.p. Kennecott Copper Corp., N.Y.C., 1945-48; dir. and v.p. Nev. Northern Ry., Ely (Nev.) Nat. Bank. Pres. Nev. Mine Operators Assn.; chmn. Gov. Adv. Mining Bd., Nev.; dir. Am. Mining Congress; pres. Nev. State Bd. of Edn. Mem. Am. Inst. of Mining and Metall. Engrs., Mining and Metall. Soc. of Am. (pres.), Mining Club, Inc., N.Y. Republican. Conglist. Mason (K.T., Shriner), Elk, Royal Order Jesters (Nev.). Clubs: University (N.Y.C.), Bankers of New York, Co-inventor: Patent Selective Converting. Home: McGill, Nevada. *

KINNEY, DONALD RICHARD, educator; b. E. Sparta, Ohio, June 21, 1923; s. Hobart Harry and Hope (Rice) K.; B.A. summa cum laude, Mt. Union Coll., Alliance, Ohio, 1954, L.H.D., 1966; L.H.D., Loyola U., Chgo., 1977; m. Dora Evelyn Davis, June 16, 1962 (dec. 1965); 1 son, Allan Clark. With Hadley Sch. for Blind, Winnetka, Ill., from 1954, exec. dir., 1973-75, pres., from 1975; cons. adv. com. Nat. Center Deaf-Blind Youths and Adults. Chmn. com. services for deaf-blind world council Welfare of Blind; exec. com. Internat. Assn. Edn. Deaf-Blind. Recipient Anne Sullivan Macy centennial award, 1966, citation Dwight Eisenhower, 1959, citation Midland Authors Soc., 1968, Helen Keller gold medal, 1948, Francis Joseph Campbell award ALA, 1978, Man of Year award Nat. Home Study Council, 1978. Mem. Am. Assn. Workers for Blind (dir.), U.S. Chess Fedn., Pi Gamma Mu, Sigma Alpha Epsilon. Lion (internat. Goodwill ambassador 1971). Author: Flight of Arrows, 1950; Flutes Beyond the Day, 1953; Encore, 1954; Independent Living Without Sight and Hearing, 1967; Harp of Silence, 1967; Relevant Braille, 1975. Home: Winnetka Ill. Died Feb. 1979.

KINNEY, THOMAS DEARMAN, physician; b. Franklin, Pa., Mar. 19, 1909; s. Thomas Andrew and Minnie (DeArman) K.; A.B., U. Pa., 1931; M.D., Duke, 1936; m. Eleanor Shepard Roberts, July 9, 1939; children—Thomas Roberts, Eleanor DeArman, Hannah Chase, Janet Shepard. Intern, Johns Hopkins Hosp., Balt., 1936-38; asst. pathologist Mallory Inst. Pathology, Boston City Hosp., 1943-44; asso. pathologist Peter Bent Brigham Hosp., Boston, 1944-47; pathologist in chief Cleve. Met. Gen. Hosp., 1947-50, dir. pathology, 1950-60; sr. cons. Crile VA Hosp., Cleve., 1947-60; asst. pathology Yale, 1938-39; instr. pathology Boston U., 1940-41; asst. prof. pathology Tufts Coll. Med. Sch., 1943-44; instr. pathology Harvard Med. Sch., 1944-47; asso. prof. pathology Western Res. U. Med. Sch., 1947-50, prof. pathology, 1950-60; prof. chmn. dept. pathology Duke Med. Center, dean 1960-75; med. and allied health edn., 1969-74, asso. provost Duke U., 1973-74; cons. Armed Forces Inst. Pathology, Washington, 1960-77, mem. sci. adv. bd. cons., 1964-77. Mem. pathology study sect. USPHS, 1956-63, chmn., 1959-62; mem. council Inst. Gen. Med. Scis., 1963-66; prin. cons. pathology Nat. Inst. Gen. Med. Scis., 1967-77, chmn. automation med. lab. scis. rev. com., 1969; mem. sci. adv. bd. Armed Forces Inst. Pathology; adv. council pathology Allied Scis. Service Am.; mem. spl. med. adv. group VA, 1966-71; com. div. med. scis. Nat. Acad. of Sci., NRC. Bd. dirs. Univs. Asso. for Research and Edn. in Pathology, 1966-77, pres., 1971-74; trustee Cleve. Center Alcoholism, Cleve. Health Mus., Cleve. Zoo, Cleve. Med. Library Assn., Cuyahoga unit Am. Cancer Soc.; v.p., trustee Cleve. Chamber Music Soc. Fellow A.A.A.S., Coll. Am. Pathologists; mem. Cleve. Acad. Medicine (pres. 1957-58, trustee), Cleve. Area Heart Soc. (trustee), Council Internat. Acad. Pathology, Soc. Exptl. Biology and Medicine (council 1955-56), Am. Assn. Pathologists and Bacteriologists (pres. 1965-66), Am. Soc. Exptl. Pathology (pres. 1972, mem. council 1964-77), Ohio Med. Assn., A.M.A., Am. Soc. Clin. Nutrition, Inter-soc. Com. Research in Pathology (sec.-treas. 1962-77), Inter-soc. Com. Pathology Information (sec.-treas. 1964-65, 73-77), Mass. Med. Soc., Soc. Exptl. Pathologists and Bacteriologists, N.C. Soc. Pathologists, So. Med. Soc., Am. Soc. Cell Biology, Am. Soc. Clin. Nutrition, Tissue Culture Assn., Am. Assn. Cancer Research, Am. Heart Soc., Diabetes Assn., Assn. Am. Med. Colls. (exec. council 1968-71, trustee), Council Acad. Socs. (pres. 1972-73, chmn. liaison com. med. edn. 1971-74), Greater Cleve. (trustee), Inter-soc. Cytology Council, Am. Soc. Human Genetics, Soc. Geog. Pathology, Sigma Xi, Nu Sigma Nu, Theta Delta Chi, Alpha Omega Alpha. Editor: Laboratory Investigation, 1952-66, Am. Jour. Pathology, 1967-77. Home: Durham, N.C. Died June 12, 1977.

KINSEY, VICTOR EVERETT, ophthalmic chemist; b. Pitts., Aug. 4, 1909; s. William L. and Grace (Everett) K.; student Carnegie Inst. Tech., 1927-28; B.A., U. Pitts., 1931, Ph.D., 1935; m. Irene Mackey, Aug. 22, 1935. Research asso. Grad. Sch. Medicine U. Pa., 1935-36; biochemist Sharp and Dohme Biol. labs., 1936-38; research asso. Med. Sch. U. Pitts., 1938-40; research asso. Howe Lab., Harvard Med. Sch., 1940-43, instr., 1944-46, asst. prof., 1946-50; asst. dir. research Kresge Eye Inst., Detroit, 1950-68; prof. ophthalmic chemistry Wayne State U. Med. Sch., 1950-78; prof., dir. Inst. Biol. Scis., Oakland U., Rochester, Mich., 1968-75, dir. emeritus, 1975-78. Mem. research exec. council Nat. Soc. Prevention Blindness; mem. com. ophthalmology and radiation cataracts Nat. Acad. Scis., NRC, 1951-78. Dir. Nat. Found. for Eye Research; mem. sci. adv. com. Nat. Council to Combat Blindness, Inc.; mem. nat. adv. neurol. diseases and blindness council USPHS, 1962-66, nat. adv. eye inst. council, 1967-68, mem. bd. sci. counsellors, 1971, chmn. eye inst., 1972; exec. editor Exptl. Eye Research, 1961-78. Dir. Detroit Opera Theatre, Inc. Co-recipient of the Warren Triennial award Mass. Gen. Hosp., 1943; recipient Proctor award, 1952, Lasker award, 1956; Modern medicine Distinguished award, 1959; Commemorative Issue Investigative Ophthalmology, 1976; award Internat. Soc. Eye Research, 1978. Mem. Fedn. Am. Socs. Exptl. Biology, Assn. Research Ophthalmology (trustee, chmn. 1960), New Eng. (hon.) Detroit (hon.) ophthalmology socs., Am. Chem. Soc., Am. Soc. Biol. Chemists, Sigma Xi. Club: Torch (dir.) (Detroit). Author numerous papers on ocular physiology and biochemistry. Home: Troy, Mich. Died July 23, 1978; buried Grosse Pointe Farms, Mich.

KINSOLVING, ARTHUR LEE, clergyman; b. Huntington, L.I., N.Y., Aug. 24, 1899; s. Arthur Barksdale and Sally Archer (Bruce) K.; B.A., U. Va., 1920; Rhodes scholar from Va., Christ Ch., Oxford U., 1920-23, B.A., 1923, M.A., 1925; B.D., Va. Theol. Sem., 1924; D.D., Amherst Coll., 1931, U. Vt., 1937, Boston U., 1939; Princeton, 1945; L.H.D., Rollins Coll., 1938; m. Mary Kemp Blagden, Sept. 4, 1937. Ordained deacon Episcopal Ch., 1923, priest, 1924; rector Grace Ch., Amherst, Mass., 1924-30, Trinity Ch., Boston, 1930-40, Trinity Ch., Princeton, N.J., 1940-47, St. James Ch., N.Y.C., 1947-69; dean Convocation of Manhattan, from 1959. Mem., dept. evangelism Nat. Council Chs.; pres. Protestant Council City N.Y., 1962-65; v.p. N.Y. P.E. City Mission; chmn. Nat. Commn. on Coll. Work; former chmn. U. Christian Mission Trustee Cathedral St. John the Divine, Chapin Sch. Mem. Phi Beta Kappa, Delta Kappa Epsilon. Mason. Clubs: Century Assn., Hay Harbor, Fisher Island Yacht. Home: Baltimore, Md. Died Mar. 28, 1977.

KINTNER, ROBERT EDMONDS, government ofcl.; b. Stroudsburg, Pa., Sept. 12, 1909; B.A., Swarthmore Coll., 1931; m. Jean Rodney, Mar. 9, 1940; children—Susan, Michael, Jeffry. Reporter, New York Herald Tribune, N.Y. City, 1933-35; Washington bureau, N.Y. Herald Tribune, 1933-37; partner in Joseph Alsop and Robert Kintner, Washington columnists, 1937-41; pres. Am. Broadcasting Co., Inc., 1950; executive v.p. National Broadcasting Co., 1957-58, pres., 1958-66, chmn., 1966; special assistant to the President U.S., 1966-67. Served as lt. col., U.S. Army; executive, War Dept. Bureau of Public Relations, Washington. Recipient Keynote award Nat. Assn. Radio and TV Broadcasters. Author: (with Joseph Alsop) Washington White Paper; Men Around the President. Home: Washington, D.C. Died Dec. 22, 1980.

KIPNIS, ALEXANDER, Russian basso; b. Zhitomir, Ukraine, Russia, Feb. 1, 1891; naturalized, 1934; grad. Warsaw Conservatory as condr., 1912; studied voice, Berlin, Germany 1912-15; m. Mildred Levy, Apr. 7, 1925; 1 son, Igor. Debut, Hamburg, 1915-17, Wiesbaden Opera, 1917-22, Berlin Staedtische Opera, 1922-30, Berlin State Opera, 1932-35; first U.S. appearance, Manhattan Opera House, N.Y., 1923; concert appearances, Buenos Aires, Paris, London, Milan, Germany, Scandinavia, Australia, including Bayreuth Festival, 1927-33, 33, Salzburg Festival, 1937, Chgo. Civic Opera, 1923-32, Australia, 1938, New Zealand; recitals throughout U.S., 1938-48; mem. Met. Opera, 1939-46. Extensive recordings include vocal compositions from Mozart to present day composers, opera, including Wagnerian basso roles, Hugo Wolf and Schubert Lieder; also 2 vols. Brahms records, Russian operatic arias, and Boris Godounoff. Mem. Juilliard Sch. Music. Mem. Am. Acad. Singing Tchrs. Address: Westport, Conn. Died May 14, 1978; interred Westport, Conn.

KIRK, RONALD T. (RAHSAAN ROLAND KIRK), musician, music publishing exec.; b. Columbus, Ohio, Aug. 7, 1937; s. Theodore and Gertrude (Broaddus) K.; ed. Columbus Sch. for Blind; m. Edith Hasking, Feb. 6, 1962; 1 son, Rory. Performer tenor sax, manzello, flute, U.S., Europe, Japan, 1949-77; leader Roland Kirk Quartet, 1954-77; writer Broadcast Music, Inc., 1962-77; pres. Rokir Music Corp., N.Y.C., 1964-77. Recipient 1st place award Downbeat Mag., 1962, 63, 64, 65, Melody Maker Mag., 1963, 64, 66; named Musician of Yr., Melody Maker, 1964, 66, World New Star in German Jazz Poll, 1964, 65. Mem. Am. Fedn. Musicians. Composer: You Dig It, 1961; Three in One Without the Oil, 1962; Reeds and Deeds, Lonesome August Child, 1963; April Morning, Abstract Improvisations, Gifts and Messages, Hipchops, 1964; Ruined Castles, Serenade to a Cuckoo, Mystical Dream, 1965; RipRig and Panic; For Bechet, Byas and Fats; Hippery Slippery, Flippery; Jurez; Shakey Money; Nothin' But the Truth, 1966. Address: New York, N.Y. Died Dec. 5, 1977; interred Columbus, Ohio.

KIRK, WILFRED BERNARD, banker; b. Narrowsburg, N.Y., Oct. 12, 1913; s. James H. and Laura (Gebhart) K.; grad. Notre Dame U., 1937, Harvard Bus. Sch., 1948; postgrad. Columbia, 1937-38; m. Eleanor Schnell, Apr. 17, 1939; children—Peter W., James P., Mark, Anne, Camille. With First Nat. City Bank, N.Y.C., 1937-52; adminstrv. v.p. Emigrant Savs. Bank, N.Y.C., 1952-54; sr. v.p., mgr. nat. accounts Tex. Bank & Trust Co., Dallas, 1954-77. Trustee Catholic Charity Found. Mem. N.Y. State Savs. Bank Assn. (past chmn. commerce financial pub. relations), Master Knights Sovereign Mil. Order Malta, East Side C. of C. (past chmn. Bowery improvement com.). Home: Dallas, Tex. Died Feb. 27, 1977.

KIRKPATRICK, DONALD, legal counsel, business exec.; b. Oakland, Calif., Dec. 29, 1884; s. James Henry and Mary Adel (Johnstone) K.; A.B., Ohio State U., 1910, LL.B., 1912; m. Anna Bertha Adams, Jan. 1, 1916; children—Donald, Mary Phyllis, Price Adams, Rosamond Rogers. Admitted to Ohio bar, 1912, gen. practice of law, Springfield, O., 1912-22; prosecuting atty., Clark County. O., 1922; dir. legal dept., Ill. Agrl. Assn. and affiliated cos., Chicago, Ill., 1923-50; gen. counsel Am. Farm Bur. Fedn., Ill. Agrl. Assn., Country Life Ins. Co., County Life Casualty Co., County Life Fire Co., Ill. Farm Supply Co. since 1931. Republican. Mem. Methodist Ch. Has organized, developed, operated gen. farm orgns., mutual ins. cos. for farm people and farmer cooperative assns. Home: Evanston, IL. *

KIRKPATRICK, WILLIAM HUNTINGTON, judge; b. Easton, Pa., Oct. 2, 1885; s. of Hon. William S. (former atty. gen. of Pa.) and Elizabeth H. (Jones) K.; A.B., Lafayette Coll., 1905, LL.D., 1944; student law dept., U. of Pa., 1905-06, LL.M., 1937; m. Mary Stewart Wells, May 17, 1913; children—William S., Miles. Admitted to Pa. bar. 1908; mem. 67th Congress (1921-23). 26th Pa. Dist.; U.S. dist. judge for Eastern District of Pa., 1927-58, sr. dist. judge, 1958—. Trustee Lafayette Coll. Lt. col. Judge Adv. Gen's Dept., and mem. Bd. of Review of Courts Martial. World War. Republican. Presbyn. Home: Harwood, Md *

KIRKS, ROWLAND FALCONER, govt. ofcl.; b. Washington, Nov. 15, 1914; s. Allie Harrison and Ella Davidson (Falconer) K.; A.B., Va. Mil. Inst., 1935; LL.B., Nat. U., 1939, M.P.L., S.J.D., 1940, LL.D., 1951;

grad. Indsl. Coll. Armed Forces, 1961, Command and Gen. Staff Coll., 1953, 63; LL.D., St. John's U., 1974; m. Virginia Louise Potter, June 15, 1940; children—Virginia Louise, Rowland Falconer II. Admitted to D.C. bar, 1939, practiced in Washington, 1939-40, 46-48; asst. prof. law Nat. U., Washington, 1940-41, prof., 1948-49, dean law sch., 1949-53, prof., 1949-54, pres. univ., 1953-54; legis. counsel Nat. Automobile Dealers Assn., Washington, 1954-60; gen. counsel Am. Textile Mfrs. Inst., Washington, 1960-70; apptd. by Supreme Ct. dir. adminstrv. office U.S. Cts., Washington, 1970-77; apptd. by Pres. Truman asst. atty. gen. U.S., dir. Office Alien Property, 1952. Past chmn., life mem. adv. bd. Salvation Army, Washington. Comdg. gen. 97th U.S. Army Res. Command, 1967-70. Mem. Bd. Edn. Washington, 1953-62. Served from lt. to lt. col. AUS, 1941-46; ETO. Mem. Am. Bar Assn., Bar Assn. D.C., Barristers, Kappa Alpha Order (past province comdr.). Presbyn. (trustee, elder). Kiwanian. Clubs: University, Lawyers, Vinson, Metropolitan. Home: Washington, D.C. Died Nov. 2, 1977; interred Arlington Nat. Cemetery (Va.).

KIRSCH, ROBERT, author, critic; b. Coney Island, N.Y., Oct. 18, 1922; s. Abraham and Pauline (Alterwein) K.; B.A., U. Calif. at Los Angeles, 1949, M.A., 1951, C.Phil., 1970; Litt.D., U. Redlands, 1970; m. Nancy Harris; children—Paul, Eric, Jonathan, Marya. Reporter, Sun Star, Merced, Calif., 1940, U.P., 1946; reporter, feature writer Hollywood (Calif.) Citizen-News, 1947-52; lit. editor, book columnist Los Angeles Times, 1952-80; lectr. journalism U. Calif. at Los Angeles, 1953, 59-60, 61-72; vis. prof. Calif. State U., Northridge, 1976-77, U. Iowa Writing Program, 1979-80. Served with USNR, 1941-45. Mem. Phi Beta Kappa, Sigma Delta Chi, Kappa Tau Alpha. Democrat. Jewish religion. Author: Do Not Go Gentle, 1958; In the Wrong Rain, 1959; Madeleine Austrian, 1960; The Wars of Pardon, 1965; (pseud. Robert Dundee) The Restless Lovers, 1960, Pandora's Box, 1961, Inferno, 1962; (pseud. Robert Bancroft) The Castilian Rose, 1961; Knight of the Scimitar, 1965; West of the West: Witness to the California Experience (with William F. Murphy), 1968; Lives, Works and Transformations: 25 Years of Essays and Reviews, 1978. Editor: Night of the Aurochs (Dalton Trumbo), 1979; Casino, A Novel of Las Vegas, 1979. Home: Santa Barbara, Calif. Died Aug. 16, 1980.

KIRSTEN, FREDERICK K., research professor; born in Saxony, Germany, March 13, 1885, son of Albert and Marie (Muller) K.; came to U.S., 1903, naturalized, 1911; B.S., U. of Wash., 1909, E.E., 1914; m. Agatha Helen Frey, October 8, 1911; children—Dorothea Marie (Mrs. Herschel Charles Hardisty), Frederick Eugene. Began as electrician Stone & Webster Engring. Corp., 1909; designer Summer hydroelectric power station, 1911; chief designer White Salmon River power plant, Big Creek development, 1912; equipment engr., design of new bldg. group of Mass. Inst. Tech., 1914; asst. prof. elec. engring., U. of Wash., 1915-18; design special smelting transformer for Gray & Barash Co., 1917; chief engr. Nitrogen Products Co., Seattle, 1918-21; asso. prof. elec. engring., in charge development aeronautic courses, U. of Wash., 1921-24; prof., 1924-28, prof. aeronautical engring. since 1928; v.p. Kirsten-Boeing Engring. Co., 1921; cons. engr. Tacoma-Lake Cushman transmission lines, 1923; designer Kirsten-Boeing propeller for dirigible Shenandoah, 1924; research for Gen. Electric, summer 1928; designer Guggenheim Aeronautics Hall equipment, 1929; established research lab. for Elec. Products Co., Seattle, 1930; pres. Kirsten Lighting Corp., Seattle, 1932 (introduced Kirsten high tensity display lighting in U.S., Can., etc.); pres. Kirsten Research Corp. of Seattle (designed 1000 horse power wind tunnel for U. of Wash. 1934); pres. Kirsten Pipe Co.; consultant in mfr. fluorescent tubing. Mem. Am. Inst. Elec. Engrs., Am. Soc. Mech. Engrs., Inst. Aeronautical Science, Am. Soc. Professional Engrs., Research Soc. U. of Wash., Steuben Soc., Sigma Xi, Tau Beta Pi. Club: Lions. Contbr. to engring. jours.; holds approximately 75 patents. Home: Seattle, Wash. *

KIRWAN, MICHAEL JOSEPH (KÛR'WAN), congressman; b. Wilkes-Barre, Pa., Dec. 2, 1886; s. John and Mary (Duddy) K.; m. Alice Kane, Sept. 15, 1920; children—John Joseph, Michael Joseph, Mary Alice. Member Youngstown City Council, 1932-36; mem. 75th to 91 congresses, 19th Ohio District. Asst. Chmn. V.I. and Guam office of territories. Served with 64th Artillery, United States Army, with A.E.F., 1917-19. Mem. Am. Legion, Vets. of Fgn. Wars. Democrat. Home: Youngstown, O. *

KISKADDON, ANDREW HENRY (KIS-KAD'DUN), lawyer; b. Washington, Mo., April 15, 1884; s. James Caldwell and Matilda Mary (Gunn) K.; A.B., and LL.B., Mo. U., 1910; m. Annette Eilts, June 10, 1914; 1 dau., Annette Elizabeth (Mrs. John J. Seery III). Admitted to Mo. bar, May 1910; mem. firm Kiskaddon, Shackelford and Kiskaddon, St. Louis, 1910-11, Nolte & Kiskaddon, 1912-17; asst. pros. atty., St. Louis County, Mo. 1917-19, first asst., 1919; asst. atty. St. Louis Southwestern Ry. Co., 1920-22, asst. gen. solicitor, 1922-33, gen. solicitor, 1933-47, gen. counsel for trustee, 1936-47, ret.; corporation and commerce counsel since 1947. Mem. Am., Mo. and St. Louis bar assns., U. of Mo. Union, Assn. of Practitioners before the Interstate Commerce Commn., Mo. State Hist. Soc., Delta Sigma Rho. Mason (32 degree, Scottish Rite), Eastern Star. Clubs: Missouri Athletic (St. Louis). Address: Kirkwood, Mo. *

KITCHEL, ALLAN F., business exec.; b. East Liverpool, O., Dec. 28, 1885; s. Farrand Deforest and Flora (Porter) K.; student Andover Acad.; B.A., Yale, 1909; m. Helen Binney, July 6, 1909; children—Barbara, Happy, Allan F., Douglas Binney. Clerk, Binney & Smith Co., crayon mfrs., N.Y.C., 1909-11, chemist, 1911-16, sales manager, 1916-22, v.p., 1922-35, pres., 1935-56, chmn., 1956—; pres. and dir. Florindia Farms Corp. and Indian River Refrigeration Terminal Company, Fort Pierce, Florida, 1935—. Former member of the Veterans Home Commn. of Conn. Republican. Conglist. Clubs: Union League, Yale, Uptown (New York); Riverside Yacht (Riverside, Conn.); Portage Country (Akron, O.). Home: Old Greenwich, Conn. *

KITTRELL, FLEMMIE PANSY, home economist; b. Henderson, N.C., Dec. 25, 1904; d. James Lee and Alice (Mills) Kittrell; B.S., Hampton Inst., 1928; Ph.D., Cornell U., 1936; L.H.D., U. N.C., 1976. Dean students, dir. home econs. Bennett Coll., Greensboro, N.C., 1928-40; dean women, dir. div. home econs. Hampton Inst., 1940-44; prof. home econs., head dept. Howard U., 1944-72, emeritus, 1972-80; vis. prof. Coll. Human Ecology Cornell U., 1974-75; Fulbright lectr. Baroda (India) U., 1950-51; mem. ICA mission to India, 1953-55. Condr. nutrition survey in Liberia, W. Africa for State Dept., 1947; nutrition of India Survey in edn. for FOA UNICEF, 1960; cons. home econs. program to Congo, 1961-62; mem. Airlift Team of Understanding to Bangladesh, 1972; del. Internat. Devel. Conf., Abidjan, Ivory Coast, 1974; participant UNICEF tour of Upper Volta, African drought land, 1974; vis. fellow Coll. Human Ecology, Cornell U., 1974-75. Trustee, Freedom from Hunger Found., Inc., Sibly Hosp., Washington, Hampton Inst.; UN observer Conf. for New Horizons for Women of Africa, Morocco, 1971; AID observer to Zaire, 1972; mem. home econs. coll. council Cornell U. Recipient Liberian award, Alumni award Hampton Inst., Internat. Club award Howard U., Meritorious award OPA, 1st Internat. award Century Club, 1965, Alumni award Coll. Home Econ. Cornell U. for contbn. to human devel. and quality environment, 1968, Centennial medal Hampton Inst., 1968. HEW postdoctoral research fellow Cornell U., 1975-76; Moton Center for Ind. Research fellow, Phila., 1976-77. Fulbright lectr. Indian univs., 1978. Fellow AAAS; mem. AAUW, NEA (life), Am. Dietetics Assn., Am. Home Econs. Assn. (life), Assn. Child Edn., Soc. Prodigal Son, Sigma Xi, Omicron Nu, Pi Lambda Theta, Phi Kappa Phi, Sigma Delta Epsilon, Beta Kappa Chi. Home: Gloucester, Va. Died Oct. 1, 1980; buried St. James Cemetery, Henderson, N.C.

KIZER, BENJAMIN HAMILTON, lawyer; b. Champaign County, O., Oct. 29, 1878; s. Benjamin Franklin and Mary Louise (Hamilton) K.; LL.B., U. Mich., 1902; LL.D., Linfield Coll., McMinville, Ore., Reed Coll., Portland, Ore.; m. Helen Bullis, May 19, 1915 (dec. Sept. 1919); m. 2d, Mabel Ashley, Mar. 12, 1921 (dec. Oct. 1955); 1 dau., Carolyn Ashley (Mrs. Stimson Bullitt. Admitted to Mich. bar, 1902, Wash. bar, 1902, U.S. Supreme Ct. bar, 1936; practice in Spokane, 1902—; spl. master U.S. Circuit Ct. Appeals, 9th Circuit, 1942-44; dir. China Office, UNRRA, 1944-46; Walker-Ames prof. internat. relations U. Wash., 1946-47, Pres. Spokane City Plan Commn., 1928-44; chmn. Wash. Planning Council, 1933-44; chmn. Pacific N.W. Regional Planning Commn.; former pres. Am. Soc. Planning Ofcls.; chmn. World Affairs Council of Inland Empire. Asso.; chmn. W. coast lumber commn. Nat. War Labor Bd.; Wash. chmn. Crusade for Freedom, 1950; chmn. Rhodes Scholars Exam. Com. for 6 Pacific N.W. States 1932-64. Bd. regents Reed Coll., Portland. Recipient Auspicious Star, Grand Cordon (China). Mem. Am., Wash. (past pres.), Spokane County (past pres.) bar assns., Phi Beta Kappa, Order of Coif, Author: The U.S. Canadian Northwest. Home: Spokane WA. *

KIZER, EDWIN DICKEN, college pres.; b. at San Diego, Cal., Dec. 3, 1882; s. C. Edwin and Nancy A. K.; B.Litt., Central Coll., Ind., 1905; Ph.D., Oskaloosa Coll., Ia., 1908; J.D., Western Coll. of Law, 1909; Litt.D., Potomac U., 1909; grad. student, U. of Cal., 1907; grad. Federate Sch. of Theology, 1907; unmarried. Ordained M.E. ministry, 1905; Pastor St. Paul's Ch., San Francisco, 1907-9; pres. and trustee Oskaloosa (Ia.) Coll. since July, 1909. Dir. Western U. Asso. Victoria Inst. Independent Republican. Author: Results of Belief, 1907. Address: Oskaloosa, Iowa*

KLARAGARD, SEVER (KLÄ'RÅ-GÅRD), coll. prof.; b. Austerjord, Norway, Jan. 14, 1884; s. Sivert Erikson Kalvatn and Johanne (Maaen) K.; A.B., St. Olaf Coll., 1917; Ph.D., U. of Il., 1922; unmarried. Came to U.S. 1902, naturalized 1914. Engaged in farm work, lumbering and logging until 1909; ednl. work, 1911-21; teacher economics, St. Olaf Coll., 1921, prof. since 1926. Pub. panel mem. 6th Regional Nat. War Labor Bd., 1943-44. Mem. Midwest Econ. Assn. (v.p. 1948-49), Am. Econ. Assn. Univ. Profs., Norwegian Am. Hist. Assn. Lutheran. Contbr. articles to jour. of marketing; author prize essay, Sons of Norway, 1917. Home: Northfield, Minn. *

KLASSEN, KARL PETER, educator, physician; b. Spat, Crimea, USSR, Oct. 25, 1908; s. Peter and Anna Maria (Warkentin) K.; B.S., Wheaton (Ill.) Coll., 1941; M.D., U. Chgo., 1936; m. Elvera Ann Hertz, May 28, 1938; children—Peter, Kristina Ann (Mrs. Edwin Owen). Intern, Billings Hosp., Chgo., 1927; fellow surg. research Ohio State U. Coll. Medicine, Columbus, Ohio, 1938, resident surgery, 1938-41, mem. faculty, from 1941, prof., dir. div. thoracic surgery, from 1960; chmn. thoracic surgery Children's Hosp., Columbus, from 1967. Trustee Center Sci. and Industry, Columbus; mem. pres.'s club Ohio State U. Chair of thoracic surgery established in his name, 1975. Diplomate Am. Bd. Surgery, Am. Bd. Thoracic Surgery. Fellow AMA., A.C.S., Am. Coll. Chest Physicians; mem. Internat., Columbus surg. socs., Central Ohio Heart Assn. (trustee, past pres.), Am. Assn. Thoracic Surgery, Soc. Thoracic Surgery, Central Surg., Assn., Alpha Omega Alpha, Sigma Xi. Contbr. articles to med. jours. Home: Columbus, Ohio. Deceased.

KLASSEN, PETER PIERRE, educator; b. Simferopol, Crimea, Russia, Oct. 17, 1904; s. Peter P. and Anna (Warkentin) K.; came to U.S., 1925, naturalized, 1941; B.A., Denison U., 1931; M.A., U. Chgo., 1938, Ph.d., 1949; m. Elsie May Woodward, Dec. 27, 1939; children—Peter Thomas, Ruth Ann (Mrs. George Jackson), Richard William. Instr. sociology Coll. of Ozarks, 1938-39; mem. faculty Pa. State U., 1939-41; social sci., analyst U.S. Govt., 1942-46; asst. prof. U. Fla., 1947-48; asst. prof. U. Ill., Chgo., 1948-51, asso. prof., 1951-54, prof., 1954-77, head dept. sociology and anthropology, 1964-68, dir. Office Demographic Studies, 1968-77; lectr. Sch. Financial Pub. Relations, Northwestern U., 1954-70; lectr. Sch. Bank Marketing, U. Colo., 1970-77; faculty Sch. Mortgage Banking Calif. Poly. U., Pomona; pvt. cons., 1960-77; profl. lectr. Mem. tech. staff Higher Edn. Commn. Ill., 1955-57; cons. Bd. Higher Edn. Ill., 1958-62. Fellow Am. Sociol. Assn.; mem. Am. Statis. Assn., A.A.A.S., Am. Population Assn., Chgo. Statis. Assn., Am. Assn. U. Profs. Club: American Commoner (Granville, O.). Author: (with D.C. Poole) Handbook of Foreign Nationalities, 1943; (with James McKenzie) Illinois Looks to the Future in Higher Education, 1957; also monographs. Home: Oak Park, Ill. Died Sept. 20, 1977.

KLAVAN, ISRAEL, clergyman; b. Zaskevitch, Lithuania, June 9, 1915; s. Joshua and Fannie (Sheifer) K.; came to U.S., 1924, naturalized, 1927; B.A., Yeshiva Coll., 1937; rabbi, Rabbi Isaac Elchanan Theol. Sem., 1940; student Bernard Revel Grad. Sch., Yeshiva U., 1938-40; D.D. (honoris causa), Yeshiva U., 1970; m. Sadie Rabinowitz, Feb. 22, 1942; children—Avram Macy, Judith Rachelle. Ordained rabbi, 1940; rabbi in Fitchburg, Mass., 1940-42, Williamsport, Pa., 1942-46, Mt. Vernon, N.Y., 1946-53; exec. v.p. Rabbinical council Am., 1953-80. Mem. commn. Jewish chapplaincy Nat. Jewish Welfare Bd. Recipient Bernard Revel Meml. award Yeshiva Coll. Alumni Assn., 1963; award Fedn. Jewish Philanthropies, 1967, Ann. Tzdakah award, 1974; Mordecai Ben David award Yeshiva U., 1974. Home: Forest Hills, N.Y. Died Mar. 7, 1980.

KLECZKA, JOHN C., congressman; b. Milwaukee, Wis., May 6, 1885; s. Michael and Agnes K.; A.B., Marquette U., 1905, A.M., 1906, LL.B., 1909; m. Wanda Lukomski, of Milwaukee, Oct. 18, 1911. Began practice at Milwaukee, 1909; mem. Wis. Senate, 1909-13; court commr. Circuit Court of Milwaukee Co., 1914-18; mem. 66th and 67th Congresses (1919-23), 4th Wis. Dist. Republican. Home: Milwaukee, Wis. *

KLEIN, ARTHUR JAY (KLIN), educator; b. Sturgis. Mich., Dec. 10, 1884; s. John G. and Eva J. (McCradit) K.; B.A., Wabash Coll., 1906, LL.D., 1932; B.D., magna cum laude, Union Theology Sem., 1909; M.A., Columbia, 1909, Ph.D., 1916; m. Marian Annis Smith, July 2, 1912. Instr. history, New York U., 1909-10, Coll. City of New York, 1910-15; head dept. of history and economics, Wheaton Coll., Norton, Mass., 1915-18; asst. dir. Service Bur., U.S. Com. on Pub. Information, Mar.-Oct. 1918; capt. A.G.D., in charge orgn. of War Dept. Pub. Information Services, at Washington, D.C., Oct. 1918-Jan. 1, 1919; asso. dir., Div. of Ednl. Extension, U.S. Bur. Edn., Jan.-June 1919; exec. sec. Nat. Univ. Extension Assn., 1919-20; executive of Research and Development Service, U.S. Army Education and Recreation Div., Camp Grant, Rockford, Ill., 1920-21; ednl. advisor U.S. Army Corr. Courses, on mil. subjects, 1921-24; lt. col. O.R.C., staff specialist on active duty in Edn. and Schools' Sect., Gen. Staff, U.S. Army, Sept. 1, 1924-Dec. 31, 1925; chief of Div. of Higher Edn., U.S. Bur. of Edn., 1926-30; dir. Survey of Land Grant Colls. and Univs. authorized by Congress; dir. survey of higher instns. Ore., and survey of pub. higher edn., Ark., U.S. Office of Edn.; mem. staff, survey of U. of Chicago, 1931-32; prof. of edn. Ohio State U., 1931-37, dean College of Edn. 1937-45, dean emeritus since 1945; asso. director Survey of Public Education in State of Wash., January-September 1946; specialist in higher edn. in surveys of edn. in W.Va.; 1945; Needs of Calif. in Higher Edn. (survey), 1947-48; Public Schs. of D.C., 1948; dir. survey O. Wesleyan Univ., 1947, U. of Wyo., 1947-48. Mem. Ohio Citizens Council (dir.). Fgn. Policy Assn. Phi Beta Kappa. Presbyterian. Author: Intolerance in the Reign of Elizabeth, Queen of England, 1916. Report on Survey of Rutgers University; dir. and editor Survey of Negro Colleges and Universities. Editor: Adventures in the Reconstruction of Education, 1941. Home: Worthington, O. *

KLEIN, WALTER CONRAD, clergyman; b. Bklyn., May 28, 1904; s. Louis William and Lillian (Sommer) K.; B.A., Lehigh U., 1924; B.D., Gen. Theol. Sem., 1929, S.T.M., 1932; S.T.D., 1933; Ph.D., Columbia, 1940; S.T.D., Seabury-Western Theol. Sem., 1957; D.C.L., Nashotah House, 1964; m. Helene M. Rosentreter, Apr. 24, 1935; children—Katherine Joanna, John Conrad. Asst., St. Mary the Virgin Ch., N.Y.C., 1930-33; curate Grace Episcopal Ch., Newark, 1934-35; vicar St. Paul's Ch., Morris Plains, N.J., 1935-37, St. Augustine's Chapel, Norristown, Pa., 1937-38; lectr. Phila. Div. Sch., 1937-38, chmn. grad. dept., 1938-42; rector St. Barnabas' Ch., Haddington, Phila., 1942-43; spl. preacher St. Mark's Episcopal Ch., Phila., 1946; Am. rep. on staff Anglican bishop of Jerusalem, 1946-50; canon residentiary St. George's Cathedral, Jerusalem, 1948-50; prof. O.T., Seabury-Western Theol. Sem., 1950-59, asst. dean, 1952-59; pres., dean Nashotah House, 1959-63, trustee, 1959-67; bishop coadjutor No. Ind., bishop, 1963-72. Served to lt. comdr., chaplain, USNR, 1943-46. Mem. Phi Beta Kapp. Author: The Elucidation of Islam's Foundation, 1940; Johann Conrad Beissel: Mystic and Martinet, 1942; Clothed With Salvation, 1953; The Psychological Pattern of Old Testament Prophecy, 1956; Jeremiah, 1963; The Dying Lord, 1963; A Priest Forever, 1964; also popular and sci. articles. Home: La Porte, Ind. Died Mar. 1, 1980; interred Crypt of St. James' Ch., Howe, Ind.

KLEIN, WILLIAM HENRY, pub. co. exec.; b. Chgo., Jan. 2, 1916; s. William M. and Elsie Claire (Nathanson) K.; A.B., U. Mich., 1937, J.D. with honors, 1940; m. Ruth Eleanor Goldman, Oct. 6, 1940; children—Lori (Mrs. Charles Andrew Adamek), Barbara Claire, William M. Admitted to Ill. bar, 1940; atty. Office of William E. Lane, Chgo., 1940-41; title examiner Chgo. Title & Trust Co., 1941-42; atty. OPA, Chgo., 1942-43; gen. counsel, asst. sec. Spiegel, Inc., 1943-52; v.p., gen. counsel Bishop Freeman Co., Evanston, Ill., 1952-61; atty. Office of Maurice Rosenfield, Chgo., 1961-62; v.p., sr. counsel Playboy Enterprises, Inc., Chgo., 1962-79. Republican precinct capt., Wilmette, Ill., 1950-60; chmn. Sch. Bd. Caucus, Wilmette, 1960. Mem. Am., Ill., Chgo. bar assns., Phi Epsilon Pi. Home: Wilmette, Ill. Died Dec. 21, 1979; buried St. Augustine's Ch., Wilmette, Ill.

KLEINMAN, ABRAHAM MORRIS, physician; b. N.Y.C., May 30, 1907; s. Sam and Sima (Reich) K.; B.S., Coll. City N.Y., 1926; M.D., U. Md., 1930; m. Lillian Doris Rabinowitz, June 24, 1934; children—Leonard I., Sylvia (Mrs. Bernard Grossfeld). Intern Beth David Hosp., N.Y.C., 1930-31; asst, pathologist Cumberland Hosp., Bklyn., 1932-46, asso. attending in medicine, 1939-46; dir. profl. services VA br. office 2, N.Y.C., 1946-48; chief med. service VA Hosp., S.I., N.Y., 1948-49; dir. profl. services VA Hosp. Bklyn., 1949-57; hosp. dir. VA Hosp., Bronx, N.Y., 1957-72, cons., 1972-78; clin. asso. prof. internal medicine N.Y. Downstate Med. Center, Bklyn., 1950-57; lectr. pub. health and administrv. medicine Columbia, 1961-73; prof. administrv. medicine Mt. Sinai Sch. Medicine, 1969-72, prof. emeritus, 1972-78. Pres. Kingsbridge Heights Jewish Center. Served from 1st lt. to maj., M.C., U.S. Army, 1942-46. Fellow A.C.P., N.Y. Acad. Medicine; mem. A.M.A., N.Y. Acad. Scis., Harvey Soc., Am. Fellowship of Israeli Med. Assn. Zionist Orgn. Am. Home: Bronx, N.Y. Died Aug. 22, 1978.

KLEINWAECHTER, LUDWIG PAUL VIKTOR (KLIN-VEK'-TER), Austrian govt. official; b. Czernowitz, Austria, Oct. 9, 1882; s. Dr. Friedrich K.; ed. Univ. of Czernowitz, Austria; LL.D., U. of Berlin, 1908; LL.D. (hon.) U. of Southern Calif., 1946; m. Anna Neschuetz, Dec. 14, 1921; children—Gunda, Ebba. Entered Austro-Hungarian foreign service, 1911; vice consul at New York, 1912; with Austro-Hungarian Embassy, 1915, Austro-Hungarian Ministry Fgn. Affairs, Vienna, 1917; sec. legation, Rome, 1920; consul gen. Republic of Austria, 1921-25 (Chicago); counsellor of legation, Austrian Legation, Washington, 1925-27; fgn. office, Vienna, 1927-29; Austrian consul gen., Ottawa, 1929-31; Fed. Press Bur. of Austrian Fgn. Office, Vienna, 1932-38; sent to Dachau, later Buchenwald concentration camps for anti-Nazi activities in 1938, released, 1939; reentered Fgn. Office, Vienna, 1945; acted as liaison officer between the Austrian govt. and U.S.; Austrian political rep. to U.S. with rank of envoy extraordinary and minister plenipotentiary, Jan. 1946 to Dec. 1946, Austrian minister to U.S. since Dec. 1946. Address: Washington. *

KLEYLE, HELEN MURRAY, univ. dean; b. Pitts., Jan. 26, 1912; d. Michael Joseph and Eleanor Clare (Connelly) Murray; B.S., Duquesne U., 1933, M.Ed., 1949; postgrad. Carnegie Inst. Tech., 1934; Ph.D., U. Pitts., 1958; m. Francis X. Kleyle, Sept. 1, 1936; children—Robert M., James F., Mary Margaret (Mrs. Patrick J. Kearney). Music tchr., group leader Settlement Houses, 1932-35; field worker pub. and pvt. social agys. in Allegheny County, 1936-38; lectr. St. Josephs Hosp. Sch. Nursing, 1948-52; instr. Coll. Liberal Arts and Scis., Duquesne U., Pitts., 1946-51, asst. prof., 1951-55, asso. prof., dir. student teaching, 1955-65, prof., dir. tchr. edn., 1965-69, prof., acting dean, 1967-69, dean Sch. Edn., 1969-80, exec. asst. to pres., 1975-80, acting acad. v.p., 1977. Mem. Pa. Gov.'s Authority on Tuition Reimbursement for Parents, 1971-80, various coms. Pa. Dept. Edn. Bd. dirs. St. Anthony Sch. for Exceptional Children, Frick Edn. Commn.; trustee Immaculata Coll., Marywood Coll., St. Fidelis Coll. Mem. Am. Assn. U. Profs., Am. Assn. U. Women, Assn. for Student Teaching (nat., regional and state divs.), Pitts. Doctoral Assn., Middle States Assn., Nat. Council for Accreditation Tchr. Edn., Adminstrv. Women in Edn., Kappa Delta Epsilon. Club: Zonta Internat. Home: Pittsburgh, Pa. Died Feb. 23, 1980; buried Calvary Cemetery, Pitts.

KLIMAS, JOHN EDWARD, educator; b. Ansonia, Conn., Mar. 10, 1927; s. John Edward and Ann (Zemaitus) K.; B.S., Fairfield U., 1953; M.S., Boston Coll., 1956; Ph.D. (USPHS fellow), Iowa State U., 1958; m. Antonia Comcowich, Aug. 7, 1954; children—John Anthony, Ann Christine, Rose Marie. Mem. faculty Fairfield (Conn.) U., 1958-68, 69-75, asso. prof. biology, 1961-67, prof., 1969-75; asst. program dir., NSF, Washington, 1968-69; cons. NSF, Interior Dept. Human Life Found., Tchr. mag., Ednl. Directions, Inc. Vice chmn. Conservation Commn. Fairfield, 1965-68. Served with USAAF, 1945-49. Mem. Nat. Assn. Biology Tchrs., Nat. Sci. Tchrs. Assn., A.A.A.S., Sigma Xi. Roman Catholic. Author: Wildflowers of Connecticut, 1968; Life-A Question of Survival, 1972; Wildflowers of Eastern America, 1974. Home: Fairfield, Conn. Died Oct. 28, 1975.

KLING, SAMUEL GROVER, lawyer, author; b. N.Y.C., Feb. 4, 1910; s. Morris and Mary (Schilling) K.; student Balt. City Coll., U. Balt. Law Sch.; m. Esther C. Beierfeld, June 26, 1936 (dec. 1953); m. 2d, Rena Levine, Jan. 1, 1964. Feature article writer Balt. Sunday Sun, 1929-31; admitted to Md. bar, 1933, Fed. bar, 1940; began practice in Balt., 1933; book reviewer N.Y. Herald Tribune, Harvard Law Rev., N.Y. Times, Sat. Rev. of Lit.; dir. radio program Crime Clinic, MBS, 1936-38; cons. U.S. Prison Industries Reorgn. Administrn., 1936; spl. writer Fed. Prison Bur., 1938; lectr. marriage and divorce, from 1940; nat. syndicated columnist Your Marriage, 1948-56; conductor daily radio program Your Marriage, MBS, 1949. Mem. Am., Md., Balt bar assns. Author: Your Legal Rights, 1945; The Marriage Reader, 1947; For Better, For Worse, 1947; Adventures in Love, 1948; The Art of Being Happy, 1948; Your Marriage Counselor, 1949; Handy Legal Adviser, 1949; The Marriage Guide, 1950; Your Legal Adviser, 1955; How to Win and Hold a Mate, 1957; Popular Legal Encyclopedia, 1957; The Legal Encyclopedia for Home and Business, 1959; The Complete Guide to Divorce, 1963; Complete Guide to Everyday Law, 1965; Sexual Behavior and the Law, 1965; Legal Encylclopedia and Dictionary, 1970; Your Will and What to do About It, 1971; contbr. legal articles Ency. Americana. Contbr. to nat. mags. Home: Baltimore, Md. Died Mar. 29, 1974.

KLINGBERG, FRANK JOSEPH, prof. history; b. Dillon, Kan., Feb. 25, 1883; s. William August and Hannah K.; A.B., U. of Kan., 1907, A.M., 1908, fellow in European history, 1907-08; graduate study, U. of Wis., 1909; A.M., Yale Univ., 1909, Bulkley fellow in history, 1908-11, Ph.D., 1911; LL.D., U. Cal. at Los Angeles, 1960; married Elizabeth Ammen Wysor, June 27, 1914; 1 son, Frank Wysor. Began in research work for census bur. and for Carnegie Endowment for Internat. Peace, 1911; prof. history, U. of Southern Calif., 1912-18; war work and lecturer for League to Enforce Peace, 1918-19; chmn. of history dept., U. of Calif., at Los Angeles; 1919-37, also prof. history since 1925. Lectured in summer sessions, Ohio State U., 1917, U. of Calif. (Berkeley), 1923, 27, 32, U. of Wash., 1929, U. of Pa., 1931. Spl. writer for Yale Univ. Press, 1921-22; research in archives of Great Britain, 1926; feature writer for the Los Angeles Times. Fellow Royal Historical Society (Great Britain); mem. several profl. assns. Episcopalian. Clubs: Lincoln (Los Angeles); Authors' (London). Author: The Carolina Correspondence of Dr. Francis Le Jan, 1706-1717, 1956; also the author of numerous works generally in sociological and historical fields; editor, co-editor, contbr. many books; regular contbr. several nat. mags. Feature writer Los Angeles Times, 1917-19, 1952—. Received citation from Knights of Columbus for distinguished service in British Humanitarianism. Home: Los Angeles, Calif. *

KLINGENSTEIN, JOSEPH, Investment banker; b. N.Y. City, June 4, 1891; s. Jacob and Clara (Buttenwieser) K.; A.B., Columbia, 1911; m. Esther Helen Adler, Nov. 14, 1922 (dec. 1974); children—John, Frederick A. With Hallgarten & Co., N.Y.C., 1911-20; mem. stock exchange firm Arthur E. Frank, 1920-27; with Wertheim & Co. from 1927, sr. partner 1950—; dir. Bond Stores, Inc., Continental Baking Co., Erlangen Corp., Gen. Realty & Utilities Corp., Abacus Fund. Gov. N.Y. Stock Exchange, 1938-44, 1947-55. Trustee, Mount Sinai Hosp., 1941-76, v.p. 1944-56, pres., 1956-62, chmn. emeritus at time of death. Home: New York, N.Y. Died Nov. 11, 1976.

KLOEB, FRANK LE BLOND, U.S. judge; b. Celina, Ohio, June 16, 1890; s. Charles A. and Emma (Le Blond) K.; student Ohio State U., 1908-09; law study Ohio State U., U. Wis., 1915-17; LL.D. (hon), U. Toledo; m. Florence Root, Sept 2, 1930; 1 dau., Carol Le Blond. Law practice, Celina, 1919; mem. Loree & Kloeb, 1921; pros. atty. Mercer County, Ohio, 1921-24; mem. 73d 74th and 75th Congresses, Ohio 4th Dist.; judge U.S. Dist Ct., No. Dist. Ohio, 1937-75, sr. dist. judge, 1964-75. Served as ensign U.S. Navy, World War 1. Mem. Am., Ohio, Lucas County, Toledo bar assns., Am Legion (post comdr.), Sigma Alpha Epsilon, Phi Delta Phi. Democrat. K.C. Home: Toledo OH. Died Mar. 11, 1976.

KLOEFFLER, ROYCE GERALD, educator, engineer, author; b. Armada, Mich., June 18, 1890; s. Galenus W. and Dora (Powell) K.; student Mich. State Coll., 1908-09; B.S., U. Mich., 1913; student Columbia, summer, 1927; M.S., M.I.T., 1930; m. Hazel Marguerite Davis, Oct. 14, 1915; children—Doris May (Mrs. William Braden), Gale Davis. Engring trainee Gen. Elec. Co., 1913-15; instr. elec. engring. U. Idaho, 1915-16; asst. prof. elec. engring. Kans. State U., 1916-22, asso. prof., 1922-25, prof., 1925-60, emeritus 1960-75, head dept. elec. engring., 1927-55; prof. M.I.T., summers 1933, 35; br. chief and engr. Nat. Security Agy., 1955-62. Fellow I.E.E.E.; mem. Am. Soc. Engring. Edn., Nat. Soc. Profl. Engrs., Sigma Xi, Phi Kappa Phi, Eta Kappa Nu, Sigma Tau. Author: Telephone Communication Systems, 1925; Direct Current Machinery (with Kerchner and Brenneman), 1934; Principles of Electronics, 1942; Industrial Electronics and Control, 1949; Basic Electronics (with Horrell), 1949; Electric Engeering Economics and Practice, 1952; Basic Theory in Electrical Engineering (with Sitz), 1955; Basic Electronics (with Hargrave), 1963; Electron Tubes, 1966; Americanism versus International Communism, 1967. Home: Clearwater, Fla. Died July 29, 1975; interred Armada, Mich.

KLUTTZ, JERRY, former news columnist; b. Clinton, Mo., May 27, 1907; s. Lawson Milo and Adelia (McKinney) K.; student Central Coll., Fayette, Mo., 1925-26, U. Mo., 1927-28; B.S., George Washington U., 1931; m. Electa Tassin, Mar. 19, 1935 (dec. 1971); children—Gerald Eugene, John Lawson, James Edward; m. 2d, Virginia W. Thatcher, Aug. 26, 1972. Reporter, Washington Herald, 1931, Washington Daily News, 1932-40; editor Fed. Diary column Washington Post, 1940-70; founder Fed. Employee Newsletter, 1948, editor, 1948-70; conducted radio news programs, 1934-46; dir. FEDCO, Inc., Los Angeles. Bd. dirs. Nat. Civil Service League. Recipient awards Washington Newspaper Guild, 1947, 53, Clapper-Edson award, 1949. Mem. Nat. Press Club, Fed. (pres.), White House corrs. assns., Internat. Platform Assn., Sigma Delta Chi, Sigma Chi. Club: Washington Golf and Country. Home: Arlington, Va. Died Dec. 22, 1976.

KLÜVER, HEINRICH, psychologist; b. Holstein, Germany, May 25, 1897; s. Wilhelm and Dorothea (Wübbers) K.; student U. Hamburg (Germany) and U. Berlin, 1920-23; Ph.D., Stanford, 1924; M.D. (hon.), U. Basel, 1965, U. Kiel, 1971; Ph.D. (hon.), U. Hamburg, 1969; m. Cessa Feyerabend, Feb. 4, 1927 (dec. 1967); m. 2d, Harriet E. Schwenk, Aug. 16, 1977. Came to U.S., 1923, naturalized, 1934. Instr. psychology U. Minn., 1924-26; Social Science Research Council fellow, 1926-28; research psychologist Behavior Research Fund, Chgo., 1928-33; asso. mem. Otho S.A. Sprague Meml. Inst., U. Chgo., 1933-38, mem. Inst., 1938-46, prof. exptl. psychology, div. biol. scis. at univ., 1938-57, Sewell L. Avery distinguished service prof. biol. psychology, 1957-62, emeritus, 1963-79. Mem. Armed Forces-NRC Com. on Vision, 1960-65; mem. program project com. Nat. Inst. Gen. Med. Scis., NIH, 1963-66; prin. investigator NIMH, 1963-72. Recipient Karl Spencer Lashley award neurobiology Am. Philos. Soc., 1960; Samuel W. Hamilton award Am. Psychopath. Assn., 1963; Gold medal award Am. Psychol. Found., 1965; Modern Medicine Distinguished Achievement award, 1969; Gold Medal award Eastern Psychiat. Research Assn., 1969. Mem. Nat. Acad. Scis., Am. Acad. Arts and Scis., Am. Psychol. Assn., AAAS (55 Year mem.), Am. Physiol. Soc., Am. Neurol. Assn. (hon.), Soc. Exptl. Psychologists, Midwestern Psychol. Assn., Neuroscis. Research Program at M.I.T., Chgo. Psychol. Club, Optical Soc. Am., Soc. Biol. Psychiatry (hon.), Am. Soc. Human Genetics, N.Y. Acad. Sci., Assn. Research Nervous and Mental Disease, Am. Philos. Soc., Am.

Soc. for Cybernetics, Internat. Brain Research Orgn. (hon.), Royal Soc. Medicine, Pavlovian Soc. N. Am., Am. Acad. Neurology, Internat. Primatol. Soc., Am. Coll. Neuropsychopharmacology (hon.), Soc. Exptl. Biology and Medicine, Inst. Medicine Chgo., Psychonomic Soc., Eastern Psychiat. Research Assn., Animal Behavior Soc. Am., Pan Am. Med. Assn. (life mem. sect. neurology). Club: Quadrangle (Chgo.). Author: An Experimental Study of the Eidetic Type, 1926; Mescal, 1928; Behavior Mechanisms in Monkeys, 1933; Mescal and Mechanisms of Hallucinations, 1966. Asso. editor Jour. Psychology, from 1935, Jour. Comparative Physiol. Psychology, 1947-50, Exptl. Neurology, 1959-70, Psychopharmacologia, 1959-68, Jour. Genetic Psychology, Biol. Psychiatry, Internat. Jour. Neurosci., Perspectives in Biology and Medicine, Genetic Psychology Monographs, from 1960, Neuropsychologia, others. Discovered Klüver-Bucy Syndrome; developed Klüver-Barrera technique for staining nervous system tissue; devised method of equivalent and non-equivalent stimuli for analysis of behavior; discovered free porphyrins in central nervous system; researched role of brain in vision. Contbr. articles to sci. jours. Home: Chicago, Ill. Died Feb. 8, 1979; buried Bellefontaine Cemetery, St. Louis.

KNAPP, GEORGE C., savs. and loan exec.; b. Salt Lake City, 1895. Chmn. bd., pres. Honolulu Savs. & Loan Co. Home: Honolulu, Hawaii. Died May 1979.

KNAPP, WILFRID MCNAUGHT, railway exec.; b. Atlanta, Ga., Oct. 3, 1883; s. Reginald Herbert and Euphemia (McNaught) K.; ed. pub. schs. of Atlanta, Ga.; m. Isabel Stevens, Aug. 19, 1925; 1 son, Wilfrid McNaught. Vice president Central of Georgia Ry., Savannah, Ga. since 1945. Dir. Fruit Growers Express Co., Washington, D.C. since 1942. Democrat. Protestant Episcopalian. Clubs: Oglethorpe, Savannah Golf. Home: Savannah, Ga. *

KNAUSS, FRANCIS J(ACOB), justice; born Chicago, Aug. 30, 1884; s. Jacob H. and Dora (Gerbing) K.; LL.B., U. Colo., 1905; m. Emma M. Gurr, Dec. 22, 1908; 1 dau., Dorothy (Mrs. Frederick L. Reid). Admitted to Colo. bar, 1905; law practice, Denver, 1905-46; judge Denver Dist. Ct., 1946-51; justice Colo. Supreme Ct., 1951-61. Mem. Denver Bd. Adjustment and Zoning, 1943-46; senator Denver dist. Colo. State Senate, 1915-31. Dir. Salt Lake City Unit Shriners Hosp. Crippled Children. Mem. Am., Denver, Colo. bar assns., Sigma Phi Epsilon, Phi Alpha Delta, Order of Coif (hon.) Elk, Mason (past grand master). Clubs: Denver Athletic, Lions. Home: Denver, Colo. *

KNEELAND, ROBERT SHEPHERD, lawyer; b. Northampton, Mass., Apr. 26, 1883; s. Frederick Newton and Adelaide F. (Dyer) K.; B.A., Amherst Coll., 1905; LL.B., Harvard, 1908; m. Annie Peters, Oct. 4, 1911 (deceased June 14, 1964); m. second, Madeleine E. Aldrich, August 1965. Admitted to the Massachusetts bar, 1908, practiced in Northampton, 1908-09, Springfield, 1911—; pres. Holden Patent Book Cover Co. to 1959; dir. Buxton, Inc.; hon. dir. Third Nat. Bank of Hampden County. Member Longmeadow Park Bd., 1931-39. Director Richard Salter Storrs Library. Member Phi Beta Kappa, Beta Theta Pi. Conglist. Club: University (Springfield). Home: Longmeadow, Mass. *

KNEUBUHL, EMILY (NU'BUL), civic work; b. Burlington, Ia., Aug. 16, 1883; d. Benjamin and Emma C. (Kupper) Kneubuhl; grad. Teachers' Coll., Winona, Minn., 1902, U. of Minn., 1923; M.A., Syracuse, 1927; unmarried. Prin. Minneapolis elementary schs., 1908-17; organizer war camp community service, 1917-20; dir. polit. edn. Minn. League Women Voters, 1920-23; directed successful campaigns for city mgr. govts., Cincinnati, 1924, Rochester, N.Y., 1925; mem. Faculty Sch. Citizenship and Pub. Affairs, Syracuse, 1926-27; exec. sec. Nat. Fed. Business and Professional Women's Clubs, Inc., 1927-35; in charge ednl. program Rural Electrification Administrn., 1935-37; pub. relations counsellor. Minneapolis, since 1938; mem. White House Conf. on How Women May Share in Post War Policy Making (chmn. Minneapolis conf.), 1944-46; mem. Mayor's adv. com. for revision Minneapolis city charter; sec. Sch. Interest Com.; sec. Minn. Women's Action Com. for Lasting Peace; mem. planning com. U. of Minn. Alumnae Inst. on Edn., 1942-46. Member League of Women Voters, Am. Assn. Univ. Women; hon. mem. Alumnae Assn. of U. of Minn. N.Y. League of Bus. and Professional Womens Clubs. Home: Minneapolis, Minn. *

KNIGHT, CHARLES STRONGMAN, agronomist; b. Mineral Point, Wis., July 11, 1885; s. John and Amelia E. (Coad) K.; B.S. Agr., U. of Wis., 1907; m. Virginia C. Kemler, of Platteville, Wis., Sept. 8, 1908; children—Charles Stuart, Virginia, Douglas Kemler. Asst. in feed and fertilizer inspection, U. of Wis., 1907-08; asst. in agronomy, Kansas State Agrl. Coll., 1908-09; instr. agronomy, U. of Nev., 1910-12; chief agriculturist, Nev. Sugar Co., 1912-13; prof. agronomy since 1913, dir. agrl. extension, 1914-15, dean Coll. of Agr., 1914-20, U. of Nev. Pres. and mng. dir. Reno Chamber of Commerce, 1920; dir. industrial dept. Calif. Development Assn., since 1923. Mem. Sigma Nu. Club: Commercial. Author bulls. on agrl. topics. Home: Berkeley. *

KNIGHT, EUGENE HERBERT, architect; b. Jacksonville, Fla., Nov. 30, 1884; s. Albion Williamson and Anna (Bishop) K.; student Atelier Hornbostel, Soc. Beaux Arts Architects, N.Y.C.; m. Nellie Rae Reeder, July 10, 1907; children—Marguerite Naomi, Louise Alberta, Albion Williamson; m. 2d, Elizabeth Jane Ward, July 7, 1957. With Harry B. Wheelock, 1902, Clinton & Russell, 1910, later York & Sawyer, William C. Weston; architect Eugene H. Knight, 1914-16, Warren & Knight, 1916-21, Warren, Knight & Davis since 1921. Fellow A.I.A. (Past sec., pres. Ala. chpt., chmn. Ala. centennial com. 1957); mem. Birmingham C. of C., Soc. Colonial Wars, Nat., Ala. assns. registered architects, Nat. Inst. Archtl. Edn., Birmingham Art Assn., Y.M.C.A., 365 Crippled Childrens Clinic Club. Awarded gold medal and hon. mention. So. Archtl. Exhbn., 1929; hon. mention, Gulf State regional exhbn., Am. Inst. of Architects, 1954. Presbyterian (elder). Mason. Clubs: Mountain Brook, Engineers, The Club (Birmingham). Home: Birmingham. *

KNIGHT, RALPH T(HOMAS), physician; b. Minneapolis, June 20, 1886; s. Charles Wisner and Alma Phoebe (Roberts) K.; B.A., U. of Minn., 1908, M.D., 1912; m. Clara Hill, June 4, 1918; children—Barbara (Mrs. Gordon R. Coffin), James Wisner, Thomas Hill. Dir. hygiene, Lincoln (Neb.) pub. schs.; instr. anatomy, U. Neb., 1913-15; gen. practice, asst. to surgeon, Mpls., 1915-17; surg. practice, Mpls., 1919-36; 1st asst. in anesthesia, Mayo Found., Rochester, Minn., 1936-37; dir. anesthesiol. Charles T. Miller Hosp., St. Paul, 1938-51, St. Mary's Hosp., 1945-50, Mpls. VA Hosp., 1945-54, Mpls. Gen. Hosp., 1928-54, Deaconess Hosp., Mpls., 1952-60; sr. mem. Doctors Knight and Baird Anesthesiol. Group, 1944-54, Anesthesia Associates, 1954—; profl. work devoted to anesthesiology, 1936—; instr., asst. professor surgery director division anesthesiology, University Minnesota, 1920-36, asso. professor, clin. prof., dir. div. anesthesiol., grad, sch. med., and U. Minn. hosps., 1936-54, prof. emeritus, 1954—. Served from lt. to maj. M.C., U.S. Army World War I; maj. to lt. col., Med. Res., U.S. Army, to 1933, col. M.C., AUS, 1933-53, ret. as col. 1953. Recipient St. Barnabas Hosp. award, 1958; Distinguished Service award, Am. Soc. Anesthesiol., 1960. Diplomate Am. Bd. Anesthesiology. Fellow A.C.S., Internat., Am. colls. anesthesiologists; mem. Am., Minn. med. assns., Am. (pres. 1953), Minn. (pres. 1948) socs. anesthesiologists, Internat. Anesthesia Research Society, Beta Theta Pi, Nu Sigma Nu. Republican. Presbyn. Kiwanian. Author: chapters in medical textbooks; articles med. jours. Home: Mpls. *

KNIGHT, THOMAS J., judge; b. Sharpsburg, Ky., Sept. 14, 1884; s. Thomas J., Sr., and Evelyn (Matthews) K.; grad. Sharpsburg Acad., 1902; LL.B., Jefferson Sch. Law, Louisville, 1912, LL.M., 1913; m. Elsie McLellan, Apr. 18, 1918; children—Thomas J., Eleanor M. Admitted to Ky. bar, 1912, practiced in Louisville, 1912-47; judge Ct. of Appeals of Ky. since 1947; prof. law Jefferson Law Sch., 1944-47. Mem. Ky. State Legislature, 1924-26. Served as 1st lt. F.A., U.S. Army, World War I. Mem. Am. Judicature Soc., Am., Ky. State, Louisville bar assns., Am. Legion. Democrat. Baptist, Mason. Author articles in legal jours. Home: Louisville. *

KNOPF, WILLIAM CLEVELAND, JR., univ. dean; b. Louisville, Dec. 13, 1910; s. William Cleveland and Anne (Flood) K.; B.S., Washington and Lee U., 1932; M.S., Vanderbilt U., 1941; Ph.D., Northwestern U., 1950; m. Mary Gene Herren, Jan. 18, 1941; children—Katherine Herren (Mrs. H. James Stadelman), Gene Miller. Asst. dean Northwestern U., 1945-51; asst. dir. research Internat. Minerals and Chem. Corp., Skokie, Ill., 1951-59; dir. research U.S. Industries Tech. Center, Pompano Beach, Fla., 1959-61; prof. elec. engring. U. Fla., 1961-63; prof. elec. engring. and ocean engring. U. Miami (Fla.), 1963-70, dean Sch. Engring., 1965-70; lectr., research asso. Ill. Inst. Tech., 1941-43; cons. to govt. and industry, 1945-70. Chmn. sci. and oceanography Dade County (Fla.) Com. 21, 1966-70; mem. Fla. Tech. Services Program, 1966-70, Fla. Articulation Com. Engring., 1965-70; chmn. oceanography Fla. Space Eta Study Task Force, 1962-63. Mem. A.A.A.S., I.E.E.E., Instrument Soc. Am. (chmn. marine sci. div. 1964-66), Am. Soc. Engring. Edn., Miami-Dade County C. of C., Sigma Xi, Tau Beta Pi, Eta Kappa Nu, Alpha Tau Omega. Rotarian. Club: Riviera Country. Contbr. profl. jours. Home: Coral Gables, Fla. Died Feb. 7, 1970.

KNORPP, WALTER WESLEY, pub., bank dir.; b. Chgo., May 19, 1891; s. John Walter and Eda Clara (Young) K.; grad. Phoenix High Sch., 1909; m. Anna Pearl Stauffer, Nov. 19, 1920; children—Betty Ann (dec.), Mary Jane (Mrs. Courtlandt Van Voorhis), Margaret Eda (Mrs Elbert Haven Neese). With Ariz. Republic successively as carrier, mailer and circulation mgr., 1905-09; circulation mgr. San Bernardino Free Press, 1909-10: advt. mgr. San Diego Tribune, 1910-17; asst. bus. mgr., then bus. mgr. Ariz. Republic, 1917-29; negotiated purchase Phoenix Gazette, 1930; gen. mgr., pub. Republic and Gazette, 1930-46; pres. Ariz. Pub. Co.; v.p., dir. Republic and Gazette Engraving Co.; organized Ariz. Broadcasting Co., radio network, 1930-46; dir. First Nat. Bank Ariz., 1956-65. Chmn. Phoenix Civilian Def. Com., 1941-44; mem. A.P., 1940-46, Instrumental in municipal, civic and polit. cleanup. Chmn. Phoenix U.S. Army Adv. com., 1948-50; civilian aide to sec. U.S. Army, 1950-64; Vice pres., dir. Ariz. State U. Found.; adv. bd. St. Lukes Hosp., Phoenix YMCA; hon. curator Heard Mus.; hon. trustee Good Samaritan Hosp.; bd. dirs. Neurol. Scis. Found.; past dir. Nat. Assn. Better Bus. Burs.; bd. advisers Indsl. Coll. Armed Forces. Served with U.S. Army, 1918-19; AEF. Recipient Outstanding Civilian medal U.S.A., 1964. Mem. Def. Orientation Conf. Assn., Am. Legion, English Speaking Union (past dir.), Navy League, Fraternal Order Police, Ariz. Newspaper Assn. Democrat. Methodist; Mason (Shriner), Kiwanian. Clubs: Hiram (past pres.), Executives (dir.), Phoenix Country, de Concho, Symphony, Fine Arts, Civic Opera (Phoenix); Arizona Automobile, Paradise Valley Country. Home: Phoenix, Ariz. Died Apr. 20, 1975.

KNORR, NATHAN HOMER, clergyman; b. Bethlehem, Pa., April 23, 1905; s. Donel Ellsworth and Estella (Bloss) K.; grad. Allentown (Pa.) High Sch., 1923; m. Jan. 31, 1953. Began with Watch Tower Bible and Tract Soc., Bklyn., 1923, gen. mgr. pub. office, 1932; dir. People's Pulpit Assn. (now Watchtower Bible and Tract Soc. N.Y., Inc.), 1934; v.p., dir. Watch Tower Bible and Tract Soc. Pa., 1940, pres., 1942-77. Pres. Internat. Bible Students Assn., London, 1942-77. Mem. Jehovah's Witnesses. Home: Brooklyn, N.Y. Died June 8, 1977; buried Wallkill, N.Y.

KNOWLES, JOHN HILTON, physician, found. adminstr.; b. Chgo., May 23, 1926; s. James and Jean Laurence (Turnbull) K.; A.B., Harvard, 1947; M.D. cum laude, Washington U., St. Louis, 1951, Sc.D. (hon.), 1970; LL.D., Northeastern U., 1969, Babson Coll., 1971, U. Pa., 1972, Suffolk U., 1975, Williams Coll., 1976; Sc.D., Hahnemann Med. Coll., 1971, Albany Med. Coll., 1972, Pratt Inst., 1973, Middlebury Coll., 1975, N.Y. Med. Coll., 1975; D.C.L. (hon.), Union Coll., 1970; D.H.L., Ithaca Coll., 1971, Boston U., 1972, Ohio Wesleyan U., 1973, Pace U., 1975, Rush U., 1975; m. Edith Morris LaCroix, June 13, 1953; children—Edith LaCroix, John Hilton, Charles Paine, James Turnbull, Jean Laurence, Robert Munroe. Intern medicine Mass. Gen. Hosp., 1951-52, asst. resident medicine, 1952-53, resident medicine, 1955-56, chief resident medicine, 1958-59, asst. medicine, chief pulmonary disease unit, 1959-61, asst. physician, dir. med. affairs, 1961-62, asso. physician, 1962-64, gen. dir., 1962-72, physician, 1964-72, also mem. bd. consultation, mem. corp.; teaching fellow medicine Harvard Med. Sch., 1952-53, asst. medicine, 1958-59, instr. medicine, 1959-60, asso. in medicine, 1960-63, lectr. medicine, 1963-72, prof. medicine, 1969-72; prof. medicine N.Y. U. Med. Center, 1972-79; USPHS postdoctoral fellow dept. physiology U. Rochester Med. Sch., also dept. physiology U. Buffalo, 1956-57; pres., trustee Rockefeller Found., N.Y.C., 1972-79. Dir. Gen. Tel. & Electronics Corp., Irving Trust Co., N.Y.C., Technicare, Charter N.Y. Corp. Trustee Duke U., Washington U., St. Louis, Boston U., Mus. Sci., Belmont Hill Sch.; bd. overseers Harvard U.; mem. corp. vis. com. Center for Internat. Studies, Mass. Inst. Tech., 1976-79. Served as lt. M.C., USNR, 1953-55. Fellow A.C.P., Am. Acad. Arts and Scis.; mem. Am. Pub. Health Assn., Assn. Am. Med. Colls., Am. Hosp. Assn., Soc. Med. Adminstrs., Am. Fedn. Clin. Research, Nat. Acad. Scis. Inst. Medicine, Council Fgn. Relations, Harvard Alumni Assn. (dir.), Boston Library Soc., Kappa Pi Eta, Alpha Omega Alpha. Clubs: Tavern, Tennis and Racquet, Harvard, Aesculapian, Somerset (Boston); Country (Brookline, Mass.); Myopia (Mass.) Hunt; Century Assn., Brook, Links (N.Y.C.). Author: Respiratory Physiology and its Clinical Application, 1959. Editor: Hospitals, Doctors and Public Interest, 1965; The Teaching Hospital, 1966; Views of Medical Education and Medical Care, 1967; Doing Better and Feeling Worse: Health in the United States, 1977; China Diary, 1977. Home: New York, N.Y. Died Mar. 6, 1979.

KNOX, CLINTON EVERETT, ambassador; b. New Bedford, Mass., May 5, 1908; s. William Jacob and Estella Jane (Briggs) K.; B.A., Williams Coll., 1930; M.A., Brown U., 1931; Ph.D., Harvard, 1939; m. Clementine Elizabeth Murphy, Nov. 24, 1934; children—William Everett, Karen Louise. Instr. history Morgan State Coll., Balt., 1931-43; with State Dept., 1945-80; dep. chief Western European sect., div. research, 1945-46, chief No. and Western European br., 1947-52, asst. chief div. research for Western Europe, 1952-55, chief div., 1955-57; 1st sec., consul Am. embassy, Paris, France, 1957-63; counselor, Tegucigalpa, Honduras, 1963-64; ambassador to Dahomey, Cotonou, 1964-69, Port-au-Prince, Haiti, 1969-73; lectr., writer on internat. relations, African and

Caribbean affairs, 1973-80. Served with AUS, 1943-45. Mem. Phi Beta Kappa. Home: Silver Spring, Md. Died Oct. 16, 1980; buried Rock Creek Cemetery, Washington, D.C.

KNOX, WILLIAM EDWARD, bus. exec.; b. Somerville, Mass., June 24, 1901; s. Willian H. and Elizabeth E. (Berry) K.; B.S. in E.E., U. N.H., 1921, D.Eng., 1954; Dr. Honoris Causa, U. Uruguay, 1946; m. Ella C. Griffin, June 10, 1927; 1 son, William Edward. Entered grad. student tng. course Westinghouse Electric & Mfg. Corp., East Pittsburgh, Pa., 1921; became sales clk. Westinghouse Electric Internat. Co., N.Y.C., 1922, salesman, 1925-32, asst. to gen mgr., 1932-36, asst. gen. mgr., 1937-44, v.p., 1944-46, pres., 1946-63, chmn., 1963-66; v.p. Westinghouse Electric Corp., 1959-65; vice chmn., dir. Techint Inc., N.Y.C. Decorated comdr. Order Al Merito (Chile), 1942; knight comdr. Order of Sun (Peru), 1947; officer Legion of Honor (France); Knight of Magistral Grace, Soverign Mil. Order of Malta, 1949; knight Order of St. Olav (Norway), 1947; comdr. Order Al Merito della Repubblica (Italy), 1954; comdr. Order of Isabel la Catolica (Spain), Order Sacred Treasure (Japan), 1956; Order Brilliant Star (Republic China), 1956; officer Order of Cruzeiro do Sul (Brazil), 1958, comdr. Order of Leopold (Belgium), 1962, comdr. Nat. Order Ivory Coast, 1962, comdr. Phillippine Legion Honor, 1963; recipient Westinghouse Order of Merit for Outstanding Accomplishments, 1940, Capt. Robert Dollar Meml. award, 1962. Mem. Regional Export Expansion Council, Far East-Am. Council of Commerce and Industry (vice chmn.), S.R. in State of N.Y., Pi Kappa Alpha. Republican. Clubs: Sky (gov.), Wall Street (N.Y.C.). Home: Jamesburg, N.J. Died Dec. 28, 1978.

KNOX, WILLIAM FRANCIS, ret. lawyer; b. Connellsville, Pa., Jan. 29, 1885; s. Alfred C. and Annie Ewing (Wilson) K.; A.B., Yale, 1907; LL.B., U. Pitts., 1910; m. Ruth Thoburn, June 29, 1916 (dec. Apr. 1950); children—William F. (dec.), James Thoburn; m. 2d, Margaret Thoburn, June 21, 1951 (dec. Sept. 1969). Admitted to Pa. bar, 1910; mem. firm, sr. partner Moorhead & Knox, Pitts., 1917-74. Vice pres., dir. Homewood Cemetery. Mem. Am., Pa., Allegheny County bar assns. Methodist. Clubs: Duquesne, Fox Chapel, Harvard-Yale-Princeton (Pitts). Home: Pittsburgh PA. *

KNUDSON, CHARLES ANTHONY, educator; b. Sheboygan, Wis., Nov. 23, 1903; s. Charles Anthony and Caroline (Hanson) K.; B.S. summa cum laude, Dartmouth Coll., 1924; A.M., Harvard, 1925, Ph.D., 1929; student Sorbonne, 1926-28; m. Donna D. Finger, Jan. 28, 1960. Instr. Romance langs. U. Buffalo, 1928-29; asst. prof. French, U. Mich., 1929-37, prof., 1937-40; prof., head dept. Romance langs. Hamilton Coll., 1940-46, dir. mil. programs, 1943-44; prof. French, U. Ill., 1946-72, prof. emeritus, 1972-76, head dept., 1954-65. Served with O.W.I., Gt. Britain, France, 1944-46, regional dir. S.W. France, 1945. Decorated Legion of Honor, 1951, Officer, 1959. Mem. MLA, Medieval Acad., Am. Assn. Tchrs. French, Assn. Internationale d'Etudes Francaises, Phi Beta Kappa, Delta Upsilon. Author: (with Louis Chapard) Introduction to French Pronunciation, 1934. Editor: (with Jean Misrahi) Jehan de Saintré, 1965. Contbr. articles French, Am., Canadian periodicals. Home: Urbana, Ill. Died Feb. 25, 1976.

KNUDSON, LEWIS, prof. plant physiology; b. Milwaukee, Wis., Oct. 15, 1884; s. John and Pauline Olivia (Portruid) K.; B.S.A., U. of Mo., 1908; Ph.D., Cornell, 1911; m. Carolyn Belle Ingels, Sept. 21, 1913; children—Louis Ingels, Giltner John. Began teaching at Cornell University, 1908, now prof. plant physiology and head of the Department of Botany. Invited to establish plant physiology in Spain; lecturer on the subject at Museo Nacional de Ciencias Naturales, Madrid, and at Barcelona, spring term, 1920 and 1921. Y.M.C.A. dir. entertainment and ednl. activities, Camp de Souge, France, Dec. 1917-Nov. 1918. Fellow A.A.A.S.; mem. Bot. Soc. America, Am. Soc. Naturalists, Orchid Society of Am. (honorary vice president), Real Sociedad Española de Historia Natural, Alpha Zeta, Gamma Alpha, Sigma Xi, Phi Kappa Phi. Researches in fermentation, enzyme production, organic nutrition of plants, germination of orchid seeds, symbiosis, wilt disease of banana, X-rays, chloroplasts, native plants as sources of rubber, etc. Home: Ithaca, N.Y. *

KOCH, ARNOLD THEODOR, lawyer; b. Bklyn., Mar. 30, 1900; s. Otto and Adele F. (Eschen) K.; A.B., Columbia, 1921, LL.B., 1923; m. Jean Von der Lancken, June 1, 1929 (dec. Apr. 1969); 1 son, Arnold Theodor; m. Marye-Stuart Gress, June 5, 1971. Admitted to N.Y. bar, 1924, Mass. bar, 1955; asso. firm Haight, Smith, Griffen & Deming, 1923-25; asso., trial counsel Roosevelt & O'Connor, 1925-32; asso., trial counsel O'Connor & Farber, 1932-37, mem. firm, 1937-50; trial counsel, mem. firm Myles, Wormser & Koch, 1950-60, Wormser, Koch, Kiely & Alessandroni, 1960-71; of counsel Wormser, Kiely, Alessandrani, & McCann, 1971-79; lectr. trial practice Practising Law Inst.; dir. Beneficial Corp. Past chmn. fair rents com., chmn. planning bd., Montclair; chmn. Montclair com. for revision N.J. constn.; mem. Montclair Housing Authority; past pres. Montclair Assn. Trustee Montclair Art Mus.; chmn. Columbia Coll. Fund, 1951. Served as cadet Coast Arty. Sch., Fortress Monroe, Va., 1918. Mem. Am. Bar Assn., Soc. Older Grads. Columbia, Delta Upsilon. Congregationalist. Author: Depositions and Discovery Under the Federal Rules, 1951. Home: Delray Beach, Fla. Died June 7, 1979; buried Delray Beach.

KOCH, JOHN, artist, painter; b. Toledo, Aug. 18, 1909; s. Edward John and Marion (O'Hara) K.; ed. pub. schs. and high sch., Ann Arbor, Mich.; m. Dora Zaslavsky, Dec. 23, 1935. Resident in Paris, 1929-33, N.Y.C., 1933—; entirely self-taught as artist; exhibt. Salon de Printemps (hon. mention) and Salon de Tuilleries, 1929, and in all leading exhbns. of Am. painting, from 1939; one-man shows include Valentine Gallery, N.Y.C., 1935, Kraushaar Gallery, N.Y.C., 1939, 41, 43, 46, 49, 51, 58, 61, 65, 69, 72, 74, Meml. Exhbn., 1980, Nelson Rockhill Found., Kansas City, Mo., 1940, Hudson Gallery, Detroit, 1941, Whyte Gallery, Washington, 1944, Art Alliance, Phila., 1945, Portraits, Inc., N.Y.C., Courie Galleries, Los Angeles, Provo, Utah, Suffolk Mus., Stonybrook, N.Y., Syracuse (N.Y.) Mus., 1951, Speed Mus., Louisville, 1971, Akron (Ohio) Inst. Arts, 1971, N.Y. Cultural Center, 1973, Picker Art Gallery, Colgate U., 1977, Pa. State U. Mus. Art, 1977; represented Met. Mus. Art, Bklyn. Mus. Art, Boston Inst. of Arts, William Rockhill Nelson Gallery, Kansas City, Mo., museums of Canajoharie, N.Y., Bennington, Vt., New Britain, Conn., Springfield, Mass., Newark, Parrish Mus., South Hamp- ton, N.Y., U. Ga. Recipient 1st hon. mention Carnegie Inst., 1943; hon. mention Audubon Artists, 1950; mus. purchases Omaha, Toledo Mus.; mus., Mus., 1954, 57; Des Moines Art Center purchase, 1954; Legion of Honor, San Francisco, 1952; Grumbacher award Audubon Artists, 1958; Ranger Fund purchase prize Nat. Acad., 1951, Altman prize, 1959, Gold Medal award, 1962; 1st award in oils and John J. McDonough M.D. award 27th Ann. Butler Inst.; Lotus Club award of merits, 1964; Artists Fellowship medal, 1964; Century Club medal, 1967; Sammuel Finley Breese Morse Medal in oil painting, 1968. Mem. NAD (academician), Allied Artists Am. (dir.), Nat. Inst. Arts and Letters. Club: Century Assn. (N.Y.C.). Home: New York, N.Y. Died April 20, 1978.

KOCH, RAYMOND JOSEPH, bus. exec.; b. Chgo., Apr. 19, 1892; s. Nicholas and Annie Virginia (Finkler) K.; B.S. in C.E., Armour Inst. Tech., 1913, C.E., 1918; LL.D., Ill. Inst. Tech., 1968; m. H. Virginia Felt, Apr. 30, 1918 (dec. Jan. 1955); children—Raymond Felt, Mary Elizabeth (Mrs. Alfred C. Schmidt), Virginia H. (Mrs. Allen C. Senear), Ruth A. (Mrs. Ronald L. Allen). Designer concrete structures bridge dept. C.M., St. P. & P. R.R., 1913-16; sales engr. Ilg Electric Ventilating Co., Chgo., 1917-20, credit mgr., 1920-29, asst. treas., 1925-29; treas., dir. Comptometer Corp. (formerly Felt and Tarrant Mfg. Co.), Chgo., 1930-34, pres., 1934-55, dir., 1934-61, chmn. bd., 1955-61; vice chmn. bd. Victor-Comptometer Corp., 1961-70, dir., 1961-74. Pres., Employers' Assn. Chgo., 1938-40, dir., 1938-58; dir. Ill. Mfrs. Assn., 1940-70, pres., 1947; industry panel mem., region 10, War Labor Bd., 1944-45. Trustee, Hadley Sch. for Blind, Winnetka, Ill.; trustee Ill. Inst. Tech., 1937-75, sec., 1948-75, also mem. exec. com.; trustee ITT Research Inst. Mem. Am. Ordnance Assn., Tau Beta Pi, Delta Tau Delta. Republican. Roman Catholic. Clubs: Executives, Union League (past treas., v.p.) (Chgo.); Indian Hill (Winnetka); Skokie Country (Glencoe, Ill.). Home: Winnetka, Ill. Died May 11, 1977.

KOCH SUMNER LEIBNITZ, surgeon; b. Cavalier, N.D., July 15, 1888; s. Leon S. and Sarah S. (Stegner) K.; A.B., Hamline University, 1908, Doctor of Science (honorary), 1958; M.A., Northwestern U., M.D., 1914; m. Lucille Baumann, Sept. 7, 1921; children—Robert, Caroline, John; Practiced at Chicago, 1914-76; clin. asst. Northwestern U. Med. Sch., 1912, became full prof., 1947-53, prof. emeritus, 1953-76; attending surgeon Passavant Memorial Hosp. Served as capt. and major, Med. Corps, A.E.F., 1917-19. Awarded President's Certificate of Merit contbns. on treatment of burns, 1945. Fellow American College Surgeons, Am. Surg. Assn., Western Surg. Assn.; mem. A.M.A., Ill. State and Chicago med. socs., Inst. of Medicine, Chicago Surg. Soc., Soc. Clin. Surgery, Am. Bd. Surgery (a founder), Am. Bd. Plastic Surgery (a founder), Am. Assn. Plastic Surgeons, Alpha Omega Alpha, Sigma Xi, Clubs; University, Barrington Hills. Home: Barrington, Ill. Died Nov. 1, 1976.

KOEGEL, OTTO ERWIN, lawyer; b. Boonville, Ind., Nov. 23, 1891; s. Henry and Laura Carolyn (Coe) K.; J.D., George Washington U., 1915, LL.M., 1916 (first honors highest average during course); D.C.L., Am. U., 1921; m. Rae Fisher, Sept. 30, 1916; children—James Erwin, Ruth Ann, William Fisher. Practiced in Washington, from 1916, also Chgo., 1924-31; mem. Matthews & Koegel, Chgo., 1926-31; mem. Hughes, Schurman & Dwight, 1931-37; mem. Rogers & Wells (and predecessor firm), N.Y.C.; chief counsel Twentieth Century-Fox Film Corp.; asso. counsel Bur. War Risk Ins., Treasury Dept., 1918-23; asst. gen. counsel U.S. Vets.' Bur. 1923; asst. U.S. atty. for D.C., 1924; prof. law domestic relations, torts and criminal law Nat. U., 1920-24; dir., counsel several corps. associated with motion picture and ins.; propr. Kaywood Farm. Active in civic affairs of Westchester County; former chmn. Citizens Com. for Fusion, Bronxville, and for Twp. of Somers; chmn. War Meat Com., World War II; legal mem. of Com. on Hereditary Defectives in U.S. of 2d Internat. Congress Eugenics, N.Y., 1922; mem. com. on marriage laws Am. Assn. for Family Social Work (allied with Russell Sage Found.); mem. Commn. N.Y. State to Commemorate 200th Anniversary of Our Independence. Trustee Am. U., Washington. Recipient 1st Bishop's medal N.Y. Episcopal Diocese, 1957, citation and gold medal Republic of Korea, 1971. Mem. Am., N.Y., Chgo. bar assns., Am. Judicature Soc., Am. Scenic and Hist. Preservation Soc. (exec. com.), John Jay Homestead Assn. (pres.), Sigma Nu Phi, Pi Gamma Mu (hon.). Methodist. Mason (32 deg.). Clubs: University (Washington); Siwanoy Country (Mt. Vernon, N.Y.). Author: Common Law Marriage and Its Development in the United States, 1922; Walter S. Carter, Collector of Young Masters, 1952; articles in legal periodicals. Home: Granite Springs, N.Y. Died Apr. 13, 1975.

KOEHLER, WALTER ALLOS, prof. chem. engring.; b. Mishicot, Wis., Mar. 25, 1893; s. Louis Carl and Ottilie (Dallmann) K.; B.S., in Chem. Engring., U. of Wis., 1919, Ch. E., 1920, Ph.D., 1923; M.S., U. of Ill., 1922; m. Laura Harker, Aug. 11, 1923; children—Elizabeth Louise, Walter Harker. Engr. research lab., Carborundum Co., Niagara Falls, N.Y., 1920-21; instr. to prof. and head dept. chem. engring., W.Va. U., 1924-59; acting dir. Engring. Expt. Sta., 1938-40, 1946-52, dir. 1952-79, acting dean grad. sch., 1960-61, asso. dean coll. engring., W.Va. U., 1961-79. Spln. in chem. engring. processes and electrochem.; mem. Pub. Land Corp. of West Va., 1946-79. Mem. Am. Inst. Chem. Engr., Nat. Soc. Profl. Engrs., Am. Soc. Engr. Education, Am. Ceramic Soc., Electro-chem. Soc., Am. Chem. Soc., W.Va. Acad. Sci., Tau Beta Pi, Sigma Xi Phi. Lambda Upsilon, Sigma Gamma Epsilon. Registered professional engr., W.Va. Presbyterian. Club: Kiwanis. Author: Applications of Electrochemistry, 1935, 1944, French ed., 1952. Contbr. tech. articles on ceramics, electrochemistry, chemical engring. Home: Morgantown, W.Va. Died Jan. 12, 1979.

KOENIG, FREDERICK GILMAN, JR., mfg. exec.; b. Birmingham, Ala., Oct. 1, 1915; s. Frederick Gilman and Myra (Browne) K.; A.B., Birmingham-So. Coll., 1935; LL.B., Harvard, 1938; m. Mary Anne Geisking, June 30, 1946; 1 son, Donald C. Admitted to Ala. bar, 1938; pvt. practice, Birmingham, 1938-41; atty. TVA, 1941-42, 46-47; with Ala. By-Products Corp., Birmingham, 1947-78, exec. v.p., mem. exec. com., dir., 1954-68, pres., 1968-78; pres., dir. Ketona Chem. Corp. (Ala.), 1968-72; dir. 1st Nat. Bank of Birmingham. Dir. Asso. Industries Ala.; mem. Ala. Water Improvement Commn., 1962-65; mem. adv. bd. Salvation Army, Birmingham; v.p. Ala. Mining Inst.; pres., dir. Am. Coke and Coal Chems. Inst.; Bituminous Coal Research, Inc., dir. Bituminous Coal Operators Assn., Nat. Coal Assn., Warrior-Tombigbee Devel. Assn. U.S. Indsl. Council. Bd. dirs. Jefferson County Community Chest; trustee Gorgas Scholarship Fund; bd. visitors Coll. Commerce and Bus. Administrn., U. Ala. Served from pvt. to capt., inf., AUS, 1942-46; ETO. Decorated Bronze Star. Mem. Am., Ala., Birmingham bar assns., Soc. Mayflower Desc., Soc. Colonial Wars, SAR, SR, Birmingham Better Bus. Bur. (dir.), Ala., Birmingham (dir. 1968-70) chambers commerce, Newcomen Soc., Omicron Delta Kappa, Tau Kappa Alpha, Sigma Alpha Epsilon. Presbyn. Kiwanian (dir. Birmingham 1966-67). Clubs: Birmingham Country, Mountain Brook, The Club, Downtown, Relay House. Home: Birmingham, Ala., Died Apr. 9, 1978; buried Elmwood Cemetery, Birmingham.

KOGSTAD, ARTHUR WOODROW, real estate adminstr., ret. army officer; b. Chgo., Nov. 5, 1918; s. Casper Arthur and May (Brady) K.; B.S. in Commerce, Loyola U., Chgo., 1940; grad. Nat. War Coll., 1960; M.A. in Internat. Affairs, George Washington U., 1964; m. Mary Lou Bell, Mar. 4, 1946; children—Marylou Michele, Marsha Anne. Commd. 2d lt. U.S. Army, 1942, advanced through grades to brig. gen., 1967; various troop assignments, 1942; asst. chief staff XIX Corps, 2d Armored Div., ETO, 1948-49; battalion comdr. 3d Armored Div., 1948-49; mem. armistice team Far East Command, 1951-54; tactics chief Armored Sch., Ft. Knox, Ky., 1954-56; prof. mil. sci. Pa. State U., 1956-59; dep. chief staff personnel Hdqrs. U.S. Army, Europe, 1960-61; brigade comdr. 4th Armored Div. 1962-63, asst. div. comdr., 1968; dep. dir. personnel Joint Chiefs Staff 1963-65; chief staff Area Command, Saigon, Vietnam, 1966; dir. personnel Hdqrs. European Command, 1967; dir. maintenance Army Material Command, Washington, 1969-70, dir. Internat. logistics, 1970-72; ret., 1972; officer cons. Internat., Inc., Washington, 1972-80; spl. projects cons. Beech Aircraft Corp., 1972; exec. v.p. No. Va. Bd. Realtors, 1972-80. Decorated D.S.M., Legion of Merit with 2 oak leaf clusters, Bronze Star with 2 oak leaf clusters, Joint Service medal, Army Commendation medal; Croix de Guerre with gold and silver stars (France). Mem. Assn. U.S. Army, Armor Assn., Ret. Officers Assn., Nat. Assn. Realtors, Va., Fairfax

County, Arlington County, Alexandria, Falls Church chambers commerce, Blue Key, Beta Pi, Alpha Sigma Nu, Pi Gamma Mu, Lambda Alpha. Club: University (Chgo.). Home: Annandale, Va. Died Dec. 5, 1980.

KOHLER, WALTER JODOK, JR., mfg. exec.; b. Sheboygan, Wis., Apr. 4 1904 s. Walter Jodok and Charlotte (Schroeder) K.; grad. Philips-Andover Acad., 1921; Ph.B., Yale, 1925; LL.D., Beloit Coll., 1951, Northland Coll.; D.C.L., Ripon Coll., 1953; L.H.D., Lakeland Coll., 1961; m. Charlotte McAleer, Nov. 8, 1948; children—Terry Jodok, Charlotte Nicolette. Employed Kohler Co. (Wis), 1925-47; pres. Vollrath Co., Sheboygan, 1947-68, chmn., 1959-76; dir. Security First Nat. Bank, Mrs. Paul's Kitchen, Phila. Gov. of Wis. 1951-56. Chmn. Am. Cancer Soc., 1952-59, dir., 1949-63. Served to lt. comdr. USNR, 1942-45. Republican. Clubs: University (Milw.); River (N.Y.C.); Mill Reef (Antigua). Home: Wis. Died Mar. 21, 1976.

KOK, BESSEL, plant physiologist; b. Hardinxveld, Netherlands, Nov. 7, 1918; s. Johannes Evert and Cornelia (Grondys) K.; came to U.S., 1958, naturalized, 1963; Ph.D., U. Utrecht (Holland), 1948; m. Cornelia Hendrika Vogelesang, Feb. 12, 1943; children—Cornelie, Johannes, Allart. Mem. biophysics dept. Utrecht U., 1942-49; with Lab. Plant Physiology U. Wageningen (Holland), 1949-58, Carnegie Inst. Washington, 1951-52; with Martin Marietta Labs., Balt., 1958-79, head dept. bioscis. Recipient Charles F. Kettering awards Nat. Acad. Scis.-NRC, 1963; Stephen Hales award, 1978. Mem. Am. Assn. Plant Physiologists (Charles F. Kettering award 1972), Am. Soc. Exptl. Biology, AAAS, Am. Acad. Arts and Scis., Nat. Acad. Scis. Contbr. numerous articles to profl. publs. Research light energy in photosynthesis of plants. Home: Baltimore, Md. Died Apr. 27, 1979; inurned Balt.

KOLETSKY, SIMON, pathologist; b. New Haven, Dec. 3, 1910; s. Jacob and Lena (Rubin) K.; B.A., Yale U., 1930, also M.D.; m. Jewel Klein, Feb. 28, 1950; children—Richard, Alan, Joy, Carol. Intern in medicine Sinai Hosp., Balt., 1934-35; resident in medicine Mission Hosp., Asheville, N.C., 1935-36; intern in pathology Cleve. City Hosp., 1936-37, resident in pathology, 1937-38; resident in pathology Univ. Hosps. Cleve., 1938-39, pathologist-in-charge, 1950-80; from instr. to asst. prof. pathology Case Western Res. U., 1939-50, prof., 1950-78, prof. emeritus, 1978-80. Served with M.C., U.S. Army, 1942. NIH grantee, 1945. diplomate Am. Bd. Pathology. Mem. Am. Heart Assn. (past pres. N.E. Ohio affiliate past pres. Ohio affiliate), Am. Soc. Exptl. Pathology, AAAS, N.Y. Acad. Scis., Am. Assn. Pathologists, Internat. Soc. Pathologists, Internat. Soc. Hypertension, Phi Beta Kappa, Sigma Xi. Author: Calcific Disease of Aortic Valve, 1947; contbr. articles to med. jours.; research in hypertension, arteriosclerosis. Home: Cleveland, Ohio. Died May 16, 1980.

KOLLER, E. FRED, economist, educator; b. Turtle Lake, Wis., Apr. 3, 1907; s. Fred W. and Elizabeth (Prosser) K.; A.B. summa cum laude, Augustana Coll., 1929, LL.D., 1957; A.M., U. Minn., 1933, Ph.D., 1938; m. Ethel M. Eliker, Aug. 25, 1935. Asst. U. Minn., 1930-34, instr., 1934-38, asst. prof., 1938-42, asso. prof., 1942-46, prof., 1946-75; head project for Nat. Bur. of Econ. Research entitled Financing of Farmer's Cooperatives in the U.S., 1946-47; tax analyst U.S. Treasury, Washington, 1934. Vice pres. Experience, Inc., Mpls., Coop. Found., St. Paul; trustee Am. Inst. Coop. Recipient Alumni Achievement award Augustana Coll., 1969; Outstanding Contbn. to Am. Agr. award, 1967; Outstanding Tchr. award, U. Minn., 1972; Nat. Coop. Edn. award, 1976. Mem. Am. Econ. Assn., Am. Agrl. Econ. Assn., Internat. Assn. Agrl. Economists, Pi Kappa Delta, Gamma Sigma Delta, Alpha Zeta. Mem. Am. Lutheran Ch. Author numerous bulls. Minn. Agr. Expt. Sta., numerous articles tech. and profl. jours. Home: Saint Paul, Minn. Died Sept. 3, 1980; buried Sioux Falls, S.D.

KOLSTER, FREDERICK AUGUST (KOL'STER), radio engr.; b. Geneva, Switzerland, Jan. 13, 1883; s. August and Henrietta K.; brought to U.S., 1885; spl. course, Harvard, 1904-08; m. Lillian G. Ricker, Dec. 11, 1908; children—Muriel, Fredericka. With Stone Telegraph & Telephone Co., 1902-09; De Forest Radio Co., 1909-11, Bur. of Standards, Washington, since 1912, chief of radio section; cons. engr. Designated by State Dept. as tech. adviser to U.S. delegates representing Dept. of Commerce to Internat. Radio Conf., London, 1912. A pioneer in development of radio communication; inventor Kolster decremeter, radio compass, directional systems for radio communication, etc. Fellow Inst. Radio Engrs., A.A.A.S.; mem. Am. Inst. of E.E. Clubs: Bohemian (San Francisco); Harvard (New York). Author: (brochures) Distributed Capacity of Coils; Measurement of Logarithmic Decrement; The Radio Compass and Its Application to Navigation; Generation and Utilization of Ultra-Short Waves in Radio Communication. Home: Palo Alto, Calif. *

KOMATSU, TAKASHI, business exec.; b. Mishima, Shizuoka-Ken, Japan, Mar. 20, 1886; s. Mikisaburo Komatsu; A.B., Monmouth Coll., 1910, LL.D., 1940; A.M., Harvard, 1911; m. Oriko Takahashi, 1917; children—Hisake, Emiko, Masayoshi, William Ryuji. Sec. to pres. Oriental S.S. Co., 1914-24, mem. staff Japanese delegation Washington Conf. on Limitation Naval Armaments, 1921; mgr. Toyo Kisen Kaisha, San Francisco, 1922-26; mem. Japanese delegation Three Power Naval Conf., Geneva, 1927; mgr., dir. Asano Shipbldg. Co., 1928-40; dir. Nippon Steel Tube Company, 1940-46, v.p., 1945, ret. 1946. Advisor, Iino Kaiun Kabushiki Kaisha. Member of the World Fedn. Ednl. Assns. (chmn. Japanese exec. com. Seventh World Conf. 1937), Am.-Japan Soc. Tokyo (pres.), Fedn. Econ. Orgns. (vice chmn. 1945). Mason (32 deg., Shriner). Clubs: Rotary, Harvard, Tokyo, Tokyo American, Tokyo Golf, Hodogaya Golf. Home: Ota-ku. *

KOMPFNER, RUDOLF, physicist, educator; b. Vienna, Austria, May 16, 1909; s. Bernhard and Paula (Grotte) K.; came to U.S., 1951, naturalized, 1957; Dipl. Ing., Technische Hochschule, Vienna, also D.Sc. (hon.); D.Phil., Oxford (Eng.) U., D.Sc. (hon.), 1969; m. Peggy Mason, Apr. 29, 1939; children—Paul, Helen. Dir. Almond Franey & Son, London, Eng., 1936-41; with Bell Labs., Murray Hill, N.J. and Holmdel, N.J., 1951-73; prof. applied physics Stanford, 1973-77; prof. dept. engring. sci. Oxford U., 1973-77. Trustee Asso. Univs. Inc. Served with Royal Naval Sci. Service, Eng., 1941-51. Fellow I.E.E.E. (medal of honor 1973, Nat. Medal of Sci. 1974), All Souls Coll Oxford U.; mem. Nat. Acad. Scis., Nat. Acad. Engring., Am. Acad. Arts and Sci. Inventor electron tubes for communications tech. Home: Stanford, Calif. Died Dec. 3, 1977.

KONDRASHIN, KIRILL PETROWICH, conductor; b. Moscow, USSR, Feb. 21, 1914; defected to Netherlands, 1978; s. Petr Andreewich and Anna (Michailovna) K.; student Moscow Conservatory, 1936; m. Nina Leonzdowha Varlamorta, Dec. 18, 1931; children—Petr, Sergei, Andrej; m. 2d, Nolde. Conductor, Mail Opera Theatre, Leningrad, 1937-43, Bolshoi Theatre, Moscow, 1943-56, Moscow Philharmonic Orch., 1956-78; condr. Concertgebouw Orch., Amsterdam, 1979-81; appearances in Eng., France, Italy, Germany, Yugoslavia, Hungary, N. and S. Am. Named Nat. Artist of USSR; recipient Govt. prize. Mem. Communist Party. Home: Amsterdam, Netherlands. Died Mar. 8, 1981.

KOOKER, ARTHUR RAYMOND, educator, historian; b. Matchwood, Mich., Feb. 25, 1907; s. David Arthur and Grace Agnes (Geroux) K.; A.B. in Edn., U. Mich., 1931, A.M., 1933, Ph.D., 1941; m. Miriam Jane Highley, Dec. 24, 1941; children—Jane Anne, Elizabeth Margaret, John Nelson. Tchr. social studies Forest Park Jr. High Sch., Crystal Falls, Mich., 1928-31; supt. McMillan Twp. schs., Ewen, Mich., 1932-33; univ. fellow U. Mich., 1935-36, teaching fellow history, 1938-41, resident adviser Chicago House, West Quadrangle, men's dormitories, 1939-41, vis. asso. prof. history, summer 1951; regional dir. for Mich., WPA sponsored survey Fed. Archives outside D.C., 1936-37, chief editor inventories of Fed. Archives in the states, 1937-38; asst. prof. history U. So. Cal., 1941-46, asso. prof. 1947-55, prof., 1955-73, prof. emeritus, 1973-78, chmn. dept. history, 1955-69; expert cons. Air. U., Maxwell AFB, Montgomery, Ala., 1947-54. Served from 2d lt. to maj., USAAF, 1943-46. Mem. Am. Hist. Assn. (council Pacific Coast Br. 1949-50, 59-60), Orgn. Am. Historians, Los Angeles Civil War Round Table (exec. com. 1957-58, pres. 1959-60), Athletic Assn. Western Univs. (faculty athletic rep. 1959-65), Soc. Am. Archivists, Blue Key, Skull and Dagger, Phi Alpha Theta, Phi Kappa Phi. Democrat. Mason. Contbr. to Men and Planes, History of Army Air Forces in World War II (vol. 6), 1955. Home: Harbor City, Calif. Died Sept. 29, 1978; buried Green Hills Meml. Park, San Pedro, Calif.

KOPPLE, ROBERT, lawyer; b. N.Y.C., Nov. 26, 1910; B.A., N.Y.U., 1932, J.D., 1934; m. Dorothy Stuhlbarg, July 22, 1944 (dec.); children—Ann Howard, Nancy Dunn; m. 2d, Marie M. VanDervort, Oct. 7, 1978. Admitted to N.Y. bar, 1934, practiced in N.Y.C.; gen. mgr. Columbia Aircraft Products, Somerville, N.J., 1939-42; exec. v.p. Midtown Realty Owners Assn., Inc., N.Y.C., 1953-77; pres. Quick Response Service, Inc., N.Y.C., 1953-79, chmn. bd., from 1979. Exec. v.p. Owners Com. on Electric Rates, N.Y.C., 1954—; exec. v.p. Com. for Adequate Supply of Energy, from 1971; mem. N.Y.C. Midtown Devel. Council, 1970—; spl. adviser Mayor City N.Y. for Tercentenary Celebration, 1959-60; organizer, 1st exec. v.p., 1964-65 N.Y. World's Fair Corp., 1958-60; employer trustee Bldg. Service Welfare Fund, 1953-77, Bldg. Service Pension Fund N.Y., 1958-77, Nat. BSEIU Pension Fund, 1968-76; mem. N.Y. Am. Revolution Bicentennial Commn., 1968-69; chmn. N.Y.C. Planning Bd. 5, 1962-71. Mem. Nassau County Democratic Com., 1946-51; Nassau County candidate N.Y. State Senate, 1950. Served as 2d Lt. Signal Corps, AUS, 1942-46; charge contract termination Gen. Electric Corp. Mem. Little Neck Bay Power Squadron (comdr.), U.S. Power Squadrons (rear comdr., nat. pub. relations officer), Tau Delta Phi, Am. Soc. Mil. Engrs., N.Y. State Bar Assn., Real Estate Bd. N.Y., Mutual Admiration Soc. N.Y. (pres.). Home: Roslyn, New York. Died Oct. 6, 1979.

KORBEL, JOSEF, educator; b. Kysperk, Czechoslovakia, Sept. 20, 1909; s. Arnost and Olga (Ptackova) K.; J.D., Charles U., Prague, 1933; student Sorbonne, Paris, 1928-29; m. Anna M. Spieglova, Apr. 20, 1935; children—Madeleine Jana (Mrs. Joseph M.P. Albright), Anna Katherine, John Joseph. Came to U.S., 1948, naturalized, 1957. With Czechoslovak Diplomatic Service, 1934-48; with Ministry Fgn. Affairs, Prague, 1934-36; press attache legation, Belgrade, 1937-38; personal sec. to Jan Masaryk, London, 1940-42; head broadcasting dept. Czechoslovak Govt.-in-exile, London, 1940-45; chef de cabinet to Jan Masaryk, Prague, 1945; ambassador to Yugoslavia, Belgrade, 1945-48; mem. Czechoslovak Delegation to Paris Peace Conf., chmn. econ. com. for Balkan countries and Finland, 1946, mem., chmn. UN Commn. for Kashmir, 1948-49; prof. internat. relations, mem. staff Social Sci. Found., U. Denver, 1949-77, dir. Social Sci. Found., 1959-69, dean Grad. Sch. Internat. Studies, 1964-69, Andrew W. Mellon prof. internat. studies, 1969-77; research fellow Russian Research Center, Harvard, 1957; sr. vis. fellow St. Antony's Coll., Oxford, Eng., 1962; sr. research fellow European Inst., Columbia, 1968. Mem. Council Fgn. Relations, N.Y.C., Denver Com. Fgn. Relations. Served as lt. Czechoslovak Army, 1933-34. Recipient U. Denver Lectureship award for research, 1958. Mem. Rocky Mountain Assn. Slavic Studies (pres. 1973-74), Am. Assn. Advancement Slavic Studies, Czechoslovak Soc. Arts and Scis. in Am., Phi Beta Kappa. Author: Tito's Communism, 1951; Danger in Kashmir, 1954; Communist Subversion of Czechoslovakia, 1959; Poland between East and West, 1963; Détente in Europe, 1972; Twentieth Century Czechoslovakia (The Meanings of Its History), 1977; also articles. Home: Denver, Colo. Died July 18, 1977.

KORN, BERTRAM WALLACE, rabbi, historian; b. Phila., Oct. 6, 1918; s. Manuel and Blanche (Bergman) K.; student U. Pa., 1935-36, Cornell U.; A.B. with honors, U. Cin., 1939; rabbi, M.H.L., Hebrew Union Coll.-Jewish Inst. Religion, 1943, fellow, 1946-48, D.H.L., 1949, D.D., 1968; LL.D., Temple U., 1957; D.Litt., Delaware Valley Coll., 1967, Dropsie U., 1976; children—Judith Carole, Bertram Wallace. Ordained rabbi, 1943; rabbi Govt. St. Temple, Mobile, 1943-44; asst. prof. Am. Jewish history Hebrew Union Coll., 1948-49; sr. rabbi Reform Congregation Keneseth Israel, Elkins Park, Pa., 1949-79; vis. prof. Am. Jewish history Hebrew Union Coll.-Jewish Inst. Religion, N.Y.C., from 1962, Dropsie U., Phila., from 1970. Past chmn. Reform del. to Commn. Jewish Chaplaincy, Jewish Welfare Bd.; v.p. Jewish Hist. Commn. of Civil War Centennial, 1961-65; adv. bd. Fed. Civil War Centennial Commn., 1961-65; mem. Pres.'s Commn. on Observance of 25th Anniversary of UN, 1970-71; past mem. com. Jewish Americana, B'nai B'rith; past v.p. Phila Bd. Rabbis; past grand chaplain Pa. Grand Lodge Masons; chaplain Navy League of U.S., 1963-65, Golden Slipper Club, from 1965; vis. preacher Valley Forge Mil. Acad.; chmn. com. contemporaneous hist. Central Conf. Am. Rabbis, 1952-58, chmn. com. on chaplaincy, 1965-69, mem. exec. bd., 1969-71; mem. rabbinic adv. council United Jewish Appeal; mem. Phila. Bicentennial Religious Liberties Commn.; mem. steering com. Nat. Rabbinic Cabinet, Bonds for Israel; mem. adv. com. historians Phila. '76, Inc.; nat. chmn. alumni centennial campaign Hebrew Union Coll-Jewish Inst. Religion. Trustee Delaware Valley Coll., Pep Boys Ednl. Found.; bd. govs. Reconstructionist Rabbinical Coll., Phila.; bd. dirs. Fedn. Jewish Agencies, Phila.; mem. bd. Chamber Symphony Phila. (past pres.); hon. bd. overseers Gratz Coll., Phila. Served as chaplain USNR, 1944-46; rear adm. Res., 1975. Recipient numerous awards for hist. contbns.; elected to Order of Anthony Wayne, Valley Forge Mil Acad., 1969, Mem. Am., So. hist. assns., Am. Jewish (past pres.), Ill. hist. socs., Orgn. Am. Historians, Jewish Publ. Soc. Am. (publs. com.), Chapel of Four Chaplains Phila. (life), Jewish Hist. Soc. of Israel, Am. Legion (past dept. chaplain Pa.), Alumni Assn. Hebrew Union Coll.-Jewish Inst. Religion (past pres.), Assn. Jewish Chaplains Armed Forces of U.S. (pres. 1967-69), Jewish War Vets. Am. (nat. chaplain 1974-76), Am. Antiquarian Soc. (councilor 1969-75). Author: American Jewry and the Civil War, 1951; Jewish Roots in America, 1953; Eventful Years and Experiences: Studies in 19th Century American Jewish History, 1954; Carvalho's Incidents of Travel and Adventure in the Far West, 1955; The American Reaction to the Mortara Case: 1858-1859, 1957; Handbooks for Naval Reserve Chaplains, 1959; Benjamin Levy: New Orleans Printer and Publisher, 1961; Jews and Negro Slavery in the Old South, 1962; The Middle Period of American Jewish History (in Hebrew), 1972; The Early Jews of New Orleans, 1969 (Merit award Am. Assn. For State and Local History 1970); The Jews of Mobile, Alabama, 1763-1841, 1970; also articles, essays and revs. in scholarly publs., Ency. Judaica. Editor: Central Conf. Am. Rabbis Yearbook, 1953-54; 75th Anniversary History, Central Conf. Am. Rabbis, 1965; (with Cecil Woolf) Letters of Baron Corvo to Leonard Moore, 1960; Bicentennial Festschrift for Jacob Bader Marcus, 1976; mem. editorial adv. com. Civil War History, 1955-60, Jewish Digest, Jewish Social Studies; contbg. ed. Phila. Jewish Exponent, 1958-61. Home: Wynecote, Pa. Died Dec. 11, 1979.

KORN, RICHARD, symphony condr.; b. N.Y.C.; A.B., Princeton, 1928; LL.B., Yale, 1931; student Juilliard Grad. Sch., 1937-39; m. Peggy Lashanska Rosenbaum (Mrs. Peter G. Lehman), Nov. 14, 1945; children—Penelope (Mrs. Stanley Karp), Wendy (Mrs. Stephen Lash), Lehman. Mem. Nat. Symphony Orch. (clarinet), Washington, 1939-40; asst. condr. Nat. Orchestral Assn., N.Y., 1940-42; founded Alumni Orch. of Nat. Orchestral Assn., conducted it in N.Y. concert and R.C.A. Victor record albums, 1941; fellowship in conducting with Serge Koussevitzky, 1941; asst. condr. N.Y. City (Center) Opera Co., 1945-46; condr. Original Ballet Russe, 1947; mus. dir. Orch. of Am., 1959-65; guest condr. Boston Pops Orch., Lewisohn Stadium Concerts, Czech. Philharmonic (Prague), philharmonic orchs. of Stockholm, Copenhagen and Oslo, Conservatoire Orch. of Paris, Carnegie Hall Pops London Symphony Orch., etc. 1945-50, New Orleans summer concerts 1949, NBC Symphony, Buffalo Philharmonic Orch., 1951-52, Lena concerts, also 1962 Montreal summer concerts; condr. Baton Rouge Symphony Orch. 1950-51; Cin. Symphony Orch., 1956, Asahi Broadcasting Symphony Orch. Japan, 1957, Phila. Dell Concerts, Kol Yisroel, Israel, Haifa Symphony, Israel, 1958, Carl Schurz Park concerts, 1962; condr. on records, notably Am. Music. Mem. faculty New York Coll. Music, 1965-81. Mem. exec. com. Nat. Music Council; pres. Am. Council Judaism, 1966-68. Chmn. Music School Com. Henry St. Settlement. Bd. dirs. Hosp. for Joint Diseases, N.Y.C., Musicians Found.; bd. govs. Bohemians, 1964-72; trustee Temple Emanu-El, N.Y.; mem. adv. com. to dept. astrophysics Princeton U.; mem. Hayden Planetarium com. N.Y. Mus. Natural History. Served as lt., USCG, 1942-45. Fellow World Acad. Arts and Scis. Author: Orchestral Accents. Clubs: Lotos, Century Assn., Princeton (N.Y.C.); Century Country. Address: New York, N.Y. Died Apr. 27, 1981.

KOSHLAND, DANIEL EDWARD, business exec.; b. San Francisco, Mar. 16, 1892; s. Marcus S. and Corinne (Schweitzer) K.; A.A. (hon.), Coll. of San Mateo, 1964; B.S., U. Calif., Berkeley, 1913, LL.D., 1965; m. Eleanor Haas. Sept. 26, 1918 (dec.); children—Daniel Edward, Frances C. (Mrs. Theodore H. Geballe), Phyllis R. (Mrs. Friedman); m. 2d, Lucile Wolf Heming, July 9, 1959. Asst. mgr. fgn. dept. Equitable Trust Co. of N.Y., 1914-16; exec. Lazard Freres, bankers, N.Y.C., 1919-22; joined Levi Strauss & Co., San Francisco, 1922, pres., 1956-58, chmn. exec. com., from 1958, hon. chmn. at time of death, also dir.; dir. emeritus Wells Fargo Bank. Former mem. Indsl. Welfare Commn., commr. State of Calif.; chmn. Dr. Henry Harris Meml. Library Fund, Rehovot, Israel; hon. chmn. Israel 25th Anniversary Com., San Francisco, 1972; founder, mem. distbn. com. San Francisco Found.; mem. investment adv. com. San Mateo Coll. Found.; mem. nat. found. com. United Negro Coll. Fund, Inc. Bd. dirs. Browning Inst., Inc., N.Y.C., Ind. Colls. No. Calif., Inc., Jewish Welfare Fedn., San Francisco, San Francisco Devel. Fund; trustee Union Am. Hebrew Congregations. Served with U.S. Army, 1916-19. Recipient Torch of Learning award Hebrew U., 1972, Alumnus of Year award U Calif., Berkeley, Calif. Grad. Schs. Bus Adminstrn., 1972; Meritorious Service award Multiple Sclerosis Soc., 1967. Fellow, Brandeis U. Mem. Robert Gordon Sproul Assos., Berkeley Fellows, Calif. Acad. Scis. (hon. mem. bd. trustees), Nat. Multiple Sclerosis Soc., Phi Beta Kappa, Beta Gamma Sigma (dirs.' table). Jewish religion (past v.p. congregation). Clubs: Peninsula Golf and Country (San Mateo, Calif.); Commercial, Concordia-Argonaut (San Francisco). Home: Hillsborough Calif. Died Dec. 10, 1979.

KOSMAN, WILLIAM FRANKLIN (KOZ'MÅN), clergyman; b. Catasauqua, Pa., Mar. 29, 1882; s. Thomas Franklin and Lillian Jane (Mantz) K.; A.B., Franklin and Marshall Coll., Lancaster, Pa., 1906, D.D., 1929; B.D., Theol. Sem. of Evangelical and Reformed Ch., Lancaster, Pa., 1909; post grad. student Lehigh U., 1935-36; m. Margaret Jacoby, June 24, 1914; children—Barbara Kehm, Jane Jacoby. Ordained to ministry of Reformed Ch., 1909; pastor, Sellerville, Pa., 1909-13, Riegelsville, Pa., 1913-17. Altoona, Pa., 1917-20, Pottsville, Pa., 1920-23; pastor Salem Evang. and Reformed Ch., Allentown, Pa., 1923-46; prof. of systematic theology Sem. of Evang. and Reformed Ch., Lancaster, Pa., since 1946. Past president board of visitors, Theol. Sem. Evang. and Reformed Ch. Mem. commn. on higher edn.; mem. (past chmn.) Western Section of Alliance of Reformed and Presbyterian Chs.; mem Fed. Council Chs. in America (mem. exec. com.; mem. dept. internat. justice and goodwill). Del. to Gen. Synod of Evang. and Reformed Ch. Mem. Phi Sigma Kappa. Mason. Address: Lancaster, Pa. *

KOSOLAPOFF, GENNADY MICHAEL, educator, chemist; b. Viatka, Russia, Sept. 2, 1909; s. Michael Paul and Alexandra Vasily (Shikhova) K.; came to U.S., 1924, naturalized, 1942; B.S. in Chem. Engring., Cooper Union, 1932; M.S. in Biochemistry, U. Mich., 1933, Sc.D. in Chemistry, 1936; m. Dorothea W. Bouton, July 20, 1934; children—Alexandra, Michael, Patricia. Research chemist Libby-Owens-Ford Glass Co., 1936-38, Monsanto Chem. Co., 1938-48; asso. prof. Auburn U., 1948-53, research prof., 1953-76; research cons. indsl. and govtl. agys., 1943-76; dir. chem. research F.J. Seiler Research Lab. Office of Aerospace Research, Colo., 1963-64; cons. AEC; lectr. chemistry of phosphorus, 1949-76. Mem. Chem. Soc. London. Author: Organophosphorus Compounds, 1950, co-author 2d edit., 1972; also sects. books and encys. Abstractor, sect. co-editor Chem. Abstracts. Contbr. articles to profl. jours. Home: Auburn, Ala. Died Jan. 1, 1976.

KOSTELANETZ, ANDRE, orch. condr.; b. Leningrad, Russia; s. Nachman and Rosalie (Dimscha) K.; student St. Peter's Sch., 1911-18, St. Petersburg Conservatory Music, 1920-22; Mus.D. (hon.), Albion (Mich.) Coll., 1939, Cin. Conservatory Music, 1945; m. Lily Pons, June 2, 1938 (div.); m. 2d, Sara Gene Orcutt, 1960 (div.). Came to U.S., 1922, naturalized, 1928. For many years conducted own shows over CBS; directed music for several motion pictures; made overseas tours conducting soldier orchrs. organized and trained by him, North Africa, Persian Gulf, Italian theatre, summer 1944, CBI and ETO, Winter 1944-45; guest condr. N.Y. Philharmonic, also all leading orchs. in U.S. and abroad; prin. condr., artistic dir. N.Y. Philharmonic Promenades; rec. artist Columbia Records. Awarded Asiatic-Pacific ribbon by Army for overseas services; selected by radio editors of U.S. and Can. for Fame Award as leading condr. for past several years. Commd. modern works by Copland, Thomson, Kern, Grofe, Creston, William Schuman, Hovhaness, Archibald MacLeish-Laderman. Address: New York, N.Y. Died Jan. 13, 1980.

KOSTMAYER, HIRAM WATKINS (KOST'MI-ER), gynecologist; b. 1883; A.B., Tulane, 1904, M.D., 1909. Prof. gynecology, vice-dean Tulane U. of La. Sch. of Medicine, ret. 1949, sr. consulting gynecologist Charity hosp. Mem. A.M.A., F.A.C.S., Am. Bd. of Obstetricians and Gynecologists, etc. Address: Waveland, Miss. *

KOSYGIN, ALEXSAI N., premier of USSR; b. Leningrad, 1904; ed. Leningrad Coop. Tech. Inst., Leningrad Textile Inst., 1935. Worker in consumer cooperatives various dists. Siberia, 1924-49; foreman, dept. head Zhelyabov textile factory, Leningrad, 1935-37; dir. October Textile mill, Leningrad, 1937-38; chmn. exec. com. Leningrad City Council of Workers' Deputies, 1938-39; dep. of Supreme Soviet, 1938—; people's commissar Textile Industry of USSR, 1939-40; dep. chmn. Council People's Commissars of USSR, 1940-46; chmn. Council of People's Commissars of RSFSR, 1943-46; dep. chmn. Council of Ministers of USSR, 1946-60; minister of finance USSR, 1949-54, chmn. state planning commn., 1959-60, 1st dep. chmn. Council of Ministers, 1960-64, chmn. 1964. Mem. Communist Party of Soviet Union, 1927-80, mem. Central Com., from 1939; candidate mem., then mem. Politburo of Central Com., 1946-52, mem., from 1966, candidate mem., then mem. Presidium, 1952-53, 57-66. Decorated Hero of Socialist Labor, Order of Lenin (4), Gold Star Hammer and Sickle, Order of Red Flag, 9 medals. Address: Moscow, USSR. Died Dec. 19, 1980.

KOTTLER, FRIEDRICH, scientist; b. Vienna, Austria, Dec. 10, 1886; Ph.D. in Physics, U. Vienna, 1911; m. 1925. Naturalized citizen. Lectr. mathematical physics U. Vienna, 1916-23, asso. prof., 1923-38; research asso. Research Lab., physics div. Eastman Kodak Co., 1939—. Comdr. arty. and mil. research, Austrian Army, 1914-18. Mem. Am. Optical Soc., Am. Soc. Testing Materials. Address: Rochester, N.Y. *

KOUCHAKJI, FAHIM JOSEPH, art collector; b. Aleppo, Syria, Mar. 17, 1886; s. George A. and Emilia (Sharki) K.; student Ecole Grèque Episcopal St. Nicolas, Aleppo; studied banking, Credit Lyonnaise, Cairo, Egypt, 1904-09; m. Evelyn Curtis, 1930. Naturalized citizen U.S. Mgr. Kouchakji Fr$012res, Paris, N.Y. and Aleppo, 1909-24; pres. Kouchakji Fr$012res, Paris N.Y., 1924-25. Fellow in perpetuity Met. Mus. of Art. Mem. Met. Mus. of Art, Cleve. Museum of Art, Coll. Art Assn., Walter's Art Gallery, Friends Fogg Art Mus., Am. Italy Soc., Archaeol. Inst. Am., Asia Inst., Am. Acad. Polit. Sci., Iranian Inst. of Art and Archaeology, Nat Geo. Soc., Iran-Am. Soc. Roman Catholic. Author: (with G.A. Eisen) Glass, 1927. Former owner Great Chalice of Antioch; pub. The Great Chalice of Antioch (2 vols). 1925, popular edit. (1 vol.), 1933, and lectr. on that subject. Collaborator with G.A. Eisen: Portraits of Washington, 3 vol., 1933; Ancient Oriental Cylinder and other Seals, 1940. Collector of Greek, Egyptian Roman, Syrian, Persian and Arabic art, glass, Faience. Home: New York, N.Y. Died Aug. 19, 1976.

KOUNTZ, CLARK HARRY (KOONTZ), oil transportation executive; b. nr. Bradford, Pa., Aug. 24, 1883; s. Frank P. and Margaret E. (Boulton) K.; ed. pub. schs.; m. Agnes Casebeer, Dec. 21, 1907; 1 dau., Marjorie. Messenger boy and office clk., Ohio Oil Co., Findlay, 1901-05; sec. to gen. mgr. Prairie Oil & Gas Co., Independence, Kan., 1905-06, asst. sec. same co., 1906-10, sec. and dir., 1910-15; v.p. and dir. Prairie Pipe Line Co., 1915-32; pres. and dir. Pure Oil Pipe Line Co. of Tex., 1926-32; chmn. bd. Sinclair Prairie Pipe Line Co., 1932-36, vice-pres. Sinclair Refining Co., 1936-48; director Consol. Oil Corp., New York, 1932-35; v.p. and dir. Commonwealth Transportation Co., Independence, Kan., 1932-39, pres. and dir. 1939-42; dir. Tex. N.M. Pipe Line Co., Houston, 1937-48; retired 1948. Republican, Mason (32 degree, K.T.). Home: New York. *

KOUWENHOVEN, WILLIAM BENNETT, elec. engr.; b. Bklyn., Jan. 13, 1886; s. Tunis Gerrit Bergen and Phebe Florence (Bennett) K.; E.E., Bklyn. Poly. Inst., 1906, M.E., 1907; Diplom Ingenieur, Karlsruhe Technische Hochschule, Baden, Germany, 1912, Doktor Ingenieur, 1913; LL.D., Johns Hopkins, 1962, M.D. (hon.), 1969; D.Sc. (hon.), Syracuse U., 1970; m. Abigail Baxter Remsen, June 22, 1910; 1 son, William Gerrit. Asst. in physics Bklyn. Poly. Inst., 1906-07, instr. in physics and elec. engring., 1907-10; instr. in elec. engring. Washington U., 1913-14; instr. Johns Hopkins, 1914-17, asso. in elec. engring., 1917-19; engring. supt. Winchester Repeating Arms Co. (leave of absence from Johns Hopkins), 1919-20; asso. prof. elec. engring. Johns Hopkins, 1919-30, prof., asst. dean Sch. Engring., 1930-38, prof., dean Sch. Engring., 1938-54, prof. emeritus, 1954—; lectr. in surgery Johns Hopkins Sch. Medicine, 1956—; cons. engr. U.S. Bureau of Mines, U.S. Bureau Standards; arbitrator Nat. Assn. Arbitration. Instr., rank of capt., R.O.T.C., World War I. Recipient Ludwig Hekton Gold medal A.M.A., 1961; Edison medalist Am. Inst. E.E., 1962; Distinguished Contbn. in Sci. award A.C.P., 1969; Distinguished Service award Underwriter Labs., 1969; Helen Taussig award, 1970; Power Life award Power Groups of I.E.E.E., 1970; Sci. Achievement award A.M.A., 1972; Lasker award, 1973; named hon. mem. faculty Med. and Chir. Soc., 1970. Fellow A.A.A.S., Am. Inst. E.E. (v.p. 1931-33; dir. 1935-39; chmn. Balt. sect. 1922-31); mem. Am. Soc. Testing Materials, Edison Electric Inst., Am. Welding Soc. (exec. com. research council), Nat. Acad. Sci., Am Heart Assn. (award of merit 1969), Eta Kappa Nu. Tau Beta Pi, Sigma Xi, Pi Kappa Phi. Democrat. Presbytn. Clubs: Johns Hopkins, Baltimore Engineers; Gibson Island. Contbr. numerous articles and papers on elec. measurements, also on electric shock, magnetic analysis, electric welding, effect of electricity on heart, elec. defibrillation, closed chest cardiac massage, effects of high voltage electric fields on human beings, treatment of atrial fibrillation. Trans. American Inst. Elec. Engring., Elec. World, proc. Am. Soc. Testing Materials, Welding Journal, med. and surg. jours. Home: Baltimore MD. *

KOWALSKI, FRANK, govt. ofcl.; b. Meriden, Conn., Oct. 18, 1907; s. Frank and Mary (Miller) K.; B.S., U.S. Mil. Acad., 1930; M.S;, Mass. Inst. Tech., 1936; student Columbia, 1945; m. Helen Amelia Bober, Oct. 20, 1931; children—Carol Helene, Barry Frank. Commd. 2d lt., inf., U.S. Army, 1930, advanced through grades to col., 1944; various co., bn., regt. assignments, 1930-44; chief tng. G-3 sect. Hdqrs. European Theater, 1944; dir. Disarmament Sch., London, Eng., 1944-45; dep. chief information and edn. div. Hdqrs. European Theater, 1945; chief mil. govt. of Kyoto, Osaka prefectures, Japan, 1948-49; dep. chief civil affairs, Japan, 1949-50; chief staff Mil. Adv. Group, Japan, 1950-52; comdt. U.S. Army Command Mgmt. Sch., 1954-58; ret, 1958; mem. 86th-87th Congresses, Conn-at-Large; mem. Armed Service, Manpower Utilization coms.; mem. Subversive Activities Control Bd., from 1963. Decorated Legion of Merit with cluster, Bronze Star. Aurthor articles on mil. mgmt. Holder patents for mil. items. Home: Alexandria, Va. Died Oct. 11, 1974.

KOYL, GEORGE SIMPSON (KOIL), architect, educator; b. Evanston, Wyo., Feb. 8, 1885; s. Rev. Charles Henry and Caroline (Emigh) K.; B.S. in Architecture, U. of Pa., 1909, M.S., in Architecture, 1911; Hon. Doctor of Fine Arts, Univ. of Pa., July 1, 1944; fellow Am. Acad. in Rome, 1911-15; m. Adelaide Wight Howard, Oct. 10, 1924. Began as archtl. draftsman, in office of F. E. Edbrooke, Denver, 1902; with Cass Gilbert, architect, N.Y. City, 1915-17 and 1919, McKim, Mead and White, 1920-24; chief designer and consultant County and City Bldg., of Denver, 1925-27; practiced alone, 1928-29; mem. Rich. Mathesius & Koyl, 1929-32; critic in design, Columbia, N.Y., 1928, Princeton, 1928-30; instr., asst. prof. U., 1929-32; prof. architecture, dean Sch. Fine Arts, U. of Pa., since 1932, retired as dean as of June 30, 1950. Member board managers House of Detention for Witnesses and Untried Prisoners for the County of Philadelphia; mem. architects advisory com. Phila. Housing Authority, 1937-38. Prin. works; Ridgewood (N.J.) Woman's Club Bldg.; Hospital, Littleton, N.H.; memorial to James Cardinal Gibbons, Washington, D.C. Received certificate in camouflage, Engrs. Sch., Ft. Belvoir, Va., July 1942. Mem. com. on camouflage, Phila. Council of Defense; chairman Eastern Dist. tech. com. Penna. State Council of Defense. Served as lieutenant Air Service, A.E.F., 1917-18. Fellow A.I.A. (past v.p. Phila. chpt.); mem. Am. Acad. in Rome (life), Pa. State Soc., T Square Club, Archaeol. Inst. Am. (past pres. Phila. Soc.), Art Alliance of Phila., Sigma Xi, Tau Sigma Delta. Republican. Clubs: Lenape, Century Association (N.Y.C.). Editor Am. Architects Directory. Home: Phila. *

KRACKE, EDWARD AUGUSTUS, JR., educator, historian; b. N.Y.C, Jan. 22, 1908; s. Edward Augustus and Leonora (Share) K.; A.B., Harvard, 1932, A.M., 1935, Ph.D., 1941; postgrad. U. Paris, 1935-36; m. Joan Hocking, June 8, 1935; children—Waud Hocking, Ernesta Henrietta. With OSS, 1942-45, Dept. State, 1945-46; vis. asst. prof. Chinese, U. Chgo., 1946-47, asst. prof., 1947-53, asso. prof. Chinese lit. and instns., 1953-60, prof., 1960-73, prof. emeritus, 1973-76, chmn. com. on Far Eastern civilizations, 1957-63, dir. Far Eastern Lang. and Area Center, 1959-63, 69-71, mem. council of Senate, 1959-62, chmn. com. on Far Eastern studies, 1970-71, chmn. Far Eastern Program in Coll., 1970-71; mem. vis. com. for East Asian studies Harvard, 1960-66; mem. adv. com. on Chinese and Japanese studies Evanston Twp. High Sch., 1963-66; adviser East Asian Studies Program, U. Miami, 1966, Mich. State U., 1967. Mem. Far Eastern Assn. (past dir., editor monograph series), Comparative Studies in Soc. and History (past v.p., mem. editorial com.), Am. Council Learned Socs. (past sub-com. chmn.), Internat. Conf. on Instl. Change in China (past chmn.), Am. Oriental Soc. (past pres.), Am. Hist. Assn., Assn. Asian Studies, Societe Asiatique (Paris). Unitarian. Club: Chicago Literary. Author: Civil Service in Early Sung China, 960-1067, rev. edit., 1968. Contbr. Ency. Brit., 1962, 65, 71. Contbr. articles profl. jour. Died July 8, 1976; buried Madison, N.H.

KRAFT, LOUIS, social worker; b. Moscow, Russia, Jan. 2, 1891; s. Abraham and Etta (Gellis) K.; came to America 1895; naturalized, 1902; B.A., Coll. of City of N.Y.; spl. courses Sch. of Architecture, Columbia University; Dr. Humane Letters, Jewish Theol. Sem., 1964; children—Stephen, Barbara. Exec. dir. Bronx Y.M.H.A., 1914-17; dir. Welfare activities Jewish Welfare Board, 1917-20; dir. Jewish Center Work, Jewish Welfare Bd., 1921-39; exec. dir., 1939-47, became gen. sec. nat. council, 1947; sec. World Federation of YMHAs; cons. to American Joint Distribution Com., Geneva, Switzerland. Former pres. Nat. Conf. Jewish Social Welfare; hon. pres., past pres. Nat. Assn. Jewish Center Workers, then exec. sec.; chmn. Internat. Conf. Jewish Social Work. Author: Jewish Community Center. Home: New York, N.Y. Died July 11, 1975.

KRAMER, ALEX, food vending co. exec.; b. Russia, May 1, 1912; s. Frank and Sarah (Gold) K.; came to U.S., 1912, naturalized, 1918; ed. pub. schs.; m. Rose Rosenthal, Feb. 6, 1944; children—Myra Ilene, Joel Herbert. Engaged in wholesale milk and dairy bus., 1938-62, food vending bus., 1948-80; founder, 1954, since pres. Autonatic Caterers Corp., Detroit; pres. Interstate Detroit Coffee Co., 1954-80; became pres. Interstate United Corp., and predecessors, 1960, chmn. bd., 1966-68; dir. Petroleum Exploration & Devel. Funds, Abilene, Tex.; chmn. bd. Georgetown Assos., Denver; dir. Bally Case & Cooler Co. (Pa.). Active local fund raising drives. Bd. govs. Culinary Inst. Am. Served with USAAF, 1942-46; PTO. Mem. Nat. Automatic Merchandising Assn. (dir., mem. spl. com. vending problems). Home: Fort Lauderdale, Fla. Died Dec. 12, 1980; buried Machpelah Cemetery, Ferndale, Mich.

KRAMER, BARRY DAVID, pub. co. exec.; b. Detroit, Feb. 25, 1943; s. Harold and Helen (Jackman) K.; student Wayne State U., 1961-64; Ph.B., Monteith Coll., 1967; m. Connie Warren, Feb. 4, 1973; 1 son, J. Justin. Mgr., buyer Marwil Book Co., Detroit, 1967-69; pres. Motor City Music, music pub., artist mgmt., N.Y.C., 1969-73; pres., chmn. Creem Mag., N.Y.C., Detroit, 1970-81; pres. Mixed Media, Inc. Cons. Am. Bicentennial Commn., 1974-81. Mem. Nat. Assn. Musical Mchts., Nat. Assn. Recording Merchandisers, Periodical and Book Assn. Am. (dir.), Hi Fi Inst., Metamora-Dryden Horse Owners Assn. (founder, pres.). Clubs: Detroit Press, Friars, Cavandish Backgammon, Cricket. Home: Dryden, Mich. Died Jan. 29, 1981.

KRAMER, CHARLES RUSSELL, lawyer, univ. trustee; b. Newark, Aug. 17, 1910; s. Charles and Gertrude V. (Porter) K.; A.B., Rutgers U., 1931, LL.B., 1934; m. Mary A. Paxton Apr. 22, 1939; children—Carol B. (Mrs. William E. Britten, Jr.), Charles Russell. Admitted to N.J. bar, 1935, U.S. Supreme Ct., 1957; practice in Newark, 1935-79; partner firm Smith, Kramer & Morrison, 1953-79; judge Municipal Ct., Cedar Grove, N.J., 1947-52. Mem. Bd. Edn., Cedar Grove, 1952-55. Trustee, Rutgers U., 1960-79, chmn., 1976-79. Served to capt. AUS, 1943-46. Mem. Am., N.J., Essex County bar assns., Phi Beta Kappa, Tau Kappa Alpha, Alpha Sigma Phi. Club: Down Town (Newark). Home: Chatham, N.J. Died Nov. 11, 1979.

KRAMER, MILTON JOSEPH, hotel cons.; b. N.Y.C., Aug. 6, 1904; s. Max J. and Yetty (Hauser) K.; grad. Peekskill Mil. Acad., Stamford Mil. Acad.; A.B., Rollins U., 1923; m. Louise Dunagan, 1955. Builder hotels, 1923-30, theatres and office bldgs., 1931-46; ownership-management, 1946-69; former pres. Hotel Edison, Max J. Kramer and Sons Corp.; formerly pres. Monterey and Greystone hotels; engaged various bldg. enterprises; hotel cons. Address: New York, N.Y. Died Mar. 17, 1977.

KRATZ, JOHN AUBEL (KRÄTZ), b. Baltimore, Md., Feb. 20, 1884; s. John and Jennie Elizabeth (Aubel) K.; A.B., Johns Hopkins, 1906; married Mary Luella Hunter, November 25, 1913; children—Jean Aubel (Mrs. J. William Frey), Elinor Hunter (Mrs. Luther C. Conant, Jr.), John Hunter, Martha Bacon (Mrs. Richard J. Shuck). Instructor and head Department of Commerce, Baltimore City College, until 1920; dir. Rehabilitation Division, U.S. Office of Education until Sept. 1943; asso dir., Office of Vocational Rehabilitation, Federal Security Agency since 1943. Life mem. Nat. Rehabilitation Assn. Author: Standard Shorthand, 1916; Vocational Rehabilitation of the Physically Handicapped, 1936. Home: Morton, Pa.

KRAYBILL, DAVID BARTO (KRA'BIL), educator; b. Maytown, Pa., Dec. 28, 1886; s. Franklin Engle and Adeline (Barto) K.; A.B., Franklin and Marshall Coll., 1911; A.M., Columbia, 1916; Ph.D., Pa. State Coll., 1927; m. Ellen Kathryn Millar, July 25, 1917; children—Margaret Adeline, William Henry. Teacher rural schs., Lancaster County, Pa., 1905-08; prin. high sch., Lampeter, Pa., 1911-18; state supervisor Bur. of Vocational Edn., Dept. Pub. Instrn., Harrisburg, Pa., 1919; dir. rural community vocational sch., Lampeter, 1919-24; asst. in dept. rural edn., Pa. State Coll., 1924-25; supt. pub. schs., Redstone Tp., Republic, Pa., 1925-29; supt. schs., Wheeling, W.Va., 1929-33; dean of instrn., W. Va. Inst. of Tech., Montgomery, W.Va., 1933-45; vocational advisor, Veterans Adminstrn., Huntington, W.Va., 1945-51; now mgr. Am. Legion Home, Huntington, W. Va. Attended O.T.C., Camp Lee, Va., 1918. Chmn. Vets. Adminstrn. Regional Rehabilitation Bd. since 1946. Mem. N.E.A. National Vocational Guidance Association America, American Vocational Association, W.Va. State Edn. Assn., Am. Assn. Sch. Adminstrs., Am. Legion, Lambda Chi Alpha, Kappa Delta Pi. Pa. del. to N.E.A. Conv., Minneapolis, Minn., 1927. Republican. Lutheran. Mason. Clubs: Rotary (pres. 1941-42). Home: Huntington, W.Va. *

KRECH, DAVID, educator, psychologist; b. Russia, Mar. 27, 1909; s. Joseph and Sarah (Rabinowitz) Krechevsky; came to U.S., 1913, naturalized, 1925; B.S., N.Y. U., 1930, M.A., 1931; Ph.D., U. Calif., Berkeley, 1933; Philosophia Doctorem (hon.), U. Oslo (Norway), 1976; m. Hilda Sidney Gruenberg, Sept. 17, 1943; 1 son, Richard Joseph. NRC fellow biol. scis. U. Chgo., 1933; research asso. Swarthmore Coll., 1937-38, asst. prof. psychology, 1945-47; instr. psychology U. Colo., 1938-39; mem. faculty U. Calif., Berkeley, 1947-71, prof. psychology, 1949-71, prof. emeritus, 1971-77, Miller Research prof., 1960, 61; lectr. William Alanson White Sch. Psychiatry, Washington, 1945-46, Bryn Mawr Coll., 1945-46; vis. prof. Harvard, 1950-51, U. Oslo (Norway), 1949-50, U. Nijmegan (Holland), 1963; Fulbright prof., 1949-50, 63-64; Jacob Ziskind vis. prof. Brandeis U., 1968. Served with U.S. Army, 1941-45. Recipient achievement citation N.Y. U. Alumni Assn., 1965, ann. award Internat. Forum Neurol. Orgn., 1969; cert. of merit Math. and Sci. Center, Richmond, Va., 1969. Fellow Soc. Psychol. Study Social Issues (past pres.), Am. Psychol. Assn. (Disting. Sci. Contbn. 1970), Soc. Exptl. Psychology, Am. Coll. Neuropsychopharmacology, AAAS; mem. Western Psychol. Assn. (past pres.), Internat. Brain Research Orgn., Soc. for Neuroscis., Internat. Soc. Psychoneuroendocrinology, Sigma Xi. Author: (with R.S. Crutchfield) Theory and Problems of Social Psychology, 1948; Elements of Psychology, 1958; (with Crutchfield and N. Livson) Elements of Psychology, 3d edit., 1974; (with Crutchfield and E. L. Ballachey) The Individual in Society, 1963; (with Joseph L. Hodges, Jr., and Crutchfield) StatLab: An Empirical Introduction to Statistics, 1975. also numerous articles. Mem. adv. bd. Internat. Jour. Neurosci. Home: Berkeley, Calif. Died July 14, 1977; buried Berkeley.

KREECK, GEORGE LEWIS, b. Clifton, Kan., Sept. 30, 1882; s. Lewis and Emma Ellen (Timmons) K.; ed. public schools and University of Kan. m. Ethel Frances Robinson, Oct. 4, 1916; 1 dau., Harriet Ellen (dec.). Long in banking business in Kan.; 1st v.p. Nat. Reserve Life Ins. Co.; mayor of Lawrence, Kan., 7 yrs.; E.E. and M.P. to Paraguay, 1925-30; del. to 2d Internat. Conference of American History and Geography, 1926; served as spl. Am. ambassador to South America. First chmn. Am. Red Cross, Douglas County, Kan., World War, and active speaker in war loan campaign; pres. League of Kansas Municipalities. Mem. Am. Acad. Polit. and Social Science, University Memorial Bd. Republican. Presbyn. Internat. lecturer. Home: Lawrence, Kan., and San Diego, Calif. *

KREISSL, FRANK NICHOLAS (KRI'SL), business exec.; b. Chicago, Jan. 27, 1883; s. Frank and Gertrude (Ebert) K.; ed. pub. schs. of Chicago; m. Helene McCashin, Aug. 17, 1921. Mgr., Am Optical Co., Chicago, 1910-26, Chicago zone mgr., 1926-46, regional mgr., 1946-47, trustee since 1947. Member Optical Wholesalers Nat. Assn. (dir. 1935-45), Chicago Jewelers Assn. (dir. 1943-44). Home: Chicago. *

KRETZMANN, PAUL EDWARD, clergyman, sem. pres.; b. Dearborn County, Ind., Aug. 24, 1883; s. Carl H. E. and Elizabeth (Polack) K.; grad. Concordia Coll., Ft. Wayne, Ind., 1902; student Concordia Sem., St. Louis; M.A., U. of Minn., 1913; Ph.D., 1915; B.D., Chicago Luth. Sem., 1920, D.D., 1922; student La Salle U., Chicago, Washington U., St. Louis; Ed.D., 1936; m. Louise Schroeder, Aug. 29, 1907; children—Dorothea, Eleonora, Theodor, Caroline, Hilda. Served as teacher in states of Colorado and Kansas until 1907; ordained Lutheran ministry, 1906; pastor St. Peter's Ch., Shady Bend, Kan., 1905-07, Emmaus Ch., Denver, Colo., 1907-12; prof. sciences and mathematics, Concordia Coll., St. Paul, Minn., 1912-19, also asst. pastor 2 chs.; editor, later production mgr. Concordia Pub. House, St. Louis, 1919-23; asst. pastor Immanuel Ch., St. Charles, Mo., 1919-38; prof. theology, Concordia Sem., 1923-46; pastor St. John Ev. Luth. Church, Forest Park, Illinois, 1946-48; past pres. Orthodox Luth. Seminary, Mpls. Past pres. Orthodox Lutheran Conference. Member Am. Rockies Alpine Club, Mo. and St. Louis acads. sci., Mo. Hist. Society, Lambda Alpha Psi (U. of Minn.), Pi Gamma Mu; honorary corr. member Institut litteraire et artistique de France. Author: Keuschheit und Zucht, 1915; Edn. Among the Jews, 1916; The Liturgical Element in the Early Drama, 1916; Die Pastoralbriefe, 1918; Concordia Teachers' Library (5 vols.); Christian Art, 1921; Popular Commentary of the Bible (4 vols.), 1921-24; Knowing and Doing, 1923; The Problems of Adolescence and Youth, 1925; The Mysterious Ways of God, 1925; While It Is Day, 1926; Knowledge unto Salvation, 1927; Missionary Stories for Young People, 1927; Heroes of Missions and Their Work, 1927; A Few Pages from the Life of Luther, 1927; The Mountain School, 1928; John Ludwig Krapf, 1928; The Religion of the Child, 1929; The Pot of Gold, 1929; The Christian Woman as a Social Worker, 1929; Great Missionary Women, 1930; From Heaven Above, 1932; Story of the German Bible, 1933; A Believer's View of the New Testament, 1933; Preaching Christ Crucified, 1934; The Doctrine of the Call, 1934; It Is the King, Up to Jerusalem, The Foundations Must Stand, 1936; Guiding the Junior, 1937; Finding Our Way Into the Bible, Knowing the Truth, 1938; That Vexing Problem, 1940; My Job as Youth Counselor, 1942; The God of the Bible and Other "Gods," 1943; In Fellowship with the Savior; Table Prayers, 1945; A Short History of the Orthodox Lutheran Conference, 1953; The Church, the Christian Congregation, and Ministerial Office, 1959. Sermons: Jesus Only, 1955; also articles, brochures, poems, etc. Co-editor of Concordia Cyclopedia, 1927, Orthodox Luth. Theologian, Conservative Lutheran Defender. Home: Mpls. *

KROCH, ADOLPH, business exec.; b. Austria, Jan. 7, 1882; s. Rudolph and Dorothy (Pliple) K.; student U. Vienna, also L.H.D. (hon.); m. Gertrude Horn, June 1, 1909; children—Carl, Gretchen. Came to U.S., 1902, naturalized, 1908. Established Kroch's Bookstores, Inc., booksellers and pubs., Chgo., 1907, chmn. bd., 1949-78; chmn. Kroch's & Brentano's Inc. Hon. fellow Am. Booksellers Assn.; mem. Art Inst. Chgo., Chgo. Hist. Soc., Chgo. Mus. Natural History. Republican. Mason. Author: A Great Bookstore in Action, 1939; Bookstores Can Be Saved, 1952. Home: Tucson, Ariz. Died Nov. 19, 1978; interred Melrose Abbey, Anaheim, Calif.

KROGSTAD, ARNOLD NORMAN (KROG'STÄD), army officer (ret.); b. Lanesboro, Minn., Aug. 28, 1885; s. Christoffer Ole and Nina Bergine (Nelson) K.; B.S., U.S. Mil. Acad., 1909; student Air Corps Tactical Sch., Langley Field, Va., 1927-28; m. Julia Rozelle, Oct. 6, 1917; children—Stanley Foster, Arnold Norman. Commd. lt. Inf., U.S. Army, 1909, capt. Air Corps. 1916, and advanced through the grades to brig. gen., 1938; began pilot training, 1916, and served successively as jr. mil. aviator, airplane pilot, mil. airplane pilot, observer, comdt. Sch. of Mil. Aeronautics, U. of Calif., 1916-17; wartime pilot Regular Army during World War; comdr. Army Air Corps Advanced Flying Sch., Kelly Field, Tex., 1936-38; comdg. gen. 2d Wing, Gen. Hdqrs. Air Force, U.S. Army, Langley Field, Va., 1938-41; comdg. gen. 1st Bomber Command, 1941-42; comdg. gen. First Air Force to Mar. 1942; comdg. gen. Hdqrs. Second Dist., A.A.F. Tech. Training Command, Mar.-July 1942; comdg. gen. Chicago Schs., July-Dec. 1942; comdg. gen. Hdqrs. Fifth Dist., A.A.F. Tech. Training Command, Dec. 1942-44; retired as brig. gen. July 31, 1944. Mem. Order of Daedahans. Home: Miami Beach, Fla. *

KROLL, WILLIAM, violinist; b. N.Y.C., Jan 30, 1901; s. Adolph and Fanny (Braham) K.; student Royal Acad., Berlin, Germany, 1911-14; grad. with highest honors Inst. Mus. Art, N.Y.C., 1917-22; m. Pearl Friedman, June 7, 1922; 1 dau., Barbara. Debut in N.Y.C., 1915; violinist with Elshuco Trio, 1923-29; 1st violinist with Coolidge Quartet, 1935-45; founder Kroll Quartet, 1945; tchr. violin and chamber music Mannes Coll. Music, N.Y.C., 1943-76, Peabody Conservatory, Balt., 1947-65; chamber music Tanglewood, Berkshire Music Center, from 1949; head string dept. Cleve. Conservatory Music, 1965-68; prof. violin Queens Coll., 1969-76; teaching asso. in music Boston U., 1977-80; soloist with orchs., U.S., Europe; soloist with Nat. Symphony Orch., White House, 1966. Recipient Collidge medal Library of Congress, 1942. Mem.

Musicians Guild (co-founder 1947). Club: Bohemians (N.Y.C). Composer violin and chamber music. Home: Boston, Mass. Died Mar. 10, 1980.

KRON, ARTHUR ADAM, advt. exec.; b. Union City, N.J., Feb. 7, 1901; s. Charles J. and Lillian (Wick) K.; A.A. in Bus. Adminstrn., N.Y. Inst., 1926; LL.D., Fairleigh Dickinson U., 1957; m. Ruth Mandeville Snyder, June 26, 1926; children—Arthur Adam, Constance Ruth (Mrs. Robert E. DeMott). With Gotham-Vladimir Advt., Inc., 1916-66, exec. v.p., mng. dir., 1950-58, pres., treas., 1958-60, chmn. bd., 1960-66; vice chmn. bd. Van Brunt & Co., Advt. Marketing, Inc., N.Y.C., 1966-72; chmn. bd. Bus. Publs. Audit of Circulation, Inc., 1955-56; pres. Office Certified Circulation, Inc., 1957-62. Chmn. No. Valley chpt. A.R.C., 1950-57, mem. Eastern adv. council, 1955-58; pres. Englewood (N.J.) Hosp., 1957-66; pres. N.J. Partners of Alliance; chmn. Allied Services Orgn. Group Ins. Fund, 1957-60; chmn. bd. Bergen County chpt. Am. Heart Assn. Trustee Fairleigh Dickinson U., Rutherford, N.J.; bd. dirs. Am. Hosp., Istanbul, Turkey; chmn. bd. Bergen Jr. Coll.; bd. advisers Valparaiso (Ind.) U. Recipient Man of Year World-Wide award Internat. Advt. Assn., 1958. Mem. Internat. Advt. Conv. (founder), Internat. Advt. Assn. (pres. 1948-49, chmn. N.Y. chpt. 1959-60, chmn. regional export expansion com. 1960-61). Republican. Rotarian (pres. N.Y. 1969-70). Home: Teaneck, N.J. Died Jan. 1, 1980; buried George Washington Meml. Park, Paramus, N.J.

KRONENBERGER, LOUIS, writer, critic; b. Cin., Dec. 9, 1904; s. Louis and Mabel (Newwitter) K.; student U. Cin., 3 years, Litt.D.; m. Emmy L. Plaut, Jan. 29, 1940; children—John, Elizabeth (Mrs. George A. Wanklyn). Editor, Boni & Liveright, 1926-33, Alfred A. Knopf, Inc., 1933-35; editorial staff Fortune, 1936-38; drama critic Time mag., 1938-61; drama critic for PM, 1940-48; lectr. English, Columbia, 1950-51; Brandeis lectr., 1951-53, prof. theatre arts, librarian Brandeis U., Waltham, Mass., 1953-70; A Lawrence Lowell vis. prof. Harvard, 1959; vis. lectr. Oxford (Eng.) U., 1959; Christian Gauss Seminar lectr. Princeton, 1961; adj. prof. English, Columbia, 1959; vis. prof. English, Stanford, 1963; Regents prof. U. Calif. at Berkeley, 1968; dir. Corp. Yaddo. Guggenheim fellow, 1969. Fellow Am. Acad. Arts and Scis.; mem. Nat. Inst. Arts and Letters, Authors League Am. Jewish religion. Clubs: Century Assn. (N.Y.C); St. Botolph (Boston); Athenaeum (London). Author: The Grand Manner (novel), 1929; Kings and Desperate Men, 1942; Grand Right and Left (novel), 1952; The Thread of Laughter: Chapters on English Stage Comedy, 1952; Company Manners, 1954; The Republic of Letters, 1955; A Month of Sundays (novel), 1961; The Cart and The Horse, 1964; numerous articles in mags. Editor: An Anthology of Light Verse, 1934; An 18th Century Miscellany, 1936; The Viking Portable Reader's Companion, 1945; The Pleasure of Their Company, 1946; Portable Johnson and Boswell, 1947; Cavalcade of Comedy, 1953; G.B.S.: A Survey, 1953; The Maxims of La Rouchefoucauld, 1937. Contbr. to After the Genteel Tradition, 1937; Books that Changed Our Mind, 1939; Selected Works of Alexander Pope, 1948; Robinson Crusoe, 1948; Don Juan, 1949; Pride and Prejudice, 1950; Tom Jones, 1952; The Way of the World, 1959; She Stoops to Conquer, 1964; Best Play Series, 1953-62; Sheridan, 1957; Marlborough's Duchess, 1958; Plays of G.B. Shaw, 1958; Novelists on Novelists, 1962; Plays of Oscar Wilde, 1962; Sense and Sensibility, 1962; Emma, 1963; The Great World (Greville's Memoirs 1814-1860), 1963; Hamlet, 1964; Quality: Its Image in the Arts, 1969; The Polished Surface, 1969; No Whippings, No Gold Watches, 1970; The Cutting Edge, 1970; Animal, Vegetable, Mineral, 1972; The Last Word, 1972; A Mania For Magnificence, 1972; The Extraordinary Mr. Wilkes, 1974; Biography of Oscar Wilde, 1976. Gen editor: Great Letters Series: Masters of World Literature Series, co-editor: The Viking Book of Aphorisms, 1962; editor: Atlantic Brief Lives: A Biographical Companion to the Arts, 1971. Contbr. to The State of the Nation, 1965, For W.H. Auden, 1972; frequent contbr. Atlantic Monthly. Home: Brookline, Mass. Died Apr. 30, 1980.

KROOTH, DAVID LOUIS, lawyer; b. Chgo., July 15, 1907; s. Louis and Fannie (Wolf) K.; student Crane Jr. Coll., 1925-26; Ph.B., U. Chgo., 1928, J.D., 1930; m. Molly Rand, Apr. 8, 1933; children—Dorothy, John David. Admitted to Ill. bar, 1930, U.S. Supreme Ct., 1936, Ct. Appeals D.C., 1947; in pvt. practice, Chgo., 1930-33; counsel Fed. Emergency Adminstrn. of Pub. Works, Washington, 1933-37; asso. gen. counsel U.S. Housing Authority, 1937-42; gen. counsel Fed. Pub. Housing Authority and Def. Homes Corp., 1942-46; gen. counsel Nat. Housing Agy. and Nat. Housing Expediter, 1946; mem. Washington law firm Krooth and Altman; pres. Nat. Housing Conf., 1950, chmn. bd. dirs., 1951, chmn. legislative policy com.; mem. Consumer Interest Adv. Com. FHA, 1951-62; mem. Housing Finance Mission to Chile, ICA, 1958; head coop. housing team to Honduras, AID, 1963. Mem. Washington Bd. Trade, Am. (chmn. com. on housing and urban renewal sect. local govt. law 1962-71, mem. council sect. local govt. law 1970), D.C. bar assns., Nat. Assn. Housing and Redevel. Ofcls., Nat. Housing Conf., Order of Coif, Phi Beta Kappa. Club: Woodmont Country. Contbg. editor on ct. decisions Jour. Housing. Home: Washington, D.C. Died Dec. 7, 1978.

KROOTH, ROBERT SCHILD, physician; b. Chgo., Jan. 2, 1928; s. Albert and Emily (Schild) K.; A.B., Stanford U., 1948; Ph.D., U. London, 1952; M.D. (Population Council Inc. fellow), Harvard U., 1957; m. Diane Marie Powell, Dec. 21, 1970. Intern, U. Utah Med. Center, Salt Lake City, 1957-58; resident in internal medicine U. Rochester (N.Y.) Hosps., 1961-62; asst. prof. human genetics U. Mich., Ann Arbor, 1962-65, asso. prof., 1965-67, prof., 1967-70; prof. human genetics Columbia U., N.Y.C., 1971-79, chmn. dept. human genetics and devel., 1972-79; attending physician Presbyn. Hosp. N.Y., 1972-79; mem. genetics tng. com. Nat. Insts. Gen. Med. Scis., 1966-70; mem. genetics study sect. NIH, 1971-75. Served with USPHS, 1958-61. Diplomate Nat. Bd. Med. Examiners. Mem. AAAS, Am. Soc. Human Genetics, Genetics Soc. Am., N.Y. Acad. Sci., Harvey Soc. Clubs: Harvard, Princeton, Brit. Schs. and Univs., Columbia U. (N.Y.C.). Editor: Somatic Cell Genetics, 1964; contbr. articles to med. jours. Home: New York, N.Y. Died Oct. 20, 1979.

KRUEGER, KARL, orchestral condr.; b. Atchison, Kan., Jan. 19, 1894; s. Carl and Sophie (Sprick) K.; M.A., Kan. State U., 1913; studied law, U. Vienna, Heidelberg U.; studied composition under Robert Fuchs and Charles Skilton; studied conducting under Nikisch, Weingartner; m. Emita McCormick Jewett, Apr. 14, 1923; 1 dau., Theresa. Condr., Seattle Symphony Orch., 1926-32, Kansas City Philharmonic, 1933-43; Detroit Symphony Orch., 1943-49; guest condr. leading orchs., Europe, U.S., S.A. Founder, dir. Soc. Preservation Am. Mus. Heritage, 1957. Author: The Way of the Conductor, 1958. Died July 21, 1979.

KRUG, EDWARD AUGUST, educator; b. Chgo., Sept. 26, 1911; s. Rudolph Hugo and Anna (Wendt) K.; B.S. in Edn., Northwestern U., 1933, M.S., 1934; Ed.D., Stanford, 1941; m. Annie Ellen McDonald, Apr. 10, 1937; children—Elizabeth Anne, Margaret Jean, Peter. Tchr. social studies Evanston (Ill.) Twp. High Sch., 1935-38; evaluator motion picture project Am. Council Edn., 1938-39; research asso. Stanford, 1939-41, acting asst. prof. edn., 1941-43, asso. prof., 1947-48; asst. prof. edn. Mont. State U., 1943-45; asso. prof. edn. U. Wis., 1945-47, 48-49, prof., 1949-79. Mem. Am. Ednl. Studies Assn., History Edn. Soc. Episcopalian. Author: (with F.L. Bacon) Our Life Today, 1939; (with I.J. Quillen) Living in Our Communities, 1945, Living in Our America, 1951; Curriculum Planning, 1950, 2d edit., 1957; Secondary School Curriculum, 1960; Charles W. Eliot and Popular Education, 1961; The Shaping of the American High School, Vol. I, 1880-1920, 1964, 69, Vol. II, 1920-1941, 1972; Salient Dates in American Education, 1966. Home: Madison, Wis. Died July 30, 1979.

KRUMBEIN, WILLIAM CHRISTIAN, geologist; b. Beaver Falls, Pa., Jan. 28, 1902; s. Charles J. and Hattie (Mauch) K.; Ph.B., U. Chgo., 1926, M.S., 1930, Ph.D., 1932; m. Marjorie Kamm, Sept. 21, 1946. Auditor, U.S. Nat. Adjustment Co., Chgo., 1924-26, comptroller, dir., 1926-30; research geologist Gulf Research and Devel. Co., Pitts., 1945-46; instr. geology U. Chgo., 1932-38, asst. prof., 1938-44, asso. prof., 1944-45; prof. geology Northwestern U., 1946-70, William Deering prof., 1960-70, Pres.'s fellow, 1965-66; geology cons. Brookhaven Nat. Lab., 1947-55; cons. Beach Erosion Bd., Corp. of Engrs., from 1951. John Simon Guggenheim fellow, 1941-42; Fullbright lectr. Queen Mary Coll., U. London, 1960. Recipient War Dept. Commendation for meritorious civilian service, 1945. Fellow Am. Acad. Arts and Scis.; mem. Geol. Soc. Am., Am. Geophys. Union, Internat. Assn. for Math. Geology (exec. com. from 1968), Am. Assn. Petroleum Geologists (editor 1955-57), Soc. Econ. Paleontologists and Mineralogists (pres. 1950, Twenhofel medal 1977), Phi Beta Kappa, Sigma Xi. Club: Cosmos. Author: (with Carey G. Croneis) Down to Earth, 1936; (with F.J. Pettijohn) Manual of Sedimentary Petrography, 1938; (with L.L. Sloss) Stratigraphy and Sedimentation; (with F.A. Graybill) Statistical Models in Geology, 1965. Contbr. articles to sci. jours. Home: Wilmette, Ill. Died Aug. 18, 1979.

KRUMGOLD, JOSEPH, film producer, author; b. Jersey City, Apr. 9, 1908; s. Henry and Lena (Gross) K.; B.A., N.Y. U., 1928; m. Helen Litwin, Jan. 11, 1946; 1 son, Adam. With press dept. Metro-Goldwyn-Meyer Studios, 1928-31, studio adminstr., Paris, France, 1934-36; asso. producer Paramount Pictures, 1931-34; film writer, producer Paramount Pictures, Columbia Pictures, Republic Pictures, RKO, 1936-40; v.p. Film Assos., N.Y.C., 1940-42; film producer OWI, 1942-45; v.p. Palestine Films, Inc., N.Y.C. and Jerusalem, 1948-52; pres. Krumgold Prodns. Co., producing for CBS and NBC TV, Hope, N.J., 1952-80. Mem. bd. edn. Freling Huysen Twn., Warren County, N.J., 1959-80. Films have received 1st prizes at Venice Bienale Festival, Edinborough Fair, others. Mem. Pi Lambda Phi, Pi Delta Epsilon. Author: (novel) Thanks to Murder , 1936; (juveniles) Sweeney Steps Out, 1942, And Now Miguel (Newberry medal A.L.A. 1954), 1954, Onion John (Newberry medal 1959), 1955. Home: Hope, N.J. Died July 10, 1980.

KRUSE, HARRY DAYTON, med. researcher; b. Bridgeton, N.J., July 9, 1900; s. Charles and Emma Margaret (Woodruff) K.; A.B., Dickinson Coll., 1922, A.M., 1926, Dr. Chem., 1955; Sc.D., Johns Hopkins, 1926, M.D., 1932; m. Mary Helen Grayston, July 28, 1944; children—H. Dayton, Douglas, Duncan. NRC fellow in biochemistry, 1926-28; asso. in biochemistry Johns Hopkins U., Balt., 1928-33, asso. prof., 1933-37; med. research with Milbank Meml. Fund, N.Y.C., 1937-52; exec. sec. Com. on Public Health, N.Y. Acad. Medicine, 1952-68; dir. div. research and planning Med. Soc. State of N.Y., 1968-72; med. dir. Med. World News, 1972—; councilor Am. Inst. Nutrition, 1953-56. Mem. food and nutrition bd., chmn. com. on diagnosis and pathology of nutritional deficiencies NRC, 1942-48; mem. nutrition com. N.Y.C. chpt. ARC, 1940-53; v.p. Welfare and Health Council, N.Y.C., 1954-55; mem. Mayor's Commn. on Narcotics Addiction, 1965, Mayor's Task Force on Air Pollution, 1966. Vice pres., mem. bd. dirs. Community Council of Greater N.Y., Inc., 1956-57. Served as cons. to Surgeon Gen., U.S. Army World War II. Fellow N.Y. Acad. Medicine; mem. AMA, Am. Soc. Biol. Chemists, Phi Beta Kappa, Sigma Xi, Alpha Chi Rho, Delta Omega. Author: Nutrition, Its Meaning, Scope and Significance. Editor books on alcoholism and mental disease. Contbr. articles on deficiency diseases and diagnosis of malnutrition to profl. jours. Home: Bronxville, N.Y. Died July 13, 1977; interred Long Branch, N.J.

KUBITSCHEK (DE OLIVEIRO), JUSCELINO, President of Brazil; b. Diamantina, Minas Gerais, Brazil, Sept. 12, 1902; s. Joan Cesar de Oliveiro and Julia Kubitschek de Oliveiro (early decided to use maternal name only); student Diamantina Sem.; M.D., Med. Coll., U. of Minas Gerais, 1927; m. Sarah Lemos, 1931; children—Marcia, Maria Estela. Intern in hosps., Paris, Vienna, Berlin; entered practice as surgeon, Belo Horizonte, Brazil, 1929; apptd. head surg. div. Med. Corps, Minas Gerais Mil. Forces, 1932; named govt. sec., 1933; elected mem. Fed. Chamber of Deputies, 1934; resumed practice of surgery, 1937; mayor, Belo Horzonte, 1940-45; elected mem. Chamber of Deputies, 1946; gov. of Minas Gerais, 1950-55; elected president of Brazil, 1955, certified to office for 5 yr. term, Jan. 1956. Home: Rio de Janiero, Brazil. Died Aug. 22, 1976.

KUEST, FRANK, editor; b. Bakersfield, Calif., July 22, 1917; s. Frank Henry and Anna Frances (Baumgartner) K.; A.A., Glendale Coll., 1937; m. Elizabeth Krantz, Jan. 31, 1948; children—Martin, Elizabeth Ann, Sally. City editor Glendale (Calif.) News-Press, 1946; corr. Washington bur. Copley Press, 1947-58; press attache Am. embassy, Karachi, Pakistan, 1959-64, Tehran, Iran, 1965-67; dep. chief info. U.S. Mil. Assistance Command, Vietnam, 1967-68; editor Am. Legion mag., Indpls., 1976-79; with Paris edit. Stars & Stripes. Served with U.S. Army, 1943-45. Recipient Meritorious Honor award USIA, 1968. Republican. Roman Catholic. Home: Indianapolis, Ind. Died Dec. 25, 1979.

KUEVER, RUDOLPH ANDREW (KE'VĚR), coll. dean; b. Lowden, Ia., Oct. 27, 1886; s. August Andrew Bartol and Caroline Margret (Hensch) K.; ed. Evang. Acad.; Ph.G., State U. of Ia., 1907, Ph.C., 1911; m. Ruth Wilberta Hindman, June 20, 1914; children—Gretchen Louise (Mrs. William O. Merritt), Mary Carolyn (Mrs. Hamilton H. Ries). Pharmacist Univ. Hospital, State University of Iowa, 1907-14, asst. prof. of pharmacy, 1913-16, associate professor, 1916-25, prof., 1925-37, dean of coll. of pharmacy since 1937; member board in control of athletics, State University of Iowa, 1916-37; gen. cons. practice in pharm. chemistry since 1913. With S.A.T.C., World War I. Mem. A.A.A.S., Am. Chem. Soc., Am. Assn. of Colls. of Pharmacy (pres. 1941), Am. Assn. of Univ. Profs., Am. Pharmaceutical Assn., Iowa Pharm. Assn., Am. Legion, Chamber of Commerce, Sigma Xi, Rho Chi, Sigma Alpha Epsilon, Phi Delta Chi. Presbyterian. Mason (32 degree). Club: Triangle. Author: Pharmaceutical Laboratory Manual, 1944. Adv. Editor. American Pharmacy, Vol. 1, 1945, Vol. II, 1947; Pharma. Comp. and Disp., 1949. Contbr. 48 contributions to professional jours. Home: Iowa City, Ia. *

KUFFLER, STEPHEN WILLIAM, neurophysiologist; b. Tap, Hungary, Aug. 24, 1913; s. William and Elizabeth K.; student Gymnasium, Kalksburg, 1923-32; M.D., U. Vienna, 1937; M.A. (hon.), Harvard, 1959; M.D. (hon.), Bern, 1964; Sc.D. (hon.), Yale, 1972, Washington U., 1974, U. London, 1974, U. Chgo., 1977, Pierre and Marie Curie U., Paris, 1977; m. Phyllis Shewcroft, Apr. 25, 1943; children—Suzanne Elizabeth, Damien Paul, Julian Philip, Eugenie Gabrielle. Came to U.S., 1945, naturalized, 1954. Staff depts. medicine and pathology U. Clinic, Vienna, 1937-38; mem. Kanematsu Inst., Sydney (Australia) Hosp., 1938-45; NRC fellow, Australia, 1943-45; Seymour Coman fellow dept. physiology U. Chgo., 1945-47; asso. prof. ophthalmology Wilmer Inst., Johns Hopkins, 1947-56, prof. ophthalmic physiology and biophysics, 1956-59, research on function nervous system Johns Hopkins Hosp.; prof. neurophysiology Harvard Med. Sch., 1959-64, Robert Winthrop prof. neurophysiology, 1964-66, Robert Winthrop prof. neurobiology, chmn. dept., 1966-74, John Franklin Enders Univ. prof.,

1974-80, Harvey lectr., 1959-80; non-resident fellow Salk Inst., LaJolla, Calif., 1966-80; Ferrier lectr. Royal Soc., 1965; Silliman Meml. lectr. Yale U., 1971; Sherrington lectr., 1972. Trustee Marine Biology Lab., Woods Hole, Mass. Recipient Passano award, 1971; Louisa Gross Horwitz prize, 1972; Proctor award in ophthalmology, 1973; Dickson prize in medicine, 1973, Wakeman award, 1976; Armin von Tschermak-Seysenegg prize Austrian Acad. Scis., 1977; Ralph Gerard prize, 1978; F. O. Schmitt prize M.I.T., 1979; Guggenheim fellow, 1956. Mem. Am. Physiol. Soc., Physiol. Soc. Eng., Nat. Acad. Scis., Am. Acad. Arts and Scis., Royal Soc. (fgn. mem.), Royal Danish Acad. Arts and Letters (fgn.), Austrian Acad. Scis., Sigma Xi. Author: (with J. G. Nicholls) From Neuron to Brain, 1976. Contbr. articles to profl. jours. Home: Newton, Mass. Died Oct. 10, 1980.

KUHLER, OTTO AUGUST, engr.-designer; b. Remscheid, Germany, July 31, 1804; s. Otto August and Amalie Helene (Sieper) K.; m. Simonne Louise Eugénie Gillette, Apr. 29, 1920; children—Winona José Helene (Zabriskie), Ronald. Came to U.S., 1923. naturalized, 1928. Asso. with Snutsel Bros., Brussells, Belgium; pioneer designer streamlined automobile, 1912-16; asso. editor Motor mag., Germany, 1916; pres. Das Plakat, graphic arts publ., 1917; publicity and advt., Krupp, Stinnes, Thyssen, Germany, 1919; independent artist, 1920-22; commercial artist, Pittsburgh, Pa., 1922-28; pioneer design streamlined locomotive, 1928, streamlined train, 1931; designer Am. Locomotive Co., 1931; co-designer Hiawatha trains; cons. engr., supervising conversion B. & O. R.R. trains; designed Royal Blue, Rebels, John Wilkes, Black Diamond trains, also bus for White Motor Co.; designer subway car for City of Phila., stations for Milwaukee R.R. and Rock Island R.R.; became design engr. passenger car equipment for postwar period Am. Car & Foundry Co., 1944; painter scenes of Historial Western Railroad; breeder of Hereford Cattle at KZ Ranch. Served as special asst., engr. corps, German Army, 1917-19. Awarded gold medal pioneer enclosed European limousine, 1912. Mem. Newcomen Soc. (Eng.). Ry. and Locomotive Hist. Soc. (hon.). Antique Engines and Threshers Assn. (hon.). Author: On the Railroads, 1938; Portraits of the Iron Horse (with Robert S. Henry), 1938; In the Steel Mill, 1940. Home: Lakewood, Colo. Died Aug. 1977.

KUHLMAN, KATHRYN, clergyman, religious assn. exec.; b. Concordia, Mo.; d. Joe and Emma (Walkenhorst) Kuhlman; D.H.L., Oral Roberts U., 1972. Ordained to ministry Evang. Ch. Alliance; minister radio broadcasts, pub. services, U.S. and Can., Sweden, Jerusalem, Israel; minister CBS-TV, Los Angeles, 1966—. Participant tour, Vietnam, 1970. Decorated Medal of Honor (Vietnam); recipient U.S. Capitol Bldg. flag commemorating 25 years of preaching in Pitts. Speaker of House, 1972, keys to cities, Pitts., 1967, Los Angeles, 1973; named Ky. col.; named mem. Rangers, guerilla fighting forces, Vietnam, 1970. Meml. chs. erected in Nairobi, E. Africa and El Salvador, C. Am. Author: I Believe in Miracles, 1962; God Can Do It Again, 1969; Captain Le Vrier Believes in Miracles, 1973; 10,000 Miles For A Miracle, 1974; How Big Is God?, 1974; Nothing Is Impossible With God, 1974; Standing Tall, 1975; Never Too Late, 1975; Twilight and Dawn, 1976; From Medicine to Miracles, 1978. Office: Pittsburgh, Pa. Died Feb. 20, 1976; interred Forest Lawn Cemetery, Glendale, Calif.

KUHN, FERDINAND, writer; b. N.Y.C., Apr. 10, 1905; s. Ferdinand and Johanna (Loeb) K.; A.B., Columbia, 1925; m. Delia E. Wolf, Aug. 28, 1931; children—Philip Alden, David Antony. With N.Y. Times as reporter, 1925-28, mem. London staff, 1928-36, chief London corr., 1937-39, editorial and spl. writer, 1939-40; asst. to sec. treasury, 1941-42; dep. dir. OWI (overseas br.) and chief Brit. div., 1943-45; head, internat. information service Dept. State, 1945-46; internat. affairs reporter Washington Post, 1946-53; free lance contbr. to newspapers and mags., 1953-78; lectr. Salzburg Seminar Am. Studies, 1967. Pres. Assn. Am. Corrs. in London, 1937-38. Decorated chevalier Legion of Honor (France); recipient Columbia medal distinguished service, 1939, Sigma Delta Chi award best fgn. corr., 1951. Mem. Washington Inst. Fgn. Affairs. Clubs: National Press, Cosmos (Washington). Author: Commodore Perry and the Opening of Japan, 1955; The Story of the Secret Service, 1957; (with wife) Borderlands, 1962, The Philippines, Yesterday and Today, 1966, Russia on Our Minds, 1970, rev. edit., 1976. Editor: (with wife) Adventures in Public Service, 1963. Home: Washington, D.C. Died Oct. 17, 1978.

KUHN, REINHARD, educator; b. Berlin, Germany, Sept. 6, 1930; s. Helmut and Kaethe (Lanke) K.; came to U.S., 1938, naturalized, 1942; A.B., Princeton, 1952, M.A., 1954, Ph.D., 1957; M.A. ad eundem, Brown U., 1965; m. Ira Astride Ameriks, June 15, 1963; children—Bernhard Helmut, Nicholas Peter. Asst. prof., then asso. prof. U. Kans., 1958-63; prof. U. Buffalo, 1963-64; prof. French, Brown U., 1964-77, prof. French and comparative lit., 1977-80, chmn. dept., 1967-76; mem. adv. com. Sweetbriar Jr. Year in France, 1968-80. Mem. tech. com. on R.I. Coastal Zone. Fulbright research scholar France, 1964-65; sr. fellow Nat. Endowment for Humanities, France, 1972-73, cons.-panelist, 1976-80; fellow John Carter Brown Library, 1973, Camargo Found., 1978-79, Inst. Advanced Study, Princeton, N.J., 1979-80. Served with AUS, 1954-56. Fellow Am. Council Learned Socs.; mem. Modern Lang. Assn., Am. Assn. Tchrs. French, Modern Humanities Research Assn., Acad. Lit. Studies (sec.-treas.), Assn. Study Dada and Surrealism, A.A.U.P., Pawtuxet-Edgewood Preservation Soc. (sec.). Author: The Return to Reality, 1962; Correspondence de Francis Jammes et de Francis Viele-Griffin, 1966; L'Esprit Moderne dans la Litterature Francaise, 1972; The Demon of Noontide: Ennui in Western Literature, 1976; co-author: Panorama du Theatre Nouveau, 4 vols., 1966-67. Translator: New Ways of Ontology, 1952; Dying we Live, 1957. Asso. editor: Novel. Home: Edgewood, R.I. Died Nov. 6, 1980.

KUHN, TERRY W., aluminum and brass mfg. cons.; b. Johnstown, Pa., June 20, 1900; s. Christian Walter and Jessie (Terry) K.; B.S., Washington and Jefferson Coll., 1923; m. Jewel Baker, Jan. 9, 1943; 1 dau., Terry. Dist. traffic supt. Mich. Bell Telephone Co., 1923-25; salesman Walter Hagen Golf Co., 1926, Udylite Corp., 1927; salesman Bohn Aluminum & Brass Co., Detroit, 1928-49, v.p. 1949-54, dir., from 1950, exec. v.p., 1954-58, pres., 1958-68, cons., from 1969; former v.p., dir. REO Motors, Inc., Del. Mem. Phi Kappa Psi. Clubs: Royal Palm Yacht and Country (Boca Raton); Country of Detroit (Grosse Pointe Farms, Mich.). Home: Boca Raton, Fla. Died Feb. 26, 1978.

KUNSTADTER, SIGMUND, apparel mfg. co. exec.; b. Chgo., Aug. 31, 1901; s. Albert and Hortense (Simon) K.; A.B., U. Mich., 1922; m. Maxine H. Weil, Jan 30, 1926; children—John Weil, Peter. With Formfit Co. (now Formfit/Rogers Co.), Chgo., 1922-66, successively mdse. mgr., asst. treas., v.p., pres., 1926-64, chmn., 1964-66, also dir.; dir. Urban Dynamics. Bd. dirs. Mus. Contemporary Art, Donor's Forum, chmn., 1975; governing life mem., trustee Art Inst. Chgo., Chgo. Hort. Soc.; trustee Monmouth Coll. Mem. Soc. Contemporary Am. Art (pres. 1959-60, dir.), Phi Beta Kappa. Clubs: Standard Metropolitan (Chicago); Lake Shore Country (Glencoe, Ill.). Home: Highland Park, Ill. Died Sept. 29, 1977.

KUPCHAN, S. MORRIS, educator, chemist; b. N.Y.C., Nov. 10, 1922; s. Hyman and Rebecca (Fishgold) K.; B.S., CCNY, 1941; M.A., Columbia U., 1942, Ph.D., 1945; Dr. honoris causa, Uppsala (Sweden) U., 1975; m. Nancy R. Slater, Mar. 28, 1954; children-Clifford, Charles. Research asso., lectr. Columbia U., 1945-48; research fellow, instr. chemistry Harvard U., 1948-55; mem. faculty U. Wis., 1955-69, prof., 1961-69; John W. Mallet prof. chemistry, mem. Center Advanced Studies, U. Va., Charlottesville, 1969-76 plenary lectr. internat. symposia, 1955-76. Mem. pharmacology, exptl. therapeutics study sect. NIH, 1963-67, mem. medicinal chemistry study sect., 1967-71, chmn, 1970-71; chmn. drug devel. panel NICHD, NIH, 1972-73, mem., 1975-76; mem. U.S. del on herbal pharmacology People's Republic of China, 1974; sci. adv. com. Am. Cancer Soc., 1975-76. Recipient Ebert prize, 1960, Research Achievement award in natural products Am. Pharm. Assn., 1965. Mem. Am. Chem Soc. (Ernest Guenther award 1975), Am. Pharm. Assn., Chem. Soc. London, Soc. Econ. Botany (past pres), N.Y. Acad. Scis., Mexican Chem, Soc (hon.). Contbr. numerous articles to profl. jours; Home: Charlottesville, N.C. Died Oct. 19, 1976.

KURTZ, WILBUR G., SR., artist, historian; b. Oakland, Ill., Feb. 28, 1882; s. George Heelen and Amanda Helen (Baum) K.; student art DePauw U., 1901-02, Art Inst., Chgo., 1904-09; m. Annie Laurie Fuller, June 14, 1911 (dec. Oct. 1946); children—Wilbur G., Nell Louise, Henry H., Annie Laurie, Eugene Allen; m. 2d, Annie R. Pye, Feb. 9, 1949. Art studio, Chgo., 1910-12, Atlanta, 1912—; tech. advisor Gone with the Wind, Selznick Internat. Pictures & Metro-Goldwyn-Mayer, Culver City, Cal., 1939, Walt Disney Studios, Burbank, Cal., Song of the South, 1944, Great Locomotive Chase, 1952; murals, easel paintings permanent collections Atlanta Woman's Club, Clark Howell Sch., Capitol Homes Auditorium, Fed. Res. Bank, First Nat. Bank, First Fed. Loan & Savs. Co. (all Atlanta), Abbeville (S.C.) Nat. Bank, others. Writer hist. roadside markers in area of Atlanta Campaign of 1864, Ga. Hist. Commn., 1952-55. Mem. Atlanta Hist. Soc., Atlanta Civil War Round Table, Atlanta Symposium. Author: Cyclorama of the Battle of Atlanta, 1954. Contbr. hist. publs. Home: Atlanta. *

KURTZMAN, DAVID HAROLD, educator; b. Russia, Jan. 11, 1904; s. Maurice and Hannah (Wolfson) K.; came to U.S., 1921, naturalized 1926; B.S., Temple U., 1930, LL.D., 1967; M.A., U. Pa., 1931, PhD., 1935; LL.D., U. Pitts., 1967; L.H.D. (hon.), Jefferson Med. Coll., 1968; D.Sc., Pa. Coll. Optometry, 1969, other hon. degrees; m. Celia Buchdrucker, July 24, 1927; children—Rochelle (Mrs. Rochelle K. Feinberg), Marshall K. Instr. polit. sci. Temple U., 1931-33; asst. dir. and dir. research Western div. Pa. Economy League, 1933-59; sec. adminstrn. Pa., 1959-63; sr. research and edn. asso. Fels Inst. Local and State Govt., U. Pa., 1963-65; vice chancellor finance U. Pitts., 1965-67, acting chancellor, 1966-67, chancellor, 1967, chancellor emeritus, 1967-77, prof. higher edn. and pub. adminstrn., 1972-75; supt. pub instrn. Pa., 1967-69, sec. edn., 1969-71; vis. lectr. Grad. Sch. Pub. and Internat. Affairs, U. Pitts., 1958-59. Sec. Pitts. Met. Study Commn., 1951-55; chmn. Mayor Pitts. Mgmt. Adv. Com., 1951-59; chief staff Gov. Pa. Tax Adv. Commn., 1956, 58; chmn. Gov. Pa. Tax Study and Revision Commn., 1966; research dir. Pa. Constl. Conv. Prep Com., 1967; mem. Pres.' Commn. on Sch. Finance 1970-72; mem; Pa. Commn. on Sch. Finance, 1971. Trustee Community Coll. Allegheny County, 1973-77; bd. dirs. Met. Pitts. Pub. Broadcasting. Mem. Phi Beta Kappa, Omicron Delta Kappa, Phi Eta Sigma, Beta Gamma Sigma, Druids. Home: Pittsburgh, Pa. Died Feb. 22, 1977.

KUTER, LAURENCE SHERMAN, air force officer, aviation cons.; b. Rockford, Ill. May 28, 1905; s. Maynard Washburn and Minna (Beiser) K.; B.S., U.S. Mil. Acad., 1927; grad. Air Corps Primary Flying Sch., 1929, Air Corps Advanced Flying Sch. (bombardment), 1930, Air Corps Tactical Sch., 1935; D.Mil. Sci. (hon.), U. Md.; m. Ethel Lyddon, Sept. 8, 1927; 1 dau., Roxanne (Mrs. R.B. Williamson). Commd. 2d lt. Field Arty., U.S. Army, 1927, trans. to Air Corps, 1930, Advanced through grades to gen., 1955; chief bombardment sect. Air Corps Tactical Sch., 1935-37, instr. air warfare, 1937-39; mem. air br., operations and tng. div. War Dept. Gen. Staff, 1939-41; asst. sec. War Dept. gen. staff, 1941-42; dep. chief air staff, 1942; comdr. 1st Bomb. Wing, 8th Air Force, 1942-43; dep. comdr. N.W. African Tactical Air Force during Tunisian campaign; asst. chief of air staff for plans, 1943-45; dep. comdr. Army Air Forces, Pacific Ocean area, also duty with U.S. Army Strategic Air Forces in Pacific, 1945; comdg. gen. Atlantic div. Air Trans. Command, 1945-46; rep. U.S. on council Internat. Civil Aviation Orgn., 1946-48; chmn. CAB by Pres. Truman, not confirmed by Senate; comdr. Mil. Air Transp. Service, 1948-51; dep. chief staff, personnel, Hdqurs. USAF, 1951-53; comdr. Air U., 1953-55, CINC Far East Air Forces, 1955-57; comdr. in chief Pacific Air Forces, 1957-59; comdr. in chief NORAD, Colorado Springs, Colo., 1959-62; ret., 1962; v.p. Pan Am. World Airways, Inc., N.Y.C., 1962-65, v.p. tech. staff, 1965-68, exec. v.p., 1968-70; mem. adv. bd. Air Acad. Nat. Bank. Trustee, past chmn. Aerospace Edn. Found. Decorated D.S.M. with 2 oak leaf clusters, Legion of Merit, Bronze Star; Croix de Guerre with palms, Legion of Honor (French); comdr. British Empire; knight grand officer Order of Christ (Portugal), other Am., fgn. decorations. Mem. Air Force Assn., Nat. Def. Transp. Assn., Order of Daedalians, Am. Legion, S.A.R., Sigma Alpha Tau. Episcopalian. Clubs: Army-Navy (Washington); Wings (past council), (N.Y.C.); Royal Poinciana Golf, Collier County Conservancy (Naples, Fla.). Author: Airman at Yalta, 1955; The Great Gamble: The Boeing 747, 1973; numerous articles. Address: Naples, Fla. Died Nov. 30, 1979; buried Air Force Acad. Cemetery, Colo.

KUYKENDALL, RALPH SIMPSON, educator; b. Linden, Calif., Apr. 12, 1885; s. John Wesley and Marilla Persis (Pierce) K.; A.B., Coll. of the Pacific, San Jose, Calif., 1910; student Stanford U., 1910-11; M.A., U. of Calif., 1918; m. Edith Clare Kelly, Aug. 11, 1919; children—John Richard, Delmar Leur. Field agt. Calif. Hist. Survey Commn., 1916-18; asst. in hist., U. of Calif., 1919-21; exec. sec. Hist. Commn., Ty. of Hawaii, 1922-32; asst. prof. hist., U. of Hawaii, 1932-38, professor 1949-50. Member American Historical Assn., American Association for State and Local History, Hawaiian Historical Soc. (trustee 1926-38; pres. 1940-43), Institute of Pacific Relations, Pi Gamma Mu, Phi Kappa Phi. Republican. Methodist. Club: Round Table. Author: A History of Hawaii (with H. E. Gregory), 1926; Hawaii in the World War (with L. T. Gill), 1928; The Hawaiian Kingdom (1778-1854). 1938; Constitutions of the Hawaiian Kingdom, 1940; Hawaii, A History (with A. G. Day), 1948. Member board editors Pacific Historical Review, 1935-37. Contributor articles on Pacific and Hawaiian Island History.*

KWALWASSER, JACOB, educator; b. N.Y.C., Feb. 27, 1894; s. Louis and Lena (Greenberg) K.; B.A., B.E., Pitts U., 1917; M.A., State U. Ia., 1923, Ph.D., 1925; m. Pearl T. Little, Dec. 21, 1919; children—Edgar, Robert, Helen. Vis. prof. music edn., Columbia, U. Iowa, U. Tex., U. Ark., U. Minn., Julliard Sch. Music; lectr. Assn. Am. Colls., Chgo. Mus. Coll., U. Idaho, Temple U., from 1926; research prof. music edn. Syracuse U., 1926-54, thereafter prof. emeritus. Pioneer research prof. music edn. in U.S.; builder music edn. tests. Mem. Music Educators Nat. Conf., Music Tchrs. Nat. Assn., Sigma Xi, Phi Mu Alpha, Kappa Phi Kappa. Jewish religion. Author: Kwalwasser-Ruch Achievement Test, 1925; Tests and Measurements in Music, 1927; Kwalwasser Dykema Music Tests, 1932; Two Hundred Songs for Junior and Senior High Schools, 1929; Problems in Music Education, 1950; Kwalwasser Music Aptitude Tests, 1953; Exploring the Musical Mind 1955; also articles. Home: Pittsburgh, Pa. Died Aug. 7, 1977.

KWAPISZEWSKI, MICHAEL, diplomat, minister plenipotentiary, counselor Polish Embassy; b. Gorlowka, Poland, August 23, 1884; s. Charles and

Paulina K; ed. High Sch., Warsaw, 1902; Imperial Coll. of Tsarskoe Selo (Russia), 1905; U. of Kharkoff, 1905-07; U. of Warsaw, 1907-09; Royal Tech. Coll., 1909-12; m. Clara Swenson, August 16, 1913. Called in 1916 by Hon. Ignace Jan Paderewski to collaborate with him in U.S.A. in his work for Poland; after restoration of Poland was apptd. counselor of Polish Legation in Washington, remaining until 1923; recalled to Ministry of Foreign Affairs in Warsaw, apptd. Chief of Div. of Americas and Far East; Polish envoy to Norway, 1924-27; envoy to Jugoslavia, 1928-29; sent to establish first diplomatic relation with govt. of Union of South Africa, Capetown, 1929-30; with Polish Delegation to Disarmament Conf., Geneva, 1932; special mission to U.S.A., 1932-35. Resigned from diplomatic service, 1935, to devote his time to promotion of closer relations between U.S.A., and Poland, as vice-pres. and gen. mgr. of Polish Am. Chamber of Commerce in Warsaw, and vice-pres. Polish-American Soc. High Commissioner for Polish participation at N.Y. World's Fair, 1939. Returned to Foreign Service of Poland, Dec. 1939; counselor of Polish Embassy in Washington with title of M.P. and E.E. since 1939. Decorations: Order of Polonia Restituta, Polish medal of merit, Grand Officer of Norwegian St. Olaf's Order; Grand Officer of Jugoslav Order of St. Sava, etc. Roman Catholic. Home: Washington, D.C. *

KYRIDES, LUCAS PETROU (KE-RE'DES), (SURNAME ORIGINALLY KYRIAKIDES), research chemist; b. Broussa, Asia Minor (Turkey), April 13, 1883; s. Petros and Theodora (Johnides) Kyriakides; came to U.S., 1905; naturalized, 1913; A.B., Anatolia Coll., Merzifon, Turkey, 1902; A.B., U. of Mich., 1907; Sc.D., 1909; m. Alma Collins, Sept. 19, 1925 (div.); children—Helen Lee (Mrs. Goodwin), Phyllis Jane. Research assistant, Univ. of Ill., 1909-10; analytical chemist, Queen Anne Soap Co., Detroit, 1910-11; research on synthetic rubber, Hood Rubber Co., Watertown, Mass., 1911-14; research on chemotherapeutic agents, Parke, Davis & Co., Detroit, 1914-16; operated own plant on aniline, 1916; research chemist, Gen. Chem. Co., 1917-19, Nat. Aniline and Chem Co., 1919-28; asst. research dir. Monsanto Chem. Co., St. Louis, Mo., 1928-29, research dir., organic chemicals div., 1930-47; pres. Chemical Specialties, Inc., Zeeland, Mich., since 1947, Sumner Chem. Co. since 1947. Fellow N.Y. Acad. of Sci. Mem. Am. Chem. Soc. (recipient Midwest Award 1944), Sigma Xi, Phi Lambda Upsilon. *

LACHER, WALTER SCOTT, assn. secretary; b. Winona, Minn., Apr. 7, 1884; s. John Henry Alois and Louisa (Krumrey) L.; B.S. in C.E., U. of Wis., 1907; m. Winona Alice Hammitt, Mar. 14, 1908; children—Jack Hammitt, Robert Baker, Karl Krumrey, Richard William. Asst. engr. C.&A. Ry., 1907-08; asst. engr. Ill. Highway Commn., July-Jan. 1908; office engr. C.,M.&St.P. Ry., 1909-15; western engring. editor Railway Age, 1915-30, engring. editor, 1930-38; mng. editor Railway Engineering and Maintenance, 1917-38; sec. engring. div., Assn. of Am. Railroads 1938-50. Mem. Am. Soc. C.E., Am. Ry. Engring. Assn. (sec. 1938-50), Western Soc. Engrs., Am. Ry. Bridge and Bldg. Assn., Tau Beta Pi. Club: Engineers. Home: Hinsdale, Ill. *

LACHMAN, HAROLD, founder, pres., chmn. John Plain & Co., Chgo. mail-order firm. Benefactor, Michael Reese Hosp., Chgo., Loyola Hosp., Chgo., M.D. Anderson Hosp., Houston. Home: Cuernavaca, Mexico. Died Nov. 26, 1978; interred Basilica of Our Lady of Guadalupe, Mexico City.

LACHMAN, HARRY, landscape painter; b. La Salle, Ill., June 29, 1886; s. Benjamin and Augusta (Neustadt)L; student U. of Mich.; unmarried. Settled in Paris, 1912; four paintings bought by French Govt. for the MusÉe du Luxembourg and one for the Petit Palais; represented in Art Inst. Chicago, Delgado Mus. (New Orleans), etc. Connected with Am. Red Cross, World War, with A.E.F. Engr. Corps, chief instr. landscape painting at A.E.F. art training centre, Bellevue, after the Armistice, later with Am. Com. for Devastated France; production mgr. Rex Ingram Productions, Nice, 3 yrs; now dir. and producer at own studios in Nice. Chevalier Legion of Honor (France). *

LACROSSE, EMMART, mech. engr.; b. Washington, Mar. 7, 1886; s. John F. and Lillian (Wallace) LaC.; student U. Tenn., 1907-09, Lowell Inst., 1912-14; E.D., Tufts Coll., 1946; m. Clara Harner, July 30, 1910; children—Emmart Jr., E. Robert. Mem. Turbine dept. Westinghouse Electric & Mfg. Co., East Pittsburgh, Pa., 1904-07; designer ordnance U.S. Army, 1909-10; factory, power plant designer Watertown (Mass.) Arsenal, 1910-15; mech. engr. S.M. Green Co., Springfield, Mass., 1915-16; joined Stone & Webster Engring, Corp., Boston, 1916, v.p., 1933, v. chmn. bd., 1944, dir. engring. since 1945; dir. Power Condenser & Electronics Corp., Boston. Fellow American Society Mechanical Engs., A.A.A.S.; member National, Mass. socs. profl. engrs., American Society Testing Materials, Newcomen Soc., Beacon Soc. Clubs: Brae Burn Country, Algonquin, Downtown (Boston). Home: Waban, Mass. *

LACY, BENJAMIN RICE, JR., clergyman, educator; b. Raleigh, N.C., July 30, 1886; s. Benjamin Rice and Mary (Burwell) L.; grad. Raleigh Male Acad., 1902; A.B., Davidson (N.C.) Coll., 1906, D.D., 1919; B.A. in Modern History, Oxford U., Eng., 1910; B.D., Union Theol. Sem. in Va., 1913, Hoge fellow, 1913-14; LL.D., Hampden-Sydney Coll., 1928; D.D., Duke University, 1934; LL.D., University of North Carolina, 1948; Doctor honoris causa, Theological Faculty of the University of Montpellier, Montpellier, France; married Emma Elizabeth White, April 19, 1919; children—Benjamin Rice III, William White, Emma Elizabeth, Robert Burwell. Ordained ministry Presbyn. Ch. in U.S., 1914; home missionary, Wake County, N.C., 1914-17; chaplain, capt. 113th F.A., 30th Div., U.S. Army, July 1918-Apr. 1919; pastor Central Ch., Atlanta, 1919-26; pres. Union Theol. Sem. Va., 1926-56; pastor Coll. Ch. and chaplain of Hampden-Sydney Coll., 1956—. Moderator Gen. Assembly, Presbyn. Ch. in United States, 1950. Member of the Kappa Alpha, Phi Beta Kappa, Omicron Delta Kappa. Democrat. Clubs: Longwood, Hermitage Country. Author: Revivals in the Midst of the Years, 1943. Address: Hampden-Sydney, Va. *

LACY, MICAJAH PENNINGTON, coll. dean; B.S., Va. Poly. Inst., 1951, M.S., 1954; Ph.D., U. Wis., 1961. Dean admissions and records Va. Poly. Inst., Blacksburg. *

LACY, O(RLANDO) J(OSEPH), life ins. exec.; b. Prairie du Chien, Wis., Aug. 20, 1884; s. Thurlow and Rachael (Cherrier) L.; student ins. Carnegie Inst. Tech., 1920; m. Helen Elizabeth Davis, Jan. 19, 1907. Locating and constrn. engr. C.M. & S.P. R.R., and in ranching and banking in Mont.; dist. agt., later state mgr. New World Life Ins. Co., Billings, Mont., 1914-20; agency mgr. Shenandoah Life Ins. Co., Roanoke, Va., 1920-22; 2d v.p. Minn. Mut. Life Ins. Co., St. Paul, 1922-29, v.p., 1929-32, exec. v.p., 1932-34, dir., 1925-34; became pres., 1934; mem. exec. com. Life Underwriters Tng. Council since 1950. Mem. Golden Empire Council, Nat. Council Boy Scouts of Am. Elk. Clubs: Rotary, Sutter, Del Paso Country. Home: Sacramento, Cal. *

LACY, WILLIAM STERLING BYRD, govt. ofcl.; b. Mesa County, Colo., Feb. 5, 1910; s. Sterling Byrd and Della Margaret (Lumsden) L.; A.B., U. Colo., 1932; m. Margaret Agnes Innes, July 24, 1935; 1 son, Sterling Byrd Innes; m. 2d, Kirsten Magelssen, Sept. 24, 1943; children—Rolf Gordon Franks (stepson) (dec.). Kirsten Linn (Mrs. Charles F. Bagley III). Sec. to Senator Alva B. Adams, 1933-34; economist A.A.A., Dept. Agr., 1934-36; exec. Colo. Life Ins. Co., Denver, 1936-37; cons. Nat. Resources Com., 1937-38; financial economist SEC, 1938-40; dir. fgn. information br. Nat. Def. Adv. Council, WPB and OPA, 1940-44; asst. dept. dir. UNRRA, 1944-45; asst. chief div. S.E. Asia, Dept. State, 1946-49, dir. Office Philippines and S.E. Asia, 1950-52; counselor, dept. chief mission Am. Embassy, Manila, 1952; U.S. ambassador to Republic Korea, 1955; spl. asst.to sec. state for East-West exchanges, 1956-61; dep. comdt. Nat. War Coll., 1960; ret., 1961. Decorated officer Order Orange Nassau; comdr. Philippine Legion of Honor; recipient Norlin award, 1960; Golden Heart medal, Presdl. award. Mem. Phi Gamma Delta. Episcopalian. Clubs: 1925 F Street, Metropolitan (Washington). Author: British Wartime Economic Controls During World War II, 1942. Home: Washington, D.C. Died Dec. 11, 1978.

LADAS, STEPHEN PERICLES, internat. patent, trademark and copyright lawyer; b. Grevena, Greece, July 11, 1898; s. Pericles C. and Anastasia (Pattajo) L.; LL.D., Athens U., Greece; A.M., Sch. Polit. Sci., Paris, 1923; LL.B., Harvard, 1926, S.J.D., 1927; m. Christine C. Douropulos, Sept. 7, 1929; children—Natalie Elizabeth, Cornelia Ann. Mem. Greek bar, 1920; attaché Greek Embassy, Paris, 1921-22; sec. Bur. Internat. Research, Harvard and Radcliffe, 1928-30; admitted to N.Y. bar; mem. firm Ladas, Perry, Von Gehr, Goldsmith & Deschamps, N.Y.C. Chmn. commn. indsl. property U.S. Council, 1947-73, and hon. chmn. commn. indsl. property Internat. C. of C. Trustee, Am. Friends of Greece, Athens Coll., Anatolia Coll. Decorated Silver Cross of Savior, comdr. Royal Order of Phoenix (Greece). Mem. Internat. Assn. Protection Indsl. Property (treas.; hon. mem.), Am. Patent and Trademark Assn. (hon.), Inter-Am. Indsl. Property Assn. (hon.), Near East Coll. Assn. (hon. mem., trustee); corr. mem. Acad. Athens, Instituto Argentino de Derecho Intelectual. Clubs: Harvard, N.Y. Athletic (N.Y.C.); Manchester (Mass.) Bath and Tennis. Author: The International Protection of Trade-Marks by American Republics, 1929; The International Protection of Industrial Property, 1930; The Exchange of Minorities: Bulgaria, Greece and Turkey, 1932; The International Protection of Literary and Artistic Property, 1939; Patents, Trademarks and Related Rights-National and International Protection, 3 vols., 1974. Home: New York, N.Y. Died Mar. 13, 1976.

LA DUE, JOHN SAMUEL, physician; b. Minot, N.D., Sept. 6, 1911; s. Samuel and Edith Woodsworth (Mann) La.D.; A.B., U. Minn., 1932, S.M. in Medicine, 1940, Ph.D. in Medicine, 1941; M.D., Harvard, 1936; m. Margaret Ruth Stokes, Apr. 24, 1937. Intern L.I. Hosp., 1936-37; resident Mpls. Gen. Hosp., 1937-40, adj. staff physician, 1940-41; asst. vis. physician Charity Hosp., New Orleans, 1941-43, vis. physician, 1943-45, dir. lung sta., 1943-45; clin. asst. Meml. Hosp., N.Y.C., 1945-46, asst. attending physician, 1946-48, asso. attending physician, 1948-80, physician to outpatient dept. N.Y. Hosp., 1946-47, asst. attending physician, 1948-80; tchr. fellow U. Minn. Med. Sch., 1937-40, instr. medicine, 1940-41; instr. La. State U. Sch. Medicine, 1941-43, asst. prof. medicine, 1943-44, asso. prof. clin. medicine, 1944-45; clin. asst. Cornell U. Med. Coll., 1945-46, faculty, 1946-80, asso. prof. clin. medicine, 1958-80; dir. heart sta. Meml. Center, N.Y.C., 1955-57; dir. cardiovascular sect. Meml. Center and Sloan Kettering Inst., 1957-66; sr. attending cardiologist St. Barnabas Hosp. Chronic Diseases. Bd. dirs., sec., past pres. med. staff Doctors Hosp., N.Y.C. Recipient Hektoen medal A.M.A., 1955; Alfred P. Sloan award clin. investigation, 1955; Cummings Humanitarian award, 1963, 64. Diplomate Nat. Bd. Med. Examiners, Am. Bd. Internal Medicine. Mem. Am. Coll. Cardiology (pres. 1962-63), Academia Nacional de Medicina do Brazil, Am. Fedn. Clin. Research (past pres.), A.M.A., A.C.P., Am. Coll. Chest Physicians, Harvey Soc., Soc. Exptl. Biology and Medicine, Am., N.Y. heart assns., N.Y. Acad. Med., N.Y. Acad. Sci., James Ewing Soc., N.Y. Cardiological Soc. (past pres.), N.Y. State Soc. Internal Medicine (past pres.), Harvard Med. Soc. N.Y., Academia Nacional de Medicina de Peru (hon.), Sigma Xi, Sigma Chi. Episcopalian. Contbr. articles to profl. jours., sects. several med. text books. Home: New York, N.Y. Died Apr. 18, 1980; buried Lakewood Cemetery, Mpls.

LAHEY, RICHARD FRANCIS, artist; b. Jersey City, June 23, 1893; s. Richard and Elizabeth (Adäms) L.; student Art Students League, N.Y.C., 1913-17; traveled and studied abroad, summers, 1920-25; m. Carlotta Gonzales, Dec. 19, 1931. Instr. Mpls. Art Sch., 1921-22, Art Students League, 1923-35; dir. Corcoran Sch. Art, Washington, 1935-63, prin. emeritus, 1963-78; artist in residence U. Ga., 1968; prof. fine arts Goucher Coll., Balt., 1937-60; prof. George Washington U.; Ford Found. grantee, artist in residence Parrish Art Mus., Southampton, 1965, Hamilton Easter Field, Ogunquit, Me., 1965; rep. permanent collection Nat. Collection Fine Arts, also large museums and galleries of U.S.; one-man shows Va. Mus. Fine Arts, Corcoran Gallery of Art, 1944, Goucher Coll., 1959, U. Ga., 1968, Patrick Henry Library, Vienna, Va., 1971; commd. with wife to execute mural for Hawaii Meml., Honolulu, 1960, portrait U.S. Treasury Dept., 1962; exhibited Retrospective Exhbn., Corcoran Gallery, 1963, U. Ga., 1968; portrait dedicated to Dean J.W. Whittemore, Dept. Engring., Va. Poly. Inst., 1967. Mem. Fine Arts Commn. of Va., 1942-44. Served with camouflage sect. U.S. Navy, 1917-19. Mem. Am. Soc. Painters, Sculptors and Gravers, Salons of Am., Soc. Ind. Artists, Art Students League, Washington Soc. Artists, Artist's Guild, Washington. Lectr. art subjects. Commd. to write Picasso His Life and Art; Rembrandt His Life and Art (with wife). Home: Vienna, Va. Died Aug. 1, 1978; buried Arlington Nat. Cemetery, Arlington, Va.

LAIDLAW, ROBERT ALEXANDER, financier; b. Barrie, Ont., Jan. 10, 1886; s. Robert and Jessie (Cameron) L.; B.A., U. Toronto, 1908, LL.D., 1951; m. Julia I. Cayley, Feb. 12, 1913; children—Katherine J., R. G. Nicholas, Roderick W. Hon. chairman Nat. Trust Co., Ltd., 1951—; mem. bd. directors R. Laidlaw Lumber Co., Ltd., British-Am. Oil Co., Ltd., Moore Corp., Ltd., Maple Leaf Gardens, Steel Company of Canada. Honorary life chmn. bd. of governors Upper Canada College; honorary chmn. bd. trustees Hosp. for Sick Children. Clubs: Toronto, York, University (Toronto); Mount Royal (Montreal). Address: Toronto, Can. *

LAIDLAW, ROBERT W., physician; b. Englewood, N.J., Feb. 26, 1901; s. Walter and Jennie Louise (Childs) L.; A.B., Princeton, 1924; M.D., Coll. Phys. and Surg., N.Y.C., 1931; m. Elizabeth Hale, July 13, 1930 (div. 1940); 1 son, Donald Hale; m. 2d, Beatrice Snedeker, Mar. 22, 1940 (div. 1968); 1 dau., Patricia Mott; m. 3d, Priscilla Gatling Spilman, Feb. 20, 1971. Intern, Presbyn. Hosp., N.Y.C., 1931-32, asst. attending neurologist Vanderbilt Clinic, 1934-49, chief vets. rehab. clinic, 1945-48; postgrad. tng. Neurol. Inst., N.Y.C., 1932-37, asst. attending neurologist, 1934-49; cons. psychiatry N.Y. State Tng. Sch. for Boys, Warwick, 1933-37; psychiat. cons. wards, outpatient clinic Roosevelt Hosp., N.Y.C., 1933-40, asst. attending psychiatrist, 1940-47, asso. attending psychiatrist, 1947-49, attending psychiatrist, 1949-66, chief psychiat. div., 1950-66, cons. dept., 1966-78; instr. neurology Coll. Phys. and Surg., 1934-39; pvt. practice psychiatry, N.Y.C., 1937-78; neuropsychiatrist Induction Center, N.Y.C., 1943-45; cons. psychiatry Union Theol. Sem., 1949-58; mem. N.Y. State Bd. Social Welfare, 1958-65. Diplomate Am. Bd. Psychiatry and Neurology. Life fellow Am. Psychiat. Assn., N.Y. Acad. Medicine; fellow Am. Assn. Marriage and Family

Counselors (founder, pres. 1950-52); mem. A.M.A., Assn. Research Nervous and Mental Diseases, N.Y. State, N.Y. County med. socs., N.Y. Psychiat. Soc. N.Y. Soc. Clin. Psychiatry, N.Y. Neurol. Soc. Contbr. articles to profl. publs. Home: New York, N.Y. Died June 25, 1978.

LAIDLER, HARRY WELLINGTON (LAD'LER), author, economist; b. Brooklyn, N.Y., Feb. 18, 1884; s. William Ebenezer and Julia (Heary) L.; A.B., Wesleyan U., Middletown, Conn., 1907; hon. A.M., 1933; LL.B., Brooklyn Law Sch., 1910; Ph.D., Columbia, 1914; m. Agnes Fuller Armington, Nov. 5, 1919; children—John Armington, Rosamond. Reporter, staff Brooklyn Daily Eagle, 1907-10; a founder, 1905, sec., 1910-21, Intercollegiate Socialist Society; executive director of the League for Industrial Democracy, 1921-57; emeritus 1957—; editor Intercollegiate Socialist, 1913-19; editor Socialist Rev., 1919-21. Coll., univ. lectr.; dir. Nat. Bureau Economic Research since 1920, v.p., 1928, pres., 1930-32, 1948-49, chmn. bd. dirs., 1932-34; member Industrial Division, Federal Council Chs., 1924-51; mem. dept. social welfare, National Council Churches, 1951-53. Socialist candidate for gov. of N.Y., 1936; FOR U.S. senator from N.Y., 1938. Mem. N.Y. City Council from Brooklyn, 1940-41. Mem. program committee Institute for Social Progress, 1936-57; member Public Affairs Committee since 1943; dir. Nat. Housing Conf., 1931-65, hon. dir., 1963—; lectr. economics, N.Y.U. 1942, Brooklyn College, 1943-44, College City of New York, 1942-45. Member New York Bar, Phi Beta Kappa, Phi Delta Phi, Commons. Club: Nat. Arts. Socialist. Author many books in field, 1914—, latest being: Social-Economic Movements, 1944; History of Socialism, 1968; Boycotts and the Labor Struggle (first edition 1913), 1968; co-author: What Do You Know About Labor, 1956; author economic brochures; latest being: Socialism in U.S., Brief History, 1952. Editor books and brochures in field, latest include: John Dewey at Ninety, 1950; Needed: A Moral Awakening in America, 1952; How Free is Free Enterprise, 1954. Home: Bklyn. *

LAING, ALEXANDER KINNAN, author; b. Great Neck, N.Y., Aug. 7, 1903; s. Edgar Hall and Mary Adeline (Pray) L.; student Dartmouth, 1921-25, 32-33, A.B. as class 1925, 1933, A.M.; m. Isabel Lattimore Frost, June 10, 1930 (div.); m. 2d, Dilys Bennett, May 30, 1936 (dec. Feb. 1960); 1 son, David; m. 3d, Veronica Ruzicka, Mar. 22, 1961. Tech. editor Radio News, 1925-26; editor The Power Specialist, 1927-28; copy writer Erwin, Wasey & Co., 1929; tutorial adviser English dept. Dartmouth, 1930, adviser to the arts, 1930-34, asst. librarian, 1937-50, dir. Pub. Affairs Lab., Great Issues Course, 1947-52, ednl. services adviser Coll. Library, 1952-66, lectr. English, 1965, prof. belles lettres, 1966-68, prof. belles lettres emeritus, 1968-76. Guggenheim Meml. Found. fellow for creative writing abroad, 1934-35. Editor: The Cadaver of Gideon Wyck, 1934; The Life and Adventures of John Nicol, Mariner, 1936; The Haunted Omnibus, 1937; The Collected Poems of Dilys Laing, 1967; co-editor Betrayal, 1967-68; Groundswell, 1968-75. Author: Fool's Errand, 1928; End of Roaming, 1930; The Sea Witch, 1933; Wine and Physic, 1934; Dr. Scarlett, 1936; The Methods of Dr. Scarlett, 1937; Sailing In, 1937; Way for America, 1943; Clipper Ship Men, 1944; Jonathan Eagle, 1955; Matthew Early, 1957; American Sail, a pictorial history, 1961; Clipper Ships and Their Makers, 1966; American Ships, 1971; Seafaring America, 1974; Brant Point: Poems, 1975; (with R. A. Lattimore) Hanover Poems, 1927; (with Thomas Painter) The Motives of Nicholas Holtz, 1936. Home: Norwich, Vt. Died Apr. 23, 1976.

LAING, ARTHUR, Canadian govt. ofcl.; b. Richmond, B.C., Can., Sept. 9, 1904; s. Thomas and Marion Brown (Mackie) L.; B.S. in Agr., U. B.C., 1925; m. Elma Geraldine Hyland, July 17, 1938; 1 dau., Linda Laurine (Mrs. David Billingsley), Mgr. fertilizers dept. Vancouver Milling & Grain Ltd., 1926-33; mgr. agrl. chems. div. Buckerfield's Ltd., 1933-51; mem. Ho. of Commons for Vancouver S., 1949-53, 62-72, Senate, 1972-75; leader Liberal party in B.C., 1953; mem. Vancouver Legislature for Point Grey, 1953-56; mem. Privy Council, minister No. affairs and natural resources Can., 1963, Indian affairs and No. devel., 1966, pub. works, 1969-72, vets. affairs, 1972-75; mem. Senate of Can., 1972-75. Chmn., Richmond Bd. Sch. Trustees, 1930-43. Pres., B.C. Young Liberal Assn., 1947, B.C. Liberal Assn., 1947-49. Mem. Canadian Soc. Tech. Agr. (past pres. B.C. br.), Agrl. Inst. Can., Phi Kappa Pi, Sigma Tau Upsilon. Mem. United Ch. Can. Home: Vancouver, B.C., Can. Died Feb. 13, 1975.

LAING, JAMES TAMPLIN, educator; b. Montgomery, W.Va., Aug. 26, 1899; s. James McAlpin and Annie (Tamplin) L.; A.B., W.Va. U., 1924; M.A., Ohio State U., 1929, Ph.D., 1933; m. Claire Lenila Thomas, Aug. 2, 1927; 1 son, James Thomas. Instr., Dunbar (W.Va.) High Sch., 1924-25, Charleston, W.Va., 1926-28; asst. instr. Ohio State U., 1929-33; prof. sociology Holbrook Coll., 1933-34; asso. prof. W.Va. Inst. Tech., 1934-35; asso. prof. sociology Kent (Ohio) State U., 1935-37, prof., head dept., 1937-59, chmn. dept. sociology and anthropology, 1937-67, prof. sociology, 1967-69, prof. emeritus, 1969-79; vis. prof. various summer assignments. Pres. Kent Welfare Bd., 1944-45, 45-46. Mem. Am., Ohio Valley (past pres.) sociol. socs., W.Va. Acad. Sci., AAUP, Alpha Kappa Delta, Pi Gamma Mu, Phi Sigma Kappa (dep. regional dir. region IV). Methodist. Rotarian (past pres.). Club: Wranglers. Co-author: Sociological Foundatios of Education, 1942; also articles, monographs. Home: Kent, Ohio. Died Jan. 1, 1979; buried Lansing, W.Va.

LAIRD, JOHN KING, coll. prof.; b. Cincinnati, O., Oct. 21, 1884; s. John King and Laura Esther (Smith) L.; A.B., Dartmouth, 1904, A.M., 1907, Ph.D., 1909; LL.D., Dartmouth, and U. of Me., 1911; m. Emma Fuller, Jan. 20, 1906; children—King, Frederic, Laura, Arthur. Taught Appleton Acad., New Ipswich, Mo.; tutor Latin, asso. prof. Latin and rhetoric, prof. oratory and belles lettres, asso. prof. Latin lang. and lit., prof., prof. emeritus, acting pres., and acting pres. of the faculty, trustee, since 1917, St. Olaf's Coll. Editor: Cicero, Laelius, Livy, books XXL, XXII, History of Monmouth College. Author: Atlas of the Geography and History of the Ancient World. Home: Chicago, Ill. *

LAIRD, JOHN WESLEY, clergyman; b. in Scotland, Oct. 5, 1882; s. Thomas and Jane (Patterson) L.; brought to U.S., 1888; grad. Wyoming Sem., Kingston, Pa., 1905; Ph.B., Syracuse U., 1909, D.D., 1916; student Yale Divinity School (class of 1916); LL.D., Albinon Coll., 1921; m. Margaret Lila Keller, June 13, 1908. Supplied Congl. Ch., W. Pittston, Pa., 1904-05, M.E. Ch., Vernon Center, N.Y., 1905-06; ordained, 1908; pastor Vernon, N.Y., 1907-10, Grace Ch., Bronx, 1910-12, Winsted, Conn., 1912-14, First Ch., New Haven, 1914-18, Mt. Vernon Place Ch., Baltimore, Md., 1918-21; pres. Albion Coll., Mich., 1921-24; minister Brighton Presbyn. Ch., Rochester, N.Y., 1925-37, Port Kennedy (Pa.) Presbyn. Ch., 1938; prof. philosophy and social ethics, Sch. of Theology, Temple U., Phila., since 1937. Visiting preacher to Scotland, 1926; dir. religious work, Y.M.C.A. at Camp Meade, Md., 1917, Mem. Phi Gamma Delta. Mason. Odd Fellow. Author: The Role of the Educated Man, 1921. Home: Philadelphia, Pa. *

LAIRD, WILLIAM J., business cons.; b. Newark, July 7, 1918; s. William R. and Winifred (Joyce) L.; B.A., Cath. U. Am., 1941; postgrad. Northwestern U., 1946-49; m. Constance A. Kretschmer, Jan. 5, 1945; children—Robert J., Christine C., Theodore T. High sch. tchr., Bklyn., 1941-43; accountant Haskins & Sells, Chgo., 1946-47, Toni Co., Chgo., 1947-50; asst. to v.p. fin. Signode Steel, Chgo., 1950-55; partner Duff, Anderson Clark, Chgo., 1955-59; v.p. internat. Sci. Research Assos., 1959-68; pres. Howard W. Sams & Co., Indpls., 1968-72; pres. National Student Mktg. Corp., 1972-75; bus. cons., 1975-77. Instr. evening sch. Northwestern U., 1951-55. Served to lt. (j.g.) USNR, 1943-46. C.P.A., Ill. Mem. Phi Beta Kappa. Home: Chicago, Ill. Died Nov. 27, 1977; buried Chgo.

LAKE, HARRY BEASTON, investment banker; b. Port Norris, N.J., Jan. 24, 1886; s. Henry H. and Emma (Sheppard) L.; Ph.B., Brown Univ., 1909; m. Jane Cooper, Oct. 14, 1921 (dec.); 1 dau., Nona (Mrs. Lloyd P. Tevis, Jr.); m. 2d, Dulce Simoes-Correa. Partner Ladenburg, Thalmann & Co., N.Y.C., 1921—; former chairman of bd. Guerdon Industry; director Cooperstown Corp. (Md.), Sutton Pl. South Corp. Mem. of American Soc. French Legion of Honor, Inc. (dir.), Republican. Episcopalian. Clubs: City Midday, Metropolitan, N.Y. Yacht, Recess, Knickerbocker (Y.Y.C). Home: N.Y.C. Died Nov. 1969. *

LALLEY, JOSEPH M(ICHAEL), journalist; b. Phila., Pa., Nov. 9, 1896; s. Michael Joseph and Annie (Hart) L.; m. Spalding Parker, Nov. 1, 1924; children—Joseph Michael, Jr., John Spalding, Thomas Lea, Stephen Fenwick, Richard Plowden, Anne Hart Lalley de Alvear. Reporter, Philadelphia Press, 1916-17; in mil. service, 1917-18; Washington corr., Philadelphia North American, 1919-20; Philadelphia Public Ledger, 1922-23; Baltimore Sun, 1923-24; in advt. business, Baltimore and New York, 1925-31; editorial writer for the Washington Post, Washington, 1937-61, lit. editor in charge book page, 1937-42; asso. editor, lit. editor Modern Age, in charge book revs., 1963-80. Contbr., essays, stories and articles in various publs., including New Yorker; contbr. History of The Smart Set to O'Brian's Anthology. Author (with Wm. Franklin Sands), Our Jungle Diplomacy, 1944; The Nature of Authority, 1946. Editor: Roy Campbell: Selected Poetry, 1968; book rev. editor Human Events, 1947-50. Home: Baltimore, Md. Died Aug. 16, 1980.

LALLEY, WILLIAM H., pres. Kelly-Springfield Tire Co.; b. Cambridge, Mass., July 22, 1886; s. Frank E. and Mary (Rowe) L.; student Mass. Inst. Tech., 1902-06; unmarried. With Kelly-Springfield Tire Cos. since 1931, pres. since 1931; pres. and treas. Kelly-Springfield Co. of N.J. since 1932; pres. and treas. Lalley Realty Co.; pres. Donco Co., Oxford Corpn.; v.p. and treas. Donander Co.; v.p. Huntington Beach Co. Mem. Rubber Mfrs. Assn. (1st v.p.), Sigma Chi. Clubs: Hangar, India House, Circumnavigators (New York); Detroit, Detroit Athletic (Detroit); Essex Golf (Sandwich, Ont.,); Detroit Country. Home: New York, N.Y. *

LAMARSH, JUDY (JULIA VERLYN), barrister, solicitor; b. Chatham, Ont., Can., Dec. 20, 1924; d. Wilfrid Clayton and Rhoda Elizabeth (Conibear) LaMarsh; B.A., U. Toronto, 1947; Barrister-at-Law, Osgoode Hall, Toronto, 1950. Called to Ont. bar, 1950, named Queen's counsel, 1963; partner firm LaMarsh & LaMarsh, Niagara Falls, Ont., 1950-63; mem. Canadian Parliament for Niagara Falls, 1960-69; mem. Canadian Privy Council, 1963-68; minister Canadian Dept. Nat. Health and Welfare, 1963-65, sec. of state, 1965-68; law firm J.V. LaMarsh, St. Catharines, Ont., 1969-80. Served with Canadian Women's Army Corps., 1943-46. Mem. Canadian Bar Assn., Royal Canadian Legion. Mem. Liberal Party. Presbyn. Club: St. Catharines Golf and Country. Author: Memoirs of a Bird in a Gilded Cage, 1969. Home: Ont., Canada. Died Oct. 28, 1980.

LAMB, B(URLEY) F(RANK), ch. official; b. on farm, Wheatland Tp., Hillsdale County, Mich., May 29, 1886; s. Benjamin Soul and Amelia (Lyon) L; A.B., Albion (Mich.) Coll., 1913; fellow in economics, polit. science and sociology, U. of Ill., 1913-15, A.M., 1914; fellow in economics, polit. science and sociology, U. of Pa., 1915-16; D.D., Heidelberg College, Tiffin, O., 1925; LL.D., Albion (Mich.) College, 1933; m. Marjorie Coors, Dec. 29, 1915; 1 son, Burjo Lemar. Supt. Schs., Mosherville, Mich., 1906-09; pastor M.E. Ch., Montgomery, Mich., 1910-12; Chautauqua lecturer, Washington, D.C., 1916-18; ordained minister, M.E. Ch., 1918; community organizer, Portsmouth, O., 1918-19; dir. surveys in Ohio for Inter-church World Movement, 1919-20; executive secretary of the Ohio Council of Churches, 1920-49, pres., 1949-52; pres. The Temple of Good Will since 1952. Editor of the Ohio Christian News, 1922-52. Member Association Executive Secs. State and Local Councils of Chs. (pres. 1928-30), Ohio Pastors' Assn., Delta Sigma Rho, Kappa Delta Pi. Mason (32 deg.). Pioneer in interdenominational Protestant cooperation. Home: Columbus. *

LAMB, FRANKLIN, mfg. co. exec.; b. Bridgeton, N.J., Aug. 31, 1898; s. George Winchester and Amy Layton (Matlack) L.; student George Washington U.; m. Jessie McLeod, June 11, 1921; children—Robert F., Joan Marie (Mrs. Bernard S. Bernard). Co-founder, pres. Reynolds Ball Pen Co.; with advt. dept. R.H. Macy Co., N.Y.C., 1929-33, also mgr. Macy Thanksgiving parade; planned and managed Round the World record breaking fights of Reynolds-Odom-Sallee in Bombshell in 1947, also Odom on solo round world flight, 1947; acted as asst. dir. of ODM on spl. project, 2 mos.; v.p. Pa. Broadcasting Co. W.I.P.; formerly chmn. bd. dirs. Teleking Corp.; asst. to pres. Dynamics Corp. Am., 1956-57; then pub. relations counsellor N.Y. and Palm Beach; then pres. Kleer-Site Corp., mfrs. lens cleaners, Newark; cons. Treasury Dept. (helped promote idea of twice a year drives versus enforced savs.), World War II. Exec. asst., chmn. Am. Cancer Soc. Palm Beach Golf Classic, 6 yrs. Hon. exec. bd. Mommouth Med. Center, Long Branch, N.J.; pres. Salvation Army Assn. Palm Beach. Served as army field clk. U.S. Army, World War I. Recipient Silver medal for outstanding service Treasury Dept., 1945; others award Salvation Army. Mason. Clubs: Old Guard of Fla.; Kiwanis (pres.) (Palm Beach). Home: Palm Beach, Fla. Died Aug. 3, 1977.

LAMB, HORACE RAND, lawyer; b. Sandusky, Ohio, July 7, 1892; s. Burt Israel and Harriett (Davis) L.; A.B., Cornell U., 1916, LL.B., 1920; m. Beatrice Pitney, Feb. 8, 1930; children—Barbara Pitney (Mrs. Tristam Johnson), Dorothy Davis (Mrs. John Crawford). Admitted to N.Y. bar, 1920; with law firm Sullivan and Cromwell, N.Y.C., 1920-26; spl. asst. U.S. Atty. Gen., anti-trust div., Washington, 1926-29; partner William J. Donovan, 1929-34, partner Le Boeuf, Lamb & Leiby, 1934-68, cons., 1968-77; dir., mem. exec. com. St. Regis Paper Co. Mem. Council Fgn. Relations. Served as 1st lt., U.S. Army Inf., 1917-19; mem. Squadron A., N.Y.C., 1923-26. Fellow Am. Coll. Trial Lawyers; mem. Am., N.Y. State bar assns., Bar Assn. City N.Y. Republican. Presbyterian. Clubs: Univ., Wall St., Down Town Assn. (N.Y.C.); New Canaan Country, Noroton (Conn.) Yacht. Home: New Canaan, Conn. Died Nov. 11, 1977.

LAMB, JOHN WALLACE, grain broker; b. Green Bay, Wis., March 6, 1885; s. George Wallace and Elizabeth (Butler) L.; student, Englewood High Sch., 1900-03, Morgan Park Mil, Acad., 1904; m. Faye Elder, July 28, 1926; one dau., Joann Carol (Mrs. Herbert Land Lowry). Asso. in grain bus. with George W. Lamb's Sons, 1903, David L. Barsaloux, 1912-44; established firm Miller & Lamb, 1944; dir, Open Bd. Trade, 1935-43; pres. 1943, 44, 45, 46. Republican. Presbyterian. Clubs: South Shore Country, Beverly Country (charter mem.). Home: Chicago *

LAMB, WILLIAM HOLLINSHEAD, lawyer; b Phila., Pa., Apr. 17, 1885; s. John Gordon and Abbie (Browning) H.; grad. Germantown Acad., 1902, Univ of Pa., 1906, College of Law, 1907; m. Edith Cochran May 15, 1918; children—Pauline Cochran, Jane

Browning. Engaged in bus., 1907-10; entered father's law office, 1910; admitted to Pa. bar, 1911, in gen. practice of law, 1911-17; asst. counsel Bell Telephone Co. of Pa., 1917-19; atty. Bell Telephone Co. of Pa. and Diamond State Telephone Co., 1919-33, gen. counsel, 1933-50; dir. Bell Telephone Co. of Pa., 1936-50. Mem. Phila. com. asso. Pa. clubs on post-war edul. policy of Univ. of Pa., Founders' Day com., Inter-Frat. Alumni Council of Univ. of Pa. Mem. Am. Bar Assn., Phila. Bar Assn., Pa. Bar Assn., Chamber of Commerce, Bd. of Trade of Phila., Telephone Pioneers of Am., Federal Communication Bar Assn., Beta Theta Pi. Republican. Protestant Episcopalian. Clubs: Art Alliance, Plays and Players, Philadelphia Country, Bay Head Yacht. BynMawr Kennel. Home: Wynnewood, Pa. *

LAMBERT, JOE CALVIN, army officer; b. Washington, Ark., Aug. 3, 1908; s. Walter Samuel and Maude (Johnson) L.; student pub. schs., Ark. and Tex.; grad. Command and Gen. Staff Coll., 1943, Armed Forces Staff Coll., 1952, Indsl. Coll. Armed Forces, 1958; m. Dora Mae M. Gehee, Sept. 2, 1936; 1 son, Joseph Calvin. Enlisted U.S. Army, 1925, commd. 2d lt. Res., 1934; active Res. duty, 1940-46, regular Army, 1946-68, advanced through grades to maj. gen., 1961; various adminstrv., intelligence, operations and exec. staff positions, 1940-46; assigned successively U.S., Germany, SHAPE, 1946-61; adj. gen., U.S. Army, 1961-66; comdg. gen. IV U.S. Army Corps, Birmingham, Ala., 1967-68; ret., 1968. Exec. com. USO, Paris; exec. council Boy Scouts Am., Birmingham, past commr. Boy Scouts Am., France. Decorated Silver Star, Legion of Merit, Bronze Star with cluster, Purple Heart; Croix de Guerre (France). Episcopalian. Kiwanian. Home: Falls Church, Va. Died Apr. 23, 1979.

LAMBIE, WILLIAM S., banker; b, Alleghany Pa., Sept. 17, 1886; s. Joseph G. and Mary Kate (Siebert) I A.B., Yale, 1912; m. Ruth Lee Wallace, May 7, 1913; children—Ruth Lee (Mrs. Edward L. Bond, Jr.), Nancy Lee (Mrs. Grayson F. Lathrop), William S. Jr., Kate (Mrs. Robert F. Loree, Jr.), Margaret (Mrs. James F. Jaffray), Assistant cashier, Union National Bank, Schenectady, New York, 1912-14, cashier, 1914-18; assistant cashier, National City Bank of New York City, 1918-19, assistant vice pres., 1919-23, v.p., 1923-40, senior v.p., 1940-49; retired Oct. 1, 1949; dir. Geo. S. Armstrong & Co., Inc., Witherbee-Sherman Corp., Campbell Wyant Foundry Co. Mem. Phi Beta Kappa, Psi Upsilon. Clubs: Elihu, Elizabethan(Yale); University (New York). Home: Portsmouth, R.I. *

LAMPE, M(ATTHEW) WILLARD (LAMP), religious educator; b. Bethlehem, Conn., Aug. 4, 1883; s. Joseph J. and Emma (Willard) L.; A.B., Knox Coll., 1904, D.D., 1919; grad. Omaha Theol. Sem., 1909; Ph.D., University Pennsylvania, 1912; D.D., Drake University, 1954; married Lydia Vallentyne, Jan. 2, 1912 (dec. June 1929); children—Alice Margaret (Mrs. John B. Heidel), Elizabeth Emma (Mrs. Sheldon E. Erickson), Marion Willard (dec.), Virginia Vallentyne (Mrs. Wilson K. Weatherly); married second, Dorothy McGlone, August 21, 1935. Instructor history Knox Coll., 1904-06; sec. Christian Assn. and Presbyn. univ. pastor U. Pa., 1912-21; gen. dir. dept. univ. work Bd. Christian Edn. Presbyn. Ch. U.S.A., 1921-29; dir. Sch. of Religion at State U. Ia., 1927-53, prof. emeritus, 1954—; exchange director and prof. sch. religion U. Hawaii, first semester 1954-55; John Hay Whitney Foundation vis. prof. Skidmore Coll., 1955-56. Former mem. Bd. Christian Edn. Presbyn. Ch. U.S.A., Westminster Found. Ia.; moderator Presbyn. (U.S.A.) Synod Ia., 1949-50. Former trustee Coe Coll., Cedar Rapids, Ia.; dir. Presbyn. Theol. Sem., Omaha, Neb. Author: Limitations Upon the Power of the Hebrew Kings, 1912; Annual Reports, other papers dealing with subject of religion in tax-supported higher edn. Home: Iowa City, Ia. *

LAMPE, WILLIAM BLAKEMAN, clergyman; b. Galesburg, Ill., Aug. 19, 1885; s. Joseph Joachim and Emma Almira (Willard) L.; A.B., Knox Coll., 1907, D.D., 1946; grad. Presbyterian Theol. Sem., Omaha, Neb., 1910; D.D., Park Coll., Parkville, Mo., 1918, Coe Coll., 1952; LL.D., Lafayette Coll., 1945; m. Minnie Estelle Avery, June 16, 1910; children—John Avery Willard Vincent, Barbara Blakeman (Mrs. Dudley Wolfe). Ordained Presbyn. ministry, 1910; pastor First Church, Shelby, Iowa, 1910-13, First Church, Winfield, Kan., 1913-18, Third Church, Chicago, 1918-20, West Church, St. Louis, 1920-56, honorably ret. by St. Louis Presbytery, 1956. Pres. Metropolitan Church Federation of St. Louis, 1929. Director St. Luke's Hospital, St. Louis, 1949-56. Trustee Westminster College (Fulton, Mo.) Knox Coll., 1935-38, Bible Coll. of Mo. (Columbia); pres. Westminster Foundation of Mo; mem. permanent judicial commn. of Gen. Assembly Presbyn. Ch. in U.S.A., 1929-37. Mem. Gen. Council of Presbyn. Ch. in U.S.A., 1942-48; moderator of the 157th Gen. Assembly of the Presbyn. Ch. in the U.S.A.; mem. spl. com. on Structure, Orgn. and Functioning of Presbyn. Ch. in the U.S.A. Member S.R. Home: Decatur, Ill. *

LAMPERT, JAMES BENJAMIN, univ. adminstr., ret. army officer; b. Washington, Apr. 16, 1914; s. James Gillespie Blaine and Sarah Katharine (Barr) L.; B.S., U.S. Mil. Acad., 1936; M.S. in Civil Engring., Mass. Inst. Tech., 1939; grad. Army Engr. Sch., 1940, Nat. War Coll., 1958; m. Margery Frances Mitchell, June 26, 1937; children—James B., Richard B., Hester A. (Mrs. Hill). Commd. 2d lt. U.S. Army, 1936, advanced through grades to lt. gen., 1966; served S. and S.W. Pacific, 1942-45; exec. officer Manhattan Project, 1946-47; army engr.-in-charge Ark.-White-Red River Basin study project, Tulsa, 1950-52; officer-in-charge Joint Army-AEC Nuclear Power Program, 1952-57; dep. chief U.S. Mil. Assistance Adv. Group, Vietnam, 1958-60; dir. mil. constrn. Office Chief Army Engrs., 1961-63; supt. U.S. Mil. Acad., 1963-66; dep. asst. sec. def. (manpower), 1966-69; U.S. high commr. Ryukyu Islands, comdg. gen. U.S. Army, Ryukyu Islands, 1969-72; ret., 1972; v.p. resource devel. Mass. Inst. Tech., 1972-78, dir. Fairchild Camera & Instrument Corp. Decorated D.S.M. with 2 oak leaf clusters, Silver Star, Legion of Merit, Bronze Star, Army Commendation medal; Order Rising Sun 1st class (Japan). Registered profl. engr., D.C. Fellow ASCE, Soc. Am. Mil. Engrs.; mem. Assn. U.S. Army, Ret. Officers Assn., Council Fgn. Relations, Assn. Grads. U.S. Mil. Acad. (pres. 1978). Episcopalian. Home: Concord, Mass. Died July 10, 1978; buried West Point, N.Y.

LAMPERTI, A. CHARLES, elec. co. exec.; b. Riverton, Vt., Mar. 1, 1901; s. Angelo and Caroline (Comi) L.; student pub. schs., Montpelier, Vt.; m. Edna Dillon, Oct. 1, 1925; 1 son, Robert C. With Graybar Electric Co., from 1920, beginning as sr. auditor, successively sr. accountant, asst. sec., sec. employees benefit com., gen. auditor, sec., comptroller from 1943, dir., from 1946, exec. com., from 1948, voting trustee, from 1954, ret., 1960. Member Am. Mgmt. Assn. Elk. Home: North Plainfield, N.J. Deceased.

LAMPORT, HAROLD, research physician, investment mgmt. exec.; b. N.Y.C., Feb. 16, 1908; s. Arthur Matthew and Sadie (Payson) L.; B.S. cum laude, Harvard U., 1929; postgrad. U. Göttingen (Germany), 1928-29; M.D., Columbia U., 1934; m. Golden R. Siwek, Mar. 27, 1933; children—Anthony Matthew, Stephanie Payson. Inter 1, resident physician Beth Israel Hosp., N.Y.C., 1935-3'; dir. Koster Research Lab., N.Y.C., 1937-39; research asst., then asso. neurology Columbia, 1939-42; mem. faculty Yale U. Sch. Medicine, New Haven, 1942-67, research asst., 1942-44, research asso., asso. prof. physiology, 1944-65, pathology, 1965-66, lectr., 1966-67, research prof. physiology Mt. Sinai Sch. Medicine, City U. N.Y., 1966-75; research asso., then med. dir. mil. research projects Pierce Found., New Haven, 1942-45. Cons. Rand Corp., 1959-63; mem., asst. sec. com. missile casualties NRC, 1943-47; responsible investigator OSRD, 1942-45. Dir. Consol. Gas Utilities Corp., Oklahoma City, 1940-60, chmn. bd., 1942-60; dir. Ark. La. Gas Co., Shreveport, 1960-75. Bd. dirs. Child Guidance Clinic Greater Bridgeport (Conn.), 1960-65; pres. Sadie and Arthur Lamport Found., 1939-75, Lamport Found., 1960-75. Recipient ultrasonic med. research prize Birtcher Found., 1955; posthumous award as Disting. Sci. Prof., Mt. Sinai Sch. of Medicine, 1976. Fellow AAAS (life), N.Y. Acad. Medicine, N.Y. Acad. Sci.; mem. Am. Physiol. Soc., Biophysics Soc., Microcirculation Soc., Am. Heart Assn. (basic sci. council), Biomed. Engring. Soc., Internat. Soc. Biorheology, Phi Beta Kappa (pres. Western Conn. 1958-59), Sigma Xi. Clubs: Harmonie, Bankers (N.Y.C.). Author articles on biophysics, physiology, blood circulation, fin. Inventor pneumatic lever suit for altitude and blackout protection aviators. Home: Westport, Conn. Died Dec. 27, 1975.

LAMPTON, DINWIDDIE, ins. exec.; b. Springfield, Ky., April 21, 1885; s. James II. and Olivia (Dinwiddie) L.; ed. pub. schs.; m. Johanna Karaft, Nov. 12, 1912; children—Dinwiddie, Mary Jane. With Prudential Life Ins. Co., 1906-10; organized Union Life Ins. Co., 1910, merged with Am. Life & Accident Ins. Co., and pres. of same since 1913; purchased assets of Ky. State Life Ins. Co., 1930. Mason, (Shriner; mem. Red Cross of Constantine). Baptist. Clubs: Bankers, Lotus (New York). Pendennis. Home: Louisville. *

LAMPTON, ROBERT BENJAMIN, banker; b. Magnolia, Miss., Oct. 26, 1920; s. Robert Benjamin and Gertrude (Thompson) L.; B.S. in Engring., Princeton, 1942; m. Katherine Anderson Bryan, Aug. 17, 1950; children—Kathy, Mary, Bob, Bryan, Jim. Instr. math. McCallie Sch., Chattanooga, 1946-49; with First Nat. Bank Jackson (Miss.), 1949-80, exec. v.p., 1967-69, pres., 1969-76, vice chmn. bd., 1976-80, also dir.; vice chmn. bd., dir. 1st Capital Corp., 1976-80; dir. Entex, Inc.; lectr. Sch. Banking, La. State U., 1966-80. Campaign chmn. United Givers Fund Jackson, 1962, v.p., 1963, pres., 1964; Miss. chmn. Radio Free Europe Fund, 1970; chmn. Miss. Arts Commn., 1967-70, Jackson City Planning Bd. Pres., bd. dirs. Pearl River Valley Water Supply Dist. Trustee Piney Woods (Miss.) Country Life Sch.; mem. lay adv. bd. St. Dominics Jackson Meml. Hosp. Served to lt. USNR, 1942-46. Mem. Newcomen Soc. N. Am. (treas. Miss.), Am. Bankers Assn. (governing council 1978), Miss.), Am. Bankers Assn. (governing council 1978), Miss. Bankers Assn. (pres. 1974-75), Jackson C. of C. (pres. 1973), Phi Beta Kappa. Kiwanian (pres. 1962). Club: River Hills (pres. 1967) (Jackson). Home: Jackson, Miss. Died 1980.

LANCASTER, BILLY JACK, oil co. exec.; b. Cross Plains, Tex., Apr. 29, 1924; s. Benton Hale and Allie Frances (Gee) L.; B.S., U. Tex., 1948; m. Jeanne Marie Murphy, Oct. 28, 1944; children—Lynda (Mrs. Laurence K. Gustafson), Deborah. Mgr. engring. Atlantic Richfield Co., Dallas, 1963-68, v.p. research and engring., 1968-73, sr. v.p., 1973-78; pres. ARCO Oil and Gas Co., 1978-80. Served to 1st lt. USAF, 1943-45. Decorated Purple Heart, Air medal. Mem. Am. Petroleum Inst., Mid Continent Oil and Gas Assn., Soc. Profl. Engrs., Dallas Petroleum Club. Club: Brook Hollow Golf. Home: Dallas, Tex. Died Sept. 30, 1980.

LANCE, THOMAS JACKSON, former state ofcl.; b. Choestoe, Ga., Jan. 31, 1886; s. James Washington and Verissa Jane (Henson) L.; A.B., Young L.G. Harris Coll., 1908; postgrad. Emory Coll., 1909-10; A.B., U. Ga., 1912-13, A.M., 1917; Pd.D. (hon.), Oglethorpe U., 1936; m. Annie Rose Erwin, May 3, 1914; children—Jack Junior (dec), Robert Park (killed in action Tyrrhenian Sea 1943), Alice Rose (Mrs. Frank McAfee), Thomas Bertram. Prin. high sch., Hopewell, Ga., 1908-10; tchr. langs. Young Harris Coll., 1911-12, head English dept., 1910-16, pres. of coll., 1930-42; head English dept. Richmond Acad., Augusta, 1916-17; supt. pub. schs., Waynesboro, 1917-30, Calhoun, 1942-44; sch. supr. Ga., 1944-60. Del. Gen. Conf. Meth. Ch., 1934, 38, 40, 48, 52, 66, Uniting Conf., 1939, Jurisdictional Conf., 1940, 44, 48, 52, 56, 60, 64. Del. Democratic Nat. Conv., Chgo., 1940. Mem. bd. regents U. Ga., 1936-40. Mem. Phi Beta Kappa, Kappa Phi Kappa. Democrat. Rotarian. Author: History of Young L.G. Harris Coll., 1936; Biography of Joseph Astor Sharp, 1961. Joint author series English textbooks. Contbr. profl. jours. Home: Calhoun GA. *

LANCEFIELD, REBECCA CRAIGHILL, microbiologist; b. Ft. Wadsworth, N.Y., Jan. 5, 1895; d. William Edward and Mary Wortley Montague (Byram) Craighill; A.B., Wellesley Coll., 1916, D.Sc. (hon.), 1976; A.M., Columbia U., 1918, Ph.D., 1925; D.Sc. (hon.), Rockefeller U., 1973; m. Donald E. Lancefield, May 27, 1918; 1 dau., Jane Lancefield Hersey. Tech. asst. Rockefeller U., N.Y.C., 1922-25, asst., 1925-29, asso., 1929-42, asso. mem., 1942-58, mem., prof., 1958-65, prof. emeritus bacteriology and immunology dept., 1965-81. Recipient T. Duckett Jones Meml. award Helen Hay Whitney Fund, 1960; Achievement award Am. Heart Assn., 1964; medal N.Y. Acad. Medicine, 1973. Hon. fellow Royal Coll. Pathologists; mem. Nat. Acad. Scis. Home: Douglaston, N.Y. Died Mar. 3, 1981; buried Woodshole, Mass.

LANDAUER, JERRY GERD, journalist; b. Stuttgart, Germany, Jan. 16, 1932; s. Adolph and Meta (Marx) L.; came to U.S., 1938, naturalized, 1943; B.A., Columbia, 1953. Reporter, Washington Post, 1956-60, U.P.I., 1960-62, Wall St Jour., Washington, 1962-81. Recipient Distinguished Service award Sigma Delta Chi, 1963; Raymond Clapper Meml. award, 1963; Drew Pearson prize, 1973; Worth Bingham prize for investigative reporting, 1973. Club: Nat. Press. Home: Washington, D.C. Died Feb. 27, 1981.

LANDIS, MARK HOMER, mech. engr., mfr.; b. Lancaster, Pa., Dec. 16, 1885; s. Frank Frick and Elizabeth (Hershey) L.; prep. edn., high sch., Waynesboro Pa., and Mercersburg (Pa.) Acad.; M.E., Cornell U., 1908. M.M.E., 1909; m. Ethel Marie Hartman, June 16, 1910 (died Jan. 17, 1937). Machinist apprentice, summers, 1899-1902. full time, 1902-04; secretary, treas. Fred Frick Clock Co., 1909-13; gen. mgr. and mech. engr. Landis Engring. & Mfg. Co., 1913-20, pres. and gen. mgr. 1920-39; pres. and gen. mgr. Geiser Mfg. Co., 1928-39: pres. and treas. Frank F. Landis Patents, Inc., 1928-39; pres. Erd Co., Inc.; dir. and exec. com. Landis Machine Co. Trustee Waynesboro Hosp. Mem. American Society Mech. Engrs., Soc. Automotive Engrs. Republican. Mason (Shriner), Elk, Clubs: Sinfonia, Waynesboro Country; Fountain Head Country (Hagerstown). Home: Waynesboro, Pa. *

LANDSBERG, MORTIMER, investment exec.; b. N.Y.C., May 22, 1903; s. William and Alice (Merkel) L.; m. Mary Cribbin, June 26, 1943; children—Mortimer, Eugenia A., Alice M. Pres. Landsberg & Co., brokerage firm, N.Y.C., from 1952; dir. Internat. Base Metals, Ltd. Mem. Am. Stock Exchange, v.p., 1949, chmn., 1950-51, gov., treas. Clubs: Downtown Athletic, Madison Square Garden, Elks (N.Y.C.); Plandome (N.Y.) Country. Home: New York, N.Y. Died 1978.

LANDSMAN, HERBERT SAMUEL, dept. store exec.; b. N.Y.C., Nov. 17, 1918; s. Nathan M. and Sara (Damsky) L.; student U. Paris (France), 1939; B.A., Dartmouth, 1940; M.A., Harvard, 1941; m. Claire Zimmerman, Aug. 2, 1942 (dec. Oct. 1949); 1 son, John; m. 2d, Madeline Rollman Stricker, June 27, 1951;

children—Herbert Samuel, Margaret, Julie. With Wm. Filene's Sons Co., Boston, 1940-42, R.H. White Co., Boston, 1946-50; with Federated Dept. Stores 1950-79, v.p., 1957-65, exec. v.p., 1965-79, dir., 1971-79; dir. Clopay Corp., Keyes Fibre Co., Holiday Inns, Inc., Asso. Merchandising Corp. Mem. com. on continuing edn. Dartmouth Coll. Trustee Cin. chpt. ARC, Children's Hosp. Med. Center, Cin. United Appeal, Nat. A.R.C. Retirement System. Mem. Submarine Vets. World War II, Nat. Retail Mchts. Assn. (dir.), Phi Beta Kappa. Club: Queen City (gov.). Home: Cincinnati, Ohio. Died May 28, 1979.

LANE, ARTHUR WILLIS, army officer; b. Gorham, N.H., Aug. 22, 1883; s. Virgil Willis and Carrie Ada (Willis) L.; B.S., U.S. Mil. Acad., West Point, 1905; grad. Gen. Staff Sch., Ft. Leavenworth, 1922, Army War Coll., Washington, D.C., 1923, Naval War Coll., Newport, R.I., 1927; m. Frances Duncan Burgoyne, June 17, 1913; children—Robert Burgoyne, Rilla Frances (wife Capt. Parker Calvert, U.S. Army), Nancy Willis (dec.). Commnd. 2d lt. inf., U.S. Army, 1905; advanced through ranks to brig. gen., 1940; regtl. duty at Ft. Thomas, Ky., Ft. Brady, Mich., 1905-08; Philippine Islands, 1908-09, Ft. Crook, Neb., 1909-11, Philippine Islands, 1913-16; staff duty at Washington, D.C., 1917-18, in France, 1918, in Washington, 1919-21 and 1923-26; batn. comdr., 26th Inf., Plattsburg Barracks, N.Y., 1927-29; instr. Command and Gen. Staff Sch., Ft. Leavenworth, 1929-34; Office Chief of Inf., 1934-37; comdr. 23d Inf., Ft. Sam Houston, Tex., 1937-39; Chief of Staff, 4th Army, 1940-41, and comdr. Ninth Corps Area, Oct. 1941, at Presidio of San Francisco, Calif.; comdr., Camp Roberts, Calif., 1942; chmn. IX Sect., War Dept. Manpower Bd., San Francisco, Calif., since Mar. 1943. Club: St. Francis Yacht (SanFrancisco, Calif.). Home: San Francisco, Calif. *

LANE, DONALD EDWARD, U.S. judge; b. Chevy Chase, Md., June 10, 1909; s. John Albert and Virginia Louise (Payson) L.; B.S., Yale, 1931; ed. George Washington U. Law Sch.; m. Virginia Plugge, Sept. 1, 1938; children—Diana Randall (Mrs. Louis A. Ebersold), Adair Payson. Admitted to D.C. bar, 1935; individual practice law, Washington, 1935-41, 45-54; commr. U.S. Ct. Claims, 1954-69; judge U.S. Ct. Customs and Patent Appeals, 1969-79. Patent adviser Manhattan Project, 1943. Served to comdr. USNR, 1941-45. Mem. Am. Bar Assn., Am. Patent Law Assn. (past sec., bd. mgrs.), Bar Assn. D.C., Washington Patent Lawyers Club (past pres.). Clubs: University, Cosmos (Washington). Home: Washington, D.C. Died May 30, 1979; buried Arlington Nat. Cemetery, Arlington, Va.

LANE, ERNEST PRESTON, mathematician; b. Russellville, Tenn., Nov. 28, 1886; s. Garrett Murph and Mary Miriam (Haun) L.; A.B., U. of Tenn., 1909; A.M., U. of Va., 1913; fellow in mathematics, U. of Chicago, 1917-18, Ph.D., 1918, Guggenheim research fellow, univs. of Rome, Bologna, Turin, 1926-27; m. Annie Laura Godbey, June 11, 1914. Prof. mathematics, Milligan Coll. (Tenn.), 1909-11, State Normal Sch. for Women, Radford, Va., 1913-14; instr. in mathematics and physics, U. of Tenn., 1914-16; instr. in mathematics, Rice Inst., Houston, Tex., 1918-19; asst. prof. mathematics, U. of Wis., 1919-23; asst. prof. mathematics, U. of Chicago, 1923-27, asso. prof., 1927-28, prof., 1928-52, prof. emeritus since 1952, chmn. dept., 1941-46. Mem. Am. Mathematics Soc. (v.p. 1930-31), Math. Assn. Am. (v.p 1934), Sigma Xi,Phi Beta Kappa, Phi Kappa Phi, Raven Soc U. Va. Home: Rich Creek, Va.*

LANE, OLEN, oil co. exec.; b. Shawnee, Okla., May 18, 1896; s. Llewellyn C. and Frances L. (Slover) L.; student Okla. A. and M. Coll., 1918; m. Georgia L. Livingston, Aug. 31, 1922; children—Olen, George L. Vice pres., dir. Marland Oil Co. of Cal., 1925-28; Marland Co. merged with Continental Oil Co., 1928, v.p. charge Western Region Continental Oil Co. until 1961. Asst. chief auxiliary police, Glendale, Cal., World War II. Served as capt., inf., U.S. Army, World War I. Mem. Western Oil and Gas Assn. (dir. past pres.). Clubs: Petroleum (president, past dir.), California (Los Angeles). Home: Glendale, Calif. Died Oct. 18, 1978.

LANE, WILLIAM DANIEL, advt. exec.; b. Hartford, Conn., Aug. 1, 1922; s. Thomas Henry and Grace (O'Brien) L.; B.S., U.S. Naval Acad., 1944; postgrad. Columbia Sch. Bus., 1950-52; m. Jean Marcell, Nov. 15, 1947; children—Mary Louise, W. Marcell, Brian Thomas, Elizabeth Ann, Elisa Jean. Account exec. Batten Batton Durstine Osborn, 1947-52; account exec. Young & Rubicam, 1952-63, v.p., supr., N.Y.C., 1965-68, sr. v.p., 1968-77; dir. client services Young & Rubicam Ltd., London, 1963-65. Mem. Franklin Lakes (N.J.) Bd. Edn., 1969-77. Served to lt. USNR, 1944-47. Home: Franklin Lakes, N.J. Died Feb. 6, 1977; buried Christ the King Cemetery, Franklin Lakes.

LANE, WILLIAM H., food co. exec.; b. Greenback, Tenn., Nov. 22, 1923; s. William Quincy and Vola (Stone) L.; student Ga. Inst. Tech., 1941-43; B.S., U. Tenn., 1946-47; m. Dorothy Dew, July 24, 1948; children—William H., Peggy Tipton, Timothy Dew. Sales engr. Ingersoll Rand Co., 1937-50; sales mgr. Woodman Co., Decatur, Ga., 1950-54; exec. v.p., gen. mgr. Red Dot Foods, Madison, Wis., 1954-60; pres. River Brand Rice Mills, Inc. (co. name now Riviana Foods, Inc.), Houston, 1960-80, also dir.; dir. Colgate-Palmolive Co.; mem. bd. Tex. Commerce Bank. Trustee, Rice U.; mem. devel. council U. Tenn. Mem. Young Pres. Orgn., Sigma Chi. Episcopalian. Clubs: Augusta (Ga.) National Golf (chmn.); Houston Country, River Oaks Country, Ramada, Allegro (Houston). Home: Houston, Tex. Died June 28, 1980.

LANEY, BEN T., gov. of Ark.; b. Ouachita County nr. Smackover, Ark., Nov. 25, 1896; s. Benjamin Travis and Martha Ella (Saxon) L.; A.B., Ark. State Teachers Coll., Conway, 1924; grad. student U. of Utah; m. Lucile Kirtley, Jan. 19, 1926; children—Ben. T., William David, Philip Edward. Began as teacher and thereafter engaged in various businesses, including farming, banking, retail drugs, motor finance, real estate, timber, oil and gas leases and investments; mayor of Camden, Ark., 1935-39; gov. of Ark., 1944-49. Served with U.S. Navy during World War I. Democrat. Methodist. Club: Rotary (Camden, Ark). Home: Camden, Ark. Died 1977.

LANG, FRITZ, motion picture dir.; b. Vienna, Austria, Dec. 5, 1890; s. Anton and Paula Lang; student Coll. Tech. Sci., Vienna, 1908, Acad. Graphic Art, Munich, Germany, 1911; student as painter, Paris, 1912-14. Came to U.S., 1934, naturalized, 1939. Film script writer, 1916-76, film dir., 1919-76; feature films include The Spiders, 1919, Destiny, 1921, Mabuse, 1922, Nibelungen, 1923-24, Metropolis, 1926, Spies, 1927, Woman in the Moon, 1928, M, 1932, Testament of Dr. Mabuse, 1932-33, Liliom, 1934, Fury, 1936, You Only Live Once, 1937, You and Me, 1938, The Return of Frank James, 1940, Western Union, 1941, Man-Hunt, 1941, Hangmen Also Die, 1942, Ministry of Fear, 1943, Woman in the Window, 1944, Scarlet Street, 1945, Cloak and Dagger, 1946, Secret Behind the Door, 1947, House by the River, 1949, American Guerrilla in the Phillippines, 1950, Rancho Notorious, 1951, Clash by Night, 1951, Blue Gardenia, 1952, Big Heat, 1953, Human Desire, 1953, Moonfleet, 1954, While the City Sleeps, 1955, Beyond a Reasonable Doubt, 1956, Der Tiger von Eschnapur, 1958, Das Indische Grabmal, 1958-59, Die Tausend Augen des Dr. Mabuse, 1960; voice in in film Mépris (Jean Luc Godard), 1963; lectr. in field. Decorated comdr.'s. cross Order of Merit (Fed. Republic of Germany); Golden ribbon Motion Picture Art (German Fed. Govt.); officer Order Arts and Letters (France); Order Yugoslav Flag with golden wreath, 1971; named hon. prof. U. Vienna, 1973. Home: Beverly Hills, Calif. Died Aug. 2, 1976; interred Forest Lawn-Hollywood Hills, Calif.

LANG, GORDON, investment co. exec.; b. Sayre, Pa., Nov. 3, 1895; s. Herman and Martha (Levis) L.; B.S., Denison U., 1918; m. Harriet Kendig, Aug. 2, 1927 (dec. Mar. 1964); 1 son, Gordon; m. 2d, Constance W. Bates, Oct. 1965. Sales corr. B.F. Goodrich Rubber Co.; Later bond salesman for Borton & Borton; then mgr. bond dept. Guarantee Title & Trust Co.; subsequently dir. sales devel. Gorham Co.; v.p., mgr. Black Starr & Frost-Gorham; pres. Spaulding-Gorham; dir. Spaulding-Gorham, Black Starr & Frost-Gorham, Gorham, Inc., Gomanco, Inc.; pres., owner Spaulding and Co., Chgo., 1943-73, cons., 1973-75; owner Loring Andrews Co., jewelers, Cin., 1953-64, Rattermann & Co. (now Loring Andrews & Rattermann), 1958-64, Spaulding & Tatman, Evanston, Tatman, Chgo., 1958-60; pres., owner Gordco Inc., investments, from 1972. Dir., past pres. Chgo. Better Bus. Bur.; dir. Chgo. Area Project; past dir. Chgo. Crime Commn., Chgo. Retail Mchts. Assn.; past chmn. city planning adv. com., mem. exec. com. Chgo. Plan Commn.; mem. North Michigan Av. Assn. (1st pres.). Sec., dir. Chgo. Clubs Baseball for Boys. Past pres. Chgo. Latin Sch. Boys. Served as 2d lt. U.S. Army, World War I. Clubs: Chicago, Chicago Racquet (Chgo.); Old Elm, Commercial, Commonwealth; Onwentsia (Lake Forest); Bath and Tennis, Everglades (Palm Beach, Fla.). Developed place-setting method for sale flat silver. Home: Palm Beach, Fla. Died Jan. 28, 1980.

LANG, JOHN WALTON, army officer, author; b. Pass Christian. Miss., Feb. 26, 1884; s. John H. and Nellie (Nelson) L.; graduate U.S. Military Academy, 1907, Infantry Sch., 1924; distinguished grad. Command and General Staff School, Fort Leavenworth, Kansas, 1927; graduate Army War College, 1931; m. Edith Harmon, May 31, 1911; children—John Walton (dec.), Cornélis de Witt Willcox, Madelin (wife of Col. William S. Biddle), Edith Louise. Commd. 2d lt., 23d Inf., June, 1907; advanced through grades to bring. gen., ret. 1946; mil. attaché Am. Embassy, Madrid, Spain, 1917-19; asst. dep. provost marshal gen. A.E.F., 1919; assigned as prof. mil. science and tactics, Lehigh U., Sept. 18, 1949; senior instr. in training management, drill and command, psychology, and Army of the U.S., at Infantry Sch., 1924-26; chief of pub. relations, War Dept. Gen. Staff, 1929-30; prof. mil. science and tactics, The Citadel (state mil. coll.), 1931-36; commanding Fort McClellan, Ala., 22d Infantry, 1936-38; dir. Command and Gen. Staff Sch., Ft. Leavenworth, Kan., 1938-39; chief U.S. Mil. Mission to Colombia, 1939-41; military attaché, Buenos Aires, 1941-45, Mexico July-Nov. 1945. Democrat. Clubs: Army and Navy (Washington); Army and Navy Country (Arlington, Va.). Author: Sketching for Scouts, 1923; (with Col. J. A. Moss) Spanish for Soldiers, 1916; Manual of Military Training (2 vols.), 1921; also short stories and professional articles. Contbr. to The Am. Hist. Assn. and Dictionary of Am. Biography. Awarded Legion of Merit. Home: PassChristian, Miss.*

LANGEN, ODIN ELSFORD STANLEY, govt. ofcl.; b. Mpls., Jan. 5, 1913; s. Joe and Selma (Almquist) L.; ed. high sch., Dunwoody Inst.; m. Lillian Clauson, Dec. 23, 1939; children—Wayne, Lynden, Lois. Rep. Kittson County, Minn. Ho. Reps., 1950-58, minority leader, 1957-58; mem. 86th-87th Congresses, 9th Dist. Minn., 88th-91st Congresses, 7th Minn. Dist.; adminstr. Packers and Stockyards Adminstrn. Dept. Agr., Washington, 1970—. Chmn. Kennedy (Minn.) P.T.A.; chmn. Red River town bd.; chmn. bd. Kennedy Sch. Mem. Prodn. and Marketing Assn. (chmn. Kittson County). Republican. Lutheran. Mason. Clubs: Red River Farmers (chmn.); Lions. Home: Kennedy, Minn. Died July 6, 1976.

LANGER, WILLIAM LEONARD, educator; b. Boston, Mar. 16, 1896; s. Charles Rudolph and Johanna (Rockenbach) L.; A.B., Harvard, 1915, A.M., 1920, Ph.D., 1923, LL.D., 1945; postgrad. U. Vienna, 1921-22; Ph.D. (hon.), U. Hamburg, 1955; L.H.D., Yale, 1956; Litt.D., Alma Coll., 1961; LL.D., Mills Coll., 1965; m. Susanne Knauth, Sept. 3, 1921; children—Leonard Charles Rudolph, Bertrand Walter; m. 2d, Rowena Morse Nelson, Apr. 9, 1943. Instr. modern langs. Worcester Acad., 1915-17; asst. prof. history Clark U., 1923-25, asso. prof., 1925-27; asst. prof. history Harvard, 1927-31, asso. prof., 1931-36, Coolidge prof. history, 1936-64, prof. history emeritus, 1964-77, dir. Russian Research Center and Center for Middle Eastern Studies, 1954-59; fellow Center Advanced Study in Behavioral Scis., 1959-60; vis. prof. Columbia, 1931; lectr. U. Chgo., summer 1926; Harvard lectr. Yale, 1933; prof. Fletcher Sch. of Diplomacy, Medford, Mass., 1933-34, 36-41; mem. bd. analysts Office of Coordinator of Information, 1941-42; chief research and analysis br. OSS, 1942-45; spl. asst. to sec. state, 1946; asst. dir. nat. estimates CIA, 1950-51; mem. adv. bd. Nat. War Coll., 1946-51; mem. President's Fgn. Intelligence Adv. Bd., 1961-69. Trustee Carnegie Endowment Internat. Peace, Harvard-Yenching Inst.; pres. Harvard Pierian Found., 1969-73. Served to master engr. 1st Gas Regiment, U.S. Army. World War I; participated in St. Mihiel and Argonne engagements. Recipient Medal for Merit, 1946. Mem. Am. Hist. Assn. (pres. 1957), Mass. Hist. Soc., Soc. Am. Historians, Am. Philos. Soc., Council on Fgn. Relations, Am. Acad. Arts and Scis., Phi Beta Kappa. Clubs: Harvard (N.Y.C.); Essex County. Author several books; co-author The Challenge of Isolation, 1947-40, 1952; The Undeclared War, 1940-41, 1953; Political and Social Upheaval, 1832-1852, 1969. Editor: Ency. of World History, 5th edit., 1972. Contbr. to Am. and European jours. Home: Cambridge, Mass. Died Dec. 26, 1977.

LANGFORD, WILLIAM SIDDON, physician; b. Lakewood, N.J., Aug. 15, 1906; s. George Philip and Edith Mary (Siddon) L.; A.B., Harvard, 1928; M.D., Columbia, 1931; m. Rebecca A. Beeman, June 30, 1928; children—Eric Siddon, Mary Ellis. Intern St. Elizabeth's Hosp., Washington, 1931-33; resident Babies Hosp., N.Y.C., 1933-34, dir. pediatric psychiat. clinic, 1935-72, asso. attending pediatrician, 1946-55, attending pediatrician, 1955-72, cons., 1972-76; fellow Johns Hopkins Hosp., Balt., 1934-35; attending psychiatrist N.Y. Psychiat. Inst., 1955-72; clin. prof. psychiatry Columbia Coll. Phys. and Surg., 1940-52, prof. clin. psychiatry, 1952-53, prof. psychiatry, 1953-72, emeritus, 1972-76; cons. children's services Columbia Presbyn. Med. Center, 1972-76. Served from capt. to maj., M.C., USAAF, 1943-45. Diplomate in psychiatry and child psychiatry Am. Bd. Psychiatry and Neurology. Life fellow Am. Orthopsychiat. Assn. (past pres.), Am. Acad. Child Psychiatry (past pres.), Am. Psychiat. Assn.; mem. Am. Acad. Pediatrics, Group for Advancement Psychiatry (life), Am. Pediatric Soc. (life), N.Y. Acad. Medicine, N.Y. Psychiat. Soc. Contbr. articles to med. jours. Home: New York, N.Y. Died Oct. 4, 1976.

LANGLAIS, BERNARD, artist; b. Old Town, Maine, July 23, 1921; s. Maurice and Jane (Pelletier) L.; student Cocoran Sch. Art, 1948-50, Bklyn. Mus. Sch., 1949-51, Skowhegan Sch. Painting and Sculpture, 1949-50, Grande Chaumier, Paris, France, 1952-53, Art. Acad., Oslo, Norway, 1954-55; D.F.A. (hon.), U. Maine, 1973; m. Helen Elisabeth Friend, Jan. 15, 1955. One-man shows Leo Castelli Gallery, Gov. Dummer Acad., Allan Stone Gallery, Grippi & Waddell Gallery, Lee A. Ault & Co., Inc., Alpha Gallery, Phillips Exeter Acad., Seton Hall U., Bklyn. Mus., Area Gallery, U. Maine, others; exhibited group shows Mus. Modern Art, Carnegie Internat., Whitney Mus., Colby Coll., Art in Embassies, XX Siecle Gallerie, Hobe Sound Gallery, Dallas Mus. Contemporary Art, San Francisco Mus. Art Assemblage, Art. Inst. Chgo., Barone Gallery, Bklyn. Mus., Kornblee Gallery, Martha Jackson Gallery, Camino Gallery, others; represented permanent collections Phila. Mus. Art, Phila. Zool. Gardens, Art Inst. Chgo., Olsen Found., Whitney Mus., Singer Sewing Machine Coll., Chrysler Mus., others, also numerous pvt. collections; vis. artist Pa. State U., 1971. Mem. Maine Arts and Humanities Commn., 1972-77. Served with USNR, 1942-48. Recipient Maine Arts and Humanities award, 1971, Ford Found. Purchase award, 1963, Skowhegan Sch. Painting Maine Artist award, 1975. Fulbright scholar, 1954-55; Guggenheim fellow, 1972-73; Nat. Endowment for Arts award, 1977-78. Bernard Langlais scholarship Skowhegan Sch. Painting and Sculpture, endowed 1979. Died Dec. 26, 1977; buried Norton Cemetery, Cushing, Maine.

LANGLER, WILLIAM J., ins. co. exec.; b. Eng., Sept. 30, 1882; student Willesden Poly. With Munich Reinsurance Co., London and Hartford, 1902-17, Travelers Ins. Co., Hartford, 1917-18, Am. Equitable, N.Y., 1918-24; with Northeastern Ins. Co., Des Moines, Ia., 1924—, pres., 1947—, vice chmn., 1953—, also dir. Home: Wethersfield, Conn. *

LANGSTON, RUSSELL LEE, elec. engr.; b. Cape Girardeau, Mo., Nov. 15, 1931; s. Roland H. and Stella Jewell (Hicklin) L.; B.Elec. Engring., U. Mo. at Rolla, 1955; m. Betty Sue Johnston, Feb. 15, 1964; children—Russell Lee, Lyle Mark. With Gen. Motors Corp., 1954-57, Davis Electric Co., 1957-58; with U.S. Army Missile Command, Redstone Arsenal, Ala., 1958-77, electronic engr. program mgmt., 1972-77; cons. in field. Served with AUS, 1955-57. Recipient letter appreciation Office Sec. Def., 1970. Registered profl. engr., Ala. Mem. Nat., Ala. socs. profl. engrs. Methodist. Author tech. reports. Home: Huntsville, Ala. Died Jan. 31, 1979.

LANHAM, EDWIN MOULTRIE, writer; b. Weatherford, Tex., Oct. 11, 1904; s. Edwin Moultrie and Elizabeth (Stephens) L.; student Tome Sch., Port Deposit, Md., Polytech. Prep. Country Day Sch., Bklyn., Williams Coll., 1923-26; study art, Paris, 1926-30; m. Irene Stillman, June 3, 1940; 1 dau., Evelyn Linda (Mrs. Kazuto Ohira). Entered newspaper work, 1930; with N.Y. Eve. Post, 1930-33, N.Y.C. News Assn., 1934-39, N.Y. Herald Tribune, 1939-44; free lance writer, 1944-79. Guggenheim fellow, 1940. Mem. Author's Guild, Mystery Writers Am., Phi Gamma Delta. Democrat. Author: Sailors Don't Care, 1929; The Wind Blew West, 1935; Banner at Daybreak, 1937; Another Ophelia, 1938; The Stricklands, 1939; Thunder in the Earth, 1941 (ann. award Tex. Inst. Letters 1942); The Iron Maiden, 1954; Slug It Slay, 1946; Politics is Murder, 1947; One Murder Too Many, 1952; Death of a Corinthian, 1953; Death in the Wind, 1956; Murder on My Street, 1958; Double Jeopardy, 1959; Six Black Camels, 1961; Passage to Danger, 1962; No Hiding Place, 1962; Monkey on a Chain, 1962; Speak Not Evil, 1964; The Paste-Pot Man, 1967; The Clock at 8:16, 1970. Contbr. short stories to nat. mags. Home: Clinton, Conn. Died July 24, 1979; buried Weatherford, Tex.

LANNAN, EDWARD PHILIP, paper mill exec.; b. Topeka, Kan., July 4, 1883; s. Thomas Francis and Alice (Dolan) L.; student pub., parochial schs., Topeka; m. Lora Neil, May 23, 1908; 1 dau., Catherine Jane. Various r.r. positions, St. Louis; with North Star Egg Case Co., Quincy, Ill., 1911-31; with Central Fibre Products Co., Quincy, 1931—, sec.-treas., 1931—, dir., 1952—, now chmn. bd. Home: Quincy, Ill. *

LANNING, JOHN TATE, educator; b. Linwood, N.C., Sept. 13, 1902; s. Baxter Franklin and Carrie Aletha (Smith) L.; A.B., Trinity Coll., Duke, 1924; A.M., U. Cal., 1925, Ph.D., 1928; m. Elizabeth Baxter Williams, June 4, 1932; children—John Tate, Lucy Hampton, Thomas Pinckney. Teaching fellow U. Cal., 1924-26; research, Brit. Mus., pub. record office, archives of the Indies, archives of Simancas, nat. hist. archives of Madrid, 1926-27; instr. history Duke, Durham, N.C., 1927-34, asst. prof., 1934-36, asso. prof., 1936-42, prof., 1942-76, James B. Duke prof. history; lectr. seminar conf. on Latin Am., George Washington U., 1935; Trumbull lectr. Yale, 1943; asso. mng. The Hispanic Am. Hist. Rev., 1935-39, mng. editor, 1939-45; Latin-Am. exchange fellow of Guggenheim Found., 1930-31; lectr. Nat. U. of Chile, Nat. U. of Córdoba, Argentine, 1931. Recipient awards of Am. Council Learned Socs., 1932, Social Sci. Research Council, 1941, com. Inter-Am. Artistic and Intellectual Relations, 1942; 1955 award Carnegie Revolving Fund, Am. Hist. Assn. and Herbert Eugene Bolton Meml. award, 1956; Serra award Ams., 1958; award merit U. Ariz., 1960. Has travelled in and conducted research in most Latin Am. countries. Corr. mem. Sociedad de Géografia e Historia de Guatemala; mem. Am. Hist. Assn. (mem. com. Albert J. Beveridge award 1952-53, chmn. 1954-55; mem. nominating com. 1962-63, chmn. com. 1963-63), Sociedad Cubana de Estudios Historicos e Internacionales, Phi Beta Kappa, Tau Kappa Alpha, Omicron Delta Kappa. Author: The Spanish Missions of Georgia, 1935; The Diplomatic History of Georgia, 1936; Academic Culture in the Spanish Colonies, 1940; Dr. Narciso Esparragosa y Gallardo, 1953; The University in the Kingdom of Guatemala, 1955; The Eighteenth-Century Enlightenment in the University of San Carlos de Guatemala, 1956. Editor: The St. Augustine Expedition of 1740, 1954. Compiler and editor of the Reales Cédulas de la Real y Pontificia Universidad de México de 1551 a 1816, 1946; Reales cédulas de la Real y Pontificia Universidad de San Carlos de Guatemala, 1954. Contbr. The Enlightenment in Latin America, 1942 (A. P. Whitaker, editor); The Hispanic Am. Hist. Rev., Revista do la Universidad de Córdoba Revista Bimestre Cubana, Revista de Historia de América, other periodicals. Home: Durham, N.C. Died Aug. 15, 1976; buried Sandy Creek Cemetery, Davidson, N.C.

LANSING, MARION FLORENCE, author; b. Waverly, Mass., June 10, 1883; d. John Arnold and Jenny H. (Stickney) L.; A.B., Mt. Holyoke Coll., 1903; A.M., Radcliffe Coll., 1905. Clubs: Pen and Brush, Boston Authors. Author hist. books for boys and girls including: Calling South America, 1945; Makers of the Americas, 1947; America in the World, 1949; Liberators and Heroes of the West Indian Islands, 1953: When Washington Traveled, 1954. Address: Cambridge, Mass., (summer) Hyannis, Mass. *

LANSKOY, ANDRE, artist; b. Moscow, Russia, 1902. Resident of Paris, 1921—; exhbn. of theme of figures in interiors Galerie Bing, 1925; first semi-abstract paintings created, 1938; totally abandoned figurative painting, 1942; exhbns. at Galeries Louis Carre, 1948, 52, 57; work includes tapestry designs. Illus. books; LaGenese; Le Journal d'un fou, Cortege. Address: France. Died Aug. 22, 1976.

LAPENTA, VINCENT ANTHONY (LAPEN'TA), surgeon; b. Naples, Italy July 4, 1883; s. Biagio and Catherine Conte Lapenta; M.D., Univ. of Naples, 1906; came to U.S., 1907; studied Harvard, 1910, Ill. Post-Grad. Sch., 1911; m. Rose Mary Mangieri, Mar. 1908; children—Catherine Elizabeth, Biagio Esculapio. In practice of abdominal surgery, Indianapolis, since 1911; surgeon in chief St. Francis Hosp.; mem. State Governing Com. of Gorgas Memorial Inst. of Tropical and Preventive Medicine. Discoverer of a serum for control of hemorrhage. Royal consul of Italy in Ind. Assigned, 1915, to reservists of Italian Army in Ind. Decorated Knight Officer of Order of Crown of Italy, Knight Comdr., 1939; Knight Comdr. Order of Crown of Roumania. Fellow Am. Med. Assn. Royal Soc. of Arts (Eng.), Internat. Coll. Surgeons, Geneva (chmn. bd. trustees and council of examiners, U.S. chapter, 1936-41); mem. Ind. Med. Assn., Indianapolis Med. Soc., A.A.A.S., Am. Medico Legal Assn., Am. Congress Phys. Medicine, Ind. Acad. Sciences. Catholic. Club: Indianapolis Athletic. Contbr. numerous articles on med. and surg. subjects. Home: Indianapolis, Ind. *

LAPIDUS, LEON, educator; b. Syracuse, N.Y., Sept. 26, 1924; s. Jacob and Libbie (Dressner) L.; B.S. in Chem. Engring., Syracuse U., 1945, M.S., 1947; Ph.D. in Chem. Engring., U. Minn., 1950; m. Elizabeth Kalmes, Aug. 12, 1950; children—Mary K., Jon J. Postdoctoral fellow M.I.T., 1950-51; mem. faculty Princeton (N.J.) U., 1951-77, prof. chem. engring., 1962-77, chmn. chem. engring., 1968-77, Class of 1943 prof., 1970-77; cons. to bus., 1953-77; mem. research adv. bd. Cities Service Co. Mem. Am. Inst. Chem. Engrs., Am. Chem. Soc., Assn. Computing Machinery, Nat. Acad. Engring. Author: Digital Computation for Chemical Engineers, 1962; Optimal Control of Engineering Processes, 1967; Numerical Solution of Ordinary Differential Equations, 1971; Process Modeling, Estimation and Identification, 1973; Chemical Reactor Theory, 1977; Numerical Solutions of Partial Differential Equations, 1981, also articles. Asso. editor Am. Inst. Chem. Engrs. Jour., Chem. Engring. Jour., Internat. Jour. Systems Sci. Home: Princeton, N.J. Died May 5, 1977; interred Princeton Cemetery.

LAPOINTE, LOUIS A., corp. exec.; b. Montreal, Que., Can., 1910; ed. U. Montreal, 1934. Pres., Miron Co., Ltd., Montreal, also chmn. bd.; dir. Hilton Can. Ltd., Toronto-Dominion Bank, Brascan Ltd., Alliance compagnie mutuelle d'assurance-vie, Fraser-Brace Engring. Co. Ltd., Canadian Arena Co., Rio Algom Mines Ltd., Indsl. Acceptance Corp. Ltd., Internat. Paints (Can.) Ltd., Goodyear Tire & Rubber Co. Can. Ltd., Fraser Brace Maritimes Ltd., Ronalds Federated, Ltd., Mines de Poirier, Inc., Sky Shops Export Ltd., I.O.S. Regent Fund Ltd., Inter City Paper Ltd., Comml. Union Group of Ins. Cos. Address: Montreal, Que., Canada. Died May 23, 1978.

LAPORTE, EWING, ex-asst. secretary U.S. Treasury; b. of Am. parents, Normandy, France, Oct. 16, 1894; s. Alphonse Adolph and Nina Agnes (Mitchell) L.; LL.B., George Washington U., 1916; student Yale, 1917-18; A.B., U. of Pittsburgh; m. Mildred Massey, Nov. 6, 1918; children—Lucile, Nancy, Jacqueline; married 2d Thelma Williams, July 5, 1950; 1 dau., Ann. Dep. sgt. at arms, U.S. Senate, 1913-16; repeatedly disch. from mil. service during World War on account of physical disability; was connected with supervision of bureaus of internal revenue, war risk ins. and customs of U.S. Treasury; apptd. asst. sec. Treasury, by President Wilson, Dec. 4, 1920, reapptd. by President Harding, resigned, June 1, 1921; financial sec., U. of Pittsburgh, June 1921-Oct. 1922; exec. sec. Dem. Nat. Conv., 1932, and exec. sec. Arrangements Com. for same. Pa. State mgr. Home Owners' Loan Corp., 1934, regional mgr. N.Y., N.J., Conn., 1935. Mem. bar of D.C., and Pa., Am. Bar Assn. Democrat. Club: Nat. Press (Washington). Home: Washington, D.C. Died Apr. 21, 1980.

LAPP, JOHN CLARKE, educator; b. Ottawa, Can., Dec. 25, 1917; s. Charles Albert and Margaret (Waddell) L.; B.A., Queen's U., 1939, M.A., 1940; Ph.D., Cornell U., 1942; m. Margaret Smail, Sept. 12, 1941 (dec.); 1 son, Harvey; m. 2d, Danielle Cauquil, Feb. 28, 1969. Instr. French, Cornell U., 1940-42, U. Ill., 1942-43; asst. prof. French, Bucknell (Pa.) U., 1945-47; asst. prof. Oberlin (O.) Coll., 1947-49, asso. prof., 1949-55, prof., 1955-56; prof. French, U. Cal. at Los Angeles, 1956-63, chmn. dept., 1956-61; Fulbright lectr. to France, 1961-62; exec. head dept. French and Italian, Stanford, 1963-68, 1st William H. Bonsall prof. French, 1968-77. Served with USNR, 1943-45. Decorated Officer d'Academie, 1955; chevalier de la Legion d'Honneur, 1961; Fulbright research grantee, 1966-67; Guggenheim fellow, 1966-67, 73-74. Mem. Modern Lang. Assn. Author: Contes Divers de Trois Siecles, 1948; The Universe of Pontus de Tyard, 1950; (with H. A. Grubbs) French Reviewed for Colleges, 1952; Notes and Commentary on Madame Bovary, 1952; Aspects of Racinian Tragedy, 1955, rev. edit., 1964; Zola Biefore the Rougon-Macquart, 1964; The Esthetics of Negligence: LàFontaine's Contes, 1971; Les Racines du Naturalisme, 1972. Editor: OEuvres poétiques complètes de Pontus de Tyard, 1966; The Brazen Tower: Essays in Mythological Imagery in the French Renaissance and Baroque (1550-1670), 1977; translator: Le Cid (Pierre Corneille), 1955. Modèles de Phrases, suivis d'un recueil de modéles de lettres d'amour de Pontus de Tyard, 1967; also articles. Home: Stanford, Calif. Died Sept. 19, 1977; buried San Bruno (Calif.) Mil. Cemetery.

LARABEE, BYRON HANLY, banker; b. Osgood, Ind., July 4, 1904; s. Edgar James and Florence Emma (Christie) L.; B.S., U. Akron, 1926; LL.B., Western Res. U., 1929; LL.D., U. Liberia, 1956; m. Helen Evelyn Chenot, Aug. 22, 1931; children—John Edgar, Dale Robert. Admitted to Ohio bar, 1930; gen. practice law, Akron, 1930-35; asst. dir. law City Akron, 1936; exec. sec. Greater Akron Assn., 1937-38; with Firestone Tire & Rubber Co., 1939-65, asst. sec., 1956-61, v.p., 1961-65; with Firestone Plantations Co., 1942-65, pres., 1956-65; pres., dir. U.S. Liberia Radio Corp., 1946-65; v.p. Akron Nat. Bank, 1966-70, dir., 1966-79. Mem. Nat. Adv. Health Council, 1950-56, Nat. Adv. Allergy and Infectious Diseases Council, 1956-57; mem. indsl. council tropical health Harvard Sch. Pub. Health, 1950-65. Bd. dirs. Am. Found. Tropical Medicine. Decorated knight comdr. Liberian Humane Order African Redemption; grand comdr. Order Star Africa; Grand Cordon with Liberia Star, Pioneers of Liberia; recipient Alumni Honor award U. Akron, 1976. Mem. Nat. Planning Assn., Phi Kappa Tau, Delta Theta Pi, Phi Sigma. Republican. Presbyn. Mason. Clubs: City, Portgage Country (Akron). Home: Akron, Ohio. Died Feb. 12, 1979; buried Rose Hill Cemetery, Akron.

LARGE, (JOHN) JUDSON, business exec.; b. Rock Valley, Ia., Dec. 26, 1903; s. John Jacob and May (McQuilkin) L.; student Dartmouth Coll., 1921-23; U. of Ia., 1923-24; Morningside Coll., Sioux City, Ia., 1924-25; m. Winifred Ward, Dec. 28, 1927 (divorced); 1 son, John Judson; m. 2d, Della Kropp, Oct. 10, 1936. Accountant United Gas Improvement Contracting Co.; Central West Pub. Service Co., 1926-35; sec.-treas. McGraw-Edison Co., 1928-56, v.p., sec., 1956-68, dir., 1929-68, chmn. executive com., 1964-68; sec. and treas. Western Power & Gas Co., 1936-49, pres., 1949-68, chmn., 1965-68, dir.; pres., dir. Middle States Telephone Co. Ill., LaCrosse Telephone Corp., Va. Tel. & Tel. Co.; Central Telephone Co., Southeastern Telephone Co. Mem. Beta Theta Pi. Conglist. Clubs: Mid-Day, Attic, Exmoor (Chgo.). Home: Chicago, Ill. Died Jan. 4, 1981.

LA RIVERS, IRA (JOHN), entomologist, biologist; b. San Francisco, May 1, 1915; s. Ira John and Yvonne (Grouix) La R.; B.S., U. Nev., 1937; Ph.D., U. Calif., Berkeley, 1948; postgrad. (Acad. fellow) Acad. Zoology, Agra, India, 1960; m. Marian Byrd Ballinger, Dec. 21, 1951; 1 son, Ira John III. Field agt. Dept. Agr., 1936, 37, 39, 42; teaching asst. N.C. State Coll., Raleigh, 1937-38, U. Calif., Berkeley, 1947-48; entomologist U. Nev., 1939-42, 48-54, asso. prof. entomology and biology, 1954-61, prof., 1961-77, chmn. dept. biology and dir. museum, 1953-63; cons. in field. Served to ensign USNR, 1942-46. Mem. Am. Entomol. Soc., Am. Inst. Biol. Scis., Paleontol. Soc., Entomol. Soc. Washington, Ecol. Soc. Am., Soc. Vertberate Paleontology, Soc. Systematic Zoology, Am. Malacological Union, Coleopterists Soc., Nev. Acad. Natural Scis. (pres. 1940-41), Nev. Audubon Soc. (pres. 1940), Oahu Micros. Soc. (pres. 1944-45), Nev. Wildlife Conservation Soc. (pres. 1949), Calif. Acad. Sci. (spl. wildlife observer Nev. area), Western Soc. Naturalists, Biol. Soc. Nev. (founder and pres. 1962-77, editor Occas 1963-77), Sigma Xi, Phi Kappa Phi, Alpha Epsilon Delta. Author: Fishes and Fisheries of Nevada; Algae of Nevada; author lab. manual; contbr. numerous articles to profl. publs. Home: Verdi, Nev. Died Oct. 11, 1977; buried Crystal Peak Cemetery, Verdi.

LARMON, RUSSELL RAYMOND, educator; born Red Oak, Ia., Mar. 6, 1897; s. Peter John and Sophia (Peterson) L.; A.B., Dartmouth Coll., 1919, M.C.S., 1920, A.M., 1934; Dr. Civil Law, New England Coll., 1963; m. Katharine Graves, December 20, 1938; children—John Russell, Jane Russell. Sec. to pres., Dartmouth Coll., 1919-22, exec. asst. to pres., 1922-26, prof. adminstrtn., 1934-63; asst. sec. Dept. Health Edn. and Welfare, 1953-54; cons. orgn. and adminstrn. N.H.; state dir. OPA, 1942-43; dir. No. R.R.; chmn. bd. Rumford Press, 1951-52. Mem. Nat. Adv. Heart Council, 1955-58, Nat. Adv. Health Council, 1959-63. Trustee Mary Hitchcock Meml. Hosp. Served with USN, 1917-18. Mem. Phi Gamma Delta. Republican. Home: Hanover, N.H. Died Jan. 4, 1973; buried Hanover, N.H.

LARMON, WILLIAM ALEXANDER, physician; b. Sunnyvale, Calif., Oct. 23, 1916; s. William A. and Eleanor (Bradford) L.; student San Jose State Coll., 1933-36, Stanford, 1936-37; B.S., Northwestern U., 1941, M.B., M.D., 1942; m. Irene Traska, Oct. 13, 1945 (dec. Oct. 1976); m. Jane Alderson, Mar. 14, 1977. Intern, Harper Hosp., Detroit, 1941-42, asst. resident pathology, 1942; Kemper fellow bone and joint dept. Northwestern U. Hosp., 1942-45, fellow bone and joint dept., 1945-46; faculty Northwestern U. Med. Sch., 1947-80, prof. bone and joint surgery, 1974, acting chmn. dept. orthopedic surgery, 1971; pvt. practice, Chgo., 1947-80; chief staff Northwestern Meml. Hosp., 1974, bd. dirs., 1974-80; attending staff VA Hosp., Hines, Ill. Orthopaedic rep. Adv. Bd. Med. Specialists, 1962-80; chmn. nat. adv. com. orthopaedic surgery VA, 1969-80; Bd. dirs. Nat. Interne and Residency Program. Diplomate Am. Bd. Orthopaedic Surgery (sec.-treas. 1962-68). Fellow A.C.S. (gov. 1968-80); mem. A.M.A., Ill., Chgo. med. socs., Am. Acad. Orthopaedic Surgery, Clin-Orthopaedic Soc., Am. Rheumatism Soc., Chgo. Rheumatism Assn., Chgo. Orthopaedic Soc. (pres. 1961-62), Chgo. Surg. Soc., Am. Assn. Ry. Surgeons, Hines Surg. Assn., Assn. Bone and Joint Surgeons, Am. Orthopaedic Assn., Alpha Kappa Kappa. Contbr. articles to profl. jours., chpts. to books. Editor instructional course vol. 15, Am. Acad. Orthopaedic Surgeons, 1958. Home: Chicago, Ill. Died July 17, 1980.

LA ROCHE, CHESTER J., ret. advt. exec.; b. Boston, Aug. 24, 1892; s. John James and Mary (Boyle) LaR.; grad. Tilton, 1913, Exeter, 1915, Yale, 1918, U.S. Naval Academy (sr. lt. U.S. Navy); m. Mathilde Hopkins (dec.); children—Joan (dec.), Chester; m. 2d, Clara Russell (dec.); children—Sean, Rosalind; m. 3d, Ritchey Farrell, Mar. 7, 1961. Successively reporter for Boston Post, sales promotion Gen. Motors; coach Yale Freshman football team and Yale Varsity, advt. mgr. The Mentor; So. advt. mgr. Collier's Weekly; with Young & Rubicam, Inc., advt., N.Y.C., successively as account exec., v.p., exec. v.p., pres., later chmn. bd.; chmn. advt. Research Found.; vice-chmn. ABC Network, to 1945; organizer Advt. Council, Inc.; chmn. War Advt. Council, 1942-44 (Gold medal for distinguished services to advt. 1942-43); chmn. LaRoche, McCaffrey & McCall, Inc.; chmn. Peoples Capitalism Commn., Dorchester Corp.; dir. United Shareowners Am. Hon. chmn. Yale Football Assn., Yale Film Com.; chmn. info. com., Yale, mem. endowment com., alumni Bd., alumni sch. com.; adv. council to sec. commerce. Past bd. dirs. Am. Ballet Theatre, Nat. Acad. Sports; trustee, vice chmn. bd. Fairfield Country Day Sch., Tilton Sch. (N.H.); co-chmn. Gen. MacArthur com. Nat. Football Found. and Hall of Fame, N.Y.C., chmn. Center for Leadership; organizer chmn. Am. Round Table; exec. com. Yale Alumni Bd. Recipient Nat. Football Found. Gold medal, Walter Camp Gold medal N.Y. chpt., Distinguished Am. award N.Y., Columbus, Cin. chpts.; Plimpton medal Tilton Sch.; LaRoche, McCaffrey & McCall award Yale; Yale Gold medal, 1972; Football award Exeter; Pat-on-Back award Sports Illustrated; Harvard Club Boston award; U.S. Treasury award; Res. AC U.S. Army award. Mem. Council Fgn. Relations, Nat. Acad. Scis., Pilgrims. Clubs: Fairfield County Hunt; Berzelius; Torch; Bathing Corp., Meadow (Southampton); Bath and Tennis, Everglades (Palm Beach); Knickerbocker, River, Squadron A., Yale, Racquet and Tennis, Sky (N.Y.C.) Home: Palm Beach, Fla. Died Aug. 21, 1977; buried Palm Beach.

LARRABEE, HAROLD ATKINS, educator; b. Melrose, Mass., Aug. 20, 1894; s. John and Mary Edna (Atkins) L.; A.B., Harvard, 1916, Ph.D., 1925; A.M., Columbia, 1918; diploma Union Theol. Sem., 1920; L.H.D., Union Coll., 1960; m. Doris M. Kennard, Dec. 27, 1917 (dec. Mar. 1965); children—Eric, Sylvia; m. 2d, Dorcas Morgan, Oct. 1, 1965. Asst. prof. philosophy Syracuse (N.Y.) U., 1920-21; asst. philosophy Harvard and Radcliffe colls., 1921-23; Rogers traveling fellow Harvard, 1923-24; asst. prof. psychology U. Vt., 1924-25; asst. prof. philosophy Union Coll., 1925-27, asso. prof., 1927-28, prof. 1928-40, Ichabod Spencer prof. philosophy, 1940-60, prof. emeritus, 1960-79, chmn. div. social studies, 1945-50, 55-56, chmn. sesquicentennial celebration, 1945. Vis. prof. Columbia, summer 1948, 53-55; Ingraham lectr. Colby Coll., 1958-59; mem. Fulbright Screening Bd. in Philosophy, 1957-59; bd. dirs. Editorial Center, U.S.A., Bibliography of Philosophy, 1953-56. Pres. bd. trustees Schenectady Pub. Library, 1959-61. Psychol. examiner at Camps Greenleaf and Beauregard, La., and U.S. Army Gen. Hosp. No. 19, Oteen, N.C., 1918-19. Mem. Am. Philos. Assn. (sec.-treas. Eastern div. 1932-34, v.p. 1941), Am. Assn. U. Profs. (pres. Union chpt. 1951-52), Société des Americanistes-de Paris, Mohawk Valley Library Assn. (pres. bd. trustees 1960-61), Phi Beta Kappa (pres. Union chpt. 1930-32, 58-60). Clubs: Appalachian Mountain (Boston); Club Alpin Français (Grenoble, France). Author: What Philosophy Is, 1928; Rhymes About College, 1936; Reliable Knowledge, 1945, rev. edit., 1964; Decision at the Chesapeake, 1964; Sesquicentennial History of Alpha New York, Phi Beta Kappa, 1817-1967, 1967. Editor: Selections from Bergson, 1949; Bentham's Handbook of Political Fallacies, 1952. Translator: Man: Mind or Matter, 1951; In Quest of New Ethics, 1953; Sensation The Origin of Life, 1960. Bd. editors N.E. Quar. Contbr. Am. Heritage, Philos. Rev., Ethics, others. Home: Austin, Tex. Died Feb. 5, 1979.

LARSELL, OLOF (LÄR-SEL'), anatomist; b. Rättvik, Sweden, Mar. 13, 1886; s. John and Anna (Anderson)L.; came with parents to U.S., 1891; B.S., Linfield Coll., Ore., 1910; M.A., Northwestern U., 1914, Ph.D., 1918; Sc.D., Linfield Coll.; m. Leo Dorcas Fleming, June 22, 1911; children—John Fleming, Franklin Sherman (dec.), Robert, Instructor in biology, Linfield College, 1910-15; instructor in zoÖlogy, Northwestern University, 1915-18; asst. prof. anatomy, U. of Wis., 1918-20; asso. prof. zoölogy, Northwestern U., 1920-21; prof. anatomy, U. of Ore. Med. Sch., 1921-52; prof. neuranatomy University Minn. since 1952; visiting prof. anatomy, Northwestern U. Medical School, 1927. Guest of Wistar Inst., 1929, 34, 35; lecturer in neuroanatomy, U. of Calif., 1931, 32; dean grad. div. Ore. State System of Higher Edn., 1938-46. Trustee Linfield Coll. (pres. bd. 1931-38). Fellow A.A.A.S.; hon. fellow Am. Acad. Ophthalmology and Otolaryngology; mem. Am. Assn. Anatomists, Soc. Exptl. Biology and Med., History of Science Soc., Am. Assn. University Professors Lärdomshistoriska Samfundet of Upsala, American Neurol. Assn. (assoc. mem.), Sigma Xi, Gamma Alpha, Phi Beta Pi. Awarded Casselberry prize (with R. A. Fenton), American Laryngological Assn., 1928. Baptist. Contributor research articles on anatomical subjects and papers on history of science and of medicine, to scientific and medical journals, also spl. monographs. Author: (translator) Autobiographical Notes of Jöns Jacob Berzelius; Neuro-Anatomy and Sense Organs; Anatomy of the Nervous System; Morris Human Anatomy (contbr.), The Doctor in Oregon, a Medical History. Mem. bd. of editors Jour. of Comparative Neurology. Cons. editor: Jour- of History of Medicine and Allied Sciences. *

LARSEN, NIELS HJALMAR, architect; b. Copenhagen, Denmark, May 17, 1885; s. Lars Peter and Elna (Johnson) L.; came to U.S., 1891, now naturalized citizen; student Harvard, 1908-09, Am. Acad., Rome, Italy, 1910-11; m. Bessie H. Cassidy, October 10, 1910 (deceased); married 2d, Amelia R. Och; children—Dorothy Hazen (Mrs. William Waldo Nelson), Paul Winthrop, Nancy Ann, Marjorie (Mrs. Wilber Ross Bowen), Eleanor Ochs (Mrs. Alfred F. Latimer II). Architectural draftsman, 1902; practiced architecture and engineering Leland and Larsen and successor firm Larsen, Bradley and Hibbard, Boston, 1921—, now partner; consulting architects University Massachusetts; vice consul for Denmark and Iceland, 1931-41. teacher of design, Mass. Inst. Tech., 1937-41. Chmn. Town Planning Board, Watertown, Mass. Trustee Russell Sage College, Troy, New York. Decorated Order of Dannebrog (Denmark); Medal for Distinguished Meritorious Service (USN). Former mem. vis. committee Sch. of Design, Harvard U. Fellow Am. Inst. Architects; mem. Boston Soc. Architects, Mass. State Assn. Architects. Mason (Shriner). Club: Boston Swedish Square and Compass (pres.). Contbr. articles to archtl. publs. Home: Belmont, Mass. *

LARSEN, ROY EDWARD, publisher; b. Boston, Apr. 20, 1899; s. Robert and Stella (Belyea) L.; grad. Boston Latin Sch., 1917; A.B., Harvard, 1921, LL.D., 1953, N.Y. U., 1952; m. Margaret Zerbe, June 20, 1927; children—Anne (Mrs. Drew Simonson), Robert, Christopher, Jonathan. Vice chmn. bd. Time, Inc. Organizer, chmn. Nat. Citizens Commn. for Pub. Schs., 1959-66; mem. Pres.'s Com. for White House Conf. on Edn. and Conf. on Edn. Beyond High Sch. Bd. dirs. United Hosp. Fund N.Y.; chmn. bd. Fund for Advancement Edn., 1955-67; trustee Ford Found., 1957-69, N.Y. Public Library, N.Y.C.; bd. overseers Harvard, 1940-46, 53-59; vice chmn., chmn. arts com. U.S. Adv. Commn. on Internat. Ednl. and Cultural Affairs, 1963-69. Chmn. bd. Nantucket Conservation Found. Clubs: Harvard, Century, River, University, Links (N.Y.C.). Home: Fairfield, Conn. Died Sept. 9, 1979.

LARSH, EVERETT PAUL, business exec.; b.Richmond, Ind., June 16, 1886; s. John Henderson and Mary Elizabeth (Posther) L.; student Internat. Corr. Schs; m. Mabel Wilcox, June 15, 1918. Successively with Remy Electric Co., M. Rumley Co., Burnett Larsh Co., Day-Fan Motor Co., 1919-20; with Master Electric Co., Dayton, 1920-57, pres., 1920-41, chmn. bd., 1940-57; pres., owner Tungston Plantation, Inc., 1937-60, Miami Ships (formerly Newport Ships), 1941-54; operator MiLarsh Lab., Miami, Fla., 1941-64; pres. Daytrol Corp. (now The Larsh Corp. 1969), Dayton, 1955—. Served with USN, 1907-11. Fellow I.E.E.E. Mason (Shriner). Club: Engineers (Dayton); Kings Bay Yacht and Country (Miami, Fla.). *

LARSON K(ARL) G(OTTFRID), prof. physics; b. Föra, Sweden, Nov. 5, 1883; s. Nils August and Tilda Maria (Nilsson) L.; arrived in U.S., May 21, 1900, naturalized 1905; A.B., Augustana Coll., Rock Island, Ill., 1915; A.M., U. of Wis., 1929. Successively instr., asst., asso. prof. physics, Augustana Coll., 1923-42, prof., head dept., since 1943. Fellow A.A.A.S.; mem. Am. Phys. Soc., Am. Assn. of Physics Teachers. Lutheran. Contbr. articles. Home: Rock Island, Ill. *

LARSON, MARTIN MAGNUSS, judge; b. Pleasant Grove, Utah, July 11, 1885; s. Thomas Christian and Karen Marie (Hansen) L.; A.B., Brigham Young U., 1910; student Mo. Law Sch., 1910-12, U. of Utah, 1912-13; m. Leah R. Smart, Sept. 2, 1917; 1 dau., Norma Rae. Admitted to Utah bar, 1913, and began practice at Provo; county atty., Utah County, 1917-19, 1923-25, judge 4th Judicial Dist., Utah, 1927-29, 1933-36; justice Supreme Court of Utah, since 1937. Served in U.S. Army, 1917-19; commd. 2d lt. June 1918. Mem. Am. Bar Assn., Utah State Bar Assn., Utah County Bar Assn. Democrat. Mem. Ch. of Jesus Christ of Latter Day Saints Club: Lions (Provo). Home: Salt Lake City. *

LARSON, RAYMOND HOWARD, coll. dean; b. Wolback, Neb., Aug. 28, 1910; s. Arthur Lawrence and Dagny (Haggstrom) L.; B.S., U. Neb., 1937; M.S., U. Minn., 1939, Ph.D. in Indsl. Edn., 1952; m. G. Louise Bunde, Aug. 11, 1940; children—Sharon (Mrs. Gary R. Parker), Joan (Mrs. Bruce G. Ferrario), Marian (Mrs. Marvin Hutchens). Instr. indsl. arts N. Platte (Neb.) pub. schs., 1931-34; teaching asst. U. Minn., 1939-40; acting head dept. indsl. arts St. Cloud (Minn.) State Coll., 1940-41; instr. Univ. High Sch., U. Minn., 1941-42; chmn. dept. indsl. arts St. Cloud State Coll., 1946-66, chmn. div. arts and music, 1951-63, dean Sch. Industry, 1966-72, prof. indsl. edn., 1972-74, ret., 1974. Chmn. precinct and county Republican orgns. Served as officer AUS, 1942-46. Mem. Nat., Minn. edn. assns., Minn. Indsl. Assn., Miss. Valley Indsl. Arts Assn., Am. Soc. Engring. Edn., Am. Council Indsl. Arts Tchr. Edn., Phi Delta Kappa. Home: St. Cloud, Minn. Died Mar. 5, 1979; buried Fort Snelling Nat. Cemetery, St. Paul.

LASHINSKY, HERBERT, educator; b. N.Y.C., Dec. 14, 1921; s. Isodore Meyer and Leah (Abrams) L.; B.Sc., Coll. City N.Y., 1950; Ph.D., Columbia U., 1961; div.; 1 dau., Karen. Engr., Western Electric Co., 1940-43; research asso. Princeton, 1961-64; prof. Inst. Phys. Sci. and Tech., Math., U. Md., College Park, 1964-80. Served with AUS, 1943-46. Mem. Am. Phys. Soc., IEEE. Editor: Soviet Physics-Tech. Physics. Translator Review of Plasma Physics. Patentee in field. Home: Bethesda, Md. Died Apr. 2, 1980.

LASKER, EDWARD, elec. engr.; b. Kempen, Germany, Dec. 3, 1885; s. Sigismund and Flora (Bornstein) L.; Mech. Engr., Charlottenburg Tech. Inst., Berlin, Germany, 1904, E.E., 1911; m. Cecile Heller, Apr. 20, 1920 (dec. 1920); m. 2d, Hertha Furth, 1927 (div. 1937). Came to U.S., 1914, naturalized, 1921. Engr., A.E.G. Electric Co., Berlin and London, Eng., 1911-14; civilian prisoner-of-war, Eng., 1914; safety engr. Sears, Roebuck & Co., Chgo., 1915-19, Burton Page Co., Chgo., 1919-21; inventor, mfr. electric breast pump for hosp. use, 1921-29; organizer electromed. dept. Lepel High Frequency Lab., N.Y.C., 1931-41; chessmaster, writer of books, 1941—; known as chess champion of Berlin, 1909, Paris, 1912, London, 1914, N.Y.C., 1915, Chgo., 1916, Western States, 1917, 19, 20, 21, 22, Mexico, 1954; winner N.Y. Masters Tournament, 1922; only amateur invited to play in Internat. Grand Masters Tournament, N.Y.C., 1924; winner Internat. Chess Master title, Scheveningen, 1913; recipient Ohkura prize Japanese Go Assn., 1971. Arbiter Internat. Chess Fedn., 1958—; hon. pres. Marshall Chess Club, N.Y.C. Author: Chess for Fun and Chess for Blood, 2d edit., 1962; Chess and Checkers, the Way to Mastership, 2d edit., 1948; Modern Chess Strategy, 1945; The Adventure of Chess, 1950; Chess Secrets, 1951; The Game of Chess, 1972. Introduced Japanese nat. game of Go in Europe and Am.; pub. Go and Gomoku, the Oriental bd. games, 1934; founder Am. Go Assn., 1915. Home: New York City NY. *

LASS, ERNEST WILLIAM, newspaper and radio sta. exec.; b. Roselle, N.J., Jan. 7, 1907; s. Ernest Charles and Elizabeth (Otter) L.; Litt.B., Rutgers U., 1928; L.H.D. (hon.), Monmouth Coll., 1971; m. Frances F. Felger, Apr. 14, 1933; children—E. Donald, Barbara Ann Lass Carr. With Asbury Park Press, Inc. (N.J.), 1928-80, sec.-treas. 1945-74, pub., 1974, chmn. bd., 1974-80; dir. emeritus Midlantic Nat. Bank-Mchts.; dir. F. & F. Felger, Inc. Mem. N.J. Water Resources Com., 1952, N.J. Commn. to Study Adminstrv. and Profl.

Salaries, 1958; chmn. Monmouth County (N.J.) Welfare Bd., 1962-68. Recipient Brotherhood award NCCJ, 1972; Disting. Citizen award Boy Scouts Am., 1977; Achievement award State of Israel, 1968. Mem. N.J. Press Assn. (pres. 1957-58, Four Freedoms award 1942), Am. Newspaper Pubs. Assn., Internat. Press Inst., Asbury Park C. of C. (pres. 1955-56). Club: Deal Golf and Country. Home: Interlaken, N.J. Died Sept. 8, 1980.

LASSWELL, HAROLD DWIGHT, educator; b. Donnellson, Ill., Feb. 13, 1902; s. Linden Downey and Anna (Prather) L.; Ph.B., U. Chgo., 1922, Ph.D., 1926; postgrad. univs. London, Geneva, Paris, Berlin, 1923-24, 25; D.Litt., Jewish Theol. Sem., N.Y.C.; LL.D., U. Ill., U. Chgo., Columbia U.; Sc.D., U. Pa. Asst. dept. polit. sci. U. Chgo., 1922-24, instr., 1924-27, asst. prof., 1927-32, asso. prof., 1932-38; polit. scientist Washington Sch. Psychiatry, 1938-39; dir. war communications research Library Congress, Washington, 1939-45; prof. law Yale, 1946—, prof. law and polit. sci., 1952-61, Edward J. Phelps prof. law and polit. sci., 1961-71, emeritus, 1971-78, Ford Found. prof. law and social sci., 1971-78; fellow Branford Coll., 1946-78; prof. John Jay Coll. Criminal Justice, N.Y.C., 1970-73, Temple U., 1973-75, 75-78; co-chmn. Policy Scis. Center, N.Y.C. Vis. prof. Syracuse (N.Y.) U., 1926, Western Res. U., Cleve., 1929, U. Calif., 1935, Yenching U., 1937, Tokyo, 1955; vis. Sterling lectr. Sch. Law, New Haven, 1938-45; lectr. New Sch. for Social Research, N.Y., 1939-46; vis. prof. U. Patna (India), U. Santiago (Chile); fellow Center for Advanced Study in Behavioral Scis., Stanford, Calif., 1954—, Social Sci. Research Council, 1928-29. Mem. research adv. bd. Com. for Econ. Devel.; Commn. on Freedom of Press (auspices U. Chgo.). Recipient prize Am. Council Learned Socs., 1960. Fellow World Acad. Art and Sci., Nat. Acad. Scis.; mem. Am. Soc. Internat. Law (pres. 1970-72), Am. Econ. Assn., Am. Acad. Arts and Scis., Am. Polit. Sci. Assn. (pres. 1955-56), Am. Sociol. Soc., Phi Beta Kappa, Delta Sigma Rho, Tau Kappa Epsilon. Clubs: Cosmos (Washington); University (N.Y.C.); Graduates (New Haven). Author books including: Propaganda Technique in the World War, 1927; Psychopathology and Politics, 1930; World Politics and Personal Insecurity, 1935; Politics: Who Gets What, When, How, 1936; Democracy Through Public Opinion, 1941; Politics Faces Economics, 1946; The Analysis of Political Behaviour, 1948; Power and Personality, 1948 (the Salmon Meml. Lectures, N.Y. Acad. Med.); (with N. Leites, assos.) Language of Politics: Studies in Quantitative Semantics, 1949; (with A. Kaplan) Power and Society: A Framework for Political Inquiry, 1950; World Revolution of Our Time, 1951; (with D. Lerner) The Policy Sciences: Recent Developments in Scope and Method, 1951; World Revolutionary Elites: Studies in Coercive Ideological Movements, 1966; (with R. Arens) in Defense of Public Order, 1961; The Future of Political Science, 1963; (with M.S. McDougal, I. Vlasic) The Public Order of Space, 1963; (with A. Rogow) Power, Corruption and Rectitude, 1963; (with R. Rubenstein) The Sharing of Power in A Psychiatric Hospital, 1966; Pre-View of Policy Sciences, 1973; (with others) Policy Sciences and Population, 1975; Power and Personality, 1976; Values and Development: Appraising Asian Experience, 1977; The Signature of Power: Buildings, Communication, and Policy, 1979; (with others) Human Rights and World Public Order, 1980, numerous others; co-editor: Propaganda and Communication in World History, 3 vols., 1979-80; adv. editor Policy Sciences (Amsterdam). Home: New Haven, Conn. Died Dec. 18, 1978; cremated.

LATHAM, EARL, educator; b. New Bedford, Mass., Oct. 28, 1907; s. Artemas Leroy and Irene Florence (Ganson) L.; A.B., Harvard, 1930, Ph.D., 1939; A.M. (hon.), Amherst Coll., 1949; m. Margaret Victoria Perrier, Aug. 21, 1935; children—Peter Samuel, Susan Gail. Asst. dept. govt. Harvard, 1933-35, instr. and tutor, 1936-40, lectr., summer 1947, vis. prof., 1959-60, summer 1947, 49, 53, 54, 55, 56, 58; instr. and tutor govt. Radcliffe Coll., 1938-40; asst. prof. polit. sci. U. Minn., 1940-44, asso. prof., 1944-48; Joseph B. Eastman prof. polit. sci. Amherst Coll., from 1948, chmn. dept., 1949-73, distinguished lectr., from 1973; Sperry-Hutchinson Found. lectr. U. Fla., 1962; vis. prof. polit. sci. Mt. Holyoke Coll., 1951-52; former polit. sci. editor Harcourt, Brace & Co.; sr. adminstrv. analyst U.S. Bur. Budget, 1942-43, asst. chief field service, 1943-46, chief budget examiner, 1946, cons., 1946-47, mem. adv. com., from 1952; cons. OPS, O.D.M., 1951-53, to statis. office UN, 1948; mem. exec. council Adminstrv. Office of U.S., 1961-63. Del. 4th Congress, Internat. Polit. Sci. Assn., Rome, 1958; bd. dirs. Social Sci. Research Council, 1954-60, chmn. com. social sci. personnel, 1952-60; dir. N.E., Western Mass. citizenship clearing houses. Social Sci. Research fellow N.Y., 1935-36, recipient award for research govtl. affairs, 1961-62. Fellow Am. Acad. Arts and Scis.; mem. Am. (exec. com. 1953-55, program chmn. 1955-56, v.p. 1957-58), New Eng. (pres. 1953-54) polit. sci. assns., Am. Soc. Pub. Adminstrn., A.A.U.P., Psi Upsilon, Pi Sigma Alpha. Club: Cosmos (Washington). Author: Federal Field Service, 1947; Group Basis of Politics: A Study in Basing Point Legislation, 1951; Massachusetts Politics, 1956; Philosophy and Policies of Woodrow Wilson, 1958; The Politics of Railroad Coordination, 1933-36, 1959; (with others) Public Policy, 1942; Ideas and Issues in Public Administration, 1953; Political Behavior, 1956; The Corporation and Modern Society, 1959; American Politics and Government, 1965; Teaching Political Science, 1965; The Communist Controversy in Washington, 1966 (David Demarest Lloyd cash prize Harry S. Truman Library Inst. 1967). Editor: John D. Rockefeller, Robber Baron or Industrial Statesman, 1949; The Declaration of Independence and The Constitution, 1949, rev. edit., 1957, 75; The Meaning of McCarthyism, 1965; J.F. Kennedy and Presidential Power, 1972. Contbr. articles and books revs. to profl. jours. and reports. Polit. sci. editor St. Martin's Press, 1962-66. Home: Amherst, Mass. Died May 6, 1977.

LATHROPE, GEORGE HAINES, physician; b. Wilkes Barre, Pa., July 19, 1878; s. William W. and Mary Overton (Maxwell) L.; A.B., Princeton, 1900; M.D., Columbia, 1904; m. Elisabeth Mecabe, Dec. 10, 1910; children—John, Barbara (Mrs. Herbert D. Merrick). Intern Presbyn. Hosp., N.Y.C., Lying-in-Hosp., N.Y.C., 1904-07; practice medicine Binghamton, N.Y., 1907-09, Morristown, N.J., 1909-17, cons. practice internal medicine, 1919—, med. cons. N.J. State Hosp., Greystone Park, Dover Gen. Hosp., All Souls Hosp., Meml. Hosp., Morristown, St. Barnabas Hosp., Newark, St. Clare's Hosp., Denville, N.J. Trustee Morristown Library 1921—, pres. bd., 1930-46. Served as lt. col., M.C., U.S. Army, 1917-19. Fellow A.C.P. (gov. N.J. 1939-50 regent 1950-54, v.p. 1954-55; Alfred Stengel Meml. award 1952); mem. A.M.A., Am. Clin. and Climatol. Assn., N.J. Heart Assn. Clubs: Princeton (N.Y.C.); Nassau (Princeton); Morristown. Home: Morristown, N.J. *

LAUCKS, IRVING FINK (LOUKS), chemist; b. Akron, O., July 3, 1882; s. Morris B. and Louisa M. (Fink) L.; B.S., Case Sch. of Applied Science, Cleveland, 1904, M.S., 1909; m. Helen Viola Thompson, June 30, 1909; children—Helen Virginia (Mrs. R. W. Cool), John Thompson; m. 2d, Eulah A. Croson, Nov. 9, 1942; 1 dau., Mary Lisa. Chemist, Schoelkopf, Hartford & Hanna, Buffalo, N.Y., 1904, Grasselli Chem. Co., 1905, Diamond Rubber Co., 1906, Anaconda Mining Co., 1907-08; Falkenburg & Laucks, testing lab., 1908-18; pres. I. F. Laucks, Inc., 1918-44, Laucks Labs., Inc., 1927-45, Laucks Laboratory, Ltd., I. F. Laucks, Ltd. (Vancouver, B.C., Can.), I. F. Laucks, Inc. (Portsmouth, Va.), Lauxite Corp. (Lockport, N.Y.), The Speedwall Co. (Seattle, Wash.) until 1944. Member American Chemical Society A.A.A.S., Am. Inst. Chem. Engrs., Kappa Sigma. Author: Commercial Oils; A Speculation in Reality. Co-inventor Greene-Laucks process for low temperature carbonization of coal: also sova bean glue,Lauxein. Address: Healdsburg, Cal. *

LAUDEMAN, RANDOLPH DOUGLASS, lawyer; b. Balt., Apr. 8, 1909; s. Randolph and Mary M. (Treut) L.; LL.B., U. Balt., 1929; m. Dorothy Irving Remington, Sept. 24, 1935; children—Arthur N., Dorothy L. (Mrs. Frank L. Mitchell). With B. & O. R.R., Balt., 1926-31; admitted to Md. bar, 1931, Ill. bar, 1951, also Fed. Ct., U.S. Tax Ct., U.S. Ct. of Claims; practice in Balt., 1931-35, Bloomington, Ill., 1951-80; pvt. practice, 1931-35, 51-80; investigator alcohol tax unit Treasury Dept., Balt., 1934-35, Raleigh, N.C., 1935, Balt., 1936, Salisbury, Md., 1937-38, examiner, revenue agt. estate and income tax unit, Bloomington, 1939-51. Auditor, Bloomington-Normal Community Chest, 1940; first aid instr. McLean County chpt. ARC, 1942-65, first aid chmn., 1945, disaster chmn., 1947-49, chpt. chmn., 1949; chmn. McLean County unit Am. Cancer Soc., 1964-70; pres. McLean County Hist. Soc., 1967-69; chmn. Bloomington-Asahigawa Sister City Com., 1969-74; bd. dirs. Credit Bur. of Bloomington. Republican precinct committeeman, 1960-65. Mem. Am., Ill., McLean County bar assns. Presbyn. (elder, trustee). Mason (Shriner). Home: Bloomington, Ill. Died Dec. 22, 1980.

LAUER, EDWARD HENRY (LOU'ER), univ. prof.; b. Peru, Ill., Feb. 24, 1885; s. Otto, Jr., and Mary (Bellinghausen) L.; A.B., U. of Mich., 1906, M.A., 1909; Berlin U., Germany. 1909-10; Ph.D., U. of Mich., 1916; m. Edna J. Mayworm, Aug. 27, 1912; children—Eleanor C., Paul R., Thomas W., David A. Teacher Modern Langs., Mich. Mil. Acad., Orchard Lake, Mich. 1906-07; acting head, dept. modern-langs., Denison U., Granville, O., 1907-08; fellow Germanics, U. of Mich., 1908-09; Ottendorffer Memorial fellow, New York U., study at Berlin, 1909-10; instr. German, U. of Ia., 1910-23, asst., asso. prof., dir. extension div., 1923-29, dir. div. phys. edn. and athletics, 1929-34; dean, Coll. Arts and Scis., 1934-50, prof. of German. U. of Wash., Seattle, since 1934. Conglist. Home: Seattle, Wash. *

LAUHOFF, HOWARD JOSEPH, grain co. exec.; b. Detroit, Apr. 7, 1912; s. Henry A. and Cecilia (Denk) L.; grad. pub. schs. Detroit; m. Bernice De Clerq, July 9, 1936. Chmn. bd. Lauhoff Grain Co., Danville, Ill., 1961-78. Bd. dirs. Lauhoff Found. Mem. U.S., Danville chambers commerce. Republican. Roman Catholic. Home: Hamden, Conn. *

LAURENCE, WILLIAM LEONARD, journalist; b. Salantai, Lithuania, Mar. 7, 1888; s. Lipman and Sarah (Preuss) Siew; came to U.S., 1905, naturalized, 1913; student Harvard, 1908-11, 14-15, Law Sch., 1921; LL.B., Boston U., 1925, Sc.D., 1946; U. Besancon (France), 1919; Sc.D., Stevens Inst. Tech., 1951; D.H.L., Grinnell Coll., 1951, Yeshiva U., 1957; m. Florence Davidow, Dec. 19, 1931. Staff, N.Y. World, 1926-30; sci. reporter N.Y. Times, 1930, sci. editor, 1956-64, emeritus, 1964-77; cons. sci. affairs Nat. Found.-March Dimes, 1964-66; sci. cons. N.Y. World's Fair, 1964-65; sec. bd. trustees Hall Sci. City N.Y., from 1966. Served with 301st Field Signal Bn., 76th Div., U.S. Army, 1917-19; with AEF, 1 year. Recipient Pulitzer prize for reporting Harvard Tercentenary Conf. of Arts and Scis., 1937; 2d Pulitzer prize for eye-witness account of atom-bombing of Nagasaki, 1946; ann. award Soc. of Silurians, 1946; George Westinghouse Distinguished Sci. Writers award A.A.A.S., 1946; U. Mo. medal for Distinguished Service to Journalism, 1947; Lasker, George Polk, Page One awards, 1950; Grady gold medal Am. Chem. Soc., 1958; Med. Writers award; Wisdom award of Honor. Fellow A.A.A.S.; mem. Nat. Assn. Sci. Writers (pres. 1939-40), Dramatists Guild of Authors League Am., P.E.N., Sigma Delta Chi. Clubs: Players, Harvard (N.Y.C.); Overseas Press, Dutch Treat, Society of Silurians, National Press (Washington). Wrote first comprehensive accounts of significance of discovery of uranium fission as an explosive and source of power, 1940; only journalist present at first test of atomic bomb, N.M., 1945; with atomic bomb mission in the Marianas, 1945; with mission that dropped atomic bomb over Nagasaki; witnessed explosions of both atomic bombs at Bikini, 1946, atomic bomb tests, Nev., 1952, 53, 55; pool corr. hydrogen bomb tests in Pacific, 1956. Author: Dawn Over Zero-the Story of the Atomic Bomb, 1946; The Hell Bomb, 1951; Men and Atoms, 1959; New Frontiers of Science, 1964. Home: New York, N.Y. Died Mar. 19, 1977.

LAURITIS, JOSEPH ALOYSIUS, univ. administr.; b. Shenandoah, Pa., June 23, 1909; s. Joseph A. and Rosalie (Witkowski) L.; B.A., St. Mary's Sem., Norwalk, Conn., 1936, B.D., 1940; M.A., U. Pa., 1942, Ph.D., 1958. Ordained priest Roman Catholic Ch., 1939; mem. faculty Duquesne U., Pitts., 1944-80, prof. English, 1958-80, chmn. dept., 1947-48, dean Coll. Arts and Scis., 1965-68, v.p. univ. relations, 1962-65, 68-74, corps. sec., 1962-80, founder dept. journalism, dept. chmn., 1948-50; asst. sec. Duquesne U. Found., 1968-80; founder, dir. radio sta. WDUQ-FM, 1949-50; dir. pub. information Am. Province, Congregation of Holy Ghost, 1952-58. Mem. Modern Lang. Assn., Medieval Acad. Am., Nat. Assn. Tchrs. English. K.C. (4 deg.), Rotarian. Clubs: University, Press (Pitts.). Gen. editor: Life of Our Lady (Lydgate), 1961; editor Paraclete. Contbr. articles to profl. jours. Home: Pittsburgh, Pa. Died June 25, 1980; buried St. Mary's Cemetery, Sharpsburg, Pa.

LAURSON, PHILLIP GUSTAVE (LÔR'SUN), civil engr., b. Oneida, Ill., Dec. 10, 1885; s. John Peter and Emma Louise (Nelson) L.; B.S., Dakota Wesleyan U., 1907; B.S., in C.E., Mass. Inst. Tech., 1910; M.S., Yale, 1926; m. Myrtle Potter, June 1915. Draftsman and asst. engr. with Am. Bridge Co., Federal Shipbuilding Co. and other cos., 1910-20; asst. prof. engring. mechanics, Yale, 1920-22, asso, prof. since 1925. Dir. and v.p. Hamden (Conn.) Chamber of Commerce, 1928-33. Mem. Am. Soc. Civil Engrs. (pres. Connecticut Section, 1947), Connecticut Soc. Civil Engrs., Soc. for Promotion Engring, Edn., Sigma Xi, Tau Beta Pi, Theta Xi. Mason. Clubs: Graduate, Elizabethan. Author: Properties and Mechanics of Materials (with W. J. Cox), 1931; Early Years of Modern Civil Engineering (with R. S. Kirby), 1932; Mechanics of Materials (with W. J. Cox), 2d edit., 1947; and tech. arts. in engring. jours. Home: Hamden, Conn. *

LAVELLE, JOHN DANIEL, air force officer; b. Cleve., Sept. 9, 1916; s. John Francis and Rose (Carlisle) L.; B.S., John Carroll U., Cleve., 1938; postgrad. George Washington U., 1953, Air War Coll., 1956-57; m. Mary Josephine McEllin, June 22, 1940; children—Barbara A. (Mrs. Robert U. Foster), Geraldine M., John Daniel, Patricia E., Michael J., Timothy W., Dennis K. Commd. 2d lt. USAAF, 1940, advanced through grades to maj. gen. USAF, 1965; comdr. 6411th Supply Group FEAMCOM, Tachikawa Air Base, Japan, 1951-52, 568th Air Def. Group, comdr. McGuire AFB, N.J., 1952-53; dep. comdr., comdr. 1611th ATWg, McGuire AFB, 1954-56; dep. dir. requirements DSC/O Hdqrs. USAF, Washington, 1957-58, sec. Weapons Bd., 1959-61; dep. dir. programs Hdqrs. USAF, Washington, 1961-62, dir. aerospace programs DCS/P&R, 1964-66; dep. chief staff for operations Hdqrs. 4th Tactical Air Force (NATO), Ramstein Air Base, Germany, 1962-64, comdr. Hdqrs. 17th Air Force, from 1966, later comdr. 7th Air Force, Southeast Asia, ret. as lt. gen., 1972. Decorated Legion of Merit with 2 oak leaf clusters, Air Medal with cluster; Belgian Fourragere. Mem. Order Daedalians, Holy Name Soc. Lion. Home: Fairfax, Va. Died July 10, 1979.

LAVINO, EDWIN M., business exec.; b. Smyrna, Turkey, Sept. 9, 1885; s. Edward Joseph and Alma (Joly) L.; student Lawrenceville (N.J.) School, 1905; U. Pa., 1909; m. Constance Muller Hunter, June 23, 1925 (dec. Apr. 28, 1944; children—Edward Joseph, 2d, Constance Hunter, 2d (Mrs. James E. Bell, Jr.). Joined E. J. Lavino & Co., 1906, pres., dir., 1926-58, chairman of the board, 1958-67, hon. chmn., 1967-76; chairman, director Lavino Shipping Co., Lavino & Company, Inc., Rogers Brown Co., Lavino Refractories Co., Balsam Gap Company; chairman and director of Lavship of Balt., Inc., Chesapeake Operating Corp., Hampton Rds. Operating Co.; dir. Lavino (London) Ltd., Girard Trust Corn Exchange Bank. Philadelphia, Lehigh Valley R.R. Co. Mayor of Longport, N.J., 1921-43. Pres. bd. trustees The Lawrenceville Sch. Trustee, Germantown Academy, Philadelphia. Served as 1st lt. U.S. Q.M.C., World War I. Mem. Phi Kappa Psi. Episcopalian. (pres. board trustees Church of Redeemer, Longport, N.J.) Clubs: Rittenhouse, Racquet, Union League, Art Alliance, Mask and Wig, Fourth St. (Phila.); Seaview (Absecon, N.J.); The Island (Hobe Sound, Fla.). Home: Philadelphia, Pa. Died July 8, 1976.

LAW, MARIE HAMILTON, educator; b. Pittsburgh, Pa., Dec. 3, 1884; d. Benjamin Snodgrass and Mary (Thompson) Law; student Wellesley Coll., 1902-03; AB, Washington Coll., 1905; A.M, U. of Pa., 1926, Ph.D., 1932; B S. in library science, Carnegie Inst. Tech., 1931; Litt.D., Drexel Institute of Technology. 1949; unmarried. Assistant, Carnegie Library, Pittsburgh, 1907-17; registrar and inst. Carnegie Library Sch., 1912-18, asst. to prin. 1918-20; librarian Employers Assn., Pittsburgh, 1920-22; instr. Sch. Library Science, Drexel Inst. Tech., 1922-25, vice director and asso. prof., 1925-36, professor and dean, 1937-49; librarian, Drexel Inst. Tech., 1937-1949. Mem. Assn. Am. Library Schs., Am. Library Assn., Pa. Library Association. Special Libraries Council, Eastern College Librarians, Phi Kappa Phi. Republican. Presbyterian. Clubs: Women's University, Drexel Women's, Pennsylvania Library (Phila.). Home: Philadelphia, Pa. *

LAWLAH, JOHN WESLEY, radiologist, educator; b. Bessemer, Ala., Aug. 12, 1904; s. John Wesley and Mattie Mae (Lindsey) L.; grad. Morehouse Acad., Atlanta, 1922; B.Sc., Morehouse Coll., 1925, D.Sc., 1941; M.S., U. Wis., 1929; M.D., Rush Med. Coll., 1932; m. Leora Frances McCarrell, Feb. 9, 1933; children—Evelyn Frances, John Wesley III. Intern, Provident Hosp., Chgo., 1931-32; fellow in radiology Billings Hosp., U. Chgo., 1932-35; radiologist Provident Hosp., Chgo., 1935-36, med. dir. and supt., 1936-41; dean Howard U. Med. Sch., also prof. radiology, 1941-46, clin. prof. radiology, 1946-73; supt. Freedmen's Hosp., Washington, 1942-44, then radiologist, appointed mem. Freedmen's Hosp. Commn., 1955; cons. radiologist Mt. Alto Vets. Hosp., from 1957. Sec.-treas. Nat. Conf. Hosp. Adminstrs., 1936-41; mem. panel med. experts selected to draw up preliminary regulations and procs. for med. sect. WHO, 1946. Diplomate Am. Bd. Radiology, Pan Am. Med. Assn. Fellow Am. Coll. Radiology, Internat. Coll. Surgeons; mem. Radiol. Soc. N.A., Am. Coll. Hosp. Adminstrs., A.M.A., Am. Roentgen Ray Soc., A.A.A.S., Sigma Xi, Alpha Omega Alpha, Sigma Sigma, Alpha Phi Alpha, Sigma Pi Phi. Clubs: Forty (Chgo.); Brookland Literary and Hunting (Washington). Contbr. articles to profl. jours. Home: Washington, D.C. Died June 15, 1976.

LAWRENCE, ALEXANDER ATKINSON, judge; b. Savannah, Ga., Dec. 28, 1906; s. Alexander Atkinson and Isabel (Paine) L.; A.B. magna cum laude, U. Ga., 1929; m. Margaret T. Adams, Apr. 18, 1933; children—Alexander Atkinson, Margaret (Mrs. Brooks Binder) (dec.). Admitted to Ga. bar, 1930; practiced in Savannah, 1930-68; judge U.S. Dist. Ct., So. Dist. Ga., 1968-78, sr. judge, 1978-79. Mem. Jud. Conf. U.S., 1974-79. Mem. Bd. Bar Examiners Ga., 1951-58. Mem. Ga. Hist. Commn., 1951-67. Pres. Ga. Hist. Soc. Mem. Am. Coll. Trial Lawyers, Ga. Bar Assn. (past pres.), Phi Beta Kappa. Episcopalian. Club: Oglethorpe (past pres.). Author: James Moore Wayne, Southern Unionist, 1943; Storm Over Savannah, 1951; James Johnston, Georgia's First Printer, 1956; A Present for Mr. Lincoln, 1961; Johnny Leber and the Confederate Major, 1962. Home: Savannah, Ga. Died Aug. 20, 1979.

LAWRENCE, ARTHUR BREWSTER, banker; b. Smithtown, L.I., N.Y., Sept. 6, 1886; s. Charles Embree and Julia (Strong) L.; student Friends Acad.; grad. Bryant Stratton Bus. Coll., 1904; m. Gertrude Fellow Foos, Dec. 6, 1913; children—Arthur Brewster, Carteret. Asso. Ingersoll Sergeant Drill Co. (consol. into Ingersoll Rand Co.), 1905, asst. mgr. pneumatic tool dept., 1907-09, asst. mgr. Boston office, 1909-10; handled family estate, 1910-14; asso. F. S. Smithers & Co., 1914-21, mem. firm. 1921-39, senior partner, 1939—; board of directors Continental Oil Co., N.Y.C.; dir. Consol. Electronics Industries Corporation (New York City), 417 Park Av. Corp. (N.Y.C.), Hayes Industries, Inc. (Jackson, Michigan). Served as captain USAC, 1917-19. Member New York C. of C., Suffolk County Antiquities Soc., Americans Armorial Ancestry. Colonial Lords of Manners. Democrat. Presbyn. Clubs: Racquet and Tennis, The River, Metropolitan, India House (N.Y.C.); Missequogue Point Beach; Hunting Camp Creek Hunting and Trout (Bluefield, W.Va.); Smithtown Polo. Home: Smithtown, L.I., N.Y. *

LAWRENCE, GEORGE HILL MATHEWSON, bot. bibliographer; b. East Greenwich, R.I., June 19, 1910; s. Dana and Anna M. (Mathewson) L.; B.S., R.I. State Coll., 1932, M.S., 1933; Ph.D., Cornell, Ithaca, N.Y., 1939; D.Sc., U. R.I., 1952; m. Miriam G. Boothby, Oct. 13, 1934; children—Dana Boothby, Celia Ann (Mrs. John R. Rice). Dir. Bailey Hortorium, Cornell U., asst. to and asso. of Liberty Hyde Bailey, Ithaca, N.Y., 1937-43, 45-50, dir., 1951-60, prof. botany, 1947-60; dir. Rachel McMasters Miller Hunt Bot. Library, Carnegie-Mellon U., 1960-70, research fellow bot. history, 1970; hon. fellow Gray Herbarium, Harvard, 1970-78; research fellow bot. history Carnegie-Mellon U. Hunt Bot. Library, Pitts., 1971-75; dir. emeritus Hunt Inst. for Bot. Documentation, Carnegie-Mellon U., 1975-78. Mem. bd. mgrs. Fairchild Tropical Garden, Coconut Grove, Fla., 1959-71, pres., 1968-71; mem. Internat. Commn. Nomenclature Cultivated Plants, 1957-66; chmn. Liberty Hyde Baily Meml. Fund, 1954-70; bd. dirs. Robert H. Montgomery Found., 1955-71; past chmn. AHC Commn. Nomenclature and Registration Cultivated Plants; mem. adv. council U.S. Nat. Arboretum, 1967-71. Mem. corp. Kent County Meml. Hosp., 1974-78; trustee U. R.I. Found., 1976-78. Served as lt. USNR, 1943-45. Recipient Gold medal Arthur Hoyt Scott Found., Swarthmore Coll., 1973; Liberty Hyde Bailey medal Am. Hort. Soc., 1968. Hon. life fellow Bot. Soc. of Edinburgh; fellow Linnean Soc. (London); mem. Mass. Hort. Soc. (trustee 1970-73), Am. Inst. Biol. Sci. (mem.-at-large bd. govs. 1966-69), Am. Soc. Econ. Botany (pres. 1971-72), Herb Soc. Am. (pres.-at-large 1970-71), Am. Hort. Soc. (sec. 1969-71), Societe Nationale d'Horticulture de France (hon.) Hort. Soc. N.Y. (hon. life; dir. 1969-70), Bot. Soc. Am., Bot. Soc. Brit. Isles, Royal Hort. Soc. (London), Bot. Soc. S. Africa, Am. Hort. Council (sec. 1952-54, dir. 1949-56), Internat. Soc. Plant Taxonomists, Am. Soc. Plant Taxonomy (pres. 1962), Torrey Bot. Club, Garden History Soc. (London) (v.p. 1966-78), Bibliog. Soc. Am., Internat. Bibliophile Assn., Sigma Xi, Phi Kappa Phi, Phi Gamma Delta. Presbyterian. Clubs: Masons, Grolier. Author: Keys to Cultivated Plants, 1946; Taxonomy of Vascular Plants, 1951; Introduction to Plant Taxonomy, 1955; Contemporary Botanical Art and Illustration, 1968; also sci. papers. Am. editor Gardening Week by Week, 1974; editor Baileya, 1954-60, Hunt Facsimile Series, 1962-72, Huntia: a yearbook of bot. bibliography, 1964-70; sr. editor Botanico-Periodicum-Huntianum, 1968; editorial adv. Horticulture mag., 1967-73. Home: East Greenwich, R.I. Died June 11, 1978; interred Quidnessett Cemetery, East Greenwich.

LAWRENCE, JOHN HENRY, engineer; b. Albany, N.Y., Sept. 5, 1886; s. Richard and Anna (Galvin) L.; grad. high sch., Albany, 1904; M.E., Cornell U., 1909; m. Evelyn C. Crotty, of Albany, N.Y., June 2, 1915. With engineering department of New York Edison Co., 1909-20; v.p. Thomas E. Murray, Inc., New York, 1920-28, pres. since 1928. Mem. Am. Soc. M.E., Nat. Electric Light Assn. Catholic. Clubs: Engineers, Cornell University (New York); Westchester Country. Home: Bronxville, N.Y. *

LAWRENCE, JOSEPHINE, author; b. Newark; d. Elijah Wiley and Mary Elizabeth (Barker) L.; ed. pub. schs. and spl. course N.Y. U.; m. Artur Platz, Oct. 19, 1940. Former mem. staff Newark Sunday News. Author novels including: Years Are So Long, 1934; If I Had Four Apples, 1935; Double Wedding Ring, 1946; The Pleasant Morning Light, 1948; My Heart Shall Not Fear, 1949; The Way Things Are, 1950; The Picture Window, 1951; Song in the Night, 1952; The Web of Time, 1953; The Gates of Living, 1955; The Empty Nest, 1956; The Prodigal, 1957; The Ring of Truth, 1958; All Our Tomorrows, 1959; Hearts Do Not Break, 1960; The Amiable Meddlers, 1961; I Am In Urgent Need of Advice, 1962; In the Name of Love, 1963; Not A Cloud in the Sky, 1964; In All Walks of Life, 1968; Remember When We Had a Doorman?, 1971; All the Years of Her Life, 1972; Retreat With Honor, 1973; Under One Roof, 1975. Died Feb. 22, 1978.

LAWRIE, HAROLD NEWBOLD, economist; b. N.Y. City, Mar. 9, 1883; a. s. Francis and Annie Gertrude (Baker) L.; desc. Gawen Lawrie, gov. of N.J.; grad. Montclair (N.J.) Mil. Acad., 1901; E.M. Sch. of Mines (Columbia), 1905; M.A. in Public Service, U. of Ore., 1920; m. Cora Columbia Cameron, of White Salmon, Wash., Aug. 5, 1908; children—George F. (dec.), Margaret Anne, Clementena Newbold. Consulting geologist and chemist in Western States and B.C., 1905-17, Portland, Ore., 1917—. Active in securing passage of laws creating and maintaining Ore. Bureau of Mines and Geology (chmn. bur. commn.); active in matters pertaining to nat. legislation regulating and promoting the development of the natural resources U.S. and Alaska. Economist, Am. Mining Congress, Washington, 1919-21; mng. dir. Am. Gold and Silver Inst., 1922—. Asst. to U.S. Senate Commn. of Gold and Silver Inquiry, 1922-25; Washington rep. Portland (Ore.) Chamber Commerce, 1922-27; mem. firm Wilson, Lawrie & Osborn since 1927; economic adviser U.S. Shipping Bd. Merchant Fleet Corpn. Mem. Nat. Assn. for Constl. Govt., Alumni Assn. of Schs. of Mines, Engring. and Chemistry (Columbia), Am. Soc. Polit. and Social Science, Nat. Geog. Soc., Am. Inst. Mining and Metall. Engrs., Am. Economic Assn., Acad. Polit. Science, Theta Delta Chi (Columbia). Home: Portland, Ore.

LAWSON, ANDREW WERNER, JR., physicist, educator; b. San Francisco, Mar. 3, 1917; s. Andrew Werner and Teresa (Harrison) L.; A.B., Columbia, 1936, Ph.D., 1940; m. Mary Ann Wyman, Apr. 7, 1945; children—Andrew Cowper, Ann McDoel, Katharine Kerr. Instr. physics U. Pa., 1940-41, asst. prof., 1941-44; staff radiation lab. Mass. Inst. Tech., 1944-46; asst. prof. physics U. Chgo., 1946-47, asso. prof., 1947-50, prof., 1950, chmn. dept., 1950-56, asso. dir. Inst. Metals, 1952-56; chmn. dept. physics U. Calif., Riverside, 1961-64, 67-70, prof. physics, 1961-78, chmn. applied sci. program, 1971-74. Bd. dirs. Block Found. Recipient Presdl. certificate of merit work on microwave radar, 1947. Fellow Am. Phys. Soc.; mem. Am. Physics Tchrs. Assn., AAAS, Am. Geophys. Union, Phi Beta Kappa, Sigma Xi, Delta Upsilon, Contbr. articles to sci. jours. Home: Riverside, Calif. Died Feb. 27, 1978.

LAWSON, FRED ALEXANDER, pharm. mfg. co. exec.; b. Merimac, Mass., Jan. 23, 1891; s. Andrew Duncan and Mary Ella (Small) L.; ed. pub. schs., Boston; D.Sc., Mass. Coll. Pharmacy, 1963; m. Edith Langley Buxton, Sept. 20, 1916; children—Donald A., Ruth E. (Mrs. Robert E. Hitchcock). With E.L. Patch Co., Boston, 1908-61, pres., 1951-61; ret., 1961; hon. trustee Stoneham Savs. Bank (Mass.), 1950-70. Chief air raid warden, Stoneham, World War II, also mem. Nat. Drugs Resources Adv. Com.; registrar for voters, Stoneham, 1932-43; pres. Stoneham Community Concerts Assn., 1946-57; treas. Boston Arena Authority, 1955-58; commr. Mass. Employees Group Ins. Commn., 1961-64; chmn. Stoneham Sch. Survey Com., 1949; bldg. com. Stoneham High Sch., 1953-55. Mem. Stoneham Rep. Town Com., 1936-64. Mem. civic adv. bd. New Eng. Meml. Hosp. Chmn. trustees Stoneham Pub. Library, 1943-60; trustee, v.p., chmn. bldg. com. Mass. Coll. Pharmacy, 1957-70. Recipient Horatio Alger award Am. Schs. and Colls. Assn., 1954; spl. citation Mass. Legislature, 1954. Mem. Am. Pharm. Mfrs. Assn. (pres. 1939-40), Am. Pharm. Assn. Stoneham Hist. Soc. (dir.), Phi Delta Chi, Kappa Mu Lambda. Conglist. Rotarian (pres. Stoneham 1950-51, dist. gov. 1963-64). Club: Century. Address: Stoneham, Mass. Died Oct. 10, 1980.

LAWTON, ROBERT OSWALD, educator; b. Greenwood, S.C., Dec. 28, 1924; s. Robert O. and Anne (Simpson) L.; student Wofford Coll., 1941-43, Litt. D., 1969; A.B., Duke, 1946, M.A., 1947, Ph.D., 1953; m. Elise Bates Nicholson, Aug. 15, 1946; children—Robert O., Elise Bates. Mem. faculty Fla. State U., Tallahassee, 1949-80, prof. English, 1964-80, dean Coll. Arts and Scis., 1966-72, v.p. acad. affairs, 1977-80. Profl. cons. So. Assn. Colls. and Secondary Schs., 1960—. Served with AUS, 1943-45. Decorated D.S.C. Mem. S. Atlantic Modern Lang. Assn., Shakespeare Assn., So. Conf. Acad. Deans, Am. Assn. Acad. Deans, Council Arts and Scis., Omicron Delta Kappa. Home: Tallahassee, Fla. Died Oct. 8, 1980.

LAX, STEPHEN GIRARD, lawyer, business exec.; b. Phila., Oct. 11, 1919; s. Harry K. and Mildred (Goldschild) L.; B.A. magna cum laude, Swarthmore Coll., 1941; J.D., Harvard, 1948; postgrad. U. Calif., Berkeley, 1940, Nat. U. Mex., 1941, Am. U., 1949; m. Frances R. Reiner, June 1, 1947; children—Jonathan R., Stephen Girard, Andrew R., Charles Reiner. Admitted to D.C. bar, 1949; practice corp. law, Washington, from 1949; co-founder, chmn. bd. SGL Industries Co., Inc., Haddonfield, N.J., 1956-76, pres., 1961-76; pres., dir. Refractory Metals Corp. (Pa.), 1955-63; sec., dir. Magnetics, Inc., Butler, Pa., 1953-56; chmn. bd. Am. Research and Mfg. Corp., Rockville, Md., 1958-65, Alpha Properties, Inc., Westville, N.J., 1960-76, Modular Molding Corp., West Trenton, N.J., 1961-63, Delta Plastics Co., Somerdale, N.J., 1958-74, Reinforced Plastics, Inc., Warminster, Pa., 1963-76, H & R Plastics Industries, Inc., Nazareth, Pa., 1963-76, Homalite Corp., Wilmington, Del., 1964-76, B & S Screw Machine Products, Inc., Glenolden, Pa., 1965-76, Mercury Packaging Machinery Corp., Westville, N.J., 1966-76, Modern Hard Chrome Service Co., Camden, N.J., 1967-76, Dependable Printed Circuit Corp., Wayne, N.J., 1967-76, G-L Microwave Corp., Wayne, 1968-70, Galaxie Mfg. Co., Inc., Wilmington, also Newport, Del., 1968-76, Du-Mor Hard Chrome Co., Pennsauken, N.J., 1969-76, Modern Creative Corp., Elmwood Park, N.J., 1969-76, Gen. Grinding Wheel Corp., Carlisle, Pa., 1971-76, Batteries Mfg. Co., Detroit, 1974-76; dir. Revere Mut. Fund, Phila., Teleflex, Inc., N. Wales, Pa. Trustee, Trenton State Coll., 1968-70; chmn. bd. mgrs. Swarthmore Coll.; bd. mgrs. Cooper Hosp., Camden. Served from pvt. to capt., inf. U.S. Army, 1941-46. Decorated Bronze Star with V and oak leaf cluster; recipient Ames Competition prize Harvard Law Sch., 1948. Mem. Am. Bar Assn., Am. Judicature Soc., Bar Assn. D.C., Mil. Order World Wars, 75th Inf. Div. Assn. (nat. judge adv. 1954-55),

Am. Acad. Polit. and Social Sci., Franklin Inst., Phila. Art Alliance, Phi Beta Kappa, Phi Kappa Psi. Unitarian (trustee So. N.J. 1960-67, chmn. bd. trustees 1965-67). Clubs: Harvard, Downtown (Phila.); Army and Navy, Swarthmore (pres. 1957) (Washington). Home: Haddonfield, N.J. Died Oct. 3, 1976.

LAY, TRACY HOLLINGSWORTH, consular service; b. Gadsden, Ala., Nov. 5, 1882; s. William Patrick and Laura Josephine (Hollingsworth) L.; student Ala. Poly. Inst., Auburn, Ala.; George Washington U., Sch. of Polit. Science and Diplomacy, Washington, D.C. (non-grad.); m. Marcia Bliss, of Washington, D.C., Oct. 5, 1921. Reporter and editor, 1904; adv. mgr. dept. store, Montgomery, Ala., 1904-07; mgr. dept. store, Birmingham, Ala., 1907-08; sec. to member of Congress, 1908-11; elk. to Com. on Immigration and Naturalization, Nat. Ho. of Rep., 1911-12; dep. consul gen., London, Eng., 1912-14; vice and dep. consul, Dublin, 1914; vice and dep. consul gen., Paris, 1914-15; consul, Paris, 1915-19; assigned to Dept. of State, Washington, D.C., 1919; detailed to Conf. on Limitation of Armament, 1921; consul gen., Munich, 1923-25, at Buenos Aires, 1926-28. Served as capt. Ala. N.G. Mem. Am. Foreign Service Assn., Am. Polit. Science Assn., Am. Economie Assn., Sigma Nu. Mem. M.E. Ch., S. Author: The Foreign Service of the United States, 1925. Home: Washington, D.C. *

LAY, WALTER E., educator, automotive engr.; b. Fulton, Mich., Feb. 5, 1889; s. Frank E. and Christie A. (Martin) L.; B.M.E., U. Mich., 1915; m. Thryza L. Spracklin, July 17, 1915; children—Frances Eileen, Shirley Lenore. Mem. faculty U. Mich. since 1915, prof. mech. engring. in charge automotive lab., 1930-60, prof. emeritus mech. engring., 1960-74; supervisor auto mechanics sch., 1917-18; consultant in automotive engring. and research work. Served as major, Ordnance Res., 1932-41. Mem. Highway bd., Nat. Research Council, 1922-44 (mem. com. on transportation economics, tractive resistance, chmn. 1930-43, transportation costs), Soc. Automotive Engrs. (mem. com. highways riding comfort and seating; delegate to the Internat. Roads Congress 1930), Franklin Institute, Pi Tau Sigma, Sigma Xi, Tau Beta Pi. Iota Alpha (pres. 1931-32), Kappa Delta Rho, Triangle. Methodist. Club: Science Research (pres. 1921-22). A pioneer anthropometrist. Home: East Lansing, Mich. Died Aug. 28, 1974.

LAYBOURNE, LAWRENCE EUGENE, instn. exec.; b. Springfield, O., Mar. 15, 1913; s. Lawrence Everett and Jean (Broadstone) L.; A.B., Ohio State U., 1934; m. Dorothy Nesbit, May 30, 1936; children—Lucinda, Lawrence Christopher Nesbit, Anne Nesbit. News staff St. Louis Post-Dispatch, 1934-44; staff Time Inc., from 1944, news bur. chief, Ottawa, Can., 1944-46, dep. bur. chief, Washington, 1946-49, chief Life Mag. news bur., 1949-50, chief corr. U.S.-Canadian News Service, 1950-57; mng. dir. Time Internat. of Can., Ltd., 1957-62; asst. pub. Time mag., 1962-67, Asia mng. dir., 1967-69; internat. editor Time-Life Books, 1969-70, v.p., dir. corp. affairs, Washington, 1970-75; dir. membership and devel. Smithsonian Instn., Washington, 1975-76. Chmn. bd. trustees Washington Journalism Center. Mem. Ohio State U. Assn. (pres. 1965-67), Phi Beta Kappa, Beta Theta Pi. Episcopalian. Home: Washington, D.C. Died Feb. 12, 1976.

LAYLIN, JOHN GALLUP, lawyer; b. Norwalk, Ohio, Aug. 9, 1902; s. John and Mabel Parker (Gallup) L.; student Deep Springs (Calif.) Jr. Coll., 1920-22; A.B., Cornell, 1925; LL.B., Harvard, 1928; m. Dorothy Adams Lewis, Sept. 11, 1930; children—John Gallup, Louise Elizabeth, David Lewis; m. 2d, Diana Morgan, Aug. 29, 1942; children—Diana, Laura. Pres. the Telluride Assn., 1927-28; admitted to bars of N.Y., 1932, Supreme Ct., 1943, D.C., 1951; jr. legal adviser Ambassador Dwight Morrow, Mexico, 1928; asso. Sullivan & Cromwell, N.Y.C., 1929-33, internat. law work, Argentina, Chile, Uruguay, 1929-30, Cuba, 1932; spl. asst. under sec. Treasury Dept., also asst. gen. counsel, 1933-35; mem. Covington & Burling, specializing corporate, financial, internat. law, Washington, 1935-79, legal adviser various Latin Am., European, Middle Eastern S. Asian govts. problems U.N. and its specialized agencies. Hon. trustee Deep Springs Jr. Coll. Decorated comdr. Order of Lion (Finland); comdr. Order of Dannebrog (Denmark); Sitara-I-Pakistan (Pakistan); comendador Order San Carlos (Colombia). Mem. Inter-Am., Am. bar assns., Internat. Law Assn. (exec. com. Am. br.), Am. Soc. Internat. Law, Washington Inst. Fgn. Affairs (v.p., dir.). Episcopalian. Clubs: 1925 F Street, Metropolitan, River Bend Golf and Country (Washington); Century Assn. (N.Y.C.); Home: Great Falls, Va. Died Feb. 16, 1979; buried Norwalk, Ohio.

LAYTON, CALEB S., lawyer; b. Georgetown, Del., Apr. 1, 1886; s. Caleb R. and Anne E. (Sipple) L.; grad. Mercersburg (Pa.) Acad., 1903; B.S., U. of Pa., 1907; student U. of Pa. Law Sch., 1908-10; m. Helene H. Mustard, Dec. 31, 1913; children—Virginia L., Ann S., Rodney M. Practiced at Wilmington, Del., since 1910; city solicitor, Wilmington, 1923-31; mem. firm, Richards, Layton & Finger; dir. Equitable Trust Co.; represented Weirton Steel Co. in case against NRA, challenging right of Congress to enact statutes affecting commerce not of an interstate or foreign nature. Episcopalian. Clubs: Wilmington, Wilmington Country.

LAZARSFELD, PAUL FELIX, sociologist, educator; b. Vienna, Austria, Feb. 13, 1901; Ph.D., U. Vienna, 1925; L.H.D., Yeshiva U., 1966; LL.D., U. Chgo., 1966, Columbia, 1970; 1 dau., Lotte (previous marriage); m. 3d, Patricia Kendall, Nov. 21, 1949; 1 son, Robert. Came to U.S. on traveling Rockefeller Found. fellowship, 1933, naturalized, 1943. Tchr. math. Jr. Coll. Vienna, then instr. psychology Psychol. Inst., U. Vienna, 1929; studies in social psychology U.S. govt. and Am. bus. concerns, 1929-37; dir. radio research Princeton, office transferred to Columbia, 1937-40; prof. sociology Columbia, 1940-67, Quetelet prof. social sci., 1967-76, chmn. dept. sociology, 1950-59, asso. dir. bur. applied social research. Vis. prof. U. Oslo (Norway), 1948-49; Sorbonne, Paris, France, 1962-63, 67-68 (on leave from Columbia); cons. agys. concerned with problems of communication by radio, newspaper or mag. Recipient variety of research awards. Fellow Am. Statis. Assn.; mem. Am. Assn. Pub. Opinion Research (past pres.), Acad. Arts and Scis., Am. Sociol. Assn. (past pres.), Nat. Acad. Edn., Am. Psychol. Assn., Am. Marketing Assn., other profl. orgns. Author numerous books; contbr. articles to jours. on social research techniques. Home: New York, N.Y. Died Aug. 30, 1976.

LAZARUS, JEFFREY L., mcht.; b. Columbus, O., June 20, 1894; s. Fred and Rose (Eichberg) L.; grad. Ohio State U., 1915; LL.D., Salem Coll., 1964; m. Adelaide Ormont, Oct. 26, 1925; children—Jeffrey L., Ruth (Mrs. Edward H. Cole), Frank, David, Betty (Mrs. Donald J. Wineman). With F. & R. Lazarus & Co., Columbus, O., 1915-28, John Shillito Co., Cin., 1928, pres., 1947-60, chmn. bd., 1960-65, hon. chmn. bd., 1965-76. Chmn. bd. Cin. Jewish Welfare Fund, 1938-46, Cin. Community Chest, 1947, pres. 1948; hon. life mem. Community Chest and Council; co-chmn. Capital Fund Drive, 1958; life mem. nat. exec. bd. Boy Scouts Am., chmn. nat. Jewish com. on scouting, 1958-64, life mem. com. Region Four; v.p., mem. exec. com. Dan Beard council Boy Scouts Am., Cin., 1963-65. Vice pres., mem. exec. com., hon. life mem. Am. Humanics Found.; bd. dirs. Nat. Fund for Med. Edn. Served with USNR, 1917-19. Recipient Silver Beaver, 1963, Silver Antelope, 1956, Silver Buffalo, 1959; Cin. Sertoma award, 1956; Good Citizenship award Nat. Conf. Christians and Jews, 1965; Good Neighbor award Isaac M. Wise Temple, 1966; Am. Artificers award, 1972; Shofar award, 1972. Clubs: Losantiville Country, Queen City, President's, University (Cin.). Home: Cincinnati, Ohio. Died July 9, 1976.

LAZENBY, MARION ELIAS (LAZ'EN-BI), clergyman, b. Forest Home, Ala., Feb. 8, 1885; s. James Elias and Elizabeth (Greene) L.; prep. edn., Forest Home Acad.; A.B., Southern Univ., 1907; D.D., Birmingham-Southern Coll., 1925; Litt.D., Bob Jones Coll., 1930; m. Mary Feagin, June 17, 1908; children—Marion Candler, Ora, Rosalyn; married 2d Mrs. Doris H. Chervase, November 15, 1949. Ordained ministry M.E. Ch., S., 1907; pastor successively Havana, Cuba, Forest Home, Centreville, Midway, Dothan, Deniopolis, and Opelika, Ala., until 1922; asso. editor Ala. Christian Advocate, 1921, editor and business mgr., 1922-35; pastor First Methodist Ch., Bessemer, Ala., 1935-36; dist. supt., Decatur Dist., 1936-40; pastor First Methodist Church, Florence, Ala., 1940-43. Pastor at Camp Sheridan, Montgomery, Ala., 1918. Agent for Superannuate Endowment Fund for Ala. Conf., M.E. Ch., S., 1919; dir. of publicity of Ala. Conf. for Southern Meth. Missionary Centenary Movement, 1920; chmn. Epworth League Bd. of Ala. Conf. Trustee Shofner-Downing Inst., Brewton, Ala., 1924-29. Mem. Southern Meth. Press Assn. (press.), Anti-Saloon League of Ala. (trustee), Alpha Tau Omega. Democrat. Mason. Transferred to N.Ala. Conf., Nov. 1928. Mem. Hosp. Commn. N.Ala. Conf.; del. to Gen. Conf. M.E. Ch., S., 1930, 34, 38, Ecumenical Meth. Conf., Atlanta, 1931; del. to Uniting Conf. of Meth. Ch., Kansas City, 1939; mem. bd. temperance and social service, M.E. Ch., S.; chmn. Joint Commn. for Ala. and N. Ala. Conf. Ednl. Survey; del. to first Gen. Conf. of Meth. Ch., Atlantic City, 1940, and to Jurisdictional Conf., Asheville, N.C., 1940; trustee Athens Coll. Ala. Temperance Alliance; member bd. of directors Nat. Temperance Movement; mem. Bd. of Publs. of Meth. Ch., 1940-44; editorial asso. Christian Advocate, Chicago, 1943-49; dist. supt. Huntsville dist. N. Ala. Conf. Methodist Ch. since 1949; bus. mgr. and editor Ala. Christian Advocate since 1950. Home: Birmingham, Ala. *

LAZRUS, OSCAR M., lawyer; b. Jassy, Rumania, July 12, 1887; s. Israel and Ella (Cohn) L.; came to U.S. 1889, naturalized citizen; LL.B., St. Lawrence U., 1909; m. Paula Kronheim, Feb. 11, 1913 (dec. 1952); children—Julian, Jay K.; m. 2d, Anna Leitner, 1953 (dec. 1961); m. 3d, Rose Lazrus, 1962. Apprentice law office Samuel Untermeyer, 1905-06; pvt. practice, N.Y.C., 1909-24; a founder, past pres., past chmn. bd. Benrus Watch Co. Nat. sec. NCCJ; mem. exec. com. Am. Jewish Com.; mem. pres.'s council Brandeis U. Bd. dirs. Am. Joint Distbn. Com.; life trustee Fedn. Jewish Philanthropies N.Y.; bd. govs. Union Am. Hebrew Congregations. Recipient certificate of appreciation Mayor John V. Lindsay of N.Y.C., 1967; cited by NCCJ, gifted $100,000 to Conf. for Oscar M. Lazrus Center for Interreligious Affairs, 1972. Mem. Am. Bar Assn. Jewish. Clubs: Harmonie, Bankers, 24 Karat. Home: N.Y. Died June 5, 1981.

LAZZARI, PIETRO, painter, sculptor; b. Rome, Italy, May 15, 1898; s. Pietro and Maria (Giacomelli) L.; Master Artist, Ornamental Sch. of Rome, 1920; m. Evelyn Cohen, Dec. 1, 1934; 1 dau., Nina. Came to U.S., 1929, naturalized, 1936. Free-lance painter, sculptor; executed murals, fine arts sect. U.S. Treasury Dept., 1936-42; faculty Am. U., Washington, 1943-48; head art dept. Dumbarton Coll., Washington, 1948-50; instr. Corcoran Gallery Sch. Art, Washington, 1966-69; executed sculptured busts of Eleanor Roosevelt, Norman Thomas, Adlai Stevenson, Edward Steichen, Alexander Kerensky, Pope Paul VI; bronze monuments to Edward Miner Gallaudent, Walter Reuther; 100-ft. sculpture frieze lobby Watergate West, Washington; mural for Central States Joint Bd., AFL-CIO, 1977; exhibited Mus. Modern Art, Whitney Mus. Am. Art, Met. Mus., NAD, Venetian Biennial, Art Inst. Chgo., Musee National d'Art Moderne, Paris, Corcoran Gallery, Washington, Pa. Acad. Fine Arts, Parsons Gallery, N.Y.C.; represented in permanent collections Am. U., Art Inst. Chgo., Corcoran Gallery, Howard U., Smithsonian Instn., Balt. Mus., Mus. Honolulu, Truman Library, Independence, Mo., San Francisco, Mus., Franklin Delano Roosevelt Library, Hyde Park, Whitney Mus., Okla. Art Center, Library of Congress, Nat. Collection Fine Arts, Washington, Nat. Air and Space Mus., Washington. Fulbright research fellow ancient art media, 1950; recipient prizes Ornamental Sch. Rome, Balt. Mus., Corcoran Gallery, Washington Water Color Soc., Soc. Washington Artists. Developer of polychrome concrete medium for painting and sculpture. Home: Washington, D.C. Died May 1, 1979; buried Nat. Meml. Park, Falls Church, Va.

LEACH, AGNES BROWN (MRS. HENRY GODDARD LEACH) (LECH), civic leader; b. Villa Nova, Pa., Oct. 16, 1884; d. Thomas Wistar and Mary (Farnum) Brown; ed. in private schools; m. Henry Goddard Leach, February 20, 1915; children—(adopted) Annis Leach (Mrs. Charles W. Young), Jeffrey E. Fuller. Acted as State chmn. N.Y. League of Women Voters, 1925-30, member advisory council since 1937; mem. N.Y. State Health Commn., 1930-32; mem. N.Y. State Commn. on Adminstrn. of Justice, 1930; mem. N.Y. State Commn. on Cost of Pub. Edn., 1933; mem. Com. for Inquiring into Conditions on Ellis Island, 1933; mem. Minimum Wage Bd. of State of N.Y., 1935-37; active in Dem. campaigns, 1930, 32, 36. Vice chmn. and dir. Training Borough of Manhattan, Civilian Defense Volunteer Office, 1943-45. Trustee, see. bd. dirs. Bryn Mawr Coll. Dir. Alumnae Adv. Center, Inc., Am. Com. for Emigre Scholars, Writers and Artists, Inc. Decorated by King of Sweden for activities in connection with Swedish Tercentenary, 1938; received Gold Medal, Am. Scandinavian Foundation. Dir. Foreign Policy Assn., Pub. Edn. Association. Mem. Colonial Dames of Am. Mem. Soc. of Friends. Clubs: Colony, Cosmopolitan (pres. 1933-37), Jr. League, Women's City (N.Y.); Acorn (Phila.). Home: New York, N.Y. *

LEAF, ERLE MERVIN, b. Idaho Falls, Ida., Dec. 25, 1886; s. Edward George and Madge (Mann) L.; A.B., Stanford, 1910, J.D., 1912; m. Italja M. Bower, Oct. 8, 1913; children—Gordon Erle, Harriet Italja, Erlda. Admitted to Calif. bar, 1912, U.S. Supreme Court, 1921; practiced with Charles L. Batcheller, Los Angeles, until 1916; apptd. trust counsel Title Ins. & Trust Co., Los Angeles, 1916; organized Los Angeles Shipbuilding & Dry Dock Corp., 1917, elected v.p., gen. mgr., 1920; an organizer, 1919, dir. and sec. The Los Angeles Steamship Co.; an organizer, 1922, Los Angeles Lumber Products Co. and elected exec. v.p. of this and of 7 subsidiary cos., pres., 1923-25 (resigned); pres. Standard Mortgage Corp. since 1925; pres. Nat. Bank of Commerce, Calif. U.S. Bond and Mortgage Corp., Standard Holding Co.; v.p. Fidelity Savings & Loan Assn. Mem. Calif. State and Los Angeles bar assns., Delta Chi. Republican. Conglist. Mason. Clubs: California, Los Angeles Country. Home: Los Angeles. *

LEAF, MUNRO, author, illustrator; b. Hamilton, Md., Dec. 4, 1905; s. Charles Wilbur and Emma India (Gillespie) L.; A.B., U. Md., 1927; M.A., Harvard 1931; grad. Army Staff and Command Sch., 1943; m. Margaret Butler Pope, Dec. 29, 1926; children—Andrew Munro, James Gillespie. Tchr., coach Belmont Hill Sch., Belmont, Mass., 1920-30, Montgomery Sch., Wynnewood, Pa., 1931; editor, dir. F.A. Stokes Co., N.Y.C., 1932-39; author, illustrator, 1934-76. Made 3 cultural and ednl. exchange program tours for State Dept. Served as maj. AUS, 1942-46. Mem. Kappa Alpha. Clubs: Cosmos (Washington); The Players, Dutch Treat, Century Assn. (N.Y.C.). Author: Story of Ferdinand, 1936; Manners Can Be Fun, 1936; The Watchbirds, 1937; Three Promises to You (for UN), 1957; Science Can Be Fun, 1958; Being an

American Can Be Fun, 1964; Turnabout, An Animal Story, 1967; Arithmetic Can Be Fun; Metrics Can Be Fun, 1976; (with William Menninger) You and Psychiatry, 1948, many others. Illustrator over 30 books of own authorship. Address: Garrett Park, Md. Died Dec. 21, 1976; buried Stowe, Vt.

LEAK, CLARENCE ELMER, ins. exec.; b. N.C., Dec. 10, 1882; s. James N. and Sadie (Poe) L.; B.S., Guilford Coll., 1902; m. Cammie Lindley, Nov. 20, 1907. With Security Life & Annuity Co., 1911; with Jefferson Standard Life Ins. Co., Greensboro, N.C., since 1912, successively as clerk, asst. sec., 1921, sec., 1931, v.p. and dir., 1932-47, exec. v.p. since 1947, also mem. exec. com. Mem. Am. Life Convention. Mason (Shriner). Club: Civitan (past pres.). Home: Greensboro, NC. *

LEAKE, CHAUNCEY D., educator; b. Elizabeth, N.J., Sept. 5, 1896; s. Frank Walker and Helen Caroline (Luttgen) L.; Litt.B., Princeton, 1917; M.S., U. Wis., 1917, Ph.D., 1923; L.H.D., Kenyon Coll.; D.Sc. (hon.), W. Med. Coll. Pa., Ohio State U., LL.D., U. Calif.; Sc.D., Phila. Coll. Pharmacy and Sci.; m. Elizabeth Nancy Wilson, Oct. 1, 1921 (dec. May 1977); children—Chauncey, Wilson Walker. Instr. physiology U. Wis., 1920-23, asst. prof. pharmacology, 1923-28; prof. pharmacology (organized dept.), U. Calif., 1928-42; exec. v.p. charge Med. Br. U. Tex., 1942-55, spl. lectr., 1970; prof. pharmacology Ohio State U. 1955-62, coordinator student research tng., 1962-65; sr. lectr. pharmacology, history, philosophy of medicine U. Calif., San Francisco, 1962-78; prof. med. jurisprudence Hastings Coll. of Law, 1963-65; med. research dir. wine adv. bd. Calif. Dept. Agr., 1965-68. Vis. mem. Inst. Advanced Study, Princeton, 1950-52, 56; lectr. human relations and librarian U. Calif. Med. Sch., 1932-42; Clendening lectr. U. Kan., 1951; Miller lectr. U. Wis., 1952, Waters lectr. 1970; Trent lectr. Duke, 1953, 69, Kaufman lectr., Ohio, 1975; spl. lectr. Motorola Exec. Inst., from 1968; dir. Carter-Wallace, Inc.; cons. NRC, USPHS; hon. cons. Army Med. Library, 1946-50 (pres. 1948), Sci. Adv. Baruch Com, 1946-49. Served with Chem. Warfare Service, 1918-19. Recipient spl. award Internat. Anesthesia Research Soc. 1928, Distinguished Service award, 1975. Hon. fellow Am. Coll. Dentists; mem. A.A.A.S. (v.p., chmn. sect. hist. sci. 1940; pres. 1960), A.M.A. (chmn. sect. pharmacology 1937), Am. Physiol. Soc., Soc. Exptl. Biol. Medicine (chmn. Pacific sect. 1936-38, pres. 1962-63), Am. Assn. History Medicine (pres. 1961-62), History Sci. Soc. (pres. 1936-39), Calif., Tex., Ohio acads. sci., Philos. Soc. Tex., Am. Acad. Arts and Scis., Am. Soc. Pharmacology (pres. 1958-59), Med. Library Assn. (hon.), Nat. Assn. Sci. Writers (hon.). Clubs: Bohemian, Chit-Chat, Cosmos, Kit-Kat. Author: Letheon 1947; Can We Agree?, 1950; Old Egyptian Medicine, 1952; Ashbel Smith and Yellow Fever, 1951; Some Founders of Physiology, 1956; The Amphetamines, 1958; (with M.S. Silverman) Medical Uses of Alcoholic Beverages, 1966; Practical Philosophy: The Ethics, 1973, The Logics, 1974, The Esthetics, 1976; History of Pharmacology, 1975. Translator: Harvey's De Motu Cordis, 1928, 6th edit., 1978. Editor: Percival's Medical Ethics, 1927, 2d edit., 1975; Tex. Rep. Biol. Med., 1943-55. Contbr. articles med. and sci. periodicals. Address: San Francisco, Calif. Died Jan. 11, 1978.

LEAKE, GERALD, artist; b. London, Eng., Nov. 26, 1884; s. John William and Jane (Owens) L.; naturalized Am. citizen. Artist, 1905—; exhibited Royal Acad., Royal Soc. Brit. Artists, Walker Art Gallery, Liverpool (Eng.), Nat. Acad., Allied Artists Am., Boston Mus., Chgo. Art Inst., Pa. Acad., Corcoran Gallery, Washington, Albright Gallery, Buffalo, and others. Recipient $1000 prize, Salamagundi Club, 1923, Shaw $1000 prize, 1925, Plimpton prize, 1925, small picture exhbn. prizes, 1926, 27; gold medal Allied Artists Am., 1926; Clark prize figure painting Nat. Acad., 1934, Gold Medal, 1937; Grumbacher award of merit, 1953; 1st prize Key West Art and Hist. Soc., 1952, 53. Bd. dirs. Island City Art Sch., Key West art and Hist. Soc. (hon. life.) Mem. N.A.D., Royal Soc. Arts (Eng.), Soc. Illustrators, Nat. Arts Club. Club: Salamagundi. Home: Marathon FL.

LEAR, WILLIAN POWELL, elec. engr.; b. Hannibal, Mo., June 26, 1902; s. Reuben Marion and Gertrude Elizabeth (Powell) L.; student pub. schs.; E.D. (hon.), U. Mich., 1951; D.Sc., Los Angeles Art Center Coll., 1969; m. Moya Marie Olsen, 1942; children—William Powell, Shirley P., John Olsen, Shanda, David R., Valentina Moya. Pres., Quincy Radio Lab. Ill., 1922-24, Lear Radio Lab., Tulsa, Okla., 1924-28; with Radio Coil & Wire Co., Chgo., 1928-31; chief engr. Calvin Mfg. Co., 1931; with Lear Devels. Co., Chgo., N.Y.C., 1931-34, Lear Avia, Dayton, 1934-49; pres. Lear, Inc., Grand Rapids, Mich., Los Angeles, 1939, then chmn. bd., dir. research and devel.; co-designer Learcat, a catamaran sailboat; designer Learstar Airplane; designer, builder Lear Jet 23-24-25; chmn., pres. Lear Jet Corp., Wichita, Kan., 1963-67, chmn., 1967-69; chmn. Lear Motors Corp.; pres. Wm. Lear Enterprises; chmn. Microcam, Inc.; pres. Reno-Stead Devel. Corp.; adv. dir Kan. State Bank. Recipient Frank M. Hawk meml. award, 1940; Horatio Alger award, 1954; Collier trophy, 1950; Great Silver medal City of Paris, 1960; Thulin medal Sweden, 1960. Mem. Nat. Aero. Assn. (dir.). Am. Inst. Aeros. and Astronautics, I.E.E.E., Soc. Automotive Engrs. Elk. Clubs: Lambs (N.Y.C.); Masquers (Los Angeles). Author Franklin Inst. paper on electro-mech. controls for aircraft. Home: Verdi, Nev. Died May 14, 1978.

LEATH, EDWARD MAGRUDER, JR., air line exec.; b. Birmingham, Ala., June 15, 1923; s. Edward Magruder and Rebecca (Hill) L.; B.S., U. Ala., 1949; m. Nina Cecile Pharr, June 7, 1946; children—Edward Magruder III, Linda Cecile. Staff accountant Price Waterhouse & Co., Atlanta, 1950-57; asst. comptroller Airlift Internat., Inc., Miami, 1958, comptroller, 1958-59, v.p., treas., 1959-70, sr. v.p., treas., 1970-77, exec. v.p. fin., treas., 1977-78. Served with USNR, 1942-45, 50-51. Mem. Nat. Assn. Accountants. Democrat. Presbyn. Home: Miami, Fla. Died July 29, 1978; buried Woodlawn Park Cemetery South, Miami.

LEAVELL, HUGH RODMAN, physician, cons.; born Louisville, Ky., Nov. 17, 1902; s. Hugh Nelson and Harriet Virginia (Rodman) L.; B.S., Univ. of Va., 1925; M.D., Harvard, 1926; Dr. P. H., Yale, 1940; m. Barbara Peace Hazard, June 24, 1924 (dec. 1958); children—Hugh Nelson, Barbara, Rodman; m. 2d, Esta Carter Holt, Nov. 22, 1958. Intern, Mass. Gen. Hosp., Boston, 1926-27, Presbyterian Hosp., New York, 1927-28; interne Johns Hopkins Hosp., Baltimore, 1928-29, asst. resident, 1929-30; pvt. practice, Louisville, Ky., 1930-37; instr., Johns Hopkins Med. Sch., 1929-30; instr., U. of Louisville Sch. of Medicine, 1930-34, prof. pub. health, head of dept., 1938-45; lecturer in pub. health, Yale Med. Sch., 1942; prof. pub. health practice, Harvard Sch. of Pub. Health 1946-63; univ. physician, U. of Louisville, 1930-34; dir. of health, Louisville, Ky., 1934-42; dir. of health, Louisville and Jefferson County Health Dept., 1942-45; USPHS Res., from 1942, med. dir., 1949-67, active duty, 1944-45, dep. director Health European Regional Office UNRRA; assistant director div. for med. sciences The Rockefeller Foundation, 1945-46, bd. cons. medicine and public health, 1952-54; member public health advisory committee W. K. Kellogg Foundation, 1944-51; consultant on health Ford Found., India, 1956-57, 59, from 1963; then cons. Va. Dept. Health and Dept. Preventive Medicine, Med. Coll. of Va. until 1976. Mem. board dirs., Louisville Community Chest, budget com., 1939-45; vice pres., Louisville Health Council, 1939-45; president of Mass. Central Health Council, 1946-49; mem. bd. dirs. United Community Services of Met. Boston, 1949-53, chmn. div. health, 1949-51. Recipient Lemuel Shatuck medal, 1961; Prentiss award in health education, 1963. Diplomate National Board Medical Examiners, member, 1948-54; certified American Bd. Internat. Med., 1937, cert. Am. bd. Preventive Medicine. Director National Health Council, president, 1955-56, director National Adv. Mental Health Council 1950-52. Fellow A.C.P., Am. Pub. Health Assn. (mem. exec. bd. and governing council 1943-54, chmn. exec. bd., 1948-52, president 1953-54); member American Academy Arts and Sciences, Medical Services Committee, Commission Orgn. Executive Branch Govt., 1948-49, 1953-54; mem. Mass. Med. Soc., So. Med. Assn. (sec., sect. of pub. health, 1940-42, chmn., 1942-44), Mass. Pub. Health Association (pres. 1962-63), Phi Beta Kappa, Alpha Omega Alpha, Delta Omega, Phi Kappa Phi, Delta Tau Delta, Phi Rho Sigma. Episcopalian. Mason (32 degree, Shriner). Clubs: Lancet; Aesculapian. Co-author text book; numerous med. articles. Home: Richmond, Va. Died Aug. 7, 1976.

LEDDY, RAYMOND G(REGORY), fgn. service officer; b. N.Y.C., Dec. 18, 1912; s. James F. and Mary V. (Walsh) L.; A.B., Coll. Holy Cross, 1933; LL.B., Fordham U., 1936; m. Janet Graham, Oct. 30, 1948; children—Gregory, John, Suzanne, George, Paul. Admitted to N.Y. bar, 1937; with firm Graves & Yawger, N.Y.C., 1937; atty. Dept. Justice, 1938-40; entered fgn. service, 1940; assigned Am. Embassy, Madrid, Spain, 1940-42; legal attache, Havana, Cuba, 1942-44; attache, Madrid, 1944-45; assigned Washington, 1946-48; 2d sec. Am. Embassy, Caracas, Venezuela, 1948-51, 1st sec., 1951-52; officer charge Central Am. and Panama affairs Dept. of State, 1952-55; assigned Nat. War Coll., 1956; 1st sec., Buenos Aires, Argentina, 1957; counselor of Embassy, Mexico City, 1957-61; State Dept. Faculty adviser Army War Coll., 1961-76. Recipient Superior Service award Dept. of State, 1956. Mem. Am. Soc. Internat. Law. Club: Army-Navy (Washington). Home: Carlisle, Pa. Died Mar. 4, 1976.

LEDERER, LUDWIG GEORGE, physician; b. Chgo., Jan. 19, 1911; s. John Jacob and Frances (Tscherney) L.; B.A., U. Ill., 1931; M.S., Northwestern U., 1932, M.D., 1938, Ph.D., 1939; m. Netta Kathryn Olsen, June 3, 1939; children—Ludwig Bert, Jack Lawrence, Lyle George, David Eric, Susan Kay. Intern, resident West Suburban Hosp., Oak Park, Ill., 1938-39; practice medicine, 1939-78, specializing internal and aviation medicine, 1942-78; researcher, mem. faculty Northwestern U. Med. Sch., 1931-39; med. dir. Capital Airlines, 1942-60; asst. prof. medicine George Washington U. Hosp., 1952-60; med. examiner and physician in chief Washington Nat. Airport, 1942-60; med. dir. Am. Airlines, 1960-77; med. cons. Am. Standard Corp., 1977-78; founder, mem., past pres. Med. Execs., N.Y.C.; cons. CAB; industry rep. Conf. on Internat. Standards for Airmen, meeting Internat. Civil Aviation Orgn., Montreal, Que., Can., 1953. Chmn. med. adv. panel to adminstr. FAA, 1964-66. Mem. Internat. Acad. Aviation and Space Medicine, Airline Med. Dirs. (past pres.), Aerospace Med. Assn. (past pres., recipient Howard K. Edwards award, Theodore C. Lyster award), Air Transport Asso. (chmn. med. com.), Am. Physiol. Soc., Am. Coll. Preventive Med. for Aviation Medicine (v.p. 1962), Phi Beta Kappa, Sigma Xi, Phi Kappa Phi. Home: Stamford, Conn. Died Nov. 10, 1978.

LEE, C(HARLES) O(REN), univ. prof.; b. McCune, Kan., Nov. 25, 1883; s. Oren Dayton and Emma Florilla (Peairs) L.; student. Baker U., 1908-10; B. S., U. of Kan., 1913; M.S., U. of Chicago, 1917; Ph.D., U. of Wis., 1930; m. Esther Margaret Haggard, Feb. 2, 1924 (dec. May 28, 1928); children—Noel Dayton, Ruth Lois (Mrs. Elerington Saunders); m. 2d Edith Palmer, Jan. 3, 1930. Pharmacist by examination 1911; asso. materia medica, Med. Co I. of Va., Richmond. 1913-15; p of. pharmacy, Purdue U., 1915 20, since 1926; pha macist, Wuhu Gen. Hosp., China, 1920-23: prof. chemistry. U. of Nanking. China, 1923-25; in charge of dispensary, U. of Wis., 1926. Mem. Ind. Council Religious Edu., since 1938; mem. com. of revision, U.S. Pharmacopeia, 1940-50. National Formulary, since 1939. Life mem. Am. Pharm. Assn. (chmn. hist. sect., 1934-35, 2d v.p., 1942-43); mem. Am. Assn. Univ. Profs., AA. A.S., Am. Inst. History Pharmacy, History of Sci. Soc., Ind. Acad. Sci., Am. Assn. Coll. Pharmacy (chmn. ecm. on libraries, since 1933), Sigma Xi. Rho Chi. Methodist. Co-author: Fundamental Principles and Practices of Pharmacy, 1949. Author: The Official Preparations of Pharmacy, 1949. Contbr. articles to prof. jours. Home: West Lafayette, Ind. *

LEE, GEORGE JOSEPH, curator art; b. Boston, July 14, 1919; s. George J. and Pauline (Hartmann) L.; A.B. cum laude, Harvard U., 1940, A.M., 1947. Mem. staff Fogg Mus., Harvard U., 1943-45, Chinese govt. cultural fellow, 1945-48, asst. curator Oriental art, 1948-49; curator Oriental art Bklyn. Mus., 1949-59, Yale U Art Gallery, New Haven, 1959-76, fellow Morse Coll., 1965-76; one-man exhbn. color photography Corcoran Gallery Art, Washington, 1969. Mem. Asia Soc. (editorial bd.), Oriental Ceramic Soc. London, Oriental Club N.Y.C. Author: Selected Far Eastern Art in the Yale U. Art Gallery, 1970; co-author, editor: The Edo Culture in Japanese Prints, 1972; also articles scholarly jours. Home: New Haven, Conn. Died Mar. 10, 1976.

LEE, HOWARD BURTON, lawyer; b. Wirt County, W.Va. Oct. 27, 1882; s. Stephen S. and Virginia (Quick) L.; student Marshall Coll., Huntington, W.Va., 1902-05; LL.B., Washington and Lee U., 1909; m. Ida Hamilton, Mar. 5, 1907. Admitted to W.Va. bar, 1909, and began practice at Bluefield; referee in bankruptcy, Southern Dist. of W.Va., 1912-16; pros. atty. Mercer County, W.Va., 1912-24; atty. gen. of W.Va., 2 terms, 1925-33. Republican, Presbyterian. Mason. Author: The Criminal Trial in the Virginias; The Story of the Constitution. Home: Charleston, W.Va. *

LEE, MILTON OLIVER, physiologist; b. Conneaut, Ohio, Sept. 8, 1901; s. Malcolm Anthony and Jennie Viola (Hazeltine) L.; A.B., Ohio State U., 1922, A.M., 1923, Ph.D., 1926; postgrad. Marine Biol. Lab., 1923, 27; m. Helen Isabel Mayhew, June 21, 1923. Instr. physiology Ohio State U., 1923, Iowa State Coll., 1925; research fellow in physiology, asso., Meml. Found. Neuro-Endocrine Research, Harvard, 1927-42; chief labs. Worcester State Hosp., 1946-47; exec. sec., div. biology and agr. NRC, 1948-52, mem.-at-large, from 1952, exec. sec. Am. Inst. Biol. Scis., 1948-50; exec. dir. Fedn. Am. Socs. Explt. Biology, 1947-49, sec., 1949-60, exec. officer, 1963-65. Vice pres. bd. Am. Documentation Inst., 1952, pres., 1954; treas. Inter. Fedn. of Documentation, 1952-62, mem. bur., from 1951; mem. nat., exec. coms.; co-chmn. orgn. com Internat. Conf. Sci. Information, 1958; gen. sec. 5th Internat. Congress Nutrition, 1960; mem. panel sci. information President's Sci. Adv. Com., from 1961; sec.-treas. Sci. Manpower Commn., 1953. Served as major San. Corps AUS, 1942; nutrition cons. 4th Service Command, 1943, Lt. Col., CMP, comdg. officer Hokkaido mil. govt. team (Japan), 1944-46. Recipient award of excellence in sci. communication Council Biology Editors, 1975. Mem. Am. Physiol. Soc. (exec. sec. 1947-56), Am. Inst. Nutrition, Soc. for Exptl. Biology and Med., Assn. for the Study of Internal Secretions (v.p., 1929), Phi Beta Kappa, Sigma Xi, Gamma Alpha. Clubs: Cosmos, Harvard; Ivy League (Sarasota, Fla.). Mng. editor Endocrinology, 1935-42, Jour. Clin Endocrinology, 1938-42, Am. Jour. Physiol., Physiol. Reviews, Jour. Applied Physiology, Jour. Neurophysiology Fedn. Procs. Home: Sarasota, Fla. Died Nov. 19, 1978; buried Dorset Cemetery, Dorset Ohio.

LEE, MORRIS MATTHEWS, JR., pub. relations counsel; b. Phila., Oct. 28, 1907; s. Morris M. and Mary (Walter) L.; A.B., Swarthmore Coll., 1929; m. Margaret Pennington Losey, Oct. 5, 1935; children—Margaret Pennington (Mrs. Blaine A. Braniff), Robert Losey. With pub. relations dept. ITT, N.Y.C., 1929-32; mgr. creative dept. Edward L. Bernays, N.Y.C., 1932-35;

pub. relations dept. N.A.M., 1935-39; partner Selvage & Lee, N.Y.C., 1939-43; asst. to pres. Carrier Corp., 1943-46; exec. v.p. Selvage & Lee, Inc., 1946-69, pres., 1961-78, vice chmn. Selvage, Lee & Howard, Inc., 1969-72; chmn. Manning, Selvage & Lee, Inc., 1972-73, chmn. exec. com., 1973-78. Mem. Pub. Relations Soc. Am. Author: (with James P. Selvage) Making the Annual Report Speak for Industry, 1937. Home: Hartsdale, N.Y. Died Sept. 18, 1978.

LEE, ROBERT GREENE, clergyman; b. Fort Mill, S.C., Nov. 11, 1886; s. David Ayers and Sarah Elizabeth (Bennett) L.; A.B., Furman U., Greenville, S.C., 1913, D.D., 1937; Ph.D., Chicago Law Sch., 1919; studied Tulane U., summer; D.D., Union U., Jackson, Tenn., 1929; LL.D., 1934; Litt.D., Bob Jones College, Cleveland, Tenn.; D.D., Stetson University, DeLand, Fla., 1944, Litt.D., Houghton College Houthton, N.Y., 1952. m. Bula Gentry, Nov. 28, 1913; children—Bula Gentry, Roy DeMent. Ordained ministry Southern Baptist Church, 1910; pastor successively Edgefield and Chester, S.C., and First Church, New Orleans. La., until 1926, Citadel Sq. Ch., Charleston, S.C., 1925-27, Bellevue Bapt. Ch., Memphis, Tenn., since 1927. Pres. Baptist State Conv. of Tenn., 1932-35. Trustee Bapt. Bible Inst., New Orleans, 1923-25, Greenville Woman's Coll., Union U. and Bob Jones Coll. President of Southern Bap. Cenvention, 1948-50. Baptist. Author numerous books since 1929; latest publs.: Pulpit Pleadings, 1948; The Sinner's Saviour, 1949; The Bible and Prayer, 1950. Home: Memphis. *

LEEBRICK, KARL CLAYTON (LE'BRIK), coll. pres.; b. Burlington, Ia., Oct. 20, 1885; s. John Philip and Mary Detweiler (Rosenberger) L.; student Tempe (Ariz.) Normal Sch., 1902-06; B.S., U. of Calif., 1911, M.S., 1913, Native Son traveling fellow to Europe, 1915-16, Ph.D., 1916; m. Beryl Mae Fountain, Sept. 25, 1913; children—Henrietta Mae, Karl Clayton. Teacher, pub. sch., Clifton, Ariz., and Covina, Calif., 1906-09; supervisor of boys, Calif. Instn. for Deaf and Blind, Berkeley, 1909-11; U. of Calif., 1916-17, instr., 1917-19, asst. prof. history, 1919-20; prof. polit. science and history, and head of dept., U. of Hawaii, 1920-28; acting prof. internat. affairs, Syracuse U. Sch. of Citizenship and Pub. Affairs, 1928-29; prof. same and dean of Coll. Liberal Arts, Syracuse U., 1929-38; pres. Kent (O.) State U., 1938-43; major, Lt. Col. Specialists Reserve, Army U.S., May 1943-Nov. 1945, foreign service European theatre, 1944-45, Dept. of State Fgn. Div., Japan, 1945-46. U.S. alternate commr. S. Pacific Commn.; mem. U.S. Navy adv. ednl. commn., Guam and trust territories. Vice pres., prof. govt., veterans adv., U. of Hawaii 1946-51; liaison ofcr., U.S. Trust Terrs. of Pacific, 1951-53. President of Maunaolu College, Paia, Maui, Hawaii, since 1953. Japan-Am. Soc. invitational lectr. Japan, 1924; exec. sec. Nat. Conf. Edn., Reclamation and Recreation, Honolulu, 1926; dir. Inst. of Internat. Relations of Pacific Coast, 1926-30; member Institute of Politics, 1930-31. Member American Political Science Association, American Society Internat. Law, Am. Acad. Polit. Science, Am. Acad. Polit. and Soc. Sci., Pan-Pacific Union, Pi Gamma Mu. Pi Delta Epsilon, Pi Kappa Delta (hon.), Acacia. Republican. Mason. Clubs: Rotary, City and Univ. (Cleveland). Author: History of Brewer & Co.—100 Years of Business in Hawaii, 1926; Proceedings of the Institute of International Relations (with J. E. Harley), 1927; Implications of the Annexation of Hawaii, 1928; The Pacific Area (with C. E. Martin). Contbr. to Contemporary World Politics; Introduction to Politics; also to Political Science Quarterly, Sunset Mag., Pan-Pacific Mag. Address: Maui, Hawaii. *

LEEMAN, CHARLES WILLIAM, bus. exec.; b. Honey Grove, Tex., July 21, 1893; s. Charles A. and Molly (Ernst) L.; ed. Burns Bus. Coll., Tyler, Tex.; m. Marjorie Mae Wilson, Dec. 24, 1938. Salesman, Cudahy Packing Co., Wichita, Kans., 1917-18, Wapples Platter Grocery Co., Ft. Worth, 1918-19; spl. rep. Businessmen's Assurance Co., Kansas City, 1919-23; v.p., sales mgr. Union Ins. Co., Wichita, 1923-33; organized Met. Accident and Health Ins. Co., Omaha, pres., gen mgr., 1933-55, chmn. bd., from 1955; gen. agt. Benefit Assn. Ry. Employees for State of Nebr.; pres., gen. mgr. Union Pacific Finance Corp., from 1937. Mayor, Omaha, 1945-48; mem. exec. com. U.S. Conf. of Mayors, 1947, 48; chmn. Omaha Downtown Ration Bd., World War II; Nebr. State chmn. Rheumatoid Arthritis Com., 1950-51; govtl. appointee Nebr. State Bd. of Control, 1956-61, chmn., 1959-61. Mem. Nebr. Accident and Health Underwriters (pres. 1941-42), Nat. Accident and Health Underwriters (law and legis. com. 1942-46), Peoples Forum, Ad-Sell League, YMCA, Omaha C. of C., Nat. Aeros. Assn., Marine Corps League (hon.), Air Res. Assn. (hon.), PTA (life mem.); hon. chief Arapahoe Indian Tribe; adm. Nebr. Navy. Democrat. Methodist. Mason (32 deg., Shriner), Elk, Eagle, Odd Fellow, Order of Ahepa. Clubs: Omaha Optimist (pres. 1942-43), Business Men's Breakfast (pres. 1939-40), Variety, Omaha Field, Highland Country, Better Omaha, South West Improvement, North West Improvement. Home: Omaha, Nebr. Died July 4, 1979; interred Forest Lawn Cemetery, Omaha.

LEESON, ROBERT, business exec.; b. Newton, Mass., May 4, 1907; s. Robert Ainsworth and Mildred Carruth (Dix) L.; A.B., Harvard, 1929, postgrad. Sch. Bus. Adminstrn., 1930-31; m. Evelyn Talbot, June 11, 1931; children—Robert, Richmond Talbot. With Leesona Corp., 1931-78, asst. to pres., 1934, sales mgr., 1935-37, pres., 1937-41, 46-67, chmn. bd., 1953-76, also dir.; hon. trustee Citizens Sav. Bank. Past trustee, sec. corp., exec. com. R.I. Sch. Design, emeritus trustee; past bd. dirs., v.p. United Fund Southeastern New Eng.; incorporator, past trustee Naval War Coll. Found.; founding mem., dir. Urban Coalition R.I. Past chmn. R.I. Republican Finance Com. Served to comdr. USNR, 1941-45; PTO, ATO; capt. Res. ret. Decorated Silver Star, Legion Merit. Mem. Am. Textile Machinery Assn. (past pres., dir.), Machinery and Allied Products Inst. Home: Boca Grande, Fla. Died Mar. 28, 1978; buried Mt. Auburn Cemetery, Cambridge, Mass.

LEFLER, MILLARD CHARLES, supt. schs.; b. Springfield, Neb., Oct. 5, 1882; s. William and Nettie (Phelps) L.; A.B., Peru State Teachers Coll., 1910; A.M., Univ. of Nebraska, 1916; Ed.D., Nebraska Wesleyan University, 1942; m. G. Adalyn Blankenship, Aug. 12, 1915; children—Millard William (dec.), Esther Louise. Rural teacher, Neb., 1902-05; supt. schs. Elmwood, 1906-07; prin. Training High Sch., Teachers Coll., Peru, 1910-15, asso. dir. of training, 1917; asst. supt. schs. Lincoln, 1918-19, supt. Lincoln since 1920. Mem. N.E.A. (life. Neb. dir. 1922-31, v.p. 1927), Neb. State Teachers Assn. (pres. 1933), Neb. Schoolmasters Club, Lincoln Chamber of Commerce, Izaak Walton League, Phi Delta Kappa. Democrat. Methodist. Mason (32 deg., K.C.C.H.). Club: Kiwanis. Writer on ednl. subjects, Home: Lincoln, Neb.

LEFTWICH, JAMES T(HOMAS), chain store exec.; b. Malden, W.Va., Feb. 20, 1889; s. James T. and Katherine L. (Stanley) L.; student pub. schs. of W.Va.; m. Rita A. Somerville, Aug. 28, 1917; 1 son, James T. III. With F. W. Woolworth Co. since 1913, starting as bookkeeper at Chicago, sec., comptroller and dir., N.Y.C., 1947-52, became exec. vice pres., treas., 1952, then pres., chairman of the board until 1959, now director and cons.; sec., controller, treas., dir. Woolco Realty Corp., 1947-52, became v.p., dir., 1952, now pres.; sec., vice pres., treas., dir. F. W. Woolworth Co., Ltd., Can., 1947-52, became v.p., dir., 1952, now pres.; sec., treas., dir. F. W. Woolworth Co. of France, 1947-52, v.p., dir., 1952-54, pres. 1954-56, chmn., 1956-59; pres. F. W. Woolworth Co., S.A. de C.V. Mexico; dir. Osmose Wood Preserving Co. Am. Home: Glen Ridge, N.J. Died July 6, 1980.

LEGER, ABEL NICHOLAS (LA'GER), Haitian lawyer and public official; b. 1886; s. Jacques Nicholas Léger; ed. St. Johns' College, Wash., D.C.; Lycée Michelet, Paris; Faculty of Law, Paris; School of Political Science, Paris; bachelor of law from U. of Paris, licentiate in law; m. Lisa Bourke; children—Jacques, Lucienne, Madelaine, Yvonne. Attaché, Haitian Legation, Paris, 1906-09; sec. Haitian Legation, 1909; sec., Haitian delegation, 2d Hague Conf., 1907; legal consultant, dept. fgn. relations, 1911-13; prof. international and civil law, Faculty of Law, Port-au-Prince, 1918-26; pres. International Claims Commn. at Port-au-Prince (1923-26), del. to Internat. Commn. of American jurists at Rio (1927); sec. of state of fgn. relations, 1931-32; pres. Haytian sect., mixed commn. of conciliation for settlement of frontiers between Hayti and Santo-Domingo (1934); mem. Hague Permanent Court of Arbitration (since 1930). Pres. Haitian delegation to permanent Wash. commn. for regulation of controversies between Haiti and Dominican Republic, 1938; pres. Haytian sect. mixed commn. for delimitization of borders between Santo-Domingo and Haiti (1938). Minister plenipotentiary to Paris and the Vatican (1938-41); first del. to Society of Nations (1938). Awarded medal, 2d Peace Conf. of the Hague; Grand Officer, Order of St. Gregory the Great; Legion of Honor (France); Order of Saints Maurice and Lazarus (Italy). Mem. Société de Législation (Portau-Prince), Haitian Soc. Internat. Law, Inst. of Internat. Law, Académie Vattel et Académie Diplomatique, Internat. de Paris, Cercle Bellevue. Author: La Doctrine Drago et la deuxieme Conférence de la Paix, 1915; Le Codification du Drout des Gens et les Conferences des Juristes Americains, 1929; Le Droit Internationale Privé en Amerique, 1929; Histoire Diplomatique d'Haiti, 1931; Code Civil d'Haiti, 1931. Address: Port-au-Prince, Haiti. *

LEGER, JULES, former gov. gen. of Can.; b. St. Anicet, Que., Can., Apr. 4, 1913; s. Ernest and Alda (Beauvais) L.; B.A., Coll. of Valleyfield, 1933; postgrad. U. Montreal, 1933-36; LL.D., U. Sorbonne, 1938; m. Gaby Carmel, 1938; 1 dau., Helene. Asso. editor Ottawa daily Le Droit, 1938-39; prof. history of diplomacy U. Ottawa, 1939-42; 3d sec. Dept. External Affairs, 1940-43; mem. Canadian mission in Chile, 1943-47; 1st sec. to London, 1947; adviser Canadian del. Gen. Assembly UN, Paris, 1948-49; exec. asst. to prime minister, 1949; participant Commonwealth Prime Ministers Meeting, London, 1950; chief European Div., 1950; asst. under-sec. state for external affairs, 1951-53; ambassador to Mexico, 1953-54; under-sec. state for external affairs, 1954-58; ambassador, permanent rep. N.Atlantic Council, Canadian rep. OEEC, Paris, 1958-62; participant ministerial meetings NATO, 1958-62, Atlantic Congress, London, 1959; ambassador to Italy, 1962-64, to France, 1964-68; under-sec. state in fields of arts and cultural support, bilingualism, edn. and citizenship, 1968-73; ambassador to Belgium and Luxembourg, 1973-74; gov. gen., comdr.-in-chief of Can., 1974-79; apptd. to Privy Council, 1979. Decorated companion Order of Can., comdr. Order Mil. Merit. Home: Ottawa, Ont., Canada. Died Nov. 22, 1980.

LEGGE, WALTER, artistic director; b. London, Eng., June 1, 1906; s. Harry Walter and Florence (MOrris) L.; ed. privately; m. Elisabeth Schwarzkopf, Oct. 1952. Recording mgr. His Masters Voice, also Columbia Records, 1931-79, Angel Records until 1964; founder Hugo Wolf Soc., Beethoven Sonata Soc.; mus. critic Manchester Guardian, 1930-37; asst. artist dir. Royal Opera House, London, 1938-39; founder Philharmonia Orch. London, 1945, artistic dir., 1945-64; founder Philharmonia Chorus, 1957, dir. Mem. Gesellschaft der Musik, Vienna. Address: St Jean-Cap Ferrat France. Died Mar. 22, 1979.

LEGGETT, WILSON DURWARD, JR., engring. exec.; b. Tarboro, N.C., Mar. 18, 1901; s. Wilson Durward and Katherine (Howard) L.; student Severn Sch., Severna Park, Md., 1916-17; B.S., U.S. Naval Acad., 1920; M.S., Columbia, 1927; student U.S. Navy Postgrad. Sch., 1925-26; D.Sc. (hon.), N.C. State Coll., 1957; married Mary Chamberlain Howard, Oct. 2, 1924; children—Elizabeth Howard (Mrs. Homer B. Sewell, Jr.), Wilson Durward. Commd. ensign, U.S. Navy, 1920, advanced through grades to rear adm., Jan. 1951; duty Bur. Engring., Dept. Navy, 1931-33; repair supt. Mare Island Naval Shipyard, 1940-44; fleet maintenance officer, 7th Fleet, 1944-45; planning officer, Charleston, 1946, Engring. Expt. Sta., Annapolis, Md., 1947-51; comdg. officer, dir. U.S. Naval Engring. Expt. Sta., 1947-51; dep., assistant chief Navy's Bureau of Ships, 1951-53, chief, 1953-55; v.p. engring. Alco Products, Inc. Schenectady, 1955-64, dir., 1955-64; asst. to chmn. bd., v.p. IMODCO Internat., 1964-77; dir. Schenectady Trust Co., Mech. Tech., Inc., Schenectady, Runnymede Mills, Tarboro, N.C. Decorated Legion of Merit, Commendation ribbon, World War I (star), World War II victory medals, Am. Def. Service medal, Am. Area, Asiatic-Pacific Area (star), Philippine Liberation (star); recipient David W. Taylor medal for achievement in navy architecture and marine engring., 1967; registered profl. engr., N.Y. Mem. Am. Soc. Naval Engrs., Soc. Naval Architects Engrs., Soc. Marine Engrs., Newcomen Soc., Naval Order World War. Presbyn. Operator farm near Tarboro, 1930-77. Home: Washington, D.C. Died Jan. 1, 1977; buried U.S. Naval Acad., Annapolis, Md.

LEGRAND, DUARD MADISON, JR., newspaper editor; b. Macon, Ga., Feb. 9, 1915; s. Duard Madison and Annie (Crawford) LeG.; A.B., Birmingham-So. Coll., Ala., 1934; postgrad. U. Ala., 1934-35; m. Elna Row Sessions, Sept. 4, 1942; 1 dau., Lissa. Reporter, Eufaula (Ala.) Tribune, 1936-38; reporter Birmingham (Ala.) Post (name changed to Birmingham Post-Herald, 1950), 1939-41, news editor, 1946-49, city editor, 1949-63, mng. editor, 1963-67, editor, 1967-78. Served to maj. USAAF, 1941-46. Mem. Am. Soc. Newspaper Editors, Phi Beta Kappa, Sigma Delta Chi, Delta Sigma Phi. Rotarian. Club: Birmingham Country. Home: Birmingham, Ala. Died May 15, 1978.

LEHMAN, ARNOLD JOHN, physician, pharmacologist; b. Good Thunder, Minn., Sept. 2, 1900; s. John Frederick and Bertha Wilhelmina (Ladwig) L.; B.S., U. Wash., 1925, M.S., 1926, Ph.D., 1930; M.D., Stanford, 1936; m. Harriet Vivian Snidow, June 24, 1928; children—Eleanor Irene, John Frederick. Asst. in instrn., instr. pharmacology Stanford Med. Sch., 1931-37; asst. prof. pharmacology U. Okla. Med. Sch., 1937-39; asso. prof. Med. Sch., Wayne U., 1939-44; prof., dir. dept. pharmacology U. N.C. Med. Sch., 1944-46; dir. div. pharmacology FDA, HEW, Washington, 1946-69. Mem. subcom. toxicology, com. food protection Food and Nutrition Bd.; com. toxicology, div. chemistry and chem. tech. NRC; mem. WHO Expert Adv. Panel on Food Additives; corr. mem. European Com. Med. Sch. at U. Miami has established Arnold J. Lehman prize in pharmacology. Fellow Royal Soc. Medicine, Am. Coll. Clin. Pharmacology and Chemotherapy, A.A.A.S.; mem. Soc. Toxicology, Canadian Pharm. Soc., Pan. Am. Med. Assn., A.M.A., Soc. Pharmacology and Exptl. Therapeutics, Soc. Exptl. Biology and Medicine, Assn. Food and Drug Ofcls. U.S., Sigma Xi, Kappa Psi, Phi Rho Sigma. Lutheran. Mason. Home: McLean, Va. Died July 10, 1979; cremated.

LEHMAN, CHESTER HAMILTON, business exec.; b. Pittsburgh, Pa., 1886; grad. Harvard, 1909. Vice chmn. bd., exec. vice pres. and dir. Blaw-Knox Co., Pittsburgh; v.p. and dir. Blaw-Knox Constrn. Co., Hoboken Land Co., Blaw-Knox Internat. Corp.; dir. Blaw-Knox, Ltd. Home: 5440 Darlington Rd. Address: Pittsburgh. *

LEHMANN, JOHN S(TARK) (LAYMAN), corporation exec.; b. Des Moines, Ia., Jan. 18, 1886; s. Frederick W. and Nora (Stark) L.; A.B., Harvard, 1907; LL.B., Washington U., 1910; m. Anne S. Lionberger, Jan. 7, 1925; 1 son, John Stark. Admitted to Mo. bar, 1910, practiced St. Louis, 1910-55; partner Lehmann & Lehmann, 1910-43, Lehmann & Allen, 1943-55; honorary chairman of the board Petrolite Corporation; president of Wm. S. Barnickel & Co.; mem. bd. directors Boatmen's Nat. Bank. Dir. Washington U. Central Inst. for the Deaf; trustee Mo. Botanical Garden. Mem. C. of C., Am. Petroleum Inst., Ind. Petroleum Assn. Home: Clayton, Mo.

LEHMANN, LOTTE, soprano; b. Perleberg, Germany, Feb. 27, 1888; d. Carl and Marie (Schuster) Lehmann; m. Otto Krause, Apr. 28, 1926 (dec. Jan. 1939). Opera and concert singer; U.S. debut Town Hall, 1932; mem. Met., San Francisco and Chgo. civic opera cos.; made debut Met. Opera Co., Jan. 11, 1934, as Sieglinde in Die Walkuere; scored notable success as Eva, in Die Meistersinger, Die Marschailin in Der Rosenkavalier, and other standard operas. Hon. membership State Opera, Vienna; decorated officer Legion of Honor (France); recipient Medal of Art (Sweden); Ring of Honor (Vienna Philharm. Orch., Vienna Opera and City Vienna); hon. pres. Music Acad. West. Author: Eternal Flight, 1937; Midway in My Song, 1938; More Than Singing; My Many Lives, 1948; Five Operas and Richard Strauss, 1964; 18 Songcycles, 1971. Known as First Lady of Song. Home: Santa Barbara, Calif. Deceased; buried Vienna, Austria.

LEHNHOFF, SHEPPARD, musician; b. Chgo., Nov. 12, 1905; s. Charles Samuel and Rose (Klein) L.; grad. Chgo. Mus. Coll., 1926; student Curtis Inst. Music, 1927-29; pupil William Primrose, 1940; m. Anna Kurgans, Aug. 10, 1937; children—Charlotte, Trudy, Nora. Dir. band and orch. Murray (Ky.) State Tchrs. Coll., 1926-27, mem. Curtis Quartet, 1927-29; mem. Phila. Orch., 1928-29, 32; violist Fine Arts Quartet, 1937-41, 46-53; mem. Chgo. Symphony Orch., 1929-45, 53-78; 1st violist Nat. Symphony Orch., Washington, 1945-46, ABC Staff Orch., 1946-53; also appeared tours; mem. applied music faculty U. Chgo., 1930-32, 55-56; lectr. in field. Recipient certificate of merit Chgo. Mayor Daley, for European tour, 1971. Compiler, arranger albums string music. Home: Chicago, Ill. Died Jan. 22, 1978.

LEICH, CHESTER (LIK), artist; b. Evansville, Ind., Jan. 31, 1889; s. Charles and Wilhelmine (Lemcke) L.; ed. in U.S. and abroad; studied in Italian and German art schs., 1911-15; grad. work, U. of Munich, 1911; m. Jean Graham Townley, July 8, 1927; 1 dau., Mary Townley. One man show George Washington U. Library, 1958; works Landing at Ulvik and Village Street, Bedford, reproduced in Fine Prints of Year, 1930, 32; etchings in permanent collections National Collection of Fine Arts, Washington D.C.; Library of Congress; Museum of New Mexico at Santa Fe; Society of Am. Etchers; Evansville Mus.; Nat. Acad. of Design Library; Newark Pub. Library; Public Museum, Evansville, Ind.; Swope Museum, Terre Haute, Ind., Met. Mus. Art, N.Y.C., Montclair Art Mus. Recipient Award, Merit Exhbn. Artists of N.J., 1932; medal of merit for black and white, Exhbn. of Artists of N.J., Montclair Art Mus., 1938, for drypoint "Rio Grande Country," price for black and white, Fine Arts Assn., Tucson, Ariz., 1938, for drypoint "Village Street, Bedford"; diploma for silver medal, Paris Expn., for drypoint "Fishing Fleet"; 1st hon. mention for black and white, Exhbn. Artists of N.J., 1940, for Going to Town. Mem. Soc. Am. Graphic Artists, Soc. Washington Printmakers. Author: Descriptive Exhibits on the Graphic Arts; Descriptive Exhibits on Techniques of Painting. War service appointment to U.S. Coast and Geodetic Survey, 1942. Home: Arlington, Va. Died Nov. 9, 1978.

LEIGHTON, HENRY, univ. prof.; b. Canandaigua, N.Y., Feb. 20, 1884; s. Peter and Jeanie (Hall) L.; A.B., Cornell U., 1906, grad. study, 1906-08; m. Jessie Cipperly, Aug. 25, 1909; children—Helen (Mrs. Ralph Cannon), Harry. Instr. geology, Cornell U., 1906-08; asst. geologist, N.Y. State Museum, 1908-10; instr. U. of Pittsburgh, 1910-12, asst. prof., 1912-17, prof., 1917-49, retired, head dept. geol., 1928-45. Fellow A.A.A.S., Geol. Soc. Am.; mem. Soc. Econ. Geologists, Pa. Acad. Sci., Sigma Xi, Republican. United Lutheran. Author: History of the Clay Working Industry, 1909; N.Y. State Museum bulls.; Pa. Geol. Survey. Home: Ithaca, N.Y. *

LEIGHTY, CLYDE E(VERT), agronomist; b. Lawrence County, Ill., May 7, 1882; s. George Henry and Lucretia (Vandermark) L.; A.B., Ill. Wesleyan U., 1904; Ph.D., Cornell, 1912; m. Ollie Edna Harris, Oct. 13, 1908; children—Florence Lucretia (Mrs. Raymond Colton), Raymond Vandermark. Soil chemist, Ill. Agr. Expt. Sta., 1905; investigated arrival condition Am. grain at European ports for U.S. Dept. Agr., 1906; established and in charge U.S. Dept. Agr. Grain Standardization Labs., New Orleans, St. Louis and New York, 1906-09; grad. work, Cornell U., 1909-12; in charge eastern wheat investigations, Bur. Plant Industry, U.S. Dept. Agr., 1912-30, in charge div. dry land agr., 1930-45, retired 1945; apptd. collaborator, U.S. Dept. Agr. Fellow A.A.A.S.; member Am. Genetic Assn. (sec. since 1926), Agrl. History Soc., Am. Soc. Agronomy, Bot. Soc. of Washington, Genetic Assn. of Am., Wash. Acad. Science, Tau Kappa Epsilon, Sigma Xi, Phi Kappa Phi. Club: Cosmos (Washington). Author numerous bulls., U.S. Dept. Agr., also professional sci. papers relating to plant breeding, etc. Home: Arlington, Va. *

LEITH-ROSS, HARRY, artist; b. Mauritius (Brit. colony), Jan. 27, 1886; s. Frederick Arbuthnot and Sina (van Houten) L.; ed. U. Birmingham (Eng.), 1901-02, Académie Delécluse and Académie Julian, Paris, 1909-10, Art Students League, N.Y.C., 1910-13; m. Emily Slaymaker, July 20, 1925; 1 dau., Emily Elizabeth. Came to U.S., 1903, naturalized 1918. Served as 2d lt., inf., U.S. Army, World War I. Recipient important prizes in art, 1913-. Nat. Academician. Mem. Am. Water Color Soc. Clubs: Salmagundi; Phila. Water Color; Balt. Water Color. Author: The Landscape Painter's Manual. Home: New Hope PA. *

LELAND, GEORGE HAVENS, cons. engr.; b. Warwick, R.I., June 7, 1926; s. Richard Cutler and Katherine (Havens) L.; B.S., Harvard, 1946, M.S., 1947; m. Virginia Saxe Kelcey, June 30, 1951; children—David Kelcey, Ann Louise, Suzanne. From asst. engr. to project engr. Edwards and Kelcey, engrs. and cons., Newark, 1947-51, asso., 1953-58, partner 1958-78; pres. Edwards and Kelcey, Inc., 1963-78, chmn. bd., 1973-78, also dir.; adminstrv. and tech. work urban transp. systems, rail transit, structures, recreation facilities, mil. installations, express hwys., communications, parking facilities, site and regional planning, traffic studies, U.S. and abroad. Vice chmn. adv. bd. hotel and multiple-dwelling health and safety N.J. Dept. Community Affairs, 1968-72; adv. com. civil engring. dept. N.J. Inst. Tech., 1967-73; mem. nat. def. exec. res. U.S. Dept. Transp., 1970-78; chmn. adv. com. planning and design HUD, 1967-70, mem. design awards jury, 1968; mem. advisory council Princeton Transp. Program, 1976-78. Mem. Chatham (N.J.) Bd. Edn., 1969-75. Served to lt. comdr. USNR, 1945-46, 51-53. Registered profl. engr., 11 states, D.C. Fellow ASCE (pres. N.J. 1964), Inst. Traffic Engrs.; mem. Soc. Harvard Engrs. and Scientists (v.p. 1965-66), Am. Cons. Engrs. Council (v.p. 1973-75, pres. elect 1978), N.J. Cons. Engrs. Council (pres. 1965-66), Am. Inst. Cons. Engrs. (mem. council 1972-73), Internat. Road Fedn. (dir. 1972-78), Hwy. Users Fedn. (dir. 1972-78), Nat. Soc. Profl. Engrs., Soc. Am. Mil. Engrs., Chi Epsilon (hon.). Episcopalian. Clubs; Minisink (pres. 1968-69) (Chatham); Harvard (N.Y.C. and N.J.); Essex (Newark). Contbr. articles to profl. publns. Home: New Vernon, N.J. Died Sept. 17, 1978.

LEMBERGER, ERNST, Austrian diplomat; b. Vienna, Austria, July 9, 1906; s. Adolf and Bertha (Wiesberg) L.; Dr., U. Vienna Law Sch., 1930; m. Martha Wobisch, Nov. 24, 1947; children—Ernst Peter, Kurt Robert, Erich Walter, Gerhard Wolfgang. Engaged in legal practice, Vienna, 1931-36; tourist officer, Paris, France, 1936-39; vol. French Fng. Legion, 1939-40; mem. French and Austrian underground, 1940-45; 1st sec. embassy, Paris, 1946-48; counsellor embassy, Washington, 1948-55; minister Fgn. Office, Vienna, 1956-58; A.M. and P. to Brussels, 1958-65, to Washington, 1965-70. Decorated Medal of Freedom with star (U.S.); Croix de Guerre with plam (France); grande croix de l'Ordre de Leopold, grande croix de l'Ordre de la Couronne (Belgium); grand cross Order Oak-leaf (Luxembourg); knight comdr.'s cross (badge and star) Order Merit Fed. Republic Germany; comdr. Order Golden Cross Honor (Lower Austria). Home: Vienna, Austria. Died Dec. 3, 1974.

LEMIEUX, ALBERT ARBY, clergyman; b. Wallace, Idaho, Sept. 13, 1908; s. Albert and Clara (Gingras) L.; A.B., Gonzago U., 1931, A.M., 1932; S.T.L., Alma Coll., 1939; Ph.D., U. Toronto, 1945. Faculty mem. Gonzaga U., 1932-35, dean sch. philosophy, 1946-47, dean faculties, 1947-48; pres. Seattle U., 1948-65, chancellor, 1976-79; rector sem. Mt. St. Michael, Spokane, 1966-68. Trustee St. Louis U. Home: Seattle, Wash. Died 1979.

LEMIRE, CLARENCE PLATO, lawyer; b. Martinsville, Mo., Apr. 13, 1886; s. Oscar and Abiah (Smith) L.; LL.B., U. of Mo., 1912; m. Winnifred Erville Delavan, Sept. 1, 1915; 1 dau., Margaret Erville (Mrs. Verrell F. Ashburn). Practiced law, Fulton, Mo., 1913-17; asst. atty. gen. of Mo., 1917-20; mem. Mo. Legislature, 1927, 1928; gen. practice law, Kansas City, Mo., 1920-46; judge, Tax Court of U.S., since 1946. Mem. Am., Mo. State, Kansas City bar assns., Phi Alpha Delta, Pi Kappa Alpha. Democrat. Presbyn. Home: Washington. *

LEMKAU, HUDSON BARDON, investment banker; b. Montclair, N.J., Dec. 27, 1910; s. J.H. Walter and Edith (Hudson) L.; grad. Montclair Acad., 1928; B.A., Princeton, 1932; m. Janet Loasby, June 2, 1936; children—Arthur L., Alison (Mrs. Alex B. Vaughn), Hudson B. With Bonbright & Co., Inc., 1932-42; with Morgan Stanley & Co., N.Y.C., 1942-44, 46-74, partner, 1956-74; mng. dir. Morgan Stanley & Co., Inc., 1970-74; mgr. Morgan & Cie Internat. S.A., Paris, France, 1971-74. Hon. mem. exec. bd. Greater N.Y. council Boy Scouts Am. Served to lt. USNR, 1944-46. Mem. Investment Bankers Assn. Am. (gov. 1957-59), Nat. Assn. Securities Dealers (gov. 1961-63, vice chmn. 1963). Clubs: Bond (gov. 1954-56, 67-69), N.Y. Yacht, Princeton, City Mid-day (N.Y.C.); Manhasset Bay Yacht (Port Washington, N.Y.); The Creek (Locust Valley, N.Y.); Princeton (N.J.) Charter (gov. 1959-69); Nantucket (Mass.) Yacht; Travellers (Paris). Home: Plandome, N.Y. Died Sept. 15, 1974.

LEMMON, ALLAN HAZLETT, ins. co. exec.; b. Kingston, Ont., Can., July 26, 1908; s. Allan and Martha Violet (Hazlett) L.; B.A., Queen's U., Kingston, 1929; m. Eleanor Margaret Scott, June 6, 1935 (dec. Jan. 1979); 1 son, 1 dau. With Can. Life Assurance Co., Toronto, Ont., from 1928, asst. treas., 1940-46, treas., 1946-53, v.p., treas., 1953-63, exec. v.p., treas., 1963, pres., 1964-73, chmn. bd., from 1973, also dir.; v.p., dir. Nat. Trust Co. Ltd. Clubs: Granite, Toronto, York, York Downs Golf and Country; Mt. Royal (Montreal). Home: Willowdale, Ont., Canada. Deceased.

LEMMON, ROBERT STELL, author; b. Englewood, N.J., June 26, 1885; s. William and Caroline (McCulloh) L.; prep. edn., Englewood (N.J.) Sch. for Boys; A.B., Yale, 1909; m. Florence G. Edwards, of N.Y. City, May 14, 1920; 1 dau., Ann Rutledge. Asst., Rhoades-Phila. Acad. Sciences zoöl. expdn. to Ecuador, 1911; asso. editor Travel Mag., 1911-14; asso. editor House and Garden Mag., 1915-18, mng. editor, 1918-37, garden editor since 1937. Republican. Clubs: Yale, Dutch Treat New York). Author: Training the Dog, 1914; The Puppy Book, 1924; About Your Dog, 1928; Old Doc Lemmon, 1930. Contbr. to Delineator, Scribner's, Country Gentleman, Woman's Home Companion, Ladies' Home Journal, etc. Lecturer, garden clubs and hort. socs. Home: New Canaan, Conn.

LEMON, HAL YATES, past v.p. Nat. Bank of Detroit; b. St. Joseph, Mo., Apr. 11, 1883; s. John Strother and Anne (Samuel) L.; ed. Princeton U., 1905; m. Mable Bartlett, June 24, 1911. Began with Tootle-Lemon Nat. Bank, St. Joseph, Mo., 1906, asst. cashier, 1914-17; asst. cashier Southwest Nat. Bank, Kansas City, Mo., 1917; bank later merged with Commerce Trust Co., Kansas City, v.p. and dir., 1923-33; assisted in organization Nat. Bank of Detroit, v.p., 1933-49; dir. Missouri Valley Trust Co., The Lemon Estate. Pres. Assn. of Reserve City Bankers, 1926; treas. Am. Bankers Assn. (1934-35). Club: Country; Benton (St. Joseph). Home: St. Joseph, Mo. *

LEMON, JAMES HANSON, investment banker; b. Washington, May 14, 1903; s. Hanson Thomas Asbury and Maud (Duvall) L.; B.S., Princeton, 1925; m. Martha Lane McGehee, Sept. 13, 1928; 1 son, James Hanson. With Johnston, Lemon & Co., Inc., and predecessors, 1925-77, chmn. bd., 1967-77; chmn. bd., dir. Washington Mut. Investors Fund., Inc., D.C. Paper Mills, Inc.; dir. Dist. Theatres Corp., Pep Com Industries, Inc., Internat. Bank of Washington, MIW Advisors, Inc.; trustee Mortgage Investors of Washington, Inc. Dir., past pres. Children's Hosp. of D.C. Mem. Am. Contract Bridge League (past pres.). Clubs: Princeton (past pres.), Chevy Chase, Metropolitan, Burning Tree, University (Washington); Home: Washington, D.C. Died July 20, 1977.

LENNARTSON, NILS ANDREW, assn. exec.; b. Webster, Mass., Aug. 9, 1915; s. Andrew L. and Anna (Skoglund) L.; student Pembroke (N.H.) Acad., 1928-32; A.B., Bates Coll., Lewiston, Maine, 1936; m. Emily Elizabeth Weston, Jan. 27, 1943. Newspaper reporter Portland (Maine) Press-Herald, 1937-42; asst. publicity mgr. Maine Central R.R., 1945-47; asst. dir. pub. relations N.E. dist. U.S. Steel Corp., 1947-48; dep. dir. pub. relations Dept. Air Force, Washington, 1948-52, spl. asst. sec. air force, 1951-52; dir. pub. info. Dept. Commerce, 1952-53; asst. to sec. treasury, 1953-61; dep. asst. sec. def. for pub. affairs, 1961-65; pres. Ry. Progress Inst., Washington, 1965-77. Served to capt. Air Trans. Command, USAAF, 1942-45. Recipient Exceptional Civilian Service award Dept. Air Force, 1952, Exceptional Service certificate Treasury Dept., 1961. Mem. Ry. Pub. Relations Assn., Pan Am. Ry. Congress, Am. Soc. Assn. Execs., Pub. Relations Soc. Am. (Harriman Safety awards com.), Western Ry. Club. Clubs: Union League, Chicago (Chgo.); Metropolitan, Capitol Hill, Nat. Press, University (Washington): Dalmatian of Am. Home: Alexandria, Va. Died May 31, 1977; cremated.

LENNON, JOHN WINSTON ONO, musician, author, artist; b. Liverpool, Eng., Oct. 9, 1940; s. Alfred and Julia (Stanley) L.; student Quarry Bank, Liverpool Art Coll.; m. Cynthia Powell, 1962; m. 2d, Yoko Ono, 1969; 1 son, Sean Ono; 1 stepdau. Founder musical group The Quarreymen, 1955; appeared with various groups until forming The Beatles. Home: New York, N.Y. Died Dec. 8, 1980.

LENSEN, GEORGE ALEXANDER, historian, educator; b. Berlin, Germany, Nov. 5, 1923; s. Alexander and Charlotte (Baruchson) L.; came to U.S.

1939, naturalized, 1943; A.B., Columbia, 1947, M.A., 1948, Ph.D., 1951; divorced; children—Karen Meng-mel, Kristin Chung-Mel; m. 2d, Rumlya Shahbey Lensen, Aug. 17, 1969. Mem. faculty Fla. State U., 1949-79, prof. history, 1959-79; vis. prof. Columbia U., summers 1962-63; pres. Diplomatic Press, Inc., 1966-79. Served to 1st lt. AUS, 1943-46. Grantee Social Sci. Research Council, 1957-58, Am. Philos. Soc., 1958, 61, 67, Am. Council Learned Socs. and Social Sci. Research Council, 1959, 61, Ford Found., 1975-78; Fulbright research scholar Hokkaido (Japan) U., 1953-54; postdoctoral researcher Leningrad (USSR) State U., 1961; sr. fellow Nat. Endowment Humanities, 1967-68; sr. scholar exchange Am. Council Learned Socs.-Acad. Sci. USSR, 1973, 74. Author: Report from Hokkaido: The Remains of Russian Culture in Northern Japan, 1954; Russia's Japan Expedition of 1852 to 1855, 1955; The Russian Push Toward Japan: Russo-Japanese Relations 1697-1875, 1959; The World Beyond Europe: An Introduction to the History of Africa, India, Southeast Asia and the Far East, 2d edit., 1966; The Soviet Union: An Introduction, 1967; The Russo-Chinese War, 1967; Japanese Recognition of the USSR: Soviet-Japanese Relations, 1921-30, 1970; Faces of Japan: A Photographic Study, 1968; April in Russia: A Photographic Study, 1970; The Strange Neutrality: Soviet Japanese Relations during The Second World War, 1972; The Damned Inheritance: The Soviet Union and the Manchurian Crises, 1924-35, 1974; Balance of Intrigue: International Rivalry in Korea and Manchuria 1884-1899, 2 vols., 1979; co-author; The Meaning of Yalta: Big Three Diplomacy and the New Balance of Power, 1966. Editor: Revelations of a Russian Diplomat: The Memoirs of Dmitril J. Abrikossow, 1964; Russia's Eastward Expansion, 1964; Korea and Manchuria between Russia and Japan, 1895-1904: The Observations of Sir Ernest Satow, 1968; The d'Anethan Dispatches from Japan 1894-1910: The Observations of Baron Albert d'Anethan, 1967; Trading under Sail off Japan 1860-1899: The Recollections of Captain John Baxter Will, Sailing Master and Pilot, 1968; (handbook) Japanese Diplomatic and Consular Officials in Russia, 1968; (handbook) Russian Diplomatic and Consular Officials in East Asia, 1968; War and Revolution: Excerpts from the Letters and Diaries of the Countess Olga Poutlatine, 1971; Japanese Foreign Policy on the Eve of the Pacific War: A Soviet View by Leonid N. Kutakou, 1972; Home: Tallahassee, Fla. Died Jan. 5, 1979.

LENZEN, THEODORE LOUIS, oil co. exec.; b. San Jose, Cal., Aug. 5, 1905; s. Louis Theodore and Rose Helen (Hennessy) L.; A.B. summa cum laude, Stanford, 1927, E.E., 1928; m. Geneva Christmas, June 20, 1931; children—Jean, Louis. Engr., Standard Oil Co. Cal., 1928-38, engring. work for fgn. interests, Europe, Middle East, 1938-39, asst. to mgr. fgn. producing dept. 1940-44, asst. to v.p., 1945-46, gen. mgr. Eastern Hemisphere operations, 1947-51, vice pres., 1952-70, dir., 1955-70; dir. Cal. Tex. Oil Corp., 1947-70 Mem. Phi Beta Kappa, Tau Beta Phi. Clubs: Bohemian, Pacific Union (San Francisco); Burlingame (Cal.) Country. Home: Atherton, Calif. Died Oct. 24, 1977.

LEO, BROTHER AMANDUS (WILLIAM PATRICK CALL), coll. dean; b. N.Y.C., Feb. 14, 1901; s. William and Mary Elizabeth (Casey) C.; B.S.C.E., Manhattan Coll., Bronx, N.Y., 1928, postgrad., 1929; student Columbia, 1929-32; D.Sc., Catholic U. Am., 1958. Teacher, grammar and high sch., 1920-28; instr. civil engring. Manhattan Coll., 1928-29, asst. prof., 1929-30, prof. and dean, 1930-61, dean engring. emeritus, 1961-80; mem. Inst. Bros. of Christian Schools (religious teaching congregation). Trustee, Manhattan Coll., 1934-54, Assn. Engring. Deans of N.Y. State; mem. Mayor's Adv. Planning Bd., Borough of Bronx, N.Y.C., chmn., 1944-63; chmn. grievance com. Concrete Industry Bd., N.Y.C.; mem. mayor's adv. council spl. com. on tech. and profl. manpower. Licensed engr., N.Y. Fellow N.Y. Acad. Scis., ASCE, mem. Am. Soc. Engring. Edn., Am. Soc. Metals, ASTM, Highway Research Bd., Am. Concrete Inst., Am. Road Builders Assn., Soc. Profl. Engrs., Manhattan Engrs., Tau Beta Pi, Chi Epsilon. Club: K.C. Address: Bronx, N.Y. Died Apr. 8, 1980.

LEONARD, JOY LUTHER, economist; b. Spring Hills, Champaign County, O., Feb. 28, 1884; s. Joseph Benjamin and Ella Norah (Carlo) L.; A.B., Ohio Wesleyan U., 1907; A.M., Yale, 1911, Ph.D., 1929; m. Vera Annette Price, June 25, 1916; 1 son, Luther Harry. Asso. prof. of history and the social sciences, also athletic dir., Hendrix Coll., Conway, Ark., 1907-09; instr. in economics and athletic dir., Birmingham (Birmingham-Southern) Coll., 1909-10; instr. in econ., Yale, 1911-13; prof. econ., Wabash Coll., Crawfordsville, Ind., 1913-28, mgr. Wabash Coll. endowment campaign, 1920-21; supply prof. econ., Trinity Coll., Hartford, Conn., 1928-29; prof. banking and finance, U. of So. Calif., 1929-30, prof. and head dept. of econ., 1930-50, prof. emeritus, 1950; visiting prof. Harding Coll. 1950-52; visiting prof. Boston Univ. summer sch., 1933. Chmn. arbitration bd. Los Angeles Garment Strike, 1933; chmn. Los Angeles Regional Labor Bd., Nat. Labor Bd., 1933-35; chmn. Pres. Roosevelt's Commn. on Labor Conditions in Imperial Valley, 1934; mem. mediation bd. Pacific Coast Longshore Strike, 1934; pub. panel mem. Tenth Regional War Labor Bd., 1943-45. Mem. American Economic Association, Pacific Coast Econ. Assn., Southern Calif. Econ. Assn. (past pres.), Economists Nat. Com. on Monetary Policy, Am. Arbitration Assn., Am. Assn. Univ. Profs., Southern California Associates (secretary-treasurer), Phi Kappa Phi, Beta Gamma Sigma, Alpha Pi Zeta, Alpha Sigma Phi, Acacia, Order of Artus. Mason. K.P. Reviser and editor: Money, 1930; Banking, 1930. Address: Culver City, Cal. Retired. *

LEONARD, WILLIAM DANIEL, drama critic, columnist; b. Chgo., Aug. 24, 1912; s. Edward Francis and Nellie (Fraser) L.; student Northwestern U., 1934-36; m. Evelyn Otten, May 3, 1941; children—Gretchen, Regina. With Chgo. Evening Post, 1929-32, Chgo. Am., 1932-37; with Chgo. Jour. Commerce, 1937-51, drama critic, 1941-51; with Chgo. Tribune, 1951-77, drama critic, from 1965. Recipient Page One award Chgo. Newspaper Guild, 1950. Mem. St. Louis Browns Fan Club. Editor Chgo. Stagebill Yearbook, 1947. Home: Chicago, Ill. Died Jan. 6, 1977.

LEONID, painter; b. St. Petersburg, Russia, June 6, 1896; s. Gustave Berman and Lydia (Manassevitch) Berman; student, University of St. Petersburg, 1912, Acad. Ranson, Paris, 1919-20; married Sylvia Marlowe, January 6, 1948. Became United States citizen, 1951. Known as Leonid, from 1925. Exhibited Paris, Brussels, London, from 1930; 1st U.S. show, Julien Levy Gallery, 1933, private shows Washington, Boston, Phila., Mpls., Dulacher Gallery, N.Y., and others. Work included in N.Y. Metropolitan Mus., Mus. Modern Art, Wadsworth Athaneum, Hartford, Conn., N.Y. Mus., Phillips Gallery, Mus. Fine Art, Houston; others. Home: New York, N.Y. Died Oct. 1, 1977.

LE PAGE, SAMUEL MAYNARD, lecturer, educator, clergyman; b. Cumberland, Ohio, Sept. 28, 1884; s. Peter Marquin and Leah Jane (Downey) L.; grad. Cumberland (Ohio) High School, 1904; A.B., Ohio Wesleyan University, 1909; S.T.B., Boston University, 1911, Ph.D., 1915; graduate student, University of Berlin, 1913-14; m. Rosette Pearl Jones, of South Hamilton, Mass., Jan. 29, 1912; 1 son, Clifford Bennett. Ordained M.E. ministry, 1911; pastor Ray, N.Dak., 1912-13, Charleston, O., 1914-15, Tallmadge, 1915-18, Salineville, 1918-20, Holliston, Mass., 1920-22, Arlington Hgts., Mass., 1922-23; prof. history, Ia. Wesleyan Coll., 1923-25, Ottawa U., 1925-31, Penn Coll., Ia., 1931-32; pastor Byfield Parish since 1934. Member contest committee League of Nations Assn. Mem. National Economic League, Am. Geog. Soc., Conseil Historique et Heraldique de France, Pi Gamma Mu. Republican. Mason, Odd Fellow, K.P. Author: The Relationship Between the Earlier Experiences of St. Augustine and His Later Religious Conceptions, 1915; A History of Ottawa University, 1928; Laying the Corner Stone, 1929; also articles in mags. Home: South Byfield, Mass. *

LERNER, DANIEL, social scientist, educator; b. N.Y.C., Nov. 3, 1917; s. Louis and Yetta (Swiger) L.; A.B., N.Y. U., 1938, M.A., 1939, Ph.D., 1948; m. Jean Weinstein, May 16, 1947; children—Louise, Thomas, Amy. Instr. modern European history and lit., 1939-42; European rep. Library of Congress Mission, 1946-47; exec. sec. and research dir. internat. studies project, 1947-53; acting prof. sociology Stanford, 1951-53; vis. prof. sociology Columbia, 1951; prof. sociology Mass. Inst. Tech., 1953-78, Ford prof. sociology and internat. communications, 1958-78, chmn. polit. and social sci. dept., 1963-64; dir. Institut de Recherches Sociales, Paris, France, 1955-65; vis. prof. U. Paris (Sorbonne). Served to capt. AUS, 1942-46; chief editor intelligence br. Psychol. Warfare Div., SHAEF; chief intelligence Info. Control Div., Office of Mil. Govt. U.S. Decorated Bronze Star, Purple Heart; Palmes Academiques, officier d'Academie (France). Fellow Conf. Sci., Philosophy and Religion; mem. Internat. Soc. Polit. Psychology (a founder), Am. Sociol. Soc., Soc. for Psychol. Study Social Issues (life), Am. Polit. Sci. Assn., World, Am. assns. pub. opinion research, Am. Psychol. Assn. Author: Psychological Warfare Against Nazi Germany, 1949; Propaganda in War and Crisis, 1951; (with H.D. Lasswell) The Policy Sciences, 1951; The Nazi Elite, 1951; (with Raymond Aron) LaQuerrelle de la CED, 1956; France Defeats E.D.C., 1957; The Passing of Traditional Society, 1958; The Human Meaning of the Social Sciences, 1959; Evidence and Inference, 1960; Quantity and Quality, 1961; Parts and Wholes, 1963; Cause and Effect, 1965; (with H.D. Lasswell) World Revolutionary Elites, 1965; (with Wilbur Schramm) Communication and Change in the Developing Countries, 1967; (with Morton Gorden) Euratlantica; Changing Perspectives of The European Elites, 1969; (with Wilbur Schramm) Communications and Change: The Last Ten Years-and the Next, 1976; Values and Development: Appraising Asian Experience, 1976; (with L.M. Nelson) Communication Research-A Half-Century Appraisal, 1977; (with Harold D. Lasswell and Hans Speier) Propaganda and Communication in World History, 3 vols., 1979; editor: M.I.T. Studies in Comparative Politics, 1965-75. Home: Santa Cruz, Calif. Died May 1, 1980.

LERNER, I. MICHAEL, geneticist, educator; b. Harbin, Manchuria, May 15, 1910; s. Michael and Cecelia (Sudja) L.; B.S.A., U. B.C., 1931, M.S.A., 1932, Sc.D. (hon.), 1962; Ph.D., U. Calif., 1936; D.Sc. (hon.), U. Edinburgh, 1973; m. Ruth A. Stuart, June 9, 1937. Came to U.S., 1933, naturalized, 1942. Instr. poultry husbandry U. Calif. at Berkeley, 1936-41, asst. prof., 1941-46, asso. prof., 1946-51, prof., geneticist in expt. sta., 1951-58, chmn. dept. genetics, 1958-63, prof. genetics, 1958-73, prof. emeritus, 1973-77; research geneticist Inst. Personality Assessment and Research, 1970-76; Canadian Club lectr. U.B.C., 1950; specializing in population and behavior genetics, selection, evolution. Guggenheim fellow, Edinburgh, Scotland, 1948, Pavia, Italy, 1953, 57; fellow Stanford Center Advanced Study Behavorial Sciences, 1967-68; recipient Poultry Sci. Research prize, 1937, Belling prize, 1940, Borden award and medal, 1951, Mendel Meml. medal Czechoslovakian Acad. Sci., 1965, Weldon Meml. medal Oxford U., 1969. Fellow Eugenics Soc., Poultry Sci. Assn., A.A.A.S.; mem. Nat. Acad. Scis., Am. Soc. Naturalists (v.p. 1957), Am. Philos. Soc., Soc. Study Evolution (pres. 1964), Italian Soc. Genetics, Permanent Internat. Com. Genetics (sec. 1953-58, U.S. rep. 1958-63), Am. Acad. Arts and Scis., Am. Soc. Human Genetics, Am. Genetics Assn., Acad. Georgofili Florence (fgn. mem.), Am. Eugenics Soc., Behavior Genetics Soc. Author: Population Genetics and Animal Improvement, 1950; Genetic Homeostasis, 1954, 70; The Genetic Basis of Selection, 1958, 74; (with H. P. Donald) Modern Developments in Animal Breeding, 1966; Heredity, Evolution and Society, 1968, 2d edit. (with W.J. Libby) 1976; also tech. articles biol. jours. Translator, editor The Rise and Fall of T.D. Lysenko, 1969. Editor: Evolution, 1959-61. Home: Berkeley, Cal. Died June 13, 1977.

LERNER, MICHAEL, bus. exec.; b. Phila., Sept. 5, 1891; s. Charles and Sophia (Eisenberg) L.; student pub. schs., Bklyn.; Sc.D., U. Miami, 1952; m. Helen Samuels, Nov. 10, 1921. One of founders Lorraine Stores Corp. (now Lerner Stores Corp.), 1917, various exec. positions, 1917-40, retired 1940. Collector specimens game and fish Am. Mus. Natural History; organizer, head 7 sci. expdns. to Cape Breton, N.S., Bimini, Bahamas, Australia-New Zealand, Peru-Chile, others, 1937-41; established Lerner Marine Lab. as field sta., Bimini, 1947; devel. recreational fishing tackle for overseas servicemen; devel. emergency life saving fishing gear adapted to rafts and life boats for U.S. Govt.; lectr. with Mrs. Lerner for U.S.O. overseas. Trustee Am. Mus. Natural History. Recipient Presdl. Certificate of Merit; named hon. citizen N.S., also France; various citations, scrolls, honors; decorated comendador Al Merito (Chile). Mem. Internat. Game Fish Assn. (organizer, founder 1939; pres. 1951-52); hon. mem. assns. and clubs in U.S., France, Australia, Panama, Scandinavian, South Am. nations. Clubs: Explorers, Circumnavigators (N.Y.C.); Westchester Country. Home: Miami, Fla. Died Apr. 16, 1978.

LERT, RICHARD JOHANNES, conductor; b. Vienna, Austria, Sept. 19, 1885; s. Adolf and Libussa (Bruell) L.; student Vienna Conservatory, 1900-04, U. Vienna, 1904-08; m. Vicki Baum, July, 1916; children—Wolfgang, Peter. Came to U.S., 1931, naturalized, 1938. Comdr. orchs. in Duesseldorf, Germany, 1910-12, Darmstadt, Germany, 1912-16, Frankfurt, Germany, 1915-16, Kiel, Germany, 1916-17, Hannover, Germany, 1917-23, Mannheim, Germany, 1923-28, Breslau, Germany, 1928-29, Berlin State Opera, 1928-32, Hollywood (Cal.) Bowl, 1932-42, Pasadena (Cal.) Symphony, 1936—, guest condr. in Paris, Oslo, Washington, Mexico City, San Francisco, Los Angeles; condr. Conductor's Workshop, Cal. and Vienna, summers 1956—. Bd. dirs. Am. Symphony Orch. League, Young Musicians Found. Los Angeles; hon. bd. dirs. Music Acad. West, Santa Barbara, Cal.; adviser Huntington Hartford Found. Recipient Arthur Noble award City Pasadena, 1951, Concert Artists Guild award, 1959, Golden Baton award Am. Symphony Orch. League, 1964; comdr's cross Order of Merit (German Republic). Home: Pasadena CA.

LESAGE, JEAN, prime minister; b. Montreal, Can., June 10, 1912; s. X. and Cecile (Cote) L.; B.A., Quebec Sem., 1931; LL.L., Laval U., Que., 1938; LL.D., Bishop's University, Lennoxville, 1961; doctorate honoris causa, University Montreal, 1961; m. Corinne Legarde, July 2, 1938; children—Jules, Rene, Marie, Raymond. Mem. Canadian Ho. of Commons, 1945, 49-53, 54-58; leader Liberal Party, Quebec, 1958-70; prime minister of Province of Quebec, 1960-66; parliamentary asst. to Sec. of State for External Affairs, Canadian Govt., 1951-53, to Minister of Finance, 1953; Minister of Resources and Development, 1953; Minister of No. Affairs and Nat. Resources, Ottawa, Canada, 1953-57; minister of federal provincial affairs, 1961-70, also minister of the Department of Finance; practice of law, Crown atty., 1939-44, vice chmn. Com. on Banking and Commerce, chmn. Com. on Old Age Security. Canadian rep. to UN Gen. Assembly, 1950, v.p. Canadian delegation, 1952; pres. Canadian Delegation to ECOSOC, Geneva, 1951, N.Y.C., 1952; pres. UN Tech. Assistance Conf., Paris, 1952. Clubs: University (Que. and Ottawa); Garrison (Que.); Reform

(Que. and Montreal). Roman Catholic. Home: Quebec, Can. Died Aug. 11, 1980.

LESCOHIER, DON DIVANCE, prof. economics; b. Detroit, Mich., Feb. 20, 1883; s. Alexander and Minnie (Judge) L.; A.B., Albion Coll., 1905, A.M., 1907; Ph.D., U. of Wis., 1919; m. Ethel Mae Robinson, Dec. 7, 1905 (died Oct. 9, 1946); children—Eric Robinson, Josephine Jean, Philip Robinson, Roger Paul; m. 2d, Mary E. Amend, Aug. 21, 1948. Spl. agt. Wis. Dept. of Labor, 1908; expert, Minn. Dept. of Labor, 1909-11; chief statistician Minn. Dept. Labor and Industry, 1911-17; also prof, social sciences, Hamline U., 1911-18, and lecturer in economics, U. of Minn., 1912-15; supt. Minneapolis Pub. Employment Office, 1917-18; prof. economics, U. of Wis., since 1918. Collaborator, farm labor investigations, U.S. Dept. Agr., 1920, 21; exec. sec. Wis. Citizens Com. on Unemployment, 1930-31; dist. supervisor U.S. Bur. Labor Statistics, 1932; cons. Works Progress Administration, New York City, 1238-39. Fellow American Statistical Association; mem. Am. Econ. Association, American Association for Labor Legislation, American Management Association, Phi Beta Kappa, Sigma Nu, Phi Kappa Phi, Delta Sigma Rho, Alpha Kappa Delta, Artus, Conglist. Author several books relating to field; also contributor articles on economics. Home: Madison, Wis. *

LESHER, CARL EUGENE, engineer, economist; b. La Junta, Colo., Nov. 20, 1885; s. David and Rosa Clair (Barnes) L., grad. Colo. Sch. of Mines, 1908; m. Lois Quick, Mar. 1911 (died 1937); children—Carl E., Barbara; m. 2d, Lois F. McCombs, 1939. With U.S. Geol. Survey, Washington, D.C., 1910-17; dir. statistics U.S. Fuel Adminstrn., 1917-18; again with U.S. Geol. Survey, 1919; dir. Bur. of Economics, Nat. Coal Assn., 1920; editor Coal Age, New York, 1920-23; chief engr. U.S. Coal Commn., 1923; with Pittsburgh Coal Co., 1924-50, asst. to pres. until 1927, exec. v.p., 1927-38; president Disco Company, successor to Pittsburgh Coal Carbonization Co., 1939-50; pres. Lesher & Associates, Inc. Mem. American Institute of Mining and Metallurgy Engineers, American Economic Association, Engineering Society Western Pa. Methodist. Clubs: Shannopin Country, Duquesne. Author of Govt. repts. on coal covering years 1915-19, also Geol. Survey repts. on coke and by-products for same period; History of Coal Distribution (3 vols.); Prices of Coal and Coke (1913-19), 1920. Contbr. to "What Coal Commission Found," 1925; "Marketing of Minerals," 1925, and technical papers on low-temperature carbonization, Am. Inst. Mining and Metall. Engrs. Home: Pittsburgh, Pa. *

LESLIE, JOHN WOODWORTH, steel corporation executive; born Chicago, Ill., May 1, 1886; s. John Hampton and Sally (Woodworth) L.; A.B., U. of Wis., 1907; m. Alma Bertles, Aug. 29, 1908 (dec.); children—Katharine, John Hampton, II: m. 2d, Elizabeth Allen, Apr. 6, 1940. Pres. Signode Corp. (formerly Signode Steel Strapping Co.), Chgo., 1916-49, chmn, bd., 1949-62, chmn. exec. com., 1962-64, hon. chmn. bd., 1964—; dir. of Signode, Ltd., London. Trustee Ill. Inst. Technology, Armour Research Found.; hon. dir. Council Profit Sharing Industries; dir. World Press Inst.; chmn. Profit-Sharing Research Found.; dir. Community Hosp., Evanston. Exec. com. of internat. com. YMCA of U.S. and Can.; hon. chmn. International Mass Education Movement. In 1917 enlisted in the AUS, commd. 2d lt. AS, 1918. Mem. Alpha Delta Phi. Clubs: Glen View Golf; University, Tavern, Commercial, Mid-America (Chgo.). Home: Evanston, Ill. *

LESSER, LAWRENCE STANLEY, lawyer; b. N.Y.C., Feb. 16, 1907; s. Jacob Joseph and Rae Virginia (Goldstein) L.; student Ethical Culture Sch., N.Y.C., 1916-24; A.B., Yale, 1928; LL.B. cum laude, Harvard, 1931; m. Frances A. Doolittle, Apr. 28, 1939; children—Margaret Doolittle (Mrs. Robert C. Hamm erling), George Hulett. Admitted to N.Y. bar, 1932, D.C. bar, 1946; mem. Pehle & Lesser and successor firms, 1946-60; mem. Phillips, Nizer, Benjamin, Krim & Ballon, 1960-68, counsel, 1968-77; legal asst. Joint Legis. Com. to Investigate Affairs City N.Y., 1931-32; spl. dep. asst. dist. atty., N.Y. County, 1934-37; atty., spl. counsel SEC, 1937-42; spl. asst. to gen. counsel for Treasury, chief counsel procurement div., asst. chief counsel Bur. Internal Revenue, Treasury Dept., 1942-46; asst. exec. dir. U.S. War Refugee Bd., 1945-46; lectr. Coll. Law, Am. U., 1951-56, 62. Mem. Internat., D.C., Am., N.Y.C. bar assns., Am. Law Inst., Am. Soc. Internat. Law. Clubs: Lawyers, Harvard (N.Y.C.): Corinthian Yacht, Cottagers' (Cape May, N.J.); Yale, Cosmos, Harvard (Washington). Editor: Harvard Law Rev., 1930-31. Address: Washington, D.C. Died June 20, 1979; interred Lake View Cemetery, Cleveland, Ohio.

LESSER, SOL, motion picture exec.; b. Spokane, Feb. 17, 1890; D.F.A., U. Redlands, 1973; M.Film Scis., U. So. Calif.; children—Mrs. Marjorie Fasman, Julian. Co-founder Fox West Coast theatres (name now Mann Theatres), later becoming producer; became exec. charge feature prodn. R.K.O. Radio, 1941; creator Sol Lesser Prodns., Inc., 1945; founder Standard Theatres, Inc., 1947, Prin. Theater Corp. Am., Prin. Mgmt. Co., Prin. Securities Corp.; producer numerous feature pictures including 11 Tarzan features, Stage Door Canteen, Our Town, The Red House, Oliver Twist, Kon-Tiki. Prof. creative motion picture, profl. TV prodn. Sch. Cinema, U. So. Calif. Bd. dirs. Motion Picture and TV Relief Fund, Permanent Charities Com. Motion Picture Industry, Palm Springs Desert Mus.; founder-mem. Los Angeles County Mus. Art, Los Angeles Music Center. Recipient Jean Hersholt Motion Picture Acad. humanitarian award, 1960, also Oscar award for Kon-Tiki; Silver platter Sch. Performing Arts, U. So. Calif., 1973; named Patriarch of Theatre Industry, Nat. Assn. Theatre Owners, 1976. Clubs: Hillcrest Country; Tamarisk Country (Palm Springs, Calif.). Home: Los Angeles CA. *

LESTER, EDWARD, lawyer; b. Hope, Ark., Nov. 18, 1921; s. Chester D. and Mary (White) L.; A.B., Hendrix Coll., 1943; LL.D., U. Ark., 1949; m. Mary Evelyn Markham, June 12, 1944; children—James Edward, Vernon Markham. Admitted to Ark. bar, 1949; partner firm Wright, Lindsey, Jennings, Lester & Shults, Little Rock, 1950-65, Lester & Shults, Little Rock, 1965-79. Pres. Ark. Conf. Local Bar Assns., 1960-61; vice chmn. Ark. Turnpike Authority. Mem. Ark. Ho. of Reps., 1949. Chmn. bd. trustees Hendrix Coll. Mem. Am., Ark. bar assns., Am. Judicature Soc. Home: Little Rock, Ark. Died Apr. 6, 1979.

LÉVECQUE, MARCEL AMÉDÉE, mfg. co. exec.; b. Paris, July 15, 1922; s. Anatole Louis and Marguerite Adéle (Robineau) L.; Engring. degree Conservatoire National des Arts et Métiers, 1945; m. Régine Louise Lardeux, Mar. 11, 1944; children—Aliette, Jean-Luc, Marc. Asst. dir. metals lab. Laboratoire du Bâtiment et des Travaux Publics, Paris, 1941-42; asst. to tech. dir. Manufacture Nationale de Porcelaine de Sèvres (France), 1942-44, chief chemist, 1944-47; research engr. L'Office National d'Etudes et de Recherches Aéronautiques, Paris, 1947-50; research engr. Saint-Gobain Industries, Neuilly-sur-Seine, France, 1950-52, head research group, 1952-56, dir. devel. dept. for glasses, 1956-60, dir. research and devel. dept. of plate glass div., 1960-63, tech. mgr. Société d'Etude pour le Développement de la Fibre de Verre, 1963-68, tech. and research and devel. dir. of insulation, strand and asbestos-cement div., 1969-76; sr. v.p., chief technology Certain Teed Corp., Valley Forge, Pa., 1976-77, exec. v.p., 1977-78, pres., chief exec. officer, 1978—, chief of technology, 1977-78, chmn. operating com., 1978—, also dir. Recipient Prix du Cercle Republicain, 1945, Prix de la Société d'Encouragement pour l'Industrie et le Commerce, 1957; decorated chevalier du Mérite Industriel et Commercial, 1962, chevalier du Mérite National, 1974; prix de l'Energie, 1975. Patentee fiber glass insulation (30). Address: Valley Forge, Pa. Deceased.

LEVENE, GEORGE, cons. radiologist; b. N.Y.C., Aug. 10, 1897; s. Samuel and Celia (Newman) L.; M.D., Boston U., 1925; m. Helen Matthews, Jan. 9, 1937. Asst., Boston U. Sch. Medicine, 1925-31, instr., 1931-33, asst. prof. radiology, 1933-38, asso. prof. radiology, 1938-45, prof. radiology, 1945-62, prof. radiology emeritus, 1962-76; chief dept. radiology Mass. Meml. Hosp., 1932-62, cons. radiologist, 1962-76; radiologist Martha's Vineyard Hosp., 1962-72, cons. radiologist, 1972-76; cons. radiologist Sturdy Meml. Hosp., Attleboro, Mass. Recipient sci. awards AMA, Am. Roentgen Ray Soc., Internat. Congress Radiology, Radiol. Soc. N. Am. Fellow Am. Coll. Radiology; mem. Mass. Med. Soc., Am., N.E. roentgen ray socs., Radiol. Soc. N. Am., Am. Cancer Soc., Am., Mass. heart assns., AAAS, AAUP, Panama Radiol. Soc., Sigma Xi, Alpha Omega Alpha. Author articles on signs and methods in x-ray diagnosis. Inventor med. apparatus for instrn. x-ray appearances in heart disease. Home: Vineyard Haven, Mass. Died Apr. 19, 1976.

LEVENE, RICARDO (LEVENE), Argentine lawyer, historian and educator; b. Buenos Aires, 1885; s. Jacinto Gabriel Levene and Rosa Sassone; ed. Colegio Nacional de Buenos Aires, B.A., 1901; Faculty of Law and Social Sciences, U. of Buenos Aires, Ph.D., 1906; m. Amelia Rosa Peyloubet; 1 son, Ricardo. prof. of law, dir. history of law, Institut. Faculty of Law, Univ. of Buenos Aires; pres. U. of La Plata; pres., 2d Internat. American History Congress, Buenos Aires, 1937. Honorary prof. of Universities of San Marcos, Lima, Santiago de Chile and Rio de Janeiro; Pres., mem. Junta de Historia y Numismática Am., now Academia Nacional de la Historia; Academia de Ciencias Económicas; Academia de Filosofía y Letras; Academia de Derecho y Ciencias Sociales. Author: Ensayo sobre la Revolución de Mayo y Mariano Moreno; Historia del Derecho Argentina; Mitre y los estudios historicós en la Argentina, and numerous other books. Address: Buenos Aires, Argentina. *

LEVENE, SAM, actor; b. Russia, Aug. 28, 1905; s. Harry and Beth S. (Weiner) Levine; came to U.S., 1907, naturalized, 1937; student Am. Acad. Dramatic Arts, 1925-27, U. S.C., summer 1940; m. Constance Hoffman, 1953 (div.); 1 son, Joseph Kenneth. First Broadway appearance in Wall Street, 1927; other starring roles include Jarnegan, 1928, Street Scene, 1929, This Man's Town, 1930, Wonder Boy, 1931, Dinner At Eight, 1932, Yellow Jack, 1934, Spring Song, 1934, Three Men on a Horse (also USO, movies, radio and TV), 1935, 69, Room Service, 1937, Margin for Error, 1939, Grand Guignol Plays, 1943, Sound of Hunting, 1945, Light up the Sky, 1948, 71, Guys and Dolls, 1940 (also London and Las Vegas), The Matchmaker (London), 1954, Hot Corner, 1956, Fair Game, 1957, Make a Million, 1958, Heart Break House, 1959, The Good Soup, 1959, The Devil's Advocate, 1961, Let it Ride, 1961, Seidman and Son, 1962, Cafe Crown, 1964, Last Analysis, 1965, Nathan Weinstein's Daughter, 1966, The Impossible Years, 1966, Don't Drink the Water, 1968, Paris is Out, 1970, Light Up the Sky, 1970, 74, 75, A Dream out of Time, 1970, The Sunshine Boys, 1972, 73, 74, 75, Dreyfus, 1976, The Royal Family, 1976-77, The Merchant, 1977, The Prince of Grand Street, 1978, The Good-bye People, 1978; Goodnight Grandpa, 1979, Horowitz and Mrs. Washington, 1980; films include The Champ, 1979, And Justice for All, 1979, Last Embrace, 1979. Home: New York, N.Y. Died Dec. 28, 1980.

LEVENSON, SAMUEL, humorist; b. N.Y.C., Dec. 28, 1911; s. Hyman and Rebecca (Fishelman) L.; B.A., Bklyn. Coll., 1934, D.H.L., 1976; M.A., Columbia, 1938; L.H.D., St. Francis Coll., 1973; D.H.L., St. John's U., 1978; m. Esther Levine, Dec. 27, 1936; children—Conrad, Emily. Tchr., Abraham Lincoln High Sch., Bklyn., S.J. Tilden High Sch., Bklyn., 1934-46; comedian radio, theatre, TV, 1946-80; star Sam Levenson Show, CBS, 1951; moderator Two for the Money, 1955-56; guest star Ed Sullivan Show; panelist This is Show Business, 1951-54; also Match Game, To Tell The Truth; also several guest appearaces. Bd. dirs. League Sch. Seriously Disturbed Children. Recipient citation of honor N.Y. U. Jewish Culture Found., 1952; citation Anti-Defamation League of B'nai B'rith, 1956; Meritorious Service award Nat. Press Club, 1957; medal of honor Nat. Acad. TV Arts and Scis., 1961; Disting. Service award City of N.Y., 1973; Cultural award State of Israel, 1975; award of merit Lotus Club, 1975; Man of Distinction award S. Shore Child Guidance Assn., L.I., N.Y., 1977, others. Mem. B'nai B'rith (dist. bd. govs.). Author: Everything but Money; Sex and the Single Child, 1969; In One Era and Out the Other, 1973; You Can Say That Again, Sam, 1975; A Time for Innocence, 1976; You Don't Have to be Who's Who to Know What's What, 1979. Address: Neponsit, N.Y. Died Aug. 27, 1980.

LEVENTHAL, ALBERT RICE, publisher; b. N.Y.C., Oct. 30, 1907; s. Philip and Ida F. (Rice) L.; A.B., U. Mich., 1928; m. Janis H. Hilpp, Mar. 14, 1934; children—Barbara, Jane, John Philip. Reporter, Bklyn. Times-Union, 1928-30, Sunday editor, 1930-32; promotion mgr. Simon & Schuster, Inc., N.Y.C., 1933-38, sales mgr., 1938-44, v.p., 1945-52, exec. v.p., 1952-57; pres. Artists & Writers Press div. Western Printing & Lithographing Co., 1958-68; pres. Golden Press, Inc., 1958-68, Am. Heritage Press, 1968-70; group v.p. McGraw-Hill Co., Inc., 1970-72, sr. cons., 1973; pres. Vineyard Books, Inc., 1973-76; partner Sandpiper Press, 1945. Mem. Am. Book Pubs. Council (bd. dirs.), Phi Beta Kappa, Phi Kappa Phi, Zeta Beta Tau. Club: Regency (N.Y.C.). Author: I Wish I'd Said That (pen name Albert Rice), 1934; False Colors, 1941; War: A Photographic History, 1973; Book Publishing in America, 1973. Contbr. articles nat. mags. Home: Mamaroneck, N.Y. Died Jan. 6, 1976; buried Chilmark, Mass.

LEVENTHAL, HAROLD, judge; b. N.Y.C., Jan. 5, 1915; s. Jules Joseph and Sadie (Wolcher) L.; A.B., Columbia U. (Green prize), 1934, LL.B. (Toppan and Ordronaux prizes), 1936; m. Kathryn Kumler, Sept. 18, 1948; children—Philip Henry J., Anne K. Admitted to N.Y. bar, 1936, D.C. bar, 1946; law sec. to Justice Harlan F. Stone, Supreme Ct. U.S., 1936-37, to Justice Stanley Reed, 1938; staff Office of Solicitor Gen., 1938-39; chief of litigation bituminous coal div. U.S. Dept. Interior, 1939-40; asst. gen. counsel OPA, 1940-43; staff Justice Jackson, Nuremberg Trials, 1945-46; exec. officer, task force on ind. regulatory commns. Hoover Commn., 1948; chief counsel OPS, 1951-52; mem. law firm Ginsburg & Leventhal and successor firms, 1946-65; gen. counsel Dem. Nat. Com., 1952-65; judge U.S. Ct. of Appeals, D.C. Circuit, 1965-79; vis. lectr. Yale Law Sch., 1957-62; Regents lectr. U. Calif. at Los Angeles, 1974; Mooers lectr. Am. U., 1975; Sulzbacher lectr. Columbia, 1976; lectr. Notre Dame U. Law Sch., London, summer 1979. Served to lt. comdr. USCGR, 1943-46. Recipient Columbia U. Law Sch. Alumni Assn. medal for excellence, 1979. Mem. Fed. (past mem. nat. council), Am., D.C. bar assns., Nat. Lawyers Club, Phi Beta Kappa. Club: Cosmos (Washington). Author articles in legal jours. Contbr. to history OPA. Home: Washington, D.C. Died Nov. 20, 1979; buried Arlington Nat. Cemetery.

LEVERAGE, (CARL) HENRY, author; b. London, Eng., 1885; s. of John Henry and Susie (Grove) L.; brought to U.S. in infancy; Denver Manual Training High Sch.; E.E., U. of Colo., 1906; m. Mary Alice Collins, of Middletown, N.Y., July 31, 1920. Elec. engr., Magnetic Transmission Co., New York, 1912. Inventor of various elec. devices for magnetic transmission on automobile. Mem. Authors' League America, The Writers, South Shore Yacht Club. Author: Whispering Wires, 1918; The White Cipher, 1919; Where Dead Men Walk, 1920; The Shepherd of the Sea, 1920; The Ice Pilot, 1921; Phantom Alibi, 1926; Purple Limited, 1927; also many serial novels and nearly 200 short stories. Co-Author: Whispering Wires (play), 1922.Address: New York, N.Y.*

LEVET, RICHARD HARRINGTON, U.S. dist. judge; b. Geneva, N.Y., Jan. 24, 1894; s. Alfred Barlow and Jennie Alice (Harrington) L.; A.B., Colgate U., 1916, A.M., 1917; J.D., N.Y. U., 1925; m. Ida C. Guldi, Aug. 21, 1918; 1 dau., Eleanor Harrington (Mrs. Thomas J. Harriman) L. Tchr. high schs., 1916-26; admitted to N.Y. bar, 1926, practiced in White Plains, 1926-56; U.S. dist. judge So. Dist. N.Y., 1956-80; instr. law N.Y. U. Sch. Commerce, 1946-51. Mem. Westchester County Bd. Suprs., 1938-56, chmn., 1945-46. Mem. Am., N.Y. State Westchester County (ex-counsel), Congregationalist. Author: Ambrose L. Jordan, Lawyer, 1975. White Plains bar assns., Phi Beta Kappa. Home: White Plains, N.Y. Died Feb. 11, 1980.

LEVI, WENDELL MITCHELL, lawyer, naturalist; b. Sumter, S.C., Sept. 28, 1891; s. Mitchell and Estella (D'Ancona) L.; A.B., Coll. Charleston, 1921, Litt.D., 1968; Ph.B., U. Chgo., 1915, J.D. cum laude, 1915; m. Bertha Cecil London, June 20, 1921; children—Estella D'Ancona (Mrs. Robert P. Kirchheimer), Patricia London (Mrs. Henry D. Barnett), Wendell Mitchell. Admitted to S.C. bar, 1915; pres. Palmetto Pigeon Plant, 1923-56, chmn. bd., from 1956; pres. Wen-le Corp., Levi Pub. Co., Inc. Merit badge counselor Boy Scouts Am., from 1934, mem. council exec. bd. Pee Dee area; v.p. Sumter County Community Chest, 1954, gen. chmn. drive, 1952-53; v.p. United Appeal Bd., 1955. Bd. dirs. Carolinas United Community Services, from 1957. Commd. 1st lt. inf., Ft. Oglethorpe O.T.C., 1917; spl. duty in charge pigeon sect. Signal Corps, U.S. Army, 1917-18; capt. comdg. Co. L, 323d Inf., 81st Div.; with A.E.F., Vosges and Meuse-Argonne, 1918-19. Recipient Cross of Mil. Service U.D.C., 1920. Founder bird egg collection Charleston (S.C.) Mus., 1910. Named First Man of Year, Internat. Fedn. Am. Homing Pigeons, 1968; recipient testimonial Los Angeles Pigeon Club, 1971. Mem. Am., S.C., Sumter County (pres. 1970-71) bar assns., Nat. Pigeon Assn. (pres. 1931-33, recipient First Hall of Fame award, 1958, Nat. Pigeon Assn. Service award 1967), Am. Pigeon Club, Am. Carneau Assn. (pres. 1942). V.F.W. (comdr. Sumter County post 1946, dept. S.C. 1948-49, chmn. nat. membership com. 1949-50), Am. Poultry Hist. Soc. (life mem.), S.C. Camellia Soc. (pres. 1954), Am. Legion, Alumni Assn. Coll. Charleston (hon. life). Mason (32 deg., Shriner), Kiwanian (Legion of Honor 1972), Elk. Author: The Pigeon, 1941, rev., 1957-63, 69, 74; Making Pigeons Pay, 1946, rev. 1955, 58, 68, 72; The Visible Pigeon, An Introduction to the World of Birds, 1963; Ency. of Pigeon Breeds, 1965. Editor question and answer dept. Am. Pigeon Jour., 1927-75. Home: Sumter SC.

LEVIN, RUBEN, editor; b. Warsaw, Poland, Aug. 2, 1902; s. Benjamin D. and Ida (Gochlik) L.; brought to U.S., 1904, naturalized, 1917; B.A., U. Wis., 1930; m. Bertha Greenberg, June 7, 1931; children—Hilda Tanenholtz (dec.), David A., Jonathan H. Reporter, copyreader on various dailies, 1924-38; writer Labor Newspaper, 1938-81, mgr., 1953-81, editor, 1953-81. Recipient Achievement awards U. Wis. Journalism Sch., Sidney Hillman Found., Internat. Labor Press Assn., Eugene V. Debs Found.; named Dean of U.S. Labor Editors, Internat. Labor Press Assn. Mem. Indsl. Relations Research Assn., Assn. R.R. Editors (pres.), Am. Newspaper Guild. Democrat. Jewish. Contbr. articles to profl. jours., Grolier-Americana Ann. Ency. Yearbook. Home: Chevy Chase, Md. Died Jan. 29, 1981.

LEVINE, IRVING ABRAHAM, judge; b. Washington, July 10, 1924; s. Benjamin and Minnie (Cohen) L.; LL.B., George Washington U., 1949; m. Shirley Routhenstein, Sept. 10, 1947; children—Susan Joy, Karen Beth. Admitted to D.C. bar, 1950, Md. bar, 1955; mem. firm Chasen & Levine, Washington, Md., 1952-66; judge Md. Tax Ct., 1965-67, 6th Jud. Circuit Ct. Md., 1967-72; asso. justice Md. Ct. Appeals, Annapolis, 1972-78; professorial lectr. Am. U. Sch. Law, 1971-74. Del. Md. Democratic Conv. 1960; mem. Md. Dem. Central Com., 1962-65. Served with USAAF, 1943-45. Mem. Am., Md., Montgomery County (Md.), D.C. bar assns., Nat. Conf. Appellate Judges, Am. Judicature Soc., Nu Beta Epsilon. Jewish. Clubs: Masons, B'nai B'rith. Home: Bethesda, Md. Died Oct. 2, 1978.

LEVINE, ISAAC DON, writer; b. Mozir, Russia, Feb. 1, 1892; s. Don and Sarah (Maloff) L.; came to U.S., 1911; grad. Westport High Sch., Kansas City, 1914; m. Mary Leavitt; 1 son, Robert V.; m. 2d, Ruth Newman, Dec. 14, 1936. Contbr. spl. articles to Kansas City Star, 1914; became editor fgn. news dept. N.Y. Tribune, 1917; fgn. corr. Chgo. Daily News, 1919-21, Hearst newspapers, 1922-24; mng. editor Book League Am., 1928-29. European dir. Am. Com. for Liberation Peoples of Russia, Munich, Germany, 1951-52. Hon. mem. staff and faculty U.S. Army Command and Gen. Staff Coll., Ft. Leavenworth. Recipient Freedom Found. medal. Club: Overseas Press (founder mem.) (N.Y.C.). Author: The Russian Revolution, 1917; Resurrected Nations, 1919; Man Lenin, 1924; Stalin, 1931; (with V. Zenzinov) The Road to Oblivion, 1931; Red Smoke, 1932; Mitchell, Pioneer of Air Power (biography of General Billy Mitchell), 1943; Stalin's Great Secret, 1956; The Mind of An Assssin, 1959; I Rediscover Russia, 1964; Intervention, 1969; Eyewitness to History (autobiography), 1973; Hands Off the Panama Canal, 1976. Transcribed Yashka, autobiography of Maria Botchkareva, Commander of Russian Women's Battalion of Death, 1918. Compiler: Letters from Russian Prisons, 1925. Editor: Willy-Nicky Letters (Kaiser-Czar corr.), 1920; Out of the Night, by Jan Valtin, 1941. Collaborator of Gen. Walter G. Krivitsky, 1939; collaborated with Oksana Kosenkina, Russian school tchr. in publ. of her story. Editor: Plain Talk, 1946-50. Address: Waldorf, Md. Died Feb. 15, 1981.

LEVINSON, BERNARD HIRSH, lawyer; b. Austin, Tex., Sept. 2, 1907; s. Samuel and Rebecca (Lewin) L.; B.A. with high honors, U. Cin., 1929; J.D., Harvard, 1932; m. Carlyn Virginia Krupp, Dec. 20, 1940; children—Peter Joseph, Brent Lewin. Admitted to Wash. bar, 1933, Supreme Ct. U.S., 1937, Hawaii bar, 1946; with firm Grosscup, Morrow & Ambler, Seattle, 1933-39; atty. Dept. Justice, Washington, 1939-42, Dept. Interior, Washington, 1942-45, Surplus Property Office, Dept. Interior, Honolulu, 1945-47; dep. atty. gen. T.H., 1947; partner firm Levinson & Cobb, Honolulu, 1949-64, Levinson, Cobb & Gould, Honolulu, 1964-65; judge 1st Circuit Ct Hawaii, 1966-67; asso. justice Supreme Ct. Hawaii, 1967-74; practiced in Honolulu, 1974-79; partner firm Levinson & Levinson, 1977-79; vis. prof. law U. Hawaii, 1975. Mem. Bd. Bar Examiners, Hawaii, 1956-62; mem. liaison com. Nat. Conf. Bar Examiners, 1968-74. Chmn. Psychiat. Commn. T.H., 1952-53; sec. Hawaii Jewish Welfare Fund, 1956-62, treas., 1962-69; nat. exec. council Am. Jewish Com., 1967-79; Oahu pres. Nat. Soc. Crippled Children and Adults, 1960-64, Hawaii pres., 1964-66; mem. com. mgmt. Armed Forces YMCA, 1957-64; chmn. Hawaii adv. com. U.S. Commn. Civil Rights, 1964-65, Hawaii chpt. World Brotherhood, 1954-55; bd. mgrs. Hawaii P.T.A., 1957-59; law com. Union Am. Hebrew Congregations, 1962-74. Recipient award of merit United Jewish Appeal, 1959, Leadership award, 1976; award of merit B'nai B'rith, 1961, A.C.L.U. Hawaii, 1975. Mem. Phi Beta Kappa. Jewish (pres. temple 1950-60). Mason (33 deg., Shriner), Rotarian (pres. Waikiki club 1959-60); mem. B'nai B'rith (pres. Hawaii 1961-62). Home: Honolulu, Hawaii. Died Mar. 13, 1979.

LEVINTHAL, LOUIS EDWARD, lawyer; b. Phila., Apr. 5, 1892; s. Bernard Louis and Minna (Kleinberg) L.; student Central High Sch., Phila., 1906-10; A.B., U. of Pa., 1914, LL.B., 1916, LL.M., 1918; D.H.L. (hon.) Jewish Theol. Seminary of America, 1948; LL.D., Dropsie College, 1956; LL.D., Hebrew University of Jerusalem, 1966; married Lenore Chodoff, December 5, 1916; children—Sylvia Betty (Mrs. Herbert I. Bernstein), Cyrus. Awarded Corpus Juris Scholarship and Gowen Fellowship for post-graduate studies at law school, University of Pennsylvania (1916-18). Admitted to Pa. bar, 1916; member Phila. County Bd. of Law Examiners, 1917-37; lecturer on bankruptcy and corporate reorganization, University of Pennsylvania Law Sch., 1933-36; spl. counsel to Pub. Service Commn. of Pa. in connection with reorganization of Phila. Rapid Transit, 1935-37; judge Common Pleas Court No. 6, Phila., 1937-59, ret., 1959; counsel Dilworth, Paxson, Kalish, Kohn & Dilks, from 1959. Appointed by Secretary of War Patterson as advisor on Jewish affairs to General Lucius Clay in Germany, June 1947-Jan. 1948. Chairman administrative committee Zionist Organization of America, 1939, pres. of orgn., 1941-43. Mem. Pa. Gov's. Commn. on Constl. Revision, 1935. Dir. Fedn. of Jewish Charities; mem. World Zionist Congress Court, 1946-56; dir. Jewish Welfare Soc. of Phila. (hon.); pres. Gratz Coll., 1945; chmn. publ. com. Jewish Pub. Soc. Am., 1939-49, 54-62, pres., 1949-54; nat. chmn. Guardians of Israel, 1954-59. Director Asso. Talmud Torahs Phila. (pres. 1929-34), Zionist Orgn. of Phila. (pres. 1926-29); v.p. Am. Assn. of Jewish Edn. since 1940. Co-Chairman, United Jewish Appeal; co-chairman, United Palestine Appeal; chmn. bd. govs. Hebrew U., Jerusalem; v.p. Am. Fund for Palestinian Institutions; trustee conference of Jews and Christians; chmn. Phila. regional Nat. Conf. Christians and Jews, 1957-60, hon. pres. Am. Jewish League for Israel, from 1957. Mem. praesidium Am. Jewish Conf., 1942-43; mem. Am. Law Inst., Order of Coif, Phi Beta Kappa, Sigma Alpha Mu. Democrat. Jewish religion. Hon. chmn. Brandeis lawyers society. Member American Assn. of Political Science; member, American, Pennsylvania and Philadelphia bar associations. Author: Land Laws of Turkey, (1916), Justice Louis D. Brandeis, 1942; Credo of an American Zionist, 1942; Mayer Sulzberger, P.J., 1927; History of Bankruptcy Law, 1918. Home: Jerusalem, Israel. Died May 16, 1976.

LEVISON, JACOB L., forester, arboriculturist; b. Riga, Russia, Jan. 1883; s. Julius and Esther L.; brought to U.S., 1893; B.A., Coll. City of N.Y., 1902; M.F., Yale, 1905; traveled and studied in most important bot. gardens, parks, forests, Am. and Europe; m. Rae B. Haskell, June 6, 1915; m. 2d, Myrtle Powell Lader, Jan. 23, 1946. With U.S. Forest Service, under Gifford Pinchot, 1905-06; forester in charge Brooklyn (N.Y.) and Queens parks, 10 1/2 yrs.; chief forester City of N.Y. to May 1917; now cons. forester, Sea Cliff, L.I., in general charge of many large estates of L.I. and vicinity, including those of H. M. Lehman, Otto H. Kahn, Gilbert Kahn, Walter P. Chrysler, C. Oliver Iselin, William L. Harkness, Nicholas P. Brady, H. L. Pratt; also of Greenwood Cemetery and other orgns. and developing new estates and ornamental woodlands; responsible for development of Marshall Field Place, L.I., and many similar estates. Lectr. on ornamental and shade trees Yale U. Forest Sch., The New Sch. for Social Research. Member council University, N.Y.C., Brooklyn Institute Arts and Sciences, colleges, civic orgns., etc. Forester for Am. Assn. for Planting and Preservation of City Trees. Sr. fellow Am, Inst. of Park Executives; sr. mem. Soc. Am. Foresters; mem. Nat. Geog. Soc., Am. Forestry Assn., Am. Civic Assn., N.Y. Tree Planting Assn. (v.p.), Am. Acad. Arborists (sec.). Recognized as an authority on naturalistic planting, developing and maintaining private places and on town development. Jewish religion. Mason. Clubs: Yale, City Athletic. Author: Studies of Trees, 1914; Home Book of Trees and Shrubs, 1940; revised 1949. Home: Sea Cliff, L.I., N.Y. *

LEVIT, BERT WILLIAM, lawyer; b. San Francisco, Feb. 16, 1903; s. Morris and Fannie (Jacobs) L.; A.B. magna cum laude, Stanford, 1924, J.D., 1925; m. Thelma Clumeck, May 10, 1928 (dec. 1970); children—Victor Bert, Roger Clumeck; m. 2d, Edith I. Garland, Oct. 4, 1972. Admitted to Calif. bar, 1925; sr. partner firm Long & Levit, San Francisco and Los Angeles, from 1927, gen. counsel, from 1977; lectr. Stanford Law Sch., 1932-45. Spl. asst. to U.S. atty. gen., Washington, 1925-26; chief asst. dist. atty. San Francisco, 1944-45; chief dep. atty. gen. Calif., 1951; dir. finance State of Calif., 1959. Commr. edn. San Francisco pub. schs., 1948-58; charter mem. Calif. Law Revision Com., 1953-58, Calif. Scholarship Com., 1955-58; Calif. del. White House Conf. on Edn., 1955; pres. Calif. Sch. Bds. Assn., 1956-57; chmn. Gov.'s Com. on Calif. Govtl. Reorgn., 1959-60; pub. mem. Calif. Coordinating Council for Higher Edn., 1962-67. Pres. San Francisco br. Am. Cancer Soc., 1968-70, bd. dirs. Calif. div., 1971-74, recipient Pres.'s Gold award, 1978; legal counsel San Francisco Conservatory Music, from 1971, bd. dirs., 1971-77; bd. govs. Internat. Ins. Seminars, from 1976. Fellow Am. Coll. Trial Lawyers; mem. World Assn. Lawyers (founding mem.), Order of Coif, Phi Beta Kappa, Delta Sigma Rho. Clubs: Bankers, San Francisco Comml. Home: San Rafael, Calif. Deceased.

LEVITT, ARTHUR, state ofcl.; b. Bklyn., June 28, 1900; s. Israel A. and Rose (Daniels) L.; A.B., Columbia, 1921, LL.B., 1924, LL.D., 1970; LL.D., Sienna Coll., 1967, Union U., 1967, Yeshiva U., 1968, St. Johns U., 1970, Jewish Theol. Sem., 1970, Pace U., 1971; m. Dorothy Wolff, June 30, 1929; 1 son, Arthur. Admitted to N.Y. bar, 1924; gen. practice law, 1925-55; comptroller State of N.Y., 1955-79; trustee Lincoln Savs. Bank of Bklyn., 1959-80. Mem. commn. on ednl. orgns. NCCJ, 1951-80. Mem. Bd. Edn., N.Y.C., 1952-54, pres., 1954; pres. Union Temple, Bklyn.; bd. dirs., vice chmn. Bklyn. chpt. ARC, 1950-80. Served as pvt., U.S. Army, 1917, capt. to col., AUS, 1941-46; col. Res. Decorated Legion of Merit. Mem. Judge Advs. Assn. (dir.), N.Y. State, Bklyn. bar assns., Assn. Bar City N.Y., Nat. Dem. Club (dir.), N.Y. Acad. Pub. Edn. (pres. 1953), Phi Sigma Delta. Clubs: Masons, K.P.; Union League; Glen Oaks Country. Home: New York, N.Y. Died May 6, 1980.

LEVY, CHARLES MARION, fgn. service officer; b. N.Y.C., July 31, 1895; s. Max and Ida (Korn) L.; A.B., Cornell U., 1916; certificate U. Lyon (France), 1919; m. Eleanor Griggs, Oct. 24, 1946. With Joint Distbn. Com., 1920-23, 30-41; editor Voice of Am., N.Y.C. and Washington, 1942-57; pub. affairs officer USIA, Am. Embassy, Lille, France, 1957-61, Strasbourg, France, 1961-64, ret., 1965. Vol. interpreter in French and German, Internat. Visitors Service, Washington. Served with U.S. Army, 1917-19. Mem. Pi Lambda Phi. Home: Washington, D.C. Died June 1, 1978.

LEVY, DAVID MORDECAI, psychiatrist; b. Scranton, Pa., Apr. 27, 1892; s. Benno C. and Sarah (Breakstone) L.; A.B., Harvard, 1914; M.D., U. Chgo., 1918; m. Adele Rosenwald, June 2, 1927. Resident physician Chgo. Psychopathic Hosp. and Cook County Hosp., 1918-20; instr. criminology U. Ill., 1920-22; lectr. psychiatry U. Chgo., 1923-27; attending neurologist, dir. mental hygiene clinic children Michael Reese Hosp., 1923-26; acting dir. Ill. Inst. Juvenile Research, 1923; lectr. Smith Coll., 1924-30; chief staff N.Y. Inst. Child Guidance, 1927-33; lectr. New Sch. Social Research, 1928-39; instr. N.Y. Psychoanal. Inst., 1936-41; cons. psychiat. personnel OSS, 1944-45; dir. inf. control div. Screening Center, Germany, 1945-46; mem. Nat. Adv. Mental Health Council, USPHS,

1946-48; attending psychoanalyst Psychoanal. Clinic Tng. and Research, from 1945; mem. Inst. Advanced Study, Princeton, 1951-53; attending psychiatrist N.Y. State Psychiat. Inst., from 1949; pvt. practice N.Y.C., from 1935; research prof. psychiatry and mental hygiene Yale, 1947-51; prof. clin. psychiatry Columbia, 1955-57; cons. USPHS, Rockland State Hosp.; program cons. Henry Ittleson Center Child Research, 1956-69. Mem. U.S. Com. Care European Children. Recipient Thomas W. Salmon award, 1946, Samuel W. Hamilton award, 1952, Sandor Radio award, 1961, Emil A. Gutheil award, 1963, Agnes Purcell McGavin award, 1965, Founders award Am. Orthopsychiat. Assn., 1968. Diplomate Nat. Bd. Med. Examiners, Am. Bd. Psychiatry and Neurology. Organizer Chgo. Psychol. Club. Assn. Psychoanalytic and Psychosomatic Med., Am. Orthopsychiat. Assn. (past pres.); fellow N.Y. Acad. Scis., N.Y. Acad. Medicine; mem. Soc. Research Child Devel. (pres. 1965-67), Royal Soc. Medicine (London), Am. Psychiat. Assn., Am. Psychol. Assn., Am. Neurol. Assn., N.Y. Psychiat. Soc. (past pres.). Author: Sibling Rivalry, 1937; Maternal Overprotection, 1943; New Fields of Psychiatry, 1947; The Demonstration Clinic, 1959; Behavioral Analysis, 1958. Home: New York, N.H. Died Mar. 1, 1977.

LEVY, GUSTAVE LEHMANN, investment banker; b. New Orleans, May 10, 1910; s. Sigmund and Bella (Lehmann) L.; student Tulane U., 1927-28, N.Y. U., 1928-32; LL.D., Syracuse U., Tulane U.; m. Janet Wolf, Mar. 7, 1934; children—Peter A., Betty (Mrs. Rodger H. Hess). With Newborg & Co., 1928-32; with Goldman, Sachs & Co., 1933-76, partner, 1945-69, sr. partner, from 1969; dir. N.Y. Telephone Co., Diebold, Inc., Witco Chem. Co., May Dept. Stores Co., Deltec Pan Am., S.A., Deltec Internat., Ltd., Foster Grant Co., Inc., Keebler Co., Ling-Temco-Vought, Inc., Maxwell Labs., Inc., Samsonite Corp., Studebaker-Worthington, Inc., Norton Simon, Inc., Patagonia Corp., Talcott Nat. Corp., Technicon Corp., Trans World Life Ins. Co. N.Y., Weis Markets, Inc., Westmount Life Ins. Co.; trustee Bowery Savs. Bank. Commr., Port of N.Y. Authority, 1970-76. Chmn. bd. govs. N.Y. Stock Exchange, 1967-69; mem. Am. Stock Exchange. Pres., Fedn. Jewish Philanthropies N.Y., 1957-59; chmn. Mt. Sinai Hosp. and Med. Center, N.Y.C., from 1962; treas., Lincoln Center Performing Arts, Inc. Bd. visitors Tulane U.; bd. govs. Tulane Med. Center; bd. dirs. N.Y. Urban Coalition. Served to lt. col. USAAF, 1942-45. Clubs: Bond, Economic, Harmonie, Madison Square Garden (N.Y.C.); Century Country (Purchase, N.Y.); University; Burning Tree. Home: New York, N.Y. Died Nov. 3, 1976.

LEVY, HARRY LOUIS, univ. dean; b. N.Y.C., Dec. 5, 1906; s. William W. and Bertha D. (Haber) L.; A.B., Coll. City N.Y., 1925; A.M., Columbia, 1926, Ph.D., 1936; diploma Mandarin Chinese, Mil. Intelligence Chinese Lang. Sch., 1945; m. Muriel Erdreich, Apr. 12, 1928 (div. Sept. 1942); children—Charles S., Ann (Mrs. Arthur L. Lathrop); m. 2d, Ernestine Friedl, Sept. 27, 1942. Mem. faculty Hunter Coll., N.Y.C., 1928-64, prof. classics, 1953-64, dean students, 1952-53, 59-63; dean, studies City U. N.Y., 1963-81, U. professor classics, 1964-81; visiting professor University Mich., 1958, 60. Editor reports of working coms. N.E. Conf. Teaching Fgn. Langs., 1958, dir., 1962-64, chmn. bd. dirs., 1962-63; editor Classical Weekly, 1949-52; cons. revision Latin exam. N.Y. State Regents, 1958-62; mem. advance placement com. Latin, Coll. Entrance Exam. Bd., 1956-59, vis. rep., 1960-81; mem. adv. council jr. sci. and humanities symposia U.S. Army Research Office, 1960-81, acting chmn., 1962; Greek lang. lectr. for Voice of Am., 1956-81; mem. mng. com. Am. Sch. Classical Studies in Athens, 1962-81; mem. steering com. social studies and humanities curriculum program, Am. Council Learned Socs.-Ednl. Services, Inc., 1962-81. Served inf., AUS, 1943-45; CBI; lt. col. Res. ret. Mem. Am. Council Learned Socs. (sec. conf. secretaries constituent socs. 1961-63), Am. Philol. Assn. (sec.-treas. 1959-62), Phi Beta Kappa. Author: The Invective in Rufinum of Claudius Claudianus, 1935; A Latin Reader for Colleges, 2d edit., 1962; also articles profl. jours. Home: Durham, N.C. Died Jan. 11, 1981.

LEVY, I. HERBERT, lawyer; b. Trenton, N.J., Dec. 8, 1894; s. Louis and Elizabeth (Abrahams) L.; student Temple U. Law Sch.; m. Elizabeth Closson, Aug. 20, 1937. Admitted to N.J. bar, 1920, practiced in Trenton; mem. firm Levy, Levy, Albert & Marcus, 1957-73. Dir. Stacy Savs. and Loan Assn.; adv. bd. N.J. Realty Title Ins. Co. Mem. Trenton Bd. Edn., 1936-60, pres., 1942-43. Served with U.S. Army, World War I. Mem. Am., N.J., Mercer County (pres. 1945-46) bar assns. Jewish religion (hon. trustee temple). Home: Trenton, N.J. Died Feb. 20, 1981.

LEVY, LEON, bus. exec.; b. Phila., June 6, 1895; s. David and Fannie (Feigenbaum) L.; D.D.S., U. Pa., 1915, LL.D., 1973; D.Sc., Widener Coll., 1933; Dr. Pub. Service, Temple U., 1972; m. Blanche Paley, Sept. 22, 1927; children—Robert Paley, Lynne Frances. Practiced dentistry, 1915-25; pres., gen. mgr., radio and TV broadcasting sta. WCAU, Inc., Phila., 1925-49, dir., from 1925; one of original owners and dir. CBS, 1927-77, sec. and treas., 1927-35; one of original owners and chmn., dir. Atlantic Racing Assn.; entered bus. of thoroughbred breeding and racing of horses, 1947. Trustee emeritus Albert Einstein Med. Center. Served dental corps, USNR, 1917-19; with USNR, 1941-42. Radio cons. Office of War Info., 1942-45. Recipient Poor Richard medal, 1937; Gen. Alumni award U. Pa., 1970; Broadcast Pioneers Delaware Valley gold medal, 1968. Hon. fellow Internat. Coll. Dentists. Reformed Jewish. Clubs: Thoroughbred Club Am. (Lexington, Ky.); Locust, Variety, Poinciana, Palm Beach Country. Home: Philadelphia, Pa. Died Aug. 9, 1978.

LEVY, LLONEL FARADAY, mfr.; b. Phila., Sept. 13, 1884; s. Louis E. and Pauline (Dalsheimer) L.; B.S., U. Pa., 1908; m. Margaret Wasserman, Feb. 11, 1926; children—Joan, Louis, Edith, Carol. Erecting engr. Graphic Arts Co., 1908-15; partner, tech. dir. Repro Art Machinery Co. 1915-62; partner, tech. dir. Max Levy & Co., 1920—, pres., dir., 1958-62, chmn., 1962—; dir. Investment Corp. Phila. Dir. Ednl. Radio and TV Sta. WHYY, Phila., 1960-65. Bd. mgrs. Franklin Inst. Pa.; dir. Art Alliance of Phila., White Williams Found., Com. of Seventy Phila., Hias (Phila.), Technion (Phila.). Mem. Am. Soc. M.E. Clubs: Chemists (N.Y.C.); Engineers (Phila.). Home: Philadelphia PA.

LEVY, MILTON, educator; b. St. Louis, July 13, 1903; s. Herman and Jennie (Leventhal) L.; B.S., Washington U., 1925; Ph.D., St. Louis U., 1929; m. Helen N. Class, Oct. 26, 1924; children—Rosalyn A. (Mrs. Sam Howell Wood) (dec.), Robert. Fellow NRC, Harvard, 1929-30; instr. biochemistry N.Y. U., 1930-56, prof., head dept. biochemistry Coll. Dentistry, 1956-71, prof. emeritus, 1971-76, research prof. biochemistry Sch. Medicine, from 1971; guest prof. Weizmann Inst. Scis., Israel, 1970. Mem. corp. Marine Biol. Lab., Woods Hole, Mass. Recipient Great Tchr. award N.Y. U., 1964; Distinguished Alumnus award, Washington U., 1966; Guggenheim fellow, 1956. Fellow N.Y. Acad. Sci.; mem. Internat. Assn. Dental Research, Soc. Exptl. Biology and Medicine, Research Soc. Am., Am. Chem. Soc., Am. Soc. Biol. Chemists, A.A.A.S., Harvey Soc., Sigma Xi, Omicron Kappa Upsilon. Home: Long Island City, N.Y. Died Oct. 30, 1976.

LEWIN, ROBERT M., journalist; b. Prentice, Wis., Oct. 3, 1904; s. Harry and Minnie Evelyn (Neimark) L.; student Ripon (Wis.) Coll. Sch. of Music, U. Wis., Madison, 1922-26, U. Wis., Milw., 1934-36; m. Hannabelle Primakow, Oct. 6, 1929. Reporter, Berlin (Wis.) Eve. Jour., 1926-28, Milw. Jour., 1928-44, Chgo. Daily News, 1944-69, labor writer, 1947-69; labor editor, columnist Jour. Commerce, N.Y., from 1969. Recipient Freedom Found. award, 1951. Mem. Sigma Delta Chi. Clubs: National W. Headline, Press (Chgo.); Milwaukee Athletic. Chgo. YMCA badminton singles champion, 1947. Contbr. articles to mags. on labor subjects. Home: Glencoe, Ill. Died June 17, 1979.

LEWIS, ARTHUR LEON, mfg. exec.; b. Laconia, N.H., June 25, 1885; s. Orin Hartley and Sarah (Yeaton) L.; B.S., Darmouth, 1908; m. Eva Hilton, June 1, 1911 (div. 1937); children—Carolyn, Virginia (dec.), Sarah, John H.; m. 2d. Naomi Kirchner, Jan. 1, 1941. Pres. Lewis-Shepard Co., Watertown, Mass., 1915-65; chmn. bd., 1965—; chmn. bd. Lewis-Shepard Products, Inc., Trustee Children's Hosp (Boston). Mem. Newcomen Soc. Clubs: Norfolk Hunt; Dedham Country and Polo. Home: Medfield, Mass.

LEWIS, AUSTIN WARREN, lawyer; b. Sulphur, La., Sept. 23, 1910; s. William Warren and Lula (Vaughan) L.; student Southwestern La. Inst., 1926-29; LL.B., Tulane U., 1932; m. Natalie Scott, July 30, 1935; children—Jerry S., Sallye L. (Mrs. John E. Hammett). Admitted to La. bar, 1932; practice in Lake Charles, 1932-35; mem. Liskow & Lewis, Lake Charles, 1935-64, New Orleans, 1964—. Mem. jud. council La. Supreme Ct., 1960-64. Served with USMCR, 1942-45. Fellow Am. Coll. Trial Lawyers; mem. Am. (mineral law and adminstrv. law sects), La., Southwestern La. (past pres.) bar assns., Order of Coif. Home: New Orleans, La. Died Nov. 18, 1974; interred Lake Lawn Park Mausoleum, New Orleans.

LEWIS, B(ENJAMIN) ROLAND, prof. English; b. St. Marys, O., Dec. 3, 1884; s. Samuel and Katherine (Fox) L.; B.S., Ohio Northern U., 1905, M.S., 1907; grad. study, University of Chicago, 1907-08; A.M., Harvard, 1915; D.Litt., Ohio Northern University, 1941; D.Litt., University of Utah, 1943; research at British Museum, Bodleian Library (Oxford) and Bibliothèque Nationale, Paris, 1925-26, Huntington Library, San Marino, Calif., 1929, 30, 31, 34, 35, 37, 39, 41, 47; m. Bessie Blanche Collins, 1906; children—Anna Katherine, Ruth Geraldine. Supt. schs., Hammond, La., 1905-07; prof. English, Grand Island (Neb.) Coll., 1907-08, Ellsworth Coll., Iowa Falls, Ia., 1908-13, U. of Utah since 1915; dir. Shakespeare Laboratory, U. of Utah. Visiting prof. English, Grad. Sch. of Catholic U. of Am., 1932-33; research Shakespeare scholar, the Folger Shakespeare Library, Washington, 1932-33. Mem. Modern Lang. Assn. of America, Scholars' Facsimiles and Reprints, Shakespeare Assn. America (v.p. 1935), Institut Littéraire et Artistique de France (D.Litt. 1938), Sigma Tau Delta, Phi Kappa Phi. Republican. Unitarian. Clubs: Harvard, Timpanogos, Author: The Technique of the One-Act Play, 1917; The One-Act Play in Colleges and High Schools, 1920; Contemporary One-Act Plays, 1922; Effective Writing, 1924; University of Utah Plays, 1928; Creative Poetry, 1930; Shakespeare Documents, 2 vols., 1942. Home: Salt Lake City, Utah. *

LEWIS, CHARLES FREDERICK, cement co. exec.; b. Phila., July 28, 1886; s. Frederick Humphreyville and Alice (Law) L.; student Germantown Acad., 1892-96, 1898-1900, Bordentown Mil. Inst., 1901-03, Civil Engrng. Sch., U. Pa., 1904-08; m. Fanny Lou Morris, Aug. 18, 1919; children—Frederick H., William C., Margaret L. (Mrs. R. L. Stephenson), Robert M. Engr., Standard Portland Cement Co., Leads, Ala., 1908-17; plant mgr., asst. gen. supt. Atlas Portland Cement Co., 1919-27; constrn. engr. Volunteer Portland Cement Co., Knoxville, Tenn., 1927-28, plant mgr., 1928-53, v.p., 1953-54, pres., mgr., 1954-58, pres., 1958—; v.p., dir. Ideal Cement Co., Denver; cons. for design and location initial operation, plant of Puerto Rico Cement Co., Coterno, P.R. Served from capt. to maj., U.S. Army, 1917-19. Mem. Am. Soc. C.E., Soc. Am. Mil. Engrs. (charter), Am. Ceramic Soc., Knoxville C. of C. (dir.). Presbyn. Clubs: Deane Hill Country; Optimist. Home: Knoxville, Tenn. *

LEWIS, CLEONA, economist; b. Concordia, Kan., Aug. 30, 1885; d. Thomas William and Louise Marie (Dorner) Lewis; Ph.B., U. of Chicago, 1917, A.M., 1921; Ph.D., Brookings Instn., 1930; unmarried. Teacher, grades and high sch., 1903-13; head comml. dept. State Coll. for Women, Denton, Tex., 1917-18; statistician with Am. sect., Allied Maritime Transport Council, London, 1918-19; with Am. Commn., to Negotiate Peace, Paris, France, Feb.-July 1919; research and lab. asst. U. of Chicago, 1919-22; mem. staff Inst. of Econs. (now Brookings Instn.), 1922-50. Member Am. Statis. Assn. Author: The International Accounts, 1927; America's Stake in International Investments, 1938; Nazi Europe and World Trade, 1941; Debtor and Creditor Countries, 1938, 1944, 1945; The United States and Foreign Investment Problems, 1949; co-author: The French Debt Problem (with H. G. Moulton), 1926; America's Capacity to Consume (with E. G. Nourse and others), 1934; Capital Expansion, Employment and Economic Stability (with H. G. Moulton et al), 1940; World Minerals and World Peace (with C.K. Leith and J.W. Furness), 1943. Home: Bethesda, Md. *

LEWIS, DALE MORGAN, banker; b. East St. Louis, Ill., July 24, 1911; s. David Morgan and Carrie (Goeglein) L.; grad. Stonier Grad. Sch. Banking, Rutgers U., 1948; m. Florence Marie Walter, Nov. 25, 1933 (dec.); children—Anne Carol (Mrs. Louis D. Sebold), Thomas David, Kay Marie (Mrs. C. DeWayne Jones); m. 2d, Mae Margaret Harbaugh, Jan. 8, 1972. With Tabler Cleaning Co., St. Louis, 1930-32, Fed. Res. Bank St. Louis, 1926-30, 32-48, 49-71, v.p., 1951-66, 1st v.p., 1966-71, ret. Mem. staff bd. govs. Fed. Res. System, 1948-49; lectr. Grad. Sch. Banking, U. Wis., 1953-67. Home: Saint Louis, Mo. Died Apr. 28, 1976; buried Calvary Cemetery, St. Louis.

LEWIS, DOROTHY MOORE, broadcasting exec.; b. Albany, N.Y., Dec. 22, 1896; d. Howard Parker and Annie M. (Hoyt) Moore; grad. Rye Sem., 1916; student U. Vt., 1916-17, U. Colo., 1919; m. Edwin C. Lewis, June 24, 1920; children—Charlotte (Mrs. Thomas A. Gage), Barbara (Mrs. Dean M. Schmitter) (dec.). Piano debut U. Vt., 1917, voice debut, Steinway Hall, 1919; mgr. radio sta., 1929; founder Radio Council on Children's Programs, 1939-42; with import-export firm, 1934-38; coordinator listener activity Nat. Assn. Broadcasters, 1942-48; rep. broadcasting industry, orgn. UN, San Francisco, 1945, FAO Conf., Que., 1945; coordinator Am. broadcasts for UN, 1948-54, liaison officer nongovtl. orgns. Office Pub. Information, 1954-56; exec. dir. covering UN, Press Service, 1956-59; world study of women in radio and TV, UNESCO, from 1959. Chmn. adv. council Am. Mothers Com., also nat. chmn. bicentennial com.; mem. George Peabody awards commn., 1940-75. Bd. dirs. Internat. Cultural Centre for Youth. Named woman of achievement Theta Sigma Phi, 1952; woman of the year N.Y. State Bus. and Profl. Women, 1956; recipient citation acievement mass communication United Ch. Women, 1958; citations Nat. Conf. Christians and Jews, Nat. Assn. Broadcasters, Community Chest. Mem. Internat. Assn. Women in Radio and Television (hon. pres. 1962-78), Advt. Women N.Y. (v.p. 1943-45), Am. Mothers Com. (pres. 1963-71), Women United for UN (past pres.), Nat. Soc., N.E. Women United Ch. Women (bd.), Women Execs. Pub. Relations (past chmn.), Nat. Council Women U.S. (named a Woman of Conscience 1968), Internat. Assn. Former UN Civil Servants. Author: Broadcasting to Youth of America, 1943; Program Patterns for Young Radio Listeners, 1945; Radio and Public Service, 1946. Editor UN News for Women Broadcasters, 1947-56; coordinator publishing Famous Mothers in American History 1776-1976, 1976. Home: Concord, N.H. Died Jan. 1, 1978.

LEWIS, ERVIN EUGENE, educator; b. Orwell, N.Y., July 20, 1882; s. Rolland O'dell and Mary Estelle (Vannier) L.; A.B., Stanford, 1907, A.M., 1909; grad. State Normal Sch., San Jose, Calif., 1907; Ph.D., Columbia, 1920; m. Elizabeth Jane Bozarth, Sept. 1, 1913; 1 son, Robert Allen. Instr. in psychology and manual training, State Normal Sch., San Jose, 1907-10; instr. San Diego Normal Sch., summer 1908; research scholar and fellow, Columbia, 1910-12; instr. Ind. U., summers 1911, 12; prin. Training Sch. of Eastern Ill. State Teachers Coll., 1912-13; asst. prof. edn. State U. of Ia., 1913-20; supt. schs., Rockford, Ill., 1920-23; prof. edn., U. of Chicago, summers 1921, 22; supt. schs., Flint, Mich., 1923, 26; prof. edn., U. of Mich., summers 1923, 24, U. of Wyoming, summer 1925; professor Hawaiian University, 1926; head of department and professor of sch. adminstrn., Ohio State U., since 1926; mem. J.F. E.L. of C.E. & I., GHQ, SCAP, Tokyo, Japan, 1948-49. Mem. N.E.A., Nat. Vocational Edn. Assn., Nat. Soc. for Sci. Study of Edn., Phi Delta Kappa, Sigma Phi Epsilon; pres. Div. No. 2, Mich. State Teachers' Assn., 1925. Author of several books relating to ednl. subjects. Home: Columbus, O.

LEWIS, FRANK M(ENDELL), univ. prof., consulting engr.; b. N.Y.C., Sept. 26, 1895; s. John Henry and Cornelia Francis (Jennings) L.; student Webb Inst. Naval Architecture, N.Y.C., 1913-17; m. Marie C. Eckes, Aug. 12, 1927; children—John M., George E. Prof. engring., Webb Inst. Naval Arch., 1918-36; prof. marine engring., Mass. Inst. Tech. from 1936; consulting engr. from 1924. Mem. Soc. Naval Archs. and Marine Engrs. (v.p., from 1942), ASME. Home: Weston, Mass. Died 1976.

LEWIS, FREEMAN, publisher; b. St. Cloud, Minn., Jan. 6, 1908; s. Claude Bernard and Wilhelmina Rosalia (Freeman) L.; student Phillips Exeter Acad., 1925-26, B.S., Harvard, 1930; m. Julia Wight Jennison, Jan. 20, 1934 (dec. 1974); children—Jennifer, Jeremy, Bradford. Salesman, John Day Co., 1930-31; exec. v.p. Blue Ribbon Books, Inc., 1931-39; editor Garden City Pub. Co., Inc., 1939-45; exec. v.p. Pocket Books, Inc., N.Y.C., 1945-66; v.p. publ. Simon & Schuster, Inc., N.Y.C., 1966-69; past pres. Washington Sq. Press, Inc. Mem. Signet Soc., Kex Club (Harvard). Club: Seawanhaka-Corinthian Yacht. Home: Glen Head, N.Y. Died Aug. 15, 1976.

LEWIS, HARRY REYNOLDS, poultry husbandman; b. Providence, R.I., Oct. 14, 1885; s. Frank Levit and Harriet Elizabeth (Reynolds) L.; B.S., R.I. State Coll., 1907, M.Agr., 1916; m. Alice Belle Mattison, Dec. 25, 1907. Prof. poultry husbandry, Baron De Hirsch Agrl. Sch., Woodbine, N.J., 1907-09; prof. agr., same, 1909-11; instr. poultry husbandry and dairying, 1911-13, asso. prof. poultry husbandry, 1913-16, prof., 1916-21, N.J. State U.; poultry husbandman N.J. Agrl. Expt. Stas., 1911-13; state commr. of agr., R.I., 1927-35; pres. treas. Harry R. Lewis & Co., Inc. Mem. R.I. Ho. of Rep., 1926-28. Mem. com. Nat. Survey Secondary Edn. Pres. Nat. Poultry Council and chmn. agrl. com. N.E. Council; mem. R.I. Poultry Council, Northeastern Poultry Producers Council, Am. Standard Bred Poultry Assn., R.I. State Grange, Varnum Continentals, Am. Poultry Assn., Am. Genetic Assn., East Greenwich Chamber of Commerce (ex-pres.), Kappa Sigma, Beta Phi, Phi Beta Kappa, Phi Kappa Phi, Sigma Nu. Republican. Baptist. Mason. Clubs: Lions, Pottowamut Golf. Author: Poultry Laboratory Guide, 1911; Productive Poultry Husbandry, 1913; Poultry Keeping, 1915; Poultry Laboratory Manual and Note Book, 1918; Making Money from Hens, 1919; Poultry Enterprises, 1931; also numerous bulls., reports, etc. Established, 1921, Lewis Farms, East Greenwich, R.I., one of largest poultry breeding farms in N.E. Home: East Greenwich, R.I. *

LEWIS, JOHN, clergyman; b. Brecon, Wales, 1885; s. John and Mary (Williams) L.; studied Presbyn. Coll., South Wales, and U. of Edinburgh, Scotland; M.A., U. of Glasgow, 1910; Ph.D., U. of Manchester, England, 1924; m. Sarah S. Daniel, Oct. 21, 1910; children—Cyril Penry, Constance Mary. Came to U.S., 1930, naturalized, 1941. Pastorates in Manchester, London, Cardiff (Great Britain), to 1930; pastor, Scranton, Pa., 1930-35, Calvary Presbyterian Ch., Milwaukee, Wis., since 1935. Dir. Calvary Sch. of Religion; lecturer at Welsh Univ., King's Coll., London, Cornell U. Clubs: Interprofessional, City, Optimist (Milwaukee). Author: Vital and Social Factors in Religious Belief; Pathway of God in Hebrew Life; Passion for Life; Windows of the Soul; New Signposts on Old Bible Trails. Home: Milwaukee, Wis. *

LEWIS, NOLAN DON CARPENTIER, M.D., psychiatrist; b. Coudersport, Pa., Nov. 22, 1889; s. Fowler and Della Adelia (Carpentier) L.; M.D., U. of Md., 1914; fellow in psychology, Johns Hopkins U., 1914-17; student U. of Vienna, 1927-28; m. Anna I. Horn, June 2, 1920; children—Nolan Don Carpentier, Mary Ann. Pathologist Md. Gen. Hosp., 1914, State Hosp. Mental Diseases, Crownsville, Md., 1915-17; asso. in psychiatry Phipps Psychiatric Clinic, Baltimore, 1918; neuro-pathologist Surgeon General's Lab., Washington, D.C., 1919; pathologist St. Elizabeth Hosp., Washington, D.C., 1919-22, dir. clin. psychiatry, 1923-33, dir. labs., 1933-35; asso. dir. Neurological Inst. N.Y. City, 1938; dir. N.Y. State Psychiatric Inst. and Hosp., 1936-53; dir. and attending psychiatrist, Dept. Psychiatry, Vanderbilt Clinic Presbyn. Hosp., New York City, 1936-53; professor exptl. pathology, George Washington U., 1920-24, prof. clin. psychiatry, 1925-35; prof. neurology, Columbia U., 1936, prof. psychiatry, 1936-53; dir. of research in neurology and psychiatry New Jersey Institutions and Agencies, from 1953; cons. N.Y. State Dept. Mental Hygiene, from 1959; research cons. in psychiatry Jefferson Med. Coll.; field rep. and coordinator research in dementia praecox, Supreme Cl., 33 deg. Northern Masonic Jurisdiction, U.S.A. 1935-50. Consultant Memorial Center for Cancer since 1951. Mem. Am. Chem. Soc., Am. Psychiatric Assn., Am. Genetic Assn., Am. Psychopathological Assn., Assn. for Research in Nervous and Mental Diseases, Assn. for Study of Internal Secretions, Am. Mammalogical Soc. A.A.A.S., Am. Neurol. Assn., Internat. Psychoanalytic Assn., Am. Psychoanalytic Assn., Phi Chi. Club: Cosmos of Washington, D.C. Author: Constitutional Factors in Dementia Precox, 1923; Research in Dementia Precox, 1936; History of Psychiatric Achievement, 1941; Pathological Firesetting, 1951; War Time Psychiatry, 1954, Editor, Year Book in Psychiatry, 1939-54; mng. editor Jour. of Nervous and Mental Disease, Psychoanalytic Rev., Monograph Series, 1942-57; quarterly jour. Child Behavior. Contbr. to jours. Home: Frederick, Md. Died Dec. 18, 1979.

LEWIS, RALPH FERGUSON, editor, publisher; b. Dayton, Ohio, Jan. 21, 1918; s. Mark C. and Marguerite (Ferguson) L.; A.B. cum laude, Amherst Coll., 1939; M.B.A. (Baker scholar), Harvard U., 1941; m. Thelma Linke, Oct. 27, 1941; children—John, Barbara, Virginia. Spl. agt. FBI, 1941-45; asst. controller Time, Inc., 1945-51; asst. mng. editor Fortune Mag., 1951-52; mgmt. cons. Booz, Allen & Hamilton, N.Y.C., 1952-54; nat. dir. mgmt. services Arthur Young & Co., C.P.A.'s N.Y.C., 1954-61, gen. partner charge N.Y.C. office, 1962-70, mem. mgmt. com., 1965-70, dir. govt. relations, 1970-71; editor, publisher Harvard Bus. Review, Boston, 1971-79. Dir. Houghton Mifflin Co., Paine, Webber, Jackson & Curtis, Inc., Frank B. Hall & Co., Inc., Twentieth Century-Fox Film Corp., SCA Services Inc. Mem. Nat. Commn. on Electronic Fund Transfers, 1975-79. Pres. sch. bd., Briarcliff Manor, N.Y., 1954-57; mem. vis. com. Harvard Bus. Sch., 1967-71, mem. exec. council, 1961-69; gen. chmn. Nat. Bus. Conf., 1961; dir. Harvard Asso. Alumni 1967-69; treas. Berkshire Sch. Boys; trustee Babson Coll., 1975-79. C.P.A., N.Y., Tex., La. Mem. Am. Inst. C.P.A.'s (exec. council), Harvard Bus. Sch. Alumni Assn. (pres. 1965-66). Clubs: Sleepy Hollow Country, Scarborough-on-Hudson; Harvard, Sky (N.Y.C.); Metropolitan (Washington); Brae Burn Country (Boston); Mid-Ocean (Bermuda). Author: Management Uses of Accounting, 1961; Planning and Control for Profit, 1970. Contbr. articles profl. jours. Home: Cambridge, Mass. Died June 8, 1979.

LEWIS, RICHMOND, steel industry exec.; b. Springfield, Mass., Mar. 19, 1901; s. Charles Cottrell and Irene (Pratt) L.; student Phillips Andover Acad., 1916-18; A.B., Williams Coll., 1922; m. Laura S. Dwight, Oct. 25, 1924 (div.); children—Richmond, Larry Dwight; m. 2d, Elizabeth Shaffner, Dec. 31, 1952. With Charles C. Lewis Co., Springfield, Mass. and Hartford, Conn., 1922-76, v.p., 1923-26, pres., treas., 1926-67, chmn. bd., treas., 1967-76; pres., treas. Lewis Boiler & Iron Works, Inc. (now Lewis Steel Fabricators, Inc.), Springfield, 1926-76; dir., mem. exec. com. Mass. Mut. Life Ins. Co., 1948-73; dir., mem. finance com. Am. Mut. Liability Ins. Co.; dir. Bay State Corp., Mass. Mutual Corporate Investors, 1972-73. Cons. iron and steel div. Bus. and Def. Services Adminstrn., Dept. Commerce, 1956-70. Chmn. exec. com. Steel Service Center Inst., 1940-41, 64-65; trustee Wesson Meml. Hosp. Mem. Sigma Phi. Clubs: Metropolitan, Williams (N.Y.C.); Colony (Springfield, Mass.); Algonquin (Boston). Home: Suffield, Conn. Died Oct. 6, 1976.

LEWIS, ROGER LABAREE, newspaper man; b. Weymouth, Mass., July 13, 1884; s. Frank Wesley and Mary Burr (White) L.; A.B., Harvard, 1905; unmarried. Instr. in English, Cedarcroft Sch., Kenneth Square, Pa., 1905-7, Harvard, and Radcliffe Coll., 1908-12; reporter Boston newspapers, 1907-8, New York Evening World, 1912-14; with Associated Press, 1914-16; with German Army in advance through southern Belgium into France; went to Russia, Sept., 1914; later in Scandinavian countries and London; in Russia, Jan.-Oct. 1916; since free lance newspaper and mag. writer. Club: Harvard. Address: New York, N.Y. *

LEWIS, WILMARTH SHELDON, author, editor; b. Alameda, Calif., Nov. 14, 1895; s. Azro Nathaniel and Miranda (Sheldon) L.; B.A., Yale, 1918, hon. M.A., 1937, LL.D., 1965; Litt.D., Brown U., 1945, U. Rochester, 1946, Nat. U. Ireland, 1957, U. Del., 1961, U. Cambridge (Eng.), 1962, U. Melbourne, 1972; L.H.D., Trinity Coll., 1950, Bucknell U., 1958; LL.D., U. Hartford, 1972; m. Annie Burr Auchincloss, Jan. 25, 1928 (dec. 1959). Asso. Yale U. Press, 1920-22; research asso. Yale U., 1933-38; chief info. div. OSS, 1941-43. Chmn. John Carter Brown Library Assos., 1944-47, mem. bd. mgmt.; chmn. Yale Library Assos., 1933-45; hon. fellow Pierpont Morgan Library; trustee Inst. Advanced Study, Watkinson Library, Hartford, Redwood Library, Newport, Thacher Sch. Ojai (Calif.), Henry F. DuPont Mus., Winterthur, Historic Deerfield (Mass.), John F. Kennedy Library; mem. Nat. Portrait Gallery Commn., Nat. Collection Fine Arts; founder chmn. librarians council Library of Congress, 1942-46. Served as 2d lt., 144th F.A., U.S. Army, 1917-19. Fellow Yale, 1938-64. Recipient Yale medal, 1965, Donald F. Hyde award Princeton, 1968; Gleeson Library Assos. medal U. San Francisco, 1969; Benjamin Franklin gold medal Royal Soc. Arts, 1975; Nathan Hale award Yale Club Hartford, 1975. Fellow Am. Philos. Soc., Am. Acad. Arts and Scis., Royal Soc. Lit.; mem. Soc. Colonial Wars, Soc. Cin (hon.), Soc. Antiquaries, Royal Soc. Arts, Holland Soc. N.Y., Phi Beta Kappa (hon.), Beta Theta Pi, Scroll and Key. Clubs: Pacific Union (San Francisco); Athenaeum (London); Century, Grolier, Yale (N.Y.C.); Tavern (Boston); Metropolitan (Washington). Author: Tutor's Lane, 1922; Three Tours Through London in the Years 1748, 1776 and 1797 (Colver lectures Brown U.), 1941; The Yale Collections, 1946; Collector's Progress, 1951; Horace Walpole's Library (Sandars lectures Cambridge U.), 1957; Horace Walpole (Mellon lectures), 1960; One Man's Education, 1967; See For Yourself, 1971; Read As You Please, 1977; Rescuing Horace Walpole, 1978. Editor: A Selection of Letters of Horace Walpole, 1926, 1951, 73; Horace Walpole's Fugitive Verses, 1931; Private Charity in England, 1947-57 (with Ralph M. Williams), 1938; Yale edition Horace Walpole's Correspondence, 42 vols., 1937-80. Contbr. Atlantic Monthly, Am. Scholar, Va. Quar., Yale Rev., other mags. Home: Farmington, Conn. Died Oct. 7, 1979; interred Riverside Cemetery, Farmington.

LHEVINNE, ROSINA, concert pianist, music educator; b. Moscow, Russia, Mar. 29, 1880; ed. Moscow Conservatory Music (gold medallist); Mus. D. (hon.) U. Denver; m. Josef Lhevinne; children—C. Don, Marianna (Mrs. Donald Graham). Numerous recital performances with Josef Lhevinne and appearances with European orchs; made Am. debut in 1906, thereafter performed with chamber music ensembles, including Julliard String Quartet, various U.S. orchs. and European groups; also performed with Felix Salmond, Joseph and Lillian Fuchs, Leonard Rose; soloist N.Y. Philharmonic Orch., 1962; mem. piano faculty Julliard Sch., 1925-76, mem. faculty Grad. Sch. from inception; mem. faculty Aspen Music Sch., 1956-70, annual soloist with orch., chamber ensemble, and hon. trustee, 1965-76. Tchr. summer master class U. So. Cal., from 1971, also UCLA, U. Calif., Berkeley. Home: New York, N.Y. Died Nov. 9, 1976.

LIBBEY, FAY WLLMOTT, engr., adminstr.; b. Macwahoc, Me., Oct. 11, 1882; s. Charles Otis and Josephine Relief (Chadbourne) L.; B.S., Mass. Inst. Tech., 1906; m. Marion E. Stewart, June 10, 1908 (dec. Dec. 20, 1910)); m. 2d Rose C. Kaiser, Dec. 12, 1913 (deceased December 22, 1952); one daughter, Rosalie (Mrs. John Leroy Swanson). Assayer Nipissing Mining Co., Cobalt, Ont., Can., 1906; supt. Vulture Mines Co., Wickenburg, Ariz., 1912; owner chemical labatory, Phoenix, 1916; supt. Pinto Valley Co., Miami, Ariz., 1924; cons. mining engr., Ariz., 1933, Ore. C.E., 1937; mining engr. Ore. State Dept. Geology and Mineral Industries, 1938-44, director, 1944-54, retired November 1, 1954; now cons. mining engr. Served as 1st lt., C.E., U.S. Army, 1918. Mem. Profl. Engrs. Ore., Geol. Soc. Ore. Country, Ore. Acad. Sci., Ore. Hist. Soc., Ore. Mus. Sci. and Industry, Am. Inst. Mining and Metall. Engrs. (dir. 1951-53), Assn. Am. State Geologists, Sigma Xi. Republican. Author reports and articles tech. jours. Home: Portland, Ore.

LIBBY, RAYMOND LORING, educator; b. Portland, Maine, Aug. 26, 1903; s. Samuel Butterfield and Ann (Frausing) L.; B.S., Rutgers U., 1925, M.S., 1937, Ph.D., 1938; m. Bessye Drury, Oct. 14, 1933; 1 dau., Barbara Jeanne (Mrs. Thomas C. Raup). Asst. dir. biol. research Lederle Labs., 1937-48; chief radiation biology div. atomic energy project UCLA, 1948-50, prof. radiology, chief div. radiation biology Med. Center, UCLA, 1950-71; cons. to pvt. cos., govt. agys.; adv. Govt. of Greece, 1961-62. Cited by Greek AEC, 1962. Fellow N.Y. Acad. Scis., AAAS; mem. Am. Assn. Immunologists, Soc. Nuclear Medicine, Soc. Exptl. Biology and Medicine, Sigma Xi. Contbg. author: Nuclear Medicine, 1965. Research and publs. in immunochemistry, instrument for measuring antigen-antibody reactions; developed scintillation counting and scanning instrumentation for nuclear medicine; designed and developed extracorporeal irradiator for exptl. use in organ transplants and leukemia. Home: Williamsport, Pa. Died Oct. 24, 1976; buried Williamsport, Pa.

LIBBY, WILLARD FRANK, educator, chemist; b. Grand Valley, Colo., Dec. 17, 1908; s. Ora Edward and Eva May (Rivers) L.; B.S., U. Calif., 1931, Ph.D., 1933; Sc.D., Wesleyan U., 1955, Syracuse U., 1957, Trinity Coll., U. Dublin, 1957, Carnegie Inst. Tech., 1959, Georgetown U., 1962, Manhattan Coll., 1963, U. Newcastle-Upon-Tyne (Eng.), 1965, Gustavus

Adolphus Coll., 1970, U. South Fla., 1975, U. Colo., 1977; m. Leonor Hickey, Aug. 9, 1940 (div. 1966); children—Janet Eva, Susan Charlotte; m. 2d, Leona Woods Marshall, 1966. Instr. chemistry U. Calif., 1933, asst. prof., 1938, asso. prof., 1945; chemist Columbia War Research Div. (S.A.M. Labs.), 1941-45; prof. chemistry Inst. Nuclear Studies and dept. chemistry U. Chgo., 1945-59; prof. chemistry UCLA, 1959-80, dir. Inst. Geophysics and Planetary Physics, 1962-80; research asso. Geophys. Lab., Carnegie Instn. Washington, 1954-59; spl. vis. prof. chemistry, physics, astrophysics and aero-engring. U. Colo., 1967-70; spl. vis. prof. chemistry U. South Fla., Tampa, 1972; dir. Sci. Research Instrument Corp., Hedge Fund Am., Summit Capital Fund. Inc., Nuclear Systems, Inc., Research Cottrell, Inc., W.F. Libby Labs., Douglas Aircraft Co., Data Design Labs.; mem. acad. adv. bd. RAND Corp., 1968-77. Mem. com. sr. responsible reviewers AEC, 1945-52, mem. gen. adv. com., 1950-54, 60-62, mem. Plowshare adv. com., 1959-72, mem. AEC, 1954-59; mem. Calif. Air Resources Bd., 1967-72; mem. com. selection Guggenheim Meml. Found., 1959-77; mem. Pres.'s Task Force Air Pollution, 1969-70, U.S./Japan Com. Sci. Cooperation, 1970-73; mem. vis. com. Jet Propulsion Lab., 1968-72; sci. adviser State of Idaho, 1969-72; mem. Calif. Gov.'s Earthquake Council, 1972-80. Bd. dirs., pres. Isotope Found. Recipient Research Corp. award, 1951; Chandler medal Columbia, 1954; Am. Chem. Soc. award, 1956; Remsen Meml. lecture award, 1955; City Coll. N.Y. Bicentennial lecture award, 1956; Elliott Cresson medal Franklin Inst., 1957; Williard Gibbs medal, 1958; Albert Einstein award, 1959; Priestly award Dickinson Coll., 1959; Nobel prize for chemistry, 1960; Day medal Geol. Soc. Am., 1961; Calif. Alumnus of Year award, 1963; Gold medal Am. Inst. Chemists, 1970. Guggenheim fellow, 1941-42, 51, 59. Fellow Am. Nuclear Soc., Am. Inst. Chemists, Brit. Acad. (corr.); mem. Am. Philos. Soc., Am. Acad. Arts and Scis., Nat. Acad. Scis., Heidelberg Acad. Sci., AAAS, Am. Phys. Soc., Am. Inst. Chem. Engrs., Am. Chem. Soc., Am. Geophys. Union, Am. Inst. Aeros. and Astronautics, Bolivian Soc. Anthropology, Berkeley Fellows (charter), Geochem. Soc., Geol. Soc. Am., Royal Swedish Acad. Sci., Phi Beta Kappa, Sigma Xi, Pi Mu Epsilon. Alpha Chi Sigma, Phi Lambda Upsilon. Clubs: Explorers; Cosmos (Washington); Metropolitan, Century Assn. (N.Y.C.). Author: Radiocarbon Dating, 1955. Editorial bd. Science, 1962-70, Space Life Scis., 1970-80, Sci. of Total Environment, 1973-80, Environ. Geology, 1973-80; editorial adv. bd. Indsl. Research, 1967-73. Contbr. articles to chem. jours. Home: Santa Monica, Calif. Died Sept. 8, 1980; cremated.

LICHT, SIDNEY, physician; b. N.Y.C., Apr. 18, 1907; s. Herman Selig and Julia (Frank) L.; B.S., City Coll. N.Y., 1927; M.D., N.Y. U., 1931; m. Elizabeth Schweitzer, Mar. 16, 1937; children—Vera Hermine, Phyllis Roxanne, Jeffrey Louis. Intern, Mt. Sinai Hosp., N.Y.C., 1931-32, Sea View Hosp., N.Y.C., 1932-33, Beth Israel Hosp., N.Y.C., 1933-35; practice medicine, 1935—, N.Y.C., 1935-42; mem. staff VA Hosp., Boston, 1946, VA Hosp., West Haven, Conn.; cons. phys. medicine Gaylord Hosp., Wallingford, Conn., from 1961; cons. Beth Israel Hosp., 1967, Inst. Crippled and Disabled, 1967, Montefiore Hosp. (all N.Y.C.); asst. clin. prof. med. Yale Med. Sch., 1955-64; prof. med. lit. U. Miami, 1975—. Served with AUS, 1942-46. Recipient Krusen award, 1974. Hon. mem. Argentine, Brit., Canadian, Danish, French, German, Italian and Polish socs. phys. medicine, Argentine Assn. Kinesiology, Canadian Occupational Therapy Assn., Asian-Pacific League Phys. Medicine and Rehab.; mem. Am. Soc. Med. Hydrology (pres. 1962-65), Am. Congress Rehab. Medicine (pres. 1967-68), Internat. Rehab. Med. Assn. (sec. 1968-70), Internat. Congress Phys. Medicine (v.p. 1968). Club: City Athletic (N.Y.C.). Author: Music in Medicine, 1946; Occupational Therapy Source Book, 1947; co-author: Occupational Therapy, 1950; Physical Medicine in General Practice, 1952; Electrodiagnosis and Electromyography, 1956; Therapeutic Heat, 1958; Therapeutic Exercise, 1958; Therapeutic Electricity and Ultraviolet Radiation, 1959; Massage Manipulation and Traction, 1960; World Directory of Physical Medicine Specialists, 1960; Medical Hydrology, 1965; Medical Climatology, 1964; Orthotics Etcetera, 1966; Rehabilitation and Medicine, 1968; Arthritis and Rehabilitation, 1969; Stroke and Its Rehabilitation, 1974. Emeritus editor Am. Jour. Phys. Medicine; editor Occupational Therapy and Rehab., 1947-51. Address: Coral Gables, Fla. Deceased.

LICHTENSTEIN, MANUEL E., surgeon; b. Chgo., Aug. 15, 1900; s. Samuel and Catherine (Klatzkin) L.; B.S., U. Chgo., 1922; M.D., Rush Med. Coll., Chgo., 1925; M.S., Northwestern U., 1936; D.h.c., U. Brazil, 1961; m. Isabelle Garland, Oct. 2, 1926; children—Robert, William, Richard. Pvt. practice gen. surgery, Chgo.; vol. attending surgeon Cook County Hosp., 1932-69, former prof. surgery Northwestern U. Med. Sch., also Cook County Grad. Sch. Medicine, chmn. dept., 1959-65. Served to col., M.C., AUS, 1942-46. Decorated Bronze Star; War medal (Brazil). Mem. A.C.S. (pres. Chgo. Met. chpt. 1954), Chgo. Surg. Soc. (pres. 1965). Contbr. med. jours. Home: Chicago, Ill. Died Dec. 3, 1977.

LICHTNER, WILLIAM OTTO (LIKT-NER), cons. engr.; b. Chicago, Ill., Aug. 25, 1883; s. William W. and Johanna G. (Otto) L.; B.S. in C.E., Illinois Inst. Technology, 1907; m. Evelyn Rodgers, June 9, 1915; children—William Otto, Jr., Virginia M., Marilyn. Estimator and construction engineer on concrete bridges, 1905-07; associated with Sanford E. Thompson, Boston, 1907-15; partner The Thompson & Lichtner Company, 1916, vice-president and treasurer since 1925; pres. The Wm. O. Lichtner Associates, management counsellors, 1932-41; chief engineering consultant, WPB, 1942; chief of technicians, American Technical Mission to Brazil, 1942; resigned Government service, May 1943, to resume engineering business. Lecturer on management and labor problems at Massachusetts Inst. Technology, Harvard, Syracuse University, etc. Mem. Assn. of Consulting Management Engrs., Inst. of Management, Phi Kappa Sigma. Catholic. Author: Plain and Reinforced Concrete, Time Study and Job Analysis, Planned Control in Manufacturing; also numerous professional papers. Home: Brookline, Mass. *

LICK, CHARLES JACOB, mfg. exec.; b. Fredericksburg, Pa., Jan. 7, 1882; s. Jacob and Rebecca (Wise) L.; student pub. schs.; m. Rose Zobelein, May 5, 1910; children—Paquita (Mrs. Maurice Machris), Rosemary. Owner, operator Lick Pier, Ocean Park, Cal., 1920—; v.p., gen. mgr. Los Angeles Brewing Co., 1930-50, pres., gen. mgr., 1950-53, dir., 1930-53; chmn. exec. com., exec. vice pres., Pabst Brewing Co., 1953—; director Farmers & Mchts. Nat. Bank of Los Angeles, Pabst Brewing Co., Douglas Aircraft Co. Hon. life dir. U.S. Brewers Found., Inc. Mem. Mchts. and Mfrs. Assn. (dir.). Home: Beverly Hills, Cal.

LIDDEL, URNER, cons. physicist; b. Butler, Mo., Sept. 3, 1905; s. Robert Lee and Lutitia Emily (Urner) L.; A.B., Central Coll., Fayette, Mo., 1926; student U. Chgo., 1928; Ph.D., George Washington U., 1941; Sc.D. (hon.), Central Meth. Coll., 1963. Phys. chemist Fixed Nitrogen Research Lab., U.S. Dept. Agr., 1929-36; physicist Stamford Labs., Am. Cyanamid Co., 1936-42; head physics br. Office Naval Research, 1946-48, head nuclear physics br., 1949-51, dir. phys. scis. div. 1949, 51-52; dir. product devel. Bendix Aviation Corp., 1952-55; biophysicist NIH, 1955-56, chief bionucleonics, 1957-60; asst. dir. gen. research Advanced Research Projects Agy., 1960-61; asst. dir. Hughes Research Labs., Malibu, Calif., 1961-62; asst. dir., chief scientist lunar and planetary program Office Space Scis., NASA, 1962-67, spl. asst. to dep. asso. adminstr. space sci. and applications (sci.), 1967-70; cons. physicist. Program dir. div. sci. personnel and edn. NSF, 1956-57; chief physics br. AEC, 1952. Served to lt. Bur. Ordnance, USNR, 1942-43, Bur. of Ships, 1943-44, Service Forces Pacific Fleet, 1945; comdr. Office Research and Inventions, 1945-46; comdg. officer Naval Research Res. Co. W-1, 1951-52, Co. 5-10, 1958-60. Named Distinguished Alumnus, Central Coll., 1950. Fellow Am. Phys. Soc., Phys. Soc. London, A.A.A.S.; mem. Internat. Astron. Union, Md., Washington acads. sci., Optical Soc. Am., Philos. Soc. Washington (pres. 1965), Sigma Xi. Club: Cosmos (Washington). Author: (with others) Infrared Spectroscopy, 1944. Contbr. papers to profl. jours. Home: Washington, D.C. Died Sept. 30, 1979.

LIEBER, LILLIAN R(OSANOFF), writer, educator; b. Nicolaiev, Russia, July 26, 1886; d. Abraham H. and Clara (Bercinskaya) Rosanoff; brought to United States, 1891; B.A., Barnard, 1908; M.A., Columbia, 1911; Ph.D., Clark University, 1914; Huff Meml. Fellow, Byrn Mawr College, 1915-17; married Hugh Gray Lieber, Oct. 27, 1926. Head, physics dept. Wells Coll., Aurora, N.Y., 1917-18; Conn. Coll. for Women, 1918-20; dir. Galois Inst. Math. and Art, 1932—; head dept. math. Long Island U., 1945-54, asso. prof. math., 1945-46, prof., 1946-54. Fellow A.A.A.S. Mem. Am. Math. Soc., Math. Assn. Am. Democrat. Jewish religion. Author: Non-Euclidean Geometry, 1931; Galois and the Theory of Groups 1932; The Einstein Theory of Relativity, Special Theory, 1936; General Theory, 1945; The Education of T. C. Mits, 1942; Mathematics for the Two Billion 1944; Mits, Wits and Logic, 1947; Infinity, 1953; Human Values of Modern Mathematics, 1956; Introduction in A Book of Abstract Drawings (by Hugh Gray Lieber); Lattice Theory, 1960. Editor: publs. Galois Inst. of Math. Address: Bklyn.

LIEBERSON, GODDARD, composer, critic, bus. exec.; b. Hanley, Staffordshire, Eng., Apr. 5, 1911; s. Davis and Rachel (Lewis) L.; student U. Wash., Eastman Sch. Music; hon. doctorate, Temple U., 1957, Cleve. Inst. Music, 1965, Lincoln Coll., Ill.; D.H.L., U. Rochester; m. Vera Zorina; children—Peter, Jonathan Sears. Came to U.S., 1915, naturalized, 1936. Tchr. music Harley Country Day Sch.; music critic Rochester (N.Y.) Jour.-Am.; lectr. colls. in N.Y.; radio critic Modern Music; founder and officer Am. Composer's Alliance; asso. editor Internat. Cyclopedia of Music and Musicians, 1955-66; pres. Columbia Records, 1956-66. CBS Records Group, 1973-77, CBS Group, 1966-71, sr. v.p., 1971-77, dir. CBS, Inc., 1956-77; program annotator New York Philharmonic Broadcast, 1943, Phila. Orch. Broadcasts, 1954. Chmn. bd. overseers Hopkins Center, Dartmouth Coll., U. Pa. Adv. Council Performing Arts; mem. Yale Council Com. on Music; bd. dirs. Met. Opera Assn.; mem. planning sect. Music Adv. Panel, Nat. Endowment for Arts. Recipient 7 Grammy awards Nat. Acad. Rec. Arts and Scis. Mem. Civil War Round Table, Record Industry Assn. Am. (past pres., chmn., recipient 7 gold record awards), Country Music Assn. (v.p.). Author: (novel) Three for Bedroom C; Columbia Book of Musical Masterworks; (book and record sets) the Confederacy, 1953; the Union, 1956; the Revolution, 1960; the Mormon Pioneers, 1965; Mexico, 1964; the Badmen, 1963; John Fitzgerald Kennedy-As We Remember Him, 1965; the Irish Uprising, 1916-22, 1966; Medicine, Mind and Music, 1972. Composer: String Quartet and Piano Pieces for Advanced Children or Retarded Adults; Homage to Handel. Contbr. articles to N.Y. Times Mag., Reporter, Saturday Rev., Gramophone. Address: New York, N.Y. Died May 29, 1977.

LIEBOW, AVERILL ABRAHAM, physician, educator; b. Austria, Mar. 31, 1911; s. Charles and Emma (Wagner) L.; came to U.S., 1920, naturalized, 1926; B.S., Coll. City N.Y., 1931; M.D., Yale, 1935; m. Carolyn Booth Gott, Feb. 16, 1946; children—Paul Averill, Milton Charles, Robert Everton. House officer pathology Yale, 1935-37, Charles Linnaeus Ives fellow pathology, 1936-37, faculty Sch. Medicine, 1937-68, prof. pathology, 1951-57; John Ely prof. pathology, 1957-68; prof., chmn. dept. pathology U. Calif. San Diego, La Jolla, 1968-77, prof. emeritus, 1977-78; house officer pathology New Haven Hosp., 1937-37; pathologist Meriden (Conn.) Hosp., 1937-42. Chmn. com. pathology NRC, 1958-63; expert com. cancer WHO, 1958-78; Nat. Acad. Sci.-NRC adv. com. to Atomic Bomb Casualty Commn., 1956-63; mem. pathology study sect. USPHS, 1960-64, mem. heart program-project com., 1964-68, mem. cardiopulmonary adv. com. NIH; mem. pathology adv. council VA Central Office; mem. Joint Commn. for Investigation Effects of Atomic Bomb in Japan, 1945-46; cons. Surgeon Gen., Armed Forces Inst. Pathology, 1947-78. Served from capt. to lt. col., AUS, 1942-46. Recipient Middleton Goldsmith medal N.Y. Path. Soc., 1968; Calif. Physician of Year award Am. Coll. Chest Physicians, 1975; gold medal Calif. Lung Assn.; Liebow Auditorium at U. Calif. Sch. Med., San Diego, named in his honor, 1978. Mem. Internat. Acad. Pathology (pres. 1953-54), Phi Beta Kappa, Sigma Xi, Alpha Omega Alpha. Author: (with Lindskog) Thoracic Surgery and Related Pathology, 1953; (with W.E. Bloomer and M.R. Hales) Surgical Anatomy of the Bronchovascular Segments, 1960; (with G.E. Lindskog and W.W.L. Glenn) Thoracic and Cardiovascular Surgery and Related Pathology, 1962, 3d edit., 1975; Encounter with Disaster A Medical Diary of Hiroshima 1945, 1971; (with Colin M. Bloor) Pulmonary and Bronchial Circulations in Congenital Heart Diseases, 1980. Editorial bd. Lab. Investigation Circulation Research, Ann. Rev. Medicine, Am. Jour. Pathology, Virchows Archiv, Am. Rev. Respiratory Disease. Home: La Jolla, Calif. Died May 31, 1978; buried Cranberry Isles, Maine.

LIERLE, DEAN MCALLISTER, physician; b. Marshalltown, Iowa, May 21, 1895; s. Fredrick Perkins and Laura (Ralston) L.; student Stanford, 1914-16; B.S., U. Iowa, 1919, M.D., 1921, M.S., 1923; postgrad. Boston U., 1921-22, U. Pa., 1928, U. Vienna (Austria), semester, 1929; D.Sc. (hon.), Wayne U., 1950; m. Pauline Thompson, Feb. 24, 1923; children—Dean McAllister, Richard, Burton, William Bayard. Practice of medicine, Iowa City, from 1921; instr. otolaryngology and oral surgery U. Iowa, 1923-26, asst. prof., 1926-28, prof. otolaryngology and maxillofacial surgery, 1928, then emeritus. Cons., Surgeon Gen. Recipient Distinguished Merit award U. Iowa, 1974. Diplomate Am. Bd. Otolaryngology (sec.-treas. emeritus), Am. Bd. Plastic Surgery (founders group). Fellow A.C.S. (v.p., regent); mem. Am. Hearing Soc. (bd. mgrs.), A.M.A., Am. Laryngological Assn (Newcomb award 1956, Roaldes award 1960), Am. Acad Ophthalmology and Otholaryngology (sec. of home study, former chmn. com. on conservation of hearing), Am. Coll. Allergists, Am. Assn. U. Profs., Audiology Found., Iowa Acad. Sci., Am. Laryngol., Rhinol. and Otolaryngol. Soc., Am. Otol. Soc., Soc. for Research in Child Devel., Ia. Acad. Ophthalmology and Otolaryngology, Iowa, Johnson County med. socs., Am. Broncho-Esophagological Assn., Am. Coll. Chest Phys., Am. Speech Corr. Assn., A.A.A.S., Sigma Xi, Alpha Omega Alpha. Republican. Episcopalian. Clubs: University Athletic, Country, Contbr. articles to profl. publs. Home: Iowa City, Iowa. Died Aug. 9, 1976.

LIGGIT, CLARENCE REED, fgn. service officer; b. Hebron, Neb., Sept. 6, 1908; s. Clark Manifold and Grace (Cooke) L.; student U. Miami, 1930-32; LL.B., Miami Coll. Law, 1932; m. Jeannette Elizabeth Cain, Nov. 30, 1934. Admitted to Fla. bar, 1932; practiced in Miami, 1932-42; prosecutor War Crimes Trials, Tokyo, Japan, 1947-48; dept. chief legal sect. Supreme Comdr. Allied Powers, Tokyo, 1948-51; spl. asst. sec. navy, Washington, 1953-53; legal counsel U.S. Operations Mission to Iran, 1954-56, dep. dir. to Iraq, 1957-58, acting dir., 1958-60, dir. to Israel, Tel Aviv, 1960-61;

dir. AID mission to Cyprus, 1961-62; with AID Dept. State, Washington, 1962-74. Served to lt. col. USAAF, 1942-46. Club: International (Washington). Home: Arlington, Va. Died Dec. 23, 1978.

LIGHT, CHARLES PORTERFIELD, JR., educator; b. Martinsburg, W.Va., Dec. 29, 1902; s. Charles Porterfield and Margaret Hunter (Harlan) L.; A.B., Va. Mil. Inst., 1923, M.A., 1928; LL.B., Harvard, 1926; m. Ethel Pearcy Kinnear, July 10, 1942; children—Elizabeth Harlan (Mrs. Cressor), Winifred Pearcy (Mrs. Flippen). Asst. prof. law Washington and Lee U., 1926-27, asso. prof., 1927-37, prof. law, 1937-47, prof. law on the Thomas Ball Found., 1947-60, dean Sch. Law, 1960-68, prof. law, 1960-73, dean emeritus, 1973-76. Vis. prof. law U. Va., spring 1947; practice of law, Washington, summers 1930-36. Served with AUS, 1940-46, as maj. office of Judge Advocate Gen.; lt. col., J.A.G.D., staff judge adv., Bermuda Base Command, U.S. Army; col. Gen. Staff Corps, adviser and liaison officer on legal and leased base Matters for the Operations Div., War Dept. Gen. Staff. Decorated Legion of Merit, Army Commendation medal. Mem. Va. (mem. exec. com. 1970-71), Am. bar assns., Am. Law Inst. (life), Order of Coif, Phi Beta Kappa, Sigma Nu, Phi Delta Phi, Omicron Delta Kappa. Episcopalian. Club: Alfalfa (Washington). Contbr. articles profl. jours. Home: Rockbridge Baths, Va. Died Nov. 19, 1976.

LIGHT, ENOCH HENRY, rec. co. exec.; b. Canton, Ohio, Aug. 18, 1905; s. Morris and Rose (Feiman) L.; B.A., Johns Hopkins, 1926; M.A., N.Y. U., 1953; student Mozarteum, Salzburg, Austria, 1929; m. Mary Danis, Nov. 18, 1927; children—Julie Light Klages, Mary Jack Light Wald. Mus. condr. in France, Germany, Italy, also rec. artist for RCA Victor and Columbia records, 1938-40; pres. Waldorf Music Hall Records, N.Y.C., 1954-59, Award Record Co., N.Y.C., 1959-65; exec. v.p., mng. dir. Command Record Co., N.Y.C., 1959-65; dir. Grand Award Record Co., Inc., N.Y.C., 1959-65; pres., chief exec. officer Total Sound, Inc., N.Y.C., 1966-78, also Record Songs, Inc., N.Y.C.; producer Persuasive Percussion, Stereo 35, also Broadway shows, 9 Beethoven symphonies; tchr. N.Y. U., 1959; pioneer 4 channel rec., 1963-78; Mem. nat. resources com. Johns Hopkins, 1963-78; mem. pres.'s council N.Y. U., 1967-78. Recipient Record Achievement award Indsl. Dept. N.Y.C. Dept. Commerce, 1964; award for finest Beethoven recs. N.Y. Times, 1970; award for outstanding contbn. to music Inst. High Fidelity, 1972; Distinguished Alumni Achievement award N.Y. U., 1976; Disting. Alumni award Johns Hopkins U., 1978. Mem. A.S.C.A.P., Profl. Music Men, Nat. Assn. Condrs. and Composers, Pi Lambda Phi. Clubs: Johns Hopkins, N.Y. Univ. (N.Y.C.); Redding (Conn.) Country. Composer popular songs; innovator new devel. multi-microphone rec., stereo rec., magnetic film rec. Home: West Redding, Conn. Died July 31, 1978; buried Umpawaug Burial Ground, Redding, Conn.

LILIENFIELD, HENRY JACOB, fgn. service officer; b. Jersey City, N.J., Oct. 29, 1905; s. Isaac and Rebecca (Bienstock) L.; LL.B., St. John's U., 1931; grad. student Columbia, 1932-33, 42-43, Fordham U., 1933-34, N.Y.U., 1934-35, 39-40; m. Lee Markman, Dec. 4, 1925; children—Laurence S., Barbara (Mrs. Robert B. Balter), Gerald S. Successively investigator, case supr., office mgr., field office supr., asst. dir. N.Y.C. Dept. Welfare, 1932-41; spl. research asso. State Charities Aid Assn., N.Y.C., 1941-42; research asso. Community Service Soc., N.Y.C., 1942-43; sr. analyst Exec. Office President, Bur. Budget, 1943-48; asst. dir. VA, 1948-51; chief mgmt. Internat. Ednl. and Cultural Exchange Program, State Dept., 1951-56; consul, 2d sec. embassy, Bonn, Germany, 1956-58; adminstr. U.S. Escapee and Refugee Program for Germany, 1958-60; consul, 1st sec. embassy London, Eng., from 1960. Group discussion leader 5th dist. (Md.) Farm Bur. Fedn., 1954-55; pres. Howard County (Md.) Planning Assn., 1955-56. Mem. Am. Fgn. Service Assn., Am. Soc. Pub. Adminstrn. Am. Soc. Advancement Mgmt., Am. Pub. Welfare Assn., U.S. Interagy. Records and Archival Adminstrn. Conf. Author numerous articles, manuals. Home: Fulton, Md. Died Jan. 5, 1980; buried Har Sinai Cemetery, Baltimore, Md.

LILIENTHAL, DAVID ELI, bus. cons., writer; b. Morton, Ill., July 8, 1899; s. Leo and Minna (Rosenak) L.; A.B., DePauw U., 1920, LL.D., 1945; LL.B., Harvard, 1923; LL.D., Lehigh U., 1949, Mich. State Coll., 1949, Boston U., 1952, Universidad de los Andes, Columbia, 1954, U. Calif. at Los Angeles, 1964, Ind. U., 1965; Dr. Pub. Adminstrn., U. Ill., 1967; m. Helen Marian Lamb, Sept. 4, 1923; children—Nancy Alice (Mrs. Bromberger), David Eli Jr. Admitted to Ill. bar, 1923; practice law, Chgo., 1923-31; mem. Wis. Pub. Service Commn., 1931-33; dir. TVA, 1933-41, chmn. 1941-46; chmn. A.E.C., 1946-50; chmn. bd., chief exec. officer Devel. and Resources Corp., 1955-79; adviser pres. Republic Colombia, 1954, co-chmn. Joint Postwar Devel. Group, Vietnam, 1967-70 chmn. U.S. State Dept. bd. cons. Internat. Control Atomic Energy, 1946; mem. Council Fgn. Relations. Trustee Twentieth Century Fund, Com. Econ. Devel. Recipient Progressive Farmer award, 1945; Cath. Com. South award, 1946; Freedom award, 1949; Pub. Welfare medal Nat. Acad. Sci., 1951; comendador de la Orden el Sol del Peru, 1964; comendador Orden de Rio Branco (Brazil), 1972. Mem. Am. Acad. Arts and Sci., Am. Philos. Soc., Authors Guild, Phi Beta Kappa. Club: Century (N.Y.C.). Author: TVA; Democracy on the March, 1944; This I Do Believe, 1949; Big Business A New Era, 1953; The Multinational Corporation, 1960; Change, Hope and the Bomb, 1963; Journals of David E. Lilienthal, Vols. I and II, 1964, Volume III, 1966, Vol. IV, 1969, Vol. V, 1971, Vol. VI, 1976; Management: A Humanist Art, 1967. Home: Princeton, N.J. Died Jan. 14, 1981.

LILJE, JOHANNES ERNST RICHARD, bishop; b. Hannover, Germany, Aug. 20, 1899; s. Theodor and Maria (Gottschalk) L.; student Göttingen U., Leipzig U., Kloster Loccum, Hannover, Germany; Th.D., U. Zürich (Switzerland) 1932; D.D. (hon.), U. Edinburgh, 1947, Thiel Coll., 1957, Augustana Coll., 1954, Oberlin Coll., 1957; Th.D., Goettingen (Germany), 1947; LL.D., Wittenberg Coll., Springfield, O., 1948, Muhlenberg Coll., Allentown, Pa., 1948: L.H.D., Concordia Coll., 1953, Rockford Coll.; Dr. theol. h.c., Helsinki, Finland, 1963. Student pastor at Technical Hochschule, Hannover, 1924-26; gen. sec. German Student Christian Movement, 1927-35; v.p. World Student Christian Fedn., 1932-35; gen. sec. Luth. World Conv., 1935-45; arrested in Berlin by the Gestapo, 1944-45; pres. central com. for inner mission German Evang. Ch., 1945-57; Luth. bishop, Hannover, 1947-71; mem. Council Evang. Ch. in Germany, 1945-73, v.p., 1949-67; abbot, Loccum, 1950-77; presiding bishop Evangelical Luth. Ch. of Germany, 1955-69; Harry Emerson Fosdick vis. prof. Union Theol. Sem., N.Y.C., 1960. Mem. exec. com. Luth. World Fedn., 1947-70, pres., 1952-57, a pres., 1968-70; mem. central com. World Council Churches, 1948-75, mem. exec. com., 1961-75. Served with German Army, 1917-18. Mem. Brit. and Fgn. Bible Soc., Am. Bible Soc. Author: Luther Now, 1946; The Valley of the Shadow, 1947; and others. Editor of Die Furche, 1934-42, Die Junge Kirche, 1933-35, Deutsches Allgemeines Sonntagsblatt, 1948-77; The Last Book of the Bible, 1940; Welt unter Gott, 1956; Kirche Und Welt, 1956; Christianity in a Divided Europe, 1964; Martin Luther, 1964. Address: Hannover, Federal Republic of Germany. Died Jan. 6, 1977; buried Kloster Loccum.

LILLARD, WILLIAM PARLIN, food corp. exec.; b. Lawrenceburg, Ky., Sept. 16, 1898; s. William and Louise (Parlin) L.; grad. U. Pa., 1921; m. Alma Shanks, Nov. 13, 1937; children—Parlin, Peggy, Peachy, John. Salesman, Snow King Baking Powder Co., Cin., 1922-28, sales mgr., v.p., 1928-37, pres. 1937-40 (became part of Gen. Foods 1937); nat. mgr. spl. coffees Gen. Foods Co., N.Y.C., 1941, dist. sales mgr., Phila., 1941-43, Western sales mgr., N.Y.C., 1943-45, div. mgr. spl. products, N.Y.C., 1947-49, sales promotion mgr. Gen. Foods Sales, 1949-53, pres., gen. mgr. Perkins div. Gen. Foods, Chgo., responsible for corp. packaging, indsl. and internat. devel. Gen. Foods Kitchens, Corp. new products, frozen prepared foods, corp. devel. and comml. evaluation, acquisitions, 1959-63; pres. Lillard Syndications, Inc., 1964-66, Lillard-Berry, Bishop & Parker, Inc., from 1966; pres. Francis-Lillard Assos., Inc., N.Y.C., 1968-79; former dir. Burgoyne Index, Inc., Security Storage Co., Emery Industries, Inc. Trustee Graham Home for Children, St. Johns Coll., Annapolis, Md., 1947-50. Served USNRF, 1918-19. Clubs: Sky (N.Y.C.); St. Anthony (Phila.); Coral Beach. Home: New York, N.Y. Died May 8, 1980; buried Grove Hill Cemetery, Cin.

LILLEHEI, RICHARD CARLTON, surgeon, med. researcher, educator; b. Mpls., Dec. 10, 1927; s. Clarence I. and Elizabeth L. (Walton) L.; B.A. magna cum laude, U. Minn., 1948, B.S., 1949, M.D., 1951, Ph.D., 1960; m. Betty Jeanne Larsen, Dec. 20, 1952; children—Richard Carlton, Theodore J., John C., James L. Intern, Hennepin County Gen. Hosp., Mpls., 1951-52; resident surgeon U. Minn. Health Scis. Center, Mpls., 1952-54, 56-59, resident cardiovascular surgeon, 1959-60, asst. prof. surgery, 1960-62, asso. prof., 1962-66, prof., 1966—. Served as capt. M.C., AUS, 1954-56. Recipient Hektoen gold medal AMA, 1964, Irving S. Cutter gold medal Phi Rho Sigma, 1976; named Man of Year, Minn. Jr. C. of C., 1962. Mem. Phi Beta Kappa, Sigma Xi, Alpha Omega Alpha. Contbr. articles to profl. jours., chpts. in books. Finished Boston Marathon, 1972-80, N.Y. Marathon, 1978-80. Home: Minneapolis, Minn. Died Apr. 1, 1981.

LILLEY, ALEXANDER NEIL, oil co. exec.; b. San Francisco, Oct. 28, 1905; s. Alexander S. and Marie Juliette (Williams) L.; grad. Lawrenceville Sch.; student Princeton, 1924-25; m. Elena Musto, Mar. 2, 1935; children—Alexander, Elena Maria. With Sperry Flour Co., 1925-29, Chase Securities Corp., 1929-33; dir. Societé des Raffineries de Petrole de la Gironde, Paris, France, 1945-1949, v.p., 1948-49; with Pacific Coast region Texaco, Inc., 1933-42, gen. mgr. Eastern Hemisphere operations, 1949-51, v.p., 1951-57, dir., 1954-57; pres. Texaco Can., Ltd., Montreal, 1957-63; pres. Cal. Tex. Oil Corp., 1963, chmn. bd., 1964-70. Served with USAAF, 1942-45. Home: New York, N.Y. Died Mar. 17, 1976.

LILLIE, RALPH DOUGALL, pathologist; b. Cucamonga, Calif., Aug. 1, 1896; s. William Adam and Ida Ford (Howell) L.; A.B., Stanford U., 1917, M.D., 1920; m. Ethel Astrup Christensen, May 14, 1920; children—Margaret Alice (Mrs. Thomas Rogers Lusk), Susan, Ida (Mrs. Herbert Herman) (dec.), Mary (Mrs. Thomas E. Wallace), Ralph Dougall, William, Andrew, Ruth (Mrs. William J. Welty). Intern, San Francisco Hosp., 1919-20; pvt. practice, Monterey, Calif., 1920; with USPHS, 1920-60, asst. surgeon (res.), 1920, regular, 1921, asst. surgeon, 1925, surgeon, 1932, sr. surgeon, 1940, med. dir., 1945-60, ret.; served at VA Hosp., Tacoma, San Francisco Quarantine, Relief Sta., Seattle, Stapleton (N.Y.) Marine Hosp., Ellis Island (N.Y.) Immigration Sta., Hygienic Lab. (now NIH Bethesda, Md.), Washington, 1925, in pathology lab., 1926-60, acting chief, 1937, chief, 1938-48; chief div. pathology and pharmacology, 1948-52, chief pathology dept. Clin. Center, 1952-53, chief lab. pathology and histochemistry, 1952-60; research prof. pathology La. State U., New Orleans, from 1960. Mem. study sect. on pathology USPHS, 1946-52; Am. v.p. 2d Internat. Congress Histochemistry and Cytochemistry, Frankfurt am Main, Germany, 1964, hon. v.p. 3d Congress, N.Y., 1968, 4th Congress, Kyoto, Japan, 1972. Served as pvt. U.S. Army, 1918. Fellow Am. Inst. Chemists, Phillipine Soc. Pathologists (hon.); mem. AMA, Internat. Acad. Pathology (pres. 1948), Am. Soc. Exptl. Pathology (hon.), Histochem. Soc. (pres. 1957-58), Biol. Stain Commn. (pres. 1959-63, trustee, rep. Am. Assn. Pathologists and Bacteriologists), Washington Soc. Pathologists, Am. Assn. Pathologists and Bacteriologists, Assn. Mil. Surgeons U.S. (first sustaining mem.'s award 1958), Pan Am. Med. Soc., Argentine Soc. Pathology (hon.), Phi Beta Kappa, Sigma Xi. Author: Histopathologic Technic, 1948; Histopathologic Technic and Practical Histochem., 1953, 4th edit., 1975; also numerous sci. papers. Editor in chief Jour. Histochemistry and Cytochemistry, 1952-64; editor Conn's Biological Stains, 8th edit., 1969, 9th edit., 1977. Home: New Orleans, La. Died Oct. 5, 1979; buried St. Mary Cemetery, Barnsville, Md.

LILLY, ELI, pharm. co. exec.; b. Indpls., Apr. 1, 1885; s. Josiah Kirby and Lilly Marie (Ridgely) L.; Ph.C., Phila. Coll. Pharmacy and Sci., 1907, Ph.M., 1935; LL.D., Wabash Coll., 1938; Litt.D., Butler Coll., 1940; D.C.L., U. of South, 1940; D.Sc., Transylvania U., 1941; LL.D., U. Ky., 1945, Ind. U. 1949, U. Pitts., 1952, Ball State U., 1972; D.H.L., Union Coll., 1948, De Pauw U., 1948, Kenyon Coll., 1956; m. Ruth Allison, Nov. 7, 1927 (dec. Mar. 1973); 1 dau., Evelyn (dec.). Entire bus. career with Eli Lilly & Co., Indpls., from 1907, supt. mfg. div., 1909-15, gen. supt., 1915-20, v.p., 1920-32, pres., 1932-48, chmn. bd. 1948-66, hon. chmn. bd., 1966-77. Pres. Lilly Endowment, 1966-72, chmn. bd., 1972-75, hon. chmn. bd., 1975-77. Recipient Remington Honor medal N.Y. br. Am. Pharm. Assn. 1958; named hon. comdr. Mil. Order Loyal Legion U.S., 1971. Mem. Ind. Hist. Soc. (pres. 1933-46). Am. Pharm. Assn. (hon. pres. 1953). Episcopalian. Author: Prehistoric Antiquities of Indiana, 1937; The Little Church on the Circle, 1957; Early Wawasee Days, 1960; Schliemann in Indianapolis, 1961. Home: Indianapolis, Ind. Died Jan. 24, 1977.

LIMB, BEN C., Korean public official; born Seoul, Korea, Oct. 26, 1893; s. Yunsang Limb, educator and Shusi Limb; ed. Seoul School of Chinese Classics, Posung Junior College, Royal Foreign Language Sch.; Mt. Hermon Preparatory Sch., Mass., and Ohio State U. (non-grad.); LL.D., Gustavus Adolphus Coll., 1951, Fairleigh Dickinson Coll., 1955. Came to U.S. in 1913 and worked almost continously for Korean independence, first as secretary to Dr. Syngman Rhee, now President of the Republic of Korea; then Dr. Rhee's successor as Chairman, Korean Commission to the U.S.; appointed Minister of Foreign Affairs, Republic of Korea, 1949, and Chief of Mission to United Nations Security Council and General Assembly, 1950; apptd. ambassador-at-large of Rep. of Korea, 1951; apptd. permanent rep. of Rep. of Korea, to U.N., 1951; apptd. A.E. and P. Republic of Korea to U.N., 1953. Appointed lt., Korean Unit, Cal. Nat. Guard, 1942; apptd. col. in Army of Korean Provisional Government, 1945. Traveled widely through Asia, Europe and North Am. on various missions for his government. Lectured widely in Am. Attended Japanese Peace Treaty Conf., San Francisco, 1951; U.S.-Korean Mut. Def. Treaty Conf., Seoul, 1953; Geneva Conf. on Asia, 1954; accompanied Pres. Syngman Rhee on state visit to U.S. 1954; chief del. of Korea to U.N. Atomic Energy Conference, Vienna, 1957, Korea-Japan Peace Negotiations, Tokyo, 1958. Author: Collection of Speeches by Ben C. Limb, 1958. Address: Seoul, Korea. Died Sept. 21, 1976.

LIMING, MELVILLE DARST (LI-MING), ret. sec. mng. dir. Boston C. of C.; b. Brown County, O., Dec. 10, 1882; s. James O. and Sabrah (Oursler) L.; A.B., Miami U., 1906; A.M., Harvard, 1910; spl. student Harvard Law Sch., 1910-12; m. Marjorie Odlin, Oct. 21, 1916; children—Elizabeth (Mrs. Robert E. Rew, Jr.), Robert Warren. Began as teacher of history, Todd School, Woodstock, Ill., 1906-08, Michigan City (Indiana) High School, 1908-09; Adams Woods fellow, Harvard, 1910-12; asst. in government, Harvard, 1910-11; instr. polit. science, Tufts Coll., 1912-14, and one of counsel for Boston Legal Aid Soc.; admitted to Mass. bar, 1913; organized Brown County (Ohio) Nat. Bank and served as an officer. and dir., 1915-17; mem. staff Nat. Industrial Conf. Bd., 1918-20; mgr. Bur. Commercial and Industrial Affairs, Boston Chamber Commerce, 1920-27; exec. sec., mng. dir. and mem. exec. com. Boston Chamber Commerce, 1927-49; sec. Boston Chamber Commerce Realty Trust since 1927; president N.E. Assn. Comml. Execs., 1929-31; dir. Nat. Assn. Commercial Orgn. Secs., 1931-34 and 1936, 39, v.p. 1932-33, pres. 1937-38; mem. Naval Offices Procurement Adv. Com., 1st Naval District and mem. Mass. Food Adv. Com. during World War II; dir. Mass. Safety Council; mem. bd. of mgrs. Northeastern Institute, 1945-50. Awarded Distinguished Service Certificate, Northeastern Institute, 1950. Mem. Delta Upsilon. Author various articles on commerical organizations, industry and commerce. Home: Newton Centre, Mass. *

LINCOLN, DANIEL WALDO, lawyer, museum trustee; b. Worcester, Mass., Sept. 2, 1882; s. Waldo and Fanny (Chandler) L.; student France and Germany; grad. Pomfret Prep. Sch., 1900; A.B., Harvard, 1904, LL.B., 1907; m. Harriet Brayton Nichols, Dec. 29, 1917; 1 son, Brayton. Admitted to Mass. bar, 1907, since practiced Worcester; also trustee real estate, other trustees, fed. receiverships; referee bankruptcy Worcester Co., 1921-47; mem. Mass. Appellate Tax Bd., 1947-53. Mem. Worcester City Govt., 1913-15, Mass. Ho. Reps., 1916-17. Honorary trustee of Worcester Art Mus.; council, recording sec. Am. Antiquarian Soc., 1938—; adv. trustee Meml. Hosp., Worcester. Served as 1st lt., inf., U.S. Army, 1917-19; AEF in France, 1918-19. Mem. Am., Mass. (past v.p.), Worcester Co. (past president), bar associations, American Judicature Soc., also Worcester Fire Soc., St. Wulstan Soc. Unitarian. Clubs: Harvard (N.Y.C.); Worcester City, Harvard (Worcester); Tatnuck Country. Home: Worcester. *

LINDENMUTH, TOD (LIN'DEN-MOOTH), artist; b. Allentown, Pa., May 4, 1885; s. Arlington Nelson and Hattie Louise (Helfrich) L.; ed. pub. schs., Allentown; art. edn., New York Sch. of Art; m. Elisabeth Boardman Warren, Oct. 28, 1925; children—Peter Lane, Anne Warren. Painter and block printer. Represented by paintings in Newark (N.J.) Museum, Pa. Acad. Fine Arts. Phila.; block prints in Rochester (N.Y.) Memorial Museum, New York Pub. Library, Toledo (O.) Museum, Houston (Tex.) Museum of Art, Bibliothèque Nationale, Paris, Los Angeles Museum of Art, Springfield (Mass.) Museum Fine Arts; paintings and block prints in Museum of Fine Arts, Allentown, Pa. Mem. Rockport Assn. Episcopalian. Address: (winter) St. Augustine, Fla., (summer), Rockport, Mass. *

LINDLEY, ALLEN LEDYARD, life ins. co. exec.; b. Englewood, N.J., Oct. 17, 1909; s. Allen L. and Elizabeth (Ellsworth) L.; grad. Hotchkiss Sch., 1928; B.A., Yale, 1932; m. Lucille Bertolette, Sept. 10, 1934. With Chase Nat. Bank, 1932-39; v.p., dir. Douglas T. Johnston & Co., Inc., investment counsel, 1939-52, Johnston Mut. Fund, 1947-52, v.p., treas. Mut. Life Ins. Co. N.Y., 1952-61, sr. v.p., 1961-67, exec. v.p., 1967-72, vice chmn. bd., from 1972, trustee, from 1969; chmn., trustee MONY Mortgage Investors; chmn exec. com. Lincoln First Banks Inc., Rochester, N.Y.; dir. Nat. Bank of Westchester, N. Am. Life and Casualty Co. Served as lt. USNR, 1943-45. Home: Rye, N.Y. Died May 29, 1978.

LINDLEY, ERNEST KIDDER, writer; b. Richmond, Ind., July 14, 1899; s. Ernest Hiram and Elisabeth (Kidder) L.; student Ind. U., 1916-17; A.B., U. Idaho, 1920, D.Litt., 1960; B.A. (Rhodes scholar), Oxford U. (Eng.), 1923, M.A., 1953; D.Litt., L.I. U., 1958; LL.D., Lehigh U.; m. Betty Grimes, Oct. 25, 1929 (dec. Mar. 1976); children—Jonathan, Christopher, Mark; m. 2d, Jean Rasch Gehman, Oct. 30, 1976. Reporter, Wichita Beacon, 1924; reporter, polit. writer, N.Y. World, 1924-31, polit. writer N.Y. Herald Tribune, 1931-37, Washington Bur., 1933-37; chief Wash. Bur., Newsweek, 1937-61; polit. commentator Washington Post, 1938-43, Register and Tribune Syndicate, 1938-52; radio and TV commentator various networks, 1938-61; spl. asst. to the sec. of state, mem. policy planning council State Dept., 1961-69; SEATO traveling lectr., 1959. Mem. delegation various ministerial council meeting NATO, SEATO, CENTO, ANZUS, 1961-68; adv. meetings U.S.-Japan Joint Cabinet Com., 1961, 64, 66. Served as 2d lt. U.S. Army, World War I. Recipient Overseas Press Club award for TV reporting, 1953; Chubb fellowship Timothy Dwight Coll., Yale U., 1952; Overseas Press Club of Am. award for best interpretation of fgn. affairs in press, 1957; Distinguished Alumni award Ind. U., 1956; Superior Honor award Dept. State, 1966; William Allen White Found. award, 1968; medal honor U. Evansville, 1970; elected Distinguished Alumni Scholar, DASA Club, Ind. U., 1974; elected charter mem. Washington Corrs. Hall of Fame, 1971. Decorated Order of St. Olav (Norway). Mem. Council Fgn. Relations, Am. Fgn. Service Assn., Washington Inst. Fgn. Affairs, Ind. Acad., Soc. Silurians, Phi Kappa Psi, Sigma Delta Chi, Phi Beta Kappa. Clubs: Cosmos, Nat. Press, Internat. (Washington); Overseas Writers (pres. 1948-49). Author: Franklin D. Roosevelt-A Career in Progressive Democracy, 1931; The Roosevelt Revolution-First Phase, 1933; Half Way with Roosevelt, 1936; (with Betty G. Lindley) A New Deal for Youth, 1938; (with Forrest Davis) How War Came, 1942. Editor and author intro.: The Winds of Freedom by Sec. State Dean Rusk, 1963. Contbr. to mags. Home: Washington, D.C. Died June 30, 1979.

LINDNER, RICHARD, painter; b. Hamburg, Germany, Nov. 11, 1901; s. Julius and Mina (Bornstein) L.; ed. in Nuremburg, Germany, also Munich (Germany) Acad.; D.F.A., 1977. Came to U.S., 1941, naturalized, 1948. Prof., Staatliche Hochschule für bildende Künste, Hamburg, 1965; prof. Pratt Inst., N.Y.C., 1952-64; lectr. Yale, 1965; exhbns. throughout U.S., France, Belgium, Eng., Italy, Germany, Can., Switzerland, Holland, Japan, also Mus. Modern Art, Whitney Mus. Recipient Lichtwerk award, Hamburg, 1970. Mem. Nat. Inst. Arts and Letters. Home: New York, N.Y. Died Apr. 16, 1978.

LINDQUIST, EVERET FRANKLIN, educator; b. Gowrie, Iowa, June 4, 1901; s. Jonas Algot and Hannah Olivia (Anderson) L.; A.B., Augustana Coll., Rock Island, Ill., 1922, Litt.D., 1964; student U. Chgo., 1922; Ph.D., State U. Ia., 1927; m. Marguerite Liebig, Aug. 31, 1927; 1 dau., Louise Joanne (Mrs. Walter Dobrian). High sch. tchr., Macoutah, Ill., 1922; prof. edn. U. Iowa, 1927-69, emeritus, 1969-78; dir. Iowa Testing Programs, 1929-69; in charge constrn. and standardization tests Gen. Ednl. Devel. for U.S. Armed Forces Inst., 1942-44; founder, pres. Measurement Research Center, 1953-68; pres. Iowa Measurement Research Found., 1968-78; co-founder, gen. cons. Am. Coll. Testing Program; originator Iowa Ednl. Information Center. Bd. dirs. U. Iowa Found., 1969-78, U. Iowa Research Found., 1975-78. Recipient Phi Delta Kappa-Am. Ednl. Research Assn. award, 1967; Ednl. Testing Service award for distinguished service to measurement, 1970. Fellow Am. Statis. Assn.; mem. Inst. Math. Statistics, A.A.A.S., Am. Assn. Sch. Adminstrs., Am. Ednl. Research Assn., Psychometric Soc., Sigma Xi. Editor: Iowa Tests of Basic Skills and Iowa sts of Ednl. Development; The Constrn. and Use of Achievement Exams., 1936; Educational Measurement, 1952. Author: A First Course in Statistics, 1938; Statistical Analysis in Educational Research, 1940; Design and Analysis of Experiments in Psychology and Education, 1953. Co-author: Statistics for Economics and Business, 1951; Elementary Statistical Methods, 1959. Designer and developer electronic test scoring machine, 1953. Coll. Edn. bldg., U. Iowa, named in his honor. Home: Iowa City, Iowa. Died May 13, 1978.

LINDSAY, MARTIN, business exec.; b. Newport, Scotland, 1884. Chmn. bd. Middle West Corp.; v.p. and dir. Automatic Electric Co., Associated Telephone & Telegraph Co., Philippine Long Distance Telephone Co.; dir. Chicago Mill & Lumber Co. Ill. *

LINDSLEY, THAYER, mining exec.; b. Yokohama, Japan, Aug. 17, 1882 (parents U.S. citizens); student Milton, (Mass.) Acad., 1895-1900; A.B., S.B., Harvard, 1904; student Columbia U. Sch. Mines, 1910. Founder, dir. of Ventures, Ltd.; president of Westfield Minerals, Limited, Eureka Corporation. Served to capt. Arty., U.S. Army, World War I. Mem. American Inst. Mining and Metall. Engrs. Home: New York, N.Y. Died May 29, 1976.

LINFORD, HENRY BLOOD, educator; b. Logan, Utah, Apr. 23, 1911; s. James Henry, Jr. and Mary Hooper (Blood) L.; B.S., Utah State Agrl. Coll., 1931; M.S., Wash. State Coll., 1933, Ph.D., 1936; postgrad. Columbia, 1936-37; m. Rebecca Marian Ririe, Sept. 4, 1936; children—Henry Larry, Marian, Alan Kenneth. Research chemist Am. Smelting & Refining Co., Perth Amboy, N.J., 1937-41; instr. chem. engring. Columbia, 1941-46, asst. prof., 1946-49, asso. prof., 1949-52, prof. chem. engring., 1952-76, prof. emeritus, 1976-80; asst. to pres. Polychrome Corp., Yonkers, N.Y., 1976-80, acting dir. research and devel., 1977-78, dir. research and devel., 1978-80; electrochem. cons., 1941-80. Recipient Acheson medal Electrochem. Soc., 1960, Sci. Achievement award Am. Electroplaters Soc., 1967, Great Tchr. award Soc. Older Grads. Columbia, 1968; Harold C. Urey award Phi Lambda Upsilon, 1977; Distinguished Service award Utah State U., 1978. Fellow N.Y. Acad. Sci., Am. Inst. Chemists; hon. mem. Electrochem. Soc. (sec. 1949-59, pres. 1961-62); mem. Am. Inst. Chem. Engrs., Am. Chem. Soc., Am. Electroplaters Soc. (bd. dirs. 1966-69), Nat. Assn. Corrosion Engrs. Home: Closter, N.J. Died Feb. 3, 1980.

LINK, KARL PAUL, educator, agrl. chemist; b. LaPorte, Ind., Jan. 31, 1901; s. George and Fredericka (Mohr) L.; B.S., M.S., Ph.D., U. Wis., 1918-25; postgrad. U. St. Andrews, Fifeshire, Scotland, 1925-26; microanalyst's certificate, U. Graz (Austria), 1926; student U. Zurich (Switzerland), 1926-27; m. Elizabeth Feldman, Sept. 20, 1930; children—John Kailin, Thomas Paul, Paul Konrad. Began as asst. asso. prof. agrl. chemistry, U. Wis., 1927-30; prof. biochemistry, from 1931; cons. chemistry and tech. plant products, 1933; collaborator Dept. of Agr. soy bean lab., 1937-40, No. Regional Lab., Peoria, Ill., 1940-45; cons. Clinton Foods, Inc., (Iowa), from 1933, Pabst Brewery Co., Milw., from 1944. Recipient Cameron prize U. Edinburgh, 1952; Albert Lasker award med. research, 1955; John Scott award, 1959; Albert Lasker award Am. Heart Assn., 1960. Mem. Harvey Soc. (hon.), Nat. Acad. Sci. (Kovalenko medal 1967), A.A.A.S., Am. Chem. Soc., Fedn. Am. Socs. Exptl. Biology, Sigma Xi. Contbr. sci. papers on chemistry of sugars, disease resistance of plants to profl. jours. Headed team of scientists that developed drug Dicumarol, a blood anticoagulant used to combat intravascular clotting, thrombosis and pulmonary embolism; developed the anticoagulant Warfarin and Warfarin Sodium. Home: Madison, Wis. Deceased.

LINNELL, IRVING NELSON (LIN-NEL'), fgn. service officer; b. Boston, Mass., Jan. 27, 1881; s. Joseph W. and Harriett F. (Huff) L.; A.B., Harvard U., 1904, LL.B., 1907; m. Lilian B. Fisher, June 27, 1914; children—Robert Irving, Gertrude Harriet. Admitted to Mass. bar, 1907, also U.S. Circuit and Dist. courts; practiced in Boston, 1907-11; pres. Common Council, Cambridge, Mass., 1910-11; moved to Prince Rupert, 1911; apptd. consular agt. there, Sept. 23, 1914, v.consul, Apr. 20, 1915; v.consul, at Vancouver, B.C., Mar. 16, 1916, consul, Feb. 19, 1918; consul at Plymouth, Eng., 1919-20; consul detailed at London, Eng., 1920-23; detailed to div. of Western European Affairs, Dept. of State, 1923; consul gen. at Ottawa, Can., 1927-31, Cape Town, S. Africa, 1932-Feb. 1935, Johannesburg, S. Africa, Feb. 1935-Jan. 1936, Canton, China, July 1936-Nov. 1938; became consul gen., Prague, Bohemia, Mar. 1939; assigned to Dept. of State, Aug. 26, 1940; consul gen., Yokohama, Japan, Dec. 9, 1940, to outbreak of war; interned in Japan, Dec. 8, 1941-June 17, 1942; consul gen., Luanda, Angola, Nov. 1942-Sept. 1943; now consul gen., Capetown, South Africa, 1943-Nov. 1944; retired June 30, 1945. Mason. Clubs: Harvard, University (Washington). Home: Medina, Wash. *

LINSKY, JACK, mfr. office specialties; b. Russia, Jan. 1, 1897; s. Zus and Rose (Linsky) L.; came to U.S., 1905, naturalized, 1917; ed. pub. schs., N.Y.C.; m. Belle Karasik, June 14, 1925. Trustee Beth Israel Hosp., N.Y.C.; bd. dirs. Brotherhood-in-Action. Served with U.S. Army, World War I; AEF in France. Jewish religion. Home: New York, N.Y. Died June 3, 1980.

LINSLEY, EARLE GARFIELD (LINZ'LE), prof. astronomy; born in Wetmore, Colo., June 19, 1882; s. Harvey and Rachel (Keyes) L.; A.B., Colgate U., 1904; M.S., Univ. of Calif., 1908; LL.D., Berkeley Baptist Divinity School, 1947; studied Harvard, 1911-12; m. Marguerite Vesper, Sept. 19, 1907; children—Earle Gorton, Katherine Ray, Robert Edward. Instr. in Calif. Coll., Oakland, 1904-08, U. of Calif., 1908-11; mem. staff Blue Hill Meteorol. Obs. of Harvard U., 1911-12; prof. astron., Mills Coll., 1912-47, dir. Chabot Observatory, Oakland, 1923-47, emeritus, 1947. Y.M.C.A. ednl. sec., Camp Fremont, Calif., 1917-18; ednl. sec. with U.S. Army Ednl. Corps, A.E.F., U. of Beaune, France, 1918-19; ordained chaplain (Baptist), Sept. 1918. Fellow A.A.A.S., Royal Astron. Soc.; mem. Calif. Acad. Sciences, Astron. Soc. Pacific, Am. Meteorol. Soc., Delta Upsilon, Pi Gamma Mu. Baptist. Lecturer Berkeley Bapt. Div. Sch. since 1923, pres. bd. of trustees since 1945. Home: Oakland, Calif. *

LINSON, JOHN HENRY, U.S. Pub. Health Service; b. Syracuse, Neb., Mar. 16, 1886; s. Henry Ludlow and Mary Amelia (Scott) L.; B.Sc., U. of Neb., 1910; M.D., Rush Med. Coll. (U. of Chicago), 1912; grad. student U. of Philippines, 1914-15, U. of Vienna, 1921-22; Northwestern U. Med. Sch., 1928; m. Helen Pauline. Satre, Sept. 13, 1930; children—Dorothy Ann, Jane Helen. Interne St. Johns Hosp., Springfield, Ill., 1912, Cook County Hosp., Chicago, 1912-14; commd. asst. surgeon, U.S.P.H.S., 1914, passed asst. surgeon, 1918, surgeon, 1922, sr. surgeon, 1934, med. dir., 1940; practiced in serveral branches of the service including 3 yrs. service in the Philippines and 3 yrs. in Europe; in charge U.S. Marine Hosp., Detroit, 1930-35; med. dir. Tuberculosis and Health Soc. of St. Louis, Inc., 1935-39; senior instr. in preventive medicine and public health, St. Louis U. Sch. of Medicine, 1935-39; in charge U.S. Marine Hosp., St. Louis, Mo., 1935-39; chief quarantine officer, Honolulu, T.H., Aug. 1939-June 1943; also Dist. Coast Guard Med. Officer, 14th Naval Dist., Oct. 15, 1942-June 1943. Transferred to Charleston, S.C., July 1943, as Dist. Coast Guard med. officer for 6th Naval Dist.; also chief quarantine officer, med. officer in charge U.S.P.H.S. relief station and Port Med. Representative, War Shipping Adminstrn. Transferred to Detroit, Mich., Jan. 1945, as med. officer in chg. Marine Hosp. Quarantine and Med. Inspection of Aliens; Chief quarantine officer Fisher's Island, Quarantine Sta., Miami Beach, 1947-49, also med. officer in charge U.S.P.H.S. Relief Station, Miami; med. dir. Orange County (Calif.) Hosp. since 1950. Chairman Rat and Mosquito Control Committee, Honolulu C. of C. Fellow A.M.A., Med. Assn. of Vienna; mem. Assn. Mil. Surgeons of U.S., Honolulu Soc. for the Hard of Hearing (bd. dirs.), Honolulu County Med. Soc., Acad.

of Medicine (Detroit), Phi Rho Sigma, Asso. mem. Wayne County Medical Soc. (Detroit). Republican. Conglist. Mason. Clubs: Sojourners, Rotary (Honolulu); Detroit Yacht; Propeller of U.S., Port of Detroit. *

LINVILL, WILLIAM KIRBY, elec. engr.; b. Kansas City, Mo., Aug. 8, 1919; s. Thomas Grimes and Emma Kirby (Crayne) L.; A.B. in Math. and Physics, William Jewell Coll., 1941; A.B./S.M. Elec. Engring., M.I.T., 1945, Sc.D. in Elec. Engring., 1949; m. Bessie Blythe Burkhardt, June 28, 1942; children—Barbara, Mary Lou, Thomas, Anne, Carl. Asst. prof. elec. engring. M.I.T., 1949-53, asso. prof., 1953-56; project leader Inst. Def. Analysis, Pentagon, Washington, 1956-58; sr. staff mem. electronics Rand Corp., Santa Monica, Calif., 1958-60; prof. elec. engring. Stanford U., 1960-64, chmn., prof. Inst. in Engring.-Econ. Systems, 1964-67, now prof., chmn. dept. engring. econ. systems; Battelle fellow, Columbus, Ohio, 1971-72; mem. vis. com. Nat. Bur. Standards, Dept. Commerce; mem. adv. com. on space and terrestrial applications NASA; mem. Westinghouse Electronics Research Adv. Council, Pitts.; vis. prof. elec. engring. U. Tex., Austin. Fellow IEEE; mem. Nat. Acad. Engring., AAAS. Democrat. Home: Portola Valley, Calif. Died Aug. 17, 1980.

LINZ, CLARENCE E., insurance official; b. St. Louis, Mo., May 24, 1884; s. Joseph and Ella B. (Cole) L.; ed. Western Mil. Acad. (Alton, Ill.), Blees Mil. Acad. (Macon, Mo.), and Cascadilla Sch. (Ithaca, N.Y.); m. Lois Sanger, Feb. 24, 1908; 1 son, Joseph Sanger. Organized, with others, 1911, the Dallas Automatic Telephone Co., the first successful operating company of the automatic system in the South; company merged later with Bell Telephone Co.; former 1st v.p. Southland Life Ins. Co., Dallas; former pres. Sanger Bros. Inc., now dir.; former dir. and vice chmn. Federal Reserve Bank of Dallas; former publisher Dallas Journal; dir. Missouri-Kansas-Texas Railroad; pres. Sanger Investment Co., Ice Sports, Inc. Pres. "Texans" (Dallas Hockey Club). Republican. Mason (32 deg., Shriner). Clubs: City, Columbian, Lakewood Country. Home: Dallas, Tex.

LIPPERT, ROBERT LEONARD, motion picture producer; b. San Francisco, Mar. 11, 1909; s. Leonard and Esther (Meyers) L.; m. Ruth E. Robinson, Aug. 30, 1926; children—Robert Leonard, Judith (Mrs. Arthur Gutzman). Started Robert L. Lippert Theatre Circuit with opening of Grand Theatre, Richmond, Calif., 1942, grew to include 104 ops.; pioneered drive-in theatres, 1945; producer, exec. producer Lippert Pictures, Inc., 1946-55, 20th Century Fox Film Corp., 1956-66. Paramount Pictures, 1964, United Artist Pictures, 1965, Warner Brothers, 1965, Am. Internat. Pictures, 1969; builder first multiple theatre, Alameda, Calif., 1965. Home: San Francisco, Calif. Died Nov. 16, 1976.

LIPPHARD, WILLIAM BENJAMIN (LIP-HÄD'), editor, author; b. Evansville, Ind., Oct. 29, 1886; s. Rev. William Augustus and Martha Auguste (Liefield) L.; B.A., Yale, 1908, M.A., 1910; B.D., Colgate-Rochester Div. Sch., 1920; D.D., Franklin Coll., 1932; Litt.D. (hon.) Ottawa (Kansas) University, 1949; m. Helen Stella Dickinson, Oct. 15, 1914; children—Dickinson, Stella D. (Mrs. L. D. Clarke). Asst. sec. Am. Bapt. Foreign Mission Soc., 1913-19, recording sec., 1918-33, asso. sec., 1919-33. asso. editor "Missions," 1922-32, editor, 1932-52, retired as editor emeritus for life; secretary program committee American Baptist Convention, 1928-32 Mem bd. mgrs. Am Baptist Hist. Soc. Relief work Europe in coöperation with Am. Relief Administration, 1920-21; del. to Bapt. World Congress, Stockholm, 1923, Toronto, 1928, Berlin (Germany), 1934, Atlanta, 1939, Copenhagen (Denmark), 1947, Cleve., 1950, London, 1955. World Conf. on Ch. and State, Oxford, 1937, World Conf. on Faith and Order, Edinburgh, 1937, World Council Chs., Holland, 1948; Evanston, Ill., 1954; visited Far East, 1925; in the interests of mission work; Eng., 1928, in interest of John Bunyan Tercentenary; Soviet Russia, 1930, Germany, 1933, Mexico, Italy, 1935, Rumania, 1937, Czechoslovakia, 1938, in special study of conditions. Sec. World Relief Com. of American Bapt. Conv., 1940-52. Church press Rep. United Nations Conf., San Francisco, 1945. U.S. War Corr., Germany. 1946 Mem. National Council of Churches Dept. Internat. Affairs; pres. Asso. Ch. Press, 1947-49, exec. sec., 1951-61. Mem. Fgn. Policy Assn., Am. Com. World Council Chs. Received Church Press award, 1951, for eminence in editorial writing. Fellow American Geographical Society; member of New York Baptist City Soc. (life), Alpha Sigma Phi, Am. Baptist Hist. Society (vice president 1948-50), Republican. Clubs: Authors (London); Yale, Quill, Clergy. Author: The Ministry of Healing, 1920. The Second Century, 1926; Communing with Communism, 1931; Out of the Storm in China, 1932; Fifty Years on Editor, 1963; A History of the Associated Church Press, published 1965; Disillusioned World, pub. 1967. Contributor to The Religions of America, 1954, Why I Am a Baptist, 1957, We Believe in Prayer, 1958. Dir. Ch. Press World Council Chs., 1954. Home: Yonkers, N.Y. *

LIPPINCOTT, JOSEPH WHARTON, author, pub.; b. Phila., Pa., Feb. 28, 1887; s. Joshua Bertram and Joanna (Wharton) L.; B.S. in Economics, University of Pennsylvania, 1908; m. Elizabeth Schuyler Mills (deceased Nov. 30, 1943); children—Joseph Wharton, M. Roosevelt Schuyler, Elizabeth Schuyler; m. 2d, Virginia Jones Mathieson, Sept. 20, 1945. With J. B. Lippincott Co. from 1908, v.p., 1915-16, pres., 1926-48, chmn. bd. from 1948; pres. Frederick A. Stokes Co., and Hibernia Mine R.R. With U.S.N.R. during the World War. Trustee, v.p. Moore Inst.; Free Library of Phila.; trustee, mem. bd. libraries U. Pa.; dir. Athenaeum of Phila. Philadelphia Zoölogical Soc., Free Library of Phila., Phila. Aquarium Soc., Council on Books in Wartime, Inc.; chmn. exec. com. Schuylkill River Valley Restoration Assn. Mem. Pa. Soc. Mayflower Descs. (gov. 1926-27), S.R., Franklin Inst. Acad. Natural Scis., Zeta Psi, Nat. Assn. of Book Publishers (pres. 1929), Am. Booksellers' Assn.; honorary mem. Nat. Council, Boy Scouts of Am. Clubs: Explorers, Philadelphia, The Brook, Pubs. Lunch, Franklin Inn, Pohoqualine Fish assn., Wilderness, Masters of Foxhounds Association, Racquet. Author: Bun, A Wild Rabbit, 1918; Red Ben, the Fox of Oak Ridge, 1919; Gray Squirrel, 1921; Striped Coat, the Skunk, 1922; Persimmon Jim, the Possum, 1924; Long Horn, Leader of the Deer, 1928; The Wolf King, 1933; (with G. J. Roberts) Naturecraft Creatures, 1933; The Red Roan Pony, 1934; Chisel Tooth, the Beaver, 1936; Animal Neighbors of the Countryside, 1938; Wilderness Champion, 1944, Black Wings, The Unbeatable Crow, 1947; The Wahoo Bobcat, 1950; The Phantom Deer, 1954. Home: Bethayres, Pa. *

LIPSCOMB, CHARLES THOMAS, JR., association exec.; b. Greensboro, N.C., Mar. 4, 1908; s. Dr. Charles Thomas and Elizabeth (Patterson) L.; A.B., U. N.C., 1928; student King's Bus. Coll., Greensboro, 1929; extension courses Columbia; m. Caroline Knowlton, June 15, 1935; children—Caroline, Claudia, Charles T. Salesman, sec. to execs. Vick Chem. Co., Greensboro, 1928-39; with Coca-Cola Co., Atlanta, 1939-42, nat. sales dept. charge nat. chain stores, 1941-42; with McKesson & Robbins, Inc., N.Y. City, 1942-50, v.p. charge indsl. chem. div., 1942-45, asst. gen. sales mgr. wholesale drug div., 1945-48, v.p., gen. sales mgr. drug div., 1948-50; pres. Pepsodent div. Lever Bros. Co., N.Y. City, 1950-55; pres., dir. J. B. Williams Co., Glastonbury, Conn., 1955-57; pres. Bur. Advt., Am. Newspaper Assn., Inc., 1957—. Mem. Advt. Council (bd. dir.), Brand Names Found. (bd. dir.). Nat. Sales Execs., Am. Mgmt. Assn. (dir.). Sigma Chi. Episcopalian. Clubs: Sales Execs. (pres., dir.), Canadian, University (N.Y.C.); Pequot Yacht, Fairfield Country. Home: Conn. Died Aug. 27, 1979.

LISAGOR, PETER IRVIN, newspaperman; b. Keystone, W.Va., Aug. 5, 1915; s. Paris and Fanny (Simpkins) L.; student Northwestern U., 1933; A.B., U. Mich., 1939; Nieman fellow, Harvard, 1948-49; m. Myra K. Murphy, Feb. 14, 1942; children—P. Scott, Diane M. Sports reporter Chgo. Daily News, 1939-41; gen. news reporter U.P.I., 1941-42; news editor Paris Post, 1945; gen. news reporter Chgo. Daily News, 1945-48, UN corr., 1949, diplomatic corr., Washington, 1950-59, chief of Washington bur., 1959-76. Served with AUS, 1942-45; mng. editor Stars & Stripes, London edit., 1944-45; editor Stars & Stripes mag., Paris, 1945. Recipient Page One award Newspaper Guild, 1948, 49; Peabody award in broadcasting, 1974, Headliners award, 1974; Edward Weintel Prize for diplomatic reporting, 1976. Clubs: Nat. Press, Overseas Writers (pres. 1960-61 Washington); Gridiron. Co-author: Overtime in Heaven, 1964. Home: Arlington, Va. Died Dec. 10, 1976.

LISSIM, SIMON, painter, designer; b. Kiev, Russia, Oct. 24, 1900; s. Michel and Anna Maria (Schorr) L.; student Art Sch. of Alexander Monko; grad. Naoumenko Sch., 1919; student Sorbonne, Ecole du Louvre; m. Irene Zalchoupine, 1925 (dec. 1945); m. 2d, Dorothea Howson Waples, January 25, 1946. Came to U.S., 1941, naturalized, 1946. Stage designer Theatre de l'Oeuvre, 1923, Theatre de L'Atelier, Theatre National de l'Opera Comique, Theatre des Nouveautes, Paris, 1931, Theatre Michel, Theatre Antoine, 1932; head art edn. project N.Y. Pub. Library, N.Y.C., 1942-66; faculty French Lycee, N.Y.C., 1943-49, Horace Mann-Lincoln High Sch., Columbia; faculty Coll. City N.Y., 1944, art. supr. adult edn. program, 1945-47, asst. prof. art, 1947-54, asso. prof., 1954-60, prof., 1960-71, prof. emeritus, 1971, asst. dir. evening session charge adult edn. program, 1948-50, asst. dir. Sch. Gen. Studies, div. adult edn., 1950-64; faculty French Summer Sch., McGill U., 1949; works include painting, stage designs, ceramics, gouaches, china; works permanently exhibited N.Y. Pub. Library, Bklyn. Mus. Art, Hyde Park Library, Met. Mus. of Art, Boston Mus. Fine Arts, Fogg Mus. Art, Cleve. Mus. Fine Arts, Santa Barbara Mus. Art, Cooper Mus., Columbus (Ohio) Gallery Fine Arts, Fla. So. Coll., Va. Mus. Art, Phila. Mus. Art, Victoria and Albert Mus., London, Eng., Shakespeare Meml. Mus., Stratford-on-Avon, Eng., Nat. Gallery of Can., Ottawa, Musee Nat. du Jeu de Paume, France, Nat. Collection Fine Arts, Washington, Cal. Palace Legion Honor, San Francisco, others, museums in Eng., France, Prague, Holland, Austria, Can., Denmark, Switzerland, Italy, Portugal, Spain, Belgium, Latvia, Norway; illustrator several books; has given over 80 one- man shows in various countries. Chmn. nat. selection com. Fulbright awards in painting, sculpture, graphic arts, 1956. Served as vol. French Army, World War II. Recipient silver medal Internat. Exhbn., Paris, 1925, gold medal, Barcelona, 1929; two grand Diplome d'honneur, Paris, 1937. Hon. fellow Am.-Scandinavian Found. U.S.A.; mem. Royal Soc. Arts (v.p. council), Société du Salon d'Automme, Société des Artistes Decorateurs (Paris), Royal Acad. Fine Arts St. George (Barcelona, Spain) (hon. corr.), AAUP, Coll. Art Assn., Am., Theatre Library Assn. Am., Royal Soc. Miniature Painters (hon.), Audubon Artists. Club: Century (N.Y.C.). Contbr. articles to books, periodicals. Home: Naples, Fla. Died May 11, 1981.

LIST, GEORGE MILTON, entomologist, educator; b. Southport, Ind., Apr. 14, 1885; s. Cornelius A. and Martha Jane (Norwood) L.; B.S., Purdue, 1909; M.S., Colo. A. and M. Coll., 1924; Ph.D., Ia. State Coll., 1932; m. Ruth Ann Moore, July 24, 1912; children—Laura Alice (Mrs. James B. Ward), Ruth Leone. Fruit grower, Grand Junction, Colo., 1909-13; mem. faculty, Colo. A. and M. Coll. since 1913, head dept. entomology, 1944-50, emeritus head dept. and spl. research since July 1950; staff Expt. Sta., 1913-50, entomologist, 1937-50; chief deputy state entomologist, 1913-31, state entomologist, 1931-37. Mem. Nat. Plant Bd., 1934-35, Western Plant Bd., 1918-37 (pres. 1924). Fellow A.A.A.S., Entomol. Soc. Am.; mem. Am. Assn. Econ. Entomol. (1st v.p. 1938; pres. Pacific Slope br. 1932, pres. Central States br., 1950); Colo.-Wyo. Acad. Sci. (pres. 1940), Rocky Mountain Conf. Entomol. (sec. since 1923), Colo. Forestry and Hort. Assn., Western Colo. Hort. Soc., Sigma Xi (local pres. 1948), Phi Kappa Phi (local pres. 1947), Alpha Zeta, Gamma Sigma Delta, Alpha Gamma Rho. Club: Rotary. Author or co-author many tech. bulletins and articles. Home: Fort Collins, Colo. *

LITTEL, CHARLES LESTER, educator; b. Bertrand, Neb., Aug. 13, 1885; s. Charles and Amanda (Atkinson) L.; A.B., U. of Neb., 1912; A.M., Stanford U., 1926; Ed.D., New York U., 1935; m. Bernice Warner, May 26, 1907; 1 dau., Estella Marie; m. 2d, Mrs. Elva C. Rauch Humphrey, Dec. 6, 1953. Engaged in teaching rural schs., then prin. sch. and acad., supt. schs., in Neb., 1902-22; teacher and supt. schs. in Wash., 1922-30; instr. New York U., 1930-31; prin. high sch., Teaneck, N.J., 1931-33; pres. Jr. Coll. of Bergen Co., 1933-53, president emeritus since July 1953; also president of bd. trustees; lecturer on India and Far East, 1954—; established first junior college in state of Washington at Centralia, 1925; first coeducational junior coll. in New Jersey, 1933. Served as Dist. Red Cross chmn. and Four-Minute Man during World War I; chmn. Selective Service Bd. No. 6, Teaneck, N.J., World War II. Mem. bd. dirs. Teaneck Bd. of Commerce; dir. Bergen County Chamber of Commerce. Mem. N.E.A. (life), Am. Assn. Sch. Adminstrs., N.J. State Jr. Coll. Assn. (pres.), Phi Delta Kappa. Republican. Presbyterian (chmn. bd. trustees). Mason (32 deg., Shriner), K.P., Elk, Odd Fellow. Clubs: Rotary (Hackensack), Bergen County Schoolmasters; Teaneck Men's Club (pres.). Contbr. to ednl. jours. Organizer first jr. Coll. in Washington, 1925, Yakima Valley Jr. Coll., 1928, Grays Harbor Coll., 1930; also organizer first co-ednl. jr. coll. in N.J., 1933. Address: Teaneck, N.J. *

LITTLEFIELD, ROBERT CRANDALL, savs. and loan exec.; b. Monterey, Calif., Jan. 18, 1930; s. Glenn Crandall and Mary (Hill) L.; A.A., Monterey Peninsula Coll., 1950; student Stanford, 1951; B.A., San Jose State Coll., 1953; m. Mary Ortman, Feb. 28, 1954 (dec.); 1 dau., Susan Marie; m. 2d, Patricia R. Hodgson, Oct. 24, 1976. Pres., dir. Monterey Savs. and Loan Assn., 1948-80; pres., dir. First Monterey Co., 1954-80; pres., dir. Bessemer Oil Co., 1948-80. Sec.-treas., dir. United Fund Monterey Peninsula, 1955-75; vice chmn. Monterey City Planning Commn., 1961-72; bd. dirs. Monterey History and Art Assn., 1970-80; trustee Eskaton Monterey Hosp., 1977-80. Served with AUS, 1951-53. Named Young Man of Year, Jr. C. of C., 1961. Mem. Monterey Peninsula C. of C. (treas., dir. 1955—, named citizen of year 1977), Calif. Savs. and Loan League (dir. 1976-80). Republican. Methodist (treas.). Elk, Kiwanian (treas.). Home: Monterey, Calif. Died Oct. 10, 1980.

LITTLEJOHN, CHARLES EDWARD, JR., educator; b. Spartanburg, S.C., Sept. 28, 1918; s. Charles Edward and Marion Clifton (Brown) L.; B.S., Clemson Coll., 1940; M.S., N.C. State Coll., 1941; Ph.D., Va. Poly. Inst., 1952; m. Doris Asbill McMillan, Dec. 15, 1946; children—Patricia Carol, Anne Olivia. With Goodyear Tire & Rubber Co., 1941-42; tchr. Va. Poly. Inst., 1946-47; asst. prof. chem. engring. Clemson Coll., 1946-49, asso. prof., 1949-55, prof., acting head dept. chem. engring., 1955-56, prof., head dept. chem. engring., 1956-75; research participant Oak Ridge Nat. Lab., 1954. Served with AUS, 1942-46; ETO. Mem. Am. Inst. Chem. Engrs., Am. Chem. Soc., Am. Soc. Engring. Edn. (vice chmn. chem. engring. sect. 1960-61), Tau Beta Pi. Co-author: An Introduction to Chemical Engineering. Home: Clemson, S.C. Died May 27, 1975.

LITTLETON, A. C., prof. accountancy; b. Bloomington, Ill., Dec. 4, 1886; s. Robert and Mary (Sholtey) L.; B.A., U. of Ill., 1912, M.A., 1918, Ph.D., 1931; m. Bonnie Ray, Aug. 21, 1916; children—Barbara, Scott. C.P.A., State of Ill., 1919. Mem. staff Deloette, Plender, Griffith & Co., Chicago, 1912-15; mem. faculty U. of Ill. since 1915, prof. accountancy since 1931. Mem. Am. Inst. Accountants, Am. Accounting Assn., Ill. Soc. C.P.A., Beta Gamma Sigma, Beta Alpha Psi, Delta Chi. Republican. Episcopalian. Author: Accounting Evolution to 1900, 1933. Co-author: An Introduction to Corporate Accounting Standards, 1940. Editor of Accounting Review, 1943-47. Contbr. articles to various accountancy jours. Home: Champaign, Ill. *

LITTLEWOOD, GEORGE, publisher, editor; b. Barrow-in-Furness, Eng., Feb. 3, 1917; s. George Francis and Jane Elizabeth (Wilkinson) L.; came to U.S., 1921, naturalized, 1943; student Columbia U. Sch. Gen. Studies, 1951-56; m. Evelyn Lucia Lindner, June 19, 1942; children—George Frederic, Deborah Mary. Mktg. dir. Indl. Press, Inc., N.Y.C., 1965-72; v.p. Gordon Publs.; pub. Metalworking Digest, Mining/Processing Equipment, Morristown, N.J., 1972-81. Welfare dir. Kinnelon, N.J., 1965-71; v.p. Fayson Lakes Assn., 1960, 64; sec. Zoning Bd., Cresskill, N.J., 1953-56. Served with AUS, 1942-45. Republican. Presbyn. Home: Kinnelon, N.J. Died Feb. 20, 1981.

LITTON, JERRY, congressman; b. nr. Lock Springs, Mo., May 12, 1937; B.S. in Agrl. Journalism, U. Mo., 1961; m. Sharon Summerville; children—Linda, Scott. Formerly co-owner Litton Charolais Ranch, nr. Chilicothe, Mo.; past editor Charolais Bull-O-Gram; farm dir. Columbia Missourian, Radio KCHI, 1955, KBIA, 1960; mem. 93d and 94th Congresses from 6th Mo. dist., mem. agr. com., D.C. com. Mem. Mo. Gov.'s Adv. Council Agr., 1967, Mo. State Council Edn., 1968; pres. Performance Registry Internat., 1964. Pres. Livingston County (Mo.) Young Democrats, 1954, U. Mo. Young Dems., 1960. Recipient citation merit Mo. Coll. Agr. Mem. Future Farmers Am. (Mo. pres. 1956; nat. sec. 1957), U. Mo. Alumni Assn., Omicron Delta Kappa, Alpha Zeta. Home: Washington, D.C. Died Aug. 3, 1976.

LIVENGOOD, CHARLES ALFRED (LIV'EN-GOOD), ret. career minister; b. Dayton, Wash., Aug. 15, 1886; s. George and Sylvia (Hopkins) L.; B.S., Whitman Coll., Walla Walla, Wash., 1908; summer courses, U. of Wash., and Columbia U.; m. Adelaide Lamphere, Aug. 14, 1912; 1 dau., Sarah Adelaide (Mrs. William Luther Finger). Began as high sch. instr., 1908-09; prin. Dayton (Wash.) High Sch., 1909-10; superintendent schools, Dayton, 1910-20; in export-import business, 1920-21; entered Bureau Foreign and Domestic Commerce, 1921; assistant trade commissioner and trade commissioner, Havana, Cuba, 1921-25; with Bur. Fgn. and Domestic Commerce, 1925; trade commr., Rome, Italy, 1925-27; commercial attaché, Madrid, Spain, 1927-33; also commercial attaché attached to American Legation at Lisbon, Portugal, 1927-33; commerical attaché, Rome, 1933-34; Bur. Fgn. and Domestic Commerce, 1934-35; commercial attaché, Rome, from 1935 until severance of diplomatic relations between U.S. and Italy, Dec. 1941; returned to U.S. on S.S. Drottningholm, May 1942; commercial attaché, Bogota (Colombia), 1942; counselor embassy for economic affairs, Bogota, 1942-43; assigned to staff of American rep. to politicomilitary mission, Algiers, Oct. 1943; econ. counselor to Am. rep. on adv. council for Italy, 1944-45; econ. counselor, Am. embassy, Rome, 1945; counsel gen., Batavia, N.E.I., 1947 (career minister); United States representative on Council of International Authority for the Ruhr, 1950-51. Del. 6th Internat. Rd. Congress, 1930, 6th Congress of Tech. Edn., Rome, 1936. Mem. Phi Beta Kappa Assos. (life mem.), S.A.R., Nat. Geneal. Soc. (councilor), Phi Beta Kappa, Pi Gamma Mu. Conglist. Mason. Address: Washington. *

LIVERMORE, GEORGE GRISWOLD, author; b. Melrose, Mass., Oct. 7, 1886; s. Charles Cunningham and Mary Howlett (Griswold) L.; A.B., Williams, 1910; unmarried. Mem. staff Youth's Companion, Boston, 1914-18; circulation mgr. Boys' Life, New York, 1918-21, American Boy, 1921-24, Modern Priscilla, 1924-27. Member Sigma Phi. Republican. Episcopalian. Clubs: Williams College (New York); Brae Burn Country (West Newton, Mass.). Author: Take It From Dad, 1920; Team Play, 1921. Contbr. short stories to mags. Home: Newtonville, Mass. *

LIVERMORE, KENNETH CARTER, grower certified seeds; b. Watertown, Mass., Jan. 3, 1886; s. Charles Edward and Caroline Brackett (Russell) L.; N.Y. State Coll. Agr., 1904-09; B.S. in agr., Cornell U., 1909; m. Madeleine S. Avery, N.Y., June 18, 1914; children—Carter, Avery. With Cornell U., 1909-20, prof. farm management, 1912-20. Mem. Am. Farm Economics Assn., Sigma Xi, Alpha Zeta. Republican. Baptist. Aurthor: Laboratory Exercises in Farm Management, 1910. Has specialized in production of pedigreed and hybrid seeds. Home: Honeoye Falls, N.Y. *

LLOYD, NORMAN, musician, found. exec.; b. Pottsville, Pa., Nov. 8, 1909; s. David and Annie Sarah (Holstein) L.; B.S., N.Y. U., 1932, M.A., 1936; Mus.D., Phila. Conservatory Music, 1963, New Eng. Conservatory, 1965, Peabody Inst., 1973; grad. piano study with Abbey Whiteside; study in music composition with Vincent Jones, Aaron Copland; m. Ruth Dorothy Rohrbacher, Apr. 10, 1933; children—David Walter, Alex. Instr., Ernest Williams Band Sch., 1935-37; lectr. N.Y. U., 1936-45; faculty Sarah Lawrence Coll., 1936-46, condr. chorus, 1945-49; dir. edn. Juilliard Sch. Music, 1946-49, faculty, 1949-63; dean Oberlin Coll. Conservatory Music, 1963-65; dir. arts program Rockefeller Found., 1965-72, cons., 1973-75; cons. Nat. Assn. Schs. Music, 1973-76, Mary Flagler Cary Charity Trust, 1974-80; composer, condr. dance scores for Martha Graham, 1935, Hanya Holm, 1937, Doris Humphrey, 1941-46, 49, Jose Limon, 1949; composer, condr. numerous music scores for exptl. and documentary films OWI, Internat. Film Found., Shirley Clarke-Halcyon Films, Mus. Modern Art, others; compositions include Song for Summer's End, 1951, Nocturne for Voices, 1953, 3 Pieces for Violin and Piano, 1957, A Walt Whitman Overture for Band, 1962, Sonata for Piano, 1963, Three Scenes from Memory, 1963, Episodes for Piano, 1964; Rememories for Wind Orchestra, 1974. Mem. vis. com. humanities Mass. Inst. Tech., 1973-75; vis. com. arts Tufts U., 1976-80; bd. dirs. Nat. Music Council. Mem. ASCAP, Am. Fedn. Musicians, Pi Kappa Lambda. Compiled: (with M. Boni) Fireside Book of Folk Songs, 1947, Fireside Book of American Songs, 1952, Fireside Book of Love Songs, 1954, Favorite Christmas Carols, 1957, Songs of the Gilded Age, 1960; (with Arnold Fish) Fundamentals of Sight Singing, 1963 (with Ruth Lloyd) The American Heritage Songbook, 1969; Creative Keyboard Musicianship, 1975; with Ruth Lloyd and Jan DeGaetani) The Complete Sightsinger, 1980. Author: Golden Ency. of Music, 1968. Home: Greenwich, Conn. Died July 31, 1980; buried Pottsville, Pa.

LLOYD, ORSON GUNNELL, univ. prof.; b. Wellsville, Utah, Jan. 8, 1884; s. Joseph Benjamin and Martha Ann (Gunnell) L.; student Brigham Young U., Provo, Utah, 1903-05; B.S., Utah Agrl. Coll., Logan, Utah, 1910; M.S., U. of Wisconsin, 1912, grad. student, 1929-30; m. Ella Winona Jensen, Nov. 28, 1918; children—Joanne Jensen (Mrs. Robert Griffin Molitor), Frances Winona (Mrs. Trevor Dale Reiley), Martha Marilyn (Mrs. James Ruple Abernethy). Mgr., with brother, livestock and grain farms, 1900-02; prin., Plano (Ida.) Pub. Sch., 1905-06; instr., Ricks Acad., Rexburg, Ida., 1906-07; research in farm tenancy and land values, Iowa State Coll., 1912-20; prof. agrl. econ., Purdue University, since 1920; head dept. agricultural econ., 1920-46, also professor agrl. econ. and head of dept. Agrl. Experiment Station. Head of Rural-Urban Relations for Indiana Dist., 1925-29. Mem. Am. Farm Econ. Assn., Am. Soc. Farm Mgrs. and Rural Appraisers, Rotary Internat., Sigma Xi, Gamma Sigma Delta. Author of numerous agrl. bulletins. Home: West Lafayette, Ind. *

LLOYD, RUSSELL G., mayor Evansville (Ind.); b. Plymouth, Pa., Mar. 29, 1932; s. Russell and Margaret (McCluskey) L.; B.A., Kings Coll., Pa., 1949; LL.B., Notre Dame U., 1961; m. Genevieve Anne Ragunas, 1956; children—Russell G., Michael, Joel, Daniel, Mary, Julie. Admitted to Ind. bar; atty. Legal Aid Soc., Evansville, 1961-62; atty. F. Wendell Lensing, Atty., Evansville, 1962-66; individual practice law, Evansville, 1966-68; partner firm Trockman, Lloyd, Flynn & Swain, Evansville, 1969-71; county atty. Vanderburgh County, 1969-71; mayor, Evansville, 1972-80. Bd. dirs. St. Citizens' Center, Evansville, 1961-63, Evansville chpt. ARC, Vanderburgh County Heart Assn., 1968, Legal Aid Soc. Evansville; sec. bd. dirs. Tri-State Epilepsy Assn.; legis. co-chmn. Evansville Future, Inc., 1965-66; exec. sec. Vanderburgh County Republican Com., 1965-66, treas., 1966-68, campaign chmn., 1968; chmn. platform com. Ind. Rep. Conv., 1972; alternate del. Rep. Nat. Conv., 1972; chmn. Ind. Mayors and Municipal Officers Com. for Reelection of Pres., 1972; hon. chmn. Easter Seal Campaign, 1973. Served with U.S. Army, 1952-54. Named Man of Year Notre Dame U., 1972. Mem. Evansville Bar Assn., Ind. Assn. Cities and Towns (2d v.p. 1972—), VFW, ACLU, Center for Study Democratic Instns. Roman Catholic. Home: Evansville, Ind. Died Mar. 21, 1980.

LLOYD, SHERMAN PARKINSON, congressman; b. St. Anthony, Idaho, Jan. 11, 1914; s. Charles Edward and Lucy (Parkinson) L.; A.B., Utah State U., 1935; LL.B., George Washington U., 1939; m. Edith Ann Gunn, Sept. 25, 1935; children—Sherman G., Kathryn, Diane, Elizabeth. Admitted to Utah bar, 1940; sec., gen. counsel Utah Retail Grocers Assn., Salt Lake City, 1940-62, also editor, gen. mgr. ofcl. publ.; dir. Beehive State Bank, Certified Warehouse & Transfer Co. (both Salt Lake City), mem. Utah Senate from Salt Lake County, 1954-62, pres., 1959; mem. Utah Legislative Council, 1957-61, chmn., 1959-61; mem. 88th, 90th-92d congresses from 2d Dist., Utah. Utah chmn. March of Dimes, 1958-60. Rep. for Utah on bd. mgrs. Council State Govts., 1959-61, chmn. com. state taxation of interstate income, 1960-62; Republican majority leader Utah Senate, 1957, pres., 1959, minority leader, 1961; candidate for U.S. Ho. of Reps., 1960. Mem. Salt Lake City C. of C. (gov.), Sigma Chi. Mem. Ch. of Jesus Christ of Latter-day Saints. Clubs: Salt Lake Country, Kiwanis. Home: Salt Lake City, Utah. Died Dec. 14, 1979.

LLOYD, WESLEY PARKINSON, educator; b. Ogden, Utah, June 16, 1904; s. Charles E. and Lucy (Parkinson) L.; B.S., Brigham Young U., 1927, M.S., 1934, LL.D., 1969; Ph.D., U. Chgo., 1937; m. Lillie Murdock, Dec. 30, 1926; children—Kent M., Gary M. Athletic coach, 1927-28; prin. high sch., 1929-30; prin. sem., 1930-33; dean of men, prof. edn. Brigham Young U., 1937-44, dean of students, 1944-60, chmn. dept. philosophy edn., 1937-50, dean Grad. Sch., 1960-69; dean Grad. Sch. Arts and Scis., U.S. Internat. U., 1969-71; dir. Calif. Western Coll., 1972-74; prof. edn. and human behavior U.S. Internat. U., 1969-75; dir. Japanese Insts. Student Personnel Services, 1951-52, 54-55. Cons. student personnel services in Europe, Asia, Africa, 1955; cons. higher edn. in Burma, 1961; Asia Found. cons. for counseling project U. Rangoon, 1958; higher edn. confs. Japanese Univs., 1958; ednl. cons., American specialist Dept. State, Am. embassy, Tokyo, 1962; condr. seminars Colombian (S.Am.) educators, 1962; participant confs. Venzuelan educators, 1963; cons. Bahamas, 1967; pres. Utah Conf. Higher Edn., 1946-47; chmn. acad. council Western Personnel Inst. Mem. Young Men's Mut. Improvement Assn. (gen. bd. 1940-41), Provo City Community Welfare Council, 1941-42; chmn. Utah County chapter of A.R.C., 1961-62. Chmn. bd. trustees Center for Ednl. Leadership, 1974-77. Mem. Nat. Assn Student Personnel Adminstrs. (pres. 1949-50), Utah Acad. Sci., Arts, and Letters, N.E.A., N.Y.A., Utah Edn. Assn., Am. Coll. Personnel Assn. (com. on internat. relations 1964-66), Western Assn. Grad Schs. (pres. 1967-68), Nat. Assn. Deans and Advisers Men (nat. com. on student orientation 1940, mem. exec. com.), Am. Personnel and Guidance Assn. (chmn. com. internat. relations 1955-56). Mem. Ch. of Latter-day Saints (bishop). Clubs: Rotary, Timpanogas Knife and Fork (bd. dirs.). Author: Learning to Live, 1940; Student Counseling in Japan: A Two-Nation Project in Higher Education, 1953; Student Personnel Services in Japan, 1957; Student Personnel Services in Universities of the World, 1957; The University in the Changing Community, 1961. Contbr. articles to mags., ednl. bulls. Home: La Jolla, Calif. Died Mar. 7, 1977.

LOBINGIER, JOHN LESLIE, clergyman; b. Chicago, Ill., Jan. 1, 1884; s. Rev. Henry Schell and Annie H. (Sinclair) L.; A.B., New York U., 1905; grad. Coll. of the Bible (Ky.), 1907; B.D., Yale U., 1915; M.A., U. of Chicago, 1916; D.D., Elon Coll., N.C., 1933; m. Elizabeth Erwin Miller, Aug. 7, 1918; 1 son, John Leslie. Pastor Disciples chs., Los Angeles and Santa Monica, Calif., 1907-14; Y.M.C.A. war work, Great Lakes Naval Training Sta., 1917-19; dir. religious edn., Chicago Ch. Federation, 1919-20; ednl. pastor, United Ch. (Congl.), Oberlin, O., 1921-26; sec. Dept. of Missionary Edn. and World Friendship, Congl. Edn. Soc., Boston, 1926-36, Depts. of Adult Edn. and World Fellowship, 1936-42; ednl. sec. Mass. Congl. Conf. since 1942. Editor, Pilgrim State News since 1942. Mem. board Religious Education Association, 1925-28, editorial com., 1925; mem. bd. mgrs. Missionary Edn. Movement (pres. 1939-43), Fed. Council of Churches (commn. on Christian edn. 1925-29, department of internat. justice and goodwill, 1934-38; Com. on Bases of a Just and Durable Peace since 1941); Internat. Council Religious Edn. (ednl. commn. 1928-32 and 1939-43; chmn. com. on Rel. Edn. of Adults, 1939-42; chmn. 1937 Conf., United Christian Adult Movement; chmn. exec. com., United Christian Adult Movement, 1939-42; chmn. Com. on Internat. Relations, Mass. Council of Churches, 1939-40; chmn. Dept. Religious Edn., 1940-44; pres. Winchester Art Assn., 1939-42; Dean, Northfield Conf. Rel. Edn., 1946, 47. Received citation from Gen. Conf. Congl. Christian Chs., 1948. Mem. Delta Theta Chi, Phi Beta Kappa, American Association Adult Education. Club: Boston City. Author: World Friendhsip Through the Church School, 1923; Projects in World-Friendship, 1925; Our Church, 1927; Youth and the World Outlook, 1929; Educating for Peace (with Elizabeth M. Lobingier), 1930; How Big Is Your World?, 1931; What Shall We Do About Missions?, 1933; Is War the Way?, 1935; The Missionary Education of Adults, 1938; The Better Church School, 1952. Home: Winchester, Mass. *

LOCKE, ARTHUR WARE, educator; b. Cambridge, Mass., Oct. 30, 1883; A.B., Harvard, 1905, A.M., 1915. Prof. music, Smith Coll. Author: Music and the Romantic Movement in France. Home: Northampton, Mass. *

LOCKE, AUGUSTUS, mining geologist; b. North Adams, Mass., Aug. 22, 1883; s. Augustus Woodbury and Martha Payson (Perkins) L.; B.A., Harvard, 1904, S.B., 1905, E.M., 1909, Sc.D., 1913; m. Helen Alma Lincoln, Dec. 18, 1915; children—Caroline, Gardner Lincoln, Elizabeth Garland. Resident geologist, Goldfield Consolidated Mining Co., 1910; Sheldon traveling fellow, Harvard, 1910-11; resident geologist Cia Minera Las Dos Estrellas, 1911; field geologist Secondary Enrichment Investigation, 1913-15; exploration and examination of mines and prospects since 1915. Mem. Geol. Soc. America, Soc. Economic Geologists, Am. Inst. Mining and Metall. Engrs., Phi Beta Kappa; mem. Nat. Research Council (div. of geology, 1926-29). Author: Leached Outcrops as Guides to Copper Ore, 1926; also papers on structural localization of ore. Address: Menlo Park, Calif. *

LOCKE, HARRY LESLIE FRANKLIN, pediatrician; b. Hudson, Mass., Oct. 30, 1886; s. Frank Daniel and Carrie Louise (Woodward) L.; M.D. cum laude, Tufts Coll., 1912; grad. student Trinity Coll., 1922-24; m. Katherine Elizabeth Entress, Nov. 11, 1914; children—Carolyn Elizabeth de Kanter, John Dustin, Janet Page. Supt., res. physician Hartford Isolation Hosp., 1914-21; in pvt. practice, specializing in pediatrics, since 1921; pres. Hartford Tuberculosis and Pub. Health Soc., 1931-32; attending pediatrician Hartford Municipal Hosp. (name changed to McCook Memorial Hosp.) since 1922, chief-of-staff, 1938-48; physician-in-charge Children's Village, Hartford, 1932-50; cons. pediatrician St. Francis Hosp., Manchester Memorial Hosp., New Britain Gen. Hosp., Bristol Hosp., Windham County Hosp. Mem. Med. Reserve Corps, U.S. Army, 1918. Sec. and dir. Hartford Citizens' Com. for Civic Progress, 1935 to 1938; pres. Civitan Club of Hartford, 1940-41; pres. Civitan Internat., 1942-43. Fellow Am. Acad. Pediatrics; licentiate Am. Bd. Pediatrics; mem. A.M.A., Psi Upsilon, Soc. Founders and Patriots (Conn.; gov. 1945-46); S.A.R. Ind. Republican. Mason (K.T., Shriner). Clubs: Civitan, Hampsted Hill. Home: Elmwood, Conn. *

LOCKE, JOHN LOOR, holding co. exec.; b. Cambridge, Ohio, June 1, 1896; s. John L. and Sophronia Thorn (White) L.; A.B., Stanford, 1918; m. Irene Fisher, Sept. 21, 1920; children—Peggy (Mrs. Newman), John Loor III (dec.), Evelyn Thorn (Mrs. Dreitzler). With Fisher Flouring Mills Co., Seattle, 1919-71, clk., salesman, purchasing agt. sec., mgr. feed div., 1919-48, pres., gen. mgr., 1948-60, pres., 1960-65, chmn., dir., 1965-71; dir. Societe Candy Co.; pres., dir. O.D. Fisher Investment Co.; dir. Oreg. Aqua-Foods, Inc., Fisher's Blend Sta., Inc. (KOMO TV-Radio Seattle, KATU-TV Portland), Fisher Mills, Inc.; past pres., dir. Fisher Properties Inc.; dir. Technovators, Inc.; past trustee Washington Mut. Savs. Bank. Trustee Seattle First Meth. Home, Inc.; pres., dir. O.D. Fisher Charitable Found. Mem. Flour Millers Export Assn., Millers' Nat. Fedn., Protein Cereal Products Internat. Stanford Alumni Assn., Seattle C. of C., Navy League U.S. Methodist (ch. trustee). Clubs: China, Rainier, Seattle Tennis, Seattle Yacht, Broadmoor Golf; Harbor. Home: Seattle, Wash. Died Apr. 2, 1976.

LOCKWOOD, LEE, financier; b. Waco, Tex., Nov. 11, 1900; s. James H. and Gussie (Doss) L.; student U. Tex., 1918-22; LL.D., Baylor U.; m. Marie Coates, Oct. 3, 1923; children—Ann Marie (Mrs. Duncan C. Howard), Laurine Lockwood Dosher. Chmn., Waco Mortgage Co., First Waco Co., Inc., Waco Savs. & Loan Assn.; owner Waco Lumber Co.; vice chairman Farm & Home Savs. Assn.; dir. Citizens Nat. Bank Waco, Merc. Nat. Bank Dallas. Past chmn. Commn. Higher Edn. Tex.; mem. Tex. com. on church and state Baylor U. Del. Democratic Nat. Conv., 1940, 44, 48, 52. Pres. Masonic Home and Sch. Tex., 1951-60; chmn. emeritus Scottish Rite Found. Tex., Scottish Rite Ednl. Assn. Tex., Scottish Rite Hosp., Dallas; bd. dirs. Community Chest, Waco, Waco Boys Club, Waco Growth Found.; dir. George Washington Nat. Meml. Assn.; bd. regents U. Tex., 1953-59; trustee Freedoms Found., Valley Forge. Recipient George Washington award. Mem. Waco C. of C., S.A.R. (gold citizenship medal Tex. chpt.), Soc. Colonial Wars. Mason (33 deg.; past dep. grand comdr., mem. emeritus Supreme Council); mem. Order De Molay (past grand master), Order Red Cross of Constantine (past grand sovereign). Home: Waco, Tex. Died Aug. 6, 1980; buried Oakwood Cemetery, Waco, Tex.

LOCKWOOD, MAURICE HERBERT, chem. cons.; b. New Britain, Conn., Aug. 1899; s. Herbert Newton and Bertha Adele (Doolittle) L.; B.S., U. Conn., 1921; m. Elena Mae Crough Aug. 15, 1927 (dec. Feb. 1962); m. 2d, Phyllis Helena Phelan, Dec. 14, 1965. County agrl. agt., Conway, N.H., 1921-24; mgr. Western Res. Farmers Coop. Assn., Unionville, Ohio, 1924; fieldman Eastern States Farmers Exchange, 1924-26, mgr. fertilizer div. West Springfield, Mass., 1926-46; pres. Nat. Fertilizer Assn., Washington, 1946-48; v.p. in charge plant food div. Internat. Minerals & Chem. Corp., Chgo., 1948-58; cons. to chem. fertilizer industry, from 1958. Leader fertilizer industry study team for Taiwan, 1964. Past mem. and chmn. bd. dirs. Nat. Fertilizer Assn.; past bd. dirs., life mem. U. Conn. Found. Served as pvt. Inf., U.S. Army, World War I. Recipient alumni award U. Conn., 1958. Mem. Am. Chem. Soc., Am. Soc. Agronomy, Gamma Sigma Delta. Author articles. Promoted prodn. and distbn. higher analysis fertilizers. Home: Ridgefield, Conn. Died Sept. 15, 1977.

LOCKWOOD, WARREN J., govt. official; b. Montclair, N.J., Nov. 29, 1884; s. Jesse H. and Sarah (Ketcham) L.; student Nat. Acad. of Design, 1903-05 Art Students' League 1906-09, Columbia Sch of Architecture, 1910-11; m. Helen H. Robinson, July 10, 1917; 1 son, Warren S. Sec. to agt. of Astor Estate, N.Y. City, 1902-17; mgr. real estate dept. Ward & Gow, 1919-26; pres. Leonia Heights Investment Co., and Real Properties, Inc., Leonia, N.J., 1926-34; sec. and v.p. W. S. Davidson, Inc., Leonia, 1926-34; chief underwriter Fed. Housing Adminstrn., Newark, N.J., 1934-36, asst. dep. commr., mortgage ins. div., Washington, 1936-38, dep. commr. in charge of mountain and Pacific states, 1938-41, in charge Midwestern states, Jan.-Apr. 1941, state dir. for N.J., Newark, 1941-47, asst. to commr. Washington, 1947-48, asst. commr. in charge field operations, 1948-50, asst. commr. in charge cooperative housing since 1950. Conglist. Home: Washington; also Newton, N.J. *

LOCKWOOD, WILLIAM WIRT, educator; b. Shanghai, China, Feb. 24, 1906; s. William Wirt and Mary Rebecca (Town) L.; A.B., DePauw U., 1927; M.A., Harvard, 1929, Ph.D., 1950; m. Virginia Chapman, Oct. 23, 1934; children—William W., Stephen C., Julia D. Instr. Bowdoin Coll., 1929-32, asst. prof., 1932-34; research sec. Am. Council, Inst. of Pacific Relations, 1935-40, exec. sec., 1941-43; exec. sec. Am. Com. for Internat. Studies, 1940-41; cons. U.S. Office of Export Control, 1941; asst. chief Far East Div., Research and Analysis Br., OSS, 1943; asst. chief div. of Japanese and Korean Econ. Affairs, Dept. of State, 1946; asst. dir. Woodrow Wilson Sch. of Pub. and Internat. Affairs, Princeton, 1946-57, asso. prof. pub. and internat. affairs, 1949-54, prof. politics and internat. affairs, 1955-71, prof. emeritus, 1971-78, dir. program in East Asian studies, 1970-71; mem. editorial bd. Princeton Univ. Press. 1962-65; cons. Ford Found., 1953-55, Fgn. Area Fellowship Program, 1971-72, Asia Found., 1976—; sr. specialist East West Center, 1969-70. Fulbright scholar to Japan, 1961-62; McCosh fellow, 1965-66. Dir. Assn. Asian Studies, 1948-49, 57-59, pres., 1963-64, trustee Am. Inst. Pacific Relations, 1946-53, 55-61; trustee Princeton-in-Asia, Inc., 1947-78, v.p., 1954-78; dir. Japan Soc., 1967-76; mem. Am. Com. on U.S.-Japan Ednl. and Cultural Cooperation, 1967-68; mem. Social Sci. Research Council-Am. Council Learned Socs. Joint Commn. on Japanese Studies, 1967-68; mem. East Asia panel U.S. Dept. State, 1968-69; mem. Nat. Com. on U.S.-China Relations, 1969-78; mem. exec. com. internat. affairs div. Am. Friends Service Com., 1970-75. Served capt. to maj. AUS, 1943-45. Mem. Council Fgn. Relations, Asia Soc., Phi Beta Kappa, Phi Kappa Psi. Author: The Economic Development of Japan, 1954; co-author, editor: The State and Economic Enterprise in Japan, 1968. Mem. editorial bd. Asian Survey, Asian Forum, 1974-78. Home: Princeton, N.J. Died Dec. 30, 1978; buried Princeton Cemetery, Princeton, N.J.

LODEN, BARBARA ANN, actress; b. N.C.; d. George T. and Ruth (Nanney) Loden; m. Laurance Joachim; children—Leo Alexander, Jon Marco. Appearances on Broadway include Out of This World, Compulsion, Look After Lulu, The Long Dream, 41 in the Sack; motion pictures include Wild River, Splendor in the Grass; permanent mem. Repertory Theatre of Lincoln Center, N.Y.C.; created role of Maggie in After the Fall (1963 Tony award for supporting actress). Died Sept. 5, 1980.

LOEB, JOSEPH PHILIP, lawyer; b. Los Angeles, Calif., Dec. 11, 1883; s. Leon and Estelle (Newmark) L.; B.A., U. of Calif., 1905; m. Amy C. Kahn, Jan. 24, 1909; children—Kathleen (Mrs. Edward J. Bernath), Margaret (Mrs. Edward J. Soares). Admitted to Calif. bar, 1906, and since practiced in Los Angeles; former sr. partner Loeb & Loeb, ret., 1965, now of counsel. Member California Board of Edn., 1943-56, past pres. Jewish Orphans' Home of So. Cal., So. California Chapter Arthritis and Rheumatism Foundation; adv. com. Am. Council for Judaism, v.p. philanthrop fund. Bd. fellows Claremont Grad. Sch. and U. Center. Mem. Am., Cal., Los Angeles bar associations, Claremont Colleges Faculty Club, Phi Beta Kappa, and Phi Beta Kappa Associates, Republican. Mason (32 deg., Shriner); past master. Clubs: Los Angeles Athletic, Town Hall. Home: Los Angeles. *

LOEB, LEONARD B(ENEDICT), physicist; b. Zurich, Switzerland, Sept. 16, 1891; s. Jacques and Anne (Leonard) L.; brought to U.S., 1891; student U. Cal., 1908-10, Columbia, 1910-11; B.S., U. Chgo., 1912, Ph.D., 1916, NRC fellow, 1919-23; post doctoral fellow U. Manchester, 1919; married Lora Lane, 1928 (div. 1940); children—Anne L., Jacqueline L.; m. 2d, Charlotte Pearson, May 1941; children—Diana B., Valerie J. Asst. physics U. Chgo., 1916-16; lab. asst., asst. physicist U.S. Bur. Standards, 1916-17; asst. prof. physics U. Cal., 1923-25, asso. prof., 1925-29, prof., from 1929; coop. expert Internat. Critical Tables; staff electronics inst. U. Mich., summer 1937; Kelvin lectr. Inst. Elec. Engrs., London, Eng., 1947. Mem. subcom. physics of com. electric insulation NRC; chmn. No. Cal. adv. com. tech. and sci. personnell SSS, from 1954. Served as 2d lt., air service, U.S. Army, 1917-19; AEF; from comdr. to capt., USNR, 1941-45; ETO. Recipient citation for anti-aircraft machine gun mount for night def., French Ministry War; named Useful Citizen, U. Chgo., 1944. Fellow Am. Phys. Soc., A.A.A.S., Phys. Soc. London, Philos. Soc. Washington; mem. Optical Soc. Am., Franklin Inst., French, German phys. socs., Am. Assn. Physics Tchrs., Phys. Soc. Japan, Geophys. Union, S.A.R., Soc. Mayflower Descs., Phi Beta Kappa, Sigma Xi; asso. mem. U.S. Naval Inst., Scabbard and Blade. Clubs: Faculty (U. Cal.); Cosmos (Washington); Monterey Peninsula Yacht. Author: Basic Processes of Gaseous Electronics, 1955; Static Electricication. 1958; numerous others, also articles, chpts. in books. Home: Berkeley, Calif. Deceased.

LOEB, VIRGIL (LOB), stomatologist; b. Columbia, Mo., Feb. 28, 1883; s. Bernhard and Bertha (Myer) L.; A.B., U. of Mo., 1903; M.D., St. Louis U., 1906, D.D.S., 1906; studied, Berlin, Vienna and London; m. Therese M. Meltzer, Jan. 20, 1913; children—(Mrs. Norman Bierman), (Mrs. Max Deutch), Virgil. Practiced, St. Louis, since 1907; professor oral surgery, St. Louis U., 1907-19; prof. stomatology, Wash. U. Dental School, 1921-34; lecturer on stomatology, Wash. U. Medical School, since 1925; mem. staffs of St. Louis Maternity, St. Louis Children's and Jewish hospitals, United States Marine Hospital, Evangelical Deaconess Hospital. Captain Medical Reserve Corps, 1917; maj. Medical Corps, U.S. Army, 1919; in France, July 1918-April 1919; consultant, facial surgery, Mesves Hospital Center, France, Fellow Internat. Coll. Dentists, Am. Acad. Periodontology, A.A.A.S.; mem. St. Louis Dental Soc. (pres. 1916), St. Louis Medical Soc., A.M.A. (chmn. sect. on stomatology, 1912-13), Mo. Med. Assn., Mo. Dental Assn. (pres. 1935-36), Am. Pub. Health Assn., Am. Soc. for Dentistry For Children, Federation Dentaire Internationale, Phi Beta Pi, Delta Sigma Delta, Omicron Kappa Upsilon, Pi Gamma Mu. Author of numerous scientific articles dealing with diseases of the mouth. Clubs: Westwood Country, University (St. Louis). Home: St. Louis, Mo. *

LOEBL, JERROLD, architect-planner; b. Chgo., Sept. 2, 1899; s. Max M. and Nettle (Sobel) L.; Art Inst. travelling scholar, 1921; B.S., Armour Inst. Tech., 1921, M.A., 1922; m. Ruth Well, Feb. 25, 1926 (dec. Apr. 1971); children—James D., Nancy H.; m. 2d, Minnabel Coleman, Mar. 4, 1973. Dir. dept. architecture Armour Inst. Tech., 1935-38; mem. Loebl & Scholossman, Chgo., 1925-46, Loebl, Schlossman & Bennett, 1946-65, Loebl, Schlossman, Bennett & Dart, 1965-78; architect-planner Park Forest, Ill.; architect Old Orchard Shopping Center, Skokie, Ill., Oakbrook (Ill.) Shopping Center, Michael Reese Hosp., Louis A. Weiss Meml. Hosp., River Oaks Shopping Center, Water Tower Place; asso. architect Chgo. Civic Center; architect Fine Arts-Performing Arts and Student Union Complex, Northwestern U. Mem., past chmn. architects exam. com. State Ill. Trustee Ill. Inst. Tech., Brandeis U., Barat Coll., Lake Forest, Ill. Fellow A.I.A. (pres. Chgo. chpt. 1940-43, Honor award 1968); mem. Chgo. Assn. Commerce, Chgo. Bldg. Congress (pres. 1944-46). Clubs: Arts, Tavern (Chgo.); Lake Shore Country. Home: Chicago, Ill. Died Oct. 1, 1978.

LOENING, GROVER, aircraft engr., author; b. of Am. parents (father U.S. consul), Bremen, Germany Sept. 12, 1888; s. Albert and Hermine (Rubino) L.; prep. edn. Cutler Sch., N.Y.C. and Lawrenceville (N.J.) Sch.; B.S., Columbia, 1908, A.M., 1910, C.E., 1911; m. Marka Truesdale, June 28, 1930 (div. 1940); children—Michael T., Mrs. William Prickett, Jr., Mrs. John Hanford. Gen. mgr. Wright Co., Dayton, Ohio, 1913-14; chief aero. engr. U.S. Army Air Corps, 1914-15; v.p., gen. mgr. Sturtevant Aeroplane Co., Boston, 1916-17; pres. Loening Aero. Engring. Corp., N.Y., 1917-28; dir., cons. engr. Custiss-Wright Corp., 1928-29; pres. Grover Loening Aircraft Co., aircraft mfrs., 1928-38; cons. engr. Fairchild Engine & Aircraft Corp.; cons. engr. Curtiss-Wright Corp.; chmn. bd., cons. engr. N.Y. Airways Corp., then chmn. bd. emeritus Aero. adviser U.S. Maritime Commn., 1937-38; cons. on aircraft War Prodn. Bd., 1942-45; mem. seaplane and helicopter coms. and aero. cons. NACA, 1945-49; mem. bd. Nat. Air Mus., 1946-68; cons. specialist Pres.'s Air Policy Commn., 1948. A founder, 1922, first pres. Aero. C. of C. Am.; mem. adv. com. Daniel Guggenheim Sch. Aeros., N.Y.U., 1950-60; chmn. adv. council Columbia U. Inst. of Air Flight Structures. Dir. Flight Safety Found. Inventor strut-braced monoplane and Loening amphibian airplane; holder many airplane patents. Winner Wright Trophy, 1921, Collier Trophy, 1922. Recipient Distinguished Service award for design and completion of Loening two-seater fighting plane, U.S. War Dept., 1919; awarded Medal for Merit by Pres. Truman, 1948; Wright Brother Meml. Trophy, 1950; Exceptional Civilian Service medal USAF, 1955, Guggenheim medal, 1960; mem. Aviation Hall of Fame. Fellow Am. Inst. Aeros. and Astronautics (hon.), Royal Aero. Soc.; mem. Soc. Automotive Engrs., Early Birds, Order Quiet Birdmen, Soc. Exptl. Test Pilots, Order Daedalians (hon.), Sigma Xi; hon. pres. Nat. Inter-Collegiate Flying Assn. Episcopalian. Clubs: Racquet and Tennis, Wings, New York Yacht; Aero Club of Washington; Army and Navy, Metropolitan (Washington); Committee of 100,

Key Biscayne (Fla.) Yacht; OX-5, Silver Wing. Author: Monoplanes and Biplanes, 1911; Military Aeroplanes (9 editions), 1915-18; Our Wings Grow Faster, 1935; Takeoff Into Greatness, 3 edits., 1968; Conquering Wing, 1970; Amphibian, 1973. Home: Key Biscayne, Fla. Died Feb. 29, 1976.

LOEW, EDGAR ALLEN (LO), coll. dean; b. Wash. County, Wis., Feb. 8, 1882; s. Henry and Louise (Boehner) L.; grad. Normal Sch., Oshkosh, Wis., 1901; B.S. in Elec. Engrg., U. of Wis., 1906, E.E., 1922; m. Minnie Rehfeld, Aug. 10, 1911; children—Edgar Allen, Henry Rehfeld, Richard Thomas. Facility engr., Chicago Tel. Co., 1906; with D.C., and Wm. B. Jackson on appraisal of utilities, summers 1907-08; instr. in elec. engrg., U. of Wis., 1906-09; instr. in elec. engrg., U. of Wash., 1909-11, asst. prof., 1911-16, asso. prof., 1916-17, 1920-23, prof., 1923-26, dean, prof. elec. engring. Coll. Engring., U. of Wash., and dir. Engring. Expt. Sta., 1935-48, dean emeritus and prof. elec. engring. since 1948. elec. engr. and supt., Am. Nitrogen Products Co., 1917-20; cons. engr. for same, 1920-29; for U.S. Engr. Office, Grand Coulee Development, 1932-33; professional engr., State of Washington, since 1936. Cons. engr., Bonneville Power Administrn., 1941-46; consultant, field service, Div. of Priorities, O.P.A., 1942-43; institutional rep. Engrg., Science, Management Defense Training, 1941-45, regional adviser for same, 1944-45. Fellow Am. Inst. Elec. Engrs., mem. Soc. for Promotion Engrg. Edn., (mem. of council, 1944-47), Newcomen Soc., Tau Beta Pi, Sigma Xi, Clubs: Faculty Men's, Municipal League (Seattle). Author: Electrical Power Transmission, 1928; Direct and Alternating Currents, 1933; Cost of Power Transmission from Columbia River Plants to Market Centers (House Document No. 103, 73d Congress, first session); also expt. sta. bulls.; contbr. to tech. jours. Home: Seattle, Wash. *

LOEWENSTEIN, RUDOLPH MAURICE, psychoanalyst, author; b. Lodz, Poland, Jan. 17, 1898; s. Maurice and Charlotte (Taube) L.; M.D., U. Berlin, 1923, U. Paris, 1935; m. Elisabeth R. Geleerd; children—Dominique-Thérèse Loewenstein Kulko, Elisabeth-Charlotte Loewenstein Novick, Marie-Françoise Loewenstein Galizia, Richard Joseph. Came to U.S., 1942, naturalized, 1948. Asst. Berlin Psychoanalytic Inst., 1923-25; asst. to Prof. Henri Claude, out-patient dept., clinic psychiatry, med. faculty, U. Paris, 1925-39; tng. analyst. lectr. Paris Psychoanalytic Inst., 1925-40; tng. analyst, instr. N.Y. Psychoanalytic Inst., from 1943, v.p. 1948-50, pres., 1950-52; asso. clin. prof. psychiatry Med. Sch. Yale, 1948-52; pvt. practice psychoanalysis, N.Y.C., from 1943. Served as Medecin de Bataillon with French Army, 1939-40. Decorated Croix de Guerre (France). Mem. A.M.A., N.Y. State, New York County med. socs., N.Y. Psychoanalytic Society (life mem., pres. 1959-61), Am. Psychoanalytic Assn. (life mem., pres. 1957-58), Internat. Psycho-Analytical Assn. (v.p. 1965-67), N.Y. Soc. Clin. Psychiatry, A.A.A.S., Conf. Jewish Social Studies, Paris (founding), Israel (corr.) psychoanalytic socs.; life mem. Royal Soc. Health. Author: Christians and Jews: A Psychoanalytic Study, 1951; articles profl. jours. Editor: Drives, Affects, Behavior, 1953. Home: New York, N.Y. Died Apr. 14, 1976.

LOGAN, GARRETT, lawyer; b. Poteau, Indian Ty., July 3, 1901; s. William Thomas and Mary (Garrett) L.; student Washington U., 1918-19; LL.B. U. Okla., 1923; m. Esther Reeves, Apr. 17, 1921; children—Esther Elizabeth (Mrs. T. M. Johnston), Christine, Geraldine (Mrs. H.B. Hunt). Admitted to Okla. bar, 1923; gen. practice law, Muskogee, 1923-25, Tulsa, 1925—; counsel firm Martin, Logan, Moyers, Martin & Conway. Served from capt. to lt. col., USAAF, 1942-45. Decorated Legion of Merit. Fellow Am. Bar Found., Am. Coll. Trial Lawyers; mem. Am. (ho. dels. 1958), Okla. (pres. 1958, chmn. com. to investigate Supreme Ct. Okla. 1964-65), Tulsa County (past pres., Senior award 1965) bar assns., Phi Beta Kappa, Order of Coif, Phi Delta Phi. Presbyn. Mason. Club: Tulsa. Author: (with Dr. J. B. Cheadle) Casebook on Indian Land Titles, 1923. Contbr. articles to profl. jours. Home: Tulsa, Okla. Died Dec. 5, 1975.

LOKEY, HULSEY SAWTELL, restaurant exec.; b. Decatur, Ill., Apr. 10, 1910; s. Robert R. and Myrtys (Sawtell) L.; student U. Fla., 1929-31; m. Edith C. Swarth, Feb. 24, 1940 (dec.); children—Sally Teresa, Linda Myrtys, Robert Hulsey; m. 2d, Rosemarry Kraemer, Feb. 5, 1966. Began with Host Internat., Inc., Los Angeles (formerly Interstate Co., Chgo.), from 1931, gen. mgr., 1938-41, pres., 1953-69, chmn. bd., chief exec. officer, from 1969, also mem. exec. com.; v.p. Liggett Drug Co., N.Y., 1947-50; dir. Union Bank, Union Bancorp, Inc. Bd. dirs. Los Angeles Conv. Bur., Inc., Crippled Childrens Soc. Chmn. bd. Pepperdine U. Served as lt. col. USAAF, 1942-46; CBI. Decorated Bronze Star. Mem. Nat., So. Calif. (dir.) restaurant assns., Los Ranchero Visitadores (dir.), Calif. C. of C. (v.p.), Alpha Tau Omega. Presbyn. Clubs: Chicago Athletic Assn.; Los Angeles Country; Outrigger (Honolulu). Address: Santa Monica, Calif. Deceased.

LOMBARD, NORMAN, b. Creston, Ia., Apr. 13, 1884; s. James Lewis and Eva (Stiles) L.; S.B., Mass. Inst. Tech., 1905; LL.B., Kansas City Sch. of Law, 1908; m. Ellen McKeighan, June 10, 1908 (died 1931); children—Norman, Elisabeth, Ellen, John Cutler, Barbara; m. 2d, Evelyn Owens Stringham, 1935. Admitted to Mo. bar, 1907, Calif. bar, 1909; farm mortgage, exporting and importing, mfg. and investment banking business 1908-26; exec. dir., later exec. v.p. The Stable Money Assn., 1926-31; spl. assignment Treasury Dept., 1935. Pres. Inst. Applied Citizenship, 1950, chmn. interim com., 1953. Founder Internat. Inst. Monetary Econs., 1934; pres. Tues. Forum, Incorporated, and chairman Nationwide Discussion-by-Mail Com., 1939. Mem. exec. com. Com. for Economic Stability, 1940; sec.-treas. Owens Industries, Inc.; managing trustee Owens Industries Trust; founder, pres. Inst. for Co-op. Stock Market Forecasting, 1949; chmn. Americans for Gwinn, 1950; mem. adv. com. Assn. Former Polit. Prisoners of Soviet Labor Camps. Mem. Delta Kappa Epsilon, Phi Alpha Delta (member board directors, Alumnia chapt.), Empire State Society, S.A.R. Republican. Club: National Republican. Author: Monetary Statesmanship, 1934; Letters of Prophecy, 1935. Author numerous pamphlets and articles on finance and economics. Home: Scarsdale, N.Y. *

LOMBARDO, GUY ALBERT, band leader; b. London, Ont., Can., June 19, 1902; s. Guy and Lena (Paladine) L.; student St. Peter's London, Ont., 1909-20; Mus.D., U. Western Ont., 1971; m. Lilliebell Glenn, Sept. 9, 1926. Came to U.S., 1923. Musician, 1916-77; began radio broadcasting in U.S., 1924; played at important theatres and hotels throughout U.S. and Can.; well known rec. artist; appeared in M.G.M. and Paramount Pictures; producer musical Arabian Nights, Jones Beach, N.Y., 1954-55, Around the World in 80 Days, Jones Beach, 1963-64, Mardi Gras, Jones Beach, 1965, 66, Hawaiian Mus. Paradise Island, summer 1961, Arabian Nights, 1967, South Pacific, 1968-69, Sound of Music, 1970-71, The King and I, 1971-72, Carousel, 1972-73, Fiddler on the Roof, 1973-74, Oklahoma, 1974-75; appeared N.Y. World's Fair, 1964-65. Accorded recognition from 1930 by radio editors of U.S. and Canada as being outstanding orch. leader. Sec. Am. Power Boat Assn. Winner Gold Cup Speedboat Race and Nat. Sweepstakes, 1946, all Am. speedboat trophies including Nat. Championship 1946, 47, 48, President's Cup, 1955. Also music publisher. Roman Catholic. Author: Auld Acquaintance, 1975. Home: Freeport, N.Y. Died Nov. 5, 1977.

LOMER, GERHARD RICHARD, univ. librarian; b. Montreal, P.Q., Mar. 6, 1882; s. Adolf and Ellen Adele (Lafleur) L.; A.B., McGill Univ., 1903, M.A., 1904; acad. diploma McGill Normal Sch., 1904; Ph.D., Columbia, 1910; unmarried. Instr. in English, McGill Univ., 1903-04, 1906-07, English and edn., 1906-07; instr. in English, Univ. of Wis., 1909-12, sch. of journalism, Columbia, 1912-18, asso., 1919; asso. editor Warner Library, 1916-17, asst. editor Chronicles of America, 1918-20; asst. instr. McGill Summer Library Sch., 1903-04, instr., 1907, 10, 13, dir. of library sch., 1920-24, and 1926-48, univ. librarian, 1920-47. Carnegie Corp. Survey of Prince Edward Is. Libraries, 1932; dir. summer library sch., Charlottetown, P.E.I., 1933, Banff, 1941. Fellow Am. Library Inst., Library Assn. (Eng.); hon. pres. Quebec Library Assn.; hon. mem. L'Academie Latine des Sciences, Arts, et Belles-Lettres. Mem. A.L.A. (liaison com., exec. bd. since 1946), Can. L.A. (mem. Can. Library Council, mem. liaison com.), Spl. Libraries Assn., Phi Kappa Sigma, Sigma Delta Chi. Author: (with J. W. Cunliffe) Writing of Today, 1915-23; (with M. Ashmun) Study and Practice of Writing English, 1947. Address: Montreal, Que. *

LONG, BENJAMIN HANNA, lawyer; b. Logansport, Ind., Apr. 7, 1906; s. Benjamin F. and Lucy (Nichols) L.; A.B., Ind. U., 1926; LL.B., Harvard U., 1929; m. Henrietta Craig Rossiter, Sept. 7, 1956; Admitted to Mich. bar, 1929; practiced in Detroit, 1929-75; sr. partner Long, Preston & Kinnaird, 1956-75. Mem. Atty. Gen.'s Nat. Com. Study Antitrust Laws, 1953-55. Mem. adv. com. Arts Commn. Detroit. Bd. dirs. Ind. U. Found.; bd. visitors Ind. U. Sch. Law. Served to lt. col. U.S. Army, 1942-46. Mem. Am. Bar Assn., Detroit Bar Assn., State Bar Mich., Beta Theta Pi. Republican. Clubs: Country, Detroit, Athletic, University (Detroit); Grosse Pointe (Grosse Pointe Farms). Home: Grosse Pointe Farms, Mich. Died Aug. 12, 1975.

LONG, EARL CECIL, officer U.S. Marine Corps; b. Clayton, N.J., Nov. 4, 1883; s. John H. and Margaret (Van Natten) L.; student U. of Calif., 1901-05; m. Fay Fairbanks, June 16, 1915. Engr., 1905-09; commd. 2d lt., U.S. Marines, 1909, and advanced through the grades to maj. gen., 1944. Decorated Nicaraguan Campaign, Mexican Campaign, World War, and China medals; Legion of Merit. Retired since Aug. 1, 1946. Clubs: Bohemian, Commercial, Yacht (San Francisco). Home: Menlo Park, Calif. *

LONG, ESMOND RAY, pathologist; b. Chgo., June 16, 1890; s. John Harper and Catherine Belle (Stoneman) L.; A.B., U. Chgo., 1911, Ph.D., 1919; M.D., Rush Med. Coll. (U. Chgo.), 1926; postgrad. German U. of Prague; Sc.D. (hon.). U. Pa., 1948; m. Marian Boak Adams, June 17, 1922; children—Judith Baird (Mrs. R.W. Neal). Esmond Ray. Asst. in pathology U. Chgo., 1911-13; asst. desert lab. of Carnegie Instn. of Washington, Tucson, 1914-15; Trudeau fellow Saranac Lab., Saranac Lake, N.Y., 1918, 20; instr. pathology U. Chgo., 1919-21, asst. prof., 1921-23, asso. prof., 1923-28, prof., 1928-32; prof. pathology U. Pa., 1932-55; also dir. lab., Henry Phipps Inst. for Study, Treatment and Prevention of Tb, 1932-35, dir. Inst., 1935-55, emeritus prof. pathology U. Pa. and dept. community medicine, from 1955; trustee Leonard Wood Meml., Am. Leprosy Found., 1970-72; traveling rep. Pan-Am. San. Bur., 1941. Pres. Wistar Inst. Anatomy and Biology, 1939-42. Served from lt. col. to col. M.C., AUS, 1942-46; chief cons. on Tb. Office of Surgeon Gen., U.S. Army, Washington, 1942-45; chief Tb sect. Pub. Health Br., Office of Mil. Govt., U.S. Zone, Germany, Aug-Nov. 1945; acting chief Tb Service, VA, Nov. 1945-Jan. 1946. Mem. NRC, 1932-55 (chmn. div. med. sci. 1936-39, chmn. sub-com. Tb, 1940-42, 46-47, 55-60, chmn. com. on vets. med. problems 1956-60), Nat. Tb Assn. (pres. 1936-37, dir. med. research 1947-55), A.A.A.S. (v.p., chmn. sect. on med. scis. 1936-37), Am. Thoracic Soc., Assn. Am. Physicians, Am. Assn. Pathologists and Bacteriologists (pres. 1936-37, Gold Headed Cane 1971), Am. Soc. for Exptl. Pathology, Am. Philos. Soc., Am. Assn. for History Medicine (pres. 1939-41), A.C.P., Nat. Acad. Scis., Coll. of Physicians (Phila); hon. mem. European and S. Am. med. and tuberculosis socs. Awarded Trudeau medal Nat. Tb Assn., 1932; Legion of Merit, 1946; Strittmatter award, Phila. County Med. Soc., 1950; Phila. award, 1954. Mem. U.S. nat. commn. on UNESCO, 1951-54. Author: The Chemistry of Tuberculosis, 1923; A History of Pathology, 1928; Selected Readings in Pathology, 1929; Antonio Benivieni; The Hidden Causes of Disease (with Charles Singer), 1954; Tuberculosis in the Army of the United States in World War II (with Seymour Jablon), 1955; History of the Therapy of Tuberculosis and the Case of Frederic Chopin, 1955; Tuberculosis Medical Research NTA, 1904-55 (with Virginia Cameron), 1959; A History of American Pathology, 1962; History of the American Society for Experimental Pathology, 1972; History of the American Association of Pathologists and Bacteriologists, 1974. Editor: Internat. Jour. Leprosy, 1964-69. Contbr. articles to med. jours. Home: Philadelphia, Pa. Died Nov. 11, 1979.

LONG, HERMAN HODGE, coll. pres.; b. Birmingham, Ala., May 2, 1912; s. Osie and Ella (Hodge) L.; A.B., Talladega (Ala.) Coll., 1935; A.M., Hartford Sch. Religious Edn., 1936; Ph.D. in Psychology, U. Mich., 1949; m. Henrietta Louise Shivery, May 3, 1938; 1 dau., Ellen. Instr. Miles Coll., 1937-39, dir. summer sch., 1940; field rep. race relations dept. Am. Missionary Assn., Congl. Christian Ch., 1943, field dir., 1944-47, asso. dir., 1947, dir., 1948-64; pres. Talladega Coll., 1964-76. Pres. United Negro Coll. Fund; v.p. Nat. Assn. for Equal Opportunity in Higher Edn. Bd. dirs. Carnegie Found. for Advancement Teaching, So. Fellowships, So. Regional Council. Rosenwald fellow and Gen. Edn. Board fellow, 1939-43. Author: (with C.S. Johnson) People Versus Property. Home: Talladega, Ala. Died Aug. 8, 1976.

LONG, JAMES BLAIR, civil engr.; b. Springfield Twp., Pa., Mar. 8, 1884; s. Thomas and Sarah (Kratz) L.; student Peirce Sch. Bus. Adminstrn., 1902-03; B.S., Pa. State Coll., 1907; m. Elizabeth M. Budding, Nov. 12, 1912; children—Elizabeth B. (Mrs. John O. Chambers), Josephine B. Sales engr. Nelson-Merydith Co., 1907-13; chief engr. Whittaker & Diehl, 1913-19; pvt. practice civil engring., Blue Bell, Pa., 1919—; dir. J. C. Budding Co., Lancaster and Harrisburg, Pa. Mem. Bd. Arbitration Claims Pa., 1950-54. Trustee, past pres. trustees Pa. State U. Registered profl. engr., Pa. Fellow Am. Soc. C.E.; mem. Nat. Soc. Profl. Engrs., Phi Kappa Psi. Republican. Presbyn. Home: Blue Bell, Pa. *

LONG, LOUIS JEFFERSON, coll. pres.; b. Belle Fourche, S.D., July 13, 1908; s. Berry Manley and Nellie Edith (Wade) L.; B.B.A., U. Colo., 1930, M.A. (teaching fellow), 1931; Ph.D. (teaching fellow) U. Ill., 1935; m. Margaret Frances Railsback, June 28, 1935; 1 son, Barry Jefferson. Prof. econs. Allegheny Coll., Meadville, Pa., 1935-41, bus. mgr.-treas., 1941-51; pres. Wells Coll., Aurora, N.Y., 1951-69, emeritus, 1969-77; mng. dir. Cornell U. Research Park; treas. 1st Industry Park Devel. Corp.; sec. Tompkins County Area Devel. Corp. Dir. Nat. Bank Auburn, N.Y. Trustee Cazenovia Coll., 1972. Mem. Am. Econ. Assn., Phi Beta Kappa, Phi Kappa Phi, Sigma Phi Epsilon. Episcopalian. Clubs: Owasco (Auburn); Ithaca Country. Home: Ithaca, N.Y. Died Mar. 22, 1977.

LONG, RALPH HENRY, JR., educator, mech. engr.; b. Ipswich, Mass., Nov. 27, 1922; s. Ralph Henry and Nellie Waterman (Pitstick) L.; B.S. in Mech. Engring. magna cum laude, Tufts Coll., 1943; M.Engring., Yale, 1949, D.Engring., 1952; m. Beatrice Jeannette Frum, Aug. 21, 1943; children—Marsha Ann, Ralph Henry III. Jr. engr. Curtiss-Wright Corp., 1943-44; lab. asst. mech. engring. Yale, 1946-47, asst. in instrn. mech. engring., 1947-49; mech. engr. Sargent & Co., New Haven, summer 1948; asso. prof., then prof. mech.

engring. U. Md., 1949-58; prof. mech. engring. Ill. Inst. Tech., 1958-59; asst. program dir. engring. scis. program NSF, 1959-61, asso. program dir. engring. sect., 1961-63; prof. mech. engring., head dept. Lehigh U., 1963-67; staff asso. NSF, 1967-70, program mgr., from 1970. Summer cons. to govt. and bus., from 1951. Served as ensign USNR, 1944-46. Registered profl. engr., Md. Mem. Am. Soc. M.E. (treas. Washington 1956-57, sec. 1957-58), Am. Soc. Engring. Edn., Combustion Inst., Sigma Xi, Phi Kappa Phi, Tau Beta Pi, Pi Tau Sigma. Contbr. articles to profl. jours. Home: Adelphi, Md. Deceased.

LONG, ROWLAND HORNSHAW, lawyer; b. Waterbury, Conn., Jan. 13, 1898; s. Rowland and Mary Hutchinson (Peggie) L.; LL.B., Fordham U., 1924; LL.M., N.Y. U., 1925; m. Ruth Stoddard Way, Feb. 1928; children—Nelson Way, Ruth Stoddard, Jane Long Hadley, and Jonathan Hutchinson. Admitted to N.Y. bar, 1926, Mass. bar, 1948; trial lawyer, N.Y.C., 1926-48; asst. counsel Mass. Mut. Life Ins. Co., Springfield, 1948-50, asso. counsel, 1950-52, counsel, 1952-54, gen. counsel, 1954-57, v.p., gen. counsel, 1957-63; asso. prof. law St. Johns U., 1927-38; lectr. forensic medicine N.Y. U., from 1955, asst. prof. forensic medicine, from 1959; trial lawyer, Mass. and N.Y.; dir. First Investors Life Ins. Co., Fla. Mortgage Funding Corp., Thomas S. Wood Inc. Trustee Wilbraham and Monson Acad. Mem. Boston, N.Y., Mass., Hampden County bar assns., Am. Acad. Forensic Scis., Assn. Life Ins. Counsel, Ins. Soc. N.Y., Internat. Assn. Ins. Counsel, Am. Life Ins. Assn. (legal sect.). Mason (Shriner, 32 deg.). Author books, including: Richards Law of Insurance, 4th edit., 1932; The Physician and the Law, 1955, 3d edit., 1968; Long on the Law of Liability Insurance; Long, Actions on Life Insurance Policies. Contbr. articles to legal and med. jours. Club: Appalachian Mountain. Home: Watertown, Conn. Died July 24, 1979; buried Riverside Cemetery, Waterbury, Conn.

LONG, S(AMUEL) BURMAN, clergyman; b. Carlisle, Pa., May 31, 1883; s. Samuel Theodore and Sarah Jane (Stout), L., B.A., Lebanon Valley Coll., 1908; B.D., Union Theol. Sem., 1911; M.A., Syracuse U., 1932, D.D., 1940; m. Margaret Mae Hough, Sept. 21, 1911; children—Margaret Mae (Mrs. Dexter Otis Arnold), Catherine Bonnita (Mrs. John W. Glendening, Jr.). Telegraph operator, Philadelphia and Reading Railroad, 1901-04; ordained Congregational ministry, 1911; pastor, Lusk, Wyo., 1911-15; Yorkville, Ill., 1915-19; Marlboro, N.H., 1919-26; Geddes Congl. Ch., Syracuse, N.Y., 1926-43; pastor, Old South Union Congl. Ch., South Weymouth, Mass., since May 1, 1943; grad. asst., Dept. of Bible, Syracuse U., 1920-31; supt. N.Y. State Fair inspirational service since 1932. Moderator New York Congl.-Christian Conf., 1938-39, Union Assn. of Congl. Chs., 1934-35. Mem. Crime Prevention Bur. and Council of Social Agencies. Trustee Aged Ministers Home. Director Crusade for a United Church of America. Mem. Council of Chs., Syracuse Ministers Assn. (pres., 1933-34), Nat. Soc. of Biblical Instrs., Nat. Soc. Biblical Lit. and Exegesis, Weymouth Hist. Soc., Rotary Internat., Phi Kappa Phi, Theta Beta Phi, Theta Chi Beta. Mason (32 deg.); chaplain, Wessagussett Lodge. Clubs: Pilgrim, Fortnightly, Boston Congl. Member Weymouth Ministers Association, Boston Ministers Assn. Contbr. to The Advance (New York), Pulpit Digest (Great Neck, L.I.). Author: Be Ye Comforted. Address: South Weymouth, Mass.

LONGACRE, J. JAMES, plastic surgeon; b. Northampton, Pa., July 26, 1907; s. Jacob E. and Anne Koehler (Beitel) L.; B.A. magna cum laude, Lehigh U., 1927; M.D. cum laude, Harvard, 1932; m. Margaret Suzanne Gruen, Oct. 21, 1939; children—Frederick Gruen, James Gruen. Intern, Geisinger Meml. Hosp., Danville, Pa., 1932-33; surg. resident Cin. Gen. Hosp.; practice medicine, specializing plastic and reconstructive surgery, from 1946; dir. plastic surg. dept. Christ and Bethesda hosps., Cin.; asso. ending staff Good Samaritan Hosp., Cin.; cons. staff St. Luke Hosp., Ft. Thomas, Ky., also William Booth Meml. and St. Elizabeth hosps., Covington, Ky.; sr. plastic cons. Vets. Hosp., Cin.; dir. Cleft Palate Rehab. Clinic, Children's Hosp., Cin.; asso. clin. prof. surgery dept. surgery U. Cin.; adv. com. crippled children Ohio Welfare Dept. Chmn. program planning com. NRC-NIH; chmn. Internat. Symposium on Craniofacial Anomalies. Trustee Am. Found. Plastic and Reconstructive Surgery; chmn. exam. com. Am. Bd. Plastic Surgery. Served from capt. to lt. col. M.C., AUS, 1942-46. Diplomate Am. Bd. Surgery, Am. Bd. Plastic Surgery (vice chmn.). Mem. Am. Soc. Plastic and Reconstructive Surgery, Am. Assn. Plastic Surgeons, Am. Assn. Cleft Palate Rehab. (past pres.), Head and Neck Soc., Ohio Valley Plastic Surg. Assn. (past pres.), A.M.A. (mem. council med. edn.), Cin. Acad. Med., Ohio Med. Assn., Am. Assn. Thoracic Surgery, Ohio Hist. and Philos. Soc. Presbyn. (trustee, elder). Clubs: Queen City, Cincinnati Country (Cin.); Harvard, Lake Placid., Skytop. Author: Cleft Palate Deformation; Scar Tissue-It's Use and Abuse; Rehabilitation of the Facially Disfigured. Editor: Craniofacial Antomalies: Pathogenesis and Repair, 1968; The Ultra Structure of Collagen-It's Relation to Wound Healing and the Management of Hypertrophy Scar. Home: Cincinnati, Ohio, Deceased.

LONGINO, JAMES CHARLES, JR., naval officer; b. Fairburn, Ga., Apr. 23, 1918; s. James Charles and Elizabeth (McLarin) L.; B.S., U.S. Naval Acad.; M.I.A., Columbia; student Georgetown U.; m. Helen O'Brien, Aug. 1, 1943; children—Helen, Michele, Virginia, James. Commd. ensign U.S. Navy, 1940, advanced through grades to rear adm.; assigned U.S.S. Pensacola, U.S.S. Suwanee; asst. naval attache, Paris; assigned Office Chief Naval Operations, Fighter Squadron 61, U.S.S. Lake Champlain; mem. staff comdr. Central Mediterranean; assigned Office Chief Naval Operations; grad. Nat. War Coll.; comdg. officer U.S.S. Canisteo, U.S.S. Lake Champlain; assigned Office Chief Naval Operations; dep. dir., then dir. intelligence U.S. European Command; comdr. Fleet Air San Diego, comdr. Anti-Submarine Warfare Group 3; dep. dir. for plans Def. Intelligence Agy.; then def. attache Am. Embassy, London, Eng. Decorated Legion of Merit (2), D.F.C. (3), Bronze Star, Air medal; chevalier Legion of Honor (France). Mem. Pi Sigma Alpha. Home: London, England. Died Mar. 13, 1977.

LONGLEY, JAMES BERNARD, gov. of Maine; b. Lewiston, Maine, Apr. 22, 1924; s. James Bernard and Catherine (Wade) L.; student Bowdoin Coll., 1947; LL.B., U. Maine, 1957; m. Helen Walsh, Sept. 3, 1949; children—James Bernard, Kathryn M., Susan Marie, Stephen J., Nancy E. Gen. agt. New Eng. Mut. Life Ins. Co., Lewiston, 1963; admitted to Maine bar; pres. Longley Assos., Lewiston, 1948-74; partner Longley & Buckley, Lewiston, 1958-74; gov. Maine, 1975—. Dir., Casco Bank & Trust Co.; treas., dir. First Fed. Savs. & Loan Assn.; guest lectr. univs. Wis., Colo., Ark., Conn., Wharton, Purdue. Athletic dir. Healey Home for Boys, 1958-70; chmn. Maine Mgmt. and Cost Survey State Govt., 1972-73. Bd. dirs. Child and Family Services of Maine; trustee Central Maine Gen. Hosp. Mem. Million Dollar Round Table (past pres., life mem.), Androscoggin Valley (past pres.), Maine (past pres.) life underwriters Am. Soc. Chartered Life Underwriters (past chmn. bd. editors. Home: Lewiston, Maine. Died Aug. 16, 1980.

LONGLEY, JAMES FARR, former utility co. exec.; b. Seymour, Tex., Aug. 11, 1903; s. George and Hallie (Farr) L.; B.S. in Elec. Engring., Tex. A. and M. Coll., 1924; m. Hazel E. Powell, Apr. 20, 1924; children—James Farr, Jo Joyce (Mrs. Ernest F. Mullikin). Instr., Tex. A. and M. Coll., 1924-26; with W. Tex. Utilities Co., Abilene, 1926-68, v.p., gen. supt., 1960-64, exec. v.p., 1964-68, also dir.; retired, 1968. Registered profl. engr., Tex. Methodist. Home: Abilene, Tex. Died Dec. 24, 1976.

LONGLEY, RAYMOND IRVING, state ofcl.; b. Hartford, Conn., Oct. 10, 1885; s. Thomas Elijah and Elizabeth (Tuttle) L.; student Rochester Bus. Inst., 1905-06; m. Elizabeth Valentine Lilly, Apr. 12, 1913; children—Raymond, Harriet (Mrs. R. C. Draper), Charles, Rodman. Comptroller, U. Conn., 1913-43; rep. Conn. State Gen. Assembly, 1945-49, judiciary com., 1945, appropriations com., 1947-49; auditor Conn. State since 1951; dir. Williamantic Savs. Inst. Mem. Joint Bd. Mental Hosps., Mansfield-Southbury Joint Bd., Penal and Correctional Com. of 15, Humane and Welfare Instn. Bldg. Commn., 1947-51. Pres. bd. trustees Mansfield Tng. Sch. and Hosp., 1945-51. Republican. Conglist. Mason (32 deg., K.T.). Home: Stafford Springs. *

LONGSTRETH, THOMAS MORRIS, author; s. Benjamin Taylor and Frances (Haldeman) L.; A.B., Haverford Coll., 1908. Travel tutor, 1908-12; with De Lancey Sch., Phila., 1912-13, Wynnewood, Pa., 1917; free-lance writer, 1917-75. Mem. Phi Beta Kappa. Mem. Soc. Friends. Latest publs.: The Great Venture, 1948; Mounty in a Jeep, 1949; Showdown, 1950; Gallows Rock, 1951; Elephant Toast, 1952; Camping Like Crazy, 1953; The Scarlet Force, 1953; Time Flight, 1954; The Force Carries On, 1954; Dangerline, 1955; Doorway in the Dark, 1956; The MacQuarrie Boys, 1957; Bull Session, 1958; Michel of Ironwood, 1959; Trouble Guaranteed, 1960; That Williams Boy, 1961; The Calgary Challengers, 1962; Henry Thoreau: American Rebel, 1963; The Comeback Catcher, 1965. Contbr. to Christian Sci. Monitor. Home: Haverford, Pa. Died Dec. 21, 1975.

LONGWELL, CHESTER RAY, geologist; b. Spalding, Mo., Oct. 15, 1887; s. John Kilgore and Julia (Megown) L.; A.B., U. Mo., 1915, A.M., 1916, hon. LL.D., 1940; Ph.D., Yale, 1920; m. 2d, Irene M. Moffat, June 18, 1935; children—Mari Louise, Flora May, Ray Megown. Asst. prof. geology Yale, 1920-26, asso. prof., 1926-29, prof., 1929-56, emeritus, 1956, chmn. dept., 1938-46; on staff U.S. Geol. Survey, 1920-45, 48-75; research asso. Stanford U., 1955-75, cons. prof., 1975; chmn. div. Geol. and Geography, NRC, 1937-40. Served as capt., F.A., A.E.F., World War I. Fellow A.A.A.S. (v.p., chmn. sect. E 1942), Geol. Soc. Am. (councilor 1937-39, v.p. 1942, 48, pres. 1949); mem. Am. Philos. Soc., Nat. Acad. Scis. (chmn. sect. geol. 1942-45), Seismol. Soc. Am., Am. Acad. Arts and Scis., Am. Geol. Inst. (pres. 1954), Phi Beta Kappa, Sigma Xi, Delta Sigma Rho. Author: Geology from Original Sources (with W. M. Agar and R. F. Flint), 1929; Physical Geology (with A. Knopf and R. F. Flint), 1932, 39, 48; Walks and Rides in Central Connecticut (with E. S. Dana), 1932; Outlines of Physical Geology (with A. Knopf and R. F. Flint) 1934, 41; Introduction to Physical Geology (with R. F. Flint), 1955, 1962; (with R.F. Flint and J.E. Sanders) Physical Geology, 1968; author monographs and articles in field. Home: Palo Alto, Calif. Died Dec. 15, 1975.

LONGWORTH, ALICE LEE ROOSEVELT, b. N.Y.C., Feb. 12, 1884; d. Theodore (pres. U.S. 1901-09) and Alice Hathaway (Lee) Roosevelt; studied with tutors and governesses; m. Nicholas Longworth, Feb. 17, 1906 (dec. Apr. 1931); 1 dau., Paulina (Mrs. Alexander McCormick Sturm) (dec. Jan. 1957). Former columnist Ladies Home Jour. Mem. Nat. Com. on Food for Five Small Democracies, 1940. Mem. bd. counselors women's div. Republican Nat. Com., 1932; del. from Ohio to Rep. Nat. Conv., 1936. Author: Crowded Hours, 1934. Editor: (with Theodore Roosevelt, Jr.) The Desk Drawer Anthology: Poems for the American People, 1937. Home: Washington, D.C. Died Feb. 20, 1980.

LOOK, ARNOLD E., educator; b. Bath, N.Y., Oct. 6, 1896; s. Newman Simmons and Lydia Ella (Shults) L.; student U. Toronto and Wycliffe Coll., 1914-15; B. Th., So. Baptist Theol. Sem., 1917; B.A., McMaster U., 1919; B.D., Crozer Theol. Sem., 1920, M.Th., 1922; M.A., U. Pa., 1920; fellow Dropsie Coll., 1921-22; Ph.D., Yale, 1927; m. Lillian Mildred Lupton, May 7, 1920; children—Arnold Evert, Donald Lupton, Lillian Emma. Ordained to ministry, 1917; pastor Upland Baptist Ch. and instr. Crozer Theol. Sem., 1923-25; pastor Shelton Congl. Ch., instr. Yale Theol. Sem., 1925-27; prof. Internat. YMCA Coll., 1927-31; pres. Charles E. Ellis Sch., Newton Square, Pa., 1931-61, asst. to pres., chmn. communications dept. and social sci. div. Talladega Coll., 1961-66; lectr. English, Edison Jr. Coll., 1967-68; founder Camp Ellis, Ellis Summer Sch., lectr. Grad. Sch. Edn., U. Pa., 1946-47, 49-50, 52-53. Chmn. adv. com. on pvt. schs., children's instns. and camps Joint State Govt. Commn. of Pa.; pres., trustee and chmn. program services com. Pa. State YMCA (mem. nat. program services com.). Mem. Headmasters Assn. Republican. Conglist. Clubs: Rotary, Philadelphia District Headmaster's (past pres.). Author: The History of Abba Marcus, 1927; Student Religion, 1928. Contbr. articles to various publs. Address: Daytona Beach, Fla. Died Aug. 22, 1978; buried West Brookfield, Mass.

LOOS, KARL DICKSON, lawyer; b. Iowa City, Feb. 10, 1891; s. Isaac Althaus and Mary Alice (Dickson) L.; A.B. State U. Iowa, 1911, LL.B., 1914; m. Zera Randall Harries, Feb. 25, 1922 (dec. Oct. 1951); children—Howard Harries, Dickson Randall. Admitted to Ill. bar, 1914, D.C. bar, 1921; practiced law, Chgo., 1914-20; partner firm Pope, Ballard & Loos, Washington, 1921-73; ret., 1973; chmn. legal and tax com. Nat. Council Farmer Coops., 1944-50; solicitor Dept. Agr., 1953-54. Served as gunnery sgt., USMC, 1917; capt., inf., U.S. Army, 1918. Mem. Am., Ill., Md., D.C., Chgo. bar assns., Assn. ICC Practitioners, Nat. Rifle Assn. (treas., 1921-26), Order of Coif, Phi Beta Kappa, Beta Theta Pi, Delta Sigma Rho. Republican. Congregationalist. Clubs: Rotary, Army and Navy, Metropolitan (Washington); University (Chgo.); Jonathan (Los Angeles). Home: Chevy Chase, Md. Died June 13, 1978.

LOOSE, JOHN G., ins. exec.; b. Palmyra, Pa., Aug. 7, 1884; s. Jacob A. and Emma (Spangler) L.; M.E., Lehigh U., 1907; m. Aimee H. Collier, Apr. 14, 1951; children (by former marriage)—John F., Robert J. Joined Gt. Am. Ins. Co., N.Y. City, 1907, insp., 1907-08, engr., 1908-17, spl. agt., 1917-20, sec., 1931-40, v.p., 1940-49, exec. v.p. since 1949. Home: Jackson Heights, N.Y. *

LOOSLI, CLAYTON G., physician; b. Marysville, Idaho, Mar. 18, 1905; s. Dimond and Hattie (Salisbury) L.; B.S., U. Idaho, 1930, M.S. (fellow) 1931, D.Sc. (hon.), 1958; Ph.D. (fellow), U. Chgo., 1934, M.D. (J. H. Koessler fellow, Douglas Smith fellow), 1937; m. Jean Russell Pederson, Sept. 15, 1933; children—Alvin Russell and Edward Salisbury (twins). Intern, Johns Hopkins Hosp., Balt., 1937-38; asst. anatomy U. Chgo., 1934-35, asst. medicine, 1938-40, instr., 1940-42, asst. prof., 1942-43, asso. prof. medicine, 1946-49, dir. student health service, 1946-49, prof., chief sect. preventive medicine, 1949-58; prof. medicine, dean Sch. Medicine, U. So. Calif., 1958-64, Hastings prof. medicine, 1964-76; mem. commns. on influenza, pneumonia and airborne infections under Surgeon Gen. M.C., U.S. Army, 1941-46; mem. com. influenza Armed Forces Epidemiol. Bd., from 1948, mem. bd., from 1957; cons. USPHS, Communicable Disease Center, from 1952, cons. div. hosp. and med. facilities, from 1964; mem. nat. adv. council Inst. Allergy and Infectious Diseases, NIH, from 1961. Served from capt. to maj. M.C., U.S. Army, 1943-46. Recipient Commonwealth Fund Sr. award for support creative research, 1956-57. Diplomate Am. Bd. Preventive Medicine and Public Health. Fellow A.C.P. (master),

Am. Geriatric Soc., Am. Acad. Microbiology (charter), Am. Public Health Assn.; mem. Am. Assn. Ry. Surgeons, Assn. Am. Med. Colls., Am. Assn. Anatomists, Am. Soc. Exptl. Pathology, Am. Soc. Clin. Investigation, AAAS, AMA, Am. Epidemiol. Soc., Assn. Am. Physicians, Central Soc. Clin. Research (pres. 1955), Soc. Exptl. Biology and Medicine, Calif Med. Assn., Los Angeles County Med. Assn., Am. Lung Assn., Am. Clin. and Climatological Assn., Am. Assn. Immunologists, Sigma Xi, Alpha Omega Alpha. Editor Jour. Lab. and Clin. Medicine, 1949-54. Contbr. articles to med. publs. Home: South Pasadena, Calif. Died June 27, 1976.

LOPATNIKOFF, NICOLAI, composer; b. Reval, Russia, Mar. 16, 1903; s. Lev and Ida (Feitelberg) L.; student high sch., Petrograd and conservatories in Petrograd and Helsingfors; grad. (engr.'s diploma), Tech. U. Karlsruhe, 1928; m. Nora Laschinsky, Aug. 17, 1926 (dec. July 1945); m. 2d, Sara Henderson Hay, Jan. 27, 1951. Came to U.S., 1939, Am. citizen. Asso. prof. composition, music dept., Carnegie Inst. Tech. (now Carnegie Mellon U.), 1945-48; prof. composition, music dept., 1948-69, prof. composition emeritus, 1969-76. Compositions: Opera Danton; Four Symphonies; Concertos for Piano and Orch.; Concerto for Violin and Orch.; also symphonic pieces, string quartets, sonatas for various instruments, piano music, etc. Compositions since coming to U.S.: Second Symphony (premiere in Boston, 1939); Violin Concerto (Boston, 1942); Symphonietta (N.Y.C. 1942); Concerto for 2 pianos and orchs., 1952; Divertimento for Orch., La Jolla, Calif. 10th ann.; Third Symphony (Pitts. 1954); commd. to write compositions for Pitts. Symphony, Louisville Orch., 1958 and composition for Nat. Automobile Show, Detroit, 1960, Concerto for Wind orch. for Am. Wind Symphony, 1962, Fourth Symphony (Pitts. Symphony Commn. Premiere 1972 in Pitts.). Represented on festivals of Internat. Soc. for Contemporary Music, Vienna, 1932, Berkeley, Calif., 1942. Compositions have been performed by orchs. of Europe and U.S. under direction of Koussevitsky, Stokowski, Bruno Walter, Gabrilowitsch, and others. Received award from Belaieff Pub. House for Second String Quartet, 1929; from German Radio Corp. for First Symphony, 1930; won the 25th Anniversary competition, Cleve. Orch., for his Opus Sinfonicum, 1943; Koussevitzky Found. award, 1944; award and citation Nat. Inst. Arts and Letters, 1953. Awarded Guggenheim Meml. Found. fellowship, 1945; Nat. Endowment for the Arts grant, 1966. Mem. ASCAP, Internat. Soc. Contemporary Music, Nat. Inst. Arts and Letters. Contbr. to Modern Music. Home: Pittsburgh, Pa. Died Oct. 7, 1976; buried Homewood Cemetery, Pittsburgh.

LORD, ARTHUR RUSSELL, civil engr.; b. Ipswich, Mass. Aug. 8, 1886; s. Aaron and Catherine Elizabeth (Underhill) L.; B.S. in C.E., U. of Me., 1907, C.E., 1911; M.S. in Theoretical and Applied Mechanics, U. of Ill., 1911., m. Ruth Mitchell Burns, Sept. 22, 1915. Began in employ of Am. Bridge Co., of New York, Brooklyn offices, 1906; instr. in civil engring., U. of Me., 1907-08, U. of Ill., 1908-09; research fellow, U. of Ill. Engr. Expt. Sta., 1909-11; chief engr. Leonard Construction Co., at Chicago, 1911-12; consulting civil engr. since 1912; formerly pres. Tait & Lord, Inc., structural building designers; became pres. Lord & Hollinger, Inc., 1925; chief engr. Cook County Civil Works Adminstrn., Nov. 1933-Mar. 1934; state adminstr. Work and Rehabilitation Div., Ill. Emergency Relief Commn., Apr. 1934-July 1935; asst. state adminstr. Works Progress Adminstrn. for Ill., 1935-40; asst. to dir. Bd. Yards and Docks, United States Navy, 1940-45; retired, October 1945. Captain engineers, United States Army, Aug. 1917-July 1918, maj. July 1918-May 1919. Mem. Am. Soc. Civil Engrs., Am. Concrete Inst. (pres.), Sigma Xi, Phi Kappa Phi. Mem. Nat. Joint Com. on Specifications for Concrete and Reinforced Concrete; representative of Am. Concrete Inst. on Building Code Com. of U.S. Dept. Commerce. Made first test for actual stresses on reinforced concrete building. Republican. Baptist. Author: Bulletin No. 56, Univ. of Ill. Engr. Expt. Station, 1912; Structural Members and Connections, 1923; Handbook of Reinforced Concrete Building Design, 1928; also numerous published books, papers, etc. Home: Palos Park, Ill. *

LORD, CLIFFORD LEE, former hist. soc. exec.; b. Mt. Vernon, N.Y., Sept. 4, 1912; s. Charles Clifford and Bertha Eunice (Lee) L.; A.B., Amherst Coll., 1933, A.M., 1934, L.H.D., 1958; Ph.D., Columbia U., 1943; LL.D., Lawrence Coll., 1948, U. Buffalo, 1962, Adelphi U., 1965; L.H.D., Rider Coll., 1970; m. Elizabeth Sniffen Hubbard, June 12, 1937 (dec. Jan. 1979); children—Charles Hubbard, Helen Patricia. Amherst Meml. fellow in history, 1934-36; instr. Am. history Columbia, 1936-41; cons. Hist. Records Survey, N.Y.C., 1936-39, N.J., 1940-42; dir. N.Y. State Hist. Assn., 1941-46; organized Farmers' Mus., Cooperstown, N.Y., 1942; dir. State Hist. Soc. Wis., 1946-58, Circus World Mus., 1955-58, now hon. dir.; v.p. Nat. R.R. Mus., 1956-63, now hon. trustee, dean Sch. Gen. Studies, prof. history Columbia, 1958-64: pres., prof. history Hofstra U., 1964-72, chancellor, 1972-73; pres. Hudson Inst., Croton-on-Hudson, N.Y., 1973-75; cons. N.Y. State Maritime Mus., 1975-76, Phila. Maritime Mus., 1976; dir. N.J. Hist. Soc., 1977-79. Cons. Western Heritage Center, 1960-64, Nat. Archives, 1962-64; mem. N.J. Tercentennial Commn., 1961-64, N.Y. Adv. Commn. Higher Edn., 1965-68; chmn. Commn. on Ind. Colls. N.Y., 1966-68; mem. council Smithsonian Instn., 1966-72, hon. 1972-80; bd. dirs. Regional Plan Assn., 1967-77; trustee Rider Coll., 1977-80. Served from lt. (j.g.) to lt. comdr. USNR, 1943-46, with Naval Aviation History Unit, 1944-46, head, 1945-46. Mem. Am. Assn. Museums (council 1943-49), Am. (chmn. com. on territorial papers 1962-64), Western, Wis., N.J., N.Y. State hist. assns., Orgn. Am. Historians, Am. Assn. State and Local History (pres. 1056-60, council 1950-56, 60-67, chmn. adv. council Am. History Research Center 1950-59), Newcomen Soc. N. Am., Phi Beta Kappa (hon.). Episcopalian. Clubs: Century (N.Y.C.); Rock Spring; Rotary. Author: History of U.S. Naval Aviation, 1949; Teaching History with Community Resources, 1964; Clio's Servant, 1967. Editor: Historical Atlas of U.S., 1943, 54, 69; List and Index of Presidential Exec. Orders: Unnumbered Series, 1942, Numbered Series, 1944; Atlas Congressional Roll Calls, 1st vol., 1943; Ideas in Conflict, 1958; (with H. Graff) J. A. Krout's American Themes, 1963; Localized History Series, 1964—; Keepers of the Past, 1965; New York Hist., quarterly mag., 1941-43, Wis. Mag. of History 1946-56; mem. adv. bd. America, History and Life, 1964-68. Address: West Orange, N.J. Died Oct. 22, 1980.

LORD, JOHN SOLON, lawyer; b. Buena Vista County, Iowa, June 8, 1881; s. Augustus Warner and Mary Elizabeth (Crowell) L.; B.A., U. Wis., 1904, hon. LL.D.; student Harvard Law Sch., 1904-06; m. Marion M. Green, Oct. 6, 1915; children—Jane Crowell (Mrs. Herbert C. Brook), John Mason (dec.). Admitted to Ill. bar, 1906, since practiced in Chgo.; mem. Richberg, Ickes, Davies & Lord, 1915-23, Lord, Wire & Cobb, 1924-30, now Lord, Bissell & Brook; atty. in fact London Lloyds (Ill.), 1932-62; past dir., v.p. Marquis-Who's Who, Inc. Chmn. bd. Meml. Union Bldg. Assn., U. Wis.; bd. dirs. Wis. Alumni Research Found. Fellow Am. Coll. Trial Lawyers; mem. Am., Ill., Chgo. bar assns., Law Club (past pres.), Chgo. Law Inst., Gen. Alumni Assn. Wis. (pres. 1916-18), Art Inst. Chgo., Chgo. Natural History Mus., Order of Coif (hon.), Phi Delta Phi (hon.). Republican. Mem. Hinsdale Union Ch. Clubs: University, Chicago, Attic (Chgo.); Hinsdale Golf; Oak Brook Polo. Home: Hinsdale, Ill. Died Apr. 15, 1979; buried Bronswood Cemetery, Hinsdale.

LORD, MARY PILLSBURY (MRS. OSWALD BATES LORD), civic worker; b. Mpls., Nov. 14, 1904; d. Charles Stinson and Nelle Pendleton (Winston) Pillsbury; B.A. cum laude, Smith Coll., 1927, LL.D., 1953, Syracuse U., 1954, Temple U., 1956, Wilmington Coll., 1961, Lindenwood Coll.; L.H.D., Wheaton Coll., 1953, Russell Sage Coll., 1954, Western Coll., 1962, Pratt Inst., 1967, Tufts U., 1966; m. Oswald Bates Lord, Dec. 7, 1929; children—Charles Pillsbury, Winston. Vol. social worker, Mpls., 1927; family welfare work, Mpls., 1927-29; vol. case worker Charity Orgn. Soc., N.Y.C., 1930-31; v.p., dir. East Side Settlement House, 1939-43; mem. N.Y. Def. Recreation Com., co-chmn. 1941-42; mem. Women's Council Greater N.Y. Fund; chmn. women's div. N.Y. War Fund, 1943; hon. chmn. women's div., 1944, mem. Com. for Winning the Peace, President's Commn. for Observation 25th Anniversary of UN; vice chmn. Citizen's Com. for Peace with Freedom in Viet Nam. Bd. dirs. and com. Nat. War Fund, Jan. 1944, chmn. women's activities 1944; mem. N.Y. Woman's Council, 1945; bd. Atlantic Council U.S.A.; hon. gov. Atlantic Inst., (Paris); past bd. Women's Africa Com.; bd. dirs. People-to-People Com., U.S. Com. Refugees, N.Y. World's Fair, chmn. nat. adv. com. women's participation, 1939-40; asst. dir. Civilian Def., Region II, Sept. 1941-43; adviser to Housing Commn. sec. def., 1950; chmn. Gov's. Com. Edn. and Employment Women, 1963-64; bd. dirs. Nat. Com. Internat. Devel.; U.S. Rep. human rights commn. ECOSOC, UN, 1953-61; U.S. alternate rep. UN Gen. Assembly, 1953-59; U.S. del. Gen. Assembly UN, 1958, 60; mem. Jr. League of N.Y., pres. 1936-38; nat. chmn. Civilian Adv. Com. for Women's Army Corps, 1944; pres. bd. RESCUE com. Former trustee Smith Coll., Town Hall, Inc.; trustee Am. U. in Cairo; past mem. vis. com. Sch. Pub. Health, Johns Hopkins; mem. vis. com. Fletcher Sch. of Tufts U.; bd. dirs. Sch. Advanced Internat. Studies, WHO U.S. past bd. dirs. Planned Parenthood Assn.; U.S. Mem. Nat. Colonial Dames N.Y., Phi Beta Kappa. Conglist. Clubs: Smith Coll.; Women's City (v.p., dir. 1940-42); Cosmopolitan; Nat. Women's Republican. Recipient citation by Gen. Omar Bradley, 1948, ofcl. ribbon Office Civilian Def. (for 5,000 hrs. vol. service), 1943. Author: (with Oswald B. Lord) Exit Backward Bowing, 1970. Contbr. several articles relating to N.Y. World's Fair, 1939-40. Home: New York, N.Y. Died July 21, 1978.

LORD, ROBERT OWEN, banker; b. Evanston, Ill., Apr. 11, 1886; s. George S. and Eda (Hurd) L.; ed. The Hill Sch., Pottstown, Pa.; m. Marie Luise Leopold, of Burlington, Ia., June 11, 1914; children—Marie Luise, Robert Owen. With Armour Grain Co., Chicago, 1904-05; jr. clk., real estate mortgage business, 1905-06; with security dept. N. W. Harris & Co., investment bankers, 1906-18, cashier, 1918-19, v.p., 1919-27; pres. Guardian Detroit Union Group, Inc.; pres. Guardian Nat. Bank of Commerce; dir. Leopold Desk Co. (Burlington), Nat. Surety Co., Universal Credit Corpn., Nat. Investors Corpn. and subsidiaries. Trustee The Hill School. Republican. Presbyn. Clubs: Detroit, Recess, Downtown; Grosse Pointe, Country (Grosse Pointe); Grosse Point Hunt (Grosse Pointe Farms); Les Cheneaux (Mich.); Bankers, Attic (Chicago); Hangar (New York). Home: Grosse Pointe Farms, Mich. *

LOUCKS, VERNON REECE, lawyer; b. Chgo., Feb. 23, 1886; s. Charles N. and Mary Ellen (Reece) L.; A.B., Northwestern U., 1908, LL.B., 1910; m: Sue Burton, Jan. 29, 1923; children—Catherine (Mrs. Richard W. Whitten) (dec.), Sue Ellen (Mrs. Fred R. Williamson), Vernon Reece. Admitted to Ill. bar, 1910, U.S. Supreme Ct. bar; mem. firm Atwood, Pease, Loucks & Peterson, 1915-23, Loucks, Eckhart & Peterson, Chgo., 1923-33, individual practice, 1933—; dir. Victor Comptometer Corp., Chgo., Salerno-Megowen Biscuit Co., Chgo. Pres., Chgo. Meml. Hosp., 1944-54; chmn. organizing com. Irving Park Blvd. YMCA, Chgo., 1926; pres. Kenilworth (Ill.) Community Chest, 1949-50, Kenilworth Sch. Bd., 1946-49. Trustee Northwestern Meml. Hosp., Meth. Ministers Endowment Fund, Victor Found., A.C. Buehler Found. Served as ensign USN, 1918-19. Recipient Alumni medal Northwestern U., 1963. Mem. Am., Ill., Chgo. bar assns., Northwestern U. Club Chgo. (past pres.), Northwestern U. Alumni Assn. (past pres.), Phi Beta Kappa. Clubs: Kenilworth; Indian Hill (Winnetka, Ill.); Union League Chicago (past pres. 1952-53). Author: James Alton James, 1963. Home: Wilmette IL. *

LOUGHRY, HOWARD K. (LO'RI), army officer; b. in Ind., Mar. 21, 1882; B.S., U.S. Mil. Acad., 1906; grad. Coast Arty. Sch., 1911, Field Officers Course, 1922, Command and Gen. Staff Sch., 1923, Army War Coll., 1927, Naval War Coll., 1928. Commd. 2d lt., U.S. Army, June 12, 1906; promoted through grades to maj. gen., Apr. 23, 1940; now chief of finance and budget officer. *

LOUHI, KULLERVO, univ. adminstr.; b. Helsinki, Finland, Apr. 7, 1918; s. Arvo Henrik and Selma (Selin) L.; came to U.S., 1923, naturalized, 1928; B.A., U. Chgo., 1939, M.B.A., 1940, Ph.D., 1955; C.P.A., Ill.; m. Ellen L. Rafalson, Aug. 28, 1952; 1 dau., Karen Alicia. Instr., U. Kans., 1940-43; instr., then asso. prof. U. Chgo., 1947-58; prof. bus. adminstrn. Mich. State U., East Lansing, 1958-75, dean, 1969-74, asst. to provost, 1974-75; ret., 1975. Served with AUS, 1943-46. Mem. Am. Inst. C.P.A.'s, Am. Accounting Assn., Phi Beta Kappa, Beta Gamma Sigma, Beta Alpha Psi, Alpha Kappa Psi. Home: Chapel Hill, N.C. Died Apr. 8, 1976.

LOUIS, JOE, heavyweight boxing champion; b. Lexington, Ala., May 13, 1914; s. Munn and Lilly (Reese) Barrow; m. Martha Jefferson, Mar. 11, 1959; children by previous marrige—Joe, Jacqueline. Winner light heavyweight championship Nat. Amateur Athletic union, 1934; world profl. heavyweight champion, 1937-49; greeter Caesar's Palace, Las Vegas, Nev. Author: My Life Story, 1947; The Joe Louis Story, 1953. Home: Las Vegas, Nev. Died Apr. 12, 1981.

LOUISELL, DAVID WILLIAM, educator, lawyer; b. Duluth, Minn., Dec. 2, 1913; s. Medor Ewing and Mary (Tallon) L.; B.S.L., U. Minn., 1935, J.D., 1938; m. Dorothy Jane Lynott, Aug. 14, 1950; children—William D., Mark N. Admitted to Minn. bar, 1938, N.Y. bar, 1940, D.C. bar, 1946, U.S. Supreme Ct. bar; practice in N.Y.C., 1938-41, Washington, 1941-42, 46-50; prof. law U. Minn., 1950-56, Alumni prof., 1971-72; prof. law U. Calif. at Berkely, 1956-77, Elizabeth Josselyn Boalt prof., 1964-77. Exec. sec. Minn. Jud. Council, 1952-56; chmn. P.R. Dept. Labor Indsl. Commn., 1957, 58, 60; mem. com. rules civil procedure Jud. Conf. U.S., 1960-70. Dir. Grad. Theol. Union, Berkeley, 1965-70. Mem. Nat. Commn. for Protection of Human Subjects of Biomed. and Behavioral Research, 1974-77. Served with USNR, 1942-45. Decorated Knight of St. Gregory (Pope Paul VI). Mem. Am. Bar Assn., Am. Law Inst., Order of Coif, Cath. Commn. on Intellectual and Cultural Affairs. Author: Modern California Discovery, 1963. Co-author: Trial of Medical Malpractice Cases, 1960, rev. as Medical Malpractice; 1970; The Parenchyma of Law, 1960; Pleading and Procedure, State and Federal, 3d edit., 1973; Jurisdiction in a Nutsell, 3d edit., 1973; Cases and Materials on Evidence 3d edit., 1976; Principles of Evidence and Proof, 2d edit., 1973; Modern California Discovery, 2d edit., 1972; Organ Transplantation, 1970. Author, narrator ann. cassette program on work U.S. Supreme Ct. Contbr. articles to profl. jours. Home: Berkeley, Calif. Died Aug. 21, 1977.

LOUTTIT, THOMAS ROBLEY, ins. co. exec.; b. Providence, Feb. 24, 1909; s. William Easton and Sophia (Robley) L.; student Brown U., 1928-29; m. Charlotte Anne Gies, Sept. 8, 1930; children—Lee Anne (Mrs. Tauck), Thomas Robley. Chmn. bd. Louttit Corp., Providence; dir., mem. exec. com. Allendale Mut. Ins. Co., Providence; dir. Appalachian Ins. Co.,

Providence, Union Mut. Ins. Co., Providence, Affiliated FM Ins. Co., New Providence Corp. Mem. Theta Delta Chi. Club: Turks Head (Providence). Home: Bristol, R.I. Died Jan. 28, 1980.

LOVEJOY, THOMAS EUGENE, JR., ins. co. exec.; b. Hawkinsville, Ga., Mar. 3, 1906; s. Thomas E. and Frances (Brown) L.; grad. Riverdale Country Sch., N.Y.C., 1924; Ph.B., Yale, 1928; m. Jeanne B. Gillette, May 26, 1939 (dec.); 1 son, Thomas Eugene; m. 2d, Audrey Paige Reidemeister, Apr. 3, 1947. With Guaranty Trust Co., N.Y.C., 1928-32; comptroller Manhattan Life Ins. Co., 1932-39, treas., 1937-80, v.p., 1939-44, 1st v.p., 1944-50, pres., 1950-67, chief exec. officer, 1955-77, chmn. bd., 1966-77, chmn. exec. com., 1978-80, also dir.; trustee Manhattan Savs. Bank. Mem. Zeta Psi. Clubs: Recess, Yale (N.Y.C.); Mill Reef (Antiqua, W.I.). Home: New York, N.Y. Died Aug. 13, 1980; buried Hawkinsville, Ga.

LOVELAND, CHESTER H., corp. official: b. Utica, N.Y., Dec. 13, 1886; s. James H. and Katherine Victoria (Dixon) L.; C.E. Cornell U., 1910; m. Mary E. Miller, Nov. 24, 1911: children—Katherine Virginia, Myrle; m. 2d, Emma M Lamp. May 29, 1924. Practiced engring in N.Y., Ohio, Wash, Ind. Calif. and Hawaiian Islands since 1910; chief hydraulic engr. Calif. State RR. Commn. 1914-21: cons. engr. in pvt practice since 1921; registered engr in State of Calif.: pres. Loveland & Co. Ltd., Calif. Water & Telephone Co., West Coast Telephone Co. Western Utilities Corp.: chmn. bd. and pres. West Coast Utilities Corp.; pres. Southwestern States Telephone Co., dir. Argonaut Investment Co. Mem. American Water-works Assn., Am. Society Civil Engrs. Clubs: Family. Commercial. Commonwealth. St. Francis Yacht, San Francisco Golf and Country. Home: San Francisco. *

LOVELL, STANLEY PLATT, chemist; b. Brockton, Mass., Aug. 29, 1890; s. Gustavus Crocker and Ella May (Platt) L.; student Dartmouth, 1908-09; B.S., Cornell, 1912, postgrad., 1912-14; m. Mabel L. Bigney, June 26, 1915; 1 son, Richard Hallett. Chemist, Geo. E. Keith Co., Brockton, Mass., 1914-18; gen. mgr. Celastic Corp., Arlington, N.J., 1918-24; pres. Arden-Rayshine Co., Watertown, Mass., 1924-43, Castex Labs., Watertown, 1925-43; v.p. Beckwith Mfg. Co., Boston, 1930-43; pres. Lovell Chem. Co., Newtonville, Mass., 1945-76; dir. McCord Corp., Detroit, Lukon, Inc., Leominster, Moore Drop Forging Co., Springfield, Mass. Cons., Investors Mgmt. Corp., Chem. Corps Dept. Army; spl. asst. to dir. OSRD, 1942-45; dir. research and devel. OSS, Washington, 1942-45. Mem. city govt. planning bd., Newton, Mass. Recipient Presdl. Medal for Merit, 1948. Registered patent atty. Inventor precipitated colloids, 1918, long-chain synthetic waxes, 1945. Pioneer application organic chemistry to shoemaking, orthopedic surgery, 1926, mfr. of clothing, 1940. Holder more than 70 U.S. and fgn. patents. Mem. Am. Chem. Soc. Republican. Conglist. Clubs: Cosmos (Washington); Algonguin (Boston). Author: Of Spies and Stratagems. Home: Newtonville, Mass. Died Jan. 4, 1976.

LOW, CLARENCE HARRY, retired exec.; b. N.Y. City, June 10, 1884; s. Rudolph A. and Sophie F. (Baer) L.; student Columbia, 1906; m. Madeleine E. Mayer, Dec. 28, 1915 (div.); children—Stuart M., Robert A., Doris M.; m. 2d, Margaret O. Ernst, July 19, 1947. Officer, dir., U.S. Rubber Reclaiming Co., Flents Products Co., Inc., since 1927. Pres., bd. of visitors, Rockland State Hosp., N.Y., 1932-47; reapptd. mem. bd. of visitors, Rockland State Hosp.; mem. Emergency Unemployment Relief Com., New York, 1931-33; treas. Dem. State Com., N.Y., 1934-41; dir. Am. Arbitration Assn., 1933-36; mem. Gov. Lohman's Post-war Employment Com., 1941-42; asst. petroleum co-ordinator, N.Y., 1941-42; chmn. salvage com., Greater New York, 1942; mem. Dept. of Def. Housing Commission, 1949-51; dir. Greater N.Y. Bldg. Defense (Civilian Defense) since Jan. 1951. Democrat. Clubs: Plymouth (Mass.) Yacht (commodore, 1941-42); Harmonie (N.Y.C.). Home: N.Y.C. *

LOW, LAWRENCE DAVID, govt. ofcl.; b. Butler, Pa., June 11, 1916; s. Lawrence Flemming and Adella Gertrude (Aiken) L.; LL.B., Nat. U., 1941; m. Elinor Boterweg, Mar. 23, 1940; children—Thomas Aiken, Robert Chapman, Michael David. Various positions ICC, Bur. Internal Revenue, Civil Service Commn., VA, Dept. State, 1937-47; admitted to D.C. bar, 1941; asst. chief Washington area security operations AEC, 1947-50, dir. security div. Savannah River operations office, Aiken, S.C., 1950-56, inspection specialist, 1956-59, chief materials inspection br. div. inspection, 1959, dir. div. compliance, Washington, 1960-72, cons. indsl. security for nuclear facilities, 1972-80. Past pres. Savannah River council Girl Scouts, Aiken, S.C. Served with USNR, 1942-45; capt. Res. Recipient Superior Performance award AEC, 1955-59. Mem. Delta Theta Phi. Presbyn. Club: Argyle Country (Washington). Home: Damascus, Md. Died Aug. 4, 1980.

LOWE, FRANK MELVILLE, JR., clergyman; b. Kansas City, Mo., Oct. 10, 1888; s. Frank Melville and Ona May (Lowe) L.; student Kansas City Sch. of Law, 1910-12, Bible Coll. of Mo., Columbia, Mo., 1916-19; B.S. in Edn., U. of Mo., 1919; A.M., Harvard, 1921, Ph.D., Columbia, 1923; unmarried. Field sec. Mo. Christian Endeavor Union, 1915; Nat. Christian Endeavor sec. Disciples of Christ Ch., 1916; student pastor, 1916-19; ordained to ministry Disciples of Christ Ch., 1919; asso. pastor Central Ch., N.Y. City, 1922-23; pastor First Ch., Mexico, Mo., 1923-29, Central Ch., Wichita, Kan., 1929-34, Central Ch., San Diego, Calif., 1934-39; founder and dir. Nat. Christian Inst. of Am. Leadership from 1939; chmn. San Diego Co. Coordinating Councils, 1946-49; pastor Peoples' Radio Pulpit from 1951. Regular radio speaker, news commentator, condr. religious programs, stations KFSD and KGB, from 1935. Chief San Diego Civilian Defense Chaplain Corps, organized Jan. 1943; forum leader, San Diego Pub. Schs. Chmn. Am. Red Cross, Mexico, Mo., 1928, Wichita, 1932-33; chmn. San Diego County Am. Red Cross, 1947-51; mem. Pacific Area adv. council A.R.C., 1949-51; honorary v.p. S.D. C. of C.; director San Diego Y.M.C.A. Has made 7 trips abroad, including 1 year in Europe and 6 months' journey around the world. Donor to San Diego of Balboa Park Peace Chimes, honoring his mother, Ona May Lowe, dedicated, Christmas, 1946. Mem. Phi Alpha Delta, Delta Sigma Rho, Phi Delta Kappa, Phi Delta Theta. Republican. Club: Kiwanis of San Diego (pres.). Author: The Passion Play, 1910; Religious Vocations, 1921; Pastorage Among Disciples of Christ, 1923; Preacher by Proxy, 1934; A Warrior Lawyer (The Life of Frank M. Lowe), 1942, Author: "Royal Highway of Prayer, 1944. Conducted community wartime worship services from 1944; established Sept. 1945, as a permanent Christian preaching mission Contbr. articles to jours. Home: San Diego, Calif. Died June 1977.

LOWE, JOHN ZOLLIKOFFER, lawyer; b. Norfolk, Va., July 25, 1884; s. John Zollikoffer and Quill Ella (Jenkins) L.; ed. pub. schs.; m. Mignon Wildy Archer, Dec. 6, 1907. Admitted to N.Y. bar, 1908, and began practice at N.Y. City; mem. Lowe, Dougherty, Hart & Marcus; collector internal revenue, 2d Dist., N.Y., and Puerto Rico, 1915-17. Served as maj. U.S. Army, judge adv. 76th and 82d Divs., A.E.F., World War. Episcopalian. Home: New York City. *

LOWELL, RALPH, banker; b. Newton, Mass., July 23, 1890; s. John and Mary Emlen (Hale) L.; student Volkmann Sch., Boston, Mass., 1900-07, El Ranch Bonito, Mesa, Ariz., 1907-08; A.B., Magna cum laude, Harvard, 1912, LL.D., 1952; L.H.D., Tufts U., 1949; LL.D., Northeastern U., 1950, Bates Coll., 1955, Emerson Coll., 1960, Brandeis U., 1961, Boston Coll., 1962, Boston U., 1967; D.Sc., Lowell Technol., Inst., 1956; D.C.S., Suffolk U., 1964; m. Charlotte Loring, Sept. 1, 1917; children—Charlotte (dec.), John, Ralph, Mary Emlen, Lucy, Susan, James Hale. With Curtis & Sanger, brokers, 1913-16, First Nat. Bank, 1916-17, Lee, Higginson & Co., 1919-32; partner Clark, Dodge & Co., 1932-43; chmn. bd. Boston Safe Deposit & Trust Co., 1943-46, pres., 1946-49, chmn. bd. exec. com., 1959-66; trustee, former mem. investment com. Provident Instn. for Savings; trustee Amoskeag Co.; hon. dir. John Hancock Mut. Life Ins. Co.; dir. Globe Newspaper Co.; mem. corp. Suffolk Savs. Bank, Dedham Instn. Savs. Life mem. emeritus Mass. Inst. Tech.; treas. Lowell Inst. Coop. Broadcasting Council; incorporator Ednl. Assos. Treas. Civic Edn. Found. Inc.; hon. dir. Mass. div. Am. Cancer Soc.; mem. finance com. House of Good Samaritan. Served as 1st lt., U.S. Res., 1917, major Inf., later lt. col., U.S. Army, 1918-19; civilian aide sec. war Mass., 1919-23. Trustee Gould Acad., Lowell Inst., Mass. Gen. Hosp., McLean Hosp., Boston Mus. Fine Arts (pres.), Bingham Assos. Fund; hon. trustee Boston U.; mem. bd. govs. New Eng. Med. Center Hosps.; treas., class agt. Harvard Class 1912; trustee Masonic Edn. and Charity Trust; treas. Tufts-N.E. Med. Center; mem. corp. Northeastern U.; mem. bd. Old Sturbridge Village, Retina Found.; chmn. WGBH Ednl. Found.; past chmn. Ednl. TV and Radio Center; mem. exec. com. Mass. Com. Cath., Protestants and Jews. Fellow Am. Acad. Arts and Scis.; mem. Boston C. of C. (hon. v.p.), Nat. Inst. Social Scis., Mass. Soc. Cin., Mass. Hist. Soc., Navy League U.S. (v.p. Boston council), Phi Beta Kappa. Republican. Episcopalian. Mason (33 deg.). Clubs: Associated Harvard (past pres.); Harvard (past pres.), Tavern (Boston). Home: Westwood, Mass. Died 1978.

LOWELL, ROBERT (TRAILL SPENCE, JR.), poet; b. Boston, March 1, 1917; s. Robert Traill Spence and Charlotte (Winslow) L.; student Harvard U., 1935-37; A.B. summa cum laude, Kenyon Coll., 1940; m. Jean Stafford, Apr. 2, 1940 (div. June 1948); m. 2d, Elizabeth Hardwick, July 28, 1949 (div. 1972); 1 dau., Harriet Winslow Lowell; m. 3d, Caroline Blackwood, 1972; 1 son, Robert Sheridan. Editorial asst. Sheed & Ward, N.Y.C., 1941-42; cons. poetry Library of Congress, 1947-48. Conscientious objector, 1943-44. Recipient Pulitzer prize (poetry), 1947; Guinness poetry award, 1959, Sarah Josepha Hale award, 1965, Guggenheim fellow, 1947-48. Mem. Am. Acad. Arts and Letters (prize), Phi Beta Kappa. Author: Land of Unlikeness, 1944; Lord Weary's Castle, 1946; The Mills of the Kavanaughs, 1951 (winner Harriet Monroe Poetry award); Life Studies (Nat. Book award), 1959; Phaedra; Imitations (transl. from Racine) (Bollingen transl. prize 1962), 1961; For the Union Dead, 1964; The Old Glory, 1965 (Obie award); Near the Ocean, 1967; Notebooks, 1967-68, 69; History, 1973; For Lizzie and Harriet, 1973; The Dolphin, 1973 (Pulitzer prize); Day by Day, 1977 (Nat. Book Critics Circle award). Home: New York, N.Y. Died Sept. 12, 1977.

LOWENFELS, WALTER, author, editor; b. N.Y.C., May 10, 1897; s. Frederick F. and Edith (Ahrens) L.; grad. Kelvin Preparatory Sch., N.Y.C., 1914; m. Lillian Apotheker, June 19, 1926; children—Michal Lowenfels Kane, Judy Lowenfels Jacobs, Manna Lowenfels Perpelitt, Angela Lowenfels Schwartz. Author books of poetry: Episodes & Epistles, 1925; Finale of Seem, 1929; Apollinaire, 1930; Elegy for D. H. Lawrence, 1932; The Suicide, 1934; Sonnets of Love and Liberty, 1955; American Voices, 1959; Song of Peace, 1959; Some Deaths, 1964; Land of Roseberries, 1965; Found Poems, 1972; Translations from Scorpius, 1966; Thou Shalt Not Overkill, 1968; author prose books: To an Imaginary Daughter, 1964; Robert Grover's The Portable Walter, 1968; The Poetry of My Politics, 1968; The Life of Fraenkel's Death, 1970; The Revolution Is to Be Human, 1973; Reality Prime, 1974; Love Letters, 1976. Editor: Walt Whitman's Civil War, 1960; Selections from Leaves of Grass, 1961; Poets of Today, 1964; Where is Vietnam?, 1967; New Jazz Poets, 1967; In the Time of Revolution, 1969; The Writing on the Wall, 1969; The Tenderest Lover, 1970; From the Belly of the Shark, 1973; For Neruda, For Chile, 1975; The Autobiography of an Empire, 1976. Served with AC, U.S. Army, 1917-18. Mem. P.E.N., Author's Guild, Poetry Soc. Am. Address: Peekskill, N.Y. Died July 7, 1976.

LOWENSTEIN, ALLARD KENNETH, lawyer, former congressman; b. Newark, Jan. 16, 1929; s. Gabriel Abraham and Augusta (Goldberg) L.; grad. Horace Mann Sch., 1945; B.A., U. N.C., 1949; LL.B., Yale, 1954; children—Frank Graham, Thomas Kennedy, Katharine Eleanor. Admitted to N.Y. bar, 1958; mem. faculty Stanford, N.C. State U., City Coll. N.Y., Yale Sch. Urban Studies, U. Mass., New Sch. Social Research, various times 1961-74; vis. fellow John F. Kennedy Sch. Govt., Harvard, 1971, Ezra Stiles Coll., Yale, spl. asst. to Senator Frank P. Graham, 1949; fgn. policy asst. to Senator Hubert H. Humphrey, 1959; mem. 91st Congress 5th Dist. N.Y.; adviser to Gov. Edmund G. Brown, Jr. of Calif., 1975; U.S. rep. UN Commn. on Human Rights, 1977; U.S. rep. UN Trusteeship Council, 1977; U.S. ambassador to U.N. for spl. polit. affairs, 1977-78. Alternate del. Democratic Nat. Conv., 1960, del., 1968, 72; mem. Dem. Nat. Com., 1972-76; chmn. Students for Stevenson, 1952, Americans for Dem. Action, 1971-73; co-chmn. Conf. Concerned Dems., 1967. Served with AUS, 1954-56. Recipient Eleanor Roosevelt peace award, 1971; Jefferson award for public service, 1980; nominated posthumously for Nobel Peace Prize, 1981, for Martin Luther King, Sr. and Grenville Clark Peace Prize, 1981. Author: Brutal Mandate, 1960. Home: New York, N.Y. Assassinated Mar. 14, 1980; buried Arlington (Va.) Nat. Cemetery.

LOWENSTEIN, LEON, business exec.; b. N.Y.C., June 14, 1883; s. Morris and Elizabeth (Sloman) L.; student Coll. City N.Y., 1898; Dr. Textile Industries, Clemson (S.C.) Coll., 1951; m. Gloria Elizabeth Perry, July 29, 1937. With M. Lowenstein & Sons, Inc., N.Y.C., 1899-71, treas., 1918-36, pres., 1936-47, chmn. bd., 1947-59, exec. chmn., 1959-71, hon. chmn., from 1971; chmn. bd. or chmn. bd. and pres. of all subsidiary corps. Mem. N.Y. Cotton Exchange. Chmn. bd. Leon Lowenstein Found., Inc.; trustee Fedn. Jewish Philanthropies of N.Y., from 1942, St. Vincent's Hosp.; hon. chmn. Joint Defense Appeal, from 1951, Hillside Hosp.; hon. vice chmn. Anti-Defamation League, from 1957, United Jewish Appeal; lay trustee Fordham U.; bd. dirs. Brotherhood-in-Action, Mt. Sinai Hosp., Miami, from 1957. Mem. N.A.M. Clubs: Westview Country (Miami Beach); Metropolis Country (White Plains, N.Y.); Weavers (N.Y.C.). Home: New York, N.Y. Deceased.

LOWENTHAL, ESTHER, coll. prof.; b. Rochester, N.Y., Sept. 15, 1883; d. Max and Louisa (Oberfelder) Lowenthal; A.B., Bryn Mawr Coll., 1905; Ph.D., Columbia, 1911. Began as asst. Smith Coll., 1911, prof. of economics on Robert A. Woods Foundation since 1921, dean of faculty, 1946-48. Mem. Am. Econ. Assn., Am. Assn. Univ. Women. Clubs: College (Boston). Author: Ricardian Socialists, 1911. Home: Northampton, Mass. *

LOWERY, PERCIVAL C., dentist; b. Harbor Beach, Mich., Mar. 26, 1885; s. Robert and Mary (Falls) L.; D.D.S., U. Mich., 1910, M.S. (hon.), 1940; post-grad. Royal Coll., Toronto, 1917; m. Myrtle A. King, June 29, 1912; 1 dau., Marie Elizabeth (Mrs. Fred H. Rollins, Jr.). Practice dentistry, Detroit, 1910-68; lectr. U. Mich. Dental Sch., 1921-23, prof. prosthetic dentistry, 1923-30; head Dental Group, Detroit, 1913—. Maj. U.S. Army, chief of dental service Army Hosp. No. 36 (Res.). Mem. Mich. governing com. Gorgas Meml. Inst., sr. dental surgeon USPHS (Res.). Mem. Mich. State Council of Health, Com. for Coordination of Pub. Health Activities in Mich.; mem. NRC sub-com. on plastic and maxillo-facial surgery. Named Dentist of

1953; recipient Pierre Fauchard gold medal, 1954; Meritorious award Mich. Dental Assn., 1964; Sesquicentennial award U. Mich., 1967; meritorious award, surgeon gen. USPHS. Diplomate Am. Bd. Prosthodontics (charter). Fellow Am., Internat. (pres., regent) colls. dentists, A.A.A.S.; mem. Royal Soc. Health, Fedn. Dentaire Internat., Am. Assn. Pub. Health Dentists (hon.), Am. Dental Assn. (v.p.; chmn. research commn.), Acad. Denture Prosthetists (hon. life mem., hon. pres.), Am. Acad. Restorative Dentistry, Mich. (past pres.), Detroit Dist. dental socs., Internat. Dental Research, Pierre Fauchard Acad. (pres. 1952-53), Nat. Adv. Dental Research Council, U. Mich. Alumni Adv. Council, U. Detroit Dental Alumni Assn. (hon.), Mich. Pioneer and Hist. Soc., Detroit Mus. Art Founders Soc., U. Mich. Union (life), Internat. Assn. Torch Clubs, Delta Sigma Delta, Omicron Kappa Upsilon (hon.). Republican. Mason (32 deg., Shriner). Clubs: Presidents (U. Mich.); Dental Clinic, Eastern Dental (hon. pres.), Northwestern Dental (hon.), University of Michigan, Detroit Yacht, Players, Detroit Athletic (Detroit). Author of chapter in Nichols' Prosthetic Dentistry, 1930, American Textbook of Prosthetic Dentistry, 1932, 42; chapter on Maxillofacial Prothesis in The Manual of Standard Practice of Plastic and Maxillofacial Surgery (mil. surg. manual of the Nat. Research Council); also papers and articles on dental subjects. P.C. Lowery award in full denture prosthesis established at U. Mich. Sch. Dentistry, circa 1935. Home: Detroit MI. *

LOWMASTER, A. T., ry. official; b. McCutchensville, O., Aug. 29, 1882; student high sch. and business coll. Vice-pres. and gen. mgr. C.&O. Ry.Co. Address: Richmond, Va.*

LOWREY, FREDERICK DWIGHT, business exec.; born Honolulu, Hawaii, June 6, 1885; s. Frederick Jewett and Cherilla (Storrs) L.; A.B., Harvard, 1908; m. Leila Parsons, Feb. 15, 1911. Began as clerk Lewers and Cooke, Ltd., Honolulu, 1907, 1st vice pres. and mgr., 1927-41, pres. and mgr. since 1941; dir. Bank of Hawaii, Bishop Trust Co., Ltd., Hawaiian Pineapple Co., Ltd., von Hamm-Young Co., Ltd. Trustee Punahou Sch. since 1925; mem. House of Rep., Territorial Legislature Sessions 1920, 21, 23, 29. Mem. C. of C. (pres., 1944). Home: Honolulu. *

LOWRIE, SELDEN GALE (LOU'RE), prof. emeritus; b. Mt. Sterling, Ill., Aug. 13, 1884; s. James Gibson and Caroline Ferris (Gale) L.; B.A., Knox Coll., 1907, LL.D., 1937; M.A., Univ. of Ill., 1908; Ph.D., U. of Wis., 1912; m. Agnes Potter van Ryn, Jan. 21, 1932. With Wisconsin Legislative Reference Library, 1908-11, Wis. State Bd. of Public Affairs, 1911-12; dir. O. Legislative Reference Bur., 1913-14, Cincinnati Municipal Reference Bur., 1914-17; prof. polit. science U. Cin., 1912-54; emeritus, 1954. Captain Ordnance Dept., U.S. Army, 1918-19; dir. Reference Library, same dept., 1918-19; spl. rep. Am. Red Cross in Turkey, 1919; admitted to bar, 1921; lecturer and administrative adviser, Tsing-Hua. Coll., Peiping, 1922-23, Canton Christian Coll. (China), 1923, Clark U., summer 1926, Sch. of Citizenship and Pub. Affairs, Syracuse U., summer, 1927, U. Hawaii, 1948; Whitney Found. vis. prof., Rollins Coll., 1955-56. Organized courses in tng. for pub. service, U. Cin. in cooperation with city govt. Awarded Fulbright Grant for study in New Zealand, 1949. Mem. Am. Group first Inst. Pacific Relations, Honolulu, 1925; mem. Am. Assn. U. Profs., Am. Polit. Science Assn., Cinn. Foreign Policy Assn. (pres. 1923-25), Cincinnatus Assn., Phi Beta Kappa, Phi Delta Theta, Phi Eta. Presbyterian. Clubs: University (Cincinnati); president City Club, 1920-21. Author: The Budget (Wis. State Bd. Pub. Affairs), 1912. Contbr. to tech. jours. on econ. and polit. subjects. Home: Cincinnati, O. *

LOWTHER, FLORENCE DE LOISELLE (LOU'THER), prof. zoology; b. New York, N.Y., Sept. 23, 1884; d. Ezra and Minnie E. (Cornell) de Loiselle; student Packer Collegiate Inst., Brooklyn, N.Y., 1898-99, Nat. Cathedral Sch., Washington, D.C., 1900-01; A.B., Barnard Coll. of Columbia U., 1912, M.A., 1915, Ph.D., 1926. Asst. dept. zoology. Barnard Coll., Columbia, 1912-16. instr., 1916-26, asst. prof. zoology, 1926-41, asso. prof., 1941-48, prof., 1948-50, asso. dean of faculty. 1948-50; organized dept. of sci., Finch Sch., 1913-15; instr. protozoology, Marine Biol. Lab., Woods Hole, Mass. summers 1923-25; zool. field expdn. to South Africa, British East Africa and Belgian Congo, 1936. Served with Woman's Land Army, 1918. Fellow N.Y. Acad. of Sci.; mem. A.A.A.S., Am. Museum Nat. History (N.Y.), Am. Soc. Zoologists, League of Women Voters, Am. Assn. Univ. Women, Society Woman Geographers (N.Y. and Washington), Asso. Alumnae Barnard Coll. (pres. 1927-29. organizer alumnae fund and chmn. 1932-35), Kappa Alpha Theta, Sigma Xi. Republican. Clubs: Barnard College of New York (vice pres. and pres. 1926-28), Women's Faculty of Columbia University (pres. 1928-30), Cosmopolitan (bd. govs. 1935-38). Author of articles, Protozoa) Mack Printing Co., 1925). African Lemuroids (Zoologica. 1939, 1940). also co-author articles on women in medicine. Home: New York (summer) Moneterey, Mass. *

LUBALIN, HERBERT FREDERICK, graphic designer; b. N.Y.C., Mar. 17, 1918; s. Joseph and Rose J. L.; B.F.A., Cooper Union, 1976; m. Sylvia Kushner, Oct. 5, 1940; children—Peter J., Robert H., David O. Designer, Display Guild, 1939; art dir. Deutsch & Shea Advt., Inc., 1940, Men's Wear mag. Fairchild Publs., 1942, Reiss Advt., Inc., 1943; v.p., creative dir. Sudler & Hennessey, 1945-64; pres. Herb Lubalin, Inc., 1964-68, LSC, Inc., 1968-76, LSC&P Design Group, Inc., N.Y.C., 1976-81; exec. v.p. Lubalin Burns, 1970, Lubalin, Delpire et Cie, Paris, 1971, Lubalin Maxwell Ltd., London, 1971, Internat. Typeface Corp., 1971; v.p. D.P.I. Inc., N.Y.C., 1977; one-man shows: Overseas Press Club, 1964, Gallery 303, 1968, TGI Gallery, 1975, Ryder Gallery, Chgo., 1975, Hampshire Coll., Mass., 1976, Centre Georges Pompidou, 1979; group shows include: Am. Inst. Graphic Arts, 1952-81, New York Art Dirs. Club, 1952-81, C.A. Mag., 1958-81, Soc. Publ. Designers, 1962-81, Type Dirs. Club, 1952-81, Whitney Mus., 1974; represented in permanent collections: Smithsonian Instn., Library of Congress, Nat. Gallery, Washington; tchr. graphics Cornell U., 1973; prof. design Cooper Union, 1974-81; lectr. numerous univs.; lectr., juror numerous art dirs. clubs throughout U.S., Can. and Europe. Mem. adv. bd. Hampshire Coll., Kean Coll., N.J. Recipient Cleo award for best TV comml. Am. TV Festival, 1963, Lotus Club award, 1973, Cooper Union Profl. Achievement citation, 1972, U.S. Govt. citation for design of airmail stamps, 1963, Augustus St. Gaudens medal for profl. achievement Cooper Union Alumni Assn., 1973; named to Art Dirs. Club Hall of Fame, 1977. Mem. Am. Inst. Graphic Arts (dir.), N.Y. Art Dirs. Club (past pres., 7 Gold medals, 3 Silver medals), N.Y. Type Dirs. Club, Soc. Publ. Designers, Soc. Illustrators, Nat. Soc. Art Dirs. (Art Dir. of Year award 1962), Scandinavian Soc. Designers (hon.), Soc. Typographic Artists Chgo. (hon.), Alliance Graphique Internat. (internat. v.p.). Democrat. Contbr. articles to mags. and newspapers. Home: New York, N.Y. Died May 24, 1981.

LUBIN, ISADOR, economist; b. Worcester, Mass., June 9, 1896; s. Harris and Hinda (Francke) L.; A.B., Clark Coll., Worcester, 1916, LL.D., 1941; student U. Mo., 1916-17, U. Mich., 1919-20; Ph.D., Robert Brookings Grad. Sch., 1926; LL.D. (hon.), Brandeis U., 1966; m. Alice Berliner, Sept. 14, 1923 (div. 1928); 1 dau., Alice (Mrs. A.L. Everitt); m. 2d, Ann Shumaker, Feb. 29, 1932 (dec. Nov. 1935); 1 dau., Ann (Mrs. L. Buttenwieser); m. 3d, Carol Riegelman, Jan. 30, 1952. Instr. econs. U. Mo., 1917-18; statistician U.S. Food Adminstrn., 1918; spl. expert U.S. War Industries Bd., 1918-19; asst. prof. econs. U. Mich., 1920-22; asso. prof. econs. U. Mo., 1924; mem. staff Brookings Instn., 1922-33; mem. teaching staff Robert Brookings Grad. Sch., 1923-26; U.S. commr. labor statistics, 1933-46; econ. asst. to White House, 1941-45; dir. Confidential Reports, Inc., pres., chmn. bd. 1946-51; U.S. rep. with rank of minister Econ. and Social Council UN, 1946-63, alternate del. Gen. Assembly, 1951-53; indsl. commr. State N.Y., 1955-59; Arthur T. Vanderbilt prof. pub. affairs Rutgers U., 1959-61, dir. urban fellowship div. Urban Center, 1961-62; econ. cons. Twentieth Century Fund, 1960-76; cons. United Israel Appeal on Programs in Israel, 1961-78. Dir. Eastern Life Ins. Co., 1960-72. Former spl. asst., adviser numerous govtl. agys., ILO, UN, other internat. bodies; mem. Council on Fgn. Relations, 1949-78; mem. Nat. Com. Money and Credit, 1958-61; cons. Office Statis. Policy, U.S. Bur. Budget, 1946-63; chmn. Amalgamated Shirt Industry Pension Fund; chmn. Pres.'s Railroad Marine Workers Commn., 1963; Columbia Seminar asso. Mem. Nat. Capitol Democratic Club; trustee Cornell U., 1955-59, Weitzmann Inst., Brandeis U., New Sch.; chmn. exec. com. Franklin D. Roosevelt Found., 1950-78; mem. exec. com. Am. Joint Distbn. Com.; bd. govs. Am. Jewish Com. Fellow Internat. Inst. Statistics, Am. Statis. Assn. (v.p. 1937-38, pres. 1946); mem. Am. Econ. Assn. Jewish. Clubs: Cosmos (Washington); Faculty (Columbia). Author of numerous books, monographs and reports; contbr. econ. jours. Home: New York, N.Y. Died July 6, 1978; buried Annapolis, Md.

LUCAS, ALBERT A., clergyman; b. Snook, Texas, July 17, 1886; s. Gus and Caroline (Dabney) L.; grad. Conroe (Tex.) Coll., 1915, hon. D.D., 1919; m. Rena Etta Utley, Nov. 15, 1915. Ordained to ministry, Bapt. Ch.; moderator Hope Western Bapt. Assn.; now pastor Good Hope Bapt. Ch., Houston. Has served as vice pres. Missionary Bapt. Gen. Conv. of Texas; treas. Nat. Bapt. Conv. of Am.; mem. exec. com. Bapt. World Alliance. Awarded U.S. Certificate of award, O.P.A., 1945. Mem. Nat. Assn. Advancement Colored People. Home: Houston. *

LUCAS, HENRY GAILLARD, pecan grower; b. Black Creek, N.C., Jan. 6, 1882; s. Henry Dearborn and Monticello (Boyette) L.; student U. of N.C., 1900-01; m. Alba Capps, Aug. 28, 1912; 1 dau., Martha Louise. Hotel business, 1901-15; began ranching, West Tex., 1915; engaged in pecan raising and diversified farming since 1919; owner Lucas Pecan Orchards, Brownwood. Pres. Southwestern Pecan Growers Assn.; mem. Am. Country Life Assn.; mem. Tex. Social Welfare Conf.; dir. Lone Star Wool-Mohair Coöperative Assn. Democrat. Episcopalian. Club: Rotary (ex-pres.). Home: Brownwood, Tex. *

LUCAS, HENRY LAURENCE, JR., educator; b. Pasadena, Calif., Jan. 8, 1916; s. Henry L. and Lilla Alice (La Spada) L.; student Chaffey Jr. Coll., Ontario, Calif., 1932-35; B.S. in Animal Husbandry, U. Calif. at Davis, 1937; Ph.D. in Animal Nutrition, Cornell U., 1943; m. Jane Marie Murray, Jan. 20, 1945; children—William Henry, Carole Jane (Mrs. Barney P. Woodward), Robert Murray, Barbara Ann, Janet Louise. Supr. advanced registry cow testing, Calif., 1938; research asst. animal nutrition U. Calif. at Davis, 1938-39; dairy cattle feed investigator Cornell U., 1940-43, research asso. animal nutrition, 1943, instr. animal physiology, 1944, research asso. poultry nutrition, 1944-45; asso. prof. statistics N.C. State U. at Raleigh, 1946-48, prof., 1948-77, William Neal Reynolds prof. statistics, 1957-77, dir. biomath. program, 1961-77. Mem. com. feed composition NRC, 1946-58; mem. program com. Internat. Grassland Congress, 1952; mem. Gov. N.C. Sci. Adv. Com., 1961-64; mem. com. internat. exchange of persons Asso. Research Councils, 1961-63; mem. President's Study Com. on NIH, 1964, Pres.'s Study Com. Environmental Pollution, 1965; mem. biometry tng. com. Nat. Inst. Gen. Med. Scis., 1965-70, chmn., 1969-70; mem. U.S. nat. com. Internat. Union Biol. Scis., 1973-77; mem. com. for minority access to research careers Nat. Ints. Gen. Med. Scis., 1974-77. Fellow AAAS, Am. Statis. Assn.: mem. Am. Soc. Range Mgmt., Math. Assn. Am., Inst. Math Statistics, Am. Inst. Nutrition, Am. Soc. Animal Prodn., Am. Dairy Sci. Assn., Biometric Soc. (pres. Eastern N.Am. region 1962, internat. council 1972-74), N.C. Acad. Scis., Sigma Xi, Phi Kappa Phi, Alpha Zeta, Gamma Alpha, Gamma Sigma Delta. Roman Catholic. K.C. Contbr. articles to sci., tech. publs. Home: Raleigh, N.C. Died June 8, 1977; buried Raleigh, N.C.

LUCAS, HOWARD JOHNSON, chemist; b. Marietta, O., Mar. 7, 1885; s. William W. and Marian (Curtis) L.; B.A., Ohio State U., 1907, M.A., 1908, D.Sc., 1953. Asst. chemistry Ohio State U., 1907-09; fellow in chemistry U. Chgo., 1909-10; asst. chemist U.S. Govt., 1910-13; instr. chemistry Cal. Inst. Tech., 1913-15, asso. prof., 1915-40, prof., 1940-55, emeritus prof., 1955—; vis. prof. chemistry U. Hawaii, 1953, Ohio State U., 1954-55. Chmn. com. nomenclature NRC, 1952-53. Mem. A.A.A.S., Am. Chem. Soc. (Sci. Apparatus Makers award 1953), Nat. Acad. Scis., Am. Assn. U. Profs., Phi Beta Kappa, Sigma Xi, Phi Kappa Sigma. Author: Organic Chemistry, 1935, rev. 1953; Principles & Practice in Organic Chemistry Laboratory (with D. Pressman), 1949. Contbr. articles Jour. Am. Chem. Soc., Indsl. and Engring. Chemistry. Home: Pasadena, Cal. *

LUCEY, WILLIAM S., business exec.; born Natick, Mass., 1885; grad. Mass. Inst. Tech., 1907; Exec. vice pres. Rayonier Incorporated, N.Y. City; v.p. and dir. Grays Harbor Pulp & Paper Co., Hoquiam, Wash. Home: N.Y. *

LUDDEN, ALLEN ELLSWORTH, TV producer; b. Mineral Point, Wis., Oct. 5; s. Homer Jameson and Leila Matilda (Allen) L.; B.A., U. Tex., Austin, 1940, M.A., 1941; m. Betty White, June 14, 1963; children—David, Martha (Mrs. Robert McAndrews), Sarah. Author, emcee Mind Your Manners, NBC radio, 1948-52, producer Monitor, 1954-56; exec. CBS Radio Network, 1956-60; emcee GE College Bowl, 1958-63; host Password, TV show, 1961-67, 71-75; partner Eltee Prodns., Los Angeles, 1968-81. Served to maj. U.S. Army, 1942-47. Decorated Bronze Star; recipient Horatio Alger award Am. Schs. and Colls. Assn., 1962. Author: Plain Talk for Men Under 21; Plain Talk for Women Under 21; Plain Talk About College; Plain Talk for Young Marrieds; (novel) Roger Thomas, Actor. Rec. album songs RCA. Home: Los Angeles, Calif. Died June 9, 1981; buried Mineral Point, Wis.

LUDGIN, EARLE, advt. exec.; b. Chgo., July 22, 1898; s. Louis and Bessie L.; student U. Chgo., 1916, 18, 22; m. Mary King MacDonald, Nov. 14, 1923 (dec. Sept. 1962); children—Mary, Earle, Donald, Roger (dec.), Quentin. Founder advt. agy. Earle Ludgin & Co., 1927, pres., treas., 1927-54, chmn. bd. 1954-76; hon. chmn. bd. Stern Walters/Earle Ludgin, Inc., 1976-81. Chmn. Ravinia Festival Assn., 1962-65; chmn. fine arts com. Ill. Sesquicentennial Commn. Trustee Art Inst. Chgo., U. Chgo., Chgo. Planetarium Soc.; chmn. U. Chgo. Alumni Found., 1951-54; past pres. Soc. Comtemporary Am. Art. Mem. Chgo. Orchestral Assn., Am. Fedn. Arts. Clubs: Arts, Commercial, Tavern (Chgo.). Home: Hubbard Woods, Ill. Died Apr. 15, 1981.

LUDVIGSEN, ELLIOT LEON, mfg. exec.; b. Jackson, Minn., Sept. 28, 1902; s. Eric and Caroline (Nelson) L.; B.S., U. Minn., 1925; m. Virginia A. Smith, Feb. 6, 1927 (dec. 1952); children—Karl Eric, Eric Case; m. 2d, Constance Kelley Ehrman, Sept. 16, 1953 (dec. Feb. 1960); children—Kelly Adam, Coniele Michele, Melody Lee; m. 3d, Molly Ford, Feb. 10, 1962. Asst. to chief insp. White Motor Co., Cleve.,

1925-28; with Fuller Transmission div. subsidiary Fuller Mfg. Co., Kalamazoo, 1928-48, pres., 1948-60; dir. Eaton Mfg. Co. (now Corp.), Cleve., 1958, v.p. adminstrn., 1960-62, group v.p., 1962-63, pres., 1963-67, chmn. bd., chief exec. officer, 1967-69, chmn. exec. com., 1969-72; dir. Simpson-Lee Paper Co., San Francisco, Truck Engring., Ltd., Woodstock, Ont., Can. Chmn. bd. trustees Tri State Coll. Mem. Soc. Automotive Engrs. Clubs: Union, Kirtland Country, Pepper Pike. Home: Cleveland, Ohio. Died July 26, 1978; buried Kalamazoo, Mich.

LUDWIG, LOUIS, business exec., inventor; b. Russia, Mar. 9, 1899; s. David and Fanny (Swedorsky) Grushevsky; student Columbia, 1916-20; m. Miriam F. Fischer, Sept. 20, 1953; children by previous marriage—Melvin S., Doris. Pres. Eagle Electric Mfg. Co., Inc., Long Island City, N.Y., 1920-69, chmn. bd., 1969-80; pres. Eagle Plastics Corp., 1938-69, chmn. bd., 1969-80; pres. 24th St. Plaza Corp., 1938-69, chmn. bd., 1969-80; pres. Eagle Electric Mfg. Co., Ltd. Can.; v.p. charge Israel industrialization Ampal-Amer Israel Corp., N.Y.C., 1953-80, also chmn. exec. com.) treas.; sec. Israel Mineral Devel. Corp., 1953-80; dir. Israel Am. Indsl. Devel. Bank, Ltd. Bd. dirs. N.Y. United Jewish Appeal, Israel Bond Drive; bd. dirs., v.p. Am. Com. for Weizmann Inst. Sci.; bd. govs. Weizmann Inst., Rehovot, Israel. Home: Hallandale, Fla. Died 1980.

LUEBKE, WILLIAM FERDINAND (Leb'ke), prof. English lang.; b. Juneau, Wis., Mar. 28, 1882; s. Carl Ludwig Erdman and Emilie (Stueber) L.; A.B., Northwestern Coll., Watertown, Wis., 1903; A.B., U. of Wis., 1904; F. W. Allis grad. scholar same, 1904-05; fellow University of Chicago, 1909-11, Ph.D., magna cum laude, 1911; post graduate study same university; married Klaerchen D. Streckfuss, June 17, 1908 (died August 1945); children—Ruth (Mrs. A. F. Bulmahn), Gertrud, M.D. (dec). Began as high school teacher, Waukesha, Wis., 1905-06; assistant professor German, Miami University, 1906-09, State U. of Ia., 1911-18; acting prof. English, Ill. Coll., 1918-19; head of English dept., Westminster Coll., New Wilmington, Pa., 1919-21; prof. English lang. and head of Dept., U. of Denver, 1921-47, now emeritus; vis. prof. Miami U., summer, 1915. Translator Post Office Department, 1918. Manager of vault Am. Nat. Bank, Denver, since 1951. Trustee Meeker Home, 1921-26. Mem. Modern Lang. Assn. America (life), Linguistic Soc. America (foundation mem., del. to regional conf., U.N.E.S.C.O., Denver, 1947), Am. Dialect Society, Am. Assn. Univ. Profs. (sec. Denver chapter, 1927-36), Shakespeare Assn. America, Internat. Phonetic Assn., Nat. Council Teachers of English, Colo. Edn. Assn. (pres. English sec. 1925, 26), Modern Humanities Research Assn., Early English Text Soc., Anglo-Norman Text Soc., Pro Musica, Colo.-Wyo. Acad. Arts and Letters Civic Symphony Soc., Phi Beta Kappa (v.p. Gamma of Colo., 1945-46). Lutheran. Clubs: Research, Buchtel. Author: The Language of Berthold von Chiemsee, 1912. Editor: Scheffel's Ekkehard (with C. H. Handschin), 1911; Seidel's Leberecht Huehnchen, 1915. Contbr. to Modern Philology, also to Dictionary of Am. English on Hist. Principles, Early Modern English Dictionary, Middle English Dictionary, Pronouncing Dict. of American English. Mem. pronunciation advisory com., Thorndike-Century dictionaries. Home: Denver, Colo. *

LUECK, ARTHUR W. (LUK), lawyer; b. Juneau, Wis., July 19, 1885; s. F. William and Phillipine (Schauer) L.; student U. of Wis. Law Sch., 1904-07; m. Wanda Krueger, Aug. 20, 1908; children—William O., Arthur G. Admitted to the Wis bar, 1907, and began practice of law in Beaver Dam. Mem. firm Burke & Lueck, later Lueck, Clark & Lueck; sr. partner firm Lueck, Skupniewitz & Lueck, since 1935; Dem. candidate for gov., 1936. Served as ch. commr. City of Beaver Dam, 1916-22. Mem. Am., Wis., State and Dodge County bar assns. Home: Beaver Dam, Wis.*

LUEDERS, CHARLES W(ILLIAMSON) (LE'DERZ), gastroenterologist; b. Phila., Pa., Aug. 14, 1883; s. Charles Henry and Edith (Williamson) Lüders; A.B., Lehigh Univ., 1904; M.D., U. of Pa., 1908; post grad. study in tropical medicine, London, Eng., Hamburg, Germany, 1911-12; m. Anne Smyth Everitt, 1911; children—Charles Williamson, Everitt H., David C. Intern. Episcopal Hosp., Phila. 1909-1911, Lying-In-Charity Hosp., 1908-Feb. 1909; research fellow in gastro-enterology Jefferson Med. Coll., 1920-22, Pa. Hosp. for Mental Diseases, 1922,26; chief gastro-intestinal clinic Pa. Hosp., 1927-34; private practice of gastro-enterology, internal medicine, since 1934. Served as capt. med. corps U.S. Army, 1917-19; maj. med. res. corps; clinical pathologist Med. Bd. Induction Centre, Phila., World War II. Fellow A.M.A.; asso. Am. Soc. of Clin. Pathologists; mem. Coll. of Physicians of Phila., Am. Gastro Enterological Assn. (mem. com. on research of pancreatic enzymes). Republican. Episcopalian. Clubs: Aesculapian; Meridian. Contbr. to gastro-intestinal section Cyclopedia of Medicine; also articles to med jours. Developed Lueders-Bergeim method for quantitative estimation of external pancreatic enzymes. Home: Bala-Cynwyd, Pa.

LUEHRING, FREDERICK WILLIAM (LOOR'ING), prof. physical edn.; b. near Hanover, Kan., Dec. 11, 1882; s. William and Emelia (Werner) L.; Ph.B., N. Central Coll., Naperville, Ill., 1905; Ph.M., U. of Chicago, 1906; Ph.D., Columbia, 1939; m. Emma Amanda Hatz, June 26, 1907 (died 1929); children—Mary Emmeline, Frederick William (dec.); m. 2d, Ellen Andrea Davidson, Dec. 5, 1930: 1 son, Davidson. Prof. and dir. phys. edn. and athletics, Ripon (Wis.) Coll., 1906-10; asst. prof. and asso. dir. hygiene and phys. edn., Princeton, 1911-20; prof. and dir. phys. edn. and athletics, U. of Neb., 1920-22, U. of Minn., 1922-30; prof. phys. edn., University of Pa., 1931-45; specialist and consultant on plant and facility problems. Member National Collegiate Swimming Rules Com. since foundation, 1913, chmn., 1914-35; mem. Am. Olympic Com., X and XI Olympiads; chmn. Olympic men's swimming com., 1934-36; mem. White House Conf. on Child Health and Protection, 1930-31. Life mem. and fellow Am. Assn. Health, Phys. Edn. and Recreation; mem. Coll. Phys. Edn. Assn. (ex-pres.), Am. Assn. School Adminstrs., Am. Assn. Univ. Profs., Nat. Collegiate Life Saving Soc., Am. Acad. of Phys. Edn., Am. Camping Assn., Am. Pub. Health Assn., Nat. Workshop on Facilities for Athletics, Phys. Edn. and Recreation, Pa. Acad. Science, Phi Delta Kappa, Kappa Delta Pi, Phi Epsilon Kappa, Phi Kappa Sigma. Episcopalian. Mason (32 deg.). Club: Lenape (Phila.). Author of Swimming Pool Standards, and various pamphlets on swimming, life-saving; contributor to phys. edn. jours. Home: Swarthmore, Pa. *

LUKE, CHARLES DANIEL, chem. engr.; b. Coin, Iowa, Oct. 4, 1907; s. Edward Louis and Delia (Johnson) L.; B.S., U. Iowa, 1929; S.M., Mass. Inst. Tech., 1931, Sc.D., 1934; m. Minerva Eagan, May 29, 1941 (dec. June 1967); m. 2d, Anne Pariza, Sept. 8, 1970. Process engr. Standard Oil Co. La., 1933-35; chem. engr. de Florez Engring. Co., 1935-37; asst. prof. chem. engring. Syracuse (N.Y.), U., 1937-39, asso. prof., chmn. chem. engring. dept., 1940-41, prof., chem. engring. dept., 1941-54; dir. div. classification AEC, Washington, 1954-55, tech. asst. to dir. for hazard evaluation, 1955-60, chief criticality br., 1960-70, cons., 1970-76. Served as maj. Manhattan Dist., AUS, 1942-46. Mem. Am. Inst. Chem. Engrs., Am. Chem. Soc., Sigma Xi, Tau Beta Pi, Phi Lambda Upsilon, Alpha Chi Sigma. Methodist. Home: Washington, D.C. Died Apr. 18, 1976.

LUKOFF, HERMAN, computer co. exec.; b. Phila., May 2, 1923; s. Aaron and Anna (Shlemovitz) L.; B.S. in Elec. Engring., U. Pa., 1943; m. Shirley Rosner, Dec. 5, 1948; children—Arthur, Barry, Carol, Andrew. Research asso. eniac project U. Pa., 1943-44, 46-47; engr. Eckert Mauchly Computer Corp., Phila., 1947-50; project engr. Sperry Univac Co., Phila., 1950-59, chief engr., 1959-68, dir. research, 1968-70, dir. tech. operations, 1970-79. Served with USNR, 1944-46. Recipient McDowell award IBM Corp., 1969; Univec Presdl. Excellence award, 1976. Fellow IEEE; mem. Am. Radio Relay League. Author: From Dits to Bits...A Personal History of the Electronic Computer, 1979. Contbr. articles digital computers to profl. publs. and tech. mags. Patentee in field. Home: Fort Washington, Pa. Died Sept. 24, 1979; buried Shalom Meml. Park, Philadelphia.

LUMMIS, FREDERICK RICE (LUM'MIS), physician; b. Houston, Tex., Nov. 1, 1884; s. Henry Holt and Charlotte Minerva (Rice) L.; A.B., Univ. of the South, Sewanee, Tenn. 1906; M.D., Jefferson Med. Coll., Phila. 1913; post grad. student, Univ. of Pa., 1926-27; m. Annette Gano, June 30, 1923. Interne Jefferson Hosp., Phila. 1913-15; in practice of medicine Houston, Tex.; clin. prof. of medicine, Baylor Med. Coll., Houston, 1943-47, now emeritus. Dir. Union Nat. Bank, Houston. Served with U.S. Army World War I. Fellow Am. Coll. of Physicians. Trustee Rice Inst., Houston Acad. of Medicine. Episcopalian. Home: Houston. *

LUND, CURTIS JOSEPH, obstetrician and gynecologist; b. LaSita, Kan., June 8, 1907; s. Frank Julius and Ida (Lund) L.; B.S., Kan. State Coll., 1929; M.S., U. Wis., 1930, M.D., 1935; m. Constance Graham, Aug. 29, 1931; 1 son, Graham Curtis. Intern, Cin. Gen. Hosp., 1935-36; asst. resident obstetrics and gynecology U. Hosp., Madison, Wis., 1936, resident, 1938-39; asst. resident obstetrics and gynecology Chgo. Lying-In Hosp., 1937; asst. research fellows Med. Sch. U. Wis., 1939-41, asso. research fellow, 1941-43; instr. Med. Sch. U. Minn., 1943-44, asst. prof., 1944-46, asso. prof., 1946-47; prof. obstetrics and gynecology La. State U. Sch. Medicine; 1947-52; vis. surgeon, obstetrician in chief La. State U. unit Charity Hosp., New Orleans, 1947-50, sr. vis. surgeon, obstetrician and gynecologist in chief 1950-52; prof. obstetrics and gynecology U. Rochester Sch. Medicine and Dentistry, also obstetrician and gynecologist in chief U. Rochester Med. Center, 1952-72; prof. emeritus, 1972-79; prof. obstetrics and gynecology U. Minn. Med. Sch., Mpls., 1972-79; also chmn. dept. Diplomate Am. Bd. Obstetrics and Gynecology (dir. exams., dir.). Mem. Am. Gynecol. Soc. (pres. 1971), Am. Assn. Obstetricians and Gynecologists, Am. Coll. Obstetrics and Gynecology, Soc. Gynecol. Investigation, Sigma Xi, Alpha Omega Alpha. Contbr. profl. jours. Home: Edina, Minn. Died Feb. 8, 1979.

LUND, ELMER I., physiologist; b. Springfield, Minn., Dec. 13, 1884; s. Peter A. and Ceceila (Person) L.; Ph.B., Hamline U., 1910, D.Sc., 1935; grad. study U. of Chicago, summer 1911; Ph.D., Johns Hopkins, 1914; m. Barbara Marion Lee, Aug. 19, 1914. Instr. in zoölogy, U. of Pa., 1914-15, asst. prof. zoölogy, U. of Minn., 1915-19, asso. prof., 1919-26; prof. physiology, Puget Sound Biol. Lab., summers 1921-31; prof. physiology, Univ. of Texas, 1926-50. director Institute of Marine Science until 1950; now real estate investor and operator. Fellow A.A.A.S.; member American Society Zoölogists. Soc. Experimental Biology and Medicine, Am. Physiol. Soc., Am. Soc. Plant Physiology, Phi Beta Kappa Assos., Sigma Xi. Author: Bioelectric Fields and Growth. Contbr. to Biol. Bulletin, Am. Jour. Physiology, Bot. Gazette, Jour. Gen. Physiology, etc. Home: Austin, Tex. *

LUND, GAGE, business exec.; b. Clinton, Ia., Oct. 25, 1901; s. Virtus and Carrie (Gage) L.; student Mont. State Coll., 1920-22, Stanford, 1922-24; m. Mary Frances Lamar, Jan. 23, 1931; children—James G., Lamar, Mary Gage. Geologist, Standard of Calif. and subsidiaries, San Francisco, 1925-29, drilling foreman, Texas, 1929-31, geologist The California Co., Dallas, 1931-36, div. supt., Gulf div., Houston, 1937-41, asst. mgr. all operation in Tex., N.Mex., La., Miss., Ala., The Calif. Co., Standard Oil Co. of Tex., 1938-41; pres. Califco, New Orleans, 1941-45, chmn. bd. Standard Oil of Tex., 1945-55, San Francisco, from 1946, v.p., dir. Standard Oil of Calif., from 1948; chmn. bd. Richmond Exploration Co.; 1948-55, The Cal. Co., 1945-55, The Cal. Standard Oil Co., 1949-76; bd. directors FMC Corp., San Jose, California. Recipient Order of Grizzly, U. Mont., 1970. Clubs: Pacific-Union, Stock Exchange, Commonwealth Bohemian, Claremont Country. Home: Piedmont, Calif. Died Aug. 26, 1976; buried Mountain View Cemetery, Piedmont.

LUND, JOHN M., mfg. exec.; b. Sweden, 1882. Chmn. exec. com., dir. Friden, Inc., San Leandro, Cal. Mason (Shriner). Home: Berkeley, Cal. *

LUND, SWEN WILLIAM, meat packing; b. Enviken, Sweden, Feb. 27, 1886; s. Rev. Emil Lund; ed. Business Coll.; m. Agnes Ellen Jones, Dec. 14, 1919. Associated with Swift & Co. since 1902; mgr. Swift Canadian Co., Ltd., Edmonton, Canada, 1924; dept. head Swift & Co., Chicago, 1927, v.p. pork operations since 1937. Mem. Chicago Bd. Trade. Home: Chicago. *

LUNDBERG, MELVIN EDWARD, utility exec.; b. Woods Cross, Utah, Apr. 13, 1904; s. Alfred A. and Margaret (Southworth) L.; B.S., U. Utah, 1930; m. Reva Rowe, June 15, 1926. Illuminating engr. Utah Power & Light Co., 1930-31; sec., treas., gen. mgr. Uintah Power & Light Co., 1932-39; sec., treas., gen. mgr. Elko Lamoille Power Co. (Nev.) (merged with So. Nev. Power Co. to become Nev Power Co. 1961), 1940-60, v.p., mgr. Elko div., 1961-73, dir., 1961-79; owner Lundberg Apts., 1946-63, Lundberg's, 1949-67; v.p. Transwester Life Ins. Co., 1958-63, dir., 1958-63; dir. Elko Broadcasting Co., 1948-74. Mem. Columbia Interstate Compact Commn. Nev., 1951-58; chmn. Gov.'s Sch. Survey Com., 1953-57; mem. Nev. Planning Bd., 1947-56; chmn. Nev. delegation White House Conf. on Edn., 1955; past chmn. Nev. Council on Edn.; mem. Nev. Bd. Parole Commrs., 1957-70, Gov.'s Com. on Edn. in Nev., 1965-72, Nat. Citizens Council Better Schs., Citizens Conf. Nev. Cts., 1968; mem. citizens adv. com. U. Nev. Coll. Engring., 1960-74; mem. Gov.'s Salary Study Commn. for Elected State Ofcls., 1969-70; mem. Nev. Civil Def. Commn., mem. regional adv. group Intermountain Regional Med. Program, 1972-75; adv. bd. No. Nev. Community Coll., 1973-79. Mem. Republican Nat. Com., 1964-68. Mem. Nev. Congress Parents and Tchrs. (hon. life), Nev. Taxpayer's Assn. (dir. 1945-79, pres. 1954-74), Nev. Soc. Profl. Engrs. (pres. Elko chpt. 1971), Elko C. of C. (past pres.). Club: Elks (past exalted ruler, Nev. dist. dep. grand exalted ruler 1959-60, hon. life mem.), Lions (past pres.). Home: Elko, Nev. Died Sept. 25, 1979; entombed Bldg. of Memory, Burns Meml. Gardens.

LUNDBORG, LOUIS BILLINGS, banker; b. Billings, Mont., Mar. 31, 1906; s. Andrew John and Emma Louisa (Karlson) L.; student Stanford, 1923-26; LL.D., Rocky Mountain Coll., 1965, Occidental Coll., 1971; m. Barbara Ann Wellington, June 25, 1926; 1 son, Bradford Wellington. Research chemist Cal. and Hawaiian Sugar Refining Corp., 1926-27; with research dept. Cal. C. of C., 1927-29, dist. mgr. San Joaquin Valley, Fresno, 1929-32, Central Coast, San Francisco, 1932-39, asst. gen. mgr., 1939-43; gen. mgr. San Francisco C. of C., 1943-48; v.p. Stanford 1948-49; v.p. Bank Am., 1949-59, exec. v.p., 1959-65, chmn. bd., 1965-71, mem. mng. com. and adv. council to dirs., 1957-71, dir., from 1964; chmn., dir. Bank of Am. (Internat.), Bamerical Internat. Finance Corp., 1965-71, Bank Am. Corp., 1968-71; dir. MCA, Inc., Envirotech Corp.; regents prof. U. Cal., 1975. Pres., United Way, 1966-68; cons. to Nat. Park Service, 1946-47. Bd. dirs. Stanford Research Inst., from 1948, San Francisco Community

Chest, 1954-56; trustee World Affairs Council 1947-63, pres., 1969-70; trustee Huntington Library, San Marino, chmn., 1971. Mem. Am. Bankers Assn. (pres. savs. and mortgage div. 1958-59), U.S. C. of C. (dir. 1955-60, v.p. 1960-63, treas. 1963-66, chmn. Mexico-U.S. com. 1957-61, 65-66), Newcomen Soc., Assn. Res. City Bankers. Republican. Conglist. Clubs: Cercle de l'Union, Pacific Union, Bohemian, Villa Taverna (San Francisco); California (Los Angeles); Links (N.Y.C.). Author: Practical Psychology for the Organization Executive; Public Relations in the Local Community; Up to Now; Japan-U.S. Dialogue on Management; The Art of Being an Executive. Home: Belvedere, Calif. Died Jan. 11, 1981; buried Cypress Lawn Cemetery, San Francisco.

LUNDIN, ALFRED HELMER (LUN'DEN), lawyer; b. Lead, S.D., Mar. 17, 1884; s. Andrew H. and Helen (Brakke) L.; A.B., U. of Neb., 1906, LL.B., 1906; m. Julia Deweese, June 8, 1909; 1 son, Daniel Howard. Practiced in Seattle, Wash., since 1906; pros. atty. King County, Wash., 1915-19; mem. firm of Lundin & Barto since 1919. Chmn. Community Chest, 1926-27. Mem. Seattle Chamber of Commerce (pres. 1934-35). Pres. Social Welfare League, 1923; mem. Am. and Wash. State bar assns., Seattle Bar Assn. (pres. 1925). Given Distinguished Service Award by U. of Neb., 1942. Republican. Conglist. Mason (Shriner). Clubs: College, Rainier. Home: Seattle, Wash. *

LUNDY, GEORGE EVERETT, pub. relations cons.; b. Manson, Ia., June 3, 1882; s. Nathan Warren and Loueria J. (Williams) L.; student Ia. State Coll., 1902; m. Nellie M. Carwood, Oct. 24, 1906; children—Margaret (Mrs. R. J. Humbert), Catherine (Mrs. D. L. Rossuier), Sec. YMCA, Waterloo, Ia., Chattanooga and Bristol, Tenn., also Canton, O.; 1906-23; campaign dir. Ward, Wells, Dreshman, ,.Y.C., 1923-26; with Marts & Lundy, Inc., N.Y.C., 1926—, v.p., 1926-56, treas., 1926-56, vice chmn., Canton O., 1956—; pub. relations, fund raising counsel, colls. and chs., 1926—. Republican. Methodist. Mason (32 deg., Shriner). Clubs: Rotary, Canton, Executives (Canton, O.). Contbr. articles religious mags. Home: Canton. *

LUNSFORD, OMER CLARENCE, business exec.; b. Anderson, Ind., Sept. 2, 1905; s. John and Eddith (Stanley) L.; student U. Wis., Coll. Armed Forces; m. Belle F. Feller, Aug. 2, 1926; children—John B., Suzanne (Mrs. David A. McElvain), Angela (Mrs. Robert E. Dowling III). With Standard Oil Co. (Ind.), 1924-70, asst. v.p. Am. Oil Co., Chgo., until 1970; exec. v.p. Soil Enrichment Materials Corp., Chgo., 1970-72; assisted in orgn. Internat. Exec. Service Corps., Central Am., 1964-65, spl. assignment, Brazil, 1966, exec. vol., Panama, 1970. Pres., United Fund of Arlington Heights (Ill.). Served to lt. USNR, World War II. Methodist. Mason (Shriner). Clubs: Lake Shore, Sales Executives (Chgo.). Contbr. bus. articles to profl. jours. Home: Arlington Heights, Ill. Died May 10, 1975; buried Mt. Pleasant Cemetery, Terre Haute, Ind.

LUNT, BERNARD JOSEPH, banker; b. Many, Louisiana, September 22, 1903; m. Clarence L. and Eunice Ursula (Tetts) L.; student U. Tex., 1922-23, U. Mo., 1923-24; LL.B., N. Tex. Sch. Law, 1935; grad. Am. Inst. Banking, 1937; m. Helen Dinan, Oct. 11, 1941; children—Mary T., Edward J., Eugene G., John J. With Ft. Worth Nat. Bank, 1924-72, asst. v.p., 1952-60, v.p.; regent Grad. Sch. Banking, 1954-56. Co-chmn. Ft. Worth sect. NCCJ, 1948-54; chmn. finance com. United Fund Ft. Worth, 1954-60; v.p. Tex. United Fund; treas., dir. Tarrant County Crime Commission. Adv. com. S.W. Center Human Relations. Nat. council U.S.O.; nat. trustee NCCJ, 1957-60. Mem. adv. bd. U. Dallas. Mem. American Bankers Assn. (exec. council 1954-57), Soc. Residential Appraisers (past pres.) Am. Inst. Banking (nat. pres. 1955-56), C. of C. (life), K.C. Home: Fort Worth, Tex. Died Oct. 7, 1978.

LUPTON, DILWORTH, clergyman; b. Cincinnati, O., Sept. 15, 1883; s. Henry Buck and Fanny (Richardson) L.; prep. edn. Shady Side Acad., Pittsburgh, and Hackley School of Tarrytown, New York, B.S., Sheffield Scientific School (Yale), 1905; graduated Meadville Theol. Sch., 1916, D.D., 1936; married Marie Helen Bell. July 2, 1918 (died December 17, 1936); married 2d, Elisabeth Hall Lewis, Jan. 9, 1939; stepdaughter, Sara Elisabeth. Ordained Unitarian ministry, 1916; minister First Unitarian Ch., Louisville, Kentucky, 1916-19, First Unitarian Ch. (Unitarian-Universalist), Cleveland, O, 1919-42, First Parish, Unitarian, Waltham, Mass., since September 1947. Chaplain United States Army, 1918. Author: "Dilworth Lupton Says Today." daily column in The Cleveland Press, 1942-47. Holds ministerial fellowship with Unitarian and Universalist denominations and in Congl. Union; also has fellowship with Society of Friends. Mem. Unitarian Ministers Assn. Author: Religion Says You Can. Contbr. to Christian Register, Christian Leader, etc. Home: Richmond, Va. *

LUSK, HALL STONER, judge; b. Washington, D.C., Sept. 21, 1883; s. Charles Stoner and Florence (Speake) L.; student Georgetown Prep. Sch., Washington, D.C., 1897-1900; A.B., Georgetown U., 1904, LL.B., 1907, Doctor of Laws (honorary), 1954; Doctor of Laws (honorary), University of Portland, 1941; m. Sara Catherine Emmons, September 30, 1914; children—Polly Carpenter (Mrs. Lloyd Appleman), Catherine Holmead, Margaret Addison (Mrs. Edgar Framm), Mary Emmons (Mrs. Glenn Meade), Jeanne Van Wyck (Mrs. Donald Fox). Admitted to bars of District of Columbia, 1907, Ore., 1910; sec. to Chief Justice Shepard, Court of Appeals, Wash., D.C., 1906-09; practiced in Protland, Ore., alone, 1910-12; in office of Dolph, Mallory, Simon & Gearin, 1912-18; asst. U.S. atty. Dist. of Ore., 1918-20; mem. firm Emmons Lusk & Bynon, 1920-30; circuit judge Multnomah County, Ore., 1930-37; appointed justice Supreme Court of Ore., July 21, 1937, and elected to same office, Nov. 1938, 44, 50, 56, chief justice, 1949-50, judge protem, 1961—; U.S. senator from Ore., Mar.-Nov. 1960; formerly instr. corp. law, N.W. Coll. Law, Portland. Mem. American Bar Association, Oregon State Bar, Multnomah County Bar Assn., Delta Chi, Delta Theta Phi (hon.). Democrat. Catholic. Clubs: University, Multnomah Athletic, Arlington (Portland). Home: Salem, Ore. *

LUSK, HAROLD F., legal educator; b. Owosso, Mich., Oct. 25, 1893; s. Walter Scott and Elizabeth Alma (Farver) L.; life cert. Central Mich. Normal Coll., 1914; A.B., U. Mich., 1921, J.D., 1925, S.J.D., 1941; m. Vera Miller Ricker, June 3, 1922; children—Betty Jane (Mrs. Guy Wm. Leonard, Jr.), Barbara Jean (Mrs. Richard H. Buskirk). Admitted to Mich. bar, 1925; practice in Grand Rapids, 1925-31; asst. prof. bus. law Ind. U., 1931-36, asso. prof., 1936-39, prof., 1939-64, emeritus; lectr. bus. law U. S. Fla., 1964-65; legal asso. Ind. U. Found., 1965-76; dir. Office Mil. Info., Ind. U., 1943-45; vis. prof. bus. law CCNY, summer 1936, Nat. Bur. Econ. Research, Cambridge, Mass., summer 1938; teaching fellow U. Mich. Law Sch., 1938-39; vis. prof. bus. law Ohio U. Law Sch., summer 1939. Served as ensign USN, 1917-18. Mem. Am. Bus. Law Assn. (pres. 1940-41), Beta Gamma Sigma, Acacia, Sigma Delta Kappa, Delta Sigma Pi. Republican. Clubs: Rotary (pres. Bloomington 1958-59), Masons. Author: Business Law, Principles and Cases, 7th edit., 1963; Legal Aspects of Business, 1949; Law of Real Estate Business, rev. edit., 1965; Indiana Supplement to Law of Real Estate business, 2d edit., 1965; Cases in Law of the Real Estate Business, 1961; Business Law Principles and Cases, Uniform Commercial Code Edition, 1966, (with others) 3d edit., 1974. Contbr. Nat. Ency., 1957, also legal periodicals. Home: Bloomington, Ind. Died Sept. 28, 1976; interred Valhalla Memory Gardens, Bloomington.

LUSK, WILLIAM THOMPSON, business exec.; b. N.Y.C., Mar. 30, 1901; s. Graham and May (Tiffany) L.; A.B., Yale, 1924; m. Katharine Adams, June 25, 1931; children—William Thompson, Hunt Adams, Charles Tiffany. With Tiffany & Co., N.Y.C., 1925-78, became asst. treas., dir., 1930, asst. sec., 1931, v.p., 1932, exec. v.p., 1952-55, pres., 1955-67, dir. to 1978; dir. Jewelers Vigilance Com. Trustee New Canaan Country Sch., 1943-56, v.p., 1944-46, pres., 1946-48. Mem. Gemological Inst. Am. (bd. govs.). Republican. Episcopalian. Clubs: Century, Yale, University (N.Y.C.); Country (New Canaan); Elizabethan (New Haven). Home: New Canaan, Conn. Died Mar. 5, 1978; interred Christ Ch., Winnetka, Ill.

LUSSIER, JEAN-JACQUES, med. sch. dean; b. Montreal, Que., Can., Apr. 23, 1920; s. Louis-Philippe and Aglaee (Sicotte) L.; B.A., U. Montreal, 1940, M.D., L.Sc., 1945, M.Sc., 1949; Ph.D., U. Cambridge (Eng.), 1951; m. Raymonde LeGendre, Oct. 26, 1946; children—Michel, Dominique, Benoit, Francois. Mem. faculty medicine U. Montreal, 1944-74, prof. physiology, asst. dean faculty, 1955-57, dean, 1957-74; dean medicine U. Ottawa (Ont.), 1974-75. Sec. Redaction de la Revie Canadienna de Biologie, 1951-55; mem. com. local orgn. XIXe congress Internat. Physiology, Montreal, 1952-53; sec. gen. Assn. Canadienne-francaise pour l'Advancement des Scis., 1952-55, pres., 1963-64; councillor adminstrv. com. Fedn. Panamericana de Associaciones de Facultades de Medicina, 1964-69; pres. Assn. des Facultes de Medecine du Can., 1966-68; fiduciaire King George V Silver Jubilee Sander Fund Can., 1964-75. Recipient medal coronation Queen Elizabeth II, 1953; medal Pro-Hungaria de l'Ordre de Malte, 1959; chevalier de grace magistrale de l'Ordre Souverain et Militaire de Malte, 1961; officer au merite de l'Ordre Malte, 1964; medal Centennial Can., 1967; fellow Nat. Research Council Can., 1949-51. Hon. fellow Internat. Coll. Surgeons; mem. Canadian (treas. 1957-58), Montreal (sec. 1952-53) physiol. socs., Canadian, Ont. med. assns., La. Soc. heraldique Can., Heraldy Soc. (Grande Bretagne). Club: Le Cercle (Ottawa). Contbr. to med. jours. Home: Ottawa, Ont., Can. Died Oct. 31, 1975.

LUSSKY, ALFRED EDWIN, prof. German, author; b. Sterling, Ill., Oct. 17, 1885; s. Rev. Fredrick and Anna Catherine (Beyer) L.; diploma, Concordia Coll., Ind., 1906; diploma, Concordia Theol. Sem., St. Louis, 1910; M.A., U. of Ill., 1911; Ph.D., U. of Mich., 1919; m. Matha Ann Drittler, Aug. 26, 1931; children—Katherine Louise, John Frederick. Asst. in German, U. of Mich., 1911-13; prof. German, Lake Forest Coll., 1913-14; asst. prof. German, U. of Ark., 1915-18, prof. German and head of dept. since 1921. Mem. Modern Lang. Assn. America, Am. Assn. Univ. Profs., Ark. Edn. Assn. Lutheran. Author: Tieck's Approach to Romanticism, 1925; Tieck's Romantic Irony, 1932. Contbr. to publs. of Modern Lang. Assn. of America, Modern Language Jour. Home: Fayetteville, Ark. *

LUTKIN, HARRIS CARMAN, lawyer; b. Chicago, Oct. 20, 1886; s. Peter Christian and Nancy Lelah (Carman) L.; A.B., Northwestern U., 1908, LL.B., 1910; m. Hazel Hackshaw, June 30, 1917; 1 son, Peter Christian II. Admitted to Ill. bar, 1910; city atty. Evanston, Ill., 1911-15; asst. gen. counsel U.S. Shipping Bd. Emergency Fleet Corp., 1918-19; former mem. McConnell, Lutkin, Van Hook & Paschen; lectr. on real property and Ill. law, Northwestern U. Law School, 1911-18. Dir., gen. counsel Poor & Co. Mem. Am., Ill., Chgo. bar assns., Law Club, Beta Theta Pi. Episcopalian. Home: Evanston, Ill.; (summer) Northport Point, Mich.

LUTKINS, CLINTON STEPHEN, business exec.; b. Bklyn., 1885. Hon. chmn. R.W. Pressprich & Co., Inc.; dir. Adams Express Co. Mem. Soc. Colonial Wars. Clubs: Brook, Bond, Downtown Assn., Racquet and Tennis (N.Y.C.); Maidstone (East Hampton, N.Y.); Manursing Island (Rye, N.Y.). Home: New York City NY 10021.

LYDON, JAMES PATRICK, aircraft mfg. co. exec.; b. Buffalo, July 10, 1907; s. James Martin and Mary Ann (Peyton) L.; student U. Notre Dame, 1925-29; LL.B., Chgo. Kent Coll. Law, 1930; m. Martha E. Adams, June 20, 1936. Admitted to Ill. bar, 1930, Ind. bar, 1934; with indsl. relations dept. Western Electric Co., Chgo., 1930-33, 37-41; pvt. practice, Chgo., 1933-34; asst. to dir. Ind. Dept. Pub. Welfare, Indpls., 1935-37; with Lockheed Aircraft Corp., 1941-68, corp. dir. indsl. relations, 1959-61, v.p. indsl. relations, 1962-68. Pres., Lockheed Leadership Fund, from 1964. Home: Escondido, Calif. Died Dec. 9, 1978.

LYE, LEN, motion composer; b. Christchurch, New Zealand, July 5, 1901; s. Harry and Rose Ann (Cole) L.; m. Jane Thompson, 1934; children—Bix, Yancy; m. 2d, Ann Zeiss Hindle, 1948. Came to U.S., 1944, naturalized, 1947. Became interested in composition of motion, 1916; developed models of practice which led to cinema and kinetic sculpture; fine art films include Tusalava, 1928, Colour Box, 1935, Rhythm, 1957, Free Radicals, 1958; invented direct film technique of inscribing designs on film without use of camera; one man shows include: Mus. Modern Art, Cin. Art Center, Howard Wise Gallery, Govett-Brewster Art Gallery, New Plymouth, N.Z., 1977; tchr. creative imagination N.Y.U. Sch. Performing Arts, 1966-80; featured lectr. on genetic element in art Berkeley Centennial celebrations, 1968, Animal Inst. Genetics, Edinburgh, 1968, Buffalo 2d Festival Arts, 1967, Internat. Animation Festival, Cambridge, Eng.; pres. jury Internat. Film Festival, Annecy, France. Recipient spl. catagory award for Colour Box, Brussels Internat. Film Festival, 1936; N.Y. TV Dirs. award for Rhythm, 1957; Silver medal for Free Radicals, Brussels World's Fair, 1959. Address: Warwick, N.Y. Died May 15, 1980.

LYLE, JOHN FREDERICK, banker; b. Whistler, Ala., Nov. 20, 1905; s. Frederick Henry and Annie Agnes (Murray) L.; grad. Sch. Banking, Rutgers U., 1948; m. Olive Isabel Palmer, May 2, 1928; children—John Frederick, Mary Olive (Mrs. James Cooke Wood). With Mchts. Nat. Bank, Mobile, Ala., 1922-73, sr. v.p., 1966-73; ret., 1973; treas. Ernest F. Ladd Meml. Stadium Corp., 1945-73. Tchr., Am. Inst. Banking, 1932-40; pres. Mobile Clearing House Assn., 1958. Past pres. Mobile Assn. for Blind, Allied Arts Council, Council Social Agys.; chmn. budget com. United Fund, 1952-56; treas. Salvation Army, Sr. Bowl, Mobile Historic Devel. Commn., Ala. Soc. Crippled Children; sec.-treas., v.p., pres. Mobile Mystic Socs.; trustee Mobile Arts and Sports Assn. Recipient Ann. Lay Award Ala. Recreation Soc., 1958. Episcopalian (del. Diocese Ala.). Kiwanian (pres. Mobile club 1953, Legion of Honor award 1967, Man of Week award 1972). Club: Touchdown (pres., dir., recipient certificate of appreciation). Home: Theodore, Ala. Died Jan. 5, 1976.

LYMAN, CHARLES BISHOP, army officer; b. Kukaian, Hamakue, Hawaii, Aug. 20, 1888; B.S., U.S. Mil. Acad., 1913; grad. Inf. Sch., 1922, Cav. Sch., 1925, Command and Gen. Staff Sch., 1927, Army War Coll., 1936. Commd. 2d lt., U.S. Army, 1913, and advanced through the grades to brig. gen., 1944; command, Maui Dist., Wailuku, Hawaii, 1941-42, 21st Inf. 1942-44, asst. div. comdr. 32d Div. 1944-45. Retired 1946. Decorated Silver Star, Legion of Merit with oak leaf cluster, Silver Star, Bronze Star with oak leaf cluster (U.S.) bdon Calderon 2d class (Ecquador). Home: Pennsbury Township, Pa. Died Apr. 15, 1981; buried Arlington Nat. Cemetery.

LYMAN, JOHN CUSHMAN, surgeon; b. Dayton, Wash., Aug. 3, 1885; s. Cornelius and Tryphena S. (Pond) L.; B.S., Whitman Coll., 1909, D.Sc. (hon.); M.D., Johns Hopkins, 1913; m. Elizabeth H. Harlan, June 30, 1920; children—Elizabeth (Mrs. Robison), Mary (Mrs. Archer). Resident surgeon Hebrew Hosp., Balt., 1915-16; asst. surg. pathology Johns Hopkins, 1917; instr. anatomy U. Neb., 1919-20; now practicing surgeon, Walla Walla, Wash. Pres. bd. trustees Whitman Coll. Served as capt., M.C., U.S. Army, World War I. Diplomate, founders group Am. Bd. Surgeons. Fellow Spokane Soc., A.C.S., A.M.A.; mem. Walla Walla Valley Med. Assn. (past pres.), Wash. State Med. Soc. (past trustee), North Pacific Surg. Assn. Spokane Surg. Soc., Phi Delta Theta, Phi Chi. Club: Inquiry (president). Home: Walla Walla, Wash. *

LYNCH, BERNARD W., b. Ottawa, Ill., Nov. 15, 1883; s. James W. Lynch; student Christian Bros. Sch., Brown's Business Coll. and Y.M.C.A. Sch.; m. Mary M. Maguire, July 8, 1910; children—Mary, Helen, William, Joseph. Vice-pres. in charge of finance and accounting Byllesby Engring. & Management Corp., 1922-36; chmn. finance com. Standard Gas & Electric Co., 1928-36, pres. 1936-39; now chmn. finance com. San Diego (Calif.) Gas & Electric Co.; dir. various corps. Home: Chicago. *

LYNCH, RUSSELL GEORGE, writer; b. Racine, Wis., June 27, 1899; s. George Edward and Flora Grace (Cooper) L.; student pub. schs., Racine; m. Esther Lillian Smith, Oct. 14, 1924; 1 son, Richard George. Sports editor Racine Times Call, 1917-18; city editor LaPorte (Ind.) Herald, 1919-20; reporter Racine Jour.-News, 1920, Racine Times Call, 1920-22; rewrite man Milw. Jour., 1922-33, sports editor, 1933-56, spl. reporter on natural resources, 1956-64. Mem. Wis. Resource Devel. Bd., 1966-68; 1st chmn. Wis. Natural Resources Bd., 1967-69; pres. Ice Age Park and Trail Found., 1971-74. Served as yeoman 3d class USNRF, World War I. Recipient 1st MacQuarrie award for conservation writing, 1958; Thomas L. Stokes award for writing on natural resources, 1963. Mem. Soil Conservation Soc. Am., Wis. Acad. Sci., Arts and Letters, AAAS. Author: Maybe I'm Wrong; Our Growing Water Problem; Ditches, Dust and Ducks; Linguistic Barriers in Science Writing; co-author The Milwaukee Braves. Home: Wauwatosa, Wis. Died May 12, 1979.

LYNCH, WARREN, pub. co. exec.; b. Chgo., Jan. 9, 1915; s. James Joseph and Laura (Healy) L.; B.A., Williams Coll., 1936; m. Jane Bethge, Aug. 26, 1940; children—Richard W., Timothy Scott. Advt. writer Lord & Thomas, Chgo., 1936-39, Batten, Barton, Durstine & Osborn, Inc., N.Y.C., 1940-50; v.p. charge advt. Book of Month Club, Inc., N.Y.C., 1950-61, exec. v.p., 1961-73, vice chmn. bd. dirs., chmn. exec. com., 1973-77. Adv. com. Center for Info. on Am. Clubs: Publishers Lunch, Coffeehouse, Century Assn. (N.Y.C.). Home: New York, N.Y. Died May 8, 1977.

LYNCH, WILLIAM JOSEPH, judge; b. Chgo., June 6, 1908; s. William Joseph and Catherine (Tynan) L.; grad. Loyola U. Sch. Law, 1931. Admitted to Ill. bar, 1931; partner Lynch, Fazio & Cullen, Chgo., 1931-33; asst. states atty., Cook County, Ill., 1933-38; pvt. practice law, Chgo., 1938-42; gen. counsel Cartage Exchange of Chgo., Inc., 1938-42; partner Daley & Lynch, Chgo., 1946-55, Lynch & Schaller, Chgo., 1955-62, Lynch, Schaller & Reilly, 1962-66; judge U.S. Dist. Ct., No. Dist. Ill., Chgo., 1966-76. Gen. atty. Chgo. Transit Authority, 1957. Mem. Ill. senate from 9th Dist., 1950-57, minority leader, 1953, 55, 57. Served to lt. comdr. USNR, 1942-46. Mem. Am., Ill., Chgo. (bd. mgrs.) bar assns. Home: Chicago, Ill. Died Aug. 9, 1976.

LYNEN, FEODOR, biochemist; b. Munich, Germany, Apr. 6, 1911; s. Wilhelm and Frieda (Prym) L.; Dr. phil., U. Munich, 1937; Dr. med. h.c., U. Freiburg (Germany), 1960; hon. doctorates U. Seoul (Korea), 1967, U. Miami (Fla.), 1968, U. René Descartes, Paris, 1976, U. Fed. Rio de Janeiro, 1977, U. Regensburg (w. Ger.), 1978; m. Eva Wieland, May 14, 1937; children—Peter, Annemarie, Susanne, Eva-Marie, Heinrich. Lectr. chemistry U. Munich, 1942-47, prof., from 1947; dir. Max-Planck-Inst. Zellchemie, Munich, 1954-72, Max-Planck-Inst. für Biochemie, from 1972. Recipient Neuberg medal Am. Soc. European Chemists and Pharmacists, 1954; Liebig-Denkmünze medal Gesellschaft Deutscher Chemiker, 1955; Carus medal Deutsche Acad. der Naturforscher Leopoldina, 1961; Otto Warburg medal Gesellschaft für Physiolog. Chemie, 1963; Nobel prize for medicine, 1964; Normann medal Deutsche Gesellschaft Fettwissenschaft, 1967; Orden pour le Merite, 1971. Hon. fellow Indian Acad. Sci., Bangalore, Royal Soc. Edinburgh; mem. Bayerische Acad. der Wissenschaften, Deutsche Acad. der Naturforscher Leopoldina, Osterreich Acad. der Wissenschaften (corr.); hon. mem. Acad. Nacional de Medicina de Colombia; fgn. mem. Royal Soc., Am. Biol. Chemists, Nat. Acad. Scis., Am. Acad. Arts and Scis., Am. Philos. Soc.; corr. mem. Acad. der Wissenschaften Göttingen. Home: Starnberg, Federal Republic of Germany. Died Aug. 6, 1979.

LYON, ARLON EVERETT, labor union exec.; b. Thedford, Nebr., Oct. 15, 1899; s. Alfred S. and Mable (Wright) L.; ed. public schs. Signalman, So. Pacific, 1919-24; gen. chmn. Brotherhood of R.R. Signalmen of Am., 1924-27, asst. to pres., 1927-34, pres., 1934-45, pres. emeritus; exec. sec. Ry. Labor Execs. Assn., 1945-62; mem. U.S. R.R. Retirement Bd., 1962-69. Home: Arlington Heights, Ill. Died July 10, 1976; buried Memory Gardens, Arlington Heights.

LYON, HARLEY WESLEY, prin. schools; b. Plainview, Minn., Oct. 14, 1886; s. John Wesley and Alice (Newland) L.; student Oshkosh (Wis.) Teachers Coll., 1904-06; Ph.B., U. of Wis., 1915; grad. study U. of Chicago, 1920-21; A.M. in Edn., U. of Southern Calif., 1929; m. Elsie M. Parratt, Sept. 1, 1915; children—Robert Harley, John Wesley. Prin. pub. sch., Greenbush, Wis., 1906-07; teacher high sch., Hayward, Wis., 1909-11; supt. schs., W. De Pere, Wis., 1911-13; prin. high sch., Roswell, N.M., 1913-14; high sch. teacher, Milwaukee, 1917-19, Oak Park, Ill., 1920-21; prin. Jr. High Sch., Kenosha, Wis., 1921-23; high sch. teacher, Pasadena, Calif., 1923; prin. elementary schs., Pasadena, since 1924. Mem. N.E.A. (life) Nat. Dept. Elementary Sch. Prins. (pres. 1935-36), Calif. Elementary Sch. Prins. Assn. (pres. state and southern sect.; editor yr. book and news bull.), Calif. Teachers Assn., Pasadena Teachers Assn., Calif. Congress of Parents and Teachers (life), Fathers Councils (state chmn.), Round Table Internat. (v.p.), Pasadena Round Table (pres.), Internat. Assn. Civic Service Club Execs. (hon.), Pasadena Service Club Officers Assn. (pres.), Boy Scouts of America, Y.M.C.A.; Pasadena Coordinating Council of Agencies Related to Youth, Schoolmasters Club of Southern Calif., Phi Delta Kappa. Republican. Baptist. Mason. Contbr. to ednl. jours. Home: Pasadena, Calif. *

LYON, HARRIS MERTON, writer, editor; b. at Santa Fé, N.M., Dec. 22, 1883; s. Mary (Merton) L.; A.B., U. of Mo., 1905; unmarried. Newspaper work in West and Southwest; dramatic critic Houston (Tex.) Post; asso. editor and dramatic critic Hampton's Magazine, and dir. corpn., since 1909. Author: Sardonics, 1909; also short stories and articles for various English and Am. mags. Address: New York, N.Y. *

LYONS, LEONARD, newspaper columnist; b. N.Y.C., Sept. 10, 1906; s. Moses L. and Bronna (Harnick) Sucher; student CCNY, 1924-25; LL.B., St. John's U. Coll. Law, 1928; LL.D., Wilberforce U.; m. Sylvia R. Schonberger, Nov. 29, 1934; children—George Martin, Warren Hay, Jeffrey, Douglas Bronn; grandchildren—Pamela Jamie, Paul Gregory, Eric Jordan. Admitted to N.Y. bar, 1928, Fed. bar, 1929; practiced in N.Y.C., 1929-34; spl. asst. atty. gen., N.Y., 1954-68; writer column The Lyons Den, N.Y. Post, syndicated 1934-74. Home: New York, N.Y. Died Oct. 8, 1976.

LYONS, RICHARD THOMAS, gas co. exec.; b. East Weymouth, Mass., Dec. 4, 1895; s. Daniel and Abbie Agnes (Lynch) L.; B.S., Mass. Inst. Tech., 1917; S.B., Harvard, 1917; m. Sammie Wamble, June 15, 1922. Petroleum geologist in S.W. states and in Venezuela, 1919-24; v.p., dir. Skelly Oil Co., Tulsa, 1924-36; pres. Tide Water Oil Co., 1936-52; pres., chief exec. officer Union Tex. Nat. Gas Corp., Houston, 1952-60. Mem. Independent Petroleum Assn. Am. (dir.), Am. Assn. Petroleum Geologists, Am. Inst. Mining Metall. and Petroleum Engrs. Home: Houston, Tex. Died June 10, 1979.

LYONS, THOMAS DANIEL, lawyer; b. Burr Oak, Ia., July 2, 1883; s. Richard Francis and Sarah (Donlan) L.; A.B., U. of Notre Dame, Ind., 1904; LL.B., U. of S.D., 1907; m. Clara, d. Thomas F. Kennedy, Sept. 2, 1915 (died June 13, 1939); 1 dau., Mary Kennedy. Admitted to bar, 1907, to Supreme Court of U.S., 1917; mem. firm Rice & Lyons, Tulsa, Okla, since 1907; pres. Lee Oil Co.; dir. First Nat. Bank; del. at large Dem. Nat. Convention, San Francisco, 1920. Mem. Charter Commn. to provide city mgr. plan for Tulsa. Nominated by Democratic State Conv. of S.D. for state supt. of schs., 1906; mem. Supreme Court Commn. of Okla. (Supreme Bench), apptd. by gov. and unanimously confirmed by Supreme Court for 4-yr. term, Apr. 9, 1923; resigned from Supreme Court Commn. and resumed law practice at Tulsa, Okla., Dec. 1, 1925; apptd. judge Dist. Court of Okla., May 5, 1933; apptd. mem. Charter Revision Commn., by Mayor of Tulsa, June 1927; regent U. of Okla., by apptmt. of Governor Murray, since 1932; del. Dem. Nat. Conv., Chicago., 1932. Apptd. receiver in river bed cases, Okla., Oct. 1, 1919. Lecturer on Law of Oil and Gas, Notre Dame U. Law Sch., Oct.-Nov. 1938; convocation day lecturer, U. of S.D. Law Sch., May 1939. Enlisted in U.S.A. as pvt. and hon. discharged from Inf. Central Officers' Training Sch., Camp Pike Ark., Dec. 7, 1918; capt. Co. C, 3d Inf., Okla. N.G. Mem. Okla. Hist. Soc., Internat. Law Assn., Delta Theta Pi. Catholic. Democrat. Clubs: Petroleum, Country University (Tulsa, Okla.); Bankers of America, New York Athletic (New York). Wrote: (with Benjamin F. Rice) The Law of Oil and Gas; The Oil Operator in Oklahoma; Schools and School Districts of State of Oklahoma; Effect of "Dred Scott" Decision on Career of Stephen A. Douglas and Abraham Lincoln. Home: Tulsa, Okla. *

LYSENKO, TROFIM DENISOVICH, biologist, agronomist; b. Poltava Oblast, Russia, 1898; grad. Uman Sch. Horticulture, 1921, Kiev Agrl. Inst., 1925. With Belaya Tserkov Selection Sta., 1921, Exptl. Selection Sta., Kirovobad, 1925-29; sr. specialist phusiology All-Union Selection and Genetics Inst., Odessa, 1929-34, sci. dir., 1934-36, dirs., 1936-38; pres. All-Uinon Lenin Acad. Agrl. Sci., 1938-56, 61-62, mem. presidium, from 1935; dir. Inst. Genetics, USSR Acad. Scis., 1940-65; spl. research heredity, individual devel. organisms, laws formation of species, crop nutrition. Head USSR delegation to All-Hungarian Conf. Maize Cultivation Problems, 1960. Decorated Order of Lenin (8), Order Red Banner of Labor, Stalin Prize (3); named Hero of Socialist Labor, 1945; hon. mem. Czechoslovakian Acad. Agrl. Sci. Mem. USSR Acad. Sci., Ukranian Acad. Sci. Author: Work During the Great Patriotic War, 1943; Agrobiology, 1952; Phase Plant Development, 1952; Selected Works, 1953. Home: Moscow, USSR. Died Nov. 20, 1976.

LYTTLE, CHARLES HAROLD, clergyman, educator; b. Cleve., July 16, 1884; s. George Herbert and Arabella Eleanor (Jones) L.; A.B., Adelbert Coll. (Western Reserve U.), 1907; A.M., Western Reserve U., 1908; B.D., Meadville Theol. Sch., 1910, Th.D., 1923; studied univs. of Berlin and Marburg, 1911; S.T.M., Harvard Div. Sch., 1913; m. Marcia Taft Janes, July 1, 1922; children—David Janes, Bradford Janes. Ordained Unitarian ministry, 1914; pastor 2d Ch., Bklyn., 1914-24, First Unitarian Ch., Geneva, Ill., 1927—; prof. Church history, Meadville Theol. Sch., 1924—; prof. Modern Church His., Federated Theol. Faculty U. Chgo., 1943-49, now prof. emeritus, lectr. University Coll., 1954-55. Dir. Unitarian Hist. Soc.; pres. Theol. Faculties Union, 1936; pres. Am. Soc. Ch. Hist., 1939-40; exec. sec. Chgo. Unitarian Council, 1937-43, pres., 1946-49; archivist Western Unitarian Conf., 1951—. v.p., Citizens Schs. Com., Chg., 1947-49, mem. bd. of advisors, 1949—. Mem. Fellowship of Reconciliation. Mem. Wider Quaker Fellowship, Masaryk Institute, Geneva (pres. 1946—). Chgo. hist. socs., Unitarian-Universalist Hist. Soc. Am. (v.p.). Author: Pentecost of American Unitarianism, 1918. Editor: The Liberal Gospel (Channing Anthology), 1925. Part author of Humanist Sermons, 1927; The Religion of Early Freemasonry, 1939; Emerson's Self Reliance, 1942; Freedom Moves West, 1953. Club: Quadrangle. Address: Chgo. *

MABON, JOHN SCOTT, publisher; b. Yonkers, N.Y., Dec. 26, 1909; s. Arthur Frederick and Elizabeth Prescott (Noyes) M.; B.A., Columbia, 1931; m. Inés Camprubí, Aug. 7, 1936; 1 son, Ferdy. Engaged in real estate and transp. bus., N.Y.C., 1932-34; asst. editor D. Appleton Century Co., Inc., N.Y.C., 1935-38; free-lance reviewer and pub.'s reader, 1938; asso. editor Alfred A. Knopf, Inc., N.Y.C., 1940-41; dir. Atlantic Monthly Press, Boston, 1942-44; asso. editor Ladies Home Jour., Phila., 1945-46; v.p., editor Peoples Book Club, N.Y.C., 1947-52; v.p. La Prensa, N.Y.C., 1952-60; asso. dir. U. Mich. Press, Ann Arbor, 1965-72, 74-75, acting dir., 1972-74. Bd. dirs. Merc. Library Assn., 1948-65. Mem. Delta Psi. Clubs: P.E.N.; Princeton (N.Y.C.) Contbr. book revs. to Saturday Rev., N.Y. Herald-Tribune. Home: Greenwich, Conn. Died May 5, 1980.

MABRY, THOMAS JEWETT, ex-gov.; b. Carlisle Co., Ky., Oct. 17, 1884; s. Jesse J. and Onie Lillian (Nance) M.; ed. U. of Okla., 1904-06, U. of N.M., 1908-09; m. Winifred White, June 20, 1907 (died June 16, 1912); 1 son, Scott Harvey; m. 2d, Katherine Burns, June 10, 1915; children—Katherine Louise (Mrs. Phillip W. Eagan), Thomas Jewett. Admitted to N.M. bar, 1915; practiced in Albuquerque, 1915-36; mem. Albuquerque City Commn., 1926-27; dist. atty. 2d judicial Dist. of N.M., 1932-36, dist. judge, same dist., 1936-38; elected justice Supreme Court of N.M., 1938, for term 1939-47; served as chief justice of the supreme court 1944-46; elected governor of New Mexico, 1946, 48. Mem. N.M. Constl. Conv., 1910; mem. N.M. State Senate, 1912-17 (youngest member of both). Former pres. N.M. Bd. Paroles and Pardons; pres. bd. N.M. Boys' Industrial Sch. Democrat. Presbyterian. Mason (Shriner), Elk. Address: Santa Fe, N.M. *

MACARTHUR, JOHN D., ins. co. exec.; b. Pittston, Pa., Mar. 6, 1897; s. William Telfer and Georgiana (Welstead) M.; student pub. schs.; m. Catherine Hyland, Aug. 30, 1937; children by previous marriage—John Roderick, Virginia de Cordova. Ins. bus., 1916-78; chmn. bd. Bankers Life & Casualty Co., 1936-78, Citizens Bank & Trust Co., Park Ridge, Ill. Home: Chicago, Ill. Died Jan. 6, 1978.

MACAUSLAND, EARLE RUTHERFORD, mag. editor, pub.; b. Taunton, Mass., May 15, 1893; s. William and Millicent Jane (Burns) MacA.; student Mass. Inst. Tech. Vice pres. Priscilla Pub. Co., 1920-29, Parents Pub. Co., 1929-33, Butterick Pub. Co., 1933-35, pub. Nat. Parents-Tchrs. Mag., 1935-37; founder, editor, pub. Gourmet mag., 1940-80. Mem. Confrerie des Chevaliers du Tastevin (grand comdr.). Clubs: Wine and Food Soc. (N.Y.C.); Paris-Am. Home: New York, N.Y. Died June 4, 1980.

MACBAIN, GAVIN KEITH, corp. exec.; b. Closter, N.J., July 9, 1911; s. William and Isabella (Lamb) MacB.; A.B., Columbia, 1932; m. Margaret Gristede, Apr. 9, 1935; 1 dau., M. Alison (Mrs. Richard S. Fay). Sales rep. Wood Struthers & Co., N.Y.C., 1933-44; with Bristol-Myers Co., N.Y.C., 1944-61, 65-78, treas., 1947-61, pres., chief exec., former chmn.; pres., chmn. bd. Gristede Brothers, N.Y.C., 1961-65; dir. U.S. Trust Co. N.Y., Simplicity Pattern Co., Kennecott Copper Co., United Mut. Savs. Bank, First Fed. Savs. & Loan Assn., J.C. Penney Co. Inc. Bd. dirs. N.Y. Stock Exchange. Former nat. chmn. United Community Campaigns Am. Mem. Sigma Nu. Clubs: Tuscarora, Anglers, Economic (pres.) (N.Y.C.); Bedford (N.Y.) Golf and Tennis. Home: Mt Kisco, N.Y. Died Mar. 31, 1978.

MACBETH, NORMAN, electro-optical instrumentation co. exec.; b. N.Y.C., Mar. 23, 1917; s. Norman and Caroline (Fraser) M.; student M.I.T.; m. Helen Vaniman, May 26, 1945; children—Norman, III, Bruce V. Pres., Macbeth Corp., electronic photometers and densitometers, 1936-67; gen. mgr., then pres. Hellige, Inc., 1942-45; sec. Brandywine Fibre Products Co., Inc., 1943-44; chmn. bd. dirs. Kollmorgen Corp., Hartford, Conn., 1967-79; dir. Empire Nat. Bank, 1970-79, vice chmn., chmn. exec. com., 1970-73. Recipient Armin J. Bruning award, Godlove award. Fellow Illuminating Engring. Soc., Optical Soc. Am.; mem. Inter-Soc. Color Council (past treas., dir.), Soc. Motion Picture and TV Engrs., Am. Inst. Physics. Clubs: Metropolitan (N.Y.C.); Crater (Essex, N.Y.); Wee Burn Country (Darien, Conn.). Home: Darien, Conn. Died Mar. 13, 1979.

MACCAFFREY, ISABEL GAMBLE, educator; b. Balt., Aug. 2, 1924; d. Thomas O. and Isabel (Davidson) Gamble; B.A., Swarthmore Coll., 1946; M.A., Radcliffe Coll., 1947, Ph.D., 1954; m. Wallace T. MacCaffrey, June 16, 1956. Faculty, Bryn Mawr Coll., 1949-69, prof. English, 1966-69; prof. English Tufts U., Medford, Mass., 1969-71; William R. Kenan, Jr. prof. history and lit. Harvard, 1971-78. Fulbright scholar Cambridge (Eng.) U., 1950-51; Guggenheim fellow, 1971-72. Mem. MLA, English Inst. (exec. com. 1967-70). Author: Paradise Lost as Myth, 1959; Spencer's Allegory, the Anatomy of Imagination, 1976. Contbr. articles to profl. jours. Home: Acton, Mass. Died May 19, 1978; buried Annapolis, Md.

MACCHESNEY, (ALFRED) BRUNSON, III, lawyer, educator; b. Chgo., May 21, 1909; s. Nathan William and Lena (Frost) MacC.; grad. Hill Sch., 1926; student Univ. World Cruise, 1926-27; B.A. cum laude, Yale, 1931; J.D., U. Mich., 1934 (editor Mich. Law Rev.); postgrad. (fellow) Carnegie Endowment Internat. Peace, 1934; m. Ruth Eastwood, June 5, 1948; children—Bruce Eastwood, Deborah Frost. Admitted to Ill. bar, 1935; instr., tutor, dept. govt. Harvard, 1935-36; asso. prof. law U. Calif. Sch. Jurisprudence, 1936-38; asso. prof. law, Northwestern U., Chgo., 1940-46, prof., from 1946, Williams Meml. prof. law, from 1969, prof. emeritus, to 1978; Fulbright research prof. Cambridge U., adviser Brit. Digest Internat. Law, 1961-62; asso. Sidley, McPherson, Austin & Burgess, Chgo., 1940; occupant chair internat. law U.S. Naval War Coll., 1955-56. Legal sec. SEC commr., Landis, Wash., 1934-35; spl. asst. atty. gen. U.S. Anti-Trust Div., 1938-40; acting chief, wages and hours unit Dept. Justice, Washington, 1939-40; asst. gen. counsel OPA, 1941-43; acting chief, F.E.A., Dakar; chief Procurement and Devel. div. North African Econ. Bd.; rep. for FEA, Algiers, 1943-44; spl. rep. FEA, spl. asst. to ambassador, Paris, 1944-46; spl. cons. U.S. Select (Herter) Com. on Fgn. Aid, 1947; mem. regional loyalty bd., 7th region, 1948-50, loyalty rev. bd., 1950; U.S. rep., claims com. Intergovtl. Study Group for Germany, London, 1950; mem. U.S. Nat. Commn. for UNESCO, 1966-71. Asso. mem. adv. bd. 46th Ward, Chgo. Selective Service. Pres. bd. trustees Library of Internat. Relations, 1950. Commd. ensign USNR, 1931, re-commd., 1940; active duty, 1941. Decorated chevalier Legion of Honor (France), 1946. Mem. Am. (chmn. internat. comparative law sect. 1954-55), Ill., Chgo. bar assns., Am. Soc. Internat. Law (pres. 1964-66, acting editor in chief Am. Jour. Internat. Law 1971-72), Order Coif, Phi Delta Phi, Beta Theta Pi. Democrat. Presbyn. Clubs: Metropolitan (Washington); University, Legal, Law (Chgo.); Yale (N.Y.C.); Onwentsia (Lake Forest, Ill.). Author: International Law Situation and Documents, 1956; Recent Developments in the International Law of the Sea, 1957. Contbr. articles to profl. mag. Home: Lake Forest, Ill. Died Mar. 9, 1978.

MACCORMICK, AUSTIN HARBUTT, penologist; b. Georgetown, Ont., Can., Apr. 20, 1893; s. Rev. Donold and Jean (Green) MacC.; came to U.S., 1893; A.B., Bowdoin Coll., Brunswick, Maine, 1915, hon. Sc.D., 1934; A.M., Columbia, 1916; hon. LL.D., St. Lawrence Univ., Canton, N.Y., 1937; m. Gertrude Albion, Dec. 15, 1917; children—Joan, James A.; m. 2d, Patricia Welling,,Jan. 6, 1936. Instr., Bowdoin College, 1916-17; exec. officer U.S. Naval Prison, Portsmouth, N.H., 1917-21; alumni sec. Bowdoin Coll., 1921-28; asst. to pres. Bennington (Vt.) Coll., 1928-29; asst. dir. U.S. Bur. Prisons, 1929-33; commr. of correction, N.Y.C., 1934-40; exec. dir. The Osborne Assn., Inc., N.Y.C., from 1940; prof. criminology University of California, 1951-60. Cons. Pres.'s Crime Commn., 1966; chief consultant Arkansas Penitentiary Study Commission, 1967. Served in U.S.N.R.F., 1917-21, ensign to lt. senior grade. Mem. bd. dirs. Madison Sq. Boys Club, Children's Village, Wiltwyck Sch. for Boys, City-wide Citizens' Com. on Harlem, mem. exec. com., Nat. Com. for Edn. on Alcoholism. Mem. Social Hygiene Com., N.Y. Tb and Health Assn.; mem. com. on youth and justice, Community Service Soc., mem. Citizens' Com. on Children of N.Y.C. Mem. bd. overseers Bowdoin Coll., Brunswick, Maine. Pres. Am. Prison Assn., 1938-39, Nat. Prisoners' Aid Assn., 1941-42, Am. Assn. Adult Edn. 1943-44, Nat. Conference Juvenile Agencies 1943-44; non-alcoholic trustee Alcoholics Anonymous; chmn. bd. Natural Sci. for Youth Found., Citizen's Com. for Children of N.Y.; mem. Pres.'s Adv. Commn. on Narcotic and Drug Abuse, 1963. Recipient Distinguished Service awards Nat. Council on Crime and Delinquency, 1963, Am. Soc. Criminology, 1963, Correctional Service Fedn., 1964. Mem. Nat. Jail Assn. (exec. bd.), Soc. Prevention of Crime (exec. bd.). Chmn. N.Y. State com. on youth correction authority plan, com. on Mental Hygiene Services in Manhattan Children's Court, Am. Prison Assn. Com. on Postwar Planning, chmn. bd. consultants to under-sec. of war on mil. prisons; vice chmn. under-sec. of war's adv. bd. on clemency. Chmn. Cal. Study Commn. Correctional Facilities and Services, 1955-57; chmn. No. Sect. Atty. Gen.'s (Cal.) Com. Crime Prevention, 1955-58; dir. Nat. Council on Alcoholism, former president. Member Citizens Union (executive board). Research Council on Problems of Alcohol (exec. com.), Delta Upsilon, Phi Beta Kappa. Conglist. Author: Handbook of American Prisons (with Paul W. Garrett), 1926; Handbook of American Prisons and Reformatories (with Paul W. Garrett), 1929; The Education of Adult Prisoners, 1931. Editor: Handbook of American Institutions for Delinquent Juveniles, 1943. Consultant to sec. of war, from 1942; chmn. war dept. adv. bd. on parole. Mem. sec. of Navy's adv. com. on confinement policies, 1948. Received war dept. exceptional civilian service award, 1945; medal for merit, 1947. Contbr. articles to handbooks and jours. Home: New York, N.Y. Died Oct. 24, 1979.

MACCRATE, JOHN, jurist; b. Mar. 29, 1885; prep. edn. Commercial High Sch., Brooklyn; LL.B., New York U., 1906; m. Flora Mae Nicholl, Nov. 23, 1911. Practiced in N.Y. City since 1906; endorsed by both Dem. and Rep. primaries and elected mem. 66th Congress (1919-21), 3d N.Y. Dist.; became justice Supreme Court of N.Y., 2d Dist., 1920. Home: Brooklyn, N.Y. Died June 9, 1976.

MACCREAGH, GORDON (MAK-KRA'), explorer, author; b. Perth, Ind., Aug. 8, 1886; s. George MacCreagh; ed. pub. schs., Perth, also Aldenham and Glenalmond, Scotland; student at Hanover and U. of Göttingen,Germany; m. Helen Komlosy, June 1923. Engaged in explorations in Borneo, South America and Africa most of time since 1905; two explorations in Abyssinia, 1927-29. Served in United States Air Force, World War I; Special Service (overseas), 1943. Member of American Society Mammalogists. Created Chevalier Star of Ethiopia by Haille Selassie (emperor). Clubs: Explorers', Ends of the Earth. Author: Big Game in the Shan States, 1909; White Waters and Black. 1926; The Last of Free Africa, 1928. Lecturer on Ethiopian and Mexican affairs. Address: St. Petersburg, Fla. *

MACDONALD, D(ELOSS) K(ENT), ins. broker; b. Victoria, B.C., Can., Apr. 28, 1886 (parents U.S. citizens); s. Joseph Edgar and Elizabeth Virginia (Crosley) MacD.; student pub. schs.; m. Elise Curtis, Mar. 26, 1913; children—Gregg Crosley, Janet W. (Mrs. Chester Paulson). With Seattle-First Nat. Bank, 1901-08; with Carter, MacDonald & Co., 1908-45, with D. K. MacDonald & Co., 1945-65, chmn. bd., 1954-65; cons. Marsh & McLennan-D. K. MacDonald & Co., Inc.; partner Yates, Wood & MacDonald, property mgmt.; dir. Smith-Berger Mfg. Corp., Pioneer Sand & Gravel, Puget Sound Power & Light. West Coast Airlines, Washington Title Ins. Co., United Pacific, Equity Fund. Regent, Seattle U. Pres. United Good Neighbor Fund; adv. bd. Children's Orthopedic Hosp., Seattle Municipal League. Mem. Am. Automobile ASSN. (v.p.), Auto Club of Wash. (pres.), C. of C. (pres. 1942-43). Clubs: Rainier, Overlake Golf, Seattle Golf (pres. 1946-47), Wash. Athletic (pres. 1938), Rotary (pres. 1926-27). Home: Bellevue, Wash. *

MAC DONALD, DANIEL JOSEPH, Can. govt. ofcl.; b. Bothwell, P.E.I., Can., July 23, 1918; s. Daniel Lauchlin and Elizabeth Margaret (Fisher) MacD.; student Bothwell schs.; m. Pauline Peters, Nov. 13, 1946; children—Blair, Heather, Gail, Daniel, Leo, Walter, Gloria. Engaged in farming, Bothwell, 1938-40, 45-80; pres. local Coop. Assn., 1955-60; mem. Legis. Assembly for First Kings, 1962-72; minister of agr. and forestry, 1966-72; mem. Parliament for Cardigan, 1972-80; minister vets. affairs, 1972-80. Mem. South Lake Sch. Bd., 1960's. Served with Can. Army, 1940-45; Italy. Recipient Confedn. Centennial medal, 1973; hon. col. P.E.I. Regt. Mem. War Amputations Can., Royal Can. Legion (past br. pres.). Liberal. Roman Catholic. Clubs: Lions, K.C. Home: Bothwell, P.E.I., Canada. Died Sept. 30, 1980.

MACDONALD, GORDON ANDREW, educator, geologist; b. Boston, Oct. 15, 1911; s. John A. and Grace B. (Griffin) M.; B.S., U. Calif. at Los Angeles, 1933, M.A., 1934, Ph.D., at Berkeley, 1938; m. Ruth Carol Binkley, May 22, 1938; children—John Alan, James Gordon, Duncan Edwin, William Andrew; m. 2d, Virginia S. Brooks, Dec. 27, 1975. Asst. geologist Shell Oil Co., 1938-39; from asst. geologist to geologist U.S. Geol. Survey, 1939-47, geologist, 1948-58; asst. prof. U. So. Calif., 1947-48; sr. prof. geology U. Hawaii, 1958-77, emeritus, 1977-78; dir. Hawaiian Volcano Obs., 1951-56. Bd. dirs. Hawaii chpt. ARC, 1958-60. Fellow Geol. Soc. Am., AAAS, Mineral Soc. Am.; mem. Am. Geophys. Union, Internat. Volcanological Assn. (pres. 1967-71). Home: Volcano, Hawaii. Died June 20, 1978; cremated, ashes interred, Mauna Loa, Hawaii.

MACDONALD, H. E., corp. exec.; b. Brockton, Mass., Sept. 29, 1901; s. Charles Edward and Georgiana (Wilcox) M.; m. Marian Bliven, Feb. 22, 1929 (dec.); 1 son, Raymond (dec.); m. 2d, Bernice Agnes Woodword, May 21, 1969. Trainee, W.T. Grant Co., Waterbury, Conn., 1922-24; store mgr. Lincoln Stores, Inc., Norwich, Conn., 1924-33; asst. regional mgr. Montgomery Ward & Co., Chgo., 1933-38, v.p., sales mgr. 1938; v.p. Schenley Distillers Corp., 1944-48; pres., chief exec. officer, dir. Household Finance Corp., 1951-67, chmn. bd., 1966-67, chief exec. officer, 1967-71, chmn. bd., 1967-72; dir. Household Finance Corp. Mem. Alumnus Mass. Inst. Tech. Republican. Episcopalian. Clubs: Skokie Country (Glencoe, Ill.); Chicago. Home: Boca Raton, Fla. Died Jan. 8, 1981.

MACDONALD, JOHN WINCHESTER, educator, lawyer; b. Albany, N.Y., Mar. 29, 1905; s. John Winchester and Catherine C. (Burns) M.; A.B., A.M., J.D., Cornell U., 1921-26; grad. Army Indsl. Coll. (indsl. reconversion), 1944; LL.D., Canisius Coll., 1959; m. Mary Elizabeth Brown, Sept. 26, 1927; children—John Winchester, Mary (Mrs. O'Connell; dec.), Catherine (Mrs. Wigsten), Virginia (Mrs. Lindseth), Rita. Admitted N.Y. bar, 1926; asso. Hun Parker & Reilly, Albany, N.Y., 1926-27; clk. court of claims, State of N.Y., 1927-30; asst. prof. law, Cornell U., 1930-35, sec. Cornell Law Sch., 1932-35, prof. law, 1935-73, Edwin H. Woodruff prof. law, 1960-73, emeritus, 1973-81, acting prof. govt., 1951, faculty rep. bd. trustees, 1951-55, chmn. adminstrv. com., 1954-56; vis. prof. law Columbia, 1947, 52, N.Y. U., 1957; lectr. St. Lawrence U. Inst. Crime and Delinquency, 1951-58; gen. counsel, dir. Therm, Inc.; dir. other corps.; staff gen. counsel Asso. Gas & Electric Corp. in reorgn. 1942; spl. asst. U.S. Atty. Gen., 1942; dir. N.Y. Legislative Service, Inc. Research asso. N.Y. Commn. on Adminstrn. of Justice, 1932-33; exec. sec., dir. N.Y. State Law Revision Commn., 1934-56, commr., 1956-81, chmn., 1958-73; del. N.Y. Constl. Conv., 1967, dir. com. on style and arrangement; vis. prof. St. Johns U., 1959; bd. visitors, Elmira (N.Y.) State Reformatory, 1942-47; del. from Cornell U. to N.Y. Joint Conf. on Legal Edn. Mem. Cornell Law Assn. (sec. 1932-35). Mem. Am. Acad. Polit. Sci., Scribes, Am. Judicature Soc., Am., N.Y. State, Tompkins County bar assns., Assn. Bar City N.Y., Am. Law Inst. (permanent editorial bd. uniform comml. code), Am. Assn. U. Profs., Cath. Commn. Intellectual and Cultural Affairs, John Henry Newman Soc., Phi Beta Kappa, Delta Sigma Rho, Order of the Coif. Democrat. K.C. (4 deg.). Roman Catholic. Clubs: Cornell (New York); Country; Yacht (Ithaca). Editor: vols. 1 and 2, N.Y. State Constitutional Convention Committee Reports, 1938 (with Horace E. Read) Cases and Materials on Legislation, 1947; (with Horace Read and Jefferson B. Fordham) Cases and Materials on Legislation 2d edit., 1959, 3d edit. (with Read, Fordham and Pierce), 1973; (with Horace E. Read, Jefferson B. Fordham, William J. Pierce) Material on Legislation, 3d Edit., 1973. Reports, Recommendations and Studies New York Law Revision Commission since 1934-81. Co-editor (with Robert S. Stevens, Arthur E. Sutherland and Harrop Freeman) Materials on Introduction to Study of Law. Contbr. articles to profl. jours. Home: Ithaca, N.Y. Died Mar. 14, 1981.

MACDONALD, LILLIAS MARGARET, educator; b. Buffalo, Nov. 25, 1885; d. John and Lillian (MacKenzie) M.; B.A., Oberlin Coll., 1908; certificate phys. edn. Oberlin, 1908; Phys. dir. Y.W.C.A., Scranton, Pa., 1908-09; supervisor phys. edn. Buffalo (N.Y.) Pub. Schs., 1909-14; playground dir. Buffalo, 1908-12; dir. phys. edn. women Masten Park High Sch., Buffalo, 1914-22; dir. Lake George (N.Y.) Camp. Gen. Electric Co. Women Employees, 1917-22; dean women, asst. prof. hygiene U. of Buffalo since 1922. Mem. Nat. Assn. Deans Women, Am. Assn. U. Women, N.Y. Assn. Deans, N.E.A., Buffalo Pub. Library Assn., Albright Art Gallery, League Women Voters, Pi Lambda Theta. Republican. Presbyn. Home: Buffalo. *

MACDONALD, MALCOLM JOHN, privy councillor, govt. ofcl. United Kingdom; b. Lossiemouth, Scotland, Aug. 17, 1901; s. James Ramsay and Margaret

(Gladstone) MacD.; M.A., Queen's Coll., Oxford; LL.D., Litt.D. (hon.), U. Malaya, U. Hanoi, Hongking U., and various North Am. universities; m. Audrey Fellowes Rowley, 1946; 1 dau., Fiona. Mem. London County Council, 1927-30; Labour mem. Parliament, Bassetlaw Div. Nottinghamshire, 1929-31, Nat. Labour mem., 1931-35, Nat. Govt. mem., Ross and Cromarty, 1936-45; parliamentary under-sec. Dominions Office, 1931-35, sec. state for dominion affairs, 1935-38, 38-39, sec. state for colonies, 1935, 38-40, minister health, 1940-41; United Kingdom high commr. Can., 1941-46; gov.-gen. Malayan Union, also Singapore, 1946; gov. gen. of Malaya and Brit. Borneo, 1946-48; commr.-gen. for United Kingdom in South East Asia, 1948-55; high commr. in India, 1955-60; leader British delegation, co-chmn. Internat. Conf. on Laos, 1961-63; gov. Kenya, 1963-64, gov.-gen., Kenya, 1964-65; high commr. in Kenya, 1965-66; Brit. spl. rep. East and Central Africa, 1966-67, spl. rep. in Africa, 1967-69; spl. envoy Sudan, Somalia, 1967. Vis. U. Coll. in Nairobi, Kenya, 1963-64. Rhodes trustee, 1948; special ambassador at the inauguration of Indonesian Republic, 1949; chancellor U. Malaya, 1949-60. Author: Down North, 1945; The Birds of Brewery Creek, 1947; Borneo People, 1956; Angkor, 1958; Birds in My Indian Garden, 1961; Birds in Sun, 1962; Treasure of Kenya, 1965; People and Places, 1969. Address: Kent, England. Died Jan. 11, 1981.

MACDONALD, TORBERT HART, congressman; b. Boston, June 6, 1917; s. John G. and Harriett (Hart) M.; A.B., Harvard, 1940, LL.B., 1946; m. Phyllis Brooks, June 1944; children—Torbert Hart, Laurie, Brian, Robin. Admitted to Mass. bar, 1946; legal asst. Eric Johnston Motion Picture Producers Assn., 1946-47; trial atty. New Eng. NLRB, 1948-52; mem. 84th to 87th congresses from 8th Mass. Dist., 88th-94th Congresses from 7th Mass. Dist. Served as lt. (j.g.) USNR, 1942-44, comdr. PT boat. Decorated Silver Star, Presdl. Citation. Mem. Fed., Mass., Middlesex County bar assns. Capt. Harvard Football Team, 1939, All Eastern Selection Football, 1939. Home: Malden, Mass. Died May 21, 1976.

MACDONALD, WILLIAM ROSS, Canadian provincial govt. ofcl.; b. Toronto, Ont., Can., Dec. 25, 1891; s. George and Julia (Bulley) M.; B.A., U. Toronto; LL.B., Osgoode Hall; LL.D., McMaster U. Waterloo Luth. U.; m. Muriel Whitaker, June 15, 1921 (dec.); children—Esther (Mrs. John Marshall), Muriel (Mrs. Douglas Haldenby). Pvt. practice law, Simcoe, Ont.; successively crown atty. County of Norfolk, mem. firm Macdonald, Brown, Binkley, McIntosh & Daboll, Brantford, Ont.; chancellor Waterloo Luth. U., from 1964; lt. gov. Province of Ont., Toronto, 1968-74. Former gen. counsel Canadian Order Foresters; solicitor gen. of Canada, 1954-57. Mem. Canadian House of Commons, 1935-53, speaker, 1949-53; mem. Canadian Senate, 1953-67; del. UN Assembly, 1960. NATO Paliamentary Assn., Paris, 1962. Served as lt. inf. Canadian Army, World War I. Created Kings' Counsel, 1934. Mem. Royal Canadian Legion (past pres. Brantford br.), Nat. Council Women (hon. life). Liberal. Mem. United Ch. of Can. Mason, Kiwanian (past pres.). Ofcl. Canadian rep. to Coronation of Queen Elizabeth II, 1953. Home: Brantford, Ont., Canada. Died May 28, 1976; interred Farringdon Burial Ground, Brantford.

MACDONELL, JAMES DONALD, ins. co. exec.; b. Westboro, Wis., 1903; s. Alexander and Sarah Bella (McDonald) M.; A.B., M.A., LL.B., U. Wash.; m. Ellen Miller, Dec. 9, 1933; 1 dau., Leslie. Admitted to Wash. bar, 1930; practice law, Seattle, Tacoma, 1930-35; with Employers Reins. Corp., San Francisco, 1940-68, v.p., dir., 1955-68. Mem. Calif., San Francisco chambers commerce, Fedn. Ins. Counsel, Am. Judiciary Soc., Delta Upsilon, Phi Alpha Delta. Clubs: College (Seattle); San Francisco Commercial; Jonathan (Los Angeles). Home: Atherton, Calif. Died July 30, 1979.

MACDOUGALL, MARY STUART, biologist; b. Laurinburg, N.C., Nov. 7, 1885; d. James and Sarah (Williams) MacDougall; A.B., Randolph-Macon Coll., 1912; M.S., U. of Chicago, 1917; Ph.D., Columbia U., 1925; ScD., Université de Montpellier, 1935. Research and instr. in protozoology, Marine Biol. Lab., Woods Hole, Mass., 14 summers; prof. zoology and head dept. biology, Agnes Scott Coll., 1920-52, ret.; research asso. Johns Hopkins Sch. Hygiene and Pub. Health, 1927; research Kaiser Wilhelm Inst., 1931, Coll. de France and U. of Montpellier, 1932 and summers 1932-35. Pres. Southeastern Biologists, 1942. Mem. Am. Soc. Zoologists, A.A.A.S., Georgia Acad. Sciences (pres. 1927), Phi Beta Kappa, Sigma Xi. Guggenheim fellow for study abroad, 1931-32. Author: Biology, The Science of Life, 1943; also 16 articles on cytology and genetics of Protozoa and Malaria published in jours. Address: Decatur, Ga. *

MACDOWELL, NOAH, company dir.; b. Paterson, N.J., Nov. 26, 1884; s. Noah and Anetta (Hopper) MacD.; m. Christine Sawyer Taylor, Apr. 21, 1914; children—Noah III (dec.), Annetta (Mrs. John P. McDonnell), Noah. Dir. W. F. Hall Printing Co., Chgo., North River Ins. Co., Am. Equitable Assurance Co. Address: Old Lyme, Conn. *

MACGILL, CHARLES FREDERICK, educator; b. Keeseville, N.Y., Feb. 11, 1886; s. Charles Frederick and Charlotte Emily (Keeler) MacG., student Union Coll., Schenectady, N.Y., 1907-10; A.B., U. of Minn. 1911; student Harvard, 1912-15; m. Helen Fay Jewett, of Newton, Mass., June 29, 1922; children—Charles Frederick, Elizabeth Fay. Asst. trust officer Exchange Trust Co., Boston, 1915-20; trust officer Mass. Trust Co., Boston, 1920-26; treas. Mount Ida Sch., 1926-27; prin. Mount Ida Sch., Newton, since 1927. Mem. Alpha Delta Phi. Episcopalian. Clubs: Alpha Delta Phi, Charles River Country. Home: Newton, Mass. *

MAC GOVERN, STAN(LEY RAYMOND EUGENE), cartoonist; b. N.Y.C., May 4, 1903; s. James Archibald and Olive Ida Katherine (Lake) MacG.; grad. Lynbrook (L.I.) High Sch., 1919; m. Olive Constance Irwin, July 1, 1929; 1 son, Terry Archer. Staff artist N.Y. Herald, from 1920, N.Y. Sun, from 1922, Phila. Ledger, from 1924, N.Y. Post, from 1927; art dir. N.Y. Post Home News, also polit. cartoonist; free lance cartoonist for mags.; creator of comic strip Silly Milly, 1939; pres. Stan Mac Govern for Gifts, from 1950. Mem. Nat. Cartoonists Soc. Home: Malverne, N.Y. Died Aug. 1975.

MACHADO, LUIS, diplomat; b. Guanabacoa, Cuba, Sept. 25, 1899; s. Luis and Maria L. (Ortega) M.; student Candler Coll., Havana, Cuba, 1916; A.B., Inst. Havana, 1917; degree civil law, U. Havana, 1920, degree pub. law, 1922; m. Genoveva Silva y Murray, Feb. 7, 1925; children—Irene (Mrs. Julio Castellanos), Elena (Mrs. Andreas F. Lowenfeld), Natalia (Mrs. Agustin Maruri). Admitted to Bar of Cuba; practiced in Havana; mem. law firm Nunez Mesa y Machado; exec. dir. Internat. Bank for Reconstrn. and Devel., 1946-48, gov. for Cuba, 1949; pres. Econ. Commn. for Latin Am., 1949; Cuban ambassador to U.S.A., 1950-52, exec. dir. Internat. Bank of Reconstrn. and Devel., Internat. Finance Corp., Internat. Devel. Assn., 1953-70, representing Mexico, Peru, Nicaragua, Venezuela, Haiti, Costa Rica, Guatemala, El Salvador, Honduras and Panama. Mem. Cuban delegation to Peace Conf., Versailles, 1919; Cuban del. to Financial and Monetary Conf., Bretton Woods, 1944, Internat.-Am. Conf. on Problems of War and Peace, Chapultepec, Mexico, 1945, 3d Internat. Conf. on Radio Communications, Rio de Janeiro, 1945, Conf. on Trade and Employment, Havana, 1948, Japanese Peace Conf., San Francisco, 1951. Pres. Good Neighbor Found., 1936. Decorated comdr. Order of Merit, Chile, 1938; Order of El Sol del Peru, 1945; Great Cross, Carlos Manuel de Cespedes, Cuba, 1950; Great Cross of Quetzal, Guatemala, 1962; Order of Balboa, Republic Panama, 1963. Mem. Nat. Mfrs. Assn. Cuba (pres. 1941-45), Nat. Tourist Commn. (pres. 1937-39), Geog. Soc. Cuba, Cuban Inst. Internat. Law, Bar Assn. Havana (mem. governing bd. 1936). Rotarian. Clubs: Country of Havana, Miramar Yacht, Havana Yacht, Vedado Tennis, Union, Havana Biltmore Yacht and Country, International Nautical, American, British, Ateneo (Havana); Lawyers, Metropolitan (N.Y.C.); Chevy Chase Country, Burning Tree, Metropolitan (Washington). Author: The Platt Amendment, 1922; International Legislation of the Air, 1923; Necessity for the Adoption of a Policy on Foreign Trade, 1929; Cuba, the Cork Island, Essay on Cuban Economy, 1936; Cuban Fiscal Index, 1944. Home: Washington, D.C. Died Feb. 5, 1979.

MACHLIS, LEONARD, plant physiologist, educator; b. Seattle, Apr. 13, 1915; s. Samuel and Beatrice (Lapiroff) M.; B.S., State Coll., Wash., 1937; M.S., U. Hawaii, 1939; Ph.D., U. Calif., Berkeley, 1943; m. Gertrude Therese Rafferty, June 28, 1946; children—Lee Ellen, Joan Louise, Paul Laurence, Gail Elizabeth. Instr., U. Ill., 1945-46; faculty U. Calif., Berkeley, 1946-76, prof. botany, 1959-76, chmn. dept., 1961-67, acting chmn., 1973, chmn., 1974-76, Miller research prof., 1959-61, 67-68, asst. chancellor ednl. devel., 1968-70. Guggenheim fellow U. Upsalla (Sweden), 1957-58. Mem. Am. Soc. Plant Physiologists. Scandinavian Soc. Plant Physiology, Bot. Soc. Am., Phi Beta Kappa. Author: (with John G. Torrey) Plants in Action, 1956. Asso. editor Ann. Rev. Plant Physiology, 1950-58, editor, 1959-72. Contbr. articles to profl. jours. Home: Berkeley, Calif. Died Mar. 23, 1976.

MACHUM, WALDO CARSON (MA-KUM), clergyman; b. Saint Mary's N.B., Can., Dec. 20, 1885; s. John Carson and Sarah Elizabeth (Hamilton) M.; A.B., Univ. of N.B. Fedn., 1907; grad. Colgate Theol. Sem., Hamilton, N.Y., 1910; D.D., Acadia Univ., Wolfville, N.S., Can., 1946; m. Julia Elizabeth Bailey, June 26, 1912. Ordained to the ministry of the Baptist Ch., 1910; minister Hantsport, N.S., Can., 1911-15, Port Maitland, N.S., 1915-19, Kentville, N.S., 1931-43; field sec. Bd. of Religious Edn. Maritime United Baptist Conv., 1919-24; gen. and boys' work sec. Maritime Religious Edn. Council, 1924-30, chmn. Maritime Boys' Work Bd. since 1932, chamn. Nat. Boys' Work Bd., 1935, 1942-43; pres. Maritime United Baptist Conv., 1936; mem. Baptist Pub. Com. of Can. since 1937; gen. sec. Maritime United Baptist Conv. since 1943; sec. Baptist Fedn. of Can. since 1944. Mem. Can. Council of Chs. (mem. exec. com. since 1944), Acadia Univ Senate. Independent. Home: Kentville, N.S. *

MACIVER, ROBERT MORRISON (MAK-KE'VER), sociology; b. Stornoway, Scotland, Apr. 17, 1882; s. Donald and Christine (Morrison) MacI.; M.A., Edinburgh U., 1903, D.Ph., 1915. LL.D., 1952; B.A., Oxford U., 1907; Litt.D., Columbia U., 1929. Harvard, 1936. Princeton, 1947; Jewish Theol. Sem. Am., 1950; D.Sc., New Sch., 1950; L.H.D., Yale, 1951; LL.D. (honorary), University of Toronto, 1957; married Ethel Marion Peterkin, Aug. 14, 1911; children—Ian Tennant Morrison, Christine Elizabeth, Donald Gordon. Lecturer on polit. science, Aberdeen U., 1907, on sociology, 1911; prof. polit. science, U. of Toronto, 1915-22, head dept. polit. science, 1922-27; prof. social science, Barnard Coll. (Columbia), 1927-36. Lieber professor political philosophy and sociology, Columbia U., 1929-50; dir. City of N.Y. Juvenile Delinquency Evaluation Project, 1956-61; president of New School for Social Research, 1963-65, chancellor, 1965-66; vice chairman of the Can. War Labor Bd., 1917-18. Fellow Royal Society Can., World, Am. acads. Arts and Scis., Am. Philosophical Society; member of American Sociol. Soc., British Academy (corresponding member), Inst. Internationale de Sociologie, Phi Beta Kappa. Author: Community—A Sociological Study, 1917; Labor in the Changing World, 1919; Elements of Social Science, 1921; The Modern State, 1926; Relation of Sociology to Social Work, 1931; Society—Its Structure and Changes, 1931; Economic Reconstruction, 1934; Society—A Textbook of Sociology, 1937; Leviathan and the People, 1939. Social Causation. 1942, Toward an Abiding Peace, 1943; The Web of Government, 1947; The More Perfect Union, 1949; The Ramparts We Guard, 1950; Democracy and the Economic Challenge, 1952; Academic Freedom in Our Time, 1955; The Pursuit of Happiness, 1955; Life: Its Dimensions and Its Bounds, 1960; The Challenge of the Passing Years, 1962; Power Transforms, 1964; The Prevention and Control of Delinquency, 1966; (autobiography) As a Tale that Is Told, 1968. Home: Palisades, N.Y. *

MACK, CLIFTON EUGENE, educator; b. Lynn, Mass., June 4, 1898; s. John Eugene and Margaret Elizabeth (Fuller) M.; LL.B., Suffolk Law Sch., 1927; L.H.D. (hon.), Denison U., 1964; m. Louise Upton, June 14, 1924; children—Lucia, Leslie; m. 2d, Emma Gholston; 1 son, Clifton Dabney. Salesman, sales mgr. Am. Woolen Co. and Payne & Stillman, 1920-27; admitted to Me. bar, 1929; spl. agt. IRS, 1927-40; commr. fed. supply service GSA, 1940-58; prof. Ohio State U. Coll. Adminstrv. Sci., 1958-69, prof. emeritus, 1969-78; pres. Profl. and Tech. Ednl. Services, 1969-78; adj. prof. Am. U. Sch. Pub. Affairs and Social Sci. sr. cons. UN. Mem. Pres.'s Soviet Protocol Com.; chmn. Fed. Supply Bd. Mem. com. on purchases Blindmade Products, 1940-49; vice chmn. Presdl. Com. on Purchases of Blind Made Products. Trustee Eastern Bapt. Coll. and Sem. Served as aviator, U.S. Army, 1918-19. Recipient Presdl. Citation and Medal for Merit, 1947; Eccles medal. Fellow Soc. Logistics Engrs.; mem. Aviators' Post, Am. Legion, English Speaking Union, Daedalians, Pi Sigma Alpha. Baptist (nat. pres. Am. Bapt. Men 1962-63, mem. exec. com. gen. council Am. Bapt. Conv.). Clubs: Washington Athletic, National Press (Washington); Beaumont, Congressional Country, World Economic Soc. (N.Y.C.). Author: Federal Procurement, 1943. Cons. editor: McGraw-Hill Book Co. Address: Dayton, Ohio. Died Dec. 2, 1978.

MACK, TED, radio, TV entertainer; b. Greeley, Colo., Feb. 12, 1904; s. John Peter and Ivy (Broach) Maguiness; student Sacred Heart High Sch., U. Denver, 1924; m. Marguerite Overholt, Mar. 27, 1926. Joined Ben Pollock's Orch., 1926-27; master of ceremonies introducing acts Los Angeles vaudeville theatre, 1927-28; toured U.S. and Can. with own band, 1928-35; musical condr. Metro-Goldwyn-Mayer movies, 1935; chief talent scout Maj. Bowes Original Amateur Hour, 1935-46; succeeded Bowes in presiding over Original Amateur Hour program, in both radio and TV, 1948; re-established Family Hour radio-TV, 1950; conducted Great Ted Mack Talent Search in colls. and univs. U.S., 1973-75; staged charity broadcast spectacles throughout U.S., also shows for U.S. Armed Forces in Europe, Korea, from 1948; pub. speaker; established Ted Mack Found. for Young Ams., Ted Mack TV Awards, 1973, also Co-ed Children's Camp at Great Barrington, Mass., Ann. Ted Mack Award of Excellence, 1967. Recipient numerous awards. Mem. Internat. Platform Assn. (pres.), Sigma Phi Epsilon. Home: Westchester County, N.Y. Died July 12, 1976.

MACKALL, COLIN MACKENZIE (MAK'AL). prof. chemistry; b. Baltimore, Md., Dec. 26, 1884; s. Charles and Eliza Bowie (Mackenzie) M.; grad. Baltimore City Coll., 1904; B.A., U. of Va., 1909, B.S. in Chemistry, 1910; M S., George Washington U., 1913; Ph.D., Johns Hopkins, 1920; studied in Universities of Paris, Strasbourg, Toulouse and College of France; 1 daughter, Marie-Antoinette Caussia de Manvoisin. Assistant in chemistry, University of Va., 1907-09; asst. chemist, Bur. of Chemistry, Dept. of Agr., 1910-11; prof. chemistry, U. of the South, 1911-16; chemist Edgewood Arsenal, 1922-23, summer 1924; prof. chemistry, St. John's Coll., Annapolis, Md., 1923-25; prof. chemistry, George Washington U., 1925-50, emeritus; vis. prof. chemistry U. of N.C., summer 1937; visiting prof.

chemistry, U. of Southern Calif., summer, 1938. University fellow Johns Hopkins, 1919-20; Am. field service fellow in French univs., 1920-22. Capt. Coast Arty. Corps, U.S. Army, 1917; capt. and maj. Chem. Warfare Service, 1918, then maj. C.W.S. Res. Served with Batt. A Trench Mortars, AEF, as asst. gas officer 1st Corps, A.E.F., then gas officer 2d Div., AEF., and as asst. chief and chief of CW.S., 2d Army, Am. Expeditionary Force, 1918. Mem. Am. Chemical Society, Delta Tau Delta, Gamma Alpha, Alpha Chi Sigma, Phi Beta Kappa, Sigma Xi. Episcopalian. Home: Washington DC. *

MACKALL, HENRY CLINTON, lawyer; b. Moorhead, Minn., Feb. 18, 1885; s. Benjamin Franklin and Mary Wright (Kurtz) M.; student Moorhead State Tchrs. Coll., 1902; A.B., U. Minn., 1906; LL.B., Harvard, 1909; m. Louise C. Jamison, May 10, 1916 (dec. 1945); children—Nancy Lou (dec.), Henry C. (dec.); m. 2d, Margaret Robertson, Apr. 22, 1947. Admitted to Minn. bar, 1909, since practiced in Mpls.; sr. mem. Mackall, Crounse & Moore; dir. Day Devel. Co., Retailings, Inc., Stockpiles, Inc., Nat. Realty Co., Princeton State Bank. Minn. Rep. Nat. Commn. on Uniform Laws, 1931-37; chmn. Am. Bar Center Drive for Minn.; charter mem. World Peace through Law Center. Hon. trustee St. Mary's Hall, Faribault, Wells Meml.; trustee Mpls. Found., 1935-73, Minn. State Bar Found.; chmn. bd. trustees U. Minn. Found., 1962-65, treas., 1965-69, trustee, from 1962, hon. life mem. bd., 1975-79. Recipient Outstanding Achievement award U. Minn., 1965; Distinguished Alumnus award Moorhead State Coll. Served as capt. 4th Minn. Inf., 1917-20. Fellow Am. Bar Found. (life mem.); mem. Am., Minn., Mpls. mycol. socs., Am. Law Inst. Am. (asso. editor jour. 1965-66), Minn. (SE counsel), Hennepin County bar assns., U.S. (exec. com. 1927-30), Western (dir. 1925-32), Trans Miss. (dir. 1921-37, pres. 1928-32) golf assns., Am. Philatelic Soc., Hennepin County Hist. Soc. (trustee, life mem.), Nat. Planning Assn., Am. Judicature Soc., Scabbard and Blade, Delta Chi, Sigma Alpha Epsilon. Episcopalian. (chancellor N.W. province 1951-66). Clubs: Minneapolis (pres. 1941, life mem.), Minikahda (pres. 1924, hon. life gov.); U. Minn. Alumni. Home: Minneapolis, Minn. Died Oct. 5, 1979.

MACKAY, ALBERT GEORGE, med. educator; b. Peacham, Vt., Oct. 5, 1907; s. Albert James and Mary C. (Blair) M.; B.S., U. Vt., 1929, M.D., 1932; postgrad. U. Chgo., 1942; m. Lois Elizabeth Fisk, Jan. 20, 1932; children—Alan Blair, Carol Ann (Mrs. Leonard M. Beams), Margaret Louise (Mrs. Raymond W. Trombley). Intern Mary Fletcher Hosp., 1932-33, resident, 1933-35; resident Boston City Hosp., 1937-39; practice medicine, specializing in surgery, Burlington, Vt., 1939-78; prof. surgery U. Vt., 1942-78, attending surgeon Med. Center Hosp., 1941-78, past chmn. dept. surgery. Vice pres., trustee Farmers Trust Co., Burlington; dir. Wizard Corp., Burlington. Bd. dirs. United Community Services of Chittenden County. Served to capt., Med. Res. Corps, U.S. Army, 1939-46. Fellow A.C.S. (past gov.); mem. New Eng. (past pres.), Internat. surg. socs., Soc. for Surgery Alimentary Tract, Am. Geriatric Soc., Am., Internat. broncho-esophagological assns., AMA, Vt. Med. Soc. (Distinguished Service award 1969). Mason (32 deg.), Rotarian. Contbr. articles to profl. jours. Home: Burlington, Vt. Died Apr. 27, 1978.

MACKENZIE, COMPTON, author; b. West Hartlepool, Jan. 17, 1883; ed. St. Pauls Sch.; B.A., Magdalen Coll., Oxford; LL.D., U. of Glasgow, 1932; m. Faith Stone, 1905. Rector Glasgow U., 1931-34; literary critic London Daily Mail, 1931-35. Pres. Dickens Fellowship, 1939-46; editor of the Gramophone since 1923. Fellow Royal Soc. Literature. Decorated Order of the British Empire. Author: The Passionate Elopement, 1911; Carnival, 1912; Sinister Street, 1913; Plashers Mead, 1915; Sylvia Scarlett, 1918; Vestal Fire, 1927; Extraordinary Women, 1928; Gallipoli Memories, 1929; For Sale, 1931; Santa Claus in Summer, 1931; Our Street, 1932; Prince Charlie, 1932; Water on the Brain, 1933; Darkening Green, 1934; Literature of My Time, 1934; Prince Charlie and His Ladies, 1935; Catholicism and Scotland, 1936; Figure of Eight, 1937; The Four Winds of Love, published in several books between 1937 and 1943; Windsor Tapestry, 1938; Wings of Freedom, 1943; Mr. Roosevelt, 1944; Dr. Benes, 1945; also numerous other books. Address: Wantage, Berks, Eng. *

MACKENZIE, HAROLD ORVILLE, diplomatic service; b. Trenton, N.J., Apr. 21, 1886; s. Thomas H. (M.D.) and Helen Gray (Buchanan) M.; grad. Lawrenceville (N.J.) Sch., 1904; Ph.B., Sheffield Scientific Sch. (Yale), 1907; grad. study Paris, Munich, Bavaria, Germany; unmarried. Formerly in mfg. business, N.J., public utility service work, Calif., also ranching and fruit growing, Tulare Co., 1914-20; E. E. and M. P. to Siam since Mar. 17, 1927. Mem. Phi Kappa Psi. Republican. Clubs: Yale (New York); Metropolitan (Washington). Address: U.S. Legation, Bangkok, Siam.

MAC KENZIE, OSSIAN, ednl. cons.; b. Hampden, Me., July 26, 1907; s. L. Robert and Evangeline Marion (Taylor) MacK.; B.A., U. Mont., 1928; postgrad. Harvard, 1928-31; J.D., Fordham U., 1938; LL.D., Rider Coll., 1962; m. Kyle Habberton, June 16, 1934; 1 dau., Robin (Mrs. Lucien E. Ferster). Estate supr. Guaranty Trust Co. of N.Y., 1931-39; admitted to N.Y. bar, 1938; head state and local tax dept. Allied Chem. & Dye Corp., N.Y.C., 1939-43; head tax dept. West Penn Electric Co., N.Y.C., 1946-47; univ. devel. officer Columbia, 1947-50; asst. dean Grad. Sch. Bus., asst. to exec. dir. Am. Assembly, 1950-53; dean Coll. Bus. Adminstrn., Pa. State U., 1953-73, asst. to pres., 1956-57, v.p., 1957-58, ednl. cons., 1977-80, prof. mgmt., chmn. dept. bus and econs. Rutgers U., Camden, N.J., 1973-77. Cons., Dept. of State, 1955-57, U. Costa Rica, 1964-65, Dept. of Health, Edn. and Welfare, 1967, Comptroller Gen. U.S., 1968-74, Ala. A. and M. U., 1968-80, Esan U., Lima, Peru, 1971-80; dir. Corr. Edn. Research Project, 1964-68. Served with USMCR, 1943-46. Recipient Disting. Alumnus award U. Mont., 1979. Mem. Middle Atlantic Assn. Colls. Bus. Adminstrn. (pres. 1961), Am. Assembly Collegiate Schs. Bus. (pres. 1973), Council for Profl. Edn. for Bus. (pres. 1962), Verband der Hochschullehrer fur Betriesbswirtschaft, Beta Gamma Sigma (pres. 1966-70), Pi Gamma Mu, Sigma Delta Chi, Sigma Chi. Republican. Protestant. Mason. Clubs: Harvard (N.Y.C.); Pa. State Faculty. Author books, articles in field. Home: State College, Pa. Died July 25, 1980; buried Hampden, ME

MACKICHAN, KEITH B., consulting engr.; b. Shabbona, Mich., Mar. 4, 1913; s. John Allan and Anna (Brooks) MacK.; B.S. in E.E., U. of Mich., 1935, M.S. in E.E., 1936, M.B. Ad., 1937; m. Ruth B. Johnson, June 11, 1938; children—Alan, Barry, Elec. engr. Niagara Falls Power Co., Buffalo, N.Y., 1937-40; instr. elec. engring., Ohio U., 1940-42, Mass. Inst. Tech., summer 1942; asst. prof. elec. engring., Bucknell U., Lewisburg, Pa., 1942-45, Duke U., 1945-47; prof. elec. engring. and head dept. U. of N.D., 1947-54; cons. engr. K. B. MacKichan & Assos., from 1954; pres. Forx-Stanley Engring. Co., Inter-Am, Engring., Inc., Ingenieria Interamericana, S.A., Panama, Registered profl. engr. N.D., S.D. and Minn. Mem. Am. Inst. Elec. Engrs., N.D. Assn. Cons. Engrs., Sigma Xi. Methodist. Club: Lions. Home: Grand Forks. N.D. Died Sept. 15, 1974.

MACKINNEY, PAUL R., pres. United Dyewood Corp.; b. Providence, R.I., Aug. 27, 1885; s. Herbert G. and Mary (Bartlett) MacK.; ed. Brooklyn High Sch., 1899-1902; m. Abigail McKelvey Dates, June 25, 1908; 1 son, Francis P. With United Dyewood Corp., New York, 1927-50, beginning as v.p., pres., 1938-50; pres. and dir. Tanimex Corp., N.Y. City; dir. Wallace & Tiernan Co., Belleville, N.J. Republican. Clubs: Union League, Montclair Golf, Oakmont Shooting, Canadian Salmon. Home: Essex Fells, N.J. *

MACKLIN, JOHN FARRELL (MAK'LIN), corp. official; b. Worcester, Mass., Oct. 17, 1883; s. Robert and Margaret (Wray) M.; student St. Paul's Sch., 1904-06, U. of Pa., 1906-10; m. Phoebe Mildred Weaver, June 12, 1915 (died 1936); children—Ida Weaver (Mrs. Lilley), John Heisley Weaver. Athletic dir. Pawling (N.Y.) Sch., 1910-11; dir. of athletics, coach, and professor of physical culture, Michigan State College, East Lansing, Mich., 1911-16; associated with J. H. Weaver & Co., coal producers, since 1917, pres. since 1934; also pres. associated and affiliated companies; pres. W.Va., Northern R.R. Co.; v.p. Cambria & Ind. R.R. Co.; dir. Phila. Nat. Bank. Trustee Bucknell U.; advisory trustee Villanova Coll. Stadium of Mich. State Coll. named "Macklin Field" in recognition of his services as football coach. Dir. Nat. Coal Assn.; mem. Phi Gamma Delta,Republican. Episcopalian. Mason, Elk. Clubs: Union League, Racquet, University, Penn Athletic, Phila. Country. Bala Golf, Overbrook Golf (Phila.); Pine Valley Golf (Pine Valley, N.J.); Seaview Golf (Absecon, N.J.); Spring Lake (N.J.) Golf; Westchester Country (Rye, N.Y.); Downtown Athletic (New York). Home: Phila. *

MACLAREN, GAY, dramatic recitalist; b. Readstown, Wis., July 20, 1886; d. Anthony Wayne and Epsie (Drake) MacL.; dramatic training, Manning Coll. of Dramatic Art, Minneapolis, Minn.; m. Carl Backman, of Chicago, Oct. 20, 1937. At 15 heard "The Sign of the Cross" and reproduced entire play from memory at Brooklyn Institute of Arts and Sciences, Brooklyn, N.Y.; toured U.S. giving play recitals on Chautauqua and for colleges and clubs; known as "One-Girl Play Company." Author: (book) Morally We Roll Along (personal reminescences of trouping on Chautaugua). *

MAC LEAN, GRACE EDITH, college prof.; b. Vineland, N.J., June 5, 1883; d. Calvin Barber and Caroline Frances (Dayton) MacL.; A.B., Temple U., Phila., 1903; A.M., U. of Pa., 1905; A.M. and Ph.D., Univ. of Heidelberg, Germany, 1909; unmarried. Asst. prin. high sch., Milford, Del., 1904; prof. English and German, Brown Prep. Sch., Phila., 1905-6; prof. German, Birmingham (Pa.) Sch. for Girls, 1910-12; dean and prof. English, Oxford (O.) Coll., 1912-15; head of dept. English lang. and lit., Friends U., Wichita, Kan., since 1915. Author: Uncle Tom's Cabin in Germany (Vol. X Americana Germanica), 1910. Address: Wichita, Kan. *

MACLEISH, BRUCE, retail merchant; b. Chicago, Feb. 22, 1882; s. Andrew and Marie Louise (Little) MacL.; prep. edn. Rugby Sch. and Morgan Park Acad., Chicago; A.B., U. Chicago, 1903; m. Elizabeth Jane Moore. Oct. 26, 1907; children—Jean, Hugh. With John Wanamaker, 1903-06; with Carson, Pirie, Scott & Co., Chicago, since 1906, now pres. Mem. Phi Delta Theta. Republican. Clubs: Commonwealth, Indian Hill. Home: Hubbard Woods, Ill. *

MACLEOD, ANNIE LOUISE (MA-KLOUD'), educator; b. Economy, N.S., Can., Feb. 7, 1883; d. Malcolm Charles (M.D.) and Margaret Adelaide (Mackeen) Macleod; A.B., McGill U., 1904, M.S., 1905, Ph.D., 1910; fellow in chem., Bryn Mawr (Pa.) Coll., 1909-12. Teacher of chemistry, McGill U., 1905-08, Barnard Coll., N.Y. City, 1908-09; reader, Bryn Mawr Coll., 1912-14; mem. chemistry staff, Vassar Coll., 1914-28, prof. chemistry and dir. euthenics, 1924-28; dean of Coll. of Home Economics, Syracuse U., 1928-48. Fellow A.A.A.S.; mem. Am. Home Economics Assn., American Assn. University Women, American Humane Society (hon. v.p.). Presbyn. Cons. editor McGraw-Hill Book Co. Author: Textbook of Chemistry for Nurses, 1920; Vital Factors of Foods (with Carleton Ellis), 1922; Chemistry and Cookery (with Edith Nason), 1930, rev. edit., 1937. Home: Fayetteville, N.Y.

MACLIN, EDWARD SILVER, educator; b. Keeling, Haywood Co., Tenn., Dec. 13, 1885; s. William Henry and Mary Alethea (Minor) M.; B.S., U. of Tenn., 1905, I.E., 1916; U. of Wis., 1910-14; M.A., Peabody Coll. for Teachers, 1932; U. Chicago summer 1940; m. Anne Luttrell, 1907 (dec.); m. 2d, Pauline Spangler, 1931; children—Mary Minor (wife Capt. Marcus L. Aderholdt, Jr.), James Luttrell. Draftsman, 1905; teacher Boys High School, Atlanta, Georgia, 1908-10; University Wisconsin, engineering, drawing and descriptive geometry, 1910-14; Tech. High School, Atlanta, Ga., 1914-18; prof. vocational edn. and State supervisor trade and indsl. edn., U. of Tenn., 1918-20; asst. corps area cons. in edn., Camp Jackson, Columbia, S.C., 1920-21; prof. trade edn. and State supervisor trade edn., W. Va. U., 1921-33; pres. W.Va., Inst. Tech., 1933-45; engring. coordinator, Marshall Coll., Aug. 1945-July 1948; dir. evening program, since July 1, 1948. Bd. dir., State Edn. Assn., 1938-40 (pres. 1940); mem. Nat. Edn. Assn., Am. Vocational Assn., Am. Soc. for Engring. Edn. Laureate mem., Epsilon Pi Tau, Kappa Delta Pi, Lion's Internat. Elder Presbyn. Ch. Author: Descriptive Geometry (with A. V. Millar), 1912; Leadership Conference Training (with P. T. McHenry), 1945. *

MACMAHON, ARTHUR W., educator; b. Bklyn., May 29, 1890; s. Benjamin and Abbie (Duke) M.; B.A., Columbia, 1912, M.A., Columbia, 1913, Ph.D., 1923, Doctor of Laws (honorary), 1 Columbia, 1913, Ph.D., 1923, Doctor of Laws (honorary), 1959; married to Edna Cers on August 14, 1929; children—Gail (Mrs. Christoph Cornaro), Alan. Instr. govt. Columbia, 1913-17, 20-23, asst. prof., 1923-27, asso. prof., 1927-31, prof., 1931-45, Eaton prof. public adminstrn., 1945-58, emeritus, 1958-80, dir. univ. self survey, 1956-58; vis. prof. Stanford, 1931, Yale, 1939, 55-56, Princeton, 1950. Coll. of Europe, 1954, U. Istanbul (Turkey), 1959, Ind. School Public Administration, 1960, U. Buenos Aires, 1962, U. of East Africa, 1963; associate Brooking Graduate Sch. Econ. and Govt., Washington, 1926-27; pres. Hessian Hills Sch., 1937-47. Staff, asst. sec. chief field div., Council Nat. Defense, 1917-19; editor N.Y.C. Charter Revision Commn., 1921-23; staff President's Com. on Adminstrv. Management, 1936; cons. U.S. Dept. State, 1943-45; mem. Loyalty Bd., U.S. Civil Service Commn., 1947-50; staff Commn. Intergovtl. Relations, 1955. Fellow American Academy Arts and Sciences; member of Am. Polit. Science Assn. (pres. 1947), Soc. Pub. Administrn. (bd. editors 1945), Phi Beta Kappa, Delta Sigma Rho. Clubs: Century Association (New York City), Cosmos (Washington). Author: Statutory Sources of N.Y. City Govt., 1923; Dept. Management, 1937; The Postwar International Information Program of the United States, 1945; Administration Foreign Affairs, pub. 1953; Delegation and Autonomy, published in 1961. Co-author: Federal Administrators, 1939. Administration of Federal Work Relief, 1941; Federalism: Mature and Emergent, 1955. Contbr. to Ency. of Social Sci. and various journals. Home: Poughkeepsie, N.Y. Died Feb. 4, 1980.

MACMILLAN, NORMAN JOHN, transp. co. exec.; b. Bracebridge, Ont., Can., Apr. 8, 1909; s. John Malcolm and Ida Alberta (Brown) MacM.; B.A. with Honors, U. Man. (Can.), 1930, LL.B. with honors, 1934, LL.D., 1967; m. Doris Maude Horne, Aug. 28, 1937; children—Elizabeth Anne (Mrs. Brian E. Denyar), Ian Malcolm. Read law with R.D. Guy, King's Counsel Winnipeg, Man., 1930-34; called to Man. bar, 1935 mem. law dept. Winnipeg Electric Co., 1930-37; asso. firm Guy, Chappell, DuVal, McCrea, barristers and solicitors, Winnipeg, 1930-37; solicitor law dept. Canadian Nat. Rys., Winnipeg, 1937-43, asst. gen. solicitor, Montreal, Que., 1943-45, gen. counsel, 1945-49, v.p., gen. counsel, 1949-56, exec. v.p., 1956-67, ret. chmn., pres. 17 prin. affiliated cos., 1967-74; gen. counsel Trans-Can. Air Lines, 1945-56; dir. Price Co. Ltd., Canadian Exec. Services Overseas, Abitibi Paper Co., Consumers Glass Co. Ltd. Apptd. Queen's Counsel, Manitoba, 1954. Mem. adv. com. Canadian Standards Assn. Mem. exec. council St. Paul's Cathedral Appeal; hon. v.p. St. John council Boy Scouts Can. Bd. govs. Canadian Export Assn., Montreal Gen. Hosp., Olympic Trust Can. Decorated companion Order of Can.; knight of grace Order St. John; recipient Distinguished Service award Am. Ry. Devel. Assn., 1972; named Man of Year Traffic Clubs Internat., 1974. Mem. Can., Man. bar assns., Law Soc. Man., McGill, U. Montreal assos., Canadian Ry. Club, St. Andrews Soc. Montreal, Delta Upsilon. Clubs: Mount Royal; St. James' (Montreal, Que.). Home: Town of Mount Royal, Montreal, Que., Can. Died Oct. 30, 1978.

MACMILLEN, FRANCIS, violinist; b. Marietta, O., Oct. 14, 1885; s. Samuel Melvin and Ella Iiams (Hill) M.; at age of 7 became student Chicago Coll. of Music; later studied in Berlin, Brussels, St. Petersburg, under Joachim, César Thomson, Flesch, Aller, and others; was awarded 1st prize "With greatest distinction" and Var Hol cash prize, Brussels Royal Conservatory, at the age of sixteen yrs.; m. Lillian More, June 19, 1923. Made his first professional appearance in Brussels, 1903; sucessfully toured England, Belgium, France and Germany; début in America in Carnegie Hall, New York, Dec. 7, 1906; made many tours of prin. cities of America, playing with leading orchestras; has appeared in all prominent cities of Europe; toured Poland in the spring of 1930, and the autumn of 1931; also toured Germany and France, 1930-31. Was greeted by 5,000 people at his "home coming," Marietta, Ohio, Jan. 23, 1907. Enlisted in A.E.F., Dec. 1917; commd. 2d lt.; served 18 months in France in corps of interpreters; cited by General Pershing for "meritorious and conspicuous service"; promoted 1st lt. and was asst. provost marshal Base 6, hdqrs.Marseilles.*

MACNAUGHTON, BOYD, sugar exec.; b. Portland, Ore., Oct. 6, 1908; s. Ernest B. and Gertrude H. (Hutchinson) MacN.; B.A., Stanford U., 1930, M.B.A., 1932; m. Roberta R. Pittock, Aug. 14, 1935; children—Gertrude, Boyd, Matilda Ann, Duncan, Robert. Vice pres. Hawaiian Pineapple Co., Ltd., 1945-52; sr. v.p. C. Brewer & Co., Ltd., Honolulu, 1952-56, pres., 1956-70, chmn. fin. com. bd. dirs., 1971-73, dir., from 1952; chmn. bd. dirs. Calif. & Hawaiian Sugar Co., 1971-75; chmn. bd. dirs. Olokele Sugar Co., Ltd.; dir. Hilo Coast Processing Co., Hawaiian Trust Co., Ltd. Vice chmn. bd. trustees Hawaii Loa Coll. Clubs: Pacific, Waialae Country (Honolulu); Salmagundi (N.Y.); Pacific Union (San Francisco). Home: Honolulu, Hawaii. Died Dec. 4, 1975.

MACNUTT, J(OSEPH) SCOTT, artist; b. Fort D. A. Russell, Wyo., Jan. 11, 1885; s. Albert Scott and Helen Marie (Patterson) MacN.; A.B., cum laude, Harvard, 1906; B.S., Mass. Inst. Tech., 1908; student Sch. of Museum of Fine Arts, Boston, 1916-18; m. Agnes Cady, May 27, 1924; children—Francis Scott, Margaret Alexandra. Began as sanitarian with Pittsburgh Typhoid Fever Commn., 1908; became health officer, Orange, N.J.; then lecturer at Mass. Inst. Tech.; also engaged in writing and research; portrait painting since 1920; instr. St. Louis Sch. of Fine Arts (Washington U.), 1927-28; mem. staff Woodbury Sch., Boston and Ogunquit, Me., 1928, 29; asso. dean School of Art Inst., Chicago, 1929-30. Served as 1st lt. San. Corps, U.S. Army, 1918-20. Mem. St. Louis Municipal Art Commn., St. Louis Artists' Guild, Sigma Alpha Epsilon. Catholic. Author: A Manual for Health Officers, 1915; The Modern Milk Problem, 1917 (both books out of print). Portraits: Prof. Walter R. Spalding (Harvard); Dr. Arthur E. Bostwick, E. J. Russell, Dr. Harry Sturgeon Crossen, Dr. Isidor Loeb, Dr. Geo. T. Moore (Mo. Botanical Garden), Albert P. Greensfelder, Dr. E. V. Cowdry, Dr. Sherwood Moore, Leif J. Sverdrup (St. Louis). Has visited Europe several times. Home: St. Louis, Mo. *

MACOMBER, WILLIAM BUTTS, JR., govt. ofcl.; b. Rochester, N.Y., Mar. 28, 1921; s. William Butts and Elizabeth Currie (Ranlet) M.; grad. Phillips Andover Acad., 1940; A.B., Yale, 1943, M.A., 1947; LL.B., Harvard, 1949; M.A., U. Chgo., 1951. Freshman counselor Yale, 1946-47; lectr. govt. Boston U., 1947-49; resident head Hitchcock House, U. Chgo., 1950-51; with C.I.A., Washington, 1951-53; spl. asst. to spl. asst. to sec. for intelligence, U.S. Dept. of State, 1953-54; adminstrv. asst. to Sen. John Sherman Cooper, 1954; spl. asst. to under sec. of state Herbert Hoover, Jr., 1955, to sec. of state John Foster Dulles, 1955-57; asst. sec. of state (for congl. relations), 1957—. Rep. committeeman, Rochester, N.Y., 1946-51. Served as lt. USMC, 1943-46. Mem. Am. Polit. Sci. Assn. Republican. Episcopalian. Club: Genesee Valley (Rochester). Home: Rochester, N.Y. *

MACPHERSON, DANIEL ALLAN, bacteriologist; b. Providence, June 6, 1896; s. Neil and Elizabeth (McKinnon) MacP.; Ph.B., Brown U., 1919, Sc.M., 1920; Ph.D., U. Chicago (fellow in bacteriol., 1920), 1929; m. Elizabeth Wolf, Sept. 10, 1924; 1 son, Carl. Asso. Rockefeller Inst. for Medical Research, 1921; asso. instr. in bacteriology, Chicago, 1922; asso. prof. bacteriology, U. N.C., 1923-29, prof. bacteriology and head dept., 1929-66, prof. emeritus, 1966-77. Recipient Disting. Service award U. N.C., 1966. Fellow Am. Acad. Microbiology; mem. Soc. Am. Bacteriologists, Am. Assn. Bacteriol. Am. Pub. Health Assn., AAUP, A.A.A.S., Alpha Tau Omega, Sigma Xi. Presbyn. Home: Chapel Hill, N.C. Died Mar. 1977.

MACPHERSON, THOMAS GEORGE, editor, author; b. Barrow-in-Furness, Eng., Oct. 28, 1915; s. Hugh Glenn and Mary Hudson (Galston) MacP.; came to U.S., 1921, naturalized, 1933; grad. high sch.; m. Mary Elizabeth Young, June 18, 1939; children—Thomas Douglas, Gary Andrew, Judith Marie (Mrs. John E. Schumacher). Public relations Gilliams Service, to 1941; with Scouting mag., 1941-43, 45-51; photo-reporter to exec. editor Boys Life, 1951-61; dir. juvenile dept. G.P. Putnam's Sons, N.Y.C., 1961-74, v.p., dir., 1964-74; free-lance author and editorial cons., Jamesburg, N.J., 1974-76. Boro councilman, Jamesburg, 1965-67. Trustee, Library at Jamesburg. Served to 2d lt. U.S. Army, 1943-45. Mem. Am. Polar Soc., Mystery Writers Am. Home: Jamesburg, N.J. Died May 7, 1976.

MACRAE, DURANT LOOMIS, publisher; b. Winooski, Vt., Apr. 19, 1883; s. Frank William and Caroline Ann (Austin) M.; A.B., U. Vt., 1904; m. Rebecca Fowler Anderson, Nov. 1, 1911 (dec.); children—Robert Mansfield, Jean Anderson, Donald Pollard. With Bobbs-Merrill Co., Indpls., 1905-08; sales mgr. George W. Jacobs Co., pubs., Phila., 1908-25; organizer Macrae Smith Co., 1925, president, 1925-63, chairman of the board of directors, 1963—. Mem. Alpha Tau Omega. Episcopalian. Clubs: Tavistock Country (Haddonfield); Century. Home: Haddonfield, N.J. *

MACWHITE, MICHAEL, diplomat; b. Glandore, County Cork, Ireland, on May 8, 1883; LL.D.; m. Paula Asta Grüttner, of Hilleród, Denmark, Sept. 22, 1921; children—Irene (dec.), Eoin. Served with French Foreign Legion, World War; rep. of Dail Eireann, Paris, 1920-21; rep. Irish Free State, Geneva, 1921-29; E.E. and M.P. to U.S., 1929-37, to Italy since 1937. Vice pres. Internat. Labor Conf., Geneva, 1928; mem. of the Academie Diplomatique International, Paris. Catholic. Address: Rome, Italy. *

MACY, CLARENCE EDWARD, foreign service officer; b. St. Joseph, Mo., Nov. 9, 1886; s. Charles Edward and Violet (Turner) M.; student State Preparatory Sch., U. of Colo., 1901-05; m. Marie-Therese Billuart, Nov. 27, 1919. Railway Mail Service, Post Office Dept., Denver, Colo., 1907-10, examiner, 1911-14; chief clerk to mgr. mail and express traffic, Frisco Lines, St. Louis, Mo., 1914-16; mgr. mail traffic, D.&R.G.W.R.R.Co., Denver, Colo., 1916-18; vice consul, Coblenz, Germany, 1921; has served as vice consul, consul at Dakar Monrovia, Port Elizabeth, Tampico and Karachi; consul general Istanbul, Turkey, 1947; retired from active service, Nov. 1948. Served with U.S. Army, 1918-21; with Postal Express Service, U.S. Army, Le Mans, Paris and Coblenz, 1919-21. Mason (32 deg.). Address: Denver. *

MACY, JOSIAH, JR., educator, biophysicist, mathematician; b. N.Y.C., Dec. 17, 1924; s. Josiah Noel and Mary (Martin) M.; S.B., M.I.T., 1949, Ph.D. in Math., 1954; postgrad. Harvard, 1950-51; m. Elizabeth Weston Murray, Sept. 12, 1945; children—Barbara Weston, Josiah III, Elizabeth Martin, Ann Murray. Staff, Research Lab. Electronics, M.I.T., 1951-54; analyst Operations Research Office, Johns Hopkins, 1954-58; faculty Albert Einstein Coll. Medicine, Yeshiva U., N.Y.C., 1958-67, asso. prof. physiology, 1961-67; prof. bio-math. and biophysics, dir. div. biophys. scis. U. Ala. Med. Center, Birmingham, 1967-79; mem. adv. com. on computers in research and computer research study sect. NIH, 1960-66; mem. biomed. library rev. com. Nat. Library of Medicine, NIH, 1973-77. Mem. Am. Math. Soc., Soc. Indsl. and Applied Math., Biophys. Soc. (mem. council 1964-67), Biometric Soc., N.Y. Acad. Scis., Biomed. Engring. Soc. (dir. 1968-74), AAAS, Sigma Xi. Contbg. author: Operations Research for Management, 1956; Computers in Biology and Medicine, 1965; also articles. Research on theoretical models for information transfer in human groups and in central nervous system, application of hybrid analog-digital computing methods to physiol. expts. and simulation. Home: Mountain Brook, Ala. Died Mar. 25, 1979.

MACY, JOSIAH NOEL, newspaper publisher; b. N.Y.C., Dec. 24, 1900; s. Valentine Everit and Edith Weisman (Carpenter) M.; A.B., Harvard, 1922; Litt.D. (hon.), Wagner Coll., 1951; m. Mary T. Martin, May 26, 1923; children—Josiah, Archer Martin, Noel Everit; m. 2d, Mary Minot Cabot, Feb. 18, 1933; m. 3d, Elena Aldcroftt Kohler, Sept. 10, 1945. Reporter, Yonkers (N.Y.) Statesman, 1924; gen. mgr., pres. Westchester County Publs., Inc., 1926-45; Inducted fed. service, capt. 101st Cav., 1941; transferred to Bur. of Public Relations, War Dept., 1941; asst. chief of internat. info. div., Dept. State, 1945-46, chief internat. press and publs. div., 1946-48; dir. printing and publishing div. N.P.A., 1951-52; chmn. bd. Vision, Inc., 1950-73. Formerly commr. Interstate Sanitation Commn., mem. Westchester Planning Commn., dir. Audit Bureau of Circulations (resigned all positions on entering Fed. service). Clubs: University, Metropolitan; Mill Reef, Masons. Home: Washington, D.C. Died Aug. 24, 1977; buried Sleepy Hollow Cemetery, Briarcliff, N.Y.

MADDEN, CARL HALFORD, economist; b. Balt., Feb. 14, 1920; s. John Thomas and Russell Mae (Morissett) M.; B.A. with honors in philosophy, U. Va., 1942, M.A. in Econs. 1952, Ph.D. in Econs. 1954; m. Joan Lysbeth Clarke, Dec. 26, 1944; children—John Thomas, James Morrissett, Martin Clarke, Corey Beth. Instr. English, Va. Poly. Inst., 1946-48; research asst., asso. Bur. Population and Econ. Research, U. Va., 1952-54; with Fed. Res. Bank N.Y., 1954-60, mgr. pub. information dept., 1956-60; dean Coll. Bus. Adminstrn., Lehigh U., 1960-63; economist U.S. Sen. Banking and Currency Com., 1963; dir. econ. research U.S. C. of C., 1963-66, chief economist, 1966-76; prof. bus. Sch. Bus. Adminstrn. Am. U., Washington, 1976-78; lectr. at Rutgers U., 1954-55; lectr. N.Y. chpt. Am. Inst. Banking, 1956-57, Grad. Sch. Banking, N.Y. U., 1959-60, Stonier Grad. Sch. Banking, Rutgers U., 1958-65. Econ. cons. Office Sec., Treasury Dept., 1962-63; dir. Joint Council Econ. Edn., also corp. exec. Served to lt. USCGR, 1942-46, comdr. Res. Mem. Am. Econ. Assn. Am. Statis. assn., Am. Finance Assn., Phi Beta Kappa, Omicron Delta Kappa. Author: Money Side of the Street, 1960; The Economic Process, 1969; Understanding Economics, 1967; Decisions for the Seventies, 1970; Clash of Culture, 1972; also articles. Syndicated feature It's Your Economy, 1969. Home: Alexandria, Va. Died Oct. 8, 1978; interred at Danville, Va.

MADISON, JAMES BUFORD, ex-mem. Federal Farm Loan Bd.; b. Indianapolis, Ind., Apr. 28, 1885; s. Charles and Genevieve (Drake) M.; ed. pub. schs.; m. Lilla Ashe, June 12, 1905; 1 son, James Buford. Began as life ins. salesman, Indianapolis, 1903; in life ins. and farm mortgage business until 1915; organizer, 1916, sec.-treas. until 1925, pres.-treas., 1925-31, The Virginian Joint Stock Land Bank, Charleston, W.Va.; mem. Federal Farm Loan Bd. Sept. 1931-May 27, 1933; organizer and pres. Madison & Co., dealers in tax exempt bonds. Associated with G. M.-P. Murphy & Co., members N.Y. Stock Exchange, since May 15, 1934. Member City Council, Charleston, 1923-31, pres. 1923-31; chmn. Kanawha Co. (W.Va.) Rep. Exec. Com. Ex-pres. Charleston Chamber Commerce. Catholic. Club: Rotary of Charleston (ex-pres.). Home: New York. *

MAERZ, JOSEPH, pianist; b. Buffalo, N.Y., Dec. 23, 1883; s. Aloys J. and Mary (Dory) M.; ed. Canisius Coll.; studied piano with Carlos de Serrano; m. Glenn Priest, violinist, of Boston, Mass., 1909; children—Lucian Carlos, Paul Julian, Début in Buffalo, at age of 8; frequently appeared as child prodigy; made 6 trans-continental tours, also toured in Can. and Mexico; daily recitals at Jamestown Expn., 1907; teacher of piano at New York Inst. of Music, 3 yrs., Syracuse U., 6 yrs.; dir. of music, Wesleyan Coll., Macon, Ga., since 1914. Repertoire includes old and modern classics. Composer: 2 works for large orchestra; Sonata for violin and piano; German lieder and English songs; about 100 pieces for piano; many pieces for violin. Home: Macon, Ga. *

MAFFETT, MINNIE LEE (maf'fet), physician and surgeon; b. Falls County, Tex., Sept. 9, 1882; d. Samuel Benton and Alice Clementine (Keller) Maffett; grad. Sam Houston State Coll., 1902; undergrad. student U. of Tex.; spl. work U. of Chicago; student Med. Coll. of U. of Tex., 1910-14. Began as teacher pub. schs., 1900; prin. Ward Sch., Cleburne, Tex., 1906, State Orphan Home High Sch., Corsicana, Tex., 1907-10; in practice medicine as physician and surgeon since 1915, at Dallas since 1915; asso. prof. gynecology, Baylor Med. Coll., Dallas, 1926-43; prof. of clinical gynecology, Southwestern Medical Foundation School of Medicine, Dallas, since 1943; mem. staff Baylor Hosp., Parkland Hosp., Med. Arts Hosp., Dallas; physician for women, Southern Methodist University, 1915-46, director of Health Center since 1946. Fellow Texas Association of Obstetricians and Gynecologists (sec. and treas. 1930-39, pres. 1940-41), Am. Coll. Surgeons; mem. Am. Bur. for Med. Aid to China (nat. Chairman), Dallas County Med. Soc., Tex. State Med. Assn., A.M.A., Central Assn. Obstetricians and Gynecologists (v.p. 1940-41), Southern Med. Assn., Med. Women's Nat. Assn., Tex. Fed. Business and Professional Women's Clubs (pres. 1919-20, hon. pres. since 1930), Nat. Fed. Business and Professional Women's Clubs (health chmn. 1935-37, 2d v.p. 1937-39, pres. 1939-40 and 1941-43), Zonta Internat., Alpha Epsilon Iota, Delta Kappa Gamma. Club: University Woman's Club of Southern Methodist University. Author articles on med. and current subjects. Home: Dallas. *

MAG, EDWARD ARNOLD, legal cons.; b. New Britain, Conn., Sept. 16, 1899; s. Nathan Elihu and Rebecca (Goldberg) M.; B.A., Yale, 1921, LL.B., 1923; m. Marian Spater, Jan. 30, 1940 (div. Aug. 1955); m. 2d, Mary C. Walker, Sept. 10, 1960. Admitted to Conn. bar, 1923, U.S. Supreme Ct. bar, 1936; asso. firm Rushmore, Bisbee & Stern, N.Y.C., 1923-24; practice in New Britain, 1924-34, 36-42; asst. litigation atty. NRA, Washington, 1935-36; asst. gen. counsel Lend-Lease Adminstrn., Washington, 1943, prin. rep., Cairo, Egypt, 1943-45; internat. law expert, chief of counsel br. U.S. Forces in Austria, 1946-47; legal attache Am. Legation, Budapest, Hungary, 1948-49, Vienna, Austria, 1950-51; econ. controls officer Am. embassy, Tokyo, 1952-54; 1st sec., consul Am. embassy, Rome, Italy, 1954-62; Am. agt. Italian-Am. Conciliation Commn., 1956-62; now cons. Am. and internat. law. Chmn. New Britain Pub. Housing Authority, 1938, 40-41. Mem. mgmt. com. Anglo-Am. Nursing Home, 1956-77; chmn. adv. bd. Temple U., Rome, 1968-77. Mem. adminstrv. tribunal Inst. for Unification Pvt. Internat. Law, Rome, 1972. Mem. Am. Soc. Internat. Law, Phi Beta Kappa. Clubs: Rome American, Rome Golf. Home: Rancho Santa Fe, Calif. Died July 5, 1980; buried Rock Creek Cemetery, Washington, D.C.

MAGEE, JAMES CARRE, former surg. gen., U.S.A.; b. Jan. 23, 1883; s. Edward Carre and Elizabeth (Armstrong) M.; M.D., Jefferson Med. Coll., 1905; hon. Sc.D., Jefferson Medical College, 1940; m. Irene Mackay, July 22, 1908 (now deceased); children—Mervyn Mackay, James Carre, Jr. Contract surgeon, U.S. Army, 1907-08; commd. 1st lt. Med Corps, U.S. Army, 1909, advancing through the grades to col.; appointed major gen., surgeon gen., June 1939; tour expired May 31, 1943. Retired maj. gen., U.S. Army, 1943. Served in San Francisco, Philippine Islands, Kan., and Mexican border; with A.E.F. in France, 1917-19; Walter Reed Gen. Hosp., Washington, D.C., 1935-39. Mem. various boards and medical societies. Military decorations; Distinguished Service Medal; Purple Heart, Protestant. Address: Washington, D.C. *

MAGNA, EDITH SCOTT (MRS. RUSSELL WILLIAM MAGNA) (MAG'NA), hon. pres. D.A.R.; b. Boston, Mass., Nov. 15, 1885; d. Walter and Sarah Dean (Campbell) Scott; A.B., Smith Coll., 1909; LL.D., Am. Internat. Coll., Springfield, Mass., 1932; L.H.D., Lincoln Memorial U., Harrogate, Tenn., 1934; m. Russell William Magna, Mar. 28, 1910. Pres. gen. Nat. Soc. D.A.R., 1932-35, also v.p. 3 yrs., librarian 3 yrs., nat. chmn. Constitution Hall Finance Com. 9 yrs., Mass. state counselor 9 yrs.; pres. National Officers' Club, National Society D.A.R., 1942-46; mem. Mass. State Tercentenary Com., 1930; served on Com. of Sulgrave Instn. (for restoration and preservation of Sulgrave Manor, Northamptonshire, England); chairman Women's Div. of War Savings Com., Holyoke, Mass., since 1943. Mem. Mass. Soc. Mayflower Descendants, Soc. Mayflower Descendants State of N.Y., Nat. Soc. Colonial Descendants of America, Daughters of Colonial Wars, Mass. Soc. Daughters of Am. Colonists, Boston Colony Nat. Soc. N.E., Women, Clan Campbell Soc. (Scotland), Valley Forge Hist. Soc., Daughters of Mass., N.E. Historic Geneal. Soc., Soc. for Preservation N.E. Antiquities, Knox Memorial Assn. (Me.), Old Glory Club (Boston), Daughters of the Union, Kenmore Assn., Smith Coll. Alumnae Assn., Am. Assn. Univ. Women (past pres. Com. Valley Br.), Nat. League Am. Pen Women, Nat. Fed. Business and Professional Women's Club, A.L.A., Western Mass. Br. of Smith Coll. Clubs (ex-pres.), Betsy Ross Flying Corps (hon.). Pres. Walter Scott Foundation for the Aid of Crippled Children, Incorporated, New York City; v.p. American International College, Springfield, Mass.; trustee Clarke School for the deaf, Northampton, Mass., Lincoln Memorial U., Harrogate, Tenn. Decorated Legion of Honor (France). Republican. Conglist. Clubs: Professional Women's, Women's Republican (Boston); Quota, Holyoke Women's, Westminster, Business and Professional Women's Club (Holyoke); Women's Press (New York); Newspaper women's (Washington, D.C.). Author: We Traveled Together, 1925; Camp Rustle, 1928; Collected Verse, 1934. Home: Holyoke, Mass. *

MAGNER, JAMES EDMUND, steamship exec.; b. N.Y. City, Feb. 24, 1898; s. John Mannix and Mary Margaret (Haettinger) M.; student Xavier Mil. Acad., 1913-16; m. Lillian Elizabeth Campbell, Dec. 15, 1923; children—Evelyn Margaret (Mrs. Thomas F. Byrne), James Edmund, Bruce Campbell. Exec. v.p. in charge traffic, passenger and freight, dir., Grace Line, Inc., N.Y. City, since 1940; dir. Huron Stevedoring Corp., Panama Agencies Inc., since 1940. Civilian shipping adv., U.S. Maritime Commn., 1941-45. Mem. Pan-Am. Soc., Inter-Am. Arbitration Assn. Clubs: India House, Downtown Athletic, Foreign Commerce. Home: New Rochelle, N.Y. Died 1979.

MAGNEY CLARENCE REINBOLD (MAG'NI), judge; b. Trenton, Pierce County, Wis., Jan. 11, 1883; s. Jonas and Hilda C. (Edholm) M.; A.B., Gustavus Adolphus Coll., St. Peter, Minn., 1903; LL.D., 1939; LL.B., Harvard, 1908; m. Lillian C. Lundgren, Apr. 26, 1911; children—John Reinhold, Mary, Charles Fred. Admitted to bar, 1909, and practiced law, Duluth, Minn., 1909-17; mayor of Duluth, 1917-20; judge of Dist. Court, 11th Judicial Dist. of Minn., 1921-43; asso. justice Supreme Court of Minn. since 1943. Mem. Minn. State Bar Assn. Club: Athletic (St. Paul). Home: Duluth, Minn. *

MAGNUS, FINN HAAKON, organ and toy mfr.; b. Bergen, Norway, Aug. 14, 1907; s. Finn Sverre and Sigrid (Christiansen) M.; ed. tutors, pvt. schs. abroad; m. Elsie Wittenberg, May 18, 1940; 1 son, Kenneth. Jr. exec. trainee Ford Motor Co., 1929; machine operator Button Corp. Am., 1930, plant supt., 1934-39, gen. mgr., 1939-43; pres. Magnus Research, Inc., 1946-76, Magnus Oceanic Corp. 1957-76, Norske Organ Corp., 1966-76, Odin Press, Inc. Chmn., Treasury Dept. Def. Bond Com., Essex County, N.J. Recipient Meritorious Service plaque for outstanding achievement Modern Plastic mag., 1948; Horatio Alger award Am. Schs. and Colls. Assn., 1951; Outstanding Naturalized Citizen award, Newark, by Unico Nat., 1951; Self-Made Man award Working Press of N.J. Assn., 1952; U.S. Treasury award, 1953, trophy for exploration of Hudson Canyon, Barnegat Marlin and Tuna Club, 1962. Mem. N.A.M., N.J. C. of C., Soc. Plastics Industry, Toy Mfrs. Assn. Am. Inc. Episcopalian. Mason (Shriner). Clubs: Newark Athletic (hon.), Essex (Newark); Brielle (N.J.) Marlin and Tuna, Brielle Yacht. Inventor all-plastic musical reed plate and all-plastic diatonic harmonica, 1942, all-plastic chromatic harmonica, 1947, accordion, 1948, keyreed organ, 1950, portable self-player organ, 1952. Home: Myrtle Beach, S.C. Died Aug. 29, 1976.

MAGNUS, PERCY CECIL, drug exec.; b. N.Y. City, Oct. 22, 1893; s. Percy Cecil and Lucy (Gartrel) M.; ed. Manual Training High Sch. and Euclid Secretarial Sch., Brooklyn; m. Margaret Ames, May 22, 1918. Began as messenger Metropolitan Trust Co., of New York; with Magnus Mabee & Reynard, Inc., dealers in drugs, chemicals and essential oils, N.Y. City, from 1911, pres., from 1917; dir. mem. exec. com. Underwriters Trust Co.; trustee East River Savings Bank (member exec. com.), Kings County Trust Co., Brooklyn, New York. Episcopalian. Clubs: Drug and Chem., India House, Metropolitan (N.Y.C.); Thames (New London, Conn.); Manhatten; Merchants. Home: New York, N.Y. Died 1979.

MAGNUSON, DONALD HAMMER, congressman; b. Freeman, Wash., Mar. 7, 1911; s. Ellis William and Ida (Hammer) M.; student Spokane U., 1926-28; A.B., U. Wash., 1931; m. June Elizabeth von der Hellen, June 3, 1944 (div. 1961); children—Craig, Terry Lynn (Mrs. Robert B. Cairns), Joel Ellis, Mary Elizabeth, Erik George. Reporter, Daily Olympian, Olympia, Wash., 1934-41, Seattle Times, 1941-52; mem. 83d-87th Congresses, congressman at large, Wash.; staff asst. Office Sec. Interior, 1963-69; editor deptl. publs. Dept. Labor, 1969-73. Mem. Am. Newspaper Guild, Theta Xi. Presbyn. Home: Seattle, Wash. Died Oct. 5, 1979.

MAGNUSON, PAUL BUDD (MAG'NU-SON), surgeon; b. St. Paul, Minn., June 14, 1884; s. Charles A. and Melinda (Graham) M.; M.D., U. of Pa., 1908; D.Sc., Duke U.; LL.D., Baylor U., Western Res. U.; m. Alice L. Hasson, June 14, 1910; 1 son, Paul B.; m. 2d, Laura Thompson, Sept. 27, 1931. Practiced in Chicago since 1908; formerly chief surgeon Chicago & Alton and Chicago Junction R.R.; first med. dir., Ill. Industrial Commn.; attending surgeon, Passavant Memorial Hosp.; sr. consulting surgeon, Wesley Memorial Hosp.; prof. surgery, chmn. dept. bone and joint surgery, emeritus Northwestern U.; on leave since 1945; apptd. head commr. on Health Needs of the Nation; former chief med. dir. Vets. Administration, Washington, D.C. Civilian cons. to Surgeon Gen., U.S. Army, 1941-46. Major, Medical Corps, U.S. Army, 1917-18. Founder mem. Am. Board Surgery; mem. Am. Bd. Orthopedic Surgery; mem. Am. Coll. Surgeons (sec. and regent); mem. Am., So. surg. assns. Am. Orthopedic Assn., Western Surg. Soc., Am. Assn. for Surgery of Trauma (pres. 1949), Clinical Orthopedic Soc., Am. Assn. Indsl. Surgeons, A.M.A., Internat. Soc. Orthopedic Surg. and Traumatol., Internat. Soc. Surgery, Am. Acad. of Orthopedic Surgeons, Nat. Research Council (co-chmn. subcom. skeletal system), Chicago Orthopedic Soc., Chicago Surgical Soc., Inst. of Medicine of Chicago, Ill. State and Chicago Medical Socs., Sigma Xi. Republican. Presbyn. Clubs: Metropolitan (Washington); Century Assn. (N.Y.C.); Racquet (Chicago). Author: Fractures, 1933, 5th edit., 1949; sect. on Ununited Fractures, Orthopedic Subjects, by direction Nat. Research Council. Home: Dundee, Ill. *

MAGNUSSON, LEIFUR (MAG'NU-SON), social econ.; labor; b. Iceland, July 7, 1882; s. Sigfus and Gudrun (Benediktsdottir) M.; came to U.S., 1886; A.B., U. of Minn., 1905; grad. study in economics George Washington U., 1910-11; LL.B., Georgetown Law Sch., 1915; m. Sarah Bement Swain, 1912; children—Jon, Ruth, Frederick. Teacher, high sch., Minn., 1906-09; in Govt. library work, 1910-11, Govt. labor research, 1912-20; also editor English edition Proceedings of First Internat. Labor Conf. in Washington, 1919; admitted to D.C. bar, 1915; asso. statistician Nat. Bank Commerce, N.Y. City, 1920-21; English editor Internat. Labor Rev., 1921-23; Am. rep. Internat. Labor Office, 1924-38; ex-pres. Nat. Inst. of Immigrant Welfare, N.Y. City; retired; returned to active duty as chief of Defense (War) Service Sect., Legislative Reference Service, Library of Congress, 1941-44; asst. dir. manpower studies, Indsl. Coll. Armed Forces, 1944-47; asso. prof. Georgetown Sch. of Fgn. Service, 1947-48. Decorated 1939, Grand Knight of the Cross with the Icelandic Falcon. Fellow A.A.A.S.; mem. American Econ. Assn. Author: Housing by Employers in the U.S., 1919; Historical Survey of International Action Affecting Labor, 1920. Home: Alexandria, Va. *

MAGOUN, FRANCIS PEABODY, JR., educator; b. N.Y.C., Jan. 6, 1895; s. Francis Peabody and Jeanne Cassard (Bartholow) M.; prep. edn., St. Andrew's Sch., Concord, Mass., and Noble and Greenough Sch., Boston; A.B., Harvard, 1916, Ph.D., 1923; Trinity Coll., Cambridge, Eng., 1919; Ph.D. (hon.), Helsinki U., 1969; m. Margaret Boyden, June 30, 1926; children—Francis Peabody III, William Cowper Boyden, Margaret Boyden, Jean Bartholow. Instr. English, Harvard, 1919-20, 1923-27, asst. prof. English, 1927-30, asso. prof. comparative lit., 1930-37, prof. comparative lit., 1937-51, prof. English, 1951-61, emeritus, 1961-79; Harvard exchange prof. to U. Paris and U. Strasbourg, 1931-32; spl. univ. lectr. U. London, 1951; Guggenheim fellow, 1955-56. Mng. editor of Speculum, a Jour. of Mediaeval Studies, 1926-30; editor Harvard Studies and Notes in Philology and Lit., 1934-35. Field service with Am. Ambulance Corps, France, 1916-17; cadet. later 2d lt. and lt. Royal Flying Corps., R.A.F., B.E.F., France, 1917-19. Awarded Mil. Cross (Brit.), 1918; Medaille de l'Universite de Strasbourg, 1932; comdr. Order of Lion of Finland, 1964. Fellow Mediaeval Acad. Am.; mem. Modern Lang. Assn. Am., Soc. Neophilogique de Helsinki, Kalevala Soc. Helsinki. Club: Faculty (Harvard University). Author: The Gests of King Alexander of Macedon, 1929. Rev. editor: The Founders of Eng., F.B. Gummere, 1930; History of Football from the Beginnings to 1871, 1938; Survivals in Old Norwegian (with H. M. Smyser), 1941; transl. and adapter (with H. Kökeritz) of Gösta Bergman, A Short History of the Swedish Language, 1975; Walter of Acquitaine (with H.M. Smyser), 1977; A Grouped Frequency World-List of Anglo-Saxon Poetry (with J.F. Madden), 1954; Anglo-Saxon Poems, 1969; Graded Finnish Readers 1-4 (with T.J. Heiskanen); Beowulf and Judith, 1962; The Vercelli Book Poems, 1965; A Chaucer Gazetter, 1961; Agricola's Gospel of Mark, 1967. Translator: (with A. H. Krappe) Grimm Brothers German Folk Tales, 1960; Eyvind of the Mountains (Sigurjonsson), 1961; The Kalevala (Lönnrot), 1963, The Old Kalevala, 1969; contbr. to Otfrid von Weissenburg, 1978; also articles to Am. and European philol. jours. Recipient hommage vol. Franciplegius: Medieval Studies in Honor of Francis Peabody Magoun, Jr., 1965. Home: Cambridge, Mass. Died June 5, 1979.

MAGOVERN, JOHN J., JR., lawyer; b. South Orange, N.J., Dec. 28, 1905; s. John J. and Elizabeth (Walraff) M.; LL.B., Fordham U., 1929; m. Kathleen V. Doyle, May 3, 1934; children—Margaret (wife of George F. Cummings, Jr.), John J., Thomas. Admitted to N.J. bar, 1930; asso. Pitney, Hardin & Skinner, Newark, 1929-37; atty. Mut. Benefit Life Ins. Co., 1942-44, asst. counsel, 1944-47, asso. counsel, 1947-51, counsel since 1951, v.p., 1952-60, exec. v.p., 1960-62, pres., also chief exec. officer, 1962-72, dir., 1972-74, hon. dir., 1974-76; trustee Phila. Nat. Bank Mortgage & Realty Co. Chmn. bd. control N.J. Dept. Instns. and Agys.; chmn. bd. Life Ins. Med. Research Fund; bd. dirs. N.J. Safety Council; trustee Nat. Carmel Guild, Greater Newark Hosp. Devel. Fund, C.F. Mueller Scholarship Found.; chmn. N.J. Econ. Policy Com., Task Force Public Credit Tax Policy Com.; mem. adv. bd. Anti-Defamation League of B'nai B'rith; mem. fin. council com. Cath. Archdiocese. Recipient Brotherhood award NCCJ. Mem. N.J. C. of C. (chmn. bd. dirs.), Greater Newark C. of C. (exec. com.), Assn. Life Ins. Counsel, Am., Essex County (chmn.) bar assn., Life Ins. Assn. Am. (dir.), N.J. Tax Policy Com. Club: Essex. Home: Summit, N.J. Died Oct. 26, 1976; buried Holy Sepulchre Cemetery, East Orange, N.J.

MAGRISH, ALFRED E., mgmt. cons.; b. Cin., Aug. 13, 1912; s. Louis and Kate (Toby) M.; A.B., Yale, 1932; m. Shirley Misrach, Mar. 10, 1946; children—David, Lewis, Emily, Kathryn, James. Mdse. exec. John Shillito Co., Cin., 1932-42; mdse. mgr. Foley's, Houston, 1946-49; v.p. Loveman Joseph & Loeb, Birmingham, Ala., 1949-52, Federated Dept. Stores, 1952-56; owner, exec. v.p. Jenny Co., Cin., 1956-66; pres. Gidding-Jenny Co., 1962-64; asso. dir. retail coordination Genesco, 1964-66; mgmt. cons., 1966-77; owner, pres. Magrish Internat. Inc., 1966-77. Served as lt. (s.g.), USN, 1942-46. Mem. A.I.M., Phi Beta Kappa. Rotarian. Club: Cincinnati. Home: Cincinnati, Ohio. Died July 9, 1977.

MAGRUDER, CARY WALTHALL, naval officer; b. Vicksburg, Miss., Apr. 7, 1886; s. Lawson William and Jessie (Kilpatrick) M.; student La. State U., 1903-04; grad. U.S. Naval Acad., 1908, B.S., 1938; m. Charlotte Barnard England, Sept. 27, 1913; 1 dau., Charlotte England (Mrs. Duncan Buttrick). Commd. ensign, U.S Navy, 1910, and advanced through grades t commodore, 1944, comd. destroyer (French Coast) World War I; commanded U.S. Naval Training Sta., Newport, R.I., 1941-45, U.S. Naval Operating Base, Dec. 1944-Mar. 1945; ret. May 1946. Decorated Navy Cross. Home: Jamestown, R.I. *

MAGRUDER, MARSHALL, army officer; b. Washington, D.C., Oct. 12, 1885; s. George Corbin Washington and Eleanor Anne Helen (Marshall) M.; student George Washington U., 1904-07; grad. Army War Coll., 1932, Naval War Coll., 1933; m. Anne Louise Peyton, Dec. 18, 1909; children—Peyton Marshall, Anne Marshall (wife of Capt. Loren L. Cole, U.S. Army ret.), Margaret (wife of Col. Wm. H. Craig, U.S. Army). Commissioned 2d lt., Field Artillery, U.S. Army, 1908, promoted through grades to brig. gen., 1940. Served with 1st Div., Army of Occupation, World War; organized and comd. first armored arty. regt., U.S. Army, 1939; with 7th Mechanized Brigade, 1937, and Armored Force since its inception 1940; arty. officer, Headquarters of Armored Forces, 1940; apptd. comdg. officer 21st F.A. Brigade, Camp Roberts, Calif., 1940-41; 14th F.A. Brig., Camp Forrest, Tenn., 1942; chmn. IV sect. War Manpower Bd. for Southeastern States, 1943-46. Mem. Theta Delta Chi, Scabbard and Blade. Mason. Clubs: Army and Navy (Washington, D.C.); Pendennis (Louisville, Ky.). Address: Atlanta, Ga. *

MAGUIRE, JOHN MACARTHUR, lawyer, educator; b. Denver, Oct. 9, 1888; s. William Miguel and Emily Mallet-Prevost (MacArthur) M.; A.B., Colo. Coll., 1908, LL.D., 1949; LL.B., Harvard, 1911; m. Mary Ballantine Hume, June 22, 1923; children—Catherine Hume (Mrs. Edward Henry Cumpston, Jr.), Nancy Ballantine (Mrs. Theodore B. Hoffman). Admitted to Mass. bar 1911; with firm Hale & Grinnell, Boston, 1911-16; partner Hale, Grinnell & Swaim, 1916-17; mem. war emergency div. Dept. of Justice, Washington, 1917-19; partner Hale & Dorr, Boston, 1919-23, counsel, 1957-73; prof. law Harvard, 1923-57, Royall prof. law, 1950-57, Royall prof. emeritus; cons. expert, U.S. Treasury Dept., 1938, 1943; asst. reporter Am. Law Inst. Code Evidence, 1939-42; cons. Am. Law Inst. Fed. Income Tax Statute, 1949-54. Mem. Am., Mass., Boston bar assn., Phi Beta Kappa. Republican. Episcopalian. Clubs: Faculty; Harvard (Boston). Author: Casebooks on Evidence and Taxation; The Lance of Justice (history of New York Legal Aid Soc.); Evidence: Common Sense and Common Law (text book); Evidence of Guilt; Restrictions upon Its Discovery or Compulsory Disclosure; also articles in field. Home: Cambridge, Mass. Deceased.

MAHER, FRANK BARRY, ins. co. exec.; b. N.Y.C., Mar. 14, 1906; s. William Francis and Margaret Barter (Carroll) M.; student Regis Prep. Sch., N.Y. U., 1930, 34-37; m. Josephine Loveday, June 27, 1931; children—Joanne E. (Mrs. T. K. Wilson), Denise C. (Mrs. J.R. Dunne), Frank B., Peter S., Jennifer D'A. (Mrs. Stephen Dibble). With John Hancock Mut. Life Ins. Co., 1923-80, became supt. agts., 1942, dir. agys., 1946, 2d v.p., 1951, v.p., 1953, exec. v.p., 1967-70, pres., chief operational officer, 1970-74; pres. Family Counseling and Guidance Centers, Inc. Trustee Mus. Fine Arts, Boston, Holy Cross Coll., Worcester, Mass., Lahey Clinic, Boston; pres. Boston Pub. Library; adv. bd. Salvation Army. Mem. Life Underwriter Tng. Council (past pres.), Life Ins. Agy. Mgmt. Assn. (past pres.), Nat. Assn. Life Underwriters. Home: Weston, Mass. Died Nov. 19, 1980.

MAHON, J. D., casualty co. exec.; b. Ellicott City, Md., Apr. 15, 1885; s. John J. and Bridget (Nee) M.; student Rock Hill Coll.; m. Gertrude E. Ells, Jan. 29, 1913 (dec. 1946); children—Gertrude E. (Mrs. G. E. Martin), Dorothy A. (Mrs. John Kenney), Joseph E. Spl. agt. Fidelity & Deposit Company, Baltimore, 1905-12, asst. sec., 1912-14; vice president New Amsterdam Casualty Company, New York City, 1914-48, president since 1948; president Commercial & Farmers Bank, Ellicott City, 1934-45; v.p. U.S. Casualty Co., N.Y., since 1937. K.C. Club: Rolling Road Golf. Home: Ellicott City, Md. *

MAHORNER, HOWARD RAYMOND, surgeon; b. Mobile, Ala., Feb. 11, 1903; s. Matthias and Catherine (Glennon) M.; A.B. maxima cum laude, Spring Hill Coll., Mobile, 1921; M.D. cum laude, U. Pa., 1925; M.S. in Surgery, U. Minn., 1929; m. Stella Hebert, June 19, 1935; children—Marie Elise Mahorner Carbone, Stella Ann (Mrs. James Hanemann, Jr.), Elizabeth (Mrs. James Landis, Jr.), Howard (dec.). Intern Mercy Hosp., Pitts., 1925-26; resident, fellow surgery Mayo Clinic, 1926-30, asst. div. surgery, 1929-30; instr., then asst. prof. surgery Tulane U. Sch. Medicine, 1932-46; clin. prof. surgery La. State U. Sch. Medicine, 1950-77; founder Mahorner Clinic, New Orleans, 1950; vis. surgeon Touro Infirmary, New Orleans, 1932-77; surgeon Baptist Hosp., 1939-77, chmn. surg. dept., 1947-51; surgeon Mercy Hosp., 1953-77; sr. vis. surgeon Charity Hosp., 1932-77; cons. surgeon Ear, Eye, Nose and Throat Hosp., 1937-77, DePaul Sanitarium, 1939-77. Cons. surgeon gen. U.S. Army, 1960. Mem. Citizens Com. Planning and Zoning, New Orleans, 1947-77. Bd. dirs. United Fund Greater New Orleans Area; bd. dirs., exec. com. New Orleans Opera House Assn. Served to maj. U.S. Army Res., 1939-43. Named King of Carnival, New Orleans, 1973. Diplomate Am. Bd. Surgery (a founder). Fellow A.C.S. (pres. La. 1950-53, sec. bd. govs. 1958-63, chmn. bd. govs. 1963-65, regent 1965-77, pres. 1970-71); mem. So. Surg. Assn. (pres. 1956-66), A.M.A., Southeastern Surg. Congress (pres. 1957-58), Am. Goiter Assn. (pres. 1960), Am. Cancer Soc. (pres. Orleans Parish 1951-53), La., Orleans Parish (v.p. 1954) med. socs., New Orleans Grad. Med. Assembly, Surgeons Travel Club (pres. 1950), Soc. Surgery Alimentary Tract, Am., La. heart assns., Council Cardiovascular Surgery, Societe Internat. de Chirurgie, Royal Soc. Medicine, Mobile Acad. Sci. (hon.), Alumni Assn. Mayo Clinic (pres. 1964), Phi Chi, Alpha Omega Alpha. Clubs: Rabelais (Univ. Pa.); Boston, Louisiana, Lake Shore, Round Table (New Orleans). Author: (with others) Thrombo-Angitis Obliterans, 1928, Varicose Veins, 1939; also numerous articles in field. Home: New Orleans, La. Died Oct. 27, 1977.

MAIDEN, ARTHUR LEE, coll. pres.; b. Rockingham Co., Va., Aug. 31, 1886; s. John William and Polly B. (Long) M.; student Shenandoah Coll., Dayton, Va., Bridgewater (Va.) Coll. and Harrisburg (Pa.) State Teachers Coll.; B.D., Bonebrake Theol. Sem., Dayton, O.; m. Minnie V. Coleman, of Shenandoah, Va., Feb. 16, 1906; children—Virginia Lee, Jeanne. Now pres. Shenandoah Coll. Mem. Pi Gamma Mu. Republican. Mason (Shriner). Home: Dayton, Va. *

MAIDMAN, IRVING, real estate investor and builder; b. N.Y.C., Feb. 25, 1897; s. Barnett and Rebecca (Schleffar) M.; student N.Y. U. Sch. Commerce, 1920; m. Annuta Kaufmann, 1920; children—Robert, Matthew; m. 2d, Edith H. Shivitz, Sept. 28, 1945; children—Rebecca, Ellen, Barnett L. Real estate broker, appraiser, N.Y.C., 1920-40; expert for tax div., law dept. City of N.Y., 1936-45; owner, builder Biltmore, Maidman Playhouse, Mayfair, Masque, Midway, Garrick, Mermaid theatres, Excelsior, Alden, Nat., Beverly hotels, West Side Air Lines Terminal, N.Y.C., 1954, Maidman Motor Hotel, 1960, Tappan Zee Motor Inn, Rockland County, 1968; owner Freedom Tower, U.S. Customs bldgs., Maimi, Fla.; owner-builder Spring Rock Country Club, pres. Tri Terminal Corp.; owner former Ford Motor Co. Assembly Plant, also Aluminum Co. plants, Edgewater, N.J.; chmn. bd., chief exec. officer N.Y., Susquehanna & Western R.R., Antilles Air Boats, Inc.; pres. Rockland Corp., Enjay Realty Co., Inc. Chmn., Mayor's Com. N.Y. Shakespeare Festival, 1962-63. Bd. dirs. Am. Israel Culture Found., Am. Coll. In Jerusalem, Parkinsons Disease Found., Rockland County Center for Physically Handicapped, Optometric Center, Inst. for Advanced Study Theatre Arts, Realty Found. N.Y., Nyack Hosp., U. Settlement, Suburban Symphony Assn.; bd. overseers Jewish Theol. Sem. Founder, Albert Einstein Coll. Medicine. Recipient Madden Meml., N.Y. U. Sch. Commerce, 1957, Nat. Community Service award Jewish Theol. Sem., 1962, Realty Man of the Year, 1961, Mr. Times Sq., 1961. Mem. Real Estate Bd. N.Y., West Side Assn. Commerce (dir.), Broadway Assn., N.Y. Hotel Assn., Commerce and Industry Assn., N.Y., N. Atlantic Ports Assn., Investing Builders Assn., Am. Legion. Mason, Knight of Malta. Clubs: The Lambs, N.Y. Railroad, N.Y. University. Home: Nyack, N.Y. Died Oct. 7, 1979; buried Mt. Hebron Cemetery, Queens, N.Y.

MAIER, NORMAN RAYMOND FREDERICK, psychologist; b. Sebewaing, Mich., Nov. 27, 1900; s. Charles and Emma C. (Cramer) M.; student Wayne U., 1919-21; A.B., U. Mich., 1923, A.M., 1925, Ph.D., 1928; grad. work U. Berlin, 1926-27; m. Ayesha Frances Ali, Feb. 17, 1930; children—Richard A., Carl C., John L. Asst. prof. L.I. U., 1928-29; Nat. Research Council fellow U. Chgo., 1929-31; instr. psychology U. Mich., 1931-35, asst. prof., 1935-39, asso. prof., 1939-45, prof., 1945-71, prof. emeritus, from 1971; research Worker on reasoning, animal behavior, brain physiology, frustration, indsl. psychology, human relations; indsl. cons., exec. devel. programs. Cons. European Productivity Agy., 1959-60. Recipient Newcomb Cleveland prize A.A.A.S., 1938, Henry Russel award U. Mich., 1939; award Soc. Humanistic Mgmt., 1974. Diplomate in Indsl. Psychology. Fellow A.A.A.S., Am. Psychol. Assn.; mem. Midwestern Psychol. Assn. (council 1939-42), Soc. Psychol. Study of Social Issues (rep. to NRC 1943-45). Episcopalian. Author: (with Reninger) Psychological Approach to Literary Criticism, 1933; Principles of Animal Psychology (with Schneirla), 1935; Studies of Abnormal Behavior in the Rat, 1939; Psychology in Industry, 1946; Frustration: the Study of Behavior without a Goal, 1949; Principles of Human Relations; Applications to Management, 1952; (with A.R. Solem and Ayesha A. Maier) Supervisory and Executive Development: A Manual for Role Playing, 1957; The Appraisal Interview: Objectives, Methods and Skills, 1958; (with J.J. Hayes) Creative Management, 1962; Problem-Solving Discussions and Conferences, 1963; (color film) The New Truck Dilemna, 1966; Problem Solving and Creativity: In Individuals and Groups, 1970; Psychology in Industrial Organizations, 1973; (with A.R. Solem and Ayesha A. Maier) The Role-Play Technique, 1975; The Appraisal Interview: Three Basic Approaches, 1976; Appraising Performance: An Interview Skills Course, 1976. Contbr. articles to sci. jours. Home: Ann Arbor, Mich. Deceased.

MAIN, LEE ROY, dean; b. St. Louis, Mo., Jan. 6, 1885; s. Stephan H. and Sarah (Walker) M.; D.D.S., St. Louis Univ., 1907; post grad. student, Northwestern, 1919; LL.D., Baylor University, 1958; married to Iva B. Barton, June 6, 1917; children—Dorothy June (Mrs. Robert Bethune Johnson), Donald LeRoy. Gen. practice of dentistry, St. Louis, Mo., 1907-18, specialist in roentgenology, 1920-45; prof. roentgenology, St. Louis U. since 1933, dean, lectr. sch. dentistry, 1945-57, dean emeritus, 1957—; consultant roentgenology John Cochran VA Hospital, St. Louis; consultant National Board Dental Examiners, American Dental Assn. Fellow Am. Coll. Dentists (past pres.). Mem. Am. Soc. for Advancement of Oral Diagnosis, Am. Assn. of Dental Schools (president 1956-57), Am. Dental Assn. (chmn. section on roentgenology, 1948), St. Louis Acad. of Sci., A.A.A.S., Internat. Assn. of Dental Research, Mo. State Dental Assn. (1st vice pres., 1944-45), St. Louis Dental Soc. (sec.-treas., 1920, 1st, 2d, 3d vice pres. 1934-36, pres., 1937), American Dental Society of Europe, Federation Dentaire Internationale (hon.), Congreso de la Asociacion Dental Mexicana (hon. mem.), Alpha Phi Omega, Psi Omega (mem. supreme council, 1941-48), Sigma Xi, Omicron Kappa Upsilon. Republican. Baptist. Contbr. articles on various phases of oral roentgenology and on dental edn. to sci. jours. Home: St. Louis. *

MAIN, VERNER WRIGHT, ex-congressman; b. Ashley, O., Dec. 16, 1885; s. Elwyn Bishop and Margaret (Lawrence) M.; A.B., Hillsdale (Mich.) Coll., 1907; J.D., U. of Mich., 1914; m. Rose E. Hoppin, of Niles, Mich., Dec. 18, 1915; children—Marcia, Stuart, Janet, Curtis. Prin. high sch., Hudson, Mich., 1908-09, Niles, Mich., 1909-12; admitted to Mich. bar, 1914, and began practice in Battle Creek; asst. pros. atty. Calhoun County, 1926; mem. Mich. Ho. of Rep., 1927-29; mem. Battle Creek Sch. Bd., 1929-32; chmn. Mich. Bd. of strategy in opposition to repeal of prohibition sections of State Constitution, 1932; Dry candidate for del. to Constl. Conv. to Repeal 18th Amendment, 1935; elected to 74th Congress to fill vacancy, Dec. 17, 1935. Served in Field Artillery Central O.T.C., Camp Taylor, Ky., World War. Mem. Mich. State and Calhoun Co. bar assns., Delta Tau Delta. Republican. Presbyn. Clubs: Torch, Kiwanis (Battle Creek). Home: Battle Creek, Mich. *

MAIR, GEORGE F(ISK), educator; b. N.Y.C., July 22, 1922; s. George and Evelyn (Thurber) M.; A.B., Princeton, 1943, A.M., 1948, Ph.D., 1957; m. Jean Lois Baum, Dec. 27, 1947; children—Edward Macdonald, Margaret Granville. Research fellow demography Princeton, 1948-50, instr. econs. and sociology, 1950-53; mem. faculty Smith Coll., 1953-78, prof. econs., 1962-78, asst. to pres., 1966-72, dean, 1976-78; vis. prof. econs. and demography U. Cal. at Berkeley, 1965-66; vis. lectr. sociology U. Mass. at Amherst, 1964, mem. grad. faculty, 1964-78; vis. prof. econs., mem. Center for Population Studies, Harvard, 1972-73; staff asso. demographic div. Population Council, N.Y.C., 1961-62. Cons. Gen. Electric Co., 1957, Outdoor Recreation Resources Rev. Commn., 1957, Nat. Inst. Child Health and Human Devel., 1969-78. Served to 1st lt., Transp. Corps, AUS, 1943-46. Milbank fellow, 1948-50; Danforth Found. tchr. study grantee, 1956-57. Mem. Am. Econ. Assn., Soc. Study Social Biology, Am. Statis. Assn., Population Assn. Am., Internat. Union Sci. Study Population, A.A.A.S., Am. Assn. U. Profs., Guild Carillonneurs in N. Am., N. Am. Guild Change Ringers, Appalachian Mountain Club, Phi Beta Kappa. Editor: Studies in Population, 1949; cons. editor Eugenics Quar., 1956-60; editorial staff Am. Sociol. Rev., 1957-60. Contbr. to profl. jours. Home: Northampton, Mass. Died Sept. 12, 1978; buried Valhalla, N.Y.

MAJOR, HOWARD BROUGHAM, author, architect; b. N.Y. City, Nov. 21, 1883; s. Walter C. and Anna (Bryan) M.; prep. edn., Adelphi Acad., Brooklyn, and Pratt Inst. High Sch.; grad. Pratt Inst. Tech., 1903; m. Katherine Clark, of Northampton, Mass., Sept. 6, 1923; 1 son, Howard Brougham. Mgr. for firm of Charles A. Rich, architect, New York, 1903-14; practiced alone since 1914; pres. The 154 E. 61st Street Corpn.; 1st v.p. Palm Beach Harbor Corpn. Mem. Squadron A. N.Y.N.G., 1907-14; studies naval aviation at O.T.C., 1918. Mem. Am. Inst. Architects, Fla.Assn. Architects. Clubs: Metropolitan (New York); Everglades, Bath and Tennis, Oasis (Palm Beach). Author: The Domestic Architecture of the Early American Republic, 1926. Contrbr. to Country Life, Vogue, House and Garden, House Beautiful, etc. Home: Palm Beach, Fla. *

MAJOR, JUDITH, univ. prof.; b. Livonia, La., March 27, 1882; d. J. B. and Adele (David) Major; Diploma, La. State Normal, 1901; A.B., La. State U., 1914; A.M., Columbia, 1915, grad. student, 1930-31; Diplome de Phonetique and Certificat, Sorbonne, Paris, 1928; Certificat, Univ. of Poitiers, 1928; 1 adopted son, James R. Demonstration teacher, Tulane U., summer 1907; teacher and prin., La. pub. schs., 1901-12; post-master, Maringouin, La., 1917-18; teacher French and Spanish,

Ark. pub. schs., 1919-24; instr. French, La. State U., 1924-28, asst. prof., 1928-31, asso. prof., 1931-46, prof. since 1946. Democrat. Roman Catholic Co-author: Parlor Lire Ecrire, 1947. Home: Baton Rouge, La. *

MAJOR, RALPH HERMON, physician; b. Clay County, Mo., Aug. 29, 1884; s. John Sleet and Virginia (Anderson) M.; A.B., William Jewell Coll., 1902, LL.D.,1933; M.D., Johns Hopkins, 1910; D.Litt., University of Cincinnati; 1952; student universities of Chicago, Leipzig, Munich and Heidelberg, 1903-1906; married Margaret Norman Jackson, Dec. 11, 1915; children—Ralph Hermon, John Keene, Margaret Virginia (Mrs. Downing A. Thomas). Interne, Johns Hopkins Hospital, 1910-12; assistant in clinic, Vienna, Austria, and Munich, 1912-13; with dept. of pathology, Stanford University, 1913-14; prof. pathology, Univ. of Kan., 1914-18; physician to Henry Ford Hosp., Detroit, Mich., 1919-21; prof. internal medicine, U. of Kan., 1921-49, professor of history of medicine since 1949. Served as capt. Med. Corps, U.S. Army, 1918-19; maj. Med. R.C. Mem. A.M.A., Am. Assn. History Medicine (pres. 1950-52), Association American Physicians, Am. Climatol. and Clin. Assn., Am. Assn. Pathologists and Bacteriologists, Am. Soc. for Clin. Investigation, Nu Sigma Nu, Alpha Omega Alpha, Phi Beta Kappa, Sigma Xi, Sigma Nu. Episcopalian. Club: Kansas City Country. Author: The Doctor Explains (translated into German), 1931; Classic Descriptions of Disease, 1932; Disease and Destiny (translated into German, Dutch, Hungarian), 1936; Physical Diagnosis, 1937; Faiths That Healed, 1940; Fatal Partners: War and Disease, 1941; Hippocrates and the Isle of Cos, 1946. Contributor to medical journals, results of investigations on high blood pressure, also on diabetes and metabolic diseases; articles on med. history. Home: Kansas City, Mo. *

MAJOR, RANDOLPH THOMAS, educator, chemist; b. Columbus, O., Dec. 23, 1901; s. David R. and Mary Randolph (Campbell) M.; A.B., U. Neb., 1922, M.S., 1924, D.Sc. (hon.), 1949; Ph.D., Princeton, 1927; m. Grace E. Lowe, July 7, 1928; children—Mary E., Randolph T., Anne C., Jane W. High sch. tchr. Albion, Neb., 1922-23; research Pasteur Inst., Paris, France, 1926-27, Pharm. Inst., Berlin, summer 1927; research asso., instr. Princeton, 1927-30; dir. pure research Merck & Co., Inc., Rahway, N.J., 1930-36, dir. research and devel., 1936-47, v.p., sci. dir., 1947-53, sci. v.p., 1953-56, sci. adviser, 1956-67; sci. adviser Merck Inst. Therapeutic Research, 1967-74; prof. chemistry U. Va., Charlottesville, 1957-67, research prof. chemistry, 1967-70; research prof. chemistry U. Conn., Storrs, 1970-76. Chmn. adv. council to dept. chemistry Princeton, 1941-51; adv. com. research div. Coll. Engring., N.Y.U., 1949-56; vice chmn. com. on research Nat. Assn. Mfrs., 1951-57. Trustee Experiment in Internat. Living. Putney, Vt., 1955-57. Mem. Am. Chem. Soc. (dir. 1955-60; rep. to div. chem. and chem. tech. NRC 1952-55, councilor 1965-68). Am. Soc. Biol. Chemists, A.A.A.S., N.Y. Acad. Sci., Phi Beta Kappa, Sigma Xi. Club: Chemists'. Holder patents in field of medicinal chemistry. Home: Storrs, Conn. Died Nov. 1, 1976.

MAJTHENYI, LADISLAUS D., mgmt. cons.; b. Kiscell, Hungary, Jan. 13, 1903; s. Alexander de and Maria (de Skublics) M.; student Acad. Commerce, Budapest, Hungary and Graz, Austria, 1920-24; m. Gabriella de Roboz, July 9, 1934; children—Klara, Alexander. Came to U.S., 1949, naturalized, 1954. With Nat. Bank Hungary, 1924-44, sect. chief Presdl. Dept., 1938-44; rep. of Austro-Impex, Linz, Austria, 1946-49; with affliated companies Hambros Bank Ltd. (London, Eng.) in U.S., 1950-53; sr. partner Hambar Co., White Plains, N.Y., 1953-58, 69; v.p. Pergamon Press Inc., 1954-63, pres., 1963-67, dep. chmn. bd., chmn. exec. com., 1967-69. Mem. com. to establish free port in Linz, 1948. Pres. Szechenyi Istvan Soc., Inc., N.Y.C., 1968-80. Bd. dirs. Am. Found. for Hungarian Lit. and Edn., Ltd., N.Y.C., 1970-80. Mem. AAAS, Am. Forestry Assn., Nat. Soc. Lit. and Art, several Am.-Hungarian socs. Club: K.C. Home: White Plains, N.Y. Died Feb. 25, 1980; buried Gate of Heaven Cemetery, Hawthorne, N.Y.

MAKI, T(ENHO) EWALD, educator; b. Newton Twp., Minn., Mar. 29, 1907; s. Karl Victor and Ida Sofia (Nissi) M.; B.S., U. Minn., 1930, M.S., 1931, PhD., 1951; m. Laurencia Bernadette Landry, May 9, 1936; children—Wilma Lee, (Mrs. Richard R. Weidman), Marilyn Carol (Mrs. Don W. Kim). Caleb Dorr fellow U. Minn., 1932-34; technician Intermountain Forest Expt. Sta., 1934-35; jr. forester So. Forest Expt. Sta., New Orleans, 1935-36; asst. forester, then asso. forester Intermountain Forest and Range Expt. Sta., Ogden, Utah, 1936-40; forester, then sr. forester Beltsville (Md.) Forest Lab., 1940-45; officer-in-charge Gulfcoast br. So. Forest Expt. Sta., 1945-51; prof. forest mgmt. Sch. Forestry, N.C. State U., 1951-54, Carl Alwin Schenck prof. forest mgmt., 1954-80, head dept. forest mgmt., 1958-70, also mem. adminstrv. bd. Grad. Sch.; Fulbright research scholar U. Helsinki (Finland), 1965-66; vis. lectr. Royal Coll. Forestry, Stockholm, Sweden, Forest Research Inst., Vollebekk, Norway, U. Aberdeen (Scotland), U. Coll. N. Wales, Bangor, 1966; cons. to industry, 1956-65, 67-80, FAO, 1966. Dir. NSF-Undergrad. Research participation programs in forest biology, 1960-64, 67-70. Recipient N.C. Gov.'s award in foresty conservation, 1971, Bicentennial award for outstanding service in forestry practices N.C., 1976, Outstanding Tchrs. award N.C. State U., 1975-76. Fellow Soc. Am. Foresters (chmn. Appalachian sect. 1957-58); mem. Soc. Forestry Finland (hon.), Soil Sci. Soc. Am. (vice chmn. div. 7 1967-70, chmn. 1970-71), Internat. Soil Sci. Soc., N.C. Acad. Sci., Sigma Xi, Gamma Sigma Delta, Xi Sigma Pi, Alpha Zeta, Phi Kappa Phi. Presbyn. (past deacon). Author numerous articles in field. Editor proc. Spl. Field Inst. Forest Biology, 1960. Home: Raleigh, N.C. Died Aug. 9, 1980.

MAKTOS, JOHN, lawyer, educator; b. Greece, Nov. 21, 1902; s. John and Eugenia (Antoniades) M.; A.B., Harvard, 1927, LL.B., 1926; postgrad. in law Oxford (Eng.) U., 1926-27; postgrad. U. Paris, Oxford U. (Carnegie fellowship in Internat. law), 1927-28; S.J.D., Harvard (Hyman fellow Law Sch.), 1929; m. Bernice Virginia Wallace. Admitted to Mich., D.C., U.S. Supreme Ct. bars; asst. solicitor Dept. of State, Washington, 1929-31; asst. counsel for U.S. in arbitration of claim on behalf of P.W. Shufeldt against Guatemala, asst. legal adviser Dept. of State, 1931-41; counsel for U.S. Govt. jud. ofcl. U.S.-Turkish Joint Claims Commn., Istanbul, Turkey and Washington, 1933-35; chmn. Interdepartmental Visa Rev. Com., Washington, 1941-43; prin. divional asst., div. internat. security and orgn. Dept. of State, 1943-44; gen. counsel Am.-Mexican Claims Commn., Washington, 1944-45; asso. chief and chief legal sect., div. of internat. orgn. affairs Dept. of State, Washington, 1945-47; asst. legal adviser Dept. of State in charge internat. orgn. affairs, 1947-51, in charge Near Eastern, South Asian and African affairs, 1951-62; practice law, Washington, 1963-69; asst. prof. law Columbus U. Law Sch., 1941-43, prof., 1943-77. Participated San Francisco Conf. on Internat. Orgn., 1945; legal adviser to U.S. delegation World Health Conf., N.Y.C., 1946; legal adviser U.S. delegation to UN Gen. Assembly, N.Y.C., 1946, 3d Gen. Assembly, Paris, 1948, 4th Gen. Assembly, 1949; U.S. rep., chmn. U.N. com. on genocide, 1948; U.S. rep. UN com. on internat. criminal jurisdiction, 1951, com. on agression, 1953. Decorated comdr. Order of George I (Greece); knight Patriarchal Order St. Andrew. Mem. Harvard Law Sch. Assn. (life), Assn. Internat. Droit Penal (hon.), Am. Bar Assn. (com. on terr. limits of jurisdiction, 1938-39), Fed. Bar Assn., Am. Soc. Internat. Law (life mem., mem. exec. council, chmn. com. on nominations and reorgn. of membership), Am. Arbitration Assn. (arbitrator), Soc. Descs. King William I The Conqueror and Companions at Arms, Soc. Friends of St. George's Chapel, Descs. Order of Garter (life), Sigma Epsilon Phi (Pres. 1924-25). Clubs: Cosmos, Internat., Harvard (Washington). Author: Federal Legal Functions, 1930; Comparative Conflict of Laws, 1929. Asso. editor Fed. Bar Assn. Jour., 1930-45. Contbr. to legal periodicals. Home: Washington, D.C. Died Feb. 26, 1977; buried Ft. Lincoln Cemetery, Washington.

MALAND, OSWALD, lawyer; b. Elmore, Minn., Oct. 25, 1891; s. Berent J. and Matilda (Finhart) M.; J.D., U. Minn., 1915; m. Ruth E. Anderson, Oct. 14, 1916; 1 dau., Dorothy Carlene (Mrs. Paul F. Ilg). Admitted to Iowa bar, 1915, Ill. bar, 1924; practice in Mason City, Iowa, 1915-24, Chgo., from 1924; sr. partner firm Chapman & Cutler, from 1943; dir. United Cities Gas Co. Trustee, v.p. Meth. Found. of Rock River Conf., 1948-51, Superannuates Relief Assn., 1952-62. Mem. Am., Ill. bar assns., Delta Chi. Author: Revision of Fletcher Cyclopedia Corporations, vol. on corporate practice, 1959. Home: Evanston, Ill. Died Sept. 21, 1979.

MALCOLM, WALTER DAVID, lawyer; b. Chgo., July 30, 1904; s. Matthew Davis and Margaret (Hancock) M.; B.S., U. Ore., 1926; LL.B., Harvard, 1929; m. Violet Prouty Harris, Aug. 31, 1930; children—Walter David Jr., Nancy Lydia (Mrs. Joseph R. Odell). Admitted to Mass. bar, 1929, since practiced in Boston; partner firm Bingham, Dana & Gould, 1937-75; lectr. uniform comml. code, uniform consumer credit code, 1946-79; commnr. Mass. Uniform State Laws, 1955-73. Mem. Hingham (Mass.) Sch. Com., 1937-46; chmn. Hingham Zoning Bd. Appeal, 1941-44. Bd. dirs. Internat. Friendship League, Boston. Fellow Am. Bar Found.; mem. Am. Law Inst., Am. Bar Assn. (pres. nat. conf. commnrs. uniform state laws 1963-65), Phi Delta Theta. Unitarian. Editorial bd. Uniform Comml. Code, 1954-74. Home: Hingham, Mass. Died Nov. 17, 1979.

MALCOLM, WILBUR GEORGE, company dir.; b. Moscow Mills, Md., June 22, 1902; s. William Henry and Annie (Thomas) M.; B.S., U. Md., 1922, Ph.D., 1930, LL.D., 1958; m. Gwennie Bennie, Jan. 11, 1928; children—Bryant, Peter Malcolm. Instr. U. Md., 1922-24; sr. bacteriol., anti-toxin and vaccine labs., Forest Hill, Mass., 1930-34; v.p., gen. mgr. Lederle Labs, Pearl River, N.Y., 1946-55; chmn., dir., mem. exec. com., chief exec. officer Am. Cyanamid Co., N.Y.C.; dir. Irving Trust Co., So. Minerals Corp., So. Petroleum Corp., So. Pipe Line Corp. Mem. Internat. Coll. Surgeons, Soc. Am. Bacteriologists, Mfg. Chemists Assn. (dir.), N.Y. Acad. Sci. Clubs: University (N.Y.C.); Rockland County (Sparkill, N.Y.). Home: Grand View-on-Hudson, N.Y. Died Dec. 29, 1979; buried Rockland Cemetery, Sparkill, N.Y.

MALCUZYNSKI, WITOLD, pianist; b. Warsaw, Poland, Aug. 10, 1914; s. Witold and Maria (Bortkiewicz) M.; grad. Warsaw Conservatory, 1936; studies with I.J. Paderewski in Morges, Switzerland, 1937; student law, philosophy, Warsaw U.; m. Corlette Gaveau, Oct. 1939; children—Marie Pierrette, Christine. Internat. debut, Pasdeloup Orchestra, Paris, 1940, S.A. debut, Buenos Aires and Rio de Janeiro, 1941, Am. debut, Carnegie Hall, N.Y.C., 1942; concert tours throughout world, world tour to celebrate 100th anniversary of Chopin's death, 1949; played with major orchestras; numerous recordings for Columbia Records, Angel Records. Recipient prize Internat. Chopin Contest, 1937. Hon. citizen Cracow, Poland, 1959, State of Tex., 1959; hon. mem. Chopin Soc., Warsaw. Home: Montreux, Switzerland. Died July 18, 1977.

MALEK, MINA LENA, educator, lecturer; b. Woodbine, Kan., Oct. 17, 1885; d. William and Caroline (Von Heske) Steckel; ed. Allen Commercial Coll. (Abilene, Kan.), Moody Bible Inst. (Chicago), Kan. State Teachers Coll. (Emporia), Passavant and Children's Memorial hosps. (Chicago), Woman's Med. Coll. (Phila.); m. Rev. Rudolph Malek, of British E. Africa, Dec. 10, 1913; children—Rudolph Gray, Patricia Ann. Ordained deacon M.E. Ch., 1925, elder, 1930; served as med. missionary in Africa 9 yrs.; Red Cross work Women's Prison of War Camp, Tanga, German East Africa, 1916-20; supt. Jennings Sem., Aurora, Ill., since 1933. Mem. Delta Kappa Gamma. Republican. Mem. Eastern Star. Clubs: Aurora Woman's, Business and Professional Women's (Aurora). Address: Aurora, Ill. *

MALIN, JAMES CLAUDE (MA LIN), educator; b. nr. Edgeley, N.D., Feb. 8, 1893; s. Jared Nelson and Emma Jane (McChristy) M.; A.B., Baker U., 1914, LL.D. (hon.), 1962; A.M., U. Kans., 1916, Ph.D., 1921; m. Pearl Ethel Keene, 1920; 1 dau., Jane Wofford. Asst. prof. U. Kans., 1921-27, asso. prof., 1927-38, prof. history, 1938-63, prof. history emeritus, 1963-79. Fellow A.A.A.S.; mem. Am., Kans. (pres. 1940-41), Agrl. (pres. 1943-44) hist. assns., Assn. Am. Geographers, Am. Studies Assn., Midcontinent Am. Studies Assn., Soc. for Advancement Scandinavian Study. Author: The United States after the World War, 1930; An Interpretation of Recent American History, 1926; Indian Policy and Westward Expansion, 1921; John Brown and the Legend of Fifty-Six, 1942; Winter Wheat in the Golden Belt of Kansas, 1944; Essays on Historiography, 1946; The Grassland of North America: Prolegomena to its History, 1947; Grassland Historical Studies: Natural Resources Utilization in a Background of Science and Technology, Vol. I, 1950; The Nebraska Question, 1852-54, 1954; On the Nature of History, 1954; The Contriving Brain and the Skillful Hand, 1955; Confounded Rot about Napoleon, 1961; Ironquill-Paint Creek Essays, 1972; Doctors Devils and the Woman, Fort Scott, Kansas, 1870-1890, 1971; H.H. Sargent and Eugene F. Ware on Napoleon: Professional and Amateur Military Historians, 1980; Power and Change in Society, 1981. Home: Lawrence, Kans. Died Jan. 26, 1979.

MALIPIERO, G. FRANCESCO, composer; b. Venice, Italy, Mar. 18, 1882; s. Luigi and Emma (Balbi) M.; m. Anna Wright. Mem. Nat. Inst. Arts and Letters (hon.), Academie Flamand Brussells, Institut de France, Royal Acad. Music (London). Composer 10 symphonies, 8 quartets, sonatas for 3 4, 5 instruments, 10 works for orchestra, 4 oratorios, 14 operas. Address: Asolo (Treviso), Italy. *

MALLON, FRANCIS BERNARD, ret. army officer; b. Middletown, N.Y., Sept. 17, 1886; s. Bernard James and Ella Marie (Koch) M.; cadet U.S. Mil. Acad., 1908-09; grad. Command and Gen. Staff Sch., 1923, Army War Coll., 1927; m. Eunice Marion Casey, Oct. 21, 1916 (dec.); 1 son, Richard. Pvt. and cpl., 5th Inf., 1909-12; commd. 2d lt. U.S. Army, 1912, advanced through grades to maj. gen., 1944; comdr. Replacement Tng. Center, Camp Jos. T. Robinson, Ark. and Army Ground Forces Replacement Depot No. 1, Fort George G. Meade, Md., World War II; mem. War Dept Gen. Staff, 1927-30, 1939-41; gen. staff with troops, 1933-37; acting comdr. VII Corps, 1945-46; ret., 1946. Clubs: Army and Navy (Washington); Bohemian (San Francisco). Home: San Mateo CA. *

MALLORY, JASPER NEWTON, coll. pres.; b. La Grange, Ga., Apr. 1, 1883; s. James Thomas and Georgia (Wheeless) M.; student Weatherford (Tex.) Coll., 1889-1902; grad, N. Tex. State Normal Sch., 1912; A.B., U. of Okla., 1916; A.M., Baylor U., 1919; Ph.D., Peabody Coll. for Teachers, 1922; m. Quinnie M. Karr, Aug. 6, 1902; children—William Martin (dec.), Mary Lou and Martha Lee (twins). Teacher pub. schs. of Tex. 15 yrs.; prof. science, Coll. of Marshall, Tex., 2 yrs., 1916-18; mem. faculty, Peabody Coll. for Teachers, 4 summers; prof. mathematics, Union U., Jackson, Tenn., 5 yrs., 1919-24; pres. Jonesboro Coll. since 1924. Mem. Phi Delta Kappa. Democrat. Baptist. Rotarian. Author: Relation of Order of Birth to School Progress, 1922; Relation of Physical Defects to School Progress,

1922; Some Formulae for Finding and Checking Multiple Correlation, 1922. Home: Jonesboro, Ark. *

MALLORY, PHILIP ROGERS, mfg. exec.; b. Bklyn., Nov. 11, 1885; s. Henry Rogers and Cora (Pynchon) M.; student Hill Sch., Pottstown, Pa.; B.A., Yale U., 1908; student law sch. Columbia U., 1908-10; m. Dorothea Barron, 1912; children—Henry Rogers, Dorothea (Mrs. Ward Grantham), George Barron; m. 2d, Mildred Courtney, June 24, 1930 (dec. Mar. 1961); m. 3d, Louise Sobotka Steffe, Nov. 1, 1961. Admitted to N.Y. bar, 1910; engaged in bond and security bus., 1910-14; gen. mgr., treas. Comml. Research Co.; organizer P.R. Mallory & Co., Inc., 1916, with plants throughout world, chmn. bd., 1946-65, hon. chmn. bd., from 1965; chmn. P.R. Mallory Internat. Inc., 1959-66, hon. chmn. bd., from 1966; officer, dir. subsidiaries. Chmn. emeritus, trustee Mystic Seaport, Inc. Clubs: N.Y. Yacht, Am. Yacht (Rye, N.Y.); Yale, Metropolitan, Links (N.Y.C.); Fishers Island (N.Y.) Country, Fishers Island Yacht; N. Am. Yacht Racing; Cruising of Am. Home: Fishers Island, N.Y. Died Nov. 16, 1975.

MALLORY, WALTER HAMPTON, exec. dir., author, editor; b. Newburgh, N.Y., July 27, 1892; s. Edward Wolcott and Mary (Gray) M.; ed. Columbia, 1913-15; m. Alice Evans, May 13, 1919; children—Walter Hampton (dec.), George Wolcott. Leader of Columbia Relief Expdn. to Serbia, 1915; first exec. officer Near East Relief, 1915-16; spl. asst. to Am. ambassador at Petrograd, 1916-17; fgn. rep. U.S. Shipping Bd., 1919; exec. sec. China Internat. Famine Relief Commn., Peking, 1922-26; spl. lectr. Columbia, summer 1926; exec. dir. Council Fgn. Relations, 1927-59, dir., 1945-80; del. Internat. Studies Conf., Paris, 1934. Mem. adv. com. fgn. participation N.Y. World's Fair, 1939; chmn. SSS local bd. 44, World War II; trustee China Inst. in Am. (pres. 1943-47); mem. China Med. Bd., 1947-58; mem. Allied Mission to Observe the Elections in Greece, rank minister, 1946; U.S. del. European-Am. Assembly, 1962. Mem. vis. com. dept. Far Eastern civilizations Harvard; dir. Asia Found. Served as lt. 18th F.A., 3d Div. Am. Expdnry. Forces, 1917-19, participated in St. Mihiel, Defensive Sector and Meuse-Argonne battles. Decorated Order of Pure Gold (China); grand officer Order of Cristóbal Colón (Dominican Republic); Cross Order of Mercy (Yugoslavia); also Yugoslav Red Cross Decoration. Mem. Am. Asiatic Assn., Pilgrims, Soc. Mayflower Descs., S.R. Republican. Episcopalian. Mason. Clubs: Century Assn., University (N.Y.C.); Cosmos (Washington); Ekwanok Country (Vt.). Author: China, Land of Famine, 1926. Editor: Political Handbook and Atlas of the World (with Malcolm W. Davis), 1928-29, alone 1929-68. Contbr. mags. on Far Eastern affairs and internat. relations. Home: Fredonia, N.Y. Died June 17, 1980.

MALONE, CARROLL BROWN (MA-LON), coll. prof.; b. Cleveland, O., Nov. 25, 1886; s. John Walter and Emma Isabel (Brown) M.; A.B., Western Reserve U., 1908; A.M., U. of Mich., 1909; A.M., Harvard, 1920; Ph.D., U. of Ill., 1928; m. Alma Earl, July 27, 1916; children—Thomas Earl, Robert Franklin. Teacher, Gallipolis, O., 1909-10; prof. Tsing Hua Coll. and Tsing Hua U., Peiping, China, 1910-27; prof. of history, Denison U., 1924-25, Ohio State U., summer 1925; asso. prof. Oberlin Coll., 1928-29, Miami U., 1929-30, Stanford U., summer 1930; prof. of history, Colo. Coll., since 1930; prof. of history, U. of Colo., summer 1935. Mem. Am. Hist. Assn., Colo.-Wyo. Social Science Assn. (pres. 1939-40), Phi Beta Kappa, Beta Theta Pi. Conglist. Author: History of the Peking Summer Palaces under the Ch'ing Dynasty, 1934. Contbr. to professional jours. *

MALONE, HENRY THOMPSON, coll. dean; b. Albany, Ga., July 4, 1916; s. Henry and Corrie (MacIver) Thompson M.; B.S., Clemson U., 1937; M.A., Emory U., 1949, Ph.D., 1952; m. Alice Clark Young, Feb. 26, 1977. Tchr., Monticello High Sch., Stother, S.C., 1937-39, Boys High Sch., Rome, Ga., 1939-42, Ga. Mil. Acad., College Park, 1942-43, Calhoun (Ga.) High Sch., 1947-48; asst. circulation mgr. Stars & Stripes, Frankfurt, Germany, 1946-47; mem. faculty Ga. State U., Atlanta, 1952-77, prof. history, 1960-77, dean Sch. Gen. Studies, 1970-77, mem. urban life faculty, 1971-77, book reviewer Atlanta Jour.-Constn., from 1960; cons. regional history Six Flags Over Ga., 1972; cons. Nat. Endowment for Humanities, 1974-77. Chmn. edn. Ga. Heart Fund, 1972-77; chmn. exec. com. Annual Ga. Leadership Inst., from 1955; mem. exec. com. Atlanta CARE, 1972-77: commr. Ga. Hist. Commn., 1968-73. Bd. dirs. G.M. Sparks Scholarship Fund, Inc. Served with AUS, 1943-45. Decorated Bronze Star; recipient M.L. Britain Service award Emory U., 1951, Distinguished Lit. Achievement award Ga. Writers Assn., 1956, McClung award E. Tenn. Hist. Soc., 1956; named ambassador Cherokee Nation, 1971, Outstanding Educator for 1972. Mem. Ga. Soc. Fund Raisers (pres. 1969-70), So., Ga., Western hist. assns., Omicron Delta Kappa (nat. scholarship com. 1970-74, nat. Distinguished Service Key 1974), Phi Kappa, Phi Eta Sigma, Gamma Alpha Mu, Delta Sigma Pi. Kiwanian (gov. Ga. 1967; pres. Ga. Kiwanis Meml. Found. 1972-73). Club: Ansley-Atlanta (pres. 1973-74). Author: Cherokees of the Old South, 1956; The Episcopal Church in Georgia, 1733-1957, 1960; background narrative for Civil War in Ga. audio-visual display, Stone Mountain, from 1960; Ga. Heritage series, over 100 newspapers Ga., 1963-64. Home: Atlanta, Ga. Died Oct. 5, 1977; buried Darlington, S.C.

MALONEY, FRANK EDWARD, educator; b. Niagara Falls, N.Y., Mar. 27, 1918; s. Frank E. and Florence (Bielman) M.; B.A., U. Toronto (Can.), 1938, grad. student philosophy, 1938-39; LL.B., U. Fla., 1942; m. Lucille Tinker, Feb. 20, 1943; children—Frank Edward, Jo Ann, Elizabeth. Admitted to Fla. bar, 1942, also Supreme Ct. U.S.; with firm Jordan, Lazonby & Dell, Gainesville, Fla., 1942; asso. prof. law U. Fla., 1946-50, prof. law, 1950-58, acting dean Law Sch., 1958-59, dean Law Sch., 1959-70, dean emeritus, 1970-80, prof. law, 1959-80, dir. Center of Expertise for Southeastern Water Law, 1965—; grad. fellow Sch. Law, Columbia, 1950-51; vis. prof. N.Y. U. Law Sch., 1957-58, Vanderbilt Law Sch., 1970-71, George Washington Law Center, summers 1968, 69, Tex. Tech. U., summer 1971; cons. internat. water law problems U.S. Dept. State. Chmn. Gov.'s resource com. to study effects of rapid growth on Fla.'s South Gulf Coast, 1979-80. Served to maj. USAAF, 1942-46; CBI; col. USAF Res. ret. Fellow Am. Bar Found.; mem. Am. Law Inst., Am. Bar Assn., Fla. Bar, Assn. Am. Law Schs. (chmn. com. fed. legislation 1964-70), Internat. Assn. Water Law, U. Fla. Law Center Assn. (vice chmn. 1961-70), Bar Assn. 8th Jud. Circuit Fla., Nat. Conf. Bar Examiners (chmn. torts com. multistate bar exam.), Fla. Soc. Profl. Land Surveyors (hon. life), Phi Beta Kappa, Order of Coif, Fla. Blue Key, Phi Kappa Phi, Phi Alpha Delta, Pi Kappa Phi. Rotarian. Co-author: Water Law and Adminstration, 1968; A Model Water Code, 1972; drafted Fla. Water Resources Acts, 1957, 72, Tenn. Water Quality Act, 1971. Co-author 3 books; contbr. numerous articles to profl. jours. Home: Gainesville, Fla. Died Apr. 23, 1980; buried Forest Meadows Meml. Park, Gainesville.

MALONEY, JAMES LOY, newspaper editor; b. Mt. Carroll, Ill., Oct. 21, 1891; s. James Sumner and Bess Agnes (Tressler) M.; student Denison U., 1910-11, Dartmouth, 1912-13, Pulitzer Sch. Journalism (Columbia U.), 1914-15; m. Hilda Gladys Blackburn, Mar. 17, 1919 (dec.); children—Betty Jean (died 1927), Patricia B., Barbara Joan. With City News Bureau, Chicago, 1915-16; reporter Chicago Tribune, 1917-25, day city editor, 1926-36, city editor, 1937-38, mng. editor, 1939-52, exec. editor, from 1952. 1st lieut. Air Service, U.S. Army, 94th Squadron, 1917-18. Mem. Sigma Delta Chi, Sigma Chi. Republican. Club: Flossmoor Country. Home: Flossmoor, Ill. Died Nov. 28, 1976.

MALRAUX, ANDRE, writer, govt. ofcl.; b. Paris, Nov. 3, 1901; s. Fernand and Berthe (Lamy) M.; ed. Ecole d'Art et d'Archéologie, Ecole des Langues Orientales; Dr. honoris causas, from 7 univs.; m. Madeleine Lioux. Novelist, writer, specializing in essays on art and thought of Far East. At the beginning of Naziism entered revolutionary activities, becoming pres. of Comité de Libération de Dimitroff; with Andreé Gide, was charged with delivery to Hitler of petitions against legal procedure of the Reichstag, also because pres. Comité de Libération de Thaelmann; organized and commanded fgn. aviation service for republicans since first week of Spanish war, 1936; served in campaign for France, 1939-40; taken prisoner, June 1940; escaped, Nov. 1940; participated in one of first dynamiting by French Resistance, Dec. 1940; under pseudonym Colonel Berger became inter-regional chief of Resistance, in Dept. de la Correze de la Dordogne et du Lot, and organized dynamiting in these depts., 1942-43; engaged in harassment of enemy and stoppage and destruction of Div. Das-Reich, June 1944; wounded and prisoner of Gestapo, July 1944; liberated at Toulouse, Aug. 1944; elected Chief of Brigade Alsace-Lorraine by Alsatian an Maquis, joined with depts. of center; fought on Vosges front; comdt. of commandos that supported tanks at capture of Damnemarie; in charge defense of sector south of Strasbourg; entered Germany with first French troops. Served as minister of information during presidency of Gen. Charles de Gaulle; minister delegated to Presidence of Council, from 1958; sec. state, Fourth Republic of France, 1958—; minister of state in charge of the cultural affairs of the Fifth Republic of France, from 1959. Former pres. Comité Mondial Antifasciste, Comité de Libération de Dimitroff; v.p. Ligue contre l'Antisémitisme. Decorated Compagnon de la Libération, Légion d'Honneur, Officier de la Résistance, Croix de Guerre (France); Distinguished Service Order (Great Britain); Comdr. Republic of Spain, Grand Cross (from 17 fgn. orders). Hon. mem. Am. Acad. Arts and Letters, Nat. Inst. Arts and Letters. Author: La Tentation de l'Occident, 1926; Les Conquérants, 1927; La Voie Royale, 1929; LaCondition Humaine (awarded Goncourt prize; translated into 18 langs.), 1933; Le Temps du Mépris, 1935; L'Espoir, 1938; La Lutte avec l'Ange, 1943; The Voices of Silence, 1953; La Métamorphose des Dieux, 1957; Antimémoires, 1967; also film Espoir, drawn from book L'Espoire. Address: Le Buisson, France. Died Nov. 23, 1976.

MANARD, HAROLD A. W., b. Rockford, Ill., Sept. 26, 1884; s. Alpheus B. and Alice Zoe (Wright) M.; prep. edn., Northwestern Mil. Acad. (Highland Park,Ill.) and Chicago Latin Sch.; student Sheffield Scientific Sch. (Yale), 1904-05; unmarried. Was with E. I. duPont de Nemours, Wilmington, Del.; later contractor in explosives, North Yakima, Wash., and Denver, Colo.; with H. W. Moore & Co., Denver, 1917-24; owner and manager of the Manard Machinery Co., and dist. representative of the Mattison-Greenlee Service Corpn., all wood working and metal working machinery and supplies; founder and owner, Chappell Sch. of Art, Denver, which was sold to U. of Denver, 1929. Mem. Colo. Yale Assn., Denver Chamber of Commerce. Mem. Nat. Guard, 1918-19. Republican. Home: Denver, Colo. *

MANDELL, SAMUEL PHILIP, business exec.; b. Phila., Jan. 6, 1911; s. Morris and Rebecca (Tecker) M.; m. Ida Slutsky, Sept. 10, 1932; children—Morton, Seymour and Ronald (twins), Gerald and Judith (twins). Engaged in fresh fruit and produce bus., 1927-78; pres. Samuel P. Mandell and Co., also six other corps. dealing in receiving and distbg., 1927-58; dir. Food Fair Stores, Inc., 1958-78; chmn. bd. Carlton Industries, Inc., Vanzetti Infrared & Computer Systems, Inc.; dir. Central Penn Nat. Bank, CP Nat. Corp. Trustee Samuel P. Mandell Found., LaSalle Coll., Albert Einstein Med. Center, Northeastern Hosp., Delaware Valley Coll., Drexel U., Downtown Jewish Home for Aged; sponsor Samuel P. Mandell Lab. Surg. Research. Mem. Pa. Soc. Jewish (dir. synagogue). Address: Philadelphia, Pa. Died May 4, 1978.

MANDERINO, LOUIS LAWRENCE, state Supreme Ct. justice; b. Monessen, Pa., Nov. 16, 1929; s. Anthony Frank and Angelina (Reda) M.; B.A. cum laude, St. Vincent Coll.; Latrobe, Pa., 1951; LL.B., Harvard, 1954, J.D., 1969; children—Susan, Laurie, Amy, Admitted to Pa., bar; law clk. U.S. Ct. Appeals, Phila., 1954-56; partner firm Manderino & Manderino, Monessen, 1956-66; mem. law sch. faculty Duquesne U., Pitts., 1956, prof. law, 1964-70, dean law sch., 1968-70, adj. prof. law, 1970-73; judge Commonwealth Ct. of Pa., 1970-72; asso. justice Supreme Ct. of Pa., 1972-79. Cons. budgetary and legal matters fed., state loan and grants to municipal bodies, 1963-79; solicitor City of Monessen, 1964-67, Monessen Redevel. Authority, 1964-79, Monessen Library Bd., 1964-79, Mon Valley Sewage Authority, 1965-79; del., co-chmn. local govt. com. Pa. Constnl. Conv., 1968. Adv. bd. Pa. Program for Women and Child Offenders. Mem. Am. Bar Assn. Home: Monessen, Pa. Died Nov. 8, 1979.

MANDEVILLE, HUBERT CARPENTER, lawyer; b. Elmira, N.Y., Aug. 26, 1903; s. H.C. and Mary (Stoops) M.; A.B., Yale, 1924; LL.B., Harvard, 1927; m. Lucy Holden, May 1937; children—Mary (Mrs. Herbert I. Willetts), Hubert, John, Jane (Mrs. Thomas G. Wetsel). Counsel. Beekman & Bogue; vice chmn. Conn. Ry. & Lighting Co.; dir. Am. Export Lines. Mem. Am. N.Y. bar assns., Assn. Bar City N.Y., N.Y. County Lawyers Assn. Republican. Clubs: Broad Street, Yale, Down Town Assn. (N.Y.C.); Larchmont Yacht; Algonquin (Bridgeport, Conn.). Home: Larchmont, N.Y. Died Oct. 12, 1976.

MANGANO, PHILLP AUSTIN, fgn. service officer; b. Richmond Hill, L.I., N.Y., Mar. 23, 1910; s. Dr. Antonio and Mabel Austin (Farnham) M.; studied in Rome, Paris; B.A., Yale, 1932, grad. student 1940-42; M.A., Rochester U., 1934; m. Mollie Slaughter, June 25, 1936 (div. Mar. 1948); children—Kathryn F., Marilyn S. Tchr. history, secondary pvt. schs., 1932-42, then Mt. Hermon Sch. for Boys, Mass., 1935-40; with Dept. State, Washington, 1942-44, research specialist Italian affairs, 1945-46, specialist internat. security affairs Bur. UN Affairs, 1947-54, adviser U.S. delegation UN Gen. Assembly, 1949, 51-52, dep. U.S. rep. in Greece on spl. UN com. on Balkans, 1950; fgn. service officer, from 1954; 1st sec. embassy, Tunis, 1955-57; consul and prin. officer Am. consulate, Haifa, Israel, 1957-61; chief division research for North, East and South Africa, Department of State. Served to lieutenant (s.g.) USNR, OSS, 1944-45. Member of New Eng. Hist. Assn. Club: Yale (N.Y.C.). Contbr. articles govt. bulls. Home: Bethesda, Md. Died Sept. 30, 1980.

MANIER, WILL R(UCKER), JR. (MA-NER'), lawyer; b. Nashville, Tenn., Jan. 3, 1885; s. Will Rucker and Mary (Owsley) M.; student Nashville Pub. Schs. (Elliott Medallist, Tarbox), Wallace U. Sch. and U.S. Naval Acad., 1903-06; LL.B., Vanderbilt U., 1908; m. Ruth Solom, Dec. 18, 1925; children—James Wyche, Robert Salom, Katherine Salom. Admitted to Tenn. Bar, 1908, and since practiced in Nashville; mem. Manier & Crouch since 1914; v.p. Commercial Law League of America, 1925-26; chmn. Rule Revision Com. of Davidson County Circuit Courts, 1939-40; spl. judge Tenn. Supreme Court, 1941. Served as lt. and capt. inf., U.S. Army, with A.E.F. in 5 maj. operations, 1917-19; officer in charge civil affairs 3rd U.S. Div. Area in Germany, 1918-19, Awarded D.S.C. (U.S.); comdr. Legion of Honor (France); Order of St. Sava (Jugoslavia); comdr. Order of Carlos Manuel de Cespedes (Cuba). Pres. Nashville Rotary Club, 1921-22; gov. 23rd Rotary Dist. (Tenn. and Ky.), 1923-24; chmn.

various Rotary Internat. Committees, including Extension (twice), Constitution and By-Laws, Community Service, Internat. Service, Convention (Dallas), Resolutions (St. Louis, Ostend, Belgium, Boston, and Mexico City conventions); draftsman of Rotary Internat. policy in Community Service and in Internat. Service; dir. Rotary Internat., 1933-34, pres., 1936-37. Mem. organizing com., sec. and dir. Nashville Commercial Club, and draftsman of plan under which Commercial Club and other civic organizations were combined to form Chamber of Commerce. Initiated campaign for Vanderbilt stadium. Initiated Boys' (now Youth) Week in Nashville. Presided at organization meeting Tenn. Valley Assn.; later pres. Organized Nashville Inst. of Internat. Affairs; and, as pres. of Rotary Internat., initiated promotion by Rotary Clubs of Institutes of Internat. Understanding. Founder Tenn. Soc. for Crippled Children; dir. Nat. Soc. Crippled Children; mem. bd. trustees U. of Nashville (Montgomery Bell Acad.). Founder and past pres. Nashville Iris Soc. Commr. Nashville area (Middle Tenn.) Council Boy Scouts of Am. Apptd. by gov., co-ordinator of State agencies for Red Cross in disaster relief. State director Office of Civilian Defense; state chairman Child Care Committee, Junior Service Corps. Colonel governor's staff. Conductor weekly Public Forum sponsored by Watkins Institute. Commentator on war and diplomacy over radio station WSM. Mem. Nashville, Tenn. and Am. bar assns., Commercial Law League of America, Internat. Assn. of Ins. Counsel, Board of Transportation Trustees of City of Nashville, Nashville Chamber of Commerce, Soc. S.A.R., Am. Legion, Phi Delta Theta (past. prov. pres), Phi Delta Phi. Democrat. Episcopalian (vestryman Christ Ch.). Mason (32 deg., K.T., Shriner). Clubs: Rotary, Old Oak (past pres.), Y.M.C.A. Health (past pres.), Nashville Vanderbilt (past pres.). Home: Nashville, Tenn. *

MANN, CONKLIN, editor; b. Ballston Spa, N.Y., Dec. 20, 1884; s. Jeremiah S. and Dorcas Ella (Riggs) M.; 9th generation from Richard Mann, Scituate, Mass., 1636; A.B., Hamilton Coll., Clinton, N.Y., 1906; m. Maude A. Thomson, of Utica, N.Y., 1906. Editorial staff New York Evening Sun. 1908-11; advertising staff Collier's Weekly, 1911-14; eastern adv. mgr. Leslie's Weekly, 1914-15, Cosmopolitan Mag. 1915-17; mng. editor Leslie's Weekly since 1917. Mem. Chi Psi. Republican. Episcopalian. Clubs: Ft. Schuyler (Utica), New York Athletic (New York), Contbr. articles in Century, Harper's Weekly, Leslie's, Outlook, etc. Home: Pelham Manor, N.Y. *

MANN, MARTY, founder Nat. Council Alcoholism; b. Chgo., Oct. 15, 1904; d. William Henry and Lillian (Christy) Mann; student Chgo. Latin Sch., Santa Barbara (Calif.) Girl's Sch., 1921-22, Montemare, Adirondacks and Fla., 1922-24, Miss Nixon's Sch., Florence, Italy, 1924-25; D.Hum., Adelphi U., 1975; divorced. Asst. editor Internat. Studio, 1928-30; contbr. Town and Country mag., 1929-34; partner photography bus., London, Eng., 1930-36; publicity for jubilee season Covent Garden Opera, 1935; fashion publicity dir. R.H. Macy & Co., N.Y.C., 1940-42; research dir., radio script writer ASCAP, 1942-44; exec. dir. Nat. Council on Alcoholism, 1944-68, now founder-cons.; lectr. alcoholism, profl. and lay orgns.; cons. on alcoholism, social agys., ednl., indsl., med., ch. groups; ofcl. del. Internat. Congress on Alcoholism, Luzerne, Switzerland, 1948; guest of Govt. Union S. Africa to advise on govt. action on alcoholism, and to address 1st Nat. Conf. on Alcoholism, 1951; guest lectr., adviser alcoholism groups, New Zealand, Australia, 1961, London, Eng., Belfast and Dublin, Ireland, 1964; addressed joint sessions state legislatures, S.C., 1946, Mich., 1952, Utah, 1957, Tenn., 1965; lectr. Sch. Alcohol Studies, Yale, U. Wash., U. Utah, U. Tex., U. Colo., U. Ga., U. La., Menninger Found.; research asso. Columbia Tchrs. Coll.; lectr. pharm. scis. U. Ariz.; del. Third Conf Internat. Union for Health Edn. of Pub., Rome, Italy, 1956; spl. cons. to dir. Nat. Inst. on Alcohol Abuse and Alcoholism; cons. on alcoholism Silver Hill Found. Recipient Elizabeth Blackwell award Hobart and William Smith Colls., 1963. Hon. fellow Am. Psychiat. Assn.; fellow Am. Pub. Health Assn., Soc. Pub. Health Educators, Royal Soc. Health, London. Author: Primer on Alcoholism, 1950 (pub. Eng. 1952, Afrikaans trans. pub. S. Africa), 1954; Marty Mann's New Primer on Alcoholism, 1958 (Finnish transl. 1962, Spanish transl. 1969, Japanese transl. 1973); Marty Mann Answers Your Questions About Drinking and Alcoholism, 1970. Contbr. articles popular, profl. jours. Home: New York, N.Y. Died July 22, 1980.

MANN, WILLIAM LEAKE, JR., naval officer; b. Georgetown, Tex., July 26, 1884; s. William Leake and Annie (Taliaferro) M.; grad. Naval War Coll., Naval Med. Sch., Sch. Aviation Medicine, Med. Field Service Sch.; Ph. B., Southwestern U. of Tex., 1903, A.M., 1904; M.D., Harvard, 1908; m. Ann Margaret Fegan, Nov. 23, 1913; 1 dau., Beverly (wife of Major W. C. Chamberlin, U.S.M.C.). Commd. lt. Medical Corps, U.S. Navy, 1908, and advanced through the grades to rear admiral, June 1943. Has had service at sea, in China, Philippines, Haiti; medical director, Gendarmerie d'Haiti, 1919-22; post surgeon, Marine Barracks, Quantico, Va., 1917-19 and 1934-36; force surgeon, Fleet Marine Force, comdg. officer, Naval Hosp., Corpus Christi, Tex., 1940-42; med. officer in command, Naval Med. Research Inst., Bethesda, Md., 1942-43; now dist. med. officer, 13th Naval Dist. Del. to Internat. Congress of Mil. Medicine. Bucharest, Rumania, 1937. Awarded spl. letter of Commendation by Navy Dept. for Service in World War I; World War I medal, Medal Militaire (Haiti), Haitian Campaign medal. Fellow Am. Coll. Surgeons; mem. Assn. Mil. Surgeons (pres. 1943). Internat. Coll. Surgeons Presbyn. Mason (Shriner). Club: Army and Navy. Contbr. articles to med. jours. and navy bulletins. Address: Georgetown, Tex. *

MANNING, ARMIN WILLIAM, educator; b. Milw., Aug. 22, 1913; s. Herman August and Amanda (Steuck) M.; B.A., Valparaiso U., 1936; B.D., Concordia Theol. Sem., 1937; M.A., U. Mich., 1939; Ph.D., Fordham U., 1958; m. Anita Louise Spannagel, Sept. 7, 1940; children—Judith, Peter. Asst. prof. physics and math. Concordia Jr. Coll., Bronxville, N.Y., 1939-56; prof. physics, chmn. dept. Valparaiso U., 1956-77; asso. research physicist Brookhaven Nat. Labs., summers, 1956-58; cons. nuclear physics U.S. Army Terminal Ballistics Lab., Aberdeen Proving Ground, Md., 1959-71; radiation expert radiol. div. Ind. Health Dept. Mem. Am. Assn. Physics Tchrs., IEEE, Ind. Acad. Sci. Contbr. articles on nuclear or neutron physics to sci. jours. Address: Valparaiso, Ind. Died Aug. 1977.

MANNIX, HENRY, lawyer; b. Bklyn., Feb. 26, 1898; s. John F. and Delia (Walker) M.; A.B., Coll. City N.Y., 1917; LL.B. cum laude, Fordham U., 1920, LL.D., 1956; m. Mary Margaret Friel, June 16, 1926; children—Henry, Joseph Friel, John, Frances (Mrs. Victor D. Ziminsky, Jr.), Mary Margaret (Mrs. Richard L. Hughes, Jr.), Aileen (Mrs. Richard H. Schaefer), Sheila, James (dec.), Charles Gordon, Delia (Mrs. John B. Burke). Tchr. Latin, Manual Tng. High Sch., Bklyn., 1917; admitted to N.Y. bar, 1920, U.S. Supreme Ct., 1938; lectr. law Fordham U. Law Sch., 1923-26; with firm White & Case, N.Y.C., 1917-74, partner, 1931-74, charge Paris office, 1931-33. Dir. Cranshaw Corp. Chmn. appeals bd. SSS, World War II. Vice pres. United Hosp. Fund, 1950-52, dir., 1946-52, chmn. Bklyn. adv. com., 1948-52; dir., treas. Interfaith Com. on Released Time Religious Edn., N.Y.C.; bd. dirs. St. Catherine's Hosp., Bklyn., 1937-55; bd. dirs. John Polachek Found. Med. Research. Henry M. Blackmer Found., Marquette League for Indian Missions; pres. Family Communion Crusade, 1960-64, dir., from 1951; dir. Emerald Assn. L.I., from 1940, pres., 1939. Recipient Fordham Law Alumni Achievement award 1964. Served with C.E., U.S. Army, W.W. I. Mem. Assn. Bar City N.Y., Am., N.Y. State bar assns., Manhattan, Bklyn. guilds cath. lawyers, Friendly Sons St. Patrick (pres. Bklyn. 1953), Fordham Law Sch. Alumni Assn. (dir.), Phi Beta Kappa. Clubs: Down Town Assn. (N.Y.C.); Cathedral (Bklyn.); Mt. Kisco Country. Home: Mount Kisco, N.Y. Died June 9, 1980.

MANSFIELD, LUTHER STEARNS, educator; b. Arlington, Nebr., Apr. 25, 1906; s. Albert Bruce and Lula Elizabeth (Stearns) M.; A.B., Tex. Christian U., 1927, A.M., 1928; Ph.D., U. Chgo., 1936. Teaching fellow English, Tex. Christian U., 1927-28; instr. English, Ill. Mil. Sch., Abington, Ill., 1928-29; asst. prof. English, Jamestown Coll., 1929-36; instr. English, Williams Coll., 1936-39, asst. prof., 1939-47, asso. prof. history and lit., 1947-52, prof. history and lit., 1952-62, prof. Am. history and lit., 1962-71, prof. emeritus, 1971-78; vis. asst. prof. English, Swarthmore Coll., 1944-45; vis. asso. prof. English, Duke U., summer 1947; vis. asso. prof. Am. lit. Johns Hopkins, summer 1950, vis. prof. U. Buenos Aires, Argentina, 1956; guest prof. English, Tex. Christian U., summer 1962; vis. lectr. English, U. Minn., 1964-65; vis. lectr. English. U. N.D., summer 1966. Recipient Distinguished Alumnus award Tex. Christian U., 1973. Mem. Emerson Soc., Modern Lang. Assn., Am. Assn. U. Profs., Am. Studies Assn., Scholarship Soc. of South, Melville Soc., Sigma Tau Delta. Club: Williams (N.Y.C.). Contbr. to Literary History of U.S., 1948. Editor: Centennial edit. Moby-Dick, 1952. Contbr. ednl. jours. Home: Williamstown, Mass. Died Apr. 6, 1978.

MANSON, ALEXANDER MALCOLM, Justice, Supreme Court, B.C.; b. St. Louis, Mo., U.S.A., Oct. 7, 1883; s. Malcolm and Katherine (MacTavish) M.; student Collegiate Inst., Niagara Falls, Ont., 1896-1901; B.A., University of Toronto, 1905; Osgoode Hall, Toronto, 1905-08; married Stella Beckwith, June 29, 1909; Children—Malcolm Alexander, Katherine Marguerite (Mrs. Godfrey Noel Harrison), Marion MacTavish, Called to Brit. Columbia bar, June 1908, barrister and solicitor; mem. Legislature, B.C., 1916-35, deputy speaker, 1918-20, speaker, 1921; atty-gen. and minister Labor, 1922-28; King's Counsel, 1922; Justice Supreme Ct., B.C., since 1935. Chmn. Bd. Eugenics, B.C., since 1936; p.p. Vancouver Inst., 1939, 41. Awarded King George V Silver Jubilee medal, 1935; King George VI Coronation medal, 1937. Former mem. Liberal Party. Presbyterian (elder). Mason (Past Grand Master, B.C., 1925-26, P.G.Z.R.A.M.). Home: Vancouver, B.C., Can. *

MANTELL, JOHN J., ry. official; b. Elmira, N.Y., June 24, 1884; s. Paul M.; ed. Elmira Acad. Began as clk. and stenographer supt.'s office Erie R.R., at Elmira, June 1899, and continued with same rd. consecutively as yard clk., chief yard clk., yardmaster and gen. yardmaster, trainmaster Delaware and Jefferson divs., terminal trainmaster at Jersey City, and supt. Wyoming div. until 1915, supt. terminals, at Jersey City, 1915-17, gen. supt. Lines East, 1917-18; terminal mgr. under R.R. Administration, Port of New York, 1918-20; mgr. New York region Erie R.R., 1920-22, became v.p. New York Region, 1922; consulting mgr. Chinese rys. since 1929. Home: Jersey City, N.J. *

MANTHORNE, MARY ELIZABETH ARNOLD, publisher; b. Haverhill, Mass., Oct. 5, 1909; d. Asher Burton and Elizabeth (Cooke) Arnold; A.B., Russell Sage Coll., 1932; m. Gordon Clarke Manthorne, June 25, 1938; children—Arnold, William Davis. With Horn Book, Inc., Boston, 1956-78, pres., 1962-78. Mem. Ashburnham (Mass.) Sch. Com., 1943-48, chmn., 1946-48. Chmn. trustees Stevens Pub. Library, Ashburnham, 1952-70; exec. com. Mass. Library Trustees Assn., 1953-58; pres. Mass. Library Aid Assn., 1958-70. Episcopalian. Home: Ashburham, Mass. Died Aug. 24, 1978.

MANTOVANI, ANNUNZIO PAOLO, conductor; b. Venice, Italy, Nov. 15, 1905; s. Benedetto Bismark Mantovani and Iparia Manfrin; studied schs. in London; studied music with father, also Trinity Coll. of Music (London); m. Winifred Kathleen Moss, Aug. 4, 1934; children—Kenneth Paolo, Paula Irene. Naturalized Brit. citzen, 1933. Formed orch. Midland Hotel, Birmingham, Eng., 1923, gave recitals at Wigmore Hall, played Concerto at Queens Hall, London; condr. orch. Hotel Metropole, London, Eng.; began recording, broadcasting for BBC, 1927; formed Tipica Orch., 1932; became theatre condr., 1940; toured Brit. Isles, made broadcasts, World War II; musical dir. for Noel Coward, 1945, also London performances Ace of Clubs. Pacific 1860 (starring Mary Martin), Sigh No More, And so to Bed, Bob's Your Uncle; formed present concert orch., 1950, numerous recordings, TV, concert tours in Europe, from 1954, ann. tour Am. and Can.; recordings include Charmaine, Dancing with Tears in My Eyes, It Happened in Monterey, Mexicali Rose, Greensleeves, La Cumparsita; recording artist London Records. Recipient gold disc of record Charmaine, also 8 golden discs of long-playing records; Ivor Novello award for artist who had done most for Brit. music in 1956. Clubs: Savage, Variety of Great Britain (London). Home: Dorset, England. Died Mar. 29, 1980.

MANUEL, HERSCHEL THURMAN, educator; b. Freetown, Ind., Dec. 24, 1887; s. Asbury Hill and Sarah Jane (Brown) M.; A.B., De Pauw U., 1909; A.M., U. Chicago, 1914; Ph.D., U. Ill., 1917; m. Dorothy Broad Beaird, July 23, 1928; children—Jane (Mrs. W. D. McKernon), Eleanor (Mrs. DeForrest Jackson), Thomas. Tchr., adminstr., public schs., Indiana, 1909-13; spent time in grad. study, 1913-17; part time instr. in psychology, education, Clark College, 1915-16; teacher, Western State Coll. Colo., 1919-25; asso. prof., U. of Tex., 1925-27, prof. ednl. psychology, from 1927, emeritus, to 1976, dir. testing and guidance bur., 1946-58; regional dir. qualifying test for civilians, Army and Navy coll. programs, 1943-45; dir. Inter-Am. test construction project for com. on modern langs. Am. Council on Edn., 1941-44; pres. Nat. Council Measurements Used in Edn., 1954-55. Served as 1st lt., U.S. Army, psychol. examiner, then adminstr. in ednl. service of hospital, 1917-19. Dir. research, Tex. Com. on Coordination in Edn., 1935-58; cons. Inter-American Ednl. Found., 1944. Editor Yearbook of Tex. Soc. for Mental Hygiene, 1936-42. Editor Research Bulletins of the Texas Commission on Coordination in Education, 1936-58. Member American Psychol. Assn., Am. Ednl. Research Assn., Nat. Soc. for Study of Edn., Sigma Xi. Methodist. Author: Talent in Drawing, 1919; Education of Mexican and Spanish-Speaking Children in Texas, 1930; Spanish and English editions of the Stanford-Binet in Relation to the Abilities of Mexican Children, 1935 (with others) Cooperative Inter-American Tests, 1950; (with R. H. Fife) Teaching of English in Puerto Rico, 1951; Taking a Test, 1956, Contbr. articles to profl. mags. Home: Austin, Tex. Died Mar. 21, 1976.

MANUEL, WILEY WILLIAM, asso. justice Calif. Supreme Ct.; b. Oakland, Calif., Aug. 28, 1927; s. Curtis W. and Gradella M.; A.B., U. Calif., 1951; LL.B., Hastings Coll. Law, 1953; LL.D. (hon.), U. San Diego Law Sch., 1978; m. Eleanor Williams, June 20, 1948; children—Yvonne Temple, Gary Manuel. Admitted to Calif. bar, 1954; dep. atty. gen. State of Calif., 1953-70, asst. atty. gen., 1970-71, chief asst. atty. gen., 1971-76 judge Superior Ct. of Alameda County (Calif.), 1976-77 asso. justice Calif. Supreme Ct., 1977-81; mem sentencing adv. com. Jud. Council Calif., 1976-81 Served with U.S. Army, 1946-47. Mem. Charles H Houston Bar Assn. (pres. 1962), Calif. State Employees Assn., Calif. Judges Assn., Calif. Jud. Council, U. Calif Alumni Assn., Thurston Soc., Order of Cirf. Democrat Roman Catholic. Club: K.C. Home: Oakland, Calif Died Jan. 5, 1981; buried St. Mary's Cemetery Oakland.

MAO, TSE-TUNG, Chinese Communist polit. leader; b. Shao Shan, Hunan Prov., China, 1893; student many subjects in various schools; degree, Hunan Normal Sch., 1918; m. Yang Kaihui, 1920 (dec.); m. 2d, Ho Tzu-chien, 1929. Joined revolutionary army of Sun Yat Sen, 1911; polit. leader and adviser, as well as army officer; active in Chinese Communist Party since 1920; helped form revolutionary army (Peasants and Workers Army), 1927; this army joined forces of Chu Teh to form 4th Red Army, 1928; by 1929, the Chinese Soviet Govt. controlled over two million people; chmn. first All-China Congress of Soviets, which formed Soviet Rep. of China, 1931; Central Soviet Govt. was set up, 1934; the Communist group (or nation), including the Red Army, moved en masse from Kiangsi to Yenan, 1934 and 1935; 1st Front Red Army (under Mao) joined 4th and 2d Red armies, Shensi, 1935, and reorganized as 8th Route Army (under Chu Teh), 1937; chmn. Central Com. of Polit. Bur., 1943, 45; The People's Republic of China, a Communist regime, was proclaimed in Peiping, Sept. 1949, chmn. Central People's Govt., 1949-54, chmn. People's Republic of China, 1954-76. Author: Selected Works of Mao Tse-Tsung (4 vols.). Address: Peking, China. Died Sept. 9, 1976.

MARAIS, JOSEF, guitarist, singer, composer; b. South Africa, Nov. 17, 1905; s. Max and Annie (Highman) Pessach; student South African Coll. of Music, 1923, Royal Acad. Music, London, 1928; violin studies with Otokar Sevcik, Jeno Hubay, 1930; m. Rosa Lily Odette Baruch, July 18, 1947. Came to U.S., 1939, naturalized, 1945. Radio program African Trek, Blue Network, 1939-41; head Afrikaans and Dutch broadcasts, O.W.I., 1941-45; partner Marais and Miranda, folk ballad singers, from 1945; pres. Fideree Music Corp.; appeared in Hollywood Bowl; recs. Decca, Kapp, Motivation, MGM records; writer music Africana Suite for Broadway play Too Late the Phalarope; composer opera Tony Beaver, Paul Gauguin Suite for art film The Noble Savage, Hebraic Rhapsody for film Land of the Book; creator popular songs Sugarbush, Around the Corner, Marching to Pretoria; first symphonic appearance with Franz Allers, Lewisohn Stadium, N.Y., also Grant Park, Chgo., 1957. Faculty, adviser Idyllwild Arts Found., U. So. Calif. Idyllwild Sch. Music and Arts, Idyllwild, Calif. Mem. Am. Guild Musical Artists, Am. Fedn. TV and Radio Artists, Am. Fedn. Musicians, Am Camping Assn. (hon.). Lion (hon.). Author: (with wife) Folk Songs Jamboree, 1960; World Folk Songs, 1964; (with Miranda Marais) Long Live The Bruegel People. Home: Hollywood, Calif. Died Apr. 27, 1978.

MARBLE, HENRY CHASE, surgeon; b. Worcester, Mass., Jan. 5, 1885; s. Edwin Henry and Emma Caroline (Moulton) M.; A.B., Clark U., 1906, D.Sc., 1956; M.D., Harvard 1910; m. Alice Eachus Ingram, Nov. 25, 1916; children—Joan (Mrs. Robert H. Cook, Jr.), William Ingram, Peter. Surg. intern Mass. Gen. Hosp., 1910-12, surg. staff, 1916—, also chief fracture service, chief hand service; alumni asst. surgery Harvard, 1912-14, asst. surgery courses for grads., 1925—, asst. indsl. surgery Sch. Pub. Health; consulting surgeon VA, since 1921—. Alumni trustee Clark U., 1951-55. Served as maj., med. dept. U.S. Army, World War I; chief orthopedic service U.S. Base Hosp. 6, AEF. Diplomate Am. Bd. Surgery. Mem. A.M.A., Boston Surg. Soc., A.C.S. (gov.), Am. Assn. Surgery Trauma (founder, past pres.), Am. Assn. Surgery Hand (founder). Clubs: Harvard (Boston); Editor: Surgical Treatment Motor Skeletal System 2 vols. Author a manual and med. articles; The Hand Manual and Atlas for the Surgeon General. Home: Newton Centre, Mass. *

MARBURY, OGLE, retired judge; b. Howard County, Md., Aug. 23, 1882; s. Ogle and Eleanora Brevitt (Mackenzie) M.; A.B., Johns Hopkins U., 1902; LL.B., U. Md. Law Sch., 1904; m. Eliza G. Cronmiller, Aug. 17, 1915 (dec. Aug. 28, 1955); 1 d. Anne T. Ogle (Mrs. David E. Oberweiser). Admitted to Md. bar, 1904, and in general practice at Baltimore and Laurel, Md., until 1941; mem. Md. Ho. of Dels., 1910-12; asst. atty. gen. of Md., 1916-20, actg. atty. gen., 1918; chmn. State Bd. Prison Control of Md., 1920-23; del. at large Dem. Nat. Conv., 1920; atty. bd. edn. Prince George County, Md., 1916-37; city solicitor of Laurel, 1929-41; atty. county commrs. Prince George Co., 1914-16, 1937-41; apptd. asso. judge 7th Judicial Circuit, Jan. 1941; apptd. chief judge 7th Jud. Circuit, judge of Court of Appeals of Md., July 1941; elected chief judge 7th Judicial Circuit and judge of Court of Appeals of Md., for 15 year term, Nov. 1942. Chief judge Ct. of Appeals of Md., 1944-52; ret. 1952. Chmn. Hall of Records, Commn. of Md., 1944-52. Mem. Am., Md. (pres. 1946-47), Prince George Co. bar assns., Order of Coif. Democrat. Episcopalian. Home: Laurel, Md. *

MARCH, CECIL CLIFFORD, mfr., found. exec.; b. Slayton, Minn., June 10, 1910; s. Richard C. and Marie (Lindscheid) M.; B.Ch.E., U. Minn., 1932, postgrad. 1933; m. Lenore R. Wells, July 8, 1939. Formerly with Minn. Mining & Mfg. Co., St. Paul, from 1933, lab. technician to group v.p. coated abrasives and related products div., adhesives, coatings and sealers div. and chem. div., from 1959; 1st v.p. The Bush Found., St. Paul. Mem. Tau Beta Pi. Home: St. Paul, Minn. Died June 26, 1976.

MARCH, WILLIAM A., army officer; b. Pa., Jan. 1, 1884; C.E., Princeton U., 1908; commd. 1st lt. Inf., Pa. Nat. Guard, and advanced to brig. gen., Jan. 2, 1941; entered Federal service, Jan 13, 1941, and now in command of 73d Field Arty. Brigade, Camp Shelby, Miss. Address: CampShelby, Miss.*

MARCUS, SUMNER, educator; b. New Brunswick, N.J., Sept. 23, 1912; s. Abraham and Lena (Wolfson) M.; A.B. cum laude, Harvard U., 1931, M.B.A., 1933, J.D. cum laude, 1936; Ph.D., U. Wash., Seattle, 1958; m. Elizabeth Tribby Caldwell, Jan. 1, 1938. Admitted to Mass. bar, 1937, Wash. bar, 1954; atty., field examiner NLRB, 1938-43; asso. counsel Navy Price Adjustment Bd. and Bur. Ships, 1946-49; counsel renegotiation div. Navy Dept., 1949-51; asst. gen. counsel Renegotiation Bd., 1951-53; lectr. Seattle U., 1954, U. Wash., 1955-57; asso. prof. U. Mont., 1957-58; mem. faculty U. Wash., 1955-79, prof. bus. and pub. policy, 1961-79, chmn. dept. bus., govt. and society, 1959-60, 61-64, 69-73, 77, asso. dean Sch. Bus. Adminstrn., 1964-67, univ. ombudsman, 1977-79; vis. asso. prof. Stanford U. Grad. Sch. Bus., 1961; vis. prof. Amos Tuck Sch. Bus. Adminstrn., Dartmouth Coll., 1965. Served with AUS, 1943-46. Ford Found. faculty research fellow, 1960-61. Mem. Acad. Mgmt. (chmn. div. social issues in mgmt. 1970-73), Am. Arbitration Assn. (nat. labor panel 1972-79), Wash. State Bar Assn. Author: The Law of Small Business, 1958; How Small Business Firms in the State of Washington Cope With Their Legal Problems, 1963; Competition and The Law, 1967; also articles, chpts. in books. Home: Seattle, Wash. Died July 28, 1979.

MARCUSE, HERBERT, educator; b. Berlin, July 19, 1898; s. Carl and Gertrud (Kreslawsky) M.; Ph.D., univs. Berlin and Freiburg, 1922; m. Erica R. Sherover, June 21, 1976; 1 son, Peter. Came to U.S., 1934, naturalized, 1940. With Inst. Social Research, Columbia, 1934-40, Russian Inst., Columbia and Harvard, 1951-53; prof. politics and philosophy Brandeis U., 1954-65; prof. philosophy U. Calif. at San Diego, 1965-70; served with OSS and State Dept., 1941-50. Author: Reason and Revolution, 1941; Eros and Civilization, 1954; Soviet Marxism, 1958; One-Dimensional Man, 1965; Negations, 1968; Essay on Liberation, 1969; Five Lectures, 1970; Counterrevolution and Revolt, 1972; Studies in Critical Philosophy, 1972. Home: La Jolla, Calif. Died July 29, 1979.

MARDER, ARTHUR JACOB, educator, author; b. Boston, Mar. 8, 1910; s. Maxwell J. and Ida (Greenstein) M.; A.B., Harvard, 1931, A.M., 1934, Ph.D., 1936; M.A., Oxford U. (Eng.), 1969, D.Litt. (hon.), 1971; m. Jan North, Sept. 13, 1955; children—Toni Anne, Tod Allen, Kevin North. Asst. prof. history U. Oreg., 1936-38; research asso. Bur. Internat. Research, Harvard and Radcliffe colls., 1939-41; research analyst OSS, 1941-42; asso. prof. history Hamilton Coll., 1943-44; asso. prof. history U. Hawaii, 1944-51, prof., 1951-58, sr. prof., 1958-64; prof. history U. Calif. at Irvine, 1964-77; vis. prof. Harvard, 1949-50; George Eastman prof. Oxford, 1969-70. Decorated hon. comdr. Order Brit. Empire; recipient George Louis Beer prize Am. Hist. Assn., 1941; Bd. Admiralty citation, 1970; Distinguished Faculty Lectureship award U. Calif., Irvine, 1977; fellow John Simon Guggenheim Found., 1939, 45-46, 58, Am. Philos. Soc., 1956, 58, 63, 66, Rockefeller Found., 1943, Japan Found., 1976; U.K. Fulbright fellow alt., 1954; Chesney Meml. gold medal Royal United Service Instn., 1968. Fellow Royal Hist. Soc., Am. Acad. Arts and Scis.; corr. fellow Brit. Acad.; mem. Am. Philos. Soc., Am. Hist. Assn. (pres. Pacific Coast br. 1971-72, council 1973-75), Phi Beta Kappa, Phi Kappa Phi. Author: The Anatomy of British Sea Power, 1940; Portrait of an Admiral, 1952; Fear God and Dread Nought, 3 vols., 1952, 56, 59; From the Dreadnought to Scapa Flow, vol. 1, 1961, vol. 2, 1965, vol. 3, 1966, vol. 4, 1969, vol. 5, 1970; From the Dardanelles to Oran, 1974; Operation Menace, 1976. Home: Santa Barbara, Calif. Died Dec. 25, 1980.

MAREMONT, ARNOLD HAROLD, mfg. exec.; b. Chgo., Aug. 24, 1904; s. Myer D. and Kate (Wolens) M.; Ph.B., U. Chgo., 1924, J.D., 1926; LL.D., So. Ill. U., 1968; m. Virginia Weisels, Apr. 2, 1928; 1 son, Michael; m. 2d, Adele Heineman, Dec. 24, 1937; children—Madelon, Nicholas; m. 3d, Eileen Adler, Oct. 18, 1968. Admitted to Ill. bar, 1926; exec. v.p., dir. Maremont Corp., Chgo., 1941-52, pres., 1952-69, chmn. exec. com., dir., 1969-70, also dir.; chmn. bd. Allied Paper Corp., 1956-65, chmn. exec. com., dir., 1965-66; chmn. bd., dir. Eckmar Corp., Chgo., 1961-69. Trustee Lyric Opera, Chgo., 1959-68, Community Music Center of North Shore; dir., chmn. Ill. Pub. Aid Commn., 1962-63; bd. dirs., 1st v.p. Nat. Assn. Mental Health, 1963-66, mem. exec. com., 1966-67; trustee N.Y.C. Center Opera and Ballet Co., Hull House; gov. life mem. Art Inst. Chgo.; bd. dirs., vice chmn. Planned Parenthood-World Population, 1964-68; dir., chmn. bd. Nat. Council on Aging, 1965-66, chmn. bd., mem. exec. com., 1966-67; mem. Western Hemisphere gov. body Internat. Planned Parenthood Fedn., 1964-78; trustee, mem. exec. com. Am. Fedn. Arts, 1958-65; asso. trustee Bard Coll., 1960-64; trustee So. Ill. U., 1961-67; pres. Kate Maremont Found., 1948-78. Recipient Distinguished Service award U. Chgo., 1951; decorated knight Order of Merit (Italy). Clubs: Lotos (N.Y.C.); Tavern, Arts (Chgo.); Bridgetown (Barbados). Home: Palm Beach, Fla. Died Nov. 1, 1978.

MARES, JOSEPH R., chemical cons.; b. Helena, Mont., Apr. 13, 1903; s. Joseph and Antonette, M.; Mont. State Coll., Mass. Inst. Tech., Akron Law Sch., N.Y. U., Toledo Law Sch.; m. Delia Nichols Smith, Aug. 3, 1935; children—Jan, Thomas, William. Dir. patent dept. Monsanto Chem. Co., 1929-46, dir. development dept., 1943-46, gen. mgr. Texas div., 1947-53, v.p., 1948-53; indsl. chem. cons. Regent Lamar State Coll. Tech. Mem. Am. Patent Law Assn., Am. Chem. Soc., Am. Bar Assn., Soc. Chem. Industry, Ethical Soc. Republican. Clubs: Athletic (Mo.); Houston, Ramada (Houston). Home: Dickinson, Tex. Died Apr. 13, 1976.

MARGOLIUS, SIDNEY SENIER, journalist, author; b. Perth Amboy, N.J., May 3, 1911; s. Max and Helen (Senier) M.; B.A., Rutgers U., 1934; m. Esther Papert, Nov. 14, 1942; 1 son, Richard. Asso. editor Retail Exec., N.Y.C., 1937-40; consumer editor Newspaper PM, N.Y.C., 1940-42, 45-48; syndicated columnist trade union newspapers, 1949-80, United Features Syndicate, N.Y.C., 1971-80; author 20 books, including: Consumers Guide to Better Buying - The Innocent Consumer vs. The Exploiters, 1967, new edit., 1972, Your Guide to Successful Retirement, 1969, How to Make the Most of Your Money, 1970, Great American Food Hoax, 1971, Health Food Facts and Fakes, 1973 (Nat. Press Club award 1973); former bd. dirs. Consumers Union; mem. Pres.'s Consumer Adv. Council-Nat. Comml. Product Safety; cons. Pres.'s Commn. on Consumer Interests, FTC; mem. N.Y. State and Nassau County Consumer Adv. Com. Recipient Media award Family Service Assn. Am., 1969, award Consumer Fedn. Am., 1972, Internat. Labor Press Assn., 1962, N.Y. Central Labor Council, 1962, Nat. Council Sr. Citizens. Home: Washington, N.Y. Died Jan. 31, 1980.

MARIN, WILLIAM PEYTON, lawyer; b. Albany, N.Y., Sept. 12, 1908; s. Ezrael and Bertha (Golin) M.; B.A., N.Y.U., 1929, J.D., 1931; m. Blanche Harris, Jan. 31, 1931; children—Peter Michael, Jonathan Keith. Admitted to N.Y. bar, 1932; pvt. practice, 1932-37; trial asso. to Isidor J. Kresel, 1937-42; mem. firm Kresel, Hershkopf, Marin & Meyerson, N.Y.C., 1942-48; pvt. practice, N.Y.C., 1948-76; legal counsel to Joseph P. Kennedy and family, gen. counsel Joseph P. Kennedy Enterprises; adviser to U.S. Atty. Gen. on disposition of Gen. Aniline & Film Corp. Dir., exec. com. GAF Corp. chmn. bd. visitors Washington Sq. Coll. of N.Y.U. Recipient Alumni Meritorious Service award N.Y.U., 1949. Mem Am., N.Y., State bar assns., Assn. Bar City N.Y., N.Y. County Lawyers Assn., N.Y. U., Club (founder), Bklyn. Lawyers Club, N.Y.U., Alumni Fedn. (pres. 1965-67), Phi Sigma Delta. Eta Sigma Phi. Home: Brooklyn, N.Y. Died Dec. 16, 1976.

MARINE, DAVID, pathologist; b. Whiteleysburg, Md., Sept. 20, 1880; s. David and Nancy (Baynard) M.; A.B., Western Md. Coll., 1900, A.M., 1907; M.D., Johns Hopkins Univ., 1905; ScD., Western Reserve Univ., 1931; m. Mary Elizabeth Nuttle, Dec. 16, 1922; 1 son, David Nuttle. Resident pathologist, Lakeside Hosp., Cleveland, O., 1905-07; instr. in pathology, Western Reserve U., 1907-08; instr., asst. prof. and asso. prof. exptl. medicine, same, 1908-20; asst. prof. pathology, Columbia, 1920-39; dir. labs. Montefiore Hosp., 1920-45; cous. pathologist Montefiore Hosp. Capt., maj. and lt. col. Med. Corps, U.S. Army, May 1917-Aug. 1919; lt. col. Med. O.R.C.; served at Ft. Benjamin Harrison, Camp Sherman, Camp Custer, also in France and with Army of Occupation in Germany, Fellow A.M.A.; mem. Assn. Am. Physicians, Am. Physiol. Soc., Am. Fisheries Soc., Assn. Am. Pathologists, Soc. Exptl. Pathologists, Am. Coll. Physicians, N.Y. Acad. Medicine, Mem. Christian Ch. Contbr. papers dealing with glands of internal secretion. Home: Rehoboth, Del. Died Nov. 26, 1976.

MARINO, ANTHONY WAYNE MARTIN, intestinal surgeon; b. N.Y.C., Jan. 5, 1894; s. Francis and Camille (Jarratan) M.; M.D., L.I. Coll. Medicine, 1916; m. Doris Guarin, Oct. 31, 1923; 1 son, Martin. Intern St. Mary's Hosp., 1916-17, 1919; postgrad. study surgery Mayo Clinic, 1917-18, clin. asst. medicine, 1919-21, gastroenterology, 1922-24, chief rectal clinics, 1925, asst. surgeon, 1930-31, asso. surgeon, 1932-33; attending surgeon Bklyn. Hosp., 1933-63, sr. attending surgeon, from 1963; proctologist Kingston Ave. Hosp., 1933-43, Bushwick Hosp., 1934-56; cons. proctologist Wyckoff Heights Hosp., from 1940, Kingston Av. Hosp., 1943-56, St. Mary's Hosp., Bklyn., 1951-70; instr. L.I. Coll. Med., 1930-43, asst. clin. prof. surgery, 1943-48, asso. prof. clin. surgery, 1948-54; clin. prof. surgery State U. N.Y. Coll. Medicine, 1954-66, clin. prof. emeritus surgery, 1966-80. Served as 1st lt. M.C., AUS, 1918-19. Decorated Fatiga di Guerra, Zona di Guerra (Italian govt.); Order Crown of Italy. Diplomate Am. Bd. Surgery (founders group proctology), Am. Bd. Colon and Rectal Surgery (pres. 1958-59, 63-64). Fellow A.C.S., N.Y. Acad. Medicine, N.J. (hon.), New Eng. (hon.) proctologic socs., Pa. Soc. Colon and Rectal Surgery (hon.), Am. (v.p. 1939-40, pres. 1954), N.Y.

(pres. 1941-45) proctologic socs.; mem. AMA (past chmn. sect. gastroenterology and proctology, Physician's award 1971-73), Med. Soc. County of Kings (pres. 1948), Med. Soc. State N.Y. (v.p. 1966), Alumni Assn. L.I. Coll. Medicine (pres. 1948), Pan Am. Med. Assn. (pres. Bklyn. and L.I. chpt.), Bklyn. Surg. Soc., Research Soc. State Med. Center in N.Y., N.Y. Soc. Ind. Research, Bklyn. Assn. Mental Health. Mem. editorial bd. Diseases of Colon and Rectum, from 1957. Contbr. articles med. jours. Home: Brooklyn, N.Y. Died Oct. 5, 1980.

MARIS, PAUL VESTAL, agrl. economist; b. Newberg, Ore., Sept. 5, 1886; s. Newton Clark and Luetta (Swalm) M.; B.S., Pacific Coll., Newberg, 1907; B.S. in Agr., U. of Mo., 1914; student U. of Wis., summer, 1913; m. Mary Elizabeth Davis, June 5, 1915; children—Lucile Elizabeth, Mary Pauline. Dep. dairy and food commr., Ore., 1908-10; dairy extension specialist, Colo., 1911; county agrl. agt., Saline County, Mo., 1914-15; county agt. leader, Ore., 1916-20; dir. agrl. extension, 1920-34; prin. agrl. economist, A.A.A., 1934-35; actg. dir. Rural Rehabilitation Div., Resettlement Adminstrn., 1935-36; cons. Farmers Home Adminstrn., since 1937; sec. Ore. Coöp. Council, 1917-25; mem. State Unemployment Relief Com., 1933-34; exec. sec., Am. Country Life Assn. Mem. Am. Acad. Polit. and Social Sciences, Alpha Zeta, Epsilon Sigma Phi, Alpha Gamma Rho, Mu Beta Beta, Patron of Husbandry. Presbyterian. Mason. Club: Country. Home: Arlington, Va. *

MARITAIN, JACQUES (MA-RE-TAN), prof. emeritus; born in Paris, France, Nov. 18, 1882; son Paul and Genevieve (Favre) M.; received degrees Agrege de Philosophie and Licencie en Sciences Naturelles, U. of Paris; Doctor in Philosophy, Roman Universities; student biology sciences, Heidelberg University; m. Räissa Oumansoff. Converted to Catholicism, 1906, and began study of scholastic philosophy, 1908; became prof. philosophy, Institut Catholique de Paris, 1914, and launched first serious criticism of Bergsonism; founded Bibliothèque Française de Philosophie, 1923; directed for Plon, Paris pubs., series of books, "Roseau d'or," for 7 yrs.; directed series, "Les lies," for Desclée de Brouwer, since 1934; has specialized in scholastic system of St. Thomas and has lectured on Thomist philosophy at univs. of Louvain, Geneva, Fribourg, Milan, Bonn, Oxford, Santander, Chicago, Angelicum in Rome, and Inst. of Mediaeval Studies, Toronto, Can. Fr. ambassador to the Holy See, 1945-48. Prof., Princeton Univ., 1948-53, professor emeritus, Princeton, 1953—. Mem. (hon.) American Acad., Nat. Inst. Arts and Letters. Author numerous books; late publs.: The Person and the Common Good, 1947; Existence and the Existent, 1948; Man and the State, 1950; The Range of Reason, 1952; Creative Intuition in Art and Poetry, 1953; Approaches to God, 1954; On the Philosophy of History, 1957; Reflections of America, 1958; The Degrees of Knowledge, 1959; The Responsibility of the Artist, 1960; On the Use of Philosophy, pub. in 1961; Moral Philosophy, 1964; The Peasant of the Garrone, pub. 1968; and also works in French, La Philosophie Bergsonienne, La Philosophie Morale, Le Paysan de la Garonne, 1966, and articles and pamphlets. Address: Princeton, N.J. *

MARK, PETER HERMAN, educator, elec. engr., physicist; b. Mannheim, Germany, Apr. 8, 1931; s. Hermann Francis and Maria (Schramek) M.; came to U.S., 1940, naturalized, 1945; B.A., Harvard, 1953; M.S., Yale, 1954; Ph.D., N.Y. U., 1958; m. Delia Henderson, Dec. 17, 1955; 1 dau., Catherine Virginia. Sr. research physicist Polaroid Corp., 1958-62; mem. tech. staff RCA Labs., Princeton, N.J., 1962-66; mem. faculty Princeton, 1966-79, prof. elec. engring., 1972-79; dir. Internat. Rectifier Corp., 1975-79; cons. in field of electronic materials. Fellow Am. Phys. Soc.; mem. Am. Vacuum Soc. (sr., dir. 1974-75), IEEE (sr.), AAAS. Author: Current Injection in Solids, 1970. Contbr. numerous articles to profl. jours. Editor: Jour. Vacuum Sci. and Tech., 1975-79. Home: Princeton, N.J. Died Sept. 26, 1979; buried St. Stephen's Church, Forest, Va.

MARKEL, LESTER, editor; b. N.Y.C., Jan. 9, 1894; s. Jacob Leo and Lillian (Hecht) M.; student CCNY, 1912-13; Litt.B., Columbia Sch. Journalism, 1914; Litt.D. (hon.), New Sch. for Social Research, 1953; D.H.L. (hon.), Bates Coll., 1953; m. Meta Edman, Apr. 3, 1917; 1 dau., Helen. Reporter, N.Y. Tribune, 1914-15; night city editor, later night editor, 1915-19, asst. mng. editor, 1919-23; Sunday editor N.Y. Times, 1923-65, asso. editor, 1965-69; cons. N.Y. Times Public TV. Asso. journalism Columbia; Disting. vis. prof. Fairleigh-Dickinson U., 1969-77. Mem. Am. Soc. Newspaper Editors, Council on Fgn. Relations: founder Internat. Press. Inst. Democrat. Author: Background and Foreground; What You Don't Know Can Hurt You. Contbr. to While You Were Gone, The Newspaper-Its Making and Its Meaning; contbr. and editor Public Opinion and Foreign Policy. Editor: World in Review. Moderator, editor News in Perspective (TV program), 1963-69. Home: New York, N.Y. Died Oct. 25, 1977.

MARKEY, GENE, writer; b. Jackson, Mich., Dec. 11, 1895; s. Eugene Lawrence and Alice (White) M.; B.S., Dartmouth, 1918; student Art Inst. Chgo., 1919-20; L.H.D., Rollins Coll., 1957; m. Joan Bennett, 1932 (div. 1937); 1 dau., Melinda Markey Bena; m. 2d, Hedy Lamarr, 1939 (div. 1940); m. 3d, Myrna Loy (div. 1950); m. 4th, Lucille Parker Wright, 1952. Served as 1st lt., 19th Inf., AUS, 1917-19; with USNR 1930-55; on active duty, 1941-46; promoted commodore, 1945; ret. rear adm., 1955. Spl. asst. Sec. of Navy, 1944, 46. Decorated Legion of Merit, Bronze Star, Navy Commendation Medal (U.S.); Star of Solidarity (Italy); Legion of Honor (France). Mem. Delta Kappa Epsilon. Mem. Roman Catholic Ch. Clubs: White's (London); Army and Navy (Washington); Knickerbocker, Brook, Jockey (N.Y.C.). Author: Literary Lights, 1923; Men About Town, 1924; The Dark Island (with Charles Collins), 1928; Mabel, 1928; Stepping High, 1929; The Road to Rouen, 1930; His Majesty's Pyjamas, 1934; The Great Companions, 1949; Kingdom of the Spur, 1953; Kentucky Pride, 1956; That Far Paradise, 1960; Women, Women, Everywhere, 1964; The Little Emerald, 1978; (plays) Right You Are, 1925, (with Samuel Hoffenstein) The Eskimo, 1926. Contbr. short stories to mags. Home: Miami Beach, Fla. Died May 1, 1980; buried Lexington Cemetery, Lexington, Ky.

MARKHAM, EDGAR (MÄRK'M), newspaper man; b. Bardolph, Ill., Dec. 22, 1885; s. Harvey and Sarah (Seybold) M.; A.B., U. of Kan., 1910; m. Frances Hart, Aug. 30, 1919. Reporter Kansas City Star, Leavenworth Times, Sioux City Journal, and Des Moines Register and Leader, 1910-13; copy reader and news editor, St. Paul Pioneer Press, 1914-16; Washington corr. St. Paul Pioneer Press-Dispatch, 1917-29; apptd. asst. to chmn., in charge of press relations, Federal Farm Board, 1929; apptd. Washington rep. Grain Com. on Nat. Affairs, 1933; apptd. exec. sec. Nat. Grain Trade Council, 1936; apptd. asst. dir. Nat. Highway Users Conf., 1938; Washington corr., St. Paul Pioneer Press-Dispatch, 1942; Washington Corr., Farm Journal, 1943. Member Phi Delta Theta, Sigma Delta Chi. Republican. Presbyterian. Clubs: National Press, Gridiron. Home: Washington, D.C. *

MARKS, JAMES HARMON, ret. cons. engr.; b. Grand Rapids, Mich., Jan. 6, 1887; s. Warren LeRoy and Isabella (Huff) M.; B.S. in Mech. Engring., U. Mich., 1908, postgrad., 3 yrs.; D.Sc. (hon.), Ricker Coll., 1971; m. Cora H. Matson, Sept. 12, 1908; m. 2d, M.R. Elisabeth La Rocheslle, Jan. 3, 1966. Cons. engr. bldg. and grounds U. Mich., 1908-10, supt. bldgs. and grounds, 1910-16; mech. engr. in charge plant Packard Motor Car Co., 1916-19, supt. mfg. div., 1919-22, indsl. engr., 1922-25, purchasing mgr., 1925-40, v.p., 1940, exec. v.p., 1944-46; formerly cons. in mgmt. engring. with assos.; chmn. bd. Luis Garavaglia Contractors, Inc., 1958-59. Chmn. com. termination and indsl. rehab. Automotive Council for War Prodn., 1942-46. Registered profl. engr., Mich. Mem. Am. Soc. M.E., Soc. Automotive Engrs., Sigma Xi (chmn. emeritus com. membership-at-large, mem. exec. com., citation for service 1970). Clubs: Detroit Athletic; Grosse Pointe (Mich.) Yacht (commodore 1944-45). Author: Challenges! Challenges!, 1977. Home: Grosse Pointe Woods, Mich. Died Feb. 6, 1979; buried White Chapel Meml. Cemetery, Birmingham, Mich.

MARKS, LEWIS HART, executive, indsl. consultant; b. New Orleans, La., July 14, 1883; s. Ferdinand and Fanny (Bensadon) M.; M.D., Tulane U., 1906; post-grad. Johns Hopkins and Harvard univs.; m. Miriam Sears (playwright), July 19, 1931. Supt. Emergency (yellow fever) Hospital, New Orleans, epidemic of 1905; voluntary asst. Royal Inst. for Exptl. Therapeutics, Frankfort-on-the-Main, 1907, asst., 1908, mem. Inst., 1910, being first foreigner and youngest man ever apptd. to this position in Germany; resigned 1912 to become dir. Inst. for Med. Research, Frankfort (an instn. founded for Dr. Marks, by a com. of Am. philanthropists); instn. closed on account of war; returned to U.S., 1917; founder and mgr. pharmaceutical div., Nat. Aniline & Chem. Co., 1920-25; exec. sec. Industrial Alcohol Inst., 1926-33; pres. Continental Distilling Corporation, 1933-Jan. 1940 (resigned); became exec. v.p. Publicker Commercial Alcohol Co., Sept. 1940, also president Bigler Chemical Corporation; consultant in chemical, distillery and pharm. industries. Officer Order of Mil. Merit, 1st Class (Spain); holder of Red Cross Medallion, 1st Class (Germany), Red Cross Officer Cross (Austria). Fellow A.A.A.S.; hon. mem. German Soc. for History of Medicine; mem. Am. Inst. Chemists, Am. Chem. Soc., Soc. Am. Bacteriologists, Phi Rho Sigma. Clubs: Chemists of New York (pres. 1933-35). Author scientific publs., appearing chiefly in German med. periodicals, also in Am. publs. Home: Paoli, Pa. *

MARKS, MARY E(LLA), librarian; b. Davenport, Ia., June 12, 1886; d. Watson Henry and Grace Elizabeth (Hammond) M.; ed. Univ. of Wis., 1904-06; Univ. of Chicago, 1906-08; Ph.B., Univ. of Ill. Library Sch., 1908-09; B.L.S., 1910-11. With Davenport (Ia.) Pub. Library, 1909-10, Ia. State Traveling Library, Des Moines, 1911-18; librarian, U.S. Gen. Hosp. Library, Asheville, N.C., also U.S. Tubercular Hosp., Oteen, N.C., 1918; cataloger, Univ. of Wyo. library, 1919-26, asst. librarian and cataloger, 1926-29, librarian, since 1929. Mem. A.L.A., Am. Assn. Univ. Profs., Wyo. Library Assn., Coll. and Reference Librarians, Unitarian. Home: Laramie, Wyo. *

MARKS, MARY HELEN, educator; b. Burgettstown, Pa. Jan. 3, 1886; d. Samuel Ferree and Sara Eliza (Fredericks) Marks; A.B., Smith Coll. 1909; hon. A.M., Pa. Coll. for Women, 1927; L.H.D., Pa. Coll. for Women, 1938; unmarried. Began as teacher Latin and mathematics, Tidioute (Pa.) High Sch., 1910; field sec., Pa. Coll. for Women, 1916-19, registrar, 1919-22, dean 1922-32, dean, acting pres., 1932-35, dean since 1935; mem. Sch. of Nursing com., Allegheny Gen. Hosp., Pittsburgh; pres. Assn. of Liberal Arts Colls. of Western Pa., 1940-41, Mem. N.E.A., Am. Assn. Univ. Women. Nat. Assn. Deans, Pa. State Edu. Assn. Pa. Dean's Assn., Western Pa. Dean's Assn. (v.p. 1932-35). Pittsburgh Council on Adult Edn.; Y.W.C.A. (bd mgs. 1937-40. Pittsburgh). Phi Beta Kappa. Presbyterian. Clubs: Pittsburgh Coll (v.p. 1931-33), Colloquium (pres. 1922-23). Monday Luncheon (pres. 1928-29) Address: Pittsburgh. *

MARKS, SAM REYNOLDS, lawyer; b. Orlando, Fla., Nov. 17, 1885; s. Matthew R. and Mary (Parramore) M.; student Washington & Lee U., 1909; LL.D. (hon.), Stetson U., 1946; m. India Ingalls. Admitted to Fla. bar, 1909, Supreme Ct. U.S., all Fed. cts., since practiced in Jacksonville; sr. mem. Marks, Gray, Conroy & Gibbs, 1914—. Gen. counsel, dir. Winn-Dixie Stores, Inc.; gen. counsel, chmn. bd. Title & Trust Co. Fla. Chmn. bd. dirs. Boys Home Assn. Mem. Alpha Tau Omega. Presbyn. Mason. Clubs: Rotary; Timuquana (Fla.) Yacht; Ponte Vedra (Fla.) Surf; River (Jacksonville). Address: Jacksonville FL. *

MARKWARD, JOHN OLIVER, paper co. exec.; b. Ft. Worth, June 30, 1921; s. Martin Forrest and Ada (Moore) M.; B.S.M.E., U. Tex., 1947; m. Joyce Reid Ingalls, Feb. 3, 1951; children—John Oliver, Anne. With S.D. Warren Co. (became div. Scott Paper Co.), Westbrook, Maine, from 1949, salesman, 1954-67, v.p., 1967-69, v.p. research, from 1972; exec. dir. Scott Graphics Internat., Bornem, Belgium, 1969-72. Alderman, City of Westbrook, 1951-53; mem. exec. bd. Pine Tree council Boy Scouts Am. Served with C.E. U.S. Army, 1943-46; Guam, Okinawa. Mem. Sales Assn. Paper Industry (pres. 1967), TAPPI. Club: Rotary. Home: Windham, Maine. Deceased.

MARLATT, EARL BOWMAN, clergyman, educator, curator, author; b. Columbus, Ind., May 24, 1892; s. Rev. Abram Newton and Anna Maria (Collins) M.; A.B., DePauw U., 1912, Litt.D., 1931; S.T.B., Boston U., 1922, Ph.D., 1929; postgrad. U. Berlin and Oxford U., 1922-23; nat. fellow in religion, 1924-25. Asso. editor Kenosha (Wis.) News, 1917-18; asso. prof. philosophy Boston U., 1923-25, apptd. prof., 1925; apptd. lectr. in religious edn. Wellesley Coll., 1928; George A. Gordon Meml. lectr. New Old South Ch., Boston, 1932-35; Mendenhall lectr. DePauw U., 1941; prof. philosophy of lit. Boston U. Sch. Theology, dean, 1938-45; prof. philosophy of religion Perkins Sch. of Theology, So. Meth. U., 1946-58; curator Treasure Room and Hymn Mus., Interchurch Center, N.Y.C., 1958-76. Served as 2d lt., F.A., AUS, 1919. Winner of Golden Flower May Day Poetry Tournament, Boston, 1925; Poet laureate, Ind., 1970-71; named to Wisdom Hall of Fame, 1970. Fellow Internat. 1st. Arts and Letters (life); mem. Am. Philos. Assn., Medieval Acad. Am., Acad. Am. Poets, Calvert Round Table Assn., New Eng. Poetry Assn., Boston Browning Soc. (pres. 1917-30, 42-46), Boston Authors Club (pres. 1934-36), Kant-Gesellschaft, Internat. Congress of Philosophy, Phi Beta Kappa, Pi Gamma Mu, Phi Delta Kappa, Delta Kappa Epsilon. Mem. New Eng. Conf. M.E. Ch. Republican. Mason, Elk. Clubs: Harvard Faculty, Bostonian Soc., Eire Soc. Author: Chapel Windows (verse), 1924; Protestant Saints, 1928; Cathedral (verse), 1937; Lands Away, 1944. Asso. editor The American Student Hymnal, 1928. Contbr. to Poetry, Jour. of Expression, Christian Century, Methodist Rev., Religion in Life, High Road S.W. Rev. Author hymns; Are Ye Able, Spirit of Life, Deepen My Music, Through the Dark the Dreamers Came, Vision of Truth, God of the Spirit Wind. Behold the Fields, Shining Armor. Home: Winchester, Ind. Died June 13, 1976.

MARLENS, AL, editor; b. N.Y.C., May 13, 1927; s. Louis and Anna (Madiefsky) M.; B.S.Sc., CCNY, 1948; M.S.Sc., New Sch. Social Research, N.Y.C., 1951; m. Hanna Steiner, Apr. 8, 1950; children—Steve, Neal. Reporter, Park Row News Service, N.Y.C., 1948-52; with Newsday, Garden City, N.Y., from 1952, asst. mng. editor, 1966-67, mng. editor, 1967-70; editor Time Mag., 1970-72; travel editor N.Y. Times, from 1972, editor N.Y. Times Week in Review, 1973-77. Mem. adv. panel urban coalition Skills Bank, N.Y.C., 1969-77. Home: Huntington, N.Y. Died Feb. 22, 1977.

MARMORSTON, JESSIE, physician; b. Kiev, Russia, Sept. 16, 1903; d. Aaron and Ethel (Wark) M.; B.S., M.D., U. Buffalo, 1924; m. Lawrence Weingarten, Feb. 2, 1945; children—Lailee Bakhtiar Marmorston Mommaerts, Elizabeth Marmorston Horowitz, Norma Marmorston Pisar. Intern, Montefiore Hosp., N.Y.C.,

1924-25; bacteriologist, 1924-32; asso. bacteriology and exptl. pathology Cornell U., Ithaca, N.Y., 1931-38; attending staff Dr.'s Hosp., N.Y.C., 1938-80; sr. attending staff Los Angeles County Hosp., 1943-80; attending staff Cedars-Sinai Med. Center, Los Angeles, 1944-80, research staff, 1948-80; research staff Med. Reserach Inst., Los Angeles, 1948-80; asso. prof. medicine U. So. Calif., 1943-53, prof. exptl. medicine, 1953-57, clin. prof. medicine, 1957-80; supervising dir. Calif. Found. Med. Research, Los Angeles. Adv. com. emergency med. care Los Angeles County, 1972-80; bd. dirs. Research Found., St. Joseph Hosp., Burbank. Recipient numerous awards. Fellow A.C.P., N.Y. Acad. Medicine, Am. Geriatrics Soc., Am. Coll. Cardiology, Royal Soc. Promotion Health; mem. N.Y. Acad. Scis., Am., Los Angeles County heart assns., Soc. Exptl. Biology and Medicine, N.Y. Pathol. Soc., Gerontol. Soc., Reticuloendothelial Soc., Assn. Immunology, AMA, Calif., Los Angeles County med. assns., other orgns. Author: (with David Perla) Spleen and Resistance, 1935; Natural Resistance and Clinical Medicine, 1941; (with E. Stainbrook) Psychoanalysis and The Human Situation, 1964; (with J. Weiner and M. Allen) Manuel of Computer Programs for Preliminary Multivariate Analysis, 1965; (with J. Weiner and P. Geller) Scientific Methods in Clinical Studies, 1970. Contbr. numerous articles to profl. publs. Home: Los Angeles, Calif. Died Oct. 21, 1980.

MARNEY, LEONARD CARLYLE, clergyman; b. Harriman, Tenn., July 8, 1916; s. John Leonard and Sarah Victoria (Mays) M.; A.B., Carson Newman Coll., 1938; Th.M., So. Bapt. Theol. Sem., 1943, Th.D., 1946; Litt.D., Wake Forest Coll., 1963; D.D., Johnson C. Smith U., 1964, Kalamazoo Coll., 1967, U. Glasgow, 1976; m. Rita Elizabeth Christopher, June 20, 1940; children—Rita Christopher, Susan Elizabeth. Ordained to ministry Bapt. Ch., 1941; pastor 1st Bapt. Ch., Austin, Tex., 1948-58; prof. Christian ethics Austin Presbyn. Sem., 1951-57; pastor Myers Park Bapt. Ch., Charlotte, N.C., 1958-67; founder, dir. ecumenical center Interpreters House, Lake Junaluska, N.C., 1967-78. Lectr. Colgate-Rochester U., Princeton Sem. Inst., Union Sem. Inst., Chautauqua, Drew Sem., U. Chgo.; vis. prof. Duke Div. Sch., 1972-78; occasional univ. and coll. preacher including Yale, Harvard; missioner for USAF to Korea, Japan, other Am. bases; mem. study commn. World Council Chs., 1957; mem. theol. commn. Bapt. World Alliance, 1957; mem. exec. com. Charlotte-Mecklenburg Council Human Relations, 1964; mem. Fed. Commn. Rural Poverty, from 1967; v.p. Nat. Council Chs., 1967-68. Trustee The Christian Century. Author: Faith in Conflict, 1957 (Religious Book Club selection); Beggars in Velvet, 1960; Structures of Prejudice, 1961 (Religious and Psychology book club selection); Recovery of the Person, 1963; The Coming Faith, 1970; Priests to Each Other, 1973; (sermons) These Things Remain, 1953, He Became Like Us, 1964, The Suffering Servant, 1965; The Carpenter's Son, 1967; The Crucible of Redemption, 1968. Mem. editorial bd. Theology Today, Religion in Life. Home: Waynesville, N.C. Died July 3, 1978; buried Charlotte, N.C.

MARQUIS, FRANKLIN WALES, prof. mech. engring.; b. Bloomington, Ill., May 27, 1883; s. Franklin DuBois and Caroline Agusta (Brush) M.; B.S. in M.E., U. of Ill., 1905, M.E., 1909; m. Elisabeth Parr, June 12, 1912 (died Feb. 1947); children—Franklin Parr, Donald Hall; m. 2d, Margaret Allen, March 22, 1948. Draftsman and designer, Kerr Turbine Co., Wellsville, N.Y., 1905-07; asst. and asso. railway engineering department, Engineering Experimental Sta., U. of Ill., 1907-13; prof. steam engring., Ohio State U., 1913-29, prof. mech. engring. since 1929, chmn. dept., 1929-46. On leave from univ. as statistician and asst. mgr. fuel conservation sect., U.S.R.R. Admstrn., Washington, July 1918-August 1919, as development engineer, B. F. Goodrich Co., Akron, Ohio, Jan.-Oct.1927, and as prin. specialist in engring. edn., Engring. Science and Management War Training Program, U.S. Office of Edn., Washington, D.C., 1942-45. Member Am. Soc. Mechanical Engineers, American Soc. for Engring. Edn., Sigma Xi, Alpha Delta Phi, Theta Tau, Tau Beta Pi. Presbyterian. Home: Columbus, Ohio. *

MARR, GIBSON ATHERTON, lawyer; b. Washington, D.C., Oct. 4, 1885; s. James Hoover and May (Atherton) M.; student Miami U., Oxford, O., 1901-03; B.A., U. of Minn., 1905; student law dept., same univ., 1908-09; m. Grace Elliott, June 28, 1911; children—Eliot, Jean, Marguerite. Began practice of law at Salt Lake City, Utah, 1909; now mem. firm Marr, Wilkins and Cannon; gen. counsel War Finance Corp., Washington, D.C., July 1922-July 1, 1923 (resigned); gen. counsel Reconstruction Finance Corp., Feb.-Apr. 1932 (resigned). Mem. Am. Bar Assn. Republican. Clubs; Alta, Salt Lake Country. Home: Salt Lake City. *

MARRIN, PAUL S., lawyer; b. Hyannis, Nebr., May 18, 1894; s. T.L. and Ida T. (Watts) M.; A.B. and J.D., U. Calif.; m. Mary Fair, Aug. 29, 1932; children—Robert S., Suzanne F. Gen. law practice in San Francisco, 1919-80; gen. counsel Henry J. Kaiser Co. and amnates. Mem. Am., San Francisco bar assns., Calif. Bar, Phi Alpha Delta. Republican. Club: Bohemian. Address: San Francisco, Calif. *

MARSH, CLARENCE STEPHEN, educator; b. Peoria, Ill., Sept. 15, 1882; s. James Daniel and Hannah Jane (Simpson) M.; B.A., Northwestern Univ., 1910. M.A., 1920; LL.D., Yankton (S.D.) Coll., 1934; m. Fern Emily Greene, Aug. 25, 1916; children—Jane (dec.), Margaret Fern, James Thomas, David Stuart. Teacher of English, high sch., Danville, Ill., 1910-11; registrar Northwestern U., 1911-19, asst. dean Sch. of Commerce, 1919-23, dir. summer session, 1920-22; dean of evening session, U. of Buffalo, 1923-35, dean of Sch. of Business Administration, 1927-35, dir. summer session, 1931-34; ednl. dir. Civilian Conservation Corps, U.S. Office of Edn., Washington, Jan 1, 1934-Apr. 1935; v.p. Am. Council on Edn., Washington, 1935-43. Consultant, War Dept., and Office of Inter-American Affairs; lecturer in extension div., U. of Calif., Los Angeles. Dir. survey of adult edn., Buffalo, 1926. Sec.-treas. Am. Assn. of Collegiate Registrars, 1919-20; pres. Am. Assn. Collegiate Schs. of Business, 1932-33; sec.-treas. Assn. Urban Univs., 1926-35. Mem. Am. Assn. for Adult Education, Nat. Edn. Assn. (ex-president Adult Dept.). Am. Assn. Univ. Profs., Phi Delta Kappa, Delta Mu Delta, Beta Gamma Sigma. Del. to meeting of Executive Council of the World Assn. for Adult Education in Belgium, Aug. 1932; del. to Fifth Internat. Conf. on Public Instruction, Geneva, Switzerland, July 1936. Awarded Cross of Polish Legion. Club: National Press. Author: Adult Education in a Community, 1926. Editor Ann. Procs. Assn. Urban Univs., 1926-35; Am. Univs. and Colls., 1936, 40; Educational Broadcasting, 1936, 37; all publs. Am. Council on Edn., including The Ednl. Record, quarterly, 1936-43. Contbr. to nat. mags. and ednl. journals. Home: Los Angeles, Calif. *

MARSH, GEO(RGE) HENRY, agrl. chemist; b. Hector, Ala., Sept. 4, 1883; s. Spencer Jackson and Sarah Roseana (Morgan) M.; B.S., Ala. Poly. Inst., 1908, M.S., 1909, grad. student, 1910; student summer sessions, Columbia, 1920-22, U. Cal., 1923; m. Dolly D. Love, June 20, 1929; children—Dolly L., Georgia A. (Mrs. Russell A. Long), Sarah J., Geo. H., Spencer J. Instr. in pharmacy Ala. Poly. Inst., 1910, instr. chemistry, 1912-16, asst. prof. organic chemistry and food chemist, 1920-24; pharmacist Collier Drug Co., Birmingham, 1911; asst. to state chemist, 1912-16; chemist Swift & Co., Bartow, Fla., 1917-18, asst. supt., 1919; food and drug chemist, Dept. of Agr. and Industries, Montgomery, Ala., 1925-29, chief div. agrl. chemistry and head chem. lab., 1930-38, dir. div. agrl. chemistry, 1939—. Mem. Assn. Ofcl. Agrl. Chemists (pres. 1948), Assn. Food, Dairy and Drug Ofcls. U.S. (past pres.), Assn. Am. Feed Control Ofcls. (past pres.), Am. Pub. Health Assn., Am. Pharm. Assn. (awarded membership for excelling in scholarship 1908), A.A.A.S., Am. Chem. Soc., Assn. Am. Fertilizer Control Ofcsl., Assn. Am. Economic Poison Control Ofcls., S. Central States Assn. Food, Drug, Feed and Health Ofcls. (past pres.), Assn. Southern Feed Control Ofcls. (past pres.), Assn. So. States Food and Drug Ofcls. (v.p. 1954), So. Assn. Sci. and Industry, So. Feed Fertilizer Assn. (chmn. feed standards com.), Phi Delta Chi, Gamma Sigma Epsilon. Democrat. Methodist. Mason (K.T., Shriner). Club: Lions. Research in the chemistry of fats, and fixed oils, also volatile oils. Home: Montgomery. *

MARSH, HOMER ELLSWORTH, tax research cons.; b. Plymouth, Ind., Apr. 19, 1912; s. Marion Oscar and Pearl Ione (Ritter) M.; B.S., Ind. U., 1935, grad. study, 1935-36; m. Hazel Gladys Monce, May 24, 1941. Instr. Ind. U. Sch. Bus. Adminstrn., 1935-36; dir. research and statistics, unemployment compensation div. State of Ind., 1936-44; cons. bur. labor statistics, U.S. Dept. Labor, 1942-44; dir. research Nat. Tax Equality Assn., Chgo., 1944-60, exec. sec., 1960-70, 72-75, pres., 1975, cons., 1970-71; dir. research Nat. Assn. Businessmen, Inc., Washington, 1948, exec. sec., 1972-75, pres., 1975, cons. Mem. Govtl. Research Assn., Nat. Tax Assn., Beta Gamma Sigma. Author: (with Thomas W. Rogers) Bibliography of Public Employment Offices, 1935; Solvency of Indiana Unemployment Compensation Fund, 1943; Cooperative Expansion in the Petroleum Industry, 1944; Super-Cooperatives in the Field of Purchasing, 1944; Tax Free Manufacturing Cooperative Corporations, 1945; Subsidized Cooperatives in the Marketing Field, 1945; Cooperative Competition in New England, 1946; The Facts in the Matter, 1947; The Other Tax Exempts, 1947; Tax Escaping Cooperatives Engaged in Grocery Distribution, 1949. Contbr. articles to trade publs. Home: Plymouth, Ind. Died Nov. 5, 1978.

MARSH, RICHARD OGLESBY, engr.; b. Washington, D.C., Mar. 27, 1883; s. Benjamin Franklin and Jennie Elizabeth (Coolbaugh) M.; student Mass. Inst. Tech., 1901-05, Universite de Lausanne, Switzerland, 1905-06; m. Helen Louise Cleveland, Sept. 15, 1909; children—Helen, Richard Oglesby, Jane, Gladys, Sec. of Legation and chargé d'affaires U.S. Legation, Panama, 1909-10; attaché Latin-Am. Div. of State Dept., 1910, near East Div., 1911; sec. U.S. Embassy at St. Petersburg, Russia, 1912; made engring. and scientific exploration trips, 1907-32, in Rio Mesquital Canyon in W. Mexico, from Bolivia over Andes in Amazon headwaters, from Peking, China, into Mongolia, in Arabia, Somaliland, Morocco and the Riff; also leader of Darien expdn., sponsored by Smithsonian Inst., Am. Mus. Natural History and U. of Rochester, and in Nicaragua; has done engring. work in U.S., Mexico, Bolivia, P.L.; junior partner Gen. G. W. Goethals, 1923-27; research engr. E. I. du Pont de Nemours, 1927-29; pres. Richard O. Marsh & Co., Inc., N.Y., 1929-33; with Pub. Works Administrn., 1933-35; with Land Utilization Div., U.S. Dept. of Agr. as chief engr., 1935-39; cons. engr. Federal Nat. Defense Bd., 1939-40; apptd. hydro electric expert Fed. Power Commn. 1940; consultant War Department, 1941; reconnaissance engr. for U.S. Mil. N. African Mission, Dec. 1941-Apr. 1943, with field service in N. Africa; returned U.S., April 1943, for convalescence from wound received in N. African campaign; cons. engr. to U.S. Rubber Development Corp.; chief U.S. Special Mission to Ethiopia, Jan. 1944 consultant to U.S. war and Navy Depts. and various foreign govts. since 1944. Commd. admiral of the Flagship Fleet, American Airlines, Inc. for "meritorious service to air transportation," July 1941. Awarded resolution of thanks from American and British associations for advancement of science for contbns. to ethnology. Fellow Am. Geographic Soc. etc. Hon. staff mem. Science Service, Nat. Acad. Science, since 1924, Pan-Am. Soc. Tropical Research since 1938. Club: Explorer (New York). Author: The White Indians of Darien, 1934; contbr. articles to mags and jours. Officially credited with responsibility for design and construction of over 3,000 impounding dams for flood control, waterpower, water conservation, irrigation, recreation, wild life.*

MARSHALL, BURKE, educator; b. Plainfield, N.J., Oct. 1, 1922; s. Henry Place and Dorothy Louise (Burke) M.; B.A., Yale, 1943, LL.B., 1951; m. Violet Person, June 20, 1946; children—Josephine Holcomb, Catherine Cox, Jane Montgomery. Admitted to D.C. bar, 1951; mem. firm Covington & Burling, Washington, 1951-61; asst. atty. gen. U.S. for civil rights div. Dept. Justice, 1961-65; v.p., gen. counsel IBM Corp., 1965-69, sr. v.p., 1969-70; prof. law, dep. dean Yale Law Sch., 1970-76. Chmn. Nat. Adv. Commn. on Selective Service; chmn. bd. Vera Inst. Justice. Clubs: Century (N.Y.C.); Federal City (Washington). Author: Federalism and Civil Rights, 1964; also articles. Home: Newtown, Conn. Died Mar. 29, 1976.

MARSHALL, CHARLES A(LEXANDER), lawyer; born Baltimore, Feb. 14, 1883; s. Charles and Rebecca (Snowden) M.; A.B., Johns Hopkins U., 1903; LL.B., U. of Md., 1907; m. Lillie H. Cunningham, April 26, 1911; children—Elizabeth C. (Mrs. Hardie Shepard), Ann S. Admitted to bar of Md., 1908, bar of New York, 1914; mem. law firm Rearick, Dorr, Travis & Marshall (later Hines, Rearick, Dorr, Travis & Marshall), and successor firms to 1948; on leave of absence as chief spl. mission to Denmark for Econ. Co-op. Adminstrn., since 1948. Participated in orgn., dir. and counsel in management of Atlantic and Pacific Internat. Corp., 1928-32; engaged in legal affairs and practical adminstrn. of properties controlled by British Financial instns. in Mexico and Costa Rica, 1941-44; gen. counsel and dir. Hunter Mfg. Corp., 1931-48. Represented flat glass industry in N.R.A. code formulation and adminstrn. Served as lt. to capt., Inf., U.S. Army, World War I. Member N.Y. State Bar Assn., Assn. Interstate Commerce Commn. Practitioners. Democrat. Episcopalian. Asst. in editing and pub. of An Aide-de-camp of Lee, by Gen. Sir Frederick Maurice, 1924. Home: N.Y. City. *

MARSHALL, CLARENCE G., newspaper editor; b. Columbus, Ind., Oct. 25, 1884; s. Gideon T. and Dora B. (Hughes) M.; ed. Newport News (Va.) High Sch.; m. Mrs. Pocahontas H. Booker, Mar. 20, 1929; (died May 29, 1933); m. 2d, Mrs. Alice P. Day, July 5, 1938. Reporter Newport News Times Herald until 1904, city editor, 1904-06; telegraph editor Norfolk (Va.) Ledger-Dispatch, 1906-07; joined Washington staff of Associated Press, as night mgr., 1907; mem. Capitol staff Associated Press, 1908-11; news editor southern div. Associated Press, 1911-13, day mgr. Chicago Office, 1913-15, and again news editor southern div., hdqrs. in Washington, 1915-18; resigned to enter U.S. Navy; v.p. and editor Newport News Record, 1919-20; mng. editor Petersburg Index Appeal-Progress, 1921; mgr. Chicago office Consolidated Press Assn., 1922, mgr. New York office, 1923-26; apptd. news mgr. U.S. Daily, Washington, Apr. 5, 1926, name changed to U.S. News, 1933, mng. editor until 1938; asso. pub. Pathfinder Mag., 1938-39; public relations adviser, Am. Export Airlines, 1939-40; chief, Division of Current Information, U.S. Dept. of Commerce, 1941-45; information specialist, Reconstrn. Finance Corp., 1945-46; senior editor Kiplinger Magazine since 1946. Clubs: Chevy Chase, National Press, Overseas Writers. Home: Washington. *

MARSHALL, HENRY SMITH, heating and cooling equipment mfr.; b. Marshall Co., Ill., Nov. 27, 1884; s. Frank and Christiana (Smith) M.; B.S., Highland Park (Ia.) Coll., 1907. Admitted Ill. bar, 1916; former mem.

Marshall, Murtaugh and Burgeson, Chicago; chmn. bd. Dunham-Bush, Inc., 1956—. Mem. Chgo. Bar Assn. Conglist. Mason. Home: Winnetka, Ill.

MARSHALL, JOHN SEDBERRY, educator; b. Fullerton, Calif., May 25, 1898; s. John Lundy and Emma Elizabeth (Gawley) M.; A.B., Pomona Coll., 1921; Ph.D., Boston U., 1926; student Harvard U., 1924-25, U. Basel (Switzerland), 1923-25, U. Calif., 1928, Russ. U. Prague (Czechoslovakia), summers 1935-36; m. Elizabeth Southard, May 26, 1923; 1 son, James Edward. Instr. philosophy Syracuse (N.Y.) U., 1926-29; prof. philosophy Albion Coll., 1929-46; prof. philosophy U. of the South, Sewanee, Tenn., 1946-68, prof. emeritus, 1968-79, prof. grad. sch. theology, 1950-62. Editor, Anglican Theol. Rev., 1959-65. Mem. Am. Philos. Assn., AAAS, AAUP, Brit. Inst. Philosophy, So. Soc. for Philosophy of Religion (past pres.), Guild of Scholars (past pres.), Realist Soc., Phi Beta Kappa, Lambda Chi Alpha. Democrat. Episcopalian. Author: (with N.O. Lossky), Value and Existence 1935; Hooker's Polity in Modern English, 1948; The Genius and Mission of the Episcopal Church, 1949; The Word Was Made Flesh, 1949; Hooker's Theology of Common Prayer, 1953; Hooker and the Anglican Tradition, 1963; contbr. various articles to The Anglican Theol. Review, The Sewanee Review, The Monist, The Personalist, The Review of Politics, Ency. Brit. Address: Sewanee, Tenn. Died Nov. 5, 1979.

MARSHALL, LAWRENCE MARCELLUS, educator, chemist; b. Pitts., Mar. 31, 1910; s. James Henry and Mary (Mosby) M.; B.S., Duquesne U., 1932, M.S., 1940; Ph.D. (USPHS fellow 1945-48), Wayne State U., 1949; m. Mary C. Williams, June 6, 1939; children—Lawrence Marcellus, Gwendolyn, Judith. Asst. prof. chemistry Clark Coll., Atlanta, 1937-39; prof. chemistry and biology Ark. State Coll., Pine Bluff, 1940-44; asst. chemist Pine Bluff Arsenal, 1942-44; asso. chemist Jeffersonville Q.M. Depot, 1944-45; mem. faculty Howard U. Med. Sch., 1948-77, prof. biochemistry, head dept., 1959-77. Recipient Lederle Med. Faculty award Lederle Lab. div. Am. Cyanamid Co., 1954; Disting. Service award Wayne State U. Sch. Medicine, 1977. Fellow Am. Inst. Chemists; mem. Am. Soc. Biol. Chemists, Am. Chem. Soc., Sigma Xi. Home: Washington, D.C. Died July 30, 1977.

MARSHALL, LEROY T(ATE), ex-congressman; b. nr. Bellbrook, Ohio, Nov. 8, 1883; s. Willis and Emma (Tate) M.; Ph.B., Cedarville (O.) Coll., 1907; m. Nellie C. Turnbull, June 4, 1909; children—Maxwell, Jean (Mrs. Fred Clark). Teacher pub. schs., 1903-07; clk., Common Pleas Court, Greene Co., 1907-11; practiced law at Xenia, O., since 1911; mem. law firm Marshall & Marshall, Mem. Ohio State Senate, 1924-28; mem. 73d and 74th Congresses (1933-37), 7th Ohio Dist. Republican. Presbyn. Home: Xenia, O. *

MARSHALL, SAMUEL LYMAN ATWOOD, mil. critic and historian; b. Catskill, N.Y., July 18, 1900; s. Caleb C. and Alice A. (Beeman) M.; student Tex. Coll. Mines, 1919-20; L.H.D., Wayne State U.; LL.D., St. Bonaventure U.; m. Catherine Finnerty, Mar. 10, 1954; children—Sharon, Catherine, Bridget; 1 son (by previous marriage), Samuel Lyman Atwood. Juvenile actor Western Essanay Co., 1913-15; sports editor, later city editor El Paso Herald, 1923-27; commd. maj. to brig. gen., U.S. Army, 1942-52, chief orientation, 1942, chief combat historian, Central Pacific area, 1943, dep. theater historian, ETO, 1944, chief theater historian, 1945, assigned to Korea, 1950-51; war corr. Korea, 1953, Sinai War, Israel-Egypt, 1956, Lebanon, 1958, South Vietnam (Dept. Def., 1962, ret., 1960; with U.S. Army, Vietnam, 1966-67, cons. chief staff, 1970, sr. cons. Army Materiel Command, 1971-77; fgn. corr., mil. critic, chief editorial writer Detroit News, 1927-62; now syndicated columnist Washington Post-Los Angeles Times; corr. Middle East and Congo, 1961. Mem. U.S. Army hist. adv. commn., Pub. Relations Com., Mich. Civil Def. Commn. Trustee Detroit ARC; mem. Chancellor's Council U. Tex. Served from pvt., engr. corps to 1st lt., inf., U.S. Army, 1917-19. Decorated D.S.M., Legion of Merit, Bronze Star medal with oak leaf cluster, Citation Medal with oak leaf clusters, Combat Inf. Badge, Victory, Pacific, Africa-Middle East-European, Korean, UN Korean medals (U.S.); Legion of Honor, Croix de Guerre with Palm, Ordre d'Armee (France); Order d'Leopold with Palm, Croix de Guerre with Palm, Ardennes medal (Belgium); Croci di Guerra, Fatigue di Guerra (Italy); Inf. Combat medal (Ethopia); Medallion of Valor (Israel); elected to Nat. Cowboy Hall of Fame, 1972. Hon. fellow Bar Ilan U., Israel. Mem. S.A.R., Soc. Am. Historians, Mil. Order World Wars, Assn. U.S. Army, Am. Legion, V.F.W. Clubs: Coffee House (N.Y.C.); Detroit Press; Bloomfield (Mich.) Hunt. Author: Blitzkrieg, 1940; Armies on Wheels, 1941; Island Victory, 1944; Bastogne, 1946; Men Against Fire, 1947; Makin, 1947; The Mobility of One Man, 1949; The Armed Forces Officer, 1950; Critique of Weapons and Tactics in Korea, 1952; Hill 440, 1952; The River and the Gauntlet, 1953; Tactics in Defense Against Atomic Attack, 1954; Pork Chop Hill, 1956; Sinai Victory, 1958; Night Drop, 1961; Battle at Best, 1964; First Book on Korea, 1964; Heritage History of World War I, 1964; The Officer as a Leader, 1966; The War to Free Cuba, 1966; Battles in the Monsoon, 1967; Vietnam Primer, 1967; Bird, 1968; West to Cambodia, 1968; Ambush, 1969; History of World War II, 1969; The Fields of Bamboo, 1971; Crimsoned Prairie, 1972; On Urban Warfare, 1973; Bringing Up the Rear, 1980; also ofcl. mil. texts and manuals. Mil. contbr. to Am. Coll. Dictionary, Crowell-Collier, Ency. Brit., U.S. Navy Ann. Rev.; contbr. to nat. mags. Address: El Paso, Tex. Died Dec. 17, 1977; buried Nat. Cemetery, Ft. Bliss, Tex.

MARSTON, FRANK ALWYN, cons. civil engr.; b. Worcester, Mass., Sept. 21, 1885; s. Charles F. and Abbie Mary (Smith) M.; B.S., Worcester Poly. Inst., 1907; E.D. (hon.), Worcester Poly. Inst., 1960; married Bertha Wheeldon, April 17, 1911; children—Ruth Alice (Mrs. Forrest P. Dexter, Jr.), Priscilla (Mrs. William R. Stewart), Alwyn Franklin, Frances Wheeldon, Philip Lincoln. Resident engr. L. D. Thorpe, 1907; asst. engr. Metcalf & Eddy, 1908-20, partner, 1920—; pres. Wollaston Fed. Savs. & Loan Assn. Registered profl. civil engr., Me., N.H., Vt., R.I., Conn., D.C., N.Y., Del., Pa., Ky., Ohio, Mich., Ill., Va., Mass. Diplomate Am. Acad. San. Engrs. Fellow Am. Soc. C.E. (pres., dir.); member Massachusetts Society Professional Engineers, American Soc. Testing Materials, Am., New Eng. water works assns., Boston Soc. C.E., Pub. Works Assn., New Eng. Sewage Works Assn. Home: Quincy, Mass. *

MARSTON, HUNTER SYLVESTER, former banker; b. St. Louis, May 5, 1885; s. Edgar Lewis and Jennie Colorado (Hunter) M.; student Hill Sch., Pottstown, Pa., 1900-04; Ph.B., Brown U., 1908, LL.D. (hon.); m. Mary A. Vanderhoef, Apr. 17, 1909; children—Mary Hunter, Edgar L. II, Elisabeth Jennie, George V.W., Hunter Sylvester. Began with Blair & Co., 1908, spl. partner, 1917-20; syndicate mgr. in consol. W. L. Solomon & Co., 1920, v.p., 1920-30; v.p. Bancamerica-Blair Corp., 1929-30, pres., 1930-32; dir. Am. Home Products Corp. Trustee Westerly Hosp. Served as maj. Intelligence Corps, mem. Gen. Staff, AUS; selected to accompany Pres. Wilson to Peace Conf., Paris, 1919. Clubs: Union, Brown University, Down Town Assn., Brook, Racquet and Tennis, Creek, River, Riping Rock (N.Y.C.). Republican. Baptist. Home: Watch Hill, R.I. Died Oct. 16, 1979.

MARSTON, JOHN, ret. marine corps officer; b. Somerset Co., Pa., Aug. 3, 1884; s. John and Mary (Roberts) M.; student Univ. of Pa., 1901-04; hon. LL.D., Calif. Coll., China, 1942; m. Elizabeth Barroll Worthington, June 8, 1910; children—Elizabeth Baroll (Mrs. J. S. Letcher), Mary Roberts (Mrs. Manly Lamar Curry), John. Commd. 2d lt., U.S.M.C., May 25, 1908, and advanced through grades to maj. gen., Mar. 20, 1942; dir. Marine Corps schs., 1933, personnel hdqrs., 1934-37; comdg. officer, Marine forces, North China, 1937-39; comdg. gen., 1st Marine Brigade, Iceland, 1941-42, 2d Marine div., 1942-43, dept. of the Pacific, 1943-44, Camp Lejeune, N.C., 1944-46; retired from active service Aug. 1, 1946. Decorated as Grand Officer of Mil. Order of Orange Nassau (Netherlands), 1946, Comdr. Order of Brit. Empire, 1946. Mem. Mil. Order of the Loyal Legion Soc. of Colonial Wars. Sons of the Revolution. Republican. Episcopalian. Home: Lexington, Va. *

MARSTON, MORRILL W., army officer; b. Ames, Iowa, Jan. 30, 1896; s. Anson and Mary (Day) M.; B.S. in Civil Engring., Iowa State Coll., 1917; grad. Inf. Sch., 1919, 27, Engrs. Sch., 1928, Command and Gen. Staff Sch., 1936, Army War Coll., 1939, Nat. War Coll., 1947; m. Lucy F. Mead, 1917; children—Morrill E., Arthur A. Commd. 2d lt. U.S. Army, 1917, advanced through grades to brig. gen.; instr. Engr. Sch., 1928-32; asst. chief staff for intelligence, Hawaiian Dept., 1939-41, for supply, Hawaiian Dept., Central Pacific Area, and U.S. Army Forces, Pacific Ocean Areas, 1941-47, Replacement Tng. Center, Fort Lewis, Wash., 1947, 4th Div., Fort Ord, Calif., 1947-48; with U.S. Forces in Austria, 1948-52, 1st Log Comd., Fort Bragg, N.C., 1952-53. Recipient D.S.M., Legion of Merit with oak leaf cluster, Bronze Star medal, Greek Cross of Grand Comdr. Royal Order of George I. Mem. Ret. Officers Assn., Mil. Order World Wars, Theta Xi. Clubs: Masons (32 deg.), Shriners, Nat. Sojourners, Commenwealth of Calif. Home: Saratoga, Calif. Deceased.

MARTIN, ALLIE BETH (MRS. RALPH F. MARTIN), librarian; b. Annieville, Ark., June 28, 1914; d. Carlton G. and Ethel (McCaleb) Dent; A.B., Ark. Coll., 1935; B.L.S., George Peabody Coll., 1939; M.S., Columbia, 1948; m. Ralph F. Martin, Oct. 6, 1937 (dec.); 1 dau., Elizabeth Erhard. Librarian Batesville (Ark.) Pub. Library, 1935-36, Little Rock Jr. Coll., 1936-37; asst. to exec. sec. Ark. Library Commn., 1937-38, 42-47; librarian Mississippi County Library, 1941-42; head children's and extension depts. Tulsa Pub. Library, 1950-62; acting dir. Tulsa City-County Library, 1963; dir. Tulsa City-County Library System, 1963-76; vis. asso. prof. U. Okla. Sch. Library Sci., 1957-76. Library bldg. cons. Library Design Assos.; dir. Study Continuing Edn. Librarians S.W. Mem. Am. (mem. council, coordinator pub. library goals study, exec. bd., pres.), Ark. (pres.), Okla. (pres.) library assns., Southwestern Library Assn. (pres.), Delta Kappa Gamma. Methodist. Author: A Strategy for Public Library Change. Editor Ark. Libraries, 1945-47, Okla. Librarian, 1953-55. Contbr. to profl. publs. Home: Tulsa, Okla. Died Apr. 11, 1976.

MARTIN, BENNETT SEEBERT, real estate exec.; b. Oregon, Mo., Mar. 6, 1904; s. Morton R. and Elsa (Bennett) M.; B.S., U. Nebr., 1925; m. Dorothy Bridgmon, June 19, 1926; children—Mary Anne, Bennett T., M. Bruce. Vice-pres., dir. 1st Nat. Bank Co., Lincoln, Nebr., 1925-53; organizer, pres., dir. Martin Investment Co., Lincoln, 1953-61; chmn. bd. Lincoln Terminal Co., from 1943; vice chmn., dir. Central Telephone & Utilities Co., Lincoln; dir., mem. exec. com. First Nat. Bank & Trust Co., Lincoln. Adv. com. St. Elizabeth Hosp., 1962-63; finance com. U. Neb. Found.; chmn. Neb. Resources Found., 1961-67. Mem. Lincoln City Council, 1955; mayor City of Lincoln, 1956-59; del. Nat. Republican Conv., 1960. Pres. bd. dirs. Lincoln Gen. Hosp. Recipient Distinguished Citizen award Nebr. Wesleyan U., 1963; Nebr. Builder award U. Nebr., 1963. Mem. Lincoln C. of C. (chmn. bus. expansion com. 1960-63, dir., treas. 1961-62), Nebr. Assn. Commerce and Industry (pres. 1967), Newcomen Soc. N.Am., Delta Sigma Phi, Sigma Chi. Republican. Presbyn. Elk. Clubs: Lincoln Country, Lincoln University. Home: Lincoln Nebr. Died Jan. 3, 1975.

MARTIN, CALDWELL, lawyer; b. Little Rock, Ark., Aug. 29, 1883; s. George Wingfield and Margaret (Caldwell) M.; LL.B., Cornell U., 1906; m. Harriet S. Platt, July 31, 1912 (died Apr. 8, 1919); children—Sarah Platt (Mrs. Carlton Harrington), Harriet Mayes (Mrs. W. G. Foeppel); m. 2d, Ethel Adams, Apr. 30, 1921. Admitted to Colo. bar, 1907, began practice as asso. firm of Vaile & Waterman, Denver, later with Charles W. Waterman; gen atty. Great Western Sugar Co., 1917-25, gen counsel 1925-55; general counsel and ex-dir. Great Western Railway Co.; member of law firm of Martin & Holt. Ex-vice-pres. and ex-sec. Denver Community Chest. Ex-dir. and ex-chmn. Denver Chap., Am. Red Cross. Past trustee Cherry Hills Village. Mem. Am., Colo. State bar assns., Denver Bar Association. State (Colo.) Hist. Soc. (trustee), Cornell Alumni Assn. of Colo., Theta Delta Chi, Sphinx Head (Cornell). Republican. Episcopalian. Clubs: Denver, Mile High, City, Law, Cherry Hills Country (Denver); Savage (Ithaca, N.Y.). Home: Denver. *

MARTIN, CHARLES EMANUEL, polit. scientist; b. Corsicana, Tex., Sept. 11, 1891; s. Emanuel Cobb and Roxie Annie (Moon) M.; A.B. U. Calif., 1914, A.M., 1915; Ph.D., Columbia, 1918; LL.D., U. So. Calif., 1942; m. Jewell Boone, June 13, 1921. Fellow in internat. law, Columbia, 1916-17; Carnegie Endowment fellow in internat. law, 1919; lectr. on politics and internat. law, U. Calif., 1919-20; head polit. sci. dept. UCLA, 1920-25; prof. internat. law and polit. sci., 1925-62, prof. emeritus, 1962-79, head dept. polit. sci. U. Wash., 1925-51, also dean faculty social sci., 1926-29, dir. Inst. Internat. Affairs, 1935-62; vis. or exchange prof. several univs. both U.S. and fgn.; prof. Am. studies U. Philippines, 1962-63; Distinguished Haynes prof. internat. law Whittier (Calif.) Coll., 1964; research study Japan, Southeast Asia and India, 1954-55. Has served as labor and indsl. arbitrator; spl. lectr. several confs., congresses, spl. schs., govt. burs. and meetings; adv. govtl. orgns.; lectr. Inter Am. Acad. Internat. and Comparative Law, Havana, Cuba, 1957; visited S.A. as guest Sec. Navy, 1958. Del. internat. confs. assns. and pvt. orgns. Has practicpated in numerous govtl. and civic orgns. Served in C.A.C., U.S. Army, 1918-19. Decorated by French Govt., 1948; recipient 1st Raymond J. Huff award Seattle World Affairs Council for distinction in internat. affairs, 1958. Mem. Am. Soc. Internat. Law (pres. 1960-61), North West Polit. Sci. Assn. (pres. 1960-61), also mem. sci. and profl. assns. and orgns. Episcopalian. Mason. Clubs: Rainier, Monday, China, Faculty (Seattle); Cosmos (Washington); Army and Navy (Manila, Philippines). Author several books in field, 1921-36, latest being Universalism and Regionalism in International Law and Organization, 1960; also many articles and pamphlets. Editor several vols. Contbr. on world affairs to Ency. Brit., Ency. Americana. Home: Seattle, Wash. Died Jan. 12, 1977.

MARTIN, CHARLES LOUIS, physician; b. Massey, Tex., Dec. 2, 1893; s. James Madison and Emma (Auerbach) M.; E.E., U. Tex., 1914; M.D., Harvard, 1919; m. Mabelle Ober, July 17, 1920; 1 son, James Addison. Radiol. resident Mass. Gen. Hosp., Boston, 1919-20; radiologist Baylor Hosp., Dallas, 1920-40; prof. radiology med. sch. Baylor U., 1925-42; cons Martin X-ray and Radium Clinic, Dallas from 1940, prof. radiology Med. Sch., U. Tex., 1950-66, emeritus prof., 1966-79; radiol. consultant Gaston, Baylor, Parkland vets. hosps., Dallas, from 1943; bd. dirs Gaston Hosp., from 1959. Recipient Janeway medal Am. Radium Soc., 1949; Marchman award, Dallas So Clin. Soc., 1953. Diplomate Am. Bd. Radiology; hon diplomate Pan Am. Med. Assn. Mem. So., Dalla County (pres. 1951) med. socs., Am. Radium Soc. (pres

1947), Am. Roentgen Ray Soc. (pres. 1952), A.M.A., Dallas Better Bus. Bur. (dir.), Dallas So. Clin. Soc., Am. Club Therapeutic Radiologists, Boylston Med. Soc., Delta Kappa Epsilon, Alpha Omega Alpha. Rotarian. Author: (with James A. Martin) Low Intensity Radium Therapy, 1959, also 2 vols. illustrated articles on radiation therapy, 1972. Home: Dallas, Tex. Died May 4, 1979; buried Hillcrest Meml. Park, Dallas.

MARTIN, CLARENCE R., jurist; b. Aberdeen, Brown County, O., Dec. 10, 1886; s. Reuben and Marianna (Brown) M.; grad. Manual Training High School, Indianapolis, Ind., 1904; LL.B., Ind. Law Sch., Indianapolis, 1906; LL.B., U. of Mich., 1907; m. Ethel B. Melvin, Mar. 9, 1914 (died Feb. 9, 1920); 1 dau., Jane (Mrs. Max White); m. 2d, Nellie L. Pape, Indiana. August 9, 1922; children—Virginia Lee (Mrs. Jack C. Daw), Claribel (Mrs. Paul W. Stewart) Edmund William. Admitted to Ind. bar, 1907, and began as law clerk, Appellate Court of Ind.; engaged in gen. practice of law at Indianapolis; justice Supreme Court of Ind., 1926-1933; chief justice, 1928-29 and 1931. Served as major 111th Inf., 28th Div., U.S. Army, 1918; asst. inspector gen. A.E.F., 1919. Counsel for U.S. Senate com. investigating radical activities, 1920. Chmn. speakers' bur., Rep. State Com., Ind., 1922; compaign mgr. for Senator Albert J. Beveridge, 1922. Mem. Ind. State Bar Assn., Am. Legion (past comdr. Indianapolis Post). Republican. Baptist. Mason, 33 deg. (hon.); grand master Ind. Grand Lodge, 1942-43; past officer Scottish Rite; K.T.; Shriner. Clubs: Columbia, Mercator (ex-pres.); Lawyers of Ann Arbor, Mich. (hon.). Home: Washington, D.C. *

MARTIN, CLYDE SAYERS, forester; b. Waynesburg, Pa., Sept. 19, 1884; s. Charles Alexander and Florence Adelaide (Sayers) M.; B.Sc., DePauw U., 1905; M.F., Yale Forest Sch., 1907; m. Gertrude Graves, Dec. 20, 1924; 1 son, Charles Alexander (dec.). Cruising and forest engr. Weyerhaeuser Timber Co., 1907-20; cons. forest engr., govt. of India and later chief forest engr., govt. of Madras, 1920-30; sawmill bus. in Oregon, 1930-33; chief forester, Western Pine Assn., Portland, 1934-39; chief forester, Weyerhaeuser Timber Co. since 1939. Pres. Soc. of American Foresters since 1947. Trustee, Washington and Oregon Forest Fire Assns., Washington Forestry Conf., Am. Forest Products Industries (dir since 1947). Fellow Soc. of Am. Foresters; mem. A.A.A.S., Beta Theta Pi. Clubs: Tacoma, Lumberman's, Lawn Bowling (Tacoma, Wash.); University (Portland, Ore.); Washington Athletic (Seattle, Wash.). Home: Tacoma. *

MARTIN, DWIGHT, editor; b. Washington, May 27, 1921; s. Lorenzo Woodhouse and Julia Hays (Worthington) M.; student George Washington U., 1940-43; m. Elizabeth Julia McNair, May 18, 1946 (div. 1952); children—Arthur, Neil; m. 2d, Emilie Lee, June 25, 1957; children—Claudia, Sarah; m. 3d, Karin Susan Smith, Aug. 9, 1965; children—Christopher Hays, Timothy Hugh. Copyboy Washington Post, 1938; reporter, rewrite man, asst. city editor Washington Times-Herald, 1942-48; fgn. news writer Time mag., 1948; covered closing months Communist Revolution in China, 1949; war corr. assigned Korean war, 1950; chief Tokyo Bur. Time-Life Internat., 1951-54, chief Bur. for Singapore and S.E. Asia, 1954-57, chief Bur. for Central and Eastern Europe, Vienna, 1958-59, chief Caribbean Bur., Havana, Cuba, 1959-60; chief Bur. for Bonn-Berlin, Newsweek, N.Y.C., 1960-62, editor Latin Am. and Canadian affairs, 1962-63; co-editor Reporter mag., 1963-64; gen. editor Newsweek mag., 1964-66, sr. editor, 1966-78. Served as spl. agt. C.I.C., U.S. Army, Germany, 1946. Mem. Kappa Sigma. Clubs: Nat. Press (Washington); Correspondents (Tokyo, Japan); The Players (N.Y.C.). Home: Millbrook, N.Y. Died Apr. 9, 1978; buried Nine Partners Burial Ground, Millbrook.

MARTIN, FLETCHER, artist; b. Palisade, Colo., Apr. 29, 1904; s. Clinton Howard and Josephine (Reed) M.; grad. Clarkston (Wash.) High Sch., 1921; m. Cecile Booth, 1925 (div.); 1 son, Robin, m. 2d, Helen Donovan, 1946 (div. 1962); children—Clint, Donovan; m. 3d, Jean Mele, 1963. Began as printer, 1916; self-taught painter; first exhbn. Fine Arts Gallery, San Diego, 1934, since shown in all leading museums in U.S.; rep. exhbns. S.A., South Africa and Europe including the Venice Biennial (1950); taught drawing and painting Art Center Sch., Los Angeles, 1938-39; artist-in-residence U. Iowa, 1940-41; dir. painting and graphic arts Kansas City Art Inst., 1941-42; artists war corr. Life mag. on African and Normandy campaigns, 1943-44; tchr. painting Art Students League of N.Y., 1948-49; vis. prof. art U. Fla., 1950-52; vis. artist Mills Coll. Calif., 1951; tchr. Albany (N.Y.) Inst. History and Art, 1952-53, Claremont (Calif.) Coll., summer 1953; Duluth br. U. Minn., summers 1954-57, North Mich. Coll., San Antonio Art Inst., 1958; head dept. drawing Los Angeles County (Calif.) Art Inst., 1958-59; tchr. Rochester (Minn.) Art Center, 1963; Am. Fedn. Art-Ford Found. artist-in residence Roswell (N.M.) Mus., 1964, Art Students League N.Y., 1965, Roberson Meml. Center, Binghamton, N.Y., 1967-68; represented in many important pub. collections including Met. Mus., Mus. Modern Art, Whitney Mus. Art, N.Y.C., Witte Meml. Mus., San Antonio. Prizes include 1st mus. award Los Angeles Mus., 1935, 2d mus. prize, 1939; U.S. sect. Fine Art mural award, 1936; Lippincott prize for figure painting Pa. Acad., 1947; Altman prize N.A.D., 1949; Clark prize, 1953; numerous honorable mentions. Painted several murals in the west. Mem. N.A.D., Woodstock Artists Assn. Democrat. Work reproduced in mags. including Life, Newsweek, Time, Art News, Art Digest; book illustration The Jungle (Upton Sinclair), 1965, Of Mice and Men (John Steinbeck), 1969; books pub. on his life and works by Barbara Eversole, 1954, H. Lester Cooke, Jr., 1977. Home: Mexico and Sarasota, Fla. Died May 30, 1979; buried Artists Cemetery, Woodstock, N.Y.

MARTIN, GEORGE WILLARD, mycologist; born Bklyn., N.Y., Oct. 27, 1886; s. George Augustus and Sarah Ann (Harned) M.; Litt.B., Rutgers U., 1912, M.S., 1915; Ph.D., U. of Chicago, 1922; student Marine Biol. Lab., Woods Hole, Mass; student Sorbonne, Paris; m. Mary Gillespie, Dec. 23, 1916; children—Elizabeth Gillespie (Mrs. Edwin S. McCollister), Ann Harned (Mrs. Richard J. Edelman). Engaged as assistant in plant pathology at New Jersey Agr. Experiment Sta., 1912-15; asst. in botany, Rutgers Coll., 1913-15; instr. botany, Massachusetts Agrl. Coll., 1916-17; asst. prof. botany, Rutgers U., 1919-23; asst. prof. botany, U. of Iowa, 1923-26, asso. prof., 1926-29, prof., 1929-55, head dept., 1953-55, prof. emeritus, 1955—; dir. Ia. Lakeside Lab., 1928-34; chief biol. lab., Jeffersonville Q.M. Depot, 1944-45; vis. prof. mycology U. Ill., 1956-57. Served as 1st lt., U.S. Army, 1917-19. Fellow A.A.A.S. (sec. Sect. G 1940-47); mem. Bot. Soc. Am., Mycol. Soc. Am. (pres. 1944 editor-in-chief Mycologia 1951—), Washington Acad. Scis., Am. Soc. Naturalists, Am. Assn. U. Profs., Am. Micros. Soc., Phi Beta Kappa, Sigma Xi. Democrat. Episcopalian. Author: The Myxomycetes (with T. H. Macbride); also bot. papers. Home: Iowa City, Ia. *

MARTIN, JOHN ARTHUR, educator; b. Westmont, Que., Can., Dec. 11, 1912; s. John James and Harriet (Hewitt) M.; came to U.S., 1913; A.B. summa cum laude, Harvard, 1934, M.A., 1936, S.T.B. cum laude, 1939, S.T.M., 1941, Th.D., 1947; m. Virginia Knowles Crosby, Sept. 17, 1938; children—Helen Knowles Martin Makela, Elizabeth Martin O'Toole, William Henry, Kenneth Hewitt. Ordained to ministry Conglist. Ch., 1940; pastor chs. in Mass., 1937-48; mem. faculty Wheaton Coll., Norton, Mass., 1948-80, coll. chaplain, 1949-57, prof. religion, chmn. dept., 1951-80. Sheldon fellow, 1934-35; grantee Danforth Found.-Wheaton Coll. Fund Advanced Study, 1960; Fulbright grantee, India, 1962; grantee Ella Lyman Cabot Trust, 1962. Mem. Am. Acad. Religion, Assn. Asian Studies, AAUP, Phi Beta Kappa. Republican. Contbr. to profl. publns. Home: Hingham, Mass. Died Dec. 22, 1980.

MARTIN, PAUL LOGAN, mag. editor; b. Fort Worth, Dec. 23, 1912; s. Rev. Logan and Julia (Pritchard) M.; A.B., Tex. Christian U., 1933; postgrad. Harvard, 1935-36; m. Kathleen Gibbs, June 17, 1950; 1 dau., Susan P. Reporter Oklahoma City Times, 1933-35; rewrite man Boston Herald, 1935-36; mng. editor Quincy (Mass.) Evening News, 1936-37; rewrite man Boston Am., 1937; polit. and legal corr. AP, Harrisburg, Pa., 1937-40; radio news editor Press Assn., Inc., AP, N.Y.C., 1940-42; reporter Los Angeles Examiner, 1946; polit. and legal corr. Gannett Newspapers, Washington, 1947-50, chief bur., 1950-66; gen. editor nat. staff U.S. News & World Report, after 1965, polit. editor. Served to maj. USAAF, 1942-46. Recipient Raymond Clapper award, 1950. Mem. White House Corr. Assn., Overseas Writers, Senate and House Press Galleries, Sigma Delta Chi. Clubs: Washington Golf and Country, Nat. Press, Gridiron, Metropolitan, 1925 F Street. Home: Arlington, Va. Died May 5, 1978; buried Columbia Gardens, Arlington, Va.

MARTIN, STROTHER, actor; b. Kokomo, Ind.; student U. Mich. Films include The Asphalt Jungle, Storm Over Tibet, The Big Knife, The Shaggy Dog, Invitation to a Gunfighter, The Sons of Katie Elder, Harper, Nevada Smith, Cool Hand Luke, True Grit, Butch Cassidy and the Sundance Kid, The Ballad of Cable Hogue, Fool's Parade, Pocket Money, Rooster Cogburn, Hard Times, The Great Scout and Cathouse Thursday, Slap Shot, The End, Cheech and Chong's Up in Smoke, The Champ, Love and Bullets, Nightwing, The Villan. Home: Thousand Oaks, Calif. *

MARTIN, SYDNEY ERRINGTON, architect; b. Phila., Pa., Sept. 6, 1883; s. Robert Thomas and Bertha (Neidhard) M.; B.S., U. of Pa., 1908; study in Europe, 1910; Dr. Fine Arts, University of Pennsylvania, 1957; m. Margaret Crozer Fox, Oct. 16, 1915 (dec. Dec. 1950); children—Margaret Crozer (dec.), Sydney Errington, Crozer Fox, Harriet. Mem. firm Martin, Stewart, Noble & Class, and predecessors, architects, Phila., 1912—. Chmn. architects com. Restoration Independence Hall; v.p. Phila Mus. Art, Univ. Mus.; mem. Independence Nat. Park Com. Bd. dirs. Pa. Acad. Fine Arts. Life trustee U. Pa. Served as capt., Engrs. Corps, U.S. Army, World War I. Recipient award of merit U. Pa., 1941; named one of 50 Phila.'s Foremost citizens Phila. Mag. Fellow A.I.A. (pres., Phila. Chapter, 1940-42); mem. Fairmount Park Art Assn. (pres. 1943-54), Am. Philos. Soc., Carpenters Co., Nat. Soc. Interior Decorators (asso.), N.A.D., U. Pa. Gen Alumni Soc. Hist. Soc. Pa. (councilor), Athenaeum (dir.). Republican. Episcopalian. Clubs: Sunnybrook Golf; Rittenhouse, Prin. works include: St. Christopher's Hosp., Phila.; Crippled Children's Hosp., Elizabethtown, Pa.; YMCA bldgs., Easton, York, Williamsport, Norristown, Germantown, Pa.; coll. bldgs. at Bryn Mawr, U. Pa., Dickinson, Swarthmore colls.; Phila. Free Library; Farmers Nat. Bank, Bristol, Pa.; library bldg. Am. Philos. Soc. Home: Phila. *

MARTIN, WILLIAM THORNTON (PETE MARTIN), editor, writer; b. Charlottesville, Va., Apr. 3, 1901; s. William Thornton and Cornelia (Janney) M.; student U. Pa.; m. Virginia Evelyn Bird, June 6, 1925; children—Peter Bird, Margery Mitchell (Mrs. Norton Downs Fern III). Art editor College Humor mag., 1924-25; asso. editor Sat. Eve. Post, 1929, art editor, 1929-42, sr. editor, 1958-80. Author numerous short stories, mag. serials, mag. articles, also non-fiction, books; collaborator with Bing Crosby, Bob Hope, Ethel Merman, Arthur Godfrey, Jerry Giesler on autobiographies. Home: Birchrunville, Pa. Died Oct. 13, 1980.

MARTINET, MARJORIE DORSEY, artist; b. Balt., Nov. 3, 1886; d. Oscar Conway and Anna Cora (Walker) Martinet; extensive study art museums, galleries Europe, U.S.; grad. Md. Inst., 1904; student Rhinehart Sch. of Sculpture, 1904-05, Pa. Acad. Fine Arts (Thouron prizeman, Cresson European scholar 1909), 1905-10; studied with William M. Chase and Cecelia Beaux; Instr. drawing, Drexel Inst., Phila., 1908, advanced life class drawing and painting, 1910-11; dir., instr. Martinet Sch. Art, Balt., 1912-69; instr. art Oldfields Sch., Glencoe, Md., 1925—. Exhibited Peabody Inst., Pa. Acad. Fine Arts, Plastic Club, Art Club of Phila., Sesqui-Centennial Expostion, Phila., 1926, (one-man show) Balt. Mus. Art, 1930. Nat. Assn. Women Artists, N.Y.C., 1960, 61, 62. Exhibited 49 paintings at Newman Galleries Phila., 1936; group include portraits, landscapes, character portraits, still life and compositions, including Spring, An Autumn Song, Orange and Gold, A Spaniard, The Half Breed, Chief White Wing. In Old Seville, Jim Tree, A Cowboy, Wholesale Fish Market, Baltimore, Japanese Persimmons; Old Slave Quarters, Gwynn's Falls Md. was one of 20 selected in 1937 to represent U.S. by jury of Nat. Assn. of Women Painters and Sculptors for Internat. Exhibition of Women's Art at Toronto, Can. (25 countries exhibiting). Works: The Court Robe, Singing Leaves, Gwynn Falls Winter, Justina Albereda and her Parrot, Enrique, Chestnut Lane in December, Indian Runner at Rest, Chief Star Eagle, Kathleen, My Grandmother, Baltimore Harbor. Chmn. art com. of Lizette Woodworth Reese Meml. Assn., Balt., for Reese Symbolic Meml. Tablet for Pratt Library, Balt. Replica of Old Slave Quarters, Gwynns Falls, Md. donated by request to Md. Br. Brit. War Relief for exhbn. and sale, 1941; purchased by Mr. Sidney Hollander and hung permanently in the Assn. of Jewish Charities Bldg., Balt. Martinet Sch. of Art, and Marjorie D. Martinet, dir., approved by Md. State Bd. Edn., and Vets. Adminstrn. to instruct veterans under G-I Bill of Rights, also approved to instruct Korean Vets. Mem. Fellowship Pa. Acad. Fine Arts, Pa. Acad. Fine Arts (life), Phila. Art Alliance (profl. artist mem.), Balt. Mus. Art, Fedn. Arts (Washington), Nat. Assn. Women Painters and Sculptors N.Y., Woman's Lit. Club of Balt. Home: Philadelphia PA. *

MARTINEZ, MARIA ANTONITA, potter; b. San Ildefonso Pueblo, N.M., Apr. 5, 1887; d. Thomas and Reyes (Pena) Montoya; LL.D. (hon.), St. Catherine Indian Sch., Santa Fe, 1953, U. Colo., 1954, N.M. State U., 1971; m. Juliam Martinez, May, 1913; children—Adam, John (dec.), Popovi Da, Phillip (dec.). Recipient Achievement award, Ford Exposition medal, 1934; Named Outstanding Indian Woman, Indian Council Fire, Chgo., 1934; decorated palmes academiqua French Ministry Edn., 1954; recipient Craftsmanship award A.I.A., 1954, Jane Addams award Rockford (Ill.) Coll., 1960, award Am. Ceremic Soc., 1969. Symbol of Man award Minn. Mus. Art, 1969. Home: Santa Fe, N.Mex. Died July 20, 1980; buried San Ildefonso Pueblo Cemetery.

MARTINEZ, MAXIMILIANO H. (MÄR-TE'NAZ), President of El Salvador; b. 1882; ed. Military Polytechnic School, Guatemala. Became President by coup d'etat, 1931; has put country into fine financial shape; has best record in road building and pub. works in Central Am. Address: El Salvador. *

MARTINEZ-VARGAS, RICARDO, economist, diplomat; b. Cochabamba, Bolivia, S.A., Mar. 13, 1885; s. Juan Martinez and Balvina Vargas; student Univ. of Cochabamba, Bolivia, 1896-1900, Univ. of LaPaz Bolivia, 1901-02; m. Maria Castanos, Dec. 23, 1912; 1 son, Antonio. First officer, Department of Pub. Works, Govt. of Bolivia, LaPaz, 1905-1906, sec. Div. of Pub. Work, 1907-18, minister of Pub. Works and Mines, Bolivian Govt., LaPaz, 1919-20; minister of war, 1920; nat. rep. LaPaz (Bolivia), 1921-23; in private bus., 1923-26, 1938-46; financial rep. in U.S.A., 1926-28; Bolivian del. to Internat. Tin Com., London, 1931-38; ambassador of Bolivia to U.S. since 1946. Decorated

Comendador Condor de los Andes, Bolivia. Liberal. Roman Catholic. Home: Cochabamba, Bolivia, S.A. *

MARTINEZ ZUVIRIA, GUSTAVO (HUGO WAST, NOM DE PLUME) (MAR-TE'NAZ), Argentine lawyer and writer; b. Córdoba, 1883; s. Zenón Martinez and Carolina de Zuviría; ed. Colegio Nacional, Córdoba; Colegio de la Immaculada, Santa Fé; Faculty of Law, Universidad del Litoral, Santa Fé (degree of lawyer, 1907); m. Matilde Iriondo; 12 children. Prof. of political economy, Universidad del Litoral, 1911; nat. deputy, 1916-20; dir. nat. Library, Buenos Aires; provisional pres. of Comisión Nacional de Cultura, 1937. Ministro de Justicia e Instrucción Publica (1943). Awarded Gold Medal, Academia Española de la Lengua, 1923; grand literary prize of Argentine govt., 1926. Mem. P.E.N., Jockey and Rotary Clubs, Buenos Aires, Academia Española de la Lengua, Madrid, Academia Argentina de Letras; Academia Columbiana de la Lengua. Commendador de la Orden de San Gregorio Magno, por Pió, XI. Author: Cindad turbulenta, ciudad alegre, 1919; Le que no perdonó, 1923; Pata de zorra, 1924; Navesoro-suenos, 1936; El camino de las llamas, 1939. Was founder and dir. of Revista de la Biblioteca Nacional, Buenos Aires since 1937. Address: Buenos Aires, Argentina. *

MARTING, WALTER ADELBERT, mining, shipping exec.; b. Columbus, O., Feb. 1, 1910; s. George Henry and Anna (Harris) M.; grad. Phillips Exeter Acad., 1930; B.S., Yale, 1934, LL.B., 1937; m. Margaret Brown, Oct. 2, 1943; children—Walter A., Michael G. Dir., chmn. exec. com. Hanna Mining Co.; dir. Bankers Trust Co., N.Y.C., Nat. City Bank Cleve., Bankers Trust N.Y. Corp., Eaton Corp., Nat. Steel Corp. Served to lt. comdr. USNR, 1941-45. Decorated Legion of Merit. Mem. Am. Mining Congress (dir.). Republican. Clubs: Pepper Pike, Kirtland Country, Union (Cleve.); University, Links (N.Y.C.); Augusta (Ga.) Nat. Golf. Home: Gates Mills, Ohio. Died June 17, 1980; buried Cleveland, Ohio.

MARTINS, JORGE DODSWORTH, naval officer; born Ponte Nova, State of Brasil, S.A., Feb. 19, 1884; s. Dr. Custodio Jose Ferreira and Georgina (Dodsworth) M.; grad. Naval Acad., Rio de Janeiro, 1903; Naval War Coll. and High Command; civil engr., Nat. Engring. Univ., Rio de Janeiro, 1922; m. D. Risa Batista Feb. 19, 1929. Commd. officer Brazilian Navy 1903, advanced through grades to fleet admiral, 1946; extensive service at sea and handling personnel, holding commands on entire Brazilian Coast; naval aide to president of Brazil, 1914; flag sec., Adm. Comdr. Brazilian Naval Div., World War I, operating in European and African war zones; in comd. Cruizer Div. 1942; active service, World War II, in cooperation with U.S. Navy patrolling and escorting convoys; hydrographic services in delta of Amazon River; also functioned as chief, Bur. Navigation, Naval Dist. Comdr.; dir. Merchant Marine; pres. Maritime Court of Justice; Minister of Marine; chief Brazilian del. on Joint Brazilian U.S. Defense Commn., Washington; now vice pres. Admiralty Bd. Decorations; Victory (Allied Nations); Fatigue De Guerra (Italy), World War I; Commemoration Brazilian Republic; Gold Medal Brazilian Armed Forces; Brazilian War Cross (World War I); War Duty, World War II; Baron Rio Branco, Distinguished Services (World War II). Comdr. Chile's Legion of Merit, France's Legion of Honor, Italy's Order Saint Maurice and Lazare (World War I); Brazil's Naval Order Merit, Mil. Order Aycucho of Peru, Naval Legion of Merit (U.S.A.). Mem. Geographic Soc. Rio de Janeiro (v.p.), Brazilian Oceanographic Inst. (pres.). Served as official Navy rep. in Internat. Congress of Life Saving at Sea, Dauville, 1929; in II Pan-Am. Hydrographic and Chartographic Congress, 1944 (v.p.), and 10th Nat. Congress of Geog. (v.p.); rep. Navy, Rotary Club of Rio de Janeiro; dir. publication general Map of Brazil, Paris, France, 1922. Democrat. Roman Catholic. Club: Engineering. Home: Rio de Janeiro. *

MARTINSON, HENRY R., state govt. ofcl.; born Mpls., Mar. 6, 1883; s. Gunerous and Karina M.; grad. sch. agr., U. Minn., 1905; m. Melba Cooke, June 18, 1927. Editor Iconoclast, 1916; labor commr. Dept. Agr. and Labor, N.D., also pub. Labor Bull. since 1937. Mem. Sons of Norway, Painters and Decorators Union, Non-partisan League, Farmers Union. Contbr. poetry publs. Home: Bismarck, N.D. *

MARTZLOFF, KARL H(ENRY), surgeon; b. Portland, Oreg., Oct. 30, 1890; s. Henry and Magdalena Rosina (Steiner) M.; A.B., U. Oreg., 1913; M.D., Johns Hopkins, 1917; m. Sarah Jane Goodpasture, Aug. 23, 1923; children—Thomas Henry, Albert Dillen. Intern surgery Lakeside Hosp., Western Res. U. Med. Sch., 1917-18; asst. resident pathologist Johns Hopkins Hosp., 1918-19, resident house officer pathology, 1918-20, asst. resident, then resident surgeon gynecology, 1920-23; asst. pathology Johns Hopkins Med. Sch., 1918-20, instr. gynecology, 1922-23; pvt. practice surgery, Portland, 1924-78; mem. staff Good Samaritan Multnomah hosps.; faculty U. Ore., 1924-78, asso. clin. prof. surgery, 1951-60; Charles Sumner Bacon lectr. U. Ill., 1951-52. Regional rep. Johns Hopkins Med. Sch., also Duke Med. Sch.; trustee Northwestern Med. Pub. Assn., 1936-62, pres., 1951-60; mem. Johns Hopkins Nat. Resources Com., 1963-78. Served with M.C., U.S. Army, 1917-18. Fellow A.C.S. (bd. govs. 1947-50); mem. N.Y. Acad. Scis., AAAS, Am. Gynecol. Soc. (pres. 1959-60), Soc. Pelvic Surgeons (a founder, pres. 1954, 55), Howard A. Kelly Soc., Johns Hopkins Surg. Assn., Oreg. Med. Soc. (pres. 1940, hon. mem. citation 1960), Portland Acad. Medicine (pres. 1957), Phi Beta Kappa, Sigma Xi, Alpha Omega Alpha, Beta Theta Pi, Nu Sigma Nu. Contbr. textbooks, jours. Home: Portland, Ore. Died Apr. 1, 1978.

MARVEL, ROBERT WILEY, coll. dean, composer; b. Webster City, Iowa, Aug. 3, 1918; s. Ralph Loren and Lela (McNee) M.; B.A., U. San Antonio, 1939; M.A., Eastman Sch. Music of U. Rochester, 1940, Ph.D., 1948; m. Kay Marguerite Mason, Sept. 3, 1940; 1 son, Kenneth R. Tchr. Tex. pub. schs., 1940-42; instr. music Trinity U., 1943-44; teaching fellow Eastman Sch. Music, 1947-48; prof. music, chmn. music theory and lit. SUNY, Fredonia, 1948-59, asso. dir. dept. music, 1959-63, dir., 1963-69, dean fine and performing arts, 1969-74; composer orchestral pieces performed by Buffalo Philharmonic, Erie Philharmonic, Eastman Rochester Symphony, Montreal Symphony orchs.; cons. Nat. Assn. Schs. of Music, Nat. Music Council-Ford Found., Young Composers Project, N.Y. State Council on the Arts. Served with USAAF, 1943-46. Mem. Music Tchrs. Nat. Assn., Music Educators Nat. Conf. (pres. Eastern div. 1961-63), Music Library Assn., Internat. Council Fine Arts Deans, Nat. Assn. Schs. of Music. Rotarian. Club: Torch (Fredonia). Home: Fredonia, N.Y. Died 1974.

MARVEL, WILLIAM WORTHINGTON, ednl. adminstr.; b. Balt., May 15, 1920; s. Norman Clyde and Marguerite May (Hogg) M.; A.B., Princeton, 1941, M.A., 1949, Ph.D., 1951; m. Marjory Jean Gillingham, June 14, 1947; children—Nancy Jean, Thomas Edward. Cultural relations officer U.S. Dept. State, Managua, Nicaragua, 1941-44; instr. Princeton, 1946-48; instr. internat. relations Yale, 1949-50; instr. dept. social scis. U.S. Mil. Acad., West Point, N.Y., 1951-52; program officer Office Dir. Mut. Security, Exec. Office Pres., Washington, 1952; exec. asso. Carnegie Corp. N.Y., 1952-62; pres. Edn. and World Affairs, N.Y.C., 1962-70; pres. Acad. Natural Scis., Phila., 1971-74; spl. cons. edn. to pres. Univ. City Sci. Center, Phila., 1974-78. Mem. adv. council Woodrow Wilson Sch. Pub. and Internat. Affairs, Princeton, 1954-60, chmn. cons. group Robertson Found., 1965-78; mem. Presdl. Task Force on Internat. Exchange Persons, 1961; mem. com. on coll. and world affairs Hazen Found., 1962-64; vice chmn. Task Force AID-Univ. Relations, 1963-64; panel mem. White House Conf. on Edn., 1965; mem. Presdl. Task Force Internat. Edn., 1966; cons. AID, 1965, HEW, 1966, Williamsburg World Conf. Edn., 1967, Commn. Internat. Edn., Am. Council Edn., 1966-69, Mich. State U., 1970; research asso. Inst. War and Peace Studies, Columbia, 1953-57, seminar asso., 1954-56. Mem. Princeton Twp. Com., 1959-61; mem. Princeton Regional Bd. Edn., 1968-73, v.p., 1969-71; mem. Mercer County (N.J.) Recreation Com., 1960-61, N.J. State Capitol Devel. Commn., 1960, N.J. Citizens Com. Higher Edn., 1962-65. Chmn., Greater Phila. Cultural Alliance, 1972-73; bd. dirs. Phila. '76, Inc., 1973, Girl Scouts, Phila., 1973-78, Phila. Conv. and Tourist Bur., 1973-74, Union Library Catalogue, 1973-78, World Affairs Council Phila., 1973-78; trustee Wistar Inst., U. Pa., 1971-73, Princeton-in-Asia, 1965-75. Adv. bd. mgrs. Morris Arboretum, Chestnut Hill, Pa., 1972-78. Mem. AAAS, Nat. Com. U.S.-China Relations, Phila. Com. Fgn. Relations, Council Fgn. Relations N.Y.C., Common Cause, Phi Beta Kappa. Presbyn. (elder). Clubs: Rittenhouse, Franklin Inn, Midday, Sunday Breakfast (Phila.); Princeton (N.Y.C.). Home: Villanova, Pa. Died June 7, 1978.

MARVIN, BURTON WRIGHT, educator; b. Somerville, Mass., Dec. 23, 1913; s. Henry Howard and Alma Ethel (Wright) M.; A.B., U. Nebr., 1935; M.Sc., Columbia U., 1937; Dr. Journalism, Southwestern Coll., 1964; m. Margaret Fiske Medlar, Jan. 15, 1938; children—Mary (dec.), Charles, Robert, Anne. Reporter, Lincoln (Nebr.) Star, 1935-36; reporter, copyreader, asst. city editor, cable editor, telegraph editor Chgo. Daily News, 1937-46; lectr. Medill Sch. Journalism, Northwestern U., 1945-46, asst. prof., 1946-47; asso. prof. Columbia U. Grad. Sch. Journalism, 1947-48; dean William Allen White Sch. Journalism and Pub. Info., dir. William Allen White Found., U. Kans., 1948-65; asso. gen. sec. for communication Nat. Council Chs., N.Y.C., 1966-68; prof. journalism Syracuse (N.Y.) U., 1968-79, dir. mental health info. program, 1968-71, head religious journalism program, 1969-79, asst. dean Sch. Pub. Communications, 1970-79; vis. prof. Tel Aviv U., 1965-66; Fulbright lectr. U. Tehran (Iran), 1960-61; lectr. journalism African-Am. Inst., summer 1963; mem. Nat. Commn. on Pub. Relations and Meth. Info., 1956-68. Bd. dirs. Laubach Literacy Internat., Inc., 1970-79; mem. interpretation and support conf. U.S. Conf. World Council Chs., Inc., 1969-75. Hitchcock scholar Columbia U. Grad. Sch. Journalism, 1936, recipient Alumni Achievement medallion, 1963. Mem. Am. Assn. Schs. and Depts. Journalism (pres. 1953), Assn. Edn. Journalism, Am. Council Edn. Journalism (chmn. accrediting com. 1956-60), Kappa Tau Alpha, Sigma Delta Chi, Theta Chi Beta. Universalist. Home: Syracuse, N.Y. Died Mar. 8, 1979; buried Wyuka Cemetery, Lincoln, Nebr.

MASLACH, GEORGE, lawyer, ins. co. exec.; b. Los Angeles, Mar. 15, 1915; s. George Michael and Anne (Scalla) M.; student U. Calif. at Los Angeles, 1932-34; J.D., Loyola U., Los Angeles, 1938; m. Daisy Lu Condon, Feb. 15, 1942; children—Michael James, Anne. Admitted to Calif. bar, 1938; mem. firm Early, Maslach, Leavey & Nutt, Los Angeles, 1950-79; chmn. bd., pres., dir. Farmers Group, Inc.; v.p., dir. Investors Guaranty Life Ins. Co., New World Fund, Inc.; dir. Mid-Century Ins. Co., Ohio State Life Ins. Co. Bd. councillors U. So. Calif. Law Center. Mem. Assn. So. Calif. Def. Counsel (past pres., dir.), Calif. Ins. Fedn. (v.p., dir.), Phi Alpha Delta. Home: Los Angeles, Calif. Died July 3, 1979.

MASON, AUGUST H(OWARD), teacher; b. Columbus Grove, O., Aug. 4, 1895; s. Franklin R. and Anna L. (Campbell) M.; A.B., Ohio Wesleyan U., 1919; Docteur d'Université, U. Paris, 1924; m. Bennie Hope Spinks, July 11, 1927; 1 son, Howard Spinks. Tchr. Latin, Williamsport-Dickinson Sem., Williamsport, Pa., 1919-20; tchr. English, Wilbraham (Mass.) Acad., 1920-21; instr. English, Syracuse U., 1921-22; appointee Inst. Internat. Edn. (N.Y.) in France, 1922-23; prof. English, Howard Coll., Birmingham, Ala., 1925-35; prof. English, U. Ala., 1935-66, prof. emeritus, 1966-80. Served as flying cadet U.S. AS, 1918-19. Mem. Coll. English Assn., Am. Assn. U. Profs., Democrat. Presbyn. Author: Walter Savage Landor, Poéte Lyrique, 1924; Landor and Lady Blessington, 1929. Editor: A Poetry Miscellany, 1938; Second Poetry Miscellany, 1939; These Unmusical Days, 1951; A Page of Poetry (in classmate monthly), 1954-57. Contbr.: Introduction To Literature, 1952; poems in The Tigers Eye, Word Study, The Montevallo Review. Contbr. verses to Literary Digest, Sewanee Rev., English Jour., The Bookman, The Step Ladder, Verse-Craft, others. Home: Tuscaloosa, Ala. Died Aug. 26, 1980; buried Tuscaloosa Meml. Park Cemetery.

MASON, CHARLES ELLIS, trustee; b. Boston, Mass., Apr. 21, 1884; s. Mortimer Blake and Mary Emma (Phillips) M.; prep. edn., Noble and Greenough Sch., Boston; A.B., Harvard, 1905; m. Elizabeth Andrew, of Boston, July 15, 1905; children—Harriet, Charles Ellis, John Andrew. V.p. and mem. bd. mgrs., Farm and Trade Sch.; v.p. Permanent Charity Fund; trustee Tuskegee Normal and Industrial Inst.; sec. and trustee St. Luke's Home for Convalescents; treas. Trinity Ch. Episcopalian. Clubs: Union, University, Exchange (Boston); Country (Brookline, Mass); Cohasset Golf; Harvard (Boston and New York). Home: Hingham, Mass. *

MASON, FRANCIS VAN WYCK, novelist; b. Boston, Nov. 11, 1901; s. Francis Payne and Ermengarde Arville (Coffin) M.; B.S., Harvard U., 1924; m. Dorothy Louise Macready, Nov. 26, 1927 (dec. Mar. 1958); children—F. van Wyck II, Robert Ashton; m. 2d, Jeanne-Louise Hand, Oct. 3, 1958. Importer 1925; pres. and treas. Van Wyck, Inc.; pres. Van Wyck Mason & Co., Inc.; author, 1928-78. Served as 2d lt. as interpreters A.E.F., U.S. Army, 1918-19; sgt. Squadron A, 101st Cav., N.Y. Nat. Guard, 1924-29; 1st lt. F.A., Md. Nat. Guard, 1930-33; maj. AUS, Jan. 1942, lt. col., Dec. 1942, Sch. of Mil. Govt.; col., May 1945; with Gen. Staff Corps, SHAEF, 1943-45. Decorated Medaille de Sauvetage, Croix de Guerre, Palmes Académique, officer Legion of Honor. Fellow Am. Geog. Soc., Boston U. Libraries; mem. Loyal Legion (jr. comdr.). Republican. Clubs: Harvard (N.Y.C.); Union (Boston); Royal Bermuda Yacht. Author numerous books including: Valley Forge, 1777, 1950; Proud New Flags, 1951; Himalayan Assignment, 1952; Golden Admiral, 1953; Winter at Valley Forge, 1954; Blue Hurricane, 1954; Two Tickets for Tangier, 1955; Silver Leopard, 1955; Our Valiant Few, 1956; The Gracious Lily Affiar, 1957; The Young Titan, 1958; Secret Mission to Bangkok, 1960; Manila Galleon, 1961; The Battle on Lake Erie, 1960; The Battle for New Orleans, 1961; The Sea Venture, 1962; Trouble in Burma, 1962; Zanzibar Intrigue, 1963; Rascals' Heaven, 1964; The Siege of Quebec, 1965; American Men-at-War (anthology), 1965; Maracaibo Mission, 1965; Wild Horizon, 1966; Deadly Orbit Mission, 1967; The Maryland Colony, 1969; Harpoon in Eden, 1969; Brimstone Club, 1971; Roads to Liberty (anthology), 1971; Log Cabin Noble, 1973; Trumpets Sound No More, 1975; Guns for Rebellion, 1977. Home: Southampton, Bermuda. Died Aug. 28, 1978.

MASON, JOHN RUSSELL, librarian, curator; b. Phila., Jan. 1, 1900; s. Charles Lincoln and Martha Ann (Taylor) M.; A.B., George Washington U., 1923, A.M., 1925; Summer Library Sch., U. Birmingham (Eng.), 1930; B.S. in L.S., Columbia, 1933; unmarried. Asst. in library George Washington U., 1920-23, asst. librarian, 1923-29, asso. librarian, 1929-33, librarian, 1933-65, curator of art, 1944-65; organist, commencements and convocations, 1930-65. Reorganized geo-phys. lab. library Carnegie Inst., Washington, 1928-29; profl. organist for churches, Washington, 1920-81, Central Presbyn. Ch., 1926-44. Trustee Powder River Found., Inc. Recipient Alumni Achievement award George Washington U., 1951. Mem. A.L.A., Library Assn. Great Britain, D.C. Library Assn. (pres. 1940-42), Am. Guild Organists, Theta Delta Chi. Clubs: Washington Arts, Cosmos. Home: Washington, D.C. Died Feb. 28, 1981; buried Oak Hill Cemetery, Washington.

MASON, KARL ERNEST, educator; b. Kingston, N.S., Can., May 30, 1900; s. Ernest Seymour and Una (Lent) M.; B.A., Acadia U., 1921, D.Sc. (hon.), 1949; Ph.D., Yale, 1925; m. Pearl Sanders, Aug. 30, 1927; 1 dau., Donna Jean. Came to U.S., 1921, naturalized, 1941. Nat. Research Council fellow Yale University, 1925-26; instructor Vanderbilt U. School of Medicine, 1926-29, assistant professor, 1929-30, associate professor of anatomy, 1930-40; professor anatomy chairman dept. U. Rochester Sch. Medicine and Dentistry. Mem. A.A.A.S., Am. Assn. Anatomists Am. Inst. Nutrition, Brit. Nutrition Soc. Contbr. articles sci. jours. Home: Rochester. *

MASON, LUCIUS RANDOLPH, lawyer; b. Frederick, Md., Jan. 23, 1886; s. William Pinckney and Elizabeth R. (McGill) M.; student lit. dept. George Washington U., 1903-04, law dept., 1905-08, LL.B., 1908; m. Sophy Stanton Johnston, De. 3, 1918; 1 dau., Sophy (Mrs. Caperton Burnam). Began practice Washington, 1910; asst. U.S. atty. for D.C., 1919-21; asst gen. counsel Fed. Res. Bank of N.Y.C., 1921, gen. counsel, 1922-28; practice law, N.Y.C., 1928-37; counsel Turk Marsh, Kelley and Hoare, and predecessor firms, 1937—. Mem. local bd. 15 SSS, 1942-43. Served as capt. inf. O.R.C., U.S.Army, 1916-18. Mem. Am. Bar Assn., N.Y. County Lawyers Assn., S.A.R., Downtown Assn. Democrat. Episcopalian. Clubs: Port Royal (Naples, Fla.); Chevy Chase (Md.). Home: New York City NY. *

MASON, MARY STUARD TOWNSEND, artist; b. Zanesville, O., Mar. 21, 1886; d. Charles Edwin and Jessie F. (Easton) Townsend; ed. Leachwood Sch., Norfolk, Va., Md. Inst. of Art, and Pa. Acad. of Fine Arts; m. William Clarke Mason, Dec. 22, 1909; children—Mary Kathleen (Mrs. Henry Lea Hudson), William Douglas. Works: permanent collections, Fellowship Pa. Acad. of Fine Arts; Pa. Acad. of Fine Arts; Albright Art Gallery; also pvt. collections. Awards: Cresson Scholarship, Pennsylvania Acad. of Fine Arts, 1909; Plastic Club gold medal, 1921 and 1924; Mary Smith prize, 1922, 1939; Philadelphia Sketch Club gold medal, 1929; New Orleans Garden Club prize, S.S.A.L. Exhbn., 1930; Women's Internat. Exhbn. hon. mention, 1929; Phila. Art Club gold medal, 1930; 1st Philadelphia Exhibition of Am. Painting, McClees 1st prize, 1933; gold medal, Fellowship Pa. Acad. Fine Arts, 1934; 1st prize Germantown Art Club, annual exhbn., 1938. Member of the Norfolk Museum of Arts and Sciences. Fellow Pa. Acad. of Fine Arts; vice pres. F.P.A.F.A; mem. Phila. Art Alliance. Republican. Episcopalian. Clubs: Cosmopolitan, Phila, Cricket (Phila.); Phila. Water Color Club. Home: Chestnut Hill, Philadelphia. *

MASON, WILLIAM D(ANIEL), indsl. exec.; b. Hanford, Calif., Feb. 23, 1885; s. Daniel Cordery and Martha Jane (Sumner) M.; ed. pub. schools, Tulare and Lindsay, Calif.; student, courses in elec. and mech. engring. and chem.; m. Josephine Lynn Rickenbaugh, Apr. 3, 1910; children—William Daniel, Jr., Marjorie Jane (Mrs. John G. Pew, II). Electrician, Standard Oil Co. of Calif., 1904, mgr. refinery, Richmond, Calif., 1924; mgr. Marcus Hook refinery, Sun Oil Co., Philadelphia, 1926, asst. to pres. in chg. of indsl. relations, 1943, mem. bd. dirs.; 1947; dir. National Bank, Clifton Heights, Pa. Dir. Crozer Hosp., Chester, Pa. Dir. facility security div. Petroleum Adminstrn. for War, Washington, 1942-43; assisted in orgn. Civil Air Coastal Patrol, 1942; apptd. lt. col., consultant to nat. comdr., 1947, promoted col., 1948. Mem. nav. commn. of Del. River and its navigable tributaries, 1944-49; chmn. Del. River Conservation Assn., 1930. Mem. C. of C. of City of Chester and Del. County (v.p.), Am. Petroleum Inst., Am. Geophys. Union, Aircraft Owners and Pilots Assn., Port of Phila. Maritime Soc., Hist. Soc. of Pa., Del. County Hist. Soc., Atlantic County (N.J.) Histor. Soc., (hon. life) Am. Pilots' Assn. Republican. Presbyterian. Mason. Clubs: Union League, Racquet, Automobile (dir.), Philadelphia Country, Philadelphia Aviation Country, Quiet Birdmen (Phila.); Rotary International (hon. mem. Rotary, Chester, Pa.); Chester River Yacht and Country (Chestertown, Md.); Springhaven (Wallingford, Pa.). Home: Philadelphia, Penn. *

MASSECK, CLINTON JOSEPH, author; b. Grand Rapids, Mich., Feb. 24, 1886; s. Clinton Sewall and May (Elmore) M.; A.B., cum laude, Tufts Coll., 1908; A.M., Harvard, 1911; Docteur de l'université de Paris, 1913; m. Annie Laurie Danforth, of Norway, Me., June 26, 1911; 1 dau., Ruth. Instr. English, Tufts Coll., 1908-11, Washington U., 1913-17; editor The Dial, summer 1916; spl. investigator, adv. dept. Capper Farm Press, Topeka, Kan., 1919-20, dir. of sales, 1920-22. Lecturer in advertising N.Y. Univ. since 1924; adv. account executive the Borden Company, H. K. McCann Co. Commissioned capt. 353d Inf., 89th Div., U.S.A., Aug. 15, 1917; arrived in France, June 1918; maj., Apr. 30, 1919; served as adj., later operations officer of regt. during trench development period. Euvezin Sector, St. Mihiel, and Meuse-Argonne offensive; comdt. at Neuenberg and elsewhere in Army of Occupation, Germany, 5 mos.; grad. Army Sch. of the Line, Langres, France; hon. discharged, June 19, 1919; major O.R.C. Awarded Croix de Guerre with gold star; citation from comdg. gen. 32d French A.C. Mem. Delta Upsilon; v.p. Soc. Mil. Intelligence Officers Army U.S. Republican. Club: Harvard. Author: Richard Jefferies—Etude d'une personnalité, 1913; Brief Official History of the 89th Division, 1919. Contbr. to Forum, Poetry, and adv. trade papers. Founder and dir., 1916-17, St. Louis Little Playhouse. Lecturer on lit. and ednl. topics. *

MASSELL, BENJAMIN JOSEPH, realtor, builder; b. Vilkomir-Lithuania, Apr. 14, 1886; s. Raphael Moses and Clara (Mitnick) M.; ed. pub. and boys high schs. of Atlanta; m. Fanny Wolfson, Feb. 8, 1916 (dec. 1941); children—Ben Joseph, Carolyn (Mrs. Simon S. Selig, Jr.); m. 2nd, Helen E. Massell. Came to U.S., 1888, naturalized, 1900. Engaged in real estate bus. and builder as Massell Cos., Atlanta, 1910—; pres. Massell Cos., Consol. Realty Investments, Inc., Realty Operations, Inc., C.M.S. Realty Co., Inc., Peachtree-Seventh, Inc., Peachtree-Whitehall, Inc. Pres. Atlanta Jewish Welfare Bd.; regional pres. Bonds for Israel; hon. pres. B'nai B'rith, Recipient citation by Atlanta City Council, 1950; outstanding achievement. Testimonial Dinner, Atlanta Real Estate Bd., 1950; Testimonial Bronze plaque, Jewish War Vets, 1950; Citation Nat. Jewish Welfare Bd., 1955, Zionist Orgn. Am., 1956; life mem. Brandeis U. Club, 1956, fellow univ., 1957; Nat. award for outstanding leadership, Am. Jewish Theol. Sem. Am. Life hon. mem. Atlanta Real Estate Bd. Mem. Hebrew Benevolent Congregation, Atlanta, Philanthropist. Club: Standard Town and Country (pres., 1924, v.p., 1949, bd. dirs.). Home: Atlanta. *

MASSINE, LEONIDE, choreographer; b. Moscow, Russia, Aug. 9, 1896; s. Teodor Affanasievitch and Eugenia Nikolaevna; ed.- Imperial Ballet Sch., Moscow; pupil of Domashoff, Enrico Checchetti and Nicolas Legat; m. Tatiana Vladimirouna Milisnikova, Mar. 14, 1939; children—Tatiana, Leonide, Choregrapher and prin. dancer, Diaghilev Ballet Russe, 1914-20; choreographer, dancer and artistic dir., Ballet de Monte Carlo, 1932-41, Ballet Nat. Theatre, N.Y., 1941-44; organized Ballet Russe Highlights, 1945-46; guest artist, choreographer Sadlers Wells Ballet, Convent Garden, Royal Opera House, Copenhagen, Teatro alla Scala, Milan, Opera-Comique, Paris, 1947-51. Ballets; Soleil de Nuit, Las Meminas, 1915; Good Humored Ladies, Children's Tales, Parade, 1917; La Boutique Fantasque, Le Tricorne, 1919; Le Sacre du Printemps, Cimarosiana, Pulcinella, Le Rossignol, 1920; Salade, Gigue, Mercure, Le Beau Danube, 1924; Les Matelots, Sephire et Flore, 1925; Le Pas d'Acier, Ode, 1927; Les Enchantements d'Alcine, Le Roi David, Amphion, 1929; Le Beau Danube (2d version), 1932; Les Presages, Les Jeux d'Enfants, Belkis Vecchia Milano, La Belle Helene, The Miracle, 1933; Choreartium, Scuola di Ballo, 1934; Le Bal, Union Pacifique, 1935; Symphony Fantastique, 1936; Gaite Paristienne, Seventh Symphony, St. Francis, 1938; Camppriccio Espagnol, Rouge et Noir, Bogatiry, Bacchanal 1939; Wien 1814. New Yorker, 1940; Labyrinth, Saratoga, 1941; Aleko, Don Domingo, 1942; Mlle. Angot, 1943: Antar, Daphnis et Chloe. Unfortunate Painter, Rêverie Classique, Moonlight Sonata, Mad Tristan, 1944; Bullet in the Ballet, Les Arabesques (revived), Les Matelots (revived), 1945-46; Boutique Fantasque, Tricorne (revived), 1946; Mam'selle Angot (2d version), 1947; Capriccio (de Stravinsky), Episode de la Via d'un Artiste, Clock Symphony, Sacre du Printemps (revived), 1948; Quattro Stagioni, Mad Tristan (revived), Good Humored Ladies (revived), Suite Bergamasque, Le Peintre et son Modele, 1949; La Valse (de Ravel), 1950. Films: Carnival in Costa Rica (produced dances and appeared), 1945; (composed and danced) Red Shoes, 1948; Tales of Hoffmann, 1951; Carosello Napolitano, 1953; appeared at La Scala, Milan, 1953-54; Teatrodel Opera. Rome: sacred drama Resurrection and Life, Foundazione Cini, Venisei; made other choreographic creations and appearances including: The Fall of the House of Usher, 1955; Marco Eil Mago, 1956; Symphony Fantastique, 1957. Home: Borker, West Germany. Died Mar. 15, 1979.

MAST, CASPER LEO, JR., editor, publisher; b. Quincy, Ill., Aug. 28, 1909; s. Casper Leo and Nellie (Chase) M.; student Gem City Bus. Coll., 1927-28; B.S., U. Ill., 1933; m. Maurene June Frey, Feb. 1,1936; children—Marilynn Alice (Mrs. Melvin Long), Maurene Gayle. Asst. farm adviser, county 4-H club leader LaSalle County (Ill.) Farm Bur., 1930-35; asst. editor Prairie Farmer, 1936-37; dir. field services Ill. Agrl. Assn., 1937-39, dir. info. and publicity, 1940-44; editor The Business of Farming, U.S. Gypsum Co., 1944-46; editor, pub. Agrl. Leader's Digest, 1946-58, County Agts. Directory, 1948-78; sec.-treas. Millers' Nat. Fedn., 1958-59, exec. v.p., 1959-62, pres., 1962-74; dir. Szabo Food Service, Inc., 1963-71. Mem. sponsoring com. Future Farmers Am. Found., 1946-58; mem. council pub. relations Nat. 4-H Found.; vice chmn. Nat. Agrl. Savs. Bonds Com., 1949-52; mem. Nat. Com. Farm Safety, 1948-58; exec. sec. Agrl. Relations Council, 1976-78. Pres., Flossmoor Police Pension Bd.; bd. govs. Glenwood Sch. Boys; v.p. Chgo./Cook County 4-H Club Found. Hon. Am. Farmer degree Future Farmers Am.; cited Friend of 4-H Clubs, Nat. 4-H orgn.; recipient 4-H alumni award. Mem. Am. Agrl. Editors Assn. (sec.-treas. 1946-58), Chgo. Assn. Commerce and Industry (chmn. agrl. council 1949-50), Am. Soc. Assn. Execs., Nat. Agrl. Mktg. Assn. (founder, hon. mem.), Am. Agrl. Coll. Editors, Am. Assn. Cereal Chemists (hon.), Recreation Assn. Flossmoor (pres. 1953), U.S. C. of C. (mem. assn. com. 1963-68), Internat. Platform Assn., Sigma Delta Chi, Phi Kappa Tau. Republican. Clubs: Flossmoor Mens (pres. 1953-54), Flossmoor Country (pres. 1958, 59); Chicago Agrl. (pres., 1961-63); Union League. Author articles agrl. mags. Home: Flossmoor, Ill. Died May 14, 1978.

MASTEN, SAMUEL WILLIAM, lawyer; b. Nemo, S.D., July 27, 1915; s. James V. and Edna (VanHorn) M.; student S.D. Sch. Mines, 1933, U. Wyo., 1940; J.D. magna cum laude, U. S.D., 1946; m. Kathryn Kaltsulas, Dec. 29, 1944; children—Jeffrey, Stephanie, Mary, Allison, Monte. Admitted to S.D. bar, 1946, practiced in Canton. Mem. S.D. Ct. Study Commn., 1962-63. Served with USAAF, 1941-42. Mem. Am. Coll. Trial Lawyers, Am. Trial Lawyers Assn. (bd. govs. 1968-80), Am. Judicature Soc., (dir. 1967-70), Am. Bar Assn. (mem. ho. dels. 1973-80), State Bar S.D. (pres. 1965), Internat. Acad. Trial Lawyers, Internat. Soc. Barristers, Delta Theta Phi. Republican. Lutheran. Mason (Shriner). Home: Sioux Falls, S.D. Died Jan. 4, 1980.

MASTERS, FRANK MILTON, consulting engr.; born Meyersdale, Pa., June 18, 1883; s. Clarendon Gideon and Eliza (Beachly) M.; student Mercersburg Acad., 1900-04, Cornell University, 1904; Dr. Engring. (honorary), Lehigh University; married Margaret Eleanor Wilson, Feb. 14, 1925; children—Frank Milton, Margaret Ann. Supervisor constrn. and bridge design, Ralph Modjeski, in west and northwest U.S., 1904-07, asso. in charge Pittsburgh office, 1907-12, charge N.Y. City and Pittsburgh offices, 1912-17, partner, hdqrs., N.Y. City, 1924-36; pvt. practice as consulting engr., Harrisburg, Pa., 1919-24, 36—. Maj. U.S. Army, 1917-19; mem. Claims Bd., World War I; designer and supervisor constrn. of large Army and Navy depots, LST boatyards, etc., World War II. Recipient Citations from Chief of Ordnance. Awarded Certificate of Merit, Am. Soc. Metals, 1948. Mem. Column Research Council and spl. com. for the Investigation of the Design of Long Span Suspension Bridges. Mem. Am. Inst. Cons. Engrs., Am. Soc. Testing Materials (life), Am. Soc. C.E. (hon., life), Am. Ry. Engring. Assn. (life), Am. Concrete Inst., Am. Welding Soc., A.A.A.S., Symphony Soc., Franklin Inst. (Gold mem.), Pa. Soc. Prof. Engrs., Am. Legion. Clubs: Engineers and Architects (hon.) (Louisville); Engineers (N.Y.C.); International House (New Orleans); Engineers (Phila.). Author tech. reports used as textbooks. Contbr. engring. publs. Home: Harrisburg, Penn. *

MASTERSON, ROBERT ERNEST, lawyer; b. Woodville, Tex., Aug. 23, 1883; s. Marshall Lewis and Sarah (Cruse) M.; LL.B., U. of Tex., 1914; m. Kate Selman, Apr. 23, 1905; children—Bobby (dec.), Dan K. Admitted to Tex. bar, 1914, and since practiced in Beaumont; dir. Am. Nat. Bank, Norwell-Wilder Supply Co., Tyrrell Hardware Co., Industrial Investment Co., First Federal Savings & Loan Assn., Keith Co., all of Beaumont. Dir. Beaumont Chamber of Commerce, 1923-29; chmn. Library Commn., Beaumont, 1932-33; organized Citizen Com. to help Beaumont city govt. overcome financial embarrassment, 1933. Mem. Tex. State and Jefferson County bar assns., chancellor's Club (U. of Tex.). Baptist. Mason (K.T., Shriner, Dist. Dep. Grand Master, 1923, 25, 35). Contbr. legal and Masonic articles to newspapers. Home: Beaumont, Tex. *

MASUR, GERHARD STRASSMAN, educator; b. Berlin, Sept. 17, 1901; came to U.S., 1947, naturalized, 1953; s. Emil and Frieda (Strassman) M.; student U. Berlin, 1919-21, U. Marburg, 1921; Ph.D., summa cum laude, 1925; m. Helen Gaylord, Aug. 29. 1960. Research asso. Historische Zeitschrift, 1925-35; privatdozent for medieval and modern European history U. Berlin, 1930-35; cons. to minister edn., Bogota, Colombia, 1936-38; prof. Escuela Normal Superior, Bogotá, 1938-45; prof. history, Sweet Briar Coll., Lynchburg, Va., 1947-66, prof. emeritus, 1966-75. Vis. prof. U. Va., 1949, 50, 51, U. N.Mex., 1953, Free U. Berlin, 1956, 60, 65, U. Calif., Berkeley, 1963-64, 67, U. Calif., San Diego, 1968. Rockefeller grantee, 1945-47, 54-55; Guggenheim fellow, 1956; Fulbright award, 1960; Research-fellow Free Univ., Berlin, 1969-70. Mem. Am. Hist. Assn. Conf. on Latin Am. History, Academia Nacional de la Historia, Buenos Aires, Argentina. Club: 13 (Lynchburg). Author: Rankes Begriff der Weltgeschichte, 1926; Friedrich

Julius Stahl, Geschichte seines Lebens, 1930; Goethe, La Ley de su Vida, 1939; Simon Bolivar, 1948; Simon Bolivar und die Befreiung SudAmericas, 1949; Simon Bolivar, 1960; Prophets of Yesterday, 1961; Nationalism in Latin America, 1966; Imperial Berlin, 1970; Geschehen und Geschichte, 1972. Contbr. articles to profl. jours. Home: Lynchburg, Va; buried North Beverly Cemetery, Beverly, Mass.

MATCHETT, GERALD JAMES, economist, educator; b. Fruita, Colo., Sept. 29, 1912; s. Andrew T. and Elma Ellsworth (Long) M.; B.A. magna cum laude, U. Colo., 1934; M.A., Clark U., 1935, Ph.D., 1939; m. Margaret Ellen Stump, Aug. 27, 1942; children—Andrew James, Susan Ellen. Instr. Cornell, 1937-39, Ind. U., 1939-41; economist Dept. Commerce, 1942, also Dept. Agr.; asso. prof. econs. Ill. Inst. Tech., Chgo., 1946-55, prof., from 1955; dir. Nat. Center for Edn. and Research in Equipment Policy, 1953-60; instr. Biarritz Am. U., France, 1945-46; vis. prof. Johns Hopkins, summer 1950, Stanford, summers, 1963-69; lectr. Indsl. Mgmt. Center, Lake Placid, N.Y., 1961-69. Chief rev. div. 9th region War Labor Bd., 1943-44; financial economist Monetary Commn. for Germany, 1946. Recipient Distinguished Alumnus award Mesa Coll., 1971. Mem. Am., Midwest econ. assns., Am. Soc. Engring. Edn. (chmn. engring, economy div.), Indsl. Relations Research Assn., AAUP, Phi Beta Kappa, Delta Sigma Rho, Sigma Iota Epsilon, Pi Gamma Mu. Unitarian. Author: (with Moffat, others) Economics, Principles and Problems, rev. edit., 1947; (with Pearce Davis) Modern Labor Economics; An Analysis of Labor Management Relations, 1954. Asso. editor Engring. Economist, from 1956. Contbr. articles to profl. jours. Home: Chicago, Ill. Died Oct. 11, 1977.

MATECHECK, RICHARD VINCENT, wholesale food co. exec.; b. Massillon, Ohio, Nov. 29, 1927; s. Vincent Stephen and Loretta (Happoldt) M.; B.S. in Bus. Adminstrn., Miami U., Oxford, Ohio, 1952; m. Helen Louise Saunders, Aug. 15, 1953; children—Stephen C., John J., Mary Kay. Sr. accountant firm Peat, Marwick, Mitchell & Co., C.P.A.'s Cleve., 1952-55; accountant, sec. The McLain Grocery Co., Massillon, 1955-77, also dir. Mem. budget com. United Fund. Trustee Massillon City Hosp. Served with AUS. Mem. Massillon Area C. of C. (v.p., dir.). Lion. Home: Massillon, Ohio. Died Jan. 8, 1977; buried Rose Hill Meml. Park, Massillon.

MATHER, KIRTLEY FLETCHER, geologist; b. Chgo., Feb. 13, 1888; s. William Green and Julia S. (King) M.; B.S., Denison U., 1909, Sc.D., 1929; Ph.D., U. Chgo., 1915; Sc.D., Colby Coll., 1936; Litt.D., Union Coll., 1942; L.H.D., Bates Coll., 1943; LL.D., Beloit Coll., 1949; D.Sc. of Oratory, Curry Coll., 1966; m. Marie Porter, June 12, 1912 (dec. Sept. 1971); children—Florence Margaret (Mrs. Sherman A. Wengerd), Julia Carolyn, (Mrs. LeRoy G. Seils), Jean Marie (Mrs. Dean W. Siebel); m. 2d, Muriel S. Williams, May 31, 1977. Instr., U. Ark., 1911-12, asst. prof., 1912-14; fellow U. Chgo., 1914-15; asso. prof. geology Queen's U., Kingston, Ont., Can., 1915-17, prof. paleontology, 1917-18; prof. geol. Denison U., 1918-24; asso. prof. physiography Harvard, 1924-27, prof. geology, 1927-54, prof. emeritus, 1954-78; dir. Harvard Summer Sch., 1934-42; vis. prof. U. N.Mex., Albuquerque; geologist several explorations, 1911-60. World Alliance of YMCAs rep. at UN, 1957-60. Trustee Childrens Mus., Boston, Curry Coll.; pres. Nat. Council YMCA, 1946-48; mem. exec. com. World's Alliance YMCA, 1947-55; chmn. Civil Liberties Union Mass., 1946-49, numerous other civic and community activities. Phi Beta Kappa Vis. Scholar, 1960-61, 66; Danforth vis. lectr. Assn. Am. Colls., 1961-62. Pres. Found. for Integrative Edn., 1946-69. Recipient Washburn Medal Boston Mus. Sci., 1964; Cullum medal Am. Geog. Soc., 1965. Fellow Geol. Soc. Am., Am. Acad. Arts and Scis. (pres. 1957-61), A.A.A.S. (pres. 1951), Royal Geog. Soc., Am. Geog. Soc., Ohio Acad. Sci. (pres. 1923-24); mem. Oliver Wendell Holmes Assn. (pres. 1962-70), also numerous profl. and sci. socs. and assns. Baptist. Mason (32 deg.). Clubs: Twentieth Century (pres. 1930-35), Acacia, Torch, Harvard Travellers, Harvard Mountaineering, Boston Authors' (Boston); Century (N.Y.C.). Author numerous books, 1915-64; The Earth Beneath Us, 1964; Source Book in Geology, 1900-1950, 1967; govt. bulls., papers in tech. periodicals and popular articles. Home: Albuquerque, N.Mex. Died May 7, 1978.

MATHEWS, EDWARD JAMES, architect; b. N.Y.C., Jan. 27, 1903; s. Wilbur Knox and Currie (Duke) M.; student Yale Archtl. Sch., 1924-25; m. Mary Burchell, May 29, 1929; 1 son, Harry Burchell. With Bertram G. Goodhue, architect, N.Y.C., 1919-23; designer Rockefeller Center Architects, 1929-30; individual practice, 1931-41; mem. spl. panel to prepare charter provision N.Y.C. Planning Commn., 1933; mem. bd. N.Y. Regional Plan Com., 1935-41; gen. partner Skidmore, Owings & Merrill, architects, N.Y.C., 1953-66; charge planning studies lower Manhattan, Morningside and Midtown areas, N.Y.C.; asso. bldgs. for Conn. Gen. Life Ins. Co., Chase Manhattan Bank, N.Y.C., Marine Midland Bank, N.Y.C., IBM hdqrs. bldg., Armonk, N.Y., Library and Museum for Performing Arts, Lincoln Center, also Hunts Point Terminal Market. Mem. N.Y. Hort. Soc. (dir.). Served with USNR, 1942-45. Clubs: Century Assn., Knickerbocker (N.Y.C.). Address: New York, N.Y. Died Mar. 28, 1980.

MATHEWS, ELBERT GEORGE, fgn. service officer; b. Troy, N.Y., Nov. 24, 1910; s. Samuel Blumenthal and Anna Margaret (Jordan) M.; student Kidder (Mo.) Acad. and Jr. Coll., 1924-28; A.B., U. Calif., Berkeley, 1930; South Asia area study U. Pa., summer 1947; m. Maomi Meffert, Aug. 20, 1934. Research asst. Inst. Child Welfare, U. Calif., 1930-33; acct. Golden State Co., Ltd., San Francisco, 1933-35; vice consul, Vancouver, 1935-36, Sydney, Australia (temporary duty Brisbane and Adelaide), 1937-40; 3d sec., Managua, 1941-42; divisional asst. Dept. State, 1943; 2d sec., Kabul, 1944-46; consul, Calcutta 1946-47; asst. chief div. S. Asian Affairs, Dept. State, 1947-48, chief, 1948-49, dir. Office of South Asian Affairs, 1950-51; consul gen., Istanbul, 1951-52; assigned Imperial Def. Coll., London, 1953; counselor Am. embassy, Oslo, 1954-55; mem. policy planning staff Dept. State, 1955-59, dep. asst. sec. policy planning, 1957-59; ambassador to Liberia, 1959-62; dir. Office Inter-African Affairs, Dept. State, 1962-64; ambassador to Nigeria, 1964-69; coordinator Sr. Seminar in Fgn. Policy, Dept. State, 1969-72. Mem. Acad. Polit. Sci. Club: Internat. (Washington). Home: Washington, D.C. Died Nov. 30, 1977; buried Rock Creek Cemetery, Washington.

MATHEWS, JACKSON, writer, translator, editor; b. Griffin, Ga., Oct. 18, 1907; B.A. magna cum laude, U. Ga., 1928, M.A., 1930; Ph.D., Columbia U., 1947. Instr. French, U. Ga., 1930-32; instr. French, Latin and English, U. Oreg., 1932-35; instr. to asso. prof. French and English lit. Central Wash. Coll. Edn., Ellensburg, 1935-41; asso. prof., chmn. comparative lit. U. Wash., 1949-51, prof., chmn. comparative lit., 1951-55; editor Collected Works of Paul Valery (Bollingen series), 15 vols., 1953-75, vols. include Dialogues, 1956, The Art of Poetry, 1958, Plays, 1960, Degas, Manet, Morisot, 1960, History and Politics, 1962, Aesthetics, 1964, Idee Fixe, 1965, Masters and Friends, 1967. Vice pres. Bollingen Found., 1957-67; chmn. bd., exec. com. Nat. Translation Center, U. Tex., 1965-66; vis. prof. English and comparative lit. U. Wash., 1967; fellow Belgian-Am. Ednl. Found. in Belgium, 1938-39; Univ. fellow in French lit. Columbia U., N.Y.C., 1941-42; Fulbright fellow, Paris, 1951, Bollingen Found. fellow, Paris, 1955-57; fellow Sch. Letters, Ind. U., summer 1967; field officer OSS, N. Africa, Italy, France, Germany, 1943-45; vice consul for cultural affairs U.S. Fgn. Service, Geneva, 1946-48; Morris Grey lectr. Harvard U., Cambridge, Mass., 1967; lectr. Sch. Letters, Ind. U., 1967. Decorated chevalier des Arts et des Lettres, French Govt., 1972; Bronze Star. Mem. Phi Beta Kappa. Author: La Wallonie: The Symbolist Movement in Belgium, 1946. Translator: Monsieur Teste, ltd. edit., 1947, complete edit. (Nat. Book award, 1973), 1973; My Theatre, 1952; Flowers of Evil, 1955, rev. edit., 1962; Hypnos Waking, 1956. Contbr. articles, poems, and revs. to profl. publs. Home: New Windsor, Md. Died Dec. 15, 1978.

MATHEWS, JON, physicist; b. Los Angeles, Feb. 10, 1932; s. John H. and Grace (Logie) M.; B.A., Pomona Coll., 1952; Ph.D., Calif. Inst. Tech., 1957; m. Charlotte Dallett, June 10, 1952 (div. 1976); children—Valerie, Jancis, Richard Hays, William Salisbury; m. 2d, Jean Vontobel, Oct. 15, 1977. Mem. faculty Calif. Inst. Tech., Pasadena, 1957-79, prof. physics, 1966-79. Mem. Am. Phys. Soc., AAAS. Author: (with R.L. Walker) Mathematical Methods of Physics, 1964; contbr. articles to profl. jours. Home: Pasadena, Calif. Died Dec. 24, 1979.

MATHEWS, JOSEPH JAMES, educator; b. Campton, Ky., Sept. 14, 1908; s. Joseph Moreau and Nancy (Houtchens) M.; student Ky. Wesleyan Coll., 1925-28; A.B., Duke U., 1930, A.M., 1931; Ph.D., U. Pa., 1935; m. Marie Marcia Mayfield, May 31, 1938; 1 son, Timothy Mayfield. Instr. history U. Chattanooga, 1931-32; asst. instr. history U. Pa., 1932-35; instr. history Duke, 1935-36, vis. lectr., 1941; asst. prof. U. Miss., 1936-38, asso. prof., 1938-42, acting dean grad. sch., 1941-42; asso. historian U.S. War Dept., 1942-43; prof. history Emory U., Atlanta, 1946-60, Charles Howard Candler prof. of history, after 1960, chmn. dept., 1948-58. Vis. lectr. or prof., summers, U. Mo., 1947, U. N.C., 1949, U. R.I., 1959, others; Fulbright lectr. Robert Coll., Istanbul, 1962-63; George A. Miller vis. prof. journalism U. Ill., Urbana, 1966-67. Dir. wartime hist. project Bur. Ordnance, U.S.N., 1943-46; disch. as lt. comdr. Carnegie Research grantee-in-aid, 1948, 1950; Guggenheim Meml. Found. fellow, 1951-52; Fulbright research fellow, U.K., 1955-56; summer fellowship, Am. Philos. Soc., 1956. Mem. Am., So. (pres. 1964) hist. assns., Phi Beta Kappa, Sigma Alpha Epsilon, Kappa Tau Alpha. Author: Egypt and the Formation of the Anglo-French Entente of 1904, 1939; Reporting the Wars, 1957; George W. Smalley: Forty Years as a Foreign Correspondent, 1973. Home: Durham, N.C. Died Aug. 16, 1976.

MATHEWS, JOSEPH WESLEY, educator, theologian; b. Breezewood, Pa., Oct. 8, 1911; s. James Donaldson and Laura (Wilson) M.; A.B., Asbury Coll., Willmore, Ky., 1936; B.D., Drew U., 1939; student Union Theol. Sem., N.Y.C., 1939-41; student Yale Grad. Sch., 1948; m. Evelyn Johnston, Jan. 3, 1942; children—Joseph Wesley, James Johnston, John Donaldson (dec.). Prof. philosophy and religion Colgate U., 1948-52; prof. Christian ethics Perkins Sch. Theology, So. Meth. U., 1952-56; dean studies Christian Faith and Life Community, Austin, Tex., 1956-62; dean Ecumenical Inst., Chgo., 1962-77; exec. dir. Inst. Cultural Affairs, to 1977; nat. lectr. theology, ethics, edn., 1948-77. Mem. S.W. Conf. Meth. Ch. Served as chaplain AUS, 1942-46; PTO. Address: Chicago, Ill. Died Oct. 16, 1977.

MATHIEU, BEATRICE, writer; b. Seattle, Nov. 7, 1904; d. Michel and Azilda Fontaine (de Beaulieu) M.; student U. Wash., 1919-20, U. Chgo., 1921, Sorbonne, 1926-27; A.B., New Sch. Social Research, 1951; m. Andre DaMiano, Dec. 31, 1935 (div. 1950); married second Dr. Allan Roos, May 22, 1954. Writer New Yorker Mag., 1928-76; columnist King Features, 1927-32, N.Y. World, 1928-30, Asso. Press, 1926-27; lectr., radio talks, Paris, 1926-39. Mem. council of Atlantic Union Com., 1952-76; trustee Am. br. Anna Freud Found., 1955-59; trustee Inst. Dermatalogical Communication and Edn. Mem. Nat. Assn. Sci. Writers, Authors League, Nat. Council Tchrs. Math. (life), Am. Assn. UN, A.A.A.S. (life), Internat. Council Women, Am. Fedn. Arts, N.Y. Psychoanalytic Inst. (aux.), Am. Med. Writers Assn., James Joyce Soc., Theta Sigma Phi. Clubs: Press (San Francisco); Cosmopolitan, Harvard, Overseas Press (gov. 1948-51, v.p. 1952, trustee corrs. fund 1959-60, phys. sci. study com. 1954-76) (N.Y.C.). Author articles U.S., fgn mags. Address: New York, N.Y. Died July 12, 1976.

MATLES, JAMES JOSEPH, labor union exec.; b. Rumania, Feb. 24, 1909; s. Joseph and Anna (Kuhle) M.; ed. in Rumania; m. Esther Gross, Aug. 11, 1933; 1 dau., Joan (Mrs. Robert Rosen). Came to U.S., 1929, naturalized, 1934. Machinist, Nash Motors and Pontiac Motor Co., 1928-36; grand lodge rep. Internat. Assn. Machinists, AFL, 1936-37; dir. orgn. United Elec. Radio and Machine Workers Am., 1937-62, gen. sec.-treas., 1962-75. CIO rep. War Manpower Commn., also WPB, 1941-43. Served with AUS, 1943-45. Author: Automation and the New Technology; co-author Them and Us. Home: New York, N.Y. Died Sept. 15, 1975.

MATLOCK, RALPH S., educator; b. nr. Norman, Okla., Aug. 24, 1921; s. Stanley G. and Mahala Lee (Lessly) M.; B.S., Okla. State U., 1948, M.S., 1949; Ph.D., U. Neb., 1952; m. Geraldine E. Evans, Oct. 31, 1944; children—John R., Steven Randolph, Kenneth E., Donald W. Sci. aide, agr. research staff. U.S. Dept. Agr., Lincoln, Nebr., 1949-51; instr. genetics dept. agronomy U. Nebr., Lincoln, 1951-52; mem. faculty Okla. State U., Stillwater, 1952-77, asso. prof., 1954-68, prof., 1957-68, head dept. agronomy, 1968-77; cons. oilseed AID, West Pakistan, 1967. Scoutmaster, chmn. com. Boy Scouts Am. Served to 1st lt., inf., AUS, 1944-47. Decorated Bronze Star, Purple Heart. Fellow Am. Soc. Agronomy; mem. Crop Sci. Soc. Am., Soil Conservation Soc. Am., Okla. Acad. Sci., Okla. Edn. Assn., Sigma Xi, Alpha Zeta, Phi Kappa Phi. Recipient Golden Peanut Research award Nat. Peanut Council, 1967; named Outstanding Tchr. Coll. Agr., 1967. Fellow Am. Soc. Agronomy. Lion. Home: Stillwater, Okla. Died Mar. 23, 1977.

MATSCHAT, CECILE HULSE, author; b. Binghamton, N.Y.; d. James Matthew and Emma Jane (Welling) Hulse; ed. pvt. tutors and spl. courses Pratt Inst., Brooklyn, N.Y.; m. Louis Jean Matschat, Sept. 15, 1925. Editorial asst. Nat. Com. Maternal Health, 1929-32; editor Internat. Com. for Study Infantile Paralysis, 1932-33; free lance writer since 1933. Mem. Nat. Assn. Women Painters and Sculptors, Soc. Woman Geographers. Author: Mexican Plants for American Gardens, 1935; Garden Calendar, 1936; How to Make a Garden, 1937; Planning the Home Grounds, 1937; Annuals and Perennials, 1937; Shrubs and Trees, 1937; Bulbs and House Plants, 1937; Suwanee River, 1938; Seven Grass Huts, 1939; Preacher on Horseback, 1940; Murder in Okefenokee, 1941; American Butterflies and Moths, 1942; Highway to Heaven, 1942; Tavern in the Town, 1942; Murder at the Black Crook, 1943. Contbr. to Garden Dictionary, also articles to jours. Address: New York, N.Y. Died Mar. 4, 1976.

MATTHEW, ROBERT JOHN, educator; b. Easton, N.H., Feb. 14, 1907; s. William and Stella Ada (Little) M.; A.B., U. N.H., 1928; Diplome d'Etudes Francaises, Institut Franco-American de Vichy, France, 1931; student U. Geneva, 1931-32; Doctorat d'Universite, Mention Lettres, 1932, U. de Clermont, Clermont-Ferrand, France, 1932; m. Helen Margaret Gunder, July 29, 1939; 1 son, John Little. Master in French and Spanish schools in Va., N.H., N.Y.C., 1928-34; instr. Ecole Internationale, Gland, Switzerland, 1931; Hunter Coll., N.Y.C., 1936; lectr. Am. U., Washington, 1944-45; instr. Coll. City of N.Y., evening sessions, 1933-36, mem. grad. adv. com. and supr. fgn. lang. tchr. tng., 1936-38, instr. Romance langs., 1938-42, 1946-47, asst. prof., 1947-57; prof. French, Sweet Briar (Va.) Coll., 1957-75, dir. Jr. Year in France, 1952-53, gen. dir., 1957-72. Pres., v.p. Books Across the Sea, 1941-43; mem. regional com.

interchange of tchrs. under Fulbright Exchange Program. Served as 2d lt., Army Specialist Corps, U.S. Army, 1942; 1st lt., G2, Gen. Staff, Washington, 1942-44; capt. air intelligence div. AAF, Washington, 1944-45; chief counter-intelligence div. Hdqrs. Continental Air Forces, Bolling Field, 1945-46. Decorated Chevalier Palmes Academiques; Chevalier Ordre National du Merite; gold medal City of Paris, 1972. Member Mutual Aid Soc. of City Coll., English-Speaking Union, (founder and editor 1st number News), Fedn. French Alliances in U.S. and Can. (mem. bd. dirs.), Am. Assn. Tchrs. French, Am. Assn. Tchrs. Spanish, AAUP, MLA, Fgn. Policy Assn., France-America Soc. Republican. Episcopalian. Author books, from 1932, including: Language and Area Studies in the Armed Services, 1948; Universities of the World Outside of the U.S.A., 1950. Contbr. to profl. jours. and reviews. Address: Sweet Briar, Va. Died Jan. 29, 1975.

MATTHEWS, A(LAN) BRUCE, corporate exec.; b. Clarksburg, W.Va., Dec. 11, 1923; s. Ezra Wilson and Hilma (Nelson) M.; B.S., Ohio U., 1945; m. Marjorie Phillips, 1944 (div. 1962); m. 2d, Marjorie Nelson, Dec. 31, 1963; children—Bruce, Thomas, Jennifer, David, Michelle, Bradford, Christopher. Partner Authur Andersen & Co., Detroit, 1945-56, mng. partner, Denver, 1956-65; v.p. finance and adminstrn. Communications Satellite Corp., Washington, 1965-70; pres., dir. Bliss & Laughlin Industries, Inc., Oak Brook, Ill., 1970-71; sr. v.p. CNA Financial Corp., Chgo., 1972-75; chmn., pres. Larwin Group, Inc., Beverly Hills, Calif., 1974-75; chmn. bd., dir. Healthco, Inc., 1972-75, 1st Healthcare Corp., 1972-75, Coaxial Communications, Inc., 1973-75, CNA Mgmt. Corp., 1973-75; pres. The Matthews Group, Washington, Cairo and London, 1975-80; chmn. bd. Egyptian Service & Supply Co., Cairo, 1975-77, Washington Communications Group,1Group, 1977-80. Pres., Jr. Achievement Met. Denver, 1960-62, chmn. bd., 1962-64, chmn. bd. Western Region, 1964-66, mem. nat. exec. com., 1962-80; pres. bd. trustees Graland County Day Sch., Denver, 1960-61, trustee, 1959-65; treas. Denver Symphony, 1964-65, trustee, 1958-65; chmn. Red Rocks Music Festival, 1960-61; treas., dir. Chgo. Crime Commn., 1970-72; trustee Nat. Symphony Orch., Washington, 1966-70; trustee Avery Coonley Sch., 1971-74, pres., 1973-74; bd. govs. Chgo. Symphony Orch. Assn., 1972-80. Served with AUS, 1942-43. Mem. Financial Execs. Inst., Am. Inst. C.P.A.'s, President's Assn., Am. Mgmt. Assn., Nat. Assn. Bus. Economists, Newcomen Soc. Clubs: Chicago, Mid-America, Economic (Chgo.); Mile High (Denver); Hinsdale Golf; Met., Congressional Country, Internat. (Washington); Sky (N.Y.C.). Home: Washington, D.C. Died June 6, 1980.

MATTHEWS, ANNABEL, lawyer, ex-pub. official; b. Culloden, Ga., Dec. 31, 1883; d. Alphonso Houghton and Augusta Louise (Vaughan) Matthews; A.B., Brenau Coll., Gainesville, Ga., 1901; student U. of Tenn., 2 summers; LL.B., Washington (D.C.) Coll. of Law, 1921; spl. courses George Washington U. Teacher pub. schs., Ga., 1901-14; clerk income tax div., Bur. Internal Revenue, 1914-25; admitted to D.C. bar, 1921, Ga. bar, 1928; spl. atty. in office of gen. counsel, Bur. Internal Revenue, 1925-30; apptd. by sec. of Treasury as asst. to del. representing U.S. at internat. confs. on double taxation held under auspices of League of Nations, London, 1927, Geneva, 1928; mem. Bd. of Tax Appeals (1st woman mem.), 1930-36. Chief Counsel's Com. Bur. Internal Revenue, 1936-38; mem. U.S. Processing Tax Board of Review, 1938-42; attorney, chief counsel's office, Bureau of Internal Revenue, Washir.gton, D.C., 1943-44; pvt. practice since 1945. Apptd. to Fair Employment Bd. of Civil Service Commn., 1948. Trustee Brenau College. Member American Bar Association, D.C. Bar Assn., Women's D.C. Bar Assn. (pres. 1937-39), D.C. Bus. and Professional Women's Club, D.C. League of Women Voters, Am. Assn. Univ. Women (Washington br.), Phi Mu, Phi Delta Delta. Democrat. Methodist. Home: Washington. *

MATTHEWS, HERBERT LIONEL, former newspaper editor, author; b. N.Y.C., Jan. 10, 1900; s. Samuel and Frances (Lewis) M.; A.B., Columbia, 1922; m. Edith Crosse, Feb. 21, 1931; children—Eric, Priscilla. With N.Y. Times, 1922-67, reporter, fgn. editor and war corr., corr. Paris Bur., 1931-34, Abyssinian War, 1935-36, Spanish Civil War, 1936-39, Rome, 1939-42, India, 1942-43, Italian campaign, 1943-45, chief London Bur., 1945-49, editorial staff, N.Y.C., 1949-67. Trustee, Radcliffe Coll. Served with Tank Corps, U.S. Army, 1918; AEF. Decorated Italian War Cross, grand officer Crown of Italy, commendatore Order of Merit (Italy); officer Order Condor of Andes (Bolivia); chevalier Legion of Honor (France); officer Order of So. Cross (Brazil); officer Order of Boyaca (Colombia). Recipient Columbia Medal of Excellence; Maria Moors Cabot award, 1956; George Polk Mem. award, 1957; Newspaper Guild N.Y. Page One award, 1957. Mem. Yale Polit. Union (hon. life mem.) Phi Beta Kappa. Presbyn. Author: Eyewitness in Abyssinia, 1937; Two Wars and More to Come, 1938; The Fruits of Fascism, 1943; The Education of a Correspondent, 1946; Assignment to Austerity (with Edith Matthews), 1950; The Yoke and the Arrows, 1956; The Cuban Story, 1961; Cuba, 1964; Fidel Castro, 1969; A World in Revolution, 1972; Half of Spain Died, 1973; Revolution in Cuba, 1975. Address: New York, N.Y. Died July 29, 1977.

MATTHEWS, MARK ALLISON, dairy co. exec.; b. Seattle, Apr. 14, 1909; s. Mark Allison and Grace Owen (Jones) M.; B.A., U. Wash., 1931; M.B.A., Harvard, 1933; m. Rachel Fenton Brown, June 16, 1933; children—Marcia Allison (Mrs. David Redick), Mark A., Richard F. With Carnation Co., Seattle, after 1933, Los Angeles, after 1936, gen. sales mgr., asst. gen. mgr. So. Calif. fresh milk and ice cream div., 1941-50, sales mgr., gen. offices, 1950-56, asst. v.p., 1956-59, v.p. charge div., 1959-74. Mem. Psi Upsilon. Home: San Clemente, Calif. Died Dec. 26, 1977.

MATTHEWS, MARY LOCKWOOD, home economist; b. Louisville, Ky., Oct. 13, 1882; d. John E. and Harriet (Beach) Matthews; grad. Sch. of Agr., St. Anthony Park, Minn., 1900; B.S., in Home Economics, U. of Minn., 1904; unmarried. Instr. in clothing, Lafayette Industrial Sch., 1906-09, U. of Minn., 1909-10; extension worker, Purdue U., 1910-12; head dept. home economics, same univ., 1912-26, dean of the School of Home Economics since 1926. Dir. home economics for Ind. Food Administration, World War, also mem. State Council of Defense. Fellow A.A.A.S.; life mem. N.E.A.; mem. Am. Home Economics Assn., Gen. Fedn. of Clubs, Am. Assn. Univ. Women, Pi Gamma Mu, Omicron Nu, Pi Beta Phi. Republican. Presbyn. Author: Elementary Home Economics, 1921, rev., 1936; The House and Its Care, 1926, rev., 1940; Clothing—Selection and Care, 1935; sect. on house furnishings in the Book of Rural Life, 1925. Home: West Lafayette, Ind. *

MATTHEWS RODERIC D(ONALD), educator; b. Clear Lake, Ia., Apr. 8, 1899; s. Burtis Homer and Annette Marie (Jackson) A.; A.B., Grinnell Coll., 1920; A.M., U. Pa., 1927, Ph.D., 1931; m. Eunice Tyrrell, Aug. 29, 1924; 1 dau., Jessica T. (Mrs. William B. Skelton, Jr.). Instr., Am. U. Cairo, 1920-23; high sch. tchr., Clear Lake, Ia., 1923-24, Woodbury, N.J., 1924-27; instr. to asso. prof. edn. U. Pa. 1927-47, prof. edn. since 1947, v. dean charge grad. program, sch. edn. 1949-52. Exec. sec. Nat. Study Secondary Sch. Evaluation, 1960. Field rep. Coop. Study of Secondary School Standards, 1938-39; exec. sec. commn. on secondary schs. Middle States Assn. Colls. and Secondary Schs., 1940-43, chmn., 1947-62; director American Council on Edn. Commn. to study edn. in Arab Countries of Nr. East 1945-51; dir. revision program Coop. Study Secondary School Standards, 1948-50, 55-60; mem. bd. visitors Marine Corps Inst., 1951-57; cons. on accreditation, veterans educational affairs, U.S. Office of Education, 1952-53. Commanding officer Navy V-12 units, Mt. St. Mary's Coll., Johns Hopkins, U. Md., 1942-45; lieutenant comdr. U.S.N.R., Member Nat. Vocational Guidance Assn. (local pres. 1949-51), Am. Assn. University Profs. (pres. U. Pa. branch), Phi Delta Kappa. Republican. Presbyn. Author: Education in Arab Countries of Near East (with Matta Akrawi), 1949. Directed devel. Evaluative Criteria for Junior High Schs. Home: Drexel Hill, Pa. *

MATTHIAS, BERND TEO, physicist; b. Frankfúrt on Main, Germany, June 8, 1918; s. Ludwig and Marta (Lippman) M.; Ph.D. in Physics, Fed. Inst. Tech., Zürich, Switzerland, 1943; Sc.D. (hon.), U. Lausanne, 1978; m. Joan Trapp, Aug. 5, 1950. Came to U.S., 1947, naturalized, 1951. Sci. collaborator Fed. Inst. Tech., 1942-47; mem. staff,, div. indsl. coop. Mass. Inst. Tech., 1947-48; mem. tech. staff Bell Labs., Inc., Murray Hill, N.J., 1948-80; asst. prof. physics U. Chgo., 1949-51; prof. physics U. Calif. at San Diego, 1961-80, also dir. Inst. for Pure and Applied Phys. Scis., 1971-80. Recipient Research Corp. Found. award, 1962; John Price Wetherill medal Franklin Inst., 1963; Indsl. Research Man of Year award, 1968; Oliver E. Buckley solid state physics prize, 1970; Internat. prize for new materials Am. Phys. Soc., 1979. Fellow AAAS, Am. Phys. Soc.; mem. Nat. Acad. Scis., N.Y. Acad. Scis., Am. Acad. Arts and Scis., Swiss Phys. Soc., Sigma Xi. Home: La Jolla, Calif. Died Oct. 10, 1980.

MATTICK, HANS W., educator, criminologist; b. Dresden, Germany, Feb. 4, 1920; s. Walter S. and Frieda (Olle) Rheiner; came to U.S., 1926, naturalized, 1939; B.A., U. Chgo., 1948, M.A., 1956; m. June Virginia Pasdeloup, Feb. 16, 1946. Research sociologist Ill. Parole and Pardon Bd., Chgo., 1950-52; sociologist-actuary Stateville Penitentiary, Joliet, Ill., 1953-54; asst. warden Cook County Jail, Chgo., 1955-58; research asso. Inst. Social Research, U. Mich., 1960-66; asso. dir. Center for Studies in Criminal Justice, Law Sch., U. Chgo., 1966-69, co-dir., 1969-72, lectr. criminology, 1956-57, 71; prof. criminal justice U. Ill. at Chgo. Circle, 1972-78, also dir. Center for Research in Criminal Justice; lectr. sociology Ind. U., Calumet-Gary, 1953-54; dir. action and research Chgo. Youth Devel. Project, 1960-66. Mem. Ill. Legislative Sex Offenders Commn., 1963-65; sec. Ill. Com. Abolish Capital Punishment, 1959-68, pres., 1969-78; chmn. prof. adv. com. John Howard Assn., 1960-67, mem., 1968-72; mem. adv. bd. St. Leonard's House, 1958-72; chmn. adv. bd. Ill. Dept. Corrections, 1974-78; chmn. Ill. Criminal Justice Info. System Policy Com., 1973-75; mem. Chgo. Crime Commn., 1974-78; exec. com. tech. adv. panel Survey Research Lab., U. Ill., 1974-78. Served with AUS, 1941-45. Recipient Ann. award John Howard Assn., 1966; Gov.'s Justice award, 1972; Profl. Achievement award U. Chgo. Alumni Assn., 1975. Mem. Ill. Acad. Criminology (pres. 1959-60, citation 1959, Commendation citation 1960), Am. Sociol. Assn., Am. Soc. Criminology, Am. Correctional Assn., Art Inst. Chgo., Dirs. Criminological Research Insts. U.S. and Can. (chmn. 1968), Nat. Council Crime and Delinquency, Internat. Soc. Criminology, Law and Soc. Assn., Soc. for Study of Social Problems, Phi Beta Kappa. Author: Parole To The Army, 1956; The Cook County Jail, 1957; (with N.S. Caplan) Street Work, Community Organization and Research, 1962. Editor: Key Issues, jour., 1961-71; The Unexamined Death, 1963, 3d rev. edit., 1966; (with N.S. Caplan) The Chgo. Youth Devel. Project, 1964; (with F.J. Carney, J.D. Callaway) Action on the Streets, 1969; (with R.P. Sweet) Illinois Jails, 1969; (with M. Gold) Experiment in the Streets, 1974; The Contemporary Jails of the United States, 1974; (with C. Olander, D. Baker, H. Schlegel) Evaluation of Operation Identification, 1974. Home: Chicago, Ill. Died Jan. 26, 1978.

MATTIMORE, JOHN CLARKE, marketing exec., writer; b. Albany, N.Y., Aug. 20, 1916; s. Horatio Seymour and Grace (Stevens) M.; A.B., Dartmouth, 1938; m. Jean Meyer, Feb. 16, 1946; children—Patrick S., Bryan and Karen (twins). Eastern advt. mgr. Glamour mag., 1948-52; mng. dir. Ind. Adv. Com. to Trucking Industry, 1953-55; account exec. Kenyon & Eckhardt Advt. Agy., 1955, became v.p., 1957; pres. Robert Mullen, Inc., pub. relations, 1960-62; cons., 1962-65; pres. Selling Areas Marketing, Inc. subsidiary Time Inc., 1965-72, vice chmn., 1972-73, v.p. parent co., 1971-73; exec.-in-residence U. New Haven, 1972-75, bd. govs., 1974-75. Exec. com. bd. dirs. Muscular Dystrophy Assns. Am. Nat. dir. Orgn. Citizens for Eisenhower 1952. Served as lt., USNR, 1942-46. Mem. Authors Guild. Mem. Dutch Reformed Ch. Clubs: Stamford Yacht (dir.); Hemsphere, Dartmouth (N.Y.C.). Author: (with Jean Mattimore) Cooking by the Clock, 1948. Home: Stamford, Conn. Died Nov. 16, 1975.

MATTIS, JAY HOWARD, former ednl. adminstr.; b. Royersford, Pa., Aug. 28, 1897; s. George R. and Mattie (McBride) M.; certificate U. Pa., 1922; m. Elma H. Buerdsell, June 15, 1927. Teller, Royersford Trust Co., 1915-24; gen. accountant Pub. Ledger Co., Phila., 1924-36; mem. staff Curtis Inst. Music, Phila., 1936-70, treas., 1940-73, also dir.; mem. staff Mary Curtis Bok Found., Phila., 1936-70, treas., 1940-73, also dir. Mem. Phila. Art Alliance. Republican. Mason. Home: Philadelphia, Pa. Died Apr. 20, 1979.

MATTISON, GEORGE AUGUSTUS, JR., slag and aggregate co. exec., Shrine ofcl.; b. Talladega, Ala., Nov. 5, 1898; s. George Augustus and Mary (Ferguson) M.; B.S. in Elec. Engring., Auburn U., 1919, D.Sc. (hon.); m. Ernestine Carriger, Dec. 20, 1923 (dec.); children—George Augustus III (dec.), William Ernest, Mary. Co-founder Woodstock Slag Corp., Anniston, Ala., 1919, pres., 1937-56; partner Houston Slag Materials Co., 1944-79; pres. Hurock, Inc., Houston, 1952-79; mem. So. adv. bd. Am. Mut. Liability Ins. Co.; dir. Ala. Gt. So. R.R. Co. Mem. Anniston lodge Masons, 1922-79, Scottish Rite, Birmingham, 1949-79, Anniston Commandery K.T., 1922-79, Red Cross of Constantine (past sovereign St. Dunstan Conclave), 1956-79, Royal Order Jesters (past dir. Court 127), 1944-79; mem. Ancient Arabis Order Nobles of Mystic Shrine for N.A., 1922, potentate Zamora Temple, 1947, imperial potentate Imperial Council, 1960-61; trustee, chmn. bldg. and equipment com. Shriners' Hosps. for Crippled Children. Chmn. Ala. Community Chest appeal, 1943, Ala. March of Dimes, 1943, USO Appeal, Birmingham, 1942, Birmingham Committee of 100, 1958-59. Former mem. bd. dirs. Auburn Research Found.; bd. dirs. Birmingham Boys Club, Boys Club Am.; trustee, past pres. Crippled Childrens Clinic, Birmingham. Served to 2d lt., inf., U.S. Army, World War I. Recipient Algernon Sydney Sullivan medallion award for humanitarian traits Auburn U., 1958, Disting. Engr. award Auburn U., 1978; named to Ala. Acad. Honor, 1976. Mem. Am. Concrete Inst., Am. Soc. Testing Materials, So. Research Inst., So. Assn. Sci. and Industry, Nat. Slag Assn. (past pres.), Auburn Alumni Assn. (past pres.), Newcomen Soc., Am. Legion (past post comdr.), 40 and 8 (post chef passe), Birmingham C. of C. (past pres.), Ala. Acad. Honor, Omicron Delta Kappa. Episcopalian (past sr. warden, vestryman). Clubs: A Club (Auburn U.); Mt. Brook, The Club (past pres.), Engineers, Kiwanis (past pres.), Traffic and Transportation (past pres.), Monday Morning Quarterback (past capt.) (Birmingham). Home: Birmingham, Ala. Died Feb. 23, 1979.

MATZ ROBERT LUKE (MATZ), univ. prof.; b. Alburtis, Pa., Jan. 21, 1886; s. Davilla and Sarah (Cook) M.; A.B., Ursinus Coll., Collegeville, Pa., 1912, A.M., New York U., 1919, M.B.A., 1926, Ph.D., 1928; student Columbia, 1925; m. Bessie B. Mapes, May 28, 1921; 1 dau., Barbara. Teacher, Bloomfield (N.J.), High Sch., 1912-21, W.Va. Wesleyan Coll., Buckhannon, W.Va., 1921-23; salesman and asst. to pres., W. H. Mapes Co.,

New York, N.Y., 1923-25; prof. business adminstrn., Bucknell U., Lewisburg, Pa., since 1925; dir. and vice pres. Lewisburg Nat. Bank. Mem. Lambda Chi Alpha, Odd Fellow. Home: Lewisburg, Pa. *

MAU, HAVETH ELMER (MOU), lawyer; b. Dayton, O., July 4, 1886; s. Julius Frederick and Martha Matilda (Gronman) M; ed. high sch., Wittenberg Coll. (Springfield, O.) and Ohio Northern U. (non-grad.); m. Louise Caverley, Apr. 25, 1911. Admitted to Ohio bar, 1907, and began practice at Dayton; pros. atty., Montgomery County, O., 1919-22; 1st asst. U.S. atty., 1923-25; U.S. dist. atty. Southern Dist. of Ohio, by apptmt. of President Coolidge, 1925-33; in practice at Cincinnati since 1933, also at N.Y. City since 1935; vice president of Pinnacle, Inc., Dayton, O. Mem. Am., Ohio State and Montgomery County bar assns., Federal Bar Assn. Republican. Episcopalian. Club: Metropolitan (N.Y.). Home: Cincinnati. *

MAUCH, HANS RUDOLF (FRACK), ice skater; b. Basel, Switzerland, May 2, 1919; s. Karl Otto and Emilie (Schaffner) M.; ed. Basel pub. schs.; student bus. coll., 1935-37; m. Mary M. Elchlepp, Jan. 13, 1944; children—Marlies K. (Mrs. Glen Smith), Jennie J., Michael S. Debut with Frick and Frack team Patria Ice Show, Brighton, Eng., 1937, then with Ice Ballet, London, Eng., 1937; appeared ice show, Los Angeles, 1938; with Ice Follies, 1939-53; appeared in motion pictures Silver Skates, 1942, Lady Let's Dance, 1943; tchr. ice skating, Los Angeles, 1953-55. Home: Long Beach, Calif. Died 1975.

MAULE, HARRY EDWARD (MAWL), editor; b. Fairmont, Neb., July 13, 1886; s. John Penrose and Mary Katherine (Finigan) M.; ed. common schs. and E. Denver High Sch.; m. Edna J. O'Dell, July 12, 1910; 1 dau., Katherine E. Reporter Denver and N.Y. City, 1903-05; corr. and feature writer in Mexico, 1906-07, mgr. of N.Y., Boston, Detroit, New Haven burs., United Press Assn., 1907-11; editor book dept. Doubleday, Page & Co., v.p. and editor book dept. Doubleday, Doran & Co. to June 1939; now with Random House, Inc., book pubs.; trustee Village of Garden City, 1942-47. Member Authors League America. Episcopalian. Clubs: Century Association (New York); Dutch Treat, Cherry Valley. Editor: A Book of War Letters, 1943, Great Tales of the American West, Modern Library, 1945, The Pocket Book of Western Stories. Pocket Books, 1945. Author: Boys' Book of New Inventions, 1912. Co-editor: The Man From Main Street: A Sinclair Lewis Reader, 1953. Contbr. to mags. Home: 108 Arthur St., Garden City, N.Y. Address: N.Y.C. *

MAURAULT, JEAN LEON OLIVIER (MOR-RO'), clergyman; b. Sorel, P.Q., Can., Jan. 1, 1886; s. Elie and Lucie (Boucher) M.; B.A., Coll. of Montreal, 1906; B.Th., Grand Sem. of Montreal, 1910; student Issyles-Moulineaux, 1911; joined Soc. St. Sulpice; student Inst. Catholique of Paris, 1911-13; hon. LL.D., Ottawa Univ., 1935, LL.D., McGill Univ., 1936, Litt.D., Laval Univ., 1937; D.C.L., Bishop University, 1938; LL.D., University of Manitoba, Canada, 1948. Ordained priest Roman Cath. Ch., July 1910 prof. Coll. Montreal, 1913-15; vicar St. James of Montreal, 1915-26; parish priest Notre Dame, Montreal 1926-29; superior Andre Grasset Coll., Montreal, 1929-34; rector Univ. of Montreal since 1934; Roman Prelate, 1937. Decorated: Officer of Public Instruction, Officer of Black Star (France); medals of the Jubilee of George V, of Coronation of George VI, Companion Order of St. Michael and St. George, 1943 (Eng.); Officer of Latin Order; Comdr. of the Order Honours and Merits (Haiti); Comdr. de l'Ordre du Libérateur San Martin, 1948; Kornmann Médaille of l'Académie Francaise, 1948; Maître ès jeux floraux, Toulouse, France, 1949. Member Royal Society of Can. (pres. 1943), Hist. Soc. Montreal (pres. since 1941), Soc. Canadian Writers (pres. 1944-46), Group of Ten (ten historians), Prior to chapter body of the Holy Sepulchre. Author: Le Petit Seminaire de Montreal, 1918: Saint-Jacques de Montreal, 1923; Saint-Francois d' Assise de la Longue-Pointe, 1924; Brievetes, 1928; Marges d'histoire, 1929-30; (3 vols.); La Paroisse, 1929; Centenaire de Notre-Dame, 1929; Nos Messieurs, 1936; French-Canadian Backgrounds (in collaboration), 1940; Propos et Portraits, 1941; Moisson de Ville-Marie, 1943; Aux Louisianais, 1943; Le Mexique de mes Souvenirs, 1945; M. Henri Gauthier, prÊtre Saint Sulpice, 1945; Par voies et par chemins de l'air, 1947; L'ecole Polytechnique, 1948. Home: Montreal. *

MAURIOCOURT, FLORY, former r.r. ofcl.; b. Weston, W.Va., Nov. 29, 1906; s. Florimond and Ida (Delwarte) M.; ed. pub. schs.; m. Mary Constance Coleman, Feb. 4, 1933 (dec. Oct. 1964); 1 dau., Patricia Ann (Mrs. Patricia M. McGovern); m. 2d, Grace Harriet Mackenzie, 1966. With A.T. & S.F. Ry., 1924-69, asst. gen. auditor, 1957-64, v.p., gen. auditor, 1964-68, v.p. information systems, 1968-69; dir. Lake Hinsdale Village Condominium J-A Corp. Mem. Assn. Am. Railroads. Home: Clarendon Hills, Ill. Died Oct. 12, 1977.

MAURY, REUBEN, editorial cons.; b. Butte, Mont., Sept. 2, 1899; s. Henry Lowndes and Anne Henderson (Perkins) M.; LL.B., U. Va., 1924, J.D., 1970; m. Thomasine Lafayette Rose, July 21, 1928. Admitted to Mont. bar, 1923; mem. firm Maury & Maury, Butte, 1923-26; reporter N.Y. Daily News, 1926, movie critic, 1926, chief editorial writer, 1926-72, editorial cons., 1973-81. Mem. S.A.T.C., U. Va., 1918. Decorated Order Brilliant Star, Taiwan (Republic of China), 1972. Recipient Pulitzer Prize for editorials printed in 1940, also Christopher editorial award, 1954; award Assembly Captive European Nations, 1965; George Sokolsky award Am. League Against Communism, 1965; Freedoms Found. at Valley Forge editorial honor certificate, 1973. Mem. Beta Theta Pi, Sigma Delta Chi, Silurian Soc. Club: Dutch Treat (N.Y.). Roman Catholic. Author: The Wars of the Godly: The Story of Religious Conflict in America, 1928; Americans to Remember, 1958; (with Karl G. Pfeiffer) Effective Editorial Writing, 1960; What Made the U.S. Great, 1968. Contbr. articles, short stories, editorials, etc., to Collier's Weekly, Woman's Home Companion, Red Book, Blue Book, Old Scribners, Old American Mercury, Liberty, Adventure, Sea Stories, Chicago Tribune-N.Y. News Blue Ribbon Fiction Features. Address: Saugatuck, Conn. Died Apr. 23, 1981; buried Willowbrook Cemetery, Westport, Conn.

MAVOR, JAMES WATT (MA'VÛR), prof. biology; b. Glasgow, Scotland, Dec. 13, 1883; s. James and Christina Gordon Balfour (Watt) M.; King's Coll., London, 1901-02; B.A., Cambridge U., Eng., 1905; M.A., Harvard U., 1910; student U. of Munich, 1911-12; Ph.D., Harvard U., 1913; m. Dorothy Jessup, Aug. 25, 1921; children—James Watt, Huntington Mavor. Came to U.S., 1907, naturalized citizen, 1924. Began as teacher, 1906; lecturer in science and mathematics, King's Coll., Can., 1906-07; instr. zoölogy, Syracuse U., 1910-11; teaching fellow, Harvard U., 1912-13; curator Biol. Station, Georgian Bay, Can., 1913; instr. zoölogy, U. of Wis., 1913-16; curator Marine Biol. Station, St. Andrews, Can., 1914; asst. prof. Union Coll., New York, 1916-21, asso. prof., 1921-24, prof., 1924-45, research prof., 1945-49. Awarded Warren Triennial Prize, Mass. Gen. Hosp., 1922; Leonard Prize, Am. Soc. Roentgenology, 1923. Member A.A.A.S., Am. Assn. Anatomists, American Physiol, Soc., Am. Soc. Naturalists, Am. Soc. Zoölogists. Marine Biol. Assn. Club: Harvard Faculty. Author: General Biology, 1936; General Biology, 3d edit., 1947; Laboratory Exercises in General Biology, 1942; A Brief Biology, 1948; A Lab. Manual for a Brief Course in Biology, 1948. Contbr. to scientific periodicals. Home: Cambridge, Mass. and (summer) Woods Hole, Mass. *

MAY, CLARENCE E(ARL), univ. prof.; b. Bloomington, Ind., Mar. 3, 1884; s. John L. and Estella (McCollough) M.; A.B., Ind. U., 1904, A.M., 1905; Ph.D., Columbia, 1908; m. Frederica Kirby, Sept. 3, 1914; children—Elizabeth, Margarellon, Charles. Inst., Indiana U., 1904-06, asst. prof. 1908-12, asso. prof. 1912-26, prof. organic chemistry since 1926; mem. com. for selection of new dean of Coll. Liberal Arts, Indiana U. 1944; abstrator for Chemical Abstracts 1908. Served with S.A.T.C., Co. 20, Fort Sheridan, 1918. Mem. Am. Chem. Soc., Sigma Xi (pres. Ind. U. chapter 1935), Alpha Chi Sigma, Phi Lambda Upsilon. Author: System of Organic Chemistry, 1949; also various papers publ. in chem. jours. Home: Bloomington, Ind. *

MAY, H(AROLD) CAMERON, surgeon; b. Ottawa, Can., Mar. 22, 1883: s. George and Sarah Elizabeth (Hibbard) M.; grad. Los Angeles High Sch., 1902; M.D., Hahnemann Med. Coll. of Pacific, San Francisco, 1907; m. Alice Gertrude Hammond, of Decatur, Ill., Sept. 2, 1910. Interne County Hosp., San Francisco, 1906-7; emergency and police surgeon subsequent to San Francisco fire; removed to Los Angeles, 1909; chief surgeon, Mutual Hosp. Assn., 1909. Member Am. Inst. Homoeopathy, Cal. State, Southern Cal. and Los Angeles Co. Homoe. socs., Phi Alpha Gamma, Hahnemannian Soc. Clubs: Gamut, Knickerbocker, Union League. Home: Los Angeles. *

MAY, HERBERT GORDON, clergyman, educator; b. Fair Haven, Vt., Dec. 26, 1904; s. Charles Leon and Mabel Maria (Cottrill) M.; A.B., Wesleyan U., 1927; A.M., U. Chgo. Div. Sch., 1929, Ph.D., 1931; B.D., Chgo. Theol. Sem., 1930; D.D., Wesleyan U., 1952; L.H.D., Oberlin Coll., 1976; m. Helen Isabelle Porter, Feb. 11, 1928 (dec. Nov. 1977); children—Gola Joyce Kina, Helen Emily. Minister, First Congregational Ch., Melvin, Ill., 1928-29; fellow Oriental Inst., U. of Chgo., 1930-31, traveling fellow, epigrapher Megiddo Expdn., Haifa, Palestine, 1931-34; faculty Oberlin (Ohio) Coll., 1934-70, emeritus, 1970-77, Distinguished vis. prof. religion, 1972-73; asso. prof. Old Testament lang. and Lit., 1938-46, prof., 1946-67; prof. O.T., Oberlin College and Vanderbilt U. Div. Sch., 1967-70; vis. prof. O.T., Yale Div. Sch., 1970-71. Lectr. Summer Sch. for Clergy, Macdonald Coll., Quebec, Can., 1938; Carew lectr. Hartford Theol. Sem., 1939; tchr. Garrett Bible Inst., summer, 1947, Union Theol. Sem., summer 1952, 56, 59; lectr. Am. Sch. Oriental Research, Jerusalem, 1960; Crozer lectr. Crozer Theol. Sem., 1950; hon. asso. Am. Sch. Oriental Research, Jerusalem, 1966-67. Vice-chmn. Standard Bible Com. Blatchford fellow Chgo. Theol. Sem., 1930. Mem. Am. Soc. for Study of Religion, Am. Oriental Soc. (v.p. Mid-west br. 1940-41, 46-47). Soc. Bibl. Lit. and Exegesis (nat. pres: 1961-62), Am. Oriental Soc. (pres. Mid-West br., 1947-48), Archeol. Inst. Am., Am. Acad. Religion, Nat. Assn. Profs. of Hebrew, World Union Jewish Studies, Internat. Orgn. for Studo O.T., Phi Beta Kappa. Conglist. Rotarian. Author: Material Remains of the Megiddo Cult, 1935; Culture and Conscience (with W.C. Graham), 1936; Remapping the Bible World (with C.C. McCown), 1949; Our English Bible in the Making, 1952; Introduction and Exegesis of Ezekiel (Interpreter's Bible), 1956; also work on 3 vols. publs. by Oriental Inst. of U. Chgo. (Vols. 32, 33, 42); articles in numerous prof. jours. Editorial bd. Jour. Religious Edn., 1948-56, Vetus Testamentum, 1959-72; O.T. book rev. editor Jour. Bibl. Lit., 1948-52; co-editor Oxford Bible Atlas, New Oxford Annotated Bible, 1973; asso. editor Interpreter's Dictionary of the Bible; editor maps Nelson Bibles, 1953; editor Abingdon Maps of Bible Lands, 1966. Home: Jacksonville, Fla. Died Oct. 3, 1977; buried Westwood Cemetery, Oberlin, Ohio.

MAY, KENNETH OWNSWORTH, mathematician, historian, educator; b. Portland, Oreg., July 8, 1915; s. Samuel C. and Eleanor (Parkin) M.; A.B. with highest honors in Math., U. Calif., Berkeley, 1936, M.A., 1937, Ph.D., 1946; postgrad. U. London, 1937-38, U. Paris, 1938-39; m. Miriam Dyer-Bennett, Nov. 2, 1963. Fellow, Inst. Current World Affairs, 1937-38; instr. U. Study Center, Florence, Italy, 1945; asst. to asso. prof. Carleton Coll., 1946-52, chmn. dept. math., 1951-61, prof., 1952-66; prof. math. U. Toronto (Ont., Can.), 1966-77, dir. Inst. for History and Philosophy of Sci. and Tech., 1973-75; lectr., U. Minn., 1947, 61, Okla. A. and M. Coll., 1948, Iowa State Tchrs. Coll., U. Mich., 1956; vis. lectr. Math. Assn. Am., 1962-67; research mathematician U. Calif., Berkeley, 1964-66; research cons. Cowles Commn., 1946-47; cons. Internat. Milling Co., 1950-54. Served to 2d lt. AUS, 1942-45. Fund for Advancement Edn. fellow, 1953-54; NSF Sci. Faculty fellow, 1962-64; Killam fellow Can. Council, 1971-73. Fellow AAAS; mem. Math. Assn. Am. (gov. 1953-56, 64-66), Inst. Current World Affairs (gov.), Internat. Union for History and Philosophy Sci. (chmn. commn. on history math. 1968-77), Internat. Acad. History Sci. (corr.). Club: Sierra (co-founder rock climbing sect.) (San Francisco). Author: Elementary Analysis, 1952; Elements of Modern Mathematics, 1959; Bibliography and Research Manual of the History of Mathematics, 1973. Asso. editor Econometrica, 1951-53, Am. Math. Monthly, 1963-70, Archive for History Exact Sci., 1972-75, Internat. Jour. Math. Edn. in Sci. and Tech., from 1972, Jour. Undergrad. Math., 1970-77; editor Delta Epsilon, 1960-66, Historia Mathematica, 1972-77; contbr. articles to math., econ. and hist. jours. Address: Toronto, Ont., Canada. Died Dec. 1, 1977.

MAY, ORVILLE EDWARD, chemist; b. New Albin, Iowa, Aug. 22, 1901; s. George Burton and Frances Margaret (Dailey) M.; student Loras Coll., 1918-20, U. Minn., 1920-23; A.B., George Washington U., 1924, M.S., 1926, Ph.D., 1929; m. Katherine Marie Barrett, Oct. 27, 1926; children—Elaine Marie, George Barrett. Research chemist on fermentation U.S. Dept. Agr., Washington, 1923-36, dir. U.S. Regional Soybean Lab., developing wider uses for soybeans at U. Ill., Urbana, 1936-39, dir. U.S. No. Regional Research Lab., Peoria, Ill., 1939-42, coordinator for chem. research U.S. Dept. Agr., Washington, 1942-44, chief Bur. Agrl. and Indsl. Chemistry, U.S. Dept. Agr., 1944-46; tech. exec. Coca-Cola Co., Atlanta, 1946-48, v.p., tech. dir., 1948-66. Bd. regents Loras Coll., 1965-67, hon. life mem., 1972-81. Recipient Alumni Achievement award George Washington U., 1962; gold medal award Am. Inst. Chemists, 1968. Hon. life mem. Am. Inst. Chemists, AAAS; mem. Am. Chem. Soc. (emeritus), Inst. Food Technologists (emeritus), Sigma Xi, Alpha Chi Sigma, Phi Lambda Upsilon. Clubs: Cosmos (Washington); Capital City (Atlanta). Home: Marietta, Ga. Died Apr. 3, 1981.

MAYER, ARTHUR L., author, educator; b. Demopolis, Ala., May 28, 1886; s. Simon and Rachel (Bernheim) M.; A.B., Harvard, 1907; L.H.D., 1972; m. Lillie Stein, May 16, 1931; children—Peter A., Michael F., Nora Simon. Dir. publicity, advt. and exploitation Paramount Pictures, 1930-33; operator Rialto Theatre, N.Y.C., 1933-48; asst. coodinator, treas. War Activities Com., Motion Picture Industry, 1942-46; film cons. to sec. war, 1943-46; pres. Mayer-Burstyn Film Corp., 1933-50; exec. v.p. Council Motion Picture Orgns. 1950-52; pres. Mayer-Kingsley 1950-54; dir. advt. and publicity Paramount Pictures Corp., 1956; guest lectr. Brandeis U., 1961-62; Instr. cinema Dartmouth, U. So. Cal., Stanford, 1964-75. Chmn. exec. com. Will Rogers Meml. Hosp., 1953; dep. commr. A.R.C., Pacific Ocean Area, 1944-45, asst. to chmn. European Theatre, 1945-46; chief motion picture br. info. control div. OMGUS (Army), 1948-49. Recipient medal of merit, 1947. Pres. Ind. Motion Pictures Distbrs. Assn., 1951-57. Author: Merely Colossal, 1953; The Movies, 1957. Address: New York City NY.

MAYER, HERBERT CARLETON, educator; b. Chgo., Nov. 6, 1893; s. Frank Edward and Ella M. (Knecht) M.; A.B., Oberlin Coll., 1915; A.M., Boston

U., 1923, Ed.D., Harvard U., 1940; m. Elsie Hauser, Mar. 19, 1919 (dec. Dec. 1965); children—Jane (Mrs. Shovell), Herbert C., Ann (Mrs. W.W. Wattman); m. 2d, Muriel L. Howard, Nov. 6, 1968. Reporter, Cleve. Press, 1914-15; supt. secondary div. Chgo. Council of Religious Edn., 1916-17, Ohio Council of Religious Edn., 1919-20; prof. secondary edn., Boston U., 1920-29; dir. tng., Curtiss-Wright Flying Service, 1928-30; pres. Aeronautical Service, Inc., 1930-34, A.D.M. Corp. 1931-45, Avite Products, Inc., 1932-37; instr. aeronautical engring., Northeastern U., Boston, 1931-39; guidance dir. Bentley Sch. of Acctg., 1939-40; v.p. Council for Democracy, N.Y., 1940-42; pres. Parsons Coll., Fairfield, Iowa, 1941-47; specialist in higher edn. U.S. Office Edn., 1947; Quadri partite Policy Officer, Office Mil. Govt., U.S., Berlin, 1947-48; pres. Am. Viewpoint, 1949-73, cons., 1973-78. Served as pilot with rank of 2d lt., U.S. Army Air Service, 1917-18. Founder and dir., Summer Camp Conf., Internat. Sunday Sch. Assn., and Am. Youth Found.; mem. adv. council Nat. Planning Assn.; dir. Lincoln Ednl. Found., 1969; Manhattan Borough Com. N.Y.C. Youth Bd., 1959-64; hon. marshall Oberlin Coll., 1965; co-chmn. All German-Am. Heritage Conf., 1970; chmn. bd. dirs. German Am. Council. Recipient Medallion of Space and Rocketry German-Am. Nat. Congress for Most Outstanding German-Am. Post-War era, 1970. Mem. NEA, Nat. Council Social Studies, Adult Edn. Assn., Am. Legion, Phi Delta Kappa, Phi Kappa Phi. Presbyterian. Clubs: Rotary (pres. 1945-46), Masons. Author: The Church Program for Young People, 1925; Community Youth Councils, 1927; Introduction to Aeronautics, 1930; New Footprints of the Trojan Horse, 1952; Young People in Your Church, 1953; Toward the Prevention of Juvenile Crime, 1954; Who? Me?, 1954; Diplomacy and World Security, 1960; (with Ruth F. Towne) The Good American Program-The Direct Teaching of Citizenship Values in the Elementary Grades; German Recovery and the Marshall Plan, 1969. Editor: Manual for Flying Instructors, 1929. Contbr. to aviation and edn. mags. Home: Springfield, Mass. Died Feb. 7, 1978; buried Ferncliff Cemetery, Hartsdale, N.Y.

MAYNARD, A. ROGERS, fin. exec.; b. South Sudbury, Mass., Nov. 5, 1907; s. Henry T. and Bessie (Rogers) M.; B.A., Harvard, 1930; m. Olive Fisher, Sept. 17, 1928; children—Joyce (Mrs. Thomas Bagg) (dec.), Deborah (Mrs. G. Brenton Creelman III), Thomas F., John R. With Met. Life Ins. Co., 1930-77, 2d v.p., 1953-63, v.p. field mgmt., 1963-65, sr. v.p., 1965-70; pres. Boston Group Inc., 1971-77. Chmn. life ins. industry com. careers for coll. grads. Life Ins. Agy. Mgmt. Assn., 1956-62, chmn. agy. officers round table, 1962-63, chmn. relations with univs. com., 1955-57; pres. Buffalo Life Underwriters, 1941-42. C.L.U. Mem. Nat. Assn. Life Underwriters, Am. Coll. Life Underwriters. Republican. Clubs: Harvard (Boston, N.Y.C.); Cummaquid Golf (Mass.). Home: Yarmouth Port, Mass. Died Dec. 27, 1977; buried Sutton, Mass.

MAYNARD, GILBERT P., educator, accountant; b. Indianola, Iowa, Jan. 2, 1917; s. Gilbert Perry and Christine (Staats) M.; B.S., Simpson Coll., 1936; M.B.A., U. Mich., 1939; Ph.D., U. Iowa, 1951; m. Barbara Jeanne Gilchrist, Feb. 28, 1942; children—Terrill Davisson, Marcia Jeanne. Asst., Simpson Coll., 1936-37; accountant Briggs & Iceman, C.P.A.'s Ann Arbor, Mich., 1939-41; instr. accounting U. Mo., 1940-41; instr. accounting U. Iowa, 1941-42, asst. prof., 1946-49, lectr., 1949-51, asso. prof., 1951-57, head dept., 1955-64, prof. accounting, 1957-73; cost accountant OPA, Washington, 1942-43. Served from ensign to lt., USNR, 1943-46. C.P.A., Iowa. Mem. Am. Inst. C.P.A.'s, Am. Accounting Assn. (v.p. 1959), Iowa Soc. C.P.A.'s, Nat. Assn. Accountants, Delta Upsilon, Epsilon Sigma, Beta Gamma Sigma, Alpha Kappa Psi, Beta Alpha Psi, Omicron Delta Epsilon. Mason. Rotarian. Co-author: Elementary Accounting, 1956; Intermediate Accounting, 1958. Contbr. articles profl. jours. Home: Iowa City, Iowa. Died Dec. 10, 1977; interred Memory Gardens, Iowa City.

MAYNE, WALTER R., lawyer; b. St. Louis, Jan. 20, 1893; s. Adolph F. and Bertha L. (Holthaus) M.; LL.B., Benton Coll. Law, 1915; m. Helene Balliett, Apr. 24, 1923; 1 dau., Margaret Manson (Mrs. James A. Kridel). Admitted to Mo. bar, 1914; practiced in St. Louis, 1914-75; sr. mem. Fordyce, Mayne, Hartman, Renard & Stribling. Dir. Champ Spring Co., Champ Fin. & Investment Co., Measuregraph Co., Edmu Realty Co. Mayor, Ladue, Mo., 1928, councilman, 1935-56, mem. sch. bd., 1929-33. Served with U.S. Army, 1917-19, with 103 U.S. Inf., 26th Div., AEF, 1918-19. Fellow Am. Coll. Trial Lawyers; mem. Internat. Assn. Ins. Counsel (past pres.), Am., Mo. (past pres.), St. Louis (past pres.) bar assns., Am. Legion (past post comdr.), Phi Delta Phi. Presbyterian. Clubs: University, Mo. Athletic (past pres.), Noonday, Old Warson Country, Clayton, Media, Masons (32 deg.). Home: Clayton, Mo. Died Dec. 3, 1975; buried St. Louis.

MAYO, ARTHUR H., naval officer; b. Ottawa, Ont., Can., June 9, 1884 (Am. parents); s. Warren Spear and Ella (Fuller) M.; student Ottawa Collegiate Inst., 1898-99; Army and Navy Acad., 1911; m. Geraldine Anna Faust, Mar. 8, 1915. Tally clk. Export Lumber Co., 1899. Entered Navy, 1911; promoted through grades to rear adm., Supply Corps, 1942; shore duty in Samoa, Santo Domingo, New York, Washington, San Diego, Oakland; retired. Decorations: World War Medal (Atlantic Fleet clasp), Legion of Merit, Expeditionary Medal, World War II medal, Mem. S.A.R. Mason. Clubs: Army and Navy (Washington, D.C.); Army and Navy Country (Arlington, Va.); New York Athletic; Chevy Chase. Home: Coronado, Calif. *

MAYO, BERNARD, historian; b. Lewiston, Me., Feb. 13, 1902; s. Frank Harry and Margaret (Donovan) M.; student U. Me., 1920-22; A.B., George Washington U., 1924, A.M., 1925; Ph.D., Johns Hopkins, 1931; m. Margaret McClure Macleod, 1952. Asso. prof. history Nat. U. (merged with George Washington U. 1954), 1926-27, prof. Am. history, 1927-37, dean sch. econs., 1929-33; lectr. Am. U., 1928-29, lectr. in history Grad. Sch., 1936; prof. Am. history Grad. Sch., Georgetown U., 1937-40; prof. Am. history U. Va., 1940-80; summer teaching George Washington U., 1940, Columbia, 1946, U. Mo., 1961; vis. prof. history, Harvard, 1946-47; Lamar Meml. lectr. Mercer U., Macon, Ga., 1958; Thomas Jefferson scholar U. Va. 1962-63. Recipient Alumni Achievement award George Washington U., 1943. Mem. Am., So. (exec. council 1941-44, editorial bd. jour. 1944-47), Miss. Valley hist. assns., Va. Social Sci. Assn. (exec. council 1954-57, v.p. 1959-60, pres. 1960-61), Soc. Am. Historians, Albemarle County Hist. Soc., Raven Soc., Phi Beta Kappa, Kappa Sigma, Pi Delta Epsilon (hon.), Omicron Delta Kappa. Club: Colonnade. Author: Henry Clay, Spokesman of the New West, 1937; Jefferson and the Way of Honor, 1951. Editor (for Am. Hist. Assn.); Instructions to the British Ministers to the United States, 1791-1812, 1941; Thomas Jefferson and His Unknown Brother Randolph, 1942; Jefferson Himself; The Personal Narrative of a Many-Sided American, 1942; Myths and Men; Patrick Henry, George Washington, Thomas Jefferson, 1959. Mem. adv. com. for publ. Papers of Thomas Jefferson, 1943-80. Home: Charlottesville, Va. Died Aug. 20, 1979.

MAYO, BRAXTON DAVIS, coll. prof.; b. Shenandoah, Va., May 24, 1884; s. Stephen Lacy and Anna (Davis) M.; B.S., Va. Mil. Inst., 1909; m. Jennie Ludwell Earnest, June 29, 1918; 1 dau., Sarah Elizabeth (Mrs. Louis Bruno Sohn). Asst. prof. mathematics, Va. Mil. Inst., 1910-16, adj. prof., 1917-19, asso. prof., 1920-24, prof., 1925-31), and head dept. of mathematics 1931-54, ret. 1954. Home: Lexington, Va. *

MAYO, EARL EDMUND, engineer; b. Springfield, Mo., Sept. 13, 1885; s. Jacob Tipton and Jennie (McKinney) M; B.S., U. Ore., 1909; m. Edith Shannon, Mar. 15, 1915; 1 dau., Barbara (Mrs. Robert C. Schulze). Rodman S.P. Co., 1907-08, instrumentman, 1908-09, resident engr., 1909-13, roadmaster, 1913-20, asst. div. engr., div. engr., 1920-23, constrn. engr., 1923-34, asst. chief engr., 1934-44, chief engr. since 1944; chief engr. Central Pacific Ry. Co., San Diego & Ariz. Eastern Ry. Co., Northwestern Pacific Ry. Co.; v.p. So. Pacific Pipe Lines, Inc., 1955—. Mem. Am. Soc. C.E., Am. R.R. Engring. Assn., Seismol. Soc. Am., Phi Gamma Delta. Home: San Francisco. *

MAYOR, A. HYATT, former museum curator; b. Gloucester, Mass., June 28, 1901; s. Alfred Goldsborough and Harriet (Hyatt) M.; A.B., Princeton, 1922; B.Litt., (Rhodes scholar), Oxford U., 1926; student Am. Sch. Classical Studies, 1926-27; m. Virginia Sluder, June 22, 1932; children—Alfred, Martha. Tchr. history of art Vassar Coll., 1922-23; tchr. sch. Am. Lab. Theatre N.Y.C., 1927-31; co-editor Hound and Horn, 1929-32; staff dept. prints Met. Mus. Art, N.Y.C., 1932-66, curator prints, 1946-66. Trustee Instituto de Valencia de Don Juan, Madrid, Brookgreen Gardens, Georgetown, S.C., Sorolla Mus, Madrid; hon. fellow Morgan Library, N.Y.C. Recipient Boston Mus. award, 1971. Mem. Am. Fedn. Arts (trustee), Hispanic Soc. Am. (pres. 1955-80), Real Acad. de Bellas Artes, Madrid, Real Academia de Santa Isabel de Hungria, Seville. Clubs: Grolier; Century Assn. (N.Y.C.). Author: The Bibiena Family, 1945; Baroque and Romantic Stage Design, 1950; Giovanni Battista Piranesi, 1952; Prints and People, 1971; Popular Prints of the Americas, 1973; 67 Goya Drawings, 1974; American Art in the Century Association, 1976. Contbr. articles mus. bulls., mags. Home: New York, N.Y. Died Feb. 28, 1980.

MAYROSE, HERMAN EVERETT, cons. engr.; b. Terre Haute, Ind., Feb. 18, 1893; s. Henry David and Myra Louise (Killon) M.; B.S., Rose Polytech. Inst., Terre Haute, Ind., 1915, M.E., 1935; M.S.E., U. Mich., 1932; m. Ina Maud Smith, Sept. 14, 1915 (dec. Oct. 5, 1915); m. 2d, Hazel Ursula Guirl, June 19, 1919 (dec. June 19, 1962); m. 3d, Mabel Agnes Guirl, July 18, 1963. Began as engineering apprentice and tool designer Ingersoll Milling Machine Co., Rockford, Ill., 1915-17, 19-21; dir. dept. engring. drawing U. Detroit, 1921-40, prof. and chmn. dept. engring. mechanics, 1927-64; cons. engr. exptl. stress analysis, 1964-79. Vol., ARC, 1969-79. Served as cpl., Co. H., 129th U.S. Inf., U.S. Army, A.E.F., 1917-19. Mem. ASME, Engring. Soc. Detroit. Methodist. Author: Engineering Mechanics Laboratories, 1950. Contbr. Design Data Sheets, ASME. Address: Mobile, Ala. Died Aug. 15, 1979; interred Pine Crest Cemetery, Mobile.

MAZUR, PAUL MYER, investment banking; b. Boston, Dec. 9, 1892; s. Louis and Eva (Siskin) Mazur; A.B., Harvard, 1914; D.C.S., N.Y. U., 1960; L.H.D., Rutgers U., 1961; m. Adolphia Kaske, June 21, 1922; children—Peter, Ann. Partner of Lehman Bros., investment bankers, N.Y.C., 1927-69, ltd. partner, 1969-79; vis. prof. investment banking Wharton Sch., 1965-67. With AUS, 1917-19. Recipient Tobe award for contbn. to nation's system of distbn. Clubs: Harvard, Lotos, Wall Street (New York). Author: Principles of Organization Applied to Modern Retailing, 1927; American Prosperity, 1928; America Looks Abroad, 1930; New Roads to Prosperity, 1931; The Standards We Raise, 1953; The Dynamics of Economic Growth, 1965; Unfinished Business: A Banker Looks at the Economy, 1973. Home: New York, N.Y. Died July 30, 1979.

MCAFEE, ALMER MCDUFFIE (MAK'A-FÉ), chem. engr.; b. Navarro Co., Tex., Sept. 24, 1886; s. Cicero and Margaret (Terry) McA.; B.A., U. of Tex., 1908; Ph.D., Columbia, 1911; married Marguerite Calfee, January 11, 1916; children—Jerry, Marguerite, Jack. With Gulf Oil Corporation as a chemical engineer since 1913; discovered the action of aluminum chloride on petroleum hydrocarbons, 1912, introduced same in petroleum refining, 1915, began mfr. of same from Bauxite on large scale, 1918, and greatly expanded its mfr. and use, 1924; announced its availability at 5 cents per pound, 1929, stimulating its use in the dye and other industries; holder of some 50 U.S. patents. Mem. bd. edn. Port Arthur pub. schs., 1931-41 (chmn. 1934-41); mem. council U. of Tex. Ex Students Assn. since 1941 (pres. 1941-43); mem. U. of Tex. Development Bd. since 1948; chmn. bd. of regents Lamar State Coll. of Technology. Mem. Am. Chem. Soc., Am. Inst. Chem. Engrs., Sigma Xi. Democrat. Presbyterian. Mason (K.T., Shriner). Club: Rotary (pres. 1938-39). Work on aluminum chloride listed by Chem. and Metall. Engring. in Chronology of Scientific Achievements; listed in Indsl. and Engring. Chemistry as one of 37 notable Am. Chem. inventors. Address: Port Arthur, Tex. *

MCAFEE, HELEN, editor; b. New Milford, Conn., June 1, 1884; d. William and Flora (Ackley) McAfee; A.B., Smith Coll., 1903, A.M., 1915, L.H.D., 1935; A.M. honoris causa, Yale, 1944, Teacher of English, Miss Johnstone's Sch., New Haven, Conn., 1904-08; head of English dept., Constantinople (Turkey) Coll. for Women, 1909-12; asst. editor The Yale Review, 1913-20, associate editor, 1920-24, mng. editor, 1924-50. Mem. Phi Beta Kappa, P.E.N. Club (New York). Club: Faculty (New Haven). Editor: Pepys on the Restoration Stage, 1916; Yale Review Anthology (with Wilbur L. Cross), 1942. Home: New Haven (Yale Station), Conn. *

MCAFEE, LARRY BENJAMIN, army med. officer; born Delphi, Ind., July 3, 1883; s. Delano Benjamin and Mary Lanphear (Ryan) McA.; M.D., George Washington U., 1906; student Army Med. Sch., 1909-10, Army Industrial Coll., 1925, Army War Coll., 1929-30; m. Marjorie Deshon, July 7, 1911 (dec.); children—Marjorie, George Deshon. Began practice of medicine, 1906; entered Med. Corps, U.S. Army, Sept. 1, 1909; promoted through grades to brig. gen., March 1942; retired Nov. 1946. Decorated-French Legion of Honor, Medaille des Epidemie, Legion of Merit, Distinguished Service medal, Victory medal. Fellow Am. Coll. Surgeons; mem. A.M.A., Assn. Mil. Surgeons, Alpha Kappa Kappa. Presbyterian, Clubs: Army and Navy Country (Washington); Denver Country. Address: Denver. *

MCATEE, WALDO LEE (MAK'A-TE), biologist; b. Jalapa, Grant County, Ind., Jan. 21, 1883; s. John Henry and Anna (Morris) M.; grad. high sch., Marion, Ind., 1900; A.B., Ind. U., 1904, A.M., 1906; m. Fannie Eldridge Lawson, Sept. 13, 1906 (divorced, 1939); children—Alice Elfrida, Robert Bruce. Curator of Mus., Ind. U., 1901-04; asst. biol. expert, U.S. Biol. Survey, 1903, asst. biologist, 1904-16, in charge economic ornithology, 1916-21, in charge food habits research, 1921-34, technical advisor office of chief, 1934-40; tech. adviser U.S. Fish and Wildlife Service since 1940; acting custodian Hemiptera U.S. Nat. Mus., 1920-42. Mem. U.S. Dept. Agr. Com. on Land Utilization, 1922-30. Recipient Distinguished Service Award, Dept. Interior. Fellow Emeritus Am. Ornithologists' Union; mem. Cooper Ornithol. Club, Wilson Ornithol. Club, Entomol. Soc. Washington, Biol. Soc. Washington, Free Thinkers of America, Ind. Acad. of Science, N.E. Bot. Club, Pacific Northwest Bird and Mammalogical Soc., Am. Society of Naturalists, Wildlife Soc. (editor, 1937-42), Am. Biol. Soc., American Dialect Soc., American Folklore Soc., Sigma Xi; hon. mem. Fortean Soc.; corr. mem. Royal Hungarian Ornithological Inst. Club: Washington Biologists' Field Club. Author: A Sketch of the Natural History of the District of Columbia, 1918; Wildfowl Food Plants, 1939; also more than 800 scientific papers, minaly on birds, insects and plants, folklore and dialect articles, and many popular articles. Home: Chicago. *

MCAUSLAND, ROBERT DONALD, bag mfg. exec.; b. Omaha, Neb., Dec. 26, 1883; s. Robert R. and Mary (Lounsbury) McA.; student pub. schs.; m. Orpha Helen Meacham, Nov. 23, 1914; children—Mrs. L. M. Dorn, Donald M., Robert R. With Bemis Bro. Bag Co., 1900—, v.p., 1947—. Clubs: Rainier, Broadmoor Golf. Home: Seattle. *

MCBRIDE, KATHARINE ELIZABETH, educator; b. Phila., 1904; d. Thomas Canning and Sally Hulley (Neals) McBride; A.B., Bryn Mawr Coll., 1925, A.M., 1927, Ph.D., 1932; postgrad. Columbia U., 1928-29. Research in psychology, Phila., 1929-35 (with Dr. Theodore Weisenburg, 1929-34); lectr. in edn. Bryn Mawr (Pa.) Coll., 1935-36, asst. prof. edn. and psychology, 1936-38, asso. prof., 1938-40, pres., 1942-70; dean Radcliffe Coll., Cambridge, Mass., 1940-42; dir. N.Y. Life Ins. Co. Chmn., Montgomery County (Pa.) Commn. on Mental Health and Mental Retardation; bd. dirs. Phila. Savs. Fund Soc.; trustee Rider Coll. Mem. Am. Psychol. Assn., AAUW. Author: (with Theodore Weisenburg) Aphasia, 1935; (with T. Weisenburg and Anne Roe) Adult Intelligence, 1936. Home: Bryn Mawr, Pa. Died Apr. 7, 1976; buried West Shokan, N.Y.

MCBRIDE, MARY MARGARET, writer; b. Paris, Mo., Nov. 16, 1899; d. Thomas Walker and Elizabeth (Craig) McBride; student William Woods Coll., Fulton, Mo., Litt D., 1970; B.J., U. Mo., 1919. Reporter Cleve. Pres, 1919; spl. and feature writer N.Y. Evening Mail, 1920-24; writer for Cosmopolitan, Sat. Eve. Post, Good Housekeeping, other mags., from 1926,; woman's page editor Newspaper Enterprise Assn., N.Y.C., 1934-35, broadcaster as Martha Deane for WOR, 1934-40; radio broadcaster CBS, 1937-41, NBC Sta. WEAF, 1941-50, with ABC, 1950-54, NBC, 1954-60; syndicated newspaper columnist A.P., 1953-56; broadcaster N.Y. Herald Tribune Radio, after 1960. Awarded Women's Nat. Expn. of Arts and Industries medal for greatest contbn. to radio for year, 1936; Wall Paper Inst. medal for outstanding contbn. to stimulation of interest in the home, 1937; U. Mo. award for distinguished service in journalism, 1938; Radio Guide award for distinguished service to radio, 1940, Gov. Mo. proclaimed Nov. 22, 1940, Mary Margaret McBride Day in Mo.; King Haakon Award for war broadcasting, 1946; Distinguished Honor award Haitian Govt.; silver medallion Gov. V.I.; One World Award, 1950; chosen as one of America's Twelve Master Salesmen, 1952. Clubs: Advt. Women N.Y., Overseas Press, Nat. Press Women, N.Y. Newspaper Women's Club, Washington Women's Press Club. Author: (with Paul Whiteman) Jazz: A Story of Paul Whiteman, 1926; (with A. Williams) Charm, 1927; (with Helen Josephy) Paris Is A Woman's Town, 1929; The Story of Dwight Morrow, 1930; (with Helen Josephy) London Is A Man's Town, 1931; (with Helen Josephy) New York Is Everybody's Town, 1931; (with Helen Josephy) Beer and Skittles-A Friendly Modern Guide to Germany, 1932; Here's Martha Deane-presented by Mary Margaret McBride, 1936; How Dear to My Heart, 1940; America for Me, 1941; Tune In for Elizabeth, 1945; Harvest of American Cooking, 1957; A Long Way from Missouri, 1959; Out of the Air, 1960; The Growing Up of Mary Elizabeth, 1968. Winner All-Am. Rose, 1943, named the Mary Margaret McBride in her honor. Home: West Shokan, N.Y. Died Apr. 7, 1976.

MCCABE, THOMAS BAYARD, JR., educator; b. Phila., May 13, 1926; s. Thomas Bayard and Jeanette (Laws) McC.; B.A., Swarthmore Coll., 1949; M.B.A., Harvard, 1954; m. Yvonne Motley, June 18, 1949; children—Thomas Bayard 3d, Marcia Bishop, Jeannette Laws. Asst. to dir. advt. Jewel Tea Co., Inc., Chgo., 1950-52; with Scott Paper Co., 1954-72, dir. advt., 1957-59, dir. mktg. services, 1960, v.p. charge internal mktg., 1961-63, v.p. mktg. dir. 1963-72, group exec., 1965-72, also dir.; pres. Marketing Sci. Inst., Cambridge, Mass., from 1972. Vis. lectr. Harvard Bus. Sch. Dir. Cooper Labs., Inc. Former chmn. bd. Advt. Council. Trustee Phila. Coll. of Art. Mem. Assn. Nat. Advertisers (past chmn. bd., mem. adv. com., past chmn.). Clubs: Nantucket Yacht; Union League (Phila.); Harvard (Phila., N.Y.C. and Boston). Home: Wallingford, Pa. Died Feb. 22, 1977.

MCCABE, WILLIAM GORDON, JR., textile co. exec.; b. Petersburg, Va., July 11, 1911; s. William Gordon and Frances C. (Spicer) McC.; grad. Woodberry Forest Sch., 1930; B.S., U. Va., 1933; m. Lydia Phillips, Apr. 14, 1936; children—Katharine Gordon, Mary Scott. Asso., Am. Cotton Coop. Assn., New Orleans, 1933-36, mgr. Greenville (S.C.) office, 1936-39; partner Donkle & McCabe, Inc., Greenville, 1939-48; dir. raw cotton purchases J.P. Stevens & Co., Greenville, 1948-51, dir. raw cotton and wool policies and procurement, 1951-52, v.p., 1952-76, group v.p., dir.; pres. W. Gordon McCabe & Co., Inc., 1976-79; dir. S.C. Nat. Bank, Columbia, Piedmont & Laurens Ry., Bibb Mfg. Co.; pres. bd. mgrs. N.Y. Cotton Exchange, 1977-79; adviser Nat. Cotton Council, Am. Cotton Shippers; del. Internat. Fedn. Cotton and Allied Textile Industries. Bd. dirs. Greenville County Found., 1959-79; chmn. bd. Greenville Gen. Hosp., 1950-56; chmn. Greenville Community Corp.; trustee Clemson U. Served to lt. (s.g.) USNR, 1943-46. Mem. Am. Textile Mfrs. Inst. (mem. various coms.) Greenville C. of C. Episcopalian. Clubs: Boston (New Orleans); Biltmore Forest Country (Biltmore, N.C.); Poinsett (past pres.), So. Cross, Carolina Yacht (S.C.); Ponte Vedra (Fla.); Cotillion (past pres.), Green Valley Country (dir.) (Greenville); Algonquin. Metropolitan (N.Y.C.); Ocean Reef (Fla.); Soc. of the Cin. of State of Va. Home: Greenville, S.C. Died Aug. 26, 1978; buried Christ Episcopal Ch. Cemetery; Greenville.

MCCAHILL, DAVID IGNATIUS BARTHOLOMEW (MAK-KA'IL), lawyer, ry. official; b. Warren County, Ia., Feb. 25, 1884; s. Matthew and Catherine Josephine (Donovan) McC; LL.B., Drake U., 1907, LL.D., 1931; LL.M., Yale, 1908; grad. study U. of Pittsburgh, 1914; m. Marie Eleanor Kaye, Sept. 9, 1909; children—David Ignatius Bartholomew, Marie Kaye and Marguerite Katherine (twins). Admitted to Ia. bar, 1907, and began practice at Des Moines; moved to San Francisco, Calif., 1908, to Pittsburgh, Pa., 1913; law partner U.S. Senator W. E. Crow, 1916-19; mem. firm David I. McCahill; gen. counsel West Penn. Rys. Co., West Penn Power Co., and affiliated cos., 1913-36; pres. West Penn Power Co., 1916; became owner Pitts., Harmony, Butler & New Castle Ry. Co., Pitts., Mars & Butler Ry. Co., Harmony Electric Co., 1919, pres., gen. counsel, 1919-28; pres., sole owner Pitts., Butler & Harmond Consol. Ry. & Power Co., and successor, Harmony Short Line Ry. Land & Bus Co., Harmony Realty Co. Short Line Land Co., 1919—, Harmony Short Line Motor Transportation Co., 1922—; gen. counsel utility properties of Asso. Gas & Electric Co., 1916-40. Served as apprentice and master-at-arms USN, 1898-1904; in Spanish War, Philippine Insurrection, Boxer Rebellion; capt. inf. Cal. N.G., 1911-13. Trustee Drake U., 1923-41. Trustee Western Penitentiary, 1924-25, treas., 1924, chmn. bd., 1925. Dir. Boys Clubs Am., 1924—; founder, pres. emeritus, dir. Boys Club Pitts. Mem. White House Conf. Child Health and Protection, 1930. Vice pres., mem. bd. Pitts. Symphony Soc., 1927-41. Mem. Delta Theta Phi. Republican. K.C.; grand viceroy Imperial Order Dragon. Clubs: Duquesne, Rotary, Pitts. Field (life), Longue, Pitts. Polo and Riding (Pitts.); Surf, Committee of 100 (Miami Beach, Fla.). Home: Fox Chapel Borough, Pa.; also Miami Beach, Fla. *

MCCAIN, DONALD ROCKEFELLER, business exec.; b. Mt. Pleasant, Pa., July 12, 1885; s. George Nox and Mary Virginia (Overholt) McC.; B.S., Bucknell University, 1905, Doctor of Laws (honorary), 1960; m. Leila Preston, June 4, 1913 (dec. 1955); children—Donald R., Leila P. (Mrs. James Howard Dawson); m. second, Ann M. Jackson, 1961. Traveled in Europe, Yucatan, Central America, assisting in preparation of Nox McCain lectures; studied new types of concrete constrn., Panama Canal, 1912; various engring. Positions, Pa. R.R., maintenance of way and transportation depts., 1906-21; with George W. Helme Company (name changed to Helme Products, Inc. in 1964), 1921, branch mgr., Helmetta, 1935, mgr., dir., 1940, vice pres., 1947-51, pres., 1951-56, chairman of the board, 1956-65, hon. chairman board, 1965—; trustee of First National Bank, Jamesburg, N.J., 1933-42. Mayor of Helmetta, N.J., 1924-38. Vestryman St. Georges Episcopal Ch., Helmetta, 1922-49. Mem. Gen. Soc. of War of 1812, Asso. Tobacco Mfrs. (pres. and dir. 1963-65), Phi Kappa Psi. Mason (32 deg., Shriner). Republican. Clubs: University (N.Y.C.); Wilmington Country, Wilmington (Willmington, Del.). Home: N.Y.C. *

MCCAIN, JOHN SIDNEY, JR., naval officer; b. Council Bluffs, Ia., Jan. 17, 1911; s. John Sidney and Katherine (Vaulx) McC.; B.S., U.S. Naval Acad., 1931; m. Roberta Wright, Jan. 21, 1933; children—Jean Alexandra (Mrs. Henry Morgan), John Sidney III (USN), Joseph Pinckney. Commissioned ensign USN, 1931, advanced through grades to admiral; comdg. officer U.S.S. Gunnell, 1942-44, U.S.S. Dentuda, 1944-45; staff Office Chief Naval Personnel, 1945-48; assigned Submarine Div. 71, Pacific 1949-50, CA St. Paul, 1950; staff Office Chief Naval Operations, 1950-53, 55-57, 58; squadron comdr. CSS 6, 1953-54; comdg. officer Monrovia, 1954-55, U.S.S. Albany, 1957-58; chief legislative affairs Office Sec. Navy, 1958-60, comdr. Amphibious Group Two, 1960-61, comdr. amphibious tng. Atlantic, 1961-62, chief of naval information, 1962-63; comdr. Amphibious Forces, Atlantic, 1963-65; comdr. Eastern Sea Frontier, 1965-67; comdr. in chief USN Forces Europe, 1967-68; comdr. in chief Pacific, 1968-72; ret., 1972. Pres., U.S. Strategic Inst.; chmn. monuments and cemeteries commn. VA. Home: Washington, D.C. Died Mar. 22, 1981; buried Arlington Nat. Cemetery.

MCCALL, CHARLIE CAMPBELL, lawyer; b. Causeyville, Miss., Mar. 23, 1895; s. Charles Edward and Mary Rebecca (Collins) McC.; student Meridian (Miss.) Male Coll., 1909; grad. Massey's Bus. Coll., Montgomery, Ala., 1909; student Starkes U. Sch., 1909-10; grad. Edgars Prep Sch., 1912, Ga. Mil. Acad., 1914; J.D., Georgetown U., 1921, LL.M., 1922, M.P.L., 1922; LL.M., Nat. U., 1922, M.P.L., 1922, S.J.D., 1936; LL.M. in Diplomacy, Am. U., 1923; studied law U. Ala., 1915, 17; grad. Sch. Mil. Govt., U.S. Army, Charlottesville, Va., 1944, AAF Sch. of Applied Tactics, Orlando, Fla., Sch. of Applied Personnel Mgmt., 1945; m. Nellie Curtis Cave, Apr. 16, 1924; 1 dau. by previous marriage, Mrs. Dorothy Brown. Admitted D.C. bar, 1920, Ala. bar, 1920, U.S. Ct. Claims, 1921, Supreme Ct. U.S., 1926, Va. bar, 1957; pvt. sec. to Congressman John McDuffie of Ala., 1919-20; state examiner pub. accounts Ala., 1924-27; atty. gen. Ala., 1927-31; spl. asst. atty. gen. of Ala., 1931-32; counsel RFC, Washington, 1932-33; chief counsel pub. bodies sect. legal div. Fed. Emergency Adminstrn. Pub. Works, 1933-34, chief legal adviser N.Y. State Office, 1934-35; counsel Pub. Works Adminstrn., 1935-38; acting gen. counsel P.R. Reconstrn. Adminstrn., San Juan, 1937; asst. gen. counsel Pub. Works Adminstrn., Washington, 1938-39, acting gen. counsel, 1939-40, gen. counsel, 1940-45; spl. asso. gen. counsel Fed. Works Agy., 1941-42, asst. gen. counsel, 1945-48; pvt. practice law, Birmingham, Ala., 1948-49; chief financing atty. div. law slum clearance staff HHFA, Washington, 1949-54, spl. counsel office gen. counsel, 1954-57, spl. asst. to gen. counsel, 1957-58; ret., 1958; pvt. law practice, from 1958. Served to 1st lt. cav. U.S. Army, 1917-19, capt., cav., U.S. Army Res., 1920; 1st lt. cav. U.S. Army, 1920-21; capt., cav., judge adv. on detail in Judge Adv. Gen.'s Dept., U.S. Army, Washington and Ft. Benning, Ga., 1921-23; capt. and maj. cav., U.S.R., 1924-34, maj., cav., Ala. N.G., 1925-34; maj. and lt. col., Air Corps, U.S. Army, Hdgrs. 1 Troop Carrier Command, Washington, D.C. and Stout Field, Indpls., 1942-45; lt. col. USAF Res. (ret. 1955). Mem. Am., Va., Fed., Birmingham bar assns., Bar Assn. D.C., Ala. State Bar, Nat. Assn. Attys. Gen. (sec. 1928, pres. 1929), Mil. Order World Wars, Animal Protective Assn., Nat. Anti-Vivesect. Soc., Res. Officers Assn., Ret. Officers Assn., Belgian Sheepdog Club Am., Sigma Nu Phi, Chi Psi Omega. Mason (32 deg., Shriner). Author many state statutes for revenue bond financing. Home: Fairfax, Va. Died Sept. 25, 1977.

MCCAMBRIDGE, JOHN, mfg. exec.; b. Braidwood, Ill., June 29, 1901; s. Richard and Martha (Stewart) McC.; student Joliet Jr. Coll., 1919-24, advanced mgmt. program Harvard, 1948; m. Viola Marie Lubs, Aug. 23, 1930; children—Donald Wayne, Robert Jack. With Am. Can Co., N.Y.C., 1920-75, beginning as office boy, successively cost accountant, internal auditor, asst. gen. auditor, gen. auditor, asst. gen. mgr., mfg., asst. comptroller, 1920-56, comptroller, 1956-61, v.p.-finance, 1961-75. Mem. Fin. Execs. Inst. (pres. N.Y.C. chpt. 1963-64, mem. nat. bd. dirs. 1965), N.J. C. of C. (dir.), Nat. Assn. Accountants. Mason (32 deg., Shriner). Club: Union League. Home: Glen Rock, N.J. Died July 3, 1980.

MCCANCE, THOMAS, banker; b. Edgewood, Pa., Aug. 25, 1902; s. William James and Nancy (Hodge) McCance; attended Phillips-Exeter Sch., 1918-21; Ph.B., Yale, 1925; m. Elizabeth Day Ferguson, Sept. 10, 1932; children—Thomas, Jr., Ellen Margaret (Mrs. Harry S. Parker, III), Henry Ferguson. With Brown Bros. Harriman & Co., N.Y.C., 1929-45, partner, 1945-79; pres. Bedgolton Corp., Bedford, N.Y.; trustee, mem. exec. com. Provident Loan Soc. N.Y.; voting trustee SKF Industries Phila.; mem. N.Y. Stock Exchange. Mem. Yale Devel. Bd. Bd. trustees Fgn. Parishes, P.E. Ch. in U.S.A. Mem. Downtown Lower Manhattan Assn. (dir., mem. exec. com.), Psi Upsilon. Wolf's Head Society. Clubs: Golf and Tennis (Bedford); Yale, Links, Down Town Assn. Home: Mt. Kisco, N.Y. Died Mar. 28, 1979; buried Bedford, N.Y.

MCCANDLESS, BOYD ROWDEN, psychologist; b. St. John, Kan., Aug. 18, 1915; s. Homer H. and Ada (Rowden) McC.; A.B., Ft. Hays Kan. State Coll., 1936; A.M., State U. Ia., 1938, Ph.D., 1941; m. Elinore Olson, June 14, 1941; children—Beth, Mark, Christine. Research asst. Ia. Child Welfare Research Sta., 1936-39, 1940-41, research prof., dir., 1951-62; research fellow Rockefeller Found. Office Radio Research, 1939-40; mental hygienist Wayne County Tng. Sch., Northville, Mich., 1941-42; selection, classification officer U.S. Maritime Service, Alameda, Calif., 1942-46; asst. and asso. prof. psychology, chmn. gen. edn. com. San Francisco State Coll., 1946-48; asso. prof. clin. psychology Ohio State U., 1948-51; dir. Iowa Child Welfare Research Sta., U. Iowa, 1952-60; Carnegie vis. prof. of psychology U. Hawaii, 1957; on leave as prof., head psychology Inst. Edn. and Research, U. Punjab, Lahore, West Pakistan, 1960-62; prof. edn. and psychology, dir. univ. sch. clinic complex, chmn. dept spl. edn. Ind. U., 1962-66; prof., dir. developmental psychology Emory U., Atlanta, 1966-75. Mem. Nat. Council on Research and Evaluation, Project Head Start. Sr. scholar U. Sydney (N.S.W.), Macquarie U., N.S.W., U. Queensland (Australia), 1974. Seminar and colloquium established in his honor Emory U. Mem. Soc. Research Child Devel., Am. Psychol. Assn. (mem. bd. profl. affairs, past pres. divs. devel. psychology and sch. psychology, Disting. Service award Young Scientist award), Sigma Xi. Author: Children and Adolescents, 1961; Children: Behavior and Development, 1967; Adolescents: Behavior and Development, 1970; (with Evans) Children and Adolescents: A Psychosocial View, 1973; posthumous books include:

Children—Behavior and Development, 1977; Children and Youth—Psychosocial Development, 1978; Adolescents, 1979; also articles in field. Editor: Developmental Psychology, 1968-74. Home: Atlanta, Ga. Died Dec. 5, 1975.

MCCANLISS, LEE, lawyer; b. Rockville, Ind., July 20, 1883; s. Samuel and Sarah (Neet) McC.; A.B., Wabash Coll., 1907; A.M., Columbia, 1910, LL.B., 1910; Doctor of Laws, Wabash College, 1941. Admitted to N.Y. bar, 1910, since practiced in N.Y.C.; charge Guaranty Trust Co. N.Y., 1933; dir. Interlake Iron Corp. Former Dem. Committeeman 15th Assembly Dist., Manhattan. Pres. bd. trustees Wabash Coll., 1939-55. Mem. Am., N.Y. State, N.Y. Co. bar assns., City N.Y. Bar Assn., Phi Beta Kappa. Home: New York. *

MCCARDLE, DOROTHY BARTLETT (MRS. CARL WESLEY MCCARDLE), columnist; b. Jonesboro, Tenn., July 25, 1904; d. George Edwin and Kate (Deaderick) Bartlett; student Smith Coll., 1922-23; B.A., U. Pa., 1927; m. Carl Wesley McCardle, Sept. 15, 1934; 1 dau., Marcia (Mrs. Sterling R. Maddox, Jr.). Free lance writer for mags., 1941; newspaper columnist Washington Post and Washington Post-Los Angeles Times Syndicate. Mem. Alpha Omicron Pi. Club: Washington Press. Home: McLean, Va. Died Nov. 1, 1978.

MCCARTHY, CHARLES E., univ. ofcl.; b. N.Y.C. June 15, 1902; s. Jere F. and Catherine (Flynn) M.; student N.Y. U. Sch. Commerce, Accounts and Finance; D.C.S. (hon), St. John's U., Bklyn.; m. Loretto MacDonald, Aug. 11, 1923; children—Jo Ann (Mrs. Charles Donnelly) Mary Catherine (Mrs. Richard Burns). Vice pres., treas. St. John's U.; dir. Allied Stores Corp., Syska & Hennessy, N.Y.C.; trustee N.Y. Bank for Savs. Decorated knight Grand Cross Holy Sepulchre, Knight of Malta. Mem. Sco. Friendly Sons St. Patrick, N.Y.C. Roman Catholic. Clubs: Union League, Economics (N.Y.C.); Spring Lake (N.J.) Golf and Country; Spring Lake (N.J.), Bathing and Tennis; Lyford Cay. Home: Westhampton Beach, N.Y. Died June 25, 1979.

MCCARTHY, JOSEPH WESTON, editor and writer; b. Cambridge, Mass., Mar. 6, 1915; s. Dennis Francis and Elizabeth (Doyle) McC.; A.B., Boston Coll., 1939; m. Mary Dunn, Dec. 21, 1941; children—Susan (Mrs. Michael Todd, Jr.), Elizabeth Doyle (Mrs. John Huckel), Dennis, Mary Dunn (Mrs. Richard Giza). Sports writer and reporter Boston Post, 1936-39; radio and publicity writer, Boston, 1940-41; in mil. service, 1941-45; pvt., 97th F.A. Bn. (pack), U.S. Army, 1941-42, promoted staff sgt., tech. sgt., master sgt.; sports editor, Yank, Army weekly, 1942, mng. editor, 1942-45; on editorial staff Cosmopolitan mag., 1946-48; free lance writer. Decorated Legion of Merit. Roman Catholic. Democrat. Author: The Remarkable Kennedys, 1960; In One Ear, 1962; Ireland, 1964; New England, 1967; Hurricane, 1969; (with Kenneth P. O'Donnell, David F. Powers) "Johnny, We Hardly Knew Ye", Memories of John Fitzgerald Kennedy, 1972; Days and Nights at Costellos, 1980. Editor: Fred Allen's Letters, 1965. Contbr. to nat. mags. Home: Blue Point, N.Y. Died Jan. 29, 1980.

MCCARTHY, WILLIAM T., judge; born Somerville, Mass., Dec. 5, 1885; s. John and Catherine (Rourke) McC.; A.B., Holy Cross Coll., 1905; J.B., Boston University. 1908; married to Nellie S. Sullivan, April 22, 1914; children—Kathryn C. (Mrs. James J. Doyle), John, Marion (Mrs. Foster McCafferty), Anne (Mrs. Joseph Monahan), Ellen (Mrs. Harry Toner). Admitted to Mass. bar, 1908, and since practiced in Boston. Alderman, Somerville, 1911-13; asst. dist. atty., Middlesex Co., 1913-15; mem. Somerville Sch. Bd., 1920-21; asst. U.S. atty., Dist. of Mass., 1934-47, U.S. atty., 1947-49; judge U.S. District of Massachusetts since Mar. 4, 1949. Mem. Fed. Bar Assn., Boston Bar Assn., Middlesex Bar Assn. Mass. Law Soc. Roman Catholic. Club: Clover. Contbr. article, A Prosecutor's Viewpoint on Narcotic Addiction, Fed. Probation Mag., 1943. Home: Cambridge, Mass. *

MCCASLIN, DAVIDA, prof. rhetoric; b. Pullman, Ill., Oct. 4, 1885; d. Rev. David Serril and Harriet Barrett (Studley) McC.; B.A., Coe Coll., Cedar Rapids, Ia., 1904; M.A., U. of Minn., 1912. Began teaching at Millikin U., 1907, prof. rhetoric since 1918. Mem. Nat. Council Teachers of English, Delta Delta Delta. Presbyn. Author: Reaching Other Minds, 1928. Contbr. short stories, articles, and verse to mags. Home: Decatur, Ill. *

MCCAUGHEY, WILLIAM JOHN (MIK-KAW'E), prof. mineralogy; b. Phila., Pa., June 21, 1882; s. Adam John and Katherine (Elliot) McC.; B.S., U. of Pa., 1906; grad. study, Johns Hopkins, part time, 1910; Ph.D., George Washington U., 1912; m. Emma R. Wilson, Nov. 25, 1908; children—Elizabeth Elliot, Emma Ruth. Assayer, U.S. Mint, 1906-08; scientist, U.S. Bur. Soils, 1908-11; became asst. prof. metallurgy and mineralogy, Ohio State U., 1911, prof. mineralogy and chmn. dept. since 1916. Mem. U.S. Assay Commn., 1909. Mem. Am. Mineral. Soc., Am. Geol. Soc., Am. Geophysical Union, Am. Inst. Mining Engrs., Am. Chem. Soc., A.A.A.S., Am. Assn. Univ. Profs., German Mineral. Soc., Tau Beta Pi, Sigma Xi, Alpha Chi Sigma. Republican. Congregationalist. Clubs: Faculty, Stone Harbor Yacht, Torch. Contbr. bulletins and articles on mineralogy and metall. slags and refractories. Home: Columbus, Ohio. *

MCCLATCHY, ELEANOR, publisher; pres., dir. McClatchy Newspapers. Newspapers Pulitzer prize, 1935 (for exposing polit. corruption in Nev.) Home: Sacramento, Calif. Died Oct. 17, 1980.

MCCLELLAN, HAROLD CHADICK, mfr., govt. ofcl.; b. Crows Landing, Calif., Aug. 20, 1897; s. Edward Leander Barker and Ada (Small) McC.; A.B., Occidental College, 1922, LL.D. (honorary), 1959; m. Katherine Elizabeth Stone, June 29, 1923; 1 daughter, Martha Louise. Sales manager Crescent Creamery Co., Los Angeles, 1923-27; founder, pres., gen. mgr. Old Colony Paint & Chem. Co., 1927-62, chmn. of the bd., 1962-66; dir. Knudsen Creamery Co., Transit Mix Corp., Inter-state Engring. Corp. Industry mem. 10th regional War Labor Bd., 1944, 12th regional W.S.B., 1951. Mem. San Marino City Council 1952, Los Angeles met. transit authority, 1952; chmn. met. traffic and transit com. of Los Angeles, 1952; mem. pub. adv. bd. Fgn. Operations Adminstrn., 1954; asst. sec. commerce of internat. affairs, 1955-57; mem. bd. Nat. Merit Scholarship Corp., 1958-64. Dir. Town Hall, 1952, 54; pres. bd. trustees Occidental Coll., 1951-54, 62-65; trustee Haynes Found., 1950-54. Named Cal. Industrialist of Yr., 1960; received Calif. Museum of Science and Industry award, 1960. Mem. N.A.M. (bd. 1952, regional vice pres. 1953, pres. 1954, chmn. bd. 1955), Los Angeles C. of C. (bd. 1952-54, pres., 1961), Los Angeles Paint Varnish and Lacquer Assn. (pres. 1934-35), Mchts. and Mfrs. Assn. (pres. Los Angeles 1949-50, chmn. exec. com. 1951-52, mng. dir. Am. Nat. Exhibition Moscow, 1959, dir.), Occidental Alumni Assn. (pres. 1941-42), Los Angeles World Affairs Council (pres. 1964-65), Kappa Sigma. Republican. Clubs: Country (San Gabriel); California (Los Angeles). Organized U.S. exhbn. in Moscow, 1959, scene of Khrushchev-Nixon "kitchen debate". Home: San Marino, Calif. Died Aug. 2, 1979.

MCCLELLAN, JOHN LITTLE, U.S. senator; b. Sheridan, Ark., Feb. 25, 1896; s. Isaac Scott and Belle (Suddleth) McC.; ed. pub. schs.; m. Eula Hicks, Nov. 2, 1913 (dec.); children—Max Eldon, Doris; m. 2d, Lucille Smith, Nov. 8, 1922 (dec.); children— John L., James, Mary Alice; m. 3d, Mrs. Norma Myers Cheatham, Nov. 10, 1937. Admitted to Ark. bar, 1913, began practice at Sheridan; pros. atty. 7th Jud. Dist. of Ark., 2 terms, 1927-30; mem. 74th-75th Congresses (1935-39), 6th Ark. Dist.; U.S. senator from Ark., 1942-77. Served 18 months as 1st lt., A.S.S.C., World War I. Recipient Distinguished Pub. Service award Nat. Tax Found., 1957; George Washington award Am. Good Govt. Soc., 1959; Hatton W. Sumners award S.W. Legal Found., 1959. Democrat. Baptist. Home: Camden, Ark. Died Nov. 28, 1977.

MC CLELLAND, JOHN MORGAN, publishing co. exec.; b. Washington County, Pa., Oct. 4, 1885; s. William and Martha (DeVore) McC.; ed. pub., schs; m. Adlyn Hayes Morris, Nov. 15, 1911 (dec.); children—Mrs. Sue Natt, John Morris; m. 2d, Ruth M. Pepper, Jan. 1, 1937. Began newspaper business, Washington, Pa., 1906; mgr. Daily Notes, Canonsburg, Pa., 1908; later engaged in pub. business in Ark.; editorial writer and contbr. econ. subjects; a founder City of Longview, Wash., 1923; pres. emeritus Longview Pub. Co., publishers Daily News, Daily News Press; v.p. Sentinel Mist Pub. Co., St. Helens, Ore., Port Angeles Evening News Corp. Mem. Asso. Property Pacific N. W. Newspaper Assn., Allied Daily Newspapers, Longview (Wash.) C. of C., Sigma Delta Chi. Republican. Presbyn. (elder). Mason (K.T.), Elk. Clubs: Rotary (past pres.), Longview Country. Wrote series articles reflecting Nazi and Fascist philosophies. Home: Longview WA. *

MCCLELLAND, THOMAS BROWN, horticulturist; b. Lexington, Ky., Feb. 7, 1886; s. Thomas Nesbit and Mary Marshall (Marrs) McC.; ed. Miss Colliers Private Sch. and Ky. U. (now Transylvania U.) Acad.; A.B., Ky. State Coll. (now U. of Ky.), 1907; m. Florence Wilson Blodgett, Oct. 6, 1920. Teacher, pub. schs., Puerto Rico, 1907-08; asst. horticulturist, Puerto Rico Agrl. Expt. Sta., Mayaguez, 1909-18, horticulturist, 1918-28, sr. horticulturist, 1928-30, prin. horticulturist and dir., 1930-34; sr. horticulturist in charge U.S. Plant Introduction Garden, Coconut Grove, Fla., 1934-43; specialist in tropical horticulture. Member War Price and Rationing Bd., 1944-46. Patron Miami Opera Guild. Fellow A.A.A.S.; mem. Lamp and Cross, Fairchild Tropical Garden, Am. Orchid Soc., Kappa Sigma; charter mem. South Fla. Orchid Assn., Orchid Soc. of Fla. Mem. Christian (Disciples) Ch. Rotarian. Club: Century (Coral Gables). Writer of bulletins and papers on coffee, vanilla, coconuts, photo-periodism, etc. Originator of numerous varieties of hibiscus. Home: Miami, Fla. Died July 22, 1980.

MCCLENON, RAYMOND BENEDICT, prof. mathematics; b. Yankton, Dak. Ty., Aug. 4, 1883; s. Rufus Buel and Mary Adeline (White) McC.; B.A., Yankton Coll., 1902; Ph.D., Yale, 1905; studied U. of Munich, 1910, Columbia, 1918; m. Else Hannah Weber, June 22, 1912 (died May 17, 1933); m. 2d, Erika Weber, June 16, 1934; one son, John Raymond. Instructor of mathematics at Grinnell College, 1905, assistant professor, 1907, associate prof., 1910, professor since 1918; with Biarritz Am. U. Biarritz, France, 1945-46. Mem. Am. Math. Soc., Math. Assn. America, A.A.A.S., Am. Assn. Univ. Profs., Am. Statistical Assn., Ia. Acad. Science (pres. 1939-40), Phi Beta Kappa, Sigma Xi. Conglist. Author: Introduction to the Elementary Functions, 1918; also articles and revs. in Am. Math. Monthly, Bulletin American Mathematical Society, etc. Asso. editor Am. Math. Monthly, 1919-24. Home: Grinnell, Ia. *

MCCLINTOCK, CHARLES ARBUTHNOT, found. exec.; b. Pitts., June 15, 1883; s. Jonas Roup and Elizabeth (Arbuthnot) McC.; A.B., Princeton U., 1907; LL.D., Waynesburg College. Advisory director of Pittsburgh Nat. Bank; trustee Kiski School; pres. Carnegie Hero Commission. Served as major, Infantry, U.S. Army, World War I. Trustee Carnegie Hero Corp.; trustee West Pa. Hospital. Mem. Hist. Soc. Western Pa. (vice president). Presbyterian. Mason (Consistory, Shriner). Clubs: Duquesne, Pittsburgh Athletic Assn., Harvard-Yale-Princeton, Fox Chapel Golf, Pittsburgh Golf (Pitts.); Rolling Rock (Ligonier, Pa.); University (N.Y.C.). Home: Pittsburgh. *

MCCLINTOCK, CHARLES BLAINE, ex-congressman; b. Paint Tp., Wayne Co., O., May 25, 1886; s. James W. and Emma (Huguelet) McC.; grad. high sch., Beach City, O., 1901; student Wooster (O.) U.; LL.B., Western Reserve U., 1911; m. Ruth M. Grant, of Wilmot, O., Nov. 16, 1912. Admitted to Ohio bar. 1911, and began practice at Canton; pros. atty. Stark Co., O., 1923-27, spl. atty., 1927-29; mem. 71st and 72d Congresses (1929-33), 16th Ohio Dist. Mason (32 deg.). Mem. Jr. Order Am. Mechanics. Republican. Methodist. Spl. prosecutor in the Don R. Mellett murder case, 1926. Home: Canton, O. *

MCCLINTOCK ROBERT MILLS, fgn. service officer; b. Seattle, Aug. 30, 1909; s. John Mills and Christine (Chamberlain) McC.; A.B., Stanford, 1931; spl. studies, Geneva, Switzerland, 1929; m. Elena Barrios, Apr. 29, 1936; children—John Martin, Robert David. Joined U.S. Fgn. Service, 1931; vice consul, Panama City, Panama, 1932; attended Fgn. Service Sch., State Dept., 1932; vice consul, Kobe, Japan, 1933-35; 3d sec. Am. embassy, Santiago, Chile, 1935-37; sec. legation, Ciudad Trujillo, Dominican Republic, 1937-39, Helsinki, Finland, 1939-42; charge d'affairs ad interim, Helsinki, 1942-44; sec. legation, Stockholm, 1944; mem. Internat. Secretariat, spl. asst. to exec. sec. UN Conf. on Internat. Orgn., San Francisco, 1945; adviser U.S. delegation UN Prep. Commn., London, 1945-46; polit. adviser U.S. delegation UN Gen. Assembly, N.Y.C., 1946, spl. sessions, 1947-48; sec. Am. embassy, Brussels, Belgium, 1949-51; assigned to Nat. War Coll., 1951-52; dep. chief mission, counselor Am. embassy, Cairo, Egypt, 1952-53; dep. chief mission, Saigon, Vietnam, 1953-54; A.E. and P. to Cambodia, 1954-56, to Lebanon, 1958-61, to Argentina, 1962-64, to Venezuela, 1970-75; chmn. U.S. govt. delegation 19th Internat. Conf. Red Cross, New Delhi, India, 1957; alternate del. U.S. to 9th UNESCO Gen. Conf., New Delhi, 1956; mem. policy planning staff State Dept., 1957, mem. policy planning council, 1961; State Dept. adviser Naval War Coll., 1964-66; sr. fgn. service insp., 1966-67; co-dir. Spl. State-Def. Study of U.S. Overseas Bases, 1968-69; coordinator preparations, chmn. interdepartmental group Symington Subcom. on Overseas Commitments, 1969-70. Recipient Superior Service award Dept. State, 1959. Life mem. U.S. Naval Inst. (Gold medalist 1941); mem. Phi Beta Kappa, Sigma Chi. Clubs: Metropolitan, Chevy Chase (Washington); Annapolis Yacht; Explorers (N.Y.). Writer, lectr. on diplomacy and naval subjects. Home: Washington, D.C. Died Nov. 1, 1976.

MCCLURE, FRANK JAMES, biochemist; b. W. Lafayette, Ind., Dec. 30, 1896; s. Lawrence James and Eliza Jane (Parker) McC.; B.S., Purdue U., 1919, M.S., 1924; Ph.D., U. Ill., 1930. Nutrition research asso. Pa. State U., 1930-35; biochemist NIH, 1936-48; chief lab. biochemistry Nat. Inst. Dental Research, NIH, 1948-66; spl. research physiol. effects fluoride, benefits flouridation drinking water. Recipient Superior Service award Dept. Health, Edn. and Welfare, 1955; initially made land available to Purdue Research Found. for McClure Indsl. Research Park, 1959. Fellow Am. Coll. Dentists; hon. mem. Am. Dental Assn. Exhbns. of block prints at Washington Water Color Club, Soc. Washington Print Makers. Author numerous articles in field. Home: Washington, D.C. Died Mar. 1979.

MCCLURE, HARRY A., naval officer (ret.); b. Buffalo, N.Y., May 31, 1884; s. Harry Everet and Anna Marion (Willis) Mc C.; B.S., U.S. Naval Acad., 1907; m. Lucy Middleton Williams, Sept. 24, 1913. Commd. ensign U.S. Navy, 1909, and advanced through grades to commodore, 1944; ret. from active duty, Sept. 1946. Awarded Navy Cross, Victory medals (World Wars I and II), Mexican campaign and China campaign medals, commendation from Sec. of Navy. Republican. Mason. Clubs: Union League (San Francisco), Meadow (Fairfax, Calif.). Home: San Francisco. *

MCCLURE, JOHN ELMER, lawyer; b. Lincoln County, W.Va., Nov. 27, 1893; s. John W. and Lucy (Vickers) McC.; LL.B., George Washington U., 1922, LL.M., 1924; m. Helen Pendleton, Aug. 25, 1920; children—John Pendleton, William Pendleton; m. 2d. Helen Muller, Jan. 1, 1944; children—Joan Vickers, Arthur Acklin, John Elmer. Admitted to D.C. bar, 1923, U.S. Ct. Claims, 1924, Supreme Ct. U.S., 1926, Ct. Appeals Md., 1933, Ill. bar, 1940, practicing in Washington. Spl. ambassador to Mexico, 1960. Mem. Am. Fed., D.C., Ill., Chgo. bar assns., Am. Judicature Soc., Nat. Lawyers Club. Baptist. Mason (32 deg.). Clubs: Burning Tree, Nat. Press, Congressional; Larry's Creek Fish and Gun (hon.). Home: Chevy Chase, Md. Died Feb. 19, 1981.

MCCLURE, RUSSELL SCHEE, disaster mgmt. cons.; b. Seattle, Dec. 26, 1915; s. Worth and Pearl Agnes (Russell) McC.; A.B., Stanford, 1937; M.A., U. Wash., 1939; student Ohio State U., 1939-42; m. Mary Helen Pruitt, Aug. 12, 1939; children—Charles Russell, James Worth, Andrew Wilson. Analyst, State Dept., 1942-43; transp. attache embassy, Paris, France, 1945-47; chief transp. div. Office U.S. Spl. Rep., ECA, Paris, 1948-49; also transp. adviser U.S. resident delegation Econ. Commn. Europe, Geneva, Switzerland; dep. head, then head U.S. resident delegation Econ. Commn. Europe, Geneva, 1950-51; dir. Office Programs and Reports, UN Korean Reconstrn. Agy., Seoul, 1951-54; dep. dir. U.S. Interagy. Program Fgn. Econ. Research, 1954-61; dir. AID mission to Jordan, Amman, 1962-65, AID mission to Afghanistan, Kabul, 1965-70, AID mission to Congo, Kinshasa, 1970-71; fgn. disaster relief coordinator AID Dept. State, Washington, 1971-75; dir. relief coordination div. Office UN Diaster Relief Coordinator, Geneva, 1975-77; disaster mgmt. cons., 1977-80; U.S. rep. Central Rhine Commn., 1946-51; fellow Harvard Center Internat. Affairs, 1960-61. Served with USNR, 1943-46. Mem. Am. Fgn. Service Assn., Foyer Interalliee Des Chemins De Fer (Paris). Clubs: American (Paris and Geneva); Cercle de Kinshasa. Home: Olympia, Wash. Died Oct. 8, 1980.

MCCOLL, CLARKE MUNRO, physician; b. Elkton, Mich., Feb. 13, 1898; s. Duncan John and Helen (Clarke) McC.; student Hillside (Mich.) Coll., 1916-18; M.D., U. Mich., 1922; m. Amanda E. McKinney, July 9, 1925; 1 dau., Mary (Mrs. Hugh Prentice). Intern Henry Ford Hosp., Detroit, 1922-23, (resident div. gastroenterology, 1923-24, mem. staff, 1925-71, chmn. dept. medicine, 1963-66, sr. cons., 1966-71. Mem. adv. bd. 3 Detroit area SSS. Diplomate Am. Bd. Internal Medicine. Fellow A.C.P.; mem. A.M.A., Am. Soc Internal Medicine, Mich., Wayne County med. socs., Detroit Acad. Medicine, Am. Rheumatism Assn., Prismatic Club, Royal Soc. Medicine (affiliate), Alpha Tau Omega, Phi Rho Sigma. Baptist. Contbr. med. jours. Home: Birmingham, Mich. Died May 19, 1976.

MCCOLL, ROBERT BOYD, locomotive mfg.; b. Kilmarnock, Scotland, Jan. 1, 1882; s. Hugh and Jane (Boyd) McC.; student Kilmarnock Acad., Science and Art Coll., 1897-1902; m. Mary Ann MacLennan, June 24, 1908. Came to U.S. 1905; naturalized citizen, 1929. Apprentice Glasgow Southwestern R.R., Kilmarnock, Scotland, 1897-1902; draftsman Robert Stephenson & Co., Darlington, Eng., 1904-05; successively small tool supervisor, gen. machine shop foreman, asst. supt., supt. and works mgr. Montreal Locomotive Works, Ltd., Montreal, Can., 1905-18; gen. mgr. Sir K. G. Armstrong Whitworth Co., Newcastle-on-Tyne, Eng., 1919-22; mgr. Schenectady plant Am. Locomotive Co. 1922-31, pres. McIntosh & Seymour Diesel Engine Corp., Auburn, N.Y., and Alco Products, Inc., subsidiaries, 1931-40; v.p. in charge mfg. Am. Locomotive Co., also Montreal Locomotive Works, Ltd., Mar. 1940-Sept. 1945, exec. v.p. (both cos.), Sept.-Dec. 1945, pres. both cos. 1945-50, also dir.; dir. Schenectady Trust Company, Beaumont (Tex.) Iron works, Gen. Steel Castings Corp. Mem. Inst. Mech. Engrs. (London), Newcomen Soc., St. Andrews Soc., A.S.M.E. Presbyn. Clubs: Metropolitan, Railroad-Machinery, Blind Brook, Westchester Country, Mohawk, Mohawk Golf. Home: New York. *

MCCONE, ALAN, design-constrn. co. exec.; b. Phila., Sept. 7, 1908; s. H.E. and Ida (Thomas) McC.; student Northwestern U., 1925-26, Stanford, 1926-29; m. Virginia Green, Nov. 2, 1929 (dec. Feb. 1975); children—Alan, Deborah Louise; m. Alice Schureman Vogdes, July 1976. Engaged in investment banking, 1929-40; dept. supt. Sun Oil Co., 1940-46; with Catalytic Constrn. Co., 1946-61, asst. to pres. for labor, sales and indsl. relations; asst. Sec. for Inst. Dept. USAF, 1961-64; sr. v.p., dir. Day & Zimmerman, Phila., 1964-78. Mem. Am. Inst. Chem. Engrs., Am. Inst. Plant Engrs., Am. Ordnance Assn. Clubs: Stanford (pres. 1930), Exchange (pres. 1947) (Phila.); Pa. Athletic (pres. 1971); University (Washington); Merion (Pa.) Golf. Author articles. Home: Philadelphia, Pa. Died July 19, 1978.

MCCONKEY, GEORGE MCDONALD, architect, educator; b. Clifton, O., Aug. 16, 1886; s. Milton M. and Azilla (Wingate) McC.; student Wittenberg Coll., 1904-05; B.Arch., U. Mich., 1914; m. Eleanor Eberle, Sept. 23, 1910; children—Ruth (Mrs. Rodney DeVore), Florence (Mrs. John S. Hafer), George McDonald. Engr., Detroit River Tunnel Co., N.Y.C. R.R., 1905-09; instr. U. Mich., 1911-14, asst. prof., 1914-18, asso. prof., 1918-28, prof. architecture since 1928; also practicing architect, Ann Arbor, since 1915; cons. architect. Assisted Mich. State Bd. Architects in establishing state examination standards; served on state and local bldg. code commns., 1944-46; Pres. Ann Arbor Hills Homes Assn., 1941-43. Mem. A.I.A., Mich. Soc. Architects (dir.1940, 1943), Mich. Acad. Arts Scis. and Letters, Engring. Soc. Detroit, Am. Assn. U. Profs., Alpha Rho Chi, Tau Sigma Delta, Phi Kappa Phi, Iota Alpha. Republican. Presbyn. Author archtl. articles. Home: Ann Arbor. *

MCCONNELL, RAYMOND ARNOTT, JR., newspaperman; b. North Ridgeville, Ohio, Dec. 31, 1915; s. Rev. Raymond Arnott and Anna Bell (Lee) McConnell; A.B., Williams Coll., 1936; LL.D., Doane Coll., 1951; m. Maren Ellen Dobson, May 31, 1940; children—Alice Maren, Raymond Arnott III, Judity Dobson, Christine. Reporter, Troy (N.Y.) Record, 1936-37; telegraph and news editor Nebr. State Jour., Lincoln, 1937-39; asso. editor Lincoln Evening Jour., 1940; mng. editor The Jour. Newspapers, Lincoln 1941-57, editor 1943-57; news exec. Twin Coast Newspapers, Inc., 1958-79; mng. editor Pasadena Star-News, The Independent, 1966-72, exec. editor, 1972-75; exec. editor Pasadena Star-News and Foothill Intercity newspapers, 1975-79. Commr. Joint U.S.-Mexico Commn. Migrant Labor, 1954. Mem. natural conservation adv. commn. U.S. Dept. Agr., 1955-57. Studied Brit. agrl. war effort on invitation, 1943; instr. journalism, 1944-45. Bd. dirs. Pacificulture Found. and Asia Mus., bd. govs. Pasadena-Foothill Urban League. Organizer, Nebr. All Star presdl. primary for which Journal awarded Pultizer prize for dist. pub. service, 1948; named Outstanding Young Man of Nebr., Nebr. Jr. C. of C., 1950 Outstanding Young Man of Lincoln, Jr. C. C., 1951; one of 10 Outstanding young men of U.S., U.S. Jr. C. of C., 1951; recipient Distinguished Service award Nat. Watershed Congress, 1973. Mem. Gargoyle Soc., P.E.N., Sigma Delta Chi, Zeta Psi. Presbyn. Mason (32 deg.). Author: Trampled Terraces, 1950. Contbr. to nat. mags. Home: Pasadena, Calif. Died Oct. 22, 1979.

MCCONOCHIE, WILLIAM ROBERT, cons. engr.; b. Rock Island, Ill., July 7, 1906; s. William Henry and Edith (Fitzpatrick) McC.; B.S. in Civil Engring., U. Mich., 1928; m. Marian Brenckle, July 6, 1935; children—Jean A., William A., Roger P., Carol Ann. Engr., U.S. Corps Engrs., Rock Island, 1928-30; traffic engr. Chgo. Surface Lines, 1930-44; chief transp. engr. DeLauw, Cather & Co., Chgo., 1944-61, sr. v.p., dir., 1961-72; pvt. cons.; cons. English Channel Tunnel, Bosphorus Straits Bridge, Sydney (Australia), Expressways, Manchester (Eng.) rapid transit study, San Juan (P.R.) rapid transit plans; guest lectr. U. Ill., Northwestern U., U. Cin., U. Mich., U. New South Wales (Australia). Registered profl. engr. Mem. Inst. Transp. Engrs., Tau Beta Pi. Contbr. to publs. in field. Home: Glen Ellyn, Ill. Died July 24, 1978.

MCCORD, CAREY PRATT, med. indsl. hygienist; b. Bibb County, Ala., Sept. 25, 1886; s. James Milton and Florence Davis (Pratt) McC.; A.B., Howard Coll., Birmingham, Ala., 1907, LL.D., 1933; M.D., U. Mich., 1912; m. Catherine Mackay. Sept. 22, 1916; children—James Mackay, Malcolm Christian, Mackay. Mem. staff research labs. Parke-Davis & Co., 1912-16; dir. research Mich. Home and Tng. Sch., 1914-16; dir. Indsl. Health Conservacy Labs., 1919-51; asso. prof. preventive medicine U. Cin., 1920-35; med. adviser Chrysler Corp. to 1951; dir. Bur. Indsl. Hygiene and Occupational Diseases, City of Detroit, 1937-40; prof. occupational medicine Wayne U. Med. Coll. Detroit, 1937-40; lectr. on occupational diseases Sch. Pub. Health, U. Mich., 1941—, cons. Inst. Indsl. Health, 1951—, resident lectr., dept. internal medicine Med. Coll., 1951-62; cons. USPHS, 1962-64. Served as 1st lt. Med. Res. Corps, U.S. Army, World Way I; col., Med. Res. Corps, ret. 1948. Recipient William S. Knudsen Award, 1947. Diplomate Am. Bd. Preventive Medicine. Fellow Am. Pub. Health Assn. (chmn. indsl. hygiene sect., former sec.), Am. Acad. Occupational Health (dir. 1946); mem. A.M.A., Acoustical Soc. of Am., Internat. Congress Indsl. Medicine (U.S. rep.), Ramazzini Soc., Am. Indsl. Hygiene Assn. (hon.), Finnish Indsl. Health Assn. (hon.), Delta Omega, Phi Chi. Dem. Baptist. Investigated Am. Leishmaniasis in tropics of Yucatan Peninsula, 1939. Author: Industrial Hygiene for Engineers and Managers (with Floyd P. Allen, 1931; A Blind Hog's Acorns, 1935; Medical Uses of Soap (with Morris Fishbein and others), 1945; Blind Hog's Acorns, 1946; (with Wm. N. Witheridge) Odors, 1949; also numerous brochures on indsl. hygiene and occupational diseases. Contbr. to med. reference books and jours. editor Jour. Indsl. Medicine and Surgery, 1951-64; editor Jour. Occupational Medicine, 1964-67, editor emeritus, 1967—. Home: Glendale OH. *

MCCORKLE, DONALD MACOMBER, musicologist, educator; b. Cleve., Feb. 20, 1929; s. Paul and Maude Alma (Atcheson) McC.; student Mt. Hermon Sch., 1945-47, Brown U., 1947-48; B.Mus., Bradley U., 1951; M.A., Ind. U., 1953, Ph.D., 1958; m. Margit Emily Lundstrom, Aug. 18, 1968; 1 dau. by previous marriage, Karen Lyn. Asst., then asso. prof. music Salem Coll., 1954-64; prof. musicology U. Md., College Park, 1964-72; prof., head dept. music U. B.C. (Can.) Vancouver, 1972-75, prof. musicology, 1975-78; founding dir. Moravian Music Found., Winston-Salem, N.C., 1956-64, gen. cons., 1970-78; contbg. music critic Washington Evening Star, 1964-66, Washington Post, 1968-72; cons. Peabody Conservatory Music, 1968-69. Bur. research field reader U.S. Office Edn., 1964-72; grad. record exam. Advanced Music Test Com., 1970-74, chmn., 1973-74. Bd. dirs. Vancouver Symphony Orch., 1972-78. Recipient Moramus award distinguished service to Am. music, 1964. Charles H. Babcock, Jr. research grantee Am. Moravian music, 1954-56; Can. Council Research grantee, 1975-76. Mem. Am. (council 1959-61, 66-68), Internat. musicological socs., Coll. Music Soc. (editor Coll. Music Symposium 1961-63, 69-70; pres. 1967-69, permanent mem. council 1975-78), Music Library Assn., Canadian Assn. U. Schs. Music, Brahms Soc. Hamburg (Germany). Author numerous studies and edits. 18th-century German Am. Moravian Ch. music, also critical studies on compositions of Brahms. Editor: The N. Simrock Thematic Catalog of the Works of Johannes Brahms, 1973; Brahms-Variations on a Theme of Haydn, 1976. Home: Vancouver BC, Canada. Died Feb. 6, 1978; buried Winston-Salem, N.C.

MCCORMACK, JOHN W., congressman; b. Boston, Dec. 21, 1891; s. Joseph H. and Mary E. (O'Brien) McC.; ed. pub. schs.; LL.B., Boston U., Holy Cross Coll., 21 others; m. Harriet Joyce, 1920 (dec. 1971). Admitted to Mass. bar, 1913, began practice in Boston; mem. firm McCormack & Hardy; mem. Mass. Constl. Conv., 1917-18; mem. Mass. Ho. of Rep., 1920-22, Mass. State Senate, 1923-26 (Dem. leader); mem. 70th-87th Congresses from 12th Mass. Dist. (majority leader), 88th-91st Congresses from 9th Mass. Dist. (speaker of house). Mem. South Boston Citizens Assn., Am. Legion. Clubs: K.C., Elks, Moose, Cath. Order Foresters, Ancient Order of Hibernians. Knight of Malta first class, Knight St. Gregory. Home: Jamaica Plain, Mass. Died Nov. 22, 1980.

MCCORMICK, CHARLES O(WEN), obstetrician, gynecologist; b. Monitor, Ind., Feb. 9, 1886; s. John and Pauline (Sautermeister) McC.; A.B., magna cum laude, Ind. U., 1911; M.D., Harvard, 1913; m. Elizabeth Frances Maines, Sept. 10, 1913; children—Charles Owen, Gene Elton. Surgical intern Boston City Hosp., 1913-15. Boston Lying-in Hosp., 1915-16; practice, Indianapolis, since 1916; clin. prof. obstetrics, Ind. U. Sch. of Medicine, since 1936; mem. obstet. staff William H. Coleman Hosp. for Women; mem. visiting staff Meth., St. Vincents, Indianapolis City hosps; obstetrical consultant Sunnyside Tuberculosis Sanitarium. Chairman of the Advisory Medical Committee of the Maternal Health League of Ind. Fellow Am. Coll. Surgeons; hon. fellow Internat. Coll. Anesthetists; mem. A.M.A., Am. Bd. Obstetrics and Gynecology, Am. Assn. Obstetrics, Gynecology and Abdominal Surgeons, Central States Assn. of Obstetrics and Gynecology, Indianapolis Obstet. and Gynecol. Soc. (pres.). Unitarian (trustee of All Souls Unitarian Ch.). Clubs: Rotary Internat., Highland Golf and Country. Author of Indiana 1935 act for sterilization of the Insane; Pathology of Labor, Puerperium and the Newborn, 1939; twenty-five scientific papers; originator of Modified Gwathmey rectal ether analgesia. Home: Indianapolis. *

MCCORMICK, HARRY BENTON, clergyman; b. Allen County, Ind., Oct. 27, 1883; s. Thomas Hormes and Rosina (Yagerlehner) McC.; A.B., Hiram (O.) Coll., 1908; B.D., Union Theol. Seminary, N.Y. City, 1915; D.D. (honorary), Chapman College, Calif., 1946; m. Edna Grace Templin, Dec. 31, 1908. Ordained to ministry of Disciples of Christ Ch., 1908; pastor Lexington, O., 1908-10. Norwalk, O., 1910-12, Second Christian Ch., N.Y. City. 1912-15, Crawford Road Ch., Cleveland, O., 1915-18, Woodward Av. Ch., Detroit, 1918-23; head of promotion dept. United Christian Missionary Society, 1923-30, pres., 1945-51; ch. wide ministry Disciples of Christ since 1951; made administrative visit to Orient, 1949; pastor Lakewood (Ohio) Ch., 1930-46. President of Internat. Conv. of Disciples of Christ, 1939; chairman commission of structure and function. 1935-39; dir. Greater Cleveland Ch. Fed., 1932-46, pres., 1935; director Ohio Christian Missionary Soc., 1930-46. Director Lakewood C. of C., 1943-44. Trustee Hiram Coll.; former trustee Disciples House, Chautauqua, N.Y., Coll. of the Bible (Lexington, Ky.); del. World Council of Churches, Amsterdam, 1948. Independent Republican. Mason; Club: Kiwanis. Recipient Hiram College Award for Distinguished Service, 1951. Home: Indpls. *

MCCORMICK, WASHINGTON JAY, ex-congressman; b. Missoula, Mont., Jan. 4, 1884; s. Washington J. and Kate (Higgins) M.; student U. of Mont. and U. of Notre Dame, Ind.; A.B., Harvard, 1906; LL.B., Columbia, 1910; m. Edna Theresa Fox, of Twin Bridges, Mont., Sept. 21, 1915; children—Washington Jay, Angela Catherine, Camilla Fox. Admitted bar, N.Y., 1910, Mont., 1911; mem. Mont Ho. of Rep., 1919; mem. 67th Congress (1921-23), 1st Mont. Dist. Republican. Catholic. Mem. Am. Legion, Delta Upsilon, Phi Delta Phi. Elk. Clubs: Army and Navy (Washington); Kiwanis (hon.), Missoula Country. Home: Missoula, Mont. *

MCCORMICK, WILLIAM THOMAS, engring. corp. exec.; b. Girardville, Pa., May 19, 1914; s. Patrick Joseph and Mary Catherine (McLaughlin) M.; B.S., Georgetown U., 1936, J.D., 1941; m. Lucy Valentine Offutt, Apr. 20, 1940 (dec. 1976); children—Kathleen Ann, William Thomas, Brian Joseph, Lucy Valentine. Fgn. aid and affairs adminstr. Dept. Def., FOA, ECA, Dept. State, Fgn. Econ. Adminstrn., Lend Lease Adminstrn., Washington, 1941-52; fgn. affairs adv. internat. concerns, N.Y.C., Washington, Zurich, Switzerland, Tokyo, Japan, 1952-56; dep. dir. Far Eastern affairs, Office Sec. Def., Washington, 1956-76; dep. dir. Washington ops. Burns and Roe, Inc., 1976-78; lectr. fgn. aid and affairs to fgn. trade councils, univs., Mil. Assistance Inst., fgn. orgns.; fgn. aid adviser Senate and House coms. Editor, dir. publ. English, German, French and Italian editions of directory U.S. firms interested in fgn. trade and investments (Marshall Plan); founder Contact Clearing House Service. Mem. Delta Theta Phi. K.C. (4 deg.) Home: Arlington, Va. Died Apr. 8, 1978.

MCCOY, ERNEST B., athletic dir.; b. Pitts., July 20, 1904; s. Jarrett Ernest and Jennie (Browning) McC.; A.B., U. Mich., 1929; A.M., Columbia, 1932; m. Elizabeth Hemenger, Aug. 27, 1932; 1 son, Ernest Hemenger. Securities salesman First Detroit Co., 1929-31; tchr., coach Montclair (N.J.) schs., 1932-40; asst. football coach U. Mich., 1940-52, basketball coach, 1948-52, asst. athletic dir., 1946-52; dean Coll. Phys. Edn. and Athletics, dir. athletics Pa. State U., 1952-70; dir. athletics Miami U., Coral Gables, Fla., 1971-74. Pres. Eastern Coll. Athletic Conf. Served to lt. comdr. USNR, 1942-45; lt. comdr. Res. Mem. Nat. Collegiate Athletic Assn. (dist. v.p. 1964-66, sec.-treas. 1966-68), Phi Sigma Kappa. Home: Miami, Fla. *

MCCOY, SAMUEL DUFF, journalist, author; b. Burlington, Ia., Apr. 17, 1882; s. Rev. Daniel Charles and America Holderby (Pollock) M.; student Princeton, 1901-03; m. Ella, d. Henry B. Neely, of Germantown, Phila., June 16, 1915. Began contributing to mags., 1898; engaged in newspaper, magazine and publicity work since 1903. Was sent by The New York World to Florida in February, 1923, to investigate death of Martin Tabert, flogged to death by a "whipping boss" in a lumber camp, leasing convict labor; wrote 50 articles exposing abuses in the state's prison system, resulting in revision of Fla. laws relating to convict leasing and corporal punishment of prisoners; annual gold medal of Cross, 1917; rep. Am. Com. for Relief in Ireland, at grave, first pres. of Irish Free State, and other Irish leaders, the two Americans negotiating with British Cabinet and mil. officers until consent was won for the Irish com. to relieve distress of non-combatants in Ireland by means of $5,000,000 contributed by the Am. public for that purpose. Apptd. asst. N.Y. State dir. Federal Writers' Projects, under Works Progress Adminstrn., for compilation first official guide New York City, as section of projected Am. Guide, 1935. Presbyn. Author: Tippecanoe (novel), 1916; Merchants of the Morning (poems), 1919: This Man Adams, 1929. Home: New York. *

MCCOY, TIM, motion picture actor; b. Saginaw, Mich., Apr. 10, 1891; s. Timothy H. and Katherine (Fitzpatrick) MC.; student St. Ignatius Coll., Chgo.; m. Inga Arvad, Feb. 14, 1946; children—Ronald Timothy, Terrence Michael. Commd. capt. cav. U.S. Army, 1917, advanced through grades to col., 1943; served in World war I and II; active with Indians between wars; ret., 1951; head Indian Commn., 1920; adj. gen. Wyo. with rank brig. gen., 1919; authority on Indian sign lang.; tec. dir., star film Covered Wagon, 1922; our of Europe with Indians, 1923-24; motion picture appearances include War Paint, 1925, Winners of the Wilderness, 1926; Around the World in 80 Days, also 90 other films; TV program on factual Western history, 1950-55; tours U.S. with Tommy Scott and Tim McCoy's Country Caravan, from 1961. Decorated legion of Merit, Army Commendation medal, Bronze Star, Legion of Honor, Medialle d'l'Areanautique (France); recipient Emmy award, 1952. Mem. Company Mil. Historians. Home: Nogales, Ariz. Died Jan. 29, 1978.

MCCREA, ALLAN, b. New York, June 10, 1886; s. John and Mary (Jones) McC.; academic edn. Inventor mining machinery. Address: Chicago, Ill. *

MCCREADY, J(AMES) HOMER (MAK-KRE-DI), otolaryngologist; b. Wellsville, O., Feb. 18, 1882; s. James Campbell and Mary Ann (MacIntosh) M.; M.D., Jefferson Med. Coll., 1906; studied Univ. of Vienna, 1908-09; m. Jean Brown, Dec. 3, 1912; children—James H., William B., Emily Jean. Prof. otolaryngology, U. Pitts., 1932-50, emeritus since 1950. Fellow A.C.S.; mem. Am. Laryngol., Rhinol. and Otol. Soc., Am. Acad. Ophthalmology and Otolaryngology, Am. Bd. Otolaryngology, A.M.A., Pa. State Med. Soc., Allegheny County Med. Soc., Pittsburgh Otol. Soc., Pittsburgh Acad. Medicine. Republican. Clubs: Faculty, University, Pittsburgh Field. Home: Pitts. *

MCCREARY, JOHN FERGUSON, educator, physician; b. Eganville, Ont., Can., Jan. 22, 1910; s. James and Anne (Ferguson) McC.; M.D., U. Toronto, 1934; D.Sc., Meml. U., Nfld., 1968; LL.D., U. Toronto, 1970; D.Sc., U. B.C., 1975; m. Dorothy Dowling, Mar. 23, 1970; 1 son, by previous marriage, James Richard. Milbank research fellow Harvard Med. Sch. and Boston Children's Hosp., 1939-41; practice pediatrics, Toronto, 1945-51; attending physician Hosp. for Sick Children, 1945-51, cons. physician, 1951; cons. newborn nurseries Wellesley Hosp., Toronto, 1946-51, newborn nurseries Grace Hosp., Toronto, 1947-51; cons. nutrition Def. Research Bd., 1949-79, Armed Forces Med. Council, 1956; asst. prof. U. Toronto, 1949-51; prof., head dept. pediatrics U. B.C., 1951-59, dean faculty medicine, 1959-72, coordinator health scis., 1971-75; pediatrician-in-chief health centre for children, Vancouver Gen. Hosp., 1951-59; cons. pediatrician Children's Hosp., Vancouver, 1952-75, St. Paul's Hosp., Vancouver, 1952-75. Mem. Canadian Council Nutrition, 1955-59; chmn. adv. com. Canadian Conf. Children, 1960-66; mem. med. team sponsored by Colombo plan studying med. ednl. methods in India, 1957; chmn. Queen Elizabeth II Fund for Research Diseases Children, 1960-74; med. adv. bd. Canadian Physiotherapy Assn., 1960-79; chmn. med. div. Royal Commn. Govt., 1961-62; pres. Assn. Canadian Med. Colls., 1963-66; pres. St. John Council B.C., 1971-76; adv. fellow World Fedn. Occupational Therapists, 1972; chmn. edn. com. B.C. Med. Centre, 1973-75. Bd. dirs. B.C. Med. Research Found., Leon and Thea Koerner Found., Hamber Found., Inst. for Research on Pub. Policy, Mr. & Mrs. P.A. Woodward's Found. Served to wing comdr. Royal Canadian Air Force, 1942-45; capt. Res. Decorated officer Order Orange-Nassau (Netherlands); Order Can.; knight St. John Jerusalem. Diplomate Am. Bd. Pediatrics. Fellow Royal Coll. Physicians and Surgeons (certified pediatrics; Duncan Graham award 1977), Am. Coll. Hosp. Administrs. (hon.); mem. Canadian (chmn. com. nutrition 1954-59), B.C. med. assns., Am. Acad. Pediatrics, Am., Canadian (Ross award 1977), N. Pacific pediatrics socs., Western Soc. Pediatric Research, Canadian Dietetic Assn. (life), Alpha Omega Alpha. Home: Gibsons, B.C., Canada. Died Oct. 14, 1979.

MCCREEDY, JOHN, metals co. exec.; b. Winnipeg, Man., Can., Mar. 23, 1917; s. William McNeilly and Mary Black (McInnes) McC.; B.Applied Sci., U. Toronto, 1949; m. Ila Elizabeth Maxwell, Apr. 29, 1942; 1 dau., Bonnie Franklyn. With Inco Ltd., 1949—, pres. Ont. div., 1970, sr. v.p. then chmn., chief exec. officer Inco Metals Co., 1977, vice chmn. Inco Ltd., Toronto, 1979—, also dir.; dir. St. Lawrence Cement Ltd., Bramalea Ltd.; bd. dirs. Centre Resource Studies, Queens U. Served with RCAF, 1942-45. Mem. Mining Assn. Can. (pres. 1979), Assn. Profl. Engrs. Ont., Can. Inst. Mining and Metallurgy, AIME. Mem. United Ch. Can. Clubs: Toronto, Toronto Golf, Copper Cliff. Home: Toronto, Ont., Canada. Died Dec. 1979.

MCCROSSEN, VINCENT ALOYSIUS, educator, author; b. Meshoppen, Pa., Nov. 21, 1918; s. Edward Henry and Alice Bridget (Hope) McC.; A.B., Dickinson Coll., 1932; Ph.D., U. Pitts., 1936; student Naval Sch. Oriental langs., U. Colo., 1944; m. Rose Mary Bunnell, Oct. 25, 1930. Head dept. langs. Aliquippa (Pa.) High Sch., 1932-33; instr. German and world lit. jr. coll., Bucknell U., 1933-35, asst. and later asso. prof. modern langs., 1936-46; instr. modern langs. Creighton U., 1935-36; prof. modern langs. Marietta Coll., 1946-49; prof. comparative lit. and modern langs. Boston-Harvard-Tech., 1949-70; vis. chmn. dept. of lit. Wilkes Coll., 1965-66, chmn. dept. English, 1964-66; mil. student and tutor in Navy Sch. Oriental langs., U. of Colo., 1944. Mem. Cath. Commn. on Intellectual and Cultural Affairs; chmn. Mass. Gov.'s Com. on Migratory Labor. Life fellow Centro di Studii e Scambe Internazionali, Zürich Acad.; mem. Modern Lang. Assn. (sec. Franco-Ger. div. 1950-52, pres. 1953, chmn. 1954, chmn. adv. and nominating com. after 1955), Central States, Pa. (former mem. exec. council) modern lang. assns., Assn. Am. Colls. (mem. distinguished lects. and campus visitors), N.Eng. Assn. Colls. and Secondary Schs., Am. Assn. of Teachers Slavonic and E. European Langs. (pres. Mass. and New Eng. chapters 1950-52), A.A.U.P., Delta Phi Alpha, Phi Beta Kappa. Author: French Translations of Goethe's Faust, 1937; The New Renaissance of the Spirit, 1949; New Wine in New Containers, 1950; Public Aid to Religious Schools, 1951; And After This Our Exile, 1952; And Again to See the Stars, 1953; Not With a Bang But a Whimper, 1953; The Empty Room; Mary Magdelene; Judas Iscariot; The Two Loves; Call to Revolution; The Elms Too are Dying; Die Bedeutung des Franziskaner Daseins;, 'Twixt Earth and Heaven; What Comparative Literature Might Be; Zo'la, Werfel, and The Song of Bernadette; If in the Beginning the Word Was False; Confrontations in American-European Literary Relations; also articles. Home: Dallas, Pa. Died Apr. 26, 1976.

MCCRUMB, FRED RODGERS, JR., physician, educator; b. Havre de Grace, Md., Dec. 23, 1925; s. Fred Rodgers and Phebe (Riley) McC.; student Loyola Coll., Balt., 1942-44; M.D., U. Md., 1948; m. Gloria Elaine Frizzell, Aug. 18, 1950; children—Sharon Elizabeth, Fred Rodgers III, Mariet Francesca. Resident internal medicine U. Md. Hosp., 1948-50, mem. faculty, 1956-76, prof. internal medicine, 1963-76, dir. Inst. Internal Medicine, 1963-65; spl. asst. to dir. Fogarty Internat. Center, NIH, Bethesda, Md. Asso. mem. commn. epidemiol. survey Armed Forces Epidemiol. Bd., 1959-76; cons. NIH, 1960-65. Served to capt. M.C., AUS, 1951-56. Recipient certificate of honor U. Md., 1948; La medaille d'Honneur des Epidemies, 1954. Mem. Am. Acad. Microbiology, Am. Epidemiol. Soc., Am. Pub. Health Assn., Am. Soc. Tropical Medicine and Hygiene, Infectious Diseases Soc. Am., N.Y. Acad. Scis., Royal Soc. Tropical Medicine and Hygiene, Acad. Nationale de Medicine. Research on ecology and treatment of plague; investigation diseases mil. importance in S.E. Asia; devel. and application measles vaccination techniques. Home: Libertytown, Md. Died Jan. 5, 1976; buried Balt. Nat. Cemetery.

MCCULLOCH, WILLIAM M., congressman; b. Holmes County, O., Nov. 24, 1901; s. James H. and Ida Fay (Moore) McC.; student Coll. of Wooster (O.), 1919-21; LL.B., Ohio State U., 1925; LL.D., Ohio No. U.; m. Mabel Pauline Harris, Nov. 8, 1926; children—Nancy Jane, Adah Ann. Admitted to Ohio Bar, 1925; mem. Ohio House of Reps., 1933-45; minority leader. Republican, 1936-39, speaker, 1939-44; mem. 80th to 92d Congresses, 4th Ohio Dist., mem. com. on judiciary, joint com. on atomic energy, joint com. on immigration and nationality policy. Dir. Piqua Nat. Bank & Trust Co., Third Sav. & Loan Co. (both Piqua, O.). Mem. Commn. on Western Hemisphere Immigration; past mem. Pres.'s Commn. on Civil Disorder, Pres.'s Commn. on Causes and Prevention of Violence. Vice chmn. Nat. Republican Congl. Campaign Com. Mem. Am., Ohio, Miami County bar assns., Am. Legion. Republican. Rotarian. Home: Washington, D.C. Died Feb. 22, 1980.

MCCULLY, ALICE WOODRUFF ANDERSON ("ANDERSON MCCULLY"), writer; b. Seattle, Wash., Dec. 15, 1882; d. Oliver Phelps and Ada Augusta (Woodruff) Anderson; grad. Annie Wright Sem., Tacoma, Wash., 1901; student U. of Wash.; m. Marshall H. McCully, of Philadelphia, Pa., May 20, 1903 (divorced); children—Dorothy Woodruff (Mrs. Harry Albert Achenbach), Louise Phelps. Formerly writer of fiction for mags. but during recent yrs. has devoted time to horticultural articles, specializing on rockgraden lines; studied alpine plants, particularly the alpines of the Northwest mountain ranges and experimented in their growth under cultivation; studied mountain flora of Southern Calif. and Mexico, 1930-31. Mem. League Am. Penwomen, Alpine Garden Soc. of England, Phi Gamma Mu. Republican. Episcopalian. Author: American Alpines in the Garden, 1931. Contbr. to Ladies' Home Jour., House Beautiful, House and Garden, American Homes, Country Gentleman, Horticulture, New York Times, and others. Regarded as an authority on rockgardens and alpines, experimenting with cacti and writing on that subject; also doing pvt. research work in growing plants from seed of Tibet, China, and other little known mountain flora. Mem. advisory board Yenching U., Peiping, China. Home: Westwood, Bainbridge Island, Wash. Address: Port Blakeley, Wash. *

MCCURDY, GILBERT JAMES CATHCART, dept. store exec.; b. Phila., Mar. 29, 1895; s. John Cooke and Florence A. (Cathcart) McC.; B.A. summa cum laude, Williams Coll., 1917, LL.D. (hon.), 1964; m. Virginia A. Geier, Sept. 25, 1920; children—Gilbert Geier, Patricia. With McCurdy & Co., Inc., Rochester, N.Y., 1919-78, successively salesman, credit mgr., sec., treas., gen. mgr., 1919-31, pres., 1931-62, chmn. bd., 1962-78; chmn. bd. Community Savs. Bank, Rochester, to 1954, mem. adv. com.; pres. Midtown Holdings Corp., to 1971, chmn. bd., 1971-78; adv. com., past chmn. bd. Lincoln First Bank of Rochester. Past pres. Rochester YMCA; hon. trustee U. Rochester, Rochester Inst. Tech. Mem. Rochester C. of C. (past pres.), Phi Beta Kappa, Zeta Psi. Republican. Baptist. Clubs: Genesee Valley, Country, University (Rochester). Home: Rochester, N.Y. Died July 8, 1978.

MC CUSKEY, RICHARD GEORGE, lawyer; b. Canton, Ohio, Mar. 23, 1912; s. Emery Andrew and Margaret (George) McC.; student Wooster (Ohio) Coll., 1930-31; grad. Mt. Union Coll., Alliance, Ohio, 1934, LL.D., 1979; grad. U. Mich. Law Sch., 1937; m. Eleanor E. Mumaw, Sept. 9, 1938; 1 son, Thomas G. Admitted to Ohio bar, 1937, practiced in Canton, to 1978; of counsel firm Black, McCuskey, Souers & Arbaugh, 1946-78; dir. Union Metal Mfg. Treas., Canton Police Boys Club, 1952-80; trustee Canton Scholarship Found., 1952-80, Canton Pub. Library,

1950-63, pres., 1958-63; trustee Mt. Union Coll., 1953-80, pres., 1964-72; trustee Aultman Hosp., 1971-80, Canton Med. Edn. Found., 1978-80. Served to maj. AUS, 1943-46. Decorated Bronze Star. Fellow Ohio Bar Found.; mem. Am., Ohio, N.Y. State bar assns., Am. Judicature Soc., Sigma Nu. Republican. Methodist. Clubs: Canton, Brookside Country (Canton). Home: Massillon, Ohio. Died Dec. 20, 1980; buried Canton, Ohio.

MCCUTCHEON, JAMES, dentist, educator; b. Elizabeth, N.J., July 10, 1920; s. Andrew and Matilda (Huff) McC.; B.A., McGill U., 1942, D.D.S., 1945; M.S.D. in Prosthetic Dentistry, U. Mich., 1948; m. Geraldine Frances Berteau, Oct. 20, 1945; children—John Gerald, Nancy Andrea. Mem. faculty dentistry McGill U., Montreal, 1948-70, dean, 1956-70, prof., 1960-70; dental surgeon in chief, dir. dept. dentistry Montreal Gen. Hosp., 1955-70; dean faculty dentistry U. Alta., Edmonton, Can., 1970-76; cons. Royal Canadian Dental Corps. Pres., Assn. Canadian Faculties Dentistry, 1972-74. Fellow Am. Internat. colls. dentists, Royal Coll. Dentists Can.; mem. Coll. Dental Surgeons Que. (bd. govs.), Montreal Dental Club (exec. com. 1948-51), Canadian Dental Assn., Montreal Endodontia Soc., Am. Acad. Dental Medicine, Canadian Acad. Prosthodontics (pres. 1964-65), Internat. Dental Fedn., Sigma Chi, Phi Kappa Phi. Mem. United Ch. Can. Home: Edmonton Alta., Can. Died Dec. 20, 1976.

MCDANIEL, JOSEPH MILTON, JR., corp. exec.; b. Balt., Mar. 1, 1902; s. Joseph Milton and Georgia DeSalles (Katzenberger) McD.; A.B., Johns Hopkins 1924, Ph.D., 1930; M.A. (hon.), Dartmouth, 1939; LL.D., Trinity Coll., Dublin, Ireland, Davis and Elkins Coll.; D.H.L., Lewis Coll.; m. Eileen Dorothy Driver, Sept. 4, 1930; 1 son, John Milton. Prof. econs. U. Del., Newark, 1928-29, Dartmouth, 1930-42; spl. asst. to sec. of commerce, 1946-47; prof. econs. Northwestern U., Evanston, Ill., 1947-48, dean sch. commerce, 1949-50; asst. to dir. Ford Found., 1950-52, sec., 1953-67, cons., 1967-69; chmn. bd. Ford Fund for Adult Edn., 1965-67, Andrews Hart Corp., N.Y.C.; dir. emeritus United Brands Corp., Revco D.S., Inc., Cadence Corp., Oppenheimer Fund, Oppenheimer Time Fund, Oppenheimer AIM Fund, Oppenheimer Spl. Fund, Oppenheimer Tax-Free Bond Fund. Cons. U.S. Nat. Resources Planning Bd., 1939-41; mem. N.E. Labor Supply Bd., 1940-41; asst. to U.S. spl. rep. in Europe, ECA, also asst. to adminstrn., Washington, 1949-50; asst. U.S. rep. 4th session Econ. Commn. Europe, Geneva, 1949; mem. U.S. Civil Service Com. on Expert Examiners. Trustee Johns Hopkins U. Served from lt. to comdr., USNR, 1942-46. Mem. Council on Fgn. Relations, Kappa Sigma, Omicron Delta Kappa. Clubs: Johns Hopkins (N.Y.C.); Tudor and Stuart; Nassau (Princeton). Author: Introduction to Social Sciences, 2 vols., 1939; Don't Bank on It, 1969. Home: Lexington, Va. Died May 16, 1980; buried Outer Banks, N.C.

MCDERMID, WILLIAM ALBERT, b. Winnipeg, Man. Can., Oct. 25, 1886; s. Andrew (M.D.) and Emma (Brett) M.; student commerce and administration, U. of Chicago, 1903-07; m. Marian Vesta Lusk, Sept. 10, 1912; children—Dorothy Marise, Elizabeth Ann. Industrial management counsel; pres. and dir. Famous Books and Plays, Inc. Organizer and director N.J. Div. Am. Protective League and spl. agt. U.S. Dept. of Justice, 1917-19. Mem. Assn. of Nat. Advertisers, 1915-24, dir., 1916-21, pres., 1919. Mem. Am. Soc. Sales Executives (exec. com.), New York Sales Managers' Club (pres. 1921 and 1939), Phi Gamma Delta. Presbyn. Mason. Author of papers and articles on economic aspects of merchandising, sales engring., etc. Consultant War Production Board since Feb. 1942. Home: New York, N.Y.

MCDERMOTT, MALCOLM, lawyer, educator; b. Rogersville, Tenn., Aug. 7, 1885; s. Thomas and Ann McNeil (Kirkpatrick) McD.; grad. Mt. Hermon (Mass.) Sch., 1906; A.B., Princeton, 1910; LL.B., Harvard, 1913; m. Gladys Willingham, Nov. 24, 1915; children—Malcolm, Raymond, Rose. Admitted to Tenn. bar, 1913, and began practice at Knoxville; mem. Webb, Baker & McDermott, 1917-20, Lee Price, McDermott & Meek, 1925-30; dean Coll. Law, U. of Tenn., 1920-30; prof. law, Duke U., since 1930; visiting lecturer universities of Krakow and Warsaw, Poland, 1936; mem. Commn. on Revision of the Laws of N.C. Relating to Estates. Mem. Com. on Revision of the Laws of N.C. Relating to Insurance; vice chmn. Gen Statutes Commission North Carolina. Dem. presidential elector, 1928; mem. Tenn. Dem. Exec. Com., 1928-32; legal consultant Dept. of Defense, 1951. Awarded Ross Essay Contest prize, American Bar Assn., 1939. Member Am., N.C. bar assns., Tenn. Bar Assn. (pres. 1920-21). Presbyn. Home: Durham, N.C.

MCDEVITT, RUTH THANE SHOECRAFT, actress; b. Coldwater, Mich., Sept. 13, 1895; d. John B. and Elizabeth C. (Imber) Shoecraft; student Wooster U., 1912-13, Bowling Green Normal Coll., 1913-14, Am. Acad. Dramatic Arts, N.Y.C., 1916-17; m. Patrick John McDevitt, Dec. 10, 1926 (dec. 1936). Made Broadway debut in Young Couple, 1940; appeared in Goodbye in the Night, 1940, Arsenic and Old Lace, 1941, Meet a Body, 1944, I'll Be Waiting, 1945, Harvey, 1944, Darling, Darling, Darling, 1947; on tour in Arsenic and Old Lace, summer 1947, Sleepy Hollow, N.Y.C., 1948; summer tour Harvey, 1949, The Silver Whistle, 1950, Picnic, N.Y.C., 1953, The Solid Gold Cadillac, 1953 (also tour 1955), Dairy of a Scoundrel, Phoenix, N.Y.C., 1956, Clerambard, 1957, The Best Man, 1960 (also tour 1961-62), Save Me a Place at Forest Lawn, N.Y.C., 1963; appeared in motion pictures The Guy Who Came Back, 1951, The Parent Trap, 1961, Boys Night Out, 1962, Love is a Ball, 1962, The Birds, 1962, The Out of Towners, 1963; TV appearances include Mister Peeper series, NBC, 1953-54, Route 66, Doctor Kildare, The Nurses, Alfred Hitchcock Presents, The Ed Sullivan Show. Mem. A.F.T.R.A. Clubs: St. Petersburg (Fla.) Woman's (life, past pres.). Home: Hollywood, Calif.

MCDONAGH, VINCENT GEORGE, accountant; b. Toledo, Mar. 21, 1912; s. James Joseph and Edna (Cook) McD.; student pub. schs., Toledo; m. Lois Waters, Aug. 22, 1935; children—Lois Ann (Mrs. Glen Schwartz), Dennis James, William Edward, James Vincent. Accountant, Ernst & Ernst, C.P.A.'s, Toledo, 1935-41; pub. accountant Alexander Grant & Co., Chgo., 1941-42; controller Trane Co., LaCrosse, Wis., 1942-51, Gar Wood Industries, Wayne, Mich., 1951-53; sec.-treas. Charles Bruning Co. div. Addressograph-Multigraph Corp., Mt. Prospect, Ill., 1953-63; treas., dir. Charles Bruning Co., Ltd., Toronto Ont., Can., until 1964, sec. until 1965; treas. Victor Comptometer Corp., 1965-69; pvt. practice as C.P.A. and investor, Toledo, 1969-71; partner Leisk, McDonagh & Co., C.P.A.'s, 1972-74; individual practice accounting, 1974-78; dir., mgr. Toledo office Walter Gons & Co., C.P.A.'s, 1971. Vol. cons. for fiscal affairs Northwest Ohio area A.R.C., 1971-78. C.P.A., Wis., Ohio. Mem. Am. Inst. C.P.A.'s, Fin. Inst., Ill., Ohio socs. C.P.A.'s. Club: Chgo. Athletic Assn. Home: Toledo, Ohio. Died Oct. 8, 1978; buried Calvary Cemetery, Toledo.

MCDONALD, DAVID JOHN, union exec.; b. Pitts., Nov. 22, 1902; s. David and Mary (Kelly) McD.; student Duquesne U., 1921; grad. Carnegie Inst. Tech., 1932; Ph.D. in Industrial Relations, St. Martin's Coll., 1959; LL.D., U. N.H.; D.H.L., Alliance Coll.; m. Emily Price, Aug. 4, 1937; 1 son, David J.; m. 2d, Rosemary C. McHugh, Jan. 3, 1950. Steelworker, sec. and asst. to v.p. United Mine Workers Am. Washington, 1923-36, sec.-treas. Steel Workers Organizing Com., 1936-42; internat. sec.-treas. United Steel Workers of Am. (CIO), Pitts., 1942-53, pres. 1953-65; v.p. AFL-CIO, sec.-treas. Polit. Action Com.; lectr. Mem. Pres.'s Labor-Mgmt. Adv. Com., Randall Com. on Fgn. Econ. Policy, Intercontinental Def. Com., Govt. Salaries Commn.; asst. econ. dir., 1953; del. to Chapultepec Conf., World Food Conf., Rome, 1965. Active A.R.C., Community Chest. Mem. bd. visitors U.S. Naval Acad.; v.p. Internat. Boxing Hall Fame. Mem. Am. Arbitration Assn. (dir.). Roman Catholic. Author: Coal and Unionism, 1939; Union Man, 1969. Home: Palm Springs, Calif. Died Aug. 8, 1979.

MCDONNELL, JAMES SMITH, aerospace co. exec.; b. Denver, Apr. 9, 1899; s. James Smith and Susan Belle (Hunter) M.; B.S., Princeton, 1921; M.S. in Aeronautical Engring., Mass. Inst. Tech., 1925; grad. Army Air Corps Flying Sch., San Antonio, 1923-24; D.Eng., Washington U., St. Louis, 1958, M.D., 1977; D.Eng., U. Mo. at Rolla, 1957; LL.D., Princeton, 1960, U. Ark., 1965; D.Sc., Clarkson Coll., 1976; m. Mary Elizabeth Finney, June 30, 1934 (dec. July 1949); children—James Smith III, John Finney; m. 2d, Priscilla Brush Forney, Apr. 1, 1956; children—George David, Susan Brush Boyd, Priscilla Young Canny. Aero. engr., pilot Huff Daland Airplane Co., 1924; stress analyst, draftsman Consol. Aircraft Co., 1925; asst. chief engr. Stout Metal Airplane Co., 1925; chief engr. Hamilton Aero Mfg. Co., 1926-27, McDonnell & Assos., 1928-29; v.p. Airtransport Engring. Corp., 1930-31; engr., test pilot Great Lakes Aircraft Corp., 1932; chief project engr. for landplanes Glenn L. Martin Co., 1933-38; pres. McDonnell Aircraft Corp., St. Louis, 1939-62, chmn., chief exec. officer, 1962-67; chmn., chief exec. officer McDonnell Douglas Corp., St. Louis, 1967-72, chmn., 1972-80. Mem. adv. council Center for Strategic and Internat. Studies, Washington; mem. Civic Progress, Inc., St. Louis. Bd. dirs. Atlantic Council, Population Crisic Com., UN Assn. U.S.A.; hon. chmn. bd. St. Louis Country Day Sch. Recipient St. Louis award, 1959, Daniel Guggenhiem medal, 1963, Robert J. Collier trophy, 1966, Founders medal Nat. Acad. Engring., 1967, Forrestal award, 1972; named to Nat. Aviation Hall of Fame. Fellow Am. Inst. Aeros. and Astronautics (hon.); mem. St. Louis C. of C., St. Louis Com. Fgn. Relations, Mo. Acad. Squires. Clubs: Log Cabin, Old Warson Country, Noonday, University, Racquet, St. Louis Country, Bellerive Country, Saint Louis, Washington University, Mo. Athletic (St. Louis); University (N.Y.C.); Met. (Washington). Home: Saint Louis, Mo. Died Aug. 22, 1980.

MCDOUGALD, JOHN ANGUS, industrialist; b. Toronto, Ont., Can., Mar. 14, 1908; s. Duncan J. and Margherita Emelie (Murray) McD.; student Upper Can. Coll., St. Andrews Coll.; m. Hedley Maude Eustace Smith, Nov. 6, 1934. With Dominion Securities Corp., Ltd., 1926-45; v.p. Taylor, McDougald Co. Ltd., from 1945; pres. Ravelston Corp. Ltd., Taymac Investments Ltd., Sugra Ltd., Thermax Ltd.; chmn. bd., pres. Argus Corp. Ltd.; chmn. bd., chmn. exec. com. Dominion Stores, Ltd., Avco of Can. Ltd.; chmn. bd. Standard Broadcasting Corp. Ltd., Grew Ltd., Standard Broadcast Sales (U.K.) Ltd.; chmn. adv. bd. Crown Trust Co.; chmn. exec. com. Massey-Ferguson Ltd., chmn. bd., 1978; chmn. exec. com. Gen. Bakeries Ltd.; v.p., chmn. exec. com. Hollinger Mines, Ltd.; dir., mem. exec. com. St. Lawrence Corp., Ltd., Domtar Ltd.; v.p., mem. exec. com. Canadian Imperial Bank of Commerce; adv. bd. First Nat. Bank, Palm Beach, Fla.; dir. CFRB Ltd., Canadian Mining & Finance Co. Ltd., Avco Corp. (N.Y.), Hollinger North Shore Exploration Co. Ltd., Hinde & Dauch Ltd., Iron Ore Co. Can., Labrador Mining & Exploration Co. Ltd., Massey-Ferguson Holdings Ltd., Massey-Ferguson (Australia) Ltd., Massey-Ferguson Holdings (Australia) Ltd., Sangamo Co. Ltd., Standard Broadcast Sales Co. Ltd., Standard Broadcasting Corp. (U.K.) Ltd., Stone & Webster Can. Ltd.; trustee Ont. Jockey Club; gov. Jockey Club Can. Hon. pres., dir., mem. exec. com. Royal Agrl. Winter Fair. Bd. govs. Good Samaritan Hosp., Palm Beach, Fla. Clubs: Rolling Rock (Ligoniar); Metropolitan, N.Y. Yacht (N.Y.C.); Toronto (pres.), York, Toronto and North York Hunt, Eglinton Hunt (Toronto); Mount Royal (Montreal); Buck's, Turf, White's (London, Eng.); Bath and Tennis (v.p.), Everglades (gov.), Seminole Golf (Palm Beach); Lyford Cay (Nassau). Home: Willowdale, Ont., Can. Died Mar. 15, 1978.

MC DOWELL, REMICK, pub. utility exec.; b. Chgo., Feb. 10, 1909; s. Irvin and Ethel (Remick) McD.; M.B.A., U. Chgo., 1954; m. Susan J. Rawson, Mar. 8, 1934; children—Catherine, Jane. Accountant Commonwealth Edison Co., Chgo., 1928-40; with Peoples Gas Light & Coke Co., Chgo., 1940, chmn., chief exec., 1961-73; chmn. exec. com. Peoples Gas Co., 1973-74; ret., 1974; dir. AMSTED Industries, Inc., Harris Bankcorp, Inc., Harris Trust & Savs. Bank. Trustee, pres. Field Mus. Natural History. Mem. Am. Gas Assn. Clubs: University, Commonwealth, Commercial, Chicago, Cliff Dwellers (Chgo.); Woodstock Country. Home: Woodstock, Ill.; also Longboat Key, Fla. Died Sept. 29, 1979.

MCEACHIN, ARCHIBALD BRUCE, lawyer; b. Tuscaloosa, Ala., Jan. 19, 1910; s. Archibald Bruce and Katie (Melton) McE.; A.B., U. Ala., 1931, LL.B., 1933; m. Charlotte Cammack, June 30, 1934; 1 dau., Charlotte Cammack (Mrs. James E. Park, Jr.). Admitted to Ala. bar, 1933, since practiced in Tuscaloosa; admitted to practice before U.S. Supreme Ct.; sr. partner McEachin, Ormond, Fulton & Lake. Dir. Tuscaloosa chpt. A.R.C., 1948. Served to capt. AUS, 1943-46; PTO. Mem. Am., Ala., Tuscaloosa County (past pres.) Tuscaloosa bar assns., Tuscaloosa Jr. C. of C. (past pres.), Internat. Assn. Ins. Counsel, Nat. Assn. R.R. Trial Counsel, V.F.W., Am. Legion, Tuscaloosa Hist. Soc., Warrior Tombigbee Devel. Assn., Tuscaloosa C. of C., Ala. Claims Assn., Kappa Alpha, Phi Delta Phi, Omicron Delta Kappa, Blue Key, Jasons. Elk. Clubs: Tuscaloosa Country, Civitan (past pres.), Gulley Hunting (Tuscaloosa). Home: Tuscaloosa, Ala. Died Aug. 30, 1978; buried Tuscaloosa.

MCELDOWNEY, HAROLD BATCHELDER, architect, educator; b. Chgo., May 7, 1896; s. Walter T. and Anna M. (Batchelder) McE.; B.S. in Architecture, Ill. Inst. Tech., 1920; student Art Inst. Chgo., 1918-19. Pvt. practice architecture, 1927-30, 44-47; dep. dir. Ill. Historic Am. Bldg. Survey, 1931-32; supt. painting Century of Progress, Chgo., 1933; dep. chief architect for Ill., Fed. Housing Adminstrn., 1934-39; prof., head dept. architecture U. Ill. at Chgo., 1947-64, professor emeritus, from 1964, assistant dean of the College of Architecture and Art, 1963-64. Registered professional engr., Ill. Fellow A.I.A.; mem. Ill. Soc. Architects, Assn. Collegiate Schs. Architecture, Scarab, Tau Beta Pi, Phi Eta Sigma. Club: Cliff Dwellers (Chgo.). Home: Douglas, Mich. Died July 5, 1979.

MCELFRESH, ARTHUR EDWARD, JR., physician, educator; b. Louisville, Feb. 27, 1923; s. Arthur Edward and Sarah (Moore) McE; M.D., Cornell U., 1947; m. Mary Stafford June 19, 1948; children—Peter, Duncan, Stuart, Bruce. Intern, N.Y. Hosp., 1947-48; asst. resident Children's Hosp., Columbus, Ohio, 1948-49, chief resident, 1950-51; research fellow Children's Med. Center, Boston, 1949-50; asst. prof. pediatrics U. Ala. Med. Sch., 1953-54; mem. faculty Temple U. Sch. Medicine, 1954-65, asso. prof. pediatrics, 1962-65; prof. pediatrics, chmn. dept. St. Louis U. Sch. Medicine, from 1965. Mem. adv. com. for study profl. communications in radiologic health Columbia Sch. Pub. Health, from 1966. Served to capt. MC. AUS, 1951-53. Mem. Soc. Pediatric Research, Am. Pediatric Soc., Soc. Human Genetics, A.A.A.S., Alpha Omega Alpha. Asso. editor Jour. Pediatrics, from 1967. Home: St. Louis, Mo. Died Oct. 29, 1977.

MCELROY, CLARENCE HAMILTON, educator; born Tulsa, Okla., Mar. 26, 1886; s. George H. and Joanna (Hodge) McE.; B.S., Okla. A. and M. Coll., 1906; D.V.M., St. Joseph Vet. College, 1919; married Maggie W. Allnut, August 22, 1906; children—Buel, Geraldine (Mrs. N. G. Blankenship). Instr. vet. med. and physiology, Okla. A. and M. Coll., 1909-12, asst.

bacteriologist, 1912-16, asst. prof. vet. med. bacteriology, 1921-23, prof. and head bacteriol. dept. since 1924, dean sch. sci. and lit., 1925-35, dean of men, 1928-47, acting dean sch. veterinary medicine, 1947-48, dean, 1948-53, emeritus dean of veterinary medicine. President of the Stillwater YMCA, 1960-61. Member American Vet. Med. Assn., Nat. Assn. Deans Men, C. of C. (dir. and past pres.), Sigma Nu, Phi Sigma, Phi Eta Sigma, Phi Kappa Phi, Blue Key. Mem. Christian Ch. Mason (K.T.). Club: Lions. Contbr. articles to various publs. Home: Stillwater, Okla. *

MCELROY, DENNIS LEE, mining engr.; b. Moundsville, W.Va., Oct. 19, 1904; s. Arch Jones and Ella Mae (Dorsey) McE.; B.S. in Mining Engring., W.Va. U. Sch. Mines, 1927, M.s., 1930; m. Opal Lucille Hall, June 2, 1926; 1 son, Arch Leslie. Mine foreman Penn-Pitt Coal & Coke Co., Greensboro, Pa., 1927-28; research fellow in mining W.Va. U., 1928-30, asst. dir. mining extension, 1930-38; head dept. mining engring. Va. Poly. Inst., 1938-39; dir. Sch. Mines, dir. Indsl. Extension, prof. mining engring. W.Va. U., 1939-43; chief coal sect. WPB, 1941-43; chief engr., v.p. engring., v.p. operations, exec. v.p., dir. Consol. Coal Co., Pitts., 1943-65; ret., 1965; dir. Rochester & Pitts. Coal Co., Nat. Mine Service Co. Mem. survey team U.S. Bur. Mines, 1953-54; mem. Dept. Commerce Indsl. Com. to Philippines, 1965; chmn. Fed. Coal Mine Safety Bd. Rev., 1967-69. Bd. Dirs. Salem Coll. Mem. Soc. Mining Engrs. (dir., past pres.), Am. Inst. Mining, Metall. and Petroleum Engrs. (dir., past pres.; Erskine Ramsay Gold medal 1972, hon. mem.), W.Va. Coal Mining Inst. (past pres.), Engrs. Soc. Western Pa. (past pres.), W.Va. U. Alumni Assn., Order of Vandalia, Sigma Xi, Kappa Kappa Psi, Phi Kappa Tau, Tau Beta Pi, Sigma Gamma Epsilon. Democrat. Presbyn. Mason. Clubs: University, Duquesne (Pitts.); Lakeview Country (Morgantown, W.Va.). Asso. editor Mineral Industry, 1939-40, 41. Contbr. articles to profl. jours. Home: Pittsburgh, Pa. Died Dec. 22, 1978.

MCENTEE, JAMES JOSEPH (MAK'EN-TE), dir. Civilian Conservation Corps; b. Jersey City, N.J., Sept. 19, 1884; s. James Lawrence and Mary (Sullivan) McE.; ed. public schools; m. Alice Donovan, Jan. 18, 1905; children—Marie (Mrs. Edwin Callahan), Alice Therese, Gertrude (Mrs. Charles J. Mahieu), Dorothy, James Joseph, Frank. Began as machinist, 1902; rep. of Internat. Assn. Machinists in industrial relations; exec. asst. dir. Civilian Conservation Corps, 1933-40, dir. since Mar. 5, 1940. Served as mem. N.Y. Arbitration Bd. to adjust hours and wages disputes in munition factories during World War. Democrat. Catholic. Home: Jersey City, N.J. *

MCEWEN, GEORGE FRANCIS, prof. physical oceanography; b. Manchester, Ia., June 16, 1882; s. John Fremont and Lillian (Dodson) McE.; student Ia. State Coll. of Agr. and Mech. Arts, 1901-05; A.B., Stanford, 1908, Ph.D., 1911; m. Mae Alice Winner, June 18, 1912; children—Paul Albert, Dora Ellen. Asst. in physics, Stanford U., 1907-10, asst. in applied mathematics, 1908-10, instr. in applied mathematics, 1910-11; physicist Marine Biological Assn., San Diego, summers 1908-12; instr. in mathematics, U. of Ill., 1911-12; instr. in physical oceanography, Scripps Instn., U. of Calif., 1912-18, asst. prof., 1918-22, asso. prof., 1922-27, prof. since 1928, also mem. faculty of extension div., San Diego dist., since 1924. Del. to 1st Pan-Pacific Science Congress, Honolulu, T.H., 1920. Internat. Math. Congress, Toronto, Can., 1924, 3d Pan-Pacific Science Congress, Tokyo, Japan, 1926; chmn. nat. sub-com. for U.S., Physical and Chem. Oceanography of Pacific, 1927; mem. Nat. Research Council, Am. Com. on Oceanography of the Pacific, Internat. Com. on Unification of Methods and Instruments of Physical Oceanography. Fellow A.A.A.S., Am. Acad. Arts and Sciences, Math. Assn. America, Am. Meteorol. Soc. (councilor 1935-37, v.p. 1938-39, chmn. San Diego branch 1939-41), Calif. Acad. of Science, San Diego Natural History Soc., Am. Physical Soc., Am. Math. Soc., Inst. of Math. Statistics, Am. Geophys. Union (sub-com. on evaporation, hydrol. sect. 31 and chmn. 1931-35; sub-com. on statis. methods of sect. of hydrology, 1934), Am. Statis. Assn., Am. Geog. Soc., Am. Assn. Engrs. (award of merit 1927), Polish Inst. of Arts and Sciences in America, Engineers Club of San Diego (president 1935), S.A.R., San Diego Chapter (pres. 1945-46), Sigma Xi, Phi Beta Kappa, Democrat. Unitarian. Clubs: University of California, Faculty, Writers Club of San Diego. Address: La Jolla, Calif. *

MCFADDEN, ARTHUR JAMES, fruit grower; b. Santa Ana, Calif., Aug. 2, 1881; s. Robert and Flora (Babcock) McF.; B.S., Pomona Coll., 1901, LL.D., 1950; LL.B., Harvard, 1904; m. Anna Jane Kelso, May 18, 1905 (dec. 1953); children—Mary (Mrs. G. W. Hinds), Edith Eleanor (Mrs. W. K. Lindsay), Annabel (Mrs. Geo. Rassmussen), Robert (killed in Germany 1945), Flora Mina (Mrs. Robert Safford); m. 2d, Mabel T. Henderson, Jan. 30, 1954. Admitted Calif. bar, 1904, practiced in Santa Ana, 1904-08; fruit grower since 1908; dir. Southern Calif. Edison Company, Pacific Mutual Life Insurance Co., director Founders Fire & Marine Ins. Co., The Irvine Co., pres. 1960-61. Vice pres. James Irvine Found. Pres. Irvine Valencia Growers Assn. and Irvine Walnut Growers Assn., Cal. Persimmon Growers Assn.; past pres. Nat. Council Farmer Coops., 1949-50; past v.p. Cal. Walnut Growers Assn.; director California Fruit Exchange; hon. president Agricultural Council of California. Ex-pres. Calif. Agrl. Pro-rate Commn.; pres. Calif. State Board of Agr. 1943-60; pres. Santa Ana Valley Hospital, 1926-33. Vice pres. and trustee, Pomona College; mem. bd. regents University of California, 1943-60. Dir. California State Chamber Commerce (pres. 1937-40; past treas.). Republican. Mem. U.P. Church. Lion. Club: University (Los Angeles). Home: Santa Ana, Cal. *

MCFADYEN, NEIL MATHIESON, hosp. exec., physician; b. Glasgow, Scotland, June 7, 1923; s. Neil and Sarah Murphy (Lothian) McF.; came to U.S., 1955, naturalized, 1961; M.B., Ch.B., U. Glasgow Med. Sch., 1951; m. Mary Eunice Stockdale, July 30, 1945; 1 dau., Barbara (Mrs. John Calhoun Sterritt, Jr.). Intern, So. Gen. Hosp., Glasgow, 1951; resident in gen. medicine Hairmyres Hosp., East Kilbride, Scotland, 1952; resident in psychiatry Hawkhead Mental Hosp., Glasgow, 1952-55; supt. Weston (W.Va.) State Hosp., 1961-63; chief psychiatry VA Hosp., Clarksburg, W.Va., 1963-70; chief of staff VA Hosp., Augusta, Ga., 1970-73, VA Center, Leavenworth, Kans., 1977; dir. VA Hosp., Battle Creek, Mich., 1973-75, VA Hosp., Palo Alto, Calif., 1975-77; clin. asst. prof. psychiatry W.Va. med. Sch., Morgantown, 1965-69; clin. prof. psychiatry Med. Coll. Ga., Augusta, 1971-73, Mich. State U. Med. Coll., Lansing, 1975-77; mem. adv. bd. Spl. Program Alcohol and Drug Addiction, Western Mich. U., Kalamazoo, 1974-77. Pres., Augusta-Richmond County (Ga.) Alcohol and Drug Council, 1971-73. Bd. dirs. Easter House, Inc., Battle Creek. Served with Royal Navy, 1942-46. Decorated 1939-45 Star, Atlantic Star, France and Germany Star. Recipient Clin. Surgery prize Dr. A.J. Hutton, 1949; Americanism medal DAR, 1977. Am. Psychiat. Assn. fellow, 1973; 1st class certificate in dermatology, psychiatry, clin. surgery. Fellow Am. Geriatrics Soc., Internat. Assn. Social Psychiatrists, Royal Soc. Health; mem. World Psychiat. Assn., Brit. Med. Soc., Am. Coll. Hosp. Adminstrs., Harrison County (W.Va.) Assn. Mental Health (vice-chmn. 1964-69), Harrison County Assn. Fgn. Med Grads. (pres. 1966-67). Clubs: Elks, Moose, Rotary. Home: Troy, Mich. Died Dec. 2, 1977.

MCFARLAND, EARL, army officer; b. Topeka, Kan., July 7, 1883; s. James Davis and Mathilda (Steele) McF.; B.S., U.S. Mil. Acad., 1906; grad. Ordnance Sch. Tech., 1911, Ordnance Sch. of Application, 1912; M.E., Worcester Poly. Inst., 1923, Command and Gen. Staff Sch., 1931., Army Industrial Coll., 1933, Army War Coll., 1934; m. Mary Edith Cole, June 30, 1911; children—Mary Ann (Mrs. Hamilton Austin Twitchell), Cole, Earl. Commd. 2d lt., arty., 1906, and advanced through grades to brig. gen., 1938; prof. ordnances and gunnery and head dept. U.S. Mil. Acad., 1924-29; asst. Chief of Ordnance, U.S. Army, 1938-42; became comdg. officer Springfield (Mass.) Armory, June 1942; retired from active service, 1943. Elected supt. Staunton (Va.) Mil. Acad. Awarded D.S.M., Legion of Merit, Army Citation. Clubs: Army and Navy, War College (Washington); Colony (Springfield) Author of a U.S. Mil. Acad. textbook. Address: Staunton, Va. *

MCFARLAND, FRANK T(HEODORE), botanist; b. Sunbury, O., May 12, 1886; s. Samuel Burton and Rebecca (Miller) McF.; B.S., Ohio State U., 1912; M.S., U. of Mich., 1916; Ph.D., U. of Wis., 1921; student U. of Chicago, summer 1917; m. Leona Moody, June 7, 1913; children—John Moody and Mary Louise, twins. Instr. in botany, U. of Ky., 1913-21; asst. prof. 1921-42; prof. and head of dept., 1942-51; research prof. bot., 1942-51. Curator of Herbarium. Owner of Lomond Hill Arboretum, Irvine, Ky. Fellow A.A.A.S.; mem. Nat. Geog. Soc., Am. Phytopath. Soc., Am. Rose Soc., Soc. Applied Bot. Club, Mycol Soc. Am., Bot. Soc. Am., Am. Fern Soc., Am. Soc. Plant Taxonomists, N.E. Bot. Club, Torrey Bot. Club, Sigma Xi. Democrat. Presbyterian. Author: A Catalog of the Vascular Plants of Kentucky, 1942. Research: Studies of the vascular flora and its distribution in Ky. Address: Irvine, Ky. *

MCFARLAND, ROSS ARMSTRONG, educator; b. Denver, July 18, 1901; s. James and Helen (Russell) McF.; A.B., U. Mich., 1923; Ph.D., Harvard, 1928; Sc.D. (hon.), Park Coll., 1942, Rutgers U., 1964, Trinity Coll., 1965, U. Denver, 1971; research fellow Trinity Coll., Cambridge, Eng., 1927-28; m. Emily Frelinghuysen, Oct. 14, 1950. Instr. psychology Columbia, 1928-37; with Internat. High Altitude Expdn. to Chile, 1935; asst. prof. indsl. research Fatigue Lab., Harvard, 1937-39; mem. faculty Harvard, 1937-72 prof. environmental health and safety, 1958-62, dir. Guggenheim Center for Aviation Health and Safety, 1957-72; Guggenheim prof. aerospace health and safety, 1962-72, emeritus, after 1972; Lester D. Gardner lectr. aeros. Mass. Inst. Tech., 1972. Cons. Office Surgeon Gen., Dept. Army, 1951-69; dir. commn. on mil. accidents Armed Forces Epidemiol. Bd., Dept. Def., 1950-69, Exec. Office Pres., 1969-70. Served as lt. comdr. USNR, 1940. Cons. air lines, USPHS, NRC, others; mem. Com. Operating Problems, NACA, 1947-53, NASA, 1963-66, com. on Research, President's Conf. Indsl. Safety, from 1948; adv. com. U.S. Nat. Health Survey, 1957-63. Recipient Longacre award in Aviation Medicine, 1947; Flight Safety Found. award, 1953; John Jeffries award Inst. Aero. Scis., 1956; Walter M. Boothby award Aerospace Med. Assn., 1962, Arthur Williams Nat. Safety award, 1965; Taylor award in engring. psychology Am. Psychol. Assn., 1968; Exceptional Service awards U.S. Air Force, 1969, Dept. Army, 1971; Annual award Airline Med. Dirs. Assn., 1970; Godfrey L. Cabot award Aero Club New Eng., 1971; Laura Taber Barbour Air Safety award, 1974. Fellow Am. Acad. Arts and Scis. Am. Physiol. Soc., Am. Psychol. Assn., Gerontol. Soc., Royal Aero. Soc., N.Y. Acad. Scis. (v.p. 1935-36), Aero. Med. Assn. (v.p. 1970-71); mem. Soc. Engring. Psychologists (pres. 1971-72); Human Factors Soc. (pres. 1970-71), Sigma Xi, Theta Chi. Presbyn. Clubs: Harvard (Boston, N.Y.C.); Century, Explorers (N.Y.C.); Tavern, Somerset, Odd Volumes (Boston). Author numerous books, latest, Human Factors in Air Transportation, 1953; The Human Body in Equipment Design, 1966; also numerous articles in profl. jours. Directed studies of effects of high altitude and human aspects of air transport design and operation. Home: Dublin, N.H. Died Nov. 7, 1976.

MCFARLANE, STUART GORDON, govt. exec.; b. Maldon, Victoria, Australia, May 4, 1885; s. John James and Jane (Matthews) McF.; M. Mary Grace McDermott, 1923; 1 son, Ian. Dir. military accountants (lt. col.) Dept. of Defence, 1916-19; asst. sec. (finance), Commonwealth Treas., 1926-32, asst. sec. (adminstrn.) 1932 35; official sec., Commonwealth in London, 1936-38; sec. Commonwealth Treas., 1938-48; mem. oversea telecom. com., 1948; exec. dir. Internat. Monetary Fund and Internat. Bank for Reconstrn. and Development, Wash., 1948-50; former sec. Australian Loan Council. Nat. Debt. Com.; former mem. adv. Council, Commonwealth Bank; mem. del., formulated United Kingdom—Dominions Joint Wool Orgn. and arrangement with U. K. on Australian Sterling Balances. Club: Australian (Sydney and Melbourne). Home: Canberra, Australia. *

MCFARLANE, WILLIAM DODDRIDGE, ex-congressman; b. Greenwood, Ark., July 17, 1894; s. Robert William and Maggie (Harris) M.; student U. of Ark., 1909-14, A.B., 1919; LL.B., Chgo. Kent Law Sch., 1921, J.D., 1969; m. Alma Ellen Carl, Dec. 25, 1923 (died Apr. 6, 1938); children—Mary Ellen, Alice Jean (dec.), William D., Betty Ann, Barbara Frances, Robert Carl; married 2d, Inez Bishop, June 2, 1945. Began law practice at Graham, Texas, 1921; member law firm McFarlane & McFarlane from 1921. Served as private, advancing to 2d lieut., 1918. Mem. Tex. Ho. of Rep., 1923-27, Tex. State Senate, 1927-31; mem. 73d to 75th Congressgs (1933-39), 13th Tex. Dist; spl. asst. to atty. gen. of U.S., 1939 to June 1940, July 1941-Jan. 1945; and from Jan. 1946; dir. of surplus property, Smaller War Plants Corp., 1945-46. Recipient Cert. of Service, U.S. Congress, 1970; Citation of Merit, Chgo.-Kent Coll. of Law Alumni Assn., 1971. Mem. State and Young County bar assns., Former Mems. of Congress, Inc. (charter mem.), Am. Legion, Forty and Eight, SAR, Delta Chi, Tau Kappa Alpha. Democrat. Methodist. Mason (32 deg., Shriner, recipient Master Mason 50-Yr. award 1969), K.P. Home: Graham, Tex. Died Feb. 18, 1980; buried Oak Grove Cemetery, Graham.

MC FEATERS, MARVIN CLYDE, fgn. service officer; b. Kingman, Kans., Dec. 21, 1914; s. Ralph Clyde and Mary Jane (Beitler) McF.; B.C.S., Strayer Coll. Accountancy, Washington, 1939; B.A., George Washington U., 1942; M.A., 1948; student Sch. Advanced Internat. Studies, Johns Hopkins U., 1959; m. Verna Marjorie Smith, Sept. 5, 1936; children—Marvin Clyde, Carol Elaine (Mrs. David P. Dunlap). City editor Alva (Okla.) Daily Record, 1933-35; clk. various govt. agys., Washington, 1935-42; economist, editor Bavarian Economist, Office Mil. Govt., Munich, Germany, 1946-47; commodity analyst ECA, Mut. Security Agy., Washington, 1948-55; chief procurement analysis br. ICA, Washington, 1955-56; controller U.S. Ops. Mission to Thailand, Bangkok, 1957-59; program officer USOM Lebanon, Beirut, 1960-62; became regional liaison officer AID, Lebanon, 1962; mem. Fgn. Affairs Info. Mgmt. Project, 1966; internat. trade adv. AID mission to Brazil, 1966-70; fin. analyst AID, Washington, 1971-76; participant spl. procurement mission to Bolivia, 1954, Pakistan, 1955, spl. econ. trade survey, Korea, South Vietnam, Thailand and Pakistan, 1960; mem. econ. study team Dept. of State, Laos, Cambodia, 1956; mem. nat. bd. dirs. Mil. Govt. Assn., 1950-54; nat. editor Mil. Govt. Jour. and Newsletter, 1948-54. Served with U.S. Army, 1943-45. Mem. Am. Econ. Assn., Soc. Internat. Devel., Pi Gamma Mu. Congregationalist. Club: Propeller U.S. (Beirut). Home: Falls Church, Va. Died June 24, 1976; buried Arlington, Va.

MCFIE, MAYNARD (MAK-FE'), b. Clearwater, Kan., Mar. 5, 1886; s. William Thomas and Elizabeth Jane (Ross) McF.; A.B., U. of Calif., 1907; unmarried. Mgr. W. T. McFie Supply Co., Wholesale distributors of steel products, 1907-27; director Security First Nat. Bank of Los Angeles, Marblehead Land Co., Los Angeles Transit Lines. V.pres. for Western States, of

Chamber Commerce U.S., 1920-21; pres. Los Angeles Chamber Commerce, 1920, treas., 1921. Mem. Phi Beta Kappa, Psi Upsilon. Republican. Mason (32 deg. Shriner). Clubs: California, Sunset, (Los Angeles); Bohemian (San Francisco). Home: Los Angeles, Calif. *

MCGARRAGHY, JOSEPH C., judge; b. Washington, Nov. 6, 1897; s. Andrew and Mary Imogene McGarraghy; LL.B., Georgetown U., 1921; m. Marian Boyd Cameron, Feb. 24, 1939 (dec.). Asst. corp. counsel, 1924-25; mem. law firm Colladay, McGarraghy, Colladay & Wallace, 1925-40, Wilkes, McGarraghy & Artis, 1940-54; judge U.S. Dist. Ct., Washington, from 1954. Pres., Washington Bd. trade, 1946-47. Chmn. Greater Nat. Capital Com., 1947-50. Chmn., Republican State Com., D.C., 1949-54; del. Rep. Nat. Conv., 1952; chmn. Eisenhower-Nixon Inaugural Com., 1953. Served with C.E., U.S. Army, 1917-20. Mem. Barristers (pres. 1937-38), Am., D.C. (1st v.p. 1941-42) bar assns., Gamma Eta Gamma. Clubs: Metropolitan, Columbia Country (Washington). Home: Washington, D.C. Deceased.

MCGARRY, PATRICK STEPHEN, coll. adminstr.; b. N.Y.C., Sept. 10, 1929; s. Joseph J. and Catherine V. (Woods) McG.; B.A., Manhattan Coll., Bronx, N.Y., 1951; M.A., Columbia U., 1953, Ph.D., 1963. Instr., Manhattan Coll., 1955-60, De LaSalle Coll., Washington, 1961-65; asst. editor Renaissance ch. history New Catholic Ency., Washington, 1963-65; mem. faculty Manhattan Coll., from 1965; prof. history, exec. v.p., provost, 1975-80; mem. Bros. Christian Schs., Roman Catholic Ch., from 1960; cons. Office Film and Broadcasting, U.S. Cath. Conf. Acad. intern, fellow Am. Council on Edn., 1969-70. Mem. Am., Cath. hist. assns., Nat. Cath. Edn. Assn., Middle Atlantic Radical Historians Orgn., Phi Alpha Theta, Theta Alpha Kappa. Democrat. Contbr. articles to profl. publs. Home: Bronx, N.Y. Died May 17, 1980.

MC GAVOCK, WILLIAM GILLESPIE, educator; b. Franklin, Tenn., Dec. 31, 1909; s. John and Mary (Gillespie) McG.; B.S., Davidson Coll., 1930; M.A., Duke, 1933, Ph.D., 1939; student Princeton, 1936-37, U. Wis., 1954-55, Cornell U., 1967; m. Sarah Herbert Nolen, June 11, 1931; children—David Nolen, Martha Randal. Tchr., Branham and Hughes Mil. Acad., Spring Hill, Tenn., 1930-32, Morgan Sch., Petersburg, Tenn., 1933-34; mem. faculty Davidson (N.C.) Coll., 1934-70, prof. math., 1946-70, Dana Distinguished prof. math., chmn. dept., 1949-67; vis. prof. Duke, 1943-44, Emory U., 1944-45. Mem. So. Regional Selection Com. Ford Faculty Fellowships, 1951-54. Chmn. Mecklenburg County Civil Service Bd.; mem. Mayor Davidson Community Com.; moderator Concord Presbytery, Presbyn. Ch.; active local Boy Scouts Am. Dir. Charlotte Fresh Air Camp. Recipient Thomas Jefferson Distinguished Prof. award, 1964; Gen. Edn. Bd. fellow, 1936-38; Ford faculty fellow, 1954-55; Grantee NSF, 1956, 62, 64. Mem. Math. Assn. Am., N.C. Acad. Sci. (chmn. math. sect. 1940, 53), AAUP, Phi Beta Kappa, Omicron Delta Kappa, Sigma Pi Sigma, Kappa Alpha. Democrat. Presbyn. (elder). Author articles. Home: Davidson, N.C. Died Feb. 23, 1980; buried Franklin, Tenn.

MCGAW, CHARLES, educator, theatre dir.; b. Grand Rapids, Mich., Aug. 30, 1910; s. Robert W. and Minnie (Clapp) McG.; A.B., U. Mich., 1932, M.A., 1937, Ph.D., 1940. Asso. prof. theatre Ohio State U., 1947-57; lectr. contemporary drama U. Chgo., 1957-64; head of edn. Goodman Theatre and Sch. Drama, Art Inst. Chgo. 1957-66, dean Goodman Sch. Drama, 1966-77. Vis. summer prof. U. Minn., 1965, Northwestern U., 1962-63, U. Hawaii, 1968, U. Wis., 1975; U.S. specialist U. Bahia (Brazil), summer 1959, 61; vis. prof. Tulane U., spring 1965; guest dir. San Diego Shakespeare Festival, summer 1958. Served with USNR, 1942-46. Mem. Am. Ednl. Theatre Assn., ANTA. Author: Acting is Believing, rev. edits., 1966, 75; Working a Scene, 1977. Home: Chicago, Ill. Died Apr. 8, 1978.

MCGEHEE, DANIEL RAYFORD (MAK-GE'HE), congressman; b. Little Springs, Miss., Sept. 10, 1883; s. William Calvin and Lenora (Lumpkin) McG.; B.S., Mississippi Coll., Clinton, Miss., 1903; LL.B., U. of Miss., 1909; m. Dorothy Dean Hunt, June 23, 1915; children—Lena Deane, Dorothy Ann, Gloria, Patricia. Began practice at Meadville, Miss., 1909; pres. Bank of Franklin, Miss., since 1918; planter; mem. Miss. State Senate, 1924-28 and 1932-34, Miss. Ho. of Rep., 1928-32; mem. 74th to 78th Congresses (1935-45), 7th Miss. Dist. Democrat. Baptist. Mason (Shriner); mem. Woodmen of the World. Home: Meadville, Miss.*

MCGEHEE, ROBERT BRUCE, educator; b. Bingham, Ala., Mar. 29, 1884; s. Oliver Clark and Mary Linton (Henderson) McG.; A.B. Southern U., Greensboro, Ala., 1905; M.A., Vanderbilt, 1910; m. Frances Tempest Herndon, of Nashville, Tenn., Oct. 4, 1911. Co-founder, 1912, and pres. Gulf Coast Military Acad. Mem. Alpha Tau Omega. Democrat. Methodist. Mason (K.C.C.H.). Club: Rotary (pres.). Home: Gulfport, Miss. *

MCGERVEY, WALTER EDMUND, banker; b. Xenia, O., May 20, 1883; s. Frank E. and Julia (Dean) McG.; ed. University Sch., Cleveland, O., and Culver Mil. Acad.; m. Esther Huber, Jan. 21, 1922. Entered employ Citizens Nat. Bank, Xenia, 1901; with auditor's office, Green County, O., as deputy and chief dep., 1909-12; cashier East Dayton Savings & Banking Co., 1912, later pres. until merger, 1921, with Dayton Savings & Trust Co., of which was v.p., 1921-25, and pres., 1925-29; exec. v.p. and dir. Third Nat. Bank & Trust Co., Dayton, since Jan. 14, 1931; dir. Maude Muller Candy Co., Dayton. Republican. United Presbyterian. Clubs: Moraine Country, Engineers', Dayton Country. Home: Oakwood. *

MCGINLEY, PHYLLIS, writer; b. Ontario, Oreg., Mar. 21, 1905; d. Daniel and Julia (Kiesel) McGinley; student country schs. in Colo., Ogden (Utah) High Sch., Sacred Heart Acad., Ogden, U. Utah, U. Calif.; D.Litt., Wheaton (Mass.) Coll., 1956, St. Mary's Coll., Notre Dame, 1958, Marquette U., 1960, Dartmouth, 1961, Boston Coll., 1962, Smith Coll., Wilson Coll., St. John's U., 1964; m. Charles Hayden, June 25, 1937; children—Julia Elizabeth McGinley Hayden, Phyllis Louise (Mrs. Charles Blake). Writer of light verse, articles and literary criticisms for nat. mags. Recipient Christopher medal, Cath. Writers Guild award, Poetry Soc. award, all 1955, St. Catherine Sienna medal, 1956; Cath. Inst. Press award, 1961; Pulitzer prize for poetry, 1961; Laetare medal U. Notre Dame, 1964; Campion award, 1967. Mem. Nat. Inst. Arts and Letters, Poetry Soc. Am., P.E.N., Kappa Kappa Gamma. Roman Catholic. Author: (collections of verse) On the Contrary, 1934; One More Manhattan, 1937, Pocketful of Wry, 1940; Husbands Are Difficult, 1941; Stones From a Glass House; 1946, A Short Walk from the Station, 1951; Love Letters of Phyllis McGinley, 1954; (children's book) The Horse Who Lived Upstairs, 1944; The Plain Princess, 1945; All Around the Town, 1948; The Most Wonderful Doll in the World, 1950; Blunderbus, 1951; The Horse Who Had His Picture in the Paper, 1951; Make Believe Twins, 1952; The Year Without a Santa Claus, 1957; (collections of verse) Merry Christmas, Happy New Year, 1958; (lyrics for revue) Small Wonder, 1948; (film narration) The Emperors Nightingale, 1951; (children's Book) Lucy McLockett, 1959; The Province of the Heart (collections of essays), 1959; Times Three (collections verse), 1960; (children's Book) Sugar and Spice, 1960; Mince Pie and Mistletoe, 1961; Boys Are Awful, 1962; The B Book, 1963; A Little Girl's Room, 1963; Sixpence in her Shoe, 1964; Wonderful Time, 1966; A Wreath of Christmas Legends, 1967. Home: New York, N.Y. Died Feb. 22, 1978.

MCGINTY, CLAUDIS LAMAR, educator; b. Norwood, Warren County, Ga., Feb. 9, 1885; s. Cornelius Stephens and Lucy Ann (Elliott) McG.; B.S., Mercer U., Ga., 1904, A.B., 1912; Th.B., Southern Bapt. Theol. Sem., Ky., 1911, Th.M., 1912, Th.D., 1913; D.D., John B. Stetson U., 1926; m. Ruby Herndon, Sept. 8, 1909; 1 dau., Marion Lamar (Mrs. Carey T. Vinzant). Ordained Bapt. ministry, 1911; pastor 5th Av. Ch., Rome, Ga., 1913-15, 1st Ch., Cartersville, Ga., 1915-19; dean Theol. Sem. and prof. Old Testament interpretation and systematic theology, Mercer U., 1919-26; prof. English Bible, Bapt. Woman's Missionary Union Training School, Louisville, Ky., 1926-37; pres. Bessie Tift Coll., 1938-47; pastor Crawfordsville Baptist Ch., 1947-50; pastor Norwood Baptist Ch. since 1947. Democrat. Author: From Babylon to Bethlehem, 1929; A Guide in the Study of the New Testament, 1935. Address: Decatur, Ga. *

MCGOODWIN, ROBERT RODES, architect; b. Bowling Green, Ky., July 7, 1886; s. Isaac Daniel and Virginia Walker (Wooten) McG.; B.S., U. of Pa., 1907, M.S., 1908; Cresson traveling scholar in architecture, 1909; m. Kate Hampton Bryan, Nov. 5, 1910; children—Robert Rodes, Daniel. Architect, Phila., 1910-52; mem. design staff Sch. of Fine Arts, U. of Pa., 1910-25. Constituent Bd. of Trustees, U. of Pa. Fellow A.I.A. (pres. Phila. chapter). Clubs: Charleston; Sunnybrook Golf (Phila., Pa.). Author: (monograph) The Work of Robert R. McGoodwin, Architect, 1943. Home: Philadelphia, Pa. *

MCGOORTY, JOHN PATRICK, JR., lawyer; b. Chgo., Aug. 28, 1902; s. John Patrick and Mary Elizabeth (Wiggins) McG.; Ph.B., U. Notre Dame, 1924; LL.B., Chgo. Kent Coll. Law, 1926; m. Josephine Alberta Lewis; children—Barbara Therese (Mrs. Starshak), Mary Ellen (Mrs. Picard), Kathleen (Mrs. Selfridge). Admitted to Ill. bar, 1926; with Mayer, Meyer, Austrian & Platt, 1924-31, Altheimer, Mayer, Woods & Smith, 1931-34; mem. firm Downs, McGoorty & Howe, 1934-37, McGoorty & McGoorty (all Chgo), 1947-53; pvt. practice, 1937-47, 53-65, 69-76; mem. firm Rooney, McGoorty, Finnegan & Bradtke, 1965-69. Mem. com. on character, fitness Ill. Supreme Ct., 1943-54, chmn. 1952-53. Mem. exec. com. South Shore dist. Boy Scouts, 1935-48; mem. Ill. Ednl. Facilities Authority; mem. exec. bd. Chgo. chpt. Nat. Conf. Christians and Jews. Trustee Chgo.-Kent Coll. Law, 1945-75; bd. dirs. Cath. Charities Chgo. Fellow Am. Coll. Probate Counsel; mem. Chgo. (grievances com. 1937-41, bd. mgrs. 1953-55, com. legal edn. 1943-54, chmn. 1952-53), Am., Ill. bar assns., Cath. Lawyers Guild (chmn. bd. govs. 1945-48), Am. Judicature Soc., Cath. Interracial Council, Chgo. Assn. Commerce (Ill. com. 1945-55), Phi Alpha Delta. K.C. (4 deg.), Order Foresters. Clubs: Serra Internat. (sec. 1946-48, pres. Chgo. chpt. 1946), Law, Forty (trustee), Irish Fellowship (pres. 1948), Notre Dame (hon. pres. 1974-75), Chgo. Athletic Assn. (Chgo.); Golf (White Lake, Mich.). Home: Evanston, Ill. Died Aug. 18, 1976.

MCGOURTY, JOHN JAMES, soft drink co. exec.; b. N.Y.C., Dec. 19, 1926; s. Myles and Delia (McGuinnes) McG.; B.S., Fordham U., 1951; M. Joan M. Conway, May 9, 1964. Prin. auditor Ernst & Ernst, N.Y.C., 1953-58; prin. auditor, asst. controller, controller, v.p. and controller Coca-Cola Export Corp., Atlanta, 1958-72; v.p., controller Coca-Cola Co., 1972-74, sr. v.p., controller, 1974-77. Served with USNR, 1944-46; with U.S. Army, 1951-53. Mem. Financial Execs. Inst. Clubs: Capital City, Ansley Golf (Atlanta); New York Athletic. Home: Atlanta, Ga. Died June 6, 1977.

MCGRATH, THOMAS AQUINAS, finance co. exec., b. Jersey City, Nov. 30, 1903; s. Patrick and Mary (Doherty) McG.; grad. Pace Coll., 1924; m. Mary Keane, Nov. 16, 1935; children—Thomas Aquinas, Joseph Patrick, Maureen Anne. With Beneficial Co., Wilmington, Del., 1924-69, 1st v.p., 1959-62, pres., 1962-69, also dir. Trustee Hodson Trust. Home: Summit, N.J. Died Sept. 19, 1976.

MC GRAW, CHARLES FRANCIS, actor; b. N.Y.C., May 10, 1914; s. Francis Park and Beatrice (Crisp) McG.; grad. high sch.; m. Freda A. Choy, Oct. 12, 1938; 1 dau., Jill McGraw Gregson. Appeared in Broadway plays Jazz Age, 1935, Dead End, 1936, Boy Meets Girl, 1936, The Night of January 16, 1936, Golden Boy, 1937-38, Native Son, 1941; motion pictures include: The Killers, 1946, The Gangster, 1947, Roses are Red, 1947, Blood on the Moon, 1948, Border Incident, 1949, His Kind of Woman, 1950, Loophole, 1953, The Bridges of Toko-Ri, 1954, Toward the Unknown, 1956, Joe Dakota, 1956, Slaughter on Tenth Avenue, 1957, Spartacus, 1960, Cimmaron, 1960, Pendulum, 1968, In Cold Blood, 1967, Johnny Got His Gun, 1971, River Blood, 1973, Twilight's Last Gleaming, 1977, others; appeared on radio for 30 years, now on TV. Served with AUS, 1943-45. Mem. Screen Actors Guild, Actors Equity Assn., AFTRA. Home: North Hollywood, Calif. Died July 29, 1980.

MCGREEVY, MILTON, business exec.; b. Chgo., Jan. 27, 1903; s. Milton C. and Dora (Achenbach) McG.; A.B., Harvard, 1924, M.B.A., 1926; m. Barbara James, Apr. 17, 1929; children—Jean, Thomas James, Barbara Ann, Gail. Partner, McGreevy & Co. (mem. N.Y. Stock Exchange), 1929-30, Harris, Upham & Co. (inc. 1965), Kansas City, Mo., 1930-65, vice chmn., 1965-76; v.p. sales Smith Barney, Harris Upham & Co., Inc., Kansas City, 1976-79; chmn. bd. Jackson County Nat. Bank & Trust Co., Prairie Village, Kans., 1979-80. Trustee Linda Hall Library, William Rockhill Nelson Gallery of Art. Mem. N.Y. Stock Exchange. Clubs: University, Kansas City, Kansas City Country, Mission Hills, River (Kansas City). Home: Shawnee Mission, Kans. Died July 1, 1980.

MCGREGOR, FRANK RUTHERFORD, mgmt. cons.; b. Punxsutawney, Pa.; s. John R. and Margaret Isabella (Branch) McG.; student Bucknell U.; m. M. Louisa Luckenbill. Steel worker Vandergrift (Pa.) plant U.S. Steel Corp., 1922-24; pres., dir. Schultz-McGregor Corp., N.Y.C., 1924-28; v.p. Alfred Wallerstein, Inc., N.Y.C., 1928-30; v.p., dir., gen. mgr. Town House Constrn. Co., N.Y. Town House, Inc., 1928-32; pub. relations, indsl. relations counsel to mfg., comml. cos., 1932-39; cons. indsl. relations 18 cement cos., eastern U.S., 1936-39; exec. N.A.M., 1939-41; asst. to pres., dir. pub. relations Gaylord Container Corp., St. Louis, 1946-49; apptd. spl. adviser to St. Louis mayor and City Airport Commn., 1946; partner Earle & McGregor, pub. relations, 1949-53; pres. Frank R. McGregor Co., mgmt. cons., 1953-78. Exec. v.p., trustee Council for Ind. Bus., Washington, 1949-78; chief field mgmt. WPB., Washington, 1941-42; cons. for small bus. to sec. def., 1951, organizer office small bus. Dept. Def.; apptd. field counselor for small bus. Mut. Security Agy., Washington, 1952; apptd. v.p. Commodity Credit Corp., dept. adminstr. operations and mgmt. U.S. Commodity Stblzn. Service, 1955-60. Served from lt. comdr. to comdr. USNR, 1942-46; comdg. officer industry cooperation div. Exec. Office of Sec. Navy, Washington, 1943-46; Navy liaison officer to spl. com. U.S. Senate to study, survey problems of small bus. enterprises and select com. of small bus. U.S. Ho. of Reps., 1942-46; mem., comdr. for Navy presdl. mission to China, Japan, Korea, Formosa, P.I., Australia, New Zealand, in survey of small bus., 1945-46; comdg. officer Naval Res. Materials Co., 1956-57. Chmn. legislative and tax com., v.p. Small Bus. Assns. Am., 1951. Recipient commendation with ribbon Sec. Navy James Forrestal, 1944; Legion of Merit, 1946; Distinguished Service award with gold medal Dept. Agr., 1959. Mem. Newcomen Soc. N. Am., Clan Gregor Soc. Am. (chieftain), St. Andrews Soc. (chmn. bd. trustees), Mil. Order World Wars, Naval Res. Assn., Res. Officers

Assn. U.S., Mil. Order of the Carabao, I.O.O.B., Sigma Chi (pres. N.Y. club 1930-32), Delta Sigma, Tau Kappa Alpha. Clubs: City Tavern (Washington); Advertising (N.Y.C.); Bison (Lewisburg, Pa.); Navy League, Noonday, University (St. Louis). Home: Washington, D.C. Died Nov. 16, 1978.

MCGUIRE, JOHN ANDREW, congressman; b. Wallingford, Conn., Feb. 28, 1906; s. John Joseph and Katherine Agnes (Barry) McG.; student Lyman Hall, Wallingford, 1924; grad. Dartmouth Coll., 1928; m. Dorothy May Martin, July 6, 1936; children—John Martin, Lois Ann. In gen. ins. bus. under name of John A. McGuire, from 1935; town clerk, Wallingford, from January 1, 1934; member 81st and 82d Congresses, 3d Conn. District. Member Nat. Assn. Town and City Clerks, Cann. Town Clerks Assn. (pres. from 1941), Conn. Assn. Ins. Agts. (mem. legislative com. since 1948), Central Conn. Boy Scout Council, Lambda Chi Alpha. Democrat (chmn. state central com.) Roman Catholic. K.C. (4 degrees), Knight of St. Patrick, Elk, Redman. Clubs: Wallingford, Nat. Exchange. Home: Wallingford, Conn. Died May 28, 1976.

MCGUIRE, JOHNSON, physician; b. Alexandria, Va., Oct. 21, 1899; s. Hugh Holmes and Sara Elizabeth (Johnson) McG.; B.S., U. Va., 1920; M.D., Johns Hopkins, 1924; M.A., U. Cin., 1930; m. Elizabeth Treon Livingood, Aug. 5, 1932; children—Treon, Mary, Sara, Anne. Intern, Johns Hopkins Hosp., 1925, Jacques Loeb fellow internal medicine, 1926, instr. pathology Johns Hopkins Med. Sch., 1927; asst. resident, resident physician Cin. Gen. Hosp., 1927-30, attending physician, 1945-70; staff mem. Christian R. Holmes Hosp.; cons. VA, Cin., 1954-77, Jewish Hosp. Cin., from 1965; asso. prof. medicine U. Cin., 1935-54, prof. clin. medicine, 1954-58, prof. medicine, 1958-70, prof. emeritus, 1974-77, cons. internal medicine Christ Hosp.; cons. 5th Service Command and 1st Army, 1943-46. Served from lt. col. to col. M.C., AUS, 1943-46. Decorated Legion of Merit. U. Cin. fellow cardiac research, Vienna, 1929-30. Diplomate Am. Bd. Internat. Med. Fellow A.C.P.; mem. Assn. Am. Physicians, Am. Clin. and Climatol. Assn., Central Soc. Clin. Research, AMA, Am. Heart Assn., Heart Assn. Greater Cin. (pres. 1954-55). Club: Camargo (Cin.). Contbr. articles to profl. jours. Home: Cincinnati, Ohio. Died May 14, 1977.

MC HALE, FRANK MARTIN, lawyer; b. Logansport, Ind., Mar. 4, 1891; s. Martin and Margaret (Farrell) McH.; A.B., U. Mich., 1914, J.D., 1916; LL.D. (hon.), St. Joseph's Coll., 1963, Marion Coll., 1970, Butler U., 1974; m. Mabel Elizabeth Corriden, June 25, 1924. Admitted to Ind. bar, 1915; mem. Kistler, Kistler & McHale, 1919-32, Fansler, McHale & Douglass, 1932-33, McHale, Douglass & Myers, 1933-35, McHale, Arthur, Myers & Patrick, 1935-45, McHale, Patrick, Myers & Cook, 1945-52, McHale, Patrick, Cook & Welch, 1952-60, with McHale, Cook & Welch, 1960-75; chmn. bd. So. Ind. Ry., Inc., Nat. Bank of Logansport; exec. com. dir. Am. Fletcher Corp.; chmn. Nickel Plate Road, Norfolk & Western Ry.; v.p., dir., mem. exec. com. Transway Internat. Corp. Mem. bd. lay trustees St. Joseph's Coll. Served as pvt. Signal Corps and later lt. Air Service, World War I. Decorated knight of St. Gregory; named to Ind. Football Hall Fame, 1975; Ky. col.; Sagamor of Wabash. Mem. Am., Ind., Indpls., Cass County (pres. 1927-31) bar assns., Am. Judicature Soc., Am. Legion (1st comdr. Cass County post 1919, 20, 21; Ind. dept. comdr. 1928; nat. exec. committeeman 1928-29), Sigma Chi (recipient Significant Sig award), Gamma Eta Gamma. Roman Catholic. Democrat (mem. nat. com. 1937-52). Club: Indpls. Athletic. Home: Indianapolis, Ind. Died Jan. 26, 1975; buried Mt. Hope Cemetery, Logansport, Ind.

MCHATTON, THOMAS HUBBARD, prof. horticulture; b. Brooklyn, N.Y., Nov. 12, 1883; s. Henry Chinn and Eliza (Hubbard) McH.; B.S., Springhill, Coll., Mobile, Ala., 1903, Sc.D., 1907; B.S., Mich. Coll. Agr., 1907, M. of Hort., 1921; studied Cornell U., Ia. State Coll. Agr.; m. Marie Lustrat, June 14, 1911; children—Marie Lustrat, Eleanore (dec.). Horticulturist, Expt. Sta. of Ga., Jan.-Nov. 1908; adj. prof. horticulture, U. of Georgia, 1908-11, prof. and head division of horticulture, 1911-50, director teaching, 1933. Hort. editor Southern Ruralist (semi-monthly), Atlanta, Ga., 1908-28. Lt. cadets Mich. Agrl. Coll., 1906, capt. 1907; capt. Air Service Production, U.S. Army, Jan.-Dec. 1918; col. C.O. 301st Chem. Regt. to 1941; col. Chem. Warfare Service; dir. War Dept. Civilian Protection Schools, Edgewood Arsenal, Md., Univ. of Florida and Stanford U., Jan. 1942-Nov. 1943; inactive status since 1943. Mem. Cath. Commn. on Intellectual and Cultural Affairs. Member American Society Horticultural Science (president 1931), Am. Pomol. Soc. (exec. com.), Hort. Sect. Southern Agrl. Workers (ex-sec.; chmn. 1927), Ga. State Hort. Soc. (pres. 1925), Ga. Acad. Science (pres. 1928), Nat. Pecan Grower's Assn. (pres. 1929), Am. Assn. Univ. Profs., Alpha Zeta, Phi Kappa Phi; fellow A.A.A.S. Mem. Am. Legion (comdr. local post, 1925), Reserve Officers Assn. (pres. Dept. of Ga., 1933; 4th Corps pres. 1933; chmn. Nat. Legislative Com., 1934-36), S.A.R., Soc. Colonial Wars. Democrat. Knight of Columbus. Clubs: Athens Country, Army and Navy (Washington, D.C.).Part Author: Land Teaching, 1910; Armchair Gardening, 1947. Contbr. to Am. Cyclo. Horticulture, Book of Rural Life—Garden History of Georgia, also numerous bulletins and articles in scientific and tech. jours. Home: Athens, Ga. *

MCHUGH, DOROTHY BARBREE, mem. Republican Nat. Com.; b. Oakland, California; d. Joseph and Nellie (Snowden) Barbree; student U. Cal. at Berkeley; m. Harry G. Miller, July 4, 1932 (dec. 1947); children—Michael B., Harry; m. 2d, Keith S. McHugh, Dec. 14, 1957. Republican County campaign mgr. for New York City Mayoral Campaign, 1961, N.Y. State Gubernatorial Campaign, 1962; co-campaign dir. Gubernatorial Campaign N.Y. State, 1966; mem. rep. Nat. Com. for N.Y., 1963-80; mem. conv. reform committee, 1966-80; mem. adv. bd. N.Y.C. Rep. Women, 1963-80. Pres. Assistance League, Glendale, Cal., 1940-41, Inwood Home for Unwed Mothers, 1974; dir. Women's aux. Inst. Phys. Medicine and Rehab., 1959-80, Assn. Homemaker Service, N.Y.C., 1961-62, N.Y.C. Conv. and Exhbn. Center Corp., 1971-80. Mem. Sigma Kappa. Home: New York, N.Y. Died May 8, 1980.

MCINNIS, EMMETT EMORY, lawyer; b. Monticello, Miss., Oct. 12, 1882; s. William Francis and Caroline Keteurah (O'Mara) McI.; B.S., Austin Coll., Sherman, Tex., 1901; LL.B., U. of Tex., 1904, grad. study, 1905; m. Helen Franc Kohler, June 14, 1919 (died 1926); children—Emmett Emory, Kohler, Mary Elizabeth; m. 2d. Grace Williams, Jan. 20, 1943. Admitted to Indian Ty. bar, 1905, and began practice at Coalgate; moved to McAlester, Okla., 1911, and Oklahoma City, 1921; atty. A.T. & S.F. Ry. Co., 1921-22, state solicitor, 1923-25, gen. solicitor, Chicago, 1926-33, gen. counsel, 1933-46, vice pres. and gen. counsel, 1946-48; retired. Pvt., F.A., U.S. Army, 1918. Mem. Am., Chicago and Okla. bar assns., Kappa Alpha (Southern). Presbyn. Clubs: Chicago, University (Chicago); Chicago Farmers, Glen View. Home: Evanston, Ill. *

MC INTIRE, JOHN ALBERT, lawyer, educator; b. Galveston, Tex., Nov. 4, 1907; s. John D. and Anna Belle (Parker) McI.; A.B. magna cum laude, Wittenberg Coll., 1929; J.D., U. Cin., 1931; postgrad. Harvard Law Sch., 1935-36; LL.D., Wittenberg U., Springfield, Ohio, 1954; m. Elsie Anna Wetzel, June 19, 1932; children—Elizabeth (Mrs. Robert T. Fifer), Janet (Mrs. Richard Abbott von Doenhoff), Paula (Mrs. James T. Eaton). Admitted to Ohio bar, 1933, U.S. Circuit Ct. Appeals D.C., 1938, U.S. Supreme Ct., 1939, D.C. bar, 1952; instr. law George Washington U., 1931-32, asst. prof., 1933-38, asso. prof., 1938-46, prof., 1946, professorial lectr. law, 1946-73, faculty editor Law Rev., 1932-42. On staff solicitor Dept. of Agr. and War Food Adminstrn., 1942-44; chief prodn. loan div. Office of Solicitor, Dept. of Agr., 1946-47; mem. U.S. Office Contract Settlement Appeal Bd., 1947-49; mem. excess profits tax council Bur. Internal Revenue, 1949-52; spl. asst. to chmn. Renegotiation Bd., 1952; gen. counsel Armed Services Textile and Apparel Procurement Agy., 1952-53; chmn. civilian legal personnel com. Dept. Army, 1953-58; civilian counselor to navy judge advocate gen., 1958-77. Exec. v.p. Montgomery County (Md.) Community Chest and Council, 1951-53; pres. Montgomery County Council Parent Tchr. Assn., 1949-50; life mem. Md. Congress of P.T.A.'s. Bd. dirs. Wittenberg U., 1964-77. Served with USNR as lt. (j.g.) to lt., 1944-45, with aviation ordnance div. Naval Gun Factory, Washington, 1944-45, staff Army Indsl. Coll., Washington, 1945. Mem. Fed. (nat. pres. 1950-51), Am. (ho. dels. 1951-52), D.C., Interam. bar assns., Order of Coif, Phi Delta Phi, Phi Mu Alpha, Theta Chi Delta, Tau Kappa Alpha, Omicron Delta Kappa, Delta Sigma Phi. Conglist. (trustee). Clubs: Nat. Lawyers, Cosmos, George Washington University (Washington). Author articles, casebooks on mcpl. corps., on govt. contracts. Home: Washington, D.C. Died Jan. 23, 1977.

MCINTYRE, JAMES FRANCIS ALOYSIUS, clergyman; b. N.Y.C., June 25, 1886; s. James F. and Mary (Pelley) McI.; student City Coll., Cathedral Coll. and St. Joseph's Sem., 1915-21. Runner, Curb Exchange, 1899-1902; with H.L. Horton Co. (later absorbed by Fahnestock & Co.) 1902-15, advancing to office mgr.; ordained priest Roman Cath. Ch., 1921; asst. St. Gabriels Ch., N.Y.C., 1921-23; apptd. asst. in chancery office, 1923, chancellor, 1934, domestic prelate, 1936; aux. bishop N.Y., titular bishop Cyrene, 1946-48; archbishop Los Angeles, 1948-53, cardinal 1953-70. Home: Los Angeles, Calif. Died July 16, 1979.

MCINTYRE, JAMES PETER, Canadian senator; b. St. Andrews, Can., July 19, 1883; s. William D. and Elizabeth (McKinnon) McI.; m. Marion Storey, Apr. 28, 1908. Pres. Savage Harbour Packing Co.; dir. Charlottetown Can Co., McDonald & Romey Woodworking Co. Ltd. Engaged in polit. work since 1919; minister of pun. works, 1927-31, later minister pub. works and highways; senator since 1942. Mem. Liberal Party. Roman Catholic. K.C. Home: Mount Stewart, P.E.I.*

MCIVER, ANGUS VAUGHN, architect; b. Great Falls, Mont., Apr. 29, 1892; s. Kenneth B. and Viola Jane (Vaughn) McI.; B.C.E., U. Mich., 1915; m. Loneta Eileen Kuhn, Mar. 19, 1915 (dec.); 1 dau., Margo (Mrs. James Thomas Shorney); m. 2d, Valborg H. Graham, Nov. 10, 1966. Archtl. practice as prin., Great Falls, from 1915, now engaged in cons. work. Mem. Bd. Archtl. Examiners, Mont., 1953-61. Served as lt. U.S. Army, 34th Div., 1918-19. Licensed architect, Mont., civil engr., 1948. Fellow A.I.A. (dir. 1945-47, past pres. Mont. chpt.), Am. Soc. C.E.; mem. Am. Legion (past post comdr.), Chi Phi. Mason (Shriner), Rotarian. Home: Great Falls, Mont. Died July 24, 1974; interred Hillcrest Lawn Meml. Mausoleum, Gt. Falls.

MCIVOR, IVOR KEEN, educator; b. Kirkland, Wash., Sept. 8, 1934; s. David Lyle and Louise Margaret (Keen) McI.; B.S. in Civil Engring., U. Wash., 1958; M.S., Stanford, 1959, Ph.D., 1962; m. Elizabeth Norine Vanderford, Oct. 6, 1952; children—Mary Lynn, Marci Beth, Ivor Scott. Research asst. Stanford, 1961-62; asst. prof. U. Mich., Ann Arbor, 1962-65, asso. prof., 1965-69, prof. applied mechanics and engring. sci., 1969-77, chmn. dept., 1972-78. Cons. FTC, Dept. Transp., Aerospace Corp., Sandia Corp., Dow Chem. Co., Gen. Motors. Recipient Pres.'s medal U. Wash., 1958; NSF grad. fellow, 1958-61; NSF research grantee, 1966-75. Mem. ASCE (chmn. com. on elastic stability 1966-68, mem. exec. com. engring. mechanics div. 1976-77), ASME (membership devel. com.), Am. Acad. Mechanics, Column Research Council (task group on dynamic instability), Phi Beta Kappa, Sigma Xi, Tau Beta Pi. Research, publs. on applied mechanics. Home: Ann Arbor, Mich. Died Apr. 17, 1978.

MCKAY, HAMILTON WITHERSPOON, urologist; b. Sumter, S.C., Sept. 10, 1885; s. Wilson James and Sarah Knox (Witherspoon) McK.; student Kings Mountain Mil. Acad., 1899-1902; B.S., Davidson (N.C.) Coll., 1906; M.D., Jefferson Med. Coll., Phila., 1910; m. Katherine W. Whitner, Nov. 15, 1923; children—Katherine R. W., Hamilton Witherspoon. Intern Presbyterian Hosp., Phila., 1910-12, Willard Parker Hosp., N.Y. City, 1912; prof. physical diagnosis, N.C. Med. Coll., 1913-17, post grad. work, Sorbonne, Paris, 1919; asst. urol. surgeon Crowell Clinic of Urology and Dermatology, Charlotte, N.C., 1919-28; member staff Presbyterian Hosp., Charlotte Memorial Hospital, Good Samaritan Hospital, Charlotte. An organizer and chairman of Medical Advisory Council of Charlotte Memorial Hospital, Inc., 1947. Mem. directors Chamber of Commerce, Charlotte Community Chest. Served as maj. Med. Corps, U.S. Army, 1919; former lt. col. Med. Res. Corps. Mem. Bd. Med. Examiners for N.C., 1931-38, pres. 1936; pres. Charlotte branch Am. Red Cross. 1935-36. Mem. bd. dirs. and exec. com. Davidson College. Diplomate Am. Bd. Urology; mem. Mecklenburg County Med. Soc. (ex-pres.), Seventh Dist. Med. Soc., N.C. Med. Assn., N.C. Urol. Assn. (ex-pres.), Tri-State Med. Soc., Southern Med. Assn. (ex-chmn. sec. on urology, chmn. council, 1st v.p. 1948, pres., 1949-50); member Southeastern Surgical Cong.; fellow Am. Coll. Surgeons, Southern Surg. Assn., Am. Med. Assn. (chmn. urology sect. 1948-49), American Urological Association (mem. exec. com.; ex-pres. Southeastern Branch), Mil. Order World War (charter mem.). Mem. bd. trustees Union Theol. Sem., Richmond, Va. Presbyn. (ruling elder). Clubs: Rotary (pres. 1926-27), Charlotte Country, Charlotte City (Charlotte). Contbr. many articles to med. jours. Home: Charlotte, N.C. *

MCKAY, MARION K., univ. prof.; b. Condit, O., Jan. 5, 1883; s. George and Letitia (Huddlestun) McK.; S.B., Ohio Northern U., 1907, Pd.D. (hon.), 1947, Ph.D. (hon.), 1949; A.B., Ohio State, 1910; A.M., Harvard, 1912, Ph.D., 1918; married Alma Bailey, November 30, 1912; 1 daughter, Marian. Teacher in pub. schs. of O., 1900-04, Isheming (Mich.), High Sch., 1910-11; grad. asst. in economics, Harvard, 1912, 14-16; teacher in Canfield (O.) High Sch., 1912-13; prof. of economics, Univ. of N.H., 1916-20, Univ. of Pittsburgh, since 1920. Mem. Pa. State coms.; tax, 1924-27, finance and taxation, 1935, unemployment compensation (chmn.), 1938-39; O. river basin compact, 1938, Pittsburgh civil service since 1940 (pres. since 1943); mem. Pa. State Sanitary Water Bd., 1936-40; Pa. State Council of Edn., 1936-40; mem. Pres. Hoover's com. on Home Finance and Taxation, 1930. Financial adviser dept. of pub. instrn., Pa., 1936-39. Mem. Nat. Tax Assn., Am. Econ. Assn., Am. Assn. Univ. Profs. Democrat. Baptist, Club: Civic, Allegheny County, Pa. (pres. 1930-34). Author: History of the Poll Tax in the New England, Middle and South Atlantic States, 1918; Monograph on Forest Taxation, 1921; Financing Education in Pennsylvania, 1937. Home: Pittsburgh. *

MCKEAN, DAYTON DAVID, educator; b. Longmont, Colo., Dec. 4, 1904; s. Thomas D. and Mary L. (Dobbins) McK.; A.B., Colo. U., 1927, A.M., 1929; Ph.D., Columbia, 1938; M.A. (hon.), Dartmouth, 1946; m. Margaret Walrod, Aug. 27, 1931; children—Mary Margaret, Paul Arthur. Instr., U. Colo., 1927-29; instr., asst. prof. Princeton, 1929-37; asst. prof. and prof. Dartmouth, 1937-52, chmn. dept., 1947-51; on leave of absence 2 years as dept. commr. finance for N.J., 1941-43. Chmn. Midwest Conf. on Grad. Study and Research, 1957-58; cons. Western Interstate Commn. on Higher Edn., 1958. Mem. N.J. House of Assembly,

1933-34; apptd. N.J. Social Security Commn., 1935; dist. dir. 7th N.J. dist. WPA, 1937. Democratic chmn. Town of Hanover, 1946-47, Grafton County, 1947-48, N.H., 1948-52. Polit. sci. editorial adviser Houghton Mifflin Co., from 1951; prof. polit. sci. U. Colo., 1952-73, dean grad. sch., 1952-62; vis. prof. Johns Hopkins U., 1962-63. Mem. various coms. Nat. Municipal League. Recipient Sr. Research award Social Sci. Research Council, 1960. Mem. Am., N.E. (past pres.) polit. sci. assns. Phi Beta Kappa, Pi Sigma Alpha, Delta Sigma Rho. Democrat. Congregationalist. Author: Pressures of the Leg. of N.J., 1938; the Boss: The Hague Machine in Action, 1940; Party and Pressure Politics, 1949; The Integrated Bar, 1963; also mag. articles, monographs, revs. Home: Boulder, Colo. Died Nov. 5, 1977.

MCKECHNIE, ARNOLD WILFRED, naval officer; b. Trent, S.D., Oct. 3, 1903; s. Wilfred and Anna Maude (Burnside) McK.; B.S., U.S. Naval Acad., 1927; grad. Nat. War Coll., 1953; m. Harriot Wheelihan, June 22, 1929; children—Harriot Anna (Mrs. R. C. Jacobson), Marion (Mrs. W. P. Flynn), Marjorie Helen (Mrs. B. W. Hughes), Arnold Wilfred. Commnd. ensign U.S. Navy, 1927, advanced through grades to rear adm., 1956; designated comdr. submarines, 1931, naval aviator, 1935; comdr. patrol squadron, 1942-43; exec. officer Naval Air Sta. Adak, 1943-44, U.S.S. Bon Homme Richard, 1945; commdg. officer Naval Air Transp. Service, Pacific Wing, 1947-48, U.S.S. Bairoko and Badoeng Straight, 1949-51, U.S.S. Yorktown, 1953-54, Naval Air Sta. N. Island, Calif., 1954-56; sr. naval aide to asst. sec. navy for air, 1951-52; comdr. Carrier Div. 15, 1956-57, Alaskan Sea Frontier, 1958-59, Naval Air Res. Tng. Command, 1960-61, ret., 1961. Decorated Legion Merit, Bronze Star, Navy Unit citation. Mem. Navy League U.S. (nat. dir.), Naval Res. Assn. (exec. com.), Naval Acad. Alumni Assn. (nat. dir.). Mason. Clubs: Calif. Indians, Chicago Press. Home: Coronado, Calif. Died Jan. 19, 1979.

MCKEEN, CARL W., banking; b. Russell, Kan., Aug. 27, 1883; s. Dean W. and Ella (Loring) McK.; student Kan. State Agrl. Coll., 1899-1902; m. Stell Morton, Mar. 20, 1913; 1 dau., Jean Clare. With Farmers State Bank, Russell, Kan., 1903-14; pres. Merchants Nat. Bank, Lawrence, 1914-20; v.p. Western Exchange Bank, Kansas City, Mo., 1920-22; pres. Nat. Bank of Topeka since 1922. Mem. Sigma Nu. Democrat. Presbyn. Mason. Home: Topeka, Kan. *

MCKEEN, JOHN E., business exec.; b. N.Y.C., June 4, 1903; s. William E. and Mary V. (Donovan) McK.; student St. John's Prep. Sch.; Chem.E., Poly. Inst. Bklyn., 1926; student Columbia U., 1930; LL.D., St. John's U., Bklyn., 1950; m. Noreen F. Condon, July 3, 1927. Dept. head, Chas. Pfizer & Co., 1935-38, asst. supt., 1938-42, supt., 1942-45, v.p., 1945-49, pres., 1949-65, chmn. bd., 1950-68, hon. chmn. bd., 1968-72, chmn. exec. com., 1965-68. Trustee Poly. Corp. Mem. Am. Chem. Soc., Am. Inst. Chemists, Am. Inst. Chem. Engrs., Bklyn. C. of C., Sigma Xi. Clubs: Chemists, University (N.Y.C.); Montauk (Bklyn.). Assisted in design and construction of fermentation plant in London, England, 1936-37; author paper on penicillin. Home: Palm Beach, Fla. Died Feb. 23, 1978.

MCKELVEY, FRANK HOTCHKISS, farm mgr.; b. Sparta, Ill., June 16, 1882; s. Sydney Algernon and Hattie Frances (Hotchkiss) McK.; B.S., U. of Ill., 1907; m. Gertrude Ann Lee, Feb. 9, 1909; children—Mary Frances (Mrs. Thornton O. Waller), Lt. (j.g.) Franklin Hotchkiss (missing in action). Farmer, 1907-17; appraiser, Fed. Land Bank, 1917-19; bank officer and farm mgr., First Nat. Bank of Springfield, Ill., since 1920. Trustee U. of Ill. Mem Am. Farm Managers and Rural Appraisers' Assn., Ill. Farm Mgrs.' assn., Phi Delta Theta, Alpha Gamma Rho. Republican. Presbyterian. Mason (32 deg., K.T.). Club: Kiwanis Springfield, Ill.). Home: Springfield, Ill. *

MCKELWAY, BENJAMIN MOSBY, newspaperman; b. Fayetteville, N.C., Oct. 2, 1895; s. Alexander Jeffrey and Lavinia Rutherford (Smith) McK.: ed. Va. Poly. Inst., George Washington U.; m. Margaret J. Prentiss, Sept. 14, 1920; children—Benjamin Mosby, William Prentiss, John MacGregor. Reporter, Washington Times, 1916; editorial writer, news editor New Britain (Conn.) Herald, 1919-20; reporter, city editor, news editor, mng. editor, asso. editor Washingotn Star, 1921-46, editor, 1946-63. editorial chmn., after 1963. Pres. A.P., 1958-63, Washington Bd. Trade, 1945-46. Trustee George Washington U., D.C. Pub. Library. Served to 1st lt. U.S. Army, 1917-18. Mem. Washington Nat. Monument Soc., Am. Soc. Newspaper Editors (pres. 1949-50), Nat. Geog. Soc. (trustee), Delta Tau Delta. Presbyn. Clubs: Cosmos, Nat. Press, Metropolitan, Chevy Chase, Alibi, Gridiron (pres. 1958). Home: Washington, D.C. Died Aug. 30, 1976.

MC KELWAY, ST. CLAIR, writer: b. Charlotte, N.C., Feb 13, 1905; Alexander Jeffrey and Lavinia Rutherford (Smith) McK.; ed. pub. schs., Washington; m. Estelle Cassidy, Dec. 8, 1929; 1 son, St Clair (dec.). From office boy to asst. city editor Washington Times-Herald, 1919-24; reporter N.Y. World, also N.Y. Herald Tribune, 1925-28; corr. in Tokyo, Japan, for Chgo. Tribune, 1929-30; editor-in-chief Bangkok (Thailand) Daily Mail, 1930-33; editor, staff writer New Yorker mag., from 1933, mng. editor, 1936-39. Served to lt. col. USAAF, 1942-45. Clubs: Century, Coffee House (N.Y.C.). Author: Gossip: The Life and Times of Walter Winchell, 1940; True Tales from the Annals of Crime and Rascality, 1954; The Edinburg Caper, 1962. Contbr. to anthologies, textbooks. Home: New York-N.Y. Died Jan. 10, 1980.

MCKENNA, DANIEL JOHN, judge; b. Toledo, July 26, 1899; s. John Francis and Mary Matilda (Purtil) McK.; A.B., St. Johns Coll., Toledo, 1918; LL.B., Harvard, 1922; A.M., St. Johns Coll., 1923. Admitted to Ohio bar, 1922; practiced at Toledo, 1922-27; prof. law Marquette U., 1927-29; asst. reporter Wis. Supreme Ct., 1929; prof. law DePaul U., 1929-31, became prof. law Detroit U., 1931, dean Law Shc., 1932-55; in pvt. practice of law, Toledo, 1955-63; judge Maumee (Ohio) Municipal Ct., 1964-70. Served as pvt. U.S. Army, 1918, World War I; on duty with U.S. Army, as maj., then as lt. col., Judge Adv. Gen.'s Dept., Oct. 1941-June 1945, in South Pacific Kingdom of Tonga and at Headquarters 6th Service Command in Chicago, World War II. Mem. Am. Bar Assn., Mich. State Bar, Ohio State Bar Assn., Parsons Law Club, Am. Legion, Pierian Sodality, Pl Gamma Mu. Democrat. Roman Catholic. Mem. K.C. Contbr. articles and verse to various publs. Home: Maumee, Ohio. Died June 1978.

MCKENNA, F(RANCIS) E(UGENE), chemist, library assn. exec.; b. Globe, Ariz., July 29, 1921; s. Patrick and Eugenia (With) McK.; B.A. with honors in Chemistry, U. Calif., Berkeley, 1941; Ph.D. in Phys. Chemistry (Procter and Gamble research fellow), U. Wash., 1944. Research chemist S.A.M. Labs., Manhattan Project, Columbia, N.Y.C., 1944-45; research supr. Manhattan Project, Carbide & Carbon Chems. Co., N.Y.C., 1945-46; postdoctoral research fellow Inst. for Nuclear Studies, U. Chgo., 1946-47; sr. chemist central research labs. Air Reduction Co., Inc., Murray Hill, N.J., 1948-53, sr. info. specialist, 1953-59, supr. info. center, 1959-67; editor Special Libraries, Spl. Libraries Assn., N.Y.C., 1967-70, exec. dir. Spl. Libraries Assn., 1970-78; mem. adv. bd. Rutgers U. Grad. Sch. Library Sci., 1959-61; John Cotton Dana lectr. Pratt Inst., 1961; mem. N.J. Council Research and Devel., 1964-65; mem. U.S. Del. in U.S.-USSR Exchange in Sci. Libraries and Info. Centers, 1965; mem. liaison com. Library of Congress, 1965-67; vis. prof. U. Tokyo, Osaka (Japan) U., Nat. Coll. Librarianship, Tokyo, 1972; Alberta L. Brown lectr. Western Mich U., 1974; witness relating to copyright before Senate Com. on Judiciary, 1974, House Subcom. on Cts., Civil Liberties and the Adminstrn. of Justice, 1975; chmn. com. on copyright practices and interpretation Council of Nat. Library Assns., 1976—; cons. revision of U.S. copyright law. Recipient Centennial citation ALA, 1976; Spl. citation Spl. Libraries Assn., 1977. Fellow AAAS; mem. Am. Chem. Soc., Am. Soc. Info. Sci., Internat. Fedn. Library Assns. (chmn. spl. libraries div. 1976-78), Spl. Libraries Assn. (pres. N.J. chpt. 1959-60, dir. 1965-68, pres. 1966-67), Sigma Xi, Phi Lambda Upsilon. Contbr. numerous articles in fields of chemistry, library and info. sci. to profl. jours. Home: New York, N.Y. Died Nov. 10, 1978.

MCKENNA, JOHN REDMOND, coll. librarian; b. Ottawa, Ont., Can., May 19, 1917; came to U.S., 1948; s. Arthur Charles and M. Eileen (Kelly) McK.; B.A., Queen's U., 1947; B.L.S., McGill U., 1948; m. M. Constance Duclos, Aug. 7, 1954; 1 dau., Anne Marie. Reference asst. U. Maine Library, 1948-49; head readers' services Bowdoin Coll. Library, 1949-53, asst. librarian, 1953-57; librarian Colby Coll., 1957-64, asso. prof. bibliography, bus. mgr., pres., 1957-64; librarian Middlebury (Vt.) Coll., 1964-75. Served with RCAF, 1943-45. Mem. ALA, Maine Library Assn. (pres. 1957-59), New Eng. Library Assn. (treas. 1962-63, pres. 1969-70). Contbr. articles to periodicals. Home: Middlebury, Vt. Died Sept. 30, 1975; buried Westbrook, Maine.

MCKENNEY, PAUL KERNS, mfg. exec.; b. Manatee Co., Fla., Sept. 10, 1882; s. Benjamin Ivy and Mary Mariah (Johnson) McK.; B.S., Ga. Tech., 1902; m. Etta Lawrence Williams, Apr. 14, 1909; children—Mrs. Sidney Hays Dykes, Paul Kerns. Dyeing dept. Eagle & Phenix Mills, Columbus, Ga., 1903-04; salesman Atlanta Compound Co., 1905-06; supt. Miss. Mills, Wesson, 1906-08; Elizabeth Mills, Egan, Ga., 1909-10; supt., mgr., treas. Tex. Cotton Mills Co., McKinney, 1910-18; v.p. Swift Mfg. Co., Columbus, 1918-37, pres., 1937-50, chmn. bd., 1950-60, ret., 1960, now dir. Presbyn. Home: Columbus, Ga. Retired. *

MCKENNEY, THOMAS KENNETH, sch. pres.; b. Milw., Jan. 5, 1914; s. William Fergus and Agatha Margaret (O'Connor) McK.; A.B., Marquette U., 1933; M.A., St. Louis U., 1948. Joined Soc. of Jesus, 1933, ordained priest Roman Cath. Ch. 1945; asst. prin. Creighton Prep. Sch., Omaha, 1948-49; prin. Regis High Sch., Denver, 1949-51, Marquette U. High Sch., Milw., 1951-54, Campion Jesuit High Sch., Prairie du Chien, Wis., 1954-56; asst. dean Coll. Arts and Scis., Creighton U., Omaha, 1958-61, dean, 1961-72, tchr. English and theology, 1956-58, bd. dirs., 1961-76; pres. Creighton Prep. Sch., Omaha, 1972-76. Sec.-treas. Omaha Adult Edn. Council, 1963-64, pres., 1964-65; mem. citizens adv. group Nebr. Dept. Rds.; mem. citizens adv. bd. Omaha-Council Bluffs Met. Area Planning Agy. Mem. Assn. Higher Edn., Mo. Valley Adult Edn. Assn., Jesuit Secondary Edn. Assn. Club: Rotary. Home: Omaha, Nebr. Died Mar. 29, 1976.

MC KERNAN, DONALD LYNN, fishery biologist; b. Eugene, Ore., Jan. 29, 1918; s. Charles Ross and Marie (MacLean) McK.; B.S. in Fisheries, U. Wash., 1940, postgrad., 1940-42, 48-49, 51; m. Patricia Geraldine O'Connor, Nov. 28, 1940; children—Barbara Lynne, Rebecca Jane, Kathy Marie, Deborah Kaye, Cynthia Anne. Fisheries research biologist Wash. State Fisheries Dept., 1940-45; dir. research Ore. Fish Commn., 1945-52; fisheries expert U.S. Army in Japan, 1950; lectr. sch. fisheries U. Wash., 1951; asst. dir. Pacific Oceanic Fishery Investigations, U.S. Fish and Wildlife Service, 1952-55; adminstr. Alaska Comml. Fisheries, 1955-57, dir. Bur. Comml. Fisheries, Washington, 1957-66, spl. asst. sec. state for fish and wildlife Dept. State, Washington, 1966-74; prof. marine affairs, dir. Inst. Marine Studies, U. Wash., Seattle, 1974-79. Fellow Am. Inst. Fish Biologists; mem. A.A.A.S., Pacific Fishery Biologists, Am. Soc. Limnology and Oceanography, Am. Fisheries Soc., Sigma Xi, Phi Sigma. Club: Cosmos. Home: Seattle, Wash. Died May 10, 1979.

MCKNIGHT, SUMNER THOMAS, b. Milwaukee, Wis., Apr. 6, 1884; s. Sumner Thomas and Eugenie (Manville) McK.; grad. St. Paul's Sch., Concord, N.H., 1903; B.A., Yale, 1907; m. Henriette D. Turney, June 8, 1912; children—Henry Turney, Edith; m. 2d. Helen Shevlin Beckwith, Oct. 4, 1932. Settled in Minneapolis, Minn., 1890; pres. S. T. McKnight Co., real estate, since 1908; dir. First National Bank of Minneapolis, First Produce State Bank, Minneapolis-Moline Power & Implement Company, Northwest States Portland Cement Co., N.W. Bell Telephone Co., Farmers and Mechanics Savings Bank.; mem. Minn. Ho. of Rep., 1921-27; mem. State Senate, 1927-29. Served as capt. inf., U.S. Army, 1917-19. Mem. Nat. Crime Commn. to study pardons, paroles, 1927; mem. Minneapolis Council of Social Agencies; dir. Orchestral Assn. of Minneapolis, Inc. Mem. Alpha Delta Phi. Republican Episcopalian. Clubs: Minneapolis, Minnesota, Chicago, Woodhill Country, Gulf Stream Golf. Home: Wayzata, Minn. *

MCLAREN, ARTHUR DOUGLAS, biophysicist, educator; b. Ipava, Ill., Sept. 27, 1917; s. Homer D. and Matilda (Rose) McL.; B.A., Park Coll., 1939; Ph.D., U. Mo., 1943; m. Alice Gray Jones, Feb. 3, 1940; 1 son, Gordon Douglas; m. 2d, Helen Rodina, Sept. 21, 1965. Research chemist E.I. duPont de Nemours & Co., Buffalo, 1943; asst. prof. Poly. Inst. Bklyn., 1946; prof. soil biochemistry U. Calif. at Berkeley, 1951-79, prof. biology, chmn. dept., 1969-74. Vis. prof. U. Sydney, 1959, U. Tex., Dallas, 1966, Tuskegee Inst., 1968; mem. com. on photo-biology NRC, 1960-68. Trustee Starr King Sch. for Ministry. Rockefeller Found. fellow, Scandinavia, 1949-50, Fulbright fellow, Australia, 1959, Guggenheim Meml. Found. fellow, Eng., 1966; Swedish Nat. Research Council grantee, Uppsala, 1967. Fellow A.A.A.S.; mem. Am. Soc. Biol. Chemists, Am. Biophys. Soc., Arms and Armour Soc. (Eng.), Am. Soc. Photobiology, Soil Sci. Soc. Am. Author: (with David Shugar) Photochemistry of Proteins and Nucleic Acids, 1964; (with George Petersen) Soil Biochemistry, 1966; (with J. Skujins) Soil Biochemistry, vol. 2, 1971, (with E. Paul) Vols. 3-4, 1975. Founder, exec. editor Photochemistry and Photobiology, 1961-66; regional editor Soil Biology & Biochemistry, 1969-79; editorial bd. Environmental Letters, 1971; editor books on soils and environment for Marcel Dekker, Inc., N.Y.C. Contbr. articles to profl. jours. Home: Inverness, Calif. Died Jan. 21, 1979.

MCLAREN, NORMAN LOYALL, accountant; b. San Francisco, Jan. 23, 1892; s. Norman and Linie Loyall (Ashe) McL.; student Taft Sch., Conn., 1907-10; A.B., U. Calif., 1914, LL.D., 1961; LL.D., U. San Francisco, 1963, Whittier Coll., 1972; m. Marguerite Amoss, Jan. 15, 1916 (dec. 1956); children—Kenneth Loyall, Thomas Loyall; m. 2d, Elizabeth Page Sproul, 1957 (dec. 1965); m. 3d, Mary Stillman Butterworth, 1966. Investment banking clk., July 1914; with McLaren, Goode & Co. from 1918, partner 1920-42; partner Haskins & Sells. after 1952; chmn. The Irvine Co. Comdr., USNR, Jan. 1942; capt., Dec. 1943. Chmn. N.Y. div. Navy Price Adjustment bd.; ret. as rear adm. Treas. UN Conf. Com. San Francisco, 1945; accounting adviser to U.S. delegation Allied Commn. or Reparations, 1945. Mem. group surveying Internal Revenue Bur. for Congress, 1947-48. Pres. and dir. James Irvine Found. Chmn. concessions com. Golden Gate Internat. Expn., 1939. Mem. exec. com. San Francisco Community Chest 1934-42; mem. Cal, Bd. State Harbor Commrs., 1945; mem. adv. council U. Calif. Sch. Bus. Adminstrn.; regent U. San Francisco; mem. pres.'s council Calif. Inst. Tech.; mem. adv. bd. Hoover Instn., Stanford U. Recipient Am. Inst. Accountants annual award for best book in accounting field, 1948. Mem. Am. Inst. Accountants (pres. 1941, v.p. 1935-36; mem. council, com. on auditing procedure and spl. com. on nat. def.), Cal. Soc. C.P.A.'s (pres. 1928-29), Soc. Cal. Pioneers, Order of Cincinnati (N.C.), Order Ky. Colonels, Order St. John Jerusalem, Newcomen Soc. N.A., Psi Upsilon. Republican. Episcopalian. Clubs: Pacific-Union, Bohemian, San Francisco Golf; Links (N.Y.C.). Author: California Tax Laws of 1929 (with Vincent K. Butler, Jr.), 1929; Income Tax Management for Individuals (with B.J. Feigenbaum), 1936; Annual Reports to Stockholders, 1947; also plays for Bohemian Club. Contbr. to Jour. Accountancy, Home: Greenbrae, Calif. Died Oct. 23, 1977.

MCLAREN, RICHARD WELLINGTON, judge; b. Chgo., Apr. 21, 1918; s. Grover C. and Nita (Waggoner) Mcl.; B.A., Yale, 1939, LL.B., 1942; m. Edith Gillett, Sept. 20, 1941; children—Patricie, Richard Wellington, Sandra, James Gillett. Admitted to N.Y. bar, 1944, Ill. bar, 1950; with firm Hodges, Reavis, Pantaleoni & Downey, N.Y.C., 1946-49; mem. firm Chadwell, Keck, Kayser, Ruggles & McLaren, Chgo., 1950-69, asst. atty. gen. anti-trust div. Justice Dept., 1969-72; judge U.S. Dist. Ct., No. Dist. Ill., Eastern Div., Chgo., from 1972. Served to capt. USAAF, 1942-46. Mem. Am. (ho. of dels. 1963-66, vice chmn. antitrust sect. 1966-67, chmn. 1967-68), Fed., Ill., Chgo. bar assn., Am. Coll. Trial Lawyers. Clubs: Law, Legal, Union League, Yale (Chgo.). Home: Winnetka, Ill. Died Feb. 25, 1976.

MCLARNAN, CHARLES WALTER, univ. dean; b. Mt. Vernon, Ohio, Mar. 13, 1928; s. John Walter and Cora Marie (Conard) McL.; B.A., Ohio Wesleyan U., 1951; B.M.E., Ohio State U., 1954, M.S., 1955, Ph.D., 1960; m. Marjorie Lucile Roseboom, June 15, 1952; children—Timothy, Linda, Margaret, Kenneth, William. Instr., Ohio State U., 1954-60, asst. prof., 1960-64, asso. prof., 1964-68, prof. mech. engring., 1968-72, exec. asst. to provost and v.p. acad. affairs, sec. univ. faculty, 1969-72; v.p., dir. instl. services Macalester Coll., St. Paul, 1972-73, v.p., exec. officer, 1973-74, interim pres., 1974-75, spl. asst. to the pres., 1975-76; dean sci. and engring. U. Tex. of Permian Basin, Odessa, 1976-79; vis. scholar Columbia, 1965-66; cons. Nat. Cash Register, Western Electric, Bell Telephone Labs., Diamond Power Specialty Corp., Battelle Meml. Inst. Served with USAAF, 1946-47. NSF Sci. Faculty fellow, 1965-66; registered profl. engr., Ohio, Tex. Mem. ASME (exec. com. design engring. div.), Am. Soc. Engring. Edn., AAAS, Soc. Petroleum Engrs., Sigma Phi Epsilon. Methodist, Mason, Kiwanian. Tech. editor ASME transactions Jour. Mech. Design. Home: Odessa, Tex. Died Apr. 10, 1979.

MCLAUGHLIN, CHARLES BORROMEO, clergyman; b. N.Y.C., Sept. 26, 1913; ed. St. Joseph Sem. Ordained priest Roman Cath. Ch., 1941; titular bishop Risinium, aux. bishop Raleigh, 1964; bishop Diocese St. Petersburg, Fla., 1968-78. Home: St. Petersburg, Fla. Died Dec. 15, 1978.

MCLAUGHLIN, JOHN, artist; b. Sharon, Mass., May 21, 1898; s. John Dwyer and Harriet (Attwood) McL.; m. Florence Emerson, Apr. 14, 1928. Fourteen one-man shows; numerous group exhbns. throughout U.S. and other countries; represented in permanent collections Bowdoin Coll. Mus. Art, Long Beach Mus. Art, Los Angeles County Mus. Art, Mass. Inst. Tech., Met Mus. Art, Nat. Collection Fine Arts at Smithsonian Instn., Oakland Mus. Art, Pasadena Art Mus., U. Art Mus. U. Calif., Berkeley, Wadsworth Atheneum, Mus. Modern Art, N.Y.C., Santa Barbara Mus. Art, Stanford, U. N. M., Corcoran Gallery Art, Addison Gallery Am. Art. Served with U.S. Navy, World War I, AUS, World War II. Decorated Bronze Star, Recipient award Nat. Found. Arts and Humanities. Home: Dana Point, Calif. Died Mar. 22, 1976.

MCLEAN, ROBERT, newspaper exec.; b. Phila., Oct. 1, 1891; s. William L. and Sarah Burd (Warden) McL.; Litt.B., Princeton, 1913, LL.D., 1947; LL.D., Franklin & Marshall, 1940, Litt.D., Columbia U., 1947, Drexel Inst. Tech., 1954; L.H.D., Temple U., 1952; m. Clare Randolph Goode, Apr. 28, 1919; children—Donald, Jenepher (Mrs. Edward J. Kelly, Jr.). Pres., pub. Evening & Sunday Bull. Phila., 1931-59, chmn. bd., 1959-80; chmn. bd. Santa Barbara News Press, 1964-80; dir. A.P., 1924-68, pres., 1938-58. Commd. maj. U.S. Res. F.A., 1918. Recipient Gold Medal of Achievement, Poor Richard Club, 1947; Edward Powell award for 1955 (Phila.). Hon. mem. Poor Richard Club, Phila., Acad. Stomatology. Presbyn. Home: Montecito, Calif. Died Dec. 5, 1980.

MC LEAN, WILLIAM BURDETTE, missile engr.; b. Portland, Oreg., May 21, 1914; s. Robert N. and Clara (Blohm) McL.; B.S. (scholar), Calif. Inst. Tech., 1935, M.S., 1937, Ph.D., 1939; fellow U. Iowa, 1939-41; m. La Verne Jones, June 25, 1939; children—William R., Donald M., Mark A. Nuclear physicist Nat. Bur. Standards, 1941-45; with Naval Ordnance Test Sta., China Lake, Calif., 1945-67, head aviation ordnance dept., 1950-54, tech. dir. sta., 1954-67; tech. dir. Naval Undersea Center, San Diego, 1967-74, cons., 1974-76. Recipient Fed. Govt. award for developing Sidewinder air-to-air Missile, 1956, President's award for Distinguished Fed. Civilian Service, 1958, Resolution of Commendation, Calif. Legislature, 1957; Blandy Gold Medal award Am. Ordnance Assn., 1960; Rockefeller Public Service award for sci. and tech., 1965; Alumni Distinguished Service award Calif. Inst. Tech., 1969. Fellow IEEE (Harry Diamond award 1972); mem. Am. Soc. Public Adminstrn., Am. Physics Soc., AAAS, Research Soc. Am., Am. Ordnance Assn., Nat. Acad. Engring., Nat. Acad. Scis., Marine Tech. Soc., Am. Soc. for Oceanography, Sigma Xi, Tau Beta Pi. Home: San Diego, Calif. Died Aug. 25, 1976; buried Grants Pass, Oreg.

MC LELLAN, ADRIAN OSWALD, banker; b. Minto, N.D., July 25, 1914; s. Alexander and Oline (Sund) McL., B.S., U. N. D., 1937, LL.B., 1939, J.D., 1969; m. Ada Thompson, June 8, 1938; children—Donn, Mary (Mrs. David Durham). With Mchts. Nat. Bank & Trust Co., Fargo, N.D., 1939-42, 46-65, trust officer, 1947-50, v.p;., 1950-53, pres., 1953-65; spl. agt. FBI, 1942-45; pres., dir. First Nat. Bank of Gt. Falls, Mont., 1965-75; exec. v.p., dir. First Bank System, Mpls., 1975-79; dir. First Computer Corp., St. Paul, First System Agys., Mpls., 1975-79. State coordinator U.S. Savs. Bonds, 1973-74. Gt. Falls Credit Bur., United Fund Cascade County; trustee Coll. of Gt. Falls, Heisey Found. Served with USNR, 1945-46. Mem. Am. Bankers Assn. (past pres. nat. bank div.), Gt Falls C. of C. (pres., dir., mem. exec. com.), Assn. Mil. Banks U.S.(pres., dir.). Presbyn. Mason (Shriner), Clubs: Meadow Lark Country, Interlachen Country; Minneapolis; Minnesota (St Paul). Home: Edina, Minn. Died June, 1979.

MCLEMORE, RICHARD AUBREY, orgn. exec.; b. Perry Co., Miss., June 6, 1903; s. Hezekiah and Tabitha (Small) McL.; A.B., Miss. Coll., 1923; A.M., George Peabody Coll., 1926, Ph.D., Vanderbilt U., 1933; Lit.D., Miss. Coll., 1969; m. Nannie Pitts, 1927; 1 son, Harry Kimbrell. Supt. village schs., Paynes, Sandersville, Miss., 1923-26; instr. history, dean Jones Co. Jr. Coll., 1926-30, 1933-34; prof. history, dean Judson Coll., 1934-38; foreign research Brit. Mus., also Archives du Ministere des Affaires Estrangeres, summer 1938; prof. Miss. So. Coll., 1938-57, acting pres., Jan.-Sept. 1955, dean coll., prof. history, 1945-57; pres. Miss. Coll., Clinton, 1957-68, pres.-emeritus, 1968-76; exec. sec.-treas. Miss. Baptist Hist. Commn., 1968-76. Bd. trustees Miss. Dept. Archives and History, 1950-69, pres., 1957-69, dir., 1969-76; chmn. edn. com. Miss. Assn. for Mental Health; mem. exec. board Andrew Jackson Area council Boy Scouts Am.; mem. gov.'s com. on pvt. colls. Mem. War Fund Board Miss., 1943-44. Mem. Am., So., Miss. hist. assns., So. Bapt. Hist. Commn. (exec. com. 1969-76), So. Bapt. Hist. Soc. (pres. 1973-76), Miss. Assn. Colls. (pres. 1949), Newcomen Soc. N. Am., Phi Delta Kappa, Omicron Delta Kappa, Kappa Delta Pi. Democrat (chmn. Forrest Co. exec. com. 1944-48), Baptist (mem. Miss. edn. com. 1945-51). Mason (33 deg., Shriner). Club: Lions (dist. gov. 1950-51, internat. counselor 1951-76). Author: Franco-American Diplomatic Relations, 1816-1836, 1940; Mississippi Through Four Centuries (with Nannie Pitts McLemore), 1945, rev. edit. 1964, 68; Outline of Mississippi History, 1941, rev. edits. 1944, 46, 51; Fundamentals of Citizenship (with Blough, Switzer), 1950; Our Nation's Story (with Everett Augspurger), 1954, rev. edit., 1963; The Natchez Country, 1956; United States History for Schools (with Boyd C. Shafer and Everett Augspurger), 1966; A High School History of Modern America (with others), 1966; History of Mississippi Baptists 1971. Editor-in-chief Jour. Miss. History, 1969-76. Editor: A History of Mississippi, 2 vols., 1973. Hist. editor: Official Map of Mississippi, 1953. Contbr. articles to hist. jours., Americana Ency., World Book, Ency. Brit. Home: Clinton, Miss. Died Aug. 31, 1976.

MC LEOD, JAMES CURRIE, clergyman, educator; b. Buffalo; s. Dugald and Mary Holmes (Currie) McL.; B.S., Middlebury Coll., 1926, D.D., 1950; B.D., Yale U., 1929; D.D., Alfred U., 1941; m. Emily Louise Johnson, Aug. 24, 1929; children—Mary Louise (Mrs. James S. Aagaard), Adrienne (Mrs. Craig Heatley), James Currie. Ordained to ministry Presbyn. Ch., 1929; univ. chaplain Alfred (N.Y.) U., 1929-40; minister to students Ohio State U., Columbus, 1940-43, univ. chaplain, prof. history and lit. of religion Northwestern U., 1946-50, prof., 1950-71, dean students, 1952-67; research fellow Yale Div. Sch., 1963-64; vis. scholar Colgate-Rochester Div. Sch., 1967-68; guest preacher Presbytery of Glasgow, Scotland, 1950, also at Syracuse, Chgo., Rutgers, Lake Forest, Middlebury, Stanford, Howard, others. Pres., trustee Evanston (Ill.) Pub. Library. Served as lt. comdr., chaplain USNR, 1943-46. Mem. Nat. Acad. Religion, Nat. Assn. Student Personnel Adminstrs. (pres. 1963-64), Religious Edn. Assn. (v.p. 1963-64), Presbytery of Chgo., Delta Upsilon (internat. pres. 1972-73). Republican. Mason. Clubs: Rotary (past pres.), University (Evanston); St. Andrew Soc. (pres. 1973-74); Yale (Chgo.). Author: Fruits of Faith (symposium); also articles various jours. Home: Evanston, Ill. Died Apr. 15, 1981.

MC LUHAN, HERBERT MARSHALL, communications specialist, educator, writer; b. Edmonton, Alta., Can., July 21, 1911; s. Herbert Ernest and Elsie Naomi (Hall) McL.; B.A., U. Man. (Can.), 1932, M.A., 1934, Litt.D., 1967; B.A., Cambridge (Eng.) U., 1936, M.A., 1939, Ph.D., 1942; D.Litt. (hon.), U. Windsor (Ont., Can.), 1965, Assumption U., 1966, Simon Fraser U., 1967, St. John Fisher Coll., 1969, Grinnell Coll., 1967, U. Western Ont., 1972, U. Toronto, 1977; LL.D., U. Alta., 1971, Niagara U., 1978; m. Corinne Keller Lewis, Aug. 4, 1939; children—Eric, Mary Colton, Teresa, Stephanie, Elizabeth (Mrs. Sean O'Sullivan), Michael. Faculty U. Wis., Madison, 1936-37; instr. English, St. Louis U., 1937-44; asso. prof. English, Assumption U., Windsor, 1944-46; faculty St. Michael's Coll., U. Toronto (Ont.), 1946-80, prof. English, 1952-80, dir. Centre for Culture and Tech., 1963-80; Albert Schweitzer prof. humanities Fordham U., N.Y.C., 1967-68; Pound lectr. The Possum and the Midwife, 1978. Chmn. Ford Found. seminar on culture and communication, 1953-55; dir. media project U.S. Office Edn.-Nat. Assn. Ednl. Broadcasters, 1959-60. Consultor, Pontifical Commn. for Social Communications, 1973. Decorated companion Order of Can., 1970; recipient hon. award in culture and communications Niagara U., 1967; Molson award in social scis., 1967; Carl-Einstein-Preis, West Germany Critics award, 1967; Christian Culture award Assumption U., 1971; Gold medal Pres. Italian Republic, 1971; Pres.'s award Inst. Pub. Relations Gt. Britain, 1970; Pres.'s Cabinet award U. Detroit, 1972. Fellow Royal Soc. Can. Roman Catholic. Author: The Mechanical Bride: Folklore of Industrial Man, 1951; Selected Poetry of Tennyson, 1956; (with E.S. Carpenter) Explorations in Communications, 1960; The Gutenberg Galaxy: The Making of Typographic Man (Gov. Gen.'s literary award for critical prose 1963), 1962; Understanding Media, 1964; (with R.J. Schoeck) Voices of Literature, 3 vols., 1964, 65, 70; The Medium is the Massage, 1967; War and Peace in the Global Village, 1968; (with Harley Parker) Through the Vanishing Point: Space in Poetry and Painting, 1968; Literary Criticism of Marshall McLuhan 1943-62, 1969; Counterblast, 1969; Culture is Our Business, 1970; From Cliche to Archetype, 1970; (with B. Nevitt) Take Today: The Executive as Dropout, 1972; (with Eric McLuhan and Kathy Hutchon) The City as Classroom, 1977; Dóeil á oreille, 1977; (with P. Babin) Autre homme autre chrétien á l'âge électronique, 1977. Co-editor Explorations, 1953-59, editor, 1964-80. Home: Toronto, Ont., Can. Died Dec. 31, 1980; buried Toronto.

MCLYMAN, BENJAMIN MURRAY, lawyer; b. Newport, R.I., May 4, 1886; s. Benjamin Marsh and Nellie Irving (Campbell) McL.; Ph.B., Brown U., 1913; LL.B., Harvard, 1916; m. Nina B. Horgan, June 23, 1913; 1 dau., Nina Horgan (Mrs. Colin Gardner, III). Began practice at Providence, 1917; associated with Gardner, Moss & Haslam until 1924; then practiced alone; asst.-atty. gen. of R.I., 1925-29, atty. gen., 1929-33; pub. utility adminstr. of R.I., 1939-41; dir. Dept. Business Regulation, of Rhode Island, 1941; dir. Civilian Defense (Providence); mem. Bur. of License, Jamestown Ferry Authority. Member Beta Theta Pi. Republican. Episcopalian. Public Utility Administrator until August 1941 (2d appointment); Mem. Bur. of Police and Fire of Providence, R.I. since 1945. Clubs: University, Beavertail Country. Home: Providence, R.I. *

MCMAHON, JOHN LASALLE, coll. pres.; b. LaSalle, Ill., Mar. 30, 1908; s. Timothy and Alice (Lukken) McM.; student Ill. Wesleyan U., 1925-27; A.B., St. Viator Coll., 1929; M.A., Catholic U. Am., 1930, Ph.D., 1933; LL.D. (hon.), St. Edwards U., 1954; LL.D., St. Mary's U., San Antonio, 1967; student U. Ill., summer 1930, U. Mich., summer 1933; m. Katharine Beilman, Sept. 1, 1934; children—John L., Katharine, Stephen, Michael, Dennis. Instr., Our Lady of Lake Coll., San Antonio, 1933-39, pres., 1941-73, now pres. emeritus; asst. prof. Cath. U. Am., Washington, 1939-41; prof. Columbus U. Coll., 1940-41. Adviser to Office Mil Govt. in Ednl. Matters, 1947. Past chmn. bd. trustees San Antonio Pub. Library; pres. Tex. Conf. Ch. Related Colls., 1947; pres. Assn. Tex. Colls., 1947; co-pres. Tex. Found. of Voluntary Supported Colls. and Univs.; mem. Charter Commn. San Antonio, 1951. Mem. city council of San Antonio, 1958-61. Bd. dirs. Oblate Coll. of S.W., 1968-76. Recipient Pro Ecclesia et Pontifice medal, 1954; Order of Balboa (Republic of Panama), 1961. Mem. Am. Polit. Sci. Assn., Theta Chi, Alpha Chi (pres. nat. council). Author: Recent Changes in the Recognition Policy of the United States, 1933; Outlines in American Government, 1942. Home: San Antonio, Tex. Died Jan. 5, 1976.

MC MANUS, JAMES EDWARD, clergyman; b. Bklyn., Oct. 10, 1900; s. William and Elizabeth (O'Laughlen) McM.; student St. Mary's Coll., North East, Pa., 1915-21, Mt. St. Alphonsus, Esopus, N.Y., 1922-28. Entered Congregation of the Most Holy Redeemer, 1922; ordained priest Roman Catholic Ch., 1927; missionary, P.R., 1929-34; prof, canon law Mt. St. Alphonsus, 1937-40; pastor, Aquadilla, P.R., 1940-45, Mayaquez, P.R., 1945-47; bishop Ponce, P.R., 1947-63; pastor St. Cecilia's Parish, Manhattan, vicar Sullivan and Ulster counties, 1963-70; titular bishop of Benda, aux. bishop N.Y. until 1976. Home: New York, N.Y. Died July 1, 1976.

MCMANUS, JOHN B., JR., justice N.Mex. Supreme Ct.; b. 1919; grad. U. N.Mex.; LL.B., Georgetown U. Admitted to bar, 1947; now chief justice N.Mex.

Supreme Ct. Address: Santa Fe, N.Mex. Died July 6, 1979.

MCMENIMEN, WALTER L., mem. U.S.R.R. Labor Bd.; b. Cambridge, Mass., Sept. 12, 1883; s. William H. and Mary E. (Powers) M.; ed. grammar sch., Cambridge; m. Nellie Bly Savage, of Louisville, Ky., Feb. 9, 1921. Postoffice spl. delivery messenger, 1896-1900; trainman, B.&M. R.R., 1900-12; chmn. Mass. Legislative Bd., Brotherhood of Ry. Trainmen, 1912-18; dep. pres. B.R.T., 1918-21, assigned as legislative rep. and mem. Ry. Bd. of Adjustment No. 1, U.S. R.R. Administration; mem. U.S. R.R. Labor Bd., term 1921-26; Labor Board discontinued in 1926; chmn. Exemption Bd. No. 8, Cambridge, during war period, also mem. Mass. Com. Public Safety and mem. Com. on War Efficiency. Dir. N. Cambridge Coöperative Bank. Republican. Catholic. Elk. Club: Traffic (hon.). Home: Cambridge, Mass. *

MCMILLAN, FRANKLIN R., dir. of research, Portland Cement Assn.; b. Worthington, Minn., Oct. 7, 1882; s. Charles Edwin and Lois Velma (Richardson) McM.; C.E., U. of Minn., 1905; m. Luvena L. Bronkway, Oct. 15, 1907. Engaged in railroad engring., building constrn. and irrigation engring., 1905-09; instr. and asst. prof. U. of Minn., 1909-17; research eng. U.S. Emergency Fleet Corp., 1918-20; in building constrn. and gen. engring., 1920-24; asso. engr. Portland Cement Assn., 1924-26; mgr. structural and tech. bureau of same, 1926-27, dir. of research, 1927-47, asst. to vice pres. for development and research, Jan. 1947-Nov. 1948. Vice-pres. Am. Concrete Inst., 1934-35, pres. 1936; mem. Am. Soc. Civ. Engrs., Am. Soc. for Testing Materials. Home: Asheville, N.C. *

MCMILLAN, JOHN LANNEAU, congressman; b. Mullins, S.C. Apr. 12, 1902; s. M.L. and Mary Alice (Keith) McM.; student Univs. N.C. and S.C., Nat. Law Sch., Washington; m. Margaret English, Oct. 31, 1936; 1 son, John Lanneau. Mem. 76th to 92d congresses from 6th S.C. Dist.; chmn. Ho. Dist. Com., 1945-46, 49-52, 55-70; vice chmn. Agr. Com., after 1969, also chmn. forestry subcom., vice chmn. tobacco subcom. Congressional del. Interparliamentary Union, London, Eng., 1960, Tokyo, Japan, 1961. Served in USN, 1918. Mem. Jr. Order United Am. Mechanics, Blue Key, Am. Legion, 40 and 8. Democrat. Baptist. Clubs: Masons, Elks. Home: Florence, S.C. Died Sept. 2, 1979.

MCMILLAN, THOMAS M., physician; b. Mobile, Ala., Jan. 27, 1892; s. Thomas Murphy and Margaret Lane (Parker) McM.; A.B., Princeton, 1913; M.D., U. Pa., 1917; m. Julia Talcott, Nov. 12, 1919; children—Thomas M. III, Frances McMillan Russell, Julia McMillan Turnbull. In practice medicine, Phila., from 1924; physician Pa. Hosp., 1925-57; cons. cardiology Burlington County Hosp., Phila. Gen. Hosp.; hon. cons. Mobile (Ala.) Gen. Hosp.; prof. clin. cardiology U. Pa. Grad. Sch. Medicine, 1948-58, emeritus prof., after 1958; Mem. bd. Museum of City of Mobile. Trustee Princeton Theol. Sem., 1948-67, trustee emeritus, from 1967. Recipient Alfred Stengel Meml. award A.C.P., 1954, gold heart award Am. Heart Assn., 1955. Master A.C.P. (gov. 1950-58, 3d v.p. 1958; regent 1960-64); mem. Am. Climatol. and Clin. Assn. Author; Blood Pressure, Its Clinical Applications (with George W. Norris and H.C. Bazet). Editor-in chief Am. Heart Jour., 1946-49, Circulation, 1950-55, Bull. Am. Coll. Physicians, 1960-64. Contbr. to med. jours. Home: Mobile, Ala. Died Oct. 19, 1976.

MCMILLAN, WILLIAM BENTON, business exec.; b. Chgo., June 8, 1901; s. William M. and Winona (Eberhart) McM.; M.E., Cornell U.; m. Arla Avery, 1925; children—Nancy Jean, William Benton, Jr., Arla (dec.), Sewell L. Avery. Treas., W. McMillan & Son, 1922-26, partner W.B. McMillan & Co., 1926-30; chmn. Hussmann Refrigerator Co., St. Louis, 1932-66, pres., 1931-60, 63-64; chmn. Hussmann Refrigeration, Inc., St. Louis, 1944-66, Hussmann Refrigerator Co. Ltd., Can., 1950-66, Duro-Consol., Inc., Menlo Park, Calif., 1958-66; ret. Pres., St. Louis Community Chest, 1951-52; mem. Civic Progress, Inc., 1959-66, mem. emeritus, 1966-78. Hon. life dir. Municipal Theatre Assn., St. Louis; adv. council Jr. Achievement, Inc.; dir. United Fund Greater St. Louis, 1955-68; exec. bd. St. Louis Council Boy Scouts Am. (pres. 1956-58); pres. Met. St. Louis Hosp. Planning Commn. (now ARCH), 1961-63, dir., 1961-69. Trustee The David Ranken Jr. Tech. Inst. (pres. 1970-71), Govtl. Research Inst., Mo. Public Expenditure Survey, McMillan-Avery Found. Mem. NAM. Presbyn. Clubs: Racquet, St. Louis; Automobile of Mo. (bd. govs.). Home: Clayton, Mo. Died Aug. 28, 1978; buried Bellefontaine Cemetery, St. Louis, Mo.

MCMINN, BRYAN TOWNE, educator; b. Superior, Wis., Feb. 29, 1896; s. Martin L. and Phoebe Jane (Conant) McM.; B.S., Oreg. State Coll., 1918; M.S., U. Wash., 1926, M.E., 1931; m. Louise Odell, July 23, 1924; children—Stephanna, Marjorie, Lucinda. Engr. Meese & Gottfried Co., Portland, Ore., 1919-20; instr. U. Wash., 1920-26, asst. prof., 1926-31, asso. prof., 1931-39, prof. mech. engring., 1939-64, prof. emeritus, 1964-79, exec. officer, from 1946. Served with U.S.N.R.F., 1918-19. Fellow ASME; mem. Instrumentation Soc. Am., Am. Soc. Engring. Edn., AAUP, Sigma Xi, Tau Beta Pi, Phi Kappa Phi, Sigma Tau. Home: Seattle, Wash. Died, Nov. 5, 1979.

MCMULLIN, JOSEPH J(OHN) A(NTHONY), ret. navy med. officer; b. Philadelphia, Dec. 5, 1885; s. John and Mary (Larkin) McM.; M.D., Jefferson Med. Coll., 1908; student graduate courses in general surgery at universities of Pa. and Vienna and Mayo Clinic; m. Elizabeth McClintock Hinkle, Feb. 3, 1935; children—John Joseph, Elizabeth Gertrude. Interne Phila. Gen. Hosp.; grad. Navad Med. Sch., 1910; chief surgical service, naval hosps., Phila., Brooklyn and Norfolk; comdg. officer hosps.: Canacao, Boston, Aiea, Pearl Harbor; promoted through grades to rear adm., 1943; ret. Adjunct prof. surg., U. of Philippines, 1938-40. Decorations: Legion of Merit; Order of the Red Cross (Netherlands). Fellow Am. Coll. Surgeons. Contributor numerous articles to medical jours. Address: San Diego, Calif. *

MC NAGNY, PHIL MCCLELLAN, JR., U.S. judge; b. Ft. Wayne, Ind., July 16, 1924; s. Phil McClellan and Lucy (Cole) McN.; LL.B., Ind. U., 1950; m. Patricia Gates, Feb. 24, 1951; children—Julia, Elizabeth, Carolyn, Marcia. Admitted to Ind. bar, 1950; asst. U.S. atty., 1953-55; U.S. atty. No. Dist. Ind., 1955-59; partner firm Gates, Gates & McNagny, Columbia City, Ind., 1960-76; U.S. dist. judge No. Ind., 1976-81. Served with USMCR, 1942-45. Mem. Am. Coll. Trial Lawyers, Am., Ind., Whitley County bar assns., Phi Delta Phi. Episcopalian. Club: Rotary (pres. Columbia City chpt. 1962). Address: Hammond, Ind. Died Mar. 28, 1981.

MC NAIR, ANDREW HAMILTON, geologist, educator; b. Victor, Mont., May 29, 1909; s. A.H. and May (Rohrbach) McN.; A.B., U. Mont., 1931, M.A., 1933; Ph.D., U. Mich., 1935; m. Evelyn Lyford, Jan. 28, 1939; children—Ann, Jane, Peter, Chmn. dept. geology Dartmouth, 1939-43, 1951-55, prof. geology, 1945-74; geologist U.S. Geol. Survey, Stategic Minerals Investigations; 1942-45; cons. geologist indsl. minerals, from 1946; geologist Phillips Petroleum Co., 1949-50, Gulf Oil Co., 1952; with Internat. Geol. Field Inst., Gt. Britain, summer 1961. Party chief Dominion Explorer's Ltd., 1959-60, Canadian Artic Islands, 1960; participant 1st Internat. Symposium on Artic Geol., Calgary, 1960., head Dartmouth Coll. Victoria Island Geol. Expdn., 1964, 65, 66. Chmn. Hanover Conservation Commn., 1967-68. Fellow Geol. Soc. Am., Paleontol. Soc.; mem. Dartmouth Sci. Assn. (pres. 1950-51). Am. Assn. Petroleum Geologists. Sigma Xi, Phi Sigma, Gamma Alpha. Author sci. articles paleontology, stratigraphy, econ. geology, Arctic geology. Home: Hanover, N.H. Died. May 1, 1978.

MCNAIR, LAURANCE NORTH, naval officer; b. May 30, 1884; entered U.S. Naval Acad., 1901; commd. in U.S. Navy, and advanced through the grades to capt.; retired, 1941; immediately returned to active duty; advanced to rear adm., 1943; wholly retired from active duty, 1946; comd. U.S.S. Chauncey (destroyer), Destroyer Div. 31, U.S.S. Reina Mercedes, U.S.S. Richmond, U.S.S. Tennessee; during World War I, comd. U.S.S. Ericsson, operated in European waters, and was later on staff of U.S. comdr. U.S. Naval Forces in Europe; served twice as naval attaché, Italy, being on duty there when World War II was declared; returned to U.S., June 1942; chief, U.S. Naval Mission to Peru, chief of Peruvian Naval Gen. Staff and Inspector Gen. of Peruvian Navy, Sept. 1942-Jan. 1946. Awarded Navy Cross (World War I), Crown of Italy, Grand Official of Order of Ayachuco (Peru). *

MCNALLY, HAROLD JOSEPH, educator; b. Phila., Jan. 3, 1913; s. George J. and Ethel V. (Quigley) McN.; student Phila. Normal Sch., 1931-34; B.S., Columbia, 1938, M.A., 1940, Ph.D., 1942; m. Marya A. Ostasheski, Aug. 24, 1940; children—Janet A. Becker, Douglas W., Judith E. (Mrs. Fred Warner). Tchr., Georgetown, Del., 1934-36, Maywood, N.J., 1936-37; research asst. ednl. psychology Columbia Tchrs. Coll., 1938-40; dir. spl. edn., Allegany County, Md., 1940-46; asst. prof. edn. Columbia, Tchrs. Coll., 1946-49, asso. prof., 1949-52, prof., 1952-64, exec. officer Agnes Russell Center, 1950-53; chief edn. div. US. Tech. Assistance Mission to Burma, 1953-54; cons. U.S. Edn. Mission to Lebanon, 1954; research asso. Burma Research Project, 1955-56; dir. ednl. services Field Enterprises Ednl. Corp., 1964-65, dir. research, 1965-66; prof. adminstrv. leadership U. Wis.-Milw., 1966-79, prof. emeritus, 1979; chmn. dept. ednl. adminstrn. and supervision, 1969-72; dir. numerous sch. system surveys; bd. cons. Asso. Ednl. Cons., Inc. Bd. dirs. Wis. Sch. Adminstrs. Found., Inc. Served to lt. USNR, 1943-46; PTO. First ann. Hanne J. Hicks Meml. lectr. Ind. U., 1967. Mem. N.E.A., Am. Assn. Sch. Adminstrs., Am. Ednl. Research Assn., ACLU, Assn. for Supervision and Curriculum Devel., Nat. Assn. Elementary Sch. Prins., Nat. Soc. for Study Edn., Phi Delta Kappa, Kappa Delta Pi. Author: (with A.H. Passow) Improving the Quality of Public School Programs, 1960; (with M. Finocchiaro) Educator's Vocabulary Handbook, 1965; (with W.S. Elsbree and D.R. Wynn) Elementary School Administration and Supervision, 3d edit. 1967. Contbr. articles and revs. to profl. jours., chpts. to books and yearbooks. Home: Milwaukee, Wis. Died Sept. 16, 1979.

MCNAMARA, FRANCIS JOSEPH, lawyer; b Watertown, Mass., Oct. 23, 1896; s. John Edward anc Katherine Gertrude (Dwyer) McN.; A.B., Boston Coll. 1918; J.D., Boston U., 1921; m. Louise A. English, Nov 25, 1926; children—Francis J., Lois Anne, Jeanne Mem. bar N.Y., Conn. supreme cts., U.S. Ct. Appeals Mass. Supreme Jud. Ct., U.S. Dist. Ct., Supreme Cour U.S., U.S. CT. Claims; practiced law, Boston; head atty Alien Property Bur., 1935; became spl. asst. to atty. ge of U.S., 1936; in charge alien property div. Dept. o Justice from 1938; became asst. to Alien Propert Custodian, 1942; dep. alien property custodian 1944-46; gen counsel Remington Rand, Inc., 1946-61 V.P., 1954-61; v.p., gen. counsel Remington Rand div of Sperry Rand Corp., 1956-60; counse Cummings&Lockwood, attys., Stamford, Conn., als Frost & Towers, attys., Washington, from 1961 founder, pres., dir. The Villas Inc., Palm Beach, Fla Chmn. finance com., Watertown, Mass., 1930-32 counsel for Watertown, 1932-35. Served at F.A Officers Tng. Sch., Camp Taylor, Ky., 1918. Mem. Am Legion, Phi Delta Phi, Exec. Council of Fed. Bar Assr Democrat. Roman Catholic. Clubs: Bath and Tennis Everglades (Palm Beach, Fla.); Wee Burn Countr (Darien, Conn.); Manhattan (N.Y.C.). Home: Nev Canaan, Conn. Died Sept. 14, 1979.

MCNAMEE, DANIEL V., JR., investment banker; b Hudson, N.Y., June 24, 1916; s. Daniel V. and Susan F (Dardis) McN.; A.B., Yale U., 1936, J.D., 1941; M.A Oxford (Eng.) U., 1938; m. Barbara Burroughs Cooley Nov. 14, 1942; children—Daniel V., George Cooley Dardis, Roger Burroughs, Giles Webb. Admitted t N.Y. bar, 1941; asso. firm Cravath, DeGersdorf, Swain & Wood, N.Y.C., 1941-42, Cleary, Gottlieb, Friendly & Cox, N.Y.C., 1946-49; v.p., dir. George R. Cooley & Co., Inc., Albany, N.Y., 1949-52; pres. First Alban Corp., Albany, 1952-75, chmn., 1975-77; pres., di Triton Corp., 1963-67; chmn. bd. Schenectad Discount Corp.; dir. Delaware and Hudson Corp. Pre Urban League, Albany, 1969-71, bd. dirs., from 196 parent trustee Albany Acad. Girls, 1961-62; sec. Yal Coll. Class of 1936. Served to lt. USCGR, 1942-4 Mem. Yale Alumni Assn. N.E.N.Y. (pres. 1966-6 1936 class treas. 1966-71; chmn. fund drs. 1961-6 75-77. Clubs: Ft. Orange (trustee) (Albany); Schuyle Meadows Country (Loudonville); Yale (N.Y.C.); Arm and Navy (Washington). Home: Loudonville, N.Y Died Oct. 31, 1977.

MCNEIL, ARCHIBALD, retired newspaper pub.; b Bridgeport, Conn., June 1, 1883; s. Archibald and Jen McKenzie (Randall) McN.; ed. pub. schs.; m. Ine Townsend. In newspaper business, 1911-19; former pub. Bridgeport Post, Bridgeport Telegram, Palm Beac (Fla.) Post, Lake Worth (Fla.) World. Served as l U.S.N., 1918-19. Mem. Conn. Senate, 1911-1 formerly mem. Dem. Nat. Com.; chmn. Conn. Advisor Bd. Pub. Wks. Administration, N.I.R.A. Hom Bridgeport, Conn. *

MCNEIL, ROBERT LINCOLN, pharm. mfr.; b Phila., Pa., May 4, 1883; s. Robert and Mary Hubbar (Urwiler) McN.; B.S. in economics, U. of Pa., 190 D.Sc. (hon.), Phila. Coll. Pharmacy and Sci., 1964; m Grace Fannie Slack, Oct. 2, 1914; children—Robe Lincoln, Jr., Henry Slack. Executive partner in firm Robt. McNeil, 1914-33; founded McNeil Labs., 193 pres., 1933-55; an organizer of Pharm. Contact Com. (cooperate with U.S. Dept. of Agr. for establishir standards of nonofficial pharm. preparations co-chmn., 1924-27. Hon. dir. U.S. committee of Worl Medical Assn.; member of Am. Drug Mfrs. Assn. (di 1929-58; treas. 1936-44; v.p. 1944-48; pres. 1948-50 Mem. American Pharm. Mfrs. Assn. (dir. 1919-58; pre 1927-29; chmn. bd. dirs. 1929-33), Drugs Resourc Committee (advisory to U.S. Army and Na Munitions Bd.), 1939-44, Pharm. Industry Adviso Com. U.S. W.P.B., 1944-45; mem. Pharm. Drug Mfr industry adv. com. U.S. O.P.S., 1951-53; mem. b grants Am. Found. Pharm. Edn., 1952—. Recipie Procter medal Phila. Drug Exchange, 1961. Mem. Cl Macneil Assn. Am. (hon. v.p. 1960—), Kappa Sigma, S Andrew's Soc.; hon. mem. Phila. Drug Exchange, V Guard of Nat. Guard of Pa. Presbyn. Mason. Club Union League. Home: Phila. *

MC NEIL, WILFRED JAMES, s.s. co. exec.; Boone, Iowa, Feb. 21, 1901; s. William H. and Alice R (Pittman) McN.; ed. pub. schs.; m. Olga Harris, Dec. 1919; children—Wilfred James, Edwin E., Ol Patricia. Cashier, Bank of Searsboro (Iowa). 1920-2 pres. 1st State Bank, Brandon, Colo., 1923026; distb Nash Motors, North Central Iowa, hdqrs., Am 1926-30; promotion, distbn. Des Moines Register Tribune Co., 1930-34; country div. mgr. Eugene Mey & Co., Washington, D.C. Post, 1934-38, country a city circulation mgr., 1938-41; fiscal dir. (civilian) US 1945-47; spl. asst. to sec. def., 1947-49; asst. sec. d and comptroller Dept. Def., 1949-59; pres. Grace Li Inc., 1959-67, Gulf & S.Am. S.S. Co., 1959-67; di cons. Fairchild Industries, Inc., Tipperary Corp.; me adv. bd. Chem. Bank N.Y.C., 1965-72. Chmn., Co Am. S.S. Lines, 1963-64; bd. advisers U.S. Mc Marine Acad., 1969-73; pres. Tax Found. Trustee We Inst., 1965-74, Naval Acad. Found. Served wi USNRF, 1918-20; to rear adm. USNR, 1941-4

Decorated El Merito (Ecuador); Gran Odicial Orden del Sol (Peru); Legion of Merit, Civilian Distinguished Service medal Navy, Def. Depts. Mem. Navy League (adv. council, pres. N.Y. 1962-63). Republican. Clubs: India House, Metropolitan (N.Y.); Army-Navy (Washington). Home: New York, N.Y. Died Aug. 30, 1979.

MCNIECE, RENWICK SLOANE, foreign service officer, b. Salt Lake City, Utah, June 28, 1886; s. Robert Gibson and Sara Jane (Irwin) McN.; A.B., Princeton, 1907; student U. of Utah Law Sch., 1912-14; married Ruth A. Storer, December 11, 1917 (died September 23, 1948); m. 2d, Mrs. Hazel Morse Hartley, October 1, 1950. Instructor Salt Lake City High School, 1907-17; teaching fellow (political science), U. of Calif., 1919-20; apptd., to foreign service after examination, June 4, 1920; assigned successively to Penang, St. Michael's, Stoke-onTrent (Eng.), Karachi, Vigo, Valparaiso, Chile; consul at Maracaibo, Venezuela, 1940; consul general, Oct. 1945; Am. consul, Horta, Fayal, Azores, 1944-46; consul gen., Am. Consulate Gen., Palermo, Italy, 1946-48. Retired from fgn. service, Nov. 1948. Served in World War as 1st lt. and capt. F.A.; survivor of Tuscania, torpedoed Feb. 5, 1918; in France, on Gen. Staff, Mar. 1918-July 1919. Presbyn. Home: Los Angeles. *

MCNULTY, WILLIAM CHARLES, artist; born Ogden, Utah, Mar. 28, 1884; s. James and Anna (Altstadt) McN.; student Art Students League, N.Y., 1908-09; m. Ann Brockman, March 28, 1914 (died Mar. 29, 1943; m. 2d, Beatrice Gellman, Aug. 10, 1945; 2 foster daus., Diana (Mrs. Murray Drexler List), Madge. Instr., Art Students League, N.Y., since 1931; represented in permanent collections U. Neb., Met. Mus. Art, Mus. City of N.Y., Newark Mus., Detroit Mus., Whitney Mus., N.Y. Public Library, Addison Gallery of Am. Art, Canajoharie Mus., Mus. of Fine Arts, Boston, N.Y. Hist. Soc., Library of Congress. Home: N.Y.C. *

MCORMOND, RAYMOND RICHARDS, educator; b. Clinton, Massachusetts, Apr. 17, 1886; s. William and Emma Eugenia Richards (Wood) McO.; A.B., Yale, 1907; studied Harvard, summer, 1908; m. Alice Bishop, d. Frank Eddy Dudley, of Haverhill, Mass., June 26, 1913; children—Alice Dudley, Raymond Richards, Jean. Instr. in mathematics and phys. dir. Woodberry Forest Sch., Orange, Va., 1907-09; with Choate Sch., Wallingford, Conn., 1909-23, respectively as head dept. mathematics, dir. athletics, head coach football, dir. music, also head master and founder Choate Summer Sch. (later McOrmond Sch.); head master The Westminster School since 1923, also a trustee of school; director of the Mutual Bank & Trust Company. Examiner in mathematics, College Entrance Bd., 1916-22. Capt. Choate Sch. Batt., corpl. C Co., Harvard Regt., Cambridge, and student Camp Thayer R.O.T.C., World War. Mem. Conn. Math. Assn., Cum Laude Soc. Republican. Episcopalian. Clubs: Graduate (New Haven); University, Twentieth Century (Hartford); Yale (New York); Sachem's Head Yacht of Guilford, Conn. (commodore 1933, 34). Author: Outline of Plane Trigonometry; Outline of Elementary Algebra, 1921. Address: Simsbury, Conn. *

MCQUEEN, STEVE, actor. Race car, motorcyle racer and enthusiast; TV actor Wanted-Dead or Alive; motion pictures include The Great Escape, The Magnificent Seven, Love with the Proper Stranger, Baby, the Rain Must Fall, Soldier in the Rain, Cincinnati Kid, Nevada Smith, The Sand Pebbles, The Thomas Crown Affair, Bullitt, The Reivers, Le Mans, Junior Bonner, The Getaway, Papillon, The Towering Inferno, Enemy of the People. Served with USMC. Home: Santa Paula, Calif. Died Nov. 7, 1980.

MCSHERRY, FRANK DAVID, lawyer; b. Toledo, Nov. 20, 1891; s. Dennis and Mary (Casaver) McS.; M.A., Catholic U. Okla. (Sacred Heart Coll.), 1909; student AAF contract termination, Harvard, 1945; student internat. law Nat. U., Washington, 1946; m. Mary Bridges Clinton, July 18, 1926 (dec. Dec. 1960); children—Frank David, Walter Clinton, Anne Laura, Mary Glynn, James Casaver. Admitted to Okla. bar, 1915; stenographer, chief clk., atty. office Gen. Atty. MK & T R.R., 1912-17; gen. practice corp. law, McAlester, 1919-77; spl. master Supreme Ct. Okla., 1934; apptd. atty., claims commr. Sec. War for Manila, P.I., 1946-48; atty. U.S. Allied Commn., Vienna, 1949-50; U.S. atty., Eastern Dist. Okla., 1953-61. Served as 2d lt., flying officer 90th Aero Squadron AEF, 166th Aero Squadron OA, U.S. Army, 1917-19; col. USAAF, 1946, dep., acting chief orgn. planning ATSC, 1945-46, chief bonds sect. contracts div. Office Judge Adv. Gen., 1946; now col. USAF Res. Mem. Am., Okla. (mem. spl. com. which drafted Okla. Bus. Corp. Act; chmn. corp. law sect. 1939, 1942), Pitts. Co. (pres.) bar assns., Am. Legion (past post comdr.), 40 and 8 (grand chef de gare Okla., 1938), World War I Overseas Flyers. Republican (co. chmn. 1935-42). Elk. Home: McAlester, Okla. Died Dec. 15, 1977; buried Memory Gardens Meml. Park, McAlester.

MCSWEENEY, JOHN MORGAN, internat, affairs cons.; b. Boston, June 9, 1916; s. Eugene M. and Margaret M. (McCarthy) McS.; A.B., Brown U., 1938; m. Henrica Moorman, Oct. 15, 1949; children—Brian M., Dennis M. Appointed fgn. service officer, 1940; vice consul, Montreal, 1940-41, Lagos, Nigeria, 1942, Accra, Gold Coast, 1943; 3d sec. and vice consul, Cairo, 1943-44; 2d sec. and vice consul, Moscow, 1946-48; consul, Vladivostok, 1947; USSR desk officer, officer in charge of USSR Affairs, 1948-50; study assignments Paris, Regensburg, 1950-51; counselor of Embassy and consul Moscow, 1951; student Nat. War Coll., 1953-54; sr. polit. advisor U.S. Mission to UN, 1954-56; U.S. liaison officer to NATO-CIC, Naples, Italy, 1956-58; dep. dir. and dir. Office of Soviet Union Affairs. Dept. of State, 1959-61; minister-counselor, dep. chief of mission Am. Embassy, Moscow, 1961-63; polit. adviser to CIC, SAC, 1963-64; counselor, dep. chief mission Am. embassy, Brussels, Belgium, 1964-66; U.S. misnister to Bulgaria, 1966, ambassador, 1967-70; sr. fgn. service insp., 1970-73; cons. Bd. for Internat. Broadcasting, 1974-75. Bd. dirs. Sr. Friendship Centers, Inc. Served as ensign, USNR, 1944-46. Clubs: Sarasota Yacht, Dacor. Home: Sarasota, Fla. Died Dec. 12, 1979.

MCWHIRTER, FELIX MARCUS, banker; b. Greencastle, Ind., June 14, 1886; s. Felix Tony and Luella Frances (Smith) McW.; Student De Pauw Univ., 1903-06; m. Alma Phillips, June 12, 1908 (dec.); children—Alma Jane (Mrs. W.C. Ousley), Felix Tony, Luella Frances (Mrs. Wesley P. Martin); m. 2d, Marguerite Graham, Sept. 19, 1953. Pres., chmn. bd. Peoples Bank and Trust Co., Indpls., 1915-59, chmn. bd., 1959-72, chmn. exec. com., 1972—; pres. Peoples Bldg. Co. Mem. nat. bd. field advisers Small Bus. Adminstrn., 1954-59; pres. Indpls. Clearing House Assn., 1956-57. Treas. Ind. Rep. State Com., 1937-40; chmn. Rep. United Finance Com. for Ind., 1940. Indiana civilian aide to sec. of war, 1925-27. Comdg. officer Third Naval Res. Area, Ninth Dist., Nov. 1940-Nov. 1941; capt. U.S.N.R., on active duty, 1941-45; dist. security officer Ninth Naval Dist., 1941-44; adminstrv. officer on staff of Adm. T.C. Kincaid, comdr. 7th Fleet, S.W. Pacific, 1944-45. Maj., attached to Gov. Goodrich's mil. staff, 1917-22. Mem. Indpls. Bd. Pub. Safety, 1918-22; chmn. Marion County War Savings Com., 1918; dir. Ind. chpt. A.R.C., 1926-41, 1946-55; treas. Ind. State com. Near East Relief, 1925. Del. to Internat. C. of C. orgn. meeting, Paris, 1920, London, 1921, Rome, 1923, Brussels, Belgium, 1925, Stockholm, Sweden, 1927, Amsterdam, Holland, 1929, Washington, 1931. Dir. Indpls. Day Nursery Assn., 1926-41; mem. bd. Dept. Community Welfare, Indpls.; mem. adv. com. Nat. Rivers and Harbors Congress; treas. Marion Co. chpt. Nat. Orgn. to Combat Infantile Paralysis, 1939-40, mem. exec. com., 1941; mem. Ind. com. Franklin D. Roosevelt Library, Inc., 1939-40; bd. mem. Moore Found., Indpls. Decorated Legion of Merit, Philippine Liberation medal. Mem. U.S. C. of C. (dir. 1921-37, v.p. 1932-37, chmn. com. finance, budget and audit, 1930-37; past chmn. com. on edn.; chmn. nat. def.; nat. policy council), Indpls. C. of C. (pres. 1923), Am. Bankers Assn. (state legislative com.; pres. state bank div. and ex-officio mem. exec. com. of state bank div. 1931-32; membership com. 1935, exec. council 1939-42, 49-50), Ind. Bankers Assn. (pres. 1933-34; mem. council adminstrn. 1934-36), Boy Scouts Am. (Indpls. council), Delta Kappa Epsilon. Republican. Methodist. Clubs: Kiwanis, Optimist, Columbia. Home: Indianapolis IN. *

MC WILLIAMS, CAREY, writer; b. Steamboat Springs, Colo., Dec. 13, 1905; s. Jerry and Harriet (Casley) McW.; LL.B., U. So. Calif., 1927; m. Iris Dornfeld, Sept. 10, 1941; children—Wilson Carey, Jerry Ross. Admitted to Calif. bar, 1927, practiced in Los Angeles, 1927-38, mem. firm Black, Hammack & McWilliams; commr. immigration and housing State of Calif., 1938-42; contbg. editor The Nation, N.Y.C., 1945-51, asso. editor, 1951-52, editorial dir., 1952-55, editor, 1955-75. Author: Ambrose Bierce: a Biography, 1929; Factories in the Field, 1939; Ill Fares the Land, 1942; Brothers Under the Skin, 1943; Prejudice, 1944; Southern California Country: An Island on the Land, 1946; A Mask for Privilege: Anti-Semitism in America, 1948; North from Mexico: The Spanish-Speaking People of the United States, 1949; California: The Great Exception, 1949: Witchhunt: The Revival of Heresy, 1950. Editor: The California Revolution, 1968; The Education of Carey McWilliams, 1979; contbr. to Dictionary of Am. Biography, numerous mags. Home: New York, N.Y. Died June 27, 1980; cremated.

MC WILLIAMS, JOHN WESLEY, lawyer; b. Phila., Aug. 7, 1892; s. Richard B. and Mary (Wesley) McW.; grad. cum laude, U. Pa. Law Sch., 1915; m. Margaret Duffus, Apr. 20, 1918; children—Edith (Mrs. Ralph C. Carroll, Jr.), John Wesley, Jr. Admitted to Pa. bar, 1915, since practiced in Phila., specializing corp., ins., comml., decedents' estate law; dir. C.J. Webb Inc. Mem. Citizens' Crime Commn. Phila., Jud. Conf. U.S. Ct. Appeals, 3d circuit. Served as lt. (j.g.) USNRF, World War I. Fellow Am. Coll. Trial Lawyers; mem. Am. Bar Assn. Found., Internat., Inter-Am., Am. (past chmn. sect. internat. law, vice chmn. com. model jud. article sect. jud. adminstrn.), Pa. (past pres.), Phila. (past chmn. bd. govs.) bar assns., Am. Law Inst., Inst. Jud. Adminstrn., Am. Soc. Internat. Law, Am. Judicature Soc., Seldon Soc. Eng., Scribes of Am. Bar Assn., Scotch-Irish Soc. U.S. (pres.), Kappa Sigma, Order of Coif. Clubs: Union League, Racquet, Philadelphia Cricket, Lawyers (Phila.); Riomar of Fla. Home: Philadelphia, Pa. Died Sept. 2, 1977.

MEACHAM, HARRY MONROE, author; b. Petersburg, Va., July 19, 1901; s. Benjamin Thomas and Julia (Webb) M.; student St. Johns Coll., Annapolis, Md., 1941-42, Richmond Profl. Inst., 1950; m. Lucy Allen Davies, Mar. 8, 1924; 1 dau., Frances Christian (Mrs. Daniel R. Strickland). Financial reporter Dun & Bradstreet, Inc., Washington, 1928-38, salesman, Balt., 1938-41, sales mgr., Richmond 1944-48, dist. mgr., Richmond, 1948-60; lectr. sales mgmt. U. Richmond. 1948-52. Mem. bd. Small Bus. Adminstrn., 1952-60; res. Richmond Import-Export Club, 1955-56; chmn. Port Richmond Adv. Commn., 1954-62; cons. small bus. mgmt., 1960-75; chmn. service corp. ret. execs. Small Bus. Adminstrn., 1964-67; mem. bd. Richmond Profl. Inst., 1952-62. Pres Richmond Federated Arts, 1956-58; mem. bd. Poe Found., from 1952; poetry critic Richmond News-Leader, from 1956; editorial bd. Va. Lives, adv. 9 Lyric mag., from 1948; adv. bd for poetry Nat. Recreation Assn., 1964-65; chmn. affiliated socs. Acad. Am. Poets, from 1961; mem. bd. James Branch Cabell Library. Mem. Soc. Study So. Lit., Va. Hist. Soc., Va. Writers Club (past pres.), Am., Va. (past pres.) poetry socs., N.H. (hon. life), Distributive Edn. Clubs Am. (hon. life), New Eng. Poetry Club (hon. life), Nat. Fedn. State Poetry Socs. (hon, chancellor 1969-70). Author: The Caged Panther: Ezra Pound at St. Elizabeth's, 1967. Editor: Lyric Virginia Today, 1956; One Hundred Years of Alaska Poetry, 1967; The Detonator, 1964; contbr. to numerous nat. lit. jours. Home: Petersburg, Va. Died 1975.

MEACHAM, MALCOLM, real estate; b. Como, Miss., August 9, 1884; s. Elzey Eugene and Lula (Gilchrist) M.; student New York U., 1903-05; m. Dorothy Hurt, Jan. 17, 1925. Began in real estate business with father's firm, E. E. Meacham & Son, 1905; pres. Malcolm Meacham, Inc., New York, since 1919; v.p. Meacham Realty Corpn.; organizer and 1st v.p. Palm Beach (Fla.) Nat. Bank, 1924, 25; organizer, and pres. Olympia Improvement Corpn., 1923 (resigned as pres. 1925); organizer and pres. Key West Foundation Co., 1925; dir. Duval Mortgage Co. (Key West). Mem. Psi Upsilon. Democrat. Presbyn. Clubs: Ardsley, Metropolitan Riding, Nassau Country (New York); Bath and Tennis, Gulf Stream, Key West Country, etc. Home: New York. *

MEACHAM, WILLIAM SHANDS, journalist, penologist; b. Petersburg, Va., Jan. 15, 1900; s. Benjamin T. and Julia Amanda (Webb) M.; student Coll. of William and Mary (Richmond Div.), 1918-21; student N.Y. U. Sch. of Journalism, 1925; m. Margaret Ball Henkel, Sept. 17, 1931 (div.); m. 2d, Margaret Upshur Ault, May 15, 1955; stepsons—Robert Bowen Ault, William Upshur Ault. Reporter, Norfolk Ledger Dispatch, 1925-26; editor Danville (Va.) Register, 1926-36; asso. editor Richmond Times-Dispatch, Sept. 1936-42; first parole commr., 1942-47; editorial contbr. N.Y. Times, 1947-64; editorial page editor Norfolk Virginian-Pilot, 1960-63, vis. lectr. Grad. Sch., N.Y.U. First chmn. Housing Authority City of Richmond, 1940-41; vice chmn. Norfolk Pub. Library System, 1973, chmn., 1946-76; pres. Mental Health Assn. Va., 1946. Trustee Norfolk Historic Found., Assn. Preservation Va. Antiquities; chmn. research com. Va. Edn. Commn., 1944; mem. Va. Social Sci. Assr. (pres. 1941), Va Conf. Social Work (pres. 1939-40); bd. dirs. Nat. Assn. Mental Health representing So. region U.S., 1951-54; mem. Internat. Penal and Penitentiary Commn. 1950; chmn. Am. Congress Corrections, Long Beach, Calif., 1947; mem. White House Conf. on Parole, 1939. U.S. del. World Penal Congress, The Hague, 1950; mem. 5th White House Conf. on Children, 1950. Recipient Lee Editorial award for distinguished editorial writing, 1938; Distinguished award Am. Cancer Soc., 1962, Distinguished Citizenship award Norfolk-Portsmouth Bar Assn., 1968; citation City of Norfolk, 1975; decorated officer Order Brit. Empire, 1963. Mem. English-Speaking Union (pres. Norfolk-Portsmouth 1960). Episcopalian. Author: (with D. R. Pound and others) Society's Stake in the Offender. Contbr. N.Y. Times Mag. and Book Rev., Sat. Rev. Lit., Va. Quar. Rev. Jour. Social Forces, other periodicals. Home: Norfolk, Va. Died Sept. 15, 1979.

MEAD, MARGARET, anthropologist; b. Phila., Dec. 16, 1901; d. Edward Sherwood and Emily (Fogg) M.; student De Pauw U., 1919-20; B.A., Barnard Coll., 1923; M.A., Columbia U., 1924, Ph.D., 1929; 1 dau., Catherine Bateson. Fellow NRC., Samoa, 1925-26; asst. curator ethnology Am. Mus. Natural History, 1926-42, asso. curator, 1942-64, curator ethnology, 1964-69, curator emeritus, 1969-78; chmn. social scis. div., Fordham U., 1968-70, prof. anthropology, 1968-70; adj. prof. anthropology Columbia U., 1954—; spl. lectr. anthropology; exec. sec. com. on food habits NRC, 1942-45; fellow Sci. Research Council, in Admiralty Islands, 1928-29; expdns. to New Guinea, 1931-33-38-53-64-65-67-71-72, to Bali, 1936-38, 57-58, 77; dir. Columbia U. Research in Contemporary Cultures, 1948-50; vis. prof. dept. psychiatry U. Cin., 1957-78; Sloan prof. Menninger Found., 1959; Alumni Assn. distinguished lectr. U. R.I., 1970-71; Fogarty scholar in residence NIMH, 1973. Mem. Am. Anthrop. Assn. (pres. 1960), Am. Ethnol. Soc., N.Y. Acad. Scis., AAAS (pres. 1975, chmn. bd. 1976), AAUW, Am. Orthopsychiat. Assn., Soc. Applied Anthropology (pres. 1940), Soc. Women Geographers, Inst. Intercultural Studies, World Fedn. Mental Health (pres. 1956-57), Scientists Inst. Pub. Info. (pres. 1970-73), World Soc. Ekistics (pres. 1969-71), Soc. Gen. Systems Research (pres. 1972-73), Phi Beta Kappa. Episcopalian. Author: Coming of Age in Samoa, 1928; An Inquiry into the Question of Cultural Stability in Polynesia, 1928; Growing up in New Guinea, 1930; The Changing Culture of an Indian Tribe, 1932; Sex and Temperament in Three Primitive Societies, 1935; And Keep Your Powder Dry, 1942; (with Gregory Bateson) Balinese Character: A Photographic Analysis, 1942; Male and Female, 1949; Soviet Attitudes Toward Authority, 1951; (with Frances Macgregor) Growth and Culture: A Photographic Study of Balinese Childhood, 1951; (with Rhoda Metraux) Themes in French Culture, 1954; New Lives for Old, 1956; People and Places, 1959; An Anthropologist at Work, 1959; Continuities in Cultural Evolution, 1964; (with Ken Heyman) Family, 1965; Anthropologists and What They Do, 1965; (with Paul Byers) The Small Conference, 1968; Culture and Commitment, 1970, rev. editor., 1978; (with Rhoda Metraux) A Way of Seeing, 1970; (with James Baldwin) A Rap on Race, 1971; Twentieth Century Faith, 1972; Blackberry Winter: My Earlier Years, 1972; Ruth Benedict, 1974; (with Ken Heyman) World Enough: Rethinking the Future, 1975; editor: Cooperation and Competition Among Primitive Peoples, 1937; (with Nicholas Calas) Primitive Heritage, 1953; (with Martha Wolfenstein) Childhood in Contemporary Cultures, 1955; (with Ruth Bunzel) The Golden Age of American Anthropology, 1960; Letters from the Field: 1925-1975; contbr. articles on Oceanic ethnology and relationship between psychology and culture to profl. jours. Home: New York, N.Y. Died Nov. 15, 1978.

MEAD, ROBERT GILLESPIE, 2D, investment banker; b. Hackensack, N.J., June 17, 1895; s. Gabriel and Virginia (Whitbeck) M.; C.E., Pa. Mil. Coll., 1914, Cornell U., 1917; m. Mary A. Cooke, Feb. 21, 1925; children—Robert G., 3d, George C., Mary C., Judith E. Vice pres. Stone & Webster Securities Corp., Chgo., 1954-63, also mem. bd. of directors. Served as capt. F.A., U.S. Army, 1917-19, A.E.F., 1918-19. Mem. Investment Banking Assn. (gov. 1952-55), Kappa Alpha, Episcopalian. Clubs: Bond, Mid-Day (Chgo.); Darlington (S.C.) Country. Home: Santa Fe, N.Mex. Died Jan. 21, 1977.

MEADE, ELEANORE HUSSEY, educator; b. Huntsville, Alabama, August 17, 1884; the daughter of William Baker and Ella (Moss) Hussey; grad. of George Peabody Coll. of Tchrs., 1904, student summers, 1906-08; student U. Mich., summer 1914; m. George Peterkin Meade, Aug. 7, 1912. Tchr. English, Gastonia (N.C.) High Sch., 1904-06, Abbeville (La.) High Sch., 1906-09; asst. prin. Lutcher (La.) High Sch., 1909-12; tchr. English, Presbyn. Sch., Cardenas, Cuba, 1914-17; tchr. bible class Lutcher Community Ch., 1925-56; mem. La. State Bd. Edn., 1927-63, v.p., 1936-53, pres., 1953-54. Mem. Gov.'s Adv. Commn. Higher Edn. Sec., home service chmn. St. James chpt. A.R.C., 1939-56; trustee Peabody Coll. Tchrs. Mem. P.T.A. (state pres. 1928-32, state treas 1945-54, state historian 1954-56), New Orleans Philharmonic, New Orleans Opera House Assn., Le Petit Theatre du Vieux Carre, New Orleans Edn. TV. Found., U.D.C., D.A.R., Am. Assn. U. Women, Nat., La. edn. assns., Delgado Mus. Art Assn., Delta Kappa Gamma, Phi Lambda Pi. Ind. Democrat. Episcopalian. Club: Orleans (New Orleans). Home: New Orleans. *

MEADE, GEORGE PETERKIN, ret. sugar refiner; b. Cumberland, Md., Dec. 26, 1883; s. Rev. Philip N. and Sarah (Rannells) M.; B.S., N.Y. U., 1905, Chem. E., 1921, D.Eng., 1955; postgrad. U. Mich., summer 1914; D.Sc. (hon.), La. State U., 1954, Tulane U., 1970; m. Eleanore Felicia Hussey, Aug. 7, 1912 (dec. Dec. 1969). Asst. chemist Nat. Sugar Refinery, Yonkers, N.Y., summers 1901-05, full time, 1905-07; same, Fajardo (P.R.) Sugar Co., 1908; chemist and asst. supt. Colonial Sugars Co., Gramercy, La., 1909-13; supt. and mgr. Cuban Sugar Refining Co., Cardenas, also dir. Central Control Lab. Cuban-Am. Sugar Co., 1913-23; gen. supt. Colonial Sugars Co., 1923-28, mgr. 1928-56, bd. dirs., 1950-59; bd. dirs. Cuban-Am. Sugar Co., 1950-59; pres. Bone Char Research Project, 1950. Mem. sugar com. 8th Internat. Congress of Applied Chemistry, N.Y., 1912; del. Internat. Commn. Uniform Methods of Sugar Analysis, London, 1936, Brussels, Belgium, 1949, chmn. U.S. del., Paris, 1954, Washington, 1958, v.p. Internat. Commn., 1954, hon. life v.p. Hamburg, 1962. Mem. tech. adv. com. Sugar Research Found.; mem. bd. trustees La. Pub. Affairs Research Council. Pres. St. James Parish Sch. Bd., 1932-56. Fellow A.A.A.S., Am. Inst. Chemists, Herpetologists League, N.Y. Acad. Scis.; mem. Am. Chem. Soc., La. Engring. Soc., Am. Inst. Chem. Engrs., Internat. Soc. Sugar Cane Technologists, Am. Soc. Ichthyologists and Herpetologists (v.p. 1953), N.Y. Zool. Soc., Phi Beta Kappa, Tau Beta Pi, Alpha Chi Sigma. Democrat. Episcopalian. Clubs: Chemists (N.Y.); Louisiana, Round Table (New Orleans). Author: Cane Sugar Handbook, 9th edit., 1963 translated into Spanish, Japanese, Hindi); Athletic Records: The Whys and Wherefores, 1966. Asso. editor: Sugar Jour. (New Orleans), 1956—. Contbr. tech. articles Indus. and Engring. Chemistry, Internat. Sugar Jour., Ency. Brit., etc.; also articles on Habits of Louisiana Harmless Snakes. Home: New Orleans LA. *

MEADE, ROBERT HEBER, cons. engr.; b. Newark, May 8, 1905; s. John Heber and Lucie Barnard (Haring) M.; student Stevens Isnt. Teach., 1922; B.S., U.S. Naval Acad., 1926; C.E., Rensselaer Poly. Inst., 1929, M. C.E., 1930; m. Mrs. Ruth Chamberlain, Sept. 28, 1945 (dec. Feb. 1976); children by previous marriage-Robert Heber, Billie Temple (Mrs. Charles E. Roath); 1 stepson, William Warren Chamberlain; m. Dorothy Louise Russek, June 18, 1977. Apptd. midshipman USN, 1922; trans, to C.E. Corps 1929, advanced through grades to rear adm.; officer-in-charge 1st Naval Constrn. Brigade (Seabees), Alaska, 1943-44, 7th Naval Constrn. Brigade, Pearl Harbor amd P.I., as commodore, 1944-45; asst. chief Bur. Yards and Docks for Bus. Mgmt., 1947-50; dir. Naval Petroleum Res., Exec. Office of Sec., Navy Dept., Denver, 1950; officer in charge Bur. Yards and Docks Contracts Joint U.S. Mil. Group, Spain, 1953; dir. constrn. and dep. chief for constrn., 1954; chief Bur. Yards and Docks, chief civil engrs. USN, 1955-57; cons. engr. City N.Y. Dept. Marine and Aviation, 1958-60; asso. cons. Parsons, Brinckerhoff, Quade & Douglas, engrs., 1960-62, 70-77, partner, 1962-70. Decorated Legion of Merit. Fellow ASCE, Soc. Am. Mil. Engrs. (past nat. dir.), Am. Cons. Engrs. Council; mem. Engrs. Joint Council (past nat. dir.), Sigma Xi. Home: New York, N.Y. Died Dec. 23, 1977.

MEADER, CLARENCE LINTON (ME'DER), coll. prof.; b. Battle Creek, Mich., Aug. 12, 1868; s. John Murray and Maria A. (Fredericks) M.; A.B., U. of Mich., 1891, Ph.D., 1902; Elisha Jones classical fellow, 1891-93; at Am. Sch. Classical Studies at Athens, 1892; U. of Bonn, Germany, 1893; U. of Munich, 1898-99; fellow in Christian archaeology, Am. Sch. Classical Studies at Rome, 1899; m. Virginia Davis Farmer, Sept. 19, 1894; m. 2d, Xenia Ethel Burt, 1926. Instructor in Latin, U. of Mich., 1893, prof. of Latin, Sanskrit and gen. linguistics, 1904-38, in charge of instruction in Russian, 1908, professor emeritus since 1938. Mem. Am. Philol. Assn., Modern Lang. Assn. America, American Dialect Soc., Linguistic Soc. America, U. of Mich. Research Club, Technocracy, Inc., Delta Upsilon. Author: An Outline of the Roman Law, 1985; The Latin Pronouns, 1901; University of Michigan Studies—Humanistic Series, Vol. III, 1910; The Psychology of Language, 1929; also writer book revs. and various articles on Russian politics and literature, gen. semantics. Translator of "Plays by Andreyev," 1915. Lecturer on Semantics. Home: Ann Arbor, Mich. *

MEADER, STEPHEN WARREN, author; b. Providence, May 2, 1892; s. Walter Sidney and Lucy Jones (Hawkes) M.; A.B., Haverford (Pa.) Coll., 1913; m. Elizabeth White Hoyt, Dec. 16, 1916; children—Stephen Warren, Jane Annesley, John Hoyt, Margaret Lucy; m. 2d, Patience R. Ludlam, Sept. 7, 1963. Case worker, Newark, 1913-14; sec. Exsex County Big Bro. Movement, Newark, 1915; publicity dept. Reilly & Britton, Chgo., 1916; editorial work Curtis Pub. Co., Phila., 1916-21; advt. writer Holmes Press, Phila., 1921-27; copy writer N.W. Ayer & Son, Phila., 1927-57, asso. copy dir., 1941-57. Trustee Moorestown Free Library Assn. Republican. Mem. N.J. Library Commn. unitl 1957. Mem. Soc. of Friends. Author: The Black Buccaneer, 1920; Down the Big River, 1924; Longshanks, 1928; Red Horse Hill, 1930; Away to Sea, 1931; King of the Hills, 1933; Lumberjack, 1934; The Will to Win, 1936; Trap Lines North, 1936; Who Rides in the Dark, 1937; T-Model Tommy, 1938; Bat: The Story of a Bull Terrior, 1939; Boy with a Pack, 1939; Clear for Action., 1940; Blueberry Mountain, 1941; Shadow in the Pines, 1942; The Sea Snake, 1943; The Long Trains Roll, 1944; Skippy's Family, 1945; Jonathan Goes West, 1946; Behind the Ranges, 1947; Cedar's Boy, 1949; Whaler Round the Horn, 1950; Bulldozer, 1951; The Fish Hawk's Nest, 1952; Sparkplug of the Hornets, 1953; The Buckboard Stranger, 1954; Guns for the Saratoga, 1955; Sabre Pilot, 1956; Everglades Adventure, 1957; The Commodore's Cup, 1958; The Voyage of the Javelin, 1959; Wild Pony Island, 1959; Buffalo and Beaver, 1960; Snow on Blueberry Mountain, 1961; Phantom of the Blockade, 1962; The Muddy Road to Glory, 1963; Stranger on Big Hickory, 1964; A Blow for Liberty, 1965; Topsail Island Treasure, 1966; Keep 'Em Rolling, 1967; Lonesome End, 1968; The Cape May Packet, 1969. Contbr. juvenile and adult fiction to mags. Home: Cape May Court House, N.Y. Died July 18, 1977.

MEADOR, CLIFTON KIRKPATRICK, physician, educator; b. Selma, Ala., Sept. 7, 1931; s. Daniel John and Mabel (Kirkpatrick) M.; B.A. (Walter O. Parmer scholar), Vanderbilt U., 1952, M.D., 1955; m. Helen Allen, June 17, 1955; children—Clifton Kirkpatrick, Aubrey Allen, Ann Graham, Elizabeth Garrett. Intern, Presbyn. Hosp., N.Y.C., 1955-56, asst. resident medicine, 1956-57; asst. resident medicine Vanderbilt U. Hosp., 1959-60; fellow endocrinology Vanderbilt U., 1960-61, instr. dept. medicine Sch. Medicine, 1960-61; practice medicine, specializing in endocrinology, Selma, 1961-62, pvt. practice; asst. prof. medicine Sch. Medicine, U. Ala., 1962-64, asso. prof., 1964-66, prof., after 1966; asst. chief-of-staff U. Ala. Hosp., 1966-68; dean Sch. Medicine, U. Ala., 1968-73; prof. medicine Vanderbilt U., from 1973; chief medicine St. Thomas Hosp., Nashville, from 1973. Served as capt., M.C., AUS, 1957-59. Recipient Founders medal for scholastic honors Vanderbilt Sch. Medicine, 1955. John and Mary R. Markle scholar, 1963. Fellow A.C.P.; mem. Am. Diabetes Assn., Am. Fedn. for Clin. Research, Endocrine Soc., N.Y. Acad. Sci., Phi Beta Kappa, Sigma Xi, Alpha Omega Alpha. Mem. editorial bd. So. Med. Jour., after 1969; contbr. articles profl. jours. Home: Nashville, Tenn. Died Mar. 18, 1973.

MEADOWS, ALGUR HURTLE, oil co. exec.; b. Vidalia, Ga., Apr. 24, 1899; s. John Morgan and Sally (Dailey) M.; grad. Centenary Coll. Law Sch., 1926, LL.D. (hon.), 1969; D.Hum., So. Meth. U., 1965; m. Virginia Garrison Stuart, Dec. 11, 1922 (dec. 1961); 1 son, Robert Al.; m. 2d, Elizabeth Boggs Bartholow, July 12, 1962. Accountant, Standard Oil Co. La., 1921-29; v.p. Gen Finance Co., 1929-30, Gen. Am. Finance System, Inc., 1930-36; v.p. Gen. Am. Oil Co. Tex., 1936-41, pres., 1941-50, then chmn. bd. and exec. com.; dir. Republic of Tex. Corp., Dallas. Trustee So. Meth. U.; bd. dirs. St. Mark's Shc., Dallas, Wadley Research Center. Mem. Am. Petroleum Inst., Ind. Petroleum Assn. (bd. dirs.), Dallas Petroleum Club, Dallas Art Assn., Sigma Nu. Democrat. Presbyn. Mason (Shriner). Clubs: Gun, Petroleum, Dallas Country, Brook Hollow Golf, Preston Trails Cöuntry (Dallas); Blind Brook (N.Y.); Everglades, Seminole, Bath Tennis and Jupiter Hills Golf (Palm Beach). Home: Dallas, Tex. Died June 10, 1978.

MEADOWS, JOHN CASSIUS, educator; b. Kenton, Tenn., May 27, 1887; s. John Augustus and Mary Elizabeth (Brents) M.; A.B., Georgie Robertson Christian Coll., Henderson, Tenn., 1908; grad. study, U. Chgo., 1908-17; M.A., Peabody Coll. for Tchrs., 1921, Ph.D., 1926; m. Emma Andrew, June 11, 1908; children—Andrea (dec.), Ruth Elizabeth (Mrs. P. B. Stephens, Jr.), John. High sch. prin., Wingo, Ky., 1908-09; supt. schs. various cities, Miss., 1909-22; asso. prof. edn. Northwestern U., 1926-29; prof. edn., head dept. Shorter Coll., Rome, Ga., 1929-30; prof. edn., Coll. of Edn., U. Ga., 1930-38; dean of coll., 1932-38; prof. sociology, 1938-54, prof. emeritus, from 1954. Mem. Dept. Superintendence N.E.A., Am. Assn. Univ. Profs., Kappa Delta Pi, Phi Delta Kappa. Democrat. Mem. Christian Ch. Mason (32 deg., Shriner), K.P., Knight of Khorassan. Kiwanian. Author books, from 1924; latest: Modern Georgia, 1946 (3 rev. edits.). Contbr. Americana Ency. Ann., from 1955; Ga. editor Ency. Americana, Ency. Internat. Home: Athens, Ga. Deceased.

MEADOWS, LEON RENFROE, educator; born Lafayette, Ala., Apr. 14, 1884; s. Simeon Joseph and Temperance Peninah (Daniel) M.; L.I., Peabody Coll., Nashville, Tenn., 1906; Ph.B., Baylor U., Waco, Tex., 1908; A.B., Yale U., 1909, M.A., 1913, student Teachers Coll., Columbia U., 1913-14, Ph.D., 1928; m. Lida Hill, Sept. 3, 1919 (died May 11, 1925); children—Leon Renfroe, Jr., Lida Elizabeth, May Temperance; m. 2d, Frances Louise Goggin, Sept. 10, 1927. Teacher, English, Crockett, Tex., 1909-10; head English Dept., East Carolina Teachers Coll., Greenville, N.C., 1910-40, dir. summer sch., 1922-44, pres., 1934-44, retired since 1944. Served in World War, 1917-19, Member American Association Teachers Colleges (executive committee; vice pres. 1941-42), N.E.A., North Carolina Education Assn. (chmn. dept. higher edn.), Am. Legion, Phi Delta Kappa, Phi Sigma Pi. Pres. N.C. College Conf., 1943. Democrat. Baptist. Author: The Teaching of Composition in Teachers Colleges, 1928. Home: Greenville, N.C. *

MEANS, FLORENCE CRANNELL, author; b. Baldwinsville, N.Y., May 15, 1891; d. Philip Wendell and Fannie Eleanor (Grout) Crannell; student Henry Read Sch. Art, 1910-11; spl. student Kansas City Bapt Theol. Sem., 1912, U. Denver, 1923-24, McPherson (Kans.) Coll., summers 1922-29; m. Carleton Bel Means, Sept. 19, 1912 (dec. Oct. 1973); 1 dau., Eleanor Crannell (Mrs. Angus C. Hull, Jr.). Lectr. Writers' Conf of Rocky Mountains, U. Colo., 1947, 48, Colo Woman's Coll. Writers' Workshop in Children's Lit. 1965. Mem. Authors' League Colo., Internat. Inst. Art and Letters (asso.), Delta Kappa Gamma (hon.), Zet Tau Alpha. Recipient ann. nat. award Child Stud Assn., 1945, Nancy Bloch award, 1957; Florenc Crannell Means Meml. Library dedicated 1975. Baptis Clubs: Denver Woman's Press, Soroptimis International Club. Author: Rafael and Consuelo (wit

Harriet Fullen), 1929; A Candle in the Mist, 1931 (reprinted in Riverside Reading Series); Children of the Great Spirit (with Frances Somers Riggs), 1932; Ranch and Ring, a Story of the Pioneer West, 1932; Dusky Day, 1933; A Bowlful of Stars, 1934; Rainbow Bridge, 1934; Penny for Luck, 1935; Tangled Waters, 1936; The Singing Wood, 1937; Shuttered Windows, 1938; Adella Mary in Old New Mexico, 1939; Across the Fruited Plain, 1940; At the End of Nowhere, 1940; Children of the Promise, 1941; Whispering Girl, 1941; Shadow Over Wide Ruin, 1943; Teresita of the Valley, 1943; Peter of the Mesa, 1944; The Moved Outers, 1945; Great Day in the Morning, 1946; Assorted Sisters, 1947; The House Under the Hill, 1949; The Silver Fleece (with Carl Means), 1950; Hetty of the Grande Deluxe, 1951; Carvers' George, 1952; Alicia, 1953; The Rains Will Come, 1954; Sagebrush Surgeon, 1956; Knock At the Door, Emmy, 1956; Reach for a Star, 1957; Borrowed Brother, 1958; Emmy and the Blue Door, 1959; Sunlight on the Hopi Mesas, 1960; But I Am Sara, 1961; That Girl Andy, 1962; Tolliver, 1963; It Takes All Kinds, 1964; Us Maltbys, 1966; Our Cup Is Broken, 1969; (audiotape) Biography of Frederick Douglass, 1970; Smith Valley, 1973; (cassettes) The Author Speaks, 1973. Contbr. articles and verse to mags. Home: Boulder, Colo. Died Nov. 19, 1980.

MEANS, HUGH J(ACKSON), physician; b. Christiansburg, O., Aug. 20, 1883; s. William J(ackson) (M.D.) and Stella (Thomas) M.; A.B., Ohio State U., 1905; M.D., U. Pa., 1908; m. Eleanor Hammond, 1910 (dec. 1934); 1 dau., Sara (Mrs. Stuart D. Eagleson); m. 2d Katherine Carmack, Feb. 1, 1936. Radiologist since 1910; radiologist, dir. radiology U. Hosp., Columbus, 1926-53, emeritus, 1953—; mem. faculty Ohio State U. Coll. Medicine, 1914—, professor and chmn. dept. of radiology, 1947-53, emeritus prof., 1953—; cons. radiologist White Cross Hosp. Diplomate Am. Bd. Radiology. Fellow A.M.A., Am. Coll. Radiology; mem. Am. Roentgen Ray Soc., Radiol. Soc. N.Am., Sigma Xi, Kappa Sigma, Alpha Kappa Kappa. Mason. Clubs: Scioto Country, Faculty. Home: Columbus. *

MEANY, GEORGE, labor ofcl.; b. N.Y.C., Aug. 16, 1894; s. Michael Joseph and Anne (Cullen) M.; ed. pub. and high sch., N.Y.C., LL.D., Seton Hall, U.; L.I. U., Cath. U., 1956, U. Pa., DePaul U., St. John's U., 1957, Boston Coll., 1959, U. Mass., 1963, Fordham U., Iona Coll., 1964, Georgetown U., 1965, Gonzaga Coll. High Sch., 1971; L.H.D., Oblate Coll., 1970; m. Eugenia A. McMahon, Nov. 26, 1919; children—Regina Clare Meany Mayer, Eileen Meany Lee, Genevieve Meany Lutz. Began career as apprentice plumber, 1910, journeyman plumber, 1915; bus. rep. Plumbers Local Union No. 463 N.Y.C., 1922-34; pres. N.Y. State Fedn. of Labor, 1934-39; sec.-treas. AFL, 1940-52, pres., 1952; pres. combined orgn. AFL-CIO, 1955-79. Mem. Nat. War Labor Bd., 1942-45; mem. bd. dirs. Communications Satellite Corp. Del. 12th, 14th Gen. Assembly UN. Recipient Laetare medal, 1955; Americanism award Amvets, 1963; Presdl. Medal of Freedom award, numerous others; decorated Cross of Merit with Star and Ribbon (Fed. Republic Germany); grand ofcl. Order of Merit (Italy). Democrat. Roman Catholic. Died Jan. 10, 1980; buried Gate of Heaven Cemetery, Silver Spring, Md.

MEARNS, DAVID CHAMBERS, librarian, writer; b. Washington, Dec. 31, 1899; s. William Andrew and Mary Beard (Chambers) M.; student George Washington U., 1916-17, U. Va., 1918; Litt. D., Lincoln Coll., 1960; diploma of honor, Lincoln Meml. U., 1961; m. Mildred Sellers Haines, Nov. 27, 1929 (dec. 1945); 1 dau., Anne Almy (Mrs. Richard Allen Jacoby); m. 2d, Mary Hume Richardson, Feb. 27, 1951. Reference asst., order div. Library of Congress, 1918-20, stack insp., spl. asst., chief asst., reading rooms, 1920-39, supt., 1939-41, chief reference librarian, 1941-43, dir., reference dept., 1943-49, asst. librarian 1949-51; asst. librarian for Am. collections, chief manuscripts div., and encumbent Chair of Am. History, 1951-67, hon. cons. humanities, 1967-81; lectr. various colls. and univs. Former gov. St. Albans Sch. Recipient award of merit Civil War Centennial Commn. Ill., 1965; citation N.J. Civil War Centennial Commn., 1965; Medallion of Honor, Lincoln Sesquicentennial Commn., also Nat. Civil War Centennial Commn. Fellow Soc. Am. Archivists; mem. Orgn. Am. Historians, Bibliog. Soc. Am., D.C. Library Assn. (pres. 1942-44), Manuscript Soc. (pres. 1962), Nat. Hist. Publs. Commn., Nat. Civil War Centennial Commn., Am. Hist. Assn., Am. Antiquarian Soc., A.I.A. (joint com. archtl. archives), Phi Beta Kappa. Clubs: Cosmos; Ampersand (Mpls.-St. Paul); Literary Society (Washington). Episcopalian. Author: The Constitution of the U.S., An Account of Its Travels (with Verner Warren Clapp), 1937, Magna Carta: The Lincoln Cathedral Copy, 1939, Lincoln Collections in the Library of Congress, 1942, The Story Up to Now, 1947, The Lincoln Papers, 1948; Morsels of History, 1949; Declaration of Independence: The Story of a Parchment, 1950; Jefferson's Other Seedling, 1951; The Story of the Queen's Letter, 1952; Lincoln and the Image of America, 1952; Three Presidents and Their Books (with Arthur E. Bestor and Jonathan Daniels), 1955; Herbert Putnam: Librarian of the United States, 1955; Largely Lincoln, 1961; Long Remembered (with Lloyd A. Dunlap), 1963; Lincoln and the Gettysburg Address (with Allan Nevins and others), 1964. Contbr. book revs. to N.Y. Times, New York Herald Tribune, Washington Post and profl. jours. Specializes in studies of Lincoln. Home: Alexandria, Va. Died May 21, 1981, cremation, Alexandria, Va.

MECK, JOHN FOSTER, coll. adminstr., lawyer; b. Altoona, Pa., Mar. 24, 1912; s. J. Foster and Margaret (Hazlett) M.; A.B., Dartmouth, 1933; student U. of Pa. Law Sch., 1933-34; J.D., Yale, 1936; m. Jean Elizabeth Anderegg, Sept. 7, 1940; children—Sarah Jean (Mrs. John B. Pinkham), John Foster, III, Julie Hazlett (Mrs. Charles B. Hamlin). Admitted to N.Y. State bar, 1937, practiced as asso. Winthrop, Stimson, Putnam, & Roberts, N.Y.C., 1936-37; asst., asso. prof. law Yale Law Sch., 1937-41, asst. dean, 1939-41; atty. Covington & Burling, Washington, 1941-43, Douglas & Proctor, 1946-48; chief counsel Bur. Naval Personnel, 1945-46; exec. sec., staff dir. Fng. Affairs Com., Hoover com. on Orgn. Exec. Br. 1948-49; treas. Dartmouth Coll., 1949-70, v.p., 1952-77, chmn. trustees investment com., 1970-77; investment cons., 1975-78. Chmn. bd. Dartmouth Nat. Bank; dir. United Life & Accident Ins. Co. Adv. com. Energy Fund, Colonial Income Fund; trustee Hubbard Real Estate Investments. Trustee, Coll. Retirement Equities Fund, Emma Willard Sch., Troy, N.Y., Fgn. Bondholders Protective Council; investment cons. Trinity Coll., 1975-78; pres. bd. trustees Common Fund for Nonprofit Orgns. Served as lt. USNR, W.W.II; counsel's office, Bur. Naval Personnel, 1943-45. Mem. Council on Fgn. Relations, Phi Beta Kappa, Theta Delta Chi, Casque and Gauntlet. Congregationalist. Clubs: Metropolitan (Wash.); Union (Boston); Canadian (N.Y.C.). Contbr. articles on legal, pub. adminstrn. subjects in law revs., other publs. Home: Hanover, N.H. Died Mar. 2, 1978.

MECLEARY, HOWARD BLAINE, naval officer (ret.); b. Phila., Sept. 1, 1884; s. John and Ida May (Waldrop) M.; B.S., U.S. Naval Acad., 1908; m. Ann Virginia Beard, July 1, 1915; children—Elmer Read, Ann Virginia wife of Comdr. R.R. Pratt, U.S. Navy). Commd. ensign U.S. Navy, 1910, and advanced through grades to commodore, 1944; served in various types of ships; navigator, U.S.S Nevada, World War I; comdr., U.S.S. Stewart, 1919-20, U.S.S. Sands, 1926-27, U.S.S. Omaha, 1936-37; chief of staff, 14th Naval Dist., 1938-39; port director, Phila., Pa., 1939-41; comdr., Naval Base, Cape May, N.J., 1941-43, Naval Advanced Base and Island Comdr., Espiritu Santo, New Hebrides, 1943-45; ret. from active duty, Nov. 16, 1945. Awarded Legion of Merit, commendation ribbon, Am. Theatre, Pacific Theatre, World Wars I and II, Mexican campaign, Nicaraguan campaign medals, Al Merito 1st class (Chile). Republican. Presbyterian. Clubs: Yacht (New York), Army Navy (Washington), Spouting Rock Beach and Clambake (Newport). Home: Newport, R.I. *

MEDALIE, CARRIE KAPLAN (MRS. GEORGE Z. MEDALIE), education; b. New York, N.Y., Sept. 25, 1884; s. Benjamin and Frances (Oberstein) K.; A.B., Barnard, 1905; student woman's law class New York U., 1911-12; Arts Master (honorary), Hunter College, 1950; married George Z. Medalie, June 30, 1910 (died Mar. 5, 1946); children—Alice Victoria (dec.), Arthur Hamilton, Gladys Vivian (wife of Dr. Julius D. Heldman). Began as high school teacher, New York, N.Y., 1905; asst. in Latin, Bay Ridge High Sch., 1908-18, chmn. dept., 1916-18; instr. in English to foreign classes, evening schools, 1904-09. Mem. local school board New York City, 1920-22; treas. Assn. Local Sch. Bds. of N.Y. City, 1922. Chmn. student interest and facilities in the four city colleges of N.Y. City since 1938. Mem. Bd. Higher Edn., City of N.Y., since 1938, sec. since 1941; memb. bd. N.Y. Adult Edn. Council (dir.), Com. for Adult Refugee Edn. (dir.). Del. Rep. Nat. Conv., Phila., 1948. Mem. Am. Acad. Polit. and Social Science, Phi Beta Kappa, Ion Soc. Club: New York Classical. Home: New York, N.Y. *

MEDSKER, LELAND L., educator; b. Guilford, Mo., July 8, 1905; s. Tilghman and Elizabeth (Beggs) M.; B.S., N.W. Mo. State U., 1928; M.B.A., Northwestern U., 1935; grad. work U. Chgo., 1946-47; Ed.D., Stanford, 1954; m. Mary Thompson, April 14, 1933; children—Susan, Linda. Instr., Arthur Hill High Sch., Saginaw, Mich., 1928-30; instr. Proviso Twp. High School, Maywood, Ill., 1930-36; chmn. dept. of Wilson Jr. Coll., Chgo., 1936-38; asst. dir. Bur. Occupational Research and Guidance, Chgo. Pub. Schs., 1938-46; dean Wright Jr. Coll., Chgo., 1946-50; dir. East Contra Costa (Calif.) Jr. Coll. 1950-56; instr. Sch. Edn. Stanford, 1950-52, lectr., part time, 1950-56 research cons. on higher edn. U. Cal. at Berkeley, 1956-58; summer instr. dept. edn. U. Chgo., 1947-48; lectr. U. Calif., 1955-60, prof. higher edn., 1960-73, emeritus, 1973-78, vice chmn. Center for Research and Devel. Higher Edn., 1958-66, acting chmn., 1966-67, dir., 1967-72, project dir., 1973-78. Mem. Nat. Commn. on Accrediting 1954-56; trustee Coll. Entrance Exam. Bd., 1962-65. Mem. Am. Assn. Jr. Colls. (sec. commn. on terminal edn., 1940-45, v.p. 1947, pres. 1948), Chgo. Guidance and Personnel Assn. (pres. 1945), North Central Assn. Colls. and Secondary Schs. (commn. on colls. and univs. and bd. rev.), Am. Council Edn., NEA (pres. Assn. for Higher Edn. 1962-63). Author: The Junior College; Progress and Prospect, 1960; The Global Quest for Educational Opportunity, 1972; co-author: From Junior to Senior College: A National Study of the Transfer Student, 1965; Beyond High School, 1968; Breaking the Access Barriers: A Profile of the American Junior College, 1971; (with others) Extending Opportunities for a College Degree; Practices, Problems, and Potentials, 1975. Home: Walnut Creek, Calif. Died July 7, 1978; buried Hazelwood Cemetery, Springfield, Mo.

MEECH, CHARLES BRADDOCK, mfg. exec.; b. Mpls., Oct. 24, 1915; s. Robert Lyon and Rose Estelle (Baldwin) M.; B.A., Princeton, 1936; m. Nanette Harrison, Apr. 6, 1940; children—Julia Baldwin, Charles Edward, Laurie, Christopher Harrison. With Mpls.-Honeywell Regulator Co. (name changed to Honeywell, Inc.), Mpls., 1936-80, successively sales engr., mem. staff Toronto office, mgr. Honeywell A.G. and Internat. div. Europe, Zurich, Switzerland, mgr. Internat. div., Mpls., 1936-56, v.p. Internat. div., 1956-64, v.p. Far East, Honeywell, Inc., 1964-70, v.p. internat., 1970-80. Served 2d lt. CAC to maj. AUS, 1941-46. Recipient Bronze Star and arrowhead. Episcopalian. Clubs: Minneapolis, Woodhill. Home: Wayzata, Minn. Died Sept. 6, 1980.

MEEK, FREDERICK MAYER, clergyman; b. Audley, Staffordshire, Eng., May 28, 1902; s. Peter Johnson and Gertrude Jane (Mayer) M.; A.B., Mt. Allison U., 1924, LL.D., 1957; B.D., Yale, 1929; D.D., Bowdoin Coll., 1939; student Yale Grad. Sch., 1929-31; Litt.D., Norwich U., 1959; m. Amy May Hunt, June 29, 1932; children—Sheila, Peter. Came to U.S., 1926, naturalized, 1942. Ordained to ministry Congl. Ch., 1929; asst. minister Dwight Place Congl. Ch., New Haven, 1928-30; minister Second Congl. Ch., Biddeford, Maine, 1932-36, All Souls Ch., Bangor, Me., 1936-43, Plymouth Ch., Des Moines, 1943-46, Old South Ch., Boston, 1946-73, emeritus, 1973; interim minister Chestnut St. Ch., Worcester, 1973-74, First Ch., Malden, Mass., 1974-75, Lynnfield (Mass.) Center Ch., 1975-76, Quincy Point Ch., Quincy, Mass., 1976-79. Preacher, Congl. Gen. Council, 1950; pres. Me. Council of Chs., 1939-43; memb. bd. dirs, Chgo. Theol. Sem., 1944-46, Mass. Council of Chs.; chmn. Council for Social Action of Congl. Christian Chs., 1946-48; trustee Bangor Theol. Sem.; past chmn. bd. trustees Andover Theol. Sem.; past chmn. adminstrn. com. Andover Newton Theol. Sch.; trustee Piedmont Coll., 1950-75; bd. preachers Harvard, 1955-75; acting chmn., 1972-75. Recipient Freedoms Found. award for sermons, 1952-58-72-73-77. Mason. Clubs: Odd Volumes; Harvard, Wedgewood (Boston). Author: This Is the Church, 1947; Monday to Friday Is Not Enough, 1951; The Life to Live, 1955; The Bethlehem Inn, 1972. Mem. editorial bd. Advance, 1944-53. Contbr. articles to periodicals. Collector John Greenleaf Whittier material. Home: Brookline, Mass. Died Sept 7, 1979.

MEEK, THOMAS BRADFIELD, stock broker; b. Columbus, Ohio, Nov. 22, 1898; s. William W. and Mary K. (Bradfield) M.; B.S. in Journalism, Ohio State U., 1920; m. Elizabeth Woodward, Oct 12, 1922 (div. 1934); children—Mary E., Thomas Bradfield; m. 2d, Edith W. Havenstrite, June 7, 1959. Exec. sec. Ohio State U. Stadium Campaign, 1921; asst. sales mgr. S. W. Straus & Co., 1922-27; br. mgr. Orvis Bros. & Co., 1929-42, Francis I. du Pont & Co., 1942-54; br. mgr. Harris, Upham & Co., 1954-70, fgn. rep., 1964-67, dir. internat. dept., from 1967, v.p., from 1965. Founder, past pres. Assn. Customers Brokers N.Y.C., Nat. Assn. Investors Brokers. Chmn. devel. fund bd. Ohio State U., also alumni adv. com. Coll. Journalism; trustee Ithaca (N.Y.) Coll. Mem. Ohio Soc. N.Y. (past pres.), Sigma Delta Chi, Phi Gamma Delta, Mason. Clubs: Metropolitan, River (N.Y.C.); Santa Barbara, Birnam Wood Golf (Santa Barbara, Calif.) Co-author: Beat the Rising Cost of Living with Vantage Stocks, rev. edit., 1959; also brochures. Home: Montecito, Calif. Died Jan. 12, 1976.

MEEK, TOM JONES, b. Nashville, Tenn., Dec. 15, 1882; s. Thomas Shephard and Eula Virginia (Jones) M.; student Dickinson Coll., Carlisle, Pa.; Ph.B., U. of Chicago, 1904; student law dept. same, univ., 1905, J.D., 1917; m. Clara May Long, Sept. 7, 1907. Teacher high sch., Aurora, 1905-06; sec. and gen. mgr. Orr's business colleges, 1908-10; mgr. salesman, later general sales manager, The Spirella Co., 1911-16; admitted to Illinois Bar, 1917; associate national director Four Minute Men, Com. on Pub. Information, 1917-18; nat. extension dir. League to Enforce Peace, 1918-19; nat. dir. speakers Roosevelt Memorial Assn., 1919; sales organizing mgr. The Spirella Co., 1920-25, gen. sales mgr., 1925-28; v.p. The Hirschy Co., 1928-29; gen. sales mgr. Marshall-Wells Co., 1928-33; v.p. and gen. mgr. The Spirella Co., Western, Inc., 1933-39; nat. sales mgr. retail portable typewriter, Remington Rand Inc., 1940-42, job instr. trainer, training within industry division, W.P.B., 1942-45, sales consultant since 1945. Member the Civil Legion (vice pres. 1926-27). Member Chicago Bar Assn., Phi Delta Theta, Delta Sigma Rho. Clubs: Niagara, Athens Athletic. Author: Handbook League to Enforce Peace; Working for the League of Nations, etc. Home: Oakland, Calif.

MEHAFFY, PAT, circuit judge; b. Little Rock, Oct. 8, 1904; s. Thomas Miller and Annie (Poe) M.; student Hendrix Coll., Conway, Ark.; LL.B., Ark. Law Sch., 1927; m. Kathryn Kurtz, June 4, 1932; children—Thomas Michael, Kathryn. Admitted to Ark. bar, 1927; asst. atty. gen., 1929-34; chief dep. pros. atty., 1934-38; pros. atty. 6th Jud. Dist. of Ark., 1939-40; practiced in Little Rock; circuit judge U.S. Ct. of Appeals for 8th Circuit, Little Rock, 1963-74. Dir., mem. exec. com. First Nat. Bank of Little Rock. Chmn. appeal bd. Selective Service System. Democratic Nat. Committeeman, 1960-63. Trustee Ark. Law Sch. Fellow Am. Coll. Trial Lawyers. Home: Little Rock, Ark. Died Jan. 31, 1981.

MEHL, JOSEPH MARTIN, lawyer; born near Arcola, Ill., September 9, 1886; s. Iver Johnson and Julia (Hanson) M.; B. Accounts, Jewell Lutheran Coll., Jewell, Ia., 1905; LL.M., Georgetown U. Law Sch., Washington, D.C., 1919, M.P.L., 1919; m. Lenora Eveline Charlson, Jan. 6, 1911; children—Joseph Martin, Charlson Iver. Bank messenger, Des Moines, Ia., 1905; clerk U.S. Reclamation Service, Yuma, Ariz., 1906-07; accountant Union Pacific R.R. Co., Omaha, Neb., 1907-08; accountant Farmers Grain Co., Story City, Ia., 1908-09; mgr. Garwin Farmers Elevator Co., Garwin, Ia., 1909-12; admitted to Iowa State Bar 1916 after 4 yrs., supervised study in law office, D.C. Bar, 1919, Illinois Bar, 1922; investigator Cooperative Organization, U.S. Dept. Ag Washington, D.C., 1917-21; asst. to pres. and late exec. sec. U.S. Grain Growers, Inc., Chicago, Ill., 1921-24; investigator in future trading, later grain exchange supervisor, U.S. Dept. Agr., Chicago, Ill., 1924-29; asst. chief Commodity Exchange Adminstrn. and predecessor bur., Grain Futures Adminstrn., U.S. Dept. Agr., Washington, D.C., 1929-40; chief Commodity Exchange Adminstrn., 1940-43; Commodity Exchange Adminstrn., 1940-43; chief Compliance Branch, F.D.A., 1943-45; dir. Office of Investigatory Services, War Food Adminstrn., 1945-46, also adminstr. Commodity Exchange Act; dir. Compliance and Investigation. P.M.A., and Adminstr. of Commodity Exchange Act, U.S. Dept. Agr., Washington, D.C., 1946-47; adminstr. Commodity Exchange Authority, U.S. Dept. Agr., Washington, 1947-54, ret.; commodity exchange cons., 1955—, Recipient U.S. Dept. Agr. Distinguished Service Award, 1953. Mem. Am. Bar Assn. Clubs: Brook Manor, Cosmos. Contbr. articles to govt. bulls. Home: Washington. *

MEHL, ROBERT FRANKLIN, research metallurgist, educator; b. Lancaster, Pa., Mar. 30, 1898; s. George H. and Sarah W. (Ward) M.; B.S., Franklin and Marshall Coll., 1919, D.Sc., 1938; Ph.D., Princeton U., 1924; D. honoris causa, U. São Paulo (Brazil), 1944; Eng.D., Stevens Inst. Tech., 1944, Colo. Sch. Mines, 1952, Case Inst. of Tech., 1959, Carnegie-Mellon U., 1973; D.Sc., U. Pa., 1959; m. Helen M. Charles, Dec. 27, 1923; children—Robert F., Marjorie Ward, Gretchen. Prof. chemistry Juniata Coll., 1923-25; nat. research fellow Harvard U., Cambridge, Mass., 1925-27; supt. div. phys. metallurgy Naval Research Labs., 1927-31; asst. dir. research Am. Rolling Mill Co., 1931-32; dir. Metals Research Lab., Carnegie Inst. Tech., 1932-59, head dept. metallurgy, 1935-59, dean grad. studies, 1953-60; cons. U.S. Steel Corp., Zurich, 1960-65; prof. Coll. Engring., U. Del., Newark, 1965-67; vis. prof. Coll. Engring., Syracuse U., 1967-76; chmn. Inst. Metals div. AIME, 1938; tech. cons. Am. embassy, London, 1945; cons. Inst. for Tech. Research, São Paulo, 1949; chmn. met. adv. bd. NRC, 1951; cons. State Dept. Point 4 Program, Brazil, 1952; spl. lectr. Royal Sch. Mines, London, 1955; Priestly lectr. Pa. State Coll., 1938; Ann. Inst. of Metals lectr. AIME, 1936; Campbell Meml. lectr. Am. Soc. Metals, 1941; lectr. Escola Politecnica, U. São Paulo, 1944; 1st ann. lectr. Associação Brasileira de Metals, 1944, 20th, 1964, 25th, 1969, other lectures. Recipient John Scott medal, 1934; Howe medal Am. Soc. Metals, 1939; prize award AIME, 1934, 39, 44, 47; medalist Am. Ind. Radium and X-ray Soc., 1943; Associação Brasileiro de Metals, 1944, 45; James Douglas gold medal AIME, 1945; Sauveur Achievement award, 1951; Gold medal, 1952; Clamer medal Franklin Inst., 1953; LeChatelier medal Société Française de Metallurgie, 1956; Vincent Bendix award Am. Soc. Engring. Edn., 1959; Platinum medal Inst. of Metals, London, 1960; Albert E. White Disting. Tchr. award Am. Soc. Metals, 1967. Fellow AIME; mem. Am. Chem. Soc., Nat. Scis., Am. Soc. Metals, Brit. Iron and Steel Inst. (hon.), Brit. Inst. Metals, Associação Brasileira de Betais, AAAS, Phi Beta Kappa, Sigma Xi, Phi Lambda Upsilon, Delta Sigma Phi, Phi Kappa Phi, Tau Beta Pi. Clubs: University (Pitts.); Cosmos (Washington); Athenaeum (London). Translator: Tammann's The States of Aggregation. Author: Metallurgia de Aco; History of Physical Metallurgy. Contbr. numerous research articles to tech. jours. Home: Pittsburgh, Pa. Died Jan. 29, 1976.

MEHRBACH, ALBERT, JR., ins. exec.; b. N.Y.C., Feb. 2, 1909; s. Albert and Eldora (Elliott) M.; student U. Ill., 1927-28; m. Marie M. Riordan, Dec. 3, 1932; children—Marilyn Ann (Mrs. Hamilton), Joy (Mrs. William Ruane), Stephen Albert, Doreen (Mrs. William Errickson). Home office employee Prudential Ins. Co., Newark, 1927-37, life ins. brokerage supr., N.Y.C., 1937-44, spl. agt., Newark, 1947-48, asst. mgr., 1948-52, mgr., 1952; life ins. mgr. Feist & Feist Agy., Newark, 1944-47; regional v.p. Franklin Life Ins. Co., Boston, 1952-58; field v.p., The Variable Annuity Life Ins. Co., 1958; former gen. agt. Franklin Life Ins. Co. and Equity Annuity Life Ins. Co., Washington; now gen. agt. All Am. Life & Casualty Co. Home: Morristown, N.J. Died Dec. 16, 1976.

MEHRING, HOWARD WILLIAM, artist; b. Washington, Feb. 19, 1931; s. Charles Fred and Florence Anna Mehring; B.S., Wilson Tchrs. Coll., 1953; M.F.A., Cath. U. Am., 1955. One-man shows: Origo Gallery, Washington, 1959, Jefferson Place Gallery, 1960, 62, 69, 72, 73, Adams Morgan Gallery, Washington, 1963. A.M. Sachs Gallery, N.Y.C., 1965, 66, 68, 70, Gallerie Heseler, Munich, W.Ger., 1970, Pyramid Galleries, Ltd., Washington, 1975; group shows include: Corcoran Gallery, Washington, 1956, 66, 73, Nat. Collection Fine Arts, Washington, 1966, Solomon R. Guggenheim Museum, N.Y.C., 1966, 67, Whitney Mus. Am. Art, N.Y.C., 1967, Mus. Modern Art, N.Y.C., 1967, Edmonton (Can.) Art Gallery, 1970; represented in permanent collections including: Solomon R. Guggenheim Mus., Mus. Modern Art, Whitney Mus. Modern Art, Woodward Found., Washington, Riverside Mus., Corcoran Gallery, Nat. Collection Fine Arts, Los Angeles County Mus., Tate Gallery, London, also pvt. collections; mem. faculty George Washington High Sch., Alexandria, Va., Montgomery Jr. Coll. Recipient 1st prize in painting Corcoran Biennial, 1965. Home: Washington, D.C. Died Mar. 21, 1978.

MEHRTENS, WILLIAM OSBORNE, dist. judge; b. Savannah, Ga., Jan. 24, 1905; s. Leo W. and Cornelia (Millen) M.; J.D., U. Fla., 1932; m. Jaime H. Hancock, Nov. 4, 1936; 1 son, William Osborne. Admitted to Fla. bar, 1932; mem. firm Mershon, Sawyer, Johnston & Simmons, 1933-42, partner Mershon, Sawyer, Johnston, Dunwody, Mehrtens & Cole, and predecessor, Miami, Fla., 1942-65; U.S. dist. judge, 1965-80. Mem. permanent adv. com. on appellate rules Fla. Supreme Ct., 1958-80. Bd. dirs. Miami Heart Inst. Served from lt (j.g.) to lt. comdr. USNR, 1942-45. Fellow Internat. Acad. Trial Lawyers, Am. Coll. Trial Lawyers, Acad. Fla. Trial Lawyers; mem. Fla. Bar (bd. govs. 1955-65, past pres. jr. sect., past dir.), Am., Fed., Internat., Dade County bar assns., Internat. Law Assn., Am. Trial Lawyers Assn., Internat. Oceanographic Assn. (dir.), Phi Beta Kappa, Sigma Alpha Epsilon, Phi Kappa Phi, Phi Delta Phi, Blue Key. Clubs: Riviera Country (Coral Gables, Fla.); Coral Reef Yacht (Miami); Palm Bay; Bermuda Anglers; Miami Beach Rod and Reel; Panama Marlin. Home: Miami, Fla. Died July 16, 1980; buried Woodlawn Cemetery, Miami.

MEID, GEORGE DONALD, instl. adminstr.; b. Laurel, Ind., Sept. 10, 1909; s. George and Anna (Secrest) M.; B.S., Butler U., 1931; M.S., U. Ill., 1932; m. Alice Irene Lowe, May 28, 1938; children—John Michael Lowe, Elizabeth Susananna. Asst. chief acct. Purdue U., 1932-42; business mgr. Nat. Acad. Sci., 1942-71. Active, Boy Scouts Am. C.P.A., Ind. Republican. Unitarian (trustee 1966-70). Home: Chevy Chase, Md. Died Jan. 10, 1978.

MEIGS, CORNELIA LYNDE, author; b. Rock Island, Ill., Dec. 6, 1884; d. Montgomery and Grace Cornelia (Lynde) Meigs; A.B., Bryn Mawr, 1907. Prof. emeritus of English, Bryn Mawr Coll. Employee of War Dept., Washington, D.C., 1942-45. Republican. Episcopalian. Author since 1915; latest publ.: The Violent Men, 1949; The Dutch Colt, 1952. Part author and editor: A Critical History of Children's Literature, 1953; Fair Wind to Virginia, 1955; What Makes a College: A History of Bryn Mawr, 1956; Wild Geese Flying, 1957; Mystery at the Red House, 1961; The Great Design-Men and Events in the United Nations, 1945-61, 1964. Home: Havre de Grace, Md. *

MEINECKE, WILLARD HENRY, govt. ofcl.; b. Herkimer, Kans., Aug. 19, 1916; s. Louis P. and Kathryn (Shcierkolk) M.; B.S. in Milling Kans. State U., 1941; postgrad. U. Okla., 1942-43, Sch. Advanced Internat. Affairs, Johns Hopkins U., 1968-69; children by previous marriage—Joel Willard, Steven Lee; m. 2d. Mary Jane Lewis, June 13, 1959; 1 son, Douglas Louis. With Gen. Mills, Inc., 1941-62, community rep., Buffalo, 1956-62; dir. U.S. AID mission to Ethiopia, 1962-66, dir. N. African affairs AID, Washington, 1966-68, project mgmt. survey, 1969, dir. South East Asia, 1969-70, dep. asst. adminstr. East Asia/AID, 1970-72, dep. asst. admistr. program and mgmt. services, 1972-74; asst. dir. administrn. and fin. ACTION, Washington, 1974-78. Mem. sch. bd. Tacoma, 1949-52, Mpls., 1955-56; active United Fund drives, Tacoma, Buffalo, Washington. Mem. Assn. Operative Millers (pres. 1953-54). Episcopalian. Club: Kiwanis. Contbr. articles on manpower tng., fgn. aid, food devel. to jours. Home: Bethesda, Md. Died Oct. 29, 1978.

MEINERS, (HENRICH) WILLIAM W., university pres.; b. Union City, Allamakee Co., Ia., Mar. 21, 1884; s. Johann Gerhard and Adelheide (Schoo) M.; life diploma, Neb. and Minn.; B.S., Southern Minn. Normal Coll., Austin, 1906; A.B., U. of Man., 1908; A.M., James Millikin U., Decatur, Ill., 1911; Ph.D., Campbell U., Holton, Kan., 1914; (LL.D.); m. Hilda Katinka Wolden, of Spring Grove, Minn., June 29, 1910. Prof. edn., 1908-10, 1912-13, dean, 1913-15, pres., Malcolm, Ia., 1909-10; crop expert, U.S. Dept. Agr., 1913; lecturer on ednl. and religious subjects. Mem. Am. Acad. Polit. and Social Science, Minn. Assn. Charities and Correction. Republican. Address: Austin, Minn. *

MEIR, GOLDA, (CHANGED NAME FROM GOLDA MYERSON 1956), Israeli premier; b. Kiev, Russia, May 3, 1898; brought to U.S., 1906; ed. pub. schs., Milw.; m. Morris Myerson, 1917; children—Menachem, Sara. Active Zionist Labor Party, Milw.; immigrated Palestine, 1921; mem. collective farm village, 1921-24; with the Solel Boneh, 1924-26; sec. Women's Labor Council, Histadruth, 1928; mem. exec. and secretariat, Fed. Labour, 1929-34; chmn. bd. dir. Workers Sick Fund, 1936; head polit. dept. Fedn. Labour, Labour party del. Actions Com., World Zionist Orgn., 1936; mem. War Econ. Adv. Council, Palestine Govt., 1939; leading mem. Hagana struggle; head polit. dept. Jewish Agy. for Palestine, 1946-48; ambassador to USSR, 1948; minister labor and social ins., 1949-52; minister of labour, 1952-56; minister fgn. affairs, 1956-66; sec. gen. Israel Labour Party (Mapai), 1966-69; prime minister of Israel, 1969-74. Home: Jerusalem, Israel. Died Dec. 9, 1978.

MELAUGH, EDWARD GERARD, razor co. exec.; b. Boston, Feb. 3, 1917; s. John A. and Mary (Gately) M.; B.B.A., Boston U., 1941; m. Juliette Fauroux, Dec. 23, 1944; children—Michael G., Anne Marie, Patricia D. With Gillette Co., Boston, 1954-79, controller, v.p., treas. Gillette Safety Razor Co. subs., 1960-65, asst. corporate controller and controller Gillette Products group, v.p., 1965-68, v.p. control and mgmt. services parent co., 1968-70, sr. v.p. fin., 1970-79; dir. Shawnut Needham Bank N.A. Bd. dirs. Mass. Taxpayers Found. Served to maj. AUS, 1941-45, 50-52. Decorated Silver Star, Bronze Star; C.P.A., Mass. Mem. Am. Inst. C.P.A.'s, Fin. Execs. Inst., Mass. Soc. C.P.A.'s, Nat. Assn. Accountants. Clubs: Charles River Country, Algonquin (Boston). Home: Needham Heights, Mass. Died Oct. 28, 1979; buried St. Mary's Cemetery, Needham.

MELHORN, KENT C., naval med. officer; b. Kenton, O., Dec. 9, 1883; s. Charles M. and Laura M.; student Ohio Northern U., 1901-02; M.D., U. of Pa., 1906; student U.S. Naval Med. Sch., 1907-08, Harvard Med. Sch., 1923; m. Jeanne Andrews, June 19, 1912; children—Elsa Ruth (wife of Lt. Comdr. Horace V. Bird, U.S. Navy), Charles Mason (U.S. Naval Res.). Commd. med. officer, U.S. Navy, Aug. 12, 1907, and advanced through the grades to rear adm., Med. Corps, Sept. 15, 1942; med. officer in command U.S. Naval Med. Supply Depot, Brooklyn, N.Y. Mem. Am. Coll. Surgeons, Am. Coll. Physicians, Assn. Mil. Surgeons; life mem. Los Angeles County Med. Soc. Home: Brooklyn, N.Y. *

MELLMAN, WILLIAM JULES, geneticist, educator; b. Phila., May 7, 1928; s. Martin William and Freda (Haas) M.; A.B., U. Pa., 1948, M.D., 1952; m. Ruth Behnke, Aug. 30, 1963; children—Lewis Alfred, Andrea Kay. Intern, Phila. Gen. Hosp., 1952-53; resident Hosp. of U. Pa., 1955-58; prof. dept. pediatrics U. Pa., Phila., 1955-72, chmn. dept. human genetics, 1972-80. Mem. genetics study sect. NIH, 1974-79. Served with AUS, 1953-55. Mem. Am. Pediatric Soc., Am. Soc. Human Genetics, Phi Beta Kappa. Editor-in-chief Am. Jour. of Human Genetics, 1975. Home: Philadelphia, Pa. Died Feb. 27, 1980.

MELOY, FRANCIS EDWARD, JR., fgn. service officer; b. Washington, Mar. 28, 1917; s. Francis Edward and Anne Teresa (Connor) M.; B.A., Am. U., 1939; M.A., Yale, 1942. Mem. Diplomatic Service, 1946—; vice consul, Dhahran, Saudi Arabia, 1946-49; assigned Office of Sec. of State, Washington, 1949-53; detailed to NATO Def. Coll., Paris, France, 1953; 2d sec. and consul Am. embassy, Saigon, Vietnam, 1953, 1st sec. and consul, 1954; 1st sec., consul, Paris, France, 1956-57; mem. U.S. Mission to NATO, Paris, 1957-58; detailed Imperial Def. Coll., London, 1959-60; spl. asst. to dep. under sec. of state for polit. affairs, 1960-62; dir. Office Western European Affairs, 1962-64; minister, dep. chief mission Am. embassy, Rome, Italy, 1964-69; ambassador to Dominican Republic, 1969-73, to Guatemala, 1973-75, to Lebanon, 1975-76. Mem. various U.S. delegations including 1st A.N.Z.U.S. Council Meeting, Honolulu, 1952, 10th NATO Council Meeting, Paris, 1952. Served as lt. comdr. USNR, 1942-46. Clubs: Metropolitan, City Tavern Assn. (Washington). Home: Washington. Died June 16, 1976.

MELROSE, ALICE GUNHILD, orgn. exec.; b. Cold Spring Harbor, N.Y., Apr. 10, 1919; d. John George and Signe (Carlson) Melrose; B.A., Randolph-Macon Woman's Coll., 1938; M.A., N.Y. U., 1940. Asst. tchr. jr. high sch., Manhasset, N.Y., 1938-39; tchr. St. Margaret's Sch., Mendham, N.J., 1939-41, Gardner Sch., N.Y.C., 1941-42; research and office mgr. OSRD project Tiffany Found., 1942-45; with Doubleday & Co., 1945-47; asst. to dir. N.A.D., N.Y.C., 1947-67, dir., 1967-77. Sec., Dr. E.A. Abbey. Meml. Scholarship Mural Painting, from 1949; fm. sec. St. John's Episcopal

Ch., 1947-77. Recipient 150th Anniversary medal N.A.D., 1975. Episcopalian. Home: Huntington, N.Y. Died Dec. 9, 1977.

MELTZER, DORIS, artist; b. nr. Ellenville, N.Y., Jan 1, 1908; d. Meyer and Anna (Doberiski) Meltzer; B.S., N.Y. U., 1933; student Art Students League. Prints exhibited Nat. Print Shows. 1940-55; founder traveling exhbn. service, sch. and gallery; prepared ednl. exhbns. Am. Serigraphy, fgn. travel, 1950; dir. exhbns. sent fgn. countries founder, Overseas Program, USIS, 1955, 56, 57-58; supervised publication 300 exhbns., 20th Century Highlights Am. Painting, 1958; founder, dir. Nat. Serigraph Soc., 1940-62; founder Meltzer Gallery, 1954; owner, dir. Doris Meltzer Gallery, N.Y.C., 1963-76; art cons., from 1963. Home: New York, NY. Died Oct. 18, 1977.

MELVILLE, WARD, shoe mcht.; b. Bklyn., Jan. 5, 1887; s. Frank and Jennie Florence (Macconnell) M.; A.B., Columbia, 1909; LL. D., Bard Coll., 1950, Hofstra Coll., 1954, Poly. Inst., 1961; L.H.D., Dowling Coll., 1973; m. Dorothy Bigelow, Apr. 30, 1918; children—Margaret, Ruth, Frank III, David Bigelow. Began as retail shoe salesman, 1909, successively mgr., buyer, adv. mgr. John Ward stores, then v.p., pres. Melville Shoe Corp., chmn. bd., 1956-77; dir. J.F. McElwain Co. Served to capt. Q.M.C., U.S. Army, 1917-18. Mem. St. Andrews Soc., Am. Bible Soc. (v.p.). Republican. Episcopalian. Clubs: University, Century, Union (N.Y.C.); St. George's, Nissequogue, Old Field (Stony Brook). Home: Stony Brook, N.Y. Died June 5, 1977.

MENCHER, ELY, educator; b. N.Y.C., Dec. 14, 1913; s. Morris and Rachel (April) M.; B.S., CCNY, 1934; Ph.D., M.I.T., 1938; m. Miriam B. Pollak, May 10, 1951; 1 son, Frederick Marshall. Prof. geology Central U., Caracas, Venezuela, 1938-43; sr. field geologist and research geologist Socony-Mobil Oil Co., Venezuela, 1943-52; asso. prof. M.I.T., 1952-67; prof. geology CCNY, 1967-78, chmn. dept., 1968-72, 77-78, cons. in field. Coordinator First Venezuelan Nat. Petroleum Conv., 1951. Recipient Ward medal CCNY, 1934. Mem. Geol. Soc. Am., A.A.A.S., Am. Assn. Petroleum Geologists, Soc. Econ. Paleontologists and Mineralogists, N.Y. Acad. Sci., Venezuelan Assn. Advancement Sci., Am. Geophys. Union. Contbr. articles profl. jours. Home: White Plains, N.Y. Died Dec. 11, 1978.

MENDEL, ARTHUR, musician, educator; b. Boston, June 6, 1905; s. Philip and Gertrude (Newman) M.; B.A., Harvard, 1925; student Ecole Normale de Musique, Paris, Nadia Boulanger, 1925-27; Mus.D. honoris causa, Rutgers U., 1973; L.H.D. (hon.), Brandeis U., 1976; m. Elsa M. Wissell, Aug. 23, 1934. Tchr., Dalcroze Sch. Music and Diller-Quaile Sch. Music, N.Y.C., 1938-50; lit. editor G. Schirmer, Inc., 1930-38; music critic Nation, 1930-33; editor Am. Musicological Soc., 1941-44; editor Assn. Music Pubs., Inc., 1941-46; prof. music Princeton, 1952-73, chmn. dept. music, 1952-67, Henry Putnam univ. prof., 1969-73; lectr. Columbia, 1949, U. Cal., 1951; condr. Cantata Singers, small chorus specializing in 17th and 18th century music, N.Y.C., 1936-53. Guggenheim fellow, 1949-50; Am. Council Learned Socs. fellow, 1962-63; sr. fellow Nat. Found. Arts and Humanities, 1968; recipient Medal of Honor, Handel and Haydn Soc., 1979. Fellow Am. Acad. Arts and Scis.; mem. Am. Musicol. Soc. (hon., v.p. 1962-63), Internat. Musicol. Soc., Am. Fedn. Music. Author: Studies in the History of Musical Pitch (with A.J. Ellis), 1969. Contbr. numerous articles to music jours. Editor: The Bach Reader (with Hans T. David), 2d edit., 1966; J.S. Bach Cantata 174, 1962-63, Passion According to St. John, 1973; Kritischer Bericht, 1974; other choral works. Translator: Paul Hindemith's Craft of Musical Composition, Theoretical Part 1942, other books. Mem. editorial bd. Neue Bach-Ausgabe, 1962-79; com. for preparation New Josquin Edit., 1973-79. Home: Princeton, N.J. Died Oct. 14, 1979.

MENDELL, WAYNE, banker, industrialist; b. Moran, Kan., Dec. 22, 1886; s. Charles and Mary (Carmain) M.; ed. pub. and pvt. schs.; m. Marguerite Meeker, Apr. 29, 1910 (dec. 1939); children—Wayne, Donn, Nadine (Mrs. A. J. Lotito); m. 2d, Charlotte Knorr, Mar. 15, 1940. Pres., dir. hardware bus., Indian Territory, 1905-14; founder-dir. Bartlesville (Okla.) State Bank, Bartlesville Water Co., 1911-14; mem. advt. dept. Nat. Cash Register Co., Dayton, O., 1914-16; founder NCR Mchts. Service Bur.; sales and advt. mgr. W.T. Grant Co., N.Y.C., 1916; with Am. Internat. Corp., 1918, exec. v.p. subsidiary, Internat. Steel Corp., 1919-21; assisted in reorganizing Brantford Computing Scale Co., 1922; with Allied Chem. Corp., 1923, sales mgr., v.p., Canadian subsidiary Barrett Co., Ltd.; dir. gen. Canadian Asphalt Roofing Industry, 1926-28; v.p. U.S. Hoffman Machinery Corp., N.Y.C., 1928-33; dir. Fletcher Works, Inc., Phila.; pres., dir. Fletcher Machinery Corp., 1934-39; with Am. Machine & Metals, Inc. (name later changed to Ametek, Inc.), N.Y.C., 1939-48, V.P. charge sales, also pres., dir. Canadian subsidiary; pvt. cons. banks and indsl. corps., 1948-52; v.p. San Diego Fed. Savs. and Loan Assn., 1952-65. Republican. Presbyn. Clubs: Metropolitan, Bankers (N.Y.C.); Tavern (Chgo.); University, Cuyamaca (San Diego). Lectr. business tng. and fgn. trade, 1918-22. Author: The Steel Industry (with H.A. Knight); also numerous monographs on bus. management, notably, Appraisal of Intangibles. Home: LaJolla CA. *

MENDELS, WALTER BASS, (MEN'DELZ), educator; b. Newark, N.H., July 25, 1886; s. Emanuel S. and Mary Jane (Carlisle) M.; ed. Newark pub. schs.; m. Katherine Wallace Taylor, Feb. 9, 1908; children—Katherine Wallace (Mrs. Albin Douglas Peden), Muriel Jean (Mrs. James Dayton Hedges). Began as brokerage runner, 1902; partner E. S. Mendels Co., brokers, N.Y. City, 1907-32; purchased Florida Mil. Acad., St. Petersburg, Fla., 1932, now pres. Mem. bd. govs. N.Y. Curb Exchange. Republican. Methodist. Mason (32 degree, K.T.). Clubs: Newark (N.J.) Athletic (founder); Maplewood (N.J.) Country; Bayhead (N.J.) Yacht; American (Havana, Cuba). Home: St. Petersburg, Fla. *

MENEFEE, F(ERDINAND) N(ORTHRUP), (MEN'E-FE), coll. prof.; b. Columbus, Kan., Jan. 7, 1886; s. Harry Bostwick and Alice DiaDame (Hodgen) M.; B.S. in C.E., U. of Neb., 1908, C.E., 1932; C.E., Cornell, 1910; D.Engring., Lawrence Inst. Tech., Detroit, 1937; m. Lucile Cull, Sept. 17, 1909; children—Charles Cull, Ruth. Great variety of practical work along with teaching; instr. civil engring., Cornell U., 1910; instr., U. of Mich., 1910-13, asst. prof. drawing, 1914, asst. prof. engring. mechanics, 1915-16, prof. since 1919; served with Ordnance Dept. during war, rising to rank of maj.; sec. United Engring. Corp., Detroit and Ann Arbor, 1919-20, v.p., 1920-29; firm Menefee and Dodge, 1925-35. Mem. Bd. Pub. Works, Ann Arbor, 1925-40, pres. 1935-40; mem. Y.M.C.A. (on nat. council 1927-32, state com. 1927-35, pres. Ann Arbor Y.M.C.A., 1923 and dir. 1921, 1922); mem. bd. dirs. Student Christian Assn., 1929-36; mem. U. of Mich. Fresh Air Camp Com. (chmn. 1923-46). Pres. Oak Park Land Co. since 1925. Pres. Community Fund Assn., Ann Arbor, 1927, treas. Dana Fiduciary; dir. Peerless Cement Corp.; pres. Lus-Trus. Extruded Plastics, Inc. Mem. Am. Soc. C.E. (pres. Mich. sect. 1948, v. chmn. com. on water diversions), Am. Soc. Testing Materials, Am. Concrete Inst. (chmn. precast floor constrn. com., dir. since 1952), Mich. Engring. Soc. (pres. 1930), Mich. Patent Law Assn., Engring. Soc. Detroit, Kappa Sigma, Sigma Xi, Sigma Tau, Sigma Rho Tau (former nat. pres.). Mem. Christian Ch. Rep. Clubs: Rotary (dir. 1932), Am. Legion, Michigan Union. Author: Materials Testing Manual, 1932; St. Lawrence Seaway, 1940; Structural Members and Connections (co-reviser with R. R. Zipprodt), 1943. Editor: Michigan Engineer, 1927-37. Contbr. numerous learned reports and engring. articles. Home: Ann Arbor, Mich. *

MENEFFE GUY CLIFTON (MEN'E-FE), clergyman; b. Albert Lea, Minn., Feb. 10, 1886; s. John Henry and Elizabeth Jane (Clifton) M.; B.A., U. of Minn., 1912; B.D., Seabury Div. Sch., Faribault, Minn., 1917; D.D., Seabury Western Theol. Sem., 1934; m. Marie Thorndike Curial, Sept. 5, 1917; children—Elizabeth Clio, Edward Curial, John Henry, Dorothy Frances. Deacon, 1916, priest, 1917, Protestant Episcopal Church; instr. in Greek and N.T., Seabury Divinity Sch., 1917-20, prof., 1920-26, also rector All Saints Ch., Northfield, Minn., 1917-23; rector St. Paul's Ch., Owatonna, 1923-25; Calvary Ch., Rochester, since Sept. 15, 1926. Mem. Standing Com. Diocese of Minn., P.E. Ch., 1932-41, examining chaplain since 1923; dep. to Gen. Conv., 1928, 34, 37, 40, alternate, 1931. Mem. Phi Beta Kappa, Lambda Alpha Psi. Republican. Mason. Home: Rochester, Minn. *

MENGE, EDWARD JOHN VON KOMOROWSKI, psychobiologist; b. Fond du Lac, Wis., June 25, 1882; s. Theodore Edward von Komorowski and Josephine (Wurzburger) M.; grad. commercial coll.; studied law 2 yrs.; student univs. Ariz., Dallas, Wis., and Chicago, all credits transferred to U. of Dallas, B.A., 1914 M.A., 1915 Ph.D., 1916, M.Sc., 1917; Sc.D., De Paul U., 1926; m. Jessica Belle Crofoot, of Fond du Lac, Wis., Sept. 16, 1903. Pvt. sec. to receiver Little Wolf River Telephone Co., 1902-04; telephone accountant, 1904-06; asst. to gen. mgr. Consolidated Telephone, Telegraph & Electric Co. of Ariz. and Imperial Valley, Calif., 1906-07; lecturer on popular biol. subjects, 1907-10; studied scientific and educational methods at univs. of Eng., Germany,Austria, France, Switzerland, Italy, Belgium, and U.S., 1910-11, also of Brazil, Uruguay, Argentina, Chile, and Peru, summer 1927; prof. biology, University of Dallas, 1917-19; dir. dept. biology and lecturer on racial psychology in the Graduate School, Marquette University, 1919-21, dir. dept. zoölogy 1922-33; demonstrator in anatomy, Central School of Nursing, 1922-33, Milwaukee, chairman department of biology. College of St. Francis, Joliet, Ill., since 1935; vice consul of Costa Rica. Founder and president Baconia Science Corporation (to aid scholarly men and women of exceptional talents). Special appointments—Univ. of Wis. departmental grad. student representative for psychology at All University Exhibit 1915; professional lecturer for Dallas Sch. of Civics and Philanthropy, 1916: one of two science representatives of U. of Dallas to give Tirads Herald Univ. lectures, 1916; professional lecturer to Franklin Union and to Social Workers of Boston, spring 1919; for Brooklyn Cathedral Club, spring 1925; for People's Inst., N.Y., spring 1927, 29. Named as chief biol. writer for Universal Knowledge, 1927; first North American biologist to be internat. guest-lecturer (subject, "National Trends in Biology") at the Nat. univs. of Cordoba (Argentina), Montevideo (Uruguay), Santiago (Chile), and for the Sociedade de Medicina e Cirugia, of Rio de Janeiro (Brazil); apptd. internat. guest-lecturer to nat. univs. of Republic of Poland, 1934; asso. organizer and first pres. University Friends of Poland, 1932; chmn. com. selecting Am. students for free internat. European grad. scholarships awarded by the Union of the World's Polish Cultural Societies since 1933; chairman "World in Milwaukee" celebrations, 1934, 35 (only one so chosen by 2 foreign language groups—Spain and Poland); mem. National Council Pilsudski Memorial Association; recommended by leders of 6 Am. and European Universities for Nobel prize in medical biology, 1934. Made following investigations: a survey of the more than 166,000 positions in U.S. which require biol. training; a survey of all outstanding biol. advances made throughout the lifetime of the present generation; and a survey of all scientific findings affecting philosophy and psychology since the scientific revolution of 1917. Mem. Wis. Acad. Sciences, Am. Soc. Zoölogists, Am. Soc. Parasitologists, Am. Assn. Univ. Profs., Phi Chi, Pi Gamma Mu; fellow A.A.A.S.; hon. fellow Internat. Faculty of Sciences (Gt. Britain); hon. mem. Asociacion Cooperadora de Concordia Americana (Argentina); corr. mem. Sociedade de Medicina e Cirurgia do Rio de Janeiro (Brazil); academician of National Academy of Natural Science (Chile), and similar organizations in Colombia, Ecuador, Paraguay, Uruguay, Venezuela, Mexico, Puerto Rico and Spain. Created Knight Commander of Order of Polonia Restituta (Poland), 1933. Catholic. Club: Business Men's Art (president 1926-27). Author: The Beginnings of Science, 1918; Backgrounds for Social Workers, 1918; General and Professional Biology, 1922, 27 (this work and the one following were the only American college texts on biology chosen by the Com. of Louvain Univ. when selecting best books for newly completed library); Introductory Embryology and Comparative Anatomy, 1922, 24; The Laws of Living Things, 1926; Your Child from Twelve to Twenty-two, 1934; A Survey of National Trends in Biology (internat. South Am. lectures), 1928; Laboratory Studies, Demonstrations and Problems in Biology (with N.H. Kingsley), 1930; Jobs for the College Graduate in Science, 1931; Biological Work as a Career, 1931; Behind that Mental Curtain, 1936; A Critique of Presentday Biophilosophy (a comparative study of Latin, Slavic and Anglo-Saxon scientific and philosophical reactions—arranged for the Nat. Universities of Poland), 1936; Just What the Latin Thinks of Us, 1936; What Parents and Students Should Know about High Schools, 1936; What Parents and Students Should Know about Colleges and Universities, 1934. Contbr. numerous articles to Am., English and South American jours. and revs. Home: Joliet, Ill. *

MENGERT, WILLIAM FELIX, obstetrician, gynecologist; b. Washington, Nov. 13, 1899; s. Ulric T. and Margaret (Johnson) M.; S.B., Haverford (Pa.) Coll., 1921; M.D., Johns Hopkins, 1927; m. Ida Gaarder, June 14, 1924; children—Eric John, Ann Katharine. Interne and resident obstetrician and gynecologist Univ. Iowa Hosp., 1927-32; research fellow Gynecean Hosp. Inst. Univ. Pa., 1932-34; asst. prof. obstetrics and gynecology, Univ. Iowa, 1934-38, asso. prof., 1938-43; prof. and chmn, dept. obstet. and gynecol. Southwestern Med. Sch. U. Tex. and Parkland Meml. Hosp., Dallas, Tex., 1943-55; prof. and head dept. obstetrics and gynecology coll. med. U. Ill., 1955-68; vis. Prof. Chgo. Med. Sch.; 1970-76. Med. adv. bd. Planned Parenthood Chgo., 1956-67, chmn., dir., 1956-61. Gen. program sec. 2d Am. Cong. Obstetrics, Gynecology, St. Louis, 1941, gen. program chmn. 3d Congress, 1947. Fellow A.C.S.; mem. A.M.A. (sec. sect. obstetrics and gynecology 1944-47, chmn. 1947-48), Am. (pres. 1957-58), Central (pres. 1947-48), Tex. assns. obstetricians and gynecologists, Am. Coll. Obstetricians and Gynecologists (president 1955), American, Chicago (president 1962-63) gynecological socs., N.D., Dallas, Ft. Worth obstet. and gynecol. socs., Alpha Omega Alpha, Sigma Xi, Nu Sigma Nu. Clubs: University (Chgo.); Cosmo (Washington). Author: Postgraduate Obstetrics, 1947. Contbr. med. jours. Home: Oak Park, Ill. Died Mar. 23, 1960.

MENN, JOE KARL, coll. pres.; b. Yorktown, Tex., Dec. 28, 1933; s. Hubert L. and Martha (Poch) M.; B.A., Tex Lutheran Coll., 1955; B.D., Capital U., 1960; M.A., U. Tex., 1962, Ph.D., 1964; m. Myrtle Vassberg, Sept 1, 1957; children—Esther, Kristine, Jonathan. Instr. English, Capital U., Columbus, Ohio, 1959-60; instr, history Tex. Luth. Coll., Seguin, Tex., 1957-59, 62-63, asst. to pres., 1962-63, dean coll., 1968-69, pres., 1969-76; asst. prof. history Augustana Coll., Sioux Falls, S.D., 1964-67, asso. prof., 1967-68; vis. prof., lectr. U. Maine, summer 1967. Mem. Orgn. Am. Historians,

Assn. So. Historians. Author: The Large Slaveholders of Louisiana, 1964. Home: Seguin, Tex. Died May 12, 1976.

MENN, THORPE, editor; b. Lakin, Kans., Nov. 10, 1912; s. Roy E. and Georgia (Thorpe) M.; student Coll. Emporia, 1931-33, 35-36, Stanford, 1943-44, Rockhurst Coll., 1947, U. Kansas City, 1950; m. Helen Lockwood Miller, July 16, 1937; children—Richard, Mary Rebecca, Gretchen, Donald, Eric. Editor-pub. Chetopa (Kans.) Advance, 1938-40; exec. sec. Lyons (Kans.) C. of C., 1941-43; asst. wire editor Kansas City (Mo.) Star, 1945-58, lit. editor, 1958-79, asso. editor arts and entertainment sect., 1964-68; editor, 1968-79; pres. emeritus Kansas City Jazz, Inc.; adv. bd. Cochefair chair U. Mo. at Kansas City. Nat. pres. bd. Panel Am. Women, 1965-71; adult edn. Instr. Coll. St. Teresa, 1959-62; judge Nat. Book Awards, 1971; mem. adv. bd. Nat. Book Critics Circle, 1973-76. Bd. dirs. Am. Poets Series, Kansas City Poetry Contests, 1964-72, Knights of Sabenadica. Served with AUS, 1943-45. Democrat. Club: Blue River Golf. Home: Kansas City, Mo. Died Jan. 28, 1979.

MENSHIKOV, MIKHAIL ALEKSEEVICH, Soviet diplomat; b. Moscow, USSR, Nov. 21, 1902; diploma econs., specializing in internat. trade, Plekhanov Inst. People's Economy, Moscow, 1929; m. Yevgenia Nicolayevna. Dir. Arkos, Ltd., London, Eng., 1930-36, USSR Dir. Exportkhleb, 1936-37; chairman USSR Assn. Exportles, 1937-43; mem. Soviet delegation to 1st UNRRA, conf., Atlantic City, 1943, dep. to dir.-gen., 1943-45, head delegation to Poland, 1945-46; dep. minister fgn. trade, 1946, then 1st dep. minister, and minister fgn. trade, 1949-52; chief com. pertaining to econ. coop. other countries USSR Council Ministers, 1952-53; USSR ambassador to India, 1953-57, to Napal, 1957, to U.S.A., 1957-62; fgn. minister Russian Soviet Federative Socialist Republic, 1962-68. Mem. Soviet delegation UN Gen. Assembly. Home: Washington, D. C. Died July 21, 1976.

MENZEL, DONALD HOWARD, astrophysicist; b. Florence, Colo., Apr. 11, 1901; s. Charles Theodore and Ina Grace (Zint) M.; A.B., U. Denver, 1920, A.M., 1921, Sc.D. (hon.), 1954; A.M., Princeton, 1923, Ph.D., 1924; A.M. (hon.), Harvard, 1942; m. Florence Elizabeth Kreager, June 17, 1926; children—Suzanne Kay, Elizabeth Ina. Field Scout exec., Denver, 1920; summer and part time tchr. math. Denver pub. schs., 1921; instr. math. U. Denver, 1919-21; asst. Princeton, 1921-22, Thaw fellow, 1922-23, Procter fellow, 1923-24; summer asst. Harvard Obs., 1922-24; instr. astronomy U. Ia., 1924-25, asst. prof. Ohio State U., 1925-26; asst. astronomer Lick Obs., 1926-32; exchange prof. U. Calif., 1928, 31; asst. prof. astronomy, Harvard U., 1932-35, asso. prof. astrophysics, 1935-38, prof. astrophysics, 1938-71, Paine prof. practical astronomy, 1956-71, emeritus 1971-76, chmn. dept. astron., 1946-49, asso. dir. Harvard Obs. for solar research, 1947-54, acting dir., 1952-54, dir., 1954-66; research scientist Smithsonian Astrophys. Obs., 1966-71; chmn. council Boyden Obs., 1954-73; chief scientist G.C.A. Corp., 1959-69; sci. dir. Electronic Space Systems Corp., 1972-76; Rushton lectr. Birmingham So. Coll., 1954; vis. prof. U. Chile, 1963; State Dept. specialist for Latin Am. affairs, 1964-76; hon. prof. physics, engring. and math. Universidad Nacional de San Agustin, Arequipa, Peru, 1972, also awarded gold medal, 1975. Bd. dirs., mem. exec. com. Assn. Univs. Research in Astronomy, Inc., 1957-66; bd. dirs. Washington Planetarium and Space Center, 1961-71; vis. com. Nat. Bur. Standards, 1951-54, chmn., 1953-54; founder, mem., chmn. bd. dirs. Nat. Radio Astronomy Obs., 1952-59; mem. Lick Obs.-Crocker eclipse expdns., Calif., 1930, Maine, 1932; dir. Harvard-M.I.T. eclipse expdn., USSR, 1936; dir. U.S.-Brit. eclipse expdn. Can., 1945, Harvard Obs. Expdn. to observe Occultation of Regulus by Venus, 1959, eclipse expdns. Minn., 1954, Italy, 1961, Mass., 1959, Greece, 1966, Peru, 1966, Mexico, 1970, Mauritania, 1973, Costa Rica, 1973. Served as corporal R.O.T.C., 1917-18; served from lt. comdr. to comdr., USNR, 1942-45; mem., chmn. radio propagation com. Joint and Combined Chiefs of Staff, 1943-45. Recipient A. Cressy Morrison award N.Y. Acad. Sci., 1926, 28, 47; James H. Rand scholarship in astrophys. computations, 1955; Thomas Alva Edison Found. award, 1957; Disting. Citizens award Denver, 1958; Outstanding Profl. Achievement award U. Denver, 1973, Mem. Am. Astron. Soc. (pres. 1954-56, dir.-at-large 1959-61), Am. Geophys. Union, Am. Assn. Variable Star Observers, Astron. Soc. Pacific, Am. Acad. Arts and Scis., Royal Astron. Soc., Internat. Astron. Union (pres. commn. 13 on eclipses, 1948-55, pres. commn. 17-the moon 1964-67), Am. Philos. Soc. (v.p. 1965-68), IEEE (sr. mem.), Internat. Geophys. Union, Internat. Radio Sci. Union, Nat. Acad. Scis., Internat. Joint Commn. for High Altitude Research Stas. (pres. 1950-54), Am. Math. Soc., Phi Beta Kappa, Sigma Xi (pres. Harvard chpt. 1941-42). Club: Harvard Wireless (trustee). Author: A Study of the Solar Chromosphere, 1931; Stars and Planets, 3d edit., 1938; The Story of the Starry Universe, 1941; Elementary Manual of Radio Propagation, 1948; Our Sun, rev. edit., 1959; Flying Saucers, 1953; Theoretical Physics, 1938; Fundamental Formulas of Physics, rev. edit., 1960; Mathematical Physics, 1953; The Universe in Action, 1957; The Radio Noise Spectrum, 1960; (with H. M. Jones and L.G. Boyd) Writing a Scientific Paper, 1961; (with P.L. Bhatnagar and H. K. Sen) Stellar Interiors, 1963; Selected Papers on Physical Processes in Ionized Plasmas, 1962; The Friendly Stars, 1964; (with Lyle G. Boyd) The World of Flying Saucers, 1963; Selected Papers on The Transfer of Radiation, 1966; (with B. Shore) The Principles of Atomic Spectra, 1968; Astronomy, 1970; (with others) Survey of the Universe, 1971. Bd. editors The Telescope, 1937-41, Sky and Telescope, 1941-59; editor Prentice Hall Physics Series, 1947-54; Field Guide to the Stars and Planets, 1964. Research work in field of astrophysics. Home: Cambridge, Mass. Died Dec. 14, 1976; interred Mt. Auburn Cemetery, Cambridge.

MENZIES, ROBERT JAMES, educator, oceanographer; b. Denver, Dec. 2, 1923; s. Walter and Florence (Lundberg) M.; A.B., Coll of Pacific, 1945, M.A., 1948; Ph.D., U. So. Calif.; 1951; m. Joan Patch; children by previous marriage—Diana, Stephen, Christopher. Zool. asso. U. Calif.; Davis, 1951-52; grad. research biologist U. Calif. Scripps Inst. Oceanography, 1953-55; dir. biology program Lamont Geol. Obs., Columbia, 1955-60; dir. Cientifico Estacion Investigaciones Marinas de Magarita Venezuela Fund, LaSalle de Ciencias Naturales, Caracas, 1960; research asso. U. So. Calif.; 1960-61, asso. prof. biology, 1961-62; prof., dir. oceanography Duke, 1962-67; prof. oceanography Fla. State U., Tallahassee, 1967-76. Mem. Expdns. of Vema, Anton Brunn, Velero IV, Eastward; chief scientist offshore ecology investigation Gulf Universities Research Corp., 1972-76. Served with USNR, 1943-45. Ellsworth fellow Arctic Inst. N.Am. Fellow A.A.A.S.; hon. mem. N.C. Shell Club; mem. Nat. Acad. Engring. (panel mem.), Phi Beta Kappa, Sigma Xi, Phi Gamma Mu, Phi Sigma. Author: Abyssal Environment and Ecology of the World Oceans. Contbr. articles to profl. jours. Home: Tallahassee, Fla. Died Dec. 18, 1976.

MERCADANTE, JOSEPH (MER-KÄ-DÄN'TE), pres. Am. Isteg Steel Corp. b Italy, Nov. 27, 1884; s. Antonio (Count di Pilo, Baron di Mattei) and Diodora Misseri Lagumina (of Dukes of Lagumina) M.; ed. mil. sch. in Italy 8 yrs., in medicine 2 yrs; m. Mary Germaine Brennan Saitta, Sept. 19, 1908; children—Dorothy Anne (Mrs. Julius George Forstmann), Mary Victoria. Came to U.S., 1905, naturalized citizen, 1916. Pres. and dir. Am. Isteg Steel Corp.; pres. The Nafra Co., Inc., Maple Gardens, Inc. Awarded silver medal by Italian Red Cross; Knight Comdr. Crown of Italy; gold medal, Opera Nazionale Balilla, conferred by Mussolini, 1929. Mem. N.Y. Chamber Commerce. Clubs: Bankers, Metropolitan Opera, New York Athletic, Automobile, Barracks, Hommocks Country, Seaview Country, Larchmont Yacht, Rochester Yacht; Westchester Country; Yorktown Country of Va. (life). Home: New Rochelle, N.Y. *

MERCER JOHNNY (JOHN H.), musician; b. Savannah, Ga., Nov. 18, 1909; student Woodbury Forest Sch., Orange, Va.; m. Ginger Meehan; children—Amanda, John. Actor, bit player, N.Y.C., 1927-29; vocalist, master ceremonies, writer mus. sketches Paul Whiteman orch.; singer Benny Goodman orch. CBS network, 1938, Bob Crosby orch. NBC, 1939-40; master ceremonies Army-sponsored program Mail Call, also master ceremonies, singer Lucky Strike Hit Parade; organizer Capitol Records, Inc. (with Glenn Wallichs, Buddy DeSylva), 1942, past pres. Writer lyrics for songs including: Pardon My Southern Accent, Jeepers Creepers, You Must Have Been a Beautiful Baby, Too Marvelous for Words, Angels Sing, Blues in the Night, You Were Never Lovelier, Accentuate the Positive, Laura, Skylark, Lazybones, Fools Rush In, Autumn Leaves, Goody Goody, Day In, Day Out, One for My Baby, I Wanna Be Around, Come Rain or Come Shine, Satin Doll, I Remember You, That Old Black Magic, others; writer lyrics, music Something's Gotta Give, GI Jive, Dream, I'm An Old Cowhand; writer lyrics for motion pictures including: Daddy Long Legs, Here Comes the Waves, Star Spangled Rhythm, Ready Willing and Able, Harvey Girls, others; plays St. Louis Woman, Li'l Abner, Foxy, Life is What You Make It for film Kotch (Golden Globes award 1972). Recipient Acad. Award for lyrics Atchison, Topeka, and Santa Fe, 1946. Pres., Songwriter's Hall of Fame, prom 1967. Mem. A.S.C.A.P. Home: Hollywood Calif. Died June 25; 1976.

MERCHANT LIVINGSTON TALLMADGE, govt. ofcl.; b. N.Y.C., Nov. 23, 1903; s. Huntington Wolcott and Mary Floyd (Tallmadge) M.; ed. Hotchkiss Sch., Lakeville, Conn.; A.B., Princeton, 1926, LL.D., 1960; LL.D., Hofstra U., 1959, Queen's, 1961, Harvard, 1968; D.C.L., Bishop's U., 1962; m. Elizabeth Stiles, Dec. 10, 1927; children—Elizabeth G. (dec.), Mary Tallmadge, Livingston Tallmadge. Asso., Scudder, Stevens & Clark, investment counsel firm. 1926-30, partner, 1930-42; with U.S. Dept. State, 1942-62, asst. chief div. def. materials, 1942, chief war areas Div., 1945; counselor for econ. affairs with rank of minister Am. embassy, Paris, 1945-46; chief aviation div. State Dept., 1946-48; apptd. fgn. service officer, 1947; counselor Am. embassy, Nanking, China, 1948-49; dep. asst. sec. state for Far Eastern Affairs, 1949-51, dep. for polit. affairs to U.S. spl. rep. in Europe, alternate U.S. permanent rep. N. Atlantic Council, Paris, rank ambassador, 1952-53; asst. sec. state for European Affairs, 1953-56, 58-59; ambassador to Can., 1956-58, 61-62; under sec. state for polit. affairs, 1959-61; ret fgn. service, 1962; U.S. exec. dir. IBRD, 1965-68. Del. or adviser numerous internat. confs. Charter trustee emeritus Princeton. Republican. Episcopalian. Clubs: Metropolitan, Alibi, Alfalfa, Chevy Chase, Princeton (Washington); Cottage (Princeton); Princeton (N.Y.C.). Home: Washington, D.C. Died May 15, 1976.

MERIAM, LEWIS (MER'I-AM), statistician; b. Salem, Mass., Oct. 5 1883; s. Horatio Cook and Edith Worcester M.; A.B., Harvard, 1905, A.M., 1906; LL.B., Nat. Law School, Washington, D.C., 1908; B.L. George Washington University Law School, 1909; Ph.D., Brookings Institution, 1936; m. Pink Wilson, Aug. 25, 1909; 1 dau., Adele Stuart. Editorial and statis. asst., U.S. Bur. of Census, Washington, 1905-07; acting chief, Div. of Revision and Results, same, 1907-12; asst. chief U.S. Children's Bur., 1912-15; mem. staff, New York Bur. Municipal Research, 1915-16; mem. sr. staff, Inst. for Govt. Research, 1916-18; production mgr. div. of planning and statistics of U.S. Shipping Bd., 1918-19; statistician Joint Congressional Commn. on Reclassification of Salaries, 1919-20; mem. sr. staff, Brookings Instn., 1920-46; vice president since 1946; tech. aid U.S. Senate and House committees on civil service in matters relating to Classification Act of 1923; tech. aid to Salary and Wage Commn. of North Carolina, 1925; tech. dir. survey of Indian affairs, made by Inst. for Govt. Research, at request of sec. of interior, 1926-28; mem. President's Emergency Com. for Employment, 1930-31; visiting prof. pub. adminstrn., U. of Chicago, 1935-36. Clubs: Cosmos (Washington); Harvard (New York). Author: Principles Governing the Retirement of Public Employes, 1917; (with associates) The Problem of Indian Administration, 1928, A Social Outlook on Indian Missions in Facing the Future in Indian Missions, 1932; Public Service and Special Training, 1936; Public Personnel Problems, 1938; Reorganization of the National Government (with L. F. Schmickibier), 1939; (with others) The Government of Montgomery County, Maryland, 1941; Relief and Social Security, 1946; The Issues of Compulsory Health Insurance, 1948; The Cost and Financing of Social Security, 1950. Home: Kensington, Md. *

MERK, FREDERICK, educator; b. Milw., Aug. 15, 1887; s. Frederick and Katharine (Klein) M.; A.B., U. Wis., 1911, L.H.D., 1971; Ph.D., Harvard, 1920, Litt.D., 1958; L.H.D., Clark U., 1977; m. Lois A. Bannister, June 21, 1931; children—Katharine Merk McNally, Frederick. Mem. editorial staff State Hist. Soc. Wis., 1911-16; Edward Austin fellow Harvard, 1916-18, Sheldon traveling fellow, 1920-21, tutor in history, govt. and econs., 1918-20, instr. Am. history, 1921-24, asst. prof., 1924-30, asso. prof., 1930-36, prof., from 1936, Gurney prof. history and polit. sci., from 1946, head dept., 1941-46, emeritus; exchange prof. Carleton, Grinnell, Pomona colls., 1927-28. Recipient Toppan prize Harvard, 1920. Fellow Am. Acad. Arts and Scis.; mem. Am. Antiquarian Soc., Am., Miss. Valley (pres. 1959), Mass. hist. socs., Agrl. Hist. Soc. (pres. 1948), Phi Beta Kappa, Delta Sigma Rho. Club: Harvard Faculty. Author: Economic History of Wisconsin During the Civil War Decade, rev. edit., 1971; (with Frederick J. Turner) List of References on the History of the West, 1922; Albert Gallatin and the Oregon Problem, 1950; Manifest Destiny and Mission in American History, 1963; The Monroe Doctrine and American Expansionism, 1843-1849, 1966; The Oregon Question, 1967; Fruits of Propaganda in the Tyler Administration, 1971; Slavery and the Annexation of Texas, 1972; History of the Westward Movement, 1978; co-author: Harvard Guide to American History, 1954, rev. edit., 1974; Dissent in Three American Wars, 1970. Editor: Civil War Messages and Proclamations of Wisconsin War Governors, 1912; Fur Trade and Empire: George Simpson's Journal, 1824-25, rev. edit., 1968. Contbr. to reviews. Home: Belmont, Mass. Died Sept. 24, 1977.

MERMOD, CAMILLE, physician; b. Sainte Croix, Switzerland, 1900; d. Leon Marcel and Helene (Paillard) Mermod; naturalized, 1926; B.A., Mills Coll., 1922, LL.D., 1967; M.D., Stanford, 1932. Clin. instr. medicine Stanford Med. Sch., 1932-38; pathologist St. Joseph Hosp., Lancaster, Pa., 1939-42; asst. pathologist St. Barnabas Hosp., Newark, 1942-46; pathologist St. James Hosp., Newark, 1942-50; chief dept. medicine St. Barnabas Med. Center, Newark, 1955-57; Pvt. practice pathology, internal medicine, Orange, N.J., 1946-72. Diplomate Nat. Bd. Med. Examiners, Am. Bd. Pathology and Clin. Pathology. Fellow A.A.A.S., Acad. Medicine N.J.; mem. A.M.A., Am. Med. Women's Assn. (pres. 1954-55, 1956-57, editor jour. 1963-71), Essex County Med. Soc. (reporter 1953-57). Contbr. med. articles profl. jours. Home: Maplewood, N.J. Died Apr. 28, 1976.

MERRIAM, ALAN (PARKHURST), educator; b. Missoula, Mont., Nov. 1, 1923; s. Harold Guy and Doris (Foote) M.; B.A., Mont. State U., 1947; M Music, Northwestern U., 1948, Ph.D. in Anthropology 1951; m. Barbara Anne Williams, Aug. 29, 1947 (div Sept. 1974); children—Virginia Claire, Paige Alison

Cynthia Williams; m. 2d, Valerie Ann Christian, May 6, 1977. Instr. anthropology Northwestern U., 1953-54, asst. prof., 1956-58, asso. prof., 1958-62; asst. prof. sociology and anthropology U. Wis.-Milw., 1954-56; asst. prof. anthropology and Am. studies U. Minn., summer 1957; prof. anthropology Ind. U., 1962-80, chmn. dept., 1966-69, asso. chmn., 1978-80; disting. vis. prof. U. Mont., summer 1965; vis. scholar UCLA, 1978; field research in Western Mont., Belgian Congo, Ruanda Urundi, Republic of Zaire. Mem. com. human resources in Central Africa, NRC, 1958; mem. President's Task Force for Africa, 1960; mem. joint com. African studies Social Sci. Research Council-Am. Council Learned Socs., 1960-66, chmn., 1962-65; adv. bd. Inter-Am. Inst. Musical Research, Tulane U., 1961-70; U.S. del. 1st Internat. Congress Africanists, Accra, Ghana, 1962, 2d Internat. Congress Africanists, Dakar, Senegal, 1967; bd. dirs. Com. on Research in Dance, 1975-76; U.S. del. Baghdad Internat. Conf. on Arabic Music, 1975. Served with USAAF, 1942-45. Grantee Mont. State U. Music Found., 1950, Grad. Sch. Northwestern U., 1958, Belgian Am. Ednl. Found. and Wenner Gren Found. Anthrop. Research, 1951-52, NSF-Belgian Am. Ednl. Found., 1959-60, African Studies Program, Ind. U. and joint African studies com. Social Sci. Research Council-Am. Council Learned Socs., 1973; Guggenheim fellow, 1969-70; Australian-Am. Ednl. Found. sr. scholar in anthropology U. Sydney (Australia), 1976. Fellow Am. Anthrop. Assn., AAAS; founding fellow African Studies Assn. (chmn. com. fine arts and humanities 1960-62, 65-66, dir. 1962-65); mem. Am. Folklore Soc. (councilor 1956-58, rev. editor jour. 1957-58), Internat. Folk Music Council (corr. 1956-60), Soc. Ethnomusicology (co-founder 1952; editor ofcl. publ. 1953-58, mem.-at-large exec. bd. 1956-65, 70-72, mem. council 1958-70, 71-74, 75-78, pres. 1962-64, editor spl. series 1972-77, 1st v.p. 1977-79), Central States Anthrop. Soc. (pres. 1960-61, exec. com. 1961-63, 78-80), Sigma Xi. Author: (With R.J. Benford) A Bibliography of Jazz, 1954; Congo: Background of Conflict, 1961; The Anthropology of Music, 1964; (with Frank Gillis) Ethnomusicology and Folk Music, 1966; Ethnomusicology of the Flathead Indians, 1967; African Music on LP: An Annotated Discography, 1970; An African World: The Basongye Village of Lupupa Nyge, 1974; Culture History of the Basongye, 1975; Perspectives in African Music, 1981; also monographs. Home: Bloomington, Ind. Died Mar. 14, 1980.

MERRIAM, (SYMS) ALLEN, editor; b. Good Hope, Ill., July 7, 1886; s. Syms Allen and Mary Angeline (Shields) M.; student U. of Kan. m. Mildred Anna Miller, Jan. 5, 1915; children—Jean (Mrs. Ralph W. Ater), Helen (Mrs. Frank C. Ebaugh, Jr.). In newspaper bus., since 1906; with Winfield (Kan.) Free Press, 1906; roving reporter, 1907-12; news editor San Antonio Light, 1912-21; mng. editor, Dallas Times Herald, 1923-41, editor, 1941-52, editor-in-chief, 1952—; dir. Times Herald Printing Co., radio sta., KRLD, Dallas. Mem. Tex. Soc. S.A.R. Clubs: Brookhollow Golf, City (Dallas). Home: Dallas. *

MERRIAM, CHARLES J., lawyer; b. Chgo., Feb. 4, 1903; s. Charles E. and Elizabeth (Doyle) M.; B.S., U. Chgo., 1922, J.D. cum laude, 1925; m. Kathryn Cheney, May 15, 1926; m. 2d, Ethelmae Sturgeon Haskell, Mar. 14, 1946; children—Dorothy (Mrs. Kenneth Venolia), Carol (Mrs. Theodore Bockman), Elizabeth (Mrs. Mason Thomas), Charles E., Robert C. Admitted to Ill. bar, 1925, since practiced in Chgo.; sr. partner firm Merriam, Marshall, & Bicknell, 1965-76, of counsel, 1976-79; pres., dir. Pine Trees Inc., 1968-79; dir. Continental Gas Transmission Co., Inc., 1973-79. Mem. panel on patents, trademarks and copyrights Bur. Nat. Affairs, 1972-79. Mem. Winnetka Sch. Bd., 1945-48, U. Ill. Citizens Com., 1965-79. Dir., v.p. U. Ill. Found., pres., 1976-79. Mem. Am., Fed., Chgo. bar assns., Order of Coif, Phi Beta Kappa, Sigma Xi. Republican. Clubs: University, Law, Chicago (Chgo.); Moon Valley (Phoenix). Home: Phoenix, Ariz. Died Nov. 4, 1979.

MERRIAM, HAROLD GUY, educator, editor; b. Westminster, Mass., Sept. 6, 1883; s. Joel Hervey and Anna Parkhurst (Mansfield) M.; A.B., U. of Wyo., 1905; Rhodes scholar, Wyoming to Oxford Eng., 1904-07, B.A., 1907, M.A., 1912; studied Harvard Univ., 1910, Columbia, 1925-26, British Museum, 1926; Ph.D., Columbia, 1939; m. Doris Woodward Foote, 1915; children—Alison Woodward, Alan Parkhurst. Mem. faculty, Whitman Coll., Walla Walla, Wash., 1908-10; faculty, Beloit (Wis.) Coll., 1911-13; prof. English, Reed Coll., Portland, Ore., 1913-19; prof. English, Montana State U., 1919-39 and since 1940 (chairman of department and of division of humanities); professor of English, University of Oregon, 1939-40. Y.M.C.A. service in France, with French Army 6 mos., Army Ednl. Commn., London, 4 mos., 1918-19. Montana director Federal Writers' Projects, under W.P.A., 1937. Co-founder Mont. Inst. Arts, 1948, pres., 1948-50. Mem. N.W. Assn. Secondary and Higher Schs., Phi Beta Kappa. Author: Edward Moxon, Publisher of Poets. Editor of The Frontier and Midland (lit. mag., 1920-39), Northwest Verse, and Northwest Books; Readings for an Air Age (in collaboration); contbr. to mags. Home: Missoula, Mont.

MERRIAM, KENNETH GERALD, educator; b. Belfast, Maine, Nov. 11, 1901; s. Eli Carr and Addie (Ranger) M.; S.B., M.I.T., 1922; M.S., Worcester Poly. Inst. 1935, D. Engring. (hon.), 1964; m. Alice Eugenia Blandin, July 24, 1929; children—Janet (Frank Cornell), Joyce. Instr. mech. engring. U. Maine, 1922-23; mem. faculty Worcester (Mass.) Poly. Inst., 1923-69, prof. aeromechanics, 1938-56, dir. summer sch., 1954-58, prof. engring. mechanics, 1956-69, Fuller prof. mech. engring., 1968-69, emeritus, 1969-77, chmn. research com., 1935-42. Served with AUS, World War II. Decorated Legion of Merit; recipient Outstanding Tchr. award Worcester Poly. Inst., 1961; Merriam Professorship established. Registered profl. engr., Mass. Fellow ASME, AIAA (asso.); mem. Am. Soc. Engring. Edn. (life), Sigma Xi, Tau Beta Pi, Pi Tau Sigma, Sigma Phi Epsilon. Republican. Unitarian. Mason. Contbr. papers to profl. lit. Home: Worcester, Mass. Died Oct. 17, 1977.

MERRILL, EDWARD D., transportation exec.; b. Des Moines, Ia., Dec. 11, 1885; s. Samuel Adams and Fanny Rainey (Hyde) M.; Ph.B., Grinnell Coll., 1907; B.S., Mass. Inst. Tech., 1909; m. Florence Southgate Hurst, Sept. 20, 1916; 1 dau., Florence (Mrs. Richard B. Pilkinton). Asst. engr. U.P. R.R., 1909, later with light, power traction cos.; traffic engr. Chicago Motor Coach Co., 1924-25; pres. and gen. mgr. Washington Rapid Transit Co., 1926-36; v.p. and gen. mgr. Capital Transit Co., 1936-37, pres., and gen. mgr., 1937-47, pres. and chmn. bd., 1947-51, ret. 1951, dir. since 1936; dir. Transit Research Corp. since 1940; dir. The Riggs Nat. Bank of Washington, Mem. A.R.C. (dir. D.C. chpt.), Am. Transit Assn. (past pres.), Washington Bd. Trade (pres. 1952-53), Mass. Inst. Tech. Alumni Assn. Clubs: Roaary, Cosmos, Metropolitan (Washington). Home: Washington. *

MERRILL, MELVIN CLARENCE, editor; b. Richmond, Utah, Apr. 6, 1884; s. Marriner Wood and Maria Loenza (Kingsbury) M.; B.S., Utah Agrl. Coll., 1905; student, Cornell U., 1910-11; S.M. in Botany, U. of Chicago, 1912; A.M., in Chemistry, Harvard, 1913; Ph.D. in Plant Physiology, Washington U., 1915; m. Amy Lyman, Sept. 9, 1914; 1 dau., Betty Jane. Teacher natural science, high sch., Springville, Utah, 1905-06; agrl. insp., supt. Agrl. Expt. Sta., Philippine Islands, 1906-10; research asst. Mo. Bot. Garden, St. Louis, 1913-15; dir. dept. agr. Ida, Tech. Inst., 1915-17; prof. horticulture, Utah Agrl. Coll., horticulturist Utah Agrl. Expt. Sta., 1917-22; dean and horticulturist, Coll. Applied Science, Brigham Young U., 1922-24; dir. forestry publs. of Forest Service, Washington, D.C., 1924-25; editorial chief of publs., 1925-28, chief of publs. since 1928, U.S. Dept. Agr. Member Botanical Society Washington (v.p., 1927-28, pres., 1940), Botanical Society America, Washington Acad. Sciences, N.E.A., Sigma Xi, Gamma Sigma Delta, Phi Kappa Phi; fellow A.A.A.S. Mormon. Clubs: Washington Torch, Harvard. Home: Washington, D.C. *

MERRITT, HIRAM HOUSTON, educator, physician; b. Wilmington, N.C., Jan. 12, 1902; s. Hiram Houston and Dessie (Cline) M.; A.B., Vanderbilt U., 1922; M.D., Johns Hopkins, 1926; A.M. (hon.) Harvard, 1942; Sc.D. (hon.), N.Y. Med. Coll., 1967, Columbia, 1971; m. Mabel Carmichael, Aug. 2, 1930. Intern New Haven Hosp., 1926-27; various hosp. and univ. assignments, study and fellowships, 1927-42; asso. prof. neurology Harvard Med. Sch. 1942-44; vis. neurologist Boston City Hosp., 1934-42; cons. neurologist Peter Bent Brigham Hosp., 1939-44; cons. in neuropsychiatry U.S. Marine Hosp., 1937-44; dir. neuropathol. labs. Boston Psychopathic Hosp., 1943-44; mem. med. adv. bd. No. 12 SSS, 1940-44; prof. clin. neurology Columbia Med. Sch., 1944-68, chmn. dept., 1948-68, Moses prof. neurology, 1963-70, emeritus, 1970-79, dean faculty medicine, v.p. charge med. affairs, 1958-70, dean, v.p. emeritus, 1970-79; chief neuropsychiat. service Montefiore Hosp., 1944-48; dir. service of neurology Neurol. Inst., Presbyn. Hosp., 1948-68; cons. various govtl. agys. Decorated grand officer Portuguese Order of Santiago; recipient George W. Jacoby award Am. Neurol. Assn., 1965; Bronze Hope Chest award Nat. Multiple Sclerosis Soc., 1967; Lennox award Am. Epilepsy Soc., 1967; North Carolina award, 1967; Golden Anniversary medal Assn. for Research in Nervous and Mental Disease, 1970; Thomas W. Salmon Distinguished Service award in psychiatry and mental hygiene, 1973. Diplomate Am. Bd. Psychiatry and Neurology (dir. 1942-50, pres. 1950). Mem. A.M.A., various other gen. and spl. med. and profl. assns. and orgns. Author: Cerebrospinal Fluid, 1937; Neurosyphillis, 1946; Textbook of Neurology, 6th edit.; articles in profl. jours. Home: Bronxville, N.Y. Died Jan. 9, 1979; buried New Haven, Conn.

MERRITT, RALPH PALMER, b. Rio Vista, Calif., Feb. 26, 1883; s. Charles S. and Ella S. (Palmer) M.; B.S., U. of Calif., 1907, LL.D., 1919; m. Varina Morrow, 1910. Comptroller and sec. Bd. of Regents, U. of Calif., 1912-20 (resigned). Pres. and gen. mgr. Rice Growers' Assn. of Calif., Sacramento, 1921-24 (resigned); pres. and mng. dir. Sun-Maid Raisin Growers, Fresno, 1923-28; pres. and mng. dir. Sunland Sales Coöperative Assn., 1924-28, farming. Engaged in mine development and operations in Inyo and Mono counties, California, 1934-41; project dir., War Relocation Authority, Manzanar, 1942-46; field director War Assets Adminstrn. since 1946. Federal food adminstr. for Calif., 1917-19. Regent U. of Calif., 1924-30. Dir. Chamber Commerce of U.S., 1925-28. Mem. Alpha Delta Phi. Republican. Conglist. Home: Fort Huachuca, Ariz. *

MERTZ, HENRY OLIVER (MERTZ), urol.; b. Roundhead, O., Apr. 5, 1884; s. James Edwin and Alice Jane (Bowdle) M.; grad. in music, Ohio Northern Conservatory of Music, 1904; M.D., Indiana U. 1908; m. Ida Ethel Fullerton, Sept. 17, 1912; children—Ellajane (Mrs. Fred W. Dickson), James Richard, John Henry Oliver, Ida Katharine (dec.). Began practice medicine, 1908; partner La Porte (Ind.) Clinic, 1912-18; Wishard, Hamer & Mertz, Indianapolis, 1918-52; asst. prof. genito-urinary diseases, Indiana U., 1929-36, prof. and dean of dept. since 1936. Fellow Am. Coll. Surgeons; mem. Am. Assn. Genito-Urinary Surgeons, Am. Urol. Assn., Internat. Soc. Urology, A.M.A., Ind. Stat Med. Assn., Marion County Med. Soc. Republican. Presbyterian. Clubs: Columbia, Contemporary (Indianapolis). Writer of scientific articles. Home: Brendonwood. *

MERWIN, FREDERIC EATON, educator; b. East Palestine, Ohio, Apr. 27, 1907; s. Charles Lewis and Estella Dora (Meek) M.; B.A., Ohio Wesleyan U., 1929; M.A., U. Wis., 1935, Ph.D., 1937; m. Jacqueline Olver Schmitt, Aug. 12, 1939; children—Miles Michael, Frederic Eaton. With East Palestine (Ohio) Daily Leader, 1922-29; reporter Indpls. Times, 1929; night bur. mgr. United Press, Cleve., 1930; telegraph editor Canton (Ohio) Repository, 1930-33; grad. asst. lectr. Sch. Journalism, U. Wis., 1933-37; asst. prof. Syracuse Sch. Journalism, 1937-40; mgr. N.Y. Press Assn., 1940; prof., dir. Sch. Journalism, Rutgers U., 1940-69, Pres. Am. Assn. Tchrs. Journalism, 1944-46; asst. chief div. information channels Office Facts and Figures, Washington, 1942. Recipient Nat. Merit award Am. Legion Press Assn., 1958. Mem. N.J. Press. Assn., Assn. Edn. Journalism, Sigma Delta Chi, Phi Gamma Delta, Kappa Tau Alpha (nat. pres. 1952-54). Republican. Methodist. Editor bibliography Journalism Quar., 1935-45; editor annual Research in Progress for Nat. Council on Journalism Research, 1940-49, Journalism Series of Rinehart & Co.; mem. editorial bd. Journalism Quart., Jersey Publisher, 1958; co-editor: The Newspaper and Society, 1942; The Press and Society, 1951. Home: Metuchen, N.J. Died Oct. 28, 1975.

MERYMAN, RICHARD SUMNER, artist; b. Boston, Mass., Apr. 4, 1882; s. Richard and Charllote (Wigglesworth) M.; grad. Boston Art Mus. Sch. of Painting; studied with Abbot H. Thayer, Edmond C. Tarbell and Frank Benson; m. Dorothea Bates, of Santa Barbara, Calif., June 1919; children—Harold Thayer, Richard S. Prin. Corcoran Sch. of Art, Washington, D.C., 1918-35; portrait painter. Awarded silver medal, Panama-Pacific Expn., 1915; silver medal, Sesquicentennial Expn., 1926. Served as 1st lt., Engr. Corps, U.S.A., World War. Home: Dublin, N.H. *

METCALF, FRANK ALBERT, civil and mining engr., govt. ofcl.; b. Bardolph, Ill., July 22, 1882; s. Henry K. and Ella (Robinson) M.; B.S. in civil engring., Cornell, 1910, C.E., 1912; m. Ruth W. Grefe, June 17, 1913; 1 dau., Mrs. E.S. Turley (adopted). Locating engr. Milw. R.R. extension, Bitter Root Mountains, 1906-07; engr. City of Wallace, Ida., 1907-10, Bunker Hill and Sullivan Mine, Kellogg, Ida., 1910-13, Alaska Juneau Gold Mine, 1913-15; pvt., also city engr. Juneau, Alaska, 1915-47; territorial highway engr., supt. pub. works, chief Alaska Highway Patrol, custodian Territorial Bldgs. since 1947, Served as capt. C.E., U.S. Army, World War I. Registered engr. Alaska. Mem. Juneau C. of C., Vets. Fgn. Wars, Am. Legion (past comdr.). Elk, Lion, Moose. Home: Juneau, Alaska. *

METCALF, LEE, U.S. senator; b. Stevensville, Mont., Jan. 28, 1911; s. Harold and Rhoda Metcalf; A.B., Stanford, 1936; LL.B., Mont. State U., 1936; m. Donna Hoover, 1938; 1 foster son, Jerry. Admitted to Mont. bar, 1936, rep. Ravalli Co. to Mont. Legislature, 1937; asst. atty. gen. of Mont., 1937-41; asso. justice Mont. Supreme Ct., 1946; mem. 83d-94th Congresses, 1st Mont. Dist.; U.S. senator from Mont., 1961-78. Served tank destroyers, World War II. Mem. Mont. Bar Assn., D.A.V., V.F.W., Am. Legion, AMVETS. Democrat. Methodist. Mason. Elk. Home: Helena, Mont. Died Jan. 12, 1978.

METCALFE, RALPH H., congressman; b. Atlanta, May 30, 1910; s. Clarence and Marie (Attaway) M.; Ph.B., Marquette U., 1936; M.A., U. So. Calif., 1939; H.H.D. (hon.), Ill. Coll. Podiatric Medicine, 1977; m. Madalynne Fay Young, July 20, 1947; 1 son, Ralph H. Track coach, instr. phys. edn. and polit. sci. Xavier U., New Orleans, 1936-42; dir. dept. civil rights Commn. on Human Relations, Chgo., 1945-49; commr. Ill. Athletic Commn., 1949-52; Democratic committeeman 3d Ward, Chgo., from 1952, alderman, 1955-71; mem.

92d-95th congresses from 1st Dist. Ill.; mem. com. on interstate and fgn. commerce, com. on post office and civil service, com. on merchant marine and fisheries, chmn. subcom. on Panama Canal, mem. Democratic Steering and Policy Com., mem. Congl. Black Caucus, Dir. Ill./Service Fed. Savs. and Loan Assn. Mem. U.S. Olympic team, Los Angeles, 1932, Berlin, Germany, 1936; mem. Am. track team touring Europe, 1933, Far East, 1934; past pres. Midwest chpt. U.S. Olympians; co-chmn. 3d Pan Am. Games, mem. organizing com., 1959; mem. Pres.'s Commn. on Olympic Sports, 1975-77. Mem. Northeastern Ill. Plan Commn., 1967-70, Chgo, Com. Urban Opportunities, 1964, Chgo. Commn. Devel. and Planning, 1964; pres. Joint Negro Appeal, 1963. Served to 1st lt. AUS, 1943-45, Decorated Legion of Merit; set former World records for 220 yard dash around curve, 100 yard dash, 100 meter dash; mem. Helms Athletic Found., Wis. Hall of Fame, Nat. Track and Field Hall of Fame, U.S. Track and Field Hall of Fame, Black Athletes Hall of Fame, Mem. Am. Vets. Com., Am. Legion, Amvets, Chgo. Urban League, NAACP, Cosmopolitan C. of C., Alpha Sigma Nu, Alpha Phi Alpha. Clubs: Masons, Elks, Varsity (pres. 1962) (Chgo.). Home: Chicago, Ill. Died Oct. 10, 1978.

MEYER, ANDRE, banker; b. Paris, France, Sept. 3, 1898; m. Bella Lehman, Dec. 23, 1922; children—Philippe, Francine. Sr. partner Lazard Frères & Co., N.Y.C., Lazard Frères Cie., Paris; dir. Lazard Bros. & Co., Ltd., London. Trustee Mt. Sinai Hosp. Decorated grand officer Legion of Honor. Home: New York, N.Y. Died Sept. 9, 1979.

MEYER, EVERETT, investment company executive; born at Seymour, Indiana, December 5, 1884; son of George Henry and Emma K. (Stellter) M.; student pub. schs., Seymour; m. Mina Helen Weaver, Mar. 21, 1909; children—Charlotte Ann (Mrs. Theodore Sitterley), Thomas Weaver (dec.); married 2d, Janet H. R. Powell, December 28, 1957. Sales field mgr. American Tobacco Company, 1906-11; with P. Lorillard Co., 1912-36, vice president in charge sales, also advt. director, 1920-36; president, chairman bd., dir. Webster Tobacco Company, Inc., 1936-52; chmn. bd., director Webster Investment Company, Inc (now Webster Investors, Inc.), 1952-61; director American Manufacturing Company; member board directors Tobacco and Allied Stocks, 1937-40, Huyler Candy Company, 1950-51. Vice president Cigar Institute of America, 1947-50. Member Cigar Manufacturers Assn. (dir. 1943-48). Elk. Clubs: Seymour (Ind.) Country; Siwanoy Country (Bronxville). Home: Bronxville, N.Y. *

MEYER, GEORGE RALPH, army officer; b. Montgomery, Minn., Nov. 27, 1886; s. Christian Wendlyn and Ellen Loretta (Carroll) M.; student U. of Minn. 1904-05; B.S., U.S. Naval Acad., 1910; grad. Command and Gen. Staff Sch., 1925, U.S. Army War Coll., 1935, U.S. Naval War Coll., 1936; m. Virginia Roget Robb, Oct. 11, 1911; children—Virginia Roget (Mrs. R. F. Moran), Carroll Louise (Mrs. W. E. Dickinson). Midshipman, resigned from Navy, Mar. 1911; commd. 2d lt., Coast Arty. Corps, U.S. Army, Aug 1911, and advanced through the grades to brig. gen., Aug. 1941, and major general, April 2, 1943. Served in Hawaii during World War and with A.F.G. in Germany at the base in Antwerp, returning to U.S. in Oct. 1920; inst. Coast Arty. Sch., Ft. Monroe and at C.&G.S. Sch., Ft. Leavenworth; chief of staff, 9th Corps, in maneuvers in Tex. and La., Apr. 1940; comdr. Pacific Brigade of Panama Coast Arty., Aug. 7, 1941; comdr. Panama Coast Artillery Command since Feb. 18, 1943. Decorated Officer of Order of Leopold II (Belgian). K. of C. Contbr. to ornithol. jours. and servicepubls. Address: Panama Canal Zone. *

MEYER, JACOB GIBBLE, textbook writer; b. Fredericksburg, Pa., Mar. 16, 1884; s. Jacob W. and Leah (Gibble) M.; Pd.B., Elizabethtown (Pa.) Coll., 1905; A.B., Franklin and Marshall Coll., 1910; A.M., Columbia, 1913; Ph. D., New York U., 1925; student U. of Pa., summers 1905, 07. Teachers Coll., Columbia, 1916-18, Northwestern U., 1938-39, U. of Chicago, 1939-40; m. Anna Royer, Oct. 13, 1940 (died Mar. 5, 1941); children—Leah Mildred (wife of Dr. Kenneth Kintner), Helen Grace, (wife of Prof. Max Kraning), Jacob Gibble, Anna Charlotte (wife of Robert A. Emmons), Mary Janet; m. 2d, Martha Marie Nelson, June 4, 1942. Began as pub. school teacher, 1902; instr., Acad. of Elizabethtown Coll., 1905-07; instr., mathematics, Millersville (Pa.) State Teachers Coll., 1910-11; prof. of chemistry and physics, Elizabethtown Coll., 1911-16; instr. of gen. science, Horace Mann Sch. for Boys, N.Y. City, 1916-18; prof. of edn. and psychology, Elizabethtown Coll., 1918-24, pres., 1920-24; dean of school of edn., Manchester Coll., North Manchester, Ind., 1924-38; extension lecturer, Fort Wayne, Ind., 1925-38; pres., Milton (Wis.) Coll., 1940-1944, trustee Am. Christian Benevolent Soc. Mem. N.E.A., Am. Sch. Adminstrs., Adult Edn. Assn., Am. Acad. Science. Fellow, National Geographic Society. Mem. Church of the Brethren (ordained minister, 1910). Author: Small Colleges and Teacher-Training, 1928; Principles of Secondary Education, 1935; The Old World and Its Gifts, 1938; The New World and Its Growth, 1941; Our Southern Neighbors, 1942; Friends Near and Far, 1943. Home: Chicago, Illinois. *

MEYER, JOHN EDWARD, hotel exec.; b. Birmingham, Ala., Aug. 27, 1918; s. Robert Randolph and Cora (Gregg) M.; B.A., Princeton, 1939; m. Stella Cutrer, Mar. 9, 1945 (div. 1965); children—Jane Cutrer, Nancy Cook, Stella Gregg; m. 2d, Margaret M. Whitman, Dec. 20, 1965. Pres. Meyer Hotels, 1947-61, chmn. bd., from 1961; dir. First Nat. Bank of Birmingham. Trustee So. Research Inst., Children's Hosp. Served as maj. USAAF, World War II. Decorated Air medal with oak leaf cluster, D.F.C. with 2 oak leaf clusters, Purple Heart; Breast Order of Yun Hui. Episcopalian. Home: Birmingham, Ala. Deceased.

MEYER, KARL FRIEDRICH, pathologist, bacteriologist; b. Basel, Switzerland, May 19, 1884; s. Theodor and Sophie (Lichtenhahn) M.; D.V.M., U. Zurich, 1909, Ph.D., 1924; postgrad. univs. Munich, Paris, Zurich, Bern; M.D. (hon.), Coll. Med. Evangelists, 1936, U. Basel, 1952; M.D. (hon.); U. Zurich, 1937, D.V.M., 1949; LL.D., U. So. Cal., 1946, U. Cal., 1958; D.Sc., Ohio U., 1958, U. Pa., 1959; m. Mary Elizabeth Lindsay, July 16, 1913 (dec. 1958); 1 dau., Charlotte; m. 2d, Marion Lewis, Feb. 26, 1960. Came to U.S., 1910, naturalized, 1922. Pathologist dept. agr., Transvaal, 1908-10; asst. prof. pathology and bacteriology U. Pa., 1910-11, prof., 1911-13; dir. lab., expt. farm Pa. Livestock San. Bd., Phila., 1912-13; prof. bacertiology, protozoology U. Cal., 1914-15; asso. prof. tropical medicine Hooper Found. Med. Research, U. Cal., 1915-21, prof. research medicine and acting dir., 1921-24; dir., 1924-54, now emeritus; cons. Cal. Dept. Pub. Health, S.P. Ry., 1920-74; prof. bacteriology No. U. Cal., 1924-48, prof. exptl. pathology, 1948-54, now emeritus; lectr. large univs., other orgns., 1931—. Mem. nat. adv. health council NIH; mem. nat. med. and health adv. com. A.R.C.; cons. to sec. war; mem. U.S. Army Epidemiol. Bd. Recipient many honors, awards. Fellow Nat., N.Y. acads. sci., A.A.A.S., Am. Acad. Arts and Scis., Am. Pub. Health Assn.; mem. Am. Assn. Pathologists and Bacteriologists, Am. Soc. Microbiology, Am. Assn. Immunologists, Soc. Exptl. Biology, Am. Soc. Tropical Medicine, Am. Vet. Med. Assn., Inst. Food Technologists, Inter-Am. Soc. Microbiology, Sigma Xi. Clubs: Commonwealth, Family (San Francisco). Author: Practical Bacteriology, 1923; Disinfected Mail, 1962. Home: San Francisco, Cal. Died Apr. 24, 1974.

MEYER, MALCOLM, mfg. exec.; b. Alameda, Calif., June 23, 1915; s. Albert C. and Cora (Fetzer) M.; B.S., U. Calif., Berkeley, 1937; postgrad. Columbia, 1953; hon. dr. Villanova U., 1972; m. Vera C. Vogel, July 8, 1939; children—Philip, Jeffrey, Mimi. Asso. Certain-teed Products Corp., Richmond, Calif., 1937-49, asst. to pres., Ardmore, Pa., 1949, gen. sales mgr., 1950-53, v.p., 1953-55, pres., dir., 1955-74, chmn. bd., Valley Forge, Pa., 1970-74, dir., cons., 1976-78 chmn. Builders Investment Group; dir. ASG Industries, Inc., Fidelity Corp. of Pa., Fidelity Bank, Health Tech. Labs. Chmn. devel. council, trustee Villanova U.; chmn. bd. trustees Lebanon Valley Coll., Annville, Pa.; bd. dirs. Livengrin Found.; chmn. Nat. Council Alcoholism. Mem. Asphalt Roofing Mfrs. Assn. (past pres.), Gypsum Assn. (pres. 1959). Home: Birchrunville, Pa. Died Apr. 4, 1978.

MEYER, OVID OTTO, educator, physician; b. Stevens Point, Wis., Dec. 17, 1900; s. Otto F. and Elmere E. (Belanger) M.; S.B., U. Wis., 1924; M.D., Columbia, 1926; m. Lyda Ann Henry (dec. Aug. 1968), June 24, 1932; children—Nancy A., Mary L. Lynn, Ralph H.; m. 2d, Irene Hite Thompson, May 5, 1972. Intern, Wis. Gen. Hosp., 1926-27, resident, 1927-29; asst. in medicine Collis P. Huntington Meml. Hosp. and Harvard Med. Sch., 1929-32; asst. physician Thorndike Meml. Lab., 1932; asst. prof. medicine U. Wis. Med. Sch., 1932-37, asso. prof., 1937-44, prof., 1944-71, emeritus, 1971-77, chmn. dept. medicine 1945-64; asso. physician Univ. Hosps., 1937-44, physician, from 1944; cons. research, edn. VA Hosp., Madison, Wis., 1971-77. Fellow A.C.P.; mem. A.M.A., Internat. Soc. Hematology, Am. Soc. Clin. Investigation, Central Soc. Clin. Research, Soc. Exptl. Biology and Medicine, Assn. Am. Physicians, Sigma Xi, Alpha Omega Alpha, Phi Kappa, Alpha Kappa Kappa, Sigma Sigma. Roman Catholic. K.C. Clubs: Madison, Blackhawk. Contbr. many articles to sci. publs. Home: Madison, Wis. Died Sept. 22, 1977.

MEYER, SCHUYLER MERRITT, lawyer; b. N.Y.C., Oct. 27, 1885; s. Charles B. and Virginia H. (Hoyt) M.; A.B., Yale, 1907; LL.B., N.Y.U., 1910; m. Helen Martin, Sept. 19, 1914. Admitted to N.Y. State bar, 1910, since practiced in N.Y.C.; mem. firm Seward & Kissel, (and predecessor), 1917—. Chairman New York State Joint Legislative Com. to Investigate Affairs City N.Y., 1920-21. Mem. N.Y. State Assembly, 1914-17, 21, N.Y. State Senate, 1920-21. Trustee Edwin Gould Services for Children. Edwin Guild; board dirs. Sheltering Arms Childrens Service, N.Y.C. Mem. Am. Bar Assn., Assn. Bar City N.Y. Clubs: Yale, Down Town Assn. (N.Y.C.). Home: Sharon, Conn. *

MEYERS, MILTON KAYTON (MI'ERZ), neurologist, psychiatrist; b. 1882; s. Sigmund and Rebecca (Kayton) M.; M.D., U. of Pa., 1902; m. Ethel K. Altshuler, 1914. Practiced in Phila. since shortly after graduation from U. of Pa. Mem. A.M.A., Med. Soc. State of Pa., Phila. Neurol. Soc., Pathol. Soc. of Phila. No. Med. Soc. of Phila., Anthropol. Society, Benjamin Franklin Institute Am. (asso.). Phila. psychiat. socs. Emeritus vis. psychiatrist Phila. Psychiatric Hosp., cons. neurologist Albert Einstein Med. Center; clinic asst. psychiatric clinic for children and psychiat. clinic Jefferson Med. Coll., neuropsychiatrist Am. Oncologic Hosp. Translator and editor of Falta's Endocrine Diseases, Including Their Treatment (with E. A. Strecker) H. Curschmann's Clinical Neurology; editor of Lang's German-English Medical Dict. Contbr. chpt. on nervous diseases in Lowenberg's Diagnostic Methods of Internal Med. *

MEYLAN, PAUL JULIEN, illustrator; b. Brassus, Canton of Vaud, Switzerland, May 17, 1882; s. Louis Julien and Jenny Henriette (Capt) M.; studied art at Nat. Acad. Design, 1896-99; special studies, Harvard, 1902-03; m. New York, Adrienne Boos. of Nancy, France, May 17, 1906; 1 dau., Lorraine Desirée. Artist on staff New York Evening World, 1900, Boston Herald, 1900-03; illustrator of "Scattergood Baines" stories by Clarence Budington Kelland; went to England to make series of drawings for Harper's Mag., 1921. Mem. Soc. of Illustrators, Artists' Aid Soc., Authors' League America. Winner of nat. amateur championship in fencing, 1913. Episcopalian. Clubs: Fencers, Players. Home: Redding, Conn. *

MEZ, JOHN, author, lecturer; b. Freiburg in Baden, Germany, Feb. 15, 1886; s. Oscar and Ida (Wild) M.; ed. univs. of Leipzig, Heidelberg and Munich; Ph.D., Heidelberg, 1907; unmarried. Came to U.S., 1913; pres. Central Com. International Federation of Students "Corda Fratres." Mem. Am. Sociol. Soc. Author: Der Internationale Postscheck-Verkehr (Tiibingen, Germany), 1910; also various pamphlets on international polity and peace movements. Has traveled and lectured extensively in interests of the peace movement. Office: Am. Assn. for International Conciliation. Home: New York, N.Y. *

MICHAELSON, CHARLES DONALD, mining co. exec.; b. Sycamore, Ill., June 28, 1911; s. Charles Henry and Josephine Elisabeth (Bosch) M.; E.M., Colo. Sch. Mines, 1932; m. Barbara Hemenway, Nov. 29, 1937 (dec.); m. 2d, A. Olive Gray, Nov. 21, 1967; children—Sean D., Carol Ann. Tin mines adminstrn. Patino Mines & Enterprises, 1934-41; mining and product processing U.S. Gypsum Co., 1941-44; labor and govt. relations Nicaro Nickel Co., Cuba, 1944-48; gen. mgr., v.p., dir. Braden Copper Co., Chile, 1948-55; gen. mgr. Western mining div. Kennecott Copper Corp., 1955-61, v.p., 1961-66, v.p. mining, 1966-69, pres. metal mining div., from 1969; dir., from 1964. Mem. Am. Inst. Mining, Metall. and Petroleum Engrs., Tau Beta Pi. Clubs: Mining (N.Y.C.); Alto (Salt Lake City); Union (Santiago, Chile); Pinnacle (N.Y.C.). Home: New York, N.Y. Died Feb. 9, 1977.

MICHALEK, BOHUMIL, concert violinist; b. Chicago, Mar. 11, 1885; s. James and Theresa Marie (Zelliuger) M.; pupil and protégé of Jan Van Oordt, in U.S.; studied in Brussels, Belgium, Prague, Bohemia; pupil and asst. Prof. Otakar Sevcik; unmarried. Apptd. concert master New Bohemian Opera, Prague, Apr., 1907; declined professorship in Prague Conservatory of Music, and other similar offers in Russia, Germany, France and Switzerland. Returned to U.S. fall of 1908 and founded the Michalek Master School for Violinists (dir.). Contbr. to mus. jours. Home: Chicago. *

MICHEL, CLARENCE WILLIAM (ME' SHEL), railroad exec.; b. N.Y.C., Sept. 21, 1883; s. Joseph Louis and Mary (Phleger) M.; student pub. schs., N.Y., N.J.; also grad. studies bus. adminstrn. and r.r. accounting; m. Matilda Elsie Moore, Oct. 3, 1908; 1 son, Clifford W. Asst. sec. St.L.-S.F. R.R., 1916-21, v.p., asst. to chmn., 1921, dir., 1921-30, exec. rep. bankruptcy trustees, 1932-46, v.p. new co. since 1947; dir. J. F. Tapley Co. Long Island City. Club: Manhasset Bay Yacht (Port Washington, N.Y.). Home: Bellerose, L.I., N.Y. *

MICHELMAN, HERBERT, pub. co. exec.; b. Harrisburg, Pa., Mar. 26, 1913; s. David I. and Sara (Robbin) M.; B.A., Bklyn. Coll., 1934; m. Blanche Krainin, May 14, 1941; children—Faith Michelman Lennon, Frances. With Gimbel Bros. Co., N.Y.C., 1929-41, book buyer, 1938-41; asst. to pres. World Pub. Co., Cleve., 1941-42; with Crown Pubs. Inc., N.Y.C., 1943-79, v.p., editor-in-chief, 1952-79; pub. Herbert Michelman Books, N.Y.C., 1979-80; lectr. adult edn. City Coll. N.Y. Editor, Laurelton (N.Y.) Civic News. Served with U.S. Army, 1943-46. Jewish. Co-author: Body Control, 1964; International Guide to Physical Fitness, 1973. Home: New York, N.Y. Died Nov. 11, 1980.

MICHTOM, BENJAMIN FRANKLIN, mfg. co. exec.; Bklyn., July 13, 1901; s. Morris and Rose (Katz) M., B.S., U. Pa., 1921; m. Hadassah Feil, June 14, 1925; children—William A., Mark Feil. With Ideal Toy Corp., Holis, 1923-80, exec. v.p., chmn. bd., 1938-78, chmn. emeritus, 1978-80; exec. v.p., chmn. Ideal Plastics Corp., Hollis, 1939-80; v.p., dir. U.S.-Israel Plastics Corp., 1952-67; chmn. Kamiro Trucking Co., Ideal Wares, Inc.; dir. Ideal Toy Corp. (Can.), Ideal Toy Corp. (Japan), Ideal Toy Corp. S.A. (France), Ideal Toy Corp. (Gt. Brit.). Trustee Phi Sigma Delta Found.; bd. dirs. Am. ORT Fedn., Am. Jewish Com.; fellow Brandeis U. Mem. Am. Arbitration Assn. (arbitrator, panelist), Toy Mfrs. U.S. (dir., treas.), Benjamin Franklin Soc. (U. Pa.), Zeta Beta Tau. Clubs: Metropolis Country, Fifty Avenue, Sales Executives, Advertising (N.Y.C.). Home: Harrison, N.Y. Died Nov. 10, 1980.

MIDDLETON, RODERICK OSGOOD, naval officer; b. Pomona Park, Fla., Jan. 23, 1919; s. William Spencer and Lizzie (Williams) M.; B.S., U.S. Naval Acad., 1941; M.S., Harvard, 1946; m. Ethel Adele Bellows, Sept. 23, 1939; children—Rodney Anne (Mrs. William H. Kuenstler), Roderick Osgood (dec.), Stephanie Adele (Mrs. William G. Kussmaul III). Commd. ensign U.S. Navy, 1941, advanced through grades to rear adm., 1967; asst. navigator, turret officer U.S.S. Washington, 1941-43; precommissioning detail and turret officer U.S.S. Alaska, 1944-45; gunnery officer U.S.S. Little Rock, 1946-48; Terrier anti-aircraft missile project officer Bur. Ordnance, 1949-52; asst. ordnance officer, then ordnance officer Staff Comdr. Service Squadron 3, 1952-54; comdg. officer U.S.S. Benham, 1954-56; dep. chief Navy Office, Army Ballistic Missile Agy., 1956; head missile br. Spl. Projects Office, Navy Dept., 1957-61; comdr. Destroyer Div. 142, 1961-62; chief staff Carrier Div. 14, 1962-63; comdg. officer U.S.S. Observation Island, 1963-64, U.S.S. Little Rock, 1964-65; Apollo mission dir. Office Manned Space Flight, NASA, 1965-67; Apollo program mgr. John F. Kennedy Space Center, Fla., 1967-69; comdr. Cruiser Destroyer Flotilla 12, 1969-70; mil. asst. to dep. dir. research and engring. (S and SS), Office Sec. Def., Washington, 1970-72; asst. ocean systems mgr. Lockheed Missiles and Space Co., Sunnyvale, Calif., 1973-78. Decorated Legion of Merit with 3 oak leaf clusters Navy Commendation medal with combat V, 2 NASA Exceptional Service medals. Conglist. Home: Los Altos, Calif. Died Jan. 10, 1978.

MIDDLETON, TROY HOUSTON, educator; b. Miss., Oct. 12, 1889; s. John Houston and Kathryne (Thompson) M.; B.S., Miss. State U., 1909; grad. Inf. Sch., 1922; honor grad., Command and Gen. Staff Sch., 1924; grad. Army War Coll., 1929; D.C.L., U. South, 1955; LL.D., Tulane, 1957, La. State U., 1962; m. Jerusha Collins, Jan. 6, 1915; children—Lt. Col. Troy Houston, Bernice Collins (Mrs. Ashton Stewart). Comm. 2d lt., United States Army, 1912, and advanced through the grades to lt. general; now retired; dean of adminstrn. La. State University, 1937-39, comptroller, 1939-51, president, 1951-62, president emeritus, 1962-76; on active duty United States Army, January 20, 1942, and advanced through the grades to lieutenant general June 5, 1945; commanding general 45th Inf. Div. during invasion of Sicily and Italy; comd. VIII Corps throughout operations in France, Belgium, Luxembourg and Germany, 1944-45. Relieved active duty August 1945. Decorated D.S.M. with oak leaf cluster, Silver Star; Order of Black Star (France); Victory Medal with 5 battle stars, Mexican Campaign, Army of Occupation in Germany medals, Legion of Merit with oak leaf cluster, Bronze Star medal, Legion of Honor, Croix de Guerre with Palm (France), E.T.O. ribbon with seven battle stars and bronze arrow, Comdr. Order of St. Maurice and Lazarus (Italy), Grand Officer Order of Leopold II with Palm (Belgium), Croix de Guerre, 1940, with Palm (Belgium), Am. Theater Medal, World War II Medal. Member Phi Kappa Phi, Kappa Alpha, Omicron Delta Kappa. Episcopalian. Clubs: Army and Navy Country (Washington, D.C.); Rotary (Baton Rouge, La.), Baton Rouge Country. Mem. bd. visitors U.S. Mil. Acad., 1951-53. Home: Baton Rouge, La. Died Oct. 9, 1976; buried National Cemetery, Baton Rouge.

MIEROW, CHARLES CHRISTOPHER (ME'E-RO), author, educator; b. New York, N.Y., June 16, 1883; s. Charles Bernhard William and Katherine Marie (Cramer) M.; A.B., Princeton, 1905, Latin salutatorian, A.M., 1906, Ph.D., 1908; LL.D., Univ. of Colo., 1927; L.H.D., U. of Denver, 1933; student at Am. School of Classical Studies in Rome, 1933-34; Ed.D., Colorado Coll., Colorado Springs, 1934; m. Bernardine Susan Beecher, June 12, 1911 (died June 28, 1952); children—Barbara (deceased), Dorothy. Instructor in Latin, Phillips Academy, Andover, Massachusetts, 1908-09; instructor classics, Princeton, 1909-16; professor classical language and literature, Colo. Coll., 1916-34, research prof., 1934-36, in absentia, dean and acting pres., 1925-34, prof. biography, Carleton Coll., since 1934, on Ambrose White Vernon Foundation since 1945; visiting prof. of Latin, summers, Syracuse U., 1939, Univ. of N.C., 1940, 41, 42; also visiting prof. biography, University of Denver, 1912. Member American Philol. Association, Classical Association Middle West and South (pres. 1936-37), Am. Classical League, Archaeol. Inst. America (lecturer, 1935-37), Cliosophic Soc., Mediaeval Acad. America, British Classical Assn., Classical Society of American Academy in Rome, Rice County Hist. Assn., Phi Beta Kappa, Kappa Sigma, Delta Epsilon, Eta Sigma Phi. President Association Colleges of Congregational and Christian Affiliation, 1929-30. Congregationalist; ordained to the Christian ministry of teaching, 1936 (St. Paul Assn. Congl. Chs.). Republican. Mason (32 degree, K.T.; Grand Master Grand Council, Minn., 1947-48). Club: Lions (past pres.). Author several books and translator of others; latest translation: The Deeds of Frederick Barbarossa, by Otto of Freising, 1953. Home: Northfield, Minn. *

MIERS, EARL SCHENCK, author; b. Bklyn., May 27, 1910; s. William Schenck and Emma (Swannell) M.; Litt.B., Rutgers U., 1933, M.A., 1943, Litt.D., 1963; L.H.D., Lincoln Coll., 1962; m. Agnes Starling Wyckoff, Aug. 25, 1934; children—David, Meredith, William. Asso. editor Univ. Publs., Rutgers U., 1935-42; editor Westminster Press, Phila., 1942-44; dir. Rutgers U. Press, 1944-49, editor Alfred A. Knopf, Inc., 1949-51, World Pub. Co. 1951-54. Mem. Nat. Soc. Crippled Children and Adults. Mem. N.J. Hist. Commn., Phi Beta Kappa. Clubs: Cosmos (Washington); University (N.Y.C.). Author: (with Ernest E. McMahon) The Chronicles of Colonel Henry, 1936; Backfield Feud, 1936; Composing Sticks and Mortar Boards, 1941; Career Coach, 1941; Bookmaking and Kindred Amenities, 1942; Big Ben, 1942; Valley in Arms, 1943; Grass Roots, 1944; The Ivy Years, 1945; (with Richard A. Brown) Gettysburg, 1948. The General Who Marched to Hell, 1950; The Christmas Card Murders (pseud. David Wm. Meredith), 1950; Monkey Shines, 1952; Touchdown Trouble, 1953; The Kid Who Beat the Dodgers, 1954; The Rainbow Book of American History, 1955; Web of Victory, 1955; The Story of Thomas Jefferson, 1955; (with Paul M. Angle) The Living Lincoln, 1955; Robert E. Lee, 1956; Ball of Fire, 1956; The American Story, 1956; Rebel's Roost, 1956; The Guns of Vicksburg, 1957; Mark Twain on The Mississippi, 1957; Blood of Freedom, 1958; Why Did This Have to Happen?, 1958; When Washington Won at Yorktown, 1958; The Great Rebellion, 1958; America and Its Presidents, 1959; Billy Yank and Johnny Reb, 1959; The Storybook of Science, 1959; When Grant Met Lee at Appomattox, 1960; (with Paul M. Angle) Tragic Years 1860-1865, 1960; The American Civil War, 1961; Our Fifty States, 1961; With Lincoln in the White House, 1963; Yankee Doodle Dandy, 1963; Golden Book of American History, 1963; Wild and Woolly West, 1964; The Story of John F. Kennedy, 1964; Where the Raritan Flows, 1964; New Jersey and the Civil War, 1964; Abraham Lincoln in Peace and War, 1964; Freedom, 1965; Men of Valor, 1965; Where Liberty Stands Guard, 1966; The Trouble Bush, 1966; Baseball, 1967; Football, 1967; That Lincoln Boy, 1968; The Bill of Rights, 1968; The Magnificent Mutineers, 1968; Basketball, 1969; The Night We Stopped the Trolley, 1969; Emancipation, 1969; Black Americans, 1969; A Blazing Star, 1970; The Golden History of the United States, 1970; That Jefferson Boy, 1970; Crossroads of Freedom, 1971; The Last Campaign, 1972; Down in Jersey, 1973. Editor: When the World Ended, 1957; A Rebel War Clerk's Diary, 1958; Lincoln Day by Day, 1960; Ride to War, 1961. Home: Edison, N.J. Died Nov. 17, 1972; buried Piscataway, N.J.

MIESSNER, BENJAMIN FRANKLIN, radio engr.; b. Huntingburg, Ind., July 27, 1890; s. Charles and Mary (Reutopohler) M.; grad. U.S. Navy Elec. Sch., Bklyn., 1909; student elec. engring., Purdue U., 1913-16; m. Eleanor-Marguerite Schulz, June 13, 1916; children—Jane Eleanor, Mary Elizabeth. Wireless operator U.S. Navy, 1909-11; charge radio torpedo control invention and devel. with John Hays Hammond, Jr. and Dr. Fritz Lowenstein, 1911-13; expert radio aide for aviation U.S. Navy, in charge devel. radio for aircraft, Pensacola, Fla., 1916-18; radio engr. with Emil J. Simon, N.Y.C., charge aircraft radio and transoceanic receiver devel., 1918-20; dir. acoustical research lab. Brunswick, Balke, Collender Co., Chgo., 1921-22; cons. engr. Wired Radio, Inc., 1922-25; pres. Miessner Radio Corp., 1925; chief engr. Garod Corp., Belleville, N.J., 1926-27; pres. Miessner Inventions, Inc.; pioneer research and invention electronic musical instruments; pioneer aircraft radio, elec. phonography, radio dynamics, elec. radio receivers, directional microphones for aircraft or submarine location. Mem. ad. hoc patent system reform panel U.S. Dept. Commerce, 1963. Recipient De Forest Audion gold medal for inventive achievement in radio and electronics, 1963; Distinguished Service award Boys Clubs Am., 1964. Gellow Fellow Club Am. I.R.E., Acoustical Soc. Am.; mem. Am. Phys. Soc., A.A.A.S., Vet. Wireless Operators Assn., Benjamin Franklins Chgo., Patent Equity Assn. (pres.), Miami Mus. Sci. and Natural History (life; past trustee), Acad. Applied Sci. (bd. govs.), Sigma Pi. Club: Purdue (Miami). Author: Radio Dynamics, 1916; Hum in All-Electric Radio Receivers, 1929; On the Early History of Radio Guidance, 1964. Contbr. papers to sci. publs.; granted approx. 200 patents U.S. and fgn. countries; inventor Wurlitzer organ, electronic piano. Home: Morristown, N.J. Died Mar. 25, 1976.

MILES, ARTHUR PARKER, educator; b. Princeton, Ill., Feb. 26, 1911; s. Edward and Myrtle (Wilson) M.; A.B., U. Ill., 1933; A.M., U. Chgo., 1936, Ph.D., 1940; m. Julia Louise Beatty, Feb. 23, 1935; children—Nancy Ann (Mrs. Peter W. Townsend), Sarah (Mrs. John Gerken), James. Case aide, later county adminstr. Ill. Emergency Relief Commn., 1933-36; resident Hull House, Chgo., 1936-37; instr. U. Mo., 1937-38, La. State U., 1938-39; asst. prof. Tulane U., 1940-42; regional social statistician Social Security Bd., Denver, 1942-44; lectr. social work U. Wis., 1944-45, asso. prof., 1945-47, chmn. dept., 1946-52, dir. Sch. Social Work, 1952-57, prof., 1947-80, sec. faculty div. social studies, 1947-48, research prof. Inst. for Research on Poverty, 1966-67; research cons. div. corrections Wis. Dept. Pub. Welfare, 1961-66. Fellow Am. Sociol. Assn.; mem. Internat. Soc. Criminology, Am. Correctional Assn., Nat. Council Crime and Deliquency, Soc. Study Social Problems, Am. Acad. Polit. and Social Sci., Delta Kappa Epsilon, Alpha Kappa Delta. Unitarian. Author: Federal Aid and Public Assistance in Illinois, 1941; An Introduction to Public Welfare, 1949; American Social Work Theory: A Critique and a Proposal, 1954. Contbr. articles profl. jours. Home: Madison, Wis. Died May 1, 1980.

MILES, EDWIN KENNETH, educator; b. Ashland, Wis., July 7, 1908; s. Kirk Lee and Helen Louise (Metzdorf) M.; B.A., Lawrence Coll., 1929; M.A., Northwestern U., 1930; student U. Munich (Germany), 1930-31, U. Paris (France), 1931; Ph.D., U. Pa., 1933; m. Evelyn Buck Adriance, June 17, 1937; children—David Holmes, Nancy Adriance. Mem. faculty U. Maine, 1933-74, prof. German, 1955-74, head dept. fgn. langs. and classics, 1960-65. Mem. Modern Lang. Assn., Am. Assn. Tchrs. German, Phi Beta Kappa, Phi Kappa Phi. Author: The Strong Verb in Schottel's Ausführliche Arbeit von der Deutschen Hauptsprache, 1933. Home: Orono, Maine. Died June 25, 1976.

MILES, SHERMAN, army officer; b. Washington, Dec. 5, 1882; s. Nelson Appleton and Mary (Sherman) M.; B.S., U.S. Mil. Acad., 1905; student Army War Coll., 1921-22, Command and Gen. Staff Sch., 1926-27; m. Yulee Noble, Nov. 24, 1909; children—Nanita (Mrs. Allen Richmond Wight), Nelson. Commd. 2d lt., U.S. Army, 1905, and advanced through grades to maj. gen., 1942; served successively in Cav., Coast Atry., and F.A., also several times on Gen. Staff and as mil. attaché in Europe, 1912-40. Mem. Ho. of Reps., Mass. Legislature, since 1947. Awarded Distinguished Serv. Medal (U.S.), Legion d'Honneur (France). Clubs: Somerset; Tavern (Boston). Home: Boston. *

MILES, WALDO GARLAND, lawyer; b. Wise, Va., June 12, 1911; s. Wade M. and Mollie S. (White) M.; student U. Richmond, 1930-33; A.B., Washington and Lee U., 1934, LL.B., 1938; m. Christine Junchen, Feb. 9, 1944; children—LaRue Carter (Mrs. Edward A. Hicks), Christine Mollie. Admitted to Va. bar, 1937; asso. firm Carter & Williams, Danville, 1938-41; partner firm Williams, Miles & Williams, Danville, 1941-48, firm Woodward, Miles & Flannagan, and predecessor, Bristol, Va., 1948-73. Pub. mem. Va. Tax Study Commn., 1956-57, 62-63; mem. Bristol Sch. Bd., 1958-63, chmn., 1962; mem. Va. State Bd. Edn., 1963-73, pres., 1970-71; mem. Va. Mental Health Study Commn., 1963-64; vice chmn. Va. Pub. Defender Commn., from 1972. Mem. Va. exec. com. Dem. Central Com., 1960-68. Pres. Bristol Mental Health Clinic, 1957; pres. Bristol Meml. Hosp., 1958-60, past dir., mem. exec. com. Bd. dirs. Bristol chpt. A.R.C. 1954-60; bd. visitors Sullins Coll., 1966-73; bd. Va. Poly. Inst., 1966-70; trustee Va. Council on Health and Med. Care, 1970-73. Served to lt. comdr. USNR, 1942-45. Mem. Va. C. of C. (dir. 1972-73), Bristol C. of C. (dir. 1952-54, 56-58, 68-73, exec. com. 1960-73), Am., Bristol (past pres.) bar assns., Va. State Bar Assn. (pres. 1962-63), Omicron Delta Kappa, Pi Delta Epsilon, Phi Delta Phi, Phi Gamma Delta. Methodist. Clubs: Country (Bristol); Commonwealth, Downtown (Richmond, Va.). Home: Bristol, Va. Died Sept. 18, 1973.

MILES, WALTER RICHARD, psychologist; b. Silverleaf, N.D., March 29, 1885; s. Thomas Elwood and Sarah Caroline (White) M.; B.S., Pacific Coll., Newberg, Oreg., 1906; A.B., Earlham Coll., 1908, ScD. (hon.), 1952; M.A., Iowa State U., 1910, Ph.D., 1913; M.A., hon., Yale U., 1931; m. Elizabeth M. Kirk, Sept. 1, 1908 (died July 2, 1925); children—Thomas Kirk, Caretta (Mrs. F. L. Capers), Marjorie (Mrs. R. D. McClelland); married 2d, Dr. Catharine M. Cox, Sept. 9, 1927; children—Anna (Mrs. E. O. Jones III), Elwood Morris (dec.). Instr. psychology and in education, Penn College, Oskaloosa, Iowa, 1908-10: asst. and fellow in psychology. State U. of Iowa, 1911-12; asso. prof. psychology, Wesleyan U., Conn., 1913-14; psychologist at Nutrition Lab. Boston. Carnegie Instn. of Washington, D.C., 1914-22; prof. experimental psychology, Stanford U., 1922-32; prof. psychology, Yale U., 1931-53, emeritus, 1953-78; prof. psychology Istanbul U., 1954-57: sci. dir. USN Med. Research Lab.. USN Submarine Base, Gorton, Connecticut, 1957-65; fellow Jonathan Edwards College, Yale, 1935-53; attending psychologist, New Haven Hosp. and

Dispensary, 1932-54. Mem. U.S. dels. to internat. confs. Howard Crosby Warren Medal (exptl. psychology), 1949, gold medal Am. Psychol. Found., 1962. Mem. Am. Philos. Soc., Am. Psychol. Assn., Nat. Acad. Scis., Optical Soc. Am., and others, past officer several. Democrat. Mem. Society of Friends. Club: Cosmos (Washington). Author several works in psychology. Editor: Psychological Studies of Human Variability. Editor, contbr.; Istanbul Studies in Experimental Psychology. Home: Gales Ferry, Conn. Died 1978.

MILGRAM, LESTER, food co. exec.; b. Kansas City Mo., 1917; grad. U. Mo., 1939; m. Ann Louise Kaplan, 1949; children—Nancy Sue, Betsy Ann, Nat Lester, Sally Anne. Chmn. bd. Milgram Food Stores, Inc., Kansas City; dir. United Mo. Bank of Kansas City. N.A., Kansas City Royals Baseball Club, Safety Fed. Savs. & Loan Assn. Home: Kansas City, Mo. Died June 19, 1976.

MILHOUS, KATHERINE, author, artist; b. Phila., Nov. 27, 1894; d. Oscar Thomas and Katie Arey Daly (McGuckin) Milhous; student Phila. Coll. Art, Pa. Acad. Fine Arts; Cresson traveling scholarship in sculpture. Staff artist Phila. Record, 1925-29; painted abroad and at home touring Pa. in a caravan; studied Pa. Dutch life which resulted in books and series of posters exhibited at N.Y. World's Fair; sent by Scribners on plane trip with Alice Dalgliesh around South Am. to illustrate her books. Recipient citation Drexel Inst. Tech., 1967. Mem. Am. Inst. Graphic Arts, Independence Hall Assn., Soc. Archtl. Historians, United World Federalists, Authors League Am., Booksellers' Assn. Phila. (hon.). Author and illustrator: Lovina, 1940; Herodia The Lovely Puppet, 1942; Corporal Keeperupper, 1943; The First Christmas Crib, 1944; Snow Over Bethlehem, 1945; The Egg Tree (Caldecott medal), 1950; Patrick and the Golden Slippers, 1951; Appolonia's Valentine, 1954; With Bells On, 1955; Through These Arches, The Story of Independence Hall, 1964. Home: Philadelphia, Pa. Died Dec. 5, 1977.

MILKS, HAROLD KEITH, fgn. corr.; b. South Milford, Ind., June 28, 1908; s. Len H. and Flossie Glen (Smith) M.; student Lombard Coll., 1927-28; m. Evelyne Elam, Oct. 10, 1929. With AP, 1934-79, beginning in Chgo. bur., successively staff Columbus (Ohio) bur., N.Y.C. bur., corr. in Buenos Aires, chief of bur., Bogota, corr., Nanking, London, regional chief of bur., New Delhi, chief of bur., Moscow, 1956-59, chief of Caribbean services, hdqrs., Havana, 1959-61, chief Spain and Portugal bur. at Madrid, 1961-67, Latin Am. editor Ariz. Republic, Phoenix, 1967-71, 78-79, mng. editor, 1971-78. Served as maj. USAAF, 1942-45. Mem. Fgn. Corr. Assn. (past pres. New Delhi), Fgn. Press. Assn. Spain (pres. 1965-66), Sigma Delta Chi. Clubs: Army-Navy (Washington); Internat. Press (1st pres.) (Madrid); Phoenix Press, Phoenix Country, Arizona (Phoenix). Home: Phoenix, Ariz. Died Dec. 12, 1979.

MILL, EDWARD WILLIAM, educator, diplomat; b. Mason City, Ill., June 14, 1916; s. Edward Jesse and Christine (Christensen) M.; B.A., U. Wis., 1940; M.A., U. Mich., 1941; M.A. Princeton, 1953, Ph.D., 1954; m. Virginia D. Nowotny, Dec. 20, 1952. With OSS, 1943-45; with Dept. State, 1945-48, including dir. Philippine Fgn. Affairs Tng. Program; fgn. service res. officer, 1948-51; chief polit. sect. Am. embassy, Manila, P.I., 1948-49; del. Fgn. Service Conf., New Delhi, India, 1949; prin. officer and Am. consul, Surabava, Indonesia, 1950-51; lectr. polit. sci. U. Calif., Berkeley, 1952; vis. Ford Found. fellow, Princeton, 1953-54, vis. prof. polit. sci. U. Philippines, 1953-54; prof. polit. sci., chmn. div. social scis., asst. to pres. Rockford Coll., 1955-59; prof. polit. sci., founder and chmn. dept. L.I. U., Bklyn., 1959-62; prof., chmn. Chevalier program in diplomacy and world affairs Occidental Coll., Los Angeles, 1962-77. Decorated Order Sikatuna (Philippines). Mem. Am. Acad. Polit. Sci., -AAUP, Assn. for Asian Studies. Clubs: Cosmos (Washington); Princeton (N.Y.C.); Internat. Los Angeles). Author: The Conduct of Philippine Foreign Relations, 1954; (with William Ebenstein) American Government in the Twentieth Century, 1968, 2d edit., 1971, 3d edit., 1973; Liberty and Law, 1971; Politics and Progress, 1971. Contbr. articles to editorial dept. Los Angeles Times, 1967-71, also to profl. publs. Home: Los Angeles, Calif. Died July 13, 1977.

MILLAR, DONALD GORDON, metal cutting tools exec.; b. Westwood, N.J., Aug. 31, 1897; s. William Mitchell and Janet (Brown); M.; B.A., Brown U., 1919, LL.D., 1959; m. Brenda Howard, Sept. 11, 1923 (dec.); children—Brenda, Nancy; m. 2d. Anne Holliss Howard, Jan. 1963. With Am. Internat. Corp., 1920-36, sec., v.p., dir., 1926-36; reorganized Greenfield Tap and Die Corp., pres., 1937-58, merged co. with United Drill & Tool Corp. as United-Greenfield Corp., chmn, exec. com., 1958-68; ret. Mem. WPB adv. com. on metal cutting tools, 1941-45; industry adv. com. metal cutting tools NPA; chmn. Metal Cutting Tool Inst., 1949-51; pres. Western Mass. Employers, 1951-52. Trustee Brown U., 1944-69, vice chancellor, 1964-68; bd. dirs. Greenfield YMCA, 1953-56. Served overseas with Battery C, 103 F.A., 26th Div., 1917-19. Mem. Delta Upsilon. Club: University. Home: Madison, Conn. Died Apr. 30, 1976.

MILLAR, MOORHOUSE IGNATIUS XAVIER, educator; b. Mobile, Ala., Mar. 7, 1886; s. Stocks and Margaret (Richards) M.; student Saint Gregoire de Tours, France, 1895-99, Real Gymnasium Hildesheim, Germany, 1899-1901, Loyola Coll., 1901-03; A.B., Woodstock Coll., 1911, M.A., 1920; Ph.D., Gregorian, Rome, 1931. Entered Jesuit order, 1903; teacher Greek, German, math. Holy Cross, 1911-12, history Canisius Coll., 1912-16, Georgetown U., 1922-23, constl. law Fordham U. Law Sch., 1923-27, originated, organized dept. polit. philosophy, social scis. grad. sch., chmn. polit, philosophy, constl. history, theory since 1923. Mem. Am. Polit. Assn., Acad. Polit. Sci., Am. Acad. Polit., Social Scis., Am. Hist. Soc., Am. Soc. Internat. Law. Author: Unpopular Essays, 1928; The State and the Church, 1922 (with John A. Ryan). Asso. editor: Thought, 1926-50. Address: N.Y. City. *

MILLARD, WILLIAM JAMES (MIL'ARD), judge; b. Bismarck, Mo., Jan. 30, 1883; s. Benjamin and Mary Elizabeth (Toler) M.; LL.B., Georgetown U., 1910, LL.D., 1935; LL.D., Coll. of Puget Sound, Tacoma, 1934; m. Bertha G. Neuhauser, 1908; children—Gertrude (Mrs. Robert Chisholm), William J. Millard, Alice Ruth, Jean, Admitted to the bar, 1910; apptd. to Supreme Court of Wash., 1928, elected, 1930, re-elected 1936, 1942; chief justice, 1935-37. Mem. Phi Delta Phi. Republican. Mason. Club: Rainier (Seattle). Home: Olympia, Wash. *

MILLER, ALBERT HOWARD, paper mfg. co. exec.; b. Neenah, Wis.; s. Roy F. and Jennie (Iverson) M.; student Lawrence Coll., 1923-24, Columbia, 1928-29; m. Mildred Wallace Wilson, June 18, 1931; 1 dau., Patricia Ann (Mrs. Patricia Reed). Successively mfg. trainee, salesman, Eastern sales mgr. specialty paper div. Kimberly-Clark Corp., Neenah, 1925-38; gen. sales mgr. J.P. Lewis Co., N.Y.C., 1938-43; pres., dir. Lewis-Brownville Sales, Inc., N.Y.C., 1943-61; pres., chief exec. officer, Manning Paper Co. div. Hammermill Paper Co., Troy, N.Y., 1961-72; dir. Internat. Purchasing Co., Ayer, Mass., 1961-72, pres., 1963-72; mem. adv. bd. Troy office State Bank Albany (N.Y.). Bd. dirs. United Community Services Mohawk-Hudson Area, Inc., Albany Boys' Club, Albany, N.Y. Trustee Albany Med. Coll. Mem. Newcomen Soc., Am. Paper Inst. (bd. dir. specialty paper and bd. affiliates div. 1965-72). Episcopalian. Clubs: University (Albany); Schuyler Meadows (Loudonville). Home: Jamesburg, N.J. Died July 24, 1979.

MILLER, ALBERT VAN COURT, newspaper exec.; b. New Orleans, Nov. 20, 1892; s. Daniel Van Court and Belle Rose M.; student, Hoffman Prep. Sch., Chgo., m. Hermine A. Abbe, Mar. 29, 1923; children—Albert Van Court, Jacqueline Orth. Accountant, statistician, traveling auditor Ill. Central Railroad, 1908-17; asst. sec., auditor Morse Dry Dock Repair Co:, Bklyn., 1917-27; mng. dir., treas, J. C. Haartz Co., New Haven, 1928-30; special tax and management consultant Courtland Palmer, law firm, N.Y.C., 1931; treas., bd. dirs. N.Y. Herald Tribune, 1932-55, treas., sec., 1955-56, v.p., treas., 1956-60, dir. press Wireless, Inc., N.Y.C. Mem. Nat. Assn. Cost Accountants, Soc. Advancement of Management. Republican. Methodist. Mason. Home: Garden City, N.Y. Died Oct. 30, 1976.

MILLER, BERTHA EVERETT MAHONY, editor, publisher; b. Rockport, Mass., Mar. 13, 1882; d. Daniel and Mary Lane (Everett) Mahoney; grad. secretarial course, Simmons Coll., 1903; m. William D. Miller. Sept. 7, 1932. Organized bookshop for boys and girls for Women's Ednl. and Indsl. Union Boston, 1916, editor Horn Book mag., pub. by union, 1924-36; purchased mag. from union, 1936; editor Horn Book mag., 1924-50; chmn. Horn Book, Inc., 1963—. Recipient Constance Lindsay Skinner award Simmons Coll., 1955, citation children's services div. A.L.A., 1959; Regina award Catholic Library Association, 1967. Mem. Am., Mass. library assn., New Eng. Round Table Children's Librarians, Am. Assn. UN, Mass., Fla. Audubon socs., Am. Civil Liberties Union, Mass. Hor. Soc. Conglist. (auxiliary). Clubs: College (Boston); Ashburnham Olio Woman's Compiler; (with Elinor Whitney) Realms of Good in Children's Books, 1929, Five Years of Children's Books, 1936; with (Louise P. Latimer and Beulah Folmsbee (Illustrators of Children's Books, 1947); others. Home: Ashburnham, Mass. *

MILLER, CLEMMY OLIN, science adminstr., chemist; b. Henry County, Ind., Dec. 27, 1896; s. Charles W. and Dora (Johnsonbaugh) M.; A.B., Manchester Coll., 1920, D.Sc. (hon.), 1967; student Johns Hopkins U. 1920-21; Ph.D., U. Chgo., 1926; m. Cora Mae Couser, May 25, 1920 (dec. 1922); 1 dau., Rose Evelyn (Mrs. Walter J. Sullivan); m. 2d, Sara Beahm, July 22, 1926; children—Marianne (Mrs. Richard Speicher), Philip Clement. Instr. chemistry U. Chgo., 1924-28; asst. prof. physiol. chemistry Northwestern U. Med. Sch., 1928-36; v.p., dir. research Lakeside Labs., Milw., 1938-46; pres. Kremers-Urban Co., Milw., 1947-51, chmn. bd., 1951-57; exec. sec. div. chemistry and chem. tech. Nat. Acad. Scis.-NRC, 1957-61; exec. sec. predoctoral research fellowships program Nat. Inst. Gen. Med. Scis., NIH, 1961-63; coordinator adv. coms. FDA, 1963-66, com. mgmt. officer, 1966-70, coordinator fgn. visitors program, 1970-76. Recipient Alumni award Manchester Coll., 1961; Honor award Wash. chpt. Am. Inst. Chemists, 1965. Mem. Am. Pharm. Mfrs. Assn., Am. Inter-Profl. Inst. (pres. 1951, dir. 1953-54), Am. Chem. Soc. (chmn. Milw. 1957), Am. Inst. Chemists (pres. Washington 1960-62), A.A.A.S., Washington Acad. Scis., Sigma Xi. Clubs: Chemists (Chgo.); Cosmos (Washington); Internat. Torch. Author articles carbohydrates, proteins in liquid ammonia, metalbolism glucuronic acid, vitamin C and gastric mucin. Home: Falls Church, Va. Died Jan. 20, 1978; interred Nat. Meml. Park, Falls Church, Va.

MILLER, DAVID P., arbitrator, assn. exec.; b. Cleve., June 21, 1919; s. Frank O. and Charlotte C. (Pry) M.; student Ohio State U., 1937-38; B.S., U. Ariz., 1948; M.B.A., U. Calif., Berkeley, 1950; m. Hazel J. Proctor, Dec. 12, 1942; children—Lynda S., Kathleen J., Stephen D., Christine E. Engaged as arbitrator with labor and mgmt.; sec. Nat. Acad. Arbitrators, 1962-68, exec. sec., gov., 1968-75, v.p., 1972, pres. 1974-75. Mem. Soc. Profls. in Dispute Resolutions, Indsl. Relations Research Assn. Home: Detroit, Mich. Died Mar. 22, 1975.

MILLER, EDWARD GODFREY, business exec.; b. New Orleans, La., Feb. 3, 1885; s. William P. and Elizabeth (Murray) M.; ed. pub. schools, New Orleans, La.; m. Nora Elzardi, Nov. 20, 1907; children—Elizabeth, (Mrs. Harold W. Knight), Edward Godfrey, John Elizardi, Margaret Patricia. Began business career as mechanic, 1903; sugar engineer, Central Guanica, Puerto Rico, 1905-08, Central Esperanza, 1908-09; superintendent, Central Juncos, Puerto Rico, 1909-13; with Miller Brothers, engineers, Havana, Cuba, 1913-15; vice pres. and gen. mgr. Rio Cauta Sugar Co., Oriente, Cuba, 1915-20; pres. Sugar Plantations Operating Co., Havana, 1920-28; v.p. Cuba Cane Sugar Corp. and Cuban Cane Products Co., 1928-33; pres. Compania Azucarera Atlantica del Golfo, Havana, since 1934; vice pres. Cuban Atlantic Sugar Co., (N.Y. City), Soledad Trading Corp. (N.Y. City), Central Violeta Sugar Co. of S.A. (Havana). Mem. Cuban Inst. for Stabilization of Sugar (mem. exec. com.), Am. Soc. Mech. Engrs. Home: Havana, Cuba. *

MILLER, FRANCIS PICKENS, govt. ofcl.; b. Middlesboro, Ky., June 5, 1895; s. Henry and Flora (McElwee) M.; A.B., Washington and Lee U., 1914; B.A. (Rhodes scholar), Oxford U., 1921, M.A., 1923; student Grad. Inst. Internat. Studies, Geneva, Switzerland, 1927-28; LL.D. (hon.), Centre Coll., 1954, Davis and Elkins Coll., 1964; D.Litt. (hon.), Washington and Jefferson Coll., 1959; m. Helen Day Hill, Aug. 25, 1927; children—Andrew Pickens, Robert Day. Asso. with YMCA, 1914-26; sec. World's Student Christian Fedn., Geneva, Switzerland, 1927-28, chmn., 1928-38; field sec. Fgn. Policy Assn., 1934-35; with Raymond Leslie Buell organized Nat. Policy Com., 1935, sec. 1935-38, vice chmn. 1938-42; organized Pub. Affairs Com., 1936, exec. sec. 1936-37; sec. Southern Policy Com., 1935-40; orgn. dir. Coms. on Fgn. Relations of Council on Fgn. Relations, N.Y., 1938-41. With Henry P. Van Dusen and Herbert Agar organized movement to secure transfer destroyers to Britain in return for bases, 1940; nat. vice chmn. Fight for Freedom Com., 1941; mem. bd. Freedom House, 1958-78; chmn. planning bd. Fgn. Information Service of Coordinator of Information, 1942; cons. Dept. State, 1950-52; mem. Nat. Com. for Effective Congress, 1966-78, Am. Revolution Bicentennial Commn., 1967-69; past mem. bd. visitors Davidson (N. C.) Coll.; bd. visitors Fla. Presbyn. Coll. (Fla.); past mem. bd. colls. and univs.; moderator Presbyn. Synod of Va., 1953-54; mem. Central Com. World Council Chs., 1954-61; pres. Va. Council Chs., 1957-59; exec. sec. Friends of Presbyn. Union. 1954-55; coordinator Va. Com. on Religious Freedom, 1960; mem. bd. So. Regional Council, 1959-76; mem. Va. Ho. of Dels., 1938-41; candidate for gov. Va., 1949, U.S. Senate, 1952; spl. asst. Ednl. and Cultural Affairs, Dept. State, Washington, 1961-65. Served to sgt. maj. 3d Bn. 5th FA 1st div., then 2d and 1st lt. 58th CAC AEF, 1917-19; commd. lt. col. AUS, 1943, col. Gen. Staff Corps., 1945; on staff G-2, SHAEF, 1944-45, and O.D.I. Office Mil. Govt., Germany, 1945-46. Decorated Legion of Merit with cluster (U.S.); Order Brit. Empire; Legion of Honor, Croix de Guerre with palms (France); Order Leopold I with palm; Croix de Guerre with palm (Belgium). Mem. Soc. Cin., Oxford Soc., Phi Gamma Delta, Omicron Delta Kappa. Democrat. Presbyn. Clubs: Century, Yale, Cosmos, City Tavern. Author: (with Helen Hill) The Giant of the Western World, 1930; (with H. R. Niebuhr, W. Pauck) The Church Against the World, 1935; The Blessings of Liberty 1936; Man From the Valley, 1971. Contbr. chpts. to Church and Campus, 1956, Christians are Citizens 1957, What the Christian Hopes for in Society, 1957 We Dissent, 1962. Address: Kitty Hawk, N.C. Died Aug. 3, 1978; buried Lexington, Va.

MILLER, HAROLD WILLIAM, educator; b. Union, S.C., Jan. 4, 1910; s. Samuel Neely and Mathilde (Croxton) M.; B.A., Wofford Coll., 1931; M.A., Duke, 1932, Ph.D., 1935; postgrad. (univ. fellow) Johns Hopkins U., 1937-38. Asst. rare book room Library of Congress, 1936-37; asst. prof. classics, Furman U. Greenville, S.C., 1939-49; mem. faculty Bucknell U., Lewisburg, Pa., 1949-76, prof. classics, chmn. dept., 1951-76, chmn. acad. honors council, 1959-76, dir. honors program, 1962-76. Recipient research awards Carnegie Found., 1944-49; Class 1956 Lectr. award Bucknell U., 1958, Lindback award, 1959. Mem. Am. Philol. Assn., Archaeol. Inst. Am., Classical Assn. Atlantic States, Am. Classical League, Classical Assn. Gt. Brit., Brit. Soc. Hellenic Studies, Soc. Ancient Philosophy, Am. Soc. Papyrologists, Assn. Internationale de Papyrologues, Am. Assn. U. Profs., Phi Beta Kappa, Pi Kappa Phi. Baptist. Spl. research Greek tragedy and comedy, Hippocratic corpus. Contbr. articles to profl. jours. Home: Lewisburg, Pa. *

MILLER, HARRY WILLIAM, ins. exec.; b. Richmond, Va., Aug. 9, 1897; s. Henry William and Anna Bromley (Farley) M.; student pub. schs.; m. Ruth Edith Peterson, Sept. 1, 1920; children—Marilynne (Mrs. John K. Olson), Joanne (Mrs. Wayland R. Bourne). Joined Comml. Union Group, ins., 1914; spl. agt. Central N.Y., Syracuse, 1919, sec., N.Y. City office, 1935, asst. U.S. mgr., 1938, U.S. mgr., pres., from 1948; president Columbia Casualty Co.; gen. U.S. atty. Comml. Union-North British Group; pres. Oil Ins. Assn.; v.p. Underwriters Salvage Company Chgo.; dir. California Insurance Company, American Central Insurance Co., Comml. Union Insurance Co., Columbia Casualty Co., Gen. Adjustment Bur., Inc., Nat. Bd. Fire Underwriters Bldg. Corp., Stock Co. Association, Factory Ins. Association, Sanborn Map Company; president Underwriters Salvage Company of New York, Inc.; trustee Underwriters Lab. Chgo. Mem. Nat. Automobile Underwriters Association (director). Mason (32 deg.). Clubs: Union League (New York City and Chicago); Knollwood Country (White Plains, New York); New York Athletic, Gyro, New York State Ex-Fieldmen's (N.Y.C.), Siwanoy Country (Bronxville, N.Y.); Economic, Pilgrims of U.S. Home: Bronxville, N.Y. Died July 29, 1975.

MILLER, HENRY (VALENTINE), author; b. N.Y.C., Dec. 26, 1891; student Coll. City N.Y., 1909; m. Beatrice Sylvas Wickens, 1917 (div. 1924); 1 dau., Barbara; m. 2d, June Smith, 1924 (div. 1934); m. 3d, Janina Lepska, Dec. 18, 1944 (div. 1952); children—Valentin, Tony; m. 4th, Eve McClure, Dec. 1953 (div. 1962); m. 5th, Hoki Tokuda, Sept. 10, 1967. Various odd jobs in U.S. until 1930; lived in Paris, 1930-39, in Greece, 1939; while living in Paris was mem. editorial staff lit. rev. Booster, also contbg. editor French rev. Volontes; living in U.S., 1940-80; author: Tropic of Cancer, 1934; Topic of Capricorn, 1939; Black Spring, 1936; Max and the White Phagocytes, 1938; Money and How It Gets That Way, 1938; The Cosmological Eye, 1939; The Wisdom of the Heart, 1941; The Colossus of Maroussi, 1941; (with M. Fraenkel) Hamlet: a Philosophic Correspondence, 2 vols., 1939-41; Sunday After the War, 1944; The Air-Conditioned Nightmare Remember to Remember, 1945-47; The Smile at the Foot of the Ladder, 1948; Sexus, 1949; Plexus, 1949; The Books in My Life, 1952; Quiet Days in Clichy, 1956; Nexus, 1957; Bug Sur and the Oranges of Hieronymus Bosch, 1958; Stand Still Like the Hummingbird, 1962, Watercolors, 1962; Lawrence Durrell and Henry Miller: A Private Correspondence, 1963; Greece, 1964; World of Sex, 1965; Plight of the Creative Artist in the United States of America, 2d edit., 1969; My Life and Times, 1971; Books Tangent to Circles, 1963; First Impressions of Greece, 1973; Henry Miller's Book of Friends, 1976; Gliding into the Everglades and Other Essays, 1977; My Bike and Other Friends, 1978, Joey, 1979, many others; exhibited paintings, Los Angeles, 1966. Decorated Legion of Honor (France), 1975. Mem. Nat. Inst. Arts and Letters. Died June 7, 1980.

MILLER, HENRY WILLARD, b. Hagerstown, Md., July 12, 1884; s. Charles Albert and Mary Katherine (Spielman) M.; B.S., Washington and Lee U., 1907. M.E., 1910; m. DeEtta Barbara Stapleton, June 30, 1917; 1 son, Jerome Stapleton. With C. A. Miller Constrn Co., Hagerstown, Md., 1907-09; asst. prof. engring. drawing, U. of Ill., 1909-11, prof. and head of dept., also asst. dean of Coll. Engring., 1912-17; chief engr., Baltimore Copper Smelting & Rolling Co., 1920-21; prof. mechanism and engring. drawing and head of dept., U. of Mich., since 1921. Pres. acad. bd. and organizer Sch. of Mil. Aeronautics, 1917; capt., Ordnance, on design of ry. arty., Washington, D.C., 1917; maj., ordnance chief of ry. afty. unit France, 1918; lt. col. ordnance, chief of heavy arty. sect., 1918-19; asst. to chief of arty. div., Washington, 1919-20; col. Ordnance R.C. Mem. Am. Soc. M.E., Am. Soc. for Engring. Edn., Army Ordnance Assn., Phi Gamma Delta, Phi Beta Kappa, Phi Kappa Phi, Theta Tau, Pi Tau Sigma, Cosmopolitan, Hindustani, Scabbard and Blade. Decorated Chevalier Legion of Honor (France); Order of the Purple Heart. Republican. Presbyterian. Clubs: University (Ann Arbor); University (Chicago). Author: Descriptive Geometry, 1911; Mechanical Drafting, 1912; Railway Artillery (2 vols.), 1921; American Seacoast Artillery, 1923, Mobile Artillery, 1926; The Paris Gun, 1930. Address: Ann Arbor, Mich. *

MILLER, J(OHN) WESLEY, dir. philanthropies; b. Stouffville, Ont., Can., Jan. 13, 1875; s. Noah E. and Susanna Catherine (Pipher) M.; pub. schs., Can. and Mich.; D.D., Ia. Wesleyan Coll, Mt Pleasant, 1924; LL.D., Geneva Coll., Beaver Falls, Pa., 1941; m. Ann Marie McKague, Sept. 2, 1899; children—Edna Faye (Mrs. Earl Cantrell), John Wesley. Ordained ministry M.E. Ch., 1905; successively pastor Hoyteville, Mich., Long Valley, Ida., Ontario, Ore., Joseph, Ore., Nampa, Ida., American Falls, Ida., until 1917; field sec. Gooding (Ida.) Coll., 1917-22; staff rep. dept. finance, bd. of edn., M.E. Ch., 1922-28; staff rep. Philanthropic Finance, 1928-31; mem. Genesee Conf. M.E. Church; dir. dept. of finance, Alfred (N.Y.) Univ., 1931-36; counselor and dir. Institutional Financing, 1937-59; The J. Wesley Miller Agency, Gooding, Ida., 1944-59; now retired. Mayor, City of Gooding, 1947-49. Rotarian. Dir. Chamber of Commerce, Gooding, Ida. Tb. Assn. (pres., dir.). Mem. Soc. of Genesee. Republican. Mason. Home: Gooding, Ida. *

MILLER, JAMES ROSCOE, univ. chancellor, b. Murray, Utah, Oct. 26, 1905; s. Leroy Cromwell and Marjorie (Sidley) M.; B.A., U. of Utah, 1925, LL.D., 1949; M.D., Northwestern U., 1930, M.S., 1931, LL.D., 1949; Sc.D., U. Ariz., 1951; LL.D., Williams Coll., 1950, Bradley U., 1950, Knox Coll., 1957, U. Mich., 1957, Ohio Wesleyan U., 1960, Notre Dame, 1964, U. Denver, 1964; L.H.D., Loyola U., Chgo., 1970; Litt.D., Jewish Theol. Sem. Am., 1974; m. Berenice Johannesen, Sept. 27, 1928; children—Roxelyn (Mrs. Richard S. Pepper), Jacquelyn (Mrs. Robert M. James), James Randall. Asst. dean Northwestern U. Med. Sch., Chgo., 1933-41, dean 1941-49, asst. prof. medicine, 1938-41, asso. prof., 1941-49, prof., 1949-74, prof. emeritus, 1974-77, pres. Northwestern U., 1949-70, chancellor, 1969-74, chancellor emeritus, 1974-77, dir. Am. Hosp. Supply Corp., 1st Nat. Bank & Trust Co. Evanston (hon.), Fidelity Life Assn., Fed. Kemper (life); former mem. Com. on Vets, Med. Problems, NRC; former mem. res. cons. bd. USN. Hon. bd. dirs. Northwestern Meml. Hosp., Prentice Women's Hosp. and Maternity Center of Chgo., Evanston Hosp.; trustee Mus. of Sci. and Industry, Field Mus. Natural History; bd. overseers Hoover Instn. on War, Revolution, and Peace; former mem. bd. visitors Air U. Served to lt. col., Med. Res. Corps, U.S. Army, Nov. 1940-42, comdr. USNR, 1942-49; head med. br., profl. div., Bur. Med. and Surgery, 1944-45. Diplomate Am. Bd. Internal Medicine. Fellow A.C.P., AMA, Am. Heart Assn., Am. Coll. Cardiology (hon.); mem. Central Soc. Clin. Research, James IV Assn. Surgeons (hon.), Chgo. Med. Soc. (pres. 1948-49), AAAS, Assn. Am. Med. Colls. (pres. 1948-49), Sigma Xi, Alpha Omega Alpha, Sigma Chi. Clubs: University (Chgo., Evanston); Glen View; Economics, Executives, Commercial, Old Elm. Home: Evanston, Ill. Died Oct. 16, 1977.

MILLER, JOHN L., judge; b. Pitts., Mar. 24, 1901; s. Lewis W. and Mary (Lester) M.; B.S., Westminster Coll., New Wilmington, Pa., 1923; LL.B., U. Pitts., 1926; m. Mary Louise Paff, Dec. 27, 1928 (dec. Oct. 1953). Admitted to Pa. bar, 1926, practiced in Pitts., 1926-54; U.S. judge Western Dist. Pa., from 1954, Sr. judge until 1978. Trustee Westminster Coll., New Wilmington. Mem. Sigma Nu, Delta Theta Phi. Home: Pittsburgh, Pa. Died July 20, 1978.

MILLER, JULIAN MALCOLM, educator; b. Berkeley, Calif., Aug. 5, 1922; s. John Benjamin and Pauline (Goldman) M.; B.S., U. Calif., Berkeley, 1944; Ph.D., Columbia, 1949; m. Prudence Loeb, July 26, 1960; children—Susan, Christopher. Mem. faculty, Columbia, N.Y.C., 1949-76, prof. chemistry, 1960-76, chmn. dept., 1970-73. Cons. Brookhaven Nat. Lab., 1950-76. NSF fellow, 1965; Guggenheim fellow, 1973. Fellow Am. Phys. Soc.; mem. Am. Chem. Soc., Am. Acad. Arts and Scis. Author: (with G. Friedlander, J. Kennedy) Nuclear and Radiochemistry, 1964. Contbr. articles to profl. jours. Home: Leonia, N.J. Died Dec. 14, 1976.

MILLER, LESLIE ANDREW, ex-governor; b. Junction City, Kan., Jan. 29, 1886; s. Andrew Early and Anna Belle (Orr) M.; ed. business coll. and commercial dept. of U. of Wyo., 1900-02; m. Margaret Morgan, of Laramie, Wyo., Mar. 31, 1909; children—Katherine Florence (Mrs. John Darrow Mabee), John Selden. Brakeman, U.P. and C.B. & Q. railroads, 1909-11; state employe, 1911-16; oil operator, 1916-17; collector of internal revenue, Cheyenne, Wyo., 1919-21; pres. Aero Oil Co., distributor of petroleum products. *

MILLER, M. CLARE, contractor; b. McPherson, Kan., Apr. 23, 1907; s. Lee and Lora (Webb) M.; student McPherson Coll., 1925-28; m. Sadie Louise Halfin, Dec. 27, 1950; children—Marka, Lance, Brent, Stephen. Asst. county engr. McPherson County, 1928-30; with San Ore Constrn. Co., Inc., McPherson, 1930-80, pres., 1955-80, sec.-treas. Miller Bros. Inc.; dir. McPherson State Bank & Trust Co., KARD TV Co., Wichita, Gt. Plains Life Ins. Co., Wichita, Sherwood, Inc., Topeka, Pioneer Savs. & Loan, McPherson, Pacific Western Corp., Cheyenne, Wyo. Past pres. Methodist Youthville, Newton, Kan.; trustee McPherson Coll. Served to maj., C.E., AUS, World War II; to lt. col., Korea. Decorated Bronze Star, Legion of Merit; recipient Highway award Kan. Constrn. mag., 1960. Registered profl. engr., Kan. Mem. Asso. Gen. Contractors Am. (pres. 1961), Kan. Contractors Assn. (pres. 1950-53, 54, dir. 1938-80), U.S. (dir.), Kan. (past dir.) chambers commerce, Kan. Engring. Soc., Am. Legion (past dist. comdr.), Vets Fgn. Wars. Elk. Mason. Home: McPherson, Kans. Died June 21, 1980.

MILLER, MAX, physician, educator; b. New Haven, June 22, 1910; s. Morris and Bessie (Shulim) M.; B.S., Yale U., 1931, M.D., 1935; m. Barbara Ann Foster, June 29, 1940; children—Claire Louise, Eric Foster. Asst. in medicine Yale U., 1936-37; teaching fellow in medicine Western Res. U., 1937-40, instr., 1940-42, sr. instr., 1942-47, asst. prof., 1947-51, asso. prof., 1951-67, dir. clin. research center, 1962-72, prof. Case Western Res. U., 1967-78, also physician Univ. Hosps. Cleve. Chmn. univ. group diabetes program Nat. Inst. Arthritis and Metabolic Disease, NIH, 1950-78, cons., 1965-78; mem. gen. med. study sect. NIH, 1957-59; cons. VA Hosp., Cleve.; cons. in diabetes, mem. policy adv. bd. diabetic retinopathy study Nat. Eye Inst., NIH, 1972-78. Mem. health council Welfare Fedn., 1964-66; trustee Cleve. Chamber Music Soc. Recipient Cleve. Honor award Med. Mut. Acad. Medicine. Mem. Am. Soc. Clin Investigation, Central Soc. Clin. Research, N.Y. Acad. Scis., Am. Diabetes Assn., Soc. Exptl. Biology, Medicine, AAAS, Endocrine Soc., Soc. Epidemiol. Research, Phi Beta Kappa, Sigma Xi, Alpha Omega Alpha. Editor: (with Dr. Peter Bennett) International Studies in the Epidimeology of Diabetes, 1976. Contbg. author chpts. on diabetes and renal diseases to textbooks. Editorial bd. Diabetes, 1955-70. Research, numerous publs. on diabetes, carbohydrate metabolism, renal disease and epidemiology. Home: Cleveland Heights, Ohio. Died Mar. 25, 1978; buried Lake View Cemetery, Cleveland, Ohio.

MILLER, NEVILLE, lawyer; b. Louisville, Feb. 17, 1894; s. Shackelford and Mary Floyd (Welman) M.; A.B., Princeton, 1916; J.D., Harvard, 1920; m. Katherine Castleman Wilson, Sept. 20, 1924; children—Barbara Neville, Gale, Katherine Wilson, Mary Welman. Admitted to Ky. Bar. 1920; mem. firm Miller & Miller, 1920-30; dean U. Louisville Law Sch., 1930-33; mayor Louisville, 1933-37; asst. to pres. Pinceton, 1938; pres. Nat. Assn. Broacasters, 1938-44; sr. dep. chief Balkan Mission, UNRRA, 1944-45; practice law, 1945-74, ret., 1974; pres. Broadcast Music, Inc. Chmn. bd. Redevel. Land Agy. D.C., 1960-71; mem. bd. Nat. Capital Housing Authority. Trustee Fed. City Council. Mem. Am., Fed., D.C., Fed. Communications (past pres.), Ky., Louisville (past pres.), Ky. bar assns., Washington Planning and Civic Assn. (trustee). Democrat. Presbyn. (elder). Elk (past exalted ruler Louisville lodge). Clubs: Ivy (Princeton); Yacht (Hyannisport, Mass.); Princeton, Chevy Chase, Nat. Press (Washington). Home: Washington, D.C. Died Mar. 27, 1977.

MILLER, OGDEN DAYTON, educator; b. Southington, Conn., Jan. 26, 1905; s. Alonzo Fyler and Susan Marion (Dayton) M.; grad. Williston Acad., Easthampton, Mass., 1926; Ph.B., Yale, 1930, M.A. (hon.), 1938; m. Anne Carolyn Sheafe, June 18, 1932; children—Ogden Dayton, David Porter II, Dwight Daniell. Factory hand, 1921-24; mem. exec.-adminstrv. staff Yale, 1930-45, asso. dean freshmen, dir. athletics, ednl. adminstrn., then headmaster The Gunnery, Washington, Conn., 1945-69; interim headmaster Ethel Walker Sch., Simsbury, Conn., 1972-73. Co-founder Pop Concerts, New Haven, 1940; co-founder, asso. dir. New Haven Hosp. Mens Volunteer Corps, 1942; co-founder, 1st pres. New Haven Jr. C. of C., 1940-42. Bd. dirs. New Haven Hosp., 1942-45, New Haven Symphony Orch. Assn., 1941-45; trustee Center for Information on Am. Williston Acad. Recipient Ward Melville gold medal award for community improvement, 1961. Mem. Conn. Assn. Ind. Schs. (co-founder, sec. 1949-61), Conn. Found. Ind. Schools (co-founder, pres. 1961-65), Headmasters Assn. (pres. 1968-69), New Eng. Assn. Coll. and Secondary Schs., Nat. Assn. Ind. Schs., Zeta Psi. Mason. Clubs: Elihu, Litchfield Couny, University (past pres.). Address: Washington, Conn. Died Feb. 11, 1978.

MILLER, ORIE OTIS, shoe mfr.; b. Middlebury, Ind., July 7, 1892; s. Daniel D. and Jeanette (Hostetler) M.; B.A., Goshen (Ind.) Coll., 1915; m. Susan Elta Wolf, Aug. 26, 1915 (dec. Feb. 1958); children—Lois Wolf (Mrs. Ronald Beach), Albert Wolf, Daniel Wolf, John Wolf, Robert Wolf; m. 2d, Elta Myers Sensenig, Jan. 9, 1960. With Miller Hess & Co., Akron, Pa., 1916-70, pres., 1954-62, chmn. bd., 1962-70, dir. 1970-72. Trustee Eastern Mennonite Bd. Missions and Charities, 1925-77, sec., charge overseas devel. and operations, 1935-58, asso. sec., 1959-68; pres. Mennonite Mut. Aid, Inc., 1945-62, trustee, 1946-65; bd. dirs. Am. Leprosy Missions, Inc., 1950-77, chmn. bd., 1960-65, vice chmn., 1965-77; Mennonite religion Central Com., 1920-77, trustee, 1922-77, exec. sec.-treas., 1935-58, asso. sec.-treas., 1958-63); bd. dirs. N.Y. Theol. Sem., 1940-42; dir. Mennonite Central Com. Relief, 1920-21, asst. to exec. sec., 1921-35. Address: Lititz, Pa. Died Jan. 10, 1977; buried Wolf Cemetery, Ephrata, Pa.

MILLER, ROBERT LEE, geophysicist, educator; b. Chgo., Apr. 6. 1920; s. Fred Lee and Gertrude (Byron) M.; A.B., U. Ill. 1942; Ph. D., U. Chgo., 1950; m. Dorothy L. Schick, June 12, 1942; children—Dolores (Mrs. Robert Pekrul), Doretta Doralee Doricia. Research asso. U. Chgo., 1950-52. mem. faculty, 1953-76, prof. geophys. scis., 1965-76, admission counselor, from 1968; vis. prof. Frankfort (Germany) U., 1958, Brown U., Providence, 1963; asso. Woods Hole Oceanographic Instn., 1957-76. Cons. to pvt. cos., govt. agy. Mem. Am. Geophys. Union (mem. commn. for erosion and sedimentation Hydrology sect.), Marine Tech. Soc., N.Y. Acad. Scis., Council for Wave Research, Sigma Xi. Author: (with E.C. Olson) Morphological Integration, 1957; (with J. S. Kahn) Statistical Analysis in the Geological Sciences, 1962; Papers in Marine Geology, 1964. Editor Jour. Geology, 1957-62; reviewer Earth Sci. revs. Contbr. articles to profl. jours. Home: Glen Ellyn, Ill. Died July 25, 1976.

MILLER, THOMAS WOODNUTT, ret. nat. comdr. Am. Legion; b. Wilmington, Del., June 26, 1886; s. Charles Robert and Abigail Morgan (Woodnutt) M.; Ph.B., Yale, 1908; m. Katharine Tallman, 1913 (dec. 1945); children—Thomas L., Mrs. George P. Bissell, Jr.; m. 2d, Eleanor Taylor, 1946. Miner, rancher in Nev.; sec. of state, Del., 1913-15; mem. 64th Congress, 1915-17; rep.-at-large (Del.), Plattsburg Tng. Camp, 1915; chmn.Del. Council of Def. until enlisted as pvt. in inf. U.S. Army, July 1917; hon. discharged as lt. col., Sept. 1919; served 11 months with 79th Div., A.E.F. in France; cited in divisional orders and by comdr. gen. A.E.F. Awarded Order of the Purple Heart (U.S.), 1933. An incorporator Am. Legion, vice-chmn. Paris Caucus, 1919, nat. exec. com., Del., 1919-28, re-elected, Nev., 1946-72, awarded title past nat. comdr., 1968, dep. comdr. Del., 1932-33, Nev., 1943-44. Mem. other nat. and dept. coms., Del. and Nev.; alien property custodian of U.S., 1921-25; mem. Am. Battle Monuments Commn., 1923-26; supr. U.S. Grazing Serv., Nev. and Cal. until 1942, when returned to pvt. bus.; staff rep. U.S. Vets. Employment Service 10 western states, 1946-56; past mem. adv. bd. Nev. State Council of Def., mem. Nev. Civil Def. Commn., 1951-59. Founder of Nev. State Park System, 1935; chmn. Nev. State Park Commn., 1935-37, 52-59, 67-72; chmn. City of Reno Park Commn., 1963-68. Del. or alt. to Republican nat. convs., 1912, 16, 20, 24. Chmn. Nev. Vets. Service Coordinating Comn., 1944-46. Pres. F. I. D.A.C. (interallied vets. fed.), Paris, France, 1924-25. Nev. State chmn. Crusade for Freedom and Am. Korean Found., 1953-54; trustee Epsicopal Found. Nev., 1954-57; mem. bishop's exec. council, 1962-66; bd. dirs. Reno Chpt. A.R.C., 1952—, chmn. bd., 1968-69. Mem. Delta Phi (pres. nat. orgn. 1916-17). Episcopalian (vestryman, sr. warden). Mason (Shriner). Clubs: St. Elmo (Yale;) University (Chgo.); Reno Press. Home: Reno NV. *

MILLER, THURMAN ("DUSTY" MILLER), lecturer, editor; b. nr. Marshall, Highland County, O., Dec. 28, 1881; s. James Fenton and Louella (Martin) M.; student Ohio U., Miami U. and Ohio Northern U.; B.Sc., Wilmington (O.) Coll., 1907, B.A., 1909; m. Grace Robuck, Aug. 7, 1907; children—Eugene James, Thurman. Teacher pub. schs. 5 yrs.; editor Daily News Journal, Wilmington, 1910-24; pres. News-Journal Co. Lecturer before business and professional groups; also known as after-dinner speaker. Republican. Quaker. Mason (K.T.). Home: Wilmington, O. *

MILLER, W. EARL, merchandising exec.; b. Clinton, Tenn., July 1, 1903; s. Harvey Fletcher and Margaret Miller; B.S., U. Tenn., 1923; M.B.A., Harvard, 1925; m. Gail Calhoun, Jan. 29, 1935 (dec.); children—William E., Sandra G.; m. 2d, Beverly Bogda, With Asso. Dry Goods Corp., James McCreery & Co., N.Y.C., 1925-28, Wm. Hengerer Co., Buffalo, 1928-29, Willian Taylor Son & Co., Cleve., 1929-40, LaSalle & Koch Co. (Macy affiliate), Toledo, 1940-46, Foley Bros. (Federated Dept. Stores), Houston, 1946-48; pres. Ed. Schuster & Co., Inc., Milw., 1948-62; v.p. Carter Hawley Hale Stores Inc., Los Angeles, 1962-65, pres. Broadway div., 1965-68, v.p. corp., 1968-72, now cons., also dir. emeritus. Home: Pasadena, Calif. Died Oct. 31, 1980.

MILLER, WALTER RICHARD, banker; b. Bklyn., July 3, 1903; s. Paul and Margaret (Robbins) M., B.S., N.Y. U., 1925; m. Anne M. Phelan, Apr. 5, 1929; children—Walter Richard, Peter Paul. Chmn. bd. trustees Met. Savs. Bank, N.Y.C., cons., trustee; adv. bd. Mfrs.-Hanover Trust Co., N.Y.C.; dir. Madison Life Ins. Co., Interbore Indemnity Mut. Ins. Co., Atlantic Bank. Vice chmn. council regents St. Francis Coll.; trustee Village Old Westbury; bd. dirs. Bklyn. chpt. A.R.C., Brotherhood in Action N.Y.C. Mem. Bklyn. C. of C. (dir.), Psi Upsilon. Home: Westbury, N.Y. Died May 19, 1976.

MILLER, WILBUR K., judge; b. Owensboro, Ky., Oct. 9, 1892; s. Reuben A. and Margaret (Morehead) M.; ed. U. Mich.; m. Marie Louise Hager, June 2, 1917. Admitted to Ky. bar, 1916, and practiced in Owensboro; county atty., Daviess County, Ky., 1922-30; chmn. Pub. Service Commn. of Ky., 1934-35; judge Spl. Ct. Appeals of Ky., 1940-41; judge U.S. Ct. of Appeals for D.C., 1945-76. Served in field arty. U.S. Army, World War I. Mem. Phi Delta Phi, Phi Kappa Sigma. Home: Alexandria, Va. Died Jan. 24, 1976.

MILLER, WILLIAM ERNEST, judge; b. Johnson City, Tenn., Feb. 3, 1908; s. Samuel Ernest and Grace (Barlow) M.; A.B., U. Tenn., 1930, J.D. (hon.), 1968; LL.B., Yale, 1933; m. Carolyn Gies, Dec. 1, 1934; 1 dau., Susan (Mrs. Charles E. Wright, Jr.). Admitted to Tenn. bar, 1933; mem. Cox, Epps, Miller & Weller, Johnson City, 1933-55; chancellor First Chancery Div. Tenn., 1939; chief judge U.S. Dist. Ct., Middle Dist. Tenn., 1955-70; mem. U.S. Ct. Appeals 6th Circuit, Cincinnati, 1970-76. Lectr. law Vanderbilt Law Sch. Chmn., Tenn. Rhodes Scholarship Selection Com. Presdl. elector, 1940; mem. Constl. Conv. Tenn., 1953. Chmn., Washington County chpt. A.R.C., 1938-40; trustee, mem. athletics bd. U. Tenn. Served as maj. USAAF, World War II. Recipient award of merit U. Tenn. Law Sch., 1966, Wisdom award of Honor, 1970. Mem. Am. Law Inst., Am., Fed. (hon.), Tenn., Va. (hon.), Nashville, Washington County (past pres.) bar assns., Am. Counsel Assn., Am. Judicature Soc., Tenn. Hist. Assn., Am. Legion, Order of Coif, Scabbard and Blade, Phi Beta Kappa, Phi Alpha Delta, Sigma Alpha Epsilon. Republican. Methodist. Rotarian. Clubs: Cumberland, Belle Meade Country, Round Table (Nashville); National Lawyers (Washington); University (Cin.). Contbr. articles to law revs. Home: Nashville, Tenn. Died Apr. 12, 1976; interred Oakhill Cemetery, Johnson City, Tenn.

MILLER, WILLIAM WHIPPLE, lawyer; b. Chgo., Feb. 17, 1906; s. William Southworth and Susan (Whipple) M.; B.A., Yale, 1928; J.D., Northwestern U., 1931; m. Helen S. Robbins, Nov. 28, 1935; children—William Peter, Thomas Robbins, Susan Jane (Mrs. Land Morrow Lindbergh), Mary Owen, James Whipple. Admitted to Ill. bar, 1931, Calif. bar, 1975; practiced in Chgo.; mem. firm Tenney, Harding, Sherman & Rogers 1931-42; head legal dept. Stewart-Warner Corp., 1942-53, dir. indsl. relations, 1943-53, v.p. indsl. relations and legal dept., 1953-71; instr. John Marshall Law Sch., 1965-74; partner firm Miller & Miller, Berkeley, Calif., 1974-78; instr. Golden Gate Law Sch., 1976-78. Past chmn. gov.'s adv. bd. Ill. Dept. Personnel Mem. Better Govt. Assn. Chgo. (dir. 1943—, past pres.), Am. Bar Assn., State Bar Calif., Order of Coif. Address: Berkeley, Calif. Died Sept. 5, 1978; buried Greenough, Mont.

MILLET, JOHN ALFRED PARSONS, psychiatrist; b. Broadway, Worcestershire, Eng., July 8, 1888; s. Francis Davis and Elizabeth Greeley (Merrill) M.; student Marlborough Coll., Eng., 1902-06; A.B., Harvard U., 1910, M.D., 1914 m. Alice Murrell, May 21, 1913 (div.); children—Jeanne Alice (Mrs. William T. King), John Bradford, Elizabeth (Mrs. Henry Sanford); m. 2d, Carmen deGonzalo Manice, Aug. 7, 1941. Began practice medicine, 1914; gen. practice later specialist in psychiatry hosps., clinics and univs., N.Y., asst. clin. prof. psychiatry Columbia Coll. Phys. and Surg., 1952; clin. research on allergic disturbances; organized neuropsychiat. clinic Lake George Found., Glens Falls, N.Y., 1940; asso. attending psychoanalyst Columbia Dept. Psychiatry, 1947-54; chmn. Mental Health Bd. Rockland County, 1955-58; supervising psychiatrist Rockland County Mental Health Clinic, 1973-76, psychiat. cons. Rockland Children's Psychiat. Center, 1974-76; pres. Assn. Psychoanalytic Medicine, 1954-57; chief psychiat. service, Am. Rehab. Com., 1946-73, pres., 1970-72; lectr. psychiatry Columbia, 1956-59; attending psychiatrist N.Y. State Psychiat. Inst., 1957-60; prof. psychiatry, asst. dean N.Y. Sch. Psychiatry, 1959-64; prof. emeritus, 1965-76, also in pvt. practice; hon. cons. Columbia Clinic, 1962-76. Dir. Ruth M. Knight Counseling Service, Manhattan Sch. Music, 1965—. Served from 1st lt. to capt., MC, AUS, 1917-19; A.E.F. Decorated Officer d'Academie with Silver Palms. Trustee Manhattan Sch. of Music, N.Y.C. Diplomate Am. Bd. of Neurology and Psychiatry. Fellow A.M.A. (life), Am. Psychiat. Assn., N.Y. Acad. Medicine; mem. nat., state and local profl. and med. assns. in gen. and spl. fields, Acad. Psychoanalysis (pres. 1959), World Fedn. Mental Health (U.S. mem. exec. com. 1972-74, mem-at-large 1974-76 Episcopalian. Clubs: Hasty Pudding, Delphic (Cambridge, Mass.); Harvard, Century Assn. (N.Y.). Author book, chpts. in books, numerous articles. Home: Nyack, N.Y. Died Feb. 18, 1976.

MILLING, ROBERTS CLAY, lawyer; b. Winnfield, La., Nov. 2, 1885; s. Robert Edward and Ida (Roberts) M.; student La. State U., 1903-06, LL.B., 1909; B.A., Washington and Lee U., 1908, student Law Sch., 1908-09; m. Dorthy Sharp, June 16, 1936. Admitted to La. bar, 1909; practice in Franklin, 1909-14, New Orleans, 1915—; partner firm Milling, Saal, Benson, Woodward & Hillyer and predecessors, 1915—. Mem. Am., La., New Orleans bar assns. Home: New Orleans LA. *

MILLOR, WILLIAM JAMES, educator, clergyman; b. Detroit, Jan. 6, 1899; s. Robert James and Margaret Mary (Roberts) M.; grad. U. Detroit High Sch., 1918; A.B., U. Detroit, 1922; A.M., St. Louis U., 1929; S.T.L., St. Mary's (Kan.) Coll., 1935; Ph.D., U. London (Eng.), 1939. Joined Soc. of Jesus, 1925, ordained priest Roman Catholic Ch., 1934; instr. classics St. Xavier High Sch., Cin., 1930-31; asst. prof. classical langs. Loyola U., Chgo., 1939-44; pres. U. Detroit, 1944-49; prof. classical langs. John Carroll U., Cleve., from 1949, dir. classical langs., 1951-57, again from 1967, exec. dean, 1956-61, dean Grad. Sch., 1957-58, 61-62, v.p. univ., 1961-64. Mem. Am. Philos. Assn., Delta Epsilon Sigma, Delta Alpha Phi, Magi. Clubs: Chicago Classical; Detroit Athletic, Detroit Golf. Home: Cleveland, Ohio. Died Oct. 19, 1977.

MILLS, ALFRED S., banker; b. Morristown, N.J., Aug. 12, 1909; s. Edward Kirkpatrick and Laura (Slade) M.; grad. Phillips Exeter Acad., 1927; A.B., Princeton, 1931; m. Ruth Mountain, Sept. 11, 1959; children—Edward K. II, Alfred S., Henrietta Wise (Mrs. Robert H. Mead). Mortgage appraiser Prudential Ins. Co., 1931; mortgage loan mgr. The N.Y. Bank for Savs., N.Y. C., 1939-42, pres., chmn. bd., chief exec. officer; dir. Colonial Real Estate Assn., N.Y., M.S.B. Fund. Mem., dir. The Battery Park City Authority, Nat. Urban Coalition, Nonprofit Housing Center, Fedn. Protestant Agys. Bd. dirs. Woodlawn Cemetery, N.Y.C.; mayor Morris Twp. (N.J.). Served as lt. comdr. USNR, 1942-45. Mem. Internat. Savs. Bank Inst. (dir.). Home: North Salem, N.Y. Died May 8, 1978; buried Nantucket, Mass.

MILLS, CHARLES BRIGHT, seed co. exec.; b. Marysville, Ohio, May 14, 1896; s. Dr. Charles Drake and Ella Ann (Stewart) M.; A.B., Ohio Wesleyan U., 1920; m. Rachel Long, June 25, 1924; children—Rachel, Mary, Charles. Chmn. bd. dirs. First Nat. Bank, Marysville. County chmn. War Fund Am. Red Cross, 1942-44; chmn. Central Ohio Heart Assn.; Alternate del. Republican Nat. Conv., 1936. Bd. dirs. Central Ohio Area Boy Scouts Am.; past chmn. bd., trustee Ohio Wesleyan U.; trustee Lakeside Assn., Ohio Meth. Theol. Sem. Mem. Am. Seed Trade Assn. (past pres., life dir.), Am. Legion, Ohio Soc. N.Y., Am. Newcomen Soc. (chmn. Columbus com.), Pi Delta Epsilon, Phi Gamma Delta, Omicron Delta Kappa. Methodist (trustee Ch.). Mason (33 deg., Shriner). Clubs: Kiwanis, Marysville Golf, University, Columbus, Scioto Country. Home: Marysville, Ohio. Died Mar. 13, 1980.

MILLS, EDWARD S., publisher; b. Orange, N.J., Mar. 3, 1883; s. Charles James and Mary F. (Quimby) M.; grad. Hill Sch., Pottstown, Pa., 1902; B.A., Yale, 1906 m. Marion Elizabeth Partridge, Dec. 31, 1907; children—George Partridge, Edward Ensign, Charles James. Vice-pres. Longmans, Green & Co., New York, 1916-27, pres., 1927-60. Mem. Nat. Assn. Book Publishers (v.p. 1923-24; pres. 1930-32), Psi Upsilon, Scroll and Key (Yale U.) Republican. Clubs: Yale Maidstone, Links. Home: Bridgehampton, L.I., N.Y. Died Oct. 10, 1976.

MILLS GORDON HARRISON, educator; b. Mt. Pleasant, Mich., Feb. 9, 1914; s. Fredrick H. and Maude Pearl (Harrison) M.; B.A., U. Iowa, 1939, M.A., 1940, Ph.D., 1942; m. Violet G. Anderson, June 1, 1941; 1 son, David K. Instr. English and physics Army Specialized Tng. Program U. Iowa, 1943-44, mem. tech. staff Physics and Engring. Devel. Project, 1944-45; instr. English, U. Tex., Austin, 1945-47, asst. prof., 1947-55, asso. prof., 1955-66, prof., 1966-78; vis. prof. La State U., summer 1964. Mem. AAAS, AAUP, Am. Studies Assn. (mem. nat. exec. council 1961-64, pres. Tex. sect. 1963-64), Coll. English Assn., Conf. Coll. Tchrs. of English (pres. 1960-61), Melville Soc., Modern Lang. Assn. Author; (with John A. Walter) Technical Writing, 4th edit., 1978; Hamlet's Castle: The Study of Literature as a Social Experience, 1976; editor: Innocence and Power, 1965. Home: Austin, Tex. Died Sept. 11, 1978.

MILLS, RAY JACKSON, ins. co. exec.; b. Hale, Iowa, June 8, 1893; s. William J. and Margaret (Inglis) M.; LL.B., J.D., U. Mich., 1916; m. Marie Breyman, Nov. 5, 1919; children—William J., Robert E. Admitted to Iowa bar, 1916; practice of law, Cedar Rapids, 1916-20; claims mgr. Iowa Nat. Mut. Ins. Co., 1920-36, sec., gen. mgr., 1936-41, pres. Cedar Rapids, Iowa, 1941-51, chmn., 1951-68, vice chmn., from 1968; hon. life dir., 1975-81; hon. dir. Mchts. Nat. Bank. Served with U.S. Army, 1917-19. Mem. Delta Chi. Mason, Elk. Club: St. Petersburg (Fla.) Yacht. Home: St. Petersburg, Fla. Died Feb. 27, 1981.

MILLS, ROBERT H., army dental officer; b. Decatur County, Ga., July 29, 1883; s. William Hilliard and Frances Anne (Byran) M.; student Southern Dental Coll., Atlanta, 1904-06; D.D.S., U. of Md., 1907, Sc.D. 1946; married, May 22, 1909; 1 dau., Frances (Mrs Robert Gordon Pendleton); m. 2d, Anne Hyatt, Sept 16, 1922. Practiced dentistry, Monticello, Fla., 1907-09 contract dental officer U.S. Army, May 17, 1909 advancing through grades to maj. gen., 1943; asst. to The Surgeon General; retired as maj. gen. U. S. Army 1946. Decorated D.S.M., Philippine Campaign Mexican Border and Victory medals. Hon. Alumnu Northwestern U. Dental Sch. Mem. Assn. of Mi Surgeons, Nat. Bd. of Dental Examiners, Am. Denta Assn., Psi Omega. Mason (Scottish and York Rites

Shriner). Clubs: Army and Navy (Washington, D.C.); Columbia Country (Chevy Chase, Md.). Home: Washington, D.C. *

MILNER, BENJAMIN HUDSON, utility co. exec.; b. Louisville, Nov. 23, 1916; s. Charles Whitner and Josephine (Hudson) M.; A.B. with highest honors, Princeton U., 1938; LL.B., U. Louisville, 1941; LL.D. (hon.), U. Ky., 1975; m. Betty Dennis, July 2, 1938 (dec.); children—H. Hudson, F. Dennis, Cathcart; m. 2d, Mina B. Jones, Feb. 28, 1975. Admitted to Ky. bar, 1940; partner firm Middleton, Seelbach, Wolford, Willis & Cochran and predecessors, Louisville, 1940-57; with Louisville Gas & Electric Co., 1957-78, exec. v.p., 1962-63, pres., 1963-78; also dir.; dir. First Nat. Bank, Louisville, Ky. Trust Co., Ohio Valley Electric Corp., East Central Aara Reliability Group. Chmn. Ky. Arts Commn. Bd. dirs. Louisville Fund, Louisville Philharmonic Soc. Served with USNR, 1944-46. Mem. Ky., Louisville chambers commerce, Ky. Bar Assn., Phi Beta Kappa. Clubs: Wynn Stay, Jefferson, Louisville Country, Pendennis (Louisville); Princeton, Regency Whist (N.Y.C.). Home: Glenview, Ky. Died Nov. 15, 1978.

MILOSLAVICH, EDWARD LUCAS, pathology, criminology; b. Oakland, Calif., Dec. 20, 1884; s. Lucas and Vincenza (Milcovich) M.; taken by parents to Austria, 1889, returned to U.S., 1921, naturalized 1928; grad. Gymnasium, Dalmatia, Austria, 1903; student U. of Vienna, 1903-08, M.D., 1908; U. of Naples, summer 1907; post-grad. work in biology and anthropology, U. of Vienna, 1911-14 and 1919-20; m. Kathryn Blaschek, Dec. 18, 1918. Asst. Pathol. Inst., Mil. Hosp., Vienna, and lecturer in mil. legal medicine, 1910-14; war pathologist, Austrian Army, Balkan territories, and medico-legal expert, 1914-18; asso. prof. (docent), pathol. anatomy, U. of Vienna, 1917-21; dir. Pathol. Inst., Mil. Hosp., and affiliated war hosps., Vienna, 1918-21; prof. pathology and bacteriology and dir. depts., Marquette U., Milwaukee, Wis., 1921-28; pathologist Marquette U. Hosp., 1922-28, Evang. Deaconess Hosp., 1923-28 and cons. pathologist since 1928; cons. pathologist St. Michael's Hosp., Stevens Point, Wis.; dir. dept. clin. pathology and med. research, St. Mary's Hosp., Milwaukee; head sect. clin. pathology and post mortem pathology, Milwaukee County Hosp., dir. pathol. labs., St. Joseph's Hosp., and mem. exec. bd. St. Joseph's Nursing Sch.; attending specialist in pathology, U.S. Vets.' Hosp., Waukesha, Wis.; pathologist Johnston Emergency Hosp.; med. adviser to dist. attorney, also coroner's physician, Milwaukee. Fellow A.M.A., Am. Soc. Clin. Pathologists, A.A.A.S. (life); mem. Internat. Medico-Legal Assn., Am. Assn. Pathologists and Bacteriologists, Chicago Pathol. Soc., Am. Soc. Parasitologists, Am. Pub. Health Assn., Nat. Tuberculosis Assn., Wis. Acad. Sciences, Arts and Letters, Milwaukee Acad. Medicine, Wis. Med. Soc., Am. Anthropol. Assn., Gesellschaft der Aerzte (Vienna), and other Am. and foreign socs. Served as maj. Austrian Army. Received many decorations from Austro-Hungary, Germany, Serbia and Bulgaria. Catholic. Club: Milwaukee Athletic. Contbr. to archives of Pathology, also to various publications, on subjects relating to own original research work. *

MILSTONE, JACOB HASKELL, physician, educator; b. St. Louis, June 30, 1912; s. Maurice and Sadie (Mackler) M.; A.B., Johns Hopkins, 1933, M.D., 1937; m. Vivian Kaufman, Dec. 9, 1942; children—Leonard Matthew, Alan David. Mem. faculty dept. bacteriology N.Y. U. Coll. Medicine, 1937-40; Commonwealth fellow Rockefeller Inst. Med. Research, Princeton, N.J., 1940-42; mem. faculty dept. pathology Yale Sch. Medicine, 1946-77, prof. pathology, 1967-77; attending pathologist Yale-New Haven Hosp. Mem. subcom. on blood coagulation NRC, 1950-54. Served to maj. AUS, 1942-46; PTO. Mem. A.A.A.S., Soc. Exptl. Biology and Medicine, Am. Assn. Pathologists and Bacteriologists, Am. Soc. Exploratory Pathology, A.M.A., N.Y. Acad. Scis., Phi Beta Kappa, Sigma Xi. Contbr. to sci. publs. Research in blood coagulation and fibrinolysis. Home: New Haven, Conn. Died Jan. 27, 1977.

MILTON, ABBY CRAWFORD, writer; born at Milledgeville, Georgia, Feb. 6, 1886; dau. Capt. Charles P. and Annah (Orme) Crawford; ed. Ga. Mil. Coll. and Ga. Woman's Coll., Milledgeville, and Chattanooga Coll. of Law; m. George Fort Milton, pub. of Chattanooga News, and Knoxville Sentinel, Sept. 19, 1904 (died Apr. 23, 1923); children—Corinne, Sarah Annah, Frances Fort. One of owners and publishers Chattanooga News. Chmn., 1920, Tenn. League of Women Voters when 19th Amendment to Constitution of U.S. was ratified by Tenn. legislature (name upon Honor Roll of Am. Suffrage leaders, in Washington, D.C.). Last pres. Tenn. Equal Suffrage Assn.; first pres. Tenn. League of Women Voters (now hon. life pres.); first pres. Tenn. Legislative Council. Established first Dem. women's clubs of Tenn.; v.p. Dem. Exec. Com. of Tenn., 1921; alternate del. at large, Dem. Nat. Conv., San Francisco, 1920, del. New York, 1924, Phila., 1936. Nat. chmn. women's div. Nat. Chickamauga Battle. Celebration, Chattanooga Centennial; state chmn. N.Y. World's Fair, women's participation; mem. League of Am. Penwomen, League of Women Voters, Hermitage Assn., Soc. Colonial Dames, D.A.R., U.D.C., New York Pen and Brush Club. Episcopalian. Clubs: Authors and Artists (chairman), Democratic Woman's Writers, Tenn. Press and Authors, etc. Author: The Magic Switch (children's verse), 1924; Ceasar's Wife and Other Poems, 1930; Lookout Mountain (verse), 1934. Editor: Strains from a Dulcimore (by Emma Bell Miles), 1930. Home: Dunedin, Fla. *

MILTON, DAVID MERRIWETHER, business exec.; b. N.Y.C., 1900; grad. Williams Coll., 1920; LL.B., Columbia, 1924; children—Abby (Mrs. George D. O'Neill), Marilyn (Mrs. William Kelly Simpson). Chairman of the board and dir. of Equity Corporation, N.Y.C., 1933-66; dir. Stokely-Van Camp, Inc., Bell Intercontinental Corp., Signode Steel Strapping Co., Wheelabrator Corp., Commercial Controls Corp., Friden, Inc. Home: Oyster Bay, N.Y. Died July 6, 1976.

MINAR, DAVID WILLIAM, educator; b. Portland, Oreg., Apr. 12, 1925; s. Edwin LeRoy and Alma (Jackson) M.; student Oreg. State Coll., 1942-43, 46-47; B.A., Reed Coll., 1949; M.A., U. Calif., Berkeley, 1951, Ph.D., 1956; m. Carola Neel Hays, June 20, 1948; children—Edward Hays, Thomas Jackson. Adminstrv. asst. U. Calif., 1955-56; instr. govt. Columbia, 1956-58; asst. prof. dept. polit. sci. Northwestern U., Evanston, Ill., 1958-68, prof., 1970-73, chmn. dept., 1970-73; prof. polit. sci., chmn. dept. U. Wash., Seattle, 1968-70. Cons. ednl. orgns., govt. Mem. Bd. Edn., Wilmette, Ill., 1966-68. Served with USAAF, 1943-46. Decorated Air medal. Mem. Am. Polit. Sci. Assn., Am. Ednl. Research Assn., Phi Beta Kappa, Pi Sigma Alpha. Author: Ideas and Politics: the American Experience; Educational Decision-Making in Suburban Communities; co-author: Education and State Politics. Co-editor: The New Urbanization; The Concept of Community. Home: Wilmette, Ill. Died May 21, 1973.

MINDA, ALBERT GREENBERG, rabbi; b. Holton, Kans., July 30, 1895; s. Hyman L. and Rachel Leah (Greenberg) M.; B.H., Hebrew Union Coll., 1919, D.D., 1947; B.A., U. Cin., 1918; postgrad. Columbia, 1922, U. Minn., 1924, U. Chgo., 1929; m. Frances G. Salinger, Nov. 14, 1922; 1 son, Roland L. Rabbi, 1919; rabbi Temple Beth El, South Bend, Ind., 1919-22; rabbi Temple Israel, Mpls., 1922-63, rabbi emeritus, 1963-77; dir., mem. adv. com. Pres., Central Conf. Am. Rabbis, 1922-63; v.p. World Union Progressive Judaism, 1961-63; chaplain Phi Epsilon Pi; trustee Union Am. Hebrew Congregations; 1st pres. Minn. Rabbinical Assn., Mpls. Fedn. Jewish Service; founding mem. Round Table Christians and Jews. Exec. com. United Fund of Hennepin County, an organizer Mpls. Urban League; founding mem. Mpls. Safe Halloween Com.; chmn. pub. library com. for new library Mpls. Citizens League. Recipient Distinguished Service award Mayor of Mpls., citation Gov. Minn.; citation Mpls. Fedn. Jewish Service; nat. award Phi Epsilon Pi; Distinguished Service award Community Chest of Hennepin County, 1967; selected one of 100 living great Minn. Territorial Centennial; Humanitarian award Mt. Zion Men's Club, St. Paul; award NCCJ, Mpls. Urban League; citation Queen and Govt. of Holland. Mason (32 deg., Shriner), Elk; mem. B'nai B'rith. Author: Fire on the Altar, 1946; Ministering to the Religious Needs of the Jewish Patient, 1954; Sanctuary of the Home, 1956; Over the Years, Vol. 1, 1957, Vol. II, 1959; The Story of Temple Israel of Minneapolis, Minn., 1970; America, America A Bicentennial Anthology, 1974. Forest in Israel dedicated in his honor by Jewish Nat. Fund. Home: Minneapolis, Minn. Died Jan. 15, 1977; interred Temple Israel Meml. Park, Minneapolis.

MINER, LEROY MATTHEW SIMPSON, oral surgeon; b. Chicago, Ill., Apr. 13, 1882; s. Clarence Horatio Gilbert and Jennie May (Macfarland) M.; grad. Boston Latin Sch., 1901; D.M.D., Harvard Dental Sch., 1904; M.D., Boston U. Sch. of Medicine, 1907; hon. Sc.D., U. of Pa., 1933; hon. Dr. P.H., Temple Univ., 1938; m. Edna Winifred Dailey, Oct. 25, 1911; children—Richard L., Robert C., Dorothy. Prof. clin. oral surgery emeritus Harvard; mem. board consultation Mass. Gen. Hospital. Reserve officer U.S.P.H.S. Trustee Forsyth Dental Infirmary for Children. Fellow Am. Coll. Surgeons; mem. Am. Med. Assn., Am. Acad. Arts and Scis., A.A.A.S. Harvard Odontol. Soc., Am. Acad. Dental Science, Mass. Dental Soc., Am. Dental Assn. (pres. 1936-37), Mass. Home. Med. Soc., Delta Sigma Delta, Chi Phi, Sigma Xi, Omicron Kappa Upsilon. Republican. Methodist. Mason. Clubs: Algonquin, Harvard, Authors (Boston). Author: The New Dentistry, 1933; Why the Teeth (National Health Series); Dental Education in the United States (with John T. O'Rourke), 1941. Contbr. on professional subjects and dental edn. Home: Boston. *

MINGUS, CHARLES, composer; b. Nogales, Ariz., Apr. 22, 1922; student schs., Los Angeles; studied with H. Rheinschagen, N.Y. Philharmonic; hon. degree Brandeis U., 1974. Appeared with Buddy Collette, with Lee Young, 1940, Louis Armstrong, 1941-43, Kid Ory, Alvino Rey, Lionel Hampton, 1946-48; record debut with Hampton, Decca Records, 1947; with Red Norvo Trio, 1950-51, Billy Taylor Trio, 1952-53; also appeared with Charlie Parker, Stan Getz, Duke Ellington, Bud Powell, Art Tatum; organized record co. Debut, 1952; concert appearances Philharmonic Hall, N.Y.C., 1972, Symphony Hall, Boston, 1975, Kennedy Center, Washington, 1975, Lincoln Center, N.Y.C., 1975; appearances throughout U.S., tour, Japan, 1972, European tour, 1972; holder Slee Chair in Music, SUNY, Buffalo, 1972; motion pictures include Higher and Higher, Road to Zanzibar, All Night Long (Brit.); appeared on CBS-TV with Mel Torme; recs. include Jazz Composers Workshop, Modern Jazz Concert, Tijuana Moods, The Black Saint and the Singer Lady, Let My Children Hear Music, Charles Mingus and Friends in Concert, Mingus Moves, Charles Mingus at Carnegie Hall, Changes I and II. Co-recipient New Star award Down Beat critics poll on bass, 1953. Guggenheim Found. grantee, 1971-72. Author: (autobiography) Beneath the Underdog, 1971. Home: New York, N.Y. Died Jan. 5, 1979.

MINTEER, EDWIN DILLIN, editor; b. Gallatin, Mo., Nov. 2, 1891; s. Joseph C. and Martha (Richardson) M.; B.A., U. Okla., 1912; m. Laura Estelle Enochs, Nov. 12, 1919; 1 son, Edwin Drew. Mng. editor Okla. News, Oklahoma City, 1920-23; editor, pres. Terre Haute (Ind.) Post, 1923-29; editorial staff Cleve. Press, 1929-30; editor Fort Worth Press, 1930-32, El Paso (Tex.) World News, 1933-36; editor, pub. Las Cruces (N.Mex.) Sun-News, 1937-39; mng. editor Rocky Mountain News, Denver, 1939-45; asso. editor, columnist Albuquerque Jour., 1945-64, editor, 1964-67, editorial counselor, 1967-79. Home: San Francisco, Calif. Died Sept. 1979.

MINTER, MERTON MELROSE, physician, univ. regent; b. Jewett, Tex., Jan. 3, 1903; s. Percival A. and Louella (Owens) M.; B.A., U. Tex., 1924, M.D., 1928; m. Katherine Huntress, Sept. 25, 1932; children—Merton Melrose, Alan Huntress. Intern, Research Hosp., Kansas City, Mo., 1928-29; pvt. practice medicine, San Antonio, 1930-76; staff Nix Southwest Meth. Meml., Bapt., Santa Rosa hosps. Dir. First Nat. Bank of San Antonio. Bd. regents U. Tex., 1955-61, chmn. med. affairs com., 1957-58, chmn. bd. regents, 1955-61; chmn. devel. com. S. Tex. Med. Center and Sch., 1962-76; chmn. com. on hosps. Internat. Good Neighbor Commn., 1963-76; mem. regional bd. Med. Program for Heart Disease, Cancer and Stroke; chmn. bd. govs. S.W. Found. Research and Edn.; chmn. San Antonio Med. Found., 1971. Bd. dirs. Tex. Law Enforcement Found. Recipient Distinguished Service award U. Tex., 1970; Outstanding Service award U. Tex. Med. Br., Galveston.Diplomate Am. Bd. Internal Medicine. Fellow A.C.P.; mem. Tex. Acad. Internal Medicine (pres.), Internat. Med. Assembly S.W. Tex. (past pres.), Tex. Med. Assn. (past chmn. bd. trustees), Bexar County Med. Soc. (past pres.), Alumni Assn. Med. Br. U. Tex. (past pres.), Tex Diabetes Soc. (pres.), Tex. Philos. Soc., Order of Alamo, Tex. Cavaliers, Phi Chi, Alpha Omega Alpha. Clubs: Conopus, Argyle, Rotary. Home: San Antonio, Tex. Died 1976.

MINTZ, HERMAN ARTHUR, lawyer, corp. exec.; b. Russia, Mar. 18, 1886; s. Fishel T. and Rosa (Shapiro) M.; brought to U.S., 1892, naturalized, 1907; A.B., Harvard, 1908. LL.B., 1910; m. Esther M. Gordon, Oct. 11, 1915; children—Marjorie Gordon (Mrs. Theodore Deltz), Richard Gordon. Admitted to Mass. bar. 1909, since practiced in Boston as sr. partner Mintz, Levin & Cohn. Member of the board directors Boston Municipal Research Association; trustee Children's Cancer Research Found., Inc., Beth Israel Hosp. Fellow Brandeis U. Home: Boston. *

MIRGAIN, FRANK CHARLES, coll. dean, engr.; b. Chgo., Oct. 19, 1909; s. Charles and Julia (Gilson) M.; B.S., Purdue U., 1931; M.S., Rutgers U., 1933; m. Velma N. Chase, Sept. 3, 1931; children—Cheryl Louise, William Chase, Judith Aileen. Instr. civil engring. Rutgers U., 1933-39, asst. prof. civil engring., 1939-42, asso. prof., 1942-47, prof., 1947-49; prof. and head dept. civil engring. Cooper Union, 1949-54; dean Coll. Engring., N.D. State U., 1954-75, dean emeritus, 1975-77. Mem. N.D. Civil Rights Adv. Com., N.D. Comprehensive Health Planning Adv. Com. Mem. Am. Soc. C.E., Nat. Soc. Profl. Engrs. (v.p.), Am. Soc. Engring. Edn., N.J. (pres.), N.D. (pres.) socs. profl. engrs., Fargo C. of C. (past dir.), Tau Beta Pi, Chi Epsilon. Elk (trustee N.D.). Home: Fargo, N.D. Died Feb. 16, 1977.

MIRICK, GEORGE HAMMOND, lawyer; b. Worcester, Mass., Sept. 7, 1885; s. Albert Henry and Anita Leonora (Henry) M.; A.B., Clark Coll., 1907; student Harvard Law Sch., 1907-10; m. Ruth Lois Goodnow, Oct. 11, 1915; children—Susannah, Richard Walter, Sally Anita, Albert H., II. Admitted to Massachusetts bar, 1910, and since in general practice; partner Mirick, O'Connell & De Mallis; dir. Worcester County Trust Co.; chmn. bd. dirs. M.J. Whittall Assn., Inc.; trustee Worcester County Instn. for Savings. Member Worcester City Council, 1914-16. Pres. bd. trustees, Clark U. Mem. Am., Mass. and Worcester County bar assns. Republican. Mason, Clubs: Worcester, Economic. Home: Worcester, Mass. *

MIROVITCH, ALFRED BERNARD, pianist; b. Leningrad, Russia, May 4, 1884; s. Bernard and Emma (Meyrovitch) M.; student Coll. of St. Peter to 1901; studied at Imperial Conservatory of Music, Russia to 1909; m. Mercedes Olds, of Portland, Ore., Oct. 24, 1926. Came to U.S., 1921, naturalized, 1936. Made debut as concert pianist in Russia, 1913; toured China, Japan, Java and India, 1914-21; Am. debut at Carnegie Hall, New York, 1921; appeared with New York Philharmonic Orchestra in Phila., Boston, Detroit, Minneapolis, Los Angeles; toured Europe and the Orient, 1926-31; concert tours in U.S. since 1931; also lecturer and educator. Home: New York, N.Y. *

MIROYIANNIS, STANLEY DEMETRIUS, anatomist; b. Metelin, Greece, Nov. 24, 1908; s. Demetrius George and Androniki John (Mandanis) M.; naturalized U.S. citizen; ed. Gymnasium of Metelin, Greece, 1917-21; S.B., Northwest Nazarene Coll., Nampa, Idaho, 1927; student Mass. State Coll., 1927-28; A.M., Boston U., 1929, Ph.D., 1939; m. Ruth E. Nemmers, Nov. 24, 1958. Grad. asst. biology Boston U., 1939-31, teaching fellow, 1931-36, lectr. summers, 1933-36; lectr. and head dept. gross anatomy New Eng. Inst. Anatomy, Boston, 1935-49; cons. in biology Northeastern U., Boston, 1935-36, asst. prof., 1936-38, asso. prof., 1938-40, prof. and head dept., 1940-48; prof. advanced biology Grad. Sch. Mass. Coll. Pharmacy, Boston, 1948-52; prof. anatomy Des Moines Still Coll., 1952-72, chmn. dept. anatomy, 1953-72, chmn. div. basic scis., 1954-72, also mem. student loan, ednl. policies, admissions com., pres. faculty senate. Lt. col. M.S.C., USAR. Fellow AAAS, Iowa Acad. Sci., Am. Med. Writers Assn., Acad. Zool., Royal Soc. Health (Eng.), Royal Soc. Medicine (London), Midwestern Assn. Anatomists, So. Soc. Anatomists; mem. Inst. Nuclear Medicine (London), N.Y. Acad. Scis., Teratology Soc., Assn. Tropical Biology, Mus. Natural History, Nat. Soc. for Med. Research, Am. Inst. Biol. Scis., Am. Soc. Exptl. Biology, Nat. Assn. Biology, Am. Soc. Mammalogists, Am. Assn. Profl. Biologists, Assn. Mil. Surgeons U.S.A., AAUP, Am. Soc. Zoologists, Soc. Systematic Zoology, Gen. Research System Soc., Mil. Govt. Assn., Res. Officers Assn., Med. Service Corps Assn., Am. Assn. Developmental Biology, Am. Micros. Soc., Am. Soc. Morphologists, So., Japanese, Mexican assns. anatomists, Sigma Xi, Iota Tau Sigma, Kappa Phi Kappa. Author: A Laboratory Course in General Zoology; The Cell and Fundamental Tissues; Microscopic Anatomy; 501 Questions and Their Answers in Gross Anatomy, 1959; also sci. papers. Home: Des Moines, Iowa. Died June 1, 1980; buried Mt. Calvary Cemetery, Dubuque, Iowa.

MISCHAKOFF, MISCHA, (ADOPTED NAME), violinist; b. Proskourov, Russia; s. Issac and Massia Fishberg; grad. Imperial Conservatory, St. Petersburg, Russia, 1912 (gold medal, Rubinstein prize); Ph.D., Eastern Mich. U., 1965, m. Hortense Moritz, Sept. 30, 1937; children—Paul, Anne, Matthew. Came to U.S., 1921, naturalized, 1927. Debut as violinist at Lipetzk, 1905; prof. Govt. Conservatory, Nizhni-Novgorod, 1918-20; concert master Moscow Grand Opera, 1920-21, Warsaw Philharmonic Orch., 1921-22; appeared as soloist in Petrograd, Moscow, Warsaw, Berlin; soloist with leading orchs. in U.S.; winner N.Y. Stadium Audition, 1923; concertmaster N.Y. Symphony Orch., 1924-27, Phila. Orch., 1927-29; became concertmaster Chgo. Symphony Orch., 1930, head violin dept. Am. Conservatory Music, Chgo., 1930; concertmaster NBC Symphony under direction of Arturo Toscanini, 1937-52, also leader of NBC String Quartet; concertmaster Detroit Symphony Orch., 1952-68; dir.-founder Mischakoff String Quartet; head violin dept. Chautaugua Instn., N.Y., 1926-65; concertmaster, soloist Meadow Brook Festival; mem. faculty Juilliard Sch. Music, 1940-52; faculty Oakland U., 1965-68; now prof. Wayne State U.; guest prof. Aspen Music Festival, 1970-73, spl. guest concertmaster, 1973; spl. guest concertmaster Balt. Symphony, 1969-70; guest prof. U. Colo., U. Mich., Boston U., 1971; prof. Peabody Conservatory, 1969-70. Mem. Soc. Am. Musicians (Chgo.). Club: Bohemians (N.Y.C.). Home: Detroit, Mich. Died Feb. 1, 1981.

MISER, HUGH DINSMORE, geologist; b. Pea Ridge, Ark., Dec. 18, 1884; s. Jordan Stanford and Eliza Caroline (Webb) M.; A.B., University of Arkansas, 1908, A.M., 1912, Doctor of Laws, 1949; m. Mary Kate Goddard, Sept. 21, 1910 (dec. 1963); d., Mrs. Catherine E. Kayser. Joined U.S. Geol. Survey, as field asst., 1907, jr. geologist, 1911, asst. geologist, 1912, asso. geologist, 1913-18, geologist, 1919-54, in charge sect. areal geology, 1927, regional geologist for eastern United States, 1942; chief fuels sect., 1928-47, staff geol., 1947-54, scientific staff assistant Office of Dir., 1955—; cons. geologist Ark. Geol. and Conservation Commission, 1959—; geologist Ark. Geological Survey, 1907-10; geologist Tenn. Geol. Survey, 1912 and 1917; state geologist of Tennessee, 1926; acting prof. geology, U. of Ark., and state geologist of Arkansas, 1920. Made investigation of manganese deposits in U.S. during World Wars I and II; author first multicolored geologic map of Okla., 1926, 2d, 1954; geologist to engring. party that explored and mapped San Juan Canyon, Utah, 1921. Dir. Sibley Memorial Hosp. (1925-44; chmn. bd. 1936-37). Recipient Distinguished Service Medal, U.S. Dept. Interior, 1955. Mem. Am. Assn. Petroleum Geologists (hon. mem. 1948), Soc. Econ., Geologists, Geol. Soc. Am., Geol. Soc. Washington (pres. 1938), Washington (v.p. 1939), Tenn. acads. scis., Mineral. Soc. Am., N.M. (hon.), Tulsa (hon.), Oklahoma City (hon.) geol. socs., Okla. Mineral and Gem. Soc. (hon.), Okla. Acad. Sci., Sigma Gamma Epsilon (hon.). Donated collection of 5700 rare and select Ark. quartz crystals to U. Ark. Mus., 1954. Home: Washington. *

MITAU, G. THEODORE, educator; b. Berlin, Germany, Apr. 4, 1920; s. Alexander and Rosel (Streim) M.; B.A., Macalester Coll., 1940; M.A., U. Minn., 1942, Ph.D., 1948; m. Charlotte Cutts, Sept. 7, 1941; children—Lee, Andrea Mitau Kircher. Mem. faculty Macalester Coll., St. Paul, 1940-68, James Wallace prof. polit. sci., 1963-68, chmn. dept. polit. sci., 1956-68; chancellor Minn. State U. System, St. Paul, 1968-76, distinguished service prof. polit. sci., 1976-79. Adj. prof. pub. affairs U. Minn.; vis. prof. U. Nebr.; chmn. task force on innovation and change in higher edn. Am. Assn. State Colls. and Univs.; chmn. Middle States accreditation com. Empire State Coll., State U. N.Y.; nat. program chmn. ann. conf. Soc. Coll. and Univ. Planning; cons. intergovtl. relations U.S. CSC; research cons. Minn. Legislative Commn. on Election Laws, Minn. Hist. Soc.; mem. com. appeals N. Central Accrediting Assn.; adv. com. Edn. Commn. States; adv. com. higher edn. Midwestern Conf. Council State Govts.; higher edn. adv. council Minn. Higher Edn. Coordinating Commn.; mem. Minn. Council Econ. Edn., Minn. Coll. Govt. Council. Mem. Gov.'s Council on Exec. Reorgn.; mem. St. Paul Charter Commn. Bd. dirs. Fund for Improvement Post-Secondary Edn., Twin City Area Ednl. TV Corp., Minn. Edn. Computing Consortium, North Star Research and Devel. Inst., Dynamy Minn., United Hosps., St. Paul; bd. dirs., exec. council Nat. Center for Higher Edn. Mgmt. Systems. Served to capt. AUS, World War II. Recipient Thomas Jefferson award for distinguished teaching McConnel Found. Mem. Am. Council Edn. (sec., exec. com.), Minn. Hist. Soc. (council), Phi Beta Kappa. Author: Politics in Minnesota, 1960; Proximate Solutions, Case Problems in State and Local Government (with Harold W. Chase), 1964; Insoluable Problems, 1966; Decade of Decision: The Supreme Court and the Constitutional Revolution, 1967; State and Local Government: Politics and Processes, 1966. Book rev. editor Midwestern Jour. Polit. Sci. Home: Saint Paul, Minn. Died July 5, 1979.

MITCHELL, H(ARRY) A(LOYSIUS), ry. official; b. San Francisco, Calif., June 20, 1883; s. Thomas and Susan T. (Breslin) M.; ed. pub. schs.; m. Myrtle E. Kerr, Oct. 5, 1927. Clk. with Equitable Gas Co., 1898-1903; with San Francisco Gas Co., 1903-06; with Thompson-Starrett Co., 1906-07; auditor City Electric Co., 1907; auditor Central Calif. Traction Co., 1907-09, gen. mgr. and sec., 1909-12; gen. mgr. San Francisco-Sacramento R.R. Co., 1913-20, vice pres., 1920-29; pres. and dir. Sacramento Northern Ry., 1929-46; v.p. and gen. mgr. Western Pacific R.R. Co., 1946-48, pres. 1949. Chmn. exec. com. Calif. Transit Assn.; chmn. San Francisco Bay area Rapid Transit Commn.; dir. Cal. C. of C.; exec. com. Nat. Soc. for Crippled Children and Adults; president Calif. Soc. Crippled Children. Roman Catholic. Clubs: Rotary, Bohemian, Sutter. Home: Atherton, Calif. *

MITCHELL, J. RONALD, broadcasting co. exec.; b. Winnipeg, Man., Canada, June 23, 1933; s. Clifford and Clarice (Way) M.; diploma in accounting U. Man., 1957; children—J. Clifford, Grant E., Donna G. Auditor, Deloitte, Plender, Haskins & Sells, Winnipeg, 1951-56, Haskins & Sells, Chgo., 1956-58; prin. Deloitte, Haskins & Sells, Toronto, 1958-60, Winnipeg, 1960-63; asst. to pres. Moffat Communications Ltd., Winnipeg, 1963-64, exec. v.p., 1964-70, pres., chief exec. officer, 1970-79; dir. CTV TV Network Ltd., Sta. CHED. Registered indsl. accountant. Mem. Canadian Assn. Broadcasters, Major Mkts. Broadcasters., Inst. Chartered Accountants. Liberal. Mem. United Ch. Can. Clubs: St. Charles, Winnipeg Winter, Mason. Home: Winnipeg Man., Canada. Died Aug. 20, 1979; buried Garry Meml. Park, Winnipeg.

MITCHELL, NICHOLAS PENDLETON, educator; b. Seymour, Tex., Apr. 25, 1911; s. Nick P. and Maude Amanda (Head) M.; B.A., U. Tex., 1929, M.A., 1930; Ph.D., Duke, 1934; m. Gartha Lena Morgan, Nov. 11, 1930; children—Nicholas Pendleton, III, Morgan Head, Maude Amanda. Instr. in govt. La. State U., 1930-31; teaching fellow in govt. Duke, 1931-34, part time instr., 1934-35; acting prof. history and polit. sci. U. Richmond, 1935-36; prof., head dept. polit. sci. Furman U., 1936-46; chmn. grad. dept., 1942-46; prof. govt., extension dept. U. S.C., 1939-50, dir. news service, 1956, dir. extension, 1957-65, dean Coll. Gen. Studies, 1965-71, asso. provost, 1971-74, v.p., 1974-76, distinguished prof. adult and continuing edn., 1973-76, prof. emeritus, 1976-79; asso. editor Greenville News, 1950-55; editor, pub. Fla. Keys Keynoter, 1955-57; editor Furman Univ. Press, 1940-45. Founder, pres. Greenville Town Hall; chmn. S.C. Com. on Humanities, 1971-77, adminstrv. officer, 1977—. Mem. Am. Polit. Sci. Assn., AAUP, So. Polit. Sci. Assn., Am. Soc. Internat. Law, Am. Assn. U. Adminstrs., S.C. Adv. Council on Adult Edn. (chmn. 1951-60), Nat. Univ. Extension Assn. (pres. 1969-70), Adult Edn. Assn. U.S., S.E. Adult Edn. Assn. (pres. 1953-55), Internat. Platform Assn., Sigma Alpha Epsilon, Phi Beta Kappa, Pi Sigma Alpha, Sigma Delta Pi, Alpha Epsilon Rho, Pi Gamma Mu. Democrat. Presbyn. Clubs: Rotary (gov. 1959-60), Thirty-nine, Poinsett. Author: Land Problems and Policies in the African Mandates of the British Commonwealth, 1931; State Interests in American Treaties, 1936. Co-author: Government in the City and County of Greenville, S.C., 1941. Radio news commentator, 1941-79. Editor: Adult Leadership, 1957-79. Home: Columbia, S.C. Died Aug. 26, 1980; buried Greenlawn Cemetery, Greenlawn.

MITCHELL, SHEPARD, lawyer; b. Sebetha, Kan., May 12, 1884; s. W. C. and Jessie (Shepard) M.; A.B., Stanford, 1908; student U. Chgo., m. Ruth Wattes, May 21, 1937; 1 dau., Caroline (Mrs. Caroline Hardy). Admitted to Cal. bar bar, asso. office John W. Kemp, 1908-10; partner Kemp, Mitchell & Silberberg, Los Angeles, 1910-25, Mitchell, Silberberg & Davis, 1925-32, Mitchell, Silberberg & Knupp, 1932—. Dir. Utah Constrn. Co. Mem. Am., Cal., Los Angeles bar assns. Home: Beverly Hills CA. *

MITCHELL, WALLACE MACMAHON, artist; b. Detroit, Oct. 9, 1911; s. Arthur and Edith (MacMahon) M.; student Hamilton Coll., 1931-33; B.A., Northwestern U., 1934; student Cranbrook Acad. Art, 1935; M.A., Columbia, 1936; m. Virginia Mills, 1941 (div.); children—Dinah, Jeffrey; m. 2d, Mary Stringer, Mar. 22, 1956; children—Daniel, Patrick. Instr. drawing and painting Cranbrook Acad. Art, Bloomfield Hills, Mich., 1936-54, sec., registrar, 1944-56, dir. galleries, 1954-71, pres., 1970-77; one-man exhbns. Bertha Schaefer Gallery, N.Y.C., 1950, 57, U. Minn., Mpls., 1954. Cranbrook Acad. Art, 1947, 53, 71, 77, Detroit Artists Market, 1939, 56, Ill. Inst. Tech., 1963, Flint (Mich.) Inst. Arts, 1971; paintings in permanent collections Detroit Inst. Arts, Cranbrook Acad. Art, Solomon Guggenheim Mus., N.Y.C., Kalamazoo Art Center, mural Gen. Motors Tech. Center, U. Ky. Med. Center. Home: Bloomfield Hills, Mich. Died Jan. 13, 1977.

MITCHELL, WILLIAM ARTHUR, banking; b. Hamilton, Can., June 6, 1892; s. Robert and Janet (Ewing) M.; student Hamilton Collegiate Inst., 1904-07, Queens Univ., Kingston, Can. (extra-mural), 1912-15; LL.D., Mount Union Coll., Alliance, O., 1938; m. Georgie Linn Brown, Nov. 2, 1920; children—David Lindsay, Robert G. B. (dec.), Janet, Elizabeth Ann. Came to U.S., 1925, naturalized, 1936. Asso. with Traders Bank of Can. and Royal Bank of Can., 1908-25; asso. with J. P. Morgan & Co., New York, 1925-49, former partner, served as v.p., dir. and mem. exec. com.; chmn. Central Trust Co., Cin., 1949-62, then dir.; chmn. adv. com. Export-Import Bank, Washington; dir., mem. exec. com. Asso. Dry Goods Co.; dir. Earthage Mills, Inc., Cin., Am. Bankshares, Inc., Lunkendeimer Co., Cin. Gas & Electric Co., D. H. Baldwin Co., Natl. Starch & Chem. Co., N.Y., Lindsay Wire Weaving Co., Cleve.; mem. adv. bd. Lord & Taylor, N.Y.C. Trustee Nat. Conf. of Christians and Jews, Salvation Army, Cincinnati; president Greater Cin. Hosp. Funds, Inc., Mental Health Assn.; chairman Cincinnati Council World Affairs. With Can. Army, 1914. Mem. Assn. Res. City Bankers (pres. 1948-49). Trustee U.S. Council of Internat. C. of C. Mem. Am. Arbitration Assn. (dir.). Presbyn. Mason. Clubs: Queen City, Commercial, Bankers (Cin.); Links, Canadian Society (N.Y.). Home: Cincinnati, Ohio. Died Mar. 1, 1980.

MITCHELL, WILLIAM JOHN, educator; b. N.Y.C., Nov. 21, 1906; s. Philip Alfred and Louise (Goering) M.; A.B., Columbia, 1930, A.M., 1938; m. Adelheid Ida Wagner, 1933 (div.); children—Judith Ann, Thomas William; m. 2d, Alice Levine; children—Philip Andrew and Aaron Peter (twins), Susan. Instr. music Columbia, 1932-41, asst. prof., 1941-47, asso. prof., 1947-52, prof., 1952-69, asst. to dean, 1948-58, mem. com. on instrn., 1957-63, chmn. dept. music, 1962-68; prof. State U. N.Y., Binghamton, 1969-71; vis. prof. U. Cal. at Los Angeles, 1950, 57, U. Ore., 1964, U. So. Cal., 1970; U.S. specialist musicology Office Cultural Exchange, Dept. State to visit Soviet Union, 1961; lectr. Mannes Coll. Music; cons. Dept. Health, Edn. and Welfare, Nat. Endowment for Humanities. Bd. dirs. Walter W. Naumburg Found., v.p., 1968-71. Recipient grant Council Research Humanities, Columbia, 1962. Sec., 8th Congress Internat. Musicol. Soc., 1961. Mem. Am. Musicol. Soc. (pres. 1965-66), Coll. Music Soc., Soc. for Music Liberal Arts Coll. (chmn. 1953). Author: Elementary Harmony, 1939, 3d edit., 1965; Essay on the True Art of Playing Keyboard Instruments, 1949. Contbg. editor Piano Quar. Newsletter, 1954-71; editor Pianist's Page, Etude, 1956-57; co-editor Music Forum. Contbr. ednl. jours. Home: Binghamton, N.Y. Died Aug. 17, 1971.

MITTELSTAEDT, RICHARD E., army officer; b. Calif., Apr. 28, 1884; commd. 2d lt. Inf., Calif. Nat. Guard, Aug. 1905, and advanced to brig. gen. of the line, Oct. 1938; entered Fed. service Mar. 1941; in command, 79th Inf. Brigade, 40th Div., in training

Camp Merriam. San Luis Obispo, Calif. Address: San Luis Obispo, Calif. *

MOCK, GLADYS, painter, engraver; b. N.Y.C.; d. Eugene W. and Rina (Walter) Mock; ed. Calhoun Sch., Art Student League, N.Y.C.; m. Pierce Trowbridge Wetter, 1924; children—Renice Telfair, Pierce Trowbridge. Exhibited Internat. Exhbn., Carnegie Inst., Corcoran Gallery, Phila. Acad. Fine Arts, Chgo. Art Inst., Nat. Acad. Design, N.Y. World's Fair, Exhbn. of Contemporary Art, 1939-40, Portrait of Am. Exhbn., 1944-45; work represented in public galleries Mountain Lake, A.M. Todd collection, Kalamazoo, Mich., The Spring, Pa. Acad. Fine Arts, Phila., engravings Library Congress, Ft. Hays State Coll., Telfair Acad. Art, Savannah, Ga., N.Y. Public Library. Syracuse U., Smithsonian Inst., Washington, Met. Mus. of Art, N.Y.C.; charge sales service Bur. Am. Fedn. Arts and N.Y. rep. Am. Mag. of Art at Met. Mus. of Art. 1918-28. Recipient award for engraving Lifting Clouds, Assn. Print for Year, 1948; 1st prize Pen and Brush Club, 1948, for graphics, 1959, 65, 68, 71; Medal of Honor, Nat. Assn. Women Artists, 1951, 54, Katheryn Colton prize graphics, 1971; 1st prize black and white Champliain Exhbn. (Vt.), 1951; hon. mention Audubon Artists, 1960, 64; Margaret Lowengrund Meml. prize Nat. Assn. Women Artists Ann. Exhbn., 1962; John Taylor Arms medal and purchase award Audubon Artists 1968; purchase award Huntington Nat. Graphics Exhibit, 1968; purchase prize N.Y. Pub. Library, 1971. Mem. Soc. Am. Graphic Artists (pres. 1959, 60, 61), Nat. Assn. Women Artists, Audubon Artists (dir., v.p.), Library of Congress, Painters and Sculptors Soc. N.J., Huntingdon County Art Center, Pen and Brush Club. Home: New York, N.Y. Died Oct. 29, 1976.

MOEHLMAN, ARTHUR HENRY, educator, author; b. Rochester, N.Y., Feb. 19, 1907; s. Conrad Henry and Bertha (Young) M.; A.B., U. Rochester, 1928; A.M., Ph.D., U. Mich., 1932; internat. fellow, U. Basel (Switzerland), 1929; m. Marguerite Carolyn Reichenbourg, Dec. 22, 1933; children—Michael Scott, Stephen Mackaye, Patricia des Roses, Jacqueline Arnauld. Instr. history and social science U. Mich., 1929-32; asst. prof. history and social sci. Ohio State U., 1932-36, asso. prof., 1937-40; prof. history and philosophy of edn. U. Iowa, 1946-54; prof. history and philosophy of edn. U. Tex., from 1954, emeritus until 1978, dir. Center History of Edn., from 1966; cultural attache Am. embassy, Bonn, Germany, 1962-64; research prof. history philosophy of edn. Sorbonne, U. Paris, 1951-52; Fulbright lectr. contemporary Am. civilization Göttingen, Germany, 1961-62, State Dept. lectr. comparative edn.; guest lectr. U. Basel, 1962, U. Hamburg, 1964, also U. Heidelberg, U. Bonn; field reader, cons. U.S. Office Edn. Mem. Commn. Internat. Edn., P.D.K., from 1948; exec. bd. History of Edn., ASCTE, from 1948, completion of survey in U.S. and Canada for ASCTE, 1951; expert cons. to FCC on TV in Higher Edn., 1951; population research mem. Ohio Planning Commn., 1935; del. Regional and Town Planning Internat. Meeting, London, Eng., 1936; field survey of European ednl. systems, 1936. Served to col. AUS, 1941-46; chief German sect. Mil. Intelligence Div., G-2, assisted planning and writing estimates German mil. situation; mission to India, 1944; U.S. Group Control Council for Germany; demobilization rep. at Potsdam Conf. Fellow Am. Geog. Soc., Philosophy Edn. Soc., Royal Geog. Soc., Comparative Edn. Soc.; mem. Am. Hist. Assn., AAAS, Res. Officers Assn., Inst. Latin Am. Studies (exec. sec.), All U. Research Council, Phi Beta Kappa. Episcopalian. Kiwanis. Author: A History of Dur Times, Vol. 1 and 2, 1937; Comparative Educational Systems, 1963; monographs in history and philosophy of edn. Editor Our Times, 1936-37; The German Armed Forces, 1941; Comparative Education, 1952; Comparative Educational Systems, 1963, trans into Spanish and Japanese; A Guide to Computer-Assisted Historical Research in American Education, 1969; Vol. XVIII, Theorien der Demokratischen Erziehung und Bildung, 1977-78. Contbr. articles to profl. jours. Research history and philosophy edn., comparative edn.; (with wife) joint research higher edn. field trips Ecology and Axiology of Universities American and European, summers 1967, 70, 72, 73; Japanese research journey, 1974; survey St. Andrews Boy High Sch., Osaka, Japan; contbr. hist. geog. and ednl. revs. to Our Times, 1937; author manuals and handbooks for armed forces. Writer, instr. TV project Adventures in Edn., 1957-58. Inventor computer-data mgmt. system's research technique, Morphology of Categories; MORC Fourteen Fator systems analyst; comparative hist. studies internat. higher edn., comparative studies in planning ednl. policy; devel. (with C. Yurkanan, J. Edmondson) Data Entry Template; also interdisciplinary Omega Project. Home: Austin, Tex. Died Feb. 8, 1978.

MOELLER, WILLIAM, JR., public utilities; b. Mount Vernon, N.Y., June 18, 1886; s. Wm. Moeller; student Stevens Inst. of Technology; m. Irene Bonetti, Apr. 11, 1918. Engr. in motive power dept. Buffalo & Susquehanna R.R., Galeton, Pa., 1906-07; engr., asst. chief engr. and chief engr. Kansas Natural Gas Co., Independence, Kans., 1907-13; chief engr. Empire Co. (H. L. Doherty), Bartlesville, Okla., 1913-14; chief engr. and gen. mgr. Midway Gas Co., Los Angeles, Calif., 1914-27; mgr. and vice-pres. in charge of natural gas production and transmission Southern Calif. Gas Co. since 1927; also mem. management com., and past chmn. natural gas dept. Am. Gas Assn. Advisory com. Pacific Coast Gas Assn. (past pres.), Am. Gas Assn., Am. Petroleum Inst. Mem. exec. com. and dir. Calif. Natural Gasoline Assn. Mason (Shriner). Clubs: Wilshire Country, California Club. Home: Los Angeles. *

MOFFITT, FREDERICK JAMES, editor, educator; b. Ellicotville, N.Y., Feb. 23, 1896; s. John Aaron and Mary Gertrude (Canfield) M.; A.B., Hobart Coll., 1918, Litt.D. (hon.), 1933; M.A., U. Buffalo, 1930; student New Coll., Oxford (Eng.) U., 1919, Syracuse U., 1921-23; m. Georgia Frank, Sept. 11, 1916; 1 dau., Sue (Mrs. Orman Billings). Classroom tchr., 1923-25; sch. supt., 1925-40; dir. pub. relations N.Y. State Tchrs. Assn., 1941-42; N.Y. state supr. elementary edn., 1942-52; exec. asst. to N.Y. State Commr. Edn., 1952-54, asso. commr. edn., 1954-56; editor profl. publs. Silver Burdett Pub. Co., 1956-59; spl. asst. to U.S. Commr. Edn., 1959-61; cons. U.S. Office Edn., 1962; editor Jack and Jill mag., 1963-80; cons. editor, author Gen. Learning Corp., 1967-68; contbg. editor Mags. for Children. Served with U.S. Army, 1917-19; AEF in France. Recipient medal S.A.R., 1956, Distinguished Teaching medal L.I. U., 1957; decorated Verdun medal; Freedoms Found. award; award SAR; hon. chief St. Regis Indians. Mem. Kappa Sigma. Republican. Protestant Episcopalian. Author: Chalkdust, 1939-80; Study of School Superintendency, 1930; Reading Interests of Young Children, 1956; Legends of the Iroquois, 1957; Children of the World (series); Indian Tales Retold; Egyptian Legends; The Warrior King. Home: Madison, N.J. Died Mar. 30, 1980.

MOFFITT, JAMES P., foreign service officer; b. Albany, N.Y., Mar. 18, 1886; LL.B., Fordham U., 1910; married. Sec., teacher, librarian, 1907-10; law practice, 1910-17; lt. U.S. Army, 1917-19; consul. Brussels, 1920; consul. Rangoon, 1921; detailed to Cape Town, 1924, consul, 1925; consul, Johannesburg, 1925, Lourenco Marques, 1925; Dept. of State, 1928; consul, Marseilles, 1930. Stuttgart, 1933. Amsterdam, 1936, Caracas, 1941; consul general, Caracas, 1944; consul gen., Monterrey, Mexico, 1946-48; retired. Clubs: Army-Navy Country (Arlington, Va.); University (Washington). Home: Alexandria, Va. *

MOISE, WILLIAM SIDNEY, artist, educator; b. Carlinville, Ill., Feb. 22, 1922; s. Lionel and Maryon Virginia (Mounts) M.; B.A., U. of the South, 1943; C.F.A., Cooper Union Art Sch., N.Y.C., 1949; M.A., Columbia, 1952; 1 dau., Renata Reich. Art tchr. Downtown Community Sch., N.Y.C., 1950-52; art tchr. Mt. Desert (Maine) Island Schs., 1952-54; art tchr. Grovetown (Va.) High Sch., 1955-58; art instr. No. Conservatory Music, Bangor, Maine, 1960-69; works exhibited Selected Artists Galleries, N.Y.C., 1973, Venable-Neslage Galleries, Washington, 1974, Las Baux de Provence, France, 1975. Sec.-treas. Oranur Weather Control, Inc., 1955-56. Sec. Wilhelm Reich Found., 1954-57. Served with USNR, 1943-45. Wilhelm Reich Found. grantee, 1954-56. Mem. Maine Art Tchrs. Assn. (v.p. 1951-52), Artist Equity Assn., Bangor Art Soc. (pres. 1969-70). Author: The Taste of Color, A Touch of Love, 1972. Address: Hancock, Maine. Died Aug. 6, 1980.

MOLINA, JUAN BAUTISTA (MO-LĒ'NÄ), leader Argentina Alliance of National Youth; b. Salta, Argentina, Aug. 29, 1882; student Officers Sch., Marksman's Sch., War Coll.; m. Adelaida Tamborini. Mem. German Army, 1911-13; prof., company comdt., Mil. Coll., 1915-16; comdt., head of batn., prof., Marksman's Sch.; dir. Officers Training Sch., sec. to pres., 1930-32; pres., noncommissioned Inf. and Arty.; pres., fgn. Supply Commn., Brussels and Paris; mil. attaché, Germany, 1933; dir. gen., War Ministry of Engrs., 1936-38. Pres. Mil. Circle, 1937-39. Took up leadership of Alliance of Nationalists Youth, modelled on Spanish Falange, 1940*

MOLLISON, CLARENCE LONGMAN, lawyer; b. West View, Ohio, May 31, 1906; s. Alexander D. and Maria (Knight) M.; student Cleve. Coll. of Western Res. U., 1924-26; J.D., Cleve.-Marshall Law Sch., Cleve. State U., 1930, LL.M., 1932; m. Ethel Denman, Dec. 24, 1930 (div.); 1 dau., Marlene Joyce (Mrs. David Alan Baker); m. 2d, Charlotte Yorke, Dec. 9, 1969. Admitted to Ohio bar, 1930; mem. Payer, Bleiweiss, Crow & Mollison, 1931-51; asst. law dir. City of Cleve., 1945-51; mem. Hauxhurst, Sharp, Mollison & Gallagher, Cleve., 1951-81. Mem. Am., Ohio, Cleve., Cuyahoga County bar assns., Internat. Assn. Ins. Counsel (state chmn.), Maritime Law Assn. U.S., Am. Coll. Trial Lawyers, Citizens League Cleve. Democrat. Baptist. Mason (32 deg., Shriner), Lion (past pres.). Clubs: Shrine Luncheon. Author articles in field. Home: Painesville, Ohio. Died Jan. 1, 1981.

MOLLOY, ERNEST LAWRENCE, retail co. exec.; b. Cambridge, Mass., May 11, 1906; s. Ernest Lane and Gertrude (Sprague) M.; A.B., Harvard, 1929; m. Julia A. Wall, Sept. 3, 1932; children—Juliana (Mrs. John Shields), Sheila (Mrs. Robert Gast II), Molly (Mrs. Michael Linneman, Jr.), Michael W. With R.H. Macy & Co., Inc., 1929-76, pres., dir. Cal. div., San Francisco, 1952-66, dir. parent company, N.Y.C., 1961-71, pres., 1966-68, pres., chief exec. officer, 1968-71, cons., dir., 1971-76; cons., dir. W.R. Grace Co. Dir., mem. exec. com. Cal. Retailers Assn., 1948-66; v.p. dir. San Francisco Downtown Assn., 1952-66. Trustee Presbyn. Hosp., San Francisco, 1962-66; trustee St. Mary's Coll., Moraga, Calif., 1964-76. Clubs: Harvard, Pacific-Union (San Francisco); Union League, Winged Foot Golf, N.Y. Athletic, Harvard (N.Y.C.); Pine Tree Golf (Delray Beach, Fla.). Home: Incline Village, Nev. Died Nov. 23, 1976.

MOLLOY, ROBERT, author; b. Charleston, S.C., Jan. 9, 1906; s. Robert William and Edith Estelle (Johnson) M.; ed. in pvt. and pub. schs., Charleston, Phila. and N.Y.C.; m. Marion Knapp Jones, June 29, 1929; children—Brian Frederick, Thomas Lawrence. Book editor The New York Sun, 1943-45; copy editor Daily News. Author: Pride's Way, 1945; Uneasy Spring, 1946; Charleston: A Gracious Heritage, 1947; The Best of Intentions, 1949; Pound Foolish, 1950; A Multitude of Sins, 1953; An Afternoon in March, 1958; The Reunion, 1959; The Other Side of the Hill, 1962. Translator various works from German, French, Spanish, including Dona Barbara (Romulo Gallegos), 1931. Contbr. articles Columbia Ency. Home: Paramus, N.J. Died Jan. 27, 1977.

MOLONY, WILLIAM HAYES, clergyman, physicist; b. Crawfordsville, Ind., Dec. 4, 1884; s. James Sullivan and Mary (Hayes) M.; Litt.B., Notre Dame, 1907; student Catholic U. of Am., Washington, 1907-10. Dir. studies, St. Edward's Coll., Austin, Tex., 1912-19, dir. studies and registrar, 1934-43; prof. physics and math., Notre Dame, 1912-32, dir. studies and registrar, 1933-34, prof. physics since 1943. Address: Notre Dame Ind. *

MOLYNEAUX, PETER (MOL'I-NO), journalist; b. New Orleans, La., Apr. 18, 1882; s. James and Rosana (Lawlor) M.; student parochial schs., New Orleans, Meadville (Pa.) Theol. Sch.; LL.D., Southern Methodist University, Dallas, Tex., 1935; reporter Daily News, Item and Daily States, New Orleans, 1902-08, Phila. Record, 1911, San Antonio (Tex.) Express, 1913-14, Houston (Tex.) Post, 1914-15; chief editorial writer Ft. Worth (Tex.) Star-Telegram, 1915-24; editor Tex. Monthly, 1928-30; editor and pub. Tex. Weekly, 1930-40; editor, Texas Digest since 1940; editor Southwestern Banking & Industry Mag. since 1935; editor the Southern Weekly, 1943; pres. Southwest Economic Bur. since 1941. Trustee Carnegie Endowment for International Peace. Mem. Acad. Polit. Science, Am. Acad. Polit. and Social Science, Council on Foreign Relations, Southwestern Social Science Assn., Philos. Soc. of Tex., Phi Beta Kappa Assos. Democrat. Unitarian. Clubs: Advertising (N.Y.); Town and Gown. Author: The Romantic Story of Texas, 1936, The South's Political Plight, 1947; and economic pamphlets. Radio commentator; lecturer. Home: Dallas. *

MONNET, JEAN, French statesman. French rep. Inter.-Allied Maritime Commn., World War I; 1st dep. sec. gen. League of Nations; chmn. Franco-British Econ. Coordination Com., 1939; mem. Brit. Supply Council, Washington, 1940-43, Algiers, 1943-44; commr. armament, supplies and reconstrn. French Com. Nat. Liberation, 1943-44; gen. commr. modernization plan; chmn. European Coal and Steel Community, 1952-55; pres. Action com. U.S. of Europe, 1955-79. Decorated Grand Cross Brit. Empire; recipient Charlemagne prize; U.S. Presdl. Medal of Freedom. Home: Houjarray, France. *

MONOD, JACQUES LUCIEN, educator; b. 1910; Sc.D. (hon.), U. Chgo., 1965, Rockefeller U., 1970. Mem. staff Pasteur Inst., 1945-76, dir. Decorated Bronze Star. Co-recipient Nobel prize in medicine and physiology, 1965. Fgn. mem. Nat. Acad. Scis., Royal Soc. (London), Am. Acad. Arts and Scis. Home: Cannes, France. Died May 31, 1976.

MONRONEY, AIMER STILLWELL MIKE, U.S. senator; b. Oklahoma City, March 2, 1902; s. Almer Ellis and Mary Wood (Stillwell) M.; A.B., U. of Okla., 1924; m. Mary Ellen Mellon, July 3, 1932; 1 son, Michael. Reporter and polit. writer, Oklahoma News, 1924-28; member 76th to 81st Congresses (1939-51), 5th Oklahoma Dist.; U.S. senator from Okla., 1951-69, chmn. Senate post office and civil service com.; co-chmn. joint com. on organization of Congress, 1965-66; aviation-transportation consultant. Mem. Phi Beta Kappa, Phi Gamma Delta, Sigma Delta Chi. Received Collier's award for distinguished congressional service, 1945; Wright Bros. Meml. trophy (aviation), 1961. Democrat. Episcopalian. Home: Washington, D.C. Died Feb. 13, 1980; buried Washington Nat. Cathedral.

MONSARRAT, NICHOLAS, writer; b. Liverpool, Eng., Mar. 22, 1910; s. Keith and Marguerite (Turney) M.; student, Winchester Coll., 1923-28, Cambridge U., 1928-31; m. Eileen Rowland, Sept. 1939; one son; m. 2d, Philippa Crosby, Dec. 1952; two sons; m. 3d, Ann

Griffiths, Dec. 1961. Writer, broadcaster, 1934-79; dir. United Kingdom Information Office, Johannesburg, South Africa, 1946-53, Ottawa, 1953-56. Mem. Kensington Borough Council, 1946. Served as lt. comdr., Royal Navy, World War II; comdg. officer corvette, also frigate, in Atlantic. Fellow Royal Soc. Lit. Author: This is the Schoolroom, 1939; Depends What You Mean by Love, 1947; Three Corvettes, 1948; My Brother Denys, 1949; The Cruel Sea, 1951; The Story of Esther Costello, 1953; The Tribe That Lost Its Head, 1956; The Ship That Died of Shame and Other Stories, 1959; The Nylon Pirates, 1960; The White Rajah, 1961; The Time Before This, 1962; Smith and Jones, 1963; A Fair Day's Work, 1964; The Pillow Fight, 1965; Life is a Four-Letter Word, 1966; Richer Than All His Tribe, 1969. Address: London, England. Died Aug. 8, 1979.

MONTGOMERY, EMERY W(ATKINS), educator; b. Newberry, Ind., Nov. 18, 1882; s. John and Elizabeth Anne (Taylor) M.; A.B., Ind. Univ., 1909, A.M., 1913; D. Humanics, Coll. Osteopathic Phys. and Surg., Los Angeles, Calif., 1946; grad. work Univ. of Chicago, summer 1915, Columbia, summer 1918, 28, Yale, summer 1932; LL.D., U. of Arizona, 1949; m. Adda Alta Smiley, Dec. 24, 1908; children—Berneth Smiley (Mrs. Francis H. Eyre), Mary Elizabeth (Mrs. John Devens Gust). Teacher elementary schs. of Ind., 1901-04; supervising teacher Philippine Islands, 1904-07; teacher and prin. Sheridan (Ind.) High Sch., 1908-10; asst. history dept. Ind. Univ., 1910; teacher Washington (Ind.) High Sch., 1911; prin. Mt. Vernon (Ind.) High Sch., 1911-13, Bedford (Ind.) High Sch., 1913-16, Brazil (Ind.) High Sch., 1916-17; supt. Bedford (Ind.) City Schs., 1917-25; pres. Phoenix (Ariz.) Jr. Coll. and supt. Phoenix Union High Sch. since 1925; mem. council advisors, office edn., U.S. Office of Edn. Member board of directors Good Samaritan Hosp., Phoenix. Del. to World Fedn. Edn. Assn., Geneva, Switzerland, 1929. Life mem. N.E.A. (dir. for Ariz., 1929-30; mem. Nat. Assn. Secondary Sch. Prin. (pres. 1946-47, exec. com. 1942-46, leg. com. since 1945), Am. Assn. Sch. Adminstrs., North Central Assn. Coll. and Secondary Schs. (past vice pres.); Ariz. State orgns.: Teachers Retirement bd. (chmn. since 1943), Bd. Edn. (1929-32), Ednl. Council (past pres.), Assn. Sch. Adminstrs., Ednl. Assn. (pres. 1932-33), Interscholastic Assn. (past pres.), Sch. Adminstrs. (past pres.), Anti-Tuberculosis Assn. (bd. dirs.); mem. Maricopa County Red Cross (past dir.); Phoenix Community Chest (pres. 1932-33), C. of C. (pres. 1932-33, dir. 1931-46); past pres. Arizona Tuberculosis and Health Assn.; vice chmn., Phoenix Army Adv. Com.; mem. Nat. Safety Council (hon. mem. bd. trustees), Phi Delta Kappa. Methodist, Mason (K.T., Shriner). Clubs: Rotary, Phoenix Dons (hon. mem.). Home: Phoenix, Ariz. *

MONTGOMERY, HARRY, newspaper exec.; b. Leon, Okla., July 28, 1902; s. Jesse A. and Willie Ann (Flanagan) M.; student Tex. Tech. Coll., 1925-27; m. Pauline Trippet, Jan. 22, 1926; children—Harry Thomas, Samuel Overton. Editor, Memphis (Texas) Democrat, 1922-25; founder, editor campus newspaper The Toreador, Tex. Tech. Coll., 1925-26; reporter Amarillo (Tex.) News and Globe, 1927-31; corr. A.P., Amarillo, 1931-34; A.P. chief of bur., Phoenix, 1934-44, Mpls., 1944-45, Albuquerque, 1945-47; exec. editor Ariz. Republic and Phoenix Gazette, Phoenix, 1947-51, asst. to pub., 1951-57; asst. pub., 1957-66, co-pub., 1966-79. Named City of Hope Man of Year, 1967, Phoenix Man of Year, 1972; recipient Distinguished Service Cross Salvation Army, 1971. Clubs: Phoenix Rotary, Phoenix Press, Phoenix Country, Arizona. Home: Phoenix, Ariz. Died Jan. 19, 1979; interred Greenwood Mausoleum, Phoenix.

MONTGOMERY, HENRY CLOSE, JR., educator; b. Seymour, Ind., Aug. 1, 1901; s. Henry Close and Jennie (Swope) M.; Ab., Hanover Coll., 1921; M.A U. Ill., 1926, Ph.D., 1945; postgrad. U. Rome (Italy), 1924, U. Vienna (Austria), 1928-29, Heidelberg (Germany) U., summer 1926; L.H.D., Miami U., Oxford, Ohio, m. Margaret E. Stuart, Dec. 22, 1927; children—Ann (Mrs. Brock Brower), Henry Close III, Virginia S. (Mrs. William Melin). Dir. athletics Divernon (Ill.) High Sch., 1921-24; from asst. prof. classics to asso. prof. Wabash Coll., 1926-40; asso. prof. classics Miami (Ohio) U., 1940-46, 24 prof., 1946-79, chmn. dept., 1940-79; asst. dir. Miami U. Abroad, 1956-58. Condr., 1962; lectr. Archaeol. Inst. Am., 1954-55, 58-59; vis. prof. U. Ill., summer 1945; mgr. Crawfordsville (Ind.) Symphony Orchestra, 1933-40; mem. Hamilton (Ohio) Symphony Orch., 1954-69. Fellow to Rome, Italy, summer 1961. Mem. Ohio Classical Conf. (pres. 1949), Classical Assn. Middle West and South (mem. exec. council 1949-53, pres. 1965). Oxford (Ohio) Archaeol. Soc. (sec.-treas. 1941-69), NAACP (pres. Oxford br. 1953-55), Phi Delta Theta, Omicron Delta Kappa, Eta Sigma Phi, Pi Kappa Epsilon. Presbyn. Club: Miami Mens. Contbr. publs. in field to jours. ency. Home: Oxford, Ohio. Died Mar. 23, 1979; buried Oxford.

MONTGOMERY, JAMES ALAN, JR., lawyer; b. Phila., Aug. 18, 1904; s. James Alan and Edith (Thompson) M.; A.B., Princeton, 1925; LL.B., U. Pa., 1928; m. Kathleen M. Keates, Sept. 15, 1931. Admitted to Pa. bar, 1928; law clk. Supreme Ct. Pa., 1928-30; asso. firm Pepper, Hamilton & Scheetz and predecessor, Phila., 1930-36, partner, 1936-74. Spl. asst. to dep. dir. intelligence OSS, 1943-44; chmn. com. on appellate court rules Pa. Supreme Ct. Pres., trustee Free Library Phila.; trustee Phila. Mus. Art, Bur. Municipal Research, Harriton Assn. Chmn. Lower Merion Planning Commn. Mem. Am. Law Inst., Pa. (mem. ho. dels., former chmn.), Phila. (past sec.), Am. bar assns., Pa. Economy League (past chmn. Eastern div., bd. govs., exec. com.). Clubs: Merion Cricket, Midday; Franklin Inn (Phila.). Home: Gladwyne, Pa. Died Jan. 31, 1980.

MONTGOMERY, PAUL VAUGHAN, ins. co., cons. actuary; b. Ft. Worth, Tex., Oct. 10, 1886; s. John Thirison and Sallie (Vaughan) M.; B.A., U. Tex., 1907; m. Mabel Chilton, Apr. 8, 1914 (dec. Aug. 19, 1971); children—Mary Vaughan (Mrs. Richard G. Fuller), Jean (Mrs. C.Z. Stevens III). Actuarial clk. Ft. Worth Life Ins. Co., 1907-09, v.p., actuary, 1914-23; actuarial clk., asst. actuary Southwestern Life Ins. Co., Dallas, 1909-14; v.p., actuary Southland Ins. Co., Dallas, 1923-49; cons. actuary, Dallas, 1949—. Dep. commr. ins. div. Bur. War Risk Ins., Washington, 1918. Mem. town council City of Highland Park, Tex., 1928-34, mayor, 1930-34. Fellow Conf. Actuaries Pub. Practice, Soc. Actuaries; mem. Acad. Actuaries, Kappa Sigma. Democrat. Episcopalian. Mason (32 deg.). Clubs: City, Dallas Country. Home: Dallas TX. *

MONTGOMERY, T. T., coll. pres.; b. Greenfield, Mo., Oct. 9, 1882; s. Philip Reynolds and Sallie (Tucker) M.; M.S., U. of Okla., 1926; m. Blanche Corbin (dec.); children—Phil, George, Jo Anne. Rural sch. teacher in Mo., 1901-05; supt. schs. Miami, Madill, Crickasha (Okla.), 1905-39; pres. Southeastern State Coll., Durant, since 1939. Dir. Red River Council, Boy Scouts of America (past pres.); life mem. Okla. Edn. Assn. (pres. 1937); mem. Kappa Delta Pi. Presbyterian (elder, Ist. Ch., Durant). Mason (32 deg.). Club: Lions (past. pres.). Author: State Government of Oklahoma; An Elementary History of Oklahoma, 1924. Home: Durant, Okla. *

MONTOYA, JOSEPH M., U.S. senator; b. Pena Blanca, N.Mex., Sept. 24, 1915; s. Thomas and Frances Montoya; student Regis Coll., Denver, 1931, 33, 34; LL.B., Georgetown U., 1934-38; m. Della Romero, Nov. 9, 1940; children—Joseph M., Patrick James, Linda Jean. Admitted to N.Mex. bar, 1939, since practiced in Santa Fe; owner Western Freight Lines, 1945; U.S. Senator from N.Mex., 1965-76, mem. Select Com. to Investigate Campaign Practices. Served as rep. from Sandoval County, N.Mex., State Legislature, 1937-40. Dem. floor leader, 1939-40; mem. N.Mex., Senate, 1940-46, Dem. whip, 1945-46; lt. gov. N.Mex., 1947-51, 55-57; senator from Sandoval County to N.Mex. Legislature, 1954-55; congressman-at-large from 85th-88th Congresses. Elk, K.C. Club: Optimist. Home: Santa Fe, N.Mex. Died June 5, 1978; interred Rosario Cemetery, Santa Fe.

MOONEY, GEORGE AUSTIN, bank exec.; b. N.Y.C., Nov. 23, 1911; s. Thomas Patrick and Sarah Cecilia (Armstrong) M.; B.S., Fordham U., 1936; m. A. Charlotte Strom, Nov. 13, 1938; children—Laura, George, Katherine. With N.Y. Times, 1926-54, successively mem. secretarial staff, news bureau staff, London, Eng., other fgn. assignments, writer gen. news, police precincts and features, N.Y.C., staff radio news dept., asst. bus. news editor, financial news dept., asst. bus. and financial news editor; supt. banks, State of N.Y., 1955-58; exec. dir. Investment Co. Inst. 1959-63; chmn., former chief exec. officer Wash. Fed. Savs. & Loan Assn.; former dir., vice chmn. Fed. Home Loan Bank N.Y.; past dir., exec. com. Savs. Assn. League N.Y. State. Trustee Savs. and Loan Found., Inc. Recipient ann. award for outstanding public service Fordham Alumni Assn., 1958; Savs. Assn. League Man of Year award, 1975. Mem. World Trade Writers Assn. (1st pres.), N.Y. Fin. Writers Assn. (past gov.), U.S. Savs. and Loan League (mem. legis. com.). Clubs: Athletic (N.Y.C.); Garden City Country (L.I.). Author articles on fin. bus. subjects. Home: Forest Hills, N.Y. Died Sept. 3, 1979.

MOONEY, HENRY KEPPLER, air force officer; b. New Orleans, Mar. 13, 1910; s. Henry and Clara (Keppler) M.; student Tulane U., 1926; B.S., U.S. Mil. Acad., 1931; grad. Nat. War Coll., 1950; m. Sarah Williford, Nov. 21, 1933; 1 dau., Marilyn. Commd. 2d lt. Cav., U.S. Army, 1931, advanced through grades to maj. gen. USAF, 1951; with 20th Pursuit Group, 1932-36, Chanute Field, 1937, March Field, 1937-39, Panama, 1940-43; during World War II, bomb comdr. in Panama, Italy, and U.S.; USAF hdqrs., 1946-50; div. comdr. Strategic Air Command, 1951-55; deputy comdr. 15th Air Force, 1955-57; comdr. 16th Air Force, 1957-60; vice comdr., Air Tng. Command, Randolf AFB, Tex., 1960-65; commdr. Lackland Military Tng. Center, from 1965. Decorated Legion of Merit, D.F.C., Air Medal with clusters (U.S.); Croix de Guerre with palm (France). Mem. Am. Legion, Air Force Assn., Res. Officers Assn., Armed Forces Mgmt. Assn. Democrat. Episcopalian. Clubs: Masons (32 deg.), Shriners. Home: Universal City, Tex. Died May 29, 1976.

MOORE, BARRINGTON, forester; b. Ossining, N.Y., Sept. 25, 1883; s. Clement Clarke and Laura M. (Williams) M.; A.B., Yale, 1906, M.F., 1908; spl. studies, forests of France, Germany, India, Japan, Philippines. With U.S. Forest Service, 1909-14; pvt. research, 1914-17; asso. curator woods and forestry, American Museum Natural History, 1917; formerly editor Ecology; asso. editor Jour. of Forestry until 1924. Served as captain of Engineers, U.S.A., with A.E.F. in France, June 1917-Sept. 1918; maj., Sept.-Dec. 1918. Mem. Nat. Research Council, 1919-22; sec. Council on Nat. Parks, Forests and Wild Life (formerly Nat. Park Commn.). Mem. bd. mgrs. New York Bot. Garden, 1922-30. Fellow New York Acad. Sciences; sr. mem. Soc. Am. Foresters (chairman Washington section, 1929-30); mem. Ecological Society America (pres. 1919-20), Bot. Soc. America, Torrey Bot. Club, Am. Geog. Society, A.A.A.S. Chevalier Légion d'Honneur (France), 1919. Republican. Episcopalian. Clubs: Boone and Crockett, Century, Yale (New York); Somerset County (England); Cosmos (Washington). Address: New York, N.Y. *

MOORE, BENSON B(OND), etcher, painter; b. Washington, D.C., Aug. 13, 1882; s. John Benson and Ella Francis Moore; ed. pub. schs., Corcoran Sch. of Art and Linthicum Inst., all of Washington. Has exhibited in larger galleries and museums of U.S. and Europe; represented in notable collections. Mem. Am. Artists Profl. League, Southern States Art League, Miss. Art Assn., Soc. Washington Artists, Washington Water Color Club, Washington Landscape Club, New Haven (Conn.) Paint and Clay Club, New Orleans Art Assn., Baltimore Water Color Club, Royal Soc. of Miniature Painters, Sculptors and Gravers, London, Soc. of Washington Etchers, Washington Soc. of Miniature Painters, Sculptors and Gravers. Home: Washington. *

MOORE, BRUCE, sculptor; b. Bern, Kans., Aug. 5, 1905; s. Elmer Bowdle and Edna Browning (Wooten) M.; student Pa. Acad. Fine Arts, 1921-25; vis. sculptor Am. Acad. in Rome, 1937-39; m. Alice Hügli, Apr. 2, 1931. Works in plaster, stone, bronze, clay, terra cotta; portrait busts, figures, animals, medals, drawing; Guggenheim fellow, 1929-31; tchr. modeling, history of sculpture U. Wichita, 1927-28; tchr. cast drawing N.Y. Sch. Applied Design for Women, 1941-42; dir. Rinehart Sch. Sculpture, Md. Inst., Balt., 1942-43. Work represented in pub., pvt. collections; works include sculpture for Nat. Meml. of Pacific, Honolulu, 2 heroic tigers Princeton, 1970, Hooker Meml. Doors, Grace Cathedral, San Francisco, 1965, King Doors, 1970, Fountain Group for Wichita Art Assn., heroic statue Gen. Billy Mitchell, D.C. Space Mus.; designer Samuel F.B. Morse medal NAD. Served with AUS, 1943-46. Recipient numerous prizes and awards; Widener gold medal Pa. Acad. Fine Arts, 1929. Fellow Am. Numis. Soc. (awarded J. Saltus Medal, 1952); mem. NAD, Nat. Inst. Arts and Letters, Nat. Sculpture Soc., Wichita Artists Guild, Wichita Art Assn. Address: Washington, D.C. Died Jan. 24, 1980; buried Old Mission Cemetery, Wichita.

MOORE, CHARLES NAPOLEON, mathematician; b. Cincinnati, O., Nov. 14, 1882; s. Gideon and Rose (Brignole) M.; B.A., U. of Cincinnati, 1903; M.S., George Washington U., 1905; hon. Sc.D., 1932; Ph.D., Harvard University, 1908; studied University of Paris, 1911-12; married Mabel Rena Heckler, June 13, 1914 (deceased Apr. 1960); children—Eugene Carroll, Betty Jane (Mrs. Walter L. Pritz). Computer United States Naval Observatory, 1903-05, instructor mathematics, University of Cincinnati, 1908-09, asst. prof., 1909-17, asso. prof., 1917-24, prof. 1924-53, emeritus, 1953, dir. grad. studies mathematics, 1937-53; vis. prof. U. of S.C., 1957, Antioch Coll., 1958. Director research project USAF, 1953-54. Fellow A.A.A.S. (council; sec. Sect. A, 1928-32; v.p. 1933); mem. Am. Math. Soc. (council; v.p. 1926-28; del. to Internat. Congress of Mathematics, Zurich, 1932), Math. Assn. America (nat. com. on math. requirements; v.p. 1931), Am. Assn. Univ. Profs., Soc. Mathématique de France, Deutsche Mathematiker-Vereinigung, Sigma Xi. Asso. editor Trans. Am. Math. Soc., 1917-35. Author: Summable Series and Convergence Factors, 1938. Contbr. to jours. of America and Europe on math. and ednl. subjects. Clubs: Harvard, Alliance Francaise. Home: Cincinnati, O. *

MOORE, DAVID CHANNING, travel corp. exec.; b. Mt. Vernon, N.Y. Sept. 20, 1910; s. T. Channing and Bertha (Stone) M.; Ph.B., Brown U., 1934; m. Harriet H. Hamilton, Oct. 26, 1934; children—Lynton (Mrs. William Littell White), Ashley (Mrs. Hoyt Ammidon, Jr.), Thomas Channing. With IBM, 1934-55, salesman N.Y. br., div. mgr., Buffalo, dist. mgr., eastern div. mgr., 1939-41, asst. div. sales mgr., 1941-42, nat. div. sales mgr., 1947-55; spl. asst. to asst. sec. air force, 1955-56; pres. Transcontinent TV Corp., N.Y.C., 1956-64; dir. IBM World Trade Ams./Far East Corp. Served from 2d lt. to lt. col. USAAF, 1942-45; lt. col. Res. Decorated Bronze Star medal. Mem. Broadcast Music, St. Nicholas Soc. N.Y., Soc. Colonial Wars, SR, Soc. Mayflower Descs., Loyal Legion, Huguenot Soc. Am., Psi Upsilon. Republican. Clubs: Metropolitan; Royal Bermuda Yacht, Mid-Ocean, Gulf Stream Golf. Home: Gulf Stream, Fla. Died Oct. 14, 1980.

MOORE, HAROLD EMERY, JR., systematic botanist, educator; b. Winthrop, Mass., July 7, 1917; s. Harold Emery and Helen Jane (Margeson) M.; B.S., U. Mass., 1939; M.A., Harvard, 1940, Ph.D., 1942. Tech. asst. Gray Herbarium, Harvard, 1947-48; mem. faculty L.H. Bailey Hortorium, Cornell U., 1948-80, prof., 1960-80, dir. hortorium, 1960-69. Bd. dirs. Fairchild Tropical Garden, Miami, Fla., 1965-71, Orgn. Tropical Studies, 1970-80; mem. com. to visit Arnold Arboretum, Harvard, 1964-70. Served to 1st lt. AUS, 1942-46. Guggenheim fellow, 1946-47, 55-56; recipient Founder's medal Fairchild Tropical Garden, 1954. Mem. Bot. Soc. Am., Am. Soc. Plant Taxonomists, Internat. Assn. Plant Taxonomy, Soc. Study Evolution, Assn. Tropical Biology, New Eng. Bot. Club. Am. Inst. Biol. Scis., Soc. Econ. Botany, Palm Soc. (dir. 1957-80), Sociedad Botánica de México, Société de Biogéographic, Sigma Xi. Author: African Violets, Gloxinias and Their Relatives, 1957; The Major Groups of Palms and Their Distribution, 1973; co-author, co-editor Hortus Third, 1976. Editor: Principes, 1957-80, Gentes Herbarum, 1973-80. Home: Ithaca, N.Y. Died Oct. 17, 1980; buried Rockridge Cemetery, Sharon, Mass.

MOORE, HARRY LEE, coll. pres.; b. Gillette, Wyo., Feb. 16, 1930; s. Harold C. and Helen A. (Fordyce) M.; A.S. summa cum laude, Cleveland State Coll., 1974; m. Glenna Jacqueline Hawkins, Dec. 13, 1952; children—Harold Blaine, Randall Craig, Valorie Kim. Internat. youth dir. Ch. of God of Prophecy, 1951-60, radio and television speaker, 1960-72; asst. pub. White Wing Pub. House, Cleveland, Tenn., 1972-75; pres. Tomlinson Coll., Cleveland, 1975-76. Pres., Cleveland Day Sch. Parents Club; chmn. bd. dirs. Tomlinson Coll., 1968-70; bd. dirs. Southeastern Travel Agys., Bradley County United Fund. Author: The Promise of His Coming, 1966; Eternal Questions, 1968. Home: Cleveland, Tenn. Died Oct. 12, 1976; interred Sunset Meml. Gardens, Cleveland, Tenn.

MOORE, HARRY T., author, educator; b. Oakland, Cal., Aug. 2, 1908; s. Harry T. and Kathryn Winifred (Moore) M.; Ph.B., U. Chgo., 1934; M.A., Northwestern U., 1942; Ph.D., Boston U., 1951; m. Winifred Sheehan, Mar. 21, 1934; children—Brian, Sharon; m. 2d, Beatrice Reynolds Walker, Oct. 12, 1946. Instr. English Ill. Inst. Tech., 1940-41, Northwestern U., 1941-42; lectr. pub. relations Air U., 1946-47; asso. prof. Babson Coll., 1947-57, chmn. dept., 1952-57; prof. English, So. Ill. U., 1957-60, research prof., 1960-62, 63-79, research prof. emeritus, 1979-81; prof. U. Colo., 1962-63; Guggenheim fellow, 1958, 60; sometime vis. prof. various univs. Served as maj. USAAF, World War II; now lt. col. USAF Res. Decorated Army Commendation medal. Fellow Royal Soc. Lit.; mem. Modern Lang. Assn., College English Assn. (nat. v.p. 1959-61, nat. pres. 1961), Am. P.E.N., Soc. Advancement Mgmt., Sigma Chi. Club: Cliff Dwellers (Chgo.). Author: The Novels of John Steinbeck, 1939; Life and Works of D. H. Lawrence, 1951; The Intelligent Heart, 1955; Poste Restante, 1956; E.M. Forster, 1965; (with Warren Roberts) D. H. Lawrence and His World, 1965; 20th Century French Literature, 2 vols., 1966; Twentieth Century German Literature, 1967; Age of the Modern, 1971; The Priest of Love, 1974; Henry James and His World, 1974; (with Albert Parry) 20th Century Russian Literature, 1974. Editor: D. H. Lawrence's Letters to Bertrand Russell, 1948; D. H. Lawrence's Essays on Sex, Literature and Censorship, 1953; The Achievement of D. H. Lawrence (with Frederick J. Hoffman), 1953; Lewis Mumford's The Human Prospect (with Karl W. Deutsch), 1955; Letters of Rainer Maria Rilke, 1960; A D.H. Lawrence Miscellany, 1959; Collected Letters of D.H. Lawrence, 1962; The World of Lawrence Durrell, 1962; Contemporary American Novelists, 1964; Elizabethan Age, 1965; (with Warren Roberts) Phoenix II: Uncollected, Unpublished and other Prose Works by D.H. Lawrence, 1968; (with Ian S. MacNiven) Literary Lifelines: The Richard Aldington-Lawrence Durrell Correspondence, 1981, The Letters of Ezra Pound and Richard Aldington, 1982; (with Dale Montegue) Frieda Lawrence and Her Circle, 1981; Crosscurrents / Modern Critiques, 1962-81. Contbr. articles to popular, profl. jours. A judge Nat. Book awards, 1963. Home: Carterville, Ill. Died Apr. 11, 1981.

MOORE, HARVEY WILSON, business exec.; b. Augusta, Ga., May 1, 1884; s. James William and Anna Patton (Wilson) M.; Student Univ. of Ga., 1901-03; Davidson (N.C.) Coll., 1903-04; m. Lucy Grattan Robertson, Oct. 14, 1909; children—Lucy Grattan (Mrs. Thomas P. Grasty), Lt. Harvey Wilson Moore, Jr., U.S.N.R. (lost in action, June 1943). Exec. vice pres., treas., gen. mgr., Brown Mfg. Co. since 1926, Roberta Mfg. Co. since 1940, White Parks Mills Co. since 1940, Concord, N.C.; vice pres. Highland Park Mfg. Co., Charlotte, N.C., since 1940, Eastern Mfg. Co., Selma, N.C., since 1940, Parks Yarn Mills, Kings Mountain, N.C. since 1947. Dir. Worth Spinning Co., Stony Point, N.C. Mayor Charlotte, N.C., 1923-26; past chmn. Pub. Library Bd., mem. Sch. Bd. and Zoning and Planing Commn. Trustee and mem. exec. com. Davidson (N.C.) Coll. Mem. N.C. Cotton Mfrs. Assn. (past pres.), Am. Cotton Mfrs. Assn. (chmn. of bd.), Cotton Textile Inst. (mem. exec. com.). Jeffersonian Democrat. Presbyterian (elder) Mason (life trustee Masonic Temple Assn.). Clubs; Country (Charlotte, N.C.); Merchants (New York, N.Y.). Home: Charlotte, N.C. *

MOORE, HENRY THOMAS, college pres.; b. Ansonville, N.C., June 27, 1886; s. Matthew Henry and Mary Eugenia (Thomas) M.; A.B., U. of Mo., 1903, A.M., 1904; A.M., Yale, 1907; Ph.D., Harvard, 1914; LL.D., Russell Sage College, 1935, Skidmore College, 1937, Dartmouth University, 1940, Union College, 1950; married Agnes Marie Blain, September 12, 1914; children—Caroline Eugenia, John Barden, Henry Thomas. Asst. in psychology, Harvard, 1912-14; lecturer on psychology, Simmons Coll., 1914-15; asst. prof. psychology, Dartmouth, 1915-17, U. of Minn., 1917-19; prof., Dartmouth, 1919-25; pres. Skidmore College, Saratoga Springs 1925—. Dir. Adirondack Trust Co. since 1948. Mem. Saratoga Springs Commn., 1941-48. Dir. Ednl. Records Bur., N.Y.C. Served as 1st lt. San. Corps, U.S. Army 1918-19; chief psychol. examiner Camp Cody, Deming, N.M., 1918; psychol. Gen. Hosp. No. 3, Colonia, N.J., 1919. Mem. Am. Psychol. Assn., Am. Assn. U. Profs., Phi Beta Kappa, Beta Theta Pi. Democrat. Club: Century Association (New York City, N.Y.). Author: The Genetic Aspect of Consonance and Dissonance, 1914; Pain and Pleasure, 1917; also numerous articles in profl. jours. Editor Jour. of Abnormal and Social Psychology, 1925-37; sec. Social Science Research Council, 1929-30. Home: Saratoga Springs, N.Y. *

MOORE, HOLLIS ANDREW, JR., univ. pres.; b. Pierce City, Mo., Apr. 3, 1923; s. Hollis Andrew and Kathleen Ruth (Jordan) M.; A.B., Baylor U., 1946; postgrad. Brown U., 1946-47; Ed.D., U. Tex., 1953; Litt.D., Hanyang U. (Korea), 1976; LL.D., Central Mich. U., 1977; m. Mabel Marian Brown, Aug. 22, 1946; children—Hollis Andrew III, Michael Brown. Adminstrv. asst. Dallas Civic Fedn., 1948; tchr. social studies Fulmore Jr. High Sch., Austin, Tex., 1949-50; dean boys Austin High Sch., 1950-51; asso. editor The Nation's Schs., 1952-55; exec. sec. Com. Advancement Sch. Adminstrn., 1955-60; dean edn. U. Ariz., 1960-64; dir. div. edn. W.K. Kellogg Found., 1964-65; v.p. acad. affairs George Peabody Coll., 1965-70; pres. Bowling Green (Ohio) State U., 1970-81; vis. lectr. Northwestern U., 1953-55, U. Va., 1954-55, No. Ariz. U., 1956, U. Denver, 1957, Stanford, 1958-60, U. Nebr., 1960, U. Tex., 1965; chmn. Inter-Univ. Council Ohio, 1974-75; chmn. Mid-Am. Conf. Council of Pres.'s., 1978-79. Bd. dirs. Coalition for Rural Devel., 1972-81, Greater Toledo Community Chest; trustee Toledo Symphony Orch., 1979-80. Served with AUS, World War II; ETO. Decorated Purple Heart. Mem. Ohio Coll. Assn. (pres. 1972-73), Am. Assn. State Colls. and Univs. (dir. 1978-81), Bowling Green C. of C., Confrerie des Chevaliers du Tastevin, Phi Delta Kappa (pres. Mu chpt. 1951), Omicron Delta Kappa. Conglist. Kiwanian. Clubs: Belmont Country (Perrysburg, Ohio); Carranor Hunt and Polo. Author: Studies in School Administration, 1957; (with others) Perspectives on Educational Change, 1957). Contbg. author: Behavioral Science and Educational Administration, 1964; contbg. author: The Administrative Team and Long Range Planning, 1967. Home: Bowling Green, Ohio. Died Apr. 19, 1981.

MOORE, HOWARD EARLE, lawyer; b. Butler, Ala., Oct. 11, 1914; s. Jacob Marvin and Martha Bruister (Mason) M.; A.A., Wesley Coll., Greenville, Tex., 1932; LL.B., So. Methodist U., 1937; m. Lettie Pauline Smith, June 8, 1943; children—Howard Austin, Martha Kathleen (Mrs. Larry B. Dwight). Admitted to Tex. bar, 1937, since practiced in Dallas; asso. with Larry B. Dwight in practice patent law, 1968-78; lectr. S.W. Legal Found., 1967-78. Pres. Victor Hexter Sch. P.T.A., 1962-63. Served with USAAF, 1942-45. Mem. Am., Tex. (chmn. patent sect. 1961-62), Dallas (chmn. ethics com. 1965) bar assns., State Bar Tex. (chmn. patent sect. 1961-62), Dallas-Ft. Worth Patent Assn. (pres. 1960), Am. Patent Law Assn. Democrat. Methodist (chmn. ofcl. bd. 1972). Kiwanian. Clubs: Optimist (pres. 1958), Dallas Athletic, Engineers (Dallas). Contbr. legal jours. Home: Dallas, Tex. Died Mar. 4, 1978; buried Restland Meml. Park, Dallas.

MOORE, HUGH RAMSAY, paper co. exec.; b. Hammond, Ind., July 17, 1916; s. Franklin and Ella F. (Ramsay) M.; B.A., U. Wis., 1938, J.D., 1948; m. Alice Bergstrom, Nov. 6, 1934 (dec. Mar. 1976); children—Mary M. (Mrs. Larry Pellegrin), Laura Lawson (Mrs. George L. Hiller). Admitted to Wis. bar, 1948; practiced in Oshkosh, 1948-52; asst. dist. atty., Winnebago County, 1951-52; with Bergstrom Paper Co. (now div. P.H. Glatfelter Co.), Neenah, Wis., 1951—, exec. v.p., 1956-62, pres. chief exec. officer, 1962-75, chmn. bd., chief exec. officer, from 1975, also dir., v.p., dir. P.H. Glatfelter Co., 1979—; dir. First Nat. Bank Neenah. Dir. Pub. Expenditure Survey Wis., 1958-69, exec. com., from 1975; mem. exec. com. Winnegago County Republican Party, 1948-55, vice chmn., 1948-53, chmn., 1953-55; mem. Winnebago County Bd. Suprs., 1957-62. Trustee Theda Clark Meml. Hosp., from 1963. Served with USNR, 1941-42; maj. USMCR, 1942-56. Mem. Am., Wis., Winnebago County bar assns., Navy League, Marine Corps League, Am. Paper Inst. (mem. exec. com. 1973-75, dir. from 1977, mem. solid waste council 1972-75). Phi Delta Phi. Republican. Presbyn. Clubs: Marine Mem. (San Francisco); Union League (N.Y.C.). Address: Neenah, Wis. Deceased.

MOORE, IRA ALLEN, banker; b. Sac County, Ia., Aug. 21, 1886; s. Rinaldo M. and Elizabeth W. (Holtz) M.; ed. Ia. pub. schs.; m. Florence L. Ellis, June 11, 1911; children—Robert E., Lee F., Alan G., Jeanne F. Teacher Neb. pub. schs., 1903-05; clk. Toy Nat. Bank, Sioux City, Ia., 1905-20, v.p., 1920-26; v.p. First Nat. Bank & Trust Co., Sioux Falls, S.D., 1926-33; pres. Peoples Nat. Bank, Grand Rapids, 1933-56, chmn. bd., 1956-58; gen. v.p. Old Kent Bank & Trust Co., 1958—; dir. Detroit br. Fed. Reserve Bank Chgo. Mgr. Reconstruction Finance Corp. (Chicago Dist.) during 1933. Republican. Presbyterian. Mason. Clubs: Rotary, Peninsular. Home: Grand Rapids, Mich. *

MOORE, JAMES PATRICK, JR., ins. exec.; b. Newark, Dec. 10, 1911; s. James P. and Regina (Rudolph) M.; student Rutgers U., Grad. Sch. Bus. Columbia; m. Evelyn Rux, Jan. 15, 1972; children by previous marriage—James Patrick III, Judith Moore (Mrs. Stage). With Mutual Benefit Life Ins. Co., Newark, 1927-78, successively clk., asst. supt. agencies, dir. agy. finance, dir. planning and methods, exec. asst., 1927-52, comptroller, 1952-78, v.p., 1955-72, sr. v.p., 1972-78. Past pres., bd. dirs. YMCA-YWCA of Newark and Vicinity; past pres. United Way of West Essex, N.J. Mem. Life Office Mgmt. Assn. (past dir.; past chmn. fin. planning and control council), Greater Newark C. of C. (past chmn. tax com.), Fin. Execs. Inst. (dir., past chpt. pres.). Kiwanian (past chpt. pres.). Home: Coral Springs, Fla. Died Jan. 6, 1978; buried Gate of Heaven Cemetery, Hanover, N.J.

MOORE, JOSEPH MARION, retired educator; b. Mingo, W.Va., Feb. 8, 1885; s. William John and Ida Ellen (Burger) M.; A.B., Washington and Lee U., 1908; B.D., Union Theol. Sem., Richmond, Va., 1914; student W.Va. U., summer, 1929; m. Margaret Taylor, July 10, 1920; children—Anne Graeme, Joseph Marion, Pamela Ross. Tchr. Greenbrier Mil. Sch., Lewisburg, W.Va., 1908-17, v.p. of corp., 1920—, supt., 1939-54, pres. sch., 1954-70. Served with French Foyer de Soldat in trenches, 1917-19. Mem. Assn. Mil. Schs. U.S., Assn. Va. Prep. Schs. Clubs: White Sulphur Springs Golf: Greenbriar Valley Country (bd. govs.), Virginia Seniors Golf, Home: Lewisburg WV. *

MOORE, OLIN HARRIS (MOR), univ. prof.; b. Mt. Airy, N.C., 1885; s. Matthew Henry and Mary Eugenia (Thomas) M.; A.B., U. of Mo., 1902; A.M., Harvard, 1904, Ph.D., 1913; studied École Pratique des Hautes Études, Paris, France; unmarried. Instr. Romance langs., U. of Ill., 1912, asso., 1915, asst. prof., 1918-19; asso. prof. Romance langs., Northwestern U., 1919-20; prof. Romance langs., Ohio State U., 1920—, emeritus, 1955—. Mem. Modern Lang. Assn. Am., Am. Association University Professors, Am. Assn. Teachers of Italian (president 1937), Phi Beta Kappa. Methodist. Club: Faculty (Columbus). Author: Elements of French, 1919; A French Reader (with Robert Fouré), 1925; The Young King, Henry Plantagenet (1155-1183) in History, Literature and Tradition, 1926; The Legend of Romeo and Juliet, 1950. Editor: Cuore of De Amicis (with D. P. Rotunda), 1924; Selected Stories of Guy de Maupassant (with George R. Havens), 1928; Victor Hugo's Ruy Blas, 1933; Easy French Readings (with George R. Havens), 1936; A travers les Ages (with George R. Havens), 1943; Onze Contes (with Walter Meiden), 1957. Contributor to Romanic Rev., Modern Philology, Romania, Modern Lang. Publs., etc. Home: Columbus, O. *

MOORE, ROBERT LEE, mathematician; b. Dallas, Nov. 14, 1882; s. Charles J. and Louisa Ann (Moore) M.; B.S. and A.M., U. Tex., 1901, fellow, 1901-02; Ph.D. (fellow 1903-05), U. Chgo., 1905; m. Margaret MacLellan Key, Aug. 19, 1910. Asst. prof. math. U. Tenn., 1905-06; instr. math. Princeton, 1906-08, Northwestern U., 1908-11; instr. math. U. Pa., 1911-16, asst. prof., 1916-20; asso. prof. U. Tex., 1920-23, prof., 1923-37, 59—, distinguished prof., 1937-53, prof. math. and astronomy, 1953; asso. editor Trans. Am. Math. Soc., 1913-26; editor Colloquium publs., 1928-36, colloquium lect., 1929; vis. lectr. Am. Math. Soc., 1931-32. Fellow A.A.A.S. (v.p. 1947); mem. Nat. Acad. Scis., Am. Math. Soc. (v.p. 1923, pres. 1937-39), Societe Polanaise de Mathematique, Acad. Tex. Author: Fundamental Theorems Concerning Point Sets, 1936; Foundatiton of Point Set Theory, rev. edit., 1962. Home: Austin, Tex. *

MOORE, ROYAL ARCHIBALD, educator; b. Jamaica Plain, Mass., July 31, 1884; s. William Archibald and Augusta May (Quigley) M.; student Adams Acad., Quincy, Mass., 1897-1901; B.A., Harvard, 1905, M.A., 1906; m. Mabel Fullerton, Aug. 10, 1910; children—Muriel Fullerton, Elizabeth Wentworth, William Everett, Roger Viets. Master in English and Greek, Adams Acad., 1904-05; in Latin, Gilman Country Sch., Baltimore, 1906-07; prin. Bacon Acad., Colchester, Conn., 1907-14; headmaster Wheeler Sch., N. Stonington, Conn., 1914-19; pres. Oak Hall (sch. for girls), St. Paul, Minn., 1919-40; asst. prof. of history, Macalester Coll., St. Paul, 1941-42. Served as chmn. Liberty Loan drives and war savings coms. and dir. Community Chorus, World War. Mem. Phi Beta Kappa. Episcopalian. Mason. Clubs: Harvard, Informal. Home: St. Paul, Minn. *

MOORE, WILLIAM J., coll. dean; b. nr. Booneville, Ky., Oct. 25, 1894; s. Henry W. and Mary (Brandenburg) M.; diploma Eastern Ky. State Coll., 1917; A.B., U. Ky., 1925, A.M., 1928, Ph.D., 1931, student Coll. Law, 1920-25; m. Nazza Kilburn, Dec. 23, 1916; children—William G., Mary Elizabeth. Tchr. pub. schs., Ky., 1913-17; supt. schs., Mancester, Ky., 1919-1923, Midway, Ky., 1925-1927; prof. econs. Eastern Ky. State Coll., Richmond, 1928-45, dean, 1945-80; dir. finance Ky. Dept. Edn., 1944; commr. revenue Ky., 1944-45. Sec. Ky. Taxation Revision Commn., 1945-46; chmn. Ky. Commn. Higher Edn., 1968-80. Mem. Ky. Ho. Reps., 1925. Mem. Am., So. econs. assns., Am. Polit. Sci. Assn., Am. Soc. Pub. Adminstrn., Am. Assn. Sch. Adminstrs., NEA, Nat. Tax Assn., Perry Victory and Internat. Meml. Nat. Monument Assn., Ky. Assn. Colls. and Secondary Schs. (pres. 1949-50), Ky. Acad. Social Sci. (past pres.), Ky. Acad. Sci. (past treas.), Phi Delta Phi, Kappa Delta Pi, Phi Delta Kappa. Republican. Mem. Christian Ch. Mason. Club: Lions Internat. (dist. gov. 1948). Home: Richmond, Ky. Died Feb. 26, 1980; buried Richmond Cemetery.

MOORE, WILLIAM TALMAN, transp. co. exec.; b. N.Y.C., Aug. 12, 1913; s. Albert Voorhis and Margaret Talman (Sterling) M.; student Lawrenceville Sch., U. Va.; m. Florence Augusta Equen (div. 1944); 1 son, William Talman; m. 2d, Jean Fisher Campbell, Nov. 18, 1944. With Moore-McCormack Lines, Inc., N.Y.C., 1935-76, pres., 1953-70, chmn., 1962-71, chmn. audit com. Moore-McCormack Resources Inc., 1975-76, chmn. exec. com., 1971-76, also dir.; dir. Combustion Engring., Inc.; trustee Bank of Savs., N.Y.C.; mem. Am. com. Lloyd's Register Shipping; mem. downtown adv. com. Chase Manhattan Bank. Trustee Lawrenceville Sch. Served with AUS, World War II. Decorated Order Southern Cross (Brazil). Mem. Nat. Fgn. Trade Council (dir.), Chi Phi. Clubs: India House, N.Y. Yacht, Leash (N.Y.C.); Seawanhaka-Corinthian Yacht; Pacific Union, Piping Rock. Home: Oyster Bay, N.Y. Died Apr. 7, 1976.

MOORE, WILLIAM TAYLOR, journalist; b. Rossville, Ill., Jan. 3, 1901; s. William Taylor and Jennie (Meridith) M.; student U. Chgo., 1924-28; m. Eloise Tasher, June 1, 1929. Feature writer Chgo. Herald and Examiner, 1924-36; mem. editorial staff Chgo. Tribune, 1936-66, mem. Washington bur., 1942-56, corr. Chgo. Tribune Press Service, Moscow, 56-57, Congressional corr., 1957-66; writer Ft. Lauderdale (Fla.) News, 1966-68. Lectr. on Russia. Mem. Sigma Delta Chi (founder Palm Beach chpt.), Phi Gamma Delta. Republican. Presbyn. Clubs: Cliff Dwellers (Chgo.); University, Nat. Press, Arts (past pres.), City Tavern Assn. (Washington). Author: Dateline Chicago, 1972. Home: Palm Beach Shores, Fla. Died May 19, 1976.

MOOT, WELLES VAN NESS, laywer; b. Buffalo, Dec. 12, 1885; s. Adelbert and Carrie A. (Van Ness) M.; A.B., Harvard, 1908, LL.B., 1911; LL.D. (hon.), Hofstra Coll., 1953; Caroline Clinton Everett, Sept. 23, 1916; children—Welles Van Ness, Richard Everett, John Rutherford, Martin Adelbert, Cecily, Mary Hurd. Admitted to N.Y. bar, 1912, also U.S. Supreme Ct., 1920; asst. dist. atty. Erie County, 1915-17; mem. firm Moot, Sprague, Marcy & Gulick, Buffalo, 1929—; pres., mng. dir. Sylvanite Gold Mines, Ltd., 1926-65, Delhite Mines Ltd., 1936-69, Tyranite Mines, Ltd., 1938-60. Chmn. City Planning Commn. Buffalo, 1941-51, City Buffalo Bd. Parking, 1952-59; mem. Citizens Com. Intermunicipal Affairs; trustee, treas. Neighborhood House Assn.; commr. Niagara Frontier State Park Commn., Niagara Frontier Authority, 1942-50. Bd. regents U. State N.Y., 1947-56, chmn. com. higher and profl. edn; mem. vis. com. Harvard Grad. Sch. Edn., 1952-62; pres. The Buffalo Sem., 1941-43; dir. Am. Unitarian Assn., 1938-41; trustee Millard Fillmore Hosp., 1938-48, 56—; bd. dirs. Canadian Metal Mining Assn., 1940-62, Blocher Homes, YMCA, 1926—; pres. trustees YMCA of Buffalo and Erie County, 1966-71; sec., dir. Creative Edn. Found., Greater Buffalo Devel. Found.; bd. dirs. Buffalo Fine Arts Acad., 1957-66; past chmn., dir. Jr. Achievement Niagara Frontier, Inc. Fellow Am. Bar Found.; mem. Am., N.Y. State, Erie County bar assns., Am. Soc. Planning Ofcls. (past v.p., dir.). Republican. Unitarian. Clubs: Saturn, Harvard (pres. 1936) Buffalo, Yacht, Canoe (Buffalo). Home: Buffalo NY. *

MOOTS, ELMER EARL, educator; b. Kirksville, Mo., Jan. 31, 1882; s. Charles Benton and Mary Ellen (Glanville) M.; B.C.E., Highland Park Coll., 1906; M.S., U. of Me., 1908; C.E., U. Wis., 1911; Ph.D., U. of Ia., 1927; m. Elpha B. Ferrel, Apr. 12, 1914; children—Max F., Elmer E., Alma D. (Mrs. Phillip A. Douglas). Instr. in math., U. of Me., 1906-09, U. Wis., 1909-11; prof. of applied mathematics, Whitman Coll., 1911-14; civil engr., Walla Walla, Wash., 1915; asst. prof. civil engring., U. Ariz., 1916; irrigation engr., Ariz., 1917-18; prof. of math. and engring., Cornell Coll., Mt. Vernon, Ia., since 1918 (on leave 1942-45); asso. dir. research on sound control, Nat. Defense Research Com., Harvard, 1942-43; stress analyst in charge of computation Douglas Aircraft Corp., Santa Monica, Calif., 1944-45; cons. municipal engr. since 1946. Awarded Certificate in appreciation of effective service, World War II, by O.S.R.D. Fellow A.A.A.S., Ia. Acad. of Sci.; life mem. Am. Soc. C.E.; mem. Am. Math. Soc., Math. Assn. of Am., Am. Geophys. Union; hon. mem. Phi Beta Kappa. Methodist. Author of tech. reports and bulletins: The Design and Construction of Anechoic Sound Chambers (with others), 1945; A Study in Flood Waves, 1938; A Study in the Theory of Flood Waves, 1938. Teacher philosophy of sci. as hobby. Home: Mt. Vernon, Ia. *

MORALES, CECILIO JOSE, economist, govt. ofcl.; b. Buenos Aires, Argentina, Mar. 18, 1921; s. Luis Morales and Jacinta Magliano de Morales; student U. Buenos Aires Sch. Engring., 1936-42; m. Amelia O. Sarlo Sabajames, 1947 (div.); 1 son, Cecilio Jose; married 2d, Susana Vivaldi. Director population research Ministry Public Health, Argentina, 1945-52; econ. counsellor Argentine delegation UN, 1952-56; del. Argentina, Internat. Wheat Confs., 1953, 55, Commodity Com. FAO, 1953-54, Inter-Am. Econ. Conf. of Rio, 1954; pvt. econ. cons., Buenos Aires, 1957-58; cons. UN sec.-gen. on commodity problems, 1958; Argentine del. UN Gen. Assembly,; 1958; attended formal meeting Fgn. Ministers of Americas, Washington, 1959; dir. dept. econ. and social affairs Pan Am. Union, exec. sec. Inter-Am. Econ. and Social Council, also exec. sec. spl. com. for charter Inter-Am. Development Bank, rep. in Bolivia. Home: Bethesda, Md. Died Nov. 15, 1980.

MORALES, FRANKLIN E., (MO'RA-LES); b. Phila., Jan. 26, 1884; s. Marcos D. and Anna Maria (Cain) M.; grad. high sch. and bus. coll., Atlantic City, N.J.; m. Mae E. Krauss, Feb. 26, 1906; 1 dau., Thelma. Export business; v.p. Internations Commercial Corp., 1916-19; rep. Am. jewelry mfrs. in Latin Am., 1919-21, E.E. and M.P. to Honduras, 1921-25; mem. Riker & Morales, Mexico City, Buenos Aires, Santiago, Chile; partner Morales & Potter, real estate and insurance brokers. Pres. Atlantic City Rep. Club, 1907-16; Rep. County Com., 1912-16. Presbyn. Mason, Odd Fellow. Clubs: Penn Athletic, Internat. of Tegucigalpa. Lakewood Country, Ocean County Shrine. Home: Toms River, N.J. *

MORALES, MIQUEL MARCOS, lawyer; b. Caguas, P.R., June 11, 1886; s. Abdon Marcos and Isabel Morales; student Instituto de P.R., 1898. Admitted to P.R. bar, 1912; practice in Ponce, 1930—; clk. charge of library Atty. Gen.'s Office, San Juan, 1912-14; mem. U.S. Food Admintrn., 1917-18; pres. Municipal Assembly, Cayey, P.R., 1918; atty. Bank Credito y Ahorro Ponceno, Ponce, 1931—, also sec., dir.; mem. bd. U.S. OPA, Ponce, 1945. Mem. Adv. Bd. for Registration, Ponce, 1940. Mem. Local Bd., Municipality of Cayey, 1918. Mem. Internat. Assn. Sci. and Law (gen assembly, Geneva, Switzerland, 1968), Bar Assn. P.R., Am. Bar Assn., Nat. Lawyers Club Washington. Clubs: Yacht, Deportivo (Ponce). Home: Ponce PR. *

MORAN, FRANK GODING, educator; b. Seattle, Wash., Sept. 23, 1885; s. Robert and Melissa Euphena (Paul) M.; Lawrenceville (N.J.) Sch.; M.A., Washington State Coll., 1918; m. Grace L. Robbins, of Valparaiso, Ind., Sept. 14, 1911; children—Robert Robbins (dec.), Mary Adelaide, Frank Robbins. Began teaching at Camden, N.J., 1906; founder, 1914, and dir. Moran Sch. for Boys, and of Junior Coll. State mgr. A.R.C., war work campaigns; western dir. in U.S. for Boys' Working Reserve and Inter Ch. World Movement; mem. Nat. Council Boys' Work Com. Republican. Conglist. Clubs: Rotary, Arctic. *

MORAN, HUGH ANDERSON, clergyman; b. Silver Creek, Ky., July 16, 1881; s. Hugh Anderson and Jennie Todd (Breck) M.; B.A., Standord, 1905; Rhodes scholar, Oxford U., 1905-08; Ph.D., Columbia U., Union Sem., 1939; m. Irene May Hornby, June 7, 1911; children—Hugh Anderson III, Irene (Mrs. Archie Van Doren), Pauline (Mrs. Harry M. Philpott), Jean Todd Myer. Ordained to ministry Presbyn. Ch., 1908; with YMCA, China, 1908-13, Siberia, 1916-19; mem. internat. com. YMCA-U.S.A., 1913-16; dir. prisoner relief, spl. adviser to Bishop Root Mission, Siberia, 1918; Presbyn. student pastor Cornell U., 1919-42; asso. pastor 1st Presbyn. Ch., Ithaca, N.Y., 1919-42; author, painter, civic leader, Palo Alto, Cal., 1947-75. East Wenatchee, Wash., 1975—. Pres., Civic League 1946-48, Palo Alto Art Club, 1946-48. Fellow Nat. Council on Religious Edn., 1923; Kent fellow, 1923-24. Fellow Nat. Council on Religion; mem. Am. Oriental Soc., Delta Upsilon. Author: Heros, 1919; Creed For College Men, 1924; Story of Santa Claus, 1952; The Alphabet and Ancient Calendar Signs (with rediscovery of Lunar Zodiac), 1953, 2d edit., 1969; David Star Jordon, 1969; (play) Oregon, 1933. Address: Wenatchee WA. *

MORANTI, PAUL JOSEPH, contractor; b. Sorrento, Italy, Dec. 7, 1884; s. Francisco and Carmella (Spinelle) M.; grad. Royal Engring. Sch., U. of Milan, Italy, 1904; m. Marietta Dwyer, Oct. 24, 1923. Came to U.S., 1906, naturalized citizen, 1910. Rodman Pa. R.R., later asst. engr. Empire Steel & Iron Co., 1906; supt. constrn. Pa. R.R. Tunnel under N.Y. City, 1906-09; same, T. A. Gillespie Co., Roundout Tunnel, 1909-11; gen. supt. constrn. Mt. Royal Tunnel, C.N. Ry., 1911-12; same, Barge Canal, 1912-13; pres. P. J. Moranti Co., gen. contractors, 1913-17; constrn. engr. Eastern Mines Development Co., 1917-20; with Replogle Steele Co., later Lehigh Coal and Navigation Co., 1920-24; pres. Moranti & Raymond, Inc., now Paul J. Moranti, Inc., engrs. and contractors, since 1924. Mem. Am. Soc. C.E. Clubs: Engineers, Engineers' Golf, Whitehall, Grassy Sprain Country. Inventor of elevator hoist. Home: New York, N.Y.; and Easthampton, L.I., N.Y. *

MORANZONI, ROBERTO, conductor; b. Bari, Italy, Oct. 1882; ed. Conservatory of Music, Pesaro, Italy, under Mascagni. Began as conductor of orchestra, at Teatro Costanzi, Rome, 1901, later at Bologne, Milan, Turin and other cities of Italy, also at Grand Opera and Champs Elysees, Paris, and Covent Garden, London; first came to U.S., 1910; with Metropolitan Opera Co., later with Chicago Civic Opera Co.*

MORAUD, MARCEL JEAN (MO-RO'), prof. languages; b. Roziers St. George, France, Oct. 19, 1886; s. Martial and Elise (Delpech) M.; A.B., Lycée Condorcet, Paris, 1908; Agrégé, U. of Paris, 1914; D.Litt., Paris, 1933; post-grad. study, U. of Edinburgh, 1910-12; m. May Middleton, Aug. 19, 1915; children—May Elise, Marcel, Jean (died September 3, 1939), Georgette; came to United States, September 1915. Instructor in French, University of Minn., 1915-16, Princeton, 1916-17. Mem. French High Commn., Washington, 1917-18; lecturer in French, U. of Toronto, 1918-19, asst. prof., 1919-21, asso. prof., 1921-24; prof. and head of dept. of Romance languages, Rice Inst., Houston, Tex., since 1924; prof. French, summer sessions, Cornell U., U. of Chicago, U. of Tex., Stanford U., also Middlebury College, summers 1937 and 1938; invited as lecturer, Madrid, London, Oxford, Glasgow, Brussels, 1933. Served in French Army, World War, Aug. 1914-July 1915. Decorated Chevalier de la Legion d'Honneur, 1936. Mem. Modern Lan. Assn. America, Assn. French Teachers (pres. Tex. chapt.), etc. Catholic. Club: Faculty. Author: Sous les Armes, 1918; French Composition, 1925; The French Classical and the Shakespearian Drama (brochure), 1928; Le Romantisme francais en Angleterre, Paris Champion, 1933; La France de la Restauration d'aprés les visiteurs anglais, Paris Champion, 1933. Home: Houston, Tex. *

MOREHOUSE, CLIFFORD PHELPS, editor; b. Milw., Apr. 18, 1904; s. Frederic Cook and Lilias E. (Macon) M.; A.B., Harvard, 1925; A.M., Marquette U., 1937; LL.D., Nashotah, 1948, Brown U., 1962; S.T.D., Gen. Theol. Sem., 1967; m. Ellen Louise Smith, Mar. 16, 1927; children—Ellen Louise (Mrs. James L. Henry), Lilias Macon (Mrs. Jackson M. Bruce, Jr.), Frederic Cook. Sec. Morehouse-Barlow Co., 1925-39, v.p., 1932-64, pres. 1964-68, chmn. bd., editorial cons., 1968-70; mng. editor The Living Ch., 1926-32, editor, 1932-52. Episcopalian; past warden, vestryman; historiographer Trinity Ch., N.Y.C., 1968-73; trustee Cathedral St. John Divine, N.Y.C., 1948-52; alternate del. Assembly World Council Chs., Amsterdam, 1948, del., Evanston, 1954, New Delhi, 1961, Uppsala, 1968; mem. standing com. Diocese Milw., 1932-43; del. Synod Midwest Province, 1930-36; dep. Gen. Conv., 1934-67; del. World Conf. on Faith and Order, Edinburgh, 1937, Lund, Sweden, 1952; del. to N.A. Ecumenical Conf., Toronto, 1941; del. Fed. Council Chs., 1940-48; vice chmn. Milw. unit U.S. Com. care European Children, 1940; mem. Nat. Com. Food for Small Democracies, 1940-41; v.p. Asso. Ch. Press, 1941-42; spl. rep. ch. press at enthronement Archbishop of Canterbury, 1942; spl. del. from Episcopal Ch. to visit and study Ch. of S. India, 1956; pres. ho. of deps. Episcopal Ch., 1961-67, mem. exec. council, 1967-73; del. Anglican Congress, Toronto, 1963. Served as 2d lt. F.A. Res., 1925-32; from 1st lt. to lt. col. USMCR, 1943-57; asst. editor M.C. Gazette, 1943-44; combat historian, Peleliu and Iwo Jima operations. Decorated King's Medal (Gt. Britain), 1946; recipient P. Chase medal Kenyon Coll., 1961; asso. comdr. Order St. John Jerusalem. Mem. Sigma Delta Chi. Clubs: Harvard (N.Y.C.); Field (Sarasota). Founder, editor Layman's mag., 1940. Author: Origins of Episcopal Church Press, 1942; Wartime Pilgrimage, 1942; (with Bishop Wilson) Outline Life of Christ, 1947; A Layman Looks at the Church, 1964; Trinity: Mother of Churches, 1973; also historical monographs for USMC. Editor: Anglican Communion Throughout the World, 1927; Episcopal Ch. Annual, History of Trinity Parish, Vol. VII, 1971. Home: Sarasota, Fla. Died Feb. 17, 1977.

MOREHOUSE, EDWARD WARD, economist; b. Yonkers, N.Y., Sept. 16, 1896; s. Rev. Daniel W. and Martha Adelaide (Bird) M.; B.A., Amherst Coll., 1918, M.A. (hon.), 1958; M.A., U. Wis., 1920, Ph.D., 1927; m. Anna Mason Ely, June 14, 1923 (dec. 1958); children—Richard Ely (dec. 1923), Nancy Anderson

(Mrs. H. J. Gordon, Jr.), Ward Ely; m. 2d, Margery Robinson Collins, Dec. 30, 1959; stepchildren—Lawrence W. Collins III (dec.), Benjamin I. Collins, and Margery C. Collins. Began career as clerk U.S. States Shipping Bd., 1918; asst. econs. U. Wis., 1919-20, 21-23; asst. labor mgr. Levy Bros. Clothing Co., Rochester, N.Y., 1920-21; research instr. Inst. Research in Land Econs. and Pub. Util., 1923-25, research asso., 1925-31; asst. prof. econs. Northwestern U., 1925-28, asso. prof., 1928-31; mng. editor Land Economics (formerly Jour. Land and Pub. Utility Econs.), 1925-32, asso. editor, 1932-34, bd. editors, 1934-71; chief economist Pub. Service Commn. Wis., dir. rates and research dept., 1931-40; chief economist Trustees of Asso. Gas & Electric Corp., 1940-45; v.p. Gen. Pub. Utilities Corp., 1945-61; econ. cons., 1961-65. Cons. TVA, 1934-46, OPM, WPB, 1941-45; chmn. elec. power adv. com. NPA, 1951; chmn. com. statistics and accounts pub. utility cos. Nat. Assn. R.R. and Pub. Utility Commrs., 1935-39; chmn. Wis. Com. Statistics, 1938-40; cons. Nat. Security Resources Bd., 1947-49; mem. com. coop, AEC and electric power industry, 1949-52; exec. adv. com. nat. power survey, Fed. Power Comn., 1962-64; ad hoc adv. com. AEC, 1964; pub. utilities and communications adv. com. on wealth inventory survey George Washington U., 1963-64; Regents lectr. U. Calif., Santa Barbara, 1966; lectr. U. Wis., 1963-66; econ. cons. corp. and engring. firms, 1962-69, AEC, 1961-62, 65-69. Bd. dirs. N.H.-Vt. Devel. Council, Inc., 1971-74; trustee Littleton Public Library Bd., 1972-74. Pres., dir. Utilities Mut. Ins. Co., 1948-62; dir. Jersey Central Power & Light Co., Pa. Electric Co., Manila Electric Co., Met. Edison Co., N.J. Power & Light Co.; dir. Atomic Power Devel. Assos., Inc., 1955-62, chmn. com. on econs., from 1955. Served as sgt., Motor Transport Corps, U.S. Army, 1918-19. Fellow A.A.A.S.; mem. Am. Econ. Assn., Am. Statis. Assn., Acad. Polit. Sci., Am. Nuclear Soc., Am. Gas Assn. (chmn. com. on econs. 1950-51), Newcomen Soc. Am., Phi Beta Kappa, Alpha Delta Phi. Unitarian. Author: (with R. T. Ely) Elements of Land Economics, 1924; (with J. B. S. Hardman, others) American Labor Dynamics, 1926. Contbr. articles jours. Home: Littleton, N.H. Died 1974.

MORELL, GEORGE FOWLER (MÔR-REL'), newspaper publisher; b. South Amherst, Mass., Sept. 24, 1886; s. John Fowler and Alice (Goodrich) M.; student Stanford Univ., 1905-10, A.B., 1930; married; children—George, Patricia, John. Successively advt. mgr., salesman, mgr. Cooperative Land Co. colonization, ranch projects, Merced, Madera Counties (all Calif.) 1910-17; own ranch projects since 1913; bought control daily Times, Palo Alto, 1919; founded daily Tribune, Redwood City, 1923; bought daily Advance, Burlingame, 1936; pres. Peninsula Newspapers Inc., pub. above, 1919-58, chmn. bd., 1958—. Recruited, trained vol. inf. co., Merced, 1917; private, lieut., capt., 20th Inf., U.S.A., 1917-19; seaman, ensign, lieut., U.S. Coast Guard, 1943-45. Dir. State Realty Fedn., 1914, Chambers of Commerce, Merced, Palo Alto, 1914-28, Merced Red Cross, 1917; comdr. Fremont Post, American Legion, Palo Alto, 1919; pres. Merced Realty Board, 1914-16, Santa Clara County Press Assn., 1921-36, Peninsula Chambers of Commerce, 1922, Veterans League, Palo Alto Rotary Club, 1927, Calif. Newspaper Publishers Assn., 1937, San Mateo County Cattlemen's Assn., 1943. Mem. bd. govs. San Francisco Bay Area Council 1946-61. Trustee Merced High Sch., 1916-17, First Congl. Ch., 1947-50, Stanford U., 1944-56, emeritus, 1956—. Home: Palo Alto, Ca. *

MORETZ, OWEN LEONARD, textile co. exec.; b. Catawba County, N.C., May 26, 1911; s. Joseph Alfred and Elizabeth (Leonard) M.; student Lenoir Rhyne Coll. Hickory, N.C.; m. Helen Schlegel, June 30, 1938; children—George, Carol (Mrs. Michael Jennings), Helen (Mrs. Kenneth Sides), Nancy (Mrs. Bill Burnside). With Carolina Mills, Inc., Maiden, N.C., from 1929, pres. after 1960; dir. Schlegel Mfg. Co., Rochester, N.Y., R.P. Caldwell Co., Gastonia, N.C., Northwestern Bank, N. Wilkesboro, N.C., Howell Mfg. Co., Cherryville, N.C.; mem. adv. bd. Liberty Mut. Life Ins. Co., Arkwright-Boston Mut. Ins. Co.; chmn. bd. Maxwell-Royal Chair Co., Carolina Maiden Corp., N.Y.C., Catawba Valley Computer Center, Maiden, N.C., MoBill Textiles, Inc., Wilmington, N.C., Alpha-Con, Inc., St Louis, Custom Brick Co., Claremore, Okla., Comml. Fabricators, Inc., Newton, N.C.; v.p. West Deal Co. Exec. com. Boy Scouts Am. southeast region, pres. Piedmont council. Trustee, treas. Lenoir Rhyne Coll.; trustee N.C. Vocat. Textile Sch., Belmont; pres., dir. Catawba County YMCA. Mem. Charlotte Textile Club, N.C. Textile Mfrs. Assn. (past pres. Charlotte 1971-72). Am. Yarn Spinners Assn. (dir.), Am. Textile Mfrs. Inst. (dir.). Rotarian. Clubs: Catawba Country, Lake Hickory Country (Hickory). Home: Hickory, N.C. Died Aug. 8, 1977.

MOREY, SYLVESTER MARVIN, advt. exec.; b. Greenwich, N.Y., Apr. 22, 1896; s. Clayton L. and Lillian H. (Phelps) M.; B.S., Dartmouth Coll., 1918; m. Minetta E. Meyer, Oct. 11, 1923; 1 son, Clayton Phelps. Copywriter George L. Dyer Co., 1920-24, Blackman Co., 1924-28, Gardner Advt. Co., 1929; advt. mgr. Sinclair Refining Co., 1930-41; pres. Hixson-O'Donnell Advt., Inc., 1941-48, Morey, Humm & Johnstone, Inc., 1949-56, Morey, Humm & Warwick, Inc., 1956-59; chmn. bd. Geyer, Morey, Madden & Ballard, Inc., from 1959. Bd. dirs. Rudolf Steiner Found., N.Y.C., Nat. Outdoor Advt. Bur., Waldorf Ednl. Found.; dir., sec.-treas. Myrin Inst.; mem. bd. Rudolf Steiner Sch., 1938-50. Mem. Anthroposophical Soc. Am. (past pres., sec.), Inst. Creative Research, Chi Phi. Clubs: Dartmouth, University (N.Y.C.), Cherry Valley Golf (Garden City). Author: Can the Red Man Help the White Man, 1970. Home: Great Barrington, Mass. Died Oct. 26, 1975.

MORGAN, BARTON, coll. prof.; b. near Jameson, Mo., Feb. 19, 1889; s. Daniel Emerson and Nancy Adeline (Stowe) M.; student Northwest Mo. State Teachers Coll. (Maryville), 1907-08; B.S., Northeast Mo. State Teachers Coll. (Kirksville), 1919; M.S., Iowa State Coll., 1922; Ph.D., U. Iowa, 1934; student U. Wash., summer 1915; m. Catherine Wallace, Aug. 18, 1914 (dec.); children—Margaret Catherine (Mrs. Warren B. Sargent), Richard Barton, Harold John, Paul Emerson; m. 2d, Helen Green, 1932 (dec.); m. 3d, Margaret Barrett, 1951. Teacher rural school, Jameson, Mo., 1908-10; prin. sch., Greencastle, Mo., 1912-13; prin. high sch., Wilson Creek, Wash., 1913-15; supt. schs., Hartline, Wash., 1915-18, Okoboji Twp. Consol. Schs., Milford, Iowa, 1918-22, Hudson, Iowa, 1922-23; asso. prof. rural edn. Iowa State Tchrs. Coll., Cedar Falls, 1922-23; prof. vocat. edn. Iowa State Univ., 1923-79, head dept., dir. tchr. edn., 1936-51; cons. agrl. edn. Inter-Am. Inst. Agrl. Scis., Costa Rica. Mem. staff of President's Com. on Vocational Edn., 1937, President's Advisory Com. on Edn., 1937; mem. White House Conf. on Rural Edn., 1944. Mem. Iowa State Teachers Assn. (pres. 1937-38), Am. Assn. Sch. Adminstrs., Nat. Soc. Coll. Teachers of Edn., Am. Ednl. Research Assn., Am., Iowa vocat. assns., Nat. Soc. Study of Edn., Phi Delta Kappa, Gamma Sigma Delta; life mem. NEA (pres. dept. rural edn. 1942-44; chmn. commn. on rural edn. and the war 1942-45); mem. bd. dirs. Am. Country Life Association, 1943-46. Conglist. Author: The Nature and Purpose of Education, 1929; History of the Extension Service in Agriculture and Home Economics of Iowa State College, 1934; A Possible Intermediate Step in the Reorganization of Rural Elementary Education in Iowa (with W. H. Lancelot), 1936; The Land-Grant Colleges (with George A. Works), 1939; Uniform County School Maps for Iowa, 1940; Learning Science; Methods in Adult Education (with G. E. Holmes and C.E. Bundy), 1960, rev. edit., 1976; Golden Nuggets of Thought; Photographing Wildlife; Before the Work Horses Went, 1978. Home: Ames, Iowa. Died Mar. 19, 1979.

MORGAN, BAYARD QUINCY, prof. German; b. Dorchester, Mass., Apr. 5, 1883; s. Miles Forrest and Fanny (Fisher) M.; A.B., Trinity Coll. (Conn.), 1904; Ph.D., U. of Leipzig, 1907; m. Johanna Rossberg, June 19, 1912; children—Annelies, Margaret. Instr., asst. prof., asso. prof., German, U. of Wis., 1907-25, prof., 1925-34; prof. and chmn. German dept., Stanford U., 1934, emeritus, since Sept. 1948. With div. mil. intelligence, 1918. Mem. Mod. Lang. Assn. Am., Am. Assn. U. Profs., Am. Assn. Teachers of German, Am. Dialect Soc., Phi Beta Kappa, Alpha Chi Rho, Mng. editor Modern Lang. Journal, 1925-30. Co-author: Introduction to German, 1923. Compiler and editor: The German Mind, 1928. Author: Nature in Middle High German Lyrics, 1912; Elementary German Syntax, 1916; Bibliography of German Literature in English Translation, 1922, 2d revised edition, 1938; German Frequency Word Book, 1928; Carl Schurz, 1939. Co-author: Neues Deutsches Liederbuch, 1931; minimum standard German Vocabulary, 1935, Reading German, 1943; various textbooks. Contbr. to pedagogical and other periodicals. Address: Calif. *

MORGAN, CLIFFORD THOMAS, psychologist; b. Minnetola, N.J., July 21, 1915; s. Samuel and Ethel Josephine (Dixon) M.; A.B., Maryville Coll., Maryville, Tenn., 1936; A.M., U. Rochester, 1937, Ph.D., 1939; m. Jean Chase Snow, Nov. 28, 1946; children—Peter Charles, Patricia Ann, Michael Thomas. Asst. psychology U. Rochester, 1936-38, research fellow, 1938-39; research asso. Psychol. Corp. New York, 1937-39; instr. in psychology Harvard and Radcliffe Coll., 1939-42, faculty instr., 1942-43; tech. aide div. physics Nat. Def. Research Com., Washington, 1943-46; asso. in psychology Johns Hopkins, 1943-45, asst. prof., 1945-46, asso. prof., 1946-48, chmn. dept. psychology, 1946-54, chmn. biol. sci. group, 1951-53, dir. Systems Research Lab., 1946-49, prof., 1948-57, fellow, 1957-60; lectr. dept. psychology U. Wis., Madison, 1959-62, U. Calif., Santa Barbara, 1962-65; adj. prof. U. Tex., Austin, 1968-76; cons. editor McGraw-Hill Book Co., 1950-59. Mem. NRC, 1950-53. Fellow A.A.A.S. (v.p. 1960), Am. Psychol. Assn. (div. physiol. and comparative psychology (pres. 1946-48, chmn. publs. bd. 1960-61); mem. Am. Physiol. Soc., Soc. Exptl. Psychologists. Methodist. Author: Physiological Psychology, 1943; textbooks in field; co-author: Applied Experimental Psychology, 1949; How to Study, 1957. Cons. editor Journal of Comparative and Physiological Psychology, 1947-54, Ann. Rev. of Psychology, 1953-59, Contemporary Psychology, 1955-60; editor Psychol. Abstracts, 1960-63; Psychonomic Sci., 1964-72, Bull. of Psychonomic Soc., 1973-76. Contbr. psychol. jours. Home: Austin, Tex. Died Feb. 12, 1976.

MORGAN, DONALD MARVIN, pvt. investor; b. Duluth, Minn., Mar. 21, 1921; s. Floyd Byron and Leanore (Kjelstrup) M.; ed. Huntington Bus. Coll., also Grad. Sch. Bus. Adminstrn., U. So. Cal.; m. Barbara Leone Proulx, Aug. 3, 1946; children—Barbara Marie, Melanie Anne, Richard Gregory. Accountant, Fluor Corp., Ltd., Los Angeles, 1941-54; controller Singmaster & Breyer, Inc., N.Y.C., 1955-59; with Fluor Corp., Ltd., 1959-72, treas., 1963-72, v.p. finance, 1966-72; v.p. finance, mem. mgmt. rev. com. Occidental Petroleum Co., Los Angeles, 1972-75. Served with AUS, 1942-45. Mem. Am. Mgmt. Assn., Financial Execs. Inst., Am. Petroleum Inst., Newcomen Soc. N.Am., Nat. Assn. Accountants. Lutheran. Home: Long Beach, Calif. Died Sept. 27, 1980.

MORGAN, GERALD DEMUTH, govt. ofcl., lawyer; b. N.Y.C., Dec. 19, 1908; s. George Wilson and Helen (Demuth) M.; A.B., Princeton, 1930; LL.B., Harvard, 1933; m. Alice Humphrey, June 25, 1932; children—Eleanor, Barbara, Gerald Demuth, Craig. Admitted to N.Y. bar, 1934, Ky. bar, 1938, D.C. bar, 1946; with solicitor's office U.S. Steel Corp., 1933-35; asst. legislative counsel U.S. Ho. of Reps., 1933-45; partner Morgan & Calhoun, Washington, 1946-50; partner Hamel, Park, McCabe & Saunders, Washington, 1950-53, 61-76; spl. asst. White House, Washington, 1953, adminstrv. asst. to President U.S., 1953-55, spl. counsel to the President of U.S., 1955-58, dep. asst. to pres., 1958-61. Cons. Commn. Orgn. Executive Br. Govt., 1947-48. Mem. Am., D.C., Ky. bar assns., Am. Law Inst. Home: Gaithersburg, Md. Died June 15, 1976.

MORGAN, INA LUCAS, prof. psychiatric social work; b. Wareham, Mass., Nov. 11, 1884; d. John Brainard and Edith Frances (Lucas) Morgan; grad. N.E. Training Sch., 1903-05, Boston Univ., 1912-15, N.Y. Sch. of Social Work, 1920, U. of Chicago, 1923-24; Bachelor in Social Science, Boston Univ., 1937; M.S., Baldwin-Wallace College, 1937. Engaged as social worker in community orgn., 1906-18; Travelers' Aid, immigrant and station worker, N.Y. City, 1918-21; Am. Red Cross psychiatric social worker, Chicago, 1921-22; same, U.S. Vets. Bur., Chicago, 1922-24; research worker Mass. Dept. Mental Diseases, Division for Examination of Prisoners, Boston, 1924-26; chief psychiatric social worker U.S. Vets. Adminstrn., Cincinnati and Boston, 1926-35; prof. psychiatric social work and dir. field work, Boston U. Grad. Division of Social Work, since 1935. Mem. Am. Assn. Social Workers, Mass. Civic League. Assn. Church Social Workers, Am. Assn. Psychiatric Social Workers (chmn. N.E. Div. 1939-40), Am. Assn. Univ. Profs., Am. Assn. University Women, Nat. Conf. of Social Work, Mass. Conf. of Social Work, Boston U. Alumni Assn., Baldwin-Wallace Coll. Alumni Assn., Pan-Am. Soc. of Mass. Republican. Contbr. professional articles. Home: Boston, Mass. *

MORGAN, J. D., athletic dir.; b. Newcastle, Okla., Mar. 3, 1919; s. David C. and Mae (Ruston) M.; B.A., UCLA, 1941; m. Cynthia Grey Crane, July 25, 1959; children—Kevin Davis, Pamela Elizabeth. Planning engr. Lockheed Aircraft Corp., Burbank, Calif., 1941-43; accountant, then asso. bus. mgr. UCLA, from 1946, tennis coach to 1963, athletic dir., 1963-80. Named Athletic Dir. of Distinction, Columbus (Ohio) Touchdown Club, Nat. Tennis Coach of Year. Mem. Nat. Collegiate Athletic Assn. (exec. com.), Nat. Athletic Collegiate Dirs. Assn., Nat. Tennis Coaches Assn. (life), Pacific Ten Council, UCLA Alumni Assn. (Profl. Achievement award). Republican. Episcopalian. Home: Northridge, Calif. Died Dec. 16, 1980.

MORGAN, JOSEPH H., lawyer; b. Roscommon, Ireland, July 23, 1884; s. John and Catherine (Fallon) M.; came to U.S., 1887, naturalized, 1905; student Lincoln Acad., Lincoln, Neb., 1903-05; LL.B., U. of Neb., 1910; m. Theola Linn, Oct. 1910 (dec. 1955); children—Catherine M. (Mrs. M. F. Delgado), Robert L., Donald J., Mary Helen (Mrs. H. M. Babcock); m. 2d to Mae Ruth Fahy, Aug. 1, 1959. Admitted to Neb. and Ariz. bars, 1910; in gen. practice of law Prescott, Ariz., since 1910; as mem. firm Morgan And Locklean, 1947-52; Justice Supreme Court of Arizona, 1945-46; regent Univ. of Ariz. 1943-45; state chmn. Ariz. State Dem. Central Com., 1942-44; practice of law, Phoenix, Arizona, 1947—; president of Yavapai-Mohave Boy Scout Council, 1928-29. Mem. Am. and Ariz. bar assns., Delta Chi. Democrat. Roman Catholic. Elk. K.C. (past state dep.). Club: Arizona (Phoenix); Rotary (past pres. Prescott). Home: Phoenix, Ariz. *

MORGAN, SAMUEL ST. JOHN, banker; b. Hartford, Conn., Apr. 20, 1882; s. William Gardner and Elizabeth Cook (Hall) M.; A.B., Trinity Coll., Hartford, 1903; m. Mary Helen Bergen, June 21, 1935. With Westinghouse Elec. & Mfg. Co., Pittsburgh, 1903, New England mgr., Boston, 1914-19; pres. Lamson & Hubbard Corp., Boston, 1919-25; v.p., dir., State St. Trust Co., Boston, since 1925; dir. Merrimac Hat Co., Loyal Protective

Life Ins. Co. Past pres. Retail Trade Board, Boston. Clubs: Country (Brookline); City Club Corporation. Home: Brookline, Mass. *

MORGAN, SHEPARD (ASHMAN), banker; b. Rochester, N.Y., June 1, 1884; s. Judge John Shepard and Lavinia (Munson) M.; B.A., Williams Coll., 1906, M.A., 1907; m. Barbara Spofford, Feb. 20, 1912; children—Mrs. John G. Laylin, Mrs. Richard T. Smyth, John Spofford. Began as teacher of political science, Williams Coll., 1906-08; reporter New York Sun, 1908-13; sec. dept. finance, later dep. comptroller, City of New York, 1913-17; comptroller Govt. Loan Orgn. 2d Federal Res. Dist., 1918-19; asst. federal reserve agt. Federal Res. Bank of N.Y., 1919-24; econ. adviser, later finance dir. Office for Reparation Payments, Berlin, 1924-30, v.p. and chmn. com. of fgn. services, Chase Nat. Bank, 1930-49; condr. banking negotiations, Berlin and Havana, 1936-38; dir. (London), research and analysis branch, Office of Strategic Services, 1943, mem. and acting chmn. Planning Group, 1944; chmn. Nat. Bur. Econ. Research, 1946-48, dir. since 1931; finance adviser Mil. Govt. of U.S. in Germany, 1949, later finance adviser to Am. High Commissioner in Germany, resigned 1949; regents' prof., sch. bus. adminstrn. U. Cal. at Berkeley, 1955-56. Past trustee Vassar College, Teachers Coll. (Columbia U.). Dir. Queen Wilhelmina Fund, 1940-43. Sec. President's Committee for Financing Foreign Trade, 1945-47. Trustee Academy of Political Science, American Historical Assn.; mem. Council on Foreign Relations, Alpha Delta Phi. Awarded D. A. Wells prize in political science, Williams College, 1907. Republican. Presbyterian. Clubs: University, Century, Williams, Metropolitan (Washington, D.C.). Wrote sections of Young Plan dealing with Bank for Internat. Settlements, Basle, Switzerland, 1929. Home: Norfolk, Conn. *

MORGAN, SHERLEY WARNER, prof. architecture; b. Cin., Apr. 4, 1892; s. Asa Bushnell and Lydia Eleanor (Moore) M.; A.B., Princeton U., 1913; B.Arch., Columbia U., 1917; m. Ethel Palmer, June 16, 1920; children—Eleanor Harrison, Arthur Palmer, Richard Sherley, Diana Melville. Engaged as draftsman, 1916; part-time instr. Princeton U., 1915-16, instr., 1916-17, asst. prof. architecture, 1919-25, asso. prof., 1925-31, prof. architecture, 1931-52, emeritus, 1952-78, dir. Sch. Architecture, 1928-52. Sec.-dir. N.J. Board Architects, from 1957. Served to capt., inf., U.S. Army, 1917-19, with A.E.F., St. Mihiel, Meuse Argonne offensives; comdg. officer U.S. Army student detachment U. Montpelier, France, 1919. Past chmn. bd. trustees Princeton Country Day Sch. Fellow AIA; mem. Assn. Coll. Schs. of Architecture (past pres.), Archaeol. Inst. Am., Phi Beta Kappa, Psi Upsilon. Sec., Nat. Archtl. Accrediting Bd., 1943-49. Honored as officer d'Academie de la Republique Français. Republican. Presbyterian. Clubs: Terrace, Nassau (Princeton); Century (N.Y.C.); Ekwanok Country (Manchester, Vt.); Yeamans Hall (Charleston, S.C.). Author: Architectural Drawing, 1950. Home: Princeton, N.J. Died Feb. 1, 1979.

MORGAN, WILLIAM JOHN, lawyer; b. Charlestown, Calumet County, Wis., Dec. 13, 1883; s. John H. and Eliza (Nicholson) M.; student U. of Wis., 1903-05; LL.B., U. of Mich., 1908; m. Mary Baker, Nov. 1, 1911; children—John Dickinson, Roger Nicholson, Richard Holden. Began practice at Milwaukee, Wis., 1908; mem. firm Morgan & Berkwich. Atty. gen. of Wis., term 1921-23; instituted suit, U.S. Supreme Court in which Sanitary Dist. of Chicago enjoined from diverting waters of Lake Mich. for sewerage and power purposes, 1929; as atty. gen. secured 20 decrees in Wisconsin anti-trust suits. Conservative candidate Rep. nom. for governor of Wisconsin, 1922. Non-resident prof. law (trusts, monopolies and unfair competition), Marquette U. Public panel chairman Nat. War Labor Bd. since 1943. Organizer and charter mem. Big Brothers and Big Sisters of Milwaukee. Mem. Motion Picture Panel of Arbitrators, Am., Wis. and Miuwaukee bar assns., Nat. Assn. Attys. Gen. (v.p. 1921-22) St. Davids Soc., Delta Chi. Dir. Am. Chess Fed. Republican. Episcopalian. Clubs: City, Chess (pres.), Church (Milwaukee); Madison (Madison). Home: Milwaukee. *

MORGENTHAU, HANS JOACHIM, educator; b. Coburg, Germany, Feb. 17, 1904 (came to U.S. 1937, naturalized, 1943); s. Ludwig and Frieda (Bachmann) M.; student U. Berlin, U. Frankfort, U. Munich, 1923-27; magna cum laude, U. Munich, 1927; summa cum laude, U. Frankfort, 1929; postgrad. Grad. Inst. Internat. Studies, Geneva, 1932; LL.D., Clark U., 1962, Ripon Coll., 1962, Alma Coll., 1965, U. Denver, 1971, U. Ill., 1978, St. Michael's Coll., 1979; Litt.D., Western Res. U., 1965; L.H.D., Hebrew Union Coll., 1975; m. Irma Thormann, June 3, 1935; children—Matthew, Susanna. Admitted to bar, 1927; practice law, 1927-30; asst. to law faculty U. Frankfort, 1931; acting pres. Labor Law Ct., Frankfort, 1931-33; instr. polit. sci. U. Geneva, 1932-35; prof. internat. law Inst. Internat. and Econ. Studies, Madrid, Spain, 1935-36; instr. govt. Bklyn. Coll., 1937-39; asst. prof. law history and polit. sci. U. Kansas., Kansas City, Mo., 1939-43; admitted to Mo. bar; vis. asso. prof. polit. sci. U. Chgo., 1943-45; asso. prof., 1945-49, prof., 1949-61, prof. polit. sci. and modern history, 1961-63, Albert A. Michelson Distinguished Service prof., 1963-68, dir. Center Study Am. Fgn. Policy, 1950-68; Leonard Davis distinguished prof. City Coll., City U. N.Y., 1968-74; univ. prof. New Sch. Socia Research, 1974-80; vis. prof. U. Calif. at Berkeley, 1949, Harvard, 1951, 59, 60, 61, Northwestern U., 1954, Columbia, Yale, 1956, U. Wyo., 1955, 58, Princeton Inst. Advanced Study, 1958, Washington Center Fgn. Policy Research, 1958-60; sr. research fellow Council Fgn. Relations, N.Y.C., 1966. Cons. Dept. State, 1949-51, 61-80, Dept. Def., 1961-65. Hon. trustee Council on Religion and Internat. Affairs. Mem. Am. Philos. Soc., Am., Internat. polit. sci. assns., Am. Acad. Arts and Scis., AAUP, Council Fgn. Relations, Fgn. Policy Assn. (hon. dir.), Johns Hopkins Soc. Scholars. Clubs: Quadrangle (Chgo.); Century (N.Y.C.). Author: Scientific Man vs. Power Politics, 1946; Politics Among Nations, rev. 1973; Principles and Problems of International Politics (with Kenneth W. Thompson), 1950; In Defense of the National Interest, 1951; Dilemmas of Politics, 1958; The Purpose of American Politics, 1960; Politics in the 20th Century, 3 vols., 1962; A New Foreign Policy for the United States, 1969; Truth and Power, 1970; Science: Master or Servant, 1971, others. Contbr. articles to philos., law and polit. sci. jours. nat. newspapers, and Ency. Brit. Home: New York, N.Y. Died July 19, 1980.

MORGULIS, SERGIUS (MOR'GOO'LIS), biochemist; b. Russia, Aug. 6, 1885; s. Samuel and Hannah (Spigel) M.; Ananieff Gymnasium; A.M., Columbia, 1907; Ph.D., Harvard, 1910; studied in Vienna, Berlin, Naples, Woods Hole, etc.; m. Fannie Bashkirtzeva, 1911. Came to U.S., 1904, naturalized citizen, 1910. Austin teaching fellow, Harvard, 1909; traveling fellow from Harvard, 1910-12; asso. in animal metabolism, Carnegie Instn., 1912-13; asso. in biochemistry, Coll. Physicians and Surgeons (Columbia), 1913-16; spl. research asso., U.S. Bur. Fisheries, 1914-16; prof. physiology and biochemistry, Creighton U., Omaha, Neb., 1916-21; prof. biochemistry, U. of Neb. Coll. of Medicine, since 1921. Fellow A.A.A.S.; mem. Soc. Biol. Chemistry, Am. Physiol. Soc., Am. Soc. Zoölogists, Biochem. Assn., Société Chimie Biologique, Paris, 1934, Biochem. Soc. (Great Britain), Sigma Xi. Author: Fasting and Undernutrition, 1923; Experiments in Physical and Physiological Chemistry, 1929; Nutritional Muscular Dystrophy, 1938; (with Oparin) The Origin of Life, 1938; Biochemical Evolution (with Florkin), 1949; also numerous exptl. and general articles in mags. Address: Omaha, Neb. *

MORIE, THOMAS ALBERT, pub. co. exec.; b. Pitts., Aug. 27, 1933; s. Thomas Adam and Edith (Gernhardt) M.; B.A., Brown U., 1955; m. Beverly Ann Kamery, June 22, 1957; 1 dau., Tara Oreen. Sales mgr. Chilton Co., Radnor, Pa., 1961-71; pub., 1971-78. Served to capt. USAF, 1955-60. Mem. Phi Kappa Psi. Club: Seaview Country (Absecon, N.J.). Home: Pocopsow, Pa. Died Aug. 22, 1978.

MORISON, H. GRAHAM, lawyer; b. Bristol, Tenn., Aug. 18, 1906; s. Hugh G. and Lucile (Barker) M.; student The Choate Sch., Wallingford, Conn., 1920-26; A.B., Washington and Lee U., 1929, LL.B., 1932, LL.D., 1966; m. Beatrice Elizabeth Keegin, June 22, 1946. Admitted to Va. Bar, 1932; practiced in Bristol, 1932-36, N.Y.C., 1936-41; mem. firm Morison, Morison, Rouse and Flannagan, 1932-36, Miller, Owen, Otis and Bailly (Willkie, Farr and Gallagher), 1936-41; asst. to gen. counsel of W.P.B., Washington, 1941-43; spl. asst. to atty. gen., 1945, exec. asst., 1945, asst. atty gen. U.S., and head of Civil Division, Dept. Justice, 1948-50, chief Am. del. Econ. and Social Council, UN, 1949; head anti-trust div., 1950-52; pvt. practice law, Washington, from 1952. Dir. Conservation Council Va.; chmn. scholarship com. Grandfather Mountain Highland Games. Trustee Nat. Conf. Christians and Jews, past chmn., bd. dirs. Nat. Conf. Christians and Jews Greater Met. Washington. Served to maj., USMC, 1943-45; PTO. Mem. Am. (vice chmn. jr. bar conf. 1939), Bristol Virginia, Tenn., Va. Tenn., N.Y. bar assns., Bar Assn. D.C., Clan Morison N.Am. (chmn.), Gt. Falls Conservation Council (chmn.), Res. Officers Assn. Marine Corps, Mil. Order Carabao, S.A.R., Am. Legion, St. Andrews Soc., Order Coif, Phi Beta Kappa, Phi Gamma Delta, Omicron Delta Kappa, Phi Delta Phi. Democrat. Presbyn. (mem. gen. council). Club: Metropolitan (Washington). Home: Great Falls, Va. Died May 1, 1976.

MORISON, SAMUEL ELIOT, historian, author; b. Boston, July 9, 1887; s. John Holmes and Emily Marshall (Eliot) M.; A.B., Harvard, 1908, Ph.D., 1912, Litt.D., 1936; M.A., Oxford (Eng.) U. 1922; student Ecole des Sciences Politiques, Paris, 1908-09; L.H.D., Trinity Coll., 1935, Amherst Coll., 1936; Williams Coll., 1950, Bucknell U., 1960; LL.D. (hon.), Union Coll., 1939, U. Me., 1968; Boston Coll., 1960; Litt.D., Yale, 1949, Oxford U., 1951, Notre Dame, 1954, Holy Cross, 1962; m. Elizabeth S. Greene, May 28, 1910 (dec. Aug. 1945); children—Elizabeth Gray (Mrs. Edward Spingarn), Emily Marshall (Mrs. H. Brooks Beck), Peter Greene (dec.), Catharine (Mrs. Cooper); m. 2d, Priscilla Barton, Dec. 29, 1949 (dec. Feb. 1973). Instr. history U. Cal., 1914; instr., lectr., prof. history Harvard, 1915-55; Harold V. Harmsworth prof. Am. history Oxford U., 1922-25. Served as pvt., inf., U.S. Army, 1918-19; attached Russian div. Am. Commn. to Negotiate Peace, Paris, 1919; Am. del. Baltic Commn. of Peace Com., 1919; historian U.S. naval operations World War II; from lt. comdr. to rear adm. USNR, 1942-51. Decorated Legion of Merit; recipient Bancroft prize Columbia, 1949, 72, Theodore Roosevelt medal, 1956, Edison award, 1957, Alfred Thayer Mahan award Navy League, 1961, Emerson-Thoreau medal Am. Acad. Arts and Scis., 1961, Gold medal history Nat. Inst. Arts and Letters, 1962, Balzan Found. award history, 1963; Presdl. medal Freedom, 1964. Fellow Soc. Antiquaries, Am. Philos. Soc., Am. Acad. Arts and Scis., Brit. Acad.; mem. Am. Antiquarian Soc. (past pres.), Colonial Soc. Mass., Mass. Hist. Soc., Soc. Cincinnati, Charitable Irish Soc., Real Academia de la Historia (Madrid), Am. Acad. Arts and Letters. Democrat. Episcopalian. Clubs: St. Botolph, Cruising Club, Somerset, Tavern (Boston). Author: Life of Harrison Gray Otis, 1913; Maritime History of Massachusetts, 1921; Oxford History of the United States, 1927; Builders of Bay Colony, 1930; Tercentennial History of Harvard University (Juserand medal and Loubat prize), 5 vols., 1930-36; Puritan Pronaos, 1936; Growth of the American Republic (with Henry Steele Commager), 1950; Admiral of Ocean Sea (Pulitzer prize), 1942; History U.S. Naval Operations World War II, 15 vols. 1947-62; By Land and By Sea, 1953; Christopher Columbus, Mariner, 1955; Freedom in Contemporary Society, 1956; The Story of Old Colony of New Plymouth, 1956; Strategy and Compromise, 1958; John Paul Jones (Pulitzer Prize 1960), 1959; The Story of Mount Desert Island, 1960; One Boy's Boston, 1962; The Two-Ocean War, 1963; Journals and other Documents of Columbus, 1963; Vistas of History, 1964; (with Mauricio Obregon) The Caribbean as Columbus Saw It, 1964; Spring Tides, 1965; The Oxford History of the American People, 1965; The Life of Commodore Matthew C. Perry, 1967; H.G. Otis, Urbane Federalist, 1969; The European Discovery of America, The Northern Voyages, 1971; Samuel de Champlain, Father of New France, 1972, The European Discovery of America, The Southern Voyages, 1974. Home: Northeast Harbor, Maine. Died May 15, 1976.

MORITZ, ERNEST A., engr.; b. Sheboygan, Wis., Aug. 30, 1882; s. Louis and Anna (Bidgenbach) M.; B.S., Univ. Wis., 1904, C.E., 1905; m. Avera C. Flint, June 30, 1909 (died Apr. 25, 1948); children—Ralph H., Robert, Bette Janet (Mrs. G. L. Jones, Jr.); m. 2d, Cora S. Trimble, Sept. 16, 1949. Instr. Univ. Wis., 1905-06; engr. United States Bur. Reclamation, Dept. Interior, Yakima, Wash., 1907-11, Washington, 1912-15, Denver, 1915-19; project mgr., St. Ignatius, Mont., 1920, gen. contracting, Effingham, Ill., 1921-34; constrn. engr., Parker Dam, Calif., 1934-38, Marshall Ford Dam, Austin, Tex., 1938-41; dir. power, Boulder Canyon Project, Boulder City, Nev., 1941-43; regional dir. U.S. Bur. Reclamation since 1943. Mem. Am. Soc. C.E., Tau Beta Pi. Club: Rotary. Author: Working Data for Irrigation Engineers, 1914. Home: Boulder City, Nev. *

MORIZE, ANDRÉ (MO-REZ'), prof. French lit.; b. Le Fleix, France, Sept. 18, 1884; s. Paul and Claire (Delhorbe) M.; ed. Lycées of Toulouse and Louis-le-Grand, Sorbonne, Ecole Normale Supérieure; Agrégé, 1907; Litt.D., Middlebury Coll., 1925; m. Ruth Muzzy, 1929. Prof. Lycée of Bordeaux, France, 1909-13; came to U.S., 1913; asst. professor Johns Hopkins Univ., 1913-14; asst. prof. of mil. science and tactics, Harvard, 1917-18, accepted chair of French lit., 1919, prof., 1925, chmn. dept. history and lit., 1931-39. Directeur at the Commissariat, then Ministry of Information, Paris, Sept. 1939-June 1940. Served with French Army as sergt., lt., and capt. of Inf., 1914-17. Decorated Officer Legion of Honor. Dir. French Summer Sch., Middlebury Coll. Mem. Modern Lang. Assn. of America, Am. Assn. of Teachers of French, Phi Beta Kappa. Clubs: Harvard (Boston); Spee (Harvard). Author: L'Apologie du Luxe au XVIIIe Siècle, 1910; Candide (Société des textes français modernes), 1914; Correspondance inédite de Montesquieu, 1914; Problems and Methods of Literary History, 1922. France: Eté 1940, 1941. Contbr. articles to jours. *

MORLAND, JOHN WALLACE (MÔR'LAND), prof. law; b. Harlem Springs, O., Oct. 28, 1886; s. John Thomas and Mary Lucille (DeFord) M.; grad. Ind. State Normal Sch., Terre Haute, Ind., 1913; A.B., Ind. U., 1916, A.M., LL.B., 1917; J.D., U. of Chicago, 1922; m. Ruth Bell, Aug. 27, 1911; children—Ruth Virginia Shimek, Mary Frances Gieseke, John Bell, Jean Bell Foreman. Public school teacher and high school principal, Indiana, until 1915; assistant in history, Indiana University, 1916-17; supervising principal high schools, Knox County, Ind., 1917-19; instr., Vincennes U., 1919; instr. history and polit. science, Valparaiso U., summer, 1919, registrar, 1919-21; registrar and instr. social science, Monmouth Coll., 1921-23; pres. Vincennes U., 1923-24; dean Lincoln Memorial U., 1924-25; with Valparaiso U. 1925—, acting dean Sch.

Law, 1928-30, prof. law and dean Law Sch. 1930-54, prof. 1954—, dean emeritus of the school of law, 1955—. With Dept. Justice, summers 1931, 33, 34, 36, 37, 38, 39, 40; visiting prof. of Law, U. of Kentucky, 1940-41 and summer 1946, U. of Oregon, Post Session, summer 1941; 1st asst. deputy reporter Indiana Supreme and Appellate Courts May-September 1944. Visited law schs. of Ga. for Am. Bar Assn., 1950. Mem. Am., Ind. bar assns., Order of Coif, Delta Theta Phi, Phi Kappa Psi. Republican. Lutheran. Clubs: Rotary (Valparaiso). Editor: Marriage and Divorce (Frank H. Keezer), 3rd edit., 1946. Home: Valparaiso, Ind. *

MORLEY, RAYMOND KURTZ, coll. prof.; b. Templeton, Mass., Oct. 28, 1882; s. Herbert Small and Sarah Elizabeth (Morton) M.; A.B., Tufts Coll., 1904, A.M., 1904; Ph.D., Clark U., 1910; m. Anne E. Thacher, Apr. 1907; 1 son, David Morton. Instr. mathematics, U. of Me., 1904-07; instr. Worcester Poly. Inst., 1910-11, asst. prof., 1912-17, prof.; 1917-49. Member Am. Math Assn., Math. Society of America, Assn. Teachers of Mathematics in N.E., Soc. for Promotion Engring. Edn., Phi Delta Kappa, Sigma Xi, Lambda Chi Alpha. Home: Worcester, Mass. *

MORONG, CARROL OSCAR, ch. assn. adminstr.; b. Rowley, Mass., June 4, 1907; s. Oscar Carrol and Myrtle (Spiller) M.; student Am. U., Washington, 1931-32, Harvard, 1932; B.D., Andover Newton Theol. Sch., Newton Center, Mass., 1935; Th.D., Boston U., 1943; D.D. (hon.), Bucknell U., 1958; m. Marion Gracia Mattinson, June 22, 1928; children—Joyce Erma, Barbara Lou, Carrol Oscar, Judith Ann. Pastor First Bapt. Ch., Waltham, Mass., 1935-41, Peoria, Ill., 1941-44; midwest dir. Bapt. World Mission Crusade, 1944-47; pastor First Bapt. Ch., Mount Vernon, N.Y., 1947-49; headmaster Peddie Sch., Hightstown, N.J., 1949-64; dir. World Mission Campaign, Am. Bapt. Conv., 1964-69; v.p. Am. Bapt. Sem. of West at Berkeley, 1969-75. Apptd. by Northern Bapt. Conv. to World Council of Chs., Amsterdam, Holland, 1948 and Second Internat. Assembly World Council Chs., Evanston, Ill., 1954-75; chmn. com. secondary edn. for bd. edn. Am. Bapt. Conv.; bd. mgrs. N.J. Bapt. Conv.; mem. Ministers Fellowship No. Bapt. Conv., N.J. Edn. Com. on U.S. Edn. Exchange Program. Mem. Oceanside-Carlsbad Ministers Assn. (pres.), Internat. Platform Assn., Cum Laude Soc. Clubs: Quill (past pres.) (N.Y.C.); Coterie, Lions (Hightstown, N.J.). Home: Oceanside, Calif. Died Nov. 25, 1975; interred Rowley, Mass.

MORRILL, CHESTER, b. Shelby County, Mo., Aug. 22, 1885; s. Flavius and Hannah (Johnston) M.; J.D., Georgetown U., 1909; m. Anna Margaret Anderson, Oct. 20, 1909; children—Margaret Nyce (dec.), Chester (dec.). Admitted to bar, 1909; began practice in Knoxville, Tenn.; asst. to solicitor Dept. Agr., Washington, 1914, charge cotton marketing and warehouse divs. Bur. Markets, 1919, apptd. asst. chief Bur. Markets and Crop Estimates, 1921, asst. to sec. agr., Sept. 1921, Feb.-Mar. 1925; ofcl. rep. of dept. at World's Cotton Conf., Liverpool-Manchester, Eng., 1921, conf. with European cotton assns., London, 1924; asst. gen. counsel War Finance Corp., Mar. 1925, gen. counsel, 1925-31; sec., gen. counsel Fed. Farm Loan Bd., 1927-31; sec. Fed. Res. Bd., 1931-45; spl. adviser to bd. govs. Fed. Res. System, 1945-50; sec. Fed. Open Market Com., 1936-50; adviser minister finance Govt. Republic of China, 1951; mem. nat. budget com. United Community Funds and Councils Am., 1953-61; chmn. hospitalization com. Fedn. Community Chests, Nat. Capital area, 1947-50, mem. budget com. Health and Welfare Council, 1958-63; mem. board number 100 (fgn.) SSS, 1961-67. Mem. Am. Bar Assn., Am. Econ. Assn. Presbyn. Clubs: Kenwood Golf and Country; Cosmos (pres. 1954). Home: Washington DC. *

MORRIS, CHARLES EUGENE, editor, pub.; b. Wapakoneta, O., May 21, 1884; s. Francis Marion and Mary Eliza (Copeland) M.; grad. high sch., Wapakoneta, 1900; student law Ohio Northern U., 1903-04; m. Clara Freda Feldheiser, of Celina, O., Mar. 5, 1907; children—Mary Elizabeth, Marian Mae. Began as news editor Wapakoneta Daily News, 1900; political writer, Toledo (O.) Blade, 1905-07; editor Wapakoneta Daily News, 1907-09; gen. mgr. Springfield (O.) Times, 1910-12; editor Ohio News League, 1912-16; sec. to Gov. James M. Cox, 1916-20; Washington corr. The News League, 1920-25; editor same (Ohio and Fla.), 1925-26; editor and pub. Canton (O.) Daily News, 1926-29; mgr. Chamber of Commerce, Canton, 1929-33; spl. insp. Div. Ins., Ohio, since 1933. Mem. Am. Inst. Polit. Science. Awarded Pulitzer gold medal, 1926, for civic cleanup of Canton, following murder of Editor Don R. Mellett. Democrat. Presbyn. Mason (Shriner). Clubs: Masonic. Torch, Rotary, City, Brookside Country; City (Washington); Athletic (Columbus, O.). Author: The New Ohio, 1914; Cox, the Man, 1920; Industrial Development, 1929, etc. Contbr. to New Republic, Forum, etc. Home: St. Louis, Mo. *

MORRIS, CHARLES MEYER, lawyer; b. Salt Lake City, Utah, June 18, 1882; s. Robert and Henrietta (Meyer) M.; student U. of Utah, 1898-1901; LL.B., George Washington U., Washington, D.C., 1908; m. Elizabeth Bowring, of Salt Lake City, Dec. 21, 1905. Sec. Congressional Printing Investigation Com., 1909; asst. county atty, Salt Lake Co., 1911-13; sec. Rep. State Com., 1916; chmn. Rep. Central Com. Salt Lake County, 1916-20; U.S. atty. for Utah, 1921-29. Mem. Am. and Utah State bar assns. Elk. *

MORRIS, EDWIN LEE, mgmt. cons.; b. Fargo, N.D., Aug. 1, 1909; s. Edwin L. and Delia (Bodkin) M.; A.B. UCLA, 1931; M.B.A. with distinction, Harvard, 1934; m. Charlotte White, 1934 (div.); children—Karen (Mrs. Allan M. Whitaker, Jr.), Deborah (Mrs. Peter H. Ross); m. 2d, Dorothy Reynolds, 1969. Asst. dean, mem. research staff Harvard Grad. Sch. Bus. Adminstrn., 1934-38; midwest sales mgr. Graton & Knight, Worcester, Mass., 1938-46; cons. Reynolds Wire Co., Dixon, Ill., 1946-47; with Booz, Allen & Hamilton, Inc., Chgo., 1947-70, exec. v.p., 1965-69, sr. v.p., 1969-70; also dir.; trustee Marketing Sci. Inst., Cambridge, Mass., 1962-77, pres., 1969-72. Mem. bus. ethics adv. council Dept. Commerce, 1961-63; dir. Chgo. Assn. Commerce and Industry, 1965-70. Bd. dirs. Lyric Opera, Chgo., 1964-70. Mem. Nat. Alumni Assn. Harvard Bus. Assn. (pres. 1955), Phi Gamma Delta. Clubs: Chicago, Attic (Chgo.); Glen View (Golf, Ill.); Duquesne (Pitts.); Country (Cleve.); Country, Ocean (Delray Beach, Fla.). Home: Wilmette, Ill. Died July 21, 1977.

MORRIS, I. SEWELL, assn. exec.; b. Federalsburg, Md., Apr. 18, 1909; s. I. Henry and Ethel (Brinsfield) S.; B.S., U.S. Mil. Acad., 1932; grad. Inf. Sch., 1937, Command and Gen. Staff Coll., 1947, Armed Forces Staff Coll., 1947, Indsl. Coll. Armed Forces, 1949; m. Harriett Melissa Joslin Fleron, June 11, 1932; 1 son, Jay Fleron. Commd. 2d lt., inf., U.S. Army, 1932, advanced through grades to maj. gen., 1959; served with inf., 1932-41; transferred to Transp. Corps, 1941; exec. dir. Mil. Traffic Mgmt. Agy., 1958-62; comdr. def. traffic mgmt. service Def. Supply Agy., 1962-63; retired, 1963; asst. v.p. Assn. Am. Railroads, 1963-69, v.p., asst. to pres., 1969-75. Chmn. bd. visitors U.S. Army Transp. Sch., Ft. Eustic, Va., 1964-75. Decorated Legion of Merit, Army Commendation ribbon with metal pendant with 2 oak leaf clusters, D.S.M.; recipient Salsberg Meml. medal, 1963. Mem. Assn. Am. Railroads, Nat. Def. Transp. Assn. (chmn. bd.), Washington Traffic Club. Clubs: Burning Tree; Army-Navy Country (Arlington, Va.). Home: Alexandria, Va. Died May 22, 1975; buried Arlington Nat. Cemetery.

MORRIS, IVAN, educator, author; b. London, Eng., Nov. 29, 1925; s. Ira Victor and Edit (de Toll) M.; B.A., Harvard, 1946; Ph.D., U. London, 1951, D.Lit., 1968; m. Nobuko Uenishi, Dec. 11, 1967. With news dept. BBC, London, 1951-52, research dept., Fgn. Office, London, 1952-56; mem. faculty Columbia, from 1960, prof. Japanese history from 1955, chmn. dept. E. Asian langs. and cultures, 1966-69. Chmn. Am. sect. Amnesty Internat., mem. nat. bd. dirs., from 1967. Served with USNR, 1942-46. Recipient Duff Cooper award lit., 1964. Mem. Assn. Tchrs. Japanese (chmn. 1962-65). Clubs: Travellers, Garrick, Savile (London), Author 17 books including: The World of the Shining Prince, 1964; The Pillow Book, 2 vols., 1967; Nationalism and the Right Wing to Japan, 1960. Home: New York, N.Y. Died July 19, 1976.

MORRIS, JOE ALEX, JR., journalist; b. Denver, June 1, 1927; s. Joe Alex and Maxine (Pooler) M.; student Carleton Coll., 1946-47; B.A., Harvard, 1949; m. Ursula Kirschbaum, Apr. 4, 1959; children—Maria, Karin, Julia. With Mpls. Tribune, 1948-49, Hartford (Conn.) Times, 1949-50, U.P.I., 1950-51, 53-57, Arabian-Am. Oil Co., 1951-53, N.Y. Herald Tribune, 1957-61, Newsweek mag., 1961-65; mem. staff Los Angeles Times, 1965-79, Mideast corr., 1965-68, Bonn. corr., 1968-79. Served with AUS, 1945-47. Contbr. articles to profl. jours. Home: West Germany. Died Feb. 17, 1979.

MORRIS, KYLE RANDOLPH, artist; b. Des Moines, Jan. 17, 1918; s. Claude Randolph and Caroline Mary (Kyle) M.; B.A., Northwestern U., 1939, M.A., 1940; M.F.A., Cranbrook Acad. Art, 1947; m. June Christophersen, Dec. 19, 1940; children—Stephen Randolph, James Geoffrey. Instr. art history and painting Stephens Coll., Columbia, Mo., 1940-41, asst. prof., 1941-42; asst. prof. U. Tex., 1945-46; asso. prof. painting U. Minn., Mpls. 1947-51, U. Calif. at Berkeley, 1952-54; lectr. art history Cooper Union, N.Y.C., 1958; vis. prof. Carnegie Mellon U., 1970; vis. critic U. Iowa, 1975; one man shows include Walker Art Center, Mpls., 1952, Guest Gallery, Des Moines, 1955, Stable Gallery, N.Y.C., 1955, Kootz Gallery, 1959-60, 62, 63, 64, Gallerie Naviglio, Milan, Italy, 1960, Berenson Gallery, Bay Shores, Fla., 1967, 69, 72, Landmark Gallery, N.Y.C., 1974, U. Iowa Art Mus., 1974, Arts Club Chgo., 1974; numerous group exhbns., 1952-79, including Brussels World's Fair, 1958, Whitney Mus. annuals, biennials U. Ill., Art Inst. Chgo., annuals U. Nebr., biennials Corcoran Gallery, Guggenheim Mus., Pa. Acad. Fine Arts, Detroit Inst. Arts, New Directions, Am. Painting, Brandeis U., 1963-64; represented in permanent collections Albright Gallery, Guggenheim Mus., Walker Art Center, Whitney Mus., others; editor, pub. Contemporary Slides, 1954-59; research, programming director Sandak, Inc., 1959. Recipient Purchase award Walker Art Center, 1948, Oil Painting award San Francisco Mus. Art, 1953, II Biennial hon. mention award Mexico City, 1960. Served with USAAF, 1942-45. Mem. Coll. Art Assn. Home: East Hampton, N.Y. Died Aug. 17, 1979.

MORRIS, LOGAN, lawyer; b. Logan, Utah, Oct. 25, 1889; s. Robert and Josephine (Meyer) M.; A.B., U. Utah, 1910; LL.B., George Washington U., 1917; m. Mildred Cooley, Nov. 19, 1919. Admitted to Utah bar, 1917, also to U.S. Supreme Ct. bar; began practice at Salt Lake City; sec. to Senator Reed Smoot, Utah, 1919-21; spl. atty. Bur. Internal Revenue, Washington, 1921-23, asst. solicitor, 1923-25; mem. U.S. Bd. Tax Appeals (now U.S. Tax Ct.), 1925-37, chmn., 1929-33, partner firm Weil, Satterlee, Nesbit & Morris, N.Y., Phila., Washington, 1937-77. Served as 1st lt. inf. U.S. Army, World War I. Mem. Am., D.C., Phila. County, Pa., Utah bar assns., Sigma Chi, Phi Delta Phi. Republican. Mason. Clubs: Nat. Press, Army and Navy (Washington); Chevy Chase (Md.). Home: Washington, D.C. Died Oct. 30, 1977; buried Rock Creek Cemetery, Washington.

MORRIS, WILLIAM JOSEPH, petroleum supply co. exec.; b. Hubbard, Ohio, July 12, 1881; s. Nicodemus and Mary Ann (Jones) M.; ed. pub. schs., Youngstown, O.; m. Alice Troutman, Mar. 31, 1910 (dec. 1924); 1 dau., Mary Barbara (Mrs. Herschel Clay Baker); m. 2d, Marian Lane Newsome, Sept. 18, 1937. Began as night time-keeper, Republic Iron & Steel Co., Youngstown, O.; became asst. treas., later treas., Youngstown Sheet & Tube Co., then v.p.; dir. Continental Supply Co., Dallas, Tex., since 1921, pres., 1932-46; pres. Continental-Emsco Co., Inc., 1932-46; dir. Dallas Nat. Bank, Republic Natural Gas Co., Emsco Derrick & Equipment Co., Internat. Petroleum Exposition, M.-K.-T. R.R. Republican. Presbyterian. Clubs: Dallas Country, Petroleum, Athletic, Idlewild, Brook Hollow Golf, Cipango (Dallas). Home: Dallas. *

MORRISETTE, JAMES E., army officer (ret.); b. Newbern, Ala., Jan. 17, 1886; s. Francis Strother and Buena Vista (Welch) M.; A.B., U. of Ala., 1906, LL.B., 1911; student Southwestern Presbyterian U., Clarksville, Tenn., 1902-03, Columbia U., 1916; m. Eleanor W. Abercrombie, May 2, 1931; 1 stepson, Daniel W. Abercrombie. Admitted to bar, 1911; practiced law as mem. firm Clarkson & Morrisette, Tuscaloosa, Ala., 1911-17, also instr., later prof. of evidence and real property, law schs., U. of Ala. Served with First Officers Training Camp, Ft. McPherson, Ga., May-Aug., 1917; commd. 2d lt., F.A., and served overseas; commd. capt., Judge Adv. Gen. Dept., U.S. Army, 1920, advancing through the grades to brig. gen., 1944; became asst. judge advocate gen., 1944; retired, 1946; now practicing law as mem. firm McQueen & McQueen. Lecturer constitutional law U. of Ala. Legal adviser to finance com. Reparation Commn., Paris, 1920. Mem. Alpha Tau Omega, Phi Beta Kappa. Club: Army and Navy (Washington). Home: Tuscalousa, Ala. *

MORRISETTE, WILLIAM LEE, JR., pub. exec.; born Beverly, W.Va., Aug. 11, 1915; s. William Lee and Mona Mae (Williamson) M.; student U. Va., 1935; m. Annette French Colbert, June 30, 1939 (div. 1963); children—William Lee, III, Michele Lee; m. 2d, Betty Lou Corley, 1964. With Am. Oil Co., 1935-37, Chevrolet div. Gen. Motors Corp., 1940; with Eastern Air Lines, 1940-63, successively dist. sales mgr. Balt., St. Louis, Boston, Miami, dir. procedures N.Y.C., New Eng. div. mgr., v.p. traffic and sales, 1954-61, v.p. sales and advt., 1961-63; pres. Business Travel, Inc., N.Y.C., 1963-64; N.Am. pres. Jamaica Tourist Bd. N.Y.C., 1964-66; v.p. Dunlap & Assos., Darien, Conn., 1966-69; pres. Intercontinental Devel. Co., New Canaan, Conn. and Coral Gables, Fla., 1969-76. Mem. Air Traffic Conf. Am. (pres.) Eaton Ednl. Found., U. Miami. Mem. Nat. Def. Transp. Assn., Am. Soc. Travel Agents, Am. Hotel Assn., Advt. Fed. Am. (dir.), English Speaking Union, Va., Fla. C. of C. Clubs: Wings, Skal, Rockefeller Centre Luncheon (N.Y.C.); Stamford (Conn.) Yacht; Rod and Reel (Miami Beach, Fla.); Coral Gables Country. Home: New Canaan, Conn. Died Jan. 13, 1976; buried New Canaan.

MORRISON, GEORGE L., baking company executive; b. Phila., May 11, 1884; s. Wesley Pierson and Jane (Murray) M.; ed. pub. schs. and private tutors in mechanical engineering; M.E. (hon.) Stevens Inst. Tech., Hoboken, N.J.; married Natalie Hansen, 1921; children—George L., Natalie Ann. Successively pres. General Cold Storage Company, Gen. Warehouse Co. (both of Phila.) and Gen. Cold Storage Co. of N.J. (Jersey City); later v.p. Harborside Warehouse Co. (Jersey City) and gen. mgr. of warehouses Pa. R.R. Co.; now chairman bd. and dir. Gen. Baking Co. (New York); dir. Van de Kamp Dutch Bakeries Los Angeles, Eddy Bakeries Co., Inc., Coca Cola, N.Y.C., Gen. Cold Storage Co., Phila. Mfrs. Mutual Fire Ins. Co., Baltimore & Eastern R.R. Co. (Phila.), Liberty Mut. Ins. Co., Boston. Trustee Stevens Inst. Tech., Hoboken,

N.J., Drexel Institute of Technology, Philadelphia, Pa. Served as 1st lieutenant, Adj. Gen. Office, World War I, capt. and 12 yrs. maj. U.S. Army inactive list. Mem. Mil. Order Fgn. Wars. Amer. Society of Refrigeration Engineers, Pa. Hist. Soc., Soc. Colonial Wars, S.R., Colonial Soc. of Pa., Pa. Soc. of N.Y., St. Nicholas Soc., St. Andrews Soc., Geneal. Soc. of Pa., Newcomen Soc., The Pilgrims, Corinthian Royal Arch. Clubs: Racquet, Union League, Merion Cricket, Merion Golf, Penn (Phila.); Union League, Knickerbocker, Veteran Corps Artillery, Links, The Brook, Racquet and Tennis, University (N.Y.C.). Home: Newport, R.I. *

MORRISON, HARRY WINFORD, contractor; b. Tunbridge Twp., DeWitt County, Ill., Feb. 23, 1885; s. George William and Amy Maria (Hawkins) M.; Dr. of Sci. (honorary), University of Idaho; LL.D., U. Portland (Ore.); LL.D., Coll. Ida., 1959; m. Anna Daly, Dec. 12, 1914 (dec. Oct. 1957); m. 2d, Velma V. Shannon, July, 1959. Water boy, later timekeeper, Bates & Rogers Constrn. Co., Chicago, 1902-05; successively axman, chainman, rodman, levelman, inspector, foreman, draftsman and supt. U.S. Bur. of Reclamation, Boise, Ida., 1906-12; partner, acting as v.p. and gen. mgr., Morrison & Knudsen, general contractors, 1912-23; v.p., gen. mgr. Morrison-Knudsen Co., Ida. corp., 1923-34, Del. corp., 1935-39, pres., gen. mgr., 1940-46, pres., 1947-60, now chmn.; organizer, pres. Six Cos., Inc., builders of Hoover and Parker Dams; past chmn., dir. Morrison-Knudsen Co., Inc.; chmn., dir. Pakistan Constructors Corp., Ltd.; dir. Ida. 1st Nat. Bank and 44 branches in Ida. Recipient Econ. Statesmanship award Seattle U., 1958; Ida. Bus. Man of Year award Ida. State U., 1963. Hon. life mem. Ida. Soc. Engrs.; hon. mem. The Moles (N.Y.C.). Home: Boise, Ida. *

MORRISON, HUGH SINCLAIR, educator; b. Portsmouth, N.H. Jan. 25, 1905; s. Henry Clinton and Marion (Locke) M.; B.S. summa cum laude, Dartmouth 1926; M.A., Princeton, 1928; Guggenheim fellow, 1948-49; m. Elizabeth Ware Newman, Dec. 21, 1929; children—Mary, Linda (div.); m. 2d, Charlotte Egan Ford, Feb. 2, 1956. Instr. art U. Chgo., 1929-32; asst. prof. art Dartmouth, 1932-38, prof., 1938-78, chmn. dept., 1953-55, 61-65, chmn. div. humanities, 1958-60, Leon E. Williams prof. art, 1963-69, prof. emeritus, 1969-78; asso. prof. Summer Sch., Harvard, 1936-37; lectr. architecture Mass. Inst. Tech., 1953-54. Mem. Hanover Town Planning Bd., 1955-60, chmn., 1955-57. Bd. dirs. Early Sites Found., 1954-78, pres., 1954-56, v.p., 1956-60. Mem. N.H. Hist. Soc., Soc. Archtl. Historians. Author: Louis Sullivan, Prophet of Modern Architecture, latest edit. 1962; Early American Architecture, 1952 (both chosen for permanent library White House); others. Home: Hanover, N.H. Died Oct. 12, 1978; buried Pine Knolls Cemetery, Hanover.

MORRISON, JOHN CAYCE, edn. cons.; b. Ramsey, Ill., Oct. 8, 1886; s. John E. and Sarah Belle (Cayce) M.; B.A., Valparaiso U., 1912; M.A., Teachers Coll., Columbia, 1916, Ph.D., 1922; LL.D., Alfred U., 1932; m. Grace Keller Doane, Aug. 27, 1916; 1 s., John Doane. Teacher and prin. schs. until 1911; supt. schs., Ramsey, Ill., 1912-14; supervising prin. schs., Chatham and Leonia, N.J., 1915-19; specialist in ednl. measurements, N.Y. State Dept. Edn., 1920-23; prof. sch. adminstrn., Ohio State U., 1923-26. Became asst. commr. for elementary edn., N.Y. State Department of Education, 1926, asst. commr. for research, 1938, coordinator of research, 1950-53; dir. Puerto Rican study, N.Y.C., 1953-57; ednl. cons. Alumni trustee Teachers Coll., Columbia, 1930-34. Mem. N.E.A., N.Y. State Teachers' Assn., Am. Assn. Sch. Adminstrs. (yearbook com., 1933, 44); Dept. Supervisors and Dirs. of Instrn. (yearbook com. 1930, pres. 1942), Ednl. Research Assn. (pres. 1929-30; chmn. editorial bd. 1943-48, chmn. bd. editors revision Ency. Ednl. Research, 1946-49, 56—); UNESCO tech. adviser on ednl. adminstrn. and finance Govt. Philippines, 1951-52. Fellow A.A.A.S.; mem. Nat. Soc. for Study End., N.Y. Acad. Pub. Edn., N.Y. Schoolmasters, Phi Delta Kappa. Presbyn. Club: University. Author: The Legal Status of the City Sch. Superintendent, 1922; The School Principalship in Ohio Cities and Exempted Village, 1926; The Morrison Spelling Series, 1930; Pub. Edn. in New York, 1935; Appraisal of Activity Program in New York City Schools, 1941; A Foundation Program for Financing Public Education in the Philippines, 1952; The Puerto Rican Study, 1958; and various other reports. Co-author: Survey of New Rochelle Schools, 1936; Roslyn Elementary Schools, 1938; A Scale for Rating Elementary School Practice. A Guide to the Development of Programs for the Institutes of Applied Arts and Sciences, 1946; Buffalo Public Schools in the Mid-Twentieth Century. Contributor ednl. journals. Trustee, Albany Exchange Savings Bank. Address: Londonville, N.Y. *

MORRISS, MARGARET SHOVE, coll. dean; b. Poughkeepsie, N.Y., June 25, 1884; d. William Hayles and Mary Elizabeth (Haviland) Morriss; A.B., Goucher Coll., 1904; grad. study, Bryn Mawr, 1904-06, 1907-08, Ph.D., 1911; grad. study, London (Eng.) School of Economics, 1906-07; LL.D., Russell Sage College, 1933. Mt. Holyoke College, 1937, Rhode Island State College, Kingston, R.I., 1943; L.H.D., Goucher College, 1938; LL.D., Brown University, 1948; Instructor history, Mt. Holyoke College, 1908-14, associate professor, 1914-17, 1920-23, also secretary bd. of admissions, 1920-23; dean of Pembroke Coll., Brown University, 1923-49. Served with war work council Y.W.C.A., France, 1917-19. N.Y. City, 1919. Trustee Rhode Island School of Design, Abbot Academy. Member Nat. Association Deans of Women, N.E.A., Am. Assn. Univ. Women (pres. 1937-41), Phi Beta Kappa, Delta Gamma. Conglist. Clubs: College Club (Boston). Author: Colonial Trade of Maryland (No. 3, Johns Hopkins University Studies in Hist. and Polit. Science), 1914. Home: Noank, Conn. *

MORRISSETT, CARLISLE HAVELOCK, lawyer; b. Richmond, Va., Jan. 25, 1892; s. William Jeter and Hattie Augusta (Nollner) M.; LL.B., Washington and Lee U., 1914; m. Gertrude Marshall Nance, May 3, 1920; children—Carlisle Nance (Mrs. Patteson Branch), Burks Laws. Admitted to Va. bar, 1914; lectr. Washington and Lee U. Summer Law Sch., 1916; reviser notes, Code of Va., 1919; dir. State Legislative Reference Bur., Va., 1919-26; state tax commr., 1926-70. Mem. and sec. Children's Code Commn., 1921-22; chmn. Commn. to Revise Tax Laws of VA., 1926-28, Commn. to Study Forestry Conditions in Va., 1930-32; mem. Commn. to Study Real Estate Taxation, 1932-34, State Compensation Bd., 1934-70, Va. Adv. Legislative Council, 1935-38. Mem. Am., Va., Richmond bar assns., S.A.R., S.C.V., Phi Beta Kappa, Delta Theta Phi. Democrat. Member Christian (Disciples) Ch. Mason. Editor of Second Edition of Burks Pleading and Practice, 1921; compiler and annotator General Laws of Virginia, 1923. Author: Notes on Statutes Subsequent to the Code of 1919, 1921. Home: Richmond, Va. Died Dec. 2, 1976.

MORROW, JAMES BAIN, exec. engineer; b. Halifax, Nova Scotia; Apr. 9, 1886; s. Matthew Richey and Ella Sarah (Neal) M.; ed. Dalhousie U., Halifax, 1906; m. Margaret Helen Baer, Apr. 26, 1940; children—Mrs. Hilary Hotchkiss, Mrs. B. C. Gardiner. Employed in various capacities from chemist to gen. outside supt., Phelps Dodge Corp., Dawson, N.M., 1908-27; preparation mgr., Pitts. Coal Co., 1927-39, operating v.p., 1939-40, pres. 1940-47; chmn. bd., 1948-49; 1st v.p. Pitts. Consol. Coal Co., 1946-51; engaged as J. B. Morrow, coal consultant, 1955—. Recipient Percy Nicholls award, 1944; Erskine Ramsay medal, 1951; Bituminous Coal Research Award, 1954. Member American Institute Mining and Metallurgical Engrs. (v.p. 1952-54), Engrs. Soc. Western Pa., Ill. Mining Inst., Rocky Mountain Coal Mining Inst., Am. Inst. Cons. Engrs. Mason. Clubs: Duquesne (Pitts.). Home: Mount Lebanon, Pa. *

MORSE, ELLSWORTH HARRY, JR., govt. ofcl.; b. Shelby, Ohio, Dec. 1, 1913; s. Ellsworth Harry and Rachel E. (Brubaker) M.; B.A., Oberlin Coll., 1935; M.B.A., U. Mich., 1937; m. Virginia F. Garbison, July 2, 1942; children—Ellen (Mrs. Donald Yokel), Jeanne. Staff accountant, auditor Arthur Andersen & Co., C.P.A.'s, 1937-42; with Gen. Accounting Office, 1946-77, dir. civil accounting and auditing div., 1956, dir. accounting and auditing policy staff, 1956-66, dir. office policy and spl. studies, 1966-71; dir. office policy and program planning, 1971-72, asst. comptroller gen. of U.S., 1972-77. Mem. adv. council Fin. Accounting Standards Bd., 1973-75; adv. bd. Paton Accounting Center, U. Mich., 1975-77; chmn. bd. auditors OAS, 1975-77. Served to lt. comdr. USNR, 1942-46. Recipient Nat. Civil Service League Career Service award, 1968. C.P.A., Mich. Mem. Am. Inst. C.P.A.'s, Assn. Govt. Accountants (nat. pres. 1970-71), Phi Beta Kappa, Beta Alpha Psi. Episcopalian. Editor The GAO Rev.; Internat. Jour. of Govt. Auditing. Home: Alexandria, Va. Died Nov. 29, 1977; buried Ivy Hill Cemetery, Alexandria.

MORSE, GEORGE FREDERICK, zoölogist and lecturer; b. Phila., Pa., May 16, 1885; s. George F. and Mary E. (Harmar) M.; grad. Phillips Exeter (N.H.) Acad., 1904; m. Elisabeth W. Taylor, Oct. 3, 1906; children—George F., III, Charles T. (dec.), John C. Engaged in nature study and fur farming, 1906-14; mem. Mass. Ho. of Rep., 1913, 14; sec. Mass. Fish and Game Protective Assn., 1915-16; pres. Mass. Sportsmen's League, 1916; curator Boston Zoöl. Park and Boston Aquarium, 1918-22; dir. Chicago Zoöl. Soc., 1922-24; dir. Shedd Aquarium, Chicago, 1925-29. Mem. staff U. of Chicago; director Wychwood Bird and Wild Flower Sanctuary. Republican. Lecturer on "Wild Animals in Captivity." Author of animal and nature books. Home: Lake Geneva, Wis.

MORSE, GEORGE W., surgeon; b. Clinton, Mass., Jan. 24, 1882; s. George W. and Lydia Ann (Bates) M.; grad. Volkmann Prep. Sch., Boston; A.B., Harvard, 1904, M.D., 1908; m. Jean Ferguson MacPherson, Dec. 17, 1913; children—George W., Jean Coates. Began practice at Boston, 1908; med. dir., in charge Dept. of Hygiene, Mass. Inst. Tech., now emeritus; surgeon in charge Brooks Hosp.; med. dir. Liberty Mut. Ins. Co. Maj. Med. U.S.R.C. Fellow Am. Coll. Surgeons; mem. A.M.A., Mass. Med. Soc. Unitarian. Home: Boston, Mass. *

MORSE, HAROLD MARSTON, educator, mathematician; b. Waterville, Maine, Mar. 24, 1892; s. Howard Calvin and Ella Phoebe (Marston) M.; grad. Coburn Classical Inst., Waterville, 1910; A.B. summa cum laude, Colby Coll., 1914, Sc.D., 1934; A.M., Harvard, 1915, Ph.D., 1917; Dr. (hon.), Paris, 1946, Vienna, 1952, Rennes, 1953, U. Md., 1955, Bklyn. Polytech., 1956, U. Notre Dame, 1956, Boston Coll., Fordham, 1958, Modena (Italy), 1975; D.Sc., Colby Coll., 1935, Kenyon Coll., 1948, Pisa, 1948, LaSalle Coll., 1960, Williams Coll., 1959, St. Peter's Coll., 1961, Harvard, 1965, U. Me., 1971; LL.D., Xavier U., 1961, Mundelein Coll., 1967; Litt.D., Yeshiva U., 1962; children (by previous marriage)—Meroe Marston (dec.), Dryden Phelps; m. 2d, Louise Jefferys, Jan. 13, 1940; children—Julia, William Marston, Elizabeth Hudson, Peter, Louise. Asst. prof. math. Cornell U., 1920-25; asso. prof. Brown U., 1925-26; asst. prof. math. Harvard, 1926-28, asso. prof., 1928-29, prof., 1929-35, chmn. tutors in math., 1933-35; prof. Inst. Advanced Study, Princeton, N.J., 1935-77; cons. Office Chief Ordnance, U.S. Army, 1943-46. Chmn. U.S. Nat. Com. Math., 1958-77; v.p. Internat. Math. Union, 1958-77; mem. bd. NSF, 1950-54; chmn. div. math. NRC, 1951-52. Served as pvt. AUS, 1918-19; 2d lt. C.A.C. Res., 1919-24. Recipient Nat. Sci. medal, 1964. Roman Catholic. Decorated Croix de Guerre with silver star, chevalier Legion of Honor (France); recipient Meritorious Service award. U.S. Army Ordnance, 1944. Fellow Am. Acad. Arts and Scis., Nat. Acad. Scis., AAAS (v.p. 1939); mem. Am. Philos. Soc., Math. Soc. Am. (v.p. 1933-35, pres. 1940-42; joint winner Bocher prize; chmn. war preparedness com., 1940-42), Circolo Mat. di Palermo, Academia delle Scienze Bologna (fgn. corr.), Internat. Math. Union (v.p. 1959-63), Phi Beta Kappa, Sigma Xi; asso. French Acad. Scis.; corr. mem. Heidelberg Acad. Scis.; Polish, Romanian acads. scis., dei Lincei Italy. Author: Colloquium Lectures on the Calculus of Variations: Functional Topology and Abstract Variational Theory. Contbr. math. periodicals. Home: Princeton, N.J. Died June 22, 1977; buried Pinegrove Cemetery, Waterville, Maine.

MORSE, ROY FRANCIS, lumberman; b. Boone Co., Ark., Mar. 23, 1885; s. Francis Joseph and Frances Josephine (Terrell) M.; student pub. schs., Lake Charles, La.; m. Inez Martin, Apr. 20, 1910; children—Jean Frances (Mrs. Edward J. Berwind, II), Nancy Ann (Mrs. John A. Moller). Mgr. export dept. Long-Bell Lumber Co., Beaumont, Tex., 1910-12, gen. mrg. mfg. dept., Longview, Wash., 1923-26, mgr. logging and timber dept., 1926-47; v.p., 1947-53, ret. Apr. 1953, now mem. adv. com., pres. Williamina & Grand Ronde (Ore.) Ry. Co. since 1942, Polk Operating Company; Grand Ronde, since 1942; v.p. Longview, Portland & No. Ry. since 1948. Dir. Pacific Lumberman's Inspection Bur., Seattle, 1932-37; president Columbia River Log Scaling and Grading Bur., Portland, Ore., 1941-42, Pacific Logging Congress, Portland, 1943-44, N.W. Log Checking Bur., Portland, since 1944. Mem. West Coast Lumbermen's Assn. (pres. 1926-27), N.W. Ore. Fire Protective Assn. (dir. since 1944). Mason (32 deg., Shriner), Elk. Home: Longview, Wash. *

MORSELL, EVERETT GRAHAM (MÔR-SEL'), naval officer; b. Washington, D.C., July 6, 1884; s. William Albion and Clara (Hodges) M.; ed. pub. schs.; m. Georgianna R. Potts, Apr. 20, 1910; 1 son, Everett Potts. Asst. paymaster, ensign, 1906; promoted through ranks to vice adm. (ret.). Supply Corps, 1946, on duty at Cavite, P.I., during Japanese attack, 1941; at Bataan and Corregidor until evacuated to Australia, Mar. 1942; dist. supply officer, 9th Naval Dist. Foreign Liquidation Commn., Manila, P.I.; Navy Claims Settlement Commn., Manila, Nicaraguan campaign, 1912; Mexican, 1914; Victory, American Defense Service, Asiatic-Pacific, Am. Theatre, Presidential Organization Citation, army, Legion of Merit, Bronze Star, letter of commendation from comdr. in chief, Southwest Pacific Area. Clubs: Army and Navy, Amry, Navy and Marine Corps Country (Washington, D.C.); Bohemian (San Francisco). Address: Vallejo, Calif. *

MORSMAN, ROBERT PORTER, banker; b. Omaha, Neb., Feb. 28, 1883; s. Edgar M. and Frances A. (Sharp) M.; A.B., U. of Mich., 1904; unmarried. In banking business in Omaha since 1904; chmn. executive com. of U.S. Nat. Bank of Omaha; director The Byron Reed Co., U.S. Securities Co., Northwest Bancorporation (Minneapolis, Minn.). Mem. Phi Kappa Psi. Republican. Presbyterian. Clubs: Omaha, University, Omaha Athletic, Omaha Country; Grolier (New York). Home: Omaha, Neb. *

MORTENSEN, OTTO AXEL, physician, educator; b. Milw., June 4, 1902; s. Morton Hans and Anna (Petersen) M.; B.S., U. Wis., 1927, M.S., 1928, M.D., 1929; m. Lila A. Embretson, Jan. 1, 1931; children—Margaret Ann, Charles Otto, Peter Andrew. Intern, Research Hosp., Kansas City, Mo., 1929-30; instr. anatomy U. Wis., Madison, 1930-31, asst. prof., 1931-37, asso. prof., 1937-46, prof., 1946-72, asst. dean

Sch. Medicine, 1949-52, asso. dean, 1952-67, chmn. anatomy, 1950-67; vis. prof. Stanford, 1972-79. Cons. med. edn., Peru, 1957-58; cons. research career awards NIH cons. anat. tng. scis. com., 1965-69. Bd. dirs. Madison Gen. Hosp., pres. Med. and Surg. Found., 1970-79. Trustee Village of Shorewood Hills, 1946, pres., 1947-49. Mem. Govs.' Ednl. Adv. Com., 1955-67; mem. Wis. Ednl. Approval Bd., 1967-79. Mem. AAAS, AAUP, Am. Assn. Anatomists (v.p. 1960-62), Wis. Med. Soc., Phi Beta Kappa; Alpha Omega Alpha. Home: Madison, Wis. Died Oct. 18, 1979.

MORTIMER, CHARLES G., foods co. exec.; b. Bklyn., July 26, 1900; s. Charles Greenough andd Cecilia Clara (Dessoir) M.; student Stevens Inst. Tech., M.E. (hon.), 1956; Eng.D., LL.D., L.I.U., 1956; LL.D. (hon.), Hamilton Coll., 1964; H.H.D., Jacksonville U., 1964; m. Elizabeth Kempley Atterbury; children—Charles G., John Atterbury, Mary Cecil (Mrs. Paul S. Bosley), Lee Reynolds. Asso. Nat. Aniline & Chem. Co., 1919-21; sales dept. R.B. Davis Co., successively dist mgr., div. mgr., charge sales, 1921-24; with advt. firm George Batten, 1924, account exec., 1924-28; with Gen. Foods Corp., 1928-65, mdse. mgr., 1935, gen. advt. mgr., 1938, v.p. marketing and operating responsibilities, 1943-52, dir., 1950-71, exec. v.p., 1952-54, pres., chief exec. officer, 1954-59, chmn., chief exec. officer, 1959-65, chmn. exec. com. bd. dirs., 1965-71, dir. emeritus, 1971-78; dir. Gen. Foods, Ltd.-Japan, 1954-65, chmn., 1961-65; dir. Fed. St. Fund. Grad. mem. Bus. Council; mem. Bus. Com. Tax Reduction in 1963. Trustee Stevens Inst. Tech; mem. corp. Presbyn. Hosp. City N.Y.; dir. Nat. Bur. Econ. Research. Served with USNRF, 1918-19. Recipient Gold medal merit, Wharton Sch. Alumni Soc. U. Pa., 1963; Silver Bowl award for pub. service Advt. Council, 1964. Mem. Nat. Grange, Advt. Council (life dir.), UN Assn. U.S.A. (dir.), Beta Theta Pi. Clubs: Links; Scarsdale Golf. Home: White Plains, N.Y. Died Dec. 28, 1978.

MORTON, JOHN JAMIESON, JR., surgeon; b. Holyoke, Mass., May 19, 1886; s. John Jamieson and Nellie Augusta (Taylor) M.; A.B., Amherst, 1907; M.D., Johns Hopkins, 1913; D.Sc., Amherst, 1947; m. Nancy Barnard, Oct. 7, 1919; 1 son, John Henderson. Interne, Peter Bent Brigham Hosp., Boston, 1913-14; fellow in pathol., Rockefeller Inst., N.Y., 1914-15; resident surgeon Mass. Gen. Hosp., Boston, 1915-16; asst. resident physician, Rockefeller Inst. Hosp., 1916; practiced orthopedic surgery, Boston, 1919-21; asst. attending surgeon in orthopedic surgery, Children's Hosp., 1919-21; asst. prof. surgery, Yale Sch. of Medicine, 1921-24; prof. surgery, U. of Rochester Sch. of Medicine and Dentistry, since 1924. Mem. growth com., Nat. Research Council, 1945; mem. Nat. Advisory Cancer Council, U.S.P.H.S., since 1948. Served as 1st lt., capt. and maj. M.C., A.U.S., Base Hosp. No. 5, in France, May 1917-Mar. 1919. Felow Am. Coll. Surgeons (mem. bone sarcoma com., 1925-40; legislative com. of N.Y. State, 1935-38; bd. govs. since 1935); mem. A.M.A. (mem. scientific com. since 1928), Med. Soc. State of N.Y. (chmn. com. on med. research), Monroe County Med. Soc., Am. Surg. Assn., Am. Soc. for Clin. Investigation, Johns Hopkins Surg. Soc., Am. Soc. for Exptl. Pathology, Robert Jones Orthopedic Soc., The Soc. Clinical Surgery (treas. 1933-35; pres. 1939-41), Am. Soc. Cancer Research, Internat. Surg. Soc., Southern Surg. Assn., Rochester Acad. Med., Am. Soc. Control Cancer (exec. com. since 1936; pres. 1938-41, chmn. bd. 1942-44), Phi Beta Kappa, Alpha Omega Alpha, Sigma Xi, Phi Gamma Delta, Nu Sigma Nu (hon.). Mem. bd. scientific advisers Jane Coffin Childs Memorial Fund for Cancer Research, Yale, since 1939, Sci. Adv. Com., Memorial Hosp., New York, Board of Visitors State Inst. for the Study of Malignant Diseases, Buffalo; bd. sci. advisors Roscoe B. Jackson since 1951, Armed Forces Inst., Phila., 1951-56. Mem. Lab., Bar Harbor, Me. Clubs: Rochester Country, Pithotomy (Balt.). Home: Rochester, N.Y. *

MORTON, LEON LINCOLN, railroad exec.; b. Mt. Eden, Ky., Apr. 2, 1884; s. Thomas Marshall and Adeline (Hedden) M.; B.S., Centre Coll., 1905; m. Katherine Driskill, June 9, 1909; 1 dau., Mary (Mrs. Baker). Engring. dept. A., B.&C. R.R., 1909; asst. engr. K.C.S. Ry., Texarkana, Tex., 1909-12; asst. mgr L.&N. R.R., 1912-17, 19, spl. engr., Louisville, 1920-28, supt. New Orleans and Mobile div., 1928-31, asst. gen. mgr., 1931-41, asst. v.p., dir. personnel, asst. gen. mgr., 1941-46, v.p. in charge operations since 1946; dir. Terminal R.R. Assn. St. Louis, Memphis Union Sta., Cin. Union Sta. Co. Served as capt. to lt. col. Engrs., U.S. Army, 1917-19. Club: Filson (Louisville). Home: Louisville. *

MORTON, ROBERT LEE, educator; b. Brownsville, Ohio, Nov. 25, 1889; s. William Archibald and Lola (Harris) M.; B.S. in Edn., Ohio Univ., 1913; student Teachers Coll. (Columbia) summers 1914, 15; A.M., Ohio State U., 1919, PdD., 1925; L.H.D. (hon.), Ohio U., 1968; m. Jean Adams, June 25, 1914 (dec.); Children—Jean (Mrs. Fredric E. Webb) (dec.), Mary Eleanor (Mrs. Herbert Kadison). Tchr. elementary schs., Ohio, 1907-09; supt. schs., Frankfort, Ohio, 1913-18; extension lectr., Ohio U., 1918-20; dir. Extension Dept., same univ., 1920-21; prof. mathematics, Coll. of Edn., same univ., 1921-36; prof. edn. from 1936; prof. edn., Ohio State U., summers, 1927, 28, 29, 30, Univ. of Washington, summer 1931. Dir. Educator and Executive Insurors, Inc., Grow Ahead Press, Inc. Recipient Certificate of Merit, Ohio U., also Distinguished Prof., 1960, Founder's citation, 1972; grad. of year, 1972. Fellow A.A.A.S.; mem. N.E.A., Cal. Mathematics Council, Ohio Ednl. Assn. (ednl. council), Ednl. Research Assn., Ohio Council Tchrs. Math., Nat. Council Tchrs. Mathematics (chmn. com. on arithmetic), Sigma Xi, Phi Delta Kappa, Phi Betta Kappa. Hon. mem. Eugene Field Soc. Mem. tech. adv. group and spl. investigator Ohio Sch. Finance Survey, 1932; cons. Ednl. Policies Commn., also mem. Ohio Com. of Nat. Survey Sch. Finance. Mem. bd. adv. Edn. Dept., Films, Inc. Republican. Presbyn. Clubs: Faculty, Athens Country. Author: Teaching Arithmetic in the Intermediate Grades, 1927; Teaching Arithmetic in the Primary Grades, 1927; Laboratory Exercises in Educational Statistics, 1928; Statistical Tables, 1928; Teaching Arithmetic in the Elementary School, vol. I. Primary Grades, 1937, vol. II, Intermediate Grades, 1938, vol. III, Upper Grades, 1939; Teaching Children Arithmetic, 1953; Helping Children Learn Arithmetic, 1960. Co-author: Ohio Curriculum Guides in Arithmetic: Mathematics Through Experience, Vols. 1-3, 1937; Making Sure of Arithmetic, Grades, 2-8, 1946, rev. 1958; Making Sure of Arithmetic, workbooks for grades 1-8, 1947-48, rev. 1953; 10th Yearbook, Nat. Council Tchrs. Mathematics, 1935, 16th Yearbook, 1941; Providing for Individual Differences with Elementary Sch.; Modern Mathematics through Discovery, Grades I and II, 1962, Grades III-VI, 1963, Grades VII-VIII, 1964, rev. edit., 1966; Modern Mathematics for Junior High School, 1962; Foundations of Secondary School Mathematics, 1968; Introduction to College Mathematics, 1972. Contbr. to report of Classification Com., Ohio State Dept. Edn. Lectr. ednl. subjects. Home: Athens, Ohio. Died May 10, 1976.

MORTON, ROGERS CLARK BALLARD, sec. of Interior; b. Louisville, Sept. 19, 1914; s. David C. and Mary (Ballard) M.; A.B., Yale, 1937; m. Anne Jones, May 27, 1939; children—David C., Anne McCance. Vice pres. Ballard & Ballard, flour miller and food mfr., Louisville, 1946-47, pres., 1947-51 (co. merged with Pillsbury Co., 1951), v.p. Pillsbury, 1951-53, dir., 1953-71; mem. 88th to 92d Congresses, 1st dist. Md., 1963-71; sec. interior, 1971-75; sec. of commerce, 1975-76; counselor to Pres. for econ. and domestic policy matters, 1976-77; dir. Pillsbury Co., Seaboard Coast Line Industries, Fla. Gas. Co. Chmn. Republican Nat. Com., 1969-71. Trustee Nat. Trust for Historic Preservation. Served as capt. F.A., AUS, 1943-45. Mem. Soc. Cincinnati. Clubs: Maryland (Balt.); Chesapeake Bay Yacht (Easton). Home: Easton, Md. Died Apr. 19, 1979; buried Old Wye Church, Wye Mills, Md.

MOSCONE, GEORGE RICHARD, mayor; b. San Francisco, Nov. 24, 1929; s. George J. and Lee (Monge) M.; B.A. in Sociology, U. of Pacific, 1952; LL.B., U. Calif., San Francisco, 1956, J.D., 1956; m. Gina Bondanza, June 19, 1954; children—Jenifer, Rebecca, Christopher, Jonathan. Playground dir. San Francisco Dept. Recreation and Parks, 1952-56; admitted to Calif. bar, 1957; instr. law Lincoln U., San Francisco; asso. firm Hanson, Bridgett, Marcus & Jenkins, San Francisco, 1968-76; mem. San Francisco Bd. Suprs., 1963-66; mem. Calif. Senate, 1966-76, floor leader, 1967-76; mayor of San Francisco, 1976-78. Served with USN. Recipient Meritorious citations Calif. Real Estate Assn., Calif. Marshal's Assn., Calif. Credit Union League; Achievement award Hamophilia Found. So. Calif., 1974; certificate of appreciation Calif. Soc. for Autistic Children, 1974; Excellence award Calif. Library Assn., 1969; named Most Effective Democratic Senator, State Capitol Press Corps, 1969, Senator of Year, Calif. Trial Lawyers Assn., 1969, Man of Year, Los Angeles Soc. Clin. Psychologists, 1973. Mem. Calif., San Francisco bar assns., Am. Bd. Trial Advocates (chmn. fed. indigent trial panel 1958), Phi Delta Phi. Died Nov. 27, 1978.

MOSELEY, EDWIN M., coll. dean.; b. Orangeburg, S.C., Sept. 12, 1916; s. John P. and Blumah L. (Sorentrue) M.; A.B. summa cum laude, Coll. Charleston, 1937; A.M., Syracuse U., 1939, Ph.D., 1947; m. Catharine Louise Fisher, June 11, 1941; children—Stephen F., Quentin B. Mem. faculty Syracuse U., 1937-42, 44-45, 46-47; asst. prof. Evansville Coll., 1947-48; asst. prof. English Washington and Jefferson Coll., 1948-49, asso. prof., 1949-55, prof., 1955-61; prof. English, dean faculty Skidmore Coll., Saratoga Springs, N.Y., 1961-78, provost, 1967-78; vis. prof. Hunter Coll. City U. N.Y., summer, 1963; chmn. cooperative program on non-Western studies N.Y. Capital Area Colls., 1967-69. Served AUS, 1943-44, 45-46. Fellow internat. Sem. on Comparative Edn., Hague, 1961, India, winter, 1968-69. Mem. Hudson-Mohawk Assn. Colls. and Univs. (bd. mgrs., exec. com., 1969, chmn., 1972-73), Modern Lang. Assn., Coll. English Assn., Am. Conf. Acad. Deans, Eastern Deans Assn., Am. Assn. U. Profs., Phi Beta Kappa. Author: Pseudonyms of Christ in the Modern Novel, 1963; The Outsider as Hero and Anti-hero, 1967; F. Scott Fitzgerald: A Critical Essay, 1967; Comparative Literature: Matter and Method, 1969; Czechoslovakia Past and Present, 1970; Religion and Modern Literature: Essays in Theory and Criticism, 1975. Author, editor (with R.P. Ashley) Elizabethan Fiction, 1953. Founder Topic, jour. liberal arts, 1960-61. Contbr. profl. jour., lit. mags., anthologies. Died Dec. 5, 1978.

MOSELEY, RAY BENJAMIN FRANKLIN, real estate broker, developer; b. Kansas City, Mo., Jan. 17, 1898; s. George E. and Mary Helen (Rose) M.; student pub. schs.; m. Lavinia Elizabeth Tobener, Sept. 2, 1919; children—Ray Benjamin Franklin, Frank William. Real estate broker, 1911-78; pres. Moseley & Co., Kansas City, 1923-58, chmn. bd., 1958-78; chmn. bd. Ray F. Mosely Mgmt. and Devel. Corp.; pres. F. & S. Devel. Corp., Bus. Properties Inc.; v.p. Westmill Corp., Indsl. Investors, Mi-Mo Investment Corp.; partner Mosely & Co. Bd. dirs. Downtown Com., Kansas City Crime Commn., Am. Heart Assn.; former pres., dir. City Union Mission; hon. trustee Kansas City council Boy Scouts Am.; mem. Heart of Am. Boys Club. Pres. Ray F. Moseley Charities Found.; co-founder, former pres., dir. Bapt. Meml. Hosp., Bapt. Found. Mo.; past pres. Am. War Dads; adv. bd. Am. Security Council; hon. dir. Rockhurst Coll. Hon. fellow Harry S Truman Library; mem. Kansas City C. of C., (past dir.), Am. Sunday Sch. Union (hon. v.p.), Kansas City Council Chs. (past dir.), Soc. Indsl. Realtors, Nat. Assn. Real Estate Bds., Mo. Real Estate Assn., Native Sons Kansas City, Christian Businessmen's Com., Kansas City Real Estate Bd., Am. Assn. Ret. Persons, Humanics Found., Conservation Fedn. Mo., Automobile Club Mo. (past dir.), Am. Assn. Retirees Club Baptist (deacon, lay preacher). Mason (Shriner, legion of honor Order of Demolay). Clubs: Kansas City, Rockhill Tennis. Author: All to God I Owe. Home: Kansas City, Mo. Died June 6, 1978; buried Mt. Moriah Cemetery, Kansas City, Mo.

MOSER, ARTHUR HURST, educator; b. Uniontown, Pa., May 27, 1904; s. Charles Smith and Adelaide (Hurst) M.; B.A., St. Stephens Coll., 1926; M.A., Cornell U., 1927; Ph.D., N.Y. U., 1931; m. Sarah Ridlehoover, June 8, 1929 (dec. June 1944); children—Charles A., Gerard S., Donald B.; m. 2d, Isabelle Johnson, Sept. 2, 1944 (dec. Apr. 1965); m. 3d, Janet T. Patterson, Aug. 29, 1969. Instr. classical langs. Vanderbilt U., 1927-29, N.Y. U., N.Y.C., 1931-32; asso. prof. U. Tenn., 1932-38, prof., 1939-72, emeritus, 1972-75, head dept. classics, 1939-68. Instl. rep. troops Great Smoky Mountain council Boy Scouts Am., 1956-75. Arthur H. Moser scholarship in classics established in his honor U. Tenn., Knoxville. Mem. Classical Assn. Middle West and South (past pres.), Tenn. Philol. Assn. (past pres.), Am. Classical League, Am. Numismatic Soc., Knoxville Stamp Club, Smoky Mountain Coin Club, and several others, Sigma Alpha Epsilon. Episcopalian. Home: Knoxville, Tenn. Died July 11, 1975.

MOSLEY, EARL LOUIS (MOZ'LI), pub. adminstr.; b. Denver, Colo., Nov. 7, 1883; s. Alfred Henry and Mary Lois (Dunn) M.; student Colo. Sch. Mines, 1901-02; B.S. in C.E., U. of Colo., 1905; m. Laura Crowe, Aug. 29, 1907; children—Earl Alexander, George Alfred, Mary Laura (Mrs. John A. Miller, Jr.). Inspector bridge and bldg. dept. I.C.R.R., Chicago, 1905-08, asst. engr. valuation dept., 1915-21; engr. transmission lines dept. Central Colo. Power Co., Denver, 1908-09; chief engr. Grand Junction & Grand River Valley Ry. Co., Grand Junction, Colo., 1909-11; div. engr. Canadian Northern Ry. Co., Winnipeg, Manitoba, Can., 1911-15; asst. engr., asst. city engr. and mgr. Light and Power Dept., City of Colorado Springs, Colo., 1921-30, city mgr. 1930-47; utilities dir. city and county of Denver, Colo., 1948-50, manager-secretary Bd. of Water Commrs. since 1950; F.W.A., 1947. First director Colorado Resources Development Council, 1948, mem. and com. chmn. exec. bd. since 1947. Served as supervising engr. war dept. U.S. Explosives Plant, Nitro, W. Va., 1918. Recipient U. of Colo. Alumni Assn. Alumni Recognition Medal. Mem. Internat. City Mgrs. Assn. (past pres.), Am. Soc. Civil Engrs. (past pres. Colo. sect.), Colo. Municipal League (past pres.), Am. Pub. Power Assn. (dir. of orgn.), Sigma Nu, Tau Beta Pi, Republican. Episcopalian. Mason (Shriner, 32 deg.). Clubs: Kiwanis (Denver and Colorado Springs), Colorado Springs Winter Nite (past pres.), Round Table of Colorado Springs. Home: Denver. *

MOSS, JOHN HALL, educator, geologist; b. Phila., Oct. 25, 1918; s. Frank Hazlett and Anna (Hunter) M.; grad. St. Paul's Sch., 1936; A.B., Princeton, 1941; M.S. (fellow) Mass. Inst. Tech., 1943; Ph.D. (fellow), Harvard, 1949; m. Margaret Stewart, June 27, 1942; children—Penney, John, Barbara, William, Jane, Frederick. Asst. prof. Franklin and Marshall Coll., 1948-51, asso. prof., 1951-59, prof., chmn. dept. geology, 1959-71, dir. environ. studies, 1971-77; vis. prof. U. Tex., Austin, 1974, Ariz. State U., 1975. Chmn. earth and space sci. adv. com. Pa. Dept. Pub. Instrn., 1958-70, mem. Lancaster County Water Adv. Commn., 1963-70; mem. policy com. Pa. Environ. Council, 1971-77; pres. Lancaster Environ. Action Fedn., 1972-73; chmn. environ. studies adv. council Pa. Dept. Edn., 1973-77; mem. sewer-water adv. com. Lancaster

County Planning Commn., 1973; mem. earth sci. adv. com. NSF, 1976-77. Served with C.E., AUS, 1943-45. Recipient Sci. Faculty fellowship NSF, 1961-62. Fellow Geol. Soc. Am. (chmn. N.E. sect. 1974, chmn. environment and pub. policy com. 1976-77); mem. Nat. Assn. Geology Tchrs. (pres. 1963-64; past pres. Eastern sect.; Ralph Digman award 1968), AAAS, Pa. Acad. Sci., Soc. Econ. Paleontologists and Mineralogists, AAUP, Phila. Atheuaeum. Home: Lancaster, Pa. Died July 28, 1977.

MOSS, ROBERT VERELLE, JR., ch. ofcl.; b. Wilson, N.C., Mar. 3, 1922; s. Robert Verelle and Constance Amelia (Bost) M.; A.B., Franklin and Marshall Coll., 1943, D.D., 1960; B.D., Lancaster Theol. Sem., 1945; Ph.D., U. Chgo. Div. Sch., 1954; D.D., Findlay Coll., 1967, Lakeland Coll., 1969; L.H.D., Catawba Coll., 1971; m. Junia Evelyn Keppel, June 20, 1946; children—Robert Verelle, John K., Timothy I. Ordained to ministry United Ch. of Christ, 1946; instr. religion Franklin and Marshall Coll., 1946-49, asst. prof. religion, 1949-50; Kunz prof. N.T., Lancaster Theol. Sem., 1951-57, pres., prof. N.T., 1957-69; pres. United Church of Christ, 1969-76. Del., Assembly of World Council Chs., 1961, 75, Internat. Congl. Council, 1962; alternate observer 2d Vatican Council, 1962; mem. central com. World Council Chs.; v.p. Nat. Council Chs. Mem. Lancaster City Bd. Edn., 1965-69; del. White House Conf. on Youth, 1971. Mem. Am. Assn. Theol. Schs. (pres. 1966-68), Roman Catholic-Ref. Dialogue Group (co-chmn. 1967-69), Phi Beta Kappa, Pi Gamma Mu. Democrat. Author: The Life of Paul, 1955; We Believe, 1957; As Paul Sees Christ, 1958. Home: Upper Montclair, N.J. Died Oct. 25, 1976.

MOSSER, SAWYER MCARTHUR, editor, numismatist; b. Chambersburg, Pa., July 16, 1905; s. Harry Samuel and Nora Rebecca (Remley) M.; A.B., Gettysburg Coll., 1927; A.M., Princeton, 1930; m. Gladys Pauline Martin, Sept. 2, 1936. Asst. librarian, The Am. Numismatic Soc., N.Y. City, 1930-37, librarian, 1938-47, secretary, from 1947, executive director, from 1955, also associate editor of the Numismatic Notes and Monographs, 1938-46, editor Numismatic Notes and Monographs, The Am. Numismatic Soc. Mus. Notes and Numismatic lit. from 1947. Mem. Am. Numismatic Soc., Am. Philol. Assn., Bibliographical Soc. of Am., A.L.A., Spl. Libraries Assn., Phi Beta Kappa (alumni mem.), Eta Sigma Phi (hon.). Compiler: A Bibliography of Byzantine Coin Hoards, 1935; The Endicott Gift of Greek and Roman Coins, 1941. Home: Chambersburg, Pa. Died Oct. 31, 1975.

MOSSTELLER, FRANK, paper mfg. co. exec.; b. Stringtown, O., Oct. 18, 1882; s. William Henry and Mary (Erwin) M.; student Miller-Droughton Coll., Cin., 1902-04; m. Gwendolyn Doolittle, May 5, 1944. With Whitaker Paper Co., Cin., 1906-18, dept. mgr., 1910-18; v.p. K.V.P. Co., Kalamazoo, 1918-27; gen. mgr. Allied Paper Mills, Kalamazoo, Mich., 1927-29. Home: Kalamazoo, Mich. *

MOSTEL, ZERO (SAM MOSTEL), actor; b. Bklyn., Feb. 28, 1915; s. Israel and Celia (Druchs) M.; grad. Coll. City N.Y., 1935; postgrad. N.Y. U., 1935-36; m. Kathryn Harkin; children—Joshua, Tobias. Traveled and painted, La. and N.Mex., 1936; various positions factories, also work as longshoreman; lectr. art various museums for WPA; debut as comedian Cafe Soc. Downtown, 1942; appeared radio program Chamber Music Soc. of Lower Bush Street; on Broadway in Keep 'em Laughing; motion pictures DuBarry Was a Lady, 1942, A Funny Thing Happened on the Way to the Forum, The Producers, The Great Catherine, The Angel Levine, Hot Rock, Marco Polo, Rhinoceros; appeared in Ulysses in Nightown, N.Y.C., 1958, London, 1959, revival Winter Garden Theatre, 1974; performed role in play Rhinoceros, 1961; on Broadway in Funny Thing Happened on the Way to the Forum, 1962, musical Fiddler on the Roof, 1964; one man art show A.C.A. Galleries, 1973. Recipient Tony award for best actor, 1961, 62, 64; Best Actor award Theatre of All Nations, Paris, 1959; Einstein medal of art. Died Sept. 10, 1977.

MOTLEY, WARREN, lawyer; b. Boston, May 14, 1883; s. Thomas and Eleanor (Warren) M.; grad. Groton Sch., 1900; A.B., Harvard, 1904, LL.B., 1906. Admitted to Mass. bar, 1906, since practiced in Boston; now partner firm Gaston, Snow, Motley & Holt, and predecessors. *

MOUAT, MALCOLM PALMER, lawyer; b. Janesville, Wis., Oct. 20, 1902; s. Malcolm O. and Eloise (Palmer) M.; B.A., Yale, 1925; LL.B., Harvard, 1928; m. Gertrude May McPherson, Feb. 6, 1932; children—Malcolm M., Lucretia. Admitted to Wis. bar, 1928; with firm Nowlan, Mouat, Lovejoy, Wood & Cripe, and predecessors, Janesville, 1928-80, partner, 1940-80; pres., dir. Mchts. Savs. Bank, Janesville; past chmn. bd., dir. emeritus Bank Janesville, 1961-80; dir. emeritus M & S BanCorp. Mem. Wis. Higher Edn. Aids Bd., 1967-77; rep. Wis. Ind. Colls., 1967-77. Vice pres., bd. dirs. Janesville Found.; life trustee Beloit Coll., 1943-80, chmn. bd., 1963-71. Fellow Am. Bar Found.; mem. Am., Wis., Rock County, Internat., Inter-Am. bar assns., World Peace Through Law, Am. Judicature Assn., Rock County Hist. Soc. (dir.), Janesville C. of C. Republican. Conglist. Mason, Rotarian. Club: Janesville Country. Author: Dr. Henry Palmer-The Fighting Surgeon, 1977. Home: Janesville, Wis. Died Mar. 11, 1980.

MOULDER, MORGAN M., congressman; born Linn Creek, Mo., Aug. 31, 1904; s. Fred J. and Margaret (Hillhouse) M.; student Missouri U.; LL.B., Cumberland U., Lebanon, Tenn.; m. Nedra White, 1928; 1 dau., Marcia. Admitted to Mo. bar, 1928; served successively as pros. atty. Camden County, Mo. (4 terms), spl. asst. to U.S. dist. atty., western dist. of Mo., judge circuit ct., 18th judicial circuit Mo.; mem. 81st and 82d Congresses, 11th Mo. District, 82d to 87th Congresses, 11th Mo. District mem. interstate and fgn. commerce committee and committee on un-Am. activity; practice law, Camdenton, Mo., after 1963. Democrat. Home: Camdenton, Mo. Died Nov. 12, 1976.

MOUNTREY, ROBERT WALTHER, business exec.; b. Hoboken, N.J., Jan. 6, 1915; s. Howard Jefferson Varick and Minerva (Walther) M.; B.S., U.S. Naval Acad., 1937; grad. Advanced Mgmt. Program, Harvard, 1950; m. Mary Elizabeth Wohlsen, Aug. 19, 1939; children—Barbara Jane, William Varick Mountrey. With Standard Oil Co. (N.J.), 1937-41, 47-56, 59-62, transp. coordinator Eastern hemisphere, 1959-62; v.p., dir. Esso Shipping, Inc., 1957-58, Esso Tankers, Inc., 1958-59, Butterworth System, Inc., 1958-68, Standard Tankers Bahamas (Ltd.), 1958-68, Transmarine Carriers, Inc., 1968-70, Ocean Industries, Inc., 1968-70, Career Assos., Inc., 1971-75; v.p. Esso Internat., Inc., 1962-68; pres. Atlantic Terminal & Tanker Services, Inc., 1970-74. Bd. mgrs. Am. Bur. Shipping, 1964-68. Served to comdr. USNR, 1941-46. Decorated Bronze Star medal (2). Home: Fort Lauderdale, Fla. Died Nov. 26, 1980.

MOWRER, EDGAR ANSEL, writer, columnist; b. Bloomington, Ill., Mar. 8, 1892; s. Rufus and Nell (Scott) M.; A.B., U. Mich., 1913; student U. Chgo., also Sorbonne, Paris, France; m. Lilian Thomson, Feb. 10, 1916; 1 dau., Diana Jane. Contbr. Am. and English mags., 1914-77; war corr. Chgo. Daily News in France and Belgium, 1914-15, at Italian front and in Rome, Italy; was chief Chgo. Daily News bur. in Berlin, 1923-33, then chief bur., Paris, 1934-39; worked in Washington, 1940-41; toured Far East 2d time, autumn 1941; dept. dir. Office Facts and Figures and OWI until 1943; columnist fgn. affairs, broadcaster; Am. editor internat. mag. Western World, 1956-60. Trustee Freedom House, N.Y. Recipient Pulitzer Prize for overseas reporting, 1932. Clubs: Century Assn. (N.Y.C.); Adventurers (Chgo.). Author: Immortal Italy, 1922; This American World, 1928; The Future of Politics, 1930; Germany Puts the Clock Back, 1932; The Dragon Awakes, 1938; (with Martha Rajchman) Global War, 1942; The Nightmare of American Foreign Policy, 1948; Challenge and Decision, 1950; A Good Time To Be Alive, 1960; An End to Make Believe, 1961; Triumph and Turmoil-a Personal History of Our Time, 1968; (with Lilian T. Mowrer) Umano and the Price of Lasting Peace, 1973. Address: Wonalancet, N.H. Died Mar. 2, 1977; buried Sao Martino Cemetery, Madeira, Portugal.

MOYER, CHARLES EDWARD, writer; b. Reading, Pa., Mar. 4, 1886; s. Edward Henry and Kate Maria (Whitman) M.; student Franklin and Marshall Coll., U. of Pa., Am. Sch. for Playwrights and Dramatists, Sheldon Sch. of Business Science; m. Marie Josephine, d. Dr. Bryan Charles Magennis, of Paterson, N.J., Nov. 20, 1920. Successively newspaper reporter, sporting editor, dramatic critic and mng. editor various Eastern newspapers; publicity campaigns, motion pictures, through Paramount Pictures Corpn., 1913, later with Famous Players-Lasky Corpn.; now foreign dir. of advertising and publicity of United Artists Corpn. Had charge of making films for Liberty Loans in U.S. and for Victory Loans, in Can., during World War; also spent some time in war countries making pictures. Episcopalian. Clubs: Pa. Wheel, North Jersey Country. Contbr. numerous articles and short stories to mags. Home: New York. *

MOYER, SHELDON, assn. exec.; b. Garrett, Ind., Dec. 11, 1920; s. Karl and Gertrude (Perry) M.; B.A., Mich. State U., 1943; m. Neva Grace Ackerman, Sept. 18, 1948; children—Marcia, Mark, Jane. With AAA Motor News Detroit, 1945-46; account exec. Prince & Co., 1947-52; v.p. Grant Advt. Co., 1952-54; v.p. Kenyon & Eckhardt, 1954-55; pres. Leo Burnett Co. Mich., Inc., Detroit, 1955-73; v.p., dir. automotive mktg. Newspaper Advt. Bur., Detroit, after 1973. Co-chmn. United Found. Detroit, 1968. Served to capt., armored div., AUS, 1943-45; ETO. Decorated Silver Star, Purple Heart. Mem. Pub. Relations Soc. Am., Am. Assn. Advt. Agys. (chmn. Mich. council). Sigma Delta Chi, Alpha Delta Sigma. Home: Birmingham, Mich. Deceased.

MOYNE, ERNEST JOHN, educator; b. Hanko, Finland, May 3, 1916; s. Ernest Alexander and Ida Sofia (Korpi) M.; B.A., Yale, 1938, M.A., 1940; Ph.D., Harvard, 1948; m. Kathleen Marie McCormick, Jan. 30, 1943; 1 dau., Elizabeth Eila. Instr. English, Williams Coll., 1942-43; mem. faculty U. Del., 1948-76, prof. English, 1964-76, Henry Francis duPont Winterthur prof., 1972-76. Mem. editorial bd. U. Del. Press, 1972-76. Served with AUS, 1943-46. Brooker scholar, 1935; Dexter travelling fellow, 1947. Mem. Modern Lang. Assn., Am. Studies Assn., Modern Lang. Soc. Helsinki, Kalevala Soc. (Helsinki), A.A.U.P., Soc. Advancement Scandinavian Study, Phi Kappa Phi. Contbr. articles to profl. jours. Translator, editor: A Half Year in the New World (Alexandra Gripenberg), 1954; Hiawatha and Kalevala: A Study of the Relationship Between Longfellow's Indian Edda and the Finnish Epic, 1963; editor: The Journal of Margaret Hazlitt, 1967; Raising the Wind: the Legend of Lapland and Finland Wizards in Literature, 1981. Home: Newark, Del. Died June 28, 1976; interred in Waterford, Conn.

MOYNIHAN, CHARLES JOSEPH (MOI'NI-HAN), lawyer; b. White Hall, Ill., Apr. 23, 1884; s. John Joseph and Ellen (Delhanty) M.; LL.B., U. of Ill., 1908; m. Marguerite Catlin, Nov. 8, 1910; children—Charles John, Alice Mae, Frank Dale, Peggy. In practice of law at Montrose, Colo., since 1908; became mem. Moynihan, Hughes & Knous, 1915; now mem. law firm Moynihan-Hughes-Sherman. Pres. Colo. Bd. of Corrections, 1917-31; mem. Pres. Hoover's Public Lands Commn. (to formulate policy for disposal of unappropriated pub. lands). Member Am. and Colo. State bar assns., Phi Delta Phi, Kappa Sigma. Republican. Episcopalian. Mason (32 deg., K.T.). Clubs: Denver, University (Denver); Rotary (Montrose). Home: Montrose, Colo. *

MUDGETT, BRUCE D. (MUJ'ET), university prof.; b. Ashland, Neb., Feb. 10, 1884; s. Joseph Edward and Delia Marilla (Grover) M.; B.A., U. of Ida., 1908; studied Columbia, 1908-09; Ph.D., U. of Pa., 1913; m. Mildred Dennett, June 3, 1916; children— Roxie Tyler, Doris Grover. Teacher, Univ. of Pa., 1910-17, Univ. of Wash., 1917-18; economist Bur. of Research, War Trade Bd., Washington, 1918-19; prof. economics and statistics, U. of Minn., since 1919. Mem. Am. Statis. Assn., Am. Econ. Assn., Royal Econ. Soc., Econometric Soc., Inst. of Math. Statistics, Phi Beta Kappa, Beta Theta Pi, Alpha Kappa Psi and Beta Gamma Sigma. Author: Life Insurance (with S. S. Huebner), 1915; Disability Provision in American Life Insurance Contracts, 1915; Insurance, 1924; War Trade Board Report (with H. F. Walradt), 1920; Statistical Tables and Graphs, 1929. Home: Minneapolis. *

MUELLER, ERWIN WILHELM, educator, physicist; b. Berlin, Germany, June 13, 1911; s. Wilhelm M. and Kathe (Teipelke) M.; diploma engring. Tech. U., Berlin, 1935, Dr.Ing., 1936, Dr.Ing. habil., 1950, Dr. rer. nat. h.c., 1968, Dr. h.c., 1975; m. Klara Thussing, Feb. 13, 1939; 1 dau., Jutta. Came to U.S., 1952, naturalized in 1962. Research physicist Siemens Research Lab., Berlin, 1935-37; head devel. lab. Stabilovolt, Berlin, 1937-46; div. chief Kaiser Wilhelm Inst. Phys. Chemistry, Berlin, 1948-52; ausser ordentlicher, prof. physics Free U. Berlin, 1951-52; prof. physics Pa. State U., 1952-55, research prof. physics, 1955-68, Evan-Pugh research prof. physics, after 1968, then prof. emeritus. Sci. mem.-at-large Max Planck Gesellschaft. Recipient C.F. Gauss medal, Braunschweig, Germany, 1952; Potts medal Franklin Inst., Phila., 1964; John Scott medal City Trust Phila., 1970; M.W. Welch award Am. Vacuum Soc., 1970; Centenary Lectureship medal Chem. Soc. London, 1969. Fellow Am. Phys. Soc. (chmn. div. electron physics 1962, Davisson-Germer prize 1972). Royal Micros. Soc. London (hon.), Acad. Deutscher Naturforscher (Leopoldina); mem. Nat. Acad. Engring., Nat. Acad. Sci. Contbr. numerous articles to profl. jours. (Müller). Inventor field emission microscope, field ion microscope, atom probe. Discoverer field evaporation. Home: State College, Pa. Died May 17, 1977.

MUELLER, FREDERICK HENRY, corp. exec.; b. Grand Rapids, Mich., Nov. 22, 1893; s. John Frederick and Emma Matilda (Oesterle) M.; B.S., Mich. State University, 1914, LL.D., 1959; m. Mary Darrah, November 6, 1915 (deceased 1958); children—Frederick Eugene, Marcia Joan; m. 2d, Mrs. Pauline Crane Kessler, May 22, 1961. General partner Mueller Furniture Co., 1914-55; pres. Furniture Mut. Ins. Co., 1941-55; pres., gen. mgr. Grand Rapids Industries, Inc., 1941-46; asst. sec. of commerce, Washington, 1955-58; under secretary of commerce, 1958-59, sec. of commerce, 1959-61; mem. board directors Detroit Edison Co., Fruehauf Trailer Co., trustee First Mortgage Corporation. President of United Hosp. Fund, Inc., 1948-55. Pres. Butterworth Hosp., 1945-55; mem. governing bd. Mich. State U., 1945-57. Mem. Nat. Assn. Furniture Mfrs. (pres. 1934-35), C. of C. (pres. Grand Rapids, 1940-41), Tau Beta Pi. Mason (33deg., Shriner). Clubs: Rotary (past dist. gov.), Peninsular (Grand Rapids); Capitol Hill, Metropolitan, Congressional Country (Washington); Detroit Athletic, Detroit Golf, Bird Key Yacht. Home: Detroit, Mich. and Venice, Fla. Died Aug. 31, 1976.

MUELLER, GILBERT JOHN, oil co. exec.; b. Hanover, Kan., May 12, 1904; s. Anton G. and Florence (Pifer) M.; A.B., U. Colo., 1928; student Yale, 1928-29; LL.B., U. Denver, 1932; m. Cornelia Pullen, Aug. 21, 1929; children—Gilbert Anton, Cornelia Florence (Mrs. George C. Gibson). Admitted to Colo. bar, 1933; asst. sec. Argo Oil Corp., Denver, 1937-40, v.p., dir., 1941-46, exec. v.p., dir., 1946-53, pres., 1953-62. Denver Mus. Natural History. Mem. Beta Theta Pi, Phi Delta Phi. Episcopalian. Clubs: Denver Country, University, Mile High (Denver). Home: Denver, Colo. Died Mar. 5, 1980.

MUELLER, JOHN THEODORE (MIL'ER), clergyman, educator, religious writer; born Janesville, Minn., Apr. 5, 1885; s. Andrew and Ernestine (Krumbholtz) M.; ed. Concordia Coll., Ft. Wayne, Ind., 1898-1904, Concordia Sem., St. Louis, Mo., 1904-07, and extension courses Tulane U., 1907-11; Th.D., Xenia Theol. Sem., 1927; m. Adeline S. Meibohm, Feb. 25, 1908; children—Armand Elmer Theodore, Irma Louisa, Norbert Carl Frederick, Arlo Max, Marilyn Emily Eugenia. Instr. Luther Coll., New Orleans, La., 1907-11, Wittenberg (Wis.) Acad., 1911-13; pastor St. John's Evang. Luth. Ch., Hubbell, Mich., 1913-17, Zion Evang. Luth. Ch., Ottawa, Ill., 1917-21; asst. pastor Bethlehem Evang. Luth. Ch. and prof. systematic theology and exegesis, Concordia Sem., St. Louis, 1920-55, teaching on modified service, 1955—. Commnr. Luth. Ch., Mo. Synod, to Theol. Confs. in Europe, 1949-50. Member Victoria Inst. (Eng.), 1919; 1 dau., Margaret Magdalene (Mrs. Armin C. Hoesch). Teacher high sch., Wis. and Minn., 1919-24; ordained to ministry Evang. Ch., 1922; pastor, Minneapolis, South Bend and Indianapolis, 1921-37; instr. North Central Coll., 1924-26; conf. supt. Evang. Ch., Ind. Conf., 1937-41; gen. sec. Christian edn. and evangelism Evang. Ch., Cleveland, 1941-46; exec. sec. Christian edn. and asso. sec. evangelism Evang. United Brethren Ch., 1946-54, bishop, 1954—, pres. bd. of bishops, 1946—, mem. gen. council of adminstrn., 1946—, pres. council, also president gen. bd. Christian edn., v.p. gen. bd. of evangelism. Vice pres. Nat. Council Chs. Christ U.S.A. *

MUELLER, KARL WILLIAM, brewery exec.; b. Stuttgart, Germany, Nov. 7, 1909; s. William and Katherine (Hurlebaus) M.; came to U.S., 1923; M.E., Cornell U., 1932; M.S., Stevens Inst. Tech., 1942; postgrad. Columbia, 1932-37; m. Ilse Gertrude Weber, Nov. 2, 1934; children—Sibyl (Mrs. Edward B. Weinstein), Todd Jeffrey, James Weber. Mgr. elevator div. Maintenance Co., N.Y.C., 1940-42; works mgr. Standard Stoker Co., Erie, Pa., 1942-46, Am. Chain & Cable Co., Reading, Pa., 1946-55; v.p. operations Trailmobile, Inc., Cin., 1955-56; exec. v.p. Crown Cork & Seal, Inc., Phila., 1956-59; pres. Clinton Engines Corp., N.Y.C., 1959-60; exec. v.p. F&M Schaefer Brewing Co., N.Y.C., 1961-74, also dir. Incorporator, bd. dirs. Community Chest, Erie and Reading. Mem. Seal and Serpent frat., Quill and Dagger Soc. Lutheran. Clubs: Huntingdon Valley Country, Palmbrook Country, Vesper. Home: Sun City, Ariz. Died Dec. 15, 1976.

MUELLER, MERRILL (RED), educator, govt. cons.; b. N.Y.C., Jan. 27, 1916; s. Carl and Kathryn (Creden) M.; spl. student Sorbonne, Paris, 1939, London U., 1946; m. Edith Nicholson, Feb. 14, 1946 (div.); m. 2d, Jane Poirson, Aug. 5, 1963; children—Kenneth Mueller, Kevin Mueller. Labor reporter Internat. News Service, 1935-36, Wash. reporter, 1936-38, fgn. corr., 1938-41; European dir. Newsweek, 1941-42; roving reporter NBC, Europe, Africa, India, Asia, Pacific, 1941-46, London dir., 1946-51, commentator, 1950-68; roving editor ABC, after 1968; Distinguished lectr. Ohio U., 1977-78, govt. cons., 1976-80; dir. Radio Corp. Am., Ltd., London, 1946-50; Syracuse (N.Y.) U., 1978-79; world radio pool voice European D-Day to D106, 1944, Japanese Surrender, U.S.S. Missouri, 1945, Astronaut John Glenn Space Flight, 1962, 1st internat. Television via Telstar, 1965, Apollo II Moonlanding. Mem. Am. Com. for UNESCO, Pres.'s Adv. Com. on Youth. Decorated Purple Heart; Order Brit. Empire; Legion of Honor (France). Recipient Polk Meml. award, L.I.U., 1953. Mem. Am. Corr. Assn. London (past pres.), Am. Radio-TV News Analyst Assn. (past pres.), Am. Ordnance Assn. (life), Congl. Corrs. Assn., Acad. Television Arts and Scis. (gov.), Sigma Delta Chi. Clubs: Overseas Press (pres. 1964-65), Dutch Treat (N.Y.C.). Home: Culver City, Calif. Died Nov. 30, 1980.

MUENZINGER, KARL FRIEDRICH (MINZ'ING-ER), psychologist; b. Speyer am Rhein, Germany, Apr. 28, 1885; s. Gottlieb and Elisabeth (Steigleiter) M.; ed. pub. schs. in Germany and Switzerland; A.B., U. of Tex., 1908; grad. study univs. of Tex., Wis.; Ph.D., U. of Chicago, 1918; m. Florence Rebecca Weaver, June 30, 1925; children—John, Lisbet, Gretel. Came to U.S., 1906, naturalized, 1924. Teacher psychology, German literature The German American Teachers Seminary, Milwaukee, 1911-13; instr. German U. Tex., 1913-17; indsl. psychologist Lakeside Press, Chicago, 1918-20; mem. psychology staff U. of Colo., since 1924, prof. psychology since 1938, chmn. dept. since 1946. Mem. Soc. Exptl. Psychologists, Am. Psychol. Assn., Soc. Psychol. Study Social Issues, Sigma Xi. Author: Psychology, The Science of Behavior, 1942. Home: Boulder, Colo. *

MUGGLETON, GERALD DEAN, paper mfg.; b. Raymond, Neb., Apr. 10, 1885; s. John Carlos and Clara (Johnston) M.; student Hiram Coll., 1905; M.S., Case Inst. Tech., 1908; m. Elizabeth Baird, Nov. 3, 1912; 1 dau., Betty (Mrs. Jere Wescott Patterson). Mech. and elec. engr. Wellman Seaver Morgan Co., Cleve., 1908-16; gen. mgr. Niagara Smelting Corp., Niagara Falls, N.Y., 1916-29; mgr. Combined Locks Paper Co., Appleton, Wis., 1930-35, Consol. Water Power & Paper Co., Wisconsin Rapids, Wis., 1935-40; exec. v.p. Combined Locks Paper Co. (Wis.), 1940-57, became president, 1957, now vice chairman bd., director president of D. M. Bare Paper Co., Roaring Spring, Pa, 1946—, South Shore Utility Co., Combined Locks, 1946—. Mem. Phi Delta Theta. Episcopalian. Clubs: North Shore Country (Menasha, Wis.); Riverview Country (Appleton, Wis.); University (Chgo.); hon. mem. Rotary (Niagara Falls, N.Y.). Home: Appleton, Wis. *

MUIR, MALCOLM, publisher; b. Glen Ridge, N.J., July 19, 1885; s. James and Susan (Brown) M.; ed. pub. and pvt. schs.; m. Lida Kelly, May 14, 1914 (div. 1942, dec. 1958); children—Malcolm Eleanor Warfield (Mrs. Collister Johnson); m. 2d, Frances Tener Brown, Aug. 19, 1943. Editor-in-chief Newsweek, pres., dir. Newsweek, Inc., 1937-59, chmn. bd., editor-in-chief, 1959-61, hon. chmn., dir., 1961-70; with McGraw-Hill Pub. Co., 1905-37, v.p., 1916-28, pres., 1928-37, founder Bus. week mag., 1929; Dir. Bullock Fund, Ltd., Carriers & Gen. Corp., Nationwide Securities Co. Inc. Dividend Shares Inc., Monthly Income Shares Inc. Dept. adminstr., div. adminstr. NRA; dir. N.A.M., 1935-43, chmn. war com., 1942-43; mem. Nat. Indsl. Conf. Bd., Labor-Mgmt. Council of WPB, 1943. U.S. chmn. council Am. Mus. in Britain; hon. trustee Com. Econ. Devel.; mem. Council on Fgn. Relations, chmn. capital fund program, 1964-67; chmn. N.Y. State Com. Med. Edn., 1962-63; chmn. Am. adv. council Ditchley Found. Eng., 1967-73; chmn. U.S. Commn. for United World Colls., 1967-73; mem. adv. com. Asso. Med. Schs. Greater N.Y., 1964-65; dir. Atlantic Council U.S. Decorated hon. knight comdr. Order British Empire; chevalier French Legion of Honor; Lebanese Order of Cedar. Mem. Internat. C. of C. (sr. trustee, mem. exec. com. U.S. council), Met. Opera Assn., Burns Soc., St. Andrews Soc., St. George's Soc., Pilgrims of U.S. (exec. com. 1959—), Am. Arbitration Assn. Republican. Episcopalian. Clubs: White's (London); Racquet and Tennis, Links, River (N.Y.C.). Home: New York, N.Y. Died Jan. 30, 1979.

MUIRHEAD, DAVID, corp. exec.; b. N.Y.C., Mar. 18, 1904; s. John and Katherine (Phillips) M.; B.C.S., N.Y. U., 1928; m. Ada Madeline Meikle, Aug. 2, 1934; 1 son, Robert Kershaw. Chmn., pres. Emhart Corp., 1964-67, chmn., 1967-71, dir., chmn. exec. com.; corporator Savs. Bank of New Britain; dir. New Britain Nat. Bank, First Conn. Bancorp. Founder, U. Hartford; bd. dirs. New Britain Gen. Hosp.; corporator Hartford, St. Francis hosps. Mem. Am. Inst. C.P.A.'s, Conn. Soc. C.P.A.'s, Conn. Sr. Golf Assn. Mason. Clubs: Shuttle Meadow Country (Kensington, Conn.); Bigelow-Howard Valley Game (Willimantic, Conn.). Home: Kensington, Conn. Died Nov. 19, 1976; interred Maple Cemetery, Kensington, Conn.

MULDER, ARNOLD, author; b. Ottawa Co., Mich., Nov. 12, 1885; s. Bouke and Jennie (Snitzler) M.; A.B., Hope Coll., Holland, Mich., 1907; student U. of Mich., Feb.-June 1909; A.M., U. of Chicago, 1910; Litt.D., Hope Coll., Holland, Mich., 1923; m. Katharine Ruth Kollen, of Holland, Mich., Apr. 4, 1911. Mng. editor Holland Daily Sentinel, 1910-15; publicity agt. State Bd. of Health, Mich., Oct. 1, 1915-July 1, 1917; editor Holland Sentinel, 1917-1929; now professor of English, Kalamazoo Coll. Editor Michigan Out-of-Doors (quarterly), 1917-22; publicity dir. Mich. Anti-tuberculosis Assn., 1917-22. Author: The Dominie of Harlem, 1913; Bram of the Five Corners, 1915; The Out-bound Road, 1919; The Sand Doctor, 1921. Writer of syndicate feature, "Adventures in the Library." Contbr. to mags. Home: Kalamazoo, Mich. *

MULHAUSER, RUTH, educator; b. Cleve., Nov. 20, 1913; d. Frederick Ludwig and Helen Elizabeth (Fletcher) Mulhauser; A.B. Oberlin Coll., 1935; A.M., Western Res. U., 1937; A.M., Radcliffe Coll., 1940, Ph.D., 1941. Instr. French, Coll. of Wooster, 1938-39; instr. Spanish and French, Hiram Coll., 1941-42; instr., asst. prof. French and Spanish, Hollins Coll., Va., 1942-46; asso. prof. romance langs. Western Res. U., 1946-55, prof. romance langs., 1955-60, chmn. dept., 1955-60, dir. Sch. French and Spanish, 1955-60. Decorated Chevalier Palmes academiques. Recipient Am. Assn. University Women Founders fellowship. Member of Am. Assn. U. Profs., Am. Assn. U. Women, Am. Assn. Tchrs. French, Am. Assn. Tchrs. Spanish, Modern Lang. Assn., Central States Modern Lang. Assn., Medieval Acad., Phi Beta Kappa, Phi Sigma Iota. Home: Cleveland, Ohio. Died Dec. 7, 1980.

MULHEARN, JOHN ROBERT, utility co. exec.; b. Jersey City, Apr. 16, 1924; s. John Joseph and Estelle Marie (Holton) M.; B.E.E., Manhattan Coll., 1948; children—Mrs. Wesley von Schack, John Robert, Patrick Francis, Michael John, Regina Mary. With N.Y. Telephone Co., 1948-58, 59-61, 63-73, 76-79, exec. v.p. corp. devel., 1971-73, pres., chief exec. officer, N.Y.C., 1976-79; staff asst. adminstrn. dept. AT&T, 1958-59, v.p., dir. corp. policy seminar, 1973-75, v.p. adminstrn. dept., 1975-76; gen. comml. mgr. Minn. area Northwestern Bell Telephone Co., 1961, v.p., gen. mgr. Iowa area, 1961-63; dir. incorporator Am. Republic Life Ins. Co. of N.Y.; dir. Allegheny Airlines, Inc., Fed. Res. Bank of N.Y., Inmont Corp., Municipal Art Soc., Econ. Devel. Council. Trustee Manhattan Coll.; mem. exec. bd. ARC in Greater N.Y.C.; chmn. I Love A Clean N.Y., Inc., Pub. Service div. Tri-State United Way; mem. cardinal's com. for edn. Archdiocese N.Y. Served with USN, 1942-46, PTO. Named First Eminent Engr., Tau Beta Pi, 1966; recipient award for accomplishment in bus. Manhattan Coll. Alumni Soc., 1972, Outstanding Exec. award Manhattan Coll. Sch. Bus., 1977. Mem. Newcomen Soc. North Am., N.Y.C. of C. and Industry, Navy League of U.S. (N.Y. council). Clubs: Econ. of N.Y., Scarsdale (N.Y.) Golf, Manhattan Coll. Spiked Shoe. Home: Bronxville, N.Y. Died Sept. 7, 1979.

MULLAHY, JOHN HENRY, educator; b. Balt., June 26, 1914; s. John Henry and Elizabeth M. (Diehl) M.; A.B., St. Louis U., 1937; M.S., Fordham U., 1941; S.T.L., St. Mary's Coll., Kans., 1946; Ph.D. Vanderbilt U., 1951; Fulbright fellow Manchester U. Eng., 1952. Joined Soc. of Jesus, 1932; instr. biology Spring Hill Coll., 1939-47, asst. prof. biology, 1947-52; asso. prof. biology Loyola U. of New Orleans, 1952-55, chmn. dept. biol. scis., 1954-78, prof. cytology, 1955-78, dir. grad. studies, biol. scis., 1956-78. Guest investigator Brit. Assn. Advancement Sci., Stazione Zoologica, Napoli, 1952; vis. prof. phycology U. Wash., 1953; asst. pastor Cathedral of the Incarnation, Nashville, 1948-51. Vice pres. New Orleans chpt. Muscular Dystrophy Assn. Fellow AAAS; mem. Am., New Orleans (pres. 1955) bot. socs., Brit. Phycology Soc., Internat. Soc. Plant Morphology, Genetics Soc. Am., Assn. So. Biologists council 1969-78), Am. Assn. Jesuit Sci., La. Acad. Sci., New Orleans Acad. Scis. (pres. 1959-60), Am. Phycological Soc., N.Y. Acad. Scis., Albertus Magnus Guild, Am. Soc. Microbiology, Internat. Phycol. Soc., La. Sci. Tchrs. Assn., Lund Bot. Soc., Nat. Assn. Biol. Tchrs., So. Appalachian Bot. Soc., Tenn. Acad. Sci., Torrey Bot. Soc., Am. Soc. Oceanography (chpt. 1st v.p. 1966), Sigma Xi, Beta Beta Beta (v.p. Southeastern region). Home: New Orleans, La. Died May 16, 1978; buried St. Charles Coll., Grand Coteau, La.

MULLEN, THOMAS FRANCIS, surgeon; b. Galesburg, Ill., Sept. 20, 1885; s. John Bernard and Catherine (English) M.; student Mt. Angel Coll., Ore., 1902-05; M.D., Jefferson Med. Coll., 1912; m. Cecile Racine, Feb. 21, 1918 (dec. 1957); 1 dau., Paule (Mrs. John R. Lehman). Intern St. Louis City Hosp., 1912; intern, resident Pa. Hosp., 1912-16; practice of surgery, Pocatello, Ida., 1920-28, San Francisco, 1928—; asso. clin. prof. surgery U. Cal., 1928—; chief surgeon Franklin Hosp, 1940-53; vis. surgeon St. Mary's Hosp., 1940—. Served from capt. to maj. M.C., U.S. Army, 1916-19. Diplomate Am. Bd. Surgery (founders group). Fellow A.C.S. (v.p. 1952-53; past gov.); mem. San Francisco (past pres.), Pacific Coast, Pan Am. surg. socs., Med. Friends of Wine (past pres.), Alpha Kappa Kappa, Alpha Omega Alpha. Club: (San Francisco). Home: Hillsborough, Cal. *

MULLER, HERBERT JOSEPH, educator; b. Mamaroneck, N.Y., July 7, 1905; s. Carl and Bessie (Fay) M.; A.B., Cornell U., 1925, A.M., 1926, Ph.D., 1932; Guggenheim fellow, 1939-40; D.Litt. (hon.), Purdue U., 1960; m. Janet Bailey, June 16, 1934; children—Richard Bailey, John Albert. Instr. English, Cornell U., 1926-35; instr., asst. prof., asso. prof. Purdue U., 1935-45, prof., 1945-56; prof. English and govt. Ind. U., 1956-59, Distinguished Service prof., 1959-80; with Fgn. Service Aux., Dept. of State, 1943; editor W.P.B., 1944; vis. prof. U. Istanbul, 1946-47, 51-52, Ind. U., 1953-54; distinguished vis. prof. at N.Y. U., 1958; Sloan vis. prof. Menninger Found., 1963, U. Ala., 1967. Mem. Am. Acad. Arts and Scis., World Acad. Art and Sci., Phi Beta Kappa (senator). Author: Modern Fiction, 1937; Science and Criticism, 1943; Thomas Wolfe, 1947; The Uses of the Past, 1952; The Spirit of Tragedy, 1956; The Loom of History, 1958; Issues of Freedom, 1960; Freedom in the Ancient World, 1961 (Phi Beta Kappa award 1962); Freedom in the Western World, 1962; Religion and Freedom in the Modern World (Frederic G. Melcher book award 1964), 1963; The Individual in a Revolutionary World, 1964; Freedom in the Modern World, 1966; Adlai Stevenson: A Study in Values, 1968; The Uses of English, 1968; The Children of Frankenstein, 1970; In Pursuit of Relevance, 1971; The Uses of the Future, 1974. Home: Bloomington, Ind. Died Jan. 27, 1980.

MULLER, JOHN H., real estate exec.; b. Newark, Apr. 28, 1899; s. John H. and Matilda (King) M.; M.E., Stevens Inst. Tech., 1921, E.D., 1959; M. Adelaide W.

Hannon, Feb. 10, 1923; children—John H., Mary A. (Mrs. Stanton S. Roller); m. Kathryn A. McLoughlin, June 7, 1969. With Equitable Life Assurance Soc. U.S., N.Y.C., 1937-66, sr. v.p., 1960-66; real estate cons., after 1966; mem. exec. com., dir. Home Title div. Chgo. Title Ins. Co., N.Y.C.; dir. First Realty Investment Corp., Miami, Fla., John Lowry Co., N.Y.C. Vice chmn. bd. trustees Stevens Inst. Tech., also chmn. exec. com.; pres. Jersey Shore Med. Center, Neptune, N.J.; past pres., bd. dirs. Speech Rehab. Inst., N.Y.C.; former pres. ACTION; past pres., bd. dirs. Ave. of Ams. Assn.; chmn., bd. dirs. West Side Assn. Commerce. Mem. Delta Tau Delta. Clubs: Univ. (N.Y.C.); Spring Lake Golf (pres.), Spring Lake Bath and Tennis (Spring Lake, N.J.). Home: Sea Girt, N.J. Died Aug. 28, 1977.

MULLIN, MARK JOSEPH, ednl. adminstr., clergyman; b. Phila., July 29, 1906; s. Mark J. and Elizabeth G. (McKeever) M.; A.B., St. Joseph's U., Princeton, N.J., 1928, M.A., 1933; grad. St Vincent's Sem., Phila., 1933; Ph.L., Angeilcum U., Rome, Italy, 1935. Joined Order of Congregation of the Mission, 1928, ordained priest Roman Cath. Ch., 1933; vice rector Lady of Angles Sem., Niagara (N.Y.) U., 1941-47, prof. philosophy at univ., 1936-50, dean Grad. Sch. and Sch. Edn., 1950-56; nat. moderator Fedn. Cath. Coll. Students, 1954-56; prof. philosophy St. John's U., N.Y.C., 1956-60, exec. v.p. univ., 1960-66; superior St. Vincent's Sem., 1966-72; office pub. relations Niagara U., after 1972. Chaplain, Internat. Narcotic Enforcement Officers Assn. after 1962; dir. Our Lady of Angels Assn., 1974. Home: Niagara Falls, N.Y. Died June 26, 1978.

MULLIN, WILLARD (HARLAN), sports cartoonist; b. Franklin, Ohio Sept. 14, 1902; s. Milo Mayberry and Edna Marie (Ballard) M.; ed. Los Angeles High Sch.; m. Helen Tousley, July 20, 1929; 1 dau., Shirley Ann. With art dept. Los Angeles (Calif.) Herald, 1922-24, 26-35; with Ft. Worth (Tex.) Record, 1925; sports cartoonist; N.Y. World Telegram 1935-66, also draws for Scripps Howard publs., Sporting News, Sport, Look, Colliers, Outdoor Life, American and others; created Brooklyn Bum cartoon character; works exhibited in athletic and sports offices throughout U.S., and in Huntington Library, Pasadena, Calif. Awarded Helms Found. prize for contribution to sports, 1947. Mem. Soc. of Illustrators, Artists and Writers. Nat. Cartoonists' Society (named Sports Cartoonist of Century 1971), Sigma Delta Chi. Clubs: Dutch Treat, Manhassett Yacht. Illustrator: Menke's Encyclopedia of Sports, 1944; It Beats Working (by John Lardner), 1947. Home: Ponte Verde Beach, Fla. Died Dec. 21, 1978.

MULLINS, CHARLES LOVE, JR., army officer; b. Gretna, Neb., Sept. 7, 1892; s. Charles Love and Katherine Belle (Coon) M.; B.S., U.S. Mil. Acad., 1917; grad. Inf. Sch., 1930, Air Corps Tactical Sch., 1932, Command and Gen. Staff Sch., 1934, Army War Coll., 1939; hon. grad. No. 2, Academia Militar de Nicaragua; m. Jane Anne Dooley, Dec. 9, 1933. Ph.D., 1932; Guggenheim fellow, 1939-40; m. Janet Bailey, June 16, 1934; children—Richard Bailey, John Albert. Instr. English, Cornell U., 1926-35; instr., asst. prof., asso. prof., Purdue U., prof. since 1945; with Fgn. Service Auxiliary, Dept. of State, 1943; editor W.P.B., 1944; vis. prof., U. of Istanbul, 1946-47. Mem. Phi Beta Kappa. Author: Modern Fiction, 1937; Science and Criticism, 1943; Thomas Wolfe, 1947. Home: San Francisco, Calif. Died Mar. 1, 1976.

MULRONEY, JOHN E., judge; b. Ruthven, Iowa, Feb. 15, 1896; s. John Edward and Anna (Foley) M.; student Creighton U., 1915; LL.B., Iowa U., 1922; m. Martha O'Connor, June 4, 1929 (dec. May 1969); m. 2d, Sonja K. Harding, Jan. 7, 1975. Admitted to Iowa bar, Jan. 1923; county atty. of Webster County, Iowa, 1929-33; asst. atty. gen. of Iowa, 1939-42; justice of Iowa, Supreme Ct., 1943-55; judge U.S. Tax Ct., 1955-79. Served as cpl. 42d Div., 1917-19. Mem. Am. Legion, Order of Coif, Am., Iowa bar assns., Phi Delta Phi. Home: Sun City, Ariz. Died May 28, 1979.

MUNGER, FRANK JAMES, polit. scientist; b. Ft. Worth, Sept. 18, 1929; s. Guy Elmer and Kathleen Grace (Gallagher) M.; B.S. in Polit. Sci., Northwestern U., 1951; M.P.A., Harvard U., 1953, Ph.D. in Polit. Sci., 1956; m. Rosemary Betty Huppert, Nov. 15, 1957; children—Daniel Allan, Laura Anne. Instr., Syracuse U., 1955-56, asst. prof. polit. sci., 1956-61, asso. prof., 1961-65, prof., 1965-70, chmn. dept. polit. sci., 1962-65; prof. U. Fla., 1970-71; prof. U. N.C., Chapel Hill, 1971-81, dir. Inst. for Research in Social Sci., 1973-81; vis. prof. U. Rochester, 1967; mem. adv. panel for polit. sci. Nat. Inst. Edn., 1973; mem. adv. com. for research NSF, 1974-77, adv. council, 1977-78. Social Sci. Research Council research grantee, 1956; Rockefeller Found. grantee, 1965-66; NSF grantee, 1967-69, 70-71. Mem. AAAS, Am. Polit. Sci. Assn., Am. Assn. Public Opinion Research, So. Polit. Sci. Assn., N.C. Polit. Sci. Assn., Phi Beta Kappa, Pi Sigma Alpha (nat. council 1964-68). Roman Catholic. Author books, most recent being: The Legitimacy of Opposition: The Change of Government in Ireland in 1932, 1975; Social Change and Community Politics in Urban Japan, 1977. Home: Chapel Hill, N.C. Died. Apr. 19, 1981.

MUNN, JOHN RANDALL, corp. exec.; b.East Orange, N.J., June 23, 1884; s. Joseph Lewis and Elizabeth (Randall) M.; C.E., Princeton, 1906; m. Harriet C. Severance, June 6, 1914; children—John Randall, Mark S., Marjorie S. Began as purchasing agt. charge London office Am. Woolen Co., later asst. selling agt. N.Y. office; chmn. Elastic Stop Nut Corp. of America, Union, N.J.; dir. Architects Samples Corp., Severance Bldg. Co. Served chief canned foods div. U.S. Food Adminstrn., World War I. Past pres. Princeton Engring. Assn. Clubs: Century, Princeton (N.Y.C.); Essex (Newark); Yeamens Hall (Charleston, S.C.). Home: Princeton, N.J. *

MUNNIKHUYSEN, HENRY D. F. (MUN'NIK-HI-ZEN), army officer; b. in Md., Dec. 28, 1886; B.S., U.S. Mil. Acad., 1909; grad. Quartermaster Corps Sch., 1926. Command and Gen. Staff Sch., 1928, Chem. Warfare Sch. (field officers course), 1929, Army Industrial Coll., 1932. Army War Coll., 1933. Commd. 2d lt., U.S. Cavalry, June 11, 1909; promoted through grades to brig. gen., U.S. Army, Oct. 2, 1940. Retired Apr. 30, 1946. Address: Washington or BelAir, Md. *

MUNOZ-MARIN, LUIS (MOON'YOTH-MA-REN'), gov. P.R.; b. San Juan, P.R., Feb. 18, 1898; s. Luis and Amalia (Marin) Munoz-Rivera; ed. pub. and pvt. schs.; Georgetown U., 1912-16; m. Muna Lee, July 1, 1919 (div.); children—Munita, Luis; m. 2d, Inés Maria Mendoza; children—Vivian, Victoria. Secretary to resident commissioner for Puerto Rico in Washington, 1916-18; editor La Revista de Indias (magazine devoted to Pan-American culture); 1918-19. Editor and publisher La Democracia (daily newspaper); elected gov. of Puerto Rico, Nov. 1948; took oath January 1949; mem. constnl. assembly of P.R., 1951; elected first governor under constitution of Commonwealth of Puerto Rico, 1952, governor until 1965. Mem. general secretariat, Pan-American Conference, Havana; formerly economic commissioner Puerto Rico in United States; elected senator-at-large, P.R., 1932, from 1965. Founder and president of Popular Democratic Party, 1938; president P.R. Senate, 1941-48; founder and editor of El Batey, rural newspaper; spl. corr. Baltimore Sun. Author: Borrones, 1917; Madre Harapos (in collaboration), 1917. Contbr. to Am. Mercury, Nation, New Republic, Foreign Affairs. Address: San Juan, P.R. Died Apr. 30, 1980.

MUNSON, CHARLES SHERWOOD, mfr.; b. Woodbury, Conn., Sept. 14, 1888; s. John Newton and Florence Averill (Seely) M.; B.A., Yale, 1912; D.S. (hon.), Clarkson U., 1971; m. Marjorie Jean Oatman, June 22, 1912; 1 son, Charles Sherwood. With Amoskeag Mfg. Co., 1912; treas. Cuban Air Products, N.Y., 1917, pres., 1919-42, chmn., 1942-76; pres. Nat. Carbide Corp., 1919-41; v.p. Air Reduction Co. Inc., 1924-37, pres., 1937-48, chmn. bd., 1948-64, chmn. exec. com., 1964-76, hon. chmn. bd., 1969-76; exec. com., dir. Baxter Labs., Inc.; pres. U.S. Indsl. Chems. Co., 1931-43, chmn., 1943-49; hon. dir. Mich. Gas Utilities, Warnaco, Inc., Greyhound Corp.; dir. adv. council Morgan Guaranty Trust Co.; dir. Gen. Fire & Casualty Ins. Co., Nat. Distillers & Chem. Corp., Greyhound Leasing & Financial Co., Compass Ins. Co., Greyhound Co. of Can., Greyhound Food Mgmt. Co., Main St. Fund. Trustee, mem. exec. com. Presbyn. Hosp., N.Y.; trustee Mus. City N.Y.; mem. adv. bd. Chem. Warfare Services. Dir. Yale Alumni Fund Assn. Recipient medal Soc. Chem. Industry, 1953. Mem. Soc. of Cin., Pilgrims U.S., Mfg. Chemists Assn. (dir.). Episcopalian. Clubs: Links (pres.), Yale, Pinnacle (organizer, 1st pres.), Cloud (gov.), Union, Church (N.Y.C.); Country of Fairfield (gov.) (Conn.). Home: Southport, Conn. Died Aug. 1, 1976; interred, Woodbury, Conn.

MUNSON, GEORGE S(HARP), lawyer; b. Williamsport, Pa., Oct. 2, 1883; s. Cyrus LaRue and Josephine (White) M.; student Lawrenceville Acad., 1900; A.B., Yale, 1904, LL.B. summa cum laude, 1907; m. Katharine A. Townsend, June 17, 1911; children—Townsend, Josephine (Mrs. Harry McD. Thayer), Katharine (Mrs. John F. Ducey, Jr.), Natalie (Mrs. Lawrence J. Brengle, Jr.), Cyrus LaRue (died in service, World War II). Admitted to Pa. bar, 1907; with Dickson, Beitler and McCouth, 1907-14; mem. firm Townsend, Elliott and Munson, since 1914; dir., mem. exec. com. Ins. Co. of N. Am. and affiliated cos., Provident Tradesmens Bank & Trust Co., Mutual Assurance Co.; mgr. Western Sav. Fund Soc. of Phila. Served as asso. gen. counsel for shipbuilding cos. organized by W. A. Harriman in Bristol and Chester, Pa.; later with F.A., Officers Training Camp, Camp Zachary Taylor, Ky., World War I. Mem. Am., Pa., Phila. (past mem. bd. govs.), bar assns. Republican. Episcopalian. Clubs: Rittenhouse (Phila.); Bar Harbor, Kebo Valley, Pot and Kettle (Me.). Home: Merion, Pa. *

MUNSON, TOWNSEND, pres. Western Savs. Fund Soc. Phila.; pres. Bellevue Stratford Co. Mem. Lower Marlon Twp. Commn., 1979. Home: Haverford, Pa. Died Nov. 1, 1979; buried Church of St. Asaph Graveyard, Bala Cynwyd, Pa.

MURANE, EDWARD E., lawyer; b. Nome, Alaska, Aug. 10, 1902; s. C.D. and Lydia (Millard) M.; LL.B., U. Mich., 1925; m. Theodora Wilson, Oct. 30, 1928 (dec. Feb. 1964); children—William, John, Mary; m. 2d, Jean Hansen, Nov. 2, 1965. Admitted to Wyo. bar, 1925, practiced in Casper; city atty., Casper, 1932-36, transp. atty., I.C.C. counsel specializing ins. def. litigation. Chmn., dir. Mid-Am. Gt. Plains Financial Corp.; pres. Wyo. Bldg. Corp. Mem. Wyo. Jr. Coll. Commn. Bd. dirs. Casper Coll. Served World War II: col. Judge Adv. Gen.'s Dept., ret. Recipient Silver Beaver award Boy Scouts Am. Fellow Internat. Acad. Trial Lawyers, Am. Coll. Trial Lawyers, Am. Bar Found.; mem. Am. Judicature Soc. (dir.), Internat. Assn. Ins. Counsel (pres. 1971-72), Fedn. Ins. Counsel, Am. (gov. 1960-63, chmn. ho. of dels. 1964-66), Wyo. (pres. 1952-53), Internat., Inter-Am., Natrona City (past pres.) bar assns., Nat. Coll. State Trial Judges (dir.), Phi Sigma Kappa, Phi Alpha Delta. Mason (32 deg., Shriner), Lion (dist. gov. Wyo.; internat. song leader 6 yrs.). Home: Casper, Wyo. Died Sept. 4, 1975.

MURCH, BOYNTON DAGGETT, investment banker; b. Cleve., June 3, 1918; s. Maynard Hale and Leah (Daggett) M.; grad. Culver Mil. Acad., 1937, Oberlin Bus. Coll., 1939; student Cleve. Coll., 1946-47; m. Rita Schmitt, Oct. 12, 1942; children—Maynard H. IV., Robert B. Security salesman Maynard H. Murch Co., Cleve., 1947-50; partner Fulton, Reid & Co., 1950-55; br. mgr. Cosgrove, Miller & Whitehead, mem. N.Y. Stock Exchange, 1955-57; pres. Murch & Co., Inc., mems. N.Y., Am. stock exchanges, 1957-73, chmn. bd., 1973-76; vice chmn. Murch Div., Parker/Hunter Inc.; chmn. bd. Robbins & Myers, Inc., Springfield, Ohio, from 1966; dir. Hunter Mfg. Co., Memphis, United Screw & Bolt Corp., Cardinal Fed. Savs. & Loan, Cleve., Whirpool Corp. Bd. govs. N.Y. Stock Exchange, 1969-72. Vice pres. Cleve. Mus. Natural History. Trustee Huron Rd. Hosp. Served to maj. AUS, 1940-45. Clubs: Kirtland Country, Union, (Cleve). Home: Kirtland, Ohio. Deceased.

MURCHISON, JOHN D., partner Murchison Bros., investments; dir. 1st Nat. Bank, Dallas, Life & Casualty Co., Nashville, Delhi Australian Petroleum Co. Address: Dallas, Tex. Died June 14, 1979.

MURDEN, FORREST DOZIER, executive; b. Norfolk, Va., Mar. 10, 1921; s. Forrest Dozier and Irene Gladys (Stavro) M.; A.B., Coll. William and Mary, 1941; M.A., Fletcher Sch. Law and Diplomacy. 1942; postgrad. summers Nat. U. of Mexico, 1947, Oxford U., 1948; fellow Columbia, 1948-50. Instr. govt. and econs. Coll. William and Mary. 1946-47; univ. liaison officer to UN. Columbia, 1949-50, lectr. fgn. trade, 1950-51; econ. adviser U.S. delegation UN, 1949-54; asst. to Henry Ford II, 1954-59; lectr. internat. orgn. Fletcher Sch. Law and Diplomacy, 1955; govt. relations counsellor Standard Oil Co. (N.J.), 1959-61; pres. Murden & Co., N.Y.C. 1962-77. Sec. Center for InterAm. Relations; U.S. com. for UNICEF; cons. Ford Found., from 1961. Served to lt. USNR, 1942-46. Recipient award Soc. Cincinnati, Coll. William and Mary; Lord Botetourt medal. Mem. Council Fgn. Relations, Accion Internat. (bd.). UN Assn. U.S.A. (bd.), Phi Beta Kappa Assos., Phi Beta Kappa, Kappa Alpha. Club: University (N.Y.C.). Author: Economic Cooperation, 1954; (with Isador Lubin) Our Stake in World Trade, 1954; Underdeveloped LandsRevolution of Rising Expectations, 1956. Home: New York, N.Y. Died Dec. 4, 1977.

MURDOCK, CARLETON CHASE, univ. prof.; b. Cooperstown, N.Y., July 29, 1884; s. Benjamin Franklin and Myrtle Emma (Chase) M.; B.S., Colgate U., 1907, A.M., Cornell U., 1910, Ph.D., 1919; m. Dorothy Lee Waugh, Aug. 28, 1923; children—Franklin Waugh, Edmund Lee. Tutor of physics, U. of Maine, 1907-08; instr. physics, Cornell U., 1909-19, asst. prof., 1919-30, prof., 1930-52, dean univ. faculty, 1945-52, prof. emeritus since 1952; researcher, Davy-Farady Lab., London, 1926-27. Fellow A.A.A.S., Am. Physical Soc.; member Am. Optical Soc., Am. Soc. for X-ray and Electron Difraction (treas. 1945-50), American Assn. of Physics Teachers, Phi Beta Kappa, Phi Kappa Psi, Gamma Alpha (pres. 1929), Sigma Xi (exec. com., 1943-48), Phi Kappa Phi. Baptist. Contbr. results of research in physics. Home: Ithaca, N.Y. *

MURDOCK, JOHN ROBERT, congressman; b. Lewis County, Mo., Apr. 20, 1885; s. John and Elizabeth (Wallace) M.; A.B., Kirksville (Mo.) State Teachers Coll., 1912; A.M., State U. of Ia., 1925; grad. work U. of Ariz., 1923, U. of Calif., 1929; m. Myrtle M. Cheney, Aug. 27, 1906; children—Rachael Weber, David Nathaniel, John Benjamin. Country school teacher, 1904-07; high sch. prin., 1908-10; instr. Tempe Teachers Coll., Tempe, Ariz., 1914-32, U. of Calif., 1929, on leave; dean Ariz. State Teachers Coll., 1933-37; mem. 75th to 82nd Congresses (1937-53), Ariz. 1st dist. Mem. Phi Delta Kappa. Democrat. Conglist. Mason (32 deg.), K.P. Author: Constitution of Arizona, 1929; Constitutional Development of Arizona, 1933. Home: Tempe, Ariz. *

MURPHY, FRANCIS S., publisher; b. New Haven, Conn., October 12, 1882; s. Henry J. and Mary A. (Dunn) M.; ed. Hartford grammar and high schs.; A.M. (honorary), Trinity College; married Iva (Marsh) Murphy, October 16, 1907; 1 son, Warner. Began as errand boy Hartford Times, 1898, and since in their employ, gen. mgr. in 1936 and sec. of corp. since Feb. 16, 1928; trustee Mechanics Savs. Bank. Life director of New England Council; chairman of Conn. aeronautics commission. Trustee Gannett Newspaper Foundation, Julius Hartt Foundation Corporation, American Sch. for the Deaf. Director Family Service Soc., Hartford County Y.M.C.A., Conn. State Chamber of Commerce, Hartford Chamber of Commerce (vice pres.); mem. U.S. Civil Service Loyalty Bd. for New England; dir. Newington Home for Crippled Children. Recipient Presidential Citation Medal for Merit. Mem. National Planning Assn. of New England. Clubs: Hartford, University (Hartford); Wings (New York); Farmington Country. Home: West Hartford, Conn. *

MURPHY, FRED P., publisher; b. Stamford, N.Y., Apr. 17, 1889; s. Thomas and Agnes (McMahon) M.; LL.B., Cornell U., 1912; D.C.L., Hartwick Coll., 1958; m. Gertrude Wheeler, Dec. 22, 1914 (dec.); children—Betty Ann (Mrs. John R. Assheton), William Joseph. Salesman, Frontier Press Co., Buffalo, 1908-11, Charles Scribners Sons, 1913; salesman Grolier, Inc., 1913, resident div. mgr., Kansas City, Mo., 1915-36, pres. N.Y.C., 1936-47, chmn., 1947-67, chmn. exec. com., 1967-79; chmn. Grolier Internat., 1964-79, Grolier Devel. Co., 1969-79; purchased Ency. Americana, 1934; pres. Americana Corp., 1938-47, chmn., 1947-52; chmn. bd. Prospect Dairies, Audio Sears Corp.; chmn. Timberland Products Co. Mem. Council State U. Agr. and Tech. Inst., Delhi, N.Y., 1958-67; mem. at large nat. council Boy Scouts Am.; chmn. Murphy Found. Decorated chevalier Des Palmes Academique (France). Mem. Phi Delta Phi. Club: Cornell (Westchester, N.Y.C.). Home: Stamford, N.Y. Died Oct. 27, 1979.

MURPHY, GLENN, engring. educator; b. Boulder, Colo., Jan. 17, 1908; s. Peter Francis and A. Myrtle (Eggleston) M.; B.S. (C.E.), U. Colo., 1925-29, M.S., 1930; M.S. in C.E., U. Ill., 1930-32; Ph.D., Iowa State Coll., 1935; C.E., U. Colo., 1937, D.Sc. (hon.), 1973; m. Frances Pearce, Aug. 18, 1934 (dec. Feb. 1976). Instr. civil engring. U. Colo. 1929-30; spl. research grad. asst. in civil engring., Engring. Expt. Sta., U. Ill., 1930-32; instr. in theoretical and applied mechanics Iowa State Coll., 1932-34, asst. prof., 1934-38, asso. prof., 1938-41, prof. theoretical and applied mechanics Iowa State U., 1941-60, in charge of nuclear engring., 1951-59, head of nuclear engring., 1959-73, prof. and head aero. engring., 1952-55, head theoretical and applied mechanics, 1955-60, coordinator engring. edn. projects office, 1972-78, sr. engr. Inst. Atomic Research, 1949-63, Anson Marston distinguished prof. engring., 1956-78. Engring. and ednl. cons. Recipient Distinguished Service award Iowa Engring. Soc., 1963; Alumni Honor award for distinguished service in engring. U. Ill.; Distinguished Alumnus award U. Colo. Fellow Royal Soc. Arts, Royal Aero. Soc. (asso.); mem. ASCE, ASME, Am. Inst. Aeros, and Astronautics, Am. Nuclear Soc., N.Y. Acad. Sci., Am. Soc. Engring. Edn. (hon.; council mem. 1946-47, 53-55; pres. 1962-63; George Westinghouse award 1951, Lamme medal 1972), Pi Tau Sigma, Tau Beta Pi, Chi Epsilon, Sigma Xi, Phi Kappa Phi. Mem. Christian Ch. Author: Properties of Engineering Materials, 1939, 46, 57; Materials Testing (with Gilkey and Bergman), 1941; Mechanics of Fluids, 1942; Advanced Mechanics of Materials, 1946; Mechanics of Materials, 1948, 59; Similitude in Engineering, 1950; Elements of Nuclear Engineering, 1962, 75; Elementos de Ingeniera Nuclear, 1963; (with Shippy and Luo) Engineering Analogies, published 1963; also various bulls. Asso. editor General Engineering Handbook, 1940. Contbr. tech. jours. Home: Ames, Iowa. Died Apr. 2, 1978.

MURPHY, JOHN JOSEPH, univ. adminstr.; b. N.Y.C., Oct. 22, 1929; s. John Joseph and Sarah Mary (Hanlon) M.; B.A., St. Joseph's Sem. and Coll., 1951; J.D., St. John's U., 1956; m. Ann Maureen Vaughn, July 12, 1958; children—Thomas James, John Joseph (dec.), Paul Andrew. Admitted to N.Y. bar, 1956; asso. atty. firm Goodwin, Savage, Clare & Whitehead, N.Y.C., 1956-61; asst. dean, asst. prof. St. John's U., Sch., of Law, Jamaica, N.Y., 1961-63, asso. prof., 1963-66, prof., 1966-80, dean, 1970-80. Spl. counsel Bd. of Edn., N.Y.C., 1965-68; appellate disciplinary hearing examiner, appellate div., State of N.Y., 1972—; examiner of attys. City of N.Y., 1966-69; insp. of law schs. for accreditation, Am. Bar Assn., 1967-80. Spl. counsel Joint Legis. Com. on Transportation, 1974—; mem. com. on ct. adminstrn. appellate div., 1973-74; mem. Pub. Employment Relations Bd., North Hempstead, N.Y., 1968-80; reporter speedy trial planning com. Fed. Eastern Dist. N.Y., 1975-80; mem. adv. council N.Y. Housing Cts., 1976-80; mem. med., moral and ethics bd. N.Y. Archdiocese, 1976-80. Founding mem., bd. dirs. Bedford-Stuyvesant Legal Services Corp.; v.p., trustee Indsl. Home for the Blind; permanent arbitrator N.Y.C. Bd. Edn. and Union Custodial Engrs.; mem. Cardinal's Task Force on Health, N.Y. Archdiocese; chmn. N.Y. State Security and Privacy Commn., 1977-80. Mem. Am. (sec. legal edn. 1965-80), N.Y. State (sect. family law 1970-80) bar assns., Am. Law Inst. Roman Catholic. Contbr. articles to profl. jours. Home: Manhasset, N.Y. Died Sept. 23, 1980; buried Nassau Knolls, Port Washington, N.Y.

MURPHY, ROBERT DANIEL, business exec.; b. Milw., Oct. 28, 1894; s. Francis Patrick and Catherine Louise (Schmitz) M.; student Marquette U.; LL.B., George Washington U., 1920, LL.M., 1928; LL.D., Marquette U., Notre Dame U., Harvard, Fordham U., N.Y.U., Georgetown U., George Washington U., Boston Coll., Louisville U., L.I.U.; m. Mildred Claire Taylor, Mar. 3, 1921; children—Rosemary and Mildred Margaret (Mrs. Geoffrey Pond). With P.O. Dept., 1916-17, Am. legation, Bern, Switzerland, 1917-19, Treasury Dept., 1919-20; vice consul Zurich, 1921, Munich, 1921-25; counsel Seville, 1925; Dept. State, 1926-30; consul Paris, 1930-36, counselor embassy, 1940; charge d'affaires, Vichy, 1940; detailed Nov. 1940 by Pres. Roosevelt to investigate conditions in French N. Africa; concluded econ. accord with Gen. Maxime Weygand, 1941; effected preparations for Allied landings in N. Africa, Nov. 1942; conducted negotiations for entry of French West Africa into war, Dec. 1942; apptd. Pres.'s personal rep. with rank of minister to French N. Africa; chief civil affairs officer on staff Supreme Comdr., AFHQ. Co-chmn. N. African Econ. Bd., Dec. 1942. Participated in negotiations for Italian armistice, July-Aug. 1943; mem. Mediterranean Adv. Commn. with rank of ambassador, Sept. 1943; apptd. U.S. polit. adviser with rank of ambassador AFHQ, Oct. 1943; apptd. U.S. polit. adviser for Germany, Sept. 1944; dir. office German and Austrian affairs Dept. State, 1949; U.S. ambassador to Belgium, 1949-52, Japan, 1952; asst. sec. state UN Affairs, 1953, dep. under sec. state, 1953, under sec. state for polit. affairs, 1959; hon. chmn. Corning Glass Internat.; dir. Corning Glass Works; dirs. adv. council Morgan Guaranty Trust Co. Bd. dirs. Japan Fund. Decorated Croix de Guerre with palm (France); Order of Leopold (Belgium); Order of Rising Sun (Japan); Order of Merit (Germany); Order of Isabella (Spain); Knight of St. Gregory, Vatican; D.S.M.; Laetare medal U. Notre Dame, 1959. Roman Catholic. Clubs: Metropolitan Alibi (Washington); Chevy Chase (Md.); Univ., Links (N.Y.C.). Author: Diplomat Among Warriors. Home: Washington, D.C. Died Jan. 9, 1978.

MURPHY, VINCENT JOSEPH, public ofcl., labor leader; b. Newark, Aug. 1, 1893; s. Thomas Francis and Sarah (Gaskin) M.; ed. St. Joseph's and St. Patrick's parochial schools, and Newark (N.J.) Bus. Coll.; m. Marie McConnell, May 30, 1917; children—Vincent Joseph, Rita, Elizabeth Louise. Began as apprentice plumber, 1913, journeyman plumber, 1917; sec.-treas., Plumbers Local Union No. 24, Newark, N.J., 1920-38; sec.-treas. N.J. State Fedn. of Labor after 1932; pres. N.J. AFL-CIO, 1961-70; past mem. Newark (N.J.) City Commn., dir. dept. of revenue and finance after 1937, also mayor of Newark, 1941-49; president Union National Bank of Newark. Served with U.S. Navy, World War I. Mem. Social Security Advisory Bd., 1936; mem. State Unemployment Compensation Commn. Trustee Newark Museum; mem. bd. trustees Newark Free Pub. Library, Newark Coll. of Engring., Newark chapter Am. Red. Cross. Chmn. joint planning com. Annual Labor Inst. of Rutgers U. Hon. vice chmn. Am.-Jewish Trade Union Council for Palestine. Member N. J. State Museum; Catholic Commn. for Human Rights, bd. sponsors Nat. Com. to Combat Anti-Semitism; Nat. Pub. Housing Conf., Nat. Indsl. Com. for Y.M.C.A. Mem. Vets. Fgn. Wars, Am. Legion, Cath. War Vets., Irish War Vets., Am. War Dads. Elk, Moose, Eagle, K.C., Kiwanian. Editor of annual report volume of N.J. State Fedn. of Labor from 1935. Home: Spring Lake, N.J. Died June 9, 1976.

MURPHY, WILLIAM THOMAS, Lawyer, congressman; b. Chgo., Aug. 7, 1899; s. William and Ida E. (Riley) M.; LL.B., Loyola U., 1926; m. Rose Mary McInerney, June 12, 1940; children—William Thomas, John P., Rosemary Blyth, Admitted to Ill. bar, 1927, U.S. Supreme Ct. bar, 1944; practice law, Chgo., from 1927; mem. 86th-91st Congresses 3d Dist. Ill., mem. house fgn. affairs com., 1959-71, chmn., sub-com. Asian and Pacific Affairs, 1969-71, mem. Can.-U.S. Interparliamentary Group, 1960-69, 16th Assembly NATO-Parliamentary Group, 1970. Alderman, 17th ward, Chgo., 1935-59, Democratic committeeman, 1940-63; del. 3d Ill. dist. Dem. Nat. Conv., 1944, 48, 52, 56; mem. Chgo. Plan Commn., 1947-59, chmn. com. planning, 1947-55, chmn. com. planning and housing, 1955-59. Served with U.S. Army, 1918. Recipient 10th Commemorative medal Assembly Captive Nations, 1964. Mem. Am. Legion, Delta Theta Phi, Lambda Alpha. Home: Hinsdale, Ill. Died Jan. 29, 1978.

MUSCHENHEIM, CARL, physician, educator; b. N.Y.C., Feb. 4, 1905; s. Frederick Augustus and Elsa (Unger) M.; A.B., Columbia, 1928, M.D., 1931; m. Haroldina Humphreys, July 18, 1929 (div. 1951); children—Linda (Mrs. Mario Perrone), Frederick; m. 2d, Ronda Keane, Apr. 5, 1951; 1 son, Dwight Keane. Intern, asst. resident physician N.Y. Hosp., 1932-35, asst. attending physician, 1938-46, asso. attending physician, 1946-50, attending physician, 1950-73, cons., from 1973; intern, asst. physician Trudeau and Loomis sanatoriums, 1936-37; chief resident physician Bellevue Hosp., 1937-38; instr. medicine Cornell U., 1938-42, asst. prof. medicine, pub. health and preventive medicine, 1942-44, asst. prof. clin. medicine, 1944-46, asso. clin. prof. medicine, 1946-60, clin prof. medicine, 1960-73, emeritus, from 1973; private practice medicine, N.Y.C., from 1944; cons. Franklin D. Roosevelt Hosp., VA, Grasslands Hosp., Valhalla, N.Y., Summit Park Hosp., Pomona, N.Y., Norwalk (Conn.) Hosp. Bd. dirs. Assn. Am. Indian Affairs, chmn. nat. com. on Indian health; hon. bd. dirs. N.Y. Lung Assn., also pres., 1957-59. Recipient Lasker award for medical research, 1955. Fellow A.C.P., N.Y. Acad. Sci., N.Y. Acad. of Medicine; mem. AMA, N.Y., N.Y. County medical socs., Am. Clin. and Climatol. Assn., Am. Thoracic Soc. Editor sect. on chest Year Book of Medicine, 1953-71; editor: (with Cranston W. Holman) Bronchopulmonary Diseases and Related Disorders, 1972. Home: New York, N.Y. Died Apr. 27, 1977.

MUSE, CLARENCE EDOUARD, actor, composer, dir.; b. Balt., Oct. 7, 1889; s. Alexander and Mary (Kellems) M.; LL.B., Dickerson U.; H.H.D., Bishop Coll. Appeared in numerous motion pictures including Hearts In Dixie, Riding High, Huckleberry Finn, Night and Day, Jamaica Run, Sun Shines Bright, Shadow of a Doubt, Porgy and Bess, Buck and the Preacher, The World's Greatest Athlete, A Dream for Christmas; Broadway plays including Dr. Jekyll and Mr. Hyde, Trilby, The Master Mind, Madame X, Thais; TV shows including Kraft Music Hall, Playouse 90, Hallmark Hall of Fame, Walt Disney Swamp Fox series; composer songs When It's Sleepy Time Down South, Liberty Road, Go Congo, Lazy Rain, Magic Lover, Alley-way of My Dreams; founder Lafayette Players of Harlem; producer-dir. Run Little Chillun, Fed. Theatre Project; dir., performer symphony Harlem Heab'n; collaborator story and screenplay (with Langston Hughes) Way Down South, 1939. Life mem. Good Hope Elementary Sch. P.T.A.; mem. Eye Dog Found, for Blind. Recipient awards U. Calif., Berkeley, mayors of Riverside and San Bernarcino (Calif.), Riverside (Calif.) City and County Public Library, Central Labor Council, Rotary, Kiwanis, Lions clubs, other awards; inducted into Black Filmmakers Hall of Fame by Cultural and Ethnic Affairs Guild, Oakland (Calif.) Mus.; cited in Congl. Record. Mem. Screen Actors Guild (pioneer life), A.S.C.A.P., Acad. TV Arts and Scis., Perris Valley C. of C., Phi Beta Sigma (social action dir. western region. distinguished service chpt., Social Action award 1967). *

MUSSER, MARC JAMES, physician, med. adminstr.; b. Terre Haute, Ind., July 3, 1910; s. Marc James and Margaret (Gallagher) M.; A.B., U. Wis., 1930, M.D., 1934; m. Sarah Ann Wiley, Sept. 23, 1933 (dec. 1944); children—Marc David, Barbara (Mrs. Frank Bilek); m. 2d, Gladys Norsetter, Feb. 22, 1946 (div. 1956); 1 son, Stephen J.; m. 3d, Alice Balcuns, Sept. 23, 1957; 1 son, William M. Intern Kansas City (Mo.) Gen. Hosp., 1934-35; resident internal medicine and neuropsychiatry Wis. Gen. Hosp., Madison, 1935-38; mem. faculty U. Wis. Med. Sch., 1938-58, prof. medicine, 1954-58; prof. medicine Baylor U. Coll. Medicine, 1958-59; with VA, 1957-66, dir. research service, asst. chief med., also dir. research and edn. in medicine, Washington, 1959-64, dep. chief med. dir., 1964-66; prof. medicine Duke Sch. Medicine, also exec. dir. N.C. Regional Med. Program, 1966-70; chief med. dir. VA, 1970-74. Served to col. M.C., AUS, 1941-45; PTO. Decorated Legion of Merit. Fellow A.C.P.; mem. A.M.A., Central Soc. Clin. Research, Sigma Sigma, Alpha Omega Alpha, Psi Upsilon, Nu Sigma Nu. Home: Arlington, Va. Died Mar. 29, 1977; buried Arlington (Va.) Nat. Cemetery.

MUSSEY, ROBERT DANIEL, physician; b. Glendale, O., Jan. 10, 1884; s. Reuben Dimond and Mary Harkness (Gano) M.; student U. Cincinnati, 1908; m. Madge Ayres, May 28, 1912; children—Dr. Mary Elizabeth, Frances Gano, Dr. Robert Delevan, Madge Ayres (Mrs. Bilka), Dr. William Clive. Interne Cincinnati General Hospital, 1908-09, receiving physician, 1909-10, intern St. Mary's Hospital, Rochester, Minnesota, 1910-11, out-patient dressing service, 1911-12; asst. in medicine, Mayo Clinic, 1912-16, head of sect., 1916, head sect. on obstetrics, 1921; prof. obstetrics, Mayo Foundation, Grad. Sch., U. of Minn., 1928-50; mem. bd. govs. Mayo Clinic, 1933-49, chmn. bd. govs., 1937-47. Capt., later maj. Med. Corps, U.S. Army, 1917-19. Mem. Olmsted-Houston-Fillmore-Dodge County Med. Soc., Minn. State Med. Assn., Minn. Soc. of Obstetrics and Gynecology (pres. 1937), Minn. Com. on Maternal Welfare (chmn. 1936), Am. Assn. of Obstetricians, Gynecologists, and Abdominal Surgeons (pres. elect 1947), Central Assn. Obstetricians and Gynecologists (pres. 1938), Am. Bd. Obstetrics and Gynecology, 1931-40, Am. Gynecol. Soc., Am. Com. Maternal Welfare (dir. 1934-52), Alumni Assn. Mayo Found., Sigma Xi, A.O.A. Republican. Presbyn. Mason. Clubs: University, Rotary (Rochester). Contbr. to mags. on profl. subjects. Home: Rochester, Minn. *

MUSSIO, JOHN KING, bishop; b. Cincinnati, June 13, 1902; s. John Edward and Blanche (King) M.; A.B., Xavier U., 1924; M.A., Notre Dame U., 1925; J.C.D.,

Angelico U., Rome, Italy, 1939. Ordained priest Roman Cath. Ch., 1935; consecrated and installed as bishop Steubenville (Ohio), 1945; ret., 1977. Address: Steubenville, Ohio. Died Apr. 15, 1978; buried Mt. Calvary Cemetery, Steubenville, Ohio.

MUTCH, THOMAS ANDREW, educator; b. Rochester, N.Y., Aug. 26, 1931; s. Thomas S. and Mildred (MacIntosh) M.; A.B., Princeton, 1952, Ph.D., 1960; M.S. Rutgers U., 1957; m. Madeline E.A. Maurer, Sept. 8, 1956; children—Patricia, Wendelin, Margaret. Asst. prof. Brown U., Providence, 1960-65, asso. prof., 1965-70, prof. geology, 1970-79, asst. dean, 1964-65, asso. dean. Grad. Sch., 1964-67, chmn. dept. geol. scis., 1968-71; geologist U.S. Geol Survey, 1967-74; asso. adminstr. for space sci. NASA, Washington, 1979-80; leader Lander imaging sci. team Viking Mission to Mars; dir. Chief Consol. Mining Co. Served with AUS, 1952-54. Recipient NASA medal for sci. achievement, 1977; various NASA group achievement awards; Cleveland-Newcomb award AAAS, 1977; Eagle award Am. Acad. Sci., 1980; Viking I lander on Mars renamed Thomas A. Mutch Meml. Sta. in his honor, 1981. Fellow Geol. Soc. Am., Am. Astronautical Soc.; mem. Sigma Xi. Club: Am. Alpine (dir. 1958-60, 78-79). Author: Geology of the Moon, 1970; Geology of Mars, 1976; The Martian Landscape, 1978. Address: Washington, D.C. Died Oct. 6, 1980.

MYERS, A(LEXANDER) J(OHN) WILLIAM, clergyman, educator; b. Lake Verd, P.E.I., Can., Dec. 17, 1877; s. Charles and Margaret Sarah Riddell (Moore) M.; B.A., Dalhousie Univ., 1902, M.A., 1904; student Knox Theol. Coll., Toronto, 1903-04, Presbyn. Theological College, Halifax, N.S., 1902-03 and 1904-05 (B.D., 1907); Ph.D., Columbia, 1912; m. Mae Ethel Dickenson, Dec. 1912 (dec. 1948). Teacher, prin. high sch. until 1899; ordained Presbyn. ministry, 1905; pastor Black River, N.B., 1905-09; ednl. sec. Presbyn. Ch. in Can., 1912-17, also sec. Canadian Com. of Religious Edn. Assn.; prof. and head dept. religious education, Hartford Sch. Religious Education (Hartford Sem. Edn.), Dec. 1917-43; acting minister First Ch., Southwick, Mass., 1923-28, Tabernacle United Ch., Belleville, Ont., 1943-45; minister Wanstrad United Church, Toronto, 1945-48. Mem. 82d Regiment Infantry (Can. militia), 1899-1902; Y.M.C.A. war work, Canada and U.S., overseas service, 1917; mem. board Religious Edn. Assn., Fedn. of Churches, Archeol. Inst. of Am., Hort. Soc., Pi Gamma Mu. Clubs: Social Service, United Empire Loyalists, Empire. Author: The Old Testament in the Sunday Sch., 1912; Teaching Values of the Old Testament, 1918; Christian Life in the Community, 1919; What Is Religious Education?, 1925; Educational Evangelism, 1925; Teaching Religion, 1928; Christian Education in the Local Church, 1929; Teaching Religion, 1928; Teachers of Religion, 1932; Teaching Religion Creatively 1932; Horace Bushnell and Religious Education, 1937; Religion for Today, 1942; Enriching Worship. Joint dir., author London Survey, 1913; Huron County Survey, 1914; Commission Survey of Religious Education in the Presbyn. Ch. in Canada; The Country Church as It Is; Living Stone, 1935; Adventuring in China with Kwo Ying. Lecturer on religious education, Reformed Theological Seminary, New Brunswick, N.J., 1922-25, Yale Divinity School, 1927, Univ. of Conn., 1925 and 1934, Auburn Theol. Sem. Summer Sch., Union Theol. Coll., Vancouver, B.C., 1938, Union Seminary, N.Y., 1945. Contbr. articles to religious and ednl. publs. Home: Toronto, Ont., Canada. Died Dec. 2, 1975.

MYERS, CAROLINE CLARK, mag. exec.; b. Morris, Pa., July 14, 1887; d. Charles Edgar and Elizabeth (Boyd) Clark; grad. Bloomsburg State Tchrs. Coll., 1905; student Ursinus Coll., 1907-08, Juaniata Coll., 1912-13, Merill Palmer Sch., Detroit, 1930-31, Tchrs. Coll., Columbia U., summers 1931-34; m. Garry Cleveland Myers, June 26, 1912 (dec. 1971); children—Jack E., Elizabeth Myers Brown, Garry C. (dec.), Laura Spellman. Rockefeller scholar, 1930; dir. parent edn. and family life Cleve. Welfare Fedn., 1931-41; instr. family life and child devel. Cleve. Coll., Western Res. U., 1931-41; leader public forums U.S. Office Edn., 1937; instr. U. Wash., Seattle, summers 1938-41; instr. Oreg. State U., 1942; asso. editor Children's Activities, 1941, 46; co-founder, mng. editor, v.p., dir. Highlights for Children, Honesdale, Pa., 1946-80, chmn. bd., 1970-80. Co-chmn. Community Fund campaign Wayne County Meml. Hosp., 1947, bd. dirs., 1946-60. Recipient Distinguished Service award Bloomsburg State Tchrs. Coll., 1953, B'nai B'rith Citizenship citation, 1971, Nat. Recognition award Freedoms Found., 1976. Mem. Nat. Council Family Relations. Co-author: Myers Mental Measure, 1920; Language of America, 1921; My Work Book in Arithmetic, 1926; Homes Build Persons, 1950; Your Child and You, 1969; compiler, editor handbooks Highlights for Children; contbr. articles and chpts. in profl. publs. Home: Milanville, Pa. Died July 3, 1980; buried Calkins (Pa.) Union Cemetery.

MYERS, DENYS PETER, publicist; born at Newton, Ia., June 26, 1884; son of Reason Watson and Arabella (Kiser) M.; A.B., Harvard, 1906; m. Ethel May Johnston, Jan. 4. 1908; children—Richard (dec.), Denys Peter. Reporter, Davenport (Ia.) Democrat, 1898-1902, Boston Herald, 1904-06, Boston Globe, 1906, Christian Science Monitor, 1908-10; with World Peace Foundation, 1910-42, dir., 1913-16, corr. sec., librarian, 1916-27, research dir., 1927-42; organized Reference Service on Internat. Affairs, Am. Library in Paris, 1924; research librarian Fletcher Sch. of Law and Diplomacy, 1933-42, Department of State, Div. of Spl. Research, June 16, 1942, Div. of Political Studies, February 1, 1943; Div. of Int. Security and Organization, Jan. 15, 1944; Div. of Int. Organization Affairs, Dec. 1944, office of legal adviser, Internat. Orgn. Br., 1947; Division Historical Policy Research, July 20, 1952. Del. Gen. Assembly, Internat. Inst. Agriculture, 1924; Am. commr. under treaty for advancement of peace with Ecuador since 1929; reference specialist, U.N. Conference on Internatl. Organizations, San Francisco, April-June, 1945. Mem. Am. Soc. Internat. Law, Am. Polit. Science Assn., Academy of Polit. Science, Council on Foreign Relations. Episcopalian. Author: Notes on Control of Foreign Relations, 1917; Manual of Collections of Treaties and Collections Relating to Treaties, 1922; Industry, Governments and Labor, 1928; Handbook of the League of Nations Since 1920, 1930; Origin and Conclusion of Paris Pact, 1929; The Reparation Settlement, 1930; World Disarmament—Its Problems and Prospects, 1932; Handbook of the League of Nations, 1935; Massachusetts and the First Ten Amendments to the Constitution, 1936 (the General Court, in consequence of a governor's message, ratified the Bill of Rights March 2, 1939); annual Documents on American Foreign Relations, 1938-42 (with S. Shepard Jones); Process of Constitutional Amendment, 1940; Treaty of Versailles and After; Annotations of Text of Treaty, 1947. Ed., compiler, World Peace Found. pamphlets, 1911-30; co-translator Secret Treaties of Austria-Hungary, 1879-1914, by Pribram; Source Material Department in Foreign Affairs, 1922-41. Contbr. to polit. science jours. Club: Cosmos. Home: Washington DC. Died Feb. 11, 1972; cremated.

MYERS, EDWARD CHARLES, steel corp. exec.; b. York, Pa., Jan. 3, 1912; s. Edward Charles and Matilda M. (Benfer) M.; A.B., Bucknell U., 1934; grad. Advanced Mgmt. Program, Harvard, 1949; m. Edna Ruth Cleckner, June 19, 1936; children—Wendy Ann, Sandra Sue. Observer, Homestead plant Carnegie Steel Co., 1934; plant dir. personnel, welfare and tng. Carnegie-Ill. Steel Corp., 1936; staff asst. pub. relations dept. U.S. Steel Corp. of Del., 1938, staff asst. pub. relations, also coordinator law, indsl. relations and pub. relations depts., 1940-42, asst. dir. pub. relations, 1942-43, asst. to v.p. indsl. relations dept. U.S. Steel Corp. of Del., 1943-51, U.S. Steel Co., 1951-53, asst. v.p. indsl. relations 1953-58, v.p. personnel U.S. Steel Corp., 1958-62, v.p., asst. to pres., 1962-69, v.p., asst. to vice chmn., 1969-74, ret. Mem. President's Com. on Employment of Physically Handicapped; exec. com. dir. Nat. Safety Council; mem. Nat. Council Crime and Delinquency; vice chmn. Greater Pitts. Airport Adv. Com. Mem. organizational services com. Community Chest Pitts.; elder Shadyside Presbyterian Ch.; mem. United Fund Allegheny County. Bd. dirs. Duquesne U., West Pa. Hosp., Pitts. Pirates Found.; v.p. Civic Light Opera Assn. Greater Pitts.; chmn. bd. dirs., mem. exec. com. Comprehensive Health Planning Assn. Western Pa., Pitts. Blind Assn.; trustee Bucknell U., Community Services Pa.; regional bd. dirs. NCCJ; v.p., bd. dirs. Pitts. chpt. Nat. Football Found. and Hall of Fame; mem. men's adv. bd. Home for Crippled Children. Named Pitts. Man of Year in Human Relations, 1968; recipient Silver Anniversary award Sports Illus., 1958; Hall of Fame, Bucknell U. Mem. Greater Pitts. C. of C., Nat. Urban League (mem. commerce and industry council), Am. Iron and Steel Inst., Pub. Affairs Council (dir., mem. exec. com.), N.A.M. (mem. pub. affairs com.). The Conf. Bd. (pub. affairs research council), Hwy. Users Fedn. (mem. program evaluation subcom.), Sigma Chi, Kappa Phi Kappa. Clubs: University, Longue Vuc, Duquesne (Pitts.); Rolling Rock (Ligonier, Pa.). Home: Ligonier, Pa. Died Mar. 17, 1975; interred St. Michael's of the Valley, Rector, Pa.

MYERS, FRANK MARTIN, exec. sec. U.S. Grain Growers; b. Adeline, Ill., Dec. 11, 1882; s. Moses W. and Ella Barbara (Jacobs) M.; B.A., State U. of Ia., 1908; m. Georgia Mae Randall, of Warren, Ill., July 8, 1915. Prin. high sch., West Liberty, Ia., 1908-9, Ft. Madison, 1909-10; partner Myers Bros., farmers, Beaman, Ia., since 1910; dir. and mgr. Farmers' Coöperative Elevator, Beaman, 1913-15; sec. Farmers' Grain Dealers Assn. of Ia., 1916-21; sec. Farmers' Nat. Grain Dealers Assn. (5,000 elevators), 1920-21, v. p. since 1921. Alternate del., later mem. Farmers' Grain Marketing Com. of 17, apptd. to devise nat. coöperative selling agency, since 1920; dir. from Iowa of U.S. Grain Growers, Inc., also exec. sec. Mem. Phi. Beta Kappa, Delta Sigma Rho. Republican. I.O.O.F. Clubs: City, Old Colony (Chicago). Home: Fort Dodge, Ia. *

MYERS, JAY ARTHUR, physician; b. Croton, Ohio, Nov. 25, 1888; s. Charlie and Clara (Baker) M.;; B.S., Ohio U., 1912, M.S. 1913, LL.D., 1954; Ph.D., Cornell U., 1914; M.D., U. Minn., 1920; m. Faithe L. McCracken, June 23, 1909 (dec. 1968); children—Wathena Fay (Mrs. Cranford W. Ingham), Marguerite LaVonne (Mrs. A. Thomas Whaley, dec.), Carlton Jay, Jack Arthur. Mem. faculty U. Minn., 1914-57, prof., 1931-57, then prof. emeritus, chief of chest clinic, 1924-57, attending specialist in diseases of chest Students Health Service, 1920-57; in practice specializing in tuberculosis and diseases of chest, 1920-66; chief of tuberculosis service Mpls. Gen. Hosp., 1924-57, cons. in tuberculosis VA, Mpls., 1946-57, Tb Therapy Study sect. NIH, 1946-68, USPHS, 1949-68. Recipient Dearholt medal Miss. Valley Conf. on Tb, 1950; Varrier-Jones Memorial award, 1956; Certificate of award Minn. State Med. Assn., 1957, U. Minn., 1957; William A. Howe Honor award, 1957; Am Sch. Health Assn. and Harrington award Minn. Junior Assn. of Commerce, 1958, Will Ross medal Nat. Tb. Assn., 1964. Mem. Selective Service Med. Adv. Bd. No. 1, Mpls., 1940-45. Mem. Nat. Tb Assn., AMA, A.C.P., Am. Assn. Anatomists, Am. Pub. Health Assn., AAAS, Am. Coll. Chest Physicians (gold medalist 1947), Am. Sch. Health Assn. (chmn. Tb com.), Am. Assn. Thoracic Surg., Am. Thoracic Soc., World Med. Assn. (a founder), Am. Coll. Health Assn., Minn. Pub. Health Assn., Minn. State Med. Assn., Phi Beta Kappa, Sigma Xi, Alpha Omega Alpha, Nu Sigma Nu, Acacia Republican. Mem Disciples of Christ Ch. Mason (32 deg., Shriner), K.P. Author of numerous books relating to field, 1924-76. Mem. editorial bd. Geriatrics, 1945-73, Sect. XV (tuberculosis) Excerpta Medica, 1949-60, Jour. of Sch. Health; editor in chief Diseases of the Chest, 1946-68, then emeritus; editor in chief Journal-Lancet, 1930-68. Home: Minneapolis, Minn. Died Sept. 11, 1978.

MYERS, RAWDON WRIGHT, ins. exec.; b. Wells, Minn., June 11, 1884; s. Walter F. and Mary Frances (Hovey) M.; student pub. schs. of Minn.; m. Emily Rulon Miller, Oct. 1, 1912. With Nat. Surety Co., N.Y. City, 1904-08; with Aetna Casualty & Surety Co. since 1908, asst. sec., 1911-20, sec., 1920-24, v.p., 1924-29, v.p. and comptroller Aetna Casualty & Surety Co., Aetna Life Ins. Co., Automobile Ins. Co. and Standard Fire Ins. Co., Hartford, Conn., since 1929. Served as capt., U.S. Army, A.E.F., World War I. Clubs: Hartford, Hartford Golf, Fenwick Golf, Fenwick Yacht. Home: West Hartford, Conn. *

MYRICK, KENNETH ORNE, educator; b. Hammonton, N.J., Mar. 10, 1897; s. Lockwood and Helen Ware (Allen) M.; A.B., Harvard, 1918, Ph.D., 1934; M.A., U. Mich., 1924; m. Hester Decker Eppens, Nov. 12, 1927; children—Katherine Hester Mulhern, Prentiss Allen, Helen Faith La Fleur, Deborah Martin. Tchr. English, Phillips Exeter Acad., 1920-21, Dummer Acad., 1921-22; instr. English, U. Mich., 1922-24; asst. prof. Grinnell Coll., 1927-29; asst. prof. English, Tufts U., 1930-39, asso. prof., 1939-46, prof., 1946-66, chmn. dept., 1957-62, now Harriet H. Fay prof. English lit. emeritus; vis. prof. Shrivenham Am. U., 1945, Biarritz Am. U., 1945-46. Served with U.S. Army, 1918-19. Mem. Modern Lang. Assn. Am. (chmn. Shakespeare sect. 1955), New Eng. Assn. Tchrs. English (past pres.), Milton Soc. Am., Renaissance Soc. Am., Am. Assn. U. Profs., Am. Unitarian Assn., Northboro Hist. Soc. Author: Sir Philip Sidney as a Literary Craftsman, 1935. Contbr. profl. publs. Home: Northboro, Mass. Died Oct. 3, 1975; buried Northboro.

MYSKOWSKI, WALTER JOSEPH, lawyer, assn. exec.; b. Lowell, Mass., Aug. 18, 1917; s. John Joseph and Olympia (Stepien) M.; A.B., George Washington U., 1944; student N.Y. U., 1943-44, Glasgow (Scotland) U., 1945; J.D., Harvard, 1948; m. Mary Ruth Funderburk, June 25, 1949; children—Patricia Lois, Janet Ruth. Admitted to Mass. bar, 1948, D.C. bar, 1957, U.S. Supreme Ct. bar, 1962; atty adviser ICC, 1950-54; asst. commerce counsel N.Y., N.H. & H.R.R., 1954-56; asso. firm LaRoe, Winn & Moerman, Washington, 1956-61; practice law specializing transp. law, Washington, 1961-80. Spl. cons. to atty. gen. State N.Y., 1961-80. Served with AUS, 1943-46. Mem. Am. Bar Assn., D.C. Bar Assn., Honorable Order Ky. Cols., Assn. ICC Practitioners (sec 1963-68), Harvard Law Sch. Assn. Republican. Author: Abstracts of Supreme Court Decisions Intepreting the Interstate Commerce Act, 1954, supplement, 1956. Editor-in-chief ICC Practitioneers Jour., 1957-58. Home: Bethesda, Md. Died May 27, 1980; buried Gate of Heaven Cemetery, Silver Spring, Md.

NABOKOV, NICOLAS, composer, writer, educator; b. Russia, Apr. 4, 1903; s. Dimitry and Lydia (von Falz-Fein) N.; student Stuttgart Conservatory, Music Acad., Berlin, Germany, 1920-23; B.A., Licence es Lettres, Sorbonne, Paris, 1924; m. Dominique Cibiel, Mar. 23, 1970; children by previous marriages—Ivan, Peter, Alexander. Came to U.S., 1933, naturalized, 1939. Composer 2 operas, 5 ballets, 3 symphonies, several maj. works for voice and orch.; prof. music history, composition and theory, head dept. music Wells Coll., Aurora, N.Y., 1936-41, St. John's Coll., Annapolis, Md., 1941-44; prof. composition Peabody Conservatory, Balt., 1943-45, 47-51; adviser for cultural affairs U.S. Mil. Govt., Germany, 1945-47; vice chief Voice of Am. to Russia, 1947; sec. gen. Congress for Cultural Freedom, 1951-63; head Berlin Festival, 1963-67; adviser for internal cultural affairs to mayor West Berlin, 1963-78; composer in residence, adviser to pres. on arts Aspen (Colo.) Inst. Humanistic Studies, 1969-78; now mem. faculty, history dept. N.Y. U. Adviser, Festival of Israel, other internat. festivals.

Decorated grand cross Order of Merit of West Germany; chevalier Legion of Honor (France). Mem. Nat. Inst. Arts and Letters, Berlin Acad. Arts and Letters; Club: Century (N.Y.C.). Author: Old Friends and New Music, 1949; Bagazh, Memoirs of a Russian Cosmopolitan, 1975. Home: New York, N.Y. Died Apr. 6, 1978; buried village cemetery, Kolbsheim, Alsace, France.

NABOKOV, VLADIMIR, author; b. St. Petersburg, Russia, Apr. 23, 1899; s. Vladimir and Helene (Rukavishnikov) N.; B.A., Trinity Coll., Cambridge (Eng.) U., 1922; m. Vera Slonim, Apr. 15, 1925 (dec. July 1977); 1 son, Dmitri. Came to U.S., 1940, naturalized, 1945. Prof. Russian lit. Cornell U., 1948-59. Author: Laughter in the Dark, 1938; The Real Life of Sebastian Knight, 1941; Nicolai Gogol, a critical biography, 1944; Bend Sinister, 1947; Spring in Fialta and Other Stories, 1956; Lolita, 1958, screenplay, 1974; Pnin, 1957; Nabokov's Dozen, 1958; Poems, 1959; Invitation to A Beheading, 1959; Pale Fire, 1962; The Gift, 1963; The Defense, 1964; The Eye, 1965; Despair, 1966; The Waltz Invention, 1966; Nabokov's Quartet, 1966; Speak Memory, 1966; King, Queen, Knave, 1968; Ada, 1969; Mary, 1970; Poems and Problems, 1971; Glory, 1971; Transparent Things, 1972; A Russian Beauty and Other Stories, 1973; Strong Opinions, 1973; Look at the Harlequins!, 1974; (stories) Tyrants Destroyed, 1975; (short stories) Details of a Sunset, 1976; The Nabokov/Wilson Letters, 1979; Lectures, vol. I, 1980, vol. II, 1981. Translator: (with commentary) Eugene Onegin, 1964; The Song of Igor's Campaign, 1960. Contbr. sci. papers to entomol. jours. Died July 2, 1977; buried Cemetery of Clarens, Clarens, Switzerland.

NACHMAN, FRED AUGUST, corp. exec.; b. Meadville, Pa., Aug. 30, 1879. s. August and Sara (Weil) N.; m. Selma Hirsch (dec.); children—Adele (Mrs. Lasalle Felheim), Fred A.; m. 2d, Anita Zeisler. Vice pres. Schultz & Hirsch Co., Chgo., 1912-15; pres. Nachman Corp., Chgo., 1916-47, chmn. bd., 1947-56, chmn. exec. com., 1956—. Home: Chicago, Ill. *

NAGY, FERENC, ex-premier of Hungary; b. Bisse, Hungary, Oct. 8, 1903; s. Ferenc and Julianna (Káta) N.; ed. pub. schs.; LL.D., Bloomfield Coll., 1948, U. Cal. at Berkeley, 1957; m. Juliette Balog, Jan. 24, 1924; children—Ferenc, Julia, László, Sophia, Maria. Sec. gen. Smallholders' party 1930; mem. parliament, 1939; prisoner of Gestapo, 1944; pres. Nat. Assembly, 1945; minister of reconstrn., 1945; prime minister Hungary, 1946-47; exile of Communism, 1947; mem. Central Eastern European Com., 1951; chmn. Assembly Captive European Nations, 1961-62; pres. Internat. Peasant Union, 1964. Lectr. colls. and univs., 1963-79. Author: Struggle Behind the Iron Curtain, 1948; articles: How the Russians Grabbed My Government 1947, Around the Iron Curtain, 1949. Home: Herndon, Va. Died June 12, 1979.

NAISH, JOHN VINCENT, airplane exec.; b. N.Y.C., 1907; grad. Fordham U., 1929, LL.D., 1960, D.Sc., 1966; m. Alice Hines; children—Richard, John. Former pres. Convair, San Diego; former sr. v.p., mem. bd. mgmt. Gen. Dynamics Corp.; pres. Electrocom., Inc.; dir. McDonnell Aircraft. Mem. Calif. State Med. Bd. Chmn. adv. bd. Mercy Hosp., San Diego; v.p., dir. San Diego United Fund; bd. lay trustees Fordham U. Decorated knight Order of Holy Sepulchre of Jerusalem. Mem. Nat. Assn. Purchasing Agts. (hon.), Nat. Security Indsl. Assn. (ordnance adv. com.), Am. Rocket Soc., Air Force Assn., Navy League, Nat. Aero. Assn., Air Force Aid Soc., Western Indsl. Nurses Assn. (mgmt. adv. board), San Diego Symphony Assn. (dir.), Aerospace Industries Assn. (bd. govs.). Clubs: Cuyumaca, La Jolla Country. Home: La Jolla, Calif. Died Dec. 10, 1978.

NANNES, CASPAR HAROLD, newspaper journalist, editor; b. Fall River, Mass., May 15, 1906; s. Max and Minnie (Silverstein) N.; A.B., Rutgers U., 1931, A.M., 1932, Litt.D., 1966; Ph.D., U. Pa., 1948. Instr. English, Rutgers U., 1931-35, 38-42, U. Ill., 1935-38; gen. reporter Washington Evening Star, 1943-49, tennis editor, 1946-60, religious news editor, 1949-66. Recipient Religious Pub. Relations Council award, 1954, Rutgers Alumni Trustees award, 1959, Religious Heritage of Am. award, 1963, W. Dickson Cunningham Sr. Tennis award, 1963, R.S. Reynolds award Presbyn. Ch. U.S., 1964. Mem. Religious Newswriters Assn. (pres. 1956-58), Lawn Tennis Writers Assn. Am. (gov. 1951), Middle Atlantic Lawn Tennis Assn. (v.p. 1948-60), Modern Lang. Assn., Nat. Press Club, Phi Beta Kappa. Clubs: Rutgers (pres. 1943-63), Edgemoor (Washington). Author: Politics in the American Drama, 1960; Cavalcade '76, 1974. Contbr. numerous mag. articles to nat. publs. Home: Washington, D.C. Died Nov. 25, 1978.

NASH, NATHANIEL CUSHING, lawyer; born Cambridge, Mass., June 19, 1885; Nathaniel Cushing and Nellie Munro (Fessenden) N.; grad. Noble and Greenough Sch., 1903; A.B., Harvard, 1907, LL.B., 1911; m. Mary Evelyn Howe, Aug. 9, 1919; children—Priscilla, Nathaniel Cushing IV. Admitted to Mass. bar, 1911, and since in gen. practice at Boston; in employ Boyden, Palfrey, Bradlee & Twombly, 1910-12; mem. firm Goodale & Nash, 1912-18; in practice alone, 1920-30; mem. firm Jones, Nash & Birmingham, 1930-54. Served as 1st lt. Ordnance Dept. U.S. Army, 1918-19; 1st lt. Ordnance O.R.C., 1920-22, Mass. N.G., 1922-23, capt., 1923-24, maj. 1924-30, lt. col. and state ordinance officer, 1930-36; col. Mass. Nat. Guard, retired, 1936-41; lieut. col. Ordnance, Mass. State Guard, div. ordnance officer, 1941-43; col. state staff, state judge advocate gen. and dept. chief of staff, 1943-44, State Judge Adv. 1944-45; col., retired, 1945. Mem. Cambridge Common Council, 1914-15. Mem. Am. Massachusetts, Boston bar assns., Military Collectors and Historians, American Ordnance Association, Nat. Rifle Assn. (ex-pres.), Massachusetts Rifle Association, Mass. Commandery Military Order of Foreign Wars (past commander), Military Order World War (past adjutant Boston chapter), Society Colonial Wars, Massachusetts, Mil. Hist. Soc. Mass., Bostonian Soc., Bunker Hill Monument Assn., Lincoln's Inn Soc. (founder), Inst. 1770, Hasty Pudding Club, Delta Kappa-Epsilon. Republican. Unitarian. Clubs: Union, Union Boat (Boston); Army and Navy (Washington); Eastern Yacht (Marblehead); Faculty, Harvard Varsity (Cambridge).*

NASH, ROBERT LEWIS, coll. pres.; b. Vernon, Wis., May 2, 1910; s. Charles Elmer and Florence Anna (Smith) N.; B.A., Muskingum Coll., 1932; M.A., Ohio State U., 1938; Ed.D., No. Colo. U., 1957; m. Mary Marie Pigman, Aug. 10, 1935. Classroom tchr. Coshocton and Columbus (O.) Bds. Edn., 1932-45; adminstr. elementary and secondary schs. Columbus Bd. Edn., 1945-57; adminstr. jr. high sch. program No. Ill. U., 1957-62; chmn. edn. dept., dean Evening and Summer Sch., Towson State Coll., Balt., 1962-66; asst. to pres. Sauk Valley Coll., Dixon, Ill., 1967-68; pres. Cecil Community Coll., North East, Md., 1968-79. Bd. dirs. North East Symphony Soc.; resident agt. Cecil Coll. Found.; sec. Md. Council Community Coll. Presidents. Recipient Outstanding Tchr. award, Columbus, 1955, Community Coll. Leadership award Mich. State U., 1968, Distinguished Service award Ohio Dept. Elementary Prins., 1965. Mem. N.E.A., Md. Tchrs. Assn., Cecil County (Man of Year, treas.), North East chambers commerce, Phi Delta Kappa. Democrat. Episcopalian. Lion. Home: Elkton, Md. Died June 8, 1979.

NASMITH, CHARLES ROY (NA'SMITH), fgn. service officer; b. Mannsville, N.Y., July 18, 1882; s. Rev. Jared Spalding and Florence Sarah (Wake) N.; prep. edn., Cary Collegiate Sem., Oakfield, N.Y., and Colgate Acad.; A.B., Colgate U., 1904, A.M., 1916; studied law, Harvard, 4 mos.; m. Evelyn Mary Kirkpatrick, June 5, 1915; 1 dau., Annette Evelyn. Apptd. vice consul at Limoges, France, Apr. 22, 1907; vice consul gen., Brussels, Belgium, 1911-17; detailed to Amsterdam, Holland, 1917; vice consul Rotterdam, 1918; detailed as consul temporarily in charge Am. Consulate Gen., at Brussels, Dec. 1918-May 1919; consul at Ghent, 1918-24, Newcastle-on-Tyne, Eng., 1924-27, reopening Am. Consulate which had been closed over 18 mos.; consul at Porto Alegre, Brazil, 1927-31, Marseilles, France, 1930-35, consul in charge, Edinburgh, Oct. 23, 1935; in charge consulate at Liverpool, Aug. 1943-Mar. 7, 1944. Re-assigned to Edinburgh; retired Dec. 1, 1946. Elected fellow of Royal Society of Edinburgh, 1937. Mem. Phi Beta Kappa, Beta Theta Pi. Clubs: University, Rotary, Royal Soc. Club (Edinburgh) Home: Marion, N.Y.*

NASON, ALVIN, educator, research biochemist; b. Coatsville, Pa., June 10, 1919; s. Samuel and Rose (Vilensky) N.; B.S., Cornell U., 1940; A.M., Columbia, 1948, Ph.D. (Lalor fellow), 1949; m. Thelma Stein, Oct. 18, 1944; children—Deborah Rose, Steffi Ruth, Jean Lenore, Gerson Samuel, Benjamin Matthew. Research asst. genetics Carnegie Inst., 1940; chemist Chromium Corp. Am., 1941-42; agt. field lab. tung investigation Dept. Agr., 1942-43; teaching asst. Columbia, 1946-48; asst. prof. biology McCollum-Pratt Inst., Johns Hopkins, 1949-54, asso. prof., 1954-58, prof., 1958-78, asso. dir. inst., 1959-78. Mem. panel NSF; cons. NIH. Mem., chmn. vis. com. biology Brookhaven Nat. Lab. Recipient travel award NRC to 4th Internat. Biochem. Congress, Vienna, Austria, 1958. Served to 1st lt. USAAF, 1943-46. Mem. Am. Soc. Biol. Chemistry, Am. Chem. Soc., Soc. Am. Bacteriology, Am. Soc. Plant Physiology, Soc. Gen. Physiologists, A.A.A.S., A.A.U.P., Phi Beta Kappa, Sigma Xi. Author: Textbook of Modern Biology; Essentials of Modern Biology; co-author: Biology, Introduction to Life: The Biological World. Editor-in-chief Analytical Biochemistry, 1959-78. Contbr. numerous articles. Home: Baltimore, Md. Died Jan. 28, 1978.

NATHANSON, DON PAUL, advt. exec.; b. Mpls., Apr. 16, 1914; s. Benjamin L. and Frances (Rosenberg) N.; B.A., U. Minn., 1937; m. Evelyn Hoberman, Aug. 27, 1939; children—Jill, Marc, Greg. Pres., Manson-Gold Advt. Agy., Mpls., 1937-46; pub. Radio Showmanship mag., 1939-44; freelance radio writer, Hollywood, Calif., 1945-46 dir. advt. and pub. relations Toni Co., 1946-52; v.p. Weiss & Geller Advt. Agy., Chgo., 1952-55; pres., chief exec. officer North Advt. Agy. of Chgo., 1955-70; pres., chief exec. officer Grey-North Inc. Advt. Agy. of Chgo., 1971-74, chmn. bd., 1974-77; exec. v.p. Harriscope Broadcasting Corp., 1956-77; chief exec. officer Falcon Communications Corp. (owners 30 CATV systems in Calif.; pres. Advance Corp. (owner Sta. KFBB-TV, Great Falls, Mont.), Eagle Communications Inc., (owners Stas. KECI-TV, Missoula, Mont., KTVM, Butte-Bozeman, Mont., KCFW, Kalispell, Mont.); dir. Films Inc. Bd. dirs. Erickson Inst. for Early Childhood Edn., Acorn Fund. Recipient various public service advt. awards Cannes Internat. Film Festival, N.Y. Internat. Film Festival, Chgo. Film Festival. Mem. Phi Beta Kappa. Home: Los Angeles, Calif. Died Dec. 24, 1980; buried Mpls.

NATTA, GIULIO, educator; b. Impwoila, Italy, Feb. 26, 1903; s. Francesco and Elena Crespi; Dr. Chem. Engring. Tchr. gen. and inorganic chemistry Pavia U.; prof. phys. chemistry Rome U., indsl. chemistry Turin U.; indsl. chemistry Milan Polytech. Pioneer devel. stereoregular (isotactic, syndiotactic and polytactic) polymers; also numerous macromolecule discoveries. Recipient Nobel prize chemistry, 1963, also various gold medals, hon. degrees. Mem. Lincei Acad., Lombard Inst. Sci. and Letters, also hon. memberships in fgn. chem. socs. Contbr. articles phys. and indsl. chemistry tech. and sci. periodicals. Home: Milan, Italy. Died May 2, 1979.

NAUMANN, OSCAR JOHN, clergyman; b. Wood Lake, Minn., June 24, 1909; s. Justus Henry and Maria (Scherf) N.; B.A., Northwestern Coll., 1931; grad. Luth. Theol. Sem., 1934; grad. student U. Minn.; m. Dorothy Wilhelmina Schwarz, Sept. 5, 1936; children—Myrna Ruth, Philip Gustav, Thomas Paul, Martin Oscar, Peter Justus, James Walter, Paul Stephen. Asst. instr. Northwestern Coll., Watertown, Wis., 1934-36; ordained to ministry Luth. Ch.; pastor Arlington Ave. Luth. Ch., Toledo, 1936-40; prof. Dr. Martin Luther Coll., New Ulm, Minn., 1940-46; pastor St. John's Luth. Ch., St. Paul, 1946-59; pres. Minn. dist. Wis. Synod, 1948-53; pres. Wis. Evang. Luth. Synod, from 1953. Home: Milwaukee, Wis. Died June 19, 1979.

NAVARRO, TOMÁS, univ. prof.; b. La Roda, Spain, Apr. 12, 1884; s. Juan and Joaquina (Tomás) N.; B.A., Instituto de Segunda Enseñanza of Alicante, 1900; M.A., U. of Madrid, 1904, Ph.D., 1905; Litt. D., Middlebury (Vt.) Coll., 1940; m. Dolores Guiaro, Dec. 4, 1914; children—Joaquina, Paquita. Prof., Centro de Estudios Históricos, Madrid, Spain, 1914-36; prof. Spanish phonetics, U. of Madrid, 1931-36, dir. courses for fgn. students, 1916-23; lecturer U. of Puerto Rico, 1925, 27-28; prof. Spanish philology, Columbia, since 1940. Mem. Spanish Acad.; corr. Hispanic Soc. Am.; hon. mem. Am. Academy Sciences and Letters. Author of several books in Spanish since 1918. Home: N.Y. City. *

NEAL, A(LFRED) G(ORMAN), public utilities; b. Upper Marlboro, Md., Aug. 22, 1886; s. John Tyler and Mary S. (Robinson) N.; educated public schools; m. Margaret McCambridge, Apr. 27, 1956; 1 dau., (previous marriage) Margaret C. (Mrs. John Charles Daly, Jr.). Steno-typist, Citizens Nat. Bank, Baltimore, 1903; clerk and cashier, National Biscuit Co. in Baltimore, Atlantic City, New Haven (Conn.), Haverhill (Mass.), 1903-06, traveling bookkeeper and auditor, 1906-12, assistant general auditor, 1912-16; assistant comptroller, Berry Brothers Varnish Co., Detroit, 1916-17; with Washington Ry. & Elec. Co. (includes Potomac Elec. Power Co.) since 1918, pres. 1939-48, chmn. bd., 1948—; member board directors, chmn. executive committee Potomac Electric Power Co. Mason. Republican. Episcopalian. Clubs: Rotary, Metropolitan (Washington); Columbia and Chevy Chase (Md.). *

NEAL, HAROLD L., JR., broadcasting exec.; b. Macon, Ga., Mar. 25, 1924; s. Harold L. and Helen (Meyer) N.; ed. Wayne State U., Mich. State U.; m. Shirley Labine, Aug. 22, 1947; children—Barbara, Nancy, David. Staff announcer radio sta. WXYZ, Detroit, 1943-51, promotion mgr., 1950, asst. sales mgr., 1951-56, dir. sales, 1956, gen. mgr. sta., 1956-60; v.p., gen. mgr. WABC, N.Y.C., 1960-63; pres. Owned Radio Stas. div. ABC, 1963-72, pres. ABC-Radio, 1972-80. Mem. N.Y. State Broadcasters Assn., Radio Advt. Bur. (dir.), Internat. Radio and TV Soc., Nat. Assn. Broadcasters, Advt. Council (dir.). Club: Country (Darien, Conn.). Home: Darien, Conn. Died Feb. 28, 1980.

NEALE, JOHN ERNEST, Brit. historian; b. Liverpool, Eng., Dec. 7, 1890; M.A., Liverpool U., 1915, D.Litt. (hon.); student Univ. Coll., London, 1914-19; D.Litt. (hon.) Birmingham, Cambridge, Leeds, Wales, London universities; Dr. Letters of Humanity (hon.), Amherst Coll.; married to Elfreda Skelton, Oct. 10, 1932; 1 dau., Stella. Asst. history dept. Univ. Coll., 1919-25. Astor Prof. English history, 1927-56, prof. emeritus, 1956-75, Creighton lectr., 1950; prof. modern history Manchester U., 1925-27; Ford's lectr. English history Oxford, 1941-42; Raleigh lectr. Brit. Acad., 1948. Mem. treasury com. House of Commons Records, Brit. Govt., 1929. Trustee London Mus., 1945—. Created knight, 1955. Fellow Brit. Acad., 1949; mem. Royal Hist. Soc. (hon. v.p. 1955); fgn. hon. mem. Am.

Acad. Arts and Scis. Author: Queen Elizabeth I, 1934; The Age of Catherine de Medici, 1943; The Elizabethan House of Commons, 1949; Elizabeth I and Her Parliaments, 1559-1581, 1953; Elizabeth I and Her Parliaments, 1584-1601, 1957; Essays in Elizabethan History, 1958. Member of the editorial board History of Parliament Trust, 1951-72. Contbr. papers hist. jours. Home: Beaconsfield, Buckinghamshire, England. Died Sept. 5, 1975; inurned Stonefall Cemetery Harrogate Yorkshire England

NEALIN, PATRICIA LORETTO, broadcasting exec.; b. Chgo.; d. Daniel Edward and Elizabeth Therese (Hallisey) Nealin; B.A., Mundelein Coll., 1949. With WGN Continental Broadcasting Co., Chgo., 1952-77, film editor, asst. film dir., dir. films, 1960-73, mgr., 1974-77, mem. editorial bd., 1971-74, chmn., 1974-77. Mem. Am. Women in Radio and TV (pres., past dir. at large, past nat. sec.-treas.), Am. Women in Radio and TV Ednl. Found. (trustee), Broadcast Pioneers, Sigma Delta Chi, Kappa Gamma Pi. Club: Chicago Headline. Home: Chicago, Ill. Died Jan. 25, 1977.

NEARING, SCOTT, sociologist; b. Morris Run, Pa., Aug. 6, 1883; s. Louis and Minnie (Zabriskie) N.; student U. Pa. Law Sch., 1901-02; B.S., U. Pa. 1905, Ph.D. 1909; B. Oratory, Temple U., 1904; D. Hum., Clark U., 1974; m. Nellie Marguerite Seeds, Juen 20, 1908; m. 2d, Helen Knothe, 1947. Sec., Pa. Child Labor Com., 1905-07; instr. econs. U. Pa., 1906-14, asst. prof., 1914-15, prof. emeritus econs., 1973—; instr. econs. Swarthmore Coll. 1908-13; prof. social sci., dean Coll. Arts and Sci., Toledo U., 1915-17; lectr. Rand Sch. Social Sci., N.Y.C., 1916; chmn. People's Council Am., 1917-18; now chmn. Social Sci. Inst. Author or co-author numerous books since 1908; latest publ.; (with Helen K. Nearing) The Maple Sugar Book, 1950; Living the Good Life, 1954; USA Today, 1955; Socialists Around The World, 1958;The Brave New World, 1958; Economics for the Power Age, 1952; Man's Search For the Good Life, 1954; Freedom; Promise and Menace, 1961; Socialism in Practice, 1962; The Conscience of a Radical, 1965; The Making of a Radical, 1972. *

NEBEL, LONG JOHN, radio show host; b. Chgo., June 11, 1911; s. John and Laura (Zimmerman) Knebel; student pub. schs., Chgo.; m. Candy Jones, Dec. 31, 1972; 1 dau., Jacqueline Nebel LaVetty. Orch. leader and musician-tenor banjo and guitar, 1930; profl. photo-journalist, mgr. Willoughby's Camera Store, 1940-48; owner, mgr. Long John's Auction, Parsippany, N.J., 1948-56; radio show host WOR, 1956-64, WNBC, 1964-72, Long John Nebel/Candy Jones Show, WMCA, N.Y.C., 1972-78. Tchr., Modern Sch. Photography, Spadra Sch. Criminology. Mem. Med. Found. Prospect Hosp., N.Y.C. Author: The Way-Out World of Long John Nebel, 1961; The Psychic World Around Us, 1969. Recs. Long John Nebel and the Phil Moore Four and Friends, 1971. Home: New York, N.Y. Died Apr. 10, 1978.

NEEB, MARTIN JACOB, clergyman; b. Augsburg, Ont., Can., Oct. 1, 1906; s. John and Lydia (Rohfrietsch) N.; came to U.S., 1913, naturalized, 1914; student Concordia Coll., 1922-24, Concordia Sem., St. Louis, 1924-29, D.D., 1972; M.A., U. Tex., 1937; LL.D., Concordia Tchrs. Coll., 1953; L.H.D., Valparaiso U., 1959; m. Severa Basilius, July 3, 1929; children—Martin John, Larry William. Prof. English, Luth. Concordia Coll., Austin, Tex., 1929-45; vis. instr. radio speech, U. Tex., 1943-45; exec. sec. bd. for higher Edn. Luth. Ch. Mo. Synod, 1945-55; pres. Concordia Sr. Coll., Ft. Wayne, Ind., 1955-72; cons. to Bd. for Higher Edn. Luth. Ch.-Mo. Synod, 1972-76. Chief narrator Tex. Sch. Air, 1942-45; exec. sec. Tex. Coll. Assn., 1936-45; pres. Nat. Luth. Ednl. Conf., 1960-76. Mem. Nat. Assn. Gen. Edn., Am. Soc. Ch. Architecture. Address: Saint Louis, Mo. Died Aug. 23, 1976.

NEELD, GEORGE AVERY, clergyman; b. Cawnpore, India (parents Am. citizens), Oct. 28, 1882; s. Frank Lawrence and Emma Leonora (Avery) N.; A.B., Wesleyan U., Middletown, Conn., 1905, A.M., 1913; B.D., Drew Theol. Sem., 1908; A.M., Harvard, 1924; m. Sarah Agnes Scudder, June 29, 1908 (died 1944); 1 dau., Leonora Agnes (Mrs. L. A. Schuttig); m. 2d Irene Marvin Eklund, Aug. 14, 1947. Pastor; Oakland M.E. Ch., Pittsburgh, Pa., 1914-19; dir. Ohio Sch. of Religion, Columbus, Ohio, 1920-21; pastor Claremont Community Ch. (Congl.), 1921-23, North Congl. Ch., St. Johnsbury, Vt., 1924-41, First Church of Christ (Congl.), New London, Conn, 1941-47; interim pastor 1st Fgn. Ch. of Hilo, Hawaii, 1947-48; now teacher lit., philosophy U. of Baltimore, First Ch. of Christ was founded in 1642 and included among its first members, the early govs. of Conn. Dir., trustee Boston Seamans Friend Soc., Vt. Congl. (chmn. exec. com.); vice pres. Vt. League of Nations Assn.; pres. bd. trustees, Learned Mission; pres. Fedn. of Chs., New London and vicinity; director South Memorial Home; v.p. League of Nations and United Nations Assn. (Connecticut branch); member Connecticut council of Congress; and Religious Edn. Del. Nat. Council of Congl. and Congl. Christian Chs. (3 times), commn. on internat. relations of Nat. Council and Conn. Council of Chs.; Vt. del. to 6th Internat. Council Congl. Ch., Wellesley, Mass.; del. Vt. League of Nations Assn. to annual meeting Nat. League of Nations Assn.; rep. Conn. Council of Chs. at Nat. Study Conf. (Protestant Chs.) on a Just and Durable Peace, Delaware, O., 1942, Del. New London Fedn. Chs. to Nat. Study Conf. on The Churches and a Just and Durable Peace, Cleveland, O., Jan. 16-19, 1945. Mem. Am. Soc. Internat. Law, Am. Polit. Science Assn., Am. Hist. Assn., Am. Soc. Ch. History, Browning Soc., Phi Nu Theta. Ind. Republican. Mason, Rotarian. Club: Sphinx. Contbr. numerous articles on internat. affairs. Speaker on internat. affairs on programs of religious confs., civic, service and edn. meetings. Traveled in Europe studying internat. relations, 1927-31-35-39. Home: Baltimore, Md. *

NEELY, FRANK H., business exec.; b. Augusta, Ga., Jan. 19, 1884; s. Benjamin and Henrietta Eve (Carmichael) N.; student Ga. Sch. Tech., 1904; m. Rae Schlesinger, Feb. 4, 1908; 1 dau. Rachel Eve (Mrs. Benjamin M. Parker). Began with Westinghouse Electric & Mfg. Co., successively draftsman, designing engr., prodn. engr.; cons. engr. factory mgmt re-orgn. So. factories, 1910-12; with Fulton Bag & Cotton Mills, 1912-24; gen. mgr., sec. Rich's Inc., Atlanta, 1924, later exec. v.p., sec., became pres. 1947, chmn. bd. 1949-61, exec. com. chmn., 1961-70, hon. chmn., 1970—, also dir.; former chmn. 6th Dist. Fed. Res. Bank of Atlanta. Regional dir. WPB, Atlanta, 1942. Past Pres. Ga. Tech. Alumni Found., Inc.; past trustee Ga. Tech. Research Inst.; adv. com. Tallulah Falls Sch.; bd. counsellors Smith Coll.; former chmn. Ga. Dept. Commerce and Ga. Better Roads Com.; former mem. Ga. Water Law Revision Commn.; chmn. Ga. Nuclear Adv. Commn., 1956—, Atlanta Area council Boy Scouts Am., Atlanta Community Chest, 3 yrs., So. unemployment Relief Com., 1932, Atlanta Bond Commn., Fulton County Pub. Welfare Bd.; mem. spl. com. on orgn. Hoover Commn., 1954-55, now mem. com. on bus. orgn. for Dept. of Def., also mem. Procurement Task Force. Recipient Gantt medal Am. Mgmt. Assn.; Taylor Key, 1958; Roy V. Wright lectr. Am. Soc. M.E., 1951. Fellow A.A.A.S., Am. Inst. Indsl. Engrs., Am. Soc. M.E.; mem. Newcomen Soc., Soc. Advancement Mgmt., Ga., Atlanta chambers commerce, Men's Garden Clubs Am., North Ga. Camellia Soc., Union Soc. Savannah, Am., Ga. heart assns., Ga. Engring. Soc. (life), Atlanta Jr. C. of C. (life), S.C.V., Nat. (past dir.), Atlanta (past pres.) retail mchts. assns., Nat. Bur. Econ. Research, Phi Kappa Phi, Kappa Phi Kappa (Distinguished Service award). Clubs: Piedmont Driving, Capital City, Standard Town and Country (Atlanta); City, Cherokee Country (Knoxville, Tenn.). Home: Atlanta GA. *

NEESER, ROBERT WILDEN, author; b. Seabright, N.J., July 16, 1884; s. John G. and Josephine C. (Wilden) N.; A.B., Yale, 1906, A.M., 1909; m. May 15, 1919, Susanne Belin; children—John S. (dec.), Odile Elvine, Beatrice, Robert M., Marie-José. Asst. to Am. naval attaché, Paris, 1917-18; 1st lt. inf., attached to G-2, S.O.S., A.E.F., France, 1918-19; liaison officer to Am. naval attaché, Paris, 1920-21; mgr. in France, Western Union Telegraph-Cable System, 1921-23. Decorated Médaille de la Reconnaissance Française, 1917; French Academic Palms, 1919, and Cross Legion of Honor (French). Mem. Am. Hist. Assn., Naval Hist. Soc. of U.S., U.S. Naval Inst. (life); asso. mem. Académie de Marine. Author: Statistical and Chronological History of the United States Navy (1775-1907), 1909; A Landsman's Log, 1913; Despatches of Molyneux Shuldham (1776), 1913; Our Navy and the Next War, 1915; Our Many-Sided Navy, 1914; Cruises of Gustavus Conyngham (1777-1781), 1915; Ship-Names of the United States Navy, 1922; American Naval Songs and Ballads, 1938; also articles in periodicals on naval subjects. Home: Rumson, N.J. *

NEET, CLAUDE CASSELL, educator, psychologist; b. Glendora, Calif., Feb. 9, 1905; s. Frederick Cassell and Mabelle (Rouse) N.; A.B., UCLA, 1930; A.M. (scholar 1930-31), Clark U., 1932, Ph.D. (fellow), 1935; m. Beulah Lillian Schurter, June 17, 1931; children—Linda Larkin (Mrs. Donald Rose), Nancy Jane (Mrs. Robert Raskevitz), Susan Elizabeth. Instr. psychology U. Nev., 1934-35; instr. edn. and psychology U. Mass., 1935-36, asst. prof. psychology, 1936-43, prof. psychology, 1943-69, prof. emeritus, 1969-78, head dept., 1947-67. Chmn. U. Mass. War Com., 1941-45. Fellow Am., Mass. psychol. assns.; mem. Eastern Psychol. Assn., Psychonomic Soc., N.Y. Acad. Scis., Am. Assn. Emeriti, Psi Chi, Sigma Xi. Contbr. articles to psychology jours. Home: Osterville, Mass. Died Oct. 30, 1978; interred Mosswood Cemetery, Cotvit, Mass.

NEFF, SHERMAN BROWN, prof. English; b. Bolton, Harrison County, Mo., Aug. 21, 1886; s. Francis Marion and Louisa Caroline (Montgomery) N.; student U. of Mo., 1904-07; A.B., Yale, 1908; A.M., 1909; A.M., Harvard, 1911, Ph.D., 1916; student U. of Paris (France), 1923-24; m. Jessie Verna Utz, Aug. 26, 1912; children—Emily (Mrs. Pierre Victor Bernard), Philip Duncan. Instr. in English, Colby Coll., Waterville, Me., 1911-12; head of English Dept., Salem (Mass) Classical and High Sch., 1912-13; prof. of English and head of dept., New Mexico Coll., of Agr. and Mechanic Arts, College Station, N.M., 1914-19, North Texas State Teachers Coll., Denton, Tex., North Texas State Teachers Coll., Denton, Tex., 1919-23; asso. prof. of English, Washington and Lee U., Lexington, Va., 1924-26; prof. English and head of dept., U. of Utah, 1926-52; prof. emeritus 1952—; prof. English, chmn. div. humanities Wayland Coll., 1955-65. Author: The Province of Art; An Approach through Literature, 1959; Lazarus and other Poems, 1962. Address: Plainview, Tex. *

NEHRLING, ARNO HERBERT, horticulturist; b. Freistadt, Mo., July 25, 1886; s. Henry and Sophia (Schoff) N.; student Shaw Sch. Botany, Washington U., 1905-09; m. Irene Dahlberg, Sept. 18, 1923; children—Arno Herbert, Dorothy Irene (Mrs. Warren P. Higgins). Asst. floriculture U. Ill., 1910-13; prof., head dept. Mass. Agri. Coll., 1914-17; pres. McDonald Floral Co., Crawfordsville, Ind., 1917-21; prof. floriculture Cornell U., 1921-27; sales mgr. Hill Floral Products Co., Richmond, Ind., 1927-33; dir. exhbns. Mass. Hort. Soc., Boston, 1933—, exec. sec., also dir. publs., 1947-63. Recipient Tessie K., Scharps Meml. membership award for outstanding service to horticulture Hort. Soc. N.Y., 1954; distinguished achievement citation and plaque for outstanding service to cause of home beauty Asso. Bulb Growers of Holland, 1954; gold medal Men's Garden Clubs Am., 1956; Arthur Hoyt Scott garden and horticulture award Swarthmore Coll., 1957; citation Am. Hort. Council, 1958; named horticulturist of the year U. Mass., 1958; large gold medal Mass. Hort. Soc., 1958; gold medal Hort. Soc. of New York, 1963. Chmn. Nat. Flower Show Com., Soc. Am. Florists (pres. 1937-38, member of the Floricultural Hall of Fame 1964); mem. Chrysanthemum Soc. America (secretary 1930-37, president 1942), Massachusetts Agricultural Club (secretary 1943-45), North America Lily Soc. (president 1954-55); Am. Hort. Council (v.p. 1954-56, dir.), Hort. Club of Boston (pres. 1955-58), Northeastern Florists Assn. (regional dir.), Am. Rose Soc. (registration com.), Am. Tulip Soc. (dir.), Am. Carnation Soc. (hon.), Kappa Sigma, Alpha Gamma Rho, Pi Alpha Xi (1st nat. pres.). Author: (with Mrs. Nehrling) An Easy Guide to House Plants, 1958; Gardening, Forcing, Conditioning and Drying for Flower Arrangements, 1958; (with Mrs. Nehrling) Peonies Outdoors and In, 1960. Propagating House Plants, 1962. The Picture Book of Perennials, 1964. Home: Needham Heights, Mass. *

NEILL, MARSHALL ALLEN, U.S. judge; b. Pullman, Wash., Aug. 23, 1914; s. Roy A. Neill and Maude (Cameron) N.; B.A. in Polit. Sci., Wash. State U., 1936; J.D., U. Ida., 1938; m. Marion Hackedorn, Aug. 15, 1938; children—Marjorie M. (Mrs. John Mitchell), Martha Anne (Mrs. Michael Vance), Howard M. Admitted to Wash. bar, 1938; practiced in Pullman, 1938-67; judge Wash. Supreme Ct., 1967-72; U.S. dist. judge, Spokane, 1972-79, chief U.S. dist. judge. Lectr. bus. law. Wash. State U., 1946-56. Mem. Nat. Conf. State Legislative Leaders, 1962-67. Mem. Wash. Ho. Reps. from Whitman County, 1949-56, Wash. Senate from Whitman-Adams-Lincoln counties, 1957-67. Served with USNR, 1944-46. Fellow Am. Coll. Probate Counsel; mem. Am. Bar Assn., Am. Judicature Soc., Am. Legion, V.F.W., Pullman C. of C. (pres. 1943), Wash. State U. Alumni Assn. (pres. 1954-55), Phi Kappa Phi, Omicron Delta Kappa, Phi Alpha Delta, Sigma Alpha Epsilon. Episcopalian. Mason. Died Oct. 6, 1979.

NEILS, PAUL, lumber co. exec.; b. Spencer, Wis., June 25, 1886; s. Julius Ferdinand Bernhard and Mary Christina (Geiger) N.; student Concordia Coll., St. Paul, 1900-04; m. Elsa Buenger, July 16, 1912; children—Ruth (Mrs. John M. Ward), Arthur, Julius, Margaret (Mrs. Vernon L. Parrington). Retail clk. J. Neils Lumber Co., Cass Lake, Minn., 1904-08, sales mgr., 1908-12, mgr., 1915-25, v.p., 1912-33, pres., Portland, 1933-57, chmn., 1957—; mgr. Libby Lumber Co., Mont., 1912-15; v.p. Klickitat Log & Lumber Co., Wash., 1925-33, pres., 1933-63; pres. Mont. Light & Power Co., Troy. Mont., 1944—. Mem. C. of C. Republican. Lutheran. Home: Portland OR. *

NELSON, CARL TRUMAN, educator, physician; b. Providence, June 27, 1908; s. Edward and Bessie (Nelson) N.; A.B., Harvard, 1935, A.M., 1937, M.D., 1941; m. Evelyn Lewis, June 26, 1937. Asst. bacteriology Harvard, 1932-35, instr., 1935-41; intern U. Minn. hosps., 1941-42; mem. faculty Columbia Coll. Phys. and Surg., from 1946, prof. dermatology, 1951-73, emeritus, 1973-78; mem. staff Vanderbilt Clinic, from 1946, attending dermatologist, dir. dermatology, 1951-73, cons., 1973-78; cons. Presbyn. Hosp. Served from 1st lt. to maj. AUS, 1942-46. Mem. Am. Acad. Dermatology, N.Y. Dermatol. Soc., Soc. Investigative Dermatology, Am. Assn. Immunologists, Am. Fedn. Clin. Research, N.Y. Acad. Medicine, N.Y. Acad. Scis., Am. Dermatol. Assn., Alpha Omega Alpha. Club:

Harvard (N.Y.C.). Home: New York, N.Y. Died Mar. 16, 1978.

NELSON, CHARLES FREDERICK, physician; b. LaFayette, Ill., Sept. 18, 1884; s. Tury and Mary (Lawson) N.; ed. Toulon (Ill.) Acad., 1905; Williams Coll., Williamstown, Mass., 1905-07; B.S., U. of Chicago, 1909; M.D., Rush Med. Coll., 1911; m. Julia Beth Prindle, Sept. 14, 1907. House physician, Los Angeles Gen. Hosp., 1911-12; police surgeon, Los Angeles Emergency Hosp., 1913; instr. therapeutics and surgery, U. of Southern Calif. Med. Sch., 1912-16; chief surgeon, Beverly Hills Emergency Hosp., 1918-43; dir. The Nelson Clinic, Beverly Hills since 1924. Chmn. Bd. Health, Beverly Hills, 1918-38; med. dir. civilian defense, Beverly Hills; on staff State Civilian Defense Council. Awarded bronze medal by A.M.A., for exhibition bone metabolism, 1940; Ling Medal (work for children), 1938; award from Calif. State Med. Soc. for physico-chemical approach to bone problems exhibit; Royal Order of Vasa, 1st class (Sweden). Fellow A.M.A., Am. Pub. Health Assn.; mem. Calif. State Med. Assn. Los Angeles County Med. Assn., Am. Acad. Gen. Practice, A.A.A.S., Phi Sigma Kappa, Phi Beta Pi. Conglist. Republican. Mason (Shriner). Clubs: University, Jonathan. Contbr. to medical jours. Home: Beverly Hills, Calif. *

NELSON, CHARLES MAURICE, banker; b. Chicago, Apr. 5, 1885; s. John H. and Maren Christine (Larson) N.; student pub. schs., Chicago; m. Martha M. Noelke, Sept. 11, 1912; children—Carol, David, Leah. Messenger Royal Trust Co., Chicago, 1902-08; with Northern Trust Co. since 1906, v.p. since 1931; v.p. and dir. The Northern Trust Safe Deposit Co. Trustee and treas. Allendale Assn. Conglist. Mason. Clubs: Union League, Mid-Day. Home: Chgo. *

NELSON, GEORGE LAURENCE, artist; b. New Rochelle, N.Y., Sept. 26, 1887; s. Carl and Alice (Kerr-Nelson) Hirschberg; student Art Students League, N.Y.C., Nat. Acad. Art Sch., N.Y.C., Acad. Julian, Paris; m. Hermine C. Redgrave, Aug. 21, 1916. Exhibited portraiture in one man shows in N.Y.C., Columbus, Ohio, Springfield, Ill., Stockbridge, Mass., New Britain, Conn.; represented in permanent collections at U. Buffalo, Nat. Arts Club, Nat. Acad. Design, Chi Psi Fraternity House, Boulder, Colo., Am. Acad. Arts and Letters, N.Y. Acad. Medicine, N.Y. Hosp., Mt. Sinai Hosp., N.Y., Meml. Library, Mt. Carmel, N.Y., Bennington (Vt.) Hist. Mus., N.Y.C. C. of C., South Kent (Conn.) Sch., Canterbury Sch., New Milford, Conn., Cochran House, Middlesex Meml. Hosp., Middletown, Conn., Fairfield Hills State Hosp., Conn., Peace Palace, Geneva, Switzerland, Shipley Sch., Bryn Mawr, Pa., New Britain (Conn.) Art Mus.; lithographs in collections of Met. Mus., N.Y. Pub. Library, Carnegie Inst., Pitts., Art Mus. New Britain, Conn., Library of Congress, Newburgh (N.Y.) Hist. Mus., N.Y. Hist. Soc.; instr. Nat. Acad. Design, 1915-41, Cooper Union, 1916-26. Recipient prizes and awards. Mem. Nat. Arts Club N.Y. (life), Allied Artists Am. (past pres.), Kent Art Assn. (pres. emeritus), Acad. Artists Assn. Springfield, Mass., Conn. Acad. Fine Arts, Am. Water Soc., Grand Central Art Galleries, N.Y.C., Meriden Arts and Crafts, Nat. Acad. Design, Nat. Academician. Clubs: Salmogundl, Nat. Arts (life mem.) (N.Y.C.). Address: Kent, Conn. Died Feb. 9, 1978.

NELSON, LAWRENCE EMERSON, university prof.; b. Clinton, Mo., July 25, 1893; s. Thomas Lee and Mary Ellen (Cowan) N.; student Bacone (Okla.) Coll., 1907-09; A.B., William Jewell Coll., Liberty, Mo., 1915; A.M., U. Kans., 1921; student Univ. of Wis., summer 1921, Univ. of Minn., summer 1924, Univ. of Mo., summer 1925; Ph.D., Stanford Univ., 1930; Litt.D., 1971; H.H.D., 1972; m. Rose Lee Stamper, June 17, 1916; children—Beatrice M. (Mrs. C.J. McLellan) (dec.), Theron Francis, Thelma (Mrs. R. C. Sheere). Prof. English, Sioux Falls Coll., 1918-25, prof. English, U. Redlands, 1925-61, dir. div. langs. and lit., 1942-52, dir. graduate studies, 1942-46 and 1952-58, dean graduate studies, 1958-61; prof. English, chmn. humanities div. Cal. Bapt. Coll., 1961—. Mem. accreditation com. Cal. State Bd. Edn., 1959—. Pres. Writers Round Table, 1943-48; dir. Cal. Writers Guild; chmn. Redlands Writers Week 1928-51, Browning Poetry awards, 1933-55. Internat. pres. Round Table-Excalibur Service Clubs, 1966-67; bd. dirs. Excalibur Found., 1966—. Mem. Western College Assn. (vice president 1956-57), P.E.N., Calif. Writers Guild (president), Sigma Tau Delta, Pi Kappa Delta, Lambda Chi Alpha. Democrat. Baptist. Clubs: Round Table (first v.p.), Forum, Fortnightly. Author: (books of verse) The Purple Feather, 1924; Dreamer's Gold, 1934; Gypsy Scarlet, 1936; (nonfictional prose) Our Roving Bible, 1945; Redlands: Biography of a College, 1958; Only One Redlands, 1963. Co-author (with T. W. Wallbank and Mary Porter), Studying Civilization, 2 vols., 1949; (with O.T. Brown) A Great Day, 1970; also booklets. Home: Redlands, Calif. Died Nov. 23, 1978.

NELSON, LAWRENCE ERNEST, clergyman; b. Des Moines, Oct. 4, 1928; s. Gerhard Ernest and Martha (Jessen) N.; B.A., Drake U., 1950; M.Div., Luth. Theol. Sem., Gettysburg, Pa., 1953; m. Mary Jane Ostrem, June 30, 1951; children—Christopher Paul, Jeffrey David, Sarah Ruth, John Martin. Ordained to ministry Luth. Ch., 1953; asst. pastor Epiphany Luth. Ch., Balt., 1953-55; pastor St. James Luth. Ch., Bettendorf, Ia., 1955-57; sec. for youth ministry, bd. parish edn. United Luth. Ch. Am., 1957-64, dir. commn. youth ministry, 1965-72, dir. dept. research and planning div. parish services, 1973-77; instr. Luth. Theol. Sem., Phila., 1970, Gettysburg, 1971; chmn. Joint Youth Publs. Council, 1967-72; facilitator staff Ch. Exec. Devel. Bd., 1971-77. Del. Nat. Council Chs., 1967-69. Chmn. Drexel Hill Interfaith Council Human Relations, 1967-72. Bd. dirs. Holden Village, 1965-72; v.p., incorporator CIStems, Inc., 1973-77. Author: Working with Young People, 1959; Planning Your Catechetical Program, 1960; Ways to Teach Teens, 1965; Creative Uses of the Youth Forum Books, 1971; Move It, 1971; Television Script, 1974. Home: Drexel Hill, Pa. Died Dec. 17, 1977.

NELSON, OLIVER EDWARD, composer, conductor; b. St. Louis, June 4, 1932; s. Eugene Cornelius and Lucilie (Wilverton) N.; student Washington U., St. Louis, 1954-58, Lincoln U., Jefferson City, Mo., 1958-59; m. Audre N. McEwen, Dec. 30, 1958; children—Oliver Edward, Nyles Oliver. Saxophone player with Bill Davis, Quincy Jones and Louis Bellson orchs., N.Y.C., 1950-60, Duke Ellington and Count Basie orchs., 1961; leader own orch. Lincoln Center Concert, 1964; CBS-TV commn. Repertorie Theatre, 1965; scored music for CBS-TV series Mr. Broadway, 1965; writer, scoring TV series Ironside for Universal Pictures, from 1967; tchr. summer session Washington U., 1966; pub. mus. ednl. material Noslen Music Co., Hollywood, Cal., Broadcast Music, Inc. Served with USMCR, 1952-54. Recipient New Star award Jazz Critics Poll, 1962, Edison award, Holland, 1965, Best Arrangement award Nat. Acad. Recording Arts and Scis., 1966; commd. by Broadcast Music, Inc. for Jazzhattan, Suite, 1967. Mem. Am. Fedn. Musicians. Author: Patterns For Saxophone, 1966. Composer: Blues and the Abstract Truth, 1960; Woodwind Quintet, 1960; Song Cycle for Contralto and Piano, 1961; Afro-American Sketches, 1961; Dirge for Chamber Orch., 1962; Soundpiece for Contralto and String Orch., 1963; Soundpiece for Jazz Orch., Piano Compositions, 1964; More Blues and the Abstract Truth, 1965; The Kennedy Dream Suite, 1967 (number 20 (tie) in Top 20 Jazz Albums); Concerto for Xylophone, Marimba and Vibraphone, 1967. Home: Los Angeles, Calif. Died Oct. 28, 1975.

NELSON, OSWALD GEORGE (OZZIE), TV actor, dir., writer, producer; b. Jersey City, Mar. 20, 1907; s. George Waldumar and Ethel Irene (Orr) N.; Litt.B., Rutgers U., 1927, L.H.D., 1957; LL.B., Rutgers U., 1930; m. Harriet Hilliard, Oct. 8, 1935; children—David, Eric. Organized dance orch. 1930, played numerous hotels, theatres, ballrooms, to 1943; radio programs include Joe Penner, Bob Ripley, Peg Murray and Red Skelton; began own radio program, Adventures of Ozzie and Harriet, 1944, producing, directing and acting in TV Adventures-series, 1951-66; dir., actor TV series Ozzie's Girls, 1973-75; recorded for Brunswick, Vocalian, Victor and Bluebird; pub. songs: And Then Your Lips Met Mine, Baby Boy, Size 37 Suit, Swinging on the Golden Gate; motion pictures: Sweethearts of the Campus, Honeymoon Lodge, Strictly in the Groove, Big City, Take It Big, People Are Funny, Here Come the Nelsons, Impossible Years; dir. motion picture Love and Kisses, 1965. Winner N.Y. Daily Mirror Popularity Contest for orch. leaders, 1931; Nat. Family Week Radio Citation by Inter-Council Com. on Christian Family Life; Distinguished Achievement Award for Comedy Script Writing, 1947 (Radio Life mag.); voted best husband and wife team in TV by readers TV-Radio Mirror mag. 7th consecutive year; Distinguished Eagle Scout award, 1973. Republican. Clubs: Ivy (Rutgers); Los Angeles Tennis. Home: Hollywood, Calif. Died June 3, 1975.

NELSON, ROWLAND WHITEWAY, educator; b. Bklyn., May 17, 1902; s. Horatio W. and Amy Roberta (Fisher) N.; B.A., Princeton, 1923; B.A., Oxford (Eng.) U., 1925, M.A., 1929; Ph.D., Northwestern U., 1938; m. Carrie Moore Neal, Sept. 5, 1927; 1 dau., Roberta Joan (Mrs. Paul Bargamin III); m. 2d, Mary G. Jones, Oct. 12, 1971. Instr. English, Northwestern U., 1926-30, fellow, 1930-32; instr. U. N.C., 1935-36; mem. faculty Washington and Lee U., 1938-79, prof. English, from 1956, prof. emeritus, to 1979. Served to lt. comdr. USNR, 1943-45. Mem. Coll. English Assn., English Speaking Union (founder Lexington br. 1950, dir. 1950-57). Episcopalian. Home: Richmond, Va. Died Jan. 19, 1979; buried Stonewall Jackson Cemetery, Lexington, Va.

NELSON, WILLIAM, educator; b. N.Y.C., Jan. 18, 1908; s. Bendet and Margaret (Ginsburg) N.; B.S., Coll. City N.Y., 1927; M.A., Columbia, 1928, Ph.D., 1939; m. Elsa Elizabeth Robinson, June 13, 1930; children—Susan Elizabeth, William. Tchr. pub. schs., N.Y.C., 1928-40; field rep., editor Amerika mag., OWI, Dept. State, 1940-46; asst. prof. English, Columbia, 1949-53, asso. prof., 1953-56, prof., from 1956, William Peterfield Trent prof., 1973-76, prof. emeritus, 1976-78. Guggenheim fellow, 1956. Mem. Acad. Lit. Studies, English Assn., Renaissance Soc. Am. (exec. dir. 1960-69, pres. 1976). Author: John Skelton, Laureate, 1939; Out of the Crocodile's Mouth, 1949; Barclay's Life of St. George, 1955; A Fifteenth Century School Book, 1956; The Poetry of Edmund Spenser, 1963; Fact or Fiction, 1973. Home: New York, N.Y. Died Oct. 26, 1978.

NELSON, WILLIAM STUART, educator; born Paris, Ky., Oct. 15, 1895; s. William Henry and Emma (Kersands) N.; A.B., Howard U., 1920, LL.D., 1936; Union Theol. Seminary, New York, 1920-21; B.D., Yale, 1924; grad. student Sorbonne and Protestant Theol. Sem., Paris, 1921-22, U. of Marburg and U. of Berlin, 1922-23, also spring and summer semesters, 1925 and 1926; LL.D., Shaw U., 1936, Daniel Payne Coll., 1962, Va. State Coll., 1967; m. Blanche Louise Wright, May 5, 1926. Instr. in religion and philosophy, Howard U., 1924-26, asst. prof., 1926-29, asso. prof. and asst. to the pres., 1929-31, dean Sch. Religion, 1940-49, dean, 1948-61, prof. Christian Theology, 1961-64, prof. emeritus, 1964-77, v.p. spl. projects, 1961-67; pres. Shaw U., Raleigh, N.C., 1931-36; pres. Dillard U., New Orleans, 1936-40; lectr. univs. in India, 1947-48. Historian Greater Washington Educational TV Assn.; bd. dirs. scholarship, edn., def. fund Congress Racial Equality, Internat. Student House Washington, Council Chs. Greater Washington. Asso. mem. Gandhi Peace Found. Fellow Sec.; vice president Am. Found. on Non Violence. Served as 1st lieutenant 367 Inf., 317 Engrs., 18 mos.; with A.E.F. 8 mos., during World War I. William Stuart Nelson Awards Fund established in his honor; Fulbright research scholar U. Delhi, India, 1958-59. Religion in Higher Edn.; mem. Religious Edn. Assn., Am. Acad. Polit. and Social Science, Fellowship Reconciliation, N.A.A.C.P., Smithsonian Associate, also member Omega Psi Phi. Baptist. Club: Cosmos. Author: Bases of World Understanding, 1949; La Race Noire dans la Democratie Americaine, 1921. Editor: The Christian Way in Race Relations, 1948; founder, editor Jour. of Religious Thought. Contbr. articles to newspapers, mags. Home: Washington, D.C. Died Mar. 26, 1977; interred Lincoln Memorial Cemetery, Suitland, Md.

NENNI, PIETRG, sec. Socialist Party Italy; b. Faenza, Italy, Feb. 9, 1891; s. Guiseppe and Angela (Castellani) N.; m. Carmen Emiliani, Mar. 9, 1911; children—Vittoria (dec.), Giuliana, Eva, Luciana. Editor (with Carlo Rosselli) Il quarto stato (newspaper); editor Avanti, ofcl. organ of Socialist Party, 1923, until suppression, 1926, and 1943-46; in exile, France, 1926-43; arrested in Vichy, France, sent to Italy where imprisoned, later released, 1943; served as a polit. commissar Garibaldi Brigade in Spain; became sec.-gen. Italian Socialist Party, 1944; served variously as vice prime minister, minister without portfolio, minister fgn. affairs, minister for Constituent Assembly, in cabinets of Bonomi, Parri, De Gasperi, 1945, 46, 47. Served with Italian Army, World War I. Author several books; 1963-69 Vice Prime Minister and Minister of Foreign Affairs of the center-left coalition government., in cabinets of Moro and Rumor. Address: Rome, Italy. Died Jan. 1, 1980, buried Cimitero del Verano, Roma.

NETZER, DONALD LEO, educator; b. Lena, Wis., Oct. 18, 1914; s. Henry Nathan and Julia Mary (Niquette) N.; Ph.B., U. Wis., 1942; M.A., U. Ill., 1946, Ph.D., 1952; m. Bernadette Brazeau, Sept. 10, 1949; children—Donald, Henry, John, Mary, Philip, Julia. Mem. faculty Atlanta div. U. Ga., 1951-55, St. Cloud State Coll., 1956-63; prof. geography Wis. State U., Oshkosh, 1963-79. Active Twin Lakes council Boy Scouts Am., 1963-71. Named Wis. Conservation Educator of Yr., Nat. Wildlife Fedn., 1977. Mem. Nat. Council Geog. Edn., Assn. Am. Geographers, Sigma Xi. K.C. Clubs: Optimist, Conservation (Oshkosh). Home: Oskosh, Wis. Died Sept. 2, 1980; buried Oshkosh.

NEU, HAROLD NICHOLAS, medical educator; b. Arcadia, Iowa, Dec. 18, 1908; s. Philip Dominic and Agnes Agatha (Dunck) N.; A.B., Creighton U., 1929, A.M., 1931, M.D., 1935; m. Othilla Anne Miller, Aug. 25, 1933; children—Harold C., John H., Mary J. (Mrs. George N. Newton). Intern Creighton Meml. St. Joseph's Hosp., Omaha, 1935-36; resident USAAF and U.S. Army hosps., 1941-46; individual practice medicine, Sac City, Iowa, 1936-41, Omaha, from 1946; instr. medicine Creighton U. Med. Sch., 1946-49, asst. prof., 1950-52, asso. prof., 1952-53, prof., 1953-74, prof. emeritus, 1974-77; med. dir. Rehab. Center Creighton Meml. St. Joseph's Hosp., 1952-64. Mem. White House Conf. Aging, 1962, White House Conf. Health, 1965. Mem. United Community Services, Omaha, 1955-64. Trustee Neb. Goodwill Industries, 1955-64. Served to col. USAAF, 1941-46. Recipient distinguished service award Arthritis Found., 1968, distinguished service award Creighton U., 1970. Diplomate Am. Bd. Internal Medicine. Fellow Am. Geriatric Soc., A.C.P.; mem. Am. Soc. Internal Medicine, Am. Congress Rehab., AMA, Nebr. Med. Assn., Omaha Mid-West Clin. Soc., Omaha-Douglas County Med. Soc., Assn. Mil. Surgeons, Am. Legion, Res. Officers Assn., Alpha Omega Alpha. Contbr. articles profl. jours. Home: Manhattan Beach, Calif. Died. Sept. 12, 1977.

NEUMAN, SIMON S., business exec.; b. 1900; m. Helen. Publicker; children—Stephen, Kenneth, Roger, Bruce, Priscilla Neuman Cohn. Chmn. bd., dir. Publicker Industries, Inc., distillers of beverage and indsl. alcohol products, until 1976. Home: Wayne, Pa. Died Aug. 29, 1976.

NEUMAN, WILLIAM FREDERICK, educator, biophysicist; b. Petoskey, Mich., June 2, 1919; s. Reinhardt F. and Louise (Grauel) N., B.S., Mich. State U., 1940; Ph.D., U. Rochester, 1944; m. Margaret Wrightington, June 10, 1943; children—W. Russell, Carol Louise, Peter David. Mem. faculty U. Rochester, 1944-81, prof. radiation biology and biophysics, chmn. dept., 1966-75, Joseph C. Wilson prof., 1972-81, prof. biochemistry and pharmacology, 1952-81; cons. in field, 1950-81. Recipient Eli Lilly award biol. chemistry, 1955, Claude Bernard medal U. Montreal, 1962, Kappa Delta award, 1964, Biol. Mineralization award Internat. Assn. Dental Research, 1965. Mem. AAAS, Am. Chem. Soc., Am Soc. Biol. Chemists, Am. Soc. Pharmacology and Exptl. Therapy, Radiation Research Soc., Urban League (dir.), Biophys. Soc., Sigma Xi, Phi Kappa Phi. Unitarian (trustee). Author: Chemical Dynamics of Bone Mineral, 1958; also numerous articles, Home: Rochester, N.Y. Died Jan. 4, 1981.

NEUMANN, EMANUEL, lawyer, Zionist leader; b. Libau, Latvia, July 2, 1893; s. Sundel Hirsch and Dannah (Esterman) N.; brought to U.S., 1893; B.A., Columbia, 1914; J.D., N.Y. U., 1928; m. Fannie Ritchik, Aug. 16, 1921; children—Gabriel J., Natanya Manson. Editor, Young Judean, 1914-15; tchr. Boys High Sch., Bklyn. 1916-17; ednl. dir. Zionist Orgn. Am., 1918-20; co-founder Palestine Found. Fund, 1921, nat. dir., 1921-25; founder United Palestine Appeal (now United Israel Appeal), 1925, chmn. appeals exec. com., 1925-28; pres. Jewish Nat. Fund, 1928-30; v.p. Century Bank N.Y., 1928-29, Interstate Trust Co., 1929-30; admitted to N.Y. bar, 1931; mem. exec. head econ. dept. Jewish Agy. for Palestine, Jerusalem, 1931-33; dir. Indsl. and Financial Corp. Palestine, Ltd., 1934-39, Migdal Ins. Co. Palestine, 1934-39, Tiberias Hot Springs Co., Palestine, 1934-39; mem. exec., polit. rep. in Washington, Jewish Agy. in U.S., 1941; head Am. Palestine Com., also mem. Am. Zionist Emergency Council, 1941-48; organizer, dir. Commn. on Palestine Surveys, 1943-46; mem. delegation Jewish Agy. in Am. to UN, 1947; pres. Zionist Orgn. Am., 1947-49, 56-68; head econs. dept., chief info. and publs. Jewish Agy. in U.S., 1951-53, chmn. Am. sect. of exec., 1953-80; organizer, 1954, since pres. Herzl Found.; pres. World Conf. Gen. Zionists, 1958-63, World Union Gen. Zionists, 1963-80; chmn. Jewish Agy.-Am. Sect., 1963-80. Organizer, 1961, hon. pres. Tarbuth Found. Advancement Hebrew Culture. Recipient Herzl gold medallion for distinguished service to Zionism, Zionist Orgn. Am., 1961. Home: New York, N.Y. Died Oct. 26, 1980.

NEWBURGER, RICHARD LANGFELD, investment banker; b. Phila., Oct. 28, 1911; s. Frank L. and Helen (Langfeld) N.; B.S., U. Va., 1933; m. Elizabeth Allman, Sept. 22, 1949. With Newburger & Co., and predecessors, Phila., from 1933, partner, from 1937. Vice pres. Phila.-Balt. and Washington Stock Exchange, 1959, then pres. Bd. dirs. Fedn. Jewish Agys. Phila., 1951; trustee Abington (Pa.) Meml. Hosp., Lower Moreland Township (Pa.) Police Pension Fund, Mt. Sinai Cemetery, Phila. Home: Huntingdon Valley, Pa. Died Aug. 22, 1979.

NEWBURGH, LOUIS HARRY, physician; teacher; b. Cincinnati, O., June 17, 1883; s. Henry and Laura (Mack) N.; A.B., Harvard, 1905, M.D., 1908; grad. study, Vienna and Berlin, 1909; m. Irene Haskell, Oct. 2, 1912; children—Henry, John David. Interne Mass. Gen. Hosp., 1908; in practice at Cincinnati, 1910; asst. in dept. internal medicine, Harvard, and mem. staff Mass. Gen. Hosp., 1912-16; asst. prof. internal medicine, U. of Mich., 1916-20, asso. prof., 1920-22, prof. clin. investigation since 1922, Sec. Spl. Med. Examining Bd., Ann Arbor, World War I. Certificate of Merit for services in O.S.R.D., World War II. Mem. A.M.A., Assn. Am. Physicians, Am. Society Clin. Investigations, A.A.A.S., Am. Inst. Nutrition. Nat. Research Council (dir. of med. sciences coms. on aviation medicine; clinical investigation; chmn. subcom. clothing), Sigma Xi, Alpha Omega Alpha, Alpha Kappa Kappa. Author or co-author several publs. in field of interest. Home: Ann Arbor, Mich. *

NEWCOMB, ERNEST HENRY, educator; b. Troutville, Va., Sept. 28, 1886; s. George Mosby and Virginia Smith (Nininger) N.; grad. State Teachers' Coll., Springfield, Mo., 1911; B.S. in Edn., U. of Mo., 1921. A.M., 1923; m. Ruby Anderson, Aug. 6, 1913; children—Norman Julien, Eldon Henry, Betty-Jo (Mrs. Boyd Vernon Rollins). Began as teacher in rural schs., prin. village schs., 1904-09; grade principal of public schools, Neosho, Missouri, 1909-11; county sch. supt., Newton County, Mo., 1911-14; supt. schs., Neosho, 1914-17; sec. and organizer Mo. Meth. Foundation, Columbia, Mo., 1919-23; pres. Central Coll., for Women, Lexington, Mo., 1923-25; organizer, co-founder and chief executive, University of Kansas City, 1925-39. President, dir., Kansas City Town Hall Ednl. Forum since 1939. Y.M.C.A. camp ednl. dir., personnel sec. Southern Dept. Y.M.C.A., 1917-19; mem. Gen. Bd. of Lay Activities of M.E. Ch., S., 1923-30; mem. Kansas City Area Council Boy Scouts Am. since 1933 (silver beaver). Supervisor U.S.O., 1942-43. Mem. A.A.A.S., C. of C., N.E.A., Phi Delta Kappa, Alpha Pi Zeta. Phi Mu Alpha, Pi Gamma Mu. Democrat. Methodist. Club: Advertising and Sales Execs. Home: Kansas City MO. *

NEWELL, WILLIAM ALLAN, mfr.; b. Ogdensburg, N.Y., Apr. 22, 1883; s. Edgar Allan and Addie Barbara (Priest) N.; A.B., Williams Coll., Williamstown, Mass., 1905; L.H.D., Clarkson Coll., 1963; m. Edith deLano Judson, Oct. 10, 1917 (dec. Oct. 1954); children—Claire (Mrs. A. M. Menkel, Jr.), Judson. Pres. Newell Mfg. Co. Ltd., Prescott, Ont.; hon. dir. Ogdensburg Trust Co.; dir., hon. chmn. Newell Nat. Mfg.Co., Freeport, Ill.; past v.p. St. Lawrence County Savs. Bank. Mayor of Ogdensburg, 1928-29; mem. Assembly of State of New York, 1933-38. Mem. Rep. State Com., N.Y., 1915-16; del. Rep. State Conv., 1914, 34, 36, 46. Mem. St. Lawrence River Bridge Commn.; past mem. adv. council N.Y. State Sch. of Agr., Canton, 1937- 38; mem. Joint Legislative Com. on Interstate Co-Operation, 1936-38; mem. for N.Y. State Am. Legislator's Assn., 1936-38. Chmn. Local Board No. 414, Selective Service Registrants Adv. Bd.; chmn. SSR Re-Employment Bd., Minute Men Def. Bond Program. Trustee emeritus Clarkson Coll., Potsdam, N.Y. Recipient citation St. Lawrence U., 1970. Mem. Acad. Polit. Sci., Williams Coll. Alumni Assn. (v.p. 1929-30), S.R., Am. Legion, Newcomen Soc. (Engl), Phi Delta Theta. Baptist. Mason. K.P., Elk; mem. Grange. Clubs: Ogdensburg Country (ex-pres.); Williams of N.Y. (a founder); Fort Orange (Albany); Pontiac Game (ex-pres.) (Que., Can.). Co-introducer Lee-Newell initial constitutional amendment creating State Dept. of Commerce; defeated, but similar amendment approved by voters, 1943. Home: Ogdensburg NY. *

NEWHOUSE, SAMUEL I., newspaper exec; Pub. Newark Star Ledger; pres. Morning Ledger Co., Long Island Daily Press, Syracuse Herald-Journal, Syracuse Post-Standard, Staten Island Advance, Harrisburg Patriot-News, Portland Oregonian, Oreg. Jour., Jersey Jour., St. Louis Globe-Democrat, Birmingham News, Huntsville Times, Times-Picayune, States and Item, New Orleans. Home: Newark, N.J. Died Aug. 29, 1979.

NEWMAN, A. JOSEPH, bus. exec.; b. Easton, Pa., Sept. 17, 1882; s. Andrew and Helen (Lanigan) N.; grad. Easton (Pa.) High Sch., 1899; m. Mary M. Hass, June 5, 1903; children—Mary A. (Mrs. Edward Donovan), Eloise C. (Mrs. Clifford Burkholder), A. Joseph, Gen. sales mgr., P. Lorillard Co., N.Y. City, 1904-24; with Bayuk Cigars, Inc., Phila., since 1924, gen. sales mgr., 1924-34, vice pres. and gen. sales mgr., 1934-38, pres., 1937, now chmn. Author: Frank Trufax Letters; Otto Noebetter; Autobiography Alex Smarts; Confessions of an Old Timer. Home: Philadelphia. *

NEWMAN, FRANK R., ry. official; b. Evanston, Ill., Nov. 6, 1883; s. E. R. and Delia (Rogers) N.; grad. Lake View High Sch., Chicago, 1901; student Northwestern U., 1901-05 (non-grad.); m. Estelle Emerson, June 9, 1908; 1 dau. Barbara. Began with Wabash R.R., June 1, 1905; traveling freight agt. M.C. R.R., 1906-15, continuing as asst. commercial agt. at Chicago, 1915-17, chief clk. to traffic mgr., 1917-18; asst. general freight agent at Buffalo, 1918-20; assistant gen. freight agt. M.C. R.R., at Detroit, 1920-22; gen. traffic mgr., M., St.P.&S.S.M. Ry., 1922-25, v.p. in charge of traffic, 1925-38; v.p. in charge traffic G.N. Ry., St. Paul, Jan. 1, 1938-May 10, 1945, retired. Vice pres. Park R. Learned Co., since Sept. 1945. Mem. Phi Kappa Psi. Republican. Methodist. Mason. (32 deg., Shriner). Clubs: Minikahda, Minneapolis, Minneapolis Athletic, Minneapolis. *

NEWMAN, JEROME A., business exec.; b. N.Y.C., 1896; LL.B., Columbia, 1919. Pres., dir. Graham-Newman Corp., N.Y.C.; chmn. of bd., dir. Govt. Employees Ins. Company; director, member of the executive committee Pepsi Cola United Bottlers, Govt. Employees Corp.; dir. Loew's, Inc., Govt. Employees Life Ins. Co., (all Washington). Home: New York, N.Y. Died Aug. 10, 1980.

NEWMAN, SAMUEL F., mfg. exec.; b. Oct. 10, 1882; student pub. schs., York, Pa.; married; 4 daus., 1 son. Mem. bd. dirs. First Nat. Bank & Trust Co. of Waynesboro. Mem. Am. Assn. M.E. (life mem.). *

NEWMARK, NATHAN MORTIMORE, educator, cons. engr.; b. Plainfield, N.J., Sept. 22, 1910; s. Abraham S. and Mollie (Nathanson) N.; B.C.E., Rutgers U., 1930, D.Sc. (hon.), 1955; M5., U. Ill., 1932, Ph.D., 1934, D.Sc. (hon.), 1978; Dr. h.c., U. Liège, 1967; LL.D. (hon.), U. Notre Dame, 1969; m. Anne Mae Cohen, Aug. 6, 1932; children—Richard Alan, Linda Beth, Susan Adele. Mem. faculty U. Ill., 1930—, research asst. civil engring., research asso., research asst. prof., research prof. structural engring., 1943-56, prof., head dept. civil engring., 1956-73, prof. civil engring., mem. Center for Advanced Study, 1973-76, emeritus, 1976-81, chmn. digital computer lab. Grad. Coll., 1951-57. Cons. structural, machine analysis and design govt. agys., indsl. orgns.; editor series of texts, civil engring. and engring. mechanics Prentice Hall, Inc., 1949-81; cons. antiseismic design Le Chateau Champlain, Montreal, Que., Can. and Latino Americana Tower, Mexico City, Mexico; prin. seismic Cons. trans-Alaska pipeline, Canadian Arctic pipeline, Bay Area Rapid Transit System, reconstrn. Managua (Nicaragua), others. Cons. NDRC, office field service OSRD, World War II; sci. adv. bd. USAAF, 1945-49; mem. U.S. Nat. Com. Theoretical and Applied Mechanics, 1953-58; tech. adv. bd. Dept. Commerce, 1963-64; mem. com. to form Nat. Acad. Engring., 1964; mem. Pres.'s Com. Nat. Medal of Sci., 1972-78, chmn., 1975-78. Recipient Presdl. Certificate of Merit; award Concrete Reinforced Steel Inst., 1956; Vincent Bendix award Am. Soc. Engring. Edn, 1961; Order of Lincoln, Lincoln Acad. Ill., 1965; Nat. Medal Sci., 1968; Washington award, 1969; John Fritz medal, 1979; named to Am. Soc. Engring. Edn. Hall Fame, 1968; Outstanding Civilian Service medal Dept. Army, 1971. Argentine Acad. Exact Natural and Phys. Scis. fellow, 1971. Fellow Am. Acad. Arts and Scis., Internat. Assn. Earthquake Engring. (hon.), Am. Geophys. Union, AAAS; mem. ASME (hon., chmn. applied mechanics div. 1954), Nat. Acad. Scis., Nat. Acad. Engring. (charter), ASCE (J. James R. Croes medal 1945, Moisseiff award 1950, Norman medal 1958, E.E. Howard award 1958, Theodore von Karman award 1962, chmn. engring. mechanics div. 1953, hon.), Am. Ry. Engring. Assn., Research Council Bolted Structural Joints, Column, Welding, Reinforced Concrete research councils, Am. Concrete Inst. (bd. dirs. 1949-52, Wason medalist 1950, hon.), Internat. Assn. Bridge and Structural Engrs., Earthquake Engring. Research Inst. (hon.), Am. Soc. Engring. Edn., Seismol. Soc. Am., Phi Beta Kappa, Sigma Xi, Tau Beta Pi, Phi Kappa Phi, Chi Epsilon. Author: (with Emilio Rosenblueth) Fundamentals of Earthquake Engineering, 1971. Editor series of civil engring., engring. mechanics texts. Contbr. articles to profl. jours. Home: Urbana, Ill. Died Jan. 1, 1981.

NEWSOM, ISAAC ERNEST, dean vet. medicine; b. Colorado City, Tex., Apr. 13, 1883; s. Eli and Lydia (Russell) N.; B.S., Colo. Agrl. Coll., 1904; D.V.S., San Francisco Vet. Coll., 1906, Kansas City Vet. Coll., 1909; student U. of Chicago, 1913, U. of Colo. Med. Sch., 1926; D.Sc., U. of Colo., 1941; m. Jessie Sarah Woods, July 8, 1905 (died May 1943); children—Fern Jessie (Mrs. Ronald Martin), Shirley; m. 2d, Mrs. Dorthy Kick, July 8, 1944. Asst. Colo. Agrl. Coll., 1904-07; state meat insp., Colo., 1907; asst. prof., Colo. A.&M. Coll., 1907-19, prof. vet. pathology, 1919-35, dean vet. medicine, 1934-48, acting dir. Expt. Sta., 1939-41, vice-pres. 1939-48, dean grad. school, 1941-48, pres., 1948-49. Member State Examining Board in Basic Sciences, 1937-48. Mem. Am. Vet. Medical Assn. (exec. bd. 1936-41), Alpha Psi, Phi Kappa Phi, Sigma Xi. Republican. Unitarian. Mason (K.T.), Grand Master, Colo., 1928-29. Contbr. many articles to professional jours.; author of tech. bulletins. Home: Fort Collins. *

NEWSOM, MARION EUGENE, banker; b. Littleton, N.C., Mar. 4, 1884; s. Marion E. and Annie S. Newsom; B.; A.B., Trinity Coll. (now Duke U.), 1905; m. Annie Laurie Long, Nov. 22, 1911; children—Marion Eugene, James Long, Annie Laurie, Mary Toms, John Walton, Ernest Edward, Nancy. Engaged in merchandising, 1907-30, in banking since 1930; pres. Citizens Nat. Bank of Durham, N.C. Former mayor of Durham, N.C. Mem. bd. trustees and exec. com. Duke U. Formerly pres. Chamber of Commerce, Durham Merchants Assn., N.C. State Merchants Assn., Durham Rotary Club, Rotary International. Home: Forest Hills, Durham. *

NEWSON, HENRY WINSTON, physicist; b. Lawrence, Kans., Nov. 26, 1909; s. Henry Byron and Mary (Winston) N.; B.S., U. Ill., 1931; Ph.D., U. Chgo., 1934; m. Meta Thode, Aug. 31, 1934; children—Meta Mary (Mrs. William D. Robb), Caroline (Mrs. James B. Barber). Research fellow Lawrence Berkeley Lab., U. Calif., 1934-36; instr. U. Chgo., 1936-42, group leader metall. lab., 1942-43; sect. chief Clinton Labs., Oak Ridge, 1943-44; tech. expert Hanford Engring. Works, Richland, Wash., 1944-45; group leader Los Alamos Sci. Lab., 1945-46; chief physicist Oak Ridge Nat. Lab., 1946-48; prof. physics Duke, 1948-78, James B. Duke prof., 1968-78, chmn. dept., 1973-75, dir. Nuclear Structure Lab., 1961-68, dir. Triangle Univs. Nuclear Lab., 1968-78; vis. prof. J.W. Goethe U., Frankfurt am Main, W. Ger., 1977-78; cons. atomic energy, 1948-78. Recipient Service award War Dept., C.E., Manhattan Dist., 1945, medal for participant 1st nuclear chain reaction expt. Stagg Field, Chgo. Fellow Am. Phys. Soc., Sigma Xi. Democrat. Unitarian. Author: (with J. H. Gibbons) Fast Neutron Physics, 1960. Home: Durham, N.C. Died May 14, 1978.

NEWTON, ALMA, author; b. Jefferson Co., Miss., Mar. 22, 1886; d. Algernon Emmett and Mattie (Hunt) N.; Newcomb Coll., New Orleans, 1902-04; grad. Cincinnati Conservatory of Music, 1908; m. James M. Anderson, of Miss., Feb. 7, 1907 (divorced 1914); 1 son,

Algernon Emmett Newton. Democrat. Author: The Love Letters of a Mystic, 1915; Memories, 1917; The Blue String, 1918; A Jewel in the Sand, 1920; Shadows, 1921; Dreaming True, 1921; An Old Fashioned Romance, 1924. Home: New York, N.Y. *

NEWTON, ANDREW E., govt. ofcl.; b. Buffalo, May 14, 1906; s. Earl B. and Elizabeth G. (Quinn) N.; evening student U. Buffalo; m. Alberta C. Zimmer, Oct. 3, 1934; children—Nancy Ann (Mrs. Robert M. Lundien), Gail C. (Mrs. Frank D. Giambattista), Cheryl K. With Post Office Dept., 1929-65, asst. dir. div. city delivery, bur. operations, 1949-61, dep. asst. postmaster gen. regional mgmt., bur. operations, 1961-62, regional dir., Washington, 1962-65; dir. postal affairs O. E. McIntyre, Inc., 1965, Metromedia, Inc., 1965; postal cons., from 1966; field rep. Congressman John O. Marsh, Jr., from 1966. Pres. for life Vets. Fleet Post Office, N.Y. Inc., from 1947. Served to comdr. USNR, 1942-46. Decorated Sec. of Navy citation, Bronze Star medal. Mem. Am. Legion. Presbyn. (elder, gen. supt. Sunday sch. 1954). Mason. Home: Falls Church, Va. Died Oct. 2, 1979.

NEWTON, ARTHUR ULYSSES, art cons.; b. N.Y.C., Mar. 31, 1892; s. Adolph and Kate (Mehesy) N.; student Univ. Coll. Sch., London, Eng., 1907-10; B.S. with 1st class honors in Chemistry, Univ. Coll., U. London, 1913; m. Grace Hamilton, Aug. 14, 1926 (dec. 1958); m. 2d, Mrs. Victor White, Jan. 8, 1959 (dec. 1960); m. 3d, Mrs. E. Kellogg Baird, Jan. 10, 1962 (dec. Mar. 26, 1975). Naturalized Am. citizen, 1954. Demonstrator chemistry Univ. Coll., 1912-13; mem. Inter-Allied Plebiscite and Govt. Commn., Upper Silesia, 1920-22; with fathers's art bus., London, 1922-25; owner Arthur U. Newton, N.Y.C., galleries, specializing in old masters, 1925-62; art cons. N.Y.C., from 1962; helped form several pvt. and mus. collections, U.S. and Can.; exhbns. old masters, lectr. on art Atlanta Mus., 1939, Charlotte (N.C.) Mus., 1941, Hagerstown (Md.) Mus., 1941, Bermuda (B.W.I.) Art Assn. 1955; exhbt. contemporary artists including Paintings of the Coronation by Frank O. Salisbury and Indian sculptor Amar Sehgal, also Views of Mallorca by Margot White, portraits by Alfred Jonniaux, Fifty American Artists. Served as lt. Border Regt., Brit. Army, 1914-22. Fellow Chem. Soc. (Eng.); asso. Inst. Chemistry; mem. Appraisers Assn. Am., English-Speaking Union (pres. Palm Beach br.). Clubs: Beach, Everglades (Palm Beach); Metropolitan, University (N.Y.C.); United Hunts, Royal Air Force (London). Contbr. articles profl. publs. Home: Palm Beach, Fla. Died Oct. 5, 1978.

NEWTON, CHARLES HOWARD, educator; b. Plattsmouth, Neb., Nov. 4, 1930; s. Edgar Sylvester and Mildred (Clark) N.; B.A. in Sociology and Psychology, U. Neb., 1956, M.A. in Sociology, 1958; Ph.D., Fla. State U., 1961; m. Janis Lea Arnold, Dec. 18, 1954; children—Charles H., Jim Harold. Asst. prof. sociology U. Richmond, 1961-63; asso. prof. Memphis State U., 1963-64, prof., 1964-75, chmn. dept. sociology and anthropology, 1970-75, chmn. research com., coordinator Bur. Social Research dept. sociology, 1970-74. Chief cons. Memphis Juvenile Ct., 1964-72, chmn. adv. com., 1966; lectr. Memphis Police Acad., 1964-70; mem. adv. com. vocational tech. tng. program Shelby County Penal Farm, 1965-75; chmn. Tenn. Assn. Advancement Child Care, 1968-72; mem. budget com. Shelby United Neighbors, 1968-74; social service service com. Family Service Memphis, 1968-74; spl. cons. commr. Tenn. Dept. Corrections, 1971-74. Served with USAF, 1948-52; Korea. Named Distinguished Educator, 1973. Mem. So., Am. sociol. assns., Alpha Kappa Delta. Author: (with Warren Chukinas, Patricia Scott) Educational Sociology: An Annotated and Cross Referenced Bibliography, 1964. Editor: Alienation in Mass Society (Paul Meadows), 1967; co-editor several pubs. proc. Law Enforcement Inst., 1967-68. Contbr. articles to profl. jours. Home: Memphis, Tenn. Died Nov. 12, 1975.

NEWTON, VIRGIL MILLER, JR., newspaper editor; b. Atlanta, Apr. 12, 1904; s. Virgil Miller and Mattie (Watson) N.; A.B., U. Fla., 1926; m. Louisa Verri, Oct. 22, 1927; 1 son, Virgil Miller. Sports editor Gainesville (Fla.) Sun, 1925-26; reporter, sports editor Tampa (Fla.) Daily Times, 1926-30; sports editor Tampa Tribune, 1930-35, asst. mng. editor, 1935-43, mng. editor, 1943-69. Chmn. Tampa Community Chest, 1949, Tampa Infantile Paralysis drive, 1950, Tampa Red Cross drive, 1950, bd. dirs., 1950-52. Recipient Free Enterprise award Nat. Assn. Mgmt., 1954, Freedoms award Va. Press Assn., 1957. Editor of Year award Nat. Press Photog. Assn., 1958; named Outstanding U. Fla. Alumnus, 1977. Mem. Asso. Press. Mng. Editors Assn. (board of directors), Am. Soc. Newspaper Editors, Phi Delta Theta, Sigma Delta Chi (mem. exec. council; chmn. nat. freedom of information com., from 1953), Blue Key. Meth. (past bd. local trustees). Mason (Shriner, Jester). Clubs: University, Tampa Yacht and Country, Ye Mystic Krewe Gasparilla (Tampa). Home: Tampa, Fla. Died Dec. 13, 1977.

NEWTON, WARREN CHILDS, feed mfr.; b. Bridgeville, Del., Aug. 17, 1896; s. Oilver A. and LeRoy (Richardson) N.; B.S., U. Del., 1916, D.Sc. (hon.), 1955; student N.Y. State Coll. Agr., 1917, Beacom Bus. Coll., Wilmington, Del., 1917-19; m. Elizabeth W. Eggert, Nov. 30, 1918; children—Elizabeth (Mrs. R. Doyle McSpadden), Jane (Mrs. Robert F. Rider), Joanna (Mrs. Robert Conaway). Partner, Newton Chem. & Supply Co., 1936-43, pres., dir., 1943-63, chmn. bd., dir., 1963-77; dir. FCA Balt., 1937-40; partner O.A. Newton & Son Co., 1940-46, pres., 1946-63, pres., chmn., 1963-70, chmn. bd., 1970-77, also dir.; pres. McSpadden Cleaners, Inc., 1953-58, v.p., 1958-63; pres., dir. Newton Realty, Inc., 1955-63, chmn. bd., dir., 1963-77; pres. Newton Leasing & Finance Co., 1952-69, Newton Farms, Inc., 1964-77, dir. Balt. Trust Co., 1945-50, 57-58, exec. v.p., 1949-50; chmn. Neppco Hatchery div. Northeastern Poultry Producers Council, 1942-43, pres., 1943-44; chmn., dir. Rust-Weir Supply Co., 1954-63, vice chmn., dir., 1963-77; pres., dir. Cedar Creek Yacht Basin, 1957-70; dir. Del. R.R. Co. Pres. Wessex Farm Labor Assn., 1946-60, Bridgeville Cemetery Assn., 1946-77; mem., chmn. Del. adv. com. Farmers Home Adminstrn., 1961-63; sec.-treas. Bridgeville Br. Tax Ditch, 1954-64, Manticoke River Tax Ditch, 1959-64; mem. Gov. Del. Citizens Adv. Com. Edn., 1955-58, Com. to Study State Hwy. Dept., 1960-61; mem. Small Bus. Adv. Com., 1951-52. Incorporator Nanticoke Meml. Hosp., 1945; trustee, v.p. U. Del. Recipient Outstanding Alumnus award U. Del. Alumni Assn., 1960; Distinguished Citizen award Delmarva Poultry Industries, 1964; Josiah Marvel Cup award Del. C. of C., 1966. Mem. Peninsula Hort. Soc., Del. Poultry Assn., Northeastern Poultry Producers Council, Delmarva Poultry Producers, Alumni Assn. U. Del. (past pres.), Grange. Methodist (trustee Peninsula Ann. Conf. 1963—). Kiwanian, Mason; mem. Tall Cedars Lebanon. Home: Bridgeville, Del. Died May 19, 1977.

NICHOLL, WILLIAM EVAN (NIK'UL), coll. dean; b. Moosomin, Saskatchewan, Can., Mar. 21, 1883; s. William and Mary Ann (Baer) N.; A.B., Bellevue (Neb.) Coll., 1904; Presbyn. Theol. Sem., Omaha, 1904-07; U. of Edinburgh, 1907-08; A.M., Columbia, 1919; m. Edith Jennie Wright, June 14, 1909; 1 son, Robert Gordon. Teacher in history and edn., Hastings (Neb.) Coll., 1909-10; prin. Acad. and instr. edn., 1910-11, prof. edn., 1911-16, Bellevue Coll., also trustee, registrar, 1912-15, acting pres., 1914-16; acting asso. prof. edn., Ind. U., Bloomington, 2d semester, 1916-17; prof. edn. and dean, Bellevue Coll., 1st semester, 1917-18; camp ednl. dir. Army Y.M.C.A., Camp Funston, Kan., Feb-July 1918; dir. training, western dept. Army Y.M.C.A., Stanford U., July 1918-July 1919; dean Pomona Coll. from 1919, now dean emeritus asst. prof. of edn., 1919-32, prof., 1932-39. Member Phi Delta Kappa. Conglist. Mason. Rotarian. Home: Claremont, Calif.*

NICHOLLS, WILLIAM HORD, educator, economist; b. Lexington, Ky., July 19, 1914; s. William Durrett and Mary Elizabeth (Hord) N.; A.B., U. Ky., 1934; M.A., Harvard U., 1938, Ph.D., 1941; postgrad. U. Chgo., 1941-42; m. Elizabeth Banfield Burwell, Sept. 5, 1936 (dec. 1969); children—David Elliot, Dorothy Louise; m. 2d, Elizabeth Carr Foote, 1970; stepchildren—Elizabeth Elaine Foote (Mrs. Babb), Robert Stephens. Statis. clk. A.A.A., summer 1934; farm worker, summer 1935; field agt. Bur. Agrl. Econs., summers 1936-37; research asst. Harvard, 1934-37; instr., research asso. Ia. State Coll., 1937-39, asst. prof., 1939-43, asso. prof., 1943-44; research asso. agrl. econs. U. Chgo., 1945-46, asst. prof. econs. 1946-48; prof. econs. Vanderbilt U., Nashville, 1948-78, chmn. dept. econs. and bus. adminstrn., 1958-61, dir. Center for Latin Am. Studies, 1965-77, Harvie Branscomb Distinguished prof., 1973. Vis. lectr., Rio de Janeiro, summer 1947; mem. faculty Salzburg seminar in Am. Studies, summer 1949; vis. prof. econs. Harvard U., 1961-62. Economist, Turkish mission Internat. Bank for Reconstrn. and Devel., 1950; staff Council Econ. Advisers, Exec. Office of Pres., 1953-54; tech. dir. 7th Am. Assembly on Agr., Columbia, 1954-55; U.S. del. profl. confs., India, 1958, Japan, 1960, Mex., 1961, Italy, 1965, Brazil, 1973; cons. Ford Found., Brazil, 1960, Vargas Found., Rio de Janeiro, 1963-64, Inst. Econ. and Social Planning Brazilian Ministry Planning, Rio de Janeiro, 1972-73; mem. com. employment security Dept. Labor, 1959-60, U.S. Com. Manpower Tng. and Devel., 1962-63; mem. U.S. Nat. Commn., UNESCO, U.S. Dept. State, 1965-68. mem. NRC, 1969-78. Recipient 1st award farm policy essay competition Am. Farm Econ. Assn., 1945; Centennial Distinguished Alumni award U. Ky., 1965. Fellow Am. Farm Econ. Assn. (pres. 1960-61); mem. Social Sci. Research Council (dir. 1956-62), Nat. Planning Assn., Am., So. (pres. 1958-59) econ. assns., Phi Beta Kappa, Delta Tau Delta, Omicron Delta Kappa. Methodist. Author 12 books. Editor: Jour. Polit. Economy, 1946-48, Jour. Farm Economics, 1958-60, Econ. Devel. and Cultural Change, from 1958; bd. editors Am. Econ. Rev., 1948-51. Contbr. articles to profl. jours. Home: Nashville, Tenn. Died Aug. 4, 1978; buried Lexington, Ky.

NICHOLS, BARBARA, actress; b. Mineola, N.Y.; d. George Adam and Julia (Wurst) Nickerauer; grad. high sch. Dancer in club acts; model for Pin-Up Photos; appeared in Broadway plays Pal Joey, 1952, Let It Ride, 1962; made 1st film, 1957; motion pictures include Miracle In The Rain, Manfish, Beyond a Reasonable Doubt, The King and Four Queens, 1956, Sweet Smell of Success, Pajama Game, Pal Joey, 1957, Ten North Frederick, The Naked and the Dead, (play) Joy Ride, 1958, Woman Obsessed, That Kind of Woman, 1959, Who Was That Lady?, Where the Boys Are, 1960, The George Raft Story, Scarface Mob, 1961, House of Women, 1962, Looking For Love, Dear Heart, Disorderly Orderly, 1964, Human Duplicators, The Loved One, 1965, The Swinger, 1966, 1967, Time, 1970; toured in stock co. in The Wonderful World of Burlesque, 1968; Charlie and the Angel, 1973. Recipient Look Mag. Best Actress award for Untouchables. Mem. Screen Actors Guild, A.F.T.R.A., Acad. Motion Picture Arts and Scis., Tail Waggers Soc. Democrat. Lutheran. Club: Astrology. Home: Los Angeles, Calif. Died Oct. 5, 1976.

NICHOLS, J(ESSE) BROOKS, mfr.; b. Dunkirk, N.Y., July 11, 1885; s. Edward and Jessie (Brooks) N.; Ph.B., Yale, 1908; m. Rosa Dunlap, of Louisville, Ky., June 3, 1908 (dec.); children—Jesse Brooks, Edward, Norval Wallace; m. 2d, Catharon Louise Dale, of Boston, Feb. 14, 1935. Formerly v.p., gen. mgr. U.S. Radiator Corporation (Detroit); dir. Red Dot Corpn. Student Plattsburg T.C.; commd. 1st lt. inf., U.S.A., 1916, later capt. and maj.; served in N. Russian Campaign, Archangel, Russia, Aug. 1918-June 1919; commdr. allied force in field. Mentioned in dispatches; D.S.O. (British); Legion of Honor and Croix de Guerre with palm and star (French); Order of St. Vladimir with swords and ribbons (Russian); lt. col. O.R.C., Feb. 1920. Mem. Mil. Order Foreign Wars. Republican. Episcopalian. Mem. S.R., Soc. Colonial Wars. Clubs: Yale, Racquet and Tennis (New York); Yondotega (Detroit). Home: St. Simons Island, Ga.*

NICHOLS, JOHN TREADWELL, ichthyologist; b. Jamaica Plain, Mass., June 11, 1883; s. John W. T. and Mary B. (Slocum) N.; A.B., Harvard, 1906 (as of 1905); m. Cornelia DuBois Floyd, June 14, 1910; children—William Floyd, Mary Blake, John Slocum, David Gelston. Asst. Dept. of Mammals, Am. Museum Natural History, N.Y. City, 1907-08; asst. U.S. Bur. Fishes, 1908-09; asst. Dept. of Fishes, Am. Museum, 1909-18, asso. curator, 1919-27, curator since 1928. Mem. Linnaean Soc. New York, also various scientific socs. Protestant. Author: Fishes of Vicinity of New York City, 1918; Fresh-Water Fishes of China, 1943; also some 950 scientific or popular articles in periodicals. Making study of certain marine fishes. Home: Garden City, N.Y. *

NICHOLS, JOSEPH CLIFFORD, coll. dean; b. Cavett, Ohio, Nov. 6, 1894; s. Legrand Byington and Fannie (Johnson) N.; A.B., Columbia U., 1920; M.A., Western Reserve U., 1928, Ed.D., 1941; m. Ethelwyne Parker, Aug. 10, 1921; children—Elizabeth Jane, Patricia Lou. Teacher, East Claridon High, 1915-16; instr. mathematics, Y.M.C.A. Tech. Sch., 1920-21, dir. trade sch., 1921-25; dean engring., Fenn Coll., 1925-31, dean, cooperative div., 1931-36, dean, student personnel services, chmn. faculty, dean coll., 1936-47, acting pres., 1947-48. Served as electrician, USN, 1917-19. Pres., Bd. Edn., South Euclid and Lyndhurst, Ohio; life trustee S. Euclid Methodist Ch.; pres. Hillcrest YMCA; bd. dirs. Human Engring. Inst., 1956-62, Pastoral Counseling Service, 1960—; mem Mayor's Com. on Ethics. Named Citizen of Yr., Cleveland Heights C. of C., 1965. Mem. Occupational Planning Com., Am. Coll. Personnel Assn., NEA, Cleve. C. of C., Ohio Coll. Assn., Iota Eta. Methodist. Republican. Mason. Clubs: Cleve. Affairs Council, Mid-day. Wrote: Faculty Participation in a College Guidance Program, 1941; subject of biog. work: Cradles of Greatness (Earl Hoover). Home: South Euclid, Ohio. Died Feb. 7, 1977; buried Roseville (Calif.) Dist. Cemetery.

NICHOLS, MARIE HOCHMUTH, educator; b. Dunbar, Pa., July 13, 1908; d. Alexander and Mary (Flydell) Hochmuth; A.B., U. Pitts., 1931, M.A., 1936; Ph.D., U. Wis., 1945; m. Alan Nichols, Aug. 18, 1960. Instr. Mt. Mercy Coll., Pitts., 1935-39; mem. faculty U. Ill., Urbana, from 1939, prof. speech, from 1958; vis. prof. U. So. Calif., summers 1957, 67, 69; lectr. La. State U., summer 1960; vis. prof. U. Hawaii, 1962. Mem. Speech Assn. Am. (adminstrv. council from 1960; pres. 1969), NEA. Author: Rhetoric and Criticism, 1963. Editor: History and Criticism of American Public Address, Vol. III, 1955; American Speeches, 1954; Quar. Jour. Speech, 1962-65. Home: Urbana, Ill. Died Oct. 7, 1978.

NICHOLS, WILLIAM ROBERT, army officer; b. Petersburg, Va. July 25, 1885; s. William Robert and Nora Desonier (Préot) N.; B.S., Va. Mil. Inst., Lexington, 1906; student Mass. Inst. of Tech., Boston, 1908-09, spl. army course, 1915-16; hon. grad. Coast Arty. Sch., Fort Monroe, Va., 1914; grad. Command and Gen. Staff Sch., Ft. Leavenworth, Kans., 1924, Army War Coll., 1930; m. Josephine Stoney Stevens, Jan. 10, 1912; children—Nora Préot (wife of Lt. Col. Marshall S. Carter), William Robert Nichols, Jr. Commd. 2d lt. U.S. Army, Apr. 1909, and advanced through the grades to brig. gen., Sept. 13, 1943; served in Germany, England, Belgium and France, 1919-22, Hawaii, 1930-32, Panama, 1939-40; chief of staff, 4th Service Command, Atlanta, Ga., since Dec. 1940.

Mem. Phi Kappa Phi, Kappa Alpha (Southern). Clubs: Hampton Yacht (Hampton, Va.); Piedmont Driving (Atlanta, Ga.). Mason. Home: Savannah, Ga. *

NICHOLSON, REX LEE, mfg. co. exec.; b. Calhoun County, Tex., Mar. 14, 1902; s. Absolom H. and Rebecca J. (Daily) N.; Structural Engr., Chgo. Tech. Coll., 1926; m. Mary Runyon, Oct. 24, 1926; children—Janice Grace, Laura Lee. With cattle ranch nr. Amarillo, Tex., 1910-24; gen. supt., partner Stabbert Constrn. Co., Tacoma, 1924-37; asst. adminstr. Fed. Works Agy., Western U.S., Alaska, Hawaii, 1937-44; mng. dir. Builders of the West, Inc., San Francisco, 1944-45; founder, 1945, thereafter pres. Pacific Tractor & Implement Co., Richmond, Calif., also chmn. bd.; organizer Indsl. Trucklease Co., San Francisco, 1948; prin. owner Columbia Tractor & Implement Co., Portland, Oreg., from 1950; pres. Liquid Carbonic Corp., 1956-57; pres. Liquid Carbonic div., sr. v.p., mem. bd. mgmt. Gen. Dynamics Corp., 1957-61; v.p., dir. Liquid Carbonic do Brazil, Inc., Manitou Carbonic Corp.; dir. Ariz.-Detroit Corp., Krueger Mfg. Co., Prather Tractor Co., Homecraft, Inc., Liquid Carbonic Canadian Corp., Ltd., Liquid Carbonic Venezolana, S.A., Gases and Chems., Internat., S.A., Liquido Carbonico Colombiana, S.A., Liquid Carbonic del Peru, S.A., Liquido Carbonic de Mexico, S.A., Liquid Carbonic West Indies Ltd., Kings Mfg. Co., Ariz.-Detroit Corp., Mile High Service Co., Croycraft Medicine Center; chmn. bd. Far-Horizons Mobile Home Parks Inc., Rex Broadcasting Corp., Cascade Builders Inc., El Dorado Lodge and Land Properties, Golden Gate Way Bldgs. Inc., Prather Ford Tractor Co., Inc.; pres. San Larendo Indsl. Park, Inc., Amphi-Plaza Shopping Centers, Inc., Tucson, Manana Land Develop. Co.; organizer Nicholson Enterprises, Inc. 1961. Engaged in reorgn. adminstrn. pub. lands, U.S. and Tys., Dept. Interior, 1946; organizer FCDA, Washington, 1951; dir. Hoover Report on Govt. Reorgn.; cons. sec. interior. Mem. U.S. Calif. chambers commerce, Newcomen Soc. N.Y. and London. Presbyn. Clubs: Kiwanis, Commonwealth (San Francisco); Chicago; Glenview (Golf, Ill.); Toastmasters Internat.; Claremont Country (Oakland, Calif.); Tucson Nat. Country, Skyline (Tucson). Author articles agrl., indsl. potentials western and pub. lands. Home: Pachaco, Calif. Deceased.

NICKERSON, WALTER JOHN, educator, microbiologist; b. Plainfield, N.J., Aug. 6, 1915; s. Walter John and Elizabeth Regina (Smythe) N.; B.S., West Chester Coll., 1937; M.A., Harvard, 1940, Ph.D., 1942; m. Helen Kelsall, Sept. 6, 1941 (div.); 1 son, Kenneth Warwick; m. 2d, Thelma Cancro, Oct. 5, 1962 (dec.); m. 3d, Shirley Hoyt, Apr. 12, 1969. Instr. Wheaton Coll., Norton, Mass., 1942-43, asst. prof., 1946-47, asso. prof., 1948-50; asst. dermatology Tufts U. Med. Coll., 1946-50; Guggenheim fellow Carlsberg Lab., Copenhagen, also Laboratorium voor Microbiologie, Delft, Holland, 1947-48; vis. prof. biology Brown U., 1948-50; asso. prof. microbiology Rutgers U., 1950-54, prof. microbial biochemistry, 1954-78; microbiologist on Blue Dolphin No. Labrador expdn., 1954. Cons. USPHS, 1955-59, 62-66, 74-77; research collaborator Brookhaven Nat. Lab., AEC, 1956-57; del. 4th Internat. Congress Microbiology, Copenhagen, 1947, Fifth Internat. Congress, Rio de Janeiro, 1950 (v.p.), 6th Internat. Congress, Rome, 1953, 7th Internat. Congress, Stockholm, 1958 (v.p.), 4th Internat. Congress Biochemistry, Vienna, 1958; plenary lectr. 2d Internat. Conf. on Yeasts, Brno, Czechoslovakia, 1968; Symposium lectr. 10th Internat. Congress Microbiology, Mexico City, 1970, French Acad. Microbiology, Paris, 1970. Mem. Sci. adv. bd. Leonard Wood Meml. Found., 1973-74, chmn., 1974-77; also Inst. Tropical Health, from 1976. Served to 1st lt. USAAF, 1943-46. Recipient Distinguished Alumni award West Chester Coll. Fellow AAAS, Am. Acad. Microbiology; mem. Soc. Am. Bacteriologists (pres. N.J. br. 1953-54), Soc. Gen. Microbiology (Gt. Britain), Am. Soc. Biol. Chemists. Editor: Biology of Pathogenic Fungi, 1947; Biochemistry of Morphogenesis, 1959. Editorial bd. Chronica Botanica, 1943-56, Science, 1952-54, Science Monthly, 1952-54, Federation Proceedings, 1973-75. Author tech. papers in sci.-jours. Home: Middlesex, N.J., also Southampton, Bermuda. Died Mar. 5, 1979; buried Lake Nelson Meml. Park, Piscataway, N.J.

NICKLESS, ALFRED SAMUEL, clergyman; b. Dawley, Shropshire, Eng., July 1, 1885; s. Benjamin S. and Annie (Beedles) N.; B.A., Lenox Coll., Hopkinton, Ia., 1913; B.D., Presbyn. Theol. Sem., Chicago, 1916; D.D., Coe Coll., Cedar Rapids, Ia., 1930; m. Ida Fishwild, June 18, 1913; children—Lester, Margaret Virginia, Helen Louise. Came to U.S., 1908, naturalized citizen, 1922. Student supply Albany Park Presbyn. Ch., Chicago, 1914-16; pastor same, 1916-23; asst. pastor Fourth Presbyn. Ch., Chicago, 1923-27; pastor Presbyn. Ch. of the Covenant, Detroit, Mich., 1927-34, 1st Ch. San Francisco, 1934-35, 1st Ch., Davenport, Ia., 1935-50, ret.; vis. lectr. in pastoral theology McCormick Theol. Sem., Chicago. Dir. Sch. of Religion, U. of Iowa. Moderator Detroit Presbytery, 1931-32, Iowa City Presbytery, 1942-43. Trustee Coe Coll., Cedar Rapids, Ia.; Sch. of Religion, U. of Ia. Mem. Commn. on Marriage and the Home of Fed. Council of Chs. of Christ in Am. Mem. Am. Arbitration Assn. Mason. Clubs: Contemporary Rotary, Davenport. Contbr. to ch. pubs. Address: Chicago. *

NICOLSON, HAROLD (GEORGE), author, critic; b. Tehran, Persia, Nov. 21, 1886; s. Lord Carnock and Rowan (Hamilton) N.; student Wellington Coll., Balliol Col. (Oxford); hon. Dr. univs. Athens, Grenoble, Glasgow, Dublin, Durham; m. Victoria Mary Sackville-West, Oct. 1, 1913; children—Benedict, Nigel. Entered Fgn. Office, 1909; service in Madrid, 1910, Constantinople, 1911; mem. Brit. delegation Peace Conf., 1919; assigned Fgn. Office, 1920, apptd. counsellor, 1925; mem. Brit. legation, Tehran, 1925, Brit. embassy, Berlin, 1927-29; resigned Fgn. Office: editorial staff Evening Standard, 1930. Mem. Parliament, West Leicester, 1935-45; parliamentary sec. Ministry Information, 1940-41; gov. BBC, 1941-46. Trustee Nat. Portrait Gallery. Decorated comdr. Legion of Honor. Mem. Classical Assn. (pres. 1950-51), Nat. Inst. Arts and Letters, N.Y. Acad (hon.). Mem. Labour Party. Clubs: Travellers', Beefsteak. Author numerous books, latest being: Why Britain is at War, 1939; (anthology with V. Sackville West) Another World Than This, 1945; The Congress of Vienna, 1946; The English Sense of Humour, 1947; Comments, 1948; Benjamin Constant, 1949; King George V: His Life and Reign, 1952; Evolution of Diplomatic Method (Chiclele Lectures), 1954; Good Behaviour, 1955, Sainte-Beuve, 1957; Journey to Java, 1957; The Age of Reason, 1960. Address: Kent, Eng.; also Piccadilly, W.1., Eng. *

NICOLSON, J(OHN) U(RBAN) (NIK'UL-SUN), author; b. Alma, Kan., Oct. 9, 1885; s. Malcolm and Olivia (Prigmore) N.; ed. pub. schs.; m. Ida May Platz, June 10, 1917. Author: (verse) The King of the Black Isles, 1924; The Sainted Courtezan, 1924; The Drums of Yle, 1925; The Road to Antioch, 1926; Sonnets of a Minnesinger, 1926; (prose) Fingers of Fear, 1937. Translator of Villon's Poems, Complete, 1927; The Canterbury Tales, Complete, 1934. Home: Mason, N.H. *

NICOLSON, MARJORIE HOPE, educator; b. Yonkers, N.Y., Feb. 18, 1894; d. Charles Butler and Lissie Hope (Morris) Nicolson; A.B., U. Mich., 1914, A.M., 1918; Ph.D., Yale, 1920, L.H.D., 1963; postgrad. Johns Hopkins 1923-26, Europe, 1926-27; Litt.D., Mt. Holyoke Coll., 1933, U. Mich., 1937, Middlebury Coll., 1941, Princeton, 1946, Mills, 1956, George Washington U., 1962, Columbia, 1963, Douglass Coll., 1964, Coll. William and Mary, 1966; LL.D., Goucher Coll., 1940, Smith Coll., 1941, Elmira Coll., 1943; L.H.D., Wilson Coll., 1940, U. Vt., 1941, Wesleyan U., 1943, Colby Coll., 1953, Yale, 1963. Tchr., Saginaw, Mich., 1914-15, Detroit, 1915-18; instr. U. Minn., 1920-22, asst. prof. English, 1922-23; asst. prof. Goucher Coll., 1923-26; fellow John Simon Guggenheim Meml. Found., 1926-27 (mem. com. on award 1930-35, 36-37); asso. prof. English, Smith Coll., 1926-29, prof., 1929-41, dean, 1929-41; prof. English, Grad. Sch. Columbia, 1941-62, William Peterfield Trent prof. emeritus, 1962-81. Luther J. Lee, Jr. vis. prof. Renaissance studies Claremont Grad. Sch., 1962-63; mem. Inst. for Advanced Study, Princeton, N.J., 1963-68. Recipient Sesquicentennial award U. Mich.; Wilbur Lucius Cross medal Yale; Crawshay prize for English lit. Brit. Acad., 1947 (for Newton Demands the Muse); Achievement award Am. Assn. U. Women, 1954; prize Am. Council Learned Socs., 1962. Mem. Modern Lang. Assn. Am., (exec. council 1929-32, v.p. 1937-38, pres. 1963-64), History of Sci. Soc., Am. Philos. Soc., Phi Beta Kappa (senator from 1937, v.p. 1937-40, nat. pres. united chpts. 1940-46), Chi Omega. Author: The Art of Description, 1926; Conway Letters, 1930; The Microscope and English Imagination, 1935; A World in the Moon, 1937; Newton Demands the Muse, 1946; Voyages to the Moon, 1948; The Breaking of the Circle, 1950; Mountain Gloom and Mountain Glory, 1959; Milton: Poems and Selected Prose, 1962; A Reader's Guide to Milton, 1963; Pepys' Diary and the New Science, 1965. Editor: Jour. History of Ideas. Contbr. to periodicals. Home: White Plains, N.Y. Died Mar. 9, 1981.

NIELSEN, ARTHUR CHARLES, business exec.; b. Chgo., Sept. 5, 1897; s. Rasmus and Harriet Burr (Gunn) N.; B.S. in Elec. Engring., U. Wis., 1918, D.Sc. (hon.), 1974; m. Gertrude B. Smith, June 15, 1918; children—Arthur Charles, Margaret Ann, Philip Robert, Barbara Harriet, Virginia Beatrice. Elec. engr. Isko Co., Chgo., 1919-20; engr. H.P. Gould Co., Chgo., 1920-23; pres. A.C. Nielsen research and bus. services, 1920-23; pres. A.C. Nielsen Co., 1923-57, chmn., 1957-75, chmn. exec. com., 1976-80, marketing research and bus. services, operators of the Nielsen Retail Index Services, Nielsen TV Index Services, Nielsen Coupon Clearing House, NEODATA Services, Petroleum Info. Corp., others; chmn. A.C. Nielsen Internat. Inc., A.C. Nielsen Co., Can., Ltd., A.C. Nielsen Pty., Ltd. (Australia and New Zealand), A.C. Nielsen Co. (Pty.) Ltd., Johannesburg, South Africa, A.C. Nielsen Nederland B.V., A.C. Nielsen (Argentina) S.A., A.C. Nielsen Co., G.m.b.H., Germany, A.C. Nielsen Mgmt. Services, Switzerland, A.C. Nielsen S.A., Switzerland, A.C. Nielsen Co., Ges. M.B.H. Austria, A.C. Nielsen Prodn. S.A., Switzerland, A.C. Nielsen Cos., France, Italy, Spain, Portugal, Japan, Mexico, A.C. Nielsen Co. Ltd. (Oxford), A.C. Nielsen Co. (Belgium) S.A., A.C. Nielsen of Ireland, Ltd. Served as ensign USNR, World War I. Recipient 1936 Silver medal Ann. Advt. Awards Com.; award Chgo. Federated Advt. Club, 1941; Paul D. Converse award Am. Marketing Assn., 1951, Marketing Man of Year award, 1970; named to Hall of Fame in Distbn., 1953, Nat. Lawn Tennis Hall of Fame, 1971; knight Order Dannebrog, 1961; Parlin Meml. award, 1963; ann. award Internat. Advt. Assn., 1966. Mem. Tau Beta Pi, Eta Kappa Nu, Sigma Phi. Clubs: West Side Tennis (Forest Hills, L.I., N.Y.); University (N.Y.C.); India Hill (Winnetka). Home: Winnetka, Ill. Died June 1, 1980; buried Chicago, Ill.

NIEPORTE, VICTOR B., clergyman; b. Norwood, Ohio, Feb. 19, 1909; s. Edward Henry and Adelaide Marie (Albers) N.; Litt.B., Xavier U., Cin., 1932; postgrad. St. Louis U., 1932-34, St. Marys (Kans.) Coll., 1938-42; M.A., Loyola U., Chgo., 1935. Mem. S.J., 1928-77; tchr. St. Xavier High Sch., Cin., 1935-38, Loyola U., Chgo., 1943-44; dean evening div. Xavier U., 1944-45, 48-53, dean Coll. Liberal Arts, 1945-48, regent evening coll., 1948-53, dir. admissions Coll. Liberal Arts 1950-53, exec. v.p., 1956-71, v.p. adminstrn., 1971-77; minister Loyola U., Chgo., 1954-56. Address: Cincinnati, Ohio. Died Nov. 21, 1977.

NILES, EMORY HAMILTON, judge; b. Balt., Oct. 15, 1892; s. Alfred Salem and Mary Hamilton (Waters) N.; A.B., Johns Hopkins, 1913; Rhodes Scholar, Oxford (Eng.) U., 1913-16, B.A., M.A., B.C.L.; LL.B., U. Md., 1917, LL.D., 1964, J.D., 1969; LL.D., Goucher Coll., 1967; m. Anne Whitridge Williams, Nov. 4, 1922; children—Anne W. (Mrs. H.C. Primrose III), Emory Hamilton, Mary Waters (Mrs. Hugh Shepley). Practice law, Balt., 1920; mem. Niles, Barton, Morrow & Yost, 1925; asso. judge of Supreme Bench of Balt., 1938-54, chief judge, 1954-62. Lectr. on law of admiralty U. Md., 1925-49, of evidence, 1941-51; lectr. med. jurisprudence Johns Hopkins Med. Sch., 1946-48; mem. U.S. Commn. Internat. Rules Jud. Procedure, 1960; mem. Jud. Council Md., 1923-34; pres. Balt. Criminal Justice Commn., 1933-34; chmn. Md. Jud. Selection Council, 1963; mem. Anglo-Am. Interchange on Criminal Justice, 1963-64. Mem. Am. Com. for Relief in Near East, Turkey, 1919; chmn. Fgn. Policy Assn., Balt., 1928-41; sec. Rhodes Scholarship Com. for Md., 1924-31, 46-69, for Middle Atlantic dist., 1946-69; ration adminstr., chmn. War Price and Rationing Bds. Balt., 1942-46; Md. Fuel Coordinator, 1948. Trustee Goucher Coll., 1934-76, pres. bd., 1936-46, Peabody Inst., 1944-46, Walters Art Gallery, 1955-76. Served from 2d lt., 313th F.A., to capt. 80th div. U.S. Army, 1917-19; AEF. Hon. fellow Hertford Coll. Oxford, 1963. Fellow Inst. Jud. Adminstrn. (pres. 1963-66), Am. Bar Assn. (chmn. jud. adminstrn. sect. 1959, gov. 1966-69; com. on minimum Standards for criminal justice 1964-76); mem. Md. (pres. 1961), N.Y., Balt. City bar assns., Assn. Am. Rhodes Scholars (pres. 1969-75), Nat. Council Crime and Delinquency (mem. judges adv. council 1954-66), Am. Law Inst., Maritime Law Assn. of U.S., Phi Beta Kappa, Alpha Delta Phi. Democrat. Unitarian. Clubs: Century (N.Y.C.); Hamilton Street. Founder, editor of American Maritime Cases, 1923-76, United States Aviation Reports, 1928-60. Address: Baltimore, Md. Died Aug. 9, 1976.

NILES, JOHN JACOB, composer, folklore collector, folk singer; b. Louisville, Apr. 28, 1892; s. John Thomas and Lula Sarah (Reisch) N.; student U. Lyon, 1919, Cin. Conservatory Music, 1920-22, Mus.D. (hon.), 1949; D.F.A. (hon.), Transylvania U., 1968; Litt.D. (hon.), Episcopal Theol. Sem. in Ky., 1970, U. Ky., 1973; H.H.D. (hon.), U. Louisville, 1971; m. Rena Lipetz, Mar. 21, 1936; children—Thomas Michael Tolliver, John Edward. Concerts Am. folk music, maj. cities, U.S., Eng. Holland, France, Germany, Scandinavian countries, 1927-78. Served to 1st lt. A.C., U.S. Army, 1917-19. Recipient nat. citation Fedn. Music Clubs, 1967. Mem. Am. Folklore Soc., Am. Dialect Soc., ASCAP. Episcopalian. Maj. compositions include Lamentation, Mary the Rose, Rhapsody for the Merry Month of May; best known songs include I Wonder As I Wander, Go 'Way from My Window, Black is the Color of My True Love's Hair, Venezuela, others; rec. artist for Tradition Everest Records, Folkways and RCA-Victor Records. Author: Singing Soldiers, 1927; Songs My Mother Never Taught Me, 1929; One Man's War, 1929; The Ballad Book of John Jacob Niles, 1961; Folk Ballads for Young Actors, 1962; Folk Carols for Young Actors, 1962; (poetry collection) Brickdust and Buttermilk, 1977. Home: Lexington, Ky. Died Mar. 1, 1980; buried St. Hubert's Cemetery, Clark County, Ky.

NILSEN, ARTHUR, physician; b. N.Y. City, July 17, 1883; s. Jonas Rein and Laura (Whittemore) N.; A.B., Yale, 1904, M.D., Columbia, 1908; m. Florence O. Zetterstrom, Oct. 2, 1915. Prof. of clin. otolaryngology and dir. of service, N.Y., Post Graduate Med. Sch. and Hosp., 1938-48; cons. otolaryngologist at the University Hospital Diplomate Am. Bd. of Otolaryngology. Mem. Am. Med. Assn., N.Y. State and County Med. Soc., N.Y. Acad. of Medicine, N.Y. Laryngol. Soc., Phi Gamma Delta. Address: New York, N.Y. *

NIN, ANAIS, author; b. Paris, France; d. Joaquin and Rosa (Culmell) Nin; ed. pub. schs. Author, Spanish dancer, lectr., dramatic reader; short stories pub. various mags. including Vogue, Harper's Bazaar. Author: D.H. Lawrence, An Unprofessional Study, 1932; House of Incest, 1936; Winter of Artifice, 1939; Under a Glass Bell, 1944; Ladders to Fire, 1946; Children of the Albatross, 1947; The Four Chambered Heart, 1950; A Spy in the House of Love, 1954; Solar Barque, 1958; Seduction of the Minotaur, 1961; Omnibus of Five Novels in One, 1961; Cities of the Interior, 1975; Collages, 1964; Diary of Anais Nin, 7 vols., 1966, 67, 69, 71, 74, 76, 80; The Novel of the Future, 1968; Anais Nin Reader, 1973; A Woman Speaks, 1975; (essays) In Favor of the Sensitive Man, 1976; Delta of Venus, 1977; Linotte: The Early Diary of Anais Nin, 1914-1920, 1978; Little Birds, 1979. Died Jan. 14, 1977.

NISWONGER, C. ROLLIN, educator; b. Pitsburg, Ohio, Mar. 24, 1907; s. Clifford O. and Edith Rose (Vance) N.; S.B., Miami U., Oxford, Ohio, 1929, LL.D., 1973; M.S., U. Ill., 1931; Ph.D., Ohio State U., 1950; m. Sue Janes, Aug. 22, 1938; children—Cynthia Sue, Thomas Rollin. Asst. instr. accounting U. Ill. 1929-31; instr. accounting Wash. State U., 1931-35; asst. prof. accounting Miami U., 1935-41, asso. prof., 1941-47, prof., 1947-72, emeritus, 1972-80, head dept., 1947-66, asst. dean Sch. Bus. Adminstrn., 1940-56, acting dean, 1954-55, dir. summer session, 1946-48; cons. Office of U.S. Comptroller Gen., 1955-58; accounting exec. OPA, 1943. Served as lt. Supply Corps, USNR, cost inspection service, 1944-46. C.P.A., Washington, Ohio. Mem. Am. Inst. of C.P.A.'s, Financial Execs. Inst., Am. Accounting Assn. (pres. 1958), Ohio Soc. C.P.A.'s, Phi Beta Kappa, Beta Gamma Sigma, Sigma Chi, Beta Alpha Psi (nat. pres. 1962-63), Delta Sigma Pi (Delta Sig of Year 1978), Omicron Delta Kappa. Co-author: Federal Tax Accounting, ann. edits., 1940-46; Income Tax Procedure, ann. edits., 1947-67; Accounting Principles, 6th thru 12th edits., 1953-77. Contbr. to jours. Home: Oxford, Ohio. Died Feb. 28, 1980; buried Oxford.

NOA, THOMAS LAWRENCE, bishop; b. Iron Mountain, Mich., Dec. 18, 1892; s. John and Magdalene (Walczak) N.; ed. St. Francis Sem., Milw., 1907-11, N. Am. Coll., Rome, 1911-17; Ph.D., Propaganda U., Rome, 1913, S.T.D., 1917. Ordained priest Roman Catholic Ch., Rome, 1916; prof. St. Joseph's Sem., Grand Rapids, Mich., 1917-46, rector, 1926-46; consecrated titular bishop of Salona, Mar. 19, 1946; coadjutor bishop, Sioux City, Iowa, Aug. 20, 1947; bishop, Marquette, Mich., 1947-68. Address: Marquette, Mich. Died Mar. 13, 1977.

NOBILE, UMBERTO, polar explorer, aeronautics officer; b. Lauro, Italy, Jan. 21, 1885; s. Vincenzo and Maria (La Torraca) N.; degree of Dr. Engring., U. of Naples, 1908; m. Carlotta Ferraiolo (dec.), June 21, 1916; 1 dau. Maria (wife of Dr. O. Schettino). Dir. Mil. Aircraft Factory, Rome, 1918, designer and builder some new types of airships for Italian, U.S., Spanish, Argentinian, Japanese govts., new type parachute, 1918, all-metal type aeroplane constrn., 1921; cons. engr. Goodyear Co., Akron, O., 1922; designer and builder new type airship (type N. Norge and Italia) used later in polar expdns., also built airship Mr, smallest in the world, 1923-24; comd. first polar expdn. with airship (the Norge expdn.) from Rome to Teller, Alaska; made the first crossing of Polar Sea accomplished by man, 1925-26; organized 2d polar expdn. in airship Italia, 1927-28, comd. expdn. to Spitsbergen Islands; from this point made 3 exploration flights over unknown parts of the polar regions, 1928; resigned as gen. in Engring. Aeronaut. Corp., Italy, 1929, reinstated and advanced, 1945; prof. aeronaut, constrn. U. of Naples, since 1926; organized constrn. of airships, Russia, 1931-36; instr. Lewis Aeronaut. Sch., Lockport, Ill., 1939-42; established in Madrid, 1942; returned to Italy; 1943. Mem. della Societá Nazionale Dante Alighieri; dell' Associazione Italiana Aerotecnica; dell' Associazione Nazionale di volontari di guerra; del Reale Istituto Beneto delle Scienze, Lettere ed Arti; della Societá Econmica di Chiavair; Casa Italiana di N.Y. (hon. vice pres.); docente dell'Universitá Italiana per stranieri, di Perugia; Accademia Pontificia delle Scienze Catholic. Author: From Rome to Teller across the North Pole, 1927; The Italia at North Pole, 1931; Preparation and Scientific Results of the Italia Expedition, 1929; I Can Tell the Truth, 1945; contbr. to numerous sci. and tech. publs. Home: Rome. *

NOBLE, ALBERT GALLATIN, naval officer; b. Preston, Tex., Dec. 14, 1895; s. Albert G. and Sally (Wilson) N.; B.S., U.S. Naval Acad., 1917; M.S. in M.E., Mass. Inst. Tech., 1923; m. Anna Madeline Martin, Aug. 9, 1917; 1 dau., Nancy Louise (Mrs. L. Andrew Reed, Jr.). Commd. ensign, USN, 1917, promoted through grades to vice adm., 1950; served in U.S.S. Delaware, Battleship Squadron 6, British Grand Fleet, World War I; comd. destroyers Dallas and Cassin, and served as fleet gunnery officer, staff of comdr. in chief U.S. Fleet, 1938-40; comd. cruiser, 1943-44; chief of staff to comdr. 7th Amphibious Force, 1944; comdr. Amphibious Group, Pacific Fleet, 1945-46; chief of Naval Bureau of Ordnance, 1947-50; chief of naval materiel, 1950-51, ret. as adm., 1951. Director Vitro Corp. Am. Decorated: Navy Cross, Navy D.S.M., Army D.S.M., Navy Legion of Merit with two gold stars, Army Legion of Merit, Atlantic and Pacific area medals, World War I medal. Clubs: Army-Navy Country, Army Navy Town (Washington). Home: Washington, D.C. Died Feb. 22, 1980.

NOBLE, DANIEL EARL, radio and TV corp. exec.; b. Naugatuck, Conn., Oct. 4, 1901; s. George and Emma (Talboy) N.; summer student Harvard; B.S., Conn. State Coll., 1929; postgrad. Mass. Inst. Tech.; D.Sc., Ariz. State Coll., 1957; m. Doraise E. Remington, July 10, 1925; (div. 1963); children—Talboy, Tryon; m. 2d, Mary Louise Lynch, Oct. 2, 1965. Asst. prof. elec. engring. U. Conn., 1923-40; radio engring. cons., Conn., 1930-40; with Motorola, Inc., Chgo., 1940—, successively dir. research, gen. mgr. communications and electronics div., v.p. charge communications and electronics div., exec. v.p., 1949-80, vice chmn. bd., chief tech. officer, 1965-70, dir., 1949-72, chmn. Motorola sci. adv. bd., 1970-80; founding dir. United Bank Financial Corp., to 1976. Mem. steering group Research & Engring. Adv. Panel, Office Asst. Seg. Def., 1957-59; mem. Army Sci. Adv. Panel, 1957-64, cons. to Panel, 1964-68; chmn. panel 13 Radio Tech. Planning Bd., 1944-48; mem. nat. TV systems com. which formulated color TV standards, 1952. Past pres. bd. Phoenix Symphony Assn., 1970-71. Bd. dirs. Ariz. State U. Found.; bd. visitors Mass. Inst. Tech. Recipient Certificate Commendation from USN and U.S. Signal Corps for service during World War II; medal Achievement, Western Electronic Mfrs. Assn., 1962; Stuart Ballantine medal Franklin Inst., 1972. Fellow I.E.E.E. (dir.); mem. Nat. Acad. Engring. Patentee electronic devices. Home: Scottsdale, Ariz. Died Feb. 16, 1980.

NOBLE, FRED B., lawyer; b. Preston, Md., April 17, 1883; s. Isaac L. and Mary Elizabeth (Corkran) N.; A.B., Wash. Coll., 1902, LL.D., 1953; student U. Md., 1904-05; LL.B., Harvard, 1907; m. Eva L. Wyand, May 20, 1910; 1 dau., Mary W. Principal, Hurlock, Md. High Sch., 1902-03; teacher of science and language, Shenandoah Collegiate Inst., Dayton, Va., 1903-04; admitted to Md. Bar, 1907, Florida Bar, 1908; Supreme Court of the United States, 1950; practice of law, Jacksonville, Fla., 1908—; special hearing officer for conscientious objectors to military service for Southern District of Florida; lecturer in Greek, Jacksonville Univ., 1957-58. Member and chmn., bd. of pub. instrn., Duval County, Fla., 1917-18, 1921-25, 1931, 1932, 1942-46; mem. Continuing Educational Council of Fla.; member board of trustees, Jacksonville Junior College, now Jacksonville University, 1936—, chairman of board, 1937-43; member United Conference, Kansas City, Mo., 1939, to unite the Methodist Episcopal Church, The Methodist Episcopal Church South and Methodist Protestant Church; mem. Gen. Confs. M.E. Church 1936 and of The Methodist Church, 1940, 44, 48, 52, 60; mem. bd. education, Methodist Episcopal Church, 1936-48, member general board of lay activiaies 1948-52; conf. lay leader, Florida Conf. of Methodist Church Dec., 1940-52; member judicial council Methodist Church, 1952-56. Served in Foyer du Soldat under auspices of American Y.M.C.A., France, 1918-19. Mem. Jacksonville (Fla.), Florida, and American bar associations. Methodist. Mason (33 deg., Grand Master, 1943), Odd Fellow. Clubs: Civitan of Jacksonville, Florida Yacht, Harvard of Jacksonville (ex-pres.). Home: Jacksonville. *

NOBLE, STUART GRAYSON, prof. edn.; b. Pasco County, Fla., May 10, 1886; s. Wylie Eli and Willie Agnes (McIntosh) N.; student Centenary Coll., Jackson, La., 1901-03; B.A., Univ. of N.C., 1907; M.A., U. of Chicago, 1910; Ph.D., Columbia, 1918; m. Annie Davis Powell, Aug. 11, 1919. Teacher rural sch., Pasco County, Fla., 1903-04; instr. in English and history, Horner Sch., Oxford, N.C., 1907-08; instr., Millsaps Prep. Sch., Jackson, Miss., 1908-11, headmaster, 1911-16; prof. edn., Millsaps College, 1916-23, Tulane U. since 1923, apptd. W.R. Irby prof. end., Tulane U., 1941; apptd. chmn. Tulane Dept. of Education, 1946; prof. edn., U. of Pa., summer, 1928, U. of Ill., summer, 1932, U. of Southern Calif., summer, 1936, U. of Washington, 1939, U. of Texas, 1940. Pvt. Coast Arty., U.S. Army, 1918. Fellow of A.A.A.S.; mem. Nat. Soc. for Study of Edn., Nat. Soc. College Teachers of Education (pres. 1933-34), N.E.A., Pi Kappa Alpha, Sigma Upsilon, Phi Delta Kappa, Kappa Delta Pi. Democrat. Methodist. Author or co-author several books relating to field. Chmn. nat. com. assisting Fed. Office of Edn. in publishing hist. treatises. Home: New Orleans. *

NODEL, SOL, artist, illuminator, lectr., art cons.; b. Washington, Sept. 29, 1912; s. Mordecai and Sarah (King) N.; student Washington U. Sch. Fine Arts, 1931-34, Grand Central Sch. Art, 1939-40; pupil with Edmund Wuerpel, miniatures with Leo Dubson; m. Shulamith Gold, Apr. 6, 1941. Instr. painting St. Louis Settlement House, 1937-39; asst. instr. Grand Central Sch. Art, 1939-40; exhibited St. Louis Art Mus., St. Louis Artists Guild, High Mus. Atlanta, Queens Coll., N.Y.C., N.Y. U., Pope Pius XII Meml. Library, St. Louis U., B'nai B'rith Museum, Washington and others; represented in permanent collections Nat. Archives, Washington, Herbert Hoover Mus., Harry Truman Library, Congress U.S., Library Congress, F.D.R. Hyde Park Library, others in U.S., Europe, Israel, and Far East, also represented numerous pvt. collections; executed 12 panel illumination of Lincoln's Gettysburg Address; commns. received and illuminations hung in 5 royal houses of Europe, also hung in Japan, Switzerland, Eng., Israel, Belgian Congo, France, Italy; designer stained glass windows Mt. Sinai Meml. Chapel, St. Louis, Hopatcong (N.J.) Jewish Community Center. Chmn. art commn. Internat. Synagogue, J.F.K. Internat. Airport, N.Y.C. Mem. fine arts com., art adviser Mary McLeod Bethune Meml. and Ednl. Center, Washington; chmn. com. on art United Synagogues; mem. Nat. Council on Art in Jewish Life; hon. adv. bd. B'nai B'rith Women Bicentennial Com. hon. founding mem. of Law Sci. Found. U. Tex. Recipient first prize Monsanto Chem. award, Proctor and Gamble award, gold medal U.S. Army, award St. Louis YMHA, St. Louis Artists Guild, others. Fellow Royal Soc. Art (Life); mem. U.S. Hall of Fame Soc., 1968. Jewish (pres. congregation). Author: Some of My Best Friends, 1942; Ketubah, 1942, 50, 61; (with Dr. Cecil Roth) Book of Grace. Home: New York, N.Y. Died Aug. 22, 1976.

NODYNE, GEORGE O., banker; b. Jersey City, May 22, 1902; s. George O. and Sarah A. (Winward) N.; grad. Grad. Sch. Banking, Rutgers U., 1941; m. Anne K. Gordon, Nov. 16, 1928 (dec. Jan. 21, 1970); 1 dau., Sandra Lyle (Mrs. J.J. Murdock II); m. 2d, Anna Cole Harman, Jan. 2, 1975. With East River Savs. Bank, 1922-72, mgr. main office, 1935-41, dir. personnel charge br. adminstrn., 1941-51, trustee, 1951-72, exec. v.p., 1951-52, pres., 1952-70, chmn. bd., 1970-71, chmn. emeritus 1971-80; faculty Grad. Sch. Banking Rutgers U., 1947-51. Mem. adv. council pres. assos. Pace U. Recipient Horatio Alger award Am. Schs. and Colls. Assn., 1963. Mem. Am. Inst. Banking (gov. N.Y. chpt. 1939-52, pres. 1948-49, hon. mem.), Hundred Year Assn. N.Y. (pres. 1957-58), Commerce and Industry Assn. N.Y., Inc. (dir., pres. 1966, chmn. bd. 1967). Clubs: Bay Head (N.J.) Yacht; Bankers of America, Union League (N.Y.C.); Nassau (Princeton, N.J.). Home: Mantoloking, N.J. Died Sept. 13, 1980.

NOE, JAMES ALBERT, former gov. La., broadcasting exec.; b. West Point, Ky., Dec. 21, 1893; s. John M. and Belle (McRae) N.; ed. country schs.; m. Anna Gray Sweeney, May 7, 1922; children—Gay, James Albert, Linda McRae. Engaged in oil and natural gas business in Ark., La., Tex., Ariz., N.M.; became mem. La. Senate, 1932, was pres. pro tem; lt. gov. La. to 1936, gov. La. to May 12, 1936, filling unexpired term of late Gov. O. K. Allen; mem. La. Senate, 1936-40; owner, operator radio stations WNOE, WNOE FM, New Orleans, KNOE, also KNOE-TV, KNOEFM, Monroe, La.; owner, operator plantations, Quachita and Tensas parishes, La. Mem. Democratic Nat. Com. for La. Enlisted as pvt. and promoted through grades to lt., 39th Inf., AUS, World War I. Presbyn. Home: Monroe, La. Died Oct. 18, 1976; interred Monroe Meml. Park Cemetery, Monroe, La.

NOFSINGER, CHARLES WILLIAM, engring. co. exec.; b. Kansas City, Mo., Apr. 26, 1901; s. Joseph L. and Lizzie K. N.; B.S. in Mech. Engring., U. Ill., 1922; children—William M., Rowland L. Process engr. Sinclair Refining Co., 1922-26; with M.W. Kellogg Co., 1926-44; chief technologist Petroleum Adminstrn. for War, 1944-45; cons. engr. Sinclair Refining Co., Stratford Engring. Co., 1946-50; founder, pres., gen. mgr. C.W. Nofsinger Co., Kansas City, Mo., 1950-78, chmn. bd., chief exec. officer, 1978-80; mem. exec. com. Fractionation Research, Inc., Heat Transfer Research, Inc. Fellow ASME, Am. Inst. Chem. Engrs.; mem. Am. Chem. Soc., Am. Petroleum Inst., Nat. Soc. Profl. Engrs., Mo. Soc. Profl. Engrs. Christian Scientist. Clubs: Rotary, Masons. Patentee in field. Home: Kansas City, Mo. Died June 23, 1980.

NOKRASHY PASHA, MAHMOUD FAHMY (NO-KRÄ-SHI), premier of Egypt; born 1886; educated Training College, Cairo (Egypt), University College, Nottingham, Eng. Teacher Ras el-Tin secondary school, 1909-14; prin. Gamalia Sch., Cairo, 1914-24; asst. sec. gen. Ministry of Edn., 1924; under-sec. of state in Ministry of Interior, 1924-30; minister of communications, 1930, 1936-37; minister of interior, 1938-39, June-Sept. 1940; minister of edn., 1939-40; minister of finance, 1940-44; fgn. minister in coalition cabinet of Ahmed Maher Pasha, Oct. 1944-Feb. 1945; apptd. premier but resigned when negotiations with British for revision of 1936 Treaty of Alliance were unsuccessful; reapptd. by King Farouk, Dec. 9, 1946; now premier, minister of interior and fgn. affairs. Expelled from Wafd Party later became dep. leader Saadist Group. Address: Cairo, Egypt.*

NOLAN, JOHN LESTER, librarian; b. Concord, N.H., Apr. 14, 1909; s. Edmund P. and Grace (Heilbrun) N.; B.S. cum laude, Harvard, 1931; B.S. in L.S., Columbia, 1938; m. Dallas Fraser, June 20, 1935; children—David Fraser, Barbara Dallas. Librarian, Adams House Library, Harvard, 1931-34; sect. head, sr. reference librarian N.Y. Pub. Library, 1935-40; with Library of Congress, 1940-69, asst. dir. reference dept., 1954-58, asso. dir. reference dept., 1958-68, dir. reference dept., 1968-69, hon. cons., 1969-80; prof.

library studies U. Hawaii, 1969-70; library cons., 1970-80; dir. library services in U.K. for USIS, 1952-54. Mem. Am., D.C., Brit. library assns. Clubs: Cosmos, Harvard (Washington). Editor: Library of Congress Quar. Jour. Current Acquisitions, 1945-51. Contbr. articles to profl. jours. Home: Kensington, Md. Died Oct. 10, 1980.

NOMER, HAROLD ADIN, educator; b. New Brunswick, N.J., Mar. 20, 1883; s. Henry Conrad and Lillie Emma (Bedford) N.; grad. high sch., Plainfield, N.J., 1902; B.A., Williams Coll., 1906, hon. M.A., 1931; LL.D., Allegheny College, Meadville, Pa., 1937; studied Columbia, summers, 1909, 1913; m. Jenny Irene Pfeiffer, June 16, 1914; children—Lois, Harold Adin, John Bedford, Howell Fitch. Master in English, Polytechnic Prep. Sch., Brooklyn, N.Y., 1906-09, Lawrenceville (N.J.) Sch., 1909-19; headmaster Shady Side Acad., Pittsburgh, Pa., 1919-37; headmaster Friends Acad., Locust Valley, N.Y., since 1938. Mem. Headmasters' Assn., Country Day Schools' Assn., Delta Upsilon. Republican. Presbyn. Clubs: Rotary. Address: Locust Valley, L.I., N.Y.*

NOOJIN, RAY O., dermatologist; b. Birmingham, Ala., Nov. 29, 1912; s. Ray Oscar and Lillian (Dunnam) N.; A.B., U. Ala., 1933; M.D., U. Chgo., 1937; m. Martha Gunning, May 12, 1938; children—Barbara Dade (Mrs. Richard LeRoy Walthall), Ray O., Martha Elizabeth (Mrs. Robert McLester Ramsay, Jr.). Instr. pharmacology U. Chgo., 1937; intern in medicine Duke U., 1938-40, resident dermatology, 1941-44, instr. dermatology, 1945; prof. dermatology U. Ala. Sch. Medicine, Birmingham, 1945-79, chmn. dept., 1945-79. Chmn. task force for allied health profls. Nat. Program for Dermatology, 1970-71; chmn. Residency Rev. Com. for Dermatology, 1969-72. Chmn. bd. trustees Brooke Hill Sch. for Girls, 1961. Diplomate Am. Bd. Dermatology (mem. bd. 1964-79, v.p. 1969-70, pres. 1970-71). Mem. AMA, Am. Dermatol. Assn. (dir. 1959-64, pres.-elect 1979), Am. Acad. Dermatology (chmn. membership com. 1954, dir. 1957-59, ednl. com. 1971-74, dir. 1975-79), Ala. Dermatol. Soc. (pres. 1947, 51), Soc. for Investigative Dermatology, Southeastern Dermatol. Assn. (pres. 1955), So. Med. Assn. (chmn. dermatology sect. 1955), Assn. Profs. Dermatology (pres. 1974-75), Phi Beta Kappa, Alpha Omega Alpha, Gamma Sigma Epsilon, Alpha Epsilon Delta, Delta Kappa Epsilon. Rotarian (pres. Birmingham 1971-72). Editor: Dermatology for Students; Dermatology, A Practitioner's Guide, 1977. Home: Birmingham, Ala. Died May 25, 1979; buried Elmwood Cemetery, Birmingham.

NORDELL, CARL JOHAN DAVID (NÔR-DEL'), artist; b. Copenhagen, Denmark, Sept. 23, 1885; s. Carl Alfred and Maria (Walkama) N.; brought by parents to U.S., 1892; grad. R.I. Sch. of Design, 1905; postgrad. scholar, Art Students League, N.Y. City, 1905-07; School of Museum of Fine Arts, Boston, 1907-09; Paige traveling scholar, in Europe, 1909-11; m. Helen Edith Eddy, Feb. 14, 1939. Recipient many prizes and awards; represented in pub. and pvt. collections in U.S. and abroad. Former mem. faculty Grand Central Sch. Art, N.Y. City; Bradford (Mass.) Acad.; Ringling School Art. Mem. Chautauqua County Society Artists (hon.); Art Students League of New York (life mem.), and Grand Central Art Gallery (N.Y. City), Soc. Am. Etchers, Print Makers Soc. of Calif., North Shore Arts Assn. Clubs: Providence Art; Boston, Art; Salmagundi (New York). Author: The Presence, The Eternal One, 1942; Cosmic Prayer (dedicated to Thomas Paine), 1942. Home: San Fernando, Calif. *

NORDOFF, PAUL, composer; b. Phila., June 4, 1909; s. Paul Bookmyer and Kathryn (Huntington) N.; Mus.B., Phila. Conservatory Music, 1927; Mus.M., 1932; Juilliard Grad. Sch., 1932; Mus.D., Combs Coll. Music, 1958, B.Music Therapy, 1960; m. Sabina Zay, 1945; children—Anthony, Sylvia, Guy. Head composition dept. Phila. Conservatory Music, 1938-43; asst. prof. Mich. State Coll., 1945; prof. Bard Coll., 1949-58; research and work music therapy handicapped children, dept. child psychiatry U. Pa., 1961-67, Devereaux Schs., Devon, Pa., 1961, Inst. Logopedics, Wichita, Kan., 1962-63; tchr.-cons. music therapy project School Dist. Phila., 1962-67; lecturing fellow Am.-Scandinavian Found., 1967-68. Recipient Guggenheim Meml. fellowship, 1933, 35; Ford Found. Faculty fellowship, 1954; Bearns prize, Columbia U., 1933; Pulitzer travelling scholarship, 1940. Mem. Anthroposophical Soc., A.S.C.A.P. Composer: Secular Mass, 1935; incidental music for Katharine Cornell's Romeo and Juliet, 1936; Every Soul is a Circus (dance for Martha Graham), 1939, 40, 41, Tallyho for Agnes deMille, 1944; The Masterpiece (1-act opera), 1941; concerto for Eugene List, 1947; incidental music for Katharine Cornell's Anthony and Cleopatra, 1948; Folly (dance for Martha Graham); Lost Summer, Winter Symphony (commd. for Louisville Philharmonic); Tranquil Symphony (commd. by New Orleans Symphony); The Sea-Change (opera commd. by Columbia U.); Robert Burns: Poems and Songs; music for children (texts by Clive Robbins); Children's Play-Songs Vol. I and II; The Three Bears, The Story of Artaban, Fun for Four Drums, The Children's Christmas Play, Pif-Paf-Poltrie, Play-Songs with Resonator Bells, Spirituals for Children to Sing and Play. Author (with Clive Robbins) Music Therapy for Handicapped Children: Investigations and Experiences, 1967, Music Therapy in Special Education, 1971, Therapy in Music for Handicapped Children, 1971. Home: Wynnewood, Pa. Died Jan. 18, 1977.

NORDSTROM, LLOYD WALTER, retail exec.; b. Seattle, June 8, 1910; s. John Wilhelm and Hilda (Carlson) N.; student U. Wash., 1928-32; m. Illsley Ball, June 3, 1933; children—Loyal (Mrs. John McMillan), Linda (Mrs. David A. Mowat), Susan (Mrs. Richard Eberhardt). With Nordstrom, Inc., Seattle, 1932-76, co-pres., co-chmn., 1970-76; trustee Wash. Mutual Savs. Bank, 1964-76; dir. Western Internat. Hotels; majority stockholder Seattle Seahawks franchise Nat. Football League. Served to lt. USNR, 1943-46. Mem. Nat. Shoe Retailers Assn. (pres. 1958-59), Central Assn. Seattle (pres. 1969-70), Beta Theta Pi. Clubs: University, Seattle Golf, Seattle Tennis, Washington Athletic (Seattle). Home: Seattle, Wash. Died Jan. 1, 1976.

NORLANDER, EVERETT C., editor; b. Chgo., Nov. 4, 1894; s. John Hjalmer and Hilda (Ostrom) N.; student Lake Forest Coll., 1916-17, U. Mo., 1919; m. Anna Hall, Sept. 12, 1923; children—Everett Charles, John Allen. Reporter City News Bur. of Chgo., 1919-21, Chgo. Daily Jour., 1921-24, Chgo. Daily News, 1924-37, polit. editor, 1937-39, news editor, 1939-44, mng. editor, 1944-60; dir. City News Bur. Chgo.; mem. bd. dir. Chicago Daily News. Served as corporal, 149th F.A., 42d Division, U.S. Army, World War I. Mem. Sigma Delta Chi. Republican. Home: Park Ridge, Ill. Died Dec. 26, 1976.

NÔRLUND, NIELS ERIK, educator, mathematician; b. Slagelse, Denmark, Oct. 26, 1885; student U. Paris, Cambridge (Eng.) U.; Ph.D., U. Copenhagen, (hon.), Lund and Oslo univs.; D.Sc. (hon.), Dijon U., London U., D.Eng. (hon.), Darmstadt U.; m. Agnete Weaver, 1912; 2 children. Prof. math. U. Copenhagen; dir. Danish Geodetic inst.; pres. Baltic Geodetic Commn. Pres. Rask-Orsted Found. Mem. Roayl Danish Acad. Sci. (past pres.), Internat. Council Sci. Unions (pres.); fgn. mem. Royal Soc., Royal Astron. Soc., Royal Instrn. (hon.; London), acads. sci. Paris, Rome, Stockholm, Oslo, Helsingfors, Uppsala, Naples. Editor Acta Methematica. Home: Copenhagen Denmark. *

NORRIS, ARTHUR HUGHES, gerontologist; b. Indpls., Apr. 25, 1925; s. Arthur Grove and Della Rice (Hughes) N.; B.A., Westminster Coll., 1947; M.S., George Washington U., 1969; m. Jean Kelley, Dec. 22, 1952; 1 son, Arthur Thomas. Biologist gerontology br. Nat. Heart Inst., NIH, 1947-65, coordinator Balt. longitudinal study, gerontology research center Nat. Inst. Child Health and Human Devel., 1958-71, chief human performance sect., clin. physiology br., gerontology research center Nat. Inst. on Aging, 1967-71, 73; commd. USPHS, 1951, advanced through grades to health services dir., 1965, ret., 1971; pvt. practice gerontology cons., 1971-73. Served in USNR, 1943-46. Recipient award merit NIH, 1978. Fellow Gerontol. Soc.; mem. AAAS, Assn. Mil. Surgeons U.S., Commd. Officer Assn. USPHS, N.Y. Acad. Scis. Republican. Contbr. papers in field of gerontology. Home: Millersville Md. Died Dec. 6, 1980

NORRIS, HOKE, publicist, univ. adminstr.; b. Holly Springs, N.C., Oct. 8, 1913; s. Cadvin Hugh and Mabel Viola (Smith) N.; A.B., Wake Forest Coll., 1934; postgrad. U. N.C., 1946; Nieman fellow Harvard, 1950-51; m. Edna Dees, Aug. 1, 1941; 1 dau., Marion Dees. Reporter, Elizabeth City (N.C.) Daily Advance, 1934-36, Raleigh (N.C.) News and Observer, 1936-37; reporter, editor A.P. Raleigh, 1937-42, Charlotte, N.C., 1946; publicity dir. Lost Colony, Manteo, N.C., 1946-47; reporter, editor Winston-Salem (N.C.) Jour.-Sentinel, 1947-55; reporter, lit. editor Chgo. Sun Times, 1955-68; editorial bd. Chgo. Daily News, 1968-70; dir. pub. info. Chgo. Pub. Library, 1971-74; instr. creative writing U. Chgo., 1959-60 asst. v.p. pub. affairs Dir. Office Pub. Info., 1974-77. Served to capt. USAAF, 1942-46. Ford Found. mass media fellow U. Chgo., 1960-61. Author: (novels) All The Kingdoms of Earth, 1956; It's Not Far But I Don't Know the Way, 1969; author, editor We Dissent, 1962. Contbr. numerous short stories to mags. Home: Chicago, Ill. Died July 8, 1977.

NORTH, EMERSON ARTHUR, physician; b. Patriot, Ind., Feb. 14, 1880; s. William Foster and Abbie Alice (Humphrey) N.; student Purdue U., 1899-1901; M.D., U. of Cincinnati, 1906; m. Edna Schwarm, Nov. 29, 1911; 1 dau., Dorothy Irine. Began as physician, 1906; practicing in Cincinnati, O.; dir. psychiatry, U. of Cincinnati, 1933; dir. Central Clinic at Cincinnati Gen. Hosp., Community Chest Hamilton County and Cincinnati. Mem. A.M.A., Am Psychiatric Assn., Central Neuro-Psychiatric Assn., Ohio State Med. Assn., Cincinnati Acad. Medicine, Nu Sigma Nu. Club: Torch (Cincinnati). Republican. Methodist. Mason. Contbr. med. subjects. Home: Cincinnati, O. *

NORTH, ERIC MCCOY, cons. Am. Bible Soc.; b. Middletown, Conn., June 22, 1888; s. Frank Mason and Louise J. (McCoy) N.; B.A., Wesleyan U., Conn., 1909, M.A., 1910, D.D., 1931; M.A., Columbia, 1910, Ph.D., 1914; grad. Union Theol. Sem., 1913; m. Gladys Haven, April 17, 1920; children—Theodora, Louise Haven, William Haven. Asst. in systematic theology, Union Theol. Sem., 1913-14; asst. prof. history of Christianity, Ohio Wesleyan U., 1915-17; asso. editor S.S. Publs., M.E. Ch., 1917-26; ordained ministry M.E. Ch., 1918; dept. sec. Bd. of Foreign Missions, M.E. Ch., 1919-26; lecturer Drew Theol. Sem., 1919-24; sec. China Union Univs., 1924-27; asso. sec. Am. Bible Soc., 1927-28, sec., 1928-56; cons., 1957-80. Asst. sec. Gen. War-Time Commn. of Chs., 1918; chaplain, 1st lt. U.S. Army, 1918-19. Trustee United Board for Christian Higher Edn. in Asia, Harvard-Yenching Institute and Drew University. Decorated Officer, Order of Orange-Nassau, The Netherlands. Mem. Phi Nu Theta, Sigma Chi, Phi Beta Kappa. Author: Early Methodist Philanthropy, 1915; Organization and Administration of the Sunday School (with J. L. Cuninggim), 1917; The Kingdom and the Nations, 1921; The Worker and His Church (with Louise M. North), 1921. Editor: The Book of a Thousand Tongues, 1939. Home: Chatham, N.J. Died July 25, 1980.

NORTH, JOHN PAUL, surgeon, assn. exec.; b. Buffalo, Jan. 25, 1901; s. Walter and Harriet S. (Foote) N.; A.B., Princeton, 1922; M.D., U. Pa., 1926; m. Grace Elizabeth Hevner, July 5, 1946; m. 2d, Eugenia Davis Liebolt, June 15, 1974. Surg. tng. Hosp. U. Pa., Phila., 1926-32; pvt. practice surgery, Phila., 1932-42; mem. faculty U. Pa. Med. Sch., 1932-46; chief surg. service VA hosps. in McKinney, Tex., also Dallas, 1946-73; clin. prof. surgery emeritus Southwestern Med. Sch., 1946-60; dir. A.C.S., Chgo., 1960-69; med. dir. Sch. Allied Health Professions, U. Tex. Southwestern Med. Sch., 1972-77. Served from maj. to col. M.C., AUS, 1942-45. Mem. A.C.S., Am., So., Western surg. assns., Am. Assn. Surgery Trauma, Tex. Surg. Soc., Alpha Omega Alpha. Episcopalian. Home: Dallas, Tex. Died Jan. 28, 1977.

NORTH, OLIVER BURNHAM, govt. official; b. New Haven, Conn., July 24, 1885; s. George Post and Margaret (Field) N.; A.B., Yale, 1908; unmarried. Successively with O. B. North & Co., New Haven, Conn.; North & Judd Mfg. Co., New Britain, Conn. Now asst. commd. attache Am. Embassy, Ottawa, Can. Republican. Episcopalian. Home: New Haven, Conn. *

NORTHCOTT, HARRY CLIFFORD, bishop; born Exeter, Ont., Can., Oct. 16, 1890; s. James Harvey and Emily (Patey) N.; brought to U.S., 1890; B.A., Northwestern U., 1918, M.A., 1919; B.D., Garrett Bibl. Inst., Evanston, Ill., 1921; D.D., Ill. Wesleyan U., 1929, LL.D., 1953; S.T.D., Northwestern University, 1952; m. Florence Engle, June 14, 1917; 1 dau., Murian Louise (Mrs. Dan Ponder). Ordained Methodist minister, 1919; pastor, Elmhurst, Ill., 1917-18; supply pastor, Chicago, 1919-21, pastor, Parkside Ch., Chicago, 1921-23; pastor, Oak Park, 1923-28; pastor First Ch., Champaign, 1928-48; consecrated bishop, Indianapolis, July 1948; resident bishop for Wis. area, 1948-60; chmn. commn. Deaconess Work Meth. Ch.; mem. commn. on chaplains Meth. Ch., mem. joint com. on cultivation Meth. Ch. Served as lt. chaplain, AEF, 1918. Mem. bd. missions Meth. Ch.; mem. bd. Evangelism Meth. Ch.; trustee Lawrence Coll., Appleton; ofcl. visitor of Meth. African Missions, 1950, S.E. Asia, 1953. Mem. Alpha Delta Phi, Delta Sigma Rho. Rep. Mason (33 deg.). Clubs: Madison. Home: Madison, Wis. Died July 18, 1976.

NORTHEY, JAMES A., business exec.; b. Toronto, Ont., July 10, 1886; s. Robert and Elizabeth (Boggs) N.; student Harbord Collegiate Inst.; m. Marjorie P. Alexander, Dec. 26, 1912; children—James A., Marjorie Patricia (Mrs. E.V. Richnitzer). Gen. mgr. Telfer Paper Box Co., Ltd., 1921-24, v.p., 1924-35, pres., 1935-56, chmn., 1957—; pres. Northey Printing Co., Ltd., 1939—, also Wellington Fire Insurance Company; member board of directors Niagara Gas Transmission Co., Consol. Fire and Casualty Ins. Co., Consumers Gas Co.; chmn. Continental Life Ins. Co.; chmn. Ont. adv. bd., dir. Guarantee Co. N.A. Chmn. centennial com., Toronto, 1934; bd. govs. Toronto Y.M.C.A., 1935—, pres. 1950-51; chmn. West End Y.M.C.A., 1942; past chmn. nat. council Y.M.C.A., now hon. vice pres.; pres. Royal Agrl. Winter Fair, 1947-48, Canadian Nat. Exhbn., 1952, 53, hon. pres., 54. Clubs: Nat., Granite, Canadian, Empire (Toronto); Gyro International (past pres.). Home: Toronto; Newmarket, Ont. *

NORTHROP, JOHN KNUDSEN, aero. engr.; b. Newark, Nov. 10, 1895; s. Charles Wheeler and Helen C. (Knudsen) N.; ed. pub. schs., Santa Barbara, Cal.; m. Inez M. Harmer, Jan. 30, 1918 (div. 1948);children—Bette (Mrs. Paul G. Johansing), John H., Ynez S. (Mrs. Robert W. Koch); m. Margaret Bateman, Dec. 23, 1950. Designer Loughead Aircraft Co., Santa Barbara, 1916-17, 19-20; designer, project engr. Douglas Aircraft, Santa Monica, Cal., 1923-26; co-founder Lockheed Aircraft, Los Angeles, 1927, chief engr., 1927-28; v.p., chief engr. Northrop Aircraft Co. div. United Aircraft, Burbank, Cal., 1929-31, The Northrop Corp. (later El Segundo div., Douglas Aircraft), 1932-37; dir. Douglas Aircraft, 1934-37; co-founder, pres., dir. Northrop Aircraft, Inc., Hawthorne, Cal., 1939-52; engring. cons., 1953-81. Hon. life trustee Occidental Coll.; trustee Northrop Inst. Tech. Served in Signal Corps, U.S. Army, 1918. Fellow Am. Inst. Aeros. and Astronautics (pres. 1948), Royal Aero. Soc. Designer. Lockheed Vega, 1927; co-designer; Northrop Alpha, 1929; Gamma, Delta, 1932; BT-1, 1935; A-17, A-17A, 1935, N3PB, 1939; P-61, 1941; Northrop Flying-Wing, Airplanes, 1940-45; F89 Scorpion, Snark, 1948. Home: Santa Barbara, Calif. Died Feb. 18, 1981.

NORTON, EDWIN MICHAEL, former assn. exec.; b. Bancroft, S.D., Sept. 11, 1910; s. Charles Edwin and Margaret Ann (Jeffrey) N.; student U. Iowa, 1929, U.S.D., 1930-32; LL.B., Cath. U. Am., 1936; m. Jane Lee, Oct. 19, 1936; children—Michael Jeffrey, Jacquelyn Lee. With Dept. Agr. 1934-54, successively staff S.D. State Conservation office, chief dairy and poultry contract div. of purchase br., chief purchase div. dairy and poultry br., asst. dir. dairy br., dept. dir., dir. dairy br. Prodn. and Marketing Adminstrn., 1950-53; exec. sec., then sec. Nat. Milk Producers Fedn., Washington, 1954-70. Dir. Nat. Agr. Hall of Fame; trustee Farm Film Found. Mem-at-large Nat. council Boy Scouts Am. Served as lt. USNR, 1944-45. Mem. S.D., Va. bar assns., Washington Bd. Trade, Disabled Am. Vets., Am. Legion. Clubs: Army Navy, University, Dairy Shrine, National Executives Assn., Washington Golf and Country. Home: Rohoboth Beach, Del. Died Sept. 2, 1976.

NORTON, HAL EARL, clergyman; b. Kinross, Ia., May 19, 1886; s. Wallace Cassius and Isabell Justina (Ferderlin) N.; B.A., Central Coll., Pella, Ia., 1914, D.D., 1929; studied U. of Chicago and Drake University, Marquette University, Milwaukee; married Stella Grau, Sept. 10, 1912; children—Elizabeth Elaine (Mrs. John N. Cooper), Ruth Isabell (Mrs. Donald M. Erikson). Ordained ministry Bapt. Ch., 1914; pastor Sandwich, Ill., 1915-21; dir. religious edn. and exec. sec. Des Moines (Ia.) Bapt. City Union, 1921-23; pastor Winfield, Kan., 1923-28; v.p. Ottawa U., 1928-29; pastor First Bapt. Ch., Janesville, Wis., 1929-39, Roundy Memorial Bapt. Ch., Milwaukee, May 1939-Dec. 1945, First Bapt. Ch., Grinnell, Ia., 1945-50; transferred to Congregational Christian denomination, Sept. 28, 1950; pastor Federated Church since 1950. Lecturer at theol. sems. and colls. Alderman, Sandwich, 1919-21. Pres. Wis. Bapt. State Conv., 1935, chmn. exec. com., 1935, 36, 37; chmn. bd. mgrs., 1935-36; mem. exec. com. Wis. Council of Churches, pres. 1937, chmn. Convocation Com., 1936, 37, 38, sec. Ch. Life Div. of same, 1936; mem. bd. mgrs. Am. Bapt. Hist. Soc.; mem. bd. mgrs. and v.p. Francis Wayland Foundation; pres. Janesville Community Union, 1937-39, also gen. chmn. 1937 campaign. Dir. Bower City Credit Union, 1938-39; sec.-treas. Janesville Rotamer Camp Assn., 1938-39; teacher Presbyn. Summer Assembly, 1940; business mgr. and registrar Green Lake Summer Assembly, 1941. Hon. mem. Boys Town, Neb. Fellow Am. Bapt. Historical Society. Mem. American Interprofessional Institute, Pi Kappa Delta (highest honors), Pi Gamma Mu; pres. Baptist Alumni of Univ. of Chicago Divinity School, 1937. Republican. Mason, Odd Fellow. Clubs: Janesville Rotary (dir. 1937-38, sec.-treas., 1938, 39; hon. life mem.). Twilight, Emerson. Author of History of First Baptist Church of Janesville, Wis.; also An Analysis of the Lyman Beecher Lectures on Preaching. Book editor of The Chronicle. Editor of The Wis. Baptist. Book reviewer for newspapers, magazines, publishing houses and over radio. Pioneer in federation of chs. Serving as guard in defense plant in addition to church work for duration of World War II. Home: Janesville, Wis. Retired 1952. *

NORTON, THOMAS LOWELL, educator; b. Saco, Me., June 19, 1900; s. Charles Henry and Edith May (Lowell) N.; B.S., Dartmouth, 1923, M.C.S., 1924; Ph.D., Columbia U., 1932; m. Verna Cutler, August 24, 1927; children—Joyce (Mrs. Donald French), Thomas Lowell. Instructor, Dartmouth, 1923-24, Brown Univ., 1924-27; univ. fellow, Columbia, 1928; asst. prof., Univ. of Buffalo, 1928-35, asso. prof., 1935-39, 20th Century Club prof. economics, 1939-45; dean, prof. business administration Bernard M. Baruch of School of Business and Public Adminstrn., City Coll. of N.Y., 1945-55; dean School Commerce, Accounts and Fin., N.Y. U., 1955-62, prof. mgmt., 1955-62. Arbitrator labor disputes; pub. mem. Fed. Adv. Council on Social Security, 1937-38; staff mem. regents inquiry into character and cost of pub. edn. in N.Y. State, 1937; commr. mediation, N.Y. State Bd. Mediation, 1939-46; with wage and hour div. U.S. Dept. Labor (chmn. enamel utensils, cigar and tobacco industry coms., mem. shoe, leather, converted paper products, carpet and rug, belts and buckles industry coms.), 1939-41; spl. indsl. consultant Bur. Labor Statistics, U.S. Dept. Labor, 1940; exec. sec. shipbuilding stabilization com., O.P.M., 1940-41; nat. panel arbitrators, Am. Arbitration Assn. since 1941; spl. mediation rep., Nat. War Labor Bd., 1942, vice chmn., Region II, 1943-44, chmn., 1944-45; pub. mem. Nat. Wage Stabilization Bd., Region II, 1946, 52; chmn. Research Adv. Com., N.Y. State Dept. of Labor, 1948. Dir. Loew's Theatres, Inc., 1954-61. Member governing com. David McCahan Foundation. Mem. Am. Econ. Assn., Am. Assn. Univ. Profs., Am. Assn. Collegiate Schools of Business, (president 1954-55), Scriptories, National Acad. of Arbitrators (charter member 1947), Indsl. Relations Research Assn. (1947), N.Y. State Assn. Colls. Bus. Adminstrn. (pres. 1951-52). Phi Beta Kappa, Beta Alpha Psi, Beta Gamma Sigma (grand president 1958-61), Sigma Alpha, Sigma Nu, Alpha Phi Omega, Alpha Delta Sigma. Episcopalian. Author: Trade Union Policies in the Mass. Shoe Industry, 1932; Old Age and Social Security Act, 1937; Edn. for Work, 1938; Public Education and Economic Trends, 1939; also contbr. articles to ednl. and econ. jours. and trade publs. Home: Scarsdale, N.Y. Died July 7, 1976.

NORTON, WILLIAM JOHN, social worker b. White-Head Island, Me., Apr. 8, 1883; s. Horace Foster and Aseneth (Elwell) N.; A.B., Bowdoin, 1905, Sc.D., 1938; LL.D., Wayne U., Detroit, 1934, U. of Mich., 1941; m. Effie Comstock, Sept. 3, 1908; children—John Comstock, James Horace, Florence, William J. Social settlement work, Brooklyn, N.Y., and Cleveland, O., 1905-09; lecturer in sociology, Western Reserve U., 1908-12, U. of Mich., 1924-29; sec. Dept. Charities and Corrections, Cleveland, 1910-12; with Cincinnati Bur. Municipal Research, 1912-13; organizer and dir. Cincinnati Council Social Agencies, 1913-17; organizer and sec. Detroit Community Union and Detroit Community Fund, 1917-30; exec. v.p. Children's Fund of Mich., 1930-54; pres. Oakland Housing, Inc.; chmn. Cranbrook Boys Sch., 1933-36; trustee Children's Fund of Mich.; pres. of Mcgregor Fund; trustee Guardian Depositors Corp.; chairman Mayor's Interracial Commission, Detroit, 1943. Director La Salle Land Co., Warren Farms Co. Chmn. Detroit Emergency Relief Commission, 1931, Michigan Emergency Relief Commission, 1933-38; chmn. Detroit chapter Am. Red Cross, 1944-45. President Ferndale-Pl. Ridge Sch. Bd., 1921-29; mem. Mich. State Hosp. Commn., 1938-45; chmn. Mich. Dept. Mental Health, 1945-47; v.p. Greater Detroit Hospital Fund. 1948—; trustee Children's Fund of Mich., Severence Pay Trust; treasurer of the Child Research Center. Member of National Conf. Social Work (pres. 1925), Am. Assn. Community Orgns. (pres. 1920-22), Mich. State Conf. Social Work (hon. pres.), Phi Beta Kappa, Beta Theta Pi, Pi Gamma Mu. Treas. Mich. Med. Service, 1939-45. Unitarian. Clubs: Detroit, Prismatic, Acanthus. Author: Coöperative Movement in Social Work; (with Wm. C. Richards) Biography of a Foundation. Home: Pleasant Ridge, Mich. *

NORVELL, WILLIAM EDMUND, JR., lawyer; b. Mobile, Ala., Mar. 1, 1885; s. William Edmund and Elizabeth Maury (Owen) N.; grad. Montgomery Bell Acad., Nashville, Tenn., 1902; B.S., Vanderbilt, 1906, LL.B., 1910; m. Martha Washington Tillman, Dec. 12, 1917. Admitted to Tenn. bar, 1910, and practiced since at Nashville; v.p. Nashville Machine & Supply Co.; dir. Commerce Union Bank, N.C. & St. L. Ry. Director Tennessee Taxpayers' Assn. Director of Transportation Association of America, Inc. Mem. adv. com. Repeal Associates. Mem. Tenn. Bar Assn. (pres. 1928-29), Phi Beta Kappa, Sigma Chi, Phi Delta Phi. Club: Belle Meade Golf and Country. Home: Nashville, Tenn. *

NOSS, JOHN BOYER, educator; b. Sendal, Japan, Oct. 5, 1896; s. Christopher and Lura (Boyer) N. (parents Am. missionaries); came to U.S., 1912; A.B., Franklin and Marshall Coll., 1916, D.D., 1964; B.D., Theol. Sem. Ref. Ch. in U.S., Lancaster, 1922; Ph.D., U. of Edinburgh, Scotland, 1928; m. Mary Williamson Bell, June 14, 1922 (dec. 1968); m. 2d, Flora B. Rudisill, Apr. 14, 1976. Ordained to ministry United Ch. Christ, 1922, and served Ephrata, Pa., 1922-26; mem. faculty Franklin and Marshall Coll., 1928-63, prof. religion, 1931-45, head dept. philosophy, 1945-63; lectr. history of religions Union Theol. Sem., N.Y., 1952-65; adj. prof. Christianity and history of religions Lancaster Theol. Sem., from 1958. Mem. Am. Philos. Assn., Phi Beta Kappa. Clubs: Torch, Sphinx (Lancaster). Author: Man's Religions, 6th edit. Past editor research abstracts in History of Religions, Jour. of Bible and Religion. Contbr. encys., dictionaries. Home: Lancaster, Pa. Died Oct. 8, 1980.

NOVAES, GUIOMAR, pianist; b. Sao Paulo, Brazil; studied with Isidore Philipp, Paris Conservatoire, winning Premier Prix du Conservatoire; m. Octavio Pinto (dec. 1950); children—Luiz Octavio, Anna Maria. Performed extensively Europe and the Americas; recordings by Vox in works by Beethoven, Chopin, Debussy, de Falla, Mendelssohn, Mozart, Schumann. Home: São Paulo, Brazil. Died Mar. 7, 1979.

NOVAK, EMIL (NO'VAK), gynecologist; b. Baltimore, Mar. 8, 1884; s. Joseph and Mary (Hajek) N.; M.D., magna cum laude, U. of Md. Med. Sch., Baltimore, 1904; A.B., Loyola Coll., 1912; hon. D.Sc., Trinity Coll., Univ. of Dublin, Eire; D.Sc. (hon.) Tulane University, New Orleans; married Elizabeth Grace Rogers, Mar. 24, 1913; children—Edmund Rogers, Mary Elizabeth (Mrs. William F. Schmick, Jr.), Thomas Emil. Resident surgeon Md. Gen. Hosp., Baltimore, 1904-05; asso. prof. gynecology, Baltimore Med. Coll., 1905-09; associate professor gynecology, Coll. of Phys. and Surgeons, 1909-15; asst. prof. gynecology, Johns Hopkins Med. Sch. since 1915. Served as mem. vol. med. service corps during World War. Hon. fellow Royal Coll. Obstetrics and Gynecology of Gt. Britain, Obstet. Soc., Edinburgh, Obstet. Soc., Glasgow, Soc. Franc de Gynecology and Obstetrics, Assn. Brazil de Obstetrics and Gynecology, Assn. Mexico of Gynecology and Obstetrics, Brit. Med. Assn., New Eng. Obstet. and Gynecol. Soc., Pacific Northwest Soc. Obstet. and Gynecol., Obstet. and Gynecol. socs. of Texas, Fla., N.J., Utah. Fellow American College Surgeons, Am. Gynecol. Society, Am. Assn. Abdommal Surgeons, Gynecologists and Obstetricians; mem. A.M.A., Am. Assn. for Study Internal Secretions, Southern Surg. Assn. Hon. fellow Soc. Reg. Med., Budapest, Soc. of Obstetrics and Gynecology, Buenos Aires, Central Assn. Obstetrics and Gynecology, Tex. State Med. Assn., Phi Beta Pi. Democrat. Clubs: University (Baltimore); Gibson Island (Gibson Island, Md.); Johns Hopkins. Author: Menstruation and Its Disorders; The Woman Asks the Doctor; Gynecological and Obstetrical Pathology; Texbook of Gynecology. Contbr. to various textbooks and about 300 articles to med. jours. Home: Baltimore, Md. *

NOVIK, YLDA FARKAS (MRS. DAVID NOVIK), pianist; b. Szatmar, Hungary, Aug. 10, 1922; d. Jack and Yolan (Zipser) Farkas; came to U.S., 1927, naturalized, 1944; B.Mus., Cleve. Inst. Music, 1943; postgrad. Juilliard Sch. Music, 1943-44; m. David Novik, June 15, 1944; children—Lewis Gregory, Jill Susan. Concert pianist, 1957-77; toured U.S., Japan, Europe, Latin Am.; adj. prof. Montgomery Coll., 1968; lectr. George Washington U., 1970; contbg. critic Washington Star-News, 1967-73; U.S. corr. Inter-Am. Music Bull., 1970-74; editor, performer series Young Pianists Guide. Hon. bd. dirs. D.C. Community Orch., Nat. Choral Found.; adv. council Washington Chamber Orch. Mem. Music Tchrs. Nat. Assn., Am. Liszt Soc., Mu Phi Epsilon. Recs. of Bartok music for Toshiba, 1972; piano editor Am. Music Tchr., 1968-72; contbg. editor Piano Quar. Address: Chevy Chase, Md. Died Mar. 17, 1977.

NOYER, RALPH, coll. dean; b. Rochester, Ind., Dec. 1, 1885; s. Lawson M. and Ella A. (Whittenberger) N.; A.B., Ind. U., 1906, A.M., 1910; Ph.D., State U. of Ia., 1922; grad. student King's Coll., Cambridge, Eng., Freiburg im Breisgau, U. of Chicago; m. Densie Oliver, Sept. 3, 1907; children—Florence Elizabeth (Mrs. R. G. Van Duyn), Robert Oliver. Prof. of public speaking, Northeast Mo. State Teachers Coll., 1914-16; head, dept. of English, Neb. State Normal Sch., Kearney, 1916-20; dir. of extension div., Neb. State Teachers Coll., Kearney, 1920-27; dean, Ball State Teachers Coll., Muncie, Ind., since 1927. Mem. local Selective Service Bd. since 1940. Chmn. state com. on antidiscrimination in coll. admissions since 1950. Mem. Phi Delta Kappa, Pi Kappa Delta, Blue Key (nat. pres.). Mason. Club: Rotary. Home: Muncie, Ind. *

NOYES, BLANCKE, investment banker; b. Montclair, N.J., Feb. 1, 1923; s. Jansen and Agnes Augusta (Blancke) N.; A.B., Cornell U., 1944; M.B.A., Harvard U., 1948; m. Margaret Thayer Talbott, June 13, 1953; children—Audrey E., Nicholas B., Talbott, Robert T. Partner, Hemphill, Noyes & Co., N.Y.C., 1951-64, Hornblower & Weeks-Hemphill, Noyes, N.Y.C., 1965-78; dir. Cascade Natural Gas Corp., King Kullen Grocery Co., Inc., Norcen Energy Resources, Ltd., Petrofina Canada Ltd., Pneumo Corp., Family Dollar Stores, Inc. Bd. govs. Nat. Assn. Securities Dealers, 1959-62, Assn. Stock Exchange Firms, 1957-62, Am. Stock Exchange, 1964-70. Bd. dirs., pres. Fresh Air Fund; trustee Sarah Lawrence Coll. Served to lt. (j.g.) USNR, 1943-46. Mem. Psi Upsilon. Clubs: Bond (past pres.), Links (N.Y.C.); Wee Burn Country (Darien); Recess; Pine Valley Golf. Home: Darien, Conn. Died Sept. 24, 1978.

NOYES, ELIOT FETTE, indsl. designer, architect; b. Boston, Aug. 12, 1910; s. Atherton and Margaret Davenport (Fette) N.; grad. Phillips Acad., Andover, 1928; A.B., Harvard, 1932, M.Arch., 1938; D.F.A., Carnegie-Mellon U., 1969; m. Mary Duncan Weed, Dec. 10, 1938; children—Mary Duncan, Eliot Fette, Frederick, Margaret Davenport. Architect on Iranian Archaeol. Expdn. of Oriental Inst. of U. Chgo., Iran, 1935-37; dir. Dept. Indsl. Design, Mus. Modern Art, N.Y., 1940-45; design dir. Norman Bel Geddes and Co., 1946-47; independent practice as architect and indsl. designer, 1948-77; asso. prof., critic in architecture Yale, 1948-53, curator of exhbns., 1948-50; cons. dir. design IBM, Mobil Oil Corp. Pres. Internat. Design Conf., Aspen, 1965-70. Served as maj. USAAF, 1941-45. Recipient top ann. award AIA, also Homes for Better Living award, 1957, Indsl. Arts medal, 1966. Fellow AIA, Royal Soc. Arts, Indsl. Designers Soc. Am. Contbr. to art publs. Home: New Canaan, Conn. Died July 18, 1977.

NOYES, LEIGH, naval officer; b. St. Johnsbury, Vt., Dec. 15, 1885; s. A. Barber and Emily (Bowles) N.; B.S., U.S. Naval Acad., 1906; m. Sue Webb Spencer, July 5, 1919. Commd. ensign, U.S. Navy, 1906; advanced through grades to rear adm., 1939; U.S. fleet communications officer, 1916-19; commanding officer, U.S.S. Biddle, 1919; Atlantic Coast communication supt., 1920-22; exec. officer, U.S.S. Colorado, 1923-26; mem. naval mission to Brazil, 1926-29; destroyer div. comdr., 1929-31; duty Bur. of Navigation and asst. budget officer, 1931-34; comdg. officer, U.S.S. Richmond, 1934-36; qualified naval aviator, Pensacola, 1937; comdg. officer, aircraft carrier U.S.S. Lexington, 1937-38; chief of staff of Comdr. Aircraft Battle Force. 1938-39; dir. Naval Communications, Navy Dept., 1939-42, also mem. Defense Communications Bd., 1940-42; comdr. Task Force in Pacific Fleet, 1942; comdr. Air at capture Guadalcanal; sr. mem. Pacific Coast, and pres. Bd. of Inspection and Survey, 1943-46; retired Nov. 1946. Decorated Navy Cross, Purple Heart, Legion of Merit, Victory, Asiatic-Pacific and North Am. Theatre medals, Order of St. Stanislaus. Home: Washington, D.C. *

NOYES, NICHOLAS HARTMAN, pharmaceuticals and biologicals mfg. co. exec.; b. Dansville, N.Y., Aug. 8, 1883; s. Frederick W. and Emma Catherine (Hartman) N.; grad. Lawrenceville (N.J.) Sch., 1902; A.B., Cornell U., 1906; LL.D., Butler U., 1960; m. Marguerite Lilly, Nov. 19, 1908; children—Nicholas Hartman (dec.), Evan Lilly (dec.), Janet (Mrs. Frederic M. Ayres, Jr.). With Crowell Pub. Co., 1906-10; with Eli Lilly & Co., Indpls., from 1910, v.p., dir., 1913-48, chmn. finance com., dir., from 1948. Mem. Bus. Council, Washington Dir. Indpls. Community Fund, 1922-42; trustee Cornell U. Mem. Am. Drug Mfrs. Assn. (pres. 1931-33, mem. exec. com.), Indpls. C. of C. (pres. 1926). Presbyterian. Clubs: University, Columbia, Meridian Hills Country, Athletic (Indpls.); Links, Cornell (N.Y.C.); Lake Placid (N.Y.); Ristigouche Salmon (Can.); Les Cheneaux (Mich.). Donated collection of rare books and documents to Cornell U. Home: Indianapolis, Ind. Died Dec. 25, 1977.

NOYES, WILLIAM ALBERT, JR., chemist, educator; b. Terre Haute, Ind., Apr. 18, 1898; s. William Albert and Flora (Collier) N.; student U. Ill., 1916-17, D.Sc., 1964; A.B., Grinnell (Iowa) Coll., 1919, D.Sc., 1946; D.-ès-Sc., U. of Paris, France, 1920, Dr.h.c.; postgrad. U. Geneva, Switzerland, 1920, U. Cal., 1920-21; D.Sc., Grinnell Coll., U. R.I., Ind. U., U. Ottawa, U. Ill., U. Montreal, U. Rochester, Carleton U., Laval U.; m. Sabine Onillon, June 10, 1921; 1 son, Claude Charles. Instr., U. Calif., 1921-22; instr. U. Chgo., 1922-23, asst. prof., 1923-29; asso. prof., Brown U., 1929-35, prof., 1935-38; prof. U. Rochester, 1938-63, emeritus distinguished prof. chemistry, 1963, chmn. dept. chemistry, 1939-55, dean Grad. Sch., 1952-56, acting dean, then dean Coll. Arts and Sci., 1956-58; vis. lectr. U. Tex. at Austin, 1958, Ashbel Smith prof. chemistry, 1963-73, Ashbel Smith prof. emeritus, 1973-81; chmn. div. Chemistry and Chemical Tech., NRC, 1947-53; chmn. com. on chem. warfare Research and Devel. Bd., 1948-50; v.p. Internat. Union of Chemistry, 1947-51; treas. Internat. Council Sci. Unions, 1952-55; exec. com. Internat. Union Pure and Applied Chemistry, 1955-59, pres., 1959-63; Montgomery lectr., U. Neb., 1956; Westman Meml. lectr., Chem. Inst. Can., 1955; Harkins lectr., U. Chgo., 1956. Trustee Sloan-Kettering Inst. Cancer Research, 1950-62. Served from sgt. to 2d lt. Signal Corps, U.S. Army, 1917-19; sect. chmn. Nat. Def. Research Com., 1940-42; div. chmn., 1942-46. On Staff of chief Tech. Div., Chem. Warfare Service, U.S. Army, 1942-46; adviser U.S. delegation 1st conf. UNESCO, 1946, alt. del., 3rd conf., 1948, alternate delegate to 10th conf., 1958; mem. Naval Research Adv. Com., 1947-52; Officer Legion of Honor, France. Received Kings Medal for Service in Cause of Freedom, Medal for Merit, Am. Philos. Soc., 1948; Priestley medal Am. Chem. Soc., 1954; Willard Gibbs medal, 1957. Mem. Société Chimique de France (hon.). Chem. Soc. London (hon.). Nat. Acad. Scis. (mem. council 1947-50), Am. Chem. Soc. (chmn. com. profl. tng. of chemists, pres. 1947, Austin M. Patterson award Dayton sect. 1963), Am. Acad. Arts and Scis., Am. Phys. Soc., N.Y. Acad. Scis., Ill. Acad. Scis., Royal Soc. Physics and Chemistry (Spain), Société Chimique de Belgique, Acad. Scis. Lisbon, Portugal (corr.), Acad. Scis. France (corr.), Am. Inst. Chemistry, Phi Beta Kappa, Sigma Xi, Sigma Alpha Epsilon, Alpha Chi Sigma, Phi Lambda Upsilon, Phi Kappa Phi. Conglist. Author: Modern Alchemy (with W. A. Noyes, Sr.), 1932; Photochimie et Spectroscopie, 1937; Photochemistry of Gases (with P.A. Leighton), 1941; Traité de Chimie Physique (with H. Weiss) (translation into French of text by E. W. Washburn), 1925; Spectroscopie et les Réactions Initiées par la Lumieré, 1938; Chemistry in World War II. Editor: (with J. N. Pitts, George Hammond) Advances in Photochemistry, vols 1-7, Editor: Chem. Revs., 1939-49, Jour. Am. Chem. Soc., 1950-62, Jour. Phys. Chemistry, 1952-64. Home: Austin, Tex. Died Nov. 25, 1980.

NUEL, (EDMOND) PERCY (NO'EL), journalist; b. St. Louis, Mo., Aug. 4, 1882; s. Henry Martyn and Julia Edwards (Graves) N.; prep. edn. Smith Acad., St. Louis, 1892-99, King Sch., Stamford, Conn., 1899-1901; student Dartmouth College, 1901-02; m. Zana Shaw, children—Henry M., Helen Vivienne (Mrs. Homer Gayne); m. 2d, Suzon Rinjonneau; son, Yves Jeffery Percy. Was reporter St. Louis Post Dispatch, 1904; with The Motor Way, 1905-06, New York Commercial, 1906-07, New York Evening Post, 1907, St. Louis Globe-Democrat, 1908-12, editor Aero (first aviation weekly mag. in U.S.), St. Louis, 1910-12; editor Acro-Hydro, Chicago, 1912-14; war corr. Chicago Daily News, 1914-19; corr. attached to British G.H.Q. in France, 1917-19; corr. Associated Newspapers in Baltic States and Russia, 1920; corr. Phila. Pub. Ledger and New York Evening Post, from 1920-26, successively at Moscow, London, Berlin, Tokyo, Geneva and Paris; Paris corr. of Phila. Record, 1927-28; with Osaka (Japan) Mainichi, and corr. N.E.A. Service, 1928-29; with Associated Press, Paris, 1930-31; Paris manager Columbia Broadcasting System, 1932-33; Tokyo correspondent Intransigeant (Paris), contributor American and British publications, 1936-38; war corr. United Press in Paris, Bordeaux, Vichy, 1939-40; corr. Internat. News Service, Vichy, 1940; successively asst. editor, asst. chief editor, chief of monitoring, Foreign Broadcast Intelligence Service, Fed. Communications Commn., Washington, D.C., 1941-43; with Washington Bureau the United Press. Washington, 1943-48. Learned to fly, 1911; made first known photographs in world from airplane, 1910. Assistant chief transport officer British Red Cross, France, 1914; awarded Mons star and British war medals as civilian. Member Am. Legion. Dartmouth Alumni Assn., White House Corrs. Assn. Dept. of State Corrs., Overseas Writers, Phi Delta Theta, Clubs: Overseas Press (N.Y.). Author of several opera libretti in English verse. Contbr. to Am. and French mags. Broadcasts and lectures. Address: Nokesville, Va. *

NUGENT, ELLIOTT, actor, author, director; b. Dover, O., Sept. 20, 1899; s. J. C. and Grace (Fertig) N.; A.B., Ohio State U., 1919, hon. degree; m. Norma Lee, 1921 (dec. Dec. 1980); children—Lee, Barbara (dec.), Nancy. Debut in New York in Dulcy, 1921; collaborated with father on Kempy, 1922, and played title role; co-author and star The Poor Nut (with J.C. Nugent), 1925; Fast Service, 1931; co-author (with James Thurber) and star The Male Animal, 1940; appeared in Without Love, 1942; The Voice of the Turtle, 1943-45; dir. Tomorrow The World, 1942; also dir. motion pictures, including Three Cornered Moon, She Loves Me Not, The Cat and the Canary, The Male Animal, Up in Arms, Welcome Stranger, My Favorite Brunette, Just For You; co-producer, actor: The Seven Year Itch (Broadway play). Served in USNR, 1918. Mem. Phi Kappa Psi. Club: The Players, Lambs. Author: A Place of Our Own, 1945; Of Cheat and Charmer, 1962; Events Leading up to the Comedy, 1965. Address: New York, N.Y. Died Aug. 9, 1980.

NUNEZ, SOLÓN, physician; b. San Jose, Costa Rica, April 29, 1885; s. José P. and Juana (Frutos) N.; Ph.B., Liceo de Costa Rica, 1902; M.D., Univ. of Geneva, 1916; student of public hygiene, Johns Hopkins, 1921; m. Oliva Rojas. Dec. 20, 1906; children—Radko Emilio, Cynthia de Villa franca. Visitor and insp., public schs., Costa Rica, 1902-09; prof. girls high sch., Costa Rica, 1906-09; physician and surgeon, Auxiliary Hosp. of St. Louis, Lyon, France, 1915-16; head of san. services, Costa Rica, 1917-36, 43-48; asst. dir., Dept. of Ankylostomiasis (under Rockefeller Found.), 1917-22; sub-sec. of State, Costa Rica, 1922-25; minister of health and public welfare, Costa Rica, 1925-36, 43-48; minister of edn. (ad interim), 1943. Del. to Med. Conf., Habana, 1922; Costa Rican rep. to League of Nations on tour of observation regarding European public health activities, 1925; del. to San. Confs., Lima, Peru, 1927, Buenos Aires, 1934, Rio de Janeiro, 1942, 46; Costa Rican del. to Hosps. and Tuberculosis Congress, Atlantic City, New Jersey, 1929, 2d Internat. Conf. of Dirs. of Public Health, Washington, 1931, 3d, 1936. Internat. Congress of Medicine, Rio de Janeiro, 1946 (served as v.p. of congress); commd. by Rockefeller Found. to study sanatorium and tuberculosis orgn. in U.S., 1931, san. orgn. of Panama and Antilles, 1934, san. orgn. in other Central Am. countries, 1934. Pres. Costa Rican Bd. of Edn., 1920 and mem. superior council of public edn., 1920—; pres. Costa Rican Bd. of Physicians, Costa Rican Red Cross; mem. bd. of dirs. Pan Am. San. Bur. Awarded 1st prize, Central Am. Med. Contest, 1921; decorated grand officer of Finlay Order, grand cross of Cuban Nat. Soc. of Red Cross, gold medal of Costa Rican Red Cross, Palms Academic (France). Mem. Pan Am. Med. Assn., Internat. Leprosy Assn., Lima Nat. Acad. of Medicine; corr. mem. Am. Assn. of Public Health, Am. Jour. of Tropical Medicine; hon. mem. Cooperating Assn. of Am. Concord, Costa Rican Red Cross. Roman Catholic. Club: Internat. Rotary (v.p., 1934). Author: Ankylostomiasis in Costa Rica, 1921, Sanitary Organization of Costa Rica; Costa Rican San. Legislation, 1922-36, 1940-48. Home: San Jose, Costa Rica. *

NUTTER, FRED JEWETT, farmer, assn. ofcl.; b. Lincoln, Maine, Mar. 21, 1893; s. H. Bartlett and Dora A. (Jewett) N.; ed. pub. schs.; M.S. (hon.) U. Maine, 1950; m. Ruth Jones, May 28, 1919; children—Dora (Mrs. Lloyd Littlefield), Effie (Mrs. Gerald Page), Robert P. Farmer and breeder registered Holstein cattle, Corinna, Maine, from 1912, later Hillsborough, N.C.; dir. Eastern States Farmers Exchange, 1931-52; pres. Bangor Prodn. Credit Assn. (Maine), 1938-44, Holstein-Friesian Assn. Am., from 1961; commr. agr. Maine, 1953-59; mem. Pres. Kennedy Agrl. Adv. Commn., from 1961. Trustee U. Maine, 1954-61. Named Outstanding Farmer in Maine, U. Maine, 1948; nominee 1980 N.C. Agrl. Hall of Fame. Address: Hillsborough, N.C. Died Aug. 13, 1980.

NUTTER, G(ILBERT) WARREN, educator, economist; b. Topeka, Mar. 10, 1923; s. Coleman Evan and Rose (Gilberg) N.; B.A., U. Chgo., 1944, M.A., 1948, Ph.D., 1949; m. Jane Calvert Couch, Dec. 24, 1946; children—Coleman Alston, Jane Terry, Anne Elizabeth, William Warren. Instr. econs. Lawrence Coll., Appleton, Wis., 1946-47; asst. prof. econs. Yale, 1949-56; asso. prof. econs. U. Va., Charlottesville, 1956-58, prof., 1958-79, Paul Goodloe McIntire prof., 1967-79, chmn. dept., 1962-66, 67-69; asso. dir. Thomas Jefferson Center, 1957-67, dir., 1967-76; asst. sec. def. for internat. security affairs, 1969-73; dir. James Madison Center, 1976-79. Div. chief CIA, 1952-53; mem. research staff Nat. Bur. Econ. Research, 1955-67; adj. scholar Am. Enterprise Inst., 1973-79. Mem. adv. com. to bd. visitors The Citadel, 1975-79; trustee Thomas Jefferson Center Found., 1976-79; mem. internat. studies program adv. com. Hoover Instn., 1976-79. Served from pvt. to staff sgt. AUS, 1943-46, 1st lt., 1948-54. Decorated Bronze Star medal with oak leaf cluster; recipient Gavel award, Am. Bar Assn., 1968. Distinguished Pub. Service medal Dept. Def., 1972. Mem. Am. Econ. Assn., Mont Pelerin Soc., Phi Beta Kappa. Author: Extent of Enterprise Monopoly in the United States, 1951; Growth of Industrial Production in the Soviet Union, 1962; The Strange World of Ivan Ivanov, 1968; Kissinger's Grand Design, 1975. Contbr. articles to profl. jours. Home: Charlottesville, Va. Died Jan. 15, 1979.

NUTTLE, HARRY (HOPKINS), business exec.; born Caroline County, Md., April 30, 1885; s. Henry T. and Emma (Hopkins) N.; Ph.B., Dickinson Coll., 1906; m. Zora Joslin, Dec. 5, 1914; children—Harry Joslin, Byron Hopkins. Teacher Dover, Del., Federalsburg, Md., 1906-08; asso. sec. Y.M.C.A., Wilmington, Del., 1908-10; farmer and canner since 1910; cannery, Hickman, Md., pres. Peoples Bank of Denton since 1945, dir. since 1925, pres. So. States Cooperative, 1944-47, dir. since 1938; dir., sec. and treas. Choptank Electric Cooperative, 1938-49. Pres., Maryland Farm Bur., 1935-38; dir., Am. Farm Bureau Fedn., 1937-44. Mem. Md. House of Delegates, 1914-15, Md. Senate, 1918-21. Regent U. of Md. Mem. Tri State Packers Assn. (pres. 1939), Sigma Alpha Epsilon. Republican. Methodist. Mason (Shriner), Odd Fellow. Clubs: Rotary, Denton (past pres.). Home: Denton, Md. *

NYDAHL, MALVIN JOHN, physician, educator; b. Mpls., Nov. 24, 1906; s. Johannes L. and Tabitha G. (Rygh) N.; B.A., U. Minn., 1928, B.Sc., 1934, M.D., 1935, M.Sc. in Orthopaedic Surgery, 1945; m. Audrey B. Bloomgren, Sept. 21, 1931; children—John, Janet. Intern U. Minn. Hosps., Mpls., 1934-35, physician and surgeon U. Minn. student health service, 1935-37; dir. hygiene and health edn. Mpls. pub. schs., 1937-40; head bur. crippled children, med. unit Div. Social Welfare Minn., 1940-43; pvt. practice orthopaedic surgery, Mpls., 1945-72; prof. orthopaedic surgery U. Minn. Med. Sch., 1958-72; former mem. staff Fairview-Southdale, Methodist. Eitel, Lutheran Deaconess, Hennepin County Gen., Abbott, Swedish hosps. Diplomate Am. Bd. Orthopaedic Surgery. Mem. A.M.A., Am. Acad. Orthopaedic Surgeons, A.C.S., Internat. Coll. Surgeons, Minn., Dakota, Manitoba, Twin City orthopaedic socs., Minn. Hennepin County med. socs., Grey Friar frat., Bone and Joint Club. Clubs: Minneapolis Athletic, Question (Mpls.); Wayzata (Minn.) Country. Contbr. articles to profl. jours. Home: Sun City, Ariz. Deceased.

NYE, ARTHUR WICKES, physicist; b. Canton, O., Jan. 28, 1882; s. Charles N. and Harriet F. (Wickes) N.; B.S., Case Sch. Applied Science, Cleveland, O., 1904, M.E., 1907; studied U. of Chicago and U. of Calif.; m. Alice L. Bird, of Lynn, Mass., Sept. 3, 1907. With Morgan Engineering Co. and Gen. Electric Co. until 1906; with U. of Southern Calif. since 1907, prof. physics and elec. engring. since 1908, also consulting practice. Physicist Ordnance Dept., U.S.A., 1918-19. Mem. Am. Physical Soc., A.A.A.S., Illuminating Engring. Soc., Am. Assn. Univ. Profs., Tau Beta Pi, Sigma Alpha Epsilon, Phi Kappa Phi. Republican. Episcopalian. Home: Los Angeles, Calif. *

OAKES, HERBERT WALTER, b. St. Paul, Minn., Aug. 10, 1882; s. George Louis and Annie Walter (Haslett) O.; ed. high sch., St. Paul, 2 yrs.; m. Goldena Ann Bilderbeck, June 14, 1915; children—Dorothy Louise, Robert Walter, Donald Herbert, Charles Richard (dec.), Peggy Jean, William George. Clerk wholesale dry goods, St. Paul, 1902-05; went on road as salesman, 1905; settled in Denver, 1907; dry goods salesman, 1907-17; associated, 1917, with R. A. Isbell and E. M. Kent in establishing the Isbell-Kent-Oakes Dry Goods Co. (pres.); pres. The Oakes Isbell Co., The Allen Mfg. Co. Republican. Baptist, Mason (K.T., 32 deg., Shriner). Clubs: Rotary, Lakewood Country. Home: Denver, Colo. *

OBEAR, HUGH HARRIS, lawyer; b. Winnsboro, S. C., Dec. 20, 1882; s. Henry Norwood and Eunice (Harris) O.; B.L., U. of Va., 1906; student U. of Paris (spl. course for officers of U.S. Army), 1919; m. Mildred Fleenor. Admitted to D.C. bar, 1907, practice Wash., 1907—; sr. partner Douglas, Obear & Campbell, 1939—. Served as maj. comdg. 1st Batt., 319th Inf., 80th Div., World War I; grad. Army Gen. Staff Coll., Langres, France, 1919. Awarded silver star with oak leaf cluster. Officer Order of Carlos Manuel de Céspédes (Cuba). Former dir. Children's Hosp., Washington; former trustee The Louise Home. Mem. Am., D.C. (pres. 1945) bar assns., Newcomen Soc. N. Am., Thomas Jefferson Soc. Alumni U. Va. (life), Phi Delta Phi. Clubs: Metropolitan (past gov. and v.p.), Army and Navy, Lawyers' (past pres.) (Washington); Chevy Chase (Md.). Home: Washington, D.C. *

OBENSHAIN, RICHARD DUDLEY, lawyer; b. Abingdon, Va., Oct. 31, 1935; s. Samuel Shockley and Josephine Mathews (Dudley) O.; B.A., Bridgewater Coll., 1956; LL.B., N.Y. U., 1959; m. Helen Nottingham Wilkins, July 15, 1961; children—Mark Dudley, Anne Scott, Kate Boyce. Admitted to Va. bar, 1959, U.S. Supreme Ct. bar, 1968; asso. firm McGuire, Woods & Battle, Richmond, Va., 1959-66, partner, 1966-69; partner firm Obenshain, Hinnant, Dolbeare & Beale, Richmond, 1970-78. Chmn. March of Dimes Va., 1970-72; chmn. Va. Republican Com., 1972-74; co-chmn. Rep. Nat. Com., 1974-76; del. Rep. Nat. Conv., 1964, 76; candidate for U.S. Ho. of Reps., 3d Va. Dist., 1964, for atty. gen. Va., 1969; chmn. Young Rep. Fedn. Va., 1961-64; bd. visitors Va. Commonwealth U., 1970-78; trustee Bridgewater Coll., 1976-78. Mem. Am., Va. bar assns., Am. Judicature Soc., Bridgewater Coll. Alumni Assn. (pres. 1971-72), Va. Hist. Soc., SAR. Presbyn. Club: Masons. Home: Midlothian, Va. Died Aug. 2, 1978.

OBERHOLTZER, EDISON ELLSWORTH (O'BER-HOLT-ZER), educator; b. Patricksburg, Ind., May 6, 1882; s. Augustus and Mary Anne (Collins) O.; student Ind. State Normal Sch., Terre Haute, 1904-05; Ph.B., U. of Chicago, 1910, M.A., 1915; LL.D., U. of Tulsa, 1921; Ph.D., Columbia University, 1934; LL.D., University of Houston, 1950; m. Myrtle May Barr, Mar. 26, 1899; children—Kenneth Edison, Esther Myrtle, Edison Ellsworth. Teacher rural schs., Ind., 1898-1901; supt. schs., Carbon, Ind., 1901-03; instr. in mathematics, Ind. State Normal Sch., 1905; supervising prin. schs., Terre Haute, 1906-09; dist. supt. schs., Evansville, Ind., 1910; supt. schs., Clinton, Ind., 1911-12; prof. edn., Ill. State Normal U., summer 1913; supt. schs., Tulsa, Okla., 1913-23; supt. schools, Houston, Tex., 1924-Apr. 1945; parttime president University of Houston, 1927-Apr. 1945; president, University of Houston, 1945-50, emeritus since 1950; univ. and pub. sch. consultant on problems of administration, orgn. and curriculum. Special lecturer George Peabody College for Teachers, Nashville, Tennessee, summer 1925, Summer School of Nova Scotia, 1929. Dir. Liberty Loan, War Savings Stamps and Am. Red Cross drives, Tulsa, World War I. Mem. library bd. trustees, Houston; chmn. 1938 Yearbook Commn. of Am. Assn. of Sch. Adminstrs.; mem. Gulf States regional council of Nat. Advisory Council on Sch. Problems; mem. Nat. Council of Edn., Nat. Com. on Illiteracy, N.E.A., Nat. Soc. for Study of Edn. (com. of 1934 yearbook), N.E.A. Department of Superintendence (pres., 1935), Horace Mann League (pres. 1933), Tex. State Teachers Assn. (exec. com.), Phi Delta Kappa, Methodist. Mason (32 deg., Shriner). Rotarian. Author: An Integrated Curriculum in Practice; and numerous reports on Houston school system. Co-author: Modern-Life Speller; Language Arts for Modern Youth. Contbr. to Nations Schools, School Executive, Journal of Edn. Home: Houston. *

OBERMAYER, LEON JACOB, lawyer; b. Sciota, Ill., Sept. 24, 1886; s. Hermann and Veronika (Lehmann) O.; A.B., Central High Sch., Phila., Pa., 1904; J.D., U. Pa., 1908, certificate of merit, 1961; D.H.L. Hebrew Union Coll., Jewish Inst. Religion, 1954; LL.D., Temple U., 1956; m. Julia L. Sinsheimer, May 24, 1923; children—Herman Joseph, Helen Adele (Mrs. Arthur M. Sellers), Arthur S. Admitted to Pa. bar, 1908; counsel firm Obermayer, Rebmann, Maxwell & Hippel, Phila. Mem. appeal bd. East dist. Pa. Selective Service, 1966-70, exec. com. Am. Heart Assn., 1963-66, chmn. bd. S.E. Pa., 1962-64; former mem. Recreational Commn. Pa.; vice chmn., Hebrew Union Coll.-Jewish Inst. Religion, Cin.; pres. YM-YWHA, Phila., 1915-26, Girls' Aid, 1921-28; mem. exec. com. Nat. Council Jewish Welfare Bd.; mem. exec. council, solicitor, hon. pres. Phila. council Boy Scouts Am., (Silver Beaver award 1941, spl. service medal, 1948). Mem. U.S. nat. commn. UNESCO, 1954-60; Pres. Bd. Pub. Edn., Phila., 1955-61. Bd. dirs. Albert Einstein Med. Center, Gov. Lucien Moss Home, United Fund Phila., Jewish Hosp. Phila.; hon. bd. dirs. Gratz Coll., Phila.; chmn.-v.p. Woods Schs., Langhorne, Pa. Brandeis U. fellow, 1968. Mem. Pa. Prison Soc. (gov.), Hebrew S.S. Soc. (gov.), Assn. Alumni Central High Sch. Phila. (hon. pres.), Inter-Am., Am. (50-Year Club), Pa. (past v.p.), Phila. (chmn. bd. govs. 1938, chmn. com. profl. guidance 1938-57, Fidelity Bank award 1972) bar assns., Am. Law Inst. (life), Acad. Natural Scis. Phila. (trustee), Ams. for Competitive Enterprise System (v.p.), Am. Jewish Hist. Soc. (pres. 1965-68; chmn. bd. govs. 1968-71), Indian Rights Assn., Phila. World Affairs Council, Franklin Inst., U. Pa. Law Alumni Assn. (pres. 1956-59), Zeta Beta Tau. Republican. Jewish religion (trustee synagogue). Mason, mem. B'nai B'rith. Clubs: Locust (gov.), Union League, Lawyers, Midday, Constitutional, Socialegal, Philmont Country, Sunday Breakfast, Peale. Home: Philadelphia PA. *

OBERON, MERLE, actress; b. Tasmania, Feb. 19, 1911; ed. India; m. Alexander Korda, 1939 (div. 1945); m. 2d, Lucien Ballard (div. 1949); m. 3d, Bruno Paglai, 1957 (div. 1973); m. 4th, Robert Wolders, 1978; adopted children—Bruno, Francesca. Film debut Service for Ladies, 1931; other appearances include The Private Lives of Henry VIII, 1932, The Private Life of Don Juan, 1934, The Scarlet Pimpernel, 1935, The Dark Angel, 1935, These Three, 1936, Beloved Enemy, 1936, The Divorce of Lady X, 1938, Over the Moon, 1939, Wuthering Heights, 1939, The Lion Has Wings, 1939, Affectionately Yours, 1941, The Lodger, 1944, A Song to Remember, 1944, This Love of Ours, 1945, Berlin Express, 1946, Temptation, 1946, Night Song, 1948, The Lady from Boston, 1951, Twenty Four Hours of a Woman's Life, 1952, Deep in My Heart, 1954, Désirée, 1954, The Price of Fear, 1956, Of Love and Desire, 1963, Hotel, 1967, others; editor, co-producer, Star Interval, 1973, also TV series Assignment-Foreign Legion, 1956, and guest appearances. Home: Los Angeles, Calif. Died Nov. 23, 1979.

OBERTEUFFER, DELBERT, educator; b. Portland, Ore., Nov. 19, 1901; s. William Gaul and Roberta (Fox) O.; A.B., U. Ore., 1923; A.M., Columbia, 1924, Ph.D., 1930; m. Katharine F. Hersey, June 10, 1935; 1 son, Theodore Kendall. Instr., asst. prof. U. Ore., 1924-28; instr. summer sessions Columbia, 1925-30; supr. phys. edn. and health edn. State of Ohio, 1929-32; prof. phys. edn. Ohio State U., 1932-66, prof. emeritus, chmn. dept. phys. edn. for men, 1933-57. Mem. joint com. health problems in edn. N.E.A., A.M.A., 1954-57, chmn., 1956-58. Recipient spl. honor award Soc. State Dirs. Health and Phys. Edn., 1953, Luther H. Gulick award, 1959. Fellow Am. Sch. Health Assn. (pres. 1957-58), Am. Coll. Sports Medicine, Am. Pub. Health Assn., Am. Acad. Phys. Edn. (pres. 1958-59), Am. Assn. Health, Phys. Edn. and Recreation, Soc. Pub. Health Educators; mem. Coll. Phys. Edn. Assn. (past pres.), Soc. State Dirs. Health and Phys. Edn., Beta Theta Pi, Kappa Delta Pi, Phi Epsilon Kappa. Episcopalian. Club: Columbus Torch (dir. 1957-58). Author: Industrial Hygiene for Schools, 1930; Personal Hygiene for College Students, 1930; Health and Physical Education, a Course of Study for Junior and Senior High Schools, Vol. III, 1932; Health in the World of Work, 1942; School Health Education, 1954; Physical Education, 1956. Editor: Jour. of Sch. Health. Home: Worthington, Ohio. Died Apr. 2, 1981.

O'BRIEN, EUGENE, actor; b. Boulder, Colo., Nov. 14, 1886; s. John H. and Katherine (McDermott) O'B.; ed. pub. schs. and prep. sch., U. of Colo.; unmarried. First appearance in minor part at Elitch's Gardens, Denver, Colo., 1900; worked way to New York and later played with Elsie Janis, Henry Woodruff, Effie Shannon, Margaret Illington, Kyrle Bellew, Frances Starr, Ethel Barrymore, Fritzi Scheff, etc.; appeared in pictures with Mary Pickford and Norma Talmadge and starred on own account; returned to stage in "Steve," 1922. Catholic. *

O'BRIEN, JOHN A., author; b. Peoria, Ill., Jan. 20, 1893; s. John Francis and Elizabeth T. (Powers) O'B.; A.B., St. Viator Coll., 1913, A.M., 1914, LL.D., 1935; Ph.D., U. Ill., 1920; postgrad. Cath. U. Am., 1916-17, U. Chgo., 1915, Oxford, Eng., 1939-40. Founded, erected Newman Found., U. Ill., 1920, dir., chaplain Cath. students, 1917-39; supt. schs. Peoria diocese, 1926-33; author-in-residence U. Notre Dame, from 1940. Established Cardinal Newman award for distinguished services, 1930; recipient Laetare medal U. Notre Dame, 1973. Roman Catholic. Author several books, latest being The Catholic Way of Life, 1962; Eternal Answers for an Anxious Age, 1962; Catching Up With the Church, 1967; The Inquisition, 1973. Asso. editor Pastoral Life. Address: Notre Dame, Ind. Died Apr. 18, 1980.

O'BRIEN, PATRICK M., abbot; b. Manchester, N.H., Oct. 29, 1885; s. Patrick and Johanna (Cronin) O'B.; ed. St. Anselm's Prep. Sch., Manchester, 1902-05, St. Anselm's Coll., 1905-07 (A.B., 1915), Holy Cross Coll., Worcester, Mass., 1907-09 (hon. A.M., 1924). Instr. St. Joseph's High Sch., Manchester, 1909-14; novitiate St. Vincent's Archabbey, Latrobe, Pa., 1914-15; professed Benedictine monk, July 22, 1915; ordained Benedictine priest, May 30, 1920; instr. St. Benedict Prep. Sch., Newark, N.J., 1920-32; pastor St. Joseph's Ch., Maplewood, N.J., 1933-37; elected abbot St. Mary's Abbey, also pres. St. Benedict's Prep. Sch., Newark, N.J., and Delbarton Sch. for Boys, Morristown, N.J., Aug. 11, 1937. Address: Newark, N.J. *

O'BRIEN, WILLIAM W., banker; born Chicago, Oct. 11, 1886; s. James and Francis M. (Chase) O'B.; ed. pub. schs. of Chicago; m. Kathleen M. Waters, Apr. 14, 1914; children—June Marion, Nancy Jean. Stock boy, J. V. Farwell & Co., Chicago, 1903-04; with The First Nat. Bank of Chicago since 1904 as clerk, 1904-19, asst. trust officer, 1919-31, asst. sec., 1931-38, asst. v.p., 1938-45, vice pres. since 1945. Club: Glen Oak Country. Home: Glen Ellyn, Ill. *

OCHELTREE, JOHN BURDON, fgn. service ofcr.; b. Riverside, Cal., Oct. 11, 1903; s. Arthur Robinson and Cora (Burdon) O.; A.B., U. of Neb., 1925; B.A., Oxford (Rhodes scholar), 1929; A.M., Princeton, 1931; m. Anna J. Stamm, July 19, 1930 (dec.); children—Ann, Lorinda; m. Frances Peebles Brown, Jr., Nov. 28, 1953. Apptd. fgn. service officer, U.S. Dept. State, 1930, vice consul, Hamburg, 1931, Seville, Spain, 1932-37; consul and 3d sec., San Jose, Costa Rica, 1937-39; Port-au-Prince, temp., 1939; consul, Curaco, temp., 1939, Habana, 1940; asst. chief Caribbean office, Dept. of State, 1941, area officer Div. Fgn. Service Personnel, 1945-47; consul at Godthaab, Greenland, 1942-45; 1st sec. and consul Rio de Janeiro, 1947-50; 1st sec. and consul gen., Rome, Italy, 1951-52; Dept. of State, retired; now real estate salesman Walker and Dunlop, Incorporated, Washington. Assisted U.S. rep. Honduran-Nicaraguan boundary mediation, 1937. Mem. Assn. Am. Rhodes Scholars. Club: University (Washington). Home: Washington, D.C. Died Dec. 21, 1979.

OCHS, PHIL, folk singer; b. El Paso; Tex.; 1941. Lyricist and recording artist Elektra Recs.; songs include: Nobody Buys from the Flower Lady, Cross My Heart, I Hope to Live, Talking Cuban Crisis, 50-Mile Hike, others. Home: Los Angeles, Calif. Died Apr. 9, 1976.

OCHSNER, ERWIN CHARLES, lawyer; b. Hermann, Mo., May 21, 1898; s. John Henry and Ida Kate (Elkermann) O.; student Ill. Coll., 1916-17; LL.B., U. Mo., 1923, also LL.D.; m. Burkella Wells, June 18, 1925; children—Frances Ann (Mrs. Sahm), Martha Jane (Mrs. Stone). Admitted to Mo. bar, 1922, Tex. bar, 1923; mem. firm Gibson, Ochsner, Adkins, Harlan & Hankins, Amarillo, Tex., 1942-78. Bd. dirs., past pres. Amarillo Regional Hearing and Speech Found., Salvation Army, Amarillo; bd. dirs. Panhandle div. West Tex. Arthritis Found., Greater Amarillo Hwy. Assn.; past bd. dirs. March of Dimes, Amarillo, A.R.C., Family Service Assn., Travelers Aid, Amarillo; mem. Potter Randall Citizens Com. Served with U.S. Army, World War I. Fellow Tex. Bar Found.; mem. Am., Inter-Am., Amarillo bar assns., State Bar Tex., Am. Counsel Assn., Tex. Ind. Producers and Royalty Owners (past dir.), Panhandle Royalty Owners Assn., Panhandle-Plains Hist. Soc. (dir., pres., exec. com.), Am. Legion (past post vice comdr.), Amarillo C. of C. (past dir.), Phi Delta Phi, Phi Alpha. Presbyn. (elder). Mason (Shriner), Kiwanian (past pres. Amarillo, lt. gov. Tex.-Okla. div.). Clubs: Panhandle Plains Auto (dir.); Amarillo. Home: Amarillo, Tex. Died May 8, 1978.

O'CONNELL, ARTHUR, actor; b. N.Y.C., Mar. 29, 1908; s. Michael and Julia (Byrne) O'C.; student St. John's High Sch. and Coll., Bklyn., 1922-28; m. Anne Hall Dunlop, June 23, 1962. Appeared in numerous motion pictures, including Citizen Kane, 1941, Naked City, 1948, Picnic (Acad. award nomination), 1955, Solid Gold Cadillac, 1956, The Man in the Gray Flannel Suit, 1956, The Proud Ones, 1956, Bus Stop, 1956, The Anatomy of a Murder (Acad. award nomination), 1959, Gidget, 1958, A Thunder of Drums, 1961, The Great Imposter, 1960, Man of the West, 1958, Seven Faces of Dr. Lao, 1963, Kissin' Cousins, 1963, The Monkey's Uncle, 1964, Fantastic Voyage, 1965, The Birds Do It, 1966, The Silencers, 1965, The Power, 1967, The Reluctant Astronaut, 1966, Suppose They Gave A War and Nobody Came, 1969, There Was A Crooked Man, 1969, The Last Valley, 1969, numerous others; stage debut in The Patsy, Dorchester, Mass., 1929; appeared in plays Remote Asylum, Los Angeles, 1970-71, Child's Play, Ft. Lauderdale and Miami, Fla., 1971; appeared on ABC-TV series The Second Hundred Years, 1967-68, Seven in Darkness, 1969; dir., actor the Army Play by Play, 1943; command performances Hyde Park for F.D.R., cabinet mems., Wilhelmina of Netherlands; actor in Army tng. films; dir. Broadway prodn. Brighten The Corner, 1945-46; toured Margaret Webster's Shakespeare Co.; studied with Mme. Ouspenskaya. Served with Signal Corps, AUS, 1940-45. Recipient certificate for profl. excellence in the theatre West Valley Coll., 1967, certificate of appreciation for efforts during Tet offensive in Viet Nam and Thailand, Dept. Def., 1968; hon. citizen N.Mex., Ky., Ala., Tenn. Mem. Screen Actors Guild, Actors Equity Assn., A.F.T.R.A., Acad. Motion Picture Arts and Scis., Nat. Acad. TV Arts and Scis., Players Club, Am. Coll. Theatre Festival (regional dir. 1968), ANTA (pres. Los Angeles chpt. 1966). Home: Beverly Hills, Calif. Died May 18, 1981.

O'CONNOR, ALBERT DENNIS, cons., former govt. ofcl.; b. Bayonne, N.J., Sept. 23, 1902; s. Matthew Dennis and Josephine (Ryan) O'C.; LL.B., Georgetown U., 1923, J.D., 1973; m. Nina Stoops, Jan. 21, 1935; 1 son, Michael Dennis. Spl. agt. Dept. Justice, 1923-27; dist. mgr. Henry L. Doherty & Co., investment bankers, 1927-31; v.p. Waggaman & Brawner, investment bankers, 1931-34; adminstr. NRA Code for Brewery Products div. Fed. Alcohol Control Adminstrn., 1934-37; mng. dir. Distilled Spirits Corp., N.Y.C., also pub. relations dir. N.Y. World's Fair Operation, 1937-41; sr. security specialist and asso. field dir. Office Sec., U.S. Treasury Dept., 1941-50; cons. NSRB, 1950; became adminstr. FCDA for N.E., N.Y., N.J., 1950, dir. Region I Office Emergency Planning, Maynard, Mass., 1950-72; cons. Council State Govts., 1973-79. Chmn., Regional Preparedness Bd.; mem. U.S. Regional Def. Moblzn. Com. for N.E. States, also com. for N.Y., N.J.; mem. port security com. Port of Boston, Port of N.Y.-N.J. Mem. Am. Soc. for Pub. Adminstrn. Roman Catholic. Home: Boston, Mass. Died Oct. 5, 1979; buried St. Joseph Cemetery, West Roxbury, Mass.

O'CONNOR, DANIEL JR., company exec.; b. N.Y.C., Jan. 5, 1882; s. Daniel J. and Katherine (Keller) O'C.; A.B., St. Francis Xavier Coll., 1903; grad. study Columbia, 1904-06; m. Ruth K. Brever, 1915 (dec. 1925); children—Daniel J., John F., Mary Helen (Mrs. G. F. Hedges), Gregory T.; m. 2d, Rebecca Jane Wakker, 1929 (dec. 1945); 1 dau., Rebecca Jane (Mrs. Henry Rollman). Mem. engring. dept. Westinghouse Elec. & Mfg. Co., Pitts., 1907-13; co-founder Formica Co., Cin., 1913, v.p., gen. mgr., 1913-34, pres., gen. mgr. since 1934; dir. Fifth-Third Union Trust Co. Vice pres., dir. Ohio Mechanics Inst.; dir. Cincinnati Indsl. Inst.; mem. adv. bd. Xavier U. Clubs: Cincinnati, Queen City (Cin.). Home: Cin. *

O'CONNOR, ELEANOR MANNING (MRS. JOHNSON O'CONNOR), architect; b. Lynn, Mass., June 27, 1884; d. James Edward and Delia Josephine (Grady) Manning; S.B., Mass. Inst. Tech., 1906; m. Johnson O'Connor, June 3, 1931. Draftsman with Lois L. Howe, 1907-13; partner firm Lois L. Howe & Manning, 1913-26, Howe, Manning & Almy, 1926-37; partner in Seventeen Asso. Architects, organized in 1935 to design Old Harbor Village, South Boston, housing project; in practice alone; special instr. in housing, Simmons Coll., Boston; lecturer on archtl. history and house planning, Chamberlain Sch. of Retailing, and house planning, Garland Sch. of Homemaking, Boston. Architect (with Lois L. Howe) of houses in Mariemont, O., restorations of old New Eng. houses, Concord Art Centre, Fitchburg Art Centre, etc.; awarded prize for design of Cape Cod Cottage. Member Mass. Federation Planning Bds. (sec. 1924-28); mem. Mass. Women's Adv. Com., N.Y. World's Fair; Nat. Assn. Housing Officials (mem. bd., N.E. div. 1944). Asst. treas. Johnson O'Connor Research Foundn., Inc.; treas. Human Engring. Laboratory, Inc. Mem. A.I.A., Massachusetts State Association of Architects, Boston Society Architeets, Mass. Civic League (chmn. com. on housing, 1937-49), M.I.T. Women's Assn. Clubs: College of Boston (pres. 1930-31), Boston, Altrusa (pres. 1932-33). Address: Boston, Mass. *

O'CONNOR, J(OHN) ROBERT, lawyer; b. Stanberry, Mo., July 13, 1885; s. Edward and Laura Belle (Fielding) O.; grad. Dallas (Tex.) High Sch., 1905; LL.B., U. of Tex., 1908; m. Marion Gray, of Midland, Tex., June 10, 1912; children—George Gray, J. Robert, Matthew Gunner, Francis Marion. Practiced at Dallas, Tex., 1908-12, Midland, Tex., Jan.-Nov. 1912, San Diego, Calif. Nov. 1912-Feb. 1914; asst. U.S. atty., Southern Dist. of Calif., 1914-17; U.S. atty., same dist., by appmt. of U.S. Dist. Court, Oct. 1917-Jan. 1918; apptd. to same office by President Wilson, Jan. 8, 1918; deputy dist. atty. Los Angeles County, July 1929-Oct. 1931. Democrat. Presbyn. Mem. Phi Delta Theta. Mason. Elk. Home: South Pasadena, Calif. *

O'CONNOR, JAMES A., army officer; b. Bay City, Mich., July 19, 1885, s. Charles and Mary Ellen (Van Paris) O;C.; student Notre Dame U., 1902-03; B.S., U.S. Mil. Acad. 1907; grad. Army Engr. Sch., 1913; hon. grad. Command and Gen. Staff Sch., 1923; grad. Army Coll. 1927; m. Marjorie Belle Allan, Sept. 26. 1912; children—Patricia (Mrs. Harry Jordan Theis), Jean Ellen (Mrs. Joseph O. Killian), Daniel Shiels. Commissioned 2d lt., U.S. Army, June 14, 1907, and advanced through the grades to brig. gen., Sept. 6, 1942; comd. Northwest Service Command, which includes Alaska Mil. Highway from Dawson Creek, B.C., to Fairbanks, Alaska; served as chief engr. China-Burma-India Theater, 1944-45; retired since 1946. Decorated D.S.M., Legion of Merit, Punitive Expdn., Army Cuban Pacification and Victory medals (U.S.), Hon. Comdr. Order British Empire. K.C. Contbr. articles to engring. jours. Home: Los Angeles, Calif. *

O'CONNOR, JOHN WOOLF JACK, author, editor; b. Nogales, Ariz., Jan. 22, 1902; s. Andrew John and Ida (Woolf) O'C.; student Ariz. State Tchrs. Coll., 1921-23, U. Ariz., 1923-24; A.B., U. Ark., 1925; A.M., U. Mo., 1927; m. Eleanor Bradford Barry, Sept. 10, 1927 (dec. July 25, 1978); children—Gerald (dec.), Bradford, Catherine, Caroline. Reporter, So. and Middle Western newspapers, 1924-26; tchr. journalism, publicity Sul Ross Coll., Alphine, Tex., corr. Tex. Big Bend country A.P. and Tex. dailies, 1927-30; dir. pub. relations Ariz. State Tchrs. Coll., Flagstaff, 1931-34; head div. journalism U. Ariz., 1934-45; exec. editor Hunting Mag., Los Angeles, 1973-78; recognized as an authority on N. Am. big game and sporting firearms. Past pres. Tucson Game Protective Assn. Served as pvt. 158th Inf., U.S. Army, 1917-18. Recipient Weatherby Hunter of Year award, 1957. Mem. Sigma Chi. Republican. Author: Conquest, 1930; Boom Town, 1938; Game in the Desert, 1939; Hunting in the Southwest, 1945; Your Sporting Gun, 1946; Hunting in the Rockies, 1947; The Rifle Book, 1949; The Big Game Rifle, 1952; Arms and Ammunition, 1952; Shotguns and Rifles, 1961; Big Game of North America, 1962; Big Game Hunts, 1963; The Shotgun Book, 1965; The Complete Book of Shooting, 1966; The Art of Hunting, 1967; Horse and Buggy West, 1969; The Hunting Rifle, 1970; Sheep and Sheep Hunting, 1974. Editor shooting dept. Outdoor Life Mag., 1939-72. Contbr. articles and stories to nat. mags. Home: Lewiston, Idaho. Died Jan. 20, 1978.

O'CONNOR, RICHARD ANTHONY, business exec.; b. San Francisco, Calif., May 22, 1900; s. Richard and Maria O'Connor; student Univ. of Santa Clara; m. Eleanor M. Sheehan, Aug. 14, 1924; children—Patricia E., Richard E., Dalton A., Eleanor M., Sheila A. Engaged in fgn. trade, traveling through and resident in Far Eastern countries, Central and S. America and Europe, 1919-24; with Magnavox Co. since 1922, now chmn. bd., dir.; also chmn. bd. dir. Magnavox Co. of Kentucky, Magnavox Co. of Tennessee, Chatauqua Plywood Corp. Clubs: Chicago Golf, Fort Wayne Country. Home: Fort Wayne, Ind. Died Mar. 5, 1981.

O'CONNOR, WILLIAM PATRICK, bishop; b. Milwaukee, Wis., Oct. 18, 1886; s. Patrick Dennis and Ellen Anna (McCarthy) O'C.; student St. Francis Sem., Wis., 1901-12; A.B., Marquette U., Milwaukee, 1916, LL.D., 1962; Ph.D., Cath. U., Washington; LL.D., Notre Dame U., 1943, Saint Norberts College; Litt. D., Loras Coll., 1947. Ordained to ministry Roman Catholic Church, 1912; assistant to pastor St. Rosa of Lima Ch., Milwaukee, 1912; prof. philosophy St. Francis Sem.; dir. Archdiocesan Socs., 1940-42; pastor Ch. of St. Thomas Aquinas, Milwaukee, 1941-42; bishop of the Superior, Wis., Diocese 1942-46; became first bishop of Madison, Wis., Mar. 12, 1946, resigned, 1967; titular bishop Diocese of Siccessi 1967—. Served as chaplain 120th F.A., sr. chaplain 32d Div., A.E.F., rank of capt., World War I. Decorated Croix de Guerre with Silver Star (France). Mem. Am. Cath. Philos. Assn. (pres. 1940), Chicago Soc. of Cath. Psychologists (pres. 1940), Am. Legion. K.C. Author: Concept of the Human Soul According to Saint Augustine, 1921. Address: Madison, Wis. *

O'DAY, JOHN, telephone exec.; b. Chicago, Ill., Sept. 16, 1885; s. Joseph and Mary (Leahy) O'D.; LL.B., Marquette U., Milwaukee, Wis., 1909. Admitted to Wisconsin bar, 1909; stenographer, later chief clerk, spl. agent legal dept., asst. to v.p. Wis. Telephone Co., Milwaukee, 1902-21, sec. and asst. treas., 1921-22, v.p., sec. and asst. treas., 1922-38, dir. since 1924, v.p., asst. sec. and asst. treas. since 1938; chief clerk Central Group of Bell Telephone Cos., Chicago, Ill., 1911-12; pvt. sec. to pres. Ill. Bell Telephone Co., 1912. Mem. Milwaukee Assn. of Commerce. Clubs: Rotary, Athletic, North Shore Country (Milwaukee). Home: Milwaukee. *

ODELL, ROBERT ALVA, lawyer; b. Port Byron, Ill., Aug. 19, 1882; s. Robert Neilson and Sarah Eliza (Ward) O.; LL.B., U. of So. Calif., 1905; m. Alice Fern Sutley, Sept. 20, 1904 (died Feb. 6, 1935); m. 2d Etta Jessamine Poe, Dec. 23, 1936. Admitted to Calif. bar, 1905, and since practiced in Los Angeles; mem. firm Tanner, Odell & Taft (Los Angeles and Santa Monica) since 1909; pres. Braille Inst. of Am., Inc., Los Angeles, 1931-56 (charter mem., trustee) pres. emeritus, 1956. Member of the Los Angeles Board of Education, 1921-27, president, 1923-27; member of gen. com. Pub. Schs. Week in Calif., 1926-50; lay member and counsel So. sect. Calif. Teachers Assn. since 1930. Mem. Los Angeles Bar Assn., Sigma Chi (awarded Significant Sig medal 1948 by Nat. Grand chpt.). Republican. Mason (32 deg., K.C.C.H.; past master). Home: Los Angeles. *

ODLE, JOE TAFT, clergyman; b. West Frankfort, Ill., Aug. 19, 1908; s. Harry Logan and Winona (Dillon) O.; B.A., Union U., Jackson, Tenn., 1930; student So. Baptist Theol. Sem., 1935; D.D., Miss. Coll., 1949; m. Clara Mabel Riley, July 17, 1930; children—Joe Thomas, Sarah Ann Odle Maddox. Ordained to ministry Bapt. Ch., 1925; pastor Bapt. Ch. Orient, Ill., 1926, Bapt. chs., Rossville and Gallaway, Tenn., 1928-29, Barlow, Bandana, Ky. Bapt chs., 1930-32; pastor East Bapt. Ch., Paducah, Ky., 1932-43, First Bapt. Ch., Crystal Springs, Miss., 1943-47, First Bapt. Ch., Gulfport, Miss., 1947-56; asso. exec. sec. Miss. Bapt. Conv. Bd., Jackson, 1956-59; editor The Bapt. Record, Jackson, 1959-76; v.p. Miss. Bapt. Conv., 1954; mem. annuity bd. So. Bapt. Conv., 1949-56; mem. Bapt. joint com. pub. affairs, Washington, 1963-69. Named Ky. col., 1961; citations Broadman Press, Nashville, 1976, So. Bapt. Theol. Sem., 1976, Miss. Coll., 1976. Mem. Evang., So. Bapt. (pres. 1971) press assns., Asso. Ch. Press (hon. life). Clubs: Kiwanis, Lions, Civitan, Rotary. Author: Church Member's Handbook, 1941; It's a Great Life-Don't Miss It, 1967; Is Christ Coming Soon?, 1971; Why I Am a Baptist, 1972; The Coming of the King, 1974. Home: Jackson, Miss. Died Mar. 24, 1980; buried Jackson.

ODLIN, RENO, banker; b. Sedro Woolley, Wash., June 26, 1897; s. William Thompson and Jessie Lee (Reno) O.; student Princeton, 1914, U. Wash., 1915-17, U. Toulouse, France, 1919; m. Edith Murphy Heston, July 12, 1922 (dec. Oct. 1964); children—Mary Lee, Reno, Richard Bingham; m. 2d, Beatrice Marshall, 1965. Clk. Pacific Tel. & Tel. Co., Seattle, 1919; clk. Citizens Bank, Anacortes, Wash., 1921-22, cashier, 1922-28; asst. v.p. Met. Nat. Bank, Seattle, 1928-32; v.p. First Nat. Bank of Seattle, 1932-36; pres., chmn. bd. Puget Sound Nat. Bank, Tacoma, 1936-74; dir. Wash. Nat. Gas Co., Pacific First Fed. Savs. & Loan, Tacoma. Exec. com. U.S. Treasury Savs. Bond div., past chmn.; dir. Fed. Res. Bank of San Francisco, 1938-44; mem. 12th Fed. Res. Dist. of Fed. Adv. Council Fed. Res. System, 1945-49. Served as 2d lt. U.S. Army, with AEF in France, World War I. Republican nominee for U.S. senator, 1934. State chmn. War Finance Com., U.S. Treasury. Recipient Distinguished Service award U.S. Treasury, 1973. Mem. Am. Bankers Assn. (pres. 1964), Wash. Bankers Assn. (pres. 1942-43), Am. Legion (state comdr. 1930-31), Wash. State Hist. Soc. (pres. 1955-76), Kappa Sigma. Republican. Rotarian. Clubs: Bohemian (San Francisco); Rainier, University (Seattle); Tacoma, Tacoma Country and Golf. Home: Tacoma, Wash. Died Sept. 15, 1979.

ODLUM, FLOYD B., finance and investments; b. Union City, Mich., Mar. 30, 1892; s. Rev. George A. and Ellen (Anderson) O.; LL.B., U. of Colo., M.B.A., LL.D. (hon.) Hillsdale College, H.H.D., Northland Coll.; m. Jacqueline Cochran; children by previous marriage—Stanley (dec.), Bruce Wendell (dec.). Chmn. bd., chief exec. officer Atlas Corp. and predecessor, U.S. Co., 1923-60; chmn. bd. Fed. Resources Corp., 1961-69; chmn. bd. RKO Radio Pictures, 1937-48, Consol. Vultee Aircraft Corp., 1947-53; past pres. Am. Arbitration Assn., N.Y. Neurol. Inst. Dir., Office Prodn. Mgmt., 1941-42; spl. adviser to chmn. WPB, 1943-44, OPA, 1940-44. Chmn. Arthritis and Rheumatism Found.; trustee, hon. life chmn. Lovelace Found. Med. Edn. and Research, Albuquerque; chmn. bd. Fannie and John Hertz Found. Sci. Fellowships, to 1964, hon. chmn., from 1964. Awarded Presdl. Certificate of Merit; French Legion of Honor; Horatio Alger award, 1972. Mem. Am. Bar Assn. Methodist. Club: Eldorado Golf (Cal.). Home: Indio, Calif. Died June 17, 1976.

O'DONNELL, CHARLES FRANCIS, insurance exec.; b. Dallas Co., Tex., 1882; ed. Univ. of Texas, 1907. Pres. and dir. Southwestern Life Insurance Co.; dir. First National Bank of Dallas. Home: Dallas. *

O'DONNELL, CHARLES ROBERT, educator; b. Pittsfield, Mass., May 3, 1926; s. Thomas Michael and Elizabeth Louise (Griffin) O'D.; B.A., U. Mich., 1950; M.A., U. Conn., 1952; Ph.D., Syracuse U., 1957; m. Janet Frances Howes, June 1948; children—David Craig, Charles Garth; m. 2d, Janet Elizabeth Miller, May 22, 1965; children—Elizabeth Ann, Paul Robert. Instr., U. Conn., 1950-52; lectr. English, Syracuse U., 1953-57; instr. U. Mich., 1957-60, asst. prof., 1960-63, asso. prof., 1963-69; vis. prof. English, Hofstra U., Hempstead, N.Y., 1965-66, prof., chmn. English dept., 1969-73; vis. prof. Am. Studies for Execs. Program, Williams Coll., summer 1969. Host, narrator, co-author television show Images of Am., 1963; host, narrator Am. Story Classics, 1966; host, narrator Understanding Our World series; cons. U. Mich. Press; cons. editor, bibliographer U. Mich. Willow Run Labs., 1958-63; tchr. U. Mich. Extension Service, supr. teaching fellows, faculty dir. Pilot Program; reader, table leader, cons. test devel. div. Ednl. Testing Service. Author: Major Authors 1914-Present, 1969. Contbr. articles to profl. jours. Home: Hempstead, N.Y. Died Oct. 3, 1979.

O'DONNELL, PAUL DANIEL, elec. mfg. co. exec.; b. Worcester, Mass., May 14, 1925; s. Daniel William and Mary Agnes (Hoey) O'D.; B.S., Worcester Poly. Inst., 1947; M.A. in Econs., Clark U., 1948; m. Clare Marie O'Donnell, Apr. 10, 1950; children—Daniel, David, Ellen, Edward. Asst. prof. Boston Coll., Newton, Mass., 1948-53; indsl. specialist USAF, Boston, 1950-52; factory mgr. Tobe Deutschmann Corp., Norwood, Mass., 1953-54; mgr. Westinghouse Electric Corp., Pitts., 1954-63, plant mgr., Muncie, Ind., 1963-66, dir. mfg., Pitts., 1966-73, gen. mgr., Blairsville, Pa., 1973-74, gen. mgr., Tampa, Fla., 1974-79; dir. IEM, Mexico City; Exchange Nat. Bank of Tampa. Lectr. prodn. Northeastern U., 1953-54; lectr. industry U. Pitts., 1955-58. Vice pres. Deleware (Ind.) council Boy Scouts Am., 1964-66. Served with USNR, 1944-46. Mem. Am.

Mgmt. Assn. (mfg. council), Am. Inst. Indsl. Engrs. (trustee, nat. pres. 1969-70), Am. Soc. Quality Control, Council on Indsl. Engring. (chmn.). Author: Production Control U.S., 1952; Production Control Japan, 1956; Production Control Argentina, 1957. Contbr. to Manufacturing Management Handbook, 1970; Ency. Sci. and Tech., 1970; Handbook of Industrial Engineering, 1971. Home: Tampa, Fla. Died Apr. 1, 1979; buried Tampa.

O'DONOHOE, JOHN FERNANDO (O-DON'O-HO), oil producer; b. Gautier, Miss., Oct. 18, 1885; s. John R. and Mina (Gautier) O'D.; ed. pub. schs.; m. Carrie Kell, Nov. 17, 1914; 1 son, Jack. Pres. Petroleum Producers Co.; dir. First Nat. Bank, First Nat. Co. Mem. Mid-Continent Oil and Gas Assn. of Tex. (ex-pres.; dir.), North Tex. Oil and Gas Assn. (dir.), Independent Petroleum Assn. of America (dir.). Democrat. Catholic. Clubs: Wichita, Wichita Falls Golf and Country. Home: Wichita Falls, Tex. *

OEHMANN, ANDREW FRANCIS, lawyer; b. Washington, Jan. 29, 1910; s. Andrew Leroy and Mary Frances (Kiely) O.; LL.B., Georgetown U., 1938; B.C.S., Benjamin Franklin U., 1948; m. Shirley Ann Morris, Nov. 20, 1940 (dec. Jan. 1956); children—Andrew Francis, Mary Ann, Deborah, Michael; m. 2d, Theresa C. Kraus, Feb. 22, 1962. Admitted to D.C. bar, 1937; with Dept. of Justice, 1941-43, atty., 1946-47, successively trial atty., exec. asst. to asst. atty. gen. (criminal), 2d asst., 1st asst. to asst. atty. gen. (tax), 1949-58, exec. asst. to atty. gen., 1961-64; asst. U.S. atty., D.C., 1948; partner Dow, Lohnes & Albertson, tax law, Washington 1958-61; private practice law, Washington, 1964-70; partner firm Oehmann and Pajak, 1970-80. Dir. Admiral Corp. Served to lt. (s.g.) USNR, 1943-46; lt. comdr. Res. Mem. Am., Fed., D.C. bar assns., John Carroll Soc., Gamma Eta Gamma. Clubs: Lawyers, Federal City. Mem. staff law jour. Georgetown Law, 1937, 38. Home: Washington, D.C. Died July 24, 1980.

OEHRLE, WILLIAM, consulting engr.; b. N.Y. City, Aug. 21, 1884; s. John and Caroline E. (Grossman) O.; prep. edn., high sch. and Pratt Inst., New York; student Columbia; unmarried. With George A. Fuller Co., contractors and builders. New York, 1901-19; New York mgr. George A. Fuller Co. of the Orient, 1919-23; cons. practice on own account since 1923. Constrn. mgr. Hotel Pennsylvania, New York, 1916-19; lecturer on building constrn., Columbia, since 1925; associated with Nat. City Bank of New York. Served as 1st lt. engineers, World War. Mem. Am. Soc. C.E., Am. Soc. M.E., Am. Concrete Inst., Am. Soc. Testing Materials, Am. Soc. Mil. Engrs., Western Soc. Engrs., Archtl. League America, A.A.A.S., Met. Mus. of Art, Acad. Polit. Science. Club: Men's Faculty (Columbia). Home: New York. *

O'GARA, JAMES VINCENT, JR., editor, writer; b. Bklyn., Mar. 26, 1918; s. James Vincent and Sarah Agnes (McEntee) O'G.; B.S., N.Y. U., 1942, M.A., 1953; m. Marguerite Helen Rohmer, May 9, 1943; children—Maureen Ellen, James Vincent 3d, Erin Anne. News editor Religious News Service, N.Y.C., 1946-50; free-lance mag. writer, 1947-79; with Advt. Age, N.Y.C., 1950-79; sr. editor charge N.Y. office, 1958-61, exec. editor, 1961-68, editor, 1969-72, editor-at-large, 1972-79; v.p. Crain Communications, Inc., 1963-79; adj. asst. prof. communication arts Fordham U., 1960-66; advt. news broadcaster Sta. WQXR, 1971-79. Served to 1st lt. USAAF, 1942-46. Recipient award of merit for outstanding journalism Asso. Bus. Publs., 1954. Mem. Kappa Tau Alpha. Roman Catholic. Club: Hempstead Golf and Country. Editor, contbg. author: The New World of Advertising, 1973; editor: How It Was in Advertising 1776-1976, 1976. Home: Hempstead, N.Y. Died Jan. 10, 1979; buried St. John's Cemetery, Middle Village, N.Y.

O'GARA, WARREN MARTIN, lawyer; b. Los Angeles, Apr. 14, 1919; s. Michael Martin and Florence (Haynes) O'G.; B.S., Utah State Agrl. Coll., 1941; M.S., U. So. Calif., 1946; J.D., U. Utah, 1952; children by previous marriage—Thomas M., Sheila G., Matthew K., Patrick B. Commd. 2d lt. U.S. Army, 1941; advanced through ranks to capt.; unit comdr. N. Africa, Italy, World War II; admitted to Utah bar, 1953, Calif. bar, 1960; practiced in Salt Lake City, 1953-59; partner firm Hampton & O'Gara, Los Angeles, 1959-78. Decorated Bronze Star. Home: La Canada, Calif. Died Sept. 21, 1978.

OGG, FRANK CHAPPELL, mathematician; b. Richmond, Va., Feb. 3, 1899; s. Oscar J. and Marcie (Chappell) O.; A.B., U. N.Mex., 1922; A.M., U. Ill., 1924, Ph.D., 1927; m. Florence Sutton, July 14, 1928; children—Frank Chappell, Virginia (Mrs. Stephen Magada), Florence (Mrs. Howard A. Smith), Andrew, Oscar. Grad. asst., fellow U. Ill., 1922-27, instr. math., 1927-31; asso. prof. math. Bowling Green (Ohio) State U., 1931-39, prof., 1939-76, chmn. dept., 1948-65; mathematician Aberdeen Proving Ground, summer 1955. Math.-Sci. Library at Bowling Green State U. dedicated to him. Mem. AAUP, Am. Math. Assn., Am. Math. Soc., A.A.A.S., Sigma Xi, Pi Mu Epsilon, Kappa Mu Epsilon, Sigma Chi. Club: Town and Gown (Bowling Green); Torch International; Toledo. Contbr. articles, revs. profl. jours. Home: Bowling Green, Ohio. Died June 9, 1976; interred Wood County Memory Gardens, Bowling Green.

OGLESBY, R(OSCOE) R(ALPH), univ. dean; b. Depoy, Ky., June 8, 1905; s. Thomas Jacob and Mary Frances (Bethel) O.; A.B., Georgetown Coll., 1925; student Harvard, 1931, Heidelberg U., 1932; M.A., University of Virginia, 1934; Ph.D., Duke Univ., 1950; married Doris Brooks, November 28, 1941. High sch. tchr., prin., Lynchburg, Va. and Graham, Ky., 1926-39; instr. Duke, 1943-44; asst. prof. Berea Coll., 1944-45; lectr. Sweet Briar Coll., 1945-47; lectr. internat. law George Washington U., summers 1946-48; asso. prof. Okla. A. and M. Coll., 1947-49, prof., acting head dept. polit. sci., 1950, dean of students, 1950-54; dean of students Fla. State U., 1954-64, prof. govt., 1964-73. Mem. Nat. Assn. Student Personnel Adminstrs., Am. Soc. Internat. Law, AAUP (exec. sec. Fla. chpt.). Baptist. Rotarian. Author: Internal War and the Search for Normative Order, 1971. Home: Tallahassee, Fla. Died Mar. 29, 1973; buried Lynchburg.

OGRYZLO, METRO ALEXANDER, physician, educator; b. Dauphin, Man., Can., Mar. 18, 1915; s. Peter and Mary (Harasym) O.; M.D., U. Man., 1938; m. Gertrude Rachel Black, Oct. 10, 1942; children—Ann, (Mrs. Kenneth R. Jeffrey), Joan, (Mrs. Steven A. McAlister), Kathryn. Mem. faculty U. Toronto Med. Sch., from 1952, prof. medicine, dir. rheumatic disease unit; sr. staff physician Wellesley Hosp., Toronto; cons. part-time practice rheumatology. Mem. med. adv. bd. Gairdner Found.; bd. dirs. Canadian Arthritis and Rheumatism Soc. Served to squadron leader RCAF, 1940-45. Fellow Royal Coll. Physicians; mem. Canadian Med. Assn., Canadian, Am. rheumatism assns., Canadian Soc. Clin. Investigation, Ont. Antibody Club, N.Y. Acad. Scis. Clubs: Donalda. Author: Amkylosing Spondylitis in Arthritis and Allied Conditions, 1972. Editor Jour. Rheumatology. Home: Willowdale, Ont., Can. Deceased.

OGSBURY, JAMES S., business exec.; b. Voorheesville, N.Y., Jan. 22, 1882; s. Junius D. and Anna M. (Ostrander) O.; m. Florence Noone, Oct. 10, 1906; children—Alva B. (Mrs. Robert P. Davies), James S. Clerk Del. and Hudson Canal Co., 1896-98; clerk N.Y. Central and Hudson Ry. Co., 1898-1900; junior official Am. Tobacco Co., 1900-09; comptroller, treas., mgr. Internat. Bus. Machines. 1910-33; gen. mgr. scale div. Hobart Mfg. Co., 1933-34; v.p., Whitman and Barnes, 1935; pres. gen. mgr., dir. Fairchild Aviation Corp. since 1936. Pres., dir. Fairchild Camera and Instrument Corp.; treas., dir. Fairchild Aerial Surveys, Inc. Lutheran. Mason. Club: Country (North Hempstead). Author of short articles. Inventor of several patented articles, improvements on tabulating machines, computing scales, time recorders. Home: Manhasset, (L.I.) N.Y. *

O'HARA, MARY, (MARY O'HARA ALSOP), author, composer; b. Cape May Point, N.J., July 10, 1885; d. Reese Fell and Mary Lee (Spring) Alsop; student Packer Inst., Brooklyn Heights; student langs., music in Europe; m. Kent K. Parrot, Oct. 1905; children—Mary O'Hara, Kent Kane, Jr.; m. 2d. Helge Sture-Vasa, Aug. 1922 (div. 1947). Author: My Friend Flicka, 1941; Thunderhead, 1943; Green Grass of Wyoming, 1946; The Son of Adam Wyngate, 1952; Novel-in-the-Making, 1954; Wyoming Summer, 1963; (mus. play) The Catch Colt, 1961, also novella, 1979; A Musical in the Making, 1966. Composer songs and piano studies. Roman Catholic. Home: Chevy Chase, Md. Died Oct. 14, 1980.

OHRBACH, NATHAN M. (OR'BÄK), mfg. exec.; b. Vienna, Austria, Aug. 31, 1885; s. Issac J. and Anna (Dickman) O.; ed. pub. and high schs., New York; m. Mathilda Kane, Feb. 24, 1907; 1 son, Jerome Kane. Began his business career in retail merchandising in 1905; opened his own store in Brooklyn, 1911; est. branch on 14th St., Manhattan, 1923; Newark Store, 1930; Los Angeles Store, 1948; La Mirada, Cal. Store, 1960; chmn. bd. Ohrbach's Inc. until 1965, Ohrtronics, Inc., N.Y.C., 1965—. Vice pres. Montefiore Hosp.; trustee, Fedn. Jewish Charities. Mem. nat. exec. bd. Boy Scouts of Am., general chairman N.Y. annual campaign fund drive, 1945-53. Former mem. Mayor's Mgmt. Survey Com.; former chmn. exec. com. Coop. Retail Tng. Sch. Bus. Civic Adminstrn., City Coll. Decorated Officer French Legion of Honor; Gold Medal of Honor (Republic of Austria); French order of Knight and Companion of Cross of Lorraine; Italian Star of Solidarity; recipient Silver Antelope, Silver Beaver, Silver Buffalo, Boy Scouts Am Eta Mu Pi. Mason. Clubs: Harmonie, City Athletic (N.Y.); Metropolis Country (White Plains, N.Y.). Author: Getting Ahead in Retailing, 1935. Home: N.Y.C.; also Westchester County, N.Y. *

O'KIEFFE, DE WITT, advt. agy. exec.; grad. Wabash Coll., 1926; m. Mary Louise; children—Charles D. III, Karen Woolard, Michael. With Homer McKee advt. agy., Indpls., then Erwin Wasey, Chgo.; a founder Leo Burnett Co., Inc., Chgo., 1935, ret. as sr. v.p., dir., 1977. Bd. dirs., exec. com. Chgo. Lung Assn., 1956-79. *

OKUN, ARTHUR M., economist, econ. cons.; b. Jersey City, Nov. 28, 1928; s. Louis and Rose (Cantor) O.; A.B., Columbia, 1949, Ph.D., 1956; M.A. (hon.), Yale, 1963; m. Suzanne Grossman, July 1, 1951; children—Lewis Edward, Matthew James, Steven John. Instr. econs. Yale, New Haven, 1952-56, asst. prof., 1956-60, asso. prof., 1960-63, prof., 1963-67; staff mem. Cowles Found. for Research in Econs., Yale, 1956-67; staff economist Council Econ. Advisers, Washington, 1961-62, mem. council, 1964-68, chmn., 1968-69; econ. cons. Donaldson, Lufkin & Jenrette, N.Y.C., 1969-80; cons. Am. Security & Trust Co., Washington, 1970-80; dir. Intercapital Funds; sr. fellow Brookings Instn., Washington, 1969-80; Godkin lectr. Harvard, 1974. Recipient medal for excellence Columbia, 1968, Frank E. Seidman Disting. award for polit. economy, 1979. Fellow Am. Statis. Assn., Am. Acad. Arts and Scis., Econometric Soc.; mem. Am. Econ. Assn. (v.p. 1972), Phi Beta Kappa. Author: The Political Economy of Prosperity, 1970 (McKinsey Found. Book award); Equality and Efficiency: The Big Tradeoff, 1975; Prices and Quantities: A Macroeconomic View, 1981. Editor: Yale Economic Essays, 1963-64; The Battle Against Unemployment, 1964, rev. edit., 1972; co-editor Brookings Papers on Economic Activity, 1970-80. Contbr. articles on econ. forecasting, potential output, fiscal and monetary policy profl. publs. Home: Washington, D.C. Died Mar. 23, 1980; buried King David Meml. Garden, Fairfax, Va.

OLEJNICZAK, JOHN JOSEPH (O-LAN'I-CHEK), pres. Polish Roman Cath. Union of America; b. Chicago, Ill., Mar. 21, 1886; s. Joseph and Mary (Gierzynska) O.; ed. South Bend (Ind.) High Sch.; m. Sophie Michalska, Aug. 17, 1909; children—John J., Martha (Mrs. Alexander Loboda). Supt. Studebaker Motor Car Co., South Bend, Ind., 1918-28; dir. Polish Roman Cath. Union of America, 1920-28, treas., 1934-38, pres., 1928-34, and since 1941. Treas. Polish Am. Council, Polish Am. Congress; mem. Ill. Pulaski Sesquicentennial Commn. Awarded Polonia Restituta, Legion of Honor (Polish Falcons of Am.). Mem. Polish Alma Mater, Polish Nat. Alliance. Home: Chicago, Ill. *

OLESEN, ANNA DICKIE (MRS. PETER OLESEN) (O'LE-SEN), lecturer; b. Waterville, Minn., July 3, 1885; d. Peter D. and Margaret (Jones) Dickie; grad. high sch., Waterville, 1904; spl. studies, Hamline U., St. Paul; m. Peter Olesen, registrar Carleton College, June 8, 1905; children—Margaret M. (dec.), Mary Winifred. Active in club work since 1912; pres. Minn. 8th Congressional Women's Fed. Clubs, 1913-16; v.p. Minn. State Federated Women's Clubs, 1916-18; del. by appmt. of gov. of Minn. to Internat. Child Welfare Congress, Washington, 1914; mem. State Americanization Com., Minn., 1918-19; mem. advisory bd. of dirs., League of Women Voters of Minn., 1920. Woman mem. Dem. Nat. Com. from Minn. 1917-24; woman speaker at Jackson Day banquet, Washington, D.C., Jan. 8, 1920; del. at large Dem. Nat. Conv., 1920 and 1932; Dem. nominee for U.S. senator, Minn., 1922; candidate for Congressional nomination in Dem. primaries, Minn., 1932; postmaster Northfield, Minn., 1933-34; state dir. NRA, 1934-35, Nat. Emergency Council, 1934-38, Office of Government Reports, 1938-42; member Minn. State Planning Board, 1937-42; mem. Minn. Resources Commn. since 1939 (mem. exec. com.). Patriotic speaker for State Safety Commn., Am. Red Cross, Y.W.C.A., and Liberty Loans during World War. Lecturer. Mem. Nat. Com. of Woodrow Wilson Foundation. Mem. League of Am. Pen Women, Women's Nat. Democratic Club (Washington). Episcopalian. Home: Northfield, Minn.*

OLIVE, JOHN RITTER, sci. orgn. adminstr.; b. Richmond, Ohio, May 26, 1916; s. Archer and Anna (Ritter) O.; B.S., Ohio State U., 1946, M.S., 1947, Ph.D., 1949; D.Sc. (hon.), Colo. State U., 1972; m. Marguerite Petty, Sept. 19, 1940; children—John Kent, Craig William. Mem. faculty Ohio State U., 1946-47, Capitol U., Columbus, Ohio, 1948-49; prof. zoology, asst. dir. Colo. Research Found., Colo. State U., 1949-59; with Am. Inst. Biol. Scis., 1959-74, acting dir., 1962-63, dir., 1963-74. Mem. bioinstrumentation adv. council Shark Research Panel, Surtsey (Iceland) Research Soc., 1965-74; liaison officer Nat. Acad. Scis.-NRC, 1963-74. Served with USAAF, 1942-45. Recipient Sigma Xi Travel award Internat. Limnology Congress, 1953; Oliver P. Pennock Distinguished Service award Abell Hanger Found., 1958; Asso. Students Top Prof. award, 1958; Distinguished Service award Abell-Hanger Found., 1958. Fellow A.A.A.S.; mem. Canadian Soc. Zoologists, Assn. Island Marine Labs., Ecol. Soc. Am., Soc. Limnology and Oceanography, Freshwater Biol. Assn., Internat. Assn. Limnology, Colo.-Wyo. Acad. Sci., Sigma Xi, Xi Sigma Xi, Phi Kappa Phi, Omicron Delta Kappa. Author articles productivity fresh water lakes. Home: Bethesda, Md. Died Mar. 30, 1974.

OLIVER, FRANK, ex-congressman; b. N.Y. City, Oct. 2, 1883; s. of Francis V. S. Oliver; student Fordham U., 1901-05, N.Y. Law School, 1906-08; m. Mrs. Viola

Morris Shelley, of N.Y. City. Began practice at N.Y. City, 1919; mem. 68th to 73d Congresses (1923-35), 23d N.Y. Dist.; resigned, 1934, to become city magistrate N.Y. City. Democrat. Catholic. Home: New York, N.Y. *

OLIVER, JAMES HENRY, historian; b. N.Y.C., Apr. 26, 1905; s. James Henry and Louise (McGratty) O.; A.B., Yale, 1926, Ph.D. (fellow Soldiers and Sailors Meml. 1926-28), 1931; student U. Bonn, 1927-28; Jesse B. Carter fellow Am. Acad. in Rome, 1928-30; m. Janet Carnochan, June 26, 1936. Instr. Latin, Yale, 1930-32; excavator, epigraphist Agora Excavations, Athens, Greece, 1932-36; asst. prof. ancient history Barnard Coll., 1936-42; prof. classics Johns Hopkins, 1946-70, Francis White prof. Greek, 1957-70, prof. emeritus, 1970-80. Guest 10th ann. congress Société des Droits de l'Antiquité, Brussels, 1955, 1st Spanish Congress Classical Studies, Madrin, 1956; organizing com. 3d Internat. Congress Epigraphy, 1956-57; sr. fellow Center for Hellenic Studies, 1962-71; posthumous contbr. Internat. Epigraphical Colloquium, Rome, 1981. Served from capt. to maj., AUS, 1943-45. Guggenheim fellow, 1946, 55-56; Fulbright grantee, Italy, 1963-64; research scholar, Athens, 1939-40, 70-71; sr. fellow Nat. Endowment for Humanities, 1973-74.) Mem. Am. Philol. Assn. (dir. 1965-70, v.p. 1972-74, pres. 1974-75), Archael. Inst. Am. (chmn. monograph com. 1957-68), Am. Soc. Papyrologists, Soc. Promotion Roman Studies, Austrian Archaeol. Inst. (hon.), Ovidianum (Bucharest). Author: (with H.G. Evelyn White) Greek Inscriptions of Hibis, 1938; The Sacred Gerusia, 1941; The Athenian Expounders of the Sacred and Ancestral Law, 1950; The Ruling Power, 1953; Demokratia, the Gods, and The Free World, 1960; The Civilizing Power, 1968; Marcus Aurelius, 1970. Hon. editor Am. Jour. Philology; adviser to Greek, Roman and Byzantine Studies, 1958-81; publs. com. Am. Sch. Classical Studies at Athens, 1952-69, exec. com., 1961-65. Contbr. articles to profl. jours. Home: Baltimore, Md. Died Apr. 3, 1981; buried Balt.

OLIVER, JEAN REDMAN, pathologist; b. Watsonville, Calif., Aug. 19, 1889; s. Cassius and Mary (Redman) O.; A.B., Stanford, 1911, M.D., 1914; m. Dorothy Franz, Oct. 10, 1926 (dec.). Instr. pathology Stanford, 1914-15, asso. prof., 1919-22, prof., 1922-29; asst. pathologist Rockefeller Inst., 1916-18, asso., 1918-19; pathologist Stanford Hosp., 1919-29, San Francisco Hosp., 1919-29; prof. pathology L.I. Coll. of Medicine, 1929-50, pathologist L.I. Coll. Hosp., 1929-50, cons. pathologist, from 1950; Distinguished Service prof. pathology State U. N.Y. Med. Coll., 1950-54, emeritus, 1954-76; cons. pathologist Kings County Hosp., from 1929, Overlook Hosp., from 1953. Trustee Hoagland Lab. Hon. pres. Internat. Congress of Nephrology, 1960. Served as lt. and lt. col. U.S. Army Res., 1916-34, AEF 1916-18. Recipient William Wood Gerhard Medal, 1952; Borden Award in Medicine, 1953; Thomas Addis Meml. medal Nat. Nephrosis Found., 1955; Purkyne medal Prague, Czechoslovakia, 1964; Gold Headed Cane award Am. Assn. Pathology, Bacteriology, 1967; Homer Smith award in renal physiology, 1967; Distinguished Service Award Modern Medicine, 1970. Fellow A.A.A.S.; mem. Am. Physiol. Soc., Am. Assn. Exptl. Pathology, Soc. Exptl. Biology and Medicine (chmn. N.Y. 1950-52), Internat. Assn. Med. Museums, N.Y. Pathol. Soc. (pres. 1941-43), Am. Assn. Pathology and Bacteriology, Am. Found. for High Blood Pressure, Am. Heart Assn. (sci. council), Gerontological Soc., Internat. Club for Research on Aging, Soc. Astronomique de la France, Soc. Internat. de Physiol. Renale (hon.), Harvey Soc. (hon.), Brit. Renal Assn. (hon.), Sigma Xi. Author: (with T. Addis) The Renal Leison in Bright's Disease, 1931; Architecture of the Kidney in Chronic Bright's Disease, 1939; Nephrons and Kidneys, 1968. Home: Chatham, N.J. Died Nov. 19, 1976.

OLIVER, JOSEPH HAYDEN, lawyer; b. Scranton, Pa., Apr. 14, 1882; s. Joseph and Mary Ann (Maschal) O.; grad. Scranton High Sch., 1899; M.E., Bloomsburg Tchrs. Coll., 1900; hon. A.M., Lafayette Coll., 1929; m. Mary Moffat Miller, Sept. 5, 1911; children—Anne Euphemia, William Joseph. Sch. teacher, 1900-07; admitted to Pa. bar, 1906; atty. D.L.&W. R.R. Co., 1907-12, asst. gen. atty., 1912-17, 1920-21; solicitor Pa. R.R. Adminstrn., 1917-20; with Glen Alden Coal Co., 1921-54, gen. counsel, 1921-29, v.p.; gen. counsel, 1930-54; now engaged in gen. law practice. Past gov. Pa. dist. Kiwanis Internat.; past pres. Pa. Self-Insurers' Assn. Mem. Pa. Bar Assn. Republican. Presbyn. Mason. Clubs: Scranton, Country (Scranton). Home: Scranton, Penn. *

OLIVIER, CHARLES POLLARD (O-LIV'I-ER), astronomer; b. Charlottesville, Va., Apr. 10, 1884; s. George Wythe and Katharine Roy (Pollard) O.; A.B., U. of Va., 1905, A.M., 1908, Ph.D., 1911; grad. study U. of Calif., 1909-10; m. Mary Frances Pender, Oct. 18, 1919 (died 1934); children—Alice Dorsey (Mrs. A.E. Hayes), Elise Pender (Mrs. H. E. Ferris); m. 2d Ninuzza Seymour, Oct. 23, 1936; m. 3d, Mrs. Margaret Ferguson Austin, July 24, 1950. Prof. astronomy and physics, Agnes Scott Coll., Decatur, Ga., 1911-14; asst. prof. astronomy, U. of Va., 1914-23, asso. prof., 1923-28; prof. astronomy and dir. Flower Obs. since 1928 and Cook Obs. since 1940 (both U. of Pa.). With U.S. Army, 1918-19. Fellow A.A.A.S., Royal Astron. Soc.; mem. Am. Astron. Soc., Internat. Astron. Union (chmn. meteor commn., 1924-34), Am. Meteor Society (founder), Am. Philos. Soc., Société Astronomique de France, Phi Beta Kappa. Sigma Xi, Sigma Alpha Epsilon. Democrat. Episcopalian. Clubs: Lenape (U. of Pa.); Colonnade (U. of Va.). Author: Meteors, 1925; Comets, 1930. Contbr. to publs. of Leander McCormick Obs., Lick Obs. Bulls., Flower Obs. publs. and reprints; also articles in jours. and encyclopedias. *

OLMSTEAD, DAWSON, army officer; b.May 21, 1884; B.S., U.S. Mil. Acad., 1906; grad. Army Signal Sch., 1909; distinguished grad. Command and Gen. Staff Sch., 1924; grad. Army War Coll., 1934. Commd. 2d lt., U.S. Army, June 12, 1906; promoted through grades to maj. gen., Oct. 1941; apptd. chief signal officer U.S. Army, Oct. 1941; assigned to Telecommunication Bd., July 1943; retired, June 1943. *

OLMSTED, CHARLES EDWARD, botanist, educator; b. Holyoke, Colo., Apr. 23, 1908; s. Charles Edward and Alice Mary (Johnson) O.; A.B., U. Neb., 1929; M.S., U. Okla., 1931; Ph.D., Yale, 1936; student U. Chgo., 1933-34; m. Hazel Wiggers Wilcox, June 27, 1937; children—Charles Edward, Joanna Belle. Instr. botany U. Chgo., 1934-41, asst. prof., 1941-45, asso. prof., 1945-48, prof. 1948-68, chmn. dept. botany, 1953-68, prof. biology, 1968-73, emeritus, 1973-76; instr. botany U. Wyo. Summer Sci. Camp, summer 1941, 59; vis. prof. botany U. So. Calif., summer 1951, U. Auckland (New Zealand), summer 1968. Mem. bd. Natural Resources and Conservation, State of Ill., from 1962. Mem. adv. panel for environmental biology NSF, 1960-63, mem. adv. com. biol. and med. scis., 1965-68. Civilian code instr. U.S. Naval Tng. Sch., U. Chgo., 1942-44; mem. adv. com. natural scis. Nat. Park Service, from 1965. Fellow A.A.A.S. (mem. commn. on sci. edn. 1962-65, v.p. and chmn. sect. G bot. scis. 1966); mem. Ill. Acad. Scis., Bot. Soc. Am., Ecol. Soc. Am. (pres. 1959-60), Am. Soc. Naturalists, Phi Beta Kappa, Sigma Xi, Phi Sigma, Gamma Alpha. Club: Quadrangle (Chgo.). Editor: Ecology, 1942-46, Bot. Gazette, 1946-59, 65-68. Home: Chicago, Ill. Died Nov. 20, 1976.

OLPP, ARCHIBALD ERNEST, congressman; b. Bethlehem, Pa., May 12, 1882; s. John and Matilda M. (Segel) O.; B.S., Lehigh U., 1903; M.D., U. of Pa., 1908; m. Beatrice S. Seiple, of Lansdale, Pa., Nov. 25, 1908. Instr. biol. chemistry, Coll. Phys. and Surg. (Columbia), 1908-09; began practice West Hoboken, N.J., 1909; surgeon North Hudson Hosp. 6 yrs. Mem. 67th Congress (1921-23), 11th N.J. Dist. Served as 1st lt. M.C., during war period. Mem. Am., N.J. State and Hudson Co. med. assns. Republican. Mason. Home: Union City, N.J. *

OLSCHKI, LEONARDO (OLSH'KE), educator, historian; b. Verona, Italy, July 15, 1885; s. Leo S. and Paula (Rosen) O.; ed. sch. of Florence; Ph.D., Heidelberg, 1908; m. Kate Mosse, Berlin, Germany, Dec. 17, 1923. Came to U.S., 1939. Instr. and prof. Romance langs., U. of Heidelberg, 1909-32; exchange and visiting prof., U. of Rome, 1932-38; lecturer Johns Hopkins U., 1939-40; research asso., dept. Oriental langs., U. of Calif. at Berkeley since 1944. Author of numerous books in field of interest; latest publications: The Genius of Italy, 1949; The Myth of Felt, 1949; also numerous articles in German, Italian and English to learned and hist. publications. Writes for publs. in four langs., Italian, German, French, English. Home: Berkeley, Calif. *

OLSON, BRUCE F., bus. exec.; b. Rockford, Ill., 1916; ed. Dartmouth. Chmn. bd., chief exec. officer Sundstrand Corp., Rockford; dir. Am. Nat. Bank & Trust Co., Ill. Bell Telephone Co. *

OLSON, CONRAD PATRICK, lawyer; b. Clay Banks, Wis., Sept. 5, 1882; s. August and Mary (Finan) O.; grad. Stevens Point (Wis.) Normal Sch., 1904; LL.B., U. of Wis., 1909; m. Nellie Frost, of Almond, Wis., Dec. 1, 1910; children—Margaret Eleanor, Conrad Patrick. Admitted to Wis. bar, 1909, and practiced at Madison and Ashland; moved to Portland, Ore., 1909; was mem. firm Duniway & Olson, later Olson, Dewart & Bain, and Olson & Bain, now alone; pres. Darnoc Corpn.; dir. Western Packing Co., Prospect Investment Co., Viking Bakery, etc. Mem. Ore. Ho. of Rep., 1913, 15, State Senate, 1917; floor leader of House, 1913, chmn. judiciary com., 1915, and had charge of road program; resigned from Senate upon apptmt. as asso. justice Supreme Court of Ore.; code commr. of Ore., 1919-21. Mem. Am., Ore. and Multnomah Co. bar assns., Phi Alpha Delta. Republican. Lutheran. Mason (32 deg., K.T., Shriner), Elk, Forester. Clubs: PortlandPress, Laurelhurst. Codifier of Oregon Laws (2 vols.), 1920.*

OLSON, GEORGE LEONARD, banker; b. Dundurn, Sask., Can., Mar. 9, 1917; s. Peter E. and Matilda (Olson) O.; came to U.S., 1918, naturalized, 1928; m. Eva Charlotte Anderson, Feb. 28, 1937; children—Larry D., Karen C. (Mrs. Roger Lee), Robert L. With Wells Fargo Bank and predecessor, 1936-78, v.p. Fairfield (Calif.) office, 1960-78. Pres. Napa-Solano United Crusade, 1965-66, mem. exec. com., 1961-78. Mem. Fairfield-Suisun C. of C. (pres. 1962-63, chmn. mil. affairs com. 1963-64), Solano Bd. Realtors, Central Bus. Dist. Assn. Lutheran. Lion (pres. Fairfield 1969-70), Elk (trustee Fairfield 1964-67). Club: Green Valley Country (Suisun, Calif.). Home: Suisun, Calif. Died Feb. 24, 1978; buried Rockville Cemetery, Solano County, Calif.

OLSON, HARRY EDWIN, educator; b. St. Joseph, Mich., June 4, 1901; s. Alfred L. and Charlotte M. (Swanson) O.; B.S.C., Northwestern U., 1925, M.B.A., 1929; C.P.A., 1940; m. Viola G. Yanaway, July 24, 1932; children—Charlotte M. (Mrs. James M. Kirby), Mary C., Thomas R. Lectr. accounting Northwestern U., 1926-29; asst. prof. business adminstrn. Parsons Coll., Fairfield, Ia., 1929-30; prof. accounting U. S.D., 1930-71, prof. emeritus, 1971-77; dir. bus. research bur., 1942, head dept. accounting, 1930-71; pres. S.D. Bd. Accountancy, 1950-52, sec.-treas., 1953-69. Finance chmn. Sioux Trails Girl Scout Council. Mem. Am. Inst. Accountants, S.D. Soc. C.P.A.'s (sec.-treas. 1946-69), Am. Accounting Assn., Mid-West Econ. Assn., Beta Gamma Sigma, Delta Sigma Pi, Beta Alpha Psi. Republican. Conglist. Mason, Rotarian. Author: Transportation Study of South Dakota, 1942; Accounting Systems, 1952; Public Accounting in South Dakota, 1956; Record Keeping for Small Business and other Enterprises, 1956; The Public Accounting Profession in South Dakota, 1880-1971, 1971; The Public Accounting Profession, Challenge and Problems, 1971. Editor: S.D. Soc. C.P.A.'s mag., 1946—. Contbr. profl. pubs. Home: Vermillion, S.D. Died May 18, 1977; interred Bluff View Cemetery, Vermillion, S.D.

OLSON, KARL JOHN, b. Grimstad, Norway, July 28, 1885; s. Ole and Anne Johnson (Christenson) O.; ed. high schools; m. Hilma A. Björk, June 3, 1916; children—Ethel Eunice, Karl Lloyd, Hazel Edna. Came to U.S., 1902, naturalized citizen, 1911. Dir. East Orange Bldg. & Loan Assn.; pres. Olson Bldg. Supply Corp.; proprietor Karl J. Olson Travel Agency. Mem. East Orange City Council, 1937-48; pres. East Orange Alcoholic Beverage Commn. Mem. Am. Scandinavian Foundn. Mem. reception com., East Orange, for visit of Crown Prince Gustaf of Sweden, June 1926, Prince William of Sweden, Feb. 1927. Ex-pres. N.Y. Conf. Luth. Brotherhood; v.p. Augustana Synod Luth. Brotherhood; treas. Upsala Coll., 1916-43, dir. 1916-46; delegate synodical meeting Augustana Synod of Am., 1922-24, 1932-41, New Eng. and N.Y. confs., 1916-41; treas. and mem. exec. com. N.Y. Conf. of Luth. Augustana Synod; mem. exec. com. of N.J. State com. for 300th anniversary of Swedish Settlement on Delaware Celebration, also mem. gen. com. Director, treas. Lutheran Memorial Hosp., Newark, N.J. Appointed mem. Goodwill Commn. of N.J. and Reemployment Com. for returned soldiers reemployment. Decorated Knight Order of Vasa,1st Class Chevalier (Sweden), 1941. N.J. chmn. John Ericsson Republican Club. Mem. New Eng. Soc. of Orange. Councilman, City of East Orange, since 1937. Club: Rotary (dir.). Home: East Orange, N.J. *

OLSON, WILLARD CLIFFORD, psychologist and educator; b. Annandale, Minn., Oct. 8, 1899; s. John A. and Anne Christine (Frykman) O.; A.B., U. Minn., 1920, A.M., 1924, Ph.D., 1926; m. Violet Hunt Pickard, June 19, 1922; 1 dau., Mary Anne Olson Hayes. Prin. high sch., Osakis, 1920-21; supt. schs., Swanville, 1921-23; instr. U. Minn., 1923-26, asst. prof. ednl. psychology, 1927-29, dir. research in child devel. U. Mich., 1929-52, asso. prof. edn., 1929-35, prof. edn. from 1935, prof. psychology, from 1946, prof. emeritus, from 1972, dean school of education, from 1952, then dean emeritus; part-time or summer instr. Ohio State U., Columbia, U. Chgo., U. Cin. Officer candidate U.S. Army, World War I; mem. emergency com. in psychology NRC, cons. Nat. Roster Sci. and Specialized Personnel, World War II. Occasional cons. Children's Bur., Office of Edn., U.S.P.H.S.; fellow Bd. of Fellowships in Biol. Scis., NRC, 1926-27, mem. div. of anthropology and psychology, 1944-47; dir. Social Sci. Research Council, 1945-48; bd. govs. UNESCO Inst. Edn., Hamburg, 1965-67. Mem. A.A.A.S. (council mem. 1943-47), Am. Edn. Research Assn. (pres. 1948-49), Am. Orthopsychiat. Assn. (v.p. 1933-36), Am. Psychol. Assn. (sec. 1937-45), Interamerican Soc. Psychology (pres. 1955), Society for Research in Child Development (pres. 1950-51), Phi Kappa Phi (pres. Mich. chpt., 1950-51), Phi Delta Kappa, Sigma Xi, Tau Kappa Epsilon. Club: University, Mich. Schoolmasters (pres. 1956-57), Rotary. Author: Child Development, 1949, rev. 1959. Contbr. sci., prof. articles, monographs to ednl., psychol. publs. Home: Ann Arbor, Mich. Died Oct. 30, 1978; interred Washtenang Meml. Park, Ann Arbor.

O'MALLEY, WALTER F., profl. baseball club exec.; b. N.Y.C., Oct. 9, 1903; s. Edwin J. and Alma (Feltner) O'M.; A.B., U. Pa., 1926; LL.B., Fordham U., 1930; m. Kay Hanson, Sept. 5, 1931; children—Terry, Peter. Admitted to N.Y. bar, 1930; practice of law in N.Y. State; atty., dir. Bklyn. Borough Gas Co., 1932-79; dir. Los Angeles Dodgers Baseball Club, (including 26 affiliates), 1932-79, v.p., 1933-49, pres., 1950-70, chmn. bd., 1970-79, v.p. pres. Ebbets-McKeever Exhbn. Co.; chmn. bd., dir. N.Y. Subways Advt. Co.; publisher Sub-Contractors Register; dir. Knudson Creamery, Kingsbury Ordnance Plant, Todd & Brown, Inc., John F. Trommer, Inc., John F. Trommer, Inc. of N.J., Union Bank, Union Bancorp. Gen. chmn. United Hosp. Fund, Bklyn., 1949. Bd. dirs. Swedish Hosp., Bklyn., Braille Inst., Arthritic and Rheumatic Found., Leisure World Found., Big Bros. Greater Los Angeles; trustee U. Pa.; lay adv. bd. Daniel Freeman Meml. Hosp. Served as 2d lt. C.W. Res., U.S. Army. Named Man of Year, B'nai B'rith, 1961. Mem. Bklyn. Bar Assn., Swedish Engrs. Soc., Downtown Businessmen's Assn. (dir.), Los Angeles Com. of 100, Theta Delta Chi, Scabbard and Blade. Democrat. Roman Catholic. Clubs: Bohemian (San Francisco); Los Angeles, Kiwanis, Vikings, Los Angeles Country, Hillcrest Country, (Los Angeles); Cathedral, Metropolitan, N.Y. Athletic (N.Y.C.); Brooklyn (dir., v.p.). Author: Sub-Contractors Begister, 1931. *

OMMERLE, HARRY GARNER, advt. exec.; b. N.Y.C., May 1, 1909; s. Harry Clay and Annye (Hardgrave) O.; Ph.B., Wesleyan U., Middletown, Conn., 1930; m. Katherine Murphy, Apr. 19, 1940; children—Gail, Stephen, Peter, Elizabeth. Asst. to head of radio N. W. Ayer & Son, 1930-35; package sales CBS Radio, 1935-36, v.p. charge TV programs, N.Y.C., 1950-58, v.p. charge TV network programs, 1958; asst. to head of radio William Morris Agy., 1936-41; v.p., account exec. Ruthrauff & Ryan, 1941-43; head radio dept. A. & S. Lyons, 1943-49; head talent and program sales H.G. Ommerle, Inc., 1947-50; sr. v.p. charge radio and TV Sullivan, Stauffer, Colwell & Bayles, Inc., N.Y.C., 1959-70, exec. v.p. charge media and broadcast ops., 1970, also dir. Home: Darien, Conn. Died Feb. 28, 1976.

O'NEAL, CLAUDE E(DGAR), univ. prof.; b. Coatesville, Ind., Jan. 29, 1884; s. Jacob E(llsworth) and Anna Jane (Harlan) O'N.; grad. Ind. State Normal Sch. (now Ind. State Teachers' Coll.), 1910; A.B., Ind. U., 1911, A.M., 1913. Ph.D., 1922; m. Mabel Loreen Hostetter, Sept. 8, 1913; children—William B., Anna Josephine (Mrs. Paul V. Wallace). Teacher, prin. Hendricks County (Ind.) schs., 1904-09; head dept. sci. Brazil (Ind.) High Sch., 1911-12; teaching fellow botany, Indiana U., 1912-13; instr. botany Ohio Wesleyan U., 1913-14, asst. prof., 1914-17, asso. prof., 1917-20, prof. since 1920, head dept. botany since 1922. Fellow Ohio Acad. Sci. (pres. 1938-39), A.A.A.S.; mem. Ind. Acad. Sci., Bot. Soc. Am., Phi Beta Kappa, Sigma Xi, Omicron Delta Kappa. Republican. Methodist. Home: Delaware, O. *

O'NEILL, C. WILLIAM, state justice; b. Marietta, Ohio, Feb. 14, 1916; s. Charles T. and Jessie (Arnold) O'N.; A.B., Marietta Coll., 1938, L.H.D., 1953; J.D., Ohio State U., 1942; LL.D., Defiance Coll., 1953, Ohio U., 1957, W.Va. U., 1957, Miami U., Oxford, Ohio, 1957, Steubenville (Ohio) Coll., 1957, Wilberforce U., 1958, Bowling Green U., 1958, Heidelberg Coll., 1958, Capital U., 1971, Bethany Coll., 1971, Dickinson Coll. Law, 1975; D.C.L., Ohio Wesleyan U., 1973; D.Pub. Service, Ohio No. U., 1973; m. Betty Hewson, July 29, 1945; children—Charles William, Peggy. Admitted to Ohio bar, 1942; mem. firm O'Neill & O'Neill, Marietta, 1942-51; instr. polit. sci. Marietta Coll., 1949-50; prof. pub. affairs Bethany (W.Va.) Coll., 1959-60; practice in Columbus, Ohio, 1959-60; judge Supreme Ct. Ohio, 1960-70, chief justice, 1970—; prof. law Capital U. Sch. Law, 1971-78. Mem. Ohio Ho. of Reps. from Washington County, 1939-50, speaker of house, 1947-48, minority leader, 1949-50; atty. gen. Ohio, 1951-57; gov. Ohio, 1957-58; v.p. Nat. Center for State Cts., 1977-78. Served with AUS, 1943-46. Named one of ten outstanding young men. U.S., Jr. C. of C. U.S., 1950, Most Outstanding State Appellate Ct. Judge in U.S., Assn. Trial Lawyers Am., 1975; recipient Centennial Achievement award Ohio State U., 1970, Ohio Gov.'s award, 1972, Columbus award Columbus Area C. of C., 1974, Outstanding Jurist award Ohio Acad. Trial Lawyers, 1974, Nat. Criminal Justice award Am. Soc. for Pub. Adminstrn., 1975, Christopher Columbus award Columbus-Day U.S.A. Assn., 1975. Mem. Am., Ohio (Ohio Bar medal 1971), Washington County, Columbus bar assns., Am. Judicature Soc. (Herbert Hawley award 1975), Nat. Conf. Chief Justices (chmn. 1977), Am. Legion, V.F.W., Soc. Benchers, Garfield Soc., Order of Coif, Phi Beta Kappa, Delta Upsilon. Republican (chmn. state conv., 1948). Baptist. Mason (K.T., 33 deg. Shriner). Home: Columbus, Ohio. Died Aug. 20, 1978; buried Oak Grove Cemetery, Marietta, Ohio.

O'NEILL, EDWARD J(OSEPH), army officer; b. St. Albans, Vt., Mar. 24, 1902; s. Jeremiah F. and Catherine (Aher) O'N.; Ph.B., U. Vt., 1924; student Inf. Sch., 1936, Command and Gen. Staff Sch., 1937, Indsl. Coll. Armed Forces, 1948; m. Marie Cronin, Nov. 6, 1933; children—Brian Richard, Kevin John, Judith Mary, Bonalyn Ann. Commd. 2d lt. inf., U.S. Army, advanced through grades to lt. gen., 1960; served, Hawaii, 1926-29, 31-35, 1st Inf. Div., 1930, 37-41; overseas combat service Hdqrs. VI Corps, also Fifth Army in North Africa, Italy, France, 1943-45; mem. G-4 div., War Dept. Gen. Staff, 1945-47; munitions bd. Office Sec. Def., 1948-50; dep. chief staff U.S. Army Europe, 1950-53; dir. supply operations Office Dep. Chief Staff for Logistics, Department of Army, Washington, 1953-57; comdg. general U.S. Army Communications Zone, Europe, 1957-59, chief of staff, Europe, 1959-60, comdg. gen. First U.S. Army, from 1960. Decorated D.S.M., Legion of Merit, Bronze Star; Order Brit. Empire; Croix de Guerre with Palm (France); Order of Crown (Italy); War Medal (Brazil); Gold Cross Merit with Swords (Poland); Legion of Honor (France). War Medal (Czechoslovakia); Lateran Medal; Papal Knight St. Gregory the Great. Home: Governors Island, N.Y. Died Jan. 9, 1979.

O'NEILL, JOHN WILLIAM, air force officer, govt. ofcl.; b. Brookline, Mass., Apr. 22, 1918; s. William H. and Mary J. (Healy) O'N.; B.S. in Bus. Adminstrn., Boston U., 1940; M.Litt., U. Pitts., 1951; grad. Air War Coll., 1955; m. Dorothea M. Howley, Nov. 22, 1941; children—Brian A., Dennis M. (dec.), Janice M., Stephen T., Kathleen A., Michael J., Peter S. Commd. 2d lt. U.S. Army, 1940, advanced through grades to lt. gen. USAF, 1967; various assignments, U.S., 1940-44; lead group pilot 28th Bomb Squadron, 19th Bomb Group, PTO, 1944-45; air operations officer, pilot command aircraft, atomic bomb tests, Bikini, 1946; liaison officer with chief naval operations Navy Guided Missile Program, 1946-47; sect. chief Hdqrs. USAF, comptroller Air Force Missile Test Center, Patrick AFB, Fla., 1951-54; comptroller in Burtonwood, Eng., also asst. dir. programs USAF Europe, Wiesbaden and Ramstein, Germany, 1955-58; dep. comdr. ballistic missiles, later dep. chief staff plans and operations Air Force Ballistic Missile Div., 1958-61; dir. staff group Office Dir. Def. Research and Engring., Office Sec. Def., 1961-64; comdr. Electronic Systems Div., Air Force Systems Command, Hanscom Field, Bedford, Mass., 1964-47; comdr. Space and Missile Systems Orgn., Los Angeles, 1967-69; vice comdr. Air Force Systems Command, Washington, 1969-72, ret., 1972; pres. Armed Forces Relief and Benefit Assn., 1972-77. Decorated D.S.M., Legion of Merit, D.F.C. with oak leaf cluster, Air Medal with oak leaf cluster, Order of Rising Sun 2d class. Address: Severna Park, Md. Died Mar. 24, 1977.

O'NEILL, MERLIN, coast Guard officer; born North Kenova, O., Oct. 30, 1898; s. John Henry and Katherine (Forgey) O'N.; student Western Ky. State Normal Sch., 1916-17, Marion (Ala.) Mil. Inst., 1918; grad. Coast Guard Acad., New London, Conn., 1921; m. Esther Emeline Tuttle, Jan. 24, 1925; children—Patricia Tuttle, Marilyn Lee. Commd. ensign, U.S. Coast Guard, 1921, and advanced through grades to rear admiral, Feb. 15, 1916; assigned to coast guard cutters, 1921-27; commandant of cadets and instr. in physics and tactics, Coast Guard Acad., 1927-30; comdg. officer Cassin, 1930-33, Apache, 1933-35; asst. operations officer, Coast Guard Hdqrs., Washington, D.C., 1935-39, chief dir. Coast Guard Auxiliary, 1939-41, chief dir. Coast Guard Reserve, 1911-12; comdg. officer U.S.S. Leonard Wood, combat duty in Atlantic-Mediterranean and central Pacific amphibious landings, 1942-44, comdr. Baltimore Sect. of 5th dist., 1944-45; asst. chief, finance and supply Coast Guard hdqrs., Washington, D.C., 1945; dist. comdr. 5th Coast Guard dist., Norfolk, Va., 1945-46; asst. commandant, Coast Guard hdqrs., Washington, 1946-49; appointed commandant with rank of vice admiral, October 1949. Served as tech. adviser to U.S. del. at Internat. Whaling Conf., London, Eng., 1937. Awarded Legion of Merit July, 1943. Mem. U.S. Naval Inst., Am. Legion. Mason. Club: Propeller, Port of Washington, D.C. Home: Washington, D.C. Died Feb. 28, 1981.

ONSAGER, LARS, educator; b. Oslo, Norway, Nov. 27, 1903; s. Erling and Ingrid (Kirkeby) O.; Ch.E., Norges tekniske hógskole, Trondheim, Norway, 1925; student Eidgenössische Technische Hochschule, Zürich, Switzerland, 1925, 26-28; Ph.D., Yale, 1935; Dr. Technicae (hon.), Norges tekniske hógskole, 1960; D.Sc., Harvard, 1954, Brown U., 1962, Rensselaer Poly. Inst., 1962, U. Chgo., 1968, Ohio State U., 1969, Cambridge U., 1970, Oxford U., 1971; Natural Scis., Rheinisch-Westfaehlisch Technische Hochschule, Aachen, 1962; Sc.D., Gustavus Adolphus Coll., 1975; m. Margaret Arledter, Sept. 7, 1933; children—Erling Frederick, Inger (Mrs. Kenneth R. Oldham), Hans Tanberg, Christian Carl. Came to U.S., 1928, naturalized, 1945. Asso. chemistry, Johns Hopkins, 1928; instr. chemistry, Brown U., 1928-33; Sterling fellow, Yale, 1933-34, asst. prof. chemistry, 1934-40, asso. prof., 1940-45, J. Willard Gibbs prof. theoretical chem., 1945-72; Univ. prof. U. Miami, Coral Gables, Fla., 1972-76; Fulbright scholar, U.K. Cambridge, 1951; vis. prof. U. Calif., San Diego, 1961, Rockefeller U., 1967, U. Goettingen, 1968, U. Leiden, 1970. Recipient Rumford medal, 1953, Lorentz medal, 1958; G. N. Lewis medal, 1962; John G. Kirkwood medal, 1962; Willard Gibbs medal, 1962; T.W. Richards medal, 1964; Debye award, 1965; Belfer award, 1966; Nobel prize in chemistry, 1968; Nat. Sci. Medal, 1968. Fellow A.A.A.S., Am. Phys. Soc., N.Y. Acad.; mem. Am. Philos. Soc., Royal Norwegian, Royal Swedish acads. scis., Norwegian Acad. Tech. Scis., Sci. Soc. Uppsala, Am. Chem. Soc., Conn. Acad., Nat. Acad., Bunsen Soc., Norwegian Chem. Soc., Norwegian Acad. Sci. in Oslo, Am. Acad. Arts and Scis., Royal Danish Acad. Scis., Royal Soc. (London), Inst. Physics (London; hon.), Neurosci. Assos., Sigma Xi. Contbr. articles to sci. jours. Home: Coral Gables, Fla. Died Oct. 4, 1976.

ONTHANK, PIERCE, banker; b. Fitchburg, Mass., Jan. 18, 1904; s. Elmer A. and Grace (Pierce) O.; grad. Philips Andover Acad., 1921; A.B., Williams Coll., 1925; M.B.A., Harvard, 1927; m. Nancy E. Fuller, June 1, 1935; children—John, Dorothy, Katherine. Pres. New London City Nat. Bank (Conn.), 1940-45; v.p. Chem. Bank N.Y. Trust Co., N.Y.C., 1946-65, sr. v.p., 1965-67; sr. v.p. nat. div. Franklin Nat. Bank, from 1967. Home: Shoreham, Vt. Died July 1, 1976.

OPLER, MARVIN KAUFMANN, educator; b. Buffalo, June 13, 1914; s. Arthur and Fanny (Coleman-Haas) O.; student U. Buffalo, 1932-34; A.B., U. Mich., 1935; Ph.D., Columbia, 1938; m. Charlotte Fox, Dec. 30, 1935; children—Ruth Ellen, Lewis Alan; m. 2d, Ruth Hyman, Dec. 23, 1973. Head sociology, anthropology dept. Reed Coll., 1938-43; chief community analysis sect. War Relocation Authority, Dept. Interior, 1943-46; asso. prof. anthropology U. Cal. at Los Angeles, Occidental, 1946-48; asso. prof. anthropology Stanford, 1948-50; lectr. Los Angeles Inst. Psychoanalysis, 1946-48; Los Angeles Neuropsychiat. Vets. Hosp., 1948; lectr., asso. prof. dept. social relations Harvard, 1950-52; prof. anthropology, social psychiatry Cornell U. Med. Coll., Payne Whitney Psychiat. Clinic, 1952-58; prof. social psychiatry, sociology and anthropology State U. N.Y. at Buffalo, 1958-81, chmn. anthropology, 1969-73; vis. prof. sociology, anthropology New Sch. Social Research, 1957-58; spl. lectr. grad. dept. psychology Clark U., 1950; vis. prof. William Alanson White Found., N.Y.C., 1957-59. Vice chmn. Portland Council Social Agys., 1938-53; chmn. social services Multnomah County chpt. ARC, 1938-43; chmn. statistics Welfare Council Greater Los Angeles, 1946-48; mem. nat. com. suicide study Nat. Inst. Mental Health. Social Sci. Research Council fellow, 1937-38, recipient award, 1946-47, grant-in-aid research, 1949. Mem. Internat. Assn. Social Psychiatry (v.p.), Am. Anthrop. Assn., Am. Sociol. Soc., Acad. Psychoanalysis, Soc. Study Social Problems, Western N.Y. Sociol. Soc., Am. Ethnol. Soc., N.E. Anthrop. Assn. (charter mem., 1st pres., 1965-66), Sigma Xi. Author: Culture, Psychiatry and Human Values, 1956; Culture and Social Psychiatry, 1967; Cultural Anthropology: Selected Themes, 1969; co-author Mental Health in the Metropolis: Midtown, 1962, rev. edit., 1977; Impounded People, 1970; North American Indians in Historical Perspective, 1971. Editor: Culture and Mental Health, 1959; asso. editor Internat. Jour. Social Psychiatry, 1957-58, editor, 1958-81; asso. editor Am. Anthropologist, 1962-81. Contbr. articles to profl. jours. Commended at death by Common Council of City of Buffalo and by meml. resolution of N.Y. State Legislature. Home: Williamsville, N.Y. Died Jan. 3, 1981.

OPPERMANN, PAUL, cons. planner; b. Saginaw, Mich., May 20, 1903; s. Gustav Frederick and Antoinette Christine (Peters) O.; student Sch. Architecture, U. Mich., 1924-28; m. Katherine Ellen Cutter; children—Kyra O. Janssen, Paula (Mrs. Davis Andrew Goddard). Asst. dir. Am. Soc. Planning Officials, Chgo., 1935-40; dir. Tri-Cities Planning Project, Johnson City, Tenn., 1941-42; urban planning adviser Fed. Housing Adminstrn., Washington, 1942-46; city planning cons. to French Ministry Reconstrn. and Urbanism, 1945; urban planning officer Fed. Works Agy., Washington, 1946-49; dir. city planning City and County of San Francisco 1949-58; exec. dir. Northeastern Ill. Met. Area Planning Commn. Chgo., 1958-64; partner Adams, Howard & Oppermann, city and regional planning cons.; Bemis vis. lectr. met. planning Mass. Inst. Tech., 1964-68; planning cons., from 1968, urban planning adviser AID, S. Vietnam, 1969-70; Coro Found. traveling fellow, summer 1955; lectr. city planning, housing and urban redevel. Am. U., 1947-49, U. Calif., 1949. Chmn. Nat. Capital Housing Authority, 1947-49, mem. Gov.'s Adv. Com. Cal. Children and Youth, 1952-58; mem. Calif. Moblzn. Service Com., 1951-52; mem. Cal. Local Planning Services Commn., 1954-58; adv. council, Land Econs.; planning adv. com. Mass. Dept. Commerce and Devel. Recipient Distinguished Service award Gt. Lakes region planning com. A.I.A., 1964. Mem. Am. Soc. Planning Ofcls., Urban Am. Inc. (dir. 1964-65), Regional Devel. Council Am., Am. Inst. Planners (bd. govs. 1946-49, editor Jour. 1944-46, pres. 1950-51), Delta Kappa Epsilon, Lambda Alpha (pres. Ely chpt. 1960-61, internat. v.p.). Democrat. Presbyn. Club: Harvard Faculty (asso. mem.). Co-editor, contbr. Environmental Engineering and Metropolitan Planning, 1964. Author research reports and articles. Home: Cambridge, Mass. Died Mar. 16, 1977.

ORCHARD, CLAUDE R., govt. official; b. Exeter, Neb., July 17, 1882; s. William James and Laura (Ewing) O.; grad. South Omaha High Sch., 1901; m. Mabelle Francisco, Nov. 7, 1906. Clerk in railroad office, 1901; live stock handler in S. Omaha Stock Yards; clerk, Armour and Co., Omaha, 1903-05; established centralized employment dept., personnel dir., 1905-34; organizer credit union in meat packing industry, May 1930; helped organize more than 100 credit unions among employes of Armour and Co. throughout U.S.; asst. dir. Fed. Credit Union Sect., Farm Credit Adminstrn., Aug. 1934; dir. Fed. Credit Union Sect., asst. chief examiner, Fed. Deposit Ins. Corp., 1941-48; dir. Bur. Fed. Credit Unions, Fed. Security Agency, since July 1948. Home: Washington, D.C. *

ORCUTT, FREDERIC SCOTT, educator; b. Sioux City, Ia., Nov. 27, 1907; s. Robert William and Florence (Waters) O.; student Antioch Coll., 1926-27; B.S. in Chemistry, U. Wis., 1931, M.S. in Biochemistry, 1933, Ph.D. in Bacteriology and Biochemistry, 1935; m. Katharine Luvinia Krauskopf, Sept. 28, 1935; children—Barbara Sue (Mrs. William T. Keeton), Frederic Scott. Research asso., Squibb fellow anesthesia and pharmacology U. Wis., 1935-36; faculty biology Va. Polytech. Inst., 1936-79, prof., 1945-79, head dept., from 1959; vis. prof. bacteriology U. Hawaii, 1953-54, U. Va. Biology Sta., 1951, 55; participant Oak Ridge Inst. Nuclear Studies, 1950-55, cons., 1949-50; vis. prof. Am. Physiol. Soc. Inst. Coll. Tchrs., summer 1957. Mem. Am. Soc. Microbiology (co-organizer Va. br. 1942, pres. 1946-49, nat. councilor 1949-52), Am. Acad. Microbiology (charter), Am. Inst. Biol. Scis. (governing bd. 1958-79), A.A.A.S., Assn. of Southeastern Biologists, Va. Acad. Sci., Sigma Xi, Phi Sigma (national executive sec.-treas. from 1952), Phi Lambda Upsilon, Gamma Alpha, Alpha Kappa Lambda. Mason (K. T.). Clubs: Shenandoah (Roanoke, Virginia); University (Blacksburg). Author articles profl. jours. Editorial bd. Jour. Applied Microbiology. Home: Blacksburg, Va. Died Dec. 19, 1979.

ORD, JAMES GARESCHÉ, army officer; b. Fort Lewis, Colo., Oct. 18, 1886; s. Maj. Edward Otho Cresap Ord II, U.S. Army, and Mary Frances (Norton) O.; is 4th in direct line of U.S. Army officers; B.S., U.S. Mil. Acad., West Point, 1909; student Sch. of Musketry, Monterey, Calif., 1910, Inf. Sch., Fort Benning, Ga., 1921-22, Command and Gen. Staff Sch., 1923-24, Army War Coll., 1928-29; m. Irene H. Walsh, Apr. 19, 1927; children—James Gareshé, Jr., Marian Eleanor, Edward Otho Cresap. Commd. 2d lt., U.S. Army, 1909, advanced through ranks to maj. gen., 1944; on Mexican border, central Alaska, 1909-17; instr. 1st Plattsburg Camp, 1916; at Culver Mil. Acad., and O.T.C., at Fort Des Moines, Iowa, 1917; with A.E.F., France, 1917-19, participated in Aisne-Marne, St. Mihiel, Argonne campaigns, occupation of Rhineland; operations staff officer, 1st Army Corps and 3d Army; on staff, 9th Corps Area, San Francisco, 1919-21; War Plans Div., War Dept. Gen. Staff, Washington, D.C., 1930-34; instr. Command and Gen. Staff Sch., 1924-28; maj., 30th Inf., 1929-30; comdg. Ft. Washington, Md., 1934-36; dir., Inf. Bd., Ft. Benning, Ga., 1936-38; comdg. 57th Inf., P.I., 1938-40; sr. instr., Pa. Nat. Guard, June to Oct., 1940; brig. gen., 1st Div., comdg. Army contingents of Spl. Task Force, specializing with Atlantic Fleet in landing operations, 1940-42; comdg. 28th Inf. Div., 1942. Chairman, Joint Brazil-U.S. Defense Commission since June 1942; U.S. Army delegate on the Inter-American Defense Board,since Feb. 1943.*

ORGAIN, WILLIAM EDMUND (OR'GAN), lawyer; b. Bastrop, Tex., Dec. 26, 1882; s. Benjamin Darby and Drusilla (Johnson) O.; student Southwestern Univ., Georgetown, Tex., 1899-1903, LL.D., 1933; B.S., U. of Tex., 1906, LL.B., 1906; m. Mary Bolinger, Dec. 2, 1908; children—Benjamin Darby, John Clinton, Drusilla Allene. Admitted to Tex. bar, 1906, and began practice at Beaumont; mem. Orgain, Bell & Tueker; dir. Am. Nat. Bank. Dir. Gulf States Utilities Co., Sabine Towing Company, Norvell-Wilder Supply Company. Member of the Texas Ho. of Rep., 1907; former mem. Tex. Civil Judicial Council; mem. Rules of Practice and Procedure Com. of Tex. Supreme Court. Mem. and former pres. bd. trustees Southwestern U. Mem. Selective Service Bd. No. 6, Jefferson County, Tex. Mem. Am. Bar Assn., Texas State Bar Assn., Jefferson County Bar Assn. (ex-pres. and dir.), Beaumont Chamber Commerce. Democrat. Methodist. Mason, Woodman of World. Clubs: Beaumont Business Men's, Beaumont Country (ex-pres.). Home: Beaumont, Tex. *

ORMOND, JOHN KELSO, surgeon; b. Princeton, N. J., Mar. 25, 1886; s. Alexander Thomas and Mary (Huston) O.; A.B., Princeton, 1906; M.D., Johns Hopkins, 1914; m. Charlotte H. Simmons, Oct. 3, 1916; children—Mary Huston, John Kelso, Robert Simmons. House officer Johns Hopkins Hosp., 1914-15; asst. resident Bay View Hosp., Baltimore, 1915-16; surg. staff Henry Ford Hosp., 1916-18 and 1919, surgeon-in-charge div. urology, 1925-52; chief dept. urology Miraj Med. Center, India, 1952-55; pvt. practice urology, 1955—. Served in U.S. Army, 1918-19, Ex-mem. bd. dirs. Cranbrook Sch.; mem. bd. management Birmingham br., Detroit Y.M.C.A.; trustee Boys Republic. Fellow A.C.S.; mem. A.M.A., Am. Urol. Assn., Am.Assn. Genito-Urinary Surgeons.*

ORMSBY, ROSS R., trade assn. exec.; b. Akron, O., Feb. 27, 1906; s. Frederick R. and Icie Dell (Royer) O.; student Akron U., 1923-24; A.B., Bucknell U., 1927; LL.B., Western Res. U., 1930; m. Agnes E. Hahn, July 11, 1931; 1 dau., Margaret Louise (Mrs. Richard A. Thompson). Admitted to Ohio bar, 1930; practiced in Akron, 1930-44; spl. counsel for atty. gen. Ohio, 1934-36, 39-42; gen. mgr. Employers Assn. Summit County, Akron, 1943-44; mem. staff Rubber Mfrs. Assn., N.Y.C., 1944-49, v.p., gen. counsel, 1949-55, pres., 1955-79, chmn. bd., 1973-79. Chmn. Tire Industry Safety Council, Washington, from 1969. Bd. mgrs. Am. Bible Soc., N.Y.C. Mem. Akron Bar Assn., Ohio Soc. N.Y. Clubs: Union League (N.Y.C.); Seaview Country (Absecon, N.J.); Akron City. Home: New Milford, Conn. Died Feb. 8, 1979.

OROVITZ, MAX, corp. exec.; b. Camden, N.J., July 28, 1904; s. Abraham and Jennie (Handelman) O.; LL.B., Emory U., 1925; m. Ruth Kaplan, Aug. 21, 1929; children—Felicia Rae, Warren James, Michael David. Officer City Nat. Bank, Miami, Fla., 1925-30; v.p. Scott-Perry Corp., builders, 1930-40; co-owner Pub. Gas Co., Miami, 1940-61; pres. Alfred Destin Co., Miami, 1945-68; vice chmn. bd. Maule Industries, Inc., 1953-68; treas., dir. Gen. Devel. Co., 1957-61; dir. City Nat. Bank, Miami Beach, Fla., City Nat. Bank of Miami. Past pres., trustee United Fund of Dade County; chmn. bd. Mt. Sinai Hosp. Greater Miami; dir. citizens bd., chmn. exec. com. bd. trustees U. Miami; former dir. Community Chest, Council Social Agys. Dade County, Fla. Mem. Greater Miami Jewish Fedn. (past pres.). Jewish (past pres. temple). Home: Miami Beach, Fla. Died Jan. 22, 1979.

ORR, JOHN, clergyman and ex-prof.; b. Ulster, Ire., June 28, 1884; s. James and Margaret Jane (McLeese) O.; brought to U.S., 1891, naturalized, 1918; student Park Coll., Mo., 1902-04; A.B., Coll. of Wooster (O.), 1907; A.M., Princeton U., 1909; B.D., Princeton Theological Seminary, 1910; grad. study, Univ. of Berlin, Germany, 1911-13; Ph.D., U. of Pittsburgh, 1931; Ped.D. (hon.) Westminster College, 1949; married Anna Mary Sauer, December 29, 1919; children—Mary Martha, Margaret Elizabeth, John William. Ordained to ministry Presbyn. Ch. in U.S.A., 1910; pastor, Middleport, O., 1913-19, Howell, Mich., 1920-28; asst. prof. Bible, Westminster Coll., 1928-31, prof. Bible and philosophy, 1938-54, acting dean 1938, 1944, 46-50; acting president, 1947-49; pastor Harlansburg Pa. Presbyterian Church, 1957—. Member of A.A.A.S., Am. Assn. Univ. Profs., Nat. Assn. Bible Instrs., Pi Gamma Mu. Republican. Presbyterian. Clubs: Clio, Calvin (Princeton, N.J.). Author: English Deism; Its Roots and Its Fruits, 1934. Home: New Wilmington, Pa. *

ORSBORN, ALBERT WILLIAM THOMAS, Salvation Army officer; b. Maidstone, Kent, Eng., Sept. 4, 1886; s. Albert and Jennie (Minshall) O.; ed. in English public schools and Salvation Army Training Coll., London; m. Phillis Ethel Taylor, Aug. 2, 1947; 6 children by previous marriage. Entered Salvation Army Training Coll., Clapton, London, 1905; became capt. to Chelmsford Corps, 1906; later transferred to staff work, becoming chief side officer Internat. Training Coll., London; chief sec. for New Zealand, 1933-36; territorial comdr. for Scotland and Ireland, 1936-40; British commr., 1940-46; elected by the High Council to be General of The Salvation Army, 1946. Pres. Salvation Army Assurance Soc., Ltd., Salvationist Pub. & Supplies, Ltd., Salvation Army Fire Insurance Company; chairman The Salvation Army Trustee Co. Composer over 200 songs and choruses used throughout world by Salvation Army and other religious societies. Address: London S.E., Eng. *

ORTMAYER, MARIE, physician; b. Chgo., Apr. 2, 1884; d. Carl and Ida (Gottfried) Ortmayer; Ph. B., U. Chgo., 1906; M.D., Rush Med. Coll., 1917. Intern Cin. Gen. Hosp., 1917-18; practice internal medicine, Chgo., since 1920; med. adv. women U. Chgo., 1921-27, asst. clin. prof. medicine, 1928-44; instr. Rush Med. Coll., 1924-28; cons. gastroenterology Cancer Prevention Center, Chgo. Diplomate Am. Bd. Internal Medicine (gastro-enterology) Fellow A.C.P.; mem. Am. Gastorenterological Assn., Alpha Omega Alpha. Home: Chgo. *

OSBORN, EDWARD BARTLEY, chem. co. exec.; b. Mpls., Apr. 13, 1907; s. Merritt J. and Susan (Bartley) O.; B.S., Dartmouth, 1928; hon. degree Hamline U.; m. Gloria M. Steele, Aug. 16, 1939; children—Susan Barrie, Steele Bartley, N.Y. mgr. Econs. Lab., Inc., St. Paul, 1928-30, gen. sales mgr., 1930-43, gen. mgr., 1943-50, v.p., dir., 1932-50, pres., dir., N.Y.C., 1950-78. Trustee Amos Tuck Sch. Bus. Adminstrn. of Dartmouth, Hamline U., Minn. Med. Found. Mem. Am. Soap and Detergent Assn. (pres. 1956-57), St. Paul Sales Mgrs. Assn. (past pres.), Nat. Sanitation Found. (vice chmn. industry adv. bd.), St. Paul Area C. of C. (dir.), Phi Gamma Delta. Clubs: Siwanoy Country, Blindbrook Country (Purchase, N.Y.); Minnesota, Somerset Country, Athletic (St. Paul); Everglades, Bath and Tennis (Palm Beach, Fla.); Apawamis. Contbr. articles trade publs. Home: Bronxville, N.Y. Died Aug. 13, 1978.

OSBORN, GARDNER, orgn. exec.; b. New Haven, June 20, 1893; s. Norris Galpin and Katherine (Gardner) O.; B.A., Yale, 1915; m. Barbara Ellen King, Dec. 3, 1958; children by previous marriage—Gardner, Nancy Lee. Engaged in advt. and pub. relations, 1915-38, preservation historic sites and their pub. interpretation to visitors, 1938-79; exec. dir. Fed. Hall Meml. Assos., Inc., N.Y.C., 1940-61; sec. Am. Scenic and Historic Preservation Soc., N.Y.C., 1946-79; v.p. Bill of Rights Commemorative Soc., Inc. (1st recipient Gold medal 1943), N.Y.C., 1960-79; pres. Am. Coalition Patriotic Societies, 1951-53; v.p. U.S. Flag Found., 1955-61; bd. dirs. Downtown-Lower Manhattan Assn., N.Y.C., N.Y. Nat. Shrines Assos., Castle Clinton Monument Assos. Founding mem. Nat. Trust for Historic Preservation; mem. N.Y. Soc. Founders and Patriots of Am. (gov. 1951-54; 1st recipient Medal of Honor 1956), S.A.R. (pres. N.Y. chpt. 1947-48, sec. Empire State chpt. 1947-59, nat. v.p. gen. 1950-51, editor nat. mag. 1949-51; Minute Man medal 1955). Home: Hartsdale, N.Y. Died July 4, 1979.

OSBORN, JAMES MARSHALL, literary historian; b. Cleve., Apr. 22, 1906; s. Clara Marshall and Mildred (Sleeper) O.; B.A., Wesleyan U., 1928; M.A., Columbia, 1934; B.Litt., Oxford (Eng.) U., 1937; D.Litt., 1968; L.H.D., Kenyon Coll., 1963; D.Litt., McGill U., 1973; m. Marie-Louise Montgomery, Nov. 20, 1929 (dec. 1968); children—Marshall, Thomas M. With Guaranty Trust Co., N.Y., 1928-32; research asso. English, Yale, 1938-72, adviser on 17th century manuscripts to Univ. library, 1954-76, curator Osborn Collection, 1962-72, curator emeritus, 1972-76; vis. lectr. English, Wesleyan U., 1939-40; dir. tng. programs Conn. War Council, 1941-44; owner Whirlwind Hill Farm, Wallingford, Conn., 1940-76. Trustee Wrexham Found., New Haven; bd. dirs. New Haven Symphony, from 1957, v.p., from 1963; v.p. New Haven Free Pub. Library, from 1959; incorporator, v.p. New Haven Preservation Trust, from 1971. Fellow Pierpont Morgan Library, Silliman Coll., Yale, from 1955, St. Catherine's Coll., Oxford U., from 1968. Recipient citation by Bruckner Soc. Am., 1969. Fellow Am. Acad. Arts and Services, Royal Soc. Arts (London), Royal Hist. Soc. (London), Soc. Antiquaries (London); mem. Yale Library Assos. (trustee 1955, chmn. 1975), Nat. Municipal League (council from 1954, Distinguished Citizen award 1962), Gentleman's Soc. Spalding (Eng.), Manuscript Soc. (past pres.), Conn. Acad. Arts and Scis., Modern Lang. Assn. (chmn. index com. from 1962), Modern Humanities Research Assn., The Johnsonians (chmn. 1958), English Inst. (chmn. exec. council 1950-51, trustee), Bibliog. Soc. (London), Oxford Bibliog. Soc., Bibliog. Soc. Am., Psi Upsilon. Clubs: Metropolitan, Grolier (N.Y.C.); Graduates, Elizabethan (past pres.), Mory's, Lawn (New Haven); Johnson, Athenaeum, Nat. Liberal (London). Author: John Dryden: Biographical Facts and Problems, 1940; The Holstein Handbook, 1947; The Beginnings of Autobiography in England, 1960; Young Philip Sidney, 1972; Neo-Philobiblon, 1972. Editor: The Queens Majesties Progress, 1960; The Autobiography of Thomas Whythorne, 1961; Work in Progress in the Modern Humanities, 1938-42; The 17th Century Newsletter, 1942-46; The New Eng. Holstein Bull., 1943-46; Spence's Anecdotes of Books and Men, 1964; Shakespeare's Poems, 1964. Contbr. articles and revs. to various lit. and agrl. periodicals. Home: New Haven, Conn. Died Oct. 17, 1976.

OSBORNE, JOHN, writer; b. Corinth, Miss., Mar. 15, 1907; s. John F. and Norma (Curry) O.; student Southwestern U., Memphis, 1925-26, U. Colo., 1926-27; m. Gertrude McCullough, May 9, 1942; 1 son, John F. Newspaper reporter Comml. Appeal, A.P., Memphis, 1927-31; pub. relations TVA, NRA, 1933-35; with Newsweek, 1936-38; writer, editor, fgn. corr. Time, Inc., 1938-61; free lance, 1961-68; asso. sr. editor New Republic, 1968-81. Clubs: Federal City, Cosmos (Washington). Author: Britain: A Country of Character, 1961: The Old South, 1965; The Nixon Watch, ann. 1970-75; White House Watch: The Ford Years, 1977. Address: Washington, D.C. Died May 2, 1981.

OSBORNE, LITHGOW, publisher; b. Auburn, N.Y., Apr. 2, 1892; s. Thomas Mott and Agnes (Devens) O.; ed. pub. schls., Auburn, and Adirondack-Florida Sch.; student Harvard, 1911-14; LL.D., Syracuse U., 1936; m. Lillie Raben-Levetzau, Mar. 12, 1918; children—Richard, Lithgow Devens, Frederik Raben-Levetzau. Private sec. to James W. Gerard, ambassador to Germany, 1914; 3d sec. of embassy, Berlin, Germany, 1915-17; sec. of legation, Havana, Cuba, 1917, Copenhagen, Denmark, 1917-19; mem. Am. Peace Commn., Paris, 1919; asst. sec.-gen. Arms Limitation Conf., Washington, D.C., 1921-22; conservation commr. New York State, 1933-42; del. at large N.Y. State Constitutional Conv., 1938; with office of foreign relief and rehabilitation operations, Dept. of State, 1943; dep. dir.-gen. European regional office (London) United Nations Relief and Rehabilitation Adminstrn., 1944; A.E. and P. to Norway, 1944-46; chmn. bd. trustees Am.-Scandinavian Found. since 1947. Pres., Auburn (New York) Publishing Company. Trustee Osborne Assn.; mem. board of directors Atlantic Council of the United States. Mem. adv. com. N.Y. State Recreation Council. Mem. Council Fgn.

Relations. Club: Harvard, Century Association (N.Y.C.). Home: Auburn, N.Y. Died Mar. 10, 1980.

OSGOOD, GILBERT HUDSON, lawyer, corp. exec.; b. Milw., Feb. 28, 1905; s. Roy C. and Ann M. (Hudson) O.; grad. Phillips Exeter Acad., 1924; A.B., Princeton, 1929; J.D., Harvard, 1932; m. Frances L. Bell, July 1, 1939; children—Christopher, Nathalie B. Admitted to Ill. bar, 1932, U.S. Supreme Ct. bar, 1945; practiced in Chgo., 1932-43, 46-48, as asso. Wilson & McIlvaine; atty., asst. gen. counsel WPB, Washington, 1943-45; partner Blunt Ellis & Simmons, securities, Chgo., 1948-68, ltd. partner, 1968-71; chmn. Boise Cascade Corp., 1955-69, dir., 1952-73; exec. v.p. Laird, Norton Co., 1957-72, dir., 1951-72; asst. sec. Laird, Norton Trust Co. Mem. Midwest Stock Exchange, 1948-68. Bd. dirs. Citizens Assn. Chgo.; pres. North Shore Country Day Sch., 1959-61, trustee found.; trustee Hadley Sch. for Blind. Mem. Investment Bankers Assn. Am. (chmn. state legis. com. 1957-60), Ill. Bar Assn. Clubs: Law, Legal, University (chmn. admissions com. 1946, colls. and degrees com. 1950, finance com. 1950, dir. 1950-53), Indian Hill, Attic (Chgo.); Tucson Nat. Golf. Co-discoverer, named Stone Man Pass, Colo. Continental Divide. Home: Winnetka, Ill. Died Nov. 12, 1977.

O'SHEA, DANIEL THOMAS (O-SHA), business exec.; b. N.Y.C., Mar. 25, 1904; s. Daniel and Margaret (Moylan) O'S.; B.A., Holy Cross Coll., 1925; LL.B., Harvard, 1930; m. Helen Convery, Sept. 4, 1926; children—Daniel Michael, Richard Michael, Terrence Patrick. Admitted to N.Y. bar, 1930, Calif. bar, 1933; atty. legal dept. RKO-Radio Pictures, N.Y.C., 1930-31, president, 1955-79, resident counsel, also asst. sec. RKO Studios, Inc., Hollywood, 1932-36; sec., Selznick Internat. Pictures, Inc., 1936-39, v.p., 1939-40; exec. v.p. David O. Selznick Prodns., Inc., 1940-42; pres. Vanguard Films, Inc., 1942-50; exec. dir. Selznick Studios, 1942-50; v.p., gen. exec. CBS, 1950-55; pres. RKO Radio Pictures, 1955-79; dir. Consol. Oil & Gas, Inc., Gen. Venture Capital Co. Knight of the Holy Sepulchre. Mem. N.Y., Calif., Los Angeles bar assns. Home: New York, N.Y. Died Dec. 13, 1979.

O'SHEEL, SHAEMAS, author; b. N.Y. City, Sept. 19, 1886; s. Henry F. and Elizabeth A. (Holmes) Shields; revived correct family name, which was legally changed, 1915; ed. grammar and high schs., N.Y. City; spl. student in English and history, Columbia, 1906-8; m. Blanche Louise Hutchinson, of Brooklyn, N.Y., Nov. 23, 1912. Critic and poet; active with Dem. Nat. Com. in presdl. campaign of 1908; active as independent in N.Y. City politics in 1909, as mem. Minute Men and People's Traction Conf. Mem. Poetry Soc. America, Gaelic Soc. Washington, Phi Alpha Sigma. Author: The Blossomy Bough (poems), 1911; The Dear Old Lady ofEighty-Sixth Street, 1912; The Light Feet of Goats (poems), 1915.*

OSTBERG, DONALD ROSS, educator, mathematician; b. N.Y.C., Oct. 8, 1929; s. O. Elmer and Marion (Ross) S.; A.B., Columbia, 1951; postgrad. U. Paris, 1957-58; M.A., U. Calif., Berkeley, 1959, Ph.D., 1960; m. Rosemarie Armstrong, Aug. 15, 1954; children—Karen Ann, Alcyone Elaine, Cynthia Lynn. Instr. math. Rutgers U., 1960-61; J.W. Young research instr. Dartmouth, 1961-63; asst. prof. Ind. U., 1963-66; asso. prof. State U. N.Y., Buffalo, 1966-67; prof. math., dept. chmn. No. Ill. U., Dekalb, 1967-78. Served to lt. (j.g.) USNR, 1951-54. Mem. Am. Math. Soc., Sigma Xi. Author: An Introduction to Linear Analysis, 1966; Elementary Differential Equations, 1968; A First course in Calculus, 1970; (with others) Calculus with Computer Applications, 1973, Achievement in Mathematics, vols. 1 and 2, 1974. Home: Dekalb, Ill. Died Oct. 20, 1978.

OSTER, JOHN EDWARD, realtor, author; b. Holgate, O., Mar. 15, 1883; s. William and Elizabeth (Fox) O.; Sc.B., Ohio No. U., 1907, Litt.B., 1908, B.Pd., LL.B., 1909; student Ohio State, Harvard and Columbia univs.; L.H.D., Lincoln Meml. U., 1917. Tchr. pub. schs., Ft. Jennings, O., 1906-07, Delphos, 1909-10, pvt. sch., Orange, N.J., 1914-15; editor World Court mag., 1915-16; lectr. politics, econs., govt. and sociology Coll. City of N.Y., 1916-63, instr. money and banking, summer sessions; lecturers before scientific socs., lyceums, chautauquas, others; pres. Real Estate Corp., 1963—; speaker Rep. Nat. Com., 1910—. Mem. Legal Advisory Bd. 166, World War; Four Minute man, Victory minute speaker; orator at Grant's Tomb 30th anniversary of his burial. Pres. Public Service Holding Corp. Fellow Am. Geog. Soc., Am. Sociol. Soc.; mem. Am. Inst. of Criminal Law and Criminology, A.A.A.S., Am. Folk-Lore Soc., Am. Econ. Assn., Stable Money Assn., Fgn. Policy Assn., Am. Acad. Polit. and Social Science, Am. Soc. Internat. Law, Harlem Bd. of Commerce, Dante League Am. (dir.), Ohio Soc., Am. Assn. UN, N.E.A., Adult Edn. Assn., Progressive Edn. Assn. Awarded medal Treasury Dept., 1919, for patriotic service, Elected to N.Y. County Rep. Com., 1916-21 inclusive. Clubs: Nat. Travel, New York Economics, Hamilton Republican, 13th Assembly Dist. Republican Club, Harvard, Athene, Verdi, Story-Tellers, etc. Author: The Political and Economic Doctrines of Chief Justice Marshall, 1915. Editor The Organization Republican, Metropolis Magazine. Lectures for New York Bd. of Edn.; specialist in debates for Hoover before colleges, others, in presdl. campaign of 1928. Lecturing on cause and cure of the financial depression. Special speaker for La Guardia in campaign for mayor of N.Y.C., 1933. Gave courses in sociology, business law and real estate law over Municipal Broadcasting Sta. (WNYC) Air College, for N.Y. Bd. of Edn., 1935; supervisor N.Y. Adult Edn. Program, 1936-37. Lectures to teachers, Adult Edn. Home: N.Y.C. *

OSTERLING, ANDERS JOHAN, author; b. Halsingborg, Sweden, Apr. 13, 1884; s. Hans and Ingeborg (Eneberg) O.; Fil. Lic., U. Lund, 1913, Ph.D. (hon.), 1927; m. Anna Margareta Sjoberg, July 12, 1916; children—Ingrid, Karin, Anna Greta. Librarian U. of Lund, 1909-19; literary critic Svenska Dagblad, 1919-35, Stockholmstidningen since 1936. Mem. Swedish Acad. 1916, permanent sec., 1941-64; president Nobel Com., 1947. Club: Swedish Pen (past pres.). Works include: Samlade dikter, 1945-46; Dagensgarning, 1921-31. Home: Sjovillan, Djurgarden. *

OSTERMANN, EDWARD ALBERT (O'STER-MAN), Marine Corps officer; b. Columbus, O., Nov. 23, 1882; s. Seigmund and Lena (Kemmerer), O.; ed. pub. schs., New York and Ohio, and Ohio Northern U.; m. Katharine Hockley Walsh, Apr. 29, 1915; children—Katharine Hockley, Margaret. Commd. 2d lt. Marine Corps, Mar. 20, 1907, and advanced through grades to brig. gen., Feb. 1, 1939. Awarded Congressional Medal of Honor. Episcopalian. Clubs: Army and Navy (Washington); Chevy Chase (Md.) Country; Racquet (Phila.). *

O'SULLIVAN, EUGENE DANIEL, ex-congressman; b. nr. Kent, Kan., May 31, 1883; s. John Edward and Josephine (Kluh) O'S.; Grad. Christian Brothers Coll., St. Joseph, Mo., 1903; student St. Benedicts Coll., Atchison, Kans.; LL.B. cum laude, Creighton U., 1910; m. Ellen K. Lovely, 1919; children—Eugene D., Mrs. Robert DeVaughn. Admitted to the Nebraska bar, 1910, and engaged in practice of law since; del. to Democratic Nat. Conv., 1924, 28, 32, 40, 44; mem. 21st Congress (1949-51), 2d Neb. dist. Mem. Am. and Douglas County bar assns., Omaha Bar Assn. (pres.), Neb. Integrated Bar, Am. Judicature Soc. Democrat. Roman Catholic. Ancient Order of Hibernians, Eagle, Elk, K.C. Clubs: Stock Yards 400 (Omaha, Neb.). *

O'SULLIVAN, JEREMIAH LEE, prof. journalism; b. Hutchinson, Kan., Apr. 28, 1894; s. Mortimer and Teresa (Decker) O'S.; St. Benedict's Coll., Atchison, Kan., 1909-11; B.J., Marquette U., 1914; honorary Doctor of Literature, Boston Coll., 1949; m. Eleanor Gavigan, Nov. 10, 1917; children— Quentin, Geraldine. Reporter, later city editor Milwaukee (Wis.) Sentinel, 1914-16; staff corr. United Press, Milwaukee, Indianapolis, Ind., Chicago, Kansas City, Mo., and N.Y. City, 1916-24; prof. journalism and mgr. Univ. Press, Marquette U., 1924-28, dean of Coll. of Journalism 1928-62. Mem. Council on Edn. for Journalism, term 1935-45; mem. National Committee on World Catholic Press Exhibit, 1936; member Gallery of Living Catholic Authors (journalism committee since 1944). Founded Catholic School Press Association (dir. since 1931); pub. Catholic School Editor from 1931; dir. Archdiocesan Cath. Charities Council, from 1931; mem. President's Com. Employment Physically Handicapped. Mem. Am. Assn. Tchrs. of Journalism (dir.), Internat. Cath. Journalists Union (pres. 1933-34), Am. Assn. of Schs. and Depts. Journalism (pres. 1941), Catholic Press Assn., Gov.'s Commn. Human Rights, from 1958, Sigma Delta Chi, Kappa Tau Alpha. Awarded Papal medal, for Catholic press work, 1938; Catholic War Veterans Wis. medal, 1952; Catholic Press Assn. medal for contbn. to Catholic Press, 1957; Knight of St. Gregory, 1961. Home: Wauwatosa, Wis. Died Dec. 21, 1976.

O'SULLIVAN, JOSEPH ANTHONY, archbishop; born Hamilton, Ontario, Nov. 29, 1886; s. Joseph and Catherine (Fogarty) O'S.; student St. Jerome's Coll., Kitchener, 1903-08, Grand Sem., Montreal, 1908-11; LL.D., Ottawa U., 1946. Ordained priest Roman Catholic Ch., 1911; rector of Cathedral, Hamilton, 1920-25; pres. St. Augustine's Sem., Toronto, 1925-31; bishop, Charlottetown, P.E.I., 1931-44; archbishop Kingston, since 1944. Mem. adminstrv. bd. Cath. Ch. Extension Soc. of Canada. Address: Kingston, Ont. Can. *

OTIS, BROOKS, educator; b. Boston, June 10, 1908; s. Edward O. and Marion (Faxon) O.; grad. Phillips Exeter Acad., 1925; B.A., Harvard U., 1929, M.A., 1930, Ph.D., 1935; D.H.D., Heidelberg Coll., 1973, Hobart Coll., 1977; m. Christine Battle Cheney, May 22, 1937; children—Brooks Adams, Marion (Mrs. Andrew E. Barnes), Franklin Carter Cheney, Irene Denny (Mrs. Michael Cosgrove), Paul Hamilton. Instr. classical langs. Earlham Coll., 1930-32; asst. prof. classics, lectr. sociology Hobart Coll., 1935-39, Hobart prof. classics 1939-57; prof. classics, exec. head dept. Stanford, 1958-63, Olive Palmer prof. humanities, 1964-70; Paddison prof. Latin, U. N.C., Chapel Hill, 1970-77. Vis. prof. U. Chgo., 1937, Ohio State U., 1949, Am. U., Beirut, 1957-58, Harvard, 1964, SUNY, Buffalo, 1968. Guggenheim fellow, 1952-53, 73-74, Fulbright fellow, 1953-54, 64, Smith-Mundt fellow, 1957-58. Fellow Am. Acad. Arts and Scis., Nat. Council Religion Higher Edn.; mem. An. Philol. Assn., Episcopal Guild Scholars. Democrat. Episcopalian. Author: Virgil, a Study in Civilized Poetry, 1963; Ovid, as an Epic Poet, 2d edit., 1970; also articles. Editor: New Frontier, 1933-35. Home: Chapel Hill, N.C. Died July 26, 1977.

OTT, ELMER B., mfg. exec.; b. Enid, Okla., Oct. 22, 1902; s. Albert C. and Hattie L. (Franzke) O.; student, U. Wis., 1918-22; m. Sabina Elizabeth Lynaugh, Aug. 6, 1927; 1 dau., Nancy Jean (Mrs. Richard Philip Trainor). With Electric Storage Battery Co., 1923-73, chmn., dir., 1959-73; dir. Mayfair Molded Products Corp., Schiller Park, Ill.; Madison Gas and Electric Company, First Nat. Bank, Madison, Wis. Home: Madison, Wis. Died Oct. 15, 1979.

OULD, EDWARD HATCHER, JR., banker; b. Middlesboro, Ky., Sept. 13, 1907; s. Edward Hatcher and Ethel Stuart (Cole) O.; B.S., Washington and Lee U., Lexington, Va., 1929; grad. Stonier Grad. Sch. Banking, 1949; m. Madolyn Burruss Airheart, Oct. 21, 1933; children—Edward Hatcher, III, Mary Robertson Ould Sabin. With First Nat. Exchange Bank Va., Roanoke, 1938-79, pres., chief exec. officer, 1956-64, chmn. bd., chief exec. officer, 1964-77, chmn. exec. com., 1977-79, also dir.; pres., chief exec. officer Dominion Bankshares Corp., Roanoke, 1967-73, chmn. bd., chief exec. officer, 1973-77, chmn. bd., chmn. exec. com., 1977-79; dir. Roanoke Valley Industries; past mem. adv. com. to comptroller currency. Pres., bd. dirs. Roanoke Pub. Library Found.; bd. dirs. Roanoke Valley Devel. Found., Roanoke Hist. Soc. Served to lt. USNR, 1943-45. Mem. Am. Bankers Assn. (past v.p. for Va.), Roanoke Valley C. of C. (past pres.), Kappa Sigma, Omicron Delta Kappa, Gamma Beta Phi, Pi Beta Epsilon. Methodist. Clubs: Shenandoah; Jefferson (Roanoke). Home: Roanoke, Va. Died Dec. 17, 1979.

OWEN, GEORGE VERNON, JR., banker; b. Akron, O., Mar. 1, 1925; s. George Vernon and Irene Gertrude (Mechlin) O.; A.B., Western Res. U., 1948; LL.B., 1951; m. Joanne Ellen Aldredge, Sept. 1, 1951; children—David Madison, Jane Elizabeth, Rebecca Irene. Admitted to Ohio bar, 1951; law dept. Fed. Res. Bank of Cleve., 1951-53, Perfection Stove Co., Cleve., 1953-54; trust officer Harter Bank & Trust Co., Canton, O., 1954-61; head of trusts Akron Nat. Bank & Trust Co., 1961-74, pres., 1974-76. Trustee Akron Community Trusts, Akron Art Inst., Akron Gen. Med. Center. Served with AUS, 1943-46. Mem. Ohio, Akron bar assns., Ohio Bankers Assn. Clubs: Akron City (Akron); Portage Country. Home: Akron, Ohio. Died Sept. 29, 1976.

OWEN, HARRY GODDARD, educator; b. Port Henry, N.Y., July 31, 1902; s. Harry Edward and Emily Goddard (Hicks) O.; A.B., Middlebury Coll., 1923, Ed.D., 1953; M.A., N.Y. U., 1924. Instr. N.Y. U., 1923-26; asst. prof. English, Middlebury Coll., 1926-28, asso. prof., 1928-32, asso. prof. fine arts, 1932-41, prof. fine arts and English, from 1941; dean Bread Loaf Sch. of English, Vt., 1928-34, dir., from 1934; mem. adminstrv. com. acting as pres. of Middlebury Coll., 1940-41; dean Coll. Arts and Scis., Rutgers U., 1945-65; adj. prof. English, Pace Coll., 1965-70. Dir. Marcella Sembrich Found., from 1938. Served to lt. comdr., USNR, 1942-45. Mem. Phi Beta Kappa, Delta Kappa Epsilon. Presbyterian. Home: New York, N.Y. Died Apr. 20, 1978.

OWEN, JOSEPH PARKES, clergyman, educator; b. Marshall Co., Ala., Mar. 14, 1886; s. Henry Clay and Eliza Eveline (Gregory) O.; student U. of Chattanooga, 1902-08; D.D., Taylor U., Upland, Ind., 1925; m. Ada Ryan, of Ala., Sept. 14, 1909; 1 son, Hubert Ryan. Ordained ministry M.E. Ch., 1910; student pastor Holston Conf., Tenn., 1904-05; evangelist, traveling extensively in United States and Canada, until 1922; pastor Boaz, Ala., 1923; v.p. John Fletcher Coll., University Park, Ia., 1924-25, pres., 1925-34; gen. evangelism, 1934-36. Author: The Unchanging God, 1929. Home: Boaz, Ala.*

OWEN, WALTER STEWART, lawyer; b. Atlin, B.C., Can., Jan. 26, 1904; s. Walter and Janet Ann (Dick) O.; grad. Vancouver Law Sch., 1927; LL.D., U. B.C., 1959; m. Jean Margaret Dowler, Nov, 8, 1929 (dec.); children—David Stewart, Philip Walter, Margaret Ann (Mrs. Jacques Barbeau), Daphne Muriel (Mrs. Michael Francis); m. 2d, Shirley Grauer, Mar. 17, 1972. Called to bar, B.C., 1928, then practiced in Vancouver; partner Hunter & Owen, 1928-32; sr. partner Campney, Owen & Murphy, 1932-69; crown prosecutor County of Vancouver, 1933-42; created Kings counsel, 1945; sr. partner Owen, Bird, from 1969. Del. numerous internat. legal confs. Dir. East Asiatic Co. (Can.), Ltd., Western Broadcasting Co., Ltd., Radio NW, Ltd., Radio OB, Ltd., Radio QR, Ltd., Radio M.L. Ltd., Northwest Sports Enterprises Ltd., Vancouver Hockey Club Ltd., Canucks Pub. Ltd., Greyhound Lines of Can., Ltd., Greyhound Computer of Can., Ltd., Brewster Transport

Co., Ltd., Eastern Canadian Greyhound Lines Ltd., Western Prodns., Ltd., Saturna Investments, Ltd., Atlin Investments Ltd. Lt. gov. Province of B.C., 1973-78. Mem. Vancouver Bd. Trade, Can.-Japan Trade Council. Premier, 1st Older Boys Parliament B.C., 1923, 2d, 1924; del. YMCA Conf., Helsinki, 1926. Chmn. bd. emeritus Found. for Legal Research in Can.; bd. dirs. Vancouver Boys Club; bd. govs. YMCA; hon. gov. Canadian Assn. for Retarded Children; mem. adv. bd. Salvation Army, Vancouver, YMCA Greater Vancouver; bd. mgmt., adv. bd. Grace Hosp.; mem. Vancouver Gen. Hosp. Health Centre for Children, Canadian Council Christians and Jews, Vancouver Masonic Temple Assn. Served with Seaforth Highlanders Can., 1942-46. Decorated Centennial medal, knight St. John Jerusalem. Mem. Can. (council from 1938, pres. 1958), Am. colls. trial lawyers, Am., Wash., Minn., Man., B.C. (bencher, past treas.) bar assns., Can. Tax Found. (past gov.). Liberal. Anglican. Mason (33 deg., Shriner, Jester). Clubs: Shaughnessy Golf and Country, Vancouver (past pres.), Union (Victoria). Home: Vancouver, B.C., Can. Died Jan. 14, 1981.

OWEN, WILBER (ALLEN), lawyer; b. Detroit, June 30, 1873; s. Charles W., Sr., and Belle J. (Allen) O.; LL.B., Columbian (now George Washington) U., 1896, LL.M., 1897. Admitted to bar, 1897; now senior patent law firm of Owen & Owen, Toledo, Ohio. Member American Bar Association, American, Toledo and Chicago patent law associations, Phi Delta Phi fraternity. Republican. Presbyterian. Author: Questions and Answers on Pleading, 1897; Questions and Answers on Evidence, 1898; Owen's Law Quizzer, 6th edition, revised and enlarged. 1932. Home: Toledo. *

OWENS, JESSE (JAMES CLEVELAND), public relations firm exec., athlete; b. Danville, Ala., Sept. 12, 1913; s. Henry and Emma (Alexander) O.; A.B., Ohio State U., 1937; m. Ruth Solom n, 1931; children—Gloria, Beverly, Marlene. Mem. U.S. Olympic Track Team, Berlin, Germany, 1936; with Office Civilian Def., Phila., 1940-42; dir. Negro personnel Ford Motor Co., 1942-46; with Leo Rose Sporting Goods Co., 1946-52; sec. Ill. Athletic Commn., Chgo., 1952-55; formerly sports specialist Ill. Youth Commn.; pres. Jesse Owens & Assos., Chgo.; briefly led orch. and acted in films; ambassador of sports U.S. Dept. State, 1955. Served with mil., World War II. Recipient 4 Gold medals for 100-meter run, 200-meter run, broad jump, relay team in Olympics, 1936. Mem. Alpha Phi Alpha. Baptist. Elk. Home: Chicago, Ill. Died Mar. 31, 1980.

PACKARD, CHARLES, biologist; b. Dorchester, Mass., Sept. 3, 1894; s. Edward Newman and Elizabeth (Ford) P.; B.S., Syracuse U., 1907, M.S., 1908; D.Sc., 1938; Ph.D., Columbia, 1913; m. Marguerite Adams Cogswell, Sept. 2, 1915; 1 dau., Priscilla Adams. Inst. in biology, Williams Coll., 1908-10; instr. in zoölogy, Columbia, 1913-18; asst. prof. biology, Perkins Union Med. Coll., 1918-23; asst. prof. cancer research, Columbia, 1923-42; instr. embryology, Marine Biol. Lab., Woods Hole, Mass., 1915-18 and 1924-34, director 1939-50, trustee since 1950. Clerk of Corporation, Marine Biol. Lab., 1931-37. Fellow A.A.A.S.; mem. Am. Soc. Naturalists, Am. Soc. Zoölogists, Sigma Xi, Psi Upsilon. Contbr. of numerous articles on effects of x-rays and radium to sci. publs. Address: Woods Hole, Mass. *

PACKARD, EARL LEROY, paleontologist; b. East Charlemont, Mass., Apr. 10, 1885; s. Everett Tower and Jennie Relief (Porter) P.; U. of Puget Sound, 1907; B.A., U. of Wash., 1911, M.A., 1912; Ph.D., U. of Calif., 1915; m. LeFay Verna Davy, Aug. 10, 1915; children—Mildred Lucy (Mrs. Ivan K. Nichols), Martin Everett. Fellow in paleontology, U. of Calif., 1912-14; instr. in geology, U. of Wash., 1915-16; asst. prof. of geology, U. of Ore., 1916-17; prof. and head dept. of geology, Miss. Agrl. and Mech. Coll., 1917-18; prof. geology, U. of Ore., 1918-32; dean school science, Oregon State Coll., 1932-38, dir. of gen. research Oregon Inst. Marine Biology and head of geology dept., Ore. State Coll., 1932-36. Dir. Gen. Research Oregon system of higher education, 1932-46. Fellow Geol. Society America. Paleontol. Soc. America; mem. Geological Soc. of Ore. Country, California Academy Sciences, Phi Sigma, Phi Kappa Phi Sigma Xi, Theta Tau. Exploration trips in Ore., Calif., Wash., B.C., Fla., Miss. and Arctic Coast of Alaska. Author of various paleontol. and biol. papers. Home: Corvallis, Ore. *

PACKARD, EDWARD N(EWMAN), physician; born Boston, May 14, 1883; s. Edward Newman and Elizabeth (Ford) P.; Ph.B., Syracuse Univ., 1906, M.D., 1909; m. Mary Bissell Betts, Nov. 28, 1919 (died 1926); children—John Mallory, Ann (now Mrs. A. T. Ladd), Mary Betts (now Mrs. J. B. Reeley. Interne at St. Lukes Hospital, New York City, 1910-12; pathologist Sloan Maternity Hosp., 1912; in pvt. practice specializing in tuberculosis, Saranac Lake, N.Y., 1913-41; med. dir. Trudeau (N.Y.) Sanatorium, 1946-50; acting dir. and director Trudeau Foundation, October 1946-May 1948; director Trudeau School of Tuberculosis, 1946-50; consultant Will Rogers Memorial Hospital; part time lecturer in medicine at the University of Rochester Sch. of Medicine and Dentistry, 1947-58; medical supvr. Saranac Lake Rehabilitation Guild. Served as med. chief, Base Hosp. No. 16, New Haven, Conn., 1919; reentered active service, 1941, and served as chief of med. services, Sta. Hosp., Ft. Dix., N.J., 1941-42, Holloran Gen. Hosp., Staten Island, N.Y., 1942-45; exec. officer and dir. professional services Holloran Gen. Hosp., 1944-46; disch. with rank of col., Apr. 1946. Awarded Legion of Merit, 1946. Fellow Am. Coll. Phys., A.M.A.; mem. Nat. Tuberculosis Assn., Am. Trudeau Soc., Am. Clin and Climatol. Assn., Am. Assn. for Thoracic Surgery. Republican. Episcopalian. Contbr. to med. jours. and systems of medicine on tuberculosis and allied subjects. Home: Saranac Lake, N.Y. *

PACKER, PAUL C., educator; b. Salem, Ia., Oct. 13, 1886; s. Mahlon Linton and Sara (Jacobs) P.; B.A., U. of Ia., 1918; M.A., U. of Mich., 1921; Ph.D., Columbia, 1923; LL.D., Cornell Coll., 1938; m. Mary C. Bliss, Dec. 31, 1913; 1 dau., Ruth Virginia (dec.). Teacher rural schs., 1905-37; prin. elementary sch., Ft. Madison, Ia., 1910-13, Iowa City, 1913-17; gen. supervisor pub. schs., later prin., Univ. Elementary Exptl. Sch., Iowa City, 1917-18; instr. Summer Sch., U. of Ia., 1918; acting dir. of ednl. research, pub. schs., Detroit, 1918-19, asst. supt. schs., 1919-21; instr. Summer Sch., U. of Mich., 1919, 20, 22; prof. administration U. of Ia., 1921-22, dean Coll. of Edn., June 1923-46; dir. summer school, 1927-45; chancellor, Oregon State System of Higher Edn., since Sept. 1946; educational adviser to University of the Philippines, 1938. Lt. col., A.U.S., Special Service Division, 1944. Mem. N.E.A., Nat. Society for Study of Edn., Am. Assn. of Sch. Adminstrs., Nat. Soc. of Coll. Teachers of Edn., Phi Delta Kappa. Republican. Conglist. Clubs: Rotary, University (Portland). Home: Eugene, Ore. *

PADÍN, JOSÉ, book editor; b. in San Juan, Puerto Rico, May 3, 1886; s. José and Francisca (Rodríguez) P.; grad. Moorestown (N.J.) Friends Acad., 1903; B.S., Haverford (Pa.) Coll., 1907, A.M., 1908, LL.D., 1931; grad. study, Columbia U., 1926-29; Litt.D., University of Porto Rico, 1933; Pd.D., Dartmouth College, Hanover, N.H., 1934; M. Paulina Cuebas, June 2, 1917; children (adopted)—Ruth Beatrice Lynch, Eleanor Judith Lynch, Edith Grace Lynch. Teacher pub. schs., P.R., 1908-09; supt. schs., Guayama, P.R., 1909-12, Arecibo, P.R., 1912-13; gen. supt. schs., P.R., 1913-16; asst. commr. of edn., P.R., 1916-17; Spanish editor, D.C. Heath & Co., pubs., N.Y. City, 1917-30; commr. of edn., Puerto Rico, 1930-36; modern language editor D.C. Heath & Co. since 1936, Pres. bd. trustees U. of P.R., Sch. of Tropical Medicine, 1930-36. Mem. Nat. Edn. Assn. Catholic. Club: University (Boston). Author: Nociones de Agricultura Tropical, 1922. Editor: El Mercader de Venecia, 1919; Misericordia, 1928. Contbr. to Puerto Rico School Review. Home: Boston. *

PADOVER, SAUL K., educator, polit. scientist; b. Austria, Apr. 13, 1905; s. Keva (Am. citizen) and Frumet (Goldmann) P.; brought to U.S., 1920; A.B., Wayne State U., 1928; postgrad. Yale U., 1928-29; A.M., U. Chgo., 1930, Ph.D., 1932; D.H.L. (hon.), New Sch., 1977; m. Margaret T. Fenwick, Apr. 13, 1957. Prof. W.Va. State Coll., summers 1930, 31; research asst. history U. Chgo., 1932; research asso. U. Calif., 1933-36, lectr., summer 1935; asst. to sec. interior, 1938-43; cons. Office Facts and Figures, 1942; dir. research unit territorial policy Dept. Interior, 1942-44; chief polit. analyst FCC, London, 1944; intelligence officer OSS, 1944; editorial writer PM Newspaper, 1946-48; prof. Grad. Faculty, New Sch. Social Research, N.Y.C., 1949-81, dean Sch. Politics, 1950-55, Distinguished Service prof., 1971-81; leader Friends Service Com. Internat. Seminars in Europe 1949-81; prof. Am. politics Sorbonne, Paris, 1949; cons. Hoover Inst., Stanford, 1948-81; lectr. State Dept. Mission to S.E. Asia, 1953, 55, 60, 74, Australian-Am. Found., 1970; vis. prof. Columbia U., 1954-55, U. Malaya, fall 1960; Fulbright prof. U. Tokyo, spring 1960, Wayne State U., 1971; project dir. Carnegie Endowment Internat. Peace, 1955-56. Served as intelligence officer U.S. Army, 1944-46. Decorated Bronze Star; Legion of Honor (France); recipient Commonwealth Silver medal, Alumni award Wayne State U., 1965, Profl. Achievement award U. Chgo., 1971; Guggenheim fellow, 1936-37; Rockefeller fellow, 1945. Democrat. Author numerous books, latest being Europe's Quest for Unity, 1953; Living U.S. Constitution, 1953; French Institutions, 1953; The Genius of America, 1960; The Meaning of Democracy, 1963; Foreign Affairs, 1964; Thomas Jefferson and American Freedom, 1965; Karl Marx: An Intimate Biography, 1978. Editor several compilations, latest being The Washington Papers, 1955; A Jefferson Profile, 1956; Confessions and Self-Portraits, 1957; The Mind of Alexander Hamilton, 1958: To Secure These Blessings, 1962; The Writings of Thomas Jefferson, 1968; editor The World of the Founding Fathers, 1958; Karl Marx on Revolution, 1972; Karl Marx on the First International, 1972; Karl Marx on America and the Civil War, 1973; Sources of Democracy, 1973; Karl Marx on Religion, 1974; Karl Marx on Freedom of the Press and Censorship, 1974; Karl Marx on Education, Women and Children, 1975; Karl Marx on History and People, 1977; The Essential Marx, 1978. Contbr. to mags. Home: New York, N.Y. Died Feb. 22, 1981.

PAEFF, BASHKA, sculptor; b. Minsk, Russia, Aug. 12; d. Louis and Fannie (Kischen) Paeff; brought to U.S. in infancy; grad. Girls High Sch., Boston, 1907, Normal Art Sch., 1911, Boston Museum Sch. Fine Arts (under Bela Pratt), 1914 (scholarships); m. Samuel Montefiore Waxman, June 1, 1940. Won competition for a war meml. placed in State House, Boston, also for World War meml. for State of Maine; The Lexington Minute Men, Lexington, Mass. Works include portraits, busts, and bas relief portraits of famous Americans, also medals, fountains, other memls., including bust Louis D. Brandeis, bas relief Martin Luther King, Jr., Oliver Wendell Holmes, Dr. Harry C. Solomon, also Shields Warren, bronze bas relief Louis B. Mayer for U. So. Cal. Med. Sch.; Elected 1 of 5 Women of Achievement, Business and Profl. Women's Club, Boston; recipient 1st and 2d prizes Scituate (Mass.) Art Festival; Daniel Chester French medal Nat. Acad. Design, 1969. Fellow Nat. Sculpture Soc.; mem. Copley Soc. Boston, Guild Boston Artists, Acad. Artists. Home: Cambridge, Mass. Died Jan. 24, 1979.

PAGE, HARRY D., lawyer; b. Milw., May 9, 1903; LL.B., U. Wis., 1929; student Advanced Mgmt. Program, Harvard, 1955; m. Martha Rowland, Jan. 7, 1927; children—Ruth (Mrs. Martin J. Lawrence, Jr.), Martha (Mrs. Henry de Forest Ralph, Jr.), Susan. Admitted to Tex. bar, 1929, Okla. bar, 1936, N.Y. bar, 1962; pvt. practice law, Dallas, 1929-36; specializing oil and gas law, Tulsa, 1936-59; sec., gen. atty. Columbian Carbon Co., 1959-64, general counsel, 1964-68. Mem. Am. Bar Assn. (chmn. sect. mineral law 1955-56, mem. ho. dels.), Order of Coif. Home: Stamford, Conn. Died Jan. 13, 1976.

PAGE, J(OHN) WATT, army officer; b. Manchester, Vt., Feb. 20, 1882; s. Dr. John Fessenden and Mary Jennie (Watt) P.; student Burr and Burton Sem., Manchester, Vt., 1899-1901; m. Elizabeth Etoile White, Dec. 28, 1909; children—John Watt, Jr., (major, U.S.A., ret.), Margaret Jane. Wholesale and retail tobacco business, 1902-11; with Armour & Co., Ft. Worth, Tex., 1912-16; personnel manager, Montgomery Ward & Co., 1928-31; associate credit manager, Washer Bros., Fort Worth, Texas, 1935-39; War Department Gen. Staff, 1920-22; initial general Staff Eligible List, 1920; asst. to chief, Nat. Guard Bureau, War Dept., 1923-27; selected by sec. of war in 1920 as one of committee of 14 officers to reorganize Army of U.S. following World War I. Brig. gen., adj. gen. of Texas, 1940-42; brig. gen. U.S. Army, Nov. 7, 1940; State dir. Selective Service for Texas, 1940-47; retired 1947. Decorated Legion of Merit, Army Commendation Ribbon Texas Meritorious Service medal with four acorns. Member Rosicrucian Order, Am. Legion (past post comdr.). Episcopalian. Address: Austin, Tex. *

PAGE, THADDEUS SHAW, archivist; b. Aberdeen, N.C., Nov. 3, 1890; s. Robert Newton and Flora Eliza (Shaw) P.; grad. Fishburne Mil. Sch., 1908; student U. N.C., 1908-12; m. Martha Macon Hinton, Oct. 29, 1913; children—Thaddeus Shaw, John (dec.). Sec. to mem. Congress, 1913-16; automobile distbr. and dealer, 1916-30; sec. to Senator Josiah W. Bailey, 1931-35; apptd. adminstrv. sec. Nat. Archives, 1935, dir. legislative service, 1947-51, chief archivist legislative and fiscal br., 1951-53, legislative, judicial and diplomatic branch, 1953-56, general records div., 1956-73; sec. Nat. Archives Council, 1936-50; trustee Nat. Archives Trust Fund Bd., 1952—. Franklin D. Roosevelt Library 1952-58. Fellow Soc. Am. Archivists; mem. Kappa Alpha. Presbyn. Democrat. Home: Alexandria, Va. Died Sept. 5, 1973; interred Bethesda Cemetery, Aberdeen, N.C.

PAINE, CLARENCE SIBLEY, librarian; b. Lincoln, Nebr., June 9, 1908; s. Clarence Sumner and Clara A. (Sibley) P.; A.B., U. Nebr., 1936, A.M., 1937; B.L.S., U. Ill., 1937; m. Ena Ruth Moore, Dec. 24, 1937; 1 dau., Lucinda Kempton. Printer, 1922-26; engaged in retail merchandising, advt. and personnel tng., 1926-33; part-time asst. Nebr. Hist. Library 1933-36; cataloger U. Ill. Library, 1937-38; dir. libraries, librarian Beloit (Wis.) Coll., 1938-48, instr. history Army Air Crew Tng. Detachment, 1943-44; vis. prof. U. Denver Coll. Librarianship, summer 1947; history research fellow Western Range Cattle Industry Study (Rockefeller Found.), summer 1944; dir. Oklahoma City libraries, 1947-59; chief librarian Lansing (Mich.) Sch. Dist. libraries, 1959-65; cons. librarian Blount County (Tenn.) Library System, 1970-74; library bldg. cons., 1960-78. Pres. Red Plains Trading Post, Ltd., 1956-57; Dir. Gt. Books Foundation, 1955-61; cons. library personnel Office Personnel, City Madison, Wis., 1944; spl. rep. Mobil Travel Guide. Chmn. county chpt. A.R.C., 1947, bd. dirs., 1948-50; mem. Alvord Meml. Commn. 1951-54. Mem. Am., Southwestern, Okla., Wis. (pres 1943-44), Tenn. library assns., Assn. Coll. and Reference Libraries (dir. 1946-47), Miss. Valley (exec com. 1951-53), Beloit (pres. 1942-43) hist. assns., The Westerners, Psi Chi. Episcopalian. Clubs: Optimist

Rotary (pres. 1947). Author: The Comedy of Manners, 1941; (with others) The Black Hills, 1952. Co-editor: Rev. Index, 1941-45. Contbr. articles and revs. to profl. and learned jours. Home: Maryville, Tenn. Died Sept. 30, 1978; buried Woodlawn Cemetery, Knoxville, Tenn.

PAINE, HARLAN LLOYD, hospital supt.; b. Rockland, Mass., Nov. 3, 1884; s. Ernest Marion and Etta J. (Hunt) P.; M.D., Tufts Coll. Med. Sch., 1908; m. Amy Yeo, June 10, 1914; children—Harlan Lloyd, Dorothy Munroe, Marion Yeo, Louis Hodgson. Intern Cambridge Hosp., 1908-09; asst. phys. Danvers State Hosp., 1909-14; asst. supt. Gardner State Hosp., 1914-18; asst. to commr. Mass. Dept. of Mental Diseases, 1918-20; chief exec. officer Boston Psychopathic Hosp., 1920-21, also acting chief med. officer same, part of time; supt. Grafton State Hosp. 1921-48; superintendant Channing Sanitarium, Inc., since 1948; clin. instr. psychiatry, Boston U. Sch. of Medicine, 1920-21. Neuropsychiatrist Med. Adv. Board, Dist. 14, Mass., 1917-18. Instr. in psychiatry, Tufts Coll. Med. Sch. Trustee Grafton Pub. Library, Westborough Savings Bank. Diplomate Am. Bd. Psychiatry and Neurology. Fellow American Psychiatric Association; member A.M.A., Massachusetts Medical Society (councillor, 1943), Worchester District Medical Society, New England Society of Psychiatry (past president), Massachusetts Psychiatric Society (past president), Massachuett Society for Mental Hygiene. Dir. Worcester Chapter Am. Red Cross, and chmn. Grafton Branch, 1940-42. Conglist. (trustee West Congl. Ch., Grafton). Address: Wellesley, Mass. *

PALFREY, JOHN GORHAM, legal educator; b. Boston, Mar. 12, 1919; s. John Gorham and Methyl (Oakes) P.; A.B., Harvard U., 1940, LL.B., 1946; m. Clochette Roosevelt, Dec. 26, 1942; children—John Gorham, Antonia Ford. Admitted to D.C. bar, 1948; mem. staff Office Gen. Counsel, AEC, 1947-50; mem. Inst. Advanced Study, Princeton, N.J., 1950-52; lectr. Columbia Sch. Law, 1952-54, asso. prof., 1954-56, prof., 1956—, dean Columbia Coll., 1958-62; commr. AEC, 1962-66; fellow Inst. Politics, Harvard U., 1966-67, Woodrow Wilson Internat. Center for Scholars, Washington, 1976-77; guest scholar Brookings Instn., Washington, 1977-78; cons. ACDA, 1975-79. Served from pvt. to 1st lt., AUS, 1943-46. Mem. N.Y. Bar Assn., Council Fgn. Relations, Internat. Inst. Strategic Studies, Phi Beta Kappa. Club: Century Assn. (N.Y.C.). Contbr. articles on atomic energy, arms control, internat. law, law and sci. to periodicals and books. Home: New York, N.Y. Died Oct. 28, 1979; buried Young's Cemetery, Oyster Bay, L.I., N.Y.

PALLISTER, HUGH DAVIDSON, b. Cleveland, O., May 31, 1883; s. John and Clara Virginia (Davidson) P.; grad. high sch., Cleveland, 1902; B.S. in Mining Engring., Case Sch. Applied Science, Cleveland, 1906, E.M., 1914; grad. study Pa. State Coll., Ohio State U.; m. Elizabeth Marion Beavis, of Cleveland, Apr. 17, 1911; children—Hugh Davidson, Marion Elizabeth (dec.). With engring. office Pittsburgh Steamship Co., Cleveland, 1906; mining engr. and asst. supt. Chisos Mining Co., Terlingua, Tex., 1906-08; cons. engr. Calif., Can., Pa. and Ohio, 1908-15; instr. in mechanics, hydraulics and mining, Case Sch. Applied Science, 1908-10; instr. and asst. prof. metallurgy, Pa. State Coll., 1910-15; head of depts. and prof. geology and mining, Sch. of Mines, U. of Tex., at El Paso, Tex., 1915-19; supt. Ky. coal mines of McKinney Steel Co., Wolfpit, Ky., 1919-21; dir. Sch. of Mines and of State Mine Expt. Sta., Ala., since 1921; cons. mining practice. Instr. engrs., R.O.T.C., World War, also spl. cons. engr. to concrete ship dept. Emergency Fleet Corpn., U.S. Shipping Bd. Mem. Am. Inst. Mining and Metall. Engrs., A.A.A.S., Ala. Acad. Science, Chi Phi, Tau Beta Pi, Sigma Tau, Theta Tau. Mason, K.P., Forester, Kiwanian. Home: Tuscaloosa, Ala.*

PALMER, DANIEL DAVID, broadcasting co. exec.; b. Davenport, Iowa, Jan. 12, 1906; s. Bartlett Joshua and Mabel (Heath) P.; B.S., Wharton Sch. U. Pa., 1929; postgrad. Grad. Sch. Bus. Adminstrn., Harvard; D.C., Ph.C., Palmer Coll. Chiropractic; H.D., Columbia Inst. Chiropractic, N.Y.C.; Ph.C., Logan Chiropractic Coll.; LL.D., Parsons Coll.; m. Agnes M. High, June 27, 1943; children—Bonnie Joan, Jenny Wren, Vickie Anne. Vice pres. Palmer Broadcasting Co., Davenport, Iowa (with stations also in Des Moines, Palm Desert, Calif., Naples, Fla., Marco Island, Fla.), 1929-61, pres., owner, chmn., 1961-78; v.p. Palmer Coll. Chiropractic, Davenport, Palmer Jr. Coll., Davenport, Clear View San., 1929-61. Pres., YMCA Davenport and Scott County, United Fund of Scott County, Tri-City Symphony Assn. Bd. dirs. Jr. Achievement Davenport, Mississippi Valley Fair and Exposition, Scott County Humane Soc., Inc., Nat. Conf. Christians and Jews, Broadway Theatre League Greater Quad-Cities, ARC, Broadcasters' Found. Inc.; trustee Lend-A-Hand Club, St. Katherine's-St. Mark's Sch., Davenport. Recipient Distinguished Service award Quad-Cities Sales Execs., 1960, Distinguished Service award Jr. C. of C., 1934, 60, Achievement award Delta Tau Delta, 1970; named Man of Year B'nai B'rith, 1967, Boss of Year Naples (Fla.) Jr. C. of C., 1970. Mem. C. of C., Friends of Chamber Music, Inc., Beaux Arts Fund Com., Inc., Hist. Soc. State Iowa, Inc., Jr. Chamber Internat., Delta Tau Delta, Delta Sigma Chi. Episcopalian. Mason (Shriner), Rotarian. Clubs: Rock Island (Ill.) Arsenal Golf; Davenport Country, Davenport; Town; Lake Shore, Union League (Chgo.); Harvard (Boston); Des Moines; Hole-In-The-Wall Golf, Naples Yacht, Royal Poinciana Golf, Country of Naples (Naples, Fla.); Crow Valley Golf (Bettendorf, Iowa); Eldorado Country (Palm Desert, Calif.). Home: Davenport, Iowa. Died May 24, 1978.

PALMER, DWIGHT MILLER, physician, educator; b. Scio, Ohio, Feb. 14, 1906; s. William Adam and Jennie Alma (Miller) P.; B.S., Ohio State U., 1929, M.D., 1932, M.S., 1933; m. Virginia Gray, Aug. 22, 1934; children—Thomas Earl, Patricia Ann, Robert Gray. Intern White Cross Hosp., Columbus, O., 1932; practice medicine, Columbus, 1935-79, specializing in neurology and psychiatry, 1937-79; mem. faculty Coll. Medicine, Ohio State U., 1927-70, prof. neurology, psychiatry and neuroanatomy, 1945-72, emeritus, 1972-79. Mem. med. adv. bd. SSS, World War II. Diplomate Am. Bd. Neurology and Psychiatry. Mem. A.M.A., Am. Psychiatric Assn., Am. Acad. Neurology, Am. Acad. Forensic Scis., Central Neuropsychiat. Assn., Ohio Med. Assn., Am. Assn. Anatomists, Sigma Xi, Alpha Omega Alpha, Nu Sigma Nu. Conglist. Mason (32 deg.). Author: The Human Nervous System, 1941. Home: Columbus, Ohio. Died Oct. 14, 1979; buried Scio.

PALMER, HOWARD SHIRLEY, railroad official; b. East Sumner, Me., Jan. 13, 1885; s. Frank W. and Sadie D. (Bonney) P.; ed. pub. schs.; m. Harriet Esther Wilson, Sept. 9, 1908; 1 son, Stuart Wilson. Clk., Portland & Rumford Falls Ry., 1901-07; clk., asst. traveling auditor, express accountant, statis. accountant, N.Y., N.H.&H. R.R. Co., 1907-15, auditor of disbursements, 1915-18, federal auditor, 1918-20, comptroller, 1920-29, v.p., 1929-34, pres. and dir., 1934-48, retired 1948; trustee, 1935-47; dir. Berkshire St. Ry. Co., Conn. Co.; Merchants Nat. Bank of Boston, Union & New Haven Trust Co., Phoenix Ins. Co., Conn. Fire Ins. Co., Nat. Savings Bank (New Haven, Conn.). Pres. Railway Accounting Officers' Assn., 1931-32. Baptist. Clubs: Quinnipiack (New Haven), Union Club (Boston). *

PALMER, JAMES LINDLEY, museum exec.; b. Waterboro, Maine, Mar. 12, 1889; s. Lindley Guy and Luella (Hill) P.; A.B., Brown U., 1919; A.M., U. Chgo., 1923; C.P.A., Ill., 1923; m. Eleanor H. Olson, Aug. 25, 1924; children—James Lindley, Jr., Donald Hill. Mem. faculty Sch. Bus., U. Chgo., 1922-44, prof. marketing, 1930-1944; business cons. various corps., 1925-36; exec. Marshall Field & Co., 1963-64, dir., 1942-64, pres., 1949-64; pres. Field Museum of Natural History, Chgo., 1964-69. Pres. Community Fund Chgo., 1946-48. Served with U.S. Navy, World War I. Mem. Kappa Sigma. Clubs: Commercial, Chicago; Onwentsia; Old Elm. Home: Lake Forest, Ill. Died Sept. 17, 1979.

PALMER, ORVILLE HENRY, educator; b. Belmont, Wis., Jan. 6, 1910; s. Howard Paine and Pearl (Ashton) P.; B.Ed., Wis. State Coll., Whitewater, 1931; M.B.A., Northwestern U., 1938; m. Mildred Lean, June 25, 1932; children—David, Richard. Tchr. bus. edn. courses West High Sch., Aurora, Ill., 1931-37; tchr. bus. edn., chmn. dept. Shorewood (Wis.) High Sch., 1937-46; mem. faculty Marquette U., Milw., 1946-63, dir. eve. div., 1950-63, prof. accounting, 1959-63, acting dean Coll. Bus. Adminstrn., 1959-62; acting chmn. commerce extension div., prof. accounting U. Wis., Milw., 1963-66, chmn. commerce extension div., prof. accounting, 1966-76, chmn. dept. bus. and mgmt. and program leader Bus. and Industry sect. Div. Econ. and Environmental Devel., U. Wis. Extension, prof. accounting, 1966-76, Citizen mem. revenue and distbn. com. Gov. Wis. Met. Study Commn., from 1956; chmn. instns. budget com. Milw. County Community Fund, from 1964; com. mgmt., also youth com. Northshore br. Milw. YMCA, from 1960. Recipient Distinguished Alumnus award U. Wis.-Whitewater, 1963, Distinguished Service award U. Wis. Extension, 1974. Mem. Am. Accounting Assn., Am. Econ. Assn., Am. Finance Assn., Nat. Bus. Tchrs. Assn., Financial Execs. Inst., Adminstrv. Mgmt. Soc. (pres. Milw. chpt. 1960, Diamond Merit award 1968), Nat. Assn. Purchasing Execs., Nat. Soc. Bus. Budgeting, Beta Alpha Psi, Beta Gamma Sigma. Editor: Selected Readings for Planning and Control Through Budgets; 1955, others. Home: Milwaukee, Wis. Died Dec. 7, 1976.

PALMER, PHILIP MOTLEY, educator; b. Bethlehem, Pa., Nov. 1, 1904; s. Philip Mason and Mary (Hodgdon) P.; A.B., Bowdoin Coll., 1926; A.M., Harvard, 1927, Ph.D., 1930; m. Dorothy Butterfield, June 21, 1944; children—Charles Motley, Philip Bartlett. Asst. prof. U. Mo., 1930-31, U. Cin., 1931-43, U. Wis., 1944-46, Clark U., 1946-48; prof. German, U. Calif. at Berkeley, from 1948. Mem. Modern Lang. Assn., Theta Delta Chi. Author: Der Einfluss der Neuen Welt auf den deutschen Wortschatz, 1933; Neuweltworter im Deutschen, 1939; The Influence of English on the German Vocabulary to 1700, 1950; The Influence of English on the German Vocabulary to 1800, 1960. Home: Berkeley, Calif. Died May 10, 1979.

PALMISANO, VINCENT L. (PÄL'ME-SÄ-NŌ), ex-congressman; b. Termini Imenese, Italy, June 13, 1883; s. Cosimo and Anna Marie (Sanzone) P.; brought to U.S. 1887; ed. parochial Schools, East Baltimore, Md.; student U. of Md.; m. Mary Fernes, Dec. 1919. Admitted to Md. bar, 1909, and began practice at Baltimore; mem. Md. Ho. of Rep., 1914; mem. city council, Baltimore, 1915-23; mem. Dem. State Central Com., Md., 1923; police examiner, Baltimore, 1925; mem. 70th to 75th Congresses (1927-39), 3d Md. Dist. Catholic. Heptasoph, Forester; mem. Federal Fraternal Assn. Home: Baltimore. *

PANTZER, KURT FRIEDRICH, lawyer; b. Indpls., Aug. 1892; s. Hugo O. and Emmy (Schmidt) P.; student Wabash Coll., 1909-11; A.B., Harvard U., 1914, LL.B., 1917, S.J.D., 1920; LL.D., Tusculum College, 1953, Ind. U., 1957, Franklin Coll., 1961, U. Evansville, 1974; Litt.D., Rose Poly. Inst., 1967; L.H.D. (hon.), Northwood Inst., 1969; m. Katharine Ferriday, Jan. 1926; children—Kurt Friedrich, Katharine, Eric. Admitted to N.Y. bar, 1920, Ind. bar, 1922; asso. Winthrop & Stimson, N.Y., 1920-22; practiced law in Indpls., 1922-79; asso. Smith, Remster, Hornbrook & Smith, 1922-38, Davis, Pantzer, Baltzell & Sparks, 1938-40, Barnes, Hickam, Pantzer & Boyd 1940-79; life dir. Am. States Ins. Co., Am. States Life Ins. Co., Am. Economy Co., Indpls.; dir. Morgan Packing Co., Inc., Lilly Indsl. Coatings, Inc., lectr. Indpls. div. Ind. U. Sch. Law, 1957-58, professorial lectr. Bloomington div. in 3 yr. required course in legal techniques, established by Inland Container Corp. Found., 1956-61. Mem. Council Fgn. Relations, Inc., N.Y.; co-founder, chmn. Indpls. Com. Fgn. Relations, 1951-58; chmn. Com. of 21 to introduce Uniform Partnership Act, Uniform Ltd. Partnership Act, Uniform Divorce Act and amendment to Bus. Corp. Act to Ind. Gen. Assmebly; co-chmn. joint com. to draft uniform act to prevent organized crime Am. Bar Assn. and Nat. Conf. Commrs. on Uniform State Laws; mem. joint com. to draft uniform comml. code Am. Law Inst. and Am. Bar Assn.; chmn. Ind. Commn. Uniform Comml. Code, 1951-63, Ind. Commn. Uniform State Laws, 1953-58; spl. master U.S. Supreme Ct. in case N.J. vs. N.Y. and Pa. involving controversy as to Delaware River 1952-54. Chmn. Ind. Republican Finance Com., 1956-66; co-founder, sec. Greater Indpls. Rep. Finance Com., 1965-66; mem. Rep. Nat. Finance Com., 1952-62; trustee emeritus Butler U., chmn. finance and bldg. coms. Clowes Meml. Hall, 1961-63; co-founder, 1st chmn. Holcomb Inst. Fundamental Sci. Research; co-founder, life gov. Asso. Colls. Ind., chmn. bd. govs., 1968-70; co-founder, pres. Ind. Acad.; incorporator finance and bldg. coms., life trustee Indpls. Museum of Art; bd. dirs. Hist. Landmarks Found., Ind. State Mus.; co-founder, life dir. Ind. Symphony Soc.; co-founder, mem. Meridian Street Found.; life trustee Indpls. Children's Mus.; mem. Ind. Gov.'s Commn. on Arts, 1965-68; co-founder Council of Sagamores of the Wabash; co-founder, chieftain Confederacy of Ind. Sachems. Served as capt., inf., U.S. Army, 1917-19; with 335th Inf., also 326th Machine Gun Bn. and 6th Inf. Fellow Royal Soc. Arts (Eng.); mem. Am. Soc. Internat. Law, Am. Judicature Soc., Am. (com. to draft Model Corp. Act), Ind., Indpls. bar assns., Assn. Bar City N.Y., Bar Assn. 7th Fed. Circuit (co-founder, pres. 1951-52), Internat. Law Assn., Am. Law Inst. (past mem. editorial bd. for Uniform Comml. Code), Fed. Communications Bar Assn., Am. Bar Found., Am. Acad. Polit. and Social Sci., Friends of Brit. Mus., Turner Soc., Old English Water Colour Soc., Walpole Soc. (London, England), Delta Tau Delta, Phi Delta Phi. Presbyn. Clubs: Athletic, Athenaeum, Players, Columbia, Dramatic, University, Woodstock; Lambs (Indpls.); University (Chgo.); Harvard, Assn. Ex-Members Squadron A (N.Y.); Ft. Benjamin Harrison Officers' (hon.). Author: The Delt House System, 1940; Preliminary Treatise on the Principles Underlying Collective Bargaining Agreement, 1947; Idea Draft of a Collective Bargaining Agreement, 1947; Preliminary Lectures and Forms in Support of a Plea for a Uniform System of Draftsmanship, 1949-50; (with Hodge O'Neal) The Drafting of Corporate Charters and By-Laws, 1951, 2d edit. (with Richard E. Deer), 1968; (with Wilbur D. Peat and David G. Carter) Turner in America, 1955; (with Wilbur D. Peat) Paintings from the Collection of George Henry Alexander Clowes, 1959; J.M.W. Turner in Indiana, 1963; Finished Watercolors of J.M.W. Turner, R.A., 1968. Home: Indianapolis, Ind. Died July 8, 1979.

PAPE, DELBERT HILL, business exec.; born Park City, Utah, Jan. 11, 1884; s. Matthew Hill and Hannah (Richens) P.; m. Neila Amanda Nelson, Sept. 2, 1914; children—Mary Jane, Patricia Anne, Helen. Sec., later Western mgr. and sales mgr. Central Coal & Coke Co., Salt Lake City, 1907-14; gen. mgr. Lion Coal Corp., Wyo. Coal Co., Wattis Coal Co., Ketchum Coal Co., Ogden, Utah, 1914-22; asst. to sec. Nat. Coal Assn., Washington, 1924-26; exec. sec. Monongahela Coal Operators Assn. of Northern W.Va., Morgantown, W.Va., 1927-28; exec. dir. Allegheny regional adv. bd. Am. Railway Assn., 1927-28; asst. to pres., later exec. v.p. sales, Cosgrove-Meehan Coal Corp., Johnstown, Pa., and N.Y. City, 1928-30; pres. Pratt Coal Co., Boston, 1930-33; chmn. bd. Marcy Bros. & Co., Boston, 1930-33; exec. v.p. Fleer Bros., Brooklyn, 1933-37; pres. Sheridan-Wyo. Coal Co., Inc., Monarch, Wyo. since

1937, Hotchkiss Coal Co., Sheridan, Wyo., since 1937. Served as fuel distbr. State of Wyo., 1918. Mem. Sheridan C. of C., Bituminous Coal Research, Inc. (dir.). Pres. Rocky Mountain Coal Mining Inst., 1944-46; mem. enec. com. Rocky Mountain Mining Inst. since 1939; chmn. Rocky Mountain div. Am. Am. Mining Congress; mem. Am. Mining and Metall. Inst.; dir. Nat. Coal Assn. since 1937. Clubs: Sheridan Country, Sheridan Rotary. Home: Sheridan, Wyo. *

PARAY, PAUL, condr., composer; b. Le Treport, France, May 24, 1886; grad. Paris Conservatory; won Prix de Rome, 1911, and spent 3 yrs. in Rome. Condr. Casino de Cauteret, 1918; asst. condr. Concerts Lamoureux Orch., prin. condr., 1923; became condr. Municipal Orchestra, Monte Carlo, 1928; condr. Paris Opera, 1930's; made Am. debut as condr. French program Lewisohn Stadium, N.Y.C., July 1939; condr. Detroit Symphony Orch., 1952-63, thereafter emeritus; condr. Concerts Colonne of Paris, 1932-52; now guest condr. various orchs. Served in French Army, World War I; captured by Germans. Decorated comdr., also grand cross Legion of Honor (France). Mem. French Acad. Composer of works for piano, violin, string quartets and voice. Home: Cincinnati, Ohio. Died Oct. 10, 1979.

PARDEE, ARTHUR MCCAY (PÄR'DE'), prof. chemistry; b. Rochester, N.Y., Mar. 27, 1885; s. John Myron and Westanna (McCay) P.; B.A., Washington and Jefferson Coll., Pa., 1907; Ph.D., Johns Hopkins, 1916; m. Gladys Marshall Stevenson, Sept. 14, 1910; children—Mrs. Genevieve Johnston, John Marshall Stevenson. Instr. chemistry, 1907-08, prof. 1908-18, Tarkio Coll.; prof. chemistry, Washington and Jefferson Coll., 1918-20; prof. chemistry, head of dept., U. of S.D., since 1920, also dir. of Grad. Sch., 1929-36, dean of Coll. of Arts and Sciences, 1936-48. Mem. Sioux Valley Sect. Am. Chem. Soc. (pres. 1921-22, 1945-46), S.D. Acad. Science (pres. 1922-23), Newcomen Soc., Phi Beta Kappa, Kappa Sigma. Republican. Presbyterian. Club: Beadle (S.D.). Contbr. chem jours. Home: Vermillion, S.D. *

PARDEE, HAROLD ENSIGN BENNETT, physician; b. N.Y. City, Dec. 11, 1886; s. Ensign Bennett and Clara (Burton) P.; A.B., Columbia, 1906; M.D., Coll. Physicians and Surgeons (Columbia), 1909; m. Dorothy Dwight Porter, Apr. 15, 1918; children—Althea, Hobart Porter, Pamela. Interne, New York Hosp., 1909-11; in practice in N.Y. City, specializing on diseases of heart and circulation, since 1911; instr. in physiology, Coll. Physicians and Surgeons, 1912-15; instr. in clin. medicine, Cornell U. Med. Sch., 1916-22, asso. in medicine, 1923-27, asso. prof. clin. medicine since 1927; asso. attending physician New York Hospital; attending phys. (cardiac diseases) Polyclinic Hosp.; cons. physician for cardiac disease, Woman's Hosp., M.E. Hosp., N.Y. City. Served as 1st lt. Med. Corps, U.S. Army, July 1917-Jan. 1918; capt. Jan. 1918-Apr. 1919. Mem. A.M.A., Am. Soc. Clin. Investigation, Assn. Am. Physicians, Am. Heart Assn., N.Y. State Med. Soc., New York County Med. Soc. Republican. Conglist. Clubs: Rockaway Hunting (Lawrence, L.I.); Union Club (N.Y. City). Author: Clinical Aspects of the Electrocardiogram, 1924, 4th edit., 1941; What You Should Know About Heart Disease, 1928. Chmn. com. which wrote Criteria for Diagnosis of Heart Disease, 1928, 4th edit., 1939. Many articles on diagnosis and treatment of heart disease in various medical journals. Home: New York. *

PARDO DE ZELA, FRANCISCO (PÄR'DO-DA-SA-LÄ), diplomat; b. Lima, Peru, Nov. 27, 1884; s. Baldomero and Carlota (Varela) P.; ed. Colegio de los Sagrados Corazones, Lima, South End Inst., London, Pitman's Sch., London; m. Maria Luisa Garland (divorced); children—Juan, Francisco. Officer, State Dept. in Peru, 1913; now minister plenipotentiary in charge of the Consulate General of Peru in the U.S. at New York. Comdr. Order Al Merito of Chile. Clubs: Nacional, Lawn Tennis (Lima); Athletic (N.Y.). Home: New York. *

PARDOE, T(HOMAS) EARL, educator; b. Ogden, Utah, Feb. 24, 1885; s, Thomas and Lenora (Farr) P.; grad. Leland Powers Sch., Boston, 1913; A.B., Brigham Young U., 1925; A.M., U. So. Calif., 1931; Ph.D., U. of La., 1936; summer study in Western Europe, 1938, 50; m. Kathryn Bassett, June 3, 1914; children—Norma (Mrs. L. Wright), William E., Catherine (Mrs. O. J. Strickland), Thomas E. With Zuahna Stock Co., Ogden, Utah, 1907-09; character parts, St. James Stock Co., Boston, 1911-13; dir. dramatic studios, Salt Lake and Ogden, Utah, 1914-16; regional dir., Four Minute Men, 1916-17; head speech dept., Brigham Young U. since 1919; dir. radio station KOVO, Provo since 1940, KBYU, Provo since 1938; ednl. advisor, Intermountain Network since 1945; instr. U. of So. Calif., 1929-31, Denver U., summer 1933, La. State U., summer 1934-36. Dir. Annual One-Act Play Festival, Rocky Mountain, since 1921; chmn. Latter Day Saints drama program for 1000 Little Theatres, 1942-49. Pres. Provo Public Library. Fellow Am. Speech Corr. Soc.; mem. Assn. Internat. Phonetique, Am. Nat. Theatre Acad., Modern Lang. Assn., Am. Edn. Radio Assn., American Linguistics Assn., Nat. Speech Assn., Western Speech Assn., Rocky Mountain Forensic League, Nat. Parks Council Boy Scouts of Am., Tau Kappa Alpha, Theta Alpha Phi, Alpha Epsilon Rho. Club: Rotary (pres., Provo). Author: The Little Theatre in U.S.A., 1923; Pantomine for Stage and Study, 1931; This Speaking World, 1934; Theatre Arts, 1942; Organized Thinking for Effective Speaking, 1947. Collector rare Western Americana. Home: Provo, Utah. *

PARDOE, WILLIAM EDWARD, corp. exec.; b. Ogden, Utah, Dec. 6, 1916; s. Thomas Earl and Kathryn (Bassett) P.; A.B., Brigham Young U., 1939; LL.B., Fordham U., 1947; m. Merle Grace Hansen, June 22, 1941; children—Kathryn Grace (Mrs. Lee M. Marshall), Sara Dianne, Billie. With Union Carbide Corp., 1939-78, treas., from 1968, sr. v.p., chief financial officer, 1971-78; admitted to N.Y. bar, 1947, Cal. bar, 1948. Served with AUS, 1942-46. Clubs: Internat. (Washington); Apawamis (Rye, N.Y.); Fox Meadow Tennis (Scarsdale, N.Y.); Stratton Mountain (Vt.) Country; Canadian, Board Room (N.Y.C.). Home: Greenwich, Conn. Died Feb. 10, 1978.

PAREDES, QUINTIN, Philippine commr.; b. Bangued Abra, P.I., Sept. 9, 1884; s. Juan Felix and Regina (Babila) P.; grad. Law Sch. of Manila, P.I., 1907; m. Victoria Peralta, 1906; children—Isidro, Quintin, Lourdes, Lucas, Guadalupe, Germelina, Victorino, Elisa, Rosario, Enes, Antonio. Admitted to Philippine bar, 1907; 4th pros. atty., 1908, advancing to 1st pros. atty., 1913; was prof. law, criminologist, dir. Law Sch. of Manila; solicitor gen., 1917; atty. gen., 1918; sec. of justice, 1920-21; nominated by Pres. Woodrow Wilson for asso. justice Supreme Court of P.I.; mem. 1st parliamentary mission to U.S., 1919; admitted to practice before U.S. Supreme Court, 1919, U.S. Dist. Court for China, 1920; resumed pvt. practice, 1921; elected mem. Ho. of Rep., 1925, re-elected, 1928, 31, 34, actg. speaker, 1929, speaker pro tem, 1931, twice speaker; elected mem. Nat. Assembly, 1935; apptd. 1st resident commr. of the Philippine Commonwealth Govt. to U.S., 1935. Served as col., judge advocate gen., Philippine N.G. Mason (32 deg.). Clubs: Philippine Columbian, Filipino, Wack-Wack Golf and Country, de Tiro al Blanco. Home: Bangued, Abra Province, P.I.*

PARGNY, EUGENE W(ILLIAM), past pres. Am. Sheet & Tin Plate Co.; b. Louisville, Ky., June 5, 1866; s. Joseph and Louise (Bennier) P.; ed. pub. and pvt. schs.; m. Emilie Tuman, June 28, 1893. In ins. business, 1884-86; sec. Belle of Nelson Distillery Company, 1886-1890; successively purchasing agent, sales agt., mgr. Apollo Iron & Steel Co., Pittsburgh, 1890-1901; mgr., in charge all plants in Pittsburgh dist., Am. Sheet Steel Co., 1901-04; v.p. Am. Sheet & Tin Plate Co., 1904-09, pres., 1909-32 (retired). Republican. Protestant. Clubs: Pittsburgh, Duquesne, Allegheny Country, Fox Chapelle, Golf, Rolling Rock. Home: Pittsburgh, Pa. *

PARHAM, WILLIAM EUGENE, educator; b. Denison, Tex., Sept. 9, 1922; s. Charles Eugene and Jewel (Looney) P.; B.S., So. Methodist U., 1942, D.D.S., 1966; M.S., U. Ill., 1943, Ph.D., 1946; m. Wilma Louise Johnston, Mar. 25, 1945; children—Janice (Mrs. Thomas A. Ophoven), Judy (Mrs. Robert Olein). Prof. organic chemistry U. Minn., 1946-72, head div., 1958-69; R.J. Reynolds prof. chemistry Duke, 1972-76; cons. E.I. du Pont de Nemours & Co., Inc. Guggenheim fellow, 1961-62. Mem. Am. Chem. Soc. (sec.-treas. organic div. 1954-59, chmn. 1959-60, mem. council 1954-57), Organic Synthesis (v.p., dir. 1971-74, treas. 1974-76). Author: Syntheses and Reactions in Organic Chemistry, 1970. Editor: Organic Synthesis, Vol. 44. Contbr. numerous articles organic chemistry to sci. jours. Home: Durham, N.C. Died May 21, 1976.

PARK, CHARLES ABRAHAM, coast guard officer; b. New Lexington, O., Nov. 30, 1882; s. Thomas and Louanna Brush (Jordan) P.; C.E., Ohio State U., 1907; m. Lela Maud Laughlin, Sept. 2, 1908; children—Geraldine Myrtle, Charles Abraham, Robert Laughlin. Draftsman U.S. Land Office, Cheyenne, Wyo., 1907, civ. engr. and supt. constrn. Q.M. dept. at large, Ft. D. A. Russell, Wyo., 1908-11; supt. constrn. U.S. Lighthouse Dist. 11, Detroit, Mich., 1911-24, lighthouse supt. in charge, 1924-33; chief engr., U.S. Lighthouse Service, 1933-35, deputy commr. lighthouses, 1935-39; capt. U.S. Coast Guard, operations officer for aids to navigation, Coast Guard Hdqrs., Washington, D.C., 1939-42; chief operations officer, U.S. Coast Guard, July 1, 1942; rank of rear admiral U.S. Coast Guard, May 1, 1943; retired Aug. 1, 1946. Awarded Legion of Merit, 1946. Received Benjamin Lamme medal from Ohio State U., June 1946, for "meritorious achievement in engineering." Transferred to United States Navy, World War I. Mem. Student Council of Ohio State U. (lt. col. in charge student regt.), Sigma Xi. Mem. Am. Soc. Civ. Engrs. Methodist. Address: Washington, D.C. *

PARK, COLIN, educator; b. Finchley, Eng., Aug. 11, 1918; s. Stanley W. and Jean (Inglis) P.; came to U.S., 1919, naturalized, 1927; grad. Ridley Coll., Can., 1937, Pace Inst., 1947; M.B.A., U. Buffalo, 1950; Ph.D., U. Chgo., 1955; m. Mildred Anne Fraser, Mar. 11, 1944; children—Andrew Fraser, Sally Joy. Various positions in bus. orgns. and univs., 1937-41, 45-56; partner Haskins & Sells, N.Y.C., 1956-73; prof. bus. adminstrn. Coll. William and Mary, 1973-77. Mem. N.Y. State Bd. Pub. Accountancy, 1965-73. Past pres. Ridley Coll. Scholarship Fund; bd. dirs. Coll. William and Mary Sch. Bus. Adminstrn. Sponsors, 1970-73; trustee organizing council Coll. Profl. Psychology, N.J., 1971-73. Served to capt. AUS, USAAF, 1941-45. C.P.A., N.Y. Mem. Am. Econ. Assn., Am. Mgmt. Assn., Am. Arbitration Assn. (panel arbitrators), Am. Accounting Assn., Am. Inst. C.P.A.'s, N.Y. State Soc. C.P.A.'s (past v.p., Achievement award 1974), Accountants Club Am. (past pres.), Pace Alumni Assn. (past pres.), Newcomen Soc. N. Am., Internat. Grenfell Assn., St. Andrews Soc. Williamsburg, Beta Alpha Psi. Clubs: Princeton (N.Y.C.); Queens Lake (Williamsburg, Va.); Chesapeake (Irvington, Va.). Author: (with John W. Gladson) Working Capital, 1963, El Capital de Trabajo, 1966. Home: Williamsburg, Va. Died Sept. 24, 1977.

PARK, LEE I., lawyer; b. Lowry City, Mo., Apr. 10, 1895; s. Thomas Benton and Martha (Bunch) P.; student Mont. State Coll., 1914-17; LL.B. cum laude, U. Chgo., 1921; m. Alice Mary Crandall, Aug. 29, 1925; children—Lee Crandall, Nancy Alice (Mrs. John W. Kern III). Admitted to Ill. bar, 1921, D.C. bar, 1927; law practice, Chgo., 1921-24; spl. atty. Office Gen. Counsel, Bur. Internal Revenue, 1924-26; mem. firm Hamel, Park, McCabe & Saunders, and predecessors, Washington, 1927-78. Mem., vice chmn. War Dept. Price Adjustment Bd., 1945-46; mem. Navy Price Adjustment Bd., 1946; dir. renegotiation and company pricing Office Surgeon Gen. Army, 1942-45; bd. dirs. Putney (Vt.) Sch., 1946-48. Served as cadet, U.S. Air Corps, 1918; from lt. col. to col., J.A.G.D. and Gen. Staff Corps, AUS, 1942-46. Decorated Legion of Merit. Fellow Am. Bar Found.; mem. Fed., Am. (vice chmn. sect. taxation 1955-57, chmn. 1957-59; ho. dels. 1960-62), D.C. bar assns., Am. Law Inst., Sigma Alpha Epsilon. Mem. Christian Ch. Mason. Clubs: Metropolitan, Washington Golf and Country (Washington); Chevy Chase (Md.); Farmington (Charlottesville, Va.). Home: Washington, D.C. Died Aug. 24, 1978; buried Culpepper (Va.) Nat. Cemetery.

PARK, RICHARD LEONARD, educator; b. Savannah, Ga., Mar. 29, 1920; s. Leonard and Alice (Farrell) P.; B.S., Northwestern U., 1942; M.A., Harvard, 1948, Ph.D., 1951; m. Donna M. Divine, May 1, 1960. Teaching fellow Harvard, 1949-50; asst. prof. polit. sci., asst. to chancellor, dir. Center for S. Asia Studies, U. Calif. at Berkeley, 1953-59; asso. prof. polit. sci., dir. Center for So. Asian Studies, U. Mich., 1959-62; rep. in India, The Asia Found, 1962-64, also cons.; dean div. social scis., prof. polit. sci. U. Pitts., 1964-66; prof. polit. sci. U. Mich., Ann Arbor, 1966-80, chmn. dept., 1971-72; prof. fgn. affairs Nat. War Coll., 1968-69. Asso., Council on Internat. Exchange of Scholars. Served to capt. Signal Corps, USAAF, 1942-46. Fellow Inst. Hist. Studies Calcutta, Social Sci. Research Council, Middle East Inst.; mem. Am. Inst. Indian Studies (past v.p., chmn. bd., now trustee), Assn. Asian Studies (sec.-treas. 1971-76, pres. 1978-79, past chmn. com. on S. Asia, past dir.), Council Fgn. Relations, Am. Polit. Sci. Assn., Am. Soc. for Internat. Law, Asiatic Soc. Bengal. Democrat. Author: State Reports on the Indian General Elections, 1951-1952, 1956; Pilot Project, India, 1958; Leadership and Political Institutions in India, 1959; Us. Foreign Policy: Asia, 1959; Modern Political Systems; Asia, 1963; India's Political System, 2d edit., 1979; India: Emergent Power?, 1978; co-author, editor: The American Revolution Abroad, 1976; also numerous chpts. and articles. Mem. editorial bd. Asian Survey, Asian Forum, 1960-80. Home: Ann Arbor, Mich. Died Sept. 8, 1980.

PARK, SAMUEL CULVER, JR., financial exec.; b. Salt Lake City, May 21, 1903; s. Samuel Sulver and Ella (Thomas) P.; Ph.B., Yale, 1925; M.B.A., Harvard, 1927; m. Katharine Anderson, Jan. 4, 1930. With J. P. Morgan & Co., N.Y.C., 1927-34, Baker, Watts & Co., Balt., 1935; financial asst. to John Hay Whitney, N.Y.C., from 1941; partner J.H. Whiteney & Co., N.Y.C., 1946-59; chmn. finance com., dir. Whitney Communications Corp., 1958-76; v.p., dir. Kern House Enterprises Ltd., London, 1965-74; partner Whitcom Investment Co., 1967-68; hon. trustee U.S. Trust Co., N.Y.C.; dir. IHT Corp. Trustee John Hay Whitney Found.; bd. dirs. Vocational Found., Inc.; pres. Fresh Air Fund, 1962-67, bd. dirs., 1960-76; hon. mem. bd. govs. N.Y. Hosp. Mem. Newcomen Soc., Psi Upsilon. Episcopalian. Clubs: Union, Links, Univ., River, Church (N.Y.C.); Piping Rock (L.I.). Home: New York, N.Y. Died July 17, 1976; interred Druid Ridge Cemetery, Baltimore.

PARKER, BERTHA MORRIS, author; b. Rochester, Ill., Feb. 7, 1890; d. Homer Darius and Margaret Elizabeth (Lawrence) Parker; student Oberlin Coll., 1908-09, Columbia, 1909; S.B., U. Chgo., 1914, S.M., 1923. Tchr. pub. schs., Springfield, Ill., 1909-12, 14-16; tchr. sci. U. Chgo. Lab Schs., 1916-55, chmn. dept., 1940-55. Cons. Rosenwald Fund, 1935; adviser Columbia Sch. for Air, 1935-38; cons. Field Enterprises, Inc., Golden Press, Western Pub. Co., Inc.; research asso. Field Mus. Natural History, 1955-80. Mem. Central Assn. Sci. and Math. Tchrs. (chmn. elementary sect. 1933-34), Nat. Council on Elementary Sci. (pres. 1935-36, editor Sci. News Notes 1934-38), Nat. Assn. for Research in Sci. Teaching, (asso. editor Sci. Edn. 1938-45), Phi Beta Kappa, Sigma Delta Epsilon. Methodist. Author numerous books, monographs on sci. edn., including The Golden Treasury of Natural History, 1952, rev. edit., 1968; The Golden Book of Science, 1956, rev., 1963; The Golden Book Encyclopedia, vols. I-XVI, 1959, rev., 1969; The Golden Book of Facts and Figures, 1962; Nature Wonderland, 1963; Wonders of Science, 1963; The Fifty States, 1965; books in Basic Sci. Edn. Series, 1941-67; Rockets and Missiles, 1961; Satellites and Space Travel, 1961; Out Into Space, 1965; Creatures of the Past, 1965; Travel Aloft, 1965; Stream of Life, 1967; Achievements of Civilization Series, 1932-33, Merrigold Activity Books, 1964-65; Science and Us, 1969; Plants, Animals and Us, 1969; (with Alice F. Martin) Exploring Chemistry I, II, Exploring Geology, 1970, The New Golden Dictionary, 1972, Dinosaurs, 1973, Rocks and Minerals, 1974. Contbr. numerous articles to jours., mags., encys. Prepared film strips on sci. subjects, 1947-62. Home: Chicago, Ill. Died Nov. 14, 1980.

PARKER, CLARENCE P(RENTICE), clergyman; b. nr. Louisville, Ky., Aug. 17, 1883; s. Rev. William Campbell and Eliza Hunt (Watkins) P.; student Wittenberg, 1902; Ohio U., 1903; Columbia (S.C.) Theol. Sem., 1906; Theol. dept. U. of the South, 1909; m. Harriet L. Coates, of Smithfield, N.C., 1915; children—Achsah J. C., William B. Became deacon, 1910, priest, 1911, P.E. Church; rector Christ Ch., Bowling Green, Ky., 1910-13, Holy Trinity Ch., Hertford, N.C., 1913-16, Christ Ch., Little Rock, Ark., 1916-17; resigned to engage in war work, principally at Camp Pike, Ark.; student chaplain, U. of Ark., 1919-25; rector Grace Ch., Chattanooga, Tenn., 1925-26, Norwood Parish, Diocese of Washington, since 1926. Trustee State Girls' Industrial Home and Sch., and City Commn. on Recreation for Soldiers, Little Rock, Ark., 1917-18; mem. Ark. Social Service Commn., and Bd. Examining Chaplains, P.E. Ch.; exec. sec. Ark. dept. of religious edn. P.E. Ch.; sec. bd. of religious edn. Province of Southwest, P.E. Ch.; mem. nat. dept. of religious edn., P.E. Ch., under religious drama and pageantry, 1923-26. Mem. Nat. Accredited Teachers' Assn., P.E. Ch. Author: Angels Unaware (novel), 1912; Mother Church is Called to the Colors (religious drama), 1922; This Good News Must Be Told! (pageant) 1923; Prepare Ye the Way! (religious drama) 1924. Home: Chevy Chase, Md. *

PARKER, DAVID BENNETT, cons.; b. Denver, June 16, 1916; s. Sam Minter and Janet (Richards) P.; B.S U.S. Mil. Acad., 1937; M.S., Mass. Inst. Tech., 1940; m. Mette Margaretha Rosencrantz, Feb. 6, 1954; children—Viveca D., Henrik D. Commd. 2d lt. U.S. Army, 1937, advanced through grades to maj. gen., 1964; engr. group comdr. S. W. Pacific, 1942-46; mil. nuclear weapons specialist, 1946-58; comdg. gen. U.S. Army Aviation Command, 1962-64, 7th Army Support Command, Germany, 1965-67; tech. cons. Research Analysis Corp., 1967-70. Decorated D.S.M., Bronze Star, Commendation medal. Mem. Inst. Aero. Scis., Am. Helicopter Soc. Republican. Episcopalian. Contbr. articles, short stories to mags., also encys. Editor: The Atomic Bombings of Hiroshima and Nagasaki, 1946; The Effects of Atomic Weapons, 1950. Home: McLean, Va. Died Mar. 30, 1980; buried West Point Mil. Acad., N.Y.

PARKER, EDWARD FOSTER, lawyer; b. Bowling Green, O., Jan. 31, 1883; s. Robert Sheldon and Susan (Thomas) P.; A.B., Univ. of Michigan, Ann Arbor, Mich., 1904, LL.B., 1906; m. Elizabeth Jane Stafford, July 12, 1907; children—Elizabeth Jane (Mrs. Robert Boyd Picking), Suzanne Ella (Mrs. Luis Odriozola). Originator, 1st pres. U. Mich. Union, 1904; adv. mgr., columnist Pomona Rev., 1908-13; admitted to Cal. bar, 1913; mem. law firm Parker and Parker, Pasadena and Los Angeles, 1913-33; counsel Parker and Irwin, Los Angeles, 1933-45; v.p., gen. mgr. Southwest Cotton Co., Ariz., 1916-22; chmn. bd. Ide-Parker Co., 1923-33; pres. Par-Associates, finance-ins., 1935, chmn., 1942, merged with Seaboard Finance Co., Los Angeles, 1945, chmn. Seaboard, 1942-48; pres. Dudley-Parker Siskiyou Hereford Ranch; 1940. Mem. bd. govs. Clements Library U. Mich. Mem. Cal. Finance Assn. (pres. 1927-37), South Orange Grove Assn. (pres. 1935-41), Mich., Cal. bar assns., U. Mich. Alumni Assn. Republican. Episcopalian. Clubs: Athletic. California (Los Angeles); Valley Hunt (Pasadena). Home: Pasadena, Cal. *

PARKER, FOSTER, engring. and constrn. co. exec.; b. Italy, Tex., Nov. 3, 1918; B.B.A., U. Tex., 1938; m. Mildred Anne Huke, Aug. 15, 1940; children—Robert Foster, Jeffry Moore, James Ayers. Mgr. Arthur Andersen & Co., Houston, 1938-50; treas., dir. Houston Oil Co., 1950-56; with Brown & Root, Inc., Houston, 1956-77, pres., chief exec. officer, to 1977; dir. Halliburton Co., Anderson, Clayton & Co., 1st City Nat. Bank of Houston. Home: Houston, Tex. Died Jan. 23, 1977.

PARKER, LOVELL HALLET, pub. taxation exec.; b. Osterville, Mass., Dec. 13, 1882; s. Charles Francis and Emma (Mathews) P.; student Tabor Acad., Marion, Mass., 1899-1901; B.S., Mass. Inst. Tech., 1905; LL.B., Nat. Univ., Washington, D.C., 1931; m. Mary Frances Murphy, of New York, N.Y., Aug. 11, 1909; children—Margaret Frances (Mrs. Armistead Williams Gilliam), Helen Matthews (dec.), Marion Elizabeth, Emma Jean. Asst., engring. corps, Pa. R.R., lines west of Pittsburgh, 1905-06; asst. engr. Pa. R.R. tunnels, N.Y. City, 1906-08; asst. engr. state engr.'s office, Albany, N.Y., 1908-09; dep. div. engr. highway dept., N.Y. State, 1909-12; contractor on pub. works, 1912-17; constrn. engr. Camp Upton, L.I., N.Y., 1917-18; material engr. Hog Island, Pa., 1918-19; field supervisor, head of inventory and appraisal sect. U.S. Shipping Bd., 1919-23; practicing as appraisal engr. since 1923; chief engr. for U.S. Senate com. investigating Bur. of Internal Revenue, 1924-26; chief of staff of joint Congressional Com. on Internal Revenue Taxation since 1926. Clubs: Burning Tree Golf, Montgomery County, Md. Author or co-author of various govt. reports on taxes. Home: Washington, D.C. *

PARKER, MORGAN, surg. instrument mfr.; born Washington, Oct. 14, 1892; s. Thomas Donaldson and Charlotte (Tiffany) P.; grad. St. George's Sch., Newport, R.I., 1911; m. Mary Welsh McLeran, Jan. 19, 1923; 1 son, Foxhall Alexander. Mech. engr. Providence Engring. Works, 1911-13; founder, 1913, since pres. Bard-Parker Co., Inc., Danbury, Conn.; chmn. bd. Becton, Dickinson & Co., E. Rutherford, N.J., 1957-65; asso. dir. Fairfield County Trust Co., Danbury. Chmn. bd. appeals Lewisboro Township, Westchester County, N.Y., 1940-76, mem. planning bd., 1937-76. Mem. Mfrs. Surg. Trade Assn. (past pres., dir.), Mfrs. Assn. Conn. (past dir.), Conn. C. of C. (dir.). Inventor Bard-Parker surg. knives and germicides. Home: Katonah, N.Y. Died Feb. 24, 1976; buried St. Matthews Episcopal Ch., Bedford, N.Y.

PARKER, ROBERT L., lawyer; b. El Paso, Tex., Jan. 29, 1920; A.B. in Chemistry, Occidental Coll., 1941; J.D., Loyola U., 1949. Admitted to Calif. bar, 1949; mem. firm Christie, Parker & Hale, Pasadena. Mem. Am., Pasadena, Los Angeles County bar assns., State Bar Calif., Am. Chem. Soc., Am. Patent Law Assn., Am. Soc. Internat. Law, Internat. Assn. for Protection of Indsl. Property, Licensing Execs. Soc., Los Angeles Council on Fgn. Relations, Phi Delta Phi. Home: Pasadena, Calif. Died June 26, 1980.

PARKER, SAM DIEHL, lawyer; b. Olathe, Kan., Nov. 10, 1906; s. John James and Ella (Diehl) P.; student Kan. U., 1925-27; LL.B., 1930; m. Maxine G. Genther, Mar. 7, 1947. Admitted to Mo. bar, 1929, Kan. bar, 1942; mem. firm Lathrop, Koontz, Righter, Clagett, Parker & Norguist and predecessor, Kansas City, Mo., 1945-80; gen. atty. Mo., A.T. & S.F. Ry., 1947-80; dir., gen. counsel Profl. Nursing Homes Am., Inc., 1968-69. Mem. Mo. R.R. Com., 1956-80, chmn., 1968-80; mem. Mo. R.R. Exec. Com., 1956-80. Hon. col. Mo., 1968-80. Mem. Am., Kansas City bar assns., Mo. Bar, Lawyers Assn. Kansas City, Kansas City C. of C. (chmn. legislative com. 1957-64). Home: Kansas City, Mo. Died May 31, 1980; buried Olathe.

PARKER, WALTER HUNTINGTON, mining co. exec.; b. Stillwater, Minn., Aug. 1, 1884; s. Reuben S. and Jennie Annette (Huntington) P.; E.M., U. of Minn. 1907; hon. grad. Sch. of Fire, Field Arty., Fort Sill, 1917; m. Veola Fourrell, Aug. 16, 1921. With Pa. Mining Co., Argentine, Colo., 1905, Bingham, Utah, 1906; mgr. Fairview Mining Co., Berlin, Wash., 1907; chief engr. Internat. Coal Co. and Mont. Coal & Iron Co., 1908-12; cons. city engr., Bearcreek, Mont., 1909; cons. structural and mining engr., Vancouver, B.C., Can., 1913-14, Mont., Colo., Minn., and Alberta, 1914-17; asso. prof. mining and head of dept., Sch. of Mines and Metallurgy, U. of Minn., 1919-23, prof. mining and head of dept., 1923-49, prof. of mining emeritus since 1949; cons. mining engr.; president San Juan Mining and Exploration Company. Mem. Minn. Nat. Guard, 1903-07; captain C.A.C., U.S. Army, World War; mem. Gen. Court Martial, 1917; mem. staff Sch. of Fire, Fort Sill, 1917; overseas, 12 mos., as bn. comdr. 69th Arty., C.A.C., and camp adjt., Romagne, France. Fellow A.A.A.S.; mem. Am. Inst. Mining and Metall. Engrs., Soc. for Promotion Engring. Edn., Am. Soc. Civil Engrs., Gen. Alumni Assn. U. of Minn. (dir.), Veterans of Foreign Wars, American Legion, Order of Founders and Patriots of America, Soc. of Colonial Wars, Engineers Club of Minneapolis, Soc. Westcott Descendants, Huntington Family Assn., Minn. Fed. Engr. Soc., New England Hist.-Geneal. Soc., Minn. Hist. Soc., Inst. of Mining and Metallurgy (England), Mining and Metall. Soc. Am., Am. Forestry Assn., Am. Mus. Natural Hist., Forty and Eight, Theta Tau. Republican. Episcopalian. Scottish Rite Mason. (K.T., Shriner). Clubs: Lions, Campus. Editor: Bluebooks. Sch. of Mines, 1922-50. Home: Phoenix. *

PARKHURST, CHARLES CHANDLER, educator, author, indsl. communications cons.; b. Somerville, Mass., Dec. 19, 1904; s. Charles Erwin and Helen Augusta (Chandler) P.; B.B.A., Boston U. Coll. of Bus. Adminstrn., 1926, A.M., 1930; D.Sc. in Bus. Adminstrn., Piedmont Coll., 1964; Litt.D. (hon.), Olivet (Mich.) Coll., 1966; m. Lillian Andrews, June 1935. With Ford Motor Co., 1926, Chrysler Motor Car sales div., 1928; dir. English, Catherine Gibbs Sch., 1929-30; instr. English, Everett High Sch., 1930-37; chmn. All-University English Dept., 1949-51; instr. English, Boston U. Coll. of Bus. Adminstrn., 1931-35, asst. prof., 1935-42, asso. prof. 1943-69, prof., head English dept. Boston U. Coll. of Practical Arts and Letters, 1944, prof. English and Bus. Communications Coll. Bus. Adminstrn., 1956-69; indsl. communications cons., lectr., 1970-77; lectr. Am. Inst. Banking; dir. English, Bentley Sch. of Accounting and Finance, 1937-48; lit. counsellor and corr. cons. for banks, ins. cos., bus. and indsl. plants; dir. edn. programs for bus. and indsl. orgns. Dir. Ware and Post-War Tng. Inst., Boston U. Coll. Bus. Adminstrn. Mem. Winchester Finance Com.; mem. Park Commn., Winchester, Mass.; pres. Hedding (N.H.) Chatauqua Assn.; trustee Hedding Camp Meeting Assn. Fellow Am. Bus. Writing Assn. (past pres.); mem. Nat. Office Mgr. Assn., AAUP, NEA, Nat. Council English Tchrs., Modern Lang. Assn., Eastern Comml. Tchrs. Assn., Newcomen Soc. of Eng., U.S. Power Squadron, USCG Aux., Francis Scott Key Meml. Assn., Lambda Chi Alpha. Methodist. Clubs: Internat. Rotary (hon.), Boston Authors, Boston University Faculty. Republican. Author: (with Grove) English Elements and Principles; (with Roy Davis) Business Writing Theory and Practice; Modern Business English; English for Business rev. 1964; Practical Problems in English for Business, rev. 1958; Using Words Effectively (vols. A. and B.), rev. 1958; A Direct Approach to Writing; Business English for College, 1957; Modern Business Communication for Better Human Relations, 1942, rev. edits., 1949, 55, 61, 66, 76; Case Studies in Business Communication, 1960; Modern Executive's Guide to Effective Communication, 1962; also articles ednl., bus. mags. Editor: Say What You See. Home: Winchester, Mass., also Cape Cod, Mass. Died Apr. 15, 1977; buried Wildwood Cemetery, Winchester.

PARKIN, GEORGE RALEIGH, organization executive; b. Toronto, Can., Feb. 25, 1896; s. Sir George Robert and Annie Connell (Fisher) P.; student Winchester College, 1909-12, Royal Military College, Kingston, Canada, 1913-14; B.A., Balliol College, Oxford U., 1922; m. Louise Margaret Gaselee Cockburn, Oct. 15, 1927; children—Elizabeth Stevenson, Jane Cockburn. Asso. with investment dept. of Sun Life Assurance Co. of Can., Montreal, since 1922, supervisor British and foreign section of investment dept. since 1940. Supervisor British and fgn. investments, 1945-77, asst. treas., 1945-58, asso. treas., 1958-61; coordinator development and extension Arctic Institute of North America, 1961-77. Served as lieutenant sixth bn. York and Lancaster Regiment, 1914-15, Gallipoli, 1915, Canadian, F.A., England and France, 1916-17, Royal Engrs. Signal Service, France, 1917-19. Mem. Canadian delegation to Inst. of Pacific Relations Conf., Yosemite, Calif., 1936, Virginia Beach, Va., 1939; mem. Harris Foundation Conf., U. of Chicago, 1941. Trustee Inst. of Current World Affairs, N.Y. City. Governor, Arctic Inst. of N.A., 1945-46. Mem. Canadian Inst. Internat. Affairs, Canadian Polit. Sci. Assn. Clubs: Century (N.Y.C.); University, Montreal (Montreal). Author (with W. E. Duffet and A. R. Hicks): India Today—The Background of Indian Nationalism, 1942. Translated into French under title L'Inde d'aujourd 'hui, 1944. Sole author: India Today—An Introduction to Indian Politics, 1945. Occasional contbr. to mags. Home: Montreal, Que., Can. Died Oct. 1977.

PARKS, GORDON ROGER, JR., motion picture dir.; b. Mpls., Dec. 7, 1934; s. Gordon Roger and Sally (Turner) P.; student Am. Sch., Paris, France, 1949, Parish English Coll., 1949. Guitarist, folksinger in Greenwich Village, N.Y.C., 1960-64; cameraman for films Africa and I, 1968, The World of Piri Thomas, Crisis in the Cities; free-lance still photographer Look, Life, Mobil Oil Co., Time, for films Burn, 1969, The Learning Tree, 1969, Godfather I, 1971; dir. movies Superfly, 1972, Thomasine and Bushrod, 1974, Three The Hard Way, 1974, Aaron Loves Angela, 1975. Served with AUS, 1956-57. Mem. Dirs. Guild Am. Photographer, author: J.T., 1969. Home: Los Angeles, Calif. Died Apr. 3, 1979.

PARMELEE, AMY OLGEN, (PAR'ME-LE), ex-coll. dean; born Chicago, Ill., Feb. 1, 1882; d. Albert Frederick and Elizabeth (Gottschall) Olgen; A.B., Northwestern U., 1904; A.M., U. of Ill., 1933; m. Egbert Nelson Parmelee, Sept. 12, 1906 (died 1922); children—Rexford Clark, Elizabeth Aletha. Y.W.C.A. sec., Northwestern U., 1904-06; traveling officer for Delta Delta Delta, 1930-33; dean of women, Colorado A. and M. College, 1934-47; retired. National pres. Delta Delta Delta, 1906-15, editor The Trident, same, 1922-36; delegate National Panhellenic Congress, 1906-25, president 1905-06, 1914-15. Member Colorado Educational Assn., American Assn. University of Women, P.E.O., Phi Beta Kappa, Delta Delta Delta, Delta Kappa Gamma. Republican. Clubs: Woman's University (Chicago). Home: Fort Collins, Colo. *

PARMELEE, MAURICE, author; b. Constantinople, Turkey, Oct. 20, 1882; s. Moses Payson and Julia (Farr) P.; A.B., Yale, 1904, A.M., 1908; PH.D., Columbia University, 1909; one daughter, Judith. Prof. sociology economics, anthropology, successively at univs. of Kan., Mo., Minn., and Coll. City of N.Y., 1909-18; rep. of War Trade Bd., London, Eng., 1918-19; spl. asst. to Sec. of State, 1920; economist consul, Berlin, Germany, 1920-23; travel in Japan, China, India, 1925-26, Russia, 1928-29, 33; research in Europe, 1936-38; principal economist, Agr., Treas., Interior Depts., Economic Warfare Board, 1935-36, 1938-42; chief economist, U.S. Railroad Retirement Board, 1942-52. Awarded Grant Squires prize for scoiological research by Columbia U., 1925. Fellow A.A.A.S.; mem. Institut International de Sociologie. Author many books relating to field of interest; including: The Science of Human Behavior, 1913; Criminology, 1918; Oriental and Occidental Culture, 1928; Farewell to Poverty, 1935. Address: Chicago. *

PARR, CHARLES MCKEW, author, historian; b. Balt, Nov. 23, 1884; s. Charles Edward and Helen B. (McKew) P.; student U.S. Mil. Acad., 1906, Columbia, 1930; LL.D., U. Bridgeport (Conn.), 1961; m. Ruth Butler, June 22, 1916; children—Charles McKew, Alexander Shipman. Dir. Thomas Y. Crowell Co., Parr Electric Co., Inc., Parr Marine & Export Corp. Spl. asst. to sec. of state, 1918; fgn. agt., War Trade Bd., Bur. Exports Washington, 1918; consular service in Spain and Canary Islands, 1919; sr. elec. cons. WPB, 1942; chmn. Industry Adv. Com., 1952; Mem. Conn. Ho. of Reps. from Chester, 1942-49, Conn. Senate from Middlesex County, 1950-54. Donated McKew Parr Magellan collection to Brandeis U., 1961; chmn. Middletown (Conn.) Library Service Center, 1955-57; chmn. trustee div. Conn. Library Assn., 1953; chmn. Chester (Conn.) Pub. Library, 1955-65. Decorated comdr. Orden Militar d Cristo (Portugal), comdr. Order Orange-Nassau (Netherlands). Mem. Am. Air Force Acad. Library, Am., Conn., N.J. Library assns., John Carter Brown Library Assns., Yale Library Assos., Am. Geog. Soc., Am., Deep River hist. socs., N.J. Hist. Soc., Hispanic Soc. Am., West Point Soc. N.Y., Bibliophile Soc. Brandeis U., S.A.R., Md. Soc. Colonial Wars, Nat. Assn. Elec. Distbrs. (bd. dirs.), Essex Elec. League (bd. dirs.), Newark C. of C. (bd. dirs.), Soc. De Geografia de Lisboa, Soc. Nautical Research, Hist. Assn. London, Hakluyt Soc. London, De Linschoten-Vereeniging, Nederlandsch Historisch Scheepvaart Museum Biblioteca Capitular Columbina Sevelle. Rotarian. Clubs: Essex (Newark); Hartford (Conn.); N.Y. Athletic, Players (N.Y.C.). Author: Over and Above Our Pacific, 1941; So Noble a Captain, 1953; Magallanes, 1955; Jan Van Linschoten, The Dutch Marco Polo, 1964; Ferdinand Magellan Circumnavigator, 1964; The Voyages of David DeVries, 1969. Address: Chester, Conn. Died Feb. 7, 1976.

PARRAVANO, GIUSEPPE, educator; b. Florence, Italy, Dec. 17, 1917; s. Nicola and Vittoria (Donati) P.; Ph.D. in Elec. Engring., U. Rome (Italy), 1940, D.Chemistry, 1942; m. Erna Paparozzi, Apr. 20, 1942; children—Nicola, Carlo, Pietro, Paolo. Came to U.S., 1946, naturalized, 1954. Postdoctoral fellow Princeton, 1948-52; prin. scientist Franklin Inst., 1952-55; asso. prof. U. Notre Dame, 1955-58; prof. chem. engring. U. Mich. 1958-78; cons. to industry and pvt. labs., 1954-78. Mem. Am. Chem. Soc., Am. Inst. Chem. Engring., Sigma Xi. Author papers in field. Address: Ann Arbor, Mich. Died Apr. 1, 1978; buried Ann Arbor.

PARRISH, JUNE AUSTIN, reins. co. exec.; b. Kansas City, Mo., June 25, 1917; d. Harry Winthrop and Marguerite Georgia (McClune) Austin; A.A., Kansas City Jr. Coll., 1935; J.D., U. Mo., Kansas City, 1950; m. Tom Howell Parrish, June 25, 1956. Admitted to Mo. oar, 1950, U.S. Supreme Ct. bar, 1958; with Employers Reins. Corp., Kansas City, Mo., 1941-81, asso. gen. counsel, 1968-73, gen. counsel, 1974-81. Mem. Jackson County Bd. Visitors, 1958-60; bd. dirs. Kansas City Assn. Blind, 1950-56, Legal Aid Soc. Kansas City, 1969-73; bd. dirs. Rehab. Inst. Kansas City, 1960-69, pres., 1966-69. Mem. Am., Mo. (chmn. ins. law com. 1975-77), Kansas City, Kansas City Women's (pres. 1956) bar assns., Lawyers Assn., Kansas City Women's C. of C. (dir. 1953-56), U. Mo.-Kansas City Law Sch. Alumni Assn. (adv. bd. dirs.), Scribes, Kappa Beta Pi. Presbyn. Club: Kansas City Soroptimist (pres. 1956). Co-author: Liability Insurance Cases, 1957-81. Home: Shawnee Mission, Kans. Died Jan. 20, 1981.

PARRISH, ROBERT MILTON, lawyer, govt. ofcl.; b. St. Paul, June 14, 1913; s. Milton Robert and Signe Marie Olivia (Carlstrom) P.; B.S.L., U. Minn., 1938, LL.B., 1938; m. Catherine Emily Brill, Mar. 22, 1941; children—Catherine Emily, Abigail Jane. Admitted to Minn. bar. 1938; atty. with several U.S. Govt. agencies, 1938-43; 45-51; counsel NPA, 1951-53; exec. dir. FTC, 1953-54, 60-72, sec., 1954-72. Mem. Phi Delta Phi, Phi Delta Theta. Episcopalian. Home: Washington, D.C. Died Feb. 1979.

PARRY, CARL EUGENE (PAR'E), economist; b. Florida, Ohio, Apr. 1, 1883; s. George William Gibbons and Flora Ellen (Halter) P.; A.B., U. of Mich., 1905, A.M., 1907, Ph.D., 1909; unmarried. Instr. in economics, U. of Mich., 1907-13; asst. prof., economics, Ohio State U., 1913-17, prof., 1917-19; prof. of economics, Tulane U. (La.), 1919-22; economist, Am. Chamber of Economics, N.Y. City, 1922-23; economist in grain futures, U.S. Dept. of Agr., 1923-24; research asst., Div. of Research and Statistics, Fed. Reserve Bd., 1924-27, asst. dir., 1927-34, director Div. Security Loans, 1934-48, in charge consumer credit regulation, 1941-47, mem. editorial com. Fed. Res. Bulletin, 1944-48; consultant Fed. Reserve Bd., 1949. Mem. Am. Econ. Assn., Am. Statis. Assn., Phi Beta Kappa. Club: Cosmos (Washington, D.C.). Home: Washington, D.C. *

PARSONS, CHARLES CUTLER, lawyer; b. Wooster, O., June 25, 1882; s. Jabez and Mary Louise (Oatley) P.; Ph.B., University of Chicago, 1905; m. Margaret Frances Harris, Feb. 8, 1910; children—Margaret Parsons Winkle, Virginia Elies (Mrs. Daniel C Forbes), Mary Frances (Mrs. George W. Wunder), Shirley (Mrs. Roger W. Sheridan). Admitted to Utah bar, 1907, since practiced in that state and before fed. cts.; now mem. Parsons, Behle, Evans & Moffat, Salt Lake City; president of Carbon Co. Railway Co., 1941—. Fellow Am. Bar Found.; mem. Am., Utah bar assns., ICC Practitioners, American Inst. Mining Metallurgical and Petroleum Engineers, American Judicature Society, also United States C. of C., Newcomen Soc., Sons Am. Revolution, Soc. Mayflower Descendants. Psi Upsilon. Republican. Episcopalian. Mason. Club: Alta. Home: Salt Lake City. *

PARSONS, DOUGLAS EUGENE, civil engr.; b. Marion, Iowa, Nov. 3, 1894; s. Samuel N. and Aley E. (Andrews) P.; A.B., Cornell Coll., Mt. Vernon, Ia., 1917, C.E., 1922; m. Lyle Chandler, Aug. 1, 1920; children—Robert Chandler, William Andrews, Mary Lyle, Margery Louise. Assistant engr. Ia. Ry. & Light Co., Cedar Rapids, 1919-23; engr. Nat. Bureau of Standards, Washington, D.C., 1923-30, chief masonry construction section, 1930-45, chief of mineral products div., 1945-46, chief bldg. research div., 1947-62; cons., from 1963. Served as 2d lt., reconnaissance officer, 314th Trench Mortar Battery, 89th Div. U.S. Army with A.E.F., 1917-19. Dir. American Concrete Institute, 1941-49; vice president, 1943-44, president, 1945-46. Bldg. research adv. bd. NRC, 1950-55, 58-63, chmn., 1954. Awarded Wason medal for noteworthy research, Am. Concrete Inst., 1936, Linden Award, 1952, Turner Medal, 1959; Award of Merit, American Society Testing Materials, 1952, Walter C. Voss award, 1963; Department of Commerce award, 1955. Mem. Am. Soc. Testing Materials (hon. life mem.); director 1954-57, Am. Concrete Inst. (hon.), Philos. Soc., Internat. Assn. Testing and Research Labs. Materials and Structures, Building Research Inst. (gov. 1959-62), Wash. Acad. Sci., Am. Soc. C.E.; chmn. Am. Standards Assn. Com., A-41 on masonry. Author of tech. publs. and reports. Home: Fort Walton Beach, Fla. *

PARSONS, TALCOTT, sociologist, educator; b. Colorado Springs, Colo., Dec. 13, 1902; s. Edward Smith and Mary Augusta (Ingersoll) P.; grad. Horace Mann Sch., N.Y.C., 1920; A.B., Amherst Coll., 1924, L.H.D., 1949; student London Sch. Econs., 1924-25; Dr. Phil., U. Heidelberg, (Germany), 1927; Dr. rer pol., U. Cologne (Germany), 1963; LL.D. (hon.), U. Chgo., 1967, U. Pa., 1974; D.Social Sci. (hon.), Boston Coll., 1968; D.Phil. (hon.), Hebrew U., Jerusalem, 1972; D.Arts (hon.), Stonehill Coll., 1974; L.H.D. (hon.), Rutgers U., 1977; m. Helen B. Walker, Apr. 30, 1927; children—Anne (dec.), Charles, Susan. Instr. econs. Amherst Coll., 1926-27; instr. econs. Harvard U., 1927-31, isntr. sociology, 1931-36, asst. prof., 1936-39, asso. prof., 1939-44, prof., 1944-73, prof. emeritus, 1973-79, chmn. dept., 1944-46, chmn. com. concentration in area social sci., 1940-46, chmn. dept. social relations, 1946-56. Fellow Ford Center Advanced Study in Behavioral Sciences, 1957-58; mem. staff Harvard Sch. Overseas Adminstrs., 1943-46; vis. prof. sociology Colombia, summers, 1933, 35, U. Chgo., summer 1937, spring 1971, fall 1972, U. Pa., 1973-76, Rutgers U., 1976-77; vis. prof. social theory Cambridge U., 1953-54; hon. fellow Trinity Hall, Cambridge, Eng., 1974. Guggenheim fellow, 1966. Fellow AAAS, Am. Acad. Arts and Scis. (pres. 1967-71), Brit. Acad. (corr.), London Sch. Econs. (hon.); mem. Am. Philos. Soc., Am. (pres. 1949), Eastern (pres. 1941-42) sociol. socs., Chi Psi, Beta Kappa. Author: Protestant Ethic and Spirit of Capitalism Breslau; (transl. Max Weber), 1930; Structure of Social Action, 1937; Toward a General Theory of Action, 1951; The Social System, 1951; Essays in Sociological Theory, rev. edit., 1954; Structure and Process in Modern Societies, 1959; Social Structure and Personality, 1964; Societies; Evolutionary and Comparative Perspectives, 1966; Sociological Theory and Modern Society, 1968; Politics and Social Structure, 1969; The System of Modern Societies, 1971; The Evolution of Societies, 1977; Social Systems and the Evolution of Action Theory, 1977. Co-author: Working Papers on the Theory of Action, 1952; Family, Socialization and Interaction Process, 1955; Economy and Society, 1956; The American University, 1973. Co-editor: Theories of Society, 1961. Contbr. to Am. Sociol. Rev., Am. Jour. Sociology, Social Forces, Psychiatry, Jour. History of Ideas, Daedalus. Home: Belmont, Mass. Died May 8, 1979; buried Jeffrey Center, N.H.

PARTCH, CLARENCE ELMAR, coll. dean; b. Rock Rapids, Ia., Mar. 12, 1884; s. Merritt Orville and Carrie M. (Schroeder) P.; B.S. in M.E., U. of Mich., 1909; Ed.M., Harvard, 1925, Ed.D., 1926; m. Vera Howard, July 31, 1912 (dec.). Teacher, high sch., Des Moines, 1909-18; soldier rehabilitation work, 1918-22; teacher training work, Northwest Mo. State Teachers Coll., 1922-24; instr. in edn., Grad. Sch., Harvard, 1925-26; asso. prof. edn., Rutgers, 1926-27, prof. edn., dean of Sch. of Edn. and dir. of summer session since 1927; now dean emeritus. Mem. State Bd. Edn., 1943. Mem. N.E.A., Nat. Vocational Guidance Assn., Nat. Soc. Coll. Teachers of Edn., Nat. Soc. for Study of Edn., Nat. Econ. League, Eastern Coll. Personnel Officers Assn., Phi Beta Kappa, Sigma Xi, Phi Delta Kappa, Kappa Delta Pi, Epsilon Pi Tau. Mason. Clubs: Michigan (New York); Kiwanis (New Brunswick). Author: Information for Prospective College Students, 1926 (Revised 1929, 1935); Case Studies in Educational and Vocational Guidance (with J. M. Brewer and others), 1926; Cases in the Administration of Guidance (with J. M. Brewer and others), 1929; Work Guide for the Study of Occupations (with Harold P. Thomas), 1936; Cost of Education in New Jersey, 1942; Analysis of the Need for Facilities to Provide Adequate Higher Educational Opportunities for Veterans and for Graduates of Secondary Schools, 1946; Facilities Needed for Higher Education, 1948. Contbr. to Industrial Arts Mag., Survey, School and Society. Home: Stelton, N.J.*

PARTRIDGE, JOHN FRANCIS, lawyer, corp. exec.; b. Chatham, Va., May 29, 1914; s. Horace E. and Mary (Johnson) P.; B.S. in Bus. Adminstrn., U. Fla., 1936; C.P.A. U. Ill., 1939; J.D., Chgo.-Kent Coll. Law, 1947; grad. Exec. Program Bus. Adminstrn., Columbia, 1956; m. Evelyn Weeks, Dec. 28, 1949; children—Lawrence Scott, Jacquelyn Mary. Accountant, Oldham & Gouwens, Chgo., summer 1936; investment analyst Welsh & Green, Inc., Chgo., 1937-38; with Welsh, Davis & Co., Chgo., 1939-51, exec. v.p., 1948-51; admitted to Ill. bar, 1947; with AMSTED Industries Inc., Chgo., 1951-80, sec., counsel, 1959-73; practice law, Chgo., 1973-80. Instr. accounting U. Iowa, 1936-37; asst. prof. law Chgo.-Kent Coll. Law, 1947. Treas. local troop Boy Scouts Am., 1962-65; mem. com. to investigate pub. transp. for handicapped Welfare Council Met. Chgo., 1966; chmn. caucus in Wilmette, Ill. for Cook County Sch. Dist., 39, 1962. Bd. dirs., sec. Rehab Inst. Chgo., 1961-80. Mem. Am., Ill. (mem. council corp. law dept. 1965-80, sec. corp. law dept. 1967-68, vice chmn. 1968-69, chmn. 1969-70), Chgo. bar assns., Am. Soc. Corp. Secretaries (sec. Chgo. regional group 1965-67, v.p. 1967-68, pres. 1969-70, chmn. mem. relations com. 1965-80, mem. adv. com 1985-86, v.p., dir. nat. 1970-80). Presbyn. (elder 1960-62, trustee sec. bd. 1966-67, pres. 1968). Home: Skokie, Ill. Died July 2, 1980.

PARTRIDGE, RICHARD CLARE, army officer; b. Boston, Feb. 15, 1899; s. George Fairbanks and Elenora Rose (Clare) P.; A.B., Harvard, 1919; B.S., U.S. Mil. Acad., 1920; grad. F.A. Sch., basic course, 1921, Command and Gen. Staff Sch., 1936, German War Acad., 1939; m. Margaret Barton, Oct. 5, 1922; children—Margaret Barton, Clare. Commd. 2d lt., United States Army, 1920, advanced through the grades to major general, 1952; attached to the American Embassy in Germany, 1938-40; military attaché Budapest, 1940-42; interned, Lisbon, Portugal, Jan.-May 1942; with Allied Force Hdqrs., England and North Africa, Aug. 1942-May 1943; with 15th Army Group, Tunisia, Sicily, Italy, June-Nov. 1943; with Hdqrs. 1st Army Group England, Dec. 1943-April 1944; with Hdqrs. VII Corps, England, France, Belgium and Germany from Apr. 1944, became chief of staff (VII Corps), Sept. 1944; wounded while comdg. 358th Inf., 90th Div., Normandy, July 1944; dep. chief of staff 7th Army, 1950-52; asst. chief of staff G-2 U.S. Army, 1952-53; div. comdr. Germany, 1954-55; chief Spl. Act. Div. Hq. USAREUR, 1955-56; chief JUSMAG, Thailand, 1956-59. Decorated Distinguished Service Medal, Legion Merit with oak leaf cluster, Bronze Star with oak leaf cluster, Purple Heart (U.S.), Comdr. Order British Empire (Gt. Britain), Legion of Honor, Croix de Guerre with palm (France), Order of Kutusov, 2d class (Russia), Croix de Guerre with palm (Belgium), Korean Distinguished Mil. Service Medal. Mem. Assn. of Grads. of U.S. Mil. Acad. Home: New London, Conn. Died July 23, 1976.

PASCHALL, NATHANIEL, business exec.; b. Seattle, June 11, 1912; s. Nathaniel and Bertha Cranston (Potter) P.; student U. Wash., 1932, Boeing Sch. Aeronautics, Oakland, Calif., 1934-35; m. Mary Katherine Price, Feb. 18, 1947; children—Nathaniel Price, Boeing C. Co-pilot United Airlines, Oakland, 1936-38; with Douglas Aircraft Co., Inc., Santa Monica, 1939-59, v.p., 1945-59, dir., 1951-61; chmn. bd. dirs. Fidelity Northwest, Seattle; chmn. Paschall Internat. Corp.; chmn. Bank of Montreal (Calif.), 1972-79. Clubs: Calif. (Los Angeles); Pacific Union (San Francisco); Annandale Golf (Pasadena, Calif.); Wings (N.Y.); Seattle Yacht; Mt. Royal (Montreal); Birnam Wood Golf (Montecito, Calif.). Home: Pasadena, Calif. Died Jan. 22, 1979.

PATCH, JOSEPH D., army officer; b. Fort Huachuca, Ariz., Dec. 8, 1885; commd. 2d lt. Inf., Aug. 1911, and advanced through the grades to brig. gen., Oct., 1941, maj. gen. May 1942; in command of 34th Inf., Ft. Jackson, S.C., June 1940-May 1942; designated comdg. gen., 80th Inf., upon its activation at Camp Forrest, Tenn., May 1942, comdg. gen. Trinidad Sector and Base Command Caribbean Defense Command, Mar. 1943; lt. gen. comdg. 7th Army, 1944. Awarded Distinguished Service Cross,Purple Heart, French Croix de Guerre, World War I.*

PATERSON, NORMAN MCLEOD, grain mcht., ship-owner, Can. senator; b. Portage La Prairie, Manitoba, Aug. 3, 1883; s. Hugh Savigny and Ella (Snider) P.; student pub. schs. Winnipeg and Toronto; LL.D. (hon.), Carleton U., Ottawa; m. Eleanor M. Macdonald, June 2, 1915; children—Elizabeth (Mrs. Eric T. Webster), Donald, John, Mary (Mrs. A. Norton Francis), Nancy (Mrs. Paul A. McFarlane), Joan (Mrs. Ayton G. Keyes). Pres., N. M. Paterson & Sons, Ltd., Western Engring. Service, Traders Building Assn.; chmn. Royal Edward Hotel. Summoned to Can. Senate, 1940. Chancellor, Lakehead U. Decorated Comdr., Officer Bro. of St. John Ambulance Assn., Knight Order of St. John (Gt. Britain). Liberal. Presbyn. Clubs: Rideau, Manitoba, Ft. William Country, Royal Lake of the Woods Yacht, Royal Ottawa Golf, Seigniory, Ottawa, Maganassipi Fish and Game. Home: Ottawa ON Canada. *

PATERSON, ROBERT, editor, author, lecturer; b. Bellefontaine, O., Nov. 17, 1885; s. Robert and (Anne) Virginia (Sharpe) P.; ed. Charlotte Hall (M.D.) Mil. Acad., 1901-02, Maplewood Classical School, Kokomo, Ind., 1903-04, Ohio State U., 1905-06, 1908; m. Eleanor de Bevoise Tunison, Oct. 27, 1926 (divorced Oct. 1940). Reporter Wilmington (Del.) Morning News, later Oklahoma City Oklahoman, 1909-10; sports editor, legislative correspondent, city editor Fargo (N.D.) Forum, 1910-14; editor Atlanta (Ga.) branch Western Newspaper Union, 1914-15; war corr. for several newspapers, 1915; Y.M.C.A. lecturer with A.E.F. in France, 1918; research editor Searchlight Library Pub. Co., New York, 1919; asst. to editor Current Opinion, 1919-22; asso. editor McClure Newspaper Syndicate, and supervisory editor Wheeler Syndicate, subsidiary, 1922-26; legislative corr. New York Herald-Tribune, 1926-27; asst. to Bernarr Macfadden, 1935-36, 1937; lecturer since 1936; editor Our State, Newark, 1939-40; staff editor Indsl. Bull., N.Y., 1948, Home Work and Unemployment Ins. divs., N.Y. Dept. Labor, 1949-55; mgr. spl. edit. Irish Echo, N.Y., 1955; dir. Pub. Housing Edn., N.J. Council of Housing Authorities, Newark, 1939-41. Dir. Vets. div., C.D.V.O., 1943; dir. pub. relations, Civilian Def. Volunteer Orgn., 1944; exec. dir. National Majority (all New York), 1945-46; chmn. Nat. Com. for Statehood for P.R., Inc., 1950. Vice chmn. board managers Army Y.M.C.A., Fort Jay, Governor's Island, N.Y., 1925-31; mem. Mayor's Com. to Welcome Distinguished Guests, New York, 1928-33. Mem. Vivisection Investigation League; director Citizens Association for Care of Animals, 1955—. Served as pvt. Tank Corps, United States Army, 1918; 2d lt. 244th C.A., N.Y. Nat. Guard, 1929-32. Recipient Liberty award Congress of Freedom, 1959; medal for upholding pub. sch. system. Am. Edn. Assn., 1963. Mem. Am. Legion (comdr. N.Y. County, 1923-25), S.A.R. Rep. Episcopalian. Mason. Club: Lambs (New York). Author: Gas Buggy, 1933; Land of the Pilgrims' Pride, 1936; Strike at the Source, 1952; Designs Upon the United States, 1955; We Believe in Prayer, 1958; Time for Scrutiny, 1958. Contbr. article on North Dakota to These United States, 1924. Contbr. jours. *

PATTEN, LEWIS BYFORD, author; b. Denver, Jan. 13, 1915; s. Lewis Byford and Anna (Miller) P.; student U. Denver, 1940-42; m. Betsy Mae Lancaster, Dec. 4, 1938 (div. 1962); children—Frances A. Patten Henry, Clifford Lewis, Lewis Byford; m. 2d, Catherine Crane Wodrich, July 11, 1963. Sr. auditor Colo. Dept. Revenue, 1942-44; ranch operator DeBeque and Evergreen, Colo., 1944-49; author 101 Western novels, 1949-80. Served with USN, 1933-37. Mem. Western Writers Am. (Golden Saddleman's award for outstanding contbn. to history and legend of Am. West 1979). Republican. Author: Red Sundown (film), 1954; Gunsmoke Empire, 1955; White Warrior, 1956; Pursuit, 1957; Five Rode West, 1958; Showdown at War Cloud, 1959; Hangman's Country, 1960; Law of the Gun, 1961; Outlaw Canyon, 1962; Guns at Gray Butte, 1963; Killer From Yuma, 1964; The Arrogant Guns, 1965; No God in Saguaro, 1966; Bones of the Buffalo, 1967; Death of a Gunfighter, 1968 (film 1969); Posse From Poison Creek, 1969; Red Runs The River, 1970; Guilt of a Killer Town, 1971; The Red Sabbath (Golden Spur award Western Writers Am.), 1969; The Meeker Massacre (Golden Spur award), 1970; The Trial of Judas Wiley, 1972; The Cheyenne Pool, 1972; A Killing in Kiowa (Golden Spur award), 1972; The Tired Gun, 1973; The Hide Hunters, 1973; The Angry Town of Pawnee Bluffs, 1974; The Gallows at Graneros, 1975; Ambush at Soda Creek, 1976; The Killings at Coyote Springs, 1977; Hunt the Man Down, 1977; Willa's Rifles, 1977; Cheyenne Captives, 1978; Death Rides a Black Horse, 1978; The Law in Cottonwood, 1978; The Trail of the Apache Kid, 1979; Ride a Tall Horse, 1980. Address: Denver, Colo. Died May 22, 1981.

PATTERSON, BRYAN, paleontologist; b. London, Eng., Mar. 10, 1909; s. Lt. Col. John Henry and Frances Helena (Gray) P.; student Malvern Coll., Eng., 1923-26, U. Chgo., 1927-33; M.A. (hon.), Harvard U., 1955; m. Bernice Maurine Caine, Apr. 14, 1934; 1 son, Alan. Came to U.S., 1926, naturalized, 1938. Asst. paleontology to curator fossil mammals Chicago Natural History Museum, 1926-55; Alexander Agassiz prof. vertebrate paleontology Harvard, from 1955. Mem. adv. panel earth scis. Nat. Sci. Found., 1956-59. Served with 16th Regt., 1st Inf. Div., AUS, 1944-45. Carnegie Corp. grant-in-aid for travel, 1938; John Simon Guggenheim Found. fellow, 1951-53, 54-55. Mem. Am. Acad. Arts and Scis., Soc. Vertebrate Paleontology (sec.-treas. 1946-48, pres. 1948-49), Geol. Soc. Am., Soc. for Study Evolution, Soc. Systematic Zoology, Am. Soc. Mammalogists, Nat. Acad. Sci., Sigma Xi. Contbr. tech. papers to sci. jours. Home: Cambridge, Mass. Died Dec. 1, 1979.

PATTERSON, CHARLES H., automobile co. exec.; b. Scotland, 1902. Exec. v.p., dir. Ford Motor Co. until 1967. Mason. Home: Dearborn, Mich. Died Jan. 24, 1977.

PATTERSON, JEFFERSON, foreign service officer; b. Dayton, O., May 14, 1891; s. Frank Jefferson and Julia Perrine (Shaw) P.; A.B., Yale, 1913; LL.B., Harvard, 1916; m. Mary Marvin Breckinridge, June 20, 1940. Admitted to Ohio bar; law clerk, Dayton, 1919-20; sec. of Legation, assigned Dept. of State, Washington, D.C., 1921; asst. sec. Conf. on Limitation of Armament, Washington, 1921-22; subsequently served as sec. of embassy or legation in various grades at Peking, Bogota, Istanbul and Ankara, Oslo and Berlin and as consul and asst. chief, Div. of Protocol, Dept. of State; chargé d'affaires ad interim at various posts; and from outbreak of World War II in charge of Prisoner of War Sect., Am. Embassy, Berlin, entrusted with protection of Belgian, British and French interests in Germany, Sept. 1939 to Apr. 1941; dep. chief of mission Embassy, Lima, Peru, 1941-45, Brussels, Belgium, 1945-46, Cairo, Egypt, 1946-49; ambassador to Uruguay, 1956-58. Member Alpha Delta Phi, Phi Beta Kappa. Clubs: Buz Fuz (Dayton); Metropolitan (Washington, D.C.). Yale and Harvard (N.Y. City). Author: Diplomatic Duty and Diversion, Diplomatic Terminus, Capitals and Captives, Family Portraits. Home: Washington, D.C. Died Nov. 12, 1977; interred Rock Creek Cemetery, Washington, D.C.

PATTERSON, MACLEAN, newspaper exec.; b. 1912. Gen. mng. editor Baltimore (Md.) Sunpapers; asst. sec., The A. S. Abell Co., Pubs.; after leaving Balt. Sun, gen. services exec. Rouse Co., Balt., until retirement in 1971. Founding mem. and past pres. Balt. Bibliophiles. Expert on H. L. Mencken; vol. editor quar. jour. Menckeniana, 1973-76. Home: Baltimore, Md. Died Aug. 27, 1976.

PATTERSON, RUSSELL, painter, illustrator, designer; b. Omaha, Dec. 28, 1894; s. William Francis and Kathleen (Callahan) P.; student St. Patricks Sch., Montreal, Can.; student Fine Arts Acad., Chgo., Chgo. Art Inst.; studied in Paris, 1920-25; study architecture Monumente National, Montreal; m. Constance Burke, 1918; 1 dau., Elinor (Mrs. James Cahill); m. 2d, Ruth Cleary, Aug. 13, 1938; 1 dau., Russelle. Comml. illustrator, later designer theatre costumes; designed and routined prodn. numbers for Stand Up and Cheer, Bottom's Up, Baby Take a Bow, Ballyhoo, Ziegfeld Follies, George White Scandals, The Gang's All Here, and others; designer hotels, restaurants, clubs, dept. store windows, etc.; head Russell Patterson Assos., Inc. Served in Royal Canadian Air Force, World War I. Received gold medal award from Acad. of Design, 1952. Mem Soc., of Illustrators (past 1st v.p.), Nat. Cartoonists Soc. (past pres.). Club: Dutch Treat, Artists and Writers. Home: New York, N.Y. Died Mar. 17, 1977.

PATTERSON, S(AMUEL) HOWARD, economist, educator; b. Phila., July 23, 1892; s. Samuel A. and Sara C. (Clagett) P.; grad. Phila. Sch. Pedagogy, 1911; B.S., U. Pa., 1914, A.M., 1916, Ph.D., 1922; m. Mae E. Griffiths, June 18, 1924. Teacher in elementary schs., Phila., 1911-14, W. Phila. High Sch., 1914-20; instr. in economics, U. Pa., 1920-22, asst. prof., 1922-28, prof. from 1928, also chmn. dept. economics, 1932-38; visiting prof. summer school, Columbia, 1935, 36, 37, 38; U.S. Army Officer School, 1918; consulting editor McGraw-Hill Book Co. and Farrar and Rinehart; editor Social Science Pub. Co.; dir. Sovereign Investors, Incorporated. Past vice pres., mem. bd. mgrs., Armstrong Assn., Phila. Public panel mem., Third Regional War Labor Board. Fellow A.A.A.S. (chmn. sect. K; v.p. 1945-46); mem. American Economics Assn., Am. Acad. Polit. and Social Sci., Nat. Council Social Studies, National Acad. Econs. and Polit. Sci. (dir.), S.A.R., Theta Chi (dir. Alumni Corporation of Kappa chapter), Pi Gamma Mu (national treasurer 1931-37; national president 1937-51, president emeritus and trustee-at-large from 1951), Phi Delta Kappa. Republican. Presbyterian. Mason. Club: Schoolmen's Overbrook Golf Club. Author or co-author numerous books relating to field from 1922. Home: Rydal, Pa. Deceased.

PATTERSON, WILLIAM ALLAN, air transportation exec.; b. Honolulu, T.H., Oct. 1, 1899; s. William Allan and Mary (Goulter) P.; educated public grammar and high schs., San Francisco, California, Military Academy, Honolulu; m. Vera A. Witt, June 20, 1924; children—Patricia Ann, William Allan. With Wells Fargo Bank & Trust Co., San Francisco, 1914-28; assistant to president Boeing Airplane Co. and Boeing Air Transport, Seattle, Wash., 1929-31; pres. Boeing Air Transport, Pacific Air Transport, Nat. Air Transport and Varney Air Lines, 1931-34; v.p. United Air Lines, Inc., 1933-34; pres. and dir. United Air Lines, Inc., Chgo., 1934-63, chmn. bd., chief executive officer, 1963-80; director Insurance Company of North America, Bell & Howell Company, Air Transport Assn. of Am., Westinghouse Electric Corp., Goodyear Tire & Rubber Co., Harris Trust & Savs. Bank Chgo. Trustee Northwestern U. Mem. Newcomen Soc. Mason. Clubs: Chicago, Executives, Economic, Commonwealth, Tavern, Commercial (Chgo.); Bohemian, Pacific Union (San Francisco); Glen View (Golf, Ill.); Old Elm (Ft. Sheridan, Ill.). Home: Wilmette, Ill. Died June 13, 1980.

PATTERSON, WILLIAM JOHN, ex-premier, Saskatchewan; b. Grenfell, Sask., May 13, 1886; s. John and Catherine (Fraser) P.; student Grenfell pub. sch., 1891-1902; m. Florence Donnelly, Aug. 14, 1937. Elected to Saskatchewan Legislature, 1921, 1925, 1929, 1934, 1938; Provincial treas., 1926-29; apptd. minister of telegraphs and telephones, 1934; became leader Liberal Party and premier of Saskatchewan, Nov. 1935, served until July, 1944; elected to Saskatchewan legislature, leader of the opposition; commr. Bd. Transport, Ottawa, Ont., Can., 1949-51; lt. gov. Saskatchewan, 1951-58. Served as lt. 3 1/2 yrs. with C.E.F., Can. Light Horse. Mem. Liberal Party. Mem. United Ch. Home: 2227 Montague St., Regina. Address: Regina, Saskatchewan, Can. Died June 10, 1976.

PATTON, KENNETH STUART, foreign service; b. Salem, Roanoke County, Va., July 22, 1882; s. John S. and Beatrice (Faber) P.; A.B., U. of Va., 1904; grad. work, Sorbonne, Paris, 1904-05; Johns Hopkins, 1905-08; student Bibliothèque Nationale, Paris, summer 1906; studied internat. law pvtly.; passed U.S. consular examinations, 1908; m. Alice Vincent Corson (artist), Oct. 7, 1908; 1 son, Kenneth Stuart. Consular asst., Dept. of State, Washington, June-Dec. 1908; with Consulate Gen., Marseilles, Dec. 1908-May 1909; v.consul, Rome, Italy, 1909-12; v.consul in charge consulate, Ceiba, Honduras, Feb.-July 1912; v.consul gen. in charge of consulate, Lisbon, Portugal, July-Oct. 1912; consul at Cognac, France, 1913-15, at La Rochelle, France, July 1915-Nov. 1916; on spl. detail at Am. Consulate-Gen., Paris. Sept.-Nov. 1916; consul at Calais, France, Nov. 1916-Feb. 1919; again on spl. detail, Paris, Feb.-June 1919; consul at Belgrade Yugoslavia, June 1919; also commercial adviser to Am. Legation, Belgrade, 1919-29; spl. detail at Consulate Gen., Paris, Aug.-Sept. 1927, returned to Belgrade as consul, Oct. 1927; consul at Leipzig, 1928-30; apptd. consul gen., Feb. 17, 1930; assigned to Batavia, Java, Mar. 26, 1930, Amsterdam, Netherlands, June 20, 1934, Singapore, Straits Settlements, Nov. 2, 1937, Calcutta, India, August, 1942; E. E. and M.P. to New Zealand, March, 1944; retired Dec. 31, 1945; apptd. adviser in foreign affairs to His Siamese Majesty's Govt., Bangkok, Siam, Feb. 11, 1946. Awarded Order of St. Sava (Jugoslavia). Mem. Foreign Service Assn. (v.p. 1944), Pi Gamma Mu. Democrat. Methodist. Mason. Author: Kingdom of Serbs, Croats and Slovenes (Yugoslavia), a Commercial and Industrial Handbook 1928. Home: Charlottesville, Va. *

PATTY, ERNEST NEWTON, mining engr.; b. La Grande, Oreg., Mar. 27, 1894; s. Thomas Franklin and Zora Euphemia (Beach) P.; B.S., U. Wash., 1919, E.M., 1925; D.Engring. (hon.), U. Alaska, 1953; m. Kathryn B. Stanton, Dec. 28, 1918 (dec. July 1961); children—Ernest N. (dec.), Stanton, Dale; m. 2d, Virginia W. Price, Jan. 20, 1968. Mining engr. Wash. State Geol. Survey, 1919-20; engr. charge Black Rock Mine, Northport, Wash., 1921; prof. geology and mineralogy U. Alaska, 1922-25, dean coll., head Sch. Mines, 1925-35, pres., 1953-60, then emeritus; pres., gen. mgr. Gold Placers, Inc., Alluvial Gold, Inc., Fairbanks, Alaska, from 1935; pres., gen. mgr. Clear Creek Placers, Ltd., 1940-53, Yukon Gold Placers, Ltd., Dawson, Yukon Ty., Can., 1946-53; cons. mining engr. various mining cos. Alaska chmn. March of Dimes. Fellow Arctic Inst. N. Am.; mem. Assn. Presidents Land Grant Colls., A.A.A.S., Am. Inst. Mining and Metall. Engrs., Am. Mining Congress, Alaska Miners Assn. (past pres., dir.), Pioneers of Alaska. Presbyn. Mason. Clubs: Explorers (N.Y.C.); Rainier (Seattle). Author: North Country Challenge; also tech. articles. Home: Seattle, Wash. Died Jan. 13, 1976.

PAUL, ALICE, b. Moorestown, N.J., Jan. 11, 1885; d. William Mickle and Tacie (Parry) P.; B.A., Swarthmore, 1905; grad. New York Sch. of Social Work, 1906; post-grad. work universities of Birmingham and

London, 1907-09; M.A., U. of Pa., 1907, Ph.D., 1912; LL.B., Washington College of Law, 1922; LL.M., American U., 1927, D.C.L., 1928. Resident New York Coll. Settlement, 1905-06, and various settlements in England, 1906-09; imprisoned in Eng. and in U.S. for activities in woman suffrage movement; chmn. Congressional Com. of Nat. Am. Woman Suffrage Assn., 1912-13; nat. chmn. Congressional Union for Woman Suffrage, from its formation, 1913, until 1917, when it was merged with the Woman's Party, forming Nat. Woman's Party; chmn. of nat. exec. com. Nat. Woman's Party, 1917-21, mem. exec. com. since 1921, also chmn. com. on internat. relations; chmn. Woman's Research Foundation, 1927-37; chmn. nationality com. Inter-American Commn. of Women, 1930-33; mem. Women's Consultative Com. on Nationality of League of Nations; mem. exec. com. Equal Rights Internat.; mem. from U.S. on laws com. Internat. Council of Women. Mem. Sons and Daughters of the Pilgrims, D.A.R., Colonial Dames of 17th Century, Ladies of G.A.R., Phi Beta Kappa, Pi Gamma Mu. Quaker. Home: Moorestown, N.J. *

PAUL, DOROTHY HITE, interior designer; b. Evansville, Ind.; student Ray-Vogue, Chgo., 1932; m. Philip Paul, 1935; children—Philip, Penelope Paul Haradon. Salesperson, Rosenbach collection Marshall Field & Co., 1934, Mary Dimery Antiques, Chgo., 1937-42; asst. Felecity Reynolds, A.I.D., Winnetka, Ill., 1942-46; owner Dorothy Paul Interiors, Los Angeles, 1954-78. Bd. dirs. Com. of Profl. Women, Philharmonic of Los Angeles. Recipient citation of merit Am. Inst. Interior Designer, 1960; Fellow Am. Inst. Design (accredited, pres. Los Angeles chpt. 1959-61; nat. bd. mem. 1960-66, nat. sec. 1968); mem. Am. Soc. Interior Designers (presdl. citation 1974). Home: Los Angeles, Calif. Died Dec. 24, 1978.

PAUL, LESTER WARNER, physician, educator; b. Everly, Iowa, Dec. 17, 1899; s. Levi W. and Sarah (Miller) P.; student North Central Coll., 1917-18; B.S., U. Minn., 1922, B.M., 1924, M.D., 1925; m. Dorothy Cole, Sept. 24, 1923; children—Lester, Susan. Intern Mpls. Gen. Hosp., 1925; gen. practice, Canby, Minn., 1925-30; residency radiology, U. Wis., 1930-31, instr. radiology, 1931-33, asst. prof., 1933-37, asso. prof., 1937-46; prof. radiology, 1946-70, prof. emeritus, 1970-75, chmn. dept., 1954-64; cons. radiology Mendota State Hosp., Madison; radiologist State Wis. Gen. Hosp. Diplomate Am. Bd. Radiology (bd. trustees). Fellow Am. Coll. Radiology; mem. A.M.A., Radiol. Soc. N.Am., Am. Roentgen Ray Soc. (past v.p.), Med. Soc., Wis. Radiol. Soc. (past pres.), Inter-Am. Coll. Radiology, Assn. U. Radiologists, Alpha Kappa Kappa, Alpha Omega Alpha. Author: (with J. H. Juhl) Essentials of Roentgen Interpretation of the Skeletal System; co-author Essentials of Roentgen Interpretation; contbg. author Diseases of the Colon. Contbr. med. articles. Home: Madison, Wis. Died Nov. 30, 1975.

PAUL, NORMAN STARK, lawyer; b. Stamford, Conn., Mar. 23, 1919; s. Dr. Voyle Abrams and Ada (Stark) P.; grad. Choate Sch., 1936; B.A., Yale, 1940; LL.B., U. Va., 1946; m. Bettie Huffard, Sept. 30, 1944; children—Margot Paul Kneeland, Susan Paul Gardner, Norman Stark, Jennifer. Admitted to N.Y. bar, 1947, D.C. bar, 1968; with Bleakley, Platt & Walker, N.Y.C., 1946-48; dep. asst. to adminstr. internat. security affairs, German affairs, ECA, 1948-52; dir. for mutual security, program adviser Middle East and Asia, 1952-54; regional dir. for Near East Africa and South Asia, dep. dir. FOA for Congl. relations, 1954-55; with CIA, 1955-60; asst. to sec. def. for legislative affairs Dept. DEf., 1961-62; asst. sec. def., 1962-65; under sec. Air Force, 1965-67; lawyer firm Chapman Duff and Paul, Washington, 1967-78. Mem. Council Fgn. Relations, Beta Theta Pi, Phi Delta Phi, Wolf's Head. Clubs: Yale (N.Y.C.); Metropolitan, Chevy Chase (Washington). Home: Washington, D.C. Died May 30, 1978.

PAULGER, LEOPOLD HOBSON (PAWL'JÛR), govt. official; b. New Hartford, Butler County, Ia., Mar. 7, 1885; s. Frederick Wheatley and Ida (Guthrie) P.; A.B., Cornell Coll., Mt. Vernon, Ia., 1905; m. Lida M. Updegraff, June 19, 1912; 1 son, John Wheatley (U.S. Army). Began as superintendent of schools at Center Point, Ia., 1905-06; teacher of mathematics, high school, Boone, Iowa, 1906-07; assistant cashier, State Bank, New Hartford, Iowa, 1907-08; successively asst. cashier, cashier and vice-pres. Security Bank, Cedar Falls, Ia., 1908-21; pres. Savings Bank, Plainfield, Ia., 1914-22; examiner and asst. to dirs., War Finance Corp., Washington, D.C., 1922-27; dir. Div. Examiners, Fed. Farm Loan Bd. and asst. to Farm Loan commr., Washington, D.C., 1927-31; chief Examining Div., R.F.C., Washington, D.C., 1932; dir. Div. Examinations, Bd. Govs. Fed. Reserve System, Washington, D.C., 1932-46; spl. adviser, since 1946. Trustee Cornell Coll., Mt. Vernon, Ia. Mem. Sons Am. Revolution. Mason. Club: Columbia Country (Washington, D.C.). Home: Washington, D.C. *

PAULSEN, MONRAD GOTKE, univ. dean; b. Clinton, Iowa, June 1, 1918; s. William H. and Esther (Gotke) P.; A.B., U. Chgo., 1940, J.D., 1942; J.D. (hon.), U. Freiburg (Germany), 1972; m. Elsa Proehl, June 23, 1955; children—Peter William, Christopher Monrad. Lectr. law U. Utah, 1945-46; asst. prof. Ind. U., 1946-50, asso. prof., 1950-51; asso. prof. U. Minn., 1951-54, prof. law, 1954-56; prof. Law Sch., Columbia, 1956-68; dean, John B. Minor prof. law U. Va., Charlottesville, 1968-80; Fulbright prof. U. Freiburg (Germany), 1964; vis. Am. prof. law U. London Inst. Advanced Legal Studies, 1966; prof. law U. Göttingen (Germany), summer 1973. Mem. Wage Stblzn. Bd. Region 8, 1951-52. Served with USAAF, 1942-46. Author: (with S. Kadish) The Criminal Law and its Processes, 1962; (with O. Ketcham) The Juvenile Court, 1967; (with W. Adlington) Cases and Materials on Domestic Relations, 1970. Home: Charlottesville, Va. Died Nov. 2, 1980.

PAUL VI, HIS HOLINESS (Montini, Giovanni Battista), Pope; b. Concesio, Brescia, Sept. 26, 1897; s. Giorgio and Giuditta (Algisi) Montini; student at Collegio Arici (Brescia), Lombard Sem., Accademia Ecclesiastica, Gregorian U., Apollinare Juridical Faculty, Rome. Ordained priest Roman Cath. Ch., May 29, 1920; attaché Apostolic Nunciature, Warsaw, Poland, 1923; staff Secretariat of State, Vatican, 1924; nat. ecclesiastical asst. Italian Fedn. Cath. U. Students, 1925; prof. history Pontifical diplomacy, 1931-37; nominated Sostituto della Segreteria di Stato, 1937; accompanied Papal Legate, Cardinal Pacelli, Internat. Eucharistic Congress, Budapest, 1938; apptd. pro-sec. state, 1952; consecrated archbishop Milan, 1954; created cardinal, 1958; elected Pope, June 21, 1963. Address: Rome, Italy. Died Aug. 6, 1978.

PAUW, ADRIAN, educator, civil engr.; b. Laren, The Netherlands, Oct. 3, 1915; s. Johanus Adrianus and Cornelia Adriana (Goethals) P.; came to U.S., 1931, naturalized, 1936; B.S. in Civil Engring, U. Wash., 1937; M.S., Calif. Inst. Tech., 1947, Ph.D., 1952; m. Alice Janet Abbott, May 30, 1941; children—Michael John, Derrick Mark, Peter George, Janet Adriana. Bridge draftsman Wash. Hwy. Dept., 1937-38; jr., then asst. engr. Bur. Reclamation, 1938-42; chief draftsman Consol. Electrodynamics Co., Pasadena, Calif., 1946; grad. teaching asst., research engr. Calif. Inst. Tech., 1946-49; asst. prof. Rice U., 1949-53; mem. faculty U. Mo., 1953-76, prof. civil engring., 1955-76, Robert Lee Tatum prof. engring., 1968-71, chmn. dept., 1963-67, acting dean Coll. Engring., 1967-68; vis. prof. U. Tex., summers 1958, 59; Fulbright lectr. Delft (The Netherlands) Tech. U., 1960-61, Fulbright researcher, vis. prof., 1974-75; structural engring. cons. R.L. Reid, Inc., Houston, from 1950. Served to lt. (j.g.) USNR, 1942-46. Registered profl. engr., Mo., Tex., Calif. Fellow Am. Soc. C.E., Am. Concrete Inst.; mem. Internat. Assn. Shell Structures, Am. Soc. Engring. Edn., Am. Assn. U. Profs., Nat. Soc. Profl. Engrs., Hwy. Research Bd., Betonvereniging, Internat. Assn. for Bridge and Structural Engrs., Am. Soc. Testing and Materials, Sigma Xi, Tau Beta Pi, Chi Epsilon. Home: Columbia, Mo. Died Sept. 25, 1976.

PAWLEY, WILLIAM DOUGLAS, business exec.; b. Florence, S.C., Sept. 7, 1896; s. Edward Porcher and Irene (Wallace) P.; ed. pvt. schs., Gordon Mil. Acad. (Ga.); A.A. (hon.), Gordon Mil. Coll., 1971; D.Aviation Mgmt. (hon.), Embry-Riddle Aeronautical U., Daytona Beach, Fla., 1975; m. Annie-Hahr Dobbs, July 25, 1919 (div.); children—William Douglas, Clifton Dobbs (dec.), Annie-Hahr (Mrs. Hobert Bommer McKay), Irene Wallace (Mrs. C. Jackson Baldwin); m. 2d, Edna Earle Cadenhead, June 30, 1943. Organized, became pres. Compania Nacional Cubana de Aviacion Curtiss, Havana, Cuba, 1928 (merged Pan Am. Airways 1932); exec. v.p. Intercontinent Corp., N.Y., 1933; pres. Intercontinent Corp., China Nat. Aviation Corp., 1933; built 3 aircraft factories in China for Nationalist Govt., 1934-38; organized Am. vol. group Flying Tigers, 1940; organized, became pres. Hindustan Aircraft Mfg. Co., Bangalore, India, 1940; built ammonium-sulfate plant, Travancore, India, 1944; Am. ambassador to Peru, 1945-46, to Brazil, 1946-48; organized, became pres. Autobuses Modernos, S.A., Havana, Cuba, 1949; spl. asst. to sec. state, Washington, 1951, spl. asst. to sec. def., 1951-52; spl. assignment Dept. State, 1954; owner, pres. Miami Beach Ry. Co., Miami Transit Co., South Miami Coach Line (sold to Met. Dade County 1962), Clifton Corp.; owner Talisman Sugar Corp., Belle Glade, Fla., 1963-76; dir. Fla. Nat. Bank & Trust Co. Del. Inter-Am. Conf. Maintenance Continental Peace and Security, Petropolis, Brazil, 1947; del. 9th Internat. Conf. Am. States, Bogotá, Colombia, 1948. Mem. Eisenhower Presdl. Library Com.; mem. sponsor's com. Cuban Families Com. for Liberation Prisoners of War (N.Y.); mem. bd. Greater Miami Philharmonic Soc., U.S. Strategic Inst. Bd. dirs. George C. Marshall Research Found., Lexington, Va.; mem. nat. bd. Boys' Clubs Am.; trustee Miami-Dade Community Coll. Decorated Medal for Merit (U.S.); Air medal (Peru); grand cross Cruzeiro do Sul (Brazil); Orden del Mérito de Duarte, Sánchez y Mella, Gran Cruz (Dominican Republic); Orden del Mérito Agrícola e Industrial, grand cross of Carlos Manuel de Céspedes (Cuba); Order of Brilliant Star with spl. grand cordon (Republic of China). Clubs: Indian Creek Country, Bath, La Gorce Country (Miami Beach); Miami; Metropolitan (Washington); Twenty-Nine, Wings, Marco Polo (N.Y.C.); Cat Cay (Bahamas). Home: Miami Beach, Fla. Died Jan. 7, 1977; interred Woodlawn Meml. Mausoleum, Miami, Fla.

PAXTON, ROBERT, mfg. exec.; b. Edinburgh, Scotland, Jan. 19, 1902; s. Robert Wilson and Annie Gordon (Johnson) P.; brought to U.S., 1904, derivative citizen; E.E., Rensselaer Poly. Inst., 1923, D.Eng., 1958; m. S. Louise Bloom, June 23, 1947. With Gen. Electric Co. since 1923, student engr., 1923, mng. engr., truck panel div., 1929, mng. engr., panel equipment div., 1932, asst. to works mgr. Phila. works, 1940, mgr. Phila. works, 1941, Pittsfield works, 1945, v.p. mfg., N.Y. City, 1950, exec. v.p., dir. 1957-58, pres., 1958-61. Life trustee Rensselaer Poly. Inst. Mem. Am. Inst. E.E., Rensselaer Poly. Inst. Alumni Assn. (pres. 1951-52). Home: Thornwood, N.Y. Died Mar. 16, 1980.

PAYER, ERNST DENIS, architect; b. Vienna, Austria, July 17, 1904; s. Ernst and Friederike (Dubsky) P.; came to U.S., 1936, naturalized, 1939; B.Arch., Acad. of Art, Vienna, 1936; Ph.D. Polit. Sci., U. Vienna, 1927; M.Arch., Harvard U., 1938; m. Dorothy G. Shepherd. Architect, N.Y.C., 1939-46; architect Ernst Payer & Assos., Cleve., 1946-81. Recipient 1st medal housing Ohio Soc. Architects, 1947; 1st medal craftsmanship Cleve. Mus. Art, 1951; 1st award Ohio Soc. Illuminating Engrs., 1966. Mem. Illuminating Engrs. Soc., A.I.A., Am. Soc. Landscape Architects. Clubs: Rowfant, Rotary (Cleve.). Contbr. to books, articles to profl. jours. in U.S. and Europe. Home: Moreland Hills, Ohio. Died Apr. 3, 1981.

PAYNE, BRITTAIN FORD, ophthalmologist; b. Madisonville, Tex., Sept. 9, 1899; s. Charles Francis and Ada Berea (Ford) P.; A.B., Rice Inst., 1922; M.D., Tex. U., 1927; m. Jessemary Donald, Mar. 12, 1932; children—Donald Remsen (dec.), Janet Ford. Interne, John Sealy Hosp., 1928; resident N.Y. Eye and Ear Infirmary, 1929-30, asst. surgeon, 1933, surgeon, dir. clinic, 1939-48, pathologist, 1940-72, cons. surgeon, 1964-72; cons. asst. clin. prof. ophthalmology N.Y. U., 1941; resumed civilian practice, 1946; clin. prof. ophthalmology N.Y. U. Med. Coll., from 1946; cons. ophthalmology Lenox Hill Hosp.; cons. Beekman-Downtown Hosp., St. Clare's Hosp., N.Y. Infirmary; attending ophthalmologist U. Hosp.; Bedell lectr. Wills Eye Hosp., Phila., 1959; past nat. cons. ophthalmology to surgeon gen. USAF. Served with U.S. Army, Officers Tng., 1918; maj., flight surgeon, later lt. col. M.C., USAAF; instr. Sch. Aviation Medicine, 1942-45, cons. PTO, 1945. Decorated Commendation Ribbon, Legion of Merit; recipient Harry Gradle medal, Pan-Am. Assn. Ophthalmology, 1960; Ashbel Smith Distinguished Alumni award U. Tex. Med. Br., 1965. Diplomate Am. Bd. Ophthalmology (past chmn.). Fellow Am. Bd. Preventive Medicine (in aviation medicine), Assn. Mil. Surgeons (hon.), A.C.S., Aero. Med. Assn. (aviation med.); mem. Pan-Am. (pres. 1956-60), N.Y. (past v.p.) med. assns., Assn. Research Ophthalmology (past chmn.), N.Y. Acad. Medicine, Soc. Med. Consultants Armed Forces, A.M.A., Pan-Am. Ophthal. Assn. (pres. 1956-60), Internat. Council Ophthalmology, Cuban Ophthal. Soc. Havana (hon.); Internat. Fedn. Ophthalmologists, others. Clubs: Metropolitan (N.Y.C.); Army and Navy (Washington). Home: Great Barrington, Mass. Died Sept. 19, 1976.

PAYNE, CHESTER H., govt. official; b. London, Ont., Can., Aug. 12, 1884; s. John Lambert and Agnes Oliver (Scott) P.; B.A., McGill Univ., 1906; m. Rita Josephine McLaren, April 30, 1921. Mem. Parliamentary press gallery, 1907-08; pvt. sec. to Rt. Hon. Richard Cartwright, Minister of Trade and Commerce, 1908-11, Rt. Hon. Sir George E. Foster, 1914-21; acting sec. Econ. Conf. of the Allies at Paris, 1916, Peace Conf. Paris, 1919; sec. Canadian Delegation to 1st assembly, League of Nations, Geneva, Switzerland, 1920-25; dir. Comml. Intelligence Service, Department of Trade and Commerce, 1927-32; reapptd., 1940; sec. to Royal Commn. on Financial Arrangements between the Dominion and Maritime Provinces, 1934-35; dep. Minister of Nat. War Service since 1943. Mem. Canadian Militia for 23 yrs. Served overseas in World War I. Recipient: Companion of the Imperial Service Order, 1946; Victory and Gen. Service Medals, 1914-18; Colonial Auxiliary Forces Long Service Medal; Kings Jubilee medal; Coronation medal. Mem. Canadian Geog. Soc., Canadian Inst. of Internat. Affairs, Phi Delta Theta. Mem. United Ch. of Can. Clubs: Rideau Royal Ottawa Golf, Rideau Curling. Home: Ottawa, Ont., Can. *

PAYNE, DONALD HUGHEL, chem. co. exec.; b. Indpls., June 22, 1928; s. Francis William and Mary Louise (Hughel) P.; student Butler U., 1945-47, Purdue U., 1947-49; B.S., U. Mich., M.S., 1951, Ph.D., 1953; m. E. Georgine Vallance, July 22, 1950; children—Beth Payne Ullom, William G., Lee C., Bruce W. Teaching fellow dept. chemistry U. Mich., Ann Arbor, 1949-51, du Pont fellow, 1951-52; successively research chemist, research supr., new product specialist, sr. research supr., planning mgr., research mgr., lab. dir., research and tech. dir. petroleum chems. E.I. du Pont de Nemours Co., Wilmington, Del., 1953-80. Active Boy Scouts

Am., Little League (past pres.); mem. businessmen's adv. com. U.S. Senate. Mem. Am. Chem. Soc., Nat. Petroleum Refiners Assn., Soc. Plastics Industries, AAAS, Am. Petroleum Inst., N.Y. Acad. Sci., Am. Mgmt. Assn., Utes, Sigma Xi, Phi Eta Sigma, Phi Kappa Phi, Phi Lambda Upsilon, Sigma Chi. Republican. Home: Wilmington, Del. Died Aug. 19, 1980.

PAYNE, EDGAR ALWIN, artist; b. Washburn, Mo., Mar. 1, 1882; s. John H. and Ellen (Reed) P.; ed. Art Inst. Chicago; m. Elsie Phillipa Palmer, Nov. 9, 1912. Exhibited in various ann. exhbns., and at San Francisco Expn., 1915. Represented in Neb. Art Assn., Lincoln; Soc. Allied Art, Peoria, Ill.; John Herron Art Inst., Indianapolis; Chicago Municipal Collections; mural decorations; American Theatre, Chicago; Hendricks County (Ill.) Court House; etc. Mem. Alumni Assn. Art Inst. Chicago, Chicago Soc. Artists, Calif. Art Club (Los Angeles), Union Internationale des Arts et des Lettres (Paris). Club: Palette and Chisel. Address: Los Angeles, Calif. *

PAYNE, ERNEST ALEXANDER, clergyman; b. London, Eng., Feb. 19, 1902; s. Alexander W. and Mary C. (Griffiths) P.; B.A., King's Coll., U. London, 1921, B.D., 1925; B. Litt., Mansfield Coll., Oxford U., 1927, M.A., 1944; D.D., St. Andrews U., 1951; student Regent's Park Coll., London, 1922-25, Marburg U. (Germany), 1927-28; LL.D. (hon.), McMaster, 1960; m. Winifred Davies, Oct. 28, 1930; 1 dau., Elizabeth Ann (Mrs. A. F. Prain). Ordained to ministry Baptist Ch., 1928; pastor Bugbrooke Baptist Ch., 1928-32; hdqrs. staff Baptist Missionary Soc., 1932-40; sr. tutor Regent's Park Coll., 1940-51; gen. sec. Baptist Union Great Britain and Ireland, 1951-67; univ. lectr. comparative religion and history modern missions Oxford U., 1947-51. Vice chmn. Central com. World Council Chs., 1954-68; pres. World Council of Chs., 1968; chmn. exec. com. British Council of Chs., 1962-71; moderator Free Ch. Fed. Council, 1958-59; v.p. Bapt. World Alliance, 1965-70. Decorated La Grande Medaille d'Argent de la Ville de Paris; Companion of Honour. Mem. Bapt. Hist. Soc. (pres.). Club: Athenaeum (London). Author: The Free Church Tradition in the Life of England, 1944; The Growth of the World Church, 1956; The Fellowship of Believers, 1944; Biography of Henry Wheeler Robinson, 1946; Biography of J. H. Rushbrooke, 1954; The Baptist Union, 1959; Free Churchmen-Unrepentant and Repentant, 1965; Violence, Non-violence and Human Rights, 1971. Home: Pitsford, Eng. Died Jan. 14, 1980.

PAYNE, FREDERICK G(EORGE), former U.S. senator; b. Lewiston, Maine, July 24, 1904; s. Frederick G. and Nellie G. (Smart) P.; grad. Bentley Sch. Accounting and Finance, Boston; m. Ella Hodgdon, Feb. 27, 1944; children—E. Thomas, Putnam. Mayor, Augusta, Maine, 1935-41; commr. fin. State of Maine, 1940-42; bus. mgr. Waldoboro Garage Co., 1945-49; gov. State of Maine, 1949-52; mem. U.S. Senate, 1953-59; dist. mgt. archtl. and engring. div. Walsh Constrn. Co., S. Portland and Waldoboro, Maine, 1959-61; indsl. cons., ret. Chmn. bd. dirs. Maine div. Am. Cancer Soc., recipient Bronze medal; trustee emeritus Bentley Coll. Accounting and Finance, Boston. Served to lt. col. USAAF, 1942-45. Recipient Silver Beaver award Boy Scouts Am. Mem. Am. Legion (Distinguished Service award). Republican. Baptist. Clubs: Kiwanis, Lions. Home: Waldoboro, Maine. Died June 15, 1978; interred German Protestant Cemetery, Waldoboro, Maine.

PAYNE, MORRIS B., architect; b. Waterford, Conn., Jan. 19, 1885; s. Charles W. and Ellen (Gillen) P.; student Coast Arty. Sch., 1914, Heavy Arty. Sch., Mailly-le-Camp, France, 1918, Army War Coll., 1924, Command and Gen. Staff Sch., 1927; m. Jeannie Crandall Nash., Oct. 14, 1909; 1 son, Harry N. Engring. training with private firm, 1901-06; U.S. Engr. Dept., 1907-12; in pvt. practice of architecture and engring. since 1912; present firm name, Payne & Keefe, New London, Conn.; dir. Am. Ordnance Co., Guardian Thrift Co. Served as maj. of arty., Mexican mobilization, 1916, World War I, 1917; maj. gen. Conn. Nat. Guard, 1924-41. Decorated Purple Heart. Awarded Pierpont Edwards Medal by Grand Lodge Masons of Conn., 1948. Mem. Conn. Soc. C.E. Mason (past grand master in Conn.). Clubs: Army and Navy (Washington, D.C.); Thames (New London, Conn.). Home: New London, Conn. *

PAYTON, RUSSELL TALBOT, lawyer; b. Montreal, Que., Can., Feb. 2, 1910; s. William Talbot and Charlotte (Whitney) P.; B.A., McGill U., 1932; postgrad. Osgoode Hall, 1933-35; m. Evlyn Beatrice Eaton, June 12, 1943; children—Evlyn Anne, Flora Constance, John Russell. Called to bar, Ont., 1935; created king's counsel, 1951; practiced in Toronto, 1935-76; asso. Alexander Stark, 1935-40; mem. firm Cassels, Brock & Kelly, 1940-42, 46-53; mem. firm Daly, Thistle, Judson & Harvey 1954-58; partner Payton, Biggs & Graham, 1958-76; mem. com. of bench and bar New Met. Toronto Ct. House, 1959-68. Past pres. Toronto YMCA, Canadian Opera Co. Trustee Canadian Opera Found., Animal Welfare Found. Can.; v.p., bd. govs. Stratford Festival. Served to maj. Canadian Army, 1942-45. Mem. Canadian Bar Assn. (past mem. council), Medico-Legal Soc. Toronto (past mem. council), County of York Law Assn. (past pres., trustee), McGill Soc. Toronto (past pres.), Delta Kappa Epsilon. Mem. United Ch. Mason. Clubs: University (past pres.) Toronto Golf, Badminton and Racquet (Toronto); Muskoka (Ont.) Lakes Golf and Country. Home: Toronto, Ont., Can. Died Feb. 5, 1976.

PEAIRS, LEONARD MARION (PERS), entomologist; b. Lawrence, Kan., June 5, 1886; s. Chalmers Addison and Susan (Banta) P.; B.S., Kan. State Agrl. Coll., 1905, M.S., 1907; student Cornell 1909; Ph.D., U. Chicago, 1925. m. Edith Pennington, June 15, 1915; children—Chalmers Addison, Jr., Dorothea Janet (Mrs. G. W. Monk). Grad. asst. Kan. State Coll., 1905-07, U. Ill., 1907-08; asst. prof. entomology U. Md., 1908-10, U. Kan., 1910-12; prof. entomology U. W.Va., entomologist W.Va. Agrl. Expt. Sta., 1912-52, ret. June 1952. Fellow A.A.A.S., Entomol. Soc. Am.; mem. Am. Assn. Econ. Entomologists (life mem.; exec. com. 1942-52), Sigma Xi, Alpha Zeta, Phi Kappa Phi. Author: School Entomology, 1917; Insect Pests Farm Garden and Orchard, 1921, 31, 41; Relation of Temperature to Insect Development, 1927. Editor Jour. Econ. Entomology since 1939. Home: Morgantown W.Va. *

PEARCY, GEORGE ETZEL, educator, geographer; b. Greencastle, Ind., May 2, 1905; s. George W. and Dora (Hodge) P.; B.E., U. Calif. at Los Angeles, 1930; M.A., Clark U., 1932, Ph.D., 1940; m. Florence E. Barili, Sept. 23, 1937. Asst. prof. U. Ala., 1939-42; instr. supervision Randolph Field, USAAF, 1942-43; geographer Trans World Airlines, N.Y.C., Kansas City, Washington, 1943-50, Dept. State, Thailand, India, U.K. and France, 1950-57, Washington, 1957-69; prof., chmn. dept. geography Cal. State Coll., Los Angeles, 1969-73. Mem. Assn. Am. Geographers (past mem. council). Author: World Political Geography, 1957; West Indian Scene, 1965; (with Louis Peltier) Military Geography, 1966; (with E. A. Stoneman) Handbook of New Nations, 1968; (with George P. Stevens) An Introduction to Geography, 1970; A 38-State U.S.A., 1973; Supercounties U.S.A., 1976; World Sovereignty, 1977. Home: Long Beach, Calif. Died June 28, 1980.

PEARL, RICHARD MAXWELL, geologist, educator; b. N.Y.C., May 4, 1913; s. Morse and Etta (Stocker) P.; B.A., U. Colo., 1939, M.A., 1940; A.M., Harvard U., 1946; m. Mignon Wardell, June 13, 1941. Instr. geology U. Colo., 1940; engaged in mineral supply bus., Denver, 1941; process engr. du Pont Co., Denver, 1941-42; geologist Shell Oil Co., Tulsa, 1944; mem. faculty Colo. Coll., Colorado Springs, 1946-80, prof., 1962-80, curator minerals, 1977-80; pub., editor-in-chief Earth Sci. mag., 1973-80, Minerals mag., Mineralogy mag., Mineral Products and Resources mag., 1977-80, Gem Studies mag., Cadillac mag., Zyzzogeton mag., 1978-80. Vis. prof. Phoenix Coll., Denver U., Pueblo Coll.; prof. extension div. U. Colo.; geol. cons. Colo. Wonderland, Walt Disney Prodns., McGraw-Hill Book Co., Aero. Library, USAF Acad.; pres. Mineral Parks of Colo.; adviser mineralogy and geology Denver Pub. Library; mem. geology adv. panel U. Tex. at Dallas; pub. Mineral Book Co., Maxwell Pub. Co. Seigneur, May Island, Gulf Islands, Can. Bd. advs. Detroit Concert Band. Served with U.S. Army, 1942-44. Am. Fedn. Mineral Socs. scholar, 1964. Fellow Gemological Assn. Gt. Britain and Ireland (with distinction), A.A.A.S., Meteoritical Soc., Am. Geog. Soc., Geol. Soc. Am., Mineral. Soc. Am., Gemological Assn. Australia (hon. v.p.); mem. Gemological Inst. Am. (cert.), Rocky Mountain Fedn. Mineral. Socs. (founder), Am. Fedn. Mineral Socs. (co-founder), Colo. Mineral Soc. (co-founder), Colo. Sci. Soc. (hon.). Republican. Unitarian. Clubs: Rocky Mountain Harvard, Explorers (fellow), Winter Night, Torch, Kiwanis. Author numerous books, syndicated newspaper columns, jour. and mag. articles. Editor: Mineral Minutes. Contbr. to several encys., anthologies. Discoverer 3 Colo. minerals. Home: Colorado Springs, Colo. Died Nov. 28, 1980.

PEARRE, SIFFORD (PARRE), business exec.; b. Balt., July 14, 1884; s. Aubrey and Anne Josephine (Sifford) P.; A.B., Johns Hopkins, 1904; m. Angelica Wirt Yonge, Sept. 9, 1930; children—Letitia Breckinridge (Mrs. Richard Eaton Burwell), Sifford, Clerk Mercantile Trust Company, Baltimore, 1906-13; sec.-treas. New Amsterdam Casualty Company 1913—, also dir., mem. exec. com.; pres., dir., mem. exec. com. Ins. Shares Certificates, Inc.; sec.-treas., dir. Am. Indemnity Co.; dir., mem. exec. com. Roland Park Co., Indsl. Bldg. Co., Syracuse Transit Co.; dir. Northwood Shopping Center, Incorporated; member board of trustees U.S. Casualty Co. Trustee Church Home and Hosp. Served as lt. USN, World War I. Mem. Delta Phi. Democrat. Episcopalian. Clubs: Gibson Island (Md.), Mchts.; Elkridge Kennels (Balt.); Green Spring Valley Hunt; Chester Yacht (N.S.). Home: Balt.; (summer) Chester, N.S., Can. *

PEARSON, IRVING FREDERICK, educator; b. Rockford, Ill., Jan. 1, 1897; s. Frank Edward and Mary Charlotte (Peterson) P.; student No. Ill. State Tchrs. Coll., 1915-17; B.S., U. Ill., 1922; M.S., Northwestern U., 1930; L.H.D., Ill. Coll., 1955; m. Erma Elizabeth Cable, Aug. 18, 1923; children—Kenneth Elmer, Irving Franklin, Donald Raymond. Prin., Cortland (Ill.) Pub. Schs., 1917-18; prin. Harlem Consol. Schs., Rockford, 1918-20, supt., 1922-27; supt. schs., Winnebago County, Ill., 1927-38; exec. sec. Ill. Edn. Assn., 1938-63; founder Horace Mann Ins. Cos. Edn. cons. U.S. State Dept., Germany, 1952. Mem. N.E.A. (exec. com., chmn. legislative commn. 1954-60), World Confedn. Orgns. Teaching Profession (past U.S. del., exec. com.), Phi Delta Kappa, Alpha Kappa Lambda, Phi Sigma Sigma. Republican. Lutheran. Author: (with Richard G. Browne) The Illinois Citizen, 1939; (with George Propeck) The History of the Illinois Education Association, 1961; Three Score Ten and More, 1971; also articles in ednl. publs. Home: Rockford, Ill. Deceased.

PEARSON, LE ROY (PER'S'N), ex-dir. selec. service Mich.; b. Urban, Mich., Oct. 12, 1884; s. Richard and Addie M. (Pope) P.; ed. Sandusky (Mich.) High Sch. and Dean Bus. Coll., Port Huron, Mich.; grad. Army Gen. Staff Coll., Langres, France, 1919, Army War Coll., Washington, D.C., 1926; m. Bertha G. Conroy, July 18, 1906; 1 son, Charles B. (officer U.S. Army). In real estate and insurance business, 1903-16; entered army service as officer Mich. Nat. Guard for duty on Mexican border; served with 32d Div., A.E.F., participating in Aisne-Marne, Oise-Aisne and Meuse-Argonne offensives, and with 7th Army Corps in Germany, 1919; commd. major, Mich. Nat. Guard, 1919, and served as Q.M. Gen. of Mich., 1919-43; U.S. property and disbursing officer for Mich., and chief of staff 32d Div., 1919-40; promoted brig. gen., 1943; adjutant gen. of Mich. and state dir. selective service, 1943-49. Retired. Dec. Medal for Merit, Silver Star (U.S.), Croix de Guerre (France). Mem. Nat. Guard Assn. of U.S. (mem. policy com.), Adjutants Gen. Assn. of U.S. Elk. Club: Lansing (Mich.) Rotary. Assisted in preparation of History of 32d Division. Home: Lansing, Mich. *

PECK, FRANCIS WINFRED, agrl. economist; b. St. Paul, Minn., May 20, 1885; s. Uri A. and Emma (Anderson) P.; B.S., Coll. of Agr., U. of Minn., 1912, M.S., 1917; m. Hazel Dell Blanchard, Nov. 7, 1912; children—Elizabeth Gail, Shirley Jane. Prof. U. of Minn., cost accounting investigations, 1912-18, dir. of agrl. extension, 1921-33; with Bur. Agrl. Economics, U.S. Dept. Agr., 1919-21; became cooperative bank commr. of U.S. Farm Credit Adminstrn., 1933; again dir. agrl. extension div., U. of Minn.; pres. Federal Land Bank, St. Paul, Minn., Feb. 1938-Oct. 1945; Mng. Dir. Farm Foundation since Oct. 1945. Mem. Alpha Zeta, Gamma Sigma Delta, Sigma Xi. Methodist. Club: Union League. Home: Chicago, Ill. *

PECK, THEODORA AGNES, author; b. Burlington, Vt., Oct. 25, 1882; d. Theodore S. and Agnes Louisa (Leslie) P.; grad. Burlington High Sch., 1900; student in U of Vt., 1901-02. Mem. Green Mountain Chapter D.A.R.; hon. mem. Vt. Soc. Daughters of 1812, and mem. No. 1, 2d class, Medal of Honor Legion of U.S.; hon. mem. Soc. Army of the Potomac. Catholic. Author: Hester of the Grants, 1905; The Sword of Dundee, 1908; White Dawn, 1914. Address: Burlington, Vt. *

PECKHAM, LAWTON PARKER GREENMAN, educator; b. Middletown, R.I., June 28, 1904; s. Reuben and Adelaide M. (Greenman) P.; Ph.B., Brown U., 1927, M.A., 1928; Ph.D., Princeton, 1931; m. Katharine H. Austin, Aug. 20, 1938; children—Katharine H., Mary A. Tchr. French, Brown U., 1931-40, asst. prof., 1936-40; asso. prof. French, U. Ill., 1940-46; faculty Columbia, 1946-71, prof. French, 1952-71, prof. emeritus, 1971-79, chmn. dept., 1963-68, dean grad. faculties, 1958-61. Decorated chevalier Legion d'Honneur, 1959. Mem. Modern Lang. Assn., Medieval Acad. Am., Linguistic Soc. Am. Home: Middletown, R.I. Died Nov. 9, 1979; buried in Middletown.

PECKWORTH, HOWARD FARON, civil engr.; b. Jersey City, July 25, 1901; s. Charles Halsey and Sallie Hann (Faron) P.; student Cornell U., 1919-22; B.S., Princeton, 1926; m. Martha Fessenden Dana, Sept. 11, 1928 (dec. Jan. 1973); children—Dana, Alice Wing (Mrs. Philip D. Leiserson), Margaret (Mrs. Alan Dean Parsons); m. 2d, Helen Schoneman Hansen, Dec. 22, 1974. Engr. charge constrn. 8th Av. Subway, N.Y.C., 1926-34; field engr. constrn. Frederick Snare Corp., on Tygart River Reservoir Dam, Grafton, W.Va., 1934-36; resident engr. charge constrn. Inland dam Birmingham (Ala.) Indsl. Water Supply Commn., 1936-38; constrn. plant designer Pacific Constructors, Inc., on Shasta Dam in No. Cal., 1938-39; sr. engr. Santee-Cooper Nav. and Hydroelectric Project, S.C., 1939-41; editor Civil Engring., Am. Soc. C.E., 1941-42, asst. to sec., 1942-45; cons. Am. Concrete Pipe Assn., Am. Concrete Pressure Pipe Assn., U.S. Steel Corp., several other large U.S. firms and various pipe mfrs. Eng., France, Australia, Japan. Cons. drainage problems Irish Govt., 1951. Mem. Northeastern Ill. Met. Area Planning Commn., 1957-65; exec. com. U.S. Com. on Internat. Commn. Irrigation and Drainage, 1961-65; mem. Washington Awards Commn., 1950-52; patron mem. Save-the-Redwoods League. Trustee Fathers Assn. Lawrenceville Sch., 1947-48. Registered profl. engr., land surveyor, N.Y. Fellow Am. Soc. for Testing Materials (award of merit 1962); mem. Am. Soc. C.E. (dir. 1956-60), Am. Water Works Assn., Princeton Engring. Assn. (past mem. exec. com.), Am. Concrete Inst., Internat. Congress Precast Concrete Industries (dir. 1962-67), Am. Orinthologist Union, Chi Epsilon. Clubs: Bohemian (San Francisco); Cosmos (Washington); Explorers (N.Y.C.); Princeton Tower; Town and Coll. (Brunswick, Maine). Author: The Engineer and Collective Bargaining, 1944; Survey of Concrete Pipe Sewers, 1948; Concrete Pipe Design Manual, 1950; Loads on Underground Concrete Conduits, 1950; The Art of Chicken Cookery, 1956; Concrete Pipe Handbook (rev. edit), 1965; Concrete Pipe Field Manual, 1960; Concrete Pipe for Irrigation and Drainage, 1961; Design Data For Reinforced Concrete Pipe to Resist External Leadings, 1966. Home: Richmond, Maine. *

PEDTKE, DANIEL HERMAN, musician, educator; b. Chgo., Jan. 6, 1906; s. Herman and Theckla (Prince) P.; Mus. B., DePaul U., 1935; m. Helen Melinski, Sept. 2, 1937; children—Dorothy, William, Mary, Theresa, Catherine, Robert, Daniel. Appeared in organ and piano concerts, from 1925; piano soloist Orch. Hall, Chgo., 1927; organist, choir dir., 1924-32; head dept. music Coll. of St. Teresa, Winona, Minn., 1932; head dept. music U. Notre Dame 1937-55, prof. emeritus, 1973-76; organist, choir dir. St. Patrick's Ch., South Bend, Ind.; dir. Notre Dame Glee Club, 1938-73. Recipient Distinguished Alumnus award DePaul U., 1963. Fellow Am. Guild Organists; mem. Assn. U. Profs., Nat. Cath. Music Educators Assn. Ind. (mem. adv. bd.) Roman Catholic. Author: (textbook) Theory of Modulation. Home: South Bend, Ind. Died Dec. 10, 1976; buried Cedar Grove Cemetery, Notre Dame, Ind.

PEEBLES, BERNARD MANN, educator; b. Norfolk, Va., Jan. 1, 1906; s. John Kevan and Sallie (Mann) P.; student Hampden-Sydney Coll., 1921-22; B.A., U. Va., 1926; A.M., Harvard, 1928, Ph.D., 1940; postgrad. (fellow in classical studies) Am. Acad. in Rome, 1932-34; m. Cary Christian Taliaferro, Mar. 21, 1942; children—Elisabeth Mann (Mrs. Michael Brownstein), Lucien Taliaferro. Instr., Schs. Greek and Latin, U. Va., 1928-29; instr. dept. classics Fordham U., 1934-35; instr., tutor dept. classics Harvard, 1937-39; asst. prof. Fordham U., 1939-41; tutor St. John's Coll., Annapolis, Md., 1941-42, 45-48; asso. prof. dept. Greek and Latin, Cath. U. Am., 1948-54, prof., 1954-71, emeritus, 1971-76, sr. lectr., 1971-72, chmn. dept., 1962-70. Mem. Cath. Commn. for Intellectual and Cultural Affairs, 1950-70. Served with AUS, 1942-45; ETO. Decorated Bronze Star; Brit. Empire medal. Mem. Am. Philol. Assn. (dir. 1967-70), Mediaeval Acad. Am., Archaeol. Inst. Am., Renaissance Soc. Am. (mem. council 1971-72), Classical Assn. Atlantic States, Assn. internationale d'études patristiques, N. Am. Patristic Soc. Author: The Poet Prudentius, 1951; also numerous articles and revs. in patristics, medieval Latin lit., Latin bibl. studies, Latin palaeography, Roman topography. Co-editor: Servius: Editio Harvardiana, vol. II, 1946; Traditio, 1952-73, emeritus, 1973-76; editor The Fathers of the Church: A New Translation, 1946-68, editorial dir., 1968-75. Home: Washington, D.C. Died Nov. 23, 1976.

PEEBLES, DICK, newspaper editor; b. Oil City, Pa., July 4, 1918; s. Herbert Lester and Sarah (Hagen) P.; student pub. schs.; m. Mary Theresa Holman, Nov. 7, 1949; children—Michael, Timothy. With Erie Dispatch-Herald, 1936-40, Sharon (Pa.) Herald, 1940-42, San Antonio Express, 1946-58; sports editor Houston Chronicle, 1958-80. Served with U.S. Army, 1942-46. Mem. Baseball Writers Assn. Am., Football Writers Assn. Am., Golf Writers Assn. Am., Delta Sigma Chi. Roman Catholic. Home: Houston, Tex. Died June 10, 1980.

PEEBLES, FRED NEAL, chem. engr., univ. dean; b Paris, Tenn., Apr. 4, 1920; s. Fred Norman and Pollye (Paschall) P.; B.S. in Chem. Engring., U. Tenn., also M.S., Ph.D. in Chem. Engring.; m. Elenor Carter, Aug. 22, 1942; children—Fred Neal, Mary, Mark, Kate. Instr. chem. engring. U. Tenn., Knoxville, 1947-50, asst. prof., 1950-54, asso. prof., 1954-57, prof., 1960-63, head engring. mechanics dept., 1963-68, dean engring., 1968-80; asst. sect. chief Oak Ridge Nat. Lab., 1957-60. Served with U.S. Army, 1945-46. Registered profl. engr. Recipient Distinguished Service Professorship award U. Tenn. Mem. Am. Inst. Chem. Engrs., Knoxville Tech. Soc. (past pres.), Sigma Xi, Phi Kappa Phi, Tau Beta Pi, Omicron Delta Kappa. Contbr. articles on hydrodynamics and chem. engring. to profl. jours. Home: Knoxville, Tenn. Died Apr. 21, 1980; buried Highland Meml. Cemetery, Knoxville.

PEEBLES, LEIGHTON H., govt. official; b. Petersburg, Va., Aug. 22, 1883; son William L. and Annie L. (Bradbury) P.; grad. Union Coll., 1906; m. Anna Erwina Ibels, May 30, 1916; children—Emilie Virginia, Leighton H. Asst. engr. to constrn. supervisor, J. G. White Engring. Co., N.Y. City, 1907-18; chief engr. and partner, Frazar & Co., internat. trade, N.Y. City, 1918-24; v.p. and treas. Parker, Peebles & Co., internat. trade N.Y. City, 1924-31; chief lumber div., Bur. Fgn. and Domestic Commerce, 1931-33; dep. and div. adminstr. Nat. Recovery Adminstrn., 1933-36; supervising utilities analyst, Security and Exchange Commn., 1937-41; prin. business specialist, fuel sect., Office Price Adminstrn. and Civilian Supply, July-Oct. 1941; chief Plumbing and Heating Br., Office Prodn. Management, Oct. 1941-Jan. 1942; dir. communications div. WPB, Jan. 1942-Oct. 1945; vice pres. Internat. Standard Electric Co., Nov. 1945-Jan. 1948; cons. to chmn. Nat. Security Resources Bd., 1948-51; consultant communications equipment division National Production Authority since 1951. Member Sigma Phi, Sigma Xi. Methodist. Author: Articles on depreciation of public utilities. Home: Chevy Chase, Md. *

PEEL, ROY VICTOR, univ. prof.; b. Des Moines, Ia., July 26, 1896; s. Victor R. and Hannah (Anderson) P.; A.B., Augustana Coll., Ill., 1920, LL.D., 1950; A.M., U. Chgo., 1923, Ph.D., 1927; m. Esther Peterson, Aug. 18, 1927; children—Sonya Frances, Peter Robert. Instr., Trinity College, Round Rock, Tex., 1920-21, college in Minn., 1921-22; instr. New York U., 1924-25, asst. prof., 1927-34, asso. prof., 1934-39, dir. research in pub. adminstrn., 1934; prof. govt., dir. Inst. Politics, Ind. U., 1939-53; dir. inst. govt., chmn. dept. polit. sci. U. Utah, 1953-61; prof. polit. sci., chmn. social sci. div. Calif. Luth. Coll., 1961-63; prof. San Fernando Valley State Coll. (name now Calif. State U., Northridge), from 1963; dir. Bur. Census, 1950-52; instr. U. Rochester, 1926-27; field research Inst. Public Adminstrn., Scandinavian countries, 1934-36; cons. Pres. Roosevelt, Pres. Truman, Gov. Adlai Stevenson, numerous others. Served as 2d lt., Air Service, U.S. Army, 1918-19; civilian service U.S. Govt., 1942-46; OSS, 1942-47; chief U.S.I.S., Copenhagen, 1945; mem. U.S. del. ILO Conf., Geneva, 1962; U.S. rep. Population Commn. UN, 1953; vis. prof. Calif. State U., Los Angeles, 1967-68. Chairman city fusion party, N.Y. City, 1934; member city plan commn., Bloomington, 1947-50. Mem. Am. Polit. Sci. Assn., Am. Soc. Pub. Adminstrn., Western Polit. Sci. Assn. (council), Western Government Research Assn. Lutheran. Club: Nat. Capitol Democratic. Author: (with T. C. Donnelly) The 1928 Campaign, 1931; (with T. C. Donnelly) The 1932 Campaign, 1935; Political Clubs of New York City, 1935; (with J. C. Roucek) Introduction to Politics, 1941; Roosevelt Talar, 1943; Plunkitt of Tammany Hall, 1938; State Government Today, 1948; contbr.: Tomorrow in the Making, 1939; Modern World Politics, 1953; editor: Better City Government, 1938; The Ombudsman, or Citizen's Defendor, 1968; contbr. articles to profl. jours. Home: Northridge, Calif. Died Aug. 31, 1978.

PEEPLES, WILLIAM GODFREY, newspaperman; b. Savannah, Ga., Sept. 26, 1924; s. Harold Gerarden and Marie (Godfrey) P.; student Emory U.; m. Edith Rule, Feb. 25, 1955; children—William Rule, Ann Lawton, Mrs. Sandra Pickrell. Editor, Hampton County (S.C.) Democrat, 1950-51; with A.P., 1951-52, Macon (Ga.) News, 1952-53; mem. news staff Louisville Times, 1953-60; asso. editor Louisville Courier-Jour., 1960-70, Lexington (Ky.) Herald Leader, 1973-74; asst. mng. editor, columnist Greenville (S.C.) News, 1974-76. Lectr., Bellarmine Coll., 1973. Mem. Nat. Conf. Editorial Writers. Sigma Delta Chi. Democrat. Author mag. articles. Home: Taylors, S.C. Died Sept. 6, 1976.

PEER, LYNDON ARTHUR, surgeon; b. Asbury Park, N.J., Dec. 12, 1898; s. Arthur M. and Madge (Clow) P.; A.B., Cornell, 1922, M.D., 1925; m. Ruth Banghart, Dec. 16, 1929; children—Lyndon Arthur (dec.), Elizabeth. Intern, New Haven Hosp., 1925-27; resident head surgery Newark Eye and Ear Infirmary, 1928; plastic surgeon N.Y. Post Grad. Hosp., 1929-31; pvt. practice as specialist, Newark, 1930-72; cons. plastic surgery St. Alban, Newark City, St. Barnabas hosps., Newark Eye and Ear Infirmary, St. Michaels, Babies, Orange Meml., East Orange Gen., Muhlenberg, Plainfield, Morristown Meml., Mountainside, Irvington Gen., N.J. Orthopedic, Montclair Community hosps.; med. coordinator, dir. research dept. St. Barnabas Rehab. Center, Newark, pres. med. staff, 1956-60, trustee, from 1958, hon. life trustee St. Barnabas Med. Center, Livingston, N.J., 1973-77; former prof. plastic and reconstrn. surgery Seton Hall Med. Coll. Recipient Edward J. Ill. award N.J. Acad. Medicine, 1961. Founder mem. Am. Bd. Plastic Surgery. Fellow A.C.S., Am. Assn. Plastic Surgeons (hon., pres. 1959); mem. Am. Soc. Plastic and Reconstructive Surgery (co-editor Jour. 1946-65, pres. 1942-44, spl. hon. citation 1971), A.M.A., N.Y. Acad. Sci., N.Y. Soc. Plastic Reconstructive Surgery (1st pres. 1960-61), N.Y. Acad. Medicine, N.J. Soc. Surgeons, N.J. Soc. Plastic and Reconstructive Surgeons. Republican. Presbyn. Clubs: Univ. (N.Y.C.); Rock Spring Country (West Orange). Author: Transplantation of Tissues, 1955, vol. II 1959. Former corr. editor Transplantation Bull.; former Am. editor Brit. Plastic Jour. Contbr. chpts. to books. Specialist in various operations in plastic surgery including reconstrn. of ear, grafts to fill skull depression; inventor ear mold, diced cartilage grafts; inventor Vitalium ear mold which was on display Smithsonian Instn. Home: Boca Raton, Fla. Died Oct. 8, 1977.

PEER, SHERMAN, lawyer; b. East Palmyra, N.Y., Sept. 11, 1882; s. Frank Sherman and Harriet (Reeves) P.; LL.B., Cornell U., 1906; student New Coll., Oxford U., Eng., 1906-07; m. Eleanor Sherman, 1921; children—George S., Emily, Mary Alice. Admitted to N.Y. bar, practiced in Ithaca, N.Y., 1907—; member board directors Nat. Cash Register Company, Dayton, Ohio; former prof. law Cornell University. Trustee of Cornell University. Served as capt., 79th Div., advancing to major, inf., U.S. Army, 1918. Trustee of the Cornell U. Research Found.; provost Cornell Univ. pro tem, 1943. Mem. Oxford Soc. (Cornell), Kappa Alpha. Republican. Presbyterian. Club: University (New York). Home: Sarasota, Fla. *

PEGRUM, REGINALD HERBERT, geologist; b. Romford, Eng., Dec. 17, 1899; s. Frank and Elizabeth M. (Keen) P.; B.Sc., U. Alta. (Can.), 1923; Ph.D., Princeton, 1927; m. M. Frieda Rapp, Mar. 28, 1929; children—Reginald F., Robert L. (dec.), Robert B. Came to U.S., 1924, naturalized, 1937. Mem. Alta. Geol. Survey, 1923, Canadian Geol. Survey, 1924-27; curator geology Buffalo Mus. Sci., 1927-29; chmn. dept. geology U. Buffalo, 1927-48, chmn. dept. geol. scis., 1948-65, prof., 1938-70, prof. emeritus, 1970-76; mem. Coop. Survey of Lake Erie, 1928; cons. geologist Labrador Mining and Exploration Corp., 1936. Served as ensign USCGR, 1943-46. Mem. Western N.Y. Weather Soc. (pres. 1951), Sigma Xi. Club: Buffalo Canoe (dir. 1950-54). Home: Buffalo, N.Y. Died July 6, 1976.

PEI, MARIO ANDREW, educator, linguist; b. Rome, Italy, Feb. 16, 1901; s. Francesco and Luisa (Ferri) P.; came to U.S., 1908, naturalized, 1925; A.B. magna cum laude, Coll. City N.Y., 1925; Ph.D., Columbia, 1932; L.H.D., Fort Lauderdale U., 1973; m. Pearl Glover, June 25, 1924. Pvt. tutor, 1920-21; instr. Regis High Sch., N.Y.C., 1921-22, Franklin Sch., N.Y.C., 1922-23, Coll. City N.Y., also Townsend Harris High Sch., N.Y.C., 1923-37; mem. faculty Columbia, 1937-70, prof. romance philology, 1952-70; ret. Linguistic cons. Army Lang. Sch., 1960; vis. Andrew Mellon prof. romance langs. U. Pitts., 1962-63; vis. prof. romance philology Rutgers U., 1963-64; vis. prof. English and linguistics Seton Hall U., 1970-72; vis. lectr. Brigham Young U., 1970, 72; NATO lectr. univs. Lisbon and Coimbra (Portugal), 1961. Mem. N.Y. County Grand Jury, 1944-62. Recipient Peace Treaty Contest award Ziff-Davis Co., 1945; George Washington Honor medal Freedom Found., 1957; Cavaliere ufficiale Order Merit Italian Republic, 1958; Oscar award for lit. Unico Nat., 1959; David McKay Humanities award Brigham Young U., 1970. Mem. Modern Lang. Assn., Am. Assn. Tchrs. French, Am. Assn. Tchrs. Spanish, Am. Assn. Tchrs. Italian, Internat. Linguistic Assn., Am. Soc. Geolinguistics, Phi Beta Kappa. Roman Catholic. Author: The Language of the Eighth-Century Texts in Northern France, 1932; The World's Chief Languages 1943; The American Road to Peace, 1945; The Story of Language, 1949; The Story of English, 1953; The Italian Language, 2d edit., 1955; All About Language, 1954; French Precursors of the Chanson de Roland, 1948; Swords of Anjou, 1953; (with R. Gaynor) Dictionary of Linguistics, 1953; Sparrows of Paris, 1958; The Consumers Manifesto, 1960; Talking Your Way Around the World, 1961; Language for Everybody, 1958; One Language for the World, 1958; Getting Along in (French, Spanish, German, Italian, Portuguese, Russian), 1957-59; The Families of Words, 1962; Voices of Man, 1962; The Book of Place Names, 1959; Our Names, 1960; Invitation to Linguistics, 1965; Glossary of Linguistic Terminology, 1966; The American Heritage, 1965; How to Learn Languages, 1966; The Many Hues of English, 1967; Language Today, 1967; The Story of the English Language, 1967; What's in a Word? 1968; The America We Lost, 1968; Words in Sheep's Clothing, 1969; Tales of the Natural and Supernatural, 1971; Double Speak in America, 1973; Dictionary of Foreign Terms, 1974; The Story of Latin and the Romance Languages, 1976; Empire Without End, 1976. Home: Glen Ridge, N.J. Died Mar. 2, 1978.

PELLETTIERI, GIUSEPPE MARIO, M.D., surgeon; b. Laurenzana, Italy, Feb 23, 1882; s. Pasquale and Anna (Nigro) P.; came to U.S., 1897; prep. edn. in Italy; registered pharmacist; M.D., Ill. Med. Coll. 1909. In drug business in Chicago since 1904; practiced medicine in St. Louis since 1915; officer Vol. Med. Corps. at St. Louis during World War. Mem. A.M.A., Mo. Med. Soc., St. Louis Med. Soc.; founder St. Louis br. Dante Alighieri Soc.; orator St. Louis Lodge, Sons of Italy in America. Republican. Odd Fellow, K.P. Writer of odes, canzoni and dramas (in Italian); contbr. to Italian newspapers in America and Italy. Widely known as speaker on subjects pertaining to Italy. Chmn. Italian Red Cross for State of Mo.; organizer Com. of Narcotic Edn., of St. Louis. Spl. corr. of several Italian newspapers. Home: St. Louis, Mo. *

PELOUBET, MAURICE EDOUARD, certified pub. accountant; b. Chgo., Jan. 7, 1892; s. Louis Gervais and Louise (Wardell) P.; student N.Y. U., 1912-14; m. Ellen Wilhelmina Ayres, May 25, 1918; 1 dau., Anna Louise (Mrs. Albert Samu); m. 2d, Louise Pedlow, July 3, 1943; 1 stepdau., Lovedy Louise (Mrs. Barbatelli). Accountant, Price, Waterhouse & Co., N.Y.C., 1911-14, London, 1914-19; with Pogson, Peloubet & Co., N.Y.C., 1919-63, partner, 1921-63; partner Price

Waterhouse & Co., 1963-64; spl. lectr. Columbia, Harvard, N.Y. U., Temple U., Wheaton Coll., Rutgers. Exec. com. 2d Internat. Congress on Accounting, N.Y.C., 1929, del. 3d Congress, London, 1933. Cons., Office Prodn. Mgmt., W.P.B., 1941-42, Navy Dept., 1942-43, subsidiaries R.F.C., 1942-44; in charge investigation accounting of civilian supplies, currency in Europe, Combined Chiefs of Staff, 1945; mem. budget and fiscal task force Hoover Commn. C.P.A., N.Y., N.J., Tex. Del. Inter-Am. Accounting Confs., 1952, 54, 57-62. Mem. Am. Inst. Accountants (chmn. bd. examiners 1933-39, v.p. 1940-41, treas., mem. exec. com. 1944-45), N.J. (pres. 1928-29), N.Y. State (bd. dirs. 1933-39, pres. 1950) socs. C.P.A.'s, Nat. Assn. Accountants, Am. Accounting Assn., Mining and Metall. Soc. Am., Am. Inst. Mining Metall. and Petroleum Engrs., Am. Arbitration Assn. (mem. bd. dirs.), Poetry Soc. Am., Beta Alpha Psi, Alpha Kappa Psi. Clubs: Harbor View, Downtown Athletic (N.Y.C.); Accountants of America. Author: Audit Working Papers, Their Function, Preparation and Content, 1937; Ballads, Songs and Snatches, 1938; Explanation of Principles for Determination of Costs under Government Contracts (with Eric A. Camman), 1942; The Financial Executive and the New Accounting, 1967. Cons. editor: Accountant's Handbook, 1943. Contbr. chpts. to textbooks in field; articles to profl. publs. Home: Cape May, N.J. Died June 1, 1976.

PELTASON, PAUL EVANS, investment banker; b. St. Louis, May 28, 1898; s. Charles and Lena (Evans) P.; A.B., U. Mo., 1919; m. Ruth Mayer, June 15, 1921; children—Ellen (Mrs. Harry Steinbaum), Paul Evans, Charles Mayer. Formerly sr. partner Peltason, Tennenbaum Co., St. Louis, from 1932; chmn. bd., dir. Signal Hill Telecasting Corp., 1952-65. Mem. Phi Beta Kappa. Club: Westwood Country (past pres.). Home: Clayton, Mo. Died Aug. 13, 1974.

PELZER, KARL JOSEF, educator; b. Oberpleis, Germany, Feb. 23, 1909; s. Friedrich and Christine (Broel) P.; Ph.D., U. Bonn, Germany, 1935; m. Elizabeth A. Clark, Mar. 21, 1936; children—Christine K., Ingrid D. Came to U.S., 1935, naturalized, 1940. Research asst. Council Fgn. Relations, 1936-37, Inst. Pacific Relations, 1938-39; research asso. Johns Hopkins, 1939-41, asso. geography, 1942-44; sr. regional specialist OWI, 1944-45; agrl. economist Office Fgn. Agrl. Relations, Dept. Agr., 1945-47; asso. prof. of geography Yale, 1947-52, prof., 1952-77, chmn. dept. geography, dir. Southeast Asia Studies Program, 1958-77. Fulbright research prof., Philippines, 1950; Ford fellow, Indonesia, 1955-56; Fulbright-Hays fellow, Malaysia, 1968. Mem. Assn. African Studies, Assn. Am. Geographers, Am. Geog. Soc., Asia Soc., Assn. for Asian Studies (pres. 1966-67), Internat. African Inst., and the Council of Fgn. Relations. Author: Population and Land Utilization, 1941; Pioneer Settlement in the Asiatic Tropics, pub. 1945; (with others) Indonesia, published 1963. Contributor of articles to professional journals. Home: New Haven, Conn. Died Nov. 9, 1980.

PEMBERTON, CYRIL E., entomologist; b. Los Angeles, Calif., Aug. 12, 1886; s. William S. and Elizabeth (Hampton) P.; Stanford, 1911; D.S.C. (honorary), University of Hawaii, 1951; married Una Craig, June 1911; 1 dau., Virginia; m. 2d, Mildred Lucas Yokom, Nov. 1935; 1 dau., Mary. With U.S. Bur. of Entomology, 1911-18, advancing to asst. entomologist; mem. 2d Hawaiian Inf., 1918-19; with Hawaiian Sugar Planters Assn. since 1919, entomologist since 1928. Engaged in citrus-fruit insect investigations, Calif., 1911-12, Mediterranean fruit-fly investigations, Honolulu, 1913-18, rat control and bubonic plague, Hawaii, 1923-24; has made explorations in relation to insect pests on principal islands of the Pacific. Commr., Hawaii Board of Agri. and Forestry since 1943. Chmn. insect control com. Pacific Science Bd., Nat. Research Council, since 1946. Mem. Am. Assn. Economic Entomologists, Internat. Soc. Sugar Cane Technologists (chmn. insect pest com.), Hawaiian Acad. Sciences, Hawaiian Entomol. Soc., Sigma Xi; fellow A.A.A.S. Contbr. on scientific subjects. Home: Honolulu. *

PENDERGRAFT, DARYL, univ. adminstr.; b. Clarinda, Iowa, July 21, 1907; s. Verdon and Crete (Douglas) P.; B.A., Buena Vista Coll., 1928; M.A., State U. Iowa, 1936, Ph.D., 1943; m. Ramona A. Shipley, June 28, 1933; children—Marcia Lu (Mrs. Athol Rogers), Mary Beth (Mrs. Dale Olson). High sch. tchr., athletic coach, Cedar Rapids, Griswold, Adair, Pacific Junction and Dow City (all Iowa), 1928-43; asst. prof. history Iowa State U., 1943-44; faculty U. No. Iowa, Cedar Falls, 1946-75, prof. history, 1950-75, exec. dean, v.p., 1950-70, acting pres., 1969-70. Cons.-examiner N. Central Assn. Colls. and Secondary Schs., Nat. Council Accreditation Tchrs. Edn. Served with USNR, 1944-46. Mem. Iowa Edn. Assn., AAUP, Phi Delta Kappa. Kiwanian (pres. Cedar Falls 1951). Contbr. articles to profl. jours., chpts. to books. Home: Cedar Falls, Iowa. Died Sept. 21, 1975.

PENFIELD, HARRY E., business exec.; b. New Britain, Conn., 1882. Dir. Standard Screw Co. Retired. Home: Chicago. *

PENFIELD, WILDER GRAVES, surgeon; b. Spokane, Jan. 26, 1891; s. Charles Samuel and Jean (Jefferson) P.; B.Litt., Princeton, 1913, D.Sc., 1939; Rhodes scholar, Oxford (Eng.) U., 1914-16, 19-20, B.A., 1916, M.A., B.Sc., 1920, D.Sc., 1935, D.C.L., 1953; M.D., Johns Hopkins, 1918; D.Sc., U. B.C., 1946, U. Toronto, 1953, Yale, U. Leeds, 1954, N.Y. U., U. Man., 1955, U. Delhi, 1957, U. Wis., 1958, Dartmouth, McGill U., 1960, McMaster U., 1962, U. N.B., 1963, Royal Mil. Coll., 1970; D.C.L., Bishops U., 1944, Ottawa U., 1966; Docteur en Medicine, U. Montreal, 1945, U. Laval, 1951; LL.D., U. Wales, Dalhousie U., 1953, St. Lawrence U., 1956, Queen's U., 1957, Edinburgh U., Sask. U., 1959, Vt. U., Melbourne U., 1962, Johns Hopkins, 1970, U. Western Ont., 1972; M.D. (hon.), U. Poland, 1960; D. de l'U. de Paris, 1954; D.U.C., Calgary U., 1967; m. Helen Katherine Kermott, June 6, 1917; children—Wilder Graves, Ruth Mary, Priscilla, Amos Jefferson. Naturalized Canadian citizen. Beit meml. research fellow, London, 1920-21; research and brain surgery Presbyn. Hosp., N.Y.C., 1921-28; neurosurgeon Royal Victoria, Montreal Gen. hosps., 1928-60; dir. Montreal Neurol. Inst., 1934-60, then hon. cons. Served in World War I with A.R.C. Hosp. No. 2. Paris, and Hosp. Militaire V.R. 76, Ris Orangis, France; col. Royal Canadian Army M.C., 1945. Guggenheim fellow, 1961-64. Decorated companion Order St. Michael and St. George, Order Merit (Brit.); Medal of Freedom (U.S.); chevalier Legion of Honor (France); Gold Cross Legion George I (Greece); recipient Lister medal Royal Coll. Surgeons (Eng.), 1961; named companion Order Canada, 1967; others. Fellow Royal Coll. Surgeons, Royal Soc. Can., Royal Soc. London, Royal Coll. Phys. and Surg. Can. (pres. 1940-44); mem. Am. Philos. Soc., Acad. Sci. USSR, Neurol. Soc. Warsaw, Am. Neurol. Assn. (past pres.), Neurol. Soc. Estonia; corr. mem. Soc. Neurologie de Paris, Academie des Sciences et des Lettres of Poland; fgn. asso. Nat. Acad. Scis. (U.S.), Am. Acad. Arts and Scis. Established Lab. Neurocytology, Presbyn. Hosp., 1925; specializes in neurol. surgery. Author: (with T.C. Erickson) Epilepsy and Cerebral Localization, 1941; Canadian Army Manual of Neurosurgery, 1941; (with T.B. Rasmussen) Cerebral Cortex of Man, 1950; (with K. Kristiansen) Epileptic Seizure Patterns, 1950; No Other Gods, 1954; (with H. Jasper) Epilepsy and Functional Anatomy of Human Brain, 1954; Excitable Cortex in Conscious Man, 1958; (with L. Roberts) Speech and Brain-Mechanisms, 1959; The Torch, 1960; The Second Career, 1963; The Difficult Art of Giving: The Epic of Alan Gregg, 1967; Man and His Family, 1967; Second Thoughts: Science, the Arts and the Spirit, 1970; Mystery of the Mind, 1975. Home: Montreal, Que., Can. Died Apr. 5, 1976.

PENNEKAMP, ARTHUR E., lawyer; s. Theodore H. and Aurelia (Klein) P.; LL.B., U. Cal. at Berkeley, 1930; m. Eleanor M. Hazen, Jan. 3, 1948; children—Carol A., Nancy J. Admitted to Cal. bar, 1930; adminstr. San Francisco region SEC, 1956-72. Served from pvt. to maj. USAAF, 1942-46. Mem. Order of Coif. Address: Piedmont, Calif. Died Nov. 8, 1977.

PENNEKAMP, JOHN DAVID, editor; b. Cin. Jan. 1, 1897; s. William Henry and Angela (Gluick) P.; student St. Francis of Assisi and pub. schs. Cin.; m. Irene R. McQuillan, Dec. 31, 1925; children—John David, Tom. Successively reporter, state editor, legislative corr., asst. city editor Cincinnati Post, 1916-18, asst. city editor, city editor, news editor, 1918-25; successively city editor, news editor, mng. editor Miami (Fla.) Herald, 1925-41, asso. editor 1941-77. Mem. Parole Com., State of Fla., 1947; cons. U.S. Fish and Wildlife Service Dept. Interior, 1954; mem. Fla. Bd. Parks and Hist. Memls., 1950-69, chmn., 1950-54; v.p. trustee Fairchild Tropical Gardens; mem. Fla. Cabinet's Com. on Seminole Affairs; member of citizens board U. of Miami; member Florida Quadricentennial Commn.; dir. El Centro de las Americas. Served as pvt. inf. U.S. Army, World War I; lt. intelligence sect. USNR, 1927-39. Mem. Everglades Nat. Park Commn. Recipient conservation awards, Nat. Audubon Soc., 1954, U.S. Dept. Interior, 1955, Sears Found., 1961, Mem. Am. Soc. Newspaper Editors. Home: Miami, Fla. Died June 17, 1978.

PEPER, JOHN HENRY (PE'PER), engring. exec.; b. Bklyn., July 4, 1886; s. John Henry and Wilhelmina (Brammer) P.; M.E., Stevens Inst. Tech., 1909; m. Mabel Brauckmuller, Sept. 25, 1913; 1 dau., Arlene (wife D. B. LaPierre, U.S.N.). Engr. Buckeye Pipe Line Co. (and subsidiaries), 1923, chief engr., 1923-48, v.p., 1938-48, pres., 1948-52, chmn., dir., 1952-54, consultant, 1954—. Recipient citation transportation div., Am. Petroleum Inst., 1952. Mem. Profl. Engrs. N.Y., Stevens Alumni Assn., Tau Beta Pi. Republican. Lutheran. Mason. Clubs: Pipe Liners president 1950), Stevens Metropolitan (N.Y.C.). Home: Glen Head, N.Y. *

PEPPER, JAMES MORGAN, church official; b. in a Mormon Camp in Southern Nev., Apr. 17, 1884; s. James Morgan and Emma (Zadow) P.; grad. high sch., St. Joseph, Mo., 1903; student William Jewell Coll., Liberty, Mo., 1904-06; Th.M., Southern Bapt. Theol. Sem., Louisville, Ky., 1909; m. Jessie May Wright, of St. Joseph, June 20, 1906; children—James, Virginia May. Ordained Bapt. ministry, 1908; missionary in lead belt of Mo., 1909, 10; pastor Festus, Mo., later Lansdowne Ch., East St. Louis, Ill., until 1926; became gen. sec.-treas. Ill. Bapt. State Assn., Apr. 1, 1926; pastor Maplewood (Mo.) Bapt. Ch., 1931-36; research and literary work, Everglades, Fla., 1936—. Pres. St. Clair Co. Law Enforcement League, 1925,26. Served as 1st lt., chaplain 10th Inf., U.S.A., with A.E.F., Aug. 15, 1918-May 5, 1919. Mem. Am. Legion. Republican. Mason; mem. O.E.S.; Woodman. Home: Maplewood, Mo.*

PEPPERDINE, GEORGE, b. Mound Valley, Kan., June 20, 1886; s. John and Mary (Lain) P.; ed. rural district schs. and business coll., Parsons, Kan.; m. Lena Rose Baker, Oct. 23, 1907 (died 1930); children—Florence May (Mrs. Randolph Crossley), Esther Louise (Mrs. Kendall Thurston); m. 2d, Helen Louise Davis, June 17, 1934; children—Marilyn, George, Wendell. Began as bookkeeper, 1905; started Western Auto Supply Co., Kansas City, Mo., 1909; sold controlling interest, 1915, and moved to Los Angeles, 1916, later starting Western Auto Supply Co. of Calif. (pres.; now retired). Pres. George Pepperdine Foundation; chmn. bd. George Pepperdine Coll. Mem. Los Angeles Chamber of Commerce. Republican. Mem. Ch. of Christ. Home: Los Angeles. *

PERELMAN, SIDNEY JOSEPH, writer; b. Bklyn., Feb. 1, 1904; s. Joseph and Sophia (Charren) P.; student Brown U., 1921-25; m. Laura West, July 4, 1929; children—Adam, Abby Laura. Artist and writer Judge, 1925-29, Coll. Humor, 1929-30; writer for motion pictures, 1930-79; contbr. to The New Yorker, 1931-79; wrote sketches for Third Little Show, Walk a Little Faster, others. Named Best Screen Writer of 1956 for Around the World in 80 Days, also Acad. award; New York Film Critics award. Mem. Screen Writers Guild, Dramatists Guild, Nat. Inst. Arts and Letters. Club: Century Assn. Author: Dawn Ginsbergh's Revenge, 1929; Parlor, Bedlam and Bath, 1930; (play) (with Laura Perelman) All Good Americans, 1934, The Night Before Christmas, 1941; Strictly from Hunger, 1937; Look Who's Talking, 1940; The Dream Department, 1943; (play) (with Ogden Nash) One Touch of Venus, 1943; Crazy Like a Fox, 1944; Keep It Crisp, 1946; Acres and Pains; Best of S.J. Perelman, 1947; Westward Ha, 1948; Listen to the Mocking Bird, 1949; The Swiss Family Perelman, 1950; The Ill Tempered Clavichord, 1953; Perelman's Home Companion, 1955; The Road to Miltown, 1957; The Most of S.J. Perelman, 1958; The Rising Gorge, 1961; (play) The Beauty Part, 1963; Chicken Inspector No. 23, 1966; Baby, It's Cold Inside, 1970; Vinegar Puss, 1975; The Last Laugh, 1981. Home: New York, N.Y. Died Oct. 17, 1979.

PEREZ, HENRY TAYLOR, magazine editor; b. Calgary, Alta., Can., Aug. 2, 1915 (parents Am. citizens); s. Henry Leslie and Annita (Taylor) P.; B.S. in Civil Engring., Cooper Union, N.Y.C., 1940; m. Rosanna M. Garrett, Feb. 21, 1941; children—Annita (Mrs. William B. Sawyer), Richard Garrett, Henry Taylor. Cost engr. Dry Dock Assos., Norfolk, Va., 1940-42; job engr. Merritt Chapman & Scott Corp., N.Y.C., 1942-43; cost. engr. Ala. Shipbldg. and Dry Dock Co., Mobile, 1943-44; with McGraw-Hill Publs. Co., N.Y.C., 1946-79, editor-in-chief Constrn. Methods & Equipment mag., 1954-79. Mem. exec. com. constrn. sect. Nat. Safety Conf. Served to lt. (j.g.) USNR, 1944-46. Fellow Am. Soc. C.E.; mem. Soc. Am. Mil. Engrs., The Moles. Clubs: Engineers (N.Y.C.); Orienta Yacht (Mamaroneck, N.Y.). Home: White Plains, N.Y. Died June 15, 1979.

PERKINS, FRED J., lawyer; b. Piedmont, Ohio, Jan. 21, 1897; s. Lewis Elwood and Alice Belle (Murphy) P.; A.B., Ohio U., 1919; J.D., Case Western Res. U., 1921; m. Virginia Zellars, May 31, 1924; 1 son, William Stephen. Admitted to Ohio bar, 1921; asso. firm Dustin, McKeehan, Merrick, Arter & Stewart, 1921; partner Arter & Hadden, and predecessors, Cleve., from 1936. Recipient Certificates of Appreciation from Presidents Eisenhower, Kennedy, Johnson, Nixon. Fellow Royal Astron. Soc. Eng. (life); mem. Nat. Legal Aid and Defenders Assn., Am., Ohio, Cleve. (life) bar assns., Am. Judicature Soc., Am. Mus. Natural History, Natural Sci. Mus. Cleve., Citizens League, Royal Astron. Soc. Can., Astron. Soc. of Pacific, Greater Cleve. Growth Assn., Cleve. Astron. Soc., Western Res. Hist. Soc., Am. Acad. Polit. and Social Sci., Ct. of Nisi Prius, Tau Kappa Alpha, Phi Alpha Delta. Clubs: Mid-Day, Shaker (Cleve.). Author articles. Home: Shaker Heights, Ohio. Deceased.

PERKINS, MAHLON FAY, foreign service officer; b. N. Adams, Mass., Nov. 23, 1882; s. Lewis and Belle Louise (Benton) P.; A.B., Harvard, 1904; m. Fanny Earp Gooden, Oct. 13, 1916; 1 son, Mahlon Fay. Student interpreter, Peking, China, 1909-11; v.consul, Chefoo, China, 1911-12; dep. consul-gen., Shanghai, 1912-14; v.consul, Shanghai, 1915-17; consul. Changsha, China, 1918-20; assigned as administrative consul, Shanghai, 1920; assigned to Far Eastern Affairs Div., Dept. of State, 1922-25; apptd. consul gen., 1925; apptd. tech. adviser to Am. delegation to Spl. Customs Conf. (Peking) and to Am. commr. investigating extraterritorialty in China, 1925; appointed sec. in Diplomatic Service and assigned as counselor of Legation at Peking, 1928, charge d'affaires ad interim,

Nov. 1929; assigned to Dept. of State, 1933, apptd. asst. hist. adviser, 1934; apptd. consul-gen. at Barcelona, 1936; counselor of Legation Copenhagen, 1937, charge d'affaires ad interim, 1940-41; assigned to Dept. of State, 1942. Served as Am. assessor, Internat. Mixed Court, Shanghai, 1913-18; also judge Shanghai Consular Court, 1915-18. Mem. Am. Hist. Assn., S.A.R., Soc. War of 1812, Phi Beta Kappa, Royal Asiatic Soc. (N. China br.), Chinese Social and Polit. Science Assn. (Peking). Episcopalian. Clubs: Shanghai; Peking; Authors', Chevy Chase, Cosmos, Harvard, Metropolitan (Washington). Home: Washington, D.C. *

PERKINS, PALFREY, college trustee; b. Salem, Mass., June 14, 1883; s. George Holten and Rebecca (Floyd) P.; prep. edn., Salem Classical and High Sch.; A.B., Harvard U., 1905, S.T.B., 1909; D.D., Meadville Theological School, 1935, Tufts College, (Boston), 1954; married Linda Wellington, Dec. 27, 1922; children—David, Arthur Wellington, Cornelia. Ordained Unitarian ministry, 1909; pastor First Parish, Brighton, Mass., 1909-16, Weston, 1916-26, First Unitarian Ch., Buffalo, 1926-33; King's Chapel, Boston, 1933-53, ret. Chmn. bd. trustees Wellesley Coll.; mem. bd. trustees Boston Symphony Orchestra. Republican. Club: St. Botolph. Home: Boston. *

PERKINS, WILMA LORD, author, editor; b. Rochester, N.Y., Apr. 27, 1897; d. Anson M. and Inez Helen (Howe) Lord; A.B., U. Rochester, 1918; student Miss Farmer's Sch. of Cookery, 1918-19; grad. work Radcliffe Coll., 1918-19; m. Dexter Perkins, 1918; children—Bradford, Dexter. Editor Boston Cooking School Cook Book, from 1929 (made 8 complete revisions of the book); operator testing kitchen; radio and TV appearances; asst. to the pres. Fanny Farmer, Inc., from 1964. Pres. Baden St. Settlement of Rochester, 1942-52. Mem. Phi Beta Kappa. Author: Fannie Farmer Junior Cook Book, 1942, rev. 1957. Contbr. articles to mags. Home: Rochester, N.Y. Died Dec. 1976.

PERLMAN, DAVID, educator; b. Madison, Wis., Feb. 6, 1920; s. Selig and Eva (Shaber) P.; B.A., U. Wis., 1941, M.S., 1943, Ph.D., 1945; m. Kato Lenard, Aug. 18, 1968. Biochemist, Hoffmann-LaRoche, Inc., 1945; microbiologist Merck & Co., 1945-47; biochemist Squibb Inst. for Med. Research, 1947-67; prof. Sch. Pharmacy, U. Wis.-Madison, 1967-81, dean, 1968-75. Chmn. 3d Internat. Congress Genetics of Indsl. Microorganisms, 1978. Fellow Am. Acad. Microbiology, N.Y. Acad. Scis., Acad. Pharm. Scis.; mem. Am. Chem. Soc., Am. Soc. Microbiology (pres. found. 1974-75), Am. Soc. Pharmacognosists, Tissue Culture Assn., Soc. for Gen. Microbiology, Am. Pharm. Assn., Am. Soc. Biol. Chemistry, Biochem. Soc., Sigma Xi. Editor: Advances Applied Microbiology, 1968-81, Ann. Reports Fermentation Processes, 1977-81. Contbr. articles to profl. jours. Home: Madison, Wis. Died Jan. 29, 1980.

PERLMUTTER, MILTON, supermarket exec.; b. Newark, June 20, 1927; s. Aaron and Genesia (Kislin) P.; B.S. with honors, Wharton Sch. U. Pa., 1950; m. Harriet Krichman, Mar. 10, 1956; children—Franklin, Genesia, David. With family owned grocery bus., 1950-55; nat. sales promotion mgr. Colgate Palmolive Co., 1955-56; asst. treas., dir. Wakefern Food Corp., 1956-68; v.p., treas. Supermarkets Gen. Corp. (formerly Supermarkets Operating Co.), 1956-63, pres., 1963-78; dir. Gen. Mills, Inc., Super Valu Stores, Inc., Pub. Service Electric and Gas Co., Newark; trustee INA Investment Securities, Phila. Pres., Jewish Community Found. Essex County. Bd. govs. Acad. St. Joseph's Coll. Phila.; trustee Pingry Sch., Jewish Community Council Essex County, Rutgers U.; bd. dirs. N.J. region NCCJ, Interracial Council for Bus. Opportunity N.J.; bd. dirs. Food Mktg. Inst., Chgo. and Washington; bd. overseers Rutgers Found., New Brunswick, N.J.; former pres., trustee Congregation B'nai Jeshurun. Served with AUS, 1944-46. Recipient Nat. Food Distbn. Educator of Year award Food Bus. Inst., U. Del., 1969; Retailer of Year award N.J. Retail Mchts. Assn., 1972. Home: Short Hills, N.J. Died Mar. 15, 1978.

PERRIGO, CHARLES R., investment banker; b. Bloomington, Ill., July 31, 1897; s. Edwin B. and Elizabeth (Ryder) P.; ed. Lake Forest (Ill.) Coll., 1915-17; m. Gertrude Cuscaden, Sept. 10, 1926; 1 dau., Jean. Office boy Chas. S. Kidder & Co., Chicago, 1919-20, Lamson Bros. & Co., 1921-23, Frazier Jelke & Co., 1924-25; with Hornblower & Weeks, Chgo., 1926—, mgr. trading dept., 1926-32, mgr. investment dept., 1933-41, gen. partner 1942-66, ltd. partner, 1966-77, v.p. Hornblower & Weeks-Hemphill, Noyes, Inc., 1972-77. Served with U.S. Army Air Service, 1918-19. Mem. Chgo. Stock Exchange (vice chmn. Central States group), Investment Bankers Assn. (gov.). Clubs: Attic, Traders, Bond (pres. 1962) (Chgo.). Home: Tucson, Ariz. Died Mar. 5, 1977.

PERRY, ALBERT RICHARD, bldg. materials co. exec.; b. Niagara Falls, N.Y., Oct. 9, 1921; s. Albert Clinton and Florence (Burkhardt) P.; student Niagara U., 1939-41; B.S., U. Ill., 1943; m. Phyllis Brewer, Nov. 4, 1944; children—Lynn Beth, Susan Lee, Richard Nelson, Clinton Brewer. Accountant, Moore Bus. Forms, Niagara Falls, 1946-48; accountant Spirella Co., Inc., Niagara Falls, 1948-52, controller, 1952-54; asst. controller Hooker Chem. Corp., Niagara Falls, 1954-60, controller, N.Y.C., 1960-69, v.p., 1968-69; controller Flintkote Co., 1969-76, v.p., 1974-76. Pres. Niagara Falls chpt. Citizens Com. for Pub. Schs. Served to 1st lt. AUS, 1943-46. Mem. Nat. Assn. Accountants, Financial Execs. Inst., Delta Upsilon, Sigma Delta Chi. Republican. Conglist. Home: Chappaqua, N.Y. Died May 22, 1976.

PERRY, ELEANOR BAYER, author; m. Frank Perry. Author play Third Best Sport; screen plays David and Lisa, 1963, Ladybug, Ladybug, 1964, Last Summer, 1969, The Swimmer, 1968, Trilogy, 1968, Diary of a Mad Housewife, 1970, The Lady in the Car, 1970, (with Truman Capote) A Christmas Memory, 1966, The Man Who Loved Cat Dancing, 1973; author: Blue Pages, 1978. Home: Los Angeles, Calif. Died Mar. 14, 1981.

PERRY, JOSEPH EARL, retired banker, lawyer; b. Shelburne Falls, Mass., Dec. 30, 1884; s. Joseph Charles and Miriam Holbrook (Packard) P.; A.B. Williams Coll., 1906; J.D., Harvard, 1909; B.B.A., Boston U., 1922; m. Bessie Luella Stanford, June 24, 1911 (dec. Oct. 1968); children—Miriam Elizabeth (Mrs. Bennett D. Bell), Joseph Earl, Walter Stanford; m. 2d, Florence S. Kuhn, May 24, 1969. Admitted to Mass. bar, 1908; practiced law, Boston, 1909—; income tax assessor Mass. State, 1917-19; mem. Mass. Ho. of Reps., 1925-30 (chmn. com. on taxation and on constl. law, vice chmn. recess com. on taxation); commr. banks Mass. State, 1940-44; pres. Newton Savs. Bank, 1944-59; chmn. Mass. Bd. Bank Inc., 1940-44. Sometime mem. faculty Boston U., Northeastern U., Grad. Sch. Banking, Rutgers U. Mem. Belmont Sch. Com., 1919-22; pres. Mass., R.I. State assns. YMCA, 1936-37; mem. budget com. Newton Community Chest, 1944; incorporator New Eng. Deaconess Hosp.; bd. dirs. Nat. Thrift Assn.; nat. bd. field advisers Fed. Small Bus. Administrn. Pres., Nat. Assn. Suprs. State Banks, 1943; mem. council Harvard Law Sch. Assn., 1942-44. Trustee Boston U., 1946-64, hon. trustee, 1964—, mem. exec. com., 1953-64, treas., 1954-57; trustee DeMolay Found. Mass., Masonic Edn. and Charity Trust (v.p.), Internat. Coll., Beirut. Mem. Mass. Savs. Bank Life Ins. Council (pres. 1949-50), Am. (pres. savs. and mortgage div. 1949-50, mem. exec. council 1951-52), Newton (pres. 1951-52) bankers assns., Boston Execs. Assn. (charter), Phi Kappa Assn. Greater Boston (past sec.), Beta Gamma Sigma (hon.). Methodist. (chmn. bd. trustees, hon. chmn. 50th anniversary com.). Mason (33 deg., grand master Mass. 1938-40, dir. grand lodge Mass., only Western Hemisphere Mason to have official part in Duke of Kent installation as Eng. Grand Master by King George VI, London, 1939), Rotarian (past pres.). Author: The Masonic Way of Life, 1968; also many articles and brochures on law, banking and masonry. Home: Belmont MA. *

PERRY, WARREN CHARLES, architect; b. Santa Barbara, Calif., May 12, 1884; s. Charles Strong and Martha Washington (Warren) P.; B.S., U. of Calif., 1907; École des Beaux Arts, Paris, 1908-11; m. Joy Wilson, July 31, 1918; children—Carolyn Joy (Mrs. Thayer Hopkins), Warren. Architect at San Francisco, 1912; architect George C. Edwards Track Stadium, Jurisprudence Bldg. University of Calif. Berkeley Potrero Hill Housing Project (with F. H. Meyer and John Bakewell, Jr.), San Francisco, 1939, also many residences; instr. in architecture, U. of Calif., 1911-18, asst. prof. architecture, 1918-21, asso. prof., 1921-27, prof. since 1927, dean Sch. of Architecture 1927-49, chmn. dept. of art. 1935-38. Mem. Calif. State Bd. Architectural Examiners from 1928 to '42. Fellow Am. Inst. Architects (pres. Northern Calif. Chapter 1938); mem. State Association California Architects, Delta Tau Delta, Tau Beta Pi. Democrat. Club: Faculty (Berkeley). Home: San Francisco. *

PERSHING, FRANCIS WARREN, broker; b. Cheyenne, Wyo., June 24, 1909; s. John Joseph and Helen Frances (Warren) P.; student Philips Exeter Acad., 1923-27, Inst. Carnal, Switzerland, 1924-25; B.S., Yale, 1931; m. Muriel Bache Richards, Apr. 22, 1938, children—John Warren, Richard Warren (killed in action Vietnam 1968). Chmn., Pershing & Co., Inc., stock brokers, N.Y.C., 1934-80; dir. Dome Mines, Ltd. Mem. Assn. Stock Exchange Firms (past gov.). Home: Palm Beach, Fla. Died June 9, 1980.

PERSHING, JOHN JAMES, educator; b. Canton, Ohio, Jan. 5, 1918; s. Benjamin Harrison and Vera (Miller) P.; A.B., Wittenberg Coll., 1939; M.Ed., Springfield Coll., 1940; D.Ed., Ind. U., 1952; m. Ruth Ann Knollenberg, Feb. 22, 1941; children—Patricia Ann, John James. Boys work sec. YMCA, Portsmouth, Ohio, 1940-42, South Bend, Ind., 1943-45; asst. dean student Ga. Inst. Tech., 1945-47, asso. dean students, 1947-60; dean men Emory U., 1960-65; dean student affairs West Ga. Coll., 1965-69, prof., 1969-78, dept. chmn., 1977-78. Mem. bd. higher edn. United Luth. Ch. Am., 1956-62, exec. com., chmn. com. colls., 1960-62; exec. council Luth. Ch. Am., 1962-68. Adminstrv. bd. Bellwood Community Center, Atlanta, 1959-65; mem. Carrollton Planning Commn., 1972-78. Trustee Newberry Coll., 1953-59, exec. com., 1954-55. Mem. Am., Ga. personnel and guidance assns., Am., So. coll. personnel assns., Nat. Vocat. Guidance Assn., Kappa Phi Kappa, Beta Beta Beta, Omicron Delta Kappa, Alpha Phi Omega, Alpha Tau Omega. Contbr. articles profl. jours. Address: Carrollton, Ga. Died Oct. 7, 1978; buried Lutherania Cemetery, Richmond, Ind.

PESHKIN, MORRIS MURRAY, physician; b. N.Y.C., May 23, 1892; s. Selig and Goldie (Feigen) P.; M.D., Fordham, 1914; m. Lillian Rapaport, Oct. 9, 1921. Intern St. Michaels Hosp., Newark, 1914-15; asst. pediatrician Mt. Sinai Hosp., N.Y.C., 1915-25; asso., 1942-52, cons. allergist, 1952; chief Children's Allergy Clinic, 1926-52, French Hosp., N.Y.C., 1934-36; attending allergist Jewish Meml. Hosp., N.Y.C., 1938-40; instr. postgrad. extension Columbia, 1926-52; clin. prof. medicine and pediatric allergies Albert Einstein Coll. Medicine Yeshiva U., 1954-60, prof. emeritus, 1960; clin. prof. emeritus Mt. Sinai Sch. Medicine, City U. N.Y.; chief cons. physician Children's Asthma Research Inst. and Hosp., Denver, 1940-62; cons. allergist Womens Service for Asthma, Inc.; vis. allergist Bronx Municipal Hosp. Center, 1955-60. Sec., trustee Allergy Found. Am., Inc., 1954-62; nat. pres. Asthmatic Children's Found., Inc., 1962-80; pres. Asthmatic Childrens Found. N.Y., Inc., 1963-80, Asthma Publ. Soc., Inc., 1963-80, chief med. cons. Asthma Treatment Center, New Castle, N.Y.; founder, past pres. Assn. Convalescent Homes and Hosps. for Asthmatic Children, Inc.; hon. pres. chief med. cons. Asthmatic Children's Found. Fla., Inc., Asthma Treatment Center, North Miami Beach; hon. pres. Soc. for Aid of Crippled in Israel, Inc., Music Lovers League, Inc. Treas. 4th Internat. Congress of Allergology, N.Y.C., 1961. Diplomate Am. Bd. Internal Medicine and Allergy. Fellow Acad. Psychosomatic Medicine (pres. 1963-64), A.C.P., Am. Coll. Allergists (pres. 1953-54, chmn. bd. 1954-55), Am. Acad. Allergy; hon. mem. French Allergy Soc.; mem. A.A.A.S., Am. Geriatrics Soc., Profl. and Bus. Men's Assn. of Am. Jewish Congress (pres. physicians chpt. 1958, chmn. bd. physicians chpt. 1959), A.M.A., Am. Assn. Study Allergy (pres. 1935-36), N.Y. Allergy Soc., N.Y. State Assn. Professions, Inc., Med. Soc. State N.Y. (life), Soc. Advancement Judaism, Collegium Internationale Allergologicum. Mason. Clubs: Friars, Fifty Rod and Gun. Contbr. med. jours. Contbg. editor Internat. Archives of Allergy and Applied Immunology; Rev. of Allergy and Applied Immunology; Clinica Europea; Psychosomatics. Hon. cons. editor Life Scis. Asso. editor: Jour. Asthma Research. Home: Weston, Conn. Died Aug. 17, 1980.

PESQUERA, JOSÉ LORENZO, former commr. from Porto Rico; b. Bayamón, P.R., Aug. 10, 1882; s. José Jesús and Inés (Dávila) P.; A.B., Provincial Inst. of P.R., 1897; student Keystone State Normal Sch., Kutztown, Pa., 1901-02; W.Va. U., 1902-04; m. Eucarnación Lopez del Valle, of Toa Alta, P.R., Dec. 25, 1908. Began law practice in P.R., 1904; mem. P.R. Ho. of Rep., 1917-20; resident commr. from P.R. in U.S., 1932-33. Mem. Bayamón Bar Assn. (v.p.), Agrl. Assn. P.R. (pres. since 1927). Dir. in chief El Agricultor Puertorriqueno (fortnightly mag.) since 1929. Home: Bayamón, P.R.

PETER, WILLIAM WESLEY, health officer; b. Elliston, Ottawa Co., O., Dec. 1, 1882; s. Henry and Alvina (Parman) P.; Ph.B., Northwestern Coll., Naperville, Ill., 1904, Ph.M., 1906; M.D., Rush Med. Coll. (U. of Chicago), 1910; C.P.H., Harvard U.-Mass. Inst. Tech. Sch. Pub. Health, 1918; Dr. P.H., Yale, 1927; m. Eleanor Elizabeth Whipple, of Chicago, Ill., May 4, 1911; children—Jane Elizabeth, Hollis William, Margaret Parman. Editor dept. preventive medicine, China Med. Jour., Shanghai, China, 1916; founder, Health Magazine, Shanghai, China, 1924, editor, 1924-26; hon. sec. China Central Com., Am. Red Cross; served with Chinese Labor Corps in France, World War; chmn. Sanitation Bd. Chinese and Foreign Famine Relief Commn.; dir. Council on Health Edn. of China, 1915-26; lecturer on pub. health, Pa.-St. John's Univ. Med. Sch., Shanghai; associate secretary American Public Health Association, 1927-29; director Department of Health Service of Cleanliness Inst. (New York); technical adviser, Ministry of Health of China, 1931; Oberlaender fellow, 1933; Near East Foundation Survey in Balkans and the Near East, 1934; medical director of the Navajo Area, Office of Indian Affairs, Dept. of the Interior, since 1934. Fellow American Public Health Association; member Arizona Public Health Association (president 1939), China Medical Assn., Shanghai Med. Soc., Am. Society Parasitologists, Royal Inst. Pub. Health (Eng.), Delta Mu, Delta Omega Epsilon; hon. mem. Nat. Med. Assn. of China, etc. Author: Broadcasting Health in China; Hitch-Hikers; The Great East Gate; Mastodons, Microbes, and Man. Contbr. on health subjects. Address: Window Rock, Ariz. *

PETERMANN, MARY LOCKE, educator, biochemist; b. Laurium, Mich., Feb. 26, 1908; d. Albert Edward and Anna (Grierson) Petermann; A.B., Smith Coll., 1929, D.Sc., 1966; Ph.D., U. Wis., 1939. Post doctoral fellow U. Wis., 1939-42, 44-45; profl. asst. com. med. research NDRC, 1942-44; research chemist Meml. Hosp., N.Y.C., 1945-46; asso. Sloan-Kettering Inst. Cancer Research, N.Y.C., 1946-60, asso. mem.,

1960-63, mem., 1963-73, mem. emeritus, 1973-76; prof. Sloan-Kettering div. Grad. Sch. Med. Scis., Cornell U., 1966-73, prof. emeritus, 1973-75. Recipient Sloan award in cancer research, 1963; Garvan medal, 1966. Fellow N.Y. Acad. Sci.; mem. Am. Soc. Biol. Chemists, Biophys. Soc., Am. Assn. Cancer Research. Republican. Presbyn. Author: The Physical and Chemical Properties of Ribosomes, 1964. Contbr. articles to profl. jours. Home: New York, N.Y. Died Dec. 13, 1975.

PETERS, HENRY DUKE, public health engr.; born Jonesboro, Ark., Oct. 6, 1886; s. George C. and Belle (Duke) P.; student Ark. State Agrl. School, 1912-15; B.S., Ia. State Coll., 1925; m. Anne Mae Gladney, July 17, 1931; children—George Thomas, Henry Duke. Rodman and instrument man Cobb & Lee, civil engrs., Jonesboro, 1915-17; rigger Townley Shingle Co., Torch, Mo., 1920; rodman and instrument man J.R. Rhyne, Corning, Ark., 1920; instrument man, party chief, J.S. Spiker, Vincennes, Ind., 1921; asst. engr. Ia. State Bd. Health, 1925-27, Mo. State Bd. Health, 1927-31; dir. div. sanitation, Jacksonville (Fla.) Health Dept. since 1931. Served as pvt. 23rd engrs., U.S. Army, 1917-19; overseas Jan., 1918-June, 1919. Fellow Am. Pub. Health Assn. (mem. Southern sect.); mem. Am. Mosquito Control Assn. (pres. 1947-48), Conf. of Municipal Pub. Health Engrs. (chmn. 1947), Inter-Am. Assn. Sanitary Engrs. Nat. Assn. Sanitarians, Engring. Soc., Pub. Health Assn., Anti-Mosquito Assn. (past pres.). Democrat. Episcopalian. Author numerous com. reports and papers delivered before tech. socs. Home: Jacksonville. *

PETERS, JAMES SOLOMON, banker; b. Nashville, Ga., Mar. 21, 1884; s. William Lot and Caroline (Walker) P.; student Emory U., 1905-06, L.D.D. (hon.), 1964; LL.D. (hon.), LaGrange Coll., 1961; m. Mary V. Jones, Nov. 28, 1910 (dec.); children—Dr. James Solomon, Mary Virginia (Mrs. S.L. Taylor); m. 2d, Mary Jane Hammack, July 23, 1965. With Bank Manchester (Ga.), from 1910, pres. 1934-58, chmn. bd., from 1958. Chmn. Ga. Democratic Exec. Com., 1941-42, 46-58, vice chmn., from 1958; chmn. Ga. delegation Dem. Nat. Conv., 1948, vice chmn., 1952; presdl. elector, Ga., 1952. Bd. regents State Ga., 1941-42; mem., vice chmn. Ga. Bd. Edn., 1947-58, chmn. from 1958. Mem. Ga. Bankers Assn. (pres. (1923-24), Ind. Bankers Assn. Am. (pres. 1952-53). Methodist. Home: Manchester, Ga. Died Dec. 6, 1974; buried Adel, Ga.

PETERS, THOMAS KIMMWOOD, educator; b. Norfolk, Va., June 22, 1884; s. William Isbestos and Laura Virginia (Logan) P.; ed. pub. and high sch., Los Angeles, Calif., 1884-94, Peace College, Mexico City, 1896-98; Ph.D., Oglethorpe University, Georgia, 1939; Doctor of Public Service, Oglethorpe University, 1940; m. Grace Margaret Price, Nov. 1, 1926. Artist with Internat. Botanical Expdn. to Yucatan, 1898; cameraman, Pathé Frères, Vincennes, France, 1899; toured Europe and N. Africa making motion pictures for Kinetoscope, 1900; freelancing, Paris, 1902; opened Peters Scenic Studio at Los Angeles, Calif., 1902; pres. Peters Photographic Expdns. and made 5 expdns. to Asiatic countries, Australia and South Seas, 1904-05; covered constrn. Panama Canal in motion pictures; art dir. N.Y.M.P., 1909; Triangle, Pathe, art and tech. dir.; dramatic dir., Cosmos, Federal, World, Famous Players and other motion picture companies. Author and correlator of standard text films for classroom use, at Palo Alto and F.B.O. Studio, Hollywood; inaugurated first regular teaching films in New York Schools, 1920. Made first commercial rare gas tubes, 1924; inventor and patentee of many vacuum and rare gas devices; made first micro-film camera, 1915. Archivist making collection and preservation of material deposited in Crypt of Civilization; prof. of audio-visual edn., Oglethorpe University, dir. China Air Force School at Oglethorpe Univ., 1945-46, formerly visual edn. consultant, former professor psychology tng. specialist Lockheed Aircraft Co., Ga.; mfg. research engineer, Lockheed; now cons., historian Los Angeles County Hollywood Museum Motion Picture TV. Owner photog. mus., Frontier Village, San Jose. Archivist, Second Crypt of Civilization; producer Southern Productions; producing and directing motion picture, Song of Dixie (author script). Author: Technique of Cinematography: Prelude to the Atomic Era; Trap to Catch a Shadow, History of Motion Picture Mechanisms; (autobiography) Portals of the Past. Home: Westport, Cal.*

PETERSEN, AAGE QVISTGAARD, business exec.; born Aarhus, Denmark, Nov. 13, 1886; s. Hans Morten Michael and Alma Katrine (Thorsen) Q-P.; ed. Fengers Private Latin Sch. and Commercial and Law Sch., Aarhus, Denmark; m. Adele L. Lange, July 31, 1913; 1 son, Morton. Came to U.S., 1907, naturalized, 1927. With Korn-og-Foderstof Kompagniet, Aarhus, Denmark, 1904-07; with New Orleans Export Co., New Orleans, and Galveston, Tex., 1907-40, with Southport Mill Co. Ltd., New Orleans, 1909-36, when liquidated. Vice pres. and dir. Wesson Oil & Snowdrift Co., Inc. from its incorporation in 1925 to 1940, president and director, 1940-56, chmn. bd., 1956-60; dir. Nat. Bank of Commerce (New Orleans), Tex. & Pacific Ry. Co., Dallas, Southdown Inc. (New Orleans), Lykes Brothers; S.S. Company; mem. bd. trustees Isaac Delgado Mus. Art, American Scandanavian Foundation, New York; board of govs. Ochsner Found. Hosp. Decorated Knight of Dannebrog (Denmark). Clubs: Boston, New Orleans Country Club, International House (New Orleans), Galveston Artillery, Royal Danish Yacht (Copenhagen, Denmark). Home: New Orleans. *

PETERSON, ARTHUR KARL, indsl. physician; born Chicago, May 3, 1907; s. Walter and Jennie (Ekblom) P.; B.S., U. of Chicago, 1932; M.D., U. of Ill., 1936; m. Mary Ann Preston, Mar. 16, 1940; children—Mary Susan, Arthur Karl. Intern Milwaukee County Gen. Hosp., 1936-37, resident medicine, 1937-38; pvt. practice medicine, Chicago, 1938-48; med. dir. R.R. Donnelley & Sons Co., Chicago, from 1947. Lt. col. M.C., U.S. Army Res. from 1945, active service 4 yrs. Diplomate Am. Bd. Preventive Medicine in occupational medicine. Fellow Am. Assn. Indsl. Phys. and Surgs. (sec.); mem. A.M.A., Ill., Chgo. med. socs., Central States Soc. Indsl. Med., Alpha Sigma Phi, Nu Sigma Nu. Home: Chicago, Ill. Died Dec. 4, 1980.

PETERSON, F. RAYMOND, banker; b. Farlington, Kan., Nov. 13, 1895; s. J. Walford and Adelaide C. (Schatz) P.; ed. pub. schs., Girard, Kan., also State Norman Sch., Pittsburg, Kan., Gem City Bus. Coll., Quincy, Ill.; D.C.S., N.Y. U.; m. Grace C. Crouch, Dec. 31, 1919. Bank examiner, Kan.; cashier First State Bank Cherokee (Kan.); v.p., cashier Citizens Nat. Bank, Okmulgee, Okla.; nat. bank examiner 10th, 8th, 11th and 2d Fed. Res. Bank dists., 1922-35; exec. v.p. 1st Nat. Bank N.J., Totowa, N.J., 1936, pres., 1937, chmn. bd., 1942-75; ret., 1975; dir. Chelsea Title & Guaranty Co., N.J. Mfrs. Ins. Co. Mem. exec. comm. Paterson Econ. Council, from 1956. Bd. govs., hon. trustee St. Joseph's Hosp., Paterson. Served as officer U.S. Army, World War I. Mem. N.J. (chmn. legislative com. 1938-44, treas. 1944-45, v.p. 1945-46, pres. 1946-47), Am. (exec. com. nat. bank div. 1939-45, chmn. com. 1941-43, pres. div. 1943-44, v.p. assn. 1948-49, chmn. finance com. 1948-49, pres. assn. 1949-50, govt. borrowing com. 1948-65, econ. policy com. 1965-71, trustee found. edn. econs. 1965-70) bankers assns., N.J. Mfg. Assn. (trustee). Clubs: Hamilton; Ridgewood Country; Union League (N.Y.C.); Seaview Country (Absecon, N.J.); Arcola Country; Charter. Home: Hackensack, N.J. Died Nov. 26, 1977.

PETERSON, FRANK J., govt. ofcl.; b. Kansas City, Mo., July 5, 1886; s. Lewis and Sophie (Mose) P.; student pub. schs. Kansas City. Bus. mgr. Kansas City Bldg. Trades Council, 1914-28; gen. organizer United Assn. Plumbers and Steamfitters, 1928-40; with W.P.B., 1943-47, Treasury Dept., 1950-51; mem. appeals bd. Nat. Prodn. Authority, Washington, since Mar. 1951. Mem. A.F. of L., United Assn. Plumbers and Pipe Fitters. Mason. Home: Washington, D.C. *

PETERSON, HENRY K., state judge; b. Council Bluffs, Ia., Mar. 16, 1884; s. Mads and Kirsten (Kaare) P.; LL.B., Drake U., 1908; m. Laura May Robinson, Aug. 5, 1911; children—Josephine (Mrs. William Eisenberry), Robert A., Richard W. Admitted to Ia. bar, 1908; practiced in Council Bluffs, 1908-55; mem. firm Peterson, Smith, Peterson, Bechman & Wilson; justice Supreme Court of Iowa, 1955—. City solicitor, Council Bluffs, 1916-20; mem. planning commn., Council Bluffs. Mem. Pottawattamie County (pres. 1930), 15th Jud. (pres. 1935) bar assns. Baptist. Kiwanian (dist. gov. 1928). Home: Council Bluffs, Ia. *

PETERSON, HOUSTON, educator, author; b. Fresno, Calif., Dec. 11, 1897; s. Nathaniel Houston and Nancy Sophronia (Blasingame) P.; A.B., Pomona Coll., Claremont, Calif., 1919; A.M., Columbia, 1920, Ph.D., 1929; m. Charlotte T. Reid, 1925; m. 2d, Martha Burlingham Berrien, Dec. 29, 1936. Asst. in philosophy, Columbia U., 1920-21, lecturer in philosophy, 1921-39; lecturer in philosophy, Rutgers U., 1929-34, asso. prof., 1934-38, prof. since 1938; chmn. Cooper Union Forum, 1934-38, prof., and head div. of social philosophy 1938-46. Public lecturer since 1926; ednl. broadcaster since 1943; weekly Rutgers U. program Speaking Acquaintance since 1950. Served with S.A.T.C., Pomona Coll., 1918. Recipient Butler Medal, Columbia U., 1931. Dir. N.Y. Adult Edn. Council, The East and West Assn. Chmn. commencement day com. Victory Book Campaign, 1942-43. Mem. Am. Philos. Assn., Am. Assn. Univ. Profs., Am. Soc. for Aesthetics, P.E.N., Phi Beta Kappa. Author: Havelock Ellis: Philosopher of Love, 1928; The Melody of Chaos, 1931; Huxley Prophet of Science, 1932; The Lonely Debate, 1938. Editor: The Book of Sonnet Sequences, 1929; Poet to Poet (with William S. Lynch), 1945; Great Teachers, 1946; A Treasury of the Great Speeches, 1954; Great Essays, 1954. Contbr. to An Introduction to Reflective Thinking, 1923. Home: New York, N.Y. *

PETERSON, ROY MERLE, univ. prof.; b. Bagley, Ia., Sept. 30, 1883; s. James Newell and Matilda Jennie (Harper) P.; B.A., Coe Coll., 1906; M.A., Harvard, 1910, Ph.D., 1912; fellow Am. Acad. in Rome, 1917; m. Bernese Loretta Barry, Oct. 4, 1917; 1 dau., Leona Bernese. Instr. langs., high sch., Oskaloosa, Ia., 1906-07; acting prof. classics, Eureka (Ill.) Coll., 1907-09; prof. Latin, Mo. Valley Coll., Marshall, Mo., 1912-14; prof. Romance langs., Sterling (Kan.) Coll., 1914-15; studied and traveled in Europe, 1915-17; prof. Romance langs., U. of Me., since 1918, acting dean Coll. of Arts and Sciences, 1931-32 and since 1942 dir. summer session since 1930, dean grad. study, 1938-46; ret. Mem. Am. Assu. Teachers of Spanish, Am. Assn. Teachers of French. Phi Kappa Phi (editor since 1925), Phi Beta Kappa. Mason. Woodman. Republican. Methodist. Author: The Cults of Campania (Vol. I of Monographs of Am. Acad. in Rome), 1923; also magazine articles. Home: Orono, Me.*

PETERSON, SHAILER, dental educator; b. Albert Lea, Minn., Oct. 12, 1908; s. P. Augustus and Annie Christine (Olsen) P.; B.A., U. Oreg., 1930, M.A., 1932; Ph.D. in Edn. Psychology, U. Minn., 1943; m. Ella Cleone Devereaux; 1 son, Devereaux Shailer. Instr., U. Minn., 1936-43; asso. prof. S.D. State Coll., 1944; asst. prof. U. Chgo., 1944-47; dir. ednl. measurements Council on Dental Edn., ADA, Chgo., 1947-48 sec., 1948-61, asst. sec. ednl. affairs, 1960-61; prof. dentistry, dean U. Tenn. Coll. Dentistry, 1961-69; prof. dental edn., asso. dir. ednl. research U. Tex. Dental Br., Houston, 1969, asso. dean, prof. Dental Sch., San Antonio, 1969-76, ofcl. advisor to dental dean, prof., 1976-78; clin. asso. prof., guest lectr. Loyola U. Dental Sch., Chgo.; mem. dental tng. com. Nat. Inst. Dental Research; hon. mem. expert com. aux. dental personnel WHO; spl. cons. USPHS. Hon. fellow Internat., Am. colls. dentists; mem. AAAS, Am. Statis. Assn., ADA (asso.), So. Conf. Dental Deans, Am. Dental Hygienists Assn., Am. Assn. Dental Examiners, Internat. Assn. Dental Research, Am. Ednl. Research Assn., Am. Assn. Med. Colls. (asso.), Am. Radio Relay League, Am. Pub. Health Assn., Am. Assn. Dental Schs. (del.), Sigma Xi, Pi Mu Epsilon, Phi Delta Kappa, Omicron Kappa Upsilon, Delta Sigma Delta; hon. mem. Chgo., Memphis, W.Va., N.C., San Antonio dental socs., Tenn. Dental Assn., Am. Acad. Gen. Dentistry, Am. Acad. Dental Medicine, Soc. Odonto Dominicano. Author: How Well Are Indian Children Educated, 1945; Manual on the Preparation of Examinations in the Field of Dentistry, 1952; Review and Test Manual for Dental Assistants, 1967; Clinical Dental Hygiene, 1959, 4th edit., 1972; Comprehensive Review for Dental Hygienists, 1964; 4th edit., 1978; The Dentist and His Assistant, 1961, 4th edit., 1977; Things to Know Before You Go for an Interview, 1974; Preparing to Enter Dental School, 1977; Preparing to Enter Medical School, 1977; Preparing to Enter Pharmacy School, 1977; Preparing to Enter Veterinary Medicine School, 1978; Preparing to Enter Osteopathic Medicine School, 1978; Preparing to Enter Nursing, 1978. Home: San Antonio, Tex. Died Oct. 24, 1978.

PETERSON, SIGURD HARLAN, educator; b. nr. Minneota, Lyon County, Minn., Dec. 27, 1886; s. Sigfinnur and Sigurbjorg (Sigurdardottir) Pjetursson; A.B., U. Minn., 1910; Ph.D., U. Wash., 1931; m. Ruth Taylor, July 31, 1912; children—Mable Maxine (Mrs. W. H. Ott), Sharoo (Mrs. Basil Hersha), Sigurd Harlan. Pub. sch. tchr., N.D., 1907-08, Colo., 1910-11; mem. faculty Ore. State Coll. since 1911, prof. English since 1933, head dept., 1933-52. Mem. Am. Assn. U. Profs. (pres. local chpt. 1933), Inland Empire Coun. Eng. (pres. 1949-50); Sigma Nu (frat. adviser, 1913-46, pat. officer (inspector), 1933-46), Phi Beta Kappa, Phi Kappa Phi, Delta Sigma Rho, Grey Friars. Democrat. Lutheran. Home: Corvallis, Ore. *

PETRI, LOUIS, bus. exec.; b. San Francisco, Oct. 13, 1912; s. Angelo and Amelia (Guidi) P.; student San Jose State Tchrs. Coll., U. Calif., also med. sch. U. St. Louis; m. Flori Cella, July 21, 1935; 1 dau., Patricia Mary. Began as gen. winery worker Petri Wine Co., 1934, pres., 1944-64, chmn. bd., 1964-68; pres., chief exec. officer United Vintners; dir., mem. exec. com., compensation and pension com. Foremost-McKesson, Inc.; dir. Bank of Am. NT & SA, Bankam. Corp., Edward D. Sultan Co., Honolulu, John Burton Machine Co., Concord, Calif. Decorated Gran Ufficiale, Order of Merit (Italy). Mem. Am.-Italy Soc. (chmn. bd. San Francisco). Clubs: World Trade, Pacific, Villa Taverna, Bohemian, St. Francis Yacht, Olympic (San Francisco); Eldorado Country, Thunderbird Country (Palm Springs, Calif.). Home: San Francisco, Calif. Died Apr. 7, 1980.

PETSCHEK, WALTER J., lawyer; b. N.Y.C., Nov. 17, 1899; s. Max and Rosa (Propper) P.; B.S., Columbia, 1919, Chem. Engr., 1921; LL.B., Fordham U., 1934; m. Paula Colin, Dec. 12, 1924; children—Willa, Xenia (Mrs. Leonard Rose). Admitted to N.Y. bar, 1934, thereafter practiced in N.Y.C.; partner firm Rosenman Colin Kaye Petschek Freund & Emil, from 1941. Home: New York, N.Y. Died Aug. 30, 1979.

PETTERSSEN, SVERRE, meteorologist; b. Hadsel, Norway, Feb. 19, 1898; s. Edward Hildor and Petronella (Petersen) P.; B.S., Oslo, U., 1924, M.S., 1926, Ph.D., 1933; m. Daisy Bonner, Aug. 16, 1925; 1 dau., Eileen (Mrs. Anton Oerbeck); m. 2d, Lilian Bye, Sept. 25, 1941; 1 son, Bernt; m. 3d Grace Beverly, Mar. 29, 1946. Came to U.S., 1948. Meteorologist Norwegian Weather Service, 1924-31, regional dir.,

1931-39; vis. prof. Cal. Inst. Tech., 1935; prof., chmn. meteorol. dept. Mass. Inst. Tech., 1939-42; advisor Meteorol. Office Brit. Air Ministry, 1942-45; chief Norwegian Forecasting Service, 1945-48; adv. Dir. Gen. Observatories, India, 1948; dir. sci. services U.S.A.F. Weather Service, Washington, 1948-52; prof. of meteorology U. Chgo., 1952-63, chmn. dept. of meteorology, 1959-61, chmn. dept. geophysical sci., 1961-63. Decorated Comdr. Order Brit. Empire; Comdr. Order St. Olaf, Liberation Cross (Norway); The Buys Ballot's Gold medal (Netherland Acad. Sci.), 1948; Letter commendation Gen. Dwight Eisenhower, 1944; Distinguished Service Award, U.S. Air Force, 1953; N.Y. Bd. of Trade Gold Award, 1958; U. Helsinki Medal, 1958; Charles Franklin Brooks award, 1962; 10th ann. prize award, Internat. Meteorol. Orgn., 1965. Pres. Internat. Commn. Maritime Meteorology, 1939-46, Internat. Commn. Aerology, 1946-51; dir. Nat. Acad. Sci. Task Force for 10 yr. plans atmospheric scis., 1961—, chmn. com. internat. programs atmospheric scis. and hydrology, 1962-63; mem. panel of atmospheric scis., Pres.'s Sci. Adv. Com., 1962—. Mem. Norwegian, Finland (fgn.) acads. sci., Acad. Sci., Ill. Acad. Sci. and Letters, Peruvian, Royal (honorary), Am. (pres. 1958-60) meterol. socs., Am. Geophys. Union, Acad. Polit. Scis., A.A.A.S., Nat. Geog. Soc. Author: Weather Analysis and Forecasting, 1940, 56; Introduction to Meteorology, 1941, 58.Co-author: The Meteorology of the Arctic, 1956.*

PETTIJOHN, EARL, univ. prof.; b. St. Peter, Minn., June 18, 1884; s. Elias Steele and Sarah Elizabeth (Hughes) P.; A.B., Univ. Minn., 1906, B.S., 1911, M.S., 1912, Ph.D., 1918; m. Clara Marie Anderson, June 10, 1913; children—Clara Elizabeth, Carol Marie, Lucile Carmen, Patricia. Chemist Bur. of Standards, Washington, D.C., 1915-18; chief chemist Firestone Steel Products Co., Akron, O., 1918-25; mem. faculty Mo. Valley Coll., Marshall, Mo., 1925-41, prof. chemistry, 1927-34, dean, 1936-41; prof. chemistry Tulsa (Okla.) Univ. since 1942. Mem. Am. Chem. Soc., Sigma Xi. Contbr. articles in Jour. Am. Chem. Soc., Bur. Standards publs. Home: Tulsa, Okla. *

PETTIT, WALTER W(ILLIAM), educator, social worker; b. Fredonia, N.Y., Aug. 9, 1882; s. William H. and Amalia (Kricheldorff) P.; grad. Fredonia Normal Sch., 1901; B.S., Teachers Coll., Columbia, 1911, A.M., 1912, Ph.D., 1918; Litt.D., Columbia, 1948. m. Katharine Fowler, Aug. 30, 1920; children—Walter Fowler, Katharine Fowler. Teacher and principal high school, Philippine Islands, 1901-09; principal Elementary Tech. School, Evanston, Illinois, 1911-13; field sec. Playground and Recreation Assn. of America, 1913-14; special asst. in relief work, Am. Embassy, Petrograd, 1916-17; attached to Am. Commn. to Negotiate Peace, 1918-19; instr. New York Sch. Social Work, 1915-16, asst. dir., 1918-39, director 1939-47; retired; dir. pub. welfare insts. in Latin-Am. countries, auspices UN, Aug.-Oct., 1947; executive dir. Temporary Emergency Relief Administration of N.Y. State, 1932-33; social welfare adviser to Guatemala, U.N., 1948-49. Mem. exec. com. Nat. Board of Review of Motion Pictures. Served as captain Military Intelligence Department, U. S. Army, 1918-19. Mem. Am. Assn. Social Workers, Am. Sociol. Soc., N.Y. State Hist. Soc., Alpha Chi Rho, Phi Delta Kappa. Episcopalian. Clubs: Columbia University, Philippine, City (New York). Author: Report of a Study of the Interrelation of the Work of National Social Agencies in 14 American Communities (with P. R. Lee and Jane M. Hoey), 1923; Social Salvage (with P. R. Lee), 1924; Russian-American Relations, 1917-20 (with C. K. Cumming), 1920; Case Studies in Community Organization, 1928. Home: N.Y. City; and Ridgefield, Conn. *

PEW, J(OHN) HOWARD (PU), industrialist; born Bradford, Pa., Jan. 27, 1882; son of Joseph Newton and Mary Catherine (Anderson) P.; ed. Shadyside Acad., Pitts., Grove City (Pa.) Coll., Mass. Inst. Tech.; m. Helen Jennings Thompson, Jan. 3, 1907 (dec. 1963). Engr. Marcus Hook Refinery, Sun Oil Co., 1901, and successively asst. supt., supt., vice pres., then president, 1912-47; chmn. bd. Sun Oil Company; director Sun Shipbuilding & Dry Dock Company. President board of trustees Grove City College. President bd. trustees United Presbyterian Found. Republican. Presbyterian. Clubs: Union League (Phila.); Merion Golf, Merion Cricket (Haverford, Pa.). Home: Ardmore, Pa. *

PEYTON, PAUL LEASON, lawyer; b. Taylorville, Ill., Sept. 5, 1895; s. Arthur Denver and Nancy Amelia (Adams) P.; B.S., U. Ill., 1921; postgrad. N.Y. U. Sch. Law, 1923-24; LL.B., Georgetown U., 1926; m. Mary L. Easby-Smith, Feb. 27, 1926; children—Paul Leason, Melanie. Admitted to D.C. bar, 1926, N.Y. bar, 1932; spl. atty. Office Gen. Counsel, Internal Revenue Service, Washington, 1926-29; asso. Breed, Abbott & Morgan, N.Y.C., 1929-71, partner, 1939-71. Adv. dir. Avon Products, Inc.; dir. Handy & Harman (both. N.Y.C.). Served with F.A., U.S. Army, 1917-19; AEF. Mem. Am. Bar Assn., Beta Gamma Sigma, Phi Delta Phi, Alpha Sigma Phi. Episcopalian. Clubs: University, Down Town Assn. (N.Y.C.). Home: Bronxville, N.Y. Died July 23, 1978.

PFATTEICHER, CARL FREDERICK (FO'IK-ER), dir. of music; b. Easton, Pa., Sept. 22, 1882; s. Rev. Phillip and Emma (Spaeth) P.; A.B., Lafayette Coll., 1903, A.M., 1908; A.M., Harvard, 1913, Th.D., 1922; Ph.D., U. Freiburg, 1931; m. Lillian Dubois Rockefeller, June 30, 1923. Instr. Latin, Lafayette, 1906-08, German, 1910-11; dir. music Phillips Acad., 1912-47, instr. philosophy, 1920-47; dir. music emeritus and vis. lectr. musicology Trinity U., San Antonio, 1947, Franklin and Marshall College, Lancaster, Pa., 1948-49; lectr. musicology, U. Pa. since 1949; has given organ recitals in larger cities of the East, several at Harvard U.; member Am. Musicological Society, Am. Hymn Soc., Delta Kappa Epsilon. Soc. of Friends. Edior of The Oxford Am. Hymnal, 1930; The Organ Works of John Redford, 1934; Introduction to The History of Music, Carl Nef, 1935; also vols. of both secular and sacred songs and chorals; The Church Organists' Golden Treasury (3 vols.) (with Prof. Davison), 1949-50; Ten Arias for Organ from the Cantatas of Bach; The Office Hymns of the Church in their Plainsoug Settings (with D. Fitts). Home: Phila. (summer) Glouceser, Mass. *

PHARR, CLYDE (FÄR), prof. Greek and Latin; b. Saltillo, Tex., Feb. 17, 1885; s. Samuel Milton and Josephine (Fleming) P.; m. Mary Elizabeth Brown, Dec. 19, 1945. B.A., Yale, 1906, Ph.D., 1910; student in Europe, 1910-12 and 1920-21; Professor Greek and Latin, Urbana (O.) Univ. School, 1906-07, 1912-13; Abernethy fellow, Yale, 1907-10; fellow Am. Inst. Archaeology, 1910-12; Am. field service fellow, 1920-21; asst. prof. Greek and Latin, Ohio Wesleyan U., 1913-17; prof. Greek and Latin, Southwestern Presbyn. U., 1918-24; asso. prof. Greek and Latin, Vanderbilt U., 1924-27, prof., 1927-50; visiting professor University of Texas, 1950-51, research professor in Roman law since 1951; prof. Latin, University of Tenn., summer 1923, Univ. of N.C., summer 1927; prof. of Latin, Language Institute, College of City of New York, summer 1932. Legal adviser, U.S. Draft Bd., 1917-18. Mem. mng. com. Am. Sch. of Classical Studies, Athens, Greece. Member American Philological Assn., Am. Inst. Archaeology, American Classical League (mem. council; sec.-treas.); mem. Am. Hist. Assn., Classical Assn. Mid. West and South (pres.; mem. exec. com.), Southern Classical Assn. (pres.), Tennessee Philological Assn. (ex-pres.), American Assn. Univ. Profs., Mediaeval Academy of America, Linguistic Society of America, Assn. Guillaume Budé (Paris), Nashville Classical Club (pres.), Eta Sigma Phi, Phi Beta Kappa, Alpha Sigma Phi. Author: Homeric Greek, 1920-22; The AEneid of Vergil, 1930; The Theodosian Code and Novels, 1952. Contributor of numerous articles to classical periodicals. Specialist in Roman law. General Editor of the Corpus Juris Romani, an enterprise for the collection, translation, and annotation of all the source material of Roman law. Home: Austin, Texas. *

PHELAN, JOHN LEDDY, educator, historian; b. Fall River, Mass., July 19, 1924; s. Joseph P. and Rose (Dunn) P.; A.B., Harvard, 1947; M.A., U. Calif., Berkeley, 1948, Ph.D., 1951. Faculty history U. Wis. Milw., 1956-58, asso. prof., 1958-60, asso. prof., Madison, 1960-64, prof., 1964-76. Mem. exec. com. Milw. Democratic County Council, 1958-60. Mem. Am. Hist. Assn., Acad. Am. Franciscan History, Conf. Latin Am. History (chmn. 1973); corr. mem. acads. history Ecuador, Colombia. Author: Millennial Kingdom of the Franciscans in the New World, 2d edit., 1970; The Hispanization of the Philippines, 1959; The Kingdom of Quito in the 17th Century; Bureaucratic Politics in the Spanish Empire, 1967. Bd. editors Hispanic-Am. Hist. Rev., 1962-70. Home: Madison, Wis. Died July 25, 1976.

PHELPS, EDWIN PHILBROOK, b. Grand Rapids, Mich., Nov. 28, 1884; s. Sebring Irving and Rosalia Katherine (Gregory) P.; student Tulane Univ., New Orleans, 1904-05, Lewis Inst., Chicago, 1905-08; LL.B., Chicago-Kent Coll. of Law, 1919; m. Vernette L. Van Deusen, Nov. 26, 1908; children—Lois Munselle, Ora Rosalia, Ruth Vernette, Lyle Loring (dec.), Gladys Irene, Edwin Philbrook, Practiced as patent atty., Chicago, 1908-23; gen. sec. Bapt. Young People's Union of America, 1923-May 1942; now associated with Soans, Pond & Anderson, attorneys and counsellors. Home: Wilmette, Ill. *

PHELPS, M(ARLIN) T(HEOPHELUS), judge; b. Dunlap, Tenn., Oct. 9, 1980; s. William A. and Rebecca (Johnson) P.; student Emory and Henry Coll., Emory, Virginia, 1905-06; Vanderbilt University, 1906-09: LL.B., 1912; married Margaret Louise Nelson, Sept. 14, 1910 (deceased, September 18, 1953); 1 son, William Nelson; m. 2d, Fae Boaedman, Sept. 4, 1956 Admitted to Ariz. bar, 1913, and practiced in Phoenix, 1913-23; judge, Superior Ct., Phoenix, 1923-49; justice Supreme Court of Ariz., 1949-61, ret., chief justice, 1954, 59. Mem. awards jury for current Freedoms Found., Valley Forge, 1954. Mem. conf. of chief justices, State Supreme Cts. of U.S.; mem. Citizens Fgn. Aid Com. Mem. Am., Ariz. and Maricopa County bar assns., Am. Acad. Pub. Affairs, John Birch Soc. (nat. council), Phi Alpha Delta (hon.). Moose. Home: Phoenix. *

PHELPS, WILLIAM RICHARD, ret. educator; b. Keyton, Va., Aug. 2, 1886; son of Thomas Key and Sarah Elizabeth (Moulton) P.; B.A., Randolph-Macon Coll., 1908; M.A., Columbia U., 1917; m. Mildred May Davis, Aug. 9, 1911; children—Rosa King, Wm. Richard (dec.) Moulton Davis. Instr. mathematics, Randolph-Macon Acad., Bedford, 1908-11; asst. prin., instr. mathematics, Randolph-Macon Inst., Danville, 1911-18; asso. prin. Randolph-Macon Acad., 1918-22, prin., 1922-33; formerly with sales department Piedmont Label Co., retired, 1956; president Bedford Tire & Rubber Company, 1929-32; dir. Bedford Trust & Savings Bank, Piedmont Label Co. Mem. Town Council, Bedford, 1924-30. Mem. national panel of arbitrators Am. Arbitration Assn. since 1943. Active in Liberty Loan and Red Cross campaigns, four minute speaker, etc., World War I. Chmn. Bedford County Citizens Com. Better Schs. 1956-58. Mem. adv. council Ferrum (Va.) Jr. Coll. Trustee Virginia War Fund, 1943 (chmn. in Bedford County, 1942-45). Recipient Alumnus award Randolph-Macon Coll., 1958. Mem. Virginia Association Prep. Schs. (pres. 1925-26), Va. Com. of Commn. on Secondary Schs. of Assn. Colleges and Secondary Schs. of Southern States (mem. standing com. on standards). Nat. Economic League (council), Bedford C. of C. (past pres.), Randolph-Macon Coll. Alumni Assn. (president 1940), Phi Delta Theta, Sigma Upsilon, Pi Gamma Mu. Democrat. Past conf. lay leader, mem. bd. missions, mem. Commn. on social concerns Virginia Conf. Meth. Ch.; trustee and exec. com. Va. Conf. Orphanage; mem. World Serv. Commn., Va. Conf., 1948-52; del. to Gen. Conf., Jackson, Miss., 1934, Birmingham, Ala., 1938; leader of lay del. to Uniting Conf. at Kan. City, Mo., 1939; del. to Gen. Conf., Atlantic City, 1940, Kansas City, 1944, Boston, 1948, Pittsburgh, 1964, Chicago, 1966, Southeastern Jurisdictional Conf., Asheville, N.C., 1940, Atlanta, 1944, Columbia, S.C., 1948, Roanoke, Virginia, 1952, Lake Junaluska, N.C., 1956, 60, 64; mem. Virginia Council Chs. (chmn. finance commn. 1951-53); mem. Gen. Bd. of Lay Activities of Meth. Ch., 1941, also sec. and mem. exec. com.; treas. Va. Meth. Adv. Bd. Elk, Rotarian (pres. Bedford 1928-29). Dir. Prohibition Emergency Movement in Va., 1933. Home: Bedford, Va. *

PHIFER, ROBERT SMITH, lawyer; b. "Burleigh," Person Co., N.C., Aug. 5, 1882; s. Prof. Robert Smith and Isabella Hunt (McGehee) P.; ed. under father (a classical scholar), and at Hampden-Sidney Coll., class of 1903; m. Corinne Elise Williamson, of Jackson, Miss., Jan. 15, 1913; children—Isabella Glenn, Calhoun Williamson. Various lines of business until 1907; city editor Danville (Va.) Daily Register; mgr. "Burleigh," 1911, 12; began practice of law at Jackson, Miss., 1913; counselor State Tax Commission of Mississippi, 1921-23; apptd. atty. for state revenue dept. of Miss., 1924; counselor of the atty. gen.'s office, Miss., 1925-27; counselor, governor's office, 1928-33; assisted attorney general in defending initiative and referendum amendment to Constitution of Miss.; defended (without pay) Charles Keller who killed 4 men in one day—now in State Insane Asylum. Atty. for Hinds Co. (Miss.) Draft Bd., World War. Served as pvt., 2d and 1st lt., Va. Vols., and a.d.c. to Gen. Vaughan; student Officers' Sch. of Instrn., Camp Zachary Taylor, Louisville, Ky., 1918; commd. capt. J.A.G.D., Res., Aug. 14, 1924. Mem. Am., Miss. and Hinds Co. bar assns., Miss. Hist. Soc., Swedenburg Scientific Assn., Nat. Single Tax League, Nat. Popular Govt. League, Soc. Colonial Wars, Soc. of the Cincinnati, S.R., S.A.R., Order of Washington, Order of LaFayette, Soc. War of 1812, Sons of Confederate Vets. (asso.), Huguenot Soc. of S.C., etc. Democrat. Presbyterian. Mason (32deg.). Home: "Burleigh," Semora, N.C.*

PHILIPPI, JULIUS EDWARD, agrl. and other projects; b. Beardstown, Ill., Oct. 2, 1882; s. Edward H. and Maria E. (Norton) P.; ed. Teachers' Normal Sch. and Ottawa (Kan.) U.; m. Eugenia Sá de Azevedo Lage, of Rio de Janeiro, Mar. 25, 1922; 1 dau., Gene-Marie. With Mexican Central Ry., 1901-06; later represented various cos. in Mexico, West Indies and S. America; apptd. commercial attaché to Am. Embassy, Rio de Janeiro, Aug. 15, 1918; resigned June 1920, re-entered industrial work connected with Brazilian development; rep. interest of Mexican Petroleum and Standard Oil Co. (Ind.) on east coast of S.A., 1920-30; now engaged in handling mining, agrl. and power projects in Brazil. Del. from Brazil to ann. meeting of Chamber of Commerce of U.S., Atlantic City, N.J., 1931, Internat. Chamber Commerce, Washington, 1931; trade adviser to Nat. Foreign Trade Conv., New York, 1931. Mem. Pan-Am. Soc., Asiatic Assn., Nat. Foreign Trade League; fellow, Am. Geog. Soc.*

PHILIPS, ALLEN GRIFFITH, business exec.; b. West Chester, Pa., Jan. 5, 1886; s. Horace Mann and Hannah Mary (Griffith) P.; B.S.A., Kansas State Coll., 1907; student Cornell U., 1907-08; m. Grace Hooker Woodward, Apr. 1, 1911; children—Helen (Mrs. Paul F. Thiele), Marion E., Paul W., Everett A. Instr. in poultry husbandry Kan. State Coll., 1908-10; prof. in charge poultry husbandry dept. Purdue U., 1910-26; vice pres. and dir. in charge of sales The McMillen Co.,

Fort Wayne, 1926-29; v.p. in charge of sales Allied Mills, Inc., since 1929, vice president and member board dirs. since 1948. Served as 1st lt., F.A., U.S. Army, World War I. Mem. Chicago Agrl. Council, Internat. and Am. Poultry Sci. Assn. (pres.), Am. Feed Mfrs. Assn., Acacia, Alpha Zeta, Gamma Sigma Delta. Clubs: Rotary, Chicago Sales Executives, Home: Kenilworth, Ill. *

PHILLIPS, BENJAMIN DWIGHT, president T. W. Phillips Gas & Oil Co.; b. New Castle, Pa., Nov. 20, 1885; s. Thomas W. and Pamphila (Hardman) P.; ed. Hiram (O.) College; m. Undine Conant, Apr. 6, 1909; children—Stella (Mrs. Rolland L. Ehrman), Clarinda (Mrs. J. F. Sprankle, Jr.), Undine (Mrs. Frank L. Wiegand, Jr.), Benjamin Dwight, Victor Karl, Donald Conant; m. 2d, Mildred Welshimer, July 11, 1963. Began in the natural gas and oil business, 1906, with T. W. Phillips Gas & Oil Co., now pres.; pres., dir. Pa. Investment & Real Estate Corp.; dir. Citizens Nat. Bank (New Castle, Pa.), Butler Consol. Coal Co., Thorofare Markets, Inc. Republican. Mem. Christian (Disciples) Ch. Clubs: Butler Country; Duquesne, Pittsburgh Athletic Assn. (Pitts.). Home: Butler, Pa.*

PHILLIPS, CABELL BEVERLY HATCHETT, journalist, author; b. Williamsburg, Va., June 4, 1904; s. Harry Newton and Annie (Maddux) P.; student U. Richmond, 1922-26; m. Syble Ruth Keeney, June 21, 1930; 1 son, Beverly Michael. Reporter, Richmond (Va.) Times-Dispatch, 1926-28, 32-36; information officer WPA, Washington, 1936-38; asst. dir. information Dept. Justice, 1940-44; Washington corr. Chgo. Herald-Examiner, 1945; mem. staff Washington bur. N.Y. Times, 1945-71. Author: Dateline Washington, 1948; The Truman Presidency, 1966; From the Crash to the Blitz, 1929-39, 1969; the 1940s: Decade of Triumph and Trouble, 1975; also articles in mags., text books. Home: Hilton Head Island, S.C. Died Nov. 14, 1975.

PHILLIPS, CHESTER ARTHUR, educator; b. Scipio, Ind., July 17, 1882; s. Jacob and Celia Celestia P.; B.A., Central Coll., Ind., 1904; B.A., Yale 1908, M.A., 1909, Ph.D., 1919; m. Mary Gordon McMurray; children—Jessie Dorothy, Gordon, Van Lehn. Prin. high sch. Weston, O., 1904-05; instr. economics, Yale, 1909-10; instr. in economics and finance, Dartmouth, 1911-13; asst. prof. same, 1913-18, prof., 1918-20; prof. economics and finance, State U. of Ia., 1920-21; dean of Coll. of Commerce, State U. of Ia., since 1921, acting pres. July-Oct. 1940; prof. economics, Columbia, summer of 1919, 20, 22, U. of Calif., summer 1923, 28, 32, 36, U. of Chicago, summer 1931; director First National Bank of Iowa City; economist Fed. Res. Bank of Chicago, 1937-42. Mem. Am. Econ. Assn., Acad. of Polit. Science, Am. Acad. Polit. and Social Science, Economists' Nat. Com. on Monetary Policy, Phi Sigma Kappa, Phi Beta Kappa, Delta Sigma Pi, Beta Gamma Sigma. United Brethren. Author: Readings in Money and Banking, 1916; Bank Credit, 1920; Banking and the Business Cycle (with McManus and Nelson), 1937. Home: Iowa City, Ia. *

PHILLIPS, DOROTHY WILLIAMS, art curator; b. Camden, N.Y., Mar. 6, 1906; d. George Henry and Edna (Burkett) Williams; B.A., Wellesley Coll., 1928; student N.Y. U. Grad. Inst. Fine Arts, 1931-36, L'Institute d'Art & Archeologie, Sorbonne, Paris, summer 1935; m. Ralph Edward Phillips, May 14, 1937 (dec. 1969); children—Diana (Mrs. Alain Berrier), Leslie Ann (Mrs. Maurice E. May), Deborah (Mrs. David Chodoff). Asst. curator Egyptian dept. Met. Museum Art, N.Y.C., 1930-48; curator collection and research, editor, compiler misc. catalogues for loan exhibitions of Am. art Corcoran Gallery Art, Washington, 1959-76. Mem. exec. bd. Japan br. Internat. Social Service, 1955-57. Carnegie fellow, 1935. Mem. Am. Assn. Museums, Washington Print Club. Clubs: City Tavern (Washington); Tokyo College Women's (pres. 1950-53). Author: Ancient Egyptian Animals, 1948. Compiler, editor: A Catalogue of the Collection of American Paintings, Vol. I, 1966, author, Vol. II, 1973. Contbr. articles profl. jours. Home: Washington, D.C. Died Dec. 15, 1977.

PHILLIPS, EDGAR JOHN, lawyer; b. Jamaica, B.W.I., Jan. 26, 1885; s. George and Emma Caroline (McIntosh) P.; came to U.S., 1905, naturalized citizen, 1911; Denison U., Granville, O., 1905-8; LL.B., U. of Chicago, 1911; m. Lois Parsons of Chicago, Ill., Feb. 20, 1914. Admitted to Illinois bar, 1911, and since practiced at Chicago; now mem. firm Phillips, Mack & O'Bryan. Four minute man, World War. Mem. Am., Ill. State and Chicago bar assns. Past dist. dep. G.M. of Masons; lecturer on Masonic topics. Republican. Baptist. Clubs: Evanston Golf (pres. 1923), Gyro of Chicago (one of the organizers, 1914, pres., 1919); pres. Internat. Assn. Gyro Clubs, 1920. Home: Wilmette, Ill. *

PHILLIPS, JAMES EMERSON, JR., educator, univ. dean; b. Los Angeles, Nov. 11, 1912; s. James Emerson and Lucy A. (Batman) P.; A.B., UCLA, 1934, M.A., 1936; Ph.D. (univ. fellow 1938-39), Columbia U., 1940; m. Geneva A. Ficker, June 6, 1955. Instr. English, U. Calif. at Los Angeles, 1939-42, asst. prof., 1946-49, asso. prof., 1949-55, prof., 1955-79, chmn. dept., 1955-60, asso. dean for honors programs, 1966-70, asso. vice chancellor for grad. affairs, 1974-79, dean grad. div., 1974-79. Organist Westwood Methodist Ch., Los Angeles, 1933-36. Mem. bd. admissions and relations with schs. U. Calif., 1954-57. Bd. dirs. Univ. Religious Conf., 1973—. Served with U.S. Army, 1942-46. Recipient UCLA Alumni Assn. Disting. Teaching award, 1969. Guggenheim fellow, 1945; Fulbright scholar, 1954-55. Mem. Modern Lang. Assn. Am., Renaissance Soc. Am., Internat. Assn. U. Profs. English (sec.), Phi Beta Kappa. Author: The State In Shakespeare's Greek and Roman Plays, 1940; Images of a Queen: Mary Stuart in Sixteenth Century Literature, 1964; Twentieth Century Interpretations of Coriolanus, 1970; also articles, revs. Home: Los Angeles. Died July 24, 1979; buried Westwood Meml. Park.

PHILLIPS, JOHN NICHOLSON, ins. co. exec.; b. Kohala, Hawaii, Jan. 31, 1919; s. John Nicholson and Mabel Ada (Joyce) P.; B.A., U. Wash., 1940; m. Natalie Klein Smith, Nov. 23, 1947; children—Marilyn (Mrs. T. Moore), Pamela, Deborah, Penny. Accountant, Pioneer Mill Co., Ltd., Lahaina, Maui, Hawaii, 1940-41; treas. Fisher Corp., Ltd., Honolulu, 1946-47; v.p., sec.-treas. First Ins. Co. Hawaii, Ltd., 1947-64, pres., dir., 1965-67; exec. v.p., dir. Gt. Am. Ins. Co., 1967-69, Am. Nat. Fire Ins. Co., 1967-69; sr. v.p., controller TICOR, 1969-79. Served to lt. comdr. USNR, 1941-45. Mem. Am. Inst. C.P.A.'s, Hawaii Soc. C.P.A.'s, Phi Beta Kappa, Beta Alpha Psi. Home: Arcadia, Calif. Died Apr. 22, 1979.

PHILLIPS, LYLE WINSTON, educator; b. Arthur, N.D., Sept. 9, 1910; s. Reuben and Sarah (Rudd) P.; B.S., N.D. State Coll., 1932; M.A., U. Buffalo, 1935; Ph.D., U. Ill., 1930; m. Audrey Flemming, Sept. 4, 1937; children—Leslie R. and Stephanie L. (twins), James W. Research fellow U. Chgo., 1939-40; instr. physics U. Ill., 1940-42, asso., 1942-44; physicist Armstrong Cork Co., 1944-46; prof. physics U. Buffalo, 1946-80, head physics dept., chmn. div. scis., 1947-80. Vice pres. Frontier Research Corp., Buffalo. Fellow Am. Phys. Soc.; mem. Am. Assn. Physics Tchrs., Phi Beta Kappa, Sigma Xi, Phi Kappa Phi. Home: Buffalo, N.Y. Died Mar. 31, 1980.

PHILLIPS, NATHANIEL, lawyer; b. Kalwarier, Lithuania, Dec. 25, 1884; s. Jacob L. and Miriam (Cohen) P.; brought by parents to U.S., 1885; A.B., Coll. City of New York, 1903; LL.B., New York U., 1907, LL.M., 1908; m. Ruth Dorothy Simon, Nov. 28, 1921. Teacher Pub. Sch. No. 20, N.Y. City, 1903-11; began law practice at N.Y. City, 1907; spl. asst. atty. gen., 1933, 35, 37, 38. Chmn. Mayor's Citizenship Com., Mayor's Com. on Reception to New Voters; mem. Mayor's Com. to Welcome British, French, Italian and Japanese Missions, City of N.Y. George Washington Bi-Centennial Commn., 1932, N.Y. Conf. for Unemployment Ins. Legislation; dir. lawyers com. on arrangement and maintenance of Dept. of Jurisprudence, Hebrew Univ. in Palestine, Mem. Nat. League for Am. Citizenship (a founder; pres. since 1913), Mitchel Memorial Commn. (mem. exec. com.), N.Y. State Commn. for Active Citizenship (dir.), Central Park Assn. (chmn. stranger's gate commn.), Arbitration Soc. America (hon. arbitration board, National Citizenship Council (hon. vice president), War Committee of the Bar, American Bar Assn., N.Y. State Bar Assn. (com. on Am. citizenship), Assn. Bar City New York (chmn. com. on round table confs.; mem. com. on courts of superior jurisdiction), N.Y. County Lawyers Assn. (chmn. on civil liberties; chmn. com. on Am. citizenship; v. chmn. com. on nominations; mem. spl. com. to consider President's proposal to reconstitute Supreme Ct.). Trade and Commerce Bar Assn. (chmn. com. on industrial relations; dir.), Soc. Med. Jurisprudence, Asso. Alumni Coll. City New York (dir.). Mem. Mayor's Com. for Observance of 150th Anniversary of Adoption of U.S. Constitution; mem. U.S. Constitution Sesquicentennial Com.; mem. Mayor's Com. to Celebrate "I am an American Day"; mem. Mayor's Com. to Celebrate "New York's Part in the War"; mem. hon. Com. for Churchman Award; mem. Textbook Commn. to eliminate from textbooks matter that breeds intolerance. Democrat. Jewish religion. Mason. Home: New York, N.Y. Died Sept. 6, 1976.

PHILLIPS, ORIE LEON, judge; b. near Viola, Mercer County, Ill., Nov. 20, 1885; s. Edward and Susan (Thompson) P.; student Knox Coll., Galesburg, Ill., 1903-04; J.D., U. of Mich., 1908, LL.D., 1935; hon. Dr. Engring., Colo. Sch. of Mines, 1940; LL.D., Colorado College, 1951, University Denver, 1951, Trinity College, 1955; married Helen M. Bissell, June 21, 1910. Admitted to bar, New Mexico, 1910, and before Supreme Court of New Mexico and United States Dist. Court, 1912; practiced at Raton; mem. Crampton & Phillips, 1915-19, Crampton, Phillips & Darden, 1919-23; gen. atty. St. Louis, Rocky Mt. & Pacific Co., 1917-23, Asst. dist. attorney 8th Jud. Dist. of N.M., 1912-16; mem. N.M. Senate, 1920-23 (Rep. majority floor leader and chmn. judiciary com.); resigned from Senate Mar. 1923, to become U.S. dist. judge, Dist. of N.M., by apptmt. of President Harding; commd. U.S. circuit judge, 10th Jud. Circuit, by President Hoover, Apr. 29, 1929; chief judge, Tenth Judicial Circuit, 1940-55, visiting professor of law, summers, Northwestern U., 1936, 37, U. of Mich., 1938. Mem. Am. Bar Assn. (exec. com. 1929-32; medal for conspicuous service for cause of Am. jurisprudence, 1950), N.M. Bar Assn. (pres. 1921-23), Am. Law Inst. (member council). Methodist. Mason (K.T., 32 deg). Clubs: Denver, Cherry Hills. Home: Denver. *

PHILLIPS, PERCY TOUMINE, dentist, dental assn. exec.; b. N.Y.C., Apr. 7, 1898; s. Percy and Mary Elizabeth (Taylor) P.; D.D.S., Columbia U., 1919, D.Sc. (hon.), 1977; LL.D. (hon.), Fairleigh Dickinson U., Rutherford, N.J., 1959; m. Henriette Otelia Boll, 1922. Practicing dentist, N.Y.C., 1920-62, sec. N.Y. State Dental Soc., 1962-77; mem. med. adv. com. Nat. Security Resources Bd., 1949-50; civilian cons. surgeon gen. Dept. Navy, 1958-59; mem. nat. adv. com. hosps. and clinics Surgeon Gen. U.S., 1959; cons. VA. Decorated chevalier del 'Ordre de la Couronne (Belgium); recipient Henry Spenadel award 1st Dist. Dental Soc., 1955; William Jarvie medal N.Y. State Dental Soc., 1957; Spl. Alumni award N.Y. U. Coll. Dentistry, 1958; William John Geis award Am. Coll. Dentists, 1959; Pierre Fauchard award Pierre Fauchard Acad., 1960; D. Austin Sniffen medal 9th Dist. Dental Soc., 1973. Fellow Am., Internat. colls. dentists, N.Y. Acad. Dentistry (dir. from 1948), N.Y. Inst. Clin. Oral Pathology, Pierre Fauchard Acad.; mem. ADA (pres. 1958-59, past trustee, speaker ho. dels.; Distinguished Service award 1976), Dental Soc. State N.Y. (sec. 1960-73; Centennial award 1958), Bronx (past pres.), First Dist. (past pres.), Bklyn. (Centennial award 1960) dental socs., Fedn. Dentaire Internat., Nat. Health Council, Am. Pub. Health Assn., Psi Omega. Home: White Plains, N.Y. Died July 22, 1979.

PHILLIPS, ROBERT ALLAN, physician; b. Clear Lake, Iowa, July 16, 1906; s. Albin Blackmore and Agnes (Allan) P.; B.S., U. Ia., 1927; M.D., Washington U., 1929; m. Hope N. Fuess, Nov. 1, 1946; children—Robert A., Wilkie McC., Hope C., Innis McF., Honor B., Abiathar. Intern Barnes Hosp., St. Louis, 1929-30; NRC fellow Harvard, also Albert Ludwig U., Freiburg, Germany, 1930-32; Lucius Littauer fellow Harvard, 1932-33, asst. fatigue lab., 1936; asst. surg. resident Yale Med. Sch., 1933-35; instr. physiology Stanford, 1935-36; asst. prof. physiology Cornell U., 1936-40; fellow Rockefeller Inst. Med. Research, 1940-46; chmn. dept. physiology Alfred I. du Pont Inst., Nemours Found., 1946; commd. lt. comdr. M.C., USNR, 1946, advanced through grades to capt. USN, 1955; comdg. officer U.S. Naval Med. Research Unit 3, 1947-49, head dept. clin. investigation, 1949-52; head medicine and surgery br., research div. Navy Dept. Bur. Medicine and Surgery, 1952-55; comdg. officer U.S. Med. Research Unit 2, Taiwan, 1955-65; ret., 1965; dir. Pakistan SEATO Cholera Research Lab., 1965-71; prof. dept. epidemiology and internat. health U. Wash. Sch. Pub. Health and Community Medicine, 1971. Treas., U.S. Ednl. Found., Egypt, 1949-52, bd. dirs., China, 1957-59, chmn., China, 1960-64. Decorated D.S.M., Certificate of Merit; hon. mem. Order Brit. Empire; recipient Egyptian Cholera gold medal, 1947, award of merit Philippines Safety Council, 1961, Stitt award, certificate of appreciation Republic Vietnam, 1964, gold Key to City of Taipei, James D. Bruce award, 1966, Lasker award for clin. research, 1967. Mem. Soc. Exptl. Biology and Medicine, Am. Physiol. Soc., Harvey Soc., N.Y. Acad. Scis., Sigma Xi, Alpha Omega Alpha. Home: Taipei, Taiwan. Died Sept. 20, 1976.

PHILLIPY, LESTER NEWTON, constrn. co. exec.; b. Greencastle, Pa., Nov. 28, 1897; s. Newton Shank and Rebecca Susan (Eshleman) P.; B.Engring., Johns Hopkins U., 1920; m. Anna Katherine Krause, Mar. 31, 1923; 1 son, Lester Newton. With Whiting Turner Contracting Co., Balt., 1920-80, gen. supt., estimator, 1928-39, sec., 1939-80, dir., 1940-80, v.p., 1947-51, exec. v.p., 1951-80; dir. Whiting Turner Consultants. Vice pres. Carroll County Hist. Soc. Served with U.S. Army, 1918. Registered profl. engr., Md. Fellow ASCE. Republican. Lutheran. Club: Kiwanis (past lt. gov. internat.). Home: Westminster, Md. Died Dec. 1980.

PHILOON, WALLACE, COPELAND, (FI'LOON) army officer; b. Auburn, Me., Oct. 13, 1883; s. Everett L. and Mary A. (Lara) P.; A.B. Bowdoin College, 1905; M.S. (hon.) 1914. B.S., United States Military Academy, West Point, 1909; attended Advanced Class, Infantry School, 1923, Command and Gen. Staff School, 1924, Army War College, 1933; m. Mary Lloyd Grayson, Oct. 20, 1921; 1 son, Wallace Copeland, Jr., Commd. 2d lt., Inf., U.S. Army, 1909, advanced through ranks to major gen. (temp.). 1945; served at various posts, continental U.S., and Hawaiian Dept., 1909-18; provost marshal, Dist. Columbia, 1918; asst. military attaché, Peking, China. 1919-23; instr. Me. Nat. Guard, 1925-27, Command and Gen. Staff Sch., 1928-32; cond. Pettit Barracks, P.I., 1933-35; Gen. Staff, War Dept., 1935-39; chief of staff, Panama Canal, 1940-41, of Caribbean Defense Command, 1941-42; comdg. Infantry Replacement Training Center, Ft. McClellan, Ala., 1942-44. Deputy Comdr., Alaskan Dept., 1944-June 1945. Served, 14th Inf., U.S. Army, Vancouver Barracks, Washington, aide to commanding general, 40th Division, Camp Kearney, California, provost marshal, office Chief of Staff, World War; ret. as maj. gen. 1945. Adminstrv. asst. to gov. of Me.,

1946-47. Overseer Bowdoin College. Member Alpha Delta Phi. Universalist. Mason. Club: Army and Navy (Washington, D.C.). Home: Liberty, Me.*

PHIPPS, LAWRENCE CLINTON, JR., utilities exec.; b. Pitts., June 30, 1886; s. Lawrence Cowle and Ibrealla (Loomis) P.; Ph.B., Yale, 1907; m. Elaine Oakes, Oct. 3, 1945; children—Mary (Mrs. Chapman Young), Diana (Mrs. Clay S. Keene), Joan (Mrs. Jack R. Pechman), Richmond (Mrs. John M. Shields), Lawrence Clinton III, Henry Richmond. Treas. Cal. Electric Power Co., 1908-19, v.p., 1919-51, also dir.; treas. Denver & Salt Lake Ry., 1925-36; dir. Mountain States Tel. & Tel. Co., 1911-65. Treas. Agnes Meml. Sanatorium, 1909-32; chmn. dist. com. Denver Found.; dir. Colo. Woman's Coll. Served as aviation cadet, World War I, as maj. Q.M.C., AUS, 1942-45. Home: Littleton, Colo. Died May 16, 1976.

PHIPPS, OVAL ALEXANDER, lawyer, educator; b. Fay, Okla., Feb. 22, 1909; s. David Alexander and Nora (Walker) P.; A.B., U. Colo., 1932, LL.B., 1937, LL.M., 1938; D.Sc. of Law, J.S.D., Yale U., 1951; m. Mabel Ravenscroft, Nov. 1, 1939 (dec. 1941); 1 son, David Alexander; m. 2d, Merle Audre Hill, June 10, 1946; children—Arral Alexander, Marion Alexander, Nancy Alexander, Nelcy Alexander, Paul Alexander. Admitted to Colo. bar, 1938; pvt. practice, Denver, 1938-43; prof. law Temple U., Phila., 1946-51; dean, prof. law U. S.D., 1951-56; prof. law St. Louis U., 1956-75. Chmn., S.D. Bd. Bar Examiners, 1952-55. Served as lt. USNR, 1943-46. Decorated Purple Heart. Mem. Colo., S.D., Mo. bar assns., Am. Judicature Soc., Am. Law Inst., C. of C. Author: Titles in a Nutshell; The Calculus of Interests, 1968. Home: University City, Mo. Died June 30, 1975; interred Jefferson Barracks Nat. Cemetery, St. Louis.

PIAGET, JEAN, educator, psychologist; b. Neuchatel, Switzerland, Aug. 9, 1896; s. Arthur Piaget; Doctoral Degree, U. Nauchatel, 1918; studied in Paris; hon. Doctor's Degree, Harvard. Asso. Theodore Simon, co-author Binet-Simon intelligence tests; with Institut J.J. Rousseau (Institut des Sciences de Education), asso. Inst. U. Geneva for Sci. study of child and tng. of tchrs., 1921-80, co-dir., 1933-80; prof. philosophy U. Neuchatel, 1926; prof. psychology U. Geneva, 1929, also U. Paris; prof. gen. phychology Lausanne U., 1937-54; mem. exec. council UNESCO; past dir. Internat. Office Edn.; established (with help of Rockefeller Found) Internat. Center Genetic Epistemology; dir. Internat. Bur. Edn. Mem. Swiss Soc. Psychology (past pres.); fgn. asso. mem. Nat. Acad. Scis. Author: The Language and Thought of the Child, 1926; Judgment and Reasoning in the Child, 1928; The Child's Conception of the World, 1929; Origins of Intelligence in Children, 1932; The Child's Conception of Numbers, 1952; The Construction of Realty in the Child, 1954; Logic and Philosophy, 1957; The Growth of Logical Thinking from Childhood to Adolescence, 1958; others. Home: Geneva, Switzerland. Died Sept. 16, 1980.

PIATIGORSKY, GREGOR, cellist; b. Ekaterinoslaw, Russia, Apr. 17, 1903; s. Paul I. and Maria (Amchislawsky) P.; student Imperial Conservatory Moscow, 1911-16; hon. degree in music Northwestern U.; D.Mus. (hon.), Phila. Mus. Acad., 1949; hon. doctorates Temple U., Columbia U., UCLA, Occidental Coll.; came to U.S., 1929, naturalized, 1942; m. Jacqueline-de Rothschild, Jan. 26, 1937; children—Jephta Maria, Joram Paul. Began as solo cellist, 1916; solo cellist Imperial Opera, Moscow, 1916-19, Berlin Philharmonic, 1923-28; prof. conservatory, Berlin, 1926-28; head cello dept. Curtis Inst. Music, Phila., chamber music dept. Berkshire Music Center; head cello dept. Performing Arts Acad., Music Center, Los Angeles; prof. U. So. Calif., to 1976; concerts in Europe, U.S. and world tours as virtuoso; tour Far East under auspices U.S. Dept. State, 1956; guest soloist with all maj. orchs., U.S., Europe; Heifetz-Piatigorsky concerts presented 1961-76; recs. for RCA Victor. Decorated Legion of Honor (France); recipient Brandeis gold medal. Hon. mem. Royal Philharmonic Soc., Royal Acad. Music, Violoncello Soc. N.Y. (hon. pres.). Author: Cellist, 1965; also mus. compositions. Home: Los Angeles, Calif. Died Aug. 6, 1976.

PICCARD, JEANNETTE RIDLON, clergywoman, former aerospace cons; b. Chgo., Jan. 5, 1895; d. John and Emily Caroline (Robinson) Ridlon; B.A. in Philosophy and Psychology, Bryn Mawr Coll., 1918; M.S. in Organic Chemistry, U. Chgo., 1919; Ph.D. in Edn., U. Minn., 1942; m. Jean Piccard, Aug. 19, 1919 (dec. 1963). Exec. sec., housing sect. Minn. Office Civilian Def., 1942-43; counselor Waldorf Paper Products, St. Paul, 1943-44; nurse's aid ARC, 1944-46; aerospace cons. Aerospace Research Dept., Gen. Mills, Inc., 1947; cons. Office Naval Research, 1955, Tex. Gulf Coast Sci. Ednl. Resources Center, 1966-70; cons. to dir. NASA Johnson Space Center, 1964-70; holder spherical balloon pilot's license Fedn. Aero. Internat., 1934; pilot stratosphere balloon flight, altitude 57,559 feet, 1934. Ordained deacon Episcopal Ch., 1971, priest, 1974. Pres. bd. dirs. St. Paul Episcopal Day Sch., St. Paul, 1961-65; hon. bd. dirs. Seabury-Western Theol. Sem., 1968-81; bd. dirs. St. Barnabas Day Sch., Houston, 1966-70; adv. council Dayton Av. Motivational-Tutorial Program, St. Paul, 1966-70. Recipient Certificate of Performance, Nat. Aero. Assn., 1934, Certificate of Honor, 1964; named One of Minn.'s Women of Distinction, 1956; recipient Harmon trophy Ligue Internat. des Aviateurs, 1934; Bronze plaque in memory of 1934 stratospheric balloon flight, Dearborn, Mich.; 1st recipient W. Randolph Lovelace II award Am. Astronautical Soc., 1965, Outstanding Achievement award U. Minn., 1968, award for personal contbns. to manned space flight NASA Manned Spacecraft Center, 1970. Asso. fellow Am. Inst. Aero. and Astronautics; mem. Bryn Mawr Coll., U. Chgo. U. Minn., Gen. Theol. Sem. alumni assns. Soc. Women Engrs., League Women Voters, AAUW, Am. Meterol. Soc. (pres. Twin City chpt. 1966-67); hon. mem. Wingfoot-Lighter-than-Air Soc., Minn. Aerostate Soc., Balloon Fedn. Am., Iota Sigma Pi, Sigma Delta Upsilon. Clubs: Soroptomists; New Century (St. Paul); Faculty Women's (U. Minn.). Author technical papers. Home: Minneapolis, Minn. Died May 17, 1981.

PICK, ALBERT, JR., hotel exec.; b. Chgo., July 2, 1895; s. Albert and Gertrude (Frank) P.; Ph.B., U. Chgo., 1917; LL.D. (hon.), U. Miami, 1973; D.H.L. (hon.), Northwestern U., 1976; m. Corinne Frada, Dec. 27, 1917; children—Gladys Vita, Albert. With Albert Pick & Co. Chgo., 1917-28, treas., dir., 1920-28; dir. Pick Hotels Corp., 1926-76, pres., 1930-72, chmn., 1972-76; dir. First Nat. Bank of Highland Park, Consol. Packaging Corp., Chgo. Hon. chmn., past pres. La Rabida Children's Hosp. and Research Center; bd. govs. Internat. House Chgo.; life trustee U. Chgo., Ravinia Festival Assn., Highland Park (Ill.) Hosp.; trustee People to People; trustee, hon. life chmn. Am. Hotel Found. Life mem. Chgo. Art Inst., Chgo. Hist. Soc., Chgo. Mus. Nat. History, Lincoln Park Zool. Soc. Served with U.S. Army, World War I. Recipient citation U. Chgo., 1952, Centennial award Mich. State Coll., 1955, USIA Distinguished Service award, 1960, Eisenhower medallion People to People, 1972. Mem. Internat. Hotel Assn. (exec. com., hon. life mem.), Am. Hotel and Motel Assn. (dir., past pres.), Hotel Greeters Assn., Ill. C. of C., Chgo. Assn. Commerce and Industry, Chgo. Acad. Scis., Chgo. Council Fgn. Relations, Am. Legion, Alpha Kappa Psi (hon.) Sigma Pi Eta (hon.; Hotelman of Year 1955). Clubs: Standard, Chicago Yacht, Mid-Am. (Chgo.); Northmoor Country. Home: Highland Park, Ill. Died Dec. 11, 1977; buried Rosehill Cemetery, Chgo.

PICKETT, TOM, congressman; b. Travis, Tex., Aug. 14, 1906; s. James D'Aubigne and Helen Augusta (Mackey) P.; ed. pub. schs., Iola, Tex., and Palestine, Tex.; Palestine Bus. Coll.; U. of Texas; m. Alice Louise Watson, Aug. 30, 1938; children—Helen Louise, Alice Melinda. Admitted to Tex. bar, 1929, and since practiced law, Palestine; co. atty., Anderson County, Tex., 1931-34, dist. atty., Third Judicial Dist. of Tex., 1935-44; member 79th to 82d Congresses (1945-52), 7th Texas District. Vice pres. Nat. Coal Assn. (Washington), 1952-61, Assn. Am. Railroads (Washington), 1961-80. Democrat. Home: Arlington, Va. Died June 7, 1980.

PIERCE, ALLIN HUGH, ret. U.S. judge; b. Graceville, Minn., Jan. 18, 1897; s. Charles Summner and Isabelle (Sanderson) P.; B.A., Swarthmore Coll., 1919; J.D. cum laude, U. Chgo., 1923; m. Florence Bennet, Aug. 15, 1938; children—Isabel Sanderson, Allin Hugh. Admitted to Ill. bar, 1923, U.S. Supreme Ct. bar, 1928, N.Y. bar, 1937; practice in Chgo., 1923-28; instr. Loyola U. Law Sch., Chgo., 1925; spl. atty. Bur. Internal Revenue, 1928-35; asso. Carter, Ledyard & Milburn, N.Y.C., 1936-43; mem. McDermott, Will & Emery, Chgo., 1943-45; practiced in Chgo., 1946-55; judge U.S. Tax Ct., 1955-68. Lectr. fed. taxation bar assns., univs., profl. assns. Served as aviation cadet USNRF, 1918. Mem. Am., Chgo. (chmn. com. fed. taxation 1949) bar assns., Assn. Bar City N.Y., Chgo. Fed. Tax Forum, Swarthmore Coll. Alumni Assn. (pres. 1939-40), Order of Coif, Delta Upsilon, Phi Delta Phi, Delta Sigma Rho. Republican. Presbyn. Mason. Clubs: National Lawyers (Washington); University (Evanston, Ill.). Home: Evanston, Ill. Died Feb. 14, 1980.

PIERCE, KATHARINE CURTIS (MRS. HENRY HILL PIERCE), church work; b. Summit, N.J., Aug. 11, 1882; d. William John and Angeline S. (Riley) Curtis; ed. Baldwin Sch., Bryn Mawr, Pa., and Bryn Mawr Coll.; A.M., Bowdoin Coll., 1933; m. Henry Hill Pierce, May 29, 1905; children—William Curtis, Henry Hill, Benjamin Thompson. Mem. nat. council Protestant Epis. Ch., 1937-43; member dept. racial and cultural relations, com. bus. and finance Nat. Council Chs. of Christ in Am.; mem. Am. Com. for World Council of Chs., 1937-48; exec. com., Episcopal Pacifist Fellowship; mem. bd. St. Christophers Coll., India; dir. Ch. World Service; mem. bd., United Bd. for Christian Colleges in China; v. chmn. Church Peace Mission. Clubs: Cosmopolitan, National Arts (N.Y.C.). Home: N.Y.C. *

PIERCE, LAWRENCE MICHAEL, airplane mfg. co. exec.; b. Bronx, N.Y., Dec. 22, 1922; s. Thomas A. and Hannah M. Pierce; m. Patricia Healy, May 5, 1951; children—Lawrence M., Nancy Elizabeth, Neil Matthew, Ellen Patricia. Claims examiner Aetna Casualty & Surety Co., N.Y.C., 1946-50; asso. firm Mendes & Mount, N.Y.C., 1951-55; asst. gen. counsel, asst. sec. McKesson & Robbins, Inc., N.Y.C., 1956-70; atty., asst. sec. Grumman Corp., Bethpage, N.Y., 1970-73, v.p., gen. counsel, 1973-79; sec., dir. Grumman Export Sales Corp.; sec. Grumman Avio Systems, Inc.; dir. Paumanock Ins. Co., Ltd. Past pres. Syosset Hills (N.Y.) Civic Assn. Served to lt. (j.g.) USNR, 1943-46. Mem. Am. Bar Assn., Assn. Bar City N.Y. Roman Catholic. Club: Huntington (N.Y.) Country. Home: Syosset, N.Y. Died Feb. 25, 1979.

PIERCE, ROBERT WILLARD (BOB), missionary, evangelist; b. Ft. Dodge, Ia., Oct. 8, 1914; s. Fred and Flora Belle (Harlow) P.; student Pasadena (Cal.) Coll., 1933-36; LL.D. (hon.), Northwestern Schs., Mpls., 1949, Yonsei U., Seoul, Korea, 1961; D.D. (hon.), John Brown U., 1967; m. Ruth Lorraine Johnson, Nov. 24, 1936; children—Sharon Ruth, Marilee, Robin. Ordained to ministry Bapt. Ch., 1942; co-organizer Youth for Christ, 1944, v.p., 1945-49, missionary to China, 1947, Korea, 1950-53; organizer 1950, pres. until 1967, World Vision, Monrovia, Cal., orgn. supports orphans in 20 nations; also broadcaster, war corr. Pres.-founder Sarmaritan's Purse, charitable trust, internat. reliefs and scholarships. Bd. reference Oriental Missionary Soc. Pres. bd. dirs. Mustard Seed. Decorated Order Cultural Merit, Nat. medal (Korea); Medal for Pub. Welfare Service, Korea, 1959, 64, 76. Author books; producer motion pictures. Address: Hollywood, Calif. Died Sept. 6, 1978.

PIERCE, WILLIAM HEFLIN, lawyer, orgn. exec.; b. Huntsville, Ala., June 30, 1908; s. Jacob Emory and Nannie (Heflin) P.; A.B., U. Ala., 1928, J.D., 1930; m. Virginia Louise Duke, June 8, 1933. Admitted to Ala. bar, 1930, also U.S. Supreme Ct. bar; practice in Huntsville, 1930-36, Montgomery, Ala., 1936-42; atty. staff gen. counsel Dept. Agr., Atlanta, 1945-58, mem. firm VanderZeyde & Pierce; municipal judge, Miami Shores, Fla., 1966-80. Mem. Knights of Pythias, 1937-80, trustee Grand Lodge of Ala., 1948-80, internat. supreme chancellor, 1958, also editor-in-chief publn., Pythian Internat.; chmn. Pythian com. Nat. Cystic Fibrosis Research Found. 1960-62. Vice chmn., exec. com. All-Am. conf. to Combat Communism, 1954-60, chmn., from 1960. Served to maj. USAAF, World War II; lt. col. Res. Decorated Air medal (6), Silver Star, Legion of Merit, Gen. Commendation ribbon with metal pendant; elected to Wisdom Hall of Fame, 1970. Mem. Am., Fed., Dade County bar assns., Fla. Bar, Am. Trial Lawyers Assn., Internat. Platform Assn., Am. Judicature Soc., Ala. Jr. C. of C. (pres. 1930-31), C. of C. Miami Shores (pres. 1966), Centennial Legion (chief staff old guard battalion 1959-60), Dramatic Order Knights Khorassan, Am. Legion, 40 and 8, V.F.W., Phi Kappa Psi, Phi Alpha Delta. Democrat. Baptist (deacon, Sunday sch. tchr.). Mason (32 deg., K.T., Shriner), Elk, Kiwanian. Clubs: Oasis Luncheon, Flamingo Dinner, Miami Shores Country. Home: Miami Shores, Fla. Died Jan. 24, 1980; interred So. Meml. Park, Miami.

PIERPONT, HARLAN TRIMBLE, corp. exec.; born Chester Hill, O., Apr. 14, 1883; s. I. E. S. and Sarah (Trimble) P.; student Albany (N.Y.) Acad.; Roxbury Latin Sch., Boston; A.B., Harvard, 1906; m. Dorothy Langley Hobson, June 1, 1910 (dec. 1957); m. 2d Janet Carter Clarke, June 25, 1958. With Springfield (Mass.) Republican, 1907-10; engaged in investment management bus., 1910—; member bd. trustee and mem. investment com. Worcester Mechanics Savings Bank; dir. American Motors Corp. Served with supply dept. Am. Red Cross, as chmn. Liberty Loan campaigns, West Roylston, Mass, vice chmn. Worcester chapter, World War II. Pres. Worcester Children's Friend Society, 1948-53. Member Welfare Federation, Worcester, Massachusetts. Clubs: Harvard, Tatnuck Country, Worcester (pres. 1931-34), Worcester University (pres. 1919). Home: West Boylston, Mass. *

PIERROT, GEORGE FRANCIS, editor, TV producer, writer; b. Chgo., Jan. 11, 1898; s. George Francis (M.D.) and Aloyse (Martin) P.; A.B. in Journalism, U. Wash., 1920; L.H.D., Wayne State U., 1978; m. Kathryn Barnhisel, Aug. 31, 1922 (div. 1929); 1 son, George Francis Jr. (dec. 1929); m. 2d, Helen Hay Reck, Aug. 3, 1935; children—Nancy Ann, Helen Jeanne, Alan Hay, Robert Charnley. Reporter, Yakima Valley Am., 1919; editor U. Wash. Daily, 1920, Canning Age, 1920; reporter Seattle Times, 1920-21; publicity sec. Seattle C. of C., 1921-22; lectr. journalism U. Wash. Extension Div., 1921-22; asso. editor Bus. Mag., Detroit, 1922; asst. mng. editor Am. Boy mag., 1922-24; editor Am. Boy-Youth's Companion, 1924-36, staff writer travelling around world, 1931; world traveller as corr. World Letters, Inc 1937-38; pres., dir. World Adventure Series Lectures, 1933-79; pres. George F. Pierrot Prodns., Inc. (TV), 1959-80; pres GFP, Inc., TV syndicated shows, 1966-73; publicity dir. Ford Motor Co. Expn., N.Y. World's Fair, 1930-40; pres editor Sprague Publs., Inc., 1940-41; traveled in Europe, Africa, Asia making ednl. films USAF, 1952; chmn. Intra-Film, 1975-76; roving editor Mich. AAA mag. Mich. Living, 1975-80. Mng. dir. Met. Detroit

USO, 1942-43; exec. sec. Med. Sci. Center of Wayne U., 1943-47; mem. Regional Loyalty Bd., US. Civil Service Commn. Candidate Central Inf. O.T.S., Camp McArthur, Tex., 1918. Trustee Cranbrook Sch. for Boys, 1935-45; trustee, v.p. Internat. Film Found., 1946-49; journalism adv. bd. Wayne State U., 1949-80; pres. Circumnavigators Club Found., 1964-80; bd. dirs. Mich. Humane Soc., 1964-80. Recipient Distinguished Service award Wayne State U., 1961; Stenius award for audio-visual service to internat. relations, 1961; award of merit Circumnavigators Club, 1964; MUCC State Conservation award, 1965; World Trader of Year award World Trade Club, Detroit, 1966; Minute Man award Gov. Mich., 1967; Significant Sig citation Sigma Chi, 1969; citation Mich. Senate, 1971, 75; Plaque Merit in Tourism, Austria, 1972; Merit award, W. Germany, 1972; Macomb Mr. Zip award, 1975; Pioneer award Detroit Producers Assn., 1978; chevalier Ordre Nationale du Merite, France, 1976, others. Mem. Detroit Zool. Soc. (dir.), Gamma Theta Epsilon, Sigma Delta Chi (internat. treas. 1923, sec. 1924, pres. 1925, editorial bd Quill Wells Key 1924). Dir., Am. Platform Guild, Am. Platform Assn., Archives Am. Art; hon. life trustee Detroit Inst. Arts Founders' Soc. Mem. Am. Polar Soc., English-Speaking Union, Ducks Unltd., Friends Detroit Pub. Library, Wilderness Soc. (life), Am. Mus. Nat. History (asso.), Mich. Outdoor Writers Assn., Detroit, Mich. hist. socs., Nat. Wildlife Fedn., Soc. Am. Travel Writers, Midwest Travel Writers Assn., Sons of Whisky Rebellion (comdr. in chief 1966-80), Profl. Travel Film Dirs. Assn. (pres. 1972). Clubs: Explorers (co-comdr. El Paricutin volcano expdn., Mex. 1944); Circumnavigators (Mich. pres. 1962, internat. pres. 1962-63, Magellan award 1973), Adventurers, Overseas Press (N.Y.C.); Detroit Press; Torch, Prismatic (Detroit); Mich. Polar Equator; Internat Skal; Economic. Author: Yea, Sheriton, 1925; The Vagabond Trail, 1935; producer World Adventure Series, WXYZ-TV, 1948-68, George Pierrot Show, WWJ-TV, 1953-76, George Pierrot Presents, WWJ-TV, 1958-75. Home: Detroit, Mich. Died Feb. 16, 1980.

PIERSON, JOSEPH BRELSFORD, reporter, editor, publisher; b. Watseka, Ill., Jan. 5, 1885; s. William Franklin and Corella (Brelsford) P.; student Ill. Wesleyan U., 1901-03; m. Josephine Lily Fritz, Feb. 7, 1910; children—Virginia (Mrs. Robert Denny), William Franklin (U.S.M.C.), Catherine (Mrs. F. T. Golden), Mary Jane (Mrs. David (Garrick), Thomas (U.S.M.C.), Homer (U.S. Army Air Corps). Founder, editor and pub. Eastland (Tex.) Co., Bulletin, 1903-05; editor Crookston (Minn.) Jour., 1905-09; reporter and news editor Pioneer Press, St. Paul Minn., 1908-10; copyreader and asst. city editor Chicago Trib., 1910-17, editor army edition, Paris, France, 1917-18, fgn. news editor, Chicago, 1918-29; chmn. and organizer Am. Newspaper Pub. Com. on Cable & Radio Communications, 1920; founder of Press Wireless, Inc., U.S., a press and broadcast carrier on every continent; pres. News Traffic Bd., Ltd., Can. 1924-45; pres. and gen. mgr. Press Wireless, Inc., 1929-44; vice pres. Raytheon Manufacturing Company, 1944-48. Mem. Inst. of Radio Engrs., Am. Physical Soc. (N.Y.). Independent. Christian. Clubs: Nat. Press (Washington, D.C.); Metropolitan, Overseas Press (N.Y.). Co-founder Trappist monastery near Evans, Mo., 1950. Address: Springfield, Mo. *

PIERSON, RICHARD NORRIS, obstetrician and gynecologist; b. Stamford, Conn., Feb. 2, 1893; s. Samuel and Caroline (Norris) P.; B.A., Princeton U., 1914; M.D., Columbia U., 1918; m. Dorothy Stewart, Oct. 8, 1927; children—Frances, Richard N., Stephen, Stewart. Cons. obstetrician and gynecologist Stamford Hosp., Huntington Hosp., North Community Hospital, Glen Cove, Long Island; formerly attending obstetrician and gynecologist Sloane Hosp. for Women (New York). Dir. Am. Hosp. of Istanbul; past pres. Planned Parenthood Fedn. America; trustee Buckley Sch. Foundation. Pres. bd. dirs. Adm. Bristol Hosp., Istanbul, Turkey. Recipient Albert and Mary Lasker Found. award for work in planned parenthood, 1948; diplomate Am. Board Obstetrics and Gynecology. Fellow A.M.A., Am. Coll. Surgeons; mem. Alpha Omega Alpha. Clubs: Piping Rock; Huntington Country; Cold Spring Harbor Beach. University (N.Y.C.). Home: Cold Spring Harbor, N.Y. Died Feb. 27, 1976.

PIERSON, WARREN LEE, corp. exec.; b. Princeton, Minn., Aug. 29, 1896; s. Louis W. and Hilda (Pearson) P.; A.B., U. Calif., 1917; LL.B., Harvard U., 1922; m. Eleanor Mehnert, Aug. 12, 1927. Admitted to Calif. bar, 1922, N.Y. bar, 1946; practiced in Los Angeles until 1933; spl. counsel RFC, Washington, 1933-34; gen. counsel Export-Import Bank of Washington, 1934-36, pres., gen. counsel, 1936-44; pres. Am. Cable & Radio Corp., Comml. Cable Co., Mackay Radio & Telegraph and All Am. Cable & Radio Corp., 1945-47; chmn. bd. All Am. Cables & Radio, Inc.; chmn. bd. Trans, World Airlines, Inc.; dir. Molybdenum Corp. Verientes-Camaguey Sugar Co. Cuba, Internat. Tel. & Tel., Tech. Studies, Inc., Twin Fair Inc. Mem. Exec. Com. on Comml. Policy, 1938-44, Inter-Am. Fin. and Econ. Adv. Com., 1940-45; adviser U.S. delegation 3d meeting Consultation of Ministers Gen. Affairs Am. Republics, Rio de Janeiro, Jan. 1942; adviser U.S. del. UN Monetary Conf., Bretton Woods, N.H., July 1944; adviser U.S. del. Inter-Am. Conf. on Problems of War and Peace, Mexico City, 1945; U.S. del. Tripartite Commn. on German Debts with rank of ambassador, 1951-52; chmn. U.S. Council, 1953-55. Served as ambulance driver French Army, 1917; grad. Saumur Arty. Sch.; 1st lt. 101st F.A., 26th Div., 1918-19. Decorated comdr. Legion d'Honneur (France); comendador Ordem Cruzeiro do Sul (Brazil); comdr. Order of White Rose (Finland); Order Mexicana del Aguila Azteca (Mexico); Order of Italian Solidarity, Order of Merit (lt.); Comdr.'s Cross, Order of Merit (Germany); comdr. Order of Christ (Portugal); grand officer Order of Merit (Italy). Mem. Internat. C. of C. (pres. 1955-57), Internat. Air Transport Assn. (pres. 1950-51), Phi Delta Theta. Clubs: Maidstone, Brook (N.Y.C.); Bohemian (San Francisco). Home: East Hampton, N.Y. Died Jan. 12, 1978; buried Further Lane, East Hampton.

PIETENPOL, CLARENCE JOHN, college professor; b. Leota, Minn., July 7, 1897; s. Henry John and Mattie (Brasser) P.; student Hope Coll., Holland, Mich., 1916-18; B.A., U. Pitts., 1920, U. Wis., 1920-21; M.S., U. Colo., 1924; postgrad. Yale, 1924-25; Ph.D., N.Y. U., 1928; m. L(inda) Claire Caflisch, June 22, 1928; children—Jack Curtis, Jerry Lewis. Instr., U. Colo., 1921-24; asst. Yale, 1924-25; instr. N.Y. U., 1925-28; asst. prof. physics L.I. U., 1928-29, asso. prof., 1929-37; asst. prof. Washington and Jefferson Coll., 1937-39, prof., 1939-46, dean engring., 1941-43, dean faculty, 1943-46, asst. to pres., 1943-45, acting pres., 1945-46; prof. Davidson Coll., 1946-63, dean of faculty, 1953-58, acting pres., 1957-58. Mem. Am. Phys. Soc., Am. Assn. Physics Profs., AAUP, Sigma Xi. Presbyterian. Author: Laboratory Physics. Home: Davidson, N.C. Died Oct. 12, 1975; cremated.

PIETENPOL, WILLIAM, BRASSER, (PE'TEN-POL) physicist; b. Newkirk, Ia., Mar. 26, 1886; s. Rev. Henry John and Mattie (Brasser) P.; A.B., Central Coll., Pella, Ia., 1909; A.M., U. of Wis., 1914, Ph.D., 1916; m. Helen Vaughn Carson, Aug. 30, 1916; 1 son, William John. Asst. in physics, U. of Wis., 1912-16; prof. physics, Hope Coll., Holland, Mich., 1916-18; asst. prof. physics, U. of Pittsburgh, 1918-20; asso. prof. physics, U. of Colo., 1920-22, prof. since 1922, assistant head of department, 1933-35, head dept., 1935-54, research professor of physics, 1954—; supervisor Airborne Coronagraph, A.M.C. rocket project, Fellow A.A.A.S., Am. Phys. Soc.; pres. Colo.-Wyo. Acad. of Science 1941-1944, mem. Am. Assn. Univ. Profs. (pres. Colo. Chapter) 1941-1943, Am. Assn. Physics Teachers (exec. com.), Colorado Wyo. Assn. Physics Teachers; S.P.E.E. Sigma Xi Sigma Pi Sigma, Rotarian, Town and Gown. Author: Notes on Electrical Measurements, 1922, (with V. P. Lubovich and M. C. Hylan) Laboratory Manual of General Physics, 1939; 1943 An Outline of General Physics, 1940, 1944. Contributor articles on absorption, electric rectifiers, electrical resistivity, linear expansion, magnetism, radiation, radio activity, surface tension, viscosity, etc. Home: Boulder, Colo. *

PIGMAN, W. WARD, educator, biochemist; b. Chgo., Mar. 5, 1910; s. James Ward and Olga (Chapple) P.; B.S., George Washington U., 1932, M.S., 1933; Ph.D., U. Md., 1936; Lalor fellow U. Leipzig (Germany), 1938-39; m. Alice Wolfe, June 6, 1933; children—James W., Jean (Mrs. Tom Helfand), John; m. 2d, Gladys Hargreaves, Oct. 26, 1973. Chemist, Nat. Bur. Standards, 1930-44; group leader Corn Products Refining Co., 1944-46, Inst. Paper Chemistry, 1946-49; asso. prof. biochemistry U. Ala. Med. Center, 1949-60, vis. prof., 1960-77; prof. biochemistry, chmn. dept. N.Y. Med. Coll., 1960-77; dir. Grad. Sch., 1963-68; pres. Apollo Solar Energy Corp. Mem. study sect. NIH, 1970-74. Recipient medal French Biochem. Soc., 1963; medal U. Milan (Italy), 1965; Distinguished Prof. award N.Y. Med. Coll. Fellow AAAS (chmn. com. social aspects sci. 1956); mem. Am. (chmn. div. carbohydrate chemistry 1949, C.S. Hudson award 1959), Am. Rheumatism Assn. (mem. council AAAS 1956-77), Am. Soc. Biochemists, Biochem. Soc. (London), Soc. for Complex Carbohydrates (pres. 1973), Internat. Assn. Dental Research, Sigma Xi (chpt. pres. 1958). Author: Chemistry of Carbohydrates, 1948. Editor: The Carbohydrate, 1957, 2d edit., 1970. Editor Advances in Carbohydrate Chemistry, 1945-49, editorial bd., 1945—; Mucus secretions, 1962; Evaluation of Agents Used in Prevention of Oral Diseases, 1968; mem. bd. editors sci. jours. Contbr. articles to profl. jours. Patentee soluble starches, solar energy utilization. Home: Jamesbury, N.J. Died Sept. 30, 1977; buried Sweetwater Cemetery, Atkinson County, Ga.

PIGOTT, REGINALD, JAMES SEYMOUR, (PIG'UT) engring, research; b. Wellington, Shrosphire, Eng., Feb. 4, 1886; s. Elphic W. S. and Lillian M. (Fance) P.; M.E., Columbia, 1906; m. Florence L. Johnston, July 2, 1908 (deceased); children—William J., Beatrice L., Elizabeth C., Patricia L.; m. 2d, Sybil Maude Harris, Dec. 1, 1946 (dec.). Came to U.S., 1891, naturalized citizen. Chief draftsman, asst. engr. chge. constrn., Interborough Rapid Transit Co., N.Y. City, 1906-11; supt. constrn., New England Engring. Co., 1911-12; prof. steam engring., Columbia, 1912-13; construction engr., Interborough Rapid Transit, 1913-15; cons. engr. and power supt. Remington Arms-Union Metallic Cartridge Co., 1915-17; cons. engr. Remington Arms and Sanford Riley Stoker Co., and supt. mills, Bridgeport Brass Co., 1917-19; with W. B. Lashar, cons. engr., 1919-20; works mgr. Crosby Steam Gage & Valve Co., 1920-22; chief engr. Stevens & Wood, engrs. and constructors, 1922-25; cons. mech. engr. Pub. Service Production Co., 1925-28; cons. mech. engr. with Stevens & Wood, 1928-29, dir. engring. Gulf Research & Development Co., 1929, later dir., now ret. Mem. A.S.M.E. (pres. 1952), Am. Petroleum Inst., Soc. Automotive Engrs. (president 1948), Instrument Soc. of Am. (pres. 1950), Pi Tau Sigma, Theta Xi, Tau Beta Pi, Sigma Tau, Sigma Xi. Rep. Episcopalian. Mason. Clubs; Engineers, Univ. Contbr. to Elec. Engrs. Standard Handbook, also tech. publs. Holder of 30 patents in vacuum trippers for turbines, rotary pumps, etc. Address: Pitts. *

PIHLBLAD, C. TERENCE, sociologist; b. Lindsborg, Kan., June 10, 1897; s. Ernst F. and Marie (Sjostrom) P.; A.B., Bethany Coll., Lindsborg, 1917; Ph.D., U. of Mo., 1925; m. Loah Lott, Sept. 18, 1920 (deceased 1956); children—Mary Louise (Mrs. Jan Roosa), Helen Kathryn (Mrs. M. C. Andrews); m. 2d, Gladys Koepke, 1959. Asso. prof. sociology Wittenberg Coll., Springfield, O., 1925-30; asso. prof. sociology U. Mo., 1930-45, prof., from 1945; chmn. dept. 1939-62; Fulbright scholar, University of Oslo, Norway, 1953-54. Served as sr. price economist, O.P.A. regional office, Dallas, 1943-44. Mem. Am. and Midwest sociol. socs., Population Assn. of Am. Am. Assn. U. Profs. Episcopalian. Author: Social Significance of Intelligence Tests (pvtly. pub.), 1926; Characteristics of Missouri Almshouse Population (Mo. Social Service Commn.) 1938; (with Gist and Gregory). Selective Factors in Migration and Occupation (U. of Mo. Studies, Vol. 18); other profl. publs. Home: Columbia, Mo. Died Aug. 4, 1978.

PIIP, ANTONIUS, diplomat; b. Tuhalaane, Esthonia, Feb. 28, 1884; s. Jaan and Ann P.; ed. univs. of Petrograd and Berlin; m. Benita Uipus, Apr. 25, 1921; 1 son, Ants Toenis. Asst. prof. Petrograd U., 1016; prof. Internat. Law, Dorpat U., 1919; admitted to bar. Served in Russian army, World War; was mem. Nat. Council, Constitutional Assembly and State Assembly, Esthonia; first diplomatic rep. of Esthonian Republic in London, 1918; mem. Esth. delegation at Paris Peace Conf., and Esth.-Russ. Peace Conf. at Dorpat, 1919; prime minister of Esthonia, 1920, and minister for foreign affairs, 1921; E.E. and M.P. from Esthonia to U.S., 1923—. Decorated Esth. Liberty Cross, Finnish Order of White Rose, Polish Order Polonia Restituta. Clubs: Metropolitan, Racquet, Chevy Chase. Address: Washington, D.C. *

PINCOFFS, MAURICE CHARLES, (PIN'KOFS) physician; b. Chicago, Ill., Aug. 6, 1886; s. Maurice and Louise (Henrotin) P.; B.S., U. of Chicago, 1909; M.D., Johns Hopkins, 1912; m. Katharine Randall, Mar. 1, 1919; children—Maurice C., Susan R., Peter II. Began practice at Baltimore, 1915; prof. medicine, U. of Md., since 1921; mem. Armed Forces Med. Adv. Com., 1949-50. Served as capt. med. Corps, U.S. Army, 1917-19; col., med. Corps, U.S. Army, 1942; chief of preventive medicine, Southwest Pacific Area; med. adv. com., sec. of war, 1946-47. Awarded D.S.C., Legion of Merit with Oak Leaf Cluster (U.S.); Croix de Guerre with palm (France). Regent Am. College Physicians; mem. Assn. Am. Physicians, Am. Climatol. and Clin. Assn. (president), Md. Mental Hygiene Soc., Delta Kappa Epsilon, Nu Sigma Nu. Club: Maryland. Editor Annals of Internal Medicine. Home: Baltimore. *

PINNEY, EDWARD LEE, educator; b. Jacksonville, Fla., Nov. 2, 1930; s. Edward Lee and Caroline (Bruner) P.; B.S., Auburn U., 1952; M.A., U. N.C., 1956, Ph.D., 1960; m. Winston Reese Withers, Apr. 27, 1956; children—Reese Bruner, Edward Lee. Instr. U. N.C. at Chapel Hill, 1956-59; mem. faculty La. State U. at Baton Rouge, 1959-63; prof. politics Washington and Lee U., Lexington, Va., 1963-80. Mem. Baton Rouge Symphony Bd., 1960-64. Chmn. Rockbridge County (Va.) Citizens for Johnson-Humphrey, Democratic Party, 1964. Served to 1st lt., AUS, 1952-54. Mem. Am., So. (exec. council, rec. sec.) polit. sci. assns., AAUP. Author: Federalism, Bureaucracy and Party Politics in West Germany, 1963. Editor: Comparative Politics and Political Theory: Essays Written in Honor of Charles Baskervill Robson, 1966. Bd. pubs. Shenandoah, 1970-76, chmn., 1973-76. Home: Lexington, Va. Died May 14, 1980.

PINNEY, EDWARD STEVENSON, lawyer; b. Bellport, L.I., N.Y., June 26, 1895; s. Edward Guy and Harriet (Stevenson) P.; B.A., Yale, 1917, LL.B., Harvard, 1921; m. Leona Hurd, Nov. 18, 1938 (dec. Nov. 1968); 1 stepdau., Joan Pierce (Mrs. Sidney Rossiter); m. 2d, Dorothy Moremen, Aug. 30, 1972; 1 stepson, Brooks. Began with Cravath, Henderson, Leffingwell & de Gersdorff, 1921; partner Cravath, Swaine & Moore, 1931-74, of counsel, 1974-78. Trustee, pres. emeritus Steep Rock Assn., Inc.; trustee Yale in China; trustee, sec. Gunnery Sch., Washington, Conn.; vis. com. Harvard Law Sch., 1959-65; bd. dirs.

C. T. Loo Chinese Ednl. Fund; mem. alumni bd. Yale. Served as 2d lt., 7th F.A., 1st Div., World War I; AEF Mem. Assn. Bar City N.Y., N.Y. State, Am. bar assns., Am. Law Inst., Harvard Law Sch. Assn. (pres. 1965-67). Clubs: University, Grolier, Century Assn., Wall Street, Down Town Assn. (N.Y.C.). Home: New York, N.Y. Died Jan. 22, 1978.

PINNEY, JEAN BURROWS, social hygiene worker; b. Beaver Creek, Minn., Oct. 14, 1886; d. Edwin Martin and Georgianna (Burrows) Pinney; ed. pub. schs., Burlington, Vt.; spl. study Emerson Coll., Boston, and Middlebury College. Mem. staff of Am. Social Hygiene Assn., 1947-50; loaned to the U.S. Army, 1917-18, Q.M. corps, duties with the Commn. on training camp activities; factory inspector, Office Commr. of Industries, State of Vt. 1919-21; sec. finance and membership cons. Am. Social Hygiene Assn., 1923-30; dir. pub. information and publications service and community orgns., 1930-42; dir. Am. Soc. Hygiene Assn.'s Washington liaison office, 1941-46, in charge spl. coop. assignments with Army and Navy, Social Protection Div., and U.S.P.H.S.; sec. com. on Internat. Relations and Activities, 1947-49, hon. life mem., cons. since 1950; dir. Regional Office for Americas, Internat. Union Against Venereal Diseases, 1947-50; served as sec. or dir. numerous nat. and regional confs. on soc. hygiene, including one in San Juan, Puerto Rico, 1944. Mem. adv. council, Women's Interest Sect., Bur. Public Relations, U.S. War Dept., Nat. Women's Adv. Council on Social Protection, Am. Pub. Health Assn., Am. Assn. of Women in Pub. Health, Vt. Council on World Affairs, Vt. Hist. Soc. Conglist. Editor Jour. Social Hygiene and Social Hygiene News, 1931. Author articles and fiction on general subjects, also film scenarios and play scripts. Home: Morrisville, Vt. *

PIPKIN, GEORGE H., banker; b. Springfield, Mo., Apr. 9, 1886; s. John P. and Vinora Ann (Wiley) P.; student Drury Coll., Springfield, Mo., Springfield (Mo.) Bus. Coll.; m. Mio Gertrude Viers, Oct. 4, 1911; 1 dau., Virginia Ann (Mrs. Harvey M. Stith). Clerk State Savings Bank, Springfield, Mo., 1909-11; asst. to executor of Benjamin Lombard Jr. Boston estate, Springfield, Mo., 1911-16; office mgr. Cochran Mortgage Co., Kansas City, Mo., 1916-18; mgr. discount dept., Fed. Reserve Bank, Kansas City, Mo., 1918-20, asst. cashier, 1920-40, vice pres. in charge of Oklahoma City, Okla. br., 1940-45, vice pres. in charge of Denver, Colo. br. since 1945. Mem. Denver Chamber of Commerce. Republican. Methodist. Club: Kiwanis (Denver). Home: Denver. *

PIPPIN, RAYMOND RUSSELL, mfg. exec.; b. Ridgeley, Md., Sept. 20, 1905; s. Herman Crossly and Viola May (Welch) P.; A.B., U. Del., 1927, LL.D., 1969; m. Bertha Chalfant Staats, June 29, 1929. With E. I. duPont de Nemours & Co., 1927-41; mgr. tax div., 1941-44, asst. comptroller, 1944-48, first asst. treas., 1948-53, treas., 1953-64, v.p., dir., mem. exec. and finance coms., 1964-70, chmn. com. on audit, 1970-77, also dir. Trustee Hampton Inst., 1961-71. Mem. Del. Accountants Assn. (pres. 1942-43), Conf. Bd. (trustee), Theta Chi, Phi Kappa Phi. Home: West Chester, Pa. Died Nov. 9, 1977.

PIRELLI, ALBERTO, rubber co. exec.; b. Milan, Italy, Apr. 28, 1882; s. Giovanni B. and Maria (Sormani) P.; grad. Sch. Econs., Milan; student Poly. Inst. Milan, Faculty of Law U. Genoa; m. Ludovica Zambelletti, July 11, 1914; children—Giovanna Maria, Elena, Giovanbattista, Leopoldo. Former pres., now hon. chmn. Pirelli Societa per Azioni, Milan, Italy. Hon. Plenipotentiary Minister. Minister of State, Italy, 1938. Mem. Internat. C. of C. (past pres.). Home: Milan Italy. *

PIRIE, JOHN T., JR., mcht.; b. Evanston, Ill., May 22, 1903; s. John T. and Sophie (Hunter) P.; m. Ginerva King; children—Suzanne Pirie Pattou, Dale Pirie Cabot, Sharon Pirie Sands. Chmn. exec. com. Carson Pirie Scott & Co., Chgo., now hon. chmn. exec. com.; dir. Universal Resources Corp. Adv. bd., officer Salvation Army; hon. trustee The Seeing Eye, Inc.; life trustee Field Mus. Natural History. Home: Lake Forest, Ill. Died Nov. 10, 1980.

PISTON, WALTER, composer, educator; b. Rockland, Maine, Jan. 20, 1894; s. Walter Hamor and Leona (Stover) P.; student Mass. Sch. Art, Boston, 1912-16; A.B. summa cum laude, Harvard, 1924, Mus.D. (hon.), 1953; m. Kathryn Nason, Sept. 14, 1920. Awarded John Knowles Paine Fellowship from Harvard, 1924-26; studied musical composition with Nadia Boulanger. Asst. prof. music Harvard, 1926-38, asso. prof., 1938-44, prof., 1944-48, Walter W. Naumburg prof. music, 1948-60, prof. emeritus music, 1960-76. Guggenheim fellow, 1935; recipient Pulitzer prize in music, 1948, 61. Mem. Nat. Inst. Arts and Letters, Am. Acad. Arts and Scis., Am. Acad. Arts and Letters, Phi Beta Kappa. Club: Harvard. Author: Harmony; Harmonic Analysis; Counterpoint; Orchestration. Composer chamber music and numerous orchestral works. Home: Belmont, Mass. Died Nov. 12, 1976.

PISTOR, WILLIAM JACOB, educator; b. Tucson, Sept. 15, 1899; s. Fritz and Eliza (Becker) P.; B.S., U. Ariz., 1922; B.S. D.V.M., Wash. State Coll., 1926; m. Virginia Pollard, June 21, 1928; 1 son, Michael Fritz. Pvt. practice veterinary medicine, Portland, Ore., 1926-30; poultry pathologist, Calif. State Dept. Agrl., 1930-33; asst. prof. vet. medicine Wash. State Coll., 1933-34; prof. animal pathology, also head of dept. animal pathology U. Ariz., 1934-71, asst. to pres. coordinator fgn. visitors program, dept. head emeritus, 1971-76; animal pathologist, dir. group AID program, Brazil, 1967-76. Mem. city council, Tucson, 1944-50; mem. Tucson Sch. Bd. Trustee Tucson Sch. Dist., 1956-70. Mem. Am. Legion, C. of C., Phi Kappa Phi, Sigma Xi, Alpha Zeta, Kappa Sigma. Rotarian (pres. 1956-57). Home: Tucson, Ariz. Died Aug. 5, 1976.

PITAMIC, LEONIDAS, diplomat; b. Postojna (Postumia), Dec. 15, 1885; s. Ivan and Irene Maricki (de Sremoslav) P.; ed. college and univ., Vienna, T.D.; LL.D., Catholic U. of America; unmarried. Formerly univ. lecturer and prof.; E.E. and M.P. from Jugoslavia to U.S. since May 24, 1929. Hon. mem. Acad. of Philosophy of Georgetown U., Am. Bar Assn.; mem. Inst. Internat. de droit public, Paris; corr. mem. Jugoslav Acad. Science and Art. Catholic. Author: The Right of Members of Parliament to Indemnity, 1913; The Coäperation of the Parliament in International Treaties in Austria, 1915; Law and Revolution, 1920; The State, 1927; Some Notions on the State and Its International Phases, 1931; A Treatise on the State, 1933. Home: Washington, D.C. *

PITCHER, ARNOLD ELLIS, retired exec.; b. South Waldoboro, Me., June 28, 1884; s. Damon W. and Livonia J. (Lawry) P.; ed. pub. schs. and high sch., Brockton, Mass.; m. Eleanor M. Lovell, June 27, 1908; 1 dau., Eleanor L. (Mrs. Ralph F. Hansen). Office boy, later salesman, Packard & Field, shoe mfrs., Brockton, Mass., 1902-10; salesman, Arlington Co., Arlington, N.J., 1910-14, dist. sales mgr., Chicago, 1914 (company purchased by E. I. du Pont de Nemours & Co., 1915), became asst. dir. sales, 1920, dir. sales, 1922-28; vice pres. du Pont Viscoloid Co. (organized, 1925), 1929, exec. vice pres., 1920-32, pres., 1932-36 (co. dissolved as subsidiary, 1936); gen. mgr. plastics dept., E. I. du Pont de Nemours & Co. since 1936; pres. Celastic Corp. (du Pont subsidiary). Mem. Plastic Pioneers Assn. (v.p.). Mason. Clubs: Wilmington (Del.) Country, Riverside Yacht (Riverside, Conn.); DuPont Country. Retired 1949. Home: Greenville, Del. *

PITT, ARTHUR STUART, educator; b. Bridgeport, Conn., May 26, 1914; s. Arthur Ernest and Ruth (Thorp) P.; B.A., Yale, 1935, M.A., 1937, Ph.D., 1939; m. Margaret Victoria Winterode, Oct. 31, 1942; children—Victoria Thorp, Robert Stuart. Instr. English, Lafayette Coll., 1939-41; mem. faculty U.S. Naval Acad., 1941—, prof. English, 1954—, chmn. dept., 1970-74. Served with USNR, 1942-45. Mem. Modern Lang. Assn., Coll. English Assn., Nantucket Hist. Assn. Club: Officers and Faculty. Author: Annapolis Today, 2d edit., 1963. Contbr. articles to scholastic jours. Home: Annapolis, Md. Died Nov. 20, 1978.

PITTENGER, BENJAMIN FLOYD (PIT'EN-JER), univ. prof.; b. Shelby, Mich., Nov. 26, 1883; s. Samuel and Lydia (Wolf) P.; A.B., State Normal Coll., Ypsilanti, Mich., 1908; M.A., U. of Tex., 1912; Ph.D., U. of Chicago, 1916; m. Katherine Bickler, Dec. 27, 1913; 1 dau., Katherine Lydia, Teacher, rural schs., Mich., 1902-04; prof. edn., Fairmount Coll., Wichita, Kan., 1908-11; instr. in edn., U. of Minn., 1913-15; adj. prof. edn., U. of Tex., 1916-17, asso. prof., 1919-25, prof. since 1925, dean Sch. of Edn., 1926-47, pres. Nat. Assn. Colls. and Depts. of Edn., 1938-40. Served as captain, later major, Sanitary Corps, U.S. Army, World War; psychol. examining service, U.S. Army, 1917-19. Mem. Texas State Teachers Assn. (pres. 1942), Phi Delta Kappa. Democrat. Conglist. Mason. Author: Introduction to Public School Finance, 1925, Indoctrination for American Democracy, 1941. Contbr. to sch. administration publs. Home: Austin, Tex. *

PITTENGER, PAUL STEWART, pharm. mfr.; born Easton, Pa., Sept. 20, 1889; s. Edward Stewart and Matilda (Riedy) P.; Ph.G., Medico Chirurg. Coll., 1909, Ph. Chemist, 1910, Pharm. D., 1911; Pharm. M., Phila. Coll. Pharmacy and Sci., 1919, Sc.D., 1940; m. Leola Bodine Welch, Sept. 10, 1913. Dir. pharmaco-dynamic research, H. K. Mulford Co., Phila., Pa., 1910-25; dir. pharmacologic research, labs., Shart & Dohme, 1927-28, asst. gen. supt., 1928-29, asst. to pres., 1929-30, v.p., 1930-55, ret.; treas. Phila. Coll. Pharmacy and Sci., 1962-64, v.p., 1964-70. Recipient Alumni award Phila. Coll. Pharmacy and Sci., 1959. Fellow A.A.A.S., mem. Am. Soc. Quality Control, Assn. of Mil. Surgeons, Biometric Society, American Drug Manufacturers Assn., Am. Pharm. Assn. (hon.) Am. Statist. Assn., Am. Chem. Soc., Phila. Chamber of Commerce (member board of directors), Phila. Drug Exchange (past president). Rep. Presbyterian. Club: Union League (Phila). Author: Biochemic Drug Assay Methods; Biologic Assays. Contbr. articles in sci. jours. Home: Phila., Pa. Died Sept. 25, 1975.

PITTMAN, CHALMERS VAN ANGLEN, geophysicist; b. Trenton, July 25, 1904; s. Raymond Hill and Evanna Catherine (Van Anglen) P.; B.S., Haverford Coll., 1925; m. Margaret Ellen Hallett, Aug. 10, 1929; 1 dau., Janet McLellan. Geophysicist, Geophys. Research Corp., Houston, 1927-30, Geophys. Service, Inc., Dallas, 1930-42; exec. v.p., chmn. bd. Geochem. Surveys, Dallas, 1942-75, cons., 1975-81; Bd. mgrs. Haverford Coll., 1971-74, also mem. corp. Mem. Am. Assn. Petroleum Geologists, Soc. Exploration Geophysicists, SAR, Soc. Colonial Wars, Hereditary Order Descs. Colonial Govs., Nat. Huguenot Soc., Soc. Descs. Colonial Clergy. Quaker. Clubs: Dallas Country, Dallas Petroleum. Home: Dallas, Tex. Died July 13, 1981; buried Trenton, N.J.

PITTS, ALICE FOX, consultant; born N.Y.C., Jan. 20, 1896; d. Arnold and Philippina (Finger) Fox; student Barnard Coll., 1912-13, Columbia Sch. Journalism, 1913-15; m. Fredric G. Pitts, Sept. 19, 1917; children—Patricia (Mrs. Werner Vellrath), Marc, Bruno, Jacquelin. Feature writer New Bedford (Mass.) Standard, 1918-19; contbr. Parents mag., also pulp mags., 1920-25; feature editor Buffalo Evening News, 1925-31; women's publicity Rep. Nat. Com., 1932, dir. women's publicity, 1936; asst. promotion mgr. Washington Post, 1932-33; asst. sec. Am. Soc. Newspaper Editors, 1934-57, exec. sec., 1958-63, cons., 1963-78. Author (with husband) syndicated column, Foxy and Freddy; Read All About It-Fifty Years of the American Society of Newspaper Editors. Home: Hockessin, Del. Died May 1978.

PITTS, ROBERT FRANKLIN, educator; b. Indpls., Oct. 24, 1908; s. John Franklin and Estella (Coffin) P.; B.S., Butler U., 1929; Ph.D., Johns Hopkins, 1932; M.D., N.Y. U., 1938; Rockefeller Found. fellow, Neurol. Inst. Northwestern, 1938-39, Johnson Found. Med. Physics, U. Pa., 1939-40; m. Marjorie Anna Wallace, Dec. 25, 1936; children—Robert Wallace, Marjorieann. Asst. physiology N.Y. U., 1932-33, instr. physiology, 1933-38, asst. prof. physiology, 1940-42, asst. prof. physiology Cornell, 1942-44, asso. prof. physiology, 1944-46, prof., chmn. dept., 1950-74, prof. emeritus, 1974-77; research prof. renal medicine and physiology U. Fla. Sch. Medicine, 1974-77; prof., chmn. dept. physiology Syracuse U., 1946-50; vis. fellow St. Catharine's Coll., Oxford U., 1967-68. Mem. physiology study sect. NIH; mem. NRC adv. com. on grad. sch. Army Med. Services; chmn. conf. renal function Josiah Macy Found.; mem. adv. bd. Life Ins. Med. Research Fund, Lederle Med. Faculty Awards, NRC Med. Fellowships. Recipient Gail Borden award Assn. Am. Med. Colls., 1960; H.W. Smith award in renal physiology N.Y. Heart Assn., 1963. Fellow A.C.P., Am. Acad. Arts and Scis.; mem. Nat. Acad. Scis., Am. Physiol. Soc. (bd. publ. trustees, mem. council; pres. 1959-60), Soc. Exptl. Biology and Medicine (chmn. N.Y. sect.), Harvey Soc. (pres. from 1960), Soc. Clin. Investigation, Phi Beta Kappa, Sigma Xi, Phi Kappa Phi, Phi Delta Theta, Alpha Omega Alpha. Author: Physiological Basis of Diuretic Therapy, 1959; Physiology of the Kidney and Body Fluids, 1963. Editor, Am. Lectures in Physiology, from 1946. Home: Gainesville, Fla. Died June 6, 1977.

PITZ, HENRY CLARENCE, artist; b. Phila., June 16, 1895; s. Henry William and Anna Rosina (Stiffel) P.; student Pa. Mus. Sch. Indsl. Art, 1914-17, Spring Garden Inst., 1919-20; LL.D., Ursinus Coll., 1971; m. Molly Wheeler Wood, June 6, 1935; children—Julia Leaming, Henry William. Illustrator of books and mags. from 1920; illustrator of over 160 books and for Saturday Evening Post, Scribners, Cosmopolitan, Country Gentleman, Good Housekeeping, others; dir. of illustration and decoration Pa. Mus. Coll. Art, 1932-60, prof. emeritus; instr. water color Pa. Acad. Fine Arts, 1939-46; vis. critic Bryn Mawr Art Center, 1939; vis. lectr. in fine arts U. of Pa., 1941, Carnegie Inst. Tech., 1964; faculty Pa. Inst. Life Culture, 1966; ofcl. artist U.S. Environmental Protection Agy., 1972. Executed 3 murals for the U.S. Govt. Bldgs. in Century of Progress, Chgo., 1933, mural for Franklin Inst., Phila.; presentation print, Rochester Print Club, 1935, Collectors of Am. Art, 1945. Represented in collections of museums, colleges, libraries. Mem. Phila. Council Def.; mem. Post War Planning Bd., Whitemarsh, Pa. Served with U.S. Army, 1918-19; AEF. Huntington-Hartford Found. fellow, 1964; recipient Salmagundi Club prize, 1951, 52; Obrig prize Nat. Acad., 1953, Harcum College prize, 1956; silver star cluster Phila. Mus., 1957; Artist award Norristown Art League, 1957, Nat. Acad. award for water color, 1960, Range Fund purchase, 1964; Samuel Morse medal, 1964; Phila. Watercolor prize Pa. Acad. Fine Arts, 1963; Atheneaum Phila. Lit. award, 1970; others. Mem. Phila. Art Alliance (v.p.), Am. Inst. Graphic Arts, Audubon Artists, Am. Water Color Soc., Soc. Illustrators, Graphic Arts Forum, Assn. for Advancement of Arts in Childhood. Episcopalian. Clubs: Folio, Sketch (pres.), Water Color (dir.), Salmagundi (N.Y.C.) Print Franklin Inn (Phila.), Newcomen Soc. of N. Am. Author: The Practice of Illustration, 1947; A Treasury of American Book Illustration, 1957; Drawing Trees, 1956; Ink Drawing Techniques, 1957; Sketching with the Felt-tip Pen, 1959; Illustrating for Children's Books, 1963; Drawing Outdoors, 1965; The Brandywine Tradition, 1968;

Charcoal Drawing, 1971; (with Edward Warwick) Early American Costume, 1929; Pen, Brush and Ink, 1949; Frederic Remington, 1972; Howard Pyle-Writer, Illustrator, Founder of the Brandywine School, 1975. Asso. editor: The American Artist. Contbr. to Am. and fgn. mags. Ofcl. artist NASA-Apollo 10, 1968. Asso. Nat. Acad., 1951, academician, 1969. Home: Philadelphia, Pa. Died Nov. 26, 1976.

PLACE, EDWIN BRAY, educator; b. La Harpe, Ill., Aug. 20, 1891; s. John and Anna (Bray) P.; A.B., U. Colo., 1913, A.M., 1916, Litt.D. (hon.), 1955; Ph.D., Harvard U., 1919; postgrad. research, Paris, Madrid, Rome, 1920, 25-26; m. Lula May Streamer, Aug. 5, 1914 (dec. Nov. 1956); children—Charles E., Dorothy-Lou (Mrs. J. D. Whicker), William O.; m. 2d, Marian Fredine, June 7, 1957. Instr., U. Colo., 1916-18, asst. prof. Romance langs., 1919-21, asso. prof., 1921-24, prof., 1924-35, head dept., 1931-35; instr. French, Harvard, 1918-19; prof. Romance langs. Northwestern U., 1935-56, emeritus, from 1956, chmn. dept., 1935-45. Vis. prof. Spanish, U. Pa., 1934; vis. lectr. Spanish, U. Calif. at Berkeley, 1956-58, vis. prof., 1966-68; vis. prof. Romance langs. U. Chgo., 1963-64. Mem. Am. Assn. Tchrs. Spanish (pres. 1937), Mediaeval Acad. Am. (councillor 1942-45), MLA (exec. council 1946-47), Am. Assn. Tchrs. French (v.p. 1939-40), Am. Assn. Tchrs. Italian (councillor 1939), Phi Beta Kappa, Sigma Chi, Phi Sigma Iota (nat. pres. 1940-46); mem. Hispanic Soc. Am. Named Officer d'Academie (France). Author: María de Zayas, 1923; (with C.C. Ayer) Un viaje por España, 1924; Manuel elemental de novelística española, 1926; (with N.B. Adams) Lecturas modernas, 1939; (with A. Torres-Rioseco) Contemporary Spanish Grammar, 1943; contbg. author: A Critical Bibliography of Old French Literature, 1947. Editor: Así se escribe la historia, 1926; La casa del placer honesto, 1927, 68; Madame Corentine, 1927; Don Gonzalo González de la Gonzalera, 1931; Gilles de Chyn, 1941; Processo de cartas, 1950; Amadís de Gaula, 1959, 62, 65, 68, 69. Translator: (with H.C. Behm) Translation of Amadís de Gaula, Books I and II, 1974, III and IV, 1975. Contbr. Am., fgn. jours., encys. Home: Oakland, Calif. Died Feb. 27, 1980; buried Green Mountain Cemetery, Boulder, Colo.

PLACHY, FRED JOSEPH, coll. pres.; b. Ponca, Nebr., Apr. 19, 1901; s. Joseph and Rose (Washicek) P.; B.S., Huron (S.D.) Coll., 1927; M.A., U. Nebr., 1931; Ed.D., Colo. State Coll., 1951; m. Margaret Rich, Jan. 1, 1927; children—Shirley Rose (Mrs. Robert W. Dunn), Fredric Rich, Jon Milton. Faculty Colegio Americano Para Varones, Barranquilla, Colombia, S.A., 1927-36; tchr., dir. Presbyn. Boys Sch., 1927-36; supt. pub. schs., Colome, S.D., 1936-39, Tyndall, 1939-43; dean Huron Coll., 1943-47; supt. pub. schs., Wilmot, S.D., 1947-49; asst. prof. edn. Colo. State Coll. Edn., 1949-51; prof. edn., dir. extension Black Hills Tchrs. Coll., Spearfish, S.D., 1951-52; pres. Adams State Coll., Alamosa, Colo., 1952-72, pres. emeritus, 1972. Mem. Alamosa C. of C. (pres.), Nat., Colo. edn. assns., S.D. Edn. Assn. (pres. Southeast dist. 1947), Am. Assn. Sch. Adminstrs., Newcomen Soc., Phi Delta Kappa. Republican. Presbyn. (elder). Rotarian (dist. gov. 1962-63). Home: Denver, Colo. Died Dec. 21, 1972.

PLASS, EVERETT DUDLEY (PLAS), univ. prof.; b. Poughkeepsie, N.Y., May 6, 1886; s. Dudley and Ida (Smith) P.; B.A., Colgate, 1907; M.D., Johns Hopkins, 1911; m. Lillian Rose Genrich, Nov. 26, 1919; children—Ruth, William Traver, Betty. With Johns Hopkins U., 1911-22, asso. prof. last 2 yrs.; obstetrician Henry Ford Hosp., Detroit, Mich, 1922-26; prof. and head dept. of obstetrics and gynecology, State Univ. of Iowa, 1926-50. Member American Society Biological Chemists, American Association of Obstetricians, Gynecologists and Abdominal Surgeons, Soc. for Experimental Biology and Medicine, Am. Gynecol. Soc., Chicago Gynecol. Soc., Central Assn. Obstetricians and Gynecologists (pres. 1933-34), Alpha Omega Alpha, Phi Beta Kappa, Sigma XI, Phi Gamma Delta, Phi Chi; fellow A.A.A.S., A.M.A. (sec. sect. obstetrics, gynecology and abdominal surgery 1934-36, chmn. 1937). Democrat. Baptist. Author: Obstetrics for Nurses, 1922; also articles on professional topics. Home: Iowa City, Ia. *

PLATT, JOHN HENRY, foods processing executive; b. Chicago, June 29, 1897; s. William Henry and Hannah Katherine (Ohle) P.; student Kent Coll. of Law, 1917, Pierson's Bus. Coll., 1919; m. Arlene Katherine Prochnow, June 1, 1920; children—Robert, John Jr., James, William. Established Elko Press, job printing co., while in sch.; engaged in auto tire bus., Chgo., 1916-17; with wholesale div. Marshall Field & Co., Chgo., 1918; with Kraft Foods Co. from 1919, advt. mgr., from 1924, dir., 1940-62, v.p. charge advt. and pub. relations, mem. exec. com., dir., 1945-62, sr. v.p., 1955-62; mem. operating com. Nat. Dairy Products Corp., 1955-62; dir. Nat. Blvd. Bank of Chgo., John Morrell & Co.; dir., mem. exec. com. Unimark Internat., Chgo., from 1967. Dir., Audit Bur. Circulations, Off-The Street Club, Chgo., Evanston Hosp. Assn., Presbyn. Home; treas. div. Christian edn., asso. treas. Nat. Council Chs.; trustee Conf. Point Camp, Nat. Council Chs.; dir. McCormick Theol. Sem., 1959-80; hon. dir. Evanston Hosp.; trustee Kendall Coll., Evanston. Presbyn. Clubs: Sunset Ridge Country, Mid-America, Economic. Home: Winnetka, Ill. Died Apr. 29, 1980; interred Meml. Park Cemetery, Skokie, Ill.

PLEASANT, EARLE BIRTRUM, ret. clergyman, religious orgn. exec.; b. Trotwood, O., Feb. 6, 1908; s. Calvin and Eva (Cassell) P.; A.B., Defiance Coll., 1932, B.D., 1952; D.D., Yale, 1935; m. Imogene Miller, Sept. 6, 1933; children—Merridee (Mrs. Frank Harris, III), Sylvia (Mrs. William E. Smith, Jr.). Ordained ministry Congl. Christian Ch., 1935; dir., pastor Western Me. Larger Parish, 1935-38; pastor First Congl. Ch., Scarborough, Me., 1939-43; acting exec. sec. Council of Chs., Portland, Me., 1942-43, exec. sec., 1943-47; nat. dir. United Ch. Canvass, N.Y.C., 1947-51; asso. exec. dir. dept. stewardship and benevolence Nat. Council of Chs., 1952; organizer, founder, exec. dir. Religion in Am. Life, Inc., N.Y.C., 1949-69. Trustee So. Union Coll., Wadley, Ala.; pub. relations com. N.Y.C. YMCA; chmn. chapel commn. Creedmoor State Hosp., Queens, N.Y.; v.p. Manhattan Kiwanis Found. Mem. Ohio Soc. N.Y. (dir.), N.Y. State Congress Parents and Tchrs. (bd. mgrs.). Clubs: Quill (dir.), Kiwanis (pres., dir.) (N.Y.C.); Newcomen, Touchdown. Contbr. articles religious jours. Home: Vandalia, Ohio. Died Dec. 15, 1978.

PLIMPTON, RUSSELL ARTHUR, art orgn. dir.; b. Hollis, N.Y., Aug. 26, 1891; s. Arthur Salem and Sarah Isabella (Tomes) P.; A.B., Princeton, 1914; M.A. (hon.), U. Minn., 1956; student art history in Europe, 50 summers. With Met. Mus. Art, N.Y.C., 1914-21, asst. curator decorative arts dept., 1916-21; dir. Mpls. Inst. Arts, 1921-56; then trustee; dir. Four Arts Soc., Palm Beach, Fla., 1956-70, emeritus dir., 1970-75. Served with F.A., U.S. Army, 1918-19; overseas. Decorated Order of Vasa (comdr.), King's Medal (Sweden). Mem. Assn. Art Mus. Dirs. (pres. 1956), Am. Assn. Museums, Am. Fedn. Arts, Soc. of the Four Arts. Republican. Clubs: Bath and Tennis, Everglades, Rotary (Palm Beach); Minneapolis', Princeton (N.Y.C.); Nassau. Lectr. on decorative arts and painting. Home: Palm Beach, Fla. Died Dec. 8, 1975.

PLYLER, EARLE KEITH, physicist; b. nr. Greenville, S.C., Apr. 26, 1897; s. John Robert and Mary (Earle) P.; A.B., Furman U., 1917, A.M., 1918; A.M., Johns Hopkins, 1923; Ph.D., Cornell, 1924; post grad. research in physics, U. Mich., 1930-31; LL.D., Furman U., 1969; m. Eleanor Mays, Sept. 3, 1925; children—Mary, Ruth. Asst. prof. physics Furman U., 1920-22, U. N.C., 1924-27, asso. prof., 1927-33, prof., 1933-41; research physicist U. Mich., 1941-45; physicist in charge infrared measurements Nat. Bur. Standards, Washington 1945-51, chief radiometry sect. 1951-61, chief infrared spectroscopy, 1961-62; prof., head dept. physics Fla. State U., Tallahassee, 1962-67, prof., 1967-70, prof. emeritus, 1970-76; cons. AEC, Oak Ridge, 1948-70; vis. lectr. Inst. Optics, Madrid, 1949. Mem. phys. sci. div. NRC. Recipient ann. award N.Y. sect. Soc. Applied Spectroscopy, 1963. Fellow Am. Phys. Soc. (mem. exec. com. southeastern sect. 1967-71, Beams medal Southeastern sect. 1973), Optical Soc. Am. (dir.), A.A.A.S.; hon. fellow Indian Acad. Scis., Soc. Applied Spectroscopy; mem. Am. Chem. Soc., Coblentz Soc. Baptist. Mason. Author articles in sci. publs. Mem. bd. editors Jour. Chem. Physics, 1954-57, Jour. Optical Soc. Am., 1962-72, Jour. Molecular Structure, 1967-71. Home: Tallahassee, Fla. Died May 8, 1976.

POE, JAMES, screenwriter; b. Dobbs Ferry, N.Y., Oct. 4, 1921; s. James and Peggy (Bobbit) P.; student St. John's Coll.; children-Lorna, Adam, Jonathan. Engaged in motion picture industry, 1941-80; pres. James Poe Co., Inc., 1967-80; credits include Around the World in 80 Days, Cat on a Hot Tin Roof, Attack!, Big Knife, Hot Spell, Summer and Smoke, Toys in the Attic, The Bedford Incident, Lilies of the Field, They Shoot Horses, Don't They?, The Gathering. Bd. dirs. Nat. Council Arts and Govt., 1965-80. Served as aviator USNR, World War II; ETO. Recipient award Am. Acad. Motion Picture Arts and Scis., 1957, also 3 nominations; award Screen Writers Guild, 1957, 63, Writers Guild Am. West, 1957, 63, 69; Laurel award, 1971. Mem. Writers Guild Am. West (pres. screen br. 1965-67), Acad. Motion Picture Arts and Scis., Screen Dirs. Guild, Film Editors Guild, Am. Film Inst. Address: Los Angeles, Calif. Died Jan. 24, 1980.

POFFENBERGER, ALBERT THEODORE, psychologist; b. Dauphin, Pa., Oct. 23, 1885; s. Albert Theodore and Lillie Jane (Umberger) P.; A.B., Bucknell U., Pa., 1909, Sc.D., 1926; A.M., Columbia, 1910, Ph.D., 1912; m. Flossie V. Kauffman, Aug. 27, 1913; children—Dora Helen, John Roberts. Instr. in psychology, Columbia, 1912, advanced prof., 1927, prof. emeritus since 1950. Capt. Sanitary Corps, U.S. Army, 1918-19. Fellow A.A.A.S. (vice pres. 1937); mem. Am. Psychol. Assn. (pres. 1934-35), Nat. Research Council (chmn. div. psychology and anthropol. 1931-33), Social Sci. Research Council (pres. 1946-48), Council for Research on Problems of Alcohol, Soc. Exptl. Psychologists (pres. 1942-43), Nat. Inst. of Psychology (pres. 1942-43), Am. Association of Applied Psychologists (pres. 1943-44), N.Y. Acad. Sciences, Phi Kappa Psi. Mason. Author: Experimental Psychology (laboratory manual), 1916; The Sense of Taste, 1917; Applied Psychology, 1917, rev. and enlarged, 1923; Psychology in Advertising, 1925, 31; Applied Psychology—Its Principles and Methods, 1927; Principles of Applied Psychology, 1942. Editor: James McKeen Cattell: Man of Science, 1947. Home: Montrose, N.Y.*

POISTER, ARTHUR (WILLIAM), organist, educator; b. Galion, Ohio, June 13, 1898; s. Theodore Henry and Sarah Caroline (Ricker) P.; B.Mus., Am. Conservatory of Music (academic work U. of Chgo.), 1925, M.Mus., 1931; student Marcel Dupré, France, 1925-26, 27-28, of Karl Straube, Leipzig, Germany, 1933-34; Mus.D. (hon.), Southwestern U., 1960, Morningside Coll., 1967; L.H.D. (hon.), Syracuse U., 1967; D.F.A. (hon.), Drake U., 1975; m. Dorothy Broeland, Dec. 20, 1941; children—Theodore Henry, Wendy. Dir. music Central High Sch., Sioux City, Iowa, also organist and dir. music First Congl. Ch., 1920-27; prof. organ and theory U. of Redlands, Calif., 1928-37; prof. organ and univ. organist U. Minn., 1937-38; prof. organ Oberlin (Ohio) Conservatory Music, 1938-48; prof. organ and univ. organist Syracuse U. 1948-67, prof. emeritus, 1967-80; vis. prof. organ Oberlin Conservatory Music, Drake U., Morningside Coll., U. Colo. at Boulder, Longwood Coll.; organ recitalist making concert tours throughout U.S. and Can., 1935-80; artist in residence Hollins (Va.) Coll., 1967-68, Meredith Coll., Raleigh, N.C., 1975-80. Asso. Am. Guild Organists; mem. Phi Mu Alpha, Pi Kappa Lambda, Phi Delta Theta. Methodist. Lectr. Arthur Porster endowed lectureship established Oberlin Coll. Conservatory, 1967; endowed Poister Scholarship Syracuse U. and St. Olaf Coll. Address: Raleigh, N.C. Died Feb. 25, 1980.

POITRAS, HERMAN ARTHUR, chem. engr.; b. Ware, Mass., Apr. 17, 1912; s. Arthur L. and Parmelia (Noreau) P.; B.S., Ch.E., Tufts Coll., 1935; student Columbia, 1943; m. Gertrude M. VanKampen, Jan. 26, 1953; children—Gail M., Robert H. With Barrett div. Allied Chem. & Dye Corp., Edgewater, N.J., 1936-42; chief process engr., project engr. Heyden Chem. Corp., Garfield and Princeton, N.J., 1942-45; asst. dept. head Chas. Pfizer & Co., Inc., Brooklyn, 1945-48; supt. Vigo Plant, Terre Haute, Ind., 1948-49, gen. prodn. mgr., 1949, v.p. charge prodn., 1949-70, dir., 1950-70; cons. chem. mfg. and chem. engring., from 1970; dir. Pfizer Fgn. Trade Subsidiaries. Mem. Pharm. Mfrs. Assn., Am. Mgmt. Assn., Am. Inst. Chem. Engrs., Am. Chem. Soc., Commerce and Industry Assn. N.Y., Tau Beta Pi. Club: Sea Pines Plantation. Patentee in field. Home: Hilton Head Island, S.C. Died Mar. 20, 1978.

POLEVITZKY, IGOR BORIS, architect; b. Leningrad, Russia, June 21, 1911; B.A. cum laude, (Mayor's scholar 1928; fgn. student scholar 1929-34; Harbeson medal 1932), U. Pa., 1934. Practiced as Igor B. Polevitzky, 1935-36, Polevitzky & Russell, 1936-41, Igor B. Polevitzky, architect, 1941-55; with Polevitzky, Johnson & Assos., Miami, Fla., from 1955; prin. works include Shelborne Hotel addition and Mardi Gras Motel, Miami, 1954, Plaza Bldg., Miami, J.R.E. Lee Sch., residence for Dr. Maurice Rich, Miami, 1955, Golden Gate Devel., Dade County, 1955, Carlton Terrace Apts. and Havana Riviera Hotel, 1957, Seaview Realty Bldg., 1960; prof. U. Ill., 1950, Cornell U., 1951, U. Fla., 1950-53, Washington U., 1955, Ohio State U., 1957, Syracuse U., 1959. Chmn. unified code com. Ofcls. of Fla., 1954-55. Recipient Centennial medal U. Fla., 1953; Concrete Man of the Year award, 1960. Fellow A.I.A.; mem. Fla. Assn. Architects (v.p. 1952, pres. 1953-54), Miami Bldrs. Exchange. Address: Estes Park, Colo. Deceased.

POLIER, SHAD, lawyer; b. Aiken, S.C., Mar. 18, 1906; s. Harris Louis and Fanny (Cohen) P.; B.S., U. S.C., 1926; LL.B., Harvard, 1929, LL.M., 1931; m. Justine Wise, Mar. 26, 1937; children—Stephen W., Trudy H. (Mrs. Festinger), Jonathon. Admitted to N.Y. bar, 1931; mem. firm Polier, Tulin, & Clark, N.Y.C.; trial, rev. atty. NLRB, 1937-40; dir. fuel and consumer goods enforcement div. OPA, 1943-44; pub. mem. War Labor Bd., N.Y. region, 1944-45; mem. Citizens Com. on Children of N.Y.C.; hon. sec., mem. exec. com. Meml. Found. for Jewish Culture; counsel Northside Center for Child Devel.; counsel Louise Wise Services; dir., mem. exec. com. Conf. Jewish Material Claims against Germany; dir. Jewish Restitution Successor Orgn.; mem. bd. Met. Applied Research Center. Served with AUS, 1942. Mem. New York County Bar Assn., Assn. Bar City N.Y., Am. Vets. Com., Am. Bar Assn., Am. Arbitration Assn., N.A.A.C.P. (legal and ednl. fund exec. com.), World (mem. governing council, budget chmn.), Am. (hon. chmn. governing council) Jewish congresses, Phi Beta Kappa. Democrat. Jewish religion. Contbr. articles to tech. jours. Home: New York, N.Y. Died June 29, 1976.

POLLAK, HARRY HAMILTON, fgn. service officer, diplomat; b. Passaic, N3., Mar. 12, 1921; s. Sigmond and Molly (Katz) P.; B.A., Rutgers U., 1948; M.A. U. Chgo., 1951; m. Suzette Lois Aldon, June 29, 1950; children—Mollyann Pollak Gassel, Daniel. Asso. dir. internat. dept. CIO, 1951-55; asso. Inter-Am. rep. AFL-CIO, 1956-58, Asian rep., 1958-62; labor adviser Am. embassy, Tokyo, 1962-65; labor editor Voice of Am., 1956-66; labor attache, polit. officer U.S. Mission to European Communities, Brussels, Belgium, 1967-73;

labor attache, first sec. Am. Embassy, London, 1973-77; dep. coordinator internat. labor affairs Dept. of State, 1977-80; vis. lectr. Am. U., 1961; pub mem. U.S Fgn. Service Selection Bd., 1951; labor adviser Peace Corps, 1961; mem. trade union advisory com. Dept. Labor and Fgn. Operations Adminstrn., 1951-55. Vice pres. Burgundy Farm Country Day Sch., Alexandria, Va., 1960; hon. sec. Tokyo Jewish Community Center, 1963. Served with USAAC, 1942-45. Decorated DF.C, Air medal with 3 oak leaf clusters; recipient certificate of merit Labor Dept., 1959. Mem. Am. Fedn. Govt. Employees, Phi Beta Kappa. Jewish religion. Editor Am. Labor Rev., Tokyo, 1962-64; asst. editor Inter-Am. Labor Bull., 1956-58. Died Sept. 27, 1980; buried Washington D.C.

POLLOCK, FRANK SCOTT, company exec.; b. Downington, Pa., Jan. 16, 1886; s. William I. and Angelica (Fondersmith) P.; B.S., Penn State Coll., 1909, M.S., 1912; m. Eva A. Allen, Sept. 15, 1910; children—Helen I., Frank Scott. Engaged in explosives and chems. bus. since 1909; dir. Atlas Powder Co. Mem. Am. Inst. Chem. Engring. Elk, Mason. Home: Wilmington. *

POLMANTIER, PAUL CHURCHILL, educator; b. Emerson, Neb., Apr. 29, 1913; s. Manley Churchill and Nellie Gertrude (Taylor) P.; A.B., U. Omaha, 1934; A.M., U. Neb., 1935; Ph.D., U. Minn., 1941; m. Gladys Evalyne Thorell, June 26, 1936; children—Joan Marie, Jean Patrice. Instr. secondary schs., Norfolk, Neb., 1935-37, North High Sch., Omaha, 1937-38; teaching asst. edn. U. Minn., 1938-40, adminstrv. fellow U. Testing Bur., 1940-41; instr. edn. W.Va. U., summer 1941, Minn. State Tchrs. Coll., Mankato, 1941-42; asst. prof. edn. Mich. State Coll., 1942-43; asst. prof. edn. U. Mo., 1946, asso. prof., 1946-49, prof. edn., 1949-77, dir. U. Testing and Counseling Services, 1946-53, chmn. dept. ednl. psychology, 1968-75; vis. lectr. Syracuse U., summer 1956; vis. prof. U. Wyo., summer 1962. Served to lt. USNR, 1943-46. Diplomate in counseling and guidance Am. Bd. Examiners in Profl. Psychology. Fellow Am., Mo. psychol. assns.; mem. Nat. Vocational Guidance Assn. (trustee 1956-59), Am. Coll. Personnel Assn., Am. Assn. U. Profs., Mo. Tchrs. Assn., Phi Delta Kappa. Baptist. Author: A Casebook of Counseling (with others), 1955. Contbr. articles to profl. jours. Home: Columbia, Mo. Died Mar. 13, 1977.

PONCE ENRIQUEZ, CAMILO, former pres. of Ecuador; b. 1912; ed. U. Quito, U. Chile. Vice pres. Quito Municipal Council, 1943; mem. Junta Gov., 1944; minister fgn. relations, leader Ecuadorial delegation San Francisco and Chapultepec confs., 1945, minister govt. and justice, 1953-56; v.p. Nat. Assembly, 1946; prof. constitutional law Cath. U. of Ecuador, 1950; senator, 1952, pres. Ecuador, from 1956. Del. UNESCO, 1952. Founder Christian Social Movement. Author: Parliamentary Speeches, 1953-54, others. Address: Quito, Ecuador. Deceased.

POND, HORACE B., pres. Pacific Commercial Co.; b. Waltham, Mass., July 21, 1882; s. George H. and Annie P.; ed. high sch.; married, June 6, 1908. V.p. Pacific Commercial Co., 1916-19, gen. mgr., 1919-25, pres. since 1925; v.p. Metropolitan Theater Co.; chmn. bd. Philippine Internat. Corp.; dir. El Hogar Filipino. Regent U. of Philippines; mem. Manila Chamber of Commerce (v.p. 1928). Baptist. Elk. Clubs: India House (New York); University, Rotary, Casino Español, Army and Navy, Manila, Elks, Polo (Manila). Home: Manila, P.I.; N.Y. *

PONIATOFF, ALEXANDER MATTHEW, magnetic tape recorder mfg. exec.; b. Kazan, Russia, Mar. 25, 1892; s. Mathew E. and Agafia (Andreef) P.; M.E., Tech. Coll., Karlsruhe, Germany, 1914; m. Hazel H. Hess, May 6, 1932. Came to U.S., 1927, naturalized, 1932. Asst. engr. Shanghai Power Co. (China), 1920-27; research and devel. Gen. Electric Co., Schenectady, 1927-30; devel. work, various orgns., San Francisco, 1930-40; devel. air-borne Navy radar Dalmo Victor Co., 1944; prodn. radar components Ampex Corp., 1944-47, pres., 1944-54, chmn., 1955-70, chmn. emeritus, 1971-80. Served as pilot Imperial Russian Navy, 1916-18, with Civil War White Russian Army, 1918-20. Fellow IEEE. Introduced 1st profl. magnetic audio tape recorder, 1947, 1st videotape recorder, 1956. Home: Atherton, Calif. Died Oct. 24, 1980; interred Alta Mesa Meml. Park, Palo Alto, Calif.

PONTI, GIO, architect, designer; b. Milano, Italy, Nov. 18, 1891; s. Enrico and Giovanna (Rigone) P.; m. Giulia Vimercati, June 24, 1921; children—Lisa (Mrs. Licitra), Giovanna (Mrs. Rosselli), Letizia (Mrs. Frailich), Giulio. Designer (with others) Pirelli Skyscraper, (with Portaluppi) Ras Palace, Secretariat Bldgs., Islamabad, Pakistan, also villas, hotels, schs., oflc. bldgs. and chs., Tehran, Rome, Italy, Milan, Italy, Padua, Voghera, Sao Paulo, Buenos Aires, Argentina, Baghdad, Stockholm, Caracas, Paris, N.Y.C.; marine decorator Andrea Doria; created frescos at Padua, scenography for LaScala; prof. architecture U. Milan; nat. academician of San Luca. Recipient Nat. Prize of Gold Compass. Mem. A.I.A., Royal Inst. brit. Architects. Author books on architecture. Editor of Domus. Address: Milano, Italy. Died Sept. 15, 1979.

POOL, LEONARD PARKER, air products mfg. exec.; b. Mpls., Nov. 5, 1906; s. Leonard J. and Emma (Ludford) P.; student Allegheny Coll., Meadville, Pa., D.Sc., 1968; Dr. Engring., Lehigh U., 1961, PMC Coll., 1962; D.Social Sci., Villanova U., 1970; D.H.L., Lafayette Coll., Easton, Pa., 1972; hon. degree Muhlenberg Coll., 1974; m. Dorothy A. Rider, Dec. 9, 1931 (dec.); m. 2d, Gloria P. Graeffe, Feb. 6, 1968. Salesman, C.H. Dockson Co., Detroit, 1927-29; asst. mgr. Burdett Oxygen Co., Detroit, 1929-36; sec.-treas. Acetylene Gas & Supply Corp., Detroit, 1936-37; mgr. railroad sales Compressed Insl. Gases, Inc., Chgo., 1937, gen. mgr., Detroit, 1937-40; founder, chmn. bd., chief exec. officer, dir. Air Products & Chems., Inc. and subsidiary firms, Allentown, Pa., 1940-73, chmn., 1973-75; dir. Am. Standard, Inc., N.Y.C. Trustee Allentown Hosp., Lehigh U. Allegheny Coll., Meadville, Pa.; bd. dirs. Boys' Club of Allentown, Good Shepherd Home and Rehab. Center, Allentown; pres., bd. dirs. Allentown and Sacred Heart Hosp. Center; bd. overseers Coll. Engring., U. Pa. Recipient Winthrop Sears medal Chem. Industry Assn., 1971, Chem. Industry medal, 1975. Internat. Acad. Law and Sci. hon. fellow, 1974. Mem. Am. Iron and Steel Inst. Clubs: Lehigh Country, Saucon Valley Country (Bethlehem, Pa.); Metropolitan (N.Y.C.); Rolling Rock (Ligonier, Pa.). Home: Allentown, Pa. Died Dec. 27, 1975.

POOL, RAYMOND JOHN, prof. botany; b. Wabash, Neb., Apr. 23, 1882; s. William H. and Mary L. (Burrows) P.; A.B., U. of Neb., 1907, A.M., 1908, Ph.D., 1913; studied U. of Chicago, 1908; m. Martha M. Stangland, June 30, 1909. Instr. botany, 1907, adj. prof., 1908-10, asst. prof. and curator Univ. Herbarium, 1910-11, asso. prof. and curator, 1911, prof., 1914, head dept. bot., 1915-48, emeritus U. Neb. Asst. prof., U. of Mich., summer, 1910; visiting prof. Southern Ill. U., 1955-56; investigator relations of indsl. operations to vegetation since 1917. Fellow A.A.A.S. (v.p., chmn. Sect. G, 1939), Bot. Soc. America (pres. syst. sect. 1925); asso. Am. Museum Natural History; mem. Torrey Bot. Club, Ecol. Soc. America, Neb. Acad. Science (pres. 1916), Am. Forestry Assn., Am. Phytopath. Soc., Am. Micros. Soc. (v.p. 1932; pres. 1941), Soc. Am. Foresters, Soc. Am.Naturalists, American Soc. Plant Taxonomists, American Inter-professional Inst. (pres. Lincoln Chapter 1940), Phi Beta Kappa (past pres. Neb. chapter), Sigma XI (past pres. Neb. Chapter), Chi Phi, Phi Sigma. Kiwanian. Author: Vegetation of Nebraska Sand Dunes; Experiments in Plant Physiology; Handbook of Nebraska Trees; First Course in Botany (with Dr. A. T. Evans); Flowers and Flowering Plants; Basic Botany for Colleges; Marching With the Grasses; also numerous articles on various phases of botany in bot. and other jours. Address: Lincoln, Neb. *

POOL, TAMAR DE SOLA, lecturer, educator; b. Jerusalem, Israel, 1890; d. Chaim and Eva (Cohen) Hirschenson; brought to U.S., 1904; A.B., Hunter Coll., 1913; student U. Paris, 1913-14 (traveling fellowship); grad. student Columbia, 1914-17; m. Rev. David de Sola Pool, Feb. 6, 1917; children—Ithiel de Sola, Naomi de Sola (Mrs. Rodstein). Tutor English lang. and lit. Lycée Lamartine, Paris, 1913-14; instr. French, Latin and Greek, Hunter Coll., 1914-17; faculty adviser Menorah Socs., Hunter Coll., 1915-16; editor Hadassah Newsletter; nat. pres. Hadassah, 1939-43, pres. N.Y. chpt., 1929-35; chmn. world praesidium Henrietta Szold Centennial, 1960; Hadassah chmn. Szold Inst.; dir. Nat. Council of Women of U.S.; hon. chmn. Jewish Nat. Fund; mem. gen. council World Zionist Orgn.; sometime mem. exec. Am.-Jewish Com.; vice chmn. Am. Jewish Conf.; mem. gov. bd. Youth Aliyah; mem. exec. com. Children to Palestine; chmn. Hebrew-University-Hadassah Med. Sch. com.; co-founder, chmn. Am. Mothers Com.; mem. bd. Sisterhood of Spanish and Portuguese Synagogue of N.Y.; pres., later hon. pres. Sifriot Libraries for Youth in Israel and U.S.; bd. govs. Hebrew U., Jerusalem; mem. bd. Union Sephardic Congregations, Am. Separdi Fedn.; women's div. Alliance Israelite Universelle. Named Virilist, World Zionist Congress. Author: Israel and the United Nations: In the Spirit of '76 (a drama); Triple Cord (novel); (with David de Sola Pool) An Old Faith in The New World, 1955; The Passover Haggadah; Is There an Answer? An Inquiry into Some Human Dilemmas; Haggadah (art edit.), 1975; (with Nima Adlerblum) David de Sola Pool. Home: New York, N.Y. Died June 1, 1981.

POOR SAMUEL SMITH, sales exec.;b. Port Chester, N.Y., Dec. 4, 1884; s. William Cheney and Harriet (Smith) P.; student pub. schs.; m. Elsie Belle Preston, dec. 4, 1911; children—Samuel S., Betsey (Mrs. Harvey S. Fisher), John Barton. With Second Nat. Bank, N.Y.C., 1900-02; salesman Am. Tobacco Co., 1902-04; with Monogrammed Cigarettes, 1904-07; sales dept. Continental Rubber Co., Hanover, Germany, later dist. mgr. U.S. Rubber Co. (purchased Continental Rubber Co.), Phila., 1907-17; sales mgr. Cleveland Pierce Arrow, 1917-19, dealer, Akron, O., 1918-19; became sales mgr. Gen. Tire & Rubber Co., 1919-32, v.p. charge merchandising, 1932-51, now dir.; propr. Gen. Tire & Rubber Service, Providence. Clubs: Portage Country (Akron, O.); N.Y. Athletic; Algonquin (Boston); Turks Head (Providence). Home: Andover, Me. *

POOS, OMER, U.S. Dist. judge; b. Mt. Olive, Ill., Aug. 22, 1902; s. Henry and Rosetta (McCann) P.; LL.B., St. Louis U., 1924; m. Virginia Van Liew, Sept. 25, 1928; 1 son, Robert Van Liew. Admitted to Mo. bar, 1923, Ill. bar, 1925; practice of law, Mt. Olive, Ill., 1924-39; pvt. practice, Hillsboro, Ill., 1939-58; U.S. dist. judge, Ill., 1958-76, chief judge of So. dist., then sr. judge So. Dist. Ill.; v.p., dir. Nokomis Coal Co., 1936-46; sec., dir. Mineralized Products Co., Inc. Pres. bd. edn., Hillsboro, Ill.; staff war finance div. U.S. Treasury Dept., World War II; war finance chmn. Montgomery County, Ill., 1941-45. Chmn. United Republican Fund of Ill., 23d Congl. Dist. Pres., dir. Hilton Football, Inc., Hillsboro Hosp. Assn. Recipient silver medallion, distinguished service citation sec. treas. Mem. Am., Ill., 2d Supreme Ct. (pres.), Montgomery County (pres.) bar assns., Delta Theta Phi, Delta Sigma Phi. Republican. K.C., Elk. Moose, Rotarian. Home: Hillsboro, Ill. Died Aug. 12, 1976.

POPE ABNER S., banker; b. Newsoms, Va., Mar. 1, 1883; s. Joseph B. and Jennie B. (Prince) P.; B.S., Richmond Coll., 1903; m. Rosa Virginia Smith, Apr. 10, 1907; children—Mrs. E. L. Woodard, Mrs. Harley F. Shuford, Mrs. Charles F. Burroughs, Jr. Cashier Seaboard Nat. Bank, Norfolk, 1912-19; pres. Savings Bank of Norfolk, 1920-21, merged with Seaboard Nat., 1922, v.p., 1922-28; exec. v.p. Seaboard Citizen's Nat. Bank, 1928-32, pres. 1932-55, chmn. bd., 1956—. Mem. C. of C. Clubs: Norfolk Yacht Country, Princess Anne Country. Home: Norfolk. *

POPE, ARTHUR EDWARD, pub. utilities; b. Burlington, Vt., Aug. 31, 1883; s. Edward Allen and Anna Maria (Root) P.; B.S. in E.E., U. of Vt., 1904, Elec. Engr., 1929; m. Elizabeth Kellogg, June 19, 1909; children—Patricia, Richard Warren. Engr. Gen. Electric Co., Schenectady, N.Y., 1904-06 inspection and constrn. engr. with J. G. White, N.Y. City, 1906-11; with N.E. Power Co. interests, Worcester and Boston, as electrical engineer, assistant general manager and assistant to president, 1911-28; pres. and director Conn. River Power Co.; vice pres., dir., N.E. Power Co. Mem. Sigma Phi, Republican. Clubs: Wellesley Country, Wellesley Hills; University, Algonquin (Boston). Home: Wellesley Hills, Mass. *

POPE, JAMES PINCKNEY, ex-senator; b. Jackson Parish, La., Mar. 31, 1884; s. Jesse T. and Lou (McBride) P.; B. of Industry, La. Poly. Inst., Ruston, 1906; LL.B., U. of Chicago, 1909; m. Pauline Ruth Horn, June 26, 1913; children—Ross P., George A. Began practice at Boise, Ida., 1909; mem. Pope & Barnes, 1910-13; dep. collector internal revenue, 1916; city atty., Boise, 1916-17; asst. atty. gen of Ida., 1917-19; elected mayor of Boise, 1929, reëlected, 1931; U.S. senator from Ida., term 1933-39; dir. Tenn. Valley Authority since 1939. Am. mem. Internat. Commn. between the U.S. and Portugal. Conglist. Mason, Elk. Club: Rotary. Home: Knoxville, Tenn. *

POPEJOY, THOMAS LAFAYETTE, educator; b. Raton, New Mexico, Dec. 2, 1902; s. Fred and Ellen (Floyd) P.; B.A., Univ. of N.M., 1925; student U. Ill., summers 1925, 26; A.M., U. N.M., 1929; student U. Cal., summers 1934, 35; LL.D., U. Ariz., 1954; LL.D., U. Albuquerque, 1968; m. Bessie Kimball, June 21, 1921; children—Jeanne Kimball, Thomas Lafayette. Instr. in econs. U. N.M., 1925-29, asst. prof., 1929-37, ass. prof., 1937-48, exec. asst. to pres., 1936-48, pres., 1948-68; comptroller, 1938-48, acting registrar, 1941-44, chmn. bd. of deans, 1944-45; research dir. N.M. Taxpayer's Assn., 1932; state dir., Nat. Youth Adminstrn., 1935-39, dep. adminstr., Washington, D.C., 1939-40; regional consumer relations rep. OPA, Denver, 1942. Mem. exec. com. Western Interstate Commn. Higher Edn., from 1953, pres., 1951-53; mem. pres.'s council Western Athletic Conf., 1961-68, chmn., 1961-62, 65-66; mem. exec. com. Asso. Rocky Mountain Univs., Inc., 1961-68, pres. 1960-61; pres. Nat. Assn. State Univs., 1963-64. Pres. Albuquerque Little Theatre, 1968-69. Mem. bd. visitors Air U., USAF, 1961-64, St. John's Coll., Santa Fe; trustee Sandia Sch. for Girls, Sch. Am. Research. Mem. Albuquerque C. of C. (dir.). Blue Key, Alpha Phi Omega, Pi Gamma Mu, Sigma Chi, Phi Kappa Phi, Tau Kappa Alpha, Alpha Kappa Psi. Democrat. Episcopalian. Clubs: Albuquerque Country, Rotary (pres. 1946-47). Author: The Causes of Bank Failures in N.M., 1920-25, 1931; The University of New Mexico, A Calculated Risk. Contbr. articles to N.M. Business Rev. Home: Albuquerque, N.M. Died Oct. 24, 1975.

POPPEN, JAMES L., neurosurgeon; b. Drenthe, Mich., Feb. 27, 1903; s. John and Ann (Slotman) P.; student Hope Prep. Sch., Holland, Mich., 1916-20; grad. Hope Coll., 1926; D.Sc., 1953; M.D., Rush Med. Coll., Chgo., 1930; m. Nancy High, Apr. 10, 1933; children—Elizabeth, John. House officer and house officer internship St. Luke's Hosp., Chgo., 1929-30;

surg. resident Ill. Research and Ednl. Hosp., 1931, 33; neurosurgeon Lahey Clinic, 1933-70, chief of neurosurgery, 1957-70; pvt. practice neurosurgery, Boston, 1970-78; neurosurgeon New Eng. Deaconess, New Eng. Baptist and Boston Psychopathic hosps., 1933-78; chmn. neurosurgery New Eng. Bapt. Hosp.; cons. Taunton (Mass.) State Hosp., Jamaica Plain (Mass.) Vets. Hosp., Sturdy Meml. Hosp., Attleboro, Mass., St. Luke's Hosp., Middleboro, Mass. Decorated cross King Alfonso X, Spain, 1947, Sword of San Martin, Argentina, Decoration of Merit; Ordem de Boyaca (Colombia). Fellow A.C.S.; mem. A.M.A., Am. Neurol. Soc., Soc. Neurol. Surgeons (pres. 1960), Argentina Sociedad de Neurologia Psiquiatria y Neurocirugla Honorario, Sociedad de Neurologia Neurocirugia Honerario Repubia Oriental del Uruguay, Soc. Neurology Rio de Janeiro, Ordem Nacional de Cruzeiro de Sul, Brazil, Am. Surg. Assn.; hon. mem. faculty medicine U. of Madrid; corr. mem. La Real Societa Italiana de Neuro-Chirurgia, Milano, Italy, Neurosurg. Soc. Brazil, Neurosurg. Soc. Venezuela; hon. mem. Nacional de Medicina, Spain; hon. mem. Societa Italiana di Neurochirurgia, Milano Italy; hon. mem. Societe de NeuroChirurgie de Langue Francaise; mem. Mass. Med. Soc., Boston Surg. Soc., Boston Soc. Neurology and Psychiatry (pres. 1951), Harvey Cushing Soc. (pres. 1959), Pan Am. Med. Assn. (N.Am. v.p. 1966), Brazilian Nueorsurgical Soc. (hon. pres. 1966), Sigma Nu. Clubs: Country (Brookline, Mass.); Punta del Esta Golf (hon. mem.; Uruguay). Contbr. articles sur. subjects. Home: Brookline, Mass. Died Dec. 8, 1978.

PORT, FREDERICK JAMES, corp. exec.; b. Parkston, S.D., Oct. 13, 1914; s. Frederick James and Gretchen (Bleser) P.; B.S., U. Ill., 1936; Sc.D., Mass. Inst. Tech., 1940; M.B.A., U. Chgo., 1946; m. Edith Ann Whitney, Sept. 14, 1940 (div. 1964); children—Robert, Thomas, Eric, David, Anthony; m. 2d, Rolanda DeWinter, Sept. 10, 1971; children—Jason, Hannah. Works mgr. Cribben & Sexton Co., 1946-49; gen. mgr. Hein-Werner Corp., 1949-50; dir. battery ops. Solar Corp., 1950-55; dir. engring. ESB, Inc., Cleve., 1955-56, mgr. mfg. and engring., 1956-58, gen. mgr. automotive div., 1958-60, v.p. automotive group, 1960-69, pres., chief exec. officer, 1971-78, also chmn.; dir. Provident Nat. Bank, SKF Industries Inc. Provident Nat. Corp., INCO (U.S.), Inc.; trustee Penn Mut. Life Ins. Co. Served from 2d lt. to capt., Ordnance Dept., U.S. Army, 1942-46. Mem. Assn. Am. Battery Mfrs. (dir., pres. 1964-65), Soc. Automotive Engrs., Electrochem. Soc. Clubs: Aronimink Golf, Pine Valley Golf. Home: West Chester, Pa. Died July 7, 1978.

PORTER, CLIFFORD LEWIS, lawyer; b. Torrington, Conn., Apr. 16, 1916; s. Gail Q. and Ethel M. (Chamberlain) P.; A.B., Dartmouth, 1936, M.C.S., Amos Tuck Sch., 1937; LL.B., Yale, 1940; m. Mary F. Pearson, Dec. 14, 1940; children—Lynn (Mrs. James W. Bodman), Lee, Mary. Admitted to N.Y. bar, 1942, D.C. bar, 1956; partner firm Cahill Gordon & Reindel, and predecessors, N.Y.C., 1940-77. Served to lt. (s.g.) USNR, 1943-46. Mem. Am. Bar Assn. (chmn. taxation sect. 1966-67), Assn. Bar City N.Y. (chmn. com. taxation 1964-65), N.Y. State Bar Assn. (exec. com. tax sect. 1971-77), N.Y. County Lawyers Assn., D.C. Bar Assn., Phi Beta Kappa, Sigma Nu. Asso. editor Yale Law Jour., 1939-40. Home: Sands Point, N.Y. Died Oct. 19, 1977.

PORTER, FREDERIC HUTCHINSON, architect; b. Salem, Mass., July 9, 1890; s. Ellis Hawthorne and Emma (Hutchinson) P.; student Wentworth Inst., Boston; m. Grace G. Wastfield, Dec. 31, 1913; 1 son, Frederic Hutchinson. Draftsman, Edward F. Stevens, Putnam and Chandler, Boston, 1917-19; partner Baerresem & Porter, Cheyenne, Wyo., 1919-21; pvt. practice, 1921-44; partner Porter & Porter, Cheyenne, 1944-61, Porter, Porter and Graves, Cheyenne, 1961-65; pvt. practice, Cheyenne, 1965-73; prin. works include women's dormitories U. Wyo., 1961, men's dormitories, 1962, service and geology bldgs., 1955-62; VA Hosp., Cheyenne, 1959, Presbyn. Ch., Cheyenne, 1961; instr. Wentworth Inst., 1917-18; lectr. archtl. engring. U. Wyo., 1952. Sec.-treas. Wyo. Bd. Architects, 1951-62; chmn. pub. adv. panel on arctl. services Region 8, GSA, 1967-76. Fellow A.I.A. (pres. Wyo. 1946-47, sec. treas. 1947-51; dir. Western Mountain region 1958-61); mem. Soc. Archtl. Historians, Cheyenne Artists Guild (pres. 1975). Author: Architecture of the Georgian Period, 1923. Home: Cheyenne, Wyo. Died July 7, 1976.

PORTER, JOHN ROGER, microbiologist; b. Alma, Nebr., Aug. 14, 1909; s. Robert William and Celia Edith (Mitchell) P.; student Westminster Coll., 1928-30; B.S., Iowa State U., 1933, M.S., 1935; Ph.D., Yale, 1938; m. Marjorie Perkins, Sept. 17, 1934; children—Roberta (Mrs. Walter W. Barbee), Carol (Mrs. Lee W. Hopkins), Katherine (Mrs. William H. Blessing), John Roger. Instr. bacteriology, coll. medicine U. Iowa, 1938-39, asso., 1939-41, asst. prof., 1941-45, asso. prof., 1945-47, prof., 1947-79, head dept. microbiology, 1949—, exec. com., 1955-59; mem. adv. microbiology panel Naval Research, 1951-59. Dir. Waverly Press Co., Balt. Mem. sci. info. council NSF, 1961-65, 66-68, chmn., 1967-68; mem. Nat. Bd. Med. Examiners in Microbiology, 1965-69; chmn. adv. com. on sci. publs. NIH, 1967-69; chmn. panel on microbiology UNEP/UNESCO, 1969-79; mem. adv. panel on sci. and tech. U.S. Ho. of Reps., 1970-74; mem. bd. on internat. orgns. and programs Nat. Acad. Scis., 1969-76; mem. U.S. del. to 18th Gen. Conf. UNESCO, Paris, 1974. Recipient Pasteur award, 1961; Stuart Mudd award World Acad. Art and Sci., 1978. Diplomate Am. Bd. Microbiology. Mem. Am. Soc. Microbiology (past nat. program chmn.; pres. 1964), Am. Chem. Soc., Soc. Gen. Microbiology (Eng.), A.A.A.S. (publs. com. 1964-74), Am. Assn. Immunologists, Soc. Exptl. Biology and Medicine, Ia. Acad. Sci., Am. Inst. Biol. Scis. (pres. 1967), Am. Biology Council (chmn. 1969), Internat. Assn. Microbiol. Socs. (adv. council 1966-70, pres.-elect 1978), Internat. Fedn. Documentation (U.S. nat. com.), U.S. Nat. Com. Internat. Union Biol. Scis. (chmn. 1967-69, del. gen. assembly 1967), Johnson County Med. Soc., Am. Acad. Microbiology (chmn. bd. govs. 1962-63), Assn. Med. Sch. Microbiology Chairmen (pres. 1975), Sigma Xi (sec. coll. chpt. 1947-49, pres. 1951-52). Presbyn. Club: Cosmos (Washington). Author: Bacterial Chemistry and Physiology, 1946; also numerous sci. papers; contbr. chpts. to books. Editor-in-chief of Jour. Bacteriology, 1951-61. Compiler, editor: 50 volume index for Jour. Bacteriology 1953, 62. Mem. editorial bd. Biomed. News, 1969-74. Home: Iowa City, Iowa. Died May 27, 1979; buried Iowa City.

PORTER, KATHERINE ANNE, writer; b. Indian Creek, Tex., May 15, 1890; d. Harrison Boone and Mary Alice (Jones) Porter; student in various pvt. schs.; D.Litt., Maryville Coll., St. Louis, 1968; L.H.D., U. Mich., 1954, U. Md., 1966; m. Albert Russel Erskine, Jr., Apr. 19, 1938; (div. 1942). Writer-in-residence and lectr. on lit. Stanford U., Calif., 1949; writer in residence U. Va., 1958-59; first Glasgow prof. Washington and Lee U., 1959. From 1920 to 1937 lived in N.Y. or in Europe and Mexico. Awarded Guggenheim fellowship for creative writing, 1931, 38; fellow of regional Am. lit. library of Congress, 1944. Recipient Book-of-the-Month Club award, 1937; first ann. gold medal for lit. Soc. for Libraries of N.Y. U., 1940, for Pale Horse, Pale Rider; Ann. prize lit. work Tex. Inst. Lit., Dallas, 1950; Emerson-Thoreau Bronze medal Am. Acad. of Arts and Sci., 1962; Nat. Book award for fiction, 1966; Pulitzer prize for fiction, 1966; gold medal for fiction Nat. Inst. Arts and Letters, 1967. Guest lectr. English dept. U. Mich. 1953-54; Fulbright lectr. U. Liege, Belgium, 1955; Ford Found. grant in literature, 1959-60. Vice pres. Nat. Inst. Arts and Letters, 1950-52. Mem. Am. Acad. Arts and Letters, Phi Beta Kappa. Author: (short story collections) Flowering Judas, 1930, Hacienda: A Story of Mexico, 1934, Noon Wine, 1937; Pale Horse, Pale Rider: three Short Novels, 1938, the Leaning Tower and Other Stories, 1944, Holiday (1st prize O'Henry Awards), 1962, Collected Stories of Katherine Anne Porter, 1964 (Book-of-the-Month Club); (novel) Ship of Fools, 1962 (Book of Month Club); (non-fiction) the Days Before: Collected Essays and Occasional Writing, 1952 (augmented edit. 1970), A Defense of Circe, 1955; The Never-Ending Wrong, a memoir of the Sacco Vanzetti case, 1977; compiler, translator French Song Book, Paris, 1933; translator the Itching Parrot (Fernandez de Lizardi), 1942. Died Sept. 18, 1980.

PORTER, LAWRENCE CHARLES, lawyer; b. Atlantic City, May 7, 1932; s. Julius J. and Hannah (Levitt) Perlmutter; B.B.A. magna cum laude, U. Miami (Fla.), 1953, M.A., 1954, J.D. magna cum laude, 1959; m. Carole Nancy Wien, Dec. 20, 1953; children—Marjorie Rose, Lawrence Charles II, Carolyn Joan. Admitted to Fla. bar, 1959, N.Y. bar, 1971, since practiced in Miami and New York; municipal judge, Fla., 1964-78; sr. partner firm Porter, Treister & Bercuson, P.A., 1966-78; Lawrence C. Porter, P.C., N.Y.C.; asst. atty. gen. Fla., 1960-61, 73-78; tchr. polit. sci. dept. U. Miami, 1953-54, 73, adj. prof. law, 1975-78; adj. prof. law N.Y. Law Sch.; Dir. So. Properties Corp., Indsl. United Corp. Participant Aspen Inst. Humanistic Studies; chmn. London Seminar, 1975. Mem. Mt. Sinai Hosp. Founders Club; chmn. steering com. St. Francis Hosp., Miami; bd. dirs. Children's Variety Hosp.; founder, pres. Porter Found. Served to 1st lt., AUS, 1955-56. Mem. Am., N.Y. State, Fla., Dade County bar assns., Oxford Soc., Iron Arrow, Omicron Delta Kappa, Scabbard and Blade (past pres.). Clubs: Standard, Westview Country (vice chmn., dir.), Jockey (Miami). Home: Palm Bay, Fla. Died Sept. 1, 1978.

PORTER, PAUL ALDERMANDT, lawyer; b. Joplin, Mo., Oct. 6, 1904; s. John J. and Dolly (Carpenter) P.; ed. Ky. Wesleyan Coll., 1923-26, LL.D., 1945; U. Ky. Law Coll., 1926-29; m. Bessie Edgar Benton, June 14, 1930 (div. June 1956); children—Betsy Gilman, Ann Dinsmoor; m. 2d, Kathleen Winsor, June 26, 1956. Newspaper reporter; city editor Lexington (Ky.) Herald, 1926-29; in practice of law, central Ky., 1928-29; editor Mangum (Okla.) Daily News and LaGrange (Ga.) News, 1929-32; spl. counsel Dept. Agr., 1932-37; Washington counsel CBS, 1937-42; lectr. on adminstrv. law Law Coll. of Catholic U., Washington, 1941-59; dep. adminstr. in charge rent div. OPA, 1942-43; asso. adminstr. War Food Adminstrn.; asso. dir. Office Econ. Stblzn., July 1943-Feb. 1944; campaign publicity dir. Dem. Nat. Com., 1944; apptd. mem. FCC and designated chmn., 1944; apptd. adminstr. OPA, 1946; apptd. chief Am. Econ. Mission to Greece with rank of ambassador, Dec. 1946; mem. firm Arnold & Porter, Washington, 1947-75; rank of ambassador, as U.S. rep. on Palestine Conciliation commn., July 1949. Mem. President's Commn. Campaign Costs, 1961-62. Mem. Nat. Press Assn., Fed. Communications, Ky. bar assns., Sigma Alpha Epsilon, Phi Alpha Delta. Democrat. Baptist. Home: Washington, D.C. Deceased.

PORTER, RAYMOND AVERILL, sculptor; b. Hermon, N.Y., Feb. 18, 1883; s. James and Meriam (Stokes) P.; ed. pub. schs.; studied Sch. of Art Inst. Chicago, 1902-04. Head of the dept. of modeling and sculpture, Mass. Sch. of Art, since 1915. Represented by "Green Mountain Boy" statue (Rutland, Vt.), monument to Pres. John Tyler (Richmond, Va.), Civil War monument (Auburn, N.Y.), World War Victory monument (Salem, Mass.), World War monument (Leominster, Mass.), Spanish-Am. War monument (Somerville, Mass.), statue of Henry Cabot Lodge (State House, Boston). Author and dir. of hist. pageants. Home: Boston, Mass. *

PORTER, WILLIAM ARNOLD, ret. lawyer; b. Chgo., Jan. 6, 1906; s. Edgar Selic and Martha (Tolleson) P.; LL.B., Nat. U., 1929; J.D., George Washington U., 1968; m. Florence Oyler, Dec. 5, 1931. Admitted to D.C. bar, 1930, practiced in Washington; partner Robb, Porter, Kistler & Parkinson, 1946-69; counsel Dempsey & Koplovitz, 1969-70. Served as lt. comdr. USNR, 1942-45; asst. dir. telecommunication ODM, as presdl. adviser on telecommunications, 1953-54. Mem. Am. (ho. of dels. 1952, chmn. standing com. on communications 1954-56), D.C., Fed. Communications (pres. 1951) bar assns., Am. Judicature Soc. Club: University (Washington). Home: Bethesda, Md. Died Jan. 10, 1976.

PORTEUS, STANLEY DAVID (PÔ'CHUS), psychologist, author; b. Box Hill, Victoria, Australia, Apr. 24, 1883; s. David and Katherine (Hebden) P.; ed. Melbourne Ednl. Inst., and U. of Melbourne, 1910-16; hon. D.Sc., U. of Hawaii, 1932; m. Frances Mainwaring Evans, July 13, 1909; children—David Hebden, John Ruxton. Came to U.S., 1919, naturalized, 1932. School teacher, Victoria, Australia, 1900-12; supt. spl. schs., Melbourne, 1912-16; govt. research scholar, U. of Melbourne, 1916-17; lecturer on exptl. edn., U. of Melbourne, 1917-19; dir. of research, Psychol. Lab. Training Sch., Vineland, N.J., 1919-25; prof. of clin. psychology, and dir. of psychol. and psychopathic clinic, U. of Hawaii, 1922-48; referee of Juvenile Court of Hawaii since 1950; leader of expdn. to N.W. Australia, 1929, expdn. to Kalahari Desert, S. Africa, 1934. Mem. American Psychol. Assn. Am. Assn. Cons. Psychologists. Author or co-author numerous books; latest publs.: The Restless Voyage, 1948; Porteus Maze Test and Intelligence, 1950; Providence Ponds, 1951. Home: Honolulu. *

POSADAS, JUAN, collector of internal revenue of P.L.; b. San Narciso, Zambales, P.I., Dec. 10, 1884; s. Juan and Eladia F. (Pablo) P.; ed. Ateneo de Manila; m. Rosario Garcia del Fierro, Feb. 22, 1905. Dep. provincial treas. Zambales, 1902-07; clk. Bur. of Audits, 1908; acting provincial treas., Antique, 1909; chief clk. and dep. provincial treas., Cagayan, 1910; clk. Exec. Bureau, 1911; chief clk. and dep. treas., Laguna, 1911-13; provincial treas. Oriental Negros, 1914-16; provincial sec.-treas. Davao, 1917; asst. dept. sec. and acting dept. treas. Mindanao-Sulu, 1918; acting dept. gov. same, 1919; dep. collector internal revenue, P.L., 1920-23, collector since 1924; also chmn. Tobacco Bd. since 1924; mem. Rural Bank Commn., 1930; treas. and dir. Philippine Safety Council, Philippine Vocational Guidance Assn. Mem. Philippine Columbian Assn., Phillipine Anti-Tuberculosis Soc. (dir.), Philippine Anti-Leprosy Soc. (trustee and treas.), Philippine Tourist Assn. (treas. and dir.). Catholic, Rotarian. Home: Manila, P.I. *

POSNER, ERNST MAXIMILLAN, educator; b. August 9, 1892; s. Carl and Sophie (Rosenberg) P.; Ph.D., U. Berlin, Germany, 1920; m. Katharina Melchior, June 10, 1929, (dec. Oct. 1979). State archivist Prussian Privy State Archives, Berlin-Dahlem, 1921-35, instr. Inst. for Archival Sci. and Advanced Hist., Studies, 1930-33; lectr. Am. U., Washington, 1939-40, adj. prof., 1940-45, prof. hist. archives adminstrn., from 1945. dean grad. div., 1945-47, dir. sch. social scis. and pub. affairs, 1947-55, dean Grad. Sch., 1955-57. Mem. Am., Cath. hist. assns., Soc. Am. Archivists, Am. Assn. State and Local History. Home: Arlington, Va. Died Apr. 18, 1980.

POST, KIRBY MARION, ry. official; b. Gatesville, Tex., Apr. 10, 1886; s. John Timothy and Martha Washington (Pouncey) P.; ed. pub. schs.; m. Enid Colgin, Sept. 24, 1906; children—John Timothy, Evelyn, Kirby Marion. With St. Louis & Soutwestern Ry. Co. since 1901; supt., 1921-29, asst. to pres., 1929-31. v.p. and gen. supt., 1931-46, chief operating officer, 1946-47, v.p. since Oct. 1947; v.p. St. Louis & Southwestern Ry. Co. of Texas; dir. Union Terminal Co.

Mem. East Tex. Chamber of Commerce, Tyler Chamber of Commerce. Democrat. Episcopalian. Mason (32 deg.. K.T., Shriner). Clubs: Willowbrook Country; Dallas Athletic. Address: Tyler, Tex. *

POTOFSKY, JACOB S., ret. labor leader; b. Radomisl, Russia, Nov. 16, 1894; s. Simon and Rebecca P.; L.H.D., Hebrew U. College-Jewish Inst. Religion, 1961, Roosevelt U., 1967, Villanova U., 1969, Brandeis U., 1969; m. Callie Taylor (dec.); children—Delia (Mrs. William Gottieb), Bruce (dec.), Jacqueline (Mrs. M. Broughton); m. 2d, Blanche Lydia Zetland, 1951. Sec.-treas. Chgo. Joint Board, Amalgamated Clothing Workers Am., CIO, 1914-16, asst. sec. treas., 1916-34, asst. pres., 1934-40, gen. sec. treas., 1940-46, gen. pres., 1946-72, pres. emeritus, 1972-79; mem. ethical practices com. AFL-CIO. Mem. bd. Amalgamated Ins. Co., Amalgamated Ins. Fund; chmn. bd. Amalgamated Bank N.Y.; pres. Amalgamated Dwellings, Inc.; treas. Amalgameted Housing Corp.; pres. United Housing Found.; dir. Hillman Housing Corp.; v.p. Riverbay Corp. Vice pres., exec. council CIO-AFL: dir. Greater N.Y. Fund, N.Y. World's Fair 1964-65 Corp., Nat. Conf. Christians and Jews, Com. Nation's Health; nat. adv. council Am. Jewish Com.; mem. nat. council U.S. Com. for Refugees; adv. com. Harvard Trade Union Program; nat. council Eleanor Roosevelt Meml. Found.; past nat. gov. A.R.C. Trustee Harry S. Truman Library, Inc.; pres. Sidney Hillman Found.; mem. nat. manpower council Columbia U.; nat. com. Am. Mus. Immigration; pres. United Housing Found.; mem. central bd. World Orgn. for Rehab. Through Tng.; bd. dirs. Am. Arbitration Assn. Decorated Order of Star Solidarity (Italy): recipient Four Freedoms award Italian-Am. Labor Council, 1964. Home: New York, N.Y. Died Aug. 5, 1979.

POTTER, ANDREY ABRAHAM, engineer, educator; b. Vilna, Russia, Aug. 5, 1882; s. Gregor and Rivza (Pelonsky) P.; came to U.S., 1897, naturalized, 1906; Bachelor of Science in Engineering, Massachusetts Inst. Tech., 1903; D.Eng., Kan. State Coll., 1925, Rose Poly Inst., 1947, South Dakota School Mines and Tech., 1949, Purdue U., 1955, Mich. State U., 1956; D.Sc., Northeastern U., 1936, Alfred U., 1947, Northwestern University, 1953; LL.D., Norwich U., 1944; Doctor of Engineering, Indiana Institute of Tech., 1964; m. Eva Burtner Potter, June 28, 1906; children—James Gregor, Helen. With Gen. Electric Co., Schenectady, 1903-05, Lynn, Mass., 1913; asst. prof. mech. engring., Kansas State Coll., 1905-10, prof., 1910-20, dean div. of engring. and dir. Engring. Expt. Sta., 1913-20; dean of engring. schs. and dir. Engring. Expt. Sta., Purdue U., 1920-53, dean emeritus of engring., 1953-79, acting pres., 1945-46; cons.; exec. dir. Nat. Patent Planning Com., 1942-45; cons. Michigan State University, 1953-54; pres. Purdue Research Foundation, 1945-46, Bituminous Coal Research, Inc., 1950-60; mem. bd. NSF, 1950-58. Cons. and mem. adv. bds. many govtl. bds., coms. and commns. Lamme Medalist 1940; Washington Award, 1943; USN distinguished pub. service award, 1952; Cyrus Hall McCormick Award, 1953; Nat. Soc. Profl. Engrs. award 1955; 75th Anniversary medal ASME, 1955; BCR award in 1964. Fellow A.A.A.S. (vice president 1939), Am. Soc. Engring. Edn. (pres. 1924-25), Am. Engring. Council (pres. 1936-38), ASME (pres. 1932-33; hon. mem. 1945); mem. numerous profl. and scientific assns. and orgns.; has served as pres. or other exec. officer of several. Republican. Mason (33 deg.). Author numerous engring. books; adv. editor pubs.; contbr. numerous mags. Home: West Lafayette, Ind. Died Nov. 5, 1979.

POTTER, CHARLES EDWARD, business cons.; b. Lapeer, Mich., Oct. 30, 1916; s. Fred and Sarah Elizabeth (Converse) P.; A.B., Eastern Mich. U., 1938, LL.D., 1954; LL.D., Hillsdale (Mich.) Coll., 1955; m. Mary Elizabeth Bryant Wismer; stepchildren—Henry R. Wismer (dec.), Wendy Cundy. Adminstr. Bur. Social Aid, Cheboygan Co., Mich., 1938-42; vocational rehab. adv., Retraining and Reemployment Adminstrn., Washington, 1946-47; elected 80th Congress, 11th Dist., Mich., to fill unexpired term, 1947; reelected 81st, 82d Congresses; U.S. senator for unexpired term of Senator Vandenberg (1952-53), elected for full term, 1953-59; chmn. 1972 Campaign Liquidation Trust; chmn. bd. Potter Internat., Inc.; vice chmn. Am. Battle Monuments Commn. Served with AUS, combat officer 28th Inf. Div., wounded at Colmar, France, 1945; disch. as maj., 1946. Decorated Silver Star (2), French Croix de Guerre with silver star, Purple Heart with two clusters, named to U.S. Junior C. of C. one of ten outstanding young men in Am., 1951; Hero of Month, D.A.V., 1951; V.F.W. award, 1951; Nat. Rehab. Assn. Pres.'s award, 1954; Goodwill award, 1957, others. Mem. Washington Real Estate Bd., Nat. Assn. Securities Dealers, Nat. Rehab. Assn. (dir.), Am. Legion, D.A.V., V.F.W., Am. Vets. Republican. Methodist. Eagle, Elk, Kiwanian. Author: Days of Shame, 1965. Home: Queenstown, Md. Died Nov. 23, 1979; buried Arlington (Va.) Nat. Cemetery.

POTTER, JAMES HARRY, educator; b. N.Y.C., Nov. 10, 1912; s. James Harry and Nina Hurlbutt (Dartt) P.; B.S., Columbia, 1935, M.E., 1936; D.Eng., Johns Hopkins, 1948; M.Engring. (hon.), Stevens Inst. Tech., 1958; Sc.D. (hon.), Lawrence Inst. Tech., 1970; m. Emma Josephine Hill, Mar. 26, 1949. Jr. engr. E.I. duPont de Nemours & Co., 1936-38; self employed, 1938-39; engr. Fed. Shipbuilding & Dry Dock Co., 1939-40, M. W. Kellogg Co., summer 1940; from instr. to asst. dean engring. Johns Hopkins U., 1940-49; prof. mech. engring. U. Ill., 1949-53; prof., head dept., asso. dean Stevens Inst. Tech., from 1953, George Meade Bond prof., 1954-78, dean grad. studies, 1955-61; edn. cons. Pa. Mil. Coll., 1962-63; with educator program E. I. du Pont de Nemours & Co., 1952-53; dir. Affiliated Fund, Inc., Lord-Abbett Income Fund, Lord-Abbett Bond Debenture Fund, Inc. Mem. U.S. Naval Acad. Bd. Curriculum Rev., 1959. Profl. engr., N.Y., N.J., Md., Ill. Decorated officier Ordre des Palmes Academique. Fellow Am. Soc. Mech. Engrs., Royal Soc. Arts (London); mem. Am. Soc. Engring. Edn., Am. Soc. Naval Engrs., Newcomen Soc., Soc. Colonial Wars, Sigma Xi, Tau Beta Pi, Theta Xi, Pi Tau Sigma, Gamma Alpha. Protestant. Episcopalian. Editor, contbr. Handbook of the Engineering Sciences, 2 vols., Steam Charts ASME, 1976. Died Mar. 15, 1978.

POTTER, PITMAN BENJAMIN, educator, author; b. Long Branch, N.J., Jan. 1, 1892; s. Joseph Covert and Louisa Ann (Lane) P.; A.B., Harvard, 1914, A.M., 1916, Ph.D., 1918; m. Jessie Isabelle Dalton, June 22, 1914 (died Jan. 9, 1940); children—Dalton, James Lane; m. 2d, Margaret Ruth Hardy, Oct. 18, 1941; children—Louisa Hardy, Charles Benjamin. Instr. in political sci., Harvard U., 1914-16; instr. in history, Yale, 1916-17; asso. in polit. science, Univ. of Ill., 1919-20; asst. prof. polit. science, U. of Wis., 1920-23, asso. prof., 1923-26, prof., 1926-32; sometimes visiting prof., U. of Chicago, Harvard, U. of Tex., U. of Calif.; prof. internat. orgn., Inst. Univ. de Hautes Etudes Internationales, Geneva, 1930-31, and 1932-41; member staff Brookings Institution, Washington, D.C., 1941-42; professor political science and chmn. dept., Oberlin College, 1942-44; Grozier prof. internat. law and chmn. dept. internat. relations and orgn. Am. U. from 1944, dean grad. sch. from 1947. Lecturer Académie de Droit International, The Hague, 1930, 38; dean Inst. World Affairs, Mondsee, Austria, 1933; dir. summer session Students Internat. Union, Geneva, 1934, 35; lecturer Institut Des Hautes Etudes Internat., U. of Paris, 1935-36. Mng. editor American Journal Internat. Law, 1943-48, mem. bd. editors, 1925-30, and from 1948. Legal adviser to government of Ethiopia, 1935; mem. Italo-Ethiopian Arbitration Commn., May-Sept. 1935; dir. and mem. governing board, Geneva Research Centre, 1939-46; gen. reporter, Internat. Studies Conf., 1939-46. Mem. American Society International Law (sec., 1945-48, vice president from 1948), Am. Polit. Science Assn., Am. Soc. Pub. Adminstrn., Phi Beta Kappa, Phi Kappa Epsilon. Author or co-author books relating to field. Mem. bd. dirs. Am. Peace Soc. Home: Washington, D.C. Died Mar. 11, 1981.

POTTER, WALDO C., army officer; b. La Moure, N.D., Aug. 27, 1885; s. Franklin and Alida (Hill) P.; B.S., U.S. Mil. Acad., 1907; married, Apr. 17, 1911; 1 son, Waldo Franklin. Commd. 2d lt., 1907; promoted through grades to brig. gen. 1943; Chairman, II Section, War Dept. Manpower Board, Governors Island, N.Y. Home: Governors Island, N.Y.*

POTTS, DAVID M., congressman; b. New York City, March 12, 1906; s. Irwin and Emma (Logan) P.; student, N.Y. City Coll., 1927-28, LL.B., Brooklyn Law Sch., St. Lawrence U., 1932, LL.M., 1933; m. Elizabeth C. Crighton, June 27, 1936; children—Audrey Crighton, David Logan. With Guaranty Trust Co., N.Y. City, 1935; admitted to N.Y. bar, 1933; asso. with Davis, Polk, Wardwell, Gardiner, Reed, lawyers (now Davis, Polk, Wardwell, Sunderland and Kiendl), 1935-46. Mem. 80th Congress (1947-49), 26th Dist., N.Y. Counsel, N.Y. State Senate Com. on Affairs of N.Y. City during 1945 session of state legislature. Mem. N.Y. State Bar Assn., Assn. of the Bar of N.Y. City, Bronx Bar Assn., Delta Theta Phi. Republican. Episcopalian. Home: Bronxville, N.Y. Died Sept. 11, 1976.

POTTS, JOSEPH MCKEAN, II, mfg. co. exec.; b. Pottstown, Pa., Sept. 3, 1918; s. Lemuel Eastburn and Sara P. (Root) P.; B.A., Princeton, 1941; m. Helen Cashwell Bolling, July 22, 1949; children—Joseph McKean III, Thomas Bolling. With Bonney Forge & Tool Works, Allentown, Pa, 1949-65, pres., 1959-65; pres. Miller Mfg. Co., Detroit, 1965-80; pres. Bonney Forge & Foundry, Inc., Allentown, 1965-69, chmn., 1969-74; pres. Bonney Group and v.p. Gulf and Western Mfg. Co., Allentown, 1972-74; pres. Taylor-Bonney Internat. and v.p. G & W Energy Products Group, 1974-77; v.p., gen. mgr. splty. products div. G & W Energy Products Group, 1977-80; chmn. Bonney Forge Internat. Ltd., Irvine, Scotland; dir. TF de Mexico, S.A., Mexico City, Metalmeg. S.A., Caracas, Venezuela, Bonney Forge Italia, Albano, Italy, Tubacex Taylor Accesorios, S.A., Llodio, Spain, John M. Henderson & Co. (Holdings) Ltd., London, 1974-77. Trustee, Hill Sch., Pottstown Pa. and Allentown YMCA, 1979-80. Served to maj. AUS, 1941-46. Mem. Allentown-Lehigh County C. of C. (bd. govs. 1964-69), Newcomen Soc., Pa. Soc. Republican. Presbyn. Mason. Clubs: Livingston, Lehigh Country, Lehigh Valley (Allentown); Mid Ocean (Bermuda); Country of N.C.; Princeton (N.Y.C.). Home: Allentown, Pa. Died Apr. 22, 1980; buried Pottstown, Pa.

POULTER, THOMAS CHARLES, explorer, dir. research; b. Salem, Iowa, Mar. 3, 1897; s. Micajah Lewis and Alberta Viola (Pool) P.; grad. Iowa Wesleyan Acad., 1918; B.S., Iowa Wesleyan Coll., 1923, hon. D.Sc., 1935; Ph.D., U. Chgo., 1933; m. Helen Elizabeth Gray. Instr. of physics Iowa Wesleyan Acad., 1916-18; asst. in biology, chemistry and physics Iowa Wesleyan Coll., 1919-23; asst. in chemistry U. Chgo., 1923-25; head dept. chemistry Iowa Wesleyan Coll., 1925-27, head dept. physics, 1927-30, head div. math., phys. sci. and astronomy, 1930-33; research U. Iowa, 1931; mem. Ariz. Meteor Expdn., 1932; John Simone Guggenheim fellow, 1933-35; with Byrd's Second Antarctic Expdn. as sr. scientist in charge of sci. program and second in command, 1933-35; asso. dir. Armour Research Found., Chgo., 1936-48; prof. Stanford, asso. dir. Research Inst., 1948-54, dir. Poulter labs., 1954-60, sci. dir., gen. mgr. phys. and life scis., 1960-63, sr. sci. adviser, 1963-78, dir. biol. sonar lab., 1963-73; research asso. U. Calif. Med. Sch., San Francisco, 1975-78; cons. U.S. Antarctic Service, Office Sci. Research and Devel., U.S. Navy and Columbia U. Nat. Def. Lab. Designed Antarctic snow cruiser and was with U.S. Antarctic Service Expdn., 1939-40. Served as mechanic 1st class and ensign USNRF, on U.S. Submarine C-4, 1918-19; lt. comdr. Engring. Div., USNR. Inventor of Poulter Seismic Method of Geophys. Exploration. Recipient Spl. Congl. medal (twice), World War Service medal; Spl. Gold medal Nat. Geog. Soc. Fellow Am. Phys. Soc., Geog. Soc. Chgo., Calif. Acad. Scis.; life mem. Nat. Geog. Soc.; mem. Soc. Exploration Geophysicists, Geophys. Union, A.A.A.S., Am. Phys. Soc., Seismol. Soc. Am., Am. Geog. Soc., Am. Polar Soc., Explorers Club, San Francisco Zool. Soc. (dir.), Sigma Xi, Lambda Chi Alpha, Sigma Pi Sigma. Contbr. many papers to tech. jours. Holds numerous U.S. and fgn. patents; preparation magnetic tape catalog of vocalization of marine mammals of world, 1964-78; engring. cons. restoring hearing in totally deaf, 1971-78. Address: Menlo Park, Calif. Died July 20, 1978.

POUND, EZRA LOOMIS, poet; b. Hailey, Ida., Oct. 30, 1885; s. Homer Loomis and Isabel (Weston) P.; U. of Pa., 2 yrs.; grad. Hamilton Coll., 1905; post-grad. U. of Pa., 2 years; m. Dorothy Shakespear, 1914; Author: Personae, 1909; Spirit of Romance, 1910; Exultations, 1910; Provenca, 1910; Canzoni, 1911; The Sonnets and Ballate of Guido Cavalcanti, 1912; Ripostes, 1913: Gaudier Brzeska (memoir), 1916. Editor: Des Imagistes (anthology), 1914; Catholic Anthology, 1915, Translator: Cathay, 1915. Lit. executor for Ernest Fenollosa's works on Chinese poetry and the classic drama of Japan. Contbr. Quarterly Review, Fortnightly Review, Blast, etc. Address: London, Eng. *

POWEL, CHARLES ALFRED, engineer; b. Rouen, France, 1884; s. Henry C. and Margaret (French) P.; ed. in elec. engring., London, Eng., and Bern, Switzerland; m. Blanche Brownrigg, 1918 (dec.). Entered elec. engring. career, 1905; asst, vice pres. in charge of engring. Westinghouse Electric Corp., Pittsburgh, Pa., since 1940. Served as chief, machinery and optics branch of mil. govt., Berlin, 1945-46. Power cons., Stillman Indsl. Survey Mission to China. ECA, 1948. Pres. Am. Inst. Elec, Engrs., 1944-45. Author of numerous papers and articles. Home: Pittsburgh, Pa. *

POWELL, BENJAMIN EDWARD, librarian; b. Sunbury, N.C., Aug. 28, 1905; s. Willis Warren and Beatrice (Franklin) P.; A.B., Duke U., 1926; B.L.S., Columbia, 1930; Ph.D., U. Chgo., 1946; m. Elizabeth Graves, Mar. 6, 1940; 1 dau., Lisa Holland. Athletic dir. Bethel (N.C.) High School, 1926-27; asst. Duke U., Library, 1927-29, reference librarian and supt. circulation, 1930-34, 1935-37; librarian, U. of Mo. Library, 1937-46; librarian Duke U., since 1946. Mem. A.L.A. (council 1947-54, v.p. 1958-59, pres. elect 1959-60, pres. 1960-61, exec. bd. 1956-58; mem. com. Co-operative Microfilm Project, 1950-54; joint com. Govt. Publications, 1955-81, Government Documents 1956-81. Spl. Com. Reorganization, 1957); Southeastern Library Assn., N.C. Library Assn., Assn. Coll. and Reference Libraries (sec. 1940-44; v.p. 1947-48, pres. 1948-49), Mo. Library Assn. (pres. 1938-39), N.C. Literary and Hist. Assn., So. Hist. Assn., Bibliographical Soc. Am., Am. Assn. U. Profs., Sigma Nu, Phi Beta Kappa. Democrat. Methodist. Clubs: Hope Valley Country, University, Rotary (Durham, N.C.). Home: Durham, N.C. Died Mar. 11, 1981; buried Maplewood Cemetery, Durham.

POWELL, EDWARD ANGUS, wood products mfg. co. exec.; b. Richmond, Va., Mar. 20, 1914; s. Louis F. and Mary Lewis (Gwathmey) P.; B.S. in Commerce, Washington and Lee U., Lexington, Va., 1936; M.B.A., Harvard U., 1938; m. Helen Elizabeth Bryson, Aug. 31, 1940; children—Helen Elizabeth, Katherine Powell Rolph, Edward Angus, Earl Bryson. With Lea Industries, Inc., and predecessor, Richmond, Va., from 1938; pres., 1951-70, chmn. bd., from 1970; pres., chmn. bd. Chesterfield Land & Timber Co., Midlothian, Va., from 1979; dir. Waste Combustion Corp., First & Mchts. Nat. Bank, Richmond, 1960-73; dir. Fed. Res.

Bank Richmond, chmn., 1976-77; bd. dirs. So. Exposition Bldg., Inc., 1970-72, U.S. Indsl. Council, So. Indsl. Relations Council, 1952-68. Pres. bd. dirs. Collegiate Schs., Richmond, 1959-62; vice chmn. trustees Union Theol. Sem., Richmond, 1969-72; rector bd. Longwood Coll., Farmville, Va., 1967-70; pres. bd. Rich-Met. YMCA, 1955-57; co-chmn. fund raising campaign Westminster-Canterbury Home, retirement home, Richmond, 1972; past elder, deacon River Rd. Presbyn. Ch., Richmond. Served to lt. A.C., USNR, 1942-45. Recipient Silver Brotherhood medallion NCCJ, 1972. Mem. Metro Richmond C. of C. (past dir.), So. Furniture Mfrs. Assn. (past dir.), Va. Mfrs. Assn. (past dir.), Phi Kappa Sigma (pres. 1935), Omicron Delta Kappa (pres. 1936). Clubs: Country of Va. (past dir.); Commonwealth (past dir.) (Richmond). Home: Richmond, Va. Died May 19, 1979.

POWELL, FRANK MARION, SR., clergyman; b. New Bloomfield, Mo., Mar. 29, 1886; s. James and Malinda (Powell) P.; A.B., William Jewell Coll., Liberty, Mo., 1912, A.M., 1915; Th.M., Southern Bapt. Theol. Seminary, Louisville, Ky., 1916, Th.D., 1917; special work in history, University of Cincinnati, 1920 and University of Chicago, 1924, research, Oxford University, Eng., 1923-24; D.D., Howard College, 1936, Georgetown Coll., 1936; m. Kathleen Stone, May 20, 1913; children—Frank Marion, Robert Stone, Virginia Ruth, Prof. ch. history Southern Bapt. Theol. Sem., 1918-41; lit. editor Review and Expositor, 1929-41; pastor Calvary Bapt. Ch., Tupelo, Miss., 1942-49; prof. ch. hist. and homiletics Golden Gate Baptist Theological Seminary, Berkeley, California, since 1949. President Kentucky Baptist Historical Society, 1940-42. Board Trustees Blue Mt. College, 1943-49. Phi Gamma Delta. Mason, Odd Fellow, Clubs: Shakespeare, Ten, Rotary. Democrat. Address: Berkeley, Calif. *

POWELL, LEGH RICHMOND, JR., ry. official; b. Portsmouth, Va., Mar. 10, 1884; s. Legh Richmond and Cora Maupin (Eastwood) P.; ed. pub. schs., Ports-1908; children—Caroline Whidbee (Mrs. E. W. Borkland Jr.), Elizabeth Blandy (Mrs. Elizabeth Powell Burke), Legh Richmond III, Entered service of Seaboard Airline Ry. Co. as clerk, accounting dept., 1902, vice-pres., 1921-27, pres., 1927-30, receiver since 1930, pres., 1946-52, chmn. bd. since 1952, dir., mem. exec. com. and voting trustee since 1946. Mem. Newcomen Soc. Republican. Episcopalian. Clubs: Princess Anne Country, Cavalier Beach (Virginia Beach, Va.). Home: Norfolk. *

POWELL, RAYMOND P., educator; b. Spokane, Wash.; grad. U. Calif., Berkeley, 1942, Ph.D., 1952; m. Sophie Zane; children—Laura Elizabeth Powell Kemper, Stephen G. Instr. econs. Princeton U., 1949-51; Social Sci. Research Council fellow Harvard U., 1951; cons. RAND Corp., 1954-62; mem. faculty Yale U., 1952-80, Henry S. McNeill prof. Russian studies, 1967-80. Author several books. Home: New Haven, Conn. Died May 28, 1980.

POWELL, SHEPPARD TAPPEN, cons. engr.; b. Troy, N.Y., Aug. 5, 1883; s. George Densmore and Mary (Johnston) P.; C.E., Rensselaer Polytech. Inst., 1908; m. Florence May Neer, May 15, 1964; 1 son, Robert Franklin. Chem. engr. Baltimore County Water & Electric Co., 1904; engaged in pvt. cons. engring, practice, 1912—; propr. Sheppard T. Powell and Assos., Balt., 1958—; cons. Nat. Resources Bd., 1934-38. TVA, 1940—; tech. adviser to sec. Dept. of Interior, 1955—; cons, AEC, 1943—; adviser Cal., N.J., Md., others; spl. lectr. Sch. Hygiene, Johns Hopkins, 1929-37. Vice chmn. Md. Bd. Registration Profl. Engrs., 1939-48; mem. Water Pollution Control Commn. Md., 1947-50; com. to study fire dept. high pressure system, City of Balt., 1960; chmn. nat. water policy panel Engrs. Joint Council, Mem. vis. com. Johns Hopkins, 1958—. Registered prof. engr., 32 states, also Can. Fellow, hon. mem. Am. Soc. M.E.; life, hon. mem. Am. Water Works Assn.; hon. mem. Am. Pub. Health Assn; mem. Am. Soc. Testing Materials, Am. Chem. Soc., Am. Inst. Cons. Engrs., Am. Inst. Chem. Engrs., Newcomen Soc. Great Britain, Md. Acad. Scis., Md. Hist. Soc., Acad. Natural Scis. Phila. Episcopalian (past vestry), Mason. Clubs: Cosmos (Washington); Maryland, Baltimore Country (Balt.). Home: Balt. *

POWELL, WESLEY, gov. N.H.; b. Portsmouth, N.H., Oct. 13, 1915; s. Samuel Wesley and Mary (Gosse) P.; student U. N.H.; LL.B., So. Meth. U.; m. Beverly Swain, 1942; children—Samuel, Peter, Nancy. Adminstrv. asst. to Senator Styles Bridges, 1940-43, 46-49; gov. N.H., 1959-63; lawyer, Portsmouth, 1963-81. Chmn. U.S. Gov.'s Conf., 1961-62; chmn. New Eng. Gov.'s Conf., 1960-63; pres. Council of State Govts., 1962. Served in AAC, 1943-46, with bomber comd. ETO. Home: Hampton Falls, N.H. Died Jan. 6, 1981.

POWELL, WILLIAM WARD, engring. exec.; b. Pa., s. William Charles and Ora Belle (Davis) P.; B.S., Carnegie Inst. Tech., 1913; Eng. D. (hon.), U. Milano; m. Martha Ariana Shaw, Dec. 27, 1917. Asst. to cons. engr. Mesta Machine Co., Pitts., 1913, dir., v.p., 1935-63, exec. v.p., 1963-77; active devel. building large steel plants Europe, Asia, Africa and U.S.; chmn. bd. Digital Graphics, Inc.; dir. Roll Mfrs. Inst. (pres.), U. Square. Dir. World Trade Council; trustee and mem. vis. com. mech. engring. Carnegie-Mellon U. Recipient Citation (Navy); Commendatore Order Al Merito Republica Italinao; Merit award Carnegie Inst. of Tech., 1964. Mem. Iron and Steel Engrs., Pitts. C. of C., Alumni Assn. Carnegie-Mellon Univ. (past pres.), Delta Upsilon. Presbyn. (chmn. finance). Mason (Shriner, Jester). Clubs: Fox Chapel Country, Duquesne, University, Athletic Assn. (Pitts.); Rancho Bernardo Country. Home: Pittsburgh, Pa. Died May 27, 1977.

POWER, ALOYSIUS FRANCIS, lawyer; b. Worcester, Mass., July 11, 1902; s. James David and Mary (Creamer) P.; A.B., Coll. Holy Cross, Worcester, 1923; student Sch. Bus., N.Y. U., 1923-24; LL.B., Fordham U., 1927; LL.D., Iona Coll., New Rochelle, N.Y., 1964; Dr. Civil Jurisprudence, Coll. Holy Cross, 1967; m. Eleanor G. Hurley, June 30, 1934; children—Patricia A. (dec.), Mary Power Monaghan, John A. Instr. math. Fordham Prep. Sch., N.Y.C., 1923-27; admitted to N.Y. bar, 1928, Mich. bar, 1938; with Gen. Motors Corp., 1927-67, v.p., gen. counsel, 1961-67. Mem. Am., Mich., Detroit bar assns., Knights of Malta. Roman Catholic. Clubs: Detroit Athletic, Recess (Detroit); Bloomfield Hills Country. Home: Bloomfield Hills, Mich. Died Oct. 3, 1977.

POWER, DONALD CLINTON, lawyer, business exec.; b. Paine Station, O., Dec. 25, 1899; s. George and Dorothy (Brooks) P.; student Denison (O.) U., 1918-20; B.S., Ohio State U., 1922, LL.B., 1926, M.A., 1927; LL.D., Upsala Coll., 1958; Doctor Bus. Adminstrn., Rio Grande Coll., 1959; m. Catherine Hamilton, July 23, 1927; children—Jane (Mrs. Peter Mykrantz), Charlotte (Mrs. John W. Kessler). Admitted to O. bar, 1926; asst. atty. gen. Ohio, atty. Pub. Utilities Commn. Ohio, 1933-36, instr., asst. prof., asso. prof. (part time) Ohio State U., 1922-39; sec. to gov. Ohio, 1939-43; pres., dir. Gen. Telephone Corp., 1951-59, chmn., chief exec. officer Gen. Telephone & Electronics Corp. (merger Sylvania Elec. Products, Inc. and Gen. Telephone Corp.), 1959-66, chmn., 1966-71; dir. Arnold Wholesale Corp. Surveyor Fund, Inc., Norton Simon, Inc., Charter N.Y. Corp., Jeffrey Co., Am. Mfrs. Mut. Curtiss-Wright Corp., Gen. Telephone Co. Ohio, Copper Range Co., Irving Trust Co., Automatic Electric Co., B.C. Telephone Co., Sylvania Electric Products, Inc., Gen. Telephone Co. Fla., Anglo-Canadian Tel. Co., Brown Steel Co., Ohio State Life Ins. Co.; mem. Eastern adv. bd. Lumberman's Mutual Casualty Co. Vice chmn. Ohio Adminstrative Law Commn., 1942-46. Mem. bd. trustees Ohio State U., 1944-51, Rio Grande Coll. 1959-79, Univ. Tampa, 1959-62. Lt. col., Ohio N.G., 1940. Recipient Ohio Gov. Award, 1959; Internat. Bus. Exec. Year, 1959; Am. Success Story award Free Enterprise Awards Assn. 1961; elected to Ind. Telephone Hall of Fame, 1975. Trustee Com. Economic Development. Mem. Ohio Soc. N.Y. (pres. 1965-66), Nat. Industrial Conf. Bd., Am. (chmn. pub. utilities sect. 1956-57), Ohio, Columbus bar assns., U.S. Ind. Telephone Assn. (pres. 1956-57), Beta Gamma Sigma, Phi Delta Phi, Sigma Chi. Republican (chmn. Ohio campaign com. 1938-42). Presbyn. Mason (32, K.T., Shriner). Clubs: University, Athletic, Faculty, Scioto Country (Columbus); The Brook, Union League, University, Fifth Avenue (N.Y.C.); Chicago. Author: The Law of Contracts Condensed, 1933. Home: Galloway, Ohio. Died Mar. 11, 1979.

POWERS, EDGAR CORDELL, clergyman; b. Glenwood, Md., Mar. 18, 1883; s. George and Sarah (Groomes) P.; A.B., George Washington U., 1909; D.D., Dickinson Coll., 1935; m. Mary Walsmith, June 30, 1908; children—Adella, Sarah. Ordained to ministry of Meth. Ch., 1908, pastor, Washington, 1905-18, Baltimore, 1918-32; exec. sec. Md. Bible Soc., Baltimore, since 1932. Served U.S. Army, 1941-42. Mem. S.A.R. Mason Contbr. articles to religions jours. Home: Towson, Md. *

POWERS, JOHN ANTHONY SHORTY, ret. air force officer; b. Toledo, Aug. 30, 1922; s. Robert Edward and Georgia Fay (Poston) P.; ed. Central Mo. State Coll., Warrensburg, 1948; m. Dorothy Ruth Schlomer, Nov. 25, 1944 (div.); 1 son, John R. Enlisted USAAF, 1942, commd. 2d lt., 1943, advanced through grades to lt. col., USAF; pilot C-47 and C-46 troop carriers, World War II, C-54, in Berlin Airlift, B-26 night intruder combat missions in Korea; bomber operations officer staff Hdqrs. 5th Air Force; dep. chief community relations div. Office Sec. Air Force, 1953-55; staff officer def. adv. com. profl. and Air Force Ballistic Missile Div., Dept. Def.; pub. affairs officer Project Mercury, NASA, 1959-64, made voice progress reports covering U.S. manned space flights; ret. as lt. col. USAF, 1964; pres. Power House, Inc.; cons. World Book Ency. Decorated Bronze Star medal. Writer weekly column Space Talk. Address: Nassau Bay, Tex. Died Jan. 1, 1980.

POWERS, WALTER, lawyer; b. Hyde Park, Mass., Aug. 3, 1885; s. Wilbur Howard and Emily (Owen) P.; A.B., Dartmouth, 1906; LL.B., Harvard, 1909; m. Ethel Louise Carver, Jan. 29, 1910; children—Wilbur Langdon, Walter. Admitted to Mass. bar, 1908; mem. firm Powers, Folsom & Powers, 1909-17, Sherburne, Powers & Needham, Boston, 1919—. Mem. Mass. Bd. Bar Examiners (sec. 1940-53, chmn. 1953—). Served to maj. Ordance Dept., U.S. Army; exec. asst. to chief ordnance officers First and Third armies, AEF, World War I. President Daylight Sav. Assn. Mass., Mass. Lawyers Postwar Inst., Inc., Frank Wood Convalescent Home, Inc. Mem. Am. Coll. Trial Lawyers, Nat. Conf. Bar Examiners (chmn. 1956-57), Am., Mass., Boston (counci. 1931-37, 38-41, 42—, chmn. grievance com. 1940-41, 42-46, pres. 1948-50) bar assns., Am. Law Inst., Casque and Gauntlet, Delta Kappa Epsilon. Republican. Unitarian. Clubs: Country (Brookline); Boston (pres. 1931-34); Union Boat; Curtis; Nisi Prius. Home: Boston MA. *

POYNTER, NELSON, editor, pub.; b. Sullivan, Ind., Dec. 15, 1903; s. Paul and Alice (Wilkey) P.; A.B., Ind. U., 1924; A.M., Yale, 1927; Litt.D., Stetson U., 1962; LL.D. (hon.), Fla. State U., 1970, Eckerd Coll., 1973, Ind. U., 1976; D.H.L. (hon.), U. South Fla., 1978; m. Henrietta Malkiel, Aug. 8, 1942 (dec. Jan. 1968); m. 2d, Marion Knauss, May 4, 1970. Reporter Scripps-Howard newspapers, Washington, 1923; news editor Japan Times, Tokyo, 1924; bus. mgr. Washington Daily News, editor Ohio Scripps-Howard, 1935-37; editor, owner St. Petersburg (Fla.) Times, 1938-78; chmn. bd. Times Pub. Co., 1968-78; owner Evening Ind., 1962-78; chmn. bd. Congl. Quar. Publs. and Editorial Research Reports, Washington, 1944-78. Named to Ind. Journalism Hall of Fame, 1976. Mem. Am. Soc. Newspaper Editors, others. Author: Post War Jobs, 1945. Contbr. to Freedom of Press, Interpretations of Journalism. Died June 15, 1978.

PRAETORIUS, ELMER WESLEY (PRĒ-ÔR'I-US), bishop; b. Dayton, O., Oct. 1, 1882; s. Eduart Herman and Anna (Roessner) P.; grad. acad. Northwestern Coll., Naperville, Ill., 1905; grad. Evang. Theol. Sem., Naperville, Ill., 1907, D.D., 1928; LL.D., North Central College, 1945; married Julia Schweitzer, June 19, 1907; children—Ruby Iola, E. Russell, Evangeline Arleta (deceased). Business, Dayton, 1897-1900; ordained minister Evang. Ch., 1908; pastor Trinity Ch., Louisville, Ky., 1907-12, Kent Av. Ch., Terre Haute, Ind., 1912-14, First Ch., Elkhart, 1914-19; founder, and gen. sec. Bd. of Religious Edn., Evang. Ch., 1919-34, now vice pres. Bd. of Christian Edn.; pres. Bd. Evangelism; bishop of Northwestern Area of Evang. United Brethren Ch. since 1934; pres. bd. trustees North Central Coll., Evang. Theol. Sem.; v.p. Bonebrake Theol. Sem. Mem. Nat. Council Chs. of Christ Am. Republican. Home: St. Paul. *

PRAGER, WILLIAM, educator; b. Karlsruhe, Germany, May 23, 1903; s. Willy and Helen (Kimmel) P.; state certificate as civil engr., 1925; Dr. Engring. Scis., Inst. of Tech., Darmstadt, 1926; hon. degrees U. Liege (Belgium), 1962, U. Poitiers (France), 1962, Case Inst. of Tech., 1963, Politeconico di Milano, 1964, U. Waterloo (Ont., Can.), 1969, U. Stuttgart (Germany), 1969, Tech. U., Hannover, Germany, 1969, Brown U., 1973, U. Manchester (Eng.), 1974, U. Brussels (Belgium), 1975; m. Gertrude A. Heyer, Sept. 16, 1925; 1 son, Stephen. Came to U.S., 1941. Instr. Mechanics, Inst. of Tech., Darmstadt, 1927-29; acting dir. Inst. Applied Mechanics, U. of Göttingen, 1929-32; prof. mechanics, Tech. Inst., Karlsruhe, 1933; structural insp. German Airsport League, Berlin, 1929-33; sci. adviser Fieseler Aircraft Co., Kassel, Germany, 1933; prof. mechanics, U. of Istanbul, 1934-41; mng. editor Revue de la Faculté des Sciences de l'Université d'Istanbul, 1935-41; prof. applied mechanics, Brown U., 1941-63, chmn. grad. div. of applied math., 1946-52, chmn. phys. scis. council, 1953-59, L. Herbert Ballou univ. prof. 1959-63, prof. engring. and applied math., 1968-73, prof. emeritus, 1973-80; cons. IBM Research Lab., Zurich, Switzerland 1963-65; prof. applied mechanics U. Calif. at San Diego, 1965-68. Recipient of Worcester Reed Warner medal ASME, 1957, Timoshenko medal, 1966; Theodore Von Karman award, ASCE, 1960; Panetti prize Turin Acad. Scis., 1963. Fellow Am. Acad. Arts and Scis.; mem. ASCE (hon.), ASME (hon.), Nat. Acad. Sci., Nat. Acad. Engring., Polish Acad. Scis., Soc. Indsl. and Applied Math. (editor jour.), Am. Math. Soc., Groupe Française de Rhéologie (hon.), Groupe pour l'AVancement des Méthodes Numériques de l'Ingénieur (hon.), Académie des Sciences de L'Institut de France (corr.). Author: (with K. Hohenemser) Dynamik der Stabwerke, 1933; Mécanique des solides isotropes, 1937; Tersimi Hendese, 1937; (with F. Gürsan) Mihanik, 1941; (with P. G. Hodge, Jr.) Theory of Perfectly Plastic Solids, 1951; Probleme der Plastizitaetstheorie, 1955; An Introduction to Plasticity 1959; Introduction to Mechanics of Continua, 1961; Introduction to Basic Fortran Programming and Numerical Methods; Introduction to APL, 1971. mng. editor, Quar. Applied Math., 1943-65. Tech. editor Jour. Applied Mechanics, 1969-72; editor Computer Methods in Applied Mechanics and Engring., 1972-80. Home: Savognin, Switzerland. Died. Mar. 17, 1980.

PRATHER, CHARLES LEE, economist, author; b. Ashmore, Ill., Aug. 14, 1899; s. William Edward and Elizabeth (Galbreath) P.; Ed.B., Eastern Ill. State Coll.,

1922, Pd.D., 1949; A.M., U. Ill., 1923, Ph.D., 1927; m. Katherine Friedrichs, Nov. 30, 1928; children—Katherine Lee Kelley, Charles Marshall, John George. Inst. U. Ill., 1924-27; asst. prof. econs. U. Pitts., 1927-29; asst. prof. econs. Syracuse U., 1929-30, asso. prof., 1930-38, prof., 1938-43; prof. finance U. Tex., 1946-66, chmn. dept., 1948-53, prof. emeritus, 1966-78; prof. U. Wash., summer 1946. Served with Co. G, 130 Inf., 33d Div., 1917-19; with AUS, 1943-45; with G-5 sect. Gen. Staff Corps (specialist econs. and finance) Hdgrs. ETO, First U.S. Army Group, Twelfth Army Group, 15th Army, col. Officers Res. Corps, ret. Decorated Bronze Star (U.S.); Grand Ducal National Ordre de la Courounne de Chene, grade de chevalier, Croix de Guerre (Luxembourg). Mem. Am. Finance Assn. (pres. 1941-42), S.A.R. Presbyn. Author: Money and Banking, 9th edit., 1969; Financing Business Firms, 3d edit., 1966; (with B.B. McNew) Fraud Control for Commercial Banks, 1962; (with G.W. Cooke and others) Financial Institutions, 1962. Home: Austin, Tex. Died Aug. 19, 1978.

PRATT, EDWARD EWING, commercial expert; b. Streator, Ill., May 11, 1886; s. Howard and Violet (Ewing) P.; A.B., Oberlin, 1906; A.M., Tulane U., New Orleans, 1907; fellow Bur. of Social Research, Russell Sage Foundation, 1908-10; diploma, New York Sch. of Philanthropy, 1909; Ph.D., Columbia, 1911; m. Helen Tredway Woodford, of New York City, May 18, 1912; children—Elizabeth Ewing, Edward Woodford. Asst. prof. economics and statistics, New York Sch. of Philanthropy, 1910-12; spl. investigator, N.Y. State Factory Investigating Commn., 1911-12; chief statistician, N.Y. State Food Investigating Commn., 1912; mgr. Industrial Bureau, Mchts. Assn. of New York, 1912-14; lecturer on commerce and statistics, New York U. Sch. of Commerce, 1912-14; chief Bur. of Foreign and Domestic Commerce, Dept. of Commerce, Washington, 1914-17; v.p. Pacific Commercial Co., New York, 1917-19; pres. E.E. Pratt & Co., Inc., 1919-20; mgr. marketing div., Frank Seaman, Inc., 1922-25; with H. K. McCann Co., 1925-27; in charge Antwerp office of J. Walter Thompson Co. since 1927. Sec. and mng. dir. Federated Am. Chamber Commerce of the Near East; lecturer on foreign trade, School of Business, Columbia U., 1921—; mem. council on foreign relations, Chamber of Commerce of New York. Mem. Am. Econ. Assn., Am. Statis. Assn., Am. Scandinavian Soc. Clubs: Columbia Univ., India House. Author: Industrial Causes of Congestion of Population in New York City, 1911; Occupational Diseases, 1912; International Trade in Staple Commodities, 1928. Editor: Course on Foreign Trade, 1917. Has written many articles on foreign trade, industrial betterment, marketing and merchandising. Home: New York, N.Y. *

PRATT, GERALD HILLARY, surgeon, educator, author; b. Montello, Wis., Dec. 15, 1906; s. Martin Henry and Margaret Anne (Farr) P.; B.S., U. Minn., 1924; M.D., State U. Ia., 1928; hon. degrees U. Bordeaux (France), U. Madrid (Spain), U. Barcelona (Spain); m. Mae Dolores Gargin, Mar. 19, 1935; children—Margaret Anne (Mrs. Thomas Taylor), Judith (Mrs. Martin Kingsley), Gerald; m. 2d, Nancy Hildegarde Brown, Mar. 22, 1956; children—Dennis Gerald, James Martin. Intern, resident L.I. Coll. Med. Sch. and Hosp., Bklyn., 1928-30; chief resident Louisville U. Med. Sch. and Hosp., 1930-31; fellow, personal asst. to W. Wayne Babcock, prof. surgery Temple U. Hosp. Med. Sch., Phila., 1931-35; instr., asst. prof., surg. tng. New York Postgrad. Hosp. and Med. Sch., Columbia, 1935-48; asso. prof. N.Y. U. Sch. Medicine, 1948-79; lectr. N.J. Coll. Medicine and Dentistry, 1965-79; mem. surg. staff St. Vincent's Hosp. and Med. Center City N.Y. St. Clare's Hosp. and Health Center, Doctors Hosp., N.Y.C. Mem. Armed Forces Cons. to U.S., 1950-79. Served to maj. M.C., AUS, 1939-41; from lt. comdr. to capt. M.C., USNR, 1941-79. PTO. Recipient Service citation for 25 years service N.Y. U., 1973. Diplomate Am. Bd. Surgery. Fellow A.C.S., Internat. Coll. Surgeons, Am. Coll. Chest Physicians, Am. Geriatrics Soc. (cons. med. adv. bd.), Am. Heart Assn. (council on circulation), Coll. Internat. de Chirurgiens; mem. N.Y. Acad. Scis., Pan Am. Med. Assn. (v.p.; chmn. vascular surgery sect.), Internat. Cardiovascular Soc. (founder), Am. Therapeutic Soc. (v.p., pres. 1955-57), N.Y. Heart Assn. (dir.), N.Y. Acad. Medicine, Navy League U.S., Nu Sigma Nu, Tau Upsilon Kappa, Phi Gamma Delta. Club: Century. Author: (textbooks) Surgical Management of Vascular Diseases, 1949; Tratamiento Quirurgico de las Enfermedades Vasculares, 1952; Cardiovascular Surgery, 1954; Vascular Surgery: Guide and Handbook, 1976; Saga of a Surgeon, 1976. Contbr. chpts. to med. and surg. books, also articles to profl. jours. Cons. for manuscripts various med. jours. Home: Sea Girt, N.J. Died Jan. 31, 1979.

PRATT, HAROLD IRVING, investment mgr.; b. Bklyn., Feb. 8, 1904; s. Harold Irving and Harriet (Barnes) P.; grad. Groton Sch., 1922; A.B., Harvard, 1926, M.B.A., 1929, LL.D., 1960; postgrad. Trinity Coll., Cambridge Eng., 1926-27; LL.D., Pratt Inst., 1968; m. Ellen Rice Hallowell, June 10, 1929; children—Harriet P. (Mrs. John B. Morris), Margaret (Mrs. Richard H. Cardozo), Ellen (Mrs. George Stoia), Harold. Clk. City Bank Farmers Trust Co., N.Y.C., 1929-31; jr. exec. Charles Pratt & Co., 1931-36, partner, 1946-75; asst. sec. U.S. Trust Co. N.Y., 1936-41; chmn. bd. Wall Street Growth Fund, Inc., 1955-73, dir., 1946-73. Pres., dir. Community Hosp., Glen Cove, 1946-61; chmn. trustees Pratt Inst., 1959-66; overseer Harvard, 1960-66; trustee Groton Sch., 1957-70. Served to lt. comdr. USNR, 1941-45. Decorated Bronze Star medal combat V (U.S.); Croix de Guerre with bronze star (France). Republican. Episcopalian (vestry). Clubs: Down Town Assn. (trustee), Harvard (pres. 1963-66), Racquet and Tennis, N.Y. Yacht (commodore 1960-63), Cruising of Am., Century Assn. (N.Y.C.); Piping Rock, Seawanhaka Corinthian Yacht (L.I.). Home: Oyster Bay, N.Y. Died Nov. 3, 1975; interred Meml. Cemetery, Oyster Bay.

PRATT, HENRY NICKERSON, physician; b. Seattle, May 9, 1902; s. Frederick Sanford and Ella Winifred (Nickerson) P.; A.B., Harvard, 1924, M.D., 1930; student U. of Chicago, summer 1926; m. Charlotte Reynolds, July 24, 1929; children—Linda, Anthony. Circulation mgr. Independent mag., 1924-26; house officer Children's Hosp., Boston, 1930-33, Bradford fellowship, 1933-35, instr. pediatrics, Harvard Med. Sch. and pvt. practice pediatrics and allergy, Boston, 1936-41; adminstr. Meml. Hosp. Center for Cancer and Allied Diseases, N.Y. City, 1946-48; dir. N.Y. Hosp., 1948-67; pres. Hosp. Bur. Standards and Supplies, 1948-52, v.p., 1952. Spl. med. adv. group VA, 1960-65. Bd. dirs. Spence-Chapin Adoption Service, 1953-80. Col. U.S. Army, ETO, 1941-45; comdg. officer 3d Gen. Dispensary, Cheltenham, Eng., 48th Gen. Hosp., Paris, 16th Gen. Hosp., Liege, Belgium. Decorated Bronze Star Medal, Medaille de Reconnaisance. Fellow Royal Soc. Medicine, N.Y. Acad. Medicine; mem. Assn. Am. Med. Colls., Internat. Hosp. Fedn., Am. Clin. and Climatol. Assn. Soc. Med. Adminstrs., Med. Soc. State N.Y., A.M.A., Am. (trustee 1961-64), Greater N.Y. (bd. govs. 1948-65, pres., 1952-53) hosp. assns., Hosp. Assn. N.Y. State (trustee), Nat. Health Council (bd. dirs. 1960-63). Rep. Clubs: University; Lake Waramaug Country (Washington, Conn.). Contbr. to profl. jours. Home: New York, N.Y. Died Apr. 7, 1980.

PRATT, JEAN PAUL, gynecologist and obstetrician; b. Wellington, O., Mar. 15, 1882; s. Jerome Benjamin and Harriett (Clark) P.; A.B., Ohio State U., 1906; M.D., Johns Hopkins Med. Sch., 1910; m. 2d. Myrtle Uline Hill, Aug. 20, 1941; children (by 1st marriage)—Jean Gardner, Charles Houghton. Interne and resident house officer, Johns Hopkins Hosp., 1910-13; instr., Surgery, U. of Calif. Med. Sch., 1913-17; asst. surgeon in chief, Henry Ford Hosp., Detroit, Mich., 1917-26 chief, Obstetrics and Gynecology, since 1926. Capt., Med. Res. Corps, 1918. Mem. Sigma Xi, Alpha Omega Alpha, Nu Sigma Nu. Protestant. Club: Detroit Golf. Contbr. papers to med. jours., and books. Home: Detroit. *

PRATT, JOSEPH GAITHER, psychologist, educator; b. Winston-Salem, N.C., Aug. 31, 1910; s. Joseph Monroe and Mattie Elizabeth (Hauser) P.; A.B., Duke, 1931, M.A., 1933, Ph.D., 1936; m. Nellie Ruth Pratt, June 14, 1936; children—John Herman, Vernon Gaither, Joseph Marion, Ellen Wilson. Research asso., research staff parapsychology lab. Duke, 1937-63; insp. engr. Gen. Motors Corp., 1942-43; research asso. psychiatry U. Va. Med. Sch., 1964-65, asso. prof. psychiatry, 1970-73, prof., 1973-79; spl. research problem extrasensory perception. Pres. Psychical Research Found., Durham. Served to lt. USNR, 1944-46. Mem. Parapsychol. Assn. (pres. 1960, mem. council 1959-62, 64-73), Am. Soc. Psychical Research, Am. Psychol. Assn., Soc. Psychical Research (London, Eng.), Phi Beta Kappa, Sigma Xi, Omicron Delta Kappa, Tau Kappa Alpha. Author: (with others) Extrasensory Perception After Sixty Years, 1940; (with J.B. Rhine) Parapsychology: Frontier Science of the Mind, 1957; Parapsychology, An Insider's View of ESP, 1964; ESP Research Today: A Study of Developments in Parapsychology Since 1960, 1973; (with Naomi Hintze) The Psychic Realm: What Can You Believe?, 1975; also numerous articles in field. Home: Keswick, Va. Died Nov. 3, 1979; buried Albemarle County, Va.

PRATT, PERRY WALTER, aircraft mfr.; b. Lompoc, Cal., Jan. 10, 1914; s. Edwin Hart and Ruth Laura (Lilly) P.; B.S. in Mech. Engring., Ore. State Coll., 1936; grad. student Yale, 1936-37, N.Y. U., 1938-39; m. Edith Margaret Abraham, Aug. 9, 1936; children—Susan Fay, Spencer George. Associated with United Aircraft Corp., East Hartford, Conn., 1939-71, beginning with Pratt & Whitney div. as test engr., successively asst. Project engr., project engr., asst. chief engr., chief engr., asst. engring. mgr., engring. mgr., 1939-58, v.p., chief sci. corp., 1958-71. Chmn. NACA subcom. on engine performance and operation, 1954-57; panel on aero. Dept. Def., 1956-58; ad hoc com. research and development Air Force Sci. Adv. Bd., 1957-58, mem. bd., 1963-64; def. sci. bd. Dept. Def., from 1965; adv. council dept. aerospace and mech. scis. Princeton, from 1961. Recipient George Westinghouse gold medal award Am. Soc. M.E., 1956. Fellow Am. Inst. Aeros. and Astronautics; mem. N.Y. Acad. Scis., Soc. Automotive Engrs., Am. Soc. ME., Tau Beta Pi. Home: Hartford, Conn. Died Feb. 6, 1981.

PRATT, ROBERTSON, educator; b. Bklyn., Oct. 28, 1909; s. Abram Johnston and Janet (Robertson) P.; B.A., Columbia, 1931, Ph.D., 1936; m. Jean Noack, Sept. 1, 1948; children—Robin Jean, David Walter. Instr. pharmacognosy U. Calif., 1938-41, asst. prof., 1941-45, asso. prof., 1945-51, prof., 1951-76, prof. pharmacognosy and antibiotics, 1954-76; penicillin research Cutter Labs., 1943-45, cons. microbiol. problems, 1945-47. Recipient Ebert Prize for research on penicillin, 1949. Fellow A.A.A.S.; mem. N.Y., Calif. acads. scis., Soc. Am. Bacteriologists (pres. No. Calif. and Hawaii br. 1952-54), Am. Soc. Plant Physiologists, Am. Pharm. Assn., Am. Soc. Pharmacognosy, Soc. Econ. Botany, Infectious Disease Soc. Am., Sigma Xi, Rho Chi, Phi Delta Chi. Author: Antibiotics (with Jean Dufrenoy), 1949; Pharmacognosy (with H. W. Youngken, Jr.), 1951. Asso. editor U.S. Dispensatory, 1955-60, co-editor-in-chief, 1960-76. Contbr. articles to profl. jours. Home: Healdsburg, Calif. Died May 21, 1976.

PRATT, ROY LESLIE, business exec.; born Grass Valley, Calif., June 22, 1885; s. George and Lucile (Morgan) P.; m. Marian Dorothy Woodside, 1913 (died 1936) m. 2d, Maud Lawton Feb. 17, 1937. Sales mgr. Griffin and Skelley Co., 1916-22; dir. Calif. Packing Corp. since 1922, gen. sales dir., 1930-48, vice pres., 1930-48, pres. since 1948; chmn. bd. dirs. and chmn. exec. com. Alaska Packers Assn. Republican. Mason. Club: Pacific Union (San Francisco). Home: Berkeley, Calif. *

PRATT, WALLACE EVERETTE, cons. geologist; b. Phillipsburg, Kan., Mar. 15, 1885; s. William Henry and Olive Belle (Bostetter) P.; A.B., U. Kan., 1908, B.S., 1908, M.A., 1909, Engr. of Mines in Geology, 1914; m. Pearl M. Stuckey, Dec. 30, 1912 (dec.); children—Fletcher Stuckey, Nancy Jane, Houston Wallace; m. 2d, Iris Calderhead, Jan. 3, 1941 (dec.); m. 3d, Suzanne d'Autremont, Nov. 4, 1966. Asst., Kan. U. Geol. Survey, 1908-09; asst. geologist Div. Mines, Bur. Sci., Govt. Philippines, Manila, 1910, geologist, 1911-12, chief div. mines, 1913-15; geologist Texaco, Houston, 1916-17; chief geologist Humble Oil & Refining Co., Houston, 1918-23, dir., 1924-33, v.p., 1933-36; dir., mem. exec. com. Standard Oil Co. (N.J.), N.Y.C., 1937-45, v.p., 1942-45, ret. 1946; spl. asst. to chmn. N.S.R.B., cons. AEC, Washington, 1948; cons. geologist, Frijole, Culberson County, Tex., 1949-66, Tucson, 1966—. Chmn., Tex. Engrs. for Hoover, 1928; elector from Tex. to Electoral Coll., 1928. Recipient Anthony F. Lucas Gold medal Am. Inst. Mining and Metall. Engrs., 1948; James Furman Kemp medal Columbia U., 1950; Am. Petroleum Inst. Gold medal, 1954; elected to Permian Basin Hall of Fame, 1969. Fellow Geol. Soc. Am.; mem. Am. Assn. Petroleum Geologists (founder mem. 1917, hon. mem. 1958; Sidney Powers Meml. medal 1945, Gold medal for Service through Geology to Human Needs 1972, pres. 1920), Soc. Econ. Geologists, Soc. Exploration Geophysicists (hon.), Houston (hon.), West Tex. (hon.) Sigma Xi, Author: Oil in the Earth, 1941. Editor: (with Dorothy Good) World Geography of Petroleum, 1950. Author papers in fields of econ. and areal geology, iron ores in Philippines, petroleum in the Arctic, 1948, petroleum on Continental shelves, 1945, distbn. of petroleum in earth's crust, vulcanology, non-metallic minerals, coal, Portland cement raw materials. *

PRATTIS, PERCIVAL LEROY, journalist; b. Philadelphia, Pa., Apr. 27, 1895; s. Alexander and Ella (Spraggins) P.; ed. Christianburg Industrial Inst., 1908-12, Hampton Inst., 1912-15, Ferris Inst., 1916-17; LL.D., Wiley Coll., 1944; m. Helen Marie Sands, Mar. 11, 1939; 1 dau., Patricia Adrienne. Editor, Mich. State News, 1919-20; city editor Chicago Defender, 1921-23; news editor Associated Negro Press, 1923-35; city editor Amsterdam News, 1935; city editor Pitts. Courier, 1936-40, exec. editor, 1940-56, editor, 1956-62, editor emeritus, asst. treas., 1962-65; covered activities of Moton Edn. Commn., Haiti, 1930, assignment to interview Haile Selassie in Bath, Eng., 1936; study tour of Near Eastern countries, 1954. Served as a bn. sgt. maj., U.S. Army, World War I. Mem. Nat. Com. to Abolish Discrimination in the Nation's Capital. Conducted survey for Pittsburgh Courier, 1949, England, France, Germany, Italy, Holland and Belgium, relative impressions made by Negro soldiers in Europe; 1st black admitted to Congressional Periodical Press Galleries, 1947. Del. Mid-century White House Conf. Children and Youth; mem. Citizen's Fed. Com. on Edn. Officer Nat. Order Honor and Merit (Republic of Haiti); most outstanding alumnus award, Hampton Inst., 1951. The Prattis Papers in archives of manuscript div. Moorland-Spingarn Research Center, Howard U. Democrat. Methodist. Contbr. chpt. to Many Shades of Black, 1969; collaborator: Perspectives of the Black Press (Henry La Brie, III), 1974. Author: Employment Opportunities Unlimited. Contbr. of articles and signed weekly column to Pittsburgh Courier. Home: Pittsburgh, Pa. Died Feb. 29, 1980; interred Homewood Cemetery, Pittsburgh.

PREACHER, GEOFFREY LLOYD, architect engineer; b. Fairfax. S.C., May 11, 1882; s. John F. and Elizabeth M. (Augley) P.; prep. edn. high sch., Fairfax

B.S., Clemson (S.C.) Coll., 1904; m. Fannie McDaniel, of Augusta, Ga., July 2, 1905; children—G. Lloyd, Jr., Mary Frances, Jack McDaniel, Margaret Elizabeth, Tom Gibson. Began practice at Augusta, 1909; moved to Atlanta, 1922; pres., treas. G. Lloyd Preacher & Co., Inc.; architect of many office, bank, hotel, school, commercial and industrial bldgs., in North and South Carolina, Ga., Fla. and Ala. Pres. Associated Enterprises, Inc.; dir. First Nat. Savings Syndicate. Baptist. Mason (K.T., 32 deg. Shriner), Elk. Clubs: Capital City, Atlanta Athletic, Kiwanis, Druid Hills Golf. Home: Atlanta. *

PREGEL, BORIS, corp. ofcl.; b. Odessa, Russia, Jan. 24, 1893; s. Jules and Rachel (Glaser) P.; C.E., U. Brussels, 1913; E.E., U. Liege, 1914; M.E., U. Petrograd, 1915; Sc.D.; Dr. Hon. Causa, U. Toulouse (France), 1964; m. Alexandra Avxentieff, July 21, 1937. Came to U.S., 1939, naturalized, 1950. Pres. Mfr. Francaise-Etablissements Laly, Paris, 1928-40; sole distbr. Union Miniere du Haut Katanga (radium dept.), Paris, 1929-40; pres. Societe Generale d'Expansion Industrielle et Commerciale, Paris, 1930-40; adminstr. Labs. Radiogene, S.R.L., Paris, 1931-40; pres. Canadian Radium & Uranium Corp., N.Y.C., 1940-60 (merged Canrad Precision Industries, Inc. 1960), Internat. Rare Metals Refinery, 1943-50 (merged Canadian Radium & Uranium Corp. 1950), Consol. Caribou Silver Mines, 1947-49, Cold Spring Tungsten, Inc., (Colo.), 1951-76, Interstate Mining & Exploration Co., Inc., 1954-56, Hetzer Mines, Inc., Colo., 1954 (merged Cold Spring Tungsten, Inc 1954); chmn. bd. Canrad Precision Industries, Inc., N.Y.C., 1960-74, now dir. Exec. pres., prof. faculty scis. Ecole Libre des Hautes Etudes (Frerh U.) N.Y.C., 1947-76; former prof. research Manhattan Coll.; expert cons. Office Chief of Staff, U.S. Army, Washington, 1944. Pres. Internat. Congress Engrs., Paris, 1953; hon. pres. Internat. Union Profl. Engrs., Paris, 1953; chmn. bd. trustees N.Y. Acad. Scis., 1959; gen. del. for U.S. Soc. d'Encouragement pour la Recherche et l'Invention, Soc. d'Encouragement au Progress; pres., gen. del. for N. Am., Inst. Internat. pour les Problémes Humains du Travail. Decorated officer Legion of Honor, Croix de Guerre with palm, Medal of Free France, grand cross Order of Merit for Research and Invention (France); recipient Laureate gold medal Assn. des Ingenieurs-Docteurs de France, 1949; gold medal French Profl. Engrs., French Assn. Inventors; medal City of Paris; grand gold medal City of Paris, 1962, medal City of St. Etienne; grand cross Order St. Dennis of Zante; grand cross Order of Cyprus; Knight of Malta; medal from the City of Tarbes (France); Laureat of Labor (Belgium); Gold medal Archimedes, Gold medal City of Athens (Greece). Fellow N.Y. Acad. of Scis. (life; counselor 1953, pres. 1958, hon. life gov., hon. chmn. bd. govs.), Royal Soc. Arts (London; Benjamin Franklin fellow), A.A.A.S., Am. Geog. Soc. (counselor, v.p.), Permanent Internat. Assn. Naval Congresses (life); mem. Academie de l'Histoire (France; life; hon. pres.), Associe Correspondant Etranger, Academie des Sciences Inscriptions et Belles-Lettres de Toulouse, Armed Forces Communications Assn. (life), Soc. Am. Mil. Engrs. (life), Am. Soc. Engring. Edn., Internat. Union French Profl. Engrs. (hon. pres.), Sci. Research Soc. Am., Am. Phys. Soc., Am. Nuclear Soc., Assn. Applied Solar Energy, Acad. Art and Sci. P.R. (asso. fgn. corr.), World Acad. Art and Sci. (pres. Am. div.), Sigma Xi; hon. mem. Soc. for Med. Jurisprudence, N.Y. Medico-Surg. Soc., Internat. Union Against Cancer (exec. com.). Clubs: Overseas Rotary Fellowship, Explorers, City (N.Y.C.); Nouveau Cercle, Union Interaliee (Paris). Author: Emploi de la Radioactive en Agriculture (Paris), 1933; Industrial Radiography with Radium (in collaboration), 1941; Peacetime Uses of Atomic Energy, 1947; Energie Atomique et l'Industrie (Paris), 1949. Contbg. author: Natural Radioactive Substances (Ency. Chem. Technology), 1953, rev. edit., 1968; Energy, Economy and Society in Transition (N.Y. Acad. Scis.), 1959; (keynote chpt.) America Faces the Nuclear Age, 1961; contbr. to Ency. Chem. Tech., 1968. Chmn. editorial adv. bd. Public Policy Toward Environment. Home: New York, N.Y. Died Dec. 7, 1976.

PRENTISS, LOUIS WATKINS, army engr., assn. executive; b. Washington, Sept. 30, 1899; s. William Clark and Julia (Watkins) P.; E.M., Colo. Sch. Mines, 1921; F.A. Sch., 1922, Signal Sch., 1923, Engr. Sch., 1931, Command and Gen. Staff Sch., 1942; m. Helen McKinstry Bowie, Dec. 28, 1921; children—Edward Bowie (dec.), Catharine (Mrs. Walter W. Plummer, Jr.), Louis Watkins. Commd. 2d lt., U.S. Army, 1921, served as 2d lt., 1st lt. F.A., 1921-29, trans to C.E., 1929, advanced through grades to maj. gen., 1954; dir. tng. and exec. officer Engr. Replacement Tng. Center, Ft. Belvoir, Va., 1941-44; office Dir. Mil. Tng. A.S.F., Washington, 1944; office chief engr. Communications Zone, E.T.O., 1944-45; acting chief engr., dept. chief engr. U.S. Forces, Frankfurt, Germany, 1945-46; dist. engr. Omaha district Missouri River Division Omaha, 1947-49; division engineer S.W. div. Dallas, 1949-52; asst. chief engrs. for personnel and adminstrn. Office Chief of Engrs., Washington, 1952-53; engr. commr. D.C., 1953-54; comdg. gen. Fort Belvoir, Va., 1954-56, ret.; exec. v.p. Am. Road Builders Assn., dir. Acadia Mutual Life Ins. Co., Potomac Electric Power Co., Pepsi Cola Bottling Co. of Washington. Dir. Washington Board Trade, Washington United Givers Fund; v.p. Fed. City Council, Washington Met. council Boy Scouts America. Hon. bd. dirs. Washington Bldg. Congress. Recipient Distinguished Grad. award Colo. Sch. Mines, 1955. Mem. Soc. Am. Mil. Engrs., Permanent Internat. Assn., Navigation Congresses, Oldest Inhabitants Association (Washington), Sigma Alpha Epsilon, Tau Beta Pi, Theta Tau. Clubs: Chevy Chase, Met., Engineers, Army and Navy (Washington); Army and Navy Country, Alfalfa, Keystone Automobile (board of advisors). Home: Washington, D.C. Died Aug. 18, 1976.

PRESCOTT, ROBERT WILLIAM, airline exec.; b. Ft. Worth, May 5, 1913; s. George Washington and Una Victoria (Stewart) P.; A.A., Compton (Cal.) Jr. Coll., 1934-36; law student Loyola U., Los Angeles, 1937-39; m. Anne- Marie Bennstrom, July 16, 1962; children (by previous marriage)—French, Kirsten. With Goodyear Tire & Rubber Co., Los Angeles, 1934-36, Challenge Cream & Butter Co., 1937-39; pilot for Transcontinental & Western Airlines, 1942-43; capt. for China Nat. Aviation Corp., transporting supplies over The Hump, 1943-44; engaged in purchasing planes and supplies for a Mexican airline, 1944-45; founder, 1945, pres., dir. Flying Tiger Line, Inc. (formerly Nat. Skyway Freight Corp.), Los Angeles. Served as ensign, instr., U.S. Naval Flying Sch., Pensacola, Fla., 1939-41; mem. Am. Vol. Group (Flying Tigers), 1941-42; flight leader participating in five maj. campaigns and shooting down 6 Japanese planes, 1942. Mem. Flying Tigers A.V.G. Group Air Transp. Assn. (dir.). Home: Burbank, Calif. Died Mar. 3, 1978.

PRESLEY, ELVIS (AARON), singer, actor; b. Tupelo, Miss., Jan. 8, 1935; s. Vernon Elvis and Gladys Presley; grad. high sch., Memphis; m. Priscilla Ann Beaulieu; May 1, 1967 (div.); 1 dau., Lisa Marie. Truck driver Crown Electric Co.; recorded for personal use My Happiness, also That's When Your Heartaches Begin, 1953; first comm. rec. That's All Right Mama, also Blue Moon of Ky., for Sun Record Co., 1954; personal appearance tour as Hilbilly Cat; weekly performances on Louisiana Hayride, radio sta. KWKH, Shreveport, La.; recs. popular music for RCA Victor, 1955, include Blue Suede Shoes, Hound Dog; first appeared TV, Jackie Gleason's Stage Show, 1956, also appeared Ed Sullivan show; actor films Love Me Tender, 1956, Loving You, 1957, Jailhouse Rock, 1957, King Creole, 1958, Kid Galahad, 1963, Blue Hawaii, Girls, Girls Girls, Paradise, Hawaiian Style, Easy Come, Easy Go, others. Numerous personal appearances. Served with AUS, 1958. Recipient Grammy award for best sacred rec. Nat. Acad. Rec. Arts and Scis., 1967. Address: Madison, Tenn. Died Aug. 16, 1977; buried Forest Hill Cemetery, Memphis.

PRESSMAN, DAVID, immunochemist; b. Detroit, Nov. 24, 1916; s. Jacob and Lottie (Frankfort) P.; B.S., Calif. Inst. Tech., 1937, Ph.D., 1940; M.S., U. Calif., Los Angeles, 1938; m. Rainie Mildred Epstein, July 11, 1940; children—Jeffrey Leonard (dec.), Adele Rhea. Sr. fellow in research Calif. Inst. Tech., Pasadena, 1940-47; head sect. immunochemistry Sloan-Kettering Inst.; N.Y.C., 1947-54; asso. prof. biochemistry Sloan-Kettering div. Cornell U. Med. Sch., 1952-54; dir. cancer research in biochemistry Roswell Park Meml. Inst., Buffalo, 1954-73, asso. inst. dir., 1967-80, dir. cancer research in immunology, 1973-80; research prof. chemistry Roswell Park div. State U. N.Y., Buffalo, 1955-80, research prof. microbiology Sch. Medicine, 1968-80; research prof. grad. faculty Niagara U., 1968-80; Canisius Coll., 1968-80; bd. sci. counselors, div. biologics standards NIH, USPHS, 1967-71; mem. breast cancer diagnostic com. Nat. Cancer Inst., 1973-75. Recipient Bertha Teplitz award Ann Langer Cancer Research Found., 1958; Service to Mankind award Sertoma Internat., 1973. Fellow AAAS, N.Y. Acad. Scis.; mem. Am. Chem. Soc. (Schoellkopf medal 1965, Morley medal 1967), Am. Soc. Biol. Chemists, Am. Assn. Cancer Research, Soc. Exptl. Biology and Medicine (pres. Western N.Y. sect. 1964-65), Am. Assn. Immunolgists, Sigma Xi, Tau Beta Pi. Author: (with Howard J. Lucas) Principles and Practice in Organic Chemistry, 1949; (with A.L. Grossberg) Structural Basis of Antibody Specificity, 1968; editorial bd. Transplant Bull., 1954-56; asso. editor Jour. Immunology, 1959-63, 65-72; editorial bd. Jour. Medicine and Pharm. Chemistry, 1962-65, Immunochemistry, 1964-71; Transplantation, 1975-78; editorial adv. bd. Immunol. Communications, 1972-80. Home: Buffalo, N.Y. Died June 16, 1980.

PREUS, JACOB AALL OTTESEN, ex-gov.; b. Columbia Co., Wis., Aug. 28, 1883; s. Christian Keyser and Louise Augusta (Hjort) P.; A.B., Luther Coll., Decorah, Ia., 1903; LL.B., U. of Minn., 1906; LL.D., Augustana Coll., 1921; m. Idella Louise Haugen, of Decorah, 1909; children—J. A. O., Robert David. Clk. to U.S. Senator Knute Nelson, of Minn., 1906-09; admitted to Minn. bar, 1906, Ill. bar, 1939; exec. clk. to gov. of Minn., 1909-10; ins. commr. of Minn., 1910-14; state auditor, 1914-20; gov. of Minn., terms 1921-23, 1923-25; mgr. The Minneapolis Com., 1925-26; v.p. W. A. Alexander & Co., Chicago, since 1926; apptd. a co-receiver Old Colony Life Ins. Co., Oct. 1932. Home: Highland Park, Ill., and Minneapolis, Minn. *

PREUSSE, CHARLES FRANCIS, lawyer; b. N.Y.C., Mar. 14, 1902; s. William and Bridget (Sheridan) P.; B.S. with honors, N.Y. U., 1925; LL.B., Columbia, 1928; m. Josephine Florence, Aug. 19, 1933; children—Sandra, Charles S. Admitted to N.Y. bar, 1929; asso. firm Baldwin, Hutchins & Todd, 1928-30; charge legal staff handling liquidation Bank of U.S., 1932-43; asso. firm Chadbourne, Wallace, Parke & Whiteside, 1943-46; 1st asst. and acting corp. counsel City N.Y., 1946-50; acting dep. mayor, part of 1949; mem. Mayor's Com. on Mgmt., Mayor's Exec. Com. on City Mgmt., 1948-53; mem. Mayor's Cabinet N.Y.C., 1954-59, 1st dept. city adminstr., 1954-55, city adminstr., 1955-59; mem. firm Whitman & Ransom, 1959-77; dir., counsel Bank of Commerce; dir. Hosp. Ins. Plan. Mem. Health Research Council N.Y.C.; br. com. N.Y. Pub. Library, 1964-66. Legal cons. Bd. Edn., 1961; counsel N.Y. World's Fair Corp., 1959-70. Bd. dirs., N.Y. Hall Sci., N.Y. Bldg. Congress, Acad. Polit. Sci. Served with 101 Cav., N.Y. N.G., 1930-33. Mem. Assn. Bar N.Y.C. (exec. com. 1963-67), Delta Upsilon, Phi Delta Phi. Clubs: Maidstone, University, Columbia University (N.Y.C.). Author municipal reports. Home: New York, N.Y. Died May 30, 1977; interred Cedar Lawn Cemetery, East Hampton, N.Y.

PREZZANO, EDWARD PETER (PRET-ZÄ'NO), pres. Westchester Lighting Co., The Yonkers Electric Light & Power Co.; b. New York, N.Y., June 17, 1884; s. Ralph and Theresa (DiGigglio) P.; student Public Schools of N.Y. City; m. Kathryn A. Carroll, June 15, 1908; children—Harold Edward, Wilbur John. Began as clerk with Standard Gas Light Co., 1902-04. With Consol. Gas Co., 1904-24, successively as filing clerk, 1904-05, gen. clerk, 1905-06, tickler's asst., Jan.-Mar. 1906, regular bookkeeper, 1906-08, deposit clerk, 1908-09, asst. chief clerk, 1909-10, chief clerk, 1910-13, asst. mgr., 1913-18, mgr., 1918-22, mgr. of 14th St. dist. office, Mar.-Dec. 1922, asst. gen. comml. mgr., gen. office, 1922-24. Sec. Westchester Lighting Co., 1924-26, vice-pres., 1926-36, pres. since Feb. 1936. Also pres. Yonkers Electric Light & Power Co. Dir. Eastchester Savings Bank, Mount Vernon, N.Y. Trustee, Consol. Edison Co. New York; dir. New Rochelle Trust Co. Was pres. Bronx Gas & Electric Co. until Dec. 1936, when company merged with the Consol, Edison Co. of New York, Inc. Clubs: Scarsdale Golf, Westchester Country. Home: Mount Vernon, N.Y. *

PRICE, EDWARD THOMAS, educator; b. Brooksville, Miss., Feb. 7, 1883; s. Walter and Bettie Caroline (Dixon) P.; ed. Webb Sch., Bell Buckle, Tenn., 1897-1900; A.B., Vanderbilt U., 1906; student U. of Chicago, 1909, Pomona Coll., Claremont, Calif., 1925-27, Claremont Colls., 1928-29 and 2932-33; m. Susan Webb, of Bell Buckle, June 21, 1911; children—Edward Thomas, Emily Clary. Instr. Webb Sch., 1902-04 and 1908-09, Polytechnic Coll., Fort Worth, Tex., 1906-08; supt. schs. Ripley, Tenn., 1909-11, Macon, Miss., 1911-13; established Price-Webb Sch., Lewisburg, Tenn., 1913, headmaster, 1913-25; asst. headmaster Webb Sch. of Calif. since 1925; mem. faculty summer sch., U. of Miss., 1910, 12. Mem. Southern Br. of Classical Assn. Pacific States (pres. 1932-33), Claremont Community Players (pres. 1932-33), Sigma Nu. Democrat. Conglist. Home: Claremont, Calif. *

PRICE, JOHN MILBURN, educator; b. Fair Dealing, Ky., Nov. 21, 1884; s. John Powers and Elizabeth Goheen (McLeod) P.; B.S., Western Ky. State Teachers Coll., 1905; A.B., Baylor U., 1911; A.M., Brown University, 1912; Th.M., Southern Baptist Theological Seminary, 1915. Th.D., 1919; Ph.D., 1930; LL.D., Baylor U., 1945; Litt.D., California Baptist College, 1965; m. Mabel Falk, July 11, 1916; children—Mabel Elizabeth, John Milburn, Jr., Joseph Wayne, James Olis. Teacher Ky. pub. schs., 1903-04; prin. Marlow (Okla.) High Sch., 1905-06; ordained Bapt. ministry, 1908; rural S.S. worker in Ky., 1912-13; acting state Bapt. S.S. sec., for Ky., 1914-15; pastor, successively, Providence, R.I., Corydon, Ky., Mansfield, Tex.; founder Sch. of Religious Edn., Southwestern Bapt. Theol. Sem., Fort Worth, dir., 1915-56, dir. emeritus; vis. prof. Hardin-Simmons U., 1958-60, Howard Payne Coll., 1962, New Orleans Bapt. Sem., 1963-64. Winnter Tex. Prohibition Oratorical Contest, 1910; winner Marston scholarship, from Baylor U. to Brown U., 1911. Mem. Southern Bapt. Association Teachers Bible and Religious Edn. (ex-pres.), So. Bapt. Religious Edn. Assn. (past president). Southwestern Bapt. Religious Education Association (founder and past pres.), American Assn. Schools Religious Education (past pres.). Democrat. Baptist. Author several books relating to field, latest being: The Unfolding Life, 1963. Contbr. religious jours. Home: Fort Worth. *

PRICE, JOHN WILLIAMSON, JR., surgeon; b. Louisville, Ky., Apr. 12, 1882; s. John Williamson and Violet Henderson (Baird) P.; A.B., University of Louisville (Kentucky), 1900; certificate of proficiency in biology, U. of Pa., 1902, M.D., 1905; grad. study U. of Vienna, 1905-06; m. Louise Reid Bruce, Apr. 26, 1911 (died 1914); 1 son, Helm Bruce; m. 2d, Barbara

Thruston Atwood, Dec. 27, 1917; children—Caroline Butler Atwood (Mrs. William M. Reid), Catherine Lytle (Mrs. R. Bruce Bass). Interne P.E. Hosp., Phila., Pa., 1906-08; instr. in abdominal surgery and gynecology, U. of Louisville, 1908-13, also instr. in surg. pathology, 1908-12, adj. prof. abdominal surgery and gynecology, 1913-23, asso. clin. prof. gynecology since 1923; visiting surgeon, Louisville City Hosp., John H. Norton Memorial Infirmary since 1908; dir., trustee First Nat. Bank, Ky. Title Trust Co., First Ky. Fire Ins. Co., First Ky. Co. Major, Med. Corps. U.S.A. with A.E.F., World War I. Fellow of Am. Coll. Surgeons, Southern Surg. Assn.; mem. A.M.A., Medico-Chirurg. Soc., Ky. State Med. Soc., Jefferson Co. Med. Soc., Beta Theta Pi, Phi Alpha Sigma. Republican. Presbyterian. Clubs: Pendennis, Pierian, Louisville Country. Home: Louisville; (winter) Delray Beach, Fla. *

PRICE, PAUL HOLLAND, state geologist; b. Uffington, Monongalia County, W.Va., Sept. 1, 1898; s. John C. and Sarah (Kinkaid) P.; A.B., U. of W.Va., 1923, M.S., 1926; Ph.D., Cornell U., 1930; m. Helen Tapp (dec.); children—Allene Helen, Joann Kinkaid, Louise Tapp, Paul H. Instr. U. of W.Va., 1930-35, asso. prof., 1936-38, head dept. geology, 1938-46, later prof.; with W.Va. Geol. Survey from asst., 1923, to State geologist, dir. since 1934. Served as 2d lt., World War I, Sept. 1918 to January 1919; lt. col., military govt., as natural resource specialist, June 1943-Jan. 1946. President Morgantown Community Assn., mem. Planning Commn., Water Resources Commission; chairman West Virginia Antiquities Commission. Member of the W. Virginia Archaeological Soc. (pres. from 1965), Association American State Geologists (president 1942-43), Geol. Soc. Am., Am. Assn. Petroleum Geologists, Am. Inst. Min. and Metall. Engrs., Am. Geophys. Union. Nat. Speleological Soc., Engrs. Soc. Western Pa., Appalachian Geol. Soc., W.Va. Acad. Sci., Sigma Xi. Epis. Rep. Clubs: Rotary (ex-pres.), C. of C. Author many tech. reports, articles, lectures. Home: The Hogback, Morgantown. Address: Morgantown, W.Va. Died Sept. 26, 1980.

PRIEBE, KARL, artist; b. Milw., July 1, 1914; s. Emil and Katherine (Wacker) P.; student Layton Art Sch., Chgo. Art Inst. Dir. Kalamazoo Inst. Arts, 1944-45; staff mem. dept. anthropology Milw. Pub. Mus., 1938-42; instr. Layton Art Sch., Milw., 1947—. Exhibited one-man shows Perls Galleries, N.Y.C., 1942, 44, 46; Vigeveno Galleries, Hollywood, 1946, Legion of Honor, San Francisco, 1946, Layton Art Gallery, 1941, 43, 46-47, Kalamazoo, 1944, Art Club Chgo., U. Wis. Union, 1958, Waterman Gallery, Paris, France, Hammer Gallery, N.Y.C., O'Brien Gallery, Scottsdale, Ariz.; exhibited Carnegie Inst., 1943-46, Va. Inst. Arts, 1944-45, Chgo. Art Inst., 1934-39, 40-46, Milw. Art Inst., 1934-46; also Corcoran Gallery, Washington, Cin. Art Mus., Pa. Acad. Arts, Katherine Kutt Gallery, Chgo., David Porter Gallery, Washington, and South Hampton, Springfield (Mass.) Inst. Arts, Art Inst. Boston, Kalamazoo Inst. Arts, Mus. Modern Art, N.Y., Renaissance Gallery, U. Chgo., Shima Mura Gallery, Tokyo, 1970, Tanglewood, Lenox, Mass., 1973. Rep. in permanent collections Milw. Art Inst., Layton Art Gallery Ency Collection, Corcoran Gallery, Washington, Bergstrom Mus., Neenah, Wis., IBM Collection, Chgo. Art Inst., Detroit Art Inst., Barnes Found. Exhibiting 1-man shows U. Ia., Springfield (Ill.) Art Inst., Art Inst., Decatur, Ill., 1947. An amateur ornithologist, relating to inclusion of birds in paintings. Home: Milwaukee, Wis. Died July 6, 1976.

PRIEST, A. J. GUSTIN, lawyer; b. Kearney, Nebr., June 9, 1897; s. Joel Lambert and Sue Alice (Gustin) P.; A.B., U. Idaho, 1918, LL.B., 1921, LL.D., 1970; m. Hartwell Wyse, Aug. 4, 1927; children—Paul, Marianna. Admitted to Idaho, N.Y., D.C., Va. bars; in gen. practice law, Boise, Idaho, 1921-22; atty. and sec. Idaho Power Co., 1922-26; atty., Elec. Bond and Share Co., N.Y.C., 1926-35; mem. firm Reid & Murphy, N.Y.C., 1935-37, Reid & Priest, 1937-53; prof. law U. Va., 1953-66, scholar-in-residence Law Sch., 1966-78. Trustee, Meadville Theol. Sch., 1961-63. Served with inf., U.S. Army, World War I; capt., Idaho N.G. 1922-23. Chmn. bd. dirs. Fed. Union, Inc. (Union Now movement), 1941-45; chmn. exec. council United World Federalists, 1948-50. Named Federalist Man of Year in 1964. Fellow Am. Bar Found.; mem. Assn. Bar City New York, Am. Bar Assn. (past chmn. sect. pub. utility law), Phi Beta Kappa, Beta Theta Pi. Unitarian. Mason. Club: Colonnade (Charlottesville). Author: The Great Ones, Old Hilarity, Principles of Public Utility Regulation, Theory and Application. Contbr. articles to legal publs. Home: Charlottesville, Va. Died Mar. 20, 1978.

PRIEST, WALTER SCOTT, physician; b. Denver, Colo., June 25, 1896; s. Walter Scott (D.D.) and Anna Ellen (Schaeffer) P.; A.B., Univ. of Kan., 1917; M.D., Wash. Univ., 1920; M.S., Northwestern, 1946; m. Ruth M. Biederman, June 12, 1923; 1 son, Walter Scott; m. 2d, Clara E. Rourke, June 7, 1939; children—David Hartzell and William Curtis (twins), Kenneth Lee. Resident pathologist Barnes Hosp., St. Louis, 1920, interne, 1920-21; resident physician Michael Reese Hosp., Chicago, 1921-22, Baer fellow in electrocardiography, 1922-24, dir. heart station, 1925-33, adjunct attending physician, 1926-33; sr. attending physician Chicago Memorial Hosp., 1927-40; physician to out patients, cardiac clinic, Evanston (Ill.) Hosp., 1935-39; asso. prof. medicine Northwestern U., 1940-62, prof., 1962-79; sr. attending physician Wesley Meml. Hosp., Chgo., 1940-79; vis. physician Passavant Memorial, Chicago, and Evanston (Ill.) Hosps. since 1940; consultant in internal medicine, St. Francis Hosp., Evanston, since 1946; cons. cardiologist United Air Lines since 1930. Served as sergt. M.C., U.S. Army, World War I. Pioneer research work on penicillin and streptomycin in the treatment of subacute bacterial endocarditis; recipient gold medal for scientific exhibit of this work, Ill. State Med. Soc., Chicago, May 1946; certificate of merit, A.M.A., San Francisco, July 1946; silver medal Miss. Valley Med. Soc., Sept. 1946. Diplomate: Am. Bd. of Int. Med., cardiovascular diseases. Fellow A.C.P., Am. Coll. Cardiology (trustee, pres. 1956); mem. A.M.A., Ill. State, Chgo. med. socs., Am. (gov.), Chicago (v.p., bd. govs.) heart assns., Chgo. Soc. Internal Med., Inst. of Med. of Chgo., Sigma Nu, Nu Sigma Nu, Phi Mu Alpha, Alpha Omega Alpha, Sigma Xi. Republican. Methodist. Club: Sigma Nu Alumni (past pres.). Editorial consultant, Am. Journal of Cardiology. Contbr. to Geriatric Medicine (edited by E. J. Stieglitz), 1943; numerous articles on internal medicine especially cardiovascular disease in med. jours. Charter mem. (1921) and past pres. Chicago Business Men's Orchestra; violinist, violist. Home: Wilmette, Ill. Died Dec. 1, 1979.

PRIESTER, GEORGE C(HARLES), educator, engr.; b. Guttenberg, Ia., Feb. 1, 1885; s. Mathias and Elizabeth Lulu (Backes) P.; B.E., U. of Ia., 1910; M.S., U. of Minn., 1916; Ph.D., U. of Mich., 1928; m. Lulu May Boller, June 6, 1911; children—Gayle Boller, Betty Lu (Mrs. Robert T. Close). Instr. mathematics and mech., U. of Minn., 1910-16, asst. professor, 1916-26; associate prof., 1924-29, professor, 1929-53, head dept. 1940-53, emeritus. President Norway Beach Improvement Assn., Cass Lake, Minn., 1935-48. Mem. Am. Soc. for Metals (pres. N.W. chapter 1925), Am. Soc. Engring, Edn., Math. Assn. Am., Sigma Xi, Tau Betz Pi Mason O.E.S. (worthy patron 1984, Worthy grand guard 1949); Job's Daughters of Minn. (asso. grand guardian, 1943-44). Clubs: Minneapolis Engineers (pres. 1941); Campus (Minneapolis). Author: engring. bulls, and articles on stress analysis in tech. jours. Constrn. engr. on projects involving stress analysis, testing and specifications. Home: Minneapolis. *

PRIMA, LOUIS, band leader, singer; b. New Orleans, Dec. 7, 1912; grad. Jesuit High Sch.; m. Gia Maione, 1963; children—Lena Ann, Louis. Trumpet player, singer local theaters, La., then night clubs, N.Y.C., Las Vegas, Lake Tahoe, Nev., Reno; band leader, from 1940, appearing with wife. Composer: Sing, Sing, Sing; Brooklyn Boogie; Marguerite; Boogie in the Bronx; Sunday Kind of Love; Robinhood, Oh Babe; Las Vegas Woman. Home: Covington, La. Died Aug. 24, 1978; buried Lake Lawn Metairie Cemeteries, New Orleans.

PRINCE, AARON ERASTUS, clergyman, educator; b. Fairfield, Ill., Jan. 1, 1887; s. Rev. Peter and Emma Jane (Young) P.; A.B., Howard Payne U.; S.T.B., LL.D., La Grange Coll.; D.D., Ewing Coll.; m. Pearl Bonner, Aug. 24, 1909; (dec. Oct. 18, 1946); children—Esther E. (Mrs. Howard L. Jackson), Ruth A. (Mrs. R. Allen Hunt), Mary L. (Mrs. Edwin F. Moore), Grace L. (Mrs. Glen Lee Greene), Dorothy E., Aaron, Jr.; m. 2d, Virginia Faye Dixon, Aug. 7, 1949. Ordained to ministry Baptist Ch., 1904; held student pastorates in Ill., 1904-10; pastor, Casey, Ill., 1910-12, Ewing, Ill., 1912-14, Charleston, Ill., 1914-16, LaGrange, Mo., 1916-19, Eldorado, Ill., 1919-21, Marion, Ill., 1921-27, Brownwood, Texas, 1927-34, Pineville, La., 1934-39, West Monroe, La., 1939-41; pastor Fifth St. Ch., Hannibal, Mo., 1941-44, pastor emeritus, 1944-80; pres. Hannibal LaGrange Coll., 1941-50; pastor First Bapt. Ch., Effingham, Ill., 1950-51; pastor Bapt. Tabernacle, Auckland, New Zealand, 1951-52; prin. Hawaiian Bapt. Acad., 1952-53; 1st pres. Honolulu Christan Coll., 1953-55; stewardship Evangelist, 1955-57; pastor 1st Bapt. Ch., Lafayette, La., 1957-58, Emmanuel chapel, Scott Field AFB, 1958-59, Maplewood Park Bapt. Ch., Cahokia, Ill., 1960-66, pastor emeritus, 1977-80; pastor Water Tower Bapt. Ch., St. Louis, 1966-68, 70-74, pastor emeritus, 1974-80; adminstr. chaplain Temple Retirement Home, Bridgeton, Mo., 1966-67. Dir. 4 Minute Speakers, Publicity Dept., U.S. Govt. for Northeast Mo., World War I, 1917-19. Chaplain U.S. Vets. Hosp., Alexandria, La., 1937-39, Central La. State Hosp., 1935-39, La. State Indsl. Sch. for Girls, 1937-39. Mem. edn. bd. So. Bapt. Conv., 1919-21, Bd. Fgn. Missions, 1921-27, Relief and Annuity Bd., 1937-40. Rec. sec. exec. bd. Ill. Bapt. State Assn., 1919-27; trustee Ewing Coll., 1919-25, pres. Ewing Coll., 1924-25; trustee Howard Payne Coll., 1927-34; mem. exec. bd. Bapt. Gen. Conv., Tex., 1927-34; moderator Brown County (Tex.) Bapt. Assn., 1929-34; mem. La. Bapt. Hosp. Bd., 1935-41; pres. exec. bd. La. Bapt. Conv., 1937-41. Mem. Ewing Coll. Alumni Assn. (pres. 1958-80). Mason (32 deg.), Odd Fellow, Rotarian. Editor: Life's Best, 1940; Meeting Life's Reverses, 1941. Author: Christ Is All, 1940 (English edit.); Cristo E. Tudo, 1941 (Portuguese edit.); Back to Bethel, 1942; To My Friends, 1943; History of Fifth Street Baptist Church, 1944; History of Ewing College, 1961; History Maplewood Park Baptist Church, 1974. Home: Saint Louis, Mo. Died Sept. 30, 1980; buired Grand View Burial Park, Hannibal, Mo.

PRINCE, SAMUEL LANDER, ednl. adminstr.; b. Williamston, S.C., Nov. 23, 1886; s. George Edward and Mattie McPherson (Lander) P.; A.B., Wofford Coll., 1907, LL.D., 1949; m. Leila Barr, Dec. 17, 1908; children—Mary Barr (Mrs. Henry S. Sullivan), Martha Lander (Mrs. Raymond A. McLees), Leila Virginia (Mrs. William F. Drew). Teacher physics and chemistry Lander Coll., 1907-11; admitted to S.C. bar, 1911; partner Watkins & Prince, Anderson, S.C., 1914-46; asst. div. counsel So. R.R., 1930-46; dean U. of S.C. Law Sch. since 1946. Spl. circuit judge Charleston, S.C., 1940-41, Columbia, S.C., 1943; mem. Jud. Conf. 4th Circuit, United States Circuit Ct. Appeals, 1934—. Mem. State Bd. Law Examiners, 1930-38; war fund chmn. A.R.C., Anderson Co., World War I, Richland Co., 1951. Mem. Assn. Am. Law Schs. (organizer, chmn. com. steering com. S.E. Regional Law Teachers Conf. since 1947), Am., South Carolina, (president 1953-54, director institute), Richland County and Anderson Co. bar assns., Jud. Council of S.C., Phi Beta Kappa, Sigma Alpha Epsilon, Phi Delta Phi, Omicron Delta Kappa. Methodist. Mason, K.P. Author articles in profl. jours. Home: Columbia, S.C. *

PRINGLE, RALPH BRADEN, business exec.; born Parker's Landing, Pa., Feb. 14, 1884; s. William and Letitia (Kistler) ed. pub. schs. of Pa.; m. Lillian Margaret Price, June 1, 1905; children—Mrs. J. S. Ford, Mrs. R. W. Simpson, Jr., Mrs. R. E. Dirickson, John P., R. Phillips, Richard B., Marguerite. With T. W. Phillips Oil and Gas Co., Butler, Pa., 1903-13; Nat. Supply Co., Tulsa, Okla., 1913-18; vice-pres. Waite Phillips Co., 1918-24; vice-pres. and gen. mgr. Independent Oil and Gas Co., 1924-29; v.p. in charge of prodn., Tide Water Asso. Oil Co., 1930-42, retired from active management, 1942, still mem. bd. dirs. Dir. Internat. Petroleum Exposition, Club: Tulsa, Southern Hills Country (Tulsa); Surf (Miami Beach, Fla.). Home: Tulsa. *

PRIOR, HARRIS KING, mus. dir.; b. Hazardville, Conn., Mar. 10, 1911; s. Leland Jay and Flora Amanda (King) P.; B.S., Trinity Coll., 1932, M.A., 1935; student Harvard, Yale, U. Paris, U. Brussels, N.Y. U.; D.F.A. (hon.), Cal. Coll. Arts and Crafts, 1959; m. Anne Foss Hirschmann, Apr. 23, 1963. Asst. instr. English, fine arts Trinity Coll., 1932-36; head Sch. Fine Arts, Olivet Coll., 1937-39; instr. fine arts Bennett Jr. Coll., Millbrook, N.Y., 1941-42; dir. community arts program Munson-Williams-Proctor Inst., Utica, N.Y., 1947-56; exec. dir. Am. Fedn. Arts, N.Y.C., 1956-62; dir. Meml. Art Gallery, U. Rochester, 1962-75, prof. fine arts, 1962-75; mem. editorial bd. The Art Gallery mag., 1973-75. Served from lt. (j.g.) to capt. USNR, World War II, Korea. Mem. Coll. Art Assn., Am. Assn. Museums Rochester C. of C., Assn. Art. Mus Dirs., Phi Beta Kappa, Alpha Chi Rho. Rotarian. Club: Century Association (N.Y.C.). Home: Rochester, N.Y. Died Mar. 18, 1975.

PRITCHARD, EDWARD KRIEGSMANN, lawyer; b. Eagle Lake, Tex., Sept. 11, 1904; s. William Richard and Eva Helena (Kriegsmann) P.; student Porter Mil. Acad., Charleston, Episcopal High Sch., Alexandria, Va.; student Union Coll., Schenectady, 1922-25; B.A. magna cum laude, U. S.C., 1927, LL.B. with honor, 1930; m. Julia Huger Myers, Apr. 22, 1933; children—Posey Bacot Myers (Mrs. Lawrence C. Bensen), Edward Kriegsmann, Julia (Mrs. David V. Haynie), Elizabeth (Mrs. Robert H. Bowles), Louisa deRosset (Mrs. J. David Hawkins). Admitted to S.C. bar, 1930, since practiced in Charleston, S.C.; with Stoney, Crosland & Pritchard, 1930-48, deRosset Myers, 1948-64, Pritchard, Myers & Morrison and Bloom, P.A., Charleston, 1964-74, Pritchard, Myers, Morrison, Bloom & Rutledge, P.S., 1974—; chmn. bd. So. Ice Co.; pres. Leeds Credit Clothiers Beaufort, Sullivan's Island Marina Co., Wando Title Co.; chmn. bd. Tri-County So. Ice Co., Charleston Ice Co.; pres., dir. Sunset Realty & Investments, Inc.; v.p., dir. Braswell Shipyards, Yellow Cab Co., Vet.'s Taxi Service, Inc., Airport Limousine & Taxi Service, Inc., Wando Leasing Co., North Charleston Leasing Co., Sullivan Island Seafood Co., Leaf'N Petal of Charleston, GBS Plant Corp., Charlotte, Wayne Homes, Ltd., Wayne Homes of Kiawah, Ltd., Southeastern Electronics, Inc., East Coast Supply Co., Lipe Sheetmetal Co., Charleston Machine & Pipe Shop, Inc., Atlantic Flooring Co.; dir. Yellow Cab Co. of Charleston, North Charleston Leasing Co., Spa Homes, Inc., New South Life Ins. Co. Chmn. Charleston County legis. del. S.C. Gen. Assembly, 1929-30; municipal recorder City of Charleston, 1948; del. Democratic Nat. Conv., 1952, 56, presdl. elector, 1952; chmn. Charleston County Dem. Exec. Com., 1954-56, City Dem. Exec. Com., 1959-63; chmn. com. on harbor pollution, 1962—. Mem. Am., S.C. (past chmn. law sch com., pres. 1962-63), Charleston County bar assns. Nat. Conf. Bar Presidents (exec. council 1964—, chmn 1969-70), St. Andrews Soc., Hibernian Soc., S.C. Soc.

Phi Beta Kappa, Omicron Delta Kappa, Kappa Alpha. Elk, Mason. Clubs: Kiwanis (lt. gov., past pres. Charleston), Carolina Yacht, Hobcaw Yacht (Charleston). Home: Mt. Pleasant, S.C.; buried St. Philips Graveyard, Charleston, S.C.

PRITCHARD, GEORGE MOORE (PRINCH'ÄRD), ex-congressman; b. near Mars Hill, N.C., Jan. 4, 1886; s. Jeter C. and Augusta (Ray) P.; ed. U. of N.C., and law dept. U. of S.C., m. Robenia Redman, Sept. 1911; children—Sarah Hulin, Louise, Helen, Jeter C. Admitted to S.C. bar, 1908, and practiced at Greenville, 1908-11; admitted to N.C. bar, 1911; rep. from Madison Co. to N.C. Gen. Assembly, 1917-19; solicitor 19th Judicial Dist., 1919-23; mem. 71st Congress (1929-31), 10th N.C. Dist. (member military affairs committee, 1928-30). Chmn. Buncombe Co. Republican Exec. Com., 1928. Republican candidate for U.S. Senate, 1930; keynote speaker at N.C. State Rep. Conv., 1932; del. at large to Rep. Nat. Conv., Chicago, 1932. Keynote speaker 11th Dist. Rep. Congl. Conv., 1942, also N.C. Rep. State Conv., 1942. Rep. candidate for Gov. of N.C., 1948, receiving 210,000 votes; now in practice of law, Asheville. Mem. bd. of trustees, U. of N.C., 1917-19. Mem. Beta Theta Pi. Mem. Junior Order. Presbyn. Mason, Elk, K.P. Mem. Asheville (N.C.) Executives' Club. Address: Asheville, N.C. *

PRITCHARD, JOHN HAYES, architect; b. Indpls., May 5, 1905; s. John M. and Leona Dell (Hayes) P.; B.Arch., Ga. Sch. Tech., 1930; m. Charlie Lowe, June 10, 1930; 1 son, John Hayes. Archtl. designer, draftsman, Beaumont, Tex., 1928-34; designer rural farm communities U.S. Govt., Austin, Tex., 1934-36; asso. bd. govs. Fed. Res. System, Washington, 1937; chief architect Nat. Youth Adminstrn., Washington, 1938-40, regional dir., Memphis, 1940-42; pvt. practice architecture, Tunica, Miss., 1946-76; asso. Pritchard & Nickles, Tunica, 1951-76. Regional chmn. Octagon Campaign Fund, 1966-76; active fund drives Boy Scouts Am., ARC, Mental Health. Mem. board aldermen, Tunica, Miss. Mem. Tunica County Indsl. Bd.; pres. Tunica County Devel. Corp. Served to major AUS, World War II. Decorated Bronze Star, recipient Silver Beaver award Boy Scouts Am.; certificate of merit for community service Gulf States Dist. A.I.A., 1955. Fellow A.I.A. (mem. nat. jud. board 1966-76, chmn. 1970); mem. Tunica County C. of C., Delta Council, Miss. Econ. Council, Soc. Friends Tewkesbury Abbey, County Farm Bur., Soc. Archtl. Historians, Am. Legion (post comdr.), 40 and 8, Vets. Fgn. Wars, Sigma Phi Epsilon. Episcopalian (bd.). Rotarian (past pres.). Home: Tunica, Miss. Died Nov. 18, 1976.

PRITCHARD, JOHN PAUL, educator; b. White Lake, N.Y., Feb. 8, 1902; s. John Henderson and Jane Margaret (DuBois) P.; B.A., Cornell U., 1922, Ph.D., 1925; m. Ruth Smith, Aug. 19, 1926; 1 son, John Paul. Prof. ancient langs. Catawba Coll., Salisbury, N.C., 1925-28; prof. classical langs. Washington and Jefferson Coll., Washington, Pa., 1928-44; prof. English, U. Okla., Norman, from 1944, research prof. English, 1956-72, prof. emeritus, 1972-76. Mem. Modern Lang. Assn., Phi Beta Kappa. Presbyn. Author: Return to the Fountains, 1942; Criticism in America, 1956; The Literary Wise Men of Gotham, 1963; August Boeckh on Interpretation and Criticism, 1968; A Literary Approach to the New Testament, 1972, paperback edit., 1981. Home: Norman, Okla. Died Nov. 2, 1976; buried Walton, N.Y., 1976.

PRITCHARD, JOHN RAYMOND, railway exec.; b. Berkley, Va., Jan. 9, 1886; s. Peleg and Mary J. (Collier) P.; student pub. schs. Norfolk, Va.; m. Lucia Privett, Apr. 11, 1917; 1 son, John Raymond. Stenographer gen. supt. office Norfolk So. Ry., 1906, sec. to gen. supt., 1906-09, sec. to receiver, 1909-10, clk. office of pres., 1910, sec. to pres., 1911, chief clk, exec. offices, 1911-25, asst. sec., 1925-32, ins. and tax agt. for receivers, 1932-39, sec. since 1939, dir. since 1948, v.p. since 1949; v.p., sec., dir. Norfolk So. Bus Corp. since 1933, Norfolk So. Warehouse Co. since 1945, N.C. Warehouse Co. since 1941, Princess Anne Power Co., Inc. since 1933, Euclid Development Corp. since 1949; treas., dir. MeGinnis Indsl. Center Inc., Norfolk, Va., since 1948; sec., treas., dir., John L. Roper Lumber Co. since 1949, Roper Realization Co., Inc. since 1949, Norfolk, So. Land Co. since 1949. Mem. Va. State G. of C. Episcopalian. Mason (K.T., Shriner) Clubs: Princess Anne Country (Virginia Beach, Va) Virginia (Norfolk. Va.) Home: Virginia Beach. *

PRITCHETT, HENRY LUCIAN (PRIT'CHET), coll. prof.; b. Glasgow, Mo., June 12, 1884; s. Henry Carr and Kate (Smith) P.; Sam Houston State Teachers Coll., Huntsville, Tex., 1901-03; B.A., U. of Tex., 1911, M.A., 1915; grad. study, summers, State U. of Ia., 1924, U. of Chicago, 1925, 1945; Ph.D., New York U., 1928; m. Mrs. Rosalie Godfrey Dorser, Aug. 15, 1911; children—Harold Godfrey Pritchett (stepson), Annie Bird, Henry Lucian II, John Carr. Teacher of science, high sch., Greenville, Tex., 1908-09; asst. in edn., U. of Tex., 1909-11; prin. Cooper Sch. for Boys, Abilene, Tex., 1911; prof. edn., Polytechnic College, Fort Worth, Tex., 1912-14; instr. in edu., U. of Tex., summers 1914, 15, 16; head of dept. of edn., Sam Houston State Teachers Coll., 1916-24; prof. sociology Southern Meth. U., 1924-44; univ. student counselor; professional counselor in problems of the family; instr. in adm. sociology, New York U (leave of absence from Southern Methodist University) 1927; visiting professor educational biology New York Univ. S.S. 1944. Mem. adv. bd. Parent Edn. Clearing House. Mem. Orthonsobiatric Assn Nat. Soc. Mental Hygiene Am. Sociol Soc. American Assn. of MaoHage Counselors, N.Y. Acad Science Tex. Soc. for Mental Hygiene, Nat. Council on Family Relations, Lambda Chi Alpha, Phi Delta Kappa, Alpha Kappa Delta, Democrat. Methodist. Mason. (Shriner). Clubs: Town and Gown, Kiwanis, Home: Dallas, Tex. *

PRITZKER, JACK NICHOLAS, lawyer; b. Chgo., Jan. 6, 1904; s. Nicholas J. and Annie (Cohen) P.; A.B., U. Mich., 1926; J.D., Northwestern U., 1927; m. Rhoda R. Goldberg, Jan. 9, 1944; 1 son, Nicholas J. Admitted to Ill. bar, 1927, since practiced in Chgo.; partner firm Pritzker & Pritzker. Dir. Hyatt Internat. Corp. Hon. dir. Jewish Children's Bur. Chgo. Served to lt. comdr. USNR, 1942-45. Mem. Ill., Chgo. bar assns. Clubs: Arts Mid-Day, Standard (Chgo.); University (Sarasota, Fla.). Home: Chicago, Ill. Died Oct. 30, 1979; buried Meml. Park Cemetery, Chicago.

PRIZER, JOHN BUTLER, lawyer; b. Lancaster, Pa., Jan. 6, 1909; s. E. Tower and Jessie (Butler) P.; student Franklin and Marshall Acad., 1924, Mercersburg Acad., 1925; B.A., Amherst Coll., 1929; B.A., Cambridge U., Eng., 1931, M.A., 1936; LL.B., Harvard, 1934; LL.D., Woman's Med. Coll. Pa., 1966; m. Charlotte Upton McNab Darling, Oct. 15, 1937; children—John Butler, Charlotte Kelsey. Admitted to Pa. bar, 1935; law sec. to justice Pa. Supreme Ct., 1934-36; asst. solicitor Pa. R.R., 1936-38, asst. gen. solicitor, 1938-42, asst. to gen. counsel, 1942-45, asst. gen. counsel, 1945-47, gen. atty., 1947-52, gen. counsel, 1952-68, v.p., 1955-68; v.p., gen. counsel Penn Central Co. (merger Pa. R.R. and N.Y. Central), 1968-69; dir. Gen. Telephone & Electronics Corp. (N.Y.C.), Reliance Ins. Co. (Phila.); bd. mgrs. Germantown Savs. Bank Chmn., Springfield Twp. Planning Commn., 1948-52; gen. chmn. Phila. area Cancer Crusade, 1952; mem. Gov.'s Commn. on Pub. Library Devel. in Pa. Bd. dirs. Fund, Phila., Am. Cancer Soc., Phila.; trustee Chestnut Hill Hosp., Phila.; exec. com. Amherst Alumni Council, chmn., 1953-60; bd. corporators Woman's Med. Coll. Pa., chmn., 1957-65. Decorated hon. comdr. Order Brit. Empire; recipient Amherst Eminent Service medal, 1961. Fellow Am. Bar Found., Royal Soc. Arts London; mem. English Speaking Union (chmn. Phila. 1957-71, pres. 1951-57), Starr Centre Assn. Philadelphia (past pres.), Harvard Law Sch. Assn. Phila. (past pres.), Council Fgn. Relations, Internat., Am. (chmn. public utility law sect. 1958-59), Pa., Phila. bar assns., Am. Law Inst., Assn. ICC Practitioners, Juristic Soc. (past pres.), Am. Acad. Polit. and Social Sci., Acad. Polit. Sci., Colonial Wars Soc. Pa. (gov. 1964-67, dep. gov. gen. 1967), Colonial Soc. Pa., Adminstrv. Conf. U.S., Athenaeum Phila., Soc. Pilgrims U.S., Phi Beta Kappa. Republican. Episcopalian. Clubs: Philadelphia, Rittenhouse, Racquet, Philadelphia Cricket, Harvard (Phila.); Nat. Lawyers, Carleton (Washington); University, Brook (N.Y.C.). Home: Philadelphia, Pa. Died Oct. 8, 1976.

PROPP, LESLIE B., assn. exec.; b. Chgo., Oct. 21, 1918; s. Irwin and Lillian P.; B.S. in Mktg., Northwestern U., 1942; m. Eileen Barkar, Jan. 12, 1947; children—Carole, Douglas, Dennis. Product group mgr. Chgo. Musical Instrument Co., 1946-53, v.p., gen. sales mgr., 1953-69; exec. v.p. Norlin Music, Inc., Lincolnwood, Ill., 1969-74, pres., 1974-76, chmn., 1976-77; pres. Am. Music Conf., from 1977. Served to capt. USAAF, 1942-46. Home: Skokie, Ill. Deceased.

PROSSER, WALTER E., army officer; b. Ind., Jan. 18, 1882; s. Evan and Sarah (Cleland) P.; B.S., U.S. Mil. Acad., 1905; grad. F. A. Sch., 1910, Army Signal Sch., 1910, Sch. of the Line, 1921, Gen. Staff Sch., 1922, Army War Coll., 1923; m. Maude Willacy, June 19, 1922. Commd. 2d lt., U.S. Army, 1905, and advanced through the grades to maj. gen., 1941; retired as major gen. Oct. 31, 1945. Clubs: Army and Navy (Washington, D.C.); Lake Shore Athletic, Chicago Athletic (Chicago). Address: San Antonio, Tex. *

PROTHRO, ADOLPHUS MAYNARD, lawyer; b. Ferndale, Ark., Dec. 20, 1914; s. George and Ida E. (Jones) P.; A.B., Baylor U., 1934; LL.B., George Washington U., 1937; m. Carolyn L. Murphy, June 18, 1941; children—Carol Dawne, Martha Grace, David George. With FHA, 1934-69, dir. legal div., 1954-61, gen. counsel, 1961-69; admitted to D.C. bar, 1937, Va. bar 1938; pvt. practice law, 1969-77; professorial lectr. Am. U., 1948-78. Active local Boy Scouts Am. Served to col. U.S. Army, World War II; col. Res. Mem. Fed. Bar Assn. Presbyn. (past pres. trustee). Club: Nat. Lawyers (Washington). Home: Silver Spring, Md. Died Dec. 13, 1978; buried Arlington Nat. Cemetery.

PROVO, LARRY SHERMAN, railroad exec.; b. Mpls., Apr. 28, 1927; s. Clarence and Alice (Iverson) P.; B.B.A. with distinction, U. Minn., 1948; m. Lorraine Rhedin, Jan. 22, 1946; children—Steven Gary, Bruce Allen, Barbara Jo. Asst. accountant Arthur Andersen & Co., 1948-51, sr. accountant, 1951-52, mgr., 1952-54; v.p., comptroller Mpls. & St. Louis Ry. Co., Mpls., 1954-56; v.p., comptroller C. & N. W. Ry. Co., 1956-63, v.p. finance, 1963-66, exec. v.p., 1966-67, pres., 1967-72, chief exec. officer, 1968-76; pres., chief exec. officer, dir. Chgo. & North Western Transp. Co., 1972-76, chmn., dir., 1976; dir. No. Ill. Gas Co. Bd. dirs. Assn. Am. R.R.s Mem. Ry. Systems and Mgmt. Assn. Clubs: Chgo., Westmoreland Country, Executive, Economic, Mid-Am., Metropolitan (Chgo.) (Washington). Home: Northfield, Ill. Died Oct. 19, 1976; buried Memorial Park Cemetery, Skokie, Ill.

PRUD'HOMME, J. ALEX, lawyer; b. Montreal. Can., Nov. 21, 1886; s. Alexandre and Adele (Picard) P.; student Montreal Coll.; B.A., LL.B., Laval U.; m. Juliette Sainte-Pierre, Jan. 18, 1909; children—Lucile (Mrs. George E. Hamilton), Jeanine, (Mrs. Paul Leman), Ghislaine (Mrs. Henri Branchaud). Read law with Beaudin, Loranger and St. Germain; called to bar of Que., 1970, created King's Counsel, 1919; practice of law with L. L. Loranger, then Aimé Geoffrion; sr. partner Geoffrion and Prud'Homme, advocates and barristers, Montreal, 1946—. Vice pres,, dir. Aluminum Co. of Can., Ltd., A. Prud-homme & Fils, Ltée, dir. Catelli Food Products Ltd., Banque Canadienne Nationale, Nat. Trust Co., Ltd., Saguenay Power Co., Ltd., Westburne Oil Co., Ltd. Mem. Canadian Bar Assn. Roman Catholic. Home: Montreal. *

PRYOR, JOHN CARLISLE, lawyer; b. Abingdon, Va., Oct. 3, 1883; s. John Clark and Melissa (Hendricks) P.; Ph.B., Simpson Coll., 1907, D.C.L. (hon.); J.D., U. Chgo., 1910; m. Elizabeth E. Smith, June 10, 1912 (dec.); children—John (dec.), Elizabeth Hacker. Admitted to Iowa bar and bars of Fed. Cts., U.S. Supreme Ct. and Fed. agys.; practice of law in Council Bluffs, Iowa, 1910-21, Burlington, Iowa, 1922-79; mem. firm Pryor, Riley, Jones and Walsh; dist. atty. C., B&Q. R.R. Co., 1922-79; asst. gen. counsel FCA, Omaha, 1938-43, Iowa State Relief Adminstr., 1935-37; mem. Iowa Uniform Law Commn., 1933—; pres. Nat. Conf. Uniform Law Commrs., 1942-46; mem. editorial bd. Uniform Coml. Code, 1943-79; mem. U.S. Supreme Ct. adv. com. on rules of civil procedure in U.S. Dist. Cts. Vice pres., now chmn., dir. Mississippi Valley Savs. & Loan Assn., 1938-79. Chief counsel preclusive operations Bd. Econ. Warfare, 1943; legal adviser Am. embassy, London; Am. mem. of Contraband Control Com., London. Chmn. adv. bd. Salvation Army, now life mem.; mem. Bd. Edn., Council Bluffs, 1918-22, pres. 1922, Burlington, 1926-32. Dem. candidate for Congress, 9th Ia. Dist., 1916; del., Dem. Nat. Conv., 1948. Trustee YMCA. Recipient award of merit Ia. Bar Assn., 1960. Fellow Am. Bar Found.; mem. Am. Bar Assn. (mem. ho. dels. 1941-44), Iowa (pres. 1936-37), Des Moines County bar assns., Am. Law Inst., Am. Soc. Internat. Law, Am. Judicature Soc. (dir. 1936-38), Burlington Lines Vets. Assn., Alpha Tau Omega. Conglist. Mason, Elk, Rotarian (pres. Council Bluffs 1921. Burlington 1932-33; mem. Internat. Com. on Constn. and Bylaws at Edinburgh Conv., 1921). Rotarian (hon.). Contbr. articles to profl. jours. Home: Burlington, Iowa. Died May 8, 1979.

PRYOR, JOSEPH WILLIAM, anatomist; b. Palmyra, Mo., Apr. 3, 1856; s. Joseph William and Frances Frazier (Bailey) P.; M.D., U. of Mo., 1876; m. Eleanor P. Hancock, 1898. Prof. anatomy and physiology, U. of Ky., since 1890. Mem. Am., Ky. State and Fayette County med. assns., Am. Assn. Anatomists, A.A.A.S., Beta Theta Pi. Democrat. Presbyterian. Clubs: Country, Research (pres.). Author monographs relating to field since 1905; latest publ.; Autobiography, 1943. Mem. Sigma Xi. Home: Lexington, Ky. *

PRYOR, THOMAS MARION, bishop; b. Cairo, Ill., Feb. 28, 1904; s. Thomas Jefferson and Esther (Handley) P.; B.A., U. Mich., 1926, M.A., 1927, Ph.D., 1933; S.T.B., Boston U., 1929; grad. student Sorbonne, Paris, France, Heidelberg (Germany) U., also Harvard; D.D., Adrian Coll., 1962; m. Alice Wuerfel, Sept. 5, 1925; children—Thomas H., Nancy Sharon (Mrs. Karl Kienholz), Mary Ann (Mrs. Roderick Daane), David Bruce. Ordained to ministry Methodist Ch., 1927; minister in Royal Oak, Mich., 1934-50, Kalamazoo, 1950-64; bishop Chgo. area, 1964-72; spl. assignment Council of Bishops, 1972—. Mem. World Council Methodist, 1944—, del. Oxford Conf., 1951, Oslo Conf., 1961; del. Gen. Conf. Meth. Ch., 1960, 64, Jurisdictional Conf., 1944, 48, 56, 60, 64; mem. gen. bd. edn. Meth. Ch.; mem. program council and ecumenical affairs commn. United Meth. Ch., then. gen. conf. com. study ministry, 1960-64; chmn. Mich. Pastor's Conf., 1959; mem. Gov. Mich. Com. Higher Edn., 1963-64; Mich. exchange minister, Nottingham, Eng., 1955; mem. Sherwood Eddy Seminar, Europe, 1951, Bd. Social Concerns Seminar, Russia, 1961; world tour for Meth. Missions, 1958. Trustee Kendall Coll., N. Central Coll., Northwestern U., Wesley Meml. Hosp., Chgo., 1964-72, Evangel. Theol. Sem., Naperville, Ill., Garrett Theol. Sem., Evanston, Ill., 1964-72. Recipient Distinguished Alumnus award Boston U. Sch. Theology, 1966. Mem. Theta Phi, Alpha Kappa Delta,

Kappa Delta Rho. Club: Union League (Chgo.). Home: Sarasota, Fla. Died July 15, 1979.

PUFFER, CLAUDE EMIGH, univ. exec.; b. Lake City, Ia., Feb. 13, 1905; s. Frank S. and Cora (Wood) P.; B.B.A., U. Wash., 1932, M.A., 1933; Ph.D., Stanford, 1941; m. Jessie A. Williams, Aug. 15, 1934; children—Frank W., John H., William C. Traffic clk. C.B. & Q. R.R., 1925-27; clk. Fruit Growers Express Co., 1927-30; state supt. U.S. Bur. Labor Statistics, 1933-34; asst. to dir. Nat. Power Survey, 1934-35; instr. econs. U. Pitts., 1935-37, research fellow Stanford, 1937-38; instr. econs. U. Buffalo, 1938-41, asst. prof., 1941-42, asso. prof., 1942, prof., 1942-73, emeritus, 1973-76, acting dean Sch. Bus. Adminstrn., 1942-45, dean adminstrn., 1945-51, treas., comptroller, 1951-56, vice chancellor, 1956-63, v.p., 1963-73. Trustee Buffalo Savs. Bank; former mem. bd. dirs. Buffalo Research Assos., Western N.Y. Nuclear Research Center; former sec., treas. U. Buffalo Found., Inc. Cons. Middle States Assn. Colls. and Univs., from 1966; former mem. finance com. of bd. trustees Coll. Entrance Exam. Bd. Econ. adv. Buffalo regional office OPA, 1941-45; mem. Niagara Frontier Post War Planning Bd., 1941-44; mem. research com. Com. Econ. Development. Erie County, N.Y., 1943-46; dir. Community Radio Exchange, Buffalo, 1943-46; dir. Bur. Municipal Research, Buffalo, 1947-51; mem. bd. community relations City Buffalo 1947-54; adv. council, former bd. dirs. Western N.Y. Ednl. TV Assn. Mem. Am. Econs. Assn., Am. Assn. U. Profs., Atlantic Union Com. (nat. council), Buffalo C. of C. (chmn. 1956-57), Eastern Assn. Coll. and U. Bus. Officers (exec. com. 1967-68), Newcomen Soc., Phi Beta Kappa, Phi Eta Sigma, Beta Gamma Sigma, Alpha Tau Omega, Presbyn. Independent. Clubs: University (Buffalo). Author: Air Transportation, 1941; Regulation of Air Carriers, 1949; Air Transportation Services, Facilities and Rates, 1949; also numerous articles. Home: Buffalo, N.Y. Died Jan. 6, 1976.

PULLEN, WILLIAM RUSSELL, librarian; b. Lexington, Va., Nov. 10, 1919; s. James Edward and Nettie Allen (Mays) P.; B.A., U. N.C., 1942, B.S. in L.S., 1947, M.A., 1948, Ph.D. in Polit. Sci., 1951; m. Pauline Purdin Evans, July 7, 1949; children—Linda Belle, Mark Evans. Asst. to dir. State Records Microfilm project Library of Congress, 1949-50; documents librarian U. N.C. Library, 1951-57, asst. librarian, 1957-58; librarian Ga. State U., Atlanta, 1959-74. Served with USAAF, 1942-45. Fellow Carnegie Project Advanced Library Adminstrn., Rutgers U., 1958; Ga. State U. Library named in his honor, 1975. Mem. A.L.A., Southeastern, Ga. library assns., Alpha Kappa Psi, Omicron Delta Kappa, Phi Kappa Phi; Methodist. Editor; Southeastern Librarian, 1961-64. Compiler: A Check List of Legislative Journals, 1955. Home: Atlanta, Ga. Died Oct. 23, 1974.

PULLING, HOWARD EDWARD, educator; b. Wausau, Wis., Feb. 3, 1886; s. Bradley Webster and Emma (Bouldrie) P.; A.B., Beloit (Wis.) Coll., 1910; Ph.D., U. of Wis., 1915, fellow, 1912-13; m. Mildred Bell Hosler, July 14, 1915; 1 son, Nathan Hosler. Instr. botany, U. of Wis., 1913-15; Johns Hopkins U., 1915-19; asst. prof. botany Wellesley Coll., 1919-20, asso. prof., 1920-23, prof. since 1923; lectr. bio-physics, 1923-33, chmn. dept. botany, 1938-45; research asst., Carnegie Inst., 1913. Mem. A.A.A.S., Am. Soc. Plant Physiology, Botanical Soc. Am., N.E. Botanical Club, Torrey Botanical Club. Contbr. articles in scientific jours. Home: Wellesley, Mass. *

PUMPIAN-MINDLIN, EUGENE, physician, educator; b. N.Y.C., July 18, 1908; s. Herman and Bessie (Levitz) P.; B.S., U. Va., 1928; M.D., U. Zurich, 1935; m. Martha Leader, Jan. 26, 1952; children—Fredric, Eva Bess, Michelle, Ilya. Resident Met. Hosp., N.Y.C., 1937, Mt. Sinai Hosp., N.Y.C., 1938-39, Bellevue Hosp., N.Y.C., 1939-40; asst. clin. psychiatrist N.Y. Med. Coll., 1941-46; dir. mental hygiene clinic VA, Los Angeles, 1946-52, chief, 1952-60; mem. faculty U. So. Calif., Los Angeles, 1952-63; dir. out-patient dept. Neuropsychiat. Inst., UCLA Med. Center, 1960-63; chief adult psychiatry div. U. Okla. Hosp., 1963-69, also chief mental hygiene clinic VA Hosp., Oklahoma City; prof. psychiatry, vice chmn. dept. psychiatry U. Okla. Sch. Medicine, 1963-69; asso. prof. Med. Sch., UCLA, 1960-63, prof. psychiatry, vice chmn. dept. psychiatry, 1969-76; tng. analyst So. Calif. Psychoanalytic Inst., 1955-76. Served to capt. M.C., AUS, 1942-46; ETO. Fellow Am. Psychiat. Assn. (life), A.A.A.S.; mem. Am. Psychoanalytic Assn., So. Calif. Psychoanalytic Inst., So. Calif. Psychiat. Soc. (pres. 1956-57), Alpha Omega Alpha. Author: Psychoanalysis as Science, 2d edit., 1956, others. Contbr. articles to profl. jours. Editorial bd. Jour. Nervous and Mental Disease, 1961-70, Jour. Am. Psychoanalytic Assn., 1966-69. Home: Beverly Hills, Calif. Died July 24, 1976.

PURDOM, JOHN LESLIE, b. Parksville, Ky., Jan. 20, 1882 s. Thomas Mark and Lucy Ann (Conder) P. AdB., Centre Coll. Danville, Ky., 1906; A. M. Harvard, 1911, PhD. 1819; m. Bessie M. Frein, Great Barrington, Mass., July 27, 1916; children—Mary Lucy Thomas Irving, Teacher dist. sch. Boy County Ky. 1901-03 Acad. of U. of Ky., 1906-09 prin. Searles High Sch. Great Barrington, 1911-14; supt sch same city, 1914-16; prof. secondary edn., U. of Ark., 1918-19; teacher of sociology, Harris Teachers Coll., St. Louis, 1919-22, prin., 1922-30; pres. Harris Teachers Coll. and Stowe Teachers Coll. since 1930; visiting prof. University of Wis., summer 1931. Mem N.E.A. and Dept. Superintendence same, Mo. State Teachers Assn., Mo. Social Hygiene Assn. (dir.), Phi Delta Kappa. Methodist. Mason (Shriner), Odd Fellow. Clubs: Harvard, Public Question. Home: St. Louis, Mo. *

PURDUM, ERNEST ALEXANDER (PÛ'DUM), physician; b. Appomattox, Va., May 13, 1886; s. Edward E. and Mattie W. Purdum; prep. education, high sch., Newport News, Va.; M.D., U. of Va., 1910; m. Nelle Ashby Martin, Dec. 23, 1912; children—Eloise Ashby, Emily Virginia. Intern Univ. of Va. Hosp. 1 yr. and instr. med. dept. of the univ., 1 yr.; settled at Hot Springs, Ark., 1912; associated in practice with late Dr. E. H. Martin for 9 yrs. Mem. Am. and Southern med. assns., Ark. State and Garland County med. socs., Am. Urol. Assn., International Soc. Med. Hydrology, Phi Beta Pi, Alpha Omega Alpha. Democrat. Presbyterian. Mason (Shriner), Elk Club; Hot Springs Country. Home: St. Louis, Mo. *

PURDY, ALEXANDER CONVERSE (PUR'DI), theol. prof.; b. West Laurens, N.Y., May 6, 1890; s. Ellison Reynolds and Amelia Frances (Converse) P.; A.B., Penn Coll., Oskaloosa, Iowa, 1910; B.D., Hartford Theol. Sem., 1913, Ph.D., 1916; studied U. Marburg, Germany, Harvard; LL.D., Earlham Coll., Richmond, Ind., 1958, Swarthmore Coll., 1964; D.D. (hon.), Penn Coll., Oskaloosa, Iowa, 1960; m. Jeannette Hadley, May 15, 1914; children—Adalyn Frances (Mrs. Edmund Jones), Thomas Ellison, Donald Alexander. Prof. Bibl. lit. and ch. history Earlham Coll., Richmond, Ind., 1916-23; Hosmer prof. N.T., Hartford Theol. Sem., 1923-60, Hosmer prof. emeritus, 1960-76, dean Hartford Theol. Sem., 1954, 60, dean emeritus, 1960-76, acting pres., 1944-45; acting chaplain Stanford U., 1939; acting dir. Pendle Hill (on leave), 1940; vis. prof. Earlham Coll., 1960-76. Chmn. of Friends Fellowship Council, Friends World Com. School minister Moses Brown Sch., Providence; dir. Foxhowe Assn., Buck Hill Falls, Pa. Mem. Soc. Bibl. Lit. and Exegesis. Quaker. Author: The Way of Christ, 1918; Pathways to God, 1922; Jesus' Way With People, 1926; Jew and Greek: Tutors unto Christ (with G. H. C. Macgregor), 1936; Jesus as His Followers Knew Him, 1944; The Gospel and Epistles of John, 1946; columnist Tchrs. Sunday Sch. Quar. Preacher and lecturer at colls., schs. and summer confs. Home: Swarthmore, Pa. Died Apr. 10, 1976.

PURDY, JOHN EARL, lawyer; b. Bklyn., Apr. 14, 1933; s. John E. and Virginia C. (Clark) P.; B.A. cum laude, Amherst Coll., 1954; LL.B., Columbia, 1960; m. Dorrit Werner, Dec. 10, 1955; children—John Christopher, Wynne Crossley. Admitted to Ohio bar, 1960, since practiced in Cleve.; asso. Lane, Krotinger, Santora, Stone & Purdy, 1960-63, partner, 1963-70; pres. Purdy & Stone, 1971-73. Sec., dir. Revco D.S., Inc.; sec. Waco Equipment Co. Served to 1st lt. USAF, 1955-57. Recipient Nathan Burkan Copyright award, 1960. Mem. Ohio, Cuyahoga County, Cleve. bar assns., Phi Alpha Psi. Presbyn. Clubs: Cleve. Athletic, Cleve. Racquet; Aurora Country. Home: Chagrin Falls, Ohio. Died Oct. 24, 1973.

PURDY, THEODORE MARTINDALE, editor; b. Short Hills, N.J., Sept. 22, 1903; s. Theodore Martindale and Helen (Van Dyk) P.; student St. Paul's Sch., Concord, N.H.; B.A., Yale, 1925; student Sorbonne, also Ecole des Sciences Politiques, Paris, 1926-27; m. Elizabeth McKee, June 14, 1946. Book reviewer, free-lance writer, N.Y.C. and London, 1933-37; asso. editor Macmillan Co., N.Y.C., 1937-42; editor-in-chief Appleton-Century-Crofts, 1946-50; editor-in-chief G.P. Putnam's Sons, N.Y.C., 1950, dir., 1952-59, v.p., 1953-57; pres. Coward-McCann, Inc., 1957-59; dir. Purdy-Carlisle-Dodds, Inc.; editor Meredith Press, 1961-70; contbg. editor Hawthorn Books, also G.P. Putnam's Sons, 1970-79. Pres. Am.-Portuguese Cultural Soc., 1970-79. Served to maj. M.I., C.E., 3d Army, AUS, 1942-46. Decorated Bronze Star. Episcopalian. Clubs: Century, Yale, P.E.N. (N.Y.C.). Home: New York, N.Y., also Roxbury, Conn. Died July 12, 1979.

PURTELL, WILLIAM ARTHUR, ex-senator; b. Hartford, Conn., May 6, 1897; s. Thomas M. and Nora (O'Connor) P.; student pub. schs., Hartford; LL.D., Trinity College, Hillyer College; married Katherine E. Cassidy, Dec. 30, 1919; children—William Arthur, Margaret Mary. Various positions mfg. concerns, Hartford, 1919-29; pres., treas., gen. mgr. Billings & Spencer Co., forging machinery and forged tools, Hartford, 1937-44, dir., chmn. exec. com., 1944-47; pres., treas., gen. mgr., dir. Holo-Krome Screw Corp., Hartford, 1929-52; v.p., treas., gen. mgr. Sparmal Engring. Corp., 1938-52; dir. Colts Mfg. Co., Connecticut Bank & Trust Company, Veeder-Root, Inc., Hartford Gas Company; National Fire Insurance Co.; apptd. interim U.S. senator from Conn. to fill unexpired term of late Brian McMahon, Aug. 1952, elected for full term November, 1952. Resigned all ofcl. positions and directorships upon election to Senate. Trustee, Robinson School. Served with the radio section, Signal Corps, AEF, 1918-19. Recipient citation NCCJ; merit award Hardware Merchants and Mfrs. Assn., 1958. Mem. Am. Soc. Tool and Mfg. Engrs. (life mem.), Am. Supply and Machinery Mfrs. Assn. (life dir.), Am. Legion. Roman Catholic. Home: Old Saybrook, Conn. Deceased.

PURVES, ROBERT OGDEN, organization exec.; b. Philadelphia, Feb. 15, 1895; s. Alexander and Helen (Ogden) P.; student, Choate Sch. (Conn.), 1912-15, Columbia, 1916-17; m. Marjorie Taylor, Oct. 23, 1926; children—Helen Ogden, Alexander. Financial sec., Hampton Inst., Va., 1918-28, asst. treas., 1929-31, treas., 1932-40, vice pres., treasurer, 1940-42, acting pres., 1951-52, now chairman of trustees; assistant manager, asst. mgr., North Atlantic area, A.R.C., 1942-46, mgr., 1946-49, nat. v.p., 1947-49; dir. field orgns. Am. Cancer Soc., 1949-50. V.p. So. Edn. Found. serving field of Negro edn.; mem. com. Youth Bur. of Community Service Soc., N.Y.; trustee, Hampton Inst., Penn Community Services, Inc. (S.C.). Served U.S. Army, 1917-18. Awarded Columbia U. Alumni medal, 1936. Mem. Delta Psi. Presbyn. (elder). Club: St. Anthony (New York). Home: New York, N.Y. Died July 6, 1976.

PURYEAR, BENNET, JR. (PÛR'REAR), marine corps officer; b. Richmond, Va., Jan. 9, 1884; s. Bennet and Ella (Wyles) P.; Tex. Agrl. and Mech., U., 1903-05, Marine Corps Sch. Application, 1905-66, Field Officers School, senior course, 1928-29; married Harriet Newell Hill (dec.), Dec. 12, 1906; 1 son, Alan Christian; married 2d, C. Elizabeth Gary, October, 1943. Commd. 2d lieut., 1905, and advanced through the grades to brig gen., Aug. 1942; retired May 1, 1944 with rank of major general; served in Cuba, Isle of Pines, 1906-09; Parris Island, 1909-11; Phillippines, 1911-14; Mare Island, 1914-17; 5th Marines, 2d Div., in France and Germany, 1917-19; hdqrs. Marine Corps, 1919-25; Haiti, 1925-28; Phila. Depot. 1929-30; hdqrs. Marine Corps. 1930-36; San Diego, 1936-37; Quantico, Va., 1937-42; hdqrs. Marine Corps, 1942-43. Decorated Navy Cross, Purple Heart, Croix de Guerre, Haitian D.S.M., Medal of Merit. Home: 918 28th St., Arlington, Va. Address: Arlington, Va. *

PUTNAM, FREDERIC LAWRENCE, investment banker; b. Salem, Mass., Oct. 15, 1895; s. Eben and Florence Maud (Tucker) P.; grad. Wellesley High Sch., 1915; war certificate, Harvard, 1919; m. 2d, Margaret E. Wilson, Oct. 1938; children—David Ward, Margaret Gail, John Stephen, Patricia Florence; children by 1st marriage—Gladys Brown, Frederic Lawrence. With banking houses R. M. Grant & Co. and Watkins & Co., 1918-23; organized banking firm Putnam & Storer, Inc., Boston, 1923, now F.L. Putnam & Co., Inc.; chmn. bd. Cape Cod Gas Co.; chmn., trustee Colonial Gas Energy System; chmn. bd. Lowell Gas Co. (Mass.), Gas, Inc.; adv. dir. Union Nat. Bank, Lowell. Trustee St. Joseph's Hosp., Lowell. Served with inf. U.S. Army, 1918. Clubs: Harvard (Boston and N.Y.C.); Yacht (Boston). Home: Newton Centre, Mass. Died May 2, 1977.

PUTNAM, ROBERT GARFIELD, educator; b. Spencer, Mass., Nov. 20, 1886; s. George Austin and Jane Stearns (Garland) P.; B.S., Worcester (Mass.) Poly Inst., 1912; M.S., U. Pittsburgh; Ph.D., U. Chicago, 1924; m. Mary Edna Schulte Oct. 9, 1919; children—Harry Reid, Robert Austin, Esther Jane. High sch. teacher, Newton, Mass., 1912-14; elec. tester and engr., Westinghouse Elec. Co., East Pittsburgh, Pa., 1915-19; instr. U. Pittsburgh, 1919-22; mem. faculty N.Y.U. since 1923, prof. mathematics since 1945, mem. research group, mathematics, 1948-49. Mem. Am. Math. Soc., Math. Assn. Am. Mem. Dutch Ref. Ch. Mason. Home: Tarrytown, N.Y. *

PUTNAM, WINDSOR BRIGGS, lawyer; b. San Francisco, Aug. 1, 1903; s. Edward Williston and Eleanor Craft (Briggs) P.; A.B., U. Cal. at Berkeley, 1925; LL.B., Harvard, 1928; m. Simone Hermine Tremblay, Dec. 31, 1949. Admitted to N.Y. bar, 1930, practiced in N.Y.C.; mem. firm Patterson Belknap & Webb, and predecessor, from 1945. Dir. Richmond-Eureka Mining Co., Boston, 1941-64, Stewart Hall, Inc., N.Y.C., 1947-50. Founder, 1st pres. Interfraternity Council U. Cal. at Berkeley, 1925. Mem. Am., N.Y. State bar assns., Assn. Bar City N.Y., Am. Judicature Soc., Nat. Legal Aid and Defender Assn., Sierra Club, Chi Phi. Made 1st ascents peaks in Sierra Nev. and Canadian Rocky Mountains, 1921-24. Contbr. mountaineering jours. Home: New York, N.Y. Died May 11, 1976; buried Jamaica, West Indies.

PYE, WILLARD DICKISON, cons. geologist, educator; b. Merzifon, Turkey, Feb. 20, 1915 (parents U.S. citizens); s. Ernest and DeEtta (Dickison) P.; A.B., Oberlin Coll., 1935; M.S., Cal. Inst. Tech., 1937; Ph.D., U. Chgo., 1942; m. Margaret M. Hurst, Dec. 25, 1940; children—Kathryne Rose, Brian Hurst, Margaret Jane. Geophysicist Shell Oil Co., 1936; geologist Carter Oil Co. div. Exxon Corp., 1937-40; research Ill. Geol. Survey, 1940-42; charge chem. warfare research Nat.

Def. Research Corp., 1942-43; charge Ida.-Utah dist. The Texas Co., 1943-46, research geologist Rocky Mountain div., 1946-47; prof., chmn. dept. geology and geography N.D. State U., 1947-57; Nat. Sci. Research asso., 1953, 54; exec. sec. Yellowstone-Bighorn Research Assn., 1954-55; dir. N.D. Inst. Regional Studies, 1955-57; pres. N.W. Investors Research, 1956-57; prof. geology U. Ariz., 1957-70; cons. geologist, 1970-81; pres. Devex Corp. Geol. adviser Ariz. Oil and Gas Commn., 1964-70. Mem. Ariz. Geological Soc., Am. Assn. Petroleum Geologists, Ariz. Oil and Gas Assn. (pres. 1965-66, dir. 1961-81), Geol. Soc. Am., Soc. Econ. Paleontologists and Mineralogists, Sigma Xi, Phi Beta Kappa. Contbr. profl. jours. Home: Tucson, Ariz. Died May 26, 1981.

PYLES, THOMAS, philologist; b. Frederick, Md., June 5, 1905; s. Joseph Thomas and Charlotte (Bowers) P.; B.A., U. Md., 1926, M.A., 1927; Ph.D., Johns Hopkins, 1938; m. Bessie Alice Yort, Dec. 21, 1929; 1 son, Thomas. With dept. English, U. Md., 1927-44; instr. English, Johns Hopkins, 1938-44; prof. English U. Okla., 1944-48; prof. English, U. Fla., 1948-66, prof. emeritus, 1972-80; prof. English and linguistics Northwestern U., 1966-71, prof. emeritus, 1971-80; guest prof. English philology U. Göttingen (Germany), 1956-57; vis. prof. N.Y. U., summer 1965, Northwestern U., 1965-66. Mem. editorial adv. bd. Funk and Wagnalls Standard Dictionary, 1963; mem. internat. editorial adv. com. World Book Dictionary, 1963, 76; editorial adv. com. Thorndike-Barnhart Coll. Dictionary, 1965-80. Mem. Am. Dialect Soc. (sec. 1952-56, v.p. 1958-60, pres. 1960-62), Linguistic Soc. Am., Modern Lang. Assn., Modern Humanities Research Assn., Am. Name Soc. (bd. mgrs 1960-63), Internat. Assn. U. Profs. English, Phi Beta Kappa. Episcopalian. Author: Words and Ways of American English, 1952; The Origins and Development of the English Language, 3d rev. edit., 1980; The English Language: A Brief History, 1968; (with John Algeo) English: An Introduction to Language, 1970; Thomas Pyles: Selected Essays on English Usage (edited by John Algeo), 1979; also articles, revs.; editorial adv. bd. Dictionary Am. Regional English; adviser to editors Ency. Brit., 1968-76; editorial adv. com. Am. Speech, 1966-67, 70-71; editor: (with S.V. Larkey) An Herbal, 1941; Home: Gainesville, Fla. Died Apr. 25, 1980; buried Gainesville.

PYNE, DAVID THOMAS, banker; b. Oneonta, N.Y., Dec. 8, 1908; s. William John and Margaret Cecelia (Callahan) P.; grad. Am. Inst. Banking, 1931; m. Anne Cecelia Clyne, Aug. 19, 1935; children—David, James, Anne (Mrs. Albert E. Altongy), Daniel, John. With Marine Midland Bank (and predecessors), Utica, N.Y., 1925-57; with Am. Nat. Bank & Trust (and predecessors), Morristown, N.J., 1960-74, First Trust & Deposit Co., Utica, N.Y., 1974-80; dir. Gillespie-Deka Corp., Lithonia, Ga., Remet Corp., Chadwicks, N.Y. Home: New Hartford, N.Y. Died Jan. 6, 1980.

QUAIL, JOHN JOSEPH, investment banker; b. Rhinelander, Wis., Sept. 17, 1893; s. Alexander Finley and Catherine (O'Connell) Q.; A.B., U. Wis., 1917; m. Rhea Bollman, Sept. 3, 1924 (dec. Sept. 4, 1957); 1 son, John Patrick; m. 2d, Mary Blake Garside, May 6, 1967. Salesman Nat. City Co. of N.Y., 1917-22; v.p. Priester, Quail & Cundy, Inc., Davenport, Ia., 1922-39; pres. Quail & Co., 1939-67; vice chmn. bd. Dain, Kalman & Quail, Inc., 1967-71, cons., 1971-77; past dir. numerous corps. Mem. N.Y. Stock Exchange 1956-67. Trustee St. Ambrose Coll., Davenport Municipal Art Gallery. Served first lt. F.A., AUS, World War I. Mem. Nat. Assn. Security Dealers (gov. 1944-46, treas. 1946), Investment Bankers Assn. (gov. 1952-54). Republican. Roman Catholic. Club: University (Chgo.). Home: Davenport, Iowa. Died May 21, 1977; buried Mt. Calvary Cemetery, Davenport.

QUAIN, EDWIN ALPHONSUS, clergyman, publisher; b. N.Y.C., Apr. 6, 1906; s. John and Nora (Cunneen) Q.; A.B., Woodstock Coll., 1929, A.M., 1930, S.T.L., 1937; Ph.D., Harvard, 1941; L.H.D., Georgetown U., 1972. Joined Soc. of Jesus, 1924, ordained priest Roman Catholic Ch., 1936; tchr. Greek and English, Georgetown Prep. Sch., 1930-33; instr. dept. classics Grad. Sch., Fordham U., 1941-45, asst. prof., 1945-48, asso. prof., 1948-55, prof., 1955-75, dean Grad. Sch., 1951-53, acad. v.p., 1952-56, dir. univ. press, 1947-52, 56-72; acting pres. U. Scranton, 1975. Bd. dirs. Georgetown U., 1966-72, chmn., 1968-72, acting pres., 1969. Mem. Am. Philol. Assn., Jesuit Ednl. Assn., Nat. Cath. Ednl. Assn., Assn. Am. Univ. Presses. Club: Grolier. Author (with others) A Monument to St. Jerome, 1952. Co-editor Traditio, 1950-75. Translator (with others) Works of Tertullian, 1950, 2d vol., 1959. Contbr. articles to learned jours. Home: Bronx, N.Y. Died Dec. 23, 1975; buried Auriesville, N.Y.

QUARLES, CHARLES SAMUEL, lawyer; b. Milw., Sept. 11, 1917; s. Louis and Inez (French) Q.; A.B., U. Mich., 1939, J.D. 1942; m. Mary Elizabeth Koch, Sept. 7, 1940; children—Sally Ann (Mrs. Francis Smith), Mary Louise (Mrs. Frank Reuter), William Louis, Nancy Alice (Mrs. Timothy Oakes). Admitted to Wis. bar, 1942, since practiced in Milw.; partner firm Quaries & Brady and predecessors, 1952-73, of counsel, 1974-76. Dir., Classified Financial Corp., Classified Ins. Corp., Classified Life Ins. Corp., Hunter Machinery Corp., Eggers Plywood Co., Eggers Hardwood Products Corp., Utility Products Co., M-B Co. Inc. Wis. Trustee, Whitefish Bay, Wis., 1949-52; chmn. Whitefish Bay Fire and Police Commn., from 1956. Bd. dirs. Wis. Heart Assn., 1951-70, pres., 1955-56, chmn. bd., 1968-70; bd. dirs. St. Mary's Hill Hosp., 1972-76. Served with USAAF, 1942-45. Mem. Am. Legion, Scimitar (pres. 1937-39), Zeta Psi (treas. 1937-38). Clubs: Univ., U. of Mich. (pres. Milw. 1949). Home: Milwaukee, Wis. Died Feb. 20, 1976.

QUICK, ARMAND JAMES, med. educator; b. Theresa, Wis., July 18, 1894; s. Gabriel and Theresa (Meixensperger) Q.; B.S., U. Wis., 1918, M.S., 1919; Ph.D., U. Ill., 1922; postgrad. U. Pa., 1924-26; M.D., Cornell U., 1928; D.Sc. (hon.), Marquette U., 1973; m. Margaret Koll, July 2, 1937; children—Elizabeth (dec.), Edith Mary Quick Ebel. Asst. in chemistry U. Wis., 1918-19; instr. chemistry Vanderbilt U., 1919-20; asst. chemist Phila. Gen. Hosp., 1921-22; instr. physiol. chemistry Sch. Medicine, U. Pa., 1922-26; intern Phila. Gen. Hosp., 1928-30; asso. in research surgery Cornell U. Med. Coll., 1930-32, also asst. physician Cornell Clinic; fellow Fifth Ave. Hosp., 1932-34; asso. prof. pharmacology Sch. Medicine, Marquette U., Milw., 1935-44, prof. biochemistry, chmn. dept., 1944-64, prof. emeritus, 1964-78, research prof. Hemostasis Research Lab., 1972-78. Recipient gold medal for sci. exhibit A.M.A., 1944, Modern Medicine award, 1954, Wis. Med. Soc. Council award, 1950; John Phillips Meml. award A.C.P., 1961, Distinguished Service award Wis. Med. Soc., 1964, Pere Marquette Faculty award Marquette U., 1964, award Alumni Assn. Cornell U. Med. Coll., 1966, James F. Mitchell Found. Internat. award for heart and vascular research, 1967, Distinguished Service award Marquette Sch. Medicine, 1970; Beaumont lectr. Wayne County Med. Soc., 1941; Lewis Linn McArthur lectr. Inst. Medicine, Chgo., 1946. Mem. Am. Chem. Soc., A.M.A., A.A.A.S., Soc. Exptl. Biology and Medicine, Am. Soc. Biol. Chemists, Am. Soc. Hematology, Am., Wis. heart assns., Milw. County Med. Soc., Milw. Internist Soc., Internat. Hemophilia Soc., European Soc. Haematology, Société Soisse d'Hématologie, Am. Soc. Pharmacology and Exptl. Therapeutics, Central Soc. Clin. Research, French Nat. Acad. Medicine (fgn. corr.), Milw. Acad. Medicine, N.Mex. Clin. Soc. (hon.), Phi Beta Kappa, Sigma Xi, Alpha Omega Alpha, Omicron Kappa Upsilon, Phi Lambda Upsilon. Author: The Hemorrhagic Diseases and the Physiology of Hemostasis, 1942; The Physiology and Pathology of Hemostasis, 1951; Hemorrhagic Diseases, 1957; Bleeding Problems in Clinical Medicine, 1970; Hemorrhagic Diseases and Thrombosis, 1966; The Hemorrhagic Diseases and the Pathology of Hemostasis, 1973; contbr. to Sahyun's Outline of the Amino Acids and Proteins, 1944; Tice's Practice of Medicine, 1947; Pharmacological Principles of Medical Practice, 1969; Coagulazione e Trombosi, 1971; numerous others. Home: Milwaukee, Wis. Died Jan. 26, 1978; buried Theresa, Wis.

QUIGLEY, ARTHUR H., business exec.; b. Litchfield, Conn., 1822. Chmn. bd. Am. Brass Co.; pres. dir. Anaconda Am. Brass Co., Ltd., New Toronto, Ont.; dir. Anaconda Wire & Cable Co., Waterbury Trust Co., Boston Mfrs. Mutual Fire Ins. Co. Address: Waterbury, Conn. *

QUIGLEY, CARROLL, historian, educator; b. Boston, Nov. 9, 1910; s. William Francis and Mary Frances (Carroll) Q.; A.B. magna cum laude, Harvard, 1933, A.M., 1934, Ph.D. (Travelling fellow), 1938; m. Lillian Fox, May 22, 1937; children—Denis Carroll, Thomas Fox. Instr. history Princeton, 1935-37; instr., tutor history Harvard, 1938-41; lectr. history and civilization Sch. Fgn. Service, Georgetown U., 1941-47, prof., 1947-76; hon. faculty Indsl. Coll. Armed Forces, 1968-77; frequent lectr., cons. Dept. Def., from 1951; cons. history Smithsonian Instn., 1957-60; cons. select com. astronautics and space exploration U.S. Congress, 1958; lectr. Brookings Instn., 1961-77; Fgn. Service Inst., Dept. State, 1961-77, Dept. Agr. Grad. Sch., 1967-77. U.S. Civil Service Commn., 1967-69; cons. USN Advanced Seabased Deterrence Project, Monterey, Cal., 1964; cons. social sci. curriculum Montgomery County (Md.) Pub. Schs., 1967-77. Recipient Vicennial medal Georgetown U., 1961, 175th Anniversary medal of merit, 1964. Fellow Am. Anthrop. Assn.; mem. Am. Hist. Assn., Am. Econ. Assn., Internat. Soc. Comparative Study Civilizations (mem. council), Con. Brit. Studies, English Speaking Union Commonwealth London (life), Anthrop. Soc. Washington, Royal Commonwealth Soc. (London), Soc. Gen. Systems Research, A.A.A.S. Club: Harvard (Washington). Author: Evolution of Civilizations, 1961; Tragedy and Hope: The World in Our Time, 1966, The World Since 1939, 1968. Mem. editorial bd. Current History, 1961-77. Home: Washington, D.C. Died Jan. 3, 1977.

QUIJANO, JUAN HORTENSIO, vice pres. Argentine Republic; b. Curuzú Cuatiá, Argentina, June 1, 1884; s. Crescencio Quijano; student Nat. Coll. of Concepcion del Uruguay; LL.D., U. of Buenos Aires, 1903. Practiced law, Goya, Argentina; lawyer Bank of the Nation; founder The Rural Soc. Foundation and Popular Bank of Goya, 1910; initiated constrn. of railway line between Lapachito and Colonia Zapallar (Chaco), 1923; in nat. politics with Unión Cívica Radical, rep. of Province of Corrientes on nat. bd. of the party; del. to nat. convs.; candidate for vice gov. of Corrientes, 1919; vice pres. Republic of Argentina since 1946. Author of articles on economic matters. Address: Buenos Aires, Argentina.*

QUINDLEN, EUGENE JOSEPH, govt. ofcl.; b. Phila., Nov. 7, 1919; s. Eugene Augustus and Catherine Josephine (O'Donnell) Q.; A.B. maxima cum laude, LaSalle Coll., Phila., 1940; M.A., Fordham U., 1942; J.D., Georgetown U., 1950; m. Katherine Marie Devine, June 23, 1943; children—Eugene, James, Carol, Maureen, Christine, Brian, Kathleen, Mark. Asst. edn., Fordham U., 1940-42; mgmt. analyst VA, 1946-47; mgmt. analyst, asst. regional rep. Office Vocational Rehab., FSA, 1947-51; admitted to D.C. bar, 1951; planning officer, dir. planning, later asst. adminstr. operations FCDA, 1952-58; staff ofcl. OCDM, 1958-61; staff ofcl. Office Emergency Planning, 1961-69, dir. Program Evaluation Office, 1962-69; dir. govt. preparedness Office Emergency Preparedness, 1969-70; asst. dir. for govt. preparedness Office Emergency Preparedness, Exec. Office Pres., 1970-73; v.p., then pres. J. M. Chambers & Co. Inc., Washington, 1973-77. Del., alt. del. NATO civil def. meetings, 1959, 61; chmn. work group Joint Bd. Fuel Supply and Transport, 1970-77. Mem. Task Force on Civil Disorders, Nat. Adv. Commn. on Criminal Justice Standards and Goals, 1971-77. Served to capt. AUS, 1942-46; Mem. Am. Soc. Pub. Adminstrn., Res. Officers Assn., Am. Legion, Delta Theta Phi. Roman Catholic. Home: Falls Church, Va. Died Oct. 17, 1977.

QUINN, JAMES LELAND, III, physican, educator; b. Pitts., July 12, 1933; s. James Leland, Jr. and Mary (Dunn) Q.; B.S., Belmont Abbey Coll., 1955, LL.D., 1973; M.D., Bowman Gray Sch. Medicine, 1959; m. Marie Magdalene Boschman, Aug. 26, 1973; children by previous marriage—Megan, Michelle Diane, James Leland IV, Michael Dennis. Intern, Pa. Hosp., Phila., 1959-60; resident radiology N.C. Baptist Hosp., Winston-Salem, 1960-63, dir. nuclear medicine, 1963-64; instr. radiology Bowman Gray Sch. Medicine, 1963-64; practice medicine, specializing in radiology, Chgo., 1964-79; dir. nuclear medicine Northwestern Meml. Hosp., 1964-79; asst. prof. radiology Northwestern U., 1964-66, asso. prof., 1966-68, prof., 1968—, asso. chmn., 1973-79, prof. pathology, 1975-79; cons. Western Med. Bd. Ireland, WHO expert Com. on radiation, 1975-79. Named Outstanding Young Man of Am., 1966. Fellow Am. Coll. Radiology, Royal Coll. Surgeons Ireland (hon.); mem. A.M.A., Assn. U. Radiologists, Soc. Nuclear Medicine (pres. 1971-72, Disting. Service award 1979), Radiol. Soc. N. Am., Soc. Clin. Research, Alpha Omega Alpha. Democrat. Roman Catholic. Editor: Scintillation Scanning in Clinical Diagnosis, 1964; Yearbook of Nuclear Medicine, 1966-79. Contbr. articles to tech. jours. Home: Chicago, Ill. Died Apr. 28, 1980; buried Calvary Cemetery, Evanston, Ill.

QUINN, JOHN J., baseball ofcl.; b. Columbus, O., Apr. 1, 1908; s. James Aloysius Robert and Margaret (Clark) Q.; student Boston Coll., 1929; m. Miriam L. Maloney, Feb. 10, 1934; children—Joan (Mrs. Timothy Quinlan), Robert, John, Margaret (Mrs. Roland Hemond), Susan. Sec. Boston Red Sox, 1929-45; gen. mgr. Boston Braves, 1945-53, Milw. Braves, 1953-59; gen. mgr. Phila. Phillies, 1959-65, v.p., 1965-73, gen. mgr., 1965-72. Clubs: Boston Coll. Alumni (Boston); Serra, Wisconsin (Milw.). Home: Santon, Calif. Died Sept. 20, 1976.

QUINN, ROBERT J., city ofcl.; b. Chgo., May 12, 1905; s. Patrick James and Nellie (O'Boyle) Q.; student evening coll. Entire career with Chgo. Fire Dept., commr., 1957-78. Mem. Chgo. Mayor's Cabinet, 1957-79. Bd. dirs. Hemophilia Found. Served with U.S. Navy, 1923; from lt. comdr. USNR, 1940-45. Decorated Army and Navy medal. Roman Catholic. Home: Chicago, Ill. Died Jan. 18, 1979.

QUIRK, ARTHUR LINCOLN, educator, physicist; b. Nasonville, R.I., Jan. 24, 1908; s. William Gerald and Alma Elizabeth (Jones) Q.; B.S., Providence Coll., 1930; M.S., Cath. U. Am., 1932, Ph.D., 1934; m. Lucy I. Fogarty, Nov. 27, 1935; children—Arthur Lincoln, William G., Mary E. (Mrs. Terrence R. Connelly), Judith E. (Mrs. William K. Hurley). Instr. Providence Coll., 1934-43; chief engr. Harvey Radio Labs., Cambridge, Mass., 1943-47; lectr. Brown U., 1947; asso. prof. U. R.I., Kingston, 1947-51, prof. physics, 1951-75; chmn. dept., 1955-69. Cons. to dir. U.S. Naval Underwater Ordnance Sta., Newport, R.I., 1960-61. Chmn. R.I. AEC, 1955-79; chmn. com. radiol. safety R.I. Council Def., from 1957. Mem. Narragansett (R.I.) Town Council, 1952-54; chmn. Narragansett Democratic Town Com., 1953-57. Bd. dirs., fellow Eppley Found. Research, Newport. Mem. R.I. Acad. Sci. (pres. 1963-68), Am. Phys. Soc., Am. Assn. Physics Tchrs., Sigma Xi (pres. R.I. chpt. 1957-58), Phi Kappa Phi, Sigma Pi Sigma, Sigma Nu. Prime responsibility design, constrn. and operation 2-megawatt R.I. research reactor, 1958-63. Home: Wyoming, R.I. Died Jan. 3,

1979; buried St. Joseph's Cemetery, West Greenwich, R.I.

QUIRK, GEORGE MARCUS, dept. store exec.; b. Edinboro, Pa., Jan. 11, 1889; s. William and Sarah (Shay) Q.; LL.B., U. Georgetown, 1915, LL.M., 1916; m. Ella Miller, June 13, 1913; children—Anna Marie (Mrs. Warren E. Tydings), Betty (Mrs. Everett R. Clarke), Eleanor (Mrs. Richard S. Abbey). Vice pres., mem. bd. dirs. Hecht Co., Baltimore from 1936; dir. Commerce & Savs. Bank, Washington since 1936. K.C., Elk. Home: Hillsborough Beach, Fla. Died Mar. 29, 1976.

QUIRK, LESLIE W., author; b. Alta, Ia., May 12, 1882; s. William F. Q. (M.D.) and Emma Elizabeth (Dudgeon) Q.; U. of Wis., 1900-02; unmarried. Pub. and editor of The Editor Magazine, 1903-08; editor, city schs., curriculum dept., San Diego, Calif., since 1935. With A.E.F. in France, 1917-19. Author: How to Write a Short Story, 1903; Baby Elton, Quarter-back, 1904; Midget Blake, 1906; Freshman Dorn, Pitcher, 1911; Tackle and Quarter-back, 1911; The Fourth Down, 1912; Freshman Friends, 1913; The Freshman Eight, 1913; Playing the Game, 1914; The Third Strike, 1914; Boy Scouts of Black Eagle Patrol, 1915; Iceboat Number One, 1916; Boy Scouts on Crusade, 1917; Boy Scouts of Lakeville High, 1920; Into Thin Air (with Horatio Winslow), 1929; Jimmy Goes to War, 1931; also many short stories in Mags. Home: Milwaukee, Wis. *

RABE, ALFRED (HERMAN), educator; b. Covington, Ky., Dec. 23, 1886; s. Frank and Bernadine (Von Wahlde) R.; student St. Mary's Normal Sch., Dayton, O.; B.A., St. Mary's Coll. (now U. of Dayton), 1906, M.A., 1916; M.A., U. of Fribourg, Switzerland, 1916. Joined Marianists (Soc. of Mary), 1903, prin. Chaminade Coll. High Sch., Clayton, Mo., 1921-27, became pres. St. Mary's U., San Antonio, Tex., 1927. Mem. San Antonio Pub. Library Bd. since 1930. Mem. Sr. Chamber Commerce. Mem. Knights of Columbus. Club: Optimist. Address: St. Louis, Mo. *

RABINER, SAUL FREDERICK, educator, physician; b. Bklyn., Aug. 11, 1926; s. Abraham M and Ella (Feldman) R.; B.S, Tulane U., 1949; M.D., State U. N.Y. at Bklyn., 1952; m. Marion Evans, Apr. 2, 1949; children—Mark, Elizabeth, David. Intern Maimonides Hosp., Bklyn., 1952, resident 1953; resident Montefiore Hosp., Bronx, 1956; attending dept. medicine VA Research Hosp., Chgo., 1960-68; asso. medicine Northwestern U. Med. Sch., 1960-65, asst. prof. medicine, 1960-69; asso. prof. medicine Pritzker Med. Sch., U. Chgo., 1970-71; asso. dir. clin. hematology Michael Reese Hosp., Chgo., 1962-63, dir., 1964-71; asso. prof. medicine U. Oreg. Med. Sch., 1971-74, prof. medicine, 1974-79; chief of medicine Good Samaritan Hosp. and Med. Center, 1971-79. Served with USAAF, 1943-45. Home: Portland, Oreg. Died Dec. 31, 1979; buried Portland.

RADEBAUGH, WILLIAM HERBERT, lawyer; b. Chgo., Feb. 22, 1899; s. William and Irene (Frankenberry) R.; Ph.B., U. Chgo., 1919; LL.B., Harvard, 1922; m. Muriel Rankin, Oct. 27, 1928 (dec. Dec. 1973); children—Julia (Mrs. Charles C. Mutti), William Herbert (dec.) m. Margaret Squibb Stokes, Apr. 19, 1975. Admitted to Ill. bar, 1922, N.Y. bar, 1931; asso. Chapman & Cutler, Chgo., 1923-29; mem. firm Chapman, Snider, Duke & Radebaugh, N.Y.C., 1933-36; partner firm Dunnington, Bartholow & Miller, N.Y.C., 1936-67, of counsel, from 1968. Chmn. Adoption Steering Com. Westchester County N.Y., 1952-53, incorporator, 1953; bd. dirs. Adoption and Children Service of Westchester, Inc., 1953-69, hon. life dir., from 1969. Club: (N.Y.C.). Home: Southport, Conn. Deceased.

RADER, JESSE LEE (RA'DER), librarian; b. Prairie Home, Mo., Apr. 20, 1883; s. Nathan Hanna and Louisa Sophia (Challes) R.; prep. sch., U. of Okla.; B.A., Univ. of Okla., 1908, M.A., 1913; studied Ind. Pub. Library Commn., Summer Sch., U. of Ill. Library Sch., 1 yr.; m. Mary Frances Simpson, July 26, 1911; 1 dau., Virginia Katherine. With U. of Okla. library since 1904, librarian, 1909-51, dir. of School of Library Sci., 1929-51, prof. library sci. and bibliographer since 1951; director City Nat. Bank, mem. Okla. Library Commn. Fellow Royal Soc. Arts, 1950; hon. mem. Okla. Hist. Society; member A.L.A., Okla. Library Assn., Phi Beta Kappa, Sigma Nu, Sigma Delta Chi, Phi Alpha Tau. Democrat. Presbyterian. Mason (K.T.). Club: Faculty. Co-author: Readings in Oklahoma History (with E. E. Dale), 1930; South of Forty, 1947. Home: Norman, Okla. *

RADIN, GEORGE, lawyer; b. Austria-Hungary, Jan. 29, 1896; s. Dobrivoj and Persida (Perin) R.; LL.B., Columbia, 1924; m. Katarina Hadji-Popovitch, June 1928; one dau., Vida (Mrs. Harry Roy Stringer, Jr.). Came to U.S. 1912, naturalized, 1921. Admitted to N.Y. bar, 1925; practiced in N.Y.C., 1925-81, Zürich, 1946-81, Washington, 1964-81, specializing internat. law; spl. rep. Govt. Yugoslavia, Washington, 1941; instr. Serbo-Croatian Columbia, 1918-21. adviser Hot Springs, Atlantic City Internat. confs., 1943, Carnegie Endowment for Internat. Peace, 1946. Founder, bd. dirs., chmn. planning and edn. com. Union Health Coops. Yugoslavia, 1921-46; chmn. bd. internat. Devel. Found., 1963-81; founder, bd. chmn., Serbian Research Found., 1972-81. Mem. Assn. Bar City N.Y., Am. Soc. Internat. Law, Am.-Yugoslav Soc. N.Y.C. (dir., exec. sec. 1923-35). Clubs: Metropolitan, Congressional (Washington). Author: The Balkan Pivot; Yugoslavia (with Charles A. Beard), 1929; Postwar Economic Reconstruction: A Practical Plan for the Balkans, 1946; Interchange of Know-How Among Nations for Raising Living Standards (adopted at Internat. Conf. on Food and Agri. 1943). Address: Washington, D.C. Died Jan. 11, 1981.

RADKE, FREDERICK HERBERT, educator; b. Jordan, Minn., Jan. 19, 1923; s. Edward Emil and Ella Hannah (Kroeger) R.; B.S., Hamline U., 1947; Ph.D., Ia. State U., 1952; m. Margaret Kathryn Hoffman, Sept. 4, 1946; children—Kathryn, Frederick, Lori, Eileen, Sharon. Grad. asst. chemistry Ia. State U., 1947-51, instr., 1951-52; asst. prof. U. Me., 1952-57, asso. prof., 1957-59, prof. biochemistry, 1959-77, head dept., 1958-77. Mem. Am. Chem. Soc., A.A.A.S., Sigma Xi, Phi Lambda Upsilon, Phi Kappa Phi. Home: Orono, Maine. Died Nov. 16, 1977.

RAEDER, OSCAR JACOB, psychiatrist; b. St. Louis, Apr. 10, 1886; s. Oscar William and Augusta (Wetzel) R.; M.D., Washington U., St. Louis, Mo., 1908; student neurology and psychiatry, Paris, France, 1920-22; m. Gladys L. Lowden, May 28, 1923 (dec. July 8, 1927); 1 son, Jon (dec.); m. 2d, Mildred Munro Woodsum, Apr. 11, 1929; children—Anne Raeder Mendler, Elizabeth Johnson (dec.), Dorothy Raeder Vegotsky, William, James. Intern St. Louis City Hosps., 1908-10; surgeon, Mo. Pacific and Frisco R.R. Hosps., 1910-12; resident physician and asst. supt. St. Louis City Sanitarium, 1912-17; asst. pathologist Mass. Dept. of Mental Diseases, 1917-20; practice medicine specializing in neuropsychiatry, after 1923; ret., 1969; instr. psychiatry Harvard Med. Sch. 1925-52; prof. psychiatry in charge of dept. Boston U. Sch. of Medicine, 1934-46, emeritus, 1946; dir. Southard Clinic, Boston, 1943-52; examining psychiatrist to Suffolk County Probate Ct., Boston, 1952-69; cons. psychiatrist New Eng. Deaconess Hosp. Served as lt. comdr. med. U.S. Naval Res., 1934-38. Mem. A.A.A.S., A.M.A., Am. Psychiat. Assn. (sec. sect. on child psychiatry 1935-47, chmn. 1948), Nat. Assn. for Mental Health, New Eng. Soc. Psychiatry, Mass. Psychiat. Soc. (pres. 1937), Boston Soc. Psychiatry and Neurology, Mass. Soc. Research in Psychiatry, Paris (France) Neurol. Soc. (corr.). Independent Republican. Mason. Clubs: Boston Univ. Faculty, Harvard (Boston). Contbr. papers and articles to neurol. and psychiatric jours. Home: Naples, Fla. Died Oct. 20, 1980.

RAGAN, CHARLES A., JR., physician; b. Washington, Dec. 21, 1910; s. Charles and Mary C. (McCue) R.; A.B., Princeton, 1932; M.D., Columbia, 1936; m. Josephine F. Parker, Feb. 3, 1937; children—Ellen M., Jody A., Charles R., Mary Ann. Intern Presbyn. Hosp., N.Y.C., 1936-38, asst. resident, 1938-39, resident, 1939-40, asst. physician, 1941-48, asst. attending physician, 1948-51, asso. attending physician, 1951-60, attending physician, from 1960, dir. med. service, 1971-75; Commonwealth fellow in medicine, instr. medicine Johns Hopkins Med. Sch., 1940-41; asst. in medicine, Columbia Coll. Phys. and Surg., 1941-46, asso. in medicine, 1946-48, asst. prof. medicine, 1948-51, asso. prof. medicine, 1951-56, asso. prof. clin. medicine, 1956-58, prof. clin. medicine, 1958-61, Lambert prof. medicine from 1961, chmn. dept. medicine, 1971-75; vis. physician, dir. First (Columbia) Med. Div., Bellevue Hosp., N.Y.C., 1961-68; dir. med. service, 1968-71, vis. physician Harlem Hosp. Center, from 1968; vis. physician Francis Delafield Hosp., 1971-75; vis. cons. medicine Roosevelt Hosp., from 1971; cons. medicine St. Luke's Hosp. Center, from 1972. Cons. USPHS; mem. com. survey of research rheumatic diseases NRC. Served to lt. col., M.C., A.U.S., 1942-45. Master A.C.P.; fellow N.Y. Acad. Medicine; mem. Assn. Am. Physicians, A.A.A.S., Am. Soc. Clin. Investigation, Am. Physiol. Soc., Am. Rheumatism Assn. (sec. 1946-51, treas. 1950-51, pres. 1953-54), N.Y. State, N.Y. County med. socs., Harvey Soc. Roman Catholic. Home: Bronxville, N.Y. Died Oct. 26, 1976; interred Gate of Heaven Cemetery, Valhalla, N.Y.

RAGATZ, LOWELL JOSEPH, educator, author, lectr.; b. Prairie du Sac, Wis., July 21, 1897; s. John and Anna (Tarnutzer) R.; A.B., U. Wis., 1920, M.A., 1921, Ph.D., 1925; postgrad. U. Pa., 1921-22, U. Grenoble, U. Paris, Collège de France, Ecole Libre des Sciences Politiques, 1922-23, London Sch. Econs., 1923; m. Mary Katheryn Parker, 1930; 1 son, Robert Lowell; m. 2d, Janet Stokes Evans, 1948; children—Veronica Anne, Jon Evans. Teaching fellow U. Wis., 1920-21, U. Pa., 1921-22; instr. history George Washington U., 1924-27, asst. prof., 1927-31, asso. prof. 1931-37, prof., 1937-49, chmn. history dept., 1934-37; prof. Ohio State U., 1949-67, emeritus prof., 1967-78, chmn. history dept., 1949-53; vis. prof. Australian Nat. U., 1955; Fulbright prof. Keio U. and Tokyo U. Edn., 1959-60, Kyoto and Kinki univs. (Japan), 1963-64; vis. prof, Alaska Meth. U., 1967-69, U. So. Cal., 1969-70; lectr. War Dept., 1942, Lend-Lease N. African Mission Sch., 1943, Am. Friends Service Com. Internat. Relations Insts., 1944, 51, 53; USIA, London (Eng.), 1947-48. Editor Am. Hist. Assn., 1929-42, 28 vols.; editorial bd. Jour. Modern History, 1937-40, Am. del., 2d Congress Pan-Am. Inst. Geography and History, 1935. Served as pvt., Q.M.C., U.S. Army, 1918-19. Recipient Jubilee medal U. Wis., 1920, Justin Winsor prize Am. Hist. Assn., 1928; Guggenheim fellow, 1933, 34. Fellow Royal Hist. Soc., Royal Soc. Arts; mem. Am. Hist. Assn., Am. Assn. U. Profs. (chpt. pres. 1943-45), Société d'Histoire Moderne, Société de l'Histoire des Colonies Françaises, Am. Bibliog. and Library Assn., Phi Beta Kappa, Omicron Delta Kappa, Pi Delta Epsilon, Pi Gamma Mu, Acacia, Phi Alpha Theta (nat. Councillor 1950-52. Unitarian. Mason. Author numerous books latest being: March of Empire, 1948; The Spud Papers, 1952; Early Philatelic Forgeries of All Countries, 1953; The Old Plantation System in the British West Indies, 1955; A Bibliography for the Study of European History; 1815-1939, 4 vols., 1957-60; The New United States, 1962. Editor: Doctoral Studies in History in Progress in the U.S., 1947. Contbr. other publs. Home: Delaware, Ohio. Died Oct. 28, 1978.

RAGLAND, JOSEPH PEMBERTON, fgn. service officer; b. Richmond, Va., May 16, 1897; s. Harry Lee and Frances Cecelia (O'Hare) R.; Ph.B., Georgetown U., 1919, A.M., 1920, M.F.S., 1923; m. Ruth Shepherd, Jan. 18, 1919; children—Frances Shepherd, Joseph Pemberton, John Christopher. Asst. investigator, U.S. Bur. of Efficiency, 1919-24; apptd. fgn. service officer, 1924, vice consul, Monterrey, Mex., 1924; fgn. service officer, State Dept., 1925; vice consul, St. John's, Nfld., 1926-28, Halifax, N.S., 1928-31, consul, 1931-36, at St. Pierre-Miquelon, terr. of France, 1935, at Brisbane, Australia, 1936-46; at Medellin, Colombia, 1946-49, at Naples, Italy, 1949-50, Southampton, Eng., 1950-53. Clubs: Rotary, Royal Southampton, Southampton Master Mariners'. Home: Washington, D.C. Died July 23, 1976.

RAGONE, STANLEY, utility co. exec.; b. Norfolk, Va., May 7, 1925; s. Vincent George and Jennie (Gross) R.; B.S., Va. Poly. Inst., 1947, M.S., 1948; m. Bertha Perlin, Sept. 5, 1954 (dec. Apr. 25, 1980); children—Vernon George, Mitchell Floyd, Sharon. With Va. Electric & Power Co., various locations, 1948-80, v.p. power, Richmond, 1967-73, sr. v.p. power group, 1973-76, exec. v.p., 1976-78, pres., chief operating officer, dir., 1978-80; dir. United Va. Bank, Richmond, Dana Corp.; instr. physics William and Mary Coll./Va. Poly. Inst. extension at Norfolk, 1948-53. Served with USNR, 1944-46; PTO. Registered profl. engr., Va. Fellow ASME, Va. Acad. Sci. (pres. 1973-74). Jewish. Clubs: Masons, Shriners. Home: Richmond, Va. Died Apr. 25, 1980; buried Forest Lawn Cemetery, Norfolk.

RAINEY, FLOYD DEAN, lawyer; b. Norcross, Ga., Feb. 1, 1904; s. Fred Eugene and Nora (Dean) R.; LL.B., Furman U., 1927; m. Margaret Smedes Rose, Apr. 17, 1932; children—Floyd Dean, Margaret Rose (Mrs. David H. Rembert, Jr.). Admitted to S.C. bar, 1927; mem. firms Haynsworth & Haynsworth, Greenville, S.C., 1927-45, Rainey, Fant & Horton, Greenville, 1946-70, Rainey, Fant & McKay, 1970-75. Dir., gen. counsel The S.C. Nat. Bank; div. counsel for State of S.C., So. Ry. Co.; dir. Greenville City Coach Co. Active United Fund. Mem. Am., S.C. bar assns., Am. Coll. Trial Lawyers, Greenville C. of C. Episcopalian. Clubs: Poinsett, Green Valley Country (Greenville). Home: Greenville, S.C. Died July 2, 1975.

RAINEY, ROBERT M., judge; b. Sherman, Tex., Sept. 29, 1882; s. Jesse G. and Annie Elizabeth (Moore) R.; student U. of Tex., 1901-03, Cumberland U. Law Sch., Lebanon, Tenn., 1903-04; m. Lillian Fryer, Aug. 12, 1905; children—Robert M., Gordon F., Dorothea, Thomas J. (dec.). Began practice at Atoka, Okla., 1904; mem. first Okla legislature, from Atoka County, 1907-08; dist. judge, 7th Jud. Dist. (later 26th Dist.), Okla., 1909-15; state chmn. Dem. State and Nat. Campaign Com., 1916; asso. justice Supreme Court of Okla., Apr. 15, 1917-May 11, 1920, chief justice May 11, 1920-Jan. 10, 1921; now mem. Rainey, Flynn, Green & Anderson. Mem. Sigma Alpha Epsilon. Methodist. Mason (K.T.). Home: Oklahoma City. *

RAINIE, HARRISON MCKINLEY, ry. exec.; b. Concord, N.H., Sept. 12, 1892; s. William and Jane (Michie) R.; student Concord Bus. Coll., 1909; Harvard U. Grad. Bus. Sch., 1931; m. Alice Bateson, June 13, 1918; children—Harrison McKinley, Jane Alice. Car dept. Boston & Maine R.R., Concord, 1909-12, stores dept., Concord, 1912-14, stores dept. Billerica shops, 1914-16, storekeeper Charlestown, Mass., 1916-17; asst. storekeeper Billerica shops, 1917-19, asst. supr. stores U.S.R.A., Eastern region, N.Y., 1919-20, traveling storekeeper, Boston, 1920-22, storekeeper Billerica shops, 1922-24, asst. to purchasing agt. 1924-33, purchasing agt., 1933-50, v.p., 1950-75; v.p. Maine Central R.R. Co., Portland Terminal Co. Mem. Gov. Com. on Standardization, State of Maine, 1958. Mem. Assn. Am. R.R.'s (chmn. purchases and stores 1953-54), Newcomen Soc. N.Am. Club: New Eng. R.R. (pres. 1945). Address: Portland, Maine. Died Mar. 5, 1980; interred North Cemetery, Billerica, Mass.

RAJAMAITRI, PHYA ABHIBAL, diplomat; b. Bangkok, Siam, Mar. 7, 1885; s. Chao Phya Surawongs and Yai Bunnag; student Malvern Coll., Eng., 1901-04; LL.B., Kings Coll., Cambridge, Eng., 1909; barrister-at-law, Inner Temple, London, Eng., 1910; m. Ruen Bunnag, of Siam, Jan. 16, 1930; 1 dau., Ramadi Teru. Barrister-at-law, Siam, 1915; E.E. and M.P. of Siam to Rome, 1930-32; state councillor of Siam for foreign affairs, 1933-34; E.E. and M.P. of Siam to Washington since 1935; mem. Assembly of Poeple's Reps., 1933-35. Awarded 1st class of Siamese Crown, 2d class of Belgian Crown, 1st class of Italian Crown. Clubs: Metropolitan, Racquet, Chevy Chase. Home: 966 Windmill Rd., Bangkok, Siam. Address: Washington, D.C. *

RALLS, CHARLES C., lawyer; b. Missoula, Mont., Mar. 29, 1904; s. Claude and Frances (Kasper) R.; LL.B., Gonzaga U., 1930; m. Alice O'Leary, Oct. 14, 1935; children—Richard Charles, Charles Patrick. Admitted to Wash. bar, and since practiced in Seattle; spl. asst. atty. gen. State of Wash.; chief dep. pros. atty. King County, 1936-42; chmn. Wash. State Census Bur.; dir. Civil Def., State of Wash., 1957-62; dir. Region 8 (Alaska, Mont., Idaho, Wash., Oreg.) Office of Civil Def., Dept. of Def., 1962-71; judge N.E. Dist. Ct., Redmond, Wash., from 1971. Mem. V.F.W., successively comdr., Seattle post, mem. nat. finance com., chmn. nat. security com., 1947, encampment at Cleve.; sr. vice comdr. Dept. of Wash., 1946-47, dept. comdr., 1947-48; jr. vice comdr., 1948, sr. vice comdr., 1949, comdr. in chief, 1950. Served from pvt. to maj., U.S.M.C.; overseas with Fifth Amphibious Corps, P.T.O. Mem. Wash., Seattle (past sec.) bar assns. Home: Redmond, Wash. Deceased.

RAMPY, EDGAR FRANKLIN, transp. co. exec.; b. Belgrade, Mont., July 4, 1939; s. Wesley Lee and Annie Laurie (Ballard) R.; B.S. in Accounting, Mont. State U., 1966; m. Barbara Jo Hammond, Dec. 20, 1963; children—Shelly, Joel, Jonathon. Sr. accountant Touche, Ross & Co., Denver, 1966-70; controller Nat. City Lines, Inc., Denver, 1970-71, v.p., treas., 1971—. Mem. Am. Inst. C.P.A.'s, Colo. Soc. C.P.A.'s. Home: Denver CO. Died June 21, 1976.

RAMPY, THOMAS RANDALL, air force officer; b. Salado, Tex., Dec. 4, 1897; s. Thomas Jefferson and Bethsaida (Underwood) R.; grad. Salado (Tex.) Coll.; grad. Advanced Management program Harvard, 1951; m. Gladys Drinkwater, Dec. 16, 1922; children—Thomas Randall, Mildred (wife of Richard Smith, U.S.M.C.), Gordon A. Commd. officer, U.S. A.A.F., 1943, chief contract audit div., 1942-47, auditor gen. USAF, 1948-54; comptroller USAF in Europe; promoted through grades to maj. gen., 1952. Decorated Legion of Merit, Commendation Ribbon. Home: Falls Church, Va. Died June 21, 1976 buried Arlington (Va.) Nat. Cemetery.

RAMSAY, GRACE KIRKPATRICK, educator; b. nr. Charlotte, N.C., Oct. 22, 1883; d. Allen Grier and Elizabeth (Gary) K.; A.B., Winthrop Coll., Rock Hill, S.C., 1904; m. Dr. William Beall Ramsay, of Salisbury, N.C., Dec. 23, 1908 (died Mar. 22, 1924). Teacher mathematics, Erskine Coll., Due West, S.C., 1904-07; pres. Mitchell Coll., Statesville, N.C., since 1929; pres. Women's Auxiliary of Presbyn. Synod of N.C., 1915-20. Mem. D.A.R., U.D.C., Am. Assn. Univ. Women. Democrat. Presbyn. Home: Statesville, N.C.*

RAMSEY, NORMAN CARNEGIE, banker; b. Bklyn., Sept. 21, 1910; s. Charles G. and Edythe (Kavanagh) R.; m. Rosalie A. Christie, Sept. 15, 1938; children—Peter C., Christie C. With Broadway Savs. Bank, N.Y.C., 1936-42, from 1945, exec. v.p., 1959-61, pres., 1961-72, trustee, from 1961, chmn., 1967-72; chmn., pres., dir. Mortgage Facilities Corp., from 1966; dir. Instl. Securities Corp., 1966-72, mem. mortgage com., 1966-71, chmn., 1970-71; chmn., trustee Prudential Savs. Bank, N.Y.C., from 1973; dir. Freeholders Service Inc., Mohawk Redevel. Co. Pres. Savs. Banks Mortgage and Real Estate Forum, N.Y., 1960-61; chmn. econ. surveys com. N.Y. Real Estate Bd., 1957-60, mem. mortgage com., 1960-72, dir. owners div., 1963-65, from 1968, gov., mem. finance com., treas., mem. com. ethics, treas., commns. and profl. practices, former mem. nominating com.; mem. adv. bd. N.Y. U. Real Estate Inst., from 1972. Chmn. savs. bank div. Legal Aid Soc. N.Y.C., 1961-62, Arthritis and Rheumatism Fund, N.Y.C., 1963; mem. nat. com. Nat. Conf. Christians and Jews, 1963; chmn. savs. banks div. Travelers Aid Soc., N.Y.C., 1963-64, 73-74, gen. appeal chmn., 1968-71, bd. govs., from 1969, sec., 1968-70, vice chmn., from 1970; mem. real estate div. Anti Defamation League, from 1965; chmn. savs. banks com. Greater N.Y. council Boy Scouts Am., 1964-65. Epilepsy Assn. Am., 1965; pres. 23d St. Assn., 1966-68, dir., chmn. exec. com.; chmn. 1967 savs. bank div. Assn. for Help Retarded Children; sponsor, com. mem. Explorers Post 310, 10th Pct., N.Y.C. Police Dept., from 1967. Trustee Marymount Manhattan Coll., N.Y.C., 1972-76; bd. dirs. Chelsea Neighborhood Center, N.Y.C., 1970-76; bd. mgrs. McBurney br. YMCA, N.Y.C., 1965-76, sec., 1967-69, vice chmn., 1969-72, chmn., 1972-76, chmn. membership and pub. relations com., 1966-73, mem. house, personnel and finance coms., 1966-76, mem. exec. search and selection com. McBurney-Seamen's House, YMCA, 1972-76; bd. govs. Riverview Hosp., Red Bank, N.J., 1966-76. Served to maj. USAAF, 1942-45. Decorated Bronze Star with cluster, Purple Heart; named Man of Year, 23d St. Assn. N.Y.C., 1969, YMCA Greater N.Y., 1970. Mem. Savs. Banks Assn. N.Y. State (past chmn. mortgage com., past chmn. exec. com. group IV, dir. group, group v.p.), N.Y.C. Chamber Commerce and Industry (com. on finance and currency 1966-76), West Side Assn. Commerce (dir. 1972-76), N.Y. State Assn. Real Estate Bds. (dir. 1972-76), Nat. Assn. Mut. Savs. Banks, Am. Legion (past post adj.), A.I.M. (fellow pres.'s council), Vets. 7th Regt. N.Y.C., Order Lafayette, St. Andrews Soc. State N.Y. (sec. 1972-76). Clubs: Army and Navy (past treas., pres., bd. gov.); Union League, Church, N.Y. Yacht (house com.) (N.Y.C.); Elgin (Morayshire, Scotland) Golf; Rumson Country; Seabright Beach (N.J.) (bd. govs., treas.). Home: New York, N.Y. Died Oct. 31, 1976.

RAMSEYER, LLOYD LOUIS, coll. pres.; b. Normal, Ill., Nov. 5, 1899; s. Michael L. and Anna (Stahly) R.; A.B., Bluffton Coll., 1924; A.M., Ohio State U., 1932, Ph.D., 1938; D.D., Bethel Coll., North Newton, Kan.; Doctor of Humane Letters, Findlay Coll., 1964; m. Ferne Yoder, June 4, 1927; children—Robert, Mary Jean, G. William. Tchr., coach Heyworth (Ill.) Community High Sch., 1924-27, prin., 1927-36; research asst. Bur. Edn. Research, Ohio State U., 1936-38; pres. Bluffton Coll., 1938-77; vis. prof. summers Bowling Green State U., 1938-39, Ohio State U., 1940-41; half-time interim pastor First Mennonite Ch., Bluffton, Ohio. Sec. Ohio Found. Ind. Colls., 1953-56, chmn., 1956-57. Mem. N.E.A., Assn. Ohio Coll. Presidents and Deans (pres. 1950-51), Ohio Coll. Assn. (pres. 1954-55), Phi Delta Kappa. Republican. Mennonite (vice chmn. sem. bd.). Clubs: Lions, Torch. Contbr. profl. jours. Editor central dist. edit. The Mennonite. Home: Bluffton, Ohio. Died June 24, 1977.

RANCK, JOHN ALLAN, clergyman; b. New Holland, Pa., Aug. 16, 1912; s. George S. and Mabel (Hoover) R.: A.B., Lebanon Valley Coll., Annville, Pa., 1934; B.D., Bonebrake Theol. Sem., Dayton, O., 1937; Th.M., Princeton Theol. Sem., 1942; D.D., Westmar Coll., LeMars, Ia., 1949; m. Mildred Arlene Stauffer, June 22, 1937; children—Mary (Mrs. Edmund J. Slezosky), Ruth (Mrs. James T. Heath), Kathleen (Mrs. Philip Jones), Ardythe (Mrs. Robert Cross); m. 2d, Kathleen Clements, July 1, 1972; m. 3d, Harriet Mae Spangler, May 29, 1975. Ordained to ministry Evangel. United Brethren Ch., 1937; pastor in Allentown, Pa., 1937-46; dir. young people's work Evangel. United Brethren Ch., 1946-53; asso. gen. dir., then gen. dir. dept. edn. for mission Nat. Council Chs., 1953-67, exec. asst. to gen. sec. council, 1967-73, asso. gen. sec. for program planning, 1973-75, asso. exec. stewardship, 1975-79; lectr. Yale Div. Sch., 1955-67. Author: Living as a Christian, 1951; Education for Mission, 1961; The Ranks of the Rancks: A Ranck/Rank Family History and Genealogy, 1978. Home: Montclair, N.J. Died Feb. 4, 1979; buried New Holland, Pa.

RAND, GERTRUDE, psychologist; b. New York, N.Y., Oct. 29, 1886; d. Lyman Fiske and Mary Catherine (Moench) Rand; B.A., Cornell U., 1908; M.A., and Ph.D., Bryn Mawr, 1911; Sc.D., Wilson College, Pa., 1943; m. Clarence Errol Ferree, Sept. 28, 1918 (died 1942). Research fellow Bryn Mawr, 1911-12, Sarah Berliner research fellow, 1912-13; demonstrator and reader in experimental and ednl. psychology, same Coll., 1913-14, and asso. in exptl. and applied psychology, 1914-25; demonstrator in exptl. psychology and research asst., Nat. Research Council's Com. on Industrial Lighting, 1925-27; asso. prof. of research ophthalmology, Johns Hopkins U. Sch. Medicine, 1928-32, asso. prof. physiol. optics, 1932-36; asso. dir. Research Lab. of Physiol. Optics, Baltimore, Md., 1936-43; research asso. in ophthalmology on Knapp Foundation, Coll. Phys. and Surg., Columbia U., 1943-57; cons. Knapp Memorial Laboratory, College of Physicians and Surgeons, Columbia University, 1957—. Mem. Armed Forces NRC Vision Com., subcom. on Color Vision and Illumination Standards. Recipient Edgar D. Tillyer Medal, Optical Soc. Am., 1959. Fellow A.A.A.S., Am. Psychol. Assn., Illuminating Engineering Society (Gold medal 1963), Optical Soc. of Am., American Acad. of Ophthalmology and Otolaryngology (hon.); mem. N.Y. State Psychol. Assn., Am. Inst. Physics, University Profs., American Assn. University Women, Inter Society Color Council (color blindness com.), Internat. Council Women Psychologists; mem. adv. com. and com. on Vision Testing Procedures, Nat. Society for Prevention Blindness. Republican. Presbyterian. Clubs: Cosmopolitan (N.Y.) Oldfield (L.I.), Women's Faculty (Columbia); Cornell Women's (New York). Author: the Factors Which Influence the Sensitivity of the Retina to Color, 1913; Radiometric Apparatus for Use in Psychological and Physiological Optics, 1917, Studies in Physiological Optics, 2 vols., 1934 (with C. E. Ferree). Co-inventor Ferree-Rand perimeter, light-sense tester, acuity projecter, multiple-exposure tachistoscope, variable illuninator, and other optical and ophthalmol. instruments. Inventor Rand Anomalscope; co-inventor Hardy-Rand-Rittler Pseudoisochromatic Plates. Contbr. mags. Home: Stony Brook, L.I., N.Y. Retired. *

RANDALL, DAVID LINDSEY, prof. chemistry; b. Athol, Mass., Dec. 8, 1882; s. George Walter and Mary Alice (Lindsey) R.; B.A., Yale, 1904; M.A., 1905, Ph.D., 1907; m. Eugenia S. Schelde, of Woburn, Mass., Aug. 17, 1910; children—Alice Evelyn, David Schelde, Helen Caroline, John Walter. Instr. chemistry, New Hampshire College (now University of New Hampshire), 1907-10; prof. chemistry, Baker University, Kansas, 1910-18; asso. prof. chemistry, Wesleyan U., Conn., 1918-19; prof. chemistry, Albion (Mich.) Coll., 1919—. Mem. Am. Chem. Soc., Sigma Xi, Sigma Phi Epsilon. Republican. Methodist. Contbr. tech. articles to scientific jours. Home: Albion, Mich.*

RANDALL, JESSE W., ret. ins. exec.; b. Hazardville, Conn., Feb. 29, 1884; s. Elmer E. and Hortense A. (Vietts) R.; ed. Enfield High Sch.; M.A., honoris causa, Trinity College, 1950; married Mary E. Holcombe, July 9, 1907; 1 dau., Eunice H. Began as mail clerk Travelers Ins. Co., 1905; spl. field agt. Travelers Indemnity Co., 1910-13, spl. agt. Liability Dept., Jan. 1913, casualty mgr., Springfield, Mass., Mar. 1913, branch mgr., Worchester, Mass., fall 1913, asst. mgr., Boston, Mass., 1914-15, transferred to home off. Aug. 1915, apptd. asst. sec. Compensation and Liability Dept., 1917, sec. of dept., 1927-34, v.p. Travelers Insurance Co., in charge of compensation and liability Sept. 1934; v.p. Travelers Indemnity Co., 1935; pres. Travelers Ins. Co., Travelers Indemnity Co., Travelers Fire Ins. Co., 1945-52; pres. Travelers Broadcasting Service Corp. and Charter Oak Fire Ins. Co. since July 13, 1945; dir. Travelers Cos., Travelers Broadcasting Service, Conn. River Banking Co., Travelers Bank & Trust Co., trustee Hartford-Conn. Trust Co., Mechanics Savs. Bank. Trustee Hartford Coll. Republican. Mem. Broadview Community Ch. Clubs: University, Winter Park Golf (Winter Park); Orlando Country. Home: Winter Park, Fla. *

RANDALL, JOHN HERMAN, JR., author, educator; b. Grand Rapids, Mich., Feb. 14, 1899; s. John Herman and Minerva I. (Ballard) R.; A.B., Columbia, 1918, A.M 1919, Ph.D., 1922, L.H.D., 1968; Litt. D., Ohio Wesleyan U., 1961; Ph.D. (hon.), U. Padua (Italy), 1967; LL.D., Temple U., 1968; L.H.D., Bard Coll., 1972; m. Mercedes Irene Moritz; Dec. 23, 1922; children—John Herman III, Francis Ballard. Asst. prof. philosophy Columbia, 1925-31, asso prof., 1931-35, prof., 1935-51, F.J.E. Woodbridge prof. philosophy, 1951-67, Woodbridge prof. emeritus, 1967-80. Fellow Am. Acad. Arts and Scis.; mem. Renaissance Soc Am. (pres. 1953-57), Am. Philos. Assn. (pres. 1956), Metaphys. Soc. Am. (pres. 1966-67), Phi Beta Kappa, Alpha Delta Phi. Mem. Ethical Culture Soc. Club: Columbia Faculty. Author: The Problem of Group Responsibility, 1922; The Making of the Modern Mind, 1926, 50th Anniv. Edit., 1976; Our Changing Civilization, 1929; The Role of Knowledge in Western Religion, 1958; Nature and Historical Experience, 1958; Aristotle, 1960; The School of Padua and the Emergence of Modern Science, 1961; The Career of Philosophy in Modern Times, Vol. I, 1962, Vol. II, 1965; How Philosophy Uses Its Past, 1963; The Meaning of Religion for Man, 1968; Plato: Dramatist of the Life of Reason, 1970; Hellenistic Ways of Deliverance and the Making of the Christian Synthesis, 1970; Philosophy After Darwin, 1977. Co-author: Introduction to Contemporary Civilization (syllabus), 1920-26; Introduction to Reflective Thinking, 1923; Studies in the History of Ideas (Vol. II), 1925; Religion and the Modern World, 1929; American Philosophy Today and Tomorrow, 1935; The Philosophy of John Dewey, 1939; The Philosopher of the Common Man, 1940; Philosophy: An Introduction, 1942; Naturalism and the Human Spirit, 1944; Preface to Philosophy, 1946; Theory and Practice in Historical Study, 1946; Freedom and Experience, 1947; Wellsprings of the American Spirit, 1948; Organized Religion in the U.S., 1948; Renaissance Philosophy of Man, 1948; The Philosophy of Ernest Cassier 1949; Freedom and Reason, 1951; Philosophy of Paul Tillich, 1952; Contemporary American Philosophy, 1970. editor Jour. History of Ideas; joint editor Jour. Philosophy. Editor: Aristotle's Vision of Nature (Frederick J. E. Woodbridge), 1965. Home: New York, N.Y Died Dec. 1, 1980; buried Peacham, Vt.

RANDOLPH, ASA PHILIP, labor leader; b. Crescent City, Fla., Apr. 15, 1889; s. James William and Elizabeth (Robinson) R.; ed. CCNY; LL.D., Howard U., 1941; m. Lucille E. Campbell, 1914. Organizer Brotherhood of Sleeping Car Porters, AFL, N.Y.C., 1925, pres. emeritus, 1968; organizer, dir. of March on Washington Movement which led Pres. Roosevelt to start Com. on Fair Employment Practice, 1941; v.p. AFL-CIO, from 1957, mem. emeritus exec. council. Mem. Mayor La Guardia's Commn. on Race, 1935; hon. chmn. White House Conf. Civil Rights, Recipient Civil Rights award Am. Fedn. Tchrs., 1973. Methodist. Mason, Elk. Contbr. to Opportunity, Survey Graphic. Address: New York, N.Y. Died May 16, 1979.

RANDOLPH, BESSIE CARTER, college pres.; b. nr. Fincastle, Botetourt County, Va., Feb. 26, 1885; d. Rev. Charles Carter and Sarah Blair (McGuire) Randolph; A.B., Hollins College, 1912; A.M., Radcliffe Coll., Cambridge, Mass., 1916, Ph.D., 1926; Carnegie fellow in internat. law, 1924-26; unmarried. Teacher various

Southern high schs., 1905-11; instr. hist., Hollins Coll., 1912-15; asso. in hist., State Normal Farmville, Va., 1916-20; adj. prof. history, Randolph-Macon Woman's Coll., Lynchburg, Va., 1921-24; prof. polit. science, Fla. State Coll. for Women, Tallahassee, Fla., 1926-33; trustee Hollins College, 1926-33, president, 1933-50, now emeritus. Instructor summer quarters, State Teachers College, Harrisonburg, and U. of Va. Mem. bd. visitors, U. of Va., 1939-42. Lecturer in internat. and ednl. subjects. Mem. Am. Assn. Univ. Women (chmn. com. on legislative program), Am. Polit. Sci. Assn. (mem. exec. council 1940-42), Am. Soc. Internat. Law (mem. exec. council 1932-35, 1937-40, 1944-47), Southern Council of Internat. Relations, Va. Edn. Assn., Southern Polit. Science Assn.. Phi Beta Kappa. Democrat. Episcopalian. Home: Lynchburg, Va. *

RANDOLPH, OSCAR DEWOLF, clergyman; b. Englewood, Ill., Sept. 28, 1884; s. Isham and Mary Henry (Taylor) R.; A.B., U. of Va., 1907; grad. Va. Theol. Sem., Alexandria, 1910; D.D., Washington and Lee U., 1929, Coll. of William and Mary, 1941; m. Alice Lawrie Crawford, June 19, 1911; children—Oscar deWolf (dec.), Angus Crawford, Mary Isham (Mrs. James E. Poindexter). Deacon, 1910, priest, 1911, P.E. Ch.; rector Luray Parish, Page and Shenandoah counties, Va., 1910-11, R. E. Lee Memorial Ch., Lexington, Va., 1911-17, St. Marys-on-the-Highlands, Birmingham, Ala., 1919-28, Va. Episcopal Sch., Lynchburg, 1928-43; civilian service, Naval Torpedo Station, Alexandria, Va., 1943-44; rector Zion Church, Rome, N.Y., 1945-46, asst. St. John's Ch., Washington, D.C., 1944-48; asst., Ch. Holy Apostles and The Mediator, Phila., since 1948. Served as capt. Inf., U. S. Army, later maj. Machine Gun Batn., Camp Funston. Ardmore, Pa. *

RANKIN, ROBERT STANLEY, educator; b. Tusculum, Tenn., Nov. 17, 1899; s. Thomas Samuel and Mary Isabel (Coile) R.; A.B. summa cum laude, Tusculum Coll., 1920, LL.D. (hon.), 1958; A.M., Princeton, 1922, Ph.D., 1924, fellow in polit. sci., 1922-24; m. Dorothy Newsom, Sept. 14, 1933; children—Dorothy Battle, Robert Stanley. Prof. history and polit. sci. Tusculum Coll., 1924-27; mem. faculty Duke, 1927-76, asst. dean Grad. Sch., 1929-36, acting dean, 1935-36, prof. polit. sci., 1934-69, prof. emeritus, 1969—, chmn. dept., 1949-64; vis. prof. polit. sci. U. Ala., summer 1945, Stanford U., 1947, Columbia U., summer 1953, Wake Forest Coll., 1972. Mem. Durham City Council, 1955-60; mem. U.S. Commn. Civil Rights, 1960-76; mem. N.C. Local Gov. Study Commn., 1967-68; dir. Johnston County Forum in Humanities, 1973, Richmond County Forum, 1974, Granville County Forum, 1975, Am. Expt., a series of bicentennial forums, 1976. Trustee, Tusculum Coll., 1950-58, 59-65. Phi Beta Kappa vis. scholar, 1964-65; Festschrift honoree Law and Justice: Essays in Honor of Robert S. Rankin, 1970; Civil Rights Library, Washington, renamed Robert S. Rankin Nat. Civil Rights Library in his honor, 1976. Mem. Am. Polit. Sci. Assn. (exec. council 1951-53), So. Polit. Sci. Assn. (a founder, pres. 1931, exec. com. 1946), Phi Beta Kappa Assos. (panel of disting. speakers 1971-76), Phi Beta Kappa, Omicron Delta Kappa, Tau Kappa Alpha, Phi Kappa Psi. Democrat. Presbyn. Clubs: Cosmos, Rotary (pres. 1946-47). Joint author: Fundamentals of American National Government, 1955, Chinese edit., 1958; Fundamentals of American Government: National, State, Local, 1957; Freedom and Emergency Powers in the Cold War, 1964; Race and the Tobacco Industry, 1970. Editor: A Century of Social Thought, 1939; The Presidency in Transition, 1949. Author: When Civil Law Fails, 1939; Readings in American Government, 1939; Political Science in the South, 1946; The Government and Administration of N.C., 1955; editorial bd. Am. Polit. Sci. Rev., Jour. Politics, Nat. Municipal Rev., S. Atlantic Quar. Book rev. editor Jour. Politics, 1942-45. Home: Durham, N.C. Died June 4, 1976; buried Maplewood Cemetery, Durham.

RANNIGER, KLAUS, physician, educator; b. Hamburg, Germany, July 4, 1926; s. Walter E. and Elisabeth (Wachholz) R.; M.D., U. Kiel (Germany), 1951; m. Renate Hartwich, Apr. 20, 1963; children—Monica A., Claudia U. Came to U.S., 1955, naturalized, 1963. Intern U. Kiel Hosp., 1951-52; intern U. Chgo. Clinics, 1955-56, resident, 1956-59; mem. faculty U. Chgo. Med. Sch., 1955-72, prof. medicine and radiology, 1968-72, chief diagnostic radiology, 1971-72; prof. radiology, chmn. dept. Med. Coll. Va., Richmond, 1972-76. Contbr. articles to med. jours. Home: Richmond, Va. Died Mar. 30, 1976; buried Haddeby, W. Ger.

RANSOM, HARRY HUNTT, univ. chancellor; b. Galveston, Tex., Nov. 22, 1908; s. Harry Huntt and Marion Goodwin (Cunningham) R.; A.B., U. of South, 1928, Litt.D., 1958; A.M., Yale, 1930, Ph.D., 1938; student Harvard, 1929-30; Litt.D., U. N.D., 1970, U. Dallas, 1971; LL.D. Baylor U., 1958, Trinity U., 1963, Tex. Christian U., 1963; L.H.D., Austin Coll., 1966, So. Meth. U., 1972; D.Eng., Colo. Sch. Mines, 1972; m. Hazel Louise Harrod, Aug. 11, 1951. Instr. English and journalism State Tchrs. Coll., Valley City, N.D., 1930-32, 33-34; instr. English and history Colo. State Coll., 1934-35; instr. English, U. Tex. at Austin, 1935-38, asst. prof., 1938-42, asso. prof., 1946-47, prof., 1947-51, asst. dean Grad. Sch., 1951-53, asso. dean, 1953-54, dean Coll. Arts and Scis., 1954-57, v.p. and provost, 1957-60, pres., 1960-61, chancellor U. Tex. System, 1961-71, chancellor emeritus, 1971-76. Dir. Southwestern Bell Telephone Co., 1967-76. Trustee Carnegie Found. for Advancement of Teaching, 1962-70; past mem. commn. on colls. and univs. So. Assn. Past chmn. hist. commn. Internat. Copyright League; past mem. Commn. on White House Fellows, Pres.'s Commn. on Patent System, Nat. Adv. Commn. on Libraries, Nat. Adv. Council for Edn. in Health Professions; mem., pres. Internat. Commn. for Library Devel., 1965; mem. com. on profl. sch. and world affairs, 1965-67, permanent com. Oliver Wendell Holmes Devise, 1964-72, Nat. Com. on Accrediting Bd. Commrs., 1966-70, commn. on acad. affairs Am. Council Edn., 1966-70. Served from 2d lt. to maj., USAAF, 1942-46. Decorated Legion of Merit. Fellow Tex. Hist. Assn.; mem. Modern Lang. Assn., Grolier Club, Tex. Philos. Soc., Tex. Inst. Letters, Phi Beta Kappa, Kappa Sigma, Episcopalian. Author: Bibliography of English Copyright History, 1948; Notes of a Texas Book Collector, 1950; The First Copyright Statute, 1955. Editor: (with J. Frank Dobie and M.C. Boatright) Texas Folklore Publications, XIV-XVII. Asso. editor Tex. Folklore Soc., 1938-41, Southwest Hist. Quar., 1952-56; English Copyright Cases, 1660-1775, 1956. Editor: Texas Quarterly, 1958—. Club: Cosmos. Home: Austin, Tex. Died Apr. 19, 1976.

RAPEER, LOUIS WIN (RA-PER'), educator; b. Cincinnati, O., Dec. 23, 1879; s. William Granville and Lissetta (Pelle) R.; grad. State Normal Sch., Terre Haute, Ind., 1902; S.B., U. of Chicago, 1904; M.A., U. of Minn., 1907; Ph.D., and Doctor's Diploma in Edn., Teachers Coll. (Columbia), 1913; hon. LL.D., Research U., 1924; children—Arthur L. (M.D.), Eugene and A. Yvonne. Teacher and supt. schools, Ind. and Minn., until 1909; asst. prof. edn., U. of Wash., 1909-10; instr. social sciences, Coll. City of New York, 1910-11; instr. N.Y. Training Sch. for Teachers, 1911-14; prof. edn., Pa. State Coll., 1914-17; pres. U. of Puerto Rico, 1917-18; research in rehabilitation for Federal Bd. for Vocational Edn., 1918-19; founder and director Research Inst., Washington, D.C., 1919-20; pres. Research U. and Research Inst., Washington, D.C., since 1920. Teacher edn., summer sessions, univs. of Minn., Ill., Kan., Mont., N.C. and Pa. State Coll. Ex-pres. Fedn. for Am. Childhood. Author: School Health Administration, 1913; Administration of School Medical Inspection, 1913; Educational Hygiene, 1916; Teaching Elementary School Subjects, 1917; The Consolidated Rural School; The Learning and Teaching Process, 1918; How to Use Your Mind, 1924; How to Think, 1929, 1935. Former asso. editor American Education; contributing editor American Journal School of Hygiene. Writer on Permanent ednl. preparedness. Home: Washington, D.C. *

RAPELYE, HARRY ANDREW, retired exec.; b. Hartford, Conn., Aug. 23, 1886; s. Charles A. and Leona (Taylor) R.; B.S., Mass. Inst. Tech., 1908; m. Alice Mahl, Apr. 8, 1913; children— Gardiner, Taylor, Sarah (Mrs. Grant Cowherd). Asst. Mass. Inst. Tech., 1909; comml. engr. Westinghouse Machine Co., 1912; mfr., 1923; pres. Continental Can Co. of Can., Ltd., 1950-52. ret. Sept. 1952. Address: N.Y.C. *

RAPER, ARTHUR FRANKLIN, social science analyst; b. Davidson County, N.C., Nov. 8, 1899; s. William Franklin and Julia Selina (Crouse); A.B., U. of N.C., 1924; M.A., Vanderbilt U., 1925; Ph.D., U. of N.C., 1931; m. Martha Elizabeth Jarrell, June 12, 1929; children—Charles Franklin, Harrison Crouse, Arthur Jarrell, Julia Margaret. Research sec. Commn. on Interracial Cooperation, Inc., Atlanta, Ga., 1926-39; acting prof. sociology, Agnes Scott Coll., Decatur, Ga., 1932-39; staff, Carnegie Corporation Study of Negro in America, 1939-40; social scientist, U.S. Dept. Agr., Bur. Agrl. Economics, 1940-52, project evaluation adviser, Foreign Operations Administration Mutual Security mission to China, 1952-54; consultant to community development div. Internat. Coop. Adminstrn., 1955; regional community development advisor in Middle East, North Africa, and Asia, ICA, 1955-57; assistant chief of orientation and counseling branch Office of Personnel, ICA, Washington, 1958-62; sr. adviser for Michigan State U. to Pakistan Acad. for Rural Devel., Comilla, E. Pakistan, 1962-64; vis. prof. dept. sociology and Asian Studies Center, Mich. State U., East Lansing, from 1965. Mem. wage earnings Industry Coms., 25, 29, 30, 56; chmn. P.R. property carrier industry hearing; spl. mediation rep. Nat. War Labor Bd.; social and econ. cons. in Japan, May-June, 1947, Oct.-Dec. 1948, 1949. Trustee Delta Cooperative Farms, Inc., 1946-52; mem. bd. Nat. Sharecroppers' Fund; exec. sec. The Council on a Christian Social Order, 1938-40); mem. Am. Sociol. Soc., So. Sociol. Soc., Rural Sociol. Soc., Southern Regional Council, Phi Beta Kappa. Methodist. Author: Tragedy of Lynching, 1933; Preface to Peasantry, 1936; Sharecroppers All (with Ira De A. Reid), 1941; Tenants of the Almighty, 1943; Rural Life in the United States (with Carl C. Taylor, et al), 1949; The Japanese Village in Transition, 1950; Guide to Agriculture U.S.A. (with Martha J. Raper), 1951; Rural Trends, 1952; Rural Taiwan—Problem and Promise, 1953; Urban and Industrial Taiwan—Crowded and Resourceful (with Han-Sheng Chuan and Shao-hsing Chen), 1954; Evaluations of Community Schools and TA Program of Taiwan, 1954; Role of Pilot and Demonstration Projects in Community Development, 1956; Function and Status of Community Development, 1957; Unique Role of Church in Village Improvements, 1958; Rural Improvement through Community Action, 1959; Technical Requisites for Socio-Economic Developmental Activities, and Some Points for Technicians Working with Villagers, 1960; Some Reflections upon Leaving Comilla (East Pakistan), 1964; Contribution of Village Development to the Modernization of Nations, 1966; Comilla: A Comprehensive Rural Development Program, 1967. Contbr, to AID Digest, 1962. Home: Oakton, Va. Died Aug. 17, 1979.

RAPER, JOHN ROBERT, biologist; b. Davidson County, N.C., Oct. 3, 1911; s. William Franklin and Julia (Crouse) R.; A.B., U. N.C., 1933, M.A., 1936; M.A., Harvard, 1939, Ph.D., 1939; research fellow botany Cal. Inst. Tech., 1939-41; m. Ruth Scholz, Dec. 19, 1936 (div. Oct. 1948); 1 son, William Thomas; m. 2d, Carlene Marie Allen, Aug. 9, 1949; children—Jonathan Arthur, Linda Carlene. Instr. botany U. Ind., 1941-43; research biologist plutonium div. Manhattan Dist., 1943-46; asst. prof. U. Chgo., 1946-49, asso. prof., 1949-53, prof., 1953-54; prof. botany Harvard, 1954-74, chmn. dept. biology, 1970-74; guest research prof. Botanisches Inst. der Universität Köln, Germany, 1961. Guggenheim fellow, 1960-61; Fulbright Research award, 1960-61. Mem. Am. Acad. Arts and Scis. (sec. 1962-64), Nat. Acad. Scis., Soc. for Study Devel. and Growth, Am. Soc. Naturalists, Bot. Soc. Am., Genetics Soc. Am., Mycol. Soc. Am. (v.p. 1957, pres. 1958), Sigma Xi. Author: Genetics of Sexuality in Higher Fungi, 1966. Home: Lexington, Mass. Died May 21, 1974.

RAPP, JOHN CYRIL, food co. exec.; b. Atlantic, Iowa, Apr. 25, 1901; s. John Joseph and Ethel G. (Sutton) R.; student elec. engring. Des Moines U., 1923; m. Mabel Ellen Azeltine, Nov. 8, 1926; 1 son, Alan Dean; m. Carolyn J. Howard, 1974. Engaged in radio engring., 1923-27; mgr. radio sta. KMA, Shenandoah, Iowa, 1927-40; a founder Tidy House Products Co., Shenandoah, 1940, v.p., 1945-47, pres., 1947-60; v.p., mgr. non-foods div. Pillsbury Co., 1960-63, also dir.; pres. Shenandoah Industries, Inc., 1954-62, Shenandoah Airways, Inc., 1948-62, Tidy House Products Co., Omaha, 1963-70; now pres. Silver Creek Lakes Inc., Colorado Springs, Colo. Mem. 7th Republican Congl. Dist. Iowa Com., 1960-62; mem. Iowa Rep. Central Com., 1960-62. Bd. assos. Chgo. Theol. Sem.; trustee Doane Coll. Mem. Am. Trapshooting Assn. Mason (Shriner), Elk, Kiwanian. Clubs: Omaha; Garden of Gods (Colorado Springs). Home: Shenandoah, Iowa. Died Sept. 28, 1979; buried Shenandoah, Iowa.

RAPPLEYE, WILLARD COLE, med. found. pres.; b. Marinette, Wis., Feb. 11, 1892; s. Albert Higgins and Elizabeth (Johnson) R.; A.B., U. Ill., 1915; M.D., Harvard, 1918; hon. A.M., Yale, 1922; hon. Sc.D., Trinity Coll., 1939, Rutgers, 1949; Med.Sc.D., hon., Woman's Med. Coll. Pa., 1950; L.H.D., N.Y. Med. Coll., 1958; Sc.D., Union U., 1962, Columbia, 1967; m. Elizabeth Cunningham, July 20, 1923, children—Willard Cole, Elizabeth Templeton. Instr. in biology U. Ill., 1914; instr. in comparative anatomy Harvard Dental Sch., 1915-17; pathologist Foxboro (Mass.) State Hosp., 1917-18; house officer Mass. Gen. Hosp., Boston, 1918-19; dir. clin. labs., instr. biochemistry U. Cal., 1919-20, dir. hosps., prof. hosp. adminstrn., 1920-22; med. adviser Cal. State Bd. Control; acting supt. Pacific Colony for Feebleminded, 1920; exec. sec. Com. on Tng. Hosp. Execs., 1922; supt. New Haven Hosp. and prof. hosp. adminstrn., Yale, 1922-26; dir. study, Commn. on Med. Edn., 1925-32; prof. med. econs., dean Coll. Physicians and Surgeons, Columbia, 1931-58; v.p. med. affairs, 1949-58; dir. N.Y. Post-Grad. Med. Sch. (Columbia) 1933-47; dean Sch. of Dental and Oral Surgery (Columbia), 1933-45; commr. hosps., City of N.Y., 1940-42. Mem. med. council State U. of N.Y. Pres. Assn. Am. Med. Colls., 1938-39; chmn. exec. council, 1942-44; chmn. bd. dirs. Health Ins. Plan of Greater N.Y., 1944-48; mem. bd. of hosps. City of N.Y., from 1950; chmn. healing arts adv. com. Selective Service Hdqrs., Washington. Trustee Roosevelt Hosp., N.Y.C., Vassar Coll., 1945-48. Columbia U. Press, 1938-49. Am. Found. for Tropical Medicine; pres. Adv. Council on Med. Edn., 1939-44; Adv. Bd. for Med. Specialties (pres., 1937-44); pres. Josiah Macy, Jr., Found., from 1941; chmn. Wm. J. Matheson Commn., 1931-54; pres. Wm. J. Matheson Found., 1954-64; mem. council United Hosp. Fund; cons. Nat. Inst. Health Nat. Cancer Inst., from 1946. Fellow Am. Coll. Physicians, A.A.A.S., N.Y. Acad. Med.; mem. A.M.A., Am. Hosp. Assn.; Coll. Hosp. Adminstrs., Alpha Omega Alpha (dir.), Phi Chi, Sigma Xi, Harvey Soc. Home: New York, N.Y. Died Aug. 19, 1976.

RASMUSSEN, ANDREW THEODORE (RAS'MUS-SEN), univ. prof.; b. Spring City, Utah, Aug. 10, 1883; s. Andreas Thustrup and Hanne (Jensen)

R,; A.B., Brigham Young U., Provo, Utah, 1909; student U. of Chicago, summers 1908, 11, 13; Ph.D., Cornell U., 1916; m. Gertrude Brown, June 24, 1909; children—Theodore Brown, Waldemar Curtis, Richard Carl, Charlotte. Instr. biology, Brigham Young U., 1909-11, head dept., 1911-13; instr. physiology, Cornell U., 1913-16; instr. of neurology (anatomy), U. of Minn., 1916-18, asst. prof., 1918-19, asso. prof., 1919-25, prof. of anatomy, since 1925; chief examiner Med. Sch., U. of Minn. Mem. A.A.A.S., Am. Assn. of Anat. (mem. exec. com. 1934-38, v.p. 1948-50), Am. Physiol. Soc., Assn. Study Internal Secretions (v.p. 1923, 36), Soc. Exptl. Biol. and Med., Sigma Xi. Author or co-author books relating to field since 1931; latest publs.: Atlas of Cross Section Anatomy of the Brain, 1951; Handbook of Neurology, 1952. Home: Minneapolis. *

RASSENFOSS, JOHN CHRISTOPHER, lumber mfg. exec.; b. Cincinnati, Mar. 21, 1886; s. John and Sally (Sommer) R.; ed. pub. schs., bus. coll. and sch. mech. arts of Cincinnati; m. Mildred A. Fitzgerald, Apr. 12, 1917 (divorced 1949); 1 dau., Mildred Jean (Mrs. R. J. Segerstrom). With Standard Lumber Co. of Sonora, Calif. and its successors, Pickering Lumber Co., and Pickering Lumber Corp. since 1907, asst. gen. mgr., 1920-37, vice pres. and gen. mgr., 1937-46, pres. and gen. mgr. since 1946; pres. Sugar Pine R.R. Co.; dir. Calif. Pine Box Distbrs., San Francisco. Dir., Forest Industries Information Com., Washington since Oct. 1946, Pacific Coast Transportation Adv. Bd., San Francisco since 1945. Mem. Calif. Forest Protective Assn. (dir.; pres., 1948-49), Calif. State C. of C. (chmn. natural resources com. Central Valley council; member statewide natural resources com. and social security com.). Elk. Clubs: Lions, Commonwealth. Home: Sonora, Calif. *

RATHBONE, MONROE JACKSON, oil co. exec.; b. Parkersburg, W.Va., Mar. 1, 1900; s. Monroe Jackson and Ida Virginia (Welch) R.; ed. Parkersburg (W.Va.) High Sch.; Chem. E., Lehigh U., 1921, Eng.D. (hon.); Sc.D., W.Va. U., Marshall U.; LL.D., Marietta Coll., U. Chattanooga, Lafayette Coll., W.Va. Wesleyan U.; L.H.D. (hon.), Pace Coll., m. Eleanor Groves, Apr. 22, 1922; children—Monroe Jackson, Eleanor Virginia. With Standard Oil Co. of La., 1921-65, chem. engr., asst. to gen. supt., 1926-31, gen. supt., 1931-33, asst. gen. mgr. mfg. dept., 1933-36, v.p., gen. mgr. in charge of mfg. operations, 1935-36; pres. Standard Oil Co. of La., 1936-44; pres., dir. Esso Standard Oil Co., 1944-49; dir. Standard Oil Co. (N.J.), 1949-65, pres., 1954-63, chmn., 1963-65, chief exec. officer, chmn. exec. com., 1960-65; dir. Nuclear Systems, Inc., Tropigas Internat. Inc., Triangle Industries, Inc., La. Nat. Bank. Trustee Lehigh U., Teagle Found.; bd. dirs. Nat. Fund Med. Edn. Served as 2d lt. inf. U.S. Army 1918-19. Decorated comdr. Order St. Olav (Norway); Order of Orange Nassau (Holland); Order of Leopold (Belgium); recipient Palladium award Societé Industrielle Chemie; award of merit Am. Inst. Cons. Engrs.; Gold medal award Wharton Bus. Sch. Alumni Soc.; Honor award Stevens Inst. Tech.; Frank H. Lahey Meml. award; named to Business Man's Hall of Fame, Fortune Mag. Mem. Am. Petroleum Inst. (past dir., past chmn.), Sigma Chi, Tau Beta Pi. Republican. Episcopalian. Clubs: University, River (N.Y.C.); Baton Rouge (La.) Country; Gulf Stream Golf, Ocean of Fla. (Delray Beach, Fla.); Baltusrol Golf (Short Hills, N.J.). Home: Baton Rouge, La. Died Aug. 2, 1976.

RATHBUN, GEORGE ST. JOHN, clergyman, educator; b. Rye., N.Y., Jan. 12, 1885; s. Rev. Scott Bogie and Julia Chalmers (Clayton) R.; B.A., St. Stephen's Coll., Annandale, N.Y., 1910; m. Gertrude Harris Reazor, Nov. 2, 1918; 1 dau., Mary Chalmers. Deacon, 1913, priest, 1914, P.E. Ch.; instr. Hoosac (N.Y.) Sch., 1910-20; headmaster Yeates Sch., Lancaster, Pa., 1920-23: master, St. James Sch., Md., 1923-29; rector St. Barnabas Ch., Detroit, Mich., 1930-40, rector, Trinity Church, Ware, Mass., 1940-44; rector, St. Mark's Church, Leominster, Mass., since 1944. Served with French Army as ambulance driver, World War. Mem. American Legion (state chaplain, dept. of Mass., 1950-51), Kappa Gamma Chi. Club: Rotary. Address: Leominster, Mass. *

RATTI, GINO ARTURO (RA'TE), educator; b. Carrara, Italy, Oct. 9, 1885; s. Cesare Augusto and Luigia (Franchini) R.; brought to U.S. at age of 3; A.B., Middlebury (Vt.) Coll., 1907, A.M., 1909; Ph.D., U. of Grenoble (France), 1911; student U. of Florence (Italy), summer, 1925; Sorbonne, Paris, 1925-26; m. Nellie Pauline Rockwood, June 28, 1912; children—Gino Arturo, Emilio Paul. Prin. high sch., Pittsford, Vt., 1907-09; instr. Romance langs., Northwestern U., 1911-13; asst. prof. Romanic langs., U. of Wash., 1913-20; head dept. Romance langs., Butler U., since 1920, actg. dean Coll. Liberal Arts and Sciences, 1935-37, dean, 1937-47, resigned; now dean emeritus. National vice president Association Cosmopolitan Clubs, 1929-31. Member American Assn. U. Profs., Modern Lang. Assn. Am., Am. Assn. Teachers of French, Ind. Hist. Soc., Nat. Fed. Modern Lang. Teachers, Phi Kappa Phi, Kappa Delta Rho (founder), Phi Eta Sigma. Republican. Conglist. Clubs: Professional Men's Forum, Allinace Francaise. Author: Idees Morales et Littéraires d'Alphonse Daudet, 1911; A Progressive Course in French Composition and Conversation, 1925. Editor: Des Histories Drôles pour la Jeunesse (by Max and Alex Fischer), 1927. Contbr. to ednl. jours. Lecturer on ednl. topics, European affairs and world peace. Home: Indianapolis, Ind. *

RATTNER, ABRAHAM, artist; b. Poughkeepsie, N.Y., July 9, 1895; s. Herman M. and Sarah (Zukerman) R.; student Corcoran Sch. Art, 1913-15, George Washington U., 1913-14, Pa. Acad. Fine Arts, 1915-17, Ecole des Beaux Arts, Paris, 1921-23, Ransom Acad., Paris, 1923-24; Acad. de la Grande Chaumiere, 1924-25; Sorbonne, Paris, 1925-26; m. Bettina Bedwell (dec. Apr. 1947); m. 2d, Esther Gentle, 1949. European traveling scholar Pa. Acad. Fine Arts, 1920, Italy, 1920, France, 1920-40; one-man shows Paris, Brussels, U.S.; exhibited Salon d' Autumn. Salon des Independants, des Surr-Independants, Paris, Julien Levy Gallery, N.Y.C., 1936-41; group shows include Miniature groups; mem. staff New Sch. for Social Research, Art Students League, N.Y.C., 1948-52; artist-in-residence, prof. painting U. Ill.; 1952-54; vis. artist Yale, Pa. Acad. Fine Arts, Bklyn. Mus.; artist-in-residence Mich. State U., 1954-60; commd., executed in Paris stained glass window design for Chgo. New Loop Synogogue, 1959. Recipient Temple gold medal Nat. Exhbn. Am. Painting, Pa. Acad. Fine Arts, 1945; 1st prize Tecla Pearls exhbn. Am. Painting, 1946; purchase prize U. Ill., Nat. Exhbn. Am. Painting, 1948; 1st prize, Corcoran gold medal Corcoran Gallery Art, nat. biennial show, 1953; Citation of Honor and retrospective exhbn. Temple U., 1954. Mem. Societe des Arts Decoratif Paris; represented in permanent collections Met. Mus. Art, N.Y.C., Mus. Modern Art, Whitney Mus., N.Y.C., Pa. Acad. Fine Arts, Chgo. Art Inst., Phila. Mus. Art, Mus. Art Balt., Des Moines Inst. Art, Albright Galleries. Buffalo, univ. and pvt. collections. Home: New York, N.Y. Died Feb. 14, 1978.

RAUCH, HARRY ERNEST, educator; b. Trenton, N.J., Nov. 9, 1925; s. James and Sara Edna (Litt) R.; student Calif. Inst. Tech., 1943-44; A.B., Princeton U., 1946, M.A., Ph.D., 1947; m. Helen Farber; children—Marc, James, Ann, Eve. Mem. Inst. Advanced Study, Princeton, N.J., 1949-51; asst. prof. math. U. Pa., 1952-56; asso. prof. Yeshiva U., N.Y.C., 1958-60, prof., 1960-68, asso. dean, 1964-67, faculty prof. math., 1969-71; prof. math. grad. div. City U. N.Y., 1971, disting. prof., 1972-79; prof. math. Coll. City N.Y., 1968-69. Served with AUS, 1944. NSF sr. postdoctoral fellow, 1958-59. Mem. Phi Beta Kappa, Sigma Xi. Author: Geodesics and Curvature in Differential Geometry in the Large, 1959; Elliptic Functions, Theta Functions, and Riemann Surfaces, 1973; Theta Functions with Applications to Riemann Surfaces, 1974. Contbr. articles to math. jours. Home: NY. Died June 18, 1979.

RAUCH, JOHN GEORGE, lawyer, b. Indpls., July 16, 1890; s. John and Mary Catherine (Schoen) R.; A.B., Harvard, 1911, student Law Sch., 1911-12; LL.D., Butler U., June 1968; m. Gertrude Alice Schnull, Apr. 14, 1914; children-Jane Catherine (Mrs. John M. Kitchen), Harriet Anne (Mrs. Alfred O. Reynolds), John George. Admitted to Ind. bar, 1913; practiced in Indpls., from 1915; partner firm Rauch, Chase & Kitchen, from 1946. Chancellor, Episcopal Diocese Indpls., 1953-65, emeritus; sr. warden Christ Ch. Cathedral, Indpls., 1951-63. Pres. bd. trustees Art Assn. Indpls., 1962-71; chmn. bd. trustees Ind. Hist. Soc., from 1950; trustee Ind. Symphony Soc., from 1957; mem. found. Park Sch., Indpls., from 1930. Served with U.S. Army, 1918. Mem. Am., Ind., Indpls. bar assns., Am. Judicature Soc., Indiana Soc. Chgo. Clubs: Harvard (N.Y.C., Boston); University, Indpls. Athletic, Woodstock, Dramatic, Athenaeum (Indpls.). Author: Bibliography of the Laws of Indiana, 1928; A Family Chronicle, 1952; A Sequel to a Family Chronicle, 1974; A Series of Essays, 1975; An Abortive Effort at the Writing of Fiction, 1976. Home: Indianapolis, Ind. Died Feb. 3, 1976.

RAUP, ROBERT BRUCE, prof. philosophy of edn.; b. Clark Co., O., March 21, 1888; s. Gustavus Philip and Fanny (Mitchell) R.; A.B., Wittenberg Coll., 1909; B.D., McCormick Theol. Sem., 1914; Ph.D., Columbia, 1926; grad. work U. of Chicago; m. Clara Eliot, August 23, 1924. Pastor, Am. Presbyterian Ch., Havana, Cuba, 1914-15, Instr. ethics, Bellvue Coll., Neb., 1916-18; instr. psychology and edn., Blackburn Coll., Ill., 1919-21; asst. prof. edn., Teachers Coll., Columbia, 1926-28, asso. prof., 1929-36, prof. since 1937. Mem. Am. Philosophical Assn., N.E.A., Philosophy of Education Soc., Nat. Soc. College Tchrs. Edn. Author or co-author several books relating to field; latest publ. (with others): The Improvement of Practical Intelligence, 1950; also profl. articles. Home: Palo Alto, Calif. Died Apr. 13, 1976.

RAUSHENBUSH, ESTHER (MRS. CARL RAUSHENBUSH), univ. ofcl.; b. Seattle, Nov. 22, 1898; d. Maurice and Anne (Suransky) Mohr.; A.B., U. Wash., 1921, M.A., 1922, Alumnus Summa Laude Dignatus award 1965; postgrad. Radcliffe Coll., 1923-24, U. Freiburg, 1925-26; Litt.D., 1962, L.H.D., 1965, LL.D., 1968, 72; m. Carl Raushenbush, Apr. 17, 1935; 1 son, John. Instr. lit. Wellesley Coll., 1923-24, 26-27, Barnard Coll., 1928-30, 32-35, Columbia, 1930-32; mem. lit. faculty Sarah Lawrence Coll., 1935-46, dean, 1946-57, prof., 1957-60, faculty trustee, 1958-60, dir. Center for Continuing Edn., 1962-65, pres., 1965-69, pres. emeritus, 1969-80; spl. cons. to chancellor N.Y. U., 1969-70; sr. adviser John Hay Whitney Found., 1970-79; vis. scholar Columbia U., 1976-80. Mem. com. on sch. and coll. relations Ednl. Records Bur.; cons. exptl. coll. program Hofstra U., 1958-60; cons. Hampshire Coll, 1966; mem. Nat. Adv. Com for Project Upward Bound, Office Econ. Opportunity; mem. Com. 2d Regional Plan of N.Y.; mem. President's Commn. Status of Women. Chmn. program com. Ellis L. Phillips Found.; trustee Marlboro Coll., Greenwood Fund. Recipient Abraham L. Sachar award Brandeis U., 1969. Mem. Assn. Higher Edn. (exec. com 1964-66), Am. Assn. Acad. Deans (sec. 1955-57), Am. Council Edn. (com. on coll. teaching 1955-58). Author: Literature for Individual Education, 1942; The Fulbright Professor Meets the American College, 1961; The Student and His Studies, 1964; Opportunity Fellows and Visiting Professors, 1972; co-author: Essays in Teaching, 1950; A Graduate Program in an Undergraduate College, 1954; Unfinished Journey, 1969. Co-author, edior: Achievement in the College Years, 1960. Contbr. articles to profl. publs. Editor: Psychology for Individual Education, 1946. Home: New York, N.Y. Died July 21, 1980.

RAVAGE, MARCUS ELI (NAME AMERICANIZED FROM REVICI TO RAVAGE), author; b. Berlad, Rumania, June 25, 1884; s. Judah Loeb and Bella (Rosenthal) Revici; came to U.S., 1900; A.B., U. of Mo., 1909; A.M., U. of Ill., 1910; studied Columbia, 1910-11, 1912-13; m. Jeanne Louise Martin, of Paris, France, Dec. 2, 1915; children—Suzanne Anna, Louise Belle, John Mark. Author: An American in the Making, 1917; The Jew Pays, 1919; The Malady of Europe, 1923; The Story of Teapot Dome, 1924; Five Men of Frankfort—The Story of the Rothschilds, 1929; Glanz und Niedergang des Hauses Rothschild, 1930; Opkomst en Bloei van het Huis Rothschild, 1930; Grandeur et Décadence de la Maison Rothschild, 1931; Cinco Hombres de Francfort, 1931; Pet Muzu z Frankfurtu, 1931; Empress Innocence—The Life of Marie-Louise, 1931; Iphigénie on Marie-Louise, 1932; La Vida de Maria Luisa, 1932; also numerous articles in mags. Address: Paris, France. *

RAVENEL, GAILLARD FITZ SIMONS, business exec.; b. St. Mary's County, Md., July 7, 1886; s. William de Chastignier and Elizabeth (Fitz Simons) R.; LL.B., U. of Va., 1908; m. Margaret Davis, Oct. 22, 1927; children—William de Chastignier, II, Margaret Davis, Helen Davis. Admitted to Washington, D.C. bar, 1909; engaged in practice of law, Washington, N.Y. City, 1909-16; ship operations in Boston, Baltimore and N.Y. City, since 1919; v.p. in charge of operations, U.S. Lines, N.Y. City, since 1942; also dir. Military service, U.S. and France, 1916-19. Mem. numerous trade assns. Episcopalian. Clubs: Racquet and Tennis, India House (N.Y. City): Maryland, Green Spring Valley Fox Hunting. Home: Garrison, Md. *

RAVIN, ARNOLD WARREN, geneticist, educator; b. N.Y.C., Aug. 15, 1921; s. Max and Rae (Levinson) R.; B.S., Coll. City N.Y., 1942; M.A., Columbia, 1948, Ph.D., 1951; m. Sophie Brody, June 11, 1956; children—Sonia, Andrea. Postdoctoral fellow Laboratoire de genetique, U. Paris (France), 1951-53; mem. faculty U. Rochester, 1952-68, prof. biology, 1962-68, chmn. dept., 1957-60, asso. dean Coll. Arts and Sci., 1960-61, dean, 1961-63; prof. biology U. Chgo., 1968-81; master collegiate div. biology, asso. dean div. biol. scis., 1968-73, chmn. com. on conceptual founds. of sci., 1973-77, Addie Clark Harding prof. biology, 1976-81, dir. Morris Fishbein Center for Study History Sci. and Medicine, 1978-81; mem. genetics tng. com. NIH, 1967-70; mem. com. biology Coll. Entrance Exam. Bd., 1956-60; mem. biology com. coll. proficiency exams. N.Y. State Edn. Dept., 1964-66; vis. prof. genetics of U. Calif. at Berkeley, 1963; Sigma Xi Bicentennial lectr., 1974-76; mem. Nat. Humanities Faculty, 1972-81. Trustee Bergey's Manual Trust, 1961, Am. Type Culture Collection, 1967-72. Recipient Edward Peck Curtis award for excellence in undergrad. teaching, 1966. Predoctoral fellow Nat. Cancer Inst., USPHS, 1949-50, post-doctoral fellow, 1951-53, spl. research fellow, 1960-61; NSF Faculty fellow, 1975. Served to 1st lt. USAAF, 1942-46. Fellow AAAS; mem. Genetics Soc. Am., Soc. Gen. Microbiology (Great Britain), Am. Soc. Microbiology, Am. Soc. Cell Biology, Am. Soc. Naturalists, Philosophy of Sci. Assn., History of Sci. Assn., AAUP, Sigma Xi. Author: Evolution of Genetics, 1965. Mem. editorial bd. Am. Naturalist, 1968-70; co-editor Genetic Orgn., 1969. Contbr. numerous articles to profl. jours. Home: Chicago, Ill. Died Feb. 28, 1981.

RAY, CHARLOTTE ELIZABETH, coll. dean; b. Titusville, Pa., Feb. 17, 1880; d. Joseph Martin and Sarah (Paulding) Ray; B.S., U. of Pittsburgh, 1919, A.M., 1924; student Columbia, 1930. Teacher in elementary and high schs., Pittsburgh and vicinity, 1900-23; dean of women, Pa. State Coll., 1923-46; social worker Morals Ct., Pittsburgh under council of Churches, since 1947. Charter trustee Westminister Found., Inc., State College, Pa. Mem. Alpha Lambda Delta, Cwens, Mortar Board, Nat. and Pa. State edn. assns., Nat. and Pa. (past pres.) assns. Deans of Women, American Assn. Univ. Women, State Coll. Woman's. Club, Pi Beta Phi, Pi Lambda Theta, Phi Kappa Phi. Republican. Baptist. Author: Key of Kappa Kappa Gamma. 1935. The Fraternity in Relation to the College. Home: Pitts. *

RAY, GEORGE WASHINGTON, JR., lawyer; b. Cripple Creek, Colo., Mar. 23, 1898; s. George Washington and Esther Livona (Magee) R.; A.B., U. Tex., 1920; J.D., M.A., Columbia, 1922; LL.D., Piedmont, 1969; m. Belle Trimble, Sept. 18, 1923; children—George Carleton, Nancy Trimble; m. 2d Bonnie Dowd Van Dyk, Aug. 31, 1946; children—James Van Dyk, Bonnie Van Dyk. Admitted N.Y. bar, 1923, U.S. Supreme Ct. bar, 1933, Conn. bar, 1963, Vt. bar, 1968; mem. legis. drafting research bur. Columbia, 1921-22; prosecuted claims by U.S. on behalf of Am. nats. against Germany, before Mixed Claims Commn., U.S. and Germany, 1922-24; counsel Tex. Co., 1922-42, gen. atty., 1942-47; gen. counsel Arabian Am. Oil Co., Trans Arabian Pipe Line Co., Aramco Overseas Co., 1947-61, internat. arbitration between Royal Govt. Saudi Arabia and Arabian Am. Oil Co., 1955-58. Chmn. adv. bd. and exec. com. Internat. Oil and Gas Ednl. Center, 1959-62, Southwestern Legal Found.; chmn. adv. bd. and exec. com. Internat. Comparative Law Center, 1962-66, mem., from 1962; counsel firm Black & Plante, White River Junction, Vt., from 1968. Served with Air Flying Corps, USNR, 1918-22. Mem. Assn. Bar N.Y.C., Am., Vt. bar assns., Acad. Polit. Sci., Am. Acad. Polit. and Social Sci., N.A.M. (dir. 1960-62, chmn. internat. econ. affairs com. 1960-61), Council on Fgn. Relations, Kappa Alpha, Phi Delta Phi. Republican. Conglist. Club: University (N.Y.C.). Author: The Law Governing Contracts between States and Foreign Nationals, 1960; Law and the Perfecting Process, 1964; numerous articles. Home: East Thetford, Vt. Died Sept. 14, 1978.

RAY, RUTH (MRS. JOHN R. GRAHAM), artist; b. N.Y.C., Nov. 8, 1919; d. Oscar Willard and Marie (Beynon) Ray; student Swarthmore Coll., 1936-38, Barnard Coll., 1938-39, Art Students League, 1938-41; m. Dr. John Reginald Graham, Jan. 3, 1948 (dec. Dec. 1964); children—Ian, Willard Reid, Lyle. Exhbtd. one man shows Norlyst Gallery, N.Y.C., 1944, Ferargil, N.Y.C., 1947, 49, Raymond and Raymond, Calif., 1947, Stamford (Conn.) Mus., 1950, Silvermine Guild Artist, 1952, 67, Darien (Conn.) Pub. Library, 1958, 59, 62, Grand Central Art Galleries, N.Y.C., 1958, 62, 66, 70, 74, Rive Gauche Galleries, Denver, 1967, Marymount Coll., 1968; was included in Whitney Ann., 1959, N.A.D., Nat. Assn. Women Artists, Pa. Acad. Ann., 1959, Allied Artists, Audubon Artists, Conn. Acad. Fine Arts, New Haven Paint and Clay Club; represented Springfield Mus. Fine Arts, Columbus (Ga.) Mus. Arts, Norfolk (Va.) Mus. Arts, Nat. Acad. of Design, Nat. Art Museum of Sports; also pvt. collections; illustrator books, comml. artists several bus. firms; radio and TV appearances, N.Y.C. Recipient Alger prize Nat. Assn. Women Artists, 1945, Marcia Brady Tucker prize, 1953; popular and purchase prize Springfield Mus. Fine Arts, 1946; purchase prize La Tausca, N.Y., 1946, Julius Hallgarten prize N.A.D., 1948; popular prize Conn. Contemporary Exhbn., 1950; prize Silvermine N.E. Ann., 1953; major award Conn. Acad. Fine Arts, 1953; medal of honor Am. Artists mag., 1956; bronze medal Allied Artists Am., 1956; Mrs. Stanley Simon award Silvermine Guild Artists, 1959, New Haven Paint and Clay Club figure prize, 1960, Lillian Cotton prize Allied Artists, 1960, Grumbacher Pruchase prize, 1960, Gloria Layton prize, 1962, Founders award for best painting Miniatures, Sculptors and Gravers Soc. Washington, 1972, 74, 76, others. Mem. Silvermine Guild Artists, Conn. Acad. Fine Arts, Allied Artists Am., Art Students League (life), Nat. Acad. (council). Presbyn. Clubs: Ox Ridge Hunt (v.p., steward), Ox Ridge Kennel (Darien). Home: Darien, Conn. Died Dec. 18, 1977.

RAY, WARD LOWE, college prof.; b. Nineveh, Pa., Dec. 21, 1883; s. John Leonard and Ella (Rush) R.; A.B., U. of Ore., 1908, A.M., U. of Wis., 1910; studied U. of Berlin, 1910-11; m. Thesie Edna Smith, of Sycamore, Pa., Aug. 23, 1910. Teacher country schs. in Pa., Wash., and Ore., 1903-5; prin. Silverton (Ore.) High Sch., 1908-9; prof. physics and chemistry, 1911-17, dean, 1913-14, pres., 1914-17, William and Vashti Coll., Aledo, Ill.; prof. physics and elec. engring., U. of N.M., 1917—. Mem. Alpha Tau Omega, Acacia. Republican. Baptist. Mason (32 deg., Shriner). Address: Albuquerque, N.M.*

RAYMOND, ANAN, lawyer; b. Rapid City, S.D., Nov. 6, 1890; s. Spencer H. and Marinda (Platt) R.; student S.D. Sch. Mines, Rapid City, 1903-07; A.B., U. Nebr., 1911, LL.B., 1913; m. Florence Hostetler, May 11, 1915; children—Margaret Marinda (Mrs. Robert J. Manning), David Hostetler (dec.), Sarah Elizabeth (Mrs. N. Peter Rathvon, Jr.), Spencer Henry. Admitted to Nebr. bar, 1913; asso. Francis A. Brogan, Omaha, 1913-14; mem. Brogan & Raymond, 1915-17, Brogan, Ellick & Raymond, 1919-29; v.p. and gen. counsel State Bank of Chicago, 1929; v.p. Foreman State Trust Savs. Bank, Chicago, 1929-31; mem. law firm Raymond, Mayer Jenner & Block, and predecessor firms, 1931-68; dir. Selected Am. Shares, Inc., State Nat. Bank of Evanston (Ill.), from 1960. Trustee U. Nebraska Found.; mem. Northwestern U. Assos.; trustee Kenilworth, Ill., 1937-45, pres. 1945-49. Served as capt. to maj. U.S. Army, World War I; col. Inf., U.S. Ret. Recipient Distinguished Service award U. Neb., 1962. Fellow Am. Bar Found.; mem. Am., Ill., Fed., Internat., Chgo., Neb. (pres. 1929) bar assns., Selden Soc., Am. Legion (comdr. Omaha post 1925), Res. Officers Assn., Order of Coif, Phi Beta Kappa, Phi Kappa Psi, Phi Delta Phi, Delta Sigma Rho. Conglist. Clubs: Chicago, Glenview, Mid-Day, Chicago Literary, Chicago Law (pres. 1956-57), Kenilworth, Caxton. Contributor of various articles to legal jours. Home: Wilmette, Ill. Died Oct. 30, 1975.

RAYMOND, ANTONIN, architect; b. Kladno, Bohemia, May 10, 1888, s. Alois and Ruzena (Tausigova) R.; student Czech Higher Tech. Inst., Prague, 1906-10; m. Noémi Pernessin, Dec. 15, 1914; 1 son, Claude Jean Francois. Came to U.S., 1910; naturalized, 1916. Office of Cass Gilbert, N.Y. City, 1910-16; with Frank Lloyd Wright, 1916-17, Japan, 1920; private practice, Japan, 1921-37; pioneer modern architecture in Orient, resulting in several hundred internationally known bldgs., including U.S. Embassy and Consular establishments (in assn. with H. Van Burren Magonigle), French Embassy, U.S.S.R. Embassy, St. Luke's Internat. Hosp. Center, Women's Christian Coll., Tokyo Golf Club, Socony Bldg., Rising Sun Bldg., etc.; Golcond Bldg., Pondicherry, India, 1937-38; mem. firm Antonin Raymond and L. L. Rado, N.Y.C., 1939-67, Tokyo, Japan, from 1967, Raymond & Rado & Partners, N.Y.C., from 1967. Recent works are recreation and indsl. bldgs. for Electrolux Corp., Reader's Digest Bldg., Housing for U.S. Embassy, Tokyo, Japan, church in Philippines, work for U.S. armed forces in U.S. and overseas, also U.S. Embassy, Djakarta, Indonesia, St. Anselm's Ch., Internat. Christian U., Rikkyo High Sch., Iranian Embassy (Tokyo), office bldg. U.S. hdqrs. KLM Royal Dutch Airlines, N.Y.C., Central Bklyn. High Sch., Gumna Music Center, Takasaki, Japan, S.V.D. Fathers Monastery, Tokyo, others. Served with the U.S. Army, 1917, 2d lt. G-2, G.H.Q., A.E.F.; Hon. consul of Czechoslovakia in Japan, 1925-57. Decorated Knight of the Legion of Honor of France; officer Order of White Lion of Czechoslovakia; knight Order of Corona d'Italia; knight Order of Dragon of Annam; Czechoslovakia War Cross; Order of Rising Sun (Japan). Registered architect, N.Y., Pa., N.J., Wis., Japan. Nagoya Internat. Sch. (Japan), Fellow A.I.A. (awarded medal honor N.Y. chpt., 1956); mem. Am. C. of C. or Tokyo, Soc. Mil. Engrs. Clubs: Architectural League, Engineers, Am. Jersey Cattle (N.Y.C.); Am., Tokyo, Tokyo Golf, Karuizawa Golf (Japan). Author: Antonin Raymond, his work in Japan, 1920-35, (Archtl. Record), 1936; "Antonin Raymond Architectural Details" (Archtl. Forum), 1938; Antonin Raymond—Autobiography. Works pub. extensively in architectural journals. Home: New Hope, Pa. Died Oct. 25, 1976.

RAYMOND, REGINALD IRVING, clergyman; b. New Orleans, May 19, 1885; s. Peter Laidlaw and Fannie (Curran) R.; B.S., Tulane U., 1905, alumni fellow in biology, 1905-7; post-graduate work same, 2 yrs.; B.A., U. of the South, 1908, B.D., 1909, M.A., 1912; grad. student for D.D., Gen. Theol. Sem., New York, 1914; for. Ph.D., U. of Chicago, 1915; m. Mary Helen Marbury, of Ruston, La., May 31, 1911. Deacon and priest, P.E. Ch., 1910; rector Trinity Church, Natchitoches, La., 1910-11, Christ Ch., Pulaski, Va., and Grace Ch., Radford Va. 1911, Otey Memorial Ch., Sewanee, Tenn., 1913; in charge Grace Ch., Memphis, Tenn., 1912, Christ Ch. Cathedral, New Orleans, 1913, 1914, St. John's Ch., Knoxville, Tenn., summer 1915; minister Plymouth Congl. Ch., Chicago, 1917—. State supt. home dept. La. State S.S. Assn., 1910-11. Asst. in biology and asso. curator Mus. of Natural History, Tulane U., 1904-6; prof. natural Science, Rugby Acad., New Orleans, 1906-7; instr. biology, 1908-10, 1911-12, asso. prof., 1912-13, prof. 1913-17, U. of the South. Lecturer bacteriology and materia medica, Emerald Hodgson Memorial Hosp., Sewanee, Tenn., 1914-17; prof. zoölogy, summer term, U. of Tenn., 1915; prof. ch. history, Congl. Training Sch., Y.M.C.A. Coll., Chicago. Clubs: University, Congregational, Kenwood, Scrooby. Mem. A.A.A.S. Am. Micros. Soc. Home: Chicago. *

RAYNER, CHARLES (RANER), petroleum adviser; b. Bloomfield, N.J., Sept. 13, 1886; s. Edwin A. and Ella Holmes (Marvin) R.; A.B., Amherst College, 1909; m. Jeanette Bennett, July 21, 1917; 1 daughter, Mary Marvin. Mgr. Standard Oil Co. of N.Y., marketing petroleum in British Malaysia. Dutch East Indies, Siam 1909-17, asst. dir., 1917-18; European rep. Bennett Tarlton & Co., Austin, Texas. 1919-23. dir., vice pres., United North & South Oil Co., United North & South Dev. Co., Luling, Texas, 1923-31; own business, dealing in oil properties, San Antonio, Luling, Texas; regional dir., U.S. Dept., Agr., 1941; chief petroleum adviser, Office of Econ. Warfare, 1941-43; petroleum adviser, Dept. of State, since Dec., 1943; v.p. American Independent Oil Co., since 1947, also subsidiary, Independent Tankships, Inc. Member American delegation to England to negotiate oil agreement, September 1945. Lieut., Transport Motor Corps., U.S., Army, World War I. Trustee Luling Foundation, privately endowed agricultural foundation, Luling, Texas, 1927-37. Clubs: India House (New York); Army and Navy Club (Washington, D.C.). Home: Washington, D.C. *

RAYNER, WILLIAM WARD, lawyer; b. Bklyn., Aug. 7, 1927; s. Edward William and Helen (Ward) R.; B.S., Georgetown U., 1950, LL.B., 1954; m. Barbara Ann Schneider, June 10, 1950; children—William Ward, Brenda Susan, Brian Carlin, Patrick Joseph, Edward Francis. Liason officer CIA, 1950-54; admitted to D.C. bar, 1954, thereafter practiced in Washington; trial atty. antitrust div. Dept. Justice, 1954-56; asso., then partner Whitlock, Markey & Tait, and predecessors, 1956-68; asst. to chmn. bd. Crowell Collier and Macmillan, Inc., London, 1968-69, v.p., 1969-76. Served with AUS, 1945-46. Mem. Am., D.C. bar assns., Brit. Inst. Dirs., Phi Alpha Delta. Republican. Roman Catholic. Editorial staff Georgetown Law Jour., 1953-54. Home: Potomac, Md. Died July 27, 1976.

REA, JAMES C(HILDS), business exec.; b. Pittsburgh, Nov. 30, 1882; s. William Holdship and Mary (Childs) Rea; grad. Shady Side Acad., Pittsburgh, 1900; B.S., Princeton, 1904; m. Julia Parish Dodge, June 8, 1911; children—William H., Cleveland D., Grace D. (Mrs. Harrison Garrett), Ruth (Mrs. Alfred H. Howell), James C., Mary C. (Mrs. Edward R. Weidlein, Jr.), John, Bayard D. Asst. chemist Colonial Steel Co., Colona, Pa., 1904-06; asst. supt. Bar Mills-Oliver Iron & Steel Corp., 1906-09; dir. Oliver Iron & Steel Corp.; v.p. and director Pittsburgh Business Properties, Inc., since 1935; trustee The Dollar Savings Bank of Pittsburgh; dir. Phelps Dodge Corp., Phelps Dodge Copper Products Corp., Montour R.R., Fidelity Trust Co. Trustee Carnegie Inst., Carnegie Inst. Tech., Shady Side Acad., Valley Sch. of Ligonier. Pres. and dir. Henry C. Frick Ednl. Commn. since 1947, Western Pa. Hosp. since 1941; mem. finance com. Home for Aged Protestant Women; treas. and mem. bd. mgrs. Homewood Cemetery; mem. adv. com. Indsl. Home for Crippled Children. Pres. Pitcairn-Crabbe Foundn. since 1942; mem. distbn. com. Pittsburgh Foundn.; treas. and trustee Y.M.C.A. of Pittsburgh. Mem. U.S. Navy V-12 Selection Com. for Western Pa., 1943-45. Trustee Princeton U., 1944-48. Presbyterian. Mason. Clubs: Rolling Rock (Ligonier, Pa.); Duquesne (pres. 1934-35, 35-36), The Golf (Pitts.); University (N.Y.C.). Home: Pitts. *

READ, FLORENCE MATILDA, ex-college pres., b. Delevan, N.Y., Nov. 12, 1885; d. William Ervin and Cornelia Minerva (Waldo) R.; B.A., Mount Holyoke Coll., 1909, hon. Litt.D., 1929; LL.D., Oberlin Coll., 1939, Atlanta University, 1953, Reed Coll., 1961. Alumnae secretary Mount Holyoke Coll., 1909-11; sec. to pres., later sec., Reed Coll., Portland, Ore., 1911-20; asst. sec., later exec. sec., Internat. Helth Bd. Rockefeller Found., N.Y.C., 1920-27; pres. Spelman Coll., 1927-53, emeritus, 1953; acting pres., Atlanta U., 1936-37. Served with med. section, Council of Nat. Defense, Washington, D.C., and with Y.M.C.A., in France, 1918-19. Trustee Atlanta University; mem. board trustees Morehouse College. Awarded the Royal Medal of Reward in Gold with Crown by Denmark in 1927. Mem. Am. Assn. Univ. Women, Mount Holyoke Coll. Alumae Assn., Phi Beta Kappa. Author: The Story of Spelman College, 1961. Club: Cosmopolitan (N.Y.C.). Address: Claremont, Cal. *

READ, HELEN APPLETON, art historian; b. Bklyn.; d. Ruel Ross and Mary (Schaumburg) Appleton; grad. Bklyn. Heights Sem.; A.B., Smith Coll., 1908; student Art Students League, 1909-12; m. Charles Albert Read, May 29, 1914; 1 dau., Helen (Mrs. Edmund K. Trent). Art critic Bklyn. Daily Eagle, 1922-38; asso. art editor Vogue mag., 1925-31; dir. Portraits, Inc., 1943-57, pres., 1957-74; dir. exhbn. 400 Years of German Painting, 1939, Am. painting sent to Latin Am. capitols, 1943, under auspices coordinator cultural relations between N.A., S.A. Recipient Medal of Honor, Salmagundi Club, 1967; medal Smith Coll., 1968. Lectr. Am. and German art, romantic art. Am. colls. and univs. Mem. Alumnae Assn. Smith Coll. Clubs: Cosmopolitan, Smith College (N.Y.C.). Author: Robert Henri, 1931; Caspar David Friedrich, 1939. Contbr, art publs. Home: Brooklyn, N.Y. Died Nov. 11, 1975.

READ, NORMAN, electrical engr.; b. Isle of Man, Eng., Apr. 25, 1883; s. Henry and Bessie C. (Ferrier) R.; B.S. (E.E.), U. of Colo., 1905; m. Ella F. Hodges, of Denver, Colo., 1910. Began with engring. dept. Denver Gas & Electric Co., 1905; consulting hydro-electric practice, 1907-9; elec. engr. and supt. of power, Denver Tramway Co., 1909-13; asst. gen. mgr. Colo. Power Co., 1913-16, v.p. and gen. mgr. since 1916. Mem. Am. Inst. E.E., Delta Tau Delta; hon. mem. Tau Beta Pi; asso. mem. Am. Inst. Mining and Metall. Engrs. Mem. Denver Civic and Commercial Assn. Republican. Episcopalian. Clubs: Denver, Cactus. Home: Denver, Colo. *

READ, WILLIAM AUGUSTUS, banker; b. Rye, N.Y., Aug. 21, 1895; s. William Augustus and Caroline Hicks (Seaman); grad. Pomfret Sch., 1913, Harvard, 1918; m. Edith Fabyan, May 10, 1917; children—William Augustus, Curtis Seaman, David Westcott, Roderick Fabyan, Peter Bancroft, Alexander Duncan, Donald Bartow, Jean, Frederick Harvey. With Dillon Read & Co., 1919-29, partner, 1921, v.p., 1922-29; v.p. Central Hanover Bank & Trust Co., 1920-40, 46-51; vice president Hanover Bank, 1951-55, senior vice president, 1955-62. Served as private, battery A, First Mass. F.A., Mexican Border, 1916; ensign Aviation Corps U.S.N.R., 1917-18 lt. comdr. to capt., 1943, commodore 1945, rear admiral, 1953. Legion Merit, Bronze Star Medal with gold star, Commendation Ribbon, Presdl. Unit Citation with two stars, Navy Unit Citation. Home: Purchase, N.Y. Died Sept. 14, 1976.

READ, WILLIAM THORNTON, SR., chemist; b. College Station, Tex., Mar. 8, 1886; s. Joseph Dotson and Belle (Thornton) R.; A.B., Austin Coll., Sherman, Tex., 1905, A.M., 1908; M.A., U. Tex., 1915; student Harvard Univ., 1915-16; Ph.D.; Yale Univ. 1921; married Roxie Clark, Sept. 9, 1918; children—William Thornton, Roxana Clark (Mrs. Otto E. Wiswell). Asst. editor Lampasas (Texas) Leader, 1905-07; sec. Austin Coll.. 1907-10; instr., U. of Tex., 1914-15. 1916-18; instr., Yale, 1919-24, asst. prof., 1924-25; head dept. of chemistry, Texas Technological College, Lubbock. 1925-30; dean school of chemistry, Rutgers U., 1930-43; section chief National Roster. 1943-46; chemical adviser, Dept. of Army, 1946-57, cons., 1957—. 1st lt. C.W.S., U.S. Army, 1918. Mem. Washington Acad. Sci., Am. Chem. Soc., Am. Inst. Chem. Engrs., Am. Inst. Chemists, Chemists Club, N.Y., Sigma Xi, Sigma Delta Chi, Alpha Chi Sigma, Phi Lambda Upsilon. Presbyn. Author: Industrial Chemistry, 1943. Contbr. Am. Ency. and Annual. Home: Pasadena, Tex. *

REAGAN, WILLIAM J., educator; b. Sheridan, Ind., Sept. 26, 1882; s. Jehu and Mary (MacMillan) R.; grad. Earlham Coll., Richmond, Ind., 1904; grad. Haverford (Pa.) Coll., 1905, A.M., 1912; m. Florence Lindley, of Fairmount, Ind., Sept. 8, 1908; children—Agnes, Caroline, James, Lindley, Robert, George. Prin. Bloomingdale (Ind.) Acad., 1905-08; teacher of philosophy and psychology, Pacific Coll., Newberg, Ore., 1908-09, acting pres., 1909-10; teacher of philosophy, Friends U., Wichita, Kan., 1910-14; prin. Oakwood Sch., Poughkeepsie, N.Y., since 1914. Mem. com. for work on boys, Nat. Council. Y.M.C.A. Republican. Quaker. Address: Poughkeepsie, N.Y. *

REARDON, JAMES G. (RERDUN), educator; b. Medway, Mass., July 22, 1901; s. William Henry and Mary Agnes (McGinnis) R.; A.B., Boston Coll., 1923, A.M., 1927, LL.D., 1937; m. Anita Thorndike, Apr. 12, 1928; children—Cynthia Ann, James Gerard, Susan Thorndike, Rosemary, Michael, Peter, Judith Anita. Engaged as tutor Latin and Greek, 1921-23; asst. prin. high sch., East Bridgewater, Mass., 1923-25, prin., 1925-28; supt. schools East Bridgewater, Mass., 1928-34; supt. schs. Adams. Mass., consultant to pvt. schs.; tech. consultant on education, Fed. Govt.; commr. of education Commonwealth of Massachusetts, 1935-39; superintendent of schools, Lenox, Mass., now on leave of absence; pres. Posse Normal Sch., Kendal Green, Mass. Served as private infantry, U.S. Army, 1918-19, World War I. Now lieut. (s.g.) U.S. Naval Aviation. Fleet Airwing Nine; now lt. comdr., U.S.N., public relations office 12th Naval District, San Francisco, Calif. Director Boston Museum of Fine Arts, Massachusetts Safety Council, Society for Prevention of Cruelty to Children. Member Boston Chamber of Commerce. Trustee Bradford-Durfee, New Bedford and Lowell textile schs., Mass. State Coll., Mass. Inst. Tech. Mem. National Educational Association, Mass. Supts. Assn., Trade Teachers Assn. of Boston, Am. Legion, Charitable Irish Soc., Catholic Alumni Sodality, Pi Gamma Mu, Robert Emmet Associates. Democrat. Roman Catholic. K.C., A.O.H. Clubs: Catholic (New York City); Clover, City (Boston.)*

REASONER, HAROLD CARLTON, utility cons.; b. Battle Creek, Mich., Apr. 10, 1908; s. Carl and Irene Pearl (Bradstreet) R.; B.S., U. Mich., 1931; m. Catherine Lewis, Sept. 20, 1932; 1 dau., Calla (Mrs. Harvey Sellner). With Detroit Edison Co., 1928-75, v.p., mgr. engring. system devel. and interconnections, 1966-70, v.p. engring., 1970, exec. v.p. prodn., 1970-73; utility cons., 1973-75. Mem. I.E.E.E., Engring. Soc. Detroit. Clubs: Detroit Athletic, Acanthus (Detroit). Home: Birmingham, Mich. Died Apr. 23, 1975.

RECINOS, ADRIAN (RE-SINOS), diplomat; b. Antigua, Guatemala, July 5, 1886; s. Teodoro M. and Rafaela (Avila) R.; grad. Law Sch., U. of Guatemala, 1907; m. Maria Palomo, of Guatemala, July 5, 1916; children—Laura, Adrian, Beatriz, Mary, Isabel. Sec. Guatemala legation, Salvador, 1908; under-sec. of state, Guatemala, 1910-20; del. 2d Pan-Am. Scientific Congress, 1915; mem. Guatemala Legislative Assmebly, 1920-21; minister of foreign affairs, 1922; M.P. to France and Spain. 1923-25; pres. Legislative Assembly, 1926-27; E.E. and M.P. to U.S. since 1928; Ambassador E. and P. to U.S., since May 1943; del. to World Economic Conf., London, 1933. Mem. Am. Soc. Internat. Law, Geog. and Hist. Soc. Guatemala, Geog. Soc., Mexico, Ateneo de Santiago, Chile, Instituto Ibero-Americano de Derecho Comparado, Madrid. Catholic. Home: Guatemala City, Guatemala. Address: Washington, D.C. *

RECORD, JAMES ROBERT, newspaper editor; b. Paris, Tex., Oct. 3, 1885; s. Julius Polk and Katie (Cross) R.; grad. Paris High Sch., 1901; student U. of Notre Dame (Ind.), 1901-04, U. of Tex., 1904-05; m. Alabell Brown, Dec. 5, 1917. Began as reporter Paris (Texas) News, 1905; reporter Star-Telegram, Fort Worth, Tex., 1907-09, sports editor, 1909-11, city editor, 1911-17, news editor, 1917-23, mng. editor, 1923-56, associate editor, 1956—. President emeritus Texas Associated Press Mng. Editors Assn.; mem. Am. Society Newspaper Assn. Mem. Kappa Sigma. Democrat. Catholic; Knight of St. Gregory. K.C., Elk. Club: Ft. Worth. Editors, Nat. Associated Press Managing Editors Home: Ft. Worth, Tex. *

RECTOR, WILLIAM GEORGE, metals co. exec.; b. Duluth, Minn., Feb. 13, 1916; s. Walter Whiting and Lillian (Post) R.; student U. Minn., 1935-36, Northwestern U., 1937; B.S., U. Ariz., 1939; m. Kathleen Spriggs Wager, Mar. 10, 1940; children—Barbara (Mrs. Robert Arnett Morken II), Susan (Mrs. Richard Carley Boynton, Jr.), Walter. Trainee, Montgomery Ward, Chgo., 1940-45; plant mgr. True Temper Corp., Evansville, Ind., also Charleston, W.Va., 1945-52, exec. v.p., 1953, pres., 1953-63; pres. Lufkin Rule Co., Saginaw, Mich., 1964-67; pres. Cooper Group div. Apex, N.C., 1967-79; sr. v.p. Cooper Industries, Inc., Houston, 1973-79. Clubs: Cleveland Union; Tucson Country, Old Pueblo (Tucson); MacGregor Downs Country (Cary, N.C.). Home: Tucson, Ariz. Died Jan. 4, 1979.

REDDICK, DEWITT CARTER, educator; b. Savannah, Ga., July 30, 1904; s. Walter Newton and Frances (Westerman) R.; student Tex. A. and M. Coll., 1921-22; B. Journalism, Tex., 1925, A.M., 1928; Ph.D., U. Mo., 1939; m. Marjorie Bryan, June 20, 1934; children—Bryan DeWitt, Frances Alicia. Reporter, Ft. Worth Star-Telegram, Austin American, 1924-26; part-time corr. Christian Sci. Monitor, 1927-31; instr. journalism U. Tex., from 1927; acting dir. Sch. Journalism, 1955-56, asso. dean Coll. Arts and Scis., 1956-59, dir. Sch. Journalism, 1959-64, dir. Sch. Communication, 1965-67, dean Sch. Communication, 1967-69, prof. journalism, 1970-75, emeritus, 1975-80, asso. prof. Columbia Grad. Sch., 1941; dean Coll. Communications, U. Tenn., 1969-70. Dir. Interscholastic League Press Conf., 1927-50; adv. edn. council Nat. Bus. Publs., 1956-80; chmn. accrediting com. Am. Council on Edn. for Journalism, 1962-64. Recipient Scarbrough award, 1955; award of honor U. Mo., 1964; award So. Ill. U., 1967; Distinguished Alumnus award U. Tex., 1972; Golden Crown award Columbia Scholastic Press Assn., 1975. Mem. AAUP, Assn. Edn. Journalism (v.p. 1954, 60-61, chmn. mag. journalism com. 1955-57, pres.-elect 1964-65, pres. 1965-66), Internat. Council Indsl. Editors (chmn. bibliog. com. 1958-63), Am. Assn. Schs. and Depts. Journalism (pres. 1961-62), Soc. Asso. Indsl. Editors, Am. Assn. Tchrs. Journalism, Sigma Delta Chi. Author: High School Newspaper Handbook, 1933; Journalism and the School Paper, rev. edit., 1964; Modern Feature Writing, 1949; (with Alfred A. Crowell) Industrial Editing, 1962; High School Journalism Work Book, 1964; Mass Media and the School Newspaper, 1975. Editor: Campus and Church, 1955. Adv. editor Tex. Presbyn.; chmn. editorial bd. Presbyn Survey, 1965-69. Contbr. articles numerous mags. Home: Austin, Texas. Died Aug. 22, 1980.

REDDIG, EDWARD STERLING, mfg. exec.; b. Centerville, Iowa, Aug. 29, 1904; s. Harry F. and Jessie (Shurr) R.; student Northwestern, 1926-30; C.P.A., Ohio U., 1943; m. Elizabeth Irene Gay, July 4, 1932 (dec.); children—Gay, Sally; m. 2d, Virginia Clark Ellingen, Jan. 17, 1973; children—Steven, Lisa, Gina, Mary, Edward. Certified pub. accountant Arthur Anderson & Co., Chgo., 1931-35; spl. auditor Pub. Service Co. No. Ill., 1935-36; asst. auditor Chgo. Surface Lines, 1936-37; asst. to v.p. and controller The White Motor Co., Cleve., 1937-44, controller, 1944-47, v.p., controller, 1947-50, v.p. finance, 1950-56; chmn. bd. Mpls.-Moline Co., 1955-58; pres. White Sewing Machine Co. (name changed to White Consol. Industries, Inc. 1964), Cleve., 1956-69, chmn. bd., from 1969, also chief exec. officer; chmn. bd. White Engines Inc., R.L. Consol. Inc., Canton, Ohio, from 1976; dir. Torcon Corp., Ashtabula, Ohio. Trustee Massanutten Mill. Acad., Woodstock Va., Gilmore Acad., Gates Mills, Ohio. Mem. Am. Inst. C.P.A.'s, Ohio Soc. C.P.A.'s C. of C. Clubs: Mid-Day, Union, Mayfield Country, Cleve. Skating, Cleve. Athletic. Home: Gates Mills, Ohio. Deceased.

REDDY, WILLIAM JOHN, educator; b. Boston, Aug. 10, 1926; s. Neil and Margaret (Doherty) R.; A.B., Harvard, 1949, M.S., 1957, Sc.D., 1960; m. Elizabeth A. Enaire, Jan. 1, 1955; children—Margaret, Elizabeth, Ann, W. John. Chemist Peter Bent Brigham Hosp., Boston, 1949-60, asso. staff, 1960-64, asso., 1964-68; dir. chemistry dept. St. Vincent Hosp., Worcester, Mass., 1968-70; prof. U. Ala. Sch. Medicine 1970-80; cons. in field. Pres. Boston chpt. Muscular Dystrophy Assn., 1965, 68; mem. exec. com. Ala. Diabetes Assn., 1971. Bd. dirs. St. Vincent Research Found., Worcester, 1967-73. Boston Med. Soc. grantee, 1966-67, Am. Heart Assn., 1967-71, NIH, 1961-73. Fellow Am. Inst. Chemistry; mem. Am. Soc. Biol. Chemistry, Am. Physiol. Soc., Am. Chem. Soc., Endocrine Soc., A.A.A.S., N.Y. Acad. Sci., Am. Assn. Clin. Chemistry, Am. Assn. U. Profs. Contrb. articles profl. jours. Home: Mountain Brook, Ala. Died Sept. 2, 1980; buried Elmwood Cemetery, Birmingham.

REDEFER, FREDERICK LOVATT, educator; b. Haverstraw, N.Y., Feb. 26, 1905; s. William and Harriet (Messer) R.; A.B., Swarthmore Coll., 1927; Ed.D., Teachers Coll., Columbia, 1952; m. Helen Sisson, 1939; 1 son, Frederick Douglas, Instr. Oak Lane Country Day Sch., Phila., 1927-28; supt. of schs., Glencoe, Ill., 1929-32; exec. sec. Prog. Edn. Assn., 1932-40, dir., 1940-43; major, U.S. Army, since 1943; chief Selection Br., Mil. Gov. Div. Mem. Wartime Commission U.S. Office of Education; chief, edn. and training, Veterans Adminstrn., B.K.R.O., 1946-47; prof. edn. N.Y. U., 1947-72, chmn. dept. higher edn., 1966-72. Phi Beta Kappa, Phi Delta Kappa, Sigma Tau. Mem. Soc. of Friends. Contbr. to Progressive Education, Frontiers of Democracy, and other ednl. publs. Home: New Milford, Conn. Died Aug. 2, 1976; buried New Milford.

REDFERN, FRANK JAMES, banker, hosp. adminstr.; b. Jersey City, July 1, 1910; s. John Joseph and Margaret Agatha (Barry) R.; grad. St. Peter's Prep. Sch., 1932; m. Gene Marie Crosby, Nov. 16, 1935; children—Peter J., James F. With Peter F. Redfern & Sons Co., constrn., Jersey City, 1932-65, pres., 1941-65; v.p., dir. Fifth Ward Savs. Bank Jersey City, 1948-66; chmn. bd., pres. Peoples Nat. Bank Sussex County (N.J.), 1964-70; sr. v.p. N.J. Bank, 1970-80; pres. Barn Hill Convalescent Center, Newton, N.J., 1972-80. Mem. Sparta (N.J.) Indsl. Commn., 1965-80. Clubs: Lake Mohawk Country (pres. 1971-72), Lake Mohawk Golf (Sparta); Carteret (Jersey City); PGA Golf (Palm Beach, Fla.). Home: Sparta, N.J. Died Jan. 8, 1980; buried Sparta.

REDHEAD, HUGH M., advt. exec.; b. St. Louis, July 18, 1920; s. Robert Carmichael and Mellie (Garland) R.; student Purdue U., 1937-41; m. Margaret Louise Davis, Aug. 20, 1943; (dec. May 1969); children—Mel Marie, Margaret Louise, Shelley Diane; m. 2d, Joan Borgman, Nov. 15, 1969. Vice pres., dir. Fuller & Smith & Ross, Inc., Pitts., 1947-60; sr. v.p. Mellon Nat. Bank & Trust Co., Pitts., 1960; pres. Campbell-Ewald Co., Detroit, 1968-75. Bd. dirs. Better Bus. Bur. Met. Detroit; trustee William Beaumont Hosp., Royal Oak, Mich. Served to capt. USAAF, 1941-45. Mem. Sales-Marketing Execs. Detroit (adv. com.), Am. Assn. Advt. Agys. (dir.), Theta Xi. Clubs: Duquesne (Pitts.); Detroit Athletic, Recess (Detroit); Bloomfield Hills Country. Home: Bloomfield Hills, Mich. Died July 11, 1975.

REDMOND, PAUL ALONZO, textile mfr.; b. Floyd County, Ga., Mar. 17, 1883; s. Gabriel Moss and Fanny Elizabeth (Wilkins) R.; student Shockley Bus. Coll., Rome, Ga., 1899-1900, Lowell (Mass.) Textile Inst., 1903; m. Sallie Agnes Burkhalter, Apr. 15, 1906; children—Verdery Inez, Alwyn Agnes, Mildred Greenwood, Paul Alonzo, Sarah Louise, Elizabeth Woodward. Law sec. Cartersville, Ga., 1900-02, Rome, Ga., 1902; paymaster Floyd (County) Cotton Mills, Rome, Ga., 1903-08; agt. Aragon (Ga.) Mills, 1908-23; treas. Brookford (N.C.) Mills, 1917-23; sales mgr. Brookford and Aragon Mills, New York, N.Y., 1923-28; exec. vice pres. Alabama Mills Co., Birmingham, 1928-30, pres., 1930-33; pres., gen. mgr., dir. and mem. exec. com. Alabama Mills, Inc. since 1933. Mem. bd. trustees Inst. Textile Technology, Charlottesville, Va. Past mem. and dir. Cotton Textile Inst., Inc. Mem. Dem. exec. com., Aragon, Ga., dist., 1912-23; county commr., Polk County, Ga., 1921-23; chmn. sch. bd., Aragon, Ga., 1909-23. Mem. Nat. Assn. Mfrs. (mem. coms.), Southern States Indsl. Council (past dir. and mem. exec. com.), Am. Cotton Mfrs. Assn. (past dir.). Ala. Cotton Mfrs. Assn. (past pres.), Associated Industries of Ala. (past pres. dir. and mem. legislative com.), Ala. State, U.S., and Birmingham Chambers of Commerce. Baptist. Mason (R.A.M., K.T., Shriner), Improved Order of Red Men, K.P. Clubs: Birmingham Country, Executives, New York-Southern Soc. Home: Birmingham. *

REED, ALAN, SR., actor; b. N.Y.C., Aug. 20, 1907; s. Henry and Rae (Greenberg) Bergman; B.A., Columbia, 1926; m. Finette Walker, Apr. 5, 1932; children—Alan, Steven Colgate, Christopher. Radio actor, 1926-50; straight man for Eddie Cantor, Bob Hope, Bert Lahr, Jimmy Durante, Al Jolson; original daddy to Fanny Brice's Baby Snooks; played Falstaff Openshaw on Allen's Alley; role as Pasquale in Life with Luigi; actor in many soap operas including Myrt and Marge, Valiant Lady, The Goldbergs; stage credits include Love's Old Sweet Song, Hope for a Harvest, The Pirate, Merry Wives of Windsor; has appeared in over 50 motion pictures; film credits include Viva Zapata, Postman

Always Rings Twice, Breakfast at Tiffanys, Dream of Kings; announcer TV commls.; voice of Fred Flintstone on The Flintstones and Pebbles and Bam-Bam cartoon series; founder Alan Reed Enterprises, specialty advt., 1954; financial dir. Theatre 40, Beverly Hills, Cal. Supplied demonstration for presdl. nomination of John F. Kennedy, 1960. Nominated for best performance in Hope for a Harvest, N.Y. Critics Drama Circle, 1941. Mem. Nat. Acad. TV Arts and Scis., Acad. Motion Picture Arts and Scis. Mem. B'nai B'rith (past pres.). Home: Los Angeles, Calif. Died June 14, 1977.

REED, ALEXANDER PRESTON, lawyer, b. Washington, Pa., Oct. 14, 1885; s. Colin and Adaline (Brownlee) R.; A.B., Washington and Jefferson Coll., 1907; Harvard Law Sch., 1907-08; LL.B., U. Pitts., 1910; LL.D., Washington and Jefferson Coll., 1943; m. Gertrude C. Shafer, Aug. 25, 1917; children—Matilda, Jane, Alice Dickey, Alexander Preston, Jr., Charlotte Claypool. Admitted to Pa. bar, 1910 and engaged in gen. practice of law at Washington, Pa., 1910-15; trust officer Fidelity Trust Co., Pitts., from 1915, v.p., dir., 1923-45, pres., 1945-53, chmn. bd., from 1954; also engaged in practice law. Trustee H.C. Frick Ednl. Commn., Pitts. Theol. Sem., Washington and Jefferson Coll., Washington, Berea (Ky.) Coll. Pitts. Bd. Pub. Edn., 1927-42, pres., 1943; bd. dirs. Community Chest, Pitts. Health and Welfare Assn. Mem. Phi Beta Kappa, Phi Gamma Delta, Phi Delta Phi. Republican. Presbyn. Club: Duquesne. Home: Pittsburgh, Pa. Died Mar. 24, 1976.

REED, ALFRED C(UMMINGS), physician; b. Pleasant Hill, Mo., Dec. 2, 1884; s. Alfred Riley and Mary Jane (Armstrong) R.; A.B., Pomona Coll., Claremont, Calif., 1906, D.Sc., 1935; M.D., Bellevue Med. Coll., 1910; London Sch. Tropical Medicine, 1928; m. Daisy C. Fredendall, June 14, 1910; 1 dau., Elizabeth Mary. Began practice, 1910; asst. surgeon U.S. Pub. Health Service, 1911-13; physician Yale Hosp., Changsha, China, 1913-15; asso. prof. medicine, Stanford University, 1916-28; assoc. clinical prof. of medicine since 1942; professor tropical medicine, University of California, 1928-42; consultant tropical medicine in Children's, Chinese, Mt. Zion, Marine hospitals; consultant and branch chief tropical med., Veterans' Adminstrn. Editor Calif. State Med. Jour., 1917-22. Lt. Med. Corps, U.S. Navy, 1917-19. Pres. Am. Soc. Tropical Medicine; councillor Am. Acad. Tropical Medicine; sec. for U.S., Royal Soc. Tropical Medicine, Far Eastern Assn. of Tropical Medicine. Mem. A.A.A.S., A.M.A. Pasteur Soc., Phi Beta Kappa, Delta Omega, Sigma Xi, Phi Beta Pi. Democrat. Episcopalian. Mason. Clubs: Olympic Club, Commonwealth. Author: Tropical Medicine in U.S.A., 1930; Health of Travelers, 1931; Manual of Tropical Diseases (with J. C. Geiger). contbr. numerous articles to med. jours. Lecturer on med. subjects. Home: Mill Valley, Calif. *

REED, ALLEN E., mfg. co. exec.; b. 1904; B.S., Harvard, 1926, M.B.A., 1928; married. Formerly with Remington Rand Corp.; with Raytheon Co., 1942-76, v.p., treas., to 1976. Address: Waltham, Mass. Died 1976.

REED, BURLEIGH, univ. prof.; born near Algona, Ia., Jan. 18, 1885; s. Albert and Alma Grace (Burtis) R.; B.S., Cornell Coll of Ia., 1909, A.M., 1919; student summer schs., U. of Denver, 1925, Western Reserve, 1929, Kan. State Coll., 1931, Columbia, 1937; m. Clara Rideout, July 30, 1923. Prof. chem. Huron (S.D.) Coll., 1919-20. Washburn Coll., Topeka, Kan., 1920-41, Washburn Municipal U. since 1941. Fellow Am. Inst. Chemists;mem. A.A.A.S., Kan. Acad. Sci., Am. Assn. Univ. Profs.*

REED, SIR CAROL, motion picture dir., producer; b. London, Eng., Dec. 30, 1906; s. Herbert Reed; ed. King's Sch., Canterbury, Eng.; m. Penelope Ward, Jan., 1948; 1 son, Max. Bagan as actor-dir. stage prodns.; became dialogue dir. Ealing Studios, 1932, dir. films, 1935-76; dir. motion pictures including Odd Man Out, 1947, Fallen Idol, 1948, Third Man, 1949, Outcast of the Island, 1951, The Man Between, 1953, Kid for Two Farthings, 1954, Trapeze, 1955, The Key, 1957, Our Man in Havana, 1959-60, Running Man, 1961-62; The Agony and Ectasy, 1964, Oliver, 1968; producer motion pictures. Served as dir. for Army Field Unit, 1942-45. Address: London, England. Died Apr. 26, 1976.

REED, CHARLES HANCOCK, textile distbg. co. exec.; b. Richmond, Va., Dec. 25, 1900; s. Charles Clinton and Lyllian (Hancock) R.; student U. Va., 1918; B.S., U.S. Mil. Acad., 1922; grad. Command and Gen. Staff Sch., 1941, Cav. Sch., 1932; m. Janice Cannon, Dec. 27, 1924. Commd. 2d lt. U.S. Army, 1922, advanced through grades to col., 1943; comdr. 2d Armored Cav. Regt., ETO, 1944-47; sec. Gen. Field Forces, 1947-49; ret., 1949; treas. Williams & Reed, Inc., Richmond, 1949-50, pres. 1950-80; George W. Delks Co., Smithfield, Va., Fosters, Mathews Co., dir. Bank of Va., Woodstock Corp., Richmond. Pres. Va. Fair, 1965-80. Bd. visitors Va. Poly. Inst., 1949-59; vice rector Radford (Va.) Coll., from 1950. Decorated D.S.C., Silver Star with clasp, Bronze Star, Purple Heart, Legion of Merit; Croix de Guerre with palms, chevalier Legion of Honor (France); cited with 2d Cavalry by U.S. Senate for heroic efforts in saving Lipizzaner horses, Vienna, World War II. Mem. Nat. Assn. Textile and Apparel Wholesalers (pres. 1965-66), Nat. Assn. Wholesaler-Distbrs. (pres. 1970). Democrat. Home: Midlothian, Va. Died Apr. 7, 1980.

REED, EDWARD U(RBANE), naval med. officer; b. Wilkes Barre, Pa., May 1, 1884; s. Charles and Nellie Wright (Dilley) R.; M.D., U. of Pa., 1905; m. Nellie Hall Bayles, May 12, 1914; children—Ellen Dilley (Mrs. William Henry Burns), Virginia Hall (Mrs. James Thomas Dale). Commd. medical officer, Navy, 1905; promoted through grades to rear adm., med. corps, 1942; instr. naval med. sch., 1919-22; sr. med. officer on U.S.S. Princeton, Ohio, Florida, Relief (hosp. ship); comdg. officer naval hosps. at Guam, Charleston, S.C., Mare Island, Calif.; med. officer 12th Naval Dist., San Francisco, Calif., 1940-43; dist. med. officer 3rd Naval Dist. 1943-45; pres. Naval Retiring Bd. 1945-46, retired. Life mem. Am. Coll. Physicians. Home: Los Angeles. *

REED, FLORENCE, actress; b. Phila., Pa., Jan. 10, 1883; m. Malcolm Williams. First appeared on stage in a monologue, Fifth Av. Theatre, New York, Apr. 1901; played in stock co. and then joined May Irwin's Co. on tour in "The Widow Jones" and "Madge Smith;" toured as Ophelia, in "Hamlet," 1907-08; played in "Girls," "The Typhoon," "The Yellow Ticket," "Chu-Chin-Chow," etc.; played as Mrs. Irene Moreland, in "The Mirage," 1920. Address: New York, N.Y. *

REED, MERLE ROLAND, railroad executive; born in Jasper County, Ill., June 26, 1883; son of William Grant and Ella Jane (Clark) R.; B.S., Rose Poly. Inst., 1905; m. Helen Margaret Duncan, Nov. 16, 1910; children—Frances Sussana, Jane McBirney. With Pa. R.R., 1905-38, successively as apprentice, draftsman, chief draftsman, foreman, gen. car inspector, supervisor of car repairs, master mechanic, supt. of motive power, gen. supt. of motive power; mem. Railroad Retirement Bd., 1938-43; returned to Pa. R.R. as asst. chief of motive power, Oct. 1943. Home: Wynnewood, Pa. *

REED, OLLIE EZEKIEL, dairying; b. on farm near Fayette, Mo., Aug. 19, 1885; s. William Lorenzo and Annie Eliza (Manion) R.; B.S., U. of Missouri, 1908, M.S., 1910; Sc.D. (hon.) Purdue University, 1947; m. Lucy Ann Lee, June 8, 1910; children—Rosa Lee (Mrs. James A. Kime), Olive E. (Mrs. Edward H. Boyle), Wilber Jackson. Asst. dairying, U. of Mo., 1908; instr. in dairying, Purdue U., 1909-10; prof. dairy husbandry, Kan. State Agrl. Coll., 1910-18, Purdue, 1918-20; farm mgr., 1920-21; prof. dairy husbandry, Mich. State Coll., 1921-28; chief of Bur. Dairy Industry, Dept. Agr., 1928-54, dir. livestock research of Agriculture Research Administration, 1954-56; now agrl. cons. (ret.). Member Kansas Council of Defense, 1917-18. Represented French High Commn. in purchase of dairy cattle, 1919; mem. of World's Dairy Congress, 1923, 28, 31, 37, 49; del. 2d Inter-American Conference of Agriculture, Mexico City, 1942, World's Dairy Congress, 1949, Inter-Am. Livestock Prodn. Meeting, Costa Rica, 1950, Buenos Aires, 1955; mem. Internat. Grassland Congress, 1952, NRC; rep. Dept. Agr. at World's Fair, New Delhi, India, 1959-60. Recipient Distinguished Service award U.S. Dept. Agr., 1952. Fellow A.A.A.S.; mem. Soc. for Internat. Development, American Dairy Science Assn. (pres. 1925-26); dir. Nat. Dairy Assn.; mem. Alpha Zeta, Sigma Phi Epsilon, Phi Kappa Phi; mem. White House Conf. on Child Health and Protection, Nat. Research Council, A.A.A.S., milk com. and com. on animal nutrition Nat. Food and Nutrition Bd., Am. Soc. Animal Prodn., Nat. Agrl. Jefferson Bicentary Committee. Mem. Christian (Disciples) Ch. (trustee). Mason. Club: Rotary. Contbr. many bulls. on dairying. Home: Washington. *

REED, STANLEY FORMAN, Supreme Ct. justice; b. Mason County, Ky., Dec. 31, 1884; A.B., Ky. Wesleyan Coll., 1902, LL.D., 1941; A.B., Yale U., 1906, LL.D., 1938; studied law U. Va., Columbia U., U. Paris; LL.D., Columbia U., 1940, U. Ky., U. Louisville, 1947; m. Winifred Elgin, May 11, 1908; chilren—John A., Stanley Forman. Practiced law, Maysville and Ashland, Ky., 1910-29; mem. Ky. Gen. Assembly, 1912-16; gen. counsel Fed. Farm Bd., 1929-32, RFC, 1932-35; solicitor gen. U.S., 1935-38; chmn. Pres.'s Com. on Civil Service Improvement, 1939-41; former dir. Commodity Credit Corp., trustee Export-Import Bank, Washington; asso. justice Supreme Ct. apptd. by Pres. Franklin D. Roosevelt, 1938-57. Home: Huntington, N.Y. Died Apr. 2, 1980.

REED, THOMAS SELDEN, wholesale food exec.; b. Bertram, Tex., Jan. 27, 1885; s. Thomas S. and Dora (Connell) R.; student Tex. Christian U., 1900-01; m. Ruby Compton, Aug. 1, 1907; children—Mary Elizabeth, Randolph Compton, Ruby Connell. Ind. crude oil producer, Beaumont, Tex., 1924—; v.p., director United Carbon Co.; dir. employers Casualty Co. Dallas, First Nat. Bank of Beaumont. Mem. U.S. C. of C., E. Tex. C. of C., Beaumont C. of C. Mem. Tex. Employers Ins. Assn. (dir.). Episcopalian (dir. Bishop Quin Found.). Club: Rotary (past pres.;. dist. gov. 1919). Home: Beaumont, Tex. *

REEDER, HOWARD CHANDLER, ins. exec.; b. Johnstown, Colo., June 2, 1906; s. Arthur J. and Maude (Swinburne) R.; A.B., U. Ia., 1927; m. Helen Macallister, Aug. 16, 1930; children—Jean Elizabeth, John Macallister. Asso. actuary Royal Union Life Ins. Co., 1927-33; actuary, mgr. Country Life Ins. Co., Chgo., 1933-41; v.p. Continental Assurance Co., Chgo., 1941-47, dir., exec. v.p., 1947-56, pres., 1956-63, also vice chmn. bd., 1962-65, chmn., chief exec. officer, 1965-71; chmn., chief exec. officer Continental Casualty Co., 1965-71; chmn. bd. Nat. Fire Ins. Co., Transp. Ins. Co., Transcontinental Ins. Co., Am. Casualty Co., Valley Forge Ins. Co., Valley Forge Life Ins. Co.; chmn. bd., pres. CNA Financial Corp., until 1971, chmn. exec. com., 1971-72; dir. Ill. State Bank Chgo. Ill. v.p. Am. Life Conv., 1950-63, pres., 1967-68; dir. Ziegler Coal Co. Fellow Soc. Actuaries; mem. Alpha Sigma Phi. Clubs: Chgo., Chgo. Athletic. Home: Wilmette, Ill. Died Oct. 24, 1977; buried Hopkinton, Iowa.

REEDER, LEO GLENN, educator; b. Chgo., Mar. 13, 1921; s. Max and Anna (Grossman) R.; A.A., Wright Jr. Coll., Chgo., 1941; M.A., U. Chgo., 1949, Ph.D., 1952; m. Sharon J. Ringholz, June 15, 1963; children—Glenn D., Susan C. (by previous marriage), Andrew D. Acting asst. prof. Wash. State U., Pullman, 1951-52; asst. prof. U. Minn., 1952-55; social scientist RAND Corp., 1955-58; prof. sociology and pub. health U. Calif. at Los Angeles, 1958-78, dir. Survey Research Center, 1969-74; cons. in field. Served with AUS, 1942-46. NIH spl. postdoctoral fellow, 1958; Milbank travel fellow, 1966. Fellow Am. Sociol. Assn., Am. Pub. Health Assn., AAAS; mem. Am. Assn. Pub. Opinion Research, Population Assn. Am., Soc. Epidemiologic Research, Delta Omega. Co-author: Handbook of Medical Sociology, rev. edit., 1972; Preceptions of Medical Care, 1974; Handbook of Indices and Scales in Health Behavior, 1976. Contbr. articles to profl. jours. Home: Pacific Palisades, Calif. Died Sept. 25, 1978.

REES, CHARLES HERBERT, fgn. service officer; b. Bklyn., May 5, 1919; s. Sherman James and Lena (Engelmann) R.; A.B., Wesleyan U., Middletown, Conn., 1940; student Grad. Sch., Am. U., 1940-41, Nat. Inst. Pub. Affairs, 1940-41; m. Jeanne Marie Fretwell, Feb. 4, 1946; children—Martha, Susan, John, David. Pub. affairs intern U.S. Govt., 1940-41; asst. to dir. personnel VA, 1946-48; with AID, and predecessor agys., 1948-76, dep. dir. orgn. and planning, 1952-55, Congressional presentation officer, 1959-61, asst. dir. mission to Pakistan for devel. planning, 1962-64; dir. South Asian affairs AID, Washington, 1964-76. Served to maj. USAAF, 1942-46. Decorated Legion of Merit; Recipient 2 Superior Honor awards, Distinguished Honor award AID. Mem. Phi Beta Kappa. Home: Arlington, Va. Died Mar. 24, 1976.

REESE, ADDISON HARDCASTLE, banker; b. Baltimore County, Md., Dec. 28. 1908; s. Gordon Lippencott and Edith Octavia (Ford) R.; grad. Marston's Univ. Sch., Riderwood, Md., 1926; student Johns Hopkins, 1926-29; LL.D. (hon.), U. N.C., 1968; m. Gertrude Craig, Apr. 22, 1936. Asst. Nat. bank examiner U.S. Treasury Dept., 1932-36, nat. bank examiner, 1936-40; v.p., dir. Nicodemus Nat. Bank, Hagerstown, Md., 1941-47; pres., chmn. bd. County Trust Co. of Md., Balt., 1947-51, exec. v.p., dir. Am. Trust Co., Charlotte, N.C., 1951-54, pres., dir., 1954-57, name changed to Am. Comml. Bank, pres., dir., 1957-60; pres., dir. N.C. Nat. Bank, 1960-67, chmn. bd., 1967-73; chmn. bd. NCNB Corp., 1968-73, also dir., chmn. fin. commn.; dir. Duke Power Co., Engraph, Inc., Ruddick Corp. Bd. dirs. Mercy Hosp.; chmn. bd. trustees, U. N.C.-Charlotte; chmn bd. dirs. U. N.C.-Charlotte Found. Served from lt. to maj. USAF, 1942-45. Mem. Assn. Res. City Bankers (past pres., past dir.), N.C. Citizens Assn., Alpha Delta Phi. Episcopalian. Clubs: Charlotte Country, City (Charlotte, N.C.); Elkridge (Balt.); Sankaty Head Golf (Nantucket, Mass.). Home: Charlotte, N.C. Died Sept. 1, 1977.

REESE, JIM EANES, educator; b. Comanche, Tex., May 29, 1912; s. Francis Jefferson and Martha (Eanes) R.; B.A., U. Tex., 1933, M.A., 1935, Ph.D., 1942; m. Sarah Burton, Sept. 1, 1936; children—Carolyn, John William, Margaret Gail, James Basset. Prin. elementary sch., Comanche, Tex., 1935-37; instr. econs. U. Tex., 1937-39; asst. prof. econs. Tex. Coll. Arts and Industries, 1939-42, So. Meth. U., 1942-46; asso. prof. econs. U. Okla., 1946-49, prof., 1949-61. David Ross Boyd prof. econs., from 1961. Economist Joint Council on Econ. Edn., 1957-58, regional rep., 1958-61. Served from ensign to lt. (j.g.), USNR, 1943-46. Mem. Am. Assn. U. Profs., Am., So. econ. assns., S.W. Social Sci. Assn. (v.p. 1973, pres. 1974-75). Author: Our American Economy, 1953; (with Gilbert Fite) An Economic History of the United States, 3d edit., 1973; Cowboys, Cattle and Commerce, 1960. Home: Norman, Okla. Died Oct. 6, 1976.

REESE, RAYMOND CASTLE, structural engr.; b. Pittsfield, Mass., Dec. 22, 1893; s. John Miles and Minnie Victoria (Castle) Rees; B.S., Mass. Inst. Tech., 1920; postgrad. Harvard U., 1916-20; D.Sc., U. Toledo, 1977; m. Florence Miller, Dec. 30, 1920; children—Carolyn Reese Clark, Allen M., Virginia Reese White. From draftsman to chief draftsman, bldg. dept. Gen. Electric Co., Pittsfield, 1907-20; pvt. practice indsl. engring., Pittsfield, 1920-22; chief engr. Bldg. Products Co., Toledo, 1922-64; pvt. practice structural engring., Toledo, 1922-80; partner, cons. Raymond C. Reese Assos., Toledo, 1960-73; lectr. Toledo U., 1924-52; chmn. bd. Nat. Bd. Accreditation in Concrete Constrn., 1973-80; mem. commn. I Recommendations pratiques Comite Europeen du Beton, mem. commn. III flexion-compression; exec. com. com. tall bldgs. Internat. Assn. Bridge and Structural Engrs.-ASCE, 1969-80, group coordinator, 1969-80; past mem. bldg. research div. Nat. Bur. Standards; past chmn. bldg. code requirements for minimum design loads in bldgs. Am. Nat. Standards Inst.; past dir. Toledo Concrete Improvement Bd.; editorial com. codes developing countries UNESCO, 1963-64. Vice pres. Northwestern Ohio chpt. Arthritis Found., 1971-75. Named Man of Year, Engring. News Record, 1966. Registered profl. engr., Ohio, Mich., Ind., Ill., N.Y., Ark., Pa., Wis. Fellow Am. Inst. Cons. Engrs., Brit. Instn. Civil Engrs.; hon. life mem. Am. Conceret Inst. (past pres.; Alfred E. Lindau award 1957, Henry L. Kennedy award 1964, Arthur Y. Moy Meml. award Mich. chpt. 1976, Henry C. Turner Nat. award 1977), ASCE (past chmn. exec. com. structural div., past chmn. com. masonry and reinforced concrete of structural div.); mem. Concrete Reinforcing Steel (past chmn. engring. practice com.; award 1953, salute 1977), ASTM (25 year award 1969), Nat. Ohio, Toledo (past pres.; Engr. of Year award 1962) socs. profl. engrs., Internat. Soc. Bridge and Structural Engrs. (past chmn. U.S. activities com.), Cons. Engrs. Ohio, Mass. Inst. Tech. Alumni Assn., Reinforced Concrete Research Council (past mem. exec. com.), Am. Soc. Engring. Edn. (life), Prestressed Concrete Inst., Internat. Assn. Shell Structures, Réunion Internationale des Laboratoires D'Essais et de Recherches Sur les Materiaux et les Constructions. Clubs: Toledo, Rotary. Author: (with Sutherland) Reinforced Concrete Design, 1943; also handbooks, reports, sects. books, articles. Home: Toledo, Ohio. Died May 1, 1980.

REEVES, FLOYD WESLEY, cons., educator; b. Castalia, S.D., Nov. 16, 1890; s. Charles Edward and Ella T. (Ogilvie) R.; B.S., Huron (S.D.) Coll., 1915; postgrad. U. Wis., summer 1916; M.A., U. Chgo., 1921, Ph.D. magna cum laude, 1925; LL.D., Albion Coll., 1932, Kent State U., 1940, Bethany Coll., 1940, Temple U., 1942, Mich. State U., 1971; m. Hazel Beatrice Flint, Sept. 11, 1915; children—Floyd Orville, Fritz Earl, Alta Mae. Tchr. rural schs., until 1912; prin. Jefferson Sch., Huron, 1915-17; supt. schs., Gregory, 1917-20, Winner, 1920-22; fellow U. Chgo., 1922-23; prof. edn., dir. Sch. Edn., adminstrv. dean Transylvania Coll., 1923-25; prof. edn. U. Ky., 1925-29, also dir. Bur. Sch. Service, 1927-29, also head dept. ednl. adminstrn.; prof. edn. U. Chgo., 1929, prof. adminstrn., 1938-53; dir. personnel, social and econ. divs. TVA, 1933-36; dir. Am. Youth Commn., 1939-42; dir. labor supply Office Prodn. Mgmt., 1940-41; cons. to pres., prof. ednl. adminstrn. Mich. State U., East Lansing, 1953-57, distinguished prof. edn., cons. to pres., 1957-62, distinguished prof. emeritus, 1962-79, dir. research projects, cons., 1962-68; cons. Ford Found., 1956-79. Trustee Huron Coll., 1925-46, Roosevelt U., 1945-46; vice chmn. bd. trustees Howard U., 1948-64, hon. trustee, 1964-79; group adviser Govt. of Pakistan, summer 1956; dir. research higher edn. Bd. Edn., Disciples of Christ; dir. surveys ednl. instns. M.E. Ch.; mem. staff Regents Inquiry into Character and Cost of Pub. Edn. in State of N.Y., 1936-37; mem. staff Pres.'s Com. on Adminstrv. Mgmt., 1936; chmn. Adv. Com. on Edn., 1936-39; mem. report com. White House Conf. on Children in a Democracy, 1939-41; mem. adv. com. on adminstrs. Pres.'s Com. on Civil Service Improvements, 1939-40; dir. studies N.Y. State Temporary Commn. on Need for a State U., 1946-48; head UNESCO Consultative Ednl. Mission to Philippines, 1949; cons. Nat. Resources Planning Bd., 1941-43; chmn. Conf. on Postwar Readjustment of Civilian and Mil. Persónnel, 1942-43. Mem. Common Cause, Center for Study Dem. Instns., N.A.A.C.P., 1942-79. Mem. Am. Assn. Sch. Adminstrs., Am. Edn. Research Assn., Am. Polit. Sci. Assn., Nat. Inst. Pub. Affairs (trustee 1961—), Am. Soc. Pub. Adminstrn., N.Central Assn. Colls. and Secondary Schs. (hon.), Mich. State U. Alumni Assn. (hon.). Author or co-author numerous books, 1924-79. Editor: U. Chgo. Survey (12 vols.), co-author 10 vols., 1933; editor, co-author Education for Rural Am., 1945. Home: East Lansing, Mich. Died Aug. 20, 1979; buried Mich. State U. Meml Gardens.

REEVES, JOHN MERCER, textile mfr.; b. Siloam, N.C., Aug. 10, 1887; s. Micajah and Mary C. (Mercer) R.; student Oak Ridge Inst. (now Oak Ridge Mil. Inst.); grad. U. N.C., 1910; student N.C. State Coll.; LL.D., Wofford Coll., Spartanburg, S.C., American University, Washington, 1952; L.H.D., High Point College; married Virginia McKenzie, 1928; children—Virginia, Ann, Emily. Principal Dothan High School, Dothan, Ala., 1910-12; with Hunter Mfg. Co., 1916; with Mooresville (N.C.) Cotton Mills, 1915-16; partner Reeves Bros., Inc., 1920-22, v.p., sec., 1920-42, treas., 1942-47, became president, 1942, chairman board directors, 1954-67; president Worth St., Inc., N.Y.C., from 1942. Executive com. Textile sect. N.Y. Bd. Trade, from 1946. Mem. exec. bd. Greater N.Y. council Boy Scouts; pres. Reeves Found, from 1944; trustee Centenary Jr. Coll.; chmn. bd. trustees Am. U. Served as ensign USN, World War I, Mem. Assn. Textile Mchts. (v.p.), Assn. Cotton Textile Mchts. N.Y. (past dir.), N.Y.C. Conf. Christians and Jews (past chmn.), N.C. State Ports Authority (chmn.), Soc. of Cin. Methodist. Home: Pinehurst, N.C. Died Mar. 16, 1976.

REEVES, NORMAN PENNINGTON, retail chain exec.; b. Knightstown, Ind., Nov. 23, 1912; s. Norman Wilmont Chesterfield and Mabell (Pennington) R.; B.S. in Pharmacy, Butler U., Indpls., 1936; m. Evelyn Fort, Mar. 16, 1935; children—Delinda Reeves Caldwell, John Douglas. With Hook Drugs, Inc., Indpls., 1945-81, v.p. ops., 1959-72, pres., 1972-81, also dir.; dir. First Nat. Bank, Knightstown, Salt Creek Realty Corp.; past mem. Ind. Bd. Pharmacy. Mem. Ind. State Police Bd., 1973-81; bd. dirs., past pres. Crossroads Rehab. Center, Indpls.; bd. dirs., exec. com. United Way Greater Indpls.; mem. finance com. Community Hosp., Indpls.; mem. dean's adv. council Krannert Grad. Sch. Indsl. Adminstrn., Purdue U., 1974-75; past mem. Knightstown Pub. Sch. Bd. Mem. Nat. Assn. Chain Drug Stores (dir. 1976-81), Ind. Retail Council (dir., exec. com.), Greater Indpls. Progress Com., Amateur Trap Shooting Assn. Clubs: Downtown Kiwanis, Columbia, Masons, K.P. Home: Knightstown, Ind. Died Feb. 22, 1981.

REFREGIER, ANTON, artist; b. Moscow, Russia, Mar. 20, 1905; s. Anton and Valentina (Besekirsky) R.; student sculpture Vasilief, Paris, France, 1920; student R.I. Sch. Design, Providence, 1920-25; studied painting with Hans Hoffman, Munich, Germany, 1927; m. Lila Kelly; children—Anton, Brigit, Aleksandre, Came to U.S., 1920, naturalized, 1930. Designer Erika Mann's review Peppermill, Chanin Theater, N.Y.C., 1937; one-man shows ACA Gallery, N.Y.C., 1942, 45, 49, 53, 58, 61, 63, 65, 68; designer, decorator Cafe Society Uptown, nightclub, N.Y.C., 1942; murals in post office Plainfield, N.J., 1943, S.S. Lurline, 1949, S.S. Independence and S.S. Constitution, 1951; spl. assignments Fortune, Red Book, What's New; artist corr. Fortune, UN Orgnl. Conf. in San Francisco, 1945; vis. prof. paintings, drawing Stanford, 1949; vis. prof. U. Ark., 1952; prof. painting Bard Coll., Annandale-on-Hudson, N.Y., 1962-64; an instr. mural painting Am. Artists Sch., N.Y.C., also Cleve. Sch. Fine Arts, designer indsl. textiles, ceramics; painter mural Phoenix Ins. Co., 1951, Hillcrest Jewish Center, L.I., 1953, Mayo Clinic, Rochester, Minn., 1954, Covington Fabrics, N.Y.C., 1954, U. Ky., P.S. 146, Bronx, Tokeneke Sch., Darien Conn.; tapestries Sheraton Cleveland Hotel, Ratron Mfg. Co., Bowery Savs. Bank, N.Y.C.; mosaic, Hotel Americana, Florida; mural Watson Hall, Syracuse U.; film Man of Art; also paintings in collections Whitney Mus. Am. Art, Waler Art Center, Mpls., Met. Mus., Mus. Modern Art, Butler Art Inst., Corcoran Gallery, San Francisco Mus. Art, Oakland (Calif.) Mus., also others; exhibited ACA Gallery, 1959, in Detroit, 1961, Phila. Art Alliance, 1962, Moscow Mus. Fine Arts, Hermitage, Leningrad, 1966, exhbn. "Chile" in Moscow, other cities in USSR, 1978; mosaics, ceramic murals (including Kingston High Sch. 1978), incidental decorative pieces, pub. and pvt. structures. Bd. dirs. Edwin Austin Abbey Meml. for Scholarships in Mural Painting, 1976-79. Awarded commn. nat. competition for murals San Francisco Post Office, 1941; 1st prize internat. Hallmark competitions, 1952; Salamagundi Club award for painting, 1977; Ward Ranger prize NAD, 1978. Mem. Nat. Soc. Mural Painters, Artists Equity, NAD, Woodstock Artists Assn., World Peace Council. Lectr. Stockholm, Moscow, Sofia, Berlin, Bucharest, 1959-60. Author: Natural Figure Drawing, 1949; An Artist's Journey; We Make Our Tomorrow; Sketches of the Soviet Union, 1978; co-author: Song of Peace. Address: Woodstock, N.Y., Died Oct. 10, 1979; buried Woodstock Artists Cemetery.

REGNIER, RAYMOND COBINGTON, JR., cons. engr.; b. Balt., July 10, 1915; s. Raymond Charles and Anna (Zimmerman) R.; B. Engring., Johns Hopkins U., 1935; m. Frances Goodwin Lockwood, Sept. 28, 1940; children—Robert L., Joanna J. Regnier Moore, Elizabeth E. Regnier Beil. Designer, engr. Whitmen Requardt & Smith, Balt., 1936-42; with Whitman, Requardt & Assos., Balt., 1946-77, engr. to asso. engr., 1946-56, partner, 1957-77. Served to maj. CWS, U.S. Army, 1942-46. Fellow ASCE (life), Royal Soc. Health, Am. Cons. Engrs. Council (life); mem. Am. Water Works Assn. (life), Nat. Soc. Profl. Engrs., Water Pollution Control Fedn., Am. Pub. Works Assn., Nat. Rifle Assn., Kappa Sigma, Engrs. Club Balt. Clubs: Center, Johns Hopkins. Home: Baltimore, Md. Died Mar. 19, 1979.

REHDER, HELMUT, educator; b. Hamburg, Germany, June 22, 1905; s. Julius Christian and Ottilie (Heyne) R.; Ph.D., U. Heidelberg, 1929; student U. Berlin, 1926-27; m. June Kruse, Apr. 4, 1931; children—Helmut Julius, Christopher Michael. Came to U.S., 1931, naturalized, 1937. Instr. U. Mo., 1931-34, asst. prof., 1934-37; asso. prof. U. Wis., 1937-42, prof., 1942-46; prof., head German dept. U. Ill., 1946-55; prof. German, U. Tex., 1955-77, Ashbel Smith prof. German, 1963-77, chmn. German, 1965-69; coll. editor, German. The Dryden Press, Inc., N.Y.C.; vis. prof. U. Colo., 1948, 56, 60, 61, 62, Northwestern, 1950, U. Tex., 1953-54, Marburg U., 1964, U. Cal. at Berkeley, 1966, Rice U., 1971-72. Mem. Modern Lang. Assn., Am. Assn. Tchrs. German, S. Central Modern Lang. Assn. (pres. 1970), Medieval Acad. Am., Am. Assn. U. Profs., Hoelderlin Gesellschaft, Lessing Gesellschaft, Phi Kappa Phi. Decorated Order Merit 1st class (West Germany). Author: Philosophie d. Unendl. Landschaft, 1932; Conversational German, 1944; German Area Readings, 1947; German, 1947, 58; Gretchen Episode from Goethe's Faust, 1950; J. Nic. Meinhard u.s. Uebersetzungen, 1953; Faust Vocabulary (with W. F. Twaddell), 1950, German Revised. 1958; Goethe's Faust, Pt. 1, 1954. Pt. II, 1955; Active German (with W. P. Lehmann and G. Schulz- Schulz-Behrend), 1958, 62; Practicing German, 1958; Review and Progress in German (with W. P. Lehmann, L. Shaw, S.N. Werbow), 1959; Deutsch; Verstehen und Sprechen (with W. F. Twaddell, U. Thomas, P. O'Connor), 1962, 70; Sprechen und Lesen, 1964, 71; Lesen und Denken, 1964; Spectrum, Modern German Thought, 1964; Denken Wissen und Kennen, 1966. Editor: Literary Symbolism, 1965; co-editor; Jour. English and Germanic Philology, 1946-55; editorial bd. Ill. Studies in Lang. and Lit., 1946-55. Contbr. Schiller bicentennial, 1959; A Schiller Symposium, 1960; A Hegel Symposium, 1963; 18th Century Symposium, 1965; Symposium on Myth and Reason, 1973; The Grad. Jour., 1968. Contbr. to numerous periodicals. Personal papers donated to Rehder Room, Library, U. Tex., Dallas. Home: Austin, Tex. Died Jan. 10, 1977; buried Forest Oaks Meml. Park, Oak Hill, Austin, Tex.

REHRING, GEORGE JOHN, clergyman; b. Cin., June 10, 1890; s. Bernard L. and Mary A. (Sander) R.; student St. Gregory Sem., Cedar Point, Ohio, 1903-08, Mt. St. Mary Sem., Cin., 1908-14; S.T.D., Collegio Angelico, Rome, 1926-28; D.C.L. honoris causa, U. Toledo, 1952. Ordained Roman Catholic Ch., 1914; adminstr. St. Mary's Ch., Hillsboro, June-Sept. 1914; asst. St. Peter and Paul Ch., Reading, Ohio, 1914-21; pastor Guardian Angels Ch., Mt. Washington, Cin., 1921-23; prof. theology, Mt. St. Mary Sem. of West, 1923-40; adminstr. Nativity Parish, June-Dec. 1925; rector Mt. St. Mary Sem., 1931-40; pastor St. Mary Ch., Hyde Park, Cin., 1940-50, domestic prelate, 1932; bishop of Cin., 1937-50; bishop of Toledo, 1950-67; titular sec. Tunnuna; asst. Pontifical Throne, 1964-76. Address: Sylvania, Ohio. Died Feb. 29, 1976.

REICHARDT, KONSTANTIN, educator; b. St. Petersburg, Russia, Apr. 30, 1904; s. Robert and Adelheid (Hoffmann) R.; student Sch. of Swiss Ref. Ch., St. Petersburg, Russia, 1912-14, Maximilians Gymnasium, Munich, Germany, 1914-15, Prinz Heinrichs Gymnasium, Berlin, Germany, 1915-23; Ph.D., Berlin U., 1927; A.M. (hon.), Yale, 1947; m. Patricia Lorraine Barker, Nov. 3, 1944; 1 dau., Maria Erica Reichardt Wilkinson. Came to U.S., 1938, naturalized, 1944. Lectr., Old Norse, U. Berlin, 1926-29; asst. and lectr. U. Cologne (Germany), 1930; prof. Scandinavian and Germanic philology, head Scandinavian dept. U. Leipzig, 1931-37; lectr. German and Norse philology U. Gothenburg (Sweden), 1938; professorial lectr. philology U. Minn., 1938-39, prof. German and Scandinavian langs., 1939-45, prof. linguistics and comparative philology, chmn. dept., 1945-47, chmn. com. Russian area studies, 1946-47; prof. Germanic philology Yale, 1947-70, Leavenworth prof. Germanic lang. and lit., 1970-72, emeritus, 1972-76, dir. grad. studies Germanics, 1961-72, acting chmn. dept. Germanic langs., 1965-66, acting chmn. dept. Medieval studies, 1967-68, adviser on Scandinavian and Icelandic lit. to Univ. Library, 1948-72, fellow Davenport Coll., Yale, from 1948. Fulbright lectr., Marburg, Germany, 1957-58, traveling fellow Norway, 1927, 28; del. Prussian Acad. Scis. to investigate German manuscripts, Royal Library, Copenhagen, 1930; del. Rask-Orsted Found, 1938, Internat. Germanists Congress, Copenhagen, 1960. Decorated knight's cross Icelandic Order Falcons, 1972. Recipient William C. DeVane medal Yale, 1973. Bollingen Found. fellow, 1955. Mem. Icelandic Acad. Sci. Unitarian. Author: Studien zu den Skalden des 9. und 10. Jahrhunderts, 1928; Thule, 1934; Runenkunde, 1936; Germanische Welt vor tausend Jahren, 1936; etc. Editor: Altnordische Uebungstexte, from 1934; co-editor Festschrift-H.J. Weigand, 1957. Translator: Sigurd Hoel, Ein Tag in Oktober (from Norwegian), 1932; Frans G. Bengtson, Karl XII (from Swedish), 1938. Contbg. author Grimms Deutsches Wörterbuch, Walde-Pokorny, Indogermanisches Wörterbuch, Hessen's Irish Dictionary; also numerous articles German, Swedish and Am. periodicals. Chmn. editorial com. William Dwight Whitney Linguistic Series, 1949-72. Home: New Haven, Conn. Died Jan. 19, 1976; buried Bethany, Conn.

REICHERT, HERBERT WILLIAM, educator; b. N.Y.C., June 5, 1917; s. William and Johanna (Schad) R.; B.A., Columbia, 1938, M.A., 1940; postgrad. U. Tubingen, 1939; Ph.D., U. Ill., 1942; m. Irene Adrienne

Nassau, Mar. 17, 1950; 1 dau., Susan Vanessa. Instr. U. Wis., 1944-45; asst. prof. Grinnell Coll., 1945-47; mem. faculty U. N.C., 1947-78, asst. prof., 1947-53, asso. prof., 1953-59, prof. German lit., 1959-78, chmn. dept. Germanic langs., 1965-70. Chmn. citizens' com. Chapel Hill Schs., 1961-63. Vice pres. Internat. A. Schnitzler Research Assn., 1963-78. Guggenheim fellow, 1958-59. Mem. Modern Lang. Assn., Am. Assn. Tchrs. German, S. Atlantic Modern Lang. Assn. (past sec., chmn. German sect.), Delta Phi Alpha (pres. 1969-78). Author: Basic Concepts Philosophy of Gottfried Keller, 1949; The Impact of Nietzsche on Herman Hesse, 1972; Friedrich Nietzsche's Impact on Modern German Literature, 1975. Editor: Deutsche Horspiele, 1959, International Nietzsche Bibliography, 1960, rev. edit., 1969; studies in A. Schnitzler, 1963. Contbr. articles profl. jours. Home: Chapel Hill, N.C. Died Mar. 15, 1978.

REID, ALFRED SANDLIN, educator; Orlando, Fla., Oct. 26, 1924; s. Ulysses Eugene and Rhoda (Wilkinson) R.; student Stetson U., 1942-44, Oxford U. (Eng.), 1945; B.Ed., U. Miami, 1948; M.A. in English, U. Fla., 1950, Ph.D., 1952; m. Nathalie Mae Rozran, July 10, 1948, children—Miriam Ruth, Martha Gene. Part-time instr. U. Fla., 1949-50; instr. English, Trinity Coll., Hartford, Conn., 1952-54; part-time asst. prof. Tchrs. Coll. Conn., New Britain, spring 1953; asst. prof. English, The Citadel, 1954-55; asst. prof. Furman U., Greenville, S.C., 1955-57, asso. prof., 1957-63, prof. English, 1963-68, Bennette E. Geer prof. Lit., 1968-76, chmn. dept. English, 1972-73; vis. prof. U. Fla., summer, 1958. Served with inf. AUS, 1944-46; ETO. Decorated Combat Infantryman's badge. Mem. Am. Assn. U. Profs. (pres. Furman chpt. 1958-59, 73-74, sec.-treas. S.C. conf. 1960-62), S. Atlantic Modern Lang. Assn. (sec. Am. lit. sect. 1965-66, chmn. Am. lit. sect. 1966-67), Am. Studies Assn., Soc. for Study So. Lit., Greenville County Hist. Soc. (dir. 1961-64). Author: The Yellow Ruff and The Scarlet Letter, 1955; (with others) The Arts in Greenville, 1960; Crumbling Stones, Poems, 1963; Lady Godiva's Lover (poems), 1969. Editor Furman Studies, 1958-74; co-editor The S.C. Rev., 1968-71, editor, 1971-73. Contbr. articles to profl. jours. Home: Greenville, S.C. Died Mar. 7, 1976.

REID, EDWY BORRADAILE, govt. official; b. Allegan, Mich., Dec. 2, 1885; s. Edwy Campbell and Adah M. (Borradaile) R.; B.S., Mich. State Coll., 1912; student, U. of Mich., 1906-07; m. Bess Marie Cornell, Sept. 9, 1908. Asso. editor 4 farm weeklies, 1 monthly, Springfield, Mass., 1910-15; chief editor, chief div. publs., dir. information, U.S. Dept. of Agr., 1915-20; Western editor Farm & Home, 1920; asst. and Washington rep. Am. Farm Bur. Fedn., 1920-25; dir. of information and advertising, 12 Fed. Land Banks and 12 Fed. Intermediate Credit Banks, 1925-33; owner and editor U.S. Banker, Washington, D.C., 1928-29; dir. of information and extension, Farm Credit Administrn., U.S. Dept of Agr., since 1933; dir. Regional Agrl. Credit Corp. Club: Corinthian Yacht (Washington, D.C.). Author: articles on agr., finance, economics. Home: Alexandria, Va. *

REID, HELEN ROGERS (MRS. OGDEN MILLS REID), b. Appleton, Wis., Nov. 23, 1882; d. Benjamin Talbot and Sarah Louise (Johnson) Rogers; student, Grafton Hall, Wis., 1893-99; A.B., Barnard Coll., 1903; Litt.D., Miami U., 1931, Columbia, 1949, Bates Coll., 1951, Manhattanville College of the Sacred Heart, 1953; Dr. Hum., Rollins College, 1933; L.H.D., Syracuse Univ., 1941, Lafayette College, 1941, N.Y.C., 1944, Yale, 1950, C. W. Post College, Long Island University, 1964; LL.D., Oglethorpe Univ., 1935, University of Toronto, Canada, 1947. Smith College, 1948. University of Wisconsin, 1953; Temple University, 1953, Mt. Holyoke College, 1954; married Ogden Mills Reid, Mar. 14, 1911 (died Jan. 3, 1947); children—Whitelaw, Elisabeth (dec.), Ogden Rogers. Newspaper work with New York Herald Tribune, 1918-58; vice president N.Y. Tribune, Inc., 1922-47, pres., 1947-53, chmn. bd., 1953-55. Trustee Metropolitan Museum of Art, Barnard College, Herald Tribune Fresh Air Fund, New York City. Republican. Episcopalian. Clubs: Colony, Women's University, Women's City. Home: N.Y.C. *

REID, JOHN THOMAS, animal scientist; b. Cumberland, Md., Mar. 14, 1919; s. Frank Ernest and Sarah Pierce (Tipton) R.; B.S., U. Md., 1941; M.S., Mich. State U., 1943, Ph.D., 1946; m. Alice Evelyn Smalley, June 8, 1945; children—J. Douglas, Sarah R., Nancy S., Gwen L., Cindy A. Asst. prof. Mich. State U., 1944-45; asso. prof. Rutgers U., 1945-48; asso. prof. Cornell U., 1948-51, prof., 1951-77, Liberty Hyde Bailey prof., 1977-79; Sir John Hammond Meml. lectr., 1972. cons. in field. Active Council Agrl. Sci. and Tech., Internat. Union Nutritional Sci., Am. Grassland Council, NSF. Recipient Nutrition Research award Am. Dairy Sci. Assn., 1950; Borden award, 1957; Merit award Am. Grassland Council, 1965; Guggenheim fellow, 1955-56. Mem. Brit. Soc. Nutrition, Am. Inst. Nutrition, Am. Soc. Animal Sci. (Morrison award 1967), Brit. Soc. Animal Prod. Methodist. Contbr. articles to profl. jours. Home: Ithaca, N.Y. Died Nov. 18, 1979.

REID, JOHN TURNER, author, ret. educator; b. Vallejo, Cal., Apr. 21, 1908; s. John Glover and Annie (Turner) R.; B.A. cum laude, Stanford, 1930, M.A., 1931, Ph.D., 1936; m. Dorcas Worsley, June 3, 1933; m. 2d, Marian Hamilton, May 21, 1947; children—Margaret Anne (Mrs. Thomas O'Connell), Sarah (Mrs. Rafael Escoto). Instr., Romance langs. and lit. Rice Inst., 1931-32, Stanford, 1933-38; asst. prof. Spanish and Spanish-Am. lit. Duke, 1938-41, U. Cal. at Los Angeles, 1946-49; spl. asst. to U.S. ambassador, Ecuador, 1942-44; cultural attache embassy, Havana, Cuba, 1943-45; pub. affairs officer embassy, Caracas, Venezuela, 1949-51; area officer State Dept., 1951-52; insp. in Germany, 1953; cultural attache embassy, Madrid, Spain, 1953-58, New Delhi, India, 1958-65, Buenos Aires, Argentina, 1965-66; lang. and area tng. officer USIA, Washington, 1966-70; asst. prof. Spanish U. Fla., Gainesville, 1970-71, asso. prof., 1972-74. Chmn. bd. U.S. Ednl. Found., India, 1958-63. Mem. Am. Assn. Tchrs. Spanish, Internat. P.E.N. Club, Phi Beta Kappa, Sigma Delta Pi (pres. 1938-40). Author: Modern Spain and Liberalism, 1937; (with E.H. Hespelt and others) An Outline History of Spanish American Literature, 1942, An Anthology of Spanish American Literature, 1946; 12 Ensayos sobre literatura de los Estados Unidos, 1952; La Cultura en una democracia industrializada, 1954; Democracy, 1960; Bridges of Understanding, 1961; Spanish American Images of the United States, 1975; also articles. Editor: Atlantico, 1955-58; Thoreau and India, 1962; Am. Rev., 1960-63; New Directions in the American University, 1963. Asst. editor Hispania, 1938-44. Home: Gainesville, Fla. Died Nov. 11, 1978; buried Oaxaca, Mex.

REIDY, DANIEL JOSEPH, Jesuit educator; b. Clare Co., Ireland, Aug. 8, 1884; s. John and Margaret (Kelly) R.; A.B., St. Ignatius Coll., Galway, Ireland, 1901; grad. study St. Andrew's Coll., Poughkeepsie, N.Y., 1903; A.M., Gonzaga U., Spokane, Wash., 1908; post-grad. study Woodstock (Md.) Coll., 1912-16, Sacred Heart Coll., Los Gatos, Calif., 1916-17. Came to U.S., 1903. Joined Soc. of Jesus (Jesuits), 1901; teacher of English, Latin and mathematics, Gonzaga High Sch., Spokane, 1903-05; prefect of Coll. of Gonzaga, 1908-12, 1919-20; prof. philosophy, Gonzaga U., 1920-27; also regent Law Sch., same univ., 1926-27, and chaplain Little Flower Industrial Sch., Spokane, 1925-27; pres. Gonzaga U. since 1927. Address: Spokane, Wash. *

REILLY, CHARLES FRANCIS, JR., newspaper editor; b. Norfolk, Va., Nov. 4, 1910; s. Charles Francis and Mary (Miney) R.; student Norfolk div. Coll. William and Mary, 1930, U. Va., 1960; m. Dorothy L. Minton, Nov. 16, 1937. With Norfolk Ledger-Star, 1929-75, news editor, 1958-61, mng. editor, 1961-75; Tidewater editor Catholic Virginian, 1975-80. Pres. for Va., A.P., 1967. Served to capt. USCGR, 1942-46. Mem. Va. Press Assn. (bd. dirs.). Home: Norfolk, Va. Died Sept. 19, 1980.

REINDEL, HAROLD FREDERICK, lawyer; b. Cleve., Jan 11, 1895; s. Frederick William and Salina (Wagner) R.; A.B., Western Res. U., 1916; LL.B., Harvard, 1919; m. Gladys McCreery, Sept. 15, 1923; children—Janet (Mrs. R. E. Tulloss), Frederick William. Admitted to N.Y. bar, 1920; partner Cahill, Gordon, Reindel & Ohl and predecessors, N.Y.C., 1926-79. Pres. West Essex Community Chest, 1947-49; trustee N.J. Symphony Orch. Mem. Phi Beta Kappa. Clubs: University (N.Y.C.); Baltusrol Golf (gov.) (Springfield), N.J.); Pine Valley (N.J.) Golf; R and A Golf (St. Andrews, Scotland). Home: Essex Falls, N.J. Died July 24, 1979.

REINEKE, ERNEST CONRAD, college pres.; b. Deerfield, Steele Co., Minn., Nov. 23, 1883; s. Conrad J. and Othelia (Wilkowske) R.; Ph.B., Baldwin-Wallace Coll., Berea, O., 1909, A.M., 1911; B.D., Oberlin Theol. Sem., 1911; m. Cora Randolph, of LeSueur, Minn., Aug. 3, 1909. Ordained M.E. ministry, 1911; pastor Glenville, Minn., 1911-13, Rushmore, 1913-15, Byron, 1915-18, Fairfax, 1918-21; pres. Parker Coll., Winnebago, Minn., since 1921. Republican. Mason. Home: Winnebago, Minn.*

REINERT, CARL M., univ. ofcl.; b. Boulder, Colo., July 4, 1913; s. Francis John and Emma Caroline (Voegtle) R.; A.B., St. Louis U., 1935, A.M., 1938, Ph.L., 1938; S.T.L., St Mary's (Kans.) Coll., 1945; student Marquette U., summer 1948. Entered Soc. of Jesus, 1931; consecrated priest Roman Catholic Ch., 1944; tchr. Creighton Prep. Sch., Omaha, 1938-41; asst. prin. Campion High Sch., Prairie du Chien, Wis. 1946-50, prin., 1950; pres. Creighton U., 1950-62, pres. Devel. Found., 1962-79. Home: Omaha, Nebr. Died Aug. 13, 1980.

REISSIG, FREDERICK E., clergyman; b. West Henrietta, N.Y., Oct. 27, 1893; s. Ernst Frederick and Dorothea (Lang) R.; student Wagner Memorial Luth. Coll., Staten Island, N.Y., 1911-17, D.D., 1943; student spl. courses, U. of Rochester, Mt. Airy Luth. Sem. (Phila.), Colgate-Rochester Div. Sch., Temple U. (Phila.); m. Florence A. Lee, Aug. 4, 1920: children—Frederick Herman, Dorothy Eleanor. Pastor, Lynbrook-Valley Stream (L.I.) parish, 1920-22, Lynbrook-St. John's Luth. Ch., 1922-23, Emanuel Luth. Ch., Rochester, N.Y., 1923-42; exec. sec. Washington (D.C.) Fedn. Chs. (now Council of Churches National Capital Area), from 1942; dean summer assembly Wagner College. Dir. Hartwick Coll., Oneonta, N.Y.; former dir. Hartwick Sem., N.Y. City. Organizer Inter-religious Court Com. (pres. 7 yrs.), Rochester. Hon. life mem. Parent Teachers Assn. N.Y. State. Mem. bd. dirs. People's Rescue Mission (Rochester, NY), Family Soc. of Rochester; mem. character building div. Council of Social Agencies (Rochester, N.Y.). Former pres. City Club (civic), also Monarch Club (civic), Rochester. Mem. bd. management Arnett Branch Y. (Rochester, N.Y.). Mem. bd. dirs. Rochester Fedn. Chs., 14 yrs.; charter mem. Ministers Round Table; pres. Ch. Conf. of Social Work, Fed. Council Chs. (1 yr.); mem. bd. dirs. and chmn. com. on adult edn. N.Y. State Council of Chs.; chmn. 3d annual regional conf. United Adult Christian Movement, Ont., Can., 1944; pres. N.Y. State Luther League, 2 yrs.; chmn. parish edn. N.Y. and N.E. Synod; chmn. parish edn. and young people's work Western Conf. United Luth. Synod of N.Y., also chmn. worship com., mem. publicity com., chmn. com. on evangelism. Pub. relations officer (9 mos. assignment) World Council chs., Geneva, Switzerland, 1948. An organizer, also secretary and member board since organization, Lutheran Inner Mission Society of Rochester. Author: Light for Today, 1940. Contbr. articles to religious publs. Corr. for Christian Century. Died Feb. 17, 1980.

REITEN, PALMER JAMES, engr.; b. Petersburg, N.D., May 1, 1917; s. Peter I. and Johanna (Knudson) R.; B.S. in Mech. Engring., U. N.D., 1943; M.S., Tex. A. and M. U., 1948; m. Beulah Jenson, June 6, 1946; 1 son, Keith Alan. Instr., Tex. A. and M. U., 1945-48; mem. faculty U. N.D., 1948-79, prof. mech. engring., 1961-79, chmn. dept. 1961-67. Cons. in field, 1952-79; tech. dir. profl. devel. service N.D. Civil Def., until 1969. Served with USAAF, 1943-44. Registered profl. engr., N.D. Mem. Nat., N.D. (pres. chpt. 1 1957-58, state pres. 1967-68, nat. dir. 1975-79, exec. bd. Profl. Engrs. in Edn. sect. 1971-74) socs. profl. engrs., ASME, Am. Soc. Engring. Edn. (pres. N. Mid-West sect. 1964-65), N.D. Acad. Sci., Am. Soc. Heating, Refrigeration and Air Conditioning Engrs., Sigma Tau. Clubs: Elks, Toastmasters (pres. Grand Forks 1961-62). Home: Grand Forks, N.D. Died Apr. 5, 1979.

REITZ, HAROLD AXTEL, bank exec.; b. Dunkirk, Ind., Nov. 1, 1891; s. George F. and Ann M. (Richter) R.; student Ohio State U., 1911-12; B.S. in Econs., Wharton Sch., U. Pa., 1916; m. Beverly Walker, June 27, 1931. With Nat. City Bank, N.Y.C., 1916-24; fgn. trader, exec., Argentina and Brazil, 1916-24; nat. bank examiner Treasury Dept., 1925-56; exec. v.p., dir. First Nat. Bank, Mt. Vernon, N.Y., 1956-63; v.p. Chem. Bank & Trust Co., N.Y.C., 1964-66; pres. Criterion Capital Corp., from 1966. Chmn. Mt. Vernon dr. A.R.C., 1956. Mem. N.Y., Westchester bankers assns., Mt. Vernon C. of C. (treas. 1956-65), Delta Tau Delta. Republican. Episcopalian. Clubs: Metropolitan (bd. govs., treas. 1962-65) (N.Y.C.); Silver Spring Country (Ridgefield, Conn.). Home: Ridgefield, Conn. Died Mar. 18, 1976; interred Columbarium, Ch. of Heavenly Rest, N.Y.C.

REMEY, GILBERT PRYCE, coal co. exec.; b. Matamoras, Pa., Nov. 24, 1912; s. Gilbert Beebe and Nancy Elizabeth (Halstead) R.; A.B., Pa. State U., 1934; m. Frances M. Snyder, May 18, 1940; children—Gilbert William, Anne M. Remey Hevner, Donald P., Catherine S. Remey Lilly. Salesman, United Eastern Coal Sales Corp., Phila., 1936-42, dist. mgr., 1947-55, v.p., gen. mgr., 1955-67, pres., 1967-72, chmn. bd., 1973-78; also dir.; pres. Merrimac Coal Co., Phila., 1942-47; pres., chief exec. officer Rochester & Pitts. Coal Co., Indiana, Pa., 1972-78. also dir. Mem. Am. Mining Congress, Nat. Coal Assn. (dir.), Delta Chi. Clubs: Merion Golf (Ardmore, Pa.); Sky (N.Y.C.); Duquesne (Pitts.); Laurel Valley Golf (Ligonier, Pa.). Home: Indiana, Pa. Died June 13, 1978.

RENALDO, DUNCAN, author, actor; b. Apr. 23, 1904; student Cooper Union Coll., 1924-25, also Santa Barbara City Coll.; m. Audrey Madalene Leonard, July 1, 1956; children—Stephanie M., Jeremy R., Richard L., Edwin. Appeared movies Fifty-Fifty, 1924, Color Art Pictures Marquita, Romany Love, Mission Bells, Verdi, Beethoven, Indian Love Lyrics, 1926-28, Bridge of San Louis Rey, 1928, Trader Horn, 1929-31, The Cisco Kid series, from 1943; producer, author Bells of San Fernando, 1946; producer Don Ricardo Returns, 1948; author Mission Bells, 1927, Marquita, 1927, The Highway Man, 1947, Dick Turpin's Ride, 1947; exhibited paintings Ebell Theater, Los Angeles, 1958. Dir. Santa Barbara (Cal.) Fiesta, 1967. Mem. Hope Ranch Assn. (dir.), Screen Actors Guild, Screen Writers Guild, Am. Guild Variety Artists Equity. Address: Santa Barbara, Calif. Died Sept. 3, 1980.

RENDLEMAN, JOHN SAMUEL, lawyer, univ. pres.; b. Anna, Ill., June 21, 1927; s. Ford Lee and Jean (Shomaker) R.; student Coll. St. Thomas, 1945, Ia. State Coll., 1945-46; B.S., So. Ill. U., 1948; J.D., U. Ill., 1951; m. Lenora Norris, Dec. 15, 1956; children—Jean Farrin, John Samuel III, Mary Elizabeth, David Scott; 1 son by previous marriage, Charles Mathew. Admitted to Ill. bar, 1951; legal counsel So. Ill. U., 1951-61, exec.

dir. bus. affairs, 1961-63, gen. counsel, 1963-64, v.p., 1964-68, chancellor Edwardsville Campus, 1968-71, pres., 1971-76. Spl. asst. atty. gen. Hodge Investigation, 1956-57; nat. chmn. Vanderbilt Traffic Survey; dir. 1st Nat. Bank, Cobden, Ill., 1st Granite City Nat. Bank; mem. com. to improve legis. processes Ill. Gen. Assembly, 1965-76. Bd. dirs. Arts and Edn. Council Greater St. Louis, St. Elizabeth's Hosp., Granite City, St. Louis Symphony, Design Sci. Inst., Washington, Kidney Found. Eastern Mo. and Met. East, 1974-76; trustee McKendree Coll.; hon. chmn. Lentz Internat. Peace Research award, 1975-76. Served with USNR, 1945-46. Mem. Am. (exec. council), Ill. (exec. com.) bar assns., St. Louis Commerce and Growth Assn. (1st v.p. 1972-76), Phi Kappa Tau (pres. 1956), Chi Delta Chi, Pi Delta Rho, Sigma Alpha Epsilon. Presbyn. Elk. Club: University. Home: Edwardsville, Ill. Died Mar. 4, 1976.

RENDON, CECIL PAUL (REN-DON), lawyer; b. Sonora, Calif., Oct. 6, 1861; s. Jesus and Dolores (Gomez) R.; ed. Santa Clara U.; m. Hannah Crowley, Sept. 5, 1887; children—Cecilia May (Mrs. Armand Woods), Anita (Mrs. Ernest F. Atkinson), Raymond, Dolores Lee, Cecil Paul; m. 2d, Emeline Olds Mitchell, June 23, 1922. Admitted to Calif. bar, 1887, and began practice at Stockton with Ex-gov. James H. Budd; now men. firm Foltz & Rendon. Sergt. Calif. N.G., 1887-92. Pros. atty., Stockton, 1890-92; city justice, Stockton, 1894-98; chief dep. dist. atty., San Joaquin County, Calif., 1906-18. Mem. Rep. County Central Com. over 40 yrs.; mem. Rep. State Central Com.; presdl. elector, Calif., 1928; del. Rep. Nat. Conv., 1932; former mem. State Civil Service Commn. Mem. Am. Bar Assn., Calif. State Bar Assn. (ex-pres.), San Joaquin County Bar Assn. (ex-pres.), San Joaquin Fish and Game Protection Assn. (ex-pres.), Young Men's Inst. (ex-grand pres.), Foresters of America (past grand chief ranger, past nat. supreme chief ranger), Elk, Red Man, Eagle (1st state pres.). Clubs: Stockton Blue Rock Gun (ex-pres.), Roberts Island Rifle (ex-pres.). Home: Stockton, Calif. *

RENEKER, ROBERT WILLIAM, diversified industry exec.; b. Chgo., Aug. 4, 1912; s. William Turner and Mary Ethel (Gilmour) R.; Ph.B., U. Chgo., 1933; spl. course Harvard, 1954; m. Eva Elizabeth Congdon, Mar. 2, 1935; children—William Carl, David Lee. With purchasing dept. Swift & Co., Chgo., 1934-44, asst. office of v.p. charge purchasing, 1944-46, tech. product sales, 1946-50, asst. in office of pres., 1950-55, 1955-64, pres., 1964-73, chief exec. officer, 1967-73, also dir.; pres., chief exec. officer Esmark, Inc., 1973, chmn., chief exec. officer, 1973-77; dir. Continental Ill. Bank, Gen. Dynamics Co., Chgo. Tribune, Trans Union Co., Jewel Cos., Inc., Morton Norwich. Nat. bd. dirs. Boy Scouts Am.; v.p. United Way; bd. dirs. Mus. Sci. and Industry; chmn. bd. trustees U. Chgo. Mem. United Ch. Clubs: Chicago, Commercial, Economics. Home: Chicago, Ill. Died Apr. 27, 1981.

RENOIR, JEAN, film writer, dir.; b. Paris, France, Sept. 15, 1894; s. Pierre Auguste and Aline (Charigot) R.; student U. Aix-en-Provence, France, 1913; D.F.A., U. Calif., 1963; m. Andree Madeleine Heuschling, 1920; 1 son, Alain; m. 2d, Dido Freire, 1944. Artist, ceramist, Cagnes, France, 1918-23; in motion picture bus. with own co. and others as dir.-writer, Paris, 1923-25; dir. films including Nana, Paris-Berlin, 1924, La Petite Marchande d'Allumettes, 1928, Tire au Flanc, 1928, La Chienne, Paris, 1929, La Nuit du Carrefour, 1932, Boudu Sauvé des Eaux, 1932, Madame Bovary, 1934, Toni, 1935, The Crime of Mr. Lange, (original story), Paris, 1935, Les Bas Fonds, 1936, Une Partie de Campagne, 1936-46, The Grand Illusion (original story), Paris, 1937, La Bête Humaine, 1938, La Marseillaise, 1938, The Southerner, Hollywood, 1943, The River, India, 1950, The Golden Coach, Rome, Italy, 1952; French Cancan, Paris, 1954, Elena (original story), Paris, France, 1955; adaption and legitimate stage dir. The Big Knife, Paris, 1957; legitimate stage dir. Julius Caesar for 2000 anniversary found. of Arles by Julius Caesar, 1954; writer, dir. Orvet, Paris, 1954; producer, dir., writer Le Dejeuner sur l'Herbe, Paris, 1959; dir. writer Le Caporal Epingle, 1962, Osella, Venice, 1968, Le Petit Theatre De Jean Renoir, Paris, 1969; Regent's prof. U. Calif. at Berkeley, 1960. Served as lt. French Calvalry and Air Force pilot, World War I. Decorated French Legion of Honor, French Cross of War, commandeur de l'Ordre des Arts et Lettres; recipient Golden Laurel trophy Brussels Fair, one of twelve best film dirs. of all times, 1958, spl. Oscar for lifetime achievement Acad. Motion Picture Arts and Scis., 1974. Fellow Am. Acad. Arts and Scis.; mem. Royal Acad. Arts (hon.) (London, Eng.). Roman Catholic. Author: Renoir, My Father, 1962 (Charles Blanc prize Academie Francaise 1963); The Notebooks of Captain Georges, 1966; My Life and My Films, 1974; Le Coeur a l'Aise, 1978; Le Crime de l'Anglais, 1978; Genevieve, 1979. Home: Beverly Hills, Calif. Died Feb. 12, 1979; buried Essoyes, France.

RENSHAW, PAUL, bus. exec.; b. 1888; grad. Columbia U., 1911. Former pres. and chmn. Gen. Ry. Signal Co., N.Y.C.; dir. Fiduciary Trust Co. Trustee, Rensselaer Polytech. Inst. Served with USN, World War I. Home: New York, N.Y. Died Dec. 17, 1976.

REPPLIER, THEODORE SILKMAN, advt. exec.; b. Yonkers, N.Y., Apr. 28, 1899; s. Francis Arthur and Elizabeth (Oakley) R.; student St. Johns Coll., 1918-19; B.S., Carnegie Inst. Tech., 1923; D.C.L. (hon.), Pace Coll., 1956; m. Martha C. Macatee, June 6, 1930 (dec. Dec. 1966); children—Theodore Silkman, Richard Oakley; m. 2d, Esmée Ertz, Dec. 12, 1967. Advt. writer Chesapeake & Potomac Telephone Co., Washington, 1923-25, advt. supr., 1925-26; copy writer Ewing, Jones & Higgins, Phila., 1926-31, Young & Rubicam, N.Y.C., 1931-38, asso. copy dir., 1938-42; campaigns mgr. War Manpower Commn., 1942; Washington mgr. War Advt. Council, 1943; Pres., dir. The Advt. Council, Inc., Washington and N.Y.C., 1946-66; mng. dir. Internat. Round Tables, 1966-69. Formerly mem. Pres.' Com. on Mental Retardation; bd. dirs. Bus. Council for Internat. Understanding. Fellow Eisehower Exchange Fellowships, Inc., 1955. Recipient Gold medal distinguished services to advt., 1948; Distinguished Service award USIA, U.S. Treasury. Mem. Delta Upsilon, Pi Delta Epsilon, Alpha Delta Sigma, Home: Silver Spring, Md. Died Nov. 7, 1976.

REQUARDT, GUSTAV JAEGER, cons. engr.; b. Balt., Nov. 11, 1886; s. John Frederick and Anna Elise Bertha (Jaeger) R.; student Balt. City Coll., 1905; C.E., Cornell U., 1909; m. Rosa Mildred Duker, Nov. 23, 1915; m. 2d, Therese M. Gerherin, January 31, 1969. Rodman to div. engr. Sewage Commn. of Balt., 1909-15; prin. engr. charge office Norton, Bird & Whitman, Balt. and Chgo., 1916-25; engr. for contractor Army Ordnance Dept., Aberdeen (Md.) Proving Ground, 1917-18; partner Whitman, Requardt & Smith, 1925-43; partner, then sr. partner Whitman, Requardt & Assos., Baltimore, 1944-66, cons. to partnership, 1967—, charge engring. designs and constrn. chem. warfare indsl. plants, Md., Ala., Colo., 1940-43. Asst. to bd. adv. engrs. Study Great Lake Levels for City of Chgo., 1924-25; mem. bd. adv. engrs., diversion waters of Delaware River, State of N.J., 1930-31, 52-53, new sources water supply City of Balt., 1934,42, 53, flood water pumping of Susquehanna River, U.S. Army Corps Engrs., 1938, sewage rental rates City of Cleve., 1938-40, study physical facilities, Balt., 1940-42, refuse disposal, 1944, new water supply and improvement existing water system, Phila., 1945-46, sewerage system and sewage treatment works, Washington, 1955-64; adv. engr. to spl. com. on water supply Delaware River and other sources, State of N.J., 1956; mem. planning council Greater Balt. Com. for Studies of Large Scale Improvements of City, 1959—; lectr. U.S. Indsl. Coll., 1950-51. Mem. Cornell U. Council, 1954—; pres. City Coll. Class of 1905, 1960—, Cornell U. Class of 1909, 1969—. Recipient Fuller award Am. Water Works Assn., 1944; citation Nat. Soc. Professional Engrs., 1969, also citation Engring. Soc. Balt., 1969. Registered profl. engr., Md., Alabama, Conn., Del., D.C., N.J., N.Y., Ohio, Pa., Va., W.Va. Mem. Am. Soc. of Civil Engrs. (hon. mem.; past dir.; past pres. Md.), Am. Water Works Assn., Am. Pub. Works Assn., Soc. Am. Mil. Engrs., Am. Soc. Planning Ofcls., Fedn. Sewage Works Assn., Am. Inst. Cons. Engrs. Nat. Soc. Profl. Engrs., Md. Hist. Soc., Balt. Assn. Commerce, Cornell Engring. Soc. (past pres.), Chi Psi. Clubs: Maryland; Engineers (past pres.), Baltimore Country (bd. govs. 1952-63), Cornell (Balt. and N.Y.C.). Contbr. articles on san. engring. to mags. Home: Baltimore MD. *

RESNICK, NATHAN, educator; b. Bklyn., June 13, 1910; s. Abraham and Fanny (Weinberg) R.; B.S., L.I. U., 1933; student Art Student's League, 1933, 1945; B.S. Columbia, 1937; M.A., N.Y. U., 1945; m. Ernestine Roberts Cederholm. May 4, 1943. Asst. librarian L.I. U., 1933-39, librarian, 1939-48, instr. English, 1938-48, dir. libraries, from 1948, dir. L.I. U. Press, from 1948, asso. prof. English, 1948-52, asso. prof. art, 1950-56, prof., from 1956, chmn. art dept., from 1961; dir. publs., exhibits, from 1962, coordinator L.I. U.-Bklyn. Museum Art Sch., 1957-68, dir. planning, from 1965, dean for devel. learning center programs. Cons., Photography in the Fine Arts; mem. internat. adv. council Fund for Concerned Photography; ednl. facilities cons., from 1969, cons. Oceanic Ednl. Found., from 1970. Sec. Leaves of Grass Centennial Com.; mem. Walt Whitman Found., Camden. Founder L.I. U.-Walt Whitman Colloquia, 1965. Trustee Walt Whitman Birthplace Assn.; bd. dirs. Internat. Cultural Centers for Youth. Mem. Am. Acad. Polit. and Social Sci., ALA, AAUP, Am. Studies Assn., AAAS (White House Conf. on Edn. 1955), N.Y. Folklore Soc., NEA, Am. Mus. Natural History, Museum Modern Art, Woodstock (N.Y.) Art Assn., Coll. Art Assn., Quill Club N.Y., Circle of Confusion. Author: Walt Whitman and the Authorship of the Good Grey Poet, 1948; co-author: The Third Eye; A New World of Exploratory Photography, 1962; also papers on art films, library service. Designed and edited: Songbirds of America in Color, Sound and Story, 1954. Photographs on world tour for USIA, 1960—; gen. editor Life, Land and Water in Ancient Peru, 1965. Home: New York, N.Y. Died Sept. 7, 1977.

RETHBERG, ELISABETH, soprano; b. Schwarzenberg, Saxony, in the Erz Mountains; d. Charles and Jenny Saettler; ed. Royal Conservatory of Music, Dresden; m. Albert E. Doman, 1923 (divorced). Admitted to Royal Opera, Dresden, at age 19; debut in the "Gypsy Baron"; sang in opera and concert in most important opera houses throughout Europe, also in South America and Covent Garden, Eng.; Am. debut as "Aida," with Metropolitan Opera Co., New York, 1922; concert tours all over the U.S. and Australia from 1925; appeared in many operatic leading roles—dramatic, lyric; first dramatic soprano in Ravinia Park Summer Opera, 1923-30. Applied for first naturalization papers, 1923; naturalized, 1939. Mem. Am. Women's Assn.; hon. mem. Sigma Alpha Iota. Guild of Vocal Teachers of America (gold medal "for perfect art of singing"); hon. mem. all state theatres of Saxony, 1930. Home: New York, N.Y. Died June 6, 1976.

REUSSER, WALTER CHRISTIAN, dean adult education; born Elgin, Iowa; son of Fred and Emma (Abbey) R.; A.B., Upper Ia. U., Fayette, Ia., 1920, A.M., State U. Ia., 1923, Ph.D., 1929; post doctoral course, Columbia Teachers Coll., 1938-39; m. Eleanor T. Bentley, Aug. 27, 1924; children—Margaret L. (Mrs. Richard Redburn), Kathryn M. (Mrs. Glen A. Pray). Asst. in chemistry, Upper Ia. U., 1918-20; instr. sci., Independence (Ia.) High Sch., 1920-22; supt. pub. schs., Oneida, Ia., 1922-24; mem. faculty, U. Wyo., from 1924, prof. ednl. adminstrn. from 1931, also dean, div. adult edn. and community service from 1948, dean emeritus, from 1962; vis. prof. edn., U. Oregon, summer 1935, W.Va. U., summer 1939, 42, Cornell, summer 1947, Syracuse U., 1952, No. Ill. U., 1962-63; dep. supt. public instrn. State of Wyo., 1963-67. Served with chem. warfare, U.S. Army, World War I. Mem. N.E.A. (dept.'s rural edn., adult edn., higher edn., Am. Ednl. Research Assn.), Am. Assn. School Admin., American Assn. U. Profs., Phi Delta Kappa, Phi Kappa Phi, Kappa Delta Pi. Presbyn. Mason. Club: Lions. Author: Public School Finance (with Paul R. Mort), rev. ed., 1951. Contbr. ednl. jours. Home: Laramie, Wyo. Died Sept. 22, 1976.

REVELL, FLEMING H., JR., publisher; b. Chicago, Ill., Nov. 29, 1882; s. Fleming H. and Josephine (Barbour) R.; ed. Lawrenceville Sch. and Yale; m. Marion Cornell, Aug. 15, 1911 (died Sept. 1, 1941); 1 dau., Muriel (Mrs. Charles E. Marshall, now deceased); married Carolyn Conner, January 27, 1949. Entered publishing company, Fleming H. Revell Company, New York, N.Y., 1907, now chairman board. Mem. Alpha Delta Phi. Clubs: Yale (New York); Los Angeles Country, Riviera Equestrian, Los Angeles Athletic, (Los Angeles). Home: Los Angeles. *

REVERCOMB, CHAPMAN, lawyer, ex-senator; b. Covington, Va., July 20, 1895; s. George and Elizabeth (Chapman) R.; student Washington and Lee U., 1914-16; LL.B., U. Va., 1919; m. Sara V. Hughes, June 9, 1926; children—William, George, Anne, James. Admitted to Va. bar, 1919, practiced in Covington, 1919-22; admitted to W.Va., bar, 1922, in gen. practice, Charleston; mem. U.S. Senate, 1943-49, 56-59. Mem. W.Va. Rep. exec. com., 1932-36; pres. state Young Rep. League, 1934-36; chmn. state jud. conv., 1936. Served as cpl. Batt. A.35th CA, U.S. Army, during World War I. Mem. Am., W.Va., Charleston (pres. 1938) bar assns., Am. Legion, Raven Soc. Republican. Presbyn. Elk. Clubs: Press, Edgewood Country (Charleston); Rotary. Home: Charleston, W.Va. Died Oct. 6, 1979.

REYBURN, WILLIAM STUART, congressman; b. Phila., Dec. 17, 1882; s. John Edgar R. (q.v.) and Margretta (Crozier) R.; Ph.B., Yale, 1904; studied law, George Washington U.; m. Georgie Fontaine Maury, of Washington, June 10, 1911. Pres. William S. Reyburn Bldg. & Loan Assn., Phila. Mem. Pa. Ho. of Rep., 1909, 1911; elected 62d Congress, May 23, 1911, 2d Pa. Dist., for unexpired term (1911-13) of Joel Cook, deceased; Republican. Episcopalian. Member Delta Psi; Mason. Clubs: Metropolitan, Chevy Chase, Century (Washington), Racquet, Phila. Country, Union League (Phila.). Home: Philadelphia. *

REYNOLDS, EMILY SIMMS BELLINGER, librarian; b. Barnwell County, S.C., Nov. 28, 1889; d. Dr. Martin and Melvina (Dunbar) Bellinger; B.A., Winthrop Coll., 1908; grad. student U. S.C.; m. John Schreiner Reynolds, Nov. 28, 1917 (dec. Oct. 1918); 1 dau., Joan (Mrs. Douglas Faunt). Engrossing dept. S.C. Gen. Assembly, 1917, 21-26, finance com., 1930-37; jour. clk., S.C. Senate, 1938-41, gen. desk clk., 1941-55; state librarian, S.C., 1956-65. Jefferson Centennial rep. for S.C. to visit battlefields of France, 1925; mem. Gold Star Mothers and Widows Pilgrimage to France, 1932. Mem. woman's div. State Nat. Def. Council, 1943-45. Mem. Am. Legion Auxiliary (dept. pres. 1926-27), Colonial Dames Am., D.A.R., A.L.A., S.C. Library Assn., Nat. Assn. Law Librarians, S.C. Hist. Soc., Alpha Delta Pi. Episcopalian. Club: New Century (Columbia). Compilor, editor: (with Joan Reynolds Faunt) Biographical Directory of South Carolina State Senators, 1776-1964, 1964, The County Offices and Officers of Barnwell County, S.C. 1775-1975, A Record, 1976. Home: Columbia, S.C. Died July 2, 1980; buried Red Hill Cemetery, Barnwell, S.C.

REYNOLDS, GRACE BANTA URBAHNS (RENOLDZ), mem. Rep. Nat. Com.; b. Rensselaer, Ind., Aug. 1, 1886; d. Bruce and Julia Frances (Gray) Banta; student Sch. of Edn., Valparaiso U., 1905-07;

summers, Valparaiso U., 1908, 10, 11, 12; m. Bernhardt Henry Urbahns, July 29, 1915 (died Jan. 21, 1926); children—John Bruce, Dorothea Frances; m. 2d, Franklin Smith Reynolds, Sept. 14, 1929. Instr., pub. schs., Porter County and Valparaiso, 1907-14; conducted 1 room model sch., connection Valparaiso U., 1911-13; instr., English and literature, pub. schs., Red Lodge, Mont., 1914-15; treas., State of Ind., 1926-31. Mem. Rep. Nat. Com. for Ind., 1936-40; elected v. chmn. Rep. Nat. Com., term 1940-44; apptd. by nat. chmn. to com. on orgn., Rep. Nat. Com., 1941; dir. women's activities, Western Div., 1936 and 1940 campaigns; co-chmn. and dir. women's activities in Wendell L. Willkie Pre-Rep. presidential campaign, Jan. 1-Apr. 4, 1944; asst. women's div. Rep. Nat. com., Rep. campaign Aug.-Nov., 1944. Vice pres., sec., Standard Mfg. Co., Cambridge, Ind., Reynolds Mfg. Co., Rushville, Ind. Treas. bldg. expansion program, Indianapolis Day Nursery, 1927-28, mem. Am. Legion Auxiliary, Rep. Women's Club (Indianapolis and Cambridge City), Kappa Kappa Kappa, Presbyterian. Address: Cambridge City, Ind. *

REYNOLDS, HORACE (MASON) (REN'ELZ), writer; b. New York, N.Y., Oct. 2, 1896; s. Horace Jackson and Margaret (Mason) R.; A.B., Harvard, 1919, A.M., 1923, postgrad. 1931-34; m. Catharine Whitford Coffeen, Apr. 29, 1922 (dec. Nov. 1962); children—John Hamilton, Margaret Whitford (Mrs. Arthur Cushing Rist). Tchr. English several universities, including Brown and Harvard, 1919-42; war work with Army Air Force, 1942-43; free lance writer from 1943; prof. English, Emerson Coll., from 1950; lectr. English, Tufts University, summers from 1954. Served in United States Army, September-November 1918. Author: A Providence Episode in the Irish Literary Renaissance (brochure), 1929; articles in the fields of Anglo-Irish lit. and Am. language, folklore, folksong, riverways and folkways. Editor: Letters to the New Island, 1934. Contbr. to N.Y. Times, Christian Science Monitor; also to Am. and fgn. mags. Home: Belmont, Mass. Died Oct. 27, 1965.

REYNOLDS, HOWARD H., educator; b. Cambridge, Mass., Jan. 28, 1916; s. Harris Aquila and Alice (Hecker) R.; A.B. cum laude Harvard U., 1936; Sc.D., Mass. Inst. Tech., 1939; m. Sarah Riley, Sept. 14, 1940; children—Howard Langdon, Jonathan, Sarah, Cynthia. Research asst. Mass. Inst. Tech., 1938-39; research engr. Wyandotte (Mich.) Chems. Corp., 1939-41; mgr. research dept. Davison Chem. Corp., Balt., 1941-44; devel. engr., mgr. quality control Dewey & Almy Chem. Co., Cambridge, Mass., 1944-49; mgr. tech. dept. and quality control Cryovac Co. div. W.R. Grace Co., Cambridge, Mass., 1949-60; v.p. research and devel. Paper & Plastics div. Ludlow Corp., Needham Heights, Mass., 1960-63; prof., head chem. engring. and paper engring. dept. Lowell Technol. Inst., 1963-76; part-time instr. Grad. Sch. Engring. Mgmt., Northeastern U., 1959-76. Regional dir. United Fund, 1958; regional dir. Mass. Inst. Tech. Fund, 1960. Registered profl. engr., Mass. Mem. Am. Chem. Soc., Am. Inst. Chem. Engrs., Tech. Assn. Pulp and Paper Industry, Soc. Plastics Engrs., N.Y. Acad. Scis. Unitarian. Club: Toastmasters' (pres. 1958). Patentee irradiated polyethylene; pigments; catalysts. Home: Belmont, Mass. Died Aug. 10, 1976; buried Mt. Auburn Cemetery, Cambridge, Mass.

REYNOLDS, JOSEPH GARDINER, JR., artist in stained glass; b. Wickford, R.I., Apr. 9, 1886; s. Joseph Gardiner and Rebecca Granger (Tillinghast) R.; ed. R.I. pub. schs.; grad. R.I. Sch. Design, 1907; studied Eng., France, Italy, Spain, 1920, 21, 35, 37; m. Bertha Clogston, Aug. 22, 1911 (dec. May 1962); m. 2d, Katherine MacKillop, June 17, 1963. Designer stained glass windows, 1907-20; opened studio, dir. partnership Reynolds, Francis & Rohnstock, designing and making stained glass windows, 1921—, Reynolds, Francis & Rohnstock, Inc. (then Joseph G. Reynolds Assos., Inc.), pres. corp., 1948-66. Prin. works appear in Princeton U. Chapel, St. Bartholmews Church, N.Y.C., Riverside Ch., N.Y.C., Cathedral St. John the Divine, N.Y.C., East Liberty Presbyn. Ch., Pitts.; Presbyn. Ch., Glens Falls, N.Y.; Mercersburg (Pa.) Acad. Chapel; Houghton Meml. Chapel, Wellesley Coll., Am. Meml. Cemetery Chapel, Belleau, France, American Church in Paris, France, Quai d'Orsay, and numerous other places; co-author apse windows and Declaration-Constitution window of Washington Cathedral; south transept Rose window and the lancets beneath Washington Cathedral, others. Awarded Medal of Merit, Boston Soc. Arts and Crafts, 1929; gold medal, Boston Tercentenary Art Exhbn., 1930; Medal of Merit. Paris Internat. Expn., 1937; A.I.A. Craftsmanship Gold Mdl., 1950; Gold Medal R.I. Sch. of Design Alumni award, 1963. Mem. Medieval Acad. of Am., Am. Fedn. of Arts, Nat. Inst. of Soc. Scis. Baptist. Mason. Clubs: Providence Art; Nat. Early Am. Glass. Home and studio: Belmont MA. *

REYNOLDS, KATHARINE (MRS. HENRY T. REYNOLDS), writer; b. Bohemia, Nov. 24, 1883; d. Thomas and Eva (Mazanec) Yirsa; brought to U.S. at 6 yrs. of age; grad. West Div. High Sch., Chicago, 1900, Chicago Teachers' Coll., 1902; m. Henry T. Reynolds, of Chicago, June 28, 1905; children—Thomas George, Henry Richard, John Robert, William David. Was teacher in pub. schs.; contbr. editorial articles and sketches to Chicago Daily News, 1908-11, later travel articles from S. America; contbr. stories to Collier's, The Green Book, Red Book, Woman's World, etc.; founded The Lombard Breeze (weekly newspaper), 1912. Author: Green Valley, 1919; Willow Creek, 1924. Spent 2 1/2 yrs. in S. America. Home: Lombard, Ill. *

REYNOLDS, MALVINA, song writer; b. San Francisco, Aug. 23, 1900; d. David and Abigail (Shenson) Milder; A.B., U. Cal. at Berkeley, 1925, A.M., 1927, Ph.D. in English Lang. and Lit., 1939; m. William Reynolds, Apr. 15, 1934; 1 dau., Nancy Schimmel. Appearances in concert throughout U.S., Japan and Europe, singing own compositions, 1950—; recordings for Folkway album of own compositions, Another County Heard From, 1960; Columbia album Malvina Reynolds Sings the Truth, 1967; Century City album Malvina Reynolds, 1970; Cassandra Records album Malvina, 1972, Held Over, 1975., Magical Songs, 1978; Mama Lion, 1980; recs. for Pacific Cascade Records, Artichokes, 1971; Funnybugs, 1972. Compositions include: Turn Around, 1958; What Have They Done To The Rain?, 1962; Little Boxes, 1962; Rand Hymn, 1961; Andorra, 1962; God Bless the Grass, 1964; Battle of Maxton Field, 1958; From Way Up Here, 1962; Let Us Come In, 1955; Bury Me in My Overalls, 1956; Monaco, 1956; Sally Don't You Grieve, 1957; Magic Penny, 1955; Vikki Duggan, 1961; Golden Bell, 1961; The Little Land, 1958; Western Wind, 1957; Morningtown Ride, 1957; Marty, 1958; Willow Tree, 1956. Collections of songs: Little Boxes and Other Handmade Songs, 1964; Tweedles and Foodles for Young Noodles, 1961; The Muse of Parker Street, 1967; Cheerful Tunes For Lutes and Spoons, 1970; The Malvina Reynolds Song Book, 1974; There's Music in the Air, 1976; also contbr. to folk jours. Mem. ASCAP, Am. Fedn. Musicians, AFTRA, Phi Beta Kappa. Address: Berkeley, Calif. Died Mar. 17, 1978.

REYNOLDS, RICHARD S., JR., business exec.; b. Winston-Salem, N.C., May 27, 1908; s. Richard S. and Louise (Parham) R.; student Davidson Coll.; B.S., U. Pa., 1930; m. Virginia Sargeant; children—Richard S. III, Sargeant (dec.). Became mem. N.Y. Stock Exchange, 1930; with two partners formed banking firm Reynolds & Co., N.Y. City, 1930; asst. to pres. Reynolds Metals Co., Richmond, Va., 1938, treas., 1938-44, v.p., treas., 1944-48, pres., 1948-63, 71-75, chmn. bd., 1963-71, chmn bd., pres., 1971-75, chmn. bd., chief exec. officer, 1975-76, chmn. exec. com., 1976-77, hon. chmn. bd., 1977—; chmn. bd. Robertshaw Controls Co., 1955-78, chmn. exec. com., 1957-59, chmn., 1959-78; dir. Central Nat. Bank, Richmond, Lawyers Title Ins Corp. Trustee U. Richmond; trustee emeritus U. Pa, Mem. Aluminum Assn. (past pres.), Bus. Council. Presbyn. Clubs: The Brook, The Jockey (N.Y.C.); Metropolitan (Washington); Country of Va., Commonwealth (Richmond); Buck's (London); Farmington Country; Deep Run Hunt. Home: Richmond, Va. Died Oct. 5, 1980.

REYNOLDS, ROLLO GEORGE, educator; b. Cambridge, Vt., Mar. 31, 1886; s. Orange W. and Mary (Morgan) R.; A.B., Dartmouth Coll., 1910; A.M., Teachers College (Columbia), 1920, Ph.D., 1923; LL.D., American International College, 1938; m. Alice Hine McCarthy, Nov. 25, 1911; children—Robert Hine, George Rollo, Mary Elizabeth. Instr. history, Juniata Coll., Huntingdon, Pa., 1910-11; prin. pub. schs. in Vt., 1911-15; exec. sec. State Bd. Edn., Montpelier, 1915-17; dir. T.N. Vail Agrl. Sch., Lyndon, 1917-18; asst. in ednl. survey schs., Greensboro, 1920, Baltimore, 1920-21; dir. Vermont State Summer Sch., 1920: with Teachers Coll. (Columbia), 1920-28, asso. in dept. of ednl. adminstrn., 1920-21, prof. edn., 1925, provost, 1926-28, also instr. Summer Sch., 1921, field sec. Alumni Assn., 1920-24, dir. Bur. Ednl. Service, 1921-28; prin. Horace Mann Sch., 1928-41; dir. of public relations 1941-43, retired. State dir. U.S. Boys Working Res., 1917-18; Vt. chmn. United War Work Drive, 1918; lecturer U.S. Army Ednl. Corps, France, Germany, 1919. Dir. Parents Pub. Assn., N.Y. City. Mem. N.E.A, Kappa Sigma, Phi Delta Kappa, Delta Pi. Conglist. Clubs: Faculty (Columbia U.), Dartmouth College. Editor Our Changing World Library for Children. Writer, radio broadcaster and pub. speaker on ednl. subjects: Home: New York, N.Y. *

REYNOLDS, THOMAS F., ins. service exec.; b. Omaha, Mar. 7, 1911; s. Thomas P. and Lenora (Hartigan) R.; student Creighton U., 1929-33; m. Helene M. McKenna, Oct. 29, 1938; children—Thomas McKenna (dec.), Helene M. (Mrs. Joseph F. Delaney). Reporter, World-Herald, Omaha, 1927; night So. divisional editor United Press Assn., Atlanta, 1935-37; Chgo. Sun, 1941, asst. mng. editor Chgo. Sun Times, 1949-50, mng. editor, 1951-58; gen. mgr. Ill. Ins. Info. Service, 1958—. White House corr., 1938-42; chief Div. Pub. Info., Office of Fgn. Relief and Rehab. Ops., Dept. of State Washington (on leave of absence from Chgo. Sun), 1943. Decorated Order of Saint Olav, Norway. Mem. White House Corrs. Assn. (pres. 1941-42), State Dept. (pres. 1945-46). Clubs: National Press, Overseas Writers (Washington); Michigan Shores (Wilmette, Ill.). Home: Evanston, Ill. Died Dec. 27, 1978; buried All Saints Cemetery, Des Plaines, Ill.

REYNOLDS, WILLIAM G., metal co. exec.; b. Bristol, Tenn., 1913. Formerly v.p., later exec. v.p. Reynolds Metals Co., also dir., mem. exec. com.; pres., dir. Reynolds Internat.; dir. Reynolds Alloys Co., U.S Foil Co., Caribbean Steamship Co., Eskimo Equipment Co., Reynolds Jamaica Mines, Reynolds Internat. of Can., Ltd., Reynolds Sales Co., Reynolds Corp., Reynolds Mining Corp., Eskimo Pie Co., Richmond Radiator Co., Reynolds Aluminum Co. Recipient Advancement of Research medal Am. Soc. for Metals, 1965. Home: Richmond, Va. Died Oct. 19, 1980.

REZNIKOFF, CHARLES, author; b. Bklyn., Aug. 31, 1894; s. Nathan and Sarah Yetta (Volvofski) R.; student Sch. Journalism U. Mo., 1910-11; LL.B., N.Y. U., 1915; m. Marie Syrkin, May 27, 1930. Admitted to N.Y. bar, 1916. Author: By the Waters of Manhattan: Selected Verse, 1962; Testimony: The United States, 1885-1890: Recitative, 1965; Family Chronicle, 1969; By the Well of Seeing and Living, New and Selected Poems 1918-1973, 1974; Holocaust, 1975. Editor: Louis Marshall: Selected Papers and Addresses, 1957. Recipient Morton Dauwen Zabel award for poetry Nat. Inst. Arts and Letters, 1971. Home: New York, N.Y. Died Jan. 22, 1976.

RHAWN, HEISTER GULE, newspaper pub.; b. Catawissa Pa., Aug. 10, 1892; s. William Howe and Anetta May (Partridge) R.; A.B., Franklin and Marshall Coll., Lancaster, Pa., 1915; student Dickinson Sch. Law, Carlisle, Pa.; m. Mary Cordelia Franklin, Feb. 12, 1918; 1 dau., Harriett V. (Mrs. James W. Behringer). Editor, Clarksburg (W.Va.) Exponent, 1924-41; pub. Clarksburg News, 1941-58, editor, mgr., from 1958; radio news editor WBLK, 1941-46. Served as pvt., World War, and mem. staff The Right About, pub. in N.Y.C. by Officer of Surgeon Gen. U.S. Army. Mem. Am. Legion, Phi Kappa Sigma. Democrat. Episcopalian. Elk, Rotarian. Author: Rimfire, Typical Mountaineer. Home: Clarksburg, W.Va. Died Sept. 10, 1973.

RHEINSTROM, CHARLES ALBERT, advt. exec.; born Phila., Jan. 10, 1902; s. Benjamin A. and Mary E. (Snyder) R.; student U. Minn., 1920-23; m. Marjorie Carolyn Gieske, Mar. 9, 1940. Automobile salesman Northwest Cadillac Co., Mpls., 1925-28; exec. Am. Airlines, Inc. and predecessor firms, 1928-37, v.p., dir., 1937-46, exec. v.p. sales, also dir., 1958-59; aviation cons., 1946-49; sr v.p. Erwin, Wasey & Co., advt., 1949-50; v.p. J. Walter Thompson Co., advt., 1950-58, 59-80, also dir.; chmn. exec. com. Helio Aircraft Corp., Bedford, Mass. Bd. govs. Flight Safety Found.; 1st pres. Air Traffic Conf. Am.; 1st chmn. traffic com. Internat. Air Transport Assn. Mem. Delta Upsilon, Scabbard and Blade, Mortar and Ball. Clubs: Racquet and Tennis, Wings (past pres.), Sky, Metropolitan (NY.C.); California. Home: New York, N.Y. Died May 27, 1980.

RHOADS, CARROLL BREWSTER, lawyer; b. Phila., July 4, 1892; s. E. Clinton and Mary Gertrude (Snyder) R.; grad. William Penn Charter Sch., 1909; B.S., U. Pa., 1912; LL.B., Harvard, 1915; m. Katharine Gage, Apr. 5, 1920 (died 1930); children—Frederic P. (U.S.N.R. killed 1943), Carroll Brewster, Margaret Gage (Mrs. James D. Evans, Jr.); m. 2d, Priscilla Chilton Stevens, June 15, 1935. Admitted to Pa. bar, 1915; practiced in Phila.; sr. partner Montgomery, McCracken, Walker & Rhoads; mem. law faculty Temple U., 1923-30; state reporter Pa. Superior and Supreme cts., 1933-42; solicitor Sch. Dist. of Phila., 1941-61; dir. Chmn. blood donor program for S.E. Pa. chpt. A.R.C., 1952-53; trustee Abington Meml. Hosp., Freedoms Found. at Valley Forge. Served as 1st lt. Field Artillery of U.S. Army, 1917-19; lt. col., U.S.M.C., active duty, 1942-44; mem. 1st Troop, Phila. City Cavalry from 1917. Awarded four Battle Stars, World War I; Navy Commendation citation for meritorious service, World War II; Penn Charter Alumni Award of Merit, 1950. Fellow Am. Bar Found. (chmn. 1967-68; Fifty Yr. award), Am. Coll. Trial Lawyers; mem. Mil. Order Fgn. Wars, Jud. Conf. 3d Circuit U.S. (permanent), Am. Law Inst., Am. (past bd. govs., chmn. budget com., former state del. to Am. Bar Assn. ho. of dels.); Pa. (pres. 1964), Phila. (chancellor 1954-55) bar assns., Am. Judicature Soc. (past dir.), Mil. Order World Wars, Phi Delta Theta. Republican. Episcopalian (rectors warden, vestryman). Clubs: Phila., Huntingdon Valley Country, Union League (pres. 1952-53). Home: Huntingdon Valley, Pa. Died Feb. 1973.

RHOADS, JOSEPH EDGAR, mfr.; b. Plainfield, Ind., Sept. 11, 1883; s. Joseph and Harriet E. (Masters) R.; ed. Westtown (Pa.) Sch. and William Penn Charter Sch. (Phila.); student spl. courses U. Pa., 1904-05; m. Edith Chambers, Sept. 28, 1909; children—Joseph, Anna Paxson (Mrs. George A. Perera, M.D.), John Biddle, Ruth Chambers (Mrs. Thomas Cooch), Edith (Mrs. Edith Weiner), Marguerite. Chemist, J.E. Rhoads & Sons, Wilmington, Del., 1905-09, asst. supt., 1909-15, partner and supt., 1915-36, partner charge sales and advt., 1936-45, sr. partner, 1945-65, dir. J.E. Rhoads & Sons, Inc., 1965—; dir., mem. exec. com. Continental Am. Life Ins. Co. (Wilmington). Bd. mgrs. Wilmington Inst. Free Library; dir. Del. Mus. Natural History trustee, dir., mem. exec. com. Bryn Mawr (Pa.) Coll. Served abroad for Am. Friends Service Com., 1920. Mem. Am. Leather Chemists Assn. (hon.), Am. Soc. M.E. (life). Rotarian. Home: Wilmington DE *

RHODES, GEORGE IRVING, engineering executive; b. Andover, Mass., Nov. 27, 1883; s. Thomas Edward and Alice (Wrigley) R.; B.S., Mass. Inst. of Tech., 1905; m. Olive Wallace, 1911 (died Apr. 1942); children—Barbara (Mrs. Gordon B. Brown), Priscilla (Mrs. William A. Salmon). Electrical engineer Interboro Rapid Transit Co., New York, 1906-11; consulting engineer White, Weld & Co., Boston, 1912-16; engring. mgr. Ford, Bacon & Davis, Inc., New York, 1917-23, now vice-pres. and dir.; vice-pres. and dir. Ford, Bacon & Davis Construction Corp. Fellow Am. Inst. E.E.; mem. Am. Soc. M.E., Am. Soc. Civ. Engrs. Republican. Conglist. Mason. Club: Glen Ridge Country. Home: Glen Ridge, N.J. *

RIBAK, LOUIS LEON, artist; b. Rozany, USSR, Dec. 3, 1902; s. Samuel and Ida (Weller) R.; came to U.S., 1912, naturalized, 1934; student Pa. Acad. Fine Arts, 1921, Art Students League, 1922-23; m. Beatrice Mandelman, Oct. 1942. Exhibited in numerous one-man shows N.Y.C., Phila., Santa Fe, elsewhere U.S., abroad, including Rhodes, Greece, 1962, Mexico, 1973; retrospective shows, Santa Fe, 1968, 75; exhibited in group shows Whitney Mus., Santa Fe Mus., Houston Mus., El Paso (Tex.) Mus., Denver Mus. and others; represented in permanent collections Whitney Mus., El Paso Mus., Chgo. Art Inst., Bklyn. Mus., U. Ariz., others. Founder, tchr. dir. Taos (N.Mex.) Valley Art Sch., 1947-53. Served with AUS, 1942-43. Mem. Taos Art Assn. Home: Taos, N.M. Died Dec. 21, 1979; buried Taos.

RICE, FRANCIS EDGAR, business exec.; b. Council Bluffs, Ia., Feb. 19, 1886; s. F. S. and Minnie H. Rice; ed. Wooster Univ.; Washington Univ., 1910; m. Ida Z. Shafer, 1917; children—Scott, Robert, Philip, Elizabeth. Began as draftsman Pittsburgh (Pa.) Filtration Plant, 1906-07; rodman Okla. Valuation Survey, Frisco R.R., June to Sept. 1909; draftsman Frisco R.R., St. Louis, Mo., 1910-15; draftsman G.C.&S.F. R.R., Galveston, Texas. 1915-16; draftsman Texas Carnegie Steel Corp., Galveston, Apr. to June 1916; chief draftsman Okla. Structural Steel Co., Tulsa, Okla., 1916-17; cons. engr. Peterson & Co., Tulsa, Okla., 1917-18; with Philips Petroleum Co. since 1918, successively as chief engr. in charge of gasoline plant construction, gen. supt. of gasoline div., v.p. in charge gasoline mfr. and gas since 1930, dir. Pres. Ind. Natural Gas Co. Home: Bartlesville, Okla. *

RICE, GEORGE ARTHUR, educator; b. Malcolm, Ia., Feb. 25, 1882; s. George Eldon and Mary (Submit) R.; A.B., Harvard, 1904, Ed.D., 1924; m. Marguerite Emma Jordan, Oct. 17, 1906; children—Margaret (dec.), George Arthur, David Wingate, Nancy, Richard Brewer. Tutor to Viconte de Naives, 1905-06; teacher, Los Angeles Pub. Schs., 1909-17, Hollywood Jr. Coll., 1917-19; asst. Harvard Grad. Sch. of Edn., 1923-24; with U. of Calif. since 1924, as lecturer and asso. prof. to 1928, prof. of secondary edn. since 1928, dir. of practice teaching since 1928, prin. Univ. High Sch. 1928-44. Trustee Menlo School for Boys. Member N.E.A., Am. Assn. Coll. Teachers, Am. Acad. Political and Social Sci., Am. Geog. Soc., Gamma Sigma, Kappa Gamma Chi, Phi Kappa Tau. Republican. Mason. Clubs: Carquinez Golf, City Commons (Berkeley). Author: Principles of Secondary Education, 1927; Specimen Objective Examination (with G. M. Ruch), 1930; Administration of Public High Schools Through Their Personnel (with C. C. Conrad and P. F. Fleming), 1933. Contributor to ednl. jours. Home: Anaheim, Calif. *

RICE, LOUISE (LOUISE GUEST), graphologist; b. New Albany, Ind., Apr. 24, 1884; d. James Harvey and Harriet Noel (Davis) Guest; grad. high sch. and St. Mary's, St. Louis, Mo., 1898. Began as reporter with St. Louis Star, 1901; reporter various newspapers of southern states and NY. City, 1901-04; practicing graphologist since 1905; founder, 1925, since pres. Louise Rice Graphological Inst., N.Y. City; also consulting psychologist. Director Foundation for Counselors of Human Relations, 1938; now president Personal Problems Institute; director National Vocational Bureau. Member Internat. Identification Assn., Am. Graphological Soc. (pres. emeritus), Am. Fiction Guild (dir.); asso. mem. French Graphological Soc. Author: Character Shown in Handwriting, 1908, 25; Girl Who Walked Without Fear, 1923; New Blood, 1926; By Whose Hand, 1930; Who Is Your Mate, 1931; also all textbooks used in Louise Rice Graphological Inst. Contbr. to leading mags. *

RICE, OSCAR KNEFLER, phys. chemist, educator; b. Chgo., Feb. 12, 1903; s. Oscar Guido and Thekla (Knefler) R.; student San Diego Jr. Coll., 1920-22; B.S., U. Calif., 1924, Ph.D., 1926; NRC fellow Calif. Inst. Tech., 1927-29, U. Leipzig, 1929-30; D.Sc. (hon.), U. N.C., 1978; m. Hope Ernestyne Sherfy, Dec. 23, 1947; children—Margarita S., Pamela S. Asso. in chemistry U. Calif., 1926-27, research asso. chem., 1935-36; instr. chemistry Harvard, 1930-35; asso. prof. chem. U. N.C., 1936-43, prof. chemistry, 1943-59, Kenan prof. chemistry, 1959-75, emeritus, 1975-78; Stewart lectr. U. Mo., 1948; Reilly lectr. U. Notre Dame, 1957; Barton lectr. U. Okla., 1967; Disting. lectr. Howard U., 1971; Robt. A. Welch Found. lectr., 1971; prin. chemist, Clinton Labs., Oak Ridge, 1946-47; vis. prof. Va. Poly. Inst., summer, 1968; Seydel-Woolley vis. prof. Ga. Inst. Tech., spring 1969. Adv. panel chemistry NSF, 1958-61; mem. gov.'s adv. group N.C. Sch. Sci. and Math., 1978. Mem. Solvay Congress, Brussels, 1962. Recipient Am. Chem. Soc. award in pure chemistry, 1932, So. Chemist Award, 1961, award Fla. Sect., 1967; N.C. award in Sci., 1966, Peter Debye award in phys. chemistry, 1970, Charles H. Stone award Carolina-Piedmont sect. Am. Chem. Soc., 1973; O.K. Rice Lectureship established at U. N.C. in his honor. Mem. Reunion Internationale de Chimie Physique, Paris, 1928. Fellow Am. Phys. Soc., A.A.A.S.; mem. Chem. Soc. London (Faraday div.), Am. Chem. Soc. (sec. 1942, chmn. 1944, div. phys. and inorganic chem., chmn. N.C. sect. 1946), Fedn. Am. Scientists (bd. sponsors), Nat. Acad. Scis., N.C. Acad. Sci., A.A.U.P., A.C.L.U., Sigma Xi. Author: Electronic Structure and Chemical Binding, 1940; Statistical Mechanics, Thermodynamics and Kinetics, 1967. Asso. editor Jour. Chem. Physics, 1934-36, 1945-47; mem. adv. bd. Philosophy of Sci. Jour., 1934-54. Contbr. articles to sci. periodicals. Home: Chapel Hill, N.C. Died May 7, 1978; buried Chapel Hill Cemetery.

RICH, DANIEL CATTON, mus. dir.; b. South Bend, Ind., Apr. 16, 1904; s. Daniel and Martha (Catton) R.; Ph.B., U. Chgo., 1926; postgrad. Harvard, 1926-27; m. Bertha Ten Eyck James, Sept. 23, 1927; children—Michael James, Stephen Ten Eyck, Penelope, Anthony Catton. With Art Inst. of Chgo., 1927-58, editor Bull., 1927-29, asst. curator painting and sculpture, 1929-31, asso. curator, 1931-38, curator, 1938-58, dir. fine arts, 1938-45, dir., 1945-58, trustee, 1955-58; dir. Worcester (Mass.) Art Mus., 1958-70, dir. emeritus, 1970-76; vis. Lectr. Harvard, 1960-61; pres. Poetry Mag., 1952; co-founder Film-Art, Inc., Chgo.; chmn. Ill. com. sect. painting and sculpture Procurement div. Treasury Dept.; mem. patrons com. Fed. Art Project of Ill.; mem. com. on art project Ill. Emergency Relief Commn.; mem. jury to select murals for Dept. Interior Building; mem. Am. nat. com. of Comité International d'Histoire de l'Art, Ill. chmn. com. selection for Exhbn. Comtemporary Am. Art, N.Y. World's Fair, 1939; chmn. jury of awards for contemporary painting exhbn. Golden Gate Internat. Expn.; mem. com. selection Am. Painting Exhbn. at Tate Gallery; mem. adv. com. on art Dept. State, Washington; mem. Am. Com. for Restoration Italian Monuments, Am. Com. for Protection and Salvage Artistic and Historic Monuments. Vice chmn. Bd. Higher Edn. Mass.; mem. citizens' bd. U. Chgo., U.S. Commr. to Venice Biennale, 1956; trustee Solomon R. Guggenheim Mus., N.Y.C. Mayors All-Chgo. Citizens Com., 1956-57; mem. adv. com. Am. Inst. France; vice chmn. Nat. Council for Nat. Art Week, 1941; chmn. jury of awards Artists for Victory, Met. Mus., N.Y. Trustee Am. Acad. in Rome; bd. overseers Brandeis U. Decorated officer Légion d'Honneur; officer Order of Orange Nassau; Cavalierie, Order Merit, Italy; Distinguished Visitor award Fulbright Program. State Dept. Mem. Council Am. Assn. Museums. Mem. com. on research in Latin Am. Art; mem. adv. com. Ency. Brit., sent by com. on Inter-Am. Artistic and Intellectual Relations for 4 months study Latin Am. art, 1943; mem. Midwest Museums Conf., Assn. Art Mus. Dirs.; mem. Art Com., A.C.S. Fellow Am. Acad. Arts and Scis.; mem. La Societé des Rosettes et Rubans de France, Internat. Council Museums (Paris), Am. Soc. Aesthetics, Am. Inst. Interior Designers, A.I.A., Am. Antiquarian Soc., Phi Beta Kappa. Democrat. Clubs: Cliff Dwellers (hon.), Art Directors (hon. life). Author: Seurat and the Evolution of La Grande Jatte, 1935; Henri Rousseau, 1942; Georgia O'Keeffe, 1915-41, 1943; Degas, 1952. Editor and compiler: Catalogue of the Charles H. and Mary F. S. Worcester Collection, 1938; contbr. to On Understanding Art Museums, 1975. Contbr. articles to art jours. Home: New York, N.Y. Died Oct. 15, 1976.

RICH, GEORGE R., engr.; b. Worcester, Mass., Nov. 3, 1896; s. Jerome Turner and Josephine (Breen) R.; B.S., Worcester Poly. Inst., 1919, C.E., 1956. Dr. Engring. (hon.), 1948; m. Embi Susannah Johnson, Sept. 8, 1925 (dec. 1959); m. 2d, Alice G. Mahan, Apr. 22, 1961. Structural designer Stone and Webster, Inc., Boston, 1919-22, McClellan and Junkersfield, N.Y., 1922-25; structural and hydraulic designer Stone and Webster Inc., 1925-28; structural engr., Jackson and Moreland, Boston, 1928-29; hydraulic engr. Stone and Webster, 1929-31; hydraulic engr., U.S. War Dept., 1931-37; chief design engr. Tenn. Valley Authority, Knoxville, Tenn., 1937-46; hydraulic engr. and dir. Chas. T. Main, Inc., 1946-77, also v.p.; partner Uhl, Hall & Rich, 1954-77; lectr. hydraulic structures Grad. Sch., Columbia; Gordon McKay vis. lectr. Harvard, from 1956. Mem. ASCE (hon.), ASME (hon.), Am. Cons. Engrs. Council, Am. Math. Soc., Seismol. Soc. Am., Newcomen Soc. England, Sigma Xi, Tau Beta Pi, Theta Chi, Chi Epsilon. Clubs: Engineers' (N.Y.); Engineers', University (Boston). Author: Hydraulic Transients, 1951. Contbr. Davis Handbook of Applied Hydraulics, 1952, also profl. jours. Home: Wellesley Hills, Mass. Died June 21, 1977.

RICH, LORIMER, architect; b. Camden, N.Y., Oct. 24, 1891; s. George W. and Sarah (Stark) R.; B.Arch., Syracuse U., D.F.A. (hon.), 1940; studied Am. Acad. in Rome, 1921, 22; m. Martha Ross Leigh, Oct. 21, 1923; 1 dau., Martha Elizabeth Gregg. In office of Charles A. Platt, N.Y.C., 1919-21, McKim, Mead & White, 1922-28; practiced alone, 1929-45; Lorimer Rich and Assos., 1945—; critic in design, Sch. of Architecture, Columbia. Critic in archtl. and city planning Pratt Inst. Architect: St. Luke's Ch., Bklyn.; Tomb of Unknown Soldier, Arlington (Va.) Nat. Cemetery (winner in nationwide competition); also approaches to Tomb and Amphitheatre; improvement of Herald Square, N.Y. City (winner of competition); Hdqrs. and Adminstrn. Bldgs., Fort Jay, Governors Island, N.Y.; Fed. Penitentiary and Narcotic Farm, Ft. Worth; 7 postal stas. in N.Y.C. and Bklyn.; Post Office and Customs House, St. Albans, Vt.; Fed. Bldgs., Gt. Barrington, Mass., and Watsonville, Cal.; U.S. post offices Johnstown, Pa., Salina, Kan.; Madison Sq. Postal Sta., N.Y. City; cons. architect U.S. Treas. Dept., Kenilworth Bapt. Ch., Lincoln U., Friends Sch., Cumberland Hosp., Bklyn., Meth. Ch. Camden, N.Y., office Suffolk County-Water Authority; new Bklyn. Civic Center and rehab. studies of downtown Bklyn.; cons. architect to N.Y.C. Planning Commn., L.I. Coll. Medicine, ARC Bldg., State Tchrs. Coll., Oswego, N.Y., N.Y. State Emergency Housing, Marine Park, Bklyn.; architect for Syracuse U. and L.I. Nat. Cemetery, Allegheny Coll., Home Office Bldg. N.Y. State Ins. Fund, Oswego State Coll. Library, Setaukey and Islip pub. schs., Fed. Ct. House and Office Bldgs., Eastern Dist. N.Y., Rome Hist. Mus., Restoration of Oneida County Court House, Rome, Bicentennial Monument to unknown soldiers of Am. Revolution, Rome, also several coll. dormitories and other bldgs. Mem. Bd. of Architect Examiners, N.Y. State. Fellow A.I.A. (chmn. competition com.); mem. Archtl. League N.Y., Municipal Art Soc., N.A.D. (asso.), Nat. Sculpture Soc. (hon.). Mem. Soc. Friends. Clubs: University (N.Y.C.); Cosmos (Washington); Rome (N.Y.). Contbr. articles to profl. jours. Hon. pres. Rich family of U.S. Address: Camden, N.Y. Died June 2, 1978; buried Arlington Nat. Cemetery.

RICHARD, DONAT RADOLPHE, pharm. co. exec.; b. St. David, Que., Can., Oct. 17, 1910; B.S., U. Montreal, 1931; M.SD., C.M., McGill U., 1937; postgrad. N.Y. Post Grad. Hosp., 1946-47; m. Mary Martin Wade; children—Ronald Robert, Dennis Raymond, Carol Ann. Extern St. Luke Hosp., Montreal, 1935-37; intern Kings County Hosp., Bklyn., 1937-39, resident, 1939-41, 46-47; practice medicine, specializing in obstetrics and gynecology, infertility, Glendale, Calif., 1947—; mem. staff Meml. Hosp. Glendale, Glendale Adventist Hosp., Verdugo Hills Hosp., Glendale, St. Joseph Hosp., Burbank, Los Angeles County Hosp., Los Angeles; asso. clin. prof. obstetrics and gynecology U. So. Calif., Los Angeles, 1947—, Loma Linda U.; founder, dir. Glendale Enterprises, Inc. (Calif.), 1958, chmn. bd., 1960; founder, dir. Houston Properties, Inc., Glendale, 1961-79; sec.-treas.; founder, dir., sec.-treas. Internat. Chem. & Nuclear Corp., Pasadena, Calif., 1961-79. Chmn. campaign United Way, Glendale, 1963; active explorer scouts Boy Scouts Am.; mem. Los Angeles World Affairs Council; active fund raising. Bd. dirs. Community Chest, 1962-65, Glendale. Served to capt. M.C., AUS, 1941-46. Diplomate Am. Bd. Obstetrics and Gynecology. Fellow A.C.S., Am. Coll. Obstetrics and Gynecology; mem. A.M.A., Cal, Los Angeles County med. assns., Am., Pacific Coast, Internat. fertility socs., Los Angeles Obstet. and Gynecol. Soc., McGill Graduates Soc. (past pres.), Princeton, Wesleyan U. parents assns. Episcopalian. Clubs: Toastmasters, Oakmont Country, Verdugo (Glendale); Canadian Los Angeles. Office: Glendale, Calif. Died Oct. 17, 1979; buried Forest Lawn, Glendale.

RICHARDS, AUTE, prof. zoölogy; b. Tekamah, Neb., Oct. 31, 1885; s. John Fletcher and Silvia Jane (McNabb) R.; B.A., U. of Kan., 1908; M.A., U. of Wis., 1909; Ph.D., Princeton U., 1911; hon. D.Sc., Marietta Coll., 1939; m. Mildred Hoge, Dec. 19, 1917; children—James Hoge, Ernest John. Teacher rural schs., Marion County, Kan., 1903-04, Sumner County High Sch., Wellington, Kan., 1907-08; grad. asst., U. of Wis., 1908-09; instr. and adj. prof. zoölogy, University of Texas, 1911-16; prof. zoölogy, Wabash Coll., 1916-20; prof. zoölogy, U. of Okla., 1920-50, dir. of Okla. Biol. Survey, 1927-49, formerly head of dept. (1920-42); dir. Sch. of Applied Biology. and Okla. Mus. Zoölogy; teacher summer schs. U. of Wash., Western State Coll., Rocky Mountain Biol. Lab. (mem. bd. trustees; ex-pres.). Fellow Am. Assn. Advancement of Science; mem. Am. Soc. Zoölogists, Am. Soc. Naturalists, Okla. Acad. (sec. 1923-27; pres. 1929-30), Am. Assn. Univ. Profs. (nat. council, 1933-36), Sigma Xi, Phi Sigma, Alpha Epsilon Delta; hon. mem. Beta Beta Beta (regional v.p.). Republican. Episcopalian. Author: Laboratory Guide in General Zoölogy, 1925; Outline of Comparative Embryology, 1931; Practical

Comparative Embryology (with A. I. Ortenburger), 1935. Contbr. to Ency. Britannica and sci. publs. Home: Tucson. *

RICHARDS, GEORGE HUNTINGTON, lawyer; b. Bath. Me., Aug. 1, 1882; s. William R. and Charlotte B. (Blodget) R.; A.B., Yale, 1903; LL.B., N.Y. Law Sch., 1907; m. Marianna M. Middlebrook, May 25, 1910; children—Marianna (Mrs. Max Bovarnick), Sarah H. (Mrs. Gifford B. Pinchot), Frederic M. Tchr., Phillips Andover Acad., 1903-05; admitted to N.Y. bar, 1907; asso. Miller, King, Lane & Trafford, 1907-11; partner Reynolds, Richards & McCutcheon, 1911-49; partner Reynolds, Richards, Ely & LaVenture, 1949—, now sr. partner. Dir. Overseas Securities Corp. Mem. exec. com. Civil Service Reform Assn., 1945—. Mem. Woods Hole Oceanographic Inst., Yale Assn. of Class Secs. (pres. 1920), Am. Bar Assn., Bar Assn. City N.Y. Club: Cruising of Am. Home: N.Y.C. *

RICHARDS, GERTRUDE RANDOLPH BRAMLETTE, author; b. Loudoun County, Va., June 11, 1886; d. John Randolph Harrison (col. C.S.A.) and Olivia (Todd) Richards; M.A., Wellesley, 1911; Ph.D., Cornell U., 1915; studied Harvard, Yale and Oxford U. Teacher pvt. schs., 1915-21; pvt. hist. research abroad, 1921-27; asso. in research, Harvard, 1927-32. Lecturer in history, Wellesley (Mass.) Coll., 1933-34. Historical assistant to Dr. D. S. Freeman, 1944—. Mem. Am. Hist. Soc. Mediaeval Acad. America, Am. Assn. Univ. Profs. Episcopalian. Clubs: Wellesley, Radcliffe, Authors' (Boston). Author: The Forerunners of St. Francis of Assisi (with Ellen Scott Davison), 1927; Florentine Merchants under the Medici, 1932; Bargaining in Benefices, 1934. In preparation: Confederate Women. Contbr. to various periodicals. Address: Richmond, Va.*

RICHARDS IVOR ARMSTRONG, educator; b. Cheshire, Eng., Feb. 26, 1893; s. William Armstrong and Mary Ann (Haig) R.; B.A., Cambridge U., 1914, M.A., 1918, Litt.D., 1932; Litt.D., Harvard, m. Dorothea Eleanor Pilley, Dec. 31, 1926. Lectr. lit. criticism, Harvard, 1939-44, prof. English, 1944-63, prof. emeritus, 1963-79. Recipient Loines Award for poetry Nat. Inst. Arts and Letters, 1962, Emerson-Thoreau medal Am. Acad. Arts and Scis., 1970. Author numerous monographs latest being: Speculative Instruments, 1955; Goodbye Earth and Other Poems, 1958; The Screens and Other Poems, 1960; (play) Tomorrow Morning, Faustus. 1962; (play) Why So, Socrates?, 1964; Plato's Republic, 1965; So Much Nearer, 1968; Design for Escape, 1968; Poetries and Sciences, 1970; (poems) Internal Colloquies, 1971; Poetries; Their Media and Ends, 1974; Beyond, 1974. Home: Cambridge, England. Died Sept. 7, 1979.

RICHARDS, JAMES PRIOLEAU, ambassador; b. Liberty Hill, S.C., Aug. 31, 1894; s. Norman Smith and Phoebe (Gibbes) R.; student U. of S.C., 1913-15, LL.B., 1921; m. Katharine H. Wylie, Nov. 4, 1925; children—Richard Evans, Norman Smith, Jane. Began law practice at Lancaster, S.C., 1921; Judge Probate Ct., Lancaster County, 1923-33. Enlisted as pvt. inf., U.S. Army, Apr. 20, 1917, advancing to 2d lt., World War. Mem. 73d to 84th Congresses, 5th S.C. Dist. Chmn. Fgn. Affairs Com., 1951-53; ambassador Am. Mission to the Middle East, from 1957. U.S. del. to UN, 1953; del. to Japanese Peace Conf. Mem. Am. Legion, Jr. O.U.A.M. Democrat. Presbyn. Mason. Home: Heath Springs, S.C. Died Feb. 21, 1979; buried Liberty Hill, SC

RICHARDS, LEGRAND, bishop; b. Farmington, Utah, Feb. 6, 1886; s. George Franklin and Alice Almira (Robinson) R.; student Salt Lake Bus. Coll., 1901-03; m. Ina Jane Ashton, May 19, 1909; children—Ina Mercedes (Mrs. J. Grant Iverson), Effie Norinne (Mrs. Reed E. Callister), Marian Louise (Mrs. Harold R. Boyer), Jane (dec.), LeGrand Ashton (dec.), George LaMont, Nona (Mrs. J. Glenn Dyer), Alden Ross. Asst. sec.-treas. Portland Cement Co. (Ore.), 1909-11; sec. George Romney Lumber Co., Salt Lake City, 1911-16; engaged in real estate bus., 1916-30; in real estate bus., Glendale, Cal., 1930-34, Salt Lake City, 1937-38. On mission Ch. of Jesus Christ of Latter-day Saints to Netherlands, 1905-08; pres. Netherlands Mission, 1913-16, on spl. mission in Eastern States, 1926; pres. Hollywood (Calif.) Stake, 1931-34; pres. So. States Mission, 1934-47; bishop in Salt Lake City, 1919-25, Glendale Calif., 1930-31, Salt Lake City, 1937-38; presiding bishop, ch. of Jesus Christ of Latter-day Saints, Salt Lake City, 1938-52, apptd. mem. Quorum of Twelve Apostles 1952. Dir. Hotel Utah, Beneficial Life Ins. Co. Pres., dir. Salt Lake Real Estate Bd., 1925, Utah State Assn., 1929; v.p., dir. Glendale Real Estate Bd., 1931. Dir. Z.C.M.I., Salt Lake City. Trustee Brigham Young U. Author: A Marvelous Work and a Wonder, 1950; Israel! Do You Know; Just to Illustrate. Home: Salt Lake City UT. *

RICHARDS, RALPH, savs. and loan assn. exec., lawyer; b. St. Paul, June 26, 1893; s. Frank Albert and Jennie Frances (Redner) R.; B.A., U. Minn., 1915; m. Harriet Maxwell Hopper, Sept. 9, 1918; 1 dau., Frances Harrison (Mrs. Thomas M. Breeden). Admitted to Fla. bar, 1927, since practiced in Clearwater; sr. partner firm Richards, Nodine, Gilkey, Fite, Meyer & Thompson; municipal judge, Clearwater, 1928-32, city atty., 1938-46; chmn. bd. Clearwater Fed. Savs. & Loan Assn., 1955-80; dir. Barnett Bank, Clearwater. Chmn. bd. Pinellas County Community Found. Trustee Bethune-Cookman Coll., Theodore Luce Found.; bd. dirs. Morton F. Plant Hosp. Served to capt. U.S. Army, 1917-21. Recipient David Bilgore award for work in race relations, 1954. Mem. Fla. (v.p. 1938), Clearwater (pres. 1938) bar assns., Kappa Sigma, Scabbard and Blade. Democrat. Presbyn. (elder), Mason, Rotarian. Clubs: Clearwater Country; Carlouel Yacht. Author: What To Do About Your Money, 1962; All About Wills, 1965; You Can't Take it With You, 1970. Home: Clearwater, Fla. Died May 23, 1980; buried Clearwater.

RICHARDSON, CYRIL CHARLES, clergyman, ch. historian, author; b. London, Eng., June 13, 1909; s. Charles Willerton and Kate Harriet (Bunker) R.; came to U.S., 1931, naturalized, 1940; B.A. with great distinction, U. Sask., 1930; Licentiate in Theol., with highest honors including Hebrew, Emmanuel Coll., Saskatoon, Sask., 1931, D.D. (hon.), 1949; S.T.M., summa cum laude, Union Theol. Sem., N.Y, 1932, Th.D., 1934; postgrad. U. Gottingen (Germany), 1933, U. Dijon (France), 1935, U. Basel (Switzerland), 1936; D.D. (hon.), Gen. Theol. Sem., N.Y., 1972; m. Louise Burbank Shattuck, Feb. 13, 1945. Ordained to ministry P.E. Ch. as deacon, 1934, priest, 1934; instr. ch. history Union Theol. Sem., 1934-35, asst. prof., 1935-39, asso. prof., 1939-49, Washburn prof. ch. history, 1949-74. Washburn prof. emeritus, 1974-76, Union scholar, 1974-76, acting librarian, 1950-51, acting dir. studies, 1952-53, dir. grad. studies, 1954-63, dean grad. studies, 1963-74; Mere preacher U. Cambridge, 1961; hon. canon St. John's Cathedral, N.YC, 1974-76; ororganizing mem. Nat. Council Grad. Study in Religion, 1963-74; adj. prof. religion Columbia U., 1963-76; mem. Commn. for Studying Spiritual Healing, Fed. Council of Chs. of Christ in Am., 1949-57; mem. N.Y. Patristics Seminar, 1968-76, Phila. Seminar in Christian Origins, 1972-76; numerous lectures including Haverford Coll., Garrett Bibl. Inst., Wycliff Coll., Seaburg-Western Sem., N.Y. U., Andover Newton Theol. Sem Gen. Theol. Sem., N.YCC., Trinity Coll., Toronto, Conn. Clergy Conf. on Sacrifice and Worship, Gettysburg Theol Sem., Theol. Soc., Cambridge U., Jewish Theol. Sem.-Inst. for Religious and Social Studies, Fordham U., Ecumenical Dialogue at Harvard (Roman Cath.-Protestant Colloquim). Mem. N.Y.C. Mayor's Com. for Police Protection and Def., 1942-43. Recipient competition award Christian Research Found., 1957; Cyril C. Richardson Meml. Lectureship established in his memory Union Theol. Sem., 1977. Mem. Am. Soc. Ch. History, Duodecim (founder, sec. 1937-43), N Am. Patristics Soc., N.Y. Soc. for Psychic Research, Am. Theol. Soc., Sigma Chi. Clubs: Episcopal, Columbia Faculty. Author: (monographs) The Christianity of Ignatius of Antioch, 1935, 67; The Church through the Centuries, 1938; The Sacrament of Reunion, 1940; The Eucharist in Zwingli and Cranmer, 1949; The Doctrine of the Trinity, 1958. Mem. editorial bd. Anglican Theol. Rev., Rev. of Religion (Columbia U.); editor: The Pocket Bible, 1951, Early Christian Fathers, 1953, 70; Collaborator: The Church and Mental Health, 1953; The Christology of the Later Fathers, 1954; A Companion to the Study of St. Augustine, 1955; Religious Symbolism, 1955; Healing: Human and Divine, 1957; Religious Experience and Truth, 1960; Living Thankfully, 1961; Christianity on the March, 1963; Ecumenical Dialogue at Harvard, 1964; Heritage of The Early Church, 1973. Contbr over 100 book revs. and articles on early ch. history, patristic theology, liturgy, history Christian worship, spirituality, and ch. unity to religious and theol. periodicals; composer (hymn) God of the Prairies, 1938. Home: New York, N.Y. Died Nov. 16, 1976; interred St. Thomas Episcopal Parish Ch., New York, N.Y.

RICHARDSON, GEORGE JAMES, def. cons.; b. Winchester, Mass., Nov. 25, 1893; s. John and Sarah (McLean) R.; ed. high sch.; m. Gertrude M. Gant, Oct. 22, 1914 (dec. 1977); children—Helen M. (Mrs. John Thompson), Howard A., Richard G. Sec.-treas. Internat. Assn. Fire Fighters, 1920-56; frat. del. AFL to Brit. Trade Union Congress, 1947; spl. representative AFL-CIO, Office of the President, 1956-63; cons. U.S. Dept. Def., 1963-72; ret., 1972. Worker adviser ILO, Geneva, Switzerland, 1952, 56, 57; head labor delegation mission to S.A., 1958; employee mem. industry com. to Am. Samoa for establishment for minimum wages. Mem. Civil Def. Adv. Council, 1951-63. Mason. Clubs: Optimist, Congressional Country. Home: Silver Springs, Md. Died Jan. 5, 1980.

RICHARDSON, JAMES MILTON, bishop; b. Sylvester, Ga., Jan. 8, 1913; s. James Milton and Pallie (Stewart) R.; A.B., U. Ga., 1934; B.D., Emory U., 1936, M.A., 1942; postgrad. Va. Theol. Sem., 1938, D.D., 1965; LL.D., John Marshall Law Sch., 1948; D.D., Episcopal Theol. Sem. Ky., 1960, U. South, 1961, Episcopal Theol. Sem. Southwest, 1976; m. Eugenia Preston Brooks, June 14, 1940; children—James Milton, Eugenia Brooks (Mrs. James W. Nash), Joan Stewart (Mrs. James R. Doty), Preston Brooks. Ordained to ministry P.E. Ch., 1938; rector St. Timothy's Ch., Atlanta, 1938-40; asst. rector, then rector St. Luke's Ch., Atlanta, 1940-52; dean Christ Ch. Cathedral, Houston, 1952-65; bishop Episcopal Diocese Tex., 1965-80, Chmn. bd. trustees St. Stephen's Episcopal Sch., 1965-80, Episcopal Theol. Sem. S.W., St. Luke's Episcopal Hosp.; trustee Ch. Pension Fund, Ch. Life Ins. Corp., Ch. Ins. Co., Ch. Hymnal Corp., Episcopal Radio-TV Found., U. of South, Baylor Coll. Medicine. Mem. Blue Key, Phi Beta Kappa, Phi Kappa Phi, Omicron Delta Kappa, Alpha Tau Omega (worthy grand chaplain 1945-52, 56-80, nat. pres. 1952-56). Home: Houston, Tex. Died Mar. 24, 1980; buried Milledgeville, Ga.

RICHARDSON, JOHN, lawyer; b. Chestnut Hill, Mass., Sept. 30, 1886; s. John and Louisa Storrow (Cabot) R.; student Noble and Greenough Sch., Boston; A.B., Harvard, 1908, LL.B., 1911; m. Hope Hemenway, Sept. 7, 1909; children—Hope, Louisa (Dreier), Hetty (Phillips), Faith (Barnett), John. practiced in Boston, 1911—; mem. firm Ropes and Gray. Dir., Gilchrist Co., Boston Filter Co. Pres. Boston Better Bus. Bur., 1926-68, now bd. dirs.; moderator, Canton, Mass., alternate years, 1919-60. Mem. Republican Nat. Com., 1932-36. Trustee Meadville Theol. Sch., Chgo., 1964-66; trustee Noble and Greenough Sch., 1913-64, pres. bd. trustees, 1921-64. Served from pvt. capt., inf., U.S. Army, 1917-19. Mem. Harvard Law Sch. Assn. (pres. 1967-69). Unitarian (treas. 1963-69). Club: Harvard (Boston, N.Y.C.). Home: Milton MA. *

RICHARDSON, JOSEPH PRIESTLEY, architect; b. Needham, Mass., Apr. 9, 1913; s. Frederick L.W. and Anne (Blake) R.; A.B. cum laude, Harvard, 1935, B. Arch., 1938; m. Margaret Stevenson, Oct. 5, 1940; children—Joseph Priestley (dec.) Philip Stevenson, Anne Blake, Alison Greenough, Emilie Randolph, Margery. Asst. resident engr. Mass. Gen. Hosp., Boston, 1938-39; pvt. practice architecture, 1939-40; partner Jackson & Richardson, Boston, 1940-41; engaged in contracting business, 1941-42; architect Coolidge Shepley Bulfinch & Abbott, Boston, 1945-50, partner, 1950-52; partner Shepley Bulfinch Richardson & Abbott, Boston, 1952-79; principle works include Wellesley Coll. dormitories (Bates, Freeman, McAfee), Quincy House at Harvard (Parker medal 1960), Div. Employment Security Bldg., Govt. Center, Mass., Ski terminal, Squaw Valley, Calif. (Honor award A.I.A. 1970). Hon mem. Boston Archtl. Center; mem. bldg. commn., Brookline, Mass.; Mem. design-visual arts vis. com. Harvard Grad. Sch. Design, 1964-70. Served to comdr. USNR, 1942-45. Fellow A.I.A.; mem. Boston Soc. Architects (pres. 1968), Mass. Assn. Architects, Harvard Grad. Sch. Design Assn., Inst. Contemporary Art. Clubs: Harvard, Somerset (Boston) Country (Brookline); Century Assn. (N.Y.C.). Home: Chestnut Hill, Mass. Died Sept. 14, 1979.

RICHARDSON, LYON NORMAN, educator; b. Andover, Ohio, July 20, 1898; s. Norman Goff and Ella (Lyon) R.; B.A., Western Res. U., 1921, M.A., 1925; Ph.D., Columbia, 1931; m. Helen Hartman, Aug. 11, 1923; 1 dau., Cora Ella (Mrs. John C. Scott, Jr.). Editor Kinsman (Ohio) Jour., 1917-22; prin. Andover (Ohio) High Sch., 1923; adv. editor The New Students' Reference Work, 1924-28; with Western Res. U., 1923, as instr. English, Adelbert Coll., 1923-25, 27-35, Sch. of Edn., 1928-33, Clev. Coll., 1927-29, asst. dean Adelbert Coll., 1929-35, asst. prof., 1935-43, asso. prof. Adelbert Coll. and Grad. Sch., 1943-46. prof., 1946-69, prof. emeritus English and Am. studies, 1969-80; chmn. grad. program Am. studies, 1947-69; dir. U. Libraries, 1946-67; vis. prof. English, Kent State Coll., 1931, Ohio U., 1938, Duquesne U., 1969-71. Served in S.A.T.C., Western Res. U., World War. Hon. fellow Cleve. Med. Library Assn.; mem. Modern Lang. Assn. (chmn. Am. lit. sect. 1965), Am. Studies Assn. (mem. nat. exec. council 1959-61), Phi Beta Kappa, Pi Kappa Alpha. Mason. Clubs: Professional, Faculty, Rowfant. Author: History of Early American Magazines (1741-89), 1931, reprinted 1966. Adv. editor: How and Why Library, 1934. Editor: The American Magazine (1741), 1937; The General Magazine (1741), 1938; Henry James, 1941, reprinted 1966; The Heritage of American Literature, 2 vols. (with G.H. Orians and H. R. Brown), 1951. Contbr. numerous reviews and articles. Home: Laguna Hills, Calif. Died Aug. 16, 1980.

RICHARDSON, W(ILLIAM) GARLAND, fgn. service officer; b. Fries, Va., Jan. 18, 1905; s. William Luke and Bertha Westmore (Muir) R.; A.B., U. Richmond, 1924; M.A., U. Va., 1934; grad. study U. Frankfort-am-Main, 1934, U. Marburg-an-der-Lahn, 1935. Yale, 1944-45; m. Edith W. Bowe, June 2, 1930 (div. 1948); children—William, Joseph White; married 2d Elizabeth Power, November 12, 1949; children—Thomas Elkins, Elizabeth Hanna. Auditor for insurance company, 1925-28; traveller coll. textbook co., 1928-30; auditor pub. utility co., Brazil, 1930-32; v. consul, sec. Diplomatic Service, 1935; lang. officer, Tokyo, Japan, 1935-37, v. consul, 1937-40, Dairen, Manchuria, 1940-41; interned by Japanese, Dec. 1941-July 42; consul, São Paulo, Brazil, 1942-44, Manila, P.I., 1945-47, 2d sec. 1946-47; consul, St. John's Newfoundland, 1948-49; consul, 1st sec., charge d'affairs, Monrovia, 1950-52; 1st sec., consul, Tokyo

1952-55; exec. sec. bd. examiners, fgn. service, 1955-57; consul Am. Consulate Gen., Munich, Germany, 1957-60; consul gen., Naha, Okinawa, 1960-62, Paramaribo, Surinam, 1962-65. Recipient Meritorious Service Award, Dept. of State, 1954. Sterling fellow Yale, 1935. Mem Asiatic Soc. Japan. Episcopalian. Mason. (32 deg.). Home: Geneva, N.Y. Died May 19, 1980.

RICHARDSON, WILLIAM ALAN, editor, pub., fin. exec.; b. Johannesburg, S. Africa, Oct. 9, 1907 (parents Am. citizens); s. Elliott Verne and Adelaide (Palmer) R.; student Harvard, 1927-30; m. Doris Ira Railing, Dec. 30, 1965; children by previous marriage—Nancy, Craig. Partner Richardson & Putnam, investment counsel, N.Y.C., 1932-33; editor Med. Econs., 1933-57; lectr. med. econs. L.I.U. Coll. Medicine, 1947-48, Yale U. Med. Sch., 1955; v.p. Soc. Bus. Mag. Editors, 1958; speaker, author, 1940-80; editor-in-chief Med. Econs., Hosp. Physician, also RN, 1957-69; v.p. Med. Econs. Book Div., Inc., 1960-69; dir. Heritage Fund, Inc., 1968-69; pres., chmn. bd. Med. Econs., Inc., 1959-68; cons. Med. Econs., Inc., 1969-73; chmn. bd. Richardson & Roebuck, Inc., asset mgmt., Greenwich, Conn., 1970-71; pres. Richardson & Co., Vero Beach, Fla., 1971-80. Asso. mem. Conn. Med. Soc., Soc. Profl. Bus. Cons. Clubs: N.Y. Yacht (N.Y.C.); Watch Hill (R.I.) Yacht; Ida Lewis Yacht (Newport, R.I.). Author: A Study of Britain's National Health Service, 1949. Editor: Personal Money Management for Physicians, 1969. Home: Vero Beach, Fla. Died Sept. 17, 1980; cremated.

RICHEY, ROBERT WILLIAM, educator; b. Russellville, Ohio, Aug. 14, 1912; s. Robert H. and Mabel (May) R.; B.S., B.S. in Edn., Wilmington (Ohio) Coll., 1933; M.A., Ohio State U., 1937, Ph.D., 1941; m. Beatrice E. Huffman, Dec. 26, 1942; 1 son, Robert. Elementary tchr., prin. New Antioch Elementary Sch., Wilmington, 1933-35; head sci. dept., critic tchr. in Wilmington City Schs., 1935-37; placement and research asst. Ohio State U., 1937-41; asst. prof. edn. U. Tenn., 1941-42; asst. prof. edn. Ind. U., Bloomington, 1946-49, asso. prof. edn., dir. elementary sch. student teaching, 1949-53, prof. edn., from 1953, campus coordinator Thailand Project, 1955-56, chief of party contract team Coll. Edn. and Chulalongkorn U., Bangkok, Thailand, 1956-59, dir. summer sessions, from 1959, dean div. continuing edn., 1970-75, dean Sch. Continuing Studies, 1975-78. Served to capt. USAAF, 1942-46; ETO. Recipient Distinguished Alumni award Wilmington Coll., 1966. Mem. Assn. Univ. Summer Sessions (pres., Distinguished Leadership and Service award 1977), AAAS, NEA, Nat. Sci. Tchrs. Assn., Nat. Soc. Study Edn., Nat. Univ. Extension Assn. (chmn. region IV, 1973), North Central Conf. on Summer Sessions (pres. 1967-68), Blue Key, Phi Delta Kappa, Chi Beta Phi, Alpha Psi Omega. Mason (32 deg.). Author: Planning for Teaching-An Introduction to Education, 5th edit., 1973; Preparing for a Career in Education—Challenges, Changes, and Issues, 1974; (with Paul R. Grim and John U. Michaelis) The Student Teacher in the Secondary School, 1953; Handbook for Supervisors of Student Teaching, 1956. Editor: Expanding Experiences in the Elementary School, 1953; The Status and Position of Teachers in the U.S. in Internat. Yearbook Edn., 1953. Contbr. articles to profl. jours. Home: Bloomington, Ind. Died May 1, 1978.

RICHMAN, BARRY MARTIN, educator, author, cons.; b. Montreal, Que., Can., Mar. 18, 1936; s. Edward I. and Belle (Dalys) R.; B. Commerce, McGill U., 1958; M.S., Columbia, 1959, Ph.D., 1962; m. Vivian Freedman, June 5, 1960; children—Viana, Stuart. Mem. faculty Columbia, 1960-62; prof. mgmt. and internat. bus. U. Calif. at Los Angeles, 1962-78, chmn. Grad. Sch. Mgmt., 1975-77; dean Faculty Adminstrv. Studies, York U., Toronto, Ont., Can., 1972-73; cons. to govt., industry and ednl. orgns., 1958-78; cons. editor Random House, Alfred Knopf, Fellow U.S. Acad. Mgmt. Internat. Acad. Mgmt. Author: Soviet Management: With Significant American Comparisons, 1965; Management Development and Education in the Soviet Union, 1967; A Firsthand Study of Industrial Management in Communist China, 1967; Industrial Society in Communist China, 1969; (with R. Farmer) Comparative Management and Economic Progress, 1965, International Business, 1966, 2d edit., 1974. Leadership, Goals and Power in Higher Education, 1974, Management and Organizations, 1975; (with R. Farmer and W. Ryan) Incidents for Applying Management Theory, 1966, Incidents for Studying Management and Organizations, 1970; (with M. Copen) International Management and Economic Development, 1972. Home: Malibu, Calif. Died June 5, 1978.

RICHTER, GISELA MARIE AUGUSTA (RICH'TER), archeologist; b. London, Eng., Aug. 15, 1882; d. Jean Paul and Louise Marie (Schwaab) Richter; Girton Coll., Cambridge U., 1901-04; British Sch. of Archaeology, Athens, Greece, 1904-05; Litt.D., Trinity Coll., Dublin, 1913; M.A., Cambridge U., Eng., 1933; L.H.D., Smith Coll., 1935; D.F.A., Rochester U., 1940. Came to U.S., 1905, naturalized, 1917. With Metropolitan Museum of Art since 1906, asst. Greek and Roman dept. until 1910; asst. curator, 1910-22, asso. curator, 1922-25, curator 1925-48, hon. curator since 1948; vis. lecturer, Columbia; Ryerson lecturer, Yale, 1938; Mary Flexner lecturer, Bryn Mawr Coll., 1941-42; Charles Beebe Martin lecturer, Oberlin College, 1943. Hon. mem. Soc. for Promotion Hellenic Studies; mem. Soc. for Promotion Roman Studies; fellow Am. Numismatic Soc.; corr. fellow, British Acad.; hon. fellow, Soc. of Antiquaries, London; mem. Archeological Institute America (exec. com., 1944-46, president N.Y. Soc., 1941-48), School of Oriental Studies, Internat. Fedn. Univ. Women (fellowships award com.), Internationaler Verband von Museumsbeamten, Deutsches archaeologisches Institut, Am. Philos. Soc., Am. Council of Learned Societies (com. on research and publs. in the Fine Arts, 1943-44; mem. Visiting Com. to Dumbarton Oaks; N.Y. City Com. of Greek War Relief Association 1942; American Friends of Greece (trustee); corr. mem. Foundation archéologique de l'Université de Bruxelles. Member adv. com., Guggenheim Foundation since 1947. Recipient of the Am. Assn. of Univ. Women Achievement Award, 1944. Clubs: Cosmopolitan (New York); University Women's (London). Author or co-author numerous books relating to field since 1915; latest publs.: Roman Portraits, 1948; Archaic Greek Art, 1949; Three Critical Periods in Greek Sculpture, 1951. Asso. editor Am. Jour. Archeology. Home: N.Y. *

RICHTER, KARL FELIX JOHANNES, organist, educator; b. Plauen, Germany, Oct. 15, 1926; s. Christian Johannes and Facilides Clara Hedwig Richter; student Leipzig (Germany) Acad. Music, 1951-56, prof., 1956—; performer numerous concerts in Germany and abroad, concert tour U.S., 1956, 58; founder, conductor Munich Bach Choir. Recipient Internat. Bach prize. Home: Zurich, Switzerland. Died Feb. 16, 1981.

RICKBEIL, RAYMOND EARL, accountant; b. Cavalier, N.D., Feb. 22, 1897; s. Henry and Elizabeth (Reichert) R.; B.S., U. Ill., 1925, M.S., 1925; m. Clara Evelyn Shellman, May 8, 1930. Farm employee and tractor mechanic, Iowa, Mont., N.D., Sask., Can., 1913-17; jr. and sr. accountant, 1925-28; practice pub. accounting, Springfield, Ill., from 1928; Springfield mgr. Ernst & Ernst, C.P.A.'s, 1961-66. Mem. Ill. Commn. Practice Accounting, 1958-59. Audit adv. Ill. Def. Council, 1941-45, Selective Service Com., 1941-45; budget, fin. chmn. Springfield Area Devel. Assn., 1963-77; mem. panel arbitrators motion picture industry, U.S. Dist. Ct. (So. Dist. N.Y.). C.P.A., Ill., Ind., Iowa. Served with M.C., U.S. Army, 1918-19. Recipient Outstanding Service award Ill. Soc. C.P.A.'s, 1956. Mem. Nat. Assn. Cost Accountants (adv. council, past pres. Decatur chpt.), Am. Inst. Accountants (past mem. council), Am. Accounting Assn., Sangamon County Hist. Soc. (dir. 1967-72), Am. Inst. C.P.A.'s (hon.), Ill. Soc. C.P.A.'s (hon.), Ill. C. of C., U. Ill. Found. and President's Club, Springfield Greater C. of C., Am. Legion Republican. Clubs: Optimist Internat. (gov. Springfield); Sangamo. Contbr. articles to profl. jours. Home: Springfield, Ill. Died July 5, 1977; buried Oak Ridge Cemetery, Springfield.

RICKETTS, HENRY TUBBS, physician, educator; b. Berlin, Germany (parents U.S. citizens), Aug. 11, 1901; s. Howard Taylor and Myra (Tubbs) R.; B.S., U. Chgo., 1924; M.D., Harvard, 1929; m. Mandeliene Franks, Aug. 1, 1931; children—Howard James, Shirley Ann, Nancy Avery. Intern, U. Pa. Hosp., 1929-31; resident Billings Hosp., Chgo., 1931-33; instr. medicine U. Chgo., 1933-39, asst. prof., 1939-43, asso. prof., 1943-49, prof. medicine, from 1949, then prof. emeritus until 1979; spl. cons. Pub. Health Service. Dir. Nat. Bank Monmouth. Exec. com. health div. Welfare Council Met. Chgo.; dir. Hosp. Planning Council Met. Chgo. Fellow A.C.P.; mem. A.M.A., Am. Soc. Clin. Investigation, Soc. Extpl. Biology and Medicine, Chgo. Soc. Internal medicine, Institute Medicine, Chicago (chairman board of governors, 1949-60), Central Society Clin. Research, Am. Physiol. Soc., Assn. Am. Physicians, Am. (pres. 1955-56), Chgo. (pres. 1958-59) diabetes Assns., Am. Clin. and Climatol. Assn., Sigma Xi, Chi Psi, Nu Sigma Nu. Methodist. Clubs: Quadrangle, University. Home: Chicago, Ill. Died Nov. 23, 1979.

RICKETTS, JAMES BREWERTON, naval officer; b. New Rochelle, N.Y., Aug. 11, 1902; s. James Brewerton and Katherine (Overton) R.; B.S., U.S. Naval Acad., 1924; student Naval Finance and Supply Sch., Phila., 1935-36; m. Catherine Stevens Ambler, Oct. 9, 1925 (dec. 1955); children—James Brewerton, David Jocelyn; m. 2d, Loretta Gilmore, Sept. 7, 1956. Commd. ensign, U.S.N., 1924, advancing through grades to rear adm. (S.C.), 1945, shifting from line to supply corps, 1935; served on U.S.S. Okla., 1924-25, U.S.S. Mervine, 1925-29, U.S.S. Md., 1929-31, at Naval Training Sta., San Diego, 1931-33, on U.S.S. Omaha, 1933-35, at Navy Yard, Phila., 1936-37, Naval Air Sta., Pearl Harbor, T.H., 1937-39, on U.S.S. Tippecanoe, 1940; supply officer, U.S.S. Augusta, Atlantic Fleet, 1941-42; aviation supply, Bur. Supplies and Accounts, Navy Dept., 1942-43; aviation supply officer, Phila. 1943, on U.S.S. Wasp, 1943-44; staff aviation supply officer, Naval Air Operational Training Command, Jacksonville, Fla., 1944-45; force supply officer with Comdr. Air Forces, Pacific Fleet, 1945-48; supply and fiscal officer, San Diego Naval Air Station, 1948-51; comdg. officer Naval Supply Depot, Great Lakes, Ill., 1951-53; promoted to rear adm., 1953; insp. gen. supply corps, Pacific Coast, 1954-57; comdg. officer Naval Supply Depot, Mechanicsburg from 1957. Decorated Nicaraguan Campaign Ribbon, Am. Def. Medal (with A), Am. and Pacific-Asiatic theater ribbons, Victory Medal. Episcopalian. Mason (Shriner), Kiwanian. Home: Harrisburg, Penn. Died Dec. 12. 1979.

RIDDLE, LAWRENCE MELVILLE, univ. prof.; b. Fork, Baltimore County, Md., Mar. 22, 1884; s. Wilbur Hicks and Maria Augusta (Payne) R.; A.B., Johns Hopkins, 1908, A.M., 1911, Ph.D., 1922; studied Marburg, Germany, summer 1907, Paris, summer 1909; m. Sara Maynadier Waters, July 17, 1912; 1 son, Laurence Maynadier. Instr. French, Allegheny Coll., Meadville, Pa., 1911-13, U. Pitts., summer 1912; prof. French, U. So. Cal., 1913-50, prof. emeritus since 1950; tchr. French, summer sessions, Johns Hopkins, 1921, 22; prof. French, summers, U. of Wash., 1927, Northwestern U., 1930, U. of Wyo., 1935, Southern Methodist U., 1936, U. of N.Carolina, 1939. Mem. Modern Lang. Assn. America, Modern Lang. Assn. Southern Calif. (pres. 1915-16), Philol. Assn. Pacific Coast, Los Angeles Chapter Archaeol. Inst. America, Alliance Francaise of Los Angeles (v.p. and sec.-treas.), Southwestern Archaeol. Federation (founder), Phi Beta Kappa, Phi Kappa Phi, Sigma Alpha Epsilon. Decorated Officer de l'Instruction publique (France); Chevalier Legion of Honor (France), Apr. 1940. Democrat. Episcopalian. Club: The Sixty-Five Club (founder and past pres.). Author: The Genesis and Sources of Pierre Corneille's Tragedies from Medée to Pertharite, 1926; articles New Century Cyclopedia of Names. Editor: Corneille's Cinna, 1934. Editor: University of Southern Calif. Studies in Romance Philology. Contbr.: Cabeen Bibliography Fr. Lit., Vol. III. Home: Los Angeles, Cal. *

RIDGE, FRANK ISAAC, physician; b. Kansas City, Mo., Sept. 17, 1885; s. Thomas Smart and Effie (Searcy) R.; student U. of Mo., 1902-06; M.D., Columbia, 1910; grad. study U. of Munich Hosp., 1910-11, Nat. Heart Hosp., London and Vienna; m. Alberta Elizabeth Sharpe, Dec. 11, 1926. Resident physician Bellevue Hosp., N.Y. City, 1911-13; gen. practice, Kansas City, Mo., since 1913; at various times physician to Kansas City Gen. Hosp., St. Joseph's Hosp., St. Mary's Hosp., Provident Hosp., Swope Settlement, Tubercular Clinic; asso. prof. medicine, U. of Kansas. Served as lt. j.g., later sr. grade, Med. Corps, U.S.N.R., Great Lakes Naval Sta., 1917-19. Fellow Am. Coll. Physicians; mem. A.M.A., Southern Med. Assn., Mo. State Med. Assn. (pres. 1928-29), Jackson County Med. Assn., Kansas City Acad. Medicine, Am. Bd. of Internal Medicine, Phi Delta Theta, Nu Sigma Nu, Med. Alumni U. of Mo. (pres.). Independent. Mem. Christian (Disciples) Ch. Club: University. Home: Kansas City, Mo. *

RIDGELY, REGINALD HEBER, JR., marine corps officer; b. Lexington, Va., Aug. 18, 1902; s. Dr. Reginald H. and Matilda (Ridgely) R.; grad. St. John's Coll., Annapolis, Md., 1923; student Staff and Command course Marine Corps Sch., Quantico, Va.; grad. Motor Transport Sch.; m. Josephine Dalton, Aug. 20, 1927; children—Johanna Waller, Reginald Heber III. Commd. 2d lt. USMC, 1923, advanced through grades to maj. gen., 1951; assigned various Marine Corps bases, including Nicaragua, Haiti, China, P.I.; mem. 4th Marine Regt., Bataan and Corregidor, World War II; Japanese prisoner of war; comdg. officer Fleet Marine Force Mediterranean, 1948; comdg. officer 8th Marines, 2d Marine Div., then U.S. Naval Disciplinary Barracks, Portsmouth, N.H.: comdr. Marine Corps Recruit Depot, San Diego, 1951-52; dir. personnel Hdqrs. USMC, Washington, 1952-55; comdr. 2d Marine Div., Fleet Marine Force Atlantic, 1955-57; comdg. gen. Marine Corps Base, Camp Pendleton, Calif., from 1957. Decorated Bronze Star with gold star, Purple Heart, Distinguished Unit Citation with cluster; Medal of Merit with citation (Nicaragua); Order of Honor and Merit (Haiti); Presidential Unit Citation (P.I.). Mem. Soc. of Cincinnati, Kappa Alpha. Address: Camp Pendleton, Calif. Died June 28, 1979.

RIEHLMAN, R(OY) WALTER, bus. exec., congressman; b. Otisco, N.Y., Aug. 26, 1899; s. Frederick and Catherine (Edinger) R.; student St. John's Mil. Acad., Manlius, N.Y., 1916-19, Syracuse (N.Y.) Bus. Sch., 1919-20; m. Lucia Sherwood, Dec. 18, 1920; children—Jane Carol (Mrs. Laurence Maxwell Downes), Royce Walter. Bookkeeper wholesale drug co., Syracuse, N.Y., 1920; operated gen. store and served as postmaster, Nedrow, N.Y., 1921-23; owner and operator Tully (N.Y.) Bakery, from 1923; v.p., dir. 1st Nat. Bank of Tully, from 1941; v.p. Lu-Mar Enterprises, Inc. Supr. (majority leader) Town of Tully, 1938-44; Onondaga Co. clerk, 1944-46; mem. 80th, 81st Congresses (1947-51), 36th Dist. N.Y.; mem. 83d-87th Congresses, 35th Dist. N.Y., member of 88th Congress 34th District N.Y. Member of re-employment com., mem. anti-discrimination bd., Selective Service Bd., World War II. Recipient citation from Gov. Dewey; awarded gold cup by people of Town of Tully for outstanding community service, Feb. 10, 1942. Dir.

Onondago County and Syracuse Community Chest; past divisional dir. Boy Scouts of Am. Mem. Bakery Engrs. of Am., Tully Chamber of Commerce, Syracuse Chamber of Commerce. Vice chmn. Rep. Party of Onondago County. Baptist. Mem. Mason (Shriner, Jester), O.E.S. (patron 1942-43, dist. grand lecturer, 1944). Clubs: Rotary, Syra-Canadian Hunting and Fishing. Home: Ormond Beach, Fla. Died July 16, 1978.

RIENHOFF, WILLIAM FRANCIS, JR., surgeon; b. Springfield, Mo., Oct. 10, 1894; s. William Francis and Sarah Aileen (Hopkins) R.; grad. Drury Acad., Springfield, 1911; A.B., Cornell U., 1915; M.D., Johns Hopkins, 1919; m. Frances Kemper Young, June 2, 1923; children—Wm. Francis III, Hugh Young, MacCallum, Francis Colston. Intern in medicine, Johns Hopkins Hosp., 1919-20, in surgery, 1920, asst. resident surgeon, 1920-23, resident surgeon, 1923-25, asst. surgeon 1925, asst. vis. surgeon, 1926-38, vis. surgeon, from 1938; also instr. surgery Johns Hopkins, 1922-30, asso. in clin. surgery, 1931-32, asso. in surgery, from 1933; asso. prof. surgery, 1933-59, prof. surgery, 1959-60, prof. emeritus, 1960-81; asso. prof. surgery, med. dept. U. Md.; attending surgeon Women's, Union Meml., Sinai Church Home and Hosp., Mercy, U.S. VA Hosps., Md.; cons. surgeon, Md. Gen. Marine, Provident, Frederick City, Emergency Hosps., Annapolis: exchange prof. Guy's Hosp., London. Moynihan Lectr. Royal Coll. Surgeons, 1948. Hon. prof. surgery U. Philippines, 1952. Trustee Gilman Country Sch. for Boys. Fellow Am. Coll. Surg., A.M.A.; mem. Med. and Chirurgical Faculty of Md., Baltimore County Med. Assn., Balt. Med. Soc., Am. Surg. Assn., Royal Soc. of Medicine, Soc. Clin. Surgery, Am. Soc. Thoracic Surgeons, Am. Bronchoscopic Soc.; So. Med. Assn., Am. Assn. Anatomists, So. Surg. Assn. (v.p. 1956), Am. Coll. Chest Phys., Internat. Soc. Surgeons, Cuban Nat. Med. Soc. (hon.), Deutsche Gesellschaft Fûr Chirurgie (hon.), Phi Beta Kappa. Alpha Omega Alpha, Phi Sigma Kappa, Sigma Xi, Pi Gamma Mu. Democrat. Episcopalian. Club: Maryland. Contbr. to Johns Hopkins, A.M.A., Archives and Annals of Surgery (asso. editor), Lewis' System of Surgery. Home: Baltimore, Md. Died Jan. 10, 1981.

RIESEN, EMIL RICHERT (RE'ZEN), coll. prof.; b. Hillsboro, Kan., Jan. 26, 1884; s. Rudolf and Sara (Richert) R.; Bethel Coll., Newton, Kan., 1904-05; A.B., U. of Kan., 1909, A.M., 1912; U. of Colo., summer 1907; grad. study, Harvard, 1911-12, U. of Chicago, 1925-26, Columbia, summer 1932; m. Rachel Penner, Aug. 27, 1911 (dec.); children—Austin H., Carl Homer. Teacher country sch., Hillsboro, Kan., 1902-04; instr., Bethel Coll., 1909-18, also registrar, 1910-18; registrar and high sch. visitor, U. of Ariz., 1918-20, asso. prof. philosophy, 1918-22, prof. since 1922; dir. summer session, 1922, dean Coll. Liberal Arts, 1930-44. Mem. American Association for the Advancement of Science, Am. Philosophical Assn., Am. Assn. Univ. Profs., Delta Chi, Phi Kappa Phi, Phi Delta Kappa. Conglist. Author: Opening College Doors. Contbr. articles on education. Home: Tucson, Ariz. *

RIGG, HORACE ABRAM, JR., educator; b. Phila., Apr. 22, 1909; s. Horace Abram and Maud (Wynkoop) R.; A.M., Harvard, 1932; guest fellow Trinity Coll., Cambridge U., Eng. 1932, 33; student Ludwig-Maximillians Universitaet, Munich, Germany, 1932-33; student in Oriental studies U. Pa., 1934-35; Ph.D., Harvard, 1937, univ. fellow in philosophy, 1931-32, traveling univ. fellow in history, 1932-33; m. Ruth Bowman Lyman, Nov. 24, 1934; children—Alexandra (Mrs. John N. Samaras), Diana, Jonathan Lyman, Margaret R. Stewart, Peter Whitney (dec.). Asso. prof. history of religion Case Western Res. U., 1937-44; prof. history of religion, 1944-47, Severance prof. history of religion, 1947-65; chmn. dept. Bibl. lit. and history religion, 1937-58; research Harvard, 1948-49, prehistoric cave research, France, 1956; prehistoric Bushmen studies So. Rhodesia, 1959, 61, 62; research asso. Carl Mackley Houses, Fed. Housing Project No. 1, Phila., 1933-34; co-ordinating editor history of religion, Ency. Americana, 1946-47. Spl. advisor Selective Service Bd. No. 41, Cleve., 1941-43; fgn. service Middle East sect. OSS, 1943-44. Mem. Archaeol. Inst. Am., Cleve. Soc. (past sec-treas. and pres.), Am. Oriental Soc., Am. Soc. Ch. Hist., Am. Geog. Soc., Am. Soc. Bibl. Lit. and Exegesis, Cleve. Chamber Music Soc., Internat. Soc. African Culture (trustee). Editor, contbr. Bibl. dictionaries. Contbr. papers, monographs, and revs. to jours., ency. Home: Union, Maine. Died Dec. 25, 1978.

RIGGS, RALPH SMITH, business executive, retired naval officer; born Paris, Texas, June 20, 1895; son of Joseph Newton and Minnie (Little) R.; B.S., United States Naval Acad., 1917; student Naval War Coll., 1929-30; m. Kathryn Pew, Dec. 3, 1929 (dec. Mar. 1981); 1 son, Ralph Smith. Commd. ensign U.S. Navy, June 28, 1917, and advanced through grades to rear adm., Dec. 12, 1944; retired with rank of vice admiral, Aug. 1951; served in U.S.S. Minneapolis, 1917-18, U.S.S. Dante Alighierl, U.S.S. Manley, 1918; fitted out U.S.S. Eagle 2 and served as comdr., 1918-19; served in U.S.S. Utah, 1919-23; Bur. of Navigation, U.S. Navy Dept, 1923-25; aide and flag lt., staff of comdr. light cruiser div., later scouting fleet, 1925-29; hydrographic office, U.S. Navy Dept., 1930-31; aide and flag lt., staff of battleship div. comdr., 1931-32; comdr. U.S.S. Zane, 1933-34; discipline div. Bur. of Navigation, 1934-36; navigator U.S.S. West Virginia, 1936-38; comdr. U.S.S. Arctic, 1938; aide to asst. secretaries of Navy, 1939-41; comdr. destroyer div., 1941-42, destroyer squadron, 1942-43; chief of staff and aide to comdr. of destroyers, Pacific fleet, 1943-44; comdr. U.S.S. So. Dakota, 1944, cruiser div., 1944-46; comdt. U.S. Naval base, Phila., 1946-47; asst. chief of naval operations and dir. naval reserves, U.S. Navy Dept., 1947-July 1951; brokerage mgr., gen. partner Washington office, Burton, Dana and Company. Navy Cross, Bronze Star with gold star, Legion of Merit with 2 gold stars, Victory medals (World Wars I and II), Navy unit commendation medal, Philippine Liberation ribbon with 2 stars, Yangtze and Am. Defense service medals, various campaign and area medals, battle stars. Christian. Clubs: Army and Navy, Army-Navy Country, Metropolitan (Washington); Chevy Chase (Md.); Yacht (N.Y. City). Home: Potomac, Md. Died Apr. 28, 1981.

RIGGS, ROBERT LANGMUIR, newspaperman; b. Joplin, Mo., Oct. 23, 1901; s. Milford and Mary Dudley (Rees) R.; student State Teachers Coll. Warrensburg, Mo., 1919-20, Georgetown (Ky.) Coll., 1920-21; A.B., U. of Mo., 1927, B.J., 1927; m. Dorothy Beth Harrison, June 18, 1930; 1 son, Russell H. Reporter, Associated Press, Madison, Wis., 1927, Milwaukee Journal, 1928-29, Associated Press, Madison, Wis., 1929; asst. state editor, Courier-Journal, Louisville, Ky., 1929-30, asst. city editor, 1930-36, night city editor, 1936-38, asst. news editor, 1938-40, asst. mng. editor, 1940-42, Washington (D.C.) correspondent since 1942. Clubs: Gridiron, National Press (Washington) Home: Washington, D.C. Died Feb. 19, 1980.

RILEY, EDWARD EDDY, JR., coll. dean; b. Greenville, S.C., Aug. 27, 1926; s. Edward E. and Ollie Anna (Glenn) R.; B.A. in Zoology, Syracuse U., 1949; M.A. in Zoology, Oberlin Coll., 1950; Ph.D. in Biology, Brown U., 1955; m. Phyllis Rose Patterson, July 20, 1955; children—Carole Helen, Marcia Glenn, Edward Eddy, III. Instr. biology Benedict Coll., Columbia, S.C., 1950-52; research scientist Walter Reed Arny Inst. Research, 1955-56; chmn. div. natural scis. Dillard U., New Orleans, 1956-59, prof. biology, 1958-73, dean instrn., 1959-73; acad. dean, prof. biology Spelman Coll., Atlanta, 1973-78. Adviser, cons. to NSF, Nat. Acad, Sci., U.S. Office Edn.; cons. United Negro Coll. Fund, Inst. for Services to Edn. Bd. dirs. UN Assn., La. Heart Assn., Greater New Orleans Ednl. TV Found., Hume Child Devel. Center, Internat. Sci. Fair; bd. govs. Isidore Newman Sch. Mem. AAAS, Am. Inst. Biol. Scis., Urban League, NAACP, NEA, Am. Soc. Zoologists, La. Edn. Assn., N.Y. Acad. Sci., Ga. Acad. Sci., Nat. Inst. Sci. (past exec. sec.), Sigma Xi, Beta Kappa Chi, Omega Psi Phi, Sigma Pi Phi, Beta Beta Beta. Contbr. articles to sci. and ednl. jours. Home: Atlanta, Ga. Died Oct. 3, 1978; buried Columbia, S.C.

RILEY, FRANK BRANCH, lectr., lawyer; b. Osceola, Iowa, Aug. 4, 1875; s. Edward Francis and Martha (Smith) R.; grad. Portland High School, 1893, Columbia Coll. of Expression (Chgo.), 1895, Portland Acad., 1896; A.B., Stanford U., 1900; student Harvard Law Sch., 1900-01; traveled and studied in Europe, 1902; m. Lotte von Strombeck Brand, Aug. 6, 1902 (dec. Nov. 23, 1929); children—William Brand, Margaret Brand (dec.); m. 2d, Elaine Strowbridge, Oct. 15, 1946. Admitted to Oreg. bar, 1902, thereafter practiced in Portlant; pres. and gen. counsel Clackamas Title Co.; admitted to the U.S. Supreme Court bar in 1918. mem. E.F. & F.B. Riley; widely known as after-dinner speaker and for illustrated travel-lectures on nat. parks and scenery of Northwest, presented on 32 transcontinental tours, also talking scenic motion pictures with world distbn.; radio addresses nationally broadcast. Chmn. Oreg.-Wash. Interstate Bridge Com. Trustee Mus. Assn. Oreg. (expres.); Rep. mem. for Oreg. Nat Gallery of Am. Indians; dir. Portland Jr. Symphony Orch. Assn.; dir. Portland Civic Theatre. Recipient Pub. Address Honor award Freedoms Found., 1970. A founder and v.p. for Oreg. of Pacific Highway Assn.; hon. asso. mem. Pacific Coast Surg. Assn.; mem. Am. Bar Assn., Oreg. Bar Assn., Nat. Parks Highway Assn., Oreg. Advt. Club, Am. Geographic Soc., Newcomen Soc. of Eng., Am. Forestry Assn., Oreg. Hist. Soc., Zeta Psi, Phi Delta Phi, S.A.R. Orator celebration 100 years peace between Great Britain and U.S. at Blaine, Wash., 1915, and dedication Columbia River Highway, 1916, dedication Oregon State Capitol, 1938, dedication of Astoria Naval Air Base, 1939, Dedication of Portland Civic Auditorium, 1968, dedication Willamette River Bridge, 1970. Republican. Presbyterian. Rotarian. Clubs: University, Harvard of Oregon, Stanford (pres.), Waverley Country, Dutch Treat (N.Y.C.); Apollo (ex-pres.). Mazamas Mountaineering (organizer, ex-pres.); Forty (Chgo.). Recipient annual award for outstanding service to Ore., Theta Sigma Chi, 1957; named hon. life mem. Portland Realty Bd. Author: Part two, We Have With Us Tonight; Obediance To Law Is Liberty; Abraham Lincoln-The Man, The Saga; A Brief For The Establishment. Contbr. to mags. Home: Portland, Oreg. Died Feb. 1975.

RILEY, PHILIP EUGENE, clergyman; b. Tehuacana, Tex., Dec. 10, 1882; s. Rev. Philip Melancthon and Josie Green (Harrison) R.; A.B., Trinity U. (Waxahachie, Tex.), 1906; Bibl. dept., Vanderbilt U., 1906-07; D.D., Southwestern U., 1925; m. Ruth Love, May 20, 1908; children—Mary Elizabeth, Philip Marshall, Ruth Clifford, Josephine Estelle; m. 2d, Ethel Isbell, June 1, 1932. Admitted on trial in Northwest Tex. Conf. M.E. Ch., S., 1907; pastor, Brownfield, Tex., 1907-09, Lockney, Tex., 1909-10, Rotan, Tex., 1910-12; prof. Latin, Clarendon (Tex.) Coll., 1912-14; pastor Weatherford St. Ch., Fort Worth, 1914-15, Itasca, 1916-19, Belton, 1919-21, Polytechnic Ch., Fort Worth, 1921-22; editor Tex. Christian Advocate, 1922-26; became presiding elder Waco (Tex.) Dist., 1926; pastor First Meth. Ch., Mineral Wells, Tex., 1931-34; presiding elder of Ft. Worth Dist., 1934-38; pastor First Meth. Ch., Corsicana, Tex., 1938-42; dist. supt., Weatherford Dist., 1942-48; now exec. sec. Res. Pension Fund, Central Tex. Conf. Mem. Gen. Conf. M.E. Ch., S., 5 times to 1938; res. del. Ecumenical Conf., Atlanta, Ga.; del. to Uniting Conf., Meth. Ch., Kansas City, 1939; del. to Gen. Conf. Meth. Ch., Atlantic City, 1940 and 1944, Boston, 1948; trustee Tex., Wesleyan Coll. (Fort Worth), Meth. Hosp., Ft. Worth; mem. bd. of pensions, Meth. Ch.; chmn. bd. of publication, Southwestern Advocate. Mason. Democrat. Lion. Home: Fort Worth, Tex. *

RILEY, PLACIDUS H., coll. dean; b. Concord, N.H., July 28, 1921; s. William Henry and Eldya (Maclean) R.; B.A., St. Anselm's Coll., Manchester, N.H., 1942; student U. Toronto (Can.), 1943-45; S.T.L., U. Ottowa (Can.), 1949; S.T.D., U. Ottawa (Can.), 1953; LL.D. (hon.), New Eng. Coll., Henniker, N.H., 1965. Joined Order of St. Benedict, 1942; ordained priest Roman Catholic Ch., 1946; mem. faculty dept. philosophy St. Anselm's Coll., 1949-54; rector St. Anselm's Sem., 1954-57; asst. to pres. St. Anselm's Coll., 1957-59, dean of coll., 1959-64, again, from 1972, pres., 1964-72. Mem. Cath. Bibl. Assn., Cath. Theol. Soc., Soc. Bibl. Lit. Address: Manchester, N.H. Deceased.

RINGLAND, ARTHUR CUMING, govt. official; born Brooklyn, New York, September 29, 1882; s. Robert Burns and Mary (Glenister) Ringland; M.F., from Yale University, 1905; m. Dorothy Gerberding, June 23, 1922; children—Peter, Susan. With U.S. Forest Service, 1905-17, regional forester in charge Southwestern Region (Ariz. and N.M.), 1908-16; capt., adj. 10th Engrs., later co. comdr. Engrs., 37th Div., France and Belgium, 1917-18; detailed Bd. of War Damages, Am. Peace Commn. (Paris), 1919, chief of U.S. Mission to Czechoslovakia, Am. Relief Administration, 1919-21; in charge Russian relief operations, Am. Relief Adminstrn., Constantinople, 1922-23; exec. sec. Nat. Conf. on Outdoor Recreation, 1925-29, also mem. U.S. Commn. on Nat. Park and Nat. Forest Boundaries; European forestry rep. Foreign Agrl. Service, U.S. Dept. Agr., Berlin and London, 1930-33; liaison officer Civilian Conservation Corps, 1933-34; chmn. Flood Control Com., U.S. Dept. Agr., 1937-39; consultant Nat. Defense Advisory Com. and President's War Relief Control Board, 1940-46; exec. dir. adv. com. on Voluntary Fgn. Aid Dept. of State, since 1946. Awarded Order of White Lion (Czechoslovakia); Order of St. Stanislaus (Russia); medal City of Prague. Episcopalian. Club: Cosmos (Washington). Home: Chevy Chase, Md. *

RIPLEY, PAUL MORTON, transportation exec.; b. Rock Island, Ill., Feb. 25, 1883; s. Joseph Pierce and Harriet (Konantz) R.; student U. Wis. Asst. gen. traffic mgr., asst. to pres. El Paso & Southwestern Ry., 1908-17; traffic mgr. Am. Sugar Refining Co., 1917-54; pres. Am. Sugar Transit Corp., 1935-49, Butler County R.R., 1928-36, Bklyn. Cooperage Co., 1941-54; dir. C.&N.-W. Ry.; trustee of Green Point Savs. Bank, Bklyn. Mem. Nat. Indsl. Traffic League (past pres.), Assn. Interstate Commerce Practitioners (past chmn.), Am. Steamship Owners Assn. (past chmn.), Nat. Freight Traffic Assn. (past pres.), Pilgrims, New Eng. Soc., Newcomen. Mason. Clubs: Traffic (sr. past pres.), Union League (past treas., chmn. bd. govs.) (N.Y.C.); Garden City Golf. Home: N.Y.C. *

RISK, THOMAS MARION, prof. edn.; b. Easton, Wis., Apr. 7, 1885; s. Thomas and Mary Elizabeth (Witter) R.; State Normal Sch., Stevens Point, Wis., 1904-07; Ph.B., U. of Wis., 1924, Ph.M., 1925, Ph.D., 1927; m. Tillie Pearl Garthwaite, July 2, 1907; children—Ellen Winifred, Dorothy June, Vivian Merle, Francis Marion, Stewart Wesley. Teacher rural schs. Adams County, 1902-03; pub. schs., Alderly, Wis., 1903-04; supt. schs. Kendall, Wisconsin Dells, Wautoma, Wis., 1907-18; editor and pub., Wautoma Pub. Co., 1918-23; asst. in edn., U. of Wis., 1924-27; prof. edn., U. of S.D., since 1927; mem. grad. council, Grad. Sch., 1930-48, dir. teacher training, Univ. High Sch., 1927-46; vis. prof. U. of So. Calif., summer 1948. Chmn. Coms. on State Revision Secondary Curricula, S.D., 1929-32; chmn. Com. on Secondary Sch. Math. Curriculum, 1929-32; chmn. S.D. Edn. Assn. Com. on Sch. Orgn. for S.D. long term program, 1933; chmn. S.D. Edn. Assn. Com. on Larger Sch. Units, 1936-42; member South Dakota H.S. Education Commission, 1944. Mem. N.E.A. and Dept. Secondary Sch. Prins. of same, S.D. High Sch. Execs. Assn., Soc. for Study, of Edn., S.D. Edn. Assn., Soc. for Curriculum Study, Supervisors of Student Teaching, Nat. Council of Teachers of English, Nat. Council for Social Studies, Am. Assn. Univ. Professors, Phi Delta Kappa, Delta Sigma Theta. Republican. Methodist. Clubs: South Dakota Hickory Stick, Beadle (hon.), U. of S.D. Research. Author: Better Teaching, 1926; Principles and Practices of Teaching in Secondary Schools, rev. edit., 1947 Editor S.D. Sch. Bd. Journal since 1948. Home: Vermillion, S.D. *

RITCHARD, CYRIL, actor, dir.; b. Sydney, New South Wales, Australia, Dec. 1, 1898; s. Herbert and Margaret (Collins) Trimmell-Ritchard; student St. Aloysius Coll. and U. of Sydney; m. Madge Elliott, 1935 (dec. 1955). State debut, Australia, 1917, appearing in various mus. comedies, 1917-24; N.Y.C. debut in Puzzles of 1925; London debut, 1925, in various prodns. including Charlot's Revue (1930), 1925-31; actor, dancer, dir. mus. comedies, including Roberta, The Gay Divorcee, in Australia, 1932-36; in London, 1936-43, leading role in revue Nine Sharp (1938); producer New Ambassadors Revue, 1941, star in Big Top, 1942, Importance of Being Earnest, 1942, The Merry Widow, 1942; toured in The Merry Widow in several countries to entertain Armed Forces, 1943-45; dir., star Gay Rosalinda, London, 1945, Noel Coward plays, Sydney, 1946; The Relapse, London, 1947, 48, N.Y. C., 1950; in Love for Love (with John Gielgud), N.Y.C., 1947, Make Way for Lucia, N.Y.C., 1948, Ann Veronica, 1949, The Schoolmistress, 1950 (both London), The Millionairess (with Katharine Hepburn), London and N.Y.C., 1952, The Pleasure of His Company (with Cornelia Otis Skinner), N.Y.C., 1958-59, Australia, 1960, Happiest Girl in the World, N.Y.C., 1961; dir. Buy Me Blue Ribbons, 1952, Jane, 1952; dir. comedy sketches in John Murray Anderson's Almanac, 1953, Missalliance, 1953, The Heavenly Twins (comedy), 1955, The Reluctant Debutante, 1956-57, also (Met. Opera prodns.) The Barber of Seville, 1954, Les Contes dHoffman, 1956, La Perichole (role of the Viceroy), Gipsy Baron; played role of Captain Hook (in mus. version of Peter Pan), 1954; star Rosalinda (Civic Light Opera Co. prodn.), Los Angeles and San Francisco, 1955; dir., singer, La Perichole (Met. Opera prodn.), 1956; leading role in Visit to a Small Planet, N.Y.C., 1957; Romulus, 1961; staged and appeared in The Irregular Verb To Love, 1963; star of musical The Roar of the Greasepaint, The Smell of the Crowd, Broadway, 1965, Sugar, 1973; star of Lock Up Your Daughters (Fla.), 1968, Rosalinda (San Francisco and Los Angeles), 1968, (with Cornelia Otis Skinner) Halfway Up A Tree, 1969; dir. The Jockey Club Stakes, N.Y.C., 1973. First appeared in motion pictures, 1929. On television in programs including the Milton Berle Show, Mr. Peepers; starred in The Good Fairy, Rosalinda, Jack and the Beanstalk, 1956; in La Perichole, 1958; as Captain Hook (Peter Pan), 1955, 56; film Half a Sixpence, 1967; dir. Midwummer Nights Dream, Stratford, Conn., 1967; dir., co-star Devil's Disciple, Stratford, 1969; co-star Sugar, 1969, A Musical Jubilee, 1975-76. Recipient Tony Award Am. Theatre Wing, 1954. Address: New York, N.Y. Died Dec. 18, 1977.

RITCHIE, HORACE BONAR, educator; b. Banks Country, Ga., Sept. 10, 1882; s. Jacob Sanford and Sarah Cornelia (Telford) R.; A.B., U. of Ga., 1905, A.M., 1920; student U. of Chicago, summers 1910, 12, 15, Ohio State U., fall 1935; m. Edith Adams, Dec. 28, 1912; children—Horace Bonar, Florence Margaret (dec.). Teacher country schs. Banks County. Ga., summers 1902-04; prin. Dallas (Ga.) Schs., 1906-07; prof. science Piedmont Coll., Demorest, Ga., 1907-09; prin. and supt. Fitzgerald (Ga.) schs., 1909-15; dean Ga. State Teachers Coll., 1915-33; prof. edn. U. of Ga. since 1933. Pres. local chapter Am. Red Cross; pres. Boy Scouts council; dir. Ga. Com. on Phonograph Records. Life mem. Ga. Edn. Assn. (pres.), N.E.A.; mem. Acad. of Sci., Am. Social Science, Am. Forestry Assn., Kappa Delta Pi, Pi Gamma Mu, Sigma Chi. Democrat. Baptist (deacon). Club: Kiwanis. Home: Athens, Ga. *

RITTENHOUSE, CONSTANCE MORGAN (MRS. PAUL LOCKWOOD RITTENHOUSE), born Great Neck, Long Island, New York, Dec. 28, 1885; d. Charles Leslie and Lucy Phelps (Allen) Morgan; privately ed.; spl. courses at Columbia and Northwestern univs.; m. Paul Lockwood Rittenhouse, June 16, 1917. Served successively as exec. sec. to pres. Farmers Loan and Trust Co., N.Y. City; rep. Minneapolis Gen. Electric Co., on Woman's Div. of Pub. Relations Com., Nat. Electric Light Assn.; sec. Minneapolis League of Women Voters, and later Ill. League; regional sec., Nat. League of Women Voters; nat. dir. Girl Scouts 1935-51. Episcopalian. Clubs: Women's City, Cosmopolitan (N.Y. City). Retired as nat. dir. Girl Scouts. Address: N.Y. *

RITTER, GEORGE WILLIAM, lawyer; b. Vermillion, O., June 30, 1886; s. John and Louise (Hauth) R.; student Cleve. Law Sch., 1903-06; LL.B., Baldwin U., Berea, O., 1906; LL.D., Baldwin-Wallace Coll., 1946, U. Toledo; m. Mary Fowler, June 30, 1911. Admitted to Ohio bar, 1907, since practiced in Ohio; dir. law City of Toledo, 1928-29; v.p., gen. counsel Overland Corp., Toledo, 1936—; partner law firm Ritter, Boesel, Robinson & Marsh. Trustee Toledo Hosp., Toledo Mus. Art, Baldwin-Wallace Coll. Mem. Toledo, Ohio, Lucas County, Am., Cleve. bar assns., Assn. Bar City of N.Y. Republican. Conglist. Clubs: Toledo, Inverness, Country (Toledo); Big Creek Hunting and Fishing (Can.); Bath, Surf, Indian Creek Country, Com. 100 (Fla.); Castalia Trout; La Gorce Country, Home: Ottawa Hills OH (winter) Miami Beach FL. *

RITTER, GERALD, apparel mfr., realtor; b. N.Y.C., Sept. 23, 1897; s. Jacob and Celia (Beck) R.; student pub. schs. N.Y.C.; m. May Ellen Thompson, Sept. 29, 1928. Founder, The Barbizon Corp., 1917, pres., from 1939; pres. Barbizon of Utah, Inc., Barbizon Lingerie & Apparel Corp., Ltd., Barbizon Sales Corp., The Barbizon Co., Inc., Jaunty Fabric Corp., Brookside Realty Co., Inc., Parkfield Realty Co., Inc., Registered Fabric Corp.; dir. Andover Advt. Agy., Inc. Bd. dirs. N.Y.C. div. Am. Cancer Soc. Mem. Acad. Polit. Sci. Club: Economics (N.Y.). Home: New York, N.Y. Died Mar. 7, 1978.

RITTER, WILLIS WILLIAM, federal judge; b. Salt Lake City, Jan. 24, 1899; s. William Wolfe and Martha May (Sykes) R.; A.B., U. Utah; LL.B., U. Chgo., 1924; S.J.D., Harvard, 1940; m. Ireta Olson, Aug. 22, 1928; children—Willis William, Nancy, Mary Lynn, John Russell. Admitted to bar, Ill. 1924, D.C., 1925, Utah, 1927; practiced in Chgo. and Washington, 1924-26, Salt Lake City, 1935-49; prof. law U. Utah, 1926-50; U.S. judge Dist. of Utah, from 1949, chief judge until 1978. Mem. Order of Coif, Phi Beta Kappa, Phi Kappa Phi. Clubs: Timpanogos, Cottonwood. Home: Salt Lake City, Utah. Died Mar. 4, 1978.

RITTER, WOODWARD MAURICE (TEX), actor, singer; b. Murvaul, Tex., Jan 12; grad. U. Tex., Austin; postgrad. Northwestern U. Law Sch.; m. Dorothy Fay Southworth; children—Thomas Matthews, Jonathan Southworth. Singer, radio actor Cowboy Tom's Round-Up, WHN Barn Dance, and others, from 1929; Broadway debut, 1930; Broadway shows include: Green Grow the Lilacs, The Roundup, Mother Lode; rec. debut, 1934; numerous hit records, including: Jingle, Jangle, Jingle, Jealous Heart, High Noon (Acad. award 1953), I Dreamed of a Hillbilly Heaven; motion picture debut in Song of the Gringo, 1936; appeared in over 60 westerns, including: Sing Cowboy Sing, 1937; Sundown on the Prairie, 1939, Old Chisholm Trail, 1942, Frontier Bullets, 1945; joined Grand Ole Opry, 1965; numerous appearances radio, TV, and touring shows; lectr. Western history and cowboy life; collector of cowboy songs and stories. Sought Republican nomination for U.S. Senate from Tenn., 1970. Elected to Country Music Hall of Fame, Cowboy Hall ofFame. Died Jan. 2, 1974.*

RITZENTHALER, ARTHUR BERNARD, appliance industry exec.; b. Rochester, N.Y., June 4, 1901; s. Bernard S. and Anna (Freund) R.; m. Edna A. Gullen, Oct. 1, 1927 (dec. Mar. 1965); children—Bruce A., Sallie (Mrs. Frank P. Waters); m. 2d, Elizabeth Coltart Brown, Feb. 11, 1969; 1 stepdau., Elizabeth (Mrs. John Roby). With Tappan Co., from 1926, v.p., 1945-65, sr. v.p., from 1965, also dir., mem. exec. com.; pres., dir. Richland Devel. Co., Mansfield, Ohio, from 1959; dir. Can. Tappan Stove Co., First Nat. Bank Mansfield; adv. bd. Farmers Savs. and Trust Co., Mansfield. Mem. Am. Gas Assn. (bd. dirs.), Gas Appliance Mfrs. Assn. (pres., dir., mem. exec. com.), Inst. Appliance Mfrs. (pres. 1966, trustee), Nat. Appliance Mfrs. Assn. (life hon., dir.), Natural LP Gas Assn. (past pres., dir., chmn. exec. com.), Mansfield C. of C. K.C. (life). Clubs: Westbrook Country, Elks (life), Our, 808, 51 (Mansfield); Oak Hill Country (Rochester); Buffalo Athletic; Union (Cleve.); Rockwell Springs Trout (Castalia, Ohio); Coral Ridge Country (Ft. Lauderdale, Fla.). Home: Mansfield, Ohio. Died Apr. 30, 1978.

RIVERS, RALPH JULIAN, lawyer, former congressman; b. Seattle, May 23, 1903; S. Julian Guy and Louisa (Lavoy) R.; LL.B. U. Wash., 1929; LL.D., U. Alaska, 1974; m. Lina Carol Caldwell, Dec. 17, 1928; children—Julian Ralph, Joyce Carol; m. 2d, Martha Wendling, Oct. 1, 1955. Gold miner, Flat, Alaska, 1921-23; admitted to Wash. bar, 1930; mem. firm Rivers & Manning, Seattle, 1930-31, alone at Fairbanks, Alaska, 1931-33; U.S. dist. atty. 4th Jud. Div., Dist. of Alaska, 1933-44, resigned; atty. gen. of Alaska, 1945-49; law practice at Fairbanks, 1949-59; mayor of Fairbanks, 1952-54; pres. League of Alaskan Cities, 1953, 54; mem. Territorial Senate, 1955; 2d v.p. Alaska Constnl. Conv., 1955-56; rep. from Alaska to Congress, Provisional basis, pending statehood, 1958-66; mem. 86th-89th Congresses, Alaska. Mem. Alaska Bar Assn. (bd. govs. 1968-69), Pioneers of Alaska, S.A.R., Soc. Mayflower Descs., Sigma Chi, Phi Alpha Delta. Democrat. Elk, Eagle. Home: Chehalis, Wash. Died Aug. 13, 1976.

RIVERS, ROBERT WHEATON, teacher; b. Milton, Mass., Aug. 13, 1882; s. George Robert Russell and Helen (Fairbank) R.; grad. Milton Acad., 1900; A.B., Harvard, 1904; m.Rosalie Channing, of Brookline, Mass., June 25, 1911. Began teaching at Boston, 1904; founder and prin. Open Air Sch. (for boys), 1915. Mem. N.E. Assn. Coll. and Secondary Schs., Mass. Soc. Mental Hygiene, Pvt. Sch. Assn. Boston (pres. 1919—). Unitarian. Clubs: Brookline Country, Oakley Country. Home: 686 Chestnut Hill Av. Address: Brookline, Mass. *

RIVERS, THOMAS ELLIS, recreation assn. exec.; b. Meridian, Miss., Oct. 6, 1892; s. Thomas Ellis and Frances (Eakins) R.; A.B., U. Wis., 1917; D.Humanics (hon.), Springfield (Mass.) Coll., 1960; m. Ruth Cunningham Harris, Oct. 26, 1923; children—Thomas Ellis, Marion Bedell, Ann Caroline (Mrs. John F. O'Brien). With Nat. Recreation Assn., 1917-56; sec. Nat. Recreation Congress, 1923-56; organizer 1st Internat. Recreation Congress, Los Angeles, 1932; an organizer Nat. Recreation Sch., 1926, sec., 1926-36; sec. Nat. and Inter-Am. Music Week Com., 1942-56; dir.-gen. World Recreation and Leisure Time Assn. (formerly Internat. Recreation Assn.), 1956-74, cons., dir., 1974-77; numerous trips abroad at request of various agencies, 1952-73. Recipient 1st class decoration Iran, 1956; Pat on Back award Sports Illus. mag., 1959; John Perry Bowditch award Sportsmanship Brotherhood, 1960; Honor of Merit, Provincial Council, Trujillo, Peru, 1963; award of merit Westchester County Recreation and Park Soc., 1967; 4th class Order Rising Sun (Japan); World Understanding citation Bronxville Rotary Club, 1970; Tom and Ruth Rivers Scholarship Fund established by Internat. Recreation Assn., 1970. Mem. Am. Recreation Soc., Nat. Recreation and Park Assn., Nat. Social Welfare Assembly, Soc. Internat. Devel., Internat. Conf. Social Work, Asia Soc., Japan Soc. Home: Bronxville, N.Y. Died Aug. 2, 1977; ashes scattered at sea.

ROACH, JAMES, newspaperman; b. Bklyn., Dec. 20, 1907; s. John Lewis and Margaret (Pilkington) R.; B.S., N.Y. U., 1929; m. Allene Zillmann, Jan. 17, 1953; children—Margaret, Marion. Sports staff New York World, 1928-31; sports staff New York Times, 1931-73, sports editor, 1958-73; pub. info. dir. N.Y. State Racing and Wagering Bd., 1973-77; free lance writer, 1977-78. Served as lt. USNR, 1943-46. Home: Douglaston, N.Y. Died Mar. 16, 1978; cremated.

ROARK, ELDON, columnist; b. Clinton, La., Aug. 24, 1897; s. Eldon Felix and Sarah Vallie (White) R.; student, La. State U., 1919-20; m. Lorena McClendon, April 17, 1925; children—Eldon Felix III (dec.), Eldon Felix IV (dec.), Selva Lorraine Rorabaugh. Newspaper and publicity work, Baton Rouge, Shreveport, New Orleans 1920-25, mem. staff Memphis Press-Scimitar 1925-79, writer column, Strolling, 1933-79. Served as pvt. USAAF, 1918. Received Nat. Headliners Club award for best feature column in U.S. during 1947, 48; Ernie Pyle award, 1954, Memphis Humane Soc. award, 1970. Served as pvt. A.A.F. U.S. Army, 1918. Baptist. Mem. Am. Newspaper Guild. Baptist. Author: Memphis Bragabouts, 1945; Just a Mutt, 1947; Work Is My Play, 1973, rev. edit. Together We Build, 1978. Author of short stories and articles in mags. Home: Memphis, Tenn. Died May 1, 1979; buried Memphis Meml. Park.

ROBB, JOHN FRANKLIN, patent lawyer; b. Wakeeney, Kan., May 16, 1884; s. Silas C. and Hattie M. R.; LL.B., Nat. Univ. Law Sch., Washington, D.C., 1902, LL.M., 1903; M.P.L., Columbian (now George Washington) U., 1904; m. Stella F. Worthington, Oct. 14, 1909; children—John W., Frank B., Winifred C. Practiced at Washington, 1900-18, Cleveland since 1918; now sr. mem. Robb & Robb of Cleveland, O., and Washington, D.C. Member Cleveland Bar Assn., Cleveland Patent Law Association, American Bar Association. Mason. Clubs: City, Kiwanis, Optimist. Author: Robb's Patent Essentials, 1922, 2d edition, 1928; (thesis) A Complete Program for the Improvement of the United States Patent Law System, 1929 (2d prize, Linthicum Fndn., Northwestern Univ.); The Arbitration of Patent Controversies, 1943. Home: Cleveland Heights. *

ROBBINS, FREDERIC JOHN, steel co. exec.; b. Kankakee, Ill., June 17, 1910; s. John F. and Rose M. (Preisel) R.; B.S., Colo. State Coll. Edn., 1933; Sc.D., Pomona Coll.; m. Doris A. Whitmer, Aug. 26, 1938; children—Franklyn W., Melodie M. (Mrs. James Rice), Phillip L. Metallurgist, Lindberg Steel Treating Co., Chgo., 1934-36; metall. engr. Bliss & Laughlin, Harvey, Ill., 1936-43; v.p., tech. dir. Pendleton Tool Industries (formerly Proto Tool Co., now Ingersoll Rand), Los Angeles, 1943-57; pres. Sierra Drawn Steel Corp., Los Angeles, 1946-60, Metall. Consultants, Inc., Montebello, Calif., 1954-60, dir., from 1954; pres. Phillips-Robbins, Inc., Los Angeles, 1958-62; pres., chief exec. officer, dir. Bliss & Laughlin Industries, Inc., Oak Brook, Ill., 1960-73; dir. Emhart Corp., Electronic Mem. and Mag. Corp., Fredor Industries. Trustee Pomona Coll., Claremont, Calif., 1976-80; past nat. trustee, del. First World Met. Congress. Registered profl. engr., Calif. Mem. Am. Soc. Metals, Newcomen Soc. N. Am., Am. Soc. Metals, ASTM, Soc. Automotive Engrs. Club: Rotary. Home: Rancho Santa Fe, Calif. Died May 10, 1980.

ROBBINS, LAURENCE LAMSON, physician; b. Burlington, Vt., Mar. 26, 1911; s. George E. and Grace L. (Lamson) R.; student Ohio Wesleyan Coll., 1929-32; BS., U. Vt., 1935, M.D., 1937, Sc.D. (hon.), 1973; m. Ruth Dick, Feb. 18, 1932; children—Dick L., Carol, Janice. Rotating intern Mary Fletcher Hosp., Burlington, 1937-38, resident, instr pathology and roentgenology, 1938-39; resident radiology Mass. Gen. Hosp., 1939-41, radiologist, 1941-46, radiologist-in-chief, 1946-71, radiologist, 1971-80, Aubrey O. Hampton lectr., 1972; asso. clin. prof. radiology Harvard Med. Sch., 1954-60, clin. prof., 1960-69, prof. radiology, 1969—. Holmes lectr. N.. Roentgen Ray Soc 1956; vis. prof Brazilian Coll. Radiology, 1972. Nat. Adv. Com. Radiation, 1964-67; adv. council radiation protection Dept. Pub. Health, 1965-80; sci. adv. bd. cons. Armed Forces Inst. Pathology, 1968-80; mem. med. radiation adv. com. Bur. Radiol Health, USPHS, 1968-80, chmn., 1962-80; cons. to surgeon gen. Navy, 1972-80. Bd. dirs. James Picker Found., 1963-80, pres. bd. 1964-69. Mem. Radiol. Soc. N.A. (pres. 1959; Gold medal 1968), N.E Roentgen Ray Soc. (pres. 1953-54), AMA (chmn. radiology 1955), Am. Bd. Radiology (pres. 1960-63, trustee 1954-72), Am. Roentgen Ray Soc., Am. Coll. of Radiology (Gold medal 1970), Alpha Omega Alpha. Author: Roentgen Interpretation, 1955 Editor: Golden's Diagnostic Radiology, 1959. Home: Winchester, Mass. Died Mar. 4, 1980.

ROBBINS, ROBERT R., educator; b. Dayton, Ohio, Feb. 17, 1909; s. Bert O. and Lulu (Beamer) R.; A.B., Ohio State U., 1932, M.A., 1934, Ph.D., 1941; grad. study, Alliance Francaise, Paris, France, 1933, Harvard, 1937-38, Acad. Internat. Law, The Hague, 1936, U. Mich.; A.M.L.D., Fletcher Sch. Law and Diplomacy, 1940; A.M., Columbia, 1943; m. Rebecca Nichols, Sept. 3, 1941 (dec. Apr. 1970); children—Sarah Brooks (Mrs. Lorenzo M. Horne), David Sears. Instr., asst. prof. govt. Tufts Coll., 1935-42; asst. prof. polit. sci. Ohio State U., 1946; specialist on dependent area affairs U.S. Dept. State, 1946-47, exec. cheif, 1948-49; exec. asst. to dir. gen. Internat. Refugee Orgn., 1947-48; officer-in-charge non-self-governing Territories Affairs, 1949-53, dep.-dir. Office Dependent Area Affairs, 1953-56; Carnegie fellow Council on Fgn. Relations, Inc., N.Y.C., 1956-57; research asso. Columbia U., 1956-57; prof. polit. sci., from 1957, chmn. dept. polit. sci. Tufts U., 1957-69, prof. Fletcher Sch. Law and Diplomacy, 1957-74, Jackson prof. polit. sci., 1958-74, prof., emeritus, 1974-80. U.S. mem. working com. Caribbean Commn., 1949-54, acting U.S. sr. commr., 1953; alternate U.S. commr. S. Pacific Commn., from 1951, acting sr. commr., 1951, U.S. acting sr. commr., 1953, to S. Pacific Conf., 1950, 53; mem. U.S. delegations U.N. meetings, including 4th, 8th, 9th, 10th Gen. Assemblies; U.S. mem. UN Vis. Mission to Togolands, 1955; 1st legistive counsel Congress Micronesia, 1965; spl. polit. adviser Trust Ty. Pacific Islands, 1965-66. Mem. corp. Lawrence Meml. Hosp; bd. dirs. Royall House Assn.; mem. alumni council Tufts U.; chmn. bd. trustees Unitarian-Universalist Ch. of Medford, vice chmn. bd. dirs. CLF Unitarian-Universalist, 1978-80. Served from lt. (j.g.) to comdr. USNR, 1942-46, comdg. officer, 1954, Internat. Affairs Co. Mem. Am. Soc. Internat. Law, Am. Polit. Sci. Assn., New Eng. Polit. Assn. (pres. 1970), ACLU, Phi Mu Alpha Sinfonia. Editor: State Government and Public Responsibility, Vol. 1, 1959, Vol. 2, 1960, Vol. 3, 1961, Vol. 4, 1962, Vol. 5, 1964, Vol. 6, 1965. Contbr. articles to profl. jours. Ency. Americana. Home: West Medford, Mass. Died May 25, 1980.

ROBERSON, FOY (ROB'ER-SUN), surgeon; b. Chapel Hill, N.C., Sept. 9, 1884; s. Abner Benton and Cornelia Adeline (Stone) R.; pre-med. student Univ. of N.C.; M.D., Jefferson Med. College, Phila., 1909; m. Helen Gribble, Dec. 10, 1914; children—Clara Cunningham, Foy (lt. U.S. Army Air Corps, killed Dec. 21, 1941), Helen Cornelia. Practiced at Durham since 1912; surgeon to Watts Hosp., State Hosp. for Insane, Raleigh; cons. surgeon Lincoln Hosp.; local surgeon Southern Ry.; mem. visiting staff Duke Hosp.; mem. State Board of Med. Examiners of N.C. (pres. 1930-31), chief surg. staff Watts Hosp., Durham, N.C. Formerly chmn. City and County Bd. of Health; ex-pres. Y.M.C.A.; trustee Lincoln Hosp. Apptd. by Gov. Gardner, mem. bd. dirs. State Prison of N.C.; v.p. Tri-State Med. Soc., 1933-34; acting dir. U. of N.C. Infirmary, 1933; mem. City Planning and Zoning Com., Durham. Chief of Med. Advisory Board Durham County, World War I. Formerly Col., M.C., Army of U.S.; chief Surgical Service, McCloskey General Hospital, Temple, Tex. Returned to civilian practice. Elected a trustee of the Univ. of North Carolina (eight year term). Member Founders' Group American Board of Surgery. Member National Subsidiary Board Medical Examiners. Fellow Am. Coll. Surgeons, Southern Surg. Assn. (v.p.); mem. A.M.A., Durham County Med. Soc., Kappa Alpha; alumni rep. U. of N.C. Athletic Council 10 yrs. Trustee U. of North Carolina (8 yr. term). Democrat. Presbyterian, Mason. Elk. Home: Durham, N.C. *

ROBERT, LAWRENCE WOOD, JR., cons. engineer; b. Monticello, Ga., Sept. 3, 1889; s. Lawrence Wood and Minnie Preston (Newton) R.; C.E., Ga. Sch. Tech., Atlanta, 1908, E.E., 1909; m. Louisa Godwin Ayres, Feb. 2, 1910; children—Lawrence Wood, III, Mrs. Grant LeRoux; m. 2d, Evelyn Walker, Oct. 11, 1935; 1 dau., Alice Birney, Practiced in Atlanta from 1919; engr. with Dallas and Co., then mem. Dallas-Robert Co.; now chmn., treas. Robert & Co., Inc., also Robert & Co. Assos., architects, engrs.; director Macon, Dublin & Savanah Ry. Co., Central of Georgia R.R. Co., Carolina Textiles, Incorporated; assistant secretary of the Treasury in charge of Public Works, 1933-36; treas. and secretary Dem. Nat. Committee, 1936-41. Director Navy League of Am.; v.p. 6th Naval Dist. Mem. bd. of regents State of Georgia. Member Am. Soc. C.E., M.E., Inst. E.E., Mgt. Soc., Am. Soc. professional Engrs. Sigma Nu, Phi Kappa Phi. Democrat. Mason. Elk. Episcopalian. Clubs: Capitol City Athletic, Piedmont Driving, Peachtree Golf (Atlanta); Arkwright, City, Twenty Nine (New York); Racquet, University, Nat. Press, Burning Tree (Wash.). Address: Atlanta, Ga. Died June 9, 1976.

ROBERT, SARAH EMILY CORBIN, teacher, lecturer; b. Williamsport, Pa., Aug. 26, 1886; d. William Wallace and Emma Flora (Hamilton) Corbin; A.B., Syracuse (N.Y.) U., 1909; student Columbia U., summers 1925, 29; hon. Litt.D., Lincoln Mem. Univ., 1940; m. Henry Martyn Robert, Jr., Aug. 26, 1919; 1 son, Henry Martyn, 3d. Taught history in pub. schs. of Brocton, N.Y., 1909-11, Rome, N.Y., 1911-14, Atlantic City, N.J., 1914-19; conducted spl. courses in parliamentary law, summers, U. of Md. and Columbia; lectured on parliamentary law before women's clubs and societies; speaker on Americanism and Am. citizenship in every state of the Union and has given radio broadcasts on same subjects frequently, 1935-41. Exec. dir. Annapolis' 300th Anniversary Celebration, 1949. Mem. Nat. Soc. Daughters Am. Revolution (treas. gen., 1935-38; pres. gen., 1938-41), Daughters of Founders and Patriots of Am. (nat. v.p. and recording sec., 1931-37), Colonial Dames of Am., Daughters of Colonial Wars, Alpha Phi. Lectured widely on adjusting meetings to the needs of war, 1942-45. Decorated Huguenot Cross (Huguenot Soc. Pa.), B.F. Goodrich award for "distinguished public service." Clubs: Arundel (Baltimore, Md.), Colonial Dames (Washington, D.C.). Author of articles on history research and parliamentary law. Home: Annapolis, Md. *

ROBERTS, ALCWYN LLOYD, clergyman, ret. church exec.; b. Youngstown, O., Mar. 9, 1910; s. Richard Lloyd and Elizabeth Ann (Lewis) R.; student Youngstown Coll., 1927-29; A.B., Ohio Wesleyan U., 1931; B.D., Yale Div. Sch., 1939; D.D., Mo. Valley Coll., 1954; m. Wilmena Barbara Rippe, Sept. 21, 1934; children—William Lloyd, Patricia Ann, David Lewis. Ordained to ministry Presbyn. Ch. U.S.A., 1939; staff Youngstown YMCA, 1927-29; pastor, also dir. religious edn. Asheville Farm Sch., Swannanoa, N.C., 1934-41; asst. sec. rural ch. Indian work Bd. Nat. Missions, Presbyn. Ch. U.S.A., 1941-42, asst. sec. dept. missionary operation, 1942-44, sec. for personnel service, 1944-47, asso. adminstrv. sec., 1947-49, asst. to gen. sec., also clk., 1951-53; field rep. Synod of Fla. Presbyn. Ch. U.S.A. 1949-51; gen. dir. Commn. on Gen. Christian Edn. also asso. exec. sec. Div. Christian Edn., Nat. Council of Chs. of Christ in U.S.A., 1953-63; sec. for inter-church agys. Commn. on Ecumenical Mission and Relations, U.P. Ch. in U.S.A., 1963-66, asso. sec. gen. council, 1968-73; archivist Warren Wilson Coll. Chmn. com. on indsl. communities Christian Commn. on Camp and Def. Communities, World War II; mem. adminstrv. and exec. coms. Home Missions Council of N.A., 1941-49; dir. Student Vol. Movement, 1944-48; exec. bd., chmn. philanthropic commn. Fla. Council Chs., 1949-51. Bd. dirs. Religion in Am. Life. Mem. Religious Edn. Assn., Phi Kappa Tau, Theta Alpha Phi. Home: Swannanoa, N.C. Died Oct. 28, 1976; buried Warren Wilson Coll. Cemetery, Swannanoa.

ROBERTS, ARTHUR EDWIN, exec. emeritus Boy Scouts Am.; b. Plymouth, Pa., June 15, 1886; s. Robert Franklin and Sarah (Evans) R.; student George Williams Coll., 1912-15, Chicago Sch. Civics and Philanthropy, 1915-16, U. of Chicago, 1916-17, war prodn. course Harvard, 1943-44; A.M., Marietta Coll., 1941; LL.D., Hanover Coll., 1949; m. Georgina Frankboner Feb. 22, 1919; children—Hugh, William, Martha Lloyd (Mrs. Tipton Sewell Ross). Pioneered youth programs on Redpath Chautauqua, 1913; surveyed youth conditions at golf clubs for Chicago Dist. Golf Assn., summers 1914-16, originating graded plan recommended by U.S. Golf Assn.; nat. field scout commr. Boy Scouts of Am., 1917-18, scout exec. Cincinnati (O.) Area Council since 1919, mem. various coms. including survey youth activities world wide, 1924-38; lecturer 1924—; began Boy's Hobby Fairs; organized Cincinnati Knot-Hole Club with 30,000 mems., 1934; mem. distinguished visitors com. Nat. Jamboree, 1937, 1950; mem. Chief Scout Execs. Staff Nat. Jamboree, 1950; made scout exec. emeritus by nat. council, 1951; now on personnel staff, mem. faculty & student advisor, Tech. Tng. Center, Cin. Milling Machine Co. Served in U.S. Army, 1918-19; with A.E.F.; hon. col., Ky. N.G., 1930. Decorated Victory medal (U.S.). Apptd. mem. naval coll. training program selection com., by U.S. Sec. of Navy, 1943. Mem. most Cinn. civic coms.; dir. Red Cross flood rescue work, Cincinnati, 1937; vice chmn. Hamilton County Scrap Conservation com. since 1941. Awarded gold medal Chicago Dist. Golf Assn., 1914, 2d Am. to receive Hornaday gold medal, 1929, civic award by Cincinnati Citizens Com., 1941. Mem. Am. Legion, Disabled Vets. of World War, Internat. Rotary, Internat. Torch. Presbyterian. Scottish Rite, Shriner. Author several books, 1914—. Home: Cincinnati, O. *

ROBERTS, CECIL, author; b. Nottingham, Eng., May 18, 1892; s. John Wellesley R.; student Kings Coll., London; hon. LL.D., Washington and Jefferson University. Literary editor Liverpool Post, 1914; dir. munitions transport, American Dept., Ministry of Munitions, 1915; official war correspondent, Brit. Navy and on Western Front, 1916-18; editor Nottingham Journal, 1920-25; literary editor Sphere, 1925-30; novelist and dramatist from 1923. Examining officer British Civil Liberties Commission, 1920. Mem. British Mission to U.S., 1940-45. Fellow Royal Geographical Society, Royal Soc. Lit. Clubs: Royal Automobile, Royal Societies, Athenaeum. Author numerous books and plays; latest publs.: And So To Rome, 1950; A Terrace in the Sun, 1951; Selected Poems, 1960; The Growing Boy, 1967; The Years of Promise, 1968; The Bright Twenties, 1970; Sunshine and Shadow, 1972; The Pleasant Years, 1974. Home: Rome, Italy, Died 1976.

ROBERTS, FLOYD MOSES, photographer; b. Ramsey, Ill., May 15, 1909; s. William Mack and Mary Elizabeth (Poland) R.; diploma Ill. Coll. Photography, 1928, Winona Sch. Profl. Photography, 1931; certificate U. Mich., 1935; M. Profl. Photography, Profl. Photographers Am., 1970, Craftsman Profl. Photography, 1968; B. Profl. Arts, Brooks Inst., 1970; m. Helen Eunice Todd, Oct. 28, 1939; children—Sharon Dee (Mrs. George Marich), Margaret Ann (Mrs. Richard Franz). Gen. asst. Covert Studio, St. Louis, Mich., 1928-31; lab. technician Dey Studio, Ann Arbor, Mich., 1931-35; Harris & Ewing, Washington, 1935-36; photographer Genelli Studio, Sioux City, Iowa, 1936-43; pres. Roberts Studio, Los Angeles, 1944-67; photo. cons., Long Beach, Calif., 1967-79; judge exhbn. photography, 1964-79; SCORE councilor for SBA, 1976-79. Vice pres. Arts and Scis. Found., 1967-71. Mem. Profl. Photographers So. Calif. (pres. 1953-54), Profl. Photographers Calif. (pres. 1955-56), Profl. Photographers Am. (portrait council 1960-71, v.p.1969-70, pres 1970-71, chmn. bd. 1971-79, Quarter Century Club). Republican. Lutheran. Clubs: Masons, Shriners, Elks. Address: Long Beach, Calif. Died July 20, 1979.

ROBERTS, HENRY LAMAR, physician; b. Macon, Ga., Sept. 2, 1919; s. Warren and Camille (Lamar) R.; A.B., U. Tex., 1941; M.D., Duke, 1944; M.Sc., McGill U., 1949, Ph.D., 1952, diploma neurosurgery, 1953; m. Louise Voelcker, Nov. 28, 1942; children—Sherry (Mrs. Clyde Martin), Lamar, Camille, Heather, Renee, Katherine, Herbert. Intern Duke Hosp., 1944-45; asst. and asso. neurosurgeon Montreal Neurol. Inst., 1955-58; neurosurgeon Univ. Hosp., Gainesville, Fla., 1958-71, Munroe Meml. Hosp., Ocala, Fla., 1971-78; lectr. neurosurgery McGill U., 1955-58; asso. prof. to prof. neurosurgery U. Fla. Served as lt. M.C., USNR, 1945-46, 53-54. Mem. Fla. Med. Assn., Marion County Med. Soc., Am. Assn. Neurol. Surgery, Congress Neurol. Surgery, AAAS, Forum Univ. Neurosurgeons, Am. Epilepsy Soc., Sigma Xi. Author: (with Wilder Penfield) Speech and Brain Mechanisms, 1959. Contbr. articles sci. jours. Home: Ocala, Fla. Died July 5, 1978.

ROBERTS, JOHN STUART, chain store exec.; b. Gloucester, Ohio; grad. high sch.; m. Therese Roberts; children—John, Karen Roberts Soeder, Holly. With FW. Woolworth Co., 1940, corp. v.p., from 1961, later pres.; dir. Crum & Forster Ins. Co., First Nat. State Bank Corp., Hamilton Investment Trust; chmn Lower Manhattan adv. bd. Chem. Bank. Clubs: Baltusrol (pres.), Pine Valley Golf (pres.), Canoe Brook Country (pres.). Home: Harding Township, N.J. Died Nov. 28, 1979.

ROBERTS, RACHEL, actress; b. Llanelly, Wales, Sept. 20, 1927; d. Richard Rhys and Rachel Ann Roberts; B.A. in English, U. Wales; student Royal Acad. Dramatic Art; m. Alan Dobie, 1955 (div. 1960); m. 2d, Rex Harrison, 1962 (div. 1971). Joined Shakespeare Meml. Theatre, Stratford-on-Avon, 1951; appeared Watergate Theatre, London, 1953; theater appearances include Alpha Beta, London, Eng., The Visit and Chemin de Fer, 1973, New Phoenix Repertory Co., N.Y.C., The Effect of Gamma Rays on Man-in-the Moon Marigolds, Los Angeles, 1971, Once a Catholic, 1979; films include The Good Companions, 1957, The Weak and the Wicked, Valley of Song, Our Man in Havana, 1959, Saturday Night and Sunday Morning, 1961, Girl on Approval, This Sporting Life, 1963, Doctors' Wives, 1971, O Lucky Man, 1973, Alpha Beta, 1976, Foul Play, 1978, others; also revues also numerous TV appearances including Jonathan North, Circus, Time, Sunday Out of Season, Shadow Squad, regular on The Tony Randall Show, ABC-TV, 1976-78. Recipient Clarence Derwent award; Brit. Acad. award for Saturday Night and Sunday Morning, This Sporting

Life; London Evening Standard best actress award Alpha Beta. Died Nov. 26, 1980.

ROBERTS, RICHARD BROOKE, scientist; b. Titusville, Pa., Dec. 7, 1910; s. Erastus Titus and Helen Troth (Chambers) R.; grad. St. Paul's Sch., 1928; A.B., Princeton, 1932, M.A. (Queen fellow 1933), 1933, Ph.D. in Physics, 1937; m. Adeline Furness, Nov. 20, 1935; children—Richard F., Helen Juliette (Mrs. James Haley); m. 2d, Irena Zuzanna Eiger, Dec. 22, 1948; 1 son, Edward Thomas; m. 3d, Josephine Taggart, Jan. 7, 1967. Fellow Carnegie Instn., Washington, 1937-39, staff mem. dept. terrestrial magnetism, 1939-80; physicist Applied Physics Lab., Johns Hopkins, 1943-46; spl. research nuclear physics, 1935-41, devel proximity fuse, fire control, guided missiles, 1941-46, biophysics, 1947-80. Vice chmn. com. sci. and tech. Democratic Adv. Council, 1959-60. Recipient Medal of Merit, 1947. Fellow Am. Phys. Soc., Washington Acad. Sci., A.A.A.S. (v.p. 1966-67); mem. Nat. Acad. Scis., Biophys. Soc. (pres. 1964-65), Am. Soc. Microbiology, Am. Soc. Cellular Biology, Biochem. Soc., Soc. Cincinnati, Phi Beta Kappa, Sigma Xi. Club: Cosmos (Washington). Co-author: Studies of Biosynthesis in E. Coli, 1955. Editor: Microsomal Particals and Protein Synthesis, 1958; Studies of Macromolecular Biosynthesis, 1964. Home: Washington, D.C. Died Apr. 4, 1980; buried Watertown, N.Y.

ROBERTS, SHEPHERD MCGREGOR, SR., steel mcht.; b. Chgo., Apr. 19, 1893; s. Charles Aaron and Cora (Hicks) R.; student pub. schs.; m. Marguerite Dixon, May 26, 1917; children—Charles S., Shepherd M., John H. With Crerar, Adams & Co., ry. supplies, Chgo., 1911-16; v.p. C. A. Roberts Co., Chgo., 1917, 1926, pres., 1926-62, chmn. bd. dirs., 1962-80. Served as lt., Ordnance Dept., U.S Army 1917-19. Mem. Steel Service Center Inst., Farm Equipment Inst. Aux. Clubs: Glen View, Question, Chgo. (Chgo.); Paradise Valley Country (Phoenix). Home: Winnetka, Ill. Died Nov. 6, 1980.

ROBERTS, WILLIAM GOODRIDGE, artist; b. Barbados, B.W.I., Sept. 24, 1904; s. Theodore Goodridge and Frances (Allen) R.; student pub. schs., also Ecole des Beaux Arts, Montreal, 1924-26, Art Students League, N.Y.C., 1927-29; LL.D., U. N.B., 1960; m. Marian Willson, Dec. 19, 1933; m. 2d, Joan Carter, July 2, 1954; 1 son, Timothy Gostwick; 1 stepdau., Glynnis Thomas. Resident artist Queen's U., Kingston, Ont., 1933-36; instr. Sch. Art, Montreal Mus. Fine Arts, 1939-52; vis. fellow U. N.B., 1959-60; over 30 one-man exhbns. in Can., one in Paris, 1954; exhibited at N.Y. World's Fair, Pitts. Internat., 26th Venice Biennale, 1st and 2d Sao Paulo Bienal, Internat. exhbn., Valencia, Venezuela, 1955, Pan Am. Exhbn., Mexico, 1958, Brussels World Fair 1958, Tate Gallery, London, 1964, Expo '67, Montreal, 1967, Nat. Gallery of Can. Retrospective, 1969-70; permanent collections Nat. Gallery of Can., Montreal Mus. Fine Arts, Que. Provincial Mus., Toronto Art Gallery, Vancouver Art Gallery, Winnipeg Art Gallery, Hamilton Gallery. Ofcl. war artist RCAF, 1943-45. Painting Quebec Landscape presented to Queen Elizabeth by RCAF Assn., 1954. Can. govt. overseas fellow, 1953-54. Mem. Can. Group of Painters, Water Color Soc. Can., Soc. Graphic Arts, Royal Can. Acad. Home: Westmount, Que., Can. Died Jan. 28, 1974.

ROBERTSON, C(HARLES) A(RCHIBALD), univ. prof.; b. Iamonia, Fla., March 20, 1895; s. William Fitzgerald and Katherine Plair (Bannerman) R.; A.B., U. of Fla., 1915, M.A., 1919; grad. student, Harvard, 1919-22, 27; Litt.D., The University of the South, 1952, U. Fla., 1969; m. Alleyne Redding, August 12, 1926. Teaching fellow, U. of Fla., 1917-19, asst. prof. Eng., 1922-27, asso. prof., 1927-28, prof., from 1928, acting head dept. of English, 1934-36, acting chmn., div. of lang. and lit., 1942-45, chmn., war training courses in English, 1943-45, chmn., division of language and literature, 1946-50, head prof. English from 1950, hon. curator rare books U. Fla. Library, 1965-75. Mem. grad. council, Univ. Fla. Mem. Modern Lang. Assn. Am., S. Atlantic Mod. Lang. Assn. (pres. 1950-51), Fla. Edn. Assn., Am. Assn. of Univ. Profs., Kappa Alpha, Phi Kappa Phi, Phi Beta Kappa. Mem. editorial bd., Southern Folklore Quarterly; Humanities Monographs, U. Fla. Contbr. articles to S. Atlantic Bull., Jour. of Politics, S. Folklore Quarterly. Home: Gainesville, Fla. Died Jan. 5, 1975; interred Tallahassee, Fla.

ROBERTSON, RALPH K., army officer; b. New York, Apr. 24, 1883; B.A., Cornell U., 1904, LL.B., 1906; commd. 2d lt. Inf., N.Y. Nat. Guard, Dec. 1906, and advanced to capt. when he entered Fed. service, June 19, 1916, for Mexican border service and World War I, commd. lt. col. Inf., N.Y. Nat. Guard, May 1922, and advanced to brig. gen. of the line, June 1937; entered Fed. service Sept. 1940 and assumed command of 87th Inf. Brigade, 44th Div. in training, Fort Dix, N.J.; transferred to Second Corps Area Service Command, Governors Island, N.Y., Sept. 1941.*

ROBEY, JOHN MURRAY, publicist, journalist; b. Billingsley, Md., Jan. 9, 1901; s. Milton and Martha Elgin (Clements) R.; attended Charlotte Hall Mil. Acad.; Western Md. Coll., 1919-23; m. Eleanor Elizabeth Glotfelty, Oct. 20, 1923; children—Eleanor Jane (Mrs. Harvey Flemister), Elizabeth Joan (Mrs. James Betsill, Jr.), John M. Jr., Elaine Joy. Asso. editor mag. Pathfinder, 1923-32, mng. editor, 1932-36, asso. editor, 1936-40, mng. editor and mem. bd. trustees, 1941; dir. (editor) Feature Div., Press Dept., Office Inter-Am. Affairs, Washington, 1942-45, directing press informational program for Western Hemisphere; chief, Editorial Branch, Div. Internat. Press and Publications, Office of Internat. Info., U.S. Dept. State, editing world-wide documentary feature program, 1946-50; chief Program Evaluation and Information Staff 1951-52; chief pubs., Latin Am. br., USIA, 1952-55, Internat. Cultural Service, 1955-57, policy application staff Press and Publs. Service, 1957-64; farmer, Md. Recipient Excellence in Journalism Award, Western Md. Coll., 1950. Episcopalian. Past grand and past chief patriarch Ind. Order of Odd Fellows. Home: White Plains, Md. Died Nov. 26, 1975.

ROBICHAUD, GERARD ALARIC, newspaperman; b. Chicopee Falls, Mass., Mar. 19, 1912; s. Joseph A. and Flordia M. (Demers) R.; B.S., N.M. Sch. Mines, 1933; postgrad. Boston U., 1934-35; m. Pauline C. Wilkinson, Oct. 15, 1938; 1 dau., Judith (deGuevara). Mining, civil engr., 1933-34; reporter Holyoke (Mass.) Transcript-Telegram, 1935-36; N.E. night mgr. United Press, Boston, 1936-37; became Washington corr. for U.P., 1937, Chgo. Sun, 1943; chief Washington bur., Chgo. Sun-Times (formerly Sun), 1946-50, editorial writer 1951-59; Latin Am. corr. for Chgo. Daily News, 1959, editorial writer, 1966-73; dir. Chgo. Daily News/Sun-Times News Service, 1973-75; free-lance fgn. corr., 1975-79. Mem. Am. Acad. Polit. and Social Sci., Mil. Order Carabao (Washington), Fgn. Corrs. Assn. Mexico, Sigma Delta Chi (profl. chpt.). Clubs: Chicago Press; American (Rio de Janiero); Nat. Press Club (chmn. bd. govs. 1950). Contbr. reviews, articles and poetry to nat. mags. Home: Oaxaca, Mexico. Died Feb. 12, 1978.

ROBIE, EDWARD HODGES (RO'BE), metallurgical engr.; b. Whitney Point, N.Y., Nov. 30, 1886; s. Harry Adams and Alma (Hodges) R.; grad. Western High Sch., Washington, D.C., 1906; student Cornell U., 1907-08; B. Chem. Engring., U. of Mich., 1911; m. Agnes Purcell Parks, Oct. 10, 1914;—children—Robert Hodges, Theodore Parks (dec.), Edward Adams, John Adams (dec.). Water softening work, with Harrison Safety Boiler Works, Phila., 1911-13; metall. work, Canadian Copper Co. and Internat. Nickel Co., Copper Cliff, Ont., 1913-19, advancing to asst. metallurgist, with spl. work in the West, investigating milling and smelting problems; with Engineering and Mining Jour., 1919-31, acting editor, 1927; asst. sec. Am. Inst. Mining and Metall. Engrs. and editor Mining and Metallurgy mag. 1932-48, sec., 1949-55, sec. emeritus, 1955-56; cons. engr., 1956-58, sec. corrosion research council, 1958-59, asst. to chmn., 1959-60. Mem. gifts com. United Engring. Center Bldg. Fund, 1958-60. Mem. Am. Inst. Mech. Engrs. (sec.), Canadian Inst. Mining and Metallurgy, Am. Inst. Mining, Metall. and Petroleum Engrs. Club: Mining. Editor: Economics of the Mineral Industries, 1959. Home: Yorktown Heights, N.Y.*

ROBINSON, ADAH M(ATILDA), univ. prof., designer; b. Richmond, Ind, July 13, 1882; d. Francis Wills and Kathryn (Haberkern) Robinson; student Art Inst., Chicago, 1904, 05, 08, 19, 21, 22; West End Sch. of Art, Provincetown, 1913-15, 1921, 22, 26, 31, 34; Tulsa Univ., 1936. Prof. art, Tulsa U., 1927-45. Trinity U., San Antonio, since 1945. Interior designer First Ch. Christ Scientist, Tulsa, 1935, Bartlesville, Okla., 1936; designer, Boston Av., Ch., Tulsa, 1928. Paintings in permanent collections, Art Center, Okla. City; Philbrook Museum, Tulsa. Mem. Coll. Art Assn. (hon.), Prairie Printers, Art League of San Antonio, Delta Kappa Gamma. Mem. Soc. of Friends. Home: San Antonio, Tex. *

ROBINSON, C(HARLES) S(UMMERS), biochemist; b. Chicago, Apr. 17, 1885; s. Joseph Sacre and Harriet Davis (Smith) R.; student U. of Ill., 1903-05; A.B., U. of Mich, 1907, M.S., 1909, Ph.D., 1917; student Cambridge U., 1928; m. Florence Sherwood, Sept. 21, 1912. Asso. chemist Mich. Agrl. Expt. Sta., 1909-27, chemist, 1927-31; asso. Rockefeller Inst., 1917-18; prof. biochem., Vanderbilt U. Med. Sch. since 1931. Mem. Tenn. Bd. basic sci. examiners since 1945. Mem. Am, Chem. Soc., Am. Soc. Biol. Chemists, A.A.A.S., Soc. Exptl. Biol. and Med., Soc. Sigma Xi, Sigma Alpha Epsilon. Author, reports of investigations in agrl. and med. biochemistry. Home: Franklin, Tenn. *

ROBINSON, DANIEL SOMMER, educator; b. North Salem, Ind., Oct. 19, 1888; s. William and Lucretia (Cassity) R.; B.A., Butler Coll., 1910; student Yale Grad. Sch. and Div. Sch., 1910-13, M.A., 1911, B.D., 1912; Dwight traveling fellow and student Breslau U., Germany, 1912-13; Ph.D., Harvard, 1917; Litt.D., Marietta (Ohio) Coll., 1937; m. Oma Glasburn, June 6, 1912 (dec.); children—Daniel Sommer (dec.), Joan (Mrs. Charles R. Clark), Sydney Caroline (Mrs. William J. Charles). Ordained Disciples ministry, 1910; pastor Christian Ch., Billings, Mont., 1913-14, S. Congl. Ch., Newport, N.H., 1917-18; instr. philosophy U. Wis., 1919-20, asst. prof., 1920-22; prof. philosophy Miami U., 1922-29; prof., head dept. philosophy Ind. U., 1929-39; pres. Butler U., Indpls., 1939-42; prof., dir. Sch. Philosophy, U. So. Calif., 1946-54, dir. emeritus, 1954-77; John Hay Whitney vis. prof. Bethany Coll., W.Va., 1954-56; lectr. Hill Family Found., Macalester Coll. and Hamline U., St. Paul, 1956-57; distinguished service prof. philosophy Bethany Coll., 1957-58; ret., 1958. Del., 9th Internat. Congress Philosophy, Paris, 1937. Mem. Ind. Hist. and Library Bd., 1940-42, Ind. Bd. Edn., 1940-42. Bd. dirs. Found. for Promotion Idealistic Philosophy Am., 1954-77. Served as lt. (j.g.) Chaplain Corps, USN, 1918-19; lt. comdr. to comdr., chaplain USNR, 1942-46. Recipient Bowdoin essay prize Harvard, 1916. Mem. Am. Philos. Assn. (pres. Western div. 1941-44, chmn. Harris centennial com. 1935), Mil. Chaplains Assn., Alpha Chi Rho, Republican. Conglist. Mason. Club: Twenty. Author: The Principles of Reasoning, 1924, 3d rev. edit., 1947; The God of the Liberal Christian, 1926; Introduction to Living Philosophy, 1932; Political Ethics, 1935; Principles of Conduct, 1948; Crucial Issues in Philosophy, 1955, Editor, compiler: Illustrations of the Methods of Reasoning, 1927; An Anthology of Recent Philosophy, 1929; An Anthology of Modern Philosophy, 1931; Royce's Logical Essays, 1951; Hoernle's Studies in Philosophy, 1952; Gomperz' Philosophical Studies, 1953; The Story of Scottish Philosophy, 1961. Contbr. chpts. to books, articles to profl. jours. Home: Los Angeles, Calif. Died Nov. 29, 1977; inurned Columbarium of the Dawn, The Great Mausoleum, Forest Lawn Meml. Park, Glendale, Calif.

ROBINSON, EDGAR EUGENE, historian; b. Oconomowoc, Wis., Apr. 5, 1887; s. George Edgar and Lydia Margaret (Bender) R.; A.B., U. Wis, 1908, fellow in Am. history, A.M., 1910, LL.D, 1942; m. Katherine Gertrude Young, Nov. 23, 1908 (dec.); m. 2d, Lisette Emery Fast, Sept. 10, 1970. Asst. in history, 1908-09, U. Wis.; instr. in history, Carleton Coll., Northfield, Minn., 1910-11; asst. prof. Am. history, 1911-18, asso. prof., 1918-23, prof. since 1923, also exec. head dept., 1929-52, Margaret Byrne prof. Am. history, 1931, Stanford U. lectr. in history U. Minn., 1915-16; acting asst. prof. history, summer session U. Mich., 1916; asst. ednl. dir. Northwestern Dist. S.A.T.C. War Dept., 1918; vis. prof. Am. history Yale, 1919-20; lectr. in Am. history U. Calif., 1924; dir. courses in problems citizenship, Stanford, 1923-35, chmn. U. com. on independent study plan, 1928-45, dir. Inst. Am. History, Stanford U., 1943-52; dir. Franklin D. Roosevelt Study under J. Brooks' B. Parker Award, 1952-54; dir. research study Commonwealth Club Calif., 1963-65; prof. history, Columbia, summer, 1926, U. Oreg., 1928, U. Calif., 1932. Adv. com. polit. statistics, U.S. Bur. Census, 1952-53. Recipient Freedoms Found. Award, 1950. Fellow Royal Hist. Soc. Gt. Britain; mem. Am. Hist. Assn., Pacific Coast Branch (pres. 1929), AAUP, English Speaking Union (pres. Cal. br. 1938-1941), Alpha Tau Omega, Phi Beta Kappa, Delta Sigma Rho. Clubs: Commonwealth of Calif. (pres. 1935, 36), Chit Chat (San Francisco) Author: The Foreign Policy of Woodrow Wilson (with V.J. West), 1917; Evolution of American Political Parties, 1924; The Presidential Vote (1896-1932), 1934; American Democracy in Time of Crisis, 1934; Independent Study at Stanford University, 1937; The Presidential Vote (1936), 1940; The New United States, 1946; They Voted for Roosevelt, 1947; Scholarship and Cataclysm, 1947; The Roosevelt Leadership (1933-45), 1955. Co-editor: The Memoirs of Ray Lyman Wilbur (1875-1949), 1960; (with V.D. Bornet) Herbert Hoover, President of the United States, 1975. Editor, contbr. Powers of the President in Foreign Affairs, 1966. Mem. editorial adv. bd. Ency. Brit., 1956-69. Died Sept. 7, 1977.

ROBINSON, ELSIE (pen name, maiden name Elsinore Justinia Robinson), newspaper columnist; b. Benicia, Calif., Apr. 30, 1883; d. Alexander and Elizabeth (Pearson) Robinson; ed. grammar and high schs. of Benicia, Calif.; m. Christie Crowell, 1903 (later divorced); 1 son, George (dec.); m. 2d, Rafael Demoro, 1926 (marriage annulled); m. 3d, Benton Fremont, (grandson of General John C. Fremont, "The Pathfinder"), 1933; one stepson, John C. Fremont. Newspaper and fiction writer since 1919; writes columns "Listen, World," and "Listen World to Young America" for King Features Syndicate. Author: I Wanted Out!, 1934. Mem. P.E.N. Club. Home: San Francisco, Calif.; also Tuolumne County, Calif. *

ROBINSON, FRANCIS ARTHUR, opera co. exec.; b. Henderson, Ky., Apr. 28, 1910; s. Robert Lee and Beulah Katherine (Cox) R.; B.A. cum laude, Vanderbilt U., 1932, M.A., 1933; Litt.D. (hon.), Westminster Choir Coll., 1969. With Nashville Banner, 1933-38, Sunday editor, 1935-38; writer, actor, producer Sta. WSM, Nashville, 1933-38; co. mgr., press rep. Cornelia Otis Skinner, 1938-39, Playwrights' Co., N.Y.C., 1938-40; pres. rep. Katharine Cornell, 1940-42, 46-48, Boston Symphony Orch., Berkshire Festival at Tanglewood, 1947-48; tour dir. Met. Opera Co., N.Y.C., 1948-80, head box office and subscription, 1950-62, asst. mgr., 1952-76, press dir., 1954-77; trustee Manhattan Sch. Music, 1969-80, Vanderbilt U., 1970-80. Chmn. music com., vestryman, warden St. Thomas Episcopal Ch., N.Y.C., 1974-80. Served to lt. USNR, 1942-45. Recipeint Handel medallion City of N.Y., 1972. Mem. Assn. Theatrical Press Agts. and Mgrs. (v.p. 1954-57). Author: Caruso: His Life in Pictures, 1957; Celebration: The Metropolitan Opera, 1979; author, narrator Biographies in Music, 1960-75, Heifetz for Bell Telephone program NBC, 1971; intermissions Met. Opera Telecasts, 1977-80, host, 1978-80; writer Bing Salute for Texaco-CBS TV, 1972. Home: New York, N.Y. Died May 14, 1980.

ROBINSON, FREDERICK FLOWER, aviation exec.; b. Watertown, N.Y., Oct. 21, 1904; s. Anson Flower and Marguerite (Williams) R.; Ph.B., Yale, 1927; m. Suzanne Spitzer, Feb. 21, 1937. With Nat. City Co., 1927-30, Tri-Continental Corp., 1930-33; treas. Continental Casuality Co., and Continentnal Assurance Co., 1934-37; asst. to pres. Libbey-Owens-Ford Glass Co., 1937-42; v.p., sec. Nat. Aviation Corp., 1942-45, pres., 1945-70, chmn. bd., 1970-71, chmn. emeritus, cons., 1971-77; dir. Collins Radio Co., Conrac Corp.; mem. adv. com. Bankers Trust Co. Bd. govs. Flight Safety Found. Dep. adminstr. NRA, 1933-34; asst. adminstr. Nat. Unemployment Census, 1937. Mem. Am. Inst. Aeros. and Astronautics, Transp. Assn. Am. (dir.). Home: New York, N.Y. Died July 7, 1977.

ROBINSON, HENRY LEON, educator; b. Los Angeles, Feb. 26, 1908; s. Joseph L. and Rosa (Alterescu) R.; A.B., U. Calif. at Los Angeles, 1928; Ph.D., U. Chgo., 1933; m. Ruth Elizabeth Cleghorn, May 21, 1939 (div. 1952); children—Penelope Carolle, Anthony Henry; m. 2d, Vernice T. Goodrich, Aug. 22, 1959. Asso. French, U. Calif. at Los Angeles, 1930-31; asst. Romance langs. U. Chgo., 1933-35; instr. Romance langs. Syracuse U., 1935-36; instr. fgn. langs. Amarillo Coll., 1936-46; asst. prof. Romance langs. U. Tenn., 1946-48; prof. French, chmn. dept. Baylor U., 1948-76, emeritus prof., 1976-80; condr. Amarillo Philharmonic Orch., 1936-38; newscaster KGNC, 1942-44; cons. French, Brit. World Lang. Dictionary. Recipient Palmes Académiques, 1965. Mem. AAUP, Am. Assn. Tchrs. French, Modern Lang. Assn., Phi Beta Kappa, Pi Delta Phi. Contbr. articles to profl. jours. Home: Waco, Tex. Died Feb. 18, 1980.

ROBINSON, JAMES JAQUESS, lawyer, judge; b. Owensville, Ind., July 14, 1893; s. Sylvester Benson and Hattie (Jaquess) R.; A.B. cum laude, Ind. U., 1914; LL.B., Harvard U., 1919, S.J.D., 1930; m. Florence Victoria Williams, Apr. 27, 1921. Admitted to Ind. bar, 1917, U.S. Supreme Ct. bar. 1943, D.C. bar, 1952; practice law, Princeton, Ind., 1919-24; prof. law Ind. U., 1924-64, on leave, 1941-64; pros. atty. 66th Jud. Circuit, Ind. 1921-22; spl. appointments as judge, and as pros. atty., 10th Jud. Circuit, Ind.; mem. and reporter Adv. Com. Rules of Criminal Procedure, U.S. Supreme Ct., 1941-44; legal counsel internat. trials at Tokyo and Manila, 1945-48; justice Supreme Ct. Libya, 1954-69; mem. U.S. Adv. Com. Internat. Rules Jud. Procedure, 1959-62. Enlisted as seaman second class, U.S. Naval Res., 1918, capt. ret.; dir., Navy dir., dep. dir. U.S. War Crimes Office, 1945-50. Recipient U.S. World War medals, 1919, 45; Commendation Ribbon (Army), 1949; Legion of Merit (Navy), 1950; Distinguished Alumni Service award Ind. U., 1972. Mem. Internat. Am. (chmn. sect. criminal law 1938-46), Ind. Fed. bar assns., Am. Soc. Internat. Law, Internat Law Assn., UN League Lawyers (sec. gen. 1952), Am. Law Inst., Am. Judicature Soc. (past dir.), World Peace Through Law Center, World Assn. Judges (Washington and Geneva), Am. Legion, Phi Beta Kappa, Phi Beta Kappa Assos., Phi Kappa Psi. Clubs: Harvard, Nat. Lawyers (Washington); Rotary (pres. Bloomington, Ind. 1934-35). Author: Cases on Criminal Law and Procedure, 1941; contbr. articles to legal jours. Draftsman state, fed. and internat. ct. charters, statutes and rules on procedure and cts., treaty plans. Home: Washington, D.C. Died May 22, 1980.

ROBINSON, JESSE SQUIBB, economist; b. Boston, Pa., Feb. 2, 1889; s. George and Annie (Divens) R.; A.B., Allegheny Coll., 1911; Ph.D., Johns Hopkins, 1917; studied London Sch. Econs. and Oxford, 1926-27; L.H.D., Allegheny Coll., 1927; m. Elizabeth Metcalf, Oct. 16, 1917 (dec. 1967); m. 2d, Freda Dungay, Sept. 1, 1967. Prin. schs., Easton, Me., 1911-13; prof. history, Summer Sch. Allegheny Coll., 1912; instr. econs. Vanderbilt, 1917-18; on leave of absence as asso. dir. edn., Fort Oglethorpe, Ga., and dir. edn., Camp Sheridan, Ala., 1917-18; expert Fed. Bd. Vocational Edn., Washington, 1918-19; prof. econs. and bus. adminstrn. Simpson Coll., Indianola, Ia., 1919-20; prof. econs. Carleton Coll., 1920-53; prof. econs. Whittier Coll., from 1953, chmn. dept. econs. and bus. adminstrn., 1953-61, chmn. div. social scis., 1954-55; prof. econs. U. Cal., summer 1926; vis. prof. econs. London Sch. Econs., spring 1934; vis. prof. econs. Rollins Coll., 1952-53; examiner U.S. Civil Service Commn., 1942-46. U.S. rep. Methodist Conf., Leicester, Eng., 1934. Panel mem. pub. disputes div. Nat. War Labor Bd., 1943-46. Fellow Royal Econ. Soc. (Gt. Britain); mem. Am. Econ. Assn., Midwest Econs. Assn. (pres. 1942-46), Nat. Econ. League (mem. nat. council), Phi Beta Kappa, Phi Gamma Delta, Pi Gamma Mu, Omicron Delta Gamma. Methodist. Mason. Club: Cosmos (Washington). Author: The Amalgamated Association of Iron, Steel and Tin Workers, 1920; (with others) Camp Reader for American Soldiers, 1918; Essentials of Economic Theory as Applied to Modern Problems of Accounting, 1932; co-author: Principles of Marketing, 1961. Asso. editor Econs. of Edn. Home: Laguna Hills, Calif. Died Apr. 11, 1976; buried Rose Hills Meml. Park, Whittier, Calif.

ROBINSON, JOSEPH LAWRENCE, engring. cons.; b. Lawrence Beach, N.Y., Sept. 6, 1900; s. Joseph Calwell and Frances D. (Marshall) R.; student Dartmouth, 1918-19; M. Mech. Engring., Cornell U., 1926; student Pratt Inst., 1928; m. Jeannette Palmer, Oct. 17, 1928; children—Palmer Hoyt, Jeremy Calwell, Beryl Ann (Mrs. Fox), Molly Jane. With Phelps-Dodge Corp., 1916-18; engaged as mining engr., 1923-28; structural engr. McClintic Marshall Co., N.Y.C., 1928-30; with Jabez Burns & Sons, Inc., N.Y.C., 1930-63, pres., 1957-63, also dir.; chmn. bd. B.F. Gump Co., Chgo., 1959-63, Tempo-Vane Mfg. Co., San Francisco, 1959-63, Tempo-Steel Corp., San Francisco, 1959-63; four companies dissolved to become part of food and chem. equipment div. Blaw-Knox Co., 1964, v.p., gen. mgr. div., 1964; dir. marketing Lummis Co., 1964-67; engring. cons., 1967-79. Registered profl. engr., N.Y. Mem. Am. Assn. Indsl. Mgmt. (pres. N.Y. and N.J., 1952-54, mem. nat. adminstrv. council 1953-54, nat. pres. 1954-57), Am. Ordnance Assn., Nat. Coffee Assn. (hon.), Sigma Alpha Epsilon. Republican. Clubs: Columbia (N.Y.C.); Buffalo Athletic; Wanakah (N.Y.) Country; Canoe Brook Country (Summit, N.J.); Hanover (N.H.) Country; Palm River Golf (Naples, Fla.); Plainfield (N.J.) Country. Contbr. profl. jours. Home: Hanover, N.H. Died Nov. 1979.

ROBINSON, WILLIAM PETERS, polit. scientist, educator, state legislator; b. Norfolk, Va., Mar. 15, 1911; s. William Carl and Avis (Peters) R.; A.B Howard U., 1932, M.A., 1935; Ph.D., N.Y. U., 1950; 1 son, William Peters. Instr. dept. polit. sci. Howard U., Washington, 1935-39; analyst program surveys div. Dept. Agr., Washington, 1939-44; prof. dept. social scis. So. U., Baton Rouge, 1944-46; dir. Sch. Arts and Scis., dir. vets. affairs Alcorn (Miss.) Coll., 1946-48; asst. to pres., prof. polit. sci. Morris Brown Coll., Atlanta, 1948-50; chmn. dept. polit. sci. Central State Coll., Wilberforce, Ohio, 1950-58, editor Research Bull., 1954-58; chmn. dept. polit. sci. Tex. So. U., Houston, 1958-62; prof. polit. sci., head dept. Norfolk (Va.) State Coll., 1962-81, chmn. div. social scis., 1965-81, pres. faculty senate, 1970-71; mem. Va. Ho. of Dels., 1970-81. Cons. Washington Office, OEO for Va., 1963-81; cons. Desegregation Inst., Elizabeth City State U., 1972-81; lectr. U. N.H., 1972. Mem. Overall Adv. Council on Needs Handicapped Children and Adults; chmn. steering com. Concerned Citizens of Norfolk; mem. Va. Adv. Legis. Council Study Commn. on Pub. Welfare; mem. exec. com. Advance Norfolk; co-chmn. Com. of 60 for Better Norfolk; mem. exec. council Tidewater council Boy Scouts Am. Coordinator, Voter Registration Project, Norfolk; chmn., dir. Conf. Newly Elected Black Local Ofcls. of Va. Bd. dirs. Med. Center Hosps. Recipient Brookings Instn. Center for Advanced Study award, 1966, award YMCA, Norfolk, 1969, Phi Delta Kappa, 1970, Lamplighter award Ednl. Assn. Norfolk, 1972, Outstanding Contbn. to Humanity award Delver Women's Club, Richmond, Va., 1972, award for distinguished achievement Howard U. Alumni Assn., 1970, certificate of appreciation Norfolk Jaycees, 1974, certificate of merit Va. State Coll., 1974, also others. Mem. Am. (exec. council), So., Southwestern polit. sci. assns., Am. Acad. Polit. Sci., Am. Acad. Polit. and Social Scis., Assn. for Study Afro-Am. Life and History (exec. council, program dir.), Am. Sociol. Assn., Assn. Social and Behavioral Scientists (Presdl. Service award 1974), Assn. Social Sci. Tchrs. (pres. 1954-55), Nat. Conf. Black Polit. Scientists (past pres.), Norfolk Mission Coll. Alumni Assn. (pres.), Nat. Municipal League (governing council), Pi Alpha Theta, Phi Sigma Alpha. Co-editor: Negro History Bull. Contbr. articles to profl. jours. Home: Norfolk, Va. Died Jan. 18, 1981.

ROBINSON, WILLIAM SMITH O'BRIEN, JR., lawyer; b. Goldsboro, N.C., June 25, 1885; s. W. S. O'B. and Grace (Moseley) R.; Ph.B., Univ. of N.C., 1907, student Univ. of N.C. Law Sch., 1906-08; student Columbia Univ. Law Sch.; 1908; m. Elizabeth E. Bridgers, Feb. 3, 1914; children—W.S. O'B., III, Grace (Mrs. W. B. MGuire), Polly (Mrs. A. G. Odell, Jr.). Admitted to the N.C. bar, 1908; in gen. practice of law, Charlotte, N.C.; became vice pres. and gen. counsel, Duke Power Company, 1927, now chairman of board and gen. counsel; gen. counsel Piedmont and Northern Ry. Co. since 1927. Trustee Duke Endownment. Mem. Am., N.C., and Mecklenburg County bar assns., Phi Beta Kappa, Omicron Delta Kappa. Home: Charlotte, N.C. *

ROBISON, URIAH JUDKIN, clergyman; b. Whatley, Ala., Sept. 15, 1883; s. Charles Lee and Corine (Starks) R.; B.D., Selma U., 1912, D.D. (hon.), 1920; LL.D., Natchez Coll., 1948; m. Mittie Kennedy, Mar. 16, 1905; children—Judkin Mathews, Marshall Foch. Ordained to ministry, Bapt. Ch., 1906; pastor Macedonia Bapt. Ch., Ft. Deposit, Ala., 1907-12, Mt. Olive Bapt. Ch., Anniston, Ala., 1912-20, Franklin St. Bapt. Ch., Mobile, Ala., 1920-51; asst. sec. Nat. Bapt. Conv., Inc., 1934-47, gen. sec., 1947-51, Ala. Bapt. State Conv., 1939-51; dean Ala. Bapt. State Sunday Sch. and Bapt. Training U. Congress. Chmn. bd. trustees Colored Old Folks Home, Mobile, 1925-51; sec. bd. trustees Selma U.; mem. bd. dirs. Am. Bapt. Theol. Sem. Served as chaplain, U.S. Army, 1917-19; capt., Reserve Chaplains, 1920-43. Mem. Nat. Council Chs. Am. (mem. exec. bd.). Mason (33 deg.), O.E.S. Home: Mobile, Ala. *

ROBITSCHER, JONAS, psychiatrist, educator; b. N.Y.C., Oct. 28, 1920; s. Jonas and Elsa (Eisinger) R.; A.B., Brown U., 1942; J.D., George Washington U., 1948, M.D., 1955; m. Jean Begeman, June 1, 1950; children—Jan, Christine, John. Intern, George Washington U., 1955-56; psychiat. resident Inst. Pa. Hosp., Phila., 1956-59; psychoanalytic tng. Inst. Phila. Assn., Psychoanalysis, 1970; practice medicine, specializing in psychiatry, psychoanalysis and forensic psychiatry, Phila., 1959-63, Bryn Mawr, Pa., 1963-72; lectr. law and psychiatry Villanova U. Law Sch., 1965-72; asst. prof. clin. psychiatry U. Pa. Sch. Medicine, 1968-72; Henry Luce prof. law and behavioral scis. Emory U., Atlanta, 1972-81. Program dir. social-legal uses of forensic psychiatry NIMH, 1970-72, prin. investigator dangerousness in psychiat. commitment study, 1974-81. Fellow Am. Coll. Legal Medicine Inst. Soc., Ethics and Life Scis., Am. Psychiat. Assn. (commn. on jud. action 1974-81, Isaac Ray award); mem. Am. Bar Assn. (commn. on mentally disabled 1973-81), Am. Acad. Psychiatry and the Law (councillor), Phi Beta Kappa, Alpha Omega Alpha. Author: Pursuit of Agreement: Psychiatry and the Law, 1966; The Powers of Psychiatry, 1980. Editor: Eugenic Sterlization, 1973. Home: Atlanta, Ga. Died Mar. 25, 1981; buried Austin, Tex.

ROBSJOHN-GIBBINGS, TERANCE HAROLD, interior designer; b. London, 1905; s. William and Miriam (Thorne) Robsjohn-G; archtl. tng. Came to U.S., 1929; naturalized, 1945. Designer contemporary interiors and funiture, fabrics, accessories; pres. Robsjohn-Gibbings, Ltd., interiors and custom made funiture, since 1936; sole designer Widdicomb Furniture Co., Grand Rapids, Mich., 1943-56. Recipient Waters award, 1950. Author: Good-Bye Mr. Chippendale, 1944; Mona Lisa's Mustache, 1947; Homes of the Brave, 1954; Funiture of Classical Greece, 1963. Contbr. popular mags. Frequent lectr. Address: New York, N.Y. Died Oct. 20, 1976.

ROBSON, MARC, film dir., producer; b. Montreal, Que., Can., Dec. 4, 1913; studied UCLA, Pacific Coast U.; m. Sara; children—Judy Lebovich, Martha Bardach, Jeanne Hearsh. With property dept. 20th Century Fox, 1932; with editing dept. RKO-Radio, 1932-43; dir. The Seventh Victim, Ghost Ship, 1944, Youth Runs Wild, 1945; pres. Red Lion Prodns., Inc.; dir. motion pictures Isle of the Dead, 1945, Roughshod, 1949, Bedlam, 1949, Champion, 1949, Home of the Brave, 1949, My Foolish Heart, 1949, Edge of Doom, 1950, Bright Victory, 1951, I Want You, 1951, Return to Paradise, 1953, Hell Below Zero, 1954, Bridges at Toko-Ri, 1955, Phfft, 1955, Prize of Gold, 1955, Trial, 1955, Harder They Fall, 1956, Peyton Place, 1957, The Prize, 1963, Valley of the Dolls, 1967, Daddy's Gone A-Hunting, 1971, Chained to Yesterday, 1973, Earthquake, 1974, others; producer, dir. The Little Hut, The Inn of the Sixth Happiness, From the Terrace, Nine Hours to Rama, Von Ryan's Express, Lost Command, Lisa, Happy Birthday Wanda June, Limbo, Earthquake. Home: Los Angeles, Calif. Died June 20, 1978.

ROCHE, JOSEPHINE ASPINWALL, labor orgn. dir.; b. Neligh, Nebr., Dec. 2, 1886; d. John J. and Ella (Aspinwall) R.; A.B., Vassar Coll., 1908; A.M., Columbia, 1910; LL.D., Smith Coll., 1931, Mt. Holyoke Coll., 1935, U. Colo., 1965; D.C.S., Oglethorpe U., 1935. Exec. sec. Colo. Progressive Service, 1913-15; spl. agt. Eng. and U.S. for Commn. for Relief in Belgium, 1915; dir. girls dept. Juvenile Ct., City and County of Denver, 1915-18, referee, 1925-27; dir. Fgn. Lang. Information Service, N.Y.C. and Washington, 1918-23; dir. editorial div. U.S. Children's Bur., Washington, 1923-25; dir. Rocky Mountain Fuel Co., 1927-50, v.p., 1928-29, pres. 1929-34, 37-50; asst. sec. U.S. Treasury, 1934-37; dir. United Mine Workers Am. Welfare and Retirement Fund, Washington, 1948-71, trustee, 1950-71. Rep. on President's Cabinet Com. on Econ. Security, chmn. interdeptl. com. to coordinate health and welfare activities of fed. govt., 1934-40; chmn. Nat. Health Conf., 1938. Recipient Chi Omega nat. achievement award, 1935. Club: Cosmopolitan (N.Y.C.). Home: Washington, D.C. Died July 29, 1976.

ROCK, JOSEPH F(RANCIS CHARLES), botanist, orientalist, explorer; b. Vienna, Jan. 13, 1884; s. Francis and Francisca (Hofer) R.; ed. Vienna Schoten Gymnasium and Vienna U.; LL.D., hon. causa, 1930; unmarried. Botanist Hawaiian Bd. of Agr. and Forestry, 1908-11, U. of Hawaii, 1911-19; prof. systematic botany, 1919; agrl. explorer with office of fgn. seed and plant introduction, U.S. Dept. Agr., since 1920; research prof. in Oriental studies, U. of Hawaii, 1938-40. Dir. Nat. Geog. Soc. Yünnan-Tibet Expedition, 1923-24; dir. Arnold Arboretum-Harvard U. Bot. and Zoöl. Expdn. to West China and Tibet, 1924-27, Nat. Geog. Soc. Southwest China-Tibet

Expdn., 1927-30; leader Zoöl. expdn., West China Mus. Comparative Zoölogy, Harvard, 1930-32, and U. of Calif. Yünnan-Tibet bot. expdn., 1932-33; leader ornithol, expdn. to Annam and Cambodia, U.S. Nat. Museum, Washington, D.C., 1940. Consultant U.S. Army Map Service, Washington, D.C., 1944-45; Research Fellow Harvard-Yenching Inst. since 1945. Formerly consulting botanist, Bd. of Commrs. of Agr. and Forestry, Honolulu, and mem. adv. com. Expt. Sta., Hawaiian Sugar Planters' Assn. Received Stanislaus Julien Award, Academic Francaise, Paris, 1948. Fellow Royal Geog. Soc., Am. Geog. Soc., Royal Asiatic Soc. of Bengal, India; mem. Bot. Soc. America, Torrey Bot. Club, Washington Biol. Soc., Royal Asiatic Soc. of N. China; hon. life mem. Nat. Geog. Soc., London Rhododendron Soc.; corr. mem. de l'Ecole Francaise d'Extrême Orient, Hanoi, Indochine, 1938. Author: The Indigenous Trees of Hawaii (Honolulu), 1913; The Ornamental Trees of Hawaii; A Monographic Study of the Hawaiian Species of the Tribe Lobelioidea, Family Campanulacea; Studies in Na-khi Literature, Hanoi, 1937; The Romance of K'a-mä-gyu-mi-gkyi, Hanoi, 1939; The Ancient Na-khi Kingdom of S. W. China (1947); Harvard University Pres; The Religious Ceremonies and the Literature of the Na-khi tribe of S.W. China, The Mûan Brö Ceremony of the Sacrifice to Heaven, Peking, 1948; The Na-Khi Naga Cult and Related Ceremonies (2 vols.); The Historical Geography of West China and East Tibet. Home: Yunnan, China. *

ROCKEFELLER, AVERY, JR., pub. co. exec.; b. Colorado Springs, Colo., Aug. 30, 1924; s. Avery and Anna (Mark) R.; grad. St. Paul's Sch., 1943; B.A., Yale, 1949; m. Lucia Ewing, July 3, 1948 (div. 1966); children—Mary, Avery III, Lucia; m. 2d, Anne Sammis Patterson, Feb. 13, 1971. With firm Dominick & Dominick, N.Y.C., 1949-73, partner, 1952-64; pres. Dominick & Dominick, Inc., 1967-71; chmn. Dominick Mgmt. Corp., 1972-73; sr. v.p. finance, dir. Grolier, Inc., N.Y.C., 1973-79; dir. Piggly Wiggly So., Inc., Grolier, Seaborad Surety Co., Home Ins. Co., Putnam Investors Fund. Bd. govs. N.Y. Stock Exchange, 1964-70. Trustee GRD Found., New Eng. Coll., Church Pension Fund. Served with USAAF, 1943-45. Mem. Nat. Assn. Securities Dealers (chmn. bd. govs. 1962-63). Clubs: Links, Bond (N.Y.C.); Field, Round Hill (Greenwich). Home: Greenwich, Conn. Died Dec. 4, 1979.

ROCKEFELLER, JOHN DAVISON, 3D, philanthropist; b. N.Y.C., Mar. 21, 1906; s. John Davison, Jr. and Abby Greene (Aldrich) R.; prep. edn., Browning Sch., N.Y.C., and Loomis Sch., Windsor, Conn.; B.S., Princeton U., 1929; m. Blanchette Ferry Hooker, Nov. 11, 1932; children—Sandra, John Davison IV, Hope (Mrs. Spencer), Alida. Trustee Rockefeller Found., 1931-71, chmn., 1952-71, hon. chmn., 1971-78; trustee Colonial Williamsburg, 1934-54, chmn., 1939-53; trustee Am. Mus. Natural History, 1933-55; founder Asia Soc., 1956, trustee, 1956-78, pres. 1956-64, chmn., 1964-74; trustee Rockefeller Bros. Fund, 1940-78, pres., 1940-56; trustee Rockefeller Family Fund, from 1967; founder The JDR 3rd Fund, 1963, pres., 1963-78; trustee Gen. Edn. Bd., 1932-71, chmn., 1952-71; trustee Princeton U., 1937-67, trustee emeritus, 1967-78; founder Population Council, Inc., 1953, trustee, 1953-78, chmn., 1957-78; dir. Lincoln Center for Performing Arts, Inc., 1956-78, pres., 1956-61, chmn., 1961-70; founder Agrl. Devel. Council, 1953, pres., 1953-67, chmn., 1967-73; founder Rockefeller Pub. Service Awards, 1952; dir. Japan Soc., 1952-78, pres., 1952-70, chmn., 1970-78; chmn. nat. council United Negro Coll. Fund, 1958-65; chmn. U.S. Commn. on Population Growth and the Am. Future, 1970-72; dir. Phelps Meml. Hosp. Assn., 1953-68; dir. Rockefeller Center, Inc., 1932-63; cons. Dulles Mission to Japan on peace settlement, 1951; adv., U.S. del. Japanese peace treaty conf., San Francisco, 1951. Chmn. Greater N.Y. Fund 1949 Campaign. Served as lt. comdr. USNR, 1942-45, working with Combined Civil Affairs Com. and State-War-Navy Coordinating Com. Recipient numerous awards and decorations, including grand cordon Order of Sacred Treasure, grand cordon Order Rising Sun (Japan); comdr. Order Thousand Elephants and White Parasol (Laos); Lasker award Planned Parenthood Fedn. Am., 1961; Order Sikatuna, Philippines; Margaret Sanger award Planned Parenthood-World Population, 1967. Baptist. Clubs: Century Assn., University, River (N.Y.C.); Metropolitan (Washington). Author: The Second American Revolution: Some Personal Observations, 1973. Home: New York, N.Y. Died July 10, 1978.

ROCKEFELLER, NELSON ALDRICH, former vice pres. U.S.; b. Bar Harbor, Me., July 8, 1908; s. John Davison, Jr., and Abby Greene (Aldrich) R.; prep. edn. Lincoln Sch. of Tchrs. Coll., N.Y.C., 1917-26; B.A., Dartmouth, 1930; m. Mary Todhunter Clark, June 23, 1930 (div. 1962); children—Rodman, Ann R. Roberts, Steven, Michael (dec.), Mary (Mrs. Thomas B. Morgan); m. 2d, Margaretta Fitler Murphy, May, 1963; children—Nelson Aldrich, Mark Fitler. Dir. Rockefeller Center, Inc., 1931-58, pres., 1938-45, 1948-51, chmn., 1945-53, 1956-58; co-ordinator Office of Inter-Am. Affairs, 1940-44; asst. sec. of state for Am. Republics affairs, 1944-45; chmn. Internat. Devel. Adv. Bd. (Point 4 Program), 1950-51; under sec. HEW, 1953-54; spl. asst. to Pres., 1954-55; gov. of N.Y., 1959-73; chmn. Commn. on Critical Choices for Am., 1973-75; vice pres. U.S., 1974-77; chmn. Commn. Water Quality, 1973-76; mem. Pres.' Adv. Commn. Intergovtl. Relations, 1965-69; mem. President's Fgn. Intelligence Adv. Bd., 1969-74. Treas. Mus. Modern Art, 1935-39, pres., 1939-41, 1946-53, chmn., 1957-58; founder Mus. Primitive Art; chmn. Pres.' Adv. Com. Govt. Orgn., 1953-58. Awarded Order of Merit of Chile, by Pres. Rios, 1945; Nat. Order So. Cross (Brazil) 1946; Order of the Aztec Eagle (Mexico), 1949; Gold medal award Nat. Inst. Social Scis., 1967; Conservation and Water Mgmt. award Gt. Lakes Commn., 1970, Medal of Freedom, 1977, others. Mem. Phi Beta Kappa, Psi Upsilon. Baptist. Clubs: Century Assn., Dartmouth (N.Y.C.); Cosmos (Washington). Author: The Future of Federalism, 1962; Unity, Freedom and Peace, 1968; Our Environment Can Be Saved, 1970. Home: North Tarrytown, N.Y. Died Jan. 27, 1979.

ROCKWELL, FLORENCE, actress; b. St. Louis, July 29, 1883; d. Theodore and Jennie R. Début in adult rôles with James O'Neill, 1897; New York debut in "Oliver Goldsmith," 1900; played with Henry Miller in "Richard Savage" and "D'Arcy of the Guards," with Nat Goodwin in "Midsummer Night's Dream"; starred in "A Doll's House," 1906; was leading woman with Richard Mansfield, 1907; starred in "The Round Up," "The Barrier," "Mills of the Gods," and "Popularity"; starred in "The Double Cross," and "Fine Feathers," 1914; with vaudeville, in "Her Awakening," 1915; starred by Oliver Morosco in plays and moving pictures, 1916; in "The Bird of Paradise," 1918-19. Address: Stamford, Conn.*

ROCKWELL, FREDERICK FRYE, author; b. Bklyn., Apr. 2, 1884; s. Frank Warren and Elizabeth Trowbridge (Hammill) R.; spl. student Wesleyan U., Conn., 1905-06; m. Marjorie Hughan, Sept. 5, 1910 (divorced); children—Wallace, Frederick F., Donald W., Margaret E.; m. 2d, Esther C. Grayson, 1933. Circulation mgr. Garden Mag., 1906-07; mgr. Wilshire Book Co., 1907-08; with New York Call, 1908-09; dir. service dept. and mgr. Burpee's Seed Farms, 1917-19; with Tuthill Adv. Agency, New York, 1919-21; mgr. nursery and bulb dept. and of publicity and advertising, Seabrook Co., Seabrook Farms, Bridgeton, N.J., 1921-25. Garden editor, The N.Y. Times garden page, 1934-43. Pres., Men's Clubs Am., founder Men's Garden Club N.Y. Author: Home Vegetable Gardening, 1911; Gardening Indoors and Under Glass, 1912; Making a Fruit Garden, 1914; The Pocket Garden Guide, 1914; The Key to the Land, 1915; Around the Year in the Garden, 1916; Save It for Winter!, 1918; Gardening Under Glass, 1921; The Book of Bulbs, 1926; Shrubs and Gladiolus, in Home Garden Handbooks series, 1927; Rock Gardening and Evergreens, 1928; Irises, 1928; Dahlias, 1929; Lawns, 1929; Roses, 1930; Peonies, 1933; Flower Arrangement (with E. C. Grayson), 1935; Gardening Indoors (with E. C. Grayson), 1938; Flower Arrangements in Color (with E. C. Grayson and F. W. Cassebeer), 1940. Editor: Ten Thousand Garden Questions Answered, 1944; The Complete Book of Flower Arrangement (with E. C. Grayson), 1947. Editor in chief: The Home Garden. Socialist. Hort. editor of McCall's Mag. Contbr. to mags. Home: West Nyack, N.Y. Died Apr. 18, 1976.

ROCKWELL, NORMAN, illustrator; b. N.Y.C., Feb. 3, 1894; s. J. Waring and Ann Mary (Hill) R.; left high sch. in second yr. to study at Art Students' League; awarded two scholarships; pupil of George Bridgeman and Thomas Fogarty: A.F.D., U. Vt., 1949, U. Mass., 1961; H.H.D., Middlebury Coll., 1954; m. 2d, Mary Rhodes Barstow, Apr. 17, 1930; children—Jarvis Waring, Thomas Rhodes, Peter; m. 3d, Mary L. Punderson, Oct. 25, 1961. Painter mag. covers and illustrations, principally for The Saturday Evening Post, also for Ladies' Home Jour., Am. Mag., Woman's Home Companion, Look mag., McCall's mag., others; mural at Nassau Tavern, Princeton, N.J.; Paintings of Four Freedoms. Represented in Met. Mus. Art, N.Y.C. Served as 1st class varnisher and painter, U.S. Navy, World War I. Recipient Presdl. Freedom medal, 1977. Mem. Soc. Am. Illustrators, Free Lance Artists Am. Author: Norman Rockwell: My Adventures as an Illustrator, 1959; Norman Rockwell, Illustrator, 1946; The Norman Rockwell Album, 1961; Norman Rockwell, Artist and Illustrator, 1970; Norman Rockwell's Americana, 1975. Home: Stockbridge, Mass. Died Nov. 8, 1978.

ROCKWOOD, NATHAN CHARMLERLAIN, editor, pub.; b. Marlboro, Mass., Sept. 9, 1884; s. Charles Henry and Abba Lawrence (Peck) R.; B.S. in C.E., Worcester Poly. Inst., 1907; m. Elizabeth Miller, June 3, 1917; children—Charles Henry, Theodore Bogart. Gen. engring. work, N.Y., Mo., Mass., Fla., Minn., and Mont., 1907-10; asst. editor, later assoc. editor Engring. News, and Engring. News Record. 1910-17; editorial consultant Rock Products; pres. Tradepress Pub. Corp., 1931-39. Mem. Nat. Lime Assn., Nat. Sand and Gravel Assn., Nat. Ready-Mixed Concrete Assn., Am. Inst. Mining and Metall. Engrs, Club: Chicago Engrs., Cumulative Index of Engring. News (1910-17), 1918. Contbr. to Ency. Brit., Dict. of Am. History. Home: Naperville, Ill. *

RODELL, FRED, educator, author, lectr.; b. Phila., Mar. 1, 1907; s. Alfred M. and Florence (Fleisher) R.: A.B., Haverford (Pa.) Coll., 1926, LL.D., 1973; U. London, 1926-27; LL.B. magna cum laude, Yale, 1931, M.A. (hon.), 1939; m. Katherine Clay Cowin, July 11, 1939 (div. 1953); 1 son, Michael; m. 2d, Janet Learned, June 12, 1954. Asst. lit. editor Century Pub. Co., N.Y.C., 1927-28; spl. legal adviser to Gov. Gifford Pinchot, Pa., 1931-33; asst. prof. law Yale, 1933-36, asso. prof., 1936-39, prof. from 1939; bd. editors, Fortune mag., N.Y.C., 1937-38; spl. feature writer Chicago Times, 1940; contbg. editor The Progressive, 1943-80, Scanlan's Mag., 1969-80; bd. dirs. Coop. Consumers, Inc., New Haven 1940-45, Scanlan's Literary House. Mem. staff of Pres. Hoover's Com. on Social Trends, 1930; cons. for com. of corr. Council for Democracy 1940-42; dir. publicity, mem. consumer com. Conn. State Def. Council, 1941-43; mem. Bethany Zoning Bd., 1957-65; mem. Bethany Dem. Town Commn., 1956-64. Dem. candidate for Conn. Gen. Assembly, Bethany, 1956. Fellow Silliman Coll., Yale. Mem Am Arbitration Assn. (nat. panel), Phi Beta Kappa, Order Coif; hon. mem. Yale Employees, Local 142, U.C.W. Author: Fifty-Five Men: the Story of the Constitution, 1936; Woe Unto You, Lawyers, 1939; Democracy and the Third Term, 1940; Nine Men: A Political History of the Supreme Court from 1790 to 1955, 1955; Her Infinite Variety, 1966. Case and comment editor Yale Law Jour., 1930-31, now contbr. Contbr. to Life, Harper's, Reader's Digest, Saturday Rev., Look, N.Y. Times mag., Atlantic, other law revs. Clubs: Founders (Haverford); Kings College (London, Eng.); Mory's (Yale); Pink Sands (Bahamas); Record Catch. Home: Bethany, Conn. Died June 4, 1980.

RODERICK, HOWARD FRANKLIN, chem. mfr.; b. Elkhart, Ind. March 24, 1908; s. William Andrew and Maude (Wheeler) R.; B.S., U. Mich., 1931; m. Emily Legate Olmsted, June 23, 1934; children—Grace, Sarah, Emily, Judith, James, Constance, Chemist Mich. Alkali Co., 1931-34; dir. research, 1934-48; prodn. sales mgr., gen. sales mgr., Wyandote Chem. Co. (Mich.) 1948-50, dir. sales, 1950-54; v.p. Internat. Minerals & Chem. Corp., Chgo., 1954-59; pres. Miles Chem. Co., 1959-62; v.p. dir. Miles Labs., Inc., 1959-62; pres., dir. Escambia Chem. Corp., N.Y.C., 1964-67, Hooker Farm Chems. Co., 1968-72; v.p. Hooker Chem. Corp. N.Y.C., 1967-72; v.p. Beker Industries, 1972-78; dir. Quimica Mexama, S.A. Miles Chems. Israel Ltd., 1960-62. Mem. adv. council Nat. 4-H Club Found. Mem. Chemurgie Council (dir.), Presidents Assn. Inc., Am. Chem. Soc., Am. Inst. Chem. Engrs., Chem. Market Research Assn. Episcopalian, Clubs: Indian Hill Country. Union League (N.Y.C.); Nutmeg Curling (Darien, Conn.). Home: Weston, Conn. Died Jan. 5, 1978.

RODGERS, CHURCHILL, lawyer; b. Bowling Green, Ky., Oct. 8, 1901; s. James Farnsworth and Mary Heugh Beall (Hedges) R.; student Ogden Coll., 1916-19; A.B., U. Louisville, 1922; LL.B., Harvard, 1926, S.J.D., 1928; m. Florence Louise King, July 24, 1927; children—Florence Louise (Mrs. Robert Fuller Anderson), John Churchill, James Anthony, Timothy King, David Brooke. Prin., tchr. Leitchfield (Ky.) High Sch., 1922-23; admitted to T.H. bar, 1926, N.Y. bar, 1931; atty. Prosser, Anderson & Marx, Honolulu, T.H., 1926-27, Cravath, de Gersdorff, Swaine & Wood, N.Y.C., 1928-33; atty. Met. Life Ins. Co., 1933-36, asst. gen. counsel, 1936-44, asso. gen. counsel, 1944-48, gen. counsel, 1948-65, sr. v.p., gen. counsel 1965-67; counsel to firm Willkie, Farr & Gallagher, 1967-76. Bd. dirs. Phelps Meml. Hosp., 1967-73; pres. bd. dirs. Tarrytown YMCA, 1947-48, trustee, to 1976; past v.p., dir. Community Chest. Fellow Am. Bar. Found. (dir. 1965-66); mem. Am. (hon. dels. 1957-74, chmn. sect. on corp. banking and bus. law, chmn. standing com. on continuing edn., gov.), N.Y. bar assns., Am. Law Inst., Assn. Life Ins. Counsel, N.Y. State C. of C. (chmn. exec. com., chmn. com. law reform; pres. 1966-68), Practicing Law Inst. (hon. chmn. nat. adv. council), Harvard Alumni Assn. (past dir.). Republican. Mem. Reformed Ch. Mason. Contbr. articles profl. jours. Home: Scarborough, N.Y. Died Jan. 6, 1976.

RODGERS, RICHARD, composer; b. N.Y.C., June 28, 1902; s. William Abraham and Mamie (Levy) R.; student Columbia, 1919-21, Mus.D. (hon.), 1954; student Inst. Mus. Art, N.Y.C., 1921-23; LL.D., Drury Coll., Springfield, Mo., 1949; D.H.L., U. Mass., 1954; Mus.D., U. Bridgeport, 1962, U. Md., 1962; hon. degrees, Brandeis U., 1965, Hamilton Coll., 1965, Fairfield U., 1968, N.Y. U., 1971; m. Dorothy Feiner, Mar. 5, 1930; children—Mary, Linda. Partner, Williamson Music, Inc.; composer songs for various musical shows and films including Poor Little Ritz Girl, 1920, The Melody Man, 1924, Garrick Gaieties, 1925, 26; Dearest Enemy, 1925; The Girl Friend, 1926; Peggy Ann, 1926; Betsy, 1926; Lido Lady (London), 1926; Connecticut Yankee, 1927; One Dam Thing After Another (London), 1927; She's My Baby, 1928; Present Arms, 1928; Chee Chee, 1928; Spring Is Here, 1929; Heads Up, 1929; Simple Simon, 1930; Ever Green, (London), 1930; America's Sweetheart, 1931; (film) Love Me Tonight, 1932; (film) The Phantom President, 1932; (film) Hallelujah, I'm a Bum, 1933; (film) Hollywood Party, 1934; (film) Mississippi, 1935; Jumbo, 1935; On Your Toes, 1936; (film) Dancing Pirate, 1936; Babes In Arms, 1937; I'd Rather Be Right,

1937; (film) Fools for Scandal, 1938; I Married an Angel, 1938; The Boys from Syracuse, 1938; Too Many Girls, 1939; Higher and Higher, 1940; Pal Joey, 1940; (film) They Met in Argentina, 1941; composer, co-author, co-producer; By Jupiter, 1942; composer, producer new version Connecticut Yankee, 1943; composer Oklahoma!, 1943, Carousel, 1945, (film) State Fair, 1945; co-producer (play) I Remember Mama, 1944; Annie Get Your Gun, 1946; Happy Birthday, 1946; John Loves Mary, 1947; Allegro, 1947, South Pacific, 1949, The Happy Time, The Heart of the Matter, Burning Bright, 1950; The King and I, 1951, Me and Juliet, 1953, Pipe Dream, 1955, Flower Drum Song, 1958, The Sound of Music, 1959; composer, lyricist producer No Strings, 1962; composer, producer Do I Hear a Waltz?, 1965, Two by Two, 1970; composer Rex, 1976, I Remember Mama, 1979; composer score TV film Victory at Sea, 1952, Cinderella, 1957; Winston Churchill—The Valiant Years, 1960, Androcles and the Lion, 1967. Recipient spl. Pulitzer award for Oklahoma, Donaldson Award for Carousel score, 1945, Allegro score, 1948, South Pacific score, 1949, Pal Joey score, 1952; recipient Pulitzer Prize for South Pacific, 1950; Antoinette Perry award for South Pacific score, 1950, The King and I, 1952; Columbia Medal of Excellence, 1949; Columbia Coll. award, 1952; Alexander Hamilton medal Columbia, 1956; Christopher award for The King and I, 1956; Emmy award for the Valiant Years, 1962; Antoinette Perry award for No Strings, 1962; U.S Navy Distinguished Pub. Service award, 1953; Creative Arts award medal Brandeis U., 1968. Trustee Barnard Coll., Actors Fund Am., N.Y. Philharmonic; bd. dirs. Juilliard Sch. Music; pres. N.Y. Music Theater, Lincoln Center. Mem. Authors' League Am., Dramatists Guild (past pres.), A.S.C.A.P., (dir.), Nat. Inst. Arts and Letters, Nat. Assn. Am. Composers and Conductors. Clubs: Columbia U., Players, Century Assn., Dutch Treat (N.Y.C.). Address: New York, N.Y. Died Dec. 30, 1979.

RODGERS, WILLIAM WOODSON, lawyer; b. Moberly, Mo., July 2, 1907; s. William and Elizabeth (Harris) R.; A.B., U. Mo., 1929; B.S., U. Okla., 1930, LL.B., 1933; m. Marguerite Louise Gurley, Mar. 9, 1935; children—William Woodson, James R. Admitted to Okla. bar, 1933; practice in Oklahoma City, 1933-37, Blackwell, 1937-80; partner firm Rodgers, Rodgers & Boyd, 1938-80. Chmn. bd. Security Bank & Trust Co., Blackwell, 1970-80. Pres., Blackwell Council Youth; bd. regents No. Okla. Coll., Tonkawa, 1951-80; past regent Okla. Baptist U.; past mayor Blackwell. Mem. Am., Okla., Kay County bar assn., Am. Judicature Soc., Blackwell C. of C., Phi Beta Kappa, Phi Delta Phi. Baptist. Rotarian (past pres. Blackwell). Home: Blackwell, Okla. Died Dec. 12, 1979.

RODIN, ROBERT JOSEPH, educator; b. Sacramento, July 15, 1922; s. Albert Henry and Hattie Viola (Sheffer) R.; A.A., Modesto (Calif.), Jr. Coll., 1942; B.A., U. Calif. at Berkeley, 1943, Ph.D., 1951; m. Elva Nellie Bain, Aug. 28, 1948; children—June Marie (Mrs. Russell Michealsen, Joy Zora (Mrs. Arden Sanders), Wanda Viola (Mrs. Brent Puder). Gen. asst. U. Calif. at Berkeley, 1942-43, asst. herbarium botanist, 1948-49, botanist U. Calif. African Expdn., 1947-48, teaching asst. botany, 1949-51; prof. botany Forman Christian Coll., Lahore, Pakistan, 1951-52; v.p. Winter & Bain, Inc., Los Angeles, 1952-53; asst. prof. botany Calif. Poly. State U., San Luis Obispo, 1953-62, asso. prof., 1962-67, prof., 1967-77. Vis. asst. prof. botany Cornell U., 1960-61; Fulbright prof. U. Delhi (India), 1966-67; vis. prof. botany Oreg. State U., summer 1971; dir. ethnobotany expdn., Ovamboland, S.W. Africa, 1973. Served with USMCR, 1943-46. NSF Research grantee, 1960-61; Am. Bot. Soc. fellow as del. to Internat. Bot. Cong., Edinburgh, Scotland, 1964; Nat. Park Service grantee to study Registered Nat. Landmarks, 1970-73. Mem. A.A.A.S., Am., Calif. bot. socs., Am. Assn. Plant Taxonomists, Am. Fern Soc., Internat. Soc. Plant Morphologists, Calif. Native Plant Soc., Sigma Xi. Author: Ferns of the Sierra, 1960, reprinted, 1967; The Ethnobotany of the Kwanyama-Speaking Ovambos, Namibia, 1981. Home: San Luis Obispo, Calif. Died June 27, 1978; buried Los Osos Valley Meml. Park.

RODMAN, BENEDICT JOSEPH, clergyman, educator; b. Lebanon, Ky., May 9, 1882; s. Hilary D. (M.D.) and Sarah H. (Webb) R.; mem. Rodman family of America; ed. St. Mary's (Kan.) Coll.; A.B., St. Louis U., 1906, A.M., 1911; studied theology, canon law, eccles. history and patrology, St. Louis U., 1913-18. Joined Soc. of Jesus (Jesuits), 1901; prof. Latin, Greek and mathematics, of U. Detroit, 1908-13; ordained priest R.C. Ch., 1916; dean St. Mary's Coll., 1918-22, pres., 1922-28; pres. John Carroll U., Cleveland, O., 1928-37; pastor Gesu Ch., Cleveland, 1937-46; pastor SS. Peter and Paul Church (Detroit) since 1946. Mem. N.E.A., Vigilance Assn. (nat. com.). Democrat. K.C. Contbg. on biog., scientific and philos. subjects. Address: Detroit, Mich. *

RODMAN, THOMAS D., railroad exec.; b. Pinckneyville, Ill., 1917; B.S. in Accounting, U. Ill., 1940; m. Sylvia S. Kuykendall, Apr. 11, 1942; children—John, Brenda, William. With Mo. Pacific R.R., St. Louis, 1940-77, asst. controller, 1959-67, controller, 1967-74, v.p., controller, 1975-77; v.p., controller Alton & Co. Ry., Mo.-Ill., Tex. Pacific-Mo. Pacific Terminal R.R. of New Orleans; v.p., controller, dir. Mo. Pacific Truck Lines, Tex. and Pacific Motor Transport Co. Served as maj. U.S. Army, 1941-46, 51-53. Mem. Pi Kappa Phi. Clubs: Mo. Athletic, Media. Home: Florissant, Mo. Died Mar. 12, 1977.

RODMAN, WILLIAM BLOUNT, JR., state justice; b. Washington, N.C., July 2, 1889; s. William Blount and Addie (Fulford) R.; A.B., U. N.C., 1910; m. Helen Farnell, Aug. 17, 1918; children—William Blount, Mary H. Rodman Hill, Marcia Rodman Lawrence, George F. and Edward N. (twins). Admitted to N.C. bar, 1911; mem. firm Rodman & Rodman, Washington, N.C., 1937-55; mayor, Washington, 1921-23; mem. N.C. Senate, 1937-39. Ho. of Reps., 1951, 53, 55; atty. gen. N.C., 1955-56; asso. justice N.C. Supreme Ct., 1956-65, emergency justice, from 1965. Served as lt. U.S. Navy, World War I. Mem. N.C. Bar Assn. (pres. 1941-42). Home: Washington, N.C. Deceased.

RODNICK, DAVID, anthropologist, educator; b. New Haven, May 10, 1908; s. Louis David and Bryna (Kaplan) R.; B.S., N.Y. U., 1931; M.A., Yale U., 1933; Ph.D., U. Pa., 1936; m. Elizabeth Wright Amis, Mar. 24, 1945; 1 dau., Amie Bowman. Asst. dir. Inst. Internat. Social Research, Princeton, N.J., 1955-59; chmn., prof. div. social scis. Inter Am. U., P.R., 1959-61; prof. sociology and anthropology Iowa Wesleyan Coll., 1961-63; sr. sociologist Ops. Research, Inc., Washington, 1963-65; prof. sociology and anthropology Tex. Technol. U., Lubbock, 1965-75; vis. prof. U. Hamburg (W. Ger.), 1975-77, cons., 1977-80; cons. Columbia U. Project in Contemporary Cultures, 1947-51. Social Sci. Research Council grantee; Fulbright Sr. Research prof. in Norway and Germany. Fellow Am. Sociol. Assn., Am. Anthrop. Assn., Soc. Applied Anthropology, AAAS; mem. Soc. Internat. Devel., Soc. History of Tech., Am. Acad. Polit. and Social Sci., Internat. Studies Assn. Author: The Fort Belknap Assiniboine, 1938, reprinted, 1978; Postwar Germans, 1948; The Norwegians, 1955; An Introduction to Man and His Development, 1966; The Strangled Democracy, 1970; Essays on an America in Transition, 1972; Man's Quest For Autonomy, 1974; A Portrait of Two German Cities; Lübeck and Hamburg, 1979; contbr. articles to profl. jours. Home: Lubbock, Tex. Died Oct. 9, 1980.

ROEDEL, JOHN W. (RO'DEL), dept. store exec.; b. Baltimore, Md., Oct. 2, 1882; s. Louis and Katherine (Heinzerling) R.; grad. Eaton and Burnetts Bus. Coll., Baltimore, 1904; m. Emma L. Behrens, Oct. 5, 1904; children—Edward (deceased), Melvin W. Accountant, The Hecht Co., dept. stores, Baltimore, 1908-29, sec., 1929-36, v.p., 1936-48, dir. since 1938, asst. treas., 1943-48; ret. Jan. 31, 1948. Mem. Nat. Assn. Cost Accountants, Controllers Congress (Nat. Retail Dry Goods Assn.), Jr. Order United Am. Mechanics (past councilor). Home: Towson, Md. *

ROEDER, ARTHUR (RA'DER), corp. executive; born Pleasantville, N.J., June 6, 1884; s. Adolph and Marie (Bonschur) R.; student civ. engring., Cornell U., 1903-07, Dr. C.E., 1907; m. Harriet K. Pupke, Feb. 15, 1913; 1 dau., Harriet A. Jr. engr., City of Newark, N.J., 1907-10; successively salesman, asst. sales mgr., production mgr., asst. to gen. mgr., Robt. H. Ingersoll and Brother, watch mfrs., N.Y. City, 1910-18; treas., later pres. U.S. Radium Corp., N.Y. City, 1918-26; exec. v.p. Am. Linseed Co., N.Y. City, 1926-29; became pres. The Colo. Fuel & Iron Co., 1929, also pres. subsidiaries of same, apptd. receiver, Aug. 1, 1933, apptd. trustee, Aug. 1, 1934, pres. reorganized company, 1936-38, chmn. bd., 1938-45, resigned Jan. 1945; formerly dir. Iron & Steel Institute; dir. Eppens, Smith Co., Inc. Mem. Sigma Alpha Epsilon. Republican. Swedenborgian. Clubs: Downtown Assn., Union League (New York). Home: Short Hills, N.J. *

ROGALSKY, GEORGE FREDERICK (RO-GAL'SKI), univ. adminstr.; b. North Tonawanda, N.Y., Feb. 15, 1885; s Frederick W. and Rosina A. (Kohl) R.; A.B., Cornell U., 1907; m. Laura C. Stutz, Sept. 17, 1913, children—Elizabeth Laura (Mrs. George A. Vikre), Margaret Stutz (Mrs. Robert T. Horn), George F., Jr. Investment banking with N. W. Halsey & Co., N.Y. City, 1910-14, Nat. City Co., N.Y. City,1914-18; asst. cashier, Tompkins Co. Nat. Bank, Ithaca, 1918-20; treas., Cornell U 1920-47, v.p. since 1947; dir. Tompkins Co. Trust Co.; dir. treas. Cornell Research Found., Inc.; dir. pres. Cornell Co-op. Soc., Inc. Served as alderman, Ithaca, 1928-38; pres. Eastern Assn. College and Univ. Bus. Officers Assn., 1935; member Financial Advisory Service, Am. Council on Edn., 1937-40. Mem. Phi Beta Kappa, Delta Chi. Republican. Lutheran. Clubs: Cornell (N.Y.); Statler (Ithaca). Home: Ithaca, N.Y. *

ROGAN, OCTAVIA FRY, librarian; b. Brownwood, Tex., Oct. 18, 1886; d. Charles R. and Frances Virginia (Stewart) Rogan; B.A., U. of Tex., 1908; B.L.S., U. of Ill. Library Sch., 1924; post-grad. study U. of Tex. and U. of Ill. Cataloguer Tex. State Library, 1911-15; asst. librarian and cataloguer, 1915-17; legislative reference librarian, Tex. State Library, 1917-25 (except 1 yr., 1923-24); state librarian of Tex., 1925-1927; reference librarian, Rosenberg Library, Galveston, 1927-31; librarian Masonic Grand Lodge of Texas Library, 1932-38; library supervisor, WPA, Tex. Dist. 9, 1928-42; librarian, McCloskey Gen. Hosp., Temple, Tex., 1942-45; now cataloger, Public Library, Houston, Tex. Member A.L.A. (life), Texas Library Assn. (president 1916-17), Southwestern Library Assn. (v.p. for Tex. 1926-28). Democrat. Mem. M.E. Ch., 8. Editor: Handbook of Texas Libraries, 1915. Address: Houston, Tex. *

ROGERS, AGNES LOW, prof. edn.; b. Dundee, Scotland, Oct. 28, 1884; d. William Thomson and Jessie (Low) R.; M.A., U. of St. Andrew's, 1908; studied Newnham Coll. (Cambridge U.), U. of Bonn, Germany; Ph.D., Columbia, 1917. Instr. English, U. of St. Andrew's, Scotland, 1906-08; lecturer in logic, ethics and psychology, Aberdeen, Scotland, 1911-14; lecturer in ednl. psychology, Columbia, 1917-18; prof. edn. and head of dept., Goucher Coll., Baltimore, 1918-23; prof. depts. of edn. and psychology, Smith Coll., 1923-25; prof. depts. psychology and edn., Bryn Mawr Coll., since 1925. Mem. Am. Psychol. Association, American Association University Women, British Association Advancement of Science, Assn. of Consulting Psychologists. Presbyterian. Club: Philadelphia College. Author: Experimental Tests of Mathematical Ability and Their Prognostic Value, 1918; also more than 30 articles on metaphysical and ednl. subjects. Home: Bryn Mawr, Pa.*

ROGERS, BENJAMIN FRANKLIN, clergyman; b. Prentiss Co., Miss., Jan. 26, 1886; a Rev. John Harbard and Willie Alice Ophelia (Gresham) R.; student Southern-Normal U. and U. of Miss.; LL.B., Cumberland U., Tenn., 1909; student Emory U. Corr. Sch. of Theology. Atlanta, Ga., 1924-28; m. Rebel Milburn, of Dallas, Tex., Sept. 25, 1915; children—Catherine Will, Benjamin Franklin, John Roland, Robert Gresham. Pub. sch. teacher in Miss., 1905-07; admitted to Okla. bar, 1909; practiced in Ardmore and Madill until 1917; asst. U.S. dist. atty., 1914; city atty., 1916; Chautauqua lecturer, 1917-18; gen. sec. Y.M.C.A., Miss. Agrl. and Mech. Coll., 1918-22; licensed ministry M.E. Ch., S., 1923, ordained deacon, 1925, elder, 1928; pastor at U. of Fla., 1923-25, Lake City, Fla., 1925-27; editor Fla. Christian Advocate, 1927-29; presiding elder Ocala (Fla.) Dist., 1929-31; pastor Carrollton Av. Ch., New Orleans, 1931-33; presiding elder Lake Charles (La.) Dist., 1934-38; pastor First Ch., Haynesville, La., since 1938. Served in army Y.M.C.A., 1918. Mem. Kappa Sigma. Rotarian. Home: Haynesville, La.*

ROGERS, DONALD IRWIN, newspaper columnist, author; b. New Hartford, Conn., Nov. 17, 1918; s. Ernest E. and Eva McClellan (Driggs) R.; pvt. tutors Fall River, Mass.; extension student Brown U. and U. Fla.; m. Marjorie Rae Lawson; children—Marilyn Lee, Donald, Mark, David, Nancy. Mgr. Fall River Bur., Providence Jour., 1936-38, spl. writer, 1938-40, financial writer, 1940-48, spcl. financial-editorial writer, 1948; editorial writer Worcester (Mass.) Telegram and Evening Gazette, 1949-50; author column The Week in Business, N.Y. Herald Tribune, 1950-65, bus. and financial editor, 1951-64; editor, pres. Independent Features Syndicate, Inc., 1964-68; editor, publisher Bridgeport (Conn.) Herald, 1965-67; editor, asso. pub. Conn. Sunday Herald, Fairfield, 1965-67; asso. publisher Wall Street Transcript, 1968-69; pres., chief exec. officer Am. Econ. Found., N.Y.C., 1972-74; columnist King Features Syndicate, Hearst Newspapers, 1974-80; partner Rogers Mfg. Co., Pine Meadow, Conn., 1946-51; dir. Scripps-Howard Investment Co. Cons., Am. Heritage Found. Served as sgt., inf., AUS, 1944-46. Mem. N.Y. Financial Writers Assn., Sigma Delta Chi. Author: Teach Your Wife To Be A Widow; Save It, Invest It and Retire; Make Your Income Count; Financial Facts of Life; Your Family's Finances; The Day the Market Crashed; How To Beat Inflation by Using It; The Trials of Jimmy Hoffa; Since You Went Away. Home: Ridgefield, Conn. Died Nov. 4, 1980.

ROGERS, HARLAN BETHUNE, lawyer; b. Portage, Wis., Dec. 9, 1886; s. Josiah H. and Viola J. (Padley) R.; B.L., U. of Wis., 1909; m. Carol R. Jones, Dec. 1, 1910; children—Harlan B., Bruce J., Marjorie E. (dec.), Blair C., John H. Admitted to Wis. bar, 1909; practiced in Wis., summer 1909, in Mexico 1909-10; asso. with father in firm Rogers and Rogers, Portage, Wis., 1910-35; formed partnership Rogers and Owens, Portage, 1930; dist. atty., 1913-17; city attorney, 1921-23 and 1943-45; member Board of Bar Commissioners, 1938-39, counsel, 1939-41 and 1947, vice president City Bank of Portage, member Portage City Council and Board of Supervisors of Columbia County; pres. Public Library. Mem. Wis. State Bar Assn. (pres. 1939-40), Am. Judicature Soc., Am. Law Inst., Wis. Alumni Soc., Beta Theta Pi, Phi Delta Phi. Republican. Presbyterian. Mason (32 deg.), Elk. Club: Madison (Madison, Wis.). Home: Portage, Wisc. *

ROGERS, HUGO EDWARD, lawyer; b. N.Y.C., Nov. 26, 1899; s. Joseph and Louise (Weiss) R.; B.S., N.Y. U., 1922, M.E., 1922; J.D., N.Y. Law Sch., 1925; m. Adele Abrams, June 16, 1929. Mech. engr., 1921-26; admitted to N.Y. bar, 1926, practiced law before State bar, U.S. dist. and circuit cts., U.S. Treasury Dept., and Bd. Tax Appeals; pres. Borough of Manhattan, 1945-49; leader Tammany Hall, 1948-49; spl. counsel to N.Y.C., 1950-54. Religious and charitable enterprises N.Y.C.; legal adviser, N.Y. County Democratic party, 1929-42; spl. N.Y. State atty. gen. for elections, 1932-38; maintained Legal Aid Soc. for Harlem, 1927-41; adviser to Indian Confedn. of Am., 1930-41; arbitrator, mem. nat. panel for Am. Arbitration Assn., 1939-74. Trustee Polyclinic Med. Sch. and Hosp. Served to col. U.S. Army, World War I, World War II. Decorated Legion of Merit, Conspicuous Service Cross; gold cross Royal Grecian Order Phoenix, grand cross Sovereign Greek Order St. Dennis of Zanta; Legion Honor, Croix de Guerre avec palme (France); chevalier Order of Merit (Republic of Italy); Grand Cross Ordre Honneur et Merité (Haiti). Licensed profl. engr. Mem. Fed. Bar Council, Internat., Am. bar assns., Assn. of U.S. Army (past pres., dir.), Def. Transp. Assn., N.Y. State Soc. Profl. Engrs., Res. Officers Assn. U.S., Mil. Order World Wars (life), Circus Saints and Sinners Assn. (life), Zeta Beta Tau. Democrat. Mason (32 deg.). Clubs: N.Y. U.; Army and Navy (Washington); Admirals. Author: Minimizing Payroll Taxes, 1935; Legal Tax Savings Methods, 1936. Editor-in-chief Whitgard Services. Home: New York, N.Y. Died Dec. 14, 1974.

ROGERS, JAMES CUNNINGHAM, lawyer; b. Livermore, Pa., July 9, 1893; s. James E. and Capitola (Cunningham) R.; student U. Pitts. Sch. Econs., 1911-12; LL.B., George Washington U., 1915; m. Marion Marguerite Mattern, Aug. 3, 1921; children—Nancy Sibley (Mrs. Reed E. Garver), Rebecca Elizabeth (Mrs. Marvin Marcus), Marion Marguerite Fieldhouse (dec.), David Lewis. Admitted to D.C. bar 1915, practiced in Washington; asst. atty. Office Solicitor Internal Revenue, 1919-21, asst. solicitor, 1921-25; mem. firm Marsh & Rogers, 1925-38, Hogan & Hartson, from 1938. Dir., gen. counsel Julius Garfinckel & Co., Washington; gen. counsel D.C. Bankers Assn.; counsel Washington Clearing House Assn. Trustee, counsel Washington Hosp. Center. Served to capt. U.S. Army, 1917-19. Republican. Unitarian. Mason. Clubs: Metropolitan, Capitol Hill (Washington). Home: Chevy Chase, Md. Died Oct. 17, 1980.

ROGERS, JAMES EDWARD, settlement worker; b. San Francisco, Mar. 22, 1884; s. James S. and Emma (Hennessey) R.; high sch., San Francisco; B.L., U. of Cal., 1908, M.L., 1909; post-grad, study same; unmarried. Headworker Sunset Boys Club, San Francisco, 1900-2; founder and pres. States of Columbia and City of Telhi, two boys self govt. summer camps in Cal., 1900-3; asst. headworker, Columbia Park Boys Club, 1902-3; dir. and acting sec. San Francisco Sch. Extension Soc., 1902-3; founder and headworker Telegraph Hill Neighborhood Boys Club, San Francisco, 1903-6; trip to Orient for study of race question, 1906; reader, 1907-8, asst., 1908-9, dept. polit. science, U. of Cal.; dir. Violet St. Playground, Los Angeles, Cal., 1909-10; social studies in Europe, 1910. Author: The State of Columbia (boys' self-governing camp), 1902; The American Newspaper, 1909. Contbr. to Sunset, Out-West, Forum, etc. Address: San Francisco. *

ROGERS, JOHN, lawyer; b. Wheatland, Mo., Apr., 4, 1890; s. Pleasant Jasper and Nancy Frances (Dent) R.; LL.B., U. Okla., 1914; LL.D. (hon.), U. Tulsa, 1958; H.H.D. (hon.), Phillips U. 1958; LL.D., John Brown U., 1966; L.H.D., So. Meth. U., 1969; m. Hazel Mallory Beattle, Feb. 19, 1921; 1 son, John. Admitted to Okla. bar, 1914; atty. McMan Oil Co., Tulsa, 1915-17, atty, and v.p. McMan Oil & Gas Co., 1919-30; receiver Superior Oil Corp., 1930-33, pres. 1933-35; atty. Chapman & McFarlin Interests, 1930-77; dean, sch. law U. Tulsa, 1948-56, spl. lectr., 1943-62; dir. Home Fed. Savs. & Loan Assn., 1950-73; adv. dir. Nat. Bank of Tulsa, 1964-72. Mem. Mayor's Com. Human Relations, 1960-66. Dir. Okla. Med. Research Found. 1950-77, pres., 1957-70. Trustee U. Tulsa, 1926-66, chmn. bd. 1950-57, hon. trustee, to 1977; trustee (hon., life) Children's Med. Center, Tulsa, regent U. Okla., 1924-31, 40-41; mem. Okla. State Regents for Higher Edn., 1940-59, chmn., 1957-59; mem. Oklahoma adv., com. Nat. Commn. Civil Rights, 1958-63, chmn., 1958-61; mem. Nat. Citizens Com. Community Relations, 1964-66; trustee John Brown U., 1960-70; mem. adv. bd. YMCA, pres. 1931-36; pres. Tulsa Council Social Agys., 1941-42; pres. (life mem.) Tulsa Community Chest, 1945; trustee United Christian Missionary Soc., 1930-57; pres. Internat. Conv. Christian Chs., 1956-57; bd. dirs. Holland Hall Sch., Tulsa, 1959-66. Southwestern Legal Found. research fellow, 1962-77; recipient Hatton W. Sumners award, 1968; named Man of Year in Tulsa, 1945. Fellow Am. Bar Found.; mem. Southwestern Legal Found., Am., Okla. bar assns. Am. Soc. Internat. Law, Am. Judicature Soc., Disciples of Christ Hist. Soc. (trustee 1960-70, mem. bd.), Nat. Benevolent Assn. Christian Chs. (trustee 1960-70), Okla. Hist. Soc. (life), Tulsa C. of C. (pres. 1938), Beta Theta Pi, Phi Delta Phi, Delta Sigma Rho. Club: Tulsa. Home: Tulsa, Okla. Died May 25, 1977.

ROGERS, JONATHAN C(LARK), coll. pres.; b. Richmond, Ind., Sept. 7, 1885; s. Jonathan Clark and Anne (Valentine) R.; B.S., Piedmont Coll., Demorest, Ga., 1905, hon. Ed.D., 1934; B.S., Earlham Coll., Richmond, Ind., 1909; Am., Columbia, 1927; m. Mary Floyd Blackshear, Aug. 23, 1911; children—Katherine Valentine (Mrs. Robert E. Williams), Laura Blackshear (Mrs. Edwin Fortson), Jonathan Clark. Mathematics master, athletic dir., Oakwood Seminary (N.Y.), 1909-11; prin., Piedmont Acad., Demorest, Ga., 1911-13; prof. mathematics, dean, Piedmont Coll., 1913-33, v.p., 1933-34; pres., North Ga. Coll., 1934-49; pres. U. of Ga., 1949-50, now emeritus. Member Assn. Ga. Colleges (president, 1931), Math. Assn. of Am., A.A.A.S., Phi Delta Kappa. Democrat. Methodist, Club: Lions (Dahlonega). Address: Dahlonega, Ga.*

ROGERS, LEON WINFIELD, educator; b. Groesbeck, Tex., May 15, 1883; s. Leonidas Gideon and Lula (Polk) R.; B.A., Southwestern U., Georgetown, Tex., 1909; M.A., U. of Tex., 1929; student Teachers' Coll. (Columbia), 1931; m. Marcia Butts, of Tyler, Tex., Dec. 23, 1914. High sch. prin., McGregor, Tex., 1909-11, Mineola, Tex., 1912-15; high sch. instr., Dallas, Tex., 1915-17; supt. schs., Huntsville, Tex., 1917-19; successively state supervisor, asst. supt. and state supt., Tex. State Dept. Edn., 1919-33; civilian ednl. adviser Civilian Conservation Corps, 8th Area, since Jan., 1934. Mem. N.E.A. (chmn. finance and budget com.), Nat. Council on Edn., Nat. Econ. League. Democrat. Methodist. Author: His Own People, 1929. Address: Ft. Sam Houston, Tex.*

ROGERS, PAUL, cons. structural engr., educator; b. Berettyoujfalu, Hungary, July 10, 1909; s. Ferdinand and Charlotte (Ehrmann) R.; B.S., Ecole du Genie Civil, Paris, 1934, C.E., 1937; postgrad. Ill. Inst. Tech., 1941; Dr.Eng., Tech. U., Jassi, Rumania, 1973; m. Charlotte S. Katz, Dec. 25, 1934; children—James Clyde, Anita Joyce. Structural designer Pub. Utility Engring. & Service Corp., 1941-42; structural engr. A. J. Boynton & Co., Inc., 1942-44, Hiram Walker & Sons, Inc., 1944-45; sr. structural engr. Roberts & Schaefer Co., 1945-46; cons engr., 1946-47; head structural dept. Ralph H. Burke, 1947-49; structural design engr. Sargent & Lundy, 1949-52; partner Rogers & Snitoff, Inc., cons., 1952-54; pres. Paul Rogers & Assos., consulting engrs., Chgo., Ill. 1954-66, Rogers-Cohen-Barreto-Marchertas, 1966-69; v.p. Hamon, Inc., 1960-69; chief structural engr. Daniel, Mann, Johnson & Mandenhall, Los Angeles, 1965-69; asst. prof. Chgo. Tech. Coll., 1941-46; prof. civil engring. Calif. State U. at Los Angeles, 1970-79; lectr. U. Calif. at Los Angeles, U. So. Calif.; pres. Paul Rogers & Assos., civil and structural engrs., Los Angeles, 1970-79. Lectr. Ill. Inst. Tech., 1951-54, Northwestern U. Grad. Sch., 1954-56. Recipient citation Western Soc. Engrs., 1950, 53, Am. Iron and Steel Inst., 1963; Eminent Engr. award Ill. Soc. Profl. Engrs., 1965; named Prof. of Year, Calif. State U., Los Angeles, 1974-75; others. Registered profl. engr., N.Y., Pa., Ind., Calif., Fla., Iowa, Oreg., Nev., Wis., Mich., Va., Colo., Ill., Hawaii, Ohio, Tex. Fellow Am. Soc. C.E. (J.J.R. Croes gold medal 1963); mem. structural engrs. assns. Cal., Ill., Nat. Soc. Profl. Engs., Am. Concrete Inst., Internat. Assn. Bridge and Structural Engring., A.I.A. (affiliate), Chambre des Ingenieurs Conseils de France, Chi Epsilon (honor mem.), Societe des Ingenieurs Civils de France. Author: Fixed End Moments; Steel Columns; Reinforced Concrete Design for Buildings; (novel) Earthquake, Sex and the Engineer from Transylvania; co-author: American Civil Engineering Practice. Contbr. numerous sci. and tech. articles to profl. publs. patentee on use of wind energy. Home: Los Angeles, Calif. Died Jan. 5, 1979.

ROGERS, RALPH KNICKERBACKER, mgmt. cons.; b. Troy, N.Y., Nov. 18, 1897; s. Howard C. and Ellen (Holton) R.; Ph.B., Brown U., 1919; M.B.A., Harvard, 1921; m. Jean Lindsay Withrow, Oct. 12, 1929; children—Jean H., Ralph W., John H. Securities analyst Henry D. Lindsley Co., 1921-25; supervising indsl. engr. Thompson & Lichtner Co., Inc., Boston, 1925-29; mfr. staff exec. Bauer & Black div. Kendall Mills, Chgo., 1929-31; cons. bus. orgn. and adminstrv. controls, 1931-39; partner Rogers, Slade & Hill, N.Y.C., 1939-62; pres. Rogers, Slade and Hill, Inc., 1962-68, chmn., 1968-76. Mayor, Village of Scarsdale, N.Y., 1963-65, trustee, 1959-63. Mem. Assn. Cons. Mgmt. Engrs., Am. Mgmt. Assn., Soc. Advancement Mgmt., Inst. Mgmt. Consultants, Newcomen Soc. N.Y. Prebyn. Clubs: Harvard (Boston); Harvard, Union League, M.I.T., Harvard Business School (N.Y.C.). Home: Greenwich, Conn. Died Apr. 9, 1976.

ROGERS, ROSWELL WESLEY, prof. edn.; b. Harrison, Ark., Apr. 27, 1883; s. Mathew Waddell and Texas Burns (Rhea) R.; student Southwestern U., Georgetown, Tex., 1900-2, 1903-4; B.S. Polytechnic Coll., Ft. Worth, Tex., 1906; studied U. of Tex., summers 1906, 07; A.M., U. of Chicago, 1911; m. Jessie Florence McCall, of Georgetown, Tex., Sept. 7, 1904. Instr. mathematics and physics, Goodnight Coll., Tex., 1902-3, mathematics, Polytechnic Coll., 1905-7; prin. high sch., Hillsboro, Tex., 1907-12; pres. John Tarleton Coll., Stephenville, Tex., 1912-13; asso. prof. edn., 1913-15, prof. since 1915, U. of Miss. Mem. Miss. State Teachers' Assn., Tex. State Teachers' Assn., Conf. for Edn. in Tex. Democrat. Mem. M.E. Ch., S. State publicity dir. for Miss. war savings orgn., 1918; spl. rep. Treas. Dept., 6th Federal Reserve Dist., 1919. Home: University Mississippi.*

ROGG, NATHANIEL H., economist, assn. exec.; b. N.Y.C., July 27, 1913; s. H.N. and Nettie (Fihrer) R.; B.A. magna cum laude, N.Y. U., 1934, M.A. with honors in Econs., 1935; postgrad. Brookings Inst., 1937-38; J.D. with honors, George Washington U., 1951; m. Genevieve DeVere, Nov. 14, 1964; children—David N., Katherine, Elizabeth, Daniel, Margaret. Econ. adminstr. Fed. Works Agy., Washington, 1935-42; econ. adviser Nat. Housing Agy., Washington, 1946-47, HHFA, Washington, 1947-54; chief economist Nat. Assn. Homebuilders, Washington, 1954-79, exec. v.p., 1965-77; dir. Universal Rundle Corp.; vis. prof. econs. Harvard, 1962-63; adj. prof. Am. U., 1965-66; cons. U.S. League Savs. Assns., 1977-79, also cons. in field. Mem. Nat. Commn. Mortgage Interest Rates, 1968-69. Served to lt. comdr. USNR, 1942-46. Mem. Order of Coif, Phi Beta Kappa. Clubs: Cosmos (Washington); Army-Navy Country (Arlington, Va.); Plantation (Hilton Head, S.C.). Home: Washington, D.C. Died Feb. 20, 1979.

ROGGE, BENJAMIN ARNOLD, educator; b. Trumbull, Neb., June 18, 1920; s. Henry Diedrich and Lulu Alice (Megrew) R.; A.B., Hastings Coll., 1940; M.A., U. Neb, 1946; student U. Minn., 1946-47; Ph.D., Northwestern U., 1953; m. Alice Mabel Landis, Sept. 23, 1942; children—Marise Lynne, Harry Landis, Benjamin Arnold, Anne Megrew, Gail Cattle; m. 2d, Sonja Staël-Holstein Taylor, June 29, 1978. Grad. asst. econs. U. Neb., 1940-41; instr. econs. U. Minn., 1946-47, Northwestern U., 1947-49; asst. prof. econs. Wabash Coll., 1949-53, asso. prof. econs., 1953-61, prof., 1961-64, distinguished prof. polit. economy, 1962-80, dir. Inst. Personal Devel., 1966-80, dean, 1956-64; vis. lectr. econs. Escola de Sociologia e Politica de Sao Paulo, Brazil, 1955; lectr. in field, 1964-80. Served to capt. USAAF, 1941-46. Mem. Am. Econs. Assn., Mont Pelerin Soc. Author: (with J.V. Van Sickle) Introduction to Economics, 1954. Contbr. articles profl. jours. Home: Crawfordsville, Ind. Died Nov. 17, 1980.

ROGGE, O(ETJE) JOHN, lawyer; b. Cass County, Ill., Oct. 12, 1903; s. Hermann and Lydia Anna (Satorius) R.; A.B., U. Ill., 1922; LL.B., Harvard, 1925, S.J.D., 1931; m. Nellie Alma Luther, Jan. 1, 1926; children—Genevieve Oetjeanne, Hermann; m. 2d, Wanda Lucille Johnston, Dec. 15, 1940. Admitted to Ill. bar, 1925; practice in Chgo., 1925-30, 31-37; counsel RFC, 1934-37; spl. counsel SEC, 1937-38, asst. gen. counsel, 1938-39; asst. atty. gen. of U.S. in charge criminal div. Dept. Justice, 1939-40; spl. asst. to atty. gen. U.S., 1943-46; former partner firm Weisman, Celler, Spett, Modlin & Wertheimer, N.Y.C.; pvt. practice, N.Y.C. Mem. Egypt Exploration Soc., Am. Bar Assn. (mem. com. internat. criminal jurisdiction), N.Y. County Lawyers Assn., Assn. Bar City N.Y., Phi Beta Kappa. Democrat. Author: Our Vanishing Civil Liberties, 1949; Why Men Confess, 1959; The First And The Fifth, 1960; The Official German Report, 1961; Obscenity Litigation in 10 American Jurisprudence Trials, 1965; contbg. author The Rights of the Accused, 1972, Equal Rights for Women, 1978. Contbr. numerous articles to legal jours. Editor Harvard Law Rev. Home: Stamford, Conn. Died Mar. 22, 1981.

ROHRBAUGH, LEWIS GUY (RO'BAW), college prof.; b. Fowblesburg, Md., Feb. 24, 1884; s. Henry and Annie (Fowble) R.; A.B., Dickinson Coll., Carlisle, Pa., 1907; B.D., Drew U., Madison, J.J., 1910; Ph.D., State U. of Iowa, 1922; m. Mae Heffelbower, June 25, 1907; 1 son, Henry Lewis. Ordained to ministry of M.E. Ch., 1910; pastorates in Kan. and Iowa, 1910-18; dir. Wesley Foundation, State U. of Ia., 1918-21; prof. philosophy and religion, Dickinson College, since 1922, dean of freshman, 1933-47; director admissions, 1942-47. Former member of educational com. Pennsylvania Council Religious Edn. Mem. Pa. Educational Assn., Am. Philos. Assn., Phi Beta Kappa, Alpha Chi Rho, Omicron Delta Kappa. Republican. Methodist. Mason (K.T.). Rotarian. Author: Religious Philosophy, 1923; The Science of Religion, 1927; A Natural Approach to Philosophy, 1934; Grandpa Weatherby (novel), 1936. Contbr. to periodicals: lecturer before religious assemblies. Home: Carlisle, Penn. *

ROKAW, DANIEL ROY, retail food co. exec.; b. N.Y.C., Oct. 8, 1917; s. Joseph E. and Dora (Rosenberg) R.; B.S. in Accounting and Finance, N.Y. U., 1941, M.B.A. in Indsl. Mgmt., 1950; certificate Signal Corps Contract Termination Sch., 1944; certificate Army Service Forces Accounting and Auditing, 1945; m. Lucille Levy, Feb. 12, 1944 (dec. 1974); children—Nanette, Elyse; m. 2d, Audrey Orenstein, 1976. Auditor Metro Goldwyn Mayer, Inc., N.Y.C., 1935-41; treas. Gen. Builders Supply Corp., N.Y.C., 1946-59; treas. Asso. Food Stores, Inc., N.Y.C., 1959-75, pres., 1975-78. Investment cons. Chmn. bd. trustees Town and Village Temple, 1960-62, treas.,

1955-60. Served to master sgt. Signal Corps, AUS, 1942-46. Mem. Golden Rule Ionic (master 1963). Home: New York, N.Y. Died Oct. 9, 1978.

ROLL, CURTIS W., judge; b. Fredericksburg, Ind., Aug. 29, 1884; s. Thomas and Lovica Frances (Adams) R.; B.S., Central Normal Coll., Danville, Ind., 1907, A.B., 1909; LL.B., Ind. U., 1912; m. Lois N. Polson, Apr. 14, 1915; children—Elta Frances, William Curtis, John Wesley. Admitted to Ind. bar, 1912; county atty., Howard County, 1913-14; in practice at Kokomo, 1912-31; judge Supreme Ct. of Ind., 2 terms, 1931-43. Democrat. Primitive Baptist. Mason. Home: Kokomo, Ind. *

ROLLINS, CHARLEMAE, author, librarian; b. Yazoo, Miss., June 20, 1897; active spl. work U. Chgo.; studied Library Sci. Columbia; m. Joseph W. Rollins; 1 son, Joseph W. Children's librarian George C. Hall br. Chgo Pub. Library, 1927-63; author: We Build Together, 1941; Christmas Gif', 1964; They Showed the Way, 1964; Famous Negro Poets, 1965; Famous Negro Entertainers, 1967; Langston Hughes, 1970. Tchr. children's lit. Roosevelt U., Chgo., 1946-60; tchr. Fisk U., Nashville, Human Relations Workshop San Francisco State Coll., library sci. Rosary Coll., River Forest Ill. Recipient Am. Brotherhood awad NCCJ, 1952; Library Letter award A.L.A., 1953, Grolier Soc. award, 1955; Good Am. award Chgo. Com. of One Hundred, 1962; Negro Centennial awards in three areas, 1963; Children's Reading Round Table award, 1963. Contbr. articles to profl. jours. Presented Jane Addams Book award to Norwegian author, Oslo, 1962. Address: Chicago, Ill. Died Feb. 6, 1979.

ROLLINS, EDWARD D. E., lawyer; b. 1899; LL.B., U. Md. Admitted to Md. bar, 1922; practiced in Elkton; atty. gen. of Md., 1953-54. Home: Elkton, Md. Died July 5, 1976.

ROLNICK, HARRY, bus. cons.; b. Bklyn., Apr. 12, 1900; s. Morris and Sarah (Stein) R.; student Dow Sch., Houston, 1916; m. Lottie Hammerstein, Dec. 27, 1919 (dec. 1928); children—Gerald, Maury; m. 2d, Rose Burr, Oct. 27, 1933; 1 dau. Barbara Ann (dec.). Established hat renovating bus., 1917; mgr. retail hat stores, Dallas, 1921-23; mgr. Florence Hat Mfg. plant, Dallas, 1923-27; formed Byer-Rolnick Hat Co., 1928, now Resistol Hats, Inc., pres., 1948-57; pres. Byer-Rolnick Hat Corp. (now Byer-Rolnick Corp.), 1957-66, chmn. bd., 1966-68, chmn. subsidiaries Ecuadorian Panama Hat Corp., N.Y.C., Weinberg Corp., Chgo., Byer-Rolnick Casual Headwear, Plainfield, N.J., Resistol Rough Hat Corp., Longview, Tex., Resistol Sales, Inc., Resistol Sales of Cal., Resistol Sales of Tex., Resistol Realty Co., Churchill Sales, Ltd.; past chmn. corp. divs., Resistol Hats, Inc., Kevin McAndrew, Hatmakers, Churchill Hats, Ltd.; past pres. Garland Indsl. Acreage, Inc.; investments and bus. cons.; dir. First Nat. Bank of Garland. Past pres. Hat Inst., Inc. Apptd. Tex. Ambassador of Good Will, 1948. Recipient Neiman-Marcus Fashion award, 1961. Mem. N.A.M., Tex. Mfrs. Assn. (dir.), Nat. Mens Apparel Clubs. Mason (32 deg.). Clubs: La Quinta (Cal.) Country; Dallas Athletic, Country, Columbia Country, Dallas, Imperial, Columbia (dir. from 1962) (Dallas); Cherokee (Longview, Tex.). Invented Self-Conforming hat constrn.; developed straight line hat prodn. methods; created flatop hat style. Home: Dallas, Tex. Deceased.

ROMANI, GEROGE THOMAS, educator; b. San Francisco, Mar. 7, 1917; s. Geroge Charles and Rose A. (Depaoli) R.; A.B., U. Calif., Berkeley, 1937, M.A., 1939, Ph.D., 1947; m. Margaret W. Lorenz, Sept. 20, 1942. Instr. history Northwestern U., Evanston, Ill., 1947-50, asst. prof., 1950-54; asso. prof., 1954-65, prof., 1965-77; cons. in history. Mem. election bd. Woodrow Wilson fellows. Served with USNR, 1942-46. Fulbright fellow, 1952-53; Guggenheim fellow, 1959-60. Mem. Am. Hist. Assn. Author: The Neapolitan Revolution, 1820-21, 1950; also articles. Home: Evanston, Ill. Died Jan. 6, 1977.

ROMNEY, JUNIUS STOWELL, lawyer; b. Colonia Juarez, Mexico, June 10, 1903; s. Junius and Gertrude (Stowell) R.; brought to U.S., 1912; student U. Utah, 1921-23; J.D. with honors, George Washington U., 1930; m. Ruth Stewart, Sept. 4, 1928; children—Junius Stewart, Joseph Barnard, Bruce Stewart, David Stewart. Asso. editor Millennial Star, Liverpool, Eng., 1925-26; asst. chief clk. Bur. of Investigation, Dept. Justice, 1927-28; admitted to D.C. bar, 1930, Utah bar, 1931 practiced in Salt Lake City; mem. Romney and Boyer, predecessor firm, 1953-70. Mem. Utah State Soc. (pres. 1927), Am., Utah, Salt Lake County bar assns., Utah Bar Found. (pres. 1964-65), Tau Kappa Alpha, Phi Alpha Delta. Mem. Ch. Jesus Christ Latter-day Saints. Home: Salt Lake City, Utah. Died Sept. 4, 1980; buried Salt Lake City Cemetery.

ROMNEY, VERNON, lawyer, mem. Republican Nat. Com.; b. Colonia Juarez, Chihuahua, Mexico, July 3, 1896; s. Miles Park and Catharine Jane (Cottam) R.; J.D., George Washington U., 1922; m. Lois Bradford, June 27, 1923 (dec. Apr. 1957); children—Vernon Bradford, Ralph Bradford, Rowena (Mrs. James D. Maher), Keith Bradford, Beverly Lois (Mrs. Robert G. Cutler), Geraldine (Mrs. Boyd Hanks Busath), Yvonne (Mrs. Grant Michael Dixon), John Bradford; m. 2d, Helen Hackett Brown, Nov. 6, 1964; stepchildren—Marilyn (Mrs. Benair Hansen), Jacqueline (Mrs. Darwin Anderson). Sec. Romney Lunt Land and Livestock Co., 1914-24; Western mgr. Nat. Wool Warehouse & Storage Co., Chgo., also Western rep. Am. Sheepbreeder, 1918-20; admitted to Utah bar, 1922, since practiced in Salt Lake City; mem. firm Romney & Nelson. First v.p., dir. State Savs. & Loan Assn., Rocky Mountain Finance Co. Chmn. Utah Com. for Internat. Contact, 1964-76. Active Republican Party; chmn. Salt Lake City County Com., 1942-44, chmn. Utah, 1944-50, 58-62, del. nat. convs., 1944-48, 52, 60, 64, mem. nat. com., 1958-62, mem. central campaign com. and mgr. N.W. states for Senator Robert A. Taft, 1952; now mem. state exec. com.; regional chmn. Rep. State Chmns. Orgn., 1949-50. Trustee Robert A. Taft Meml. Found. Recipient Wisdom award, 1969. Mem. Am. Bar Assn. (savs. and loan assns. com.), U.S. Savs. and Loan League (lawyers com.), George Washington U. Alumni Assn. (local pres., mem. gen. gov. bd. 1965-76), Utah, Salt Lake County bar assns., George Washington Law Assn. (pres. 1953), George Washington U. Alumni Assn. (local pres. gov. bd. 1965-76), Phi Delta Phi. Home: Bountiful, Utah. Died Jan. 9, 1976.

RONNE, FINN, Antarctic explorer, geographer; b. Horten, Norway, Dec. 20, 1899; s. Martin Richard and Maren (Gulliksen) R.; M.E., naval architect, Horten Tech. Coll., 1922; m. Edith A. Maslin, Mar. 18, 1944; 1 dau., Karen. Came to U.S., 1923, naturalized, 1929. Mem. Adm. Byrd's 2d Antarctic Expdn., 1933-35; 2d in command East Base, U.S. Antarctic Service, 1939-41; apptd. 1st. Am. postmaster Antarctic, 1946; leader Ronne Antarctic Research Expdn., 1946-48, claimed 250,000 sq. miles of new land, including Edith Ronne Land for U.S.; wintered four times on Antarctic Continent; expdn. to Antarctica with Argentine Navy, 1958-59, South Pole trips, 1961, 71; leader 1st Lindblad Antarctic trip, 1968; capt. USNR, cons. U.S. Dept. Def., 1949-62; comdg. officer IGY, 1956-58; mil comdr., sci. leader Ellsworth Sta., IGY, Edith Ronne Land, Antarctica, 1956-58; leader Arctic Expdn., 1962-69; lectr. hist. films Great Polar Adventures, Antarctic Challenge, North of the Circle, Ronne Antarctic Research Expdn. Mem. exec. bd. Nat. Capitol area council Boy Scouts Am. Decorated Congl. Silver medal, 1935, Gold medal, 1943, 48, 61; Argentine Govt. Decoration, 1959; Legion of Merit (USN), 1964; knight 1st class Royal Order of St. Olav (Norway); recipient Elisha Kent Kane gold medal Geog. Soc. Phila., 1966, Sons of Norway Profl. Achievement award, 1970; Ronne Ice Shelf named in his honor. Mem. Am. Geophys. Union (hon.), Am. Polar Soc. (hon., v.p.). Clubs: Explorers (dir., gold medal 1968), Adventurers (hon.) (Los Angeles); Adventurers of Norway (hon.). Author: Antarctic Conquest; Hellhole of Antarctic; Antarctic Command; The Antarctic Husky, 1968; Adventure; Antarctica Comes to Life, 1971; Giants of Polar Exploration, 1971; The Ronne Expedition to Antarctia, 1971; The Call of the Ice, 1972; Antarctic, My Destiny, 1979; also articles on Polar regions. Address: Washington, D.C. Died Jan. 12, 1980; buried Arlington Nat. Cemetery.

RONNERMANN, CHARLES, JR., investment counsellor, govt. ofcl.; b. N.Y.C., July 27, 1908; s. Charles and Katherine (Bolte) R.; B.S., St. Lawrence U., 1930; m. Edith Gardner, Jan. 5, 1935; children—Gail, Jane (Mrs. Sharat Chandra), Alan. Analyst, account exec. Standard Statistics Co., N.Y.C., 1930-40; asst. to pres., mgr. statis. dept. Calmar & Ore Steamship Corp., 1940-47; supr. bank, large pension trust and individual investment portfolios Moody's Investors Service, 1947-60; v.p., investment officer Greenwich Savs. Bank, N.Y.C., 1960-73; investment Specialist State Fla. Retirement Funds, 1973-76. Mem. Beta Theta Pi. Home: Tallahassee, Fla. Died Apr. 28, 1976; buried Greenfield Cemetery, Hempstead, N.Y.

RONNING, MAGNAR, educator; b. Norway, May 4, 1922; s. Ingvar G. and Dorothea (Fatten) R.; came to U.S., 1925, naturalized, 1945; B.S., Mont. State Coll., 1948; M.S., Pa. State U., 1949, Ph.D., 1951; hon. degree, U. Chile, 1967; m. Jane Matzke, Sept. 7, 1946; children—Karen Ann, Karl John. Asso. prof. dairy Okla. State U., 1951-57; prof. animal sci. U. Cal. at Davis, from 1957; Fulbright lectr. U. Cairo, 1963-64. Active Boy Scouts Am. Served with AUS, 1941-45. Decorated Purple Heart; recipient research award, Am. Feed Mfrs. Assn., 1969. Mem. Am. Dairy Sci. Assn., Am. Inst. Nutrition, Am. Soc. Animal Sci., Sigma Xi, Phi Kappa Phi, Alpha Zeta, Alpha Gamma Rho. Home: Davis, Calif. Died Oct. 13, 1976.

ROOSEVELT, JOHN A., investment exec.; b. Washington, Mar. 13, 1916; s. Franklin D. and Eleanor (Roosevelt) R.; B.A., Harvard, 1938; m. Irene Boyd McAlpin, 1965; children by previous marriage—Haven C., Anne S. Roosevelt Gibson, Joan L. Roosevelt Schoonmaker. With William Filene's Sons Co., Boston, 1938-41, Grayson-Robinson Stores, Inc., Los Angeles, 1946-48; with Roosevelt, Lee, Magee, Inc., Beverly Hills, Calif., 1953-61; sr. v.p., dir. Bache Halsey Stuart Shields Inc. Trustee Eisenhower Exchange Fellowship Found., State U. N.Y., Marist Coll., Roosevelt U., Chgo.; bd. dirs. Boy Scouts Am. Served as lt. comdr. USNR, 1941-46. Decorated Bronze Star. Mem. Am. Legion, Holland Soc. N.Y., Pilgrims of U.S., Huguenot Soc. Am., St. Nicholas Soc. N.Y. Republican. Episcopalian. Clubs: Leash, Racquet and Tennis (N.Y.C.); Tuxedo (N.Y.); Mid-Ocean (Bermuda). Home: New York, N.Y. Died Apr. 27, 1981; buried family burial site, Hyde Park, N.Y.

ROOT, DARRELL ASTOR, engring. co. exec.; b. West Springfield, Mass., Feb. 22, 1913; s. Raymond C. and Minnie (Pagenkopf) R.; B.S. in San. Engring., Mass. Inst. Tech., 1935, M.S., 1939; m. Margaret Felker, Oct. 12, 1939; children—Stephen C., Elizabeth Root Blackmer, Caroline. Design engr. N.H. Water Resources Bd., Concord, 1938; research asst. Mass. Inst. Tech., 1936-39, Permutit Co., N.Y.C., 1939-41; sr. civil engr. East Bay Municipal Utility Dist., Oakland, Calif., 1946-50; with Camp, Dresser & McKee, Boston, 1950-78, partner, 1952-71, sr. v.p., 1971-75, cons., 1976-78. Served to lt. col. C.E., U.S. Army, 1941-45; PTO. Registered profl. engr., Calif., N.H., Maine, Mass., Conn., N.Y., R.I., Vt., Ill., Md., Fla. Fellow ASCE, Am. Cons. Engrs. Council; mem. Am. Acad. Environ. Engrs. (diplomate), Am., New Eng. (Dexter Brackett Meml. medal 1955) water works assns., New Egn. Water Pollution Control Assn., Royal Soc. Health (Eng.), Sigma Xi, Chi Epsilon. Contbr. articles to profl. jours. Home: Longboat Key, Fla. Died Aug. 2, 1978; buried Winchester, Mass.

ROOT, FLORENCE KELLOGG (MRS JOHN BOLTON KELSO), educator; b. East Hampton, Conn., Nov. 27, 1885; d. Edward Payson and Fannie I. (Bryant) R.; student Colorado Coll., Colorado Springs, Colo., 1902-03; B.A., Smith Coll., Northampton, Mass., 1906, M.A., 1914; studied Columbia, 1916-17; m. John Bolton Kelso, June 16, 1932. Latin tutor Smith Coll., 1906-10; prof. Latin and Greek, Pa. Coll. for Women, Pittsburgh, 1910-14; instr. Latin, Smith Coll., 1915-17; dean Pa. Coll. for Women, 1917-22; dean of women, Coll. of Wooster, 1922-30; dean of women and dir. ednl. and vocational counseling, Cleveland Coll. of Western Reserve U., 1930-33. Trustee Y.W.C.A., Cleveland; mem. bd. Y.W.C.A. of St. Paul (chmn. adult edn. dept.). Mem. Nat. Assn. Deans of Women (pres. 1931-33), Am. Asso. Univ. Women (mem. coll. advisory com.), Phi Beta Kappa. Presbyn. Clubs: College (v.p.), Smith Coll. (pres.), Schubert, New Century (St. Paul). Lecturer. Home: La Jolla, Calif. *

RORER, GERALD FRANCIS, pharm. chemist; b. Wyncote, Pa., Feb. 11, 1908; s. William H. and Helen (Crawley) R.; B.S., Haverford Coll., 1929; B.S., Phila. Coll. Pharmacy and Sci., 1931, D.Sc., 1970; m. Mary Amelie Runk, Jan. 27, 1939; children—Gerald Barcroft, Edward Crawley, Herbert Taylor. Dir. William H. Rorer, Inc., Fort Washington, Pa., from 1940, v.p., 1944-50, exec. v.p., treas., 1950-59, pres., 1959-62, chmn. bd., pres., 1962-66, chmn. bd., from 1966; chmn. bd. merged co. Rorer-Amchem, Inc., from 1968. Pres. bd. dirs. Chestnut Hill Acad., 1961-64; bd. mgrs. Germantown Dispensary and Hosp., Phila., from 1964; trustee Acad. Natural Scis., Phila., from 1964, vice chmn., 1967; bd. dirs. Pa. Plan to Develop Scientists in Med. Research, U. Pa., 1962-72; bd. mgrs. Haverford Coll., 1967-73. Mem. Pharm. Mfrs. Assn. (dir. 1964-72), Am. Pharm. Mfrs. Assn. (sec. 1942-44, pres. 1944-46), Mil. Order Loyal Legion, Pa. Soc. S.R. Episcopalian. Clubs: Philadelphia Cricket (pres. 1961-64), Merion Cricket, Union League (Phila.); Royal Poinciana Golf; The Courts; Sunnybrook Golf; Merion Golf. Home: Gladwyne, Pa. Died Feb. 20, 1976.

ROSA, JOSEPH, fgn. service officer; b. Hungary, Jan. 16, 1906 (parents U.S. citizens); student Columbia, 1932; B.A., M.A., U. Wis., 1937; attended Am. U., Washington, 1948-49; m. Evelyn L. Brown, Feb. 1937 (div.); married 2d, Frances L. McConnell, 1958. Economist Resettlement Adminstrn., 1936; econ., statis. analyst Wis. State Tax Commn., 1937-38; editorial, research asst. Harold M. Groves, 1938-39; economist U.S. Dept. Agr., 1939-42; chief pub. finance br. U.S. element Allied Commn. for Austria, 1945-46; ofcl. Dept. State, 1947-80, chief econ. development policy br., 1950-53, adviser econ. development staff, 1953-55; dep. chief econ. analysis sect. Am. Embassy, Paris, 1956-58; chief econ. sect. Am. Embassy, Saigon, Vietnam, 1958-61; spl. asst. to the ambassador on mutual security affairs American Embassy, Seoul, Korea, 1961-64, counselor for econ. affairs, 1964-65. Served with AUS, 1942-45. Mem. Am. Econ. Assn., Am. Statis. Assn., A.A.A.S., Am. Polit. Sci. Assn. Club: Cosmos. Home: Washington. Died Dec. 5, 1980; buried Arlington National Cemetery.

ROSCOE, H(ARRY) L., mining exec.; b. Swanton, O., Feb. 4, 1885; s. Lucius and Harriet (Gibbs) R.; A.B., Michigan College of Mines, 1909, Doctor of Engineering, 1947; married to Edna Halsey Curry, Jan. 15, 1914; children—Harry E., Robert L., Stuart Murray, Edna Jean. Sr. v.p., dir. Noranda Mines, Ltd., Que., Can., 1940—; v.p., dir. Noranda Copper & Brass, Montreal, 1947—, Mining Corp. of Can., Toronto, 1949—, Hallnar Mines, Ltd., Toronto, 1952—; pres., dir. Normetal Mining Corp., Ltd., Quemont Mining Corp., 1949—, Canada Talc Industries, 1951— (all

Toronto); dir. Canada Wire and Cable Co., Pamour Porcupine Mines, Ltd., Kerr-Addison Gold Mines, Ltd., Torbit Silver Mines, Ltd., Waite Amulet Mines, Ltd., Amulet DeFault Mines, Ltd. (all Toronto), East Sullivan Mines (Montreal), Canadian Copper Refiners, Ltd. (Montreal East). Mem. Tau Beta Pi. Mason. Clubs: National Granite, York, Toronto. Home: Toronto. *

ROSE, ALEX (OLESH ROYZ), labor union ofcl.; b. Warsaw, Poland, Oct. 15, 1898; s. Hyman and Faiga (Halpern) Royz; ed. high sch., Warsaw; m. Elsie Shapiro, July 7, 1920; children—Mrs. Carmy Schwartz, Herbert. Came to U.S., 1913. Millinery operator; mem. Millinery Workers Union, 1914; v.p. Internat. Union, 1927; pres. United Hatters, Cap and Millinery Workers Internat. Union, 1950-76; head appeals com. 1957 conv. for expulsion Internat. Brotherhood Teamsters from AFL-CIO. Bd. dirs. Welfare Island Planning and Devel. Corp., N.Y.C. Pub. Devel. Corp. Assisted orgn. Am. Labor Party, 1936, state sec., dir., 1936-44; active Liberal Party, 1944-76, vice chmn., to 1976; del. N.Y. State Constnl. Conv., 1966, presdl. elector, 1940, 48, 64, 68. Served as pvt. Brit. Army, 1918-20. Address: New York, N.Y. Died Dec. 28, 1976.

ROSE, HANNA TOBY, museum curator; b. N.Y.C., Apr. 12, 1909; d. Jacques H. and Theresa (Toby) Rose; student Wellesley Coll., 1930. Staff, Bklyn. Mus., 1932-72, supr. lending services and spl. programs, 1941-47, curator edn., 1947-72. Mem. N.Y. State Regents Adv. Council Adult Edn., 1959-72; v.p. Community Assn. Sch. Dist. 25 and 27, Bklyn. Mem. Internat. Council Museums (pres. internat. edn. com. 1953-62), Nat. Com. Art Edn. (council), N.Y. Acad. Pub. Edn., Am. Assn. Museums, Am. Assn. UN (adv. council So. N.Y. State). Editor: Museums and Teachers, 1956. Home: New York, N.Y. Died Dec. 14, 1976.

ROSE, JOHN LAWRENCE, bus. exec., editor; b. Sioux City, Iowa, Nov. 30, 1908; s. Benjamin Ayrault and Lillian Agnes (Rollins) R.; student S.D. Sch. Mines, 1926-28, U. Ariz., 1928-29; U. Fla., 1929-30; m. Jane Pelela, July 10, 1933; children—John Thomas, Lawrence B. Reporter, asst. city editor, sports editor Sioux City Tribune, 1930-43; staffer U.P.I., Des Moines, 1942, Detroit, 1945-56; with publs. dept. Ford Motor Co., 1946-47, asst. mgr. Ford News Bur., 1947-48; mgr., 1948; asst. dir. pub. relations, 1949-51; owner-pub. Pismo Beach (Calif) Times, 1951-53; with Burroughs Corp., Detroit, 1953-68, asso. dir. pub. relations, 1957-60, dir. pub. relations, 1960-66, dir. information, 1966-68; pres. Rose Enterprises Bd. advisers Wayne State U. Press. Mem. pub. relations com. Mich. United Community Services; mem. Met. Detroit Area Planning Commn., 1966-79; mem. Police Commn., Grosse Ile Twp., 1966-74, chmn., 1970-74, chmn. Grosse Ile Twp. Bd. Assessments and Rev., 1975-79; adminstrv. mgr. Grosse Ile Twp., 1976-79; mem. exam. Bd. Mich. Civil Service Commn. Served to lt. comdr. USNR, 1942-45. Mem. Pub. Relations Soc. Am. (nat. sec. 1965, past pres. Mich.), Detroit Adcraft Club, Sigma Delta Chi. Presbyn. (elder). Mason. Clubs: Detroit Press; Grosse Ile Golf and Country. Home: Grosse Ile, Mich. Died May 30, 1979.

ROSE, W. J., bus. exec.; b. Chgo., 1902. Dir. Am. Electric Power Co., N.Y.C., to 1975. Home: New York, N.Y. Died Apr. 21, 1978.

ROSE, WILLIAM PALEN, (WILL ROSE), writer; b. Woodstock, N.Y., Mar. 17, 1889; s. Abram Dubois and Mary (Palen) R.; prep. edn., Kingston (N.Y.) Acad.; A.B., Cornell U., 1911; m. Jennie Louise Lamberson, June 14, 1913; 1 dau. Jeannette (Mrs. Glenn Stanford). With Lord & Thomas Advt. Agy., Chgo., 1911; successively with Suburban Life mag., N.Y.C., Erie (Pa.) Herald, Washington Post and Washington Times until 1916; pub. Cambridge Springs (Pa.) Enterprise-News, 1916-56, Union City Times-Enterprise 1926-56, Waterford Leader and Edinboro Independent, 1943-56, Girard Cosmopolite-Herald, 1946-56. Mem. Greater Pa. Council, 1931-34. Winner Republican Congrl. Primary 29th Pa. Dist., 1934, 36; Republican candidate for State Senate, 1926; chmn. Crawford County (Pa.) Young Rep. Com., 1935. Pres. bd. trustees Cambridge Pub. Schs. 1926-56; trustee Edinboro (Pa.) Coll., 1939-64, pres. bd., 1956-63, 1st hon. coll. trustee for life in Pa., 1964-77; corporator Meadville City Hosp., 1950-70. Mem. Pa. Newspaper Publishers Assn. (v.p. 1935; Merit (award), Acad. Polit. Sci., Sigma Delta Chi (hon.), Sigma Nu, Pi Gamma Mu, Pi Delta Epsilon. Mem. Dutch Reformed Church. Mason (32 deg.), K.P., Elk. Clubs: Rotary (pres. 1929), University; founder Cornell U. Dramatic Club, 1908. Author: Small Town Gastronomy; Big Stick of the Small Town (The Church); Rotary for Rubens; Tarnished; The Vanishing Village, 1961; Splurgin' and numerous other articles, stories and books. Contbr. to Scribner's Rotarian, Readers Digest and other mags. Dormitory at Edinboro Coll. named in his honor, 1966. Address: Annapolis, Md. Died Mar. 25, 1977.

ROSELER, R(OBERT) O(SWALD), univ. prof.; born Germany, July 30, 1883; s. Albert and Mathilde (Gundlach) R.; student, univs. of Berlin and Posen; Ph.D., Ohio State U., 1929; m. Anna Marie Metschl, Sept., 1916; children—Herbert, Nancy, Gerhart. Came to U.S., 1913. Became successively teacher at Teacher's Coll., Koschmin, Germany, Herder Inst., Riga, Russia, Nat. Teachers Seminary, Milwaukee; rector Ober-Realschule, Mexico City; asso. prof. Ohio State U.; prof. German lang. and lit. U. of Wis. since 1934. Mem. Modern Lang. Assn., Assn. Modern Lang. Teachers (pres. 1938), Wis. Modern Lang. Teachers Assn. (pres. 1943), Phi Delta Kappa. Author several books relating to field since 1931. Editor: Monatshefte (jour. on study German lang. and lit.). Home: Madison, Wis. *

ROSEN, GEORGE, historian, educator, physician; b. N.Y.C., June 23, 1910; s. Morris and Rose (Hendleman) R.; B.S. CCNY, 1930; M.D., U. Berlin, 1935; Ph.D., Columbia U., 1944, M.P.H., 1947; m. Beate Caspari, July 6, 1933; children—Paul Peter, Susan Joan. Intern, Beth-El Hosp., Bklyn., 1935-36; practice medicine, N.Y.C., 1937-42; health officer N.Y.C. Health Dept., 1947-49; dir. Bur. Pub. Health Edn., 1949-50; asso. med. dir. Health Ins. Plan Greater N.Y., 1950-57; lectr. health edn. Sch. Pub. Health Columbia U., 1949-50, prof. 1951-69; prof. history medicine and epidemiology, pub. health Yale U., 1969-77; vis. lectr. Med. Care, Harvard Sch. Pub. Health, 1956-60; Victor Robinson Meml. lectr. Temple U., 1958, Fielding H. Garrison lectr., 1961; Beaumont lectr. Yale U., 1962; Benjamin Rush lectr. Am. Psychiat. Assn., 1967; Richard H. Shryock lectr. U. Pa., 1975; cons. NIH, 1959-64; mem. med. adv. bd. Sidney Hillman Health Center. Served to maj. as med. intelligence officer, AUS, 1943-46. Recipient Grant Squires award Columbia U., 1945; Prentiss award Cleve. Health Mus. 1964; Hayhow award Am. Coll. Hosp. Adminstrs., 1965; Hafner award Am. Assn. History of Medicine and Med. Library Assn., 1966. Mem. Am. Pub. Health Assn., Am. Assn. History Medicine (William H. Welch medal 1961), Am. Sociol. Assn., N.Y. Acad. Medicine. Author: History of Miners Diseases, 1943; The Specialization of Medicine, 1944; Fees and Fee Bills, 1945; The Reception of William Beaumont's Discovery in Europe, 1942; 400 Years of a Doctor's Life, 1947; A History of Public Health, 1958; Madness in Society, 1968; From Medical Police to Social Medicine, 1974; Preventive Medicine in the United States, 1900-1975, 1975. Translator, editor: Man in Structure and Function, 1938; Einstein-His Life and Times, 1947; Democracy and Socialism, 1939; editor Ciba Symposia, 1938-44, Jour. History of Medicine, 1946-52; editorial bd. Am. Jour. Pub. Health, 1948-57, chmn. bd., 1957, editor, 1957-73. Home: North Haven, Conn. Died July 27, 1977.

ROSENBERG, ABE EUGENE, lawyer; b. Milw., May 11, 1898; s. Jacob and Jenny (Levitt) R.; B.A., U. Oreg., 1921, J.D., 1923; m. Jeane Kamusher, Feb. 14, 1924; children—Edward Alan, Susan Struck Rosenberg Struck. Admitted to Oreg. bar, 1923, since practiced in Portland; mem. firm Rosenberg, Swire & Riebe, and predecessors, 1926-77. Exec. sec. Pacific Coast regional bd. Nat. Bd. Coat and Suit Industry, 1935-68; pres. Oreg. Jewish Welfare Fund, 1940-45. Mem. Am., Oreg. bar assns., Portland C. of C. Republican. Jewish. Home: Portland, Oreg. Died Nov. 24, 1977; buried Beth Israel Mausoleum.

ROSENBERG, HAROLD, author; b. Bklyn, Feb. 2, 1906; s. Abraham Benjamin and Fanny (Edelman) R.; student Coll. City N.Y., 1923-24; LL.B.; St. Lawrence U., 1927; D.Litt., Lake Forest (Ill.) Coll., 1968; m. D.F.A., Md. Inst. Coll. Art, 1971, Parsons Coll., 1975; m. Maynatalie Tabak, Mar. 13, 1932; 1 dau., Patia Myra. Nat. art editor Am. Guide Series, WPA, 1938-42; dep. chief domestic radio bur., charge N.Y. Office, OWI, 1944-45; cons. expert Treasure Dept., 1945-46; program cons. Advt. Council, 1946-73; lectr. New Sch. Social Research, 1953-54; regents lectr. U. Cal. at Berkeley, 1962; lectr. Christian Gauss seminars in criticism, Princeton, 1963, others; vis. prof. So. Ill. U., 1965; prof. com. social thought and art dept. U. Chgo., 1966-78; art critic New Yorker mag., 1967-78. Mem. adv. council Smithsonian Instn., commr. Nat. Collection Fine Arts. Recipient Frank Jewett Mather award Coll. Art Assn., 1964. Morton Dauwen Zabel award Am. Acad. Arts and Letters, 1976. Fellow Am. Acad. Arts and Scis.; mem. Internat. Assn. Art Critics. Author: (poems) Trance Above the Streets, 1942; The Tradition of the New 1959; Arshile Gorky, 1962; The Anxious Object, 1964; Artworks And Packages, 1969; Act and the Actor, 1971; Barnet Newman Sculptures, 1972; The De-Definition of Art, 1972; Discovering the Present, 1973; Willem de Kooning, 1974; Art on the Edge, 1975. Contbr. numerous articles to profl. jours. Home: Springs East Hampton, N.Y. Died July 11, 1978; buried Springs East Hampton.

ROSENBERG, JAKOB, educator, art curator; b. Berlin, Germany, Sept. 5, 1893; s. Gabriel and Bertha (Rosenbaum) R.; student Univs. of Bern, Zurich, Frankfurt-am-Main, Munich; Ph.D., Munich, 1922; M.A. (hon.) Harvard, 1942; Arts D. (hon.), Harvard, 1961; m. Elisabeth H. Husserl, Dec. 22, 1922; children—Ruth (Mrs. Nahum Z. Medalia), Wolfgang. Asst. in print dept. State Mus., Berlin, 1925-30, keeper, 1930-35; instr. Harvard summer sch., 1936-37; research fellow, lectr. Harvard, 1937-39, curator prints, 1939, asso. prof., 1940-47, prof. fine arts, 1948-64, prof. emeritus, 1964-80; Robert Sterling Clark prof. Williams Coll., 1965-66; Kress prof. Nat. Gallery Art, 1966-67. Hon. fellow P. Morgan Library, N.Y.C. Fellow Am. Acad. Arts and Scis. Club: Harvard Faculty. Author: Die Handzeichnungen von Martin Schongauer, 1922; Jacob van Ruisdael, 1928; die Niederlaend, Handzeichnungen des Berliner Kupferstich Kabinetts (with E. Bock), 1930; Die Gemaelde Lucas Cranach D. Ae. (with M.J. Friedlaender), 1932; Rembrandt (2 vols.), 1948, rev. edit. (1 vol.), 1964; German Expressionism and Abstract Art (with C.L. Kuhn), 1957; Great Draughtsmen from Pisanello to Picasso, 1959, 2d enlarged edit., 1974; Die Zeichnungen von Lucas Cranach D. Ae., 1960; (with S. Slive) Dutch Painting from 1600-1800, 1965; On Quality in Art (A. W. Mellon lectrs. of 1964), 1965; Louis Cranach, rev. edit., 1978. Home: Arlington, Mass. Died Apr. 7, 1980.

ROSENBLOOM, CARROLL D., chmn. bd. Balt. Colts Prof. Football Team. Address: Baltimore, Md. Died Apr. 3, 1979.

ROSENFIELD, ISADORE, architect; b. Mayaky, Russia, Sept. 7, 1893; s. Haem and Rosse (Keegler) R.; B.S., Harvard, 1918, M.Arch., 1921; m. Leora Kagan, Nov. 28. 1918; children—Zachary, Lenora (Mrs. Roderick Kyle de Camp). Came to U.S., 1910, naturalized, 1916. Asst. prof. architecture N.Y. U., 1932-40; chief architect Dept. Pub. Works, N.Y.C., 1940-45; prof. med. architecture Columbia, practice arch., N.Y.C., 1945-70; sr. partner firm Isadore and Zachary Rosenfield (firm now Zachary Rosenfield & Partners), ret.; design, color cons. U. Minn., Inst. of Design, Chgo.; lectr. med. archtl. planning profl. orgns. and univs. in U.S.; designer P.R. Med. Center, San Juan, Khyber Med. Center, Peshawar, Pakistan. Served with 472d Engrs., U.S. Army, World War I. Fellow A.I.A. (lectr. med. archtl. planning N.Y. chpt. 1944, 1st chmn. com. hosp. research; various profl. honors); mem. Am. Assn. for Hosp. Planning (dir., honor award for distinguished contbn. to hosp. planning and health of Am. people 1975), Am. Hosp. Assn. Author: Hospitals-Integrated Design, 2d edit., 1951; Hospital Architecture and Beyond, 1969; Hospital Architecture-Integrated Components, 1971; Lest We Forget, Memoirs, 1977; also articles. Home: New York, N.Y. Died Mar. 6, 1980.

ROSENHAUS, MATTHEW BERNARD, toiletries and pharm. co. exec.; b. Bayonne, N.J., Mar. 19, 1912; s. Morris and Sophie (Post) R.; B.A., Rutgers U., 1933; m. Sarah Esther Pollack, Nov. 8, 1934 (dec. Feb. 1968); children—Harriet Rosenhaus Bobrow, Lawrence, Annetta Rosenhaus Chester, Albert; m. 2d, Gila Golan, Sept. 16, 1969; children—Sarita Agnes, Hedy Marisa, Loretta Sonia. Pres., chmn. bd. J.B. Williams Co., Inc., N.Y.C., 1935-80; vice chmn. bd. Nabisco, Inc., Columbia Pictures Industries, Inc. Chmn. bd. dirs. Eleanor Roosevelt Cancer Found.; bd. dirs. United Cerebral Palsy Research and Edn. Found.; trustee Fund for Peace, Huxley Inst., N.Y. Acad. Scis., Rutgers U. Found., Synagogue Council Am.; mem. exec. com. Daus. of Jacob Geriatric Center, Bronx; hon. vice-chmn. Anti-Defamation League; hon. life mem. Am. Cancer Soc. Died Aug. 26, 1980.

ROSENSOHN, ETTA LASKER (MRS. SAMUEL J. ROSENSOHN), social and civic worker; b. Galveston, Tex., Aug. 29, 1885; d. Morris Lasker and Nettie (Davis) Lasker; student U. Tex., 1901-03; certificate N.Y. Sch. Social Work; 1916; m. Samuel J. Rosensohn, Nov. 25, 1918; children—Edward (dec.), William Janet (dec.) Research worker Bur. Philanthropic Research, N.Y.C., 1916-17; organizer, dist. supervisor Home Service, A.R.C., 1917-19; bd. Nat. Council Jewish Women, 1919-30; chmn. Dept. Service to Fgn. Born, 1919-30; mem. bd. dirs. Nat. Travelers Aid Assn., 1920-47, sec., 1925-30, v.p., 1944-47; mem. nat. bd. Hadassah, Women's Zionist Orgn. Am. since 1930, nat. treas., 1933-37, 40-42, chmn. bd., 1942-44, pres. since 1952; bd. dirs. Conf. Jewish Relations since 1935; bd. govs. Hebrew U. in Jerusalem, 1939-49, since 52; bd. dirs. U.S.O., Inc., 1941-46, Jewish religion. Club: Quaker Ridge Golf (Scarsdale, N.Y.). Home: N.Y.C.; also Larchmont, N.Y. *

ROSENSTEIN, NETTIE, designer; b Vienna, Austria, Sept. 26, 1893; d. Joseph and Sara (Hoffman) Rosencrans; brought to U.S., 1899; ed. pub. schs. and normal coll., N.Y.C.; m. Saul Rosenstein, Oct. 12, 1913; children—Jerome H., Claire C. Operated own business as fashion designer, 1917-60; designer costume jewelry beginning 1942, and handbags, 1944, opened perfume dept., 1946; later dir. Nettie Rosenstein Perfumes, Inc., Nettie Rosenstein Accessories Corp. Recipient Lord & Taylor Achievement award, 1938, Nieman Marcus Achievement award, 1938; Fashion Trades award for best design of day dresses, 1946; Coty Award for consistency in good designing, 1947, for best accessories, 1960. Mem. Fashion Group. Designed Mrs. Eisenhowers inaugural gowns, 1953, 57. Home: New York, N.Y. Died Mar. 13, 1980.

ROSENTHAL, DANIEL I., lawyer; b. Pitts., June 3, 1914; s. Charles Herman and Rose (Lambie) R.; B.A., Johns Hopkins, 1934; student Harvard, 1934-36; LL.B., U. Cin., 1937, J.D., 1968; m. Mildred Goodman, Aug. 7, 1938; children—Sue Ann, Dan G. Admitted to Ohio bar, 1937, practiced in Springfield; spl. agt. FBI, 1941-45. Dir. Vining Broom Co., Inc. Vice pres. Ohio Bar Found. Past chmn. Clark County Jail Study Com. Mem. Am. (Ho. of Dels.), Ohio (exec. com., pres.-elect. 1974-75, pres. 1975-76), Clark County (past pres.) bar assns. Jewish (past bd. dirs. temple). Home: Springfield, Ohio. Died June 23, 1976.

ROSENWALD, LESSING J(ULIUS), merchant; b. Chgo., Feb. 10, 1891; s. Julius and Augusta (Nusbaum) R.; student Cornell U., 1909-11; L.H.D., U. Pa., 1947; Litt.D., Lincoln U., 1954; LL.D., Jefferson Med. Coll., 1954; m. Edith Goodkind, Nov. 6, 1913; children—Julius II, Helen R. Snellenburg, Robert L., Joan R. Scott, Janet R. Becker. Connected with Sears, Roebuck & Co. from the beginning of active bus. career until retirement, became mgr. Phila. plant at its openings, 1920, vice chmn. bd. dirs. and chmn. exec. com., 1931-32, chmn. bd., 1932-39; retired. Chmn. Am. Council for Judaism, Inc. Served as seaman, 2d class, Gt. Lakes Naval Sta., World War I. Mem. Am. Philos. Soc. Midday. Club: Grolier (N.Y.C.). Home: Jenkintown, Pa. Died June 24, 1979.

ROSNER, HAROLD, merchandising exec.; b. N.Y.C., 1901; m. Belle. Pres., dir. Robert Hall Clothes, Inc., N.Y.C. Home: New York, N.Y. Died Dec. 28, 1976.

ROSS, CHARLES ALEXANDER, clergyman; b. Newburgh, N.Y., Nov. 12, 1883; s. George Munro and Caroline (Lawson) R.; student Newburgh Free Acad., 1897-1901, Spencerian Business Coll., 1902-03, Union Theol. Seminary, 1907-09; m. Nanny MacLennan Merritt, Sept. 18, 1908; children—Jean (Mrs. Robert Frost Knox), Ruth (Mrs. Merle Alden Reed). Elizabeth (Mrs. Philip Denton Lambe), Antoinette (Mrs. Frank Oliver Kingdon.) Began with Phelps, Dodge & Co., of New York City, 1904; entered the ministry, Meth. Church; pastor East Chatham, N.Y., 1909-11, Carmel, N.Y., 1911-13; asso. with Dr. Charles Goodell, St. Paul's Ch., N.Y., 1913-15; pastor Congl. Church, Massena, N.Y., 1916-17; asso. with Dr. Parkes Cadman, Central Congl. Ch., Brooklyn. 1917-19; pastor Congl. Ch., Poughkeepsie, N.Y., 1919-22, First Presbyn. Ch., Rutherford, N.J., 1922-36; pastor First Presbyn. Ch., Elizabeth, N.J., since 1936. Chaplain, A.E.F., 1918-19. Trustee Elizabethtown Chapter, Am. Red Cross. Mem. Pi Gamma Mu. Mason (K.T.). Club: Elizabeth Rotary (pres. 1938, gov. 183d Dist., 1939-40). Home: Elizabeth, N.J. *

ROSS, CLARENCE HOPKINS, lawyer, utility exec.; b. David City, Nebr., Mar. 20, 1900; s. John Gans and Lucy (Clark) R.; A.B., U. Nebr., 1922; LL.B., Harvard, 1925; m. Elizabeth Hall, Feb. 21, 1942; children—Gwen, Elizabeth; m. Mrs. James Flower, May 4, 1973. Admitted to Ill. bar, 1926, then practiced in Chgo.; Washington counsel R.F.C., 1932-33; Washington counsel for Navy Renegotiation Bd., 1943; counsel Ross, Hardies, O'Keefe, Babcock & Parsons. Past chmn. Central Telephone & Utilities Corp. Mem. Am. (past chmn. pub. utility law sect.), Ill., Chgo. bar assns. Clubs: Gulf Stream Golf (Delray Beach); Everglades (Palm Beach, Fla.). Home: Delray Beach, Fla. Died May 14, 1981.

ROSS, EARLE DUDLEY, prof. history; b. Ross Hill, Tioga Co., N.Y., Dec. 20, 1885; s. John Warren and Fanny Jane (Coleman) R.; Ph.B., Syracuse U., 1909, Ph.M., 1910; Am., Cornell, 1912, Ph.D., 1915; U. of Wis., 1913-14; m. Ethel Eileen Newbecker, of Ord, Neb., June 27, 1917; children—Ronald Dudley, Bruce Mitchell. Prof. history and social science, Mo. Wesleyan Coll., 1915-17; prof. history, Simpson Coll., Indianola, Ia., 1917-18, Ill. Wesleyan U., 1918-19; prof. history and head of dept., N.D. Agrl. Coll., 1919-23; asso. prof. history, Ia. State Coll., 1923—. Mem. Am. Hist. Assn., Agrl. History Soc., Miss. Valley Hist. Assn., Ia. State Hist. Soc., Am. Assn. Univ. Profs., Pi Gamma Mu, Phi Beta Kappa, Phi Kappa Phi. Democrat. Methodist. Mason. Author: The Liberal Republican Movement, 1919. Editor (with L.B. Schmidt): Readings in the Economic History of American Agriculture, 1925. Asso. editor "Social Science" (mag.) since its establishment, 1925. Contbr. to various ednl. and hist. jours. Home: Ames, Ia.*

ROSS, JOHN BAYHA, univ. adminstr.; b. Painesville, O., Oct. 30, 1925; s. Clarence Crump and Florence Lois (Bayha) R.; B.S. in Bus. Adminstrn., Ohio State U., 1950, M.B.A., 1951; Ph.D., U. Ala., 1960; m. Jo Ann Kishler, Sept. 4, 1949; children—Daniel, Andrew. Mem. staff Arthur Young & Co., C.P.A.'s, Tulsa, 1951-54; instr. accounting U. Ala., Tuscaloosa, 1954-57; mem. facu.ty U. Tenn., Knoxville, 1957-76, prof. accounting, 1960-76, head dept., 1960-72, dean Coll. Bus. Adminstrn., 1972-76. Served with USNR, 1943-46. C.P.A., Okla., Tenn. Mem. Am. Inst. C.P.A.'s, Tenn. Soc. C.P.A.'s, Am. Accounting Assn. Home: Alcoa, Tenn. Died June 27, 1976.

ROSS JULIUS ROBERT, rice mill exec.; b. N.Y.C., 1885; s. Robert and Margaret R.; student of public schools. Chairman of the board and president of the River Brand Rice Mills, Inc. (consol. of Southern Rice Sales Co., Inc., N.Y., Pfeffer Rice Milling Co., Inc., Houston. River Brand Rice Mill, Inc., El Camp. Tex., Champion Rice Mills, Eunice, La., also Memphis), N.Y.C., 1946—. Home: N.Y.C. *

ROSS, MARTIN CHAUNCEY, curator; b. Moriches, N.Y., Nov. 21, 1904; s. William Edwin and Mary (Rogers) R.; A.B., Harvard, 1928, A.M., 1930; m. Lotus Robb Smith, Sept. 10, 1937 (dec. Sept. 1969). Curator mediaeval, subsequent decorative arts Walters Art Gallery, Balt., 1934-52; dep. adviser monuments fine arts, archives SHAEF, 1944-45; chief curator art Los Angeles County Mus., 1952-55; curator Hillwood, Washington, 1959-73; curator Hillwood Collections, Smithsonian Instn., 1974-77; Fulbright lectr. U. Vienna, 1960-61. Author: Catalogue of Exhibition of Byzantine Art, 1947; Catalogue of the Works of W.H. Rinehart, 1948; The West of Alfred J. Miller, 1951; The Life of Christ in Masterpieces of Art, 1957; The Art of Karl Faberge and his Contemporaries, 1965; The West of Alfred Jacob Miller, 1967; Russian Porcelains: Merriwether Post Collection, 1968. Editor: George Catlin, Last Rambles with the Indians, 1959; Migration Art in the Walters Art Gallery, 1961; Catalogue of the Byzantine Antiquities in Dumbarton Oaks Collection, Vol. I, 1962, Vol. II, 1965. Contbr. articles to art mags. Home: Washington, D.C. Died Apr. 24, 1977.

ROSS, ROBERT CRAIG, steel mcht.; b. Wingham, Ont., Can., Nov. 14, 1883; s. Alexander and Anna Jane (Wilson) R.; student London (Ontario). Collegiate Inst., 2 yrs.; m. Betsy May Albrecht, May 11, 1903 (died 1936); 1 dau., Dorothy Ellen (Mrs. Paul H. Burgert); m. 2d, Ann S. Ogden, Nov. 19, 1937. Stenographer and telegrapher Joseph T. Ryerson & Son, Inc., steel iron and machinery, Chicago, 1903, v.p. and dir. since 1931, sec., since 1939; dir. Inland Steel Co. Mem. Chicago Assn. Commerce (past v.p.). Republican. Clubs: Chicago, Union League, Traffic, Racquet (Chicago); Chicago Golf (Wheaton), La Grange (Illinois). Home: La Grange, Ill. *

ROSS, VINCENT C., publisher; b. Bklyn., Oct. 19, 1895; s. Thomas J. and Mary E. (Eagan) R.; ed. N.Y. U., 1921; LL.D. (hon.), St. Michael's, Winooski, Vt., 1960; m. Kathleen Cannon, June 13, 1935; (dec.); children—Vincent C., George Cannon; m. 2d, Anne. Dir. Prentice-Hall, Inc., Victoria Investment Co., N.Y.C. adv. bd. Chem. Bank N.Y. Trust Co.; mem. bd. Nat. Co., Malden, Mass. Trustees St. Michael's. Mem. Cardinal's Com. Laity. Mem. Financial Execs. Inst. (pres. 1950-51, chmn. bd. 1951-52), U.S. Seniors Golf Assn. (tournament com.), Met. Golf Assn. (v.p.), Westchester Srs. Golf Assn. Decorated Knight of Malta, Knight of Holy Sepulchre. Clubs: Westchester Country (Rye, N.Y.); Knickerbocker Country (Tenafly, N.Y.); Everglades, Old Guard Soc. Golfers (Palm Beach, Fla.); Union League (N.Y.C.). Home: Rye, N.Y. Died Apr. 1, 1976.

ROSSBACH, JOSEPH HOWARD, lawyer; b. N.Y.C., Dec. 19, 1913; s. Max J. H. and Mabel Minnie (Limburg) R.; A.B., Yale, 1935, LL.B., 1938; m. Eleanor A. Frank, Dec. 29, 1947; children—Anne Clara, Sarah, Howard. Admitted to N.Y. bar, 1938; with Cook, Nathan, Lehman & Greenman, N.Y.C., 1938-40, Guggenheimer & Untermyer, 1946-50; atty.-in-chief Legal Aid Soc., N.Y.C., 1950-52, 53-55; commr. SEC, 1952-53; justice Ct. Spl. Sessions, N.Y.C., 1955-62; judge Criminal Ct. City N.Y., 1962-71; practiced in N.Y.C., to 1975. Served to lt. col. AUS, 1941-46. Mem. N.Y. State, Bronx County bar assns., Assn. Bar City N.Y. Jewish. Clubs: Yale, City (N.Y.C.); Riverdale Yacht; Century Country. Contbr. articles legal jours. Address: New York, N.Y. Died Sept. 3, 1975.

ROSSITER, ROGER JAMES, educator, biochemist; b. Glenelg, S. Australia, July 24, 1913; s. James Leonard and Marguerite (Jacobs) R.; B.Sc., U. Western Australia, 1934; B.A., Oxford (Eng.) U., 1938, D.Phil., 1944, B.M., B.Ch., 1941, M.A., 1942, D.M., 1946; m. Helen Margaret Randell, Mar. 16, 1940; children—James Randell, Margaret Ruth, John Cunningham, George Mattingly. Demonstrator biochemistry, tutor physiology Oxford U., 1938-46; biochemistry U. Western Ont., from 1947, head dept., 1947-65, dean grad. studies, 1965-68, v.p. acad., provost, 1968-74, v.p. health scis., 1974-76. Cons. biochemistry Westminster Hosp.; cons. medicine Victoria, St. Joseph's hosps. Mem. research adv. group Nat. Cancer Inst. Can., 1957-67, chmn., 1960-65; mem. Med. Research Council Can., 1960-66, chmn. biochemistry grants com., 1963-66; mem. com. univ. affairs Province of Ont., 1968-74. Served to maj. Royal Army Med. Corps, 1943-46. Recipient Flavelle medal Royal Soc., Can., 1963. Mem. Biochem. Soc., Canadian Biochem. Soc. (pres. 1962-63), Am. Soc. Biol. Chemists, Internat. Soc. Neurochemistry (chmn. 1967-69). Home: London, Ont., Can. Died Feb. 21, 1976; buried Helsinki, Finland.

ROSSITER, WILLIAM THOMAS, business exec.; born Cleveland, Aug. 19, 1882; s. James C. and Katharine (Mahon) R.; ed. in pub. schs. of Cleveland; m. Margaret Andrews, Feb. 17, 1925; children—William Thomas, James Cullen, Helen Chmn. bd. The Cleve Builders Supply Co.; pres. Madison Foundry Co., Cleve., 1947—. Home: Shaker Heights, O. *

ROSSMANN, KURT, physicist, educator; b. Berlin, Germany, Mar. 20, 1926; s. Theodore and Lucie (Winkelmann) R.; came to U.S., 1948, naturalized, 1956; B.S., U. Dayton, 1951; M.S., Ohio State U., 1954, Ph.D., 1958; m. Helen Arlene Brown, Sept. 14, 1952; 1 dau., Lynn. Grad. research asst. Ohio State U., 1952-58; sr. physicist Eastman Kodak Co., Rochester, N.Y., 1958-64, research asso. research labs., 1964-67; prof. radiol. scis., dir. sect. radiol. scis. U. Chgo., 1967-76, dir. center for radiologic image research, 1972-76. Chmn. task group on radiographic image quality Internat. Commn. on Radiation Units and Measurements, 1965-75, chmn. task group on resolution of screen-film systems, 1975-76; U.S. rep. working group image quality Internat. Electrotech. Commn., 1975-76; mem. adv. com. on med. radiation Bur. Radiol. Health, Dept. Health, Edn. and Welfare, 1967-71; mem. med. radiation adv. com. Nat. Cancer Inst., 1973-75. Served with German Army, 1943-45. Hon. fellow Am. Coll. Radiology; mem. Am. Assn. Physicists in Medicine, Radiol. Soc. N. Am., Sigma Xi, Pi Mu Epsilon, Sigma Pi Sigma. Editorial bd. Investigative Radiology, 1967-76. Mem. adv. editorial bd. Radiology, 1970-76. Contbr. articles to numerous profl. publs. Home: Hinsdale, Ill. Died Oct. 16, 1976.

ROSSO, AUGUSTO, diplomat; b. Tronzano, Italy, Dec. 23, 1885; son of Pietro and Emilia (Bouchet) R.; grad. in jurisprudence, U. of Turin, 1908. Sec. of Italian Embassy, Washington, D.C., 1910-12; same, embassies at St. Petersburg and Berlin, 1913; sec. to minister for foreign affairs, 1913-14; lt. cav., Italian Army, 1914-16 (decorated with Italian War Cross and Interallied Victory Medal); sec. embassy, Oslo, Norway, 1917-18, later at Athens, 1919; counselor to embassy, Washington, 1922-25, London, 1925-27; head of League of Nations Dept., Foreign Office, rank of M.P., 1927-32; ambassador to Washington since Nov. 1932. Del. to meetings of Council and Assembly of League of Nations, 1927-32, including Reparations Conf., The Hague, 1929, Naval Conf., London, 1930. Address: Washington, D.C. *

ROSTOCK, FRANK WITTE, newspaper editor; b. N.Y. City, Sept. 16, 1882; s. Carl Friederich and Johana Mary (Rostock) Witte (adopted); student Buchtel Acad., University Sch. and Buchtel Coll.; m. Virginia Carolina Dangeleisen, Aug. 17, 1907. Reporter Akron (O.) Press, 1900-01, Akron Beacon-Journal, 1901-02; asst. sporting editor Cleveland Press, 1903-07; sporting editor Cincinnati Post, 1907-12, Cleveland Press, 1912-15; editor in chief Cincinnati Post, 1915-21; gen. business mgr. N.E.A. Service, 1921-24; gen. mgr. St. Louis Times, 1924-25; business mgr. Cincinnati Post, 1925-29, pres. and editor since 1929. Mem. Phi Delta Theta. Lutheran. Mason, Elk. Clubs: Queen City, Cincinnati, Cuvier Press, Advertisers, Automobile, Kenwood Country, Clovernook Country. Home: Cincinnati. *

ROTH, ALMON E. (ROTH), pres. S.F. Employers Council; lawyer; b. Crandon, S.D., July 31, 1886; s. Edward Herman and Magdalena (Beckley) R.; A.B., Stanford U., 1909, J.D., 1912; m. Mildred Mary Hayes, Dec. 26, 1912; children—Mary Elizabeth (Mrs. Marron Kendrick), Miriam Virginia (Mrs. Alexander Scott Gray MacKenzie), William Edward. Dean of men, Stanford U., 1909-12; comptroller and business mgr., Stanford U., 1919-37; pres. Waterfront Employers Assn. of Pacific Coast, 1937-39; also pres. Pacific Am. Shipowners Assn., 1937-39; pres. San Francisco Employers Council, 1939-44, re-elected, 1947; chmn. bd. govs., 1944-47; pres. Nat. Fedn. Am. Shipping, Inc. Washington, D.C., 1944-47; consultant and lecturer on labor relations; mem. National War Labor Board. Pres. Rotary Internat., 1930-31; presided at Internat. Conv., Vienna, Austria. Adviser to U.S. State Dept. Internat. Shipping Conf., London, 1946, Amsterdam, 1947, and Washington, D.C. Former trustee Stanford U., Industrial Relations Counselors, Inc.; former member board directors American Planning and Civic Assn., New York City; vice-pres. Calif. State Chamber of Commerce; mem. radio advisory com. America's Town Meeting of the Air; mem. advisory com. Am. Econ. Foundation; designer of Frost Memorial Amphitheater at Stanford University. Mem. Calif. Bar Assn., Phi Delta Phi. Republican. Methodist. Clubs: Rotary, Commonwealth, Bohemian; San Francisco Golf. Contbr. to Periodicals. Home: Burlingame, Calif. *

ROTH, EDWARD ULYSSES, lawyer; b. Phila., Mar. 17, 1885; s. Bernard and Rose (Silver) R.; prep. edn. N.Y. pub. and pvt. schs., also U. State N.Y.; LL.B., N.Y. Law Sch., 1906. Legal tng. with Stetson, Jennings & Russell (now Davis, Polk, Wardwell, Sunderland & Kiend), 1900-20; partner with Thomas Carmody and Chester Mayer, 1920-45, Carmondy, Roth & Francess, 1946—; appeal agt. SSS, 1941-47. Served as chief insp. ordnance shell loading sta., Morgan, N.J., Ordnance Dept., U.S. Army, World War I. Mem. Am., N.Y. State bar assns., Assn. Bar City N.Y. Mason (past master). Home: New York City NY. *

ROTH, WILLARD LAWRENCE, ins. co exec.; b. Kansas City, Mo., Feb. 24, 1914; s. Theodore and Malvina (Glatter) R.; student Northwestern U.; m. Geraldine Eisenstadt, Sept. 22, 1935; children—Rachelle A. (Mrs. Jay A. Rosenberg), Robert A. With Western & So. Life Ins. Co., Cin., 1935-78, v.p., dir. agys., 1959-70, sr. v.p., 1971-74, exec. v.p., 1974-78, dir., 1972-78; pres. RAR Operations, Inc. Mem. Life Ins. Mgmt. Research Assn. (chmn. bd. dirs., 1970), Life Underwriters Tng. Council (dir.). Clubs: Cincinnati, Crest Hills Country, Queen City. Home: Cincinnati, Ohio. Died Mar. 9, 1978.

ROTHROCK, MARY UTOPIA, librarian; b. Trenton, Tenn., Sept. 19, 1890; d. John Thomas and Utopia Ada (Herron) Rothrock; B.S., Vanderbilt, 1911; M.S., 1912; D.Litt., Univ. of Chattanooga (Tenn.), 1948; student New York State Library School, Albany, 1912-14; B.L.S., 1922; Assistant New York State Library, 1913-14; head of circulation dept., Cossitt Library, Memphis, Tenn., 1914-16; librarian Lawson McGhee Library, Knoxville, Tenn., 1916-34; supervisor of libraries Tenn. Valley Authority, 1923-48, library cons., 1948-51; librarian Knox County (Tenn.) library since 1949. Received Lippincott award, 1938. Member adv. com. on libraries, U.S. Office of Edn., 1941. Fellow. Am. Lib. Inst.; mem. A.L.A. (editorial com. 1924-29 and 1932-33; mem. exec. 1938-42; lending sect. chmn. 1922, 31; library extension bd. 1933-38; chmn. adult edn. round table, 1935-36; council, 1932-42; chmn. visual methods com., 1937-40; chmn. audio-visual com., since 1948; chmn. joint com. libraries and educational films, 1940-42; chmn. Nat. Defense activities and libraries, 1941-42, 1st vice-president, 1945-46; pres. 1946-47), Tennessee Library Assn. (sec.-treas. 1916-18; pres. 1919-20, 1927-28), South-eastern Library Assn. (chmn. 1920-22; pres. 1922-24), East Tenn. Hist. Soc. (sec. 1925-28; treas. 1929-32; pres. 1932, 37; editorial board since 1929; mem. Tennessee Hist. Commn. from 1944), Soc. Colonial Dames, Delta Delta Delta. Democrat. Presbyterian. Author: Discovering Tennessee, 1936. Editor, French Country, 1946. Contbr. to professional jours. Home: Knoxville, Tenn. Died Jan. 30, 1976; buried Old Gray Cemetery, Knoxville.

ROTHSCHILD, HERBERT M., furniture mfg. exec.; b. N.Y.C., Nov. 18, 1891; s. Morris and Carrie (Vogel) R.; student pub. schs., N.Y.; m. Nannette Friend, Feb. 27, 1917; children—Robert Friend, Judith (Mrs. Anton Myrer), Barbara (Mrs. Roger A. Michaels). Officer, dir. H. Herrmann Furniture Co., 1919-34; pres., dir. John Stuart, Inc., John Widdicomb Co., 1934-76. Dir. Friends of Whitney Mus. Art; trustee Robert D. Hirsch Estate, Herbert and Nannette Rothschild Fund. Mem. Nat. Wholesale Furniture Assn. (dir. 1955-58), Am. Fedn. Arts (dir.), N.E.A., ACLU, Americans for Democratic Action, Nat. Com. for Effective Congress, N.Y. (trustee 1928-76), Bklyn. societies ethical culture, Soc. Advancement Edn. Address: Grand Rapids, Mich. Died Oct. 28. 1976.

ROTHSCHILD, JEROME J., lawyer; b. Phila., Jan. 6, 1884; s. Solomon R. and Estelle (Goldsmith) R.; LL.B., U. Pa., 1904; m. Carrie Kohn, June 9, 1909; 1 dau., Estelle (wife of Dr. R. Lynn Roddy). Admitted to Pa. bar, 1905, and since practiced in Phila.; counsel law firm Fox, Rothschild, O'Brien & Frankel. Dir. Samuel S. Fels Fund, 1937—, pres., 1950-56; dir. Fellowship House. Mem. Am. Jewish Coms. (mem. adminstrv. and exec. bds.). Mem. Order of Coif. Home: Elkins Park, Phila. *

ROTUNNO, NOREDA ANTHONY, landscape architect; b. Fondi, Italy, June 13, 1898; s. Alberto and Teresa Maria (Velletri) R.; came to U.S., 1901, naturalized, 1906; B.S., Syracuse (N.Y.) U., 1921, M.S., 1923; M.L.A., Harvard U., 1937; m. Mildred Green, June 25, 1923; children—Madeline Green Rotunno Knafla, William Albert. Instr. landscape arch. Syracuse U., 1921-27, asst. prof., 1927-34, prof., head dept., 1937-65, emeritus, 1965-78; pvt. practice profl. landscape design, Syracuse, 1931-78; landscape arch. Syracuse U., 1942-65; works include: gardens, estates, indsl. complexes, univ. campuses, sch. pub. housing, recreation areas; v.p., dir. Thousand Island Park Corp., 1958-78; cons. restoration of Sonnenberg Gardens, Canandaigua, N.Y., 1966-78. Chmn. Syracuse Planning Commn., 1957-71, Onondaga County Planning Commn., 1967-71; bd. dirs. Council Cultural Agys., 1959-62; mem. Citizens Council Urban Renewal, 1960-68. Served with S.A.T.C., 1917-18. Recipient citation Federated Garden Clubs, 1968, Community Service award Rotary Club, 1971; Landscape Beautification award Men's Garden Club Syracuse, 1965. Fellow Am. Soc. Landscape Architects (pres. Upstate chpt. 1956-58, 66-68, trustee 1958-61); mem. Internat. Fedn. Landscape Architects, Garden Center Assn. Central N.Y. (past pres.), Phi Kappa Tau. Republican. Roman Catholic. Clubs: Mens Garden (past pres.), Univ. (Syracuse). Contbr. articles on garden subjects to periodicals. Home: Syracuse, N.Y. Died May 20, 1978.

ROUSSEAU, THEODORE, museum curator; b. Freeport, L.I., N.Y., Oct. 8, 1912; s. Theodore Duncan and Marta (Fremery) R.; student Lycee Henry IV, 1923, Eton Coll., 1924-29; A.B. cum laude, Harvard, 1934, M.A., 1937; 2 certificats d'etudes superieures, Sorbonne, 1933. Instr. dept. fine arts Harvard, 1937, Harvard Travelling fellow, 1938-39; speaker French programs C.S. Monitor Radio, 1939-40; asst. curator paintings Nat. Gallery Art Washington, 1940-41; asst. curator paintings Nat. Gallery Art Washington, 1940-41; asst. curator paintings Met. Museum Art, 1947, curator, 1948-68, vice dir., curator in chief, 1968-73. Pres. Spanish Institute, Inc. Served to lt. comdr. USNR, 1941-46; asst. naval attache, Lisbon and Madrid; art loot investigation of France, Spain, Germany, Austria for OSS, 1945-46, also service in Japan; lt. comdr. Res. Decorated Legion of Merit; chavalier Legion of Honor, chevalier de l'Ordre des Arts et Lettres (France); officer Order of Orange-Nassau (The Netherlands); Order Alfonso X el Sabio (Spain); knight officer Order Merit Republic Italy. Mem. Hispanic Soc. Am. (corr., trustee); corr. mem. Acad. San Fernando, Madrid. Clubs: Racquet and Tennis, Century (N.Y.C.); Metropolitan (Washington); Travellers (Paris). Author articles profl. jours., bulls. Home: New York, N.Y. Died Dec. 31, 1973.

ROVERE, RICHARD HALWORTH, writer, editor; b. Jersey City, May 5, 1915; s. Louis Halworth and Ethel Josephine (Roberts) R.; A.B., Bard Coll., 1937; Litt Litt.D., Bard Coll., 1962; L.H.D., Grinnell Coll., 1967; hon. degree, Haverford Coll., 1975; m. Eleanor Alice Burgess, Dec. 20, 1941; children—Ann Megan, Richard Mark, Elizabeth. Asso. editor New Masses, 1938-39; asst. editor The Nation, 1940-43; editor Common Sense, 1943-44; staff writer The New Yorker, 1944-79; U.S. corr. Spectator, London, 1954-62; contbg. editor Harper's, 1949-54, book critic, 1949-50; Chubb fellow Yale, 1951, lectr. history, fellow Ezra Stiles Coll., 1972-73; vis. prof. English, Vassar Coll., 1975-76; asso. in Am. civilization Columbia, 1957-59. Trustee Bard Coll., 1956-61. Fellow Am. Acad. Arts and Scis.; mem. Council on Fgn. Relations. Clubs: Century Assn.; Nat. Press (Washington). Author: Howe & Hummel: Their True and Scandalous History, 1947; The General and the President (with A.M. Schlesinger, Jr.), 1951; Affairs of State: The Eisenhower Years, 1956; Senator Joe McCarthy, 1959; The American Establishment, 1962; The Goldwater Caper, 1965; Waist Deep in the Big Muddy, 1968; Arrivals and Departures, 1976. Bd. editors Am. Scholar, 1958-67; chmn. editorial adv. bd. Washington Monthly, 1969-79. Home: Barrytown, N.Y. Died Nov. 23, 1979.

ROWE, GUY I., army officer; b. Peacham, Vt., Feb. 25, 1886; B.S. in C.E., Norwich U., Vt., 1909; married; 3 daus. Commd. 2d lt. Inf., Jan. 1910, and advanced through the grades to brig. gen., May 1942; mem. Supply Div. War Dept. Gen. Staff, Washington, 1932-36; Q.M., Inf. Sch., Ft. Benning, Ga., 1936-38; Corps Area Q.M., Sixth Corps Area Hdqrs., Chicago, Ill., and temp. duty with Third Army maneuvers in La., 1936-40; with Office of Q.M. Gen., 1940-42; with Q.M. Replacement Training Center, Camp Lee, Va., Apr. 1942-Mar. 1944; comd. Jeffersonville Q.M. Depot, Jeffersonville, Ind., Mar. 1944-Aug. 1946; retired. Awarded Distinguished Service Cross, Purple Heart, Legion of Honor, Legion of Merit, World War II, Croix de Guerre with Palm (France) World War I. Home: Weaverville, N.C. *

ROWE, HOWARD MARSHALL, educator; b. San Francisco, June 22, 1908; s. Harry Manuell and Josephine (Marshall) R.; B.A., U. Calif., Berkeley, 1933, certificate in Librarianship, 1935; M.A., U. Idaho, 1938; Ph.D., U. So. Calif., 1970; m. Mary Manning Reynolds, Sept. 2, 1933; children—David Crowder, Marguerette (Mrs. Byron G. Tate). Law librarian Sch. Law, U. Idaho, 1935-38; dist. librarian Coalinga (Calif.) Union High Sch. Dist. Library, 1938-44; dir. libraries Santa Barbara (Calif.) City and County libraries, 1944-50, Tacoma Pub. Library, 1950-53; librarian Humboldt County Library, Eureka, Calif., 1954-55, San Bernardino (Calif.) Pub. library, 1955-66, mem. faculty U. So. Calif. Sch. Library Sci., 1966-73, asso. prof., until 1973. Mem. Am., Calif. (past pres.) library assn. Home: San Bernardino, Calif. Died Nov. 15, 1978.

ROWE, JOHN JAY, banker; b. Cincinnati, O., Nov. 5, 1885; s. William Stanhope and Margaret (Richardson) R.; A.B., Harvard, 1907, student law, 1906-07; LL.D., Miami U., Oxford, O., 1954; D.C.S., U. of Cin., 1956; D.Sc., Hobart & William Smith Coll., 1956; m. Grace Sherlock Probasco, Nov. 24, 1909; children—Mrs. Grace Rowe Mackall, Mrs. Margaret Rowe Chatfield, William Stanhope II, John Jay. With First Nat. Bank, Cin., 1907-34, pres., 1929-34; pres. Fifth Third Union Trust Co. since Jan. 1934; vice pres. Cincinnati Industries, Inc.; director U.S. Printing & Lithograph Company, Fox Paper Co., Philip Carey Mfg. Co., Emery Industries, Inc., Cincinnati Gas & Electric Co., Cincinnati Equitable Insurance Company, Baldwin-Lima-Hamilton Corporation, Pullman Company, Sorg Paper Company, Midland Enterprises, Incorporated, Eagle Picher Company. Trustee Cincinnati Inst. Fine Arts. President Associated Harvard Clubs, 1939-40; chmn. Cincinnati and Hamilton Co. Chap. Am. Red Cross, 1937-43. Republican. Episcopalian. Clubs: University, Queen City, Commercial, Commonwealth, Camargo, Links, Skytop. Home: Cincinnati. *

ROWE, R(APHAEL) ROBINSON, civil engr.; b. Spencer, Mass., Aug. 26, 1896; s. George Edwin and Eckka M. (Robinson) R.; A.B. cum laude, Harvard, 1916; B.S., M.I.T., 1918; m. Edythe Evelyn Reily, Nov. 9, 1918; children—Edythe Almeda (Mrs. Meda Collins), Edwin Robinson, Richard Reily. With U.S. Geol. Survey, Utah, Nev., 1920-23; cons. engr. Allen & Rowe, San Diego, 1926-33; asso. bridge engr. San Francisco-Oakland Bay Bridge, 1933-37; asso. hydraulic engr. U.S. Forest Service, Juneau, Alaska, 1937-38; sr. engr. bridge dept. Calif. Div. Hwys., 1938-47, supervising engr., 1947-56, prin. engr., 1956-60; exam. commr. Bd. Registration for Civil Engrs., 1945-60; lectr. engring. Sacramento State Coll., 1954-57. Served as 2d lt. Engrs., U.S. Army, 1918-19. Mem. ASCE (nat. dir. 1955-58), Am. Geophys. Union, Internat. Assn. Hydraulic Research, A.A.A.S., Hwy. Research Bd., Engring. Council Sacramento Valley (chmn. 1955), Structural Engrs. Assn. Central Calif., Nat. Soc. Profl. Engrs., Chi Epsilon, Lambda Chi Alpha (nat. treas. 1920). Republican. Baptist. Mason (Shriner). Club: Hiawatha Sportsman's (planning cons.) (Engadine, Mich.); University (Sacramento). Columnist Civil Engineering, 1940—. Contbr. articles to profl. jours. Home: Sacramento, Calif. Died May 4, 1978.

ROWE, WILLIAM DENNISON, govt. ofcl.; b. Swampscott, Mass., Mar. 23, 1902; s. Allen Stanley and Sally Savory (Hammand) R.; grad. Phillips Exeter Acad., 1920; B.S., Mass. Inst. Tech., 1924; m. Mary Eleanore Chalmers (dec. 1945); m. Nedra Nelda Marotte, Dec. 5. 1953; children—William Dennison, Allen Stanley. Asst. to dist. sales mgr. Standard Plate Glass Co., Cambridge, Mass., 1924-26; asst. sales mgr. Chilton Pen Co., Boston, 1926-27; pres. William D. Rowe, Inc., Swampscott, Mass., 1927-35; asst. to chmn. Nat. Constrn. Planning and Adjustment Bd., 1935, chief div. data and statistics Coordinator Indsl. Cooperation, 1935-37; chief planning and survey unit Bur. Old Age and Survivors Ins., FSA, 1937-42; adminstrv. planning officer Fed. Works Agy., 1942-45; asst. dir. budget div. War Assets Adminstrn., 1945-46, spl. asst. to dep. adminstr. real property, 1946-49; orgn. and methods exam. army comptroller, Dept. Army, 1949; dep. chief for operations Office Internat. Security Affairs, Dept. State, 1950-52; dir. supply and requirements staff Tech. Coop. Adminstrn., FOA, 1952-53; civilian exec. asst. Office Chief of Ordnance, 1953-55; supply and contracts officer U.S. Operations Mission to Iran, 1955-58; supply adviser ICA, Washington, 1958; industry officer, acting dir., U.S. Operations Mission to Greece, 1958-61; industry officer and spl. asst. to rep. AID, Salisbury, Fedn. of Rhodesia and Nyasaland, 1961-63, indsl. mgmt. cons., 1963-79; U.S. adviser to Greek Govt. on econ. and indsl. development in Greece. Dir. USO, Athens, Greece; chmn. Hungarian Relief Com., Tehran. Mem. M.I.T. Alumni Assn., Hellenic-American Union, Alpha Tau Omega. Clubs: Dad-Coached Clubs Inc. (dir.); Propeller of U.S.; Propeller of Greece (Athens); Engineers (N.Y.C.). Home: Washington, D.C. Died Nov. 22, 1978.

ROWELL, FRANK WHEATON, army officer; b. Ft. Coeur d'Alene, Ida., Feb. 29, 1880; s. Capt. Charles Walter and Sarah Cooper (Wheaton) R.; grad. Army Sch. of the Line, 1909; m. Gertrude Mercer, Aug. 19, 1904; children—Gertrude Mercer (Mrs. Jesse F. Dressler), Frank Wheaton (dec.), Catherine (Mrs. Thomas A. Doxey), Virginia (Mrs. Virginia R. Ballard), Frederick Mercer. Apptd. 2d lt. inf. at age of 18, and advanced through grades to maj. general U.S. Army, Apr., 1938; retired Jan. 31, 1941. Served with 2d Inf. in N.Y., Ala., Ky., Cuba and P.I., 1898-1903; trans. to 11th Inf., P.I.; detailed for duty at La. Purchase Expn., 1904; again in P.I. with 15th Inf., participating in operations against the Moros; served in China Expdn., 1912-15, with 16th Inf., El Paso, Tex., 1915-16 and the Punitive Expdn. into Mexico; prof. mil. science and tactics, Ala. Poly. Inst., 1916-17; with 326th Inf., 82d Div., A.E.F., to July 1918, advancing to col. in Nat. Army; comd. 68th Inf., Camp Sheridan, Ala., 1918-19; with R.O.T.C. br., war plans div. of Gen. Staff Washington, D.C., 1919-20, and in office of chief of inf., 1920-24; R.O.T.C. officer, 4th Corps Area, 1924-27; comdg. officer 7th Inf., Vancouver Barracks, Wash., 1927-30; asst. chief of staff, 1st Corps Area, Boston, 1930-33, chief of staff, 1933-34; prof. mil. science and tactics, U. of Vt., 1934-35; comdr. 18th Brig., 1935-36; comdr. Atlantic Sector, Panama Canal Dept., 1936-38, 2d Div., U.S. Army, 1938-39, N.Y. Port of Embarkation, Brooklyn, 1939-40; retired, Jan. 31, 1941. Episcopalian. Home: Palo Alto, Calif. *

ROWLAND, ALBERT LINDSAY (RO'LAND), educator; b. Phila., Pa., Oct. 7, 1882; s. George Lindsay and Sarah Jones (Petty) R.; A.B., Central High Sch., Phila., 1901; grad. Phila. Sch. Pedagogy, 1904; A.B., Temple U., 1908; A.M., U. of Pa., 1911, Ph.D., 1914; m. Lillie Maria Hill, Apr. 1, 1907; 1 son, George Austin. Teacher pub. schs., Phila., 1904-18; critic teacher. Phila. Sch. of Pedagogy, 1910-11; prin. Practice Sch., same, 1911-18; supt. schs. Radnor Twp., Delaware County, Pa., 1918-19; dir. Teacher Bur., Dept. of Pub. Instrn., Pa., 1919-25; supt. schs., Cheltenham Twp., Montgomery County, Pa., 1925-32; pres. State

Teachers Coll., Shippensburg, 1932-45. Pres. Eastern States Assn. of Professional Schs. for Teachers, 1943-45; visting prof. of edn., The Pa. State Coll. since 1946. Pres. Lower Montgomery Family Service Soc., Cheltenham Twp. Community Council. Life mem. N.E.A., Pa. State Edn. Assn. (former chmn. com. on tenure problems of both orgns.), Am. Assn. Sch. Adminstrs., Am. Edn. Fellowship, Hist. Soc. of Pa.; mem. Am. Acad. of Polit, and Social Sci., Fgn. Policy Assn., Phi Delta Kappa Phi Sigma Pi, Kappa Phi Kappa, Pi Omega Pi, Kappa Delta Pi. Vestryman, St. Paul's Ch., Elkins Pk. Chmn. Dept. of Christian Social Relations, Protestant Episcopal Diocese of Pa. Bd. dirs. Health and Welfare Council (Phila. and vicinity). Episcopalian. Mason (32 Deg.). Clubs: Rotary of Jenkintown (pres. 1928-29); Rotary of Shippensburg (gov. 180th Rotary District, 1937-38); Keystone, Automobile. Author: Heroes of Early American History, 1918; (with W. D. Lewis) The Silent Readers, 1920; "England and Turkey" in Studies in English Commerce and Exploration in the Reign of Elizabeth, 1934. Address: Philadelphia, Pa. *

ROWLETT, JOHN MILES, architect; b. Jonah, Tex., Jan. 23, 1914; s. John Vincinto and Ora Tommy (Miles) R.; B.Arch., B.S. in Edn., U. Tex., Austin, 1938; m. Virginia Lavon Reinoehl, Aug. 13, 1938; children—John Charles, Karen DeLura. With Nat. Youth Adminstrn., Austin, 1938-40; mem. faculty Tex. A & M U., 1940-44, 46-52; partner Caudill, Rowlett, Scott, architects, engrs. and planners, Houston, 1946-78. Served to lt. (j.g.) USNR, 1944-46. Fellow AIA; mem. Tex. Soc. Architects. Democrat. Episcopalian. Clubs: Lions, Masons. Home: Austin, Tex. Died Nov. 22, 1978.

ROWLEY, FRANK BENJAMIN, prof. mech. engring.; b. Evansville, Wis., Apr. 3, 1882; s. Elvin Clarence and Ella (Emery) R.; B.S., U. of Wis., 1905; M.E., 1906; m. Edith Kuhlmeyer, June 24, 1908; children—Adelaide Hildegard (Mrs. Myles LaGrange Mace), Robert K. Engr. Racine (Wis.) Gas Light Co., 1906-07; with U. of Minn. since 1907, as instr. in engring., 1907-14, asst. prof., 1914-19, asso. prof. of exptl. engring. and acting head dept., 1919-20, prof. mech. engring since 1920, dir. exptl. engring. labs., 1920-38, dir. Engring. Expt. Sta. since 1938, head mech. engring. dept. since Jan. 1941; mem. adv. com. on Commercial Standards, U.S. Dept. of Commerce, Bur. of Standards, since June 1946; consultant, Dept. of Commerce Indsl. Research and Development Division, since November 1946; general consulting practice since 1916; dir. of research and production Insulite Co., Minneapolis, Minn. (on leave), 1928-29. Served as instr. in automobile work, Jr. Olattsburg Training Camp, with rank of capt., U.S. Army, 1918. Mem. sci. adv. com. war industries, State of Minn. Registered Professional Engr., Minn. Awarded F. Paul Anderson medal by Am. Society Heating and Ventilating Engrs., 1939. Fellow A.A.A.S.; mem. Am. Soc. Heating and Ventilating Engrs. (pres. Minneapolis sect. 1922-23; chmn. nat. com. on research 1929-30; mem. nat. council 1927-33, 2d v.p. 1930; 1st v.p. 1931; pres. 1932), Am. Soc. Mech. Engrs. (pres. Minn. sect. 1923-24), Soc. for Promotion Engring. Edn. (pres. Minn. sect. 1923-24), Minn. Fed. Architects and Engrs. Soc., Minn. Assn. Prof. Engrs., Nat. Soc., of Prof. Engrs., Sigma Xi, Theta Xi, Pi Tau Sigma, Tau Beta Pi. Republican. Conglist. (trustee First Congl. Ch., Minneapolis). Club: Campus (U. of Minn.). Author of Expt. Sta. Bulletins on heat transmission; contbr. many tech. articles to Jour. Am. Soc. Heating and Ventilating Engrs. and other jours. in field of air conditioning, etc. Home: Excelsior, Minn.*

ROWNTREE, LEONARD GEORGE (ROUN'TRE), medical research; b. London, Can., Apr. 10, 1883; s. George and Phoebe (Martindale) R.; M.D., Western Med. Sch., London, Can., 1905; Sc.D., Western U., London, Can., 1916; Litt.D. (honorary), Univ. of Miami, 1958: married Katherine Campbell, July 9, 1914; children—Mrs. Laird Wallace, Mrs. H. Clinton Davis. Interne Victoria Hospital, 1906; vol. assistant, pharmacology and experimental therapeutics, assistant instructor, associate and associate professor Johns Hopkins Medical School, 1907-14; asso. prof. medicine, Johns Hopkins, 1914-16; prof. medicine and chief dept., U. of Minn., 1916-20; prof. medicine and chief of div. of medicine, Mayo Foundation, Rochester, Minn., also senior med. consultant and dir. clin. research, Mayo Clinic, 1920-32; dir. Phila. Inst. for Med. Research and research clinician Phila. General Hosp., 1932-46: chmn. deans' com. VA Hosp., Coral Gables, Fla., 1946-55; adv. bd. Biochem. Research Found., Newark, Del., 1933-55. Mem. Am. Med. Assn., American Assn. for the Advancement of Science, Assn. Am. Physicians, Society Clinic Investigators, Assn. for Study of Internal Secretions, Phi Beta Kappa, Phi Beta Pi, Sigma Xi. Episcopalian. Devised and introduced the phenolsulphonephthalein test, now in universal use in renal disorders, and participated in establishing value of renal functional studies; also devised and introduced the dye method of determining liver function and determining blood volume of the body; pioneer in demonstrating water intoxication, the beneficial effect of cortin in Addision's disease and the role of the thymus and pineal glands in growth and development. Revealed the presence of a sarcogenic agent for rats in wheat germ oil made by ether extraction. Lt. col., Med. Corps., U.S. Army and exec. officer Medical Research Labs., A.E.F., 1918-19; col. Reserve Corps. Formerly dir. London Assn. for War Research, London, Ontario, Can.; chief, med. div., Nat. Hdqrs., Selective Service System, Washington, 1940-45; chmn. Nat. Joint Com. on Phys. Fitness, FSA, 1944-55; chief med. advisor and chmn. adv. med. bd. Am. Legion, 1945-50; v.p. Nat. Com. for Mental Hygiene. Recipient Presdl. Medal for merit. Author: Amid Masters of Twentieth Century Medicine, 1958. Home: Miami Beach, Fla. *

ROYAL, JOHN FRANCIS, radio exec.; b. Cambridge, Mass., July 4, 1886; s. Thomas F. and Katherine (Buckley) R.; ed. grammar and high schools of Cambridge; m. Anne Kenny, June 24, 1915 (died Jan. 26, 1942); children—Edward F., Anne (Schatzie); m. 2d, Leonora Marie Corbett, Aug. 29, 1942 (divorced July 1, 1946). Successively reporter Boston Post, public relations B. F. Keith, Boston; mgr. B. F. Keith, Cincinnati, later Cleveland; gen. midwest dir. Keith-Albee-Orpheum; v.p., gen. mgr. WTAM Sta., Cleveland; v.p. N.B.C., 1938-53, cons. since 1953. Catholic. Home: N.Y.C. *

ROYAL, WILLIAM CARSON, clergyman; b. Johnston County, N.C., Aug. 30, 1885; s. Richard and Jane (Barbour) R.; prep. edn., Benson (N.C.) Acad.; student Wake Forest (N.C.) Coll., 1907-09; m. Nellie Smith, June 8, 1908; children—Edna Mae, Virginia Nell, Joe Smith. Missionary pastor Bapt. State Mission Bd., N.C., 1907-09; missionary pastor Va. Bapt. Bd., Hampton, Va., 1910-12; pastor 4 rural chs., Accomack County, Va., 1913-15; pastor First Baptist Church, Frederick, Md., since 1916. Pres. bd. trustees Storer Coll.; director Frederick City Community Chest. President Maryland Baptist Union Association, 1932-35. Trustee Southern Baptist Theological Sem., 1932-36. Mem. Maryland Baptist Summer Assembly, Francis Scott Key Nat. Council of Boy Scouts, Frederick Charity Orgn. Chairman War Fund Drive, 1944. Received Beaver award Boy Scouts, 1942. Chaplain Fitzhugh Lee Chapter, Daughters of Confederacy; chaplain Ho. of Deis., Md. Assembly, 1939, 41; chaplain Md. Senate, 1947. Democrat. Mason, Odd Fellow. Club: Lions (ex-pres.). Home: Frederick, Md. *

ROYCE, STEPHEN WHEELER, hotel exec., lawyer; b. Liberty, N.Y., Nov. 18, 1892; s. S.A. and Louise (Clements) R.; Ph.B., Hamilton Coll., 1914, LL.D. (hon.), 1958; LL.B., N.Y. Law Sch., 1917; m. Dorothy Linnard, Aug. 8, 1918; children—Stephen W., Dorothy Royce Stimpson, Daniel Linnard. Admitted to N.Y. bar, 1917, Calif. bar, 1920; mgr. Hotel Vista del Arroyo, Pasadena, Calif., 1921-24; mng. dir. Huntington Hotel, Pasadena, 1924-55, Coronado (Calif.) Hotel, 1934-48, Fairmont Hotel, San Francisco, 1939-45, Royal Hawaiian, Moana, Surf Rider hotels, Honolulu, 1948-55; pres. Huntington Hotel Co., 1928-77; mgr., owner The Inn, Rancho Santa Fe, Calif., 1955-77; v.p. hotels div. Matson Nav. Co., 1948-54, hotel cons. hotels div., 1954-77; pres. Pasadena-Sheraton Corp.; dir. Lloyds Bank Calif., Pasadena. Chmn. Citizens Com. Air Pollution Los Angeles County; chmn. emergency action com. Air Pollution Control Dist.; mem. Calif. Olympic Commn.; trustee Hamilton Coll.; bd. dirs. Stanford Research Inst., Pasadena Tournament Roses Assn. Served as 1st lt. A.C., U.S. Army, 1917-18. Mem. Delta Kappa Epsilon, Phi Delta Phi. Address: Rancho Santa Fe, Calif. Died Apr. 12, 1977.

ROYSTER, PAUL FREEMAN, govt. ofcl.; b. Morocco, Ind., Jan. 31, 1891; s. Sigel Allen and Lydia (Freeman) R.; student Ind. U.; m. Nina Pease, June 4, 1913; children—Mary Louise (Mrs. R. H. Alexander), Rev. Robert Frank, Barbara (Mrs. B. H. Sexton). Successively telegrapher, train dispatcher, train master, acting supt. Monon Ry., 1908-40; gen, mgr. Lafayette Transit Co. & Cross Transit, 1940-51; asst. to under-sec. for transportation, Dept. Commerce, 1951-57; asst. commnr. operation, also asst. to fed. hwy. adminstr. Bur. Pub. Roads, 1957-63. Mem. U.S. study commn. Tex. land and water resources, 1958-62. Mem. Inst. Traffic Engrs., Am. Soc. Traffic and Transportation. Home: Denver, Colo. Died Sept. 15, 1976.

ROZMAREK, CHARLES, hon. pres. Polish Nat. Alliance and Polish Am. Congress, Inc.; b. Wilkes-Barre Pa., July 25, 1897; s. John and Magdalina (Chybki) R.; A.B., U. Pa., 1922; student Harvard Law Sch., 1925; LL.B., Boston U., 1927; m. Wanda Blinstrub, June 24, 1928; children—Elaine Regina, Marilyn Teresa. Admitted to Pa. bar, 1928; solicitor for Larksville, Pa., 1930-33. Pringle, Pa., 1933-35; dep. atty. gen. Pa., 1935-37; merc. appraiser of Luzerne County, Pa., 1937-39; pres. Polish Nat. Alliance, 1939-67, hon. pres., 1967-73; pres. Polish Am. Congress, 1944-68, hon. pres., 1968-73; pres. Alliance Printers and Pubs., 1939-67. Del. at large from Ill. to Nat. Democratic Conv., 1944. Vice pres. bd. dirs. Alliance Coll., 1939-67. Mem. Chgo., Ill. bar assns. Home: Chicago, Ill. Died Aug. 5, 1973.

RUBEY, HARRY, educator, civil engr.; b. St. Louis, Feb. 23, 1886; s. Thomas Thornton and Flora (Vivian) R.; B.S. in Civil Engring., U. Ill., 1905, C.E., 1925; m. Maude Harden, July 20, 1912 (dec.); children—Harry (dec.), Mildred Lovelace (Mrs. Charles H. Bartlett), Thomas Harden; m. 2d, Ann Todd, Aug. 4, 1948. From Rodman to asst. engr. M.P. Ry., 1905-09; engr., mgr. irrigation, drainage and hydro-electric projects along Pacific Coast, 1909-15; asst. prof., then asso. prof. civil engring. Carnegie Inst. Tech., 1917-19, U. Wash., 1915-17, 19-24; prof. civil engring., chmn. dept. U. Mo., 1924-56, prof. emeritus, lectr., 1956—, often acting dean engring; dir. Naval Diesel Tng. Sch. and Engring, Sci. Mgmt. War Tng. 1942-44; engring. practice, 1915—. Adv. Com. Congress on Flood Control, 1927; cons. Nat. Resources Com., 1936-37. Mem. Am. Soc. Engring. edn. (life; council 1932-35, chmn. civil engring. div. 1950-51), Am. Soc. C.E. (life), Engrs. Council Profl. Devel. (accrediting com. 1950-59), Nat. Soc. Prof. Engrs. (life), Tau Beta Pi, Chi Epsilon, Phi Kappa Psi. Club: University (Columbia). Author: Industrial Organization, 1931; Engineering Surveys, 3d edit., 1958; Route Surveys, 1938, 2d edit. as Route Surveys and Construction, 1956; Applied Engineering Surveys (with G.E. Lommel and M.W. Todd), 2d edit., 1958; The Engineer and Professional Management, 3d edit., 1961, (with John A. Logan) rev. edit., 1966-71; Supplemental Irrigation, rev. edits., 1947, 50, 53; Supplemental irrigation for Eastern United States, 1954, enlarged, 1956; (with Walker W. Milner) Construction and Professional Management, rev. edit., 1971. Contbr. Ency. Brit.; tech. press, world travel. Presbyn. Home: Columbia MO. *

RUBICAM, RAYMOND, advt. exec.; b. Bklyn., June 16, 1892; s. Joseph and Sarah (Bodine) R.; ed. pub. schs.; LL.D., Colgate U. 1947; Litt.D., Boston U., 1948; m. Regina McCloskey, Nov. 30, 1916 (div.); children—Kathleen Bodine (Mrs. John D. Witten), Jane Collins (Mrs. Judd L. Pollock); m. 2d, Bettina Hall, Sept. 16, 1940; children—Stephen Merrill, Joan Wister (Mrs. Carlton J. Kirel). Clk. and salesman, Denver, 1907-12; successively clk, automobile salesman and newspaper reporter, Phila., 1912-16; copy writer F. Wallis Armstrong Co., Phila., 1916-19; copy writer, supr. N. W. Ayer & Son, 1919-23; co-founder Young & Rubicam, Inc., advt., 1923, v.p., pres., chmn. bd., ret. as chmn. bd., 1944; dir. Valley Nat. Bank Ariz., 1951-67, hon. dir., 1967-78. Bd. dirs. Am. Grad. Sch. Internat. Mgmt.; trustee Colgate U., 1947-62, hon. trustee, 1962-78; trustee Com. Econ. Devel., 1946-52, hon. trustee, 1952-78. Spl. asst. to chmn. War Manpower Commn., 1942. Recipient gold medal for distinguished services to advt., 1938; named to Am. Advt. Fedn. Hall of Fame, 1974, Copywriters Hall of Fame, 1975. Mem. S.R., Newcomen Soc. N.A., Alpha Delta Sigma. Contbr. on pub. affairs for mags. and books. Home: Scottsdale, Ariz. Died May 8, 1978.

RUBIN, EDWARD PERRY, investment counsel; b. Payne, Ohio, Mar. 27, 1903; s. Henry E. and Blanche (Reader) R.; A.B., Heidelberg Coll., 1925, LL.D. (hon.), 1968; grad. work, Harvard, 1926; m. Mary Allene Myers, Nov. 27, 1930; 1 son, Edward P. Pres., dir. Selected Am. Shares, Inc., 1942-70; pres. Selected Investments Co., 1943-55, chmn. bd., 1955-68; chmn. bd. Selected Spl. Shares, Inc., 1968-70; adviser, dir. Security Suprs., investment counsel, 1969-70, partner, pres. predecessor orgns.; a prin. organizer Selected Am. Shares, Selected Cumulative Shares, Selected Income Shares, Selected Am. Shares, Inc., Selected Spl. Shares, Inc. Adv. gov. Midwest Stock Exchange, 1956-59. Trustee Heidelberg Coll., 1954-80, mem. fin. and investment com. 1958-80, chmn., 1958, 64-66, 70-73, 76-80, chmn. planning com., 1967; trustee Library Internat. Relations, 1960-77. Mem. Investment Co. Inst. (bd. govs. 1949-52, 58-61, 63-67, 68-70, chmn. tax com. 1958-60, 67-70, chmn. instl. studies com. 1963-66), Fin. Writers Assn. Chgo. (pres. 1965-66), Investment Analysts Soc. Chgo., Am. Rose Soc. Episcopalian. Clubs: Bond, Attic, Economic, Heidelberg, Harvard, Execs. (Chgo.); Internat.; 71; Rotary. Writer, lectr. fin. subjects. Home: Winnetka, Ill. Died Nov. 12, 1980; buried Churchyard of Christ Ch., Winnetka.

RUBIN, MORRIS HAROLD, author; b. N.Y.C., Aug. 7, 1911; s. Jacob and Leah (Abrahamson) R.; B.A., U. Wis., 1934; m. Mary Barbara Sheridan, Sept. 12, 1936. With Portland (Me.) Evening Express, 1929-34, Boston Globe, 1929-34, N.Y. Times, 1935-38, N.Y. Herald Tribune, 1939, Time Mag., 1935-38, Milw. Jour., 1933-35, Wis. State Jour., Madison, 1934-38; editor The Progressive Mag., Madison, 1940-73, pres., pub., 1973-76; editorial cons., free-lance writer, 1976-80; trustee, dir. Madison Capital Times; dir. Madison Newspapers, Inc.; aide to Gov. Philip F. LaFollette and Sen. Robert M. LaFollette, Jr., Madison, 1938-40. Founder, Wis. Civil Liberties Union, 1941, pres., 1941-47; v.p. ACLU, 1947. Recipient Sidney Hillman Found. award for outstanding journalism in domestic field for spl. issue on Senator Joseph R. McCarthy, 1954; George Polk Meml. award for distinguished fgn. reporting for spl. issue on Latin Am., 1962. Mem. Madison Newspaper Guild (founder). Editor: McCarthy-The Documented Record, 1954; The Crisis of Survival, 1970. Home: Madison, Wis. Died Aug. 8, 1980.

RUBIN, SAMUEL, found. exec.; b. Bialystock, Russia, Nov. 17, 1901; s. Julius and Lena (Sadvoransky) R.; came to U.S., 1905, naturalized, 1914; student schs., N.Y.C.; 1 dau., 1 son. Founder, pres. Spanish Trading Corp., N.Y.C., 1930-36, Fabergé Perfumes, N.Y.C. and Paris, 1937-63; pres. Samuel Rubin Found., N.Y.C., 1949-78, Fragrance Found., Inc., 1952-54; mktg. cons. to industry-consumer goods. Founder N.Y. U. Bellevue Med. Center, 1940, Postgrad. Center for Mental Health, N.Y.C., 1947; past trustee Sydenham Hosp., N.Y.C.; chmn. adv. bd. Fordham Hosp., N.Y.C. 1952-71; trustee N.Y. U. Med. Center, 1960-73, Spoleto Festival, 1966-76; pres. Am.-Israel Cultural Found., N.Y.C., 1955-64, Am. Symphony Orch., N.Y.C., 1960-70. Decorated Order of Merit (Italy); Order of Crown (Iran); recipient Presdl. citation N.Y. U., 1963. Mem. N.Y. U. Sch. Medicine Alumni Assn. (hon.), N.Y. U. Edn. Assos. Club: Rotary Internat. (hon. mem. France). Established Rubin Found. fellowships for fgn. students to study at U.S. univs., 1969. Died Dec. 21, 1978.

RUBINSTEIN, DAVID, medical educator; b. Montreal, Que., Can., Mar. 4, 1929; s. Louis and Anna (Kooperstock) R.; B.S., McGill U., 1949, M.S., 1951, Ph.D., 1953, M.D., 1957; m. Blanche Goldstein, June 28, 1952; children—Larry, Bruce, Rhonda. Intern Jewish Gen. Hosp., Montreal, 1957-58; research fellow Michael Reese Hosp., Chgo., 1958-59; asst. prof. biochemistry McGill U. Med. Sch., Montreal, 1959-63, asst. prof. exptl. medicine, 1959-70, asso. prof. biochemistry, 1966-67, asso. prof. exptl. medicine, 1970-76, prof. biochemistry, 1971-79, prof. medicine, 1976-79; prof. chmn. dept. biochemistry Dalhousie U., Halifax, N.S., Can. 1979-80; vis. prof. Hebrew U., Jerusalem, Israel, 1966-67; asso. scientist Royal Victoria Hosp., Montreal, 1968-79. Fellow Council on Arterioscloerosis; Am. Heart Found.; mem. Am. Soc. Biol. Chemists, Can. Biochem. Soc., Can. Soc. Clin. Investigation, Am. Fedn. Clin. Research, McGill Assn. Univ. Tchrs. (past pres.). Research in lipid and blood metabolism. Home: Halifax NS Canada. *

RUCHAMES, LOUIS, educator, historian; b. N.Y.C., May 25, 1917; s. Sam and Yetta (Schaeffer) R.; B.S.S., City Coll. N.Y., 1937; M.A., Columbia, 1940, Ph.D., 1951; m. Miriam Lantz, Aug. 22, 1943; children—Robert Mark, Barbara Rena. Dir. B'nai B'rith Hillel Found., U. Ala., 1943-44, Western Mass. B'nai B'rith Hillel Founds., Smith Coll., Amherst Coll. and U. Mass., 1944-66; vis. lectr. history Smith Coll., 1962-63, 65-66, U. Mass.-Amherst, 1963-64; prof. history U. Mass.-Boston, 1966-76, chmn. dept., 1967-70. Adv. com. Civil Liberties Union Mass., 1966-76. Bd. overseers Jacob Hiatt Inst., Brandeis U., 1966-70. Mem. Am., So. hist. assns., Orgn. Am. Historians, Am. Jewish Hist. Soc. (chmn. acad. council 1973-76), Americans Democratic Action, Am. Civil Liberties Union, Assn. Study Negro Life and History. Author: Race, Jobs and Politics: The Story of FEPC, 1953; A John Brown Reader, 1960; The Abolitionists: A Collection of their Writings, 1963; Racial Thought in America, From the Puritans to Abraham Lincoln, 1970; John Brown: The Making of a Revolutionary, 1970; The Letters of William Lloyd Garrison, Vol. II, 1836-1840, A House Dividing Against Itself, 1971, Vol. IV, 1850-60, From Disunionism to the Brink of War; also essays and revs. Editorial bd. Am. Jewish Hist. Quar., 1972-76. Home: Newton Lower Falls, Mass. Died June 2, 1976.

RUCKER, TRUMAN BURRIS, lawyer; b. Norman, Okla., Sept. 30, 1907; s. William Newton and Sue (Burris) R.; B.A., LL.B., U. Okla., 1929; m. Genevieve Louise Mayfield, July 22, 1941; children—Sue Burris, Victor Mayfield, Truman Burris, Lois Ann. Admitted to Okla. bar, 1929; practice in Tulsa, 1931-78; mem. firm Rucker, McBride & Hopkins and predecessor firms, 1952-78. Trustee Okla. Meth. Found. Served from capt. to lt. col. USAAF, 1942-45. Mem. Am., Okla., Tulsa County bar assns., Internat. Acad. Trial Lawyers, Am. Coll. Trial Lawyers, Order of Coif, Phi Delta Phi. Methodist (steward). Author: The Verdicts Were Just. Home: Tulsa, Okla. Died Nov. 9, 1978.

RUDDOCK, ALBERT BILLINGS, bus. exec.; b. Chicago, Ill., Jan. 13,1886; s. Charles H. and Sarah (Billings) R.; ed. Hopkins Grammar Sch., New Haven, 1903; B.A., Yale, 1907; M.A., Columbia, 1909; student, Ecole Sciences Politiques, Paris, 1911; m. Margaret Kirk, March 14, 1912; children—Merritt Kirk, Billings Kirk. Sec. Am. Embassy, Berlin, 1912-16, Brussels, 1917; in Dept. of State, Washington, 1917-20; Am. Embassy, Peking, 1920-23; resigned 1924; in private business, Los Angeles. Dir. Security First Nat. Bank, 1925-29. Trustee Occidental Coll. 1926-48, Calif. Inst. Tech., 1938—, chmn. board directors, 1954-62; member of the board of governors Los Angeles County Mus.; Southern Cal., Symphony Assn., 1934-48, Pasadena Civic Music Assn., 1944-46, Town Hall of Los Angeles, 1941-45; v. chmn. Greater Los Angeles Plans, Inc.; pres. Hollywood Bowl Assn., 1932-34, Pasadena War Chest, 1942-44, Polytechnic Elementary Sch. Pasadena, 1940-48, Pasadena Hosp., 1923-36, Calif. Grad. Sch. of Design, 1939-42; dir. Pasadena Community Chest, 1939-45; chmn. management com. Huntington Hosp., 1936-46; chmn. adv com., Los Angeles Co. Gen. Hosp., 1939-47. Mem. bd. Santa Barbara Found., Santa Barbara Mus. Art. Received Arthur Noble Pasadena award, 1943. Republican. Clubs: California, Sunset (Los Angeles); Twilight, Valley Hunt (Pasadena); Valley and The Santa Barbara (Santa Barbara); Bohemian (San Francisco); Commonwealth (Richmond). Home: Santa Barbara, Cal. *

RUDISILL, DORUS PAUL, educator; b. Cherryville, N.C., Apr. 30, 1902; s. John Henry and Sarah Frances (Rudisill) R.; A.B., Lenoir Rhyne Coll., 1922; postgrad. Mt. Airy Sem., 1922-23; B.D., Lutheran So. Sem., 1925; M.A., U. S.C., 1925; S.T.M., Hartford Sem., 1932; Ph.D., Duke, 1945; m. Robbie Ione Stevenson, Aug. 30, 1935; children—Dorus Paul, Barbara Stevenson. Ordained to ministry Lutheran Ch., 1926; minister Dallas, N.C., 1925-31, Morganton, N.C., 1932-42, Chapel Hill, N.C., 1942-46; teaching fellow Duke, 1943-45; prof. philosophy and religious studies, Lenoir Rhyne Coll., Hickory, N.C., 1946-73. Pres. Coosa Devel. Co., Inc., Goodwater, Ala., 1971-78. Rep. to Nat. Council Chs. from N.C. Council Chs. Bd. trustees Lutheran Theol. So. Sem. Recipient Distinguished Service award Lenoir Rhyne Coll., 1972, Lenoir Rhyne Coll. Alumni Assn., 1971. Mem. N.C. Philos. Soc., Soc. Bibl. Lit. Clubs: Execs., Rotary. Author: The Doctrine of the Atonement in Jonathan Edwards and His Successors, 1971; Love Activates and Acts, 1971; Thinking About Hell and Heaven, 1974. Contbr. articles profl. jours. Patentee in automotive engring. Home: Hickory, N.C. Died Aug. 10, 1978.

RUDNER, RICHARD SAMUEL, philosopher, educator; b. N.Y.C., Oct. 3, 1921; s. Irving and Fanny Rudner; A.B., Queens Coll., 1946; M.A., U. Pa., 1948, Ph.D., 1949; m. Martha Kaufman, Aug. 28, 1946; children—David West, Kathryn Ann. Instr., Cornell U., 1948-49; asst. prof. Washington U., St. Louis, 1949-52; research asst. prof. logic Naval Research Labs., Washington, also Tufts Coll., 1952-54; asst. prof. Swarthmore Coll., 1954-56; prof. Mich. State U., 1956-62; prof. philosophy, chmn. dept. Washington U., St. Louis, from 1962; cons. govt., ednl. instns. and industry, from 1952. Served with AUS, 1942-43. NSF sr. postdoctoral fellow, 1962-63; NSF research grantee, 1978-79. Fellow A.A.A.S.; mem. Am. Philos. Assn., Philosophy Sci. Assn. (gov. bd.), Phi Beta Kappa. Author: Philosophy of Social Science, 1966. Contbr. profl. jours. Editor-in-chief Philosophy of Sci. Jour., 1959-76, mem. editorial bd., 1976-79. Home: Saint Louis, Mo. Died July 27, 1979.

RUDOLFS, WILLEM, educator; b. Wageningen, Holland, Feb. 13, 1886; s. Willem and Antonia Petronella (Van Ewyk) R.; student U. Ill., 1915-18; Research fellow Pasteur Inst., Paris, 1919-20; Ph. D., Rutgers, 1921; m. Cornelia Gerdina Van Laar, Sept. 12, 1920. Came to U.S., 1915 naturalized, 1921. Soil chemist U. Ill., 1915-18; biochemist N.J. Agrl. Expt. Sta., 1921-26; prof. sanitation Rutgers U. since 1924, also research specialist; cons. engr. since 1928. Chmn. zoning bd. New Brunswick, N.J., since 1937, mem. planning bd. since 1941. Fellow Inst. Chemists, Am. Pub. Health Assn., A.A.A.S.; mem. Am. Soc. C.E., Am. Chem Soc., Profl. Engring. Soc. Nat. Malaria Soc. Fed. Sewage Works Assn., Am. Water Works Assn. Author over 300 books, bulls. and articles in tech. jours. Home: New Brunswick, N.J. *

RUDOLPH, ANDREW D., clergyman; b. Paducah, Ky., June 24, 1884; s. Ephraim Davis and Lucinda Cathrine (Phelps) R.; ed. West Ky. State Normal Sch., Bowling Green Ky., 1908-09; Bethel Coll., McKenzie, Tenn., 1910-13; B.D., Cumberland Presbyn. Sem., McKenzie, 1913; m. Myrtie Arant, Nov. 3, 1909; 1 son, Alton Dual. Teacher pub. schs. of Marshall County, Ky., 6 yrs.; ordained ministry Cumberland Presbyn. Ch., 1911; pastor successively Paducah, Brimingham, Ala., and Fulton, Ky., until 1921. chs. near Paducah, 1921-25, Fairfield, Ill., 1925-28, chs. near Paducah, 1928-31, West End Ch., Birmingham, 1931-32, Owensboro, 1932-34, Bowling Green, 1934-36, Margaret Hank Memorial Ch., Paducah, Ky., 1936-40, First Ch., Dallas, Tex., 1940-44, Russellville Ch., 1944-49; Arrington St. Church, Nashville, Tenn., since 1949. Mem. bd. trustees, Bethel Coll., McKenzie, Tenn.; moderator Ark Synod, 1947-48. Stated clk. and treas. Mayfield Presbytery of Ky. Synod, 1922-31. Pres. Cumberland Presbyn. Bd. of Edn., 1933-37. Home: Nashville. *

RUDWIN, MAXIMILIEN (JOZEF), educator and writer; b. Jan. 22, 1886; s. Léon and Gudule (de Trèves) R.; Testimonium maturitatis, Leipsic Realschule, 1906; A.B., U. of Wis., 1908; A.M., U. of Cincinnati, 1910; Ph.D., Ohio State U., 1913; studied Stanford U., U. of Chicago, univs. of Aix-Marseille and Montpellier; Ph.D., Columbia, 1922; Docteur de l'Université de Montpellier (with highest honors), 1926; m. Armelle Laure, Lefèvre, Aug. 10, 1925; children—Geneviève, Sylvère. Came to U.S., 1906, naturalized citizen, 1912. Teaching fellow Ohio State U., 1912-13; instr. modern langs., Purdue U., 1913-16; instr. German, Univ. of Ill., 1916-18; Johnston research scholar, Johns Hopkins, 1918-19; asst. prof. French, Swarthmore, 1920-23; asst. prof. modern langs., Univ. of Pittsburgh, 1923-26; prof. same, Baker U., 1926-29, U. of Wyo., 1929-32; asso. prof. modern langs., Tex. Coll. of Mines, 1932-33, St. Bonaventure Coll., 1934-36. Lecturer Middlebury Coll., summer 1916; visiting prof. Hunter College, summers 1927, 1934-39; lecturer New York colls. 1937-42. Government war agencies, 1942. Mem. Modern Language Association America, American Assn. Univ. Profs., League of Am. Writers, Kan. Modern Lang. Assn. (v.p. 1929), Kans. State Teachers; Assn. (group chmn. 1929), Am. Assn. Teachers of French, Société Anatole France, Artistes Populaires; Fédération des braves gens de France (Am. del.). Am. Friends of Lafayette, Eugene Field Society (hon. mem.). Author: The Prophet Scenes in Medieval Drama, 1913; The Devil Scenes in Medieval Drama, 1914; The Devil in the German Religious Plays of the Middle Ages and the Reformation, 1915; The Origin of the Carnival Comedy, 1920; Supernaturalism and Satanism in Chateaubriand, 1922; Historical and Bibliographical Survey of the Religious Drama, 1924; Satan et le Satanisme dans l'Oeuvre de Victor Huge; Bibliographie de Victor Hugo, 1926; Romantisme et Satanisme, 1927; The Devil in Legend and Literature, 1932; Lés Ecrivains diaboliques de France, 1937. Edition: Devil Stories—An Anthology, 1921. Contbg. editor Books Abroad, 1927-40. Am. corr. periodicals in France, Belgium, Switzerland. Lit. "Le Jour" (Montreal), Am. rep. Comp. Lit. Studies (London) since 1943. Address: New York, N.Y. *

RUGH, ROBERTS, educator; b. Springfield, O., Apr. 16, 1903; s. Arthur and Gertrude (Roberts) R.; A.B., Oberlin (O.) Coll., 1926, M.A., 1927; Ph.D., Columbia, 1935; m. Harriette Sheldon, July 24, 1926; children—Mary Elizabeth (Mrs. A.J. Downs), William Arthur. Mem. faculty Lawrence Coll., Appleton, Wis., 1927-28, Hunter Coll., NY.C., 1929-39, N.Y. U., 1939-48; prof. radiology Columbia until 1971, dir. research biol. effects of ionizing radiations, 1948-71, sr. med. cons., lectr., 1971-78; research biol. effects microwaves Bur. Radiol. Health, Dept. Health, Edn. and Welfare. Trustee Marine Biol. Lab., Woods Hole, Mass. Mem. Am. Assn. Roentgenol., Soc. Cancer Research, Radiol. Soc. N.A., Brit. Inst. Radiology, Am. Soc. Zoologists, Am. Assn. Anatomists, Soc. Exptl. Biology and Medicine, Harvey Soc., Am. Assn. for Advancement of Sci., Tissue Culture Assn., Am. Soc. Neuropathologists, Am. Teratology Soc., Teratology Soc. (Japan). Author: Experimental Embryology, rev. edit., 1962; A Laboratory Manual of Vertebrate Embryology, 6th rev. edit., 1971; The Frog: Its Reproduction and Development, 1951; Vertebrate Embryology, The Dynamics of Development, 1964; The Mouse: Its Reproduction and Development, 1967. Contbr. sci. articles profl. jours. Editorial bd. Biol. Bull., Atompraxis. Home: New York, N.Y. Died 1978.

RUKEYSER, MURIEL, poet; b. N.Y.C., Dec. 15, 1913; d. Lawrence and Myra (Lyons) R.; student Vassar Coll., Columbia U., 1930-32; Litt.D., 1961; 1 son, William L. Author poems, biographies, motion pictures, TV; lectr., tchr.; faculty Sarah Lawrence Coll., 1956-67; bd. dirs. Tchrs.-Writers Collaborative, 1967-80. Pres. P.E.N. Am. Center, 1975-76. Recipient Nat. Inst. award, 1942; Swedish Acad. Trans. award, 1968; Copernicus award, 1977; Shelley award, 1977; Guggenheim fellow, 1943; Am. Council Learned Socs. fellow, 1963. Mem. Nat. Inst. Arts and Letters, Soc. Am. Historians. Author: Theory of Flight, 1935; U.S. 1, 1938; A Turning Wind, 1939; Soul and Body of John Brown, 1941; Willard Gibbs, 1942; Beast in View, 1944; The Green Wave, 1948; Orpheus, 1949; The Life of Poetry, 1949; Selected Poems, 1951; One Life, 1957; Body of Waking, 1958; Waterlily Fire, 1962; The Orgy, 1965; The Speed of Darkness, 1968; The Traces of Thomas Hariot, 1971; Breaking Open, 1973; The Gates, 1976; Collected Poems, 1979; (children's books) Come Back Paul, 1955; I Go Out, 1959; Bubbles, 1967; Mazes, 1970; translator: Sun Stone, 1963; Selected Poems of Octavio Paz, 1963; (with Leif Sjoberg) Selected Poems of Gunnar Ekelof, 1967; Brecht's Uncle Eddie's Moustache, 1974. Address: New York, N.Y. Died Feb. 12, 1980.

RUMELY, EDWARD ALOYSIUS, manufacturer, educator; b. LaPorte, Ind., Feb. 28, 1882; s. Joseph J. and Margaret (Zimmerman) R.; ed. U. of Notre Dame, and U. of Heidelberg: M.D., U. of Freilber, 1906; m. Apr. 2, 1910. Founded and organized, 1907, The Interlaken School, of which is pres.; was sec. M. Rumely Co., Laporte, Ind.; now vice pres., sec. Mail & Express Co. Developed mechanical tractor as substitute for horsepower in plowing. Dir. and mem. state com. Nat. Assn. for Promotion of Industrial Training; mem. Am. Assn. Agrl. Engrs. Wrote, "To Teach Boys to Live," containing outline of new ideas in edn. Joint Author: (with L. W. Ellis) Power and the Plow, 1911. Address: N.Y. *

RUNNELS, HAROLD LOWELL, congressman; b. Dallas, Mar. 17, 1924; m. Dorothy Gilland, 1944; children—Michael, Phillip, Matt, Eydie. Formerly employed by FBI, Washington, mgr. Magnolia Amusement Co. (Ark.); partner Southland Supply Co., 1952; formed Runnels Mud Co. and RunCo Acidizing & Fracturing Co.; mem. N.Mex. Senate, 1960-70; mem. 92d-96th congresses from 2d Dist. N.Mex. Served with USAAF, World War II. Named Lovington Citizen of Yr., 1971. Mem. Permian Basin Petroleum Assn.

(co-founder), Am. Petroleum Inst., C. of C. Democrat. Baptist. Mason. Address: Aldie, Va. Died Aug. 5, 1980.

RUNNELS, RICHARD STITT, household products mfg. exec.; b. Wabash, Ind., Dec. 19, 1923; s. William and Miriam (Stitt) R.; B.S., Ind. U., 1947; m. Josephine Cooley, Dec. 27, 1948; children—Richard S., Miriam Ann. With Procter & Gamble Co., Cin., 1947-74, asso. comptroller, 1955-61, comptroller, 1961-67, v.p. finance, sec., from 1967, v.p. toilet goods div., 1968-70, v.p. food products, 1970-72, v.p. adminstrv. services, 1972-74. Home: Cincinnati, Ohio. Died Oct. 19, 1974.

RUPP, ADOLPH FREDERICK, basketball exec.; b. Halstead, Kan., Sept. 2, 1901; s. Henry and Anna (Lichti) R.; A.B., Kan. U., 1923; M.A., Columbia, 1930; m. Esther Smith, Aug. 29, 1931; 1 son, Adolph Frederick. Head basketball coach U. Ky., Lexington, from 1930; former pres. Memphis Tams. Dir. Central Dist. Warehousing Corp., Lexington. Mem. Nat. Basketball Rules Com., from 1961. Chmn., Shrine Crippled Childrens Hosp., from 1942. Named Southeastern Conf. Coach of Year, 1963-66, 68-72, Nat. Coach of Year, U.P.I., A.P., 1951, 59, 66, Coach of Century Columbus (O.) Touchdown Club, 1967; recipient Gov.'s medal, 1959; named to Kan. Hall of Fame, Naismith Hall of Fame, Springfield, Mass. Mem. Ky. Hereford Assn. (pres. 1953-69), Nat. Assn. Basketball Coaches (dir. from 1961, pres. 1970-71), Delta Sigma Pi (Deltasig of Year 1966) Omicron Delta Kappa. Mason. Author: Championship Basketball, 1948, 56; Adolph Rupp's Basketball Guidebook. Died Dec. 10, 1977; buried Lexington Cemetery.

RUSH, CHARLES EVERETT, librarian; b. Fairmount, Ind., Mar. 23, 1885; s. Rev. Nixon and Louisa (Winslow) R.; A.B., Earlham Coll., Richmond, Ind., 1905; U. of Wis., 1905-06; B.L.S., N.Y. State Library Sch., Albany, 1908; M.A., Yale, 1931; m. R. Lionne Adsit, Sept. 7, 1910; children—Alison Adsit, Frances Marie, Myra Lionne. Library asst., Earlham Coll. Library, 1903-05, U. of Wis. Library, 1905-06, Public Library, Newark, N.J., 1907; librarian Pub. Library, Jackson, Mich., 1908-10, St. Joseph, Mo., 1910-16, Des Moines, Ia., 1916-17, Indianapolis, Ind., 1917-28, Teachers Coll. Library, Columbia, 1928-31; asso. librarian Yale U. Library, 1931-38; librarian Cleveland Public Library, 1938-41; dir. libraries Univ. of N. Carolina Library, and Prof. of Library Science, since Apr. 1941. Adviser on reading National Council of Boy Scouts. Mem. American Library Assn., Bibliog. Soc. of America, Yale Library Associates, Am. Association for Adult Education, Am. Library Inst., Theatre Library Asso., Society American Archivists, Asso. of Research Libraries. Member Friends Ch. Clubs: Elizabethan, Grolier, Rotary, Rowfant. Joint Author: Modern Aladdins and Their Magic, The Science of Things About Us. Home: Chapel Hill, N.C. *

RUSH, FRANK NEILL, utilities cons.; b. Charles City, Ia., Apr. 11, 1886; s. John and Emma (Neill) R.; B.S., Occidental College, 1909, LL.D., 1957; married Eloise Strobridge, Oct. 29, 1912; children—Eloise N. (Mrs. H. K. Swenerton), Virginia N. (Mrs. Edward Kincaid). With Pacific Tel. & Tel. 1909; supt. traffic Southern Calif. Telephone Co., Los Angeles, 1924-26, chief engr., 1926-28, v.p., gen. mgr. The Pacific Tel. & Tel. Co., 1928-51; communications and transportation rep., staff U.S., Commissioner for Austria, 1951-53; director Farmers & Mchts. National Bank. Pres. bd. trustees Occidental Coll.; trustee Hollenbeck Home for Aged, past pres. Los Angeles Community Welfare Fedn. Mem. Phi Gamma Delta. Republican. Presbyterian. Clubs: Sunset, Cal. Home: South Pasadena, Cal. *

RUSSELL, CHARLES FRANK, naval officer (ret.); b. Wellsboro, Pa., Aug. 19, 1883; s. John Morse and Marion (Derbyshire) R.; B.S., U.S. Naval Acad., 1907; m. Florence Robinson Fischler, Dec. 26, 1910. Commd. ensign U.S. Navy, 1908, and advanced through grades to commodore, 1944; flag lt. to Adm. Fiske, 1911-12; officer, destroyer command, Queenstown, Ireland, World War I; served in battleships, destroyers; comd. various ships; insp. of ordnance, coordinator, dir. of enlisted personnel at various shore stations, 1906-35; ret. with rank of capt., 1935; recalled to post of center comdr., U.S. Naval Training Center, Bainbridge, Md., 1941-45; ret., 1945. Mem. bd., Soldiers and Sailors Memoial Hospital, Green Free Library (Willsboro, Pa.). Awarded Navy Cross (World War I), Legion of Merit (World War II). Republican. Presbyterian. Mason. Clubs: Army Navy, Army Navy Country (Washington), Tyoga Country (Wellsboro). Home: Wellsboro, Pa. *

RUSSELL, FRANKLIN FERRISS, lawyer, educator; b. Bklyn., Mar. 5, 1891; s. Isaac Franklin and Ruth (Ferriss) R.; B.A. cum laude, N.Y. U., 1911, J.D., 1915; B.A. (Rhodes scholar), Brasenose Coll., Oxford, 1913, B.C.L., 1914, M.A., 1924; m. Mildred Cutter Henry, June 25, 1917; children—Mildred, Ruth Elizabeth (Mrs. Frank Faulkner). Admitted to N.Y. bar, 1914, N.J. bar, 1934; mem. firm Zabriskie, Sage, Gray & Todd, 1925-28, Russell, Shevlin & Nussell, 1929-42; counsel to law firm Shevlin Siegfried & Shainman, N.Y.C., 1959-78. Prof. law Bklyn. Law Sch. postgrad. div., 1921-42, 47, 62-67; Owen D. Young prof. internat. relations St. Lawrence U., 1925-28; prof. law Mercer Beasley Sch. Law, Newark U., 1934-36; dep. chief legal div. U.S. element, Allied Commn. for Austria, 1945-46; with CIA, 1949-50; spl. asst. to legal adviser for aid to Greece and Turkey, Dept. of State; magister Riccobono Seminar Roman Law in Am., 1951-52; vis. instr. Greek, Va. Episcopal Theol. Sem., 1953; legal adviser, atty. gen. Govt. of Eritrea, Ethiopia, 1955-56; legal adviser to rep. Emperor of Ethiopia in Eritrea, 1957-59. Bd. visitors U.S. Naval Acad., 1931. Served with 1st N.Y. Cav., Mexican Border Campaign, 1916-17; lt. Transp. Corps, U.S. Army, 1918-19; AEF; capt. to lt. col. Signal Corps, AUS, 1942-46. Mem. Phi Beta Kappa, Phi Delta Phi, Psi Upsilon. Republican. Episcopalian. Author: Outline of Legal History, 1929; Review Guide to New Testament Greek, 1954. Contbr. numerous articles to legal, banking publs. Home: Englewood, N.J. Died Mar. 1978.

RUSSELL, JAMES ALVIN, clergyman; b. Lawrenceville, Va., June 10, 1885; s. James Solomon and Virginia M. (Morgan) R.; A.B., Oberlin Coll.; grad. Phila. Divinity Sch., 1916; A.M., U. of Pa., 1916, Columbia, 1928; L.L.D. (hon.) Va. State College, 1937; D.D., Va. Union U., 1937, Va. Theol. Sem. (Alexandria, Va.); m. Nellie Marguerite Pratt, June 12, 1916; children—James Alvin, Henry Pratt, Virginia Marguerite, Donald Churchill, Ulysses Wharton. Ordained to ministry of Episcopal Ch., 1915; instr. in history and Bible, St. Paul's High Sch., 1916-18, vice prin., 1918-29; prin., 1929-41; pres. St. Paul's Poly. Inst., Lawrenceville, Va., since 1941; rector St. Paul's Memorial Chapel. Mason, Elk. Address: Lawrenceville, Va. *

RUSSELL, JOHN BENJAMIN, JR., elec. engr.; b. Boston, Mar. 10, 1907; s. John B. and Nellie (Hodskins) R.; B.S., Mass. Inst. Tech., 1928, M.S., 1931, D.Sc., 1950; m. Mary C. Merry, Sept. 20, 1930; 1 dau., Carolyn. Research asst. Mass. Inst. Tech., elec. engring. dept., 1928-29, instr. elec. engring., 1929-31; instr. elec. engring. Columbia U., 1931-35, asst. prof., 1935-47, asso. prof., 1946-49, prof., 1949-55, head dept. elec. engring., 1952-55; mgr. engring. analysis electronics lab. Gen. Electric Co., 1955-57, gen. mgr. electronics lab., 1957-64, sr. cons. engr. electronics lab., 1964-65; dean engring. Clarkson Coll. Tech., 1965-68, prof. elec. engring., 1968-72; cons. elec. engring., radio and electronics, 1935-75; tech. aide, Div. 7, Nat. Def. Research Com., 1941-45; expert cons. Office sec. of War, 1945-46; expert cons. Office Chief of Staff, War Dept., June-Sept. 1946. Recipient Naval Ordnance Devel. award with certificate of Excellence; Army-Navy Certificate of Appreciation. Fellow N.Y. Acad. Scis., I.E.E.E.; mem. U.S. Power Squadron (past rear comdr.), Am. Soc. Engring. Edn., Tau Beta Pi. Sigma Xi, Epsilon Chi, Eta Kappa Nu. Republican. Conglist. Contbr. numerous articles to tech. jours. Home: Grahamsville, N.Y. Died Aug. 11, 1975.

RUSSELL, PERCY HICKLING, lawyer; b. Washington, Aug. 31, 1908; s. Percy Hickling, Sr., and Tuna (Saunders) R.; A.B.. Dartmouth, 1929; J.D., Harvard, 1932; m. Marjorie Allman, June 10, 1933; children—Patricia H., Percy Hickling, Andrea J.; m. 2d, Wilson Fitz, Nov. 29, 1963. Admitted to D.C. bar, 1932; law clk. to asso. justice Benjamin N. Cardozo, U.S. Supreme Ct., 1932-36; with firm Kirkland, Ellis & Rowe and predecessor, 1936-74, mng. partner, Washington office, 1964-68; dir. Gilmore Broadcasting Corp., Kalamazoo. Mem. Nat. Capital Area council Boy Scouts Am., 1951-65. Served to lt. USNR, 1943-45. Recipient Silver Beaver award Boy Scouts Am. Mem. FCC Bar Assn. (editor-in-chief jour. 1937-41, pres. 1955-56), Am. (ho. of dels. 1956-57), D.C. bar assns. Am. Legion, Zeta Psi. Republican. Methodist. Clubs: Met., Columbia Country (Washington); Ocean Reef (Key Largo, Fla.). Home: Washington, D.C. Died Jan. 3, 1978.

RUSSELL, (CHARLES) PHILLIPS, author; b. Rockingham, N.C., Aug. 5, 1884; s. Moses H. and Lucy Plummer (Phillips) R.; A.B., U. of N.C., 1904; m. 2d, Caro Mae Green, 1931; children—Leon, Claire, Avery. Asso. prof. English, U. of N.C., 1931, prof. journalism, 1936. Author: Benjamin Franklin, 1926; John Paul Jones, 1927; Fumbler, 1928; Red Tiger, 1928; Emerson, the Wisest American, 1929; Harvesters, 1932; William the Conqueror, 1934; The Glittering Century, 1936; The Woman Who Rang the Bell, 1949. Home: Chapel Hill, N.C.*

RUSSELL, ROSALIND, actress; b. Waterbury, Conn., June 4, 1911; d. James and Clara (McKnight) Russell; student Marymount Coll., Tarrytown, N.Y., 1926-28; Dr. Fine Arts, U. of Portland, 1967; m. Frederick Brisson, Oct. 25, 1941; 1 son, Lance. Played in summer stock co., Lake Placid, N.Y., 1931-32; appeared on N.Y. stage (Theater Guild), 1932; The Garrick Gaieties, Company Coming, Talent; in motion pictures for Metro-Goldwyn-Mayer, 1935-41; free lance actress from 1941; formed (with husband) producing co., Independent Artists, 1947; starred in 51 films, including Craig's Wife, Night Must Fall, The Citadel, The Women, His Girl Friday, No Time for Comedy, Take A Letter Darling, My Sister Eileen, Flight for Freedom, Sister Kenny, Mourning Becomes Electra, The Velvet Touch, Tell It to the Judge, A Woman of Distinction, Never Wave At A WAC, Picnic, Auntie Mame, A Majority of One, Five Finger Exercise, Gypsy, The Trouble With Angels, Oh Dad, Poor Dad, Mama's Hung You in the Closet and I'm Feelin' So Sad, Where Angels Go. . .Trouble Follows, Mrs. Pollifax—Spy; starred on Broadway in Wonderful Town, 1953, Auntie Mame, 1956, and on CBS-TV in Wonderful Town, 1958. Chmn. exec. com. Cedars-Sinai Hosp. Women's Guild, 1967; mem. Los Angeles Mayor's Celebrity Com., Nat. Council on Arts, 1972, Nat. Commn. on Arthritis and Related Musculo-skelatal Diseases, 1975. Bd. dirs. Center Theater Group. Elizabeth Kenny Inst., Los Angeles Internat. Film Exposition; trustee St. John's Hosp., Motion Picture Relief Fund. Recipient Jean Hersholt Humanitarian award Acad. Motion Picture Arts and Scis., 1972. Roman Catholic. Died Nov. 28, 1976; buried Holy Cross Cemetery, Los Angeles.

RUSSO, JOSEPH LOUIS (ROO'SO), univ. prof., author; b. Naples, Italy, Oct. 12, 1884; s. Federico and Concetta (Fiorentino) R.; A.B., Liceo Garibaldi, Naples, 1903; student (law), U. of Naples, 1903-06; A.M., Columbia U., 1915, Ph.D., 1921; m. Margherita Alessandri, Sept. 28, 1927. Came to U.S. 1906, naturalized 1916. Asst. prof., Hamilton Coll., 1919-21; asso. prof., Allegheny Coll., 1921-24; asst. prof., asso. prof., prof. Italian lit., U. of Wis., 1924-50. Served as pvt., lt., 1st lt., Italian Army (arty.), 1916-19; fought in battles of Valhella, Piave, Vitorio Veneto. Decorations: War Cross (Italian); Cavaliere della Corona d'Italia. Mem. Am. Assn. Teachers of Italian. Roman Catholic. Republican. Author: Lorenzo Da Ponte, 1922; Elementary Italian Grammar, 1927; Pirandello's Cosí è sevi pare, 1930; Nel paese del sole, 1934; First Year Italian, 1937; Second Year Italian, 1941; Present Day Italian, 1947; Sotto un cielo azzurro, 1950; Goldoni's I Rusteghi (to be published), 1951; also articles, reviews, etc. Address: Naples, Italy. *

RUTHERFORD, CHARLES HAYES (RUTH'ER-FERD), lawyer; b. Nelson, N.H., Dec. 1, 1884; s. John and Diana L. (Clary) R.; a direct descendant of John Howland, passenger on the Mayflower; grad. Montpelier (Vt.) Jr. College; LL.B., Marion (Ind.) Coll. of Law, 1905; m. Erie E. Dykes, Nov. 9, 1909 (died Oct. 1, 1931); children—Charles (died in infancy), John (maj. A.C. Res.). Admitted to bar Ind. Supreme Ct., 1905, to Arizona bar, 1906, bar of U.S. Supreme Court, 1912; in active practice since 1906; city atty., Jerome, Ariz., 1906-19, U.S. commr., Ariz. 1911-20. State senator, Ariz., 1917-18 and 1923-24; candidate for U.S. Senate, 1934. Aide to sec. of treasury World War I; toured U.S. for Liberty Loans. Awarded Victory medal. Apptd. maj., judge adv., U.S. Army Res., 1923, col. since 1928; civilian aide to various secs. of war since 1930. Awarded Victory; medal. Mem. Am. Bay Assn. (ex-v.p.), Ariz. Bar Assn. (ex-pres.), Ariz. Small Mine Operators Assn. (pres.), Mayflower Soc., Vets. Fgn. Wars, Sons of Revolution, Soc. of Am. Wars, Reserve Officers Assn. of Ariz. (past pres.), Nat. Reserve Officers Assn. of U.S. (past judge adv.; organizer and 1st president Ariz. chapter). Democrat. Christian Scientist. Mason (32 deg. Shriner). Inventor of method now used extensively for curing frosted fruit and vegetation. Home: Phoenix, Ariz. *

RUTHERFORD, EMERY GAYTHOR, mfg. co. exec.; b. Mt. Vernon, Ill., 1909; s. Roy Gaythor and Metta (Watson) R.; B.S. U. Ill., 1935, M.S., 1936; m. Marjorie Wham, June 9, 1936; children—James Joel, Marjorie Lynn, John Warren. Sr. auditor Lybrand, Ross Bros. & Montgomery, Rockford, Ill., 1936-39; gen. auditor Modine Mfg. Co., Racine, Wis., 1939-40, asst. sec., 1940-42, sec. 1942-44, 54-60, treas., 1944-60, v.p., 1960-63, pres., 1963-74, chmn. bd., from 1974, also dir.; dir. M&I Am. Bank & Trust Co., Racine, Twin Disc, Inc., Racine, Giddings & Lewis, Inc., Fond du Lac, Wis., Marshall & Ilsley Corp., Milw. Pres., Racine Art Assn.; sec.-treas. Racine County Planning Council. Methodist (trustee). Clubs: Country, Somerset, Racine Yacht (Racine). Home: Racine, Wis. Deceased.

RUTHERFORD, HARRY K., army officer; b. Nov. 7, 1883; B.S., U.S. Mil. Acad., 1907. Commd. 2d lt. Coast Arty. Corps, June 14, 1907; promoted through grades to col., Dec. 1, 1935; temporary rank of maj. gen. since Dec. 1941; assigned to Office of Chief Ordnance, Washington, Apr. 1942. *

RUTHERFORD, RICHARD JAMES, utilities exec.; b. Chgo., Aug. 14, 1903; s. James L. and Margaret (Dowling) R.; B.S., U. Ill., 1924; m. Mildred A. Horney, June 10, 1926; children—Judith, Jo Ann. With Pub. Service of Colo., 1924-25; v.p., gen. mgr., Union Gas & Electric Co., Bloomington, Ill., 1929-31; gen. sales mgr., New Eng. Gas & Electric Assn., Cambridge, Mass., 1931-36; v.p. Worcester Gas Light Co., 1936-51, pres., 1951-68, dir., from 1936; chmn. bd. Riley Stoker Corp., from 1968; partner Hall-Bud Assos.; dir. Negea Service Corp., Mechanics Nat. Bank, Peoples Savs. Bank, Thomas Smith Corp. Bd. dirs. local A.R.C., Boy Scouts Am.; bd. dirs., past pres. local YMCA; trustee Holy Cross Coll., Worcester Jr. Coll., Hahemann Hosp. Mem.

U. Ill. Found. Mem. C. of C., New Eng. Gas Assn. (past chmn.), Guild Gas Mgrs. (past pres.), Am. Gas Assn. (past pres.). Rotarian (past pres., past dist. gov.). Clubs: University, Worcester, Tatuuck Country (Worcester). Home: Worcester, Mass. Died Nov. 21, 1977.

RUTHVEN, ALEXANDER G(RANT) (ROOTH'VEN), univ. pres.; b. Hull, Ia., Apr. 1, 1882; s. John and Katherine (Rombough) R.; B.S., Morningside Coll., 1903; U. of Chicago, summer quarter, 1902; Ph.D., U. of Mich., 1906; Sc.D., Kalamazoo Coll., 1931, Mich. Coll. of Mining and Technology, 1937; LL.D., Albion Coll., 1930, Northwestern U., 1930, Morningside Coll., 1931, Denison U., 1933, Tulane U., 1938, U. of Calif., 1938, U. of N.M., 1944, Wayne U., 1950; Dr. Honoris Causa, Catholic University of Chile, 1944; m. Florence Hagle, September, 1907; children—Katherine Lenora, Alexander Peter, Bryant Walker. With Univ. of Michigan since 1906; successively instr. zoölogy and curator Museum of Zoölogy, 1906-11, asst. prof. and curator Museum of Zoölogy, 1911-13, asst. prof. and dir. Museum of Zoölogy, 1913-15, prof. and dir. Museum of Zoölogy, 1915-29, dir. univ. museums, 1922-36, chmn. dept. of zoölogy and dir. Zoöl. Labs., 1927-29, dean adminstrn., 1928-29, pres., 1929-51, emeritus since 1951. Chief field naturalist, Mich. Geol., Biol. Survey, 1908-12. Dir. various sci. expeditions, in North, South and Central America. Awarded Blue Grand Cordon of the Order of the Brilliant Jade, 1938. Fellow A.A.A.S., Am. Acad. Arts and Sciences; mem. Am. Soc. Zoölogists, Am. Soc. Naturalists, Mich. Acad. Science, Arts and Letters (pres. 1913-15), Am. Philos. Soc., Am. Soc. Ichthylogists and Herpetologists, Assn. Am. Geographers, Phi Sigma, Gamma Alpha, Sigma Xi, Phi Beta Kappa, Phi Kappa Phi; corr. mem. London Zoöl. Soc. Author of numerous papers on Zoöl. subjects. Home: Ann Arbor, Mich. *

RUZICKA, LEOPOLD, educator, chemist; b. 1887; ed. Tech. High Sch., Karlsruhe. Prof. organic chemistry Zürich Fed. Inst. Tech. Recipient Nobel Chemistry Prize (with Adolph Butenandt) for work on polymetylenes, higher terpen compounds, 1939. Fgn. mem. Royal Soc. London. Mem. Am. Acad. Arts Scis., Nat. Acad. Scis., Brit. Chem. Soc., Am. Soc. Biol. Chemists. Address: Zurich, Switzerland. Died 1976.

RUZICKA, RUDOLPH, illustrator, designer; b. Bohemia, June 29, 1883; s. Vaclav and Josephine (Reichman) R.; brought to U.S., 1894; ed. Art Inst. Chgo., N.Y. Sch. Art; m. Filomena Srpova, Aug. 3, 1914; children—Tatiana, Veronica. Represented in print collections of Met. Mus. Art, N.Y.C., Congl. Library, Washington, Art Inst. Chgo., Newark Mus., Dartmouth Coll. Library, Houghton Library, Harvard. Awarded Alice McFadden Brinton prize, Phila. Print Club, 1924; bronze medal, Sesquicentennial Expn., Phila. 1926; gold medal Am. Inst. Graphic Arts, 1935. Academician, NAD. Fellow Am. Acad. Arts and Scis., mem. Colonial Soc. Mass., Soc. Printers Boston (hon.), Mass. Hist. Soc. Clubs: Century, Grolier (hon.) (N.Y.C.); Club of Odd Volumes (hon.) (Boston). Illustrator books, 1915-78. Author: Thomas Bewick, Engraver, 1943; Studies in Type Design, 1968. Home: Hanover, N.H. Died July 20, 1978.

RYAN, HAROLD FRANCIS, clergyman, educator; b. Sunnyside, Utah, Mar. 9, 1908; s. James Joseph and Lillian (Bulwer-Roche) R.; B.A., Gonzaga U., 1932, M.A., 1933; postgrad. Alma Coll., 1936-40; Ph.D., St. Louis U., 1944. Joined Soc. of Jesus, 1926, ordained priest Roman Catholic Ch., 1939; instr. English Loyola U., Los Angeles, 1933-35, asst. prof., 1944-47, asso. prof., 1947-51, prof., 1951-78, dean grad. div., 1950-71; vis. prof. English, U. Detroit, 1948, U. San Francisco, 1940-41, Cath. U. Rio de Janeiro (Brazil), 1949, Cath. U. Sao Paulo (Brazil), 1949. Mem. Coll. English Assn. So. Calif. (pres. 1954), Modern Lang. Assn. Am., Renaissance Soc., Philol. Assn. Pacific Coast, Fedn. Fly Fishermen, Inglewood Fly Fishermen. Home: Los Angeles, Calif. Died Feb. 23, 1979; buried Santa Clara Mission Cemetery.

RYAN, LEO JOSEPH, Congressman; b. Lincoln, Nebr., May 5, 1925; s. Leo Joseph and Autumn (Mead) R.; B.S., Creighton U., 1949, M.S., 1951; children—Christopher, Shannon, Patricia, Kevin, Erin. Mem. South San Francisco City Council, 1956-62, mayor, 1962; mem. Calif. Legislature, 1962-72; mem. 93d-95th congresses from 11th Dist. Calif., chmn. subcom. on environment, energy and natural resources of House Govt. Ops. Com. Hon. chmn. No. Calif. Kidney Found., 1967; mem. Am. Revolution Bicentennial Commn., from 1968; adv. bd. Am. Oceanic Assn., Closeup program. Mem. Italian-Am. Fedn. San Mateo County, Sociedad Mutualista Mexicana Morelos. Clubs: Elks, Commonwealth. Home: Belmont, Calif. Died Nov. 18, 1978.

RYAN, PATRICK JAMES, clergyman; b. Litchfield, Minn., Dec. 3, 1902; s. Patrick Philip and Johanna (Cassady) R.; A.B., St. Thomas Coll., St. Paul, 1923, LL.D., 1954; S.T.B., St. Paul Sem., 1927. Ordained priest Roman Catholic Ch., 1927; priest St. Helena's Parish, 1927-28; served from 1st lt. to maj. gen. Chaplain Corps, U.S. Army, 1928-58, Office Chief of Chaplains, Washington, 1945-48, 52-58, chief of chaplains, 1954-58, ret.; exec. v.p. The Catholic Digest. Decorated Legion of Merit, B.S.M. (U.S.); Medal of War (Brazil); Order of Crown, Bronze Medal of Valor with Star (Italy); Order Brit. Empire; Legion Honor (France), 1958; Distinguished Service medal (U.S.), 1958. Elevated to rank domestic prelate by Pope Pius XII, with title monsignor, 1947, to rank of prothonotary apostolic, 1967. Grand prior Mil. and Hospitaler Order St. Lazarus Jerusalem. Home: Washington, D.C. Died June 6, 1978.

RYAN, SYLVESTER JAMES, judge; b. N.Y.C., Sept. 10, 1896; s. James S. and Julia Leone (Colemann) R.; Coll. City N.Y. (Ex. 1916); LL.B., Fordham U., 1917, LL.D., 1956; m. Mary Margaret Corcoran, Jan. 21, 1922; children—Sylvester J., Rosemary E. (Mrs. Robert Ryder Luttrell), Margaret Ann (Mrs. Dermott Gerard Foley). Admitted to N.Y. State bar, 1918, practiced in N.Y.C., 1918-47; chief asst. and acting dist. atty. Bronx County, N.Y., 1924-47; U.S. dist. judge for So. Dist. N.Y., from 1947, chief judge, from 1960. Knight of Malta. Mem. Am., N.Y. State, Bronx County (pres. 1946-47) bar assns., Am. Judicature Soc. Roman Catholic. Home: New York, N.Y. Died Apr. 10, 1981.

RYDEN, ERNEST EDWIN (RI'DEN), clergyman, editor; b. Kansas City, Mo., Sept. 12, 1886; s. August and Emma Sophia (Peterson) R.; A.B., Augustana Coll. and Theol. Sem., Rock Island, Ill., 1910, B.D., 1914, D.D., 1931; m. Agnes Elizabeth Johnson, June 23, 1914; children—Cecile Elizabeth (Mrs. Philip A. Johnson), Richard Edward (dec.), Jean Agnes (Mrs. Lewis Eley), Hope Elaine, Ernest Edwin. Reporter Kansas City (Mo.) World, 1904; with telegraph department K.C. Southern Railway, 1905-07; telegraph editor Moline (Ill.) Dispatch, 1910-11; ordained Luth. ministry at Sycamore, Ill., 1914; pastor Grace and Holy Trinity chs., Jamestown, N.Y., 1914-20, Gloria Dei Ch., St. Paul, 1920-34; editor Lutheran Companion (official organ Augustana Church), Rock Island, 1934-61; editor Lutheran Outlook (organ Am. Luth. Conf.), 1943-47; director bureau of press, radio and television Augustana Church, Minneapolis, Minn. 1961—. Lutheran camp pastor, Camp Wadsworth, Spartanburg, S.C., World War I. Mem. Jamestown Bd. of Health, 1917-19. Pres. Am. Lutheran Conf., 1938-42, Nat. Luth. Editors' Assn., 1941-43, 48-50, 53-55; Bd. Christian Service, Minn. Conf. of Augustana Ch., 1926-35, Assn. English Chs. of Augustana Synod, 1922-25, Protestant Ministers Council, St. Paul, 1932-34; mem. Bd. of Christian Edn. and Literature, Augustana Synod, 1929-35; chmn. liturgy com. Am. Luth. Conf., 1934-38; com. on congregation constitution, Augustana Synod, 1932-38; chmn. hymnal com., Augustana Synod, 1936-58; chmn. commn. on Luth. ch. unity, Am. Luth. Conference, 1942-48; sec. joint commn. on common Luth. hymnal, 1945-58; mem. permanent commn. service Book and Hymnal, 1958—; mem. bd. Augustana Coll. and Theol. Seminary, 1938-48; pres. of bd., 1944-48; president board of Augustana College, 1948-60; board of Moline Lutheran Hospital, 1938-41. Delegate and speaker Lutheran World Conv. (Paris), 1935; alternate delegate First Assembly, World Council of Chs., Amsterdam, 1948. Decorated Knight Order of North Star (Sweden). Member Augustana Hist. Soc., Hymn. Soc. Am., Am.-Scandinavian Foundation. Republican. Clubs: Rotary, After Dinner. Author: The Story of Our Hymns, 1930; Bible Study Quarterly, 1931; The Story of Christian Hymnody, published 1959. Co-editor of Augustana Hymnal, 1923-25, Jr. Hymnal, 1928. Wrote Story of Songs, broadcast over KSTP, St. Paul, 1933-34. Writer and translator of hymns. Transl. from Swedish: Captain Bright (novel) 1961. Contbr. to theol, quarterlies. Home: Rock Island, Ill. *

RYDEN, ROY WARREN, naval officers; b. Des Moines, Ia., Feb. 27, 1882; s. Charles Augustus and Christine (Johnson) R.; B.S., U.S. Naval Acad., 1903; M.S., Mass. Inst. Tech. (post grad. course in naval architecture and warship design), 1908; grad. U.S. Naval War Coll., 1925, U.S. Army Indl. Coll, 1935; m. Garnett Rainey (dec. 1948), Sept. 26, 1907; children—Garnett Ethel (Mrs. John R. Waterman), Roy Warren, Jr. Commd. ensign, U.S. Navy, 1903; capt. Constrn. Corps, 1927-40; supt. mech. div., Panama Canal, 1921-24, 1929-34; rear adm., 1941-46; mgr. Norfolk (Va.) Navy Yd., 1936-41; supervisor of shipbuilding U.S. Navy, Camden, New Jersey, 1941-46; ret. Aug. 1, 1946. Awarded Spl. letter of commendation by Navy Dept. for services during World War I; Legion of Merit, World War II. Mem. Sigma Chi. Address: Montgomery, Ala. *

RYDER, MELVIN, editor, publisher; b. Cadiz Junction, O., Jan. 26, 1893; s. Charles M. and Mary Frances (Ralston) R.; A.B., Ohio State U., 1915; m. Florence Snelling, May 11, 1936; children—Mary Jane, Susan, Molly. Mem. staff Stars and Stripes, AEF newspaper, World War I; partner Kiplinger Washington Agy., 1921-24; asso. Amos Parrish & Co., later partner McBride, Ullman & Ryder, N.Y.C., 1924-32; editor, pub. Happy Days, 1933-40; pres. Happy Days Pub. Co.; editor, pub., pres. Army Times Pub. Co., pubs. of Army Times, Air Force Times, Navy Times, Am. Weekend, Mil. Market, Washington, from 1940. Home: Washington, D.C. Died Aug. 10, 1979.

RYERSON, MARGERY AUSTEN, artist; b. Morristown, N.J., Sept. 15, 1886; d. David Austen and Mary McIlvaine (Brown) R.; A.B., Vassar Coll., 1909; studied at Art Students' League, N.Y.C., and under Robert Henri and Charles W. Hawthorne. Painter, etcher and lithographer. Represented by prints in permanent collections Smithsonian Instn., other museums in U.S. and abroad; paintings in collections N.J. Hist. Soc., Norfolk (Va.) Mus. Arts and Scis., Abbott Labs., N.A.D., Vassar Coll., Philbrook Art Center, Tulsa, Frye Mus., Seattle, Va. State Coll., others. Recipient 1st prize (oil) Hudson Valley Art Assn., 1956, 57, 58; gold medal for oil portrait prize Nat. Arts Club, 1957, 62, 69, Silver medal, 1971; Maynard portrait prize N.A.D., 1959; 1st prize Balt. Water Color Club, 1960; portrait prize (oil) Silvermine Guild, 1960; Hook Meml. award Am. Watercolor Soc.; Talens award N.J. Watercolor Soc., 1963, Winsor and Newton award, 1968; Stevenson prize (oil) Nat. Arts Club, 1967, Grumbacher award, 1972; Clinedinst medal Artists Fellowship, 1971; Holton Meml. watercolor prize Knickerbocker Artists, 1974; Dole prize Am. Artists Profl. League, 1973, prize for graphic, 1974; Albany Print Club prize, 1973. N.A., 1959; painter mem. Grand Central Art Galleries. Mem. Am. Watercolor Soc., Balt. Water Color Club, Knickerbocker Artists, Soc. Am. Graphic Artists, Allied Artists Am. (v.p. 1952-53), Audubon Artists (corr. sec. 1958-59). N.J. Water Color Soc., Print Club of Albany, Pen and Brush. Contbr. to Art in Am., The Am. Scholar, Am Artist, The Artist, N.Y. Herald Tribune, N.Y. Times Book Review. Compiler: The Art Spirit, by Robert Henri. Co-editor: Hawthorne on Painting: illustrator Winkie Boo. Home: New York City NY. *

RYLE, GILBERT, philosopher; b. 1900; ed. Brighton Coll. and Queen's Coll., Oxford U. Tutor philosophy Christ Ch., Oxford, 1924; Waynflete prof. metaphys. philosophy, also fellow Magadalen Coll., Oxford, 1945-68; hon. fellow Queen's Coll., Magdalen Coll.; hon. student Christ Church. Served as officer with Welsh Guards, World War II. Fgn. mem. Am. Acad. Arts and Scis. Author: The Concept of Mind, 1949; Dilemmas, 1954; Plato's Progress, 1965. Editor: Mind, 1947—. Address: Islip, Oxon, England. Died Oct. 6, 1976.

RYSKAMP, HENRY JACOB coll. dean; b. Grand Rapids, Mich., Nov. 3, 1893; s. Jacob and Maggie (Bolt) R.; student Calvin Coll. Prep. Sch.; A.B., U. Mich., 1916, M.A., 1917, Ph.D., 1930; m. Flora De Graaf, Aug. 3, 1923; children—Henry James, Charles Andrew, Philip John. Instr. Calvin Coll., prof. sociology, econs., 1921-24, prof., head dept., from 1925, coll. and faculty dean, from 1941; instr. history U. Mich., 1920-21, sociology, 1924-25. Del. White House Conf. as rep. nat. bd. Family Service Assn., 1950; mem. planning div. Grand Rapids and Kent County United Community Services. Bd. dirs. Kent County chpt. A.R.C.; bd. dirs. past pres. Grand Rapids Family Service Assn.; nat. board directors Family Service Assn. Am.; first chmn., past mem. bd. dirs. Council Social Agencies Grand Rapids; past mem. bd. Legal Aid Bur., Travelers Aid Soc.; mem. adv. bd. U. Mich. Extension Service, Grand Rapids. Mem. Calvin Coll. Alumni Assn. (past pres.), Am., Mich. (past pres.) sociol. socs., Mich. Coll. Assn. (exec. com., chmn. com. Mich. Secondary Sch. Coll. Agreement). Mem. Christian Reformed Ch. Club: Grand Rapids Torch (mem. bd. past pres.). Contbr. articles profl. jours. Home: Grand Rapids, Mich. Died Nov. 5, 1976.

RYTINA, ANTON GEORGE (RI'TI-NA), urologist; b. Baltimore, Md., Feb. 3, 1882; s. Anton and Anna (Hulla) R.; A.B., Loyola Coll., Baltimore, 1901; M.D., U. of Md., 1905; grad. study, Berlin, 1911; m. Katherine M. Gier, Jan. 24, 1912; children—Anthony George, Katherine Luciene. Instr., clin. lab., U. of Md., and phys. Out-patient Clinic, Johns Hopkins Hosp., 1905; physician Phipp's Tuberculosis Clinic, Johns Hopkins Hosp., 1906-07; mem. urol. dept., Johns Hopkins Hosp., 1908-15; chief of urology, Out-patient Clinic, Mercy Hosp., 1909-10, chief urologist, 1910-23; clin. prof. urology, Coll. Physicians and Surgeons (now U. of M.D.), 1910-15, prof. urology, 1915; organizer, 1919, owner and operator until 1928, Morrow (later Colonial) Hosp.; organizer Colonial Hosp. Training Sch. for Nurses, 1925; organizer, 1926, dir. until 1928, Physicians and Surgeons Casualty Clinic; organizer, 1929, since dir. med. and surg. depts. Safe Harbor (Pa.) Hosp.; visiting urologist South Baltimore Gen. Hosp., U.S. Govt. Marine Hosp., U.S. Vets. Bur. Hosp.; cons. urologist St. Joseph's Hosp. Mem. Md. State Bd. of Health since 1918 (dir. and adviser venereal disease clinics); mem. Selective Draft Bd., Baltimore, World War. Mem. Bd. Supervisors of City Charities, 1912-21. Fellow Am. Coll. Surgeons; mem. A.M.A., Am. Urol. Assn., Med. Chirurg. Faculty of Md., Baltimore City Med. Soc. Democrat. Catholic. Clubs: Rotary, Baltimore Athletic, Maryland Country. Contbr. on genito-urinary surgery. Pioneer in use of salvarsan and neosalvarsan. Home: Baltimore, Md. *

RZYMOWSKI, WINCENTY, minister of fgn. affairs, Poland; b. Warsaw, 1883. Student economics at the Univ. of Geneva and Lausanne, Switzérland; master's degree in law, Univ. of Odessa, Russia. During World War I participated actively in the Polish movement for independence. Fgn. corr. in Italy, 1923-27; in politics and journalism in Poland. Spent eight months in a German prison and in 1944, during World War I, volunteered for the Polish Army. Upon formation of the Polish Com. of Nat. Liberation apptd. head of the Dept. of Arts and Culture and remained in this position under the Polish Provisional Govt. until 1945; minister fgn.affairs since May, 1945.*

SABINI, DOMINIC JOSEPH, army officer; b. Corning, N.Y., Aug. 27, 1893; s. Anthony and Madaline (Ferranto) S.; student Canisius Coll., 1909-10, St. Bonaventure College, 1912; married Nielsine Christine Madsen. Entered United States Army, 1913, and advanced through the grades to brig. gen., 1945; served punitive expdn., World War I, 1916; in various parts of U.S. and world, 1919-45, chief army exchange service U.S. Army, 1945-46, retired 1946. Decorated Legion of Merit with oak leaf cluster, Mexican Service, World War I, Am. Defense, World War II, Asiatic Pacific. Home: Honolulu, Hawaii. Died Feb. 8, 1979.

SACHS, WALTER EDWARD, banker; b. N.Y. City, May 28, 1884; s. Samuel and Louise (Goldman) S.; prep. edn., Sachs Collegiate Inst., New York; A.B., Harvard, 1904, studied law, Harvard, 1904-05; studied foreign banking methods in London, Berlin, Paris, 1906, 07; m. Emanie Louise Nahm, July 10, 1917 (divorced); 1 dau., Jane Ellen (Mrs. Robert Hodes); m. 2d, Mary Williamson, Aug. 12, 1939 (div.); children—Katherine Russell (Mrs. Bernard D. Steinberg), Philip Williamson; m. 3d, Virginia Maitland, Oct. 21, 1961. Mem. Goldman, Sachs & Co., 1910-59, ltd. partner, 1959-80. Mem. vis. com., dept. music Harvard. Mem. N.Y. C. of C. (v.p.). Club: Harvard. Home: Darien, Conn. Died Aug. 21, 1980.

SACHSE, VICTOR A., JR., lawyer; b. Baton Rouge, Sept. 21, 1903; s. Victor A. and Fannye (Bloomenstiel) S.; LL.B., La. State U., 1925; m. Janice Rubenstein, Jan. 2, 1929; children—Victor A. III, Harry R. Admitted to La. bar, 1925, U.S. Supreme Ct. bar, 1934; practiced in Baton Rouge, 1925-79; mem. firm Breazeale, Sachse & Wilson; gen. counsel Surplus Property Adminstrn., Washington, 1945-46; dir. Fidelity Nat. Bank. Chmn. prisoner of war adv. com. to sec. of Air Force, 1963-64. Chmn. City-Parish Plan Commn., 1947-48; parish atty., East Baton Rouge, 1949-50. Bd. dirs. Council for a Better La., Found. for Better La., La. Arts and Sci. Center, 1965-67, La. State U. Found. Served to lt. col., AUS, 1942-45. Decorated Legion of Merit. Recipient Brotherhood award NCCJ, 1972. Fellow Am. Coll. Trial Lawyers; mem. Am., La. (bd. govs. 1957-58), Baton Rouge (pres. 1941-42) bar assns., Am., La. (council) law insts., Mil. Order World Wars, Am. Legion, Am. Jewish Com. (mem.-at-large ho. dels), Order Coif (hon.), Phi Delta Phi. Jewish (pres. congregation 1931, 35). Club: Mason (knight comdr. ct. honor). Home: Baton Rouge, La. Died Jan. 1, 1979.

SACKETT, ARTHUR JOHNSON, civil engr.; b. Ft. George, Fla., May 25, 1884; s. John Warren and Louise (Johnson) S.; student U. Pa., 1905-06; m. Ethel Lee Clancy, Sept. 2, 1907; 1 dau., Virginia Lee; m. 2d, Julia Hopkins, Nov. 5, 1932; 1 dau., Louise (Mrs. W.J. Hartley). Asst. engr. on constrn. East River Tunnel for Pa. R.R., 1906-11, asst. engrn. on constrn. Catskill Aqueduct, Mason & Hanger Co., 1911-17, chief engr. on constrn. Camp Taylor, 1917, chief engr. of company, 1919-29, pres. 1929-55, also dir.; chmn. bd., dir. Silas Mason Co., 1949-55, Mason & Hanger-Silas Mason Co., Inc., 1955—. Served as maj. Q.M.C., U.S. Army, 1918-19. Mem. Am. Soc. C.E., Soc. Am. Mil. Engrs. Episcopalian. Mason (Shriner). Clubs: Engineers, Turf and Field (N.Y.C.); Va. Country, Commonwealth (Richmond, Va.); U. Pa. (Phila.). Home: Charles City VA. *

SACKS, SHELDON, educator; b. N.Y.C., Feb. 20, 1930; s. Max and Pauline (Lindenbaum) S.; B.S., Northwestern U., 1952, M.A., 1953; Univ. fellow, U. Chgo., 1953-54, Vis. Com. fellow, 1954-55, Ph.D., 1959; Fulbright scholar, Univ. Coll., London, 1955-56; m. Marjorie Hamilton, May 10, 1952 (dec.); children—Colin Hamilton, James Phillip; m. 2d, Jean Karen Weber, June 2, 1967. Instr., U. Tex., Austin, 1956-58; asst. prof. U. Calif., Berkeley, 1959-65, asso. prof., 1965-66; asso. prof. U. Chgo., 1966-67, prof. English and linguistics, 1967-79; vis. Fulbright lectr. U. Rome, Italy, 1961-62. Recipient E. Harris Harbison prize for gifted teaching Danforth Found., 1970; Nat. Endowment Humanities fellow, 1978. Mem. Am. Soc. Eighteenth-Century Studies, Linguistic Soc. Am., Johnsonian Soc., Midwest Modern Lang. Assn., Modern Lang. Assn. (chmn. dir. philos. approaches to lit. exec. com. 1976, del. assembly), P.E.N. Author: Fiction and the Shape of Belief, 1964; (with R.W. Rader) An Analytic Reader, 1964; The Psychological Implications of Generic Distinctions, 1967; Golden Birds and Dying Generations, 1969; Clarissa and the Tragic Traditions, 1973; Novelists as Storytellers, 1976. Editor: Critical Inquiry, from 1973. Home: Chicago, Ill. Died Jan. 5, 1979.

SADLER, DANIEL K., judge; born in Paris, Ark., Oct. 28, 1882; s. Charles R. and Ophelia C. (Logan) S.; A.B., U. of Ark., 1906; LL.B., Washington and Lee U., 1909; m. Jessie M. McGaugh, Aug. 27, 1911; children—Daniel Kennard, Robert Granville. Justice Supreme Court of New Mexico, now serving 4th term ending Jan. 1, 1963, chief justice, 1935, 36, 1943-45, 46, 53. Address: Santa Fe, N.M. *

SADUSK, JOSEPH FRANCIS, JR., physician, health services cons.; b. Balt., Oct. 4, 1909; s. Joseph and Eva Marie (Kolita S., Sr.); student Loyola Coll., Baltimore, 1927-29; A.B., Johns Hopkins U., 1931, M.D. (Henry Strong Denison fellow, 1934-35), 1935; m. Marian Wayman Young, Dec. 28, 1938; children—Estelle, George, Barbara, Eva Mary, William. Interne Johns Hopkins Hosp., Balt., 1935-37, asst. resident in obstetrics, 1938-39; asst. resident in medicine, New Haven Hosp., 1937-38, resident in med., 1939-40, dir. med. outpatient clinic, 1941-42, asso. physician, 1939-47; asso. med. dir. Prudential Ins. Co., 1947-48; instr. Yale Sch. Med., 1939-42, asst. prof. medicine, 1946-47; adj. prof. clin. medicine George Washington U., 1948-49, prof. preventive medicine and community health, 1962-66; asso. clin. prof. medicine Stanford, 1949-62; med. dir. FDA, 1964-66; prof. medicine, asso. dean for community medicine Johns Hopkins, 1966-67; physician Johns Hopkins Hosp., 1966-67; v.p. med. and sci. affairs Parke, Davis & Co., 1967-71, dir., 1967-74; clin. prof. medicine Wayne State U., 1967-71; sr. v.p., dir. med. and sci. affairs Warner-Lambert Co., 1971-74, also dir.; sr. cons. Permanente Med. Group, Oakland, Calif., 1974-78; research cons. Peralta Hosp., 1974-75; dir. Kaiser Found. Research Inst., 1975-78. Mem. Commn. on Pneumonia, Army Epidemiol. Bd., 1940-42; cons. to Sec. of War in infectious diseases, 1940-42, in tropical diseases, 1946-47; expert cons. to sec. of Defense, 1948-52; area cons. in tropical medicine VA, 1952-62; exec. dir. com. on med. scis., Research and Development Bd., Dept. of Defense, Washington, 1948-49; mem. civilian health and medical adv. council to the sec. of def., 1961-64; medical dir. FDA Dept. of Health, Edn. and Welfare, 1964-66. Trustee St. John Hosp., 1967-71, Lindenwood Coll., 1970-71. Served to col. M.C., U.S. Army, 1942; exec. officer U.S. of Am. Typhus Commn., 1943-46; exec. officer Spl. Commn. for Study of Serub Typhus in New Guinea, 1946. Decorated Legion of Merit with Oak Leaf Cluster, 1946; U.S. of Am. Typhus Commn. medal, 1945. Fellow A.C.P.; mem. Am. Soc. Clin. Investigation, Am. Fedn. Clin. Research, Am. Soc. Clin. Pharmacology and Therapeutics, A.M.A., Sigma Xi. Republican. Catholic. Club: Cosmos (Washington). Contbr. Cecil's Textbook of Medicine, 1946; Nelson's Loose-Leaf Textbook of Medicine, 1949; Conn's Current Therapy, 1952-64. Contbr. articles on biochem. and infectious diseases and legal medicine and drug safety to med. jours. Home: Walnut Creek, Calif. Died July 3, 1978.

SAFFORD, WILLIAM CULLEN, ins. exec.; b. Columbus, Ohio, Dec. 2, 1898; s. William C. and Martha (Reese) S.; student Aquinas Coll., 1916-17, Columbus Law Coll., 1926-27; m. Frances Fobiano, July 21, 1956; children—Melissa Jane, Susan. Dep. supt. ins. Ohio, 1925-26, supt., 1927-28; v.p. The Western and Southern Life Ins. Co., Cin., 1922-57, pres. from 1957, chmn. bd., also dir. Mem. adv. council Ohio Bur. Employment Services, from 1937; vice chmn. Ohio Devel. Financing Commn., from 1965. Bd. visitors West Point Mil. Acad., 1950-52, chmn. 1952; trustee Ohio State U. Democrat. Clubs: Queen City, Hyde Park Country, Columbus, N.Y. Athletic, N.Y. Economic, Manhattan. Home: Cincinnati, Ohio. Deceased.

SAGUE, MARY LOUISE LANDON (SA-GU), prof. chemistry; b. Burlington, Vt., Sept. 29, 1885; d. Sealand Whitney and Helen Frank (Weeks) Landon; student Priscilla Braislin Sch., Bordentown, N.J., 1901-02, Trenton Model Sch., 1902-03; A.B., Vassar Coll., 1907; A.M., Columbia University, 1914, Ph.D., 1920; D. Sc., Middlebury (Vt.) College, 1946; married James Edward Sague, June 14, 1928; one step-daughter, Isobel (Mrs. Edward Sterling Carter). High sch. teacher, Bordentown, N.J., 1907-08; asst. in chemistry, Vassar Coll., 1908-10, instr., 1910-13, 1914-17, asst. prof., 1919-24, asso. prof., 1924-28, prof. since 1928, chmn. dept. of Chemistry since 1924. Goldschmidt fellowship, Columbia Univ., 1918-19; Asso. Alumnae of Vassar Coll. fellowship, 1913-14. Fellow A.A.A.S., Am. Inst. of Chemists; mem. Am. Chem. Soc. (chmn. Mid-Hudson sect.,1947-48), Biochem. Soc. (British), N.Y. Acad. of Sciences, Am. Assn. Univ. Women, Am. Assn. Univ. Profs., Sigma Xi. Club: Garden (Poughkeepsie). Home: Poughkeepsie, N.Y. *

SAINSBURY, NOËL EVERINGHAM, JR. (SANS'BUR-I), author; b. New York, N.Y., June 11, 1884; s. Noël Everingham and Pauline (Pistor) S.; student St. Gall, Switzerland, 1898-1900, Coll. Internat., Geneva, Switzerland, 1900-03, Cornell U., 1904-06; m. Bessie Slade; 1 son, John S.; m. 2d, Dorothy Wayne Illick, April 28, 1926; 1 dau., Wayne. Civil engr., 1906-08; mem. Beerman & Sainsbury, Inc., New Orleans, La. and Moscow, Russia, 1908-14; engineering work, 1914-17, 1925-30; writing juvenile fiction since 1930. Seaman 2d class, later lt. comdr. naval aviator, U.S.N.R.F., World War. U.S. Civil Service, attached U.S. Navy, since 1942. Mem. Psi Upsilon. Author: The Great Ace Series (7 books); The Bill Bolton Naval Aviation Series (6 books); The Dorothy Dixon Air Mystery Series (6 books, under pseudonym Dorothy Wayne); The Malay Jungle Series (6 books), under pseudonym of Harvey D. Richards; The Champion Sports Series (5 books); Out with Magellan; also short stories in juvenile mags. and radio scripts for children, including Billy Smith, Adventures of Patty and Jim, Bill Bolton, Dorothy Dixon, etc.; also (adult fiction) Mischief in Malaya; Mischief in Manhattan; Skin Deep. Home: Oxford, Somerset, Bermuda.*

ST. PIERRE, CHARLES, banker; b. Montreal, Que., Aug. 3, 1886; s. Charles and Marie (Racicot) St. P.; student Mont St. Louis Coll., Montreal. With Banque Canadienne Nationale since 1902, apptd. gen. mgr., 1935, elected pres., mng. dir. 1950. Home: Montreal, Que. Can. *

SAINT-QUENTIN, RENÉ DOYNEL COMTE DE, ambassador; b. Garcelles, France, Dec. 2, 1883; s. Comte Louis Doynel and Comtesse Alice (Liégeard) de Saint-Quentin; student Lycée Janson de Sailly, Paris, 1895-1901, Faculté des Lettres, Ecole de droit, Ecole des Sciences Politiques, Paris, 1901-06; LL.D., Lafayette College, 1938, Boston U., 1939. Attaché of Embassy, London, 1907-09; sec. of Embassy, Constantinople; 1909-14; attached to gen. secretariat of the Peace Conf., 1919; 1st sec., later counselor, of Embassy, Berlin, 1920-24; gen. sec. to the Protectorates Govt., Morocco, 1925-26; served in Fgn. Office, Paris, 1926-38; ambassador to Italy, 1936-38, to U.S. since Jan, 1938. Served as lt. and capt. French Army, 1914-18. Decorated Comdr. of Legion of Honor, Croix de Guerre (France); Brit. Mil. Cross. Hon. mem. Soc of the Cincinnati. Roman Catholic. Clubs: Jockey, Union (Paris). Address: Washington, D.C. *

SALANT, ROBERT STEPHEN, mfg. co. exec.; b. N.Y.C., Mar. 28, 1914; s. Gabriel and Bessie L. Salant; A.B., Brown U., 1935; m. Margaret E. Brownell, Sept. 29, 1936; (dec. 1941); children—Susan Brownell, Margaret Earle, Robert Stephen; m. 2d, Katharine Will, July 23, 1947; m. 3d, Marilyn Moffat, Sept. 12, 1970. With Salant Corp., N.Y.C., 1935-79, pres., 1946-65, then chmn. exec. com., chmn. bd., 1976-79, also dir. Served to lt. (s.g.) USNR, 1942-45. Clubs: Leash (hon.) (N.Y.C.); Piping Rock. Home: Locust Valley, N.Y. Died Jan. 28, 1979.

SALE, WILLIAM M., JR., educator; b. Louisville, Ky., Feb. 16, 1899; s. William M. and Jessie (Jennngs) B.; A.B., U. of Wis., 1922; A.M., Harvard, 1923; Ph.D., Yale, 1930; m. Helen Stearns, Jan. 28, 1929; children—William M., III, Roger, John Kirkpatrick. Instr., Yale, 1926-36; asst. prof. English, Cornell, 1936-39, asso. prof. 1939-47, prof., 1948-59, Goldwin Smith professor of English, from 1959, chmn. dept. lit., 1951-57, chmn. dept. English 1962-66; chief examiner of College Entrance Examination Bd., Princeton, N.J., 1946-50; chief reader in English, Coll. Entrance Examination Bd., 1944-60. Mem. Phi Beta Kappa, Phi Kappa Phi, Sigma Delta Chi. Democrat. Episcopalian. Author: Samuel Richardson, A bibliographical record, 1936; The Use of Language, 1946, Samuel Richardson, Master Printer, 1950. Editor: Henry James' Hawthorne, 1956; Prose Readings, 1958; Samuel Richardson's Pamela, 1958; Emily Bronte's Wuthering Heights, 1963. Home: Ithaca, N.Y. Died Jan. 6, 1981.

SALISBURY, LUCIUS A., b. Sandy Creek, N.Y., Jan. 1, 1882; s. Moreau J. and Helen M. (Warriner) S.; A.B., Brown U., 1904; M.D., Harvard, 1908; m. Margaret E. Duryee, Oct. 21, 1916 (dec.); children—Mason (dec.), Lucius, Helen M. (Mrs. Robert Ludwig), Hope F. (Mrs. Lyman F. Thompson), Joseph D.; m. 2d, Margaret V. N. Duryee, September 28, 1963. Intern Boston City Hosp., 1908-09; practice of med., N.Y.C., 1910-40; asso. prof. clin. surgery Post Grad. Med. Sch. and Hosp., 1919-35; attending and cons. surgeon Met. Hosp., 1912-36; asst. surgeon USPHS, Marine Hosp., N.Y.C., 1934-40; dir. hosp. services, Oak Ridge, 1946-49; former asst. med. dir. A.R.C., N.Y. regional blood program. Pvt., 1st Inf., R.I. N.G., 1902-03; pvt., 23d Inf., N.Y. N.G. 1910-11; 1st lt. Med. Corps, 1911, capt., 1914, maj., 1917, lt. col., 1919, col., 1921; served with Am. Ambulance Hosp., Juilly, France, 1915; Mex. Border Campaign, 1916, with AEF in France and Belgium, 1917-19; div. surgeon, 27th Div., 1921; organizer and comdr. 102d Med. Regt. (only completely organized med. regt. in U.S.), 1921-40; on active duty with N.G. 1940-46; brevet brig. gen., New York N.G., 1923—; med. insp. recruiting and induction, 2d Service Command, 1942-43; with exec. sect. Inspector Gen.'s Office, Washington, 1944-45. Decorated Silver Star, Legion of Merit, Purple Heart, Mex. Border, World War I, and Am. Defense medals (U.S.), chevalier Legion of Honor, chevalier Order of Service de Sante Publique, Commemorative medal (France), Croix de Guerre with palm (Belgium); Conspicuous Service Cross (N.Y.). Formerly trustee Northern Dispensary, also Lenox Sch., N.Y. Fellow A.C.S.; mem. Am. Assn. Mil. Surgeons (past pres.), A.M.A., Harvard Med. Soc. of N.Y. (past pres.), Med. Soc. County N.Y., N.Y. State Medical Society, American Legion (past commander of Caduceus Post Number 808). Author of numerous profl. articles on medico-military subjects. Introduced "vertical" control of evacuation of wounded, method received general recognition as greatly increasing efficiency. Address: N.Y.C. *

SALMAGGI, ALFREDO (SAL-MAD'JE), impresario; b. Aquila, Italy, Mar. 4, 1886; s. Felice and Micolina S.; ed. European conservatories; m. Elvira Canzano, 1910, children—Lina, Felix, Guido, Dora, Alfred, Henry, Mario and (twins) Robert and Edward. Presenting grand opera in U.S., Canada and S. America since 1915; presented popular-priced operatic productions at N.Y. Hippodrome, 1933-38; presenting operatic performances, Brooklyn (N.Y.) Acad. of Music since 1939; has introduced more than 500 new singers to the public; instr. of voice; editor Music and Musicians, 1914-22; editor, International Lyric Courier; author of numerous brochures on vocalization. Founder Brooklyn Opera Guild, 1948. Home: Brooklyn. *

SALMON, KURT, ret. mgmt. cons.; b. Cologne, Germany, Apr. 3, 1910; s. Morris and Mathilde (Isay) S.; student in econs., U. Cologne, 1927-28; grad. Textile Sch., Chemnitz, Saxony, 1930; D. Textiles (hon.), Phila. Coll. of Textiles and Sci.; m. Lula Maye Owen, Oct. 10, 1932; children—Eleanor Lynn (Mrs. R.L. Chartrand), Douglas Erwin, Larrine Gray (Mrs. Russell Abolt), Thomas Allen. Came to U.S., 1930, naturalized, 1936. Resident engr., plant mgr. May Hosiery Mills, Nashville, 1930-34; founder-owner Kurt Salmon Assos. (now Kurt Salmon Assos. Inc.), Nashville, from 1935, pres., chmn. bd., 1946-74, hon. chmn. bd., 1974-79. Mem. adv. com. textile and apparel research sec. commerce; spl. adv. Dept. Commerce and Office of Mgmt. and Budget. Recipient award for excellence Am. Conf. Mgmt. Cons., 1979. Registered profl. engr., D.C.; certified mgmt. cons. Asso. mem. Internat. Assn. Clothing Designers; mem. Assn. Cons. Mgmt. Engrs. (v.p. 1963-64, dir. 1963-66, pres. 1968-69); founding mem. Inst. Mgmt. Cons. (dir. from 1973). Republican. Contbr. numerous articles pub. in trade papers, mags. Home: Washington, D.C. Died Sept. 12, 1979.

SALOMON, IRVING, mfg. exec., orgn. exec.; b. Chgo., Aug. 23, 1897; s. Abraham Douglas and Ella (Polachek) S.; student Northwestern U., 1915-18; D.H.L. (hon.), Calif. Western U., 1959; LL.D., Georgetown U., 1972, Brandeis U., 1973; m. Cecile Liebowitz, Sept. 25, 1937; 1 dau., Abbe (Mrs. Wolfsheimer). With Royal Metal Mfg. Co., Chgo. from 1915, chmn. bd. from 1942; chmn. bd. Royal Metal Mfg. Co. Can., Ltd., Deluxe Metal Furniture Co., Warren, Pa.; pres. Gold Coast Prodns., Hollywood; dir. Coates Board & Carton Co., Stroudsburg, Pa., Diversified Investments, Inc., Union Bank; Under-sec. Spl. Fund of UN. Bd. dirs., mem. exec. com. UN Assn. of U.S.A.; chmn. bd. San Diego Ballet, Inc. bd. dirs. Scripps Clinic and Research Found., San Diego Balboa Park Bd., Children's Hosp., San Diego, Cons. War Dept., 1947, Munitions Bd., 1949, Fund for Adult Edn., 1952, Fund for Advancement Edn., 1952-53; cons., rep. Ford Found. UNESCO Conf.; Paris, 1951; chmn. U.S. delegation UNESCO Conf., Paris, 1953; U.S. del. ECOSOC, Geneva, 1953; U.S. del. 13th General Assembly of UN; mem. bd. U.S. Com. for UNICEF. Pres. Salomon Found.; trustee Atlanta Coll., Brandeis U., U. San Diego, Calif. Western U.; pres. San Antonio de Pala Cath. Mission; trustee Claremont Sch. Theology; pres. World Affairs Council San Diego; bd. dirs. San Diego Symphony Assn., Old Globe Theatre, YMCA, Child Guidance Clinic, trustee Georgetown U.; mem. World Fedn. UN Assn.; bd. mem. Inst. Internat. Edn., Am. Jewish Com., Inst. for Internat. Order, Trust for Support UN; mem. spl. adv. com. State Dept. Served with USMC, World War I; lt. col., AUS, World War II. Mem. San Diego UN Assn. (hon. pres.), Fgn. Policy Assn. (mem. bd.), San Diego County Hereford Assn. (past pres.). Republican. Author: Retire and Be Happy, 1951; Management Surveys in Colleges and Universities, 1955; Incidents and Coincidences, 1980. Contbr. articles to mags. and newspapers; TV commentator on fgn. affairs. Home: San Diego, Calif. Died Jan. 7, 1979; buried Home of Peace Cemetery, San Diego.

SALOUTOS, THEODORE, educator, historian; b. Milw., Aug. 3, 1910; s. Peter and Demetra (Perdikis) S.; BE., Milw. State Tchrs. Coll., 1933; student U. Wis. Law Sch., summers 1934-36; M. Philosophy, U. Wis., 1938, Ph.D., 1940; m. Florence Louise Schwefel, Sept. 21, 1940; children—Bonita Louise (Mrs. Martin Gilbert), Theodore A. Peter. Tchr., Waukesha (Wis.) Pub. Schs., 1933-36; research asst. history U. Wis., 1937-40, postdoctoral fellow history and agrl. econs., 1940-41, instr. history extension div., 1941-43; vis. lectr. Oberlin Coll., 1943-45; lectr. U. Calif. at Los Angeles, 1945-46, mem. faculty, 1946-78, prof. history, 1956-78, chmn. dept., 1962-65; vis. summer prof. U. Minn., 1947, U. Wis. at Milw., 1962; vis. prof. U. Hawaii, 1968 U. Miss., 1980. Fulbright research scholar U. Athens, 1952-53, 66-67; Fulbright lectr. U. Freiburg (W. Germany), 1959-60; Guggenheim fellow, 1966-67; cons., panelist Nat. Endowment Arts and Humanities, 1968-75; mem. nat. adv. bd. Immigration History Research Center, U. Minn., 1973-80; cons. Holloman (N.Mex.) AFB, 1958-59. Pres., Mar Vista (Calif.) Democratic Club, 1961-62, Save Cyprus Council So. Calif., 1974-77; mem. Friends of Huntington Library, 1964-80. Recipient Disting. Alumnus award U. Wis.-Milw., 1977. Mem. Am. (exec. com. Pacific Coast br. 1962-65, pres. 1980), Miss. Valley hist. assns., Agrl. History Soc. (pres. 1965-66), Immigration History Soc. (pres. 1973-76), Bus. History Soc., Econ History Assn., English Econ. History Soc., Pan Arcadian Fedn., Canadian Ethnic Studies Assn., U. Wis. Alumni Assn. (life), U. Wis-Milw. Alumni Assn. (life), U Calf. Alumni Assn. (life), Order Ahepa (chmn. edn. com. 1964-65). Club: Hellenic Univ. So. Calif. (pres. 1961-63, 69-71). Author: (with John D. Hicks) Agricultural Discontent in the Middle West, 1900-1939, 1951; They Remember America, 1956; Farmer Movements in the South, 1865-1933, 1960; The Greeks in the United States, 1964; Twentiety Century Populism, 1964; Farmer Movements in the South, 1964; The Greeks in America, 1967; Populism: Reaction or Reform, 1968; The American Farmer and the New Deal, 1981. Contbr. to encys. including American Ethnic Groups, Harvard U. Mem. editorial bd. Agrl. History, 1957-80, Jour. Am. History, Hellenic Jour. Home: Los Angeles, Calif. Died Nov. 15, 1980.

SALSINGER, HARRY GEORGE (SÄL'SING-ER), sports writer; b. Springfield, O., Apr. 10, 1885; s. Frederick John and Anna Babara (Butzer) S.; m. Elizabeth Gladys Johnson, Nov. 26, 1913; 1 son, Harry George. Sports editor and sports columnist, Detroit (Mich.) News, since 1908. Home: Detroit. *

SALTONSTALL, LEVERETT, former U.S. senator; b. Chestnut Hill, Mass., Sept. 1, 1892; s. Richard Middlecott and Eleanor (Brooks) S.; grad. Noble and Greenough Sch., Boston, 1910; A.B., Harvard, 1914, LL.B., 1917; LL.D., Northeastern U., 1935, Bates Coll., 1939, Boston U., 1940, Bowdoin Coll., 1940, Amherst Coll., 1941, Williams Coll., 1941, Holy Cross Coll., 1942, Harvard, 1942, Colby Coll., 1942, Tufts Coll., 1942, De Pauw U., 1943, Clark U., 1944, Toledo U., 1945, Franklin and Marshall Coll., 1947, Trinity Coll., 1947, Coll. William and Mary, 1948, Northwestern, 1949, Worcester Polytech. Inst., 1950, Kenyon Coll., 1953, Norwich U., 1955, Brandeis U., 1958; M.S., New Bedford (Mass.) Inst. Textile and Technology, 1955, U. Mass., 1963; J.D., Portia Law Sch., Boston, 1957; Dr. Pub. Adminstrn., Suffolk U., 1957; Dr. Bus. Adminstrn., Babson Inst., 1961; LL.D., Merrimack Coll., 1967; D.S. Oratory, Curry Coll., 1969; Sc.D., Lowell Technol. Inst., 1968; m. Alice Wesselhoeft, June 27, 1916; children—Leverett (dec.), Rosalie (dec.), Emily, Peter (dec.), William, Susan. Admitted to Mass. bar, 1919, began practice in Boston as atty. and trustee; mem. firm Gaston, Snow, Saltonstall & Hunt, 1926-28. Asst. district atty., Middlesex County, Mass., 1921-22; mem. Bd. of Aldermen, Newton, 1920-22, Mass. Ho. of Reps. 1923-36, speaker, 1929-36; gov. of Mass., 1939-44; elected to U.S. Senate, Nov. 1944, to fill unexpired term of Sen. Henry Cabot Lodge (resigned); re-elected 1948, 54, 60, ret., 1967. Former dir. Ivest Fund, Inc., Nat. Shawmut Bank Boston. Bd. dirs. Peabody Mus., Salem; bd. overseers Harvard U. Served as 1st lt., F.A., 1917-18, World War I. Mem. Am. Legion. Republican. Unitarian. Mason, Elk. Clubs: Harvard, Boston, Somerset, Tavern (Boston); Alfalfa (Washington). Govt. papers donated to Mass. Hist. Soc., Boston. Home: Dover, Mass. Died June 17, 1979.

SALTZSTEIN, BENJAMIN F(RANKLIN), lawyer, civic worker; b. Plock, Poland, Nov. 4, 1884; s. Isidore Jacob and Sarah (Goldberg) S.; LL.b., U. Mich., 1906; m. Edna Docter, June 11, 1911; children—Robert A., James I., Jean (Mrs. David A. Herman). Came to U.S., 1888, naturalized by Act of Congress. Admitted to Wis. bar, 1906; pvt. practice law, Milw., 1906—; member of firm Salzstein, Levine & Wolff. Dir. Jewish Welfare Fund, 1938—, pres., 1949-52; mem. exec. bd. Am. Jewish Com., 1949—; dir. Jewish Community Center, 1940—; mem. Jewish Tercentennary Com., 1955—; mem. nat. spl. gift com. Nat. Conf. Christians and Jews, 1952-53; pres. Federated Jewish Charities, 1929-30; dir. Milw. County Community Fund, 1933-36; regional chmn. United Jewish Appeal, 1951; mem. United Hosps. Fund Milw. County, 1952. Mem. planning com. Deaconess Hosp., 1946—; pres. Home for Aged Jews, 1939-52. chmn. bd., 1952—; trustee Union American Hebrew Congregations, 1960—, dir. Union Inst., vice chmn. bd., 1953—; dir. Am. Financial and Development Corp. for Israel, 1951-53. Mem. Am. Judicature Soc., Am., Wis., Milw. bar assns., Fgn. Policy Assn. (council mem. 1947). Brandeis U. Assn. Jewish. Mason, Elk. Club: Milwaukee Athletic. Home: Milw. *

SAMPLE, GLENN W., coll. exec.; b. Centerville, Ind., July 9, 1912; s. Alfred W. and Thersia Mae (Williamson) S.; B.S. in Agr., Purdue U., 1935, D.Agr. (hon.), 1972; m. Mary Catherine Templin, Oct. 11, 1936; children—Louise M., James A., Joseph T., Elizabeth June. Agrl. editor Purdue U., 1935-44; dir. public relations U. Md., 1944-45; v.p. Ind. Farm Bur., Indpls., 1945-75; pres. Ind. Vocat. Tech. Coll., 1975-80; dir. Farmers State Bank; bd. dirs. Channel 20 TV; chmn. bd. Ivy Tech Found. Mem. various Ind. commns. on taxing policy, ednl. structure and policies, 1948-75; active Ind. 4-H Found.; former mem. Ind. Air Pollution Control Bd. Recipient Distinction award Purdue Agrl. Alumni, 1948, Brigham award Am. Agrl. Editors Assn., 1973, Hon. Master Farmer award Prairie Farmer, 1978. Mem. Ind. Farm Bur., Ind. State C. of C., Zionsville C. of C., Ind. Vocat. Edn. Assn., Sigma Delta Chi, Alpha Zeta. Mem. Christian Ch. (Disciples of Christ). Clubs: Columbia, Indpls. Press., Shriners (Indpls.); Univ., Scottish Rite, Masons. Editor Hoosier Farmer Mag., 1945-58. Home: Zionsville, Ind. Died Jan. 5, 1980; buried Westside Cemetery, Milton, Ind.

SAMPSON, CHARLES HENRY (SAM'SUN), educator; b. Gorham, Me., June 7, 1883; s. Albert Henry and Lucy Jane (Marston) S.; B.S. in Engring., Univ. of Me., 1904; Ed.M., Harvard, 1925; m. Annie Laurie Wells, Sept. 8, 1908 (died Aug. 27, 1924); 1 dau., Ruth Eleanor; m. 2d, Helen Louise Cox, Mar. 24, 1934; 1 dau., Martha. Successively with Gen. Electric Co., Lynn, Blake Steam Pump Co., Cambridge, Great Northern Paper Co., Millinocket, Me., B. F. Sturtevant Co., Hyde Park, Mass., 1905-07; instr., U. of Me., 1907-08; teacher, high sch., Bangor, Me., 1908-12; teacher and head of math. dept., Huntington Sch. for Boys, 1912-24, headmaster, 1924-43; prof. engring, drawing and descriptive geometry, Bates Coll., since July 1, 1943, also adminstrv. asst.; dir. Huntington Summer Sch., 1913-43; prin. Northeastern Prep. School, 1923-25; actively engaged in work connected with cadet training under auspices Massachusetts Department Education; lecturer on Abraham Lincoln. Mem. N.E.A., Harvard Teachers Assn., Cum Laude Society; mem. Round Table, Bates Coll. Club: Friday Evening. Author or co-author books relating to field since 1913; also courses in related subjects for Univ. Extension Div., Mass. Dept. Edn. Home: Auburn, Me. *

SAMPSON, EDITH SPURLOCK, circuit ct. judge; b. Pitts., Oct. 13, 1901; d. Louis and Elizabeth (McGruder) Spurlock; student N.Y. Ch. Social Work, U. Chgo. Sch. Social Service Adminstrn.; LL.B., John Marshall Law Sch., Chgo., 1925, LL.D. (hon.), 1952; LL.M., Loyola U., Chgo., 1927; L.H.D. (hon.), MacMurray Coll., Jacksonville, Ill.; LL.D., North Central Coll., Naperville, Ill., Eureka (Ill.) Coll., 1968; widow. Admitted to Ill. bar, 1927; referee Juvenile Ct. Cook Country, 1930-40; asst. corp. counsel City Chgo., 1955-62; asso. judge Municipal Ct. Chgo., 1962-64, asso. judge Circuit Ct. of Cook County, 1964-78. Mem. U.S. delegation to UN, 1950, 52, mem. U.S. Citizens Commn. for NATO, 1961-62. Trustee Roosevelt U., Chgo. Mem. Am., Chgo., Cook County bar assns., Womens Bar Assn. Ill., Nat. Assn. Women Lawyers (life), N.A.A.C.P. (life), Am. Assn. UN (dir.). Home: Chicago, Ill. Died Oct. 8, 1979.

SAMPSON, HOMER CLEVELAND, prof. of botany; b. Wheeler, Ill., Jan. 21, 1885; s. Mark and Laura Ann (Welker) S.; grad. Eastern Ill. State Normal Sch., 1912; B.S., U. of Chicago, 1914, Ph.D., 1917; m. Mae Patton, Dec. 22, 1912; 1 son, Edgar Nelson, Teacher in grade school, at Dietrich, Ill., 1905-08; asst. biol. sciences, Eastern Ill. State Normal Sch., 1909-12; asst. natural sciences, Sch. of Edn., U. of Chicago, 1912-17: with Ohio State U. since 1917, as instr. in botany, 1917-19, asst. prof., 1919-22, prof. since 1922; research asst. in botany, Desert Lab. Carnegie Instn., summer 1914; investigator, Ill. State Natural History Survey, summers 1915, 16; field agent Bureau of Plant Industry, U.S. Dept. of Agr., summers, 1918, 25; member research staff Ohio Agrl. Expt. Station, summers of 1926, 27, 28; collaborator U.S. Central States Forest Expt. Sta. since 1928. Mem. A.A.A.S. (com. on improvement in science edn.), Bot. Soc. America (com. on teaching of botany in colls. and univs.), Ecol. Soc. America, Am. Soc. Plant Physiologists, Ohio Acad. Science, Phi Beta Kappa, Sigma Xi. Author: Directions for Laboratory and Field Work in General Botany (with E. N. Transeau), 1919; Textbook of Botany (with E. N. Transeau and L. H. Tiffany), 1939; Workbook for General Botany, 1941. Contbr. to bot. and ednl. jours. Home: Columbus, Ohio. *

SAMUEL, DONALD CAROL, investment co. exec.; b. N.Y.C., May 26, 1919; s. Ralph E. and Florence (Weingarten) S.; grad. Fieldston Sch., 1937; student Dartmouth; m. Berelle Katz, Sept. 28, 1947; children—Wendy B., Patricia A., Pamela J. Dist. mgr. Robert Hall Clothes, 1946-47; with Ralph E. Samuel & Co., N.Y.C., 1948-70, partner, 1949-70; exec. partner Neuberger & Berman, N.Y.C., 1970-80; asst. treas. Energy Fund, Inc., N.Y.C., 1955-60, pres., 1960-80, also dir. exec. v.p. No Load Mutual Fund Assn., N.Y.C., 1971-75, pres., 1975-78; pres. Neuberger & Berman Mgmt., 1970-80; vice chmn. Neuberger & Berman Pension Mgmt., 1976-80, dir. Partners Fund. Trustee, Jewish Bd. Family and Children's Services, Sarah Lawrence Coll., Bronxville, 1967-75; bd. govs. Investment Co. Inst., 1978-80; mem. adv. council Columbia U. Sch. Social Work. Served to maj. USAAF, 1941-45. Clubs: Harmonie (N.Y.C.); Century Country (Purchase, N.Y.). Home: New York, N.Y. Died Feb. 20, 1980.

SAMUELS, J. CLIFTON, educator; b. Bishopville, S.C., June 26, 1924; s. Isaac W. and Sallie (Henry) S.; B.S. in Elec. Engring., Bklyn. Poly. Inst., 1948; M.S., N.Y. U., 1950; Ph.D., Purdue U., 1951; children—Russell E., Frederick N. Aero. research scientist NACA, Cleve., 1948-49, 50-52; research engr. Farnsworth Electronics Co., 1952-54; prof. engring. sci. Purdue U., 1957-65; prof. elec. engring., head dept. Howard U., Washington, 1966-77; cons. to govt. and industry, 1958-77. Served with AUS, 1942-45; ETO. Mem. I.E.E.E., Acoustical Soc. Am., Soc. Engring. Sci., Am. Soc. Engring. Edn., Sigma Xi, Tau Beta Pi, Eta Kappa Nu. Contbr. articles to profl. jours. Patentee in field. Home: Washington, D.C. Died Sept. 28, 1977.

SANBORN, BRUCE WALTER, lawyer; b. St. Paul, July 11, 1882; s. Walter Henry and Emily (Bruce) S.; A.B., Dartmouth, 1904; student St. Paul Coll. Law, 1904-06, Harvard Law Sch., 1906-07; m. Conradine Schurmeier, Sept. 24, 1913 (dec. Feb. 1927); children—Conradine (Mrs. Edward Burch), Hildegarde Eunice (Mrs. Francis D. Butler), Bruce W., Jr., Theodore S.; m. 2d, Maud Moon Weyerhaeuser, May 20, 1943; stepchildren—Carl A. Weyerhaeuser, Sarah Maud (Mrs. Robert J. Sivertsen). Admitted to Minn. bar, 1906, since practiced in St. Paul; mem. firm Durment, Moore & Sanborn, 1910-13, Sanborn, Graves & Appel, 1917-20, Sanborn, Graves & Ordway, 1920-27, 1920-27, Sanborn, Graves & Andre, 1927-36, Sanborn, Graves, Appel, Andre & Morton, 1936-39, Sanborn and Andre, 1939-48, Sanborn Jackson & Biorn, 1948-54; mem. firm Sanborn Rice & Grayson, 1943-73, Sanborn & Grayson, 1973—. Hon. chmn. bd. N. Central Life Ins. Co., St. Paul. Apptd. legal mem. adv. council U.S. Vets. Bur., 1926. Mem. city council, St. Paul, 1910-11; pres. Lincoln Republican Club, St. Paul, 1926. Fellow, life mem. Am. Bar Found.; mem. Nat. Conf. Commrs. on Uniform State Laws (life; treas. 1927-37), Am. Bar Assn. (exec. com. 1928-31), Minn., Ramsey County bar assns., Am. Judicature Soc., S.A.R. (pres. Minn. chpt. 1944), Comml. Law League Am. (life). Psi Upsilon. Presbyterian. Kiwanian (pres. 1927). Clubs: Minnesota, Somerset Country, Athletic (St. Paul); University (Chgo.). Home: St Paul MN. *

SANDER, THEODORE, JR., business exec.; b. St. Paul, May 18, 1897; s. Theodore and Ida (Pause) S.; B.S.E., U. Minn., 1919; M.B.A., Harvard, 1925; m. Evelyn Wallgren, Sept. 18, 1924 (dec. Sept. 1964); 1 son, Theodore; m. 2d, Florence Scudder, May 18, 1968. Indsl. commr. St. Paul Assn. of Commerce, 1919-24; with Goldman Sachs & Co., N.Y.C., 1924-28; asst. gen. sales mgr. Royal Baking Powder Co., N.Y.C., 1928-30; with Am. Maize Products Co., N.Y.C., 1935, pres., 1942-63, chmn., 1963-64; v.p., dir. Great Island Holding Corp.; pres., dir. Huttig Mfg. Co., Muscatine, Iowa. Trustee, v.p. Corn Industries Research Found.; bd. dirs. White Plains YMCA, 1966-72, Westchester div. Am. Cancer Soc.; hon. gov. White Plains Hosp., 1966-79; mem. Westchester Republican County Com., Scarsdale Rep. Town Com. Former mayor of Scarsdale. Recipient Scarsdale Bowl, 1960. Clubs: Scarsdale Golf, Town (past pres.) (Scarsdale, N.Y.). Home: Scarsdale, N.Y. Died Apr. 23, 1979; interred Kensico Cemetery, Valhalla, N.Y.

SANDERS, HARLAND, food franchising co. exec.; b. nr. Henryville, Ind., Sept. 9, 1890; ed. grammar sch.; m. Claudia Ledington, Nov. 17, 1948; 3 children from previous marriage. Operator gas sta., then restaurant Sanders' Cafe, Corbin, Ky., 1929-56; began franchise operations Ky. Fried Chicken, 1956, owner, 1956-64, then ambassador good will. Active various charities. Named Ky. col., 1936. Recipient Horatio Alger award, 1965. Home: Louisville, Ky. Died Dec. 16, 1980; buried Cave Hill Cemetery, Louisville.

SANDERS, WALTER BENJAMIN, educator; b. Ann Arbor, Mich., July 30, 1906; s. Chauncey K. and May B. (Paine) S.; B.S. in Architecture, U. Ill., 1929; M. Architecture, U. Pa., 1930; m. Carroll Thompson, Aug. 25, 1935. Instr. architecture Columbia, 1930-36; asso. editor Am. Architect mag., 1937-38. Archtl. Forum mag., 1938-39; vis. lectr. Pratt Inst., 1939-40, Columbia, 1946-49, U. Mich., 1947-49; prof. architecture U. Mich., from 1949, chmn. dept., 1954-64, dir. doctoral program, 1966-72; partner Sanders & Breck. Architects, N.Y.C., 1938-42, Sanders & Malsin, N.Y.C., 1946-50; prin. Walter Sanders, Architects. Ann Arbor, from 1950; design cons. Albert Kahn Asso. Architects & Engrs., Detroit, from 1955. Cons. community facilities div. FHA, 1952. Served form lt. to lt. col., USAAF, 1942-46. Decorated Bronze Star medal, Legion of Merit; recipient hon. mention Smithsonian Gallery of Art, 1940, spl. commendation N.Y. chpt. A.I.A. House awards, 1940, 2d and 3d prizes Bloomingdale's House Competition, N.Y.C., 1946, gold medal Mich. Soc. Architects, 1964; Distinguished Faculty award U. Mich., 1969. Fellow A.I.A. (dir. from 1968); mem. Assn. Collegiate Schs. Architecture (dir. 1963-65, pres. 1965-67), Mich. Soc. Architects (dir. from 1968), Congresses Internationeaux d'Architecture Moderne, Bldg. Research Inst. (dir. 1959-67), Mich. Acad. Sci., Arts and Letters, Sigma Nu, Phi Kappa Phi, Alpha Rho Chi, Tau Sigma Delta, Scarab. Contbr. articles profl. jours. Home: Ann Arbor, Mich. Deceased.

SANDERS, WILLIAM, diplomat; b. Durango, Mexico, Apr. 14, 1903; s. John and Quirina (Olazabal) S.; A.B., Stanford U., 1928; A.M., George Washington U., 1936; LL.B., Columbus U., 1935; student Oxford U., Eng., 1928-29; m. Elizabeth Negley (Scully), Sept. 3, 1935; children—Quirina Harryette, William Barlow, Jonathan Scully. Mgr., agency bur., met. div. postal telegraph ITT, N.Y.C., 1929-32; admitted to D.C. bar, 1935; practiced with law firm, 1935-36; chief juridical div. Pan-Am. Union, 1936-41; prin. atty., coordinator of Inter-Am. Affairs, 1942; alternate mem. Emergency Adv. Com. for Polit. Def., Montevideo, 1942-43, mem., 1944-45; asso. chief div. internat. orgn. affairs Office of Spl. Polit. Affairs, U.S. Dept. State, 1945-48; alt. U.S. rep. Council of OAS, 1948; spl. asst. Office of UN Affairs, 1948, acting dir., 1948; dir. seminar in internat. law and orgn. Georgetown U., 1948-53; spl. asst. Bur. of UN Affairs and acting dep. asst. sec. of state, 1950-52, apptd. fgn. service officer, class 1, 1952; staff dir. Bur. UN Affairs, 1953; counselor and dep. chief mission, Santiago, Chile, 1953-56; U.S. rep. UN Com. Definition Aggression, 1956; coordinator for U.S. preparations Conf. Law of Sea, Geneva, Mar. 1958; asst. sec.-gen. OAS, 1958-68. U.S. rep. Inter-Am. Council Jurists, 1948-58. Chmn. U.S. delegation Inter-Am. Council Jurists, Brazil, 1950, Argentina, 1953, Mexico, 1956; vice chmn. U.S. delegation Conf. Plenipotentiaries on Law of the Sea, Geneva, 1958; sec. gen. 9th Meeting of Consultation of Ministers of Fgn. Affairs, 1964, 1st Spl. Inter-Am. Conf., 1964; U.S. del. to confs. and meetings OAS, UN, NATO. Pres. Pan Am. Devel. Found., 1963-72. Mem. Am. Bar Assn., Am. Soc. Internat. Law, Internat. Law Assn., Am. Polit. Sci. Assn., Phi Kappa Sigma. Clubs: Cosmos, Dacor (Washigton); Belle Haven Country (Va.). Author: Improvement and Coordination of Inter-Am. Peace Instruments, 1940, Sovereignty and Interdependence in New World, 1948. Contbr. to legal and profl. jours. and govt. publs. Home: Alexandria, Va. Died Dec. 5, 1976; buried St. John's Ch. Cemetery, Georgetown, Washington.

SANDIFER, DURWARD VALDAMIR, internat. lawyer; b. Tamalco, Ill., July 26, 1900; s. Albert Baylor and Susie Olive (Coker) S.; A.B., Eureka (Ill.) Coll. 1924, LL.D., 1947; A.M., Columbia, 1928, LL.B., 1931, Ph.D., 1939; student Sch. Internat. Studies, Geneva, Switzerland, summer 1929; m. Irene Reiterman, June 23, 1925 (dec. Apr. 8, 1977); 1 dau., Muriel Reiterman; m. 2d, Virginia Tannar, June 15, 1978. Instr. rhetoric and argumentation, debate coach, Eureka Coll., 1924-27; with Guatemalan-Honduran Boundary Arbitration, 1931-32; instr. internat. law relations Rutgers U., 1931-34; asst. to legal adviser Dept. of State, Washington, 1934-42; admitted to D.C. bar and U.S. Ct. Appeals for D.C., 1941; chmn. interdeptl. visa rev. com., 1942; asst. chief of div. working on internat. orgn., 1942-44; asso. chief div. internat. security and orgn., 1944; chief div. internat. orgn. affairs, 1945-47; tech. expert U.S. delegation Dumbarton Oaks Conf. on Internat. Orgn., 1944; sec. gen. and chief tech. expert U.S. delegation to UN conf., San Francisco, 1945; adviser to U.S. delegation UN Assembly, London, 1946, 1st and 2d sessions of UNECOSOC, London and N.Y.C., 1946; U.S. del. to World Health Conf., N.Y.C., 1946; prin. adviser U.S. delegation to UN Assembly, N.Y.C., 1946; acting legislative counsel, 1947; dep. dir., Office UN Affairs, 1947-48; prin. exec. officer and adviser U.S. delegation to UN Assembly, N.Y.C., 1947; alternate del. U.S. delegation to 1st World Health Assembly, WHO, Geneva, 1948; adviser U.S. delegation to UN Assembly, Paris, 1948; acting dir. Office UN Affairs, 1949; dep. asst. sec. of state for UN affairs 1949-54; alternate del. Conf. FAO UN, Washington, 1949, 50; sr. advisor U.S. delegation 6th session UN Gen. Assembly, Paris, 1951-52; apptd. counselor polit. affairs, Buenos Aires, 1954-57; with ICA, Dept. State, Washington, 1957-59; State Dept. and fgn. affairs adviser to Indsl. Coll. Armed Forces U.S., 1959-60; prof. Sch. Internat. Service, Am. U., Washington, 1960-70, emeritus, 1970-81; mem. Inter-Am. Commn. on Human Rights, 1960-72. Mem. Am. Soc. Internat. Law, Polit. Sci. Assn., Fed. bar assns. Mem. Disciples of Christ. Author: Evidence Before International Tribunals, 1939, rev. edit., 1975; (with L. Ronald Scheman) Foundations of Freedom, 1966. Contbr. articles to legal jours. and govt. bulls. Home: Silver Spring, Md. Died May 31, 1981; buried Rock Creek Cemetery, Washington.

SANDISON, HELEN ESTABROOK, prof. English; b. Terre Haute, Ind., Sept. 16, 1884; d. Howard and Frances (Estabrook) Sandison; A.B., Bryn Mawr Coll., 1906, A.M., 1907, Ph.D., 1911, special Bryn Mawr European fellow, Oxford, Eng., 1909-10. Asst. prin. and teacher English and Latin, Brookville (Ind.) High Sch., 1907-08; reader in English, Bryn Mawr Coll., 1911-13; instr. English, Vassar Coll., Poughkeepsie, N.Y., 1913-19, asst. prof., 1919-24, asso. prof., 1924-29, prof. 1929-50; chmn. com. on admissions, 1923-30, chmn. dept. of English, 1931-33, 1938-41 and 1943-46. Mem. Modern Language Assn. of Am. (mem. exec. council 1931-36), Shakespeare Assn. of America, Am. Assn. Univ. Profs., Am. Fd. Teachers, Soc. for Nautical Research (Great Britain). Author: Chanson d'Aventure in Middle English, 1913; Manual of Good English (with H.M. MacCracken), 1917. Contbr. articles to learned jours. since 1910. Address: Poughkeepsie, N.Y. *

SANDITEN, JULIUS, tire and supply co. exec.; b. Russia, 1903. Vice pres., chief exec. officer, dir. Okla. Tire & Supply Co., Tulsa; vice chmn., chief exec. officer Economy Auto Stores; pres., dir. JAM, Inc.; exec. v.p., mem. exec. com., dir. McCrory Corp., chmn., chief exec. officer Otasco div.; dir. Farmers & Mchts. Bank & Trust Co. Bd. dirs., mem. exec. com. Tulsa Jewish Community Council, Congregation B'nai Emunah; bd. dirs. United Jewish Appeal, United Israel Appeal, Tulsa Philharm. Soc., Tulsa C. of C., Okla. C. of C.; bd. dirs., v.p. Ark. Basin Devel. Assn.; trustee, bd. dirs. Children's Med. Center; mem. dean's adv. council Coll. Bus. Adminstrn., U. Tulsa; pres. JAM, Inc.; trustee OTASCO Employees Retirement Trust; sec. OTASCO Found. Home: Tulsa, Okla. Died Feb. 17, 1977.

SANDLIN, MARLIN ELIJAH, investment co. exec.; b. Colmesneil, Tex., July 22, 1909; s. John Mancel and Matilda F. (Mann) S.; A.B., U. Tex., 1930; m. Mary Elizabeth Brown, Dec. 17, 1931; children—Carole Elizabeth Burnett, Suzanne Sparger Sefanides, Marlin Elijah. Admitted to the Texas bar, 1930; practiced in Woodville, Tex., 1931-36; asst. sec. of state Tex., 1936-39; legal adviser to commr. Gen. Land Office, 1939; mem. firm Fountain & Sandlin, Houston, 1939-41, Fountain, Cox & Sandlin, 1941-43; sec., dir. Woodley Petroleum Co., Houston, 1944-47, v.p., 1946-58, exec. v.p., 1958-60, also dir.; pres., dir. Woodley Canadian Oil Co., 1952-60, Minn. Pipe Line Co., 1953-67, Sharpstown Tower Corp., 1962-74; vice chmn. bd., dir. Great No. Oil Purchasing Co., 1954-55; v.p., gen. counsel, dir. Great No. Oil Co., 1955-64, chmn. bd., 1960-64, dir., chmn. exec. com., 1964-65, dir. 1966-69; v.p., dir. Seven J. Stock Farm, Inc., 1948-60; chmn. Caribbean Sulphur Shipping Co., Ltd., Nassau, Bahamas, 1963-67. Pan. Am. Sulphur Sales Co., 1963-67, Pan Am. Sulphur Co., Ltd., London, 1960-72; vice chmn. bd. Fertilizantes Fosfatados Mexicanos, S.A. de C.V., Mexico, 1965-72, Compania San Noe, S.A. de C.V. Mexico, 1965-72; vice chmn., chief exec. officer Azufrera Panamericana S.A., 1967-72; v.p., dir. South Saskatchewan Pipe Line Co., 1954-67; dir. Bank of S.W. Nat. Assn., N.W. Houston Water Supply Corp., Pasco, Inc., Am. Gen. Mgmt. Co. Mem. adv. council, past chmn. Arts and Scis. Found., U. Tex., Austin; exec. com. Winston Churchill Meml. Fund; adv. bd., dir. found. St. Joseph's Hosp., Houston, Mem. Fellows Tex. Bar Found., Texas, Houston bar assns., Am. Petroleum Inst., Anglo-Texan Soc. (chmn. Houston), Houston Council World Affairs (dir.), Tex. Mid-Continent Oil And Gas Assn., English-Speaking Union U.S. (past dir. nat. bd.; dir., past pres. Houston), Philos. Soc. Tex. Methodist (steward). Mason (past master); mem. Order Eastern Star (past patron). Clubs: Coronado, River Oaks Country, Petroleum (past pres.) (Houston). Home: Houston, Tex. Died May 28, 1974.

SANDMEL, SAMUEL, educator, author; b. Dayton, Ohio, Sept. 23, 1911; s. Morris and Rebecca (Lenderman) S.; A.B., U. Mo., 1932; B.H.L., Hebrew Union Coll., 1934; student Duke, 1940-41; Ph.D., Yale, 1949; m. Frances Langsdorf Fox, June 23, 1940; children—Charles, Benjamin, David. Ordained rabbi, 1937; rabbi, Atlanta, 1937-39, Hillel Found., N.C., 1939-42, Hillel Found., Yale, 1946-49; prof. Jewish lit. and thought Vanderbilt U., 1949-52; prof. Bible and Hellenistic lit. Hebrew Union Coll.-Jewish Inst. Religion, 1952-66, Distinguished Service prof. Bible and Hellenistic lit., 1966-78, provost, 1957-66, dir. grad. studies, 1974-78; Helen A. Regenstein prof. religion Div. Sch., U. Chgo., 1978—; chmn., exec. com. Frank Weil Inst. Religion and Humanities; hon. vis. prin. Leo Baeck Coll., London, 1968-69; spl. field Hellenistic Jewish lit. and N.T. Served as chaplain USNR, 1942-45. Mem. Soc. Bibl. Lit. (pres. 1961), Central Conf. Am. Rabbis, Phi Beta Kappa. Club: Literary (Cin.). Author: A Jewish Understanding of the New Testament, 1956; Philo's Place in Judaism, 1956; The Genius of Paul, 1958; The Hebrew Scriptures, 1963; We Jews and Jesus, 1965; Herod: Profile of a Tyrant, 1967; We Jews and you Christians, 1967; The First Christian Century in Judaism and Christianity, 1969; The Several Israels, 1971; Two Living Traditions, 1972; The Enjoyment of Scripture, 1972; Alone Atop the Mountain, 1973; A Little Book on Religion, 1975; When a Jew and Christian Marry, 1977. Editor: Old Testament Issues, 1968; Hebrew Union Coll. Ann., 1970-72; Oxford Study edit. New English Bible, 1976; Judaism and Christian Beginnings, 1978; Anti-Semitism in the New Testament?, 1979; Philo of Alexandria, 1979. Home: Cincinnati, Ohio. Died Nov. 4, 1979; buried Cincinnati, Ohio.

SANDONA, MATTEO (SAN-DO-NA'), portrait painter; b. Seino, Italy, Apr. 15, 1883; s. Francesco and Teresa (Zanon) S.; student Fine Arts Acad., Verona, Italy, 1896-99; m. Gertrude A. Macfarlane, Dec. 2, 1913. Came to U.S., 1894, naturalized through father's papers. Represented in collections of large museums and galleries of U.S., also in pvt. collections. Recipient numerous medals and awards. Mem. Calif. Commn. of Fine Arts, Golden Gate Internat, Expn., 1939, 40; mem. Jury of Awards, Calif. State Fair, 1933-37. Mem. Bay Region Art Assn. of Oakland, Am. Physicians Art Assn. of San Francisco, Carmel Art Assn. Club: Bohemian (San Francisco). Mem. internat, jury of awards, Panama-Pacific Internat. Expn., 1915. Home: San Francisco. *

SANFORD, CHARLES WILSON, educator; b. Allentown, Pa., Aug. 26, 1902; s. Chester Milton and Ella (Stillson) S.; B.S., U. Ill., 1929, M.S 1930, Ph.D., 1933; m. Mary Marguerite Sharp, June 30, 1923; children—Mary Marguerite (Mrs. James Wayne Davidson), Charles Wilson. Tchr., Ogden (Ill.) Community High Sch., 1923-25, Latrobe (Pa.) High Sch., 1925-28; asst. edn. U. Ill., Champaign, 1929-32, asst. philosophy, 1930-31, prin. Univ. High Sch., 1932-43, instr. edn., 1932-33, asso. edn., 1933-35, asst. prof., 1935-41, asso. prof., 1949, prof., 1949-67, coordinator tchr. edn., 1943-46, asso. dean Coll. Edn., 1949-56, dean admissions, records, 1956-65, univ. dean admissions and records, prof. high edn., 1965-80; dean, prof. emeritus, 1967-80; chief cons. Study of Comprehensive High Sch. in Mass., 1969-70; lectr. edn. U. Mich., summers, 1939, 46. Dir. Ill. Curriculum Program, 1947-54; mem. Gen. Motors Nat. Scholarship Com., 1957-59, chmn. steering com., 1959; mem. Nat. Adv. Com. Coop. Plan for Guidance and Admissions Ednl. Testing Service, 1963-80; pres. annuitants assn. Ill. State Univs. Retirement System, 1973-80. Mem. Nat. (past com. chmn.), Ill. (past com. chmn.) assns. secondary sch. prins., Am. Assn. Collegiate Registrars and Admissions Officers, Kappa Delta Pi, Phi Delta Kappa. Presbyn. Author: (with others) Guide to the Study of the Curriculum in the Secondary Schools of Illinois, 1948, The Story in Nineteen Schools, 1950. Editor: Illinois Curriculum Program Series, 1947-54; (with H. C. Hand and W. B. Spalding) The Schools and National Security, 1951; (with others) College Admissions Policies for the 1970s, 1968. Contbr. to Ency. Ednl. Research rev. edit., 1950, Dictionary of Edn., 2d edit., 1959. Contbr. to ednl. jours. Home: Sun City West, Ariz. Died June 20, 1980.

SANFORD, JOHN BERKSHIRE, JR., investment banker; b. New Orleans, Sept. 25, 1906; s. John Berkshire and Caroline (O'Shaughnessy) S.; B.B.A., Tulane U., 1928; m. Ethel LeGardeur, Dec. 2, 1929; children—Betty (Mrs. Charles B. Molster, Jr.), John Berkshire III, Jane (Mrs. William T. Blessey). With bond dept. Whitney Nat. Bank, New Orleans, from 1938. Treas., dir. Louise S. McGehee Sch., New Orleans. Served to lt. (s.g.) USNR, 1942-45. Mem. Investment Bankers Assn. Am. (bd. govs.), Kappa Alpha. Clubs: Boston, Internat. House (New Orleans). Home: New Orleans, La. Died Mar. 30, 1980; buried New Orleans.

SANGER, RICHARD HARLAKENDEN, fgn. service officer; b. Sangerfield, N.Y., July 22, 1905; s. William Cary and Ethel (Dodge) S.; grad. St. Marks Sch., Southboro, Mass., 1924; B.A., Harvard, 1928, M.B.A., 1931; m. Marion Child, Nov. 19, 1931; children—Patience Margo, Richard Harlakenden, Anne Cary. With Dept. Commerce Fgn. Service, 1931-32; writer, reporter, 1932-36; staff Republican Nat. Com., 1936-40; econ. analyst Bd. Econ. Warfare, Fgn. Econ. Adminstrn., 1941-42; staff econ. warfare div. Am. Embassy, London, Eng., 1942; mem. Am. Econ. Mission to Algiers, 1943; staff Near East econ. div. Dept. State, 1944, staff Nr. East Polit. Div., 1945-46; mem. 1st U.S. Diplomatic Mission to Yemen, 1946; officer in charge Arabian Peninsular affairs, 1947-49; asst. chief div. Near East affairs, 1949; 1st sec., chief polit. sect. Am. Embasy, Beirut, Lebanon, 1950-51; pub. affairs adviser to Asst. Sec. State for Nr. East Affairs, 1952-55; dep. chief to mission, counsellor Am. Embassy, Amman, Jordan, 1955-58; dir. office of research and analysis Mid-East and Africa, Dept. of State, Washington, 1958; U.S. representative NATO sub-com., Paris, France, 1959-60; director office of research and analysis for Africa, Department of State, Washington, 1961-62; prof. African affairs, Fgn. Service Inst., 1962-65; special adviser to United States delegation to UN Emergency Session on Middle East, August, 1958. Bd. govs. Middle East Inst., Washington, 1952-55. Trustee Landon School, Bethesda, Md. Mem. Fgn. Service Assn., Profl. and Sci. Assn. Episcopalian. Clubs: Harvard, Chevy Chase, Metropolitan (Washington). Author: The Arabian Peninsula, 1954; Where the Jordan Flows; Insurgent Era; Holley's Hurricane. Home: Washington, D.C. Died Mar. 20, 1979; buried Rock Creek Cemetery, Washington.

SANGER, WILLIAM THOMAS, coll. prof.; b. Bridgewater, Va., Sept. 16, 1885; s. Samuel F. and Susan A. (Thomas) S.; B.A., Bridgewater Coll., 1909; M.A., Ind. U., 1910; student Columbia, summer 1911; fellow in psychology, Clark U., 1912-13 and Mar.-June, 1915, Ph.D., 1915; LL.D., Hampden-Sydney Coll., 1926, Coll. William and Mary, 1953; L.H.D., Bridgewater Coll., 1939; LL.D., U. Richmond, 1939, U. N.C., 1950, Va. Union U., 1956; D.Sc., U. Fla., 1953; D.C.L., Med. Coll. Va., 1957; m. Sylvia Gray Burns, Aug. 20, 1913; 1 son, Julian. Prof. history and philosophy Bridgewater Coll., 1910-12, prof. philosophy and edn., 1913-16; instr. edn. Madison Coll., Harrisonburg, Va., summers 1913-16, registrar and instr., 1916-17, dean, head dept. edn. and dir. summer session, 1917-19; asst. in high sch. inspection of Va., 1917-19; spl. collaborator and mem. field staff Va. State Sch. Survey, 1919; dean and prof. psychology and edn., Bridgewater Coll., 1919-21; instr. in psychology, U. Utah, summer 1920; in edn. U. Va., summers 1921, 22; exec. sec. Va. State Tchrs. Assn. and editor Va. Jour. Edn., 1921-22; sec. Va. State Bd. of Edn., 1922-25; pres. Med. Coll. Va., 1925-56, chancellor, 1956-59, chancellor emeritus, 1959-75; exec. dir. Med. Coll. Va. Found., to 1975; dir. Central Nat. Bank. Dir. Meharry Medical College, Nat., Va. socs. crippled children and adults, Nat. Health Council, Bridgewater College, Virginia Council on Health and Med. Care, Richmond Area U. Center. Mem. N.E.A., Va. Edn. Assn., A.A.A.S., Va. Acad. Sci., Richmond Acad. Medicine, Med. Soc. Va., ADA (hon.), Phi Delta Kappa, Phi Beta Kappa, Alpha Omega Alpha, Omicron Delta Kappa, Omicron Kappa Upsilon. Democrat. Presbyn. Author numerous articles in ednl. and med. jours.; author: (autobiography) As I Remember, 1972. Home: Richmond, Va. Died Apr. 17, 1975; interred Hollywood Cemetery, Richmond.

SANSOM, WILLIAM, author; b. London, Eng., Jan. 18, 1912; s. Ernest Brooks and Mabel (Clark) S.; ed. Uppingham Sch.; m. Ruth Grundy, 1954; children—Sean, Nicolas. Recipient travel scholarship Soc. Authors, 1946, lit. bursary, 1947. Mem. Royal Soc. Lit. Author: Fireman Flower, 1944; Three, 1946; Westminster in War, 1947; Something Terrible, Something Lovely, 1948; South: Aspects and Images from Corsica, Italy and Southern France, 1948; (short stories) The Passionate North, 1950; the Face fo Innocence, 1951; A Touch of Sun, 1952; A Bed of Roses, 1954; (ballads) Lord Love Us, 1954; (short stories) A Contest of Ladies, 1956; the Living Eye, 1956; The Icicle and the Sun, 1958; The Cautious Heart, 1958; Bay of Naples, 1960; Chendru: The Boy and the Tiger, 1960; Blue Skies, Brown Studies, 1961; The Last Hours of Sandra Lee, 1961; The Stories of William Sansom, 1963; (introduction) Doctor Glas, 1963; Away to it All, 1964; The Ulcerated Milkman, 1966; (novels) Goodbye, 1966; Grand Tour Today, 1968; (sociol. hist. study) Christmas, 1968. Address: London, England. Died Apr. 20, 1976.

SANTOS Y BASCO, JOSE ABAD, judge; b. San Fernando, Pampanga, P.I., Feb. 19, 1886; s. Vicente Abad and Toribia (Basco) S.; student Santa Clara Coll., Calif., 1904-05, U. of Ill., 1905-06; LL.B., Northwestern U., 1908; LL.M., George Washington U., 1909; m. Amanda Teopaco e Hizon, of San Fernando, Pampanga, Sept. 21, 1918; children—Josa, Duz, Amanda, Osmundo, Victoria. Admitted to P.I. bar, 1911, and began practice at Manila; asst. atty., Bur. of Justice, P.I., 1913-17; atty. for Philippine Nat. Bank, 1917-19; mem. firm Abad Santos & Abad Santos, 1920-21; under sec. of justice, Jan.-Apr. 1922, sec. of justice until 1923; in practice as mem. firm Santos & Benitos, later Abad Santos, Camus, Delgado & Recto, 1924-28; sec. of justice, 1928-32; asso. justice Supreme Court of Philippines since 1932. Mem. Philippine Mission to U.S., 1919; head of Philippine Ednl. Mission to U.S., 1926. Chmn. bd. trustees Philippine Women's Coll. Mem. Philippine Bar Assn., Am. Acad. Polit. and Social Science, Philippine Columbian Assn. Mem. Nationalist Party. Catholic. Club: Wack Wack Golf. Home: Manila, P.I. *

SAPIRSTEIN, JACOB, greeting card mfr., b. Grajeyve, Russian Poland, Oct. 30, 1885; s. Isaac and Molly (Berenson) S.; came to U.S., 1905; M. Jennie Kanter, June 7, 1908; children—Irving, Morris, Harry, Bernice (Mrs. David Davis). Founder, 1907, pres., 1902-60, former chmn. bd. Am. Greetings Corp., Cleve. (originally Sapirstein Greeting Card Co.), now dir. Active Hebrew Acad. Cleve., Young Israel Cleve. Mem. N.A.M., C. of C. Home: University Heights OH. *

SAPOSS, DAVID JOSEPH (SA'POS), industrial economist; b. Kiev, Ukraine, Feb. 22, 1886; s. Isaac and Shima (Erenske) S.; came to U.S., 1895; ed. Univ. of Wis., 1907-12, Columbia U., 1925-26; m. Bertha Tigay, July 3, 1917; children—Corinne Tigay, Barbara Tigay. Labor economist sonce 1911; has been identified with U.S. Commn. on Industrial Relations, N.Y. Dept. of Labor, Brookwood Labor Coll., Inter-Church World Movement, etc.; chief economist Nat. Labor Relations Bd., 1935-40; labor consultant to Coordinator of Inter-American Affairs, Washington, D.C., 1941-45; chief econ. advisor, Labor Prodn. Div., War Prodn. Bd., Washington, D.C., 1943-45; chief, Reports and Statistics Branch, Manpower Div., Office of Mil. Govt. for Germany (U.S.), Berlin, June 1945-Sept. 1946; with Bur. Labor Statistics, U.S. Department of Labor, Washington, D.C., 1946-48; with European hdqrs. E.C.A., Paris, Fr., since Sept. 1948. Mem. Am. Econ. Assn., Indsl. Relations Research Assn. Author: Left Wing Unionism, 1926; The Labor Movement of Post-War France, 1930; also other works relating to labor. Contbr. to mags. Home: Washington, D.C. *

SAPP, CLAUD NAPOLEON, lawyer; born at Sapp's Crossroads, Lancaster County, South Carolina, February 11, 1886; s. Daniel F. and Mittie (Fulp) S.; A.B., Wofford Coll., Spartanburg, S.C., 1907; LL.B., U. of S.C., 1911; m. Mary Davis, Nov. 20, 1916 (died Apr. 3, 1937); children—Claud Napoleon, Joe Daniel. Admitted to S.C. bar, 1911; mem. S.C. Legislature, 1912-14, 1920-24, S.C. Hist. Commn., 1913-16; 1st asst. atty. gen. of S.C., 1916-19. County atty, Lancaster County, 1912-14, Richland County, 1926-28; U.S. atty. Eastern Dist. of S.C. since 1934; chmn. State Dem. Exec. Com. of S.C., 1930-34; del. Nat. Dem. Convs., 1924, 28, 32 and 36; presidential elector, 1932. Trustee Cedar Springs Inst. for Deaf, Dumb and Blind. Mem. Am. and S.C. bar assns., U. of S.C. Alumni Assn. (pres. 1933-36), Omicron Delta Kappa. Democrat. Methodist. Mason, Elk. Home: Columbia, S.C. *

SAPPINGTON, A. D., ins. co. exec.; b. Columbia, Mo., Oct. 20, 1912; s. Admiral Dot and Lula Margaret (Maupin) S.; J.D., U. Mo., Columbia, 1936; m. Helen Edmiston, Sept. 30, 1936; children—Judith Ann, Kathern Lee. Admitted to Mo. bar, 1936; practiced law, Columbia, 1936-45; city atty., 1936-45; gen. atty., then gen. counsel Mo. Farmers Assn., 1943-57; gen. counsel, then gen. counsel and v.p. MFA Mut. Ins. Co. Group, Columbia, 1946-64, pres., 1964-79. Past chmn. local United Fund, ARC; mem. Mo. Hwy. Commn., 1954-63; mem. fin. com. Rock Bridge State Park. Named Man of Year, Fedn. Ins. Counsel, 1975, Bus. Man of Year, Alpha Kappa Psi, 1968; recipient Mo. Good Roads award, 1965; Mo. Law Citation of Merit, U. Mo., 1971; Distinguished Service award Mo. Farmers Assn., 1976, U. Mo. Alumni Soc., 1976. Mem. Nat. Assn. Ind. Insurers (gov. 1964-79, chmn. 1969-72), Health Inst. Inst. (past gov.). Address: Columbia, Mo. Died Feb. 27, 1979.

SARGENT, FREDERICK, II, educator; b. Boston, Jan. 11, 1920; s. Ralph and Elise Hodges (Connor) S.; student Phillips Exeter Acad., 1934-38; S.B., Mass. Inst. Tech., 1942; M.D., Boston U., 1947; m. Anne Virginia Swiedler, Mar. 29, 1968; children—Peter, Fredericka, Laura. Intern Presbyn. Hosp., Chgo., 1947-48; asst. prof. U. Ill., 1950-55, asso. prof., 1955-59, prof., 1959-67, dir. Center Human Ecology, 1965-67; dean Coll. Environmental Sci., prof. human ecology U. Wis. at Green Bay, 1968-70; provost, prof. human ecology Western Wash. U., Bellingham, 1970-72; prof. human ecology Sch. Pub. Health, U. Tex., Houston, 1972-80; cons. in field. Commr. Green Bay Met. Sewage Dist., 1969-70; mem. Wis. Environmental Health Adv. Com., 1969-70, Environmental Health Commn. Comprehensive Health Planning Council, N.W. Wash., 1970-72, environmental health study group Houston-Galveston Area Health Council, 1973. Served with USAF, 1952-54. John Simon Guggenheim fellow, 1957-58; recipient Centennial Alumni award Boston U. Sch. Medicine, 1973. Fellow Am. Public Health Assn. (food and nutrition council), Royal Soc. Health. AAAS, World Acad. Arts and Scis.; mem. Am. Meteorol. Soc. (recipient award 1960), Am. Physiol. Soc., Ecol. Soc. Am., Soc. Human Ecology (pres. from 1979), Am. Soc. Clin. Nutrition, Tex. Med. Assn. (chmn. com. on nutrition and food resources 1978-80), Internat. Soc. Biometeorology (hon., pres. 1956-66). Editor: Recent Advances in Bioclimatology, 1954; Human Biometeorology, 1964; Human Ecology, 1974; editorial bd. Bull. Environmental Contamination and Toxicology; regional editor Chemosphere. Contbr. articles to profl. jours. Home: Houston, Tex. Died Mar. 3, 1980.

SARGENT, MURRAY, business exec.; b. New Haven, Conn., Aug. 30, 1884; s. Henry Bradford and Harriet Amelia (Oaks) S.; B.A., Yale 1905; m. Mary Hale Cunningham, Jan. 18, 1913; children—Murray, James Cunningham, Henry Bradford, John Moffat. With Sargent and Co., mfrs. since 1907, sec., 1917-35, dir., 1927-47, pres., 1942-44, chmn. bd. since 1944; dir. 1st Nat. Bank, New Haven, Conn., 1927-34; adminstr. New York Hosp., 1934-44, dir., 1945-48, hon. mem. bd. govs., Soc. N.Y. Hosp., 1948—. Trustee Asso. Hosp. Service (Blue Cross Plan), 1945-56, Chief of hardware and handtool sect. War Industries Bd., Washington, World War I. Pres. Blood Transfusion Assn.; hon. trustee Knickerbocker Hosp., N.Y.C., since 1950. Mem. Am. Hardware Manufacturers Assn. (vice pres., 1919-20), Greater New York Hosp. Assn. (pres., 1947-48), St. Andrews Soc. of New York. Republican. Episcopalian. Clubs: Yale, University (N.Y.); Mountainy Pond (East Holden, Me.). Home: N.Y.C. *

SARGENT, SAMUEL S(TEGALL), educator; b. Evergreen, Miss., Dec. 15, 1883; s. Leonidas T. and Isabell (Goodwyn) S.; A.B., Union Univ., Jackson, Tenn., 1924; A.M., Peabody Coll., Nashville, Tenn., 1926; m. Lucy Terry, Dec., 1913; 1 dau., Mabel Terry (Mrs. Amos Milton Teasley). Teacher and prin. Guntown (Miss.), high sch., 1918-27; supt. Booneville city schs., 1927-37; academic dean, Union Univ., since 1937; religious lecturer and pulpit supply various chs., W. Tenn. since 1938. Mem. Miss. Accrediting Commn. for high schs., 1929-30. Mem. Nat. Assn. Academic Deans, Kappa Alpha. Democrat. Baptist. Mason. Clubs: North Eastern Miss. (pres. 1929-30; chmn. curriculum study courses, 1929-30); West Tennessee Executives; Jackson Exchange (sec. since 1939). Home: Jackson, Tenn. *

SAROYAN, WILLIAM, writer; b. Fresno, Aug. 31, 1908; s. Armenak and Takoohi (Saroyan) S. (of Bitlis, Armenia); ed. public schs., Fresno, Cal.; m. Carol Marcus, Feb. 1943 (div. Nov. 1949); children—Aram, Lucy. Co-founder Conf. Press, Los Angeles, 1936; dir. Saroyan Theatre, N.Y.C., 1942; writer-in-residence Purdue U., 1961. Author: The Daring Young Man on the Flying Trapeze, 1934; Inhale and Exhale, 1936; Three Times Three, 1936; Little Children, 1937; Love, Here Is My Hat, 1938; The Trouble with Tigers, 1938; Peace, It's Wonderful, 1939; My Name is Aram, 1940; My Heart's in the Highlands (play (play, produced by Group Theatre, N.Y.C.), 1939; The Time of Your Life (play, prod. by Theatre Guild, N.Y.C., received Drama Critics Circle Award, also Pulitzer Prize, the latter being rejected; made into film with James Cagney 1948), 1939; Love's Old Sweet Song (play, prod. by Theatre Guild), 1939; The Beautiful People (play, produced and directed by himself in N.Y.C.), 1941; Across the Board on Tomorrow Morning (play, produced by Pasadena (Calif.) Playhouse), 1941; Jim Dandy (play, presented by 60 theatre mems. of Nat. Theatre Conf.), 1941; The Great American Goof (ballet, produced by Ballet Theatre in N.Y.C.), 1940, 41; Saroyan's Fables (old country fables), 1941; Razzle Dazzle (short plays), 1942; (novel and movie) The Human Comedy, 1942; Get Away, Old Man (play, produced by George Abbott), 1944; Dear Baby (stories), 1944; The Adventures of Wesley Jackson (novel), 1946; Jim Dandy, Fat Man in a Famine (play), 1947; The Saroyan Special (selected stories), 1948; Mama, I Love You (novel), 1956; The Whole Voyald (stories), 1956; Papa You're Crazy (novel), 1957; Not Dying (autobiography), 1963; One Day in the Afternoon of the World (novel), 1964; After Thirty Years: The Daring Young Man on the Flying Trapeze, 1964; Short Drive, Sweet Chariot (autobiographical fragment), 1966; Look at Us (photographs by Arthur Rubenstein), 1967; I Used to Believe I Had Forever, Now I'm Not so Sure (stories, essays, plays, poems), 1967; Letters from 74 Rue Taitbout, or Don't Go But If You Must, Say Hello to Everybody (letter-stories), 1969; The Dogs and Two Other Plays (plays), 1959. Dir. moving picture The Good Job, 1942; opened Saroyan Theatre, N.Y.C., with Across the Board on Tomorrow Morning and Talking to You, 1942; The Twin Adventures, 1950; The Assyrian and Other Stories, 1950; Rock Wagram, 1951; Tracy's Tiger, 1951; The Bicycle Rider in Beverly Hills, 1952; The Laughing Matter, 1953; Here Comes/There Goes/You Know Who, 1961; Boys and Girls Together, 1963; Places Where I've Done Time, 1972; The Tooth and My Father, 1974. Mem. Nat. Inst. Arts and Letters. Home: Fresno, Calif. Died May 18, 1981.

SARTRE, JEAN-PAUL, author, playwright, philosopher; b. Paris, France, June 21, 1905; ed. Lycée Henri VI, and Ecole Normale Supérieure. Teacher philosophy Lycée du Havre, and Inst. Français (Berlin), 1929-34; prof. philosophy Lycée Condorcet, Paris, 1935-42 (resigned to devote entire time to literary work). Served with French army, 1939, prisoner in Germany, 9 mos.; returned to Paris and as journalist served the Resistance movement, 1941-44. Founder, 1947, editor Les Temps Modernes (monthly). Awarded 1964 Nobel prize for lit. (prize refused). Author of stories, novels, plays, film plays (many trans. and pub. under English titles), among the most notable: L'Etre et l'Néant, 1943 (English trans., Being and Nothingness, 1947, 56, 57); Les Mouches (The Files) (play), 1943; Huit Clos (No Exit) (play), 1943; La Putain respecteus (The Respectful Prostitute) (play), 1947; Les Jeux sont faits (film play); Le Diable et' le Bon Dieu; The Psychology of the Imagination, 1951; Les Main Sales, 1952; Oeuvres complets, 1952; Nebrasso (farce), 1957; The Condemned of Altona (play), 1960; The Devil and the Good Lord (play), 1960; Imagination, 1962; Huis Clos, 1962; Literature and Existentialism, 1962; The Age of Rea, 1963; The Words, 1964. During visit to U.S. lectured before univs., Harvard, Columbia, Yale, Princeton, 1947. Address: Paris, France. Died Apr. 15, 1980.

SARVELLA, PATRICIA ANN, geneticist; b. Waukegan, Ill., July 24, 1926; d. Otto O. and Ethel (Sutherland) Sarvella; A.B., Case Western Res. U., 1948, M.S., 1950; Ph.D., N.C. State U. at Raleigh, 1956. Research asst. Case Western Res. U., 1948-50, N.C. State U., Raleigh, 1953-56; research fellow Inst. Genetics, U. Lund (Sweden), 1956-57, Wash. State U., Pullman, 1958-59; asst. prof., asst. agronomist Miss. State U., State Coll., 1959-60, asso. prof., asso. agronomist, 1960-65; research geneticist Dept. Agr., Beltsville, Md., 1965-77; tchr. NSF Scieneer's Program for High Sch. Srs., Miss. State U., 1961, 62, 64, 65. Pres. Prince George's County (Md.) Sci. Fair, 1968-69, chmn. awards com., 1970-77; Dept. Agr. judge Internat. Sci. Fair, New Orleans, Oklahoma City, San Diego, and Denver 1972, 73-76; mem. Washington Met. Area Joint Bd. Sci. Edn., 1969-75, pres., 1971-72. Active YMCA, Girl Scouts U.S.A. Recipient YMCA Gold Triangle award Miss. U., 1965; Ralph Spangler, Jr. award in botany Case Western Res. U., 1948; Am. Assn. U. Women fellow, 1956-57, U. Lund Inst. Genetics fellow, 1957, Wash. State U. fellow, 1958-59. Fellow Washington Acad. Sci. (sec. 1973-74), AAAS (council 1972-73), Orgn. Profl. Employees Dept. Agr. (pub. service v.p. 1971-74, exec. v.p. 1974-76; Prince George's County recognition award 1975); mem. Genetics Soc. Am. (grantee, del. internat. congress 1963), Am. Genetic Assn. (sec. 1969-74, v.p. 1974-75, pres. 1975-76), Am. Inst. Biol. Scis., Am. Soc. Agronomy (chmn., presiding officer session on corn sterility 1965), Miss. Acad. Sci. (dir. sci. fair Starkville chpt. 1962-65, chmn. botany and plant physiology sect. 1964, 65), Finlandia Found. (sec. 1971-72), AAUW (Starkville br. higher edn. chmn. 1960-61, pres. 1963-65; Miss. div. chmn. for occident and orient 1964-65, 2d v.p. 1965; College Park Md. br. chmn. world problems 1966-68, Md. div. 2d v.p. 1970-72, pres. 1973-75; named grant 1972), Assn. Southeastern Biologists, U.S. Dept. Agr. Agrl. Research Center Employees Assn. (pres. 1971-72), Sigma Xi (treas. Miss. State U. chpt. 1960), Phi Kappa Pi, Gamma Sigma Delta, Delta Kappa Gamma, Sigma Delta Epsilon (v.p. 1973-74, pres. 1974-75), Alpha Lambda Delta (hon.), Sigma Omega. Clubs: U.S. Dept. Agr. Travel (dir. 1971-76); Pilot Washington (v.p. 1972-73, pres. 1973-74; pres. Starkville, Miss. 1964-65; membership and info. chmn. Miss. and La. div. 1963-64, lt. gov. dist. 1976). Contbr. articles to profl. publs. Home: Laurel, Md. Died Mar. 8, 1977.

SATER, RICHARD FRANCIS, lawyer; b. Columbus, Ohio, Apr. 23, 1905; s. Lowry F. and Katharine E. (Morhart) S.; A.B., Princeton, 1926; J.D., Ohio U., 1929; m. Velma I. Stevens, Oct. 3, 1929; children—Velma (Mrs. David F. Williams), Frederic S. Admitted to Ohio bar, from 1929; partner firm Vorys, Sater, Seymour & Pease, Columbus, from 1929. Recipient Ohio Bar medal, 1970. former trustee Ohio Bar Assn. Found., Am. Coll. Probate Counsel; mem. Am., Ohio, Columbus bar assns., Princeton U. Alumni Council, Phi Delta Phi. Presbyn. Clubs: Quadrangle (Princeton, N.J.); Rocky Fork Hunt and Country (past pres.), University (Columbus); Princeton (N.Y.C.). Home: Columbus, Ohio. Deceased.

SAUER, LOUIS W(ENDLIN), pediatrist, immunologist; b. Cin., Aug. 13, 1885; s. Louis W. and Caroline Mary (Muth) S.; A.B., U. Cin., 1907, A.M., 1908; student Med. Sch., U. Berlin, 1908-12; M.D., Rush Med. Coll., U. Chgo., 1913; Ph.D., U. Chgo., 1924; m. Mira Lucia Seypelt. Aug. 20, 1912; children—Miralotte Lucia (Mrs. Raymond Ickes), Paul Willibald, Gisela Josepha (Mrs. Carl Enchelmayer). Attending physician Chgo. Infant Welfare Soc., 1913-17; research fellow Sprague Inst., U. Chgo., 1914-19; asst. attending physician Children's Meml. Hosp., 1914-18; sr. attending pediatrist Evanston Hosp., 1915-30 chief dept. pediatrics 1938-51; asso. prof. pediatrics emeritus Northwestern U.; med. dir. The Cradle, Evanston; staff Evanston Health Dept., Immunization Clinic, 1932-55; past chief pediatric staff, immunologist St. Vincent's Infant and Maternity Hosp., Chgo., practice pediatrics, Coral Gables, Fla. Elected Sertoma Man of Year, 1955. Distinguished Service award U. Chgo., 1957. Fellow Am. Pub. Health Assn., Royal Soc. Health (London); mem. A.M.A., Ill., Chgo. med. socs., A.A.A.S., Inst. Medicine, Am. Acad. Pediatrics, Chgo. Pediatric Soc. (pres.1946), Alpha Omega Alpha, Pi Gamma Mu. Republican. Unitarian. Author: Nursery Guide, 1923, 26, 33; From Infancy Through Childhood, 1942, 44, 47, Contbr. articles to profl. jours. Perfected methods of whooping cough prevention, combined whooping cough and diphtheria prevention, and combined whooping cough, diphtheria and tetanus prevention. Home: Coral Gables FL. *

SAUER, WALTER CHARLES, lawyer; b. Jersey City, Mar. 5, 1905; A.B., Princeton, 1928, LL.B., Yale U., 1931. Vice chmn. bd. dirs. 1st v.p. Export-Import Bank of U.S. Home: Washington, D.C. Died Oct. 15; 1980; buried Hillside Cemetery, Plainfield, N.J.

SAUGSTAD, JESSE EDWIN, govt. ofcl.; b. Westby, Wis., June 6, 1886; s. Theodore Even and Josephine (Hagen) S.; student St. Olaf Coll., Northfield, Minn., 1903-06; m. Lucille Van Valey Woodrow, May 31, 1927; 1 son, Edgar Van Valey (foster son). Instr. U. Wis., 1910-18; traffic, operations depts. Oriental Navigation Co., N.Y.C., 1919-22; asst. dir., bur. research U.S. Shipping Bd., 1922-26; exec. asst. to v.p. Mcht. Fleet Corp., 1926-29; spl. agt., transportation div. Dept. Commerce, 1929-35; shipping adviser, trade agreement div. Dept. State, 1935-38, asst. chief div. internat. communications, 1938-44, chief shipping div., 1944-49, chief shipping policy staff 1949-54. Vice chairman U.S. delegation Safety of Life at Sea Conf., London, 1948; pres., dir. State Dept. Fed. Credit Union, 1945. Asst. dir. music Wis. N.G., 1908-10; served as ensign U.S.N., enrollment officer for colls., central div., 1918-19. Decorated Comdr. Royal Order Orange-Nassau (Netherlands), 1948, Knight Royal Order St. Olaf, 1948 (Norway); Order of the Sacred Treasure, 2d class (Japan). Mem. Acacia. Clubs: Propeller (Washington), Torch Internat. Cosmos (Washington). Author: Shipping and Shipbuilding Subsidies, 1932. Home: Washington. *

SAUNDERS, EDMUND A., life ins. exec.; b. Richmond, Va., July 20, 1886; s. Edmund A., Jr., and Martha A. (Brown) S.; grad. Va. Mil. Inst., 1906; student Cornell U., 1906-07; m. Janie L. Quinn, of Lynchburg, Va., Nov. 6, 1913; children—Jane Quinn, Ann Lee. Engaged in farming, 1907-14; with Atlantic Life Ins. Co. since 1914, successively asst. treas., asst. sec-treas., treas., v.p.-treas., pres. and chmn. bd., now dir.; also dir. First & Merchants Nat. Bank of Richmond. Mem. Kappa Alpha (Southern). Democrat. Episcopalian. Clubs: Westmoreland, Swannanoa Country. Home: Richmond, Va. *

SAUNDERS, WILBOUR EDDY, clergyman, educator; b. Warwick, R.I., Sept. 20, 1894; s. Colver L. and Harriet (Robertson) S.; A.B., Brown U., 1916; M.A., Columbia U., 1918; grad. Union Theol. Seminary, 1919; postgrad. Cambridge U. (Eng.), 1919-20; D.D., Colgate U., 1936; Dr. Edn., Brown U., 1941; LL.D., Dickinson Coll., 1943, U. Rochester, 1951; Litt.D., Keuka Coll., 1959; L.H.D., Kalamazoo Coll., 1961; D.D., Denison U., 1961; m. Mildred A. Paige, Sept. 22, 1919 (dec. 1950); m. 2d, Esther Hale Gosnell, Jan. 2, 1952; 1 adopted dau., Marjorie Luther. Ordained to ministry Baptist Ch., 1919; teacher Horace Mann Sch. N.Y.C., 1920-21; asst. pastor Marcy Ave. Ch., Bklyn., 1920-23, pastor 1927-32; pastor First Ch., Rahway, N.J 1923-27; chaplain N.J. State Reformatory, 1924-27; exec. sec., Fedn. Chs. Rochester and Monroe. County, N.Y., 1932-35; spl. lectr. Colgate-Rochester Div. Sch., 1933-35; headmaster Peddie Sch., Highstown, N.J., 1935-48; pres. Colgate-Rochester Div. Sch., 1949-60; interim sr. minister Irondequit United Ch. of Christ, 1964-79; interim pres. Keuka Coll., Keuka Park, N.Y., 1965-66, First Bapt. Ch., Rochester, N.Y., 1966-68. Past pres. Hightstown YMCA; chmn. trustees Rochester Regional Research Library; trustee Wayland Jr. Coll., Peddie Sch., Brown U., Columbia Sch., Colgate Rochester Div. Sch., Allendale Sch. Past pres. Assn. No. Bapts. Ednl. Instn. Del. Constnl. Conv., State N.J. Chmn. gov's. Com. Civil Rights, 1947-48. Mem. Acad. Polit. and Social Sci., Delta Tau Delta. Mason; mem. Royal Arcanum. Clubs: Brown (N.Y.); University, Country (Rochester). Mem. editorial bd. Crusader. Home: Webster, N.Y Died May 12, 1979.

SAUTER, EDWARD ERNEST, musician; b. Bklyn., Dec. 2, 1914; s. August and Julia (Greter) S.; student Juilliard Sch. Music, N.Y.C., 1932-33, Columbia, 1933-35; m. Margaret Charette, Sept. 6, 1938; children—Gregory Edward, Daniel Stanley. Arranger Red Norvo Orch., Mildred Bailey, 1935-39, Benny Goodman Orch., 1939-43, Ray McKinley Orch., 1946-50; arranger, composer, condr. Sauter-Finegan Orch., recordings RCA Victor, from 1952. Mem. A.S.C.A.P. Home: West Nyack, N.Y. Died Apr. 21, 1981.

SAVAGE, EUGENE FRANCIS, painter, sculptor; b. Covington, Ind., Mar. 29, 1883; s. Hardy and Ann E. (Weldon) S.; student Gonzaga Coll., Washington; student art Corcoran Art Sch., Washington, Art Inst. Chgo., Fine Arts Acad., Chgo.; studied with Von Groeber, Munich; B.F.A., Yale, 1924, M.A., 1927; D.F.A., U. Hartford, 1963; m. Matilda M. Freitag, Oct. 17, 1908; 1 dau., Dorothy Ann (Mrs. Raymond G. Crawford). Figure, portrait, mural and landscape painter; William Leffingwell prof. painting Yale, 1923-58, now emeritus. Apptd. mem. Commn. of Fine Arts (U.S.) by Pres. Hoover, 1933, by Pres. Roosevelt, 1937. Recipient prix de Rome, 1912; medal of honor Archtl. League, 1921; W.M.R. French meml. gold medal Art Inst. Chgo., 1921, Norman Waite Harris silver medal and prize, 1922, Saltus medal of merit and T.B. Clark prize N.A.D., 1923, 2d Altman prize, 1924, Frank G. Logan 1st prize and medal All-Am. Biannual, Chgo., 1924, John C. Shaffer prize, 1925, Centennial medal Artists Fellowship, 1968, Diamond Jubliee medal Am. Sculpture Soc., 1969. Painting, Arbor Day, on permanent exhbn. Art Inst., Chgo., and Elks Nat. Meml., Chgo.; Expulsion, City Art Museum, St. Louis; sculpture, Bailey meml. fountain, Grand Army Plaza, Brooklyn; Alma Mater, in Sterling Library, Yale; Videbimus Lumen in South Hall, Columbia; The Republic and The State, Centennial Hall of Tex., Dallas; Almighty Spring, in State Mus., Neb.; Spirit of Oshkosh, Fine Arts Museum, Oshkosh, Wis.; Litany of the Mail (two paintings), Post Office Bldg., Washington; exterior mural facades of Communication Bldg., and 12 murals of U.S. Govt. Bldg., New York World's Fair; north and south loggis ceilings Pa. Treasury, Harrisburg; Collection and Distributions of Taxes in Courthouse, Covington, Ind.; facade mosaic, Home State Tabernacle, Honolulu; mosaic in U.S. Meml., Epinal, France; N.Y.; Spirit of Ind. in Indpls., 1963; murals in Foyer Meml. Center, Purdue U., N.Y. State Ct. of Appeals, Albany, Ind. State Capitol; hist. mosaic in 1st Nat. Bank, N.Y.C.; others. N.A., 1924, Nat. Academician, 1926. Mem. Nat. Inst. Arts and Letters, Nat. Soc. Mural Painters, Painters' and Sculptors' Gallery Assn., A.I.A. Club: Century (N.Y.C.). Home: Woodbury CT. *

SAVANT, DOMENICO PIETRO (SA'VANT), educator; born Nole, Italy, February 17, 1886; s. Nicola and Cristina (Vigna) S.; came to U.S., 1890, naturalized, 1925; student Highland Park Coll., Des Moines, Ia., 1907-08; B.S. in Elec. Engring., Rose Poly. Tech., Terre Haute, Ind., 1912, M.S., 1914, E.E., 1916; M.S. in Elec. Engring., Harvard, 1920; m. Marie Hammond, Sept. 12, 1916; 1 son, Nicholas Hammond (killed in action, May 2, 1944). Teacher, Rose Polytechnic Institute, 1915-16 instructor University of Mo., 1916-19; instr. Harvard 1919-21; successively asst. professor, asso. professor and professor elec. engring. and head dept. Ga. Sch. of Tech., since 1922, dean of engring., 1935-50 now dean emeritus. Fellow Am. Inst. Elec. Engrs.; mem. Am. Soc. for Engring. Edn., Nat. Soc. Professional Engrs., Phi Kappa Phi, Eta Kappa Nu, Omicron Delta Kappa. Mason. Home: Atlanta. *

SAVELLE, MAX, educator; b. Mobile, Ala., Jan. 8, 1896; s. Myles Hicks and Rosabel (Pooley) S.; A.B., Columbia, 1924, A.M., 1926, Ph.D., 1932; m. Jean Happ, Mar. 18, 1950; children—David (by former marriage), Michele, Jon Marc. Instr. history Columbia, 1926-32; prof. history Stanford, 1932-47; prof. history U. Wash. 1947-67; Cutting travelling fellow, 1930-31; Social Sci. Research Council travelling fellow, 1938-39; Fulbright scholar, 1950; Fulbright lectr. U. Madrid, 1960-61; vis. prof. U. Chile, Santiago, 1963, Australian univs., 1966, U. Wis., 1968, Central Wash. State Coll., 1968, So. Ill. U., 1969, U. Ill. Chgo., 1969-74; sr. research scholar Newberry Library, 1967-68. Served with USN, 1918-19. Recipient Serra award Acad. Am. Franciscan History, 1976. Mem. Am. Hist. Assn., Orgn. Am. Historians, Am. Antiquarian Soc., Sigma Delta Pi, Phi Alpha Theta. Author: George Morgan, Colony Builder, 1932; The Diplomatic History of the Canadian Boundary, 1749-63, 1940; Foundations of American Civilization, 1942; chpt., The American Balance of Power and European Diplomacy, 1713-1778, in The Era of the American Revolution (edited by R. B. Morris), 1939; This Is My America, 1948; Seeds of Liberty, 1948; chpt. Road to Revolution, in Problems in American History (edited by Arthur Link, Richard Leopold and Stanley Coben), 1952, 4th edit., 1972; The United States, Colonial Period, 1953; Short History of American Civilization, 1957 (Spanish translation 1962); The Colonial Period in the History of the New World, 1962; A History of Colonial America, 1964, 3d edit. (with Darold Wax), 1973; The Colonial Origins of American Thought, 1964; Origins of American Diplomacy, 1967; (novel) The Gospel of Judas Iscariot, 1969; Empires to Nations: Expansion in America, 1713-1825, 1974. Gen. editor and contbr. A History of World Civilization, 1957; Is Liberalism Dead? and Other Essays, 1967. Contbr. hist. and ednl. publs. Home: Seattle, Wash. Died Aug. 12, 1979.

SAWYER, BICKFORD EDWARD, army officer; b. Melrose, Mass., Aug. 1, 1894; S Edward W. and Flora (Bickford) S.; student Norwich U., 1917; LL.B. La Salle U., 1937; student Army Indsl. Coll., 1938. Harvard, 1951; m. Grace Bell, Aug. 19, 1917; children—Capt. Bickford Edward, Richard Vincent. Enlisted Vt. N.G., 1913; commd. 2d lt. cav., U.S. Army, 1917, advanced through grades to maj. gen., 1951; with 1st Inf. Div., 1st Cav. Div.; disbursing officer, Canal Zone, fiscal dir 8th Service Com.; chief fiscal officer, Pacific Theater; comptroller Hq. 4th Army; chief accounting div. Office Chief of Finance; chief of finance, from July 1951. Vice pres., dir. Armed Forces Relief and Benefit Assn.; bd. commrs. U.S. Soldier's Home. Trustee Kermit Roosevelt Fund. Decorated Legion of Merit, Commendation with two oak leaf clusters. Mem. Soc. Mil. Accts. and Statisticians (pres.), Soc. Advancement Mgmt., Mil. Order World Wars. Club: Harvard Business School (v.p.) (Washington). Died Apr. 27, 1976.

SAWYER, CHARLES, lawyer; b. Cin., Feb. 10, 1887; s. Edward Milton and Caroline (Butler) S.; A.B., Oberlin Coll., 1908; LL.B., U. Cin., 1911, LL.D., 1950; m. Margaret Sterrett Johnston, July 15, 1918 (dec. July 1937); children—Anne Sawyer Greene (Mrs. John Bradley), Charles (dec. Sept. 1967), Jean Johnston (Mrs. Jean S. Weaver), John, Edward; m. 2d, Elizabeth L. de Veyrac, June 10, 1942. Admitted to Ohio bar, 1911, since practiced in Cin.; sr. partner law firm Taft, Stettinius & Hollister. Mem. City Council, Cin., 1911-15; lt. gov. Ohio, 1933-35; Democratic candidate for gov. Ohio, 1938; mem. Dem. Nat. Com. from Ohio, 1936-44. Ambassador to Belgium, minister to Luxembourg, 1944-45; sec. of commerce, 1948-53; dir. numerous corps. Chmn. Cin. Community Chest, 1954, United Fund, 1955-60, Citizens Development Com. Cin.; mem. Commn. on Money and Credit, 1959-60. Served from capt. to maj. U.S. Army, 1918-19. Hon. trustee Oberlin Coll. Mem. Am., Fed., Ohio bar assns. Democrat. Episcopalian. Mason. Clubs: Queen City, Commercial, Commonwealth, Cincinnati Country (Cin.); Chevy Chase, National Press (Wash.); Everglades, Bath and Tennis, Beach (Palm Beach, Fla.). Author: Concerns of a Conservative Democrat, 1968. Home: Glendale, Ohio. Died Apr. 7, 1979; buried Cin.

SAWYER, HERBERT SMITH, lawyer; b. Merrit, N.C., Dec. 12, 1889; s. William Riley and Ann Bryan (Riggs) S.; A.B., Guilford Coll., 1912; J.D., U. Fla., 1916; m. Eleanor Coffin, Dec. 25, 1920; 1 dau., June (Mrs. Wallace I. Garrick); m. 2d, Virginia Davis, Dec. 12, 1934. Tchr. subfreshman dept. U. Fla., 1913-14, 15-16; admitted to Fla. bar, 1916; practice in Jacksonville, 1916-22, Sarasota, 1922-30, Miami, 1930-78; mem. firm Mershon, Sawyer, Johnston, Dunwoody & Cole, Miami, Fla., 1933-78; pros. atty., Sarasota, 1922-25, states atty., 1929-30. Past v.p., dir. Miami YMCA. Past bd. dirs. So. Scholarship Research Found. Served as officer A.C., U.S. Army, 1918-19; comdr. 492d Squadron, USAAF, France. Mem. Am., Fla., Dade County (past dir.) bar assns., Phi Kappa Phi, Sigma Alpha Epsilon. Republican. Baptist. Kiwanian (past dist. gov.). Clubs: Riviera Country; Biscayne Bay Yacht; Flamingo Dinner (past pres., dir.). Home: Coral Gables, Fla. Died July 19, 1978.

SAWYER, MEYER JOSHUA, lawyer; b. Boston, Mass., Dec. 9, 1886; s. Mendal and Bassie (Minsk) S.; student Boston Latin Sch., 1900; grad. Boston English High Sch., 1905; LL.B., Boston Univ., 1908; m. Sara Reinherz, July 14, 1922; 1 dau., Ruth Madelyn (Mrs. Sydney Goldstein). Admitted to Mass. Bar, 1908; in practice of law in Mass.; mem. firm Brookhart Sawyer & Cannon, Washington, D.C., 1939-43; spl. asst. atty, gen., Washington, D.C. Dir. Trement Trust Co., Union Cooperative Bank, Coolidge Corner Cooperative Bank, Sawyer Real Estate Corp., Boston. Gen. counsel Nat. Small Bus, Council, Nat. Safety Highway Assn., Washington Gasoline Dealers Assn. Trustee Temple O'Habei Sholom, Boston. Mem. Am., Washington, Fed. Communications bar assns., Boston Chamber of Commerce. Vice chmn. Mass. Republican State Com., 1912-14. Mason (Shriner), Club: New Century. Home: Washington, D.C. *

SAWYER, RALPH ALANSON, physicist; b. Atkinson, N.H., Jan. 5, 1895; s. George Alanson and Lillie Elvira (Noyes) S.; prep. edn., Atkinson Acad., 1907-11; A.B., Dartmouth, 1915, Sc.D., 1947; Ph.D., U. Chgo., 1919; LL.D. (hon.), Wayne U., 1954; Sc.D., Mich. Coll. Mining & Tech., 1959; m. Martha Green, Apr. 22, 1919 (dec. 1957); children—George Alanson, II, Rosalind (Mrs. George S. Springsteen, Jr.); m. 2d, Frances Hay, 1964. Instr. field physics U. Mich., 1919-22, asst. prof., 1922-27, asso. prof., 1927-30, prof. physics, 1930-64, v.p. research, 1959-64; dean Horace H. Rackham Sch. Grad. Studies, 1946-64; cons. Goddard Space Flight Center, NASA, 1964-65; acting dir. Am. Inst. Physics, 1964-66, cons., 1965-71; J.S. Guggenheim Meml. fellow, Berlin, 1926-27; mem. NRC, 1949-52, 59-71; mem. U.S. nat. com. Internat. Commn. Optics, 1954-56; mem. sci. adv. bd. Naval Weapons Lab., 1953-65; chmn. gov. bd. Am. Inst. Physics, 1959-71; chmn. Nat. Acad. Scis. panels adv. to Nat. Bur. Standards, 1965-69; tech. cons. to dir. Navy Labs., 1965-68; asso. editor, Jour. Optical Soc. Am. Served as ensign USNRF, 1918-19; lt. comdr. and comdr. USNR, 1941-45, capt., 1950; stationed at Naval Proving Ground, Dahlgren, Va., as exptl. lab. officer; civilian tech. dir. Joint Task Force One, atomic bomb tests, Bikini Atoll, 1946. Recipient award Spectroscopy Soc. Pitts., 1961; Frederic Ives medal Optical Soc. Am., 1963; Karl Taylor Compton medal Am. Inst. Physics, 1971. Mem. A.A.A.S. (v.p. sect. B 1964), Am. Phys. Soc., Optical Soc. Am. (pres. 1955-57), Am. Assn. Physics Tchrs., Phi Beta Kappa, Phi Kappa Phi, Sigma Xi, Gamma Alpha. Universalist. Clubs: Rotary, Ann Arbor Golf and Outing. Author: Experimental Spectroscopy, 1944, rev. edit., 1951, 63. Contbr. to tech. and sci. jours. Home: Ann Arbor, Mich. Died Dec. 6, 1978; buried Atkinson, N.H.

SAWYER, ROLAND DOUGLAS, clergyman, lecturer; b. Kensington, N.H., Jan. 8, 1874; s. of Stephen C. and Maria P. (Blake) S.; studied in common and high schs. and worked in shoe shop and on farm; continued studies at Lay Coll., Revere, Mass., and Boston U.; m. Mary L. Palmer, June 29, 1898; children—Ruth Elizabeth, Rachel Nathalie, Roland Darrow, Robert Palmer, Rosalind Blake, Ramona Jeanette. Asst. pastor S. Congl. Ch., Brockton, Mass., 1898-1900; pastor First Ch., Hanson, 1900-04, Ward Hill Ch., Haverhill, 1904-09, First Ch., Ware, since 1909. Instr. dept. Bible history and criticism, Lay Coll., 1900-03. Conducted crusade against profanity, 1902-07, and organized Anti-Profanity League. Del. Manchester (N.H.) Conv., to organize Populist Party, 1894; del. various polit. convs., N.H. and Mass., 1896-1904; represented Hearst movement in Dem. State convs. of Mass., 1904, 05, 06; chmn. com. on resolutions Independent League Conv., Boston, 1907; del. Independent League Nat. Conv., Chicago, 1908, and made nominating speech for Thomas L. Hisgen as candidate for President of U.S.; lecturer Socialist Party, 1908-12; socialist candidate for gov. (Mass.), 1912; returned to Dem. party, 1913, and mem. Mass. legislature, 1914-41 (holds record of longest continuous service in 300 year-old Mass. General Court). Delegate Mass. Constl. Conv., 1917-19; candidate for Congress, 1925; delegate Dem. Nat. Conv., 1924, 28. Mem. Patrons of Husbandry, I.O.O.F., L.O.O.M. Author several books; latest publ.: History of Kensington, N.H., 1943; Words of the Lord Jesus, 1963. Contbr. scholarly reviews of N.T. study. Home: Ware, Mass.*

SAWYERS, MOTT RANDOLPH, clergyman; b. Unionville, Ia., July 5, 1870; s. Sylvester Heartwell and Mary Flavia (Miller) S.; A.B., Parsons Coll., Fairfield, Ia., 1890, D.D., 1914; student Princeton, 1891; grad. Princeton Theol. Sem., 1895; grad. study Union Theol. Sem., 1898-99; Ph.D., Western Union Coll., Lemars, Ia., 1913; m. Rebecca Margaret Taylor, July 17, 1907; 1 dau., Ruth LaRue. Ordained ministry Presbyn. Ch., 1903; pastor Unionville and Moulton, Ia., 1895-96, Centerville, 1897; state sec. Ia. Anti-Saloon League, 1899-1902; pastor Mt. Ida Presbyn. Ch., Davenport, Ia., 1902-11; gen. sec. Y.M.C.A., Davenport, 1911-13; pastor Avondale Presbyn. Ch., Cincinnati, O., 1914-15; lecturer Redpath Lyceum Bur., 1910-17; in Y.M.C.A. service at various army posts 1917-19; also lecturer on United States Constitution; pastor Centerville, 1920-40, pastor emeritus May 1, 1940: interim pastor, Congl. Ch., Anoka, Minn., 1941, First Presbyn. Ch., Rochester, Minn., Sept. 1942-Aug. 1943. Mem. bd. dirs. Greater Mpls. Council of Chs. Mem. Iowa Nat. Guard 3 years; served with Y.M.C.A., Spanish-Am. War. Awarded testimonial of good citizenship "for more than 20 years of useful public service," 1940; recipient Minute Man medal Nat. Soc. S.A.R., 1958. Mem. Internat. Magna Charta Assn. (v.p. Ia.), S.A.R. (pres. Minnesota, nat. chaplain 1949-54; chmn. Minn. observance 175th anniversary of formation of the U.S. Constitution 1959-1963), mem. Centerville Association of Commerce (life); hon. mem. Chapparal Society, Poets and Authors. Republican. Club: Commercial (ex-pres.). Writer Pep Talks, syndicated weekly newspaper feature, and contbr. stories and verse to mags. Author: Famous Friends of God, 1933; The Shepherd Who Abided, 1937; The Chaplain Speaks, 1951. Author of ofcl. nat. S.A.R. hymn, adopted 1956. Home: Mpls. *

SAXE, THOMAS EDWARD, II, bus. exec.; b. Milw., Oct. 9, 1903; s. John Edward and Elizabeth (Crosswaite) S.; A.B., U. Minn., 1925; m. Helen Duff, Feb. 6, 1940 (dec. Apr. 1950); 1 son, Thomas Brock; m. 2d, Rosalind Saindon Axton, May 5, 1962. Founder, White Tower Mgmt. Corp. 1926, pres., 1926-70, chmn. bd. 1970-75; owner T.E.S. Realty Co., Wash.; dir. State Nat. Bank Conn. Pres. Saxe Found., Inc. Bd. dirs. St. Joseph's Hosp., Stamford, Conn. Diabetes Assn., Young Women's Towne House, Stamford Boys' Club, Stamford Mus.; trustee Stamford Day Nursery; endowment trustee Stamford Cath. Library, Inc. Mem. Soc. Am. Magicians, U.S. Navy League, Nat., N.Y. State restaurant assns., Am. Inst. Mgmt. (pres.'s council N.Y.C.), New Canaan Hort. Soc., Phi Alpha Delta. Decorated knight Sovereign Mil. Order of Malta; knight of St. Gregory the Great; Star of Solidarity (Italy). Roman Catholic. Clubs: Rotary (hon.), Nat. Exchange (hon.); Country of New Canaan, Sun and Surf, Sittin' Starin' N' Rockin' (founder, pres. 1950); (New Canaan); Skeeters. Circumnavigators (N.Y.C.); Midtown; University, Field (Sarasota, Fla.). Home: New Canaan, Conn. Died Dec. 20, 1975.

SAYERS, ROYD RAY, industrial medical consultant; born Crothersville, Indiana, October 25, 1885; s. Smith and Ida May (Lewis) S.; B.A., M.A., Ind. U., 1907; M.D., U. of Buffalo, 1914; m. Edna Linnen, Feb. 26, 1923; 1 dau., Joan. Professor electrochemistry, U. of Buffalo, 1911-13; med. dir., U.S. Public Health Service since 1913; served as public health officer on U.S. Coast Guard Cutter "Comanche," 1917; detailed U.S. Bureau of Mines as chief surgeon and chief of Health and Safety Branch, 1917-33; chief, Div. of Industrial Hygiene. Nat. Inst. of Health, 1933-40; dir. U.S. Bur. of Mines, 1940-47; med. dir. U.S.P.H.S., ret.; sr. supervisor occupational disease Baltimore City Health Dept. Chmn. med. adv. bd. United Mine Workers Am. Welfare and Retirement Fund; lectr. Inst. Indsl. Med. N.Y.U. Mem. Pres.'s Com. on Nat. Employ the Physically Handicapped Week. Mem. Nat. Conf. of Govtl. Indsl. Hygienists; professorial lecturer on indsl. hygiene, George Washington Univ.; mem. Advisory Com. on Industrial Hygiene, Internat. Labor Office, Geneva, Switzerland (mem. corr. com. indsl. hygiene); mem. Indsl. Hygiene Foundation of America, Inc.; mem. Com. on Commercial Policy, Dept. of State; mem. Interdepartmental Com. on Safety, and numerous other coms. In 1923, mem. delegation of U.S. to Pan-Pacific Science Congress in Australia, serving as chmn. sect. on hygiene among workers, particularly miners; visited mines of New Zealand, Australia, South Africa, and European countries; chmn. same sect. when Pan-Pacific Science Congress met in San Francisco, 1939; chmn. Am. delegation to represent U.S. at 8th Internat. Congress for Prevention of Industrial and Occupational Diseases (Frankfort-on-Main, Germany). Chairman medical advisory board, United Mine Workers of America Welfare and Retirement Fund. Mem. Am. Public Health Assn. (chmn. pneumoconiosis com.), A.M.A., Am. Inst. Mining and Metall. Engrs., Am. Soc. Heating and Ventilating Engrs., Am. Gas Assn. (mem. various coms.), Assn. of Mil. Surgeons of the U.S., A.A.A.S., Mining Assn. of Montana, Jos. A. Holmes Safety Assn. (pres.); Washington Biophysical Inst.; Am. Assn. of Indsl. Physicians and Surgeons (past pres.). Author: numerous publs. dealing with carbon monoxide, silicosis, high temperatures and humidities, health and safety in mines, toxic dusts and gases, etc. Home: Upper Marlboro, Md. *

SAYPOL, IRVING H., justice; b. N.Y.C., Sept. 3, 1905; s. Louis and Minnie (Michakin) S.; LL.B., Brooklyn Law Sch., 1927; m. Adele D. Kaplan, Sept. 29, 1925; children—Roger L., Ronald D., Barbara Joan (Mrs. Elliott (Blinderman). Admitted to N.Y. State bar, 1928; asst. corp. counsel, law dept., City of New York, 1929-34; pvt. law practice N.Y.C., 1934-45; chief asst. U.S. atty., So. Dist. N.Y., 1945-49, U.S. atty., So. Dist. of N.Y., 1949-51; justice Supreme Ct. State N.Y. 1952-77. Asso. counsel, com. on judiciary N.Y. State Constl. Conv., 1938. Mem. Assn. Bar City N.Y., Phi Delta Phi, Omicron Delta Kappa. Home: New York, N.Y. Died June 30, 1977.

SAYPOL, RONALD DIETZ, diversified holding co. exec.; b. N.Y.C., Nov. 12, 1929; s. Irving Howard and Adele (Kaplan) S.; B.A., Dickinson Coll., Carlisle, Pa., 1951; LL.B., Bklyn. Law Sch., 1955; m. Wendy Saypol; children—Cathy Lynn, Amy Elizabeth, Natasha. Demonstrator, salesman, adminstrv. v.p., v.p.

operations Lionel Corp., N.YC., 1951-62, pres., 1968-1977; also chief exec. officer; dir. marketing Ideal Toy Corp., N.Y.C, 1962-63; v.p., exec. v.p. Topper Corp., Elizabeth, N.J., 1963-68. Toy industry chmn. Fedn. Jewish Philanthropies, 1963-64; toy industry chmn. United Jewish Appeal, 1965; mem. President's Council, Brandeis U., 1965-1977; chmn. drive Boy Scouts Am., 1971. Mem. N.Y. State Bar Assn., Air Force Assn. (Iron Gate chpt.), Mashomack Fish and Game Preserve, Phi Epsilon Pi, Phi Delta Phi. Club: Wyandanch Sportsmen's (Smithtown, N.Y.). Died June 30, 1977.

SAYRE, FRANCIS BOWES, ambassador; b. South Bethlehem, Pa., Apr. 30, 1885; s. Robert Heysham and Martha Finley (Nevin) S.; A.B., Williams Coll., 1909; L.H.D., 1937; LL.B., Harvard, 1912, S.J.D., 1918; LL.D., Ursinus Coll., 1934, Rollins Coll., 1943, Bowdoin Coll., 1944, U. Rochester, 1949, Park Coll., 1950; LL.D. (honorary), St. Paul's University Tokyo, Japan, 1959; D.C.L., U. of South, 1938; Litt. D., Bucknell College, 1942; married Jessie Woodrow, daughter President Woodrow Wilson, November 25, 1913 (deceased January 15, 1933); children—Francis Bowes, Eleanor Axson, Woodrow Wilson; m. 2d, Elizabeth Evans Graves, June 28, 1937. Dep. asst. dist. atty. N.Y. County, N.Y., 1912-13; asst. to pres., also instr. in govt., Williams Coll., 1914-17; Thayer teaching fellow Harvard Law Sch., 1917-18, assistant professor Harvard University, 1919-24, prof., 1924-34 (on leave of absence 1923-25); dir. Harvard Inst. Criminal Law, 1929-34; lectr. U. So. Cal., summer 1923; adviser in foreign affairs Siamese govt., 1923-25; E.E. and M.P. from Siam, 1925; mem. representing Siam, Permanent Ct. of Arbitration, The Hague, 1923-34; trustee Mass. State Tng. Schs., 1932-33, state commr. correction, 1933; asst. sec. state, also chmn. exec. com. on comml. policy, U.S. govt., 1933-39; U.S. high commr. to Philippines, 1939-42 (escaped from Corregidor by submarine 1942); spl. asst. to sec. State, dep. dir. Fgn. Relief and Rehabilitation Operations, 1943; head UNRRA mission to 23 countries, 1945-46; diplomatic adviser UNRRA, 1944-47; U.S. rep. Trusteeship Council UN, as ambassador, 1947-52, pres. 1947-48; head council's mission to Western Samoa, 1947; mem. U.S. del. 2d, 2d spl., 3d sessions UN Gen. Assembly, 1947-48; personal rep. in Japan of presiding bishop of P.E. Ch. in Am., 1952-54. Decorated Grand Officer Order Orange-Nassau (Netherlands). Comdr. Order of Dannebrog, 1st class (Denmark), Grand Cross Royal Order Isabella la Católica (Spain), Grand Cross Order of Christ (Portugal), Comdr. Order St. Olav, 1st class (Norway), Grand Officer Legion of Honor (France); created Phya Kalyan Maitri by King of Siam, 1924; recipient Knight Grand Cross Crown of Siam, Grand Cross of White Elephant, Knight Grand Comdr. Chula Chom Klao (Siam), Royal Cypher medal (Ratanaphon), 1st class (from King of Thailand). Trustee Woodrow Wilson Found. Fellow Am. Acad. Arts and Scis.; mem. Japan-Am. Soc. Washington (pres. 1957-59), Phi Beta Kappa, Sigma Phi. Democrat. Episcopalian. Club: Cosmos (Washington). Author books on internat. law and adminstrn., 1919-39; Glad Adventure, (autobiography), 1957. Home: Washington, D.C. Died Mar. 29, 1972; interred Washington Nat. Cathedral, Washington, D.C.

SAYRE, MORTIMER FREEMAN, educator; b. Newark, N.J., July 14, 1885; s. Joseph M. and Ella G. (Browne) S.; M.E., Columbia, 1907, A.M., 1911; m. Grace S. McKinney, Sept. 25, 1912; children—Harrison S., Penelope C. (Mrs. Edward S. Setchko). Engaged in engineering work in New York, Pa., Ariz., 1907-14; instr. Union Coll., 1914-18, asst. prof., 1918-25, asso., prof. 1925-37, prof. applied mechanics, 1937-52, dir. extension, 1945-49, head dept. mech. engring., 1952-55, now emeritus prof.; director of Mechanical Technology, Incorporated; cons. engr. Alco Products Corp., 1940-63. Pres. Schenectady Bur. Municipal Research, 1931-35, 1939-47. Fellow A.S.M.E.; mem. Am. Inst. Mining Metall. and Petroleum Engrs., Am. Soc. Metals, Am. Soc. Engring. Edn., Am. Soc. Testing Materials, Am. Assn. U. Profs., Sigma Xi, Tau Beta Pi. Contbr. articles profl. publs. Home: Schenectady. *

SAYRE, THOMAS HENRY, lawyer, utilities exec.; b. Scottown, Ohio, Sept. 15, 1904; s. John Wilson and Frances (Marks) S.; LL.B., N.Y. U., 1942; postgrad. Harvard U., 1957; m. Margaret Edwards Lothrop, June 26, 1926. With Appalachian Power Co. and predecessor cos., 1922-36; admitted to N.Y. bar, 1942; practiced in N.Y.C., to 1977; with Am. Electric Power Service Corp., 1936-69, asst. chief counsel, 1954-67, v.p., chief counsel and sec., 1967-69; past sec. Appalachian Power Co., Beach Bottom Power Co., Inc., Captina Operating Co., Cardinal Operating Co., Central Appalachian Coal Co., Central Coal Co., Central Ohio Coal Co., Central Operating Co., Franklin Real Estate Co., Ind. Franklin Realty Inc., Ind. & Mich. Electric Co., Kanawha Valley Power Co., Ky. Power Co., Kingsport Power Co., Mich. Gas & Electric Co., Mich. Gas Exploration Co., Ohio Power Co., South Bend Mfg. Co., Twin Br. R.R. Co., W.Va. Power Co., Wheeling Electric Co.; past dir. Am. Electric Power Service Corp., Central Appalachian Coal Co., Central Ohio Coal Co., Franklin Real Estate Co., Ind. Franklin Realty, Inc., W.Va. Power Co. Mem. Am. Bar Assn., Pilgrims of U.S., Phi Delta Phi, Theta Sigma Lambda. Republican. Baptist. Club: Masons. Home: Beckley, W.Va. Died Oct. 18, 1979; buried Sunset Meml. Park, Beckley.

SCAMMON, RICHARD EVERINGHAM, anatomist; b. Kansas City, Mo., July 9, 1883; s. James and Laura (Everingham) S.; A.B., U. of Kan., 1904; A.M., 1906; Ph.D. in Medical Sciences, Harvard, 1909; LL.D., St. Thomas Aquinas Coll., 1933; m. Julia Simms, June 14, 1913; children—Richard Montgomery, Jean. Instr. zoölogy, U. of Kan., 1906-07; Austin teaching fellow, Harvard Med. Sch., 1907-09; instr. same, 1909-10; asst. prof. anatomy, U. of Kan., 1910-11; asst. prof. anatomy, 1911-13, asso. prof., 1913-14; prof., 1914-30, U. of Minn.; prof. anatomy and dean of Div. Biol. Sciences, U. of Chicago, 1930-31; dean of med. sciences, U. of Minn., 1931-35, distinguished service prof., grad. school since 1935; Benjamin Radeford Knox lecturer, U. of Cincinnati; Porter lecturer, U. of Kan., 1934; De Lamar lecturer, Johns Hopkins, 1935. Pres. Minn. Bd. of Examiners in the Basic Sciences, 1927-30; chmn. Minn. State Planning Board, 1934-41; chmn. Minn. Resources Commn. since 1939; mem. advisory board of Minn. Inst. Govt. Research. Mem. Am. Assn. Anatomists (v.p. 1928-30), Am. Statis, Assn., Am. Math. Soc., Am. Soc. Naturalists, Am. Acad. Pediatrics, Math. Assn. America, Soc. Exptl. Biology and Medicine, Minn. Acad Medicine, Am. Physiol. Soc., Sigma Xi, Nu Sigma Nu, Gamma Alpha, Alpha Omega Alpha; fellow and dir. Soc. for Research in Child Development; fellow A.A.A.S. Author: Normal Plates of Acanthias, 1911; A Summary of the Anatomy of the Child (in Abt's System of Pediatrics), 1923; Growth in the Fetal Period (with L. A. Calkins), 1929; Developmental Anatomy (in Morris' Human Anatomy) since 1922; also numerous papers on comparative embryology, and on the growth and physical development of children. Asso. editor Growth, Child Development. Actuary for establishment of Univ. of Minn. Ins. and Pension System. Home: Minneapolis, Minn. *

SCARBOROUGH, JOHN BARRET, publisher; b. Chgo., Aug. 10, 1891; s. Henry and Mary (Barret) S.; student Armour Acad., 1905-08, Lewis Inst., 1908-09; m. Frances Hale, Mar. 4, 1914 (dec. Sept. 1956); children—Frances (Mrs. Naylor, dec. Feb. 1973), Suzanne (Mrs. Robert S. Edwards, Jr.); m. 2d, Elizabeth Helton, Nov. 2, 1958. With 20th Century Machinery Co., Waukegan, Chgo., Milw., 1910-15; mgr. out-of-town dept., with spl. features div.; asst. mgr. classified sales force Chgo. Tribune, 1915-17; with Crowell Pub. Co. and Crowell-Collier Pub. Co., Chgo. and N.Y.C., 1917-51; advt. salesman The Am. Mag., 1917-20, western advt. mgr., 1920-26, nat. advt. mgr., N.Y.C., 1926-46, pub., 1946-51; v.p. and dir. Crowell-Collier Pub. Co., N.Y.C., 1946-51; pres. Family Pub. Corp., Chgo., pres., pub. Am. Family mag., 1951-54; pres., pub. Everywoman's Mag., Inc., 1955-76; v.p., dir. advt. and marketing Everywoman's Family Circle Mag., 1958-76; dir. Creative Printing Sales, Cuneo Pres, Inc. Mem. nat. adv. council Jr. Achievement; mem. Darien (Conn.) Library Rd. Clubs: Chicago Athletic Assn. (Chgo.); Rifle and Pistol, Wee Burn Country (Darien); Riomar Bay Yacht (Vero Beach, Fla.). Home: Vero Beach, Fla. Died July 5, 1976.

SCARBOROUGH, WILLIAM JOHN, govt. ofcl., educator; b. Lincoln, Neb., Feb. 15, 1913; s. Ray James and Carrie (Case) S.; student Carleton Coll., 1930-31; summer Winona (Minn.) State Tchrs. Coll., 1931, U. Minn., 1932; A.B., Hamline U., 1933, LL.D., 1951; A.M., Boston U., 1935, S.T.B., 1936, Ph.D., 1940, LL.D., 1963; L.H.D., McKendree Coll., 1963; LL.D., Baker U., 1972; m. Irene Parish, May 17, 1934; children—John Samuel, Katharine Elizabeth. Ordained to ministry Meth. Ch., deacon, 1935; elder, 1936; pastor Homecroft Meth. Ch., St. Paul, 1931-32, Grace Meth. Ch., St. Paul, 1932-33, Oaklands Meth. Ch., Methuen, Mass., 1934-35, Federated Ch., Norfolk, Mass., 1935-39; prof. philosophy and religion McKendree Coll., Lebanon, Ill., 1939-42, dean of men, 1941-42; prof. psychology and religion, dean of chapel Cornell Coll., Mt. Vernon, Iowa, 1942-43; dean coll., prof. philosophy and religion Morningside Coll., Sioux City, Iowa, 1943-46; prof. N.T. lit. Garrett Bibl. Inst., Evanston, Ill., summer 1946; pres. W.Va. Wesleyan Coll., Buckhannon, 1946-56, Baker U., Baldwin, Kans., 1956-66; program officer, region VII rep. (Kansas City) Higher Edn. Facilities, U.S. Office Edn., HEW, 1965-73, program officer for vets., cost constrn. program, 1973-76, also equal employment officer, 1971-76. Mem. commn. on colls. and univs. North Central Assn. Colls. and Secondary Schs., 1954-60, examiner and cons. North Central Assn.; pres. Kansas City Regional Council Higher Edn., 1962-65; chmn. edn. com. Greater Kansas City Fed. Exec. Bd., from 1966, recipient ann. citation, from 1968. Pres. W.Va. Council Chs. and Religious Edn., 1949-51; state chmn. U.S.O., 1948-49; chmn. Gov's. Com. on W.Va. Citizens Health Planning 1950-52; pres. W.Va. Found. Ind. Colls., 1954-56; mem. W.Va. com. for White House Conf. on Edn., 1956; mem. Kans. Conf. of Meth. Ch., from 1956; pres. Nat. Assn. Schs. and Colls. of Meth. Ch., 1965-66. Mem. Am. Soc. for Public Adminstrn., NEA (life), AAUP, Soc. Biblical Lit. and Exegesis, Nat. Bibl. Assn., Am. Philos. Soc., Kappa Phi Sigma. Club: Rotary. Author: A Life of Jesus, 1950. Editor: Is It Morning Yet, 1944. Home: Overland Park, Kans. Died Mar. 19, 1976; buried Woodlawn Cemetery, Winona, Minn.

SCARFF, JOHN EDWIN, neuro-surgeon; b. Bellefontaine, Ohio, Mar. 19, 1898; s. Edwin Curl and Margaret Gorton (Riddle) S.; student Ohio-Wesleyan U., Delaware, Ohio, 1916-18; B.S. Princeton, 1920; M.D., Johns Hopkins, 1924; m. Ellen Backland, Apr. 14, 1934; children—John Edwin, Timothy Backland. Attending neurosurgeon Neurol. Inst. N.Y.; cons. Columbia-Presbyn. Med. Center, N.Y.; prof. emeritus clin. neurosurgery Coll. Phys. & Surg., Columbia U. Served as lt. col. M.C., AUS, 1942-46; dep. sr. cons. neurosurgery ETO, 1942-45. Decorated Bronze Star. Diplomate Am. Bd. Neurol. Surgery. Fellow A.C.S.; mem. Am. Assn. Neurol. Surgeons, Soc. Neurol. Surgeons, Soc. Brit. Neurol. Surgeons, Am. Electroencephalographic Soc., AMA, N.Y. Acad. Medicine, N.Y. Neurol. Society Assn. Research in Nervous and Mental Diseases, Am. Neurol. Assn., Phi Delta Theta, Phi Beta Kappa, Alpha Omega Alpha, Key and Seal. Progressive Republican. Presbyn. Clubs: University (N.Y.C.); Sleepy Hollow Country; Athenaeum (London, Eng.), Masons, St. John of Jerusalem (comdr. asso.). Author: Fifty Years of Neuro-Surgery, 1955; also numerous papers, chpts. in books. Co-author sect. on Peripheral Nerves, Military Surgical Manual, Nat. Research Council, 1942. Home: New York, N.Y. Died Aug. 8, 1978.

SCHAEFFER, ASA ARTHUR, zoölogist; b. Kunkletown, Pa., May 9, 1883; s. Peter P. and Lucinda (Engler) S.; Polytechnic Inst., Gilbert, Pa.; A.B., Franklin and Marshall Coll., 1904; Ph.D., Johns Hopkins, 1909; m. Mary Elizabeth Kresge, of Gilbert, Pa., June 13, 1908; children—Olive Kresge, Mary Elizabeth, Asa Arthur. Prof. zoöology, U. of Tenn., 1909-23, Clark U., 1923-24, U. of Kansas, 1924—. On instructional staff Biol. Lab. of Brooklyn Inst. Arts and Sciences, Cold Spring Harbor, L.I., summers 1912-18, on staff of investigators, 1925—; investigator, dept. marine biology, Carnegie Instn. of Washington. Fellow A.A.A.S.; mem. Am. Soc. Zoölogists, Am. Assn. Univ. Profs., Institut de Sociologie Solvay (Brussels), Am. Genetic Assn., Pa. German Soc., Phi Sigma, Am. Naturalists. Author: Ameboid Movement, 1920; The Taxonomy of the Amebas with Descriptions of 39 New Marine and Fresh-Water Species, 1925. Has specialized in classification of fresh-water and marine amebas; discovered the principle that all motile organisms, including man, are compelled to move in spiral paths, when the guiding senses are not functioning. Home: Lawrence, Kansas. *

SCHAEFFER, JOHN MESSMER, investment management exec.; b. Newark, Aug. 20, 1905; s. Harry and Aurelia (Messmer) S.; B.S., U. Pa., 1927; m. Alice Jane Pollock, June 1, 1929; 1 son, Alan Pollock. With Nat. City Co., 1927-28; head research J. G. White & Co., 1928-34; asst. investment mgr. Firemen's Ins. Co., Newark, 1934-37; joined Keswick Corp., N.Y.C., 1937, pres., 1942-80; sr. v.p. U.S. & Fgn. Securities Corp., to 1970, dir., to 1980; dir., mem. exec. com. Vertol Aircraft Corp., Morton, Pa., 1956-60. Vice chmn. nat. citizens com. Navy Relief Soc., 1941-42; chmn. bd. trustees First Congregational Ch., Old Lyme, Conn. Mem. Assn. Closed-End Investment Cos. (past chmn.; dir.) Nat. Assn. Investment Cos. (exec. com. 1951-54, bd. govs. 1957-60), Delta Upsilon. Episcopalian. Clubs: Riverside (Conn.) Yacht; Woodway Country (Springdale, Conn.); Pinnacle (N.Y.C.). Home: Old Lyme, Conn. Died June 3, 1980.

SCHAEFFER, PAUL NICHOLAS, lawyer; b. Reading, Pa., Aug. 11, 1884; s. D. Nicholas and Katherine (Grim) S.; A.B., Franklin and Marshall Coll., Lancaster, Pa., 1905; LL.D., 1937; LL.B., U. of Pa., 1914; LL.D., Albright Coll., 1933; m. Helen M. Burkey, Sept. 20, 1918. Admitted to Pa. bar 1914, and began practice at Reading; specialized in criminal law with spl. reference to probation and restoration of criminals; apptd. president judge Court of Common Pleas of Berks County, 1924, elected to same office, 1925, re-elected, 1935. Dir. Pa. Com. on Penal Affairs; mem. Welfare Commn. of Pa. since 1924; mem. Governor's Com. on Probation in Pa., 1934, on Pub. Assistance and Relief, 1936; pres. Pa. Conf. on Social Work, 1936; assigned by Supreme Court of Pa., to take charge of proceedings of Grand Jury Investigation in Dauphin County, Pa., 1938; dir. Nat. Probation Assn., 1943; mem. Pa. State Bd. Law Examiners, since 1946. Mem. Chi Phi, Pi Gamma Mu. Mem. Reformed Ch. Democrat. Mason. Club: Wyomissing. Home: Reading, Penn. *

SCHAFER, EDWIN GEORGE (SHAF'ER), agronomist; b. Jewell, Kan., Feb. 18, 1884; s. John Christian and Mary Louisa (Klink) S.; B.S., Kansas State Coll., 1907; M.S., U. of Ill.; 1910; m. Ella Frances Miles, Aug. 16, 1912; children—George Miles, Judith Evelyn (Mrs. Louis Chevalley), John Francis. Asst. in agronomy, Kan. State Coll., 1907-09, instr. in farm crops, 1910-13; prof. farm crops, State Coll. of Wash. and agronomist Wash. Agrl. Expt. Sta., 1913-51; head of dept. farm crops same, 1917-28. of dept. agronomy (farm crops and soils), 1928-48; asst. dean Coll. of Agr. 1947-51, emeritus prof. of agronomy 1951—; prof. c agr. Idaho State Coll., 1952-1954. Fellow A.A.A.S., Am. Soc. Agronomy (pres. Pacific sect. 1925-26); mem. Am. Assn. U. Profs., Alpha Zeta, Phi Kappa Phi, Alpha Gamma Rho. Conglist. Club: Kiwanis. Author: A Laboratory Manual of Agriculture (with L. E. Call), 1912; also various bulls. dealing with farm crops. Home: Pullman, Wash. Retired. *

SCHAFER, GEORGE EZRA, air force officer, physician; b. Cin., Aug. 9, 1922; s. Donald W. and Neoma (Pontius) S.; M.D., U. Cin., 1946. Intern St. Joseph Hosp., Ft. Wayne, Ind., 1946-47; commd. U.S. Army, 1947, advanced through grades to lt. gen., 1970; trainee Sch. Aviation Medicine, Randolph AFB, Tex., 1947; trainee preventive medicine and pub. health Nat. Naval Med. Center, Bethesda, Md., 1956; hosp. comdr. 7330th Air Force Hosp., Furstenfeldbruck, Germany, USAF Hosp., Davis-Monthan AFB, Ariz., Air War Coll., Maxwell AFB, Ala., 1962; vice comdr. aerospace med. div. Brooks AFB, Tex., 1965-67; dep. surgeon Mil. Airlift Command, 1970-71; comdr. Sch. Aerospace Medicine, 1967-69; surgeon 7th Air Force, Vietnam, 1969-70; comdr. aerospace med. div. Brooks AFB, Tex., 1971-75; surgeon gen. U.S. Air Force, Washington, from 1975. Diplomate Am. Bd. Preventive Medicine. Mem. A.M.A., Aerospace Med. Assn. (pres. 1974), Am. Coll. Preventive Medicine, Assn. Air Force Flight Surgeons (past pres.), Assn. Mil. Surgeons U.S. (pres.). Home: Washington, D.C. Deceased.

SCHAIRER, OTTO SORG, v.p. Radio Corp. of America; b. Saline, Mich., Oct. 7, 1879; s. George Edward and Sophia (Sorg) S.; A.B U of Mich., 1901, B.S. in E.E., 1902, Doctor of Engineering (honorary), 1942; admitted to Pennsylvania bar, 1912; m. Elizabeth Blanche Swift, June 28, 1905; children—George Swift, Robert Sorg, Julia Elizabeth. Engr. apprentice, Westinghouse Electric & Mfg. Co., 1902-03, with patent dept., 1903-19, dir. patent development, 1919-26, mgr. patent dept., 1926-29; dir. patent development Radio Corp. America, 1929-30, v.p. in charge patent dept., 1930-41; v.p. in charge RCA Labs., 1941-45, staff vice president, 1945, retired, 1946; consultant since 1945 Mem. Am. Institute E.E., Institute of Radio Engineers, American Bar Assn., American Patent Law Association, New York Patent Law Assn., A.A.A.S., Photog. Soc. of Am., Royal Photog. Soc. Gt. Britain. Republican. Presbyterian. Clubs: Miniature Camera (New York); Nassau, Springdale Golf, Old Guard, Highland Park, Fla., (luke (Lake Wales, Fla.). Home: Hightstown, N.J. Died Mar. 12, 1976.

SCHAPIRO, ISRAEL (SHA-PI'RO), librarian; b. Sejny, Russia, Dec. 5, 1882; s. Tobiah Petachiah and Leah (Galanti) S.; student univs. of Berlin and Strassburg, Ph. D., Strassburg, 1906; also at Hochschule für Wissenschaft des Judentums and Veitel-Heine-Ephraim'sche Beth-Hamidrasch, Berlin; m. Miriam Kirschberg, July 6, 1917 (died August 1942). Professor of Jewish history and Hebrew literature, Bible and Talmud, Lehrer-Seminar, Jerusalem, Palestine, 1907-10; co-editor Harderor (Hebrew weekly), New York City, 1911; chief division of Semitic literature, Library of Congress, Washington, 1913-44, retired; prof. Semitic langs, and lit., George Washington U., 1916-27. Mem. Am. Library Assn., Am. Oriental Soc., Soc. Bibl. Lit. and Exegesis, Am. Acad. for Jewish Research. Author: Die haggadischen Elemente im erzählenden Teil des Korans (Leipzig), 1907; Leviticus XXVII im Lichte des Talmuds, 1909; Bibliography of Hebrew Translations of English Works, 1929; Bibliography of Hebrew Translations of German Works, 1934; Schiller und Goethe im Hebräischen, 1935; A Bibliography of Supercommentaries on Rashi's Pentateuch-commentary, 1940. Editor Maimuni's Mischnah-Kommentar zum Traktat Arachin (Jerusalem), 1910; Meshal Ha-Kadmoni, 1925; Pitgamim shel Hakhamim, 1927. Translator: Bikashtikha (Sippur Biography), Tel. Aviv, 1932. Contbr. to numerous Hebrew, Yiddish, and German periodicals. Home: Los Angeles, Calif. *

SCHARY, DORE, motion picture producer, playwright, city ofcl.; b. Newark, Aug. 31, 1905; s. Herman Hugo and Belle (Drachler) S.; ed. Central High Sch., Newark; L.H.D. (hon.), Coll. Pacific, 1951, Wilberforce U.; D.F.A. (hon.), Lincoln Coll., 1960; m. Miriam Svet, Mar. 5, 1932; children—Jill, Joy, Jeb. Dir. Little Theatre; actor, playwright, publicity and newspaper work, 1926-32; with Columbia Paramount, Warner Bros. as writer of 35 screen plays, 1933-37; writer Metro-Goldwyn-Mayer studios, 1938-41, exec. producer, 1941-46; producer David O. Selznick, 1943-46; exec. v.p. in charge prodn. RKO Studios, 1947-48; exec. v.p. in charge prodn. and studio operations M-G-M Studios, Culver City, Calif., 1948-56, became head ind. producer, 1956-80; past chief exec. officer Theatrevision, Inc., also pres. Schary Prodns. Commr. cultural affairs, City N.Y Mem. Citizens Crusade Against Poverty, Pres.'s Com.-Nat. Citizens Commn., Nat. Adv. Com. Farm Labor, Nat. Com. Immigration. Fellow, trustee Eleanor Roosevelt Meml. Found. Recipient Acad. award for story Boys Town; Antoinette Perry award for Sunrise at Campobello, 1958. Mem. Author's League, Screen Writers Guild, Producers Guild, Acad. Motion Picture Arts and Scis., Dramatists Guild Fund (pres.), Anti-Defamation League (nat. chmn. 1963-69, now hon. chmn.). Democrat. Mem. B'nai B'rith. Author: Boys Town; Edison the Man; Young Tom Edison; Case History of A Movie; For Special Occasions, 1962; (with Sinclair Lewis) Storm in the West, 1963; (autobiography) Heyday, 1979. Exec. producer films Joe Smith, American, Journey for Margaret, Bataan, Lassie Come Home, Lost Angel. Producer films Spiral Staircase, I'll Be Seeing You, The Farmer's Daughter, The Bachelor and the Bobby-Soxer, Till the End of Time, Battleground, The Next Voice You Hear, Go For Broke, Plymouth Adventure, Dream Wife, Take the High Ground, Bad Day at Black Rock, The Last Hunt, Designing Woman; writer, co-producer Sunrise at Campobello, 1958; co-producer, dir. A Majority of One, 1959; writer, dir., co-producer The Highest Tree, 1959, The Devils Advocate, 1960; writer, producer motion picture Sunrise at Campobello, 1960; co-producer, dir. The Unsinkable Molly Brown, 1960, Something About a Soldier, 1962, The Zulu and The Zayda, 1965; producer, dir., writer motion picture Act One, 1963; producer, dir., playwright One By One, 1964; playwright Brightower, 1970; producer, co-playwright Herzl, 1976. Home: New York, N.Y. Died July 7, 1980.

SCHARY, SAUL, artist; b. Newark, Nov. 3, 1904; s. Rudolph and Florence (Schrier) S.; grad. Newark High Sch.; student Fawcet Art Sch., Pa. Acad. Fine Arts, Art Students League, also schs. in Paris; m. Hope Christie Skillman, Dec. 15, 1934. One-man shows at Daniel Gallery, N.Y.C., 1930; Milch Gallery, N.Y.C., 1939; Perls Gallery, N.Y.C., 1940, 1941, 1943; Joseph Luyber Gallery, N.Y.C., 1947; Asso. Am. Artists, Galleries, Los Angeles, F.A.R. Gallery; exhibited Chgo. Art Inst., Pa. Acad. Fine Arts, Whitney Museum, Carnegie Inst., Cal. Palace of Legion of Honor, M.H.D. Young Meml. Museum, others. Painting in permanent collections at Columbus Museum, Pa. Acad. Fine Arts, numerous pvt. collections. Fellow Royal Soc. Arts (London); charter mem. Artists Equity. Author: Tendencies in American Art, 1936. Paintings reproduced Scribner's, Parnassus, Art Digest, N.Y. Times, Cashiers D'Art, others. Address: New York, N.Y., also New Milford, Conn. Died May 30, 1978; buried New Milford.

SCHAUER, BENJAMIN REY, judge; b. Santa Maria, Calif., May 9, 1891; s. Samuel Benjamin and Eva Emaroy (Hayes) S.; A.B., Occidental Coll., 1912, LL.D., 1948; J.D., Southwestern U. Coll. Law, 1916, LL.D., 1937; m. Eva E. Summers, Oct 21, 1915 (dec. Jan. 1969); 1 son, Richard; m. 2d, Jean M. Dewsbury, Mar. 16, 1970. Admitted to Calif. bar, 1913; pvt. practice, Los Angeles, 1913-27; judge Superior Ct. Los Angeles County, 1927-41, assigned appellate div., 1935-41, presiding judge Superior Ct., 1941; apptd. presiding justice Dist. Ct. of Appeal of Calif., 2d Dist., Div. 3, 1941, elected, 1942, apptd. asso. justice Supreme Ct. Calif., 1942, elected, 44, 46, 58, ret. Past bd. dirs. Council Promotion Boys' Welfare. Commd. lt. comdr. USNR, 1932, comdr., 1945; served as spl. expert in nav. U.S. Shipping Bd., World War I; called to active duty with USNR, 1940; participated in conf. of joint army and navy selective service com. on Selective Service Act and Regulations; assigned liaison officer to Calif. state staff, and participated in setting up system in Calif., 1940; naval aide to gov. and gen. liaison officer to Calif. state staff for 11th Naval Dist., 1941-45. Recipient Commendation medal Sec. Navy. Mem. Am. Bar Assn., Naval Order U.S., So. Calif. Yachting Assn. (staff commodore), Native Sons of Golden West, SAR, Nat. Sojourners, Alpha Tau Omega, Phi Delta Phi. Clubs: Masons; Aviation Country (dir.); Lawyers (San Francisco); Calif. Yacht; Commonwealth of Calif.; Quiet Birdmen. Co-editor: Legal Secretary's Handbook, 1940. Home: San Francisco, Calif. Died Mar. 5, 1977.

SCHAUER, FRED HAYES (SHOUE'R), lawyer; b. Washington County, Kan., July 29, 1882; s. Samuel Benjamin and Eva (Hayes) S.; prep. edn., high schs., Santa Maria and Santa Barbara, Calif.; A.B., Occidental Coll., Los Angeles, Calif., 1903; student George Washington Law Sch., 1903-05, Stanford U. Law Sch., 1905; m. Bessie Turner, Mar. 9, 1909; 1 dau., Mary Margaret Stewart. Admitted to Calif. bar, 1906, practiced since at Santa Barbara; deputy district attorney, 1911-18; member of the firm of Schauer, Ryon and McIntyre of the firm of Schauer, Ryon and McIntyre and predecessor firms, 1922—; chmn. bd. First Fed. Savs. and Loan Assn., 1953-58, president 1942-53; director Credit Bureau of Santa Barbara, 1934-36, 1940-42. Chairman of Appeal Board No. 20, Selective Service, 1940-45; chairman Santa Barbara Veterans Service Committee Chmn, Santa Barbara County Rep. Com., 1922-31; Rep. presdtl. elector, Calif., 1928; sec. Southern Counties Rep. Central Com., 1929-30; alternate Rep. Nat. Conv., 1936. Trustee Occidental Coll., 1910-53, hon. 1953; trustee San Francisco Theol. Sem., 1940-48. Mem. Am. Bar Assn. (chmn. com. probate and trust literature, 1944-45), State Bar of Calif. (chairman administrative com.), Santa Barbara Museum Natural Hist. (pres. 1947-51, hon pres. since 1951), Santa Barbara Chamber Commerce (pres. 1919 Santa Barbara Hist. Soc. (v.p.), Calif. Hist. Assn., Pacific Southwest Acad. (affiliate Am. Acad. Social and Polit. Science), Calif. Soc. S.R. (director 1932-36; v.p. 1935-36), Am. Acad. Polit. and Social Sci., Santa Barbara Found., Alpha Tau Omega. Presbyn.; pres. Corporate Presbytery of Santa Barbara, 1934-55. K.P. Clubs: University (pres. 1940), Rotary, Commonwealth, Channel City. Home: Santa Barbara, Calif. *

SCHENCK, HARRY PAUL, otolaryngologist; b. Phila., Jan. 6, 1894; s. James Buchanan and Savilla Ettinger (Fries) S.; B.S., Haverford Coll., 1918; M.D., U. Pa., 1923; m. Edna Manvillier Leinbach, Dec. 1924. Staff U. Pa. Hosp., 1923-25, from 1938; curator Mutter Mus., Coll. Physicians of Phila., 1925-37; staff U. Pa., 1927-37, Evans Inst., 1932-59, head dept. otolaryngology U. Pa., 1938-59, prof. otolaryngology grad. sch. medicine, 1939-59, prof. emeritus, from 1959; asso. otolaryngologist Lankenau Hosp., Phila., 1949-59; research cons. New York E E Infirmary, 1956-66. Cons. in otolaryngology VA. Trustee research fund Central Bur. Research. Served as pvt. M.C., AEF, World War I; capt. M.C., USNR, World War II. Recipient Casselberry award Am. Laryngol. Assn., 1929; Newcomb award Am. Laryngol. Assn., 1959. Diplomate Am. Bd. Otolaryngol. (bd. dirs.). Fellow Coll. Physicians Phila., A.C.S. (bd. govs. 1956-66); mem. AMA, Am. (pres. 1967-58), Phila. (past pres.) laryngol. assns., Phila. Allergy Soc. (past pres), N.Y. Acad. Scis., Am. Otol. Soc., Am. Acad. Allergy, Coll. Allergists, Am. Laryngol. Rhinol. and Otol. Assn., Am. Acad. Ophthalmology and Otolaryngology, Assn. Mil. Surgeons U.S., Soc. Med. Cons. to Armed Forces. Republican. Lutheran. Clubs: University, Phila. Country, Philobiblon, Contemporary, Union League (Phila.). Editor-in-chief Cyclopedia of Diseases of the Ear, Nose and throat; contbr. articles to profl. jours. Home: Wynnewood, Pa. Deceased.

SCHEUER, SIMON HAAS, investor; b. N.Y.C., Oct. 7, 1891; s. Jonas and Olga (Haas) S.; B.A., Columbia, 1913; m. Helen Rose, Oct. 25, 1916; children—Richard J., James H., Walter, Steven H., Amy (Mrs. Saul Z. Cohen). Chmn. bd., dir. Ohio River Co., 1954-61; company merged with Eastern Gas and Fuel Assocs., Boston, 1961, trustee, mem. exec. com. Home: New York, N.Y. Deceased.

SCHIFF, LAWRENCE FRED, psychiat. hosp. adminstr.; b. Bronx, N.Y., June 21, 1937; s. Milton and Lillian (Fleischman) S.; B.B.A., CCNY, 1959; M.S., Harvard, 1962, Ph.D., 1964; m. Marcia Mandelbaum, June 14, 1959; children—Sarah, Alexandra. Asst. prof. sociology Brown U., Providence, 1964-65; psychologist Boston State Hosp., 1965-72; supt. Westboro (Mass.) State Hosp., 1973-76; lectr. psychology Harvard Med. Sch., 1973-76. Pres. bd. dirs. Freeport Inc., Newton, Mass., 1974-75. Home: West Newton, Mass. Died Oct. 7, 1976.

SCHIFF, ROBERT WILLIAM, shoe mfr.; born Leizevo, Lithuania, July 4, 1886; s. Chaim Hirsh and Ethel (Schleszinger) S.; ed. Talmudic Coll., Tolsai, Lithuania, 1902-05; m. Rebacca Lurie, 1912 (died 1927); children—Saralyn L. (Mrs. Jos. S. Blatt) (dec.), Mrs. Fredi Levin, Herbert H., Mildred (Mrs. Herbert Lee); m. 2d, Mrs. Ann Rose Neff. Oct. 21, 1930; step-daughter, Margy Neff (Mrs. Arnold Newman). Came to United States, 1905; naturalized citizen, 1919. Began as clerk in shoe store, 1911, mgr. shoe dept., 1912; opened store with partner, at Marion, O., 1913; sold interest in chain of 12 stores to partner, 1919; organizer, 1920, pres., treas. Shoe Corp. Am., 1920-65, chmn., 1965, dir. Dir. Am. Joint Distbn. Com., Inc.; trade and industry chmn. United Jewish Appeal. Hebrew religion. Mason. Club: Lions. Home: Columbus. *

SCHILD, ALFRED, physicist, educator; b. Istanbul, Turkey, Sept. 7, 1921; s. Ignaz and Fanny (Mandel) S.; student Univ. Coll., London, Eng., 1938-40; B.A., U. Toronto, 1943; M.A. (fellow), 1944, Ph.D. (fellow), 1946; m. Winnifred Zara Beames, Aug. 7, 1943; children—Carol Helen Marguerite, Frances Kathleen, John David. Came to U.S., 1946, naturalized, 1956. Instr., Carnegie Inst. Tech., 1946-47, Frank B. Jewett fellow, 1947-48, asst. prof., 1947-48, 49-51, asso. prof., 1951-56; on leave as Frank B. Jewett fellow Inst. Advanced Study, Princeton, 1947-48; asst. prof. U. Toronto, 1948-49; cons. Gulf Research & Devel. Co., 1953-56; adv. mathematician Westinghouse Research labs., 1956-57; prof. U. Tex., 1957-77, Ashbel Smith prof. physics, 1963-77, dir. Center for Relativity Theory, 1963-72; vis. prof. King's Coll., U. London, 1960-61, Dublin Inst. Advanced Studies, Ireland, 1961, Nordisk Inst. Teoretisk Atomfysik, Copenhagen, Denmark, 1965-66, 70-71, U. Sydney (Australia), 1965, Collège de France, Paris, 1973, U. Würzburg, Germany, 1975; lectr. Internat. Sch. Physics Enrico Fermi, Italy, 1961, Am. Math. Soc. Summer Seminar, Cornell U., 1965; vis. sr. fellow Cambridge U., 1970; vis. scientist U. Warsaw, 1974, Oxford U., 1974; vis. distinguished scientist Argonne Nat. Lab., 1977. Mem. organizing com. Tex. Symposia on Relativistic Astrophysics, from 1963, Am. Math. Soc. Summer Seminar, Ithaca, 1965; mem. Internat. Com. on Gen. Relativity and Gravitation, Bern, Switzerland, 1965-74. NSF sr. postdoctoral fellow, 1965-66. Fellow Am. Phys. Soc.; mem. Am. Math. Soc. (mem. com. applied math. 1963-65, chmn. 1964), Am. Assn. Physics Tchrs., Am. Astron. Soc., Internat. Soc. for Gen. Relativity and

Gravitation (exec. com.), A.A.A.S., Assn. Mems. Inst. for Advanced Study, A.A.U.P. Author: (with J.L. Synge), Tensor Calculus, 1949; Rachunek Tensorowy, 1964; Lectures on Relativity Theory, 1967; also chpts. to books. Mem. editorial bd. Jour. Math. and Mechanics, 1964-66, Jour. Math. Physics, 1965-68, Jour. General Relativity and Gravitition, from 1969. Contbr. numerous articles and revs. to profl. publs. Translator The Mission of the Vega (Friedrich Dürrenmatt) for CBS-TV, 1963. Holder patents on combustion process for prodn. of oil. Home: Austin, Tex. Died May 24, 1977; buried Austin.

SCHILLER, A. ARTHUR, ret. educator; b. San Francisco, Sept. 7, 1902; s. George Marcus and Bertha (Kohn) S.; A.B., U. Calif., 1924, M.A., 1926, J.D., 1926; fellow Columbia U., 1926-28, J.D., 1932; fellow Social Sci. Research Council, 1929-30; student U. Munich, 1929; fellow Guggenheim Found., 1949, 56, 63; Dr. iuris honoris causa, U. Erlangen (Germany), 1950; m. Irma H. Coblentz, Aug. 22, 1926 (dec. 1946); children—Donald Coblentz, Jerome Paul; m. 2d, Erna Kaske, Jan. 23, 1947. Admitted to Cal. bar, 1926; lectr. Columbia U. Law Sch., 1929, asst. prof. law, 1930-37, asso. prof. law, 1937-49, prof. law, 1949-71, emeritus, 1971-77, also dir. African Law Center, 1965-71; guest lectr. U. Indonesia, U. Graz, Austria, U. Erlangen (Germany), 1949; exchange prof. Free U. Berlin, 1953, Fulbright prof. U. Aberdeen, Scotland, 1957; U.S. observer 1st Internat. Congress Africanists, Ghana, 1962. Research asst. N.Y. State Law Revision Commn., 1935; atty., staff asst. gen. counsel Treas. Dept., 1938; legal counsel U.N. Mission, Eritrea, 1951-52, Inst. Internat. Legal Studies, U. Istanbul, 1955; Survey of African Law, travel-study grant Ford Found., 1959, 63; guest lectr. U. Cape Town, 1968; mem. Inst. for Advanced Study, Princeton, 1973. Fellow Am. Soc. Legal History; mem. Soc. Internat. d. Droits de l'Antiq., Soc. Ital. Storia d. Diritto. Internat. Assn. Papyrologists, Riccobono Seminar Roman Law (Wash.), Ancient Civilization Group, AAUP, N.Y. Oriental Club. Indonesian Acad. Arts and Scis., Accademia Naz. dei Lincei (Italy). Author or co-author books relating to field; latest publ.: Cases in the Law of Agency (with E.R. Keedy), 1948; translator and editor B. ter Haar's Adat Law in Indonesia (with E.A. Hoebel), 1948; The Formation of Federal Indonesia, 1945-49, 1955; Apokrimata, Decisions of Septimius Severus on Legal Matters (with W.L. Westermann), 1954; Syllabus on African Law, 1961; Roman Law, 1967; Military Law, 1968; An American Experience in Roman Law, 1971. Home: Oneonta, N.Y. Died July 10, 1977.

SCHILLING, EUGENE WASHBURN, engr., coll. dean; b. Whatcheer, Iowa, Dec. 23, 1897; s. Francis R. and Mary (Washburn) S.; student U. S.D., 1915-18; B.S. in E.E., U. Ill., 1919; M.S. in E.E., Iowa State U., 1930, Ph.D., 1933, E.E., 1936; m. Grace Margaret Hoyt, Oct. 12, 1927; children—Robert Eugene, Donald Hoyt. Switchboard dept. Western Electric Co., Chgo., Ill., 1917; test dept. Gen. Electric Co., Schenectady, 1918-19, tech. corr. in dept. elec. engring., 1919-20; elec. engr. Goodrich Rubber Co., Akron, Ohio, 1920; instr. elec. engring. Iowa State Coll., 1920-23, 1928-31; pvt. practice E. W. Schilling & Co., Brandon, S.D., 1923-28; asst. prof. elec. engring. Mich. Coll. Mining and Tech., 1931-34, asso. prof., 1934-38, research engr. summers, 1934-38; prof. and head dept. elec. engring. Mont. State U., Bozeman, 1938-42, acting dean engring., prof. and head dept. elec. engring., 1942-43, prof. and head elec. engrs., 1943-60, dean engring., dir. engr. expt. sta., 1943-63, prof. elec. engring., to 1968, dir. Army Specialized Tng. Program, 1943; instl. rep. engring. sci. mgmt. war tng., 1942-43. Trustee, Rocky Mountain Coll. Fellow IEEE (chmn. Mont. sect. 1940-42, sec. sects. com. 1942, v.p. Northwest dist. 1942-44); mem. Engrs. Council profl. devel. (mem. accrediting com. 1946-47), Am. Soc. Engring. Edn., Mont. Acad. Sci., Mont. Soc. Engrs., Sigma Xi, Tau Beta Pi, Eta Kappa Nu, Phi Kappa Phi, Lambda Chi Alpha. Presbyterian. Author: Illumination Engineering (textbook), 1940; Theory and Applications of Electrical Engineering, 1951; Electrical Engineering, 1958. Contbr. to tech. pubs. Home: Bozeman, Mont. Died Aug. 31, 1977; interred Bellevue, Wash.

SCHINDLER, JAMES SCHWARTZ, educator; b. Hillsboro, Ill., Sept. 11, 1917; s. Anthony and Caroline (Schwartz) S.; B.S., U. Ill., 1939; M.A., U. Wash., 1941; M.B.A., U. Mich., 1942, Ph.D., 1955; Econ.D. (hon.), Yonsei U., Seoul, Korea, 1962; m. Ailcy Josephine Bullington, July 31, 1945; children—James Anthony, Mary Ann, Steven Joseph. Teaching fellow U. Wash., 1939-41; teaching fellow U. Mich., 1941-42, instr., 1946-48, vis. lectr., 1955-56; asst. prof. U. Buffalo, 1948-49; prof. accounting Washington U., St. Louis, 1949-63, chief of party for univ.-State Dept. project, Seoul, 1960-62; prof. accounting State U. N.Y. at Buffalo, 1963-77, chmn. dept. financial accounting, 1963-66, 68-70, dean Sch. Bus. Adminstrn., 1964-68, asso. dean, 1969-71, chmn. undergrad. program, 1974-77. Served to lt. USNR, 1942-46. C.P.A., Wash. Mem. Am. Inst. C.P.A.'s, Am. Accounting Assn. (v.p. 1958), Nat. Assn. Accountants, Am. Finance Assn., Inst. Internal Auditors, N.Y. State Soc. C.P.A.'s, Am. Econ. Assn., Beta Gamma Sigma, Beta Alpha Psi, Pi Mu Epsilon, Omicron Delta Epsilon. Democrat. Roman Catholic. Author: Quasi-Reorganization, 1958; (with Mason and Davidson) Fundamentals of Accounting, 1959, 5th edit. (with Davidson and Weil), 1975; (with Davidson, Stickney and Weil) Financial Accounting, 1975; (with others) Accounting: The Language of Business, 1975, 76. Contbg. editor Accountants' Handbook, 1956, rev., 1970. Contbr. articles to profl. jours. Home: Eggertsville, N.Y. Died Dec. 4, 1977.

SCHIPPERS, THOMAS, conductor; b. Kalamazoo, Mar. 9, 1930; s. Peter and Agnes (Nanninga) S.; student Curtis Inst., Phila., 1944-45, Juilliard Sch. Music, 1945-46, Yale, 1946; m. Elaine Lane Phipps, April 1965 (dec. 1973). Piano debut in concert, Kalamazoo, 1936; appeared choir, organ, piano concerts, midwestern cities, also weekly radio program, Kalamazoo, 1938-44; organist St. Luke's Episcopal Ch., 1941; chosen nat. contest to conduct Phila. Orch. in Acad. Music, 1947; coach-pianist Met. Opera, 1947; profl. debut as condr. Lemonade Opera Co., N.Y.C., 1948; toured U.S. as piano recitalist; condr. The Consul, N.Y.C., 1949, Europe, 1949-50; appeared in concert, Europe, 1949-50; condr. music soundtrack of film The Medium, Italy; resident condr. N.Y.C. Opera Co., 1951-54; condr. Met. Opera Co., N.Y.C., from 1955; music dir. Cin. Symphony, to 1977; Distinguished prof. music, mem. faculty Coll. Conservatory of Music U. Cin., 1972-77; artistic dir. Orch. of Santa Cecilia, Rome, 1977; condr. NBC-TV premiere Amahl and the Night Visitors, 1951; premiere The Saint of Blaeker Street, 1954; appeared as condr. Lewisohn Stadium, 1952, NBC Symphony, Phila. Orch., Grant Park, Chgo., 1952-53, Boston Symphony, N.Y. Philharmonic, Spoleto (Italy) Festival of Two Worlds, 1958-77; European tour, 1954; guest condr. prin. orchs. U.S., Europe, Asia; recs. for Angle Records, 1957. Mem. Nat. Council Arts, 1975-77. Recipient Arnold Bax award, Eng., ASCAP award, 1956. Address: New York, N.Y. Died Dec. 16, 1977.

SCHLAGER, WALTER LINCOLN, JR., r.r. exec.; b. Scranton, Pa., June 30, 1918; s. Walter Lincoln and Susan (Davies) S.; B.S., Pa. State U., 1940; m. Mary Louise Bircher, Apr. 26, 1941; children—Mary Louise, Susan Bircher, Walter Lincoln III. Chief maintenance of way officer N.Y.C. Transit Authority, 1958-63, gen. mgr., exec. officer operations and maintenance, 1963-69; pres., gen. mgt. L.I. R.R., Jamaica, N.Y., 1969-76. Active Boy Scouts Am., United Fund. Lighthouse of the Blind, March of Dimes, United Cerebral Palsy. Served with constrn. Bn. USNR, 1944-46. Named Lighthouse Man of Year, 1968. Mem. Nat. Soc. Profl. Engrs., L.I. Assn. Commerce and Industry (dir.), Am. Ry. Engring. Assn., Internat. Union Pub. Transp., N.Y. R.R. Club (pres.), The Moles. Presbyn. Mason. Home: Manhasset, N.Y. Died Aug. 4, 1976.

SCHLENDORF, JOHN MARTIN, steel exec.; b. Union City, N.J., Jan. 14, 1886; s. August and Katherine (Erhardt) S.; ed. pub. schs. of Union City; m. Marguerite Mitchell, June 14, 1913; children—John W., Robert E., Jane S. (Mrs. W. J. Carter). Salesman Am. Sheet & Tin Plate Co., Detroit, 1905-15; asst. purchasing agt., Willys Overland Co., Toledo, 1915-17; vice pres. in charge sales, Central Steel Co., Massillon, O., 1917-26; v.p. in charge sales, Central Alloy Steel Corp., Massillon, 1926-30; mgr. sales alloy steel div., Republic Steel Corp., Cleveland, 1930-36, asst. vice pres. in charge sales, 1936-45, v.p. in charge sales 1945-52, cons. since. Mem. Am. Iron and Steel Inst., Am. Ordnance Assn., Am. Petroleum Inst., Farm Equipment Inst. Clubs: Union, Mayfield Country, Pepper Pike Country, The Country (Cleve.); Chicago (Chicago); Duquesne (Pittsburg); Cloud (N.Y. City); Recess, Athletic (Detroit). Home: Cleveland. *

SCHLOSSSTEIN, ADOLPH GEORGE, JR., accountant; b. St. Louis, Mar. 28, 1911; s. Adolph George and Clara (Braun) S.; B.S., Washington U., St. Louis, 1932, M.S., 1941; m. Corinne Cammann, June 15, 1937; children—Steven Braun, Stuart Wade. Staff accountant, then sr. accountant Price Waterhouse & Co., C.P.A.'s, St. Louis, 1934-38, sr. accountant, mng. accountant, Houston, 1938-50, mng. accountant, gen. partner, Dallas, 1950-71. Chmn. bd. Dallas County unit Am. Cancer Soc.; treas. Mental Health Assn. Dallas County; past pres. Friends of Tex. Libraries; vis. com. Sch. Bus. and Pub. Adminstrn., Washington U., St. Louis; treas. Friends Dallas Pub. Library; former chmn. adv. bd. accounting dept. N. Tex. State U. Recipient Elijah Watt Sells Silver medal, 1940; Alumni citation Washington U., 1973. C.P.A., Tex., N.Y. Mem. Am. Inst. C.P.A.'s, Tex. Soc. C.P.A.'s (past v.p.), Dallas Mgmt. Assn. (past pres.), Dallas Petroleum Club, Dallas C. of C. Republican. Presbyn. Clubs: Brook Hollow Golf (past gov., pres.), Chaparral, Petroleum (Dallas). Contbr. articles profl. jours. Home: Dallas, Tex. Died Oct. 12, 1980; interred Hillcrest Meml. Park, Dallas.

SCHLUETER, CLYDE FREDERICK, co. dir.; b. Rib Falls, Wis., Mar. 22, 1910; s. August H. and Anna (Schulze) S.; E.E., U. Wis., 1933; m. Ruth Brown Schlueter, Nov. 1974; children from previous marriage—James Allen, Jean (Mrs. Michael Fisher). With Employers Mut. Liability Ins. Co. of Wis., from 1933, v.p. safety and health services, 1961-64, v.p. br. operations, 1964-66, sr. v.p., 1966-67, exec. v.p., 1967-69, also dir., mem. exec. com.; pres. Employers Ins. Co., Wausau, 1969-75, chmn. bd., 1975-77; dir. Employers Ins. of Wausau, Central Wis. Bankshares, Mosinee Paper Corp., Forward Communications Corp. Bd. dirs. YMCA Found., Wausau. Fellow Am. Soc. Safety Engrs.; mem. Wis. (dir., past pres.), Wausau Area (past pres.) chambers commerce, Indsl. Conf. (hon. life), Wis. Alumni Assn., U. Wis. Found., Alpha Chi Rho. Mem. Universalist Ch. Mason (Shriner). Club: Wausau. Home: Hazelhurst, Wis. Died July 11, 1978.

SCHLUMBERGER, MAURICE, banker; b. Guebwiller, France, May 20, 1886; s. Paul and Marguerite (de Witt); B.A., Ecole des Sciences Politiques; m. Francoise Monnier, July 4, 1914; children—Odile (Mrs. Guy de Rouville), Remy, Georges (dec.), Xavier (dec.), Henriette (Mrs. Alexandre Babeanu). Partner MM.de Neutlize, Schlumberger & Cie, bankers, Paris; chmn. Cie Generale Francaise de Credit, Paris, France; dir. Societe de Gestion Mobiliere, Paris, France, also Genecredit, Paris; dir. S.A. des Eaux Minerales d'Evianles-Baines, Paris, Compagnie Parisienne de Reescompte, Paris; mgr. Petits-Enfants Maurice Schlumberger, S.a.r.l., Paris, Petits-Enfants Maurice Schlumberger, Societe Civile, Paris, Schlumberger Found., Houston, Tex. dir. Latonia Investment Trust Co. S.A., Panama; dir. emeritus Schlumberger, Ltd., Netherlands, Antilles. Served with French Army, 1914-18. Decorated Legion Honor, Croix de Guerre. Home: Marnes-la-Coquette Seine-et-Oise France. *

SCHMEISSER, HARRY CHRISTIAN (SHMISE'R), pathologist; b. Baltimore, Md., Sept. 20, 1885; s. Ernst and Louise (Gail) S.; A.B., Johns Hopkins, 1908, M.D., 1912, Ph.D., 1914; student University of Marburg and University of Freiburg, summers 1908, 1910; m. Mrs. Arthur Hall Drane (Ella Bess McMichael), June 14, 1921; children—Mary Stewart, Harry Christian, Jr. Fellow, asst., instr. and asso. in pathology, Johns Hopkins Med. Sch., 1912-19; prof. of pathology and bacteriology, Emory U. Sch. of Medicine, visiting pathologist Grady and Wesley Memorial Hosps., Atlanta, Ga., 1919-21; prof. of pathology and bacteriology and chief of div., U. of Tenn. College of Medicine, 1921-44; sec. faculty council; dir. University of Tennessee Institute of Pathology, 1921-44; prof. pathology, Univ. of Tenn. Coll. of Med., since 1944; chief of labs., mem. med. bd., John Gaston Hosp., 1921-44, attendant pathologist, since 1944. Served as major Medical Corps, United States Army, with A.E.F., 1917-19. Certified by Am. Bd. Pathology. Fellow Am. Coll. Physicians; mem. Tenn. State Med. Assn., Memphis and Shelby County Med. Soc., Southern Med. Assn., (chmn. sect. on pathology 1935; chmn. sect. on med. edn. 1936), A.M.A., Am. Assn. of Pathologists and Bacteriologists, Am. Soc. for Exptl. Pathology, Am. Bd. of Pathology (special examiner 1937), Internat. Assn. of Med. Museums, Internat. Assn. for Geographic Pathology, Phi Gamma Delta. Democrat. Methodist. Club: Memphis Country, Contbr. to med. jours. Home: Memphis, Tenn. *

SCHMID, CARL L(UITPOLD), mfg. exec.; b. Bavaria, May 27, 1904; s. Heinrich and Anna (Bader) S.; came to U.S., 1925, naturalized, 1930; student Akron (O.) U., Akron and Cleve. Law Sch.; m. Alice L. Indorf, June 16, 1934; children—Karl H., Linda Anne. Comptroller, dir. Sheffield Farms Co., Inc., 1945-50; comptroller Foremost Dairies, Inc., 1950-53; treas., dir. Congoleum-Nairn, Inc., Kearny, N.J., 1953-77. Bd. govs. West Hudson Hosp., Kearny, N.J. Home: Summit, N.J. Died Jan. 17, 1977.

SCHMIDT, EDWARD FRED, elec. wholesale co. exec.; b. Chgo., Dec. 24, 1908; s. Erdmann L. and Minnie (Burmeister) S.; B.S., U. Ill., 1931; m. Josephine Roggen, Feb. 10, 1940; children—James, John, Willard, Robert. With Alexander Grant Co., C.P.A.'s, 1931-34; with W.W. Grainger, Inc., Chgo., 1934-76, v.p., 1945-48, exec. v.p., 1948-68, pres., 1968-73, vice chmn., 1973-76, also dir.; v.p., dir. Dayton Electric Mfg. Co. Bd. dirs. Grainger Found., Inc. Club: University (Evanston). Home: Evanston, Ill. Died Mar. 30, 1976.

SCHMIDT, EMERSON P., economist; b. Tavistock, Ont., Can., July 4, 1899; s. John D. and Barbara A. (Wilhelm) S.; A.B., North Central Coll., Naperville, Ill., 1923; A.M., U. Toronto, 1924; Ph.D., U. of Wis., 1935; m. Gertrude Grace Wilson, 1926; 1 son, Wilson; married 2d Ada E. Furr, 1949. Came to The United States in 1919, naturalized, 1931. Assistant professor economics, Marquette U., Milwaukee, 1924-26; instr. in economics, U. Wis., 1926-28; asst. prof. economics, U. Ore., 1928-30; asso. prof. of economics, U. Minn., 1930-43; econ. analyst, Govt. of Alberta, 1937-38; econ. consultant and editor, Am. Legion Employment Stabilization Service, 1939-42; chmn. Manitoba Electrification Inquiry Commn., 1942; dir. econ. research C. of C. of U.S., 1943-62, economic consultant, 1962-76. Mem. Bur. Labor Statistics Bus. Research adv. council; vice chairman adv. council Fed. Reports to Bureau the Budget. Club: Cosmos (Washington). Author or co-author books relating to field; also bulls. of C. of C. Mem. editorial council, Jour. of Land

Economics, 1942-61. Home: Oakton, Va. Died Apr. 8, 1976.

SCHMIDT, EUGENE ARTHUR, JR., business exec.; b. Milwaukee, Wis., Oct. 17, 1903; s. Eugene and Lina (Linsz) S.; ed. pub. schs. Pittsburgh, Pa., m. Lola Merydith, June 26, 1929; children—Joanne Merydith (Mrs. Edward L. Madden, Jr.), Nancy Virginia (Mrs. Arthur C. Leiser). Treas., v.p., dir. Nalray Corp., New York, N.Y., 1930-32, Ry. and Utilities Investing Corp., New York, N.Y., 1930-32; dir. and mem. exec. com. C.G.W.Ry., 1941-44, chmn. reorgn. mgrs., 1940-41; mem. reorgn. com. D.&R.G.W. R.R. Co., 1944-47; v.p., treas. Metropolitan Life Ins. Co.; dir., mem. exec. com. C.&N.W. Ry. and C.,St.P., M.&O. Ry. Co.; chmn. adv. bd. Chem. Bank & Trust Co., N.Y.C.; dir. First Nat. Bank of Jersey City. Member of board of directors, mem. exec. com. Woodlawn Cemetery. Trustee Am. Mus. of Safety. Mem. N.Y. State C. of C., Ins. Soc. of N.Y., Transportation Association America (director), Newcomen Society. Republican. Methodist. Mason. Clubs: Baltusrol Golf, Treasurers, Inc. Home: Short Hills, N.J. Died Sept. 21, 1976; buried Meml. Garden of Morrow Meml. Ch., Maplewood, N.J.

SCHMITT, WALDO LASALLE, zoologist; b. Washington, June 25, 1887; s. Ewald and Fanny Mathilde (Hesselbach) S.; B.S., George Washington U., 1913, Ph.D., 1922; M.A., U. Calif., 1916; D.Sc., U. of So. Calif., 1948; m. Alvina Stumm, Nov. 19, 1914; children—Waldo Ernest (dec.), Barbara Ann (Mrs. Robert T. Lundy, USN). Aid in econ. botany, U.S. Dept. Agr., 1907-10; scientific asst., U.S. Bur. Fisheries, 1910-13, naturalist, 1913-14; asst. curator, Div. Marine Invertebrates, U.S. Nat. Museum, 1915-20, curator, 1920-43, head curator of biology, 1943-47, zoölogy, 1947-57; research asso. Smithsonian Instn., 1957-77. Walter Rathbone traveling scholar, Smithsonian Instn., in S.A., 1925-27; at Tortugas Marie Lab., 1924-25, 1930-32; with Hancock Pacific Expdns., 1932-35; Smithsonian-Hartford Expdn. to West Indies, 1937; naturalist Pres. Roosevelt's cruise to Clipperton, Cocos, and Galapagos Islands, 1938; Hancock Atlantic Expdn., N. Coast South America-Netherlands West Indies, 1939; King Crab investigation for U.S. Fish and Wildlife Service in Alaska, 1940; State Dept. detail to Latin America, 1941, 42, 43; study mus. Paris, Turin 1954; mem. Smithsonian-Bredin Expdn., Belgian Congo, Sudan, Egypt, 1955, Caribbean, 1956, and 58, 59, Tahiti and Society Island, 1957, also Quintana Roo, Yucatan, 1960, Bahamas, 1961, Palmer Peninsula Survey USARP, Antarctica, 1962-63. Mem. bd. trustees Slocum-Lunz Found., Charleston, S.C., Internat. Oceanographic Found., Serological Mus. Rutgers U. Member USN Oceanographic Conf., 1925, chmn. conf. Importance and Needs of Systematics in Biology, NRC, 1953; del. Friday Harbor Symposium on Biology of Marine Boring and Fouling Organisms, 1957, Internat. Conf., Taxonomic Biochemistry, Physiology and Serology, U. Kans., Lawrence, 1962. Fellow AAAS, Calif. Acad. Scis.; mem. Soc. Systemic Zoology, Am. Soc. Limnology and Oceanography, Am. Soc. Zool., Am. Inst. Biol. Sci., Am. Geophys. Union Biol. Soc. Washington, Washington Acad. Scis., Soc. Vertebrate Paleontology, Assn. Meiobenthologists, Assn. Tropical Biology, Cushman Found. for Foraminiferal Research, Paleontol. Research Instn., Antarctican Soc., Systematics Assn., Am. Polar Soc., Atlantic Estuarine Research Soc. (hon.), Sigma Phi Epsilon, Beta Kappa Alpha, Sigma Xi; corr. mem. Zool. Soc. London, and hon. mem. other fgn. scientific socs. Clubs: Cosmos (Washington); Explorers (New York). Author: The Marine Decapod Crustacca of California, 1921, 72; Crustaceans, 1931, 65, 68 (English edit. 1973); also numerous reports and papers on marine invertebrates. Home: Takoma Park, Md. Died Aug. 5, 1977.

SCHNARE, LESTER L. (SHNAR), consular service; b. Mondovi, Wis., May 15, 1884; s. Henry W. and Anna M. (Hefling) S.; grad. high sch., Fitzgerald, Ga., 1902; LL.B., George Washington U., 1914, LL.M., 1919; m. Margaret B. Kloss, Sept. 29, 1919. Teacher, pub. schs., Ga., 1902-05; city editor, Fitzgerald, Ga., 1905-06; stenographer, Pensacola (Fla.) Navy Yard, 1906-07. U.S. Bur. Immigration, Washington, D.C., 1907-12; law clk., same, 1912-15; vice consul, Shanghai, China, 1916-17, Canton, 1917-18, Yokohana, Japan. May July 1918; spl. asst., Dept. State, Oct. 1918-July 1919; consul, Yokohama, 1920-21; detailed to Krobe, 1921-22, consul, Swatow, China, 1922-23, Cartagena, Columbia, 1923-27, Breslau, Germany, 1927-31, Hamburg, Germany, 1931-36; Milan, Italy, 1936-41; consul gen., Rangoon, Burma, Nov. 1941-Feb. 1942, Maymyo; Brumo, Feb.-Mar. 1942, Calcutta, India, Apr.-Sept. 1942; first-sec. of Legation, Tehran, Iran, Sept. 1942-Oct. 1943; Dept. of State Oct. 1943-Dec. 1944; consul general, Rome, Dec. 1944-April 1945; consul gen., Genoa, May 1945-Nov. 1947; ret. from active service, Nov. 1947. Mason. Home: Macon. Ga. *

SCHNEIDER, HUBERT AUGUST, lawyer, airline exec.; b. Newark, Nov. 28, 1908; s. Henry and Olga (Giesen) S.; grad. Newark Acad., 1926; A.B., Princeton, 1930; student Yale Law Sch., 1930-32; LL.B., Columbia, 1933; m. Mary R. Plum, May 11, 1935; children—Peter P., Mary Ann (Mrs. Clark Hughes), Elizabeth (Mrs. Jack Frances). Admitted N.J. bar, 1933, D.C. bar, 1940, the Maryland bar, 1946; atty. various govt. depts., 1933-40; asso. Whiteford, Hart, Carmody & Wilson, Washington, 1940-48, partner, 1948-59; v.p., gen. counsel, dir. Pan Am. World Airways, from 1959. Mem. Adminstrv. conf. of U.S., 1961. Trustee Suburban Hosp., Bethesda, Md., 1946-57, v.p., 1955-57; trustee Landon Sch., 1950-53, Barker Found., 1950-56, Norwood Parish School, 1958-60. Served to lt. colonel, USAAF, 1942-45; asst. jr. intelligence U.S. Strategic Air Forces, Hawaii, Guam, Okinawa, Japan, 1944-45. Decorated Bronze Star. Mem. Am., D.C. bar assns. Clubs: Burning Tree, Chevy Chase, Princeton (pres. 1956-58), Metropolitan, International (Washington); Sky, Princeton (N.Y.C.). Home: Bethesda, Md. Deceased.

SCHNEIDER, J(OHN) THOMAS, lawyer, govt. ofcl.; b. Cedar Hill, Tenn., June 2, 1895; s. Charles and Lila (Ayers) S.; A.B., U. South, 1917; student George Washington U., 1922; J.D., Harvard, 1925; m. Sarah Thomson, June 3, 1939; children—Laura Thomson, Charles Ayers. Admitted to N.J. bar, 1930; practiced in Newark, 1930-34, Washington, 1955-59, 68—; asso. firm Pitney, Hardin & Skinner, Newark, 1930-34, Becker, Sisk & Becker, Washington; instr. law U.S. Mil. Acad., 1927-30; spl. asst. to Sec. Interior, 1934-35; counsel RFC, Washington, 1935-36; asst. agy. counsel N.Y. Loan Agy., RFC and various subsidiaries, 1936-37, agy. counsel, 1937-43; sec., gen. counsel, dir. personnel and labor dept. Standard Brands, Inc., and subsidiaries, N.Y.C., 1943-49; dir. Standard Brands subsidiaries, 1943-49; asst. sec. commerce internat. affairs, 1952-53, adv. council U.S. Internat. Monetary and Econ. Policies, 1952-53; 1st asst. and coordinator field offices Anti-Trust div. Dept. Justice, 1953-55; adminstrv. law judge ICC, 1959-68; professorial lectr. Washington Coll. Law, Am. U., 1955-60. Cons. Munitions Bd., Nat. Mil. Establishment, 1949-50, chmn. inter-agy. com. on mil.-contractor relationship, chmn. industry adv. com. on mil.-contractor relationship; chmn. personnel policy bd. Dept. Def., 1950-51, Armed Forces Policy Council, 1950-51. Mem. Bd. Fgn. Service, 1952-53; mem. interdepartmental com. on report of Randall Commn. on Fgn. Econ. Policy, 1953-55. Commd. 2d lt. U.S. Army, 1917; advanced through grades to capt. F.A., U.S. Army, 1927; served with arty. information service French Army, 1918, Arty. Regt. in France, AEF; information officer gen. staff, aide to chief of staff and sec. gen. staff G.H.Q.; served as personal aide to Gen. Pershing, 1919-24; resigned, 1929, col. JAGC, U.S. Army Res. Decorated Purple Heart, AEF for meritorious service; recipient citation Commdr. in-Chief AEF, citation for civilian service Pres. Truman, citation Dept. Army and 2d U.S. Army, 1955; Mem. N.J., N.Y., D.C., U.S. Supreme Ct. bars. Mem. Am., Fed., ICC Practioners bar assns., Alpha Tau Omega, Sigma Upsilon. Methodist. Clubs: Metropolitan (Washington); Chevy Chase; University (N.Y.C.); Tucson Nat. Golf. Author Fed. legislation preservation hist. Am. sites, bldgs., and creating div. on hist. sites and bldgs. in Nat. Park Service, 1935; also legislation providing for Nat. Park Trust Fund Bd., 1935. Mem. editorial adv. com. Food-Drug-Cosmetic Law Quar., 1944-49. Contbr. articles to profl. and popular mags. Home: Washington, D.C. Died Nov. 26, 1976.

SCHNEIDER, LOUIS, educator; b. Vienna, Austria, Mar. 22, 1915 (came to U.S 1921, naturalized 1927); s. Gustave and Frieda (Salz) S.; came to U.S., 1921, naturalized, 1927; B.A., Coll. City N.Y., 1935; M.A., Columbia, 1938, Ph.D., 1947; m. 2d, Josephine A. Sundine, Jan. 3, 1956; one dau., Valerie S.; children by previous marriage—David S., Dana A. Tutor sociology Brooklyn Coll., 1937-43; labor economist WPB, 1943-45; economist OPA, 1945-47; asst. prof. sociology Colgate U., 1947-49; asso. prof. sociology Purdue U., Lafayette, Ind., 1949-54, prof., 1954-59; prof. sociology U. Ill. at Urbana, 1960-67, head dept. 1960-64; prof. sociology U. Tex., Austin, 1967-79; vis. prof. Dartmouth, 1959-60. Fellow Center Advanced STudy Behavioral Scis., 1954-55. Fellow Am Sociol. Assn.; mem. Ohio Valley Sociol. Soc. (pres. 1959-60), Phi Beta Kappa. Author: (with Ogle and Wiley) Power, Order and the Economy, 1954; (with S. M. Dornbusch) Popular Religion, 1958; Sociological Approach To Religion, 1970; The Sociological Way of Looking at the World, 1975; Classical Theories of Social Change, 1976. Editor: Problems of Economics and Sociology (by Carl Menger), 1963; The Scottish Moralists on Human Nature and Society, 1967; editor, contbr. Religion, Culture and Society, 1964; (with C.M. Bonjean) The Idea of Culture in the Social Sciences, 1973; (with C.M. Bonjean and R. Lineberry) Social Science in America, 1976. Asso. editor Am. Sociol. Rev., 1958-61. Contbr. articles to profl. jours. Home: Austin, Tex. Died Mar. 17, 1979.

SCHNEIERSON, SOL STANLEY, physician, educator, microbiologist; b. N.Y.C., May 15, 1906; s. Isaac and Anna (Levine) S.; A.B., Cornell U., 1928; M.D., L.I. Coll. Medicine, 1932; m. Marianne Jacqueline Katz, July 21, 1950; 1 dau., Martine. Mem. staff Mt. Sinai Hosp., N.Y.C., 1935-76, dir. microbiology, 1955-74, cons. microbiologist, 1974-76; research asst. Pasteur Inst., Paris, 1938-39; cons. microbiologist Elmhurst (N.Y.) Hosp., 1964; prof. microbiology Mt. Sinai Sch. Medicine, 1966-74, emeritus, 1974-76. Served to comdr. USNR. 1941-46. Diplomate Am. Bd. Pathology, Am. Bd. Microbiology. Fellow N.Y. Acad. Medicine, A.C.P., Am. Acad. Microbiology, N.Y. Acad. Scis.; mem. Soc. Exptl. Biology and Medicine, Am. Soc. Microbiology, Am. Assn. Immunologists, Am. Assn. Pathologists and Bacteriologists, Infections Disease Soc. Am., Am. Soc. Tropical Medicine. Author: Atlas of Diagnostic Microbiology, 1966. Home: New York, N.Y. Died Jan. 30, 1976.

SCHOBINGER, GEORGE (SHO'BING-ER), civil engr.; b. Chicago, Ill., Aug. 6, 1885; s. John J. and Emily (Hildebrand) S.; A.B., U. of Chicago, 1905; S.B., Mass. Inst. Tech., 1908; m. Helen Lockwood Johnson, Aug. 28, 1913; children—Elisabeth Hall (Mrs. George T. Herschel), Gertrude Emily (Mrs. Walton F. Battershall), John Lockwood, Barbara Ann. Engr. insp. under bd. of supervising engrs., Chicago Traction, on constrn. Chicago River tunnels, 1908-11; asst. engr. U.S. Reclamation Service, on irrigation systems, Yuma, Ariz., and Rio Grande, N.M., and Tex. projects, 1911-17; progress engr. with Am. Internat. Shipbuilding Co., Philadelphia, 1917-19; engr. and rep. Dwight P. Robinson & Co., Inc., erecting U.S. Embassy bldgs., etc., at Rio de Janeiro, 1919-31; engring. mgr. United Engrs. & Constructors, Inc., Phila.; v.p. Dwight P. Robinson & Co. of Brazil, and United Engrs. & Const. of Argentina, 1929-37; v.p. Ulen & Co., N.Y., 1938-39; vice president and Day & Zimmermann, Inc., Phila., 1939-55; consulting engr., 1956—. Pres. Swarthmore School Dist., 1940-41. Mem. Am. Soc. C.E. (life mem.; Collingwood prize), Am. Soc. M.E., Am. Inst. Cons. Engrs., Phi Beta Kappa. Clubs: Meridian, Engineers (Phila.); Cosmos (Washington). Mason. Author: (with A. M. Lackey) Bus. Methods in the Building field (treatise). 1939; New Plant (monograph), 1939. Home: Swarthmore, Pa. *

SCHOEFFLER, OSCAR EDMUND, editor; b. Alton, Ill., Mar. 5, 1899; s. John William and Louise (Lutz) S.; student U. Ill.; B.S., Columbia, 1922; m. Helen M. Dwight, Oct. 6, 1923; children—Dwight, John William, Edmund Henry. Various positions trade publs., 1923-39; fashion editor Esquire mag., Esquire's Apparel Arts, 1939-57, fashion dir., 1957-69, fashion adv., 1969-72, mem. editorial bd. Esquire's Twentieth Century Ency. and Dictionary of Men's Fashions, 1969-73; v.p. and fashion dir. Esquire, Inc., to 1972; fashion dir. Gentlemen's Quar., 1957-72. Author articles on men's fashions and apparel. Home: Sarasota, Fla. Died May 6, 1979.

SCHOEMANN, PETER THEODORE, labor union ofcl.; b. Milw., Oct. 28, 1893; s. Paul and Mary (Bauer) S.; ed. pub. schs.; m. Mary Margaret Furey, Oct. 21, 1925; children—James Peter, Maryann. Mem. United Assn. Plumbers and Steam Fitters U.S. and Can. (AFL), from 1914, rec. sec., bus. rep. local 75, chmn. credentials com. assn. conv., 1928-32, chmn. laws com. 1942 conv., now nat. pres.; also pres. Milw. Bldg. and Constrn. Trade Council and chmn. labor disputes com. Fed. Trade Council Milw. Labor rep. region VI War Manpower Commn.; certifying officer Milwaukee County Civil Works Adminstrn., also mem. nat. adv. com.; mem. Milw. Sch. Bd.; v.p. Milw. Housing Authority; mem. bd. 1948 Centennial Corp., Milw.; chmn. Wis. Bd. Vocational and Adult Edn. Mem. Am. Legion. Roman Cath. Eagle, K.P. Club: Serra. Home: Milwaukee, Wis. Died Aug. 7, 1976.

SCHOENBORN, EDWARD MARTIN, JR., engring. educator; b. Columbus, Ohio, May 3, 1909; s. Edward Martin and Emma Catherine (Wolfram) S.; B. Chem. Engring., Ohio State U., 1932, M.Sc., 1934, Ph.D., 1941; m. Virginia Walter Harrington, June 18, 1940; 1 son, Edward Martin III. Mem. faculty U. Del., Newark, 1935-45, asso. prof. chem. engring., 1942-45; with engring. dept. E.I. duPont de Nemours & Co., Inc., 1959-60; prof. chem. engring., head dept. N.C. State U., Raleigh, 1945-66, Charles H. Herty prof. chem. engring., 1966-74, ret. Recipient Distinguished Alumnus award Ohio State U., 1974. Fellow Am. Inst. Chem. Engrs. (council, dir. 1964-66), Am. Chem. Soc., Am. Soc. Engring. Edn. Contbr. articles on fluid flow, heat transfer, distillation, phase equilibria to profl. publs. Home: Raleigh, N.C. Died Mar. 13, 1979; buried Raleigh Meml. Park.

SCHOENFELD, RUDOLF EMIL, diplomatic service; b. Washington, D.C., Jan. 25, 1895; s. Hermann and Johanna (Richter) S.; A.B., George Washington U., 1915; Ph.D., magna cum laude, U. of Berne (Switzerland), 1920; unmarried. With U.S. Efficiency Commn., 1915; master, Nat. Cathedral Sch., Washington, D.C., 1915-16; v. consul, Zurich, Switzerland, 1916, Berne, 1917-21; in charge office of Am. Commn. at Cologne, Germany, July-Sept. 1921; v. consul, Berlin, 1921-23, consul, Dec. 1923-Oct. 1924; consul at Cologne, 1924-25; consul and sec. Am. Legation, La Paz, Bolivia, Dec. 1925-27; sec. Am. Embassy, Rio de Janeiro, 1927-31; sec. of legation, Budapest, Jan. 1931-Oct. 1932; assigned to Dept. of State, Washington, D.C., Nov. 1932-Dec. 1936; sec. Am. Legation, Stockholm, Sweden, Dec. 1936-Sept. 1938; sec. Embassy, London, Eng., Sept. 1938-Apr. 1, 1941; apptd. charge d'affaires near govts. (in Eng.) of

Norway, Netherlands, Poland, Belgium, 1940; counselor of embassy, near govts. (in Eng.), of Poland and Belgium, 1941; 1st sec. of legation, near govts. (in Eng.), of Norway, Netherlands, Yugoslavia, Greece, Czechoslovakia, 1941; counselor of embassy, near govts. (in Eng.), of Norway, Netherlands, Greece, Yugoslavia, 1942; charge d'affaires near govts. (in Eng.), of Belgium, Czechoslovakia, Luxembourg, Netherlands, Norway, Poland and Yugoslavia, Dec. 1, 1945; rank of minister, Jan. 1944. Political adviser to U.S. delegation, 1st General Assembly of the United Nations, London, England, Jan.-Feb. 1946; appointed envoy extraordinary and minister plenipotentiary to Rumania, July 1947. Member Theta Delta Chi. Episcopalian. Clubs: Metropolitan (Washington); Athenaeum (London). Author: Main Currents in the Political and Religious Development of Maryland as a Proprietary Province (1633-1776), 1921; Taxation in Germany, 1924. Home: Washington, D.C. Died Apr. 15, 1981.

SCHOENRICH, OTTO, lawyer; b. Balt., July 9, 1876; s. Carl Otto and Lena A. (Sieck) S.; grad. with honors Balt. City Coll., 1894; LL.B., U. Md., 1897; D.C.L. magna cum laude, U. Havana, 1922, Dr. Social Scis. and Pub. Law (hon.), 1951; m. María Janer y Arias, June 10, 1902 (dec. 1939); children—Mercedes (Mrs. Fred Lynn Steely), Carlos. Practiced law in Md. and N.Mex., 1897-1900; asst. to Commn. to Revise and Compile Laws of P.R., 1900-01; dist. judge of Arecibo, P.R., 1901-04; municipal judge of Mayaguez, 1904-06; sec. Am. sp. commr. to investigate finances of Santo Domingo, 1905-06; sec. to minister of finance of Dominican Republic, 1906, to provisional gov. of Cuba, during second intervention, and mem. Adv. Law Commn. which drafted new Cuban laws, 1906-09; dist. judge of Mayaguez, P.R., 1909-11; pres. Nicaraguan Mixed Claims Commn. 1911-15; dist. judge of Humacao, P.R., 1916; asso. with law firm Curtis, Mallet-Prevost, Colt & Mosle, N.Y.C., 1916-65, sr. partner, to 1965. Arbitrator between Greek govt. and Am. cos., 1929, 34. Decorated Cruzeiro do Sul, Brazil; Lanuza, Cespedes Cuba; Cristobal Colon, Dominican Republic; Star of Africa, Liberia; Libertador, Venezuela, Honneur et Merite, Haiti; named hon. prof. law, U. of Santo Domingo, Dominican Republic. Mem. Am. Soc. Internat. Law, Am. Acad. Polit. and Social Sci., Am. Fgn. Law Assn. (past pres.), Pan Am. Soc. U.S., (past pres.), Peruvian-Am. Assn. Republican. Club: University (Washington). Author: Santo Domingo, 1918; The Legacy of Christopher Columbus, 1949; Translation of Civil Code of Mexico 1950; also reports and articles on Latin-Am. and legal subjects. Address: New York, N.Y. Died Feb. 9, 1977; buried Hartsdale, N.Y.

SCHOENY, LEO JOHN, dentist; b. Ridgeway, Ill., Oct. 15, 1896; s. John Ralph and Susan (Stringer) S.; D.D.S., Loyola U., New Orleans, 1920; m. Byrdie Marie Casso, Oct. 10, 1918. Gen. practice dentistry, Donaldsonville, La., 1920-30, New Orleans, 1930-76; mem. staff Hotel Dieu Hosp., 1930-76, instr. sch. nursing, 1931-33; mem. staff Ochsner Found. Hosp., 1955-76; mem. La. State Board Health, 1941-49, sec., 1941; chmn. health div. Council Social Agencies, New Orleans, 1947-49, dir., 1951-59; chmn. mayor's com. sch. health services, New Orleans, 1949-52; mem. nat. adv. com. Selective Service System, 1950-55, spl. cons., 1955-76; mem. health resources adv. com. ODM, 1950-55, spl. cons., from 1955; mem. Dental adv. com. Am. Korean Found., from 1954; cons. Dentistry, Med. Services Task Force, Hoover Commn., 1954; chmn. Fed. Interagency Council on Dental Affairs, 1954-55; mem. commn. on dental edn. So. Regional Edn. Bd., 1956-76. Bd. dirs. United Community and War Chest, 1944-46, New Orleans Social Welfare Planning Council, 1960-65; mem. New Orleans Found. for Research and Edn., 1961-76. Served as lt. comdr. Dental Corps, USNR, 1940-43. Fellow Internat. Coll. Dentists. Am. Coll. Dentists (chmn. La. sect. 1964-65), Am. Pub. Health Assn., A.A.A.S., Royal So. of Health, Acad. Psychosomatic Medicine; mem. Acad. Gen. Dentistry, La. State Dental Soc. (pres. 1928-29), chmn. bur. dental health edn. 1929-41), Sixth Dist. Dental Soc. La. (pres. 1923-25), Am. Dental Assn. (com. pub. health and edn. 1940-42, mem. council dental health 1942-50, chmn. council dental health 1948-50, com. nat. emergency dental services 1952, cons. council fed. dental services 1951-55), New Orleans Dental Assn. (chmn. dental conf. 1950), Am. Acad. Periodontology, Acad. Internnat. Dentistry., Pierre Fouchard Acad., Orleans Parish Med. Soc., New Orleans C. of C. (dir. 1937-40), New Orleans Mid-Winter Sports Assn. (Sugar Bowl sec. 1956-57), Fedn. Dentaire Internat., So. Acad. Periodontology, La. Pub. Health Assn., Chgo. Dental Soc., Delta Sigma Delta, Omicron Kappa Upsilon. Roman Catholic. Club: Young Men's Business (pres. 1934). Clinician and speaker before profl. groups. Contbr. articles to profl. jours. Home: New Orleans, La. Died Aug. 10, 1976.

SCHOLANDER, PER FREDRIK, physiologist, educator; b. Orebro, Sweden, Nov. 29, 1905; s. Torkel F. and Agnethe (Faye-Hansen) S.; M.D., U. Oslo, 1932, Ph.D., 1934; D.Sc., U. Alaska, 1973, U. Uppsala, 1977; m. Susan Irving, June 20, 1951. Came to U.S., 1939, naturalized, 1945. Research fellow physiology U. Oslo, 1932-39; research asso. zoology Swarthmore Coll., 1939-43, research biologist, 1946-49; research fellow biol. chemistry Harvard Med. Sch., 1949-51; physiologist Woods Hole Oceanographic Inst., 1952-55; prof. physiology, dir. Inst. Zoophysiology, U. Oslo, 1955-58; prof. physiology Scripps Instn. Oceanography, U. Calif., 1958-80, dir. Physiol. Research Lab., 1963-70; research asso. in zoology U. Wash., Seattle, 1972-80; Harvey lectr., 1962, NIH lectr., 1972. Served to maj. USAAF, 1943-46. Decorated Legion of Merit, Soldier's medal; recipient Nansen prize, Oslo, 1979; Rockefeller fellow, 1939-41; John Simon Guggenheim fellow, 1969. Mem. Nat., Norwegian, Royal Swedish acads. scis., Am. Philos. Soc., Am. Acad. Arts and Scis., Arctic Inst. N.Am., Am. Physiol. Soc., Marine Biol. Lab. Assn., AAAS, Soc. Gen. Physiologists, Sigma Xi. Clubs: Cosmos (Washington); Explorers (N.Y.C.). Author: (with others) Osmosis and Tensile Solvent, 1976. Home: La Jolla, Calif. Died June 13, 1980.

SCHOLER, CHARLES HENRY (SHOL'ER), coll. prof., cons. engr.; b. Lincoln County, Kan., Sept. 19. 1890; s. Frederick Madsen and Henrietta (Baldwin) S.; B.S., Kan. State Coll., 1914; m. Bertha Marie Frey, Sept. 5, 1916; children—Ruth Lillian (Mrs. Howard B. Liebengood, dec.), John, Charles Frey. Chainman on surveys, 1914; resident engr. for concrete pavement, 1915; asst. engr. Office of State Engr., Manhattan, Kan., 1916; asst. bridge engr. State Highway Dept. Topeka, 1917; engr. Ordnance Dept., Washington, D.C., 1918-19; with Kan. State Coll. since 1919, as engr. of tests, 1919-20, associate professor and professor applied mechanics, 1920-61, professor emeritus, 1961—, head of department, 1923-56; consultant on numerous engring. projects; consultant Portland Cement Assn., 1939-40, Cons. Kan. Turnpike Authority, 1954-55; chairman of Highway Research Board, 1958. Recipient of Wason medal American Concrete Inst., 1952. Mem. Am. Society Civil Engrs., Am. Concrete Inst. (pres. 1954), Am. Soc. for Engr. Edn., Nat. Soc. of Prof. Engrs., Kan. Engring. Soc., Am. Soc. Testing Materials, Highway Research Bd., (mem. of exec. com., distinguished service award, 1948), Sigma Xi, Phi Kappa Phi. Republican. Baptist. Club: Cosmos (Washington). Contributor to bulletins and proceedings of professional socs. Home: Manhattan, Kan. *

SCHOMBURG, AUGUST, army officer; b. Denver, July 3, 1908; s. Sam and Mary (Harms) S.; student Colo. Sch. Mines, 1926-27; B.S., U.S. Mil. Acad., 1931; M.S., M.I.T., 1938; student Indsl. Coll. Armed Forces, 1952-53; m. Fern Wynne, June 12, 1931; children—Alice (Mrs. R. W. Maher), Augusta Ann (Mrs. Mead S. Gruver), August. Commd. lt. inf., U.S. Army, 1931, advanced through grades to lt. gen. U.S. Army; asst. mil. attache, Ottawa, Canada, 1946-49; dir. research and development and engring. Watertown Arsenal, Mass., 1949-52; dir. procurement, hdqrs. U.S. Army Europe, 1953-55; asst. chief ordnance for research and development, 1956-58, deputy chief ordnance, 1958-60; comdg. gen. U.S. Army Missile Command, Redstone Arsenal, Huntsville, Ala., 1960-62; comdg. gen. U.S. Army Supply and Maintenance Command, 1962-64; comdt. Indsl. Coll. Armed Force, 1964-67; cons., from 1967. Chmn. council Sch. Govt. and Bus. Adminstrn., George Washington U. Decorated Legion of Merit with cluster; D.S.M. Mem. Am. Ordnance Assn. (dir. Washington post), Armed Forces Mgmt. Assn. (nat. bd. dirs.), Def. Supply Assn., Nat. Security Indsl. Assn. Assn. U.S. Army. Address: Arlington, Va. Deceased; buried Arlington Nat. Cemetery.

SCHOO, CLARENCE JOHN, fibre mfg. exec.; b. Louisville, Oct. 27, 1884; s. John Conrad and Josephine (Glaser) S.; student high sch.; H.H.D., Am. Internat. Coll., Springfield, Mass., 1965; m. Grace Harwood, June 10, 1911. Sales mgr. Ft. Wayne Corrugated Box Co. (Ind.), 1910-20; organizer, pres. Gen. Fibre Box Co., Springfield, Mass., 1920-29, merged with Longview Fibre Co. (Wash.), 1929, v.p., mem. exec. com. Longview Fibre Co., 1961—, also chmn. Gen. Fibre Box Co., 1956-61; dir., mem. exec. com. Third Nat. Bank & Trust Co., Springfield, Mass. Trustee, life mem. Springfield Library Assn.; trustee Eastern States Exposition, West Springfield, Mass. Mem. Augusta (Ga.) Nat. Golf Club (bd. govs., v.p.). Home: Springfield, Mass. *

SCHOOLEY, ALLEN HEATEN, govt. scientist; b. Terril, Iowa, Dec. 16, 1909; s. Alfred Heaten and Bertha Hope (Allen) S., B.S. in Elec. Engring., Iowa State U., 1931; M.S. in Elec. Engring., Purdue U., 1932, D.Eng., 1966; m. Meriel Mercedes Vestrem, Sept. 10, 1938; children—Robert Allen, Jean (Mrs. S.W. (Freeman), Mary Elena. Electronic engr. RCA, 1936-40; with U.S. Naval Research Lab., from 1940, supt. electronics div., 1954-56, asso. dir. research 1957-67, sr. research scientist, from 1967; resident adviser to Brazilian Navy, Rio de Janeiro, 1956-57; research scientist NATO Anti-Submarine Submarine Warfare Research Center, La Spezia, Italy, 1963-65; lectr. Geophysical Inst., U. Bergen (Norway), 1965. Mem. U.S. Navy Undersea Warfare Research and Devel. Planning Council, 1959-63, U.S. nat. com. Union Radio Sci. Internat., 1958-78. Decorated Knight Ordem do Merito Naval (Brazil); recipient Distinguished Civilian Service award U.S. Navy, 1946; Marston Gold medal Ia. State U., 1974, Profl. Achievement Citation, 1969; Honor Iowan award Buena Vista Coll., 1966. Registered profl. engr., D.C. Fellow IEEE (Harry Diamond Meml. prize 1963, Distinguished Service award Washington sect. 1963; chmn. Washington sect. 1957-58), AAAS, Washington Acad. Scis.; mem. Am. Meteorol. Soc., Internat. Assn. Phys. Scis. Ocean; Marine Tech. Soc., Internat. Oceanographic Found., Am. Geophys. Union, Sci. Research Soc. Am., Am. Inst. Physics, Washington Philos. Soc., Armed Forces Electronics and Communications Assn., Sci. Research Soc. Am. (Applied Sci. award 1971), Am. Assn. Physics Tchrs., U.S. Naval Inst., Sigma Xi, Phi Kappa Phi, Theta Xi. Contbr. articles on interdisciplinary fields electronics, optics, oceanography, fluid dynamics, research mgmt. to profl. jours. Patentee in field. Home: Springfield Va. Died August 3, 1979.

SCHOONOVER, LAWRENCE LOVELL, author; b. Anamosa, Iowa, Mar. 6, 1906; s. George L. and Grace (Lovell) S.; student U. Wis., 1923-26; m. Gertrude Bonn, May 29, 1938; children—Judith, Elizabeth, Caroline, Virginia. Reporter Colliers mag., 1927-28; with Batten, Barton, Durstine & Osborn, 1928-30, account exec., 1945-47; advt. mgr. Underwood and Underwood, 1931-42; copywriter Gotham Advt. Agy., 1943-45; author, 1948—. Mem. Chi Phi. Republican. Epixcopalian. Author: The Burnished Blade; The Gentle Infidel; The Golden Exile; The Quick Brown Fox; The Spider King; The Queen's Cross; The Revolutionary; The Prisoner of Tordesillas; The Chancellor; Central Passage; Key of Gold; To Love a Queen; The Cuckold King. Home: Pound Ridge, N.Y. Died Jan. 8, 1980.

SCHOPF, JAMES MORTON, geologist, educator; b. Cheyenne, Wyo., June 2, 1911; s. Ira Morton and Nettie (Bufton) S.; B.A., U. Wyo., 1930; M.S., U. Ill., 1932, Ph.D., 1937; m. Esther Julie Nissen, Apr. 7, 1934; children—Thomas Joseph Morton, James William. Asst. geologist Ill. Geol. Survey, Urbana, 1934-43; coal microscopist U.S. Bur. Mines, Pitts., 1943-47; geologist, paleontology and stratigraphy br. U.S. Geol. Survey, Washington, 1947-50, fuels br., Columbus, Ohio, 1950-76, annuitant, 1976-78; prof. geology mineralogy Ohio State U., Columbus, 1950-78, prof. botany, 1964-78; del. bot. nomenclature, U.S. Geol. Survey and Ohio State U. to Internat. Bot. Congresses, 1950-59, 64, 69, 75, Internat. Palynological Conf., 1966, Internat. Geol. Congress, 1968; mem. NSF coal research panel, 1976. Recipient Antarctic medal Dept. Interior, 1970; Mary Clark Thompson medal award Nat. Acad. Sci., 1976. Fellow Geol. Soc. Am. (Cady award 1974), AAAS, Paleobot. Soc. India; mem. Bot. Soc. Am. (Merit award 1969), Disting. Paleobotanist award 1977), Paleontol. Soc. (medal 1978), Soc. Econ. Geologists. Democrat. Methodist. Contbr. articles in field to profl. jours. and encys. Home: Columbus, Ohio. Died Sept. 15, 1978.

SCHORGER, ARLIE WILLIAM, chemist; b. Republic, O., Sept. 6, 1884; s. John Valentine and Cora Ellen (Meyers) S.; Ph.B., Wooster (O.) Coll., 1906; M.A., Ohio State University, 1908; Ph.D., University of Wisconsin, 1916, D.Sc. (honorary), 1961; D.Sc. (honorary), Lawrence College, 1955; married William Davison, John Rodger. Asst. Chemist Bur. Standards, Washington, 1908, Bur. Internal Revenue, 1909; research chemist U.S. Forest Service, 1909-17; dir. chem. research C. F. Burgess Labs., 1917-31; president of the Burgess Cellulose Company, Freeport, Illinois, 1931-50; professor wildlife management U. Wis., 1951-55, now emeritus; dir. Research Products Corporation, Burgess Cellulose Company. Member of Wisconsin Conservation Commn., 1953-60. Recipient Brewster award, 1958. Fellow Am. Ornithol. Union; mem. Am. Chem. Soc., Nat. Audubon Soc. (dir. 1957-59), Am. Soc. Mammalogy, Cooper, Wilson, Wis. ornithol. socs., Wis. Hist. Soc., Wis. Archeol. Soc., Wis. Acad. Scis. (pres. 1942-43), Phi Beta Kappa, Sigma Xi, Delta Upsilon. Republican. Presbyn. Club: Madison. Author: Chemistry of Cellulose and Wood, 1926; The Passenger Pigeon, 1955; The Wild Turkey, 1966. Author articles on chemistry, ornithology. Holder numerous chem. patents. Home: Madison, Wis. *

SCHOTT, CARL PETER, coll. dean; b. nr. Carleton, Neb., Nov. 17, 1886; s. Henry and Katie (Hagenlocher) S.; B.E., Neb. State Normal, 1909; B.P.E., Springfield Y.M.C.A. Coll., 1912; B.S., Columbia, 1925, M.A., 1926, Ph.D., 1929; m. Ivy Hall Hutchison, May 29, 1913; 1 dau., Katharine Elizabeth (Mrs. F. Graff Sinclair, Jr.). Prin. jr. high sch., Fairbury, Neb., 1909-10; dir. recreation, London, Ont., summer 1912; dir. phys. edn. and athletics, head coach football, baseball and basketball, State Normal Sch., Plattsville, Wis., 1912-16; supt. Lincoln Chautauqua, summers 1916, 17; dir. physical edn. and athletics (head baseball coach, 1916-24; head basketball coach, 1918-24), Pomona Coll., Claremont, Calif., 1916-24; dir. St. George's Boy's Club, New York City, 1924-27; head dept. phys. edn. and athletics, Western State Teachers Coll., Kalamazoo, Mich., 1927-28; dir. div. phys. edn., W.Va. U., 1928-37; dean sch. phys. edn. and athletics, Pa. State Coll. since 1937. Pres. Wis. Intercollegiate Athletic Conf., 1914-15; mem. approved list Western Conf. Football Officials, 1928; pres. W.Va. State Football Officials Assn., 1933-34; organizer and first pres., W.Va. State

Bd. Basketball Officials, 1934-36; mem. exec. com. nat. bd. Nat. Assn. Approved Basketball Officials, 1934-37, chmn. rules revision com., 1936-37; editor Annual Nat. Collegiate Athletic Assn. Boxing Guide, since 1938; mem. Nat. Collegiate Athletic Assn. Boxing Rules Com. since 1938; sec. Olympic Boxing Com., 1940; sec. Olympic Boxing Com., 1940; sec. U.S. Olympic Boxing Com. since 1946; mem. spl. com. on Survey of Phys. Training in U.S.N., 1942; mem. adv. council Physical Training Program for Naval Aviation, 1942; pres. Coll. Phys. Edn. Assn., 1942-44; pres. U.S. Intercollegiate Lacross Assn., 1945-47; mem. Nat. Council Phys. Fitness, Fed. Security Agency, 1943-45, mem. subcom. schs. and colls., 1943-44; made survey health, phys. edn. and recreation in Pittsburgh (Pa.) Pub. Schs., 1944. Received professional honor award of Pa. State Assn. Health, Physical Edn. and Recreation, 1944. Fellow Am. Assn. Health, Phys. Edn. and Recreation. Mem. Coll. Phys. Edn. Assn., Nat. Edn. Assn., Phi Delta Kappa, Kappa Delta Pi, Phi Delta Theta. Mem. Soc. of Friends. Club: Centre Hill Country (State College, Pa.). Author: Physical Education in the United Lutheran Colleges, 1929. Home: State College, Penn. *

SCHRADER, EDWARD ALBERT, business exec.; b. Kokomo, Ind., 1912; s. Edward August and Elizabeth (Leas) S.; A.B., Ind. U., 1934, LL.D., 1966; M.B.A., Harvard, 1936; LL.D., Marlboro Coll., 1969; m. Aimee St. John, 1941 (div.); children—Edmee Hollister (Mrs. Michael McCormack), Constance St. John (Mrs. Robert Rapp); m. 2d Margaret Martin Buhrman, 1976. With Goldman, Sachs and Co., N.Y.C., 1936-75, buying dept., 1936-48, partner, 1949-75, ltd. partner, 1976-78, vice chmn. mgmt. com., 1969-75; dir. Vulcan Materials Co., Birmingham, Ala., Fed. Paper Bd. Co. (Montvale, N.J.). Dir. Ind. U. Found., Mem. Phi Beta Kappa, Beta Theta Pi. Clubs: Harvard (N.Y.C.); Pine Tree Golf (Boynton Beach, Fla.); Boca Raton (Fla.) Hotel and Club. Home: Boca Raton, Fla. Died Mar. 3, 1978.

SCHRANK, HARRY PAUL, born Akron, Ohio, May 14, 1903; s. Fred J. and Ida (Rohr) S.; B.S., U. Akron, 1924; student U. Wis., 1924-25; advanced management program Harvard U., 1956; Ph.D. (hon.), U. Akron, 1970; m. J. Kathryn Palmer, Aug. 11, 1925 (dec.); children—Edwin P., Harry Paul, Frederick J., Joel P.; m. 2d, Mrs. Rachel W. Herberich, April 3, 1941; 1 stepdau., Katharine Herberich. Devel. engr. Norwalk Tire & Rubber Co. (Conn.), 1925-26; devel. engr. Seiberling Rubber Co., 1926-34, supr., 1934-36, dir., v.p. prodn., 1936-56, exec. v.p., 1956-61, pres., chief exec. officer, 1961-65; pres. Seiberling Tire & Rubber Co., 1965-67. Chmn. bd. trustees U. Akron; pres. bd. trustees Boy Scouts Am. Mem. C.E.D. com., Summit County. Harry P. Schrank Hall at U. Akron named for him, 1969; recipient joint resolution and key to city City of Akron, 1970. Mem. Lone Star frat., Omicron Delta Kappa, Beta Delta Psi. Republican. Lutheran. Clubs: Portage Country (pres.), Masons (Akron). Home: Akron, Ohio. Died Oct. 18, 1979.

SCHREIBER, LUDWIG DAVID, investment co. exec.; b. Milw., Mar. 3, 1890; s. Isidor and Henrietta (Mandel) S.; student pub. high sch.; m. Jeanette Reinstein, Dec. 12, 1918; children—Marilyn (Mrs. Jay L. Winston), Marcia (Mrs. Robert K. Deutsch). Pres. L.D. Schreiber & Co., Inc., Chgo., 1919-76, also dir.; dir. L.D. Schreiber Cheese Co., Inc., Green Bay, Wis., Albert Lea Freezer Warehouse Co. (Minn.), Worthington Freezer Warehouse Co. (Minn.), Mpls. Cold Storage Co. City clk. Chgo., 1939-55. Mem. N.Y. Merc. Exchange. Clubs: Standard (Chgo.); Westview Country (Miami Beach). Home: Chicago, Ill. Died Nov. 30, 1976.

SCHROCK, ROBERT D., orthopaedic surgeon; b. Delaware, O., Aug. 22, 1884; s. Dr. William H. and Nettie M. (Patterson) S.; A.B., Wabash Coll., Crawfordsville, Ind., 1905; M.D., Cornell U., 1912; m. Elizabeth Winslow Wetherbee, Aug. 1935; 1 son, Robert D. Interne, New York Hosp., 1913-15, resident, 1915-16; engaged in practice of orthopaedic surgery, Omaha, Neb., since 1916; prof. orthopaedic surgey, U. of Neb. Coll. of Medicine, 1932-49. Lt., capt. and maj. U.S. Army, A.E.F., base hosp. No. 9, 1917-19. Fellow Am. Coll. Surgs. (bd. govs. 1947-50), mem. Western Surg. Soc., A.M.A. (chmn., orthopaedic sect., 1935), Neb. State Assn., Omaha-Douglas Co. Med. Soc. (pres., 1946-47), Am. Assn. Ry. Surgs., Omaha Mid-West Clin. Soc. (pres. 1943), Clin. Orthopaedic Soc. (pres. 1929), Am. Acad. Orthopaedic Surgs. (pres. 1941), Am. Orthopaedic Assn., Internat. Orthopaedic Assn.; mem. Am. Bd. Orthopaedic Surg., 1943-46. Civilian cons. orthopaedics to comd. officer 3902d Med. group, Strategic Air Command, Ft. Crook, Neb.; commd. surgeon (R) U.S. Pub. Health; attending surgeon Meth. and Bishop Clarkson Hospitals, and Hattie B. Munroe Home for Convalescing Crippled Children. Mem. Phi Delta Theta, Nu Sigma Nu, Alpha Omega Alpha. Mason (Shriner). Clubs: Omaha, Omaha (Neb.) Country. Contbr. numerous scientific articles to various publs. Home: Omaha, Neb. *

SCHROEDER, JOSEPH JEROME, banking edn.; b. Chicago, Ill., May 10, 1889; s. Carl Stephen and Frances Catherine (Cornelisen) S.; grad. Am. Inst. of Banking, 1915; m. Frances Walker Noyes, Feb. 10, 1923; 1 son, Joseph Jerome. Clerk Nat. Bank of the Republic, Chicago, 1906-17; exec. sec. Chgo. chpt. Am. Inst. Banking, from 1920; editor The Bank Man, from 1921. Served as sergt. U.S. Army 149th F.A., Rainbow Div., 1917-19; capt. F.A. Reserve, 1920-40. Sec. Banking Research Fund. Sec. Chicago and Cook County Bankers Assn., 1920-21; sec. Assn. Reserve City Bankers, from 1925; member Nat. Adv. Council on Financial Research. Republican. Club: Westmoreland Country (Wilmette, Illinois). Author: Elements of Banking, 1928; Bank Administration, 1938. Home: Wilmette, Ill. Died July 22, 1976.

SCHROTH, FRANK D. (SHROTH), newspaperman, ex-pub.; b. Trenton, N.J., Oct. 18, 1884; s. John and Margaret (Donahoe) S.; L.D. (hon.) St. John's University; Litt.D. (hon.), Long Island University; married Lorette E. Nolan, July 6, 1914; children—Margaret, Lorette, Frank David, Thomas, Raymond, Gerald. Newspaper reporter, 1904-14; sec. N.J. State Bd. of Taxes and Assessments and newspaper correspondent, 1914-25; editor and pub. Trenton State Gazette, 1925-26; gen. mgr. and asso. pub. Trenton Times Newspapers, 1926-33; editor and pub. The Scranton (Pa.) Tribune, 1934-38; editor and pub. Brooklyn Daily Eagle, 1938-55; editorial cons., N.Y. News, New York City, 1955-58. Life trustee Bklyn. Inst. Arts and Scics., Pratt Inst. Mem. N.Y. com. Ednl. Finance, White House Conf. Edn. Awarded silver medal N.Y.C. Park Assn., 1951, Bklyn. C. of C. award, 1951, medal award Bklyn. Downtown Assn., 1951, annual Americanism award Flatlands Am. Legion post, 1951; Pulitzer prize to Bklyn. Eagle for pub. service, 1951. Mem. Pilgrim Soc. U.S., Am. Press Inst. (founder, sponsor). Roman Catholic. Home: Trenton, N.J. *

SCHRUTH, PETER E., broadcasting co. exec.; b. Fargo, N.D., Mar. 10, 1917; s. John Lewis and Mary (Elliott) S.; B.B.A., U. Minn., 1939; student FBI Acad., 1942; m. Anne Killmade, Aug. 3, 1946; children—Barbara, Susan, Peter, Mark. With Campbell-Mithun Advt. Agy., Mpls., St. Paul, 1939-41; sales mgr. Pepsi-Cola Bottling Co., St. Paul, 1941; Western mgr. Holiday mag., 1947-53, advt. dir., 1954-58, pub., 1962-64; advt. dir. Sat. Eve. Post, 1959-62; v.p. Westinghouse Broadcasting Co., N.Y.C., 1964-66, sr. v.p., 1966-79, v.p. western region, San Francisco, 1974-79; vice chmn. Westinghouse Learning Corp., 1967-79; v.p., gen. mgr. WINS radio. Past mem. Greenwich (Conn.) Bd. Edn. Bd. dirs. San Francisco Heart Assn., San Francisco Conv. and Visitors Bur., San Francisco Planning and Urban Renewal Assn., Bay Area Council, Calif. Instrnl. Television Adv. Commn. Served as spl. agt. FBI. World War II. Named Sales Exec. of Yr., Nat. Sales Execs., 1961. Mem. Alpha Delta Sigma, Chi Psi (exec. council), Alpha Nu. Clubs: Menlo Country (Woodside, Calif.); Bohemian (San Francisco); University (N.Y.C.). Home: Menlo Park, Calif. Died Sept. 21, 1979; buried Gates of Heaven Cemetery, Los Altos, Calif.

SCHUBERT, LEO, chemist, educator; b. N.Y.C., Mar. 1, 1916; s. Solomon and Katherine (Anker) S.; B.S., Coll. City N.Y., 1936; M.S., N.Y. U., 1943; Ph.D., U. Md., 1954; Sc.D., St. Augustine's Coll., 1964; m. Edith Broffman, Feb. 12, 1938; 1 dau., Leda Deirdre. Chemist Nat. Bur. Standards, 1942-51; mem. faculty Am. U., 1951-78, prof. chemistry, 1956-75, chmn. dept., 1951-75, Univ. prof., 1975-78; cons., 1959-78. Dir. China Closet, Bethesda, Md. Mem. Joint Bd. Sci. Edn., 1959-67, chmn. com. research participation, 1960-78. Dir. purchase guide revision project Council Chief State Sch. Officers, 1964. Trustee St. Augustine's Coll. Recipient College Chemistry Teacher award Mfg. Chemists Assn., 1968. Fellow A.A.A.S. (sec. chemistry sect. 1968-78, councillor 1973-78); mem. Chem. Soc. Washington (chmn. com. edn. 1958-61, program com. 1956-57, councilor 1960-78, bd. mgrs.; program rev. com. 1974-78, com. on chemistry and pub. affairs 1975-78, pres. 1964) Washington Acad. Scis. (chmn. com. encouragement sci. talent 1958-61, bd. mgrs. 1961-63; pres. 1965), Colloquium Sci. and Soc. (dir.), Philos. Soc. Washington, History Sci. Club, Sigma Xi (pres. 1964-66), Phi Kappa Phi. Club: Cosmos (Washington). Editor-in-chief: Jour. of Coll. Sci. Teaching, 1969-78; editor: History of Chemistry series, Am. Chem.-Soc., 1970-78. Contbr. articles profl. jours., encys. Home: Bethesda, Md. Died June 21, 1978; buried King David Meml. Cemetery.

SCHUETTE, HENRY AUGUST, chemist; born Green Bay, Wis., Jan. 11, 1885; s. Frederick and Helen (Gieseler) S.; B.S., U. of Wis., 1910; M.S., 1912, Ph.D., 1916; m. Jean Fyfe Frederickson. Nov. 2, 1918; children—Helen C. (Mrs. F. Chandler Young), John F., Henry G. Asst. chemistry, U. of Wis., 1910-14, instr., 1914-18, asst. prof., 1918-28, asso. prof., 1928-36, prof. since 1936; chem. cons. Fellow, A.A.A.S; mem. Am. Oil Chemists' Soc. (pres., 1940-41), Am. Chem. Soc. (chmn. div. agrl. and food chemistry, 1932-34), Wis. Acad. of Sciences, Arts and Letters (pres. 1944-46), Inst. of Food Technologists, Wis. Hist. Soc., Alpha Chi Sigma, Phi Lambda Upsilon, Sigma Xi. Republican. Lutheran. Club: University (Madison). Contbr. numerous papers, book revs. Home: Madison, Wis. *

SCHUETTE, OSWALD FRANCIS (SHOO'TY), newspaperman and public relations counselor; b. Chicago, Illinois, Aug. 31, 1882; s. William Henry and Caroline Anna (Bayerl) S.; grad. high sch. at 15; m. Mary Patrice Moran, June 24, 1919; children—Oswald Francis, Anne Catherine (Mrs. John J. Tkacik), Mary Patrice (Mrs. Paul B. McMahon), Patrick William (deceased), James Moran, William Henry, II. Engaged in newspaper work, Chicago, Illinois, 1902; editorial staff Milwaukee Sentinel, 1903-04; city editor Evening Wisconsin, 1905; traveling European corr., 1906-07; polit. writer, Inter-Ocean, Chicago, 1907, and Washington corr. same, 1908-14; Washington corr. Leslie's Weekly; war corr., Chicago Daily News, with armies of Central Powers, in Germany, Austria, Hungary, Belgium, France, Russia, Bulgaria, Serbia, Roumania and Turkey, Jan. 1915-17; was last Am. corr. to leave Berlin after declaration of war; then rep. Daily News in Switzerland, 1917-18; Washington corr. Leslie's Weekly, Iron Age, 1918-20, Chicago Herald-Examiner (under pen-name "Politicus"), 1921-22, Chicago Abendpost, 1921-22; editor in charge of editorial page Chicago Herald-Examiner, 1922-25; pres. Short Wave Inst. of Am., 1935-36; counselor public and govt. relations; director Staats-Herold Corporation and German Herold Publishing Company (N.Y.C). Executive head of independent radio industry in campaign to dissolve $7,000,000,000 combination of Radio Corp. America, Gen. Electric Co., Westinghouse Co., Gen. Motors Corp., Am. Telephone & Telegraph Co., which resulted in consent decree of dissolution, leaving Radio Corp. America an independent corp. Mem. Am. Sect. Internat. Com. on Radio, Electron Microscope Soc. Am., Catholic Econ. Assn. Wrote Repub. Nat Com.'s Handbook on League of Nations in 1920 campaign. Lecturer on European War and internat. affairs. Coined political phrase "the steam roller." Republican. Catholic. Clubs: Nat. Press (sec. 1912; pres. 1913); Overseas Writers, Palaver, Askeaton Country (Washington); Milwaukee Press; Mediaevalists, Press Veterans (Chicago); Inquirendo (Washington). Home: Madison, Wisc. *

SCHUETZ, ROBERT DAVID, educator, chemist; b. Mpls., June 27, 1915; s. David Aloysius and Olive Margaret (Carver) S.; B.S., Northwestern U., 1937, M.S., 1939, Ph.D., 1947; m. Maryellen Murray, Nov. 28, 1942; children—Laura Catherine, Robert Edward. Research chemist, chem. engr. Richardson Co., 1940-46; research asso. Ohio State U., 1946-47; mem. faculty Mich. State U., East Lansing, from 1947, prof. dept. chemistry, 1958-64, dir. labs., 1957-64, asst. dir. Inst. Biology and Medicine, 1964-67, asso. dir., from 1967, acting dir., from 1970, coordinator for health programs, from 1973, prof. chemistry, from 1959. Mem. Am. Chem. Soc., N.Y. Acad. Scis., Sigma Xi, Alpha Chi Sigma. Author: Organic Chemistry, 4th edit., 1972; (with H. Hart) Laboratory Manual for Study Guide and Solutions Book for Organic Chemistry, 1972; Laboratory Manual for Organic Chemistry, 4th edit., 1972; also numerous articles. Patentee polymers, polymerization, medicinal chems.; research on reaction mechanisms and kinetics catalytic hydrogenations, carbohydrate chemistry, synthesis, reaction mechanism, stereochemistry organo-sulfur compounds and sulfur heterocylic compounds, bio-synthesis naturally occuring organo sulfur compounds, photochemistry, pesticide chemistry. Home: East Lansing, Mich. Died Aug. 20.

SCHULTZ, HENRY EDWARD, lawyer; b. N.Y.C., June 18, 1906; s. Julius and Esther (Block) S.; LL.B., N.Y. Law Sch., 1928; L.H.D., W.Va. State Coll., 1961; m. Rose Jane Yellin, Oct. 16, 1930; children—Roger Anthony, Michael Edward, Jane Ellen. Admitted to N.Y. bar, 1929, practiced in N.Y.C. Vice pres., gen. counsel J.B. Williams Co., Inc. Mem. Bd. Higher Edn., N.Y.C., 1942-69, emeritus mem., 1969-79. Nat. chmn. Anti-Defamation League B'nai B'rith, 1953-63, hon. nat. chmn., 1963-79; chmn. exec. com. Eleanor Roosevelt Cancer Found., Inc. Home: Miami Beach, Fla. Died May 5, 1979.

SCHULTZ, HOWARD LOUIS, educator; b. Cassadaga, N.Y., Mar. 23, 1912; s. Louis and Antonette (Sheu) S.; B.A., U. Buffalo, 1933, M.A., 1935; Ph.D., Yale, 1937; m. Kathleen Pound, Apr. 10, 1939; 1 dau., Frances Anne. Sterling post-doctoral fellow Yale, 1937-38, instr., 1938-40, asst. prof. physics, 1945-48, prof. physics, project dir. Electron Accelerator Lab., 1951-77; instr. U. Buffalo, 1940-41, asso. prof. physics, 1945; research asso. Mass. Inst. Tech., 1941-45. Mem. Am. Phys. Soc., Conn. Acad. Arts and Scis., Phi Beta Kappa, Sigma Xi. Home: Hamden, Conn. Died Mar. 4, 1977.

SCHULTZ, SIGRID (LILLIAN), newspaper corr.; b. Chgo., 1893; d. Herman and Hedwig (Jaskewitz) Schultz; Diplôme de Certificat d'Etudes Supérieures; student Sorbonne, Paris, 1913, Berlin U., 1916. Asst. corr. Chgo. Tribune, Berlin, 1919; corr.-in-chief Central Europe, 1925-41; broadcasting for MBS, 1939-41; also war corr. Chgo. Tribune, McCalls Mag., MBS; corr., Bonn, Germany, 1952-53; now free lance news corr. Clubs: Overseas Press (bd. govs.); Pen. Author: Germany Will Try It Again, 1944. Editor: Overseas Press Club Cookbook, 1962. Contbr. articles to nat.

mags., lectr. Home: Westport, Conn. Died May 14, 1980.

SCHULZ, GEORGE J., educator, physicist; b. Brno, Czechoslovakia, Apr. 29, 1925; s. Felix and Elisabeth (Wallerstein) S.; came to U.S., 1947, naturalized, 1957; student U. Dr. E. Benes, Brno, 1945-47; B.S., Pa. State U., 1949, M.S., 1951; Ph.D., Mass. Inst. Tech., 1954; m. Rose Anfaenger, Sept. 20, 1949; children—Peter A., R. Stanley. Adv. physicist Westinghouse Research Lab., 1954-66; prof. applied sci. Yale, 1966-76. Sec. Gaseous Electronic Conf., 1963. Fellow Am. Phys. Soc. (Davisson-Germer prize 1965). Research electron collisions with atoms and molecules, mass spectrometry, gas discharge, vacuum technique. Home: Woodbridge, Conn. Died Jan. 15, 1976.

SCHUMACHER, BOWEN EMERSON, lawyer; b. Highland Park, Ill., Oct. 30, 1900; s. Bowen Wisner and Harriet Orne (Emerson) S.; B.A., U. Mich., 1922, J.D., 1924; m. Janet Dyer Lowenthal, Jan. 19, 1933 (dec. 1964); children—Janet, Bowen Emerson; m. 2d, Jean M. Gallery, Apr. 9, 1966. Admitted to Ill. bar, 1924, since practiced in Chgo.; law clk. Schumacher & Murphy, 1924-26, partner, 1926-29; partner Packard, Barnes, McCaughey & Schumacher, 1929-40, Packard, Barnes, Schumacher, Gilmore & Van Ness, 1940-50, Schumacher, Gilmore & Van Ness, from 1950 (now Schumacher, Jones Vallely Kelly & Olson); dir., atty. Highland Park Savings and Loan Assn.; atty. Gregor Jonsson Associates, Inc., Prairie Farmer Publishing Co., Wallace Homestead Co., Wis. Farmer Co. Corp. counsel, Highland Park, 1927-29, spl. counsel bd. local improvements, 1929-31; counsel park dist., Highland Park, 1927-57; mem. Ill. Commn. for Revision and Recodification Park Laws, 1947-49. Trustee Highland Park Hosp.; governing member Glenwood Sch. for Boys. Member American, Illinois State, Chgo. (chmn., mem. various coms.) bar assns., Psi Upsilon, Phi Delta Phi, Pi Delta Epsilon, Order of Coif. Republican. Presbyn. Clubs: Exmoor Country (bd. of govs. Highland Park, past pres.); Mid-Day (member of the board of trustees), Law, Legal (Chgo.). Home: Wilmette, Ill. Died Aug. 15, 1976.

SCHUMACHER, HENRY, Catholic educator; b. Ramsen, Germany, Jan. 13, 1883; s. Leonhard and Maria (Mechnich) S.; grad. Gymnasium, Speyer, Germany, 1903; student of philosophy and theology, Innsbruck, 1903-06; D.D., U. of Freiburg, 1911; spl. studies at Pontifical and Bibl. Inst., Rome, 1911-13. Came to U.S., 1913, naturalized, 1924. Prefect of Episcopal Sem., Speyer, 1907-11; vice-rector German Inst. Santa Maria dell' Anima, Rome, 1912-13; ordained priest R.C. Ch., 1907; prof. of New Testament Scripture, Cath. U. of America, Washington, D.C., 1913-31; prof. of New Testament, Regensburg, Germany, 1932. Has written many books on religious subjects in German and English langs. Contbr. articles to mags. Home: Gardenville, N.Y.*

SCHUMAKER, ALBERT JESSE RINGER (SHOO'MAK-ER), educator; b. Big Rock, Ill., Nov. 23, 1882; s. Rev. Lebbeus James and Emilie Jane (Coulter) S.; B.A., Marietta (O.) Coll., 1905, M.A., 1907; B.D., Hartford Theol. Sem., 1908; studied univs. of Leipzig and Berlin, 1908-10; Litt.D., honorary, Marietta College, 1939; married C. Agnes Donahue, January 25, 1919. Prof. psychology and edn., Grove City (Pa.) Coll., 1910-11; pastor First Ch., Coraopolis, Pa., 1912-14; ordained Bapt. ministry, 1913; asst. editor Am. Sunday Sch Union, 1914-18; again pastor First Ch., Coraopolis, 1919; dir. religious edn., Pittsburgh, 1920-29; mgr. New Eng. br. Am. Bapt. Publication Soc., Boston, 1930; dir. of leadership edn., Am. Bapt. Soc., Phila., 1930-41; sec. Leadership Training Pub. Assn., 1936-40; prof. sociology, Storer Coll., since 1941. Inventor of automatic mechanical calculator, 1943 (patent issued March 1948). Life mem. N.E.A., Phi Beta Kappa. Home: Harpers Ferry, W. Va.*

SCHUMAN, FREDERICK LEWIS, author, educator; b. Chgo., Feb. 22, 1904; s. August and Ella (Schulze) S.; Ph.B., U. Chgo., 1924, Ph.D., 1927; m. Lily Caroline Abell, June 23, 1930 (dec. 1977); children—Karl (dec.), Donald Robert, Marcia Lenore Armstrong. Instr. polit. sci. U. Chgo., 1927-32, asst. prof., 1932-36; prof. polit. sci. Williams Coll., Williamstown, Mass., 1936-38, Woodrow Wilson prof. govt., 1938-68, Woodrow Wilson prof. govt. emeritus, 1968-81; prof. polit. sci. Portland (Oreg.) State U., 1968-71; vis. prof. Harvard Summer Sch., 1938, U. Calif., 1939, 55, Cornell U., 1944, Columbia, 1946, U. Chgo., 1956, Central Wash. Coll., 1959, Portland State Coll., 1961, Stanford, 1963, others. Polit. analyst, for broadcast intelligence service. Fellow Social Sci. Research Council, 1929-30; fellow Am. Acad. Polit. and Social Sci., 1933, Found. for World Govt., 1950-51. Mem. Am. Polit. Sci. Assn., Am. Soc. Internat. Law, Am. Anthrop. Assn., Civil Liberties Union, Phi Beta Kappa. Author several books including: Soviet Politics, 1946; The Commonwealth of Man, 1952; Russia Since 1917, 1957; International Politics, 7th edit., 1969; Government in the Soviet Union, 1961; The Cold War: Retrospect and Prospect, 1962. Contbr. to mags. Home: Portland, Ore. Died May 19, 1981.

SCHURZ, WILLIAM LYTLE, author, commercial attaché; b. South Lebanon, O., Nov. 25, 1886; s. Henry Clay and Anna L. (Lytle) S.; B. Litt., U. of Calif., 1911, M.Litt., 1912, Ph.D., 1915; engaged in historical research in Spain, 1913-15; m. 2d, Marie L. Leyden, of Washington, D.C., Dec. 11, 1924. Mem. faculty, U. of Mich., 1915-18; with U.S. Dept. Commerce since 1919; trade commr.,in charge of general investigation in Paraguay and Bolivia, 1919-20; commercial attaché, at Rio de Janeiro, Brazil, since 1920; chief of Dept. of Commerce crude rubber survey in the Amazon Valley, 1923-24. Author: Paraguay (a commercial handbook), 1920; Bolivia (a commercial and industrial handbook), 1921. Joint Author: Rubber Production in the Amazon Valley, 1925. Address: New York, N.Y., or Rio de Janeiro, Brazil. *

SCHUTZ, ANTON (FRIEDRICH JOSEPH), artist, publisher; b. Berndorf, Germany, Apr. 19, 1894; s. Anton Valentine and Elizabeth (Struth) S.; M.E., U. Munich, 1920; student Munich Acad. Fine Arts, 1919-23; m. Mimi Gross, Aug. 30, 1920; children—Herbert, Beatrice; m. 2d, Christa Trapp, July 13, 1961; children—Anton Villars, Christina Villars and Linda Frances (twins); came to U.S., 1924, naturalized, 1930. Began as etcher, 1919; asso. with Joseph Pennell at Art Students' League, N.Y., 1924-25; toured Japan, China, 1929; founder, pres. N.Y. Graphic Soc., Inc., 1925-66 (merged with Time, Inc. 1966), dir., cons., from 1966 (fine art pub. in U.S. on same basis as in Europe; reprodns. old and modern masters); past pres. Inter-Am. Graphic, Ltd.; established UNESCO Art Popularization Series, São Paulo, Brazil, 1953; mem. numerous UNESCO missions gathering materials for art reprodn. books in India, Bulgaria, Ceylon, Egypt, Iran, Israel, Japan, Mexico, Rumania, Tunisia, other countries, 1953-61. Represented in collections Library Congress, Washington, Brit. Mus., London, Bibliotheque Nationale, Paris, Uffizi, Florence, Italy, Cleve. Mus. Art, Bklyn. Mus., Art Inst. Chgo., others. Served as lt. of engrs. German Army, 1914-18. Awarded Iron Cross 1st class and 2d class (Germany), Iron Half-moon (Turkey), Croce Laterane (Vatican). Mem. Soc. Am. Graphic Artists, Chgo. Soc. Etchers. Author: New York in Etchings, 1939; Fine Art Reproduction of Old and Modern Masters, 1941; Hand Book of Fine Art Color Reproductions, 1945; Blue Book Color Reproductions, 1951; Fine Art Reproductions: Old and Modern Masters, 1961, 65; Reproductions of American Paintings, 1961. Pub. and co-editor UNESCO World Art Series. Author: (autobiography) My Share of Wine, 1973. Home: Scarsdale, N.Y. Died Oct. 6, 1977; interred Ferncliff Cemetery, Hartsdale, N.Y.

SCHUYLER, GARRET LANSING, naval officer; b. N.Y.C., Mar. 18, 1885; s. James Everett and Lillian (Randolph) S.; B.S., U.S. Naval Acad., 1907; course in explosives, George Washington Univ., 1909-10; m. Beatrice Tracy, June 14, 1919. Commd. ensign U.S. Navy, 1908, and advanced through grades to rear adm., 1947; attached to U.S. Embassy, London, 1917-21, mem. Inter-Allied Naval Armistice Commn., also on Adm. Sim's staff; gunnery officer, U.S. Naval Ry. guns, France, 1918; comd. U.S. Naval Proving Ground, Dahlgren, Va., and Naval Powder Factory, Indian Head, Md., 1931-34; organized and headed research and development div., Navy Bur. of Ordnance, 1941-42; pres., spl. bd., Naval Ordnance, 1942-47; ret. from active duty, Jan. 1, 1947; explosives safety cons. Calif. Inst. Tech. and AEC, from 1947; special consultant to Civil Defense Office (National Security Resources Board) from 1951. Served on panels of Research and Development Board coms., from 1947; mem. NRC, 1941-46. Awarded Navy Cross, Legion of Merit, Order of Brit. Empire, Legion of Honor, and various campaign ribbons. Mem. Seismol. Soc. Am., Philosophical Society of Washington. Dutch Reformed Ch. Clubs: Cosmos, Army Navy (Washington). Contbr. 16 articles to U.S. Naval Inst.; other articles to various tech. and professional publs. Invented use of fuel oil tanks for torpedo protection of naval ships; delay coil; holds patents on bomb displacer, and automatic rocket launcher. Home: Washington, D.C. Died Jan. 4, 1977.

SCHWARTZ, SIDNEY L., investment banker and broker; b. San Francisco, Calif., Jan. 3, 1886; s. William and Henrietta (Gump) S.; grad. Lowell High Sch., San Francisco, 1904; student U. of Calif., 1904-06; LL.D., University of Santa Clara; married to Alice Wolff, June 22, 1913; children—Marie Louise (Mrs. Alfred Barnston), Elizabeth (Mrs. Jack Virgil Cosgriff). With Sutro & Co. (member N.Y. Stock Exchange), bankers and brokers, San Francisco, 1906, partner, 1907-29, sr. partner, 1929-60, now ltd. partner; gov. N.Y. Stock Exchange, 1944-50. Investment adviser for Hebrew Home for Aged and Disabled; pres., chmn. of bd. of Sidney L. and Alice Schwartz Found.; member bd. counsellors Sch. of Bus., U. Santa Clara. Mem. Investment Bankers Assn., San Francisco Stock Exchange (pres. 1923-30, and 1942-44), Lowell Alumni Assn. (p.p.), Old Time Athletes Assn. (past pres.), Big Bros. San Francisco (hon. dir.), Beta Gamma Sigma (hon.). Republican. Jewish religion. Mason. Clubs: Stock Exchange, Rotary (pres. found.), Commonwealth, Merced Golf and Country, Rio Del Mar Golf and Country. Home: San Francisco, Calif. *

SCHWARTZ, WILLIAM SAMUEL, artist; b. Smorgon, Russia, Feb. 23, 1896; s. Samuel and Taube Schwartz; came to U.S. 1912, naturalized, 1925; scholarship student Vilna Art Sch., Russia, 1908-12, Art Inst. Chgo., 1915-17; grad. with hon. mentions for portrait painting, life study painting, gen. excellence in painting; studied singing under Karl Stein, Auditorium Conservatory of Music, Chgo., 1915-18, under Francesco Daddi, 1918-19; m. Mona Turner, Aug. 15, 1939. Appeared in leading tenor roles in operas including The Bartered Bride, Rigoletto, La Traviata, Il Trovatore, Aida, Cavaleria Rusticana, also in operatic roles in concerts and on vaudeville stage. Art exhibited in nat. internat. exhbns. in leading museums, galleries in U.S., Can., 1918-77. Recipient 1st Albert Kahn prize, 1925, 1st prize Temple Beth El Sisterhood, 1926 (both Detroit); recipient Marshall Fuller Holmes prize, 1927, M.V. Kohnstamm prize, 1928, John C. Shafer prize, 1930, Clyde M. Carr prize, 1930, Mr. and Mrs. Jules F. Brower prize, 1945, 63, Municipal Art League Prize, 1952 (all Art Inst. Chgo.); received hon. mention Scarab Club, Detroit, 1936, First Nat. Lithograph Exhbn., Oklahoma Art Center, Oklahoma City, 1939, Fourth Exhbn., 1942, Corpus Christi (Tex.) Art Found., 1945; recipient Covenant Club prize, 1936, 41, 1st purchase, prize Monticello Coll., Godfrey, Ill., 1939, 1st prize in watercolors Union League Club, Chgo., 1st spl. hon mention, 1965, Zimmerman award Phila. Water Color Club, 1974. Represented in permanent collections Art Inst. Chgo., Ency. Brit., Am. Peoples Ency., Detroit Inst. Arts, Library of Congress and Dept. of Labor (both Washington), Art Alliance Phila., Dallas Mus. Fine Arts, Madison (Wis.) Art Assn., Tel Aviv (Israel) Mus., Biro Bidjan Mus. (Russia), Little Gallery, Cedar Rapids, Ia., Oshkosh (Wis.) Mus., Montclair (N.J.) Art Mus., Standard Oil Co. N.J., N.Y.C., San Francisco Mus., Joslyn Art Mus., Omaha, Pa. Acad. Fine Arts, Phila., U. Washington, Santa Barbara Mus. Art, Denver Art Mus., Des Moines Art Center, Ain Herod Mus., Israel, Ill. State Hist. Library, Springfield, Evansville (Ind.) Mus. Arts and Scis.; collections of univs. Ill., Neb., Mo., Wyo., Minn., State Tchr. Coll. DeKalb, Ill., Ill. State Normal U., Carbondale, Chgo. Normal Coll., Monticello Coll., Beloit (Wis.) Coll., Bradley U., Peoria, Ill., DePaul U., Chgo., Chgo. pub. schs.; pub. library collections: Davenport, Ia., Glencoe, Ill., Cin., Chgo., also in other pub., pvt. collections U.S., France, Germany, Russia, Sweden, Czechoslovakia. Murals: Mining-Chgo. Century of Progress Expn., 1933, Cook County Nurses Home, Chgo., 1935, Old P.O., Fairfield (Ill.) P.O., 1936, Mining in Ill., Eldorado (Ill.) P.O., 1937, River Boat and Bridge, Pittsfield (Ill.) P.O.; represented in permanent collections including Ill. State Mus. Springfield, So. Meth. U., Dallas, Okla. Art Center, Oklahoma City U., Chgo., Northwestern U., Chgo., Musée D'Art Juif, Paris, France, Union League Club Chgo. Subject of book: William S. Schwartz, A Study by Manuel Chapman, 1930. Address: Chicago, Ill. Died Feb. 10, 1977; buried Rosehill Cemetery, Chicago.

SCHWARTZMAN, DANIEL, architect; b. Balt., Dec. 9, 1908; s. Abraham and Ethel Bernice (Benjamin) S.; B.Arch., U. Pa., 1931; student Ecole Nat. Superieure des Beaux arts, France, 1933-34; m. Dorothy E. Kemler, Feb. 24, 1933; children—John Bennett, Ellen. Archtl. practice, N.Y.C., 1940-77; sr. partner Daniel Schwartzman & Assos.; pres. Daniel Schwartzman Cons. Inc.; prin. works include dept. stores, synagogues, shopping centers, residences, pub. schs., univ. buildings, public building for N.Y.C.; mem. faculty Pratt Inst., 1948-70, N.Y.U., 1959-61. Trustee Nat. Inst. Archtl. Edn.; chmn. architects adv. panel Union Am. Hebrew Congregations Trustee Jewish Bd. Guardians. Fellow A.I.A. (v.p. N.Y. chpt. 1950, chmn. nat. commn. on professional practice 1958-77, nat. treas. 1965-67, nat. v.p. 1968-69; Kemper award 1964, bd. spl. citation for internat. relations); mem. Internat. Union of Architects (U.S. rep. to exec. com., v.p. 1969-73 rep. to UN 1970-73), Archtl. League N.Y. (pres. 1954-55), Mcpl. Arts Soc., N.Y. State Assn. Architects (dir. 1954-55). Clubs: North Shore Country (pres. 1961-62) (Glen Head, N.Y.); City Athletic, Grolier (N.Y.C.). Contbr. articles to profl. jours., sects. to books. Home: Sea Cliff, N.Y. Died Jan. 25, 1977.

SCHWEITZER, PAUL HENRY, mech. engr.; b. Miskolc, Hungary, May 20, 1893; s. Henry and Hermin (Robitsek) S.; M.E., Royal Hungarian Tech. U., Budapest, 1917; Dr. Eng., Saeschische Technische Hochschule, Dresden; Dr.H.C., Budapest Tech. U., 1967; m. Susan Morse, Apr. 29, 1975. Came to U.S., 1920, naturalized, 1925. Asst. master mechanic, diesel engine designer De La Vergne Machine Co., N.Y.C., 1920-22; tool designer Oakland Motor Car Co., Pontiac, Mich., 1922-23; asst. prof. Pa. State U., 1923-27, asso. prof., 1927-36, prof. engring. research, 1936-57, prof. emeritus, 1958-80; partner Schweitzer & Hussmann Engring. Office, 1952-80; mfrs. cons., 1952-80; cons. Army Tank Automotive Center. Fulbright scholar, 1953-54. Served as 1st lt. F.A. and Air Corps, Austro-Hungarian Army, 1914-18; as lt. comdr. USNR, 1937-57. Fellow ASME, AAAS, Soc. Automotive Engrs.; mem. Sigma Xi.; hon. mem. Japan Soc. M.E. Author: Scavenging of Two-Stroke Cycle Diesel Engines, 1949 (in Spanish 1959); also numerous tech. bulls., papers, articles in tech. and sci. jours. Am., Eng., Germany, Japan, France, Spain, Hungary, Poland.

Holder 20 U.S., also fgn. patents. Home: State College, Pa. Died Apr. 12, 1980.

SCHWENDLER, WILLIAM THEODORE, aerospace mfg. exec.; b. Winfield Junction, N.Y., Apr. 1, 1904; s. Carl and Emilie B. (Klein) S.; B.S. in M.E., N.Y. U., 1924; D. Eng. (hon.), 1955; m. Mabel R. Jorden, Oct. 20, 1933; children—Olga E., Hazel A., William T. Jr. engr. Loening Aero. Engring. Corp., N.Y.C., 1924-25, project engr., 1926-27, asst. gen. mgr., 1928-30; chief engr. Grumman Aircraft Engring. Corp., 1930-50, dir. 1939-69, v.p., 1940-46, exec. v.p., 1946-56, sr. v.p., 1956-60, chmn. exec. com., 1960-69; chmn. exec. com. Grumman Corp., 1969-73, dir., to 1978; vice chmn. Grumman Aerospace Corp., 1969-71, sr. exec., 1971-73; dir. Sunrise Fed. Savs. & Loan Assn., L.I., N.Y. Mem. Nassau County council Boy Scouts; emeritus mem. adv. bd. Acad. Aeros. Trustee N.Y. U., 1956-78, recipient Pres.'s citation, 1965. Fellow AIAA; mem. Newcomen Soc., Soc. Automotive Engrs., Phi Kappa Tau, Pi Tau Sigma, Tau Beta Pi. Lutheran. Clubs: Ocean Reef; Unqua Corinthian Yacht: N.Y. Yacht. Home: Farmingdale, N.Y. Died Jan. 14, 1978.

SCHWIERING, OSCAR CONRAD (SWE'RING), univ. prof.; b. Peoria, Ill., Sept. 5, 1886; s. William Henry and Lydia (Wilkening) S.; A.B., Iowa Wesleyan U., 1909; grad. student U. of Ill., summer, 1911, U. of Colo., summers, 1912, 13; M.A., U. of Wyo., 1916; grad. student U. of Chicago, summers, 1917, 18, 21, Stanford U., summer, 1923; Ph.D., New York U., 1932; research asso., Teachers Coll., Columbia, fall 1943; m. Willetta B. Jamison, Jan. 4, 1910; children—Oscar Conrad, William Henry. Instr., Greek and German, Berea (Ky.) Coll., 1909-10; prin., Marengo (Ill.) High Sch., 1910-12, Cheyenne (Wyo.) High Sch., 1912-16; supt. schs., Douglas, Wyo., 1916-19, Rock Springs, 1919-25; prof. edn., U. of Wyo., 1925-39, dean, Coll. of Edn. and dir. summer session since 1939; dir. Student Welfare Foundation. Mem. Gov's. Child Welfare Com. for Wyo., State Curriculum Planning Com., pres. coordinating council; consultant Ednl. Policies Commn., N.E.A.; mem. Nat. Com. on Policies in Conservation Education. Member Colo.-Wyo. Acad. of Science, Am. Assn. Sch. Adminstrs., N.E.A. (mem. com. on ednl. standards and teacher edn.), Soc. for Curriculum Study, Soc. Study of Edn., Wyoming Ednl. Assn., Deans and Dirs. of Summer Session, Beta Theta Pi, Iota Phi, Kappa Delta Pi, Phi Delta Kappa. Presbyterian. Clubs: Lions, Jesters (Laramie), Author: College Curriculum, 1932; The Superintendent in Action, 1938; School Survey Techniques, 1937; Teacher Education Program. Home: Laramie, Wy. *

SCOTT, AUSTIN WAKEMAN, prof. law; b. New Brunswick, N.J., Aug. 31, 1884; s. Austin and Anna Prentiss (Stearns) S.; A.B., Rutgers Coll., 1903; LL.B., Harvard, 1909; LL.D., Rutgers U., 1933, Harvard U., 1944; D.C.L., Oxford U., 1954; LL.D., Brown U., 1960; m. Esther Kendall, June 12, 1914; children—Austin Wakeman, Gordon Kendall. Admitted to New York bar, 1910, Massachusetts bar, 1911, instructor Harvard Law Sch., 1909-10 assistant professor law, 1910-14, prof., 1914-20, Story prof. law, 1920-38, Dane prof. law since 1938; served on leave of absence, as dean Coll. of Law, State U. of Ia., 1911-12. Reporter for trusts, Am. Law Inst. Co-reporter for restitution and judgments. Pres. Asso. of Am. Law Schools, 1928. Fellow Am. Acad. Arts and Sciences. Editor: Cases on Civil Procedure, 1914; Cases on Trusts, 1951. Joint editor: Cases on Civil Procedure, 1950. Author: Fundamentals of Procedure in Actions at Law, 1922; The Law of Trusts, 2d edit., 1956; also various legal monographs. Home: Cambridge, Mass. Died Apr. 9, 1981.

SCOTT, JAMES T., foreign service officer; b. Eatonton, Ga., June 5, 1885. Employed by steamship company; asst. to chief of staff, U.S. Army, France, Holland, Belgium, World War I; chief Lithuanian Relief Mission, 1919; London office of U.S. Shipping Bd., rep. in Baltic States and Russia and in charge orgn. in Germany, 1922-26; trade commr., Hamburg, 1926; N.Y. office, Dept. of Commerce, 1931; coml. attaché, Copenhagen, 1933-35; Cairo, 1936; also coml. attaché, Jidda, 1940; coml. attaché, Ankara, 1941; consul, Beirut, 1941, Bombay, 1941; Dept. of State, detailed to Maritime Commn., 1942; assigned commercial attaché, Beirut and Damascus, 1942. Address: Washington, D.C. *

SCOTT, JOHN, author; b. Phila., Mar. 26, 1912; s. Scott Nearing and Nellie (Seeds) S.; student U. of Wis., 1929-31, Sorbonne, Paris, 1938-39, Russia, 1932-37; m. Maria Dikareva, June 15, 1934; children—Leigh, Elena. Worked in Siberian steel mills, 1932-37; journalist in Moscow, Paris, Balkans, Berlin, Near East and Japan, 1938-41; returned to U.S., 1941; contributing editor Time Magazine, 1942-43; war corr. Time and Life mags., 1943-48; asst. to pub. Time Mag., 1952-76. Vis. asso. prof. Fletcher Sch. Law and Diplomacy Tufts U., 1966-67. Author: Behind the Urals, 1942; Duel for Europe, 1942; Europe in Revolution, 1945; Political Warfare, 1955; Democracy is Not Enough, 1960; China—The Hungry Dragon, 1967; Hunger: Man's Struggle to Feed Himself, 1969. Home: Ridgefield, Conn. Died Dec. 1, 1976.

SCOTT, JOHN DILWORTH, mgmt. co. exec.; b. Pitts., June 23, 1911; s. John Dillworth and Clara (Moedinger) S.; student N.Y. U., 1930, U. Pitts., 1931; m. Jean Frances McIlwain, Apr. 1937 (dec. Mar. 1974); children—Jean Claire, Elizabeth, John Charles; m. 2d, Virginia Williams Swanson, July 20, 1974. With H.J. Heinz Co., Pitts., 1932-74, beginning as salesman, successively supr., br. mgr., sales promotion mgr., hotel and restaurant sales mgr., chain store sales mgr., 1932-54, gen. sales mgr., 1954-74, v.p., 1956-74; pres. J. and D. Assos., Dunedin, Fla., 1974-80; pres., dir. Point Chautauqua Land Co. Pres., Point Chautaugua Assn. Presbyterian. Mason (Shriner). Clubs: Chautauqua Golf; Dunedin Country. Home: Dunedin, Fla. Died Aug. 2, 1980; buried Pitts.

SCOTT, JOHN HULL, lawyer; b. Pittsburgh, Nov. 7, 1886; s. Charles Shiras and Mary D. (MacCloskey) S.; ed. pub. schs., Pittsburgh; A.B., Cornell U., 1909, LL.B., 1911; m. Marguerite Glafey, Dec. 10, 1917; children—John Hull, Marcia. Admitted to Pa. bar, 1912; mem. legal dept., Pittsburgh Coal Co., 1911-13; pvt. practice law, Sloan & Scott, 1913-17, Duff, Scott and Smith since 1919; mortgage investment corr., Prudential Ins. Co. since 1925, Western and So. Life Ins. Co. since 1929; dir. Union Title Guaranty Co., Am. Austrian Magnesite Co., Kahingiwerk A.G. Radenthein, Carinthia, Austria. Capt. and adjutant, 317 F.A., A.E.F., 1917-19. Mem. Am. and Allegheny Co. bar assns., The Mortgage Bankers of Am., Am. Legion, S.A.R., Pennsylvania Soc. Republican (mem. Pa. Finance Com.). Clubs: Duquesne, Rolling Rock. Home: West Woodland Rd., Pitts. *

SCOTT, JOHN IRVING ELIAS, educator; b. Jamaica, B.W.I.; s. Joseph N. and Harriet (Dawkins) S.; came to U.S., 1920, naturalized, 1932; A.B., Lincoln (Pa.) U., 1927; A.M., Wittenberg Coll., Springfield, Ohio, 1937; Ph.D., U. Pitts., 1942; m. Helen R. Timms; children—Irvlen, J. Irving E., Jr. Dean, Fla. Meml. Coll., 1927-29; prin. pub. sch., Jacksonville, Fla., 1929-44; dean Wiley Coll., Marshall, Tex., 1944-48; dean instrn. Alcorn Coll., 1948-50; prof. edn. Grad. Sch., dir. ednl. extension service (S.C.) State A. and M. Coll., 1950-53; dir. Negro edn. Jacksonville and Duval County, 1953-60; asst. dir. edn. Duval County, 1960-65, dir. spl. projects, 1965-81; dir. tchr. tng. program Fla. Normal Coll., summers 1937, 38; extension work Bethune-Cookman Coll., Daytona Beach, Fla., 1933-35; extension classes Hampton (Va.) Inst., 1942-44, Albany State Coll. Summer Sch., 1943, Fla. A. and M. Coll., 1943-44; pres. Citizens Investment Corp. Mem. Nat. Tchrs. Research Assn. (founder, pres.), A.R.C., Boy Scouts Am., Fla., Tex. tchrs. assns., N.E.A. (dept. elementary prins.), Am. Acad. Polit. and Social Sci., Am. Tchrs. Assn. (commn. teaching profession), Doctoral Assn. U. Pitts., Beta Kappa Chi, Alpha Kappa Mu, Phi Beta Sigma. Mason. Author: Living With Others, 1939; Chemistry Through Life Situation Method; Best Fields for Small Investment; Professional Functions of Negro Principals in State of Florida in Relation to Status; An Educational Point of View; Negro Students and Their Colleges, 1949; Finding My Way, 1949; Research in Negro Colleges; Foreign Students in Negro Colleges and Universities; Guide to Thesis Writing; Education of Negroes above the Master's Degree; Honorary Degrees Conferred by Negro Colleges; Getting the Most Out of High School; The Education of Black People in Florida, 1974; other publs. in field of edn. Editor-in-chief The Negro Educational Rev. Home: Jacksonville, Fla. Died Jan. 6, 1981; buried Evergreen Cemetery, Jacksonville.

SCOTT, JOSEPH WELCH, fgn. service officer; b. Houston, Sept. 15, 1911; s. Joseph Welch and Anna (Forsgard) S.; B.A., U. Tex., 1932; M.A., U. Va., 1933; traveling fellow Carnegie Endowment, 1936-37; certificate in internat. studies London Sch. Econ. and Polit. Sci., U. London, 1937; student Columbia, 1937-38; m. Ann Collins, Sept. 14, 1935 (dec. 1969); 1 dau., Joanna; m. 2d, Claretta Krueger, Aug. 1, 1970. Trainee oil co., 1938-39; instr. Columbia, 1939-40, Bklyn. Coll., 1940-41; research asso. Fgn. Policy Assn., 1941; apptd. asst. on internat. security Dept. of State, 1946, specialist internat. security affairs, 1947; adviser, dep. U.S. rep. UN Security Council com. good offices, Indonesian Dispute, 1947-49; fgn. affairs specialist, 1949; officer charge Swiss-Benelux affairs, 1950; assigned NATO Def. Coll., Paris, 1952; attache U.S. Mission to NATO and European Regional Orgns., Paris, 1953-55, 1st sec., consul, Paris, 1955, 1st sec., Ankara, 1956, counselor, Ankara 1956; assigned Canadian Def. Coll. Kingston, Ont., 1957; assigned Dept. of State, Washington 1958, spl. asst. under-sec. state, 1958-61, dep. dir. Bur. Intelligence and Research, 1961-64; U.S. minister to Can., 1964-68; country dir. Can., Dept. State, 1968-70; cons. Bur. Oceans and Internat. Environmental and Sci. Affairs, Dept. State from 1971. Mem.-at-large Alexandria (Va.) Tourist Council, 1971-79; chmn. Alexandria Sister City Com., 1974-79. Served from lt. (j.g.) to lt. comdr., USNR, 1941-45. Mem. Alpha Tau Omega. Club: Farmington Country (Charlottesville, Va.). Home: Alexandria, Va. Died Jan. 2, 1979.

SCOTT, WILLIAM EDOUARD, artist; b. Indianapolis, Ind., Mar. 11, 1884; s. Edward Miles and Caroline Gertrude (Russell) S.; grad. Manual Training High Sch., Indianapolis, 1903; studied art at Art Inst. Chicago, and at Acad. Julian, Colarossi Acad., Beaux Arts Acad., Paris, also with H. O. Tanner, Etaples, France; m. Esther Elaine Fulks, of Charleston, W.Va., Mar. 15, 1922. Exhibited at Paris Autumn Salon, 1912; Salon La Touquet, 1912; Royal Acad., London, 1913, Art Inst. Chicago, 1915, 16, 18, 27; etc. Represented by mural decorations in State House, Springfield, Ill; Allen County Court House, Ft. Wayne, Ind; Peoples Finance Corpn., St. Louis; also (with Robert W. Grafton) murals in First Nat. Bank, and High Sch., Michigan City, Ind., and First Nat. Bank, Edwardsville, Ill. Picture "Rainy Night in Etaples," bought by City of Indianapolis for permanent collection in Herron Art Inst.; "La Pauvre Voisine," purchased by Govt. of Argentine Republic. Winner Frederick Magnus Brand prize; received special gold medal and Harmon award, Harmon Foundation; Jesse Binga prize, Chicago Art League; Eames MacVeagh prize, Chicago Art League. Illustrator for mags. Mem. Soc. Western Artists, Chicago Art League (1st pres.), Sociéte des Beaux Arts (Etaples). Methodist. Clubs: Chicago Assembly, Hoosier, Appomattox. Home Chicago, Ill. *

SCOVILL, HIRAM THOMPSON, educator; b. near Leaf River, Ogle Co., Ill., Feb. 22, 1885; s. William Preston and Theresa Josephine (Thompson) S.; A.B., U. of Ill., 1908; LL.D., Ill. Coll., 1946; m. Edith Eliza Stewart, Aug. 31, 1912; children—William Stewart, Mary Josephine (Mrs. Parker R. Beamer), Janet Ruth (Mrs. J. C. Herweg, dec.). With McGregor, Chase & Co., pub. accountants, Chicago, 1908-11, Deloitte, Plender, Griffiths & Co., 1911-13; prof. accountancy and head dept. bus. orgn. and operation, U. of Ill., from Sept. 1913, acting dean, 1942-47, prof. emeritus, 1953-62; spl. accountant Ill. Pub. Utilities Commn., summer 1914; auditor for constructing contractor, Camp McClennan, Ala., 1918; cons. accountant Resettlement Adminstrn., 1935-37. Active various civic projects over 40 year period. Awarded gold medal by Ill. Soc. C.P.A. for passing exam. with highest grade; received Leading Citizen award, 1934; annual Outstanding Service award, Am. Inst. Accountants, 1949; elected to Beta Alpha Psi National Hall of Fame for Accountants, 1953, Ohio State University Hall of Fame for Accountants, 1954. Member American Economic Association, Am. Accounting Assn. (pres. 1920), Ill. Soc. Certified Pub. Accountants (pres. 1937-38), Nat. Assn. Cost Accountants, Am. Inst. Accountants (mem. bd. of examiners 1939-42, and of accounting procedure com., 1942-44); pres. Nat. Conf. State Univ. Schs. of Business, 1943-46. Phi Beta Kappa, Kappa Delta Rho, Beta Gamma Sigma (nat. pres. 1919-25), Alpha Kappa Psi, Beta Alpha Psi (nat. pres. 1919-23). Republican. Presbyn. Clubs: University (sec.), and Union League (Chicago). Author: A Uniform System of Accounts for Gas Companies, 1916; Farm Accounting, 1918; Elements of Accounting, 1919; Elementary Accounting, 1923; Accounting Procedure, 1926; Fundamentals of Accounting, 1940; also numerous articles in periodicals. Editor: Wiley Accounting Series of Text Books. Home: Urbana, Ill. Died Oct. 19, 1962; interred Rosemont Cemetery, Urbana, Ill.

SCOWDEN, FRANK F. (SKOU'DEN), army officer; b. Meadville, Pa., Aug. 18, 1886; s. Franklin Pierce and Margaret (DeArment) S.; B.S., U.S. Mil. Acad., 1910; student Ecole de l'Intendence, Paris, France, 1924; M.B.A., Harvard, 1928; grad. Army Industrial Coll., 1934, Army War Coll., 1935. Commd. 2d lt. of inf., 1910; advanced through the grades to brig. gen., 1940; served as 2d lt. in 8th U.S. Inf., Philippine Islands, 1912-15; on duty as lt., 11th U.S. Inf., with Q.M., Mexican Punitive Expdn., Apr. 1916-Feb. 1917; served as major and lt. col., as exec. officer Motor Transport Corps, with A.E.F. in France, Sept. 1918-Jan. 1920; major Q.M. Corps, 1920; now maj. gen. Decorated Distinguished Service medal, Chevalier of Legion of Honor, Mexican Punitive Expdn. ribbon, World War ribbon. Protestant. Mason. Clubs: Army and Navy, University, Army and Navy Country (Washington, D.C.). Address: Washington, D.C. *

SCRIBNER, JOSEPH M., investment banker; b. Ben Avon, Pa., June 14, 1897; s. Henry Sayre and Mary Lee (Myers) Scribner; ed. Allegheny Prep. Sch.; m. Mrs. Gwendolyn Brewster Judson, Apr. 17, 1939; children—Mrs. Judson Scribner Carstensen, Harriet (Mrs. Harriet Judson Van Ingen), Gwendolyn Brewster Judson (Mrs. E. H. Sipe, Jr.); m. 2d, Helen Orrick Morrill, June 13, 1963. With Stout & Co., investment bankers, 1919-20, Imbrie & Co., 1920-21; asso. with Wells, Deane & Singer (name changed to Singer, Deane & Scribner, 1928), Pitts., 1921-79, partner, 1925-79; past gov. N.Y. Stock Exchange, Pitts. Stock Exchange; dir. Washington Steel Corp. (Pa.), Vulcan Mold & Iron Co. Former spl. asst. to dir. gen. for industry ops. WPB, Washington; dep. dir. OSS. Past trustee St. John's Coll. Mem. Nat. Assn. Securities Dealers (past gov.), Investment Bankers Assn. Am. (past gov.), Assn. Stock Exchange Firms (past pres., gov.). Clubs: Duquesne, Harvard-Yale-Princeton (Pitts.); New York Yacht; Allegheny Country; Sewickley; Annapolis, Yacht

(Annapolis, Md.). Home: Annapolis, Md. Died May 24, 1979.

SCRIMSHAW, STEWART, economics; b. Old Leake, Boston, Eng., May 20, 1886; s. John and Hannah Maria (Gilliat) S.; B.A., Ohio Wesleyan U., 1912; Ph.D., U. of Wisconsin, 1926; LL.D., Ohio Wesleyan University, 1948; m. Harriet Fernwood Smith, Dec. 28, 1916; children—Nevin Stewart, Norman Gilliat (dec.). Came to U.S., 1906, naturalized, 1912. Grad. instr. in economics, U. of Wis., 1912-15, asst. instr. in transportation and pub. utilities, 1912-13, asst. instr. in labor economics, 1913-14; fellow with Industrial Commn. of Wis., 1914-15; state supervisor of apprenticeship, Wis., 1915-20; dir. industrial relations, Kearney & Trecker Corp., 1920-29; prof. industrial relations, in charge cooperative relations of Marquette U. Coll. of Engring., 1922-29; prof. economics and industrial relations, Marquette U., since 1922; asso. dean Coll. Business Administration, 1942-48; summer lecturer on apprenticeship edn. and industrial relations, Okla. A. and M. Coll., 1937, 38; lecturer on personnel adminstrn., U. of Wis., 1938-39; consultant on industrial relations. Mem. Milwaukee County Com. on Unemployment, 1929-30; leader of Lake Geneva (Wis.) Conf. on Human Relations in Industry, 1931; dir. Milwaukee Regional Labor Bd. of Nat. Labor Relations Bd., 1934-35; chmn. Social Action Com. of Milwaukee Council of Social Agencies, 1935-37; vice chmn. Social Planning Com., Milwaukee Council of Social Agencies; consultant to Fed. Com. Apprentice Training, 1936; public mem. panel Nat. War Labor Bd., Chicago area, 1942-44. Mem. Am. Economics Assn., Am. Arbitration Assn., Industrial Relations Assn. of Wis., Am. Management Assn., Alpha Kappa Psi, Pi Gamma Mu. Congregationalist. Clubs: City, University. Author: Apprenticeship—Principles, Relationships, Procedures, 1931; Textbook on Personnel Administrations and Labor Relations, 1934. Contbr. on subjects of apprenticeship and industrial edn. Home: Wauwatosa, Wis. *

SCRIPTURE, ELIZABETH, librarian; b. Minneapolis, Minn., Aug. 27, 1882; d. James Byron and Emma (Haskell) Scripture; A.B., U. of Minnesota, 1904; student New York State Library Sch., 1912-13. Asst., Columbia U. Library, 1913-14, Minneapolis Pub. Library, 1914-15; librarian High School Libraries, Minneapolis, 1915-30; supervisor sch. libraries, Denver, Colo., since 1930; teacher summer library schs., U. of Minn., 1920, Syracuse U., 1926, 1928, N.Y. State Coll. for Teachers, 1927, Columbia U., School for Library Service, 1929, 30. Mem. N.E.A., Am. Library Assn. (Mem. exec. bd.), Colo. Library Assn. (pres. 1933), Colo. Ednl. Assn., Administrative Women in Edn. (Denver), Kappa Alpha Theta. Club: Altrusa (Denver). Author: (pamphlet) Find It Yourself (with Margaret Greer), rev. edit. 1942. Contbr. to various library periodicals. Home: Denver. *

SEAGLE, WILLIAM, author, lawyer; b. N.Y.C., Jan. 14, 1898; s. Jacob and Yetta (Schapiro) S.; B.A., Coll. City N.Y., 1920; J.D., Columbia, 1922; m. Miriam Goldberg, Feb. 17, 1928; children—Ronah (Mrs. Richard T. Brodkin), Jonathan Judah. Practice law, 1922-24; mag. writer, 1924-28; asst. editor Ency. Social Scis., 1928-34; sr. atty. Petroleum Bd., Washington, 1934-35; trial examiner, adminstrv. law judge NLRB, 1937-40, 60-69; pvt. practice law, N.Y.C., 1940-41; asst. solicitor U.S. Dept. Interior, 1941-43, asst. chief Indian div. Office Solicitor, 1943-54, atty. adviser, mem. bd. contract appeals, 1954-60. Mem. Mystery Writers Am. Author: (with Morris L. Ernst) To the Pure-A Study of Obscenity and the Censor, 1928; Cato, or the Future of Censorship, 1930; There Ought to Be a Law, 1933; The Quest for Law, 1941; Men of Law: From Hammurabi to Holmes, 1947; Law: The Science of Inefficiency, 1952; Acquitted of Murder, 1958. Home: Washington, D.C. Died Dec. 31, 1977; buried King David Meml. Garden, Falls Church, Va.

SEAGRAM, JOSEPH EDWARD FROWDE, distilleries exec.; s. Edward Frowde and Edna Irvine (MacLachlan) S. Chmn., Canbar Products Ltd.; hon. chmn. Joseph E. Seagram & Sons, Ltd., 1937—; hon. dir. Seagram Co. Ltd. Home: Waterloo, Ont., Canada. Died Nov. 28, 1979.

SEARLE, JOHN GIDEON, mfg. pharmacist; b. Sabula, Iowa, Mar. 18, 1901; s. Claude Howard and Marion Hall (Titus) S.; B.S., U. Mich., 1923, D. Sc. (hon.), 1967; LL.D. (hon.), Northwestern U., 1969; m. Frances Louise Crow, Apr. 25, 1925; children—Daniel Crow, William Louis, Suzanne (Mrs. Wesley M. Dixon, Jr.). Became buyer G.D. Searle & Co., mfg. chemists, Chicago, 1923, later office mgr., and then treas. in charge of lab. and office, pres. and gen. mgr., 1936-66, chmn. bd., chief exec. officer, 1966-72, hon. chmn. bd. dirs., 1972-78; dir. Hobe Sound Co. Life trustee Field Mus. Natural History; life trustee, former pres. bd. trustees Northwestern U. Served as chief yeoman, USN, World War I. Awarded Citizenship Fellowship, Inst. Medicine of Chgo. Past chmn. bd. Health Information Found. Mem. Am. Pharm. Mfrs. Assn. (sec. 1926-31, pres. 1931-33), Am. Drug Mfrs. Assn. (pres. 1941-44, exec. com. 1935-58), Pharm. Mfrs. Assn., Alpha Delta Phi. Republican. Episcopalian. Clubs: Jupiter Island, Seminole, Everglades, Hobe Sound Yacht (Hobe Sound, Fla.); Casino (Chgo.); Commonwealth, Commercial, Glen View, Old Elm, Onwentsia, Shoreacres. Home: Hobe Sound, Fla. Died Jan. 21, 1978.

SEASONGOOD, MURRAY, lawyer, former mayor; b. Cin., Oct. 27, 1878; s. Alfred and Emily (Fechheimer) S.; A.B., Harvard, 1900, A.M., 1901, LL.B., 1903; LL.D., Marietta Coll., 1950, N.Y.U., 1951, Miami U., 1963, U. Cin., 1964; L.H.D., Hebrew Union Coll. Jewish Inst. Religion, 1962; LL.D., Wilmington Coll., 1963; m. Agnes Senior, Nov. 28, 1912; 1 dau., Janet (Mrs. Herbert Hoffheimer, Jr.). Admitted to Ohio bar, 1903; practiced law, Cin.; mem. Paxton & Seasongood; part time prof. U. Cin. Coll. Law, 1925-59, now prof. emeritus; vis. prof. law Harvard, 1947-48, Godkin lectr., 1933. Mayor, Cin., 1926-30, chmn. City Planning Commn. Former pres. Cin. Legal Aid Soc., Nat. Municipal League; v.p. Nat. Civil Service League; hon. v.p. Nat. Legal Aid Assn.; mem. Pres.'s Housing Conf., 1932; security cons. to personnel Clearance Security Bd., U.S. AEC, 1954-59; mem. adv. com. rules criminal procedure U.S. Supreme Ct., 1941-44, Ohio Commn. Code Revision, 1945-49; former pres. Hamilton County Good Govt. League; former mem. Hamilton County Charter Commn.; former pres. Nat. Assn. Legal Aid Orgns.; mem. U.S. Civil Service Commn. Loyalty Rev. Bd., 1947-53, Ohio Turnpike Commn., 1949-52, Task Force on Personnel Adminstrn., Ohio Program Commn. 1950-51; mem. Ohio Commn. for Blind, 1915-26. Mem. overseers com. to visit Harvard Dept. Govt.; trustee Clovernook Home and Sch. Blind, Cin., also v.p. Mem. Nat. Municipal League (life mem. council), Am. Law Inst., Am. (chmn. standing com. on civil service, 1949-53, former chmn. municipal law sect.), Cin. (past pres.) bar assns., Harvard Law Sch. Assn. Cin. (1st pres., gov.), English-Speaking Union (dir. Cin. br.), Phi Beta Kappa (past v.p. Cin. chpt., life sec. Class of 1903 Harvard Law Sch.), Delta Upsilon. Republican. Clubs: Harvard (past pres.), University (past v.p.), Literary (past pres.), Travel, Print and Drawing, Queen City, Cincinnati Art (life asso.) (Cin.); Harvard Faculty (Cambridge); Harvard (N.Y.C.). Author: Local Government in the United States: A Challenge and an Opportunity, 1933; Cases on the Law of Municipal Corporations, 3d edit., 1953; Selections From Speeches: 1900-1959 of Murray Seasongood, 1960. Contbr. articles to various publs., Ency. Americana. Home: Cincinnati OH 45208.

SEATH, JOHN, communications co. exec.; b. Edinburgh, Scotland, Oct. 25, 1914; s. John and Elizabeth A. (Sutherland) S.; came to U.S., 1915, naturalized, 1918; B.B.A. cum laude, CCNY, 1948; m. Rose A. Featherstone, June 17, 1939; children—John, Ellaine A. Mgr., Milton M. Bernard, C.P.A., N.Y.C., 1946-55; tax mgr. Gen. Dynamics Corp., N.Y.C., 1955-59, Budd Co., Phila., 1959-61; asst. v.p., dir. taxes ITT, 1961-64, v.p., 1964-73, dir. taxes, 1964-79, sr. v.p., 1973-79. Served with AUS, 1943-46. C.P.A., N.Y. Mem. Am. Inst. C.P.A.'s, Tax Execs. Inst., Fin. Execs. Inst. (tax com.), Tax Found., Tax Inst., NAM (tax com.), Nat. Fgn. Trade Council (tax com.), Internat. Fiscal Assn., Machinery and Allied Products Assn. (tax com.). Republican. Presbyterian. Clubs: Knickerbocker Country (Tenafly, N.J.); Englewood. Home: Englewood, N.J. Died Feb. 15, 1979.

SEATH, WILLIAM (SETH), clergyman; b. Widnes, Eng., March 16, 1899; s. George and Eleanor (Twiss) S.; came to U.S., 1911, naturalized; pvt. tutors, 7 yrs.; D.D., Cedarville Coll., 1944; m. Charlotte May Otto, Sept. 15, 1921 (dec. May 9, 1958); children—Dorothy Mae (Mrs. Henry H. Schwarz Jr.), Wilma (Mrs. George E. Weber); m. 2d, Katherine Alta Schwartz, June 17, 1959. Asst. supt. Union City Mission, Mpls., 1920-31; exec. dir. Chgo. Christian Indsl. League, from 1931; ordained to ministry Presbyn. Ch., 1931; tchr. summer sch. Houghton (N.Y.) Coll., 1952, 53, 55, mem. summer faculty, to 1963; stated supply pastor Barnett (Mo.)-Hopewell Presbyn. Ch.; pastor Barnett Presbyn. Ch. Exec. adminstr. Chgo. Christian Indsl. League, 1963-77. Mem. Mayor's Com. on Skid Row, 1950-77, Mayor's Commn. Rehabilitation of Persons, 1957-77. Corr. sec. Assn. Ch. Social Workers, 1939-43; pres. Internat. Union Gospel Missions, 1944-47, pres. Chgo. dist., 1954-57. Mem. Am. Legion. Served as cpl., Co. E, 48th Inf., U.S. Army, 1918-19. Contbr. articles to religious publs. Author: I Saw the Cross, 1969; Unto the Least of These, 1974. Home: Elden, Mo. Died Dec. 9, 1977.

SEATON, GEORGE, writer, dir. motion picture producer; b. South Bend, Ind., Apr. 17, 1911; m. Phyllis Loughton; children—Mary Seaton Henderson, Marc (dec.). Actor, dir. stage plays; writing staff Metro-Goldwyn-Mayer, Universal Studios, 20th Century-Fox, Paramount Pictures; screen plays for pictures include: A Day at the Races, Doctor Takes a Wife, Magnificent Dope, Coney Island, Song of Bernadette, Eve of St. Mark; writer screen play, dir. Apartment for Peggy, Anything Can Happen, Miracle on 34th Street (Acad. Award, 1947), Little Boy Lost, Country Girl (Acad. Award, 1954); co-producer Bridges at Toko Ri, 1955; Proud and Profane, 1956; dir. Teacher's Pet, 1958; producer (with William Perlberg) But Not for Me, 1959, The Rat Race, 1960; dir. and/or writer and/or producer The Pleasure of His Company, 1960, The Counterfeit Traitor, 1961, The Hook, 1962, 36 Hours, 1964, What's So Bad About Feeling Good, 1967, Airport, 1969, Showdown, 1972; dir. stage prodn. Juno and the Paycock. Vice pres. Motion Picture and TV Fund; exec. com., bd. dirs. Centre Theatre Group, Los Angeles; trustee Colonial Williamsburg. Recipient Laurel award Writers Guild Am., West, 1961, Valentine Davies award, 1968; Jean Hersholt humanitarian award, 1962; Writer-Dir. of Yr. award Nat. Assn. Theatre Owners, 1972; Morgan Cox award Writers Guild Am., 1979. Mem. Motion Picture Acad. Arts and Scis. (past pres.), Screen Dirs. Guild (pres. 1948). Home: Beverly Hills, Calif. Died July 28, 1978.

SEAVER, JAY JOHN, consulting engr.; b. Ypsilanti, Mich., Jan. 6, 1885; S. John Smith and Tracey (Geis) S.; B.M.E., U. Mich., 1912; D. Engring., Eastern Mich. U., 1968; m. Hallie Phelps, Sept. 11, 1917 (dec. 1951); children—Roberta Marie, James Phelps; m. 2d, Virginia P. Tegarden, July 1, 1965. Successively draftsman, supt. gen. supt. and v.p. Arthur G. McKee & Co., engineers, Cleve., 1912-28; pres. Pulaski Foundry & Mfg. Corp. (Va.), 1923-28, Pulaski Engring. Works, 1924-28; v.p., dir. H.A. Brassert & Co., Chgo., engrs., 1928-40; with Day & Zimmermann, Inc., engrs., Phila., 1941-46, as constrn. engr., Iowa Ordnance Plant, Burlington, then cons. engr. blast furnace and coke plant, Provo, Utah, cons. engr. blast furnace plant, Duluth, Minn., blast furnace and steel plant, Monclova, Coahuila, Mexico, 1941-43, v.p. Chgo. office, 1943-46; organizer, mgr. Jay J. Seaver Engrs., Chgo., 1946; pres., dir. Asso. Plastics Cos., Inc., 1951-52. Mem. Am., Brit. iron and steel insts., Eastern, Western blast furnace and coke assns., Inst. Iron and Steel Engrs., Am. Inst. Mining and Metall. Engrs., S.A.R., Order Founders and Patriots Am. (Ill. gov. 1952-55). Clubs: South Shore Country, Acacia, Union League, Michigan; Adventures. Republican. Patentee in field. Home: Green Valley AZ. *

SEBALD, WILLIAM JOSEPH, fin. service officer; b. Baltimore, Nov. 5, 1901; s. Frank Joseph and Elizabeth (Buerkholtz) S.; B.S., U.S. Naval Acad., 1922; J.D., U. Md., 1933, LL.D., 1949; m. Edith Frances de Becker, May 14, 1927. Commd. officer U.S. Navy, 1922-30; language officer attached to Am. Embassy, Tokyo, 1925-28; resigned commn., 1930; practiced law Kobe, Japan, 1933-39, Washington, 1939-41; commd. lt. comdr. U.S. Navy, 1941, served as chief Pacific div., Combat Intelligence, U.S. Navy, returned to inactive duty as capt., 1945; apptd. aux. fgn. service officer, Dept. State, 1945, fgn. service officer, 1947, dep. for Supreme Comdr. for Allied Powers, chmn. Allied council for Japan, 1947-52, chief Diplomatic Sect., GHQ, SCAP, 1947-52, minister plenipotentiary of U.S., 1948, acting U.S. polit. adviser for Japan, 1947; apptd. political adv. for Japan with rank ambassador, 1950; American A.E. and P. to Burma, 1952-54; deputy assistant secretary Far Eastern Affairs, 1954-57, A. E. and P. to Australia, 1957-61; ret., 1961. Decorated Legion of Merit; 1st class Order of Rising Sun (Japan). Mem. bars Maryland, Washington, U.S. Supreme Ct. Mem. Asiatic Soc. of Japan. Clubs: Met. (Washington); Naples (Fla.) Yacht. Author of books and pamphlets on Japanese law; author: With MacArthur in Japan, 1965; (with others) Japan: Prospects, Options, and Opportunities, 1967. Home: Naples, Fla. Died Aug. 10, 1980.

SEBENTHALL, ELIZABETH ROBERTA, author; b. Eau Claire, Wis., Jan. 6, 1917; d. Robert Graham and Laura Rose (Cote) Sebenthall. Recipient Nat. Endowment for the Arts award, 1970. Author numerous novels including: If the Shroud Fits, 1969; The Cold Ones, 1972; The Bronze Claws, 1972; (poetry) Acquainted with a Chance of Bobcats, 1969, Anatomy of December, 1978. Home: Mount Horeb, Wis. Deceased.

SEEDS, ASA ELMORE, obstetrician, gynecologist; b. Balt., Apr. 5, 1934; s. Asas Elmore S.; A.B., Stanford U., 1955, M.D 1958; m. Sheila Ellen Gocke, Oct. 28, 1960; children—William Asa, John Thomas, James Robert. Intern, U. Oreg. Hosp., 1958-59; resident in ob-gyn. Johns Hopkins U., 1959-64; practice medicine specializing in ob.-gyn., Cin.; fellow dept. ob-gyn. Johns Hopkins U. Sch. Medicine, 1964-66, asst. prof., 1966-69, dir. Toxemia Clinic, 1967-71, asso. prof., 1969-71; prof. dept. ob-gyn. Georgetown U. Sch. Medicine, 1971-72; prof. depts. ob-gyn. and physiology, dir. Minn. Center for Perinatal Care and Obstet. Service, Univ. Hosp., U. Minn. Med. Sch., 1972-75; prof., chmn. dept. ob-gyn. U. Cin. Sch. Medicine, 1975-80; cons. Nat. Inst. Child Health and Devel., NIH, 1973-76. Recipient NIH Career Devel. award, 1968-71. Diplomate Am. Bd. Obstetrics and Gynecology (examiner 1973-80). Mem. Am. Coll. Obstetricians and Gynecologists (editorial bd. Jour. Ob-Gyn.), Perinatal Research Soc., Soc. for Gynecologic Investigation, Am. Assn. Obstetricians and Gynecologists, Central Assn. Obstetricians and Gynecologists. Contbr. articles to med. jours. Home: Cincinnati, Ohio. Died May 12, 1980.

SEEGER, CHARLES LOUIS, musicologist; b. Mexico City, Dec. 14, 1886; s. Charles Louis and Elsie Simmons (Adams) S.; A.B., Harvard U., 1908; D.Fine Arts, U. Calif. at Berkeley, 1968; m. Constance de Clyver Edson, Dec. 22, 1911; children—Charles Louis, John, Peter; m. 2d, Ruth Crawford, Nov. 14, 1931; children—Michael, Margaret, Barbara Mona, Penelope; m. 3d, Margaret Adams Taylor, Mar. 10, 1955. Volontär condr. Cologne Opera, 1910-11; prof. music U. Calif., 1912-19; lectr. Inst. Mus. Art, 1921-33, New Sch. for Social Research, N.Y.C., 1931-35; tech. adviser spl. skills div. Resettlement Adminstrn., Washington, 1935-38; asst. to dir. Fed. Music Project, WPA, 1938-40; chief, music div. Pan-Am. Union, Washington, 1941-53; vis. prof. Yale, 1949-50; lectr. U. Calif. at Los Angeles, 1957; research musicologist Inst. Ethnomusicology, 1961-71, regent prof., 1961-62; lectr. Harvard, 1972. Decorated Comdr. Al Merito, Chile. Fellow A.A.A.S., Am. Folklore Soc.; mem. Soc. Ethnomusicology (pres. 1960-61, hon. pres. 1972-79), Am. (pres. 1945-46), N.Y. (chmn. 1930-34) musicological socs., Am. Soc. for Comparative Musicology (past pres.), Gesellschaft für Vergleichende Musikwissenschaft (chmn. 1935), Am. Council Learned Socs. (past chmn. com. on musicology), Internat. Folk Music Council. Club: Cosmos (Washington). Composer miscellaneous compositions. Author: Studies in Musicology 1935-75. Contbr. articles on music and musicology to various publs., encys. Editor: music sect. Handbook of Latin Am. Studies, 1943-50; pres., editor Am. Library of Musicology, 1932-38; Music Series (Pan. Am. Union), 1941-50; Check-List of Recorded Songs, Library of Congress, 1942; Army Song Book, 1941; Cancionero Popular Americano, 1950. Home: Bridgewater, Conn. Died Feb. 7, 1979.

SEELER, ALBERT OTTO, physician, educator; b. Derry, N.H., Dec. 25, 1915; s. Karl Emil Felix and Clara Baylies (Cornell) S.; A.B., Harvard, 1934, M.D., 1938; m. Edwina DeWitt Dusenbery, Nov. 29, 1941; children—Alan Thayer, Joan DeWitt, Marcia Drake, Karl Albert, John Henry. Intern Meml. Hosp., Worcester, Mass., 1938-40; pharmacologist Merck Inst. Therapeutic Research, 1940-44, asst. dir., 1944-45; asst. resident medicine, resident and research fellow medicine Thorndike Lab., Harvard med. unit Boston City Hosp., 1945-48; asst. prof. indsl. medicine Harvard Sch. Pub. Health, 1948-50, instr. Med. Sch., 1950-54, clin. asso. medicine, from 1954, lectr. on medicine, from 1963; practice internal medicine, 1950-56; physician Mass. Inst. Tech., 1956-59, physician-in-chief, 1959-60, prof., dir. med. dept., from 1960; physician-in-chief II Med. Service, Harvard-Boston City Hosp., 1959-73; physician Mount Auburn Hosp., from 1955. Diplomate Am. Bd. Internal Medicine. Fellow A.C.P.; mem. A.M.A., Mass. Med. Soc., New Eng. Grenfell Assn. (dir.). Club: St. Botolph (Boston). Home: Waban, Mass. Died Feb. 12, 1976; buried Derry, N.H.

SEELEY, PAUL STARK, Christian Sci. tchr.; b. Poughkeepsie, N.Y., Oct. 1, 1885; s. James Ezra and Affa (Stark) S.; A.B., Princeton, 1906; LL.B., Harvard, 1909; C.S.B., Mass. Metaphys. Coll., 1919; m. Vernita Swezea, Mar. 19, 1929; children—David Lee, John Lee. Joined Mother Ch. of Christ, Scientist, Boston, 1909, later First Ch., Portland, Ore.; began practice, 1912; tchr. Christian Sci., 1919-; mem. Ore. Christian Sci. Com. on Publn., 1912-15; 1st reader First Ch., Portland, 1915-16; mem. bd. lectureship Mother Ch., 1916-42, 48-67; asso. editor C.S. periodicals, 1942-48; pres. Mother Ch., 1944-45, tchr. Normal Class, 1961. Clubs: Harvard (Boston); University (Portland). Home: Portland OR. *

SEELY, ELIZABETH CAVEN, librarian; b. Poughkeepsie, N.Y.; d. Alexander and M.E. (Scoville) Caven; A.B., Vassar Coll.; B.S. in L.S., Columbia; m. William E. Seely. Reference librarian Tompkins Sq. br. N.Y. Pub. Library; librarian Westchester County (N.Y.) Union Catalog, Sarah Lawrence Coll. Library, Bronxville, N.Y., 1965-74, emeritus, 1974-76. Mem. Am., N.Y. State, Westchester County (past pres. editor bull.) library assns., Assn. Coll. and Research Libraries. Home: Bronxville, N.Y. Died Feb. 2, 1976.

SEELY, FRED B., univ. prof.; b. Chester, N.Y., Apr. 29, 1884; s. Fred B. and Ruth A. (Davis) S.; B.S., Worcester Poly. Inst., 1907; M.S., U. of Ill., 1915; m. Anna Roe Wood, Oct. 17, 1908; children—Ralph Wood, Irving Roe. Testing engr. and draftsman, Carpenter Steel Co., Reading, Pa., 1907; instr. in mech. engring., Villanova (Pa.) Coll., 1908; instr. in theoretical and applied mechanics, U. of Ill., 1909-15, asst. prof., 1915-21, prof. since 1921, head dept. theoretical and applied mechanics since 1934. Instr. Sch. of Mil. Aeronautics, 1917. V.p. University Dist. Building and Loan Assn., Champaign, since 1938. Alderman of Urbana, 1925-28; mem. of City Planning Commn., Urbana, 1926-31; v.p. Champaign-Urbana Council Boy Scouts America, 1931-32; dir. Family Welfare Soc., Champaign-Urbana, 1936-40. Mem. Am. Soc. M.E. (Worcester Reed Warner Medal, 1949), Am. Soc. Testing Materials, Am. Soc. for Engring. Edn. (Lamme Medal, 1950), Phi Gamma Delta, Sigma Xi, Tau Beta Pi, Phi Kappa Phi, Sigma Tau. Meth. Clubs: Univ. (Urbana); Kiwanis (Champaign); Engrs. (Chicago). Author: Analytical Mechanics for Engineers (with N. E. Ensign), 1921; Resistance of Materials, 1925; Advanced Mechanics of Materials, 1931. Contbr. to tech. periodicals. Home: Urbana, Ill. *

SEEVERS, MAURICE HARRISON, pharmacologist, educator; b. Topeka, Oct. 3, 1901; s. Giles Alpheus and Emma Mary (Dreisbach) S.; A.B., Washburn Coll., 1924; Ph.D., U. Chgo., 1928, M.D., 1930; LL.D., U. Hokkaido (Japan), 1976; m. Frances Lois Hebl, Nov. 14, 1936; children—Pamela, Giles. Research asst. U. Chgo., 1926-28; instr. pharmacology Loyola U., Chgo., 1929; intern State of Wis. Gen. Hosp., Madison, 1930-32; asst. prof. pharmacology U. Wis., 1930-34, asso. prof., 1934-42; prof., chmn. dept. pharmacology U. Mich., from 1942, prof., chmn. emeritus, asso. dean Med. Sch., 1947-50; dir. Miles Lab. Mem. Surgeon Gen.'s Com. on Smoking and Health, 1964; Nat. Commn. on Marihuana and Drug Abuse, 1971; cons. Research and Devel. Bd., Dept. Def.; mem. pharmacological study sect. NIH, com. on drug addiction, narcotics NRC. Decorated Order of Sacred Treasure 2d class, Order of Rising Sun 3d class (Japan); recipient Nathan B. Eddy Meml. award Nat. Acad. Scis.-NRC, 1974. Mem. Am. Physiol. Soc., Am. Soc. Pharmacology and Exptl. Therapeutics (council 1937, pres. 1946-48), A.M.A. (council pharmacy and chemistry; chmn. sect. exptl. medicine and therapeutics 1953), Am. Soc. Anesthetists (hon.), A.A.A.S., Soc. Exptl. Biol. and Med. Central Soc. Clin. Research, Nat. Acad. Medicine of Mexico (hon.), Sigma Xi, Alpha Omega Alpha, Phi Chi. Clubs: University, Barton Hills Country (Ann Arbor). Editorial bd. Physiol. Revs., Anesthesiology and Procs. Exptl. Biology and Medicine. Contbr. articles to physiol., med. jours. Home: Ann Arbor, Mich. Died Apr. 20, 1977; buried Forest Hill Cemetery, Ann Arbor.

SEGER, WALTER G., business exec.; b. St. Paul, Minn., March 8, 1886; s. John A. and Elvina (Yoerg) S.; student U. of Minn., 2 yrs., 1905-07; m. Nellie Ienza Luse, Apr. 14, 1909; children—Dorothea, Miriam, Helen. With Seeger Refrigerator Co., St. Paul, since 1907, beginning as metal worker and advanced through various depts. into sales dept. and exec. div., pres. since 1936; trustee Minn. Mutual Life Ins. Co., St. Paul; v.p. and dir. Anchor Casualty Co., St. Paul; dir. Empire National Bank, St. Paul; dir. Great Northern Ry. Co., N.W. Bell Telephone Co., N. W. Bauco Corp.; pres. of St. Paul Baseball Club, Inc. Trustee Shriners Hosp. for Crippled Children, Minneapolis. Pres. St. Paul Assn. Commerce, 1940. Mem. Delta Upsilon. Republican. Episcopalian. Clubs: Rotary, Minnesota, St. Paul Athletic. Home: St. Paul, Minn. *

SEIGFRED, EARL COVERT, coll. dean; b. Seneca Falls, N.Y., Feb. 18, 1901; s. Lester George and Della (Covert) S.; student Ithaca Conservatory of Music, 1919-20; A.B., Hobart Coll., 1926; M.A., Columbia Univ., 1929; student summers Syracuse U., 1934, U. Colo., 1935; Ph.D., U. Iowa, 1939; m. Ellen Louise Nuschke, June 23, 1927; children—Shirley Anne, Suzanne, Marshall. Actor, 1920-26; head dept. speech edn., secondary schs., Cortland, N.Y., 1926-29; prof. drama, head drama dept., Washburn Coll., Topeka, Kan., 1929-36, 1937-38; asst. in speech State U. Iowa, 1937; prof. speech, head of speech dept., Miss. State Coll. for Women, Columbus, 1939-41; dean, Coll. of Fine Arts, Ohio Univ., Athens, Ohio, from 1941, act. dir., Sch. Dramatic Art and Speech, 1942-47. Mem. Western Arts Assn., Am. Ednl. Theatre Assn., Ohio Edn. Assn., Nat. Collegiate Players (nat. 2d v.p. 1947-51, pres. 1954), Speech Assn. Am., Kappa Kappa Psi, Phi Beta Kappa. Home: Athens, Ohio. Died Jan. 1, 1978.

SEILER, ALEXANDER WALTER, advt. exec.; b. Arlington, Wis., Apr. 21, 1885; s. Alexander Jacob and Clara Susan (Pritchett) S.; A.B., U. Wis., 1907; m. 2d, Elsa Kroeck, Nov. 26, 1945. Copy writer, Cramer-Krasselt Co., advt. agency, Milwaukee, 1907-08, mgr. media dept., 1908-18, mgr. service dept., 1918- 24, sec., 1924-26, dir., 1926—, pres., 1934-62, chmn., chief exec. officer, 1962-68, chmn. exec. com., 1968—. State publicity dir., U.S. Savs. Bonds; dir. Greater Milw. Com., Milw. Better Bus. Bur. Recipient citation U. Wis., 1955; Advt. Fedn. Am. award, 1960. Mem. Am. Assn. Advt. Agencies, N.A.M., Wis. Mfrs. Assn., U.S. C. of C. Contbr. "Advertising Agency Functions and Relations" in Advertising Agency and Advertising & Selling; sect. on "Industrial Advertising" in Advertising Handbook, 1950; "Cooperative Advertising" and "Advertising Manager" in Printers' Ink. Methodist. Mason (32). Clubs: Milwaukee, University, Wisconsin, Rotary, Advertising, Milwaukee Country (Milw.). Home: Milwaukee, WI. *

SEITZ, WILLIAM CHAPIN, educator; b. Buffalo, June 19, 1914; s. George William and Cora Elizabeth (Chapin) S.; student Albright Art Sch., 1932-33; B.F.A., U. Buffalo, 1946; M.F.A. (Proctor fellow 1951-52), Princeton, 1952, Ph.D., 1955; m. Irma J. Seigelman, Dec. 1, 1938. Instr. art history U. Buffalo, 1946-48, asst. prof., 1948-49; critic in residence Princeton, 1952-53, asst. prof., bi-centennial preceptor, 1956-60; asso. curator painting and sculpture exhbns. Mus. Modern Art, N.Y.C., 1960-65, curator, 1965; prof. fine arts, dir. Rose Art. Mus. Brandeis U., 1965-70; vis. prof. history art Harvard, 1969-70; William R. Kenan, Jr. prof. history art U. Va., Charlottesville, 1970-74. Kress prof. Nat. Gallery Art, Washington, 1971-72; exhibited one man shows Arista Gallery, N.Y.C., 1938, Willard Gallery, N.Y.C., 1949, 51, 53, Princeton Mus., 1949, 51, Meml. Exhbn., Bayly Mus., U. Va., 1975; exhibited group shows Bklyn. Mus. Whitney Mus. Am. Art, Albright Art Gallery, Allen Meml. Art Mus., Oberlin Coll., Cleve. Mus., Milw. Art Inst., Columbus (O.) Gallery Fine Arts, U. Ill. Mus. Modern Art. Nat. Council Learned Socs. fellow, 1952-53; Fulbright fellow, 1957-58. Mem. Coll. Art Assn., Soc. for Aesthetics, Am. Assn. U. Profs., Assn. Mus. Dirs. Author: Claude Monet, 1960; Monet, Seasons and Moment, 1960; The Art of Assemblage, 1961; Mark Tobey, 1962; Arshile Gorky, 1962; Hans Hofmann, 1963; Art Israel, 1964; The Responsive Eye, 1965; Henri de Toulouse-Lautrec: At the Circus, 1965; San Paulo 9: Edward Hopper and Environment U.S.A., 1967; Seventh Biennial Canadian Painting, 1968; Kinetic Art, 1969; Sculpture, Its Image in the Arts, 1969; Turner, 1970; Manet, 1971; George Segal, 1972. Contbr. articles to profl. jours., mus. bulls. Home: Charlottesville, Va. Died Oct. 26, 1974.

SELBY, JOHN ALLEN, editor, author; b. Gallatin, Mo., Feb. 7, 1897; s. John Allen and Mary Ellen (Erickson) S.; student Park Coll., Parkville, Mo., 1915-16, U. of Mo., 1916-18, Columbia U., 1927; m. Esther Baxter, June 11, 1923 (dec. 1952). With Kansas City Star, 1918-29, various positions including music editor; literary editor Associated Press, 1932-36, arts editor and writer of syndicated columns on books, 1936-44; editor-in-chief Rinehart & Co., Publishers, N.Y City, 1945-53; lectr. in English, Columbia, 1945-59. Served in U.S Navy 6 mos., World War I. Mem. Kappa Alpha, The Players. Author: Sam, 1939 (received $1000 award as Am. Winner of the All-Nations Prize Novel Competition); Island in the Corn, 1941; Starbuck, 1943; Elegant Journey, 1944; The Man Who Never Changed, 1954; Time Was, 1956; The Days Dividing, 1958; A Few Short Blocks Between, 1959; Madame, 1961; Beyond Civil Rights, 1966. Address: New York, N.Y. Died May 7, 1980.

SELBY, ROGER A., shoe mfr.; born Portsmouth, O., May 11, 1885; s. George Dyar and Lydia V. (Webster) S.; Ph.B., Yale, 1906; m. Dorothy Oldfield, Aug. 12, 1923 (divorced Apr. 17, 1940); children—Roger A., Jr. (dec.), Lois; m. 2d Louise Wingo, December 31, 1948. Secretary to Congressman H. T. Bannon, 1906-09; sec. to Senator Theodore E. Burton, 1909-11; asst. to gen. mgr. Selby Shoe Co., Portsmouth, O., 1911-22, general manager, 1922-34, president, 1926-46, chmn. bd., 1946-56; chmn. bd., pres. Selby Internat., Inc., 1956—; pres. Pyrrole Chem. Corp., Portsmouth; dir. Physical Culture Shoes, Ltd., London, Murray-Selby Shoes, Ltd. (London, Ont., Can.), Security Central Nat. Bank (Portsmouth); officer or dir. numerous subsidiary and asso. cos., various fgn. countries; pres. Selby Realty Co., Selby Shoe Co. (Portsmouth); v.p. Selby Homes, Inc. (Ft. Lauderdale, Fla.). Mem. Pres.'s Com. of 12 for Consumers Goods Industries. Pres. Nat. Boot & Shoe Mfrs. Assn., 1931-35; chmn. Code Authority under NRA; trustee Ohio Mfrs. Assn. Republican. Methodist. Mason (Past Master). Clubs: Kiwanis of Portsmouth (past pres.); Cincinnati (Cincinnati); Athletic (Huntington). Home: Buena Vista, O. *

SELDIS, HENRY JAMES, art critic; b. Berlin, Feb. 23, 1925; s. Edward E. and Edith (Danziger) S.; came to U.S., 1939, naturalized, 1943; B.A., N.Y. U., 1946; postgrad. Columbia, New Sch. Social Research, 1946-48; m. Anna Bruni, Aug. 27, 1960 (div. June 1977); 1 son, Mark; stepchildren—Maralee Maltauro, Carol Ann Brahm. Art critic, feature editor Santa Barbara (Calif.) News-Press, 1950-58; art editor Los Angeles Times, 1958-78; lectr. art U. Calif. at Santa Barbara, 1955-58, at Los Angeles extension div., 1958-59; vis. prof. U. So. Calif., summer 1961; asso. prof. Calif. State Coll., Los Angeles, 1965-69; lectr. museums, univs. throughout U.S., 1956-78; dir. numerous exhbns., 1959-78. Mem. exec. com. Save Sam Rodia's Watts Towers, 1958; cons. Tamarind Lithography Workshop, 1960, Century City, 1967; mem. sub.-com. taxation and arts Calif. Arts Commn., 1966-67; exec. chmn. So. Calif. chpt. Com. Rescue Italian Art, 1966-67; exec. v.p. Los Angeles chpt. Venice Com. Served with AUS, World War II. Decorated cavaliere officiale Order Merit, 1967, commendatore, 1973 (Italy); grantee Schreiber Found. Mem. Coll. Art Assn. Am. (Frank Jewett Mather award 1953), Internat. Art Critics Assn. (rapporteur-gen. N.Y.C. meeting 1959), Soc. Aesthetics, Am. Fedn. Art, Amici di Brera, Milan, Dante Aligieri Soc. (dir.), Kappa Tau Alpha. Author: Rico Lebrun, Hollywood Collects; (with others) The Collector in America, Henry Moore in America; Henry Moore Sculpture, 1973. Contbr. numerous articles to various publs. Address: Los Angeles, Calif. Died Feb. 22, 1978.

SELFRIDGE, CALVIN FREDERICK, lawyer; b. Lima, O., Feb. 11, 1892; s. Oliver Boston and Anna (Brice) S.; A.B., Coll. Wooster, 1913; LL.B., Harvard, 1916; m. Violet Bradley, Dec. 30, 1924; children—Anna (Mrs. Robert F. Steinhoff), Ellen (Mrs. John C. McKeown), Calvin. Admitted to Ohio bar, 1917, Ill. bar, 1923; practice in Lima, O., 1917-22, in Chgo., 1923-72; partner firm Wilson & McIlvaine, 1937-72. Mem. appeal bd. SSS, 1944-62; commnr. Winnetka (Ill.) Park Dist., 1953-59, pres., 1955-57. Bd. dirs. Winnetka Community Chest, 1947-50, pres. 1949-50. Served as 2d lt., F.A., U.S. Army, 1917-19; AEF in France; mem. Ohio N.G., 1921-22. Mem. Am., Ill., Chgo. (bd. mgrs. 1951-57), 7th Fed. Circuit bar assns., Izaak Walton League (pres. Winnetka 1952-54), Northwestern U. Assos. Conglist. (trustee 1956-62). Clubs: Law, Legal, University (Chgo.); Indian Hill (Winnetka); Balboa (Malatlon, Mexico). Home: Winnetka, Ill. Died July 20, 1978.

SELIGMAN, ARNOLD MAX, educator, surgeon; b. St. Johnsbury, Vt., Mar. 30, 1912; s. Maurice J. and Sylvia F. (Crestin) S.; B.A. magna cum laude, Harvard, 1934, M.D. magna cum laude, 1939; m. Blume Appel, Mar. 3, 1940; children—Myron Lee, Dale Berna, Garry Alan, Stanley Fred. Research asso. dept. surgery Harvard Med. Sch., 1943-48, asst. prof. surgery, 1948-54; surg. house officer Beth Israel Hosp., Boston, 1939-41, asst. resident in surgery, 1941-42, resident in surg. research, 1942-43, resident surgery, 1945-46, asst. vis. surgeon, 1948-54, asso. dir. surg. research, 1949-54, dir. tumor clunic, 1952-54; surgeon-in-chief Sinai Hosp. Balt., 1954-72, chief research oncology and cell biology, 1972-76; asso. prof. surgery Johns Hopkins U. Sch. Medicine, 1954-67, prof. surgery, 1968-76, Am. Cancer Soc. prof. research oncology and cell biology, 1973-76. Responsible investigator research grants Nat. Cancer Inst., Bethesda, Md., 1946-76, spl. cons., 1947-48, mem. chemotherapy study sect., 1953-57, 63-65, chmn., 1965-67; mem. com. on growth Am. Cancer Soc., 1950-53, mem. adv. com. on research of therapy of cancer, 1957-59, 62-76; pres. 3d Internat. Congress for Histochemistry and Cytochemistry, N.Y.C., 1968; vis. prof. Center for Electron Microscopy, U. Los Andes, Merida, Venezuela, 1969; mem. adv. com. pharmacology-morphology fellowship program Pharm. Mfrs. Assn. Found., 1970-75. Named Md. Chemist of Yr., 1972; hon. pres. 2d Latin Am. Electron Microscopy Congress, 1974; recipient Andres Bello medal Republic of Venezuela, 1975; medal Electron Microscopy Soc. Am., 1975. Diplomate Am. Bd. Surgery. Fellow A.C.S.; mem. Am. Surg. Assn., Surg. Biology Club, Boylston Med. Soc., Mass. Med. Soc., A.A.A.S., Am. Assn. Cancer Research (dir. 1958-61), Histochem. Soc. (council 1950-53, v.p. 1953-54, pres. 1954-55, hon. pres. 1973-76), A.M.A., Am. Chem. Soc., Am. Acad. Arts and Scis., New Eng. Cancer Soc., Balt. City Med. Soc., Am. Soc. Cell Biology, Johns Hopkins Med. and Surg. Assn., Phi Beta Kappa, Sigma Xi, Alpha Omega Alpha. Asso. editor Jour. Biochem. and Biophys. Cytology, 1950-60, Jour. Histochemistry and Cytochemistry. Annales d'Histochimie, France, Histochemistry, Germany; advisor Revista de Microscopia Electronica. Contbr. articles profl. jours. Home: Owings Mills, Md. Died June 15, 1976.

SELIGMAN, EUSTACE, lawyer; b. N.Y.C., Apr. 1, 1889; s. Edwin Robert Anderson and Caroline (Beer) S.; A.B., Amherst Coll., 1910, LL.D., 1965; studied Harvard Law Sch., 1910-12, law schs., Berlin U. and Paris U., 1913; LL.B., Columbia, 1914; m. Maud Jaretzki, Aug. 16, 1917. Began practice with Sullivan & Cromwell, New York, 1914, mem firm, 1923 ; dir. Marine Midland Trust Grace Co. N.Y. Allied Stores Corp. (emeritus). Bd. dirs. Legal Aid Soc., Nat. Fund Med. Edn.; mem. Am. Jewish Com.; bd. dirs., hom. chmn. Fgn. Policy Assn.; chmn. Am. Found. for the Blind. Mem. Am. Law Inst., Am., N.Y. State, City & County bar assns., Council on Fgn. Relations, Theta Delta Chi, Phi Beta Kappa. Former pres. City Club (N.Y.), Amherst Assn. N.Y.; former v.p. Harvard Law Sch. Assn. N.Y. Served as capt., field arty., World War I. Republican. Clubs: Harvard, University, Recess (New York); Westchester Country (Rye, N.Y.); Tamarack Country (Greenwich, Conn.); Cosmos (Washington). Author: What the U.S. can do about India, 1956; The U.S. Should Change It's China Policy, 1958. Contbr. to various publs. Home: Greenwich, Conn. Died Sept. 5, 1976.

SELIGMAN, GERMAIN, art dealer, art historian; b. Paris, France, Feb. 25, 1893; s. Jacques and Blanche (Falkenberg) S.; came to U.S., 1921, naturalized, 1943; student Paris Lycee, Ecole du Louvre, also pvt. tutors; m. Ethlyne Elizabeth Jackson, June 26, 1946. With Jacques Seligmann & Co., Inc., Paris and N.Y.C. from 1914, pres., N.Y.C. from 1923; dir. Customs Expert, Paris, 1925-27. Served as capt. French, Am. and Greek armies, World War I. Decorated D.S.M., Croix de Guerre with 6 citations, comdr. Legion of Honor, knight Holy Saviour (Greece). Author: The Drawings of Georges Seurat, 1946; Oh!, Fickle Taste, 1952; Merchants of Art: Eighty Years of Professional Collecting, 1961; Roger de La Fresnaye, A Catalogue raisonne (Charles Rufus Morey award Coll. Art Assn., Academie Francaise prize Prix Broquette-Gonin 1970), 1969. Contbr. articles to profl. publs. Home: New York, N.Y. Died Mar. 27, 1978; buried Mont par nasse Cemetery, Paris.

SELLARS, WALTER BAILEY, textile co. dir.; b. Burlington, N.C., Dec. 10, 1905; s. Walter Raleigh and Lila (Bailey) S.; B.S., U. N.C., 1927, M.S., 1928; postgrad. Mass. Inst. Tech., 1928-29; m. Elizabeth Morris, June 8, 1932; children—Betty (Mrs. C. G. Wright IV), Rainey, Ann (Mrs. Robert Goodsell). Research chemist, prodn. mgr. Tubize-Chatillon Corp., Rome, Ga., 1929-36; head quality control and labs. Burlington Mills Corp., Greensboro, N.C., 1936-47, asst. v.p., 1947-49, v.p. research and devel., 1949-56: v.p. research and devel. Burlington Industries, Inc., Greensboro, 1956-63, v.p., 1963-70; dir. Sellers Mfg. Co. Bd. dirs., trustee Textile Research Inst., 1946-60; mem. exec. com., bd. govs. Research Triangle Inst., 1955-72. Mem. S.A.R., Newcomen Soc., Am. Assn. Textile Chemists and Colorists, Am. Assn. Textile Technologists, Phi Beta Kappa, Sigma Xi, Alpha Chi Sigma, Delta Tau Delta. Home: Greensboro, N.C. Died Jan. 5, 1979; buried Forest Lawn Cemetery.

SELLERS, HENRY EUGENE, grain merchant; b. Port Arthur, Ont., Can., Dec. 16, 1886; s. David Henry K. and Sarah (Tutty) S.; ed. pub. and collegiate schs., Fort William and Port Arthur, On.; LL.D., U. Manitoba, 1944; m. Irene Maulson, 1912; children—George Henry. Edward Alexander. Barbara. Honorary chairman board Federal Grain, Ltd., Winnipeg. Manitoba, Alberta Pacific Grain Co., ltd. (1943): pres Superior Feed Co. Pacific Elevators, Ltd., Westland Elevators, Ltd.; pres., dir. Sellers, Dickson Securities, Ltd.: hon. dir. The Royal Trust Co.; dir. Canadian Pacific Ry., Great West Life Assurance Company, Federal Grain Limited, Dominion Glass Company, Ltd. Commander Order British Empire; Knight of Grace, Venerable Order Hosp. of St. John of Jerusalem. Hon. capt. Royal Canadian Naval Vol. Res. Dir. Winnipeg Clinic Research Inst. Mem. Royal Commonwealth Soc., Newcomen Soc. Eng. Mem. Anglican Ch. Mason (Shriner). Clubs: Manitoba; St. Charles Country; Canadian; Lakewood Country. Home: Winnipeg, Man., Can. *

SELLERS, MARK ASHLEY, lawyer; b. Grand Bay, Ala., Mar. 24, 1902; s. James Freeman and Medora (Fort) S.; A.B., Princeton, 1924; LL.B., U. Tex., 1928; S.J.D., Harvard, 1933; m. Katherine Luther, Jan. 17, 1937; children—Katherine Ashley, Mark Ashley. Admitted to Tex. bar, 1928, Ga. bar, 1931, D.C. bar, 1947; practice law, Abilene, Tex., 1928-30; county atty., Andrews, 1930; asst. prof. law Emory U., 1931-33; spl. asst. to U.S. atty. gen., 1933-35, 45; prof. law U. Ga., 1935-38; head atty., asso. solicitor USDA, 1938-43; asst. war food adminstr., dir. price War Food Adminstrn., 1943-45; mem. McFarland & Sellers, Washington, 1947-53, Sellers & Conner, 1953-56, Cummings & Sellers, 1956-63, Sellers, Conner & Cuneo, 1964-77. Mem. Adminstrv. Conf. U.S., 1961-63, 68-74. Bd. dirs. Center for Adminstrv. Justice, chmn., 1972-73. Fellow Am. Bar Found. (chmn. 1971-72); mem. Am. (ho. dels. 1952-77, chmn. spl. com. legal services and procs. 1955-58), Fed., Ga., Tex., D.C. bar assns., Am. Law Inst., Am. Judicature Soc., Kappa Alpha, Delta Sigma Rho, Phi Delta Phi. Democrat. Methodist. Clubs: Cosmos (pres. 1966), Princeton, Harvard, Metropolitan (Washington). Contbr. profl. jours. Home: Washington, D.C. Died Apr. 7, 1977; buried West View Cemetery, Atlanta, Ga.

SELLERS, OVID ROGERS, theologian; b. Waco, Tex., Aug. 12, 1884; s. Sandford and Lucia Valentine (Rogers) S.; A.B., U. Chgo., 1904; B.D., McCormick Theol. Sem., Chgo., 1915; Ph.D., Johns Hopkins, 1922; m. Katherine Neill Wilson, June 1, 1918; children—Elizabeth Nickerson (Mrs. Richard L. Harter), Lucia Rogers (Mrs. Warwick W. Butler), Roger Wilson. Asst. prin. high sch., Rockford, Ia., 1904-05; instr. English, Wentworth Mil. Acad., Lexington, Mo., 1905-06, 09-12, headmaster, 1919-21; editor Lexington Intelligencer, 1907-12; ordained to Presbyn. ministry, 1915; instr. O.T., McCormick Theol. Sem., 1916-18, prof., 1922-54; dean, 1940-54, emeritus, 1954—; vis. prof. U. Chgo., 1925, 26, 34, 43; moderator Presbytery of Santa Fe, 1962-63. Staff, excavation Tell Beit Mirsim, 1930; Bethel, 1934, Shechem, 1957, 60, 62, 64, 66; dir. Beth-zur, 1931, 57, Silet edh-Dhahr, 1949; trustee Am. Sch. Oriental Research, 1939-54; mem. bd. fgn. mission Presbyn. Ch. U.S.A., 1941-55; vis. lectr. Sekolah Tinggi Theologia, Djakarta, 1955; dir. Am. Sch: Oriental Research, Jerusalem, 1948-49, prof. archaeology, 1957-58. Chaplain 17th F.A., U.S. Army, 1918-19. Mem. Am. Oriental Soc. (v.p. 1948), Soc. Bibl. Lit. and Exegesis, Chgo. Soc. Bibl. Research, Archaeol. Inst. Am., Am. Acad. Religion, Am. Legion, Linguistic Soc., Archaeol. Soc. N.M., Vets. World Ward I, Beta Theta Pi. Acacia. Democrat. Mason. Author: Hebrew and Homiletics (brochure), 1924; The Citadel of Bethzur, 1933; Biblical Hebrew for Beginners (with Edwin Voigt), 1941; Genesis Rhymes, 1948; The Fifth Quarter Century of McCormick, 1955; The 1957 Excavation at Beth-zur (with others), 1968. Contbr. A New New Standard Bible Dictionary; Interpreter's Dictionary of the Bible; other publs. Home: Santa Fe NM. *

SELLERS, PETER, actor; b. Southsea, Eng., Sept. 8, 1925; s. William Sellers and Agnes Marks; student St. Aloysius Coll., Highgate, Eng.; m. Anne Hayes, Aug. 15, 1951 (div.); children—Michael, Sarah; m. 2d, Britt Ekland (div.); 1 dau.; m. 3d, Miranda Elizabeth Louise Quarry, Aug. 24, 1970. With Windmill Theatre, London, 1948; appeared on The Goon Show, BBC radio, 1949-59; numerous appearances London Palladium, from 1948; pantomime debut in Mother Goose, 1954-55, royal command variety performance, 1954; other stage appearances include Brouhaha, 1958; originator, star TV comedy series The Idiot Weekly, 1958, A Show Called Fred, 1958, Son of Fred, 1959, Yes, It's the Cathode Ray Tube Show, 1959; motion pictures include Let's Go Crazy, 1950, John and Julie 1955, Order are Orders, 1955, The Ladykillers, 1956, The Smallest Show on Earth, 1956, The Naked Truth, 1957, Tom Thumb, 1958, Up the Creek, 1958, I'm Alright Jack (Best British Actor award 1959), 1959, The Battle of the Sexes, 1959, The Mouse That Roared, 1959, The Running Jumping and Standing Still Film (Golden Gate award for best fiction still San Francisco, 1960, Silver Miqueldi statuette Bilbao 1960, honor diploma Mannheim Festival 1960, 59), Two Way Stretch, 1960, Never Let Go, 1960, The Millionairess, 1960, Mr. Topaze (also dir., 1960, Lolita, 1961, The Wrong Arm of the Law, Only Two Can Play, 1962, Heavens Above, 1963, The World of Henry Orient, 1964, The Pink Panther, 1964, Shot in the Dark, 1964, What's New Pussycat, 1965, After the Fox, 1966, Casino Royale, 1966, The Bobo, 1966, The Party, I Love You Alice B. Toklas, The Magic Christian, Hoffman, There's A Girl In My Soup, 1970; rec. artist Parlophone E.MI Served with RAF, World War II. Recipient Best Film Actor award Variety Club, Gt. Brit., 1960; Silver disc. 1960. Jewish religion. Address: London, England. Died July 23, 1980.

SELLING, LAURENCE, physician; b. Portland, Ore., Mar. 18, 1882; s. Ben and Mathilda (Hess) S.; B.A., Yale, 1904; M.D., Johns Hopkins Medical Sch., 1908; m. Adelaide Lowenson, Oct. 13, 1913; children—Phillip, John, Margaret (Mrs. Labby), Ben. Prof. medicine, U. of Ore. Med. Sch., 1927-47, emertus; mem. Portland Clinic. Served as maj., M.C., World War I, 1917-18. Mem. Am. Medical Assn., Am. Neurological Assn., Portland Acad. Medicine. Republican. Contbr. various articles on medical subjects. Home: Portland. *

SELTZER, LOUIS BENSON, editor; b. Cleveland, O., Sept. 19, 1897; s. Charles Alden and Ella (Albers) S.; ed. pub. grade and high schs. until 1910; m. Marion Elizabeth Champlin, Jan. 9, 1915; children—Chester Ellsworth, Shirley Marion. Began as office boy, 1911; then reporter Cleveland Leader; advertising writer O. S. Hubbell Co., 1914-15; reporter Cleveland News. 1916-17; with Cleveland Press successively as reporter, editorial writer, city editor, news editor, asso. editor, chief editorial writer, 1916-28, and editor, from 1928; editor-in-chief Scripps-Howard Newspapers of Ohio (Columbus Citizen, Cincinnati Post, Cleveland Press) from 1937. Mem. adv. bd. Pultizer Prize, 1956. Mem. Am. Soc. Newspaper Editors (dir.). Unitarian. Clubs: Mid-Day, Union, Rotary, Advertising, City, Cleveland Club. Author: The Years Were Good, 1956. Home: Cleveland, Ohio. Died Apr. 7, 1980.

SEMENENKO, SERGE, financier; b. Russia; s. Jacques and Marie (Temeli) S.; A.B., Classical Coll., Constantinople, Turkey; B.S., Robert Coll., Istanbul; B.S., M.B.A., Harvard; D.S. in B.A. (hon.), Bryant Coll.; m. Virginia Boyd, 1948; 1 dau., Christine. Joined credit dept. First Nat. Bank of Boston, 1926, asst. v.p., 1928, v.p., 1943-47, sr. v.p., 1947, vice chmn., dir. until 1967; chmn. finance com., chmn. bd., dir. Chemway Corp.; vice chmn., dir. Columbia Pictures Corp., 1967-76; dir., mem. exec. com. City Stores Corp.; dir. Basic Resources Internat. S.A., Hilton Internat. Co., 721 Corp. (Bonwit Teller Corp.); chmn. finance com., chmn. bd. dir. Pierre Service Corp. (Hotel Pierre); chmn. Crooks-Barnes Labs. Trustee Children's Hosp. Med. Center, Boston. Clubs: Wianno Yacht (Cape Cod, Mass.); Harvard, Union (Boston); Acapulco (Mexico) Yacht; Motor Yacht (Cote Azur, France); Marks (London). Home: Boston, Mass. Died Apr. 24, 1980; buried Mt. Auburn Cemetery, Cambridge, Mass.

SEMRAD, CHARLES A., utilities exec.; b. Highland, Wis., July 5, 1885; s. John V. and Anne (Bohacek) S.; B.S., U. of Wis., 1908; m. Louise A. Wagner, June 24, 1914 (dec.); children—Charles J., Mary Lee Quinn; married second, Mildred G. Hopkins, 1958. Instructor University of Wisconsin, 1908-09; with Union Electric Company, St.Louis, 1909-10; elec. engr., Western Light & Power Co., Boulder, Colo., 1910-13, vice president, general manager, 1918-24; vice president, general manager Cheyenne (Wyo.) Light, Fuel & Power Co., 1913-18; v.p., comml. mgr. Public Service Co. Colo., Denver, 1924-27; pres., dir., St. Joseph Light & Power Co., 1927-56, dir., chmn., 1956—; dir. Asso. Industries Mo. Dir. Mo. Expenditure Surrey, Am. Humanics Found., also trustee, St. Joseph United Fund. Member American Institute E.E., K.C. Elk. Clubs: Country,

Benton, Rotary. Home: St. Joseph, Mo. *

SEMRAD, ELVIN VAVRINEC, educator, psychiatrist; b. Abie, Neb., Aug. 10, 1909; s. Theodore and Albina (Koza) S.; A.B., Peru State Tchrs. Coll., 1932; B.S., U. Neb., 1932, M.D., 1934; M.A., Harvard, 1968; m. Henrietta Stava, Jan. 9, 1936; children—Theodore, Henrietta, Elvin Lawrence, Susan. Rotating intern Univ. Hosps., Omaha, 1934-35; resident psychiatry Luth. Psychiat. Hosp., Omaha, 1935; intern Boston Psychopathic Hosp., 1935-36, asst. physician, 1936, sr. physician, 1937; resident McLean Hosp., Waverly, Mass., 1937-38; sr. physician Met. State Hosp., 1938-42; dir. clin. psychiatry Boston State Hosp., 1946, dir. research, 1948-52, cons. clin. research, 1952-76; asst. prof. psychiatry Boston U., 1946-52; instr. Boston Coll. Sch. Social Work, 1947-52; cons. 1947-76; lectr. clin. psychology Harvard Med. Sch., 1948-60, instr. psychiatry, 1949-52, asst. prof., 1952-55, asso. clin. prof., 1955-59, clin. prof., 1959-68, prof. psychiatry, 1968-76; acting chmn. dept. psychiatry Mass. Mental Health Center, 1956-58, 73-76, dir. psychiatry, 1952-76; instr. group work Mass. Soc. Mental Hygiene, 1948-52; instr. Boston Psychoanalytic Inst., 1949-76, asso. tng. analyst, 1960-62, tng. analyst, 1962-76, pres., 1968-76; instr. Judge Baker Child Guidance Center, 1949-57. Served from 1st lt. to maj., AUS, 1942-46. Diplomate Am. Bd. Neurology and Psychiatry (asst. examiner). Mem. Am. Psychiat. Assn., Am., Boston psychoanalytic assns., Boston Psychoanalytic Inst., Group Advancement Psychiatry, C. of C., Sigma Xi, Kappa Delta Pi. Contbr. articles profl. jours. Home: Waban, Mass. Died Oct. 7, 1976.

SENSENBRENNER, JOHN STILP, business exec.; b. Neenah, Wis., Apr. 20, 1886; s. Frank J. and Margaret (Stilp) S.; A.B., Princeton, 1909; m. Julia Reese Smith; children—Gretchen, Frank James, Helen Mary, John Stilp. Began as apprentice Kimberly-Clark Corp., 1907, dir., 1916, Pacific Coast sales mgr., 1921-26, gen. sales mgr. and vice pres., 1926-42, mem. exec. com., 1928-42, resigned active bus. connection to enter U.S. Army, 1942. Director Kimberly-Clark Corp., Neenah, Wis. Served F.A. U.S. Army, 1918; commd. major and assigned to purchases div., War Dept. Gen. Staff, 1942; grad. U.S. Army Sch. of Mil. Govt., U. of Va., 1943; sent to E.T.O., assigned to G-5, S.H.A.E.F., 1943-44; renegotiation div., War Dept. Gen. Staff, 1945; mem. Gen. Staff Corps and vice chmn. War Dept. Price Adjustment Bd., with rank of lt. col., 1945-46, promoted col., 1946, chmn. bd., 1947; chief of renegotiation br. and vice chmn. War Contracts Price Adjustment Bd., 1947. Decorated Legion of Merit, Army Commendation Medal. Mem. Am. Legion, Vets. Fgn. Wars, Mil. Govt. Assn. Clubs: Chicago Athletic, Chicago; Neenah, Neenah Nodaway Yacht, North Shore Golf (Neenah); University (Milwaukee); Army-Navy (Washington); Princeton (N.Y.C.); Oceanside Golf and Country (Ormond Beach, Fla.), Bath and Tennis (Palm Beach, Fla.). Address: Neenah, Wis. *

SENTNER, P. DAVID, journalist, poet; b. N.Y.C.; s. Joseph and Juanita (Brandon) S.; B.A., Columbia, 1923, B.Lit., 1923; m. Mary Southerland Steele; 1 dau., Joyce. Mem. N.Y. bur. U.P.I., 1924; spl. writer and dramatic editor Internat. News Service, 1924-35, fgn. corr. Internat. News Service, 1935-38; mem. editorial staff. N.Y. Jour.-Am., 1938-42; Washington corr., Washington bur. chief, contbg. editor Hearst Newspapers, Hearst Headline Service, 1942-75, Washington rep. Hearst Mags. Bd. dirs. Internat. Eye Found. Served with 27th Div., A.E.F., France, World War I. Recipient Alfred A. Knopf Poetry Prize; Am. Legion Medal of Merit. Mem. Dramatists Guild, White House Corrs. Assn., Am. Legion, Sigma Delta Chi. Clubs: Gridiron, Columbia University (N.Y.C.); National Press (Washington). Author: Cobblestones: Hollywood Comet; How the FBI Gets Its Man. Home: Washington, D.C. Died Apr. 22, 1975.

SENYSHYN, AMBROSE ANDREW, clergyman; b. Stary Sambor, Galicia, Feb. 23, 1903; s. Thomas and Mary (Perucka) S.; ed. monastery colls., Krechow and Lviw, Galicia; philosophy, Dobromil, Galicia, theol. Crystynopol, Galicia and Warsaw, Poland. Joined Order St. Basil The Gt., 1921; ordained priest Ukrainian Cath. Ch., 1931; curate, Warsaw, 1930-33; missionary and curate, Chgo., 1933-37; pastor St. Nicholas parish, superior Ukranian Cath. Chs. in Chgo., 1937-42; aux. bishop Ukrainian Cath. Diocese Phila., 1942-56; apostolic exarch Byzantine Rite Apostolic Exarchy, Stamford, Conn., 1956-58; bishop Diocese Stamford, 1958-61; archbishop Phila. Ukrainian Cath. Archeparchy, from 1961. Address: Philadelphia, Pa. Died Sept. 11, 1976; interred Bishops' Crypt, Ukrainian Cath. Cathedral, Phila.

SERVAAS, SANDRA JEAN, editor; b. Indpls., Feb. 22, 1947; d. John D. and Nita (Camp) Servaas; B.A., Wellesley Coll., 1969. Asso. editor Child Life mag., Indpls., 1968; asst. mng. editor Holiday Mag., Indpls., 1971-72, mng. editor, asso. pub., 1972-75; prof. English, Tokyo (Japan) Kasei Gakuin Coll., 1970-71. Durant scholar, 1969. Mem. Phi Beta Kappa. Contbr. profl. jours. Home: Indianapolis, Ind. Died Sept. 6, 1975.

SETTLE, THOMAS GREENHOW WILLIAMS, naval officer; b. Washington, Nov. 4, 1895; s. Joseph Andrew and May Curtis (Williams) S.; grad. US. Naval Acad., 1918, post grad. sch., 1923; S.M., Harvard, 1924; attended Naval War Coll., 1939-41; in Fay Brackett, June 6, 1925; 1 s., Thomas Brackett. Commd. ensign USN, 1918, advanced through grades to vice admiral, 1954. Served in war zone in U.S.S. Martha Washington and U.S.S. Sampson, 1918; U.S.S. Chew and Whipple, 1910-22; in Asiatic Fleet, 1934-38; commanded U.S.S. Portland, 1944-45; naval forces, North China, 1945-46; airship adviser to deputy chief of naval operations (air), 1946-47; comd. American naval mission to Turkey, 1947-49; comdt. 8th naval district, 1951-54, comdr. Amphibian Force Pacific Fleet, 1954-56, retired. Devoted himself to airships, 1924-34, making over 100 balloon flights; winner, distance record (952 miles), in Pittsburgh race, 1929, James Gordon balloon race, Switzerland, 1932; made ascent into stratosphere, Nov. 20, 1933, attaining height of 61,237 feet. Address: Washington, D.C. Died May 1, 1980.

SETTLEMIRE, CLAUDE LAPRELL, librarian; b. Harrisburg, Ark., Dec. 26, 1920; s. Charles and Mary Rose Blanche (Bullard) S.; B.S., Ark. State Coll., 1947; B.S. in Library Sci., Peabody Coll., 1949, M.S. in L.S., 1951; m. Helen Margaret Studlien, Apr. 14, 1950. Reference librarian Ft. Hays (Kans.) State Coll., 1951-54; librarian Hutchinson (Kan.) Pub. Library, 1954-56, Roanoke (Va.) Pub. Library, 1956-58, Boulder (Colo.) Library, 1958-66; cons. Calif. State Library, 1966-69; chief supr. St. Louis Pub. Library, 1969-71; librarian Salem (Oreg.) Pub. Library, 1971-77. Summer vis. faculty Ark. State Coll., 1948, Peabody Coll., 1950-51, U. Denver, 1956-61, U. Oreg., 1974; cons. pub. libraries Grand Junction, Colo., Laramie County (Wyo.), Lake County (Calif.). Democratic precinct committeeman, Boulder, 1955-56. Bd. dirs. Rocky Mountain Bibliog. Center, 1963-65, Freedom to Read Found. Served with USAAF, 1942-46. Mem. Am., Ore., Kan. (pres. 1955-56) library assns. Lion. Home: Salem, Oreg. Died May 14, 1977.

SETZLER, EDWIN LAKE, educator; b. Newberry, S.C., Feb. 15, 1903; s. E.B. and Una (Lake) S.; A.B. Newberry, Coll., 1922, A.M., 1923, D.H.L., 1955; M.A., U. Va., 1924; Ed.D., Lenoir Rhyne Coll., 1972; m. Nancy Martin, June, 1932; children—Alice, Edwin, John. Instr., Newberry Coll., 1922, Clemson Coll., 1924-25; prof. English, Lenoir Rhyne Coll., Hickory, N.C., 1925-35, dean, 1935-67, prof., 1935-72, registrar, 1925-67. Democrat. Lutheran. Home: Hickory, N.C. Died June 21, 1976; buried Hickory, N.C.

SEVERINGHAUS, AURA EDWARD, anatomist; b. Jeffersonville, Ind., May 5, 1894; s. Charles Edwin and Ida Henrietta (Mock) S.; student U. Wis., 1912-15; A.B., Columbia, 1916, M.A., 1919, Ph.D., 1927, Sc.D., D.H.L., LL.D.; m. Sara M. Nay, July 9, 1923. Grad. asst. dept. zoology Columbia, 1916-17, 19-20; asst. prof. biology Peking (China) Union Med. Coll., Rockefeller Found., 1920-23, dean, 1923-26; faculty Columbia, 1927-63, asso. dean in medicine, sec. faculty, 1945-62, prof. anatomy emeritus, asso. dean emeritus, 1962-79. Dir. studies neurology and neurol. scis. Nat. Inst. Neurol. Disease and Stroke, 1962-71; cons. Ford Found., 1962-63, Josiah Macy Jr. Found., 1968-70. Am del. Internat. Colloquium Les Hormones Sexuelles, Paris, 1937; v.p. Nat. Med. Fellowships, from 1950. Bd. dirs. N.Y. YMCA. Served with M.C., AUS, 1917-19. Recipient Peoples Medal of Honored Merit with citation Republic China, for efforts in rehab. med. libraries, 1943; Order Brilliant Star, 1946, with grand cordon, 1973. Mem. Harvey Soc., Exptl. Biology and Medicine, A.A.A.S., Am. Assn. Anatomists, Marine Biol. Lab. (Woods Hole, Mass.), Assn. for Study Endocrine Glands, Am. Bur. Med. Aid to China (pres.), United Service to China, Sigma Xi, Phi Beta Kappa, Alpha Omega Alpha. Clubs: Riverdale Yacht, St. Andrews Golf, Quill (N.Y.C.). Co-author: Bailey's Text Book of Histology, 1944; Preparation for Medical Education in the Liberal Arts College, 1953; Preparation for Medical Education: A Restudy, 1961; Neurology—A Medical Discipline Takes Stock, 1971. Contbg. author The Pituitary Gland (Assn. Research Nervous and Mental Diseases), 1938; Les Hormones Sexuelles, 1939; Symposia on Quantitative Biology (Cold Spring Harbor Series), 1937; Sex and Internal Secretion, 1941; numerous articles in sci., med. jours. Home: New York, N.Y. Died Apr. 7, 1979.

SEYA, CHARLES LOUIS, diplomat; b. Latvia, June 2, 1885; s. Jan and Louise (Stahlberg) S.; studied philology at Grenoble and Paris, law at U. of Riga; m. Herta Osol, of Smilten, Latvia, June 4, 1917; children—George, Mirdza, André. Teacher and prin. high sch. and university lecturer; chargé d'affaires at Washington, D.C., 1922-23; minister to Lithuania, 1923; minister of foreign affairs, Latvia, 1924; 1st del. of Latvia to Assembly of League of Nations, 1924; E.E. and M.P. to U.S. from Latvia since June 1925. Comdr. Legion d'Honneur (French). Lutheran. Clubs: Metropolitan, Chevy Chase, Congressional Country. Address: Washington, D.C. *

SEYBOLD, ROSCOE (SE'BOLD), corp. exec.; b. Rockville, Ind., Feb. 9, 1884; s. J. L. and Margaret Ellen (Neet) S.; B.S. in E.E., Purdue University, 1907; Doctor of Engineering (honorary), 1942; m. Nancy Frank, Sept. 1, 1915; children—Robert J., William V. Began as clerk Westinghouse Electric & Mfg. Co., Pittsburgh, Pa., 1907, asst. to v.p. and gen. mgr., 1926-29, asst. to pres. 1929-31, controller, 1931-34, v.p. and controller, 1934-48, vice pres. and asst. to the president, 1948-50, dir., 1939-51, retired; now vice chmn. Munitions Bd., Washington; director Union Nat. Bank (Pittsburgh), Wilkinsburgh (Pa.) Federal Savings and Loan Assn.; trustee Dollar Savings Bank, Pittsburgh. Member Controllers Inst. of America (pres. 1938-39), Phi Gamma Delta. Methodist. Mason. Clubs: Duquesne, University, Bankers (Pittsburgh); Oakmont Country. Home: Wilkinsburg, Pa. *

SEYDELL, ERNEST MORRIS (SI'DEL), oto-laryngologist; b. Chicago, Ill., Mar. 29, 1882; s. Morris and Mathilda (Probsthan) S.; M.D., Northwestern U. Med. Sch., 1909; post-grad. studies at Hamburg and Berlin, also Copenhagen, Denmark; m. Margaret Anne Carter, Aug. 8, 1911; children—Margaret Ernestine (Mrs. Verne M. Laing), Jane (Mrs. Glenn L. Milbourn), Ernest Morris. Intern, St. Francis Hospital, Wichita, Kan., 1909-10; in practice at Wichita since 1910; oto-laryngologist Wesley, St. Francis and Sedgwick County hosps. since 1911. Fellow Am. Coll. of Surgeons; mem. American Board of Otolaryngology, A.M.A., Am. Laryngol. Assn., American Otological Soc. (pres. 1941), American Laryngol., Rhinol. and Otol. Soc., American Broncho-Esophagological Assn., Am. Academy of Ophthalmology and Oto-Laryngology, Kansas City Eye, Ear, Nose and Throat Assn. (hon.), Alpha Kappa Kappa, Alpha Omega Alpha. Mason. Clubs: Wichita Rotary, Asso. editor of Archives of Otolaryngology. Writer of many articles on medical subjects. Home: Wichita, Kan. *

SEYMOUR, CHARLES, JR., educator; b. New Haven, Feb. 26, 1912; s. Charles and Gladys (Watkins) S.; student Choate Sch., 1925-30, King's Coll., Cambridge U., 1930-31; B.A., Yale, 1935, Ph.D. (Sterling fellow), 1938; postgrad. U. Paris, 1935-38; m. Charlotte Ball, May 4, 1940; children—Charlotte Elizabeth, Charles. Instr. history, history of art Yale, 1938-39, asso. prof., curator Renaissance art, 1949-54, prof., curator Renaissance art, 1954-77, prof. emeritus, 1977; chmn. dept. history art, 1956-59; curator sculpture Nat. Gallery Art, 1939-42, asst. chief curator, 1945-49. Lectr., Johns Hopkins 1947-48; vis. Mellon prof. U. Pitts., 1965, adj. prof., 1966-77. Mem. Nat. Com. to Restore Italian Art. Served with M.I. War Dept., 1943-45. Guggenheim fellow, 1954-55. Mem. Renaissance Soc. Am. (council), Coll. Art Assn., Phi Beta Kappa. Author: Notre Dame of Noyon in the Twelfth Century, 1939, 2d edit., 1969, French edit. with additions, 1976; Masterpieces of Sculpture in the National Gallery of Art, 1949, rev. edit. (with C. Douglas Lewis), 1978; Tradition and Experiment in Modern Sculpture, 1949; Art Treasures for America: S.A. Kress Collection, 1961; Italian Sculpture 1400-1500 (Pelican History of Art), 1966; Michelangelo's David, a search for identity, 1967; Early Italian Paintings in the Yale University Art Gallery, 1970; The Sculpture of Verrochio, 1971; Michelangelo-The Sistine Ceiling, 1972; Jacopo della Quercia, Sculptor, 1973. Mem. editorial bd. Renaissance Quar. Contbr. to Gen. Edn. in Sch. and Coll., 1952; articles to profl. jours. Home: New Haven, Conn. Died Apr. 7, 1977; buried Grove St. Cemetery, New Haven.

SEYMOUR, CHARLES KINNE, pres. Henry Barroll & Co., Inc., b. Chatham, N.Y., Jan. 9, 1882; s. Harvey A. and Nellie (Hawley) S.; M.E., Cornell U., 1903; m. Florence White, Nov. 1, 1910; children—Edward White, Thomas Cornell, Harold Hawley. Began as spl. apprentice Niles Bement Pond Co., N.Y. City, 1903, successively salesman, asst. sales mgr., sec., treas. and v.p. until 1930, pres. and treas., 1930-36; dir. Niles Bement Pond Co., Henry Barroll & Co., Inc., John Bertram & Sons Co., Shepard-Niles Crane & Hoist Co. Republican. Clubs: University, Engineers, Columbia Country (New York). Home: Chatham, N.Y.*

SEYMOUR, FRANK MARCELLOUS, pub. relations cons.; b. Detroit, Dec. 6, 1916; s. Perry and Ann Porterfield Traybue S.; student Wayne State U.; m. Edith Victoria Jacobsen, Feb. 4, 1956; children—Ruth Ann, Magda Lynn, Don King. Engaged in pub. relations Altes Brewing Co., 1949-52; pub. relations dir., 1952-54; mgr. radio sta. WCHB, Detroit, 1958-65; founder Frank Seymour Assos., Detroit, 1965-69; pres. Seymour & Lundy Assos. Inc., Detroit, 1969-75, Frank M. Seymour, Inc., 1975-78. Councilman Ypsilanti (Mich.) 1943-45. Mem. Pub. Relations Soc. Am. (accredited), Adcraft Club, Detroit Press Club. Mem. 1st Ch. Christ Scientist (dir. 1974-78). Home: Bloomfield Hills, Mich. Died Feb. 9, 1978.

SEYMOUR, WALTON, power economist; b. Faribault, Minn., July 10, 1909; s. Charles Walton and Margaret Lucinda (Rugg) S.; A.B., U. Wis., 1929; m. Katherine Rankine Denniston, Nov. 21, 1936 (dec. 1960); children—Martha, C. Walton; m. 2d, Sonya Thorp, Apr. 8, 1966. With N. Am. Co., 1929-34, power marketing activities TVA, including negotiation contracts, acquisition properties and econ. studies, 1934-47; power rate cons. Lower Colo. River Authority and S.C. Pub. Service Authority. 1939-40; dir. div. power and program staff Office Sec. Interior, 1947-50; mem. adv. com. cooperation between Electric Power Industry and AEC, 1949-51; power adviser M.S.A. mission to Greece, 1950-52; cons. on resource devel. including U.S., El Salvador, Guatemala, Pakistan, and Venezuela, Iran, 1952-58; v.p. indsl. devel. Devel. & Resources Corp., N.Y.C., 1958-73. Dep. leader spl. UN flood control mission, Pakistan, 1956-57, NPA project on productive uses of nuclear energy, 1954-58; cons. power econs. P.R. Water Resources Authority, 1956-58; U.S. del. UN Conf. application sci. and tech. for benefit less developed areas, Geneva, 1963; cons. Fed. Power Commn., 1963-66. Mem. Nat. Planning Assn., Am. Acad. Polit. and Social Scis., Acad. Polit. Sci. Democrat. Contbr. reports, articles. to profl. publs. Home: New York, N.Y. Died Apr. 26, 1979.

SHAFFER, JAMES GRANT, med. educator; b. Washington, Kans., Jan. 17, 1913; s. Bowen Ross and Myrtle Katherine (Worley) S.; B.S., Manchester Coll., 1935, D.Sc., 1973; D.Sc., Johns Hopkins U., 1940; m. Esther Elizabeth Willard, Sept. 3, 1939; children—Carol (Mrs. Wesley Stieg), Susan (Mrs. John Willard), Janet (Mrs. Gregory Harsha), Nancy (Mrs. James Lanier). Tchr., Jackson Twp. High Sch., Flint, Ind., 1935-36, Jefferson Twp. High Sch., Ossian, Ind., 1936-37; student instr. immunology and filterable viruses Johns Hopkins U., Balt., 1937-40, instr., 1940-42; med. research biologist Am. Cyanamid Co., Stamford, Conn., 1942-43; asst. prof. preventive medicine Vanderbilt U., Nashville, 1946-48, vis. prof. bacteriology, 1947-48; asso. prof. bacteriology and virology U. Louisville, 1948-52; dir. labs. Louisville Children's Hosp., 1948-50, microbiologist, 1950-52; prof., chmn. dept. microbiology and pub. health Chgo. Med. Sch., 1952-60, asso. dean, prof. microbiology, 1967-74; dir. microbiology and hosp. epidemiology Luth. Gen. Hosp., Park Ridge, Ill., 1960-67; cons. hosp. epidemiology 1967-74; dir. ednl. and profl. programs Mt. Sinai Hosp. Med. Center of Chgo., 1974-80; prof. microbiology Rush U., Chgo., 1975-80, dir. undergrad. med. edn., 1975-80; professorial lectr. microgiology U. Chgo., 1965-68; cons VA Hosp., Hines, Ill., 1972-80; coordinator devel. of projected urban-oriented med. sch. Mt. Sinai Hosp. Med. Center and Roosevelt U., 1974-80. Pres. PTA Lincoln Sch., Elmhurst, Ill., 1956-57. Mem. sch. bd. dist. 46 Elmhurst Elementary Sch., 1958-67. Served to maj. AUS, 1943-46. Recipient Outstanding Alumni award Manchester Coll., 1965, award of merit Chgo Tech. Socs. Council, 1969. Diplomate Am. Bd. Microbiology. Fellow Am. Pub. Health Assn. (chmn. lab. sect. 1970-71, governing council 1971-76, mem. action bd.), Am. Inst. Chemists, Am. Acad. Microbiology, Inst. Medicine Chgo.; mem. Am. Soc. Microbiology, AAAS, Am. Soc. Tropical Medicine and Hygiene, Soc. Ill. Bacteriologists, Ill. Pub. Health Assn., Assn. Tchrs. Preventive Medicine, Royal Soc. Health, Assn. Am. Med. Colls. (chmn. com. fin. problems of med. students 1971-73), Alumni Assn. Manchester Coll. (pres. 1962-63), Sigma Xi, Alpha Omega Alpha, Delta Omega. Author: Amebiasis: A Biomedical Problem, 1965. Contbr. to publs. in field. Home: Elmhurst, Ill. Died May 12, 1981; interred Hall of Remembrance, Elm Lawn Meml. Park, Elmhurst.

SHAFFER, JAMES TRAVIS, gas co. exec.; b. Athens, La., Dec. 22, 1930; s. George Henry and Dorothy Velma (Bridges) S.; B.S., La. Tech. U., 1951; postgrad. La. State U.; m. Jean Ruffin, Feb. 5, 1955; children—Cynthia, Cheryl, James. With Ark.-La. Gas Co., Shreveport, 1954-80, asst. sec., asst. treas., 1969-74, sec., asst. treas., 1974-80; mem. evening faculty Shreveport-Bossier Vocat. Tech. Sch. Past bd. dirs. Shreveport Assn. Blind, Shreveport YMCA, Shreveport Y's Men Club, Shreveport Jr. C. of C.; past mem. adminstrv. bd. Neel Methodist Ch., Shreveport. Served with USAF, 1952-54. Mem. Am. Soc. Corporate Secs., Omicron Delta Kappa. Club: Riverside Swim and Tennis (past dir.). Home: Shreveport, La. Died 1980.

SHAFFER, LAURANCE FREDERIC, psychologist; b. Johnstown, N.Y., Aug. 12, 1903; s. Mathew Thomas and Ines (Vaissiere) S.; B.S., Union Coll., 1924, LL.D., 1949; M.A., Columbia, 1927, Ph.D., 1930; m. Dorothy Rhodes, June 24, 1931; 1 son, Warren Frederic. Tchr. math. Kingsley Sch., Essex Fells, N.J., 1924-26; research asso. Inst. Ednl. Research, Columbia Tchrs. Coll., 1926-28, prof. edn., 1945-68, head dept. guidance, 1945-55, dir. doctoral studies, 1963-64, asso. dean, 1964-68, prof. emeritus psychology, 1968-76; asst. prof. to prof. psychology Carnegie Inst. Tech., 1928-41, head bur. measurement and guidance, 1940-41. Cons. clin. psychology VA, 1948-63, NIH, 1947-55, 62-64; dir. Psychol. Corp., N.Y.C., 1957-75, chmn. bd., 1965-70. Trustee Am. Psychol. Found., 1953-59, pres. 1955-56. Served from maj. to col. USAAF, 1941-45. Decorated Legion of Merit. Diplomate in Clin. Psychology, Am. Bd. of Profl. Psychology. Fellow Am. Psychol. Assn. (pres. 1952-53), A.A.A.S.; mem. Sigma Xi, Phi Kappa Phi, Kappa Delta Pi. Presbyn. Author: Children's Interpretations of Cartoons, 1930; The Psychology of Adjustment, 1936, rev. edit. (with E.J. Shoben, Jr.), 1956; co-author: Child Psychology, 1937; Fields of Psychology, 1940, rev., 1950, 66; Psychology, 1940; Foundations of Psychology, 1948. Editor Jour. Cons. Psychology, 1947-58. Home: Oradell, N.J. Died July 20, 1976.

SHAFROTH, MORRISON, lawyer; b. Denver, Oct. 27, 1888; s. John Franklin and Virginia (Morrison) S.; (father twice gov. Colo., and U.S. senator, 1913-19); A.B., U. Mich., 1910; J.D., 1927 (1912); m. Abby Staunton Hagerman, Sept. 20, 1917 (dec. Nov. 1976); children—Virginia Morrison (Mrs. Quigg Newton), Ellen (Mrs. William Dean Embree, Jr.), John Franklin, Frank Hagerman. Began practice in Denver, 1912; now mem. firm Shafroth & Toll. Vis. lectr. U. Denver Law Sch. Democratic nominee for atty. gen. Colo., 1920, for U.S. senator from Colo., 1924; mem. Dem. Club. Chief counsel U.S. Bur. Internal Revenue, Washington, 1936-37. Enlisted in 1st O.T.C., Ft. Riley, Kan., 1917; commd. 1st lt., promoted to capt. and served at front 341st F.A., 89th Div., AEF; discharged 1919. Life trustee, past pres. bd. U. Denver, Social Sci. Found. Mem. Am. Law Inst., Am. (tax council), Colo. Hist. Soc. (trustee), Colo., Fed., Denver bar assns., Am. Judicature Soc., Phi Beta Kappa, Phi Delta Theta, Michigamua. Baptist. Rotarian. Clubs: Westerners, University, Colorado Mountain, Denver Country. Died Oct. 4, 1978.

SHAKE, CURTIS GROVER, lawyer; b. Knox County, Ind., July 14, 1887; s. Daniel W. and Arminda F. (Wyant) S.; student Vincennes (Ind.) U., 1903-06; LL.B., Ind. U., 1910; m. Ann Szeleczky, June 5, 1911 (dec. Nov. 1946); 1 son, Gilbert (dec.); m. 2d, Alice K. Hubbard, Jan. 2, 1952 (dec. June 1970); 1 dau., Susan K. Admitted to Ind. bar, 1909; practice in Vincennes; dep. pros. atty., 1911-13; city atty., 1912-15; U.S. commr., 1917-21; county atty., 1923-26; state senator, 1927; Democratic nominee for atty. gen. Ind., 1928; apptd. judge Ind. Supreme Ct., Jan. 1938, elected for 6 yr. term, Nov. 1938; ret. from bench, 1945. Permanent chmn. Dem. State Conv., 1942. Referee for Nat. R.R. Adjustment Bd. in 400 labor disputes. Mem. Nat. Ry. Labor Panel; Pres.'s Emergency and Arbitration Bds.; exec. presiding judge U.S. Mil. Tribunals, presiding judge I.G. Farben Case, Germany, 1947-48. Past trustee Vincennes U. (pres. emeritus). Mem. Am., Ind. bar assns., Am. Judicature Soc., Am. Arbitration Assn., Ind. Hist. Soc., S.A.R., Soc. Ind. Pioneers, Sigma Pi, Kappa Sigma, Phi Delta Phi, Delta Sigma Rho. Democrat. Mem. Christian Ch. Mason, Kiwanian. Contbr. to legal periodicals. Wrote several pamphlets on history of Vincennes. Home: Vincennes, Ind. Died Sept. 11, 1978.

SHAKOW, DAVID, psychologist; b. N.Y.C., Jan. 2, 1901; s. Abraham and Eva (Leventhal) S.; S.B., Harvard U., 1924, A.M., 1927, Ph.D., 1942; D.Sc., U. Rochester, 1971; m. Sophie Harap, June 1, 1926; children—Alice Judith, Naomi, Alexander. Asst. psychopathology McLean Hosp., Waverly, Mass., 1923-24; asst. psychologist Worcester (Mass.) State Hosp., 1924-25, chief psychologist, dir. psychol. research, 1928-46; psychol. intern Boston Psychopathic Hosp., 1925-26; cons. psychologist Worcester Child Guidance Clinic, 1928-46, acting dir., 1945-46; prof. psychology U. Ill. Coll. Medicine, 1946-54, U. Chgo., 1948-54; professorial lectr. in psychology U. Ill., 1954-61; Collier lectr. U. Rochester, 1960; cons. mental health NIMH, 1946-54, mem. selection com. career investigators grant, 1953-57, chief lab. psychology, 1954-66, sr. research psychologist, 1967-81; scientist emeritus NIH, 1974-81; cons. clin. psychology VA, 1946-55, mem. psychiatry and neurology adv. com., 1954-55; expert cons. in psychology to surgeon gen. Dept. Army, 1948-54; cons. clin. psychology Group for Advancement Psychiatry, 1947-55; cons. Pres. Commn. on Health Needs of Nation, 1952; mem. div. anthropology and psychology NRC, 1950-53, com. psychiatry, div. med. scis., 1953-55; adv. screening com. psychology Fulbright com., 1959-62. Recipient Stanley R. Dean Research award, 1963; Helen Sargent Meml. award, 1965; Salmon medal for distinguished service in psychiatry, 1971; Spl. Recognition Mental Health award, 1971; Seymour D. Vestermark Meml. award, 1971. Diplomate clin. psychology Am. Bd. Examiners in Profl. Psychology (mem. bd. 1947-81). Fellow Am. Psychol. Assn. (Div. Clin. Psychology award 1959, 1st Ann. Distinguished Scientist award 1971, Distinguished Sci. Contbn. award 1975, Distinguished Profl. Contbn. award, 1976, assn. rep. World Fedn. Mental Health 1970—, council 1946-48, policy and planning bd. 1946-49, pres. clin. div. 1948, chmn. com. on tng. in clin. psychology), Am. Psychiat. Assn. (hon.); mem. Am. Orthopsychiat. Assn., Soc. Psychol. Study of Social Issues, Am. Psychosomatic Soc., Am Psychopath. Assn. (council mem. 1948), Eastern Psychol. Assn., Washington Psychoanalytic Soc. (hon.), Am. Psychoanalytic Assn. (hon.), Founds. Fund for Research in Psychiatry (dir. 1953-56, 57-60), Sigma Xi. Author: (with D. Rapaport) The Influence of Freud on American Psychology, 1964; Clinical Psychology as Science and Profession: A Forty-Year Odyssey, 1969; Selected Papers on Schizophrenia, 1976; also monographs; asso. editor Psychoanalytic Rev., 1966-81, Jour. Gen. Psychology, 1967-69, Jour. Genetic Psychology, 1969-81; cons. editor Psychologia, 1964-70; editor adv. bd. Schizophrenia Bull., 1969-81; contbr. articles to profl. jours. Home: Kensington, Md. Died Feb. 26, 1981.

SHAMROY, LEON, cameraman; b. N.Y.C., July 16, 1901; s. Elisha and Miriam (Soujon) S.; student Cooper Union, 1918, CCNY, 1919-20; studied mech. engring. Columbia; m. Mary Anderson, May 13, 1953. With lab. Fox Film Corp., Hollywood, 1920-24; photographed serials and stunt pictures, Charles Hutchison of Pathe, 1924-27; co-producer and photographer (with Dr. Paul Fejos) exptl. film The Last Moment (voted honor film of 1928 by Nat. Bd. of Rev.), 1927; asso. with Robert J. Flaherty in photographing a documentary film of Acoma Indians, N.M., 1928-29; cinematographer for Huntington Ethnol. Expdn., Japan, Manchurai, China, Celebes, Philippines, Bali, Malay States, Siam, Burma, India, Egypt, 1930-31; dir. photography B.P. Schulberg Prodns., 1933-37; dir. photography Selznick Internat., 1938; dir. cinematography 20th Century-Fox, from 1938; recent pictures include 12 O'Clock High, 1949 (Look award), The Robe (introduced cinemascope), 1952, Love Is a Many Splendored Thing, The King and I, South Pacific, Porgy and Bess, Cleopatra, The Cardinal, The Agony and the Ecstacy, Planet of the Apes, Justine (Laurel award Internat. Motion Picture Exhibitors 1969). Pres., Award Winners Sch. of Photography, Inc., from 1946. Recipient 18 Acad. nominations, 4 Acad. awards Acad. Motion Picture Arts and Scis.: 1st award for color photography The Black Swan, 1942; awards for color photography Wilson, 1944, Leave Her to Heaven, 1945, Cleopatra, 1963; film achievement award for creating new technique of color-photography, lighting Look Mag., 1945; Film Daily Critics award, 1949, 53, 54, 55, 63. Mem. Am. Soc. Cinematographers (past pres.), Motion Pictures Assn. Am. (chmn. Photog. com., research div. 1946-50), Soc. Motion Picture Engrs. Club: Los Angeles Press. Home: Los Angeles, Calif. Died July 6, 1974.

SHANKLIN, WILLIAM CHARLES, newspaper editor; b. Sandoval, Ill., Feb. 27, 1884; s. Philip Andrew and Mary Belle (Hyde) S.; student Knox Coll., Galesburg, Ill., 1902-06; m. Jessie Irene Pryor, June 17, 1910; children—William Charles, Jessie (Mrs. Robert Reedy), Sylvia Webb. Reporter St. Louis Globe-Democrat, 1906-08, St. Louis Republic, 1908-12, St.Louis Post-Dispatch, 1912-13; city editor Denver Republican, 1913-14; city editor and mng. editor The Rocky Mountain News and mng. editor Denver Times, 1914-22; asst. pub. The Denver Post, 1922-25; mng. editor Denver Morning Post, 1926-28; mng. editor The Wichita Beacon since 1929. Conglist. Clubs: Press (Denver); Crestview Country (Wichita). Home: Wichita, Kan. *

SHANKS, CARROL METEER, business exec.; b. Fairmont, Minn., Oct. 14, 1898; s. Edgar Beeson and Lilly (Meteer) S.; B.B.A., U. Wash., 1921; LL.B., Columbia, 1925; m. Martha S. Taylor, Apr. 7, 1921; children—Wallace Taylor, Margaret Jackson, Carrol Meteer. Admitted to N.J. and N.Y. bars; with law firm Root, Clark, Buckner & Ballantine, N.Y.C., 1925-27, 31-32; lectr. Columbia U. Law Sch., 1925-27; asso. prof. law Yale, 1929-30; asst. solicitor Prudential Ins. Co. of Am., 1932-38, gen. solicitor, 1938-44, exec. v.p., dir., 1944-45, pres., 1946-61; pres., dir. Universal Controls, Inc., 1962-67; dir. Bigelow-Sanford Carpet Co., Pub. Service Electric & Gas Co., Nat. Biscuit Co., Urethane Structures, Inc., Vesco Corp. Trustee Johns Hopkins U., Inst. for Advanced Study, Princeton, N.J. Served as pvt. U.S. Army, World War I. Mem. Beta Theta Pi, Beta Gamma Sigma, Phi Beta Kappa. Author various law sch. case and text books. Home: New York, N.Y. Died May 17, 1976.

SHANNON, JAMES COUGHLIN, state govt. ofcl.; b. Bridgeport, Conn., July 21, 1896; s. Henry Edward and Ellen (Coughlin) S.; A.B., Georgetown U., 1918; LL.B., Yale, 1921; m. Helen McMurray, Apr. 15, 1925; children—James C., John H., Helen Claire (Mrs. Robert C. Richards). Lt. gov. Conn., 1947-48, gov., 1948; judge Superior Ct. Conn., 1953-65; asso. justice Supreme Ct. Conn., 1965-66; Conn. trial referee, 1966-80. Served as aviator US. Navy, 1918. Mem. Conn., Bridgeport bar assns., Am. Legion. K.C., Knight of Malta, Kiwanian. Home: Bridgeport, Conn. Died Mar. 6, 1980.

SHAPERO, NATE S., business exec.; b. Detroit, Sept. 27, 1892; s. Samuel and Augusta (Metzger) S.; Ph.G., Ferris Inst., Big Rapids, Mich., 1921, LL.D., 1944; m. Ruth Bernstein, Jan. 27, 1924; children—Ray A., Marianne. Propr., Econ. Drug. Store, Detroit, 1918; pres. Cunningham Drug Stores, Inc. (merged with Econ. Drug Stores), Detroit, 1930-57, chmn. bd., 1957-68; chmn. bd. Marshall Drug Co. (50 stores), Cleve.; dir. Nat. Bank Detroit. Past pres. Mich. Welfare Commn., Sinai Hosp., Detroit; v.p. Greater Detroit Hosp. Fund; vice chmn. S.E. Mich. div. Am. Cancer Soc.; mem. Mich. Crippled Children Commn.; exec. com. Nat. Found. for Infantile Paralysis; past pres. Chaim Weitzman Chem. Research Found., Rehoveth, Israel; dollar a year man U.S. Treasury Dept., nat. chmn. multiple stores sect. for sale of war bonds and stamps, mem. bd. govs. War Chest of Met. Detroit, World War II. Trustee Detroit Inst. Tech.; adv. bd. trustees U. Detroit; bd. dirs. Ferris Inst., Detroit Community Fund, Boy Scouts Am., Detroit Conv. and Tourist Bur., Boys Clubs Detroit, Detroit Symphony Assn., United Fund, Detroit Bd. Commerce. Served as chief pharmacist's mate USNR, World War I. Mem. USN Adv. League, Nat. Assn. Chain Drug Stores (past pres.), Inst. Distbn. (v.p.), Mich Chain Stores Bur. (chmn.), Detroit Round Table Caths., Jews and Protestants (exec. com.), Jewish Hosp. Assn., Jewish Welfare Fedn. (bd. govs.). Jewish (past pres. Temple). Clubs: Palm Beach Country; Harmonie; Economic, Franklins Hills Country (past pres.) Standard. Home: Southfield, Mich. Died Jan. 23, 1980.

SHAPIRO, JOSEPH GEORGE, lawyer; b. N.Y.C., Jan. 18, 1886; s. Barnet and Esther Martha (Spitz) S.; LL.B. cum laude, Yale, 1907, J.D. cum laude, 1972; m. Helen Rosenstein, June 19, 1917; children—Howard Scott, Carol Ruth (Mrs. Herman R. Shepherd), Elaine Martha (Mrs. Samuel M. Silver). Admitted to Conn. bar, 1907, since practiced in Bridgeport; mem. Shapiro & Shapiro (bro. Charles H.), 1907-22, Shapiro, Goldstein & Brody, 1922-41, Shapiro & Daly, 1941-48, Shapiro & Belinkie, 1948-66, Shapiro, Belinkie & Welch, Bridgeport, 1966-69; counsel Clancy, Kenney & Scofield, 1969-75. Pros. atty. Shelton, Conn., 1913-20; corp. counsel Shelton, 1917-22; judge City Ct. Shelton, 1920-31; mem. Jud. Council Conn., 1927-31; acting judge Ct. of Common Pleas, 1928; dir. Aerosol Techniques, Inc. Spl. asst. state's atty. chmn. standing com. on admission to bar. Pres., Bridgeport Community Forum, 1926-39; chmn. Conf. of City Ct. Judges Fairfield County, Conn., 1930; mem., sec. Com. on Rules and Grievances, U.S. Dist. Ct. for Dist. Conn. Former dir., mem. exec. com. Conn. Soc. for Mental Hygiene; bd. dirs. Bridgeport Symphony Soc.; trustee Palmer Meml. Inst.; mem. exec. com. Brigeport Round Table, Conn. Valley Regional, pres. New Eng. regional council U.A.H.C.; Bridgeport War Meml. Com.; hon. life trustee Union Am. Hebrew Congregations, also rep. on Synagogue Council Am. and Nat. Com. Religious Adv. Council; gov. bd. World Union for Progressive Judaism; life mem. Rabbinical Pension Fund. Mem. Am., Conn. (ins. law com., hon. life), Fairfield County, Bridgeport (past pres.) bar assns., Assn. Bar City N.Y., N.Y. County Lawyers Assn., Comml. Law League Am., Am. Judicature Soc., Am. Law Inst. (hon. life), Internat. Assn. Ins. Counsel, Chi Tau Kappa. Jewish religion (trustee temple). Mason. Clubs: Algonquin (Bridgeport); Yale (N.Y.C.). Known as speaker on legal, social subjects. Home: Bridgeport, Conn. Died Sept. 18, 1975; buried Temple B'nai Israel Cemetery, Fairfield, Conn.

SHARP, LEWIS INMAN, psychiatrist, neurologist; b. East Orange, N.J., Nov. 5, 1907; s. Lewis I. and Helen (Tapson) S.; B.Sc., McGill U., 1930, M.D., 1935; m. Katherine Hodges, Oct. 2, 1936; children—Joan Lewis, John, Michael, Richard, Susan. Intern, McGill U., 1934-35; sr. neurology Montreal Gen. Hosp. 1935-36; Commonwealth fellow, asst. resident in psychiatry Johns Hopkins U., 1936-37; psychiatrist Inst. Living, 1937-39; resident neurologist Bellevue Hosp., 1939-40, clin. asst., vis. neuropsychiatrist, 1940-45, asst. vis. neuropsychiatrist, 1945-46, asso. vis. neuropsychiatrist, 1947-49, dir. psychiat. div., 1949-55, vis. neuropsychiatrist, 1949-78; instr. neurology N.Y. U., 1940-46; sr. attending psychiatrist Westchester br. St. Vincent's Hosp.; cons. psychiatry VA. Diplomate Am. Bd. Neurology and Psychiatry. Fellow Am. Psychiat. Assn., mem. Harvey Soc., N.Y. Neurol. Soc., N.Y. Soc. Clin. Psychiatry, Assn. Research Nervous and Mental Diseases, N.Y. Psychiat. Soc. (pres. 1966-68). Club: Vidonian. Died Apr. 7, 1978.

SHARP, MORELL EDWARD, judge; b. Portland, Oreg., Sept. 12, 1920; s. Eugene Edward and Hazel E. (Eaton) S.; student U. Oreg., 1939-41; LL.B., J.D., Northwestern U., 1948; m. Betty Marie Parker, Apr. 3, 1948; children—Laurie, John. Admitted to Ill. bar, 1948, Wash. bar, 1951; asst. gen. atty. Milw. R.R., Chgo., Seattle, 1948-52; partner Williams, Kinnear & Sharp, Seattle, 1952-56; mem. firm Graham, Dunn, Johnston & Rosenquist, Seattle, 1957-67; judge Superior Ct., King County, Wash., 1967-70; justice Wash. Supreme Ct., 1970-71; judge U.S. Dist. Ct. Western Dist. Wash., Seattle, 1971-80. Dir. Nat. Center for State Cts., 1970-71; Mayor, councilman Beaux Arts Village, Wash., 1952-56; councilman Municipality Met. Seattle, 1956-57. Served to capt. AUS, 1943-46. Fellow Am. Bar Assn.; mem. Wash., Ill. bar assns., Jud. Conf. U.S. Episcopalian. Clubs: Wash. Athletic (Seattle), Harbor, Overlake (Medina, Wash.). Bd. editors Am. Bar Assn. Jour., 1974-80. Home: Bellevue, Wash. Died Oct. 19, 1980.

SHARP, RAYMOND NEIL, naval officer; b. Maryville, Tenn., Apr. 9, 1906; s. Giffis Claton and Susan (Beeler) S.; B.S., U.S. Naval Acad., 1930; grad. Naval War Coll., 1950; m. Elizabeth Higgason, Dec. 21, 1937. Commnd. ensign U.S. Navy, 1930, designated naval aviator, 1932, advanced through grades to rear adm.; various assignment at sea and on shore, 1930-43; asst. air officer, then navigator U.S.S. Yorktown, 1943-44; mem. staff comdr. Carrier Div. 3, then chief staff comdr. Carrier Div. 5; assigned staff comdr. 2d Carrier Task Force, 1944; exec. officer N.A.S Patuxent River then successively dir. armament test Naval Air Test Center, exec. officer U.S.S. Midway, comdg. officer Naval Air Res. Tng. Unit, U.S.S. Tripoli, U.S.S. Essex, asst. chief staff operations Comdr. in Chief Atlantic Fleet, comdr. Carrier Div. 15, assigned Office Sec. Def., comdr. Carrier Div. 1; assigned ComFairWestPac, 1962-63; dep. comdr. Fleet Activities Command, Washington, 1963-65; commander of Pacific Missile Range, since 1965. Decorated Commendation ribbon, Legion of Merit, Silver Star. Home: Johnson City, Tenn. Died Dec. 3, 1980.

SHARPE, DORES ROBINSON, ch. ofcl.; b. Pembroke, N.B., Can., Jan. 23, 1886; s. Charles Frederick and Frances (Robinson) S; A.B., U. N.B., 1908, A.M., 1910, LL.D., 1943; B.D. (scholar, fellow), Rochester Theol. Sem., 1911; postgrad. U. Chgo., 1911-12; D.D., Hillsdale (Mich.) Coll., 1930; LL.D., Ark. Bapt. Coll., 1931; L.H.D., Wilberforce U., 1951; m. Harriet Maude Holdsworth, Sept. 8, 1914 (dec. 1917); children—Margaret Louise, Roger Holdsworth and Harriett Frances (twins); m. 2d, Ruth Leila Mitchell, Feb. 25, 1920 (dec. 1972). Ordained to Bapt. ministry, 1908; pastor in Edmonton, Calgary. Sask., gen. sec. Sunday Sch. Assn. Sask, 1917-19; dir. Forward Movement for Protestant chs. in Sask., 1919; gen. supt. Bapt. chs. in Sask., 1917-25; exec. sec. Cleve. Bapt. Assn., 1925-53, exec. sec. emeritus, 1953—. Rauschenbusch lectr. Colgate-Rochester Sem., 1948; cons. Grad. Theol. Union, Berkeley, Cal. Former mem. Council of Finance and Promotion and Council of World Evangelization, No. Bapt. Conv.; past chmn. Com. on City Missions, Com. on Ch. and City of Ch. Fedn., Com. on Pub. Edn. and Service; mem. speakers bur.Community Chest; founder, dir. Cleve. Sunday Evening Hour; founder ann. Theol. Conf. Roger Williams Fellowship and Div. Sch. U. Chgo., also Dores Robinson Sharpe lectureship. Past mem. Cal. Democratic State Central Com.; Dem. candidate Assembly, 47th dist., Cal.; mem. exec. com. Los Angeles County Dem. Central Com.; foreman Grand Jury Cuyahoga, Cleve., which uncovered corruption in mental hosps. (recipient Albert Lasker award). Former dir. Bapt. Home No. Ohio., Northwestern Bapt. Hosp. Assns.; trustee Grad. Theol. Union; trustee emeritus Colgate-Rochester Div. Sch.; past trustee Rio Grande Coll.; past vice chmn. Cleve. Community Relations Commn.; hon. pres. Consumers League of Ohio; founder, past pres. Ohio Mental Hygiene Assn.; exec. com. Community Relations Bd., N.A.A.C.P.; former chmn. State Hosps. Betterment Com; founder, pres. Ch. Civic League; chmn. Interaward, Nat. Com. Mental Hygiene, 1946; v.p. Rauschenbusch Fellowship; past chmn. com. Internat. Justice and Peace, Pasadena Council Chs. Mem. Pi Gamma Mu. Mason. Club: Professional, Alpine (Can.). Author: (book) Rise and Place of American City, 1959, Call to Christian Action: The Triumph of Religious Liberty, Of One Blood, The Golden Fountain; also other pageants, Biography of Walter Rauschenbusch, Lectr., writer, dir. instnl. finance, organizer. Home: Pasadena CA. *

SHARPE, MARY ELIZABETH EVANS (MRS. HENRY DEXTER SHARPE), b. Syracuse, N.Y., Oct. 23, 1884; d. William Edward George and Fanny Elizabeth (Riegel) E.; ed. grammar schs., Syracuse; m. Henry Dexter Sharpe of Providence, R.I., 1920. Began making candies for sale, 1900; now associated with sisters in "Mary Elizabeth's" candy shops and tea rooms, New York, Boston, Newport, R.I.; etc.; pres. Mary Elizabeth's, Ltd., New York. Service under U.S. Food Administration, 1917; with Am. Red Cross in France, 1918-19; organized and operated Central Diet Kitchen in Paris. Unitarian. Author: War Time Recipes, 1917; My Candy Secrets, 1919. Home: Providence, R.I. *

SHARPLEY, JOHN MILES, chem. co. exec.; b. Norfolk, Va., Jan. 28, 1918; s. John Edward and Annie Carter (Miles) S.; B.A., Hampden-Sydney Coll., 1941; M.S., U. Richmond, 1950; postgrad. USAF Command, Staff and War Coll., 1950-51; Ph.D., U. London, 1951; m. Mary Elwang Shannon, 1976. Asst. dir. Froehling & Robertson, Inc., Richmond, Va., 1945-49; chief microbiologist Buckman Labs., Inc., Memphis, 1952-62; pres. Sharpley Labs., Inc., Fredericksburg, Va., 1962-81; prof. Va. Commonwealth U., Richmond, 1967-77. Past pres. Gallery Modern Art, Fredericksburg. Served to lt. col. USAAF, 1941-45. Decorated Silver Star, Purple Heart; named Distinguished Vis. Scientist, Am. Inst. Biol. Scis., 1970. Fellow AAAS, Am. Inst. Chemists; mem. Soc. Indsl. Microbiology, Am. Chem. Soc., Am. Soc. Microbiology, Soc. Gen. Microbiology (Gt. Britain). Author: Applied Petroleum Microbiology, 1962; Elementary Hydrocarbon Microbiology, 1967; International Biodegradation Symposium, 1976. Contbr. articles to profl. jours. Home: Fredericksburg, Va. Died Jan. 5, 1981.

SHAW, ELTON RAYMOND, author, lecturer; b. Grand Rapids, Mich., Jan. 19, 1886; s. Solomon Benjamin and Etta Ellen (Sadler) S.; B.L., Ohio Wesleyan U., 1907; M.A., 1916; m. Mabel Crystal Bacon, Sept. 9, 1909; children—Everett Raymond, Evelyn Ruth (Mrs. Fred B. Arbuckle), Ralph Bacon. Pres. Shaw Pub. Co. 1907-49; Sunday lecturer Mich. Prohibition State Com., 1908-12; Sunday and summer lecturer Ohio Prohibition State Com., 1912-14, chmn. same, 1914-16; grad. student and teacher pub. speaking, Ohio Wesleyan U., 1912-16; dean Coll. of Speech Edn., Kan. Wesleyan U., 1916-18, Coll. of Commerce, 1918-19; lecturer in Kan. colls. for United Com. for War Temperance Activities in the Army and Navy, 1917-18; lecturer Kan. Wesleyan Lyceum Bur., 1916-19, mgr., 1918-19; financial sec., business sec., exec. sec. and nat. lecturer, Intercollegiate Prohibition Assn., 1919-21; dir. Methodist Ch. Life Service and Older Boys confs., 1921-24; with finance dept. Bd. of Edn. of Methodist Ch., summers, 1922-24; connected with life ins., 1924-28; field sec. Chamber Commerce U.S.A., 1928-34; exec. sec. Mich. State Chamber Commerce, 1934-37; exec. sec. Nat. Committee for Revision of "Comstock" Law since 1937, mem. Am. Acad. Polit. and Social Science. World Narcotics Research Foundation since 1939. Mem. American Philatelic Soc., Sons of the American Revolution, Delta Sigma Rho, Pi Gamma Mu. Author numerous books since 1909; also contbr. to newspapers and mags. Home: Washington. *

SHAW, F(RED) ALDEN, headmaster; b. Detroit, Minn., Dec. 20, 1885; s. Charles Joseph and Elizabeth Luella (Gahring) S.; grad. Boston Latin Sch., 1905; B.S., Harvard, 1909; student Ecole des Hautes Etudes, Paris, 1912; m. Amy Elizabeth Ellis, June 21, 1923; children—Charles Alden, Elizabeth Amy, Daniel Ellis, Joseph Herbert. Established Detroit Prep. Sch., 1914; headmaster Detroit Country Day Sch., since 1923. Field arty. officer training sch., Camp Taylor, Ky., 1917. Mem. Country Day Sch. Headmasters Assn., Pvt. Schs. Assn. Central States (exec. com., past pres.), Am. Legion (dir. Northville post, chmn. essentialist com. Unitarian. Club: Harvard of Michigan (trustee, past pres.). Home: Northville, Mich. *

SHAW, FRANK HOLCOMB, music dir.; b. Paxton, Ill., May 8, 1884; s. John Burnham and Mary Elizabeth (Holcomb) S.; Mus.B., Oberlin (O.) Conservatory, 1907; studied in Paris, 1912-13, in Stuttgart, 1913-14; m. Julia M. Seiler, Dec. 29, 1908 (dec.); children—Virginia S. Holmes, John Burnham; m. 2d, Mary S. Van Metre. Professor piano and organ, Monmouth College, Monmouth, Ill., 1907-10; prof. organ and theory, Cornell Coll., Mt. Vernon, Ia., 1910-12; dir. Cornell Coll. Conservatory, 1915-24; dir. Oberlin Conservatory, 1924-49. Director Peoples Banking Co., Oberlin, Republican. Conglist. Home: Oberlin, O. *

SHAW, HENRY SOUTHWORTH, retired business executive; b. Boston, Mass., November 29, 1884; s. Henry Southworth and Louisa Stuart (Towne) S.; A.B., Harvard, 1906; married Mary Bruce Allen, January 25, 1912 (died May 14, 1951); children—Robert Southworth (deceased). Lawrence Merrill, Treas., Gen. Radio Co., 1918-26, mem. of dirs., 1918-50, chmn., 1926-44; dir. Boston Storage Warehouse Co., 1923-46; trustee Franklin Savings Bank of Boston, 1923-27; dir. Boston Safe Deposit and Trust Co., 1926-33. Mem. bd. dirs. Mt. Washington Observatory, 1930-50, v.p. 1936-39. Councilor Am. Meterological Society, 1946-49. Fellow Am. Acad. of Arts and Sciences, Inst. of Radio Engrs., Acous. Soc. of Am. A.A.A.S., mem.American Geophysical Union.*

SHAW, HERBERT BELL, bishop; b. Wilmington, N.C., Feb. 9, 1908; s. John Henry and Lummie Virginia (Hodges) S.; student Fisk U., Howard U.; D.D., Livingstone Coll., Salisbury, N.C.; m. Sept. 1, 1931. Ordained elder African Methodist Episcopal Zion Ch., 1928, elected bishop, 1952; pastor, 1929-37; presiding elder Wilmington dist., Cape Fear Conf., 1937-43; sec.-treas. dept. home missions, pensions, and ministerial relief, 1943-52, presiding bishop 1st Episcopal Dist., 1952-56, 6th Episcopal Dist., 1956-60, 3d Episcopal Dist., 1960-68, 2d Episcopal Dist., 1968-72, 1st Episcopal Dist., 1972-80. Del. 8th World Meth. Conf., Oxford, Eng., 1950, 9th Conf., Lake Junaluska, N.C., 1956; del., v.p. 10th Conf., Oslo, Norway, 1961, del. 11th Conf., London, 1966, del., mem. presidium 12th Conf., Denver, 1971; del. 3d assembly World Council Chs., New Delhi, 1961; mem. delegation Nat. Council Chs. as spl. guest Russian Orthodox Ch. to Soviet Union, 1962; v.p.-at-large Nat. Council Chs. of Christ in U.S.A., 1970-73; mem. presidium World Meth. Council, 1971-80; chmn. curriculum com. dept. Christian edn. A.M.E. Zion Ch.; bd. dirs. Community Boys Club Am., Wilmington 4-H Club Found. N.C.; chmn. bd. trustees Livingstone Coll.; trustee Clinton Jr. Coll., Rock Hill, S.C., Lomax-Hannon Coll., Greenville, Ala., Johnson Meml. Inst., Batesville Miss. Recipient scroll of honor Omicron Alpha chpt. Omega Psi Phi, 1970, plaque of honor, 1971. Mem. Nat. Com. Negro Churchmen (pres. 1967-80, chmn. bd. dirs.), Masons (Most Worshipful Grand Master, Prince Hall Grand Lodge 1974-80). Wilmington, N.C. Died Jan. 3, 1980; interred Greenlawn Meml. Mausoleum, Wilmington.

SHAW, JOSEPH BRADFIELD, ceramics; b. West Lafayette, O., May 13, 1884; s. Seth and Nancy Ann (Hall) S.; B.S. in Ceramics, Ohio State U., 1908, Ceramic Engr., 1931; licensed professional engr., State of Pa., 1933; m. Marian M. Wilde, Dec. 20, 1906; children—Myril Clement, Lucian Bradfield, Josephine Fay, Marian Margaret, Gene Ruth. Teacher, dist. schs.,

Ohio, 1901-03; supt. Wheeler Reflector Co., Boston, Mass., 1908-09; supt. porcelain dept. Grand Rapids (Mich.) Refrigerator Co., 1909-11; ceramic engr. Andrew Ramsay Co., Mt. Savage, Md., 1911-12; supt. Sanitary Mfg. Plant, Ellerslie, Md., 1912; supt. high sch., Centreville, Pa., 1912-13; ceramic engr. Pittsburgh (Pa.) Testing Lab., 1913-16; prof. ceramic engring., N.Y. State Sch. Clay Working and Ceramics, 1916-24; head of dept. ceramics, Pa. State Coll., 1924-32; cons. engr. for many cos.; cons. engr., Harrisburg, 1932-35; asso. engr. Pub. Works Adminstrn., 1935-39; sr. industrial com. adviser U.S. Department of Labor, 1939-42; industrial consultant War Prodn. Bd. since 1942. Dist. chief U.S. Fuel Administration, N.Y., World War. Pres. village bd. and mayor of Alfred, N.Y., 1920-24. Fellow A.A.A.S., Am. Ceramic Society (mem. standards com., com. on edn.); mem. Am. Refractories Ins., Am. Soc. for Testing Materials (chmn. sub-com. on abrasion), Soc. of Rheology, Beta Phi Kappa, Delta Sigma Phi, and Sigma Gamma Epsilon. Democrat. Methodist. Mason (K.T., Shriner). Club: University. Contbr. many bulls., reports and articles on enamels, clays, glazes, etc. Home: Silver Spring, Md. *

SHAW, ROBERT, author, actor; b. Westhoughton, Eng., Aug. 9, 1927; student Royal Acad. Dramatic Art; m. Jennifer Bourke, 1952; four daus.; m. 2d, Mary Ure, 1963 (dec.); 2 sons, 2 daus.; m. 3d, Virginia Jansen, 1975. Mem. Shakespeare Meml. Theatre Co., 1949, 50, 53; appeared as Rosenkrantz in Hamlet, 1951; mem. Old Vic Co., 1951-52; appearances in West End prodns. include Tiger at the Gates, Caro William, Live Like Pigs, The Long and The Short and The Tall, One More River, A Lodging for the Bride, The Changelling: on Broadway in The Caretaker, The Physicists; motion pictures include The Dambuster, Hill in Korea, Sea Fury, The Valiant, Tomorrow at Ten, The Caretaker, From Russia with Love, The Luck of Ginger Coffee, The Battel of the Bulge, A Man for All Seasons, Custer of the West, The Birthday Party, Battle of Britain, The Royal Hunt of the Sun, Figures in a Landscape, A Town Called Bastard, Young Winston, A Reflection of Fear, The Sting, The Taking of Pelham One Two Three, Jaws, End of the Game, Diamonds, Robin and Marian, Swashbuckler, Black Sunday, The Deep; Broadway mus. Elmer Gantry, 1970, Old Times, 1971; The Dance of Death, 1974; TV series The Buccaneers, plays. Author: (play) Off the Mainland; (novels) The Hiding Place, 1959, The Sun Doctor (Hawthornden prize 1962), 1961, The Flag, 1965; (novel and play) The Man in the Glass Booth; (novel) A Card from Morocco; (play) Cato Street, Club: Savage (London). Home: Tourmakeady, Ireland. Died Aug. 27, 1978.

SHAY, FELIX, business man, author, world-traveler; b. Summit, N.J., May 27, 1885; s. David F. and Mary E. (Murphy) S.; ed. pub. schs. and pvt. tutors; m. Florence Nesbit Porter, of Andover, New Brunswick, Canada, Sept. 29, 1909; children—Felix Buckley, Ann Porter. Successor to Elbert Hubbard as editor the Roycroft publs., 1915-18, and gen. mgr. The Roycrofters, 1918-22. Made lecture tour British Isles and Continent, 1912; lecture tours prin. cities of U.S. since 1912. Author: Cairo to Cape Town Overland; Felicitations (3 vols.); Elbert Hubbard of East Aurora. Mem. bd. govs. Associated Adv. Clubs of the World, 1913-14; pres. Adv. Assn. Baltimore, 1912-14. Club: Baltimore Country. Home: Mt. Washington, Md.*

SHAY, HOWELL LEWIS, architect; b. Washington, Dec. 24, 1884; s. Aurelius King and Julia Stanford (Lewis) S.; M.S. in Architecture, U. Pa., 1913; m. Eunice Mabel Quinby, Sept. 27, 1909; children—Howell Lewis, William Dixon, Eunice Elizabeth. In practice, Phila., 1919—. Principal works include important public bldgs., hotels, hosps. Recipient A.I.A. medal for designing Packard Building, 1925. Fellow A.I.A., Pa. Assn. Architects; mem. Soc. Colonial Wars in Commonwealth of Pa. Episcopalian. Mason. Clubs: University, T-Square (past pres.), Orpheus. Home: Rose Valley PA

SHAY, JUNIOR RALPH, educator; b. Bird City, Kan., Jan. 8, 1918; s. John Wesley and Elsie (Valetta) S.; B.S., U. Ark., 1939; M.S., U. Wis., 1941, Ph.D., 1943; m. Jean Eleanor Rhode, Aug 7, 1943; children—Margaret Ellen, Linda Jean, Michael Ronald, Elizabeth Ann, Susan Diane, Jennifer Elaine. Grad. research asst. plant pathology U. Wis., 1939-43; asst. prof. plant pathology U. Ark., 1943-45; faculty Purdue U. 1945-66, prof. botany and plant pathology, 1951-66, chmn. dept., 1954-66, prof., chmn. dept. botany and plant pathology Ore. State U., Corvallis, 1966-73, asst. dean research, 1973-79, asso. dean research, 1979-80. Chmn. com. agrl. uses aerial surveys NRC, 1960-80. com. on space applications Nat. Acad. Scis., 1967-69; cons. plant sci. AID, Brazil, 1963. Mem. Am. Inst. Biol. Scis. A.A.A.S., Am Phytopath. Soc. (councillor 1955, 60, sec. 1963-66), Sigma Xi, Alpha Gamma Rho. Contbr. numerous articles profl. jours. Research on disease resistance in tree fruits, virus diseases of apples. Home: Corvallis, Ore. Died Mar. 27, 1980.

SHEA, GEORGE E., JR., editor; b. Paris, 1902; came to U.S., 1914; grad. Princeton U., 1922; children—George E. III, Mrs. S. Gilmer Towell. Joined Dow Jones Publs., N.Y.C., 1922; with Wall Street Jour., N.Y.C., fin. editor, from 1949, writer Outlook column, 1953-67. Active Atlantic Union Com. Address: New York, N.Y. Died Apr. 27, 1980.

SHEA, JAMES J., business exec.; b. Cambridge, Mass., 1889; ed. Worcester Poly Inst., 1912. Chmn. bd. Milton Bradley Co., dir. Buxton, Inc.; adv. dir. Valley Bank & Trust Co. Trustee, Old Sturbridge Village. Home: Springfield, Mass. Died Jan. 3, 1977.

SHEARD, CHARLES (SHE'ÄRD), biophysicist and physiological opticist; b. Dolgeville, N.Y., May 27, 1883; s. Charles and Frances (Scatchard) S.; B.A., St. Lawrence U., 1903, D.Sc., 1930; M.A., Dartmouth, 1907; Ph.D., Princeton, 1912; Dr. Ocular Sci., Los Angeles Coll. Optometry, 1953; m. Blanche Amaral, Dec. 31, 1907; children—Dorothy Blanche (Allen), Charles Amaral. Instr. and asst. prof. physics, Ohio State U., 1907-13, prof. physics, applied optics, 1914-19; with Am.Optical Co., 1919-24, as head div. of ocular interests and in gen. charge professional and scientific work; dir. div. physics and bio-physical research, Mayo Clinic, and prof. biophysics under the Mayo Foundation Univ. of Minn., 1924-49, director emeritus and prof. emeritus since 1949; directing mem. Mayo Aero-Medical Unit, 1941-45; prof. ophthalmic optics Rochester College since 1947; interim dean L.A. College of Optometry, 1952-53; distinguished lecturer in opthalmology, graduate school medicine Tulane University, New Orleans since 1949. Chmn. Joint County City Rochester Planning Commn., 1959. Tillyer Medal, Optical Soc. Am., 1957. Founded the Sheard Foundation for Edn. and Research in Vision, Grad. Sch. Ohio State Univ., 1943. Fellow A.A.A.S., Am. Heart Assn., Am. Acad. Optometry (founder), Am. Acad. Ophthalmology (hon.); mem. Ophthalmic Inst. Gt. Britain, Optical Soc. Am., Am. Physiol. Soc., Soc. Exptl. Biology and Medicine, Am. Soc. Plant Physiologists, Am. Congress Phys. Therapy, Am. Soc. of Clin. Pathologists, Assn. for Research in Ophthalmology; Illuminating Engring. Society, National Research Council (associate), Sigma Xi, Sigma Pi Sigma, Phi Sigma Kappa; hon. life mem. Am. Optometric Assn. Board of Directors, National Society Prevention Blindness; past pres., now sec. Am. Bd. of Opticianry; member civilian bd. consultants to Bur. Medicine and Surgery, United States Navy, 1947-54. Author: Dynamic Ocular Tests, 1917; Physiological Optics, 1919; Dynamic Skiametry, 1920; Ophthalmic Glasses, 1921; Ocular Accommodation, 1921; Practical Ocular Tests, 1924; Life Giving Light (Century of Progress Series), 1933; Ophthalmic Optics, 1944; Sheard Volume of Selected Writings in Visual and Ophthalmic Optics, 1957. Fourth Thomas Young oration, London, Eng., 1921; recipient Distinguished Service Medal in optics, 1930; Certificate of Merit, U. Minn., 1947; also recipient Ward Burdick medal, American Soc. of Clinical Pathologists, 1947. Beverly Myers Nelson Achievement award, 1951. Chief researchers on dynamic ocular tests; relationships between accomodation and convergence; effects of radiant energy on plant and animal tissues; applications of spectrophotometry and photo-electrometry to biol. and med.; dark adaptation; heat losses and temperature regulation of the body; visual problems of aviation. Designer and inventor following instruments: artificial larynx, electromotive thermometer, photolometer, Scientific and profl. cons. Home: Riverstone, Stewartville, Minn. *

SHEARMAN, ROBERT WILLIAM, assn. exec.; b. Bklyn., June 7, 1916; s. William Hugh and Florence Emily (Bell) S.; A.B., Princeton, 1937; m. Dorothy French Dodge, July 3, 1954; children—Grace Dodge, Edith Bell. Chemist, Pitts. Plate Glass Co., Newark, 1937-39; metall. observer Bethlehem (Pa.) Steel Co., 1940-41; with gen. publicity dept. Union Carbide Corp., N.Y.C., 1946-51, 53-54, sec. metals br., 1955-57, sec. Metall. Soc., Am. Inst. Mining, Metall. and Petroleum Engrs., N.Y.C., 1957-66; adminstrv. sec. Am. Soc. for Quality Control, Milw., 1966-71, exec. dir., 1971-79. Served to capt. USAAF, 1941-46, to maj. USAF, 1951-53. Mem. Am. Chem. Soc., Am. Inst. Mining, Metall. and Petroleum Engrs., Metal Sci. Club of N.Y., European Orgn. Quality Control (asso.), Am. Soc. Assn. Execs., AAAS, Council Engring. and Sci. Soc. Execs. (pres. 1973-74), Soc. Sigma Xi (asso.). Club: Appalachian Mountain (Boston). Home: River Hills, Wis. Died Sept. 16, 1979.

SHEDD, WILLIAM EDGAR, JR., army officer; born Danville, Ill., Feb. 25, 1885; s. William Edgar and Alice Mary (Scott) S.; B.S., Mil. Acad., 1907; student Coast Arty. Sch., 1925-26, Comd. and Gen. Staff Sch., 1926-27, Army War Coll., 1927-28; m. Lettie Patterson, June 29, 1914; children—William Edgar, III, George Patterson. Commd. 2d lt., C.A.C., U.S. Army, June 1907, advanced through grades to maj. gen., Jan. 30, 1941; apptd. coast defense and anti-aircraft comdr. Panama Canal dept., Aug. 1941; dep. comdr. Panama Canal Dept., apptd. comdg. gen. Antilles dept., Dec. 1, 1943; apptd. comdg. gen. Ninth Service Command, Sept. 1, 1944; served on staff, chief of arty., rank of col., with A.E.F., France, 1917-19. Decorated D.S.M. (U.S.); Legion of Merit (U.S.); Order of the Black Star (France) Order of Vasco Nunez de Balboa (Panama); Order of Boyaca (Columbia); Order of Abden Calderon (Ecuador); Order of Ayacucho (Peru); Order Condor of the Andes (Bolivia); Order of Merit Juan Pablo Duarte (Dom. Rep.). Clubs: Army and Navy (Washington, D.C.), Army-NavyCountry (Washington, D.C.), Alta (Salt Lake City, Utah).*

SHEDLOVSKY, THEODORE, chemist; b. Leningrad, Russia, Oct. 29, 1898; s. Alexander and Bertha (Weinstein) S.; S.B., M.I.T., 1918, Ph.D., 1925; m. Beatrice Paul, May 16, 1929; children—Richard E., Julian P., Alexandra E. Came to U.S., 1908, naturalized, 1927. Asst. in phys. chemistry M.I.T., 1919-21; indsl. chem. research, 1921-27; asst. Rockefeller U., 1927-29, asso., 1929-44, asso. mem., 1944-56, mem., 1956-76, prof., 1957-76; civilian cons. Navy Dept., 1944. Fellow N.Y. Acad. Scis. (asso. editor 1938-42, v.p. 1942, 60), World Acad. Art and Sci.; mem. Nat. Acad. Scis., Am. Chem. Soc. Editor, contbr. Electro-chemistry in Biology and Medicine, 1955. Author sci. articles. Home: New York, N.Y. Died Nov. 5, 1976.

SHEEHAN, PAUL VINCENT, journalist, educator; b. Everett, Wash., Aug. 7, 1904; s. Thomas Francis and Mary Anna (Winninghoff) S.; A.B., U. Wash., 1926, A.M., 1930; Ph.D., U. So. Calif., 1942; m. Mary Ann Hemenway, Aug. 19, 1932; 1 dau., Pamela Ann. Instr. journalism Fresno State Coll. (now Calif. State U. at Fresno), 1930-36, asst. prof., 1938-43, asso. prof., 1943-46, prof., 1946-69, prof. emeritus, 1969-78, chmn. journalism dept., 1951-69; vis. lectr. journalism Syracuse U., 1936-37; interim staff So. Calif. newspapers, Seattle Post-Intelligencer, San Francisco Call-Bull., Fresno Bee; chmn. state curriculum com. journalism Calif. Dept. Edn., 1951; spl. asst. to state dir. edn. and coordinator state informational program on bldg. needs Calif. instns., 1958. Mem. Assn. Edn. Journalism, Alpha Phi Gamma (Western v.p. 1951-52, pres. 1952-53), Sigma Delta Chi, Theta Chi. Club: Fresno Press (pres. 1967-68). Author: Better Business Letters, 1939; Reportorial Writing, 1972. Contbr. articles to various publs. Home: Fresno, Calif. Died July 14, 1978; buried Fresno Meml. Gardens.

SHEEN, FULTON JOHN, clergyman, educator, writer; b. El Paso, Ill., May 8, 1895; s. Newton Morris and Delia (Fulton) S.; grad. Spalding Inst., Peoria, Ill., 1913; A.B., St. Viator Coll., Bourbannais, Ill., 1917, A.M., 1919, LL.D., 1929; student St. Paul Sem., 1919; S.T.B., J.C.B., Catholic U. Am., 1920; Ph.D., Louvain (Belgium) U., 1923, Agregée Philosophie, 1925; D.D., U. Rome, 1924; LL.D., Loyola U., Chgo., 1929, St. Bonaventure Coll., N.Y.C., 1939, Notre Dame U., 1941; Litt.D., Marquette U., 1934; D.H.L., St. John's U., Bklyn., 1941. Ordained priest Roman Catholic Ch., 1919; tchr. St. Edmunds Coll., Ware, Eng., 1925; mem. faculty Cath. U. Am., 1926-50; nat. dir. Soc. for Propagation of Faith, 1950-66; bishop Rochester (N.Y.) Diocese, 1966-69; titular archbishop of Newport, Wales, 1969-79. Preacher, summer conf. Westminster Cathedral, London, 1925, 28-31; lectr. Cath. Summer Sch., U. Cambridge (Eng.), 1930-31; preacher on Catholic Hour, NBC, 1930-52; preacher St. Patrick's Cathedral, N.Y.C., 1930-52; consecrated titular Bishop Caesariana and aux. bishop of N.Y., 1951; on Commn. of the Missions, Vatican II, 1965. Recipient Cardinal Mercier prize of philosophy Georgetown U., 1936; apptd. Papal Chamberlain, 1934, Domestic Prelate, 1935. Author: God and Intelligence, 1925; Religion Without God, 1928; The Life of All Living, 1929; The Divine Romance, 1930; Old Errors and New Labels, 1931; Moods and Truth, 1932; Way of the Cross, 1932; Seven Last Words, 1933; Hymn of the Conquered, 1933; The Eternal Galilean, 1934; Philosophy of Science, 1934; The Mystical Body of Christ, 1935; Calvary and the Mass, 1936; The Moral Universe, 1936; The Cross and the Beatitudes, 1937; The Cross and the Crisis, 1938; Tactics of Communism, 1937; Liberty Under Communism, 1937; Communism Answers Questions of a Communist, 1937; Communism and Religion, 1937; Communism, The Opium of the People, 1937; Liberty, Equality and Fraternity, 1938; Lord's Prayer on the Cross, The Rainbow of Sorrow, 1938; The Way of the Cross for Our Enemies, 1938; Victory Over Vice, 1939; Whence Come Wars, 1940; The Seven Virtues, 1940; For God and Country, 1941; A Declaration of Dependence, 1941; God and War, 1942; Peace, 1942; The Divine Verdict, 1943; The Armor of God, 1943; Philosophies of War, 1943; Seven Words to the Cross, 1944; Seven Pillars of Peace, 1944; Love One Another, 1944; Seven Words of Jesus and Mary, 1945; Preface to Religion, 1946; Characters of the Passion, 1946; Jesus, Son of Mary, 1947; Philosophy of Religion, 1948; Communism and Conscience of the West, 1948; Peace of Soul, 1949; Lift Up Your Heart, 1950; Three to Get Married, 1951; The World's First Love, 1952; Life is Worth Living, 1953, Vol. II, 1954, Vol. III, 1955, Vol. IV, 1956, Vol. V, 1957; Way to Happiness, 1954; Way to Inner Peace, 1954; Thinking Life Through, 1955; God Love You, 1955; Thoughts for Daily Living, 1955; Life of Christ, 1958; The True Meaning of Christmas, 1955; (with D. Rops) This Is The Mass, 1958; (with H. Morton) This is Rome, 1960; Go To Heaven, 1960; This is the Holy Land, 1961; These Are the Sacraments, 1962; The Priest is Not His Own, 1963; Missions and the World Crisis, 1964; The Power of Love, 1964; Walk With God, 1965; Guide to Contentment, 1966; Footprints in A Darkened Forest,

1967; Easter Inspirations, 1967; That Tremendous Love, 1967; Parents and Children, 1970; Those Mysterious Priests, 1974. Editor: Mission and World-Mission. Contbr. to mags. including Commonwealth, America, New Scholasticism. Columnist religious and radio presses. On radio and TV program Life is Worth Living, after 1951. Recorded record album Life is Worth Living, 1965. Address: New York, N.Y. Died Dec. 10, 1979.

SHEETS, EARL WOODDELL, prof., agrl. leader; born at Lost Creek, W.Va., Dec. 23, 1886; s. Arthur and Annie Jane (Wooddell) S.; student W.Va. Wesleyan Coll.; B.S. in Agr., W.Va. U., 1911; M.S., U. of Ill., 1914; D. Agr., U. of Md., 1933; m. Leda Cordelia Atkeson, Oct. 29, 1912 (deceased November 19, 1949); children—Jane Atkeson, Helen Wooddel, Betty Caroline; m. 2d, Frances Clifton Mannix; children—Francine Patricia Mannix, Jojean Helen Mannix, Ralph, Edward Mannix, Jr. Teacher rural and public schs. 4 yrs.; lecturer W.Va. State Grange, 1908-11; instr. W.Va. State Normal Sch., 1911; extension specialist animal husbandry and agronomy, W.Va. U., 1911-12, instr., 1912; prof. animal husbandry and animal husbandman, W.Va. U. and Expt. Sta., 1913-18; extension animal husbandman in charge of beef cattle extension work, animal husbandry div. U.S. Dept. Agr., Washington, D.C., 1918-19; senior animal husbandman in charge beef cattle investigations, Animal Husbandry Div., Bur. Animal Industry, U.S. Dept. Agr., 1919-21; actg. chief, Animal Husbandry Div., 1921-23, asst. chief, 1923, chief, 1924-34; dir. of Agricultural Drought Relief, U.S. Department of Agr., 1935; chief of animal husbandry, Miss. Agrl. Expt. Sta. and prof. animal husbandry, Miss. State Coll. Sch. of Agr. and Agricultural Experiment Station. 1935-39; secretary livestock, fats and oils, and farm groups, 1940-41; assistant to Master National Grange, 1941-48; prof. animal husbandry, head dept. animal husbandry, College of Agriculture, Univ. of Nev. since 1948. Secretary Tri-State Sheep Breeders' Assn., 1911-17, W.Va. Live Stock Assn., 1914-18. A founder and sec. W.Va., Farmer Co., and asso. editor The Farmer, 1906-14. Mem. Am. Soc. Animal Production (sec. 1922-26; v.p. 1926-27; pres. 1928-29), Am. Genetic Assn. (sec. 1921-23), Kappa Alpha, Sigma Xi, Grange; rep. of Am. Soc. Animal Production to Nat. Research Council, 1924-35; chmn. com. on animal breeding and mem. sub-com. on animal nutrition of Nat. Research Council, 1930-35; mem. council of editorial bd. Am. Genetic Assn. Methodist. Mason. Clubs: Saddle and Sirloin, Block and Bridle. Author: Feeding Farm Livestock; numerous books, and bulletins published by expt. stations and U.S. Dept. Agr. Home: Reno. *

SHEFFER, EUGENE J., educator; b. L.I., N.Y., 1905; ed. Columbia U. Prof. French, Columbia U., N.Y.C., until 1966, prof. emeritus, 1966-81, dir. Maison Francaise, 1941-66. Awarded Knight's Cross of Legion of Honor, Govt. of France, 1960. Home: Westport, Conn. Died May 7, 1981.

SHEIB, SIMON, lawyer; b. Jan. 23, 1916; s. Benjamin and Fannie (Fine) S.; B.A., N.Y. U.; LL.B., Harvard; m. Stella Newman, Sept. 29, 1945; children—David, Fredda, Jonathan, James. Admitted to N.Y. State bar; practiced in N.Y.C.; pres., chief exec. officer, chmn. bd. Avnet, Inc., N.Y.C.; dir. Rexham Corp., Golden Crest Records, Inc. Home: Larchmont, N.Y. Died June 15, 1980.

SHEKERJIAN, HAIG (SHEK-ER-JI-AN), army officer; b. Ada Bazaar, Turkey, June 13, 1886; s. Hagop and Esther (Alexanian) S.; came to U.S., 1891; student Colgate U., 1906-07; B.S., U.S. Mil. Acad., 1911; grad. Command and Gen. Staff Sch., 1924, Chem. Warfare Sch., 1924, Army War Coll., 1931; m. Helen Russell Bain, Apr. 4, 1921. Commd. 2d lt., U.S. Army, 1911, and advanced through the grades to brig. gen. (temp.), 1942; served with troops in U.S., Hawaii and Mexico, 1916-17; served in Balkans and Russia with Allied Armies of the Orient and with Brit. Forces in Turkey, 1918-19; with Am. Mission to Armenia, 1919; transferred to Chem. Warfare Service, 1923; asst. commandant, Chem. Warfare Sch., 1925-26; instr., Command and Gen. Staff Sch., 1926-30; chem. officer First Army, 1931; chief, Personnel Chem. Warfare Service, 1931-33; chem. officer IX Corps Area, 1933-35; exec., Office of Chief, Chem. Warfare Service, 1936-40; chief, troops and training, Edgewood Arsenal, Md., 1942; comdg. gen. Chem. Warfare Replacement Training Center, 1942-43; comdg. gen. Camp Sibert, Ala., 1943-44; dep. commr. Army and Navy Liquidation Commn., Africa Middle East Theater, 1945; European dir. A.N.C.H.A., 1947-51. Congretationalist. Mason (32 deg.). Mem. Phi Gamma Delta. Clubs: Army and Navy, Chevy Chase, Army and Navy Country (Washington, D.C.). Contributor to Encyclopedia Britannica and Yearbook. Home: Washington. *

SHELDON, ARCHIBALD MCDANIELS, mfr. indsl. sewing machines; b. Rutland, Vt., Apr. 23, 1885; s. John A. and Caroline (Eastman) S.; B.A., Yale, 1908; m. Fay Crawford, Aug. 7, 1926; children—John, Archibald, Louise, Anita. With Union Special Machine Co., Chgo., 1915—, pres., 1930-53, chmn. bd., 1953—. Mem. Ill. Mfrs. Assn., Chgo. Nat. Metal Trades Assn. (past pres.). Home: St. Charles, Ill. *

SHELDON, LUTHER, JR., naval medical officer; b. Norfolk, Va., Feb. 17, 1883; s. Luther and Jane Stevens (Baldwin) S.; Norfolk Acad., 1894-96, 1898-1900, Randolph-Macon Acad., 1897-98, A.B., Hampden-Sydney Coll., 1903, LL.D., 1943; M.D., U. of Mich., 1909; m. Helen DuBose (dec.), Aug. 12, 1912; children—William DuBose (dec.), Helen (Mrs. John Frederick Taggart); m. 2d, Ruth Noyes (McDowell), Dec. 31, 1937. Commd. asst. surg., U.S. Navy, 1911, and advanced through the grades to rear admiral, Med. Corps, Nov. 17, 1947, retired Aug. 1, 1947. Mem. A.M.A., Am. Coll. of Surgeons, Kappa Alpha (Southern), Phi Rho Sigma, Omicron Delta Kappa. Mason. Clubs: Chevy Chase, Army-Navy, (Washington, D.C.). Home: Washington, D.C. *

SHELDON, WILLIAM HERBERT, medical and psychol. research; b. Warwick, R.I., Nov. 19, 1898; s. William Herbert and Mary Abby (Greene) S.; A.B., Brown U., 1918; A.M., U. Colo., 1923; Ph.D., U. Chgo., 1925, M.D., 1933; m. Louise Steger, 1925 (div. 1928); m. 2d, Milancie Hill, 1943 (dec.). Instr. psychology U. Tex., 1923-24; instr. psychology U. Chgo., 1924-26, asst. prof., 1926-27; asst. prof. psychology U. Wis., 1927-30; intern U. Chgo. Clinics, 1933-34; traveling fellow (abroad) in child psychology Nat. Council, 1934-36; prof. psychology U. Chgo. Theol. Sem., 1936-38; research asso. in anthropology, lectr. in psychology Harvard, 1938-42; dir. Constitution Clinic, Presbyn. Hosp., N.Y.C., 1946; dir. Constitution Lab., Coll. Physicians and Surgeons Columbia, 1946-59; clin. prof. medicine U. Oreg. Med. Sch., 1951-70, emeritus, 1970-77, dir. follow-up studies in constl. medicine, 1951—; research asso. U. Calif. Inst. Human Devel., Berkeley, 1956-77; attending chief research facility Rockland State Hosp., Orangeburg, N.Y., 1961-77; dir. research Biol. Humanics Found. Served as 2d lt., machine gun co. U.S. Army, 1918; maj. to lt. col. M.C., U.S. Army, 1942-44. Mem. Am. Psychol. Assn., A.M.A., Am. Soc. Phys. Anthropologists. Author: Psychology and the Promethean Will, 1936; The Varieties of Human Physique, 1940; The Varieties of Temperament, 1942; Early American Cents, 1948; Varieties of Delinquent Youth, 1949; Atlas of Men, 1954; Penny Whimsy, 1958; Prometheus Revisited, 1974. Address: Cambridge, Mass. Died Oct. 16, 1977.

SHELL, CLAUDE IRVING, JR., educator; b. Pine Bluff, Ark., Oct. 15, 1922; s. Claude Irving and Ela (Hartsell) S.; B.A., Maryville Coll., 1947; M.S., U. Tenn., 1949; Ph.D., So. Ill. U., 1966; m. Mary Frances Robinson, July 27, 1952; children—Barbara Jane, Mary Louise, James Claude, William Joseph. Partner, Shell-Ross Co., 1951-54; asst. prof. bus. adminstrn. Tenn. Tech. U., 1948-51, asso. prof., 1954-57; product planner Ford Motor Co., 1957-60; asst. dir. Small Bus. Inst., So. Ill. U., 1960-65; asst. dir. placement services, 1965-66, chmn. dept. mgmt., 1966-67; prof., head dept. mgmt. Eastern Mich. U., Ypsilanti, 1967-79, acting dean Coll. Bus., 1978-79; cons. Ill. Div. Vocational Rehab., 1964-79. Bd. dirs. Bus. Opportunities for Blind, 1965-69; mem. bd., exec. com. Visually Handicapped Mgrs. Ill., 1972-79, chmn., 1974-79. Served to lt. F.A., AUS, 1943-46; ETO. Mem. Acad. Mgmt., Internat. Council Small Bus., Beta Gamma Sigma. Phi Kappa Phi, Alpha Kappa Psi, Pi Sigma Epsilon, Sigma Iota Epsilon. Presbyn. (elder). Contbr. articles to profl. jours. Home: Ypsilanti, Mich. Died Aug. 29, 1979; buried Highland Cemetery, Ypsilanti.

SHELL, DAN HUFF, II, lawyer; b. Okolona, Miss., Jan. 2, 1918; s. Oliver Enochs and Lorette (Strong) S.; J.D., U. Miss., 1940; m. Eleanor Elease Easter; Mar. 8, 1941; children—Sally Ann Porter (Mrs. Thomas William III), Daniel Huff III. Admitted to Miss. bar, 1940; practice in Amory, Miss., 1940; spl. agent FBI, Des Moines, N.Y.C., Jackson, Miss., Miami, Fla., Milw. and Buffalo, 1940-45; mem. firm Satterfield, Ewing & Hedgepeth, Jackson, 1945-50; partner Satterfield, Ewing, Williams & Shell, Jackson, 1950-55; sr. mng. partner Satterfield, Shell, Williams & Buford, Jackson, 1955-76; prof. law Jackson Sch. Law, 1948-55. Sec. Council Sch. Found. Fellow Am. Coll. Trial Attys.; mem. Hinds County (pres. 1962), Am. bar assns., Miss. State Bar (commr. 1962-63), Fed. Ins. Counsel, Internat. Assn. Ins. Counsel, Miss. Def. Lawyers Assn., Scribes. Kiwanian (pres. 1962). Club: Knife and Fork (pres. 1962), Jackson Country, Capital City, Petroleum, Univ. (Jackson). Home: Jackson, Miss. Died Dec. 1976.

SHELLY, MARY JOSEPHINE, air force officer; b. Grand Rapids, Mich., Feb. 17, 1902; d. James Robert and Mary Isabelle (Hayes) Shelly; A.B., U. Ore 1926; M.A., Columbia, 1930. Asst. to dean students U. Chicago, 1935-38; asst. to pres. Bennington (Vt.) Coll., 1938-42, 46-51; col., dir. women U.S. Air Force, rank of col. Served as comdr., Women's Res., U.S.N., 1942-46. Recipient Citation, Sec. of Navy. Mem. Phi Beta Kappa. Died Aug. 6, 1976.

SHELTON, EDWARD NICHOLAS, ret. chem. mfr.; b. Epworth, Ga., Sept. 9, 1907; s. George H. and Margaret (Quintrell) S.; student U. Mich., 1925-29; m. Mary Longworth, September 9, 1933; children—Walter L., Emily B. Sales trainee Am. Blower Corp., 1929; salesman Dubois Co., 1930; sales mgr. H.O. Trerice Co., 1934-38; salesman Tenn. Corp. (acquired by Cities Service Co.), 1938-41, asst. sales mgr., 1941-52, sales mgr. chem. div., 1952-54, gen. sales mgr., 1954-56, v.p. charge sales, 1956-64, exec. v.p. marketing, 1964-68, sr. v.p., 1968-70, pres. agrl. chems. div. 1965-70, also dir.; ret., 1970. Mem. Mfg. Chemist Assn., Nat. Plant Food Inst., Nat. Agrl. Chems. Assn. Clubs: Bankers; Capital City, Commerce (Atlanta). Home: Atlanta, Ga. Died Sept. 1, 1980; buried Atlanta.

SHELTON, JAMES ERRETT, banker; b. Colusa, Calif., Nov. 6, 1886; s. William Thomas and Mattie (Calhoun) S.; A.B., Stanford, 1910, J.D., 1912; m. Anne Jacobson, July 6, 1928. Engaged in practice of law, Los Angeles, 1912-17; trust counsel Title Ins. & Trust Co., Los Angeles, 1917-19; with Secretary First Nat. Bank and its predecessors, 1919—, pres., 1946-55, chmn. bd., 1955-62, now chmn. emeritus, dir.; dir. Los Angeles Investment Co. Mem. Los Angeles (pres. 1946), Cal. State (pres. 1949-50), cs of c. Am. (pres. 1950-51), Cal. (pres. 1942-43) bankers assns., Mchts. and Mfrs. Assn. (dir.), Delta Chi. Clubs: California, University, Los Angeles Country, Bel-Air Bay, Rotary. Home: Los Angeles. *

SHENSTONE, ALLEN GOODRICH, educator; b. Toronto, Ont., Can., July 27, 1893; came to U.S., 1910; s. Joseph Newton and Eliza (Hara) S.; B.S., Princeton, 1914, A.M., 1920, Ph.D., 1922; B.A., Cambridge U., 1921, M.A., 1935; D.Sc. (hon.), York U., Toronto, 1972; m. Mildred Madeline Chadwick, July 28, 1923 (dec. Apr. 1967); 1 son, Michael; m. 2d, Tiffin H. Harper, Aug. 22, 1969; children—Katherine Mead, Daisy Fitch. Instr. Toronto U., 1922-25; prof. physics Princeton U., 1925-80, Class 1909 prof., 1945-62, chmn. dept. physics, 1949-60. Mem. NRC-Can. on War Work, 1940-45. Served with Royal Engrs., 1915-19. Awarded Mil. Cross, 1918; Officer Order Brit. Empire, 1943. Fellow Royal Soc. of London; mem. AAAS, Am. Phys. Soc., Am. Assn. Physics Tchrs., Optical Soc. Am. (Meggers prize 1971). Baptist. Clubs: Princeton of N.Y.; Nassau (Princeton); Athenaeum (London). Contbr. numerous papers on atomic spectroscopy to sci. jours. Home: Princeton, N.J. Died Feb. 16, 1980.

SHENTON, HERBERT NEWHARD, sociologist; b. Pottstown, Pa., July 9, 1884; s. Robert M. and Helen Louise (Scheck) S.; Ph.B., Dickinson Coll., Carlisle, Pa., 1906, M.A., 1909, L.H.D., 1926; B.D., Drew Theol. Sem., 1910; Union Theol. Sem., 1910-12; Ph.D., Columbia, 1925; m. Edna Mae Logan, of Carlisle, Pa., June 27, 1919. Student pastor, various times, in Pa. and N.J., 1905-15; ordained M.E. ministry, 1910; instr. sociology, Columbia, 1912-25, asst. prof., 1925-27; prof. sociology and head of dept., Syracuse U., since 1927; asst. to Josiah Macy, Jr. Foundation since 1934. Chief of reconstruction research div. U.S. Council Nat. Defense, World War, acting dir. same, and dir., June-Oct. 1920. Exec. sec. U.S. Bituminous Coal Commn., 1920; organizing sec. U.S. Anthracite Coal Commn., 1920; lecturer, Gen. Staff War Coll., 1920-21; director of reconnaissance study Y.M.C.A. and Y.W.C.A. relations throughout United States, 1920-30. Mem. exec. com. Meth. Federation for Social Service; vice chmn. dept. of research and edn. Federal Council of Chs. Mem. Am. Sociol. Soc. (chmn. sect. on sociology of religion, 1924-26), Am. Statis. Soc., Am. Assn. for Labor Legislation, Am. Acad. Polit. and Social Science, Am. Assn. Univ. Profs., Religious Edn. Assn. of U.S. and Canada (pres. 1933-35; mem. nat. bd. dirs.), Beta Theta Pi, Alpha Kappa Delta, Kappa Phi Kappa. Exec. sec. Internat. Auxiliary Lang. Assn. in U.S.; mem. Nat. Council and Internat. Com. of Y.M.C.A. Mason. Clubs: Faculty of Columbia Univ., Town Hall (New York); Faculty of Syracuse Univ. Author: The Practical Application of Sociology, 1926; Cosmopolitan Conversation, 1933. Co-Author: International Communication, 1931. Contbr. to Social Science and to religious publs. Home: Syracuse, N.Y. *

SHEPARD, ROGER B., business exec.; b. St. Paul, Minn., Sept. 14, 1885; s. Frank Parsons and Anna (McMillan) S.; A.B., Yale, 1908; m. Katherine Kohlsaat, July 27, 1910; children—Roger B., Blake, Constance (Mrs. Henry Gaylord Dillingham), Stanley. Clerk, Harris Trust and Savings Bank, Chicago, 1908-10; asst. treas. Finch, Van Slyck & McConville, St. Paul, Minn., 1910-14, sec. and treas., 1914-23, pres. since 1923; director and chairman Federal Reserve Bank, Minneapolis, Minn., since 1940; dir. Merchants Nat. Bank (later merged with First Nat. Bank), 1913-40. Pres. St. Paul Community Chest and Council, 1940-42. Pres. bd. trustees St. Paul Acad. Country Day Sch., since 1942. Mem. Skull and Bones. Clubs: Minnesota, Somerset Country (St. Paul), Yale (New York). Home: St. Paul, Minn. *

SHEPERD, HOWARD COTTERILL, financier; b. Vincennes, Ind., Oct. 15, 1894; s. Albert McK. and Clara (Burlingame) S.; A.B., DePauw U., Greencastle,

Ind., 1916; honorary Doctor Laws, Vincennes (Ind.) U., 1950; m. Lois von Behren, Oct. 2, 1920; children—Howard Cotterill (dec.), Jean Elizabeth (Mrs. Donald A. Tase), David Albert. Tng. class, Nat. City Bank of N.Y.C., 1916-21, asst. cashier, 1921-26, asst. v.p., 1926-29, v.p., 1929-40, sr. v.p., 1940-48, pres., 1948-52, chmn. bd., chief exec. officer, 1952-59; dir. Fundamental Investors, Inc., Diversified Investment Fund, Inc., Diversified Growth Stock Fund, Inc.; chmn. Atlas Copco, Inc.; dir. Sinclair Oil Corp., Miles Labs., Inc., Riegel Paper Co., Borden Co., Canadian Pacific Ry. Co., Corning Glass Works; mem. bd. trustees, DePauw U. Rep. Methodist. Clubs: Union League, Links (N.Y.C.). Home: Bronxville, N.Y. Died Feb. 17, 1980.

SHEPHERD, HENRY LONGDON, lawyer; b. N.Y.C., July 12, 1907; s. Henry L. and Marna (Magnussen) S.; A.M., Princeton U., 1929, Ph.D., 1932; A.B., Tex. Christian U., 1927; m. Barbara Weller, Dec. 17, 1969; children—Henry Longdon, Lynn Munroe. With Ft. Worth Star Telegram, 1923-28; instr. Tex. Christian U., 1927-28; economist U.S. Dept. Commerce, 1931-33, U.S. Treasury Dept., 1933-35; admitted to Conn. bar, 1942, practice in Hartford; prof. internat. affairs Lincoln U., San Francisco, 1971-74; prof. adminstrv. sci. Central Conn. State Coll., 1975-76; lectr. Lyme (Conn.) Acad. Fine Arts, 1976-77; dir. Crow Hill Corp.; instr. Trinity Coll., 1940-42, Hillyer Coll., 1943-45; spl. treasury agt. in Europe on monetary problems, 1935; mem. adv. group to commr. internal revenue, 1962-63; U.S. State Dept. specialist West Germany, 1960, Africa, 1966; mem. Conn. adv. council SBA, 1976-77. Mem. Am., Conn bar assns., Conn. Writers League, Wethersfield (Conn.) Art League. Author: Monetary Experience of Belgium, 1936; Default and Readjustment of Argentine Debt, 1890-1907, 1933; Visit to Eastern Africa, 1966; Litchfield, Portrait of a Beautiful Town, 1969; Marina Rhymes, 1971, 72, 73, 74, 75, 76, 77. Mem. winning crew in Newport-Bermuda sailing race, 1946. Address: Marlborough, Conn. Died Nov. 7, 1978.

SHEPPARD, ALBERT, educator; born Swansea, Wales, May 31, 1882; s. Samuel and Elizabeth (Edwards) S.; student Trevecca Coll., Wales, 1905-07; A.B., Huron (S.D.) Coll., 1911; A.M., Princeton, 1912; Ph.D., New York U., 1930: student Princeton Theol. Sem., 1911-13, Western Theol. Sem., Pittsburgh, Pa., 1913-14; m. Catherine McEwan, Aug. 19, 1914. Presbyn. minister, First Ch., Leechburg, Pa., 1914-16. Elizabeth Av. Ch., Newark, N.J., 1916-19, First Ch., Forest Hills, L.I., N.Y., 1919-26; with New York U., 1926-47, becoming prof. of history; retired since 1947. Democrat. Presbyterian. Author: A Survey of Civilization (with N. D. Godfrey), 1937. Contbr. to Essentials of World Knowledge. Co-author Through the Ages, 1931. Address: Fort Pierce, Fla. *

SHERBURN, GEORGE WILEY, univ. prof.; b. Northfield, Vt., Nov. 4, 1884; s. Joel Osmun and Mary (Gale) S.; A.B., Wesleyan U., Conn., 1906, M.A., 1909, L.H.D., 1941; Ph.D., U. Chgo., 1915; D. Litt., London, 1952. Instr., Northwestern U., 1906-10, Beloit (Wis.) College, 1910-11, Wesleyan U., 1911-12; fellow in English, U. of Chicago, 1912-13, instr., 1914-19; asst. prof., 1919-23, asso. prof., 1923-26, prof., 1926-36; visiting prof., U. of Tex., summer, 1926; prof., Columbia U., 1936-39, Harvard, 1939-52, prof. emeritus since 1952, chmn. div. Modern Languages, 1943-50, chmn. dept. English, 1945-47; directeur in Les Foyers du Soldat, France, 1917-18; visiting scholar in Henry E. Huntington Library, 1929-30; editorial staff, Modern Philology, since 1920. Fellow American Acad. Arts and Sciences, 1945. Mem. Bibliog. Soc. (London), The Walpole Soc., The English Inst. (chmn. 1941), Am. Council of Learned Socs. (rep. Modern Lang. Assn., 1939-44), Modern Language Association (president, 1949), Psi Upsilon, Phi Beta Kappa. Clubs: Odd Volumes, Grolier, Harvard (Boston). Author: The Early Popularity of Milton's Minor Poems, 1922; The Best of Pope, 1929; Eighteenth Century Prose (with Others), 1932; The Early Career of Alexander Pope, 1934; A Literary History of England (with others), 1948. Contbr. to learned mags. and jours. Home: Middleburg, Vt. *

SHERFESEE, FORSYTHE (SHER'FE-ZA), financial adviser, retired; b. Transylvania County, N.C., May 23, 1882; s. Louis and Anne (Griffith) S.; grad. high sch. Charleston, S.C., 1900; A.B., Coll. of Charleston, 1903; M.F., Yale University, 1905; married Mrs. Emily Borie Ryerson, December 10, 1927 (deceased December 28, 1939). Chief of office of wood preservation U.S. Forest Service, 1905-09; asst. dir. and dir. forestry for Philippine Islands, 1909-16; forestry adviser to Chinese Govt., 1916-25; financial adviser to same, 1925-28. Episcopalian. Author of govt. publs. issued by U.S., P.I., China. Home: Alpes Maritimes, France. *

SHERFF, EARL E(DWARD), coll. prof.; born Flint, Mich., May 18, 1886; s. John H. and Anna Linda (McHenry) S.; A.B., Albion (Mich.) Coll., 1907; S.M., U. of Chicago, 1912, Ph.D. magna cum laude, 1916; m. Fern Rosetta Seeley, June 19, 1910; 1 son, Miner Linnaeus. Asst. in botany, Albion Coll., 1905-06, instr., 1906-07; prof. biology and agr., Mt. Morris (Ill.) Coll., 1907-09; instr. chem. and physiol. Elgin (Ill.) High Sch., 1909-10; instr. biol. and agr., Deerfield Township High Sch. (Ill.), 1910-12; instr. biol. and Latin, Christian Fenger High Sch., Chicago, 1912-19, Robert Lindblom Tech. High Sch., 1919-23; instr. botany, Chicago Teachers Coll., 1923-51, head dept. sci., 1929-51; assistant Desert lab., Carnegie Inst., 1908; instr. Univ. Coll., U. of Chicago, 1917-29; pres. Plaisance Hotel Co., 1926-29, Plaisance Hotel Corp., 1930-32; vice president Newton Lumber Company since 1950. Contbg. mem. and hon. research asso. in systematic bot., Chicago Nat. Hist. Mus. since 1936. Fellow A.A.A.S. (council, 1945-46); hon. life mem. Friends of Our Native Landscape; life mem. Am. Soc. Plant Taxonomists (councilor, 1936-37, chmn. council 5 terms, pres. 1948); Hon. mem. Mu Beta Phi; mem. Sigma Xi, Am. Humane Assn., Am. Nature Study Soc., Am. Soc. Naturalists, Anti-Cruelty Soc. of Chicago, Bot. Soc. of Am., Inc. (sec. systematic sect., 1946, chmn. 1947; councilor 1947), Calif. Bot. Soc., Chicago Biol. Round Table (pres. 1932-36). Author of bot. bulletins. Asso. editor Bot. Gazette, 1925-43; mem. editorial bd. Brittonia, 1943-50, Fedn. Ry. Progress, etc. Home: Chgo. *

SHERIDAN, MICHAEL H., fed. judge; grad. Lafayette Coll., Dickinson Law Sch. Asst. U.S. atty. D.C., 1947; partner Sheridan & Flood; judge U.S. Dist. Ct. Middle Dist. Pa., 1961-76. Address: Scranton, Pa. Died Aug. 23, 1976. *

SHERMAN, LEO P(RENTISS), educator; b. Salem, N.Y., June 11, 1888; s. Charles Warner and Margaret Ann (McKee) S.; B.S., Dartmouth Coll., 1910; M.S., U. Chgo., 1917, Ph.D., 1923; m. Bertha Louise Spencer, Dec. 27, 1911; children—Margaret Louise (Mrs. David R. Bair), Elizabeth Spencer (Mrs. Joseph B. Weaver), Lucy Mason (Mrs. Paul E. Bridgham), Miriam Kellogg McEwen. Sci. tchr. Sheridan (Wyo.) High Sch., 1911-13, Paducah, Ky., 1913-16; instr. chemistry Grinnell Coll., Iowa, 1917-18, asst. prof., 1918-23, asso. prof., 1923-26, prof., from 1926, head dept., 1928-48. Mem. Am. Chem. Soc. (Gold Medal award Iowa sect. 1953), Iowa Acad. Sci. (v.p. 1935-36, pres. 1936-37). Republican. Christian Scientist. Clubs: Fortnightly, Country. Home: Grinnell, Iowa. Died Oct. 4, 1978; interred Evergreen Cemetery, Salem, N.Y.

SHERMAN, NATE H., mfg. co. exec.; m. Beatrice Sherman; children—Gordon, Sarita Sherman Warshawsky, Bette Lou Sherman Seidner. Founder Internat. Parts Corp. and Midas Co. (combined as Midas Internat. Corp.), chmn., hon. chmn. Active Jewish Fedn. Chgo.; trustee Chgo. Med. Sch., Goodwill Industries of Chgo. and Cook County; founding mem. Technion, recipient Albert Einstein award. Home: Chicago, Ill. Died July 29, 1980.

SHERRILL, HENRY KNOX, bishop; b. Bklyn., Nov. 6, 1890; s. Henry Williams and Maria Knox (Mills) S.; B.A., Yale, 1911, D.D., 1929; LL.D. 1960; B.D., Episcopal Theol. Sch., 1914; LL.D., Boston U., 1930; D.D. Harvard, 1936, Trinity Coll., 1936, Phila. Divinity Sch. 1947, Princeton, 1947, Columbia, 1948, Hobart Coll., 1948, U. Edinburgh, 1949, Seabury Western Theol. Sem., 1949, U. Rochester, 1952, Hamilton Coll., 1953, Berkeley Div. Sch., 1954; S.T.D., Gen. Theol. Sem., 1947, Russian Orthodox Theol. Acad., Paris, 1953; D.C.L. Union Coll., 1952, U. Denver, 1952, Lehigh U., 1956; Litt. D., Norwich U., 1954; m. Barbara Harris, Sept. 6, 1921; children—Henry Williams, Edmund Knox, Franklin, Barbara (Mrs. Mason Wilson, Jr.). Ordained to ministry Protestant Episcopal Ch. as deacon, 1914, priest, 1915; asst. minister Trinity Ch., Boston, 1914-17; rector Ch. of Our Savior, Brookline, Mass., 1919-23, Trinity Ch., Boston, 1923-30; bishop of Mass., 1930-1947, presiding bishop, 1947-58, ret. Pres., Nat. Council of Chs., of Christ in Am., 1950-52, World Council of Chs., 1954-61. Pres. Yale U. Council, 1960-65. A.R.C. and U.S. Army chaplain A.E.F. France, July 1917-Jan. 1919. Decorated Legion of Honor (France); medal of Merit (U.S.). Chmn., Gen. Army and Navy Commn., 1945-47; mem. pres.'s. Com. on Civil Rights, 1947. Fellow Am. Acad. Arts and Scis.; mem. Mass. Hist. Soc. Club: Union (Boston). Author: William Lawrence-Later Years of a Happy Life; The Church's Ministry in Our Time (lectures), 1948; Among Friends, 1962. Address: Boxford, Mass. Died May 11, 1980.

SHERROD, CHARLES CHESTER (SHER'OD), coll. pres.; b. Knoxville, Tenn., Sept. 13, 1882; s. Isaac and Margaret (Howell) S.; student Maryville (Tenn.) Coll., 1901-02, Tenn. Normal Coll., 1902-05; A.B., Valparaiso U., 1909, LL.B., 1909; M.A., George Peabody College for Teachers, 1921, Ph.D., 1924; LL.D., Emory and Henry College, 1950; married Carrie Lee Hood, Aug. 28, 1910; children—Isa Lee, Wilma Deen, Charles Chester, Howell Hood. Teacher and prin. pub. schs., Knoxville, until 1906; supt. schs., Millington, Tenn., 1909-12; practiced law, 1912-15; supt. schs., Madisonville, Tenn., 1915-17; instr. history and civics, Knoxville High Sch., 1917-18, East Tenn. State Normal Sch., summers, 1918, 20; supt. schs., Morristown, Tenn., 1918-22; fellowship student Peabody Coll., 1922-24; prof. edn., Peabody Coll., 1924-25, also dir. Demonstration Sch.; president East Tennessee State College, 1925-49; president emeritus and educational cons. since 1949; mem. Tenn. Ednl. Commn., 1933-35; pres. 1st Federal Savings and Loan Assn. since 1950; director of Peoples Bank of Johnson City. Mem. bd. dir. Memorial Hospital. Member State Board of Education, Tennessee, 1920-21; mem. com. on standards, Am. Assn. Teachers Colls., 1931-32, also mem. accrediting and classification com, 1934-39; pres. Am. Assn. Teachers Colleges, 1939-40; mem. commn. on instns. of higher education, Southern Assn. Colleges and Secondary Schools, 1934-39, secretary of same commission, 1940, mem. com. reports 1935-40, fraternal del. Middle States Assn. Colls. and Secondary Schs., Atlantic City, 1941; insp. of colls. for So. Assn. Colls. since 1940. Trustee Hiawassee Coll., 1937—; mem. C. of C., E. Tenn. Ednl. Assn. (pres. 1919-20), Tenn. Pub. Sch. Officers Assn., State Teachers Assn., Tenn. Coll. Assn. (acting pres. 1926-27, pres. 1948-49), N.E.A. and Department Superintendence of same, Phi Delta Kappa (nat. council 1923). Mem. Meth. Ch., S.; del. Gen. Conf., 1930, 34, 38; del. Uniting Conf., Kansas City, 1939, delegate General Conference Methodist Church, Atlantic City, 1940, Kansas City, 1944, Boston, 1948, San Francisco, 1952, del. Ecumenical Conf., Oxford, Eng., 1951; member Bd. Edn. Meth. Ch., 1940-48. Mem. Gen. Bd. of Lay Activities, 1942-44; mem. Board of Christian Education, Holston Conf., since 1931; conf. lay leader, Holston Conf., 1941-43; mem. inter-board council of Holston Conference; member of S. E. Jurisdictional Conference, 1940, 44, 48, 52; member Jurisdictional Council, 1940—. Club: Executives (president 1956-57). Author: Administrative Practices in Tenn. High Schools, 1921; Administration of State Teachers Colleges, 1925; also numerous ednl. articles. Address: Johnson-City, Tenn. *

SHERWOOD, ELMER WILLIAM, ins. and real estate exec.; b. Linton, Ind., Feb. 22, 1896; s. Elmer Tip and Hattie (Price) S.; A.B., Ind. U., 1921; m. Lucille Smith, Sept. 27, 1924; children—Joan, Robert Elmer. Tchr. English, Linton High Sch., 1923-34; pres. Sherwood Sales Co., Linton, 1932-34; pub. relations rep. Sherwood-Templeton Coal Co. and Central Ind. Coal Co., 1935-37; editor Nat. Legionaire, publ. Am. Legion, 1937-42; dir. Nat. Americanism Commn. Am. Legion, 1945-46; pres. Ind. Mut. Fire Ins. Co., Sherwood Assos., pub. relations counsellors, also Sebring Shores Devel. Corp.; treas. Am. Travelers Life Ins. Co.; dir. Midwest Devel. Co., Bloomfield State Bank. Founder, Internat. Automobile Hall of Fame, 1966. Clk., Green County, Ind., 1927-35; mem. Ind. Ho. of Reps., 1921-23; del. Republican Nat. Conv., 1936; organizer Nat. Democrats for Ike, 1952; nat. chmn. Vets. for Eisenhower, 1952. Bd. dirs. Century Council Boy Scouts Am.; treas. A.R.C.; chmn. adv. bd. Salvation Army; bd. dirs. Nat. Athletic Inst. Served with U.S. Army, World Wars I and II; brig. gen. ret.; adj. gen. Ind., 1944-45. Mem. Res. Officers Assn., Mil. Order Loyal Legion, U.S. Mil. Order World Wars, Am. Legion (del. nat. conv. 1923, 45, del.-at-large 1921-50, chmn. nat. legis. com., chief coordinator Congress and Senate com., Rep. Nat. Com.), 40 and 8, V.F.W., Ind. Soc. Chgo., Sons of Ind., N.Y.C., Nat. Ski Assn., Rainbow Div. Soc. Ind. (pres. 1922-79), Sigma Delta Chi, Beta Theta Pi. Methodist. Mason (32 deg.), Rotarian. Clubs: Army and Navy (Washington); Armed Forces (Ft. Harrison, Ind.); Writers, Aeons and Sun'n Lake Country; Sphinx (Ind. U.); Sno Birds (Lake Placid, N.Y.); Columbia (Indpls.); Sebring Shores Country (Sebring, Fla.); Emeritus (Ind. U.). Author: Rainbow-Hoosier, 1918; Diary of a Rainbow Veteran, 1928; The Shibboleth, 1942; American Citizenship, 1943; Analysis of Communism, 1946. Home: Sebring, Fla. Died Feb. 27, 1979; buried Sebring.

SHERWOOD, HENRY NOBLE, educator; b. Mitchell, Ind., Dec. 8, 1882; s. Daniel Webster and Susan Adella (Connelly) S.; A.B., Ind. U., 1909, Ph.D., 1914; A.M., Harvard, 1910; LL.D., Beaver (Pa.) Coll. for Women, 1925; m. Adda Angeline Hendrickson, Aug. 8, 1906; children—Alice Adella, Sarah Isabel. Teacher pub. schs., Ind., 1900-04; supt. schs., Jonesboro, Ind., 1906-07; acting asst. in history, U. of Cincinnati, 1911-12, also teacher Cincinnati Coll. of Finance, Commerce and Accounts; prof. history and govt., Central Normal Coll., Danville, Ind., 1912-13; prof. history, U. of Colo., summer, 1913; prof. history, State Teachers Coll., La Crosse, Wis., 1914-18, dir. Jr. Coll., same, 1915-18; prof. history Ind. U., summers 1915-17; prof. history Franklin (Ind.) Coll., 1918-24, dean 1919-23, dir. summer session, 1919-23; state supt. pub. instrn., Ind., term 1924-27; prof. history, U. of Louisville, 1927-34, dir. summer session, 1928-34; pres. Georgetown (Ky.) Coll., 1934-42; asst. editor of publication, Coll. of Agr., and prof. polit. science, Coll. of Arts and Sciences, U. of Ky., 1942-45; chancellor Transylvania Coll., 1945-46; Exec. Sec., Bd. of Higher Edn., Disciples of Christ 1945-50, president, 1950, president emeritus since 1950. Chairman Kentucky State adv. committee Nat. Youth Administrn., 1939-42; sec.-treas. Ky. Assn. of Church-Related Colls., 1930-43. Mem. State Speakers Bur., Wis., World War I. Mem. N.E.A., Eugene Field Soc. Am. Hist. Assn., Ky. Ednl. Assn., Am. Polit. Science Assn., Southern Assn. Colls. and Secondary Schs. (mem. commn. on higher instns., 1936-43), Indian Schoolmen's Club, S.A.R., Phi Beta Kappa, Phi Delta Kappa. Republican. Mem. Christian

(Disciples) Ch. Mason. Clubs: Executives, Rotary, Informal (Lexington). Author: Manual for Mediaeval and Modern History Maps, 1919; Life of Paul Cuffee, 1923; Our Country's Beginnings, 1924; Makers of America, 1929; Civics and Citizenship, 1929, Citizenship, 1934. Home: Louisville. *

SHERWOOD, THOMAS KILGORE, educator; b. Columbus, O., July 25, 1903; s. Milton Worthington and Sadie (Tackaberry) S.; B.Sc. McGill Univ., 1923, D.Sc. (hon.) 1951; S.M. Mass. Inst. Tech., 1924, Sc.D., 1929; E.D. (hon.), Northeastern U., 1948; D. Technices (hon.), Tech. U. Denmark, 1974; m. Betty Macdonald, Sept. 7, 1927 (dec. 1950); children—Thomas K. III, Richard M., Lorna Marcia; m. 2d, Virginia Howell Smith, June 17, 1953. Asst. dept. chem. engring. Mass. Inst. Tech., 1924-26, asst. prof., 1930-33, asso. prof., 1933-41, prof., 1941-69, Lammot duPont prof. chem. engring., 1965-69, also dean engring., 1946-52; asst. prof. chem. engring. Worcester Poly. Inst., 1928-30; Priestley lectr. Pa. State U., 1959; vis. prof. chem. engring. U. Cal. at Berkeley, 1970-76; cons. chem. engr., 1926-74; mem. com. div. MPE Scis., Nat. Sci. Found., 1954-58; NRC com. air quality mgmt., 1967-73. Served as tech. aide, sect. chief, div. mem. Nat. Defense Research Com. OSRD, 1940-46, as cons. to Baruch rubber com., 1942, as expert cons. (Alsos Mission) War dept., 1944. Recipient William H. Walker award, Am. Inst. Chem. Engrs., for publs. in chem. engring. 1941, Founders' award, 1963, W.K. Lewis award, 1972; U.S. Medal for Merit, 1948. Mem. Am. Acad. Arts and Scis., Nat. Acad. Engring. (founding mem.), Am. Chem. Soc. (E.V. Murphree award 1973), Am. Soc. M.E., Am. Inst. Chem. Engrs., Nat. Acad. Scis. (chmn. engring. sect. 1962-65), Canadian Inst. Chemistry (hon. life), Sigma Xi, Tau Beta Pi. Republican. Unitarian. Author: Absorption and Extraction, 1937, 2d edit. (with R.L. Pigford) 1952; (with C.E. Reed), Applied Mathematics in Chemical Engineering, 1939, 2d edit., 1957; (with C.N. Satterfield) Role of Diffusion in Catalysis, 1963; A Course in Process Design, 1963; (with R.C. Reid) Physical Properties of Gases and Liquids, 1958, 2d edit., 1966, 3d edit., 1977; (with R.L. Pigford and C.R. Wilke) Mass Transfer, 1975. Contbr. articles on various chem. engring. subjects to tech. pubs. Home: Berkeley, Calif. Died Jan. 14, 1976.

SHIELDS, LEIGHTON, lawyer; b. St. Louis, Mo., July 12, 1883; s. George Howell and Mary Harrison (Leighton) S.; A.B., Harvard Coll., 1904; LL.B., St. Louis Law Sch. (Washington U.), 1905; m. Harriette Lucille Krause, Nov. 1, 1919; children—Mary Louise (Mrs. Robert J. Wilkinson), Leighton; married 2d, Helen Frances Wilson, Sept. 28, 1947. Mem. bar of U.S. Supreme Ct.; practiced law in St. Louis, 1905-33; U.S. Commr. East Dist. of Mo., 1909-11; rep. in Mo. legislature, 1911-13; counsel R.F.C. (preferred stock sect. and bank reorganizations), Washington, D.C., 1933-36; U.S. dist. atty. for China, 1936 until U.S. relinquished extraterritoriality over China; captured and held with Am. diplomatic and consular officials by Japanese govt., Shanghai, Dec. 8, 1941; returned to U.S. on exchange ship Gripsholm, Aug. 26, 1942; spl. asst. to U.S. atty. gen. (anti-trust div., Boston, Mass.), 1943. Organized Mo. branch Am. Red Cross, 1904, sec. and v.p. St. Louis chapter, 1904-15. Chmn. St. Louis (Mo.) Draft Bd., 1917-19, Capt., Judge Adv. Gen. Dept., U.S. Army Reserve, 1919-29. Mem. Royal Asiatic Soc., Bostonian Soc., Huguenot Soc. of Am. Democrat. Presbyterian. Mason. Clubs: Harvard (Boston); Faculty of Harvard College; Cercle Sportif Français (Shanghai). Contributor to law jours. Home: Brookline, Mass. *

SHIELS, ARCHIBALD WILLIAMSON (SHELZ), v.p. Pacific Am. Fisheries, Inc.; b. Edinburgh, Scotland, May 26, 1878; s. Thomas and Mary Hannah (Kidd) S.; ed. pvt. schs.; m. Nina Belle Parsons, Mar. 4, 1913; 1 son, John Burton. Came to U.S., 1893; naturalized, 1907. Steamship purser, 1893-97; railroad constrn. in Alaska, 1898-1916; pres. Pacific Am. Fisheries, Inc., 1930-46, chmn. exec. com. 1946, now v.p.; president Pacific American Steamship Line. Member Canadian Historical Assn., Washington Historical Soc., B.C. Hist. Soc., Alaska-Seattle C. of C., Bellingham C. of C. (trustee 1922-26). Presbyterian, Mason (33 deg.), K.T., Elk. Clubs: Washington Athletic (Seattle); Terminal City (Vancouver, Wash.); Bellingham Golf and Country. Home: Bellingham, Wash. *

SHIELY, VINCENT ROBERT, mfg. co. exec.; b. St. Paul, Aug. 25, 1920; s. Joseph Leo and Mary Elizabeth (Jenny) S.; B.S. in Bus. Adminstrn., U. Notre Dame, 1942; M.B.A., Harvard, 1947; m. Mary Elizabeth Hope, Oct. 11, 1947; children—Elizabeth, Catherine, John, Maura, Judith, Vincent. With Toro Mfg. Corp., Mpls., 1947-59, v.p., sec., 1955-59; v.p. Briggs & Stratton Corp., Milw., 1959-63, exec. v.p., 1963-70, pres., 1970-77, chmn. bd., 1976-77, also dir.; dir. First Wis. Nat. Bank, Milw., First Wis. Bankshares, J.L. Shiely Co., Allen-Bradley. Served to capt. AUS, 1943-46; ETO. Clubs: Blue Mound Golf and Country, Western Racquet, Milwaukee. Home: Milwaukee, Wis. Died Aug. 1977.

SHIFRIN, SEYMOUR, composer; b. Bklyn., Feb. 28, 1926; s. Abraham and Yetta (Schultz) S.; A.B., Columbia U., 1947, M.A., 1949; m. Miriam Levine, June 6, 1947; children—Theodore, Susan. Mem. faculty U. Calif. at Berkeley, 1952-66, asso. prof., 1960-64, prof. music, 1964-66; prof. music Brandeis U., 1966—; dir. Koussevitzky Found, Inc.; adv. bd. Koussevitzky Found, Library of Congress; commd. for composition Julliard Sch. Music, 1953, Rodgers and Hammerstein, 1958, Composers Forum, 1958-59, C. F. Peters, N.Y.C., 1958-59, Fromm Found., 1961, Rosemary Harbison, 1968, Temple Emmanuel, San Francisco, 1969, Stanley Quartet U. Mich., 1970, Robert Helps, 1971, San Francisco Chamber Music Soc., 1973, Naumburg Found., Nat. Found. for Arts, 1976; compositions include: Sonata for Cello and Piano, 1948, Music for Orchestra, 1948, String Quartet, Four Cantos for Piano, Cat and the Moon, 1949, Composition for Piano, 1950, No Second Troy, 1952, Chamber Symphony, Spring and Fall, 1953, Medieval Latin Lyric, Serenade for Five Instruments, 1954, Trauermusik, 1956, Cantata, 1957, Three Pieces for Orchestra, 1958, Modern Temper, Hear O Ye Heavens, 1959, Concert Piece for Solo Violin, 1959; String Quartet No. 2; Odes of Shang, for chorus, piano and percussion, 1962; Satires of Circumstance, soprano and 6 instruments, 1964; String Quartet No. 3, 1966; String Quartet No. 4, 1967; In Eius Memoriam for Mixed Quintet, 1968; Duo for violin and piano, 1969; Chronicles for chorus, orch., soloists, 1970; String Quartet No. 5, 1972; Responses for Piano Solo, 1973; Piano Trio, 1974; A Renaissance Garland for Soprano, Tenor, Recorder and Lute, Viol, 1975; The Nick of Time, 1977; Five Last Songs, 1979. Recipient of the Seidl fellowship, 1947; recipient Bearns prize Columbia, 1950; Fulbright fellow, 1951-52; award for composition Fromm Found., Chgo., 1953; Guggenheim fellow in composition, 1956-57; 59-60; grant Nat. Inst. Arts and Letters, 1957; creative arts award Brandeis U., 1959; award Copley Found., 1961; award Koussevitzky Found., Library of Congress, 1963; Horblit merit award Boston Symphony Orch., 1963; Fine Arts Music Found. commn. String Quartet #4, 1966; Koussevitzky Internat. Rec. award, 1970. Home: Natick, Mass. Died Sept. 26, 1979.

SHILLINGLAW, CLIFFORD ALLEN, beverage co. exec.; b. Blairsburg, Iowa, Apr. 24, 1914; s. Andrew Gibson and Carrie (Manion) S.; B.S. in Chem. Engring., Iowa State Coll., 1937, M.S. in Chem. Engring. and Bacteriology, 1939, Ph.D., 1941; m. Winifred S. Moore, Sept. 27, 1941 (dec. Dec. 1957; children—Ellen G., Anne M.; m. 2d, Frances E. Marx, Aug. 9, 1958. With Coca-Cola Export Corp., 1941-42, 44-61, v.p. tech. div., 1948-61; v.p., dir. tech. research and devel. Coca-Cola Co., Atlanta, 1961-66, became v.p. tech. div., 1966, sr. v.p.; process and design engr. Petro-Chem. Devel. Co., 1942-44. Trustee Am. Assembly. Mem. Am. Chem. Soc., Inst. Food Technologists, Inter-Am. Food Inst., Soc. Soft Drink Technologists, Asia Soc., Japan Soc., Round Table. Clubs: Chemists (N.Y.C.); University; Cherokee Town and Country. Home: Dunwoody, Ga. Died Feb. 27, 1979; buried Sleepy Hollow Cemetery, North Tarrytown, N.Y.

SHINKMAN, PAUL ALFRED, journalist; b. Grand Rapids, Mich., Oct. 8, 1897; s. Joseph C. and Emeline (Boxheimer) S.; A.B., U. Mich., 1920; spl. courses Columbia U. and Sorbonne; m. Elizabeth Benn (dau. Sir Ernest and Lady Benn), 1935; children—Paul Glanvill, Christopher Joseph, Bernard Francis III. Began as cub reporter Grand Rapids Press; reporter Chgo. City News Bur., 1920-21, Paris edit. Chgo. Tribune, 1924-26; Paris corr. Italian Mail; Chicago Tribune corr. in Paris, 1927, London, 1927-29; covered Lindbergh's and Amelia Earhart's transatlantic flights, prayer book debate in the House of Commons, funeral of Thomas Hardy in Westminster Abbey, enthronement of Cosmo Lang, Canterbury Cathedral, as Archbishop of Canterbury; returned to U.S., 1929; editorial staff King Features Syndicate, N.Y.C., 1929-38; N.Y. corr. Central Press Assn.; radio commentator 2 seasons The Story Behind the News; roving corr. Internat. News Service, Central Europe, summer 1938; first interview with Lord Runciman in Prague (exclusive to U.S.), 1938, also exclusive interviews with Premier Hodza of Czechoslovakia and Jan Masaryk, Czech Ambassador to London; lectured throughout U.S. on European problems leading to World War II, 1938-42; chief, German section, Daily Report, U.S. Fgn. Broadcast Intelligence Service, 1942-44; Office of War Information 1944-46; radio news commentator Sta. WBCC, Washington, 1946-51; fgn. service officer, Vienna, Austria, 1951-53; editor N.E.A. News, asst. editor N.E.A. Jour., 1957-63; radio news commentator Stations WASH and WDON, also writer Central Press Assn., from 1963. Appointed mem. Gov. of Mich's bd. visitors Nat. Naval Med. Center, 1944; Missions to Berlin, Germany, in May and October 1950 as cons. for Dept. State. Hon. trustee Baxter Sem., from 1957. Mem. Am. Austrian Soc. (mem. bd. trustees), Acad. Polit. Sci. Clubs: National Press; Overseas Writers; Anglo-Am. Press (Paris, France); American Corr. Union (London); Sigma Delta Chi. Episcopalian. Contbr. to U.S. and British publs. Home: Washington, D.C. Died Dec. 19, 1975; buried St. Paul's Rock Creek Cemetery, Washington.

SHINNER, ERNEST G., merchant; b. St. Johns, Mich., May 22, 1883; s. Thomas and Julia Ann (Knight) S.; ed. dist. sch. Bengal Twp., Mich.; m. Emma Plato, Feb. 9, 1912; 1 son, Thomas Gardner (dec.). Organized firm of E. G. Shinner & Co., wholesale and retail meats, Aug. 1912, now operate 35 stores in Mich., Ill., Wis. and Ia.; pres., 1912-52, chmn. bd. employees' retirement fund since 1943; pres. and chmn. bd. South Shore Nat. Bank, 1947-52; pres. Lincoln Village Shopping Center, 1949-52. Chmn. bd. trustees Shinner Pol. Economy Research Found. since 1947; dir. Chgo. Boys Club. Clubs: Chicago Athletic Assn., South Shore Country. Author: The Forgotten Man, 1933; Streamlined Bridge, 1941; Prosperity Can Be Permanent, 1951. Home: Chgo. *

SHIPMAN, FRED W., archivist; b. Worcester, Mass., Mar. 9, 1903; s. Charles and Caroline A. (Wilhelmi) S.; A.B., Clark Univ., 1927, A.M., 1933; student Harvard, 1930-31; m. Ruth A. Connelly, June 4, 1932; children—Frederick W., Ruth A., James C. Research worker, Am. Antiquarian Soc., Worcester, Mass., 1918-29; library asst. Library of Congress, 1929-30; instr. history, Boston U., 1930-31; hist. expert, State Dept., 1931-35; dep. examiner, The Nat. Archives, 1935-36; chief div. of State Dept. Archives, 1936-40, dir. Franklin D. Roosevelt Library, 1940; rep. of President's Com. on Records of War Adminstrn., 1942-45; archives adviser to War Dept. on commn. to M.T.O., spring 1944, to E.T.O., fall 1944; asst. dir. gen. research and reports, Nat. Security Resources Bd. from 1948, 1st records mgmt. officer Dept. State, 1949-54, chief librarian Dept. State and Fgn. Service Posts, 1954-70, ret., 1970. Mem. Soc. Am. Archivists, Dutchess County Hist. Soc., Am. Hist. Soc., State and Local hist. socs., New York History Soc. Contbr. to Dictionary of Am. Biography. Home: Chevy Chase, Md. Died June 14, 1978.

SHIPTON, CLIFFORD KENYON, librarian; b. Pittsfield, Mass., Aug. 5, 1902; s. George and Edith May (Kenyon) S.; B.S., Harvard, 1926, M.A., 1927, Ph.D., 1933, D.Litt., 1964; D.Litt., Clark U., 1969; m. Dorothy MacKillop, June 11, 1927; children—Ann Boyd, Nathaniel Niles, George MacKay. Instr. history Brown U., 1928-30; instr. and tutor Harvard, 1933, 36; editor Sibley Publs., Mass. Hist. Soc., 1930-73; custodian Harvard U. Archives, 1938-73; librarian Am. Antiquarian Soc., 1940-68, also dir. Past chmn. finance committee Shirley, Mass.; clerk First Parish of Shirley, Mass. Trustee Fruitlands Mus., Wayside Mus. Fellow Soc. Am. Archivists (pres.); mem. Am. Antiquarian Soc., Am. Acad. Arts and Scis., Mass. Hist. Soc., Colonial Soc. Mass. (pres.), Phi Beta Kappa; hon. mem. Beverly Hist. Soc. Clubs: Grolier; Odd Volumes. Author: Biographical Sketches of the Graduates of Harvard College, Classes of 1690-1771; Roger Conant, 1945; Isaiah Thomas, 1948; New England in the 18th Century, 1963; National Index of American Imprints Short Title Evans, 1969; Sibley's Harvard Graduates, 1768-1771, Vol. XVII; Index to the Proceedings of the American Antiquarian Society, 1812-1961, 1978. Home: Shirley Center, Mass. Died Dec. 3, 1973; buried Shirley Center, Mass.

SHIRES, HENRY MILLIS, clergyman, educator; b. Bernardsville, N.J., Jan. 28, 1913; s. Henry Herbert and Mable (Millis) S.; B.A., Stanford, 1934; B.D., Ch. Div. Sch. Pacific, 1937, D.D., 1962; Th.D., Pacific Sch. Religion, 1946; m. Loie Calvert Judkins, June 29, 1941; children—Stephanie Hall (Mrs. Chester D. Hooper), Elizabeth Millis (Mrs. W. Terry Maguire), Henry Calvert. Ordained to ministry Episcopal Ch., 1937; rector chs., San Leandro, Calif., 1940-42, Alameda, Calif., 1942-51, Los Altos, Calif., 1952-54; prof. N.T., Episcopal Theol. Sch., Cambridge, Mass., 1954-76, asso. dean, 1967-69; instr. Ch. Div. Sch. Pacific, 1937-51; vis. scholar Stanford, 1971-72; ret., 1976. Trustee Mass. Bible Soc., 1963-80. Mem. Soc. Bible Lit. (sec. New Eng. 1961-63), Am. Soc. Ch. History, Phi Beta Kappa. Kiwanian (pres. Alameda 1950). Author: The Eschatology of Paul, 1966; Finding the Old Testament in The New, 1974. Home: Los Altos, Calif. Died Aug. 2, 1980.

SHIRK, GEORGE HENRY, lawyer; b. Oklahoma City, May 1, 1913; s. John H. and Carrie (Hinderer) S.; A.B., U. Okla., 1935, LL.B., 1936. Admitted to Okla. bar, 1936, also U.S. Supreme Ct.; practice in Oklahoma City, 1936-40, 46-77; sr. mem. firm Shirk, Semtner, Work & Robinson and predecessor firm. Gen. mgr. Okla. Industries Authority. Mayor, Oklahoma City, 1964-67. Former pres., Jr. Achievement of Greater Oklahoma City, Okla. div. Am. Automobile Assn., Salvation Army Adv. Bd., Consumers Credit Counseling Service of Oklahoma City, Greater Oklahoma City Safety Council, Okla. Philatelic Soc., Community Council; pres. Okla. Firefighters Found.; trustee Nat. Trust for Historic Preservation, 1972-77, United Appeal Oklahoma City, Mercy Hosp. Served to col. AUS, 1940-46; ETO. Decorated Legion of Merit, Bronze Star medal, Chevalier of French Legion of Honor; recipient Service to Mankind award Sertoma, 1966, citation Okla. chpt. A.I.A., 1964, Disting. Service award Okla. Bar Assn., 1976. Mem. Oklahoma City C. of C. (dir.), Okla. Hist. Soc. (pres.), Phi Beta Kappa, Phi Delta Phi, Phi Delta Theta. Mason (32 deg., Shriner, Jester). Author: Oklahoma Place Names, 1965, rev.

edit., 1974. Home: Oklahoma City, Okla. Died Mar. 1977.

SHISKIN, JULIUS, govt. ofcl.; b. N.Y.C., Oct. 13, 1912; s. Abraham and Bella (Bender) S.; A.B., Rutgers U., 1934, M.A., 1936; postgrad. Columbia U., 1935-37; m. Frances Levine, Nov. 21, 1937; children—Laura (Mrs. Alan Rubin), Carol (Mrs. David Warlick). Instr. econs. and statistics Rutgers U., 1934-38; research asst. Nat. Bur. Econ. Research, N.Y.C., 1938-42; head economist WPB, Washington, 1942-46; chief econ. statistician Bur. Census, Washington, 1947-68, asst. dir., 1968-69; asst. dir. statis. policy Bur. Budget, 1969-70, chief statistician Office Mgmt. and Budget, 1970-73; commr. Bur. Labor Stats., Dept. Labor, 1973-78. U.S. rep. Statis. Commn. UN, 1969-73; cons. Council Econ. Advisers, 1957-60, OECD, 1960, UN, 1962, IMF, 1964. Recipient Silver medal for meritorious Service Dept. Commerce, 1954, Gold medal for exceptional service, 1963, Spl. award for disting. achievement in fed. Service, 1969; Rockefeller Pub. Service award, 1956; ann. award Nat. Assn. Bus. Economists, 1971. Fellow Am. Statis. Assn., Brit. Royal Statis. Soc. (hon.), A.A.A.S.; mem. Internat. Statis. Inst., Am. Econ. Assn., Internat. Assn. for Research on Income and Wealth, Phi Beta Kappa. Club: Cosmos (Washington). Author: Signals of Recession and Recovery, 1961; (with G.H. Moore) Indicators of Business Expansions and Contractions, 1967; Electronic Computers and Business indicators (transl. into French, German, Spanish, Japanese, Hebrew), 1957; also articles. Contbr. to Internat. Ency. Social Scis., Time Series, Vol. 16, 1968; Internat. Ency. Stats., Time Series, Vol. 2, 1978. Home: Bethesda, Md. Died Oct. 28, 1978; buried King David Meml. Gardens, Falls Church, Va.

SHOCKNESSY, JAMES W., lawyer; b. Springfield, Ohio, Nov. 26, 1906; s. James A. and Margaret (White) S.; A.B., Notre Dame U., 1928; LL.B., Harvard, 1931, J.D., 1969; LL.D., Wilberforce U., 1957. Admitted to Ohio bar, also U.S. Supreme Ct.; state counsel, regional counsel HOLC, 1933-39; individual practice law, Columbus, 1939-76; chmn. com. bar examiners Supreme Ct. of Ohio, 1951-52. Chmn. Ohio Turnpike Commn., 1949-76; mem. Ohio Constl. Rev. Commn., 1972-76; mem. bd. tax commrs. City of Columbus, 1941-42, also trustee sinking fund. Presdl. elector, 1948, 64; vice chmn. Democratic State Exec. Com., 1948-58; del. Dem. Nat. Conv., also mem. platform com., 1960-64. Bd. trustees Boychoir Sch., Princeton, N.J., 1949-50,59-64; bd. Gilmour Acad., Cleve., 1958-65; chmn. bd. trustees Mt. Carmel Hosp., 1969-73; trustee Wilberforce U. Found., 1955-66, chmn., 1962-75; trustee Ohio State U., 1965-74, Wilberforce U., 1968-75; mem. Ohio Bd. Regents. Served with USAAF, 1942-45. Decorated knight Order of Holy Sepulchre, 1958, knight Grand Cross, 1961, Knight of Malta, 1967. Mem. Pres.'s Club Ohio State U. Home: Blacklick, Ohio. Died July 15, 1976.

SHOLES, WALTER HENRY (SHOLZ), (SURNAME CHANGED FROM SCHULZ TO SHOLES IN 1917), consular service; b. Brooklyn, N.Y., Feb. 17, 1883; s. John Peter and Agnes Emma (Brebeck) Schulz; ed. Emerson Inst. (Washington, D.C.), Columbian U., and in Berlin (no degrees); m. Isabel Nicholas Phillips, Oct. 17, 1911; children—Agnes Nicholas, Janie Belle Brebeck. Formerly polit. writer and editor in Okla., and Washington corr.; counsul at Aden, Arabia, 1911-13, Nantes, France, 1913-15, St. Michael, Portugal, 1915, Berne, Switzerland, 1915-17, Nuevo Laredo, Mexico, 1917-19, Göteborg, Sweden, 1919-26, Trieste, Italy, 1926-30, Brussels, 1930-37; consul gen., Milan, 1937-40, Lyons, France, 1940-42, at Basel, Switzerland, 1941-47, ret. 1947. Official observer, Internat. Maritime Congress, Göteborg, 1923. Mem. Pan-Am. Soc.; fellow Am. Geog. Soc.; mem.Acad. of Polit. Science, Am. Acad. of Polit. and Social Science. Home: Oklahoma City, Okla. and Washington. *

SHOR, BERNARD (TOOTS), restaurateur; b. Phila., May 6, 1905; m. Marian Volk; four children. Former salesman; propr. Toots Shor Restaurant. Address: New York, N.Y. Died Jan. 23, 1977. *

SHOREY, WINSTON KINNEY, univ. adminstr.; b. Wheelock, Vt. Sept. 14, 1919; s. Pliny J. and Leila M. (Laffo) S.; A.B., Dartmouth, 1941; M.D., U. Pa., 1943; m. Jeannette S. McConnell, Oct 2, 1948; 1 dau., Jeannette McConnell. Intern, resident internal medicine and gastroenterology Hosp. U. Pa., 1943-50; mem. faculty U. Pa. Sch. Medicine, 1951-55; asst. prof. medicine, 1954-55; asso. prof. medicine, then asso. dean, prof. medicine U. Miami (Fla.) Sch. Medicine, 1955-61; dean Sch. Medicine, U. Ark., 1961-74, dir. area health edn. centers program, 1974-76. Served to lt. comdr. M.C., USNR, 1945-46, 52-54; Winston K. Shorey Bldg. named in his honor U. Ark., 1980. Diplomate Am. Bd. Internal Medicine. Fellow A.C.P.; mem. Am., Ark., Pulaski County med. assns., Phila. Coll. Physicians, A.A.A.S., Phi Beta Kappa, Alpha Omega Alpha. Presbyn. (elder). Rotarian. Home: Little Rock, Ark. Died Jan. 11, 1976; cremated.

SHORT, DEWEY, ex-congressman, government official; born in Galena, Missouri, April 7, 1898; son of Jackson Grant and Permelia Cordelia (Long) S.; grad. Marionville (Mo.) Coll., 1917; A.B., Baker U., 1919; Frank D. Howard fellow, Boston U., S.T.B., 1922, LL.D., 1941; studied Harvard, U. of Berlin, Heidelberg, Oxford U., 1922-25; LL.D., Drury Coll., Springfield, Mo., 1930, Boston U., 1941, Baker U., 1954; J.U.D., Central Coll., 1953; m. Helen Gladys Hughes, Apr. 20, 1937. Prof. philosophy and psychology, Southwestern Coll., Winfield, Kan., 1923-24, 1926-28; mem. 71st Congress (1929-31), 14th Mo. Dist., 74th to 84th Congresses, 7th Mo. District Chmn. House Com. on Armed Services, 1953-55. Delegate Rep. National Conv., Chicago, 1932, Internat. Parliamentary Union, Oslo, Norway, 1939, Cairo, Egypt, 1947; mem. Congressional Del. to inspect Nazi atrocity camps, 1945; alternate delegate U.S.-Japanese Security Pact. President National Rivers and Harbors Congress, 1938-44, chmn. bd., 1944-48; vice chmn. Nat. Rep. Congl. Com., 1950-57; asst. sec. Army for civil-mil. affairs, 1957-60. Received 108 votes for vice-presidential nomination Rep. Nat. Conv., Phila., Pa., 1940. Served as acting lt. infantry, U.S. Army, World War. Mem. Mo. Soc., Young Rep. Assn. of Mo., Am. Legion, Nat. Rifle Assn., Delta Tau Delta, Pi Gamma Mu. Republican. Methodist. Mason. Dewey Short Scholarship established in his honor by Aerojet Gen. Corp. Home: Galena, Mo. Died Nov. 19, 1979; buried Galena Cemetary.

SHORT, OLIVER CLARK, govt. official; b. Georgetown, Del., Aug. 15, 1883; s. Eli S. and Sarah Elizabeth (Jefferson) S.; A.B., Univ. of Delaware, 1904; A.M., Univ. of Pennsylvania, 1913; L.H.D., American University, 1944; post grad. study in psychology, Johns Hopkins, 1924-27; m. Katharine Mae Alton, Jan. 30, 1909; children—Oliver Alton, Sarah Louise, Katharine Elizabeth. Teacher and commandant mil. corps, N.C. Mil. Acad., Red Springs, 1904-05; teacher and prin. pub. schs., Delaware City, Del., 1905-06; teacher and vice prin. high sch., Dover, Del., 1906-07; teacher mathematics, Bethlehem (Pa.) Prep. Sch., 1907-08; teacher mathematics and science, Sayre (Pa.) High Sch., 1908-10; teacher science High Sch., Trenton, N.J., 1910-17, Germantown (Phila., Pa.), High Sch., 1917-18; asst. chief examiner N.J. Civil Service Commn., 1918-20; sec. and chief examiner Md. Employment Commn., 1920-22, commr., 1922-35; personnel dir. Thos. Maddock's Sons Co., Trenton, part time 3 yrs.; exec. asst. to dir. of U.S. Census, 1935-37, asst. to dir., 1937-39; personnel dir., U.S. Dept. of Commerce since 1939; reemployment dir. for Md., U.S. Employment Service, 1933-35; dir. war transfers United States Civil Service Commission, March-December 1942 (on detail); lecturer on personnel administration, Johns Hopkins, University of Maryland, Univ. of Baltimore, Am. Univ.; lecturer on orgn., supervision and management, Am. Univ. Mem. Assembly of Civil Service Commns, of U.S. and Can. (ex-pres.), Personnel Administrn Group, Baltimore (ex-pres.), Society for Personnel Administration (past pres.). Member Phi Kappa Phi. Democrat. Episcopalian. Mason (Shriner); member Anchor Masonic Club (ex-president), Advisory Board of Masonic Clubs (ex-president); K.P. (past chancellor). Clubs: Gavel (ex-pres.), Schoolmasters of Trenton (ex-pres.), Ratary Internat. (ex-pres. Baltimore; ex-gov. 34th dist.), Federal Club, Inc. (past pres.). Author: The Merit System, 1928; Probation Period, 1946; Probation in the Public Service, 1946. Home: College Park, Md.*

SHORTLEY, GEORGE HIRAM, math. physicist, sci. services co. exec.; b. Mpls. Mar. 3, 1910; s. George Hiram and Mabel (Johnson) S.; B.E.E., U. Minn., 1930; A.M., Princeton, 1932, Ph.D., 1933; postgrad. (NRC fellow), Mass. Inst. Tech., also Harvard, 1933-35; m. Irene Wilson, June 17, 1955. From instr. to prof. physics Ohio State U., 1935-42, 46-49; div. chief Naval Ordnance Lab., 1942-46, Operations Research Office, Johns Hopkins, 1949-55; asso. dir. research center Borg Warner Corp., 1955-57; v.p., chief scientist Booz, Allen Applied Research, Inc., Bethesda, Md., 1957-70. Recipient Distinguished Civilian Service award Navy Dept., 1946. Fellow Am. Phys. Soc.; mem. Am. Astron. Soc., Operations Research Soc. Am. (editor, pres., mem. council). Author: Theory of Atomic Spectra, 1935; Physics, 1950; Elements of Physics, 1952; Principles of College Physics, 1959; Physical Processes in Ionized Plasmas, 1962. Home: Bethesda, Md. Died Dec. 25, 1980.

SHORTLIDGE, RAPHAEL JOHNSON, educator; b. Media, Pa., Aug. 3, 1883; s. Swithin Chandler and Mary Jane (Johnson) S.; grad. State Normal Sch., West Chester, Pa., 1901; A.B., Haverford (Pa.) Coll., 1906; A.M., Harvard, 1909; m. Helen Wetmore Houghton, Sept. 2, 1914; children—George Houghton, Anne, Margaret, Mary Jane, Raphael Johnson, Helen Houghton. Master Choate Sch., Wallingford, Conn., 1910-24, asso. headmaster, 1925-27; headmaster Storm King Sch., Cornwall-on-Hudson, N.Y., 1927-32; headmaster Tome School, Port Deposit, Md., 1932-35; headmaster Pawling (N.Y.) Sch., 1935-42; owner Hill Camp, Chesham, N.H. Mem. Nat. Headmaster's Assn. Home: Keene, N.H.*

SHOW, STUART BEVIER (SHOU), forester; b. Waco, Neb., Apr. 9, 1886; s. Arley Barthlow and Bucephalia (Wolph) S.; A.B., Stanford Univ., 1909; M.F., Yale Forestry Sch., 1910; m. Mabel J. Griffin, Dec. 25, 1910; children—Mrs. Elizabeth M. Beales, Mrs. Jean K. Clark, Stuart Bevier, Jr., Mrs. Barbara C. Volarvich. Forest asst. U.S. Forest Service, 1910-15, forest examiner, 1915-17, silviculturist in charge of research Region 5, 1917-26, regional forester in charge Calif. National Forest, 1926-46; now forestry consultant Forestry and Forest Products Div. of FAO of U.N. Mem. Soc. Am. Foresters, Calif. Acad. Science. Conglist. Clubs: Commonwealth, Sierra. Author of many govt. professional papers. Address: Palo Alto, Calif. *

SHREINER, CHARLES WESLEY (SHRIN'ER), clergyman; b. Mount Joy, Pa., Sept. 18, 1882; s. Eli and Harriet (Huffty) S.; attended U.S. Naval Acad., 1905-07, Phila. Div. Sch., 1908-11; hon. M.A., U. of Pa., 1928; D.D., Temple U., 1931; m. Mary Cardwell, Jan. 11, 1916; children—Mary Jane, Charles Wesley. Ordained ministry P.E. Ch., 1911; headmaster Church Farm Sch., Glen Loch, Pa., since 1918; also dean Convocation of Chester, Diocese of Pa.; rector Ch. of the Atonement, Phila., 1911-18. Home: GlenLoch, Pa.*

SHREVE, RANDOLPH NORRIS, chem. engr.; b. St. Louis, Mar. 9, 1885; s. Thomas Taliaferro and Mary Rhodes (McMillin) S.; A.B. summa cum laude, Harvard, 1908; Eng.D., Purdue U., 1961; Ph.D. (hon.), China Acad., 1970; m. Nancy B. Vaughan, Jan. 28, 1928 (dec. Dec. 1932); m. 2d, Eleanor Burns Mitchell, Dec. 26, 1935 (dec. Nov. 1967); m. 3d, Irene M. Strieby, June 1, 1968. In charge mfg. chems. Mallinckrodt Chem. Works, St. Louis, 1902-04, 07-11; with Lamar Chem. Works, Newark, 1911-15; bldg. and operating chem. plants for Marden, Orth & Hastings Corp., Newark, Shreve Chem. Co., Jersey City, and Calco Chem. Co., Bound Brook, N.J., 1915-19; cons. chem. engr.; asso. prof. chem. engring. in charge organic tech. Purdue U., 1930-31, prof. 1931-61, emeritus, 1961-75, head Sch. Chem. and Metall. Engring., 1947-51, dir. Formosa-Purdue Engring. Project, 1953-61. Ofcl. investigator Office Sci. Research and Devel.; dollar-a-year man in research (atomic fission engring., for bomb) WPB; observer with USN in Pacific, 1947; studied chem. industry in Europe, 1928, Japan, 1952, Formosa, 1952-59. P.I., 1955-56. Bd. dirs., mem. exec. com. Purdue Research Found., trustee Indpls. Mus. Art. Fellow A.A.A.S., Am. Inst. Chemists, Am. Inst. Chem. Engrs.; mem. Am. Assn. Textile Chemists and Colorists (charter), Am. Soc. Engring. Edn., Am. Chem. Soc. (organizer and sec. dye div. 1918-24, chmn. 1924-25, chmn. medicinal div. 1935, counselor-at-large, 1936-38, chmn. div. indsl. and engring. chemistry 1943-44; chmn. unit processes symposia 1937-53; organizer and chmn. subdiv. chem. processes 1954; adv. bd. Indsl. and Engring. Chemistry, Chem. and Engring. News, 1943-50; Scroll of Honor div. indsl. and engring. chemistry, Soc. Cin., Chinese Inst. Engring. (Formosa), Sigma Xi, Phi Beta Kappa, Tau Beta Pi, Sigma Alpha Epsilon, Phi Lambda Upsilon, Alpha Chi Sigma, Omega Chi Epsilon. Registered profl. engr., Ind. Republican. Episcopalian. Mason, Rotarian. Clubs: Harvard (Ind., N.J.); Chemists' New York; Purdue Club of Retired Personnel (pres. 1966). Author: Dyes Classified by Intermediates, 1922; Greensand Bibliography to 1930 and Zeolite Water Softeners (brochure), 1930; Intermediate Readings in Chemical German (with Fotos), 1938; Advanced Readings On Chemical and Technical German (with Fotos), 1940; also chpts. of Groggins' Unit Processes in Organic Synthesis, Comings High Pressure Technology, Rogers Manual of Industrial Chemistry, 1942. Chemical Process Industries, 1945, 56, 67; Chemical and Met. Flow Sheets (in collaboration with Olive); Selected Process Industries, 1950; Industrial Research and Development (with Ewell and Alder), 1956, and tech. articles. Home: Lafayette, Ind. Died Feb. 17, 1975.

SHRIVER, J. NICHOLAS, JR., lawyer; b. Westminster, Md., 1913; A.B., Georgetown U., 1933, J.D., 1937. Admitted to D.C. bar, 1936, Md. bar, 1937; mem. firm Ober, Grimes & Shriver, Balt. Served with AUS, 1942-46. Fellow Am. Coll. Probate Counsel (bd. regents 1966-72, sec. 1972-74, v.p. 1974-75, pres. 1976-77); mem. Am. (mem. council 1964-68, vice chmn., dir. probate law div. 1968-69, sect. real property, probate and trust law, vice chmn. 1970-71, chmn. elect 1971-72, chmn. 1972-73), Md. (chmn. sect. estates and trusts 1968-70) bar assns., Bar Assn. Balt. City, Am. Law Inst., Greater Balt. C. of C. (legislation com. 1965-68). Home: Baltimore, Md. Died Feb. 8, 1977; interred Westminster, Md.

SHUEY, HERBERT STANLEY, mfg. exec.; b. Danville, Cal., Apr. 11, 1886; s. John Adam and Lelia Alice (Mathewson) S.; B.S., U. Cal., 1909; m. Florence M. McEvoy, Dec. 26, 1919 (dec. June 1956); m. 2d, Mrs. Verland Bowen, May 26, 1962. With The Merrill Co., San Francisco, 1911-71, dir., 1913, v.p., 1943-71; dir. Merco Centrifugal Co., 1930—, v.p., 1945—; dir. Merrill Estate Co., 1923-71, v.p., 1932-71; dir., v.p. The Merrill-Brose Co., 1943-71; dir. Engrs. Investments, Inc. 1929—, v.p., 1949—; dir. Merco Trinke Machine Co., 1939—, v.p., 1948—; exec. Western Ore Purchasing Co., Nev.; dir., sec. The Alloys Co., San

Francisco, 1916-46, Nordstrom Valve Co., 1924-32; dir. Halstead Products Co., Oakland, Cal. Mem. Civil Service Commn., Piedmont, Cal.; foreman Alameda County Grand Jury, 1954. Served with U.S. Army, 1918. Recipient Silver award of merit Red Cross of Sweden, 1959. Pres. Scaife Scholarship Found., Oakland, 1947-49; pres. Oakland Forum, 1946-49; chmn. emeritus financial adv. bd. Womens Athletic Club, Oakland, 1947—. Mem. Am. Legion. Conglist. Mason (33 deg.), Rotarian (pres. San Francisco, 1943-44; dist. gov. 1949-50). Author: Follow Us. Home: Oakland CA. *

SHUFF, BENJAMIN L., banker; b. Frederick, Md., 1901. Chmn. bd., chief exec. officer, dir. Farmers & Mechanics Nat. Bank, Frederick, Md.; trustee OFB Corp. Trustee Francis Scott Key Meml. Found., Hood Coll. Moose, Elk. Home: Frederick, Md. Died Apr. 4, 1976; buried Mt. Olive Cemetery, Frederick.

SHUGERT, STANLEY PULLIAM, educator; b. Berryville, Va., Dec. 21, 1885; s. Rezin Deal and Frances Coleman (Pulliam) S.; student Charles Town (W. Va.) Male Acad.; A.B., Roanoke Coll., 1905; A.M., U. Pa., 1909, Ph.D., 1914. Tchr. pub. schs., Charles Town, W.Va., 1905-06; instr. mathematics U. Del., 1907-08; instr. mathematics U. Pa., 1908-19, asst. dir. admissions, 1919-26, asst. prof., 1919-28, prof., 1928-55, chmn. roster com., 1941-54, emeritus prof., 1955—. Served as instr. navigation, U.S. Shipping Bd., 1917-19. Mem. Sigma Xi, Phi Gamma Delta. Clubs: Lenape (Phila.), Phi Gamma Delta (N.Y.C.). Home: Phila. *

SHULMAN, KENNETH, neurosurgeon; b. Worcester, Mass., Sept. 6, 1928; s. Hyman Abraham and Sophie (Levine) S.; A.B. with highest honors Clark U., 1950; M.D. with honors, Washington U., 1954; m. Jean Carol Lewit, June 25, 1955; children—Michildren—Michael Eben, Daniel Richard. Intern, Yale-New Haven Hosp., 1954-55; resident in neurosurgery Neurol. Inst., Columbia-Presbyn. Med. Center, N.Y.C., 1957-61; asst. prof. neurosurgery N.Y. U. Med Sch., 1961-64; asst. prof. neurosurgery U. Pa. Med. Sch., 1964-65, asso. prof., 1965-67; prof. neurosurgery Albert Einstein Coll. Medicine, N.Y.C., 1967-81, chmn. dept., 1972-81; dir. neurosurgery Montefiore Hosp. Med. Center. Served with USNR, 1955-57. Mem. Am. Assn. Neurol. Surgeons (past pres. pediatric sect.), A.C.S., Soc. Neurol. Surgeons. Contbr. articles to profl. jours. Home: Scarsdale, N.Y. Died Mar. 23, 1981.

SHUMAN, RONALD BUSWELL, educator; b. Owatonna, Minn., Mar. 22, 1908; s. Milton G. and Lodema B. (Buswell) S.; A.B., Hamline U., 1928, LL.D., 1952; A.M., U. Minn., 1929, Ph.D., 1934. Instr. U. Minn., 1930-34; vis. prof. U. Wash., 1934-35; asst. prof. bus. adminstrn. U. Okla., 1935-38, asso. prof., 1938-44, prof. bus. mgmt., 1944-72, chmn. dept., 1938-41, 46-53, George Lynn Cross research prof. mgmt., 1951-72. Curator, Bass Collection in Bus. History, 1955-72. Served as col. O.R.C., AUS, 1941-46; ETO. Mem. Res. Officers Assn. U.S., Acad. Mgmt. (founding fellow, pres. 1955), Soc. Advanced Mgmt., Am. Econ. Assn., Indsl. Relations Research Assn., Phi Beta Kappa (hon.), Theta Chi, Delta Sigma Pi, Beta Gamma Sigma. Mason Clubs: Faculty (Norman, Okla.); Cosmos (Washington). Author: The Petroleum Industry, 1940; The Management of Men, 1948. Editor: On the Contracts of Merchants, 1966. Home: Norman, Okla. Died Feb. 5, 1979.

SHUMLIN, HERMAN, play producer and dir.; b. Atwood, Colo., Dec. 6, 1898; s. George and Rebecca (Slavin) S.; ed. grammar sch. and 1 year in high sch.; m. Diana. Reporter on N.Y. Clipper, theatrical weekly, 1921-24; motion picture editor for Billboard, 1924-25; theatrical press agent and business mgr., 1925-27; began producing plays, 1927, producing and directing, 1930; asst. producer for Samuel Goldwyn, 1931; producer or producer-dir. numerous successful plays, including Grand Hotel, 1930, The Children's Hour, 1934, The Little Foxes, 1939, The Male Animal, The Corn Is Green, 1940, The High Ground, 1951, Dear Me, the Sky is Falling, 1963, Bicycle Ride to Nevada, 1963, Soldiers, 1968, Transfers, 1970, Flowers, 1974; co-producer Daphne Laureola, 1950, Inherit the Wind, 1955; dir. motion pictures Watch on the Rhine, 1943, Confidential Agent, 1945; staged Tall Story (N.Y. Theatre), 1959; staged and produced Only in America, 1959, The Deputy, 1963; Bicycle Ride to Nebr.; adapted and directed Spofford, 1968. Secretary League New York Theaters. Recipient Tony award for prodn. of The Deputy, 1963. Address: New York, N.Y. Died June 14, 1979.

SHUMWAY, HARRY IRVING (SHUM'WA), writer; b. Naugatuck, Conn., Oct. 26, 1883; s. David King, Jr., and Mary Abbie (Thayer) S.; prep. edn., pub. schs., Boston, Mass.; student Art Students' League, N.Y. City, and 47 Workshop, Harvard; m. Letitia Frances Valentine, July 30, 1910; 1 dau., Hope Iris. In art dept., Doubleday, Page & Co., N.Y. City, 1902-03; engaged in business until 1917; mem. editorial staff House Beautiful, Boston, 1917-20, Youth's Companion, 1924-26; gov. Youth's Companion lab., 1925-26. Republican. Conglist. Mason. Author numerous books since 1918; latest publ.: Bernard M. Baruch, 1946. Contbr. to nat. mags. Home: Bridgewater, Mass. *

SHURCLIFF, SIDNEY NICHOLS, landscape architect; b. Boston, Mar. 24, 1906; s. Arthur Asahel and Margaret Homer (Nichols) S.; A.B. magna cum laude, Harvard U., 1927, student Sch. Landscape Architecture, 1927-28, 29-30; m. Katharine Noyes Balch, June 28, 1935; 1 foster son, James C. Heigham. Assisted Restoration of Williamsburg, Va., 1928-40; landscape architect, town planner, 1930—; partner Shurcliff and Merrill; prepared town plans for Dedham, Falmouth, Sherborn, Randolph, Marion, Mattapoisett, Needham, Mass.; adviser Boston Park Dept., Met. Dist. Commn. of Mass., 1930-81, also colls., univs., instns.; prepared recreation plan for Taiwan, 1971. Mem. adv. com. Trustees of Reservations (Mass.), 1963—; mem., sec. Commonwealth of Mass. Art Commn., 1954-77. Served as lt. comdr. USNR, 1942-45. Fellow Am. Soc. Landscape Architects (v.p. 1952-54); mem. Am. Inst. Planners, Internat. Fedn. Landscape Architects (pres. 1958-62), N.A.D. (asso.), Gore Place Soc. (gov.). Clubs: St. Botolph, Harvard Travellers, Veteran Motor Car of Am. (Boston); Country (Brookline, Mass.). Author: Jungle Islands, 1929; Upon Road Argilla, 1958; The Day it Rained Fish, 1977; Roughing It in Roughwood, 1979; contbr. to mags. Home: Ipswich, Mass. Died Jan. 19, 1981.

SHURE, RALPH DEANE, composer; b. Chillisquaque, Pa., May 31, 1885; s. George Brenton and Mary Eva (Becht) S.; Mus.B., Oberlin Coll., 1907; Mus.D., Am. U., 1953, organ and compostion with D. Felix Draeseke and Dr. Alex. Wolff, Dresden, Germany, 1912-13; composition with De Blois Rowe, London, Eng., 1915; m. Hazel E. Towne, Apr. 7, 1909; children—Ralph George, Mary Bertha. Dir. music Central, U. of Ia., 1907- 09, Clarendon (Tex.) Coll., 1909-19, State Tchrs. Coll., Indiana, Pa. 1919-21, Am. U. Washington, 1921-25, Mt. Vernon Pl. M.E. Ch., Washington, 1921—, now minister music emeritus. Chapel named in his honor. Mem. Friends of Music in Library of Congress. Washington Composers Club (pres.) A.S.C.A.P. Methodist. Composer: Through Palestine (suite for organ), 1925; Lyric Washington (piano), 1926; Symphony No. 2, Circles of Washington, played by Nat. Symphony Orch., 1935; Berkie Symphony No. 3, played by Nat. Symphony Orch., 1937; American Symphony No. 4, played by Rochester Orch., 1938; Choric Symphony No. 5, played by Harrisburg (Pa.) Symphony Orch., 1938; Symphony No. 6, played by Marine Symphony Orch., 1939; Flax Spinner, played by NBC Symphony Orch., 1941; Logan Circle, played by Stokowski Youth Orch., 1940; Chesapeake Suite for English Horn and Strings, played by Nat. Gallery Orch., 1952; Twelve Disciples of Christ (organ), 1966 (world premier Nat. Gallery of Art Symphony Orch. 1968); Nativity Carol and the Galilean Easter Carol (sung on world-wide radio broadcast by Mormon Tabernacle Choir, The Heldeberg Coll. Choir, S. Africa, Tokyo Coll. Choir, Japan, also Voice of Am. in France, The Netherlands, Germany); Setting of Palm 121 (World premiere, massed choirs Washington 1973); Circles of Washington, 1975; This is America, 1975. Pub. over 150 compositions for organ, piano and voice. Home: Takoma Park MD. *

SHURLOCK, GEOFFREY MANWARING, motion picture exec.; b. Liverpool, Eng., Aug. 10, 1894; s. Charles and Frances (Hallawell) S.; brought to U.S., 1901, naturalized, 1930; ed. pvt. schs. Lit. sec. to author Rupert Hughes, 1922-26; with Paramount Pictures, 1926-32, successively story reader, asst. to v.p. charge prodn., studio scenario editor, exec. charge fgn. lang. prodns., staff scenario dept.; mem. studio relations com. Motion Picture Assn., 1932-34, asst. to dir. Prodn. Code Adminstrn., 1934-54, acting head, 1941-42, adminstr. Prodn. Code Adminstrn., 1954-70. Mem. Motion Picture Assn. Am. Episcopalian. Address: Los Angeles, Calif. Died Apr. 26, 1976. Interred Hollywood Memorial Park Cemetery, Hollywood, Calif.

SHUSTER, GEORGE NAUMAN, coll. adminstr., author; b. Lancaster, Wis., Aug. 27, 1894; s. Anthony and Elizabeth (Nauman) S.; A.B., U. Notre Dame, 1915, A.M., 1920; Certificat d'Aptitude, U. Poitiers, France, 1919; grad. study Columbia, 1925-26, Ph.D., 1940, LL.D., 1954; LL.D., St. Thomas Coll., 1950; Mus.D., N.Y. Coll. Music, 1954; Litt.D., Jewish Theol. Sem., 1956. Loyola U., 1957; L.H.D., Dropsie Coll., 1957; Ph.D. honoris causa, U. Freiburg, 1957; LL.D., Manhattan Coll., 1958; Litt.D., Seton Hill Coll., 1958; En.d. U., U. Free Berlin, 1958; LL.D., L.I. U., 1960, Stonehill Coll., 1964; LL.D., St. Mary's Coll., 1965; L.H.D., Hunter Coll., 1960, Mundelein Coll., 1966, Ind. U., Bloomington, Ind., 1968; m. Doris Parks Cunningham, June 25, 1924; 1 son, Robert George. Head dept. English, U. Notre Dame, 1920-24; instr. Eng., Bklyn. (N.Y.) Poly. Inst., 1924-25; prof. English, St. Joseph's Coll. for Women, Brooklyn, 1924-35; asso. editor The Commonweal, 1925-29, managing editor, 1929-37, fellow Social Sci. Research Council, Columbia, 1937-39; dean and acting pres., Hunter Coll., N.Y., 1939-40, pres., 1940-60; asst. to pres. Notre Dame U., 1961-71, prof. emeritus English, South Bend campus, 1971-77; cons. Center Study Democratic Instns. Dir. Ency. Britannica Ednl. Corp., Szabo Foods, Inc. Oberlaender Trust fellow in Germany, 1932. Mem. gen. adv. com., Div. Cultural Relations, Dept. State, 1944-45; mem. Enemy Alien Bd. No. 2, New York, 1942-45. Chmn. Historical Commn. to Germany, War Dept., 1945; adviser, Am. delegation, London Conf. on Internat. Edn., 1945; del., UNESCO Conf., Paris, 1946, 1958; U.S. rep. to exec. bd. UNESCO 1958-64. Mem. U. Chicago Commn. on the Freedom of the Press, 1944-47. Chmn. Com. on Discrimination in the Nation's Capitol, 1947; chmn. bd. trustees, Inst. Internat. Edn., 1948-51; trustee U. Notre Dame, 1961-77; Land Commr. for Bavaria, 1950-51. Pres. Pestalozzi Found., 1955; dir. Fund for Republic; dir. Carnegie Endowment Internat. Peace, 1954-64, hon. dir., 1964-77. Served as sgt. Intelligence Sect., U.S. Army, World War I. Recipient Butler medal. Columbia, 1954; Pax Christi award St. John's U., 1965; decorated Chevalier, Legion of Honor, 1955; Great Gold Medal of Honor (Austrian Republic); Knight Commander's Cross of Order of Merit (Germany); Laetare medal, U. Notre Dame, 1960. Roman Cath. Club: Century. Author: The Catholic Spirit in Modern English Literature, 1922; The Hill of Happiness, 1926; The Germans, 1932; Strong Man Rules, 1934; Like A Mighty Army, 1935; Brother Flo, 1938; Look Away, 1939; The English Ode-From Milton to Keats, 1939; A Short History of Germany, 1944; Cultural Cooperation and the Peace, 1952; Religion Behind the Iron Curtain, 1954; In Silence I Speak, 1956; Education and Moral Wisdom, 1960; The Ground I Walked On, 1961; UNESCO, 1963; Catholic Education in a Changing World, 1967. Author, co-author, translator or editor numerous books, 1922-77. Editor: Freedom and Authority in the West, 1967; bd. editors Ency. Brit., 1959-68. Home: South Bend, Ind. Died Jan. 25, 1977.

SIAS, AZARIAH BOODY, educator; b. Spencerport, N.Y., Jan. 2, 1880; s. Daniel Boody and Lucy Hebarts (Burger) S.; Ph.B., U. Rochester, 1903, A.M. 1922; Ph.D., Stanford, 1926; m. Grace Mary Furbish, Aug. 31, 1904; 1 son, Charles Robert. Tchr. in dist. sch., 1899; tchr. English, Cook Acad., Montour Falls, N.Y., 1903-04, East High Sch., Rochester, N.Y., 1904-05; tchr. English and pub. speaking West High Sch., Rochester 1905-13, head of English dept., 1913-20, vice prin., 1917-24; asst. in sch. adminstrn. Stanford, 1925-26; prof. edn. Ohio U., 1926-31, prof. sch. adminstrn. and dir. tchr. tng., 1931-47, prof. emeritus of sch. adminstrn., 1947—; prof. Sch. Adminstrn., Ohio State U., summers 1926, 38; prof. Sch. Adminstrn., U. Fla., summer 1941. Pres., Athens (O.) Community Chest Bd. 1936-37, 39-40. Mem. SSS Bd., Athens County, O., 1943-47. Mem. tech. adv. group Ohio Sch. Survey Commn., also Nat. Survey Sch. Finance, 1932. Trustee Nat. Soc. S.A.R. (pres. Ohio soc., 1943-44). Fellow Inst. Am. Genealogy (certificate of merit 1954); mem. A.A.U.P. (pres. chpt. 1942-43), N.E.A., Ohio Edn. Assn., Nat. Soc. Study Edn., N.Y. State Assn. Tchrs. English (pres. 1917-19), Central Fla. Fedn. Arts and Scis. (charter), Phi Beta Kappa, Phi Delta Kappa, Alpha Delta Phi. Presbyn. (elder). Club: University (Winter Park, Fla.). Author: The Sias Family in America, 1677-1952, vol. 1, 1953, vol. II supplement, 1958, vol. III, 1968. Home: Orlando FL. *

SIBERT, FRANKLIN CUMMINGS (SI'BERT), army officer; b. Bowling Green, Ky., Jan. 3, 1891; s. Maj. Gen. William Luther and Mary Elizabeth (Cummings) S.; B.S., U.S. Mil. Acad., 1912; grad. Inf. Sch. advanced course, 1924, Command and Gen. Staff Sch., 1925, War Coll., 1929; m. Helen Mildred Rogers, Mar. 4, 1913; children—Franklin Rogers (officer, U.S. Army), Kathryn Mary (wife of Ret. Gen. Bruce Palmer, Jr., U.S. Army). Commd. 2d lt., U.S. Army, 1912; promoted through grades to maj. gen. (temp.), 1942; staff Gen. Joseph W. Stilwell, China-Burma-India, and participated in retreat from Burma, 1942; comd. 6th Inf. Div., participated in two campaigns on New Guinea, 1942-44; comdg. X Army Corps, 1944-46, participated in Philippine campaign, ret., 1946. Decorated Victory Medal with 4 bronze stars, Army of Occupation of Germany, Mexican Border Service, Am. Defense Service, European-Africa-Middle Eastern Campaign, Am. Campaign medals, Asiatic-Pacific Campaign Medal with 4 bronze stars, Legion of Merit, D.S.M., Bronze Star (medal), Silver Star, Philippine Liberation Medal with 2 bronze stars. Home: Fort Walton Beach, Fla. Died June 24, 1980.

SIBLEY, SHERMER LEE, utilitiy exec.; b. Oakland, Cal., Sept. 24, 1913; s. Edward F. and Julia F. (Moll); B.S. in Elec. Engring., U. Calif., Berkeley, 1936; m. Mary C. Horwinski, May 2, 1942; children—Peter E., Patricia Allen, Jeffrey. With Pacific Gas and Electric Co., San Francisco, 1936-76, v.p., gen. mgr., 1958-65, dir., 1963-76, pres., 1965-72, chief exec. officer, 1969-76, chmn. bd., 1972-76; chmn. bd., dir. Alta. and So. Gas Co., Ltd.; dir. Pacific Gas Transmission Co., Alta. Natural Gas Co., Gen. Motors Corp., Del Monte Corp., Stanford Research Inst. Mem. Bus. Council; vice chmn. Nat. Indsl. Pollution Control Council, 1973; mem. adv. council World Energy Conf., Detroit, 1971-74. Pres., United Way of Bay Area, 1967, chmn., 1968; mem. engring. adv. bd. Coll. Engring., U. Calif.; mem. adv. bd. Coll. Bus. Adminstrn., U. Santa Clara

(Calif.); chmn. No. Calif. council Invest-In-Am., 1974; nat. chmn. utility div. U.S. Savs. Bond Campaign, 1975-76. Bd. dirs. Mt. Zion Hosp. and Med. Center, Council Financial Aid to Edn., Calif. Council Environ. and Econ. Balance; vice chmn., bd. dirs. The Bay Area Council; mem. adv. council Grad. Sch. Bus., Stanford. Served with USAAF, 1941-45. Recipient Brotherhood award NCCJ, 1974. Mem. Am. (dir. 1961-65, adv. council 1966-69), Pacific Coast (dir. 1960-64, pres. 1963) gas assns., Edison Electric Inst. (chmn. 1975), Pacific Coast Elec. Assn. (dir. 1963-69), Electric Power Research Inst. (dir. 1972-74), Calif. C. of C. (dir. 1970-76), Tau Beta Pi, Eta Kappa Nu, Beta Gamma Sigma. Died July 16, 1976; interred B.C., Canada.

SICK, THEODORE ALFRED, life ins. exec.; b. Fontanelle, Nebr., Sept. 14, 1897; s. Christian and Mary A. (Sprick) S.; grad. Lincoln Sch. Commerce, 1916; m. Mary J. Patton, Dec. 25, 1920; 1 dau., Sandra Nadine. Began as clk. Security Mut. Life Ins. Co., Lincoln, Nebr., 1917, cashier, 1920-27, v.p., treas., 1928-42, dir., 1937-78, pres., 1943-63, chmn., 1963-78, dir. 1st Nat. Bank & Trust Co. Mem. County Real Estate Classification and Reappraisal Com., 1951; mem. Victory Loan drives, World War II; past pres. Lincoln Community Chest. Trustee, chmn. Cooper Found.; chmn. U. Nebr. Found.; trustee Tabitha Home. Recipient Builder's award U. Nebr., Distinguished Service medal Kiwanis Club. Mem. Am. Life Conv. (investment law com. 1944-45, chmn. resolutions com. 1947, mem. exec. com., bd. regents of life officers investment seminar, 1948, mem. program com. 1950-53, pres. 1952-53), Lincoln Jr. (past pres.), Lincoln Sr. (past pres.) chambers commerce, Ins. Fedn. Nebr. (past pres.), Ins. Inst. Nebr. (past pres.), Life Ins. Assn. Am. (dir., past chmn.). Conglist. Mason (Shriner). Club: University Country (past pres.) (Lincoln). Home: Lincoln, Nebr. Died Aug. 7, 1978.

SIEGEL, ELI, poet; b. Dvinsk, Latvia, Aug. 16, 1902; s. Mendel and Sarah (Einhorn) S.; came to U.S., 1905, naturalized, 1912; student Balt. City Coll., 1916-19; m. Martha Baird, Oct. 7, 1944. Contbr. Balt. Am., 1925; writer, lectr., conductor poetry readings, N.Y.C., 1926-36; book reviewer Scribner's, 1931-35; founder, 1940, since tchr. Aesthetic Realism; known for shortest poem in world, I-/Why?, 1925. Author: The Scientific Criticism, 1923; Hot Afternoons Have Been in Montana (Nation Poetry prize 1925), 1925; The Aesthetic Method in Self-Conflict, 1946; Is Beauty the Making One of Opposites, 1955; Williams' Poetry Talked About, 1964; James and the Children: A Consideration of Henry James's The Turn of the Screw, 1968; Hail, American Development, 1968; The Williams-Siegel Documentary, 1970; Goodbye Profit System, 1970; Children's Guide to Parents and Other Matters, 1971; Damned Welcome: Aesthetic Realism Maxims, 1972; The Frances Sanders Lesson and Two Related Works, 1974; The Opposites Class, 1975. Address: New York, N.Y. Died Nov. 8, 1978; buried Greenwood Cemetery, Bklyn.

SIEGEL, SEYMOUR NATHANIEL, radio exec.; b. N.Y.C., July 29, 1908; s. Isaac and Ann (Natelson) S.; B.S., U. Pa., 1929; M.A., Columbia, 1932; LL.D., Emerson Coll., 1976; m. Nancy Davids, Oct. 13, 1943; (div.); m. 2d, Frances Ladd, Dec. 21, 1959; stepchildren—John Hanan, Sarah Lavigne, Deborah Hanan. Chief statistician Morris & Smith, N.Y.C., 1929-33; program dir. radio sta. WNYC, N.Y.C., 1934-47; lectr. radio broadcasting CCNY, 1938-41; dir. radio communications, N.Y.C., 1947-71; vis. prof. mass communications Emerson Coll., Boston, 1971-78; adj. prof. tele communications City U. N.Y., 1971-78, univ. dean for ednl. tech., 1975-78; dir. UHF TV Sta. WNYC-TV; chmn. Internat. Broadcasting Council. Am. del. Universite Radiophonique Internationale, Paris, 1953, 55; Am. rep., v.p. Gen. Assembly Prix Italia, Palermo, Italy, 1953, pres., 1955, v.p., Florence, 1974; Mem. broadcasters adv. council to Pres. of U.S.; dir. Civil Def. Communications N.Y.C.; mem. Am. consultative com. French Broadcasting System; chmn. Mayor's Com. on Living Music, N.Y.C.; mem. Mayor's Task Force on Future of Sta. WNYC-AM-TV, 1976, Mayor's Task Force on CATV and Telecommunications. Pres., Broadcasting Found. Am. Bd. dirs. Community Council N.Y. Served as comdr. U.S. Navy, 1941-46; capt. USNR ret. Recipient Hearst Pub. Service Silver Medal award; officer Order of Oranje-Nassau (Netherlands), 1953; chevalier Legion of Honor, 1953; English Speaking Union Award for Internat. Understanding, 1953. Mem. Radio Pioneers, Radio and TV Execs. Soc., Radio Corrs. Assn., Radio, TV and Newsreel Working Press Assn., Nat. Assn. Ednl. Broadcasters (past pres.), Supply Corps Officers Assn. (pres. 1955-56), Joint Com. Ednl. Television, Am. Statis. Assn., Aviation Commandry, Naval Order U.S., Tau Epsilon Phi, Theta Alpha Phi. Clubs: Nat. Republican; Bohemians, Lotos, Overseas Press. Contbr. articles to profl. jours. Home: Southbury, Conn. Died July 15, 1978.

SIEMENS, CORNELIUS HENRY, coll. pres.; b. Ufa, Russia, Jan. 15, 1911; s. Kornelius Henry and Katherine (Dyck) S.; A.B., U. Cal., 1933, A.M., 1937, Ph.D., 1939, LL.D., 1964, 75; m. Olga Marie Gromer, June 16, 1936; children—Ronald Cornelius, Joan (Mrs. Laurence Fox), Mark Cornelius. Came to U.S., 1913, naturalized, 1926. Instr., Bakersfield (Cal.) Jr. Coll., 1934-36; math. fellowship U. Cal., 1936-38; sci. supr. Berkeley pub. schs., 1938-39; prof. edn. San Diego State Coll., 1939-41, U. Cal., 1941-46; West Coast cons. Dept. Commerce, 1941-46; pres. Compton Coll., 1946-50; lectr. U. Cal., summer, 1947; prof. U. So. Cal., summer 1948, 49; pres. Humboldt State U., Arcata, Cal., 1950-73, Linfield Coll., 1974-75; prof. edn. U. Hawaii, summer 1957, U. B.C., summer 1964. Chmn. Cal. com. for study of edn., sub-com. on math., 1946-50. U.S. Dept. State study tour to Poland, 1964. Vice pres. Redwood region Boy Scouts Am., from 1961. Mem. Cal. Constn. Revision Commn., 1966-70. Regent Berkeley Bapt. Div. Sch. Mem. Western Coll. Assn. (chmn. research com. 1955-58), Phi Beta Kappa, Phi Delta Kappa, Pi Mu Epsilon. Rotarian (pres. 1958-59). Author: Aeronautics Workbook, 1942; aviation corr. courses pub. by U.S. Armed Forces Inst.; edn., math., and sci. corr. courses. U. Cal. Extension. Home: Arcata, Calif. Died 1978.

SIEMS, LEONARD A. A., fin. cons. co. exec.; b. Balt., Aug. 2, 1896; s. John A. and Anna (Kohlhepp) S.; student Johns Hopkins, 1916-17; m. Marie Wekenman, Sept. 13, 1924; 1 son, Leonard A. Asst. examiner FRS, Washington, 1923-28, examiner, 1928-32, chief examiner, field orgn., 1933-38; v.p. Fidelity Trust Co., Balt., 1943-54, dir., 1945-54, Mem. exec. com., 1951-54; sr. v.p. Md. Nat. Bank, Balt., 1954-64, dir., 1963-67; pres. Siems Asso., Inc., Balt., 1964-68; vice chmn. bd. Suburban Trust Co., Hyattsville, Md., 1968-73; pres. Siems, Hammond & Assos. Inc., 1973-78; chmn. bd., chief exec. bd. Nat. City Bank, Balt.; dir. Chesapeake Life Ins. Co., Balt. Chmn., Md. Indsl. Devel. Financing Authority, 1964-70; mem., pres. CSC, 1946-62; mem. Md. Mental Hygiene Bd. Rev., 1948-52; treas. City Balt., 1962-63; mem. adv. bd. Baltimore County Redevel. Commn., 1958-62; co-chmn. Radio Free Europe Fund, 1959-60; regional chmn. NCCJ, 1959-62; treas. Md. chpt. March of Dimes, 1950-60. Bd. dirs. Luth. Hosp. of Md. Served with USNR, World War I. Mem. Navy League (past pres. Balt. council), English Speaking Union, Hist. Soc. Md. Clubs: Reciprocity of Balt., Civitan, Baltimore Country, Center, Maryland, Merchants. Home: Baltimore, Md. Died Mar. 6, 1978.

SIEVERS, HARRY JOSEPH, univ. dean; b. Bklyn., Nov. 14, 1920; s. Harry Sterling and Albertina Elizabeth (Fleck) S.; student Fordham U., 1941-43; A.B., Loyola U. at Chgo., 1945, M.A., 1947; Ph.L., West Baden Coll. (Ind.), 1947; Ph.D., Georgetown U., 1950. Mem. S.J.; instr. Canisius Coll., Buffalo, 1947-48; asst. prof., chmn. Bellarmine Coll., Plattsburgh, N.Y., 1956-64; asso. prof., chmn. history dept. Fordham U., Shrub Oak campus, 1966-69, asso. prof. Rose Hill Campus, Bronx, 1969-70, prof., chmn. dept., 1971-72, dean Grad. Sch., dean of faculty, from 1972. Hist. cons. for Venezuela in boundary dispute between British Guiana and Venezuela. Recipient Author of Year award Ind. U., 1953, Simon Bolivar award Venezuela, 1963. Mem. Am. Hist. Assn. (life), Orgn. Am. Historians (life), Am. Cath. Hist. Assn., Ind. Hist. Soc., Am. Jesuit Hist. Conf.(exec. sec.), Phi Alpha Theta. Author: Biography of Pres. Benajamin Harrison, 3 vols., 1952-68. Editor: Harrison, 1969, McKinley, 1970, both Presdl. Chronologies Series; Six Empire State Presidents, 1974. Asst. editor: America, 1967-69. Address: Bronx, N.Y. Deceased.

SIFTON, CLIFFORD, barrister; b. Brandon, Man., Can., Aug. 3, 1893; s. Sir Clifford and Lady Elizabeth (Burrows) S.; student Ottawa Collegiate Inst.; B.A., U. Toronto, 1915; student Osgoode Hall, 1925-27; m. Doris Margaret Greene, May 5, 1920 (dec.); children—Elizabeth Ann Jane (Mrs. Ernest Llewllyn Gibson Smith, Michael Clifford; m. 2d, Mrs. Elizabeth Crispo, Apr. 13, 1963. Read law Starr, Spence, Fraser & Hall, 1925-27; called to Ont. bar, 1927; Queen's counsel; chmn. bd. Armadale Co. Ltd., Armadale Pubs. Ltd. (Saskatoon Star-Phoenix), Regina Leader-Post, Armadale Enterprises Ltd., Armadale Communications Ltd. (CKCK-TV Regina, CKCK Regina, CKRC Winnipeg, CKOC Hamilton). Mem. Internat. Press Inst., 1962-71, hon. chmn., 1971-76. Life dir. Royal Agrl. Winter Fair; 1st chmn. North York Gen. Hosp., 1961-69, hon. chmn., 1969-76; an incorporator, council mem., hon. life pres. Can. Hunter Improvement Soc.; vice chmn. Quetico Found. Served from lt. to maj. Canadian F.A., CEF, 1914-19. Decorated Distinguished Service Order. Mem. Harcourt Lodge, Delta Kappa Epsilon. Mason. Clubs: Canadian; Rosedale Golf; Brockville Golf and Country, Eglinton Hunt; Cricket, Skating and Curling, Toronto and North York Hunt (joint master, hon. dir.), University (hon.). Home: Toronto, Ont., Canada. Died Apr. 1976.

SIGMON, RICHARD ROLAND, lawyer; b. Roanoke, Va., Nov. 30, 1924; s. Leonard E. and Lida (Tapley) S.; student U. Chgo., 1947-49, U. Houston Law Sch., 1953-54; LL.B., U. Md., 1957; LL.M., George Washington U., 1959; m. Maha Berniece Finley, Oct. 18, 1952; 1 son by previous marriage, Kurt Derek. Admitted to Md. bar, 1957, D.C. bar, 1966, also U.S. Supreme Ct.; atty. ICC, 1957-59; asst. gen. counsel Am. Trucking Assns. Inc., 1959-65; pvt. practice, Washington, 1965-78; mem. firm Rice, Carpenter and Carraway, 1969-78. Mem. nat. panel arbitrators Am. Arbitration Assn., 1969-78; lectr. transp. Southeastern U., Washington, 1964-66. Served with USNR, 1943-46, 50-52. Smithsonian asso., 1968-78. Fellow Internat. Oceanographic Found.; mem. Am., D.C. bar assns., Assn. ICC Practitioners (pres., chmn. exec. com. 1968-69, exec. com. 1966-71), Motor Carriers Lawyers Assn., Am. Judicature Soc., World Peace Through Law Center, Seldon Soc. Editor: Miller's Law of Freight Loss and Damage Claims, 3d edit., 1967. Home: Hyattsville, Md. Died Feb. 17, 1978; cremated.

SILING, PHILIP FRANCIS, radio engr.; b. East Orange, N.J., Aug. 14, 1897; s. William L. and Lillian (Fradenburgh) S.; Ph.B. cum laude, Yale, 1917; m. Grace R. Post, June 5, 1921; 1 dau., Jeanne B. (Mrs. Earl Palmer). Engr., AT&T, 1917-29; outside plant engr. ITT, 1929-31, supt. materials and supplies for S. Am., Buenos Aires, 1931-33; asst. dep. adminstr. NRA, 1933-35; asst. chief Internat. div. FCC, 1935-41, chief, 1941-43, asst. chief engr. in charge broadcasting, 1943-44; dir. RCA Frequency Bur., 1944-63; radio cons., 1963-79; mem. U.S. del. Internat. Radio Conf., Rio de Janeiro, 1945, Bermuda, 1945, Moscow, 1946, Atlantic City, 1947, Stockholm, 1948, D.C., 1949, Geneva, 1951, 59, Buenos Aires, 1952; mem. Panel Radio Experts, Geneva, 1961, 63. Fellow I.E.E.E.; mem. Radio Pioneers, Armed Forces Communications Assn., Sigma Xi. Mason. Clubs: Rockefeller Luncheon, Yale (N.Y.C.); Cosmos, Washington Golf and Country (Washington); Civitan (pres. Arlington, Va. 1964-65). Home: Arlington, Va. Died July 11, 1979; buried National Meml. Park, Falls Church, Va.

SILLCOX, LEWIS KETCHAM, educator; b. Germantown, Pa., Apr. 30, 1886; s. George Washington and Georgiana (Parker) S.; student Trinity Sch., N.Y. and L'Ecole Polytechnique, Brussels, 1903; D.Sc., Clarkson Coll., 1932; D.Eng., Cumberland U., 1941, Purdue U., 1951; LL.D., Syracuse U., 1948, Queen's U., 1955; D.H.L., Norwich U., 1963; m. Edna May Harris, Sept. 14, 1918 (dec. Feb. 1961); children—Elsie Winifred (Mrs. Donald G. Bridge), Esther Harris (Mrs. Stanley L. Whittemore), Enid Burnham (Mrs. Peter Darlington), Edith May (Mrs. Francis A. Kelly), Robert Lewis. Machinist apprentice N.Y.C. & H.R. R.R., High Bridge, N.Y., 1903-07; foundry apprentice McSherry Mfg. Co., Middletown, O., 1907-09; shop. engr. Canadian Car & Foundry Co., Montreal, Que., Can., 1909-12; mech. engr. Canadian No. Ry., Toronto, Ont., 1912-16; mech. engr. I.C. R.R., 1916-18; gen. supt. motive power C.,M. & St.P. Ry., Chgo., 1918-27; asst. to pres., exec. v.p., vice chmn. bd. N.Y. Air Brake Co., N.Y.C., 1927-59; dir. Office of Transp., Exec. Dept. State of N.Y., Albany, 1959-60; prof., lectr. engring. Purdue U., 1946—; lectr. transp. various colls., univs. Chmn. mech. engring. adv. com. Princeton, 1938-58; vis. com. dept. mech. engring. Mass. Inst. Tech., 1955-57; trustee, gen. chmn. vis. coms. Norwich U.; hon. curator Baker Library, Harvard, 1935—; mem. Alfred Noble Joint Prize Com. Ret. trustee Hosp. Rev. and Planning Council Central N.Y., Inc.; mem. adv. bd. Salvation Army. Recipient gold medals Am. Soc. M.E., Inst. Mech. Engrs., George Washington Honor medal, 1954, Freedoms Found. award, 1955. Fellow Inst. Mech. Engrs., I.E.E.E., A.A.A.S.; hon. mem. Am. Soc. M.E., A.R.E.A., Engring. Inst. Can.; mem. Am. Soc. C.E. (life, past pres.), Am. Inst. Mining and Metall. Engrs. (life), other nat., state, local profl. engring. socs., Sigma Xi, Pi Tau Sigma, Tau Beta Pi. Episcopalian. Mason (32 deg., K.T., Shriner). Clubs: Harvard (Boston); University (N.Y.C., Chgo. and Toronto, Can.); Black River Valley (Watertown, N.Y.); Seigniory (Can.). Author: Mastering Momentum, 1941. Contbr. to tech. publs. Home: Watertown NY. *

SILTZBACH, LOUIS ELLIOTT, physician, educator; b. N.Y.C., May 27, 1906; s. Jacob and Rose (Kreisberg) S.; student Coll. City N.Y., 1922-23, Columbia, 1923-25; M.D., L.I. Med. Coll., 1929; postgrad. U. Vienna, 1932-33. Intern Lebanon Hosp., N.Y.C., 1929-31, Montefiore Hosp., N.Y.C., 1931-32; pvt. practice medicine, 1934-80; clin. prof. medicine emeritus head Sarcoidosis Lab., Mt. Sinai Sch. Medicine of City U. N.Y., 1966-80; cons. physician Mt. Sinai Hosp., Rockefeller U.; attending physician pulmonary div. Montefiore Hosp. Exec. sec. Internat. Com. on Sarcoidosis. Nathan Hofmeimer Research fellow, 1940-44; research grantee NIH, 1958-80. Diplomate Am. Bd. Internal Medicine. Mem. N.Y. Acad. Medicine, Harvey Soc., Am. Thoracic Soc., AAAS, N.Y. Acad. Scis., Am. Coll. Chest Physicians, Royal Soc. Medicine. Contbr. textbooks. Helped to perfect skin test for sarcoidosis. Home: New York, N.Y. Died Apr. 22, 1980.

SILVER, SAMUEL, educator; b. Phila., Feb. 25, 1915; s. Boris and Molly (Agrin) S.; A.B., Temple U., 1935, M.A., 1937, D.Sc. (hon.), 1963; Ph.D., Mass. Inst. Tech., 1940; m. Marjorie Euster, Dec. 28, 1938; children—Daniel Ben, Deborah Ruth. Instr., then asst. prof. physics U. Okla., 1941-43; with radiation lab. Mass. Inst. Tech., 1943-46; physicist Naval Research Lab., 1946-47; asso. prof., prof. elec. engring. U. Calif., Berkeley, 1947-52, prof. engring. sci., 1952-76, dir. Electronics Research Lab., 1956-60, dir. Space Scis.

Lab., 1960-70. John Simon Guggenheim fellow, 1953, 60. Fellow I.E.E.E., Am. Geophys. Union, Am. Phys. Soc.; mem. Nat. Acad. Engring., Am. Meteorol. Soc., Internat. Sci. Radio Union (pres. 1966-69, hon. pres. 1972-76, commn. chmn. 1953-60), Sigma Xi. Jewish. Editor: Microwave Antenna Theory and Design, vol. 12, Mass. Inst. Tech. Radiation Lab. Tech. series, 1948; Radio Waves and Circuits, U.R.S.I. Monograph, 1963; co-editor Progress in Radio Science, vol. 8, Space Radio Research, 1964. Home: Walnut Creek, Calif. Died Nov. 5, 1976.

SILVERBERG, LORENCE A., retail exec.; b. Sioux City, Iowa, June 19, 1914; s. Abraham and Blanche (Magasiner) S.; A.A., U. Minn., 1934; m. Lillian Baker, June 14, 1936; children—Barry J., Cheri Lou (Mrs. Robin Fern), Keith C. Mgr. store Silverberg Bros., Sioux City, Ia., 1934-42; wholesale clothing distbr., 1943-46; mfrs. rep. William Schwartz & Co., Phila., 1946-50; pres. Coombs Mfg. Co., Mpls., 1950-62; chmn. Asso. Apparel Industries, N.Y.C., 1962-64; dir. restaurants concessions McCrory-McLellan-Green Stores, York, Pa., 1964-66, pres., 1966-68; exec. v.p. S. Klein Dept. Stores, N.Y.C., 1968-72; chmn. bd. Leeds Travelwear, N.Y.C., 1972; chief operating officer, pres., chmn. bd. dirs. Kenton Corp., N.Y.C., 1972-74; pres. McCrory Stores, York, Pa., chmn. bd., chief exec. officer, 1977-80; exec. v.p. McCrory Corp., N.Y.C., 1974-77, pres., chief exec. officer, 1977-80, also dir.; exec. v.p. Rapid Am. Corp., pres., 1977-80. Served with AUS, 1942-43. Mem. Sigma Alpha Mu. Home: New York, N.Y. Died Sept. 19, 1980; buried Westchester Hills Cemetery, Hastings on Hudson, N.Y.

SILVERMAN, LOUIS LAZARE, educator; b. nr. city of Kovno, Lithuania, Apr. 21, 1884; s. Abraham and Fanny (Swig) S.; A.B., Harvard, 1905, A.M., 1907; Ph.D., Univ. of Mo., 1910; A.M. (hon.), Dartmouth, 1924; m. Sonia Paeff, June 17, 1912; children—Raphael Hillyer, Michelle (Mrs. Leonard A. Goldsmith), Fedora (Mrs. Seymour Bluhm). Instr. in math., U. of Mo., 1907-09; Cornell U., 1909-17; war work, Gen. Elec. Co., 1917-18; asst. prof. of mathematics, Dartmouth Coll., 1918-24, professor of mathematics, 1924-47, prof. of mathematics on the Chandler Found. since 1947. Visited Russiia in 1924 on invitation of Russian mathematicians; lecturer at universities of Moscow, Leningrad, Prague, Budapest, Mexico and at the Hebrew Univ. in Jerusalem. Hon. mem. Moscow Math. Soc. Mem. Am. Math. Soc., Math. Assn. of Am., Sigma Xi, Pi Lambda Phi, Phi Mu Alpha. Mem. Dartmouth Symphony Orchestra. Home: Hanover, N.H. *

SILVERMAN, OSCAR ANSELL, educator; b. Uniontown, Pa., Feb. 13, 1903; s. G. M. and Leah R. (Cohen) S.; student U. Pa., 1920-21; A.M., U. Wis., 1926; A.B., Yale, 1925, Ph.D., 1941; m. Margaret de Morinni, Aug. 25, 1932 (div. Sept. 1950); children—Clare, Ansell. Asst. in English, U. Wis., 1925-26; instr. English, U. Buffalo (now State U. N.Y. at Buffalo), 1926-28, asst. prof., asso. prof., English, 1932-42, prof. English, 1942-77, chmn. dept., 1956-63, also dir. libraries, dir. libraries emeritus, 1968; fellow Yale Grad. Sch., 1928-30; instr. English, Biarritz Am. U., France, 1945-46; vis. fellow Harvard, 1953-54; radio commentator weekly program on books, WBEN, Buffalo, 1940-44, WGR, Buffalo, 1944-46, WKBW, 1946-47. Mem. AAUP, Buffalo Fine Arts Acad., Phi Beta Kappa. Clubs: Grolier (N.Y.); Thursday (Buffalo). Editor: The Management of Universities (S.P. Capen), 1953; James Joyce Epiphanies, 1956. Contbr. articles and books reviews to publs. Home: Buffalo, N.Y. Died Mar. 26, 1977.

SILVERMAN, SHIRLEIGH, physicist; b. Balt., Jan. 12, 1907; s. Louis and Minerva (Kamens) S.; A.B. with honors, Johns Hopkins, 1927, Ph.D. in Physics, 1930; m. Florence Morris, Sept. 24, 1937; children—Ann M., Leigh Silverman Tischler, Lucy Silverman Ogburn. Instr. physics Johns Hopkins, 1930-34, mem. prin. staff, research physicist and supr. Applied Physics Lab., 1943-55; research physicist E.I. du Pont de Nemours & Co., 1934-43; lectr. Catholic U., 1955-59, research prof., 1959-69; dir. phys. scis. div. Office Naval Research, 1955-61, dir. naval research group, 1958-61, research dir., 1961-64; navy liaison for phys. scis. div. NRC, 1956-63; asso. dir. profl. and academic liaison Nat. Bur. Standards, Washington, 1964-74, cons., 1975-78. Fellow Am. Phys. Soc., Optical Soc. Am.; mem. Washington Acad. Scis., Washington Philosophy Soc., A.A.A.S., Royal Instn. London, Sigma Xi. Club: Cosmos (Washington). Home: Silver Spring, Md. Died Feb. 9, 1978.

SILVERT, KALMAN HIRSCH, educator; b. Bryn Mawr, Pa., Mar. 10, 1921; s. Henry Jacob and Ida (Levine) S.; B.A., U. Pa., 1942, M.A., 1947, Ph.D., 1948; Ph.D. (hon.), Dartmouth Coll., 1962. Instito de Condido Mendes, Rio de Janero, Brazil; m. Frieda Moskalik, July 24, 1942; children—Henry Morris, Benjamin Bela, Alexander Manuel. From asst. prof. to prof. polit. sci. Tulane U., 1948-60; prof. govt. Dartmouth Coll., 1960-67; asso. Am. Univs. Field Staff, 1955-60, research dir., 1960-68; program adviser Latic Am., Ford Found., 1967-76; prof. govt. N.Y. U., 1967-76, dir. Ibero-Am. Inst., 1967-74; vis. prof. U. Buenos Aires, 1958-59, Brandeis U., 1967, Harvard, 1964, U. Chile, 1966-67. Cons. Ford Found., 1959-61, Ency. Brit., 1964-67. Served with USAAF, 1942-45. Mem. Latin Am. Studies Assn. (pres. 1966-67), Com. for Latin Am. Relations, Council Fgn. Relations, Center Inter-Am. Relations (dir.). Democrat. Jewish. Author: A Study in Government: Guatemala, 1955; The Conflict Society, 1961; Chile Yesterday and Today, 1965; Nacionalismo y la politica del desarrollo, 1965; Man's Power, 1970; Education, Class and Nation, 1976; (with Leonard Reissman) The Reason for Democracy, 1977; Essays on Latin America, 1978; also monographs, articles. Editor, contbr.: Discussion at Bellagio, 1964; Expectant Peoples, 1963; Churches and States, 1968; Soc. Reality of Scientific Myth, 1969. Home: Norwich, Vt. Died June 15, 1976.

SIM, ALASTAIR, actor, producer; b. Oct. 9, 1900; s. Alexander and Isabella (McIntyre) S.; ed. U. Edinburgh, also hon. LL.D.; m. Naomi Plaskitt, 1932; 1 dau. Fulton lectr. elocution New Coll., Edinburgh, 1925-30; rector Edinburgh U., 1948-51; stage appearances include Othello, 1930, The Venetian, 1931-33; produced and/or played in Holy Isle, Mr. Bolfry, It Depends on What You Mean, Forrigan Reel, Dr. Angelus, The Anatomist, Mr. Gillie, The Brass Butterfly, Number 10, The Magistrate, The Jockey Club Stakes, Siege, A Private Matter, Dandy Dick, The Clandestine Marriage (all London); produced A Clean Kill; produced (with George Colle) and played in The Bargain; producer and played in Windfall; played in The Tempest, Too True to be Good, Peter Pan; motion picture appearances, 1934—. Club: Garrick. Address: Henley-on-Thames, England. Died Aug. 19, 1976.

SIMENSTAD, LIEN OTIS, physician and surgeon; b. Northwood, N.D., Sept. 26, 1900; s. Martin and Laura (Lien) S.; A.B., U. N.D., 1921; M.D., Rush Med. Coll., Chgo., 1924; m. Agnes Berget, Sept. 24, 1924 (dec. 1957); children—John Otis, Paul Otis; m. 2d, Ethel Kremser, Aug. 26, 1964. Intern, Ancker City and County Hosp., St. Paul, 1923-24; individual practice, Osceola, Wis., 1924-76; chief staff Ladd Meml. Hosp., 1960-76. Pres. Bank of Osceola, 1967-76. Chmn., Aero. Commn. Wis., 1959-61; mem. med. adv. panel FAA, 1959-76; commr. Joint Commn. on Accreditation Hosps., 1964-76. Mayor of Osceola, 1948-60, 62-76. Recipient Distinguished Service citation U. N.D., 1961. Fellow A.C.S., Internat. Coll. Surgeons, Am. Indsl. Physicians and Surgeons; mem. A.M.A. (ho. of dels. 1943-63, trustee 1963-76), Wis. Med. Soc. (pres. 1956-57, speaker ho. of dels. 1954-55), Nat. Flying Physicians Assn. (v.p. 1962-63, mem. bd. 1960-76), U. N.D. Alumni Assn. (pres. 1963-65), Quiet Birdmen. Republican. Methodist. Mason. Home: Osceola, Wis. Died Sept. 12, 1976; interred Mt. Hope Cemetery, Osceola.

SIMKIN, MEYER, musician; b. Phila., Dec. 27, 1905; s. Philip and Minna (Gorelick) S.; B.S. in Edn. cum laude, U. Pa., 1929, Mus.B., 1932; postgrad. Curtis Inst. Music, 1929-31, Combs Coll. Music, 1958; m. Celia Boudov, Aug. 9, 1942; children—Phillips M., Steffi L. 1st violinist Phila. Orch., 1930-73. Home: Philadelphia, Pa. Died Apr. 5, 1976.

SIMMONS, JOHN WILLIAM, mfg. co. exec.; b. Toledo, Aug. 12, 1919; s. Francis W. and Stella (Arnsman) S.; B.A., Williams Coll., 1941; grad. Advanced Mgmt. Program, Harvard, 1958; m. Paula Marie Johnston, Oct. 10, 1944; children—Lorraine (Mrs. John Tuohy), Carol, Paula (Mrs. Mark Butler), John William Jr. With Scott Paper Co., 1945-46; with Becton, Dickinson & Co., Rutherford, N.J., 1946-72, exec. v.p., chief ops. officer, dir., chmn. exec. com., mem. finance com., 1961-72; with Morton-Norwich Products, Inc., Chicago, 1972-80, pres., chief exec. officer, dir., chmn. exec. com., mem. fin. com., chmn. bd., 1976-80; chmn. bd., dir. Eaton Labs. P.R., Inc., Canadian Salt Co. Ltd.; vice chmn., dir. Rohm Pharma GmbH; dir. Noroma Produtos Quimicos Ltd. (Brazil), Williams (Hounslow) Ltd. (Eng.), Burlington Industries, Morton Bahamas Ltd.; adv. dir. Arkwright-Boston Ins. Co. Mem. Brazil-U.S. Bus. Council; governing mem. Orchestral Assn.; mem. citizens bd. U. Chgo.; trustee Am. Health Found., Rush-Presbyn.-St. Luke's Med. Center; bd. dirs. Lyric Opera of Chgo. Served to lt. USCGR, 1941-45. Named master knight Sovereign Mil. Order of Malta, 1962. Mem. Pharm. Mfrs. Assn. (dir.). Clubs: Arcola (N.J.) Country; Casino, Glen View, Mid-America, Chicago, Metropolitan, Commercial, The Plaza, Saddle and Cycle, Economic, Tower (Chgo.); Devon Yacht (East Hampton, N.Y.); Maidstone (L.I., N.Y.); Union League, Williams (N.Y.C.); Lyford Cay (Nassau, Bahamas). Home: Chicago, Ill. Died Apr. 1, 1981.

SIMMONS, WALTER EDWIN, retail co. exec.; b. Willard, O., Sept. 26, 1905; s. Louis E. and Julia (Simmermacher) S.; student Oberlin Coll., 1923-25; B.A. cum laude, U. Mich., 1927; m. Vera Janice Wallington, Aug. 6, 1932; 1 son, Walter Edwin II. With J.L. Hudson C., Detroit, 1928-70, sr. v.p., dir. mdsg., expansion, also corporate dir.; retired; dir. First Fed. Savs. Bank of Detroit; cons. devel. program Edison Inst., 1970. Mem. Detroit Better Bus. Bur. (chmn. bd., dir., exec. com.), Warden of Goldsmiths Hall London (asso.), Phi Beta Kappa. Presbyn. (trustee). Clubs: Country of Detroit, Detroit Athletic; Grosse Pointe (Mich.) Yacht. Home: Grosse Pointe Farms, Mich. Died Jan. 18, 1979.

SIMMONS, WILLIAM P., JR., lawyer; b. Jacksonville, Fla., July 1, 1910; A.B., U. Fla., also J.D.; m. Clara Mae Noble, June 22, 1935 (dec. Feb. 1967); m. 2d, Evaline R. Underwood, Feb. 24, 1968; 1 son, William N. Admitted to Fla. bar, 1934; mem. firm Shutts & Bowen. Mem. Fla. Jud. Council, 1958-62; pres. Crime Commn. Greater Miami, 1975-77. Trustee U. Fla. Found., 1953-72. Served to lt. col. AUS, 1941-46; brig. gen. ret. Fla. Army N.G., 1966. Fellow Am. Bar Found.; mem. Fla. Bar (bd. govs. 1961-65, pres. 1967-68), Am. (ho. dels. 1968-72), Dade County (pres. 1957-58) bar assns., Miami-Dade County C. of C. (pres. 1961-62), Phi Alpha Delta. Mem. Christian Ch. (elder). Address: Miami, Fla. Died June 12, 1978; interred mil. div. Woodlawn South, Miami, Fla.

SIMONDS, GEORGE PATTON, architect; b. Chattanooga, Apr. 1, 1905; s. Royal Ambrose and Angus (Patton) S.; A.B., U. Calif. at Berkeley, 1927, M.A., 1928; m. Edith Merle Strickland, Aug. 3, 1931; children—Jean Alden, Roberta Lynn, Ann Patton. Practice architecture, Hayward, Calif., 1932-38; designer Asso. Architects, Oakland, Calif., 1938; with U.S. Pub. Housing Authority, 1939-45, acting asst. dir. devel. region X, 1945; gen. partner firm Anderson & Simonds, Oakland, 1946-65, Anderson Simonds Dusel & Campini, Oakland, 1965-72; individual practice, 1972-77, ret.; mem. faculty U. Calif. at Berkeley, 1948-73, prof. architecture, 1957-73, prof. emeritus, 1973-78, asst. dean Coll. Environ. Design, 1969-71; adv. com. Earthquake Engring. Research Center, 1968-77; works include pub. schs., coll. bldgs. Pres. Calif. Bd. Archtl. Examiners, 1954; mem. engring. adv. group joint com. seismic safety Calif. Legislature, 1970-73; engring. adv. bd. Bay Convervation and Conservation Dist., 1970-77; commr. Hayward Pub. Housing Authority, 1946-50, Hayward Planning Commn., 1946-54; mem. Hayward Fine Arts Com., 1960-70, Hayward Spl. Com. Sign Ordnance, 1966; mem. Hayward Bd. Appeals, 1968-78, Hayward Bldg. Code Adv. Com., 1968-78. Recipient BERKELEY CITATION, U. Calif. at Berkeley, 1972. Fellow AIA; mem. Earthquake Engring. Research Inst., Seismological Soc. Am., Am. Arbitration Assn., Tau Beta Pi. Methodist. Research earthquake damage. Home: Hayward, Calif. Died July 26, 1978; cremated.

SIMONS, LLOYD RHODERICK, ret. educator; b. Sardinia, N.Y., Nov. 8, 1886; s. Julian Seymour and Alice Amelia (Bigelow) S.; B.S. in Agr., Cornell U., 1911, grad. work summer sessions 1924, 27; m. Lucy Ada Phelps, Dec. 27, 1914; children—Howard Julian, Clara Pauline, Instr. agr. Gowanda High Sch. (N.Y.) 1911-14; agr. agt. Nassau County (N.Y.) 1914-16; specialist in extension orgn. and methods with U.S. Dept. Agr. 1916-20; asst. county agt. leader Cornell U., 1920-28, county agt. leader, 1928-32; dir. extension N.Y. State Colls. Agr. and Home Econs., 1932-54, now emeritus prof. Coordinator, Farm Flood Relief, 1935; dir. Farm Bur. Fedn., N.Y. State, 1932-54; mem. N.Y. State adv. coms. for Soil Conservation and Farmers Home Adminstrn., Agrl. Adjustment Adminstr., 1934-54, N.Y. Agrl and Conservation Council, 1959—; mem. N.Y. State Agrl. Adjustment Agy. Com.; former chmn. N.Y. State rural policy com. Land Grant Coll. Assn.; chmn. extension sect., 1938, chmn. Nat. Older Rural Youth Comm., 1936-38, mem. extension com. on orgn. and policy, 1939-41, 53-54, chmn. 1941; chmn. N.Y. State Victory Garden Council, 1942-46; mem. U.S. Dept. Agr. Adv. Com. on Wartime Extension, 1942-45; mem. farm labor adv. com. to Regional Manpower Commn., 1942-46; mem. sub-com. on young workers in wartime agr. U.S. Dept. Labor, 1942-46; mem. div. labor, industry and agr. State War Council, 1941-42; mem. N.Y. State Emergency Food Commn. of State War Council, 1943-46. Recipient Epsilon Sigma Phi certificate of recognition for outstanding service to agr. and rural life, 1936, hon. degree of State Farmer by Future Farmers Am., 1944, Am. Farm Bur. Fedn. Award for Distinguished Service to organized agr., 1944, citation for outstanding service to 4-H Club Work, 1946, U.S. Dept. of Agr. Superior Service award, 1951. Mem. Patrons of Husbandry, Forest City, Tompkins County, Pomona, State and Nat. granges, Epsilon Sigma Phi, Ho-Nun-De-Kah. Methodist. Mason (K.T., Shriner). Contbr. to several agrl. bulls. on extension methods, orgn., history and policy. Home: Ithaca NY. *

SIMPSON, CLAUDE MITCHELL, JR., educator; b. Kansas City, Mo., July 29, 1910; s. Claude M. and Sarah (Burks) S.; B.A., So. Methodist U., 1930, B.Mus., 1930, M.A., 1931, Litt.D., 1966; A.M., Harvard, 1934, Ph.D., 1936; m. Lucy Elizabeth Carrigan, Dec. 28, 1933. Instr. English, East Carolina Tchrs. Coll., 1935-36, U. Wis., 1936-39; instr., then asst. prof. Harvard, 1939-47; prof. English, Ohio State U., 1947-64; Coe prof. Am. lit. Stanford, 1964-73, emeritus, 1973-76. Sr. research asso. Huntington Library, 1973-76. Bd. dirs. Ohio State U. Research Found., 1959-62. Served to lt. comdr. USNR, 1943-46. Rockefeller Found. fellow, 1946-47; Fulbright research grantee, Eng., 1950-51; Folger Shakespeare Library fellow, 1955; Guggenheim fellow, 1967-68; Huntington Library fellow, 1971-72. Mem. Modern

Lang. Assn. (exec. council 1965-68), Am. Folklore Soc., Am. Acad. Arts and Scis., AAUP. Democrat. Methodist. Author: Jacobean and Restoration Musicke for the Recorder, 1941; Elizabethan and Shakespearean Musicke for the Recorder, 1941; (with Allan Nevins) The American Reader, 1941; (with Leonhard Deutsch) A Treasury of the World's Finest Folk Song, rev. edit., 1967; The Local Colorists, 1959; The British Broadside Ballad and Its Music, 1966 (U. Chgo. Folklore prize). Gen. editor Centenary edit. of Works of Nathaniel Hawthorne, 1962-76; editor: Mozart: Twelve Original Duets, 1942; Twelve Bach Chorals, 1948; Sister Carrie (Theodore Dreiser), 1959; The Story of a Country Town (E.W. Howe), 1961. Home: Pasadena, Calif. Died Apr. 6, 1976.

SIMPSON, JOHN L(OWREY), exec.; b. Woodland, Calif., Feb. 18, 1891; s. John Lowrey and Gertrude (Pendegast) S.; B.L., U. Cal., 1913, LL.D., 1960; law sch., 1913-14; m. Margarete Mandel, Apr. 19, 1924. Admitted to Calif. State bar, 1914; rep. P. N. Gray & Co. N.Y. in Vienna, 1919-21; exec. v.p. J. Henry Schroder Banking Corp. and Schroder Trust Co., N.Y.C., 1925-51, then dir.; finance chairman, dir. Bechtel Corp., 1952-61, then cons.; director Homestake Mining Company. Director of Belgian Am. Ednl. Found., Inc. Served under Mr. Herbert C. Hoover, World War I, in following orgns.: Commn. for Relief in Belgium, 1915-17, U.S. Food Adminstrn., Paris, 1917-18, Am. Relief Adminstrn., Central Europe and Yugoslavia, 1919. Financial adviser economic section Allied Control Commn., Italy, 1943-44. Decorated: Legion of Honor, France; also Officer, Order Leopold II, Belgium. Member of the Council on Foreign Relations, World Affairs Council No. Cal. (pres. 1957-58); dir. Fgn. Policy Assn. Mem. Holland Lodge, Phi Beta Kappa, Delta Upsilon. Republican. Clubs: Century Association (N.Y.C.); Recess (N.Y. City); Metropolitan (Washington); Pacific-Union, Bohemian (San Francisco). Home: San Francisco, Calif. Died Mar. 28, 1981.

SINAI, NATHAN, found. ofcl.; b. Stockton, Calif., Nov. 28, 1894; s. Max and Sadie (Cantor) S.; D.V.M., San Francisco Coll., 1915; M.S. in Pub. Health, U. Mich., 1924. Dr. P.H., 1926; m. Kathryn Maree McBarron, June 11, 1924 (dec. 1965). Dir., Div. Sanitation, Stockton, 1916-21; health officer, Stockton, 1921-23; instr. hygiene and pub. health U. Mich., Ann Arbor, 1924-27, asst. prof., 1927-29, asso. prof., 1929-32, prof., 1932-64, prof. emeritus, from 1964, ann. Nathan Sinai lectr., from 1974; dir. Bur. Pub. Health Econs., and mem. exec. bd. Horace H. Rackham Sch. Grad. Studies; cons. USPHS, Social Security Adminstrn., WHO, Ont. Med. Assn., Hosp. Study Commn. Hawaii. Pres., World Health Found., U.S.; trustee World Health Found., Can.; chmn. policy com. Fedn. World Health Founds., Geneva, Switzerland, now pres. Fellow Am. Pub. Health Assn., Am. Coll. Dentists (hon.); mem. Nat. Orgn. Pub. Health Nursing (dir., mem. exec. com.), NIH (hosp. facilities research sect.), Mich. Pub. Health Assn. (pres.), Washtenaw Med. Soc. (hon.), Oreg. Dental Assn. (hon.), Tau Kappa Epsilon, Phi Kappa Phi, Delta Omega. Club: University. Author: A Survey of the Medical Facilities of San Joaquin County, Calif., 1931; A Survey of the Medical Facilities of Philadelphia (with A. B. Mills), 1931; A Study of Physicians and Dentists in Detroit (with A. B. Mills), 1931; The Way of Health Insurance (with A. M. Simons), 1932; The Incidence of Illness and the Receipt and Costs of Medical Care (with I. S. Falk and M. Klem), 1933; Medical Relief Administration, Essex County, Ontario, 1937; Medical Relief in Michigan (with M. Hall, V. Hogue and M. Steep), 1938; Medical Relief Administration (with M. Hall and R. E. Holmes), 1939. Compiler: Report of the Survey of Medical Services and Health Agencies in Michigan, 1933; Health Insurance in the United States (with Anderson and Dollar); (with O. W. Anderson) Emergency Maternity and Infant Care, 1948; (with D. Paton) Hospitalization of the People of Two Counties, 1949; Disability Compensation, 1949; Comprehensive Medical Service Under Voluntary Health Insurance (with B. J. Darsky and S. J. Axelrod), 1958; (with B. W. Wheeler and B. S. Thomas) Disability Insurance in California, 1965; Disability Insurance and Vocational Rehabilitation, 1967; also articles. Home: Laguna Hills, Calif. Deceased.

SINCLAIR, JAMES HUNTLY, educator; b. Dorchester County, Md., Oct. 7, 1886; s. Henry and Annie (Maclean) S.; B.A., St. John's Coll., Annapolis, Md., 1906; winner of Rhodes scholarship from Md., 1908; B.A., Oxford U., Eng., 1910, M.A., 1915; Ph.D., Syracuse U., 1916; studied Columbia; m. Annie Carter, Sept. 3, 1917; 1 son, Carter. Instr., later asst. prof. psychology, Syracuse U., 1914-17; asst. prof. psychology Smith Coll., Mass., 1920-22; prof. of edn. Occidental Coll., Los Angeles, 1922-52. Mem. nat. adv. bd. Life Ins. Policyholders Protective Assn., N.Y. Entered 1st R.O.T.C., Madison Barracks, N.Y., May 1917; commd. 1st lt., Aug. 1917 and sent to G.H.Q. in France, Oct. 1917; served with G-2 Sect. Gen. Staff, 3d A.C., May 1918-Feb. 1919; promoted capt. inf., Nov. 1918; mem. Interallied Commn. for Repatriation of Prisoners in Berlin, Feb.-Sept. 1919; hon. discharged, Oct. 20, 1919. Fellow A.A.A.S.; mem. Nat. Soc. Study Edn., Nat. Soc. Coll. Teachers of Edn., Phi Beta Kappa, Sigma Alpha Epsilon. Republican. Home: Pasadena. *

SINGER, JACQUES, (KUBA), condr.; b. Przemysl, Poland, May 9, 1917; s. Mark Eli and Rachela (Bach) S.; student Curtis Inst. Music, 1926; grad. Juilliard Grad. Sch. Music, 1931; Mus.D., Corpus Christi U., 1962; m. Leslie Wright, Jan. 28, 1946; children—Claude, Mark, Lori and Gregory (twins). Came to U.S., 1921, naturalized, 1931. Music dir., conductor Dallas Symphony, 1937-42, Vancouver (B.C., Can.) Symphony, 1947-51; music dir. N.Y. prodn. Shakespeare and Shaw Cleopatras with Lawrence Olivier and Vivian Leigh, 1952, Tel Aviv (Israel) Philharmonic, Haifa, 1953; condr. 1st symphony concert in Nazareth, 1953; music dir., Corpus Christi, 1954; guest condr. Mexico, Guatemala, also Indpls. symphonies, 1956, Peru, 1957, Portugal, 1958; mus. dir. Filharmonic de Buenos Aires, 1959, 60, Havana, 1959, Caracas, 1961, Florence, Italy, 1962, London Philharmonic, 1962, Portland Symphony Orch., from 1962; condr. Columbia Sinfonica, 1966, Filharmonica de Chile, Santiago, 1966, London Royal Philharmonic, 1970, Congress of Strings, U. So. Calif., 1970, Cin., 1970, N.Z. B.C. Symphony, N.Z. and Dublin, Ireland, 1971, Ind. U. Philharmonic, Orquesta Sinfonica Venezuela, Honolulu Symphony, 1972, Filharmonia de Wroclaw, de Krakow, de Gdansk (all Poland), Sacramento Symphony, Orquestra Filarmonica de Lisboa (Portugal), 1973, Warsaw Philharmonic, Poznan Philharmonic, Lodz Philharmonic, 1975, also Louisville Philharmonic, Naumburg Orch., N.Y.C., 1976-78; gen. music dir., comdr. Oreg. Symphony Orch., 1962-73; prof. No. Ill. U., 1977-80, condr. No. Ill. U. Philharmonic, Portugal Festival, Lisbon, 1978. Served with AUS, 1942-46. Recipient gold medal Buenos Aires Filharmonica, 1959. Mem. Nat. Assn. Am. Composers and Condrs. Home: New York, N.Y. Died Aug. ll, 1980.

SINGEWALD, JOSEPH THEOPHILUS, JR. (sing'e-wald), geologist; b. Baltimore, Md., Sept. 25, 1884; s. Joseph Theophilus and Magdalena Julianna (Dreyer) S.; grad. Baltimore City Coll,, 1903; A.B., Johns Hopkins Univ., 1906, Ph.D., 1909; m. Laura Page Heroy, June 14, 1934; children—Frances, Page. Fellow, Johns Hopkins U., 1907-08, Henry E. Johnston scholar, 1910-13, asso. in econ. geology, 1913-17, asso. prof., 1917-22, prof. since 1922, chmn. dept. geology since 1939. Field asst., U.S. Geol. Survey, 1907, jr. geologist, 1910; jr. geologist U.S. Bur. Mines, 1911-20; field asst., 1906, asst. geologist, 1908-13, geologist since 1913, Md. Geol. Survey; chief prodn. specialist, Bd. of Econ. Warfare, 1942; director Department Geology, Mines and Water Resources, State of Maryland, since 1943; consulting econ. geologist. Mem. Am. Inst. M.E., Geol. Soc. Am., A.A.A.S., Geol. Soc. Washington, Freiberger Geologische Gesellschaft, Am. Assn. Petroleum Geologists. Soc. Econ. Geologists. Mining and Metall. Soc. Am., Am. Geophysical Union, Sociedad Geolojica del Peru (hon.), Gamma Alpha, Phi Beta Kappa, Sigma Xi. Clubs: Engineers (Baltimore); Explorers (N.Y.). Author of report on iron ores, also numerous papers in tech. publs. on geology and econ. geology, on geology and mineral deposits of Latin America. Home: Baltimore, Md. *

SINGSEN, ANTONE GERHARDT, health ins. co. exec.; b. Providence, July 4, 1915; s. Arthur Girard and Edith Barrett Soule (Pierce) S.; A.B., Brown U., 1938; M.S. in Journalism, Columbia, 1939; m. Mary Ellen McKee, Sept. 27, 1941; children—Antone Gerhardt III, William Dana, Sarah Ellen Singsen Nevin, Katrina Singsen Taggart, Michael Pierce. Editorial asst. Providence Jour. & Bull., 1939-41; pub. relations dir. R.I. and Conn. Blue Cross, 1939-45; with Blue Cross Commn. Am. Hosp. Assn., Chgo., 1946-57, asso. dir., 1955-57; v.p., treas. Blue Cross Assn., N.Y.C. and Chgo., 1957-69, sr v.p. 1969-74; sr. v.p. finance Blue Cross and Blue Shield Greater N.Y., 1974-77; sec. nat. retirement program Blue Cross Assn., 1953-69. Vice pres., treas. Health Services Found., 1963-72. Mem. Am. Hosp. Assn., Am. Pub. Health Assn., Group Health Assn. Am., Am. Philatelic Soc. Mem. Soc. of Friends. Home: Scarsdale, N.Y. Died Nov. 19, 1977; buried Purchase (N.Y.) Friends Cemetery.

SINGSTAD, OLE, consulting civil engr.; b. Lensvik, Norway, June 29, 1882; s. Knut and Anne (Auseth) S.; C.E., Poly. Inst. of Trondheim. Norway, 1905; D. Engring., N.Y.U., Stevens Inst. of Tech., Poly. Inst. of Brooklyn; D.Sc., St. Olaf College, Newark College of Engineering; married Else Johansen, Jan. 23, 1912; children—Rita Anna (Mrs. Henry E. Gardiner), Paul John. Came to U.S., 1905, naturalized citizen, 1911. Asst. engr. and design engineer Central R.R. of N.J., Virginian R.R., Hudson-Manhattan R.R. (Hudson River Tunnels), 1905-09; design engr., rapid transit subways and subaqeous tunnels Pub. Service Commn., 1st Dist. N.Y. (successor N.Y. City Transit Authority), 1910-17; structural and tunnel design engr. pvt. firms, 1917-19; successively engr. design, chief engr., supt. Holland Tunnel (developed and designed its novel ventilation system, now the standard method of ventilating vehicular tunnels), N.Y. State Bridge and Tunnel Commn. and N.J. Interstate Bridge and Tunnel Commn., 1919-30; chief cons. engr. on tunnels Lincoln Tunnel, Port of N.Y. Authority. 1930-35; chief engr. Queens Mid-town Tunnel, also Brooklyn Battery Tunnel, N.Y.C. Tunnel Authority, 1935-45; cons. engr. Oakland-Alameda Tunnel (Cal.), Detroit-Windsor Tunnel, Scheldt River Tunnel (Antwerp, Belgium), Baltimore (Md.) Harbor Tunnel, Boston (Massachusetts) Harbor Tunnel, redevelopment Lincoln Memorial area, Washington; consultant engineer on wide variety construction projects, U.S. and fgn. lectr. engring. subjects various univs. Member bd. dirs. American Standards Assn. Decorated Officer Order of the Crown (Belgium); Knight 1st Class Royal Norwegian Order of St. Olav; Commander Order of Merit, (Chile). Member fgn., national, state profl. engring. socs.; hon. mem. Norwegian Society of Professional Engineers, Am. Society C.E. Received 1944 Abraham Lincoln Award; James Laurie Prize American Society of Civil Engineers. Clubs: Metropolitan, Engineers (president 1942-43), Harvard, Cosmos, Whitehall. Author of many tech. papers. Asso. editor American Civil Engineering Practice. Home: N.Y.C. Died Dec. 8, 1969. *

SINK, CHARLES ALBERT, pres. University Musical Soc., U. of Mich; b. Westernville, N.Y., July 4, 1879; s. Herman and Caroline (Gleasman) S; A.B., U of Mich., 1904; hon. M.Ed. Michigan State Normal College, 1929; LL.D., Battle Creek (Mich) College, 1930; H.H.D., Wayne State University (Detroit), 1957; m. Alva Joanna Gordon, June 18, 1923. Sec. Univ. Sch. of Music. U. of Mich., 1904-07, sec. and business manager. 1907-27, pres. 1927-40. Vice pres., dir. Mich. Life Ins. Co. Mem. City Council, Ann Arbor, Mich., 1912-18; mem. Mich. Ho. of Rep., 1919-20, 1925-26, Senate, 1921-22, 1927-28, 1929-30. Candidate for lt. gov., Mich. Rep. primaries, 1932; mem. Rep. State Central Com., Mich., 1929-36; delegate or guest at most Rep. State conventions, 1912—, and most Rep. Nat. convs., 1920—. Chmn. Michigan State Teachers Retirement Fund Commn., Mich. Hist. Commn.; mem. Mackinac Island State Park Commission, George Washington Bicentennial Commission, Ann Arbor (Mich.) Historical Commission, Past mem. numerous civic orgns. and coms. Cofounder Acacia (Mich. 1904), now honorary national president; member International Association Concert Mgrs. (chmn. bd. 1962; hon. chmn.), Phi Kappa Phi, Phi Mu Alpha, Sinfonia, Alpha Epsilon Mu, numerous orgns. for promotion of music. Rep. Conglist. Mason. Clubs: Rotary, Mich. Union, Ann Arbor, University of Michigan. Author of pamphlets, Music in Our Colleges and Universities, Michigan's Teachers' Retirement Law. Recipient of King Albert medal for services in connection with starving Belgian children. World War. Home: Ann Arbor, Mich. *

SINN, FRANCIS PEIRCE, consulting engr.; b. Germantown, Phila., Pa., Oct. 7, 1882; s. Joseph Albert and Ella Thomas (Wise) S.; student Germantown Boys Combined Sch., 1889-96; A.B., Central High Sch. of Phila., 1900; E.M., Lehigh Univ., 1904; m. Margaret Cortright Convers, Oct. 10, 1906; 1 dau., Margaret Elizabeth (died 1928). Engr., summers 1902, 03; mining in Mexico, cyanide millwork, de la Mar, Nev., 1904-05; Alanwood Iron & Steel Co., Ivy Rock, Pa., summer 1905; various capacities with New Jersey Zinc Co., Palmerton (Pa.) Works, 1905-17, gen. supt. N.J. Zinc Co. of Pa. 1917-18; asst. mgr. Chestnut Ridge R.R. Co., 1917-18, asst. to vice pres., 1919-41; part time consultant Am. Smelting & Refining Co., 1928-29, Trepca Mines, Ltd., of Yugoslavia, 1938, Am. Metal Co., Ltd., 1937-41; cons. engr. Am. Metal Co., Ltd., New York City, since 1941. Dir. 1st Nat. Bank of Palmerton, Pa., 1916-26; director, vice president Palmerton Lighting, Telephone and Disposal Companies, 1917-41; director Blackwell Zinc Company. Honorary mem. Chemical Metall. and Mining Soc. of South Africa, June 30, 1946-June 30, 1947. Mem. Am. Inst. Mining and Metall. Engrs. (mem. zinc and lead com., chmn. 2 yrs.), Mining and Metall. Soc. of Am. (mem. exec. com., vice pres. 1945, pres. 1946), Montclair Society of Engineers, Am. Iron and Steel Inst., Am. Zinc Inst., Nat Safety Council (past mem. exec. com., 1st vice pres. 1919), Chi Psi, Sigma Xi. Republican. Unitarian. Mason. Clubs: University, Downtown Association, Mining (New York City); Montclair Golf. Home: Montclair, N.J. *

SIPES, LEONLESS MARCELLOUS, clergyman; b. Mineral Springs, Howard County, Ark., Sept. 12, 1884; s. William Walter and Henrietta (Green) S.; A.B., Ouachita Coll., Arkadelphia, Ark., 1911; Th.M., Southwestern Bapt. Theol. Sem., Ft. Worth, Tex., 1916 (residence work for Th. D. completed); D.D. Ouachita Coll., 1924; m. Sallie Moore, June 30, 1910; children—Leon M., William Burke, Margaret, Frank Moore. Ordained ministry Missionary Bapt. Ch., 1905; pastor successively College Hill Ch., Texarkana, Lewisville and Stamps, Ark., Mansfield, Tex., Conway, Ark., Seminary Hill, Tex., First Ch., Little Rock, 1922-29; v.p. Central Coll., Conway, Ark., 1929-31, also pastor Tillar (Ark.) Bapt. Ch.; editor Baptist Advance, 1931-33; full time pastor, Pulaski Heights Ch. Little Rock, Ark.; pres. Ark. Bapt. State Exec. Bd., 1936-37, now Ark. Baptist State Conv., 1937-38; formerly chief librarian Southwestern Bapt. Theol

Sem.; Interim Pastor Immanuel Bapt. Ch., Kansas City, Kan.; 1942-45; now prof. pastoral efficiency Central Bapt. Theol. Sem., Kansas City, Kan., also associate to pres. military training, Ouachita Coll., 4 yrs. Mem. bd. dirs. Southwestern Bapt. Theol. Sem. Mem. Am. Assn. Bibl. Research. Democrat. Mason (32 deg.). Mem. editorial com. Southwest Religious Monthly Book Club. President Kansas Baptist State Convention, 1946-47. Address: Kansas City, Kan. *

SIPLE, WALTER HELCK, museum dir.; b. Boston, May 25, 1890; s. Marvin DeForest and Caroline Elizabeth (Helck) S.; B.S., Harvard, 1915, M.A., 1917; grad. study Oxford U., 1923-24; m. Ella Simons, June 18, 1925. Master, Groton (Mass.) Sch., 1918-25; asst. to dirs. Fogg Art Mus., Harvard, 1926-29, also dir. students sent to Harvard Summer Sch. by Carnegie Found. under auspices of A.I.A., 1927, 28, 29; lectr. Mass. Div. Univ. Extension, 1926-29, 1948-78, Harvard, 1928-29; dir. Cin. Mus. and Art Acad. Cin., 1929-45, also dir. Taft Mus. and prof. fine arts Univ. Cin.; prof. fine arts Emerson Coll., Boston, 1948-55. Mem. Am. Assn. Mus., Coll. Art Assn., Assn. Art Mus. Dirs., Phi Delta Kappa. Contbr. articles on art and edn. to various mags. Home: Cambridge, Mass. Died June 7, 1978.

SIPORIN, MITCHELL, educator, artist; b. N.Y.C., May 5, 1910; s. Hyman and Jennie (Dressler) S.; student Crane Jr. Coll., Chgo., Chgo. Art Inst., 1927-30; m. Miriam Tane, Nov. 11, 1945; children—Judith, Rachel. One man shows Downtown Gallery, N.Y.C., 1938-42, 57; exhibited American Painting, Chgo. Art Inst., 1938-39, North Am. Painting, Mus. Modern Art, 1940-42; exhibited San Francisco and N.Y. world's fairs, Whitney Mus., Met. Mus., N.Y.C.; Am. drawings touring France, 1956-58; retrospective Rose Art Mus., Brandeis U., Waltham, Mass., 1976; represented permanent collections Mus. Modern Art, Chgo. Art Inst., Met. Mus., Whitney Mus., Fogg art Mus., Harvard, others; frescoes executed Decatur (Ill.) P.O., Lane Tech. High Sch., Chgo., Bloom Twp. High Sch., Chicago Heights, Ill.; mural post office frescoes, St. Louis, 1939; asso. prof. fine arts Brandeis U., 1951-60, chmn. dept. fine arts, 1951-76, prof. fine arts, 1960-76. Artist-in-residence Am. Acad., Rome, 1966-67. Trustee Boston Arts Festival. Served with 909th Engrs., Camouflage Battalion, AUS, 1942-43, 5th Army Hdqrs., 1943-45. Recipient Bertha Aberle Florsheim prize, Chgo., 1941; Pennel medal Pa. Acad. Fine arts, 1946; Logan prize and gold medal Art Inst. Chgo., 1947; prix-de-Rome, 1949-50; 2d Am. prize Internat. Hallmark Competition, 1950; award Inst. arts and Letters, 1955; 1st prize watercolor Butler Art Inst., 1959. Guggenheim fellow, 1945-46, 46-47; Fulbright research fellow, Italy, 1966-67. Fellow Am. Acad. in Rome; mem. New Eng. Contemporary artists (exec. bd.). Home: Newton, Mass. Died June 11, 1976.

SIRICH, EDWARD HINMAN (SI'RIK), prof. Romance langs.; b. Baltimore, Mar. 29, 1884; s. John Henry and Elizabeth (Hinman) S.; A.B., Johns Hopkins, 1906, Ph.D., 1914; m. Marjorie Williamson, June 16, 1923. Prof. modern langs., St. John's Coll., Annapolis, Md., 1908-12; instr. and asst. prof. Romance langs., U. of Minn. 1914-17, asst. prof. 1919-23; dean St. John's Coll., Annapolis, Md., 1923-24; asso. prof. Romance langs., U. of Minn. 1924-29, prof. of Romance langs. since 1929. Consular agent for France in Minneapolis, 1932-39. Served as lt. Ordnance Dept., U.S. Army, 1917-18; capt., 1918-19. Mem. Modern Lang. Assn., America, Modern Humanities Research Assn., Beta Theta Pi, Phi Beta Kappa. Awarded silver medal by minister of foreign affairs, France, for liaison work, World War. Democrat. Episcopalian. Author or co-author books relating to field; latest publ.: Simplified French Grammar, 1941. Home: Minneapolis. *

SISK, GLENN NOLEN, educator; b. Cookeville, Tenn., Mar. 15, 1906; s. Therman K. and Martha (Sewell) S.; B.A., U. Ala., 1933, M.A., 1935; Ph.D., Duke, 1951; m. Josephine Courtney, Aug. 22, 1940; 1 son, Courtney Sewell. Tchr. high sch., Andalusia, Ala., 1935-37; registrar, instr. history State Tchrs. Coll., Livingston, Ala., 1937-39; instr. history U. N.C. Women's Coll., Greensboro, 1941-42, Ala. Poly. Inst., Auburn, 1942-43; asst. prof. social sci. Ga. Inst. Tech., Atlanta, 1943-46, asso. prof., 1946-48, prof., head dept. social sci., 1948-56, prof., 1956-73, prof. emeritus, 1973-77. Vis. lectr. history Bklyn. Coll., N.Y.C. Coll., summer 1958. Fellow Econs.-in-Action Program, Case Inst. Tech., 1954; Ford Ednl. Forum fellow, 1955. Mem. Ga. Edn. Assn. (pres. council social studies 1956-58), So. Hist. Assn., Delta Chi. Methodist. Contbr. articles to profl. publs. Home: Atlanta, Ga. Died July 15, 1977; interred Westview Cemetery, Atlanta.

SISK, JOHN KELLY, communications co. exec.; b. Cookeville, Tenn., Mar. 3, 1913; s. Thurman Kelly and Martha Jane (Sewell) S.; B.S., U. Ala., 1934; LL.D. (hon.), Livingston (Ala.) Coll., 1975; m. Isbell Lane, Sept. 30, 1936; children—John Kelly, Lane Sisk Irick. With Greenville (S.C.) News-Piedmont Co., 1948-80; chmn. bd., 1963-80, publisher, 1966—80, chmn. bd. Miltimedia, Inc., Greenville, 1973-80; dir. S.C. Nat. Corp., S.C. Nat. Bank, Liberty Life Ins. Co., Dan River Inc. Trustee Duke Endowment, Converse Coll,; adv. trustee Furman U.; chmn. trustees Greenville Gen. Hosp., 1959. Mem. Am. Newspaper Pubs. Assn., So. Newspaper Pubs. Assn. (pres. 1963, chmn. 1964), S.C. Press Assn. (pres. 1962), Greater Greenville C. of C. (pres. 1953). Methodist. Clubs: Nat. Press (Washington); Green Valley Country, Greenville Country, Poinsett, Cotillion, Biltmore Forest Country, Plantation. Home: Greenville, S.C. Died Nov. 6, 1980.

SISSMAN, LOUIS EDWARD, poet, advt. exec.; b. Detroit, Jan. 1, 1928; s. Edward James and Marie (Anderson) S.; B.A. cum laude Harvard, 1949; m. Anne Bierman, Nov. 27, 1958. Editor Prentice-Hall, 1949-51, A.A. Wyn, 1951-52; campaign aide John F. Kennedy, 1952; advt. writer Boston agencies, 1953-56; sr. writer, supr. Kenyon & Eckhardt Advtg., Boston, 1956-65, creative v.p., 1966-72; creative v.p. Quinn & Johnson Advt., Boston, 1972-76; book reviewer New Yorker mag.; columnist Atlantic Monthly; lectr. Northeastern U. Writers' Workshop. Creative dir. United Fund, Boston, 1964; mem. bd. mgrs., chmn. publicity and community relations com. Vis. Nurse Assn. of Boston, 1962. Recipient Garrison Poetry prize, 1949, Nat. Inst. Arts and Letters award, 1969. Guggenheim fellow, 1968. Hon. mem. Phi Beta Kappa. Author: Dying: An Introduction, 1968; Scattered Returns, 1969; Pursuit of Honor, 1971; Innocent Bystander, 1975. Home: Harvard, Mass. Died Mar. 10, 1976.

SITTERLY, BANCROFT W(ALKER), ret. educator, astronomer; b. Madison, N.J., Sept. 11, 1895; s. Charles Fremont and Julia Cobb (Buttz) S.; A.B., Princeton, 1917, A.M., 1920, Ph.D. in Astronomy, 1922; m. Charlotte E. Moore, May 30, 1937. Instr. astronomy U. Mo., 1922-23; asst. prof. Wesleyan U., Middletown, Conn., 1923-45; staff mem. Radiation Lab., M.I.T., 1943-45; asso. astronomer U.S. Naval Obs., 1946-47; asso. prof. math. Am. U., 1947-50, prof. math., 1950-53, prof. physics, 1953-66, prof. emeritus, 1966-77, chmn. dept. physics, 1955-61; spl. research binary stars. Fellow Royal Astron. Soc., A.A.A.S.; mem. Am. Astron. Soc., Am. Assn. Phsyics Tchrs., Philos. Soc. Washington, Washington Acad. Sci., Phi Beta Kappa, Sigma Xi. Methodist. Home: Washington, D.C. Died Feb. 1, 1977; interred Fallowfield Friends' Meeting Cemetery, Chester County, Pa.

SIVAGE, GERALD ALBERT, retail exec.; b. Watertown, S.D., Dec. 17, 1908; s. John Wesley and Emma (Belky) S.; B.S., Caroll Coll., 1931; m. Elizabeth Kepler, Aug. 22, 1942; children—Suzanne, Elizabeth. Clk. Marshall Field & Co., Chgo., 1931-32, mem. exec. office staff, 1932-35, asst. to mgr. real estate div., 1936-37, asst. treas., 1937-41, 45, asst. sec., asst. treas., 1945, asst. to pres., 1946-48, asst. to chmn., 1949-51, treas., 1952-53, v.p., treas., 1954-56, v.p., gen. operating mgr., 1956-59, exec. v.p., dir., 1959-64, pres., dir., 1964-74, dir., 1974-77; dir. Standard Brands, Inc., Met. Life Ins. Co., 1st Nat. Bank Chgo., Gen. Motors Corp. Trustee Northwestern U., Chgo. Womens' Hosp. and Maternity Center. Served with USNR, 1942-44. Republican. Presbyn. Clubs: Racquet, Commercial, Economic, Chicago, Commonwealth Casino (Chgo.); Metropolitan (N.Y.C.); Oconomowoc (Wis.) Lake Home: Chicago, Ill. Died Sept. 26, 1977; buried Wis. Meml. Park, Milw.

SIWEK, MANUEL, publisher; b. N.Y.C., June 23, 1908; s. Abraham and Bertha (Gessler) S.; B.S., N.Y. U., 1930; m. Pauline Fancher, Nov. 24, 1945; children—Alexandra, Donald Fancher. Sales promotion Boni & Liveright, 1930-32; asst. to sales mgr. Doubleday & Co., 1932-41; v.p. Grosset & Dunlap, 1946-55, exec. v.p., 1955-62, pres., 1962-76, chief exec. officer, 1965-76, chmn. 1967-76, also dir.; pres. Wonder Books, Inc., Treasure Books, Inc., 1952-64, chmn., 1967-76; chmn., dir. Transworld Publs., Ltd., 1967-76; Bantam Books, Inc., 1967-76; v.p., dir. Nat. Gen. Corp., 1968-76; dir. Gt. Am. Ins. Co., Gt. Am. Life Ins. Co. Served as maj. USAAF, 1944. Mem. Am. Book Pubs. Council (dir. 1961-63), Beta Gamma Sigma. Clubs: New York University Players, Manhattan. Home: Rye, N.Y. Died Feb. 21, 1976.

SIZELOVE, OLIVER JAMES, ret. educator; b. Irvington, N.J., July 16, 1911; s. Oliver and Lillian (Eisenberg) S.; B.S., Newark Coll. Engring. 1934; M.A.E., N.Y. U., 1944; m. Mildred Ruthweis, Dec. 26, 1936 (dec. 1952); children—J. Douglas, J. Donald; m. 2d, Helma Roos, June 16, 1953; 1 son, J. David. Staff indsl. engring. Diehl Mfg. Co., 1934-36; instr. indsl. engring. Newark Coll. Engring., 1936-42, asst. prof. indsl. engring., chmn. dept., 1942-46, asso. prof., exec. asso. dept. mgmt. and personnel, 1946-50, prof., 1950-75, chmn. dept. mgmt. engring., grad. and undergrad. divs., 1954-60, chmn. dept. indsl. and mgmt. engring., 1960-70, distinguished prof., 1965-71, prof. emeritus, 1971-75; cons. profl. engr., 1938-75. Tech. arbitrator N.J. Bd. Mediation, 1952-75. Recipient Gilbreth medal, 1964. Fellow Am. Inst. Industrial Engrs., Am. Soc. M.E. (mem. com. mgmt. div. 1958-63, chmn. div. 1962-63), Soc. Advancement Mgmt. (pres. No. N.J. chpt. 1950-51, v.p. indsl. engring. 1961-75, internat. pres. 1965-66, chmn. bd. 1966-67); mem. Am. Soc. Engring. Edn. (nat. dir., hon. life), Tau Beta Pi. Contbr. articles to engring. jours. Home: Point Pleasant, N.J. Died Mar. 13, 1975.

SKEELS, DORR, forester; b. Grand Rapids, Mich., Mar. 6, 1883; s. Fremont E. and Matilda (Cox) S.; B.S., Mich. Agrl. Coll., East Lansing, Mich., 1904; student in forestry, U. of Mich., 1904-06; m. Blanche Covell, Oct. 3, 1907; children—Dorr Covell; Dorothy Elizabeth. With U.S. Forest Service as forest supervisor, 1908-12, logging engr., 1912-14; organizer and dean, Sch. of Forestry, U. of Mont., Sept. 1914-Sept. 1923, prof. of forestry, 1923-33; chief engr. Civil Works Administration for Montana, 1934 and 1935; dist. superviser, U.S. Dept. Agr., 1935-40, agrl. economist, 1940-49, ret. Commd. capt. Engrs., U.S. Army, Sept. 1917; served with A.E.F., in France; hon. discharged, Sept. 1, 1919. Universalist. Mason, Elk Contbr. to Jour. of Forestry, The Timberman, Land Policy Review, etc. Home: Lincoln, Nebr. *

SKEEN, DAVID ALFRED, lawyer; b. Plain City, Weber County, Utah, May 13, 1885; s. Lyman and Electa (Dixon) S.; A.B., B.S., Utah State Agr. Coll., 1909, LL.B. cum laude, U. Chgo., 1910; m. Bertha Kerr, Nov. 16, 1910; children—Priscilla (Mrs. John P. Pitts), LaRae (Mrs. Frank Fonnesbeck), Eleanor, Margaret (Mrs. Monroe B. Morton), Nancy Jane. Admitted to Utah bar, 1910 and since practiced in Salt Lake City; civil dep. county atty., Salt Lake County, 1916-20. Dir. Bamberger R.R. Co. Pres. Utah Conf. Social Work, 1937-38; chmn. bd. trustees Utah State Training Sch., 1930-40. Official cons. to Am. delegation to U.N. Conf., San Francisco, 1945, Paris Peace Conf., 1946, Lake Success, 1947. Mem. bd. trustees Utah State Agrl. Coll., 1946. Fellow Am. Assn. on Mental Deficiency; chmn. Health Welfare, Edn., Recreation and Nutrition Div., Utah State Council of Defense; mem. Nat. com. Mental Hygiene. Mem. Internat. Assn. of Lions Clubs (pres. 1944), Salt Lake City C. of C., Pi Kappa Alpha. Clubs: Elks, University (Salt Lake City); Fort Douglas Golf. Address: Salt Lake City. *

SKEHAN, PATRICK WILLIAM, clergyman, educator; b. N.Y.C., Sept. 30, 1909; s. William F. and Johanna A. (Dwyer) S.; A.B., Fordham U., 1929; student theology St. Joseph's Sem., Dunwoodie, N.Y., 1929-33; S.T.D., Cath. U. Am., 1938; LL.D., Boston Coll., 1957, Manhattan Coll., 1962. Ordained priest Roman Catholic Ch., 1933, papal chamberlain, 1954, domestic prelate, 1958; instr. Cath. U. Am., Washington, 1938-43, asst. prof., 1943-46, asso. prof., 1946-51, prof. Semitic langs., 1951-80, chmn. dept. Semitic and Egyptian langs. and lits., 1951-54, 56-65, 67-71; vis. prof. Johns Hopkins, 1947-58, Pontifical Bibl. Inst., Rome, Italy, 1969-70; ann. prof. Am. Sch. Oriental Research, Jerusalem, 1954-55, dir., 1955-56, asso. trustee, 1957-58, 60-64, cons. pontifical Bibl. com., 1965-71. Recipient Pro ecclesia et pontifice medal, 1970. Mem. Cath. Bibl. Assn. (pres. 1946-47, exec. bd. 1959-65, 73-75, treas. 1978-80), Am. Oriental Soc., Phi Beta Kappa. Author: Studies in Israelite Poetry and Wisdom, 1971. Vice chmn. editorial bd. New American Bible, 1947-70; publ. editor Cath. Bibl. Quar., 1946-49, asso. editor, 1966-73, 76-80. Contbr. articles to tech. lit. Research in Dead Sea Scrolls, 1954-80. Address: Washington, D.C. Died Sept. 9, 1980.

SKELTON, ALAN GORDON, librarian; b. Fayetteville, Ark., Aug. 3, 1912; s. James Lee and Josephine (Carter) S.; B.L.S., U. Okla., 1933, BA. in Polit. Sci., 1934; m. Martha Hope Butcher, Jan. 26, 1940; children—Ann Hope Skelton Fentress, Gordon William. Librarian pub. sch., Alice, Tex., 1934-36, Robstown, Tex., 1936-38; librarian geol. library U. Okla., Norman, 1938-44; librarian, research asst. Mid-Continent Oil and Gas Assn., Tulsa, 1944-47; head Research Center Library, U.S. Army Engrs. Waterways Expt. Sta., Vicksburg, Miss., 1947-71, chmn. expt. sta. arboretum bd., 1978-79, chief Tech. Info. Center, 1971-79, fgn. intelligence officer, 1972-79; rep. Fed. Lab. Consortium Tech. Transfer, 1978-79. Chmn., Vicksburg Municipal Rose Garden, 1957-79, Vicksburg City Beautification Commn., 1963-65; mem. exec. bd. Vicksburg-Warren Beautiful, Inc., 1969-70; mem. adv. com. for title programs Miss. Library Commn., 1969-79; pres. State Library Adv. Council, 1978-79; dep. exec. dir. Miss. Nat. Library Week, 1971, exec. dir., 1972, steering com., 1978; parlimentarian Gov.'s Conf. on Library and Info. Services, 1979. Recipient award of merit Vicksburg City Beautification Commn., 1965; Quality award Waterways Expt. Sta., 1971, Outstanding Service award, 1974, 75, 76, 77, 78. Mem. Miss. Library Assn. (pres. 1961, chmn. constn. and by-laws com. 1966, long range planning com., Miss. libraries 1972-79, elections com. 1978, parliamentarian 1975, 76, 77, 78, 79, merit award 1972, outstanding achievement award 1978), Spl. Libraries Assn. (pres. La. chpt. 1959-60, editor La. chpt. Bull. 1958-59, mem. nat. adv. council 1959-60), Am. Soc. Info. Sci., Friends of Miss. Libraries, Miss. Ornithol. Soc., Am. Rose Soc., Washington County (Ark.), Carroll County (Ark.) hist. socs., N.W. Ark., Ark. geneal. socs., Mid-Continent Oil and Gas Assn. (sec. nomenclature com. 1944-47), Phi Beta Kappa, Phi Eta Sigma, Phi Delta Kappa. Democrat. Presbyterian. Contbr. articles to profl. jours. Home: Vicksburg, Miss. Died Jan. 26, 1979.

SKIBINE, GEORGE BORIS, artistic dir. ballet; b. Yasnaya, Polyana, Russia, Jan. 17, 1920; s. Boris Nicolayevitch and Vera (Hobe) S.; ed. Lycee Albert de Mun, Nogent, France, Paris (France) Opera Sch.; pvt.

study ballet; m. Marjorie Tall Chief, Dec. 27, 1947; children—Alexandre, George T. Soloist Ballet de Monte Carlo, 1939; first dancer Ballet Theatre, 1940; mem. Grand Ballet du Marquis de Cuevas, 1947; tour U.S. with Ruth Page Co., 1956; ballet master Paris Opera, 1956-62, guest artist, choreographer, 1962-64; choreographer, artistic dir. Harkness Ballet, N.Y.C., 1964-69; artistic dir. Dallas Civic Ballet, 1969-81; vis. prof. North Tex. State U., 1970-81; free-lance choreographer, works performed Paris Opera, La Scala, Milan, Italy, Royal Ballet London (Eng.), Teatro Colon, Buenos Aires, Argentina, Teatro Municipal, Rio de Janeiro, Brazil. Adviser dance Tex. Commn. Arts and Humanities. Served with U.S. Army, 1942-46. Decorated Officer des Arts et Lettres (France), chevalier du Merit Culturel; Niham Iftikar (Tunisia); recipient Prix de la Critique Lyrique (France), 1956-58, Italia prize, 1962, Prix Diaguilef Inst. Paris, 1964. Home: Dallas, Tex. Died Jan. 14, 1981.

SKINNER, WILLIAM SHERMAN, ret. clergyman; b. Gouverneur, N.Y., Feb. 3, 1906; s. William Franklin and Katherine (Markwick) S.; student Princeton, 1923-25; A.B., Colgate U., 1927; Th.B., Princeton Theol. Sem., 1930, Th.M., 1931; student U. Berlin, 1931-32, Marburg (Germany) U., 1932; D.D., Temple U., 1941, Lafayette Coll., 1948; m. Helen M. Loetscher, June 6, 1931 (dec. 1944); children—William Franklin, Sherman; m. 2d, Frances N. Townsend, June 15, 1946; 1 dau., Sarah Skinner-Munoz. Ordained to ministry Presbyn. Ch., 1930; pastor in Bethlehem, Pa., 1933-36, Phila., 1936-47, Pitts., 1947-55, 2d Presbyn. Ch., St. Louis, 1955-70; interim exec. Synod So. Calif., U.P. Ch. in U.S.A., Los Angeles, 1970-72; vis. prof. McCormick Theol. Sem., Chgo., 1972-75. Mem. bd. pension Presbyn. Ch. U.S.A., 1937-53, pres., 1941-52, mem. bd. Christian edn., 1956-68, pres., 1965-68, chmn. comm. to produce policy statement on ch. and higher edn., 1958-61, chmn. spl. com. proposal to revise doctrinal standards, 1965-67; chmn. commn. on reorgn. gen. assembly agys., 1971-73; pres. Met. Ch. Fedn. Greater St. Louis, 1963. Bd. dirs. Bethlehem chpt. A.R.C., 1935-36; gen. chmn. campaign United Fund Bethlehem, 1935. Trustee Beaver Coll., 1937-47, Wilson Coll., 1938-50, Princeton Theol. Sem., 1940-72, Western Theol. Sem., 1948-55, Westminster Coll., 1955-66, Lindenwood Coll., 1955-69. Named Ecumenical Minister of Year in St. Louis Met. Ch. Fedn. Greater St. Louis, 1967. Author: (with L.K. Anderson) Bridge to Africa, 1952; also articles. Home: Santa Fe, N.Mex. Died Jan. 22, 1976; interred Princeton, N.J.

SKONING, WARREN GERALD, retail dept. store chain exec.; b. Elgin, Ill., Mar. 14, 1915; s. Walter and Edna (Hendricks) S.; grad. U. Chgo., 1937; m. Betty Jean Dunlap, Apr. 26, 1941; children—Gerald D. Mark S., Elissa S. With Sears, Roebuck and Co., Chgo., v.p. facilities planning; dir. Homart Devel. Co.; trustee Am. Fletcher Mortgage Investors Northwestern Mut. Life Mortgage & Realty Investors; officer, dir. Dearborn Park Corp. Trustee, Community Hosp., Geneva, Ill.; bd. dirs. Rehab. Inst. Chgo., Met. Housing Devel. Corp., Chgo., Nat. Realty Com. Served with USN; ETO. Home: Saint Charles, Ill. Died Feb. 21, 1979.

SKUTT, GILBERT LEWIS, park supt.; b. Waterloo, Ia., April 15, 1882; s. Wayne and Louise (Norris) S.; ed. pub. schs.; m. Helen Theresa Updegraff, Dec. 23, 1906; children—Miriam Constance, Forrest George. Engaged in floral and hort. bus., Denver, Colo., 1896-99; ornamental horticulture in comml. nurseries, 1900-05; park horticulturist, Minneapolis, 1906, Tacoma, Wash., 1907; parks supt., Walla Walla, Wash., 1908-09; private landscape work, 1910; propagator and salesman Wm. H. Moon Co., Morrisville, Pa., 1911-14; salesman Andarra Nurseries, Chestnut Hill, Pa., 1915; mgr. eastern br. Elliott Nursery Co., Princeton Junction, N.J., 1916-18; supt. Alto San Rafael Estates, Pasadena, Calif., 1919-22; park supt. Pasadena, 1923-36, Los Angeles since 1936. Coordinator of work projects for unemployed, Pasadena, 1930-36. Mem. Am. Inst. Park Execs. (past dir., now pres.), Western Shade Tree Conf. (past pres.), Calif. Inst. Park Execs. (past pres.), All City Employees Assn. of Pasadena (past pres.). Republican. Club: California Art (hon. mem.). Home: Pasadena. *

SLACK, JOHN M., JR., Congressman; b. Charleston, W.Va., Mar. 18, 1915; s. John M. and Jennie (Gilchrist) S.; ed. Va. Mil. Acad.; m. Frances J. Reid; 1 son. Mem. 86th-87th Congresses from 6th Dist. W.Va., 88th to 96th Congresses from 3d Dist. W.Va. Mem. Kanawha County (W.Va.) Ct., 1948-52; assessor Kanawha County, 1952-58. Mem. SAR. Democrat. Presbyterian (treas., deacon). Clubs: Masons, Shriners, Exchange. Address: Washington, D.C. Died Mar. 17, 1980.

SLADEN, FRANK JOSEPH (SLAD'EN), physician; b. West Point, N.Y., Jan. 6, 1882; s. Maj. Joseph Alton (U.S. Army) and Martha Frances (Winchester) S.; A.B., Yale 1902; M.D., John Hopkins, 1906; m. Susan Catherine Andrus, Jan. 9, 1915; children—Catherine Martha (Mrs. Rowland Lowe Hall), Frank Joseph Jr., Inin Andrus (Mrs. John Howland Wardwell). Mem. staff Johns Hopkins Hosp. and faculty of medicine, Johns Hopkins Univ., 1906-13; physician in chief, Detroit Gen. Hosp., 1913-15, Henry Ford Hosp., 1915-52; consultant to the medical services, 1952—. Mem. adv. bd. Selective Service, 1941. Mem. bd. trustees Henry Ford Hosp., 1923-53, McGregor Fund, McCormick Theol. Sem. (Chicago), McGregor Health Foundation. Mem. com. on religion and health, Fed. Council Churches; mem. bd. dirs. Mich. Soc. for Pastoral Care (pres. 1952-55); mem. gen. council Mich. synod, mem. nat. com. relating faith to health United Presbyn. Ch.; mem. steering com. Home Care Program; mem. bd. Jr. League St. Center; mem. adv. com. Visiting Nurses Assn.; mem. nat. com. Worldwide Church Canvass; mem. adv. com. Detroit Girl Scout Council; mem. alumni adv. bd. Yale. Served as capt., major M.C., U.S. Army, World War I. Diplomate American Board Internal Medicine. Fellow American Coll. Physicians; member A.M.A., A.A.A.S., Central Soc. for Clinical Research, Am. Rheumatism Assn., Detroit Com. on Aging, Wayne County Med. Soc., Zeta Psi, Alpha Omega Alpha, Phi Beta Kappa. Republican. Presbyn. Clubs: Graduate (New Haven); Detroit, University, Yale of Mich., Country, Grosse Pointe, Torch, Economic (Detroit); Cosmopolitan Medical Club (Interurban). Editor: Psychiatry and the War. 1944. Author: The Indispensable Man in Medicine, Sir William Osler, 1950. Contbr. to Faith at Work mag. Home: Grosse Pointe, Mich. *

SLATER, JOHN CLARKE, b. Oak Park, Ill., Dec. 22, 1900; s. John Rothwell and Katharine Southland (Chapin) S.; A.B., U. Rochester, 1920; A.M., Harvard, 1922, Ph.D., 1923; postgrad. Cambridge (Eng.) U., U. Copenhagen, 1923-24; Sc.D., Ripon Coll., 1946, Rochester U., 1964; U. Chgo., 1966, U. Fla., 1971; m. Helen Frankenfeld, 1926; children—Louise Chapin, John, Clarke; m. 2d Rose Mooney, 1954. Instr. physics, Harvard, 1924-26, asst. prof., 1926-29, asso. prof., 1929-30; prof. physics in charge of dept. M.I.T., Cambridge, 1930-51, staff Radiation Lab., 1940-45, inst. prof. physics, 1951-66; grad. research prof. physics and chemistry U. Fla., Gainesville, 1964-75; mem. staff Inst. Advanced Study, Princeton, N.J., 1937, tech. staff Bell Telephone Labs., 1943-44, Brookhaven Nat. Lab., 1951-52. Recipient Nat. medal of Sci., 1971. Guggenheim Meml. fellow, Leipzig, 1929. Mem. Am. Phys. Soc., Am. Acad. Arts and Scis., Nat. Acad. Scis., Am. Philos. Soc., Phi Beta Kappa, Delta Upsilon. Author: (with N. H. Frank) Introduction to Theoretical Physics, 1933; Introduction to Chemical Physics, 1939; Microwave Transmission, 1942; (with N. H. Frank), Mechanics, 1947, and Electromagnetism, 1947, Microwave Electronics, 1949; Quantum Theory of Matter, 1951, 2d edit., 1968; Modern Physics, 1955; Quantum Theory of Atomic Structure, vols. I and II, 1960; Quantum Theory of Molecules and Solids, vol. I, 1963, vol. II, 1965, vol. III, 1967, vol. IV, 1974; Solid State and Molecular Theory, a Scientific Biography, 1975; The Calculation of Molecular Orbitals, 1979. Contbr. tech. articles to profl. publs. Home: Gainesville, Fla. Died July 25, 1976; interred Evergreen Cemetery, Gainesville.

SLATER, LOUIS N., banker, merchant; b. Lithuania, Sept. 27, 1886; s. Martin and Monesh (Segal) S.; ed. Theol. Sem., Lithuania; m. Bertha Miller, Aug. 1, 1915; children—Matt, Miriam, Gerald. Came to U.S., 1907, naturalized, 1924. Pres. Slater Furniture Co., Fresno, Cal., 1912—, State Center Bank, Fresno, 1956-63; bank merged with Wells Fargo Bank, San Francisco, 1963, sr. v.p., 1963—. Chmn. local Draft Bd., 1940-46; mem. Cal. Legislative Adv. Com., 1956; mem. Cal. Social Welfare Bd., 1958-61; chmn. finance com. Fresno chpt. A.R.C., 1946—. Bd. govs. Fresno State Coll.; treas. Fresno chpt. Nat. Found. Infantile Paralysis; pres. Fresno Charities Assn.; bd. dirs. Fresno chpt. Am. Cancer Soc., Fresno United Givers Plan, Fresno council Boy Scouts Am., Fresno chpt. Am. Heart Assn., Fresno Boys Club, St. Agnes Hosp. and Blood Bank, Fresno. Recipient Outstanding Citizen Fgn. Birth award Internat. Inst., 1939, Outstanding Citizen award Fresno State Coll., 1951, Outstanding Citizen award Frat. Order Eagles, 1958. Mem. Fresno County and City C. of C. and Merchants Assn. (v.p. 1929-32). Jewish religion (hon. pres. temple 1961)). Kiwanian, Mason (Shriner); mem. B'nai B'rith (pres. Fresno 1924-26). Club: University-Sequoia-Sunnyside (Fresno). Home: Fresno, Calif. *

SLAUGHTER, ROBERT EDWARD, publisher; b. Vernon, Tex., Aug. 11, 1910; s. Robert E. and Goldie (Geingar) S.; A.B., Fresno State Coll., 1931; M.S., U. So. Calif., 1936; postgrad. Columbia U., 1942-45; advanced mgmt. program Harvard Grad. Sch. Bus., 1953; LL.D. (hon.), Rider Coll., 1960, U. N.D., 1966; m. Mary Pauline Funk, Aug. 22, 1937 (div. Oct. 1959); children—Lucretia Slaughter Gruber, Marcele Slaughter Kurz, Lynn Slaughter Rosenfeld; m. 2d, Gertrude Case, Mar. 5, 1960. Bus. tchr. Fresno (Calif.) City Schs., 1931-35; teaching fellow U. So. Calif., 1936-37; prof., head dept. commerce N.Mex. Highlands U., Las Vegas, 1937-38; prof., head dept. bus. edn. Madison Coll., Harrisonburg, Va., 1938-41; asst. mgr. N.Y. office Gregg Pub. Co., N.Y.C., 1941-44, advt. mgr., 1945-47; asst. to chief bus. and sales tng. sect., edn. div. VA, Washington, 1944-45; mgr. bus. edn. dept. McGraw-Hill Book Co., Inc., N.Y.C., 1948-49, v.p. Gregg Pub. Co. bus. edn. div. McGraw-Hill Book Co., 1949-52, v.p., gen. mgr., 1952-55, v.p., dir. McGraw-Hill Book Co., Inc., 1955-60, sr. v.p., dir., 1961-65, exec. v.p. McGraw-Hill, Inc., after 1965, dir., 1966-76; dir. Taft Broadcasting Co. Mem. Ind. Schs. Talent Search Program. Recipient Disting. Service award Nat. Assn. Council Bus. Schs., 1958, Leffingwell medal Adminstrv. Mgmt. Soc., 1964, ann. award for disting. service to edn. of pub. N.Y. Acad. Pub. Edn., 1971; Robert E. Slaughter Research award in Bus. and Office Edn. established by McGraw-Hill Book Co., 1975. Mem. N.Y. Acad. Pub. Edn. (pres.); Harvard Bus. Sch. Alumni Assn., Harvard Advanced Mgmt. Assn., Adminstrv. Mgmt. Soc., Delta Pi Epsilon, Alpha Kappa Psi. Home: Greenwich, Conn. Died May 28, 1976.

SLAUGHTER, WILLIAM HOWARD, pub. health service; b. Tensaw, Ala., Sept. 2, 1886; s. Howell W. and Eliza (Belt) S.; B.S., U. of Ala., 1909; M.D., U. of Va., 1912; m. Mary Cahalan, Aug. 11, 1914; children—William Howard, Howel William, Madeleine, Lee. Began as asst. surgeon U.S. Pub. Health Service, 1913, passed asst. surgeon, 1918-21, surgeon, 1921-33, sr. surgeon, 1933-40; became med. officer in charge of U.S. Marine Hosp., New Orleans, 1935; formerly med. officer in charge U.S. Marine Hospital, Chicago; retired as medical director, September 1, 1940. Served in Med. Corps at Fort Sill, Okla., and U.S. Navy Yard, Charleston, S.C., World War. Fellow Am. Coll. Surgeons, Am. Med. Assn.; mem. Theta Kappa Psi Democrat. Baptist. Mason. Contbr. articles to med. jours. Home: New Orleans, La. *

SLAVIT, JOSEPH (SLA'VIT), medical economist; b. Russia, June 15, 1883; s. Morris and Dinah (Goodman) S.; brought to U.S., 1890, naturalized, 1895; M.D., Cornell, 1904; grad. student Long Island Med. Coll., 1921, U. of Vienna, Austria, 1927-28; m. Charlotte Ross, Dec. 31, 1905 (dec.); children—Lester Lewis (dec.), Lewis Lester, Margaret Ross Franklin; m. 2d, Isabelle Bliden, Sept. 1, 1942. Medical inspector Dept. of Health, New York, 1908-12; attending pediatrist Jewish Hosp., O.P.D., Brooklyn, 1905-20, Samaritan Hosp., Brooklyn, 1908-22; adjunct-physician Beth Moses Hosp., Brooklyn, 1920-22, asso. physician Israel-Zion Hosp., Brooklyn, 1922, attending physician since 1928, chief of clinic since 1922; physician Union Health Center since 1929; cons. physician Maimonides Hosp., Brooklyn. Past chmn. Med. League for Socialized Medicine, Am. League for Public Medicine; past president medical staff, Israel-Zion Hosp.; member U.S. Interdepartmental Health Conference, 1938. Diplomate Am. Bd. Internal Medicine; mem. Am. Pub. Health Assn., A. Acad. of Polit. and Social Science, Brooklyn Institute of Arts and Sciences, A.M.A., New York State Medical Soc., N.Y. City Public Health Assn., Kings County Med. Soc., New Utrecht Med. Soc. (past pres.). Lecturer Rand Sch. Social Science, 1918-23, and Adult Edn. Div., New York City Bd. of Edn. Editor Am. Jour. Socialized Medicine, 1936. Author of An American Plan for Medical Care (monograph), 1935; Principles and Program of the Medical League for Socialized Medicine, 1933. Socialization of Med.; Objections and Questions Answered, (with Dr. S. Fischoff), 1933. Co-author; Gittelson-Goldstein Public Medicine Bills, New York State Legislature, 1938-41. Contributor to jours. on socialized medicine and med. econs. Address: Bklyn. *

SLESINGER, DONALD, psychologist; b. N.Y.C., Dec. 27, 1897; s. Anthony and Augusta (Singer) S.; A.B., Columbia U., 1920, postgrad., 1921-22; postgrad. Harvard U., 1920-21; m. Dorothy Eaton Avery, Sept. 3, 1921; children—Jonathan Avery, Joanna Slesinger Caproni. Served as psychologist to Judge Baker Found., Boston, 1920-21, then with Nat. Com. for Mental Hygiene, New York, 1921-23; with Cherry Lawn Sch., Darien, Conn., 1923-25; research Laura Spelman Rockefeller Meml., 1926-27; Sterling fellow Yale Law Sch., 1927-28, research asst., 1928-29; asst. prof. law Yale, 1929-30, also exec. sec. Inst. Human Relations; prof. law U. Chgo., 1930-36, asso. dean Div. Social Scis., 1931-36; dir. dept. edn. N.Y. World's Fair, 1937-38; mem. Raymond Rich Assos., 1937-38; dir. mgmt. tng. course Nat. Assn. Housing Ofcls., Washington, 1935-36; exec. dir. Am. Film Center Inc., 1938-47, exec. dir. Internat. Film Center; cons. TVA, War Dept. and Office Health, Welfare and Related Def. Activities Fed. Security Agy., 1940-42, chief visual tng. sect. U.S. Office Civilian Def., 1942-43; adminstrv. dir. Ednl. Film Library Assn., 1943-44; pub. Film News, 1945-47; analytic psychologist, 1947-77; lectr. N.Y. U. Mem. Planning Bd., Truro, Mass., 1972-77. Bd. dirs. Fountain House Found. Served with U.S. Army, 1918. Mem. Council Psychoanalytical Psychotherapists, Nat. Com. U.S.A. Internat. Intellectual Coop., Assn. Psychoanalytic Psychologists (pres.). Contbr. articles to periodicals, ency., Psychol. Review, Psychol. Bull., Am. Jour. Sociology, Harper's Scribner's, Nation, Ency. Social Sci., Modern Canterbury Pilgrims. Episcopalian (vestryman). Address: Truro, Mass. Died Oct. 13, 1977; interred St. James the Fisherman Cemetery, Wellfleet, Mass.

SLICHTER, LOUIS BYRNE, educator, geophysicist; b. Madison, Wis., May 19, 1896; s. Charles Sumner and Mary Louise (Byrne) S.; A.B., U. of Wis., 1917, Ph.D., 1922, D.Sc., 1967; LL.D., U. Cal., Los Angeles, 1969; m. Martha Merry Buell, Oct. 20, 1926; children—Susan Merry, Mary Louise (Mrs. Ward Whaling). Physicist

Submarine Signal Corp., Boston, 1922-24; geophys. prospecting, Mason, Slichter & Hay, Madison, Wis., 1924-27, Mason, Slichter & Gauld, 1927-31; research asso., Calif. Inst. Tech., 1930-31; asso. prof. geophysicis, Mass. Inst. Tech., 1931, prof. 1932-45; prof. geophysics, U. Wis., Madison, 1946-47; dir. Inst. Geophysics, U. Cal., 1947-62, prof. geophysics, 1962, emeritus, 1963. Served as ensign, U.S.N.R., 1917-19. Mem. div. 6 Office of Scientific Research and Devel., 1942-45. Recipient Presidential Certificate of Merit, 1948, Distinguished Service citation Univ. Wis., 1957; Daniel C. Jackling award, Am. Inst. Mining, Metall. and Petroleum Engrs., 1960; Alumnus of Yr. award Joint Wis. Alumni Assns. of So. Cal., 1963, William Bowie medal Am. Geophys. Union, 1966. Fellow Am. Phys. Soc.; mem. Am. Acad. Arts and Scis., Geol. Soc. Am., Nat. Acad. Sci., A.A.A.S., Am. Geophys. Union, Soc. Exploration Geophysicists (hon. life), Explorers Club, Am. Seismol. Soc., Phi Beta Kappa, Chi Phi, Sigma Xi, Tau Beta Pi, Gamma Alpha. Club: Cosmos (Washington). Contbr. articles to tech. articles. Home: Pacific Palisades, Calif. Died Mar. 25, 1978; buried Forest Hill Cemetery, Madison, Wis.

SLOAN, ARTHUR WILLIAM, chemist; b. Denver, Ill., Nov. 25, 1900; s. William Findlay and Myrtle (Cannon) S.; B.S., U. Ill., 1922; M.S., Harvard, 1924, Ph.D., 1926; m. Ruth C. McNeil, Sept. 17, 1927. Research chemist B.F. Goodrich Co., 1926-27, div. head research, 1927-40, dir. chem. research, 1940-44; requirements office Fgn. Econ. Adminstrn., Egypt, 1944-46; project dir. Engring. Research Asso., 1947-49; pres. Atlantic Research Corp., Alexandria, Va., 1949-50, chmn. bd., exec. v.p., dir. research, 1951-62, vice chmn. bd., chief exec. officer, dir. research, 1962-65, chmn. bd., chief exec. officer, 1965-67; chmn. bd., mem. exec. com. Susquehanna Corp., Alexandria, 1967-71, chief exec. officer, 1967-71; dir., mem. exec. com. Pan Am. Sulphur Co. Sci. adviser Joint Chiefs Staff, Dept. Def., 1950-51. Chmn. Fairfax County Com., United Givers Fund, 1960; mem. commn. on human resources Washington Center Met. Studies, 1961-67. Mem. president's club U. Ill. Found., 1964-80; bd. dirs. Washington Ballet Guild, Inc., 1961-64; bd. dirs. Nat. Symphony Orch. Assn., 1962-80, 1st v.p., 1970-73; trustee Washington Nat. Ballet Found., 1962-65; mem. U. Ill. Found., 1961-80; council mem. Harvard Grad. Soc. Advanced Study and Research, 1962-73; vis. com. chemistry Harvard, 1962-74. Mem. Am. Chem. Soc., A.A.A.S., Am. Inst. Chem. Engrs., Combustion Inst., Harvard Alumni Assn. (dir. 1964-66). Club: Cosmos (Washington). Home: Washington, D.C. Died June 17, 1980.

SLOAN, EDWARD RAY, lawyer; b. Seward County, Neb., Mar. 12, 1883; s. George W. and Hannah J. (McCullough) S.; LL.B., Washburn Coll. Sch. of Law, Topeka, Kan., 1905; m. Julia L. Wright, Jan. 24, 1906; children—Eldon R., Gordon W., Clarice E. Admitted to Kan. bar, 1905; atty. for Sheridan County, Kan., 1905-11, for City of Holton, Kan., 1912-31; mem. Kan. Legislature, 1923-29; asso. justice of Supreme Ct. of Kan., 1931-33; mem. Kan. Ins. Code Commn., 1926-27; sr. mem. Sloan, Hamilton & Sloan, Topeka, Kan., 1933-47; apptd. referee in bankruptcy for Dist. of Kan., 1947; chmn. State Corp. Commn. of Kan., 1937. Mem. Phi Alpha Delta. Democrat. Methodist. Mason. Clubs: Country, Knife and Fork. Home: Topeka, Kan.*

SLOAN, EVERETTE ASKINS, coll. prof.; b. Fayetteville, Tenn., Nov. 26, 1895; s. Albert Lowry and Ollie (Askins) S.; ed. Morgan Sch., Fayetteville, Tenn., 1909-11; A.B., Erskine Coll., Due West, S.C., 1915; M.S., Vanderbilt U., 1930; Ph.D., chemistry, U. of Chicago, 1938; student Columbia U., 1925; m. Ann Pressly, Aug. 10, 1923; 1 dau., Elizabeth. Chemistry teacher Principal, High Sch., Oak Hill, Ala., 1916-17; prof. chem., Bryson College, Fayetteville, Tenn., 1919-29, dean, 1925-29; prof. chem. Tenn. Polytech. Inst., Cookeville, Tenn., 1930-36; prof. chem. Erskine Coll., Due West, S.C. since 1938, dean of college, 1947-63, emeritus, 1967-76, chmn. chemistry dept. Erskine Coll., to 1967. Served as 1st lt., Ordnance Dept., A.E.F., France, World War I. Mem. S.C. Acad. Science, Sigma Xi. Democrat. Presbyn. Address: Due West, S.C. Died Apr. 14, 1976.

SLOANE, JOHN, corps. dir.; b. N.Y.C., 1883; B.A., Yale, 1905; m. Elsie Nicoll, June 23, 1917 (dec.); children—Grace Elsie (Mrs. Cyrus R. Vance), Nancy (Mrs. Benjamin Coates), Evelyn (Mrs. Percy R. Pyne III); m. 2d, Mrs. Hope Colgate Jerome, Sept. 14, 1954. Chmn. bd., dir. W. & J. Sloane N.Y.C., resigned as chmn., 1955, retired as director; dir. Centennial Ins. Company; trustee Atlantic Mutual Insurance Company of New York. Director Union Settlement. Past v.p., honorary trustee. Presbyterian Hospital, City of N.Y.; v.p., trustee Nat. Inst. of Social Science; trustee Marine Museum of City of N.Y., Cathedral of the Pines Trust (life), Served as pvt. Squadron A, N.Y. N.G., 1907-12; on gen. staff, Washington, 1918; N.Y. State Guard, 1941-46, retiring as col. Decorated Chevalier French Legion of Honor. Honorary chairman, member board of trustees Mus. of City of N.Y.; mem. bd. trustees Bennington (Vt.) Mus. Mem. N.Y. C. of C. (life), English Speaking Union, Pilgrim Soc., Soc. Colonial Wars, St. Andrews Soc. (hon.), So. Vt. Art Assn. Clubs: Union, River, University, Century, Yale, Somerset Hills Country; Mt. Anthony Country (Bennington, Vermont). Home: N.Y.C.*

SLONIM, MARC, author, educator; b. Novgorod-Seversk, Russia, Mar. 26, 1894; s. Leo and Indiana (Aikhenvald) S.; student U. Petrograd, 1915-18; Ph.D., U. Florence (Italy), 1920; m. Suzanne Campaux, 1920 (div. 1922); 1 dau., Helen (Mrs. Theodore Costinesco); m. 2d, Tatiana Lamm, Dec. 18, 1951; 1 son, Dimitry. Came to U.S., 1941, naturalized, 1957. Mem. Russian Constituent Assembly, 1917-18; editor monthly Will of Russia, Prague, Czechoslovakia, 1922-32; writer, lectr., Paris and other European capitals, 1932-40; lectr. various Am. Coll., 1941-42; faculty mem. comparative, Russian lit. Sarah Lawrence Coll., Bronxville, N.Y., 1943-62, dir. fgn. studies, from 1962; contbr. N.Y. Times Book Review. Mem. Am. Assn. Advancement Slavic Studies, League Ams. Residing Abroad, Pen Club. Author: The Epic of Russian Literature, 2d edit., 1964; Modern Russian Literature, 1953; An Outline of Russian Literature, 1957; Three Loves of Dostoevsky, 1956; Russian Theater from the Empire to the Soviets, 1962; Soviet Russian Literature, 1964. Editor: Modern Italian Short Stories, 1964. Contbr. articles Am., European mags., jours. Home: Geneva, Switzerland. Died May 8, 1976.

SMALL, ALVAH RANDALL, fire protection engring.; b. South Portland, Me., Dec. 7, 1882; s. Winfield Scott and Georgia Anna (Spear) S.; B.S., U. of Me., 1904, C.E., 1929; m. Josephine Roquetta McManus, 1906 (died 1907); 1 son, Alvah Randall; m. 2d, Carol Lynn Greegs Buchanan, 1909 (died Sept. 1928); m. 3d, Oleita Harlan Harrison, July 29, 1933. Inspector N.Y. Fire Ins. Exchange, 1904-06; with Underwriters Laboratories, Chicago, Ill., since 1906, asst. engr., also asst. elec. engr., 1906-07, special agent, 1908-09, supt. label service, 1910-16, became vice pres. 1916, pres. 1935-48, vice chairman of the board since 1948, also trustee and dir.; pres. and dir. Underwriters Lab. of Can., 1935-38. Served as expert, fire prevention sect. War Industries Bd. 1917-18. Fellow Am. Inst. E.E.; mem. Am. Soc. for Testing Materials, Am. Standards Assn. (dir.), Nat. Fire Protection Assn. (hon. life mem., dir.), Internat. Assn. Elec. Inspectors (hon. life mem.). Republican. Clubs: University, Lake Shore (Chicago); Indian Hill (Winnetka, Ill.); Drug and Chemical (New York). Home: Winnetka, Ill.*

SMALL, BURRELL LESLIE, communications exec.; b. Kankakee, Ill., Apr. 2, 1918; s. Leslie Charles and Grace Olive (Burrell) S.; B.S. in Journalism, U. Ill., 1940; m. Reva Arlene Gray, Dec. 3, 1938; children—Susanne Gray, Leslie Howard, Stephen Burrell. With Kankakee Daily Jour., 1940-69, pres., co-pub., 1957-69; pres. Mid Am. Media, Kankakee, 1947-81; pres. Mid Am. Audio-Video, Mid Am. Radio, Mid Am. Broadcasting, Imagery Corp.; dir. First Trust & Savs. Bank, First Bank of Meadowview. Fin. chmn. Asbury United Methodist Ch.; chmn. ARC. Mem. Kankakee C. of C. (pres.), U. Ill. Journalism Alumni (pres.). Republican. Home: Kankakee, Ill. Died Feb. 22, 1981.

SMALL, CHARLES HUGHEY, lawyer; b. St. Louis, Mo., Sept. 2, 1880; s. Charles Edwin and Laura A. (Hughey) S.; student U. of Pa., 1900-01; LL.B., Kansas City (Mo.) School of Law, 1903; m. Jenice Thomas Marshall, Dec. 1, 1927 (died Oct. 9, 1936). Practiced with father at Kansas City, Mo., 1903-09; U.S. vice consul gen. in charge at Bogota, Colombia, 1910-11, Guatemala City, 1911-12; attaché Am. Legation, Santa Domingo City, Dominican Republic, 1912 (resigned); resumed pratice of law, Kansas City, Mo.; moved to Denver, Colo., 1915; practiced law, 1917-28. Mem. Mo. Child Labor Com., 1903-10; Mo. del. Child Labor Conv., Washington, D.C., 1915. Mem. exec. bd. Colo. Patriotic League, 1918-19 (chmn. com. to investigate so-called German efficiency); speaker under auspices of Nat. Com. on Pub. Information, 1918; speaker under auspices various nat. and state orgns. since 1916; referee, Industrial Commn. of Colo., 1921; sec. Pub. Utilities Commn. of Colo., 1922; spl. asst. to atty. gen. of U.S., 1928-30; senior atty., Dept. of Justice, in defense of Govt. in suits brought by Indian tribes, 1930-46; retired from govt. service and moved to Little Rock, Ark., Jan. 1946; now lectr. and writer on politics, economics, etc. Mem. Acad. Polit. Sci., Nat. Council on Am. Rights (dir.), Sigma Alpha Epsilon. Republican. Methodist. Club: National Press (Washington D.C.). Home: Little Rock, Ark.*

SMALL, EDWARD, motion picture producer; b. Bklyn., Feb. 1, 1891; s. Philip and Rose Small. Began career as actor, booker and producer gen. theatrical attractions; later organized screen talent agency for actors, writers, and dirs. which operated in N.Y. and Hollywood; producer of silent pictures for First Nat. release; organized Reliance Pictures, Inc. (with Harry M. Goetz), 1932, producer pictures including Last of the Mohicans, Count of Monte Cristo, Red Salute, I Cover the Waterfront; organizer Edward Small Prodns., Inc., for United Artists release, 1938, producing numerous pictures, including: Duke of West Point, Man in the Iron Mask, My Son, My Son, Kit Carson, Son of Monte Cristo, Corsican Brothers, Twin Beds, Up in Mabel's Room, Brewster's Millions, Red River, Black Magic, Fuller Brush Man, Valentino, Lorna Doone, The Brigand, New York Confidential, T-Men, Monkey on My Back, Witness for the Prosecution, Solomon and Sheba, Jack the Giant Killer, Apache Rifles, Arizona Raiders, Frankie and Johnny, I'll Take Sweden, Boy, Did I Get a Wrong Number, The Wicked Dreams of Paula Schultz; The Christine Jorgensen Story, 1970. Address: Hollywood, Calif. Died Jan. 25, 1977.

SMALLEY, RUTH ELIZABETH, educator; b. Chgo., Nov. 14, 1903; d. Joseph Henry and Grace (Hollister) S.; B.A., U. Minn., 1924; M.S.S., Smith Coll., 1929; D.S.W., U. Pitts., 1949; LL.D., Cath. U. Am., 1968. Staff bd. edn. Bur. Child Guidance, Newark, 1929-32; mem. faculty U. Chgo., 1932-35; dir. vis. tchr. dept. Bd. Edn., Rochester, N.Y., 1935-37; faculty Sch. Social Work, Smith Coll., 1937-38; asso. prof., then prof. Sch. Social Work, U. Pitts., 1939-50; prof. Sch. Social Work, U. Pa., 1950-67, prof. emeritus, 1967-79, acting dean, 1957-58, dean, 1958-66; Fulbright lectr., Italy, 1966-67; lectr. Leader Exchange Program U.S.-South Africa, 1968. Recipient group award of merit Nat. Conf. Social Welfare, 1956; Disting. Alumni award U. Pitts., 1969. Fellow Am. Orthopsychiat. Assn.; mem. Nat. Assn. Social Workers, AAUP, Council Social Work Edn. (pres. 1960-63), Phi Beta Kappa, Gamma Phi Beta, Mortar Bd. Author: Theory for Social Work Practice, 1966; also articles. Home: Radnor, Pa. Died July 10, 197 1979; interred Valley Forge Meml. Gardens, King of Prussia, Pa.

SMART, WYATT AIKEN, clergyman, educator; b. Newberry, S.C., Oct. 22, 1883; s. Richard Davis and Ella (Aiken) S.; prep. edn., Webb Sch., Bell Buckle, Tenn.; B.A., Vanderbilt, 1904; B.D., Union Theol. Sem., 1907; spl. work, U. of Chicago; D.D., Southern Methodist Univ., Dallas, Tex., 1919, Ohio Wesleyan Univ., Delaware, O., 1930; m. Ethel Bradshaw Chappell, Dec. 30, 1909; 1 dau., Mrs. Helen Smart Rewis. Ordained ministry M.E. Ch., S., 1911; pastor Trinity Ch., Lynchburg, Va., 1907-09, Park View Ch., Portsmouth, Va., 1909-13, First Ch., Charlottesville, Va., 1913-14; prof. Bibl. theology, Emory U., since 1914. Associate Dean, School of Theology, since 1943; Chaplain of the University since 1943. Mem. Soc. Bibl. Lit. and Exegesis, Delta Kappa Epsilon, Omicron Delta Kappa, Phi Beta Kappa. Democrat. Author: The Contemporary Christ, 1942; The Spiritual Gospel, 1945; Still the Bible Speaks, 1947. Co-author:Preaching in These Times, 1940. Home: Emory University, Ga.*

SMEAD, EDWARD LEON (SMED), banker. b. Branch County, Mich., Feb. 23, 1884; s. Nelson and Mary (Smith) S.; grad. Northern Ind. Commercial Coll., Valparaiso, 1904; LL.B., Georgetown Law Sch., Washington, D.C., 1914; m. Marion E. Lake, Apr. 1906; children—Fay Agana, Richard Peer, Ward Grayson (dec.). Teacher, pub. schools, 1901-04; with Coldwater (Mich.) Nat. Bank, 1904-05; accountant, Navy Dept., Island of Guam, 1905-10; asst. to chief clerk Bur. of Navigation, Navy Dept., 1911-14; asst. chief Div. of Reports and Statistics, Federal Reserve Bd., 1914-20; chief of same div. (now known as Div. of Bank Operations, Board of Governors, Federal Reserve system), 1920-44, and director of division, 1944-48; administrator for War Loans, Board Governors of Federal Reserve System, Oct. 1942-Aug. 1946. Admitted to practice before District of Columbia Court of Appeals, 1914, and before Supreme Court of United States, 1926. Mason. Club: Pasadena. Author of chpt. on operations of res. banks, Banking Studies. Home: Coldwater, Mich.; also St. Petersburg, Fla.*

SMELSER, MARSHALL, historian; b. Joliet, Ill., Feb. 4, 1912; s. Albert Marion and Alma (Van Hook) S.; A.B., Quincy Coll., 1935; A.M., Harvard U., 1942, Ph.D., 1948; m. Anna May Padberg, Dec. 27, 1937; children—Mary Elizabeth, Mary Katherine. Teaching fellow St. Louis U., 1937-39, instr., 1939-43; with ARC, 95th Inf. Div., 1943-44, Nat. Hdqrs., 1944-46; asst. prof. Coll. St. Thomas, 1946-47; faculty U. Notre Dame, 1947-78, prof., 1956-78, head dept., 1960-63, also mem. acad. and grad. councils; Forrestal fellow U.S. Naval Acad., 1956-57. Del. Ind. Democratic Conv., 1956, 58, 60, 62, 68; del. tally clk. Dem. Nat. Conv., 1956; mem. St. Joseph County Superior Ct. Jud. Commn., 1975-78; hist. adviser Ind. Gen. Assembly, 1976-78. Recipient Commencement citation U. Notre Dame, 1972; Guggenheim fellow, 1963-64. Mem. Authors Guild, Am. Fedn. Musicians, Soc. Ind. Pioneers. Roman Catholic. Author: American Colonial and Revolutionary History, 1950; The Campaign for the Sugar Islands, 1955; American History at a Glance, 1959; The Congress Founds the Navy, 1959; The Democratic Republic, 1801-1815, 1968; Winning of Independence, 1972; The Life That Ruth Built, 1975; contbr. articles to mags. Home: South Bend, Ind. Died Jan. 19, 1978; buried Cedar Grove Cemetery, Notre Dame, Ind.

SMITH, ALFRED FORREST, polit. economist; b. San Francisco, Aug. 26, 1897; s. James Oliver and Marie Caroline (Scow) S.; student U. Calif., 1918-21; m. Emma N. Fenzl, Aug. 7, 1926. Civil engring. field asst.; granted full C.E. status by State of Calif., 1931; dir. San Francisco Bur. Govt. Research, from 1943. Mem. Nat.

Tax Assn., Am. Soc. Public Adminstrn., Nat. Mcpl. League, Govtl. Research Assn. (trustee 1946, v.p. 1947), Theta Chi. Republican. Club: Press and Union League (San Francisco). Home: Oakland, Calif. Died May 21, 1976.

SMITH, ALLAN ADOLPH, lawyer; b. Gilmore City, Ia., Apr. 15, 1885; s. Jacob and Louisa (Hoffman) S.; A.B., Humboldt Coll., 1908; m. Mabel Garrett, June 19, 1912 (dec. Jan. 1960); children—Lois M. (Mrs. R.E. Dwan), Allan Hugh. Admitted to Ore. bar, 1910; practiced in office Judge John L. Rand, Baker, Ore., 1910-16; pvt. practice law, Baker, 1910-40; mem. firm Smith, Rives & Rodgers, and predecessors, Portland, 1941-64; consultant firm of Rives & Rodgers, 1964—. President, dir. Western Loan & Bldg. Co., Salt Lake City, 1934-55; treas., dir. Collins Pine Co., 1931—; gen. counsel, dir. Ore. Water Corp., 1943-64; gen. counsel Pacific Power & Light Co., 1953-64, dir., 1957-64; v.p., dir. Eastern Ore. Light & Power Co., Baker, 1933-41. Mem. Ore. Ho. of Reps., 1919-21. Mem. Am., Ore. (bd. govs. 1935-39, pres. 1936), Multnomah Co. bar assns., Baker, Portland chambers commerce. Democrat. Roman Catholic. Elk, K.C. Clubs: Kiwanis, City, Arlington. Home: Portland. *

SMITH, ARTHUR JAMES MARSHALL, author; b. Montreal, Que., Can., Nov. 8, 1902; s. Octavius Arthur and Alexandra Louise (Whiting) S.; came to U.S., 1930, naturalized, 1941; B.S., McGill U., 1925, M.A., 1926, Litt.D. (hon.), 1958; Ph.D., Edinburgh U., 1931; LL.D., Queen's U., Kingston, Ont., 1966, Dalhousie U., 1969; D.C.L. (hon.), Bishop's U., 1967; m. Jeannie Dougall Robins, Aug. 15, 1927; 1 son, Peter George Marshall. Instr. to prof. and poet in residence English dept. Mich. State U., East Lansing, 1936-72; vis. prof. U. Toronto, 1946-47, Queens U., summers 1952, 60, U. B.C., summer 1956, Sir George Williams U., Montreal, summers 1967, 69, Dalhousie U., 1966-67, State U. N.Y. at Stony Brook, 1969, McGill U., 1969-70; Claude Bissell chair Can.-Am. studies U. Toronto, 1976-77. Recipient Gov.-Gen.'s medal for poetry, 1943, medal Royal Soc. Can., 1966, Dominion of Can. Centennial medal, 1967, Can. Council medal, 1968; Guggenheim fellow, 1941-42, Rockefeller fellow, 1945-47. Author: The Book of Canadian Poetry, 1943; News of the Phoenix (poems), 1943; Seven Centuries of Verse, 1947, 57, 67; The Worldly Muse, 1951; A Sort of Ecstasy, 1954; (with M.L. Rosenthal) Exploring Poetry, 1955, 73; (with F.R. Scott) The Blasted Pine, 1957; The Oxford Book of Canadian Verse, 1960; Collected Poems, 1962; Modern Canadian Verse, 1967; Poems, New and Collected, 1967; Towards a View of Canadian Letters, 1973; The Canadian Experience, 1973; The Colonial Century, 1973; The Canadian Century, 1973; Essays on Poetry and Poets, 1977; The Classic Shade, Selected Poems, 1978. Contbr. articles to profl. jours. Home: East Lansing, Mich. Died Nov. 21, 1980.

SMITH, AUSTIN WHEELER, coll. dean; b. Franklin Co., Tenn., Sept. 5, 1885; s. Robert George and Myra Anne (Mitchell) S.; student Middle Tenn. State Normal, 1911-13; B.S., U. of South. 1918, M.A., 1928; m. Sina Clarissa Vaden, Apr., 1919 (dec. Feb. 1936); children—Myra Isabella (Mrs. Edward C. Gracey), Clarissa Anne, Austin Wheeler; m. 2d, Altie Lorelle Hayes, Dec. 18, 1941. Tchr. elementary, high sch., 1909-10; supt. pub. instrn., Franklin County, Tenn., 1910-16; head history dept. Tenn. Poly. Inst., 1916-22, registrar, 1921-22, dean, registrar, 1922—, acting pres., 1926-27, 1940. Chmn. Putnam Co. chpt. A.R.C., 1941-46. Mem. S.A.R. (v.p. Tenn. chpt.), Middle Tenn. Edn. Assn. (pres. 1917-18), Tenn. Assn. Collegiate Registrars and Admission Officers (pres. 1949-50), N.E.A., Tenn. Edn. Assn., Nat. Assn. Collegiate Registrars and Admissions Officers. Democrat. Church of Christ. Author: Dickson-McEwen and Allied Families Genealogy, 1946. Home: Cookeville, Tenn.*

SMITH, BUDD ELMON, coll. pres.; b. Benson, N.C., Feb. 9, 1910; s. James L. and Hettie (Lee) S.; A.B., U. N.C., 1931, M.A., 1934, Ph.D., 1942; postgrad. Duke, 1950-51; LL.D., Wake Forest Coll., 1961; D.Sc. (hon.), Campbell Coll., 1973; m. Ethel Lillie Knott, Dec. 27, 1943; children—James Fielding, William Budd. Prof. biology Coker Coll., 1931-32, 34-35, 39-46; plant breeder Coker's Pedigreed Seed Co., Hartsville, S.C., 1935-39; prof. biology Wake Forest Coll., 1946-51; supt. schs. Oxford, N.C., 1951-53; pres. Wingate Coll., 1953-74, pres. emeritus, 1974-76. Mem. Nat. Accrediting Commn. Higher Edn.; mem. edn. commn. So. Bapt. Conv., 1972—. Trustee Union Meml. Hosp.; mem. indsl. commn. Union County, 1954-57; pres. Union County Indsl. Devel. Commn., 1960-64, 66-69. Served to lt. USNR, 1942-45. Named Man of Year, Union County, 1961. Mem. A.A.A.S., Am. Assn. Sch. Adminstrs., Bot. Soc. Am., Monroe-Union County C. of C. (pres. 1972), Am. Assn. Community and Jr. Colls. (dir. 1972—), Phi Beta Kappa, Sigma Xi, Omicron Delta Kappa, Alpha Sigma Phi, Alpha Epsilon Delta. Democrat. Baptist (deacon). Lion, Rotarian. Home: Benson, N.C. Died Aug. 5, 1976.

SMITH, C(HARLES) WILLARD, educator; b. Pottstown, Pa., Jan. 24, 1899; s. Charles Adam and Helen Fussell (Bierbauer) S.; A.B., Princeton, 1922, A.M., 1925, Ph.D. in English Lit., 1937; m. Florence Webster, Sept. 5, 1925; children—Alice Virginia (Mrs. George N. Barrett, Jr.), Webster. Instr. English, biology, Latin, Pingry Sch., Elizabeth, N.J., 1922-24; mem. faculty Bucknell U., 1925-79, prof. English, from 1946, prof. emeritus, to 1979, John P. Crozer prof., from 1954, chmn. dept., 1954-64, sec. faculty, 1952-79, rep. faculty to bd. trustees, 1953-55, chmn. com. acad. freedom and tenure, 1962-79, dir. Coll. Theatre, 1930-50, chmn. bd. Univ. players, 1948-52, dir. Inst. Fgn. Students, 1944-54; cons. Inst. Internat. Edn., 1950. Charter mem. Lewisburg Community Theatre Guild, 1936-50. 2d lt. F.A. Res. Officers Corps, U.S. Army, 1922-32. Recipient Lindback award distinguished teaching, 1963. Mem. Modern Lang. Assn., Shakespeare Assn., Am. Assn. U. Profs., Nat. Assn. Fgn. Student Advisers (bd. dirs. 1948-50), Phi Beta Kappa (hon.), Delta Upsilon. Baptist. Author: Browning's Star Imagery, 1941. Home: Lewisburg, Pa. Died Oct. 22, 1979.

SMITH, CHARD POWERS, author, lectr.; b. Watertown, N.Y., Nov. 1, 1894; s. Edward North and Alice (Lamon) Powers S.; A.B., Yale, 1916; LL.B., Harvard, 1921, postgrad., 1924-25; summer sch., Oxford U., Eng., 1921; M.A., Columbia, 1949; m. Olive Cary MacDonald, Sept. 10, 1921 (dec. Mar. 1924); m. 2d, Marion Antoinette Chester, Dec. 21, 1929 (div. Sept. 1957) children—Chard Powers, Marion Kendall; m. 3d, Eunice Waters Clark, Oct. 18, 1957. Lectr. poetry, hist. items; vis. prof. on N.E. culture U. Kans., 1950; fellow Huntington Hartford Found., 1956-57, 58. Del. Agrarian-Distributist Conf., Nashville, 1936, Northwestern U., 1937; trial justice, Cornwall, Conn., 1939-45. Mem. Soc. of Friends. Trustee N.Y. Friends Sem., Bklyn. Friends Sch. Served to capt. AUS, 1917-19; grad. Army Staff Coll., Langres, France, 1919. MacDowell fellow, 1924-52; guest at Yaddo, 1956. Mem. MacDowell Assn., Soc. Am. Historians, P.E.N. Soc., Conn. Hist. Soc., Vt. Acad. Arts and Scis. (trustee), Am. Legion, Wolf's Head Soc. (Yale), Zeta Psi. Clubs: Century (N.Y.C.); Elizabethan (Yale); Gilpin (Hartford). Author: (verse) Along the Wind, 1925; Lost Address (U.S. and Eng.), 1928; Hamilton (poetic drama), 1930; The Quest of Pan, 1930; Prelude to Man, 1936; (anthology) Poets of the Twenties—100 Great Poems, 1967; (prose) Pattern and Variation in Poetry, 1932; Annals of the Poets, 1935; (novels) Artillery of Time, 1939, (Eng. 1956); Ladies Day, 1941, (Eng. 1958); Turn of the Dial, 1943; He's in the Artillery Now, 1943; The Housatonic (Rivers of America Series), 1946; Yankees and God, 1954; Where the Light Falls, a Portrait of Edwin Arlington Robinson, 1965. Editorial bd. Free America, 1936-37. Address: Arlington, Vt. Died Oct. 31, 1977; interred at Watertown, N.Y.

SMITH, CHARLES ADELBERT, aluminum and chem. co. exec.; b. Corning, Ohio, Oct. 23, 1901; s. Charles Ellsworth and Sarah Augusta (Prior) S.; B.Ceramic Engring., Ohio State U., 1923; grad. student Lehigh U., 1924; m. Waldine Barnes, Apr. 16, 1931; 1 son, Charles Conard. Ceramic engr., supt. A. P. Green Fire Brick Co., Mexico, Mo., 1924-26; chief engr. Liptak Fire Brick Arch Co., Mexico, 1926-27, Bigelow Liptak Corp., Detroit, 1927-30; chief engr., v.p., dir. Mexico Refractories Co. (Mo.), 1930-57, exec. v.p., dir., 1957-59; v.p. Kaiser Aluminum and Chem. Corp., Oakland, Calif., 1959-66. Vice pres. Great Rivers council Boy Scouts Am., 1956-59; trustee Andrian County Hosp., Mexico, 1948-59. Registered profl. engr., Mo. Fellow Am. Ceramic Soc. (Plaque award 1970); mem. Nat. Inst. Ceramic Engrs., ASTM (Lamme Gold Medal award 1967), ASME, Sigma Xi, Tau Beta Pi. Presbyn. (elder). Mason (32 deg.), Rotarian. Clubs: Mexico Country; Sequoyah Country (Oakland). Home: Oakland, Calif. Died Nov. 4, 1975.

SMITH, CHARLES FREDERICK, author, educator; b. Cleveland, O., Aug. 14, 1883; s. Frank Steven and Clara Elizabeth (Albach) S.; prep. edn., high sch.; student Case Sch. Applied Science, 1903, Ohio State U., 1904-05, Teachers Coll. (Columbia), 1906-07; B.S., Columbia, 1908; m. Bertha Francis Thompson, of Hartford, Conn., June 11, 1910; children—Charles Warner, Gilbert Creig, Sylvia Christine. Instr. in manual training, high sch., Cleveland, 1908-09; instr. manual training and physical edn., high sch., Highland Park, Ill., 1909-10; instr. manual training, physical edn. and scouting, Staten Island (N.Y.) Acad., 1910-17; instr. physical and recreational edn., Horace Mann Sch., New York, 1917-20; instr. scouting and recreational leadership, Teachers Coll. (Columbia), since 1917. Exec. officer Boy Scout Internat. Jamboree, 1920; nat. ednl. dir. Boy Scouts America, 1924. Mem. 9th Coast Arty., N.Y.N.G., 1916. Mem. N.E.A., Woodcraft League, Camp Fire Girls, Nat. Camp Directors' Assn. Episcopalian. Mason. Author: Games and Recreational Methods, 1924; Scoutmaster-Patrol Leader Pow Wow, 1925; Scouting Principles and Practices, 1927. Home: Rosebank, N.Y.*

SMITH, CHARLES LAVENS, banker; b. Franklin, Pa., Mar. 9, 1885; s. Edwin D. and Sophie Jane (Rogers) S.; A.B., Allegheny Coll., 1904; m. Bess McMillan, Sept. 25, 1909; children—Virginia Wadsworth (wife of Dr. Don McCauley Curtis), Raymond McMillan, Edwin David (dec). Engaged in mfg., Franklin, 1904-07, in mining, Utah and Ariz., 1908-11; partner Ed. D. Smith & Sons, Salt Lake City, 1911-22; v.p. Central Trust Co., 1922-31; pres. Security Nat. Bank, 1931-32; pres. First Nat. Bank, 1932-48; chmn. First Security Bank; dir. First Security Corporation, Salt Lake City Branch of Federal Reserve Bank; mem. Salt Lake City Clearing House Assn. (ex-pres.). Pres. Community Chest of Salt Lake City, 1937-38; mem. adv. com. R.F.C., state chmn. Savings Bond Div. U.S. Treasury Dept. Treas. U. of Utah. Mem. bd. of Govs. Salt Lake Chamber of Commerce. Mem. Am. Bankers Assn. (mem. economic policy com.); mem. Utah Bankers Assn., (pres. 1934-35), Reserve City Bankers Assn., Sigma Alpha Epsilon, Phi Beta Kappa. Republican. Presbyn. Club: Alta (pres. 1946). Home: Salt Lake City. *

SMITH, CHARLES WILLIAM, lawyer, pub. utilities cons.; b. Balt., May 18, 1896; s. Thomas Little and Rebecca Frances (Chilcote) S.; B.C.S., Southeastern U., 1923; B.S., Nat. U., 1924; LL.B., U. Balt., 1932; m. Catherine Agusta Meehan, June 23, 1928; children—Charles W., Charlotte M. (Mrs. Joseph F. Hennessy), Frances (Mrs. Justin A. Vitrano). Millworker, 1915; successively stenographer, clk. and bookkeeper, 1916-20; auditor U.S. Income Tax Unit, 1920-29; chief auditor Pub. Serv. Commn. of Md., 1929-36; chief Bur. of Accounts, Finance and Rates, FPC, 1936-55; cons. public utilities; tchr. accounting Johns Hopkins U. Evening Sch. Econ., 1930-38; maj. role in obtaining Supreme Ct. recognition of prudent investment principle of public utility regulation; expert witness numerous public utility cases; C.P.A., N.C. and Md.; mem. bars Md. and U.S. Supreme Ct. Mem. Md. Assn. C.P.A.'s (ex-pres.), Am. Bar Assn. (mem. council pub. utilities sect.), Am. Inst. Accountants, Am. Accounting Assn., Am. Econ. Assn., Delta Sigma Pi, Beta Alpha Psi. Author: Practical Accounting Systems; also articles on accounting, financial and econ. subjects. Address: Baltimore, Md. Died Feb. 20, 1976.

SMITH, DANIEL MALLOY, educator; b. Sanford N.C., July 12, 1922; s. Daniel Malloy and Alma (Bruton) S.; A.B., U. Cal. at Berkeley, 1949, M.A., 1950, Ph.D., 1954; m. Carolyn Aladeen Brown, Jan. 11, 1946; children—Stephanie Ann, Daniel Bennett, Gregory Malloy. Instr. history Stanford, 1953-57; vis. instr. U. Cal. at Berkeley, 1954; mem. faculty U. Colo., 1957-76, prof. history, 1964-76, chmn. dept., 1969-76; vis. prof. U. Ore., 1965. Chmn. Am. history com. Coll. Level Exam. Program, Ednl. Testing Services, 1968-69. Served with USNR, 1942-46. Grantee Am. Philos. Soc.-Am. Council Learned Socs. Mem. Am. Hist. Assn., Orgn. Am. Historians, Soc. History Am. Fgn. Relations, Denver Council Fgn. Relations, Phi Beta Kappa, Phi Alpha Theta. Author: Robert Lansing and American Neutrality, 1958; Major Problems in American Diplomatic History, 1964; American Intervention 1917, 1966; The Great Departure: U.S. in World War, 1965; Aftermath of War: Bainbridge Colby and Wilsonian Diplomacy, 1970; The American Diplomatic Experience, 1972; War and Depression, 1972. Home: Boulder, Colo. Died July 28, 1976.

SMITH, EARL JONAS, govt. official; b. Ogle Co., Ill., Mar. 11, 1883; s. Jonas C. and Mary E. (Mead) S.; B.S., Mendota Coll., 1904; J.D., Univ. of Chicago, 1909; m. Ethel R. Shatto, Mar. 25, 1919; children—Sheridan, Mary Mead. Admitted to Ill. bar, 1910, and practiced in Chicago, 1910-33; with Solicitor's Office, U.S. Dept. of Agr., 1933-46, chief of office of hearing examiners, since 1946. Served in U.S. Army. 1917-19. Home: Washington. *

SMITH, EARLE SAMUEL, dental educator; b. Wenona, Ill., Mar. 27, 1884; s. Herbert Amos and Elsie Ann (Hazard) S.; B.D., Ia. State Teacher's Coll., 1903; D.D.S., State Univ. of Ia., 1914; student U. of Minn., 1920; m. Clara Bonnewell, June 7, 1905; children—Elsie Isabelle (Mrs. J. Franklin Robinson), Herbert Bonnewell. Teacher and sch. supt., Iowa, 1903-11; began private practice of dentistry, 1914; instr. dental anatomy, U. of Ia., and operative dentistry technic, Coll. of Dentistry, State U. of Iowa, asst. prof. operative dentistry, 1919-20, asst. prof. clinical prosthetic dentistry, 1920-23, prof., head of dept. since 1923. Civilian consultant in prosthetic dentistry to the Surgeon General, U.S. Army, 1944-46. Fellow American Coll. Dentistry, 1930; mem. Univ. Dist. Dental Society (pres. 1942), Ia. State Dental Soc. (sec. 1919-26, pres. 1929), Am. Acad. Prosthetic Dentistry (pres. 1940), Xi Psi Phi, Omicron Kappa Upsilon. Republican. Methodist. Mason. Club: Triangle. Contbr. to dental jours. Home: Iowa City, Ia.*

SMITH, GEOFFREY F. N., life ins. co. exec.; b. Box Hill, Eng., Mar. 11, 1926; s. Sydney A. and Phyllis I. (Elworthy) S.; came to U.S., 1963, naturalized, 1969; B.A., U. Toronto, 1946; m. Marguerite H. Scaife, Sept. 1954; children—G. Lawrence, Craig D., Gail B. Actuarial trainee, then supr. Can. Life Ins. Co., Toronto, 1947-53; sucessively asst. actuary, actuary, v.p. and actuary Sovereign Life Ins. Co., Winnipeg, Man., 1953-63; v.p., actuary Am. Mut. Life Ins. Co., Des Moines, 1963-67, pres., 1967—, chief exec. officer, 1969-80. Chmn. capital fund drive Campfire Girls, 1978; exec. com. Jr. Achievement of Des Moines, 1975-80. Fellow Soc. Actuaries, Canadian Inst.

Actuaries; mem. Am. Acad. Actuaries. Episcopalian. Clubs: Des Moines, Des Moines Golf and Country. Home: Des Moines, Iowa. Died Sept. 28, 1980.

SMITH, GEORGE FREDERICK, educator, mfr.; b. Lucasville, Ohio, July 29, 1891; s. Clarence Michel and Matilda (Pflaumer) S.; student Ohio State U., 1910-12; B.S., U. Mich., 1917, M.S., 1919, Ph.D., 1921; m. Mary Ellen Sweeny, Aug. 19, 1921; children—Ruby Mae (Mrs. Robert R. Harding), Joseph Clarence Clifton, Mary Eleanor (Mrs. S. B. Weaver). Faculty, U. Ill. 1921-76, instr. chemistry, asso., asst. prof., asso. prof., 1921-39, prof. chemistry, 1939-55, prof. emeritus, 1955-76; pres. G. Frederick Smith Chem. Co., Columbus, Ohio, 1924-68, chmn. bd. 1968-76; pres. Aeration Processes, Inc., Columbus, 1932-68, chmn. bd., 1968-76; dir. Applied Chem. Testing Lab. Recipient Fisher award Am. Chem. Soc., 1954; Ann. chem. award Am. Chem. Soc., 1959; Outstanding Achievement award U. Mich., 1974. Mem. Am. Chem. Soc. (chmn. div. analytical chemistry 1954), Am. Ceramic Soc., Soc. Chem. Industry, Electro-chem. Soc., Am. Leather Chems. Soc., Am. Inst. Chemists, Alpha Chi Sigma, Phi Lambda Upsilon, Sigma Xi, Mason (32 deg. K.T. Shriner). Clubs: University, Country (Urbana). Author: Quantitative Analysis (with Harvey Diehl), 1952. Home: Urbana, Ill. Died Sept. 23, 1976; interred Mt. Hope Mausoleum.

SMITH, GLENN J., business exec.; b. Deerfield, O., Feb. 11, 1885, s. Charles M. and Elizabeth (Card) S.; m. Bess L. Carpenter, June 3, 1908 (dec. 1968); children—Jack Carpenter, Don Carlos, Dale J., Virginia Lee (Mrs. Donald Dwyer Young) (dec.), Brooksey Nell (Mrs. Claude L. Wright), Joe Wesely. With Jennings State Bank (Okla.), 1911-16; pres. Wood Oil Co., 1929; owner Mora Ranch, Wagon Mound, N.M., Mora Ranch, Miami, Okla., Investors Royalty Co., Inc. Mem. C. of C. Republican. Mason (Shriner, Jester). Clubs: Tulsa; Summitt. Address: Tulsa OK. *

SMITH, GUY-HAROLD, prof. geography; b. La Farge, Wis., Jan. 1, 1895; s. John William and Harriet (Waddell) S.; Ph.B., U. of Wis., 1921, Ph.D., 1927; post grad. study, U. of Pa., 1922-23; m. Elizabeth Baker, Aug. 5, 1926; 1 son, John Waddell. Student asst. in geography, U. of Wis., 1920-21, grad. asst., 1921-22; instr. geography, U. of Pa., 1922-23, U. of Wis., 1923-27; asso. U. of Ill., 1928-29; asst. prof. geography, Ohio State U., 1927-28, 1929-34, asso. prof. and chmn. dept., 1934-37, prof. and chmn., 1937-63; visiting prof., summer sessions, Peabody Coll. for Teachers, 1929, 30, U. of Wash., 1935, Western Reserve U., 1937, State Teachers College, Buffalo, N.Y., 1938, Columbia U., 1939, 41, 42, 44. Served in infantry U.S. Army, World War, 1917-18, disch. as 2d lt. Mem. Ohio George Washington Bicentennial Commn., 1932. Consultant, Mil. Intelligence Service, U.S. Army Gen. Staff. 1943-44, 1948-49. Fellow A.A.A.S. (vice president 1962), Am. Geog. Soc., Ohio Acad. Science (v.p. 1935, pres. 1961); mem. Assn. Am. Geographers (v.p., 1937; treas., 1938-47), Nat. Council Geog. Education, American Polar Society, Arctic Inst. N.A., Sigma Xi, Phi Beta Kappa, Beta Gamma Sigma. Author (with Dorothy Good): Japan: A Geographic View, 1943. Editor & contbr. Conservation of Natural Resources, 1950, 58; also numerous physiographic maps; chpts. and articles various publs. in field. Republican. Clubs: Faculty; East Chop Beach (Oak Bluffs, Mass.). Address: Columbus, Ohio. Died Apr. 7, 1976; buried Union Cemetary, Columbus.

SMITH, HAROLD, lawyer; b. Chicago, Ill., Dec. 13, 1884; s. Felix F. and Claribel (Hooker) S.; LL.B., Northwestern U., 1905; LL.M., Yale U., 1906; m. Lilian Howard Wiley, Apr. 24, 1912 (died Oct. 15, 1918); 1 son, Harold; m. 2d, Pauline Virginia Curtiss, Mar. 31, 1926; children—Pauline Curtiss, Robert Imbrie. Admitted to Ill. bar, 1906; asso. with Glennon, Cary, Walker & Howe, later Glennon, Cary & Walker), 1906-12, mem. firm, 1912-19; atty. Westinghouse Electric & Mfg. Co., New York, 1919-26, gen. solicitor, 1926-30, vice pres., 1930-44, and dir. various Westinghouse companies during that period; now engaged in general practice of law. Mem. Am., Chicago Bar Assn., Assn. Bar N.Y.C., Am. Fgn Law Assn. (past pres.). Rep. Presbyterian. Mason. Clubs: Racquet and Tennis, Down Town Association, Yale (New York). Home: Washingtonville, N.Y., and N.Y.C. *

SMITH, HENRY GARFIELD, clergyman; b. Parkersburg, Ia., Sept. 2, 1885; s. Wilke Albert and Elizabeth (DeVries) S.; A.B., Shurtleff Coll., Alton, Ill., 1914; B.D., Rochester Theol. Sem., 1918; D.D., Grand Island (Neb.) Coll., 1929; m. Mary Ellen Hamil, Sept. 24, 1918; children—Marjorie Ellen, Virginia Lois, Robert Hamil. Began as clerk, 1905; ordained ministry Bapt. Ch., 1918; pastor Berwich, Ill., 1918-21, Second Ch., Lincoln, Neb., 1921-27, Temple Ch., Chicago, 1927-33, Calvary Ch., Denver, Colo., since 1933. Pres. Chicago Bapt. Ministers' Assn., 1929-30; trustee Chicago Ch. Fedn., 1928-33, Colo. Woman's Coll., Denver, since 1933; pres. Denver Ministerial Alliance, 1935, Colo. Bapt. State Conv., 1935-37; v.p. Am. Bapt. Home Mission Soc., 1935; mem. Council of Finance and Promotion of Northern Bapt. Conv., 1939-40, pres., 1940-41; member bd. mgrs. Ministers' and Missionaries Benefit Bd., Northern Bapt. Conv., since 1942; pres. Denver Bapt. Ministers' Conf., 1939-40; mem. bd. trustees Denver Y.M.C.A. since 1935. Club: Lions (dir.). Home: Denver, Colo.*

SMITH, HOWARD EVERETT, painter, etcher; b. West Windham, N.H., Apr.27, 1885; s. Charles and Sarah Jane (Goodwin) S.; student Boston Latin Sch., 1899-1902; studied Art Students' League, New York; pupil of Howard Pyle, Wilmington, Del., 2 yrs.; m. Martha Jeanne Rondelle (deceased April 1948); married second, Helen Hughes, 1949. Has exhibited in leading cities of U.S.; represented in U.S. Treasury Bldg. by portrait of William H. Osborn, portraits of Governor Eugene Foss and Governor Maurice J. Tobin, in State House, Boston, Mass., Dr. Herman C. Bumpus and Dean Otis Randall, Brown University, Dean Arthur McLean, Boston University, Gen. J. Stilwell, West Point, Chief Justice Earl Warren, California State Capitol, A. P. Giannini, Bank of America, San Francisco, California, and by portraits in Salem (Mass.) Court House, Rand School, New York, North Adams (Mass.) Pub. Library, Pa. Acad. Fine Arts, Gregg Collection, New York, University of Neb., and in many private galleries; has painted many equestrian portraits, including Man O' War, Battleship, Troublemaker, Flowing Gold, Culpepper, Colony Boy. Recipient John Wanamaker prize, Phila., Paige traveling scholarship, Mus. Art, Boston, bronze medal, San Francisco Expn., First Hallgarten prize, Isidor medal, and Maynard portrait prize, N.A.D.; Augustus S. Peabody prize, Art Inst. Chgo., illustration prize, Wilmington, Del., first prize Sacramento, Cal., first prize Santa Cruz, Cal. State-Wide Exhibit, popular print prize, Cal. State Fair, A.N.A., 1921; mem. Art Students' League (N.Y.), Am. Water Color Soc., Carmel (Cal.) Art Assn., Republican. Episcopalian. Contbr. illustrations and articles to Harper's Monthly. Address: West Chester, Pa.*

SMITH, HOWARD F(RANKLYN), surgeon, U.S. Pub. Health Service; b.Baltimore, Md., Feb. 1, 1884; s. Isaac F. and Florence I. (Evans) S.; student Baltimore City Coll., 1902-05; M.D., Baltimore Med Coll., 1909; m. Kathryn C. Cunningham, Nov. 10, 1908. Commd. asst. surgeon U.S.P.H.S., 1913, passed asst. surgeon, 1917, surgeon, 1921, sr. surgeon, 1933; quarantine officer Philippine Islands, 1913-14; stream pollution studies in Ohio River watershed, 1915-17; med. officer in charge extra cantonment zone, Camp Beauregard, La., 1917-18; chief quarantine officer, Hampton Roads, Va., 1919-22, Philippine Islands, 1923-26; Am. consulates at Dublin, Bergen, Norway, and Palermo, Italy, 1927-29; med. adviser to Pres. of Republic of Italy, 1927-29; med. adviser to Pres. of Republic of Liberia, Africa, on control of yellow fever, 1930; Am. consulates gen. at Mexico City and Havana, 1931-32; became chief quarantine office for Philippine, Islands, 1933; now chief pub. health adviser, staff U.S. ambassador of P.I., also asst. surgeon gen. for Far East. Clubs: Army and Navy, Manilo Polo, Manila Golf, Wack Wack Golf and Country (Manila).*

SMITH, HOWARD WORTH, congressman; b. Broad Run, Va., Feb. 2, 1883; s. William W. and Lucinda (Lewis) S.; grad. Bethel Mil. Acad., Warrenton, Va., 1901; B.L., U. Va., 1903; m. L. Violett Proctor, Nov. 4, 1913 (dec. 1919); children—Howard Worth, Violett Adelaide; m. 2d, Anne Corcoran, June 27, 1923. Practiced law, Alexandria, Va., 1904-22; asst. gen. counsel Alien Property Custodian, 1917-18; commonwealth's atty. of Alexandria, 1918-22; judge Corp. Court, Alexandria, 1922-28; judge, 16th Jud. Circuit of Va., 1928-30; mem. 73d Congress (1933-35), Va. at large; mem. of 72d, 74th to 89th congresses, 8th Va. Dist. Past owner and pres. Alexandria Gazette Corp.; past chmn. bd. Alexandria Nat. Bank; engaged in farming and dairying. Past mem. bd. visitors U. Va. Mem. Md.-Va. Milk Producers Assn. Democrat. Episcopalian. Mason, Odd Fellow, Elk. Home: Alexandria, Va. Died Oct. 3, 1976.

SMITH, J. JOSEPH, U.S. judge; b. Waterbury, Conn., Jan. 25, 1904; s. James Emile and Margaret Loretta (Dunn) S.; A.B., Yale, 1925, LL.B., 1927; LL.D. (hon.), U. Hartford, 1979; m. Eleanor M. Murnane, Aug. 16, 1939; children—J. Joseph, Richard P., Mary Eleanor McCarthy, Mary Martha Murphy. Admitted to Conn. bar, 1927; law practice at Waterbury; research fellow Yale Sch. Law, 1927-28; mem. 74th to 77th Congresses (1935-41), 5th Conn. Dist.; apptd. U.S. dist. judge, Conn., 1941; apptd. U.S. circuit judge, 2d circuit, 1960; sr. U.S. Circuit judge, 2d Circuit, Hartford, Conn., until 1980. Mem. Am. Conn., Waterbury bar assns., Am. Judicature Soc., Phi Delta Phi. Catholic. Home: West Hartford, Conn. Died Feb. 16, 1980; buried Calvary Cemetery, Waterbury.

SMITH, JAMES CRAIG, textile exec.; b. Birmingham, Ala., July 23, 1905; s. James Craig and Mignon (Comer) S.; A.B., Va. Mil. Inst., 1925; m. Mary Page Thompson, Dec. 11, 1928; 1 dau., Mignon Comer. Started as cotton weigher, 1925; with Avondale Mills, textiles, Sylacauga, 1925-77, v.p., dir., 1935-41, v.p., treas., dir., 1941-45, exec. v.p., dir., 1945-51, pres., treas., dir., 1951-70, chmn. bd., 1970, chmn. exec. com., dir., 1975-77; chmn. 1st Fed. Savs. & Loan Assn. Sylacauga; dir. I.C. Gulf R.R., South Central Bell Telephone Co., So. Bancorp., Birmingham Trust Nat. Bank, Protective Life Ins. Co., Gen. Machinery Corp., Ill. Central Industries. Bd. dirs., past pres. Ala. Safety Council; trustee, past chmn. Eye Found., Inc., Birmingham; chmn. Avondale Ednl. and Charitable Found.; vice chmn. Sylacauga Park and Recreation Bd.; trustee Avondale Mills Employees Profit-Sharing Trust; hon. trustee Boys' Club of Sylacauga, So. Talladega County chpt. A.R.C.; bd. visitors U. Ala. Sch. Commerce. Named Outstanding Layman, Ala. Recreation and Park Soc., 1955, Communicator of Yr., Internat. Council of Indsl. Editors, 1970, Man of South, Dixie Bus., 1970; recipient Mktg. Man of Year award Birmingham chpt. Am. Mktg. Assn., 1970; J. Craig Smith Community Center, Sylacauga Parks and Recreation Dept. named in his honor, 1976; elected posthumously to Ala. Bus. Hall of Fame, 1977. Mem. Am. Textile Mfrs. Inst., Inc. (dir., past pres.), Ala. Textile Mfrs. Assn. (past pres., Textileer award 1971), Internat. Fedn. Cotton and Allied Textile Industries (past pres.), Nat. Cotton Council Am. (dir., past pres.), Ala. C. of C. (dir., past pres., Newcomen Soc. N.Am. (Ala. chmn., nat. trustee), Liverpool Cotton Assn. (hon.), Ala. Acad. Honor, Omicron Delta Kappa (hon.), Phi Psi (hon.). Republican. Rotarian (past pres., hon. mem.). Clubs: Exchange (hon.), Coosa Valley Country (Sylacauga); Birmingham Country, Mountain Brook, Redstone, Relay House, The Club, Downtown (Birmingham). Home: Birmingham, Ala. Died May 12, 1977; buried Birmingham.

SMITH, JOHN FRANCIS, JR., steel exec.; b. Chgo., July 3, 1908; s. John F. and Matilda J. (Shanahan) S.; Certificate in advanced management, Harvard Bus. Sch., 1946; LL.D., Loyola U., Chgo., 1965; m. Mary V. Cradick, Aug. 22, 1931; children—Patricia Ann (Mrs. James Lehr), John F. III, George William. Asst. mgr., order div. Inland Steel Co., Chgo., 1937-39, mgr. order div., 1940-45, asst. mgr. sales, 1946-47, gen. mgr. sales, 1948-52, v.p. sales, 1952-59, pres., 1959-66, asst. to chmn., 1966-69, dir., 1956-80, finance com., 1959-69, exec. com., 1967-80; chmn. Inland Steel Container Co. div., 1967-80, Grotnes Machine Works, Inc., 1967-80, dir. N.P. Ry. Asst. dir., chmn. directive com. steel div. NPA, 1951. Gen. chmn. Community Fund-Red Cross Joint Appeal, 1957; dir. Community Fund Chgo., 1959-63, Jr. Achievement Chgo., 1960-64, Chgo. Assn. Commerce and Industry, 1960-65; trustee, v.p. Chgo. Joint Appeal, 1959-61; dir. Cath. Charities Corp., 1958-80, pres., 1967-68. Mem. bd. lay trustees Loyola U., 1959-80, chmn., 1966-68; mem. med. council Stritch Sch. Medicine. Decorated Knight Sovereign Mil. Order Malta; recipient Founder's Day Civic award Loyola U., 1962. Citizen fellow Inst. Medicine, Chgo. Mem. U. Chgo. Citizens Bd., Ill. C. of C., Assn. Northwestern U., Wildlife Soc., Council Fgn. Relations. Clubs: Economic, Commercial, Chicago (Chgo.); Bob O'Links Golf (Highland Park, Ill.); North Shore Country (Glenview, Ill.). Home: Wilmette, Ill. Died Feb. 10, 1980.

SMITH, JOHN JAMES, educator, physician; b. Elizabeth, N.J., Feb. 7, 1912; s. Denis J. and Wilhelmina (Ollenstaedt) S.; A.B., St. Peters Coll., 1934; M.D., Cornell U., 1938; m. Rosemary V. Gorman, Nov. 28, 1945; children—Margaret (Mrs. Allen Mitchell), Vincent, Cornelius, Denis, Rosemary, Padraic. House officer N.Y. Hosp., 1938-42; practice medicine, specializing in cardiology, N.Y.C., 1946-75; from instr. to clin. prof. medicine Cornell U. Med. Coll., N.Y.C., 1942-75, prof., 1967-75; attending physician N.Y. Hosp., 1967-75; physician-in-charge Pvt. Patients Service, 1968-75. Served with M.C., AUS, 1942-45. Fellow Am. Heart Assn.; mem. Am. Fedn. Clin. Research. Home: Elizabeth, N.J. Died Mar. 19, 1975; interred St. Mary's Cemetery, Kingston, N.Y.

SMITH, JOHN LUCIAN, JR., beverage co. exec.; b. West Point, Miss., Oct. 24, 1918; s. John Lucian and Sara Eugenia (Cottrell) S.; B.C.S., U. Miss., 1940; m. Claire Davis, Aug. 6, 1953; children—Daniel Davis, Susan Peyton. With Coca-Cola Co., Atlanta, 1940-67, field sales mgr., 1957-61, pres., 1974-79, dir., until 1980; pres. foods div. Coca-Cola Co., Houston, 1967-70; pres. Coca-Cola USA, Atlanta, 1971-74; chmn. bd. Coca-Cola Export Corp., 1976-79; dir. Phillips Petroleum Co.; adv. dir. So. Ry. System. Nat. bd. dirs., v.p. Boys' Clubs Am.; trustee Spelman Coll.; mem. adv. bd. Scottish Rite Hosp. Mem. Am. Soc. Corporate Execs., Delta Kappa Epsilon. Clubs: Capital City, Univ. Yacht, Commerce, Piedmont Driving (Atlanta). Home: Atlanta, Ga. Died July 19, 1980.

SMITH, JOSEPH EDWARD, mfg. co. exec.; b. Monroe, N.Y., July 12, 1923; s. Howard A. and Emily A. Smith; student Princeton U., 1941-42; m. Elizabeth Bennett, Sept. 6, 1947; 1 son, Joseph Edward. With Investors Diversified Service, Mpls., 1954-56, Bear Stearns & Co., N.Y.C., 1957-64; fin. cons., 1964-68; with Singer Co., N.Y.C., 1966-80, dir., 1971—, sr. v.p., 1974-80, chief fin. officer, 1975-80, vice chmn. for policy and programs, 1978-80; dir., mem. exec. com Penn Central Corp.; dir. Mass. Mut. Corp. Investors. Served with U.S. Army, 1942-45. Clubs: N.Y. Yacht, Rumson Country, Edgartown Yacht, Indian Harbor Yacht. Home: Greenwich, Conn. Died May 1, 1980; buried Edgartown, Mass.

SMITH, KENT HALE, company dir.; b. Cleve., Apr. 9, 1894; s. Albert William and Mary (Wilkinson) S.; B.S. in Physics, Dartmouth, 1915; B.S. in Chem. Engring., Case Inst. Tech., 1917; D.Eng. (hon.), 1954; LL.D. (hon.), Western Res. U., 1960, Dartmouth College, 1961; Doctor of Science (honorary), Oberlin College, 1960; m. Thelma Gertrude Samson, Jan. 3, 1946. With Dow Chem. Co., 1919-21; pres. Ce-Fair Devel. Co., Cleve., 1921-28; a founder Lubrizol Corp., Wickliffe, Ohio, 1928, pres., 1928-29, 32-51, chmn. bd., 1951-59, dir., 1928-80; acting pres. Case Inst. Tech., 1958-61; dir. Aero Distbs., Inc., Gen. Aviation, Inc., Cleve. Electric Illuminating Co., Cleve. Trust Co., Growth Capital, Inc. Trustee Case Inst. Tech., Cleve. Council World Affairs, Euclid-Glenville Hosp. (life), Holden Arboretum, Cleve. Zoo; distbn. com. Cleve. Found.; chmn. emeritus Cleve. Mus. Natural History, from 1971, Greater Cleve. Associated Found., from 1971; trustee, a founder Corp. 1% Program for Higher Edn., Inc., from 1961; hon. dir. Cleve. Growth Assn. Mem. Am. Chem. Soc., Phi Kappa Psi, Kappa Kappa Kappa, Alpha Chi Sigma. Clubs: Chagrin Valley Hunt (Gates Mills); Cleve. Skating (Shaker Heights, Ohio); Mid-Day, Rowfant, Union, University (Cleve.); Riomar (Vero Beach, Fla.). Address: Gates Mills, Ohio. Died Mar. 26, 1980.

SMITH, LELAND LESLIE, consular service; b. Portland, Ore., June 29, 1885; s. Walter Vincent and Edith Jewett (Carter) S.; student Portland Acad., Stanford, École Internationale, Paris; m. Gilberte Garros, of Versailles, France, Nov. 7, 1922. In mortgage and security business, Portland, 1908-17; served as capt. U.S.A., 1917-19; asst. mil. attaché, Rumania, 1919-20; apptd. consul, June 13, 1921, and assigned to Saigon, French Indo-China; consul at Tunis since 1924. Decorated Chevalier Legion of Honor (French); Croix de Guerre (Rumanian). Home: Portland, Ore.*

SMITH, LESTER SHERALD, lawyer; b. Granc Rapids, Mich., July 14, 1906; s. Samuel H. and Rose (Kirk) S.; A.B., U. Mich., 1927, LL.B., 1930; m. Esther Winkelman, Sept. 3, 1929; children—Suzanne (Mrs. John C. Hopp, Jr.,), Nancy (Mrs. Jerome C. Hirsch), Richard L. Admitted to Mich. bar, 1930, since practiced in Detroit; mem. firm Smith, Hirsch & Brody, 1965-69, Smith, Miro, Hirsch & Brody, 1969-73, Smith, Miro, Hirsch, Brody & Zweig, 1973-76. Dir. Allied Products Corp.; sec., dir. Hughes & Hatcher, Inc. Mem. Am., Mich., Detroit bar assns. Clubs: Standard City, Franklin Hills Country (past pres.). Home: Franklin, Mich. Died Nov. 16, 1976.

SMITH, LEVI PEASE, chmn. Burlington Savs. Bank; b. Burlington, Vt., Aug. 30, 1885; s. Charles P. and Anna (Pease) S.; Bachelor of Arts, University of Vermont, LL.D., 1950; LL.B., Harvard University; m. Julia Pease, June 20, 1914; children—Frederick Plimpton, Robert Pease, Levi Pease, Jr. v.p. Burlington Savings Bank, 1917-34, pres., 1935-58, chmn. board, 1959—; director Vermont Broadcasting Corp. Mem. Vt. House of Reps., 1923-24; state senator, Vt., 1925-26, 1927-28, 1929-30. Chmn. Vt. State Banking Advisory Bd., 1935-39. Mem. Administrative Council Nat. Assn. Mut. Savs. Banks, 1934-42, pres., 1942-43, mem. com. fed. taxation. State chmn. U.S. Savs. Bonds Div.; pres. Vt. State Bankers Assn., 1929. Mem. exec. council Am. Bankers Assn., 1930-33, 1943-44, administrative com., 1943-44; econ. policy commn., 1944-50. Pres., dir. Converse Home (Burlington, Vt.), Club: St. Botolph (Boston), Century (N.Y.). Home: Burlington, Vt.*

SMITH, LUTHER ANDREW, Masonic exec.; b. Alpharetta, Ga., Sept. 20, 1883; s. Freeman R. and Sarah Elizabeth (Alexander) S.; Ph.B., Emory Coll., 1904; LL.B., Vanderbilt U., 1909; LL.D., George Washington U., 1961, Am. U., 1963; m. Loraine McInnis, Mar. 26, 1912; children—Sarah Lou (Mrs. Burns Dews). Admitted to Miss. bar, 1909, and practiced in Hattiesburg until 1953; chancellor Ct. of Chancery for 10th Dist. Miss., 1953-55. Organized trust dept. Hattiesburg Bank, 1918; organized Hattiesburg Bldg. & Loan Assn., 1927-28; pres. Morgan Plan Bank, Hattiesburg, 1925-30; dir. Forrest Hotel Corp., Hattiesburg, 1935-55, v.p., 1945-55. Mem. Masons, 1907—, grand master in Miss., 1941-42; mem. Shriners, 1920—, K.T., 1921—; active mem. Supreme Council, 33, Ancient and Accepted Scottish Rite of Freemasonary, So. Jurisdiction, U.S.A., 1937—, grand orator, 1939-47, grand minister of state, 1947-51, grand prior, 1951-53, lt. grand comdr., 1953-55, sovereign grand comdr., 1955-69, also editor monthly publ., The New Age; advocated, secured approval establishment edn. program in pub. schs. for courses in Am. history, way of life and heritage; also sponsored fellowships at George Washington U. Sch. Govt. Chmn. Hattiesburg Democratic Exec. Com. 1930-35; mem. Forrest Country Dem. Exec. Com., 1940-58. Trustee Whitworth Coll., Brookhaven, Miss., 1935-42; chmn. trustees Hattiesburg Pub. Sch. System, 1941-45. Mem. Am., Miss., Hattiesburg bar assns., Hattiesburg C. of C. (dir) 1921-30). Kiwanian. Home: Washington, DC. *

SMITH, OSCAR ALPHEUS, ry. official; b. near Sterling, Ill., Oct. 16, 1885; s. George Washington and Anna (Vroman) S.; student Los Angeles High Sch., 1900-03, Southern Calif. Business Coll., 1904; m. Daphne May Tilley, Sept. 7, 1910; 1 son, Oscar A. Began as mfr.'s agent, 1905; soliciting agent Mo., Kan. & Tex. Ry., 1908-09; with Pacific Electric Ry. Co. since 1909, successively clk., traveling agent, asst. traffic mgr., gen. passenger agent, passenger traffic mgr. and v.p., pres. since 1937, also dir.; pres. and director Pacific Electric Land Company, Motor Transit Lines, Subway Terminal Corporation; trustee Anna V. Smith Estate; Pres. Optimist Internat., 1927-28. Rep. Meth. Mason, Forester. Clubs: California, Jonathan, Transportation, Optimist (Los Angeles); Los Angeles Athletic. Home: San Marino, Calif. *

SMITH, PAUL ALTHAUS, educator; b. Lancaster, N.H., May 18, 1900; B.S., Dartmouth, 1921; Ph.D., Princeton, 1926; NRC fellow, Harvard, 1926-27; m. Suzanne Bloch, 1935; children—Matthew, Anthony. Instr. mathematics Barnard Coll., Columbia, 1927-29, asst. prof., 1929-40, asso. prof. 1940-45, prof., 1945-77. Chmn. div. mathematics NRC, 1955-58. Mem. Nat. Acad. Scis., Math. Soc. (treas. 1937; mem. edn. bd.). Contbr. math. jours. Home: New York, N.Y. Died June 13, 1980.

SMITH, PAUL JORDAN, author; b. Wytheville, Va., Apr. 19, 1885; s. Rev. J. Wesley and Lucy (Jordan) S.; student Emory and Henry Coll., 1903-04; B.A., U. of Chattanooga, 1906, Litt. D., 1946; studied Lombard Coll., Galesburg, Ill., 1907-08, U. of Chicago, 1912, U. of Calif., 1914-15; m. Sarah Bixby, Mar. 30, 1916 (dec.); children—Isabel Jordan, Wilbur Jordan, Ralph Wendell; m. 2d, Dorothy Eads Wysor, June 26, 1934. Instr. in English, U. of Calif., 1914-16, instr. in English novel, extension liv., 1918-20; literary ed. of the Los Angeles Times, 1933-58; lectr. on American hist. novel, U. Cal., 1958—. Adv. bd. Huntington Hartford Found., 1950-65. Mem. Authors' League Am., Oxford Bibliog. Soc. Episcopalian. Clubs: Zamorano (Los Angeles); Authors' (London). Author books, latest being: On Burton's 'Anatomy of Melancholy', 1959; The Road I Came, 1960; Firm Hidden Springs, 1961; also editor or compiler several books; contbr. to newspapers and mags. Home: Los Angeles. *

SMITH, RICHARD GARBETT, mining co. exec.; b. Anaheim, Cal., Sept. 19, 1886; s. Charles F. and Henrietta E. (Bremmerman) S., A.B., Stanford, 1909; m. Ethel Anda Irwin, Mar. 23, 1913; 1 dau., Maty Anda. Jr. engr. U.S. Mineral Survey, Alaska, 1909-12; engr. gold dredging dept. Natomas Co., 1912-28, supt., 1928-32, mgr., 1932-49, pres., gen. mgr., 1949—. Mem. Am. Inst. Mining and Metall. Engrs. Lion. Home: Folsom, Cal. *

SMITH, ROBERT DWIGHT, steel co. exec.; b. Belle Center, O., Nov. 25, 1903; s. John Kerr and Edna (Bell) S.; student Chgo. Inst.; grad. sr. exec. program, Mass. Inst. Tech., 1959; m. Margaret Elizabeth Lundegard, Sept. 1, 1934; 1 son, Ronald Keith. Instr., Chgo. Inst., 1924-26; with Truscon Steel Co., Chgo., 1926-40, claims and dist. credit mgr., 1930-40; company acquired by Republic Steel Corp., 1935, asst. sec.-asst. treas., 1960-65, treas., asst. sec., 1965-70; asst. treas. Cuyahoga Corp., 1960-70; sec., treas. K & S Metal Supply Co. Bd. dirs., v.p. Midwest Credit Conf., 1963-64. Bd. dirs. PolyClinic Hosp., Cleve., 1965-77. Mem. Nat., Cleve. (bd. dirs. 1959, pres. 1962) assns. credit mgmt., Cleve. Treasurers Club (bd. dirs. 1961, sec. 1964), Cleve. C. of C., Am. Iron and Steel Inst. Mason (Shriner). Clubs: Cleve. Athletic, Mid Day (Cleve.); Chagrin Valley Country. Home: Ft Lauderdale, Fla. Died Feb. 6, 1977; buried Chgo.

SMITH, ROBERT PAUL, writer; b. N.Y.C., Apr. 16, 1915; s. Joseph Elkin and Esther (Breckstone) S.; B.A., Columbia, 1936; m. Elinor Jane Goulding, Feb. 7, 1940; children—Daniel Paul, Joseph Robert. Writer radio scripts, TV scripts, mag. articles and stories. Author: So It Doesn't Whistle, 1941; The Journey, 1943; Because of My Love, 1946; The Time and the Place, 1952; Where Did You Go Out, What Did You Do?, Nothing, 1957; How to Do Nothing with Nobody All Alone by Yourself, 1958; Translations from the English, 1958; Where He Went, 1958; (poems) And Another Thing, 1959; Crank, 1962; (play) The Tender Trap (with Max Shulman), 1954; How To Grow Up in One Piece, 1963; Nothingatall, Nothingatall, Nothingatall, 1965; Robert Paul Smith's Lost and Found. 1973. Address: New York, N.Y. Died Jan. 30, 1977.

SMITH, ROGER HASKELL, editor; b. Detroit, Apr. 25, 1932; s. Demonte Haskell and Catherine (Linn) S.; B.A., Yale, 1954; m. Beverly Chew Bates, Feb. 18, 1956; children—Roger Haskell (dec.), William Boulton. Asst. editor, news editor, exec. editor, contbg. editor Pubs. Weekly, N.Y.C., 1954-80; mng. editor Police Athletic League of N.Y., 1976-80. Bd. dirs. Am. Hist. Documents Inst., Washington, 1963-74, Council on Interracial Books for Children, N.Y.C., 1970-74. Mem. P.E.N. Am. Center N.Y.C. (sec. 1973-76, exec. bd.). Clubs: Players (N.Y.C.); Devon Yacht (East Hampton, N.Y.). Author: Paperback Parnassus, 1976. Editor: The American Reading Public, 1963. Home: New York, N.Y. Died July 12, 1980.

SMITH, ROLLIN COLEMAN, JR., advt. art exec.; b. Franklin, Pa., Mar. 9, 1913; s. Rollin Coleman and Florence Glover (Blakslee) S.; student Stanford; grad. Art Center Sch., Los Angeles, 1936; m. Kathryn Helen East, Feb. 15, 1931; children—Mary Ann (Mrs. Arthur Ober), Rollin Coleman III; m. 2d, Edythe Hardman Pulley. Oct. 14, 1949; 1 dau., Georgiana Birchard. Art dir. N.W. Ayer & Son, Phila., 1936-43, McCann Erickson, Inc., N.Y.C., 1943-50; joined Ogilvy & Mather, Inc., N.Y.C., 1950, v.p. charge art, 1952-58, sr. v.p., mem. plans bd., 1958-69, became sr. v.p., head art group, 1969. Clubs: Art Directors (N.Y.C.); Country (Darien, Conn.). Home: Darien, Conn. Died Mar. 30, 1980.

SMITH, RUFUS BURR, fgn. service officer, educator; b. Montreal, Can., Apr. 6, 1912 (parents Am. citizens); s. Rufus Daniel and Georgia Lois (Burr) S.; A.B., Princeton, 1934; A.M., N.Y. U., 1937, Ph.D., 1941; m. Maud M. Bordes, 1964; children (by previous marriage)—Rufus, Douglas, Roy. Dir. social scis. Hofstra Coll., Hempstead, N.Y., 1935-39; asst. prof. econs. U. Newark, 1939-41; with U.S. Housing Authority, 1941-42; planning com. WPB, 1942-43; coordinator research Supreme Comdr. Allied Powers, Tokyo, Japan, 1946; economist Dept. State, 1946-49, officer charge econ. affairs for South Asia, 1955-58; comml. attache Am. Embassy, Bangkok, 1950-52, econ. counselor, Karachi, 1953-55; counselor embassy, dep. chief mission, Colombo, Ceylon, 1958-60; counselor embassy econ. affairs, New Delhi, India, 1960-62; sr. inspector Fgn. Service Inspection Corps., 1963-67; William R. Kenan Jr. prof. econs. Rollins Coll., Winter Park, Fla., 1967-80. Mem. U.S. delegation Far Eastern Commn., 1947-49; chief U.S. Reparation and Restitution to Japan, 1947; mem. U.S. delegation Austrian Treaty Conf., 1949, U.S. delegation Econ. Commn., Asia and Far East, 1950-53, 57-58, alternate rep., 1960-62. Served to lt. USNR, 1943-45. Mem. Phi Beta Kappa. Home: Winter Park, Fla. Died Apr. 30, 1976.

SMITH, RUSSELL P(AUL), coll. prof.; b. Kendallville, Ind., Nov. 23, 1897; s. Isaac Walter and Susannah (Diehl) S.; A.B., Ind. Univ., 1920; A.M., U. Pa., 1930; student Oak Ridge Inst. Nuclear Studies, summer 1956; m. Doris Pauline Wasson, June 29, 1922; children—Alicia Anne (Mrs. Donald Stephens), Russell Paul, David Wasson. Instr. of physics, Univ. of Pa., 1920-39; asso. prof. physics, Grove City (Pa.) Coll., 1939-42, prof. physics, from 1942, head dept. physics, from 1945. Recipient Silver Beaver, Boy Scouts Am. Mem. Am. Assn. Physics Tchrs., Am. Phys. Soc., Am. Inst. Physics, Pa. Acad. Sci., Phi Kappa Psi. Sigma Xi. Republican. Presbyn. Mason. Rotarian. Home: Grove City, Pa. Died May 14, 1978.

SMITH, STERLING BISHOP, educator; b. New Haven, May 7, 1899; s. Herbert H. and Frederica E. (Bishop) S.; Ph.B., Yale, 1920, M.S., 1923; Ph.D., N.Y. U., 1927; m. Harriet Chamberlain, Aug. 15, 1928; children—Robert M., Edward C. Mem. faculty Trinity Coll., Hartford, Conn., 1923-72, prof. chemistry, 1952-72, chmn. dept., Scoville prof., 1955-72. Mem. Am. Chem. Soc., Am. Assn. U. Profs. Mason (K.T.). Home: Wethersfield, Conn. Deceased.

SMITH, STUART FARWELL, ins. exec.; b. Sioux City, Iowa, Sept. 27, 1898; s. William Skeldon Adamson and Zelma Melinda (Farwell) S.; student U. Pa., 1920; m. Marjorie Emily Walters, Oct. 1, 1921; children—Robert Graeme, Shirley; m. 2d Mary Amelia Ellsworth, July 11, 1950. Mgr. ins. and bond dept., B. F. Goodrich Co., Akron, O., 1920-24; field rep. Conn. Gen Life Ins. Co., Akron, 1924-32, mgr. Pittsburgh br., 1932-34, mgr. Phila. br., 1934-47, v.p., dir. home office Hartford, Conn., 1947-61; chmn. exec. com., dir. of Puritan Life Ins. Company. Mem. Million Dollar Round Table Nat. Assn. Life Underwriters (life mem.). Clubs: Golf, Hartford (Conn.); Country (Farmington, Conn.); Hole In The Wall Golf, Port Royal Beach, Yacht (Naples, Fla.). Author articles on ins. jours. Home: Farmington, Conn. Died May 14, 1976.

SMITH, T(HEODORE) TOWNSEND, univ. prof.; born Charleston, S. C., Nov. 9, 1884; s. Benjamin Pressley and Eva Rosa (Hard) S.; A.B., Harvard, 1907, A.M., 1908, Ph.D., 1916; m. Elizabeth Nowell, Aug. 3, 1916; children—Thomas Hard, Andrew Nowell. Instr. U. of Kan., 1910-13, asst. prof. physics, 1913-19; prof. physics U. of Neb. since 1919. Served as mem. and temp. acting chief optical instruments sect., Nat. Bur. Standards, Washington, Feb.-Dec. 1918; optical work U.S. Navy, Naval Obs., Washington, Sept. 1944-Aug. 1945. Mem. Am. Physical Soc., Am. Assn. Physics. Teachers, A.A.A.S., m. Assn. Univ. Profs. Democrat. Presbyterian. Author: Electricity for Students of Science and Engineering, 1949. Home: Lincoln, Neb.*

SMITH, THOMAS LATHAM, educator; b. Key, Ala., Aug. 8, 1890; s. John Long and Fannie (Smith) S.; B.S., Coll. Wooster, 1917; M.S., U. Chicago, 1926; Ph.D., Columbia, 1936; grad. Army Arty. Sch., 1918; Sc.D., College Ozarks, 1960; m. Lois Aarant, Sept. 4, 1927;

children—Thomas David, Margaret Susan. Asst. instr. zoology Columbia, 1929-33; prof. biology coll. Ozarks, Clarksville, Ark., 1919-29, 1933-73, chmn. div. natural scis. 1933-53, dean men, 1937-53, dean 1953-61, coordinator higher edn. 1950-61; regional cons. family life edn. Am. Inst. Family Relations, 1944-73. Grant from NIH, HEW. Mem. 7th International Congress of Genetics, Edinburgh, Scotland, 1939; chairman first Annual Arkansas State Conference Higher Edn., 1949, 2d Conf., 1950; gen. chmn. Ozarks Regional Conf. Higher Edn., 1948. Served as lt. F.A., U.S. Army, 1918-19. Fellow A.A.A.S.; member Ark. Acad. Sci. (pres.), Am. Assn. Plant Physiologists, Am. Genetics Assn., Genetics Society of Am., Ark. C. of C., N.E.A., Ark. Edn. Assn., Ark. Hist. Soc., Sigma Xi. Presbyn. (elder). Club: Rotary (pres. Clarksville). Author research papers. Contbr. sci. book. Home: Clarksville, Ark. Died Mar. 4, 1973.

SMITH, TOM K., banker; b. Glenwood, Schuyler County, Mo., Sept. 4, 1882; s. Ambrose Henry Flood and Celeste (O'Day) S.; A.B., U of Missouri, 1904, LL.D., 1935; LL.D., Westminster Coll., 1952; m. Jane Howard Wells, April 27, 1916; children—Tom K., Jr., Jane Howard (Mrs. Warren McKinney Shapleigh), Henry Parker, Celeste O'Day (Mrs. John S. Penney, Jr.). Bond buyer and salesman with Little & Hays, St. Louis, 1905-10; sec. and treas. William R. Compton Co., St. Louis, 1910-15; v.p. Kauffman, Smith & Co., Inc., 1915-29; pres. Boatmen's Nat. Bank, 1929-47, chmn. bd., 1947—; dir. Am. Tel. & Tel. Co., 1940-59; mem. exec. com., dir. General Am. Life Ins. Co.; dir. Fed. Res. Bank, St. Louis, 1945-50, Ann Arbor R.R. Co., Wabash Ry. Co. Vice chmn. Liberty Loan Orgn., 8th Fed. Dist., 1917-19; member St. Louis War Finance Committee 1942-45; v.p. Children's Aid Soc., 1919-33; mem. bd. govs. Investment Bankers Assn. of America, 1923-25, v.p., 1926; trustee Community Fund of St. Louis, 1923-27, chmn. budget com., 1925; mem. bd. St. Louis chapter Am. Red Cross, 1928-31; chmn. St. Louis Citizens Com. on Relief and Unemployment, 1931-32 (in recognition of outstanding work on this com. received St. Louis Civic Award, 1932); mem. Nat. and Mo. coms. on unemployment relief, 1932; mem. adv. com., St. Louis Loan Agency, R.F.C., 1932-53; spl. adv. on banks and banking matters to sec. of treas., 1933-34, 1939-40; financial adv. to Office of Procurement and Material, U.S. Navy, 1942-43; mem. adv. com. St. Louis Ordinance Dist., 1943-46; mem. bd. curators, U. of Mo., 1939-45, pres., 1944-45; pres. bd. trustees Phi Gamma Delta, 1934-46; mem. Nat. Citizens Com. on Mobilization for Human Needs, 1935-42 (chmn. 1941-42); dir. Community Chests and Councils, Inc., 1936-45, mem. Nat. Citizen's Com., Community Chests of Am., since 1946; mem. bd. dirs. Nat. War Fund, 1943-46; chmn. St. Louis Social Security Commn., 1937-39; mem. Civic Progress Inc., St. Louis, 1953-58; chmn. St. Louis Citizens Charter Com., 1956. Recipient of S.R. Modern Patriot award, 1956. Mem. Am. Bankers Assn. (v.p. 1934-35, pres. 1936-37), Phi Gamma Delta, Phi Beta Kappa, Beta Gamma Sigma. Clubs: University (pres., 1927), Noonday (pres., 1926), St. Louis Country, Cuivre. Democrat. Presbyn. Home: St. Louis. *

SMITH, TONY, sculptor; b. S. Orange, N.J., 1912; student Art Students League, N.Y.C., 1934-35; archtl. student New Bauhaus, Chgo., 1937-38; archtl. apprentice of Frank Lloyd Wright, 1938-40; married; three daus. Practicing architect, 1940-60; tchr. design Pratt Inst.; sculptor in steel plate, from 1960; prof. art emeritus Hunter Coll; exhbns. include Wadsworth Atheneum, Hartford, Conn., 1964, 67, Jewish Mus., N.Y.C., 1967, Phila. Inst. Contemporary Art, 1967; prin. works include Throne, Die, Black Box, Free Ride, The Elevens, The Marriage, Willy, Gracehoper, Cigarette, The Keys to, Given., Amaryllis, Spitball, We Lost, Playground, Wall, Snake. Home: New York, N.Y. Died Dec. 26, 1980.

SMITH, WALTER HENRY, advt. exec.; b. Pelham, N.Y., July 13, 1915; s. Richard Harrison and Mary Virginia (Kelcher) S.; A.B. cum laude, Princeton, 1936; m. Constance Rulison Righter, Apr. 17, 1937; m. 2d, Alexandra Carola Popelak Von Cranichsfeld, Oct. 26, 1946. With CBS, 1936-40, Young & Rubicam, Inc., 1940-41, FR Corp., 1947-48, Curtis Pub. Co., 1948-50, Kastor, Farrell, Chesley & Clifford, Inc., advt., 1950-54; with Young & Rubicam, Inc., 1954-65, sr. v.p., 1962-65, mem. mgmt. com., 1964-65; mng. dir. Young & Rubicam, Ltd., London, Eng., 1965-76, Mem. Mayor N.Y.C. Council Devel. and Promotion Port N.Y., 1963-76. served with AUS, 1941-47. Clubs: Univ. Cottage (Princeton, N.J.); Princeton (N.Y.C.); Westchester Country (Rye, N.Y.). Home: London, England. Died Apr. 10, 1976.

SMITH, WILBUR MOOREHEAD, clergyman; b. Chgo., June 9, 1894; s. Thomas Sylvester and Sadie (Sanborn) S.; student Moody Bible Inst., 1913-14, Coll. of Wooster, 1914-17; D.D., Evang. Theol. Coll., Dallas, 1932; Litt.D., Trinity Evang. Div. Sch., 1971; D.Litt., Trinity Div. Sch., 1971; m. Mary Irene Ostrosky, Aug. 27, 1917; 1 son, Thomas Sylvester (dec.). Ordained Presbyn. ministry, 1922; stated supply First Presbyn. Ch., Ocean City, Md., 1918-22; pastor Lafayette Square Presbyn. Ch., Balt., 1922-27, First Presbyn. Ch., Covington, Va., 1927-30, Presbyn. Ch., Coatesville, Pa., 1930-37; faculty Moody Bible Inst., Chgo., 1938-47; prof. English Bible, Fuller Theol. Sem., 1947-63, Trinity Evang. Div. Sch., Deerfield, Ill., 1963-71, emeritus, 1971-76; editor Peloubet's Select Notes on the Internat. Sunday School Lessons, 1933-72. Mem. Com. for Revision of Scofield Reference Bible. Mem. Am. Soc. Ch. History, Chgo. Soc. Bibl. Research, Nat. Assn. Bibl. Instrs., Soc. Bibl. Lit., Am. Schs. Oriental Research (asso.). Compiler; A List of Bibliographies of Theological and Biblical Literature, (Gt. Brit. and Am.), 1595-1931. Republican. Presbyn. Author: Time Periods of Prophecy, 1935; How To Study the Bible for the Enrichment of Our Spiritual Life, 1936; The Glorious Revival Under King Hezekiah, 1937; Profitable Bible Study, 1939; The Supernaturalness of Christ, 1940; The Gospel of Mark for Men in Service, 1944; Therefore Stand, 1945; D.L. Moody (a Bibliography), 1946; This Atomic Age and the Word of God, 1947; A Voice for God: the Life of Charles E. Fuller, 1949; The Approaching World Crisis, 1950; Chats from a Minister's Library, 1950; A Watchman on the Wall, 1950; The Word of God and the Life of Holiness, 1952. Egypt in Biblical Prophecy, 1957; A Treasury of Books for Bible Study, 1960; Great Sermons on the Birth of Christ, 1963; Great Sermons on the Death of Christ, 1964; Great Sermons on the Resurrection of Christ, 1965; The Biblical Doctrine of Heaven, 1967; The Israeli/Arab Conflict and the Bible, 1967; The Best of D.L. Moody, 1971; You Can Know the Future, 1971; (autobiography) Before I Forget, 1971; The Minister in His Study, 1973; also various pamphlets; contbr. religious press. Editor: Collegiate Challenge, 1961-62. Contbg. editor Bibliotheca Sacra, Moody Monthly, Christianity Today. Home: San Marino, Calif. Died May 20, 1976.

SMITH, WILFRID RUSSELL, sports editor; b. Milroy, Ind., Apr. 7, 1899; s. William Francis and Kathryn (Power) S.; B.A., DePauw U., 1920, M.A., 1921; student U. Chgo., 1923-24; m. Lillian Mason, Apr. 28, 1928; one son, Wilfrid M. Director athletics, instructor of history in the high school of Greencastle, Indiana, 1919-21, East Chicago, Ind., 1921-25, Harrison High Sch., Chgo., 1925-30; newspaper work Chattanooga Times, summers 1917-19; with Florida Metropol's, Jacksonville, 1920, Knickerbocker Press, Albany, N.Y., 1921; sportswriter Chgo. Tribune, from 1926, sports editor, 1955-66. Served as pvt., U.S. Army, 1918. Mem. Phi Delta Theta, Sigma Delta Chi. Home: Park Ridge, Ill. Died Aug. 3, 1976.

SMITH, WILLIAM HOWARD, farmer, livestock breeder; b. Prattville, Ala., Nov., 25, 1885; s. McQueen and Lila Holt (Smith) S.; student U. Tenn., 1902-04; B.S., Ia. State Coll., 1906; LL.D., Auburn U., 1961; m. Louise A. Maytag, Oct. 15, 1909; children—Dean Bergman, Don McQueen, Diane Louise (Mrs. Milton A. Wendland). With McQueen Smith Farms, Prattville, 1906—, partner, 1934—; dir. Ala. Power Co., 1943-63, Birmingham (Ala.) br. Fed. Res. Bank, 1944-51. Bd. dirs. So. Research Inst., 1958—. Recipient Achievement award Ia. State Coll., 1934, Master Farm Family award Progressive Farmer mag., 1929. Mem. Am. Cotton Assn. (pres. Ala. div. 1930), Nat. Cotton Council (bd. dirs.), Ala. (pres. 1949), Autauga County cattlemen's assns., Ala. Crop Improvement Assn. (pres. 1949), Ala., Autauga County farm burs., Ala. C. of C. Presbyn. (ruling elder, trustee). Address: Prattville, Ala.*

SMOKER, EDWARD HEISE, utility exec.; b. Columbia, Pa., Dec. 29, 1905; s. Howard Grant and Ella (Heise) S.; B.S., Franklin and Marshall Coll., 1926; M.A., U. Cin., 1927, Ph.D., 1929; m. Dorothy Conner, Sept. 1, 1927; children—Audrey (Mrs. Dominic Salerno), Dorothy (Mrs. Frederick Nielsen). With Nat. Aniline & Chem. Co., Buffalo, 1929-30; with United Gas Improvement Co. (co. name changed to UGI Corp.), Phila., 1930-79, beginning as chemist research dept., successively engr. operation dept., operation mgr., v.p., 1953-55, pres., 1955-70, chmn. bd., 1971-79; dir. Quaker Chem. Corp. Gen. chmn. United Fund, 1966. Trustee Delco Meml. Hosp., Franklin and Marshall Coll.; bd. mgrs. Franklin Inst. Profl. engr., Pa. Mem. Chem. Soc. Am. Inst. Chem. Engrs., Am. (pres. 1961-62), Pa. (pres. 1960-61, 63) gas assns., Soc. Gas Lighting, Phi Beta Kappa, Sigma Xi, Alpha Chi Sigma. Clubs: Union League (Phila.). Home: Wallingford, Pa. Died Feb. 17, 1980; cremated.

SMOOT, WILLIAM CLAY, banker; b. Sweetwater, Ill., Nov. 24, 1885; s. Charles E. and Tempe (Clarke) S.; B.S., Northwestern U., 1907; s. Carolee Alvord, Apr. 14, 1908; 1 son, Charles Alvord. Engaged in banking, Clinton, Okla., 1908-24; successively cashier, pres., chmn. bd. 1st Nat. Bank, Bartlesville, Okla., 1924-54, now dir.; dir. Phillips Petroleum Co. Trustee, sec., treas. Frank Phillips Found.; asso. Northwestern U.; exec. com. Buffalo council Boy Scouts Am. (silver beaver, silver antelope, silver buffalo). Mem. Delta Upsilon. Mem. Christian Ch. Clubs: Rotary, Hillcrest Country (Bartlesville). Home: Bartlesville. *

SMOTHERS, FRANK (ALBERT) (SMUTH'ERZ), writer, editor; b. Rossville, Ill., Feb. 9, 1901; s. Isaac Alonzo and Martha (Peters) S.; student Northwestern U., 1918-20, U. of Wis., 1922-23; m. Dorothea Ann Culkin, June 27, 1924; children—Michael Thurston (dec.), David C., Dorothea, Mrs. Nancy Abegglen, John E. Began as reporter Evanston (Ill.) News Index, 1921, Kan. City Star, 1923; with United Press Assn., 1924-25; with Chgo. Daily News 1925-42, corr. in China, 1934, in China, Manchuria and Japan, 1935-37, in Italy, 1937-38, covered Palestine strife, summer 1938, expelled from Italy by Fascist govt., Nov. 1938, for "unfriendly" dispatches, subsequently in Tunis, Catalonia with Republican forces during climax of Spanish war, France, England, Balkans, Warsaw, Berlin, Holland, Netherlands East Indies and elsewhere; editor of editorial page and columnist, Chicago Sun, 1942-46; headed survey group to Greece for Twentieth Century Fund, 1947; dir. publs. Council State Governments, and editor of State Government 1948-81; lecturer public affairs. Member of Alpha Delta Phi. Roman Catholic. Clubs: Quadrangle (Chicago). Author: Report on the Greeks (with others). Home: Chicago, Ill. Died June 12, 1981.

SMYTH, CHARLES EDWARD, ednl. publisher; b. Milton, Mass., July 23, 1931; s. Ralston Blackburn and Eleanor Rogers (Greene) S.; B.A., Ohio Wesleyan U., 1953; M.Ed., Miami U., Oxford, Ohio, 1957; m. Patricia Ann Rhodes, July 4, 1953; children—Cynthia, William, Scott, Judith. Pub. sch. prin. Spring Valley (Ohio) Schs., 1955-57; guidance dir. Upper Arlington (Ohio) City Schs., 1957-60; staff asso. sci. Research Assos., Ohio, Mich., 1960-62; rep. Learning Materials Inc., Chgo., 1961-63; dir. devel. services Ency. Brit., Chgo., 1963-65; v.p. edn. div. Random House, Inc., N.Y.C., 1965-76; v.p. Baker & Taylor, 1976-77; exec. v.p. Macdonald/Raintree, Inc., pubs., Milw., 1977-79; instr. Ohio State Guidance Inst., Columbus, Ohio, 1959-79. Chmn. Citizens Com. Quality Edn., White Plains, N.Y., 1972-79; mem. Com. Sch. Enrollment, White Plains, 1972-74. Served with USAF, 1953-55. Mem. Am. Assn. Publishers (chmn. research com. 1973-79; mem. Great Cities Com. 1973-74), Phi Delta Kappa. Home: Wauwatosa, Wis. Died Nov. 30, 1979.

SMYTHE, HUGH HEYNE, ambassador, sociologist; b. Pitts., Aug. 19, 1913; s. William Henry and Mary Elizabeth (Barnhardt) S.; A.B., Va. State Coll., 1936; M.A. (scholar), Atlanta U., 1937; Ph.D., Northwestern U., 1945; postgrad. Fisk U., 1938-39, U. Chgo., 1940, Columbia, 1950-51, Woodstock (Vt.) Sch. (grantee Am. Friends Service Com.), 1950; LL.D., Va. State Coll., 1968; honor diploma JVEK Inst., Germany, 1968; m. Mabel Hancock Murphy, July 26, 1939; 1 dau., Karen Pamela. Researcher, adminstrv. asst. Am. Youth Commn. of Am. Council Edn., 1937-38; research asst., instr. Fisk U., 1938-39; research asso. Atlanta U., 1942; asst. dir. research Negro Land Grant Coll. Coop. Social Studies Project, also prof. sociolgy Morris Brown U., 1944; prof. sociology Tenn. State Agrl. and Indsl. U., 1945-46; dep. dir. spl. research N.A.A.C.P., 1947-49; dir. research W. B. Graham & Assos., N.Y.C., 1949-50; vis. prof. sociology and anthropology Yamaguchi Nat. U., Japan, 1951-53; prof. sociology Bklyn. Coll. of U. City N.Y., from 1953; ambassador to Syria, 1965-67, Malta, 1967-69; dir. research N.Y. State Senate Finance Com. evaluation project State Commn. Against Discrimination, 1956; social affairs officer U.S. Mission to UN, 1961-62; Fulbright prof. Chulalongkorn U., also adviser NRC, Thailand, 1963-64; UN corr. Eastern World and Africa Trade and Devel. (London), from 1964; vis. prof., spl. lectr. govt., pvt. orgns., univs., from 1950; adviser, mem. delegations U.S., other internat. orgns. and meetings, from 1957. Examiner, N.Y. State Civil Service Commn., 1961-65, N.Y.C. Bd. Edn., 1970-71, 73-74; dir. research project on benefits of sch. desegregation and integration for Fleischman com. N.Y. State Commn. on Quality, Cost and Financing of Edn., 1971; cons. Ford Found., Phelps Stokes Fund, U.S. Office Edn., U.S. Dept. State, Congl. Black Caucus, Nat. Council Chs. of Christ (Middle East com.), Arab-Israeli Research and Relations (dir.), Mass. Inst. Tech. Sahel-Sudan Project, dir., mem. exec., personnel com., program com. and nat. council exec. com. U.S.O., Near East Found., UN Assn. USA, Atlantic Council, Council on Fgn. Relations, Washington Task Force on Africa. Bd. dirs. African Student Aid Fund, Internat. Center N.Y., Holy Land Center of N.Y., Internat. Med. Research Found.; trustee Luther Coll., L.I. U., Interfuture. Served with AUS, World War II. Decorated grand knight Order Royal Crown of Crete, Order of St. Agatha; Harriet N. Strong Found. scholar, 1935-37; Rosewald fellow, 1939-41; grantee Am. Council Learned Socs., 1940, 62, Social Sci. Research Council, 1960; award Brit. Colonial Office, 1948; Ford Found. fellow, 1957-58; Phelps-Stokes Fund scholar, 1975; named Distinguished alumni Va. State Coll., 1957; Distinguished alumni, citation for distinguished service in public and internat. affairs, Atlanta U., 1972; grantee State U. N.Y., 1964; guest Fellow Columbia U. Seminars, 1974-77. Fellow African Studies Assn., Soc. Applied Anthropology, Am. Anthrop. Assn.; mem. Eastern Sociol. Soc., Assn. Asian Studies, African-Am. Scholars Council (dir.), Japan Soc., Am. Assn. for Chinese Studies, UN Assn. U.S.A. (dir.), Inst. Race Relations Gt. Britain, Siam Soc., Operations Crossroads Africa (vice chmn., dir., mem. nominating com.), Sociol. Soc. Japan, Smithsonian Instn., A.A.U.P., Am. Com. on Africa (nat. council), Am. Fgn. Service Assn., Malta C. of C., Profl. Staff Congress, United Service Orgn. Malta (pres.), Mus. African Art (dir.), Frederick Douglass Inst. (dir.), Middle East Inst., N.Y. State Sociol. Assn., Near-East Found. (dir., exec., nominations coms.), Freedom House, Common Cause, N.A.A.C.P., Nat. Urban League, Western Assn. Africanists, Caribbean Studies Assn., Black Forum on Fgn. Policy, Sigma Xi, Alpha Kappa Delta, Iota Sigma Lambda, Alpha Pi Zeta, Alpha Phi Alpha, Delta Tau Kappa (hon.). Club: Union (Malta). Author: (with W.E.B. DuBois) Negro Land Grant Colls. Social Studies Project, 1944; (with M.M. Smythe) New Nigerian Elite, 1960; (with L. Crow and W. Murray) Educating the Culturally Disadvantaged Child, 1966; (with H. Petersen, et al) Foreign Policy Decision Making: The New Dimensions, 1973. also pamphlets, articles, chpts. in books. Mem. editorial bd. Jour. Human Relations, 1954-70, Africa Today, 1955-69, Sociol. Abstracts, 1956-69; asso. editor Jour. Asian and African Studies, from 1966. Home: New York, N.Y. Deceased.

SNEATH, GEORGE MARK, educator; b. Baltimore, Sept. 6, 1884; s. Rev. Isaiah W. and Ella (Mark) S; A.B., Yale, 1907, A.M., 1910; Ph.D., Boston U., 1926; m. Jessie Fowler, June 21, 1911; children—Martha F., Gordon W. Instr. in English, U. of N.C., 1910-14; asst. prof., Goucher Coll., Baltimore, 1916-18; prof. of poetry, Boston U., 1923, prof. of English since 1931, chmn. dept. since 1947, univ. dir. of debating; mem. editorial staff, Baltimore Evening Sun, 1918-23. Republican. Conglist. Home: Waban, Mass. *

SNEED, EARL, lawyer; b. Tulsa, Jan. 19, 1913; s. Earl and Nellie Frances (Johnson) S.; A.B., U. Okla., 1934, LL.B., 1937; LL.M., Columbia, 1948, S.J.D., 1961; m. Cornelia Lynde, Apr. 22, 1935; children—James Lynde, Cornelia Ann, Robert Earl. Admitted to Okla. bar, 1937; asso. Monnet & Savage, Tulsa, 1937-39; partner Biddison & Sneed, Tulsa, 1939-40; sec. civic and legislative dept. Tulsa C. of C., 1940-41; vis. asso. prof. law U. Okla., 1945-46, asso. prof., 1946-48, prof., 1948-65, dean, 1950-65; v.p., asst. to pres. Liberty Nat. Bank & Trust Co., Oklahoma City, 1965-77, formerly vice chmn.; of counsel firm Crowe, Dunlevy, Thweatt, Swinford, Johnson & Burdick, Oklahoma City, 1977-81; formerly pres. Liberty Nat. Corp, also dir.; past dir. Comml. Nat. Bank, Comml. Finance Co., Muskogee, 1st Nat. Bank, Norman, Okla., Doric Corp. Mayor, Norman, 1961-65; pres. Okla. Municipal League, 1964, 65; chmn. Central Okla. Parking and Transit Authority. Trustee U. Okla. Found.; former bd. dirs. Am. Heart Assn. Past pres. Okla. Heart Assn., Oklahoma City Symphony; past chmn. Jud. Council Okla. Served as col. USAAF, 1941-45. Decorated Bronze Star; Croix de Guerre. Fellow Am. Bar Found. (trustee); mem. Am., Okla., Oklahoma County bar assns., Am. Judicature Soc., Air Force Assn. (past nat. dir.), Am. Legion, Res. Officers Assn., Nat. Municipal League (v.p.), Okla. C. of C. (past pres.), Okla. Hall of Fame, Okla. Hist. Soc., Phi Beta Kappa. Phi Delta Phi, Beta Theta Pi, Order of Coif. Episcopalian. Clubs: Oklahoma City Golf and Country, Beacon, Whitehall, Petroleum (Oklahoma City). Home: Oklahoma City, Okla. Died 1981.

SNEED, JAMES RICHARD, clergyman; b. Moravia, Iowa, Mar. 11, 1911; s. James Bert and Helen Brown (Carson) S.; A.B., Grinnell Coll., 1932; A.M., Boston U., 1934, S.T.B., 1935; D.D., Cornell Coll., 1947; L.H.D., Calif. Coll. Medicine, 1961; m. Adelaide Baker, June 6, 1932; children—Carol (Mrs. Robert Hinds), Barbara (Mrs. Robert Knutson). Student minister, 1932; ordained to ministry Methodist Ch., deacon, 1933, elder, 1935; pastor Bryantville, West Duxbury, Mass., 1932-36, Richland, Iowa, 1936-38, Shenandoah, Iowa, 1938-42; pastor Court St. Meth. Ch., Rockford, Ill., 1942-48, First Meth. Ch., Los Angeles, 1948-63, 1st Meth. Ch., Whittier, Calif., 1963-68; minister-at-large, in charge pub. relations United Ch. of Religious Sci., Los Angeles, 1970-76. Gates lectr. Grinnell Coll., 1953. Pres. City of Los Angeles Fire Dept. Recipient Boston U. Award, 1948. Trustee Hosp. Found. of the Meth. Ch.; sec. Meth. Gen. Conf. Commn. on Public Information, 1957-1964; mem. intercultural seminar Nat. Conf. Christians and Jews, 1956; trustee Los Angeles City Missionary Bd.; Missionary sec. for Rockford Dist. of Meth. Ch.; nat. alumni chmn. Boston U. Sch. Theol. $1,500,000 bldg. campaign. Nat. radio preacher, M.B.C. Faith in Our Time series for Fed. Council Chs. of Christ in Am., 1948-54; Start to Live weekly Pub. Service broadcast KMPC, 1950-77; chmn. pub. relation chmn. So. Calif.-Ariz. Meth. Con.; Rep. Ch. World Service, N.Y., World Council of Chs., Geneva, Switzerland, 1947; del. North Central Jurisdictional Conf. of the Meth. Ch., 1948. Mason (32 deg., K.T., Shriner, Jester; chaplain Al Malaikah Shrine from 1956); hon. mem. Legion of Honor Order of DeMolay. Clubs: Professional Men's Forum, Town Hall, Kiwanis, Los Angeles Breakfast. Beyond the Facts, 1940; How to Live Effectively, 1948. Writer monthly column Start to Live, in The Al Malaikahan, Shrine. Contbr. to Good Housekeeping, Christian Herald, Christian Advocate (judge Why I Go To Church contest 1953), Christian Science Sentinel, Think Mag., Zions Herald, and others. Home: Los Angeles, Calif. Died June 23, 1977.

SNEED, M. CANNON, prof. chemistry; b. Nashville, Tenn., Jan. 2, 1886; s. William L. and Mary (Waller) S.; A.B., Peabody Coll., Nashville, 1911; A.M., U. of Cincinnati, 1913, Ph.D., 1916; studied U. of Chicago, summers, 1909, 12; m. Edna Dyer, May 30, 1912; children—Thelma, William Cannon, Mildred, Catherine. Teacher chemistry, high sch., Newport, Ky., 1911-14; head dept. of biology, West Tenn. State Normal Sch., 1914-15; teacher dept. chemistry, Univ. of Cincinnati, 1915-18; asso. prof. chemistry, U. of Minn., 1918-24; prof. chemistry and chief div. of inorganic chemistry, since 1924. Fellow A.A.A.S., Am. Chem. Soc.; mem. Sigma Xi, Alpha Chi Sigma, Phi Lambda Upsilon. Mason (32 deg.). Club: Campus. Author or co-author books relating to field; latest publ.: General College Chemistry (with Julius L. Maynard), 1944. Home: Minneapolis.*

SNIDER, ARTHUR J., journalist; b. Iowa City, Ia.; grad. U. Ia., 1939; M.S. in Newspaper Sci. Writing, Medill Sch. Journalism, Northwestern U., 1946; married; two sons. With Chgo. Daily News (later Chgo. Sun-Times) 1946-81, sci. editor, 1966-81. Served with AUS, World War II. Recipient Nat. Headliners award, 1949, 64; Open Door award Chgo. Com. Alcoholism; Helen Baker Cody award for sci. writing; Ill. State Med. Soc. award, 1964, 65, 66, 67, 68; Golden Key award Ill. Dept. Mental Health, 1968; Robert T. Morse writers award Am. Psychiat. Assn., 1968 Spl. Commendation certificate A.M.A., 1966, 67, 68; award best news story of yr. Chgo. Newspaper Guild, 1966, Page One award, 1971; 1st pl. award journalism contest Am. Soc. Anesthesiologists, 1967; G.V. Black Meml. lectr. Northwestern U. Dental Sch., 1968; Marshall Field award, 1969; Spl. award Chgo. Med. Soc., 1974; award for coverage of Heimlich Maneuver, Ill. State Med. Soc., 1974; elected to U. Iowa Journalism Hall of Fame, 1978; Disting. Service award U. Ill., 1979; Inst. Medicine fellow, 1971. Mem. Nat. Assn. Newspaper Writers (past pres.), Nat. Assn. Sci. Writers (pres. 1953-54, exec. com. 1960-81), Council Advancement Sci. Writing (pres. 1966). Home: Skokie, Ill. Died May 21, 1981; buried Memorial Park Cemetery.

SNIDER, JOHN RAYWALDT, utility exec.; b. Kilbourn, Wis., Nov. 15, 1886; s. Frank Raywaldt and Jessie Belle (Rust) S.; LL.B., University of Wisconsin, 1908, Juris Doctor degree, 1966; m. Abby Elizabeth Cundall, Jan. 26, 1923; 1 dau., Jane Cundall (Mrs. Jack K. Moore). Admitted to Wis. bar, 1908; engaged in business, 1908—; v.p., gen. mgr., dir. Grays Harbor Ry. and Light Co., also affiliated companies, Aberdeen, Wash., 1930-42; pres., dir. N.M. Power Co., Sante Fe, 1942-46; pres., dir. Tucson Gas, Electric Light & Power Co., 1946-59, chmn. bd., 1955-67, honorary chairman board, 1967—, dir. emeritus, 1967; also dir. Bd. dirs. Ariz. Research Found. Recipient medallion U. Ariz., 1960. Clubs: Old Pueblo, Tucson Golf and Country, Elks (Tucson); Washington Athletic (Seattle). Home: Tucson.*

SNOOK, JOHN LLOYD, business exec., cons.; b. Troy, Ohio, Nov. 25, 1896; s. Clarence Guy and Anna B. (Counts) S.; Ph.B., Kenyon Coll., 1919; m. Alice V. Winger, June 21, 1923 (dec. Dec. 31, 1967); children—John Lloyd, Elizabeth Anne, Julia Winger, Alice Winger; m. 2d, Mary C. Gayler, Jan. 29, 1972. Sec., treas., plant mgr. Kitchen Aid Mfg. Co., Springfield, Ohio, 1919-24; prof. indsl. research Antioch Coll., Yellow Springs, Ohio, 1924-30; pres., gen. mgr. J.L. Snook Co. (formerly Antioch Shoe Project, Inc.), 1930-60. Cons. SCORE, 1966—. Mem. dist. 11, Fla. Ancillary Manpower Planning Bd.; mem. Lakeland Creative and Performing Arts Council; chmn. Scioto County chpt. A.R.C., 1946-59; chmn. Greater Lakeland (Fla.) chpt., 1965-80, life mem., 1970-80; mem. nominating com. Am. Nat. Red Cross, 1948-49, mem. Eastern area adv. council, 1950-52, vice chmn. mems. and funds Ohio, 1953-55, mem. nat. bd. govs., 1957-61, mem. Fla. conf. com., 1965-80; chmn. Ret. Sr. Vol. Program; mem. Human Services Council; bd. dirs. YMCA, 1957-62, pres. Clay Twp. br., 1960-62; bd. dirs. Lakeland Family YMCA, 1967-80, treas., 1973-80; chmn. Scioto County Community Chest, 1950; bd. dirs. Scioto County Crippled Children's Soc., 1948-60, pres., 1950-56; active Ohio Soc. Crippled Children, 1949-55, pres., 1951-52; dir. Nat. Soc. Crippled Children, 1951-52; pres. Scioto County Council Social Agys., 1953-55; chmn. Com. for Ministry to Def. Community in Scioto Valley, 1952-56; mem. Portsmouth Town Hall Forum Com., 1942-60, chmn., 1955-59; exec. com. Ohio Citizens Council for Health and Welfare, 1954-59; bd. dirs. United Cerebral Palsy of Polk County, Fla. 1962-80; bd. dirs. Salvation Army, 1965-80, chmn. adv. bd., 1968-70; bd. dirs. Human Relations Council; pres. Lakeland Concert Assn., 1968-71; bd. counsellors Fla. So. Coll. Mem. bishop and chpt. Diocese of So. Ohio, Episcopal Ch., 1956-59, del. ho. of dels., 1955; chmn. dept. stewardship and every mem. canvass Diocese of S. Fla., 1964-80, mem. exec. bd., 1966-80, chmn. dept. communications Diocese S. Fla.; pres. Portsmouth Assn. Chs., 1949-50; adminstrv. com. Ohio Council Chs., 1954-61, trustee Found., 1961-62; dir. Fla. Council Chs., 1968-80. Mem. Portsmouth City Charter Revision Com., 1951-52. Served as ensign, aviation USN, 1918-19; lt. comdr. USNR, 1944-46. Recipient citation for outstanding performance Navy Dept., 1945. Mem. Nat. Mgmt. Assn. (charter), Mid-State Tb and Respiratory Assn. (dir. 1969-80), Imperial Polk Mgmt. Assn. (hon. life), Delta Kappa Epsilon. Episcopalian (past sr. warden, vestryman, jr. warden 1966-80). Mason, Rotarian (past pres., past dist. gov., dir. 1964-67, 68-71, Coll. Govs. 1963-80, Paul Harris Fellow award 1975). Home: Lakeland, Fla. Died May 8, 1980.

SNOW, BARON, (CHARLES PERCY SNOW), writer; b. Leicester, Eng., Oct. 15, 1905; s. William Edward and Ada (Robinson) Snow; B.Sc., U. Leicester (England), 1927, M.Sc., 1928; Ph.D., Christ's Coll., Cambridge U., 1930; LL.D., U. Leicester, 1959, U. Liverpool, 1960, Bklyn. Poly. Coll., 1962, St. Andrews U., 1962, Bridgeport U., 1966, York U., 1967; D.Litt., Dartmouth, 1960, Bard Coll., 1962, Temple U., 1963, Syracuse U., 1963, U. Pitts., 1964, Ithaca Coll., 1967; D.H.L., Kenyon Coll., 1961, Washington U., St. Louis, 1963, U. Mich., 1963; D.Philol. Scis., Rostov on Don, 1963; D.Sc., Pa. Mil. Coll., 1966; m. Pamela Hansford Johnson, July 14, 1950; 1 son, Philip Charles Hansord. Engaged as profl. scientist, 1928-40; fellow Christ's Coll., 1930-50, tutor, 1935-40, Rede lectr. Cambridge, 1959; with Brit. Civil Service Commn., 1945-60; dir. English Electric Co., Ltd., 1947-64; bd. dirs. London br. U. Chgo. Press. Parliamentary sec. to minister of tech., Eng., 1964-66. Created Knight, 1957; named comdr. Order Brit. Empire: created Baron Snow of City of Leicester, 1964. Hon. mem. Am. Acad.-Nat. Inst. Arts and Letters; hon. fgn. mem. Am. Acad. Arts and Scis. Clubs: Savile, Athenaeum, Century (N.Y.C.). Author: (novels) Death Under Sail, 1932; New Lives for Old, 1933; The Search, 1934; Strangers and Brothers, 1940; The Light and The Dark, 1947; Time of Hope, 1949; The Masters, 1951; The New Men, 1954; Homecomings, 1956; The Conscience of the Rich, 1958; The Affair, 1969; Corridors of Power, 1964; The Sleep of Reason, 1968; Two Cultures and the Scientific Revolution (Rede lecture), 1959; Science and Government (Godkin lectures), 1960; The Two Cultures and a Second Look, 1964; Variety of Men (essays), 1967; Last Things, 1970; The Malcontents, 1972; In their Wisdom, 1974; A Coat of Varnish, 1979; The Physicists, due for publication later 1981; (plays adapted by Ronald Millar) The Affair, The New Men, The Masters. Address: London, England. Died July 1, 1980.

SNOW, CONRAD EDWIN, lawyer; b. Haverhill, N.H., Aug. 6, 1889; s. Leslie Perkins and Susie Eliza (Currier) S.; A.B., Dartmouth Coll., 1912; B.A., Oxford U., 1915, M.A., 1929; LL.B., Harvard, 1917; m. Katherine Amelia Hartley, Oct. 26, 1921; children—Constance Hopkins (Mrs. Brede Klefos), Katherine Ann (Mrs. Louis Cima), Richard Currier. Admitted to N.H. bar, 1919, law practice, Rochester, 1919-40; asst. legal adviser Dept. State, 1946-56, Far Eastern affairs, 1950-56, chmn. Loyalty-Security Bd., 1947-53, U.S. rep. treaty negotiations, London, 1951; counsel Nighswander, Lord Martin & Killkelley, Laconia, N.H., 1956-75; dir. Rochester (N.H.) Trust Co., 1934-46. Rep., N.H. Legislature, 1929-30, 59-60; pres. Daniel Webster council Boy Scouts Am. Served from 1st lt. to capt. 4th F.A. Brigade, AEF, 1917-19; to col., dir. legal div. Office Chief Signal Officer, 1940-45, brig. gen. G.S.C., Office Under Sec. War, 1945-46. Mem. adv. bd. on clemency High Commr. Germany, 1950; chmn. adv. bd. on clemency for Japanese war criminals. Decorated Legion of Merit; recipient Silver Beaver award Boy Scouts Am. Mem. Am. (mem. ho. dels. 1937-42), N.H. (sec.-treas. 1932-42) bar assns., Am. Law Inst., Am. Judicature Soc., Soc. Colonial Wars, Descs. Mayflower, Newcomen Soc., Theta Delta Chi. Mason. Compiler: N.H. Annotations to Restatement of Law of Contracts, 1936. Home: Gilmanton Iron Works, N.H. Died Dec. 21, 1975; interred Rochester (N.H.) Cemetery.

SNOW, (CHARLES) WILBERT, author; b. White Head Island St. George, Me., Apr. 6, 1884; s. Forrest Alwin and Katharine (Quinn) S.; prep. edn., high sch., Thomaston, Me.; B.A., Bowdoin, 1907, hon. M.A., 1925; M.A., Columbia Univ., 1910; LL.D. (hon.) Wesleyan Univ., 1945; Litt.D. (hon.) Marietta College, 1945; m. Jeannette Simmons, Feb. 23, 1922; children—Charles Wilbert, John Forrest, Nicholas, Stephen Hopkins (deceased), Gregory Elisha. Teacher of English successively New York U., Bowdoin Coll., Williams Coll., U. of Utah, Reed Coll., and Ind. Univ. until 1921; asst. prof. and asso. prof. English, Wesleyan U., Conn., 1921-29, prof. since 1929. Eskimo teacher and reindeer agt. in Alaska, 1911, 12. Served as 2d and 1st lt. F.A., U.S. Army, 1917-19. Pres. Conn. Assn. Bds. Edn. 1940. Spl. lectr. Dept. State in Europe, Asia and Near East, 1951-52. Lieutenant governor State of Connecticut, 1945-46, governor, 1946-47. Fellow, Yale Corporation. Member Modern Lang. Assn. America, Phi Beta Kappa, Beta Theta Pi. Democrat. Club: Players (New York). Author: (verse) Maine Coast, 1923; (verse) The Inner Harbor, 1926; (verse) Down East, 1932; Selected Poems, 1936; Before the Wind (verse), 1938; Maine Tides (verse), 1940. Home: Middletown, Conn.*

SNOWDON, JOHN COLIN, physicist; b. London, June 21, 1932; s. Cecil Filis and Norah Cater (Crowhurst) S.; came to U.S., 1956, naturalized, 1965; B.Sc. in Physics and Math., U. London, 1952, B.Sc. in

Physics, 1953, D.I.C., Imperial Coll. Sci., 1956, Ph.D., 1956, D.Sc., 1965; m. Anne Joy Vickery, Sept. 8, 1956; children—Jane Louise, Mark Andrew. Research scientist Philco Corp., Phila., 1956-58; research asso. Willow Run Labs., Ann Arbor, Mich., 1958-59, asso. research physicist, 1959-60; vibration engr. Hawker-Siddeley Aviation, Ltd., Eng., 1960-61; asst. prof. engring. research Applied Research Lab., Pa. State U., State College, 1961-64, asso. prof., 1964-67, prof., 1967-80; mem. Nat. Acad. Scis.-NRC evaluation panel for Mechanics div. Inst. for Basic Standards, Nat. Bur. Standards, 1970-73, ad hoc panel for acoustics and vibration, 1972-74; chmn., organizer Pa. State U. seminars, 1972-79; program chmn. Inter-Noise 74, Internat. Conf. Noise Control Engring. Recipient Disting. Performance award Pa. State U., 1977. Fellow Acoustical Soc. Am. (pres. 1977, asso. editor jour. 1966-80, Trent-Crede Medal 1980), Brit. Inst. Physics, Brit. Inst. Acoustics, Am. Acad. Mechanics; mem. ASME (chmn. shock and vibration com. applied mechanics div. 1972-73), Sigma Xi. Episcopalian. Club: Pa. State U. Faculty. Author: Vibration and Shock in Damped Mechanical Systems, 1968. Editor: (with E.E. Ungar) Isolation of Mechanical Vibration, Impact and Noise, 1973; Proceedings of Inter-Noise 74, 1974; bd. editors Dept. Def. Shock and Vibration Digest, 1975-80; editorial adv. bd. Jour. Soc. Environ. Engrs., 1975-80. Contbr. articles to profl. jours. Home: State College, Pa. Died July 9, 1980.

SNYDER, CHARLES EDWIN, editor; b. Norwalk, O., May 30, 1886; s. Edmund P. and Annette (Tillson) S.; B.S. in Agr., Ohio State U., 1909; m. Mary Virginia Makepeace, Sept. 5, 1913; children—Stanley Makepeace, William Lewis, Ralph George, Robert Charles. With the Nat. Stockman and Farmer, Pittsburgh, Pa., 1909; U.S. Govt. service, 1910-11; editor Farmers' Review, Chicago, 1914-20; editor Chicago Daily Drovers Journal and editorial dir., Corn Belt Farm Dailies since 1920. Mem. Alpha Gamma Rho, Sigma Delta Chi (pres. 1932-33). Episcopalian. Club: Saddle and Sirloin (pres. since 1924). Home: Chicago.*

SNYDER, DANIEL J., JR., fed. judge; b. 1916; B.A., Wooster Coll.; LL.B., U. Pitts. Admitted to Pa. bar, 1941; asst. U.S. atty., Pitts,. 1957-60; judge U.S. Dist. Ct. Western Dist. Pa., 1973-80. Mem. Am. Bar Assn. Address: Pittsburgh, Pa. Died May 11, 1980; buried St. Clair Cemetery, Greensburg, Pa.

SNYDER, HENRY BURGESS, newspaper executive; born Waverly, Ohio, April 25, 1884; son of Henry Richard and Minerva (Burgess) S.; student at Drury College, Springfield, Missouri, 1903-05; A.B., Yale, 1908; married to Mary Rennels, January 15, 1930; 1 son, Burgess. Reporter Springfield (Mo.) Republican, 1902-03; editor Urbana (O.) Citizen, 1908-10, Gary Post, 1910-21, Gary Post-Tribune, 1921-56, editor-publisher, 1956-62; pres., chmn. bd. Gary Printing and Publishing Company; postmaster of Gary, 1915-20. President emeritus Gary Urban League. Methodist. Club: Tavern (Chgo.). Home: Chesterton, Ind. *

SNYDER, JOHN STEWART, publisher; b. York, Pa., May 16, 1911; s. Herbert Turner and Estelle Cobb (Herring) S.; A.B., Dickinson Coll., 1933; grad. Advanced Mgmt. Program Harvard, 1955; m. Marion Ellen Baker, June 26, 1937; children—John Stewart, Geoffrey Turner, James Norwood. With John Wiley & Sons, Inc., N.Y.C., 1935-78, sec., 1960-78, adminstrv. v.p. editorial divs., 1964-70, cons., 1970-78, also dir. Chmn. tech., sci. and med. book pubs. group Am. Book Pubs. Council, 1963-64; bd. dirs. Am. Textbook Pubs. Inst., 1954-56. Mem. Scarsdale (N.Y.) Bd. Edn., 1958-65, pres., 1962-64; mem. local govt. planning bd., 1973-78. Trustee Dickinson Coll. Mem. Alpha Chi Rho. Congregationalist (past clk., trustee). Club: Scarsdale Golf. Home: Center Lovell, Maine. Died Dec. 1978.

SNYDER, JOHN WILLIAM, surgeon; b. Vandalia, Mich., Nov. 25, 1884; s. Henry Albert and Clara (Lutes) S.; M.D., U. of Mich., 1906; M.S., Mayo Clinic Found. (U. Minn.), 1923; m. Mary E. Holden, Sept. 27, 1913 (dec. 1956); 1 s., John William. In practice, Michigan City, Ind., 1909-18; fellow in surgery, Mayo Clinic, 1918-20, surg. asst., 1920-23; surg. practice, Indianapolis, Ind., 1924, Miami, Fla., since 1925; pres. and chief of staff Dade County Hosp.; emeritus surgical staff Jackson Memorial Hospital; surgical consultant St. Francis, Mount Sinai, and Children hospitals. Trustee U. of Miami. In charge of med. relief in Miami dist. after hurricane of 1926. Fellow Am. Coll. Surgeons; mem. Southeastern Surg. Congress, Pan-Am. Med. Assn., Am. Fla. State and Dade County med. assns., A.A.A.S., N.Y. Acad. Sci., Newcomen Soc. N.A., Sigma Xi (Mayo Foundation chapter), Com. of One Hundred (Miami Beach). Mason. Republican. Club: Rotary (Miami). Home: Miami Beach.*

SNYDER, OTTO, public utilities; b. St. Louis, Mo., Apr. 24, 1884; s. John and Margaret Ann (Kiniff) S.; student Harvard Scientific Sch., 1903-05; E.E., Cornell U., 1908; m. Margaret Peabody, June 9, 1911; children—John, Robert Peabody, Ellery Peabody. Meter tester Pawtucket Electric Co., 1908-10; elec. engr. Tacoma Ry. Co., 1910-11; meter supt. Seattle Elec. Co., 1911-13; supt. Houghton County, Mich., 1913-17; commercial mgr. Adirondack Electric Power Corp., 1917-21; gen. supt. Adirondack Power & Light Corp., 1921-25; gen. mgr., 1925-27; exec. v.p. N.Y. Power & Light Corp., 1927-29, pres. since 1929; v.p. and dir. Niagara Hudson Power Corp.; dir. Nat. Commercial Bank & Trust Co. Mem. N.Y. State Soc. Professional Engrs. Clubs: Fort Orange, Albany Country, Schuyler Meadows Country (Albany, N.Y.). Home: Albany, N.Y.*

SNYDER, WILLIAM FRANKLIN, lawyer; b. Lehighton, Pa., Mar. 10, 1903; s. William F. and Charlotte A. (Strohl) S.; A.B., Pa. State U., 1925; LL.B., Harvard, 1929; m. Beatrice F. Hammond, June 25, 1930. Admitted to N.Y. bar, 1931; engaged in metall. research N.J. Zinc Co., Palmerton, Pa., 1925-26; asso. Peaslee & Brigham, N.Y.C., 1929-30, Roosevelt & O'Connor, N.Y.C., 1931-33; asso., partner O'Connor & Farber, 1934-69; partner O'Connor & Snyder, N.Y.C., 1970-76. Dir. Riddell Petroleum Corp.; dir., sec. Riddell-Thatcher Corp. Sec., treas., v.p., gen. counsel Ga. Warm Springs Found., 1944-76; past v.p., sec. Franklin D. Roosevelt Library, 1938—; gov., past pres., exec. com. New Rochelle Hosp.; past v.p., sec., trustee Nat. Found. for Infantile Paralysis (name later changed to Nat. Found.), 1938-76, past chmn., mem. exec. com. Greater N.Y. chpt. Trustee, sec., gen. counsel Internat., Poliomyelitis Congress, 1949-76, Internat. Med. Congress, Ltd., 1959-76; dir., gen. counsel Am. Nat. Council for Health Edn. Pub., Inc. Mem. Am. Judicature Soc., Am., N.Y. State bar assns., New York County Lawyers Assn., Assn. Bar City of N.Y., Harvard Law Sch. Assn., Sigma Phi Sigma, Phi Kappa Phi (hon.). Republican. Episcopalian. Mason (32 deg., Shriner). Clubs: Wykagyl Country (New Rochelle); Harvard (N.Y.C.). Home: New Rochelle, N.Y. Died Mar. 14, 1976.

SOANS, CYRIL ARTHUR (SO ANS), lawyer; b. nr. Nottingham, Eng., May 31, 1884; s. John Isaac and Martha Anne (Campion) S.; grad. mech. and elec. engring., Univ. Coll., Nottingham, 1902; student N.Y. Law Sch., 1912-13; LL.B., John Marshall Law Sch., Chgo., 1915, LL.D., 1954; m. Mary Agnes Finn, June 14, 1913; children—Jacqueline, Tracy. Came to U.S., 1904; naturalized, 1911. Engr. mining projects, B.C., Nev., 1903-05; research telephone engring., mfr. elec. supplies, Chgo., 1906-10; research elec. starting and lighting of automobiles, N.Y.C., 1911-13; practice of law, specializing patent law, Chgo., 1913—; mem. firm Soans, Anderson, Luedeka & Fitch, and predecessors, 1918-65. Mem. Am. (chmn. patent sect. 1956), Chgo bar assns., Assn. Bar City of N.Y., Chgo. Patent Law Assn. (pres. 1948), Am. Inst. of Electrical Engineers, Am. Patent Law Assn. Republican. Episcopalian. Mason (K.T., Shriner). Clubs: Oak Park (Ill.) Country; Union League (Chgo.). Home: Oak Park, Ill. *

SOBELOFF, JONATHAN, lawyer; b. N.Y.C., Sept. 29, 1934; s. Isidore and Edith (Mozorosky) s.; A.B. with high distinction, U. Mich., 1955; J.D. magna cum laude, Harvard U., 1958; m. Barbara Rich, 1961; children—Judy, Deborah, Susan. Admitted to Mich. bar, 1958, D.C. bar, 1965; individual practice law, Detroit, 1958-62, Washington, 1964-66; mem. staff Office of Tax Legis. Counsel, U.S. Dept. Treasury, 1962-64; assoc. prof. law Georgetown U., Washington, 1966-69, prof. law, from 1969; faculty adviser The Tax Lawyer, 1972-74, from 77. Mem. Am. Law Inst., Internat. Fiscal Assn., Nat. Tax Assn.-Tax Inst. Am., Assn. Am. Law Schs., Am. Bar Assn. Author: Tax and Business Organization Aspect of Small Business, rev. edit., 1974; Federal Income Taxation of Corporations and Stockholders in a Nutshell, 1978; contbr. articles to legal jours. Home: Bethesda Md. Died June 22, 1979.

SOBEY, ALBERT, engr., educator; b. Hancock, Mich., Aug. 5, 1885; s. William John and Lylie (Clymo) S.; trade apprenticeship, 1900-04; B.S., Mich. State Coll., 1909, M.E., 1930; grad. study, Univ. of Chicago, summers 1913-16; m. Bess B. Penoyar, Aug. 16, 1923; 1 son, Albert James. Engr. Mich. Power Co., Lansing, 1909-10; engr. in charge Chicago office W.H. Zimmerman Co., cons. engrs., 1910-12; instr. physics, mathematics and elec. engring., Mich. Coll. of Mines, Houghton, Mich., 1912-18; ednl. dir. Ind. Mutual Assn. (initiated ednl. and training program for industries, Flint, Mich. 1919), 1919-50; dir. Flint Inst. of Technology: pres., dir., regent Gen. Motors Inst., president emeritus and consultant since 1950. Mem. of commission on Motion Pictures in Adult Edn. since 1946: mem. nat. com. on volunteer training, Boy Scouts of Am. since 1943. Served as capt. and major S.C., U.S. Army as asst. chief and chief, radio intelligence sect., Mil. Intelligence Div., 1918-19; consultant War Manpower Commn. (training within industry) Washington and Detroit. 1940-45; mem. consultative com. War Manpower Commn. on Engrs. and Engring. Students. 1941-45; mem. adv. com. Vocational Training for Nat. Defense. 1940-45. Recipient Silver Beaver award. Boy Scouts of Am., 1947. Member national committee on industrial fatigue, National Research Council. 1944. Member American Management Association. American Soc. for Engring. Edn., Mich. Indsl. Training Council (hon. life mem.), Tau Beta Pi. Alpha Tau Iota. Independent Republican. Presbyterian. Mason. Club: Rotary. Dir. editor Gen. Motors Exec. Training Series since 1927, series include: Department Management, 1927, Factory Organization, 1928, Economics of Industry, 1929, Outlines of Industrial Development, 1929, Advanced G.M. Exec. Training Texts. Author: (with Carl Kinsley) Radio Direction Changes, 1918-19. Home: Flint. *

SOBY, JAMES THRALL, art critic, editor; b. Hartford, Conn., Dec. 14, 1906; s. Charles and Anna (Hazlewood) S.; student Williams Coll., 1924-26, L.H.D. (hon.), 1962; m. Melissa Wadley, Apr. 10, 1952; one son, Peter Allyn. Asst. dir. Mus. of Modern Art, N.Y.C., 1943-45, dir. painting and sculpture trustee, 1942, chmn. dept. painting and sculpture, 1946, became v.p. of the museum, 1968; editor Mag. of Art, Washington. Author: After Picasso, 1935; The Early Chirico, 1941; Salvador Dali, 1941; Tchelitchew, 1942; Romantic Painting in America (with Dorothy Miller), 1943; Georges Rouault: Paintings and Prints, 1945; The Prints of Paul Klee, 1946; Ben Shahn, 1946; Contemporary Painters, 1948; (with A. H. Barr, Jr.) Twentieth Century Italian Art, 1949; Amedeo Modigliani, 1951; Glorgio de Chirico, 1955; Yves Tanguy, 1955; Balthus, 1956; Modern Art and the New Past, 1957; Ben Shahn, His Graphic Art, 1957; Juan Gris, 1958; Joan Miro, 1959; Ben Shahn, 1961; Ben Shahn, 1963; Rene Magritte, 1965. Contbr. art articles to nat. mags., art jours.; monthly column art Sat. Rev. of Lit., 1946-57. Decorated Stella della Solidarieta Italiana (Italy). Home: New Canaan, Conn. Died Jan. 29, 1979.

SODERBERG, CARL RICHARD, mech. engr., educator; b. Ulvöhamn, Sweden, Feb. 3, 1895; s. Jonas Axel and Johanna Kristina (Nordquist) S.; naval architect, Chalmers Inst. Tech., Goteborg, Sweden, 1919, Tech. Dr., 1951; fellow Am.-Scandanavian Found., 1919-20; S.B., Mass. Inst. Tech., 1920; D. Eng., Tufts Univ., Medford, Mass., 1958; came to U.S., 1919, naturalized, 1927; m. Sigrid Kristina Lofstedt, May 9, 1921; children—Carl Richard, Lars Olof, Barbro Kristina. Devel. engr. for large elec. machinery Westinghouse Electric & Mfg. Co., East Pittsburgh, Pa., 1922-28, chief turbine engr., 1931-38; in charge of turbo generators ASEA, Västeras, Sweden, 1928-30; prof. mech. engring. M.I.T., 1938-59, Inst. prof., 1959-61, Inst. prof. emeritus, 1961, head dept. mech. engring., 1947-54, dean engring., 1954-59. Decorated comdr. Royal Order North Star; recipient Capt. Joseph H. Linnard prize (with Ronald R. Smith), Soc. Naval Architects and Marine Engrs., 1944; Certificate of Appreciation, Army and Navy, 1948, John Ericsson gold medal Am. Soc. of Swedish Engrs., 1952; Exceptional Service award U.S. Air Force, 1955, ASME, 1960; DeLaval medal Royal Swedish Engring. Acad., 1968; Gustaf Dalen medal Chalmers, 1970. Fellow Am. Acad. Arts and Scis., AIAA, (hon. mem.), Royal Swedish Engring. Acad., Nat. Acad. Sci., Nat. Acad. Engring.; mem. A.A.A.S., Brit. Inst. M.E., Svenska Teknologföreningen, Soc. Naval Architects and Marine Engrs., Am. Soc. Swedish Engrs. Designer, Inventor steam turbines, generators for land and marine applications. Author numerous monographs to Am. and European jours. on dynamics, vibrations, design of turbines and generators, gas turbines, etc. Address: Cambridge, Mass. Died Oct. 17, 1979.

SOFFEL, SARA MATHILDE (SO'FEL), judge; b. Pittsburgh, Pa., Oct. 27, 1886; d. Jacob and Katherine (Ulrich) Soffel; A.B., Wellesley Coll., 1908; LL.B., U. of Pittsburgh, 1916, LL.D., 1939; LL.D. Wilson Coll., Chambersburgh, Pa., 1935, Pa. Coll for Women, 1945; LL.D. (honorary), Grove City College, 1949. Admitted to Pa. bar, 1916; asst. city solicitor, City of Pittsburgh, 1922-26; dir. bur. of women and children Dept. of Labor and Industry of Pa., 1929-30; apptd. to bench, 1930; judge, county court, Allegheny County, Pa., Aug. 1930-Jan. 1942; judge, Court of Common Pleas of Allegheny County, since Jan. 1942. Member board of trustees U. Pittsburgh, Grove City College. Member American, Pa. and Allegheny County bar assns., Am. Assn. Univ. Women, Mortar Board, Phi Delta Delta, Phi Beta Kappa, Order of Coif. Clubs; 20th Century, College, Womans City, Business and Professional Women's, Wellesley (Pittsburgh). Home: Pittsburgh. *

SOINE, TAITO OLAF, educator; b. Virginia, Minn., Aug. 13, 1915; s. Henry and Aina (Rousu) Soini; A.A., Virginia (Minn.) Jr. Coll., 1935; B.S., U. Minn., 1938, M.S., 1939, Ph.D., 1943; m. A. Berenice Martin, May 21, 1940; children—John, Mary, William. Research agt. U.S. Dept. Agr., Minn., 1941; organic chemist Fed. Cartridge Corp., Anoka, Minn., 1942; instr. pharm. chemistry U. Minn., 1942-45, asst. prof., 1945-46, asso prof., 1946-50, prof. medicinal chemistry, 1950-78, head medicinal chemistry dept., 1970-74, asst. dean for grad. study and research, 1974-77; cons. USPHS, NIH. Recipient research achievement award in natural products Am. Pharm. Assn. Found., 1964. Registered pharmacist, Minn. Mem. Am., Minn. pharm. assns.,

Am. Chem. Soc., Acad. Pharm. Scis., AAUP, Sigma Xi, Rho Chi, Phi Lambda Upsilon, Phi Delta Chi. Lutheran. Author: Laboratory Manual of Inorganic Pharmaceutical Chemistry (with C. H. Rogers), 1949; Rogers' Inorganic Pharmaceutical Chemistry (with C.O. Wilson), rev. edit., 1967; Inorganic Medicinal and Pharmaceutical Chemistry (with others), 1975. Contbr. articles to profl. publs. Mem. revision com. U.S. Pharmacopoeia, 1960-70. Home: Minneapolis, Minn. Died Oct. 22, 1978; buried Virginia, Minn.

SOKOLNIKOFF, IVAN JOHN STEPHAN, educator; b. Chernigov Govt., Russia, Nov. 10, 1901; s. Stephan Ivan and Katherine (Triguboff) S.; B.S. in E.E., Ida. U., 1926; Ph.D., U. Wis., 1930; m. Elizabeth Thatcher Stafford, June 6, 1931; m. 2d, Ruth Lawyer, Dec. 23, 1947; 1 dau., Katherine Ann. Naturalized citizen, 1927. Fellow, Ida. U., 1925-27; instr. U. Wis., 1927-30, asst. prof. math., 1930-35, asso. prof., 1935-41, prof., 1941-46; prof. math. U. Cal., 1946-68, prof. emeritus, 1968-76; vis. prof. Brown U., summers 1941, 42; Fulbright prof. Middle East Tech. U. Ankara, Turkey, 1968; spl. cons. Army Air Forces, 1942. Commd. ofcl. investigator Nat. Def. Research Com., 1941; chief tech. aide Math. panel Nat. Def. Research Com., Office of Sci. Research and Devel., 1944-45; cons. Nat. Def. Research Com., 1945-46. Mem. USSR 1st All-Union Congress on Mechanics, Moscow, 1960. Awarded medal by Anders' Classical Gymnasia; Presdl. Certificate of Merit, 1948. Recipient grants from Research Corp. of N.Y., 1949, 50, 51; Guggenheim fellow in Europe, 1952-53, 59-60, Swiss Fed. Inst. Tech., Zurich, 1959-60. Mem. Circolo Matematico di Palermo, Am. Math. Soc. (Council, 1945-47), Math. Assn. Am. (gov. 1948-50), AAUP, Soc. Indsl. and Applied Math., Sigma Xi, Tau Beta Pi, Gamma Alpha. Author: Higher Mathematics for Engrs. and Physicists, 1934; Advanced Calculus, 1939; Mathematical Theory of Elasticity, 1941, Mathematical Theory of Elasticity, 1946; Matematica Superior para Ingenieros y Fisicos, 1947; Tensor Analysis, 1951, rev. edit., 1964; A Treatise on the Mathematical Theory of Elasticity, 1956; (with R. M. Redheffer) Mathematics of Physics and Modern Engineering, 1958, rev. 1966; research articles math, theory of elasticity. Contbr. Ency. Brittanica, Collier's Ency. Editor: Quar. of Applied Math., Wiley's Series in Applied Mathematics; Mathematical Reviews. Home: Pacific Palisades, Calif. Died Apr. 16, 1976.

SOLBERG, ARCHIE NORMAN, biologist, educator; b. Lemmon, S.D., Jan. 4, 1909; s. Joseph and Oline (Amundsen) S.; B.S. (Masonic scholar), N.D. State U., 1930, M.S., 1933; Ph.D. (Univ. fellow), Columbia 1938; m. Margaret Jane Olsen, Sept. 12, 1934; children—Norman, James, Mary A., Marilyn, Eric, Elizabeth. Instr. zoology N.D. State U., 1930-33; asst. in zoology Columbia, 1933-36; instr. biology U. Toledo, 1937-39, asst. prof., 1939-43, asso. prof., 1943-51, prof., 1951-71, chmn. dept., 1957-62, exec. dir. Research Found., 1946-66, exec. v.p. Research Found., 1966-70, dir. Office Spl. Services, 1952-55, dean research and spl. services, 1955-57, dean research, 1957-66, dir. grad. div., 1959-63, dean Grad. Sch., 1963-66, v.p. research 1966-71, emeritus prof., 1971-77. Mem. research rev. bd. Am. Cancer Soc., 1968-77; pres. Toledo Tech. Council, 1964-65. Bd. dirs., chmn. program com. Tb Soc., 1969-70; trustee, chmn. research com. Toledo Clinic Found.; trustee, pres. Tech. Found. Toledo, 1969-71. Served as 2d lt. inf., AUS, 1930-40 (Res.). Fellow Ohio Acad. Sci. (v.p. 1953); mem. Mich. Acad. Sci., Arts and Letters (life), Am. Soc. Zoologists, Am. Soc. for Engring. Edn., Nat. Council Univ. Research Adminstrs., Am. Ceramic Soc., AAAS, Tech. Soc. Toledo (pres. 1970-71), Scabbard and Blade, Sigma Xi (research award 1938), Phi Kappa Phi (life dir. fellowships 1963-71, exec. dir. 1971-77), Kappa Delta Pi, Blue Key, Alpha Epsilon Delta (nat. v.p. 1962-68), Beta Beta Beta, Theta Chi. Republican. Lutheran. Rotarian (dir. Toledo 1968-70, 2d v.p. 1969-70, dir. chpt. 1972-74). Club: University of Toledo Sigma Xi (pres. 1969-71). Home: Ann Arbor, Mich. Died Nov. 22, 1977.

SOLES, THOMAS FRANKLIN, business exec., b. McKeesport, Pa., June 30, 1882; s. Wesley Cramer and Emma Loraine (Smith) S.; Ph.B., Lafayette Coll., Easton, Pa., 1904, LL.B., U. of Pittsburgh, 1907; m. Terrissa Cochran Brooks, June 17, 1909 (died); children—Dorothy (Mrs. Edward T. Phillips), John Jay. m. 2d, Mrs. Jane Nicholson Koch, Aug. 10, 1955. In gen. law practice, 1907-34; pres. Bank of Glassport, Pa. since 1934; v.p. and counsel Talon, Inc., Meadville, Pa., since 1922, chmn. bd., v.p. since 1944. Trustee Lafayette Coll. Mem. Am. Arbitration Assn., Nat. Alumni Assn., Lafayette Coll. (pres. 1939), Phi Kappa Psi. Republican. Methodist. Mason. Clubs: Country, Iroquois (Meadville, Pa.); Youghiogheny Country (McKeesport); Duquesne, University (Pittsburgh). Home: McKeesport, Pa.*

SOLINSKY, ROBERT S., corp. exec.; b. Chgo., May 12, 1894; LL.D. (hon.), Elmhurst (Ill.) Coll.; m.; two children. Pres., Cans, Inc., 1939-52 (merged with Nat. Can Corp. 1952), pres., dir., 1953-58, chief exec. officer, 1953-66, chmn. bd., dir., 1958-69, mem. exec. com., 1953-78, chmn. fin. com., 1966-78, chmn. exec. com., 1968-78, hon. chmn. bd., dir., 1969-78; head metal can sect. Container Div., WPB, 1942-44. Mem. Horatio Alger Awards Nat. Com.; trustee Elmhurst Coll.; hon life trustee Meml. Hosp. of Du Page County, Elmhurst, Central Du Page Community Hosp., Winfield, Ill.; bd. dirs. Insts. Religion and Health, N.Y.C.; bd. govs. Citizens Greater Chgo.; trustee Ill. Masonic Med. Center, Chgo.; hon. life bd. dirs. Lincoln Park Zool. Soc., Chgo.; adv. bd. Salvation Army; chmn. Inst. Econ. Inquiry, Nat. Council. Recipient Horatio Alger award Am. Schs. and Colls. Assn., 1960. Mem. Can Mfrs. Inst. (pres. 1946-48, exec. com. 1946-78; hon. life mem. bd. govs.), Old Guard Soc., Nat. Canners Assn. and Allied Industries (hon. life), Carbonated Beverage Container Mfrs. Assn. (gov.), United World Federalists (nat. adv. bd.). Republican. Congregationalist. Clubs: Glen Oak Country (Glen Ellyn); Capitol Hill (Washington); Masons (33 deg.), Shriners. Home: Glen Ellyn, Ill. Died May 2, 1978.

SOLOMON, SAMUEL JOSEPH, aviation ins. exec.; b. Washington, July 11, 1899; s. Samuel and Maggie (Rosenberry) S.; grad. Central High Sch., Washington, 1918; grad. Nat. U., 1936; m. Alma Marie Garber, Dec. 26, 1923; children—Robert Franklin, Richard Joseph, William Samuel. Vice-pres. Nat. Airport Corp., Washington, 1933-42; mgr. Washington Airport, 1933-41; v.p. Northeast Airlines, and predecessor cos., Nat. Airways Inc., and Boston-Me. Airways, 1933-41; pres. Northeast Airlines, Inc., 1941-44, chmn. bd., 1944-45, pres., dir. Calif. Eastern Airways, Inc., 1949-59, chmn. bd., 1954-56; pres. Land Air, Inc., 1954-56; pres. AVEMCO Corp., AVEMCO Life Ins. Co., AVEMCO Ins. Co. Aviation Growth Investments, Inc., 1960-65, AVEMCO Finance Corp., 1960-65; pres. Aircraft Investment Corp., 1963-65; dir. Washington Helicopter Co. Pres. Airlines War Tng. Inst., Washington; chmn. Airlines Com. for U.S. Air Policy, 1943-44. Awarded Presdl. Certificate of Merit, 1947. Dir. YMCA, Washington; chmn. Aviation Hist. Found. Mem. Am. Inst. Aeros. and Astronautics, Aero. Tng. Soc. (pres. 1956-58). Clubs: Argyle Country (Silver Spring, Md.); Wings (N.Y.C.); Aviation (Washington). Home: Silver Spring, Md. Died Dec. 8, 1977; buried Parklawn Cemetery, Rockville, Md.

SOMERS, GERALD GEORGE, educator; b. Toronto, Ont., Can., Aug. 6, 1922; s. Joseph and Betty (Behr) S.; came to U.S., 1946, naturalized, 1956; A.B., U. Toronto, 1943, M.A., 1946; Ph.D., U. Calif. at Berkeley, 1951; m. Rita Schacter, July 13, 1945; children—Eric, Jonathan, Laura. Asso. prof., dir. Inst. Indsl. Relations, W.Va. U., 1956-57; prof. econs. U. Wis.-Madison, 1960-77, chmn. dept., 1968-71, dir. indsl. relations research inst. Center for Studies in Vocat. and Tech. Edn., 1964-68; cons. Office Econ. Opportunity, Dept. Labor, Nat. Council Aging, 1964-77; arbitrator labor-mgmt. disputes, 1951-77; mem. Nat. Council on Employment Policy, 1969-77. Served with RCAF, 1943-45. Guggenheim fellow for research in Western Europe, 1959-60; NATO sr. fellow in sci., 1976-77; grantee Ford Found., Dept. Commerce, Dept. Labor, Office Edn. Mem. Nat. Acad. Arbitrators (editor procs. 1968-77), Am. Econ. Assn., NAACP, Internat. Indsl. Relations Assn. (mem. exec. bd. 1967-77), Indsl. Relations Research Assn. (editor 1958-74, pres. 1975). Author: Lessons from a Decade of Manpower Policy, 1977; (with others) Contemporary Labor Economics, 1974; author, editor: (with K. Little) Vocational Education—TODAY Education—Today and Tomorrow, 1970; Retraining the Unemployed, 1968; editor, co-author: Essays in Industrial Relations Theory, 1969; editor: (with D. Wood) Cost-Benefit Analysis of Manpower Policies, 1969; editorial bd. Jour. Human Resources, 1966-77, editor, 1966-69. Home: Madison, Wis. Died Dec. 30, 1977.

SOMMERBURG, MIRIAM, artist; b. Hamburg, Germany; d. David and Nanny (Munk) Cahn; student, Hamburg, 1926-29; sculpture pupil Richard Luksch, 1926-29; design pupil Friedrich Adler, Bauhaus, 1926; m. Rudolf Sommerburg, Feb. 10, 1927 (dec.); children—Sascha, Dimitri, Sonia S. Rabin, David P., Gioconda (Mrs. Howard L. Richards). Came to U.S., 1946, naturalized, 1951. Exhbns.: New Delhi, Bombay, Calcutta, Madras, Hyderabad and Baroda, India, 1965-66, Alpes Maritimes, La Napoule, Musée de Cognac, Cannes, France, 1965-66, N.Y. World's Fair, 1965, Vera Cruz, Mexico City and Monterey, Mex., 1964-65, 75, Birmingham, Eng., 1964, Edinburgh, Scotland, 1965, Mus. Modern Art, Rio de Janeiro, 1963, Museo de Belles Artes, Buenos Aires, Argentina, 1963, S. Am. with USIA, 1963-64, Acad. Arts and Letters (grant candidate), 1960, invitation to participate in Ford Found. grant, 1959, Brussels, Antwerp, Ghent and Ostend, Belgium with USIA, 1956-57, Stedelijk Mus., Amsterdam, Netherlands, 1956, Burlington Galleries, London, 1955, Berlin Acad. Fine Arts, 1954, Whitney Mus., 1951, 54, Bklyn. Mus., 1951, 54, Pa. Acad., 1954, 66, Isaac Delgado Mus., 1947-56, Boston Art Mus., 1954, Audubon Artists, 1948-80, Nat. Assn. Women Artists, 1952-80, Soc. Am. Graphic Artists, 1947, 48, 51, 59, Am. Soc. Contemporary Artists, 1951-80, The Contemporaries, N.Y.C., 1956, 57, Nat. Arts Club, N.Y.C., 1961, 71, 74, 76, Bd. of Trade, N.Y.C., 1968, Union Carbide, N.Y.C., 1970, 72, 75, Jewish Tercentary traveling exhbn., 1954, 55, Soc. Young Am. Artists, 1955, Allied Artists Am., 1949, Grand Central Art Galleries, N.Y.C., 1952, Bergen County Mus., Paramus, N.J., 1974, New Sch. Social Research, N.Y.C., 1955, Calif. Soc. Etchers at Gumps, San Francisco, 1946, Syracuse Mus., 1945, also in Florence and Naples, Italy, 1972, Am. Drawings, Portsmouth, Va., 1976, Lever House, 1977, numerous others; one-woman shows, 1950, 51, 53, 54, 55, 58, 59, 63, 65; represented in permanent collections: Met. Mus., N.Y.C., Norfolk (Va.) Mus., Springfield (Mo.) Mus., Butler Inst. Am. Art, Fla. So. Coll., B'nai B'rith Mus., Inst. Advanced Study, Princeton, N.J., Rose Art Mus., Brandeis U., Assn. Research and Enlightenment, Va. Recipient Audubon Artists prize, 1966, Audubon award, 1978, Nat. Assn. Women Artists award, 1961, 2 awards Design in Hardwoods, Chgo., 1959, Silvermine Guild Artists award, 1959, Am. Soc. Contemporary Artists award 1958, 62, 64, Painters and Sculptors N.J. award, 1949, 55, Knickerbocker Artists award, 1954, Village Art Center award, 1946, 48, 49, 50, 51, 56, 57, 60, Creative Gallery, 1951, Fla. So. Coll., 1952, Internat. Women's Yr. award, 1976. Life fellow Intercontinental Biog. Assn.; mem. Audubon Artists, Nat. Assn. Women Artists, Am. Soc. Contemporary Artists, Print Council Am., Artists Equity Assn. N.Y., Washington Women Artists. Work reproduced in Mosaics and Design Through Discovery. Home: New York, N.Y. Died Sept. 5, 1980.

SONNEBORN, TRACY MORTON, scientist, educator; b. Balt., Oct. 19, 1905; s. Lee and Daisy (Bamberger) S.; B.A., Johns Hopkins, 1925, Ph.D., 1928, D.Sc (hon.), 1957; D.Sc. (hon.), Université de Genève, Northwestern U., 1975, Ind. U., 1978, U. Münster (W. Ger.), 1979; m. Ruth Meyers, June 6, 1929; children—Lee M., David R. Fellow, NRC, 1928-30; research asst. zoology Johns Hopkins U., 1930-31, research asso., 1931-33, asso., 1933-39; asso. prof. zoology Ind. U., 1939-43, prof., 1943-53, distinguished prof., 1953-76, distinguished prof. emeritus, 1976-81, acting chmn. div. biol. scis. 1963-64; vis. prof. U. Wash., Seattle, Battelle Research Center, 1971 vis. researcher U. Paris South, Orsay, France, Laboratoire de Génétique Moleculaire, Gif-sur-Yvette, France, 1973; vis. prof. zoology U. Geneva (Switzerland), 1979. Discoverer of mating types in ciliated protozoa, 1937, roles of genes, cytoplasm and environment, control cell heredity, 1943-81. Co-winner Newcomb-Cleveland prize for outstanding research paper AAAS, 1946; Kimber Genetics award Nat. Acad. Scis., 1959; Mendel medal Czechoslovakia Acad. Sci., 1965. Mem. Am. Soc. Naturalists (pres. 1949), Am. Soc. Zoologists (pres. 1956), Genetics Soc. Am. (pres. 1949), Soc. Study Evolution (v.p. 1958), Nat. Acad. Sci. (1946), Am. Philos. Soc. (Phila.), Am. Acad. Arts and Sci. (Boston), Am. Soc. Protozoologists (hon.), Royal Soc. London (fgn.), Am. Soc. Cell Biology, Am. Inst. Biol. Scis. (pres. 1960-61), Phi Beta Kappa (vis. scholar 1969, asso. lectr. 1975-81), Sigma Xi (nat. lectr. 1949, 68); hon. mem. Faculdad de Biologia y Ciencias Medicas, Universidad de Chile, Sociedad de Biologia de Santiago de Chile, Sociedad de Biologia de Concepcion (Chile), Sociedad Medíca de Concepcion (Chile), French Soc. Protozoology (hon.), Genetics Soc. Japan (hon.). Editor: The Control of Human Heredity and Evolution, 1965; editorial bd. Jour. Morphology, 1946-49; Genetics, 1947-62; Jour. Exptl. Zoology, 1948-60; Physiol. Zoology, 1948-60; editoral com. Ann. Rev. Microbiology, 1954-58; contbr. articles to mags. and chpts. to books on genetics. Home: Bloomington, Ind. Died Jan. 26, 1981.

SONNENBERG, BENJAMIN, publicity exec.; b. Brest-Litovsk, Poland, July 12, 1901; s. Harry and Ida Bedder) S.; ed. pub. sch. in N.Y.C. and by pvt. tutors; m. Hilda Caplan, Mar. 3, 1924; children—Helen, Benjamin II. Began as reporter Flint (Mich.) Daily Jour.; became mem. Am. Relief Adminstrn., 1922, being stationed in Constantinople (Istanbul) supervising relief work in Turkish waters and the Ukraine after World War I; fgn. corr. for Am. newspaper services in Europe, 1923-24; organized pub. relations bur. N.Y.C., 1928; pres. Publicity Consultants, Inc., N.Y.C., 1937-78; engaged in pub. relations for nationally known orgns. Decorated chevalier French Legion of Honor. Home: New York, N.Y. Died Sept. 6, 1978.

SOPER, FRED LOWE, pub. health adminstr.; b. Hutchinson, Kans., Dec. 13, 1893; s. Socrates John and Mary Ann (Jordan) S.; A.B., U. of Kan., 1914, M.S., 1916; M.D., Rush Med. Coll., U. of Chicago, 1918; CPH., Johns Hopkins U., 1923, Dr.P.H., 1925; D.Sc. (hon.), Jefferson Medical College, 1956; married Juliet Snider, Dec. 1919. Intern Cook County Hosp., Chicago, 1918-19; mem. staff Internat. Health Bd. (now Internat. Health Div.). Rockefeller Found., 1920-50; regional director International Health Division, 1927, asso. dir., 1945-50; dir. Pan American Sanitary Bus. from 1947, regional dir. World Health Orgn. for Ams. from 1949; hookworm campaigns, Brazil, 1920-22, Paraguay, 1923-27; general administration (headquarters Rio de Janeiro), 1927-42; epidemiology yellow fever; malaria and yellow fever control; species eradication of mosquitoes (Aedes aegypti and Anopheles gambiae); consultant to Sec. of War. Epidemic Diseases, 1942-46; mem. U.S.A. Typhus Commn. 1943; dir. Rockefeller Foundation Health Commn., Typhus Team, North Africa, 1943, Italy, 1943-44; typhus control Naples with Allied Military Government for Italy; malaria control. Italy and Egypt, 1944-45. Enlisted U.S. Army, 1917. transferred to Med. Res., 1917-18, Decorations: Cuba

1940, Brazil, 1942, Egypt, 1947, U.S.A., 1944, Lasker Award, 1946. Mem. American Academy of Tropical Medicine; corresponding member National Academy Medicine, Rio de Janeiro, Brazil, and Bogot.*

SORENSEN, ROYAL WASSON, prof. elec. engring.; b. Wabaunsee County, Kan., Apr. 25, 1882; s. Soren and Margaret E. (Wasson) S.; B.S., in Elec. Engring., University of Colorado, 1905, E.E., 1928. D.Sc., 1938; m. Grace Milner, Apr. 26, 1906; children—Jennie Maguerite, Grace Helen, Royal Milner. Georginia (dec.), Lewis Robert. Asst. engr. Golden Illuminating Co., 1900; testman Gen. Electric Co., 1905-06, research and design engineer in transformer dept., General Electric Co., 1906-10, asso. professor elec. engring., Throop Poly. Inst. (now Calif. Inst. Tech.), 1910-11, prof., 1911-50, chmn. faculty, 1938-39; spl. lectr. Cal. Inst., 1950-52; prof. emeritus elec. engring. Cal. Inst. of Tech. since 1952; mem. sci. adv. group to Japan, Nat. Acad., 1917; cons. engr. Cole Elec. Co. since 1951; cons. engr. U.S. Elec. Mfg. Co. till 1929; cons. engr. Gen. Electric Co., 1929-30; mem. cons. engrs. Met. Water Dist. Southern Calif. 1931-44. Planned and designed equipment of the first Am. 1,000,000 volt cascade transformer system and lab.; invented (with Dr. Robt. A. Millikan) vacuum switch for high potential electric circuit; also other inventions. Spl. radio instr., Signal Corps, S.A.T.C. and mem. Research Com. for Submarine Detection, World War I. Coordinator for radio courses and supervisor for other courses in war training program for engring. sci. and management for U.S. Office of Edn., World War II. Asso. dir. Spl. Studies Group at Columbia U., Div. of War Research, 1943-45. Member engineering division National Research Council, 1942-45. Fellow American Institution E.E. (research com.), 1923-30, chairman, 1941-43; v.p., 1933-35; dir., 1937-40; pres., 1940-41; pres. mem. bd., 1941-43; mem. Society for Promotion Engring. Edn. (mem. gov. bd., 1938-40, v.p., 1938-39; mem. com. on accelerated engring. programs, 1941-43; chmn. com. on grad. study, 1942-43), Engring. Council of Founder Socs. So. Cal., A.A.A.S., Assn. Am. U. Profs.; hon. mem. Japan Inst. E.E.; mem. Tau Beta Pi, Sigma Xi. Recipient most valuable engring. service scroll given by Engrs. and Architects of Los Angeles, 1944. Mason. Republican. Baptist. Pres. Pasadena Y.M.C.A., 1933-39. Rotarian. Clubs: Joint Tech., Sigma Xi (Los Angeles); Engineers, Twilight (Pasadena). Contbr. many articles in tech. mags. on high voltage electric power transmission and apparatus. Home: Pasadena, Calif.*

SORENSEN, SVEND OLUF, banker; b. Grenaa, Denmark, Feb. 24, 1914; s. P. and Anna (Jensen) S.; diploma banking Copenhagen Sch. Econs. and Bus. Adminstrn., 1941; m. Karen Vontillius, Nov. 12, 1949; children—Aase Hellemann, Birgit Hoffmeyer. With Den Danske Bank, Copenhagen, 1930-80, mng. dir., 1962-80; gov. Adela Investment Co. S.A. Adviser banking Govt. Pakistan, 1952-53; mem. bd. Danish Bankers Assn.; mem. bd. Banking Fedn. EEC; chmn. bd. Ship Credit Fund Denmark; chmn. bd. Den Danske Bank Internat. S.A., Luxembourg; mem. bd. Danish Agrl. Real Property Loan Fund; mem. Institut International d'Etudes Bancaires, Internat. Monetary Conf.; internat. counsellor Conf. Bd.; mem. Danish-Am. Trade Council. Mem. bd. Danish nat. com. Internat. C. of C.; mem. com. Fin. Inst. Danish Industry and Handicrafts, Ltd., Danish Soc. Preservation Bldgs. and Landscapes. Decorated comdr. Order Dannebrog (Denmark); knight 1st class Order St. Olav (Norway). Mem. Danish Acad. for Tech. Scis. Rotarian. Clubs: American (Copenhagen); Overseas Bankers (London, Eng.); Rungsted Golf. Home: Hellerup, Denmark. Died July 25, 1980.

SORENSON, CHARLES J(AMES), coll. prof., agrl. entomologist; b. Hyrum, Utah, May 3, 1884; s. Charles M. and Alice (Unsworth) S.; certificate of grad. in commerce, Utah State Agrl. Coll., 1906, B.S., 1914, M.S., 1927; student U. of Wash., summer 1916, U. of Calif., 1919; m. Lois Wallace, June 27, 1912; children—Charles Wallace, James Keith. Recorder Hyrum City, Utah, 1912-14; instr. Utah State Agrl. Coll., 1914-16, asst. prof., 1916-20, asst. entomologist, 1926-30, asso. entomol., 1931-37, research asso. prof., 1938-45, prof. agrl. entomol. since 1946; instr. U. of Wash., summer 1916; agrl. inspector Utah State Dept. of Agr., 1921-25. Member A.A.A.S., Entomol. Soc. Am., Am. Assn. Econ. Entomol., Am. Assn. Univ. Profs., Utah Acad. Sci., Arts, and Letters, Sons of Utah Pioneers, Sigma Xi, Phi Kappa Phi. Republican. Mem. Ch. of Jesus Christ of Latter-Day Saints. Clubs: Logan Men's, Knife and Fork. Contbr. articles to professional jours. Home: Logan, Utah.*

SORG, HERBERT PETER, U.S. judge; b. St. Marys, Pa., Dec. 19, 1911; s. Jacob P. and Margaret M. (Wehler) S.; student St. Vincent Coll., 1927-31; LL.B., Duquesne U., 1935; m. June Mary Storer, Dec. 31, 1940; children—Suzanne (Mrs. Gregory Tornatore), Karen (Mrs. Richard I. Thomas), June (Mrs. Daniel Lloyd Diamond), Herbert Peter, Vivian (Mrs. Daniel L. Dermyer). Admitted to Pa. bar, 1935; practiced in St. Mary's, Pa., 1935-55; judge U.S. Dist. Ct. for Pa., Pitts., 1955-79. Mem. Pa. Ho. of Reps., 1940-53, majority whip, 1945-47, majority leader, 1947, speaker, 1947-53. Mem. Pa. Bar Assn., Am. Judicature Soc. K.C. Home: Pittsburgh, Pa. Died Mar. 11, 1979; buried St. Mary's, Pa.

SORIA, DARIO, music and records cons.; b. Rome, Italy, May 21, 1912; s. Raffaello and Amelia (Padoa) S.; B.A., U. Rome, 1934; postgrad. law U. Ferrara (Italy), 1937-39; m. Dorle Jarmel, July 26, 1942. Came to U.S., 1939, naturalized, 1945. Jr. partner Raffaello Soria & Co., bank, Rome, 1930-39; treas., dir. Buitoni Foods Corp., N.Y.C., 1940-41; announcer Italian programs, dir. Italian and French programs OWI, N.Y.C., 1942-43; asst. dir., then dir. network programs CBS, N.Y.C., 1943-48; dir. radio programs D'Arcy Advt. Agy., N.Y.C. and Hollywood, 1948-50; pres., gen. mgr. Cetra-Soria Records, N.Y.C., 1950-53; pres. EMI Inc. (Angel Records), N.Y.C., 1953-57; adminstrv. dir. Festival of Two Worlds, Spoleto, Italy, 1958; ind. producer Soria Series for RCA Victor, N.Y.C., 1959-61; div. v.p. charge internat. operations and fgn. subsidiaries RCA Records, N.Y.C., 1961-70; mng. dir. Met. Opera Guild, Inc., N.Y.C., 1971-78; adv. dir. Met. Opera Assn., 1978-80; producer Met. Opera Historic Broadcasting Rec. Series, 1975-80; producer, narrator weekly radio program Festival of Opera, WOR radio, N.Y.C., 1951-56. Served to lt. Italian Alpine Troops, 1933, 35-36. Decorated War Cross of Merit, Ufficiale al Merito della Repubblica (Italy); officier Ordre des arts et des lettres (France). Clubs: Metropolitan Opera, Century. Home: New York, N.Y. Died Mar. 28, 1980.

SOSIN, ABRAHAM, educator; b. Chgo., June 23, 1925; s. Solomon and Sophia (Mason) S.; Ph.B., U. Chgo., 1948, B.S., 1949; M.S., U. Ill., 1950, Ph.D., 1954; m. Dorothy S. Simon, Sept. 23, 1947; children—Howard B., Cynthia A. Asst. prof. U. Fla., 1954-55; mem. faculty U. Cal. at Los Angeles, 1959-68; prof. physics, dir. and prof. materials sci. and engring. U. Utah, Salt Lake City, 1968-78; group leader North Am. Rockwell, Inc., 1955-68. Served with USAAF, 1943-46. Mem. Am. Phys. Soc., Am. Inst. Metall. Engrs., Am. Soc. Metals, Am. Acad. Arts and Scis., Soc. Advanced Materials and Process Engrs. Home: Salt Lake City, Utah. Died June 18, 1978.

SOTO, JUAN B(AUTISTA) (SO'TO), university prof.; b. Aguada, P.R., Feb. 24, 1882; s. Juan Bautista and Maria (Gonzalez) S.; A.B., Instituto Civil de Puerto Rico, 1899; Ph.D., J.D., U. of Madrid, Spain, 1929; m. Felícita Ramos, 1901 (now dec.); children—Juan Francisco, José; m. 2d, Josephine Eakin, 1912 (now dec.); 1 son, Russell David; m. 3d, Librada Alarcón, of San Juan, P.R., 1921; children—José Luis, Margarita. Began as elementary sch. teacher, 1901; prof. Presbyn. Sch., Aquadilla, P.R., 1904; admitted to Puerto Rican bar, 1910, and began practice as atty. and solicitor in chancery; prof. of law, U. of P.R., 1915-32, prof. philosophy, 1941-50, head dept., 1932-36, chancellor, 1936-41. Asso. mem. Board Parole of P.R. since 1948. Senator at large, Senate of P.R., 1924-32; president div. of polit. and social science, Ateneo de P.R.; former pres. Bd. of Examiners for admission to Federal Court bar; dir. San Juan Y.M.C.A. Mem. Puerto Rican Acad. of History (pres.), Am. Acad. Polit. and Social Science, Puerto Rico Bar Assn. (ex-pres.), A.A.A.S., American Philosophical Assn. Member Union-Republican party. Mason. Clubs: Casino de Puerto Rico, Casino Espanol (San Juan). Author books relating to field. Editor PuertoRico Rev. Address: Rio Piedras. P.R.*

SOUBY, JAMES MARTIN (SOO'BI), lawyer; b. Karnes County, Tex., Aug. 10, 1882; s. Armand Maxie and Emma Lowry (Rose) S.; A.B., Vanderbilt U., 1908, LL.B., 1910; m. Betty Weitzel, Jan. 17, 1916; children—James Martin, Marjorie Reeves (Mrs. Richard F. Cooper). Admitted to Mo. bar, 1912; in gen. practice of law, Kansas City, Mo., 1912-13; commerce counsel, later solicitor, Kansas City Southern R.R., Kansas City, Mo., 1913-19; with Union Pacific R.R., Omaha, Neb., 1919-37, successively asst. valuation and commerce counsel, valuation and commerce counsel, western gen. counsel; asst. gen. counsel Assn. of Am. Railroads, Washington, D.C., 1937-42, gen. solicitor since 1942. Awarded Founder's Medal in both academic and law schools Vanderbilt U. Mem. bd. trustees Vanderbilt U. Mem. Phi Beta Kappa, Phi Kappa Sigma, Phi Delta Phi, Sigma Upsilon. Home: Washington. *

SOULE, EDGAR CLARKE HUCKABEE, ex-consul, lawyer; b. Waxahachie, Tex., Dec. 9, 1886; s. Edgar Clarke Huckabee and Millicent Kathryn S.; student U. Ill., 1915; B.A., U. of Tex., 1919; M.A., George Washington U., 1920; m. Floy De Vore Perfect, Sept. 18, 1911; children—Gardner, Margaret, Patricia. Entered consular service, July 7, 1920; consul at Cartagena, Colombia, 1920-22; Dept. of State, 1922-23; consul, Cardiff, Wales, 1923-July 26, 1924 (resigned); now engaged in practice of law at Houston, Tex.; consul in Houston of Ecuador. Served as lt. Air Service, U.S. Army, Aug. 24, 1917- Mar. 16, 1920. Mem. Nat. Council Nat. Econ. League, Acad. Polit. Sci. Am. Judicature Soc., Phi Beta Kappa, Delta Sigma Rho, Pi Gamma Mu. Democrat. Mason (32). Mem. Christ Ch. Episcopal. Clubs: Cardiff Rotary, Whitchurch Golf, American Business (pres. Houston chpt. 1926). Address: Houston, TX.*

SOULE, ELIZABETH STERLING (SOL), nursing education; b. East Douglas, Mass., Oct. 13, 1884; d. Edwin (M.D.) and Adeline (Bates) Sterling; grad. Malden Hosp. Sch. of Nursing, 1907; A.B., U. of Wash., 1926, A.M., 1930; D.Sc., Mont. State Coll., 1944; m. Harry W. Soule, June 11, 1912. Engaged in public health nursing since 1909; mem. staff pub. health nursing, Mass., 1909-12; mem. Seattle, Walla Walla County, State Bd. of Health (Wash.), 1912-20; adminstrn. and teaching, Sch. of Nursing Education, U. of Wash., 1920-45, dean, 1945-50, now dean, prof. emeritus. Traveling guest of the Rockefeller Foundation to study schs. of nursing in Europe, 1930. Fellow Am. Pub. Health Assn.; mem. Am. Nurses Association, American Sch. of Nursing, Nat. Orgn. for Public Health Nursing, National League Nursing Edn., American Assn. Univ. Professors, Assn. Collegiate Schs. Nursing (past pres.), Am. Legion Auxiliary, Pi Lambda Theta, Alpha Kappa Delta, Phi Mu. Author: Community Hygiene (with Christine MacKenzie), 1940. Alumnus summa laude dignatus, U. of Wash. Home: Wash. *

SOULE, PHELPS (SOOL), director of the U. Pennsylvania Press; b. Boston, Mass., April 15, 1883; s. Edward Lincoln and Elizabeth Newhouse (Phelps) S.; A.B., Harvard, 1906; m. Doris Hill, Aug. 31, 1911; children—Elizabeth Phelps (Mrs. John R. Brownell), Edmund Foster. Accounting mgr., later editor, Yale U. Press, 1918-27; editor and mgr. U. of Pa. Press, 1927-41, dir. since 1941; sec., U. of Pa., 1941-46. Mem. Pa. Hist. Assn., Book Clinic (Philadelphia) (organizer and chmn., 1939-40). Clubs: Franklin Inn, Lenape, Art Alliance (Philadelphia, Pa.). Editor Pennsylvania Lives, since 1940. Contbr. book reviews and articles to various journals. Home: Swarthmore, Pa. *

SOUPART, PIERRE, physician, educator; b. Morlanwelz, Belgium, Oct. 1, 1923; s. Arthur and Angèle (Couteau) S.; came to U.S., 1962, naturalized, 1969; M.D., Brussels U., 1949, Ph.D., 1959, hon. prof., 1975; m. Simone Haegeman, July 23, 1949; children—Evelyne, Antoinette, Pascale. Asst. prof. dept. biochemistry Brussels U. Sch. Medicine, 1950-56, asso. prof., 1956-62; head clin. labs. Clinic for Indsl. Accidents, Brussels, 1952-62; prof. biochemistry and human nutrition Province of Brabant Inst. Tech., Brussels, 1959-62; research asso. div. reproductive physiology, dept. Ob-Gyn, Vanderbilt U. Sch. Medicine, Nashville, 1962-63, asst. prof. Ob-Gyn, 1963-66, asso. research prof., 1966-81, sr. investigator Vanderbilt Center for Population Research and Studies in Reproductive Biology, 1969-81, mem. univ. com. for protection of human subjects, 1973-76; vis. prof. Universidad Catolica de Chile and Universidad de Chile, Santiago, 1976; vis. prof. U. Calif., spring 1979; guest speaker numerous confs.; vis. prof. U. B.C., Vancouver, Can., 1979, Karolinska Inst., Stockholm, 1979, Monash U., Melbourne, Australia, 1979. Served as med. officer Belgian Army, 1949-50. Francqui Found. fellow, 1948, advanced fellow, 1961; Vanderbilt U. Centennial fellow, 1974-75; grantee NSF, March of Dimes, others. Mem. Soc. Study of Reprodn. (chmn. bylaws com. 1973-75), Société Belge de Biochimie, N.Y. Acad. Scis., Soc. Study of Fertility (U.K.), Am. Fertility Soc., Sociedad Latino Americana de Microscopia Electronica, Am. Soc. Andrology (charter), Soc. Cryobiology, Am. Assn. Tissue Banks, Internat. Embryotransfer Soc., Am. Assn. Gynecologic Laparascopists, Sigma Xi, Belgian Dietetic Assn. (hon.). Democrat. Club: Masons (Brussels). Author: Aminoaciduria of Pregnancy, 1959; editorial bd. Advances in Reproductive Biology, 1975—; contbr. articles to profl. jours. Pioneer in in vitro fertilization of human ovum. Home: Nashville, Tenn. Died June 10, 1981.

SOUSER, KENNETH, lawyer; b. Rockwell, Pa., Oct. 21, 1905; s. Russell R. and Grace (Critchfield) S.; A.B., U. Pa., 1927, LL.B., 1930; m. Margaret Smith, Oct. 9, 1930. Admitted to Pa. bar, 1930, since practiced in Phila.; asso. firm Slocum & Ferguson, and successors, 1930-37; mem. firm Saylor, Ferguson & Souser, and successors, 1938-59, Morgan, Lewis & Bockius, from 1959. Mem. Baker Street Irregulars, Phila. Bar Assn. Republican. Clubs: Lawyers, Union League (Phila.). Home: Berwyn, Pa. Deceased.

SOUTER, CLYDE DOUGLAS (SOO'TER), lawyer; b. Northampton, Mass., Sept. 21, 1885; s. William and Emma H. (Kreiger) S.; A.B., Dartmouth, 1906; student Columbia Law Sch., 1906-07; LL.B., N.J. Law Sch., Newark, 1910; m. Genevieve Dwyer, July 26, 1911; children—Edna Marion, Mary Elizabeth, Dorothy Elaine, Robert Mason; m. 2d, Evelyn Madeley Richardson, Jan. 3, 1925; children—Clyde Douglas, Eve-Lyn Sanduska. Admitted to N.J. bar, 1911, and practiced in N.J. until 1923; judge of Second Dist. Court of Jersey City, N.J., 1918-23; city atty. of Kearney, N.J., 1915-23; instr. law N.J. Law Sch., 1915-17, asst. prof., 1917-19, prof., 1919-23; admitted to Nev. bar 1923, and since practiced in Reno; lecturer on law, U. of Nevada, 1926-40. Served as chmn. Four Minute Men, local

Council of National Defense, inspector-instr. for Essex County, N.J., and chmn. legal advisory bd., Kearney, N.J., World War. Three times v. chmn. and twice sec. Rep. State Central Com. of Nev., chmn., 1936-38. Del. Republican National Convention, 1936-44-48. Mem. Am., N.J., Washoe County bar assns., State Bar of Nev., Reno Chamber Commerce, Dartmouth Assn. of Northern Calif., Delta Theta Phi. Mason (32 deg., Shriner), K.P., Eagles, Elks. Clubs: The Lawyers' (N.Y.); Dartmouth Outing of Northern Calif. Home: Reno.*

SOUTHARD, ADDISON E., diplomat; b. Louisville, Ky., Oct. 18, 1884; s. Henry C. and Sarah (Barfield) S.; ed. Lebanon U. and Univ. of St. Thomas, Manila, P.I.; m. Lucy B. Maloy, May 1913; 1 son, Patrick Hendy. With Vista Hermosa Sugar & Mercantile Co., State of Oaxaca, Mexico, 1904-05; country newspaper work, 1906; officer Govt. of P.I., 1907-15; in diplomatic and consular service in China, Arabia, Abyssinia, Somaliland, Persia, Eritrea, Palestine, Sweden and France; chief of Consular Reporting Office, Dept. of State, 1922-26; consul gen., 1924; assigned to Singapore, Apr. 7, 1926; Am. minister at Addis Ababa, Ethiopia, 1927-35; mem. with rank of E.E. and M.P. of U.S.special Mission to Imperial Coronation, 1930, palace guest Emperor Haile Selassie, Coronation Jubilee, Addis Ababa, 1955; counselor of the Legation, Stockholm, Sweden, 1935; counselor of Embassy and consul gen. Paris, 1936-37; consul. gen. Hong Kong, 1938-Dec. 1941; Dept. of State, 1941-62; Jap. prisoner 6 months after fall of Hong Kong. Decorated Grand Comdr. of Saint Trinity, 1st, Epthiopia. Mem. Am. Ffg. Service Assn., Am. Polit. Science Assn. Protestant. Clubs: Cosmos (Washington), Commonwealth, Bohemian (San Francisco), and various foreign clubs. Author: (commercial handbooks) Abyssinia, 1918; Eritrea, 1920; Palestine, 1922. Contbr. to mags. Lecturer. Address: San Francisco.*

SOWERWINE, ELBERT ORLA, mining exec.; b. Cicero, Ind., Aug. 20, 1884; s. Noah W. and Sarah May (Keesling) S.; A.B., Wabash Coll., 1905; m. Margaret Alice Evans, June 28, 1911; children—Owen E., Elbert O., Jr., Charles O., John W. High sch. teacher of Latin and German, Anaconda, Mont.; with Anaconda Copper Mining Co. beginning as metall. clerk, 1907, asst. to pres., 1937, v.p., 1945-56, ret.; dir., Internat. Smelting and Refining Co.; v.p., treas. Silesian Holding Co. Mem. Am. Mining Congress, Am. Inst. Mining and Metall. Engrs., C. of C. State N.Y., Kappa Sigma. Mason. Home: Westfield, N.J. *

SPAETH, EDMUND BENJAMIN, ophtalmologist, plastic surgeon; b. Webster, N.Y., Apr. 22, 1890; s. Philip George and Amelia Marie (Witzig) S.; M.D., U. Buffalo, 1916; post-grad. studies Army Med. Sch. (medalist), 1917, U. Vienna, Austria, 1922; m. Lea Maria Link, June 15, 1918; children—Edmund Benjamin, Philip George, Karl Henry, George Link. Intern Arnot-Ogden Meml. Hosp., Elmira, N.Y., 1916-17; pvt. practice of medicine, 1927-76; practice ophthalmology, Phila., 1927-76; prof. ophthalmology, grad. sch. medicine U. Pa., 1934-55, prof. emeritus, vice dean ophthalmology, chmn. dept. opthalmology; cons. U.S. Naval Hosp., Phila.; consulting surgeon Wills Eye Hosp., Phila.; consultant Graduate Hospital of Univ. of Pa. Served from 1st lt. to maj. M.C., U.S. Army, 1917-26. Awarded Ophthalmol. Medal, U. Buffalo, 1927; Lucian Howe medalist, Univ. Buffalo, 1927; University citation, University of Buffalo, 1958. Diplomate American Board Opthalmology, Am. Bd. Plastic Surgery. Fellow A.C.S., Internat. Coll. Surgeons, Am. Acad. Opthalmology and Otolaryngology, Phila. Coll. Physicians; mem. Pan-Pacific Surg. Soc., Pan-Am. Assn. Ophthalmology, Ophthalmol. Soc. Egypt (hon.), Ophthalmol. Society Chili, A.M.A., Oxford (Eng.) Ophthalmol. Congress. Rep. Unitarian. Mason. Author: Ophthalmic Plastic Surgery, 1927; Principles and Practice of Ophthalmic Surgery, 1939, rev. four subsequent edits.; also med. articles. Home: Philadelphia, Pa. Died Aug. 18, 1976.

SPANGLER, FRANCIS EDWIN, clergyman, educator; b. New Sheffield, Pa., July 4, 1882; s. James H. and Mary Ann Spangler; A.B., Mt. Helena (O.) Coll., 1908, A.M., 1909; student Medill Theol. Sem., 1909-10; grad. Southwestern Theol. Sem., Pittsburgh, Pa., 1911; B.D., Carelton Theol. Sem., 1916; LL.D., Coll. of Utah, 1936; D.D., Coll. of Northwest, Seattle, Wash.; m. Mary D. Scall, June 8, 1903; children—John Hancock, Elizabeth Jane, Edwin James. Ordained Presbyn. ministry, 1911; pastor, Updale, Ind., 1911-12, Coloma, Ill., 1913-16, Western Winnetka, Ill., since 1917; prof. philosophy, Carston Coll. since 1917, also dean of edn. Maj., chaplain 42d Div., N.G.; retired with rank of lt. col., 1936. Home: Winnetka, Ill.*

SPANN, WILLIAM BOWMAN, JR., lawyer; b. Savannah, Ga., June 10, 1912; s. William Bowman and Annie Elizabeth (Holversen) S.; A.B., Emory U., 1932, LL.D., 1973; LL.B., Harvard, 1935; m. Theodora Lillian Peterson, Feb. 8, 1946; children—William Bowman III, Robert Moseley, Karen Elizabeth Marion. Admitted to Ga. bar, 1935, also Supreme Ct. Ga., Ct. Appeals 5th Circuit, U.S. Supreme Ct. bar; practice in Atlanta, 1935-81; asso. Alston Foster, Moise & Sibley, 1935-41; partner firm Alston, Miller & Gaines, and predecessors, 1942-81; prof. law Woodrow Wilson Coll. Law, 1947-81. Chmn. adv. bd. Fulton County Juvenile Ct., 1953-63. Mem., dir. exec. com. Pres.' Lawyers' Com. Civil Rights under Law, 1963-81; commr., mem. exec. com. Uniform State Laws, 1965-81. Bd. dirs. Atlanta Legal Aid Soc.; trustee Atlanta Lawyers Found., Loridans Found.; mem. vis. com. U. Chgo. Law Sch., 1976-79. Served to lt. comdr. USNR, 1942-46. Fellow Am. Bar Found., Am. Coll. Trial Lawyers; mem. Internat., Inter-Am., Fed., Am. (bd. govs. 1961-64, state del. 1955-70, chmn. ho. dels. 1970-72, pres. 1977-78, life mem. ho. dels.; labor editor Law Notes 1965—), Ga. (chmn. labor sect. 1964-66), Atlanta bar assns., Am. Law Inst. (vice chmn. joint Am. Bar Assn. com. continuing profl. edn.), Am. Judicature Soc., Atlanta Lawyer's Club (past pres.), Phi Beta Kappa, Phi Beta Kappa Assos., Tau Kappa Alpha, Delta Tau Delta, Phi Alpha Delta. Lutheran. Clubs: Capital City, Commerce, Harvard (past pres.), Piedmont Driving. Home: Atlanta, Ga. Died May 17, 1981.

SPARHAWK-JONES, ELIZABETH, painter; b. Baltimore, Nov. 8, 1885; d. Rev. J. Sparhawk and Harriet Sterett (Winchester) Jones; unmarried. Winner of long term Cresson Scholarship and first Charles Toppen prize, Schs. of Pa. Acad. Fine Arts, also Mary Smith prize. 1908, 1912, Pa. Acad. Fine Arts; hon. mention, Carnegie Inst., Pittsburgh, 1909. Represented in permanent collection Art Inst., Chicago. Presbyn. Address: Philadelphia, Pa.*

SPARKS, WILLIAM JOSEPH, chemist; b. Wilkinson, Ind., Feb. 26, 1904; s. Charles Edward and Daisy (McDaniel) S.; A.B. with distinction, Ind. U., 1926, A.M., 1929; Ph.D., U. Ill., 1936; student Harvard Grad. Sch. Bus. Adminstrn., 1952; D. Sci., Ind. U., 1966, Mich. Tech. Inst., 1966; m. Meredith Pleasant, Dec. 31, 1930; children—Ruth, Katherine, Charles, John. With E.I. de Nemours du Pont Co., 1929-34; prin. chemist U.S. Dept. Agr., Peoria, Ill., 1939-40; with Esso Research and Engring. Co., 1936-38, 40-67, dir. chem. div., 1946-58, sci. adviser, 1958-67. Chmn. dir. chemistry and chem. tech. NRC, 1953-55; chmn. U.S. del. Internat. Union Pure & Applied Chemistry, Stockholm, 1953. Recipient Gold medal, Am. Inst. Chemists, 1954, Distinguished Alumni Service award, Ind. U., 1956; Charles Goodyear medal, 1963; Perkin medal Am. sect. Soc. Chem. Industry 1964; Priestley medal Am. Chem. Soc., 1965; Nat. Achievement award. Mem. Sci. Research Soc. Am. (nat. chmn. 1968-70), Am. Chem. Soc. (pres. 1966, dir. 1958-67), Armed Forces Chem. Assn. (chmn. com. chem. and biol. warfare), Am. Inst. Chemists (Pioneer award 1969), Assn. Research Dirs., Soc. Chem. Industries, Nat. Acad. Engring., Sigma Xi (nat. chmn.), Alpha Chi Sigma, Phi Lambda Upilon (hon.). Clubs: Chemists' (v.p.) (N.Y.C.); Cosmos (Washington); Riviera (Coral Gables, Fla.). Author numerous articles. Patentee. Home: Coral Gables, Fla. Died Oct. 23, 1976.

SPARROW, FREDERICK KROEBER, univ. prof.; b. Washington, May 11, 1903; s. Frederick Kroeber and Minnie (Tomlinson) S.; B.S., U. Mich., 1925; A.M., Harvard, 1926, Ph.D., 1929; m. Anna Gabler, Sept. 2, 1925; children—Frederick Tomlinson, George Burbank. Austin teaching fellow, Harvard, 1926-29; asst. in botany Radcliffe Coll., 1927; asst. in plant ecology Biol. Station, Cold Spring Harbor, N.Y., 1926-31; instr., asst. prof., biology Dartmouth Coll., 1929-36; NRC fellow in biol. scis. Cornell U., 1931-32, Cambridge U. (Eng.) and U. Copenhagen (Denmark), 1932-33; research fellowship Woods Hole (Mass.) Oceanographic Instn., 1934-36; research Atkins Gardens and Research Lab., Harvard U., Cienfuegos, Cuba, 1949, Botany Sch., Cambridge U., 1956, U. Fla., 1975; asst. prof. botany U. Mich., 1936-44, asso. prof., 1944-49, prof. botany, 1949-77, acting dir. Biol. Sta., Douglas Lake, 1967, dir., 1968-72; mem. com. on biology and agr. NRC, 1953-58; research asso. Mich. State Coll. Exptl. Sta., summers 1943-44; vis. prof. U. Hawaii, 1963, U. Calif., Berkeley, 1966, U. Wash. Friday Harbor Lab., 1968, 72, U. South Fla., 1973-74. Hon. v.p. Xth Internat. Bot. Congress, Edinburgh, 1964; chmn. Symposium I Internat. Mycological Congress, Exeter, Eng., 1971, pres. 2d Congress, Tampa, Fla., 1977; chmn. 2d Internat. Symposium on Marine Fungi, Bremerhaven, Germany, 1972. Collaborator, div. cotton and other fibre crops and plant diseases, bur. plant industry, soils and agrl. engring., agr. research adminstr. U.S. Dept. Agr. Recipient Russell award for achievement in research and teaching U. Mich., 1944; merit award Bot. Soc. Am., 1968. Fellow A.A.A.S.; mem. N.E. Bot. Club, Bot. Soc. Am., Mich. Acad. Scis., Arts and Letters (sec. 1943-47, editor 1947-52, pres. 1954-55), Mycol. Soc. Am. (sec.-treas. 1945-48, v.p. 1948, pres. 1949; Seventh Ann. lectr. 1958), Brit. Mycol. Soc., Washington Acad. Sci. Am. Soc. Limnology and Oceanography, Cambridge (Eng.), Philos. Soc., Sigma Xi, Alpha Sigma Phi, Phi Kappa Phi. Corr. mem. Third Microbiol. Congress, New York, 1939. Author: Aquatic Phycomycetes, 1943, 2d edit., 1961; (with T.W. Johnson) Fungi of Oceans and Estuaries, 1961; also of invitation papers: Sixth International Bot. Congress (Amsterdam), 1935, British Assn., Advancement Sciences (Norwich), 1935, Linnean Soc. of London, 1936; also more than 100 papers dealing with marine and freshwater fungi. Co-editor: The Fungi, Vol. IV, 1973. Home: Ann Arbor, Mich. Died Oct. 2, 1977; inurned St. Andrew's Columbarium, Ann Arbor.

SPARROW, LOUISE WINSLOW KIDDER, sculptor and writer; born at Maplewood, Malden, Massachusetts, January 1, 1884; daughter of Wellington Parker and Emma Louise (Hinckley) Kidder; grad. Quincy Mansion School, 1905, Thompson-Baldasseroni Sch. of Travel, 1907; U. of Poitiers, France, 6 weeks, 1923; studied sculpture under Henry K. Bush-Brown, 1915, Ulric S. Dunbar, Frederick W. Allen and Bela Pratt. 1916; anatomy with Phillip Hale; drawing with Edmund C. Messer, Eric Pape, 1908; m. Herbert George Sparrow, Capt. U.S. Navy, Nov. 16, 1909 (dec.); 1 son, Herbert George (col., U.S. Army); m. 2d, Paul E. H. Gripon, November 9, 1940 (divorced on June 7, 1949). Recipient of medal awarded for sculpture, Corcoran Gallery, Washington, D.C., 1930; Diplôme d'Honneur (France) for bust of Gen. Gorgas, exhibited Paris, 1932; Diplôme U. of Poitiers, France, 1923. Rep. in old National Gallery of Art, Naval Obs., U.S. Capitol, Smithsonian Inst., George Washington U., Howard U., Catholic U. (all of Washington, D.C.), San Bernardo, Chile, Oberlin Coll., Western Reserve Univ., State Capitol, Helena, Mont., Annapolis, Md., West Point, N.Y., Univ. of Ala., U. of Wis., Austen Riggs Foundation, Stockbridge, Mass., Med. Soc. Denver, etc. Mem. Prize Award Jury, Corcoran Gallery. Presented plaque of Capt. James H. Tomb to U.S. Merchant Marine Acad., Great Neck, N.Y., also to N.Y. State Merchant Marine Acad., Ft. Schuyler. Fellow Royal Soc. of Arts, London; mem. D.A.R., Ladies Auxiliary of the Sparrow-Maxwell All-Navy Post, Veterans Foreign Wars. Member World Federalist (Scarsdale, N.Y.). Republican. Unitarian. Gave ten 15-minute broadcasts on the wisdom of the classics. September-October, 1943. Author: Lyrics and Translations, 1904; The Last Cruise, 1926; also many poems. Translations from the French of Nico D. Horigoutchi, Tankas, and Air-Temples (2 books). Formerly editor of translations of Star Dust (mag. of verse). Home: Washington, D.C., also Basses-Pyré-nées, France.*

SPAUGH, W. HERBERT, bishop, newspaper columnist; b. Winston-Salem, N.C.; s. Rufus A. and Louise (Hege) S.; A.B., LL.D., Moravian Coll.; B.D. Moravian Theol. Sem.; M.A., D.D., Davidson Coll.; m. Ida Brown Efird; children—Earle, Herbert, Mrs. Robert Farmer, Jr. Furniture mfr., Winston-Salem; ordained to ministry Moravian Ch., pastor Little Ch. on Lane, Charlotte, N.C., 1924-66; columnist Charlotte News, 1933-78, also other So. newspapers; bishop, past mem. various exec. bds. Moravian Ch. Am.; bd. govs., past v.p. Moravian Ch. Am. South, mem. finance bd. Past chmn. Consol. Sch. Bd. Charlotte and Mecklenburg County; chaplain Charlotte Police Dept.; past pres. Charlotte-Mecklenburg Ministerial Assn.; past chmn. Mecklenburg ARC; organizer Charlotte Pub. Sch. Music System; mem. N.C. Sch. Bd. Assn., N.C. Council Chs., Charlotte Alcohol Edn. Com., Groves Conf. Marriage and Home, Charlotte Mental Hygiene Soc., Charlotte Family Life Council, Moravian Ch. Archives Bd. Trustee Moravian Coll., Bethlehem, Pa., Salem (N.C.) Coll. Mil. service World War I. Recipient Silver Beaver award Boy Scouts Am.; Rotary Citizenship award. Mem. Am. Legion (hon. life chaplain), Order of St. Luke the Physician. Club: Civitan (Citizenship award, past chaplain Carolina dist., past chaplain internat.). Author: The Pathway to Contentment; Everyday Counsel for Everyday Living; The Pathway to a Happy Marriage; The Boy, the Man, the Bishop; Psalms for Everyday Living; A Merry Heart. Contbr. articles to numerous mags. Home: Charlotte, N.C. Died Nov. 22, 1978; buried Evergreen Cemetary, Charlotte.

SPAULDING, CLARENCE ARTHUR (SPAWL'DING), clergyman; b. Dubuque, Ia., Sept. 24, 1886; s. Edgar Alonzo and Mary (Sheerer) S.; B.L., Occidental Coll., Los Angeles, 1907, D.D., 1919; B.A., M.A., Oxford U., (Rhodes scholar), 1908-11; B.D., Auburn Theol. Sem., 1912; m. Mary Frances Pierre, Dec. 31, 1912; children—Clarence Arthur, Frederick Pierce, Carolyn Mary. Ordained ministry Presbyn. Ch., 1912; pastor Westminster Ch., Pasadena, Calif., 1912-17, First Ch., Santa Barbara, Calif., 1919-31, First Presbyn. Ch., River Forest, Ill., 1931-45; vice pres. Presbyterian College of Christian Education, Chicago, 1945-49, Endeavor Presbyterian Church, Chicago, since 1949. War work with Y.M.C.A., 1917-19. Moderator Presbytery of Santa Barbara, Calif., 1922-23, Synod of Calif., 1930-31; mem. Nat. Commn. of Presbyn. Ch. on Marriage, Divorce and Remarriage; member Presbyterian Board of National Missions; trustee Chicago Presbytery; pres. Chicago Church Extension Board, 1933-43; v. chmn. General Assemblies Com. of Five; exchange preacher to Eng., 1935. Mem. Phi Beta Kappa. Republican. Clubs: Cleric, Union League (Chicago); Oak Park Club. Edited "Twenty-Four Views of Marriage," 1930. Home: Chicago, Ill.*

SPAULDING, THOMAS CLAUDE, b. Richmond, Ind., July 16, 1885; s. Ansel Phinney and Lida (Lattin) S.; B.S., in Biology, U. of Mont., 1906; M.S. in Forestry, U. of Mich., 1909; m. Willie Clanton, Sept. 8, 1911;

children—Kenneth Ansel, Albert Clanton, Dorothy Ethel. Field asst. U.S. Geol. Survey, 1904-05; with U.S. Forest Service, 1906-15; prof. forestry, U. of Mont., 1915-23, dean Sch. of Forestry since 1923. Correlative private forestry work with state and forestry protective assns. since 1920. Served as 2d lt., 2d Mont. Inf., Mont. N.G., 1914-16; border duty as engr. officer, 1916; 1st lt. and capt. 163d Inf., A.E.F., 1917-19; dir. Base Training Schs., Feb.-Nov. 1918; regt. supply officer 163d Inf., Dec. 1918-Mar. 1919; state adminstr., Federal Emergency Relief Adminstrn., Civil Works Adminstrn., State Planning Bd., 1932-34; v. chmn. and tech. adviser forestry and lumber industry sect., Northwest Planning Bd.; chmn. Forestry and Lumber Industry Com., State of Mont. Mem. Soc. Am. Foresters, Am. Forestry Assn., Druids, Sigma Xi, Phi Sigma, Phi Sigma Kappa. Episcopalian. Clubs: Rotary, University. Contbr. on subjectspertaining to forestry. Home: Missoula, Mont.*

SPAULDING, WILLIAM E(LLSWORTH), publishing exec.; b. Passaic, N.J., Feb. 5, 1898; s. Frank E. and Mary E. (Trow) S.; grad. Harvard, 1919; m. Caroline Pearson, June 4, 1921; children—William E., John Pearson, Donald Trow, Richard Metcalf. With Houghton Mifflin Co., Boston, 1919-79, successively college salesman, college editor, editor edn. dept. and dir., 1937-66, v.p., 1940-57, pres., 1957-63, chmn. bd., 1963-66, ednl. cons., 1966-79; chmn. bd. dirs. Franklin Publs., 1957-59, now dir. and cons.; mem. publs. com. Beacon Press. Dir. editorial staff U.S. Armed Forces Inst., 1942-44. Dir. Am. Textbook Pubs. Inst. (pres. 1950-51), 1950-58; v.p. Am. Book Pubs. Council, 1960-62, pres., 1962-64; mem. U.S. Nat. Commn. UNESCO, 1961-63; mem. com. leaders and specialists Am. Council Edn., 1961-62; dir. Council Pub. Schs., 1962-79; adv. com. new ednl. media Nat. Def. Edn. Act, Title VII, 1960-63; v.p. Boston Council International Visitors, 1965-79; bd. mem. Nat. Book Com. Trustee Center Applied Linguistics, Washington 1965-79. Mem. Pi Beta Alpha. Club: Monday (Winchester, Mass.). Home: Winchester, Mass. Died Dec. 19, 1979.

SPAVENTA, GEORGE, sculptor; b. N.Y.C., Feb. 22, 1918; s. Sylvester and Aida (Accetella) S.; student Beaux Arts Inst. Design, N.Y.C., 1939-40, Acad. de la Grande Chaumier, Paris, France, 1948-50. One-man shows include Holland Gallery, Chgo., 1962, Poindexter Gallery, N.Y.C., 1964; groups exhbns., N.Y.C., 1954-78, latest being traveling exhibit Mus. Modern Art, 1964-65; tchr. sculpture N.Y. Studio Sch., 1964-78; tchr. Skowhegan (Me.) Sch. Painting and Sculpture, 1968, Md. Inst. Art, Balt., 1969. Address: New York, N.Y. Died June 16, 1978.

SPEAR, ROGER ELIOT, investment adviser; b. Jamaica Plain, Mass., Sept. 3, 1898; s. Frank Oliver and Mae Matilda (McMullen) S.; B.C.E., Northeastern U., 1921; m. Gladys Agnes Robbins, June 30, 1925; children—Joyce Mae (Mrs. Charles M. Marshall) Roger Eliot. Advt. cons. Poor's Pub. Co., 1937-40; pres. Spear & Staff, Inc., Babson Park, Mass., 1939-72, chmn. bd., 1972-74; cons., 1974-76; advt. cons. Babson's Reports, Wellesley Hills, Mass., 1933-36; pres. Oil Statistics Co., Babson Park, 1927-68, chmn. bd., 1969-76; author, syndicated columnist, Successful Investing. Dir. Nat. Council Northeastern U., 1968-76; trustee Alpha Kappa Sigma Trust, 1923-45, hon. trustee, 1945-76. Mem. Timber Owners' New Eng. (dir.), Wildlife Conservation Trust (trustee), Alpha Kappa Sigma. Home: Weston, Mass. Died July 16, 1976.

SPEER, EDGAR B., steel co. exec.; b. Pitts., July 28, 1916; s. Edgar B. and Gladys (Kelly) S.; student U. Pa., also Harvard Bus. Sch.; m. Arlene R. Kline, Apr. 8, 1946; children—Edgar B. III, John Michael, Stephen Fox, Tony Scott. With U.S. Steel Corp., 1938-79, gen. supt. Fairless work, 1955-58, gen. mgr. steel ops., Pitts., 1958-79, exec. v.p. for prodn., 1967-69, pres., 1969-73, chmn. bd., 1973-79; dir. Am. Tel. & Tel. Co., Procter & Gamble Co. Trustee Widener Coll., Waynesburg Coll.; bd. overseers U. Pa. Mem. Am. Iron and Steel Engrs., Am. (dir.), Internat. (dir.) iron and steel insts., Bus. Council, Harvard Bus. Assn., Phi Gamma Delta. Home: Pittsburgh, Pa. Died Oct. 13, 1979.

SPEIGHT, JOHN JOSHUA, lawyer, judge; b. Eufaula, Ala., July 24, 1885; s. John Williams and Emma Elinor (Cobb) S.; student Washington-Lee Univ., 1907-08; LL.B., Georgetown U., 1911; m. Ruth Wood, Aug. 17, 1914; children—John J., Betty. Pvt. sec., Congressman Henry D. Clayton, 1902-10; exec. clerk Nat. Congl. campaign com., 1910; clerk judiciary com., U.S. House of Reps., 1911-14; referee in bankruptcy, Ala., 1915-32; mem. Ala. Dem. exec. com., 1926-32; gen. practice of law, Ozark and Dothan, Ala., 1914-46; spl. asst. to atty. gen. of U.S., 1937-39; judge Mil. Tribunal No. II. War Crimes Trials, Nurnberg, Germany, 1946. Mem. Ala. Bar, Dist. Columbia Bar, Supreme Court U.S., Phi Gamma Delta, Phi Delta Phi. Mason. Democrat. Baptist. Author: textbook for Nat. Congressional Campaign Com., 1910; (compilation) Bills and debates in Congress on trusts and monopolies, 1912; (compilation) Laws of U.S., various states, and fgn. countries on monopolies and trusts, 1912. Home: Dothan, Ala.*

SPENCE, BARTHOLOMEW JOHN, physicist; b. Chicago, Ill., June 4, 1883; s. John and Anna A. (Weck) S.; B.S., Northwestern U., 1905; studies U. of Wis.; Ph.D., Princeton, 1909; m. Frieda Louise Schneider, July 7, 1910; 1 son, Bartholomew John, Instr. physics, U. of Ill., 1907-08, Princeton, 1909-10; asst. prof. physics, 1910-13, assoc. prof., 1913-18, prof. and head of dept., 1918-20, U. of N.D.; assoc. prof. physics, Northwestern U., 1920-25, prof. and chmn. dept., 1925-48; exchange lecturer, U. of Manitoba, 1919; pres. N.D. Acad. of Sci., 1918-19. Fellow Am. Physical Soc., A.A.A.S.; mem. Optical Soc. Am., Am. Assn. Teachers of Physics, Sigma Xi, Alpha Delta Phi. Episcopalian. Clubs: University, Chaos, Physics (pres. 1939-40). Mason (32 deg., Shriner). Home: Evanston, Ill.*

SPENCE, HERSEY EVERETT, religious edn.; b. South Mills., N.C., June 12, 1882; s. Joseph Newton and Lucy Indiana (Howell) S.; A.B., Trinity Coll., Durham, N.C., 1907, A.M., 1908; B.D., Duke U. Sch. of Religion, 1927; D.D., Asbury Coll., Wilmore, Ky., 1938; Litt.D., High Point (N.C.) Coll., 1941; studied Columbia and Univ. of Chicago; m. Bessie Octavia Whitted, Oct. 4, 1913. Ordained ministry M.E. Ch., S., 1907; pastor Durham, 1907-10, Sanford, 1913-16; supt. of Sunday School work, N.C. Conf., 1916-18; asst. prof. English lit., Trinity Coll. (now Duke U.), 1910-13, professor religious education since 1918. Trustee Louisburg Coll. Mem. Kappa Delta Pi, Phi Beta Kappa, Omicron Delta Kappa, Sigma Upsilon, Pi Kappa Alpha, Theta Alpha Phi, Democrat. Mason, Odd Fellow, K.P. Clubs: University Faculty, University Monogram. Author books, also dramas andpageants since 1913. Home: Durham, N.C.*

SPENCER, DUNCAN MACGLASHAN, banker; b. Glasgow, Scotland, Aug. 10, 1898; s. William and Jessie Jenet (MacGlashan) S.; B.S., U. Pa., 1921; m. Josephine Choate, June 1937 (dec.); children—Margaret M., Duncan C., Josephine B.; m. 2d, Louisa Hunnewell Clark, June 1953; children—Louisa, Leslie, Roderick. Formerly with Lee, Higginson & Co., N.Y.C.; with Fiduciary Trust Co. of N.Y., 1931-79, hon. chmn. bd.; trustee Bowery Savs. Bank; director Martin Marietta. Served as lt., RAF, 1917-19, as col., USAAF, 1942-45. Clubs: Knickerbocker, Down Town Assn., New York Yacht (N.Y.C.); Bedford (N.Y.) Golf and Tennis. Home: Bedford Hills, N.Y. Died Nov. 10, 1979.

SPENCER, ELDRIDGE TED, architect; b. Woodland, Calif., July 31, 1892; s. William Francis and Mary Marie (Ballard) S.; A.B., U. Calif., 1917; diploma Ecole des Beaux Arts, Paris, France, 1925; m. Jeannette Dyer, June 6, 1920; children—Fran (Mrs. Valerie Reynolds), Doris (Mrs. Doris Leonard). Practice architecture, Calif., 1926-72; prin. Spencer Assos., Palo Alto, until 1972, cons., 1972-78; works include housing projects, numerous govt. bldgs., resort and recreation devel., Yosemite Nat. Park, Grand Teton, Nat. Park, sci. and ednl. research for U. Calif. and Stanford, Conf. Center for Colonial Williamsburg; lectr. emeritus on engring. Stanford U. Served as 1st lt. aviator corps U.S. Army, World War I. Fellow A.I.A.; mem. San Francisco Art Assn. (dir. 1938-44). Home: San Francisco, Calif. Died Sept. 22, 1978.

SPENCER, FLOYD ALBERT, author, army ofcr.; b. Bedford, Ia., Oct. 23, 1899; s. Orin E. and Mary Etta (Polton) S.; B.A., U. of Colo., 1919; Ph.D. summa cum laude, U. of Chicago, 1923; m. Paula Teresa Bayne, Apr. 28, 1928; 1 son, Philip Gordon Hamilton. Reporter Denver Times, 1919-20; research and teaching fellow, U. of Chicago, 1921-23; asst. prof. classics, later asso. prof. and chmn. dept. Greek, Ohio Wesleyan U., 1923-27; substitute for chmn. dept. classics (on sabbatical leave), U. of Ill., 1927-28; asso. prof., prof. and chmn. dept. classics, also prof. historical sociol., Roanoke Coll., Salem, Va., 1928-30; asst. prof. classics and hist. sociol., Washington Sq. Coll. of N.Y. Univ., 1930-36, asso. prof., 1936-38. Resigned to do full-time writing, 1938-41. Guest prof. sociol. (invitation course for officials of Egyptian Govt. Ministries, sr. course for regular students), Am. Univ., Cairo, Egypt, 1945-47; prof. sociology and chmn. dept., Queens Coll., 1951-54; cons. sociologist; exec. v.p. Execs. Assn. Balt., 1955-78; cons. on internat. affairs, Library of Congress, 1952-78. Served from pvt. to col. AUS, 1942-55; various intelligence asignments ETO, NATO USA, ret. 1955. Author or co-author several books, 1928-80; latest publ.: Agent Extraordinary (also pub. in Eng. and Argentina; syndicated in S.A. and Sweden), 1942; War and Postwar Greece, 1952. Home: Glen Burnie, Md. Died 1978.

SPENCER, JUDAH COLT, banker; b. Erie, Pa., Sept. 29, 1883; s. William and Mary Richards (DuPuy) S.; A.B., Princeton U., 1907; m. Almira Durban, 1917; children—Mary, George Colt, Thomas Durban. With Erie Foundry Co. (Pa.), mfrs., 1907-08, Fulton Mfg. Co., Erie, 1908-17; with First Nat. Bank of Erie, 1917-80, successively asst. to pres., cashier, v.p., pres., 1917-50, chmn., 1950-58, chmn. exec. com., 1958, hon. chmn. bd., 1959-80. Republican. Presbyn. Home: Erie, Pa. Died July 26, 1980.

SPICER, GEORGE WASHINGTON, educator; b. Flint Hill, Va., Oct. 31, 1897; s. Charles Edward and Ella James (Finnell) S.; A.B., Randolph-Macon Coll., 1920; Ph.D., Johns Hopkins, 1926; grad. study, U. Va., summer 1921, 22; m. Leone Irene Reaves, Sept. 1, 1928; Instr. history and govt., Randolph-Macon Acad., 1920-22; asso. prof. govt., Coll. of William and Mary, 1923-24, prof. polit. sci., 1926-28; acting prof. polit. sci., U. Va., 1928-30, asso. prof., 1930-38, prof., 1938-68, prof. govt. emeritus, 1968-80, chmn. Woodrow Wilson dept. govt. and fgn. affairs, 1966-67; summer faculty Johns Hopkins, 1930, U. Cal. at Los Angeles, 1931, U. Ala., 1947; vis. prof. Emory U., 1953, Vanderbilt, 1957; vis prof. govt. Fla. State U., 1969-70. Vice chmn. in charge research, Va. Commn. on County Govt., 1930-32, chmn., 1932-38. Mem. Am. (mem. council from 1959), So. (pres. 1951-52) polit. sci. assns., Nat. Municipal League, Am. Society for Pub. Adminstrn., Va. Social Sci. Assn. (ex-pres.), Phi Beta Kappa, Sigma Upsilon. Cons. Nat. Resources Com., 1937-38, Commn. on Civil Rights, 1959. Club: Colonnade. Author: Constitutional Status and Government of Alaska, 1927; essay in Essays on the Law and Practice of Governmental Administration, 1935; Ten Years of County Manager Government in Virginia, 1945; Fifteen Years of County Manager Government in Virginia, 1951; The Supreme Court and Fundamental Freedoms, 1959, 2d edit., 1967; also reports and articles to profl. and civic jours. Home: Charlottesville, Va. Died Mar. 9, 1980.

SPIEGELBERG, GEORGE ALFRED, lawyer, educator; b. N.Y.C., Dec. 13, 1897; s. Frederick and Terese (Goldsmith) S.; B.A., Cornell U., 1918; J.D., Harvard, 1921; m. Helen Pisek, Dec. 13, 1935 (dec. 1978); children—Frederick, Ann Marshall. Admitted to N.Y. bar, 1922; partner Mack, Taylor & Spiegelberg, 1926-43, Strasser, Spiegelberg, Fried & Frank, 1943; emeritus prof. law N.Y. U.; sec., dir. Frenchurch Corp. Vice pres., co-founder Joint Conf. Legal Edn. N.Y. Candidate 17th Congl. Dist. N.Y. State Congress, 1934. Bd. dirs. Practicing Law Inst., N.Y. U. Law Center Found. Served as dirigible pilot, U.S. Naval Air Force Reserve, World War I; spl. asst. to Atty. Gen. U.S., col., Gen. Staff Corps, U.S. Army, World War II. Decorated Legion of Merit with oak leaf cluster, Conspicuous Service medal (U.S.); Croix de Guerre with palm (France and Belgium); Officer of Comml. Merit (France). Fellow Am. Coll. Trial Lawyers (regent 1962-65, 68-70; pres. found. 1965-70), Am. Bar Found.; mem. Assn. Bar City N.Y., Am., N.Y. State bar assns., Order of Coif. Club: Harvard (N.Y.C.). Home: New York, N.Y. Died Nov. 6, 1979.

SPIEKER, EDMUND MAUTE, geologist, educator; b. Balt., Feb. 25, 1895; s. Edward Henry and Adelaide Marie (Maute) S.; A.B., Johns Hopkins, 1916, Ph.D., 1921; Sc.D., Ohio State U., 1972; m. Helen Frances Heard, Dec. 28, 1922; 1 son, Andrew Maute. Geologic aid U.S. Geol. Survey, 1917, asst. geologist, 1918, asso. geologist, 1919, geologist, 1921, geologist part time since 1924; asst. geologist Imperial Oil Ltd., N.W. Can., 1919, 1940; geologist Province B.C., 1920; asst. prof. Ohio State U., 1924-28, asso. prof., 1928-32, prof., 1932-44, chmn. dept. geology, 1944-52, research 1952-65, research prof. emeritus, 1965-78; dir. NSF summer insts. in geology and nature of sci., 1962-73. Mem. panel geology research devel. bd. U.S. Dept. Def., 1947-53, chmn., 1950-53, cons., 1953—; mem. Am. Commn. Stratigraphic Nomenclature, 1950-53; chmn. adminstrv. bd. Ohio Jour. Sci., 1948-57. Decorated comdr. Order of Lion (Finland). Recipient Distinguished Service award dept. geology Ohio State U., 1970. Fellow Geol. Soc. Am., A.A.A.S., Ohio Acad. Sci. Paleontol. Soc.; mem. History of Sci. Soc., Am. Assn. Petroleum Geologists (distinguished lectr. 1950, 52), Assn. for Edn. Tchrs. Sci., Soc. Econ. Paleontologists and Mineralogists, Am. Geophys. Union, Geol. Soc. Washington, Geol. Soc. Utah, Phi Beta Kappa, Sigma Xi, Gamma Alpha, Omicron Delta Kappa, Alpha Delta Phi. Club: Faculty (Ohio State U.). Author articles profl. jours., govt. publs. Home: Columbus, Ohio. Died Mar. 6, 1978.

SPIELMAN, JOHN PHILIP, coll. dean; b. Sleepyeye, Minn., Nov. 24, 1903; s. Robert P. and Louisa (Gutensohn) S.; B.S., N.D. State Coll., 1928; Degree of Met.E., Montana Sch. of Mines 1953; m. Lewanna Coleman, Sept. 21, 1929; 1 son, John Philip. Research metallurgist Anaconda Copper Mining Co., Mont., 1928-41; prof. metallurgy Mont. Sch. Mines, Butte, 1941; vice dir. Wash. State Inst. Tech., dean Coll. of Engring. and Mineral Tech., chmn. and prof. metallurgy Wash. State Coll. Served with U.S. Army, 1941-46. Profl. engr., Mont. Mem. Am. Inst. Mining Metall. and Petroleum Engrs., Am. Soc. Engring. Edn., Am. Soc. for Metals, Sigma Tau, Tau Beta Pi. Author articles. Home: Pullman, Wash. Died Jan. 30, 1981.

SPIELMAN, RALPH, educator; b. Leipzig, Germany, Oct. 30, 1914; s. Isaac and Rella (Spitz) S.; came to U.S., 1936, naturalized, 1943; Bacc. Phil., U. Paris (France), 1934; B.A., U. Mich., 1946; M.A., 1947, Ph.D., 1953; m. Beatrice C. Kramer, July 22, 1944; 1 son, Richard S. Mem. faculty U. Cin., 1951-52, Wellesley Coll., 1952-55, U. Ky., 1955-56, Eastern Mich. U., 1956-58; prof. sociology and demography Bucknell U., 1958-78. Served with AUS, 1943-46. Mem. Am. Sociol. Assn.,

Population Assn. Am. Home: Lewisburg, Pa. Died Nov. 27, 1978.

SPILLANE, JAMES J(OHN), govt. official; born Bloomfield, Conn., Sept. 6, 1883; s. Michael and Maria (Goss) S.; LL.B., Detroit Coll. of Law, 1915; m. Lucy Frances McGrath, Feb. 4, 1904 (died Feb. 23, 1937); children—Dorothy Francis (Mrs. J. Carl Philips), Leona Elizabeth (Mrs. Edward O. Fricker); m. 2d, Mildred Murray, Oct. 2, 1943. Gen. law practice, fed. and state, 1915-41; asst. U.S. Att., 1923-25; commr. U.S. Conciliation Service, 1941-45; regional dir. Fed. Mediation and Conciliation Service, Chicago, since Aug. 1947; Mich. dir. Near East Relief (under charter of U.S. Congress, 1922-26); mem. Integrated Mich. Bar Assn. Episcopalian. Home: Evanston, Ill.*

SPILLER, CLIFFORD, advt. exec.; b. Union, N.J., Mar. 5, 1911; s. Charles and Therese (Daum) S.; A.B., Columbia, 1931, B.S., 1932; m. Geraldine Stannek, Dec. 24, 1938; children—Jill, Peter, Susan, Nancy. Asso. Editor Conde'Nast Publs., 1932-37; asso. editor, art dir. Publisher's Weekly, 1937; dir. market research and sales promotion Am. Home mag., 1937-43; v.p. Fed. Advt. Agency, N.Y.C., 1943-47; nat. sales mgr., advt. mgr. Durkee Famous Foods Co., 1947-49; gen. mgr. Franklin Baker div. Gen. Foods Corp., 1949-54, Walter Baker div., 1954-56, dir. marketing Maxwell House div., 1956-57; vice chmn. bd. dirs. and plans bd. Sullivan, Stauffer, Colwell & Bayles, Inc., 1957-67; pres., chief operating officer Louis Sherry, Inc., 1967-71; marketing dir. Pamarco, Inc., Roselle, N.J., 1971-76; dir. Constellation Growth Fund, N.Y.C., 60 Sutton Corp., N.Y.C. Clubs: Algonquin (Boston); Yale (N.Y.C.); Morristown Field. Author, compilor, editor: Marketing Guide of the U.S., 1941. Home: Morristown, N.J. Died Oct. 29, 1976; interred Madonna Cemetery, Ft. Lee, N.J.

SPILLMAN, HARRY COLLINS, personnel dir., lecturer; b. Scottsville, Ky., Apr. 27, 1882; s. Festus Winfield and Mary Laura (Martin) S.; student Bethel Coll., Russellville, Ky., 1900-02, Bowling Green (Ky.) Business U., 1902-03; Harvard, 1910; m. Roberta Beauchamp, Dec. 26, 1930. Writer for Louisville Courier-Journal under Henry Watterson, 1903; dir. commercial edn. in pub. schs. of Rockford, Ill., Butte, Mont., and Milwaukee, Wis., 1904-10; ednl. dir. and employment mgr. Remington Typewriter Co., N.Y. City, 1910-30; dir. ednl. service Gregg Pub. Co., N.Y. City, 1930-32. Mem. Sigma Nu. Democrat. Methodist. Mason. Rotarian (hon. Internat.). Author: Personality-Studies in Personal Development, 1919; Making the Business Speech Effective, 1925; The Aristocracy of Service, 1939. Has delivered more than 5000 addresses before ednl. and business audiences throughout America and the eastern hemisphere. Home: New York, N.Y.*

SPIVACKE, HAROLD, musicologist, cons.; b. N.Y.C. July 18, 1904; s. Charles A. and Romana (Klinkowstein) S.; B.A., N.Y. U., 1923, M.A., 1924; Ph.D. magna cum laude, U. Berlin, 1933; Mus.D. (hon.), Baldwin-Wallace Coll., 1947, U. Rochester, 1955, Cleve. Inst. Music, 1969; pvt. study music with Henry Levey, N.Y.C., Eugen D'Albert, Hugo Leichentritt, Berlin; m. Carolyn Le Fevre, 1927 (div. 1953); children—Joseph L., Robert C.; m. 2d, Rose Marie Grentzer, 1955. Research asst. Olin Downes, N.Y.C., 1933-34; asst. chief music div. Library Congress, Washington, 1934-37 chief, 1937-72, hon. cons. musicology, 1972-77. Adv. com. music Dept. State, 1939-46; chmn. adv. com. music div., Pan-Am. Union, 1940-42, 47-49; chmn. subcom. music Joint Army Navy Com. Welfare and Recreation, 1941-46; mem. nat. com. of U.S. on Internat. Intellectual Cooperation, 1946; mem. U.S. Nat. Commn. UNESCO, 1950-56, 62-65, mem. exec. com., 1954-56. Artists' adv. com. Rachmaninoff Meml. Fund., 1944-49; mem. Fulbright advanced sect. Committee on Music, 1949-55, chmn. Fulbright Com., 1953-55; adv. music panel internat. exchange program ANTA, 1954-77. Awarded Ogden Butler fellowship in philosophy, 1923-24; Am.-German students exchange fellow, 1929-30, Alexander von Humboldt stiftung fellow, 1930-31, Library of Congress Distinguished Service award, 1965. Mem. Acoustical Soc. Am., Nat. Guild Community Music Schs. (adv. council 1954-77), ALA, Contemporary Music Soc., Nat. Music Council (chmn. organizing com., pres. pro tem 1939, archivist, exec. com. 1940-77), Internat. Assn. Music Libraries (pres. phonograph sect. 1962-73), Music Library Assn. (pres. 1951-53), Am. Musicol. Soc. (exec. bd. 1937, 53-77, council 1937-77, v.p. 1940-41), Music Tchrs. Nat. Assn. (exec. bd. 1937-41, 53-77, v.p. 1950-53), Am. Council Learned Socs. (adminstrv. com. Russian transl. project 1944-49), Am. Soc. Comparative Musicology (v.p. 1933-37), N.Y. Musicology Soc. (sec. 1933-34), Haydn Soc. (editorial bd.), Phi Sigma Delta. Club: Cosmos (Washington). Mem. editorial bd. Music Educators Jour., 1944-46; editorial com. Jour. Research in Music Education, 1952- 53. Contbr. profl. jours. Home: Washington, D.C. Died May 9, 1977.

SPLAWN, JENNIE LILLIAN, Coll. prof.; b. Greenwood, Tex., June 12, 1885; d. William Butler and Mary Marshall (Collins) Splawn; grad. Decatur Bapt. Coll., 1908; Ph.B., Baylor U., 1910; Ph.B., U. of Chicago, 1915, grad. student spring and summer of 1915; M.A., Columbia, 1925, grad. student, 1930-31; unmarried. Head dept. of English, Burleson Coll., Greenville, Tex., 1910-15, Amarillo (Tex.) High Sch., 1916-19, Wichita Falls (Tex.) High Sch., 1919-24; dept. of English, Tex. Coll. Arts and Industries, Kingsville, 1925-55, prof. English, 1931-55, professor of English emeritus, 1955—. Member of Albermarle County Vocational Historical Association, D.A.R. Colonial Dames of XVII century, The Dames of the Court of Honor. Democrat. Baptist. Home: Kingsville, Tex.*

SPOONER, CHESTER M., newspaper publisher; Publisher Pawtucket Times. Died Dec. 31, 1976.

SPORN, PHILIP, engr., former pub. utility exec.; b. Austria, Nov. 25, 1896; s. Isak and Rachel (Kolker) S.; brought to U.S. by parents, naturalized, 1907; E.E., Columbia U., 1917, postgrad., 1917-18; D.Eng., Stevens Inst. Tech., 1947, Ill. Inst. Tech., 1953, Poly. Inst. Bklyn., 1955, Tri-State Coll., 1959, Rensselaer, 1968; Docteur honoris causa, U. Grenoble (France), 1950; LL.D., Hanover Coll., 1953; L.H.D., Marshall Coll., 1956; D.Sc., Ohio State U., 1957, Ind. Tech. Coll., 1958, W.Va. Inst. Tech., 1967; D. Tech. Scis., Haifa Technion (Israel), 1959; LL.D., Columbia, 1966; m. Sadie Posner, Sept. 10, 1923; children—Deborah (Mrs. Andrew Gilbert), Arthur David, Michael Benjamin. With Am. Electric Power Co., 1920-71, successively protection engr., communication engr., transmission and distbn. engr., chief elec. engr., chief engr., v.p. charge engring. activities, v.p. and chief engr., 1920-45, exec. v.p. (Am. Electric Power Co. and Am. Electric Power Service Corp.), 1945, pres., chief exec. officer, 1947-61, also pres., dir. some 20 cos. in Am. Electric Power System, 1947-61, chmn. system devel. com., mem. exec. com., dir., 1961-67, dir., cons., 1967-69, cons., 1969-71; pres., dir. Ohio Valley Electric Corp., Ind.-Ky. Electric Corp., 1952-67; pres., dir. Nuclear Power Group, Inc., 1955, v.p., dir., 1957-61, chmn. working com. East Central nuclear group, 1957-58, chmn. research and devel. com., 1958-67; vis. prof. Cornell Coll. Engring., 1963, Mass. Inst. Tech. Sch. Engring., 1967-70, Manhattan Coll., 1975. Cons. WPB, 1944-45; cons. Oak Ridge Nuclear Power Project, Monsanto Chem. Co., 1947; mem. electric power com. NSRB, 1947-53; chmn. U.S. AEC ad hoc adv. com. on cooperation between electric power industry and AEC, 1949-51; mem. electric utility defense adv. coun. Def. Electric Power Adminstrn., 1950-52; vice chmn. U.S. AEC ad hoc adv. com. to evaluate Shippingport project, 1959; mem. AEC ad hoc adv. com. on reactor policies and programs, 1959, lectr. Inds. Coll. of Armed Forces, 1948-57; mem. U.S. del. Geneva Conf. for Peaceful Uses of Atomic Energy, 1955; chmn. U.S. nat. com. C.I.G.R.E., 1955-73; mem. com. on dispersal and disposal radioactive wastes Nat. Acad. Scis.-NRC; council on indsl. atomic energy Nat. Indsl. Conf. Bd.; mem. gen. tech. adv. com. Office Coal Research, U.S. Dept. Interior, 1960-78; mem. U.S. State Dept. ad hoc adv. com. on U.S. Policy toward IAEA, 1962; chmn. Nat. Acad. Scis. adv. bd. on hardened electric power systems, 1963-70; chmn. exec. adv. com. FPC, Nat. Power Survey, 1962-65. Mem. vis. com. for nuclear engring. and reactor depts. Brookhaven Nat. Lab., 1953-57. Mem. adv. groups several colls. and univs. Recipient numerous awards and honors profl. assns., also Chevalier French Legion of Honor. Mem. numerous profl. assns., former dir. or officer several. Author: The Integrated Power System; Vistas in Electric Power; Foundations of Engineering; Technology, Engineering and Economics; The Social Organization of Electric Power Supply in Modern Societies; contbr. articles to profl. jours. Inventor advanced practices elec. energy generation and ultra-high voltage transmission. Clubs: City Midday, Engineers (N.Y.C.). Home: New York, N.Y. Died Jan. 23, 1978; buried Mt. Hebron Cemetery, Flushing, N.Y.

SPRADLING, ABE, L., labor leader; b. Woodford County, Ky., June 19, 1885; s. Abe L. and Annie E. (Gilvin) S.; student of pub. schs.; m. Lula May Hutton, Sept., 1907. (died Dec. 21, 1910); 2d. Mary A. Jones, Oct. 3, 1931. Motorman, Cincinnati Traction Co., May, 1903; elected sec. treas., Div. 627, Cincinnati, Ohio Amalgamated Assn., 1915, internat. vice pres., 1927-35, elected mem. of the gen. exec. bd., 1935, gen. exec. bd. mem. Detroit, Mich., 1936-44, appointed asst. to the internat. pres., 1944; elected internat. pres., Amalgamated Assn. of Street, Electric Railway and Motor Coach Employes of Am. June 1946. Home: North College Hill, Ohio. *

SPRAGUE, HARRY A., univ. cons.; b. Ellington, N.Y., July 31, 1885; s. William Titus and Viola (Huntington) S.; grad. Fredonia State Normal Sch., 1905; student Chautauqua Inst., Cornell U.; B.S., Columbia, 1915, M.A., 1917, Ph.D., 1940, LL.D. (hon.), 1957; m. Julia Meeker Conklin, Mar. 27, 1915; 1 dau., Elizabeth Sprague Love. Prin. Union High Sch., Farmington, N.Y., 1905-06, high and grade sch., Hinsdale, N.Y., 1906-07, Schs. No. 2 and 10, Olean, N.Y., 1907-09, City Tchr. Tng. Sch., 1908-10; supr., instr., practice and exptl. sch., Teachers Coll. Columbia, 1910-11; instr. N.Y. U., 1915-16; supr., instr. City Normal Sch., Newark, 1910-14; N.J. State Normal Sch., Newark, 1914-18; prof. edn., adminstr. State U. N.J., summers 1916-23; supt. city schs., Summit, N.J., 1918-23; prin. N.J. State Normal Sch., Upper Montclair, 1924-27; pres. State Tchrs. Coll., Upper Montclair, 1927-51; cons. higher edn., 1951—; dean Grad. Sch., Fairleigh Dickinson University, 1955-65, consultant to the president, 1965—; training program director Nat. Assn. Elec. Distbrs. Mem. N.J. Council Edn., N.J. Bd. Examiners, Commn. for Internat. Ednl. Reconstrn. Mem. A.A.A.S., N.E.A., N.J. Edn. Assn., Am. Assn. Sch. Adminstrs., Soc. Study Edn., Am. Arbitration Assn., Am. Assn. Tchrs. Colls. (pres. 1935-36, del. to UNESCO), Middle States Assn. Colls. and Secondary Schls. (commission on higher edn.), Alpha Chi Rho, Phi Delta Kappa, Kappa Delta Pi. Presbyn. (ruling elder). Author: A Decade of Progress in the Preparation of Secondary School Teachers; Lakewood Schools Survey. Clubs: Rotary, Schoolmasters, Lake Mohawk. Home: Sparta, N.J. Died Apr. 23, 1977.

SPRATLEY, CLAUDE VERNON, judge; b. Surry, Va., July 16, 1882; s. Peter Thomas and Fannie Howard (Sclater) S.; A.B., College of William and Mary, 1901, LL.D., 1938; B.L., U. of Va., 1906; m. Eleshia Annie Woodward, Oct. 27, 1909; children—Katherine Woodward (Mrs. William Franklin Metts), Anne Fletcher (Mrs. John F. B. Dice), Claude Vernon. Admitted to Va. bar, 1906; city atty. Town of Hampton, 1912-23; circuit judge, 1923-36; asso. justice Va. Supreme Court of Appeals, 1936-67; vice chmn. Citizens and Marine Bank. Mem. Phi Beta Kappa, Phi Delta Phi, Kappa Alpha, Raven Soc. Democrat. Episcopalian. Mason (Shriner), Elk. Club: Commonwealth (Richmond). Home: Hampton, Va. Died Oct. 25, 1976.

SPRECKELS, ALMA DE BRETTEVILLE, b. Mar. 24, 1886; d. Viggo le Normand and Mathilde (Unserud) de Bretteville; ed. pub. schs.; m. Adolph Bernard Spreckels, May 11, 1908 (now dec.); children—Alma Emma (Mrs. John Newton Rosekrans), Adolph Bernard, Dorothy Constance (Mrs. Jean Dupuy of Paris); m. 2d, Elmer Maclay Awl, February, 1939. With first husband was builder and donor of California Palace of Legion of Honor, memorial to California soldiers who died in World War. Decorated Chevalier Legion of Honor (France). Republican. Protestant. Clubs: Burlingame, Country, Western Women's. Home: San Francisco; (country). Sonoma, Calif. *

SPRINKLE, GEORGE WESLEY, architect; b. Sweetwater, Tenn., Oct. 4, 1923; s. George Wesley and Gladys Roberta (Callahan) S.; student East Los Angeles Jr. Coll., 1946-47, U. So. Calif., 1948, 49-50, UCLA, 1948-49; m. Dorothy Ann Cope, May 29, 1953; children—Clifton Wesley, Ann Elizabeth. Archtl. draftsman McCune & McCune, Architects, Tulsa, 1950-51, So. Mill & Mfg. Co., Tulsa, 1951-53, Santa Barbara Mill & Mfg. Co. (Calif.), 1953-54; project architect Welton Becket & Assos., Los Angeles, 1954-61; office mgr. Guirey, Srnka, Arnold, Sprinkle-Architects and Planners, Flagstaff, Ariz., 1961-70, sr. v.p., sec., 1970-81. Mem. Flagstaff Planning Commn., 1966-69, chmn., 1965-67; mem. Flagstaff Water Commn., 1966-68, Flagstaff Environ. Commn., 1966-68, Ariz. Gov.'s Commn. on Environ., 1967-73; mem. nat. panel Am. Arbitration Assn., 1968-76; bd. dirs. Jr. Achievement Central Ariz., 1971-76. Served with USN, 1943-46. Fellow AIA (pres. 1973-74, chmn. nat. com. on architects for justice 1977, nat. office mgmt. com. 1976-77, Western Mountain Region Bradley P. Kidder award 1974, Ariz. Personal Contbns. award 1975, Central Ariz. award for outstanding service to profession 1975; Western Mountain Region Architects' medal 1979), Bldg. Owners and Mgrs. Assn., Ariz. Acad., Sigma Chi. Republican. Episcopalian. Clubs: Kiwanis, Masons. Home: Scottsdale, Ariz. Died Aug. 6, 1981; cremated.

SPURRIER, RICHARD ROSS (SPUR-YER), state ofcl., petroleum engr.; b. Columbus, Ohio, Mar. 16, 1915; s. John Richard and Mary (Ross) S.; B.S., N.Mex. Sch. Mines, 1940; m. Naomi Wolf, Oct. 14, 1941; children—Sarah, Sophie. State geologist, dir. N.Mex. Oil Conservation Commn., 1945-54. Chmn. research and coordinating com. Interstate Oil Compact Commn., 1949; adv. Petroleum Adminstrn. for Def., Dist. III. Served as capt. C.E., E.T.O., World War II. Decorated Purple Heart. Mem. Am. Assn. Petroleum Geologists (asso.), Am. Petroleum Inst. (hon. mem. N.Mex. chpt.). Democrat. Home: Santa Fe, N.Mex. Died Oct. 26, 1976.

SQUIRE, FAY HUFFMAN, physician; b. Lake Benton, Minn., Apr. 14, 1901; s. Melvin and Jennie (Huffman) S.; student U. Minn., 1918-19; B.A., U. Colo., 1923; M.D., State U. Ia., 1925; m. Nolene Schmitt, Dec. 8, 1926; children—Mary Ann (Mrs. A.A. Schilt), John William. Intern, St. Joseph's Hosp., St. Paul, 1925-26; fellow radiology Mayo Clinic, Rochester, Minn., 1926-29; asso. dept. radiology Presbyn. Hosp., Chgo., 1929-35, chmn. dept., 1935-68; cons. dept. radiology Presbyn.-St. Luke's Hosp. 1969-70; clin. asso. Rush Med. Sch., 1932, clin. instr., 1933, asso. clin. prof., 1934-41; asso. prof. radiology U.

Ill., 1941-48, prof. radiology, 1948-70. Diplomate Am. Bd. Radiology. Mem. Coll. Radiology (sec.-treas., recipient gold medal 1973), A.M.A., Am., Chgo. roentgen ray socs., Central Soc. Nuclear Medicine, Eastern Radiol. Soc., Radiol. Soc. N.Am. Contbr. articles to profl. jours. Home: Panama Valley, Calif. Died Oct. 9, 1976.

SRYGLEY, HUBBARD FLETCHER, ex-supt. schools; b. Bellwood, Tenn., Jan. 26, 1886; s. Filo Bunyan and Mary Bell (Hubbard) S.; B.S., George Peabody Coll. for Teachers, 1916, M.A., 1938; student Vanderbilt U., 1908-09, 1911-12; m. Nina Brown, Sept. 24, 1917; children — Hubbard Fletcher, Donald Brown, Nina Joyce. Instr. mathematics and asst. prin. Pine Bluff, Ark., 2 years, 1909-11; instr. Tyler (Tex.) High Sch., 1912-13; prin. Nashville (Tenn.) City Schs., 1913-19; supt. schs., Morgantown, N.C., 1919-22, Raleigh, N.C., 1922-30; became supt., Nashville, Tenn., 1930. Dir. Y.M.C.A. Mem. Tenn. State Teachers' Assn. (exec. com.), Peabody Alumni Assn. (past pres.), Nashville Chamber of Commerce, Middle Tenn. Edn. Assn. (pres.1934-35), N.E.A. (life), Phi Kappa Sigma, Kappa Delta Pi. Democrat. Mem. Church of Christ. Revised curricula Raleigh (N.C.), and Nashville (Tenn.) schs. Prin. George Hildebrand Sch., Connelly Springs, Burke, Co., N.C., since 1939. Home: Nashville, Tenn.*

STACE, WALTER TERENCE, prof. philosophy; b. London, Eng., Nov. 17, 1886; s. Edward Vincent and Amy Mary (Watson) S.; student Bath (Eng.) Coll., 1896-1900, Fettes Coll., Edinburgh, Scotland, 1900-02; B.A., Trinity Coll., Dublin, Ireland, 1908, Litt.D., 1929; m. Adelaide Vaughan Cooke, 1910; 1 dau., Beryl Mary Cynthia; m. 2d, Blanche Bianca Beven, 1925; children—Noel John, Jennifer Jean. In British Civil Service, Ceylon, 1910-32, holding various positions, including pvt. sec. to gov., later mayor of Colombo, and controller of revenue; came to U.S., 1932, and since prof. philosophy at Princeton U. Mem. Am. Philosophical Association (president Eastern division 1949), British Institute Philos. Studies, Mind Assn. Author: Critical History of Greek Philosophy, 1920; Philosophy of Hegel, 1924; Meaning of Beauty, 1929; Theory of Knowledge and Existence, 1932; The Concept of Morals, 1937; The Nature of the World, 1940; The Destiny of Western Man, 1942; Time and Eternity, Religion and the Modern Mind, The Gate of Silence, 1952. Home: Princeton, N.J.*

STACHIEWICZ, JULES WACLAW, educator; b. Lwow, Poland, Sept. 16, 1924; s. Waclaw T. and Wanda (Abraham) S.; B.Eng., McGill U., Montreal, Can., 1948, M.Eng., 1950; m. Halina Rozwadowska, Apr. 29, 1954; children—Barbara, Renata, Bettina. Research engr. Gas Dynamics Labs., Ste Anne, Que., Can., 1950-55; asst. prof. mech. engring. McGill U., 1955-58, assoc. prof., 1958-64, prof., 1964-76, chmn. dept. mech. engring., 1972-76. Served with 1st Polish Armoured Div., 1943-46. Decorated Cross of Valour (Polish Army); recipient numerous research grants and contracts. Mem. Am., Canadian socs. mech. engrs., Engring. Inst. Can., Order Engrs. Que. Author: (with D.L. Mordell) Experimental Coal Burning Gas Turbine, 1960 (Lt. Gov. of Que. award). Contbr. articles to profl. jours. Home: Ste Adele, Que., Canada. Died June 3, 1976.

STACK, JAMES OTTO, hotel exec.; b. Boston, June 14, 1882; s. James Henry and Ann Frances (Clifford) S.; student Hopkinson Sch. and Harvard; m. Helen Fay, Feb. 12, 1942; children—Barbara Ann, Dariel Jane, James O., Jr. With Lythgoe, Maher & Co., brokers, 1905, Hotel Knickerbocker, 1908; mem.-mgr. Harvard Club, 1910; mgr. Holland House, 1913; pres. Hotel Imperial, 1916; dir. Ritz-Carlton Hotel Corp., 1925; gen. mgr. St. Regis Hotel, 1935-40; pres. Ritz-Carlton Hotel, 1940, pres., treas. and dir. Ritz-Carlton Hotel Co., Inc., New York City, 1940-58, chairman of the board, 1959—; mem. bd. directors Ritz-Carlton Hotel Co. Boston, Astor Hotel Co. N.Y. City. Clubs: Harvard, New York Yacht, Seawanhaka Yacht, Racquet and Tennis (N.Y.). Home: Bayville, L.I., N.Y.; also N.Y.C. *

STACKPOLE, RALPH, sculptor, painter; b. Williams, Ore., May 1, 1885; s. Fremont and Ethel (Jordan); S.; ed. Mark Hopkins Inst., San Francisco, 1901-02, Ecole des Beaux Arts, Paris, 1906-08, Robert Henri Sch. of Art, New York, 1911; m. Adele Barnes; 1 son, Peter; m. 2d. Francine Mazen; children—Francis, John David. Began as sculptor, 1909; instr. in sculpture, Calif. Sch. of Fine Arts, San Francisco. Works: sculpture for Panama Pacific Expn., 1915; Coleman fountain, Sacramento, 1925; sculpture for San Francisco Stock Exchange, 1930; San Francisco Coit Tower, 1932; Sacraments Jr. Coll., 1936; sculpture for Golden Gate-Pacific Expn., 1939; sculpture John Powell, Dept. of Interior Bldg., Washington, 1940. Appointed to Commn. of Fine Arts, Washington, 1941-45. Club: Family (San Francisco). Home: San Francisco. *

STACY-JUDD, ROBERT BENJAMIN, architect; b. London, Eng., June 21, 1884; s. Benjamin and Elizabeth (Thomson) S.; student Acton Coll., Eng., Regents Street Polytechnic, London, Southend Tech. Inst., Eng.; grad. South Kensington Science and Art Institute, London, 1905; married Elizabeth Susan Schofield, Feb. 12, 1932 (divorced 1946); m. 2d, Marjorie Webster, Aug. 5, 1949 (div. 1958). Came to United States, 1913, naturalized, 1935. Architect with surveying department, Great Northern Railway Co., London, 1906-07; architect in charge grounds office constrn., Franco-British Expn., London, 1907-08; editor Eastbourne and Sussex Society Jour. and Short Story Time Table, Eng., 1909-10; also practised architecture in England until 1913; proprietor of a movie theatre, Ventnor, Eng., 1910-13; architect, Minot, N.D., 1914-19, Edmonton and Calgary, Alberta, Can., 1920-22, Los Angeles, Calif., since 1922. Principal architectural works include public buildings in various cities in California. Supervisor housing div., U.S. Emergency Fleet Corps, 1st World War, in charge all construction work for city additions to Manitowoc, Wis., Wyandotte, Mich., and Lorain, O. Mem. Am. Inst. Architects (also Southern Calif. Chapter), Calif. Council Architects, Engrs. and Architects Association, Pacific Geological Society International Adventurers (life), Eugene Field Society (life). Clubs: Knife and Fork, Platform, radio lecturer, writer on Ancient Mayan Civilization. Author several plays and other publs., also contributions to professional periodicals. Made expedition with 2 native guides into jungles of Yucatan, 1930, exploring Maya ruin area from Quintana-Roo to Campeche; first to photograph Loltun Caves. Explored all principal Aztec ruins Mexico, Guatemala. Has specialized on adaptations of Am. Indian Art and architecture and internationally known as first architect to utilize Mayan architectural motifs under modern American conditions. Inventor, Am. Cottage, rapidly erected prefabricated bldg., pre-cast concrete bldg. panels. Address: Hollywood, Cal. *

STAELIN, CARL GUSTAV, lawyer, glass products mfr., engr.; b. N.Y.C., Jan. 8, 1911; s. Richard A. and Wilhelmina (Kessler) S.; B.S., U. Mich., 1932; LL.B., Fordham U., 1935, U. Toledo, 1936; m. Margaret E. Hudson, Dec. 22, 1935; children—David H., Earl H., Mimi Margaret, Stephen H. Admitted to N.Y. bar, 1935, Ohio bar, 1936, law clk. A. W. Deller, N.Y.C. 1932-34; atty. Upham & Blasi, 1934-35; patent lawyer Owens-Ill. Glass Co., Toledo, 1935-38; head legal, patent dept. Owens-Corning Fiberglass Corp., Toledo, 1938-77, sec., 1942-65, v.p. and sec., 1965-77; instr. of law U. Toledo, 1937; dir. Asahi Fiber Glass Co. (Tokyo, Japan), Australian Fibre Glass Pty., Ltd. (Sydney), New Zealand Fibre Glass Ltd., Auckland, Owens-Corning Fiberglas (U.K.), Ltd., Eng., Owens-Corning Fiberglas Internat. Corp. Registered profl. engr., Ohio. Mem. Am., Toledo (pres. 1949-50) patent law assns., Am., Ohio, Toledo bar assns., Am. Soc. Corporate Secs., Toledo Orch. Assn. (trustee), Toledo Council World Affairs (dir. 1955-77), Chi Psi, Phi Delta Phi. Clubs: Toledo (Trustee 1953-60, pres. 1956-59), Inverness Golf (gov. 1964-77, pres. 1965-66), Toledo Ski (pres. 1948), Rotary (pres. 1965-66). Author: Toledo Highlights. Patentee in field. Home: Toledo, Ohio. Died July 15, 1977.

STAFFORD, JEAN, author; b. Covina, Calif., July 1, 1915; d. John Richard and Mary Ethel (McKillop) Stafford, A.B., U. Colo., 1936, A.M., 1936; postgrad. U. Heidelberg, 1936-37; D.H.L., Litt.D.; m. Robert Lowell, Apr. 2, 1940 (div. 1948); m. 2d, Oliver Jensen, Jan. 28, 1950 (div. 1953); m. 3d, A.J. Liebling, Apr. 1959 (dec.). Fellow Center for Advanced Studies, Wesleyan U.; adj. prof. Columbia. Author: (novels) Boston Adventure, 1944; The Mountain Lion, 1947; The Catherine Wheel; Children are Bored on Sunday; (juveniles) Elephi, The Cat With the High I.Q.; The Lion and the Carpenter; Bad Characters; A Mother in History; also Complete Stories of Jean Stafford. Contbr. to Kenyon, Partisan, Sewanee revs., Harpers, Harper's Bazaar, Vogue, Mademoiselle, New Yorker. Acad. Arts and Letters grantee, 1945; Guggenheim fellow, 1945, 48; Rockefeller Found. grantee, 1965. Recipient Nat. Press Club award, 1948; Pulitzer prize, 1970. Mem. Nat. Acad. Arts and Letters. Address: New York, N.Y. Died Mar. 26, 1979; inurned Greenriver Cemetery, East Hampton, N.Y.

STAHLMAN, JAMES GEDDES, publisher; b. Nashville, Feb. 28, 1893; s. Edward Claiborne and Mary (Geddes) S.; grad. Webb Sch., Bell Buckle, Tenn., 1912; A.B., Vanderbilt U., 1916; postgrad. U. Chgo., 1916; LL.D., Atlanta Law Sch., 1939; m. Mildred Thornton, Jan. 20, 1917; children—Ann Geddes (Mrs. George R. Hill), Mildred Stahlman; m. 2d, Effye Chumley, Jan. 10, 1939 (dec.); m. 3d, Gladys P. Breckenridge, June 1, 1953. Pres., pub. Nashville Banner, 1930-72; chmn. bd. Newspaper Printing Corp., 1937-72. Mem. nat. council Boy Scouts Am. Trustee Vanderbilt U., MacArthur Meml. Found., Freedoms Found. Served as pvt. U.S. Army, World War I; capt. USNR, World War II. Recipient Am. award Ams. Found., 1956, Freedoms Found. Washington medal, 1961, 65; Am. Legion 4th Estate award, 1970; S.A.R. Patriot's medal. 1970. Mem. Inter-Am. Press Assn. (pres. 1955-56), Am. (pres. 1937-39), So. (pres. 1932-33, chmn. bd. 1933-34) newspaper pub. assns., Phi Beta Kappa, Sigma Chi, Sigma Delta Chi, Omicron Delta Kappa, Sigma Upsilon, F.A.G.S. Presbyn. Mason (33 deg., K.T., Shriner). Clubs: Belle Meade Country, Hillsboro Hounds, Cumberland; National Press, Army and Navy, Army Navy Country (Washington); Metropolitan, Dutch Treat, University (N.Y.C.); Circumnavigators. Home: Nashville, Tenn. Died May 1, 1976.

STAKMAN, ELVIN C., plant pathologist; b. Algoma, Wis., May 17, 1885; s. Frederick and Emelie (Eberhardt) S.; A.B., U. Minn., 1906, A.M., 1910; Ph.D., 1913; Dr. Nat. Sci. (hon.), U. Halle, 1938; D.Sc. (hon.), Yale, 1950, U. R.I., 1953, U. Minn., U. Wis., 1954, Cambridge, 1964; m. Louise Jensen, Sept. 6, 1917. Mem. faculty U. Minn., 1909-53, prof. plant pathology, 1918-35, head sect. plant pathology, 1913-40, head div. plant pathology and botany, 1940-53, now prof. emeritus; pathologist, agt. U.S. Dept. Agr., 1919-55, collaborator, from 1955; Hitchcock prof. U. Calif., 1955; spl. cons. agr. Rockefeller Found., from 1953; Nat. Def. Leader rubber expdn. to S. Am., 1940; sci. mission to Japan, SCAP, 1948; guest prof. U. Halle, 1930-31. Mem. div. biology, agr. NRC, 1931-34, vice chmn., 1937-38, 47-48, mem. agrl. bd., 1950-58; mem. com. biology and medicine U.S. AEC, 1948-54, cons., 1954-59; mem. exec. com. Nat. Sci. Bd., 1950-54; mem. Nat. Commn. for UNESCO, 1950-56; del. numerous fgn. sci. confs. Decorated Cruz de Boyacá (Colombia); recipient E. C. Hansen medal and prize, 1928; Centennial award Mich. State Coll., 1955; Medalla del Merito Argónomico (Colombia), 1955; certificate of merit Bot. Soc. Am., 1956; Otto Appel medal, 1957; award Cosmos Club, 1964. Fellow Am. Acad. Arts and Scis., Bot. Soc. Edinburgh (hon.), Am. Phytopathol. Soc. (award of distinction 1967); mem. N.Y. Acad. Scis., Am. Philos. Soc., Bot. Soc. Am., Am. Genetic Assn., A.A.A.S. (pres. 1949), Brit., Am. mycological socs., Am. Soc. Naturalists, History Sci. Soc., Norwegian Acad. Sci. and Letters, Nat. Acad. Sci., Philos. Sci. Assn., Wash. Acad. Sci., Kaiser Akad. Naturf., Canadian (hon.), Japanese (hon.), Indian (hon.) phytopathol. socs., Swedish Royal Acad. Agr. (fgn. mem.), Phi Beta Kappa, Sigma Xi, Alpha Zeta, Gamma Sigma Delta (Distinguished service award 1951), Gamma Alpha. Specialist mycology, plant pathology; extensive investigations of cereal rusts and smuts. Edit-in-chief Phytopathology, 1925-29; editorial com. Ann. Rev. Microbiology, 1946-54. Author: (with J. G. Harrar) Principles of Plant Pathology, 1957; (with others) Campaigns Against Hunger, 1967; also bulls articles profl. jours. Home: St. Paul, Minn. Died Jan. 23, 1979.

STALEY, AUSTIN L., judge; b. Pitts., 1902; s. Harry M. and Millie (Boehm) S.; LL.B., Duquesne U., 1928; LL.D., St. Vincent Coll., 1963; m. Elnor Soisson, 1930; 1 dau., Mary Jane. Admitted to Pa. bar, 1928, practiced in Pitts.; asst. solicitor City of Pitts., 1934; dep. atty. gen. Commonwealth of Pa., 1935; dir. Workmen's Compensation Bur., 1936; dep. sec. Dept. of Labor and Industry, Commonwealth of Pa., 1937; judge U.S. Ct. of Appeals for 3d Circuit, 1950-66, chief judge, 1966-68; U.S. sr. circuit judge, 1968-78. Mem. Am. Law Inst., Am., Pa. bar assns. Democrat. Roman Catholic. Home: Pittsburgh, Pa. Died Aug. 3, 1978.

STALLING, BETTIN, lawyer; b. Lexington, Mo. Oct. 26, 1897; s. Diederich and Emile (Bettin) S.; student U. Mo., 1916-17, Milsaps Coll., 1918; LL.B., U. Chgo., 1923; m. Lucy Tolhurst, June 30, 1926; children—Suzanne (dec.), Richard. Admitted to Ill. bar, 1924; practice in Chgo., 1924-34; head atty. HOLC, Washington, 1934-39; regional counsel, Chgo., 1939-47, 54-55; spl. rep. dir. loan guaranty service VA, 1948-50, chief direct loan div., 1951-54; acting asst. chief investigation Gen. Accounting Office, 1955-56; counsel USN, Spain, 1956-61; lectr. law Chgo., prof. Kent Coll., 1946. Del., Internat. Bar Conf., Monte Carlo, 1954, Bonn, 1958, Salzburg, 1960; counsel, chmn. compliance bd. NRA, Chgo., 1933. Mem. Internat. (del. conv. Cologne 1958), Am. (ho. dels. 1947-49, chmn. real property div. real estate and trust sect. 1943), Fed. (mem. nat. council 1947-66, pres. 1953-54; incorporator Fed. Bar Found., treas. 1974-77), Ill. (chmn. real estate sect. 1947-48) bar assns., Pi Kappa Alpha, Phi Delta Phi. Methodist. Clubs: Cosmos (Washington), Nat. Lawyers. Contbr. articles to legal jours. Editor: Fed. Bar News, 1953-55. Address: Washington, D.C. Died Nov. 15, 1977.

STANCZYK, JAN (STAN'SHIK), U.N. representative; b. Wola Przemykowska, Poland, Dec. 24, 1886; m. Anastazia Zelcer, March 23, 1900. Sec. gen. Polish Mines Workers Union, 1919-39; mem. Polish Parliament, 1919-35; minister of labor and social welfare Polish Govt., 1939-46; principal dir. Dept. of Social Affairs, U.N. Secretariot, since 1946. Mem. Polish Socialist Party. Home: Manhasset. *

STANDLEY, PAUL CARPENTER, botanist; b. Avalon, Mo., Mar. 21, 1884; s. Ingram Calvin and Florence (Carpenter) S.; student Drury Coll., Springfield, Mo., 1903-06; B.S., N.M. State Coll., Las Cruces, 1907, M.S., 1908; unmarried. Asst. botanist N.M. State Coll., 1907-09; asst. and asso. curator div. of plants, U.S. Nat. Museum, Washington, D.C., 1909-28; asso. curator herbarium, Field Museum Natural History, Chicago, 1929-36; curator of the herbarium, 1937-50. Fellow A.A.A.S. Author: Flora of New Mexico, 1915; Flora of the District of Columbia, 1919; Trees and Shrubs of Mexico, 1920, 26; Plants of Glacier National Park, 1927; Flora of the Panama Canal Zone,

1928. Has made many bot. expdns. to western U.S., Mexico and Central America. Address: Honduras, C.A. *

STANFORD, EDWARD ROSEMOND, coll. pres.; b. Waco, Tex., June 9, 1884; s. Marshall Wright and Helen (Barcus) S.; grad. Clarendon (Tex.) Coll., 1904; B.A., Southwestern U., Georgetown, Tex., 1907, M.A., 1910; M.A., Yale, 1912, B.D., 1913; m. Elizabeth Wright, of Palestine, Tex., 1918; children—Edward Rosemond, Harry Wright, Earl Gooch, David. Asst. pastor M.E. Ch., S., Hewitt Circuit, Tex., 1908-09, Waterbury, Conn., 1911-13; dir. religious edn., 1st Ch., Ft. Worth, Tex., 1914-15; pastor Ballinger, Tex., 1916, Stanford Memorial Ch., Ft. Worth, 1917; supt. intermediate sr. work, Gen. S.S. Bd., M.E. Ch., S., Nashville, Tenn., 1918-23; pres. Westmoorland Coll., San Antonio, Tex., since June 1923. Chaplain 344th F.A., N.A., Camp Travis, Tex., 1917; served with regt. in France and with Army of Occupation, Germany. Mem. Kappa Alpha. Democrat. Mason. Kiwanian. Address: San Antonio, Tex. *

STANGER, ROBERT C., coll. pres.; b. Elmhurst, Ill., Jan. 26, 1900; s. Christian G. and Pauline (Hoeck) S.; student Eden Theol. Sem., St. Louis, 1921; B.D., Yale, 1922; M.A., U. Chgo., 1923; D.D. (hon.), Heidelberg Coll., 1941; m. Juel Elizabeth Wolf, June 20, 1931; children—Ronald Robert, Richard Leonard. Ordained to ministry Evang. and Reformed Ch., 1921; pastor, Chgo., 1923-30, 48-57, Detroit, 1933-48; instr. Bible and history Elmhurst Coll., 1930-33, pres., from 1957. First v.p. Evang. and Reformed Ch., 1953-56, mem. gen. council, 1947 53; del. 2d assembly World Council Chs., Evanston, Ill., 1954. Bd. dirs. Elmhurst YMCA. Clubs: University (Chgo.); Kiwanis (Elmhurst). Co-author: March on with Strength, 1953. Home: Elmhurst, Ill. Died Nov. 2, 1976.

STANLEY, CARLETON WELLESLEY, pres. Dalhousie U.; b. (Canadian parents) Providence, R.I., July 6, 1886; B.A., U. of Toronto (highest place in Classics and gen. proficiency, two gold medals), 1911; B.A., New Coll. Oxford, Eng. (1st class honors, Literae Humaniores), 1913, M.A., 1916; LL.D., U. of Toronto, 1933, Litt.D., U.of Colo., 1935, LL.D., U. of Maine, 1935; m. Isabel Buchen Alexander, 1918; children—Carleton Alexander, Laura. Lecturer, English literature, Victoria Coll., U. of Toronto, 1913-16; engaged in business, 1916-25; prof. Greek, McGill U., 1925-31, asst. to prin., 1930-31; pres. Dalhousie University since 1931. Fellow Royal Soc. of Can. Author: Roots of the Tree, 1936; Matthew Arnold, 1938. *

STANOYEVICH, MILIVOY STOYAN (STA'NO-YE-VICH), author, educator; b. Koprivnitsa on Timok, Yugoslavia, Feb. 14, 1882; s. Stoyan and Kupina (Radovanovich) S.; A.B., Zayetchar Coll., 1902; M.A., U. of Belgrade, 1907; LL.M., U. of Calif., 1914; Ph.D., Columbia, 1921; spl. lit. researches univs. of Munich, Paris, Vienna and Zurich; came to Am. 1908; m. Beatrice, d. of late William W. Stevenson, Nov. 15, 1917; 1 son, Nicholas. Assistant professor modern langs. and lits., Zayetchar Coll., 1907-08; lecturer on Slavonic instns., U. of Calif., 1916; polit. adviser in Slavonic affairs to consul gen. of Russia, at San Francisco, 1916-17; owner and editor of several Yugoslav journals in America, 1909-17; exec. sec. of Serbian War Mission to America, 1918; chief of the Slavic div. U.S. Censorship, 1918-19; editor of Yugoslav dept. in Ency. Americana, 1918-44; lecturer in Slavonic hist., N.Y. Bd. Edn., 1921-24; expert adviser State of N.Y. joint legislative com. to investigate exploitation of immigrants, 1923; professorial lecturer in Slavonic langs. and lit., Columbia U., 1920-25; asst. actuary, Carnegie Foundation for Advancement of Teaching, 1924; dir. and editor Slavonic dept. Universal Pictures Corp., 1925-30; pres. Universal Syndicate, 1927-37, chmn. since 1938; co-trustee, Stevenson Stanoyevich Fund, 1917-37, trustee since 1938; contbg. editor of Slavonic terminology, Webster's New Internat. Dictionary, 1938-40; special and consulting editor since 1941; president Rating Dir. Co. of New York since 1940. Fellow Am. Geog. Society; member Modern Language Association of America. Academy of Political Science. Club: Cosmopolitan (Montclair). Author several books since 1907; also numerous papers relating to field, and essays and monographs. Home: Montclair, N.J. *

STANSELL, CHARLES VERNON, newspaperman; b. Greenville, S.C., Sept. 7, 1882; s. Franklin Grant and Ellen (Hiott) S.; A.B., Furman U., 1907, Litt.D., 1945; A.M., U. Chgo., 1911; grad. study Harvard, 1907, Columbia, 1915; m. Mary Woodside, June 19, 1916; children—Laura (Mrs. W. H. Timmons), Margaret (Mrs. Walter L. North), Charles Vernon (dec.), Bettie (Mrs. Harold L. Baker). Instr. Latin, Furman U., 1907-09; prof., head English dept. Ottawa U., 1911-19; gen. writer Kansas City Star, 1919-34, chief editorial writer, asso. editor, 1934-56, contbg. editor, 1956—; news analyst sta. WDAF, 1943- 45. Regional planning council Greater-Kansas City. Trustee Ottawa U., 1945-48. Participant Pulitzer editorial award 1933; achievement award Ottawa U., 1951. Mem. Kansas City C. of C., Kansas City Art Inst., Phi Kappa Delta, Sigma Delta Chi. Congregationalist. Clubs: University Chgo.; Press (Kansas City). Author: Extraneous Elements Elizabethan Drama, 1911; More or Less Personal, 1959. Contbr. articles mags., 1915—. Home: Kansas City, MO also (winter) Boca Raton St Petersburg FL. *

STAPLES, LEONARD W., mgmt. cons.; b. Lima, O., Sept. 22, 1906; s. Edgar M. and Mildred (Starr) S.; grad. Ohio State U.; m. Rebecca E. Ewing, June 4, 1932; 1 son, William L. With H.D. Lee Co., Inc., Kansas City, Mo., 1928-72, staff sales dept., 1928-35, mgr. indsl. sales, 1942-52, sec., 1952-55, asst. to pres., 1955, pres., 1956-71, past dir.; vice chmn. bd U.F. Corp., Reading, Pa., 1970-72; mgmt. cons. Leonard Staples, Kansas City, Mo., 1972-77; dir. Rival Mfg. Co., Parkview-Gem, Inc., City Nat. Bank & Trust Co. Past pres., dir. Mo. Pub. Expenditure Survey; dir. Greater Kansas City Fgn. Trade Zone. Mem. Financial Analysis Soc. Kansas City (dir.), Am. Apparel Mfgs. Assn. (dir., past pres.), Asso. Industries Mo. (dir., past pres.). Clubs: Saddle and Sirloin; Indian Hills; Carriage; Kansas City; Sedgefield Country (Greensboro, N.C.); Eldorado Country (Palm Desert, Cal.). Home: Shawnee Mission, Kans. Died July 11, 1977.

STAPLES, STANLEY F., ins. co. exec.; b. Stillwater, Minn., Jan. 10, 1899; s. Lyle Stanley and Mabel (Fuller) S.; student U. Minn., 1923; m. Helen Schmitt, Jan. 10, 1923; children—Stanley F., John H. Salesman, Long-Bell Lumber Co., 1923-29; sales supr. Red Top post div. Indland Steel Co., 1929-33; with Employers Muts. of Wausau (Wis.), 1933-76, v.p. sales and advt., 1944-60, sr. v.p., 1960-76, also dir. Mem. mgmt. teams for ICA, Japan, Columbia. Pres., Wausau Police and Fire Commn., United Fund Marathon County, Wis. Served with U.S. Army, World War I. Mem. Am. Mgmt. Assn. (v.p. marketing dir.), Wausau C. of C. (pres.), Tuscania (World War I) Survivors Assn. (past pres.). Club: Mason (Shriner). Home: Wausau, Wis. Died Sept. 23, 1976.

STAPLEY, DELBERT LEON, business exec., ch. leader; b. Mesa, Ariz., Dec. 11, 1896; s. Orley S. and Polly May (Hunsaker) S.; student pub. schs.; m. Ethel Burdette Davis, Jan. 14, 1918; children—Berdine (Mrs. Grant A. Farley), Orley S., Phyllis (Mrs. Reed F. Mack). Missionary, Ch. of Jesus Christ of Latter-day Saints, So. States Mission, 1915-17; with O.S. Stapley Co., Phoenix, 1914-78, v.p., 1915-49, pres., 1949-66, chmn. bd., 1966-78, dir. Valley Nat. Co.; dir., mem. trust com. Zions 1st Nat. Bank, Salt Lake City. State supt. Young Men's Mut. Improvement Assn., 1919-38; chmn. Ariz. regional council Ch. of Jesus Christ of Latter Day Saints, 1944-50, pres. Phoenix stake, 1947-50, sustained mem. Quorum of 12 Apostles, 1950; trustee Brigham Young U. and Latter Day Saints Ch. Bd. Edn., 1951-75. Pres., Roosevelt council Boy Scouts Am., 1931-32, nat. rep., 1939-50, nat. rep.-at-large, mem. regional adv. bd., recipient Silver Beaver award, 1934, Silver Antelope, 1957, Silver Buffalo, 1961. Served with USMCR, World War I; maj. Ariz. N.G., 1924-34. Clubs: Lions (pres. Phoenix 1938), Salt Lake Country (Salt Lake City). Home: Salt Lake City, Utah. Died Aug. 19, 1978.

STARCH, DANIEL, psychologist, business cons.; b. LaCrosse, Wis., Mar. 8, 1883; s. Frank and Theresa Starch; B.A., Morningside (Iowa) Coll., 1903, Sc.D., 1949; MA., U. Iowa, 1904, Ph.D., 1906; postgrad. Harvard, 1907-08; m. Amy Jane Hopson, Aug. 26, 1913. Instr. psychology State U. Iowa, 1906-07, Wellesley Coll., 1907-08; instr. psychology, 1908, asst. prof., 1912; asso. prof. U. Wis., 1917-20, lectr. bus. psychology Harvard, 1919-20, asst. prof., 1920-23, asso. prof., 1923-26; dir. research dept. Am. Assn. Advt. Agys., 1924-32. Prof. psychology U. Wash., summer 1915; prof. N.Y.U., summer 1922. Capt. aviation sect. Signal O.T.C. Recipient certificate achievement U. Iowa, 1947, Distinguished Service medal, 1969. Fellow A.A.A.S., Am. Psychol. Assn.; mem. Am. Marketing Assn. (Paul D. Converse nat. award 1951), Market Research Council, Sigma Xi, Alpha Delta Sigma, Gamma Alpha, Phi Delta Kappa, Psi Chi, Beta Gamma Sigma, Kappa Tau Alpha. Club: Scarsdale Golf. Author works in psychology, advt., edn., 1905-43. Contbr. to Ency. Brit., psychol. ednl. and bus. jours.; author numerous reports on bus. research. Founder, hon. chmn. Daniel Starch and Staff, cons. bus. research. Pioneer surveys readership of advt., 1922, audience of radios, 1928, mag. advt. readership, 1931. Home: Scardsdale, N.Y. Died Feb. 8, 1979.

STARK, CHARLES J., publisher; b. Wooster, O., Oct. 8, 1882; s. Jacob and Caroline (Bringger) S.; ed. Ohio State U.; m. Penelope C. Mack, Jan. 18, 1911; 1 dau., Penelope Mack (Mrs. Robert D. Beatty, Jr.). Asso. editor Iron Trade Review, 1907-17, editor, 1917-27; v.p. Penton Pub. Co., 1924-25, pres. and treas. and officer of affiliated cos., 1925-37; supt. purchases and printing, State of Ohio, 1939-42; now v.p. and gen. mgr. Sandusky Newspapers, Inc., Sandusky, O.; sec., treas. and dir. Sandusky (O.) Broadcasting Co.; dir. Penton Pub. Co., Sandusky Newspapers, Inc. Ed. of volume, "Ohio—An Empire Within An Empire" (1944). Pres. Nat. Conf. Business Papers Editors, 1921-22; pres. Associated Bus. Papers, Inc., 1928-29; mem. Phi Kappa Psi. Episcopalian. Home. Cleveland Heights, O. *

STARKIE, WALTER FITZWILLIAM, lit. historian; b. 1894; M.A., Litt.D., Shrewsbury and Trinity Coll., Dublin, Ireland, Trinity Coll., Hartford, Conn., 1930. Lectr., Romance langs. Trinity Coll., 1920, modern Spanish drama King's Coll., London, Eng., 1923; fellow Trinity Coll., 1924-47; dir. Irish Nat. Theatre (Abbey), 1927-42; vis. prof. Romance langs. U. Chgo., 1930; Lord Northcliffe lectr. lit. Univ. Coll., London, 1936; prof. Spanish, lectr. Italian lit., Dublin U., 1926-47; dir. Brit. Inst. Madrid, Spain, 1940-54; vis. prof. U. Tex., 1957, 58, N.Y. U., 1959, Kan. U., 1960, Colo. U., 1961; lectr. throughout U.S., Europe; prof. in residence UCLA, 1961-70, emeritus, 1974. Rep. Brit. Council in Spain, 1940-54. Decorated comdr. Order Brit. Empire; knight comdr. Isabel the Cath. (Spain); companion Order St. Michael and St. George. Fellow Royal Soc. Arts, Royal Soc. Lit.; hon. mem. Hispanic Soc. Am. Author: Jacinto Benavente, 1925; Raggle-Taggle, 1933; Spanish Raggle-Taggle, 1934; Luigi Pirandello, 1937; The Waveless Plain, 1938; Grand Inquisitor, 1940; In Sara's Tents, 1953; The Road to Santiago, 1957; The Dukes of Alba, 1959; Spain: A Musician's Journey through Time and Space, 2 vols. with 6 LP records in French, 1958; Scholars and Gypsies, 1963: Translation of Don Quixote, 1964; The House of Alba, 1976. Address: Madrid, Spain. Died Nov. 2, 1976.

STARNES, JULIA BAYLIS, former librarian; b. Columbia, Miss; d. Robert Jabus and Birdie (Warren) Baylis; student Whitworth Coll., Miss.; degree in law library administrn. Columbia U., 1944. Chief dept. sheriff's office, Marion County, Miss., 1932-36; claims examiner Miss. Unemployment Compensation Commn., Jackson, 1936-39; Miss. state librarian, 1940-70. Mem. Gov.'s Commn. on Status of Women. Trustee Sch. for Cerebral Palsy. Mem. Miss. State Bar (hon.), Am. Legion Aux. Democrat. Methodist. Clubs: Mississippi Official Woman's, Jackson; As You Like It (Columbia). Home: Columbia, Miss. Died Jan. 7, 1980; buried Columbia City Cemetery.

STARR, FRANCES (GRANT), actress; b. Oneonta, N.Y., 1886; d. Charles E. and Emma (Grant) S.; ed. Albany pub. schs.; m. Haskell Coffin, artist, New York. Made 1st appearance on stage in a stock co. at Leland Theatre, Albany, N.Y., June 1901; joined Murray Hill Stock Co., New York; played in "Gallops" with Charles Richman, spring of 1906; leading lady in "The Music Master," fall of 1906; starring in "The Rose of the Rancho," 1907; "Easiest Way," 1909-11; "Case of Becky," 1912-13; "The Secret," 1914-15; "Marie Odile," 1915-16; "Little Lady in Blue," 1916-17; "Tiger, Tiger," 1919-20; "One," 1920-21; revival of "Easiest Way," 1921-22; "Shore Leave," 1922-23. Home: Garden City, L.I., N.Y. *

STARR, LOUIS MORRIS, journalist, historian; b. N.Y.C., Nov. 1, 1917; s. Howard White and Henriette (Danforth) S.; B.A., Yale, 1940; Ph.D., Columbia, 1954; m. Mary Belle Head Bancroft, Jan. 6, 1944; children—Jennifer, Carolyn, Thomas, Theodore. Editor, publisher Gallatin (Tenn.) Examiner, 1942-44; mem. editorial staff Chgo. Sun, 1944-47; mem. staff Oral History Research Office, Columbia, 1953-56, dir. office, 1956-80, dir. internat. div. Grad. Sch. Journalism, 1958-72, asso. prof. journalism, 1961; book editor Columbia Journalism Rev., 1961-71. Mem. Darien (Conn.) Bd. Edn., 1958-64. Adv. bd. Lyndon Johnson Oral History Project, 1968-80; bd. dirs. Yale Alumni Fund, 1969-80. Mem. Am. Hist. Assn., Orgn. Am. Historians, Oral History Assn. (co-founder; 1st pres. 1968). Clubs: Yale; Men's Faculty (Columbia). Author: Bohemian Brigade: Civil War Newsmen in Action, 1954; also numerous articles. Editor: The Oral History Collection, 2d edit., 1964, 4th edit., 1979; The Second National Colloquium on Oral History, 1967; Oral History in the United States, 1971. Home: Darien, Conn. Died Mar. 2, 1980; buried Mountain Grove Meml. Ch. Cemetery, Huletts Landing, N.Y.

STARR, WALTER A., business executive; b. San Francisco, Calif., Mar. 14, 1877; s. William M. and Kate F. (Calkin) S.; Ph.B., U. of Calif., 1897; m. Carmen Moore, 1902; 2 sons, Walter A., Jr., Allan M. U.S. mail carrier in Alaska by dog sled, 1898-99; in grain bus., W. A. Starr, San Francisco, 1901-17; 2d vice pres. U.S. Grain Corp. & Food Adminstrn., 1917-20; dir. Edw. L. Eyre & Co., 1921-35; dir. Soundview Pulp Co., 1932-51, chmn. bd., 1940-51; director Scott Paper Company, 1951-59; director, chairman executive committee Central Bank, Oakland, 1943-47; director Yosemite Park & Curry Co.; dir. North Am. Investment Corp.; mem. Industrial adv. com. Fed. Reserve Bank, San Francisco. Apptd. mem. industry advisory com. Pulp and Paper, WPB, April 1942. Pres. Calif. Hist. Soc., 1942, Sierra Club, 1941-42. Dir. Save the Redwoods League. Member of the Society of California Pioneers, Delta Kappa Epsilon. Republican. Episcopal. Clubs: Pacific Union, Commonwealth. Home: Piedmont, Cal. *

STAUB, MARSHAL GERALD, business cons.; b. N.Y.C., June 19, 1922; s. Irving and Mollie (Rosenberg) S.; ed. LaSalle Extension U.; m. Marilyn Carol Delaney, May 15, 1958; 1 dau., Kathy. With Merritt-Chapman & Scott Corp., 1944-69, treas., 1951-61, exec. v.p., 1955-61, pres., 1961-69, mem. exec. com., 1957-69, dir. 1955-69; v.p., dir. N.Y. Shipbldg. Corp.; pres., dir., exec. com. Tenn. Products & Chem. Corp.; pres. Revday Industries, Inc.; dir. Merritt-Chapmen & Scott Overseas. Served with AUS, World War II. Mem. Am. Legion. Clubs: Advertising of N.Y., Marco Polo. Address: Sea Girt, N.J. Died Apr. 15, 1979.

STAUDINGER, HANS, educator; born Worms am Rhein, Germany, Aug. 16, 1889; s. Franz and Auguste (Wenck) S.; student Gymnasium Darmstadt, Univ. of Munich and Heidelberg, Ph.D., Heidelberg, 1912; LL.D., New Sch. Social Research, 1959; m. Else Maier, Feb. 21, 1912 (dec. Mar. 1966); children—Ruth (Mrs. Joseph Schaffner), Frank; m. 2d, Elizabeth Todd, Oct. 29, 1966. Came to U.S., 1934, naturalized 1939. Served in Reich Ministry of Food and Agr., 1918-19, in Reich Ministry of Econs., 1919-27; in Prussian Ministry of Trade and Industry, 1927-33, from 1929 as Staatssekretär; member of the Reichsrat, 1929, Reichstag, 1932; chairman and mem. various transport, mining and elec. cos., consultant, utility cos., 1927-33; prof. econs. and bus. adminstrn. in Grad. Faculty of Polit. and Social Sci., New Sch. for Social Research, N.Y. City, 1934-59, professor emeritus, 1959-80, dean of grad. faculty, 1950-51, 53-59, dean emeritus, 1959-80; chairman council for research, Institute of World Affairs, 1943-53, director of the Institute, 1951-53. Established the foundations for a rationalized and managed electric power supply for Germany; power plant sta. Hanau-Frankfort named Staudinger Power Plant; coordinated policy for all Prussian state-owned cos.; initiated and executed reforms in indsl. and bus. edn. Permanent faculty chair named Else and Hans Staudinger at New Sch. for Social Research, N.Y.C., 1965. Mem. Am. Econ. Assn., Population Assn. of Am. Editor: Social Research, 1959-64. Home: New York, N.Y. Died Feb. 25, 1980.

STAUFFER, OSCAR STANLEY, editor, pub.; b. Hope, Kan., Nov. 26, 1886; s. Solomon Engle and Elizabeth (Conrad) S.; student U. Kan., 1908-10; m. Ethel Lucille Stone, Sept. 7, 1914 (dec. July 1964); children—Betty Stauffer Collinson, Stanley Howard, John Herbert; m. 2d, Cornelia Hardcasle, Conwell, July 15, 1965 (dec. July 1973). Reporter, Emporia Gazette, 1906-08, Kansas City (Mo.) Star, 1910-15; editor, owner Peabody (Kan.) Gazette, 1915-24; editor Arkansas City (Kan.) Traveler, 1924-40; editor, pub. Topeka State Jour. and Topeka Daily Capital; chmn. bd., exec. head Stauffer Publs., pubs. Ark. City Daily Traveler, Pittsburg (Kan.) Morning Sun, Grand Island (Neb.) Daily Ind., Maryville (Mo.) Daily Forum, Shawnee (Okla.) News & Star, Nevada (Mo.) Daily Mail, York (Neb.) News Times, Newton (Kan.) Kan., Independence (Mo.) Examiner, Capper's Weekly, Kansas City (Kan.) Kansan, Marshall (Mo.) Democrat News, Brookings (S.D.) Register, Glenwood Springs (Colo.) Post, Hillsdale (Mich.) Daily News, Hannibal (Mo.) Courier-Post; pres. KGFF Broadcasting Co., Shawnee, Okla., WIBW-TV, AM-FM, Topeka, KGNC AM-FM, Amarillo, Tex., KSOK Broadcasting Co., Arkansas City, KRNT-AM-FM, Des Moines; former v.p. A.P. Trustee Washburn U., Menninger Found. Former chmn. Kan. Indsl. Devel. Commn., Kan. State Bd. Regents; past pres. Inland Daily Press Assn. Mem. Am. Soc. Newspaper Editors, Beta Theta Pi, Sigma Delta Chi. Republican. Presbyn. Rotarian. Clubs: Topeka Country, Scottsdale (Ariz.) Villa Monterey. Home: Topeka KS. *

STAUSS, JAMES HARTMANN, coll. adminstr.; b. Buchanan County, Iowa, Apr. 4, 1914; s. George J. and Mariam (Ginn) S.; B.A., Grinnell Coll., 1936, LL.D., 1969; M.S., Iowa State U., 1937; Ph.D., U. Wis. 1945; m. Harriet Huntley Golden, June 18, 1940; children—Jane Ann, Mary Ellen, James Richard. Instr. agrl. econs. Tex. A. and M. Coll., 1937-38; asst. prof. econs. U. Tenn., 1941-46; asso. prof. econs. Grinnell Coll., 1946-50, prof. econs., 1950-69, Macy prof. social studies, 1961-69, dean coll., 1960-69, acting pres., 1964-65, provost, 1966-69; exec. v.p., provost, prof. econs. Colo. Coll., Colorado Springs, 1969-75. Trustee Colorado Springs Fine Arts Center; bd. dirs. Colorado Springs Symphony Orch. Assn. Mem. Am. Econ. Assn., Western Social Sci. Assn., Phi Beta Kappa. Contbr. articles to profl. jours. Co-editor: The Teaching of Elementary Economics, 1960. Home: Colorado Springs, Colo. Died Dec. 19, 1975.

STAYER, MORRISON CLAY (STAR), army med. officer; b. Roaring Springs, Pa., July 12, 1882; s. Andrew Snowberger and Rosa Kissecker (Brumbaugh) S.; student, Wittenberg Coll., 1899-1900; A.B., Lafayette Coll., 1903; M.D., Jefferson Med. Coll., 1906; student Army Med. Sch., 1908-09, Royal Army Med. Coll., London, Eng., 1920-21, Army War Coll., 1926-27, Inf. Sch., 1927-28; m. Edna Ingham Keller, Nov. 3, 1907; children—William Keller. Private practice, 1907-08; commd. as 1st lt., Med. Corps, U.S. Army, 1908, and advanced through grades to major gen., 1943); served in P.I., 1910-12; Dayton, O., flood region, 1913; Letterman Hosp., San Francisco, 1914-18; chief health officer, Am. Occupational Force, Coblenz, Germany, 1919-21; prof. preventive medicine, Med. Field Service Sch., 1922-26, and Army Inf. Sch., 1927-32; asst. comdt., Carlisle Barracks, 1932-36; post surgeon, Ft. Riley, 1936-39; chief health officer, The Panama Canal, 1943-44 and chief surgeon, Caribbean Defense Command, 1941-44; chief surgeon, Mediterranean Theatre of Operations, 1944-45; chief public health and welfare, edn. and religious affairs, Office Mil. Govt. for Germany (U.S.), 1945-46; dir. of Tuberculosis Control, Pa. Dept. of Health, since 1946. Mem. Am. Bd. of Preventive Medicine and Pub. Health. Fellow Am. Coll. Chest Physicians; mem. American Medical Assn., Am. Hosp. Assn., Am. Pub. Health Assn., Phi Gamma Delta. Mason. Club: Army-Navy(Washington, D.C.). Address: Carlisle, Pa. *

STE. HELENE, SISTER educator; b. Blooming Prairie, Minn., Nov. 9, 1883; d. Michael and Amelia (Vollhardt) Guthrie; prep. edn., Blooming Prairie High Sch. and St. Joseph's Acad., St. Paul; B.A., U. of Minn., 1907, M.A., 1915; studied U. of Chicago, 1915-16, Oxford U., Eng., 1924-25; joined Congregation Sisters of St. Joseph of Carondelet. Began as teacher public high school; with Coll. of St. Catherine, St. Paul, Minn., since 1911, successively instr. in English until 1917, principal of Demonstration High Sch., 1917-20, prof. English, 1920-22, registrar and head of English dept., 1922-29, dean of Coll. and head of English dept. since 1929. Mem. Am. Assn. Univ. Women, Nat. Assn. Deans of Women, Nat. Council Teachers of English, Minn. Assn. of Deans. Catholic. Club: St. Paul College Club. Has traveled widely in U.S., British Isles, Europe and Asia Minor. *

STEARNS, DON M., pres. Lansdowne Constrn. Co.; b. Humboldt, Ia., Sept. 23, 1883; s. W. W. and Emma S.; grad. high sch., Humboldt, 1900; student Ia. State Coll., 1901; m. Martha Engelbart, of Fort Dodge, Ia.; 1 son, George Frederick. Organizer Northern Ia. Power Co., 1903; organizer and head of various power cos., later combined as Ia. Pub. Service Co.; pres. same to 1928; pres. Lansdowne Constrn. Co. (holding co.), since 1928. Chmn. Ia. State Bd. Y. M. C. A. Boys' Camps. Republican. Unitarian. Mason (32 deg., Shriner). Clubs: Fort Dodge Country, Wakonda, Des Moines (Des Moines); Sioux City Country, West Okoboji Country. *

STEARNS, MYRON MORRIS, writer, editor; b. West Hartford, Conn., May 19, 1884; s. Charles Cummings and Sophia Dickerman Putnam (Seymour) S.; student Stearns Preparatory School, Hartford, 1897-1902; A.B., Stanford University,1906; married Helen Mar Gibbons, 1909; children—Helen Mar, David Mason, John Foote, Charles Miner; married 2d, Mara Evans; 1 son, Timothy Morrison. Reporter and special article writer, Los Angeles Times, 1906-10; developer of orchard land, Southern Calif., and free lance writer, 1910-17; lecturer, U. of Calif., Southern Br., 1917-18; scenario editor D. W. Griffith Corp., 1918-20; scenario adviser, Cosmopolitan Pictures, 1921; motion picture editor, Judge, 1921-22; producer, Outlook Pictures, 1922; screen editor First Nat. Pictures, 1923; mag. article writer since 1924; advisory editor, Boy's Life, 1930-32, editorial dir., 1932-35; editorial asso. Automotive Safety Foundation 1940-46. Member White House Conf. on Child Health and Protection, 1930. Author: With the Movie Makers, 1923; (with C. W. Washburne) New Schools in the Old World, 1926, and Better Schools, 1928; What Kind of College Is Best?, 1928; What Kind of School Is Best?, 1929; (with Jack Dempsey) Round by Round, 1940. Article writer for Harper's Mag., Reader's Digest, Redbook Mag., etc. Winner $25,000 for safe driving rules, 1938. Home: Greenwich, Conn. Address: N.Y. *

STECK, CHARLES CALVIN, mfg. exec.; b. Wheaton, Ill., Mar. 24, 1884; s. Calvin and Louisa Maria (Finch) S.; B.S., Wheaton Coll., 1906; M.S., U. Chgo., 1911; m. Jennie Ward Kinsman, Sept. 8, 1909; children—Helen Shirley (Mrs. Paul R. Swanson), Kenneth Kinsman, Richard Lamont; m. 2d, Etelka Holt Vincent. Instr. mathematics dept. U. N.H., 1911-19, head dept., 1917-19; with Spaulding Fibre Co., N. Rochester, N.H. 1919—, pres., gen. manager and dir., 1942-60, director and consultant, 1960—. Executive of Food Administration of N.H., 1917-18. Clubs: Park Country (Buffalo); Orchard Park (N.Y.) Country. Home: Orchard Park, N.Y. *

STECKEL, HARRY ARTHUR, psychiatrist; b. Catasauqua, Pa., Dec. 13, 1886; s. J. Henry and Martha Jane (Bartholomew) S.; M.D., U. of Pa., 1910; m. Carolyn E. Moon, Sept. 29, 1919; children—Elizabeth Ann (Mrs. Edward S. Barnard), William Henry. Interne, St. Francis Hospital, Trenton, New Jersey, 1910-11; resident physician Trenton State Hospital, 1911, Mt. Pleasant (Iowa) State Hospital, 1912; interne, asst. physician, senior asst. physician Kings Park (N.Y.) State Hosp., 1912-24; sr. asst. physician Binghamton (N.Y.) State Hosp., 1924-25, clin. dir., 1925-29; supt. Newark (N.Y.) State Sch., 1929-30; dir. Syracuse (N.Y.) Psychopathic Hosp., 1930-47; retired; prof. of psychiatry, Coll. of Medicine (Syracuse U.), 1930-47. Cons. psychiatrist, Regional Office, Vets. Adminstrn., Syracuse, N.Y. Served as 1st lt. Med. Corps, U.S. Army in France, World War I; col. Med. Res., ret. Fellow A.M.A., Am. Coll. Physicians; mem. N.Y. State Med. Soc., Syracuse Acad. of Medicine, Am. Psychiatric Assn., National Com. for Mental Hygiene, N.Y. State Com. on Mental Hygiene, Alpha Kappa Kappa. Methodist. Mason. Contbr. scientific articles to mags. Home: Syracuse, N.Y. *

STEEFEL, ROBERT DAVID, lawyer; b. Rochester, N.Y., May 5, 1901; s. Joseph D. and Sadie (Lang) S.; A.B., Harvard, 1922, LL.B., 1924; m. Margaret Lane, Dec. 18, 1929; children—Caren (Mrs. Austin K. Haldenstein), Edward R. Admitted to N.Y. bar, 1925; asso. Stroock & Stroock & Lavan, N.Y.C., 1924-36, mem. firm, 1937-79; gen. counsel, dir. Charles F. Noyes Co., Inc.; gen. counsel Durst Orgn., Hotel Pierre, Sherry-Netherland Hotel; former mem. bd. advisers Title Guarantee Co. Gov., Real Estate Bd. N.Y., chmn. legislative, arbitration coms. Trustee Hosp. Council So. N.Y.; gen. counsel Fedn. Jewish Philanthropies N.Y., 1953-58, trustee, 1952-79; trustee, gen. counsel, exec. v.p. Montefiore Hosp. and Med. Center, 1930-79. Mem. Mayor's Task Force on Child Abuse and Neglect; exec. com. Am. Jewish Com., 1944-54. Fellow Brandeis U. Mem. Assn. Bar City N.Y., N.Y. County Lawyers Assn. Clubs: Harmonie (N.Y.C.); Century Country. Home: New York, N.Y. Died July 29, 1979.

STEELE, FRANK SWARTZ, r.r. exec.; b. Winchester, Va., Oct. 29, 1908; s. Frank Kern and Lillie (Swartz) S.; student George Washington U., 1925-29; m. Grace Marie Newman, Oct. 20, 1928; 1 dau., Lorna Lee, With So. Ry. System, 1924-76, gen. account agt., 1951-53; v.p., 1963-76, v.p. Ga., So. & Fla. Ry., 1953-55, v.p., 1951-76; v.p., dir. Live Oak Perry & Gulf Ry., St. Johns River Terminal Co.; dir. S. Ga. Ry., Albany & No. R.R. Co., Ga. Midland Ry., Macon Terminal Co., Ga., So. & Fla. Ry. Home: Valdosta, Ga. Died Feb. 29, 1976.

STEELE, JACK, journalist; b. N. Manchester, Ind., Sept. 15, 1914; s. Roscoe and Dessie (Wonderly) S.; A.B., Middlebury (Vt.) Coll., 1936; M.S. in Journalism, Columbia, 1937; m. Barbara Louise Lyons, Sept. 30, 1939; children—Jeffrey L., Peter C. Reporter, N.Y. Herald Tribune, 1937-53; chief polit. writer Scripps-Howard Newspaper Alliance, 1953-67, mng. editor, 1967-74, editor, 1974-80. Recipient Raymond Clapper award, 1949, Sigma Delta Chi award, 1949, Heywood Broun award, 1951, Ernie Pyle award, 1963. Clubs: Nat. Press, Gridiron (Washington). Presbyn. Home: Washington, D.C. Died Dec. 31, 1980.

STEELE, ROBERT MCCURDY, educator; b. Jefferson County, Pa., Mar. 21, 1882; s. Joseph and Josephine Adelaide S.; Ph.B., Bucknell U., 1908; grad. study, U. of Wis., 1912-13; A.M., and Ph.D., Columbia, 1926; LL.D., Bucknell U., 1936; m. Genevieve G. Dunkle, Aug. 23, 1916; children—Joanne, Mary W. Teacher elementary schs., 1900-04; teacher Clarion (Pa.) State Normal Sch., 1908-12; supt. schs. and prin. high sch., Latrobe, Pa., 1912-20; dir. tr. sch., State Teachers Coll., Slippery Rock, Pa., 1920-26; prin. Clarion State Normal Sch., 1926-28; pres. State Teachers' Coll., California, Pa., 1928—. In ednl. service, U.S. Army, 1918-19. Mem. N.E.A., Delta Sigma, Kappa Delta Pi, Phi Delta Kappa. Republican. Presbyn. Mason (32 deg., K.T.). Club: Schoolmen's. Author: A Study of Teacher Training in Vermont, 1926. Home: California, Pa.*

STEELE, WILLARD, eye, ear, nose and throat specialist; b. Corinth, Miss., Dec. 11, 1884; s. Newton Chambers and Frances Ellen (Jones) S.; A.B., Cumberland U., Lebanon, Tenn., 1907; student Vanderbilt Med. U.; M.D., Jefferson Med. Coll., 1911; grad. study London and Vienna; m. Kate Adelle Hinds, Oct. 18, 1911; children—Willard Hinds, Mary Bashie. Began practice at Chattanooga, Tenn., 1911; oculist surgeon, Southern R.R., Central of Ga. R.R., Tenn., Ala. & Ga. R.R.; mem. staff Baroness Erlanger, Pine Breeze Tubercular, Children's hosps. First lieut. Med. R.C., 1918. Fellow Am. Coll. Surgeons; mem. A.M.A., Southern Med. Assn., Tenn. State Med. Soc. (chmn. eye, ear, nose and throat sect.), Chattanooga and Hamilton County Med. Soc. (ex-pres.), Acad. Ophthalmology and Otolaryngology, Kappa Sigma, Alpha Kappa Kappa. Independent. Democrat. Presbyterian. Mason (Shriner). Clubs: Mountain City, Fairyland. Home: Chattonooga. *

STEELE, WILLIAM OWEN, writer; b. Franklin, Tenn., Dec. 22, 1917; s. Core and Sue (Johnston) S.; A.B., Cumberland U., 1940; m. Mary Quintard Govan, June 1, 1943; children—Mary Quintard, Jenifer Susan, Allerton William. Sr. staff writer Historic Rev. and Antique Digest. Author: The Golden Root, 1951; The Buffalo Knife, 1952; Over-Mountain Boy, 1952; Wilderness Journey, 1953 (selected by Parents mag. Book Club for 1955); John Sevier, 1953; The Story of Daniel Boone, 1953; Winter Danger (N.Y. Herald Tribune Spring Book Festival award), 1954; Francis Marion, 1954; The Story of Leif Ericson, 1954; Tomahawks and Trouble, 1955; Davy Crockett's

Earthquake, 1956; We Were There on the Oregon Trail, 1955; We Were There With the Pony Express, 1956; DeSoto, Child of The Sun, 1956; The Lone Hunt (spl. citation Child Study Assn. Am.), 1956; Flaming Arrows (William A. White award 1960), 1957; Daniel Boone's Echo, 1957; The Perilous Road (Jane Addams children's book award), 1958; Andy Jackson's Waterwell, 1959; The Far Frontier, 1959; The Spooky Thing, 1960; Westward Adventure: The True Stories of Six Pioneers (Thomas A. Edison Found. award), 1962; The Year of the Bloody Sevens, 1963; Wayah of the Real People, 1964; The No Name Man of the Mountains, 1964; Trail Through Danger, 1965; Tomahawk Border, 1966; The Old Wilderness Road: An American Journey, 1968; Hound Dog Zip to the Rescue, 1970; The Wilderness Tattoo: A Narrative of Juan Ortiz, 1972; Surgeon, Trader, Indian Chief: Henry Woodward of Carolina, 1972; Triple Trouble for Hound Dog Zip, 1972; John's Secret Treasure, 1975; (with wife) The Eye in the Forest, 1975; The Man with the Silver Eyes, 1976. Mem. Tenn. Archeol. Soc., Tenn. Anthrop. Assn., Archaeol. Soc. N.C., Author's Guild, Blue Key Soc., Lambda Chi Alpha. Home: Signal Mountain, Tenn. Died June 25, 1979.

STEEVER, EDGAR ZELL, 3D, b. Scranton, Pa., Oct. 10, 1882; s. Brig. Gen. Edgar Zell S. (U.S.A.); hon. M.A., Lafayette Coll., Easton, Pa., 1927. Commd. 2d lt. 11th U.S. Inf., June 9, 1904; promoted through grades to capt., July 1, 1916. Detailed as mil. instr., State of Wyo., and developed the "Wyoming Plan" of mil. training, based on inter highschool military competition; transferred to Chicago, and Culver (Ind.) Mil. Acd., 1916, and later to other parts of the country, in same line of work. Largely instrumental in developing R.O.T.C. section military policy of U.S. Served as maj., lt. col. and col. Air Service, U.S.A., World War (resigned, 1919). With Gen. Electric Co. exec. offices, N.Y. City and Schenectady, N.Y., as consultant on labor, 1920-22, supervisor industrial relations, 1922-28 (resigned). Developed first fused quartz window ever made; presented Harriet Lane ward to Johns Hopkins Hosp., 1923, for treatment of children having tuberculosis or rickets; engaged in laboratory study of heart, nerve and rheumaticconditions. Address: Washington, D.C. *

STEEVER, MILLER DIDAMA, educator; b. Scranton, Pa., Mar. 25, 1886; s. Edgar Zell and Julia Beaumont (Collings) S.; Ph.B., Lafayette Coll., 1909; LL.B., Harvard, 1912; m. Dorothy Gladys Ingelhart, July 2, 1912; children—Andrew Beaumont, Edgar Zell, IV. Kirby prof. civil rights and head of dept. of govt. and law Lafayette College, 1921-54, prof. emeritus of civil rights, 1952—; director Kirby Political Sci. Library and Museum. City clerk, Pittsfield, Mass., 1916-19; chmn. Zoning Board of Appeals Talbot County, 1955-60; spl. rep. U.S. Sec. of War, War Dept. cases vs. Brit. French and Italian ministries of munitions Paris and London, 1919-21; counsel U.S. Liquidation Commn., London; mem. U.S. War Dept. Claims Bd. (chmn. standing com.). Mem. Mass., Dist. Columbia, Pennsylvania bars, Phi Beta Kappa (chmn. 1934-40, senator 1940-46), Delta Kappa Epsilon. Republican. Clubs: Cosmos (Washington D.C.); Chesapeake Bay Yacht. Home: St. Michael's Md.*

STEEVES, HARRISON ROSS, educator; b. N.Y.C., Apr. 8, 1881; s. John Francis and Imogene (Upson) S.; A.B., Columbia, 1903, A.M., 1904, Ph.D., 1913, Litt.D., 1972; m. Jessie Hurd, June 16, 1906 (div. 1947); children—Imogene Hurd, Harrison Ross; m. 2d, Edna R. Leake, Jan. 28, 1947. Asst. and instr. English, Columbia, 1905-13, asst. prof., 1913-19, asso. prof., 1919-26; prof. English, 1926-49, now emeritus. Mem. Nat. Conf. on Uniform Entrance Requirements in English (chmn.1925-31); pres. Coll. Conf. on English of Central Atlantic States, 1919- 20. Mem. Phi Beta Kappa, Theta Delta Chi. Author: Learned Societies and English Scholarship, 1913; The Teaching of Literature (with C.C. Fries, J.H. Hanford),1926; Literary Aims and Art, 1927; Good Night, Sheriff (fiction), 1941; Before Jane Austen, 1965. Co-author: A College Program in Action 1946. Editor: Representative Essays in Modern Thought (with F.H. Ristine), 1913; Selected Poems of Wordsworth, 1922; Three Eighteenth Century Romances, 1931; Plays from the Modern Theatre. 1931; Anatole France's Penquin Island, 1933; (with Edna L. Steeves) Wild Sports in the Far West (Friedrich Gerstäcker), 1968. Translator: Maurice Donnay's Lovers, 1931. Contbr. articles on edn., taxation to newspapers, mags., scholarly publs. Home: Kingston RI. *

STEFFEL, VICTOR LAWRENCE, dentist; b. Defiance, Ohio, May 11, 1897; s. Joseph Charles and Mary Elizabeth (Moser) S.; student Defiance Coll.; D.D.S., Ohio State U., 1926; m. Marie Isabelle Mekus, Oct. 3, 1927; 1 son, Thomas Victor. Staff mem. Columbus State Hosp., 1925-26; instr. prosthetics Ohio State U., 1926-42, asst. prof., 1942-43, asso. prof., 1943-48, prof., 1948-67, prof., chmn. partial denture div., 1945-62; engaged pvt. practice; mem. grad. dental faculty Walter Reed Army Hosp., Washington, 1952-64; hosp. staff Wright-Patterson AFB, Ohio, 1966-67. Civilian cons. prosthodontics VA Hosp., Chillicothe. Served with USN, 1918-19; to lt. USNR, 1930-40. Recipient Centennial Achievement award Ohio State U., 1970, Silver Pilgrim Medal award Defiance Coll., 1977; honored by state senate, 1975. Fellow Acad. Internat. Dentistry, Acad. Denture Prosthetics (acad. council 1957-66, pres. 1963-64), Am. Coll. Dentists, Internat. Coll. Dentists; mem. Am. Prosthodontic Soc. (pres. 1954-55, exec. dir.-treas. 1955-74; ann. Steffel lectures established 1974), Am. (del. ann. meeting), Ohio (pres. 1955-56), Australian dental assns., Am. Assn. Cleft Palate Rehab., Fedn. Dentaire Internationale, Fedn. Prosthodontic Orgns. (pres. 1973), Pierre Fauchard Acad., Nat. Bd. Dental Examiners (pres. 1954-55), Am. Assn. Dental Schs., Am. Legion, AAAS, Am. Equilibration Soc., Psi Omega (supreme council 1957-65, supreme grand master 1961-62), Omicron Kappa Upsilon. Roman Catholic. Clubs: Faculty, Scioto Country, University, Optimist, Torch (Columbus, Ohio). Co-author: McCracken's Removable Partial Prosthodontics Textbook, 1967, latest rev. edit., 1977. Contbr. articles to profl. jours. Home: Columbus, Ohio. Died May 22, 1978; buried St. Michael's Ridge Catholic Cemetery, Defiance County, Ohio.

STEIGER, G(EORGE) NYE, historian; b. Laurel, Md., Oct. 24, 1883; s. Walter Henry and Grace Houston (Nye) S.; A.B., Occidental Coll., Los Angeles, 1906; A.M., Harvard, 1914, Ph.D., 1923; m. Susan LePage Cronmiller, July 24, 1914. Prof. history, St. John's U., Shanghai, 1906-19; successively instr. in history, asst. prof., asso. prof. and prof. history Simmons Coll., Boston, 1921-50, emeritus, chmn. div. social scis. 1942-50, dean grad. div. 1946-50; visiting prof. Western Reserve U., summer 1928 and year 1929-30, Boston U. summer 1926 and extension courses, 1930-31; visiting lecturer Harvard, 1942 and 1943-45, Wellesley Coll., 1944; prof. diplomatic history Fletcher Sch. Law and Diplomacy, Medford, Mass., 1946-50. Participated sessions of Williamstown Inst. of Politics, World Peace Foundation and Inst. Pacific Relations; joined group making effort to stop shipment of war supplies to Japan, 1938-41. Mem. Am. Hist. Assn.; Am. Oriental Soc., Am. Assn. Univ. Profs., Foreign Policy Assn., Inst. Pacific Relations (mem. bd. trustees). Author: A History of the Orient (with H. Otley Beyer and C. Benitez), 1926; China and the Occident, Origin and Development of the Boxer Movement, 1927; A History of the Far East, 1936. Contbr. articles to professional jours. Home: Laurel, Md.*

STEIGER, WILLIAM ALBERT, congressman; b. Oshkosh, Wis., May 15, 1938; s. Carl Emil and Ruth (Storms) S.; B.S., U. Wis., 1960; m. Janet Dempsey, Aug. 10, 1963; 1 son, William Raymond. Pres., Steiger-Rathke Devel. Co., Oshkosh, 1963-66; mem. Wis. Assembly from 1st dist. Winnebago County, 1960-66; mem. 90th to 95th Congresses, 6th Dist. Wis.; mem. ho. com. on ways and means. Nat. chmn. Coll. Young Republicans, 1959-61; del. Rep. Nat. Conv., 1968, 1972, 76; chmn. rule 29 com. Rep. Nat. Com., 1973-76. Mem. corp. Joslin Diabetes Found.; trustee People-to-People Internat. Named One of Five Outstanding Young Men in Wis., Wis. Jr. C. of C., 1964; One of 10 Outstanding Young Men in Am., 1968. Mem. Chi Psi. Episcopalian. Home: Oshkosh, Wis. Died Dec. 4, 1978.

STEIN, CLARENCE S., architect; b. Rochester, N.Y., June 19, 1882; s. Leo and Rose (Rosenblatt) S.; student Columbia U. Sch. Architecture, Ecole des Beaux Arts, Paris, 1908-11; m. Aline MacMahon, Mar. 27, 1928. Archtl. practice, office Bertram G. Goodhue, 1911-18; sec. com. on housing, reconstrn. com. State of N.Y., 1920, chmn. commn. housing and regional planning, 1923-26; pres. Civic Films, Inc., 1938-58; archtl. works include bldgs. Calif. Inst. Tech., 1927, Wichita (Kans.) Art Inst., 1935, Temple Emanuel, N.Y.C., 1929; chief architect and planner Sunnyside Gardens, Queens, N.Y.C., 1924, Radburn, N.J., 1928, Phipps Garden Apts., Queens, 1931, Hillside Homes, Bronx, 1935; planning dir., coordinator new indsl. municipality, Kitimat, B.C., Can., 1951; archtl. planning cons. communities, Greenbelt, Md., Greendale, Wis., Greenhills, O., 1935-38, Baldwin Hills Village, Los Angeles, 1941. Cons. U.S. Housing Authority, Resettlement Adminstrn., Fed. Works Agy., Fed. Pub. Housing Authority, N.Y. State Div. Housing; lectr. community architecture Harvard, U. Calif., U. N.C., Columbia, Mass. Inst. Tech. Recipient gold medal apt. house award N.Y. chpt. A.I.A., 1940, award for distinguished work low-cost housing, 1941; award for pioneering toward new towns for Am., Am. Soc. Planning Ofcls., 1955; gold medal of honor A.I.A., 1956; Distinguished Service award, Am. Inst. Planners, 1958; Ebenezer Howard Meml. medal, 1960; Dist. Service award, N.Y. Home Builders Assn., 1965; Andrew J. Thomas award, New York chpt. A.I.A., 1967; 50th Anniversary award, A.I.A., 1967. Fellow A.I.A.; mem. Am. Inst. Planners, Am. Soc. Planning Ofcls., Regional Devel. Council Am. (pres. from 1948), Regional Planning Assn. Am. (pres. 1925-48), Internat. Garden Cities and Town Planning Fedn. (v.p. 1924), Community Planning Assn. Can.; hon. mem. Soc. Mexican Architects. Author: Towards New Towns for America, 1951. Asso. editor Jour. A.I.A., 1921-23, Town Planning Review, 1951-59. Author articles on planned community development, art mus. planning. Home: New York, N.Y. Died Feb. 7, 1975.

STEIN, JACK MADISON, educator; b. Newark, Apr. 25, 1914; s. Floyd Sweden and Florence (Sandt) S.; B.A., Rutgers U., 1934, M.A., 1936; Ph.D., Northwestern U., 1944; M.A. (hon.), Harvard, 1958; m. Isabel Smith, May 27, 1938; children—Judith, Jane. Instr. German, Northwestern U., Evanston, Ill., 1944-46; instr. Columbia U., N.Y.C., 1946-48, asst. prof., 1948-55, deptl. rep., 1949-58, asso. prof., 1955-58; prof. German, Harvard, Cambridge, Mass., 1958-76, chmn. dept. Germanic lang. and lit., 1965-73, 75-76, coordinator Germanic lang. courses, 1958-66, 73-75. Adv. editor German textbooks W.W. Norton Co.; mem. adv. com. on fgn. langs. Mass. Bd. Edn., 1963-76. Pres. Boston Musica Viva, 1970-76. Guggenheim award, 1954, 62; Fulbright sr. research grantee, 1954. Mem. AAUP, MLA, Am. Assn. Tchrs. German, Am. Council on Teaching Fgn. Langs., N.A.A.C.P., New Eng. Goethe Soc. (dir. 1964-76), Ams. for Dem. Action, ACLU, Common Cause. Democrat. Author: (with Henry Hatfield) Schnitzler-Kafka-Mann, 1953; (with Reginald Phelps) The German Heritage, 3d edit., 1970; The German Scientific Heritage, 1962; Richard Wagner and Synthesis of the Arts, 1960; Poem and Music in the German Lied from Gluck to Hugo Wolf, 1971. Home: Arlington, Mass. Died Oct. 2, 1976.

STEIN, JULES, entertainment bus. exec., physician; b. South Bend, Ind., Apr. 26, 1896; s. Louis M. and Rosa (Cohen) S.; student Winona (Ind.) Acad., summers 1911-12, U. W.Va., 1912-13; Ph.B. U. Chgo., 1915; M.D. Rush Med. Coll., Chgo., 1921; postgrad. Eye Clinic, U. Vienna, Austria, 1922; L.H.D., U. Louisville, 1966; LL.D., U. Calif. at Los Angeles, 1968; D.Sc., Med. Coll. Wis., 1975; m. Doris Jones, Nov. 16, 1928; children—Jean Babette, Susan Rosa. Resident staff Cook County Hosp., Chgo, 1921-23; ophthalmologist asst. to Dr. Harry Gradle, Chgo., 1923-25; founded MCA Inc. (Music Corp. Am.), 1924, pres. corp. and affiliated cos., 1924-46, chmn. bd. 1946-73, founder, 1973-81. Bus. mgr. Hollywood Canteen, 1942-45, chmn. Hollywood Canteen Found., 1945-66, pres., 1966-81. co-founder, chmn. Research to Prevent Blindness; mem. nat. adv. eye council NIH 1969-71. Served as 1st lt. Med. Officer Res. Corps., AUS, 1923-28. Named asso. Knight Order of Hosp. of St. John Jerusalem, Pioneer of Yr., Found. Motion Picture Pioneers, 1978; recipient Migel award Am. Found. for Blind, 1963; Humanitarian award Variety Clubs Internat., 1968; hon. Alumnus award U. Calif. at Los Angeles Alumni Assn., 1972; Albert Lasker Pub. Service award, 1975; Humanitarian award Lions Internat., 1976; Jean Hersholt Humanitarian award Acad. Motion Picture Arts and Scis., 1976; Walt Disney Humanitarian award Nat. Assn. Theatre Owners, 1976. Former fellow Am. Bd. Ophthalmology; hon. fellow Am. Acad. Ophthalmology and Otolaryngology; mem. Assn. for Research in Ophthalmology (hon.). Author: Telescopic Spectacles and Magnifiers as Aids to Poor Vision, 1924. Home: Beverly Hills, Calif. Died Apr. 29, 1981.

STEIN, WILLIAM HOWARD, biochemist; b. N.Y.C. June 25, 1911; s. Fred M. and Beatrice (Borg) S.; grad. Phillips Exeter Acad., 1929; B.S., Harvard, 1933; Ph.D., Columbia, 1938, D.Sc. (hon.), 1973; D.Sc. (hon.), Yeshiva U., 1973; m. Phoebe Hockstader, June 22, 1936; children—William Howard, David F., Robert J. Asst., Rockefeller Inst. Med. Research, N.Y.C., 1938-42, assoc., 1942-49, assoc. mem., 1949-52, mem. staff, 1952; prof. Rockefeller U., from 1954; vis. prof. U. Chgo., 1960, Harvard, 1964. Fellow Am. Swiss Found., 1956; Harvey Lectr., 1957; mem. med. adv. bd. Hebrew U. Hadassah Med. Sch., Israel, 1947-61; Phillips lectr. Haverford Coll., 1962; Philip Schaffer lectr. Washington U., St. Louis, 1965; sci. counselor Nat. Inst. Neurol. Diseases and Blindness. Trustee Montefiore Hosp., N.Y.C., 1947-74. Recipient (with Stanford Moore) Kaj Linderstrom-Lang award, 1972; (with Stanford Moore and Christian B. Anfinsen) Nobel prize in chemistry, 1972; Columbia Grad. Faculty and Alumni Assn. award excellence, 1973. Fellow AAAS; mem. Am. Acad. Arts and Scis., Nat. Acad. Scis., Am. Soc. Biol. Chemists (chmn. editorial com. 1958-61), Am. Chem. Soc. (co-recipient with Stanford Moore Electrophoresis award, Richards medal 1972), U.S. Nat. Com. Biochemistry (chmn. 1965-68), Biochem. Soc. (London), N.Y. Acad. Sci., Harvey Soc., Sigma Xi. Editorial bd. jour. Biol. Chemistry, 1962-64, asso. editor, 1964-68, editor, 1968-71. Contbr. to sci. jours. Home: New York NY. Died Feb. 2, 1980.

STEINBERG, WILLIAM, orch. condr.; b. Cologne, Germany, Aug. 1, 1899 (came to U.S. 1938); s. Julius and Bertha (Matzdorf) S.; student Sch. Higher Mus. Studies, U. Cologne; studied piano with Uzielli, composition with Boelsche, conducting with Abendroth; m. Lotti Stern, Nov. 1934;

children—Sylvia, Arthur, Richard. Condr., Cologne Opera House, 1920; opera dir. German Theatre, Prague, 1925-29; later gen. music dir. Frankfurt Opera House; guest condr. Berlin State Opera House; condr. Ceska Philaharmonic (Prague), Museumgesellschaft (Frankfurt), Palestine Orch.; guest condr. in Am. with Vancouver, Chgo., Mpls., Cleve. symphony orchs., Los Angeles Philharmonic Orch., N.Y. Philharmonic, Phila., San Francisco, Brazilian symphony orchs., Havana Philharmonic; condr. San Francisco Opera, 1944-52; music dir Buffalo Philharmonic Orch., 1945-52; mus. dir., condr. Boston Symphony Orch., 1968-72; music dir. Pitts. Symphony Orch, 1952-76. Recs. with RCA, Capitol, Command Records, Deutsche Grammophon. Home: Atherton, Calif. Died May 16, 1978.

STEINMAN, JOHN FREDERICK, newspaper pub.; b. Lancaster, Pa., Aug. 21, 1884; s. Andrew Jackson and Caroline Morgan (Hale) S.; Ph.B., Yale, 1906; LL.D., Elizabethtown Coll., 1957; m. Blanche Lazo, June 3, 1913; 1 dau., Shirley Lazo (Mrs. Alan N. Sidnam); m. 2d, Shirley Watkins, Nov. 25, 1933. Chmn. bd. Lancaster Newspapers, Inc., pubs. Lancaster New Era, Intelligencer Jour., Sunday News; chmn., dir. Steinman Stas., Intelligencer Printing Co., Gen. Engraving, Inc.; sec., dir. Meeker Co. (Ill.), Meeker Radio, Inc. Trustee Lancaster Gen Hosp. Served as civilian, Washington, World War I. Clubs: Porcupine, Nassau, Lancaster Country, Hamilton (Lancaster, Pa.); St. Elmo (New Haven). Home: Lancaster County PA. *

STEINMETZ, FERDINAND HENRY, botanist, educator; b. Edwardsville, Ill., Aug. 19, 1886; s. John Herman and Sophia Maria (Krome) S.; Diploma, Eastern Ill. State Coll., 1913; B.S.A., U. of Ill., 1915, M.S., U. of Minn., 1921, Ph.D., 1926; Ped. D. (hon.), Eastern Ill. State Coll., 1949; m. Helen Marguerite Horn, Aug. 2, 1916; children—Margaret Olive (Mrs. Ralph A. Mosher), John Ferdinand (killed in action, 1945), Harriet Ann (Mrs. Harold R. Fray, Jr.). High sch. instr., Truman, Minn., 1915-18; asst. prof. agronomy, U. of Minn., 1918-19; instr. and grad. asst., dept. agronomy, U. of Minn., 1919-26; prof. botany, U. of Me., 1927-29; prof. of botany and head dept. botany and entomology since 1929; agent, bur. agr. econ., U.S.D.A., 1924-25, collaborator, 1925-26; asso. agronomist, Me. Agr. Expt. Sta., 1943-45. Fellow A.A.A.S. Mem. Am. Phytopathol. Soc., Am. Plant Physiologists, Bot. Soc. of Am., Am. Soc. Plant Taxonomists, Josselyn Bot. Soc. of Maine (pres. since 1934), Alpha Zeta, Gamma Sigma Delta, Phi Kappa Phi, Sigma Xi. Conglist. Mason. Contbr. numerous articles to tech. jours. and agr. expt. sta. bulls. Home: Orono, Me. *

STEPÁNEK, BEDRICH (FREDERICK), diplomat, lawyer; b. Prague, Bohemia, Feb. 5, 1884; s. Václav and Marie (Kopecká) S.; grad. ácole libre des Sciences Politiques, Paris, 1906; grad. in Oriental langs., Lazarev's Inst., Moscow, 1907; LL.D., Charles U. of Prague, 1908, grad. in philosophy, 1911. Sec. of Revolutionary Czechoslovak Orgn. against Austria-Hungary, 1916-18; temporarily in charge foreign office, Prague, later asst. to Dr. Benes, 1919-20; E.E. and M.P. from Czechoslovakia to U.S., Nov. 27, 1920-June 13, 1923. Studying economic and social conditions in the U.S. Address: San Francisco, Calif. *

STEPHENS, JOHN ALLEN, steel exec.; b. Albany, N.Y., May 1, 1895; s. John A. and Anna (Mangan) S.; B.A., Columbia U., 1917; D.Sc. (hon.), Wesleyan U., 1953; Ph.D. (hon.), St. Martin's College, 1958; m. Mary Elizabeth Lathrop, Feb. 4, 1918; children—Marcia (dec.), Mary Elizabeth (Mrs. W. W. Winfree, Jr.), Nancy Lathrop (Mrs. Wallace H. Kirkpatrick). Asst. sec., treas., dir. Campbell Metal Window Corp., 1922-25; pres. dir., Research, Inc., 1925-28; pres. Celluloid Corp., 1928-31; v.p., dir., Thompson-Starrett Co., 1931-32; pres., dir., Bush Terminal Co., 1932-34; mgr. indsl. relations, Carnegie-Illinois Steel Corp. (Chicago dist.), 1935-38; dir. indsl. relations U.S. Steel Corp. of Del., 1938-43, v.p., dir., 1943-51, v.p. indsl. relations, 1951-58, v.p. advisory capacity, 1958, ret. Mem. adv. com. to mgmt.-labor policy committee War Manpower Commn.; Del., ILO Com. on Iron and Steel, 1947, 49, 52, Geneva, 54, Monterrey, 57; mem. Joint N.A.M.-C. of C. Com. on ILO, 1950-72; cons. to spl. asst. to Pres., and chmn. U.S. Council on Fgn. Econ. Policy, 1958-61; deputy chairman U.S. Steel del. to Soviet Union, 1958; cons. Internat. Cooperation Agy., Washington, 1959, Japan Productivity Center, Tokyo, 1959; mgmt. cons. to Turkey, West Pakistan, India, Thailand, Indonesia, Philippines, Japan, 1961. Member of the dept. ch. and econ. life Nat. Council Chs., 1951-54. Trustee Lake Placid Edn. Found. Commd. 1st lt., F.A., 1917, advanced to maj., 1918. Recipient Outstanding Civilian Service medal Dept. Army, 1961. Mem. U.S. C. of C., Am. Iron and Steel Inst. (chmn. indsl. relations com. 1944-58), Am. Mgmt. Assn. (v.p. charge personnel div. 1947-48, dir. 1949), N.A.M. (mem. indsl. relations com. 1946-72, Acad. Polit. Sci. (life), Charity Orgn. Society N.Y., Beta Gamma Sigma, Delta Kappa Epsilon. Clubs: Allegheny Country (Sewickley, Pa.); Duquesne (Pitts.); Cosmos (Washington); Lake Placid (N.Y.). Home: Sewickley, Pa. Died Oct. 26, 1979.

STEPHENS, RODERICK, industry cons.; born N.Y. City, Nov. 26, 1885; s. Olin James and Elizabeth (Sexton) S.; student Columbia, 1902-04; m. Marguerite Dulon, June 18, 1906 (divorced 1933); children—Olin James, Roderick, Marguerite; m. 2d, Annabel Wilson, Feb. 21, 1933. Began with Olin J. Stephens, Inc., 1904, v.p., 1910-19; v.p. Stephens Fuel Co., Inc., 1919-29, pres. and dir., 1929-36; coordinator Retail Solid Fuel Industry, New York City, 1936-39; pres. Stephens Fuel Co., Inc., 1939-48. Chairman Nat. Retail Solid Fuel Code Authority, NRA, 1933-34; pres. Bronx Bd. of Trade, 1936-39; vice chmn. Triborough Bridge Authority, 1936-46; pres. Roderick Stephens & Assos., 1947-56; exec. asst. Sparkman & Stephens, Inc., N.Y.C., 1956—. Dir. N.Y. chpt. A.R.C., 1940-52; mem. bd. mgrs. Home for Incurables. Mem. N.Y.C. council, State Com. Against Discrimination, 1946-48; chmn. N.Y.C. adv. council N.Y. Commn. Human Rights. Republican. Clubs: Phi Gamma Delta, Cruising Club of America; Royal Ocean Racing (England). Former owner, also member crew, of Dorade, winner Transatlantic race, Newport, Rhode Island, to Plymouth, England, also winner Fastnet Race, England, 1931; winner Class B and All-Amateur Crew prize, Bermuda race, 1930. Home: N.Y.C. *

STEPHENS, WILLIAM EDWARDS, educator, physicist; b. St. Louis, May 29, 1912 s. Eugene and Marie P. (Gelwicks) S.; A.B., Washington U., 1932, M.S., 1934; Ph.D., Calif. Inst. Tech., 1938; m. Helen Elizabeth Burnite, Oct. 27, 1942; children-Richard Burnite, William Massie. Westinghouse Research fellow, East Pittsburgh, 1938-40; lectr. physics U. Pitts., 1938-39; instr. Stanford U., 1940-41; instr. U. Pa., Phila., 1941-42, asst. prof., 1942-46, asso. prof., 1946-48, prof. 1948-80, chmn. dept. physics, 1955-56, 63-68, dean Coll. Arts and Scis., 1968-74. Vis. prof. U. Zurich, 1957, 69; sci. investigator NDRC, 1942-46; vis. fellow Australian Nat. U., 1974, Princeton U., 1975. Fellow Am. Phys. Soc.; mem. AAUP, AAAS, Am. Inst. Physics, Phi Beta Kappa, Sigma Xi. Author: (With G.P. Harnwell) Atomic Physics, 1955. Editor: Nuclear Fission and Atomic Energy, 1950. Home: Philadelphia, Pa. Died July 17, 1980; buried Valley Forge Gardens, King of Prussia, Pa.

STERN, ELLIS EABY, banker; b. Lancaster County, Pa., June 11, 1892; s. John W. and Susan (Williams) S.; student Clark Bus. Coll., Coatesville, Pa.; m. Anne M. Pennegar, July 20, 1921; 1 son, Ellis E. With Central Penn Bank, Parkersburg, Pa., 1957—, vice chmn. bd., 1963-75, dir. Mem. Coatesville Sch. Bd., 1936-54, Chester County Planning Commn., 1951-65. Served with U.S. Army, World War I. Episcopalian. Club: Masons (33 deg.). Home: Coatesville, Pa. Died Dec. 30, 1979; interred Fairview Cemetery, Coatesville.

STERN, HAROLD P., art museum dir.; B.A., U. Mich., 1943, M.A., 1948, Ph.D., 1959. Mem. curatorial staff Freer Gallery Art, Smithsonian Instn., Washington, 1951, asst. dir., 1962-71, dir., 1971-77. Hon. lectr. Japanese art U. Mich. Author: Masterpieces of Korean Art, 1957; Hokusai: Paintings and Drawings in the Freer Gallery of Art, 1960; Master Prints of Japan Ukiyo-e Hanga, 1960; Freer Gallery of Art: Japan, 1971; Rimpa: Masterworks of the Japanese Decorative School, 1971; The Magnificent Three: Lacquer, Netsuke and Tsuba, 1972; Ukiyo-e Painting, Freer Gallery Art, 1973; Birds, Beasts, Blossoms and Bugs: The Nature of Japan, 1976. Research on Chinese art, Japanese painting, ceramics and decorative arts. Home: Washington, D.C. Died Apr. 3, 1977.

STERN, HENRY, investment banker; b. Jochsberg, Germany, Apr. 3, 1885; s. Jacob and Rosa (Feldenheimer) S.; ed. in Germany. Chmn. Stern Brothers & Co., pres.; dir. Stern & Stern Land Co., Inland Mortgage Corp., Continental Oil and Asphalt Co.; dir. Milbank Mfg. Co. Mem. Kansas City C. of C. Clubs: Oakwood Country; Kansas City Athletic; Fulton (Mo.) Country. Home: Fulton, Mo. *

STERN, LAURENCE MARCUS, newspaper editor; b. N.Y.C., June 16, 1929; s. August L. and Masha (Markusfeld) S.; A.B., U. Mo., 1951; student Bklyn. Coll., 1946, New Sch. Social Research, 1949; m. Ann Davis Somers, June 20, 1951 (div.); children—Gunther, Marc, Catherine, Christopher. Editor-writer USIA, 1951-52; mem. staff Washington Post, 1952-79, nat. affairs reporter, 1962-65, nat. editor, 1965-68, asst. mng. editor, 1968-70, chief Saigon bur., 1970-72, diplomatic corr., 1972-77, asst. mng. editor for nat. affairs, 1977-79. Served with AUS, 1946-47. Recipient George Polk Meml. award, 1961, Nat. Headliners award, 1962, Am. Newspaper Guild Front Page award, 1958, 62, Am. Polit. Sci. Assn. award, 1962; Carnegie Endowment for Internat. Peace sr. fellow, 1974-75. Club: Federal City (Washington). Author: The Wrong Horse, 1977; contbr. articles to nat. mags. Inventor game Influence, 1964. Home: Washington, D.C. Died Aug. 11, 1979.

STERN, LEON THOMAS (LEFEVRE), social worker and criminologist; b. Phila., Pa., Feb. 27, 1887; s. Richard Craven LeFevre and Elizabeth Magee Gregg; grad. Pa. Sch. Social Work, 1908, N.Y. Sch. Social Work, 1911, Temple U. Law Sch., 1916-18; A.B., U. Pa., 1923, postgrad. after 1935; m. Elizabeth Gertrude Limburg-Morgan, Sept. 26, 1911 (dec. Jan. 1954); children—Thomas Noel, Richard Stephen. Dir. Yorkville Community, 1910-11; asst. mgr. Immigrants Information Bur., Galveston, Tex., 1911-12; dir. dept. edn. Municipal Ct., Phila., 1914-24, chief probation officer Juvenile Ct., 1924-25; dir., sec. research Pa. Com. Penal Affairs, 1924-49; cons. penal affairs Pa. Citizens Assn., 1929-52; reg. dir. U.S. Atty. Gen.'s Survey of Release Procedures, 1936-37; cons. Prison Industries Reorgn. Adminstrn., 1937-38; cons. Gov's Com. on Penal Instns., 1943; cons. Pa. Joint State Govt. Commn., from 1945, dir. Phila. Commn. on Detention and Commitment, 1951-52; dir. Phila. Adv. Commn. on Commitment, Detention and Discharge of Prisoners, 1952-55; research cons. cons., editor Youth Services Bd., 1956-60. Mem. Gov.'s Com. on Probation, 1934, Phila. Com. on Pub. Affairs from 1918; directed numerous local, state and fgn. surveys in field of prison adminstrn. Sec. Phila. Council Nat. Def., 1917-19. Mem. prison com. Am. Friends Service, from 1943; del. UN congress Crime and Delinquency, Geneva, Switzerland, 1955, Internat. Congress Criminology, London, Eng., 1955. Recipient certificate of award Pa. Assn. Probation and Parole, 1950, Joint State Govt. Commn., Pa., 1945, Pub. Service Inst., Pa., 1947, Nat. Jail Assn., 1951, Citizens Assn., 1953; certificate of award U. Pa. Soc. Social Workers; citation Columbia, 1964, U. Pa., 1964, Am. Correctional Assn., 1964. Mem. Acad. Certified Social Workers, Am. Correctional Assn. (hon. life; hon. chmn. nat. com. on citizen participation), also active com. mem., past officer nat. state and local, profl. assns. Mem. Soc. of Friends. Club: Contemporary. Author numerous works in fields of parole, sociology and prisons, 1923-80, works include: Jails; Yesterday and Today, 1945; In the Shadow of the Jail, 1946; Sixty Five and Over: Care of the Aged in Philadelphia Yearly Meeting of Friends, 1946; The Psychopathic Offender (result of survey), 1952; (with Elizabeth Stern) A Friend at Court, 1923, Capital Punishment, 1952; Survey of French Prisons, 1952; Citizen Participation in Correctional Services, 1953-54. Author of survey reports on cts. and prison mgmt; collaborator book on family history. Contbr. articles to jours. Home: South Dartmouth, Mass. Died Aug. 1, 1980; interred Friends Cemetery, Upper Darby, Pa.

STERN, WILLIAM, past mem. Republican Nat. Com.; b. Fargo, N.D., May 19, 1886; s. Alexander and Bertha (Aurora) S. Pres. Dakota Nat. Bank of Fargo; dir. Northwest Airlines, Inc., Northwestern States Portland Cement Co. Past mem. Rep. Nat. Com. for N.D. Served as 2d lt. World War. Home: Fargo, N.D. *

STERNBERG, VERNON ARTHUR, pub. exec., editor; b. Wausau, Wis., Aug. 12, 1915; s. Herman and Ella (Prahl) S.; B.A., U. Wis., 1941, M.A., 1946, postgrad., 1945-47, 50-53; m. Jean Marie Lees, June 20, 1941; 1 son, Jonathan Vernon. Asst. prof. English, U. N.D., Grand Forks, 1947-50; from asst. to asso. editor U. Wis. Press, Madison, 1953-56; dir., editor So. Ill. U. Press, Carbondale, 1956-79. Served to lt. (j.g.) USNR, 1942-45. Mem. Modern Lang. Assn. Mason (K.T.). Club: Grolier (N.Y.C.). Home: Carbondale, Ill. Died Feb. 26, 1979.

STERNER, RALF LEECH, teacher of voice; b. Lock Haven, Pa., Feb. 26, 1883; s. Henry Clay and Emma (Robinson) S.; ed. schs. and univs. at Hornell, Elmira, Buffalo and Syracuse, N.Y. Began teaching 1901; founder, 1902, and dir. New York Sch. of Music and Arts; trainer of many concert, oratorio and opera singers; in charge of music, various times, in open forums, N.Y. City. Democrat. Presbyn. Contbr. articles on voice culture to Century Opera Weekly, during 1st season of English opera, N.Y. City; formerly editor vocal dept. Cadenza; sp. writer Musical Observer; contbr. Etude, and Musician*

STERRETT, CLIFF (STER'ET), cartoonist; b. Fergus Falls, Minn., Dec. 12, 1883; s. Samuel O. and Virginia (Johnson) S.; ed. pub. schs.; studied art at Chase School of Art, New York; m. Natalie Cocks, May 17, 1906 (dec. 1948); 1 son, Paul Edmond; m. 2d, Susan Revere Winsor, Apr. 30, 1949. Cartoonist, N.Y. Herald, 1904-08, N.Y. Times, 1908-10, Rochester Democrat and Chronicle, 1910-11, N.Y. Telegram, 1911-12, N.Y. Journal since 1912. Episcopalian. Mason. Clubs: Players, Soc. of Illustrators, Dutch Treat. Creator of "Polly and Her Pals." Address: New York, N.Y. *

STERRETT, FRANK WILLIAM, bishop; b. Middleport, N.Y., Jan. 21, 1885; s. William J. and Mary Elizabeth (Spalding) S.; grad. high sch., Middleport, 1901; student Hobart Coll., Geneva, N.Y., 1902-03, U. of Buffalo Law Sch., 1904-05; A.B., U. of Pa., 1908; B.D., Philadelphia (Pa.) Divinity Sch., 1911, D.D., 1924; LL.D., Hobart College, 1924, Lehigh University, 1933; D.D., Lafayette College, 1951; m. Fredrica Lott Haring, June 18, 1910; children—Annie Lott, Margaret

Howe, Frank William. Deacon, 1911, priest, 1912, P.E. Ch.; vicar Grace Chapel, St. Stephen's Parish, Kingston, Pa., 1911-12; asst. St. Stephen's Ch., Wilkes-Barre, Pa., 1912-14; rector St. Stephen's, 1915-23; consecrated bishop coadjutor Diocese of Bethlehem, Nov. 9, 1923; bishop of Bethlehem since Feb. 27, 1928. Mem. bd. trustees Phila. Divinity Sch., Hobart Coll. and Lehigh U.; mem. gen. bd. Nat. Council Churches. Member Phi Delta Phi, Phi Phi Delta. Republican. Mason. Kiwanian. Am. chaplain Newcomen Soc. Home: Bethlehem, Pa. *

STETSON, CHANDLER ALTON, JR., coll. dean, physician; b. Boston, Nov. 3, 1921; s. Chandler Alton and Helen Winthrop (Baker) S.; B.S., Bowdoin Coll., 1941; M.D., Harvard, 1944; m. Betty Jean Dill, Jan. 13, 1948; children—Catherine Lynn, Barbara Jean, Diana, Janet. Intern, Children's Hosp., Boston, 1944-45; vis. investigator Rockefeller Inst. Med. Research, 1948-51; asso. prof. N.Y. U. Coll. Medicine, N.Y.C., 1955-57, prof. pathology, 1957-58, prof., chmn. dept., 1958-72; dean U. Fla. Coll. Medicine, Gainsville, 1972-77, univ. v.p. for health affairs, 1974-77. Cons., VA. Mem. N.Y. Path. Soc. (pres. 1965-67), Am. Assn. U. Pathologists, Am. Assn. Pathologists and Bacteriologists (council mem. 1966-77, pres. 1970), Nat. Bd. Med. Examiners (pathology test com.), Harvey Soc., Am. Assn. Immunologists, Soc. Clin. Investigation, Am. Assn. Exptl. Pathology (mem. council 1967-77, pres. 1971), Soc. Exptl. Biology and Medicine, Alpha Omega Alpha. Home: Gainsville, Fla. Died May 25, 1977.

STETSON, HENRY THOMAS, lawyer; b. Orange, N.J., Feb. 18, 1886; s. Horace and Eva Jane (Adams) S.; LL.B., N.Y. Law Sch., 1907; m. Mary Lindsley, Oct. 31, 1918 (dec. May 1954); m. second, Mary Walsh, December 30, 1959. Admitted to bar, N.Y., 1907, N.J., 1910; practice of law, N.Y.C., 1907—, Orange, N.J., 1910—; dir. The Safety Car Heating & Lighting Co., Inc., 1924-59, firm name changed to Safety Industries, Inc., v.p. atty., 1930-51, pres., 1951-54, chmn. bd., 1954-59; bd. mgrs. Half Dime Savs. Bank, Orange, 1919, v.p., 1942-44, pres., 1944-58, merger into U.S. Savs. Bank of Newark, 1958, mgr., chmn. exec. com., 1958-60, chmn. bd., 1960-61, adv. mgr., 1964—; director of Second National Bank, Orange. Trustee YWCA of the Oranges, Record Ambulance of Orange. Episcopalian. Club: Union League (N.Y.C.). Home: West Orange, N.J. *

STEVENS, ALBERT WILLIAM (STE'VENZ), stratosphere research; b. Belfast, Me., Mar. 13, 1886; s. Andrew Jackson and Nancy (Trimble) S.; B.S., U. of Maine, 1907, M.S., 1909, D.Eng., 1932; D.Sc., S.D. Sch. of Mines, 1935; m. Ruth Fischer, Aug. 5, 1938. Spent several yrs. as elec. and mining engr. in gold fields of Mont., Ida., Calif. and Alaska; experimented with photography and developed an individual technique; enlisted as pvt. in Signal Corps, U.S. Army, 1917; commd. 1st lt. at Cornell U., after taking special courses; attached to photographic sect. in France, 88th Observation Squadron; participated in most major engagements of U.S. troops; capt., chief photographic officer, 1st Army, 1918; after armistice photographed battle fronts and part of France and Germany with 24th Airplane Observation Squadron; assisted making 1st large photographic mosaics in U.S., 1919; joined Rice Expdn. to S. America, 1924, making extensive air maps of the upper Amazon; made photographic survey of large areas of S. America for Nat. Geog. Soc., 1930, getting 1st photograph showing laterally the earth's curvature; obtained 1st photographs of moon's shadow on earth during sun eclipse, 1932; obtained longest distance photograph showing Mt. Shasta's peak 331 miles from camera; made unsuccessful balloon ascension 60,600 ft. into stratosphere, 1934, the balloon exploding; made record ascent of 72,395 ft. with Capt. O.A. Anderson, 1935, flight sponsored by the Nat. Geog. Soc. and U.S. Army A.C.; gathered large amount of scientific data. Mem. Beta Theta Pi. Awarded Purple Heart, Distinguished Flying Cross, with Oak Leaf Cluster. Contbr. tech. articles to Nat. Geog. Mag. Home: San Carlos, Calif. *

STEVENS, AMBROSE E., assn. exec.; b. Savannah, Ga., June 30, 1904; s. F. E. and Marie Stevens; B.S., Princeton, 1925; m. Julia Seaman, July 15, 1946; children—Nancy, Agnese, James. Vice pres. Birdseye div. Gen. Foods Corp., 1927-45; now exec. v.p., gen. mgr. Nat. Cranberry Assn., Hanson, Mass., also exec. v.p. Ocean Spray Cranberries, Inc., Hanson, Mass.; exec. counselor, cons. mktg. and mgmt. to pvt. industry, 1963-78. Home: Duxbury, Mass. Died Sept. 26, 1978.

STEVENS, DAVID HARRISON, educator; b. Berlin, Wis., Dec. 20, 1884; s. William Waters and Katherine (McCoy) S.; A.B. Lawrence U., Appleton, Wis., 1906, A.M., 1910, LL.D., 1931; A.M., Harvard U., 1912; Ph.D., U. Chgo., 1914; m. Ruth Frances Davis, Mar. 26, 1915 (dec. Dec. 8, 1973); children—John, Anne Elizabeth, Barbara. Tchr., Latin and English high sch., Merrill, Wis., 1906-07; instr. English, Northwestern U., Evanston, Ill., 1908-11, registrar Coll. Liberal Arts, 1910-11; instr. English, U. Chgo., 1914-18, asst. prof., 1919-23, dean Coll. Arts, Lit. and Sci., 1920-22, asso. prof. 1923-25, prof., 1925-30, asst. to pres., 1926-29, asso. dean faculties, 1929-30; v.p. Gen. Edn. Bd., 1930-38; dir. div. humanities Rockefeller Found., 1932-50, research asso. Huntington Library, 1951-52; curator Wis. Hist. Soc. Lectr., English lit. U. Helsinki (Finland), 1964; adviser Chgo. Mayor's Com. Econ. and Cultural Devel., 1965; adviser programs in humanities here and abroad; mem. com. Inter-Am. artistic and intellectual relations Office Coordinator Inter-Am. Affairs, 1940-44; mem. Edn. Mission to Japan, U.S. Army, 1946. Pres., Ephraim Found., 1952-54; trustee Lawrence U., 1949-60. Served as capt. M.I. Div., U.S. Army, Washington, 1918-19. Recipient citation for aid to humanities Wis. Acad. Scis., Arts and Letters, 1974. Mem. Modern Lang. Assn., ALA (hon. life mem., chmn. Ephraim library bd. 1957-67), Phi Beta Kappa. Presbyterian. Author: Party Politics and English Journalism, 1702-1742, 1916, 2d. edit., 1967; The Home Guide to Good Reading, 1920; Types of English Drama, 1923; The Stevens Handbook of Punctuation, 1923; College Composition, 1927; Milton Papers, 1927, 2d edit., 1968; A Reference Guide to Milton from 1800 to the Present Day, 1929, 2d edit., 1967; The Changing Humanities: an Appraisal of Old Values and New Uses, 1953 (transl. into Korean by USTA), 2d edit., 1969; contbr. articles to modern lang. jours., current mags.; adviser, writer survey reports on higher edn. for instns. and founds; compiler: American Patriotic Prose and Verse (with Ruth D. Stevens), 1917; editor Ten Talents in the American Theatre, 1957, 2d edit., 1976. Home: Ephraim, Wis., also La Jolla, Calif. Died Jan. 29, 1980.

STEVENS, ERNEST JAMES, hotel mgr.; b. Colchester, Ill., Feb. 13, 1884; s. James William and Jessie Louise (Smith) S.; Ph.B., U. of Chicago, 1904; LL.B., Northwestern U., 1907; m. Elizabeth Street, of Michigan City, Ind., Apr. 17, 1907; children—Ernest, Richard James, Wm. K., John Paul. With Ill. Life Ins. Co., 1904-07; admitted to Ill. bar, 1907; pres. and mgr. Hotel La Salle Co.; pres. Stevens Hotel Co.; dir. Ill. Life Ins. Co., Charles A. Stevens & Bros., Stevens Brothers Corpn., Congress Trust & Savings Bank. Mem. Chicago Bar Assn., Psi Upsilon, Phi Delta Phi. Republican. Presbyn. Mason. Clubs: Union League, Quadrangle, Chicago Athletic. South Shore Country, Chikaming Country. Home: Chicago and Lakeside, Mich. *

STEVENS, JOHN PETERS, JR., business exec.; b. Fanwood, N.J., 1897; grad. Yale, 1919, Harvard Law Sch., 1922. Chmn. bd., dir. J. P. Stevens & Co., N.Y.C.; trustee The Hanover Bank; director Asso. Dry Goods Corp., Am. Brake Shoe Co. Pres., Edison (N.J.) Bd. Edn., 1942-59; gen. chmn. Greater N.Y. chpt. ARC, 1944; chmn. bd. trustees Phillips Acad., 1966-68; founding trustee Outward Bound; trustee Columbia-Presbyn. Med. Center, Am. Mus. Natural History, N.Y. Public Library. Home: South Plainfield, N.J. Died Nov. 14, 1976.

STEVENS, RICHARD KINGSMAN, lawyer; b. Washington, Aug. 5, 1896; s. Edward A. and Annie (Barr) S.; LL.B., M.P.L., Nat. U., 1920; J.D., M.P.L., George Washington U., 1920; m. Idell Leonell Macfarland, July 24, 1918 (dec. Apr. 1973); children—Lucinda, Mae. Admitted to D.C. bar, 1922; mgr. Washington office firm Pennie, Davis, Marvin & Edmonds, 1921-30; partner firm Stevens, Davis, Miller & Mosher, Washington, 1933-73. Chmn. bd. Modern Labs. Inc. Md., 1958-73. Served with U.S. Army, 1918. Mem. Am., D.C. bar assns., Am. Patent Law Assn. (past mem. bd.). Republican. Mem. Christian Ch. (chmn. bd. from 1950). Home: Washington, D.C. Died 1973.

STEVENSON, ARCHIBALD EWING, lawyer; b. Uniontown, Pa., Sept. 23, 1884; s. John J. and Mary (Ewing) S.; B.S., New York U., 1904; C.E., 1905; LL.B., New York Law Sch., 1909; m. Katharine DeLaVergne, of N.Y. City, Apr. 27, 1910. Instr. mineralogy, New York U., 1905; in charge dept. geology, same univ., 1909; gen. law practice until 1917; chmn. com. on aliens, Mayor's Com. of Nat. Defense, 1917; spl. agt. Bur. of Investigation, U.S. Dept. Justice, studying enemy propaganda, 1918; Mil. Intel. Div., U.S.A., 1918-19; counsel to joint legislative com. of N.Y., investigating seditious activities, 1919-20; counsel to judiciary com., N.Y. Assembly, investigating qualifications of five Socialist assemblymen. Mem. Assn. Bar City of N.Y., Seismol. Soc. America, Soc. Colonial Wars, S.R., Delta Phi. Republican. Presbyn. Clubs: Union League, Bankers, Ox Ridge Hunt. One of authors of "Revolutionary Radicalism" (rept. of Joint Legislative Com. of N.Y., investigating seditious activities), 4 vols. Chmn. com. on free speech, press and assemblage of Nat. Civic Federation. Home: New York. *

STEVENSON, CHARLES ROYAL, management engr.; b. Bradford, Pa., June 8, 1880; s. Charles Porter and Louise (Wade) S.; B.S., Harvard, 1902; m. Agnes R. Collins, Aug. 31, 1902 (divorced 1926); 1 dau., Patricia (Mrs. H. B. Strong); m. 2d, Julia McKenna, Nov. 22, 1926. Asst. metall. engr. Homestead Steel Works, 1903; supt. U.S. Steel Casting Co., 1904; partner Miller, Franklin & Stevenson, management engrs., 1904-10; gen. mgr. Thomas Motor Car Co., 1910-11; asst. to pres. Dodge Mfg. Co., 1912-15; pres. Stevenson, Jordan & Harrison, Inc., N.Y.C., 1916-58, chmn. bd., 1958—; dir. Catalin Corp. Am., The Murray Corp. Am., Marshall-Wells Co. Trustee George Jr. Republic, Freeville, N.Y. Clubs: Harvard, St. Nicholas, Regency, Whist, Links, Buffalo, Port Jefferson Yacht, Seawanhaka-Corinthian Yacht. Home: N.Y.C. *

STEVENSON, E(LIAS) ROBERT, newspaper editor; b. New Haven, Conn., Aug. 29, 1882; s. Elias Gilbert and Mary Ann (Tighe) S.; B.A., Yale, 1907; m. Alice Louise Armbruster, June 30, 1909 (dec. 1950); children—Robert Irving, Sylvia Virginia; m. 2d Margaret Doreen Edwards, May 26, 1951. Began as reporter New Haven Palladium, 1903; reporter New Haven Register and New Haven Journal Courier, 1903-07; instr. in English, Ga. Sch. of Tech., Atlanta, 1907-08; teacher English, high sch., Hartford, Conn., 1908-09; reporter Springfield (Mass.) Republican, 1909-12, feature writer, 1912-14, city editor, 1914-17; editor Waterbury (Conn.) Republican, 1917-22, mng. editor same also of Waterbury American, 1922-27, editor in chief both newspapers, 1927-49. Member Connecticut Safety Commission, American Society of Newspaper Editors, Waterbury Chamber Commerce, Mattatuck History Society. Episcopalian. Mason. Clubs: Waterbury, Rotary, University, Green Mountain, Waterbury Country. Author: The Damnation of Sandy MacGregor, 1911; Connecticut History Makers (3 vols.), 1929; At the Tables Down at Mory's, 1955; The Springfield (Mass.) Republican. Contbr. series travel articles to newspapers; short stories to mags. Home: Southbury, Conn. Died July 1978.

STEVENSON, JOHN A(LBERT), mycologist; born Woonsocket, S.D., July 16, 1890; s. Thomas Jefferson and Adda Alice (Westcott) S.; B.S., U. of Minn., 1912; grad. study George Washington U., 1921-24; m. Katherine Genevieve Thompson, Sept. 23, 1914; children—John A. Jr., Robert J., Donald T. Asst. in botany U. of Minn., 1912-13, Asst. plant pathologist Agr. Expt. Sta., Rio Piedras, Puerto Rico, 1913-14, pathologist, 1914-16; chief, dept. botany and plant pathology, librarian, editor, Insular Exptl. Sta., Rio Piedras, Puerto Rico, 1916-18; path. inspector Fed. Hort. Bd., 1918-19, chief path. inspector, 1920-25; botanist in charge Foreign Agrl. Explorations, Bureau Plant Industry, U.S. Department Agr., 1925-27, mycologist in charge, mycological collections, 1927-45, prin. mycologist in charge, div. of mycol. and disease survey, Bureau Plant Industry, 1945-53; prin. mycologist in charge sect. plant disease epidemiology and curator national fungus collections Agricultural Research Service, 1953-60. Official delegate 7th International Botanical Congress, Stockholm, 1950, 8th congress, Paris, 1954, 9th Montreal, 1959. Cons. Puerto Rican Fruit Growers Assn., 1917-18; hon. curator of fungi Smithsonian Instn. Recipient Cert. of Merit, Bot. Soc. Am., 1956; Superior Servicer award U.S. Dept. Agr., 1959; Outstanding Achievement award U. Minn., 1975. Fellow A.A.A.S.; mem. Mycol. Soc. of Am. (mem. bd. editors 1931-44; councilor 1945; vice pres. 1946, pres. 1947; councilor 1948), Bot. Soc. of Am., Am. Phytopath. Soc., Wash. Acad. Science, Bot. Soc. Wash. (archivist), British Mycol. Soc., Soc. Mycol. de France, Sigma Xi, Alpha Zeta. Mason; mem. Order Eastern Star. Torrey Bot. Club. Author: Manual of Foreign Plant Diseases, 1926; An Account of Fungus Exsiccati, 1971; Fungi of Puerto Rico and the American Virgin Islands, 1975; also series of papers on mycology and plant pathology since 1914. Editor, Jour. Wash. Acad. Sciences, 1933-35. Home: Falls Church, Va. Died Oct. 30, 1979; buried Parklawn Cemetery, Rockville, Md.

STEVENSON, STUART RIDDLE, securities broker; b. Schenectady, Nov. 14, 1896; s. S. Russell and Mary (Kennedy) S.; Litt.B., Princeton, 1918; m. Irene Davis, June 5, 1920 (dec. 1960); children—Stuart D., Kennedy, Langdon R.; m. 2d, Katherine McKee Hand, Feb. 11, 1966. With Smith & Galatin, mems. N.Y. Stock Exchange, 1919-21, Hornblower & Weeks, 1921-30; partner Montgomery Scott & Co., mems. N.Y. Stock Exchange, 1930-38, Stevenson & Bartram, N.Y.C., mems. N.Y. Stock Exchange, 1938-72, Janney Montgomery Scott, Inc., 1972-75; dir., mem. exec. com. Am. Re-Ins. Co. Served as ensign USNRF, 1917-19. Clubs: Ardsley Country (Ardsley-on-Hudson): Lunch (N.Y.C.). Home: Ardsley-on-Hudson, N.Y. Died Feb. 18, 1975.

STEVENSON, THOMAS KENNEDY, business exec.; b. Chambersburg, Pa., Nov. 10, 1883; s. Dr. Alexander Russell and Mary Margaret (Kennedy) S.; ed. Hill School, 1901; B.C.E., Princeton University, 1905; married Candace Thurber, May 21, 1912; 1 dau., Caroline Stuart (Mrs. William T. Pullman). With Am. Locomotive Co., Schenectady, N.Y., 1905-10; asst. treas. Duplex Metals Co., 1910-14; distributing dept. Western Electric Co., 1914, sales mgr., St. Louis, 1916-18, special work on sales to govt., 1918, sales statistics, 1919-21, asst. comptroller, 1921-27, personnel dir., 1927-28, comptroller of mfrs., 1928-38, pres. Elec. Research Products, Inc. (Western Electric Co. subsidiary), 1938-41; v.p. and dir. Western Electric Co., 1941-48; pres., dir. Westrex Corp., 1941-48; dir., chmn. exec. com. Griscom-Russell Company 1949—; dir. Fundamental Investors, Inc., Diversified Investment Fund, Inc., Manhattan Bond Fund, Inc., Diversified Growth Stock Fund, Inc. Mem. Council Fgn. Relations. Clubs: University, Union League, Down

Town Association, Union (N.Y.C.). Home: N.Y.C. *

STEWART, ALEXANDER COUTTS, textile co. exec.; b. Bklyn., May 1, 1924; s. Donald Barton and Jean (Coutts) S.; grad. Hotchkiss Sch., 1942; B.A., Yale, 1945; m. Lucy Ann Rockefeller, June 11, 1955; children—Alexander Coutts, Lee Rockefeller, Seth Thayer. Sec., Nylok Corp., Paramus, N.J., 1949-66; treas. Collins & Altman Corp., N.Y.C., 1960-66, v.p. fin., 1966-79, also dir.; dir. Heritage Quilts Corp., Cranston Print Works, N.Y.C., Med. Care Systems, N.Y.C., ViaCom Internat.; mem. N.Y. adv. bd. Arkwright Boston Ins. Co.; mem. Westside adv. bd. Chem. Bank. Active New Canaan United Fund. Trustee Hotchkiss Sch., Lakeville, Conn. Served to lt. USNR, World War II. Decorated Purple Heart. Clubs: Union League, Yale (N.Y.C.); Blind Brook (Purchase, N.Y.). Home: New Canaan, Conn. Died Feb. 6, 1979; buried Stamford, Conn.

STEWART, BRYCE MORRISON, economist; b. Lyn, Ont., Can., Nov. 24, 1883; s. Alexander Watt and Jemima (Morrison) S.; M.A., Queens U., Kingston, Ont., 1911; Ph.D., Columbia, 1926; m. Annabel Murray, Sept. 15, 1914. Research worker and statistician Canadian Dept. Labour, 1914-18, and editor Labour Gazette of Canadian Dept. of Labour, 1917; dir. Employment Service of Canada, 1918-22; pres. Internat. Assn. Pub. Employment Services, 1919-21; in charge adminstrn. employment exchanges and unemployment ins., Amalgamated Clothing Workers of America, 1922-27; staff mem. Indusl. Relations Counselors, Inc., N.Y. City, 1927-30, dir. research since 1930; assistant director since 1934, mem. board of trustees, since 1945; deputy minister of labor, Can., 1940-42 (on leave). Mem. President Hoover's Emergency Com. for Employment, 1930-31; member State adv. council N.Y. State Employment Service, 1930-40; council U.S. Employment Service, 1933-40; dir. unemployment compensation studies for Com. on Econ. Security, 1934; consultant N.Y. State Unemployment Ins. Adminstrn., 1935-37; rep. of Canadian Govt. on governing body Internat. Labor Orgn., 1941-42; v. chmn. Nat. War Labor Bd., Can., 1942; mem. econ. adv. com. Canadian Govt., 1941-42. Trustee Queens U. since 1939. Member American Statistical Association, American Economic Association, Royal Economic Society Gt. Britain, Canadian Polit. Sci. Assn. Author or co-author books relating to field since 1926. Home: Hartsdale, N.Y. *

STEWART, DONALD OGDEN, author, actor; b. Columbus, O., Nov. 30, 1894; s. Gilbert Holland and Clara Landon (Ogden) S.; A.B., Yale, 1916; m. Beatrice Ames, July 24, 1926 (div. Sept. 8, 1938); children—Ames Ogden, Donald Ogden, Jr.; m. 2d, Ella Winter Steffens (widow of Lincoln Steffens), Mar. 4, 1939. Appeared as Nick Potter in Philip Barry's Holiday, produced at Plymouth Theatre, New York, Nov. 1928-June 1929, and on road 1929; appeared as Les Crawford, in own play Rebound, 1930. Served as seaman, q.m. and chief q.m., U.S. Navy, World War I. Mem. Delta Kappa Epsilon. Author several books from 1921, also 3 plays and musical comedy; screen plays include: Life with Father; Without Love; Cass Timberlane; Edward My Son; The Kidders, 1951 (play prod. London 1957, 58, Hamburg 1958). Acad. Award winner for best screenplay, 1941. Home: London, England. Died Aug. 2, 1980.

STEWART, EDWARD ELLSWORTH, corp. exec.; b. Pitts., Nov. 18, 1896; s. James and Sarah Jane (Eickley) S.; student engring., Carnegie Inst. Tech.; m. Claire May Wilbert, Apr. 20, 1948; 1 son, James E. Vice pres. Telling-Belle Vernon, Nat. Dairy co. in Cleve., 1929-34; pres. Rieck-McJunkin Dairy Co., Pitts., 1934-44 (this company and Hydrox Corp., Chgo., had merged to form Nat. Dairy Products Corp., 1923); elected v.p. Nat. Dairy Products Corp., 1944, became dir. (in charge milk, ice cream operations 14 mid-western cos.), 1945, mem. exec. staff, N.Y.C., from 1946, exec. v.p., 1950-52, pres., 1952-57, pres., chmn. bd., 1957-59, chmn., chief exec. officer, 1959-61; mem. board directors Federal Street Fund, Inc., W.Va. Pulp & Paper Co., Irving Trust Co., McKesson & Robbins, N.Y.C., Mchts. Refrigerating Company, Clupak, Incorporated, A.O. Smith Corporation. Member of the corporation Presbyn. Hosp. City of N.Y. Served with U.S.N., 34 mos., World War I. Clubs: Gulf Stream Golf, Gulf Stream Bath and Tennis, Delray Beach Yacht, Ocean (Delray Beach, Fla.); Racquet and Tennis (N.Y.C.). Home: New York, N.Y. Died May 29, 1976.

STEWART, FRANCES ELIZABETH, dietitian; b. Flint, Mich., Jan. 1883; d. Damon and Frances (McQuigg) S.; graduated high sch., Flint, 1900; grad. Normal Domestic Science Course, Pratt Inst., Brooklyn, N.Y., 1903; studied U. of Chicago, Northwestern U., Chicago Normal Sch. Cooking teacher, 7th and 8th grades pub. schs., Chicago, 1903-05; critic teacher, Chicago Normal Sch., 1905-08; cooking teacher, Phillips High Sch., 1908-15, Tuley High Sch., 1916-19, Lindblom High Sch., since Sept. 1, 1919, all of Chicago. Republican. Conglist. Author: Food Economy, 1918; Diet for Adults, 1919; Diet for Children, 1919; Diet for Invalids, 1920. Home: Chicago, Ill. *

STEWART, GEORGE RIPPEY, writer, educator; b. Sewickley, Pa., May 31, 1895; s. George Rippey and Ella May (Wilson) S.; A.B., Princeton, 1917; M.A., U. Cal., 1920, L.H.D., 1963; Ph.D., Columbia, 1922; m. Theodosia Burton, May 17, 1924; children—Jill, John Harris. Mem. dept. English, U. Cal., 1920, Columbia, 1921, U. Mich., 1922-23; Dept. of English, U. Cal., from 1923, prof., 1942-62, emeritus; author books, from 1922. Fulbright prof. Am. lit., civilization U. Athens, 1952-53; resident fellow in creative writing Princeton, 1942-43; tchr. summers U. Mich., 1926, Duke, 1939; editor U. Cal., Div. War Research, 1944. Chmn. adv. com. Cal. Place-Names Project, 1944-47; collaborator U.S. Forest Service, 1945-46. Served in U.S. Army, 1917-19. Civilian technician U.S. Navy, 1944. Recipient Lit. award Commonwealth Club of Cal. (silver medal 1936, gold medal 1938), recipient Centennial citation U. Cal., 1968, Sidney Hillman award, 1969. Berkeley fellow, 1968. Fellow Cal. Hist. Soc. (Henry R. Wagner award 1973); mem. Modern Lang. Assn., Am. Names Soc., Phi Beta Kappa. Club: Bohemian (San Francisco). Author: Bret Harte, 1931; Ordeal by Hunger, 1936; Storm, 1941; Names on Land, 1945; Fire, 1948; Earth Abides, 1949; U.S. 40, 1952; American Ways of Life, 1954; The California Trail, 1962; Committee of Vigilance, 1851, 1964; Good Lives, 1967; Not So Rich As You Think, 1968; American Place-Names, 1970; Names on the Globe, 1975; American Given Names, 1979. others. Collaborator: The Year of the Oath, 1950. Home: San Francisco, Calif. Died Aug. 22, 1980.

STEWART, JAMES BOLTON, American foreign service; b. Philadelphia, Pa., Nov. 27, 1882; s. James and Sarah Jane S.; student Central High Sch., and Temple U.; m. Harriotte Stearns Goddard, Oct. 1920; 1 dau., Mary Stewart Aid. Hydrographic engring. with U.S. Reclamation Service and U.S. Geol. Survey, 1905-15; apptd. v. consul, at Pernambuco, Brazil, July 14, 1915; consul at Chihuahua, Mexico, Jan. 10, 1918-Sept. 18, 1922, at Tampico, Mexico, 1922-25; insp. Am. Consulates in Can., Mexico and West Indies, 1925-28; mem. exec. com. Foreign Service Personnel Bd. 1928-29; dir. Foreign Service Officers' Training School, 1928-33; consul. general, April 10, 1931; assigned to Budapest, June 22, 1933; apptd. counselor of Legation, Budapest, Oct. 1935; Am. Consul Gen. Mexico, D.F. May 1, 1937; Am. Consul Gen., Zürich, Mar. 5, 1940; Am. minister to Nicaragua, Mar. 5, 1942; Am. ambassador to Nicaragua, Mar. 6, 1943-Jan. 31, 1945 (retired). Mem. Denver Com. on Fgn. Relations. Mem. Am. Fgn. Service Assn. Presbyterian. Regular contbr. to Am. Fgn. Service Jour. Home: Lakewood, Colo. *

STEWART, O(LUS) J(ESSE), univ. prof.; b. Freeport, O., Jan. 27, 1884; s. John Thomas Hart and Ruth (Williams) S.; A.B., Ohio State U., 1910; M.S., Purdue U., 1912; Ph.D., Harvard, 1929; m. Ruth Powers, Dec. 25, 1914; 1 dau., Margaret (Mrs. James Randolph Simpson). Mem. faculty U. of N.H., 1914-19; with U. of Ky. since 1919, now prof. chemistry. Mem. Am. Chem. Soc., Sigma Xi, Sigma Nu. Patent on frosting glass with lithium research in matter, energy, motion. Home: Lexington, Ky. *

STEWART, ROBERT BURGESS, educator; b. Matewan, W.Va., Nov. 30, 1908; s. William Henry and Elmira (Stewart) S.; student Morehead State U., 1928-30; A.B., U. Ky., 1931, A.M., 1932, LL.D., 1962; M.A.L.D., Fletcher Sch. Law and Diplomacy, 1937; Ph.D., Harvard, 1938; Litt.B., Marshall U., W.Va., 1963; m. Charlotte Kibbe Fuller, Dec. 27, 1941; children—Robert Fuller, Jay Randolph. Instr. govt. Harvard, 1937-38; Brit. commonwealth specialist div. European affairs, asst. chief div. Brit. Commonwealth affairs Dept. State, Washington, 1938-45; mem. staff U.S. delegation Internat. Civil Aviation Conf., Chgo., 1944; asst. exec. sec. San Francisco Conf., 1945; dean, prof. internat. relations Fletcher Sch., Tufts U., Medford, Mass., 1945-65, prof., 1965-74, prof., dean emeritus, 1974-80; vis. lectr. govt. Harvard, 1947; cons. Dept. State, 1950, 64-68. Pub. mem. Fgn. Service Selections Bd., 1950, 64. Carnegie fellow internat. law for study in Europe, 1936-37. Mem. Am. Acad. Arts and Scis., Am. Polit. Sci. Assn., Am. Soc. Internat. Law, Phi Beta Kappa, Pi Sigma Alpha. Unitarian. Author: Treaty Relations of the British Commonwealth of Nations, 1939. Bd. editors Internat. Orgns., 1947-50. Home: East Orleans, Mass. Died June 8, 1980.

STEWART, SARAH ELIZABETH, research scientist, educator; b. Tecatillan, Jalisco, Mexico, Aug. 16, 1906 (father U.S. citizen); d. Arthur J. and Maria-Concha (Andrade) S.; B.S., N.Mex. State U., 1927, LL.D. (hon.), 1962; M.S., U. Mass., 1930; Ph.D., U. Chgo., 1939; M.D., Georgetown U., 1949, D.Sc. (hon.), 1972. Bacteriologist, Colo. Expt. Sta., 1930-33; research fellow U. Colo. Sch. Medicine, 1933-35; bacteriologist USPHS, Washington, 1935-44, intern USPHS Hosp., S.I., N.Y., 1949-50, head human virus studies sect. Nat. Cancer Inst., 1951-70; prof. pathology Georgetown U. Sch. Medicine, Washington, 1970-74; med. dir. Commd. Corps, USPHS. Recipient Lenghi award Accademia Nazionale Dei Lincei, 1963; Lucy Wortham James award James Ewing Soc., 1964; Med. Men. of Georgetown U. award, 1964; Fed. Woman's award, 1965; Heart award in medicine Phila. Variety Club, 1964; John Carroll award Georgetown U., 1975. Mem. Am. Assn. Cancer Research, A.A.A.S., Soc. Exptl. Biology and Medicine, Washington Acad. Sci., Med. Women's Assn., Sigma Xi, Alpha Omega Alpha. Home: New Smyrna Beach, Fla. Died Nov. 27, 1976; buried Rock Creek Cemetery, Washington.

STICHTER, WAYNE EDWIN, lawyer; b. Bradford, Ohio, Jan 22, 1901; s. George Jacob and Martha Olive (Bell) S.; A.B. cum laude, Ohio State U., 1922, J.D. summa cum laude, 1924; m. Irene L. Mason, Aug. 25, 1925; children—Richard Duane, Don Mason, John Alan, Philip Wayne. Admitted to Ohio bar, 1924, partner firm Eastman, Stichter, Smith & Bergman, Toledo. Part time instr. U. Toledo Law Sch., 1925-40; sec., dir. Sheller-Globe Corp. Chmn. advancement com. and ct. honor Toledo Area council Boy Scouts Am., 1942-47; v.p. Scottish Rite Masonic Mus. of Our Nat. Heritage. Served as signalman USN, 1917-19. Fellow Am. Coll. Trial Lawyers (bd. regents 1952-58, pres. 1955-56), Am. Bar Found.; mem. Assn. Bar City N.Y., Internat., Am (chmn. trial tactics com. ins. law sect. 1954-57, mem. council ins. law sect. 1957-65, chmn. 1963-64), Ohio (chmn. ins. law sect. Ohio 1941-42, chmn. negligence law com. 1949-50), Lucas County, Toledo bar assns., Internat. Assn. Ins. Counsel (exec. com. 1946-52, pres. 1950-51), Am. Judicature Soc., AMA (affiliate mem.), Def. Research Inst., Ohio Med. Assn. (hon.) Newcomen Soc. N.Am., Nat., Ohio, Maumee Valley hist. socs., Toledo Mus. Art, Toledo C. of C., High Twelve, Order of Coif, Torch Club Internat., Am. Legion, Phi Beta Kappa, Delta Theta Phi. Presbyn. Republican. Mason (33 deg., dep. for Ohio, grand lt. commander Supreme Council); mem. Internat. Order DeMolay (Legion of Honor). Clubs: Inverness, Toledo. Contbr. articles to profl. jours. Home: Toledo, Ohio. Died Mar. 22, 1977.

STICKLER, WILLIAM HUGH, educator; b. Cincinnati, Iowa, Jan. 16, 1910; s. Christopher Andrew and Adra Anna (Conger) S.; B.S. magna cum laude, Parsons Coll., 1931; M.S., U. Iowa, 1934; Ed.D. (Lydia C. Roberts fellow), Columbia, 1941; m. Margaret Louise Winter, Dec. 27, 1934; children—Ann Jayleen (Mrs. A.S. Potter), Sindy Lynne (Mrs. Donald R. Lumpkin). Instr. pub. schs., Clear Lake, Iowa, 1931-36; instr. sci. div. of schs., Panama, C.Z., 1936-42; prin. Cristobal High Sch., extension dir. C.Z. Jr. Coll., 1942-43; prof. sci. Stephens Coll., 1943-47; asst. dept. supt. Tenn. Eastman Corp. (Manhattan Project), Oak Ridge, 1943-45; cons. Office Naval Research, 1946; asso. dean in charge gen. edn. Fla. State U. Coll. Arts and Scis., 1947-52, dir. instl. research and service, 1952-63, prof., head dept. higher edn., 1958-70, prof. higher edn., 1970-75. Cons. higher edn. Dept. State, Germany, 1951. Recipient Disting. Prof. of Yr. award Fla. Assn. Colls. and Univs., 1975. Mem. Assn. Profs. Higher Edn. (pres. 1972-73), Iowa Acad. Sci., A.A.A.S., Lambda Chi Alpha, Phi Kappa Phi, Kappa Delta Pi, Phi Delta Kappa. Democrat. Presbyn. Author: General Education: A University Program in Action, 1950; Organization and Administration of General Education, 1951; The Year Round Calendar in Operation, 1963; Experimental Colleges, 1964; (with Maurice L. Litton) College Teachers and College Teaching, 1967. Contbr. articles to sci., ednl. publs. Trip down headwaters of Amazon River by raft, 1938. Home: Tallahassee, Fla. Died Feb. 6, 1975; interred North Page Cemetery, Villisca, Iowa.

STIEMKE, ROBERT EDWARD, engr., educator; b. Milw., Mar. 10, 1915; s. Edward Frederick and Anna (Knappert) S.; B.S., U. Wis., 1936, M.S., 1940, C.E., 1953; m. Jeanne Lenore Johnson, July 2, 1938; children—Edward George, Gwenda Jeanne, Paul Robert. Research asst. hydraulics U. Wis., 1939-40; instr. civil engring. Wayne U., engr. san. engring. design Hubbell, Roth & Clark, Inc., Detroit, 1940-42; asso. prof. san. engring. N.C. State Coll., 1942-44, 45-47, in charge N.C. State Engring. Expt. Sta., 1942-44; san. engr. USPHS, 1944-45; cons. san. engr., 1945-47; prof. san. engring. Pa. State Coll., 1947-50; dir. Ga. Inst. Tech. Sch. Civil Engring., Atlanta, 1950-61, dir. engring. expt. sta., 1961-63, asso. dean faculties, adminstr. research, 1963-66, acting dean engring., 1966, v.p. programs, 1966-69, exec. asst. to pres., 1969-70, prof. civil engring., 1970-79. Civilian adviser san. engring. edn. USPHS; mem. Nat. Adv. Com. on Pub. Health Tng.; chmn. Task Force on Environmental Health State of Ga.; rep. Univ. Space Research Assn.; mem. Ga. Gov.'s Sci. Adv. Bd., Ga. Gov.'s Commn. on Energy, 1973-79. Served as engr.-insp. C.E., U.S. Army, 1936-39; san. engr. dir. USPHS Res. Registered profl. engr., Ga. Mem. Am. Acad. Environmental Engrs., Inter-Am. Assn. San. Engring., Soc. Am. Mil. Engrs., Am. Soc. Engring. Edn., Am. Soc. C.E., Am. Water Works Assn., Water Pollution Control Fedn., Nat. Soc. Profl. Engrs. (bd. ethical rev. 1970-79), Sigma Xi, Omicron Delta Kappa, Chi Epsilon, Phi Kappa Phi. Presbyn. (deacon). Contbr. articles to profl. jours. Home: Atlanta, Ga. Died Mar. 27, 1979.

STIFEL, ARTHUR C., ret. textile finisher; b. Wheeling, W.Va., Dec. 11, 1882; s. Wm. F. and Emma (Schandein) S.; student Cornell U., 1899-1901, Phila.

Textile Sch., 1901-04; m. Adelaide Flaccus, Mar. 25, 1906; children—Wm. Flaccus, Arthur C., Joan A. Asso. with J. L. Stifel & Sons Inc., finishers cotton and mixed fibre fabrics, Wheeling, W.Va., 1903-57, pres., 1941-48, chmn., 1948-57, ret.; dir. Fostoria Glass Co., Wheeling, W.Va., 1930—. Wheeling Steel Corp., 1930—, Wheeling Tile Co., 1933—. Sterling Drug Co., Inc., N.Y. Trustee Ohio Valley Gen. Hosp. Mem. Beta Theta Pi. Republican. Episcopalian. Clubs: Ft. Henry, Wheeling Country (Wheeling); Duquesne (Pitts.). Home: Wheeling, W.Va. Retired. *

STIGER, CARL BLINN (STI'GER), judge; b. Toledo, Ia., Feb. 21, 1-83; s. Horry Jefferson and Carrie Eloise (Blinn) S.; Ph.B., Western Coll., Toledo, Ia., 1903; J.D., U. of Chicago, 1912; m. Mary Emeline Dugan, Dec. 25, 1930; children—Larry Hull Dugan, Harry Almon Dugan, Mary Katherine Dugan. Admitted to Ia. bar, and practiced at Toledo, 1913-33; mayor City of Toledo, 1916-18; mem. Ia. House of Reps., 1931-33; judge 17th Judicial Dist. of Ia., 1933-36; assn. justice Ia. Supreme Court since 1936. Served as justice of Supreme Court, 1936-43; apptd. (1943) for 6 yr. term to Ia. Employment Security Commn. Served as pvt., U.S. Army, World War I. Mem. Am. and Ia. State bar assns., Phi Alpha Delta. Democrat. Mason. Club:Lions. Home: Des Moines, Ia. *

STILES, JAMES WASHINGTON, clergyman; b. Flintville, Tenn., Nov. 5, 1886; s. Rufus Washington and Mattie Elizabeth (Knowles) S.; A.B., Bethel Coll. B.D., Vanderbilt University, 1932; married Eula Vashti Duer, May 7, 1923; one son, John William. Ordained ministry Cumberland Presbyterian Church, 1910; pastor successively Rutherford, Dyer, Trimble, South Pittsburgh and Jasper, Tennessee, until 1917, First Church, Hopkinsville, 1917-21; editor Cumberland Presbyterian, 1921; again pastor at Hopkinsville, 1923-27; pastor Grace Cumberland Presbyn. Ch., Nashville, Tenn., 1927-44; instr. in Christian Edn., Cumberland Presbyterian Theol. Sem., 1942-44. Editor in chief Cumberland Presbyterian Sunday School Literature, 1944-47; pastor Kelly's Chapel Cumberland Presbyn. Parish since 1947. Democrat. Odd Fellow. Home: Whitwell, Tenn. *

STILL, CLYFFORD, artist; b. Grandin, N.D., Nov. 30, 1904; B.A., Spokane U., 1933; M.A., Wash. State Coll.; D.F.A., Md. Inst., Balt., 1967; D.F.A. (hon.), N.D. State U., 1972, San Francisco Art Inst., 1976. Mem. faculty Wash. State Coll., 1935-41, Richmond Profl. Inst. Coll. of William and Mary, 1943-45, Calif. Sch. Fine Arts, 1946-50, (originated) Subject of the Artist, N.Y.C., 1947-48, l). Pa., 1963, Hunter Coll., 1951, Bklyn. Coll., 1952; mem. Yaddo, 1934, 35; exhibited in one-man shows at San Francisco Mus. Art, 1943, Palace of Legion of Honor, San Francisco, 1947 Betty Parsons Gallery, N.Y., 1947, 50, 51, Metart Gallery, San Francisco, 1950, Art of This Century, N.Y.C., 1946, Albright Art Gallery Buffalo, 1959, U. Pa., 1963, Marlborough Gallery, N.Y., 1969, Met. Mus. Art, N.Y.C., 1979, others; exhibited in group shows 15 Americans, Mus. Modern Art, N.Y., 1952, The New Am. Painting, Europe, 1958-69, Documenta II, Kassel, 1959, others; represented in permanent collections Balt. Mus. Art, Albright-Knox Gallery, Buffalo, Kunsthalle Mus., Basel, Switzerland, Mus. Modern Art, N.Y.C., Whitney Mus. Art, N.Y.C., Tate Gallery, London, San Francisco Mus. Modern Art, numerous others. Mem. Am. Acad. Arts and Letters (Gold medal award of merit for painting 1972). Donor paintings to San Francisco Mus. Modern Art, 1975. Address: New Windsor, Md. Died June 23, 1980; interred Mausoleum, Pipe Creek Cemetery, New Windsor.

STILLMAN, CLARA GRUENING, writer; b. New York, N.Y., Apr. 9, 1882; d. Emil and Phebe (Fridenberg) Gruening; ed. Institut des Essarts-Boblet, Paris, France, 1894-96, Miss Gerrish's Sch., Englewood, N.J., 1896-68, Park Av. Sch., N.Y. City, 1898-99, Barnard Coll., 1899-1903 (A.B.); grad. study at Columbia and New York U.; m. Louis S. Stillman, 1907 (now deceased). Substitute teacher, New York high schs., 1904-05; teacher, Miss Jacobi's Sch., N.Y. City, 1905-07; teacher of history of edn., Brooklyn (N.Y.) Coll., 1934-35; wrote column "Then and Now" for Sunday Mag. of Brooklyn Daily Eagle, 1936-37; contbr. articles, reviews to newspapers and mags. Has been active in woman suffrage, child labor, birth control, advancement of Negroes and other social movements. Mem. Com. for Cultural Freedom. Formerly mem. Socialist party. Club: Town Hall (New York). Author: Samuel Butler. A Mid-Victorian Modern, 1932. Home: New York, N.Y. *

STILLMAN, EDWIN A., mfr. hydraulic machinery; b. Brooklyn, N.Y., Nov. 13, 1886; s. Francis Hill and Irene A. (Bancroft) S.; M.E., Cornell U., 1908; m. Louise Huff, Feb. 16, 1920; children—Mary Louise, William Rogers, Nancy. Began with the Watson Stillman Co., 1908, pres. from 1912. Mem. Delta Phi. S.R. Republican. Episcopalian. Clubs: University, Railroad-Machinery, Cornell. Home: New York, N.Y. *

STILLMAN, HENRY, playwright, stage dir.; b. Brooklyn, N.Y., Apr. 10, 1884; s. Harry D. and Jennie (Bennett) S.; ed. Boys' High Sch., Brooklyn; m. Marie Sims, Dec. 8, 1908 (divorced, 1934). Began in theatrical business with David Belasco, New York, 1907; asso. with Daniel Frohman, 1910-11. Harrison Grey Fiske, 1911-15. The Theatre Guild, 1919-21. Producer of "Sun Up" and "The Dunce Boy." Director of "Cobra"; "The Wonderful Visit"; "Nocturne"; "Van Zorn"; Players production of "Milestones"; etc.; dir. dramatic prodns. with National Broadcasting Co. Club: Players. Author: (plays) Lally, 1927; Nightshade, 1920;Nocturne (dramatization), 1925. Address: New York, N.Y. *

STILLWELL, ERLE GULICK, architect; b. Hannibal, Mo., Jan. 20, 1885; s. Amos John and Francis Crooks (Anderson) S.; U.S. Naval Acad., 1904, Univ. of N.C., 1907, Cornell Univ., 1910, Univ. of Pa., 1912; m. Eva Douglas Smith. Architect since 1913; pres. Erle G. Stillwell, Inc.; pres. Six Associates, Inc., Architects-Engrs. Fellow: A.I.A. Mem. N.C. Bd. of Architectural Examination and Registration, North Carolina Chapter of the A.I.A., also Beta Theta Pi, Gargoyle. Mason. Club: Kiwanis (Hendersonville, N.C.) Address: Hendersonville, N.C. *

STILLWELL, HENRY SHELDON, aero. engr., educator; b. Kansas City, Mo., May 15, 1917; s. Henry Sheldon and Maude (Johnson) S.; B.S. in Aero. Engring., U. Minn., 1939, M.S., 1940; m. Jo Lee Graham, Nov. 9, 1940; children—Pamela Jo, Deborah, Henry III, Alan. Aero. draftsman Tipton Aircraft, Kansas City, 1936; draftsman J.D. Akerman, cons., Mpls., 1936-37; engr. Porterfield Aircraft Corp., Kansas City, 1937, chief engr., 1938; engr. Consol. Aircraft Corp., San Diego, 1939; structural engr. Vought-Sikorsky Aircraft, Stratford, Conn., 1940; instr. aero. engring. U. Minn., 1940-42; head aero. engring. dept., U. Kans., 1942-44, U. Ill., 1944-76; aerodynamics cons. Johns Hopkins Applied Physics Lab., 1945-48, USAF, 1950, Aeroproducts div. Gen. Motors Corp., 1951, N.Am. Aviation, 1952, Douglas Aircraft Corp., 1953, Gen. Dynamics Astronautics, 1961-76; cons. mechanics research div. Am. Machine and Foundry; aerodynamicist McDonnell Aircraft Corp., 1955; design specialist Convair, 1956, engring. staff specialist, summer 1960, 61; aerodynamicist Boeing Airplane Co., 1958; Boeing Co. faculty asso. summer 1962; cons. Gen. Dynamics Convair, 1967-76. Faculty rep. to Big-10 Athletic Conf., 1968-76. Bd. dirs. U. Ill. Athletics Assn. Mem. Am. Inst. Aeros. and Astronautics (chmn. ednl. activities com.), Engrs. Council for Profl. Devel. (dir.), Am. Soc. Engring. Edn., Sigma Xi, Sigma Gamma Tau, Sigma Phi Delta, Tau Beta Pi. Rotarian. Home: Champaign, Ill. Died Dec. 15, 1976; interred Mt. Hope Mausoleum, Champaign.

STINE, DAN GISH, physician; b. Hopkinsville, Ky., Oct. 24, 1884; s. Louis Henry and Cora Ellen (Gish) S.; A.B., U. of Missouri, 1907; M.D., Harvard U., 1911; m. Ellen Pearl Wylder, Dec. 23, 1916; 1 dau., Ellen Wylder. Began practice of medicine, 1913; asso. prof., Dept. of Clin. Medicine, U. of Mo., 1916, prof. 1917-30, prof. medicine since 1930; dir. medical services University Hosps., U. of Mo., since 1930; dir. student health service, U. of Mo., since 1937; chief of staff University hosps.; cons. staff Ellis Fischel State Cancer Hosp., 1946; director of university hospitals, Univ. of Missouri. Attending specialist U.S. P.H.S., 1918-20. Mem. council Am. Student Health Assn., 1939-40. Mem. exec. com. Civilian Defense, Columbia, Mo. Chmn. med. adv. bd. Dist. 27, State of Mo. Certificate Am. Bd. of Internal Medicine, 1938; pres. Miss. Valley Med. Soc., 1941-42, mem. bd. dirs., 1935-40, mem. exec. com. since 1942; fellow Am. Coll. of Physicians, Kansas City Acad. Medicine; mem. A.M.A., St. Louis Med. Soc. (hon.), Phi Beta Pi, Phi Beta Kappa, Phi Gamma Delta. Mem. Christian Ch. Mason (32 deg.). Democrat. Club: University (St. Louis). Contbr. to med. periodicals. Retired from teaching. Home: Columbia, Mo. *

STINSON, MALCOLM BEARD, educator; b. Ottumwa, Iowa, May 2, 1907; s. William Stuart and Ina (Beard) S.; A.B., Wittenberg Coll., 1929, LL.D., 1967; M.A., U. Chgo., 1937; Ph.D., U. Minn., 1951; m. Loraine Thomas, June 27, 1936; children—Thomas Malcolm, Wayne Stuart, Craig Dana, Marian Fern. Dir. county relief Wayne County, Mo., 1932-34; dir. research Old Age Assistance div. Ill. Dept. Public Welfare, 1937-39; regional research cons. FSA, Mpls., 1939-45; asso. prof. social work U. Pitts., 1945-49; prof. social work U. Minn., 1951-59; dir. Family Center Project, St. Paul Community Chest, 1953-55; cons. Sch. Social Work U. Lucknow (India), 1956-58; former dean Sch. Social Work, U. So. Calif., then prof. social work. Cons. Sch. Social Work, Ceylon, 1966-67. Mem. Nat. Accrediation Commn. Council Social Work Edn., 1962; chmn. tech. adv. com. Cal. Welfare Study Commn., 1961-62; pres. Pasadena Community Planning Council, 1970-77. Bd. dirs. Spl. Services to Families and Groups, Los Angeles. Mem. Nat. Assn. Social Workers (pres. Los Angeles), Am. Pub. Welfare Assn., AAUP, Internat., Nat. (dir.) confs. social work. Home: Pasadena, Calif. Died Jan. 9, 1977.

STIPE, J(OHN) G(ORDON), univ. exec.; b. Carrollton, Ga., Sept. 26, 1885; s. Henry Nelson and Mary Emeline (Steed) S.; A.B., Emory Coll. (now Emory U.), 1907; honorary LL.D., Mercer University, 1950; Litt.D. (hon.), Birmingham-Southern College, 1952; married Annie Zuleika Dillard, June 11, 1911 (died 1924); children—Lellita, John Gordon, Mary Steed (Mrs. Don Edgar Eyles); m. 2d, Nell Burruss Parker, Sept. 19, 1941. Teacher of mathematics Candler Coll., Havana, Cuba, 1907-10; instr. Romance langs. Emory Coll., 1911-19, registrar Emory Univ., 1919-38, registrar and dir. admissions, 1938-48, also asst. prof. Romance langs., 1919-27, prof. Romance langs., 1927-48, v.p. since 1948, dean faculties, 1948-50. Member Omicron Delta Kappa, Phi Beta Kappa. Methodist. Home: Atlanta, Ga. *

STIPPES, MARVIN CLIFFORD, educator; b. Chgo., Aug. 8, 1922; s. John and Ella (Hess) S.; B.S., U. Ill., 1943; M.S., U. Wash., 1946; Ph.D., Va. Poly. Inst., 1957; m. Patricia Kovatovich, Dec. 14, 1946; 1 son, Geoffrey Brandon. Asst. prof. math. Mont. State Coll., 1948-49; asso. prof. applied mechanics Washington U., St. Louis, 1951-53; mem. faculty U. Ill., Urbana, 1949-51, 53-79, prof. theoretical and applied mechanics, 1959-79. Co-author: Mechanics of Deformable Bodies, 1960. Editor Jour. Elasticity, 1972-79. Contbr. tech. jours. Home: Urbana, Ill. Died Apr. 20, 1979.

STOCKDALE, E(DWARD) L., ret. bus. exec.; b. Antrim, O., 1885; grad. Denison U., 1908. Former president, dir. Universal-Cyclops Steel Corp., Bridgeville, Pa., now hon. chmn. bd., cons., dir.; dir.; Union Nat. Bank (Pitts.). Recipient Denison U. citation. Clubs: Duquesne (Pitts.); Bassett (Washington, Pa.). Home: Ptts. *

STOCKER, CRAWFORD HAWKES, JR., banker, assn. ofcl.; b. Saugus, Mass., Jan 15, 1904; s. Crawford Hawkes and Louisa May (Hawkes) S.; student pub. schs.; m. Edith M. Haines, Sept. 26, 1931; children—David Bruce, Jane Lewis. With Lynn Five Cents Savs. Bank (Mass.), from 1922, pres., 1950-69, chmn. bd., chief exec. officer, 1969-72; dir. Nat. Shawmut Bank of Boston; Middlesex Mut. Fire Ins. Co., Patriot Gen. Life Ins. Co., Patriot Gen. Ins. Co. Bd. mgrs. Lynn Hosp.; v.p., bd. mgrs. Lynn Home for Elderly. Mem. Savs. Banks Assn. Mass (pres. 1952-53), Nat. Assn. Mut. Savs. Banks (pres. 1956-57). Conglist. Mason. Clubs: Tedesco Country (Marblehead, Mass.); Beach (Swampscott). Home: Swampscott, Mass. Deceased.

STOCKER, GEORGE PATRICK, dean of engring.; b. Platteville, Wis., Feb. 9, 1883; s. Frederick William and Mary Katherine (Burns) S.; grad. Platteville (Wis.) Normal Sch., 1902; B.S. in C.E., U. of Wis., 1909; M.S. in Highway Engring., Iowa Agr. and Mech. Coll., Ames, 1924; student Cornell U., 1916-17, U. of Wis., summer 1921; m. Anna Katherine Mengel, Aug. 20, 1913; children—George Francis, James William, Edward Eugene. Pub. school teacher in Wis., 1902-05; asst. prof. civil engring. and mathematics, N.M. Agr. and Mech. Coll., 1909-12, prof. and head civil engring. dept., 1912-16; instr., Cornell U., 1916-17; prof.civil engring. and head dept., Swarthmore (Pa.) Coll., 1917-18. Miss. Agr. and Mech. Coll., Starkville, 1918-19; prof. of civ. engring. and head dept., U. of Ark., 1919-36, dean engring., 1936-48, emeritus. Mem. Soc. for Promotion Elec. Engring., Tau Beta Pi, Omicron Delta Kappa, Phi Kappa Theta. Catholic. Home: Fayetteville, Ark. *

STOCKING, COLLIS, economist; b. Clarendon, Tex., Aug. 25, 1900; s. Jerome D. and Sarah M (Ward) S.; student Clarendon Coll., 1919-20, U. Kans., 1920-21, Columbia, 1921-24, Dijon U., 1924, Sorbonne, 1924-25, U. Pitts., 1925; A.B., Columbia, 1925, M.A., 1926; m. Claudia E. Roberts, Aug. 28, 1929; children—Claudia Diane (Mrs. William K. Callam), Collis Suzanne. Research economist, 7th and 8th fed. dists., Nat. Banking Study, 1924; asst. prof. econs. U. Vt., 1927-28; instr. econs. N.Y. U., 1928-35; lectr. Newark U., 1931-33; spl. investigator, N.R.A., 1934; asst. chief, div. fgn trade, U.S. Dept. of Commerce, 1935-36; chief research and statistics, asst. dir., bur. employment security, Social Security Bd., 1936-41; asst. exec. dir. War Manpower Commn., asso. dir. Bur. Program Planning, 1941-45; asst. dir. U.S. Employment Service, 1945-48; asst. dir program div., N.S.R.B., 1948-51; dir. prodn. div. and moblzn. and expansion goals div. D.P.A., 1951-53; sr. economist and adminstrv. officer of Pres.; Council Econ. Advisers, 1953-61; econ. cons. Dept. of Commerce, 1962; economist, Surveys and Research Corp., statis. advisers to Korea, 1962-63; adviser to govt. of India, 1964-65; dir. Store Radio Co. Social Security Yearbook Adv. com., 1938-40, White House Conf. on Children, 1940, U.S. ednl. com. on vocational tng. for def., 1940-41; U.S. govt. rep., commn. on employment service, Internat. Labor Conf., Geneva, 1947, San Francisco, 1948. Mem. Am. Econ. Assn., Am. Statis. Assn. Clubs: Washington Golf and Country, Cosmos. Protestant. Author: Public Dance Halls and Commercial Recreation, 1924; Economic Principles and Problems (with Walter Spahr and others), 1936; Company Script as a Form of Wage Payment, 1934; U.S. Foreign Trade, 1935. Contbr. to Ency. Social Sci., Social Work Yearbook, Nat. Bur. Econ. Research, Twentieth Century Fund, Am. Econ.

Rev., Law and Contemporary Problems, others. Home: Arlington, Va. Died Sept. 23, 1978.

STOCKLEN, JOSEPH BERNARD, physician, hosp. adminstr.; b. Nelsonville, Ohio, Mar. 26, 1906; s. John Joseph and Gertrude (Jacoby) S.; A.B., Ohio U., 1927; M.D., Western Res. U., 1930; m. Violet Freiler, Dec. 14, 1963. Resident physician Sunny Acres Hosp., Cleve., 1933-37, 40-41, med. supt., 1942-70; intern Met. Gen. Hosp., Cleve., 1937-38, asst. resident physician, 1938-40; pres. med. staff, 1963; acting v.p. community health Cuyahoga County Hosp., Cleve., 1973-75; controller Tb Cuyahoga County, 1942-75, controller chronic illness, 1959-75; asst. clin. prof. medicine emeritus Case-Western Res. U., 1976—, asso. clin. prof. community health emeritus, 1975—. Sec., Forest City Hosp. Assn., 1944-71; bd. examiners nursing home adminstrs. State of Ohio, 1970-75; pres. Mississippi Valley Conf. on Tb, 1959. Trustee, Golden Age Centers, 1974—. Recipient Dearholt medal Mississippi Valley Conf. on Tb, 1957; Will Ross medal Nat. Tb Assn., 1966; Distinguished Service award Acad. Medicine Cleve., 1975; named Med. Alumnus of Yr., Sch. Medicine, Case-Western Res. U., 1973; named to Am. Lung Assn. Hall of Fame, 1980. Fellow Am. Pub. Health Assn.; mem. A.M.A., Ohio Med. Soc., Ohio Tb and Health Assn. (pres. 1945-46, v.p. 1951-52, sec. 1952-79), Am. Thoracic Soc. (pres. 1968-69), Nat. Tb Assn. (v.p. 1970-71), Am. (pres. 1974-75, trustee 1951-75), No. Ohio (pres. 1976-78) lung assns. Contbr. articles to profl. jours. Home: Bedford Heights, Ohio. Died Mar. 3, 1981.

STOCKLY, AYRES J., lawyer; b. Smyrna, Del., Sept. 4, 1886; s. John C. and Lucy E. (Daniel) S.; A.B., U. of Del., 1908; read law under his preceptor, John Biggs, Sr., Wilmington, Del., 1908-11; m. Esther R. Wilson, June 12, 1923; children—Charles Wilson, Ayres Holmes. Admitted to Del. bar, 1911, and since practiced in Wilmington; associated with John Biggs, Sr., 1911-14, with Daniel O. Hastings, 1914-26; partner of Daniel O. Hastings since 1926, present firm Hastings, Stockly & Walz; dir., v.p. Stewart & Donahue, Inc. Mem. censor com. of Supreme Court of Del. until 1950. Mem. Am. Bar Assn. (mem. of asso. and adv. com. on the unauthorized practice of the law), Del. State Bar Assn., New Castle Co. Bar Assn. Independent Democrat. Episcopalian. Club: University (Wilmington). Home: New Castle, Del. *

STOCKTON, RICHARD FINCH, ins. co. exec.; b. Chgo., Sept. 23, 1908; s. Richard Stockton and Helen Beryl (Gove) S.; m. Veronica Myszak, Aug. 30, 1944; children—Stephen Finch, Susan Ann. With State Farm Mut. Automobile Ins. Co., 1939-77, v.p. 1954-70, treas. from 1960, chmn. bd. 1970-77, dir., to 1979; chmn. State Farm Cos. Found.; v.p., treas., dir. State Farm Investment Mgmt. Corp.; dir. State Farm Life Ins. Co., State Farm Life and Accident Assurance Co., State Farm Gen. Ins. Co. Founding mem. Center Internat. Security Studies, Fgn. Policy Research Inst. Served to col. N.G. and AUS, 1925-62; active duty, 1941-46. Decorated Legion of Merit, Army Commendation medal; officer Order British Empire; Order Phoenix (Greece); Silver medal Greek Red Cross. Mem. Am. Mil. Inst., Am. Enterprise Inst., Am. Security Council, Nat. Guard Assn., Res. Officers Assn., Ret. Officers Assn., Mil. Order World Wars, Polish-Am. Hist. Soc., Am. Legion. Episcopalian (past vestryman, synod del.). Elk. Home: Cocoa Beach, Fla. Died June 11, 1979.

STOESSEL, HANS MAX, metal products co. exec.; b. nr. Rosenheim, Germany, Dec. 6, 1910: s. Ernest Ludwig and Mathilde Bertha (Bollinger) S.; came to U.S., 1912, naturalized, 1928; grad. U. Pa., 1937; m. Roberta Carolean Spence, June 5, 1937; children—William, Stephen, Virginia. With E.I. duPont de Nemours & Co., 1929-51, asst. comptroller, 1948-51; treas., sec. Remington Arms Co., Inc., Bridgeport, Conn., 1952-65, v.p., 1965-76, treas., 1965-73, dir. finance, 1973-76; dir. Remington Arms of Can., Ltd. Mem. Am. Mgmt. Assn., Am. Ordnance Assn., Financial Execs. Inst. Clubs: Brooklawn Country (Bridgeport); Seaview Country (Absecon, N.J.); DuPont Country (Wilmington, Del.). Home: Monroe, Conn. Died Feb. 24, 1976.

STOHL, RALPH N., mgmt. cons.; b. Salt Lake City, Jan. 26, 1914; s. Lorenzo Nelson and LaVinna (Ralphs) S.; A.B., U. Utah, 1934; J.D., George Washington U., 1939; m. Phyllis Young Bennion, Jan. 8, 1935; children—Sheila (Mrs. James W. Todd), Anthony, Jeffrey, Shannon, Kristin. With FCA, Salt Lake City, 1933-35, Soil Conservation Service, 1935-40; fiscal mgmt. analyst Office Sec. Agr., 1940-41; dir. adminstrn. Office Civilian Def., 1941-42; dir. field adminstrn. WPB, 1942-44; dir. civilian manpower distbn. Office Sec. Navy, 1946-47; dir. adminstrn. Office Sec. Def., 1947-55; cons. Mass. Inst. Tech., 1956; asst. to exec. v.p. Olin Mathieson Chem. Corp., 1956-57, Washington rep., 1958-61; v.p. Southwest Center for Advanced Studies (now U. Tex. at Dallas), 1961-71, v.p. univ., exec. asst. to pres., 1971; exec. dir. Ferroalloys Assn., 1971-72; dir. exec. secretariat Health Service and Mental Health Adminstrn., Dept. Health, Edn. and Welfare, Rockville, Md., 1972-73; mgmt. cons., 1974-78. Admitted to Utah bar, D.C. bar; atty., counsellor U.S. Ct. Mil. Appeals. Served as lt. USNR, 1944-46. Mem. Am. Bar Assn., A.A.A.S., Sigma Chi. Club: University (Washington). Home: McLean, Va. Died Dec. 27, 1978; cremated.

STOKES, FREDERICK HALLOCK, lawyer; b. Brooklyn, N.Y., Dec. 25, 1892; s. Mark P. and Minnie L. (Thomas) S.; student Cornell U., 1913; LL.B., New York (N.Y.) Law Sch., 1915; LL.D. (honorary), Middlebury College, 1958; m. Gladys M. Purser, Sept. 28, 1918; children—Joan (Mrs. Frederick T. Creigh), Richard, Sally (Mrs. Elwyn Chamberlain), Barbara (Mrs. Francis H. Spitzer). Admitted to N.Y. bar, 1916; employed in law offices, New York, N.Y., 1915-17; employed by predecessor of present firm, Clark, Carr & Ellis, 1920, became partner, 1924, and since engaged in general practice of law; dir. numerous business corps. Served with Ordnance Dept., U.S. Army, 1917-19; disch. with rank of capt. Mem. bd. mgrs. and chmn. of trustees endowment fund Church Charity Foundation of Long Island. Mem. Am. and New York State bar assns., Assn. of Bar City of N.Y. Clubs: Union League Lawyers (N.Y.). Home: Forest Hills, L.I., N.Y. *

STOKES, MICHAEL FRANCIS, ry. official; b. Pittsburgh, Pa., Oct. 11, 1883; s. Daniel and Catherine (McGuire) S.; student pub. and high schs., Chicago, 1890-99, Chicago Bus. College, 1899-1900; m. Ellen Deaderick, Oct. 25, 1910. In employ Ill. Central R.R., in various clerical capacities, 1900-07, chief clk., 1911-13; various clerical positions, including chief clk. to div. supt. and station agent, Mo. Pacific Ry., 1907-11; chief clk. to gen. supt., later trainmaster, Belt Ry. of Chicago, 1913-16; with Belt Ry. of Chicago and C.&W.I. R.R. since 1916, as chief clk., and asst. to pres., 1916-35, sec., 1928-39, treas., 1935-39, pres. and gen. mgr. since 1939. Home: Chicago. *

STOKOWSKI, LEOPOLD (BOLESLAWAWICZ STANISLAW ANTONI), orch. condr.; b. London, Eng., Apr. 18, 1882; s. Boleslaw Kopernik S.; B.Mus., Oxford (Eng.) U.; D.Mus., U. Pa.; LL.D., U. Calif.; studied in France and Germany and Royal Coll., London. Naturalized Am. citizen, 1915. Organist, choirmaster St. James's, Piccadilly, London, 1902-05, St. Bartholomew's, N.Y.C., 1905-08; condr. Cin. Orch., 1909-12, Phila. Orch., 1912-36; organizer, condr. All-Am. Youth Orch., 1940-41; co-condr. NBC Symphony Orch., 1941-43; founder, condr. N.Y.C. Symphony Orch., 1944-45; condr. Hollywood Bowl Symphony Orch., 1945-46, New York Philharmonic Orch., 1947-50; music dir. Houston Symphony Orch., 1955-60; founder, music dir. Am. Symphony Orch., N.Y.C., 1962-72; films include The Big Broadcast of 1937; 100 Men and a Girl, 1937; Fantasia, 1940; Carnegie Hall, 1946. Made recordings of symphonic transcriptions of Bach; has recorded for RCA Victor Co., Columbia Recording Co., Capitol Records, Everest Records, Vanguard Records, others. Author: Music For All of Us, 1943. Address: New York, N.Y. Died Sept. 13, 1977.

STOLL, CLARENCE GRIFFITH (STO), ret. electric company exec.; b. Mount Joy, Pa., Nov. 29, 1883; s. John H. and Sallie Aurelia (Griffith) S.; B.S. in E.E., Pa. State Coll., 1903; m. Carolyn Bowman, Mar. 14, 1907; 1 son, Bruce Bowman; m. 2d, Winifred Broughton, Apr. 14, 1928. Student apprentice Western Electric Co., Chicago, 1903-05; chief of telephone apparatus design, Western Electric Co., New York, 1905-08, engr. of mfg. methods, 1908-12, asst. shop supt., 1912; shop supt. Bell Telephone Mfg. Co., Antwerp, Belgium, 1912-16; with Hawthorne Works of Western Electric Co., Chicago, 1916-26, advancing to works mgr.; v.p. in charge of mfr., 1926-28, v.p. in charge operations, 1928-39, president, 1940-47, now dir.; formerly director Teletype Corp., Bell Telephone Labs., Inc., Western Electric Co., Ltd. of Canada, Northern Electric Co. of Can. Mem. Am. Soc. Mech. Engrs., Phi Sigma Kappa. Democrat. Methodist. Mason. Clubs: University, Bankers (New York); Garden City Golf. Contbr. on tech. subjects. Home: Gloucester, Va.

STOLL, GEORGE ENGMAN, aviation exec.; b. Lexington, Ky., Nov. 2, 1906; s. George James and Tillie (Engman) S.; student Goshen Coll., 1922-26; m. Marjorie Fothergill, Oct. 14, 1937; children—Tom Fothergill, Sheila, Eric. Metallurgist Engman Range Co., Goshen, Ind., 1926-27, Long Mfg. Co., Goshen, 1927-28, The Bendix Corp. (formerly Bendix Aviation Corp.), Products Div., South Bend, Ind., 1929-33, 41, gen. mgr. Owosso (Mich.) Plant, 1943-46, gen. mgr. Bendix Products Div., 1946-49, v.p., 1949-60, exec. v.p., 1960-65, pres., chief operating officer, 1965-80, dir., 1950-80, group exec. charge automotive and midwestern divs., 1952-60; dir. Selas Corp. Am. Mem. Nat. Security Indsl. Assn. (trustee), Soc. Automotive Engrs. Clubs: Detroit Athletic, Economic (Detroit); Bloomfield Open Hunt, Bloomfield Hills Country, Recess. Home: Franklin Village, Mich. Died Apr. 27, 1980.

STOLL, NORMAN RUDOLPH, medical research; b. North Tonawanda, N.Y., Sept. 4, 1892; s. Charles J. and Fredericka (Jenzen) S.; attended Syracuse University, 1910-11; B.S., Mt. Union Coll., 1915, honorary D.Sc., 1941; M.S., U. Mich., 1918; Sc.D., Johns Hopkins Sch. Hygiene and Pub. Health, 1923; m. Estella Margaret Scott, Aug. 23, 1919 (dec. Nov. 1947); children—Henry C., Margaret Edith (Mrs. W.A. Dawson), Louise Martha (Mrs. W.S. Maddux); m. 2d, Helen Kennedy Stevens, Dec. 26, 1951 (dec. Oct. 1975). Tchr. biology high sch., Massilon, Ohio, 1915-17; head dept. biology Central High Sch. and Jr. Coll. (now Wayne U.), Detroit, 1919-21; mem. commn. to investigate hookworm disease, P.R., 1922, China, 1923-24, Panama, 1926; asso. in parasitology Peking (China) Union Med. Coll., 1923-24, asso. in helminthology Johns Hopkins, 1925-26; asso. mem. Rockefeller U. (formerly Rockefeller Inst. for Med. Research), Princeton, N.J., 1927-50, N.Y.C., 1950-62, prof., 1962-63, emeritus prof., 1963-76; Theobald Smith Meml. lectr. N.Y. Soc. Tropical Medicine, 1962; panel systematic biology NSF, 1955-58; Charles Franklin Craig lectr. Am. Soc. Tropical Medicine and Hygiene, 1960; 1st lectr. U. Ga. Faculty Parasitology, Athens, 1972. Mem. expert adv. panel parasitic diseases WHO, 1952-56, 57-61, 62-66, 67-71, 72-73; WHO cons. hookworm, W. Africa, 1961. Served as 2d lt. F.A., U.S. Army, World War I; lt., later lt. comdr. H (S), USNR, with U.S. Naval Med. Research Unit. 2, Guam, World War II. Chmn. editorial com. Jour. Parasitology, 1938-43; mem. Internat. Com. Zool. Nomenclature 1944-67, chmn. editorial com. for revision internat. code zool. nomenclature 1958-61; del. 14th Internat. Congress Zoology, Copenhagen, 1953, 15th, London, 1958. Fellow A.A.A.S., Royal, Am. socs. tropical medicine and hygiene, N.Y. Acad. Scis.; mem. Am. Soc. Parasitology (charter mem., councillor 1933-42, 1952-57, pres. 1946, emeritus 1966, editorial bd. Jour. Parasitology 1944-55), Am. Soc. Zoologists, Am. Soc. Naturalists, N.Y. Soc. Tropical Medicine (charter mem., pres. 1947-48, life), Am. Found. Tropical Medicine (sci. adv. council 1957-69), Royal Soc. Medicine London (affiliate) Brit. (charter), N.J. (charter) socs. for parasitology, World Assn. Advancement Vet. Parasitology (hon.), Helminthol. Soc. Washington (hon.), Sigma Xi (1st pres. Rockefeller U. chpt. 1958), Sigma Nu, Delta Omega, Ubiquiteers. Club: Nassau (Princeton). Author: This Wormy World, 1947. Editorial bd. Exptl. Parasitology, 1951-66. Contbr. to sci. jours. Home: Princeton, N.J. Died Dec. 30, 1976.

STONE, CHARLES BRAGDON, corp. exec.; b. Middletown, Conn., July 1, 1901; s. Berkley Charles and Annie (Bragdon) S; B.S., Wesleyan U., Middletown, 1923; m. Thyra S. Jacobson, Aug. 22, 1925; 1 son, Charles Bragdon. Sales engr. Valley Fuel Oil Heating Co., 1923-25, mgr., 1925-28; mgr. oil heating div. Meech & Stoddard, Inc., 1928-31; pres., dir. C. B. Stone, Inc., 1931-73, treas., 1931-77, chmn. bd. dirs., 1973-77; dir. Hill Devel. Corp.; mem. adv. bd. Riverside Trust Co., 1950-65. Mem. adv. bd. United Bank & Trust Co., 1965-77, chmn. adv. bd., 1974-77. Mem. bd. finance Town of Cromwell, 1955-68. Dir. Middlesex County Mfrs. Assn., 1950-52, pres., 1952; dir. Oil Heat Inst. New Eng., 1955-64, 1st v.p., 1958-60, pres. 1960-62; dir. Conn. Petroleum Assn., 1955-59, New Eng. Fuel Inst., from 1964. Trustee Wesleyan U., Middletown, from 1951, Conn. Valley Hosp., Middletown, 1963-73; corporator Middlesex Meml. Hosp., from 1940. Mem. Alumni Assn. Wesleyan U. (chmn. 1949-51), Psi Upsilon. Clubs: Exchange (pres. Middletown 1948); Madison (Conn.) Beach, Madison Winter; Hartford (Conn.); Home of Meriden. Home: Cromwell, Conn. Died Mar. 29, 1980.

STONE, DEWEY DAVID, business exec.; Brockton, Mass. Aug. 31, 1900; s. Morris L. and Idletta E. Stone; B.B.A., Boston U., 1920, D.L.H., 1950; H.H.D., Boston U., 1958; LL.D., Stonehill Coll.; m. Anne Abrams, June 28, 1923. Sales mgr. Harodite Finishing Co., North Dighton, Mass., 1919, one of prin. owners, 1922-77, pres., from 1952, chmn., to 1977; prin. Ashton Valve Co., Boston, 1945-77, Crosby Steam Valve & Gage Co., 1946-77, T. Noonan Sons Co., 1945-77, Ward Machine Co., Brockton, 1942-77; dir. Palestine Econ. Corp. Chmn bd. Jewish Agy. Israel, 1960-77, Weizmann Inst. Sci., Rohovoth Israel, 1945-77, also hon. fellow; mem. YMHA; chmn. Stone Charitable Found., Brockton, 1945-77, United Israel Appeal; New Eng. chmn. United Jewish Appeal, 1947-77, nat. co-chmn., 1955—; nat. chmn. United Israel Appeal, 1954-77. Trustee Truman Library, Independence, Mo., Boston U. (in honor of being prin. benefactors, new bldg. named Dewey D. and Harry K. Stone Sci. Bldg. 1948, asso. founder 1968), Cardinal Cushing Hosp., Jewish Inst. Religion, N.Y.C., Hebrew Tchrs. Coll., Boston, Am. Friends of Hebrew U., Zionist House, Boston. Served from sgt. to maj. AUS, 1918. Mem. Am. Legion, Jewish War Vets., A.B.C. (dir. Brockton chpt.), World Zionist Orgn. (actions com.), Zionist Orgn. Am., Zeta Beta Tau (Man of Year award 1947). Mason (33); mem. B'nai B'rith. Home: Brockton, Mass. Died Nov. 19, 1977.

STONE, EDWARD DURELL, architect; b. Fayetteville, Ark., Mar. 9, 1902; s. Benjamin Hicks and Ruth (Johnson) S.; student U. Ark., 1920-23, D.F.A., 1951; student Harvard Archtl. Sch., 1925-26, Mass.

Inst. Tech. Archtl. Sch., 1925-27; Ph.D. (hon.), U. Ark., 1951; m. Orlean Vandiver, Dec. 5, 1931 (div.); children—Edward Durell, Jr., Robert Vandiver; m. 2d, Maria Torch, June 24, 1954 (div.); 1 son, Benjamin Hicks, III, Maria Francesca; m. 3d, Violet Campbell La Stella, June 11, 1972; 1 dau., Fiona Campbell. Began as architect, Boston, 1923; archtl. design N.Y. U. Sch. Architecture. Architect residence of Richard M. Mandel, Mt. Kisco, N.Y., estate Henry R. Luce, Charleston, S.C.; asso. archt. Mus. Modern Art, John F. Kennedy Center for Performing Arts, Internat. Coll., Beirut, Lebanon, Hotel el Panama, Panama City, R.P.; architect U. Ark. Med. Center; Social Security Hosp., Lima, Peru, Works include U.S. Embassy, New Delhi, India, Phoenicia Hotel, Beirut, Lebanon, U. Ark. Fine Arts Center, Am. Pavilion, Brussels World's Fair, Stanford Med. Center, Palo Alto, Calif., G.M. Bldg., N.Y., Standard Oil Bldg., Chgo., State U. N.Y. at Albany, Nat. Geog. Bldg., and other pub., coll., univ., corp., pvt. bldgs. Prof. architecture, Yale, 1946-49; instr. advanced design, N.Y. U., 1935-40. Served as maj., Hdqrs. A.A.F., chief planning and design-sect., 1942-45. Awarded Rotch traveling fellowship in architecture, 1927. Awards: Archtl. League medal for domestic architecture, 1937, 53; Archtl. League Gold medal, Silver medal, 1950, Gold medal, N.Y. chpt. A.I.A., 1955, 1st Honor award, 1958, Award of Merit, 1958, Mem. Am. Acad. Arts and Scis., Royal Soc. Arts, Archtl. League of N.Y., A.I.A. (honor award 1967), Nat. Inst. Arts and Letters, N.A.D., Sigma Nu. Methodist. Home: New York, N.Y. Died Aug. 6, 1978.

STONE, FRED DALZELL, mfg. co. exec.; b. Evanston, Ill., Jan. 31, 1934; s. Fred L. and Elizabeth (Sweet) S.; student Princeton, 1952-54; B.S. in Indsl. Engring., Stanford, 1955, M.S. in Indsl. Engring., 1956; postgrad. in bus. Northwestern U., Chgo., 1957-58; m. Elizabeth McCollister, Mar. 28, 1956; children—Mary Elizabeth, Catherine, Charles. Mgr. Peat, Marwick, Mitchell & Co., Chgo., 1958-63; sr. v.p. White, Weld & Co., investment banking firm, Chgo., 1963-75; sr. v.p. finance Quaker Oats Co., Chgo., 1975-79, also dir.; chmn. bd. Wis. Nat. Life Ins. Co., Oshkosh, Waste Mgmt. Inc., Oak Brook, Ill. Mem. Bd. Edn., New Trier Twp., Ill.; treas. or chmn. bd. trustees Glencoe Union Ch., 1972-77. C.P.A., Ill.; chartered fin. analyst. Mem. Am. Inst. C.P.A.'s, Ill. Soc. C.P.A.'s, Fin. Execs. Inst., Am. Inst. Indsl. Engrs., Inst. Chartered Fin. Analysts, Fin. Analysts Soc., Delta Upsilon. Clubs: University, Economic (Chgo.); Princeton of N.Y., Skokie (Ill.) Country. Home: Glencoe, Ill. Died Aug. 22, 1979.

STONE, GREGORY PRENTICE, educator; b. Olean, N.Y., Oct. 28, 1921; s. Horace Prentice and Sarah Grace (Emerson) S.; B.A., Hobart Coll., 1942; certificate Turkish area and lang., Princeton, 1944; M.A., U. Chgo., 1952, Ph.D., 1959; m. Gladys Ishida, June 9, 1962; children—Mead M., Susan L. Instr., U. Ill., Chgo., 1947-49; asst. prof. Mich. State U., 1949-55; instr. U. Minn., 1955-59; vis. lectr. U. Mo., 1958-59; asst. prof. Washington U., St. Louis, 1959-61; mem. faculty U. Minn., 1961-81, prof. sociology, 1963-81; guest lectr. 6th Seminar in Honor of George Herbert Mead, U. Tokyo, 1978; cons. in field. Chmn. research com. Gov. Minn. Task Force Mental Retardation, 1966-68. Served with AUS, 1944-45. Recipient all univ. recognition U. Minn., 1967. Fellow Midwest Sociol. Soc. (bd. dirs. 1968-70), Internat., Am. sociol. assns.; mem. Soc. Study Social Problems, Soc. Study Symbolic Interaction (co-founder, co-chmn. 1974-75, pres. 1976-77), Internat. Com. Sociology of Sport (a founder, Am. rep.), AAAS, ACLU. Co-author: Being Urban, 1977. Editor: Internat. Review of Sport Sociology, 1965-71; sr. editor: Social Psychology Through Symbolic Interaction, 1970; editor: Games, Sport and Power, 1971; co-editor, translator Herman Schmalenbach on Society and Experience, 1977. Home: Hudson, Wis. Died Feb. 16, 1981.

STONE, HARVEY BRINTON, surgeon; b. Baltimore, Md., Nov. 22, 1882; s. John Theodore and Clara May (Brinton) S.; A.B., Johns Hopkins, 1902, M.D., 1906; m. Ethel Hoffman, Aug. 27, 1906; children—Brinton Harvey, Douglas Hoffman, Dorothy Ann (Mrs. George H. Yeager). Interne, Johns Hopkins Hosp., 1906-07; engaged in practice of medicine, Baltimore, Md., since 1910; asso. prof. surgery Johns Hopkins Med. Sch. since 1932. Vice chmn. directing bd., procurement and assignment service, W.M.C., 1941-46, mem. med. com., Md. State Planning Commn., mem. Md. Council for Defense. Mem. A.M.A. (council on med. edn. and hosp.), Am. Surgical Assn. (past pres.), Am. College of Surgeons, Southern Surgical Assn., Johns Hopkins Alumni Assn. (pres. 1942-46). Mem. Md. Commn. on Higher Education, Md. Commn. on Hospital Survey. Clubs: Maryland; Johns Hopkins. Contbr. to med. jours. *

STONE, JACOB CHAUNCEY, securities co. exec.; b. North Adams, Mass., June 15, 1894; s. Lewis and Kate (Bennet) S.; B.A., Williams Coll., 1914; m. Isebel Greenbaum, Apr. 3, 1921; children—Robert L., Donald, James H.; m. 2d, Beatrice Heht Marks, Feb. 27, 1937 (dec. Mar. 1962); stepchildren—Kenneth Marks, Barry A. Marks: m. 3d, Eve A. Finsterwald Oct. 10, 1963; stepchildren—Barbara F. Hess, Patricia Aks. Partner, Asiel & Co., N.E.C., from 1919, now ltd. partner; bd. govs. N.Y. Stock Exchange, 1937-40. Trustee Williams Coll. Served to 1st lt. U.S. Army, 1917-19; to lt. comdr. USNR, 1942-44. Mem. Investment Bankers Assn. Am., Assn. Stock Exchange Firms (past gov.). Clubs: Century Country, Bond, Williams, Harmonie (N.Y.C.). Home: New York, N.Y. Died Mar. 21, 1981.

STONE, L(AWRENCE) JOSEPH, psychologist; b. Washington, May 20, 1912; s. Nahum and Esther Bertha (Levinson) S.; A.B., Cornell U., 1933; A.M., A.M., Columbia, 1934, Ph.D., 1937; m. Beatrice Berlin, June 23, 1933 (dec. Sept. 1962); children—Deborah (Mrs. Nelson), Susannah (Mrs. Eldridge), Miriam (Mrs. Robert Leavitt); m. 2d Jeannette W. Galambos, May 9, 1970. Instr. psychology Columbia, 1935-37, Bklyn, Coll., 1938-39, CCNY, 1940-42; research asso. Sarah Lawrence Coll., 1937-39; research editor dept. child study Vassar Coll., 1939-41, asst. prof., 1941-47, asso. prof., 1947-49, prof., 1949-65, prof. psychology, 1965-75, acting chmn. dept. child study, 1953-55, chmn., 1955-61, chmn. dept. psychology, 1966-70, dir. Vassar film series Studies of Normal Personality Development, 1942-75. Lectr., New Sch. Social Research, 1945-56; producer films on Israeli Kibbutz for Inst. Child Mental Health; dir. Com. for Certification Psychologists N.Y. State, 1954-57, mem. adv. bd. psychology bd. regents SUNY, 1958-66; mem. research career award com. Nat. Inst. Mental Health, 1962-66. Served from lt. to lt. comdr., psychobiol. unit USPHS, 1944-46, sci. dir. USPHS Res. Certified psychologist N.Y. Fullbright Research grantee U. Oslo, Norway, 1957-58; Nat. Inst. Mental Health spl. fellow, 1965; travel grantee Ford Found., Grant Found., 1970-71. Diplomate Clin. Psychology, Am. Bd. Examiners Profl. Psychology. Fellow Am. Psychol. Assn., Am. Orthopsychiat. Assn., Soc. Personality Assessment (past dir.), Soc. Research Child Devel. (past bd. govs.); mem. World Fedn. Mental Health, Eastern Psychol. Assn., Sigma Xi. Author: (with J. Church) Childhood and Adolescence: A Psychology of the Growing Person, 1957, 3d edit., 1973. Co-editor: The Competent Infant: Research and Commentary, 1973. Contbr. articles profl. jours.; many ednl. films. Address: Poughkeepsie, N.Y. Died Dec. 13, 1975.

STONE, MODE LEE, univ. dean; b. Blountstown, Fla., Oct. 11, 1902; s. John Henry and Nancy (Bauldree) S.; B.S. in Math., U. Fla., 1928; M.A., Columbia, 1935; Ph.D., Peabody Coll., 1941; m. Jeanne Compton, Aug. 17, 1942; children—Mary Lois, Mode Lee, Nancy Compton. Prin., Leon High Sch., Tallahassee, 1928-30, supervising prin. pub. schs., 1930-37; curriculum dir. Fla. Dept. Edn., 1937-40, dir. instrn., 1940-42; prof. Fla. State U. Sch. Adminstrn., 1946-51, acting dean Sch. Edn., 1951-53, asso. dean, 1953-56, dean, 1956-67, prof. sch. adminstrn., 1967-73, ret., 1973, dean emeritus, prof. edn., 1973-79. Dir. Nat. Variable Annuities Co. of Fla., First Am. Investment Corp., Sun Fed. Savs. & Loan Assn. Pres. emeritus So. Scholarship and Research Found. Served from lt. to lt. comdr. USNR, 1942-46. Mem. Nat. Council Accreditation Tchr. Edn., Am. Assn. Colls. Tchr. Edn., Nat. Commn. Tchr. Edn. N.E.A., Fla. Edn. Assn. (pres. 1957), Newcomen Soc. N.A., Tallahassee C. of C. Kiwanian. Home: Tallahassee, Fla. Died May 23, 1979; buried Oakland Cemetery, Tallahassee.

STONE, MORTIMER, lawyer; b. Mansfield, Pennsylvania, January 15, 1882; s. Norman Clark and Alice Amelia (Webster) S.; A.B., Colgate University, 1904, D.C.L. (honorary), 1953; student Columbia, 1904-05; LL.B., N.Y. Law Sch., 1910; m. Mary Lydia Hibbs, Aug. 30, 1911 (dec. 1952); children—Ruth Elizabeth (Mrs. William McCreary), Frederick Mortimer, Margaret (Mrs. Loren Swanson), Martha Lucile (Mrs. Frank D. Cooper); married second to Lottie E. Wilkerson, December 24, 1953. Teacher private boys' schools, 1905-09; admitted to Colo. bar, 1910; practiced at Delta, 1910-22, Fort Collins, 1922-44; formerly county atty., Delta County; county attorney, Larimer County, 1938-44. Sec. Selective Service Bd. of Appeal No. 1. Formerly chmn. Colo. Interim Com. on Revenue and Taxation. Rep. candidate for Supreme Court, 1938. Chmn. Rep. State Conv., 1938 and 1942; asso. justice Colo. Supreme Court, 1945-53, chief justice, 1953-55; engaged in pvt. practice law, 1955—; of counsel Yegge, Hall and Shulenburg, 1963—; referee for the National Mediation Board, also a referee Nat. R.R. Adjustment Bd. Mem. Bd. Colo. Woman's Coll. Mem. Colo. Bar Assn. (pres. 1932), Phi Beta Kappa, Alpha Tau Omega, Phi Delta Phi. Rep. Mason (32 deg., K.T.). Elk. Clubs: Mile High (Denver); Lake Shore (Chgo.); Rotary (dist. gov. 1938). Contbr. to law jours., lectr. Home: Denver. *

STONE, PAUL TIBBLES, former coll. dean; b. Lawrence County, O., Oct. 31, 1900; s. Elmer Ellsworth and Ada Louisa (Truesdell) S.; A.B., Ohio Wesleyan U., 1923; M.S., Syracuse U., 1929; student Ohio State U., 1923, Garrett Biblical Inst., 1923-25, Northwestern U., 1925; LL.D., Huntingdon Coll., 1966; m. Lessie Mae Hall, Aug. 18, 1928; 1 son, John Elmer. Teacher sci. Circleville (O.) High Sch., 1923, Hawthorne (Fla.) High Sch., 1925-26; fellow chemistry Syracuse (N.Y.) U., 1926-27, instr., 1927-28; asst. prof. chemistry Huntingdon, Coll., Montgomery, Ala., 1928-29, asso. prof., 1929-33, prof., 1933-69, business mgr., 1930-33, treas., 1933-46, dean coll., 1945-69, sec. bd. trustees, 1942-69. Fellow A.A.A.S.; mem. N.E.A., Nat. Soc. Study Edn., Assn. Higher Edn., Am. Chem. Soc., Assn. Ala. Coll. Adminstrs. (past v.p.), Alpha Chi Sigma, Phi Beta Kappa. Lion (past pres. Montgomery). Club: Knife and Fork (Montgomery, Ala.). Home: Montgomery, Ala. Died Aug. 6, 1975.

STONE, WHITNEY, engring. exec.; b. Boston, Apr. 24, 1908; s. Charles A. and Mary (Leonard) S.; student Harvard; m. Anne Minor, Mar. 12, 1932. Chmn. bd., dir. Stone & Webster, Inc.; dir. Am. Express Co., The Chase Manhattan Bank, Stone & Webster Engring. Corp., Stone & Webster Mgmt. Cons., Inc., Indsl. Gas Supply Corp., Spruce Hills Prodn. Co., Stone & Webster Internat., Inc., Stone & Webster Can., Ltd., Stone & Webster India Corp., San Salvador Devel Co., Inc., Stone & Webster Land Corp. Episcopalian. Clubs: Jockey, Recess, The Links, Knickerbocker (N.Y.C.). Home: New York, N.Y. Died Oct. 21, 1979.

STOODLEY, BARTLETT HICKS, educator; b. Somerville, Mass., July 15, 1907; s. Harry Marr and Laura (Hicks) S.; B.A. cum laude, Dartmouth, 1929; LL.B., Harvard, 1932, M.A., 1947, Ph.D. in Sociology, 1948; m. Helen Virginia Stark, Mar. 16, 1944; children—Bartlett Hicks, Ronald. Admitted to Mass. bar, 1932; practice in Boston, 1932-42; mem. faculty Wellesley Coll., 1947-73, prof. sociology, 1959-73, emeritus, 1973-78. Vis. Fulbright prof. U. Philippines, 1954-55; vis. prof. Chung Chi Coll., Hong Kong, 1962-63, Queen's U., Kingston, Ont., Can., 1973-74, 74-75, Saint Mary's U., Halifax, N.S., Can., 1975-76, U. Western Ont., London, 1977-78. Served to lt. comdr. USNR, 1942-46. Mem. Am., Eastern (exec. bd. 1958-62) sociol. assns., Asia Assn. Author: Concepts of Sigmund Freud, 1958. Editor: Society and Self, 1962. Home: Wiscasset, Maine. Died Dec. 8, 1978.

STOODY, RALPH WAINMAN, ch. ofcl.; b. Rochester, N.Y., Apr. 19, 1896; s. Rev. John Henry and Fannie (Wainman) S.; B.A., Ohio Wesleyan U., 1917; student Garrett Biblical Inst., 1917-18, S.T.B., Boston U., 1920; student Columbia, summer 1930, Harvard, summer 1938; S.T.D., Gordon, Coll., Theology and Missions, 1939; D.D., Ohio Wesleyan U., 1947; Litt. D., Am. U., 1958; m. Lucile Eloise Bennett, March 5, 1918; 1 dau., Rosemary (Mrs. Harry P. Felger). Editorial asso. Epworth Herald, Chicago, 1917-18; ordained to ministry Methodist Ch., 1920; pastor Meth. Ch., South Walpole, Mass., 1919-20, St. Alban's, Vt., 1920-23, St. Johnsbury, Vt., 1923-26, Chestnut St.,Portland, Me., 1926-34, Union Meth. Ch., Fall River, Mass., 1934-40; dir. Commn. on Pub. Relations and Meth. Information, 1940-64; bd. mem. dept. internat. justice and goodwill, and dept. religious radio, Nat. Council Chs.; cons. Ch. of Air, CBS. Mem. World Meth. Conf., 1947, 51, 56, 61; pres. Council of Secs. Methodist Agencies, 1956. Meth. rep. Nat. Council Churches. Served in U.S. Army, with A.E.F., 1918-19. War corr. Mediterranean, North African theaters. 1945; U.S. Army corr. Japan and Korea, 1953. Press corr. World Council of Churches, Amsterdam, Holland, 1948, New Delhi, India, 1961; headed press room World Methodist Conference, 1947, 51, 56, 61. Mem. Am. Coll. Public Relations Assn., Pub. Relations Soc. Am., Nat. Religious Pub. Council (p.p.), Sigma Phi Epsilon, Pi Delta Epsilon, Delta Sigma Rho. Clubs: Advertising, Publicity (N.Y.C.). Broadcast series of religious addresses over radio ABC, NBC networks. Author: Religious Journalism: Whence and Whither (dissertation). Author: Handbook of Church Public Relations, 1959. Contbr. to religious publs. Home: Jackson Heights, N.Y. Died Dec. 30, 1979.

STOPHLET, DONALD VICTOR, univ. adminstr.; b. Oak Park, Ill., Nov. 12, 1918; s. Donald Stirling and Anne (Gilmer) S.; Ph.B., U. Wis., 1941, Ph.M., 1946. Mng. dir. Central City Opera Assn., Central City and Denver, 1948-52; sec. of coll., dir. devel. Rockford (Ill.) Coll., 1952-58; dir. devel. programs U. Pitts., 1958-59; v.p. for devel. Western Res. U., 1959-63; v.p. for devel. affairs Miami (Fla.), 1963-67; v.p. for devel. Fla. Inst. Tech., 1967-80. Served as pilot USAAF, 1943-46. Mem. Am. Coll. Pub. Relations Assn., Am. Alumni Council, Nat. Collegiate Players, Alpha Delta Phi. Home: Melbourne, Fla. Died Sept. 26, 1980.

STORCH, OSCAR T., financial cons.; b. Paterson, N.J., 1900. Vice chmn. 1st Nat. Bank Passaic County, Paterson, N.J. until 1970; financial cons. until 1976. Home: Oakland, N.J. Died Oct. 3, 1976.

STORER, JAMES WILSON (STOR'ER), clergyman; b. Burlington, Kan., Dec. 1, 1884; s. Lewis Burnette and Lydia (Burnett) S.; B.S., William Jewell Coll., Liberty, Mo., 1912, D.D., 1943; D.D., Union U., Jackson, Tenn., 1920; LL.D., Okla. Bapt. U., Shawnee, 1939; m. Nora Isabel Wilbanks, Dec. 31, 1912. Ordained to ministry Bapt. Ch., 1912; pastor, Pauls Valley, Okla., 1913-15, Repley Tenn., 1915-18, Paris, Tenn., 1918-21, Greenwood, Miss., 1921-25, Grove Av. Ch., Richmond, Va., 1925-31, First Bapt. Ch., Tulsa, Okla., 1931-56; exec. sect.-treas. Southern Baptist Found., 1956—. Pres. So. Bapt. Conv., 1953-54. Mem. S.A.R., Sigma Nu, Aeons. Democrat. Mason (32 deg.). Clubs: Hi-Twelve, Tulsa Consistory, Tulsa. Author: Truth Enters Lowly Doors, 1937; By Ways to High Ways, 1938; Major

Messages of the Minor Prophets, 1940; These Historical Scriptures, 1952; The Preacher: His Belief and Behavior, 1953. Collector of Confederate items. Home: Nashville, Tenn. *

STOREY, CHARLES MOORFIELD, lawyer; b. Brookline, Mass., Mar. 4, 1889; s. Moorfield and Anne Gertrude (Cutts) S.; grad. St. Mark's Sch.; A.B., Harvard, 1912, A.M., 1913, LL.B., 1915; m. Susan Jameson Sweetser, June 24, 1913; children—Charles M., Anderson (killed in action, Jan. 17, 1943), Susan Jameson (Mrs. Ronald T. Lyman, Jr.), Gertrude Cutts (Mrs. William M. Bancroft), James Moorfield. Admitted to Mass. bar, 1915; asst. atty., later atty. U.S. Dept. Justice, Washington, 1915-18; asst. commr. Commn. Relating to Prisoners of War, also attache commn. to negotiate peace, U.S. Commn. to Austria-Hungary, Budapest, 1918-19; partner Peabody, Brown Rowley & Storey, Boston, 1920-79; head atty. N.E. regional office WPB, 1942-43; compliance commr. N.E. region, 1943-44; appeal agt. Selective Service, 1941-47, 62-69; cons. (renegotiator) Boston Q.M. price adjustment dist. office U.S. War Dept., 1943-47; chmn. bd. trustees Park Sch. Corp., 1920-30; v.p. Winsor Sch., 1930-32; pres. Mass. Soc. Prevention Cruelty to Children, 1942-49; trustee Mt. Auburn Cemetery, 1932-79; mem. Boston Finance Commn., 1932-35; past chmn.; overseer Harvard, 1945-51. Mem. Am., Mass., Boston (mem. council 1935-36) bar assns., Harvard Alumni Assn. (dir. 1935-37, v.p. 1938), Mass. Hist. Soc., Mass. Soc. Cin. (sec. 1955-72), N.E. Hist. Geneal. Soc. (pres. 1961-63). Clubs: Tavern, Somerset. Home: Chestnut Hill, Mass. Died Mar. 19, 1980; buried Mt. Auburn Cemetery, Cambridge, Mass.

STOREY, ROBERT GERALD, lawyer; b. Greenville, Tex., Dec. 4, 1893; s. Frank Wilson and Mary Edith (Thomson) S.; student U. Tex., 1911-14; LL.D., Tex. Christian U., 1947, Laval U., 1953, Drake U., 1954; D.C.L., Chungang U., Korea, 1961, So. Meth. U., 1965; H.H.D., Rikkyo U., Japan, 1961, U. Ryukyus, 1964; m. Frances Hazel Porter, July 26, 1917 (dec. 1962); children—Robert G. (dec.), Charles P.; m. 2d, Jewel Hope Osborn, 1965 (dec. 1978). Admitted to Tex. bar, 1914; city atty., Troup, Tex., 1914-17; asst. atty. gen. Tex., 1921-23; spl. asst. dist. atty., Dallas, 1924; partner Storey, Armstrong, Steger & Martin, ret.; chmn. bd. emeritus Lakewood Bank & Trust Co.; dean law sch. So. Meth. U., 1947-59; pres. Southwestern Legal Found., 1947-72. Mem. New Hoover Commn. to reorganize exec. br. of govt., 1953-55; spl. rep. of State Dept. to conduct seminars among mems. of legal profession of Friendly Free Nations, 1954-55; vice chmn. U.S. Civil Rights Commn., 1957-63; spl. counsel State Tex. Investigation Pres. Kennedy death, 1963-64; vice chmn. Atlantic-Pacific Interoceanic Canal Study Commn., 1965-81; chmn. for U.S., World Peace Through Law Center, 1966-81. Chmn. bd. fgn. scholarships Fulbright Bd., 1958-62. Served as 1st lt. U.S. Army, 1918-19; col. AUS, World War II. Decorated Legion of Merit, Bronze Star, Medal of Freedom (U.S.); Legion of Honor (France); Second Order of Merit, Japanese Govt.; recipient Linz civic leadership award, Dallas, 1955; Am. Bar Assn. gold medal, 1956. Served as U.S. exec. trial counsel to Justice Robert H. Jackson in Nuremberg trial of major war criminals, 1945-46. Regent U. of Tex., 1924-29; pres. Park Bd., City of Dallas, 1939-42. Mem. Internat. (council 1950-56), Inter-Am., (pres. 1954-56), Am. (bd. govs. 1949-54, chmn. sect. on legal edn. 1947-49, mem. ho. dels., pres. 1952-53, chmn. electoral coll. Commn. 1966-81), Tex. (pres. 1948-49), Dallas (pres. 1934) bar assns., Am. Legion (nat. exec. com. 1920-21), Order of Coif, Phi Beta Kappa, Phi Alpha Delta; hon. mem. Canadian, Peruvian, Mexican, Korean, Cuban, other nat., state bar assns. Mem. Christian Ch. Mason (33 deg., Shriner), Kiwanian (pres. 1927, dist. gov. 1931). Club: Dallas Country. Author: Professional Leadership, 1958; Our Unalienable Rights, 1965; The Final Judgement. Home: Dallas, Tex. Died Jan. 16, 1981.

STOREY, SMITH WILLIAM, orgn. cons.; b. Vernon, Ind., Dec. 27, 1893; s. Smith Willaim and Selena (Carlisle) S.; LL.B., Ind. Univ., 1917; LL.D., 1966; m. Gladys Miller, Feb. 2, 1929; 1 dau., Suzann. Mem. bd. govs. Sigma Chi Found.; bd. dirs. Ind. U. Found.; trustee Indiana Soc. of Chgo. Mem. Phi Delta Phi. Episcopalian. Clubs: Chicago, Garden of the Gods, Mid-Day, Union League, Tavern, Exmoor Country, Mid-America. Home: Kenilworth, Ill. Died 1978.

STORY, HAROLD WILLIS, lawyer, business exec.; b. Milw., June 4, 1890; s. Willis Edson and Alice Louise (Tichenor) S.; A.B., U. Wis., 1912, LL.B., 1915; LL.D. (honorary), U. Wis., 1961; m. Lina N. Duffy, Aug. 7, 1920; 1 son, Richard. Admitted to Wis. bar, 1915, practiced in Milw., 1915-19; with firm Quarles, Spence & Quarles, 1915-17, Lenicheck, Boesel, Wickhem & Story, 1919; with Allis-Chalmers Mfg. Co., 1919-57, atty., 1919-32, gen. atty., 1932-34, v.p., gen. atty. 1934-57; v.p., dir. Allis-Chalmers, Rumely, Ltd., Winnipeg, Man., Can., 1931-57, dir. Canadian Allis-Chalmers, Ltd., 1951-57; pres. Wis. Fund, Inc., 1938-69, chmn., 1969-77. Participated in Pres. Roosevelt's initial conf. on unemployment ins., 1934, in drafting Wis. Employment Relations act, 1939; dir., sec. Unemployment Benefit Advisors, Inc.; mem. legislative adv. com., Wis. Employment Relations Bd.; trustee Citizens Govtl. Research Bur., chmn. bus. gifts com. United Negro Coll. Fund., Milw., 1950; mem. adv. com. Wis. Citizens Pub. Expenditure Survey; bd. dirs. Internat. Inst. Milwaukee County; trustee Allis-Chalmers Found., Inc.; bd. dirs. Milw. Sch. Bd., 1962-77; trustee Nat. Probation and Parole Assn.; chmn. com. equal edn. Bd. Sch. Dirs. Milw. Recipient Caroline McGeogh award League Women Voters, 1958. Mem. Am., Wis., Milw. bar assns., Am. Legion, Wis. State Bd. Pub. Welfare (vice chmn.), World Affairs Council Wis. Service Assn. (dir.), NCCJ (mem. adv. com.), Ducks Unlimited (charter mem., dir. and trustee U.S. and Can. groups, chmn. liaison com.). Clubs: Gyro, Milwaukee Country, University. Home: Milwaukee, Wis. Died Oct. 28, 1977.

STOTT, ROBERT LESLIE, stock broker; b. Bklyn., Feb. 26, 1900; s. Robert Wright and Annie (Leslie) S.; student N.Y. Prep. Sch., 1917-18; m. Mary Lasse, June 28, 1928 (dec.); children—Robert Leslie, Donald Bishop. Clk., Halsted & Harrison, 1918-20, broker for same, 1920-23; joined N.Y. Curb Exchange, 1923, N.Y. Stock Exchange, 1929; former chmn. N.Y. Stock Exchange; partner Wagner, Stott & Co. Clubs: Cedar Creek, National Golf, Links Golf (L.I.); Everglades, Seminole, Bath and Tennis (Fla.). Home: New York, N.Y. Died Dec. 12, 1979.

STOUFFER, KARL J., educator; b. North Baltimore, O., June 19, 1884; s. Josiah and Phoebe Almeda (Osborn) S.; B.S., and A.M., Otterbein Coll., Westerville, O., 1910; grad. work U. of Chicago; m. Nellie Antoinette Smith, of Canton, Ill., Aug. 14, 1914; 1 dau., Alice Janet. Head dept. of science, Wayland Acad., Beaver Dam, Wis., 1910-20; headmaster, Wayland Hall, 1912-20; dean, Elgin Jr. College and principal of the Elgin Academy, 1920-36, supt. Roosevelt Mil. Acad. since 1936. Mem. Nat. Assn. Principals, Pvt. Sch. Assn. of Central States (ex-pres. 1921, 1936), Progressive Education Assn. Republican. Baptist. Mason. Kiwanian. Home: Aledo, Ill. *

STOUT, GEORGE LESLIE, museum cons.; b. Winterset, Iowa, Oct. 5, 1897; s. Abraham Lincoln and Lulu May (McBride) S.; student Grinnell Coll., 1915-17; B.A., U. Iowa, 1919-21; A.M. Harvard, 1926-28; Litt.D., Clark U., 1955; m. Margaret Hayes, June 11, 1924; children—Robert Hayes, Thomas McBride. Instr. dept. graphic and plastic arts State U. Iowa, 1921-24; lectr. U. Pitts., 1925-26; Carnegie fellow Harvard, 1926-28; fellow for research Fogg Mus. Art, Harvard, 1929-33, head dept. conservation, 1933-47; dir. Worcester (Mass.) Art Mus., 1947-54; dir. Isabella Stewart Gardner Mus., Boston, 1955-70. Hon. fellow Internat. Inst. Conservation Historic and Artistic Works. Served with U.S. Army, 1917-19; from lt. to lt. comdr. USNR, 1943-46. Mem Am. Antiquarian Soc., Am. Acad. Arts and Scis., Am. Inst. for Conservation Historic and Artistic Works (hon). Author: (with Rutherford J. Gettens) Painting Materials, A Short Encyclopaedia 1942; The Care of Pictures, 1948; Treasures from the Isabella Stewart Gardner Museum, 1969. Mng. editor Technical Studies in the Field of the Fine Arts, 10 Vols., 1932-42; editor: Color and Light in Painting, Roland Rood, 1941. Contbr. articles to various pubs. Home: Menlo Park, Calif. Died July 1, 1978.

STOUT, PERRY ROBERT, educator; b. Hughson, Calif., Feb. 9, 1909; s. Perry Elliot and Hazel Sophie (Beebe) S.; A.B., U. Calif., Berkley, 1930; Ph.D., 1939; m. Mabel Goldstein, Nov. 24, 1929; children—Robert Walter, Norman David, Carol (Mrs. David S. Duthie), Marilyn (Mrs. Robert Milhous). Analyst agr. expt. sta. U. Calif., Berkeley, 1930-40, jr. chemist, 1940-42; research asso. elec. engring. Mass Inst. Tech., 1942; staff radiation lab. U.S. Bur. Standards, 1944-45; civilian with OSRD, 1945; faculty U. Calif., Berkeley, 1945-75, prof. plant nutrition 1950-54, prof. soil sci., chemist expt. sta., 1954-75, prof. internat. agr., 1968-69, dir. Kearney Found. Soil Sci., 1954-70, chmn. dept. soils and plant nutrition Davis-Berkeley, 1949-64, chmn. dept. soils and plant nutrition. Davis, 1964-66. Ford Found. cons. Inst. Land Reclamation, U. Alexandria, Egypt, 1962-63; cons. U.S. Dept. Agr. AID, India, 1967; cons. desalination research program Oak Ridge Nat. Lab., 1968-75; adv. com. div. biology and medicine U.S. AEC, 1969-75. Fulbright scholar, 1955. Fellow Am. Soc. Agronomy; mem. Am. Soc. Plant Physiologists (Stephen Hales award 1960), Am. Chem. Soc., Soil Sci. Soc. Author: Nuclear Powered Agro-industrial complexes Designed for the Indo-Gangetic Plain. Research properties soil clays, micro nutrient element nutrition of plants, soil, plant, animal interelations, preparation radioactive isoteps for plant and soil research, mass spectrometry and x-ray fluorescent spectroscopy in biol. research. Home: Davis, Calif. Died July 14, 1975.

STOUT, REX TODHUNTER, author; b. Noblesville, Ind., Dec. 1, 1886; s. John Wallace and Lucetta Elizabeth (Todhunter) S.; student pub. schs.; m. Fay Kennedy, Dec. 16, 1916 (div.); m. 2d, Pola Hoffmann, Dec. 21, 1932; children—Barbara, Rebecca. Office boy, store clk., bookeeper, sailor, hotel mgr., inventor sch. thrift system, 1916-27; enlisted USN, 1906, purchased discharge, 1908; master ceremonies, Speaking of Liberty radio program Council for Democracy, 1941; Voice of Freedom radio program Freedom House, 1942; Our Secret Weapon radio program, 1942-43. Chmn., Writers' War Bd., 1941-46; pres. Friends Democracy, 1941-51; pres. Author's Guild, 1943-45; pres. Soc. Prevention World War III, 1943-46; chmn. Writer's Bd. World Govt., 1949-75; pres. Author's League Am., 1951-55, 62-69, v.p., 1956-61; pres. Mystery Writers Am., 1958-75; treas. Freedom House, 1957-75. Author: How Like a God, 1929; Seed on the Wind, 1930; Golden Remedy, 1931; Forest Fire, 1933; Fer-de-Lance, 1934; The President Vanishes, 1934; The League of Frightened Men, 1935; O Careless Love, 1935; The Rubber Band, 1936; The Red Box, 1936; The Hand in the Glove, 1937; Too Many Cooks, 1938; Mr. Cinderella, 1938; Some Buried Caesar, 1939; Mountain Cat, 1939; Over My Dead Body, 1939; Red Threads, 1940; Double for Death, 1940; Bad for Business, 1940; Where There's a Will, 1941; The Broken Vase, 1941; Alphabet Hicks, 1942; Black Orchids, 1942; The Illustrious Dunderheads, 1942; Not Quite Dead Enough, 1944; The Silent Speaker, 1946; Too Many Women, 1947; And Be A Villain, 1948; Trouble in Triplicate, 1949; The Second Confession, 1949; Three Doors to Death, 1950; In the Best Families, 1950; Curtains for Three, 1951; Murder by the Book, 1951; Triple Jeopardy, 1952; Prisoner's Base, 1952; The Golden Spiders, 1953; Three Men Out, 1954; The Black Mountain, 1954; Before Midnight, 1955; Three Witnesses, 1956; Might as Well Be Dead, 1956; Three for the Chair, 1957; If Death Ever Slept, 1957; And Four to Go, 1958; Champagne for One, 1958; Plot It Yourself, 1959; Three at Wolfe's Door, 1960; Too Many Clients, 1960; The Final Deduction, 1961; Homicide Trinity, 1962; Gambit, 1962; The Mother Hunt, 1963; Trio for Blunt Instruments, 1964; A Right to Die, 1964; The Doorbell Rang, 1965; Death of a Doxy, 1966; The Father Hunt, 1968; Death of a Dude, 1969; Nero Wolfe Cookbook, 1973; Please Pass the Guilt, 1973. Home: Brewster, N.Y. Died Oct. 27, 1975.

STOVER, HOLLY, railroad exec.; b. Beckley, W.Va., Mar. 12, 1883; s. Paris and Eleanor (Watts) S.; ed. country school; unmarried. Began as railroad telegrapher, 1898; engaged in coal business and holds considerable interest in coal mines; returned to railroad work with Gulf, Mobile & Ohio R.R.; with Chicago and Eastern Illinois R.R. since 1944, president 1944-47, now chmn. bd., dr. Gulf Mining Co., West Gulf Mining Co., Holly Stover, Inc. Clubs: Bath, Indian Creek country (Miami Beach, Fla.); Burning Tree, (Washington); Chicago, Glenview Golf (Chicago). Home: Washington, D.C. *

STOWELL, WILLIAM AVERILL, author; b. Appleton, Wis., Mar. 29, 1882; s. William Henry Harrison and Emma C. (Averill) S.; A.B., Princeton, 1904; Sorbonne, Paris, 1906-07; Ph.D., Johns Hopkins, 1908; married Mabel Gardner, Jan. 14, 1904 (died Jan. 4, 1943); children—Averill, Eldon; married 2d, Edith de Greve, December 14, 1944. Began as professor of Romance languages at Randolph-Macon Woman's Coll., Lynchburg, Va., 1903-09; same, Amherst Coll., 1909-20; now research advisor of Buffalo Museum of Science, also field associate in geography of same museum. Mem. Modern Lang. Assn. America, Loyal Legion, Phi Beta Kappa, Camp Fire Club of America. Democrat. Episcopalian. Author: Old French Titles of Respect, 1908; The Wake of the Setting Sun, 1923; The Mystery of the Singing Walls, 1925; The Marston Murder Case, 1930; also numerous mag. articles on French historic and lit. subjects. Attached to mil. intelligence sect. U.S. Army, at New York, 1918. Address: Vero Beach, Fla. *

STOY, JOHN METZGER, accountant; b. Arlington. Va., May 18, 1911; s. Clifford M. and Daisy (Pearson) S.; student Emory U., 1930-33; B.C.S. cum laude, Southeastern U., 1936; m. Anna L. Sanford, Oct. 3, 1936; children—John R., Judith A. Partner, Stoy, Malone & Co., C.P.A.'s, Washington, 1938-76; prof. accounting Southeastern U., 1938-43; dir. Security Bank. Pres., D.C. Bd. Accountancy, 1957-58. Mem. contract appeals bd. AEC. C.P.A., D.C. Treas. ch. sch. Mt. Vernon Pl. Methodist Ch. Mem. Am. Inst. C.P.A.'s (chmn. small bus. com.), Md. Assn. C.P.A.'s, D.C. Inst. C.P.A.'s (pres. 1946-47), Am. Inst. Accountants (council 1953-57, v.p. 1957-58, trail bd. 1956-57), Assn. C.P.A. Examiners, Washington Bd. Trade. Kiwanian. Club: Congressional Country (Washington). Contbr. articles to profl. jours. Home: Rockville, Md. Died Apr. 19, 1976.

STRACHAN, WILLIAM MELVILLE, coll. prof.; b. Cleveland, Jan. 1, 1884; s. John and Jeannette (Bell) S.; student Western Reserve University, 1902-05; A.B., University of Michigan, 1912, LL.B., 1915; A.M., 1923, Doctor Philosophy, 1929; married Mary Addeman, February 3, 1919; children—Henry, Jill. Admitted to Ohio and Mich. bars, 1915, practiced in Detroit, 1921-22. Supervisor of schs., Philippine Islands, 1905-11; comml. agt. Customhouse, N.Y. City, 1916-17; asst. mgr. fgn. trade bur. Merchants Assn., 1918; trade commr. to Central Am. U.S. Dept. Commerce, 1918, to Spain, 1919-21. Instr. polit. sci. U. of Mich., 1923-27; asso. prof. polit. sci. Ohio Wesleyan, 1927-30, prof. since 1930. Mem. Am. Polit. Sci. Assn.,

Am. Soc. Internat. Law Republican. Presbyterian. Home: Delaware, O. *

STRAIGHT, WHITNEY WILLARD, corp. executive; b. N.Y., Nov. 6, 1912; s. Willard Dickerman and Dorothy (Whitney) S.; student Trinity Coll., Cambridge 1930-32; m. Lady Daphne Finch-Hatton, July 17, 1935; children—Camilla Caroline, Amanda Betsy. Profl. motor car driver, 1931-34; founded Straight Corp. (aviation), 1934; dep. chmn. Brit. European Airways, 1946; chief exec. Brit. Overseas Airways Corp., 1947-49, dep. chmn., 1949-55; dep. chmn. Rolls-Royce Limited, 1956-71, chmn., 1971-79; dir. Midland Bank; dep. chmn. Post Office Corp., 1968-79. Chmn. exec. com Alexander Rose Day. Served with R.A.F., 1938-45; Decorated comdr. Order Brit. Empire, Mil. Cross, Distinguished Flying Cross, Legion of Merit, Norwegian Cross; hon. companion Royal Aero. Soc. Fellow Royal Soc. Arts, Royal Geog. Soc., Brit. Inst. Mgmt.; mem. Institute Transport. Clubs: International Sportsmens'; Royal Yacht Squadron, Corviglia Ski, Buck's (London); Racquet (N.Y.C.); Whites. Home: Southall Middlesex England. Died Apr. 5, 1979.

STRAIN, HARRY ARTHUR, steel exec.; b. Clinton, Ill., Feb. 18, 1886; s. Isaac Harry and Nancy (Underwood) S.; grad. Clinton (Ill.) High Sch., 1904; student Armour Inst. Tech., Chicago, Ill., 1910-13; m. Elma Bradley, Dec. 24, 1913; children—Dorothy Jean (Mrs. H. J. Katris), Jane Harriet (Mrs. J. R. Hill). Clerk, Illinois Central Railroad, Clinton, Illinois, 1904, American Steel and Wire Co., Joliet, Ill., 1905-06; laborer, blast furnace, Joliet works, Ill. Steel Co., 1906-10, foreman blast furnace, Chicago, Ill., 1913-15, supt. blast furnaces, Milwaukee, Wis., 1915-20; supt. blast furnaces, Woodward Iron Co., Woodward, Ala., 1921-22; asst. supt. blast furnace div., Ill. Steel Co., Chicago, 1922-25, div. supt. blast furnaces, 1925-36; asst. gen. supt., Carnegie-Illinois Steel Corp., Chicago, 1936-41, dir. of raw materials, fuel and power, Pitts. since 1941; pres. Fenimore Iron Mines, Ltd., 1951-52, chmn. bd., 1952-53. Member Donald Nelson Mission to China, 1944-45, Pres. Blast Furnace and Coke Assn. (Chicago dist.). Mem. Am. Inst. Mining and Metall. Engrs., Theta Xi. Mason. Club: South Shore Country (Chicago). Home: Pitts. *

STRAND, PAUL, photographer, filmmaker; b. N.Y.C., Oct. 16, 1890; s. Jacob and Matilda (Arnstein) S.; grad. high sch.; m. Rebecca Salsbury, 1922; m. 2d, Virginia Stevens, 1936; m. 3d, Hazel Kingsbury, Feb. 2, 1951. One man photog. show 291, N.Y.C., 1916; made film Mannahatta with Charles Sheeler, 1921; free-lance photographer with Akeley motion picture camera, 1922-29; exhbns. include Seven Americans, Anderson Galleries, N.Y.C., 1925, Intimate Gallery, N.Y.C., 1929 (with Rebecca Strand) An American Pl., N.Y.C., 1932, Sala de Arte, Mexico City, 1933, one-man shows: Mus. Modern Art, 1945, Worcester Art Mus., 1967, Currier Gallery, Washington, 1971, Belgium and Netherlands, 1969-70, Florence, Rome, Bologna, Naples, Turin, 1976-77, Kunsthaus, Zurich, 1979, Galerie Zabriskie, Paris, 1979, Galerie AMC, Mulhouse, 1980; group shows include: Mus. Modern Art, 1956; retrospective exhbn. Phila. Mus. Art, 1971, City Art Mus. of St. Louis, Boston Mus. Fine Arts, 1972, Met. Mus. Art, Los Angeles County Mus. Art, M.H. DeYoung Meml. Mus., 1973, Nat. Portrait Gallery, London, also museums in Stockholm, Paris, Amsterdam, Berlin, 1976-78, Edinburgh, Oxford, Glasgow, 1978, Phila. Mus. Art, 1978-79; chief dept. photography and cinematography, producer, and photographer film The Wave, Dept. Fine Arts, Secretariat Edn. Mexico, 1933-34; a photographer The Plow that Broke the Plains, 1935; pres. Frontier films, 1937-42; co-dir., photographer Native Land, 1942; photographer close-ups of plants, landscapes, individuals, numerous areas of world. Named to honor roll Am. Soc. Mag. Photographers, 1963; recipient David Octavius Hill medal Gesellschaft Deutscher Lichtbildner, Mannheim, Germany, 1967; Order Comdr. Arts and Letters, French Ministry of Culture, 1976. Fellow Am. Acad. Arts and Scis. Photographic books: Photographs by Paul Strand, Camera Work, 1916, 17; Photographs of Mexico, 2d edit., 1967; Time in New England, 1950, 2d edit., 1980; La France de Profil, 1952; Un Paese, 1955; Tir A'Mhurain, Outer Hebrides, 1962; Living Egypt, 1969; Ghana, An African Portrait, 1975; Sixty Years of Photographs, 1976; Retrospective Monograph, 1915-68, 1971; others; contbr. numerous articles to profl. jours. Address: Millerton, N.Y. Died Mar. 31, 1976.

STRANG, WILLIAM FREDERICK, lawyer; b. Junius, N.Y., Sept. 14, 1883; s. John William and Henrietta (Shear) S.; A.B., Cornell, 1904; LL.B., Albany Law Sch., 1906; m. Eugenie Degree, Feb. 22, 1919; 1 dau., Clara (Mrs. John Hurley). Admitted to N.Y. bar, 1906; practicing lawyer, Rochester, since 1907; sr. partner Strang, Wright, Combs, Wiser & Shaw, law firm; dir. Lincoln Rochester Trust Co., Monroe Abstract & Title Corp.; v.p., dir. Buffalo, Rochester & Pittsburgh Ry. Mem. Rochester C. of C. (pres. 1945, trustee), Rochester (pres. 1928), Am. and N.Y. State bar assns. Republican. Presbyn. Mason (grand master N.Y. 1942-44). Home: Rochester. *

STRANGMAN, HARRY WYMAN, aircraft co. exec.; b. Marblehead, Mass., June 16, 1886; s. William L. and Sylvania Spofford (Toppan) S.; student pub. schs., Mass.; 1 son, John. Asst. to v.p. finance Douglas Aircraft Co., Santa Monica, Cal., 1949—, hon. dir. *

STRASSBURGER, EUGENE BONN, lawyer; b. Pitts., Sept. 23, 1886; s. Samuel and Julia (Morganstern) S.; A.B., Harvard, 1908, LL.B., 1910; LL.D., Duquesne U., 1930; m. Constance Block, May 10, 1915; children—Eugene Bonn, Joan S. (Mrs. Marne Obernauer), Martha S. (Mrs. Herbert Ringel). Admitted to Pa. bar, 1910; practiced with Wilima H. Lemon, 1910-19; mem. Strassburger & McKenna, 1919-78; prof. Duquesne U. Law Sch., 1920-42; v.p., Grant Bldg., Inc., Pitts., 1927-78; atty. Pitts. Outdoor Advt. Co. Formerly standing master bd. governance Supreme Ct. Pa.; chmn. law library com. Allegheny County Cts.; chmn. Orphans' Ct. Rules Com. Formerly trustee, sec. Maurice and Laura Falk Found.; trustee Union Am. Hebrew Congs. Mem. Am. Law Inst. (exec. com., council), Am. Judicature Soc., Am., Pa., Allegheny County bar assns., Harvard Law Sch. Alumni Assn. (council, v.p.), Harvard Law Sch. Assn. Western Pa. (pres. 1951-52). Mason. Home: Pittsburg, Pa. Died Mar. 10, 1978.

STRATTON, FREDERICK P., machine tool exec.; b. 1914; s. H.M. Stratton; married. With Briggs & Stratton Corp., Wauwatosa, Wis., 1935-76, v.p. sales, 1963-72, chmn. bd., 1972-76; dir. Marine National Exchange Bank. Address: Wauwatosa, Wis. Died June 1, 1976.

STRAUMANIS, MARTIN EDWARD, metallurgist; b. Krettingen, Lithuania, Nov. 23, 1898; s. Janis and Matilde (Sviders) S.; grad. in engring. chemistry, U. Latvia, 1925, Dr. chem., 1927; m. Ieva Reinhards, Apr. 25, 1927; children—Lilita, Mara, Andrejs, Ilze, Liene. Came to U.S., 1947, citizenship applied for. Instr., asst., prof., U. Latvia, 1928-36, asso. prof., 1936-37, extraordinary prof., 1937-42, prof., 1942-44, dir. analytical lab., 1934-44; worker Inst. Metal Chemistry, U. Marburg, Germany, 1944-47; research prof. metallurgy Sch. Mines, U. Mo., Rolla, from 1947, prof. emeritus, 1969-73; participant 5th Internat. Congress Metallic Corrosion, Tokyo, 1972. Fellow, Rockefeller Foundn., Göttingen, Germany, 1927-28; mem. Am. Crystallography Association, Am. Chem. Soc., Electrochem. Soc., Deutsche Bunsen Gesellschaft, Sigma Xi, formerly member Latvian Chemical Society, Deutsche Chemische Gesellschaft, Gesellschaft für Korrosionsforschung. Evangelical Lutheran. Author: Präzisonsbestimmung von Gitterkonstanten nach der asymmetrischen Methode (with A. Ievins), 1940; Lehrbuch der Kolloidchemie (with B. Jirgensons), 1949. Contbr. to jours. on corrosion of metals, crystal growth, crystal structure and x-rays, chemistry of complex compounds. Home: Rolla, Mo. Died Mar. 19, 1973.

STRAUS, GLADYS GUGGENHEIM (MRS. ROGER W. STRAUS), b. Elberon, N.J., Aug. 15, 1895; d. Daniel and Florence (Schloss) Guggenheim; student Finch Sch., Rosemary Hall, Greenwich, Conn., 1910-13; m. Roger W. Straus, Jan. 12, 1914; children—Oscar S. II, Roger W., Florence S. (Mrs. Max A. Hart). Vice pres., asst. editor Gourmet mag., 1940-50. Nutrition commr. for met. area from N.Y. State, 1943-45, 1947-48. Hon. trustee Mt. Sinai Hosp.; trustee Inst. on Man and Sci., Rensselaerville, N.Y., Mt. Sinai Med. Sch. Chmn., Roger Williams Straus Meml. Found.; chmn. Daniel and Florence Guggenheim Found.; mem. council N.Y. State Coll. Home Econs., 1943-46. Vice pres. bd. govs. Women's Nat. Republican Club, 1936-51. Clubs: Cosmopolitan, Woman Flyfishers. Author: My Favorite Recipes; More Recipes. Home: New York, N.Y. Died Mar. 13, 1980.

STRAUS, WILLIAM LEVI, JR., phys. anthropologist, educator, anatomist; b. Balt., Oct. 29, 1900; s. William Levi and Pauline (Gutman) S.; student Harvard, 1917-18; A.B., Johns Hopkins, 1920, Ph.D., 1926; m. Henrietta S. Hecht, Sept. 19, 1926 (dec. 1954); 1 dau., Pauline Gutman (Mrs. Edward Rauh); m. 2d, Bertha L. Nusbaum, June 15, 1955. NRC fellow, 1926-27; instr. to asso. prof. anatomy Johns Hopkins, 1927-52, prof. phys. anthropology, 1952-57, prof. anatomy and phys. anthropology, 1957-66, prof. emeritus, 1966-81, adminstrv. head dept. anatomy, 1947-48. Vis. prof. anatomy Wayne U., 1950. Mem. adv. bd. Patuxent Instn., Md., 1955-60. mem. anatomy bd. State Md., 1947-52. Recipient Viking Fund medal and award in phys. anthropology, 1952; Guggenheim fellow, 1937-38. Fellow A.A.A.S., (editorial bd. 1953-64, v.p., chmn. anthropology sect. 1956), Am. Assn. Anatomists, Am. Anthrop. Assn.; mem. Am. Inst. Human Paleontology, Am. Assn. Phys. Anthropologists (pres. 1953-55), Am. Soc. Mammalogists, Corp. Marine Biol. Lab. Woods Hole, Zool. Soc. London (corr.), Am. Assn. U. Profs., Am. Soc. Zoologists, NRC (div. med. scis. 1960-64), Soc. Vertebrate Paleontology, Nat. Acad. Scis., Phi Beta Kappa, Sigma Xi. Editor: (with others) Forerunners of Darwin; 1745-1859, 1959. Editor, contbr.: (with Carl G. Hartman) The Anatomy of the Rhesus Monkey, 1933; editorial bd. Am. Jour. Anatomy, 1946-58, Human Biology, 1953-81, Sci. and Sci. Monthly, 1953-64, Folia Primatologica, 1962—. Contbr. articles to profl. jours. Home: Baltimore, Md. Died Jan. 28, 1981.

STRAUSS, ANNA LORD, civic worker; b. N.Y.C.; d. Albert and Lucretia Mott (Lord) Strauss; ed. Horace Mann Sch., Miss Marshall's Classes, N.Y.C., N.Y. Sch. for Secs.; H.H.D., Hood Coll., 1951; L.H.D., Temple U., 1953; LL.D., Western Coll. Women, 1954. Sec., N.Y. office Fed. Res. Bd., U.S. Shipping Bd., 1918, War Trade Bd., 1919, U.S. Dept. State, 1919-20, A.R.C., 1921-22; mag., sec. to mng. editor Century mag., 1923-29; librarian, employment service N.Y. Dept. Labor, 1931-33; bd. dirs. Nat. League Women Voters, 1934-38; pres. N.Y.C. League Women Voters, 1937-43; personnel dept. Chance Vought div. United Aircraft Corp., 1943-44; pres. League Women Voters U.S., 1944-50; mem. U.S. delegation Conf. FAO, Quebec, Can., 1945; mem. U.S. delegation UN Gen. Assembly, Paris, France, 1951-52; U.S. Dept. State ednl. exchange rep. S.E. Asia, 1953; cons. UN Seminar on Civic Responsibilities, Asian Women in Pub. Life, Bangkok, 1957. Mem. Pres.'s Famine Emergency Com., 1946, Citizens Food Com.; vice chmn. Pres.'s Commn. on Internal Security and Individual Rights, 1951, Pres.' Com. on Edn. Beyond High Sch., 1956; mem. Pres.' People-to-People Program, 1956; mem. bd. Women's African Com., African Am. Inst., Nat. Inst. Pub. Affairs, UN Assn. U.S., Fair Campaign Practices Com., Interchange Found., Nat. Council Negro Women Edn. Fund., Com. of Corrs., Fgn. Policy Assn., Conn. Coll.; adv. council Hampshire Coll., Center for Information on Am., U. Pitts. Grad. Sch. Pub. and Internat. Affairs. Mem. bd. Republicans for Progress. Trustee Com. Econ. Devel., Overseas Edn. Fund of League Women Voters. Recipient M. Carey Thomas award Bryn Mawr Coll., 1948; Sir James Jeans award New London Jr. Coll., 1959; Rockefeller Pub. Service award; award Conn. Coll., 1973. Mem. UN Assn. U.S.A. (mem. bd., hon. co-chmn. bd.). Club: Cosmopolitan (N.Y.C.). Home: New York, N.Y., also Newton, Conn. Died Feb. 23, 1979.

STRAUSS, JULIUS, cigar mfr.; b. Stuttgart, Germany, July 21, 1899; s. Solomon and Frieda (Neter) S.; student U. Munich, 1920-23; m. Eva Kops, Nov. 24, 1927; children—Peter, Rosemary. Partner, Gebruder Strauss, 1926-35; mgr. tobacco processing div. Gen. Cigar Co., Inc., N.Y.C., 1938-45, prodn. mgr., 1945-49, pres., 1949-63, chmn. bd., 1963-73, dir., until 1973, chmn. bd., dir. emeritus, 1973-76. Home: Great Neck, N.Y. Died Sept. 3, 1976; buried Beth Moses Cemetery, Pine Lawn, L.I.

STRAVINSKY, IGOR FEDOROVICH (STRÄ-VIN'SKE), composer; b. near St. Petersburg (Leningrad), Russia, June 5, 1882; studied law. St. Petersburg U.; studied music under Rimski-Korsakov; married 2d, Vera de Bossett, April 1940; four children by first marriage. Composer: Symphony, 1907; Fireworks; "L'Oiseau de Feu." Fire Bird Suite, 1910; Petrouchka, 1911; LeSacre de Printemps, 1917; Chant du Rossignol, 1917; Renard; Concerto for Piano and Orchestra: Oedipus Rex; Capriccio: Symphony of Psalms, Persephone; also many others. Author: Poetics of Music. 1947. Naturalized 1946. Mem. Am. Acad. Arts and Letters. Recipient Internat. Sibelius prize, 1963. Address: N.Y.C. *

STREATER, EDWARD CLARE, mfg. co. exec.; b. Pocahontas, Iowa, Jan. 14, 1903; s. Lewis E. and Clara (Propp) S.; student U. Minn., 1925; m. Alma Loen, June 9, 1928; children—Joanne Streater Scott, Janice (Mrs. John H. Kelley). Founder, 1946, Streater Industries, Inc., Mpls. (now div. Litton Industries, Inc.), chief exec. officer, 1946-72. Mem. Triangle Frat. Clubs: Mpls. Athletic; Lafayette (Minnetonka Beach, Minn.). Home: Pompano Beach, Fla. Died Jan. 24, 1980.

STREET, ALLEN M., city mgr.; b. Mexia, Tex., June 17, 1886; s. Joseph G. and Ida (Hall) S.; student Vanderbilt U.; m. Erma McElheny, June 4, 1909; 1 son, John Gordon. Asso. with Street and Draper Funeral Home, Oklahoma City, 1907—, now owner and gen. mgr. Mem. city council, Oklahoma City, 1943-47, city mgr., 1947—; served as mem. Okla. Legislature, 1919, 23-25, 29-31. Chmn. Community Fund campaign, 1949, 50; active in scouting, mem. exec. bd. Last Frontier council, 1919—, also mem. nat. council. Awarded Silver Beaver, 1939. Mem. Pres. Highway Safety Conf., 1949; Okla. Soc. for Crippled Children (pres. 1945—, nat. bd. dirs.). Mem. Kappa Kappa Sigma. Democrat. Presbyn. (trustee). Club: Rotary (charter mm., past pres., treas., dir.; dist. gov., 1st v.p. Rotary Internat). Home: Oklahoma City. *

STREET, WILLIAM EZRA, educator; b. Benfranklin, Tex., Apr. 12, 1901; s. William Dan and Josie (Cook) S.; B.S. in Elec. Engring., Tex. Tech. U., 1930, M.A., 1933; D.Eng. Edn., Harding Coll., 1947; m. Clara Johnson, June 21, 1924; children—William Elvin, Clara Louise (Mrs. Charles Beagle). Tchr. pub. schs., Tex., 1920-25; instr. Tex. Tech. U., 1928-32, asst. prof., 1932-38, asso. prof., 1938-41; prof., head engring. graphics dept. Tex. A. and M. U., College Station, 1941-65; prof. La. State U., Baton Rouge, 1965-78, head dept., 1965-72. Ind. expert Sinclair Oil & Refining Co., Waco Constrn. Co.,

Lockheed Vega Aircraft Co., Gen. Dynamics. Recipient Gen. Dynamics Convair award for excellence in engring. teachine Tex. A. and M. U., 1961, named outstanding tchr. during first 100 years; Halliburton award for excellence in engring. teaching La. State U., 1969. Registered profl. engr., Tex. Mem. La. Engring. Soc., Am. Soc. Engring. Edn. (chmn. engring. design graphics div. 1955-56; Distinguished Service award graphics div. 1961), Tau Beta Pi, Phi Kappa Phi. Rotarian (dist. gov. 1954-55). Editor: Jour. Engring. Design Graphics Jour., 1944-46. Author numerous books including: Drafting Fundamentals I, 1965; Design and Engineering Graphics Problems, 1965; Drafting Fundamentals II, 1969; Engineering Graphics Design and Analysis Problems, 1970; Design Drafting Problems I, 1973; Descriptive Geometry Problems, 1973; Design Fundamentals, 1975. Home: Nashville, Ark. Died Nov. 13, 1978.

STREETER, DANIEL DENISON, architect; b. Bklyn., Jan. 27, 1885; s. Milford Barzaleel and Sarah Maria (Wyckoff) S.; grad. Poly. Prep. Sch., 1903; student Poly. Inst. Bklyn., 1904-05; B.S., Columbia, 1909; postgrad. George Washington U., 1910-11, Columbia Sch. Architecture, 1921-24; grad. Army Sch. of the Line, Langres, France, 1918, Cavalry Sch., Ft. Riley, 1929, C. and G.S. Extension Sch., 1936; m. Gladys Marie Rudolph, June 10, 1914 (dec. Sept. 23, 1975); children—Catherine (Mrs. George M. Thorpe), Daniel Denison Jr., Samuel Schuyler (died at sea), Sarah Ann (Mrs. Harrison). With Am. Mus. Natural History fossil hunting expdn. in Wyo., summer 1903, Bur. Ethnology expdn. excavating Puye, N.M., summer 1907; with Biol. Survey in N.W. states, 1909-10, in Alaska, 1911-48, 58, 59, 63; leader expdn. Nat. Mus. to Algeria, Sumatra, Borneo, 1912, Costa Rica, Venezuela, Aruba, 1949, Lake Athabaska and Great Slave Lake, 1952, Antarctic Continent, 1961-62; with Streeter & Denison, Bklyn., 1910-11, 13-16; insp. Chevrolet Motor Co., Flint, Mich., 1920; draftsman Warren & Wetmore, 1921, Thomas W. Lamb, N.Y.C., 1923, Worcester (Mass.) City Plan Commn., 1922; Practicing architect Daniel D. Streeter, Bklyn., 1924-52. Trustee emeritus Anchor Savs. Bank, Bklyn.; corporator Mt. McKinley Mut. Savs. Bank, Fairbanks, Alaska. Bd. dirs. Hong Kong True Light Found., 1954-69; chmn. bd. trustees Wyckoff House Found., 1959-66. Pvt. cadet corps 23d inf. N.Y.N.G., 1899-1902; enlisted Troop C, 1st N.Y. Cav., 1909; on Mexican Border, 1916-17; 1st lt. 6th Cav. in Tex., Eng., France, Turkey, Greece, Bulgaria, Armenia, Caucasus, 1917-20; lt. col. Cav. at N.Y.P.E., 1941-42, in N. Africa, 1943-44, IGD, 1942-45. Mem. A.I.A. (Seattle chpt.). Am. Legion, N.Y. State Assn. Architects, N.Y. Soc. Architects, AAAS, N.Y. Zool. Soc., Soc. Colonial Wars, Arctic Inst. N. Am., Denison Soc., Wyckoff Assn. Am. (exec. v.p. 1950-67), St. Nicholas Soc. Nassau Island (pres. 1961-62), L.I. Hist. Soc. (dir.), Inst. Agrl. Research, Photog. Soc. Am., Streeter Soc., N.Y. State Rifle and Pistol Assn., Phi Delta Theta. Mem. Soc. Friends. Mason. Clubs: Camp Fire; Camp Fire Rifle; Squadron C Cavalry (Bklyn.); Explorers. Home: Seattle WA. *

STREETER, DANIEL DENISON, JR., biomechanicist; b. Bklyn., Feb. 8, 1925; s. Daniel Denison and Gladys Marie (Rudolph) S.; S.B., Mass. Inst. Tech., 1946, S.M., 1951; PhD., Catholic U. Am., Washington, 1969; m. Patricia Ann Engle, Aug. 10, 1956; children—Ann Megrath, Daniel Denison. Draftsman Douglas Aircraft Co., El Segundo, Cal., 1947; maintenance and constrn. engr. Lago Oil & Transport Co. Ltd., Aruba, Netherlands W.I., 1948-50; research asst. Cavitation Lab., Mass. Inst. Tech., 1950-51, teaching asst., in charge High Temperature Torsional-Creep Lab., 1951-52; vis. prof. mech. engring. U. Rangoon (Burma) on Mass. Inst. Tech.-State Dept. Fgn. Aid contract, 1952-54; instr. engring. scis. div. Purdue U., 1954-55; stress analyst Boeing Co., Seattle, 1955-65; USPHS trainee, spl. fellow Cardiovascular Tng. Program, U. Wash. Sch. Medicine, Seattle, 1965-66, research fellow pathology dept., 1969-71, research asso., 1971—, project dir. left ventricular fiber geometry unit, 1971—; USPHS trainee Nat. Heart Inst., Bethesda, Md., 1966-68. Engring. cons. Union of Burma Govt., Am. embassy, Burma, Knappen, Tippetts, Abbetts & McCarthy, Engrs., N.Y.C., 1952-54. Active Boy Scouts Am., 1948-52, 69—. Served with USNR, 1943-45. Recipient Order of Arrow, Boy Scouts Am., 1939, Eagle Scout, 1943. Registered profl. engr., Wash. Fellow The Explorers; mem. Am. Soc. M.E., Am. Acad. Mechanics (a founder), Am., Wash. (research fellow 1969-70) heart assns., The Mountaineers (trustee, sec. 1959-60), Wyckoff Soc. Am., Tau Beta Pi. Republican. Conglist. Contbr. articles on muscle structure of heart to profl. jours. Patentee in field. Home: Seattle WA. *

STREETER, DANIEL WILLARD (STRE-TER') author; b. Highland Park, Ill., Nov. 22, 1883; s. Harvey Benjamin and Frances Demarest (Chamberlain) S.; graduate The Hill School, Pottstown, Pa., 1903; S.B., Harvard, 1907; m. Gertrude Norton, May 30, 1908; children—Daniel Barton, Porter Norton, Gertrude. Began career with the Buffalo Weaving & Belting Co., 1907, treasurer, 1908-17, president 1917-22; retired and hunted big game, 1922-30; vice pres., Niagara Share Corp., 1930-36; president and director The Guedag, Inc., Niagara Falls, N.Y.; dir. McCall Corp., McCall Co.; Trustee Erie Co. (Savings) Bank; chmn. Mayor's Com. Unemployment, 1933-34 chmn. emergency Relief Bur., 1934-38; Municipal Civil Service Commr., 1938, pres. Commn. since 1939; chmn. Frontier Manpower Mobilization Com Bd. Mgrs. Buffalo Soc. of Natural Science. Traveler and big game hunter; dir. Niagara Frontier Planning Assn., Buffalo Fine Arts Acad.; mem.-at-large Buffalo Council of Boys Scouts of Am.; mem. bd. trustees Buffalo Gen. Hosp.; mem. adv. com. Salvation Army; pres. Buffalo C. of C.; dir. Hosp. Service Corp., Western N.Y., Am. Red Cross, Buffalo Chapt.; dir. exec. com., Council of Social Agencies, Buffalo Philharmonic Assn.; v.p. and dir. Buffalo City Planning Assn.; chmn. 2d to 8th incl., War Loans Erie Co.; mem. American Museum Greenland Expdn., 1926. Republican. Episcopalian. Clubs: Boone and Crockett, Harvard, Explorers (New York); Buffalo Tennis & Squash. Author: Denatured Africa, 1926; Camels, 1927; An. Artic Rodeo, 1929. Home: Buffalo, N.Y. *

STREETER, EDWARD, author; b. N.Y.C., Aug. 1, 1891; s. Harvey B. and Frances (Chamberlain) S.; A.B., Harvard, 1914; m. Charlotte Warren, Oct. 29, 1919; children—Claire (Mrs. C.S. Woods), Edward, William (dec.), Charlotte (Mrs. John T. Goodhue). Reporter, Buffalo Express, 1914-16; asst. v.p. Bankers Trust Co., N.Y.C., 1921-29; partner Blake Bros., mems. N.Y. Stock Exchange, 1929-30; v.p. Fifth Ave. Bank (now Bank of N.Y.), 1931-56; past trustee N.Y. Bank for Savs. Past trustee Lingnan U. (China); bd. overseers Harvard Coll., 1965-71; v.p., dir. Woodlawn Cemetery, Community Service Soc., N.Y.C. Served as lt. F.A., U.S. Army, World War I. Clubs: Century, Harvard, Coffee House, Union, Author: Dere Mable, 1917; That's Me All Over Mable, 1918; Same Old Bill, 1918; Daily Except Sunday, 1938; Father of the Bride, 1949; Skoal Scandinavia, 1952; Mr. Hobbs Vacation, 1954; Merry Christmas, Mr Baxter, 1956; Mr. Robbins Rides Again, 1957; Window on America, 1959; Chairman of the Bored, 1961; Along the Ridge, 1964; Ham Martin, Class of '17, 1969. Contbr. to Sat. Eve. Post, Red Book, McCall's mag., other periodicals. Home: New York, N.Y. Died Mar. 31, 1976.

STREIT, PAUL HENRY, physician, army officer; b. Seguin, Tex., Mar. 18, 1891; s. John and Louise (Weiss) S.; M.D., U. of Tex., 1916; interne John Sealy Hosp., Galveston, Tex., 1917; post grad. nose and throat training, U. of Bordeaux, France, 1919; graduate of Army Medical Field Service School, 1923; nose and throat student, New York Post Graduate Hospital, 1925-26; student course in bronchoscopy under Dr. Chevalier Jackson, Phila., 1929; m. Metta Miller Megeath, Sept. 15, 1926; children—John Paul, Metta Elizabeth. Commd. 1st lt., Med. Corps, U.S. Army, 1917; promoted through grades to maj. gen., 1949. Mem. Typhus Relief Expdn. in Poland, 1919-20; chief Eye, Ear, Nose and Throat Service, Army Dispensary, Washington, 1926-29, Sternberg Gen. Hosp., Philippines, 1929-31, Ft. Leavenworth, Kan., 1931-35, A. & N. Gen. Hosp., Ark., 1935-38, Letterman Army Hospital, Calif., 1938-42; surg. Central Pacific Base Command, 1943-45; comdg. officer Dibble General Hospital, Calif., 1945-46; comdg. gen. Brooke General Hospital, Tex., 1946-49, Army Medical Center and Walter Reed Gen. Hosp., Washington, 1949-53; cons. United Mine Workers of American Welfare and Retirement Fund. President of Gorgas Memorial Institute of Tropical and Preventive Medicine. Diplomate Am. Bd. Otorhinolaryngology. Fellow A.C.S.; member Alpha Mu Pi Omega, Alpha Omega Alpha, Am. Med. Assn., Acad. Medicine Washington. Awarded Commemorative Cross of Poland; Legion of Merit with Oak Leaf Cluster. Republican. Episcopalian. Mason. Home: Chevy Chase, Md. Died May 12, 1976; buried Arlington Nat. Cemetery.

STREITHORST, TOM, journalist; b. N.Y.C., June 4, 1931; s. Thomas John and Mary Agnes (O'Neill) S.; A.B., Princeton, 1953; M.A., Johns Hopkins Sch. Advanced Internat. Studies, 1954; m. Lucienne Pierre, 1963; children—Thomas Nicolas, Catherine Arlette. Asst. instr. history Am. U., Beirut, Lebanon, 1954-56; editor Middle East Forum, 1956; reporter Time-Life, 1957; reporter NBC News, 1958, Middle East corr., 1960-61, Latin Am. corr., 1964-68, Vietnam, 1968, Morocco, 1968-75, San Francisco, 1975—. Middle East corr. Newsweek mag., 1961-62; Common Market corr. Newsweek and Washington Post, 1962-64. Home: San Francisco, Calif. Died Feb. 19, 1981.

STRELSIN, ALFRED A., industrialist; b. Antwerp, Belgium, Feb. 27, 1898; s. Henry and Leah (Kunin) S.; ed. extension div. U. Wis.; m. Dorothy Dennis, May 29, 1947. Journalist, Mil. Fee Press, later advt. mgr. pharm. house; organizer Reliance Advt. Co., Chgo., chmn., to 1976; organizer merger, operator 6 German porcelain enamel industries, 1921-24; arranged hog's hair concession, Russia, 1922; purchased defunct businesses from banks, reorganized and resold, 1932-33; reorganizer Gen. Sci. Corp., Chgo., mfs. optical lenses, became pres., chmn. bd. (sold 1970); organizer Park Constrn. Co., builder sect. 6th Av. Subway, N.Y.C., 1936, later merged with Stiefel Constrn. Co., N.Y., chmn. bd. (builder Fischer Hill Mines, awarded Am. Soc. C.E. constrn. engring. prize, 1944, also Union Village Dam, participating with fgn. firms constrn. irrigation systems and hydro-electric projects Europe and Asia; with partners obtained controlling interest Central Sci. Co., Chgo., chmn. Cenco, holding co. owning this and other equities; helped establish lab., Cape Cod, Mass., for devel. new med. products by Albert Szent Gyorgyi (Nobel prize winner) and 16 asso. scientists brought from behind Iron Curtain; organized with others Electronized Chems. Corp., for devel. high-voltage intensity, pres. (sold); organizer with others Atlas Aircraft Products Co., became Induction Motors, mfrs. small motors, blower motors, dinamotors and generators; organizer Cinerama Prodn. Corp. Head Preclusive Operations, charged with stymieing enemy procurement from neutrals and non-belligerents, World War II, covered Israeli-Arab War in Near East for Internat. News Service, 1948. Address: New York, N.Y. Died Aug. 25, 1976.

STRICKLER, GEORGE ARNOLD, sports writer; b. South Bend, Ind., Aug. 12, 1904; s. William and Anna (Goetz) S.; student Ind. U., 1922-23, Notre Dame U., 1923-25; m. Amy Caroline McKay, May 31, 1940. Publicity dir., sec. to Knute Rockne, 1924; Chgo. mgr. Internat. News Service, 1925-27; sports editor Atlanta Georgian, 1929-30; asst. to commr. Nat. Football League, 1940-47; asst. gen. mgr. Green Bay Packers, 1947-50; sports editor Chgo. Tribune, 1965-69, asst. to editor, 1970-76. Dir. S. & S. Ry. Supply Co. Pres. Chgo. Tribune Charities, 1967-76. Mem. Profl. Football Writers Assn. (1st pres.). Home: Evanston, Ill. Died Dec. 8, 1976.

STRICKLIN, JAMES ALVIN, educator; b. Yazoo County, Miss., Feb. 21, 1932; s. Lee Andrew and Mattie Jane (Milner) S.; B.S., Miss. State U., 1955; M.S., Ga. Inst. Tech., 1958; Ph.D., Mass. Inst. Inst., 1964; m. Nancy Douglass Carr, Oct. 27, 1956. Asso. engr., flutter and vibrations dept. Lockhead-Ga. Co., Marietta, Ga., 1955-56; instr. Ga. Inst. Tech., 1956-58; engr. N.Am. Aviation, Columbus, O., 1958; asst. prof. aerospace engring. Ga. Inst. Tech., 1959-61; research asst. aeroelastic and structures lab. Mass. Inst. Tech., 1962-64, staff research lab., 1965; asso. prof. Tex. A. and M. U., 1965-68, prof., 1968—, chmn. interdisciplinary engring., 1970-76. Home: Bryan, Tex. Died Aug. 30, 1976; buried Bryan, Tex.

STRIKE, CLIFFORD STEWART, engr.; b. Marion, Ill., Aug. 28, 1902; s. James Matthew and Addie (Copeland) S.; B.Sc. in Engring., U. Ill., 1924; m. Ida Marie Pollitt, Aug. 28, 1924; (dec.); children—Jennie (Mrs. George T. Watkins III), Constance (Mrs. Alan G. Wadsworth); m. 2d, Sali A. Godard, Nov. 25, 1950 (div.); children—Clifford Beach, Douglas Copeland, Kerby Stewart; m. 3d, Marjorie Stanley, 1963. With Dwight P. Robinson & Co., 1924-29; asst. v.p., v.p., F.H. McGraw & Co., 1930-41, pres., 1941-62, chmn., 1962-63; partner Strike & Meissner, 1964-65; pres. Clifford S. Strike & Co., Inc., 1965-68, chmn., 1968-79; chmn. Jamaica Nat. Mortgage Assn., Ltd., 1962-67, Guaranty Home Savs. & Loan Assn., Ltd., 1962-67, Title Guaranty & Escrow Co., Ltd., 1962-67, Am. Radar Protective Devices, Montego Beach Hotel Co., Ltd.; pres., dir. Nat. Pipeline Co., Inc., 1960-62, No. Mich. Pipeline Co., 1960-62, The Unamco Corp., 1960-62; pres., chmn. Silent Sentry, Inc., 1974-79; chmn. exec. com. J.G. White Engring. Corp., N.Y.C.; dir. Kent Hotels Ltd., Caribbean Resorts Ltd. Dir. Conn. Valley Enterprises, Inc. Bd. dirs. U. Ill. Found., Def. Orientation Conf. Recipient Medal of Freedom. Mem. ASCE, ASME. Congregationalist. Clubs: Engineers, Moles, Illini, Cloud, Sky (N.Y.C.); Fairfield Country (Montego Bay, Jamaica); Rancho Santa Fe (Calif.) Golf. Contbr. articles to mags. Home: Rancho Santa Fe, Calif. Died Jan. 18, 1979; buried Hartford, Conn.

STRINGER, WILLIAM HENRY, editor; b. Randallsville, N.Y., Nov. 19, 1908; s. William Henry and Maud Amelia (Smith) S.; grad. Utica Free Acad., 1927; B.A., Colgate U., 1931; LL.B., Harvard, 1935; m. Mary Tappe, Apr. 8, 1939; children—David Llewellyn, Deborah Anne. Staff news bureaus Christian Science Monitor, Boston, N.Y.C., Washington, 1935-43, war corr. and broadcaster, Middle East, also London, Paris, 1944-45, with Washington bur., 1945-47, chief London bur., 1947-51, mng. editor Monitor, 1951-53, chief of Washington bur. 1953-64, chief London (Eng.) bur., 1965-67, later Washington columnist, until 1974; part-time columnist; sr. editor Am. Revolution Bicentennial Adminstrn., Washington, 1974-76. Mem. Phi Beta Kappa, Delta Kappa Epsilon. Clubs: Overseas Writers (past pres.), Garrick, Cosmos, Gridiron. Home: Rockville, Md. Died Mar. 31, 1976.

STRINGFELLOW, ERVIN EDWARD, educator, clergyman; b. Rose Hill, Ia., Feb. 28, 1884; s. Granvill and Florence Ann (Bacon) S.; student Penn Coll., 1903-04, A.B., Drake U., 1909, A.M., 1911; fellow in classics, Princeton U., 1911-14; student U. of Chicago, summer 1915; m. Myrtle M. Blake, June 22, 1909; children—Wilma V., Ervin R., Helen L. (Mrs. Raymond G. Hughes), Granvill B. Public sch. teacher, Iowa, 1900-03; instr. in Greek, Drake U., 1907-09, asst. prof. in classics, 1909-11, asst. prof. Biblical theology, 1914, 15, asso. prof. church history, 1915-19, prof. of New Testament lang. and lit., 1919-50, retired since 1950; chmn. Bible Coll. faculty com., 1949, 50; instr. in classics, Princeton U., 1911-13; organizer Am. Sunday Sch. Union, summers 1904, 05; teacher Polk Co. Sunday Sch. Inst. since 1925. Mem. Am Assn. Univ. Profs., Hist. Soc. of Disciples of Christ, Phi Beta Kappa, Eta Sigma Phi. Democrat. Mem. Christian Ch. (ordained. 1909, elder since 1922; pres. state conv., Disciples of Christ of Iowa, 1950). Club: University. Author: The Gospels Translation Harmony and Annotations, 1943; Acts and Epistles Translation and Annotations, 1945; Bethany Bible-Teacher, 1930-36. Home: Des Moines. *

STROCK, JOHN ROY, missionary; b. Allen P.O., Cumberland County, Pa., June 8, 1882; s. George W. and Barbara (Herman) S.; A.B., Dickinson Coll., Carlisle, Pa., 1903, A.M., 1908; B.D., Luth. Theol. Sem., Gettysburg, Pa., 1908; studied Teachers' Coll. (Columbia); D.D., Gettysburg Coll., 1925; m. Elizabeth M. Evans, Nov. 9, 1911. Ordained Luth. ministry, 1908; missionary among Telugus, India, 1908-49; professor in Andhra Christian College, Guntur, since 1909, principal, 1913-24, and 1926-39; prin. Noble Coll., Masulipatam, South India, 1924-26. Pres. Guntur Synod; pres. India Mission of United Luth. Ch. in America; convener bd. of examinations of Madras Representative Council of Missions; mem. exec. com. Missionary Ednl. Council of South India; mem. Syndicate, Senate and Academic Council of Andhra U., also of Nat. Christian Council, of which is also treas. and mem. exec. com.; sec. Andhra Christian Council; mem. All-India Central Bd. for Christian Higher Edn.; chmn. Bd. of Written Examiners for Telugu, South India Lang. Examinations for Missionaries; chmn. Bd. of Higher Edn. of the United Luth. Ch. in America Mission. Pres. Andhra Evang. Luth. Ch.; pres. Andhra Christian Council; v.p., All India Fedn. of Evang. Luth. Chs.; mem. Tambaram Meeting of the Internat. Missionary Council, Madras, Dec. 1938. Recipient (1936) from His Majesty the King Emperor of the United Kingdom of the Kaiser-i-Hind First Class (Gold) Medal in recognition of pub. service in India. Lecturer on the Holman Foundation, Lutheran Theol. Seminary, Gettysburg, Pa., 1942; prof. English Bible and Missions, Chicago Luth. Theol. Sem., Maywood, Ill., 1942-43; sec. Bd. of Foreign Missions of United Luth. Ch. in America 1943-46; adv. to Gossner Evang. Luth. Ch. (Autonomous), India, 1946-49; prof. theol. and church hist., Theol. Sem., Ranchi (India), since 1949. Mem. Phi Beta Kappa, Kappa Sigma. Republican. Author: (in Hindu language) The Spirited Experience of Martin Luther and The Doctrine of Justification by Faith;Three Lectures to Pastors. Address: Midway, Tenn.*

STRODE, HUDSON, writer, educator, lectr.; b. Cairo, Ill., Oct. 31, 1892; s. Thomas F. and Hope (Hudson) S.; A.B., U. Ala., 1913, D.Litt., 1952; M.A., Columbia, 1914; spl. study, Harvard, 1916; student, travel in Italy and Africa, 1922-23; D.Litt. (hon.), U. of South, 1960; m. Therese Cory, Dec. 20, 1924. Instr. English, Syracuse U., 1914-16; asso. prof. English, U. Ala., 1916-23, prof., 1924-63, prof. emeritus, 1963-76. Decorated knight Royal Order North Star (Sweden). Mem. Newcomen Soc. Eng., P.E.N., Phi Beta Kappa, Delta Kappa Epsilon. Author stories, books and articles, 1916—, latest being: Sweden: Model for a World, 1949; Denmark is a Lovely Land, 1951; Jefferson Davis: American Patriot, 1955; Jefferson Davis: Confederate President, 1959; Jefferson Davis: Tragic Hero, 1964; Jefferson Davis: Private Letters, 1823-1889, 1966; Ultimates in the Far East, 1970, The Eleventh House-Memoirs, 1975. Contbr. Am., European mags. Translations into German, Swedish, Danish, French and Hungarian. Known for interpretations of Mexico, S. Am., Finland, Sweden and as definitive biographer of Jefferson Davis. Home: Tuscaloosa, Ala. Died Sept. 22, 1976; inurned in Tuscaloosa.

STRONG, ALDEN GEORGE, army officer; b. Goddard, Kan., Jan. 1, 1885; s. Walter Davis and Mary Ida (Anderson) S.; B.S. in E.E., Kansas State Agrl. Coll., 1911; grad. advance course, Coast Arty. Sch., 1924, Command Gen. Staff, 1925, Army War Coll., 1933, Naval War Coll., 1934; m. Anne Gerry Butterfield, Sept. 2, 1914; children—Anne Gerry (wife of Capt. Peter Semenoff, U.S. Inf.), Nancy Alden (wife of B. T. Kinsey). Commd. 2d lt., Coast Arty. Corps, Dec. 20, 1911; promoted through grades to brig. gen., U.S. Army, Sept. 29, 1941. Commanded 1st Bn., 41st F.A., 14th Div., 1918, Camp Custer, Mich.; Adjutant Postal Express Service AEF (Paris), 1919; mem. U.S. Army of Occupation, Germany, 1919-23. Comd. 61st CA (Anti-Aircraft, 1925-28); instr. Command and Gen. Staff Sch., 1928-32; dep. chief of staff and asst. chief of staff (operations), Hdqrs. First Army, 1934-38; to overseas assignment; comdg. gen. Bermuda Base command, 1941-44; Hawaian Seacoast Arty., 1945; Western Pacific Base Command, Saipan, 1945; ret. 1946. Awarded Legion of Merit; hon. Comdr. British Empire (Mil. div.). Methodist. Club: Army and Navy (Washington). Home: Washington. *

STRONG, EARL D., educator; born Tecumseh, Neb., Feb. 15, 1885; s. William David and Kate (Nye) S.; Ph.B., Grinnell (Ia.) Coll., 1909; A.M., U. of Wis., 1912; student N.Y. Sch. of Social Work, 1914-15; Ph.D., Columbia; honorary LL.D., Grinnell College, 1950; married Margaret Ellen Bentley, September 1, 1917; children—James Bentley, Douglas Earl, Jerome Culton. Teacher, Crookston (Minn.) High Sch., 1909-11; instr., Moorhead (Minn.) State Teachers Coll., 1912-14; instr. in economics, Grinnell Coll., 1915; asso. prof., 1919, prof. since 1924, dean 1944-50; instr. in economics, Columbia, 1920-21; lecturer in economics, U. of Ia., 1923-24; asso. prof., U. of N.C., 1929-30; mem. econ. staff Ia. State Teachers Coll., George Peabody Coll., U. of Ark., summer sessions. Supervisor of auditors, War Camp Community Service, 1917-18; sr. economist Temporary Nat. Economic Com., Washington, D.C., 1938-39; dist. price exec., O.P.A., Des Moines, Ia., 1942-43. Mem. Am. Econ. Assn., Mid-West Econ. Assn., Phi Beta Kappa. Mason. Author: Amalgamated Clothing Workers of America, 1940. Home: Grinnell, Ia. *

STRONG, GEORGE FRANKLIN, librarian; b. Kents Hill Me., Aug. 12, 1882; s. William Cyrus and Sarah Adelaide (Fisk) S.; student Northwestern U., 1898-99; B.A., Wesleyan U. (Conn.), 1903; B.L.S., N.Y. State Library Sch., 1909; unmarried. Asst. Wesleyan U. Library, 1903-04; librarian U. of N.D., 1904-08; librarian in charge Boston U., 1909-10; librarian Adelbert Coll. (Western Reserve U.), 1910-36, and of Case Library, Cleveland, 1924-27; asso. dir. Western Reserve University Libraries, 1935-50, associate director emeritus since 1950. Organizer and librarian, camp libraries at Camp Beauregard, La., and Camp Bowie, Tex., 1917-18; acting exec. sec. Library War Service of A.L.A., 1918. Mem. A.L.A., Phi Nu Theta and Phi Beta Kappa fraternities. Methodist. Club: Rowfant (pres. 1925-26). Contbr. to library periodicals. Home: Natick, Mass. *

STRONG, WILLIAM AUGUSTUS, landscape architect; b. Joliet, Ill., Dec. 15, 1891; s. George Woodworth and Laurabel (Wallace) S.; B.A., U. Ill., 1914, B.S., 1916; M.L.A., Harvard U., 1920; m. Lucy Drinkwater Wensley, Oct. 28, 1920; children—Ruth Strong Hammerstrom, William Augustus, Dorcas Wensley. Draftsman, acting sec. Cleve. City Planning Commn., 1920-22; designer Albert D. Taylor, Cleve., 1922-25; partner Alexander & Strong, Cleve., 1925-44; pvt. practice, Cleve., from 1944; partner firm Strong & Hill, Cleve., 1961-76; asst. town planner, Greenhills, Ohio, 1955-57; site and planting planner Kent (Ohio) State U., 1936-68, Holden Arboretum, Mentor, Ohio, 1950-76, Lake View Cementery, Cleve., 1951-77; trustee Regional Assn. Cleve., 1937-71; mem. Cuyahoga County Planning Commn., 1934-47, Cleveland Heights City Planning Commn., 1951-71, Forest Hill Park Adv. Commn., 1951-77; cons. Fine Arts Garden Commn., Cleve., 1950-78; cons. in field. Trustee Hubbard Ednl. Trust, Boston, from 1953. Fellow Am. Soc. Landscape Architects (trustee 1940-44, 45-51; medal Ohio chpt. 1975). Club: Rockwell Springs Trout (Castalia, Ohio). Chmn. publ. bd. Landscape Architecture mag., 1948-62. Home: Shaker Heights, Ohio. Died Feb. 1980.

STROUP, RUSSELL CARTWRIGHT, clergyman; b. Cleve., Jan. 16, 1905; s. Ner Wallace and Emma (Cartwright) S.; A.B., Stanford, 1925, postgrad., 1925-26; postgrad. U. So. Calif., 1932-33, Am. U., 1952-53; D.D. (hon.), Washington and Lee U., 1947; m. Louise Wells Stroup, June 25, 1947; 1 dau., Susan Margretta. Ordained to ministry Methodist Ch., 1927; pastor in Murietta, Calif., 1927-30, Newport Beach, Calif., 1930-35, 1st Presbyn. Ch., Lynchburg, Va., 1937-50, Georgetown Presbyn. Ch., Washington, 1950-77; Instr. Am. U., 1960-68; moderator Washington Presbytery. Mem. Inter Faith, Inter Racial Com., Washington. Served as chaplain, maj. AUS, 1942-46. Decorated Bronze Star; recipient Freedom Found. award, 1952, 54; Traveling fellow to Mid East, 1960. Democrat. Contbr. articles to profl. jours. Home: McLean, Va. Died Nov. 17, 1977; buried Lynchburg, Va.

STRUB, CHARLES HENRY, exec. vice pres., Los Angeles Turf Club, Inc.; b. Hollister, Calif., Nov. 3, 1884; s. Isadore William and Rebecca (Williamson) S.; student St. Ignatius Coll., San Francisco, Calif., 1890-95; student Santa Clara (Calif.) Coll., 1896-1902; D.D.S., U. of Calif., Berkeley, 1906; m. Vera Wood, Apr. 14, 1915; children—Peter, Robert, Mary Louise, Virginia, Elizabeth. Engaged in practice of dentistry, San Francisco, Calif., 1906-15; pres. San Francisco Baseball Club, 1917-38; v.p. and gen. mgr. Los Angeles Turf Club, Inc., Arcadia, Calif., 1934-45, exec. vice pres. since 1945; pres. Sierra Nevada Investment Co., San Francisco, 1928-44. Mem. bd. dirs. Golden Gate Internat. Exposition, 1936-39, mng. dir., 1939; dir. The All Year Club of Southern Calif., Ltd. since 1938. Chmn. special events div. Southern Calif. Citizens Com. for Navy Relief Society's 1943 drive. Mem. bd. regents Loyola U. of Los Angeles since 1942; trustee Southern Calif. Symphony Assn. since 1943; v.p. and chmn. operations com. Greater Los Angeles Plans, Inc., since Feb. 12, 1945. Mem. Assn. of Professional Baseball Players of America, Xi Phi Chi. Republican. Roman Catholic. Clubs: California (Los Angeles); Annandale Golf (Pasadena). Home: San Marino, Calif. *

STRUNK, OLIVER, educator; b. Ithaca, N.Y., Mar. 22, 1901; s. William Jr., and Olivia Emilie (Locke) S. student Cornell, 1917-19, 27, U. Berlin, 1927-28; Litt.D., U. Rochester, 1936; L.H.D., U. Chgo., 1970; pvt. study music; m. Mildred Altemose, June 23, 1930 (dec. 1973). Staff music div. Library of Congress, 1928-37, chief, 1934-37; lectr. music Cath. U. Am., 1934-37; mem. faculty Princeton, 1937-66, Prof. music, 1950-66, prof. emeritus, 1966-80, acting chmn. dept., 1942-43, 51-52, 60; lectr. music Columbia, summer 1948, U. Mich., summer 1952, Harvard, fall 1974-75; editorial bd. Monumenta Musicae Byzantinae, Copenhagen, 1958-80, dir., 1961-71. Mem. Inst. Advanced Study, 1944, Internat. Congress for Sacred Music Rome, 1950. Recipient award distinguished scholarship in humanities Am. Council Learned Socs., 1961, Derek Allen Prize British Acad., 1977; traveling fellow Am. Council Learned Socs., 1934; Guggenheim fellow, 1951; Fulbright scholar, 1961-62. Fellow Medieval Acad. Am.; corr. fellow Brit. Acad.; mem. Royal Danish Acad., Music Library Assn. (pres. 1935-37), Am. Musicol. Soc. (pres. 1959-60, jour. editor 1947-48; hon. mem.), Am. Acad. Arts and Scis., Internat. Musicological Soc., Royal Mus. Assn. (hon. fgn.), Dansk selskab for Musikforskning, Gesellschaft fär Musikforschung, Vereniging voor Nederlandse Muziekgeschiedenis, Societá italiana di musicologia. Author: State and Resources of Musicology in the United States, 1932; Source Readings in Music History, 1950; Specimina notationum antiquiorum, 1966; Essays on Music in the Western World, 1974; (with Enrica Follieri) Triodium Athoum, 1975; Essays on Music in the Byzantine World, 1977. Editor: Music from the Days of George Washington (with Carl Engel, U.S. Bi-centennial Commn.), 1931. Home: Rome, Italy. Died Feb. 24, 1980.

STUART, HAROLD COE, pediatrician; b. Pocantico Hills, N.Y., Aug. 17, 1891; s. James Marshall and Jessie (Coe) S.; Litt.B., Princeton, 1914; M.D., Coll. Physicians and Surgeons (Columbia), 1918; A.M. (honorary), Harvard University, 1944; post-graduate studies in U. Kinderklinik, Vienna, spring 1921; m. to Agnes M. Brown, December 21, 1917; one daughter, Eleanor (Mrs. John Clinton Palmer). Was intern 1918-19, asst. resident phys., 1919-20, Presbyn. Hosp., N.Y. City; private practice pediatrics, Boston, 1922-28; asst. pediatrics, 1921-25, instr. pediatrics, 1925-27, Harvard Med. Sch.; asst. prof. child hygiene, 1927-31, asst. prof. pediatrics and child hygiene, Harvard Med. and Pub. Health Schs., 1931-44; asso. prof. child health Harvard Sch. of Pub. Health, 1944-46, prof. maternal and child health 1946-58, professor emeritus, 1958-76. continuing research in child health and devel., same school; staff mem. Children's and Infants' Hospital, Boston, 1921-56, cons. for child health division Children's Med. Center. In Med. R.C. during World War I. Mem. White House Conf. Child Health and Protection, 1929-30, vice chmn. com. growth and development; mem. Rockefeller Foundation Health Commn. to Europe at Marseille, France, Dec. 1940-June 1941. Med. advisor to Am. Red Cross in France, interned with the official Am. group in detention, at Lourdes, France and Baden-Baden, Germany, Aug. 1942-Mar. 1944. Consultant in nutrition to surgeon general, U.S. Army, 1944-46. Certified by Am. Bd. of Pediatrics, 1933, American Board of Preventive Medicine and Public Health, 1949. Mem. American Pediatric Society, American Academy of Pediatrics, A.A.A.S., Am. Pub. Health Assn. Soc. Pediatric Research, Soc. Research in Child Development (chmn. 1940-41), N.E. Pediatric Soc., Mass. Med. Soc. Republican. Trinity Church. Clubs: Harvard (Boston); Country (Brookline). Author: Healthy Childhood, 1933. Writer numerous articles med. subjects, child development and public health. Home: Chestnut Hill, Mass. Died Dec. 21, 1976.

STUART, JAMES MERTON, pub. utility exec.; b. Coshocton, O., Mar. 1, 1905; s. James M. and Margaret (Laird) S.; student U. Cin., 1922-24; LL.D., Wilmington Coll., 1964; H.H.D., U. Dayton, 1964; D.C.S., U. Cin., 1969; m. D. Deloris Walker, May 23, 1925 (dec.); children—James Merton, Curtiss Nolan, Charles Walker; m. 2d, Blodwyn M. Evans, July 20, 1946. Apprentice substa. operator Dayton Power & Light Co., 1923-24, constrn. helper, tech. clk., 1925-28, underground cable foreman supr. underground dept. 1929-42, mgr. electric operations, 1942-47, became v.p., 1947, asso. gen. mgr., dir., 1948, pres., gen. mgr., 1958-63, chmn., 1963-71, dir., mem. exec. com., 1971-75; dir. emeritus Winters Nat. Bank & Trust Co., State Fidelity Fed. Savs. & Loan Assn. Bd. dirs. Dayton Community Chest-Red Cross, Frank M. Tait Found., Air Force Mus. Found.; trustee, past chmn. bd. Jr. Achievement Dayton Inc.; trustee Dayton Boys' Club, Wilmington Coll., Wilberforce U., Engring. and Sci. Inst. Dayton, Sinclair Community Coll. Found.; Charles F. Kettering Found.; mem. civic adv. bd. Charles F. Kettering Meml. Hosp. mem. civic adv. bd. Cox Coronary Heart Inst. Trustee U. Dayton. Mem. Dayton Jr. C. of C. (hon.), I.E.E.E., Am. Gas Assn., Ohio Electric Utility Inst. (dir., past pres.), Edison Electric Inst. Eng., Ohio, Dayton chambers commerce, Ohio Soc. of N.Y., Newcomen Soc. Eng., Pi Kappa Alpha, Alpha Kappa Psi (hon.). Episcopalian. Rotarian. Clubs: Engineers (Dayton); Moraine Country. Home: Dayton, Ohio. Died Mar. 14, 1975.

STUART, JOHN LEIGHTON, ex-ambassador; b. of Am. parents, Hangchow, China, June 24, 1876; s. John Linton and Mary Louise (Horton) S.; A.B. and B.Litt., Hampden-Sydney Coll., Va., 1896, D.D., 1915; B.D., Union Theol. Sem. of Virginia; Litt.D., Princeton-University, 1930; LL.D., Austin College (Texas), 1949; married Aline Hardy Rodd, Nov. 17, 1904; 1 son, John Leighton. Ordained Presbyn. ministry; missionary in China, from 1905; prof. New Testament, Nanking Theol. Sem., 1908-19; pres. Yenching Univ. (Peking), 1919-46; United States ambassador to China, 1946-53. Trustee China Foundation for Promotion of Education and Culture. Mem. China Edn. Com., Sigma Chi, etc. Presbyterian. Author: Essentials of New Testament Greek (in Chinese), 1916; Greek-Chinese-English Dictionary of the New Testament, 1918; Commentary on the Apocalypse (in Chinese), 1922; Fifty Years in China, Memoirs of John Leighton Stuart, 1954. Special First Class Order of Merit, Republic of China. Address: Washington, D.C. Died Sept. 19, 1962.

STUART, MILTON C(ALEB), univ. prof.; b. Caroline County, Md., Mar. 31, 1886; s. William Johnson and Sarah Dorcas (Manly) S.; B.S., U. of Pa., 1909, M.E., 1924; m. Ethel Hinchman, May 2, 1914 (dec. Jan. 7, 1944); m. 2d, Katherine Gertrude Capel, Nov. 8, 1947. Instr., Rensselaer Polytech. Inst. Troy, N.Y., 1909-12; asst. steam engr. Cambria Steel Co., Johnstown, Pa., 1912-15; mech. engr. U.S. Navy Engring. Expt. Sta., Annapolis, Md., 1915-20; prof. mech. engring., U.S. Navy Postgrad. Sch., Annapolis, Md., 1920-26; prof. mech. engring., Lehigh University, Bethlehem, Pa., since 1926, head dept. mech. engring., since 1950; sabbatical year with Westinghouse Electric Corp. Turbine Div., South Phila., Pa., 1936-37; cons. U.S. Army Ordnance Dept. on rockets and recoiless gun research, 1942-45; prof. mech. engring. information and edn., div. U.S. Army, Am. Univ., Biarritz France, also Frankfurtam-Main, Germany, 1945-46. Registered professional engr., Pa. Fellow Am. Soc. Mech. Engrs.; mem. Am. Soc. Engring. Edn., Soc. Naval Architects and Marine Engrs., Am. Soc. Naval Engrs., Franklin Institute (Phila.), Newcomen Soc., Tau Beta Pi, Pi Tau Sigma, Sigma Xi. Republican. Methodist. Club: Bethlehem. Author: Asa Packer 1896-1879—Captain of Industry, Educator, Citizen (Am. Branch of Newcomen Soc., 1938); Principles of Engineering Thermodynamics (with Paul J. Kiefer), 1930. Editor: Naval Propulsive Power (restricted pub. Office of Naval Research), since 1947. Contbr. tech. articles to sci. jours. Home: Bethlehem, Pa. *

STUART, ROBERT LEE, clergyman, educator; b. Basham, Va., Sept. 12, 1883; s. Charles W. and Lorena Jackson (Moore) S.; student Asbury Coll., Wilmore, Ky., 1901-02; Ph.B., Taylor U., Upland, Ind., 1906, D.D., 1923; m. Josie Lena Conner, Mar. 24, 1908; children—Robert Marvin, Mary Elizabeth, Charles Conner, Paul, Josephine. Ordained M.E. ministry, 1906; pastor successively Whiting, Paulina, Akron, Humboldt, Spencer and Newton, Ia., until 1928, El Dorado, Kan., 1928-31; pres. Taylor U., 1931-45. Pastor Wesley Methodist Ch., Wichita, Kan. Home: Wichita, Kan. *

STUART, WILLIAM ALEXANDER, lawyer; b. Abingdon, Va., Oct. 24, 1889; s. John James and Kate Greenway (Preston) S.; B.A., Emory and Henry Coll., 1909; postgrad. U. Va., 1909-10, postgrad. law dept., 1914-16; postgrad. (Rhodes scholar from Va.), Oxford U. (Balliol Coll.), 1910-14, M.A., 1918; m. Ellen Pearce Bodley, Apr. 29, 1922 (dec. Nov. 1969); children—William Alexander, George Rogers Clark. Mem. firm Irvine & Stuart, Big Stone Gap, Va., 1916-20; now mem. Penn, Stuart & Eskridge and predecessor, Abingdon; pres. Stuart Land & Cattle Co. of Va., Inc.; dir. Pittston Co. Asst. U.S. atty. Western Dist. of Va., 1920-21; spl. asst. to atty. gen. of U.S., 1921-24. Chmn. bd. Johnston Meml. Hosp. 1947-57; bd. visitors U. Va., 1932-38, Emory and Henry Coll., 1934-76; bd. dirs. Va. Mus. Fine Arts 1951-55; mem. Va. State Library Bd., 1952-62, Va. Pub. Sch. Authority Bd. 1962-76; v.p., bd. dirs. Barter Theatre Va., Inc., 1941-76; Sec. 3d So. dist. Rhodes Scholarship Selection Com., 1930-33; civilian insp. U.S. Selective Service, 1941. Served from 2d lt. to maj. F.A., U.S. Army, 1917-18; assigned brigade adj. 44th Arty. Brig. Mem. Am. Legion (state comdr. 1919-20), Va. State Bar Assn. (pres. 1941), Am. Bar Found., Am. Law Inst., Va. Hist. Soc. (exec. com.), Phi Delta Phi, Beta Theta Pi, Raven Soc. (U. Va.). Democrat. Presbyn. Club: Commonwealth (Richmond, Va.). Home: Abingdon, Va. Died Aug. 10, 1976; interred Sinking Springs Cemetery, Abingdon.

STUBBEMAN, FRANK DIEDRICH, lawyer; b. Cuero, Tex., Jan. 3, 1906; s. William George and Ione Louise (Harrison) S.; A.B., U. Tex., 1929, LL.B., 1929; m. Violet Ann Graves, May 20, 1932; children—Robert Frank, David Graves. Admitted to Tex. bar, 1929; practice in San Angelo, Tex., 1929-30, Midland, Tex., 1930-78; mem. firm Stubbeman, McRae, Sealy, Laughlin & Browder, 1936-78. Mem. Tex. Legislature, 1933-34; city councilman, Midland, 1943-47. Chmn. bd. govs. Midland Meml. Hosp.; trustee Tex. Bur. for Econ. Understanding; bd. dirs. Jr. Achievement, Midland; bd. executors Permian Basin Petroleum Mus., Library and Hall of Fame. Mem. Am. Bar Assn., State Bar Tex. (dir. 1954-57, chmn. bd. dirs. 1956-57). Presbyn. (elder 1931-78, commr. Gen. Assembly 1948, moderator El Paso presbytery 1956). Mason (32 deg., Shriner), Lion (past dep. dist gov.). Home: Midland, Tex. Died Apr. 27, 1978.

STUBBLEFIELD, FRANK ALBERT, congressman; b. Murray, Ky., Apr. 5, 1907; s. Vernon C. and Virginia (Wilson) S.; student U. Ariz., 1927; B.S. in Commerce, U. Ky., 1932; m. Odessa Boaz, Feb. 4, 1934; children—Jennye Sue, Frankie Ann, Mary B. Retail druggist, Murray, Ky., 1933-77; mem. 86th-93d Congresses from 1st Ky. Dist. Councilman, Murray, 1939-43; mem. Ky. R.R. Commn., 1951-58. Served as lt. (j.g.) USNR, World War II. Mem. Murray C. of C. (dir.), Alpha Tau Omega. Democrat. Methodist. Elk. Rotarian. Home: Murray, Ky. Died Oct. 14, 1977.

STUHLMAN, OTTO, JR., physicist; b. Elberfeld, Germany, Nov. 12, 1884; s. Otto and Elizabeth (Hensman) S.; brought to U.S., 1891; grad. Woodward High Sch., Cincinnati, O., 1903, B.A., U. of Cincinnati, 1907; M.A., U. of Ill., 1909; Ph.D., Princeton, 1911; m. Cecil Craighead Wilbur, of Princeton, N.J., June 4, 1913. Instr. Stevens Inst. Tech., 1911-12, U. of Pa., 1912-18; asst. prof. physics, U. of Ia., 1918-19, U. of W.Va., 1919-20; asso. prof. physics, U. of N.C., 1920-24, prof. physics, since 1924. Fellow A.A.A.S., Am. Phys. Soc.; mem. Am. Optical Soc., N.C. Acad. Science, Sigma Xi, Sigma Phi Sigma. Presbyn. Author: Laboratory Manual of Physical Experiments, 1922. Contbr. on tech. topics especially the photo-electric effect, the electron theory of matter, and on the spectraof extra-ultra-violet radiations. Home: Chapel Hill, N.C.*

STULBERG, LOUIS, trade union ofcl.; b. Bogria, Poland, Apr. 1901; s. Benjamin and Jeanette Stulberg; S.; grad. Harbord Collegiate Inst., Toronto, Ont., Can.; student U. Chgo.; m. Bebe Friedman, Feb. 17, 1929; 1 dau., Judith (Mrs. David Crystal). Exec. v.p. Internat. Ladies Garment Workers Union, 1956-59, gen. sec., treas., 1959-66, pres., sec.-treas., 1966-75. Mem. U.S. del. UN. 1968-69; mem. Pres.'s Com. on Consumer Interests; mem. adv. bd. N.Y. Housing and Redevel. Bd., Pub. Devel. Corp. N.Y.C. Vice Pres. Liberal Party. Trustee United Housing Found., Mut. Redevel. Houses, East River Housing Corp., Fashion Inst. Tech.; exec. com. City of Hope. Fellow Brandeis U. Served with Jewish legion Brit. Army. Home: New York, N.Y. Died Dec. 14, 1977.

STULTS, WALTER ALLEN, Univ. prof.; b. Farmer City, Ill., Nov. 18, 1884; s. Allen Sylvester and Carrie Elizabeth (Haynes) S.; grad. West High Sch., Des Moines, Ia., 1900; G.M., Mus.B., Northwestern U., 1909; m. Edith Monica Graham, June 26, 1911; children—Mary Caroline, Barbara Edith, Gladys Jane. Has specialized in concert, oratorio and recital; dir. music Garrett Bibl. Inst., Evanston, 1908-11; prof. of singing, Northwestern U., since 1908, chmn. vocal dept., now emeritus; prof, singing Barat Coll., Lake Forest; mus. editor Evanston News-Index since 1910; now vis. prof. singing, music sch. N. Tex. State Coll., Denton. Mem. Nat. Assn. Tchrs. of Singing (pres.), Soc. Am. Musicians. Pi Kappa Lambda (bd. regents; pres.-gen.), Chgo. Singing Tchrs. Guild (pres.). Republican. Mason. Elk. Clubs: Cliff Dwellers (Chgo.); Evanston. Author many articles on singing. Home: Denton, Tex. *

STURC, ERNEST, economist; b. Bekescaba, Hungary, Jan. 12, 1915; s. Jindrich Jan and Regina (Atlas) S.; J.D., Comenius U., Bratislava, Czechoslovakia, 1938; postgrad. U. Chgo., 1939-42; m. Hilda Sirluck, Dec. 26, 1946; children—Marta Elizabeth, John Henry. Fgn. service officer of Czechoslovakia, 1939-46; dep. dir. Czechoslovakia Govt. Information Service, 1942-46; with IMF, 1946-80, dir. exchange and trade relations dept., 1965-80. Del. Czechoslovakia to Bretton Woods Conf. Internat. Monetary Coop., 1944, to San Francisco Conf. on UN, 1945. Mem. Am. Econ. Assn. Home: Washington, D.C. Died Oct. 27, 1980.

STYLER, WILLIAM FRANCIS, business exec.; b. N.Y.C., Aug. 10, 1917; s. William F. and Dorothy M. (Clain) S.; B.S. in Bus. Adminstrn., U. Ark., 1940; m. Meryl B. Byrns, Nov. 30, 1940; children—William Francis III, Robert F. Tchr., athletic coach Little Rock High Sch., 1940-41; sr. accountant FSA, 1941-42, Haskins & Sells, Tulsa, 1942-45; financial mgr. Nat. Asso. Petroleum Co., Tulsa, 1945-49; v.p. finance Crescent Petroleum Corp., Tulsa, 1949-62, dir., 1958-64, exec. v.p., 1962-64; vice chmn. bd. Norbute Corp., 1962-64; v.p. Apache Corp., 1964-68; v.p. sales White Shield Oil & Gas Corp., 1969-70; v.p., treas. Telex Corp., 1970-72, v.p. finance, treas., 1974-78, also dir.; pres. White Shield Corp. and subsidiaries, Tulsa, 1972-73. C.P.A., Okla. Mem. Am. Inst. C.P.A.'s, Okla. Soc. C.P.A.'s, Fin. Execs. Inst. Clubs: Cedar Ridge Country, Tulsa, Petroleum (Tulsa). Home: Tulsa, Okla. Died Sept. 18, 1978; buried Meml. Park, Tulsa.

STYRI, HAAKON (STÜRE), metallurgist; b. Christinia (now Oslo), Norway, Mar. 17, 1886; s. Nicolai Bernhard Hansen and Anna (Haug) S.; grad. high sch., 1903, mil. acad., 1904, Christiania; Mech. Engr. Tech. Sch., Christiania, 1907, Chem. E., 1909 (1 yr. shop practice); fellow Am. Scandinavian Foundation, Carnegie Inst. Tech., 1910; Dr. Ing., in Metallurgy, Technische Hochschule, Aachen, Germany, 1912; married Adele G. Aschehoug, September 15, 1945. Assistant professor metallurgy of iron, Poly. Inst., Trondhjem, Norway, 1912-16; came to U.S., 1916; asst. prof. metallurgy, Carnegie Inst. Tech., 1917-20; chief of S.K.F. Research Lab., mfrs. ball bearings, 1920-27, dir. research S.K.F. Industries, 1927-51, consultant for research and development since 1951. Decorated St. Olav Medal (Norway), 1951. Mem. Am. Inst. Mining and Metall. Engrs., Am. Soc. for Metals, A.S.M.E. Franklin Inst., Am. Society for Testing Materials, Iron and Steel Institute (Brit.). Contbr. research papers on metallurgy of steel and on ball-bearing engineering. Home: Philadelphia, Pa. *

SUGRUE, EDWARD D., newspaper exec. Former gen. mgr. Newark News. Home: Newark, N.J. Died Mar. 31, 1976.

SULLIVAN, ALOYSIUS MICHAEL, poet, editor, advt. exec.; b. Harrison, N.J., Aug. 9, 1896; s. William Henry and Mary Elizabeth (Flynn) S.; LL.D. (hon.), St. Edward's Coll., Austin, Tex., 1964; Litt.D. (hon.), Montclair State Coll., 1970; m. Catherine Veronica McNamee, Oct. 8, 1919; children—Catherine Rose, Mary Rose Sullivan Tuohy. Free lance writer, 1917; with Submarine Boat Corp., 1918-24; with J. P. Muller Advt. Agency, N.Y.C., 1924-34; with Dun & Bradstreet, 1934-61, cons., to 1971; editor Dun's Rev., 1954-61. Medalist, Catholic Poetry Soc. Am., 1958. Fellow N.J. Hist. Soc.; mem. Poetry Soc. Am. (pres. 1939-42, 50-52; exec. bd. o 1980; Gold medal 1951, 76), P.E.N., Cath. Poe.ry Soc. (pres. 1961-68), Craftsmen (pres.), Am. Irish Hist. Soc. (dir.; historiographer to 1980). Roman Catholic. Clubs: Advertising, Downtown Athletic (N.Y.C.). Author numerous books, including: Incident in Silver, 1950; Psalms of the Prodigal, 1953; The Bottom of the Sea, 1966; Songs of the Musconetcong and Other Poems of New Jersey, 1968, audio cassette edit., 1973; Selected Lyrics and Sonnets, 1970; (essays) The Three Dimensional Man, 1956; (collected editorials) Human Values in Management, 1968. Contbr. nat. mags. Founder of the New Poetry Hour, a radio forum for poets over WOR and Mutual Network. Subject of films: Songs of the Musconetcong (PBS), 1979; The Work of Love-A.M. Sullivan, Poet (CINE Golden Eagle award), 1979. Home: Montclair, N.J. Died June 10, 1980; buried Catholic Cemetery, Oxford, N.J.

SULLIVAN, C. M., coll. dean; b. Potsdam, N.Y., Feb. 20, 1884; s. Dennis F. and Mary (Lynch) S.; ed. State Normal Sch., Potsdam, 1902-05; B.S., Columbia U., 1913; M.S., Pa. State Coll., 1929; m. Mary Clare O'Malley, June 30, 1915; children—Cornelius Gerard, John Joseph, Eugene Francis. High Sch. prin., 1905-08; instr. Central State Normal Sch., Lock Haven, Pa., 1908-26; instr., head social studies dept., State Teachers Coll., Lock Haven, 1926-42, acting pres., 1942, dean instrn. since 1943. Pres. Lock Haven Community Service Assn., 1929-35. Mem. Pa. Edn. Assn. (sec. Central Conv. Dist., 1925-43), Phi Gamma Mu. Roman Catholic. K.C. Club: Kiwanis. Home: Lock Haven, Pa. *

SULLIVAN, CHARLES BRUCE, lawyer; b. Livonia, N.Y., Aug. 13, 1881; s. James D. and Hattie (Archer) S.; A.B., Hamilton Coll., 1905; LL.B., Albany Law Sch. (Union U.), 1907; m. Flora B. Randall, Aug. 18, 1910; 1 son, Bruce Randall. Admitted to N.Y. bar, 1907, and since engaged in gen. law practice in N.Y. State. Mem. judicial council of the State of New York; trustee Albany Law Sch.; mem. Am., N.Y. State, Albany County bar assns., Phi Beta Kappa. Republican. Clubs: Fort Orange, University, Wolferts Roost Country (Albany). Home: Albany, N.Y. *

SULLIVAN, GEORGE LEONARD, educator and engr.; b. Jackson, Neb., Oct. 16, 1881; s. Peter and Alice (Beacom) S.; B.Sc., U. of Neb., 1908; M.E., U. of Colo., 1910; Ph.D., U. of Santa Clara, Santa Clara, Calif., 1914; m. Eunice Lord Gale, Sept. 5, 1910; children—George Gale, Robert F. (dec.). Instr. in mech. engring., U. of Colo., 1908-11; asst. prof. mech. engring., Mont. State Coll., 1911-12; prof. mech. engring. U. Santa Clara, 1912-18, dean Coll. Engring., 1918-55, emeritus. City engr., Santa Clara, 1928-34; mem. Cal. State Bd. Registration for civil and profl. engrs., 1946-55, v.p., 1950-53. Cons. projects since 1918; consultant on saline water program Dept. of Interior, 1953—; cons. engr. Santa Clara-Alameda-San Benito Water Authority. Co-author, with Charles Gilman Hyde, of Master Plans for Sewage Disposal in Santa Clara County and in Santa Cruz County, 1946-47. Past chmn. government com. Citizens Planning Council, County of Santa Clara. Past pres. Chamber of Commerce; past chmn. planning commn. City of Santa Clara. Engring. center, U. Santa Clara named for him. Dipolomate American Academy Sanitary Engineers. fellow Am. Soc. M.E. (past chmn. San Francisco sect.; past chmn. standing com. on relations with colleges; hon. life mem.); mem. Soc. for Eng. Edn. (past mem. council), Am. Soc. C.E. (life), Cal.

Assn. Cons. Engrs., Nat. Soc. Profl. Engrs., Newcomen Soc., Sigma Tau, Sigma Xi, Tau Beta Pi,Alpha Sigma Nu. K.C. Rotarian. Home: Santa Clara, Cal. *

SULLIVAN, HAROLD JOSEPH, lawyer; b. Maysville, Okla., Nov. 26, 1909; s. Dr. Ernest and Mary Queen (Colley) S.; A.B., Washington and Lee U., 1932; LL.B., U. Okla., 1935; LL.M., Georgetown U., 1949; grad. Judge Adv. Gen. Sch., 1943; m. Mabel Gurney Wilkes, Apr. 14, 1949; children—Linda Alcock, Gurney Bartlett, Harold Joseph, Stewart Jeffress. Admitted to Okla. bar, 1935, U.S. Supreme Ct., 1947, Republic of Korea bar, 1954; practice of law, Oklahoma City, 1935-42, 65-80; commd. 2d lt. U.S. Army, advanced through grades to col. USAF, 1952; judge adv. Fifth Air Force and Far East Air Forces, 1943-45; chmn. bd. rev. Judge Adv. Gen., USAF, 1948-51, staff judge adv. Eighth Air Force, 1951-53, Fifth Air Force, Korea, 1954, Mobile Air Materiel Area, 1955-58, Eastern Air Def. Force, 1958-60, Oklahoma City Air Materiel Area, 1960-65; ret. 1965. Decorated Bronze Star. Fellow Am. Bar. Found.; mem. Am. (chmn. com. Am. Citizenship 1958, mem. com. continuing edn. 1958-59, 63-68, 74-80, ho. of dels. 1976-78), Okla. (bd. govs. 1968, exec. dir. 1969-75, dir. continuing legal edn. 1975-77) bar assns., Am. Law Inst., Beta Theta Pi, Phi Delta Phi. Democrat. Baptist. Clubs: Army and Navy (Washington); Men's Dinner; Beacon. Home: Oklahoma City, Okla. Died Nov. 3, 1980; buried Rose Hill Cemetery, Oklahoma City.

SULLIVAN, WALTER EDWARD, coll. prof.; b. Ludlow, Me., July 22, 1885; s. James Steven and Mary (Mitchell) S.; A.B., Bates Coll., Lewiston, Me., 1907; A.M., Brown U. Providence. RI 1908. Ph.D. 1912; m. Margaret Boley, 1914 (dec.); children—Ernest Walter, Mary Elizabeth (wife of Samuel H. Lerner, M.D.), Jane Freda (wife of Norman E. Jentz), Dorothy Louise; m. 2d, Caroline E. Vose, 1934. Instr. biology, Western Reserve U., 1911-13; asst. prof. anatomy, Marquette U., 1913-15; prof. anatomy, Tufts Coll., 1915-20; asst. prof. anatomy, U. of Wis., 1920-24, asso. prof., 1924-25, prof. since 1925; visiting prof., Washington U., St. Louis, 1943. Mem. (chmn.) Village Bd. Trustees, Shorewood Hills. (Mem. board of directors, Madison General Hospital. Mem. A.A.A.S., Am. Assn. Anatomists, Soc. Exptl. Biology and Medicine, Phi Beta Kappa. Protestant. Democrat. Clubs: Rotary (Madison), Chaos (Chicago). Co-author: Anatomy of the Rhesus Monkey, 1933. Contbr. anatomy papers. Home: Madison, Wisconsin. *

SULLIVAN, WALTER H., real estate investments; b. San Francisco, Oct. 28, 1884; s. Matthew J. and Mary (Feeney) S.; m. 2d, Mrs. Kenneth Dawson Nov. 3, 1952; children by previous marriage—Walter H., Thomas A. Mem. bd. of dirs. Walter H. Sullivan, Inc., Crocker First Nat. Bank of San Francisco, Santa Cruz Portland Cement Co., California, Pacific Title & Trust Co., Pacific Gas & Electric Co. Chmn. bd. Californians, Inc. Clubs: Pacific Union, San Francisco Gulf. Dir. A.R.R. Home: San Francisco. *

SULLIVAN, WILLIAM FRANCIS, assn. exec.; b. Nashua, N.H., Oct. 8, 1913; s. William Francis and Mary Elizabeth (Thomas) S.; student Phillips Exeter Acad., 1930-33; A.B., Harvard, 1938; LL.B., 1941; m. Helen B. Dolan, Feb. 27, 1943; children—Christine B., William, Mary. Admitted Mass. bar, 1941, and practiced with firm of Ropes, Gray, Best, Coolidge & Rugg, specializing in labor law practice, Boston, 1941-50; treas., pres. Nat. Assn. Cotton Mfrs. 1950-79; pres. No. Textile Assn., 1959-79. Mem. N.H., Boston bar assns. Roman Catholic. Home: Belmont, Mass. Died Apr. 12, 1979; buried Mt. Auburn Cemetery, Cambridge, Mass.

SULLOWAY, FRANK J., lawyer; b. Franklin, N.H., Dec. 11, 1883; s. Alvah Woodbury and Susan Keith (Daniel) S.; A.B. cum laude, Harvard, 1905, LL.B., 1907; m. Margaret Thayer, Sept. 24, 1913; (dec. Nov. 1967); children—Gretchen (dec.), Alvah Woodbury, Faith Thayer. Admitted to bar, 1907; with law firm Hill, Barlow & Homans, Boston, 1907-11, Streeter, Demond & Woodworth, Concord, N.H., 1911-12, Streeter, Demond, Woodworth & Sulloway, and later, with Sulloway, Jones, Hollis & Godfrey, now with Sulloway, Hollis, Godfrey & Soden, 1912—; past pres., treas. Concord Investment Corp.; dir. Concord Nat. Bank; trustee Amoskaeg Co. (Boston), Concord Savs. Bank. Former treas. Concord Hosp.; past state chmn. Harvard Coll. Fund. Rmeritus mem. investment com. N.H. Congl. Conf. Concord; N.H. chmn. 1st A.R.C. Roll Call., 1917; chmn. Concord chpt. A.R.C., 1917-39; N.H. chmn. Navy Relief Soc. campaign, 1942, Nat. War Fund, 1943. N.H. chmn. Republican finance campaign, 1937-48; Rep. nat. committeeman for N.H., 1944-56. Mem. Am. N.H. bar assns., Newcomen Soc., Harvard Alumni Assn. (v.p. 1956-57, class agt. Harvard Law Sch., 1970), U.S. Lawn Tennis Assn. (exec. com. 1939-59). Clubs. Spee, Hasty Pudding DKE, Choate (law) (Harvard); Union, Harvard, Longwood Cricket (Boston); Bow Brook (Concord). Home: Concord NH. *

SUMMERSKILL, WILLIAM HEDLEY JOHN, physician; b. London, Eng., Jan. 8, 1926; s. William Hedley and Elaine (Gerard) S.; B.A., Oxford U., 1947, M.A., 1951, M.B., 1949, D.M., 1955, D.Sc., 1975; student London U. Med. Sch., 1947-49; m. Elizabeth Anne Sheppard, Jan. 25, 1950 (dec.); 1 son, William S. Markham; m. 2d, Barbara Charlotte Helene Ehmcke, Sept. 17, 1969. Came to U.S., 1958, naturalized, 1965. Intern, St. Mary's Hosp., London, Eng., 1950; tutor Postgrad. Med. Sch., London, 1953-55; research asso. Harvard Med. Sch., 1955-56; sr. registrar Central Middlesex Hosp., London, 1957-58; cons. medicine Mayo Clinic, Rochester, Minn., 1959-77, dir. gastroenterology unit, 1962-77; asst. prof. Mayo Grad. Sch., U. Minn., 1959-63, asso. prof., 1963-67, prof. medicine, 1967-77; vis. prof. U. Colo., U. Cin., Dartmouth, Yale, London Mgd. Sch., Cleve. Clinic Found. Cons. gastroenterology and nutrition tng. com., NIH, VA; chmn. FDA Drug Evaluation Com., 1974-77. Served to capt. Brit. Army, 1951-53. Rockefeller Travelling fellow, 1955. Fellow A.C.P. (mem. sci. com.), Royal Coll. Physicians; mem. Med. Research Soc., Harveian Soc. London (v.p. 1958), Internat. Assn. Study Liver (councillor), Am. Gastroent. Assn. (research and internat. liaison com.) Am. Assn. Study Liver Diseases (pres. 1974-75), Assn. Am. Physicians, Assn. Physicians Gt. Britain and Ireland, A.A.A.S., Internat. Wine and Food Soc. (pres. Rochester chpt. 1974), Sigma Xi. Episcopalian. Club: Royal Thames Yacht. Editorial bd. Am. Jour. Digestive Diseases. Contbr. articles to profl. jours. Home: Rochester, Minn. Died Mar. 9, 1977.

SUNDSTROM, FRANK LEANDER, distillery cons.; b. Massena, N.Y., Jan. 5, 1901; s. Charles and Nora (Vandevener) S.; A.B., Cornell U., 1924; m. Jean Ross Johnstone, Dec. 26, 1936; children—Jean R., Frank L. Vice pres. Schenley Industries, Inc., N.Y.C., 1955-69; v.p., dir. Shenley Distillers, 1954-69; ltd. partner Burton, Dana & Co., stockbrokers, N.Y.C., until 1968; exec. Tobacco Inst., Washington, 1969-74; cons. Am. Distillery Co., Inc., 1974-80. Mem. U.S. Ho. of Reps., 11th Dist. N.J., 1943-49. Named to Cornell U. Hall of Fame, 1978, Nat. Football Found. Hall of Fame, 1978. Mem. Sigma Delta Chi. Phi Kappa Psi. Republican. Home: Chatham, N.J. Died May 23, 1980; buried Restland Meml. Park, Hanover, N.J.

SUNKIN, IRVING BURTON, cosmetics and pharm. co. exec.; b. N.Y.C., July 9, 1932; s. Nathan and Fay (Ackerman) S.; student Washington U., St. Louis, 1949-50; A.B., N.Y. U., 1953; J.D. (Harlan Fiske Stone scholar), Columbia, 1958; m. Mirel Jacobs, Dec. 5, 1953; children—Neil Michael, Andrew Alan, Ellen. Admitted to N.Y. bar, 1958; asso. firm Paul, Weiss, Rifkind, Wharton & Garrison, N.Y.C., 1958-65; v.p., corporate sec., counsel Revlon, Inc., N.Y.C., 1966-79; corporate sec. USV Pharm. Corp., Tuckahoe, N.Y., 1966-79, Coburn Optical Industries, Inc., Muskgogee, Okla., 1975-79, Barnes-Hind Pharms., Inc., San Francisco, 1977-79, Armour Pharm. Co., Phoenix, 1977-79. Served with AUS, 1953-55. Mem. Am. Soc. Corp. Secs., Assn. Bar City N.Y. Editor: Columbia Law Rev., 1956-58. Home: New York City, N.Y. Died Jan. 9, 1979; buried Cedar Park Cemetery.

SUNLEY, EMIL MCKEE, ret. educator, social worker; b. Paola, Kans., Apr. 22, 1906; s. George B. and Lucy M. (McKee) S.; student Kans. State Coll. Applied Sci., 1924-26; B.A., U. Kan., 1927; M.A., U. Iowa, 1934; Ph.D., U. Chgo., 1938; m. Nelle Traer, Aug. 26, 1933; children—Emil McKee, Traer Frazier. Caseworker, dist. sec. United Charities, St. Paul, 1927-30; field rep. Bur. Social Welfare, Extension Div., State U. Iowa, 1930-33, instr. dept. social adminstrn. U. Louisville, 1936-37; head dept. social work W.Va. U., Morgantown, 1938-47; dir. Grad. Sch. Social Work U. Denver, 1947-66, dean Grad. Sch. Social Work, 1966-71, dean emeritus, 1971-77. Cons. mental health tng. and research tng. Western Interstate Commn. on Higher Edn., 1955-56, mem. social work planning com., 1968-77; mem. child health council Colo. Dept. Pub. Health, 1956-58; mem. adv. bd. Denver Dept. Welfare, 1951-59, chmn., 1954-56; del. Mid-Century White House Conf. on Moving Ahead to Curb Juvenile Delinquency, Washington, 1954; del. White House Conf. Children and Youth, 1960; mem. Deans' Adv. Com. Sec. HEW, 1961-64. Mem. Am. Public Welfare Assn., Nat. Assn. Social Workers (mem. regional task force 1959-60, 1st v.p. 1957-59, mem. commn. on social policy and action 1955-58), Council Social Work Edn. (chmn. div. grad. schs. 1953-54, chmn. commn. on schs. and depts. 1953-54, gen. chmn. 13th ann. meeting, Denver 1965, chmn. nominating com. 1962-65), Colo. Conf. Social Welfare (2d v.p. 1949-50), Nat. Fedn. Settlements and Neighborhood Centers, Am. Assn. Schs. Social Work (dir. 1948-52), Phi Kappa Delta, Pi Kappa Delta. Episcopalian. Author: The Kentucky Poor Law, 1942. Home: Denver, Colo. Died Apr. 30, 1977; interred Chapel Hill Cemetery, Denver.

SUSENS, GEORGE, pres. Production Credit Corpn.; b. Germany, Oct. 22, 1885; s. Fred Marie marie (Oitken) S.; brought to U.S. by parents, 1888; ed. U. of S. Dak. and U. of Minn.; m. Bertha Martin, of Ottumwa, Ia., Aug. 6, 1909; 1 son, Morean George. Began as teacher pub. schs., 1906; connected with banking business 10 yrs., sec. Minn. Banking Assn. 5 yrs., 1928-33, apptd. pres. Production Credit Corpn. for the Northwest (a subsidiary of the Farm Credit Administra.), Nov. 1933, apptd. nat. acting dir. Emergency Crop and Feed Loan Sect. of F.C.A., June, 1934. Club: St. Paul Athletic (pres.). Home: Minneapolis, Minn. *

SUSSKIND, WALTER, orch. condr.; b. Prague, Czechoslovakia, May 1, 1913; s. Bruno and Gertrude (Seger) S.; grad. State Conservatorium, Prague, 1931, Acad. Music, Prague, 1931; Hum.D., U. So. Ill.; D.F.A., Washington U., St. Louis. Coach, Asst. condr. German Opera, Prague, 1935-38; prin. condr. English opera cos., Royal Carl Rosa, Sadler's Wells and Glyndbourne, 1940-46; mus. dir. Scottish Nat. Orch., 1946-52; music dir. Festival in Aspen, Colo., 1961-68; founder Nat. Youth Orch. Can., 1958; guest condr. symphony orchs. throughout world; prin. condr. Victoria Symphony Orch., Melbourne, Australia, 1953-55, Toronto Symphony Orch., 1956-65; concert pianist, composer, 1944-80; music dir. St. Louis Symphony Orch., 1968-75; music advisor Cin. Symphony Orch., 1978-80; faculty Washington U., St. Louis, U. So. Ill. Composer, arranger piano works for orch.; recs. for Columbia, H.M.V., Parlaphone, Everest, Pye, Angel, Capitol, Vox, others; lectr. on conducting and contemporary music. Mem. Am. Inst. Orchestral Conducting. Address: New York, N.Y. Died Mar. 25, 1980.

SUSSMAN, MORTY, fashion designer; b. N.Y.C. With volume designing houses in N.Y.C.; v.p., chief designer for Johere, N.Y.C.; pres., dir. Spartans Industries Inc. Address: New York, N.Y. Died Mar. 26, 1979.

SUTHERLAND, LOUIS W., paper co. exec.; b. Kalamazoo, Mich., Dec. 24, 1882; s. Frederick and Anna Sutherland; LL.D., Kalamazoo Coll.; m. 1907; children—Betty Race, Louis W. Chmn. bd. Sutherland Paper Co., Kalamazoo, Mich.; v.p., dir. Am. Nat. Bank & Turst Co., Kalamazoo; dir. KVP Sutherland Paper Co., Clarage Fan Co., Kalamazoo Bldg. Co., Lissner Paper Grading Co., Chgo. Mayor Kalamazoo. Mem. Mich. Mfrs. Assn. (dir.). Conglist. Clubs: Athletic (Chgo.); Country, Park. Home: *

SUTHERLAND, ROBERT LEE, educator, sociologist; b. Clarinda, Iowa, Feb. 11, 1903; s. Donald Grant and Charlotte (Cleveland) S.; A.B., Knox Coll., 1925, LL.D., 1958; A.M., Oberlin Coll., 1927; Ph.D., U. Chgo., 1930; m. Marjorie Lewis, Aug. 24, 1926; 1 dau., Elizabeth. Prof. pub. speaking Huron (S.D.) Coll., 1926-27; prof. sociology Bucknell U., Lewisburg, Pa., 1930-40, chmn. social science div., 1934-36, 38-40, dean of men, 1938-40; dir., pres. Hogg Found. and prof. sociology U. Tex., Austin, 1940-70, pres. emeritus, 1970-76; Hogg prof. sociology Hogg Found., 1970-73, emeritus, 1973-76; mem. staff Am. Studies Course, Cambridge U., summer 1954. Mem. Nat. Adv. Council Dental Research, 1960-63; asso. dir. Am. Youth Commn., 1937-41. Bd. dirs. The Woman's Found., Inc., 1946-50, United Community Services, 1966-76, Council Founds., Conf. S.W. Founds., 1973; trustee Knox Coll., 1958-63; bd. curators Stephens Coll., 1943-52. Robert Lee Sutherland chair U. Tex. established, 1980. Mem. Am., Southwest sociol. socs., Nat. Council Religion in Higher Edn., Tex. Soc. Mental Health, Tex. United Community Services, Tex. Philos. Soc., Phi Beta Kappa, Delta Sigma Rho, Sigma Delta Chi, Phi Kappa Phi, Tau Kappa Epsilon. Presbyn. Author: Introductory Sociology (with J.L. Woodward), 5th edit., 1956, 6th edit. (with Milton A. Maxwell), 1961; Color, Class and Personality (American Youth Commn.), 1941, 72. Co-editor: Personality Factors on the College Campus, 1962; Understanding Mental Health, 1965. Contbr. articles to profl. jours. Home: Austin, Tex. Died Nov. 19, 1976; interred Austin Meml. Park Cemetery.

SUTTER, CHARLES CLYDE (SUT'ER), physician; b. Punxsutawney, Pa., Mar. 22, 1885; s. Jacob Wesley and Mary Elizabeth (Schlemmer) S.; M.D., U. of Pa., 1908; unmarried. Became interne Adrian Hosp., Punxsutawney, 1908; also interne Presbyn. Hosp., Phila., and Phila. Hosp. for Contagious Diseases; mem. Staff Glen Springs Sanitarium, Watkins Glen, N.Y.; private practice, Rochester, N.Y., since 1912; practice limited to digestive and metabolic diseases; mem. med. staff and chief of staff Park Av. Hosp. Served as capt. Med. Corps, U.S. Army, during World War; with A.E.F. as dir. of lab. Base Hosp. No. 19, dir. combined labs. of Vichy Hosp. Center. Dir. Park Av. Hosp. Certified as specialist in internal medicine by Am. Bd. Internal Medicine; fellow Am. Coll. Physicians; mem. A.M.A., Rochester Acad. Medicine, Phila. Pathol. Society, Rochester Pathol. Soc., Am. Diabetes Assn. Republican. Presbyterian. Mason (32 deg., Shriner). Contbr. to medical jours. Address: Honeoye Falls, N.Y. *

SUTTIE, ROSCOE H(ENRY), educator; b. Lisbon, N. H., Feb. 24, 1886; s. H.M. and Isabelle F. (Gould) S.; Ph.B., Yale, 1911, C.E., 1913; m. Edith K. Hewitt, June 29, 1914; children—Ruth (Mrs. Robert A. Whiting), Anne Gould (Mrs. Bennet Murdock). Instr. Yale, 1913-18; asst. engr., U.S. Geol. Survey, 1918-19; asst.

prof. civil engring., Yale, 1919-28, asso. prof., 1928-44, prof. since 1944; hydraulic engr. Conn. State Geol. Nat. Hist. Survey, 1926; cons. Conn. Commn. concerning reorgn. state depts. Fellow Trumbull Coll., Yale. Mem. Pub. Health Council of Conn., Am. Soc. C.E., New Eng. Sewage Works Assn., New Eng. Water Works Assn., Am. Pub. Health Assn., Am. Geophys. Union, Am. Soc. C.E., Sigma Xi, Tau Beta Pi, Delta Omega. Republican. Clubs: Faculty, Sigma Nu, St. Elmo, Aurelian Morys. Author reports and bulletins. Home: New Haven, Conn. *

SVERDRUP, LEIF JOHN, civil engr.; b. Sulen, Norway, Jan. 11, 1898; s. John Edward and Agnes (Vollan) S.; came to U.S., 1914; B.A., Augsburg Coll., 1918; B.S. in C.E., U. Minn., 1921; D.Eng. (hon.), U. Mo. Sch. Mines and Metallurgy, 1952, Norwich U., 1969; D.Sc., Washington U., St. Louis, 1960; D.Litt. (hon.), Webster Coll., 1972; m. Helen L. Egilsrud, Nov. 26, 1924; 1 son, Johan Norman. Designer and resident engr. Minn. Hwy. Dept., 1921-22; designer Mo. Hwy. Dept., 1922-23, engr. in charge constrn. Mo. River bridges, 1922-23, chief bridge engr., 1924-28; partner Sverdrup & Parcel, cons. engrs., 1928-48; chmn. bd. Sverdrup & Parcel & Assos. Inc., St. Louis, Sverdrup & Parcel Internat., Inc., Spire Corp., Conv. Plaza East, Inc.; chmn. bd., chief exec. officer Sverdrup & Parcel and Assos. N.Y. Inc., ARO, Inc.; dir. First Union, Inc., Midcoast Aviation Services, Inc., 1st Nat. Bank St. Louis, Northwestern States Portland Cement Co., St. Louis County Water Co., St. Louis Union Trust Co., United Food Products. Spl. cons. U.S. Corps Engrs. on airports in South Sea Islands, Australia and N.Z., cons. on portable mil. bridges; spl. cons. Pub. Works Adminstrn. on Lake Washington Pontoon bridge, Seattle; mem. bd. inquiry into failure of Tacoma Narrows bridge, also mem. cons. bd. on re-design. Served in U.S. Army, 1918-19; col. to maj. gen. Engrs. Corps, AUS, 1942-46; chief engr. overseas duty PTO; comdg. gen. 102d Res. Inf. Div., 1947-58, Engr. adv., plan and devel. Idaho atomic reactor testing sta. Decorated Silver Star, D.S.M., Purple Heart, D.S.C., Legion of Merit, Philippine Disting. Service Star; comdr. Order Brit. Empire, Croix de Guerre with palm; comdr. with star Order of St. Olav. Recipient Outstanding Achievement medal U. Minn., 1950; Honor award U. Mo., 1952; Man of Yr. award St. Louis Globe Democrat, 1956; Lloyd Kimbrough medal Am. Inst. Steel Constrn., 1959; Golden Beaver award The Beavers, 1959 Outstanding Service award Nat. Soc. Profl. Engrs., 1961; Outstanding Tech. Achievement award Cons. Engrs. Council, 1964; Gold Medal Achievement award Engrs. Club St. Louis, 1966; Bronze Medal Meritorious Civilian Service award and lapel rosette Mobility Adv. Group, 1967; Disting. Exec. award Sales & Mktg. Execs.-St. Louis, 1967; Citizen of Yr. award Mo. Moose Assn., 1967; Man of Yr. award Kiwanis, 1967; Silver Beaver award Boy Scouts Am., 1967, Silver Antelope award, 1968, Silver Buffalo award, 1974; Free Enterprise award Jr. Achievement, 1969; St. Louis award, 1970; Engr. of Yr. award Mo. Soc. Profl. Engrs., 1971; Disting. Service medal Royal Arch Masons, 1971; Levee Stone award Downtown St. Louis, Inc., 1972; Brotherhood award NCCJ; Spirit of St. Louis award Conv. and Visitors Bur. Greater St. Louis. Mem. Am. Soc. Mil. Engrs. (award of appreciation 1970), Am. Soc. C.E. (hon.), Norwegian Soc. C.E., Am. Inst. Cons. Engrs., Am. Ry. Engring. Assn. Lutheran. Clubs: St. Louis, St. Louis Country, Bogey, Old Warson Country, Racquet, Noonday, Engineers (St. Louis); Links (N.Y.C.); Lyford Cay (Bahamas). Home: St Louis, Mo. Died Jan. 2, 1976; interred Valhalla Cemetery, St. Louis.

SWAIM, LORING TIFFANY, physician; b. Claitemont, N.H., Dec. 11, 1882; s. Joseph Skinner and Caroline Tiffany (Dyer) S.; student Volkman Sch., Boston, 1901; A.B., Harvard, 1995; M.D. cum laude, 1909; m. Madeleine Katherine Gill, Oct. 4, 1913; children—Shirley T. (Mrs. E. C. Nickerson), Loring T., Thomas Gill. Intern Mass. Gen. Hosp., 1909-12, surg. outpatients 1917-22; asst. to Dr. Joel E. Goldthwait, Boston, 1912; orthopaedic surgeon, Clifton Springs, Sanatorium New York, 1912-15; pvt. practice splty., N.Y. City, 1915; partner Goldthwait Osgood Brown, Boston, 1916-29; chief orthopaedic service, Robert B. Brigham Hosp., 1917-35, chief orthopaedic consultant, 1935-44, instr. orthopaedic surgery, Med. Sch., Harvard, 1926-46, ret. 1944. Active in Moral Rearmament program since 1933, traveled with Dr. Frank N.D. Buchman for program, 1944-47. Civilian instr. orthopaedic Army Officers, Mass. Gen. Hosp., World War I. Hon. mem. Royal Soc. Medicine (Eng.). Diplomate Am. Bd. Orthopaedic Surgery, 1935. Mem. A.M.A., Am. Orth. Assn., Am. Acad. Orth. Surgery. Am. Rhematism Assn., Mass. Med. Soc., Pan Am. Rheumatism Lique, Lique International Contra le Rhematism, Rhematisme Lique of Argentina. Brazil and Denmark, Phi Beta Kappa, Sigma Xi, Alpha Omega Alpha. Mem. Community Ch. Clubs: Rotary (dir., Groton); Harvard (Boston). Home: East Pepperell, Mass. *

SWAIN, CARL C., coll. pres.; b. Zumbrota, Minn., Mar. 31, 1884; s. Christian Nelson and Oline (Rud) S.; B.S., St. Olaf Coll., Northfield, Minn., 1907, LL.D., 1940; grad. study U. of Wis., 1908; A.M., Columbia, 1918; m. Mabel Elenore Swanson; 1 dau., Carol Marie. Prin. high sch., Anoka, Minn., 1907-08, Virginia, Minn., 1908-09; pres. St. Ansgar (Ia.) Sem., 1909-10; supt. schs., Goodhue County, Minn., 1910-13; state commr. rural edn., Minn., 1914-20; spl. lecturer Summer Sch., U. of Minn., 1914-19; prof. ednl. administration, Ia. State Teachers Coll., Cedar Falls, 1920-23; pres. State Teachers Coll., Mayville, 1923-38; pres. State Teachers Coll., Minot, since 1938. Chmn. Lutheran Ch. Bd. of Charities, since 1946, American Red Cross, Traill County, N. D. Member N.E.A., Nat. Soc. Teachers Colls., Nat. Country Life Assn., N.D. State Teachers Assn. (pres. n.e. sect., 1926), N.D. Edn. Assn. (pres. 1929-30), Nat. Lutheran Brotherhood (president, since 1948), Pi Gamma Mu. Republican. Lutheran. Author: Studies in Consolidation, 1916; State Reorganization of Rural Schools, 1919; (with others) Rural SchoolManagement, 1924. Home: Minot, N.D.*

SWAN, DANA MERRILL, lawyer; b. Providence, Feb. 26, 1908; s. Frank Herbert and Hannah (Dana) S.; A.B. summa cum laude, Bowdoin Coll., 1929; B.A., Oxford (Eng.) U., 1931, M.A., 1936; postgrad. Harvard, 1931-32; m. Martha Henwood, Mar. 25, 1933; 1 dau., Mary Becket (Mrs. Henry F. Anthony II). Admitted to R.I. bar, 1932, since practiced in Providence; partner firm Swan, Keeney Jenckes & Asquith, 1939—. Vice pres., sec., dir. Union Wadding Co.; sec., dir. Taylor, Symonds Co., Providence Braid Co. Sec., Providence chpt. A.R.C., 1941-45, vice chmn., 1945-46, chmn., 1946-47. Trustee Providence Pub. Library, 1947-75; trustee Emma Pendleton Bradley Home, 1942-77, v.p., 1943-51, pres., 1951-72. Rhodes scholar, 1929-31, mem. selection com. 1932-63. Mem. Am., R.I. bar assns., Estate Planning Council R.I. (sec. 1960-62; v.p. 1962-63; pres. 1963-64). Episcopalian. Clubs: Turks Head, Agawam Hunt. Home: Providence, R.I. Died May 5, 1977.

SWAN, MARSHALL, lawyer; b. Bristol, R.I., Aug. 25, 1906; s. Frank Herbert and Hannah Little (Dana) S.; A.B., Bowdoin Coll., 1929; LL.B., Boston U., 1932; m. Katharine Brusstar McLaughlin, Apr. 4, 1932; children—Henry Marshall, Susan Louise. Admitted to R.I. bar, 1932, practiced in Providence; asso. Swan, Keeney & Jenckes, 1932-37, partner, 1937-79. Bd. overseers Bowdoin Coll. Served with USNR, 1943-45. Mem. Am., R.I. bar assns., Am. Judicature Soc. Episcopalian (sr. warden emeritus). Clubs: R.I. Country; Turks Head (Providence). Home: Barrington, R.I. Died Feb. 11, 1979.

SWANN, THEODORE, mfr. chemicals; b. Dandridge, Tenn., Sept. 5, 1886; s. John S. and Sonora (Williams) S.; prep. edn., Maury Acad., Dandridge; student Carson and Newman Coll., Jefferson City, Tenn., Va. Inst., Bristol, Va.; hon. Sc.D.; m. Catherine Dunwody, Jan. 6, 1909; children—Catherine (dec.), Virginia. Elec. contractor. Bristol. Va., 1906-10; salesman with Westinghouse Electric & Mfg. Co., 1910-12; commercial mgr. Virginia Power Co. Charleston, W.Va., 1912-13; sales mgr. Ala. Power Co., 1913-17; pres. W.Va. Light & Traction Co., 1914-26; vice-pres. Anniston Ordnance Co. and Anniston. Steel Co., 1916-17; pres. Swann Corp., Swann Chem. Co., Swann Fertilizer Co., Southern Manganese Corp., Federal Abrasives Co. (until 1935); now owner Swann & Co. Asso. mem. U.S. Naval Consulting Bd., World War; col. Ordnance R.C.; chmn. adv. bd. Birmingham Ordnance Dist. Asso. mem. Am. Inst. Elec. Engrs. Republican. Home: Birmingham, Ala. *

SWART, ROBERT LEE, naval officer; b. Elizabeth, N.J., Nov. 8, 1901; s. Robert Lee and Selma (De Vantier) S.; B.S., U.S. Naval Acad., 1924, student Postgrad. Sch., 1929-30; M.S., Pa. State U., 1931; m. Eleanor R. Owings, Aug. 16, 1924; children—James Hamilton, Robert Lee (USN). Commd. ensign USN, 1924, advanced through grades to rear adm., 1953; assigned U.S.S. New York, U.S.S. Reid, 1924-26, also tng. Torpedo Sch., Newport, R.I., Submarine Sch., New London, Conn.; squadron engr. Submarine Squadron 3, Panama, C.Z., 1932-34; mgmt. prodn. diesel engines Navy power boats, 1934-36; exec. officer U.S.S. Perch, also comdr. submarine R-11, 1937-39; engr., repair officer Submarine Base, New London; budget officer Submarine Force Atlantic Fleet, 1939-41; navigator, tactical officer U.S.S. Wichita, North Atlantic patrols, 1941; force engr., material officer Comdr. Service Forces Atlantic Fleet, 1942-45; head auxiliary vessels br. Bur. Ships, asst. dir. ship tech. div. for machinery, elec. and electronics, 1945-47, dir. div., 1947-49; prodn. officer Norfolk Naval Shipyard, 1949-51; supr. shipbuilding, Newport News, Va., 1951-53; asst. chief Bur. Ships, 1954-55; vice chief naval material, 1955-81. Decorated Legion of Merit. Mem. Am. Soc. Naval Engrs., Am. Soc. Naval Architects and Marine Engrs., Am. Newcomen Soc., Am. Ordnance Assn., Nat. Sojourner, Episcopalian, Mason. Clubs: Army-Navy (Washington); Army-Navy Country (Arlington, Va.). Home: Arlington, Va. Died Feb. 7, 1981; buried Arlington Nat. Cemetery.

SWARTLEY, STANLEY SIMPSON, coll. prof.; b. North Wales, Pa., July 2, 1884; s. Mahlon R. and Mary (Godshalk) S.; A.B., U. of Pa., 1905, Ph.D., 1917; S.T.B., Boston U., 1908, A.M., 1909; Columbia, summers 1912, 13; m. Annette Miller, Apr. 12, 1909 (died Sept. 8, 1940); 1 son, David S. Master in English and Latin, Harrisburg Acad., 1908-10; Harrison fellow in Eng., U. of Pa., 1913-14, 1916-17; instr. English, Allegheny Coll., 1910-14. asst. prof., 1914-20, asso. prof., 1920-21, prof. English lang., 1921-33; prof. English, 1933-49, now prof. emeritus; on leave, 1927-28, for travel and study in Europe, also 1938-39 in Southwestern U.S. Mem. Modern Language Assn., American Association Univ. Profs., S.A.R., Phi Delta Theta, Phi Beta Kappa. Pi Delta Epsilon. Republican. Methodist. Mason (32 deg.). Clubs: Round Table, Iroquois, Rotary. Author: Life and Poetry of John Cutts, 1917; Aids to Good English, 1933, rev. edits.,1936, 38. Home: Meadville, Pa. *

SWARTZ, HAROLD, sculptor; b. San Marcial, N.M., Apr. 7, 1886; s. Charles and Carrie (Bending) S.; prep. edn., pub. and high schs., Columbus, O.; student Ohio State U., 1904-07; studied sculpture Kunstgewerbeschule, Berlin, also at Paris and Rome; m. Winifred Dunn, Nov. 9, 1927. Instr. in sculpture, Otis Art Inst., Los Angeles, Calif., 1923-25; asst. instr. Kunstgewerbeschule, Berlin, 1927; instr., Chouinard Sch. of Art, Los Angeles, 1927-28. Awarded 1st prize, Arcadia Expn., 1922; 1st prize, Pomona Expn., 1923; gold medal, Pacific Southwest Expn., 1925; 2d prize, Berlin Internationale, 1927; 1st prize, C.A.C. Expn., 1931. Represented at Los Angeles Mus. Commr. municipal art, Los Angeles, 1929; mem. Civic Bur. Music and Art; mem. com. on art and edn., Los Angeles Chamber Commerce. Mem. Sculptors Guild of Southern Calif., Painters and Sculptors Club, Calif. Art Club. Home: Los Angeles, Calif. *

SWEARINGEN, J(AMES) I(SAAC), coll. administrator; born Spencer, Ia., Apr. 8, 1898; s. Henry Franklin and Nettie (Storey) S.; B.S., Univ. of Ill., 1923, M.S., 1927; student, Univ. of Chicago, part-time, 1929-35; L.H.D. (hon.), Chgo. State U., 1974; m. Lucile G. Haworth, June 26, 1928; children—Charles Franklin, Carol Ann. Teacher, rural schs., Ill., 1916-18; coach and teacher, Morrisonville (Ill.) High Sch., 1923-24; prin., Raymond (Ill.) Community High Sch., 1924-27; geography teacher, Bay View High Sch., Milwaukee, Wis., 1927-29; with Chicago pub. schs., since 1929; dir. of instruction, Chicago Teachers Coll., 1940-42, and since 1948, acting pres., 1942-48, associate prof. geography, from 1963; acting dean Wilson Jr. Coll., Chgo., 1942-48; instr. Ind. U. Extension, E. Chgo., Ind.; v.p. Bankers Dispatch Corp. Ill., Bankers Transport Corp. Wis., Ind. In Boy Scout work since 1943; training chmn., S.W. dist., Chicago, 1946-47, and vice chmn. of training com., Chicago Council of Boy Scouts, since 1947; supt. of Morgan Park Ch. Sch., Chicago. Served A.U.S. with 10 months overseas, 1918-19. Mem. Ill. Edn. Assn., National Education Association, American Legion. Sigma Delta Sigma, Kappa Phi Kappa. Methodist. Mason. Club: Kiwanis. Home: Chicago, Ill. Died Dec. 9, 1976; buried Long Point Cemetery, Wapella, Ill.

SWEAT, HERBERT J., clergyman; b. Boyce, La., Sept. 11, 1925; s. William L. and Edna E. Sweat; student Northwestern State Coll., 1946; grad. Internat. Bible Coll., 1949; postgrad. Pitts. Theol. Sem., Duquesne U.; m. Rita A. Predajna, Sept. 5, 1949; children—Gary L., Randall D. Ordained to ministry Ind. Assemblies of God; minister ch., Madisonville, Ky., 1950-56, Calvary Temple, Washington, Pa., 1957-77; dir. Outreach Missionary Service to Haiti (built 15 chs., 5 orphanages and day schs., food distbn. centers); advisor Full Gospel Bus. Men's Fellowship, Washington, Pa.; sec. Ind. Assemblies of God, Washington, Pa. Bd. dirs. Interfaith Fellowship, Pitts. Served with inf. 34th div. AUS, 1943-46; ETO. Decorated Bronze Star with three oak leaf clusters. Home: Washington, Pa. Died Oct. 22, 1977.

SWEATT, CHARLES BAXTER, appliance mfg. co. exec.; b. Mpls., Dec. 19, 1894; s. William R. and Jessie (Wilson) S.; B.A., U. Minn., 1917; m. Margaret Lamberton, Oct. 1927; children—Charles Baxter, Henry Lamberton, Sarah Wilson, Margaret Elizabeth. With Mpls.-Honeywell Regulator Co., 1919, vice chmn. bd., 1953-58, also dir.; chmn. bd. Apache Corp., 1964-77, also dir. Former dir. and v.p. U.S. Equestrian Team; former dir. Am. Horse Show Assn.; former pres. bd. trustees St. Barnabus Hosp., pres. United Hosp. Fund, pres. Downtown Found. Mem. Newcomen Soc., Beta Theta Pi. Home: Palm Beach, Fla. Died July 31, 1977; interred Lakewood Cemetery, Mpls.

SWEDENBERG, HUGH THOMAS, JR., educator; b. Milledgeville, Ga., Aug. 2, 1906; s. Hugh Thomas and Clyde (Johnson) S.; B.A., Presbyn. Coll., 1928, D.Litt., 1972; M.A., Columbia, 1929; Ph.D., U. N.C., 1937; m. Anne Elizabeth Lilly, June 4, 1936; 1 dau., Anne Carol. Asst. prof. Presbyn. Coll., 1929-31, prof. English, 1933-36; instr., then asst. prof., asso. prof., prof. English, U. Calif., Los Angeles, 1937-74, prof. emeritus, 1974-78, Clark Library prof. 1969-71; Rushton vis. prof. Birmingham-So. Coll., 1966. Fellow John Simon Guggenheim Found., 1952-53, Folger Shakespeare Library, 1962-63. Served as maj. AUS, 1942-46. Recipient Distinguished Alumnus award U. N.C., 1973. Mem. Philol. Assn. Pacific Ocast, Modern Lang. Assn. Am., Internat. Assn. U. Profs. English, Phi Beta Kappa,

Pi Kappa Phi. Editor: (with Louis B. Wright) The American Tradition, 1941; The Theory of the Epic in England, 1650-1800, 1944. Co-founder, co-editor The Augustan Reprint Soc. Publs., 1946-78. Gen. editor: The Works of John Dryden, 1956-78. Editor: Essential Articles for the Study of John Dryden, 1966; English Poetry of the Restoration and Early Eighteenth Century, 1968; England in the Restoration and Early Eighteenth Century, 1972. Author of scholarly articles on English lit. 17th and 18th centuries. Home: Santa Monica, Calif. Died May 16, 1978.

SWEENEY, JAMES WILLIAM, educator; b. Long Island City, N.Y., July 26, 1923; s. William and Oriel Margaret (Grable) S.; B.S., M.S., Ga. Inst. Tech., 1948; Ph.D., Mass. Inst. Tech., 1954; m. Mary Mason Byrd, June 12, 1976; children by previous marriage—James Patrick, Michael Thomas, Kathleen Francis, Timothy Sean. Instr., Ga. Inst. Tech., 1946-48, asst. prof. indsl. mgmt., 1950-55, research asso. Engring. Expt. Sta., 1950-53, research asso. Rich Electronic Computer Center, 1953-55, dir. pub. utility exec. course, 1952-55; asso. prof. indsl. mgmt. Tulane U., 1955-60, dir. Computer Lab., 1958-67, prof. indsl. mgmt, 1960-67, dir. Bio-Med. Computing System, 1961-65, prof. computer medicine dept. psychiatry and neurology Sch. Medicine, 1963-67, dir. div. med. computing scis., 1965-67, prof. computing sci., 1966-67; dir. div. computer services Miss. Research and Devel. Center, Jackson, 1967; dir. U. Okla. Computing Center, 1967-72, prof. computer sci., 1968-72, prof. indsl. engring., 1968-78, cons. prof. biostatistics and epidemiology Sch. Health, Med. Center, 1969-78, prof. information and computing sci., 1969-78. Mem. health services demonstration grants rev. com. Nat. Center for Health Services Research and Devel., USPHS, 1966-78; mem. planetarium and sci. com. Okla. Sci. and Arts Found., 1969-78; mem. com. on computer centers So. Regional Edn. Bd., 1970-78; cons. Touro Infirmary, New Orleans, 1966-69; spl. cons. to Am. Psychiat. Assn. Interprofl. Adv. Council on Manpower Utilization in Mental Health Services, 1966-78. Mem. study com. New Orleans Dept. Health, 1964-67, New Orleans Dept. Finance, 1964-66. Served to lt. (j.g.) USNR, 1941-46; PTO. Mem. Am., So. econ. assns., Acad. Mgmt., Am. Inst. Indsl. Engrs. (sr.), Assn. for Computer Machinery (past chmn. Greater New Orleans chpt.), Bio-Med. Information Processing Orgn. (past sec.-treas.), Internat. Sci. Information Services, Inc., Data Processing Mgmt. Assn., Assn. Computer Mgmt., Operations Research Soc. Am., Assn. for Health Records, Frontiers of Sci. Okla. Soc., Internat. Interdisciplinary Orgn. for Medicine, Delta Sigma Pi. Contbr. numerous articles to profl. jours.; asso. editor Archives for Electronic Computing, 1968-78, Methods of Med. Information, 1967-78. Home: Atlanta, Ga. Died July 18, 1978; buried Arlington Cemetery, Atlanta.

SWEENEY, JOSEPH, fgn. service officer; b. Salem, Mass., Sept. 11, 1912; s. Patrick Henry and Mary Jane (Turner) S.; A.B., Whittier Coll., 1933; M.S., in Social Work, U. So. Cal., 1939, M.A. in Internat. Relations, 1940; Ph.D., Fletcher Sch. Law and Diplomacy (Tufts-Harvard), 1943; m. Adelaide Mary Rasin, July 6, 1936; children—Kevin, Ellen. Served with prisoner of war sect. A.R.C., 1943; with O.S.S., 1943-45; with Dept. of State, 1945-68, chief Brit. Commonwealth br. Office Research and Intelligence, 1945-50; polit. officer Am. Embassy, Union of South Africa, 1950-52; U.S. liaison officer Anglo-Egyptian Sudan, 1953-55; 1st sec. Am. Embassy, Stockholm, Sweden, 1955-57; dep. chief of mission Am. Embassy, Jidda, Saudi Arabia, 1957-59; assigned Nat. War Coll., 1959-60; officer-in-charge UN Gen. Assembly Affairs, 1960-62, U.K. and Ireland Affairs, State Dept., 1962-63; dep. chief mission Am. Embassy, Dublin, Ireland, 1963-64; Dept. of State rep. faculty Armed Forces Staff Coll., Norfolk, Va., 1964-66; bd. examiners fgn. service State Dept., 1966-67, chief of the junior officer branch, 1967-68. Mem. Internat. Secretariat, San Francisco Conf. to establish UN, 1945. Home: McLean, Va. Died Apr. 4, 1979.

SWEENEY, MARTIN L., ex-congressman; b. Cleveland, O., Apr. 15, 1885; LL.B., Cleveland Law Sch. of Baldwin-Wallace Coll., 1914. Mem. Ohio Legislature, 1913-14; admitted to Ohio bar, 1914; in gen. practice of law, 1914-23; judge Municipal Court of Cleveland, 8 yrs.; elected Nov. 1931, mem. 72d Congress (1931-33) to fill vacancy caused by death of Charles A. Mooney; mem. 73d to 77th Congresses (1933-43), 20th Ohio Dist. Democrat. *

SWEET, ARTHUR JEREMIAH, elec. engr.; b. Oneida, County, N.Y., Dec. 20, 1879; s. William Henry Seward and Emily R. (Richardson) S.; A.B., Cornell U., 1901; Mass. Inst. Tech., 1901-03; m. Dea C. McClusky, Mar. 4, 1907; children—Hubert Richardson, Arthur Pittman. Engr. with Westinghouse Elec. & Mfg. Co., 1903-06, Western Electric Co., Chicago, 1906-07, Westinghouse Lamp Co., Bloomfield, N.J., 1907-09; research and commercial engr. with Holophane Co., Newark, O., 1909-13; mem. Vaughn, Meyer & Sweet, Milwaukee, 1913-16; independent consulting practice, 1916-28; commercial engr. on lighting with Westinghouse interests, 1928-36; independent consulting practice since 1936. Research work on relation between various conditions of illumination and their effect on the human eye, and for pioneer studies on street lighting. Mem. Illuminating Engring. Soc., Phi Gamma Delta, Sphinx Head (Cornell U.), Osiris (Mass. Inst. Tech.). Presbyn. Address: New York, N.Y. *

SWEET, ONEY FRED, fiction writer; b. Hampton, Ia., Feb. 7, 1882; s. Oney Foster and Helen Matilda (Coon) S.; grad. high sch. Hampton, 1899; m. Helen Bjornson of Minneapolis, Minn. May 15, 1913; children—Ruth Helen Oney Foster (dec.) Teacher dist. schs., near Hampton, 1900-04; newspaper work, Yazoo City, Miss., 1904-06. Des Moines Capital, 1907, Minneapolis Tribune, 1908, Los Angeles Examiner, 1908, Milwaukee Sentinel, 1909, Minneapolis Tribune, 1909-12, Chicago Tribune since 1912. Mem. Am. Legion, Elks. Methodist. Known for series of pages in Chicago Sunday Tribune telling of experiences of trying out "The Other Fellow's Job." Contbr. many stories to mags. Lectures on "In Other Mem's Shoes." Home:Hollywood, Ill.*

SWEET, SIDNEY EDWARD, clergyman; b. Mackinac Island, Mich., Aug. 31, 1883; s. Edwin Forrest and Sophia (Fuller) S.; A.B., Yale, 1905; B.D., Episcopal Theol. Sch. Cambridge, Mass., 1908; D.D., Ill. Coll., 1936, Eden Theological Seminary, 1956; married Elta Mae Armstrong, September 3, 1907; children—Edwin Armstrong (dec.), Sidney Edward. Ordained deacon, P.E. Ch., 1908, priest, 1909; asst. rector St. John's P.E. Ch., Jersey City, N.J., 1908-10; rector St. Stephen's Ch., Jersey City, 1910-18; rector St. Paul's Ch., Columbus, O., 1918-31; dean Christ Church, Cathedral, St. Louis, 1931-56; mem. clergy staff Christ Ch., Grosse Pointe Farms, Mich., 1956-57, All Saints Ch., Pasadena, Cal., 1957—. Member of the executive board Pasadena Clinic. Member exec. committee and chmn. social service commn. Mo. Council of Chs. (pres. 1942-44), Church Fedn. of St. Louis (pres. 1937-38); mem. Fed. Council of Chs. Public chmn. War Labor Bd., Region VII, 1941-45. Mem. Los Angeles World Affairs Council, Pasadena Council Chs., Los Angeles Religious Com. Nat. Conf. Christians and Jews. Alpha Delta Phi. Club: Torch. Home: Altadena, Cal. *

SWEETING, ORVILLE JOHN, coll. provost; b. Rochester, N.Y., Oct. 26, 1913; s. Burton Cornelius and Rose (Bailey) S.; A.B., Cornell U., 1935, Ph.D., 1942; m. Mary Ruth Andrews, Aug. 22, 1942; children—Janet Ruth, Richard John, Barbara Rose. Tchr. LeRoy High Sch., Ludlowville High Sch., N.Y., 1935-38; instr. organic chemistry Cornell U., Ithaca, N.Y., 1942-44; instr. inorganic, indsl. chemistry Ind. U., 1944-46; asso. prof. chemistry U. Colo. at Boulder, 1946-51; asst. dir. tchr. tng., lectr. chemistry Yale, 1964-68; prof. chemistry Quinnipac Coll., Hamden, Conn., 1968-76, v.p., provost, 1969-72; asso. dir. research, devel. Olin Film Div., New Haven, 1951-64, Dir. Council for Basic Edn., Washington, 1960-73; cons. U.S. Office Edn., 1964-76, Conn. Dept. Edn., 1966-76; mem. Conn. Commn. Higher Edn., 1965-76. Mem. Charter Revision Commn., City of New Haven, 1958-59; mem. Bd. Edn., City of New Haven, 1959-73, v.p., 1962-72. Bd. dirs. New Haven United Fund, 1960-72. Mem. Conn. Assn. Bds. Edn. (pres. 1966), Edn. Improvement Assn. New Haven (dir., sec., 1969-76), Telluride Assn., Am. Chem. Soc. (pres. New Haven sect., 1963), Sigma Xi, Phi Beta Kappa. Democrat. Author: Science and Technology of Polymer Films, Vol. I, 1968. Vol. 2, 1970. Contbr. numerous articles tech. lit. Home: New Haven, Conn. Died Nov. 19, 1976.

SWEETSER, EDWIN FREDERIC, engr., govt. ofcl.; b. Colima, Mexico, July 17, 1910; (parents U.S. citizens), s. Sidney Pulsifer and Adelina (Schacht) S.; B.S., Tufts Coll., 1933; m. Irma Tharaldsen, Jan. 17, 1948; children—Perry Hart, Barbara, Catherine. Employee N.Y. Telephone Co., 1934-42; with applied physics lab. Johns Hopkins, 1946-47; dep. exec. dir. commn. guided missiles Research and Development Bd., 1947-51, exec. dir. commn. ordnance 1951-53; executive secretary coms. on ordnance Office of Asst. Sec. Defense for Research and Devel., 1953, dep. dir. Office Aeros., 1953-57; dir. Guided Missiles, Office Research and Engring., Office of Sec. Def., 1958-62, spl. assistant Tactical Warfare Programs, 1962-70, ret., 1970. Served as lt. comdr., U.S.N.R., active duty, 1942-46, now comdr. Mem. Am. Ordnance Assn., Tau Beta Pi, Zeta Psi. Club: Kenwood Golf and Country (Washington). Home: Bethesda, Md. Died Aug. 12, 1979.

SWEIGERT, RAY LESLIE, mech. engr.; b. Freeprot, Ill., Nov. 24, 1898; s. Milton Edward and Evelyn May (Reese) S., B.S. in M.E., U. Ill., 1920; M.A., U. Iowa, 1930, Ph.D., 1935; m. Edna Adella Powers, Dec. 27, 1921; children—Ray Leslie, Milton Edward. Mech. engr. Deere & Co., 1920; instr. mech. engring. Ohio State U., 1921; engr. in adminstrn. Deere & Co., 1922-26; supr. indsl. edn. East Peoria and East Chicago, Ill., 1926-29; asst. prof. mech. engring. Ga. Inst. Tech., 1929-31, asso. prof., 1931-36, prof., 1936-78, dir. freshman engring., 1934-41, dir. gen. engring., 1941-47, dean Grad. Div., 1947-61, dean emeritus, 1961-78; lectr., cons. U. South Fla., 1961-63; cons. mech. engring., 1930-78; dir. Inst. Citizenship, 1940; spl. cons. Navy Project, 1941-42, Army Project, 1943; state dir. Engring., Sci., and Mgmt. War Tng., 1941-45; mem. council Oak Ridge Inst. Nuclear Studies, 1948-61; faculty adv. council Univ. Center of Ga., 1948-53; mem. bd. Ga. Tech. Research Inst., 1948-61. Chmn., Ga. Vocat. Adv. Council, 1940; spl. cons. engring. edn. War Dept., A.S.T., 1944; mem. Ga State Tng. council, 1944-45; Fellow A.A.A.S. (nat. council 1955-56); mem. Am. Soc. of Engring. Edn. (nat. council 1936-39, chmn. ednl. methods div., 1953-54, v.p. S.E. sect. chmn. adminstrn. div., So. Conf. Grad. Deans (pres. 1953-54), Nat. Soc. Profl. Engrs. (nat. bd. 1949-50), Ga. Soc. Profl. Engrs. (sec. 1944-48, pres. 1952-53), Tau Beta Pi, Phi Delta Kappa, Sigma Xi, Phi Kappa Phi, Pi Tau Sigma. Lutheran. Author: Thermodynamics. Writer articles and bulls. on engring. subjects. Mem., sec. or chmn. various nat. coms. on engring. edn., 1934-78. Home: Atlanta, Ga. Died Jan. 29, 1978.

SWENT, JAMES WATERMAN, mining engr.; b. San Francisco, Nov. 5, 1885; s. Rudolph N. and Amy (Waterman) S.; student U. of Ill., 1908-09; B.S., Mich. Coll. Mines, 1911, E.M., 1912; m. Ursula Langan, Dec. 21, 1915; children—Langan, James. Dir. sch. undergrad. shift bosses, Cleveland Cliff Iron Co., Ishpeming, Mich., 1912-13; smelter constrn., Brit. Am. Nickel Corp., Sudbury, Ont., 1913-14; engr. Buffalo Mines Co., Ltd., Cobalt, Ont., 1914-15; shift boss engr. Goldfield (Nev.) Consol. Mines, Nov. 1915; engr. mine supt. Candelaria Co., San Dimas, Durango, Mexico, 1915-18; geol. mine supt. mgr., exec. vice pres. and pres. San Luis Mining Co., Tayoltita Durango, Mexico since 1918; cons. engr. and dir. Banco Internacional, chmn. bd. Banco Occidental; pres. Triumph Mining Co., Ida., Fluoresqueda, S.A.; v.p. Cementos del Pacifico, Homestake Mining Co. (S.D.). Mem. Am. Inst. Mining Engrs., Tau Beta Pi. Clubs: Bohemian, Pacific-Union (San Francisco). Home: Piedmont, Cal. *

SWETMAN, RALPH WALDO, coll. pres.; b. Camden, N.Y., Nov. 10, 1886; s. Frederick and Isabel (MacFern) S.; Ph.B., Hamilton Coll., 1907; M.A., Columbia, 1917; Ph.D., Stanford U., 1928; m. Alice R. Pierson, April 1916; children—Robert Pierson, Elizabeth Pierson, Katherine Pierson. Prin. at New York Mills, N.Y., 1907-08, Groton, N.Y., 1908-10, Camden, N.Y., 1910-12, Palmyra, 1912-16; dir. of training, State Normal Sch., Ellensburg, Wash., 1917-22; Cubberley teaching fellow in edn., Stanford, 1922-24; pres. Humboldt State Teachers Coll., Arcata, Calif., 1924-30, State Teachers Coll., Tempe, Ariz., 1930-33; pres. State Teachers Coll., Oswego, N.Y., 1933-47. Pres. Wash. State Edn. Assn., 1921-22; dir. Wash. Sch. equalization initiative campaign, 1922; mem. Phi Beta Kappa, Phi Delta Kappa. Republican. Unitarian. Author: Digest of California SchoolLaw, 1924. Home: Boca Raton, Fla.*

SWEZEY, ROBERT DWIGHT, lawyer; b. Somerville, Mass., Sept. 27, 1906; s. Arthur Dwight and Elizabeth (Thompson) S.; student Cambridge Latin Sch., 1923, postgrad., 1924; A.B., Harvard, 1928, LL.B., 1931; spl. courses George Washington U., 1936-37, Southeastern U., Washington, 1938, Columbia, 1939, N.Y. U., 1940; m. Helen Hyde Brereton, Apr. 29, 1938; children—Robert Dwight, Maria, William Denny. Admitted to Mass. bar, 1932, N.Y. bar, 1940, D.C. bar, 1961; practiced law with Dana T. Gallup, Boston, 1932-33; with Warner, Stackpole and Bradlee, Boston, 1933-34; legal asst. in research Chem. Bank & Trust Co., N.Y.C., 1934; atty. RFC, N.Y.C., 1934; atty., legal advisor to treas. Home Owner's Loan Corp., Washington, 1934-38; atty. Pub. Works Adminstrn., Washington, 1938-39, NBC, N.Y.C., 1939-42; gen. counsel, sec. Blue Network Co. (now ABC), N.Y.C., 1942-44; v.p., gen. mgr. Mut. Broadcasting System, N.Y.C., 1944-48; exec. v.p., gen. mgr. WDSU Broadcasting Corp., 1949-60; spl. asst. to sec. of labor Dept. Labor, 1960-62; dir. Code Authority, Nat. Assn. Broadcasters, Washington, 1962-64; sec.-treas. Corp. Pub. Broadcasting, 1968-70; pres. MCI Mid-Atlantic Communications, Inc., 1970-73; country dir. Internat. Exec. Service Corps, Riyadh, Saudi Arabia, 1974-75; dir. M.C.I. Communications Corp. Mem. Bar Assn. City N.Y., Am., Fed. Communications, Boston bar assns., N.Y. County Lawyers' Assn., Am. Arbitration Assn. Methodist. Clubs: Harvard, Lambs, Radio Executives (pres. 1946), Players (N.Y.C.); Broadcasters, Nat. Lawyers', University (Washington). Home: Leesburg, Va. Died Spet. 1979.

SWIFT, GUSTAVUS FRANKLIN, JR., archaeologist; b. Chgo., Dec. 7, 1916; s. Gustavus Franklin and Marie (Fitzgerald) S.; grad. Hotchkiss Sch., 1935; A.B., Harvard, 1939; student U. Cin., 1940-41; Ph.D., U. Chgo., 1958; m. Eleanor Browne Ransom, Aug. 19, 1939; children—Alice, Eleanor B., Gustavus F. Research analyst War Dept., 1941-46; research asso. Oriental Inst., U. Chgo., 1959-64, field work Near E. countries, Greece, 1951, 52, 54, 60-65; hon. research fel. Fogg Mus., Harvard, 1964-76. Dir. Wedron Silica Co., Chicago Brick Co. Dir. Hyde Park Neighborhood Club, settlement house; trustee John G. Shedd Aquarium. Mem. Archaeol. Inst. of America, Am. Schs. Oriental Research, Soc. Bibl. Lit. and Exegesis, Chgo. Soc. Archaeol. Inst. Am. (pres.), Hyde Park-Kenwood Conservation Community Council. Clubs: University,

Quadrangle (Chgo.). Home: Chicago, Ill. Died Oct. 1, 1976.

SWIFT, JONATHAN DEAN, educator, mathematician; b. Portland, Oreg., Nov. 12, 1918; s. Mathew Dean and Marie (Serum) S.; B.A. with highest honors, U. Calif., Berkeley, 1939; Ph.D., Calif. Inst. Tech., 1947; m. Hildegarde W. Commons, Nov. 9, 1968. Mem. faculty UCLA, 1947-75, prof. math., 1961-75, vice chmn. dept., 1963-67, chmn. Coll. Letters and Sci., 1968-69, acad. asst., v.p. acad. affairs, 1972-73; mathematician Inst. Def. Analyses, 1961-62; cons. in field. Served to capt. U.S. Army, 1941-45. Mem. Am. Math. Soc. (council 1961-67), Math. Soc. Am., Phi Beta Kappa, Sigma Xi. Author: (with L.J. Paige) Elements of Linear Algebra, 1961, rev. edit. (with L.J. Paige and T.A. Slobko), 1974. Home: Pacific Palisades, Calif. Died Sept. 16, 1975.

SWIFT, LEWIS BURRIE, business executive; b. Lyndonville, N.Y., May 17, 1885; s. Lewis B. and Effie Euphemia (Gray) S.; M.E., Cornell U. Coll. of Engring., 1912; m. Madge A. VanDresser, Sept. 9, 1913; children—Lewis B., Jr., William V. D. With Taylor Instrument Companies since 1904, in clerical work, 1904-08 (also in summer vacations 1908-12); successively mgr. recorder sales, 1912-19, mgr. sales engring. dept., 1919-28, chief engr. and dir. in charge research, engring. and patent depts., 1928-38, v.p., 1934-38, pres., 1938-51, chmn. since 1951: dir. Lincoln Rochester Trust Co., Pfaudler Co. Mem. exec. com. Indsl. Mgmt. Council Dir. Rochester Community Chest, Rochester Regional Hospital Council, Rochester Museum Assn. Vice chmn. board trustees Rochester Inst. Tech. Fellow Am. Soc. M.E.; mem. Rochester Engring. Soc., C. of C., Newcomen Soc., Tau Beta Pi. Presbyterian. Clubs: Cornell of Rochester, Rochester Ad, Genesee Valley (Rochester); Country Club of Rochester. Home: Rochester. *

SWIG, BENJAMIN HARRISON, hotel owner and operator; b. Taunton, Mass., Nov. 17, 1893; s. Simon and Fanny (Levy) S.; ed. pub. schs., Taunton; LL.D. (hon.), U. Santa Clara, 1962, Carroll Coll., 1968, Gonzaga U., 1979 L.H.D., Hebrew Union Coll., 1964, Brandeis U., 1966, John F. Kennedy U., 1979; H.H.D., Norwich U., 1967; m. Mae Aronovitz, Dec. 24, 1916 (dec.); children—Melvin M., Betty S. (Mrs. Richard S. Dinner), Richard L. Engaged in real estate, Boston and N.Y.C., 1925-45; chmn. bd. Fairmont Hotel Co. Del., Democratic Nat. Conv., 1956, 60, 64. Vice pres. Western States region Am. Friends of Hebrew U.; founder, chmn. bd. dirs. Careers Unltd. for Women; vice chmn., bd. govs. West Coast U. Judaism; soc. founders, trustee Calif. sch. Hebrew Union Coll.-Jewish Inst. Religion; hon. gov., hon. fellow Hebrew U., Jerusalem; chmn. bd. trustees, life mem. bd. founders U. Santa Clara; bd. dirs., bd. overseers Jewish Theol. Sem. Am., also hon. fellow soc. fellows; bd. dirs. Israel Devel. Corp., Israel Investors Corp.; mem. nat. adv. bd. PEC Israel Econ. Corp.; hon. chmn. No. Cal., mem. exec. com. State of Israel Bonds, San Francisco; mem. nat. council Am. Jewish Joint Distbn. Com.; pres. Greater Western region Jewish Nat. Fund; nat. bd. trustees Nat. Jewish Hosp./Nat. Asthma Center; mem. fund com. U.S. Mil. Acad.; hon. nat. chmn., co-chmn. West Coast region, mem. exec. com. United Jewish Appeal; mem. nat. com., West Coast chmn., vice chmn. soc. Founders Albert Einstein Coll. Medicine; nat. council, hon. vice chmn. West Coast div. Yeshiva U.; chmn. No. Calif. region Am.-Israel Cultural Found.; bd. dirs. Am. Friends Tel Aviv U., Brandeis Camp Inst. West, Brandeis Youth Found., Catholic Youth Orgn., Coast Guard Acad. Found., Nat. Realty Com., St. Anthony Dining Room, Exec. Council on Fgn. Diplomats; mem. adv. council Anna Head Sch., Israel Edn. Fund, Mary's Help Hosp.; hon. bd. dirs. Blackfeet Art Found., Jewish Welfare Fedn. San Francisco, Marin County and the Peninsula; financial adviser Blackfeet Indians, Browning, Mont.; mem. pres.'s council, mem. devel. council Carroll Coll.; v.p., bd. dirs. Columbia Park Boys Club; mem. adv. bd., pres. men's guild Convent of Good Sheperd; mem. nat. council, hon. chmn. Western State Joint Def. Appeal; mem. nat. adv. council Nat. Inf. Museum Devel. Program, Synagogue Council Am.; life mem. San Francisco adv. bd. Salvation Army; mem. vis. com. Stanford Sch. Medicine' alternate mem. bd. govs. Technion-Israel Inst. Tech.; nat. vice chmn. combined campaign, life hon. trustee Union Am. Hebrew Congregations; numerous other civic and charitable activities. Decorated comdr.'s cross Order of Merit of Fed. Republic of Germany; comdr. Order of Merit of Italian Republic, Star of Solidarity (Italy); knight Order St. Sylvester; recipient numerous other fgn., nat. and local awards including: Outstanding Civilian Service medal Dept. Army, 1960, 67, 71; certificates of honor Bd. Suprs. City and County of San Francisco, 1968, 69; Silver Keystone award Boys Clubs Am., 1970; Stephen S. Wise award Am. Jewish Congress, 1970; Gold award N.A.A.C.P., 1971; citation Brandeis U., 1971; Meritorious Pub. Service award U.S. Coast Guard, 1972; Silver medal City of Paris (France), 1972; Prime Minister's medal State of Israel Bonds, 1972; St. Francis of Assisi award City of San Francisco, 1972. Mem. Am. Soc. for Technion (nat. council), Am. Jewish Com. (nat. exec. council, nat. bd. dels., adv. com. San Francisco chpt.), Zionist Orgn. Am. (dir.), Civic League Improvement Clubs and Assns. (dir.), NCCJ (San Francisco adv. bd.), John Carroll Soc. (charter mem.), Soc. Hon. Fellows City of Hope, San Francisco C. of C. (chmn. mil. affairs com.), West Point Soc. San Francisco Bar Area (hon.). Jewish. Mason (33 deg.). Address: San Francisco, Calif. Died Oct. 31, 1980.

SWINEFORD, OSCAR, JR., physician; b. Richmond, Va., Jan. 12, 1897; s. Oscar and Harriet (Gardner) S.; B.S., U. Va., 1923, M.D., 1926; m. Agatha Gay Allen, Aug. 27, 1926. Interne Mass. Gen. Hosp., Boston, July 1926-Dec. 1927; practice of medicine, U. Va. Hospital, Charlottesville, Va. from 1931, specializing in internal medicine and allergy, from 1931. Instr. internal med. and clin. pathology, Med. Sch., U. Va., 1928-30, acting asso. prof. pathol., 1930-31, instr. practice med., 1931-37; asst. prof., 1937-40, asso. prof., 1940-45, prof., 1945-67, Mem. sci. and ednl. council Allergy Found. Am. Served as lt. (j.g.) U.S. Navy, World War I. Fellow A.C.P., A.M.A.; mem. So. Med. Assn. (past chmn. allergy sect.), Am. Rheumatism Assn., Am. Acad. Allergy (past pres.), Southeastern Allergy Assn. (pres. 1949), Phi Beta Kappa, Alpha Omega Alpha. Contbr. articles to med. jours. Home: Charlottesville, Va. Died Feb. 23, 1976.

SWISHER, WALTER SAMUEL, clergyman; b. Meadville, Pa., Sept. 15, 1882; s. Samuel Jefferson and Ella Electa (White) S.; B.D., Meadville Theol. Sch., 1910, D.D., 1935; Crufts fellow U. of Göttingen, Germany, 1910-11; grad. study U. of Mich. and Harvard; student Pa. Coll. of Music. Meadville; m. Marion Lord Newell, Aug. 18, 1914 (died July 5, 1945); 1 d., Rosamond Lee; m. 2d, Heeln Viola Plumly, Aug. 19, 1948. Ordained ministry Unitarian Ch., 1911; pastor Passaic, 1911-14, All Souls Ch., New London, Conn., 1914-20, Wellesley Hills, Mass., 1920-33, Ch. of the Messiah, St. Louis, 1933-37, First Congl. Ch., Freeport, Maine, 1940-45; Parish minister, Hope Congl. Ch., Springfield, Mass., 1946-47; Grace Union Church, N. Wilbraham, Massachusetts, since 1948; president Tuckerman School (normal school of religious education), 1925-29. Served as chmn. Am. Red Cross (New London), and volunteer chaplain, Camp Gordon, and capt. Conn. Reserve Corps, World War. Chmn. Freeport Chapter Am. Red Cross since 1940. Trustee Meadville Theol. Sch., 1936-41; pres. Meadville Alumni Assn., 1938-39. Club: Sandwich. Author: Religion and the New Psychology, 1920; Psychology for the Music Teacher, 1927; Music in Worship 1929. Editor (with others) Beacon Hymnal; composer hymn tunes and songs. Contbr. to Atlantic Monthly, Psychoanalytic Rev., etc. Lecturer onmusic and psychology. Address: North Wilbraham, Mass. *

SWOPE, GERARD, JR., lawyer; b. St. Louis, Dec. 13, 1905; s. Gerard and Mary (Hill) S.; A.B., Dartmouth, 1929; LL.B., Harvard, 1932; m. Marjorie Park, July 2, 1932; children—Gerard Lincoln, Stephen Park, John Franklin. Admitted to N.Y. State bar, 1932; practiced N.Y.C., firm Cahill, Gordon, Zachry & Reindel, 1932-34, 1937-40; with SEC, 1934-37; counsel to appliance and mdse. div. Gen. Electric Co., 1940-42; counsel to Internat. Gen. Electric Co., Inc., 1945-52; trade regulations counsel Gen. Electric Co., N.Y.C., 1952-60, internat. counsel, 1960-68. Trustee Bklyn. Inst. Arts and Scis., Horace Mann Sch.; chmn. Teatown Lake Reservation; hon. chmn. Woods Hole Marine Biol. Lab; trustee Woods Hole Oceanographic Inst. Served to comdr. USNR, 1942-45; counsel Bur. Naval Personnel, Navy Dept., 1942-45. Mem. Am. Bar Assn. Address: Croton-on-Hudson, N.Y. Died Sept. 27, 1979.

SWORAKOWSKI, WITOLD S., educator; b. Suceava, Rumania, Jan. 16, 1903; s. Eduard and Olga (Jarzembecki) S.; M.Polit. Sci., Acad. Polit. Sci., Warsaw, Poland, 1932; m. Helena Krzywicka, Feb. 10, 1934; 1 son, Michael Thomas. Came to U.S., 1942, naturalized, 1953. Researcher, Inst. Nationality Problems, Warsaw, 1931-34; div. chief World League Poles, Wassau, 1934-36; mem. Polish Fgn. Service, 1936-45; with Hoover Instn., Stanford, 1947-79, asst. prof., 1954-56, asso. prof., 1956-65, prof., 1965-68, curator East European collections, 1952-62, asst. dir. Hoover Instn., 1956-67, asso. dir., 1967-79. Decorated Silver Cross of Merit (Poland). Author: The Communist International and Its Front Organizations, 1965. Home: Stanford Calif. Died Jan. 15, 1979.

SWORDS, VINCENT THOMAS, clergyman, educator; b. Bklyn., Mar. 8, 1914; s. Michael J. and Margaret (Cleary) S.; A.B., St. Joseph's Coll., 1936; M.A., St. John's U., 1950; student Mary Immaculate Sem., Pa.; LL.D., DePaul U., 1959. Ordained priest Roman Cath. Church, 1941; missionary, Panama, C.Z., 1941-44; prof. prep. sch., chmn. dept. religion, asso. dir. Sch. Social Action, St. John's U., 1944-51; superior Our Lady of the Miraculous Medal, Cath. Ch. and Mission, Greensboro, N.C., 1951-55; superior Niagara U., 1955-57, pres., 1957-64, also chmn. exec. council, bd. trustees; superior, pres. St. Joseph's Coll., Princeton, N.J., 1964-68; asst. superior St. John's U., Jamaica, N.Y., 1968-76; mem. priest senate Diocese Trenton. Trustee Western N.Y. Nuclear Research Center; vice chmn. bd. trustees St. John's U., 1964-76. Served with Aux. Chaplains Corps, AUS, World War II. Recipient Outstanding Civilian Service medal, Department Army, 1962. Mem. Assn. Colls. and Univs. State N.Y. (pres.), Alpha Kappa Psi, Sigma Alpha Sigma, Scabbard and Blade K.C. (4 deg.), Faithful Friar. Address: Jamaica, N.Y. Died Sept. 29, 1976; interred St. Joseph's Seminary, Princeton.

SYLVESTER, ARTHUR, govt. ofcl.; b. Montclair, N.J., Oct. 21, 1901; s. Arthur and Natasha (Victorson) S.; A.B., Princeton, 1923; m. Kathryn Frances Ferguson, Dec. 27, 1928; children—Anthony Irving, Natasha. Shipping clerk, salesman, Macmillan Co., New York, N.Y., 1923; became reporter on suburban staff Newark (N.J.) Evening News, 1924, city staff, 1925-29, asst. city editor, 1929-32, suburban editor, 1932-34, feature editor, 1934-36, city editor, 1936-44, Washington corr., from 1944; asst. sec. of def. for pub. affairs, 1961-67. Mayor, Cold Spring, N.Y., 1970's. Mem. Sigma Delta Chi. Clubs: Campus (Princeton), National Press, Gridiron, Overseas Writers, Cosmos (Washington). Home: McLean, Va. Died Dec. 28, 1979; buried Mt. Hebron Cemetery, Upper Montclair, N.J.

SYLVESTER, RICHARD STANDISH, educator; b. St. Louis, Nov. 30, 1926; s. Kilburn Gerry and Marguerite (Fisher) S.; A.B., St. Louis U., 1949; B.A. (Rhodes scholar), Oxford (Eng.) U., 1952, M.A., 1956; Ph.D., Yale, 1956; Litt.D. (hon.), Georgetown U., 1978; m. Joyce Sandra Gurian, June 17, 1956; children—Patrice (dec.), Paul, Sara, Peter. Mem. faculty Yale, 1955-78, prof. English, 1966-78, Ford prof. English, 1978; sr. fellow Southeastern Inst. Medieval and Renaissance Studies, 1965; cons. Nat. Endowment for Humanities, 1976-78. Served with U.S. Maritime Service, 1945-46. Fellow Am. Council Learned Socs., 1964-65. Fellow Royal Hist. Soc.; mem. Renaissance Soc. Am., Modern Lang. Assn. Am., Renaissance Text Soc. (pres. 1974-78), Early English Text Soc., Conf. Brit. Studies, Amici Thomae Mori (pres. 1976-78). Author: Cavendish's Life of Wolsey, 1959; Two Early Tudor Lives, 1961; More's History of King Richard III, 1963; Pace's De Fructu, 1967; Thomas More's Prayerbook, 1969; Anchor Anthology of Seventeenth-Century Verse, 1969; St. Thomas More: Action and Contemplation, 1972; Anchor Anthology of Sixteenth-Century Verse, 1974; Richard Third and Selections from Thomas More's Poems, 1976; Essential Articles for the Study of Thomas More, 1977. Exec. editor Yale Edit. Works of St. Thomas More, 1958-78, editor Yale Studies in English, 1965-78; co-editor Archives British History, 1966-78. Mem. editorial com. various renaissance lit. edits. Home: Hamden, Conn. Died July 9, 1978.

SYMES, JAMES MILLER, railroad exec.; b. Glen Osborne, Pa., July 8, 1897; s. Frank H. and Clara (Heckert) S.; grad. Sewickley (Pa.) High Sch., 1914; hon. degrees Waynesburg Coll., Ursinus U., Duquesne U., Trinity Coll., Marietta Coll., Temple U.; m. Fern Elizabeth Dick, Sept. 27, 1919; 1 d., Jeanne Doris. With P.R.R. Co., 1916-68, beginning as clk., car tracer, car distbr. in train master's office Pitts., successively statistican, freight movement dir. in gen. supts.'s office Cleve., freight movement dir. Central region, Pitts., chief clk. to gen. mgr., Chgo.; supt. passenger transportation Western region, Chgo., Eastern region, Phila., chief of freight transportation, Phila., 1934-35, gen. mgr. Western region, Chgo., 1939-41, v.p. Western region, 1942-46, dep. v.p. charge ops., Phila., 1946-47, v.p. charge ops., 1947-52, exec. v.p., 1952-54, pres., 1954-59, chmn. bd., chief exec. officer, 1959-63, chmn. exec. com., 1963-68; also dir., dir. various subsidiary cos.; v.p. ops. and maintenance Assn. Am. R.R.'s, Wash., 1935-39; trustee Phila. Savs. Fund Soc.; dir. Wabash R.R. Co., D.T.&I. R.R. Co., First Pa. Banking and Trust Co., Ins. Co. of N.Am., Pa. Co., Manor Real Estate Co., SCM Corp. Morgan Guaranty Trust Co. Trustee Temple U., U. Pitts., Tax Found., Inc., Com. for Econ. Devel., Nat. Indsl. Conf. Bd. Mem. Am. Ry. Engring. Assn. Presbyn. Clubs: Philadelphia, Philadelphia Country, Union League (Phila.); Merion (Pa.) Cricket; Commercial (Chgo.) Home: Philadelphia, Pa. Died Aug. 3, 1976.

SYMINGTON, CHARLES JULIAN (SI'MING-TON), business exec.; b. Baltimore, Md., Feb. 2, 1883; s. William Stuart and Lelia Skipworth (Powers) S.; grad. Belleview (Va.) High Sch., 1900; student Amherst Coll., 1901-02; m. Elizabeth Lloyd, Oct. 1, 1912. Hon. chmn. bd. Symington Wayne Corp. Member adv. council, Hospital for Spl. Surgery. Trustee, mem. bus. com. Nat. Planning Assn., Washington. Clubs: Century, Down Town, Cloud (N.Y.C.). Home: N.Y.C. *

SYNDERGAARD, PARLEY REX, educator; b. Mt. Pleasant, Utah, Mar. 3, 1918; s. Parley Pratt and Ada (Kay) S.; B.A., Westminster Coll., Fulton, Mo., 1940; M.A. (Van Blarcom scholar), Washington U., St. Louis, 1941; Ph.D., St. Louis U., 1951; m. Patricia Jane Graf, June 10, 1941; children—Susan, Mary Kay, Sally, Martha. Mem. faculty Murray (Ky.) State Coll., 1946-54, asso. prof. history, 1949-54, dean of men, 1948-49; mem. faculty Eastern Ill. U., Charleston, 1956-80, prof. history, 1962-80, chmn. dept., 1961-70; editor Daily Breeze-Courier, Taylorville, Ill., 1954-56. Served with F.A., AUS, 1943-45; ETO. Newberry Library fellow, 1966; Truman Library fellow, 1962.

Mem. Am. Hist. Soc., Omicron Delta Kappa, Alpha Kappa Lambda. Home: Charleston, Ill. Died Dec. 6, 1980; buried Charleston.

SYNICK, HENRY, business executive; b. Sebastian, O., July 30, 1878; s. John and Catharine (Witte) S.; student pub. schs.; m. Wilhelmine Oppenheim, Oct. 6, 1903; children—Mary, Adolph, Sophia, Louis, Engaged in development work New Idea, Inc. (now Avco Mfg. Corp.), farm machinery, Coldwater, O., 1900, was factory mgr., became v.p., 1920, pres., 1935-48 pres. Peoples Bank Co., Coldwater, since 1932. Address: Coldwater, O. *

SZOLD, ROBERT, lawyer; b. Streator, Ill., Sept. 29, 1889; s. Adolph and Rachel (Gumbiner) S.; B.S., Knox Coll., 1909, M.S., 1909, M.A. summa cum laude, 1909, LL.D., 1953; LL.B. cum laude. Harvard, 1912; D.H.L., Brandeis U., 1956, Jewish Studies, 1959; D.J., Hebrew U. Jerusalem, 1972; m. Zip Falk, Sept. 4, 1917; children—Miriam (Mrs. Norman Seligman), Ruth (Mrs. Eli Ginzberg), Betty (Mrs. B. Krainis), Joan (Mrs. Norman L. Zheutlin). Asst. atty. gen. P.R., 1915; asst. to solicitor gen. U.S., 1915-18; mem. law firm Szold, Brandwen, Meyers & Altman and predecessor law firms, N.Y.C.; chmn. bd. Palestine Econ. Corp., 1945-60, ast pres. United Housing Found.; dir. Riverbay Corp., East River Housing Corp., Edward A. Filene Good Will Fund, Inc.; chmn. P.E.F. Israel Endowment Funds, Inc.; pres. Hillman Housing Corp. Past pres. Zionist Orgn. Am.; vice chmn. Council of Jewish Agy., 1931. Mem. Assn. Bar City N.Y., N.Y. County Lawyers Assn., Am. Bar Assn., Am. Law Inst., Phi Beta Kappa, Beta Theta Pi. Home: Pelham, N.Y. Died Nov. 9, 1977.

TABER, FREDERIC HOWLAND, lawyer; b. New Bedford, Mass., May 3, 1883; s. Frederic and Elizabeth (Howland) T.; A.B., Harvard, 1904, LL.B., 1907; m. Helen Wendell Bourne, Apr. 11, 1908; children—Helen Standish (Mrs. Arthur Mills), Frederic Howland, Philip, Standish, Elizabeth (Mrs. R. Harding, Jr.). Admitted to Mass. bar, 1907, and in practice at New Bedford; asso. with Cook, Brownell, Taber & Sherman, 1909-58; asso. with Brownell, Sherman & Whittier, 1958—; member of board Reconstruction Finance Corporation, 1933-38. President and director Bedford Storage Warehouse Company; director New Bedford Morris Plan Company. Republican. Unitarian. Mason. Clubs: Union, Harvard (Boston); Cosmos (Washington); Wamsutta (New Bedford). Home: New Bedford, Mass. *

TABER, GLADYS, author; b. Colorado Springs, Colo., Apr. 12, 1899; d. Rufus Mather and Grace (Raybold) Bagg; B.A., Wellesley Coll., 1920; M.A., Lawrence Coll., 1921; student Columbia, 1931-33; m. Frank A. Taber, Jr., June 10, 1922; 1 dau., Constance Taber Colby. Tchr. English, Lawrence Coll., 1921, Randolph-Macon Women's Coll., 1925-26; profl. writer, 1932-80; tchr. profl. short story writing Columbia, N.Y.C., from 1936; columnist Ladies Home Jour., 1937-58, asst. editor, 1946-58; columnist Family Circle, 1959-80, The Oracle, Orleans, Mass. Writer of plays, among them a one-act play which received Little Theater award in nat. contest, 1925. Mem. Authors League Am., Nat. P.E.N., Pen and Brush Club, Kappa Alpha Theta. Author numerous books, the latest being: Especially Father, 1949; Stillmeadow Seasons, 1950; Stillmeadow Kitchen, 1951; When Dogs Meet People, 1952; Flower Arranging for American Home, 1952; (with Barbara Webster) Stillmeadow to Sugarbridge, 1953; Stillmeadow Daybook; What Cooks at Stillmeadow, 1958; Mrs. Daffodil, 1958; Stillmeadow Sampler, 1959; Spring Harvest, 1959; Road to Stillmeadow, 1960; Another Path, 1963; Gladys Taber's Favorite Stillmeadow Recipes, 1965; Stillmeadow Calendar A Countrywoman's Journal, 1967; Especially Dogs-Especially at Stillmeadow, 1968; Flower Arranging, A Book to Begin On, 1969; Stillmeadow Album, 1969; Amber A Very Personal Cat, 1970; Reveries at Stillmeadow, 1970; (short stories) One Dozen and One; My Own Cape Cod, 1971; My Own Cookbook, 1972; Country Chronicle, 1974; Harvest of Yesterdays, 1976; The Best of Stillmeadow, 1976; Conversations with Amber, 1977; Still Cove Journal, 1981. Contbr. to mags. in U.S., Eng., Sweden, Australia. Home: Orleans, Mass. Died Mar. 11, 1980; buried Southbury, Conn.

TABER, STEPHEN, geologist; b. Victory, Cayuga County, N.Y., Apr. 24, 1882; s. George Albert and Caroline Lake (Crowell) T.; A.B., Stanford, 1906; Ph.D., U. of Va., 1912; m. Bessie Ray, June 1914; children—Elsie, Molly, Stephen. Field asst. to the Calif. Earthquake Investigation Commn., 1906; assayer and chemist, Santa Maria de Guadalupe, Minillas, Zac., Mexico, 1906-07; private work in Va., 1908-09; asst. geologist, Va. Geol. Survey, 1909-12; instr. economic geology, U. of Va., 1909-12; prof. geology and mineralogy, U. of S.C. Sept. 1912-47; state geologist 1914-47; asso. prof. geology, Stanford U., summer 1920. Mem. Puerto Rico Earthquake Commn., 1918-19. Fellow Geol. Soc. of America, Mineral. Soc. America, A.A.A.S.; mem. Société Géologique de France, Am. Inst. Mining Engrs. (life), S.C. Acad. Science (president 1930), Seismological Society of America (chmn. Eastern Section 1932), American Geophysical Union, Geol. Soc. of London, Phi Beta Kappa, Sigma Xi, etc. Author: Geology of the Gold Belt in the James River Basin, Virginia, 1913; Report on the Titanium and Apatite Deposits of Virginia (with T. L. Watson), 1913; also various bulletins and articles pertaining to earthquakes, mineral deposits, structural geology of Greater Antilles, perennially frozen ground. Home: Columbia, S.C. *

TABOADA, DIOGENES, fgn. minister Argentina; b. Santa Rosa, Argentina, June 18, 1885; s. Jeronimo Leon and Lucinda (Mora) T.; Lawyer, D. Jurisprudence, U. Buenos Aires; m. Maria Elia Dominguez, Nov. 11, 1917; children—Juan Carlos, Maria Leonor, Daria; Elia y Susana. Mem. panel examining magistrates Province San Luis, Argentina, 1913-17; chancellor of exchequer in Provincial Govt., 1917; mem. Parliament for San Luis, 1920-24; gen. adminstr. inland revenue, 1925; pres. Post Office Savs. Bank, 1926-28; minister of interior of Argentina, 1938-40; ambassador to Uruguay, 1958-59; now fgn. minister Argentina. Mem. bd. Nat. Ry. Pensions Funds; past mem. bd. Buenos Aires-Pacific Ry. Co., Argentine Great Western Ry. Co., Villa Maria-Rufino Ry. Decorated great cross Piana Order (Vatican); great cross Legion of Honor (France); great cross Order Leopold (Belgium); great cross of gold with ribbon Order Services to Fed. Republic (Austria); great string Order Raising Sun (Japan); ribbon 1st Class Order Aztec Eagle (Mexico); great cross Order So. Cross (Brazil); great cross Order Merit (Paraguay); great cross Order Quetzal (Guatemala); great cross Order Sun (Peru); great cross insignia and ribbon Order Milt. Merit (Malta); great cross Order Merit (Chile); great cross Order Orange Nassau (Holland); great cross Order Elizabeth the Cath. (Spain); great cross Order Civillian Merit (Fed. Republic Germany; great cross Order Civilian Merit (Italy); great cross Order Condor of Andes (Bolovia): great cross Order Boyaca (Colombia); great cross Order Merit (Ecuador); lakan Order Sakatuma (Philippines). Home: Buenos Aires. *

TAFEL, LEONARD IMMANUEL, clergyman; b. Phila., Feb. 6, 1888; s. Louis Herman and Anna Louise (Dutt) T.; M.D., Atlantic Med. Coll., Baltimore, 1912; M.D., New Ch. Theol. Sch., Cambridge, Mass., 1921-24; m. Gertrude Hommen, May 26, 1920; children—Anna Louise, John Frederick, Rudolph Edward, Louis Leonard, Walter Richard. Interne, Minn. State Hosp., Fergus Falls, Minn., 1913, pvt. practice medicine, N.W. Canada; ordained to ministry of the Swedenborgian Ch., June 22, 1924, and served as pastor Frankford (Phila.) Swedenborgian Ch. since 1926. Served as sgt., U.S. Army, 1917-21; with U. S. Army Occupation Germany 1918-21, France Mar.-Dec. 1918. Chmn. bd. mgrs. New Ch. Theol. Sch., 1938-46; chmn. council ministers, Gen. Convent of the New Jerusalem, 1937-46, pres. since 1946. Mem. Swedenborg Scientific Assn. (pres. 1938-46), Swedenborgian Foundation. Republican. Home: Phila. *

TAFT, EDWARD AUGUSTINE, lawyer; b. Boston, Nov. 30, 1882; s. Edward A. and Adelaide (Larrabee) T.; grad. St. Mark's Sch., Southboro, Mass., 1900; A.B., Harvard, 1904, LL.B., 1907; m. Gertrude Tower, Aug. 14, 1923; children—Edward A (dec.). Admitted to Mass. bar, 1907; partner firm Herrick, Smith, Donald, Farley & Ketchum, and predecessors, Boston, 1918—. Past dir., mem. exec. com. Boston Safe Deposit Trust Co. Active Boston Community Fund. Trustee Boston Symphony Doc. Home: Boston. *

TAFT, JULIA JESSIE, educator; b. Dubuque, Ia., June 24, 1882; d. Charles C. and Amanda May (Farwell) T.; A.B., Drake U., 1904; B.S., U. of Chicago, 1905, Ph.D., 1913; unmarried; children (adopted)—Martha Scott, Everett Francis. Engaged in teaching high sch., 4 yrs.; asst. supt., State Reformatory, Bedford Hills, N.Y., 1912-15; psychiatric social worker State Charities Aid Assn., N.Y. City, 1915-18; psychologist Mental Hygiene Clinic, Children's Agencies, Phila., 1918-26; supervisor child placing, Children's Aid Soc., Phila., 1927-34; asso. prof. social case work, Pa. Sch. of Social Work, 1934, prof. of social casework and dir. advanced curriculum, U. of Pa., 1947-51, retired. Mem. Am. Assn. Social Workers, Am. Orthopsychiatric Assn. Author: The Dynamics of Therapy, 1933. Editor: Journal of Social Work Process, 1938-39. Translator from the German: Will Therapy by Otto Rank, 1937; Truth and Reality by Otto Rank, 1937. Contbr. articles to mags. and jours. Home: Flourtown, Pa. *

TAFT, PHILIP, educator; b. Syracuse, N.Y., Mar. 22, 1902; s. Jeremiah and Anna (Jaegar) T.; A.B., U. Wis., 1932; Ph.D., 1935; m. Theresa Shirley Branstetter, July 30, 1936; foster dau., Marilyn Arline (Mrs. Donald A. Blake), Spl. economist Wis. Indsl. Commn., 1935; staff Regional Labor Adv. Resettlement Adminstrn., 1935-36; asso. econ. analyst Social Security Bd., 1936-37; asst. prof. econs. Brown U., 1937-44, asso. prof., 1944-47, became prof. econs., 1947, then prof. emeritus, chmn. dept., 1949-53. Chmn. trucking commn. War Labor Bd., Boston, 1943-45; chmn. Workmen's Compensation Law Commn., R.I., 1947-48. Mem. Am. Econ. Assn., Nat. Acad. Arbitrators, Am. Arbitration Assn., AAUP, Indsl. Relations Research Assn., Am. Acad. Arts and Sci. Author: History of Labor in the United States, 1896-1932 (with Selig Perlman), 1935; Economics and Problems of Labor, 1942; Movements for Economic Reform, 1950; Organized Labor in American History. Contbr. articles to profl. publs. Home: Providence, R.I. Died Nov. 17, 1976.

TAGGART, WILLIAM GILBERT, research agriculturist; born Latimer, S.C., Sept. 17, 1883; s. Dr. William M. and Carolina (Tennent) T.; B.S., Miss. Agrl. and Mechanical Coll., 1906; M.S., La State U., 1933; m. Mary Catherine Tennent, Dec. 27, 1911; children—Catherine (Mrs. John C. Monroe), Cornelia Elizabeth (Mrs. W. N. Maddox). Asst. chemist Agr. Expt. Sta., La. State U., 1906-08; asst. research chem., 1908-13; asst. dir. Sugar Expt. Sta., 1913-23; asst. dir. La. Expt. Sta., 1923-41, dir. since 1941. Life mem. Am. Sugar League, La. Sugarcane Technol., mem. Alpha Chi Sigma, Phi Kappa Phi. Democrat. Presbyterian. Home: Baton Rouge, La. *

TAIT, EDGAR WENDELL (TÄLT), lawyer; b. Bradford, Pa., June 18, 1886; s. Edwin Edgar and Mary Jane (Hamil) T.; A.B., Yale, 1908; LL.B., U. of Pa., 1910; m. Idah Katherine Beery, June 18, 1910; 1 dau., Katherine Beery. Admitted to Pa. bar, 1909, and began practice at Bradford; moved to Pittsburgh, 1915, Urbana, O., 1934; president Alleghany River Mining Company and vice-pres. Pittsburg & Shawmut R.R. Co., 1923-30; city solicitor, Urbana, O., 1936-39; with bituminous coal div., U.S. Dept. of the Interior, 1942-43; judge of the Municipal Court of Urbana, Ohio, since 1946. Served as post adjutant Park Field, Tenn., World War. Mem. Am. Bar Assn. Republican. Methodist. Clubs: Urbana Country; Springfield (O.) Country. Author of "Criminal Procedure Practice in the Municipal Courts of Ohio." Home: Urbana, O. *

TALBOT, RALPH, army officer; b. Denver, Colo., June 18, 1884; s. Ralph and Frances (Hardin) T.; B.S., U.S. Mil. Acad., 1905; grad. Cav. Sch., Fort Riley, Kan., 1906; grad. Field Arty. Sch., Fort Sill, Okla., 1924; honor grad. Command and Gen. Staff Sch., Ft. Leavenworth, 1925; grad. Army War Coll., Washington, D.C., 1928; m. Marguerite Morgan, June 19, 1907; children—Ralph III, (U.S. Army), Marguerite Lucy (wife of Capt. Claire Beverly Mitchell, U.S. Army). Commd. 2d lt., U.S. Army, 1905, and advanced through the grades to brig. gen., 1940; assigned to 12th Cav., 1906; comdt., Shattuck Sch., Faribault, Minn., 1913-14; served on Mexican border and with Punitive Expdn., 1914-15; with Philippine Scouts in Mindanao, charged with maintenance of Overton-Kiethley Trail, 1915; served in World War with Gen. Staff and Motor Transport Corps; with Army of Occupation in Germany until 1923; with 7th F.A., Fort Ethan Allen, Vt., 1925-27; on War Dept. Gen. Staff, Washington, D.C., 1928; then comd. 18th F.A., Fort Sill, later C.O. F.A. Sch. troops; instr. Command and Gen. Staff Sch., 1932, and later dir., 1935-36; then R.O.T.C. officer for 9th Corps Area, San Francisco, and later dep. chief of staff, 4th Army to 1939; chief of staff newly organized 5th Div., Fort McClellan, Ala., through 4th Army Corps and 3d Army maneuvers in South, 1939-40; chief of staff, 6th Army Corps, to Oct. 1940; comdg. gen. 6th Div. Arty., Fort Des Moines, Ia., and comdg. 6th Div., 1940-41; first comdg. gen., Trinidad Base Command, B.W.I., and comdg. gen., Trinidad Sector, Caribbean DefenseCommand, since Apr.1941. Mason. Author of Motor Transport Manual.*

TALBOT, WILLIAM HOWE MCELWAIN, sculptor; b. Boston, Jan. 10, 1918; s. John Cleveland and Dorothy Howe (McElwain) T.; student Pa. Acad. Fine Arts, Phila., 1936-41, Academie des Beaux Arts, Paris, France, 1945-46; m. Joan Sangree, Aug. 1, 1946; children—Constance, Augusta, John, Peter. Exhibited in one man shows at Carroll-Knight Gallery, St. Louis, 1948, Andrew-Morris Gallery, N.Y.C., 1963, Martin Schweig Gallery, St. Louis, 1965, 69, Frank Rehn Gallery, N.Y.C., 1968, 71, Arts Club, Chgo., 1972; exhibited in group shows at Whitney Mus. Am. Art, 1950, 61, 63, Pa. Acad. Fine Arts Ann., 1942, 49, Phila. Mus. Internat., 1949, DeCordova & Dana, Lincoln, Mass., 1949, New York World Fair, 1964; commns. include Meml. Sculpture, Rehab. Center, Barnes Hosp., Washington U., St. Louis, 1964, Fountain, Nat. Hdqrs., Nat. Council State Garden Clubs of Am., St. Louis, 1959, Fountain, Fitchburg (Mass.) Youth Library, 1950; artist-in-residence U. Mich., Ann Arbor, 1949; vis. lectr. Earlham Coll., Ind., 1964, St. Lawrence U., Canton, N.Y., 1965; pres. Sculptors Guild, 1965-68, v.p. publs., 1968-72; founder, trustee Washington (Conn.) Art Assn., 1952-58. Served with AUS, 1941-46. Recipient Prix de Rome, Am. Acad. in Rome, 1941, Sculpture award St. Louis Artists Guild, 1950, Penrose prize for sculpture Conn. Acad. Fine Arts, 1953, Am. Acad. and Nat. Inst. Arts and Letters award, 1975. Cresson traveling fellow Pa. Acad. Fine Arts, 1941. Mem. Sculptors Guild, Century Assn. Home: Washington, Conn. Died Nov. 16, 1980.

TALIAFERRO, SIDNEY FLETCHER (TOL'I-VER), banker; b. Salem, Va., Mar. 4, 1885; s. Van and Sallie (Pendleton) T.; LL.B., M.P.L., Georgetown U., 1913; m. Elizabeth Kirkwood Fulton, Oct. 3, 1916 (died 1938); m. 2d, Helen Munn Wayland Watson, Mar. 9, 1943. Practiced law in Washington, D.C., 1913-26; asst. prof. of law, Georgetown U., 1919-23; ret. v.p. and trust officer Riggs Nat. Bank, Washington; dir. Washington Gas Light Co. and subsidiary gas companies, Brooks Bros., Julius Garfinckel & Co., Inc. Commr., D.C., 1926-30; formerly member Public Utilites Commn., D.C., and Zoning Commn., D.C.; ex-mem. Board Pub. Welfare, D.C.; mem. board Washington Self-help Exch.; mem. adv. bd. Y.W.C.A. Member Am. Bar Assn., Bar Assn. D.C., Delta Chi. Episcopalian. Mason. Clubs: Cosmos, Chevy Chase, Lawyers (Washington). Home: Washington. *

TALLCOTT, ROLLO ANSON (TAWL'KUT), prof. pub. speaking; b. Constantia, N.Y., Jan. 5, 1884; s. Herbert Hudson and Harriet Isadore (Scoville) T.; A.B., Syracuse U., 1909, A.M., 1920; Litt.D., Valparaiso U., 1921; Ph.D., Cornell U., 1936; studied acting and speaking in professional schs.; m. Jennie Rebecca Witmer, June 29, 1910. Prof. pub. speaking, Hiram (O.) Coll., 1909-13, Mt. Union Coll., part of time, 1912-13; dean Sch. Pub. Speaking, 1913-21, dean Coll. Arts and Sciences, 1920-21, Valparaiso (Ind.) U.; head of pub. speaking dept., Butler Coll., Indianapolis, 1921-25; dean Williams Sch. of Expression and Dramatic Art (Ithaca, N.Y.), 1925-31; prof. oral English, State Teachers Coll., Slippery Rock, Pa., 1932-36; prof. of English, Ithaca Coll., since 1936. Mem. Am. Assn. Univ. Profs., Phi Kappa Phi, Tau Kappa Alpha, Alpha Chi Rho, Phi Mu Alpha, Theta Alpha Phi, Pi Epsilon Delta. Republican. Widely known as a reader and entertainer. Established annual summer tour to Am. and Canadian univs., reading plays. Author several books; (plays) The Scornful Lady, 1942; Pansy, For Thoughts, 1944. Home: Ithaca, N.Y. *

TALLEY, FRANZ G., business exec.; b. 1919; ed. Ind. U., Purdue U.; married. With St. Louis Ordnance Plant, 1942-43; with Hertz Engring. Co., Indpls., 1943-44; with engring. products div. R.C.A., Victor, Camden, N.J., 1944-47; mgr. part check div. Telephone & Electric Co., Meriden, Conn., 1947-49; cons. New Haven Clock & Watch Co., 1949; co-founder Talco Engring. Co., 1949-59; pres., chief exec. officer Talley Industries, Inc., after 1960, also chmn. bd., chmn. exec. com.; chmn. exec. com. Gen. Time Corp. Home: Mesa, Ariz. Died June 18, 1978.

TALLEY, LEE, soft drink exec.; b. Monroeville, Ala., June 26, 1901; s. Rev. Charles S. and Bertha (Calhoun) T.; B.S., Emory U., 1923; m. Marjorie Irene Moxam, Apr. 27, 1933; children—Mary Lee (Mrs. William G. Herbster), and John Eugene. With The Coca-Cola Co., from 1923, sales advt. rep., Atlanta, 1923-27; br. mgr. Coca-Cola, Ltd., Vancouver, B.C., 1927-30, regional mgr., 1930-36, v.p., Toronto, 1936-43; v.p. The Coca-Cola Export Corp., N.Y.C., 1943-50, pres., 1954-59, v.p. Parent Co., Atlanta, 1950, chmn. parent co., from 1961, dir.; pres. Coca-Cola Ltd., Can., from 1952; chmn. bd. Coca-Cola Cuba, 1954-58; pres. Coca-Cola Co., 1958-62; dir. Trust Co. of Ga. Trustee Emory University. Member Pi Kappa Alpha. Clubs: Capitol City (Atlanta); Newcomen. Home: St. Michaels, Md. Died Aug. 26, 1976; buried Eastern Shore, Md.

TANDY, CHARLES DAVID, corp. exec.; b. Brownsville, Tex., May 15, 1918; s. David Lewis and Carmen (McLain) T.; B.S., Tex. Christian U., 1940, LL.D., 1971; postgrad. Harvard U., 1940-41; m. Gwendolyn Purdy Johnston, Oct. 25, 1945 (dec.); stepchildren—Sherwood Johnston, Constance Johnston (Mrs. Jesse L. Upchurch); m. 2d, Anne Burnett Windfohr, June 12, 1969. Vice pres. Tandy Leather Co., Ft. Worth, 1947-55, pres., 1955-64; chmn. bd., chief exec. officer Tandy Corp., 1964-78; dir. First United Bancorp., Inc., Tandycrafts, Inc., Tandy Brands, Inc., Pier I Imports, Inc., Stafford-Lowdon Inc., Kimbell, Inc., Alcon Labs., Inc., Robintech, Inc., Dillard Dept. Stores, Inc. Trustee Tex. Christian U.; bd. dirs. N. Tex. Commn., Ft. Worth Art Assn., Ft. Worth Community Theatre, Ft. Worth Progress, Inc., Ft. Worth Jr. Achievement, Arts Council Greater Ft. Worth, Trinity Improvement Assn.; mem. founding council Rockefeller U. Served with USN, 1941-47. Recipient Distinguished Alumnus award Tex. Christian U., 1967; Ike Harrison award Tex. Christian U. Mgmt. Alumni Assn., 1972; Silver award Financial World mag., 1976; Dateline award Advt. Club Ft. Worth, 1976; Distinguished Bus. Leadership award U. Tex. at Arlington, 1976; named Newsmaker of Year Press Club Ft. Worth, 1968; Salesman of Year, Sales and Mktg. Execs. Club, 1969; Bus. Exec. of Year, Tex. Wesleyan Coll., Ft. Worth Area C. of C., 1976. Mem. Ft. Worth C. of C. (dir.), Newcomen Soc., Tex. Assn. Bus. Baptist. Clubs: Ft. Worth, Century II (dir.), Ridglea Country (dir.), Exchange (past pres., Golden Deeds award 1974), Shady Oaks Country (Ft. Worth). Home: Fort Worth, Tex. Died Nov. 4, 1978.

TANKOOS, SAMUEL JOSEPH, JR., realty investor; b. N.Y.C., Mar. 11, 1921; s. Samuel J. and Mary (Walsh) T.; grad. Mass. Inst. Tech., 1943; m. Catherine Moore; children—Dianne, Bradley Joseph, Lisa Suzanne. Adminstrn. engring. with Sperry Gyroscope Co., 1942-44; advt., pub. relations, 1946-49; real estate financing and investment, 1949-76; founder, gen. partner Tankoos & Co., N.Y.C.; chmn. bd. Tankoos Yarmon, Ltd., Toronto, Ont., Can.; pres., dir. Muss-Tankoos Corp., N.Y.C., Tankoos Yarmon Hotels, Inc., Palm Beach, Fla., 155 Hammon Avenue Corp., Palm Beach, Fla.; mng. dir. Dollar Land Corp., Ltd., 1961-67; pres., dir. County Dollar Corp., Inc., 1961-68; dir., exec. com. Fla. Capital Corp., 1959-67; dir. Western Realty Projects Ltd., Vancouver, Exec. Internat. Investors Ltd., Montreal, exec. Fund Can. Ltd., Montreal. Hon. consul Republic Panama, Palm Beach, Fla., 1964-70, Republic Nicaragua, 1970-76. Trustee Citizens Budget Commn., N.Y., 1960-70, Cancer Research Inst., Library of Presdl. Papers; mem. adv. council N.Y. State Joint Legislative Com.; mem. devel. com. Mass. Inst. Tech.; pres. Nicaraguan Relief Commn.; mem. Nat. Pub. Adv. Com. Regional Econ. Devel.; hon. commr. N.Y.C. Dept. Pub. Events. Served with Am. Field Service, attached Brit. 8th Army, 1944-46. Decorated Brit. Empire medal; 11 Cuore di rincalzo (Italy). Mem. Chi Phi. Roman Catholic. Clubs: Mass. Inst. Tech., Wall Street, Madison Square, Metropolitan, Canadian (N.Y.C.); Coral Beach, Atlantic Beach, Mid-Ocean (Bermuda); Westchester Country; Mayacoo Lakes (Palm Beach, Fla.). Home: New York, N.Y. Died Sept. 21, 1976.

TANNENBAUM, ALBERT, physician; b. Chgo.; B.S., U. Ill., 1922; M.D., Rush Med. Coll., 1930. Sr. chemist, toxicologist Cook County (Ill.) Coroner's Toxicology Lab., 1923-27; Logan research fellow, 1927-29; intern Michael Reese Med. Center, Chgo., 1930-31, asst. dir. hosp.'s dept. biochemistry, 1932-35, dir. dept. cancer research, 1935-71; cons. cancer research, La Jolla, Calif., 1971-80. Sect. chief metall. lab. Manhattan Project, 1942-46. Mem. Am. Assn. Cancer Research (pres. 1956-57), Soc. Exptl. Biology and Medicine, Am. Assn. Pathologists. Contbr. articles to profl. jours. Home: La Jolla, Calif. Died Sept. 14, 1980.

TANNER, EDWARD EVERETT, 3D (PATRICK DENNIS, VIRGINIA ROWANS), author; b. Chgo., May 18, 1921; studied pvt. sch.; m. Louise Stickney, Dec. 30, 1948; children—Michael, Elizabeth. With Stebbins Hardware Co., then bookstore clk. Columbia Ednl. Books, Inc., Chgo. account exec. Franklin Spier, Inc., advt. agy., N.Y.C., advt. mgr. Creative Age Press; promotion dir. Fgn. Affairs mag. until 1956; drama critic New Republic, 1957-71. Served as ambulance driver Am. Field Service, World War II. Author: On What a Wonderful Wedding, 1953; House Party, 1954; Auntie Mame, 1955 (adapted for Broadway prodn. 1956, motion picture 1958); An Irreverent Escapade in Biography; Guestward Ho!; (with Mrs. Barbara C. Hooton) As Indiscreetly Confided to Patrick Dennis, 1956; The Loving Couple, 1956; (with Dorothy Erskine) The Pink Hotel, 1957; Around the World with Auntie Mame, 1958; Love and Mrs. Sargent, 1960; Little Me, 1961; Genius, 1962; The Joyous Season, 1965; Tony, 1966; How Firm a Foundation, 1968; Paradise, 1971, (as Patrick Dennis) Three-D, 1972. Home: N.Y. Died Nov. 6, 1976.

TANNER, WILSON PENNELL, mcht; exporter; b. Toledo, Feb. 6, 1886; s. Frank Henry and Nina Virginia (Pennell) T.; student U. Mich., 1904-05, Western Res. U., 1906-07; m. Esther Marie Rayman, March 16, 1910; children—Wilson Pennell, Betty Chalfonte, Robert Rayman; m. 2d, Annette Ryall, 1950. Pres. Brown's Hungarian Corp. (flour millers, distbrs.), N.Y.C.; pres. dir. Tanner-Evans-Siney Corp., Esdorn-Youngs Lumber Co. Pres., N.Y. Flour Club, 1937-38; pres. Nat. Assn. Flour Distbrs., 1938-39, chmn. bd. 1940-46. Mem. Republican N.Y. County Com., 1912-19. Pres., N.Y. Meth. Social Union, 1924-26. Past pres. bd. trustees Drew Sem. for Young Women; trustee N.Y.C. Soc. M.E. Ch., Broadway Temple; pres. bd. trustees Washington Heights M.E. Ch., John St. Meth. Ch. Mem. S.R., Beta Theta Phi. Mason (32, Shriner). Clubs: Union League, New York Athletic. *

TAPLIN, CHARLES FARRAND, lawyer; b. Cleveland, O., Dec. 13, 1879; s. Charles G. and Frances (Smith) T.; Ph.B., Western Reserve U., 1901; LL.B., Harvard, 1904; m. Elsie Holliday, Sept. 8, 1908; children—Charles Farrand, Jr., Benjamin Holliday. Admitted to Ohio bar, 1904, and began practice at Cleveland; dir. Wellman Bronze and Aluminum Co. Mem. Phi Beta Kappa, Delta Kappa Epsilon. Rep. Presbyn. Clubs: Union, Mayfield Country. Home: Shaker Heights. *

TARRANT, WILLIAM THEODORE, naval officer (ret.); b. Black Hawk, Miss., July 28, 1878; s. Edward William and Anne Wilson (Spencer) T.; ed., U.S. Naval Acad., 1898; m. Ruth Gibson, June 13, 1906. Commd. ensign U.S. Navy, 1900 and advanced through grades to vice adm., 1936; comdt. 11th Naval Dist., 1933-36; comdr. scouting force, U.S. Fleet, 1936-38; comdt. 1st Naval Dist., 1938-42; ret., 1942, recalled to active duty, 1943-46. Episcopalian. Club: Army Navy (Washington). Home: Washington, D.C. *

TARUMIANZ, MESROP A., psychiatrist; b. Schuscha, Caucasus, Sept. 27, 1885; s. Avetis and Ann Tarumjanz; student Coll. in Elizabethpol, Caucasus; M.D., U. of Berlin, 1910; M.D., U. of Moscow, 1911; m. Sonia Rabus, Sept. 27, 1911; 1 son, Alexis. Received psychiatric training under Profs. Kraepelin and asst. physician Del. State Hosp., 1918-21, assistant supt., 1921-25; med. director, 1925—, supt., 1925—; director Delaware Mental Hygiene Clinics, 1929—; state psychiatrist, 1929—; superintendent, also governor Bacon Health Center, 1947—; superintendent Hosp. for Mentally Retarded, 1955—; cons. in neurology and psychiatry Wilmington Gen. Hosp., Memorial Hosp., VA Hospital, Wilmington, Del.; director Delaware Day Care Centers for Severely Mentally Retarded Children, 1957—; teacher of internes and residents; lecturer in psychiatry Sch. of Medicine, University of Pa., since 1947. Mng. editor Del. State Med. Jour.; dir. Family Service No. Dela.; exec. com. Dela. Commn. on children and Youth; bd. govs. Menninger Found.; gov., Citizens Adv. Com. for Study of Needs and Problems of Edn.; Youth Services Commn. of Del.; So. Regional Edn. Bd.; vice chmn. So. Regional Council on Mental Health Training and Research; planning committee Northeast State Governments' Conference on Mental Health; Welfare Council Dela.; chairman Gov.'s Com. on Mental Health Tng. and Research in Del., chmn. Del. Bd. Mental Health Tng. & Research. Served as field surgeon Med. Dept., Imperial Russian Army, 1914-17. Diplomate Am. Bd. of Psychiatry and Neurology. Fellow Am. Psychiat. Assn. (mem. nat., state and local profl. orgns. and assns. Clubs: Medical (Philadelphia); Rotary; Torch (Delaware). Author numerous publs. in field, latest being: Recreation in Medicine, 1957; Mental Health in Regard to Homicide Investigation, 1958. Address: Farmhurst, Del. *

TASCA, HENRY J., ambassador; b. Providence, Aug. 23, 1912; s. Julius and Phiomena (DePaulis) T.; B.S., Temple U., 1933; LL.D., 1966; M.B.A., U. Pa., 1934, Ph.D., 1937; grad. fellow Brookings Instn., 1936-37, London Sch. Econs., 1937-38; post-doctoral Social Sci. Research Council fellow, 1938-39, Penfield traveling scholar in Europe, 1938-39; m. Natalina Federici, Aug. 22, 1949; children—Ann, Eileen, Elia, John. Econ. analyst div. trade agreements Dept. State, 1937-38; asst. dir. trade regulation and comml. policy project in European countries Rockefeller Found., 1938-40; econ. adviser on fgn. trade to Nat. Def. Com., 1940-41; Dept. Treasury rep. Am. embassy, Rome, Italy, 1945-48; spl. financial adviser to Allied Commn. for Italy, 1945; alt. U.S. exec. dir. Internat. Monetary Fund, also spl. asst. to sec. treasury, 1948-49; acting tech. cons. to Herter Select Com. on Fgn. Aid, 1947; dir. plans and policy staff Dept. Econ. Affairs Marshall Plan, Paris, France, 1949-51, dep. U.S. spl. rep. Europe, 1952-53; econ. adviser, dep. to W. Averell Harriman, pres. temp. council com. NATO, 1951-52; dir. U.S. ops. mission to Italy and minister for econ. affairs Am. embassy, Rome, 1953-56; minister econ. affairs Am. embassy, Bonn, Germany, 1956-60; dep. asst. sec. African Affairs charge ops. Dept. State, 1960-65; ambassador to Morocco, 1965-69, to Greece, 1969-74; ret., 1974; engaged in internat. bus. activities, 1974-79. Spl. rep. of the Pres. for Korean econ. affairs, 1953. Served to lt. comdr. USN, 1941-45. Decorated Medal of Freedom, Distinguished Service Order (Korea); grand cordoni Quissam Alaouite (Morocco); Cavaliere di grand croce Order Merit (Italy). Clubs: Metropolitan; Parioli Tennis, Circolo della Caccia, Circolo dei Scocchi. Author: The Reciprocal Trade Policy of the U.S.: A Study in Trade Philosophy, 1948; World Trading Systems; A Study of American British Commercial Policies, 1939. Address: Rome, Italy. Died Aug. 22, 1979; buried Arlington (Va.) Nat. Cemetery.

TASHIRO, SHIRO (TA-SHI'RO), prof. biochemistry; b. Kagoshima, Japan, Feb. 12, 1882; s. Shirobe and A. (Tashiro) T.; came to U.S., 1901; B.S., U. of Chicago, 1909, Ph.D., 1912; Dr. Med. Science, Kyoto Imperial U., Japan, 1923; m. Shizuka Kawasaki, Nov. 9, 1915; children—Kiyoshi, Kazuo, Mitsu. Asst. in biochemistry, U. of Chicago, 1909, fellow in physiol. chemistry, 1910-12, asst. in same, 1912-13, asso. 1913-14, instr. in same, 1914-18, asst. prof., 1918; asso. prof. biochemistry, U. of Cincinnati, 1919-21, prof. since 1921, lecturer on Japanese lang., Evening Coll., for the duration of war. Fellow A.A.A.S.; mem. American Society Biological Chemists, American Physiological Society, American Chemical Society, Am. Soc. Naturalists, Soc. Exptl. Biology and Medicine, Cincinnati Acad. Medicine (hon.), Ohio Acad. Science (ex-v.p.), Phi Beta Kappa, Sigma Xi, Alpha Omega Alpha. Awarded Crown Prince Memorial prize, Imperial Acad., Japan. Club: Literary. Author: A Chemical Sign of Life, 1917. Editor: (with N. C. Foot) Kawamura's Studies on Tsutsugamushi Disease, 1926. Contbr. numerous articles to scientific journals. Home: Cincinnati, O. *

TASTROM, EDWARD P(HILLIP), pub. relations dir.; b. N.Y.C., Aug. 3, 1897; s. Edward T. and Louisa (Roller) T.; A.B., Columbia, 1919; m. Dorothy Easton

Blohm, Nov. 26, 1924. Reporter N.Y. Tribune, 1920-21; advt. mgr. and v.p. John Nickerson and Co. (investments), 1923-32; with Preston, James and Co. (investments), 1932-38; pres. Norman and Tastrom, Inc. (investments), 1938-41; asst. financial editor, N.Y. Journal of Commerce, 1942-44, textile editor, 1944-47, asso. editor, 1947-59; dir. pub. relations and research N.Y. Shipping Assn., 1959-72, ret., 1972; editorial dir. Jour. Commerce ann. corporate pension plan rev. and analysis from 1943; dir. Guardian Investors Trust, 1930-33, George Washington Life Ins. Co., Charleston, W.Va., 1933-38. Mem. New York Financial Writers Association, World Trade Writers Assn., Silurians, Sigma Delta Chi. Home: Forest Hills, N.Y. Died Oct. 12, 1976.

TATE, ALLEN (JOHN ORLEY), critic, poet; b. Clark County, Ky., Nov. 19, 1899; s. John Orley and Eleanor (Varnell) T.; B.A. magna cum laude, Vanderbilt U., 1922; Lit. D., U. Louisville, 1948, Colgate U., 1956, U. Ky., 1960, Carleton Coll., 1963; U. South, 1970; m. Caroline Gordon, Nov. 3, 1924 (div.); 1 dau., Nancy Meriwether (Mrs. Percy Wood, Jr.); m. 2d, Isabella Gardner, Aug. 27, 1959 (div.); m. 3d, Helen Heinz, July 30, 1966; children—John Allen, Benjamin Bogan. Free lance writer, 1924—; Guggenheim fellow, 1928-30; lectr. English lit. Southwestern (Memphis) 1934-36; prof. English, Woman's Coll., U. N.C., 1938-39; resident fellow in writing, creative arts program Princeton, 1939-42; incumbent chair poetry Library of Congress, 1943-44; editor Sewanee Rev. 1944-46, poetry and belles lettres Henry Holt & Co., 1946-48; lectr. English, N.Y. U., 1947-51; prof. English, U. Minn., 1951-66, Regents' prof. English, 1966-68, Regents' prof. emeritus, 1968—. Vis. prof. humanities U. Chgo. 1949; Fulbright prof. U. Oxford, 1958-59; vis. prof. Vanderbilt U., 1967; sr. fellow Ind. Sch. Letters; vis. lectr. U. South, 1968-69. Recipient Midland Author's prize, (Chgo.), 1933; Bollingen prize in Poetry, 1956; Brandeis U. medal award poetry, 1961; Medaglio D'Oro, Dante Soc. (Florence), 1962; $5,000 award Acad. Am. Poets, 1963; Oscar Williams award, 1976; Ingram Merrill award, 1976; Nat. Medal for Lit., 1976. Mem. Am. Acad. Arts and Letters, Nat. Inst. Arts and Letters (pres. 1968), Am. Acad. Arts and Scis., Soc. Am. Historians, So. Hist. Assn., Phi Beta Kappa, Sigma Upsilon, Phi Delta Theta (So. editor Hound and Horn, 1932-34). Democrat. Clubs: Princeton, Century Assn. (N.Y.C.); Authors (London). Author or co-author books, 1928—, latest publs.: The Fathers, 1938; On the Limits of Poetry, 1948; The Hovering Fly, 1949; (with Caroline Gordon) The House of Ficton, 1950; The Forlorn Demon, 1953; The Man of Letters in the Modern World, 1955; Collected Essays, 1960; Poems, 1960; Essays of Four Decades, 1969; The Swimmers and Other Selected Poems, 1970; Memoirs and Opinions, 1975; Collected Poems, 1977; also articles and verse in various publs. Editor: Man and His Work (T.S. Eliot), 1966. Adv. editor Kenyon Rev., 1938-42. Regular mem. CBS radio program Invitation to Learning, 1940-41. Address: Nashville, Tenn. Died Feb. 9, 1979; buried Sewanee, Tenn.

TAUBER, MAURICE FALCOLM, librarian, univ. prof.; b. Norfolk, Va., Feb. 14, 1908; s. A. Albert and Leona (Miller) T.; B.S., Temple U., 1930, M.Ed., 1939; B.S., Sch. Library Service, Columbia U., 1934; Carnegie fellow Grad. Library Sch., U. Chgo., 1938-39, Ph.D., 1941; m. Rose Anne Begner, May 15, 1932 (dec. May 1964); children—Robert M., Frederic J. Asst., Temple U. Library, 1927-35, head catalog dept., 1935-38; research asst. Grad. Library Sch., U. Chgo., 1939-41, instr., 1942-44, asst. prof., 1944; chief catalog dept. U. Chgo. Libraries, 1941-42, chief preparations div., 1942-44; asst. dir. libraries Columbia U., 1944-47, asst. prof. Sch. Library Service, 1933-46, asso. prof., 1946-49, prof., 1949-54, Melvil Dewey prof. library sci., 1954-80; survey of libraries and cons. Augustana Coll., Columbia U., U. Vt., U. S.C., Vassar Coll., N.Y. State Library, Cornell U., Union Theol. Sem., Va. Poly. Inst., Army Med. Library, Mont. State U., Dartmouth Coll., Boston U., Barnard Coll., Library of Congress, Queens Borough Pub. Library, U.S. Office Edn., Canadian Dept. Agr., McGill U., Yonkers Pub. Library, Hampton Inst., NSF, Calif. State Library, Library of Hawaii, Pace Inst., U. N.Mex., Pa. State U., Newberry Library, Union Coll., Pratt Inst., St. John's U., Bklyn., many others; mem. adv. com. descriptive cataloging to Librarian of Congress, 1946-47; mem. library adv. bd. Air U., Maxwell Field, Ala.; mem. bd. dirs. Assn. Am. Library Schs., 1948-50; mem. com. on orgn. of info. Am. Documentation Inst., 1948-58; mem. joint com. on edn. for librarianship Nat. Council Library Assns., 1949-80. Bd. advisors Naval War Coll., Newport, R.I. Recipient Margaret Mann award, 1953; Melvil Dewey medal, 1955; Fulbright scholar, Australia, 1961. Mem. AAUP, ALA (library edn. div., assn. reference libraries, pres. div. of cataloging and classification, bd. and council), N.Y. State Library Assn., N.Y. Regional Group Catalogers, Beta Phi Mu (pres. 1967-68). Club: N.Y. York Library. Author: The University Library (with L.R. Wilson), 1945; Technical Services in Libraries, 1954; The Columbia University Libraries (with C.D. Cook and R.H. Logsdon), 1959; Cataloging and Classification, 1960; (with R.E. Kingery) Book Catalogs, 1964; (with Irlene R. Stephens) Use of Printed and Audio-Visual Materials for Instructional Purposes, 1966; Louis Round Wilson: Librarian and Administrator, 1967; (with Irlene R. Stephens) Library Surveys, 1968; (with Hilda Feinberg) Book Catalogs, 1971; Library Binding Manual, 1972; editor: College and Research Libraries, 1948-62; contbr. numerous papers to profl. jours. Home: New York, N.Y. Died Sept. 21, 1980, buried N.Y.C.

TAUROG, NORMAN, motion picture dir.; b. Chgo., Feb. 23, 1899; s. Arthur and Anita (Goldsmith) T.; student pub. schs.; m. Julie Leonard, May 23, 1925 (div. 1943); 1 dau., Patricia Anne; m. 2d, Susan Ream, Sept. 16, 1944; children—Jonathan Ream, Priscilla Ream. Actor legitimate stage, 1912-16; engaged in motion picture industry, 1916-81, dir., 1919-81; films include Skippy, Adventures of Tom Sawyer, Mad About Music, Boys Town, Young Tom Edison, Yank at Eton, Presenting Lily Mars, Girl Crazy, The Beginning of the End, Words and Music, That Midnight Kiss, The Toast of New Orleans, Ricy, Young and Pretty, The Stooge, Room for One More, Jumping Jacks, The Stars Are Singing, The Caddy, Living it Up, You're Never Too Young, Birds and the Bees, Pardners, The Fuzzy Pink Nightgown, Onionhead, Don't Give up the Ship, Visit to A Small Planet, G.I. Blues, Huckleberry Finn, Adventures of Tom Sawyer, others. Prof. cinema dept. So. Calif. Recipient Acad. award for direction Skippy, 1931. Mason. Died Apr. 7, 1981.

TAUSSIG, FRANCES, social worker; b. Chicago, June 23, 1883; d. Samuel and Lena (Alexander) T.; Ph.B., U. Chicago, 1904; unmarried. Exec. dir., Jewish Social Service Assn., Inc., N.Y. City, since 1919; exec. dir. Jewish Family Service, N.Y. City, 1946-49, mem. bd. and exec. com. since 1949. Mem. Am. Assn. Social Workers (pres. 1930-32), Family Welfare Assn. Am. (v.p. and chmn. exec. com., 1939-41, mem. bd. and exec. com., 1939-44), Nat. Conf. Social Work (1st v.p., 1950-51); mem. bd. and exec. com. N.Y. Assn. for New Americans since 1950; mem. Welfare Council City of N.Y. (mem. bd. and exec. com., 1929-49). Home: N.Y. City also West Redding, Conn. *

TAUSSIG, GARFIELD JOSEPH, investment dealer; b. St. Louis, June 27, 1881; s. John Jay and Lenore (Taussig) T.; B.A., Harvard, 1902; m. Lilliam Imrie Aitken, Apr. 15, 1911; 1 dau., Carroll Wright. Chief clk. to supt. terminals, Burlington R.R., 1902-05; statistician Simon, Brookmire, Clifford, mems. N.Y. Stock Exchange, 1905-15, Brookmire Econ. Chart Co., 1905-13; v.p. William R. Compton Co., 1915-24; formed Taussig, Day, Fairbank & Co., St. Louis, investment dealers (now Taussig, Day & Co., Inc.), 1924, since partner, dir., pres.; pres., dir. Lafayette Fed. Savings & Loan Assn., 18th & Market Corp.; v.p. Sterling Aluminum Products, Inc.; dir. Terre Haute Malleable and Manufacturing Corporation. Member of Midwest Stock Exchange, Investment Bankers Assn. Am. (gov.). Clubs: Racquet, University, Noonday (St. Louis); Harvard (N.Y.C.). Home: St. Louis. *

TAVARES, CYRUS NILS, judge; b. Pukalani, Maui County, Hawaii, Apr. 12, 1902; s. Antone Ferreira and Julia Mahealani (Akana) T.; J.D., U. Mich., 1925, LL.D., 1963; m. Unita Thelma Gillett, Aug. 19, 1927; 1 dau., Shirly Ann Wetzel. Admitted to Hawaii bar, 1925; practice in Maui County, 1925-27, also 2d dist. magistrate Wailuku Dist. Ct.; dept. atty. gen. Hawaii, 1927-34; partner firm Hewitt & Tavares, Honolulu, 1934-40; individual law practice, 1940-41; spl. dep. atty. gen. Hawaii, war emergency matters, 1941-42, asst. atty. gen., 1942-43, atty. gen., 1944-47; mem. firm Pratt, Tavares & Cassidy, later Pratt & Tavares, 1947-60; U.S. dist. judge, Hawaii, 1960-72, sr. judge, 1972. Mem. Compilation Commn. to Compile Revised Laws of Hawaii, 1935; spl. counsel Senate of Hawaii, 1935, 37, 39, Ho. of Reps. Hawaii, 1935-41; counsel Honolulu Charter Revision Commn., 1937-39; chmn. social protection com. Honolulu Council Social Agys., 1949; chmn. subcom. taxation and finance Hawaiian Constn. Com., 1949; del. Hawaii Constl. Conv., 1950; mem. Fed. Loyalty Rev. Bd., 1952-53; mem. procedural rules com. Hawaii Supreme Ct., 1952-54; chmn. Hawaii Statehood Commn., 1953-56; mem. Honolulu Charter Commn., 1957-59. Mem. Bar Assn. Hawaii (past pres.), Legal Aid Soc. Hawaii (past pres.), Fed., Am. bar assns., Am. Judicature Soc., Social Sci. Assn. Hawaii, Lawyers Club U. Mich., Internat. Platform Assn., Hawaiian History Soc., Order of Coif. Republican. Conglist. Mason (33 deg., Shriner), Rotarian. Club: National Lawyer's. Home: Honolulu, Hawaii. Died Aug. 3, 1976.

TAWES, JOHN MILLARD, former state govt. ofcl.; b. Crisfield, Md., Apr. 8, 1894; s. James and Alice (Byrd) T.; m. Helen Avalynne Gibson, Dec. 25, 1915; children—Jimmie Lee (Mrs. William R. Wilson), Phillip W. Sec.-treas. Tawes Shipbldg. Co., 1917-19, Tawes Baking Co., 1919-45; dir. Bank of Crisfield; clk. of ct. Somerset County, 1930-38; comptroller Md., 1938-47, 50-58; bank commr., 1947-50; gov. Md., 1959-67; sec. Md. Dept. Natural Resources 1969-71. Dir. McReady Meml. Hosp., Crisfield. Mem. Nat. Assn. State Auditors, Comptrollers and Treasurers (past pres.), Hibernian Soc. Balt., Md. Soc. Pa., Crisfield Fire Dept., Md. Chesapeake Bay Fishing Fair Assn. (past pres.). Methodist. Elk, K.P., Rotarian, Mason (32 deg., Shriner); mem. Order Eastern Star, Tall Cedars. Club: Scimeter (Balt.). Home: Crisfield, Md. Died June 25, 1979; interred Sunnyridge Meml. Park, Crisfield.

TAYLOR, BENJAMIN BROWN, lawyer, bus. exec.; b. Jackson, La., Mar. 20, 1885; s. David H. and Callie (Brown) T.; B.S., Centenary Coll., 1904; LL.B., Tulane U., 1906; LL.B., U. of Mich,. 1907; m. May McKowen, June 7, 1910; children—Benjamin B., May M., Jane S., John M. Mem. Taylor, Porter, Brooks & Fuller; chmn. bd. Louisiana Nat. Bank; v.p. and dir. Baton Rouge Water Works Co., Capital Bldg. & Loan Assn.; pres. Mayola Realty Co. Inc., Morehouse Planting Co. Ltd.; dir. La. Fire Ins. Co. Pres. La. State Bar Assn., 1948-49; mem. council and exec. com. La. Law Inst.; trustee Southwestern U. Mem. Kappa Sigma, Phi Delta Phi, Order of Coif. Home: Baton Rouge. *

TAYLOR, C. NEWBOLD, investment broker; b. Jenkintown, Pa., Sept. 13, 1893; s. William J. and Emily (Newbold) T.; A.B., U. Pa., 1915; m. Anne W. Meirs, 1918 (dec. 1930); children—Anne (Mrs. Robert C. Richardson III), Phoebe (Mrs. Charles Biddle); m. 2d, Lydia E. Dadmun, Apr. 10, 1943. With W.H. Newbold's Son & Co., 1915-76, gen. partner, 1927-72, limited partner, 1972-76; mem. N.Y. Stock Exchange, from 1938, past gov. Bd. dirs. Pa. Acad. Fine Arts. Library Company Phila., from 1941. Served to capt., F.A., U.S. Army, 1916. Mem. Investment Bankers Assn. Am. (gov. 1945-48), Assn. Stock Exchange Firms (gov. 1945-52, 57-63). S.R. (past pres. Pa.), Soc. Colonial Wars (past treas. Pa.) Home: Philadelphia, Pa. Died Mar. 5, 1976.

TAYLOR, CHARLES, artist; b. Phila., Dec. 15, 1910; s. Andrew and Kathryn (Lohmiller) T.; student pub. schs.; m. Annette Skinner, Feb. 11, 1950; m. 2d, Patricia Cayo, May 5, 1972. Works exhibited Carnegie Inst. 1943, Phila. regional exhbn. Phila. Art Alliance, 1954-55, exhbns. Am. Water Color Soc., Audubon Artist, Nat. Acad., 1954-55, Phila. Sketch Club Show, 1975, 76; one-man show Fine Arts Co., Phila., 1975; represented collections Phila. Art Mus., Woodmere Gallery, Phila. Recipient regular oil exhbn. prize Phila. Art Alliance, 1954, regular water color exhbn. prize, 1955; B. Altman prize Nat. Acad., 1955, Ranger Fund purchase prize, 1955; Bronze medal C. Wolf prize Da Vinci Alliance, Phila., 1958; Grumbacker prize Allied Artists N.Y.; Seeley purchase prize Salmagundi Club, 1961, Mem. Audubon Artists, Phila. Art Alliance, Artists Equity, Phila., Water Color Club, Am. Watercolor Soc., Allied Artists Am. Club: Salmagundi (N.Y.C.) Address: Sarasota, Fla. Died Feb. 10, 1980.

TAYLOR, CHARLES LINCOLN, JR., clergyman; b. Hartford, Conn., Jan. 27, 1901; s. Charles Lincoln and Bertha (Smith) T.; A.B., Williams Coll., 1921, D.D., 1944; B.A., Oxford (Eng.) U., 1923, M.A., 1929; B.D., Episcopal Theol. Sch., Cambridge, Mass., 1924; Th.M., Harvard, 1929, Th.D., 1932, D.D., 1958; m. Hannah Chamberlin, June 14, 1924 (dec. 1972); children—Carolyn, Ann, Elizabeth, Mary Chamberlin, Margaret Hannah, Charles Lincoln and William Fosdick Chamberlin (twins); m. 2d Margaret R.G. Bennett, May 4, 1974. Ordained to ministry Episcopal Ch., 1924; asst., St. John's Ch., Waterbury, Conn., 1924-25; pastor St. Gabriel's Ch., Marion, Mass., 1931-44; instr., prof. O.T., dean Episcopal Theol. Sch., Cambridge, 1925-56; exec. dir. Am. Assn. Theol. Schs., 1957-66. Home: Wellesley Hills, Mass. Died Dec. 12, 1979.

TAYLOR, ELMER BRUCE, lawyer; b. Harrisburg, Pa., Oct. 15, 1886; s. Samuel Nimrod and Jane (Cashman) T.; prep. edn., high sch., Adams County, Pa.; student Sch. of Commerce, Harrisburg, 1901-02; m. Alma Euada Garverich, June 30, 1909; children—Mildred Josephine, E. Bruce. Admitted to Pa. bar, 1922, and began practice at Harrisburg; asst. city solicitor, Harrisburg, 1922-23; v.p. and trust officer, Mechanics Trust Co., 1923-26, pres., 1926-30; dir. Community Discount Co. Trustee Harrisburg Polyclinic Hosp. Republican. Presbyterian. Mason. Home: Harrisburg, Penn. *

TAYLOR, EUGENE JACKSON, health adminstr.; b. Wichita, Kans., June 26, 1913; s. Wesley E. and Lela (Brown) T.; B.S. in Edn., Kans. State Tchrs. Coll., 1936; A.M., State U. Iowa, 1939; LL.D., Chungang U., Korea, 1956; D.H.L., Adelphi Coll., 1959. Secondary sch. tchr., Kans., Iowa, N.Y., 1936-42; editorial staff N.Y. Times, 1945-70, Med. World News, 1966-69; adj. prof. rehab. medicine N.Y. U. Sch. Medicine, 1949-78, cons. Human resources Center, 1954-78, vice chmn. exec. com., 1969-78, chmn. bd. Human Resources Sch., 1969-71. Chmn., Gov. N.Y. Council Rehab., 1966-70, N.Y. State Planning Council for Vocation, 1967-70; mem. Nat. Commn. Archtl. Barriers, 1965-70; pres. Am.-Korean Found., 1968-71. Bd. dirs. Assn. Crippled Children and Adults N.Y. State, Just One Break, Soc. for Facially Disfigured, Joseph Bulova Sch. Watch Making. Served to 1st lt. USAAF, 1942-45. Decorated Legion of Merit; Nat. medal (Korea); Order Jose Fernandez Madrid (Colombia). Recipient gold key Am. Congress Phys. Medicine and Rehab., 1964; Lasker award Internat. Soc. Rehab. Disabled, 1966. Author: (with Howard A. Rusk) New Hope for the Handicapped, 1949, Living with a Disability, 1952,

Rehabilitation Medicine, 3d edit., 1971, Spanish edit., 1962, Japanese edit., 1967, Serbo-Croatian edit., 1971. Home: New York, N.Y. Died Dec. 2, 1978.

TAYLOR, FRANCIS CHARLES, librarian; b. Hartford, Conn., May 23, 1923; s. Charles Henry and Charlotte (Fitzgerald) T.; B.A., Franklin and Marshall Coll., 1947; B.S. in L.S., U. Ill., 1948, M.S., 1949; m. Jane Carolyn Stevens, June 16, 1948; children—Elizabeth Louise, Lauri Anna. Head bus. and tech. dept. Wichita (Kans.) City Library, 1949-51; chief librarian Wichita div. Boeing Airplane Co., 1951-55; asst. librarian Providence Pub. Library, 1955-59, asso. librarian, 1960-61; asso. librarian St. Louis Pub. Library, 1961-66, librarian, 1966-68; librarian Providence Pub. Library, 1968-80; co-owner bookstore, Wichita, 1952-54; lectr. library sci. Univ. Coll., Washington U., St. Louis, 1962-67; lectr. Grad. Library Sch., U. R.I., North Kingstown. Bd. dirs. Adult Edn. Council Greater St. Louis, 1964-67; bd. trustees R.I. Sch. Design. Served with USNR, 1943-46. Mem. Am., R.I., New Eng. library assns., Beta Phi Mu (founding mem.). Episcopalian. Home: Barrington, R.I. Died Mar. 17, 1980.

TAYLOR, GEORGE ALFRED, clergyman; b. Hazardville, Conn., Nov. 9, 1903; s. Frank Webb and Maude Mary (Evans) T.; B.A., Springfield (Mass.) Coll., 1925; M.Div., Yale, 1928; D.D., Gen. Theol. Sem., N.Y.C., 1967; m. Ann Gary, June 12, 1971; children—Frank Webb, Sydney Tucker. Ordained deacon P.E. Ch., 1928, priest, 1929; curate Grace Ch., N.Y.C., 1928-29; rector St. Philip's Ch., Easthampton, Mass., 1929-32, St. Paul's Ch., Albany, N.Y., 1932-47; St. David's Ch., Balt., 1947-59; bishop, Easton, Md., 1966-78. Trustee Episcopal Theol. Sem., Alexandria, Va. Mem. Yale Alumni Assn. Md. (pres. 1955-57). Rotarian. Home: Easton, Md. Died Mar. 13, 1978.

TAYLOR, GRIFFITH, prof. geography; b. Walthamstow, London, Eng., Dec. 1, 1880; s. James and Lily (Griffiths) T.; B.S., Univ. of Sydney, Australia, 1904, B.M.E., 1905, Sc.D., 1916; Exhbn. of 1851 traveling scholar, 1907-10; Sudbury-Hardyman prizeman, Cambridge, 1910, A.B., 1910; m. Doris Priestley, July 8, 1914; children—Griffith Priestley, Natalie Joyce (dec.), David Priestley. Instr. in geology, U. of Sydney, 1906-07; physiographer, Commonwealth Weather Service, 1910; sr. geologist and leader of Western Parties, Brit. Antaractic Expdn., 1910-13; acting Commonwealth geologist, 1913; lecturer at Commonwealth Flying Sch., 1914-18; lecturer in physiography, U. of Melbourne, 1915-18; head of dept. geography, U. of Sydney, 1920-28; prof. geography, U. of Chicago, 1929-35; head dept. geography, U. of Toronto, since 1935; presented Messenger lectures at Cornell, 1944. Mem. Internat. Committee on Agr., Solar Radiation and Upper Air since 1919. Mem. Australian Assn. for Advancement of Science (pres. geography sect. 1922), Geog. Soc. New South Wales (pres. 1927-28), Australian Nat. Research Council, British Assn. Advancement of Science (pres. Sect. E, 1938); fellow Assn. Am. Geographers (v.p. 1938; pres. 1941). Awarded King's Polar Medal, 1913, Royal Geog. Soc. medal, 1913, Syme prize and medal, 1915, Thomson gold medal, 1917, Livingstone gold medal of Am. Geog. Soc., 1923. Club: Hart House (U. Toronto). Author or co-author books relating to field; latest publs.: Urban Geography, 1949; Jugoslavia (joint author), 1949. Home: Toronto, Can. *

TAYLOR, H(ERMAN) MARSHALL, otolaryngologist; b. Wilmington, N.C., June 7, 1881; s. Rev. James B. Taylor and Fannie (Calendine) T.; M.D., Emory U., 1903; M.D., Med. Coll. of Va., 1910; Sc.D., John B. Stetson U., 1940; m. Pallie Elaine Dekle; children—Marshall, Coakley, Margaret, Dekle. Senior house surgeon, New York Eye and Ear Infirmary, 1908-09; practiced in Jacksonville, Fla., since 1911; now chief of department of otolaryngology, Post Graduate Sch. of Medicine, U. of Fla.; post-grad. work in Vienna, 1925; consulting otolaryngologist, St. Luke's Duval County, Riverside and Hope Haven hosps., Children's Home Soc. of Fla., Fla. East Coast R.R. Served as capt. Med. Corps, World War I. Sec. bd. of trustees, Bolles School, Jacksonville. Awarded Casselberry prize by Am. Laryngol. Assn., 1939. Certificated by the American Board of Otolaryngology. Fellow Am. Coll. of Surgeons; mem. Florida Acad. Sciences, Duval County Med. Soc. (past pres.), Fla. Med. Assn. (past pres.), Fla. Soc. Ophthalmology and Otolaryngology (past pres.), Southern Med. Assn. (past pres.), Am. Laryngol. Assn., Am. Otol. Soc. Am. Lasyngol., Rhinol. and Otol. Soc. (past pres.), Am. Acad. Ophthalmology and Otolaryngology, Am. Bronchoscopic Soc. (past pres.), Clin. Congress Surgeons of America, A.M.A. (past chmn. sect. of Otol., Rhinol. and Laryngol.), Phi Gamma Delta, Theta Nu Epsilon, Sigma Xi. Democrat. Baptist. Clubs: Florida Yacht, Timuguana Country. Mem. editorial board Annals of Otology, Rhinology and Laryngology. Home: Jacksonville. *

TAYLOR HENRY GEORGE, naval officer; b. Philadelphia, Pa., June 3, 1885; s. John Barrett and Agnes Kennedy (McGrotty) T.; B.S., U.S. Naval Acad., 1908; B.S., Rensselaer Poly. Inst., Troy, N.Y., 1913; m. Ellen Simpson Alexander, June 5, 1909; children—Jane (Mrs. Joseph White), Catharine Alexander (Mrs. Randall M. Victory), Henry George. Entered navy as ensign, 1908; promoted through grades to rear adm., 1942; served at many Navy Yards and Naval Stations both here and abroad; superintending C.E., Area V., hdqrs., Chicago, Ill. Awarded Victory Medal. Mem. Soc. Am. Mil. Engrs., Rensselaer Soc. Engrs. Mason. Clubs: Chicago, Chicago Athletic Assn. Home: San Mateo, Calif. *

TAYLOR, HERBERT JOHN, mfg. co. exec.; b. Pickford, Mich., Apr. 18, 1893; s. Frank H. and Nellie (Salkeld) T.; B.S., Northwestern U., 1917; LL.D., Houghton (N.Y.) Coll., 1947; L.H.D., John Brown U.; H.H.D., Taylor U.; Litt.D., Trinity Coll.; m. Gloria Forbrich, June 21, 1919; children—Gloria Beverly Taylor Mathis, Ramona Estellene Taylor Lockhart. Real estate, ins. bus., Pauls Valley, Okla., 1919-24; home office mgr. Jewel Tea Co., Inc., Barrington, Ill., 1924-26, asst. to pres. 1926-28, v.p., dir., 1928-31; pres. Club Aluminum Co., 1931-52, chmn. bd., 1952-68, chmn. bd. emeritus, 1968-78; dir. First Nat. Bank Barrington, Chgo. Fed. Savs. & Loan Assn. Bd. dirs., chmn. Young Life campaign, Colorado Springs, Colo., 1945-47; founder, chmn. trustees Christian Workers Found.; bd. dirs. Christian Service Brig., Chgo., Creation House, Wheaton, Ill., Nat. Meth. Found. Christian Higher Edn.; chmn. bd. Internat. Child Evangelism Fellowship, 1952-62; trustee Found. Evangelism, Nashville; chmn. Meth. Nat. Lay Com. Evangelism, 1961-66; chmn. bd. Christian Life Inc., Pioneer Girls, Chgo.; chmn. bd. Internat. Child Evangelism Inst., 1952-62; mem. bd., chmn. Inter-Varsity Christian Fellowship, Chgo., 1940-51; mem. bd. Young Life Inst., Youth for Christ, 1960-65, Christian Camps Found., Colorado Springs; mem. bd., v.p. Fuller Theol. Sem., Pasadena, Calif., 1948-58; trustee Sterling (Kans.) Coll.; bd. dirs. Cottey Coll., Nevada, Mo., 1962-67, Am. Inst. Holy Land Studies, Jerusalem; bd. govs. Ill. Crippled Children Soc., 1941-42; past mem. Ill. U. Adv. Com., 1948-54, Nat. Boys' Work and Nat. Hi-Y coms. YMCA, 1940-48; mem. Nat. CD Com., Park Ridge, 1941-43; mem. Ill. war savs. com. U.S. Treasury; mem. price adjustment bd. War Dept., vice chmn., 1943; mem. Northwestern assos. Northwestern U. Served as lt. (j.g.) USNRF, World War I. Recipient Northwestern U. Alumni medal, 1955; decorated by govts. Belgium, Chile, Ecuador, France, Italy, Lebanon, Syria, Egypt and Domincan Republic, 1954-55. Mem. Aluminum Wares Assn., Am. Mgmt. Assn. Methodist. Clubs: Rotary (dist. gov. 1941-42, chmn. Nat. Boys and Girls Week 1946-54, 1st internat. v.p. 1945-46, internat. pres. 1954-55, mem. found. bd. trustees, chmn. 1955-56); John Evans. Author: The Four Way Test; Ten Marks of a Good Citizen; Twelve Marks of a True Christian; God Has a Plan for You. Home: Park Ridge, Ill. Died May 1, 1978.

TAYLOR, HOBART, JR., lawyer; b. Texarkana, Tex., Dec. 17, 1920; s. Hobart and Charlotte (Wallace) T.; A.B., Prairie View (Tex.) State Coll., 1939; A.M., Howard U., 1941; J.D., U. Mich., 1943; L.H.D., Agrl. and Tech. Coll. N.C.; LL.D., Pacific U., Shaw U., Knoxville Coll.; m. Lynnette Dobbins, Jan. 21, 1951 (div. 1978); children—Albert, Hobart; m. 2d, Carole Angermeir Rader, Sept. 13, 1980. Admitted to Mich. bar, 1944, D.C. bar, 1968; research asst. Mich. Supreme Ct., 1944-45; jr. partner firm Bledsoe & Taylor, Detroit, 1945-48; asst. pros. atty. Wayne County (Mich.), 1949-50, corp. counsel, 1951-61; sr. mem. firm Taylor, Patrick, Bailer & Lee, Detroit, 1958-61; spl. counsel Pres.'s Com. Equal Employment Opportunity, 1961-62, exec. vice chmn., 1962-65; spl. asst. to Vice Pres. U.S., 1963; asso. counsel to Pres. Johnson, 1964-65; dir. Export-Import Bank U.S., 1965-68; partner firm Dawson, Riddell, Taylor, Davis & Holroyd, and predecessor, 1968-79; of counsel firm Jones, Day, Reavis & Pogue, 1980-81; dir. Eastern Airlines, Aetna Life and Casualty Co., Gt. Atlantic & Pacific Tea Co., Westinghouse Electric Corp., Burroughs Corp., Standard Oil Co. (Ohio). Vice chmn. bd. trustees Wolf Trap Found. for Performing Arts; mem. Pres.'s Commn. on Exec. Exchange, 1979-81; trustee Howard U. Mem. Fed., Inter-Am., Am., Mich., D.C. bar assns. Clubs: Univ. (N.Y.C.); George Town; Nat. Lawyers, Internat., Federal City (Washington); Lyford Cay (Bahamas). Home: Washington, D.C. Died Apr. 2, 1981; buried Middleburg, Va.

TAYLOR, HOY, coll. prof.; b. Boone, N.C., July 20, 1879; s. Leland and Sarah (Bumgarner) T.; A.B., Duke U., 1906; A.M., Columbia U., 1913; Ph.D., Peabody Coll., 1931; m. Lucy Cleone Liles, July 29, 1913; children—Henry Liles, Hoy, Jr., Sarah Horton. Teacher, Cary (N.C.) High Sch., 1906-07; prin., Biscoe (N.C.) High Sch., 1907-13; supt., Greenville (N.C.) pub. schs., 1913-18; supt. Franklinton (N.C.) pub. schs., 1919-27; prin., Wilson (N.C.) High Sch., 1927-28; instr., Western Ky. Teachers Coll., 1929, 30, 31; acting dean Ga. Teachers Coll., 1931-32, prof. history, 1932-34; dean instrn., prof. social science, Georgia State College for Women 1934-43; dean of instruction, registrar, professor social science, 1943-46, registrar and prof. social science, 1946-47, dean emeritus 1947, now professor Educational secretary U.S. Army Y.M.C.A., 1918-19. Member National Education Assn., Ga. Edn. Assn., Ga. Acad. Polit. Science, Phi Delta Kappa, Pi Gamma Mu, Phi Beta Kappa, Southern Hist. Assn., Southern Polit. Sci. Assn. Democrat. Club: Rotary (Milledgeville, Ga.). Author: An Interpretation of the Early Administration of the Peabody Education Fund, 1933. Home: Milledgeville, Ga. *

TAYLOR, JAMES DAVIDSON, arts cons.; b. Shelbyville, Tenn., Feb. 26, 1907; s. James Arthur and Elizabeth D. (Forbes) T.; A.B., Miss. Coll., 1927; Th.M., S. Baptist Theol. Sem., 1930; m. Mary Elizabeth Plummer, June 8, 1935; 1 dau., Alison Elizabeth. With sta. WHAS, Louisville, 1929-33; wrote critical radio column for Louisville Courier-Jour. announcer, producer CBS, 1933, asst. dir. music div. 1935-37, dir. music div., 1937-38, asst. to v.p. in charge broadcasts, 1938-42, asst. dir. broadcasts., 1942-43; v.p., dir. programs, 1945, v.p., dir. pub. affairs, 1947; spl. cons., Dept. of State, 1950; gen. prodn. exec. NBC television, 1951, dir. pub. affairs radio and television networks, 1952; v.p. in charge pub. affairs NBC, 1954-58, cons. N.Y. Public Library for Lincoln Center Library Mus. of Performing Arts, 1958-59; dir. arts center program Columbia U., N.Y.C., 1959-69, dir. Sch. Arts, 1966-69, dean Sch. Arts, 1969-71, spl. asst. on arts to pres., 1971-72; arts cons., 1972-79; mem. adv. bd. Regional Arts Center of Centre Coll., Danville, Ky.; chief of radio Phsychol. Warfare Div. SHAEF, 1944; chief of film, theater, music control Information Control Div., USFET, 1945. Mem. at large U.S. Nat. Commn. USESCO, 1950-52. Recipient Medal of Freedom, 1945. Clubs: Century Assn. Contbr. to N. Am. Rev., Mademoiselle, transition, Modern Music, Theatre Arts Monthly, Poetry, Sat. Rev., Columbia U. Forum; one-man exhbn. of collages and watercolors Newlin Hall, Regional Arts Center of Centre Coll., Danville, Ky. Home: New York, N.Y. Died July 27, 1979.

TAYLOR, JOHN EARL MAXWELL, lawyer; b. Foster, Ky., Feb. 21, 1879; s. Artemus Day and Anna Laura (Schoolfield) T.; grad. Salsbury (Mo.) Acad., 1896; m. Pearle Mae Davenport, Oct. 10, 1900; 1 son, Maxwell Davenport. Admitted to Mo. bar, 1900, and began practice at Keytesville; moved to Joplin, 1902, to Kansas City, 1903; with Bradstreet Co. 4 years, later associated in practice with Karnes, New & Krauthoff, then New & Krautoff and firm of Miller, Camack Winger & Reeder; apptd. gen. atty., K.O. & G. Ry. Co. and settled at Muskogee, Okla., Jan. 1, 1922; asst. gen. atty. for Okla. of Mo.-Kan.-Tex. R.R. Co., 1926-31, and 1936-46, gen. atty. since 1946; gen. practice of law, 1934-36; moved to Oklahoma City, 1936. Democrat. Mem. Christian (Disciples) Ch. Home: Oklahoma City. *

TAYLOR, JOHN EDWARD, clergyman; b. East St. Louis, Ill., Nov. 15, 1914; s. Daniel R. and Mary E. (Pohl) T.; student Angelicum U., Rome, 1934-37, Gregorian U., Rome, 1937-40; Ph.D., U. Ottawa, 1941; D.D., U. Rome, 1962. Mem. Oblates of Mary Immaculate; ordained priest Roman Cath. Ch., 1940; rector Order Sems., Carthage, Mo., Pass Christian, Miss.; superior of mission in Greenland, 1958; Episcopus electus, 1962; consecrated bishop, 1962; bishop of Stockholm, Sweden, 1962-76; pres. Bishop's Conf. for Scandinavia, 1965. Home: Stockholm, Sweden. Died Sept. 9, 1976; interred Stockholm Cathedral.

TAYLOR, JOSHUA CHARLES, educator, art historian; b. Hillsboro, Ore., Aug. 22, 1917; s. James Edmond and Anna L.M. (Scott) T.; student Mus. Art Sch., Portland, Ore., 1935-39; B.A., Reed Coll., 1939, M.A., 1946; M.F.A., Princeton, 1949, Ph.D., 1956. Designer for theatre, 1936-41, San Francisco Opera Ballet, 1936-37; tchr. theatre Reed Coll., 1939-41; tchr. history art Princeton, 1948-49; faculty U. Chgo., 1949-74, chmn. 1st yr. program humanities in coll., 1954-58, William Rainey Harper prof. humanities, prof. history art, 1963-74; dir. Nat. Mus. Am. Art (formerly Nat. Collection Fine Arts), Smithsonian Instn., 1970-81. Lectr. in U.S., also on TV, 1953-81; lectr. Inst. Interuniversitario, Argentina, 1962; spl. research 19th and 20th century painting and artistic theory Italy, U.S. Mem. adv. com. 20th Century art Art Inst. Chgo.; bd. dirs. Am. Fedn. Arts, Mus. Contemporary Art, Chgo.; faculty adv. com. Ency. Brit.; mem. adv. bd. Lillie P. Bliss Internat. Study Center, Mus. Modern Art; council Archives Am. Art. Served to maj., inf. AUS, 1941-46; ETO. Fellow Royal Soc. Arts; mem. bd. Coll. Art Assn. Am., Internat. Inst. Conservation Historic and Artistic Works, Assn. Art Mus. Dirs., Am. Assn. Museums, Phi Beta Kappa. Author: William Page, the American Titian, 1957; Learning to Look, 1957, 81; Futurism, 1961; Graphic Works of Umberto Boccioni, 1961; Vedere prima di Credere, 1970; To See is to Think: Looking at American Art, 1975; America as Art, 1976; The Fine Arts in America, 1979; also articles, revs. Home: Washington, D.C. Died Apr. 26, 1981; buried Portland, Oreg.

TAYLOR, KENNETH, physician; b. St. Paul, Minn., Nov. 13, 1885; s. John W. and Sarah W. (Ware) T.; B.A., U. of Minn., 1906, M.A., 1907, M.D., 1914; m. Anne Ueland, 1909; 1 dau., Carlotta. War service in Europe with French, British and U.S. armies, 1914-19; research in pathology and treatment of wounds, Am. Ambulance Hosp., Paris, 1915-16; at mil. hosp., Ris Orangis, France, 1916-17; with Am. Red Cross Mil. Hosp. No. 2, Paris, 1917-19; editor Med. Bulletin (war publ.), 1918; comdg. officer Red Cross Mil. Hosp. No. 2, Paris, 1918; also comdg. officer Base Laboratory Dist., Paris, 1918-19; med. adviser European Commn. Am. Red Cross, 1919; commd. lt. col. of M.C., U.S. Army. Dir. Robert Walton Goelet Research Fund, 1915-19; dir. of medicine Lincoln Hosp., N.Y. City; surgeon, U.S. Pub. Health Service. Fellow Am. Coll. of Physicians; mem. Acad. Medicine (New York), Chi Psi, Sigma Xi. Episcopalian. Club: Century Assn. Home: New York. *

TAYLOR, LEA DEMAREST, social settlement and civic work; b. Hartford, Conn., June 24, 1883; d. Graham and Leah (Demarest) Taylor; student Lewis Inst., 1900; A.B., Vassar Coll., 1904. Resident of Chicago Commons since its founding, 1894, head resident, 1921-54, head resident emeritus, 1954—; president of the Chicago Federation of Settlements, 1924-37 and 1939-40, National Fedn. of Settlements, 1930-34 and again 1950-52; vice president American Association of Social Workers, 1934, 1935 (v.p. Chicago Chapter 1935). Recipient Illinois Welfare Assn. Award Meritorious Service; 1954; Jane Addams Medal, Rockford College, 1953; Outstanding Achievement Award, National Fedn. Settlements & Neighborhood Centers, 1960; Jane Adams medallion, 1965. Member National Conference of Social Work (member executive committee 1932-34), Chicago Community Fund (bd. dirs. 1952-54), Chicago Council of Social Agencies (secretary 1935-41), Cook County Bureau of Public Welfare (advisory com.), Metropolitan Housing Council (bd. dirs.), Chicago Recreation Com., Immigrants Protective League of Chicago (bd. dirs.). Clubs: Woman's City (adv. bd.), Chicago Woman's, Chicago College. Contbr. article on Social Settlements in Social Works Year Book, 1935 and 1937. Home: Highland Park, Ill. *

TAYLOR, MARTIN, lawyer; b. Hereford, Eng., Dec. 15, 1885; s. James Durham and Mary (Preece) T.; L.B., Trinity Coll. (fellow 1921), Hartford, Conn., 1908; LL.B., Columbia, 1913; m. Caroline Strong Reboul, Apr. 21, 1915; 1 dau., Nina (Mrs. Jean Buchet). Came to U.S., 1890, naturalized citizen. Admitted to New York Bar, 1913, since practiced in New York, N.Y.; asso. Strong & Mellen 1913-15, De Forest Bros., 1915-16, counsel State Tax Commn., 1915; partner McKinstry, Taylor & Patterson and successor firms, 1917-34; partner Reed, Hoyt, Taylor & Washburn; counsel British financial interests. Past director of the National Jail Association Founder Village Nissequoque. Trustee, Relief for Americans in P.I. Mem. Am., N.Y. State (chmn. com. on constl. law), N.Y.C. (com. on internat. law) bar assns., Internat. Law Assn. Rep. Episcopalian. Clubs: Beef steak, Portland (London, Eng.). Union, Down Town Association River, Pilgrims (N.Y.C.); Metropolitan (Washington). Author: Reorganization of Federal Judiciary (Supreme Court controversy), 1937. Home: N.Y.C. also St. James, L.I., N.Y. *

TAYLOR, PHILIP BRODT, bus. exec.; b. N.Y.C., Mar. 7, 1899; s. Henry Ling and Daisy (Brodt) T.; Ph.B. in Mech. Engring., Yale, 1920; m. Helen Patrick, May 12, 1928; children—Philip Brodt, John Donald, Janet Patrick. Chief engr., then acting gen. mgr., v.p. Curtiss-Wright Corp., 1922-44; spl. cons. Pan-Am. World Airways, 1945-46; pres. Taylor Turbine Corp., 1946-47; partner Sanderson & Porter, engring. and constrn., N.Y.C., 1947-59; asst. sec. USAF, 1959-61; dir. Gen. Precision Equipment Corp., from 1961, Marquardt Corp., Walter Kidde Corp., Sanderson & Porter, Inc. Mem. bd. edn. Essex County (N.J.) Vocational Sch., 1942-44; commr. pub. works, Montclair, N.J., 1947-52. Chmn. Adult Edn. Center, Montclair, N.J.; trustee Montclair Pub. Library, 1942. Decorated Air Force Medal of Merit. Mem. Am. Soc. M.E., Soc. Automotive Engrs., Inst. Aero. Scis., Atomic Forum, Yale Engring. Assn., Berzelius Soc., Montclair Soc. Engrs. Club: Montclair Golf. Home: Upper Montclair, New Jersey. Died Dec. 21, 1978

TAYLOR, R. E. LEE, architect; b. Norfolk, Va., Apr. 9, 1882; s. Walter Herron and Elizabeth Selden (Saunders) T.; student Norfolk Acad., 1890-98, B.A., Univ. of Va., 1901; B.S., Mass. Inst. of Tech., 1904; m. Lelia Symington Goode, Oct. 21, 1911; children—(twins) Robert E. L. (U.S. Navy), Stuart Symington (U.S. Army). Private practice of architecture, Norfolk, Va., 1906-17, Baltimore, 1917-43; mem. bd. of review, Public Works Adminstrn., Washington, D.C., 1934-35; mem. exec. com., Advisory Bd., Rockefeller Restoration of Williamsburg, Va., 1930-40. Fellow A.I.A.; Baltimore Symphony Orchestra Assn. (chmn.), Delta Psi. Clubs: Maryland (Baltimore). Colonnade (Univ. of Va.). Home: Baltimore. *

TAYLOR, RICHARD RAY, physician; b. Prairieburg, Iowa, Nov. 21, 1922; s. Charles F. and Harriet (Sack) T.; B.S., U. Chgo., 1944, M.D., 1946; fellow tropical medicine La. State U., 1959; grad. Command and Gen. Staff Coll., 1962, Army War Coll., 1966; m. Betty Lou Simpson, 1945 (dec. 1949); m. Frances Dudley Colby, Mar. 19, 1950; children—Richard Ray, Carolyn J., Colby F., Bryan D., David W. Commd. 1st lt., M.C., U.S. Army, 1947, advanced through grades to lt. gen., 1973; chief research div. to chief program planning and dep. comdr. U.S. Army Med. Research and Devel. Command, 1959-64; staff surgeon JUSMAG/Thailand, 1964-65; chief med. scis. div. Office Dir. Def. Research and Engring., 1966-69; command surgeon U.S. Mil. Assistance Command, Vietnam, 1969-70; comdg. gen. U.S. Army Med. Research and Devel. Command, Washington, 1970-73; dep. surgeon gen. Dept. Army, 1973, surgeon gen., 1973-77; asst. prof. medicine U. Colo., 1957-59. Decorated D.S.M. with oak leaf cluster, Legion of Merit with oak leaf cluster, Bronze Star, Joint Services Commendation medal with oak leaf cluster, Army Commendation medal with oak leaf cluster (U.S.), Distinguished Service Order 1st Class, Pub. Health Services medal 1st class (Vietnam); recipient John Shaw Billings award Assn. Mil. Surgeons U.S., 1962; Distinguished Service award U. Chgo. Alumni Assn., 1976. Fellow A.C.P., Am. Coll. Chest Physicians; mem. Am. Thoracic Soc., N.Y. Acad. Scis., AMA. Contbr. articles to profl. jours. Home: McLean, Va. Died Nov. 8, 1978; buried Arlington (Va.) Nat. Cemetery.

TAYLOR, ROBERT KINDER, air force officer; b. Evanston, Ill., Dec. 30, 1902; s. George and Cora (Kinder) T.; B.S., U.S. Mil. Acad., 1928; m. Aida Pacheco, March 7, 1940. Commd. 2d lieut., 1928, advanced through grades to brig. gen., 1945; served as chief of staff, 15th Air Force, Italy, 1944-45; comdg. gen., Kelly Field, Texas, 1946; comdg. gen. Brookley Field, Ala., from 1947; ret., 1955. Decorated Distinguished Service Medal, Legion of Merit, Bronze Star and Air Medal, Hon. Officer in Order of Brit. Empire. Home: South Laguna, Calif. Died Sept. 11, 1976; buried U.S. Mil. Acad. Cemetery.

TAYLOR, RUTH, social worker; b. Cedar Rapids, Ia., July 1, 1886; d. William Kennedy and Annie Elizabeth (Ferguson) Taylor; A.B., Vassar College, 1909. Rockland County agt. for dependent children, State Charities Aid Assn., N.Y. City, 1909-10, asst. supt. county agencies dept., 1910-15; supervisor children's agts., Westchester County Supt. of Poor, East View, N.Y., 1915-16; dir. dept. child welfare, Dept. Pub. Welfare, Westchester County, White Plains, N.Y., 1917-23; research asst., Commr. Pub. Welfare, 1923-24, deputy, 1924-31, commr., 1931-50. Sec. Westchester County Recreation Commn., 1924-42; mem. Westchester County Dept. Health since 1931; mem. governor's Commn. on Unemployment Relief, N.Y. State, 1934-36; pres. N.Y. State Conf. Social Work, 1944-45; Asso. Alumnae of Vassar Coll., 1945-48. Home: Hartsdale, N.Y. *

TAYLOR, WILLIAM NEELY, urologist, educator; b. Coshocton, O., Jan. 30, 1890; s. John Hogle and Wilhelmina (Sibley) T.; M.D., Ohio State U., 1915; m. Edith Belle Pavey, June 30, 1916; children—Jack, Joan. Physician in Columbus, 1915; practice confined to urology; mem. med. faculty Ohio State U., from 1917, asst. in genito-urinary surgery, 1917-21, instr., 1921-29, asst. prof., 1929-32, asso. prof., 1932-38, prof., from 1938, then emeritus, head dept. urology, from 1929. Served as 1st lt., M.C., U.S. Army, 1917-19, Fellow A.C.S., A.M.A.; mem. Columbus Acad. Medicine, Am. Urol. Assn., Wis. Urol. Soc. (hon.), Med. Rev. Club, Phi Rho Sigma. Republican. Methodist. Mason, Rotarian. Clubs: Faculty, Columbus Athletic, Scioto Country (Columbus). Home: Columbus, Ohio. Died Sept. 9, 1976.

TAYLOR, WILLIAM SENTMAN, prof. psychology; b. Passaic, N.J., Mar. 15, 1894; s. Rev. Franklin Ellsworth and Mary Agnes (White) T.; grad. high sch., Gettysburg, Pa., 1912; B.S., Gettysburg Coll., 1916; M.A., Harvard, 1920, Ph.D., 1921; M.S., U. of Wis., 1923; m. Phoebe Louise Smith, Jan. 3, 1925; children—Phoebe Agnes (Mrs. Richard Hyatt Lansdale), Cicely Ellsworth (Mrs. Walter F. Buckley, Jr.). Lectr. in psychology, Bryn Mawr Coll., 1921-22; instr. philosophy U. Wis., 1922-23; prof. philosophy U. Maine, 1923-26; prof. psychology, Smith Coll., from 1926-1962, prof. emeritus until 1976; instr. psychology, Harvard Summer Sch., 1926, 27, U. of Chicago, summer 1928. Consultant in clin. psychology, V.A. Hosp., Northampton, Mass. Psychol. work USNRF, 1918-19. Certified psychologist Mass. Bd. Certification in Psychology. Diplomate Am. Bd. Examiners Psychological Hypnosis. Fellow A.A.A.S., American Psychol. Assn., Soc. Clin. and Exptl. Hypnosis, Mass. Psychological Assn., Am. Soc. Clinical Hypnosis, Internat. Society Clinical Exptl. Hypnosis; member Am. Psychopathol. Association, Am. Assn. Univ. Prof., Phi Sigma, Phi Kappa Phi, Phi Beta Kappa, Sigma Xi. Author: Morton Prince and Abnormal Psychology 1928; Dynamic and Abnormal Psychology, 1954. Compiler: Readings in Abnormal Psychology and Mental Hygiene, 1926. Co-editor (with Phowbe Taylor), The Human Course, 1974. Contbr. to Jour. Abnormal and Social Psychology, Psychol. Review, etc. Home: Northampton, Mass. Died Apr. 12, 1976. Interred Harvard Medical School cemetery, Tweksbury, Mass.

TAYLOR, WILLIAM TOWSON, mfg. exec.; b. Balt., Sept. 29, 1900; s. William H. and Bertha May (Towson) T.; A.B., Columbia, 1921, LL.B., 1923; m. Ethel Lewis, June 30, 1926; children—Ann Towson (Mrs. John Scudder Boyd), Ethel Lewis (Mrs. John Kirk Greer). Practice of law with firm O'Brien, Boardman, Parker and Fox, 1923-24; exec. sec. Alumni Fedn. Columbia, 1924-25, sec. faculty of law, asst. to dean Law Sch., 1924-27; sec. Indsl. Finance Corp., N.Y.C., 1927-28; v.p. Comml. Nat. Bank and Trust Co., N.Y.C., 1928-41, vice chmn. bd., 1945-51; pres. Union Trust Co. Springfield, 1941-43; v.p. Guaranty Trust Co. of N.Y., 1944-45; v.p., dir. Bankers Trust Co., 1951-57; chmn. bd. ACF Industries, Inc., 1957-67, chmn. exec. com., 1967-69; bd. dirs., exec. com. Adams Express Co., N.Y.; dir., mem. exec. audit and finance coms. Allied Stores. Pres. N.Y. State Bankers Assn., 1951-52. Mem. bd. supervising trustees Parker Sch. Fgn. and Comparative Law, Columbia. Decorated chevalier de l'Ordre de la Couronne (Belgium). Mem. Theta Delta Chi, Phi Delta Phi. Republican. Episcopalian. Clubs: University, Pilgrims, Cloud (N.Y.C.); Round Hill (Greenwich, Conn.). Home: Greenwich, Conn. Died Mar. 15, 1976; interred Putnam Cemetery, Greenwich.

TAYLOR, WILLIS HARVEY, physician; born Villisca, Ia., Sept. 11, 1886; s. William Harvey and Lusetta (Portlock) T.; S.B., U. of Neb., 1909, M.D., 1911; m. Myrtle Heacock, Feb. 4, 1914; children—Willis H., Calvin P., Elizabeth Ann (Mrs. Ketzler). Resident Lying In Hosp., N.Y. City, 1915; instr. obstetrics, U. of Neb., 1916-20, assoc. obstetrics and gynecol., 1920-24, asso. prof., 1924-29, asst. prof., 1929-35, clin. prof. since 1935; staff U. of Neb. Hosp.(past pres.), Meth. Episcopal Hosp., Immanuel Luth. Hosp., Omaha. Mem. Omaha Douglas Med. Soc., Neb. State Med. Soc., A.M.A., Central States Obstet. and Gynecol. Soc. Republican. Conglist. Club: Kiwanis (past pres. Omaha). Home: Omaha. *

TCHEREPNIN, ALEXANDER, composer, pianist, condr.; b. St. Petersburg, Russia, Jan. 21, 1899; s. Nicolai and Marie (Benois) T.; student St. Petersburg Conservatory; Mus.D. (hon.), Chgo. Mus. Coll., Roosevelt U., 1953, Music and Arts Inst., San Francisco, 1977; m. Hsien Ming Lee, Aug. 24, 1937; children—Peter, Serge, Ivan. Western debut, recital in London, 1922; composer orchestral, piano, vocal and chamber music, 1912-77; concert tours, China, Japan, 1934-37, France, 1921-77, Eng., 1922-77, Scandinavia, Egypt, 1946-48; faculty San Francisco Music and Art Inst., 1948; tchr. piano and composition DePaul U., 1949-64. Compositions include: 4 operas; 10 ballets; Piano Sonata in A Minor; Sonatine Romantique; Bagatelles; Concerto da Camera (Schott's internat. prize); 6 piano concerti; Russian Dances for Orch.; Showcase; Divertimento, 1957, Symphonic Prayer, 1959; 4 symphonies for orch.; opera The Farmer and the Nymph (David Bispham award 1960); Serenade for Strings, 1964, Flute Duo, 1977. Recipient Glinka prize (France), 1959; Achievement award Immigrants Service League, 1960; named chevalier of Arts and Letters, French Minister Cultural, 1968. Mem. Nat. Inst. Arts and Letters. Home: Marlow Buckinghamshire, England. Died Sept. 29, 1977; interred St. Geneviève des Bois Cemetery, Paris, France.

TEAGUE, OLIN EARL, congressman; b. Woodward, Okla., Apr. 6, 1910; s. James Martin and Ida (Sturgeon) T.; student Tex. A. and M. Coll., 1928-32, LL.D. (hon.); m. Freddie Dunman, Dec. 30, 1932; children—James M., John O., Jill Teague Ruth. Sta. supt. U.S. Post Office, College Station, Tex., 1932-40; elected in 1946 to fill unexpired term Luther A. Johnson as mem. 79th Congress (1945-47), 6th Tex. Dist.; mem. 80th-95th congresses, chmn. various coms.; chmn. Democratic Caucus, from 1971, caucus rep. Nat. Dem. Com., from 1972; caucus mem. com. for formation Congress. Served to col., inf., U.S. Army, World War II. Decorated Silver Star with 2 clusters, Bronze Star with 1 cluster, Purple Heart with 2 clusters, Combat Infantryman's Badge; Croix de Guerre with palm (France). Club: Lions. Baptist. Home: Washington, D.C. Died Jan. 23, 1981.

TEALE, EDWIN WAY, author, naturalist; b. Joliet, Ill., June 2, 1899; s. Oliver Cromwell and Clara Louise (Way) T.; grad. Joliet Township High Sch.; student U. Ill., 1918; A.B., Earlham Coll., 1922, Litt.D., 1957; A.M., Columbia U., 1926; L.H.D., Ind. U., 1970; Sc.D., U. New Haven, 1978; m. Nellie Imogene Donovan, Aug. 1, 1923; 1 son, David Allen (dec.). Instr. pub. speaking Friends U., Wichita, Kans., 1922-24; editoria asst. to Dr. Frank Crane, 1925-27; staff feature writer Popular Sci. Monthly, 1928-41; free lance writer, 1941-80. Revised insect-study program Boy Scouts Am., 1944. Recipient John Burroughs medal, 1943 Christopher award, 1957; Ind. U. Writers Conf. award 1960; Secondary Edn. Bd.'s Ann. Book award, 1961 Eva L. Gordon award Am. Nature Study Soc., 1965 Sarah Chapman Francis medal, 1965; Sarah Josepha Hale award, 1975; Ecology award Mass. Hort. Soc. 1975; Conservation Medal New Eng. Wildflower Soc. 1975. Fellow AAAS, N.Y. Acad. Scis. (counc 1942-49); mem. Royal Photog. Soc. (asso.), N.Y. (v.p 1943, pres. 1944), Bklyn. (pres. 1949, 50, 53) entomo socs., Am. Nature Study Soc. (pres. 1947), Baldwin Bird Club (pres. 1942-43), Nat. Audubon Soc. Thoreau Soc. (pres. 1958), Am. Ornithologists' Union, Linnaean Soc. N.Y., Conn. Entomol. Soc. (hon.). Methodist. Club: Explorers; Appalachian Mountain (corr.). Author: The Book of Gliders, 1930, rev. edit., 1939; Grassroot Jungles, 1937, rev. edit., 1944; Boys Book of Insects, 1939; Boys' Book of Photography, 1939; The Golden Throng, 1940; Byways to Adventure, 1942; Near Horizons; The Story of an Insect Garden, 1942; Dune Boy, The Early Years of a Naturalist, 1943; Armed Services Ed., 1944; Insect Life, 1944; The Lost Woods, 1945; Days Without Time, 1948; W.H. Hudson's Green Mansions, 1949 (intro.); North With The Spring, 1951; Insect Friends, 1955; Autumn Across America, 1956; Adventures in Nature, 1959; Journey Into Summer, 1960; The Lost Dog, 1961; The Bees, 1961; The Strange Lives of Familiar Insects, 1962; Wandering Through Winter, 1965 (Pulitzer prize 1966); Springtime in Britain, 1970; Photographs of American Nature, 1972; A Naturalist Buys an Old Farm, 1974; books also pub. in Brit. Swedish, Spanish, French, Finnish, Arabian and Braille edits. Editor, illustrator Walden, by Henry Thoreau, 1946; editor The Insect World of J. Henri Fabre, 1949; Green Treasury (Nature anthology) 1952; Circle of the Seasons, 1953; (Intro.) M. Maeterlinck's The Life of the Bee, 1954; The Wilderness World of John Muir, 1954; The Long Island Naturalist; The Thoughts of Thoreau, 1962; Audubon's Wildlife, 1964; The American Seasons, 1976; A Walk Through the Year, 1978; contbg. editon Audubon Mag., 1942-80. Home: Hampton, Conn. Died Oct. 18, 1980; buried North Cemetery, Hampton.

TEASDALE, SARA (MRS. ERNST B. FILSINGER), author; b. St. Louis, Mo., Aug. 8, 1884; d. John Warren and Mary Elizabeth (Willard) T.; ed. pvt. schs., St. Louis; m. Ernst B. Filsinger, of St. Louis, Dec. 19, 1914. Author: Sonnets to Duse, and Other Poems, 1907; Helen of Troy and Other Poems, 1911; Rivers to the Sea, 1915; Love Songs, 1917; Flame and Shadow, 1920; Dark of the Moon, 1926. Editor of The Answering Voice—One Hundred Love Lyrics by Women, 1917; Rainbow Gold, Poems Old and New Selected for Boys and Girls, 1922. Club: American Women's (London). Address: New York, NY Died 1933.

TEED, JOHN EDSON, lawyer; b. Pampa, Tex., Sept. 13, 1936; s. Arthur Milton and Dorothy (Stark) T.; B.A., U. Tex., 1958, LL.B., 1960; m. Cynthia Cason, May 30, 1979; 1 son, Arthur. Admitted to Tex. bar, 1960; asso. firm Royston, Rayzor & Cook, Houston, 1961-66, partner, 1966-68. Served to capt. AUS, 1960-61. Mem. Houston, Am. bar assns., State Bar of Tex., Beta Theta Pi, Phi Alpha Delta. Home: Houston, Tex. Died Oct. 5, 1979.

TEEL, ROLLAND MARSHALL, ednl. adminstr.; b. Hackettstown, N.J., Nov. 7, 1885; s. Lewis Marshall and Julia Annette (Kemple) T., Ph.B., Lafayette Coll., 1907; grad. student Law Sch., U. Md., 1909-10; m. Sue B. Ashley, Sept. 20, 1911; children—Richard Ashley, Rolland Marshall. With dept. entolology Am. Mus. Natural History, N.Y.C., 1907; tchr. U.S. Naval Acad. Prep. Sch., Annapolis, 1908-14; founder Severn Sch., country boarding sch. for boys, Severna Park, Md., 1914, headmaster, 1914-55, chmn. bd. mgrs., 1955—. Dir Soc. for Prevention Cruelty to Animals, Anne Arundel County, Md. Mem. Naval Inst., Pvt. Sch. Assn. Balt., Acad. Polit. Sci., Alumni Assn. Lafayette Coll., Md. Hist. Soc., Boarding Sch. Assn. of Phila. Area, Sigma Chi. Democrat. Presbyn. Clubs: Annapolitan (pres. 1941-43), Annapolis Yacht. Home: Severna Park, Md. *

TEETER, THOMAS ANDERSON HENDRICKS, univ. prof.; b. Rolling Prairie, Ind., Feb. 12, 1886; s. Edwin J. and Emily A. (Ocker) T.; B.S., Purdue U., 1907; m. Katherine M. Hitchcock, Sept. 1, 1915 (dec.); children—Robert Thomas, Phillip Hitchcock; m. 2d. Pauline F. Hargrave, June 30, 1933; children—William Hargrave, Pauline Ann. Instr. r.r. location and constrn., Purdue U., 1907-08; temporary lab. asst. timber tests, U.S. Forest Service, Purdue U., 1908; instr. civil engring., U. of Pa., 1908-09; instr. mechanics and materials constrn., Pa. State Coll., 1909-10; asst. prof. civil engring., U. of Southern Calif., 1910-11; computer and field asst., Los Angeles, 1911; instr. civil engring., Cornell U., 1911-13; field engr. Desert Land Bd. Central Ore., 1914-16; engr. Big Nestucca Drainage Dist., Cloverdale, Ore., 1916-19; field engr. Baar & Cunningham, Portland, Ore., 1919-20; prof. hydraulics and irrigation engring., Ore. Agrl. Coll., 1913-20; engr. salesman Spokane Culvert & Tank Co., 1920-21; asst. engr. N. Canal Co., Portland, Ore., 1922; asst. constrn. engr., Narada Cutoff Highway Nat. Park Service, Mt. Rainier, 1922; asso. prof. engring. and head engring. courses, gen. extension div., U. of Minn., 1922-39, asso. prof. and dir. summer session 1939-47; dean and prof., summer session, and exec. officer, Inst. Technology, 1947-49, dean summer session since 1949. Methodist. Club: Campus (University of Minnesota). Home: Minneapolis, Minn. *

TEISER, SIDNEY (TI'SIR), lawyer, manufacturing executive; born at Williamsburg, Virginia, August 30, 1882; son of William and Lena (Engelberg) T.; LL.B., University of Va., 1903; m. Betty Kline, July 10, 1905; children—William K., Ruth L. Admitted to Va. bar, 1903, Ore. bar, 1911; pres. Microlex Corp., Rochester, N.Y. since 1950. Commr. uniform state laws State of Ore., 1930-49. Ore. state del. Am. Bar Assn., 1936-43, mem. ho. of dels., 1936-48 and since 1949; mem. exec. com. U. of Va. Law Sch., 1941-44; chmn. Ore. com. Trust Cos. Lawyer Relationship, 1941-47, Realtor-Lawyer Relationship, 1944-47; chmn. sect. corp., banking and mercantile law Am. Bar Assn., 1945-47; mem. Nat. Bankruptcy Conf. since 1930; bd. govs. Am. Bar Assn. since 1949. Awarded Distinguished Service award Am. Inst. Cooperation, 1948. Mem. Am., Portland, Ore., Multnoman Co. and Internat. bar assns., Am. Judicature Soc., Am. Law Inst., Scribes (pres.). Mason (Shriner). Author articles in profl. jours. Inventor Microlex process. Home: Portland, Ore. *

TELFER, BRUCE THOMAS, food and products co. exec.; b. Chgo., Sept. 10, 1916; s. Thomas Arthur and Camilla H. (Wagenseil) T.; A.B., U. Mich., 1938, LL.B., 1941; m. Elizabeth Howe Whitney, June 29, 1940; children—Barbara Whitney Telfer Riedel, Marilee Whitney Luttig, Shelley Elizabeth Telfer Flynn. Admitted to Mich. bar, 1941, Ill. bar, 1948; with firm Clark, Klein, Brucker & Waples, Detroit, 1941-42, 47-48; asst. counsel Coca-Cola Co., 1948-50; regional counsel wholly-owned subsidiaries Cola-Cola Co. in Midwest, 1950-52; v.p., gen. counsel Coca-Cola Bottling Co., Chgo., 1952-62; exec. v.p. Canteen Corp., Chgo., 1967-78, also dir.; dir. Comml. Discount Corp. Pres. Kenilworth (Ill.) United Fund, 1963. Trustee Lake Forest (Ill.) Acad., 1963-65; bd. govs. in Chgo., U. Mich., 1963-65; bd. dirs. March of Dimes, Cook County, Ill., 1960-63. Served to lt. USNR, 1942-46. Mem. Am., Mich., Ill., Chgo. bar assns., Newcomen Soc. N. Am. Episcopalian. Clubs: Chicago, Chicago Athletic, Merchants and Manufacturers, Executives (Chgo.); Oakmount Game (McHenry, Ill.); Bull Valley Hunt (Woodstock, Ill.); Glen View (Golf, Ill.). Home: Kenilworth, Ill. Died May 1, 1978.

TELLER, SIDNEY A., lecturer, writer, social engr.; b. Chicago, Ill., April 4, 1883; s. George J. and Josephine (Zuckermann) T.; student Armour Inst. Tech., Chicago; grad. Chicago School Civics and Philanthropy (now a school of University of Chicago), 1909; m. Julia Pines, June 27, 1916 (deceased May 10, 1957). In chemical engring. work with C.,R.I.&P. R.R., 1903-07; supt. Deborah Boys' Club, Chicago, 1907-08; dir. playground, Butler, Mo., 1908; with United Charities of Chicago, 1908-09; dir. Stanford Park, Chicago, 1910-16; dir. Irene Kaufmann Settlement and Emma Farm Assn., Pittsburgh, 1916-42, formerly hon. mem. both bds. Lectr., 1910—, in 25 countries; on radio 1922—, TV, 1947—. Nat. Recreation Assn., Boys Clubs America: Awarded in 1941 a 40-yr. Meritorious Service medal by Boys' Club of America; Special Diploma of Honor, Mexican Dept. Pub. Edn. Hon. mem. France-U.S.A. Comite, Ananai-Kyo Internat., Japan, Community Execs. Round Table; hon. dir. Allegheny County Scholarship Assn.; hon. v.p. Hebrew Free Loan Assn. Editor Butterfly (social service mag.), 1907-17; former contbg. editor, Youth Leaders Digest. Founder Goodwill Collection Carnegie Library, Pitts.; donor (with Julia P. Teller) Teller brass and copper collection, Illinois Institute of Technology, Sidney and Julia Teller Lecture Fund, University of Chicago, Sidney and Julia Teller Cancer Research Fund, Michael Reese Hosp., Chgo., Teller Lecture Fund, U. Pitts., Teller Cancer Research Fund, Montefiore Hosp., Pitts. Spl. del. Pan-Am. Good Neighbor Forum, 1943; spl. rep. of World Fellowship, Inc., to Latin Am.; observer UNESCO Confs., 1947, 50, 52 (rep. Boys Clubs Am., Nat. Recreation Assn., Youth Leaders Digest, World Fellowship, Inc. and Ill. Inst. Tech.). Originator Pan Am. Essay Contests, Teller English Essay Contests, Japan. Lit. work pub. in Mexico. Hon. life mem. English Speaking Soc., Chuo Univ., Japan. Home: Chgo. *

TEMPLE, PAUL RUSSELL, educator; b. Williamstown, Vt., Oct. 10, 1884; s. John Milo and Emma Amelia (Reed) T.; A.B., Harvard, 1907, M.A., 1921; unmarried. Teacher Brown & Nichols Sch., Cambridge, Mass., 1907-08; with Choate Sch., Wallingford, Conn., 1908-25, sr. master, 1915-25; sr. master Tamalpais Sch., San Rafael, Calif., 1925-30, headmaster since July 1930. Mem. Calif. Headmasters' Assn., Phi Beta Kappa. Republican. Episcopalian. Club: University (San Francisco). Address: San Rafael, Calif. *

TENNANT, HENRY FRY, diplomatic service; b. Mayville, N.Y., Mar. 5, 1886; s. Willis Hale and De Emma (Van Volkenberg) T.; grad. Cascadilla Sch., Ithaca, N.Y., 1905; LL.B., Cornell U., 1909; m. Paulita, d. of Hon. Federico Mejía, ex-minister from Salvador to Washington, May 29, 1915. Admitted to N.Y. bar, 1909, and practiced in Buffalo; clk. legation, Lisbon, Portugal, 1910-11; apptd. 3d sec. of embassy, at Mexico City, Aug. 22, 1912, 2d sec., Mar. 1, 1913; sec. of legation and chargé d'affaires, Caracas, Aug. 1, 1913; sec. of legation, chargé d'affaires and consul gen., San Salvador, Feb. 11, 1914; apptd. sec. of embassy or legation of class 3, Feb. 15, 1915; resigned Mar., 1917; asst. mgr. Buenos Aires branch of Guaranty Trust Co. of New York since Apr. 1, 1917. Republican. Episcopalian. Mem. Psi Upsilon. Clubs: International, Casino (San Salvador). Home: Buffalo, N.Y. Address: Buenos Aires, Argentina, S.A. *

TENNENT, CHARLES GAILLARD, orgn. ofcl.; b. Asheville, N.C., Apr. 5, 1894; s. James E. and Annie L. (Raby) T.; A.B., U. N.C., 1918; m. Jessie L. Mercer, Apr. 5, 1923; children—M. Gail, Charles M., William G., David L. Owner, mgr. Tennent Nurseries, Asheville, from 1923; landscape cons. U. N.C., Asheville. Mem. Rotary Internat., from 1935, 1st v.p., dir., 1948-49, dir., 1958-59, pres., 1957-58. Chmn. Asheville Sch. Bd., 1958-60. Chmn. finance com. Rotary, 1951-52, 54-55, chmn. program planning com., 1950-57, trustee found., 1958-63, chmn., 1958-59, chmn. devel. com., 1962-63. Decorated Order of So. Cross (Brazil); Order of Merit (Chile); Order of Merit for Distinguished Service (Peru); Order of Merit (Ecuador); recipient Distinguished Service award U. N.C. at Asheville, 1977. Served as 2d lt., inf., U.S. Army, 1918; capt. cav., N.C. N.G., 1925. Mem. N.C. Sch. Bd. Assn. (dist. pres. 1956), Thomas Wolfe Meml. Assn. (dir. 1958-64, pres. 1963-64, vice-chmn. advisory com. 1977-79), Western N.C. Nurserymen's Assn. (pres. 1962, chmn. bd. 1963), Sigma Upsilon, Phi Delta Theta, Order Golden Fleece. Author: Little Lessons in Rotary. Address: Asheville, N.C. Died Feb. 22, 1979.

TENNENT, MELVIN GREENE, ex-mayor; b. Marietta, Ga., Sept. 10, 1885; s. Madison Greene and Sarah Ann (Bowden) T.; ed. pub. schs.; m. Agnes H. Hastings, Sept. 12, 1900. Settled in Tacoma, 1920, and bought a malleable steel and iron foundry; organized, 1921, The Tennent Steel Casting Co., of which is pres.; also acquired the Aurora Foundry, at Seattle, the Bilroe Alloys Co., and erected a modern foundry at Portland, Ore.; twice elected mayor of Tacoma; resigned in 1929 because of lack of coöperation by the city council; reëlected, Mar. 1930, by a majority of more than 5,000, for term ending May 1934; v.p. and mgr. Atlas Foundry & Machine Co.; Oct. 1940, moved to Seattle, Wash., and reopened the Tennent Steel Casting Co., Inc. Mem. Seattle Chamber Commerce. Republican. Baptist. Mason (K.T., Shriner), Eagle, Moose. Home: Seattle, Wash. *

TERRY, NATHAN MAXSON, lawyer; b. Camden, Del., Feb. 15, 1904; s. Charles L. and Elizabeth B. (Maxson) T.; certificate Sch. Bus. Adminstrn., Washington and Lee U., 1926, LL.B., 1927; J.D., 1971; m. Rebecca Dashiell Wolcott, Oct. 3, 1939; children—Nathan Maxson, Harry Kendall Fooks, Mary Elizabeth, Terry Mason. Admitted to Del. bar, 1929; mem. firm Hughes, Terry & Terry, Dover, Del., 1933-39; practiced in Dover, 1939-79; atty. levy ct. Kent County, 1936-40, 49-67; chief atty. Del. Pub. Service Commn., 1951-55; mem. Del. Bd. Bar Examiners, 1955-74; atty. for Kent County, Del. Hwy Dept., 1957-61, chmn. dept., 1961-64. Dir. Farmers Mut. Ins. Co. Del.; mem. adv. bd. Wilmington Trust Co. Pres. Del. Bd. Edn., 1951-53; mem. Gov. Del. Goals Com., 1961-65. Del., Democratic Nat. Conv., 1954. Bd. dirs. U. Del., 1964-78, Del. Steeplechase and Race Assn. Mem. Am. Law Inst. (ex-officio), Am. Judicature Soc., Del. Bar Assn. (pres. 1961-62), Soc. Colonial Wars, Phi Kappa Sigma, Phi Delta Phi. Episcopalian. Clubs: Wilmington (Del.). Home: Dover, Del. Died Sept. 12, 1979; buried Dover.

TESTER, ALBERT LEWIS, educator, marine biologist; b. Toronto, Ont., Can., Nov. 27, 1908; s. Jesse and Fanny (Kinge) T.; B.A., U. Toronto, 1931, M.A., 1932, Ph.D., 1936; m. Laura May Arnold, Apr. 21, 1934; children—Murray Arnold, Loretta May (Mrs. Edward W. Fink). Came to U.S., 1948, naturalized, 1954. Fishery scientist Fishery Research Bd. Can., 1931-48; prof. zoology U. Hawaii, 1948-55; dir. Pacific Oceanographic Fishery Investigations, Honolulu, 1955-57; chief div. biol. research U.S. Bur. Comml. Fisheries, 1957-58; sr. prof. zoology U. Hawaii, from 1958, dir. sea grant coll. program, 1968-69. Alternate U.S. del. Indo Pacific Fisheries Council, Tokyo, Japan, 1955, del. Bandung, Indonesia, 1957; chmn. standing com. fisheries 9th Pacific Sci. Congress, Bangkok, Thailand, 1957, chmn. div. maine biology and fisheries 10th congress, Honolulu, 1960, symposium chmn. 11th congress, Tokyo, 1966; mem. marine resources devel. com. Pacific Islands Devel. Commn., 1971-74. Recipient medal and award for excellence in research U. Hawaii, 1973. Grantee Office Naval Research, 1959-68, NSF, 1967-69. Mem. Am. Inst. Biol. Scis., Am. Fisheries Soc., Am. Soc. Zoologists, A.A.A.S., Am. Soc. Limnology and Oceanography. Author numerous sci. papers in field Spl. research on sharks. Home: Honolulu, Hawaii. Died Nov. 27, 1974.

TETELMAN, ALAN STEPHEN, educator, engring. cons.; b. N.Y.C., May 9, 1936; s. Harry and Leah (Markovitz) T.; B.S., Yale, 1958, M.S., 1960, Ph.D., 1961; 1 son, Michael. Research metallurgist Ford Motor Co., Detroit, 1962-63; asso. prof. Stanford U. (Calif.), 1967; dep. dir. materials Advanced Research Projects Agy., Washington, 1967-68; prof. engring. U. Calif. at Los Angeles from 1968, chmn. materials dept., 1968-74; head tech. staff Failure Analysis Assos., Palo Alto,

Calif., 1974-78. Mem. Nat. Materials Adv. Bd., 1969-73, adv. com. for research NSF, 1973-74, U.S. Army Sci. Adv. Bd., 1975. NSF fellow, 1961-62; recipient Robert L. Hardy Gold medal Am. Inst. Metall. Engrs., 1966, Engrs. Merit award Inst. for Advancement Engring., 1973. Mem. Am. Inst. Mining, Metall. and Petroleum Engrs. (pres. 1962), Am. Soc. for Metals (pres. 1964, distinguished lectr. Western congress 1974), Soc. Aerospace Material and Process Engrs. (pres. 1968), Nat. Acad. Sci., Sigma Xi (pres. 1961), Tau Beta Pi (pres. 1958). Club: Malibu Beach Racquet. Author: (with A.J. McEvily) Fracture of structural Materials, 1967; (with C.R. Barnett and W.D. Nix) Principles of Engineering Materials, 1973; also tech. articles on metallurgy and failure analysis. Home: Pacific Palisades, Calif. Died Sept. 25, 1978.

TEUBER, HANS-LUKAS, physiol. psychologist; b. Berlin, Aug. 7, 1916; s. Eugen and Rose (Knopf) T.; baccalaureat, Coll. Francais, Berlin, 1934; student U. Basel (Switzerland), 1935-39; Ph.D., Harvard, 1947; hon. degrees U. Claude Bernard, Lyon, France, 1975, U. Geneva, 1975; m. Marianne Liepe, Aug. 1, 1941; children—Andreas Wolfgang, Christopher Lawrence. Came to U.S. 1941, naturalized, 1944. Asst. psychology Harvard, 41-42; from research asso. to prof. psychiatry and neurology N.Y. U. Coll. Medicine, also dir. psychophysiol. lab. N.Y. U.; Bellevue Med. Center, 1947-61; prof., chmn. psychology dept., dir. psychophysiol. lab. Mass. Inst. Tech., 1961-77. Past mem. biol. and behavioral sci. panels Office Sci. Research, USAF; mem. bioscis. subcom. NASA; research adv. bd. United Cerebral Palsy Assn.; cons. head injury sect. NIH, 1967-77; area cons. VA; chmn. exec. council Internat. Brain Research Orgn., WHO; Eastman prof. Oxford (Eng.) U., 1971-72; James R. Killian, Jr. Faculty Achievement award M.I.T., 1976-77. Served with USNR, 1944-46. Recipient Karl Spencer Lashley award, 1966. Mem. Am. Acad. Arts and Scis., Nat. Acad. Scis. (Inst. Medicine), Am. Neurol. Assn., Am. Acad. Neurology, Assn. Research Nervous and Mental Diseases, Soc. Exptl. Psychologists, Am. Mental Diseases, Soc. Exptl. Psychologists, Am. Psychol. Assn., N.Y. Acad. Sci., Eastern Psychol. Assn., A.A.A.S., Nat. Inst. Neurology Mexico (hon. mem. faculty), French Psychol. Assn. (associe etranger), French Neurol. Soc. (hon.), Soc. Neuroscis., Sigma Xi. Author: Visual Field Defects after Penetrating Missile Wounds of the Brain, 1960; (with J. Semmes S. Weinstein and L. Ghent) Somatosensory Changes after Penetrating Brain Wounds in Man, 1960; also articles, chpts. in books. Editor: Internat. Jour. Neuropsychology, 1962-77, Jour. Psychiat. Research, 1961-64; co-editor Exptl. Brain Research Jour., 1965-77. Home: Arlington, Mass. Died Jan. 4, 1977.

TEYTE, MAGGIE, operatic soprano; b. (Tate) of Scotch-Irish descent, at Wolverhampton, Eng., Apr. 17, 1891; ed. Royal Coll. of Music, London, and full vocal training with Jean de Reske; m. Eugene Plumon, of Paris, Oct. 16, 1909. Début, as "Zerlina," at Monte Carlo, 1907; was for several yrs. mem. Opéra Comique, Paris, and at 19 sang Mélisande in "Pelléas and Mélisande"; toured Europe and Eng. in concerts; first appearance in America, at Met. Opera House, Phila., Nov. 4, 1911; created part of Cinderella in Massenet's opera: has sung in leading cities of U.S., 3d season, 1913-14; appeared frequently in U.S. for concerts from 1937. Catholic. Home: London, England. Died May 26, 1976.

THALER, ALWIN, educator; b. Hamburg, Germany, Jan. 10, 1891; s. Adolf and Rosa (von Halle) T.; B.A., Adelphi Coll., 1912; M.A., Columbia, 1914; Ph.D., Harvard, 1918; Litt.D., Adelphi U., 1967; m. Harriet Page Albright, Aug. 14, 1920; children—Richard Winston, Roderick Page. Instr. English, Adelphi Coll., 1912-13, Northwestern U., 1913-16; Sheldon traveling fellow Harvard, 1919-20; asst. prof. English, U. Calif., Berkeley, 1920-23; prof. English, U. Tenn., 1923-61, then emeritus; vis. prof. Stanford, 1925, Emory U., 1961-63, Tenn. Wesleyan, 1964, also summers Adelphi Coll., Harvard, U. Calif., U. Tex., U. Minn.; Keenan vis. prof. U. N.C., 1952; Guggenheim traveling fellow, 1929-30. Served with U.S. Navy, 1918-19. Mem. Modern Lang. Assn. (successively sec., chmn. and mem. adv. com. Shakespeare Group), South Atlantic Modern Lang. Assn., Tenn. Folklore Soc., Tenn. Philol. Assn. (pres. 1955-56), AAUP, Shakespeare Assn. Am., Phi Kappa Phi. Episcopalian, Clubs: Irving, Smokers, Faculty. Author: Shakespeare to Sheridan, 1922; Shakespeare's Silences, 1929; Shakespeare and Democracy, 1941; Shakespeare and Sir Philip Sidney, 1947; Shakespeare and Our World, 1966; Ports and Happy Havens: an autobiography, 1974, contbr. articles and reviews to philol. jours. Editor: (with C.M. Gayley) Representative English Comedies, Vol. IV, 1936; (with R.B. Davis) Tenn. Studies in Literature, Vols. I-VII, 1956-62; (with Norman Sanders) Shakespearean Essays, 1964. Home: Knoxville, Tenn. Deceased.

THATCHER, ROY DAVIS, lawyer; b. Logan, Utah, Sept. 17, 1879; s. John Bethuel and Sarah Maris (Davis) T.; student Agrl. Coll. of Utah, Logan, Utah, 1894-97; LL.B., U. of Chicago, 1909; LL.D. (honorary), University of Utah, 1947; married Diana Bean, Feb. 21, 1905; children—Paul Bean, Emerson Bean, Olive (Mrs. Ramon Lawrence Irwin), Miriam (Mrs. David Mahlon Bonner). Admitted to bar, 1909; engaged in practice of law, Logan, Utah, 1909-23, Ogden, Utah, since 1923; district atty., 1912-20; gen. atty. for banks in Utah, Idaho, and Wyoming, since 1922. Trustee Utah State Training Sch., 1929-35. Regent Univ. of Utah 1935-47, also chmn. bd. of regents 1938-47. Mem. Am. and Utah bar assns. Clubs: Timpanogos, Aztec (Salt Lake City); Rotary (Ogden). Home: Ogden, Utah. *

THATCHER, TORIN HERBERT ERSKINE, actor; b. Bombay, India, Jan. 15, 1905; s. Torin James Blair and Edith Rachel (Batty) T.; student Kensington Coll. Bus., London, 1924-25; m. Mildred Daniel, 1939 (dec. 1950); 1 son, Phillip Torin; m. 2d, Anne LeBorgne, June 12, 1952. Debut in Shakespearean Repertory at Maddermarket Theatre, Norwich, Eng., 1924-26; appeared at Cambridge (Eng.) Festival Repertory Theatre, 1926, Old Vic Theatre, 1927-29, West End Theatre, London, 1928-48; toured with Bernard Shaw Repertory throughout Eng., 1930-31; played 8 prodns. of Hamlet, 25 Shakespeare plays, 50 Shakespeare prodns., 19 Shaw plays; starred in numerous Broadway plays, from 1948, including Edward My Son, Billy Budd, Miracle Worker, The First Born; appeared in numerous motion pictures, from 1935, latest being The Robe, Love is a Many Splendored Thing, Snows of Kilimanjaro, Hawaii, Mutiny on the Bounty, Sandpiper, Helen of Troy, The Canadians, Black Shield of Falworth, King's Pirate, Crimson Pirate; appeared in numerous TV shows, latest being Night Gallery, Defenders, Daniel Boone, Chrysler Theatre, Petrocelli, Probe, Brenda Starr. Served to lt. col. Brit. Army, 1940-45. Recipient Sylvania TV award, 1957. Mem. Reunion Theatre Assn. (founder), Theatre Research Soc. London, Acad. Motion Picture Arts and Scis., Brit. Actors Equity Assn. (founder mem.), Screen Actors Guild, Am. Actors Equity, A.F.T.R.A. Address: Hollywood, Calif. Died Mar. 4, 1981.

THAXTER, SIDNEY WARREN, lawyer; b. Portland, Maine, Apr. 21, 1914; s. Sidney St. Felix and Phyllis (Schuyler) T.; grad. Phillips Exeter Acad., 1933; B.S., Harvard, 1937, LL.B., 1940; m. Willamain Cranmer McPhee, Sept. 25, 1942 (dec. Aug. 1972); children—Sandra McPhee, Sidney St. Felix II, Philip Schyler, John Cranmer; m. 2d. Jean Vernon Russert, June 22, 1973. Admitted to Maine bar, 1940; asso. briefly with N.Y.C. law firm, 1940; practiced in Portland, 1946-77; mem. firm Perkins, Thompson, Hinckley, Thaxter & Keddy, 1946-75; sr. partner firm Curtis, Thaxter, Corey, Lipez & Stevens, 1975-77. Chmn., Maine-for-Eisenhower Com., 1952, Maine Citizens for Eisenhower Com., 1956; mem. Portland City Council, 1965-67, Cape Elizabeth Town Council, 1967-71; mem. Greater Portland Council Govts., 1968-71, pres., 1969-70. Mem. Portland Soc. Art (past pres.), Greater Portland C. of C. (dir.), Cumberland County, Maine Am., Internat. bar assns. Home: Falmouth, Maine. Died Mar. 27, 1977.

THAYER, ROBERT ELLIS, mechanical engr.; b. Chelsea, Mass., Aug. 4, 1883; s. James Franklin and Cornelia May (Sessions) T.; S.B. in Mech. Engring., Mass. Inst. Tech., 1907; m. Maud J. Gilbert, of Chelsea, Mass., Sept. 1, 1910. Spl. apprentice with Am. Locomotive Co., 1907-8; instr. mech. engring., Mass. Inst. Tech., 1908-10; mech. dept. editor, Railway Age and mng. editor of Railway Mechanical Engineer, 1911-19; European editor of Railway Age and allied publs. since Apr. 1, 1919. Mem. Am. Soc. M.E. Republican. Conglist. Mason. Home: Ridgewood, N.J. *

THAYER, VIVIAN TROW, educator, editor; b. Lincoln, Neb., Oct. 13, 1886; s. Oscar Benjamin and Rose Standish (Munson) T.; A.B., U. of Wis., 1916, A.M., 1917, Ph.D., 1922; m. Florence A. Adams, Apr. 18, 1914; children—Robert Adams, Horace Standish, Lois Lillian. Supt. schs., Ashland, Wis., 1913-16, 1918-19; instr. in philosophy and psychology, U. of Wis., 1919-22; prin. Ethical Culture High Sch., New York, 1922-24; prof. secondary edn., Ohio State U., 1924-28; mng. editor American Review (bi-monthly), 1923-27, then editor; asso. editor Jour. Edn. Research, 1929-31; ednl. dir. Ethical Culture Schools, N.Y. City, 1929-48; visiting professor University of Hawaii, 1948-49. Chairman commn. on secondary sch. curriculum Prog. Edn. Assn., 1932-39. Mem. National Education Association, National Soc. for Study of Edn., Prog. Edn. Assn., Phi Beta Kappa, Phi Delta Kappa. Wrote: (brochure) Misinterpretation of Locke As a Formalist in Educational Philosophy, 1921; The Passing of the Recitation, 1928; (with H. B. Alberty) Supervision in the Secondary School; (with R. Kotinsky and C. B. Zachry) "Reorganizing Secondary Education," 1939; American Education Under Fire, 1944; Religion in Public Education, 1947. Contbr. to The Educational Frontier, The Challenge to Secondary Education; also to School and Society, Jour. Ednl. Research, Educational Administration and Supervision. Home: Arlington, Va.

THEIS, HENRY A., banker; b. Germania, Pa., May 7, 1884; s. Henry J. and Virginia (von Senden) T.; ed. Larch Prep. Sch., Easton, Pa.; Ph.B., Lafayette Coll., 1904; m. Hope Claugh-Leighter, June 15, 1918; children—Henry Grant, Virginia von Senden. With Guaranty Trust Co. of N.Y., 1904-07; v.p. Franklin Soc. for Home Bldg. and Savings, 1907-18; asst. trust officer, Guaranty Trust Co., 1918-26, asst. v.p., 1926-27, v.p. since 1927, pres. and dir. Citizens Nat. Bank & Trust Co., Englewood, N.J.; dir. and v.p. Fiduciary Fund Corp., N.Y. City; v.p. Trust Companies Assn. of State of N.Y.; pres. Corporate Fiduciaries Assn. City of N.Y. (1936-37); mem. legislative com. N.Y. State Bankers Assn.; mem. ex-officio trust div., exec. com. and mem. Nat. Conf. Group, Am. Bankers Assn. (chmn. trust div. com. on costs and charges, 1929-43; chmn. exec. com. trust div., 1941-42, v.p., 1942-43, pres., 1943-44, mem. research council). Pres. and trustee Englewood Boys Sch. Ednl. Foundation; trustee and chmn. Endowment Fund Com. Englewood (N.J.) Hosp. Assn.; trustee and mem. exec. com. Englewood Boys Country Day Sch. Mem. Sigma Nu (dir and treas. Sigma Nu Inc. Ednl. Foundation, Indianapolis). Mason. Clubs: Knickerbocker, Englewood Field (Englewood). Home: Englewood, N.J. *

THEOBALD, WALTER HENRY, ret. otolaryngologist; b. Oconomowoc, Wis., Dec. 19, 1886; s. Peter A. and Sophia (Schudderkopf) T.; S.B., U. Chgo., 1909; M.D., Rush Med. Coll., 1911; m. Mildred Morkill, 1913; children—Pierce, Harriet M. (Mrs. Hugh M. Elwood). Specialist in diseases of ear, nose and throat, Chgo., 1913-69; intern St. Luke's Hosp., 1911-12; examining surgeon I.C. R.R., 1912; otolaryngologist Municipal Tb Sanitarium, 1914; became mem. sr. attending staff St. Luke's Hosp., 1915, now emeritus staff Presbyn.-St. Luke's Hosp.; emeritus prof. dept. otolaryngology U. Ill., Research and Ednl. Hosp.; cons. Chgo. Bd. Health. V.p. Oconomowoc Canning Co.; dir. Champion Machinery Co., Joliet, Ill. Pres. Med. Center Commn. Ill., 1946—. Mem. Procurement and Assignment Comm., 1944-45. Served as med. examiner Exemption Bd., SSS, Chgo., 1917-18. Recipient George Coleman medal Inst. Medicine, 1962. Fellow Inst. Medicine (pres. 1951); mem. A.M.A., Ill., Chgo. med. socs., Otolaryngology Soc., Am. Laryngol. Assn., Am. Acad. Ophthalmology and Otolaryngology (pres. 1954), Am. Laryngol., Rhinol. and Otol. Soc., Phi Beta Pi. Contbr. to med. lit. Home: Chicago IL. *

THIBAUD, JACQUES (TE'BO), violonist; b. Bordeaux, France, Sept. 27, 1880; s. Georges and Philomene (Reverdy) T.; student Lycee of Bordeaux, 1886-94, Conservatory of Paris, 1894-96; m. Marguerite Francfort, Sept. 30, 1902; children—Roger, Philippe (killed in action 1940). Concertized violonist Europe, Asia, Africa, North and South Am., China, Japan, and India since 1908. Member Liszt Acad. in Hungary. Catholic. Home: Basses-Pyrenees, France.*

THIELE, CLAUDE MARTIN, army officer; b. Danville, Ky., Sept. 25, 1888; s. Edward B. and Emma L. (Hodges) T.; C.E., Cornell U., 1911; Coast Artillery Sch., 1924, Command and Gen. Staff Sch., 1924-25, Army War Coll., 1931-32; m. Ethel A. Wilson, June 25, 1913. Commd. 2d lt., C.A.C., U.S. Army, 1911, advanced through ranks to brig. gen., 1941; served Adj. Gen.'s Dept., France, Germany, 1919-23; War Dept. Gen. Staff, 1932-36; commd. 63d C.A. (anti-aircraft) and Ft. MacArthur, 1936-38; on staff of comdg. gen. and U.S. High Commr., Philippines, 1938-40; comdr. 77th C.A., 34th C.A. Brigade, Ft. Bragg, 1941; Anti-aircraft Region Norfolk, Anti-aircraft Command European Theater of Operations, 1942; anti-aircraft officer E.T.O., 1943; anti-aircraft officer 12th Army Group, 1944-45; comdg. gen., American Univ., Shrivenham, Eng., 1945; comdg. gen. United Kingdom Base; sr. army instr. N.M.N.G., 1947-48; ret., 1948; recalled to active duty Office of Army Field Forces, 1949. Awarded Legion of Merit with oak leaf cluster, Bronze Star Medal, Army Commendation Ribbon (U.S.), Chevalier Legion of Honor, Croix de Guerre with palm (France), Chevalier Order of Leopold I, Croix de Guerre with palm, Order Leopold II (Belgium), Croix de Guerre with palm, Grand Ducal Order Couronne de Chêne (Luxembourg), Order Orange-Nassau with swords (Netherlands), Comdr. British Empire. Mem. Seal and Serpent Soc. Presbyterian. Club: Army and Navy (Washington). Home: Lakes Wales, Fla. Died Oct. 1976.

THIELE, EDWARD HODGES, coast guard ofcr.; b. Washington, Sept. 4, 1905; s. Edward B. and Emma L. (Hodges) T.; B.S., U.S. Coast Guard Acad., 1927; B.S. in Mgmt. Engring., Rensselaer Poly. Inst., 1949; m. Vibeke Laub, Feb. 16, 1935; children—Barbara (Mrs. A. Byron Holderby, Jr.), and Vibeke (Mrs. Jerome J. Weber). Commissioned with the rank of ensign USCG, 1927, advanced through grades to rear adm., 1957; assigned various ships, 1927-29, asst. engring. officer Cutter Mendota, 1929-30; instr. elec. engring. Coast Guard Acad., 1930-33; engring. officer Coast Guard Cutter Chelan; chief internal combustion engine and small boat sect., then chief research and development div. Office Engr.-in-chief, Coast Guard Hdqrs., 1936-40; study and constrn. icebreakers; supr. design and constrn. icebreakers Office Navy Supr. Shipbuilding, N.Y.C., World War II; exec. officer icebreaker Westwind, 1944; comdg. officer troop transports U.S.S. Gen. Aultman, U.S.S. Wakefield; dist.

engr. 3d Coast Guard Dist. N.Y., then chief machinery sect. Naval Engring. Div., also safety dir., 1946-48; chief adminstrv. mgmt. div. Office Comdt., Hdqrs. Coast Guard, 1949-51; sr. Coast Guard and Merchant Marine detail officer, Europe, 1951-53; staff Comdr. 5th Coast Guard Dist., chief Merchant Marine safety div., Norfolk, Va., 1953-56, chief staff, 1957; comdr. 9th Coast Guard Dist., Cleve., 1957-58; engr.-in-chief Coast Guard, 1958-61, ret.; vice pres. Cleveland Stevedore Co., 1961-70; pres., dir. Cleveland Seamen's Service, Inc., from 1963. Trustee Port of Cleveland Information, Inc.; president of Counsel of Lake Erie Ports. Mem. Soc. Naval Architects and Marine Engrs., Am. Soc. Naval Engrs. (pres. 1961), Soc. Am. Mil. Engrs., Newcomen Soc. Eng., Nat. Def. Transp. Assn. Clubs: Westwood Country, Union (Cleve.); Army and Navy (Washington); Whitehall (N.Y.C.). Home: Cleveland, Ohio. Died Apr. 21, 1981.

THISTLETHWAITE, GLENN F., (THIS'L-THWAT), physical edn.; b. Sheridan, Ind., Mar. 18, 1885; s. Cyrus D. and Laura A. (Ramsey) T.; B.S., Earlham Coll., Richmond, Ind., 1908; grad. Chautauqua Sch. of Physical Edn., 1913; m. Esther Painter, June 22, 1911; children—Robert Painter, Glenn Edwin, James Richard. Dir. of athletics and instr. in mathematics, Ill. Coll., Jacksonville, 1908-09; dir. of athletics and dean of men, Earlham Coll., 1909-13; physical dir. pub. high schs., Oak Park, Ill., 1913-22; head football coach, Northwestern U., 1922-27; head football coach and prof. physical edn., U. of Wis., 1927-32; dir. physical edn., Carroll Coll., 1932-34; dir. physical education, U. of Richmond, 1934-42; dir. United Service Orgns., Richmond, Va., 1942-45; with Muhleman & Kayhoe, Inc., real estate, since 1945. Pres. Richmond Chapter Am. War Dads, 1945-46; mem. Am. Assn. for Health, Physical Edn. and Recreation, Assn. Secs. of Y.M.C.A. Presbyterian. Rotarian. Home: Richmond, Va. *

THODE, EVERETT WAYNE, legal educator; b. Broadlands, Ill. Apr. 30, 1920; s. Barnhart Henry and Wilma Vada (Green) T.; B.S. U. Ill., 1943; LL.B., U. Tex., 1950; S.J.D. (Ford grad. fellow), Harvard 1964; m. Betty Jane Lyle, Aug. 19, 1944; 1 dau., Sharon Lynn (Mrs. James C. Porter, Jr.). Admitted to Tex. bar, 1950, Utah bar, 1969; clk. Supreme Ct. Tex., 1950-51; asst. atty. gen. Tex., 1951-52; practice law, Austin, 1952-55; asso. prof. law U. Tex., 1955-59, prof. law, 1959-67; prof. law U. Utah, Salt Lake City, 1967-80. Commr. Uniform State Laws Tex., 1962-66, Uniform State Laws Utah, 1969-75. Served to capt. AUS, 1942-47. Recipient Teaching Excellence award U. Tex. Law Sch., 1965; Distinguished Teaching award U. Utah, 1971, Distinguished Research award, 1975; named Prof. of Yr., U. Utah Law Sch., 1973. Mem. Am. (reporter spl. com. standards of jud. conduct 1969-72), Tex., Utah bar assns., Am. Law Inst., AAUP, Chancellors, Order of Coif, Phi Delta Phi. Democrat. Unitarian. Author: Reporter's Notes to Code of Judicial Conduct, 1973. Co-author: Texas Judicial Process, 1966; Injuries to Relations, 1977; Torts Cases and Materials, 1977; Introduction to the Study of Law, 1970. Editor: Personal Injury Litigation in Texas, 1961. Home: Salt Lake City, Utah. Died Jan. 7, 1980.

THOM, WILLIAM TAYLOR, JR., geology educator; b. Roanoke, Va., June 9, 1891; s. William Taylor and Elizabeth Porter (Miller) T.; B.S., Washington and Lee U., 1913, D.Sc., 1936; Ph.D., Johns Hopkins U., 1917; m. Rachel Trimble Hoopes, Nov. 4, 1916; children—William Taylor 3d, Judith Preston, Elizabeth Pearson. Page, U.S. Senate, 1907; messenger boy Govt. Printing Office, 1908; surveyor D.C. Water Dept., 1909-10; geologic aide, asst. geologist, asso. geologist, geologist, sr. geologist, U.S. Geol. Survey, 1913-27; chief of plan sect. Bur. Statistics, U.S. Fuel Admn., 1918-19; in charge coal sect. U.S. Geol. Survey, 1923-24, fuel sect. (coal and oil), 1925-27; asso. prof. geology Princeton, 1927-35, prof., 1935-36, Blair prof. geology, 1937-56, Blair prof. geology emeritus, 1956-79, chmn. dept. geol. engring., 1940-56. Chmn., NRC Com. on Studies in Petroleum Geology, 1931-35; chmn. spl. com. geophys. and geol. study continents Am. Geophys. Union, 1935-48; spl. asst. Div. Subsistence Homesteads, Dept. Interior, Washington, 1933. Fellow World Acad. Art and Sci. (dir. Am. div.); mem. Geol. Soc. Am., Am. Inst. Geonomy and Natural Resources (pres.), Am. Geophys. Union, Yellowstone-Bighorn Research Assn., Am. Assn. Petroleum Geologists (hon.), Am. Inst. Mining, Metall. and Petroleum Engrs., Sigma Xi, Phi Gamma Delta, Gamma Alpha, Phi Beta Kappa. Author: Petroleum and Coal, The Keys to the Future, 1929; The Goal of Democracy, 1940; Tectonic Sketch of North America, 1959; The Meaning of America, 1959; Science and Engineering and The Future of Man, 1961; The Discovery, Development and Constructive Use of World Resources, 1963; also govt. reports, profl. papers, and tech. articles. Home: Ashland, Oreg. Died May 22, 1979; buried Sandy Spring, Montgomery County, Md.

THOMAS, AMOS, lawyer; b. Milwaukee, Wis., Aug. 30, 1882; s. Joseph Amos and Addie Margaret (Neilson) T.; U. of Neb., 1900-02, 1906-09, LL.B., 1909; grad Army War Coll.; m. Gertrude Owen, Aug. 25, 1917; children—Ann (Mrs. D. W. Rankin), Dorothy (Mrs. E. O. McDonald), Gay. Atty., 1909-41; asst. atty. gen. of Neb., 1921-22; atty. U. of Neb. Bd. of Regents, 1926-36; mem. Neb. Unicameral Legislature (chmn. judiciary com. and legislative council), 1936-42; brig. gen. Neb. Nat. Guard and U.S. Army, 1932-45; commanding general Camp White, Ore., 1942-44. Chairman Omaha Municipal Airport Committee, 1926-36. Awarded Order of Black Cross, French Legion of Honor. Delegate of G.H.Q., A.E.F. to Founder's Conv., Am. Legion, Paris, 1919. Mem. Nebraska and Omaha bar assns., Phi Delta Theta, Phi Delta Phi, Theta Nu Epsilon. Mason. Clubs: Montecito Country; University (Santa Barbara). Home: Santa Barbara, Calif. *

THOMAS, ARTHUR ABBOT, lawyer; b. Providence, R.I., June 13, 1878; s. Charles Lloyd and Sarah Sophia (Barstow) T.; graduate Phillips Andover, Mass., 1897; A.B., Yale, 1901; LL.B., Harvard, 1904; m. Pauline deW. Bartlett, June 1, 1910; m. 2d, Norma R. Hermann, Dec. 15, 1928. Practiced at Providence since 1905; pres., dir., treas. Westminster Real Estate Co.; secretary, director, General Insurance Agency, Inc. Mem. City Council, Providence, 1918-36. Mem. Commercial Economy Board, State Council of Defense, and govt. appeal agent, World War I; govt. appeal agent, World War II; four times a member National Conference on Street and Highway Safety under Sec. of Commerce Herbert Hoover, and apptd. by him mem. of com. to draft a model traffic ordinance, and chmn. of drafting com. Trustee Providence Lying-in Hosp., 1913-47. Dir., sec. Auto. Club of R.I.; sec.-treas. Class of 1897, Phillips Acad., Andover. Mem. Exec. Com. Andover Assn. of Class Secretaries. Exec. dir., treas. Coated and Processed Paper Assn., Laminated Foil Manufacturers Association; member Society Colonial Wars, S.A.R., Alpha Delta Phi, Elihu Club (Yale). Republican. Episcopalian. Mason (K.T.). Clubs: Yale Club, Art (Providence); Graduate (New Haven); Yale (New York); Yale, Harvard (Boston). Home: Providence, R.I. *

THOMAS, BURT RANDOLPH, cartoonist; b. Cleveland, O., Dec. 4, 1881; s. Martin Lee and Mary (Randolph) T.; grad. high sch., Cleveland, 1899; student (Cleveland Art Sch., 1899-1902, Detroit Art Sch., 1903-05; m. Margaret Yarger, June 3, 1911; 1 dau., Margaret Randolph. Newspaper artist Cleveland Press, 1900-02; advertising illustration, 1902-04; cartoonist Detroit News since 1904; has worked for Thompson Feature Service and Bell Syndicate; his political cartoons are syndicated to 57 papers of N. Am. Newspaper Alliance; made colored comic page "Mr. Straphanger" which ran for 7 years; has drawn for Life and Judge. Address: Detroit. *

THOMAS, CLARENCE DELMAR, educator; b. Bozeman, Mont., Oct. 14, 1900; s. Clarence Edwin and Anna Gusta (Fast) T.; B.S., N.E. Mo. State Teachers Coll., 1927; M.A., U. Mo., 1931, Ph.D., 1938; m. Naomi Lucy McClellan, May 25, 1924; children—Veta Arelyn (Mrs. Charles T. Mahan, Jr.), Louise Anne (Mrs. Robert B. McGill). Prin. high sch., Ewing, Mo., 1923-25, Holden, Mo., 1925-27; physics instr. Carthage (Mo.) High Sch., 1927-29; asst. dept. physics U. Mo., 1929-30; instr. Mo. Sch. Mines and Metallurgy, U. Mo., 1930-36, asst. prof. physics, 1936-42; instr. in physics, engring., sci. mgmt., def. tng. Pa. State Coll., summer 1942; instr. in physics dept. elec. engring. U.S. Naval Acad., 1942-46; asso. prof. physics, head dept. U. Tulsa, 1946-47, prof. physics, 1947-67, head dept., 1947-66; prof. physics Oral Roberts U., Tulsa, 1967-73. Instr. NSF In-Service Inst. Physics, U. Ark., 1964-65. Served to commdr. USNR, 1942-46. Mem. Am. Assn. Physics Tchrs., Am. Soc. Engring. Edn., Am. Assn. U. Profs., Am. Phys. Soc., Sigma Xi, Pi Mu Epsilon. Methodist. Contbr. to professional jours. Home: Tulsa, Okla. Died May 22, 1976; buried Meml. Park, Tulsa.

THOMAS, DONALD ROFF, educator; b. Oakland, Calif., June 11, 1924; s. Hugh Wadsworth and Lillian Hope (Wells) T.; B.A., U. Calif., 1948, M.A., Stanford U., 1955, Ed.D., 1957; m. Marilyn Zito, Aug. 3, 1947 (div. May 1963); children—Jordan, Alan, Melinda; m. 2d, Sarah Hufham, June 14, 1964; children—David, Julia. Elementary tchr.-prin. schs. in Calif., 1948-51, 53-54; dir. Colegio Bolivar, Cali, Colombia, 1951-53; demonstration tchr. San Francisco State Coll., 1954-57; asst. prof. U. Wis., Madison, 1957-60; asso. prof. U. Ariz., Tucson, 1960-61, Calif. State U., Northridge, 1961-67; prof. edn. Case Western Res. U., 1967-72; prof., dean Sch. Edn., Am. U., 1972-79; dir. OEO Tng. and Devel. Center, Northridge, 1965-67; mem. various task forces, cons. in field. Pres. Programs for Action by Citizens in Edn. (PACE), Cleve., 1971. Served with USMCR, 1943-46. Recipient Emily C. Cook prize in poetry U. Calif., 1948; grantee U.S. Office Edn., 1961. Mem. AAUP, AAAS, Am. Assn. Coll. Tchr. Edn. (instl. rep.), World Future Soc., Phi Delta Kappa. Author: The Schools Next Time, 1973; co-author: Social Foundations of Educational Decisions, 1965; also articles ednl. commn. reports. Address: Rockville, Md. Died Nov. 13, 1979; buried Parklawn Cemetery, Rockville.

THOMAS, DOROTHY SWAINE, educator, social scientist; b. Balt., Oct. 24, 1899; d. J. Knight and Sarah (Swaine) Thomas; A.B., Columbia, 1922; Ph.D., U. London, 1924; D.Sc. (hon.), U. Pa., 1970; m. W.I. Thomas, 1935 (dec.). Research asst. Fed. Res. Bank, 1924; fellow Social Science Research Council, 1925-26; research Laura Spellman Rockefeller Found., 1926; research asso., asst. prof. Tchrs. Coll., Columbia, 1927-30; research asso., asso. prof. Yale, 1931-35, dir. research in social statistics, 1935-39; staff mem. Carnegie Corp. Study of Negro in Am., 1939-40; lectr. in sociology U. Cal., 1940-41, prof. rural sociology, 1941-48; research prof. sociology U. Pa., Phila., 1948-70; professorial lectr. Georgetown U., Washington, 1972-77; vis. prof. Social Sci. Inst., U. Stockholm, Sweden, 1933, 35, 36; cons. N.Y. State Research Found. for Mental Hygiene. Spl. analyst Fed. Emergency Relief Adminstrn., 1935-36; cons. Nat. Resources Com., 1936-37; chmn. com. on migration differentials, dir. Social Sci. Research Council, demographer Tech. Assistance Adminstrn., UN, Bombay, India, 1957, 63; mem. tech. adv. com. on 1960 census, U.S. Bureau Census, until 1971; former mem. Census Adv. Com. on Population Statistics, until 1972; chmn., Pacific Coast Regional Com. Social Sci. Research Council, 1942-46; dir. U. Cal. Evacuation and Resettlement Study, 1942-48; cons. demography UN Tech. Assistance Bombay and Cairo, 1963-64; vis. prof. U. Gothenburg (Sweden), 1964, U. Uppsala (Sweden), 1971, 72, Ohio State U., 1971; cons. Central Statis. Bd., Sweden, 1965. Recipient Hutchinson Research medal London Sch. Econs., 1924. Fellow Am. Statis. Assn.; mem. Am. Sociol. Soc. (pres. 1952), Am. Philos. Soc. (councillor 1966-67), Population Assn. Am. (pres. 1958-59), Internat. Union Sci. Study Population, Phila. Author: Social Aspects of the Business Cycle, 1925; Child in America (with W. I. Thomas), 1928; Some New Techniques for Studying Social Behavior, 1929; Observational Studies of Social Behavior, 1933; Research Memorandum on Migration Differentials, 1938; Social and Economic Aspects of Swedish Population Movements, 1941; The Spoilage (with R. S. Nishimoto), 1946; The Salvage (with C. Kikuchi and J. Sakoda), 1952; Population Redistribution and Economic Growth. United States, 1870-1950 (with others), Vol. I, 1957, Vol. II, 1960, Vol. III, 1964; United Nations, Manual VI, Methods of Measuring Internal Migrations (with others), 1970. Home: Bethesda, Md. Died May 1, 1977.

THOMAS, ELEANOR WALTER, univ. prof.; b. Charlotte, N.C., Sept. 11, 1880; d. Col. John Peyre and Mary Caroline (Gibbes) Thomas; A.B., Coll. for Women, Columbia, S.C., 1900; B.S., Columbia U., 1912, M.A., 1918, Ph.D., 1930. Teacher mathematics and English St. Mary's Jr. Coll., Raleigh, N.C., 1900-1917, principal, 1908-1917; asso. prof. English Lake Erie Coll., Paimesville, O., 1917-19; instr. English Western Reserve U., Cleveland, 1919-24, asst. prof., 1924-35, asso. prof., 1935-44; Woods prof. English, 1944-49; asst. dean, 1928-44, head Eng. dept., Flora Stone Mather Coll., 1944-49. Mem. Am. Assn. Univ. Profs., Modern Lang. Assn., Coll. English Assn., Nat. Coll. Teacher's Assn. Episcopalian. Author: Christina Georgina Rossetti, 1931. Home: Cleveland. *

THOMAS, FRANK WATERS, educator; born Danville, Ind., May 14, 1878; s. Erasmus Darwin and Mary (Roseberough) T.; grad. Ind. State Normal, Terre Haute, 1902; A.B., Ind. U., 1905; A.M., U. of Ill., 1910, Ph.D., Stanford, 1926; LL.D. (honorary), Occidental College, 1945; married Ina Gregg, Sept. 2, 1908; children—Lawrence, W. Craig, Franklin. Instr., Acad. U. of Ill., 1906-10, prin. Acad., 1910-11; prin. high sch., Santa Monica, Calif., 1911-13; prin. schs. Sacramento, Calif., 1913-17; head of dept. of edn., Fresno (Calif.) State Coll., 1917-27, pres., 1927-48; lecturer in summer sessions, Stanford, Univ. of Calif., U. of Hawaii, U. of Southern California. Pres. Am. Assn. of Teachers Colleges, 1938-39; mem. Nat. Commn. on Teacher Edn., 1939-43. Administrative adv. Univ. of the Philippines, 1951-52. Member N.E.A., Phi Beta Kappa, Phi Delta Kappa, Sigma Nu. Republican. Rotarian. Author: Training for Effective Study, 1921; Principles and Technique of Teaching, 1927; (with others) The Junior College—Its Organization and Administration, 1927; Principles of Modern Education (with A. R. Lang), 1937. Editor Calif. Jour. Secondary Edn. Home: Palo Alto, Calif. *

THOMAS, FREDERIC WAGNER, banker; b. Sargent, Nebr., May 1, 1885; s. Joseph William and Idella Edith (Wagner) T.; A.B., U. Neb., 1908; m. Alyce Mongene, Nov. 9, 1947. Apprentice, Union Nat. Bank of Omaha, 1904-05; cashier Live Stock Nat. Bank of Omaha, 1909-17; joined First Nat. Bank of Omaha, 1917, cashier, 1917-25, v.p., 1925-47, pres. 1947-74, vice chmn., 1953, chmn.; v.p. Mchts. Investment Co., 1925-74, Douglas Investment Co., 1925-74; dir. North Side Bank, Met. Utilities Dist. Chmn. state adv. bd. B.F.C., 1940-52. Trustee U. Nebr. Found., Doane Coll., Clarkson Hosp., Nebr. Children's Home Soc.; former pres. Omaha Library Bd.; regent U. Nebr., 1938-40. Mem. Phi Gamma Delta. Episcopalian (vestryman). Home: Elkhorn, Nebr. Died May 13, 1976.

THOMAS, FREDERICK FOLGER, JR., lawyer; b. Oakland, Cal., Oct. 26, 1885; s. Frederick Folger and Nora (Peck) T.; A.B., U. Cal., 1908, J.D., 1911; m. Alice Louise Paine, Dec. 17, 1913; children—Elisabeth (Mrs. Norman J. Hearn), William Paine. Admitted to the California bar, 1911; associate firm McCutchen, Thomas, Matthew, Griffiths & Greene, San Francisco, and predecessor law firms 1911—, partner, 1919-58; counsel McCutchen, Doyle, Brown, & Enersen, 1958—. Member of Am. Bar Assn., State Bar Cal., Am. Petroleum Inst., Cal. Hist. Soc., Phi Delta Phi, Delta Tau Delta. Clubs: Pacific-Union, University, Commonwealth (San Francisco); Diablo (Cal.) Country; Book of Cal. Home: Berkeley, Cal. *

THOMAS, GEORGE C(ARROLL), naval med. officer; b. Lima, Pa., May 27, 1881; s. William Moore and Sarah Emma (Ogden) T.; student Swarthmore Prep. Sch., 1898; P.D., Phila. Coll. Pharmacy and Science, 1902; M.D., Jefferson Med. Coll., 1906; grad. Naval Med. Sch., 1909; registered pharmacist, Pa. and N.J., 1902; m. Bertha Leota Pratt, Sept. 15, 1913; children—Gertrude Eloise (Mrs.Clarence Moore Young), George Carroll, Richard Ogden. Apprentice pharmacist, 1898; resident physician Chester (Pa.) Hosp., 1906-07, Phila. Gen. (Blockley) 1907; Med. Corps, Navy since 1907; promoted through grades to rear adm., 1943. Dist. med. officer, 11th Naval Dist., 1943-44; chief professional div., Bur. of Medicine and Surgery, Navy Dept., 1944-45. General Inspector, 1945-46; retired, Sept. 1946. Fellow, Am. Coll. Physicians. Mem. A.M.A., Assn. Mil. Surgeons, U.S. Naval Inst., Mil. Order of the Carabao, Phi Chi. Mem. Soc. of Friends. Clubs: Army and Navy (Washington). Home: Chevy Chase, Md. *

THOMAS, GILBERT JOSHUA, urologist; b. Colby, Wis., Sept. 16, 1884; s. Daniel and Sarah (Reynolds) T.; M.D., Northwestern U., 1908; m. Ethel Fuller, Mar. 6, 1912; children—Jane (Mrs. Frederick C. Schlumberger, dec.) Gilbert L., John O., Robert D., William Henry. Intern, Mercy Hosp., Chgo., 1908-09 mem. staff dept. of surgery and urology Mayo Clinic, 1909-18; asso. clin. prof. urology Med. and Grad. Sch., U. Minn., 1918-43; asso. clin. prof. surgery (urology) U. So. Cal., 1943-50; clin. prof. surgery (urology) U. Cal. at Los Angeles, 1950—. Mem. bd. regents A.C.S., 1939-51; past pres. Am. Bd. Urology. Served on overseas duty as maj. M.C., U.S. Army, during World War I. Mem. Am. Assn. Genito-Urinary Surgery, A.M.A., Am. Urol. Assn. (past pres.), Am. Urol. Assn. (Western sect.), Clin. Soc. Genito-Urinary Surgeons, Internat. Soc. Urologists, Alpha Kappa Kappa, Delta Phi. Contbr. chpts. books, also numerous articles on urol. subjects to various publs. Cons. editor Urology, Post Graduate Medicine. Home: San Clementa CA. *

THOMAS, HAROLD ALLEN, educator; b. Ann Arbor, Mich., July 24, 1885; s. Calvin and Mary Eleanor (Allen) T.; A.B., Columbia, 1906, C.E., 1908; m. Katherine M. Sass, Feb. 5, 1910; children—Harold A., Charles Calvin, Katherine E., Mary E. Instr. civil engring., U. of Wash., 1909-10; prof. hydraulic engring., Rose Polytech. Inst., Terre Haute, Ind., 1911-22; prof. civil engring., Carnegie Inst. Tech., 1923-50, prof. emeritus since 1950. Asst. engr. Miami Conservatory Dist., Dayton, O., summer 1918; sr. engr. U.S. War Dept., Phila., summer and part time, 1928-29; hydraulic engr., City of Pittsburgh, part time, 1927-28, Mead & Scheidenhelm, summer 1936; Westinghouse Electric & Mfg. Co., part time 1937; head hydraulic research lab., Carnegie Inst. Tech. carrying on extensive model studies of dams and other hydraulic structures in various parts of U.S.; research for U.S. Navy and Army, 1945-51. Mem. Am. Soc. C.E. Auhthor: The Hydraulics of Flood Movements in Rivers (Bull. of Carnegie Institute Tech.), 1934; Cavitation in Outlet Conduits of High Dams (Trans. of Am. Soc. C.E.), 1941. Tester of golf balls for U.S. Golf Assn. Home: Murrysville, Pa. *

THOMAS, JAMES SHELBY, economist; b. Saltville, Va., Mar. 27, 1879; s. Samuel Morgan and Sarah (Vail) T.; B.A., Milligan Coll., 1900; M.A., Lynchburg Coll., 1904, LL.D., 1940; grad. work, U. of Chicago, 1919; LL.D., U. of Ala.; m. Ethel McCartney, June 18, 1902. Prof. history and Latin, Milligan Coll., 1900-03; prof. history, Lynchburg Coll., 1903-05; Va. state sch. examiner, 1905-08; state rural sch. supervisor of Va., 1908-10; dean of faculty, Lynchburg Coll., 1910-11; prof. secondary edn., U. of Ala., 1912-19; organized, and was dir. of extension div., U. of Ala., 1919-30; asso. dir. Ala. State Industrial Bd., 1928-29; chief economist Commonwealth & Southern Corp., 1931-33; pres. Clarkson Coll. of Technology, 1935-40; pres. Chrysler Inst. of Engring., Detroit. Mem. advisory council Vocational Edn. for N.Y. Civilian aide to sec. of war for Ala. Past dist. gov. Rotary Internat.; former mem. Boy's Work Com., and economic advisory com. on N. America, Rotary Internat. Mem. N.E.A., Am. Acad. Polit. and Social Science, Newcomen Soc., Phi Beta Kappa, Sigma Chi. Democrat. Mem. Christian (Disciples) Ch. Clubs: Potsdam, Potsdam Country, La Gorce Country. Author: What Machine Has Done to Mankind; New Frontiers for Smart People; This Thing Called Democracy. Contbr. to Engring. Opportunities, mags. and trade jours. Lecturer and traveler. Home: Miami, Fla. Died July 10, 1976.

THOMAS, JOSEPH ALBERT, investment banker; b. Ft. Worth, Sept. 22, 1906; s. Albert E. and Ellen (Owsley) T.; A.B., Yale, 1928; M.B.A., Harvard, 1930; m. Martha Paula Ruppanner, July 9, 1949; children—Michael Mackenzie, Jeffrey Furlough. Joined Lehman Bros., investment bankers, N.Y. City, 1930, partner, 1937-77, dir., chmn. finance and exec. coms.; adv. bd. Flintkote Co.; dir. Survival Tech. Inc., Litton Industries, Inc., Halliburton Co., Getty Oil Co., Asso. Dry Goods Corp., Black & Decker Mfg. Co.; dir., mem. exec. com. Cluett, Peabody, & Co., Inc.; mem. Lower Manhattan adv. bd. Chem. Bank. Trustee Presbyn. Hosp. Met. Mus. Art, N.Y. Zool. Soc. Clubs: Links, Brook, Jockey, Racquet and Tennis, 29 (N.Y.C.); Meadow Brooks; Pacific-Union (San Francisco). Home: Old Brookville, N.Y. Died May 28, 1977.

THOMAS, M(ILTON) HALSEY, archivist, editor; b. Troy, N.Y., Feb. 3, 1903; s. Elijah Milton and Elea (Manny) T.; B.S., Columbia, 1930, B.S. in L.S., 1931, A.M., 1942. Librarian, Butler Library of Philosophy, Columbia, 1926-28; curator Columbiana, 1928-59, mng. editor U. Quar., 1930-35; univ. archivist Princeton, 1959-69; contbg. editor Papers of Woodrow Wilson, 1968-77. Mem. Am. Antiquarian Soc., Mass. Hist. Soc., Mayflower Descs., New Eng. Hist. Geneal. Soc. Democrat. Unitarian. Clubs: Nassau (Princeton); Princeton, Grolier (N.Y.C.). Compiler: Bibliography of John Dewey (with H. W. Schneider) 1929; Bibliography of the Faculty of Political Science, Columbia U., 1931; Bibliography of Nicholas Murray Butler, 1934; John Dewey: A Centennial Bibliography, 1962. Editor: Columbia Univ. Officers and Alumni, 1754-1857, 1936; C. C. Moore's Early History of Columbia College, 1940; The Diary of George Templeton Strong (with Allan Nevins), 4 vols. 1952; Elias Boudinot's Journey to Boston in 1809, 1955; The Diary of Samuel Sewall, 1674-1729, 2 vols., 1973. Contbr. to Dictionary of Am. Biography, others. Home: Princeton, N.J. Died July 7, 1977.

THOMAS, WILLIAM MATTHEWS MERRICK, bishop; b. Mattapany, Md., May 3, 1878; s. Capt. George (C.S.A.) and Ellen Ogle (Beall) T.; B.A., U. of Va., 1901; grad. Va. Theol. Sem., 1904, B.D., 1911, D.D., 1925; m. Sara Elizabeth Cruikshank, Oct. 25, 1904; children—George Calvert (dec.), James Walter, Llewellyn Cruikshank. Deacon, 1904, priest, 1905, P.E. Ch.; prof. Theol. Sch., Rio Grande do Sul, Brazil, 1905-10; rector Ch. of Our Savior, Rio Grande, 1907-10; founder, 1912, and headmaster, 1912-25, Southern Cross Ch. (for boys), Porto Alegre; prof. canon law liturgics and ethics, Porto Alegre Theol. Sem., 1921-25, Bible in Portuguese, 1940-41; consecrated suffragan bishop of Southern Brazil, Dec. 28, 1925; missionary bishop of Southern Brazil, 1928-49. Member standing com. of diocese and examining chaplain for same, 15 yrs.; dep. to Gen. Conv., 1910, 22. Home: Avenida Belém, 254, Porto Alegre. Address: New York, N.Y. *

THOMPSON, CHARLES H(ENRY), educator; b. Jackson, Miss., July 19, 1896; s. Patrick Henry and Sara Estelle (Byers) T.; A.B., Va. Union U., Richmond, Va., 1917; Ph.B., U. of Chicago, 1918, A.M., 1920, Ph.D., 1925; D.Litt., Va. Union U., 1941; LL.D. (honorary), Morgan State Coll., 1954; married Mae Stewart, Mar. 10, 1928 (dec. 1975). Instr. psychology, Va. Union U., 1920-21; dir. instrn., State Normal Sch., Montgomery, Ala., 1922-24; instr. psychology and social science, Sumner High Sch. and Jr. Coll., Kansas City, Kan., 1925-26; asso. prof. edn., Howard U., Washington, D.C., 1926-29, prof. edn. from 1929, acting dean Coll. of Edn. 1932-33, dean. Coll. Liberal Arts, 1938-43, dean Grad. Sch., 1944-64. Served World War I. Mem. U.S. Nat. Commn. for UNESCO, U.S. Dept. of State, 1946-49; committee on discrimination in higher education American Council on Edn., 1948-57, panel education Commn. Occupied Areas, 1949-55. Fellow A.A. A.S.; member National Society College Teachers of Edn., N.E.A., Nat. Soc. for Study of Edn., Association of American Colleges (member comm. on teacher edn.), NAACP (bd. dirs. nat. defense and ednl. fund). Independent. Conglist. Editor: Journal of Negro Education, 1932-63; editor Yearbooks Jour. Negro Edn., 1932-63; editorial consultant The Nation's Schs., 1943-50, World Book Ency., 1944-60. Contbr. articles to edn. pubs. Home: Washington, D.C. Died Jan. 1980.

THOMPSON, EARLE SPAULDING, public utilities; b. Bath, Me., Mar. 2, 1892; s. George Edward and Lizzie (Low) T.; Bowdoin Coll., Brunswick, Me., A.B., 1914; M.A., 1944; LL.D., W.Va. U., 1956, Marietta College, 1959. With National Fire Insurance Co., Hartford, Conn., 1914-16, Hornblower & Weeks, 1916-22; with Am. Waterworks & Electric Co., 1923, treas., 1925-32, v.p., treas., 1932-35, exec. v.p., dir., 1935-37, pres., dir., 1937-48, chmn. and dir. successor co., Allegheny Power System, Inc.; dir. Monongahela Power Co., Potomac Edison Co., West Penn Power Co., West Penn Rys. Company. Member of the distribution committee of the N.Y. Community Trust. Trustee Bowdoin Coll., Lenox Hill Hosp. Mem. C. of C. State N.Y., Council Fgn. Relations, Pilgrims U.S., New Eng. Soc., St. Georges Soc., Alpha Delta Phi. Clubs: Century Association, University, Union, Pinnacle, Downtown Association (N.Y.C.); Blind Brook (Portchester, N.Y.); Yeamans Hall (Charleston, S.C.). Home: New York, N.Y. Died Mar. 30, 1981.

THOMPSON, GEORGE WESLEY, mfg. co. exec.; b. Syracuse, Kans., Mar. 15, 1915; s. Talmadge Dewitt and Ruth Anell (Calkin) T.; student pub. schs., Syracuse; m. Margaret Doyle, May 7, 1934; 1 dau., Sue Thompson Guenther. Laborer, Kans. Hwy. Dept., Syracuse, 1934-35, Am. Sisters Mining Co., Lawson, Colo., 1935-36, in rd. constrn. Hamilton Gleason Co., Littletown, Colo., 1936-37; with shipping and receiving dept. Montgomery Ward, Denver, 1937-41; worker transp. and purchasing Swift & Co., Denver, 1941-45, with purchasing dept. Chgo. gen. offices, 1945-47; with Indpls. Wire Bound Box Co., 1947-61, subsequently gen. mgr.; v.p., gen. mgr. box div. Altamil Corp. (merger Indpls. Wire Bound Box Co. and Altamil Corp.), Indpls., 1961-70, pres., chief exec. officer, 1970-77, chmn. bd., New Orleans, 1977-80, also dir., dir. subsidiaries Fontaine Truck Equipment Co., Aluminum Forge Co.; chmn. bd. Am. Box Co., also dir. Republican. Presbyterian. Clubs: Metairie (La.) Country, Fernwood (Miss.) Country; Plimsoll (New Orleans); Mispah (Chgo.). Home: Metairie, La. Died June 18, 1980; buried Syracuse (Kans.) Cemetery.

THOMPSON, GERSHOM JOSEPH, educator, physician; b. Cambridge, Ohio, Jan. 12, 1901; s. John William and Fanny (Gittings) T.; M.D., Washington U., St. Louis, 1925; M.S. (fellow urology Mayo Found.), U. Minn., 1930; m. Maxine Tews, July 16, 1933; children—Gershom Joseph, Pamela, Elizabeth, Victoria. Intern, St. Lukes Hosp., St. Louis, 1926; practice medicine, Webster Groves, Mo., 1926, specializing urology, St. Louis, 1930-31; mem. staff Mayo Clinic, Rochester, Minn., 1932-42, 46-69, head dept. urology, 1939-69, chief sect. transurethal surgery, 1933-66; prof. urology U. Minn. Grad. Sch., 1939-75. Served as comdr. M.C., USNR, World War II. Diplomate Nat. Bd. Med. Examiners, Am. Bd. Urology. Fellow A.C.S., Internat. Coll. Surgeons; mem. Western Surg. Assn., Clin. Soc. Genito-Urinary Surgeons, Am. Assn. Genito-Urinary Surgeons, Am. Urol. Assn., A.M.A., So. Minn., Olmsted County med. assns., Sigma Xi, Phi Rho Sigma, Tau Pi Epsilon, Alpha Omega Alpha. Episcopalian. Clubs: Rochester Country. Contbr. numerous articles to profl. jours.; contbg. author chpts. med. textbooks. Specialist in genito-urinary surgery. Inventor Thompson Resectoscope widely used in urol. surgery. Home: Rochester, Minn. Died Nov. 2, 1975.

THOMPSON, GROVER CLEVELAND, lawyer; b. Lawrence County, Ky., Jan. 10, 1885; s. James Franklin and Amanda Helen (Watson) T.; B.S., Western State Teachers Coll., Bowling Green, Ky., 1908; LL.B., U. of Ky., 1910; m. Virginia Lee Gill, May 19, 1909; 1 son Grover Cleveland. Prin. Gilbert (La.) High Sch., 1908-09, Waynesboro (Miss.), 1911-12, Brooksville (Miss.), 1912-13; admitted to bar at Lexington and before Court of Appeals, Frankfort, Ky., 1910, United States Circuit Court of Appeals, 1926, Supreme Court of the United States, 1950; practice of law in partnership with bro., Linzy O. Thompson, Lexington, 1913-30; son became asso. with firm, June 1936. Dir. and sec. bd. dirs. Lexington Y.M.C.A., 1927-31. Mem. bd. adjustment, Lexington and Fayette Co. Planning and Zoning Commn., 1928-60, chmn., 1932-60. Democrat member Fayette Co. Election Commn., 1931-33. Fayette Co. campaign mgr. for former Senator and Gov. J. C. W. Beckham, 1927. Organizer Fayette Co. Roosevelt-Garner League, 1932. Mem. bd. dirs. Ky. Bapt. Found., 1950-59. Pres. Law Alumni, U. of Ky., 1937-38. Mem. Am. (ins., bus. law sects., Bankruptcy com. 1945-53), Ky. State, Fayette Co. bar assns., Coml. Law League of Am. (v.p. 1945-46, pres. 1946-47), Internat. Assn. Ins. Counsel and Fed. Ins. Counsel. Bapt. Clubs: Ky. Mountain (pres. 1936), Blue Grass Execs. (dir. 1944-46, pres. 1951-52). Home: Lexington, Ky. *

THOMPSON, HARRY CHARLES, publishing exec.; b. Yonkers, N.Y., Jan. 16, 1921; s. Charles Henry and Adele (Gross) T.; B.A., Colgate U., 1942; grad. Advanced Mgmt. Program, Harvard U.; m. Eleanor Louise Balcke, May 25, 1946; children—Charles, Katharine. Pub. relations exec. Newell Emmett Co., 1946; free-lance mag. writer, 1946; promotion mgr. Popular Publs., 1947-49; merchandising mgr. Time mag., 1949-51; promotion dir. Newsweek mag., 1951-58, exec. dir. Newsweek Internat., 1958-62, v.p., exec. dir., 1962-64, v.p., advt. dir., 1964-69; pub. Newsweek mag., 1969-72; exec. v.p., dir. Newsweek, Inc., 1969-72; pres. Mag. Networks Inc., N.Y.C., 1972-74, The Washingtonian Mag., 1972-74; v.p., asso. pub. U.S. News & World Report, 1975-80; partner Bourne-Thompson & Assos.; pub. The Dial, 1979-80; chmn. 13th World Congress, Internat. Advt. Assn., 1961. Bd. dirs. Colgate U. Alumni Corp. Served to lt. USNR, 1942-45. Mem. Mag. Mktg. Com. (chmn. 1968-70), Mag. Pub. Assn. (vice chmn. 1970-72, chmn. 1972-74, Phi Beta Kappa, Sigma Chi. Club: Univ. (N.Y.C.). Home: Westport, Conn. Died Apr. 20, 1980.

THOMPSON, HOMER COLUMBUS, educator; b. Montgomery County, Md., Jan. 5, 1885; s. Millard Fillmore and Julia Anna (Duvall) T.; B.Sc., Ohio State U., 1909, M.S., 1923, Ph.D., 1926; m. Clara Smith, June 20, 1912; children—Homer Smith (dec.), John Fanning, David Duvall. Asst. prof. horticulture, Miss. Agrl. and Mech. Coll., 1909-10; asso. prof. Clemson (S.C.) Agrl. Coll., 1910-11; asst. horticulturist U.S. Dept. Agr., Washington, D.C., 1911-13, horticulturist, 1913-18; prof. vegetable crops, Cornell U., from 1918, head dept., from 1921. Fellow A.A.A.S.; mem. Am. Soc. Hort. Science (pres. 1924), Am. Soc. Plant Physiologists, Sigma Xi. Methodist. Rotarian. Author: Vegetable Crops, 1923, 31, 39, 49; Sweet Potato Production and Handling, 1929; Asparagus Production, 1942. Home: Ithaca, N.Y. Died Apr. 12, 1976.

THOMPSON, JOHN CHARLES, newspaper editor; b. Jarrodsburg, Ky., July 15, 1979; s. John Charles and Laetitia (Magoffin) T.; ed. pub. schs., Cheyenne, Wyo.; m., Delia May Burke, Feb. 12, 1905; children—John Charles, Samuel Shelby, Philip Burton (dec.), Burton Beriah, Edward Beyerle (dec.) and Beriah Magoffin (twins). Began as miner, 1898; employed as stenographer, 1900; reporter Wyoming Tribune, 1900-02; reporter Cheyenne Leader, 1902-08, editor, 1908-11, reporter, 1919-20; assessor, Laramie County, 1911-12; reporter, Wyo. State Tribune, 1912-17 and 1920-24, editor since 1924; editor Wyo. Stockman Farmer since 1926; sec. to gov. of Wyo., 1917-18. Mem. Wyo. Hist. Landmarks Commn., 1939-42. Mem. S.A.R. Republican. Elk, Eagle. Author of daily hist. column, in Old Wyoming, pub. in Wyo. State Tribune and Wyo. Stockman Farmer; also of other Wyo. hist. articles. Home: Cheyenne, Wyo. *

THOMPSON, JOHN IRVIN, engring. and marketing cons.; b. Bellefonte, Pa., Jan. 12, 1907; s. George B. and Magdalene (Callaway) T.; B.S. in Civil Engring., Pa. State U., 1925; m. Gwenyth Bruyere, Jan. 12, 1927; children—John I., Owen B., Daniel B. Engr. and exec. Campbell Soup Co., 1939-43, Sharp & Dohme, Inc., 1937-39, Bristol-Myers Co., 1930-37, Central R.R. Co. of N.J., 1925-30; indsl. adviser and spl. lectr. on prodn. mgmt. Wharton Sch., U. Pa., 1940-42; cons. to Bur. Ordnance, Navy Dept., 1942-47; partner John I. Thompson & Co. (now Tracor Jitco, Inc.), Bay Head, N.J., 1943-79, pres., dir., 1945-79, chief engr., 1951-79, chmn. bd., 1968-79. Asst. adminstr. for marketing prodn. and marketing adminstrn., v.p., dir. Commodity Credit Corp., U.S. Dept. Agr., Washington, 1948-51; exec. com. Nat. Conf. on Adminstrn. of Research, 1959-70, chmn., 1964; U.S., rep. OECD Conf. on Research Mgmt., Monte Carlo, 1965. Trustee Oglethorpe U. Recipient medal for Merit Bur. Ordnance U.S. Navy, 1946. Mem. ASME, Inst. Food Technologists, Nat. Soc. Profl. Engrs. Republican. Presbyterian. Clubs: Congressional Country, Admirals, Dacor House, Metropolitan (Washington); Bay Head (N.J.) Yacht; Manasquan (N.J.) River Golf. Contbr. articles to profl. jours. Patentee in field. Address: Bay Head, N.J. Died Nov. 26, 1979; buried Bellefonte, Pa.

THOMPSON, LOUIS TEN EYCK, research engr.; b. South Haven, Mich., Oct. 24, 1891; s. Ten Eyck and Lucy Maria (Hall) T.; B.S., Kalamazoo Coll., 1914, Sc.D. (hon.), 1951; A.M., Clark University, 1915, Ph.D., 1917, D.Sc. (honorary), 1954; m. May Margaret Fraser, Aug. 27, 1913; children—May Margaret (Mrs. McDonald Wellford), Joan Eileen (Mrs. Bruce L. Hicks), Anne Fraser (Mrs. Leonard L. Graves), James Fraser; m. 2d, Margaret Marsden Bowles, Dec. 21, 1944. Instr. physics Clark Coll., 1917-18, asst. prof., 1918-19; prof. physics Kalamazoo Coll., 1920-24, Nat. Research Council fellow, 1920-23; physicist Naval Proving Ground, Dahlgren, Va., 1923-42; dir. research Carl L. Norden, Inc., also Lukas-Harold Corp., 1942-45; tech. dir. Naval Ordnance Test Sta., Inyokern, 1945-51; v.p. Norden Labs. Corp., 1952, exec. v.p., 1954-55; vice pres. research Norden-Ketay Corp., 1956-58; cons. Norden div. United Aircraft Corp., from 1958, Spl. Projects Office, Bur. Weapons, U.S. Navy, 1956-63. Sci. adv. bd. USAF, 1949-52; adv. bd. Naval Weapons Lab., Geophys. Inst. U. Alaska; vice chmn. Research, Development Bd., Dept. Def., 1953; chmn. tech. adv. panel on ordnance Dept. Def., 1954-59, mem. Def. Sci. Bd., Office Asst. Sec. Def., 1956-59; mem. adv. bd. USAF, USA, USN lab. programs, 1949-63, Geophys. Inst., U. Alaska, 1961-63. Distinguished Civilian Service Award, USN, 1952, Navy Distinguished Service award, 1961. Mem. A.A.A.S., American Physical Society, Sigma Xi. Club: Cosmos (Washington). Home: Scarsdale, N.Y. Died Dec. 13, 1978.

THOMPSON, LOYD, physician; b. Mercer, Pa., June 5, 1882; s. Andrew Burgess and Eliza (Martin) T.; Ph.B., Westminster Coll., New Wilmington, Pa., 1904; student Yale U. and U. of Southern Calif.; M.D., U. of Ark., 1910; m. Corinne Scull, Aug. 16, 1911. Pathologist to St. Vincent's Hosp., Little Rock, 1910-12; city bacteriologist, Little Rock, 1911-13; pathologist to Arkansas State Hospital for Nervous Diseases, 1912-14; instr. clin. diagnosis and dir. Clin. Lab., U. of Ark. Med. Dept., 1912-14; visiting physician, St. Joseph's Hosp., Hot Springs; formerly consulting pathologist, Leo N. Levi Memorial Hosp. and syphilologist to clinic of the Govt. Free Bath House Hot Springs, Ark. Founder Am. Jour. of Syphilis, editor, 1916-20. First lt. Med. Res.-Corps. Feb. 5, 1915; maj. Apr. 15, 1918; active duty, Aug. 1916-Mar. 1919; lt. col., Mar. 20, 1920; col. May 1, 1926; Fellow Am. Coll. Physicians; mem. Am., Calif. State, and San Diego County med. assns., Nu Sigma Nu. Republican. Author: For Old Eli (play), 1909; (with Wm. H. Deaderick), The Endemic Diseases of the Southern States, 1916; Syphilis, 1916, 2d edit., 1920; King of Mapledale (novel), 1926; The Great Red Plague (a treatise on syphilis for the laity), 1931; Wide is the Gate (novel), 1937; also numerous med. and non-med. articles and short stories. Home: San Diego, Calif. *

THOMPSON, MARY WOLFE (MRS. CHARLES D. THOMPSON), author; b. Winsted, Conn., Dec. 7, 1886; d. Theodore F. (M.D.) and Gertrude (Franklin) Wolfe; grad. N.J. State Normal Sch., Trenton, 1905; grad. study, 1906; grad. New York Sch. Fine and Applied Arts, 1915; student extension courses, Columbia, 1920-29; m. Charles D. Thompson, Sept. 11, 1915. Presbyn. Author several books since 1923; latest publs.: Hillhaven, 1949; The Steadfast Heart, 1951; also 1-act comedy; writer short stories. Home: Arlington, Vt. *

THOMPSON, RALPH, editor; b. West Orange, N.J., Nov. 11, 1904; s. Hugh and Francesca (Ornstein) T.; B.S., Dartmouth, 1925; Ph.D., Columbia, 1936; m. Marcia Aldrich Thompson, Dec. 14, 1955. Instr. various univs., 1926-31, 47-48; Fulbright vis. prof. U. Sheffield, Eng., 1949-50; asso. editor Current History, N.Y.C., 1932-36; daily book columnist N.Y. Times, 1936-42; contbg. editor Time mag., 1946-47; book columnist N.Y. Times Book Review, 1948-49; editor Book-of-the-Month Club, N.Y.C. from 1951, sec. from 1956. Author: American Literary Annuals and Gift Books, 1936. Translator: Uhde, Five Primitive Masters, 1948. Contbr. articles to mags. Home: New York, N.Y. Died Nov. 12, 1979; buried Prospect Hill Cemetery, Schuylerville, N.Y.

THOMPSON, RICHARD RYAN, b. Fulton, Ky., Jan. 23, 1878; s. Samuel and Clementine (Ryan) T.; A.B., Union Univ., Jackson, Tenn., 1899; A.M., U. of Mich., 1905; m. Anne Augusta Ellis, Aug. 2, 1927. Instr. Latin and French, Jefferson Davis Coll., Pittsburg, Tex., 1890-1901; prin. Wartrace (Tenn.) Training Sch., 1901-02; gen. sec. U. of Mich. Y.M.C.A, 1903-05; dean Crescent Coll., Eureka Springs, Ark., 1908-10, pres., 1910-38. Mem. Ark. State Senate, 1935-39. Pres. Eureka Springs Water Co. Lecturer. Mem. Ark. State Highway Commn., 1914-18; pres. Lake Lucerne County, Eureka Springs Ozarka Water Co. Democrat. Episcopalian, Elk. Club: Rotary. Home: Eureka Springs, Ark. *

THOMPSON, RUTH PLUMLY, author; b. Phila., Pa., July 27, 1895; d. George Plumly and Amanda Elton (Shuff) T.; grad. William Penn High Sch., Phila. Author numerous books, from 1922, including numerous Oz books; writer verse, articles, special advt. features, movie shorts, television program ideas and sketches, also stories for juvenile mags. Home: Malvern, Pa. Died Mar. 6, 1976.

THOMPSON, STANLEY GERALD, chemist; b. Los Angeles, Mar. 9, 1912; s. Stanley Good and Bessie (Sims) T.; A.B., U. Cal. at Los Angeles, 1934; Ph.D., U. Cal. at Berkeley, 1948; m. Alice Smith, Nov. 27, 1938; children—Ruth (Mrs. Kenneth Lincoln), Joyce (Mrs. Richard McClenney). Chemist, Standard Oil Co. Cal., Richmond, 1934-42; chemist metall. project U. Chgo., 1942-44, DuPont-Hanford Engr. Works, Richland, Wash., 1944-45, Metall. Lab., U. Chgo., 1945-46; chemist Lawrence Radiation Lab., U. Cal. at Berkeley, 1946-76. Guggenheim fellow, 1955, 65. Mem. Am. Chem. Soc. (award for nuclear applications in chemistry 1965), Am. Phys. Soc. Codiscoverer berkelium and californium, 1950, einsteinium and fermium, 1954, mendelevium, 1955; developed concept of radiochem. process for 1st indsl. scale separation and isolation of plutonium, 1942; research in nuclear fission. Home: Berkeley, Calif. Died July 16, 1976.

THOMPSON, THEOS JEFFERSON, univ. dean; b. Northville, S.D., Nov. 1, 1886; s. Charles Kier and Flora Belle (Torrence) T.; student Houghton (N.Y.) Coll., 1909-12, U. of Mich., summer 1912; A.B., U. of Neb., 1913, A.M., 1915, Ph.D., 1921; student U. of Chicago, summer 1919; LL.D., Houghton Coll., 1940; m. Mabel Elizabeth Dow, May 25, 1916; children—Theos Jardin, John Rutherford, Richard Dow. Prof. of chemistry, Miltonvale (Kan.) Wesleyan Coll., 1913-14, dean and prof., 1915-18; asst. in chemistry, U. of Neb., 1918-19, instr., 1919-21, asst. prof., 1921-25, asso. prof., 1925-27, pre-medic adviser, 1925, prof. and dean of student affairs since 1927. Chmn. State Basic Science Bd. in Medicine; mem. City Council, University Place, Neb. Mem. A.A.A.S., Am. Chem. Soc., Sigma Xi. Methodist. Contbr. to jours. Home: Lincoln, Neb. *

THOMPSON, W(IRT) FURNESS, hosp. exec.; b. Phila., Feb. 20, 1907; s. Wirt L. and Kate (Furness) T.; Ph.B., Yale, 1930; m. Eleanor Lewis, Apr. 18, 1940; children—Eleanor L., W. Furness, Kate F. With John Hancock Mut. Life Ins. Co., 1930-33, J. Clark Sims Advt. Agy., 1933-36; tech. coordinator Smith, Kline & French Labs., Phila., 1936-60, successively med. adminstr., asst. dir. research, v.p. research, devel., dir., cons. 1960; dir. devel. Pa. Hosp., 1962-63, treas., 1963-79. Member board of trustees Smith, Kline and French Foundation. Clubs: Rittenhouse (Phila.); Mill Dam (Wayne, Pa.). Author articles periodicals. Home: Villanova, Pa. Died Apr. 29, 1979.

THOMPSON, WILLIAM DONALD, educator; b. Kansas City, Mo., June 27, 1921; B.A., U. Kans., 1947, M.A., 1948, Ph.D., 1954; married; 4 children. Instr. in psychology U. Kans., 1949-54; research asso. psychophysiology Fels Research Inst., Antioch Coll., 1954-57, asst. prof. psychology, 1955-57; asso. prof. Baylor U., Waco, Tex., 1957-62, prof., dir. grad. studies, 1962-69, chmn. dept. psychology, 1969-79. Served to capt. AUS, 1942-46. Mem. Am. Psychol. Assn., Soc. Psychophysiol. Research. Home: Waco, Tex. Died Nov. 29, 1979.

THOMPSON, YEWELL REYNOLDS, educator; b. Hazlehurst, Miss., Nov. 26, 1912; s. Francis G. and Lula (Donahue) T.; B.A., Millsaps Coll., 1948; M.A., George Peabody Coll. Tchrs., 1949; Ed.D., U. Fla., 1954; m. Alice E. Jenkins, June 29, 1936; 1 son, Yewell Reynolds. Elementary classroom tchr., Copiah and Yazoo Counties, Miss., 1934-42, 46-47; prin. Ga. Tchrs. Coll. Lab. Sch., 1949-51; elementary sch. supr. Brevard County, Fla., 1953-55; chmn. programs in elementary and early childhood edn. Coll. Edn., U. Ala., University, 1955-75, head area curriculum and instrn., 1975-79. Served with AUS, 1942-46; CBI. Mem. Ala., Nat. edn. assns., Assn. Supervision and Curriculum Devel., Dept. Elementary Sch. Prins., Phi Delta Kappa, Kappa Phi Kappa. Mem. Christian Ch. Rotarian. Contbr. articles to bulls., chpts. in books. Home: Northport, Ala. Died Mar. 18, 1980; buried Tuscaloosa (Ala.) Meml. Park.

THOMS, HERBERT, physician, teacher; b. Waterbury, Conn., Jan. 5, 1885; s. William Peter and Adaline Delia (Hart) T.; M.D., Yale Univ., 1910; post grad. student Johns Hopkins Univ., 1914-15; m. Edith May Comstock, Aug. 21, 1912; 1 dau., Margaret Alison. Intern. Backus Hosp., Norwich, Conn., 1910-11; asst. resident Sloane Hosp. For Women, 1912; became prof. obstetrics and gynecology, chmn. dept. Yale Univ. Sch. Medicine, 1947, now prof. emeritus; curator Yale Medical School Library; member of the staff of Grace-New Haven Hosp., Meriden Hosp., New Britain Hosp., Hungerford Hosp., Norwalk Hosp., Stamford Hosp., Backus Hosp., Milford Hosp. Awarded Lasker Award, 1953. Mem. Am. Med Assn., American Gynecological Society. Clubs: Acorn. Beaumont Medical. Elizabethan. Author: The Estimation of Pelvic Capacity, 1940; The Obstetric Pelvis, 1935; Chapters in American Obstetrics, 1933; Classical Contributions to Obstetrics and Gynecology, 1935; Training for Childbirth, 1950; Understanding Natural Childbirth, 1950; Pelvimetry, 1956; The Doctors Jared of Connecticut, 1958; The Doctors of Yale College, 1701-1815, 1960; Our Obstetric Heritage, 1960; Sanuel Seabury, Priest and Physician, Bishop of Connecticut, 1963; Jared Eliot, Minister, Doctor, Scientist and His Connecticut, 1967; Yale Men and Landmarks in Old Connecticut, 1967. Home: Stony Creek, Conn. *

THOMSEN, WELLS HAMLEN, financial cons., govt. ofcl.; b. Cleve., Oct. 26, 1912; s. Mark Lawrence and Mary Louise (Hamlen) T.; A.B., Oberlin Coll., 1934; M.B.A., Harvard, 1936, M.P.A., 1943; m. Anna-Kathrine Hickok, Sept. 15, 1935; 1 dau., Wendy Hamlen; m. 2d, Kathrine Burch, Apr. 18, 1946. Prodn. scheduling and mgmt. incandescent lamp div. Gen. Electric Co., 1936-41; Littauer fellow Harvard, 1942-43; fed. budget exam. Exec. Office of Pres., Bur. Budget, 1943-53; dir. Office of Analysis and Rev., Dept. Navy, 1953-63, dep. dir. Offices Program Appraisal and Mgmt. Information, 1964-65; dir. logistics rev. Office Asst. Sec. Navy, 1965-71; municipal financial cons., 1971-80. Vice pres. North Ridge Citizens Assn., Alexandria, Va. Recipient Distinguished Civilian Service award, U.S. Navy, Joslin Diabetes Found. award, Eli Lilly and Co. award. Mem. Am. Soc. for Pub. Adminstrn. Home: Alexandria, Va. Died Feb. 29, 1980.

THOMSON, MARY MOORE DABNEY, coll. pres.; b. Raleigh, N.C., Aug 30, 1886; d. Charles William and Mary Chilton (Brent) Dabney; student Horace Mann Sch., N.Y. City, 1902-03, U. of Tenn., 1903-04, U. of Cincinnati, 1904-05; Litt.D., Beaver Coll., 1936; m. Alexander Thomson, May 9, 1907 (died June 27, 1939; children—Alexander (dec.), Mary Moore (dec.), Charles Dabney, Lewis Clark, Chilton. Acting pres. Western Coll. for Women, June 1941-June 1942, pres., June 1942-May 1945, chmn. bd. trustees since 1946. Mem. bd. Cincinnati Community Chest, 1932-34; president Woman's Committee, Cincinnati Symphony Orchestra; pres. Cincinnati Y.W.C.A, 1930-33, mem. nat. bd., 1932-33. Republican. Presbyterian. Clubs: Cincinnati Woman's, Cincinnati Country, Town. Home: Cincinnati, Ohio. *

THOMSON, ROY HERBERT, publisher; b. Toronto, Ont., Can., June 5, 1894; s. Herbert and Alice (Coombs) T.; ed. pub. schs., Toronto; D.Litt., St. John's Meml. U., Nfld.; D.C.L., N.B. U.; LL.D., No. Mich. U.; L.H.D.,

L.I. U.; m. Edna Alice Irvine, 1916 (dec.); children—Kenneth Roy, Irma Jacqueline (Mrs. I.J. Brydson) (dec.), Phyllis Audrey (Mrs. P.A. Campbell). Chmn., Thomson Orgn., Ltd. (and subsidiaries including The Time and The Sunday Times), The Scotsman Publs. Ltd., Thomson Newspapers, Ltd., Can.; dir. Security Trust Co. Birmingham Ltd., Royal Bank of Can. Trust Corp. Ltd., Imperial Life Assurance Co. Can. Ltd., Royal Bank of Can., Abitibi Pulp & Paper Co., Ltd.; trustee Reuters. Vice chmn. council Commonwealth Press Union. Founder, Thomson Found. Former chancellor Meml. U. Nfld. Served as lt. in Can. Militia, 1914-18. Created Baron of Fleet of Northbridge, City of Edinburgh, 1964; decorated comder Royal Order of Phoenix (Greece). Fellow Royal Soc. Arts, Brit. Inst. Mgmt.; mem. Worshipful Co. Stationery and Newspaper Makers (liveryman), Periodical Props. Assn. (v.p.) Publicity Club London (v.p.), Commonwealth Press Union (vice chmn. council). Home: London, England. Died Aug. 4, 1976.

THOMSON, SAMUEL HARRISON, educator, editor; b. Pasadena, Calif., Nov. 5, 1895; s. Williell and Clara F. (Thompson) T.; B.A., Princeton, 1923; Dr.Phil., Charles U., Prague, Czechoslovakia, 1925; B.Litt., Oxford U., 1926, D.Litt., 1942; m. Rosamund Vere Dargan, Jan. 30, 1936; children—Williell Riddett, Clara Day. Tutor modern langs. Princeton summer sch., 1922-31, co-prin., 1926-31; instr. Bibl. lit. Princeton, 1926-29; asst. prof. history Calif. Inst. Tech., 1929-31; fellow medieval history Huntington Library, 1929-30; traveling fellow Am. Council Learned Socs., 1931-33; asst. prof. modern history U. Chgo., 1934-35; asso. prof. European history and dir. admissions Carleton Coll., 1935-36; prof. history U. Colo., Boulder, 1936-75, dir. Center for Slavic and East European Studies, 1960-64; vis. prof. U. Mich., 1941, Ind. U., 1950-51, U. Wash., 1964-65, UCLA, 1965-66; mem. Inst. Advanced Study, Princeton, 1955-56; Masaryk lectr. U. Toronto, Can., 1949; Fulbright prof. U. Vienna, 1959. Served with U.S. Army in France, 1917-19; chief of outpost Office War Info., Czechoslovakia, 1945, spl. asst. to Am. ambassador to Czechoslovakia, 1945; dir. USIS, Warsaw, Poland and pub. affairs officer Am. embassy, Warsaw, 1945-46. Recipient Czechoslovakia state prize for lit. 1944. Fellow Polish Acad. Scis., Mediaeval Acad. Am. (past 1st v.p. Haskins medal 1971); hon. fellow Polish Inst. Arts and Scis. (council); mem. History Sci. Soc. (councillor 1947-53), Am. Council Learned Socs. and Social Sci. Research Council (mem. combined Slavic com. 1947-51, 1955-59; chmn. of the Western Slavic Conf., 1963), Am. Hist. Assn., Soc. Mediaeval Langs. and Lit. (Oxford), Am. Soc. Ch. History, Phi Beta Kappa; asso. Soc. Philosophique, Louvain. Republican. Presbyn. Club: Town and Gown (Boulder). Author or co-author books relating to field; latest: Handbook of Slavic Studies (with others), 1949; Czechoslovakia in European History, rev. edit., 1953; M.J. Hus De Ecclesia, 1956; Guide to Historical Literature, 1961; Europe in Renaissance and Reformation, 1963; Latin Bookhands of the Later Middle Ages, 1970. Editor: Progress of Medieval and Renaissance Studies in United States and Canada, 1936; founder editor Jour. Central European Affairs, 1941-75, Medievalia et Humanistica, 1943-75; mem. editorial bd. Am. Slavic and East European Rev., 1941-61. Contbr. articles on cultural history to numerous Am. and European jours. Home: Boulder, Colo. Died Nov. 19, 1975.

THORNDIKE, DAME SYBIL, actress; b. Gainsboro, Eng., Oct. 24, 1882; d. Arthur John Webster and Agnes McDonald (Bowers) Thorndike; student Sch. Music; m. Lewis Casson, Dec. 22, 1908; children—John, Christopher, Mary (Mrs. Ian Harvey), Ann (Mrs. Douglas Campbell). Profl. pianist; with Shakespearian Repertory in Am., 1905-07, Miss Horniman's Company, Manchester, Eng., 1908-09, Charles Frohman's Repertory, 1910; Am. tour with John Drew, 1910-11; leading roles with Miss Horniman's Company, 1911-13; Shakespearian leading roles with Old Vic Theatre, 1914-18; leading roles London prodns., 1919-20, Little Theatre, 1920-22, also Grand Guignol Theatre, London; TV appearances, numerous tours throughout world. LL.D., U. Manchester, Edinburgh U., D.Litt., Southampton U.; granted Freedom City Rochester; named dame comdr. British Empire. Address: London S.W.3, Eng. *

THORNE, DAVID WYNNE, soil scientist; b. Perry, Utah, Dec. 19, 1908; s. Milton Jefferson and Elmerta (Nelson) T.; student Weber Coll., Ogden, Utah, 1926-28; B.S., Utah State Agrl. Coll., 1933; M.S., Iowa State Coll., 1934, Ph.D., 1936; D.Sc., Utah State U., 1975, Marathwada Agrl. U., India, 1976; m. Alison Comish, Aug. 3, 1937; children—Kip, Barrie, Sandra, Avril, Lance. Research asst. prof. soils Ia. State Coll., 1936-37; research asso. in biochemistry, U. of Wis., summers 1937, 38; asso. prof. agronomy, Tex. A. and M. Coll., 1937-39: asso. prof. agronomy Utah State Agrl. Coll., Logan, 1939-47, prof. agronomy and head agronomy dept., 1947-55, acting dean grad. sch., 1949, prof. emeritus soil sci., 1974-79; ret., 1974; dir. Utah Agrl. Expt. Sta., 1955-65, 73-74, v.p. research, 1965-73. Chief soils and fertilizer research br. TVA, 1953-54; mem. Nat. Soil Research Com., 1948-50, chmn. Western Soil Research Com., 1948-51; mem. soil and water study group to Russia, 1958; mem. agrl. bd. NRC, 1970-76; bd. govs. Internat. Crops Research Inst. for Tropical Agr., Hyberdad, India, 1972-79; cons. world food, 1974-79. Fellow AAAS (sect. v.p. 1961), Am. Soc. Agronomy, Soil Conservation Soc. Am.; mem. Land Grant Coll. and Univs. Assn. (chmn. agr. expt. stas. sect. 1961-62), Soil Sci. Soc. Am. (pres. 1955-56), Western Soc. Soil Sci. (pres. 1953), Utah Acad. of Sci., Sigma Xi, Phi Kappa Phi, Phi Lambda Upsilon, Gamma Sigma Delta, Alpha Zeta. Mem. Ch. of Jesus Christ of Latter-day Saints. Author: Irrigated Soils, Their Fertility and Management (with Howard B. Peterson), 1949; Soil, Water and Crop Production (with Marlowe D. Thorue), 1979. Contbr. numerous sci. articles on chemistry and fertility of arid region soils and on soil microbiology to tech. and sci. pubs. Home: Logan, Utah. Died Feb. 15, 1979.

THORNE, THOMAS ELSTON, educator; b. Lewiston, Maine, Oct. 5, 1909; s. Addison Elston and Fannie (Carter) T.; grad. Portland (Me.) Sch. Fine and Applied Art, 1932; B.F.A., Yale, 1940; m. Lelia Agry Bancroft, Feb. 12, 1934; 1 son, Bancroft Agry. Mem. faculty Coll. William and Mary, from 1940, prof. fine arts, 1965-75, prof. emeritus, 1975-76, head dept., 1943-70; exhbns. include Pa. Acad. Fine Arts, N.Y. Water Color Club, Boston Art Club, Boston Soc. Ind. Artists, Grace Horne Gallery, Boston, Gloucester (Mass.) Soc. Artists, Balt. Mus., Va. Mus. Fine Art, Norfolk (Va.) Mus. Arts and Scis., U. Ga., Hobart Coll., Tidewater Artists, others. Pres., Va. Art Alliance, 1947; dir. Va. Nat. Art Week, 1953. Chmn., Williamsburg Community Fund, 1960. Bd. dirs. Williamsburg Community Center, 1954. Recipient Purchase award Va. Mus. Fine Arts, 1945, 47. Mem. Coll. Art Assn. Episcopalian (vestryman). Contbr. articles to profl. jours. Murals in James Blair High Sch., Community Center, Maine Gen. Hosp. Home: Williamsburg, Va. Died Nov. 7, 1976.

THORNTON, ELLA MAY, librarian; b. Atlanta, Ga., Apr. 28, 1885; dau. Eugene Hascal and Emma (Neal) Thornton; student Walnut Hill Sch., Natick, Mass., 1900-03; certificate library sch., Carnegie Library of Atlanta, 1909; unmarried. With Ga. State Library since 1909, legislative reference librarian, 1914-18, asst. state librarian, 1919-26, state librarian, 1926-54, retired, named hon. state librarian for life; lecturer Emory U. School of Library Science, 1926-39. Awarded His Majesty's medal for Service in the cause of Freedom, by King George VI, 1946; citation for service Ga. Soc. Hist. Research, 1947. Hon. mem. Ga. Bar Assn. Mem. Ga. Hist. Commn. (mem. bd. 1926-31), Ga. Library Commn. (mem. bd. 1926-43), Ga. Library Assn. (planning com. 1935-43, state library survey com. 1946), Am. Assn. Law Libraries, Nat. Assn. State Libraries (sec. 1934, vice pres. 1935, pres. 1936), Atlanta Hist. Society, English Speaking Union (Atlanta branch vice president), Georgia Historical Society, Atlanta Voters Guild, Atlanta Music Club, Atlanta Art Assn. Democrat. Baptist. Atlanta Woman of the Year in Professions, 1951. Contbr. to library, law, hist. jours. Home: Atlanta. *

THORP, CHARLES M., JR., lawyer; b. Pitts., Mar. 9, 1895; s. C.M. and Jessie M. (Boulton) T.; A.B., Cornell U., 1916; LL.B., Harvard, 1919; m. Virginia G. Eicher, Feb. 16, 1933 (div. 1958); children—Winona (Mrs. Robert C. Hodgkins) (dec.), Jessie B. (Mrs. Andreae) (dec.), Charles M. III; m. 2d, Carlotta W. Samson, Sept. 15, 1964. Admitted to Pa. bar, 1919, practiced in Pitts., from 1919; partner Thorp, Reed & Armstrong, and predecessor firms; dir. Homestead Industries, Inc., West Elizabeth Lumber Co., White Consol. Industries, Inc. Mem. Republican Finance Com. Allegheny County. Mem. Am., Pa., Allegheny County bar assns., Cornell U. Council, Newcomen Soc. N.Am., Pa. Soc., Theta Delta Chi. Presbyn. Clubs: Duquesne, Oakmont Country, Fox Chapel Golf (Pitts.). Editor: Harvard Law Rev., 1917-19. Composer for piano, organ. Home: Pittsburgh, Pa. Died Nov. 5, 1976.

THORP, HARRY WEBSTER, company dir.; b. Guelph, Ont., Can., Dec. 5, 1885; s. George J. and Maud (Tanner) T.; ed. Guelph schs.; m. Martha Murdock Scott, June 1, 1914; 1 son, Harry Douglas. Past vice chmn. Canadian Pittsburgh Industries Ltd.; now dir. Texaco Can. Ltd., Foster Wheeler Ltd., Columbian Carbon (Can.) Ltd., Dominion Textile Co. Ltd. Clubs: Mt. Royal (Montreal); St. James's; Mt. Bruno Country. Home: Montreal Que., Can. *

THORSON, HARRY TORVAL, Republican nat. committeeman; b. Milan, Minn., Aug. 17, 1902; s. Gulmun and Anne (Graves) T.; m. Inga Corinne Gysland, June 24, 1929; children—James Donald, Mary Lynne, Thomas Alan. Asst. instr. commerce N.D. Agrl. Coll., 1921-22; with Ill. Pipe Line Co., 1923-32; mgr. Osage Trust, oil and gas producers, 1932-41; ind. oil producer, 1941-76; organizer Black Hills Bentonite Co., Moorcroft, Wyo., 1947, pres., 1947-76; owner, operator farm, Woodworth, N.D. Chmn. Wyo. Republican State Com. and mem. Republican Nat. Com., 1955-76; mem. Wyo. Jud. Nominating Commn., Wyo. Yellowstone Centennial Com.; bd. dirs. Fedn. Rocky Mountain States. Mem. Rocky Mountain Oil and Gas Assn. (dir.), Am. Petroleum Inst. Lutheran. Mason (Shriner), Elk. Club: Lions (Newcastle, Wyo.). Home: Newcastle, Wyo. Died Sept. 24, 1976.

THRASH, JOSEPH MERIWETHER, coll. pres.; b. Gay, Ga., Feb. 19, 1885; s. Elmore Callaway and Sara Frances (Andrews) T.; father mem. covered wagon party, driving through to Calif., 1849; college training Ga. Sch. of Tech., 1903-05; spl. studies, Mercer U., Macon, 1928; m. Jimmie Estelle Estes, Oct. 6, 1907; children—Joseph Meriwether, Elmore Callaway. Chief engr., State of Ga., 1905-06; supt. Warm Springs, Ga., summers, 1915-17; head dept. of mathematics and mechanic arts, Agrl. and Mech. Sch., Douglas, Ga., 1907-10, head of sch., 1919-27; pres. South Georgia since 1927; head dept. of mathematics and mech. arts, Agrl. and Mech. Sch., Tifton, Ga., 1910-19. In charge Ga. State Arsenal, 1905-06. Mem. Ga. Legislature, 1927-28, 1929-30, extra session, 1931, also member, 1943-46 (chmn. education com.); chmn. Univ. of Georgia and its Branches (Com.; pres. Douglas Chamber of Commerce, 1932, v.p., 1932-36. Dist. chairman Okefenokee Area Council, Boy Scouts of America; mem. state-wide com. on Kiwanis education; introduced football in South Georgia schools, 1908. Mem. Ga. Tech. Industrial Tour, apptd. by Gov. Hugh Dorsey, 1920, to visit various cities and industrial instns. throughout the North and East; apptd. del. from Ga. by Gov. Cliff Walker to Nat. Good Roads Meeting, Calif., 1926; apptd. by Gov. Hardman as mem. spl. com. to inspect all depts. of state, 1927. Apptd. by Gov. Arnall on Veterans Edn. Council, serving from 1943 to 1946. Dist. commr. Boy Scouts of America, 1942, nat. rep., 1943-47; congl. dist. chmn. Infantile Paralysis drive, 1944. Mem. adv. bd. Coffee County Bank. Mem. A.A.A.S., Am. Assn. Sch. Administrators, Georgia Education Assn. (legislative com.), National Education Assn. (membership com.), Anak Soc. Democrat. Baptist. Mason (Shriner); mem. K.P., Elks (dist. deputy grand exalted ruler for Georgia East, 1939; exalted ruler (1943) and trustee Douglas Lodge), W.O.W., Jr. Order United Am. Mechanics. Clubs: Cracker Country, Kiwanis (pres. 1925, 1936). Home: Douglas, Ga. *

THRASHER, CHARLES ORVAL, army officer; b. Paxton, Ill., Dec. 9, 1886, s. Charles Edward and Charlotte (Barnes) T.; grad. U. of Ill., Class of 1910; m. Ethel W. Rorer, Jan. 3, 1912; children—Frances, Leonard, Charles, Joan. Entered first Officers Training Camp, Fort Sheridan, Ill., 1917; commd. 2d lt., Q.M.C., U.S. Army, 1917, advancing through the grades to brig. gen., 1944; served with A.E.F. in France, 1918-19; post quartermaster, Hawaii, 1933-1936; planned supply scheme to be developed on West Coast in case of war while on tour of duty at San Francisco Port of Embarkation, 1936-40; organized and comd. Seattle Port of Embarkation, 1940-41; organized and comd. Seattle Gen. Depot, 1942; on duty overseas since 1942; as mem. staff of Gen. John C. H. Lee, Service of Supplies comdr. for European Theatre of Operations, planned supply installations supporting assault on Europe and later comd. Southern Base Sect., hdqrs. nr. Salisbury, carrying out work of Service of Supply below a line (roughly) east and west through London, 1942-43; also mounted assault on Europe for Army of Liberation, 1943-44; comdg. Oise Sect., France, since Sept. 1944. Awarded Legion of Merit Bronze Star. Protestant. Mason. Home: Gilman, Ill. *

THROCKMORTON, EDNA JENIZA DUDLEY (MRS. TOM BENTLEY THROCKMORTON), orgn. ofcl.; b. Malta, Ill., July 2, 1886; d. Homer Price and Elitha Recardo (Ginn) Dudley; student Simpson Coll., Indianola, Ia., 1903-05, Des Moines U., 1905-06, Cummings Art Sch., Des Moines, 1906-07, Louise Bennett Weber Conservatory of Music, Des Moines, 1906-07; m. Tom Bentley Throckmorton, Jan. 21, 1911 (dec. July 1961); children—Tom D., Robert B., Hobart Hare (dec.), James Priestley. Supr. music and art, pub. sch., Harlan, Ia., 1908-10; Washington Ia., 1911. Third v.p.-gen. Nat. Soc. D.A.R., 1944—, chmn. auditing Constn. Hall, resolutions coms., pres. Nat. Chmn.'s Assn., regional dir. Nat. Officer's Club; pres. Past Pres.'s Assn. Des Moines Women's Club, 1965. Mem. Abigail Adams chpt. D.A.R. (regent 1931-33, hon. regent, chmn. 1963—), Ia. Soc. D.A.R. (pres.), Colonial Dames Am., Daus. Colonial Wars, Daus. Am. Colonists (state regent, nat. historian), Daus. of Barons of Runeymede, New Eng. Women, Daus. of Founders and Patriots Am., Roosevelt High Sch. P.T.A. (pres.), Polk County Med. Aux. (pres.), State Med. Aux. (v.p., sec.), Women's Aux. to A.M.A. (com. mem.), Women's Program for Inter-State Post Grad. Med. Assn. of N.A. (arrangements chmn.), P.E.O. Mem. mil. staff Gov. of Ia., rank of lt. comdr., 1943-44. Republican. Methodist (parliamentarian Women's Soc. Christian Service). Sisterhood, Order Eastern Star. Clubs: Des Moines Women's (pres.), Chauncey Depew (parliamentarian). Home: Des Moines IA. *

THROCKMORTON, RAY IAMS, agronomist; b. Waynesburg, Pa., Dec. 10, 1886; s. James Buchanan and Nancy Clarissa (Iams) T.; student Waynesburg Coll., 1905-07; B.S., Pa. State Coll., 1911; M.S., Kan. State Agrl. Coll., 1922; post-grad. study, Cornell U., 1922-23; m. Marcia Story, June 10, 1916; children—Celeste Jane, Ray Iams, Marcia Marie. Asst. in soil survey, Kan. State Coll., 1911-12, asst. prof. soils, 1913-16, asso. prof. agronomy, 1916-18, prof. soils, 1918-25, prof.

agronomy and head dept., 1925-46, dean agriculture and dir. agrl. expt. sta. since 1946; cons. agronomist U.S. Dept. Agriculture since 1937; grad. asst. Cornell U., 1922-23. Fellow American Society Agronomy (pres. 1934), A.A.A.S., Soil Conservation Society of America; member Soil Science Society of America, Sigma Xi, Phi Kappa Phi, Alpha Zeta, Gamma Sigma Delta, Ph Kappa Alpha, Republican. Presbyterian. Contbg. author to Southern Field Crop Enterprises, 1928, and to Northern Field Crop Enterprises, 1928, consultant Country Gentleman since 1946. Author of many exptl. sta. bulletins, also popular and tech. articles on agrl. subjects. Home: Manhattan Kan. *

THURBER, HAROLD HEATH, advt. exec.; b. Terre Haute, Ind., July 7, 1905; s. Walter Dennison and Viola (Runnels) T.; student Indpls. pub. schs.; m. Marie Gilliam, July 28, 1928; 1 son, Timothy Barton; m. 2d, Carol P. Lynn, July 5, 1968; 1 son, Harold Lynn Barton. With Indpls. newspapers, 1922-24, Central Ind. Power Co., Indpls., 1924-25; mgr. radio sta. WFBM, 1924-25; with McJunkin Advt. Co., Chgo., 1926. Sweeney & James Co., Cleve., 1927, Tracy-Locke-Dawson, Inc., Dallas, 1928-34; v.p., chmn. operating com. D'Arcy Advt. Co., St. Louis, 1934-45; mng. partner Ewell & Thurber Assos., Toledo, 1945-56; exec. v.p., dir. Wade Advt. Agy., Chgo., 1956-60; pres., dir. Wade Advt., Inc., 1960-65; sr. v.p., mgr. Chgo. operations Lennen & Newell, Inc., 1965-66; exec. v.p. AM-AD, Inc., Chgo., 1967-68; adminstrv. v.p. Clinton E. Frank, Inc., 1968-71; v.p. Henderson Advt. Agy., Chgo., 1971-75. Served as maj. G-2 sect. AUS, 1942-45. Mem Am. Assn. Advt. Agys. (chmn. Chgo. council). Republican. Episcopalian. Home: Chicago, Ill. Died Nov. 24, 1976.

THURMAN, HOWARD, clergyman; b. Daytona Beach, Fla., Nov. 18, 1900; s. Saul Solomon and Alice (Ambrose) T.; A.B., Morehouse Coll., 1923, D.D. (hon.) 1935; B.D., Rochester Theol. Sem., 1926; D.D., Wesleyan Coll., Conn., 1946; D.D. (hon.), Lincoln U., Howard U., 1955; Oberlin Coll., 1958, Boston U., 1967; H.H.D., Ohio Wesleyan U., 1954, Va. State U., 1959; LL.D., Washington U., 1955, Allen U., 1954; Litt.D., Tuskeegee Inst., 1956; L.H.D., Fla. Normal Coll., 1961; m. Sue E. Bailey, June 12, 1932; children—Anne (Mrs. C. Chiarenza), Olive (Mrs. Wong). Ordained to ministry Bapt. Ch., 1925; pastor Mt. Zion Bapt. Ch., Oberlin, Ohio, 1926-28; prof. religion Morehouse Coll., 1928-31; prof. systematic theology, dean of chapel Howard U., Washington, 1932-44; pastor Ch. for Fellowship of all Peoples, San Francisco, 1944-53; dean Marsh Chapel, 1953-64, emeritus, 1964-81; prof. spiritual disciplines and resources Boston U., 1953-65, univ. minister-at-large, 1964-65; vis. prof. Sch. Religion Earlham Coll., 1966, Presbyn. Theol. Sem., Louisville, 1967; Ingersol lectr. immortality of man Harvard, 1947; Merrick lectr. Ohio Wesleyan U., 1953; Ratcliff lectr. Tufts U., 1957; lectr. Beech Quiet Hour, Bangor Theol. Sem., 1958; Earl lectr. Pacific Sch. Religion, 1959; Smith Wilson lectr. Southwestern U., 1960; Mendenhall lectr. DePauw U., 1961; Wilson lectures Nebr. Wesleyan U., 1961; Theme lectr. gen. council United Church Can., 1962; Quaker lectr. Earlham Coll., 1962; Billings lectr. U. Hawaii, 1964; Oswald McCall Meml. lectr., Berkeley, Calif., 1964; hon. canon Cathedral St. John the Divine, N.Y.C., 1975; Earl lectr. Pacific Sch. Religion, 1977. Bd. dirs. Meals for Millions, Urban League Greater Boston, Inc., Travelers Aid Soc., Hampton Inst. Fellow Nat. Council Religion Higher Edn., Am. Acad. Arts and Scis.; mem. Fellowship of Reconciliation. Clubs: Fed. City (Washington), Book of Calif., Mass. Schoolmasters. Author: The Greatest of These, 1945; Deep River, 1946, rev. 1955; Mediations for Apostles of Sensitiveness, 1947; The Negro Spiritual Speaks of Life and Death, 1947; Jesus and the Disinherited, 1948; Deep is the Hunger, 1951; Meditations of the Heart, 1953; The Creative Encounter, 1954; Apostles of Sensitiveness, 1956; The Growing Edge, 1956; Footprints of a Dream, 1959; The Inward Journey, published 1961; Temptations of Jesus, 1962; Disciplines of the Spirit, 1963; The Luminous Darkness, 1965; The Centering Moment, 1969; The Search for Common Ground, 1971; A Track to the Water's Edge, 1973; The Mood of Christmas, 1973. Contbr. Interpreter's Bible, Volume 7. Address: San Francisco, Calif. Died Apr. 15, 1981.

THURSTON, LLOYD, ex-congressman; b. Osceola, Ia., Mar. 27, 1880; s. S. and Margaret (Maloy) T.; LL.B., State U. of Ia., 1902; m. Louella Bolibaugh, 1910. Admitted to Iowa bar, 1902, and began practice at Osceola; county atty. Clarke County, Ia., 1906-10; mem. Ia. Senate, 1920-24; mem. 69th to 72d Congresses (1925-33), 8th Ia. Dist., and 73d to 75th Congresses (1933-39), 5th Ia. Dist. Successively, mem. Rules, Appropriations and Ways and Means Coms. Served in Spanish-Am. War, Philippine Insurrection and World War I. Mem. Library Bd., Farm Bureau, Am. Legion, United Spanish War Vets., Pioneer Lawmakers Assn.; Caribou Soc., Rotary Internat., Isaak Walton League of Am. Republican. Protestant. Home: Osceola, Ia. *

THURSTON, RAYMOND LEROY, ambassador, coll. ofcl.; b. St. Louis, Feb. 4, 1913; s. Charles LeRoy and Hazel May (Ruth) T.; student Washington U., St. Louis, 1930-31; B.A. with highest honors, U. Tex., 1931-34, M.A., 1935; Ph.D., U. Wis., 1937; postgrad. Russian, Fgn. Service Inst., 1948; grad. Nat. War Coll., 1951-52; m. Elizabeth Sherman, Nov. 30, 1934; 1 dau., Ruth; m. 2d, Gabriella Mariani, Jan. 29, 1970. Joined U.S. Fgn. Service, 1937; vice consul in Can., Italy, India, 1937-45; asst. chief div. Middle Eastern, later S. Asian affairs State Dept., 1945-49; 1st sec., later counselor embassy, Moscow, USSR, 1949-51; dep. dir., later dir. Office Eastern European affairs State Dept., 1952-55; counselor embassy, dep. chief mission, Athens, Greece, 1955-57; counselor embassy, Paris, France, also polit. adviser to SHAPE, 1957-61; alternate rep. U.S. delegation to NATO, 1961; dep. dir. operations center State Dept., 1961; U.S. ambassador to Haiti, 1961-63; State Dept. adviser to Air U., 1963-65; ambassador to Somali Republic, Mogadiscio, 1965-69; vis. asso. prof. polit. sci. U. Nev., 1969-70, lectr. polit. sci., 1970-71; vis. prof. govt. Chapman Coll. World Campus Afloat, Orange, Calif., 1971-76, dir. program devel., 1971-76, asso. prof. internat. studies, dean, 1972-74, East Coast rep., 1975-76; Fla. rep. Lifelong Learning, Inc., 1975-81; acad. adv. bd. Inst. Shipboard Edn., 1976-81. Adviser U.S. del. to UN Security Council and Gen. Assembly, 1947-50, U.S. dels. internat. confs. Bermuda, Berlin, Geneva, 1953-54; attached to ICA, 1956-57. Founder, Anglo-Am. Childrens Sch., Moscow, 1949. Mem. Am. Fgn. Service Assn., Am. Polit. Sci. Assn., DACOR House, Phi Beta Kappa. Editor: Fgn. Service Jour., 1952-55. Contbr. articles to profl. jours. Home: Siesta Key, Fla. Died May 12, 1981; buried Rock Creek Cemetery, Washington, D.C.

TIBBETTS, MILTON, patent lawyer; b. Washington, D.C., July 27, 1879; s. Noah V. and Ida May (Tibbetts) T.; LL.B., George Washington U., 1903; m. Anne Reville Hallam, Sept. 16, 1903; children—Alice Reville (Mrs. Roy E. Stringer), Sallie Hallam (Mrs. Gerald S. Black). Admitted to practice, U.S. Patent Office, 1903, Supreme Court Dist. of Columbia, 1903, U.S. Court of Appeals for D.C., 1903, U.S. Dist. Ct., Eastern Dist. of Mich., 1910, U.S. Supreme Ct., 1927, U.S. Ct. Customs and Patent Appeals, 1936, State Bar of Mich., 1936; practiced patent law in Washington, D.C., 1903-07; patent counsel, Packard Motor Car Co., Detroit, Mich., 1907-30, v.p. and patent counsel, since 1930. Mem. Detroit Bd. of Commerce, Sec. of Commerce's com. on patent law, 1937-45. Mem. Am. Bar Assn. (mem. patent sect.), American Patent Law Association (past president), Mich. Patent Law Assn. (president several terms), Automobile Mfrs. Assn., Nat Assn. Mfrs., Kappa Sigma. Republican. Conglist. Clubs, Golf Athletic, Detroit. Home: Detroit. *

TIBBOTT, HARVE, ex-congressman; born Ebensburg, Pa., May 27, 1885; s. Sherman and Elizabeth (Rowland) T.; Ph.G., U. of Pittsburg Sch. Pharmacy, 1906; m. Mary Eldora Humphreys, Sept. 16, 1908; 1 son, Rowland Humphreys. Engaged as pharmacist and propr. Tibbott's Corner Drug Store, Ebensburg, Pa., since 1906; pres. First Nat. Bank of Ebensburg since 1938; dir. Cambria Thrift Corp. Treas. Cambria Co., 1932-36. Mem. Rep. State Com., 1936-37. Mem. 76th to 80th Congresses (1930-49), 26th Pa. Dist. Pres. Ebensburg Y.M.C.A. Mem. Beta Phi Sigma. Republican. Mem. Christian Ch. Mason (33 deg., Shriner, Past Potentate). Club: Kiwanis of Ebensburg (past pres.). Home: Ebensburg, Pa. *

TIDBALL, VOLNEY JEAN (TID'BAWL), judge; b. Bozeman, Mont., Apr. 7, 1883; s. Lewis Cass and Jennie Elizabeth (Kelly) T.; grad. high sch., Sheridan, Wyo., 1901; A.B., U. of Wyo., 1905; LL.B., U. of Mich., 1908; m. Gertrude Ellen Ponting, July 15, 1913; children—Volney Jean, Marjorie Ellen, Mary Grace, David Charles. Admitted to Wyo. bar, 1909, and practiced at Laramie until 1913; judge, Dist. Court, 2d Jud. Dist., Wyo., since 1913; lecturer on practice and procedure, Law Coll., U. of Wyo. Chmn. legal advisory bd., Selective Draft, Albany County, Wyo., World War. Mem. bd. trustees, U. of Wyo., 1909-13. Mem. Wyo. State Bar Assn., Phi Beta Kappa, Phi Kappa Phi. Democrat. Clubs: Lions, Jesters. Home: Laramie, Wyo. *

TIDWELL, MOODY RUDOLPH, air force officer; b. Miami, Okla., Apr. 9, 1903; s. Moody Ruolph and Kate (Peebles) T.; student Western Mil. Acad., 1918; LL.B., U. Okla., 1923; m. Dorothy Thompson, Sept. 2, 1923; 1 son, Moody Rudolph III. Admitted to Okla., D.C. bars, also U.S. Supreme Ct.; with First Nat. Bank, Miami, Okla., 1923-26; partner Berry-Tidwell Motor Co., Enid, Okla., 1927-28; pvt. practice, Miami, 1928-40; commd. capt. U.S. Army, 1940, advanced through grades to maj. gen. USAF, 1958; chief claims div. Office Chief Finance, U.S. Army, Washington, 1940-42; mem. War Dept. bd. contract appeals Office Under Sec. War, 1943-49; staff judge adv. Hdqrs. Far East Air Forces, Tokyo, Japan, 1949-52, Hdqrs. Air Material Command, Dayton, O., 1952-60; asst. judge adv. gen. Hdqrs. USAF, Washington, 1960-63. Decorated Legion of Merit with 2 oak leaf clusters, Bronze Star, Army Commendation award; recipient Distinguished Service award U.S. Jr. C. of C., 1934. Mem. Am., Okla., Dayton bar assns., Judge Adv. Assn., Kappa Sigma, Phi Delta Phi. Clubs: Army Navy Country (Arlington); Army Navy (Washington). Home: Arlington, Va. Died Jan. 13, 1979.

TIDWELL, ROBERT EARL, educator; b. Blount Springs, Ala., July 21, 1883; s. Robert and Nannie (Graves) T.; B.S., U. Ala., 1905, LL.D., 1927; A.M., Columbia, 1925, supts. diploma, Teachers Coll., 1925; LL.D., Birmingham-So. Coll., Ala., 1923; m. Bessie Sargent, July 6, 1906 (dec. April 1928); m. 2d, Bessye Veach, Feb. 3, 1930. Prin. Ensley High Sch., Birmingham, Ala., 1906-12; supt. Tenn. Coal, Iron and R.R. Co. Schs., Birmingham, 1912-18; dir. tchr. tng. State Dept. Edn., Montgomery, Ala., 1918-27; asst. state supt. edn. Ala., 1920-27, state supt. edn., 1927-29; dean extension div., prof. edn. U. Ala., 1930-54, now emeritus; asst. to pres. Stillman Coll., 1954-64, acting dean, 1957-60, chmn. div. social sci., 1955-59; edn. cons. ICA, Baghdad, Iraq, 1956-57. Mem. several ednl. survey groups; mem. dept. supervision and curriculum devel.; lectr. on edn. Summer Tng. Sch., Halifax, N.S., 1928. Life deacon First Baptist Ch. of Tuscaloosa. Tidwell Hall at U. Ala., Birmingham, named for him. Mem. Ala. Ednl. Assn., N.E.A. (mem. exec. com. dept. rural edn. 1952-56), Nat. U. Extension Assn. (exec. com. 1940-41, pres. 1947-48, Julius M. Nolte award 1968), Nat. Soc. for Study Edn., Am. Assn. Adult Edn., Am. Council on Edn. (del.), Am. Assn. Sch. Adminstrs., Phi Beta Kappa, Phi Delta Kappa, Kappa Delta Pi, Kappa Phi Kappa, Kappa Sigma. Democrat. Mason, Rotarian. Club: University. Author ann. reports State Bd. Edn. Ala., 1927-30, Ala. Unified Equalization Ednl. Program, 1927; Teacher Training in Alabama; Planning Improvement in Rural Living through the Schools; Adult Education in a Free Society, 1955; also biography Pastors First Bapt. Ch., Tuscaloosa, 1968. Contbr. articles to various mags. and jours. Home: Tuscaloosa, Ala. Died Jan. 18, 1977; interred Memory Hill Gardens, Tuscaloosa.

TIFFANY, HENRY WALTER, clergyman; b. Middleburg, Va., July 23, 1885; s. William Swartz and Tacy (Hixon) T.; Th.B., Southern Baptist Theol. Seminary, 1907, Th.M., 1918, Th.D., 1920, B.A., Davis & Elkin Coll., 1915, post-grad. student, Washington & Lee University, 1922-23; m. Carrie Beatrice Engle, October 30, 1907; children—Walter Maclaren, Elizabeth Engle, Harold Boyce. Pastor of Baptist Church, New Martinsville, West Virginia, 1907-09, Baptist Church, West Union, W.Va., 1909-12, Elkins, 1912-17, Deer Park, Louisville, Ky., 1917-22, Lexington, Va., 1922-23, Ch. of the Redeemer, Brooklyn, N.Y., 1923-30; pastor Park Lace Baptist Ch., Norfolk, Va., since 1930. Mem. exec. com. of the Southern Baptist convention. Trustee Watchman Examiner, Eastern Theological Seminary, Philadelphia, Pa. Mason. Club: Norfolk Golf. Home: Norfolk, Va. *

TIGRETT, ISAAC BURTON (TI'GRET), ry. official; b. Friendship, Tenn., Sept. 15, 1879; s. Samuel King and Elizabeth Alice (Nunn) T.; ed. Union U., Jackson Tenn., 1898, LL.D., 1930; LL.D., Shurtleff Coll., Alton, Illinois, 1948; m. Mary Sue Kennedy, July 20, 1904. Cashier Bank of Halls, Tenn., 1899-1903; cashier Union Bank & Trust Co., Jackson, Tenn., 1903-12; pres. Birmingham & Northwestern Ry., 1912-19; pres. Gulf, Mobile & Northern R.R., 1919-40, Gulf, Mobile & Ohio R.R. since 1940. Trustee Union U. since 1904, acting pres., 1909-11; trustee U. of Tenn. since 1913. V.p. (for Tenn.) Am. Bankers' Assn., 1911-12; pres. Tenn. Bankers' Assn., 1908-09; mem. Sigma Alpha Epsilon. Democrat. Baptist. Mason. Clubs: Rotary (hon.), Union League (Chicago); Noonday (St. Louis, Mo.). Home: Jackson, Tenn. *

TILGHMAN, WILLIAM BELL (TIL'MAN), mfr.; b. Salisbury, Md., Oct. 30, 1884; s. William Beauchamp and Annie Esther (Bell) T.; Eastman Coll., Poughkeepsie, N.Y., 1903; m. MaBelle Gray Sterling, June 5, 1919; children—Jean Sterling (Mrs. Gary Thomas Todd), Wm. Beauchamp, Samuel Sterling. Mfg. fertilizers since 1908; now pres. W. B. Tilgham Co.; dir. Salisbury Nat. Bank, Salisbury Bldg. & Loan Assn. Mem. staff Governor Goldsborough, rank of col. Del. Rep. Nat. Conv., 1912. Methodist. Scottish Rite Mason, Rotarian. Home: Salisbury, Md. *

TILLOTSON, MINER RAYMOND, regional dir. Nat. Park Service; b. Vermillion County, Ind., Oct. 2, 1886; s. Dr. Demetrius and Eusiba (Wishard) T.; student Northwestern U., 1904-05; B.S. in civil engring., Purdue U., 1908; m. Winifred Shawcross, July 7, 1909; children—Wishard Dean, Winifred Jean. Engr. and exec. with U.S. Forest Service, 1908-19; constrn. engr. Standard Oil Co., 1920-21; resident engr. Grand Canyon Nat. Park, 1922-27, supt., 1927-38; regional dir. Nat. Park Service, U.S. Dept. of Interior, Region 1, Jan. 1, 1939-Aug. 15, 1940, Region 3 since Aug. 15, 1940. Chmn. U.S. Commission apptd. by State Dept. to meet with a similar Mexican Commission to formulate plans and policies for the development of International Parks, Forest Reserves and Wildlife Refuges along the boundary between the U.S. AND Mexico. Mem. Nat. Conf. on State Parks, Am. Planning and Civic Assn., Delta Upsilon. Mason (32 deg., Shriner). Author: Grand Canyon Country. (with F.J. Taylor), 1929. Home: Santa Fe, N.M. *

TIMM, TYRUS RAYMOND, educator; b. Hallettsville, Tex., Aug. 27, 1912; s. Adolf and Ada (Speakerman) T.; B.S., Tex. A. and M. U., 1934. M.S., 1936; summer student Iowa State Coll., 1939; M.S. Harvard, 1947, D.Pub. Adminstrn., 1950; m. Valerie Padgett, Aug. 2, 1941; 1 dau., Susan. Grad. asst. dept. agrl. econo. Tex. A. and M. U., 1934-36; asst. prof. agrl. econs. N.Mex. State Coll., 1936-37; economist farm marketing extension service Tex. A. and M. U., 1938-44; agrl. economist OPA, 1944, agrl. relations adviser, 1945; adminstry. asst., economist extension service Tex. A. and M. U., 1946, prof. agrl. econs. and extension economist, 1949-53, head dept. agrl. econs. and sociology, 1953-75, prof. emeritus, 1975-77; leader task force studying European Common Market, summer 1962; vis. prof. Colo. State U., from 1954; leadership agrl. instrn., Southwestern Grad. Sch. Banking, So. Methodist U., 1960—. Mem. nat. agrl. com. U.S. C. of C., 1947-48; mem. Nat. Agrl. Policy Com., from 1959; chmn. extension service Internat. Conf. Agrl. Economists, 1961, Nat. Study Group to Evaluate Common Market, 1969; gen. chmn. Farm and Ranch Credit Sch. for Comml Bankers, 1952-62. Dir. Houston br. Fed. Res. Bank, 1953-61, Univ. Nat. Bank, from 1963. Named hon. state farmer Future Farmers Am., 1956; recipient 30 year Service award U.S. Dept. Agr.-Tex. Agrl. Extension Service, 1968; certificate and citation Tex. Ho. of Reps., 1975; Meritorious Achievement award Tex. Fedn. Coops., Houston Bank Coops., Tex. Coop. Ginners Assn., 1977; established Tyrus R. Timm Agrl. Econs. Fellowships. Mem. Am. Farm Econ. Assn., Am. Banking Assn. (land grant coll. adviser), Southwest Social Sci. Assn. Methodist. Rotarian. Home: College Station, Tex. Died Sept. 4, 1977; buried City of College Station Cemetery.

TIMOSHENKO, V.P., economist, educator; born Czernigov prov., Ukraine, Russia, April 25, 1885; s. Prokop and Josephine (Sarnavska) T.; student of economics, Polytechnic Inst., St. Petersburg, cand. Ec. Sc., 1911; Ph.D., Cornell Univ., 1927; m. Odette A. Leger, Nov. 17, 1920; 1 dau., Pauline (Mrs. W. D. Moore). Econ. adviser, Ukrainian delegation at peace conf. (Paris), 1919-21; prof., Ukrainian Univ., Prague, Czechoslovakia, 1922-28; fellow, Internat. Education Bd., 1926-27; lecturer in economics and statistics, Univ. of Mich., 1928-34; sr. agrl. economist, U.S. Dept. of Agr., 1934-36; economist and prof. of commodity economics, Stanford Univ. Calif., 1936-50; chief, prodn. policies program, food and agr. branch, Office of Mil. Govt. for Germany (U.S.), Berlin, 1946-47; Mem. Am. Economics Assn., Am. Statis. Assn., The Econometric Soc., Sigma Xi. Contbr. articles on economics to professional journals. Home: Palo Alto. *

TINDALL, EDWIN LAMAR, steel co. exec.; b. Stuttgart, Ark., Oct. 15, 1904; s. Jerome Lamar and Grace (Sampson) T.; B.S. in Mech. Engring., U. Ill., 1929; m. Margaret Hodgkiss, July 20, 1951. Gas engr. Pub. Service Co. of No. Ill., 1929-35; with U.S. Steel Corp., 1935-69, successively combustion engr. South works of Carnegie-Ill., chief engr. Edgar Thomson, Pitts., central operations, 1935-38, v.p. design and constrn. engring., 1958-63, adminstrv. v.p. engring., 1963-69, asst. to exec. v.p. engring. and research, 1969. Served as lt. col. AUS, 1942-46. Decorated Bronze Star. Mem. AIME, ASME, Am. Iron and Steel Inst., Assn. Iron and Steel Engrs., Engrs. Soc. Western Pa., Newcomen Soc. Club: Duquesne. Home: Pittsburgh, Pa. Died Aug. 29, 1979.

TINGLEY, CLYDE, ex-gov.; b. London, O., Jan. 5, 1883; s. William and Belle T.; grad. high sch., London; m. Carrier Wooster, of Bowling Green, O., 1912. Began active career in ry. construction work, later locomotive fireman; machinist with Dayton Cash Register Co., then supt. of Gramm Motor Co., Bowling Green; settled in Albuquerque, N.M., 1910, and served as alderman and mayor; founder of park system for Albuquerque, a zoölogical collection and municipal bathing beach; elected gov. of N.M., 1934, re-elected, 1936. Served in Ohio N.G. Democrat. Conglist. Mason. Elk. Home: Albuquerque, N.M. *

TIOMKIN, DIMITRI, composer, music dir.; b. Russia, May 10, 1899; s. Zinovie and Marie (Tartakovsky) T.; student St. Petersburg Conservatory Music, St. Petersburg U.; LL.D. St. Mary's U.; m. Albertina Rasch, May 28, 1925 (dec. 1967); m. 2d, Olivia Cynthia Patch, Nov. 13, 1972. Came to U.S., 1925, naturalized, 1937. Concert pianist, conductor, 1919-79; introduced works of Gershwin in Europe, works of French and Russian composers in Am.; composer for numerous motion pictures, including: Bridge of San Luis Rey, Duel in the Sun, Mr. Smith Goes to Washington (Acad. award nomination), Corsican Brothers (Acad. award nomination), Portrait of Jennie, Lost Horizon, Cyrano de Bergerac, Dial M for Murder, The Moon and Sixpence (Acad. award nomination), The High and Mighty (Acad. award for best musical score 1954), The Champion (Acad. award nomination), High Noon (Acad. award for best musical score 1952, best theme song 1952), Wild is the Wind (Acad. award nomination), Friendly Persuasion (Acad. award nomination), Giant (Acad. award nomination), The Old Man and the Sea (Acad. award for best musical score 1958), Last Train from Gun Hill, The Alamo (2 Acad. award nominations, Golden Globe award 1961), The Sundowners, Guns of Navarone (Acad. award nomination, Golden Globe award 1961), Young Land (Acad. award nomination), Town Without Pity (Acad. award nomination, Golden Globe award 1962), Without Each Other, 55 Days at Peking (2 Acad. award nominations), Circus World (Golden Globe award 1965), Fall of the Roman Empire (Acad. award nomination, Golden Globe award 1965), The 36 Hours; producer, musical dir. joint Am.-Soviet prodn. Tchaikovsky (best film award San Sebastian Film Festival, 2 Acad. award nominations 1972. Distinguished prof. music St. Mary's U., Tex., 1961. Scored, conducted all orientation and tng. films for Signal Corps, U.S. Army, World War II. Decorated chevalier of Legion of Honor, 1960, officer, 1976, Chevalier de Belles Letters et Arts, 1967 (France); also Cruz De Caballero De La Orden De Isabel La Catolica, 1964, knight of grace S.M.O. Constantiniana de San Jorge (Spain); recipient Downbeat magazine plaque for best overall underscore of motion picture, Old Man and the Sea, 1959, plaque for best original song, Friendly Persuasion, 1956; Golden globe award Hollywood Fgn. Corrs. for best mus. score, High Noon, 1952, outstanding contbn. to internat. understanding through music, 1965, enrichment motion pictures with mus. compositions of lasting significance, 1956; scroll of appreciation Greater Los Angeles Press Club, 1959; Christopher award, 1959; Music Dept. award Loyola U., Los Angeles, 1957; Nice, France, 1955; Ind. Ch. Sacred Music award, 1955; scroll for song hit of year, Friendly Persuasion, Radio-Television Daily, 1956; Golden Recording from Dot Records for Thee I Love, 1961; Western Heritage award Nat. Cowboy Hall of Fame for Alamo, 1960; Boxoffice award for Best Composer, 1961, 62, 63; 24 Acad. award nominations, 4 Oscars; Western Heritage Wrangler Trustee award Nat. Cowboy Hall of Fame and Western Heritage Centre, 1974. Mem. Am. Inst. Fine Arts Los Angeles (hon. life 1964). Author: Please Don't Hate Me, 1959. Address: Los Angeles, Calif. Died Nov. 11, 1979; interred Forest Lawn Meml. Park, Glendale, Calif.

TIPTON, ISABEL HANSON, educator, physicist; b. Monroe, Ga., June 17, 1909; d. Wesley Turnell and Ruth (Gardner) Hanson; B.S., U. Ga., 1929, M.S., 1930; Ph.D., Duke U., 1934; m. Samuel Ridley Tipton, Dec. 18, 1934; children—Jennifer, Samuel Ridley, Hiram Gardner, Joseph Mangham. Tutor math. Ohio State U., 1935-37; spectroscopist Chrysler Corp., Detroit, 1942; instr. physics U. Ala., 1943-44; instr. physics U. Tenn., 1948-49, asst. prof., 1949-54, asso. prof., 1954-64, prof., 1964-72, emeritus prof., 1972-80; cons. Oak Ridge Nat. Lab., 1949-72; chmn. bd. dirs. Stewart Labs., Inc., 1968-72. Trustee Webb Sch., Knoxville, 1963-69, 70-72. Recipient Alumni Outstanding Tchr. award U. Tenn., 1966. Mem. Optical Soc. Am., Am. Assn. Physics Tchrs., Health Physics Soc., Soc. Applied Spectroscopy (treas. 1962-64), Tenn. Acad. Sci. (pres. 1957), Eastern Bird-Banding Assn. (councillor 1979-81), Phi Beta Kappa, Sigma Xi, Phi Kappa Phi, Sigma Pi Sigma, Phi Mu. Research, publs. on raman spectroscopy, optical spectroscopy, trace elements in humans, ornithology. Home: Southport, N.C. Died Apr. 21, 1980.

TITUS, MURRAY THURSTON, missionary; b. Batavia, O., Nov. 5, 1885; s. Frank M. and Lottie (Harrison) T.; student Lombard Coll., Galesburg, Ill.; B.Litt., Ohio Wesleyan U., 1908, D.D., 1926; student U. of Chicago, 1909; Ph.D., Hartford (Conn.) Sem. Foundation, 1927; m. Olive M. Glasgow, July 6, 1910; 1 dau., Carol Elizabeth. Principal high sch., Sleepy Eye, Minn., 1908-10; missionary, M.E. Ch., in India, since 1910; dist. supt., North India Conf., 1916-41; teacher of philosophy, Lucknow (India) Christian Coll., 1910-13; prin. Lucknow Christian Coll., 1941-43; sec. for India Meth. Bd. of Missions, 1944; sec. Nat. Christian Council of India, Burma and Ceylon, 1945; dist. supt. Meth. Ch. North India Conf., 1948-51; prof. of missions Westminster Theol. Sem. since 1951; lecturer Henry Martin Sch. of Islamic Studies; asso. editor Moslem World Quarterly; asso. editor Religious Quest of India Series, Oxford U. Press Mem. Asiatic Soc. Bengal, Phi Beta Kappa, Phi Delta Theta, Pi Gamma Mu, Rotary Club. Author: books relating to field; contbr. to other publs. on similar subjects. Address: Westminster, Md. *

TITUS, WALTER F., vice pres. Sperry Gyroscope Co.; b. Westbury, LL., June 22, 1886; s. Robert Franklin and Phebet (Carpenter) T.; m. Isabelle Lewis, June 26, 1912. Vice pres. Internat. Bus. Machines Corp., 1935-43; gen. plant mgr., vice pres. in charge of contract terminations, Sperry Gyroscope Co., Inc., since 1943. Clubs: Bohemian, Menlo Country, North Hempstead Country. Home: Manhasset, L.I. *

TJADEN, JOHN CHRISTIAN, (CHA'DEN), univ. prof.; b. Holland, Ia., Oct. 17, 1878; s. Menke J. and Menna J. (Tjaden) T.; A.B., U. of S.D., 1920, A.M., 1921; Ph.D., U. of Ia., 1923; m. Adelaide Myrtle Muma, Aug. 18, 1908; children—Lowell Edward, Elinore Adelaide. Farmer, music teacher, supt. of schs., 1918-23; dir. Extension Div. U. of S.D., 1923-50; prof. German, U. of S.D.; guest prof. philos. and psychol, 1939-40. Served as translator of secret German war documents, U.S. Army, 1946-47. Republican. Mem. Christian Ch. Home: Vermillion, S.D. *

TOBEY, MARK, artist; b. Centerville, Wis., Dec. 11, 1890; s. George Baker and Emma Jane (Cleveland) T.; student pub. schs. Fashion layout artist, Chgo., 1917; tchr. Cornith Sch., Seattle, 1922; resident artist Darlington Hall, Eng., 1931-37, Mexico, 1931-34, Far East, 1934-36; works exhibited portrait show Kurchlees Gallery, N.Y.C., three exhbns., Paris, London, Berne, 1954; one-man show at Fine Arts Gallery, Calif. State U., Northridge, 1975; works represented permanent collections Seattle Art Mus., Met. Mus., Addison, Phillips galleries, Toledo, Bklyn., Balt., Detroit, Portland Art, Abington museums, Allied Arts Soc. Seattle, Art Inst. Chgo., Pa. Acad., Whitney Mus. Am. Art. Mem. Inst. Arts and Letters. Mem. Bahai World Faith. Home: Seattle, Wash. Died Apr. 24, 1976.

TOBIAS, RUSSELL STUART, educator, chemist; b. Columbus, Ohio, Sept. 11, 1930; s. Russell Stewart and Mary (Bigger) T.; B.Sc. in Chemistry, Ohio State U., 1952, Ph.D., 1956; m. Nancy Ann Westbrook, Apr. 14, 1956; children—Janet Lenore, Douglas Andrew, Ellen Elizabeth. NSF postdoctoral fellow Royal Inst. Tech., Stockholm, Sweden, 1956-57; research asso. U. N.C., 1958-59; mem. faculty U. Minn., 1959-69, prof. chemistry, 1966-69; prof. chemistry Purdue U., Lafayette, Ind., 1969-80; NSF sr. postdoctoral fellow Technische Hochschule, Munich, Germany, also Imperial Coll., London, Eng., 1967-68; cons. Mobil Oil Corp., 1964-67. NATO sr. postdoctoral fellow Ludwig Maximilian U., Munich, Germany, 1977. Fellow Am. Soc. Biol. Chemists; mem. Am. Chem. Soc., Chem. Soc. (London), Phi Beta Kappa, Sigma Xi, Phi Lambda Upsilon. Author: (with L.E. Conroy and R.C. Brasted) General Chemistry Laboratory Operations, 1977. Editorial bd. Jour. Coordination Chemistry, 1970-80. Contbr. articles to profl. jours. Home: Lafayette, Ind. Died Feb. 19, 1980.

TOBIN, AUSTIN JOSEPH, ret. state ofcl.; b. Bklyn., May 25, 1903; s. Clarence J. and Katherine (Moran) T.; student St. John's Prep. Sch., Bklyn., 1921; A.B., Holy Cross Coll., 1925; LL.B., Fordham U., 1928; LL.D., Adelphi Coll., Tuskegee Inst., Pace Coll., St. Peter's Coll.; D. Engring., Stevens Institute of Tech.; m. Geraldine Farley, Dec. 9, 1925 (dec. July 1966); children—Austin Joseph, Stacy (Mrs. Martin Carmichael); m. 2d, Rosaleen C. Skehan, June 29, 1967. Admitted to N.Y. bar, 1928; law clk. Port of N.Y. Authority, 1928-30, real estate atty., 1930-35, asst. gen. counsel, 1935-42, became exec. dir., 1942, ret., 1972; port cons. Royal Govt. of Thailand; dir. Tricontinental Corp., C.F. Mueller Co., cons. World Bank on orgn. of Israel Port Authority. Chmn. Conf. State Def.; exec. cons. Minister Communication Republic of China, also Port of Singapore Authority, Guatemala Internat. Exec. Service Corps. Trustee Stevens Inst. of Tech., U.S. council of Internat. C. of C. Decorated French Legion Honor, Italian Order Merit. Mem. Am., N.Y. State bar assns., Am. Judicature Soc., Acad. Polit. Sci., Soc. Friendly Sons of St. Patrick, Municipal Forum of New York. Home: New York, N.Y. Died Feb. 8, 1978; buried Holy Road Cemetery, Bklyn.

TOBIN, EMERY F., publisher; b. Roxbury, Mass., Dec. 14, 1895; s. August F.L. and Emma Louise (Ericson) T.; ed. Boston and Quincy (Mass.) schs.; m. Clara Matilda Willard, Oct. 15, 1926; 1 dau., Doris L. Bordine. Reporter, Quincy Patriot Ledger, 1916-17; accountant, asst. mgr. Ketchikan br. N.E. Fish Co., 1920-32; bus. mgr. Ketchikan Crhonicle, 1932-35; founded The Alaska Sportsman, editor and pub., 1935-58. Mem. exec. com. S.E. dist. Alaska, Boy Scouts Am., after 1940; led citizen investigation of organized vice in Ketchikan, 1953. Served as sgt. Co. M. 325th Inf., 82d Div., Camp Gordon, 1917-18; in France to 1919. Recipient Jessen's Weekly plaque for Distinguished service to Alaska, 1948; Freedom Found. medal, 1950, 73, certificate 1951, 72, 75; Distinguished Citizen award Nat. Municipal League, 1962; Silver Beaver award Boy Scouts, 1962. Mem. Am. Legion, Ketchikan C. of C. (past v.p. and treas., Outstanding Service award 1966), Oreg., Tongass, Ft. Vancouver, Skamania County hist. socs., Vets. of World War I, 82d Div. Assn., Verdun-Meuse-Argonne Vets. Assn., Am. Social Health Assn., Pioneers of Alaska. Dir. amateur theatricals. Republican. Christian Scientist. Rotarian (pres. 1960-61). Contbr. to Ripley's Believe It or Not! Home: Vancouver, Wash. Died May 9, 1977.

TOBRINER, WALTER NATHAN, lawyer; b. Washington, July 2, 1902; s. Leon and Blanche (Barth) T.; A.B., Princeton, 1923; LL.B., Harvard, 1926; m. Marienne E. Smith, July 20, 1933; children—Constance E. (Mrs. David Povich), Matthew W. Admitted to D.C. bar, 1927, since practiced in Washington; prof. law Nat. U. Law Sch., 1933-50; commr. D.C. Govt., 1961-67, pres. bd. commrs., 1961-67; U.S. ambassador to Jamaica, 1967-69; cons. U.S. Dept. State, 1969; engaged in practice of law, Washington, 1969-79. Mem. Washington Bd. Edn., 1952-61, pres. bd., 1957-61; chmn. Washington Met. Area Transit Authority, 1966-67; mem. Com. of 100 on the Fed. City, 1974-79. Del. Democratic Nat. Conv., 1956, 60, 64. Pres.

Garfield Meml. Hosp., 1952-55, Lisner Home, 1954-79, Washington Hosp. Center, 1959-61; bd. dirs. Blue Cross Plan, 1953-61. Trustee Nat. Cultural Center, 1964-67. Served to lt. col. USAAF; 1943-46, chief price adjustment office Mid-Central Procurement Dist., Chgo., also chief price adjustment br. Office Plans and Policies, Washington. Mem. Phi Beta Kappa, Phi Beta Kappa Assos. Clubs: Nat. Capital Democratic, Cosmos (Washington). Home: Washington, D.C. Died July 14, 1979; interred at Nat. Meml. Park, Falls Church, Va.

TODD, FORDE ANDERSON, naval officer; b. Anderson, S.C., Feb. 20, 1881; s. Albert Whitner and Martha (Anderson) T.; student Richmond Acad., Augusta, Ga., 1896-98, Coll. of Charleston (S.C.), 1899-1900; B.S., U.S. Naval Acad., 1904; m. Sylvia Leland Barnes, June 21, 1917; children—Emily Harrison, Anderson, Dorothy Marilla, John Barnes. Commd. ensign, U.S. Navy, 1906, and advanced through the grades to rear adm., 1938; served as naval aid to Pres, Wilson; exec. officer U.S.S. Utah with Grand Fleet, during World War; naval attaché, Rome, Italy, 1926-28; comdg. officer U.S.S. Idaho, 1933-34; comdt. of midshipmen, U.S. Naval Acad., 1935-37; comdr. Atlantic Squadron, 1938; comdg. Cruiser Div. 8, U.S. Fleet, 1938-40; retired for physical disability, May 1, 1941, and ordered Governor Naval Home, Philadelphia. Decorated Victory medal for World War, Mexican Campaign medal. Mem. Alpha Tau Omega. Democrat. Presbyn. Clubs: New York Yacht (New York); Rittenhouse, Racquet (Phila.); Army and Navy, Chevy Chase (Washington, D.C.). Home: Bryn Mawr, Pa. *

TODD, FREDERICK PORTER, museum cons.; b. Richmond, Va., Apr. 18, 1903; s. William and Alice (Porter) T.; student Princeton, 1921-24; B.S. in Social Sci., Am. U., 1953; m. Maria C. Pevear, May 9, 1936. Curator, Mus. City N.Y., 1934-36; archivist Nat. Archives, Washington, 1936-42; historian Office Mil. History, 1946-53; dir. West Point (N.Y.) Mus., 1953-65, New Windsor Cantonment, Vails Gate, N.Y., 1965-67; cons. N.Y. State Historic Trust, Heritage Plantation, others; trustee Washington's Hdqrs., Newburgh, N.Y., Old Museum Village, Monroe, N.Y.; commr. Nat. Portrait Gallery, 1963-69; commr. N.Y. Bi-Centennial Commn., 1969-77. Served to col. AUS, 1942-46; PTO. Mem. Am. Mil. Inst. (sec. 1935-47), Co. Mil. Historians (pres. 1951-52, editor 1952-57, gov. 1951-74). Club: Century Assn. (N.Y.C.). Author: Soldiers of the American Army, 2d edit., 1954; Cadet Gray, 1955; Pro Patria et Gloria, 1956; Soldier Stamps, 1957; American Military Equipage, 1851-1872, 1974. Home: Cornwall-on-Hudson, N.Y. Died Nov. 9, 1977; interred Willow Dell Cemetery, Cornwall-on-Hudson.

TODD, JOHN WELHOFF, prof. psychology; b. Aurora, Ind., Nov. 20, 1880; s. John Alexander and Ellen (Welhoff) T.; a.b., in Philosophy and Psychology, Ind. U., 1905, A.M., 1910; Ph.D., Columbia, 1912; m. Helen Batchelor, August 30, 1906; married 2d, Mabel L. Wright, Aug. 13, 1943; married 3d, Florence Zoe Chase, Aug. 2, 1946; children—Helen Frances, Mary Welhoff, John Sanford. Teaching fellow and assistant in experimental psychology, Ind. and Columbia univs., 1909-12; lecturer in exptl. psychology. Columbia, 2d semester, 1912; asst. prof., asso. prof. and prof. psychology, U. of N.D., 1912-20; acting prof. psychology and dir. psychol. clinic, Ind. U. (on leave), 1915-16; prof. psychology, Indian U., summer 1916; prof. psychology. U. of Utah, summer 1924; prof. psychology, U. of So. Calif., 1920-48, retired; lecturer in psychology, U. of Chicago. first quarter (on leave), 1927-28. Made special investigation in psychology foreign langs. for Nat. Council on Edn., 1926-27. Mem. A.A.A.S., Am. Psychol. Assn., Sigma Xi, Phi Kappa Phi, Phi Delta Kappa. Democrat. Author: Reaction, to Multiple Stimuli, 1912. Co-Author: Prognosis Tests in the Modern Foreign Languages, 1929. Specializes in applied psychology and psychometry. Originator of an electro-mechanical chronoscope and compound dynamograph, and the Todd Linguistic Diagnosis Test. Home: Hollywood, Calif. *

TODD, NELSON BARNARD, lawyer; b. Lynn, Mass., Apr. 1, 1883; s. Herbert Edgar and Rose (Cashman) T.; LL.B., Northeastern U., 1908; m. Edna H. Peale, Sept. 30, 1908; children—Barnard P., Charles N., David B. Admitted to Mass. bar, 1908, since practiced in Boston; gen. counsel, v.p., dir., mem. exec. com. United Shoe Machinery Corp., Boston. Home: Lynnfield Center, Mass. *

TODD, W. PARSONS, pres. and dir. Quincy Mining Co., W. Parsons Todd, Inc., 205 W. 101st St. Realty Corp., 1440 Concourse, Inc.; v.p. and dir. Fordham Concourse Garage, Inc.; pres. dir. 693 Madison Av. Corp. Pres. W. Parsons Todd Found., Inc., Macculloch Hall Hist. Mus. Home: Morristown, N.Y. Died Sept. 28, 1976.

TODD, WALTER LEDYARD, mfg. exec.; b. Gettysburg, S.D., May 6, 1886; s. George Walter and Grace (Ledyard) T.; A.B., Cornell, 1909. Asso. with The Todd Co., Inc., Rochester, N.Y., since 1909, successivley sales mgr., gen. mgr., pres., chmn. board, 1946—, consultant Burroughs Corporation division; trustee Rochester Savs. Bank, Security Trust Co.; dir. Rochester Gas & Elec. Corp., Stromberg Carlson Telephone Mfg. Co., Widmer Wine Cellars, Inc., Naples, New York. Director Bur. of Municipal Research, Rochester Community Chest, Hillside Children's Centre (pres. 1951), Navy League of U.S. Trustee Cornell U., Rochester Inst. Tech., Rochester Y.W.C.A. (also mem. adv. bd. Y.M.C.A.), Conv. and Publicity Bur. Mem. exec. com. N.Y. State YMCA. Mem. Rochester C. of C. (pres., 1948). Clubs: University, Cornell (N.Y. City); University, Genesee Valley (Country Club of Rochester (Rochester); R.C.Y.C. (Toronto). Home: Rochester, N.Y. *

TODMAN, WILLIAM SELDEN, TV producer and program packager; b. N.Y.C., July 31, 1916; s. Frederick Simpson and Helena Diana (Orlowitz) Todman; B.S., Johns Hopkins, 1938; B.A., N.Y. U., 1941; m. Frances Holmes Burson, Dec. 17, 1950; children—Lisa Susan (Mrs. Plough), William Selden. Free lance radio writer and producer, 1938-41; writer, producer WABC, 1941-43; agy. supr. Biow Co., also writer, dir. Connie Boswell Show for Blue Network, 1943; writer, dir. Anita Ellis Sings, 1944; writer Treasury Salute dramas, 1945-46; partner Goodson-Todman Prodns., N.Y.C.; pres. Central States Pub. Co., Mid-Atlantic Newspapers, Central States Pub. Co., Inc.; v.p. New Eng. Newspapers, Capitol City Pub. Co., Inc.; developer, producer TV programs It's News to Me, What's My Line, The Web, By Popular Demand, The Name's the Same, I've Got a Secret, Two for the Money, Beat the Clock, Judge for Yourself, To Tell the Truth, The Price is Right, Play Your Hunch, Philip Marlowe, The Legend of Ethan Allen, Jefferson Drum, Split Personality, The Rebel, Password, The Richard Boone Show, The Don Rickles Show, 1968, He Said She Said, Snap Judgement; producer Get the Message, 1964, Match Game "73", 1973; producer Ride Beyond Vengeance (feature film); pres. Winner Prodns., Inc., Two for the Money, Inc.; v.p. Goodson-Todman Enterprises, Ltd., What's My Line, Inc.; lectr. Queen's Coll., 1947. Chmn. radio-TV, stage artists and musicians div., United Jewish Appeal, 1954, 56-79; chmn. broadcasting div. Am. Heart Assn. Mem. Internat. Radio-TV Soc., Phi Epsilon Pi. Club: Friars. Author: (with Mark Goodson) Winner Take All Home Quiz Book, 1949. Contbr. to Television, Advertising and Production Handbook, 1954. Home: Scarsdale, N.Y. Died July 29, 1979.

TOLL, CHARLES HANSEN (TOL), coll. prof.; b. Denver, Colo., May 21, 1882; s. Charles Hansen and Katharine Ellen (Wolcott) T.; B.A., Hamilton Coll., 1904; M.A., Harvard, 1905, John Harvard fellow, 1906-08; travelled, 1906-07; studied U. of Berlin, 1907-08; Ph.D., U. of Freiburg, 1909; hon. M.A., Amherst Coll., 1934; m. Mayes Martin, July 17, 1912; children—Katharine Wolcott, Charles Hansen, Henry Caldwell, Caldwell Martin. Asst. prof. philosophy, Amherst Coll., 1909-12, asso. prof., 1912-24, prof. psychology, 1924-48, emeritus. Enrolled 2d O.T.C., Plattsburg, 1917; chief psychol. examiner Camp Custer, Mich., Apr.-Dec. 1918; commd. capt. Sanitary Corps, 1918; maj. Sanitary O.R.C., 1922-42. Mem. Am. Philos. Assn., Am. Psychol. Assn., Psi Upsilon, Phi Beta Kappa, Sigma Xi. Home: Amherst, Mass. *

TOLSTOY, ALEXANDRA LEO, charitable found. exec., author, speaker; b. Yasnaya Polyana, Russia, July 1, 1884; d. Leo N. and Sophie A. (Bers) Tolstoy; ed. at home; D.H.L., Hobart Coll., 1962 William Smith Coll., 1962. Sec. to father Leo N. Tolstoy, 1901-10 worked preparing definitive edit. of Leo N. Tolstoy's works, 1917-29; formerly prin. sch., Yasnaya Polyana; arrested five times, spent 2 months in prison, Lubianka, and one year of convict labor; after release, left Russia to lecture in Japan, 1929-31; lectr., author in U.S. 1938-79; co-founder, with T.A. Schaufuss, of Tolstoy Found. Inc., Am. Russian refugee resettlement welfare agy., N.Y.C., 1939, now chmn. bd. Served as nurse, 1914-17; worked during German lethal gas attacks in trenches. Decorated 2 St. George's medals for valour on the battlefield. Author: Tragedy of Tolstoy, 1933; I Worked for the Soviets, 1934; Tolstoy—life of my father, 1953, 73, 76 (numerous transls.); The Real Tolstoy, 1968. Tolstoy Found. has fourteen offices and twelve homes for the aged in U.S. and abroad. Home: Valley Cottage, N.Y. Died Sept. 26, 1979; buried Cemetery of Russian Orthodox Convent of Novo Diveyevo, Spring Valley, N.Y.

TOMLINSON, JOHN DOREN, fgn. service officer; b. Wheaton, Ill., Mar. 7, 1903; s. George Horace and Marian (Doren) T.; B.S., Northwestern U., 1925; A.M., Columbia, 1927; Docteur es Sciences Politiques, Grad. Inst. Internat. Studies, U. Geneva, 1938; m. Jean Duncan-Clark, June 10, 1936; 1 dau., Elizabeth Murray (Mrs. Russell V. Theiss). Asst. prof., then prof. polit. sci. Wabash Coll., 1927-41; dir. Am. Com. in Geneva, and Geneva Inst. Internat. Relations, summers 1931-38; staff div. export controls State Dept., 1941, div. Am. Republics, 1942, div. polit. studies, 1943-44, div. internat. orgn. affairs, 1945-46, asst. chief, 1946, adviser Office UN Econ. and Social Affairs, 1948-54; U.S. mem. adv. commn. UNRRA, Beirut, Lebanon, 1954-56; Am. consul, Port Elizabeth, South Africa, 1956-58; Am. consul gen., Leopoldville, Belgian Congo, 1958-60, Casablanca, Morocco, 1960-63; exec. Church Center for UN, 1963-66; Moroccan rep. Am. Friends of Middle East, 1966-73. Adviser, U.S. delegations Gen. Council UNRRA, Atlantic City, 1943, Dumbarton Oaks Conversations, 1944, San Francisco Conf., Internat. Orgn., 1945, UN Prep. Commn., London, 1945, Prep. Commn. WHO, Geneva, 1947-48, UN Gen. Assembly, 1946, 1958, others. Mem. Delta Upsilon, Sigma Delta Chi. Methodist. Home: Washington, D.C. Died Apr. 5, 1981; buried Rock Creek Cemetery, Washington.

TOMONAGA, SIN-ITIRO, physicist; b. Tokyo, Japan, Mar. 31, 1906; degree in atomic physics, Tokyo U., 1929; children—Shigeko, Atsushi, Makoto. Prof. emeritus Tokyo U. of Edn. Recipient Lomonosov medal, USSR, 1964; co-recipient Nobel prize in physics, 1965. Fgn. asso. mem. Nat. Acad. Scis., Japan Acad., Royal Swedish Acad., Deutsche Akademie der Nuturforscher Leopoldina Bayerische Akademie der Wissenshaften. Home: Tokyo, Japan. Died July 8, 1979.

TOMPKINS, OSCAR L., lawyer; b. Belgreen, Ala., Oct. 26, 1883; s. Rufus Alonzo and Emma Weston (Gober) T. (lineal desc. Tishilingi Gates of Cherokee Indian tribe); student U. of Ala., summer 1907, U. of Tenn., summers 1908-10, U. of Ala. 1912-13; m. Lou Deason, April 29, 1916 (died Sept. 1959); m. 2d, Hazel Thomley, Oct. 1962. Prin. Dothan High Sch., 1906-11; admiteed to Ala. bar. 1914, and since practiced in Dothan; mem. Ala. Ho. of Rep., 1918-22, 1926-30; author of Anti-Ku Klux Flogging Law, which makes flogging by masked persons a felony, 1927; city atty., Dothan, 1927-28; county atty. (civil), Houston County, 1919-35; U.S. referee in bankruptcy, 1931-46; mem. Alabama Muscle Shoals Commn., 1927. Mem. Dothan Bd. of Edn., 1924-49; trustee State Training Sch. for Girls, 1929-31. Mem. Am. Bar Assn., Ala. State Bar Assn. (pres. 1928-29), Dothan Bar Assn., Internat. Assn. of Ins. Counsel. Independent Democrat. Methodist; lay del. Gen. Conf. M.E. Ch., S., 1934, 38, Uniting Conf., Meth. Ch., Kansas City, 1939, Gen. Conf. Meth. Ch. Atlantic City, 1940; lay del. Jurisdictional Conf. Meth. Ch., Southeast Jurisdiction, 1944. Author: (monographs) Some Alabama Political History, Alabama "Bolters" and "Bolting"; Wiregrass Sagas (1942); (Law); Action by Child Against Parent; And They Too Were Alabamans, 1961. Mason. Home: Dotham, Ala. *

TOMSON, BERNARD, state supreme ct. justice; b. N.Y.C., Sept. 28, 1909; s. Israel and Sarah (Sidlin) T.; A.B., City Coll. N.Y., 1929; LL.B., Columbia U., 1933; m. Rose Linchitz, Oct. 17, 1936; children—Louis R., Susan W. and Steven H. (twins), Elizabeth C. Admitted N.Y. bar, 1934, Mass. bar, 1945, U.S. Supreme Ct. bar, 1947; partner firm Bernstein, Weiss & Tomson, N.Y.C., 1934-59; chief law dept. Surrogate's Ct., Nassau County, Mineola, N.Y., 1956-59; judge Dist. Ct., Nassau County, 1959-70; judge Nassau County Ct., 1970-76; justice N.Y. State Supreme Ct., 1977-78; adj. prof. Pratt Inst. Tech., Bklyn. Mem. SS Bd. #3, Nassau County, 1949-52; mem. L.I. Regional Hosp. Planning Counsel, 1954-57; mem. Nassau County Mental Health Bd., 1956-59. Bd. dirs. United HIAS Service, 1956; v.p., trustee North Shore U. Hosp. Manhasset, N.Y. Recipient Theodore Roosevelt award Nassau-Suffolk Hosp. Council, 1963; Mental Health award Nassau County Neuropsychiat. Soc., 1964. Mem. Fed., N.Y., Mass. bar assns.; hon. mem. AIA. Author: Architectural and Engineering Law, 1951, 2d edn., 1967; It's The Law, 1960; contbg. editor Progressive Architecture, 1948. Contbr. articles to profl. jours. Home: Great Neck, N.Y. Died May 9, 1978; buried Beth Moses Cemetery, Temple Beth El of Great Neck, Pinelawn, N.Y.

TOOILL, KENNETH DU VALL, editor, writer; b. Jeffersonville, Ohio; s. George Washington and Luella (Smith) T.; grad high sch., Columbus, Ohio, 1918; student Columbia, Coll. City N.Y., Ohio State U.; m. Virginia E. Christian, Feb. 28, 1944; 1 son (by former marriage), John Pershing; 1 dau., Patricia Ann (adopted). Began as reporter Ohio State Jour., 1917; reporter successively for the Louisville Courier-Journal, Phila. Ledger, Chgo. Herald and Examiner, N.Y. Am., also N.Y. Sun until 1928; mng. editor successively Johnstown Democrat, Newark Ledger and Ohio State Jour.; asso. editor Columbus Dispatch; mng. editor Toledo Blade; editor and co-pub. Erie (Pa.) Dispatch-Herald, 1945; editor editorial page, St. Louis Star-Times; exec. editor Toledo Times, from 1948; author nat. syndicated column; with news dept. Toledo Blade, from 1966. Mem. Am. Soc. Newspapers Editors, Sigma Delta Chi. Clubs: University, Torch, National Press. Home: Toledo, Ohio. Deceased.

TOOLEN, THOMAS J., clergyman; b. Balt., 1886. Ordained priest Roman Cath. Ch., 1910; consecrated bishop, 1927; bishop of Mobile, 1927-54, archbishop ad personam Mobile-Birmingham, 1954-69, titular archbishop Glastonbury, 1969-76. Home: Mobile, Ala. Died Dec. 4, 1976; interred Bishop's Crypt, Cathedral of Immaculate Conception, Mobile.

TORRENCE, ANDREW PUMPHREY, univ. pres.; b. Little Rock, Nov. 20, 1920; s. Boston Lafayette and Nancy (Pumphrey) T.; B.S., Tenn. A. and I. U., 1948; M.S., U. Wis., 1951, Ph.D., 1954; m. Marian Salters,

June 26, 1948; children—Kenneth, Andrea. Tchr. vocat. agr. Immanuel High Sch., Almyra, Ark., 1948-50; asso. prof. agrl. edn., head dept. Tuskegee Inst., 1954-62, prof., dean acad. affairs, 1962-67, prof., v.p., 1967-68; pres. Tenn. State U., Nashville, 1968-74; provost, exec. v.p. Tuskegee Inst., 1974-80. Research asso. Center Study Edn. Adults, Chgo., 1959-60; vis. prof. U. Wis., summer 1962; participant ednl. travel groups AID, 1960, 71; cons. Negro Coll. Com. Adult Edn., 1960-64. Mem. numerous ednl. coms. and councils including Gov.'s Sci. Adv. Com., 1969-80, nat. adv. council Human Resources Devel. Center, Tuskegee Inst., 1969-74, com. on indsl. extension State Land-Grant Assn., 1969-80, joint com. Negro Coll. Fund, 1969-80, inst. policy commn. So. Regional Edn. Bd., 1970-74, Jud. Council Tenn., 1971-74; vice chmn. Coop. Coll. Devel. Program, 1970-73. Bd. dirs. Nashville Urban League, Nat. Alliance Businessmen, Heifer Project Internat.; mem. United Bd. for Homeland Ministries, 1969-74. Served with AUS, 1943-46. Recipient Alumni citation Tenn. A. and I. U., 1962. Mem. Adult Edn. Assn. Am. (sec. 1968), NEA, Rural Edn. Dept., Tenn. Edn. Assn., Tenn. Coll. Assn. (exec. com. 1969-70), Tenn. Adult Edn. Assn. (2d v.p. 1969), So. Assn. Coll. Deans, Tuskegee Civic Assn., Arnold Air Soc., Phi Delta Kappa, Alpha Phi Alpha, Sigma Pi Phi Boule, Phi Kappa Delta. Baptist (deacon, trustee). Clubs: Tuskegee Optimist, Masons. Author: (with B.W. Kreitlow and E.W. Aiton) Leadership for Action in Rural Communities, 1960; also numerous articles. Co-author: Teacher Education in Agriculture, 1967; Careers and Curriculum Change, 1968. Address: Tuskegee Institute, Ala. Died June 11, 1980; buried Oakland Fraternal Cemetery, Little Rock.

TORRES, JUAN JOSE, pres. of Bolivia; b. Cochabamba, Bolivia, Mar. 5, 1919; ed. Mil. Arty. Coll. Argentina; m. Emma Obleas de Torres; 4 children. Successively chief staff, instr. arty. regts. Mil. Coll. Bolivia; comdr. 2d Arty. Div.; comdr.-in-chief Armed Forces; permanent sec. Nat. Def. Council; mil. attaché, Brazil; ambassador to Uruguay; minister of labor; pres. Bolivia, 1970—. Home: La Paz, Bolivia. Assassinated 1976.

TORREY, JOHN STEPHEN, mfg. co. exec.; b. Los Angeles, Aug. 1, 1909; s. John Francis and Jesse M. (Farnsworth) T.; student U. Idaho, 1929-32; m. Margaret Young, Dec. 13, 1952; children—Margaret Katherine, John Stephen, Joan Stephanie, James Michael. Account exec. Erwin, Wasey & Co., Los Angeles, 1936-41; pres. Lennan Lights, Inc., Burbank, Calif., 1941-46, John S. Torrey, Inc., Burbank, 1946-47; sr. v.p. Avery Internat., San Marino, Calif., from 1948. Mem. Calif. Mfrs. Assn. (dir. 1969-71, pres. 1973-74, chmn. bd. dirs. 1974-75), Sales and Mktg. Execs. Assn. Los Angeles (dir. 1972-74). Club: Bahia Corinthian Yacht. Home: Balboa Island, Calif. Died Aug. 1978.

TORREY, PHILIP HUSTON, marine corps officer (retired); b. Ft. Douglas, Utah, July 18, 1884; s. Col. Zerah Watkins and Anna (Huston) T.; student, Lehigh Univ., 1902-04; grad. Naval War Coll. (sr. and advanced courses), 1935, 38, Field Officers course, U.S.M.C., 1931; m. Elizabeth Trescot, Nov. 10, 1909; children—Elizabeth Worthington, Philip Huston (killed in action, U.S. Navy), Rebecca Britton (wife of Lt. Col. Neil Ross MacIntyre, U.S.M.C.). Commd. 2d lt., U.S.M.C., 1905, and advanced through grades to maj. gen., 1942; served Cuba, 1906-09, France, 1918, Haiti, 1920-21, 29-31; comdr., 1st Marine div., 1941-42; comdt., Marine barracks and Marine Corps Sch., Quantico, Va., 1942-46; ret. from active duty, 1946. Awarded Cuban Pacification medal, Marine Corps expeditionary medal with 2 stars. Mexican and Haitian campaign medals, Victory medal, World War II; decorated grand officer, Order of Orange Nassau (Netherlands). Mem. Sigma Phi. Republican. Roman Catholic. Club: Racquet (Phila.). Home: Coronado, Calif. *

TORREY, THOMAS MCCHESNEY, ins. co. exec.; b. N.Y.C., Apr. 4, 1911; s. Owen Cates and Gertrude (McChesney) T.; grad. Middlesex Sch., Concord, Mass., 1929; A.B., Harvard, 1933; m. Betty Brawley, June 19, 1937; children—Hope (Mrs. Mallory S. Grantham), Betty (Mrs. S.S. Lusk), Sarah, Catharine, Thomas. With Ins. Co. N.Am., N.Y.C., 1933-80, mgr. N.Y. office, 1952-58, resident v.p., 1958-72. Pres. Am. Inst. Marine Underwriters, 1962-64, dir., 1957-68; pres. Bd. Underwriters N.Y., 1962-64, dir., 1957-58; 1st v.p. Assn. Marine Underwriters U.S., 1964-66; dir. Nat. Cargo Bur., Inc., 1958-72, treas., 1965-67, pres., 1967-69; vice chmn. exec. com. Internat. Union Marine Ins., 1966-70; dir. Maritime Assn. Port N.Y., 1964-80, also treas.; chmn. coms. marine fire protection and marine field service Nat. Fire Protection Assn., 1958-72; mem. mgmt. com. Am. Bur. Shipping, 1970-72. Trustee, 2d v.p. Leopold Schepp Found., 1964-72; bd. govs. India House, 1969-80. Home: Jamestown, R.I. Died Jan. 4, 1980.

TOUCHSTONE, OSCAR O'NEILL, lawyer; b. Grayson County, Tex., Dec. 4, 1885; s. James Nathaniel and Mary Lucy (Smith) T.; A.B., Austin Coll., Sherman, Tex., 1907; LL.B., U. of Tex., 1909; m. Ellie Mills, Aug. 3, 1911; children—Justin, Marianne (wife of Dr. John Dunlap), Eleanor (Mrs. Paul Douglas Lindsey). Admitted to Tex. bar, 1909; in office of Col. William Thompson, 1909-10; mem. Milam & Touchstone, 1910-13, Thomas, Milan & Touchstone, 1913-21; Thomas, Frank, Milam & Touchstone, 1921-27, Touchstone, Wight, Gormley & Price, 1927-40; sr. partner Touchstone, Wight, Gormley & Touchstone, Dallas, Tex., 1940-48; now in practice under name O. O. Touchstone, Dallas. Mem. bd. regents N. Tex. Agrl. Coll., 1927-31; mem. exec. com. Tex. Soc. for Crippled Children. Mem. Dallas Bar Assn (sec. 1920-22; pres. 1923), Am. Bar Assn., Austin Coll. Alumni Assn. (pres.), U. of Tex. Alumni Assn. (former mem. exec. council), Alpha Tau Omega (worthy high chancellor), Phi Delta Phi (charter mem. Roberts Inn). Democrat. Baptist. Mason (32 deg., K.C.C.H.). Clubs: Rotary, Athletic (charter mem.), Dallas Country (mem. bd. govs. 1924-29; pres. 1928), Idlewild (Dallas). Home: Dallas. *

TOURTELLOT, ARTHUR BERNON, author, broadcasting exec.; b. Providence, July 23, 1913; s. Walter Roy and Ethel Maude (Harris) T.; student Harvard Univ., 1931-35; m. Elizabeth Davis, June 21, 1941; children—Jonathan Bernon, Christopher Trayne. Author: Be Loved No More, 1938; The History of the Horse, 1940; The Charles (Rivers of America series), 1941; Woodrow Wilson Today, 1946; An Anatomy of American Politics, 1950; William Diamond's Drum, The Beginning of the War of the American Revolution, 1959; A Bibliography of the Battles of Concord and Lexington, 1960; The Presidents on the Presidency, 1963; contbr. to nat. mags., editor: Life's Picture History of World War II, 1950; Crusade in Europe (film version of Gen. Eisenhower's book made for television; winner of 1949 Peabody award); asso. producer The March of Time (film div. of Time, Inc.), 1942-50; dir. Time, Inc., TV Prodns., 1950-52, joined Earl Newsom & Co., 1952, partner, 1953-65, chmn. bd. 1965-68; v.p., gen. exec. CBS, Inc., 1968-77. Mem. Commn. to Modernize Cts. Bd. dirs., pres. CBS Found., Inc.; bd. dirs., v.p. William S. Paley Found., Green Park Found.; trustee N.Y. Cancer Research Inst.; vis. com. of bd. overseers Harvard Coll. Library, Harvard U. Press; v.p. Bus. Com. on Arts. Served with USCGR, 1942-44. Fellow Soc. Am. Historians; mem. Am. Hist. Soc., Orgn. Am. Historians, Hist. Inst. of Am. Music (trustee), Am. Antiquarian Soc. (council), Mass. Hist. Soc., Roger Williams Family Assn., Be Bernon Soc., Wilton Town Assn. (dir.). Episcopalian. Clubs: Authors (London); Harvard, Metropolitan, Century (N.Y.C.); Nat. Press (Washington); Wilton Riding. Author: Benjamin Franklin: The Shaping of Genius, 1976. Editorial bd. Columbia Bus. Quar.; chmn. editorial bd. Columbia Jour. Bus. Home: Westport, Conn. Died Oct. 18, 1977; buried Hillside Cemetery, Wilton, Conn.

TOUSTER, BEN, hat mfr.; b. N.Y.C., Apr. 9, 1893; s. Osias and Betty (Ehrlich) T.; student pub. schs.; m. Betha Landau, Feb. 22, 1920; children—Irwin, Saul. Partner Beatty Hat Co., N.Y.C., 1919-23; owner Cinderella Hat Co., N.Y.C., from 1923; pres. HIAS Immigrant Bank, from 1952. Trustee Home for Aged and Infirm Hebrews; dir. Council of Fedns. and Welfare Funds, Am. Jewish Com.; pres. Hebrew Immigrant Aid Soc. 1952-54, United HIAS Service, 1954-56; v.p. CARE, from 1953; pres. YM and YWHA, Brooklyn, 1949-55; v.p. Maimonides Hospital, Bklyn., from 1959. Trustee Fedn. Jewish Philanthropies N.Y., from 1945. Mem. Met. Mus. Art, Mus. Modern Art, Assn. Millinery Men, Grand Street Boys Assn. Clubs: Overseas Press, Advertising (N.Y.C.). Home: New York, N.Y. Deceased.

TOWE, KENNETH CRAWFORD, bus. exec.; b. Elizabeth City, N.C., Jan. 19, 1893; s. William and Katherine (Crawford) T.; ed. Trinity Coll. (now Duke); m. Betty McCarn, Apr. 28, 1934; children—Kenneth McCarn, Rolf Harvy, Teri Noel. Treas., Am. Cyanamid Co., N.Y.C., 1939-45, v.p., 1945-52, pres., 1952-57, chmn. bd., 1957-58, also dirs.; dir. Mich. Gas Utilities; dir. emeritus Campbell Soup Co., Duke Power Co.; mem. dirs.' adv. council Morgan Guaranty Trust Co. Trustee Duke Endowment and related trusts; trustee emeritus Duke U.; hon. trustee Presbyn. Hosp. N.Y.; nat. adv. dir. Boys Club Am. Mem. Omicron Delta Kappa, Kappa Alpha. Mason (Shriner). Clubs: Blind Brook (Port Chester, N.Y.); Pinnacle, Links (N.Y.C.); Indian Harbor Yacht (Greenwich, Conn.). Home: Greenwich, Conn. Died Jan. 6, 1978; interred at Rocky Mount, N.C.

TOWL, ROY NATHAN, civil engineering; b. Chicago, Ill., Mar. 29, 1881; s. Edwin B. and Charlotte (Summers) T.; student Armour Inst. Tech., 1901-03; m. Zulu Z. Renwick, Sept. 1, 1904; children—Dorothy (dec.), Andrew, Charlotte, Div. engr. C., R.I.&P. Ry., Tex., 1900-01; resident engr. I.C. R.R., Miss., 1903-04; mem. Towl, Nelson & Schwartz, cons. engrs., Omaha, 1904-35; pvt. practice, specializing in drainage, hydraulics, flood control and gen. municipal engring., since 1904; commr. of pub. improvements, Omaha, 1918-21, fire and police commr., 1930-33; mayor of Omaha, term 1933-36; commr. of parks, 1939-47; mem. Parks and Recreation Commission and acting supt., 1947-48. Member Am. Soc. of C.E., Omaha C. of C. Republican. Presbyn. Mason, Elk. Club: Engineers. Home: Omaha, Neb. *

TOWLE, SIDNEY NORWOOD, headmaster; b. Brookline, Mass., Feb. 16, 1913; s. Sidney Norwood and Hazel W.M. (Safford) T.; B.A., Yale, 1935, J.D., 1938; m. Nancy Lois Roberts, Apr. 25, 1943; children—Sidney Norwood, Alexis Charles, Diana, Christopher Philip. Admitted to Mass. bar, 1939; asso. firm Withington, Cross, Park & McCann, Boston, 1938-47, partner, 1947-59; asso. headmaster Kent (Conn.) Sch., 1959-62, headmaster, 1962-80, trustee, 1963-80. Mem. sch. com., Newburyport, Mass., 1950-52. Mem. Newburyport City Council, 1940-41. Trustee Conn. Jr. Republic, Litchfield, Conn., 1961-63, Harvey Sch., Katonah, N.Y., 1963-71, Indian Mountain Sch., Lakeville, Conn., 1965-67; v.p., trustee Ipswich Hist. Soc., 1958-59. Served to lt. col. AUS, 1941-46. Decorated Legion of Merit; recipient All Am. award Sports Illus. Silver Anniversary, 1959; Martin W. Souders award New Eng. Prep. Schs. Athletic Council, 1977. Mem. Boston Bar Assn., Conn. Assn. Ind. Schs. (v.p. 1968-69), Headmasters Assn. (v.p. 1978-79), Scroll and Key Soc. Republican. Episcopalian (vestry 1959). Clubs: Fence (Yale); Leander (Henley-on-Thames). Home: Kent, Conn. Died Nov. 5, 1980; buried St. Mark's Cemetery, Kent, Conn.

TOWNS, CHARLES HENRY, accounting firm exec.; b. Marlborough, N.H., Jan. 9, 1893; s. George Milton and Harriet (Buss) T.; B.C.S., N.Y. U., 1917; m. Eleanor E. Stearns, Apr. 18, 1921. Partner Loomis, Suffer & Fernald, N.Y.C., 1927-58; partner Lybrand, Ross Bros. & Montgomery, 1958-62. Hon. trustee Belknap Coll., Center Harbor, N.H. Mem. N.Y. State Soc. C.P.A.'s (ex-pres.), Am. Inst. Accountants (former treas.), Nat. Assn. Accountants (former v.p., treas.), Alpha Kappa Psi. Presbyn. Mason. Clubs: Accountants, New York University (N.Y.C.). Contbr. profl. jours. Home: Gilsum, N.H. Died Dec. 21, 1979; interred Woodlawn Cemetery, Keene, N.H.

TOWNSEND, JOHN WILSON, author; b. nr. Lexington, Ky., Nov. 2, 1885; s. Charles Wesley and Jeannie Frank (Wilson) T.; studied Ky. (Transylvania) U., 1902-6, Harvard, 1907. Prof. English, Fishburne Mil. Sch., Waynesboro, Va., 1908; night librarian Lexington Pub. Library, 1909-10; asso. editor publs. Ky. Hist. Soc., 1910-11. Founder and sec.-treas. King Solomon Memorial Assn. of Ky., which built monument to memory of William ("King") Solomon, hero of the 1833 cholera plague in Lexington, Ky. Mem. Ky. Hist. Soc., Ohio Valley Hist. Assn., Miss. Valley Hist. Assn., Ia. Hist. Soc. Clubs: Filson, Harvard of Ky. Author: Richard Hickman Menefee, 1907; Kentuckians in History and Literature, 1907; The Life of James Francis Leonard, 1909; Kentucky—Mother of Governors, 1910; Lore of the Meadowland, 1911. Wrote study of Thomas H. Chivers for Library of Southern Literature; wrote 36 sketches of Kentuckians for The South in the Building of the Nation. Contbr. to mags. and newspapers. Address: Lexington, Ky. *

TOWNSEND, LEE HILL, educator; b. Leland, Miss., Jan. 20, 1903; s. Newitt Lee and Mabel Lyle (McNeill) T.; B.S., U. Va., 1925; M.S., U. Ill., 1932, Ph.D., 1935; m. Anna Louise Talbott, Aug. 31, 1940; 1 son, Lee Hill. Sci. instr. Greenwood (Miss.) High Sch., 1925-27; grad. asst. entomology U. Ill., 1927-30; asst. entomologist Ill. Natural History Surveys, Urbana, 1932-36; faculty agrl. entomology U. Ky., 1936—, prof., 1948-73, emeritus, 1973-80, acting asst. dean in resident teaching Coll. Agr. and Home Econs., 1947, acting head dept. entomology and botany, 1957, head dept., 1957-73. State entomologist, adminstr. Ky. Seed Law and Plant Pest Control Law, 1957-80. Mem. Entomol. Soc. Am., Entomol. Soc. Washington, Ky. Beekeepers Assn. (v.p.), Ky. Acad. Sci., Sigma Xi (pres. 1951-52), Phi Sigma, Gamma Alpha, Phi Eta Sigma, Alpha Gamma Rho (scholarship chmn. 1946-50, province counselor 1950-58). Methodist. Home: Lexington, Ky. Died Feb. 27, 1980.

TOWNSEND, REGINALD T., bus. exec.; b. Newport, R.I., Aug. 3, 1890; s. James Bliss and Eugenie Mathilde (Gilbert) T.; A.B., Princeton, 1912; m. Madeleine Drexel Dahlgren, June 13, 1919; married 2d, Ruth Poor Blake, Sept. 17, 1951; 1 son, Wharton Anthony Duncan. With Price Brothers & Co., paper mfgrs., Quebec, Can., 1912-15; asst. editor World's Work, 1915-17; editor Red Cross Mag., 1917-19; mng. editor Country Life, 1919, editor, 1920-35; pres. Staten Island Beach Land Improvement Co., 1921-54; v.p., sec., and dir. Lennen & Mitchell, advt. agency, 1935-51; v.p., trustee Radio Liberty Com., Inc., from 1951. Private Motor Bn., N.Y. Nat. Guard, 1916-18; capt. and maj. A.R.C., service in France, 1918-19. Past pres. French Inst. in the U.S.; dir. Madison Square Boys' Club. Mem. St. Nicholas Soc. (ex-pres.), Fedn. des Alliances Francaise, Soc. Colonial Wars (ex-gov., dir.), New Eng. Soc. (ex. pres.). Created Comdr. Legion of Honor (France). Roman Catholic. Clubs: Union (past v.p.), Coffee House, Dutch Treat, Circus Saints and Sinners (past pres.) (N.Y.), Colonial (Princeton). Author: This, That and the Other Thing, 1929; Mother of Clubs, 1936; 1912—A Twenty-five Year Record, 1937; The Comical Chronicle of the Circus Saints and Sinners, 1956; God Packed My Picnic Basket, 1970. Home: Cross River, N.Y. Died Nov. 12, 1977.

TOWNSEND, WALLACE, lawyer; b. DeWitt, Iowa, Aug. 20, 1882; s. John Robinson and Katherine Italia (James) T.; A.B., Hendrix Coll., Conway, Ark., 1902; LL.B., U. of Ark., 1906; m. Bess Wells Voss, Apr. 15, 1914; children—Eleanor Katherine (Mrs. Wm. F. Rector), Elizabeth Voss (Mrs. S. C. Rowland II). In practice, Little Rock, from 1910; registrar United States Land Office, Little Rock, 1922-25; dir. Voss-Hutton-Barbee Co., Comml. Nat. Bank, Little Rock Co., Inc., Longfellow Circle, Inc.; gen. counsel Fed. Home Loan Bank Little Rock. U.S. dist. atty., Eastern Dist. Ark., 1930-34; mem. Com. on Conservation and Administration of Pub. Domain, 1930-31. Dir. Ark. State Council Defense, July 1917-May 1919. Rep. candidate for gov. of Ark., 1916, 20; mem. Rep. Nat. Com. from 1928. Ex-pres. Community Chest and Council of Greater Little Rock, Community War Chest of Pulaski County; dir. Little Rock Boys Club (ex- pres.). Dir. Nat. Rivers and Harbors Congress. Ex-pres. Little Rock Chamber of Commerce. Trustee Hendrix College. Mem. Am., Ark. State, Pulaski County bar assns., Am. Judicature Soc. Methodist. Clubs: Little Rock and Little Rock Country (past pres.). Home: Little Rock, Ark. Died Jan. 1979.

TRABER, HERMAN L. (TRA'BER), ry, official; b. Kansas City, Mo., Apr., 27, 1880; s. Lafayette and Ella A. (Langworthy) T.; ed. high sch., Kansas City; m. Hortense V. Sergeant, Jan. 14, 1903. In various capacities with K.C.,Ft.S.&M. and St.L.&S.F. rds., 1898-1905; contracting agt. St.L.&S.F. R.R., at Kansas City, 1905-08; chief clk, joint commercial office, same rd. and C.,R.I.P. Ry. Co., 1908-09; contracting agt. St.L.&S.F. R.R., 1909-11; commercial agt. M., Okla. & Gulf R.r., 1911-12; gen. freight and passenger agt. same rd., at Muskogee, Okla., 1912-19; v.p. and gen. mgr. Okla., Kan. & Mo. Ry., at Miami, Okla., May-Nov. 1919; v.p. and gen. mgr. Okmulgee Northern Ry., 1919-20; traffic mgr. Kan., Okla. & Gulf Ry., at Muskogee, Mar.-Sept. 1920; v.p. and gen. mgr. same rd., 1920-24, receiver June 1924-Aug. 1925; gen. freight agt. M.P. Ry., at Little Rock, Ark., 1925-27, at Kansas City, 1927-29, and exec. gen. agt. same ry., at Kansas City, June 1, 1929-50; industry consultant since June 1, 1950; general chairman of United Charities Campaign, 1935. Member American Railway Engineers Association, Missouri State Planning Bd., 1941-43; mem. Mo. State Dept. of Resources and Development since Nov. 1943. Pres. Native Sons of Kansas City, 1938, Provident Assn., 1939. Clubs: Rotary of Kansas City (v.p. 1939), Kansas City, Mission Hills Country. Home: Kansas City, Mo. *

TRAINER, LEONARD R., corp. exec.; b. Las Vegas, N.M., Apr. 24, 1912; s. Thomas F. and Nelly (May) T.; student N.M. Normal Univ., 1929-32; Univ. of Ill., 1932-33; Univ. Colo., 1933-34; m. Marjorie Kemper Strickfaden, Mar. 5, 1937. Regional dir. Food Distribution Adminstrn., 1941; asst. dir. food distribution br., prodn. and marketing adminstrn., U.S.D.A., Washington, 1943-46, dir., 1949-55; pres. Sierra Broadcasting Co., Hot Springs, N.M., 1946-76. Mem. Phi Delta Theta. Elk. Club: Lions Internat. Home: Hot Springs, N.M. Died Oct. 31, 1976.

TRAPHAGEN, JOHN CONSELYEA, banker; b. Nyack, N.Y., Oct. 20, 1889; s. William C. and Caroline Ross (Maxwell) T.; student N.Y. U. Sch. Commerce; LL.D., St. Lawrence U., Canton, N.Y., 1934; m. Janet McAdam Voorhis, June 1920. Began bus. career with George C. White Jr. & Co. of N.Y., dealers in bonds; pres. Bank of New York, 1931-48, chmn., 1948-57, now mem. exec. com., bd. trustees; director, member executive committee International Nickel Co. of Can., Ltd.; dir. Am. Agrl. Chem. Co., Babcock & Wilcox, Centennial Ins. Co., Fgn. Bondholders Protective Council, Inc., Hudson Ins. Co., Internat. Nickel Co., Inc., Lazard Fund, Inc., Marine Midland Trust Co. Rockland County, Prudential Ins. Co. Gt. Britain, Skandia Ins. Co.; trustee Atlantic Mut. Ins. Co. Mem. fed. adv. council 2d Fed. Res. Dist., 1944-46, dir. Fed. Res. Bank of N.Y., 1950-52. Trustee emeritus Rockefeller Inst. Med. Research. Mem. Holland Soc., Pilgrims, St. Andrew's Soc., St. Nicholas Soc. Clubs: Century Assn., India House, Links, Union (N.Y.C.). Home: West Nyack, N.Y. Died Oct. 2, 1979.

TRASK, JOHN JACQUELIN, stock broker; b. N.Y.C., May 2, 1905; s. Frederick K. and Katharines S. (Jacquelin) T.; grad. Groton Sch., 1923; B.A., Yale, 1927; m. Elsie Y. Barber, May 27, 1930; children—Elsie Y. Trask Wheeler, John Jacquelin, Richard Ten Broeck. With Farr & Co., 1927-36; mem. N.Y. Stock Exchange, 1936-59; asso. broker Jacquelin DeCoppet, 1936-41; partner, v.p. Francis I. duPont & Co., N.Y.C., 1941-71, v.p. duPont Glore Forgan Inc., N.Y.C., 1971-72; vol. photographer Mystic Sea Port, Conn., 1974-77. Served from lt. (j.g.) to lt., USNR, 1943-45. Author: Stonington Houses, 1978. Home: Stonington, Conn. Died June 3, 1977; buried Evergreen Cemetery, Stonington.

TRAVER, W. ALLEN (TRAVER), texile exec.; b. Worcester, Mass., Feb. 15, 1886; s. Lewis Hammond and Margaret R. (Allen) T.; student pub. schs.; m. Ada Adams, June 14, 1916; children—W. Allen, Eleanor M., Shirley. Supt. William Allen Sons Co., Worcester, Mass., 1908-15; mech. supt. Franklin Process Co., Providence, 1915-19, asst. mgr., 1919-29, v.p., gen. plant mgr., 1929-44, pres., 1944-52, chmn. bd. since 1952, also dir.; pres., dir. So. Franklin Process Co., Central Franklin Process Co., Franklin Process Spinning Mill; dir. Citizens Savs. Bank, Citizens Trust Co. Pres. town council, Barrington, 1949-50. Mem. Am. Assn. Textile Colorists and Chemists. Mason. Clubs: British Empire, Hope, R.I. Country. Home: Barrington, R.I. *

TRAVERS, HOWARD KARL, U.S. Fgn. Service officer; b. Central Valley N.Y., Feb. 19, 1893; s. Alvah Hiram and Adelaide (Norton) T.; grad. high sch., Central Valley, 1908, Am. Sch. Accountancy, 1911, Pace Sch. Accountancy, 1912, U.S. Sch. Mil. Aeronautics, Princeton, and Sch. of Fire for Aerial Observers, Fort Sill, Okla.; m. Helen Margaret Wildern, Nov. 18, 1920; children—Helen Elizabeth, John Howard, William Robert. Paymaster and cashier, iron mfg. co., Hilburn, N.Y., and Niagara Falls, Ont., 1914-15; bookkeeper, Newburgh, N.Y., 1918-19; U.S. vice consul, Hull, Eng., 1919-20, Naples, Italy, 1920-23, consul, 1923-27; consul. Palermo, Italy, 1927-33, Southampton, England, 1933-36; 1st Sec. of Legation and consul general, Budapest, 1936-41; chief visa div., Dept. of State, 1942-46; was consul gen. Vancouver, Canada; then chief Foreign Service Inspection Corps; nominated U.S. ambassador to Haiti, Aug. 1951. Served as pvt., infantry, United States Army, Mexican Border, 1916, cadet, later 2d lt., U.S. Army Air Service, World War. Republican. Mason. Clubs: Rotary, Royal Southern Yacht, Metropolitan; Vancouver, Capilano Country, Royal Vancouver Yacht. Home: Washington, D.C. Died Dec. 25, 1976.

TRAYNELIS, VINCENT JOHN, educator, chemist; b. Cliffside, N.J., Oct. 3, 1928; s. Kazimer A. and Anna (Petrauskas) T.; B.S. in Chemistry, Rutgers U., 1950; Ph.D., Wayne State U., 1953; m. Elaine Ann Fairbairn, Sept. 12, 1953; children—Lisa Anne, Vincent Charles, Christian Louis, Lynette Marie, Stephen Francis. Postdoctoral fellow U. Minn., 1953-54; mem. faculty U. Notre Dame, 1954-65, asso. prof. chemistry, 1962-65; asst. head dept., 1963-64; prof. chemistry, W.Va. U., Morgantown, 1965-76, chmn. dept., 1965-72. Fellow Am. Inst. Chemists; mem. Am. Chem. Soc. (sec. St. Joseph Valley sect. 1957-59, chmn. elect. program chmn. 1961, chmn. 1962), W. Va. Acad. Sci., A.A.A.S., Phi Beta Kappa, Sigma Xi, Phi Lambda Upsilon, Alpha Epsilon Delta. Contbr. articles to jours. Research in mechanistic studies certain reactions of aromatic N-oxides, synthetic studies seven-membered sulfur heterocycles, dehydration and oxidative reactions in dimethyl sulfoxides, ylid alklation of nitro-aromatic compounds. Home: Morgantown, W.Va. Died May 2, 1976; buried East Oak Grove Cemetery, Morgantown.

TREADWAY, LAURIS GOLDSMITH, hotel exec.; b. Somerville, Mass., May 13, 1884; s. Charles and Emma (Goldsmith) T.; B.S., Dartmouth, 1908; m. Helen Fowle, Apr. 10, 1911; children—Richard, John, Antoinette, David, Jane. With Williams Inn, Williamstown, Mass.; founder Treadway Inn Corp., 1912, managing director, 1912-55, chairman of the board, 1955—; director Williamstown National Bank, Williamstown Savs. Bank. Served as maj., U.S. Army Res., 1919-49. Mem. Am., N.E. (past pres.), Mass. (past pres.). Vt. (past pres.) N.Y. (hon. life mem.) hotel assns., Berkshire Inn Keepers Assn. (past pres.). Republican. Conglist. Mason (Shriner). Home: Williamstown, Mass. *

TREADWAY, WALTER LEWIS, psychiatrist; b. Arnezville, Illinois, January 16, 1886; s. Henry and Margaret (Wilson) T.; M.D., Barnes Medical College, St. Louis, 1907; Sc.D., University of Southern California, 1945; married Sylvia Houston, August 5, 1908. Assistant physician Jacksonville (Ill.) State Hospital, 1908-12; clin. psychiatrist Ill. Psychiatric Inst., 1912-13; asst. surgeon U.S. Pub. Health Service, 1913, passed asst. surgeon, 1917, surgeon, 1921, asst. surgeon gen., 1930-38, med. dir., 1939-44, retired. Assigned as asso. Dept. of Preventive Medicine, Harvard Med. Sch., 1922-25; asso. psychiatry, Calif. U. Med. Sch., 1939-41; lecturer in psychiatry, U. of So. Calif. Med. Sch.; signatory to convention on Limitation of Mfr. of Narcotic Drugs, Geneva, 1931; chief div. of Mental Hygiene Bur., U.S. Pub. Health Service, 1930, 1938. Med. mem. Permanent Retiring Bd., U.S. Navy, World War I; Port Med. Rep., U.S. Ship Adms., Los Angeles, World War II. Diplomate American Board of Psychiatry. Fellow American College Physicians, A.M.A., American Psychiatric Assn.; associate editor of Am. Jour. of Psyhicatry); mem. Royal Acad. Medicine (Ireland), Sigma Xi. Presbyterian. Address: Santa Barbara, Calif. *

TREBILCOCK, PAUL, portrait painter; b. Chgo., Feb. 13, 1902; s. William Paul and Adele Christine (Christensen) T.; grad. Oak Park and River Forest High Sch., 1920; student U. Ill., 1920-22, Art Inst. Chgo., 1922-24; m. Amaylia Chiarina Castaldo, Apr. 8, 1929; children—William Anthony, Adrienne Claire. Principal works: portraits of notable persons, including: President Franklin D. Roosevelt, Governor Albert A. Ritchie, Mrs. Reginald Vanderbilt, Viscountess Furness, Harold W. Dodds, Stephen Francis Voorhees, Charles H. Warren, Edward Shelton, Willard C. Rappleye, Charles Proctor Cooper, Dr. William G. MacCallum, Dr. Edwards A. Park, Dr. George E. Bennett, Dr. E.V. McCollum, David Kinley, George Eastman, Rush Rhees, Harvie Branscomb, Walter Dill Scott, Irving S. Cutter, George I. Haight, Oliver C. Carmichael, Francis Henry Taylor, Bishop Horace W. B. Donegan, Benjamin F. Fairless, Mrs. Benjamin F. Fairless, Wilfred S. Sykes, Cleo F. Craig, Walter S. Franklin, William B. Storey, Carle C. Conway, K. S. Adams, Harrison Jones, Charles Hayden, Lucius M. Boomer, George O. May, Harold H. Helm, Clarence C. Michalis, James E. Gowan, J. Hamilton Cheston, Edwin S.S. Sutherland, Alfred H. Cosden, C. Brewster Rhoads, others. Recipient Martin B. Cahn prize, 1925, William Randolph Hearst prize, 1926, Frank G. Logan medal and prize, 1928, William H. French gold medal, 1929, Municipal Art League Portrait prize, 1937 (all received at Chicago Art Inst.), first prize $1,000 Chicago Galleries Assn., 1926, 1st Hallgarten prize NAD, N.Y., 1931; Newport (R.I.) Art Assn. prize Mem. NAD. Clubs: Arts, Tavern, Cliff Dwellers (Chgo.); Chelsea Arts (London); Century Assn. (N.Y.C.) Home: New York, N.Y. Died Apr. 8, 1981.

TREDWELL, ROGER CULVER, consul gen.; b. Brooklyn, N.Y., Jan. 12, 1885; s. Alanson and Frances Vail (Culver) T.; A.B., Yale, 1907; studied U. of Grenoble, France, 1908; m. Winifred van Shaick Reed (died 1921); m. 2d, at Tokyo, Japan, Louise Orr, 1929, Appointed consular assistant, Apr. 14, 1909; vice and dep. consul gen., at Yokohama, Japan, 1910-11; dep. consul gen., London, Aug.-Sept.1911; vice and dep. consul, at Burslem, Eng., 1911-12, Dresden, Germany, May-July 1912; duty in London and in Dept. of State, at Washington, D.C., 1912-13; consul at Bristol, 1913-14; in charge of consulate, Amsterdam, 1914, Naples, 1914; consul at Leghorn, 1914-15, Turin, 1915-16, Rome, 1916-17; in State Dept., Washington, 1917; assigned to Petrograd, July 1917, to Vologda and Moscow, 1918; proceeded to Tashkent, Turkestan, May 1918; held under arrest by Soviet govt. for 6 months, 1918-19; ordered to American Peace Mission, Paris, May 1919, to Dept. of State, Sept. 1919; apptd. consul gen. at large, Nov. 25, 1921; foreign service insp., July 1, 1924; consel gen. at Hong Kong, 1925-30, at Sydney, Australia, 1930-31, Stockholm, Sweden, 1932-33; assigned to Dept of State, Washington, since 1933. Clubs: University, Racquet (Washington). Address: Washington, D.C. *

TREFFLICH, HENRY, animal importer; b. Hamburg, Germany, Jan. 9, 1908 (came to U.S. 1923, naturalized 1934); s. Heinrich and Carolina (Jahn) T.; student pub. schs., Hamburg; m. Alberta Stetin, June 27, 1942; children—Richard, Carol, Arno, Marlene. Animal dealer, 1928-73, established Henry Trefflich Animal Co., 1931, set up agys. in Far East for collection of animals; established collecting agys., West Africa, 1936, later worldwide; pioneer importer of monkeys in large quantities for research, importation heavy livestock by air transport; importer monkeys Nat. Found. Infantile Paralysis, 1939-42. Clubs: Adventurers, The Players (N.Y.C.). Author: (with Baynard Kendrick) They Never Talk Back, 1953; (with Edward Anthony) Jungle for Sale, 1967. Address: Whitehouse Station, N.J. Died July 7, 1978.

TREIDE, HENRY E., financier; b. Baltimore, Nov. 28, 1884; s. George Charles and Susanna (Winters) T.; ed. Deichmans Prep. Sch., 1897; A.B. Johns Hopkins U., 1903; m. Mary Bell Baker, June 11, 1912; children—George Baker (dec.), Elizabeth Baker (Mrs. Abner Mcgehee Harvey), George Baker. Asso. with father in the firm Treide & Sons, founded 1869, 1903, full partner 1912 until firm sold 1929: engaged in internat. finance specializing in acceptances, 1929-30; fgn. dir. for the Baltimore Trust Co., 1929-35; assisted in orgn., v.p., Baltimore Steamship Co., 1930; dir. Davision Chem. Co., 1931, exec. v.p., gen. mgr., chmn. bd., 1931-32, pres., 1932-33, coreceiver, 1935, trustee under 77 b. Co-trustee Standard Power & Gasn., 1938; president Presbyterian Eye, Ear and Throat Hospital. A founder night courses Johns Hopkins U. Regional dir. Manpower Commn. for the States of Md., Va., N.C., W.Va. and D.C., 1943; chief gov. aid on subsidies maritime adminstr., Dept. Commerce, 1950-51. Pres. Baltimore Art Museum, 1937-40, trustee since 1932; trustee Peabody Inst., Md. Inst., Buckingham Found., Y.M.C.A., Presbyn. Eye and Ear Hosp. Mem. Council of Civil Service (U.S.) 4th Region. Capt. Q.M.C., C.E. div., U.S. Army, 1919. Recipient medal for Outstanding Contributions to Civic Advancement by Baltimore Advt. Club, 1939. Mem. Baltimore Assn. Credit Men, Baltimore Criminal Justice Commn. (a founder), Mayer's Art Commn. Presbyn. (trustee). Clubs: American (London); Maryland, Elkridge (Baltimore). Address: Baltimore. *

TRENAM, JOHN JAMES, lawyer; b. Evanston, Wyo., July 13, 1912; s. Erwin Wayne and Leah Bush) T.; student U. Utah, 1931-33; B.S., Georgetown U., 1940, LL.B., 1944; m. Mary Eloise Smith, Oct. 31, 1935; children—John James, Patricia Adelle. Admitted to D.C. bar, 1944, Fla. bar, 1948; atty. Office Chief Counsel, Bur. Internal Revenue, 1945-47; mem. firm Fowler, White, Collins, Gillen Humkey and Trenam, Tampa, Miami and St. Petersburg, Fla., 1948-69; mem. firm Trenam, Simmons, Kemker, Scharf & Barkin,

Tampa, 1970-78; vis. prof. Stetson U. Coll. Law, St. Petersburg, from 1953. Bd. dirs. Tampa Philharmonic Assn., 1963-70; pres. Estate Planners Council Tampa, 1963-64. Mem. Tampa and Hillsborough County (pres. 1961), Fla. (bd. govs. 1963-69), Am. bar assns., Sigma Chi, Phi Alpha Delta, Pi Gamma Mu. Kiwanian. Clubs: Tampa Yacht and Country (sec. 1962-65, 71-72, vice commodore 1972-73, commodore 1973-74), University (pres. 1965, sec. dir. 1970-73). Home: Tampa, Fla. Died Mar. 23, 1978.

TRESSLER, DONALD KITELEY, pub. co. exec.; b. Cin., Nov. 7, 1894; s. Martin Luther and Florence (Mereness) T.; student Miami U., Oxford, O., 1909-10; A.B., U. Mich., 1913; Ph.D., Cornell U., 1918; m. Ella Bagley Watkins, Apr. 23, 1919; children—Eleanor Marjorie, Wilfred Watkins. Instr. chemistry Flint (Mich.) High Sch., 1913-14; asst. instr. chemistry Cornell U., 1914-17; instr. agr. and food chemistry, Ore. State Coll., 1917-18; spl. asst. U.S. Bur. Fisheries, 1918-19; fellow Mellon Inst. Indsl. Research, 1920-22, sr. indsl. fellow, 1923-29; rep. U.S. Dept. Commerce, Brazilian Centennial Expn., 1922-23; chief chemist Birdseye Labs., 1929-33; head chemistry div., chief research N.Y. State Agr. Expt. Sta., also prof. agr. and food chemistry Cornell U., 1933-43, prof. chemistry Sch. Nutrition, Cornell, 1941-43; mgr. Consumers Inst., Gen. Electric Co., 1944-45, cons. foods and refrigeration 1943-50; adj. prof. food tech. N.Y. U., 1947-50; vis. prof. Laval U., 1941, 46, 47; sci. dir. Q.M. Food and Container Inst. U.S. Army, 1950-58; pres. Avi Pub. Co., Westport, Conn., 1957-81; mgr. Donald K. Tressler & Assos., Westport. Cons. OCDM, 1958-64; cons. HEW, 1959-61. Received exhibitor's gold medal Brazilian Centennial Expn., 1923; Distinguished Service award Am. Soc. Refrigerating and Air Conditioning Engrs., 1965, F. Paul Andersen award, 1971; 25 Year Service award T.R.R.F.; Nicholas Appert award Inst. Food Technologists, 1968, Hart-Babcock award 1975. Mem. Am. Chem. Soc. (v.p. 1943, chmn. agr. and food chem. div. 1933-35, pres. Rochester sect. 1938-39, councilor 1940-43), Inst. Food Technologists (dir. 1942-43), Refrigeration Research Found. (research adv. com. 1940—), NRC (fruits and vegetables com. of food and nutrition bd. 1941-42, liaison mem. 1950-58). Fellow Am. Soc. Refrigerating Engrs. (councilor 1941-52, treas. 1951-52), Am. Pub. Health Assn. (life); mem. Alpha Chi Sigma, Phi Tau Sigma. Rotarian. Past asst. editor Food Research. Author or co-author books relating to field, latest being: (with C.F. Evers) Freezing Preservation of Foods, 1957; (with M. Joslyn) Chemistry and Technology of The Manufacture of Fruit and Juice Production, 1954; (with M.A. Joslyn) Fruit and Juice Processing Technology, 1962; (with M.S. Peterson) Food Technology the World Over, 1964; (with W.B. Van Arsdel and M.J. Copley) Freezing Preservation of Foods, 4 vols., 4th edit., 1968. Contbr. 100 tech. and sci. papers, articles to profl. jours., mags. Patentee in field. Address: Conn. Died Feb. 28, 1981.

TREVETHAN, PERCY JOHN, educator, social work cons.; b. Hancock, Mich., Mar. 12, 1899; s. John and Elizabeth (Jenkins) T.; student U. Mich., 1917; A.B., George Williams Coll., 1921; postgrad. Boston U., 1926; L.H.D., Southwestern Coll., 1963; m. Anna Marie Thompson, Aug. 21, 1925; children—John Thomas, Percy Alexander, Weldon Ray. Sales dept. Standard Oil Co. of Ind., Duluth, Minn., 1925-26; asst. mgr. Morgan Meml. Goodwill Industries, Boston, 1926-31, dir. operations, 1931-41, asst. exec. sec., 1941-46; adminstrv. asst. Goodwill Industries Am., 1946-49, exec. sec., 1949; nat. exec. sec. Goodwill Industries of Am. Inc., 1949-56, exec. v.p. 1956-66; pres. Trevethan Assos., cons., Chgo., 1966-76; asso. prof. mgmt. DePaul U., 1966-72, dir. rehab. tng. dept., 1972-76. Mem. XII World Congress Rehab. Disabled. Bd. dirs. Bethesda Eye Research Found. (pres. 1964-76), Dept. of Goodwill Industries, Bd. Missions and Ch. Extension Meth. Ch., 1949; mem. Pres.'s com. Nat. Employment Physically Handicapped; mem. adv. com. Wage and Hour Adminstr., Dept. Labor; dir. Goodwill Industries, Oakland and San Bernandino, Cal. Recipient Pres.'s Distinguished Service award, Distinguished Service award Internat. Soc. Rehab. of Disabled, Pres.'s award Nat. Rehab. Assn., Outstanding Service award Nat. Society of Crippled Children and Adults. Mem. Am. Legion, Am. Assn. Ch. Social Workers, Nat. Com. Sheltered Workshops (dir.), Nat. Com. Displaced Persons, Nat. Conf. Social Work, Internat. Conf. Social Work, Internat. Soc. Crippled and Disabled, Nat. Rehab. Assn., Internat. Soc. Rehab. Disabled (dir. U.S. Com.), World Commn. Vocational Rehab. Kiwanian. Home: Chicago, Ill. Died May 21, 1976.

TREXLER, HARRISON ANTHONY, coll. prof.; b. Freeport, Ill., Dec. 6, 1883; s. Filbert and Lelia (Perkins) T.; Ph.B., Hastings (Neb.) Coll., 1906; grad. study U. of Chicago, 1906-07; student Bonn, 1909-10; Ph.D., Johns Hopkins, 1914; m. Nell Bullard, July 12, 1916; children—James Hugh, David William. Prof. of history, Hardin Coll., 1907-09; acting prof. hist. and polit. science, Allegheny Coll., 1910-11; asst. prof. same, U. of Mont., 1913-19; prof. polit. science, Whitman Coll., Wash., 1919-23; prof. history and polit. science, Birmingham-Southern Coll., 1923-29; prof. history, Southern Methodist U., since 1929; mem. faculty, Johns Hopkins U., summer, 1924, 25. American Historical Association, Miss. Valley Historical Association, Southern Hist. Assn., Mo. Hist. Soc., Beta Theta Pi. Mason. Methodist. Author: Slavery in Missouri, 1804-65, 1914; The Confederate Ironclad "Virginia," 1938. Address: Dallas, Tex. *

TRIBBLE, HUGH WALLACE, photographer; b. Hilton Village, Va., May 8, 1920; s. Thomas A. and Irene (Cable) T.; ed. pub. schs., Va.; m. Dora Ellen Harris, Nov. 10, 1939; children—Patricia Anne (Mrs. John D. Griffin), Burton Taylor. Mold loftsman Norfolk (Va.) Naval Shipyard, 1939-50; propr. Tribble Studio, Portsmouth, Va., 1950-67; marketing mgr. Nat. Color Labs., Roselle, N.J. 1967-69, v.p. marketing, 1969-78; lectr. on control strobe light portraiture. Pres. Photog. Art and Sci. Found., Des Plaines, Ill., 1966. Served with AUS, 1944-46. Life mem. Va. Profl. Photographers Assn. (pres. 1955; award for service to profession 1960); mem. Profl. Photographers Am. (bd. dir. 1960, v.p. 1965, pres. 1966; Nat. award for service to profession 1959; Master Photography degree 1957; Hon. Master Photography degree 1966), Southeastern Profl. Photographers Assn. (pres. 1959), Profl. Photographers Assn. N.J. (hon.). Methodist. Mason (32 deg.). Home: Westfield, N.J. Died June 29, 1978.

TRIBLE, GEORGE BARNETT (TRIB"L), ear, nose and throat surgeon; b. Piasa, Ill., May 5, 1883; s. Samuel and Mattie Ellen (Barnett) T.; prep. edn., Shurtleff Acad., Alton, Ill.; student Shurtleff Coll.; M.D., Washington U. Med. Sch., 1906; grad. study U.S. Naval Med. Sch., U. of Vienna, U. of Pa.; m. Nina Alma Knecht, Dec. 8, 1906 (div.); m. 2d, Letha MacLohon Simkins; children—George Barnett (Ensign U.S.N.R., killed in action 1944), Wm. MacLohon. Clinical assistant, Washington U., 1906-07; instr, eye, ear, nose and throat, U.S. Naval Med. Sch., 1912-13, 1916-20; instr. in ear, nose and throat, Georgetown U. Sch. of Medicine, 1922-28, clin. prof. oto-laryngology, 1928-30, prof. oto-laryngology, 1930-34; asst. surgeon Episcopal Eye, Ear and Throat Hosp., 1922-27; mem. sr. staff oto-laryngology, Garfield, D.C. Med. Soc. hosps., teaching and exec. staff Doctors Hosp.; mem. consulting staff Garfield Hosp.; consultant, Annapolis (Md.) Emer. Hosp., London County Hosp. (Leesburg Va.). Member Fundacion Internacional Eloy Alfaro. Served in U.S. Naval Med. Corps, 1907-21, advanced from asst. surgeon to comdr. Med. Corps; Navy mem. Commn. Nat. Defense. Decorated Abdon Calderon 2d class, Ecuador. Past res. local chapter Pan-American Medical Assn. Fellow A.M.A., Am. College Surgeons, Internat, Coll. Surgeons, N.Y. Acad. Medicine; mem. Am. Acad. Ophthalmology and Oto-Larynogology, D.C. Med. Soc., Hippocrates-Galen, Soc., Washington Medical and Surgical Society, Am. Stomatol. Society, Assn. Military Surgeons of U.S., Washington Clinical Club (former pres.), Otolaryngol. Jour. Club, Internat. Med. Club (former pres.), former chmn. ear, nose and throat sect., D.C. Med. Soc., Washington Surg. and Med. Soc.; corr. mem. La Academia Nacional de Medicin de Mejico, Military Order of the Carbao. Phi Beta Pi, Kappa Sigma. Republican. Episcopalian. Mason (Shriner). Clubs: Army and Navy, Metropolitan, University, Army and Navy Country, Newcomers (Washington); Lions Internat. (hon. mem.). Contbr. to med. jours. Home: Washington. *

TRIEM, PAUL ELLSWORTH, author; b. Manchester, Ia., Mar. 4, 1882; s. Peter Ellsworth and Mary Augusta (Dewey) T.; student Coe Coll., Cedar Rapdis, Ia.; m. Minnie Wetzstein, of Chicago, Feb. 27, 1902; children—Francis E., Justin Dewey; m. 2d, Eva Helen Plotnik, of San Francisco, Sept. 20, 1924; children—Yvonne Patricia, Peter Dewey. Became newspaperman, 1902. Mem. Authors' League of America. Author: Direct Healing, 1914; The Mind Magnet, 1924; Psychology of Prosperity, 1925; Health and Power throughCreation; Alias, John Doe, 1930. Home: Manchester, Ia.*

TRILLING, LIONEL, author, educator; b. N.Y.C., July 4, 1905; s. David W. and Fannie (Cohen) T.; A.B., Columbia, 1925, A.M., 1926, Ph.D., 1938; D.Litt., Trinity Coll., 1955, Harvard, 1963, Case Western Res. U., 1968, Durham U., Leicester U., 1973; L.H.D., Northwestern U., 1964, Brandeis U., 1974, Yale, 1974; m. Diana Rubin, June 12, 1929; 1 son, James Lionel. Instr. English, U. Wis., 1926-27, Hunter Coll., 1927-30; mem. faculty English, Columbia, 1931-75, prof., 1939-75, George Edward Woodberry prof. lit. and criticism, 1965-70, univ. prof., 1970-74, univ. prof. emeritus, spl. lectr., 1974-75; George Eastman vis. prof. Oxford U., 1964-65; Charles Eliot Norton vis. prof. poetry Harvard, 1969-70; vis. fellow All Souls Coll., Oxford, 1972-73. Recipient Creative Arts award Brandeis U., 1968; 1st ann. Thomas Jefferson award in humanities, 1972; Lionel Trilling seminars at Columbia U., and Lionel Trilling book award established in his honor. Author: Matthew Arnold, 1939; E.M. Forster, 1943; The Middle of the Journey, 1947; The Liberal Imagination, 1950; The Opposing Self, 1955; Freud and the Crisis of our Culture, 1955; A Gathering of Fugitives, 1956; Beyond Culture: Essays on Literature and Learning, 1965; The Experience of Literature, 1967; Sincerity and Authenticity, 1972; Mind in the Modern World, 1972; also stories, essays in various periodicals. Editor: The Portable Matthew Arnold, 1949; The Letters of John Keats, 1950; The Life and Work of Sigmund Freud; Literary Criticism, 1970; The Oxford Anthology of English Literature (with others), 1973; uniform edit. of works by Lionel Trilling pub. by Harcourt Brace Jovanovich and Oxford U. Press. Fellow Am. Acad. Arts and Scis.; mem. Nat. Inst. Arts and Letters, Phi Beta Kappa. Club: Athenaeum (London); Century (N.Y.C.). Home: New York, N.Y. Died Nov. 5, 1975; buried Ferncliff Cemetery, Hartsdale, N.Y.

TRIMBEY, EDWARD JAMES, cement co. exec.; b. Utica, N.Y., Apr. 16, 1883; s. Henry J. and Nellie F. (Spratt) T.; M.E., Cornell U., 1905; m. Reba Tibbitts, July 24, 1907; children—Roger J., Ethelyn S. (Mrs. Theodore C. Swartz). Engr. bur. tests Internat. Paper Co., 1906-13, engr., 1915-18; engr. Canada Paper Co., 1913-15; supt. bur. economy Great No. Paper Co., 1918-20; propr. Trimbey Machine Works, 1920-52; dir. Gen. Portland Cement Co., Chgo. Bd. mgrs. Meth. Hosp. of Bklyn.; dir. Charlton Sch., Burnt Hills, N.Y., Am. Bur. for Medical Aid to China, N.Y.C.; trustee Green Mountain Coll., Poultney, Vt. Decorated Mil. Service medal Nationalist Chinese Republic, 1959. Club: Rotary (dist. gov. 1953-54). Home: Glens Falls, N.Y. *

TRIMBLE, HARRY EVANS, pub. health officer; b. St. Joseph, Mo., Oct. 21, 1888; s. William Sterrett and Mary Virginia (Trimble) T.; A.B., Coll. of William and Mary, 1911; M.D., U. of Va., 1916; m. Agnes Malley, Dec. 18, 1919; children—William M., Mary Ellen, John McD. Asst. surgeon U.S. Pub. Health Service, 1917-21, past asst., 1921-15, surgeon, 1925-37, senior surgeon, 1937-43, medical director since 1943; medical officer in charge Public Health Service Hospital, Washington, D.C., 1919-21, United States Marine Hospital, Detroit, Michigan, 1927-30, U.s. quarantine stas., Phila., 1926-27, Los Angeles, 1930-33, San Francisco, 1933-36, New Orleans, 1936-37, U.S. Marine Hosp., and U.S. Quarantine Station, Galveston, Tex., 1937-40, U.S. Marine Hosp., Chicago, 2ll., 1940-44. Served as med. officer, U.S. Navy, World War I; dist. med. officer, U.S. Coast Guard, 9th Naval Dist., 1942-44; dist. med. officer, U.S. Coast Guard, 7th Naval Dist., 1944-45. Med. officer in charge, U.S. Marine Hosp., Buffalo, N.Y., 1945-47; later med. officer in charge, U.S. Pub. Health Service, San Diego, Calif.; now med. dir. and adminstr. Santa Cruz Co. Hosp. Fellow Am. Coll. Surgeons; mem. A.M.A., Phi Beta Kappa.Address: Santa Cruz, Calif. *

TRIPP, CHESTER DUDLEY, mining and metall, engr.; b. Chicago, Ill., July 25, 1882; s. George A. and Marion Cora (Chester) T.; Ph.B., Yale U. (Sheffield Scientific Sch.), 1903; m. Madeline McClure Hanson June 16, 1909 (died 1955); children—Lois H., Madeline B.; married 2d, Jane B. Shiverick, Mrrch 3, 1958. Practiced as mining and metall. engr. and indsl. consultant, 1903—; pres., director Television Electronics Fund, Inc.; pres. Econ. Trend Line Studies, Greenway Mining Co.; director Television Shares Management Corporation, Heli-Coil Corp., Fiduciary Mut. Investing Co., Inc. Dir. Evanston Hosp. Mem. Art Inst. (gov. life), Chicago Museum. Natural History (life), Chicago Hist. Soc. (life). Clubs: University, Cliff Dwellers, Chicago: Yale (New York); Glen View (Golf, Ill.); Union (Cleve.). Home: Evanston, Ill. *

TRIPPE, JUAN TERRY, airline exec.; b. Seabright, N.J., June 27, 1899; s. Charles White and Lucy Adeline, (Terry) T.; Ph.B., Yale, 1921, M.A. (hon.), 1937; LL.D., U. Miami, 1941, Boston U., 1943, U. Cal., 1944; D.C.S. (hon.), N.Y. U., 1950; m. Betty Stettinius, June 16, 1928; children—Betty (Mrs. Stuyvesant Wainwright II), Charles, John T., Edward. With Lee Higginson Co., 1921-22; pres. L.I. Airways, Inc., 1922-23; mng. dir. Colonial Air Transport, Inc., 1924-26; pres., dir. Pan American World Airways, Inc., 1927-64, chmn., dir., chief exec. officer, 1964-68, hon. chmn., dir., mem. exec. com., from 1968; dir., chmn. finance com. Bermuda Properties, Ltd.; pres., dir. S. Eleuthera Properties, Ltd.; pres., dir. Liberian Development Corp.; dir., mem. finance com. Metropolitan Life Ins. Co., Chrysler Corp. (mem. exec. com.); dir. Hotel Waldorf Astoria Corp. Mem. Bus. Council (vice chmn. 1940), transp. council U.S. Dept. Commerce. Alumni trustee Yale Corp., 1949-53, successor trustee, 1953-68; trustee of the Carnegie Institn., Washington, Phelps-Stokes Funds, Nat. Safety Council, Eisenhower Exchange Fellowships, Inc. (exec. com.), Inst. Internat. Edn. Recipient numerous awards and honoraria from U.S. and fgn. govts. also numerous profl. orgns. Mem. many orgns. and assns., both domestic and fgn., profl. and trade assns. Clubs: Explorers, Economic, Cloud (honorary), Wings, Sky (honorary) (New York City); Maidstone National, Devon Yacht (Long Island, N.Y.); Mid-Ocean (Bermuda); Cotton Bay (Bahamas); Aero of New England (Boston); Maryland (Balt.); St. Andrews (Scotland). Home: New York, N.Y. Died Apr. 3, 1981.

TRITSCHLER, Y CORDOVA, GULLERMO, bishop; b. San Andrés Chalchicomula, Pueblo, Mexico, July 6, 1878; ed. in Mexico and Rome. Became Subdeacon, 1904; now bishop. Prof., Seminario Conciliar. Address: Monterrey, NuevoLeon, Mexico.*

TROSTER, OLIVER JOHN, investment broker; b. Bellflower, Ill., Aug. 13, 1894; s. John Emory and Sebra Ellen (Smith) T.; B.S. in Agr., U. Ill., 1916; m. Gretchen Louise Gooch, Nov. 6, 1919; 1 son, John Gooch. Partner firm Troster, Singer, & Co., and predecessors, N.Y.C., 1919-76; dir. Peoples Savs. Bank, Yonkers, N.Y., 1939-68, vice chmn. 1965-68. Treas. N.Y. Bd. Trade, 1937-42; bd. govs. Nat. Over-the-Counter Clearing House, 1965-71. Mem. Am. Revolution Bicentennial Com., N.Y.C., also Yonkers, from 1971. Trustee St. John's Riverside Hosp., Yonkers, 1952-68, pres., 1963-68; chmn. Yonkers Youth Bd., 1958-62; bd. govs. Yonkers Police Athletic League, 1956-62; N.Y. State commnr., treas. Interstate Sanitation Commn., from 1962; vice chmn. Boyce Thompson Inst. Plant Research, from 1963; bd. mgrs. N.Y. Baptist City Soc., 1933-69, pres., 1962-64; bd. mgrs. Ministers and Missionaries Benefit Bd., Am. Bapt. Chs., from 1934, v.p., chmn. exec. com., from 1964; bd. dirs. Hudson River Mus., Yonkers, from 1969. Served to 1st lt. Mexican Border, 1916-17, to lt. col., World War I, to col. World War II, as col. Korean War. Decorated Silver Star, Legion of Merit, Bronze Star, Army Commendation medal; named Yonkers Citizen of Year, B'nai B'rith, 1960; recipient Bill of Rights Gold Def. medal, 1966, Alumni Achievement award U. Ill., 1967; Silver Beaver award Boy Scouts Am., 1973. Mem. N.Y. Security Dealers Assn. (pres. 1934-37, bd. govs. from 1928), Bill of Rights Commemorative Soc. (pres. from 1964), Yonkers Hist. Soc. (v.p. from 1962), Vets. World War I (comdr. Yonkers barracks 1969-71, 11th dist. 1971-72), Retreads (nat. comdr. 1956-58, nat. coordinator from 1960). Clubs: City (Yonkers); Capitol Hill (Washington); Siwanoy Country (Bronxville); Downtown Athletic (N.Y.C.). Patentee last drop funnel, 1958. Home: Yonkers, N.Y. Died Oct. 2, 1976; buried Arlington Nat. Cemetery.

TROUP, RONALD MORRISON, physician; b. Kansas City, Kan., Oct. 4, 1886; s. David William and Mary Candance (Morrison) T.; M.D., Kansas City Hahnemann Med. Coll., 1909; s. Maxine Black Ashley, Oct. 17, 1943. Intern Grace Hosp., Kansas City, Mo., 1908-09; pvt. practice, Garden City, Kan., 1909-35, Berkeley, Cal., 1935—; mem. staff Hahnemann Hosp., San Francisco, Alra Bates Community and Herrick Meml. hosps., Berkeley. Served to maj., M.C., U.S. Army, World War I. Mem. Am. Inst. Homoeopathy (pres. elect, chmn. trustees 1960-61,pres. 1961-62, asso. editor jour. 1958-61), San Francisco County Homoeopathic Med. Soc. (sec.-treas.), Internat. Hahnemannian Assn. (pres. 1959-60). Republican. Presbyn. Club: City Commons (Berkeley). Contbr. profl. jours. Home: Oakland, Cal. *

TROUTMAN, HENRY BATTEY, lawyer; b. Rome, Ga., June 15, 1886; s. Marcellus L. and Elizabeth (Battey) T.; student U. Ga., 1905-06, 08-09; m. Margaret Foote, Dec. 21, 1912 (dec. June 1971); children—Laura (Mrs. Pollard Turman), Margie (Mrs. Thomas S. Harbin), Henry B.; m. 2d, Ruth Miller Shropshire, Aug. 12, 1972. Admitted to Ga. bar, 1910, since practiced in Atlanta; mem. firm Troutman, Sanders, Lockerman & Ashmore and predecessor firm, Atlanta, from 1910. Past mem. Aldermanic Bd., City of Atlanta, mem. Sch. Bd., 1920-21. Mem. Am., Ga., Atlanta bar assns. Episcopalian (vestry, diocesan fin. com.). Clubs: Lawyers of Atlanta, Piedmont Driving, Commerce (Atlanta). Home: Atlanta, Ga. Died Dec. 28, 1978; buried Westview Cemetery, Atlanta.

TROWBRIDGE, ARTHUR CARLETON, prof. geology; b. Glasgow, Mo., Mar. 4, 1885; s. Samuel Hoyt and Julia Almira (Goodhue) T.; B.S., U. of Chicago, 1907, Ph.D., 1911; m. Sue Estelle Bussey, of Minneapolis, Minn., Aug. 29, 1911; children—Charles Lambert; Carolyn Frances. Instr. geology, U. of Chicago, 1909-11, prof. geology, State U. of Ia., 1911—. Asst. geologist U.S. Geol. Survey, 1913, 19, geologist, 1921, associate geologist since 1924; geologist in Iraq for Turkish Petroleum Co., Ltd., 1925-26. Y.M.C.A. camp educational dir., Camp Dodge, Ia., 1917-18, Y.M.C.A. war personnel board New York, 1918; asso. dir. ednl. bur. War Work Council Y.M.C.A., 1918-19. Fellow A.A.A.S., Geol. Soc. America, Ia. Acad. Science; mem. Sigma Xi, Phi Kappa Sigma, Gamma Alpha. Republican. Methodist. Author: Geology of the Wheaton Quadrangle (Ill. Geol. Survey), 1912; Interpretation of Topographic Maps (with R. D. Salisbury), 1912; Studies in Geology (with same), 1913; Laboratory Exercises in Structural and Historical Geology (with same), 1913; Geology and Geography of the Galena and Elizabeth Quadrangles (with E. W. Shaw and B. Schockel), 1916; The Erosional History of the Driftless Area (State U. of Ia.), 1921; Geologic Reconnaissance in the Gulf Coastal Plain of Texas near the Rio Grand e(U.S. Geol. Survey), 1923, Home: Iowa City, Ia. my Y.M.C.A., Camp Dodge, Ia., 1917-18, N.Y. City, 1918-19. Fellow Geol.*

TROWBRIDGE, PHILIP NEWTON, business exec.; b. Chatham, N.J., Oct. 7, 1900; s. Alfred Muchmore and Edna May (Ferris) T.; student Lafayette Coll., 1918-19; m. Eleanor VanCise King, Apr. 24, 1926; children—Philip Newton, Richard King. With U.S. Cigar Stores, Inc., 1919-20, Everlasting Valve Co., 1920-21, Composers Music Corp., 1921-22; with N.J. Bell Telephone Co., 1922-67, gen. mdsg. mgr., 1955-60, sec., treas., 1960-67; past dir. First Nat. Bank & Trust Co., Camden, N.J., First Nat. Bank, Stone Harbor, N.J.; adv. com. Nat. State Bank, Summit (N.J.) br. Mem. Common Council, Summit, 1961-73. Club: Essex (Newark). Home: Stone Harbor, N.J. Died Oct. 27, 1973.

TROWBRIDGE, WILLIAM SHERMAN, ry, executive; b. Pawling, N.Y., Jan. 11, 1880; s. Belden C. and Josephine M. (Campbell) T.; ed. high sch., Pawling and Hackensack, N.J.; m. Mildred S. Warner, June 30, 1905; children—Marion Warner, Marjory Annis, Lois Sabin. With N.Y.C. R.R., 1895-1911; asst. auditor B.&A. R.R., 1911-15, auditor, 1915-18; comptroller B.&M. R.R., 1918-30, v.p. since 1930; treas. North Station Hotel Building; director Boston & Maine Transportation Company, Springfield Terminal Railway; vice president, treasurer and dir. North Station Industrial Bldg., Inc. Republican. Methodist. Mason. Clubs: Algonquin, Traffic Club of N.E. Home: Newtonville, Mass. *

TROWER, HARRY ALLAN, business exec.; b. Round Grove, Mo., May 28, 1885; s. T. J. and Virginia (Hunt) T.; ' ed. pub. schs.; m. Elsie Mae Coda, Jan. 1, 1911; children—Mrs. Merdese Morton, Thomas H., Helen Louise Walker. With Santa Fe R.R. Co., 1908-18, telegrapher, later relief agent, agent, traveling freight agent; v.p. Phillips Petroleum Co., Bartlesville, Okla., 1918-50. Club: Hillcrest Country. Home: Tulsa. *

TRUESDAIL, ROGER WILLIAMS, cons. chemist; b. Burlingame, Kans., Feb. 6, 1899; s. Ernest Leonard and Ruth (Williams) T.; B.S., U. Redlands, 1921; M.S., U. Oreg., 1922; Ph.D., U. Wash., 1926; m. Dorothy Painter, June 27, 1923; children—Betty Barbara (Mrs. George M. Fielding), Katherine Ann (Mrs. Philip J. Charley), Audrey Mae (Mrs. Roland H. McClure). Head dept. chemistry and physics Mt. Angel Coll., Oreg., 1922-23; acting head dept. chemistry U. Redlands, 1923-24; instr. chemistry U. Nev., 1926-27; asst. prof. chemistry Pomona Coll., 1927-31; lectr. chemistry U. So. Calif., 1935-44; founder, 1931, then pres., now chmn. bd. Truesdail Labs., Inc., Los Angeles. Ofcl. chemist Calif. Horse Racing Bd., 1938-79, adv. com. Nat. Conf. Adminstrn. Research, 1955-60; mem. Citizens Smog Com. Los Angeles, 1946, Pasadena Tournament Roses, 1952—. Trustee, vice chmn. exec. com., chmn. trustees faculty com. U. Redlands, 1935-74, trustee emeritus, 1974-79; trustee Sch. Theol. Claremont, 1955-65; bd. dirs. S. Pasadena YMCA, 1940-48; bd. dirs., bd. govs. So. Calif. Goodwill Industries, 1971-79. Fellow AAAS, Am. Inst. Chemists (councillor 1954-55), Am. Pub. Health Assn. (councillor food and nutrition sect. Western br. 1958-59); charter mem. Inst. Food Technologists; mem. Am. Chem. Soc. (chmn. So. Calif. sect. 1939-40), Am. Council Ind. Labs. (pres. 1949-51, sec. 1954-75, charter mem.), Assn. Ofcl. Racing Chemists (pres. 1953-54), Am. Air Force Assn., Am. Ordnance Assn., Navy League U.S., Los Angeles C. of C., Sigma Xi. Congregationalist (past moderator). Rotarian (pres. Los Angeles 1946-47). Clubs: Oneonta (pres. 1941-42) (S. Pasadena); University (Los Angeles). Author numerous papers in field. Home: Pasadena, Calif. Died Nov. 10, 1979; buried Hillside Meml. Park, Redlands, Calif.

TRUESDALE, MRS. JOSEPH R., pres. Metropolitan Opera Guild.; b. Larchmont, N.Y., Sept. 26, 1885; d. Drancis Markoe and Lucy Parkman (Higgins) Scott; m. Joseph Robinson Truesdale, Jan. 19, 1909; children—Marka (Mrs. M. T. Loening), Barbara (Mrs. Harold R. Talbot), Francis Scott, Lucy (Mrs. David S. Hemingway), Anne Robeson (Mrs. John C. Wood), Joseph Robinson, Jr. Pres. Metropolitan Opera Guild since 1942. Presbyterian. Home:Westbury, L.I., N.Y. Address: New York, N.Y. *

TRUESDELL, LEON EDGAR, statistician; b. Rowe, Mass., Mar. 15, 1880; s. Clarence and Linna V. (Streeter) T.; A.B., A.M., Brown U., 1907, Sc.D., 1931; Ph.D., Robert Brookings Grad. Sch., 1928; m. Constance Ethel Cole, 1916 (died 1957); children—Constance Emma (Mrs. Ralph B. DeLano, Jr.), Miriam Helen. High sch. prin., 1907-10; statistical editor Bureau of Census, 1911-14; agrl. statistician U.S. Dept. Agr., 1915-19; statistician Bureau of Census from 1920 to 1924, chief population division, 1925-48, chief demographer, 1948-55, cons., 1956-68. Fellow A.A.A.S., Am. Statis. Assn.; mem. Am. Econ. Assn., Population Assn. Am. (pres. 1939-40), Internat. Population Union, Inter Am. Statis. Inst. (U.S. representative on 1950 census committee), Phi Beta Kappa. Club: Cosmos. Author: Farm Tenancy in the U.S. (with E. A. Goldenweiser), 1924; Farm Population of the United States, 1926; The Canadian Born in the United States, 1943; Sex and Age of International Migrants (UN report), 1954; Early Poems, 1957; Farm Population, 1880-1950, 1960; Development of Punch Card Tabulation in the Bureau of the Census, 1890-1940, 1965; also numerous articles. Home: Washington, D.C. Died Jan. 12, 1979.

TRUMAN, HERBERT FREDERIC, lecture manager; b. Brooklyn, N.Y., July 1, 1882; s. George Richard and Clara Macklin (Eckert) T.; ed. pub. schs.; m. Vilena Wilson, of Brockville, Ont., Can., May 28, 1915. Supervisor lectures and concerts, Brooklyn Inst. Arts and Sciences, 1909-15; mgr. J.B. Pond Lyceum Bur., 1915-20; part owner and mgr. Coit-Alber, N.Y. office, 1920-22; booking mgr. Emmerich Lecture Bureau, Inc. Republican. Unitarian. Home: Flushing, N.Y. *

TRUMBO, DALTON, playwright, novelist; b. Montrose, Colo., Dec. 9, 1905; s. Orus Bonham and Maud (Tillery) T.; student U. Colo., 1924-25, UCLA, 1926, U. So. Cal., 1928; m. Cleo Beth Fincher, Mar. 13, 1938; children—Nikola, Christopher, Melissa. Nat. chmn. Writers for Roosevelt, 1944; founding editor The Screenwriter, 1944; war corr. USAAF, PTO, 1945; convicted contempt of Congress, 1948; served in Fed. Correctional Instn., Ashland, Ky., 1950-51. Spl. assignment State Dept. to UN Conf. Internat. Orgn., San Francisco, 1945. Mem. Authors League, Dramatists Guild, Writers Guild Am. (dir. 1945, Laurel award 1970), Delta Tau Delta. Club: Mulholland. Author: (novels) Eclipse, 1935; Washington Jitters, 1936; Johnny Got His Gun, 1939 (Nat. Book award 1939); The Remarkable Andrew, 1940 (also motion picture); (play) The Biggest Thief in Town (also on TV-BBC 1957), 1949; also verse; (motion picture scripts) A Man to Remember, Kitty Foyle, A guy Named Joe, Thirty Seconds Over Tokyo, Our Vines Have Tender Grapes, The Brave One (acad. award 1957), Spartacus, Exodus, Lonely Are the Brave, The Fixer, Executive Action, Papillon, Ishi; writer, dir. Johnny Got His Gun (Internat. Critics award and Spl. Grand priz Cannes Film Festival, 1971, Best of Festival and Peace award Atlanta Film Festival, 1971, Audience and Dir.'s award Belgrade Film Festival, 1972, Grand priz Japanese Internat. Festival Arts, 1972). Contbr. to Sat. Eve. Post, Vanity Fair, McCalls, Playboy, The Nation, Theatre Arts, Esquire, others. Author: Additional Diaglogue-Letters of Dalton Trumbo, 1942-62 (edited by Helen Manfull), 1970; pamphlets; The Time of the Toad, Collected Essays, 1972. Home: Los Angeles, Calif. Died Sept. 10, 1976.

TRUMBOWER, HENRY ROSCOE (TRUM'BOU-ER), economist; b. Passer, Pa., Aug. 27, 1882; s. Aaron R. and Amelia (Koch) T.; grad. Bethlehem (Pa.) Prep. Sch., 1899; B.A., Lehigh U., 1903; M.A., Princeton, 1908; grad. study, Munich, Germany, 1909-10; Ph.D., University of Wisconsin, 1924; married Josephine Allyn, June 10, 1916; one daughter, Josephine Allyn. Began as teacher, Pennington (N.J.) Seminary, 1903-07; fellow in economics, University of Wisconsin, 1910-11, asst., 1911-12, instr., 1912-15, asst. prof., 1915-16, lecturer, 1916, 20; mem. Wis. R.R. Commn., 1916-23; economist, Bur. Pub. Roads, U.S. Dept. Agr., Washington, D.C., 1923-26; cons. economist, same bur. 1926-52; prof. commerce and economics, U. Wis., 1926-52; emeritus prof. since 1952; dir. placements, School of Commerce since 1930. Trustee and member exec. com. Northwestern Mutual Life Ins. Co. Mem. Am. Economic Assn., Phi Beta Kappa, Beta Gamma Sigma, Chi Phi, Artus. Club: University. Contbr. on highway finance and highway and ry. transportation. Home: Madison, Wis. *

TRUMBULL, GROVER C., banker; b. Au Sable Forks, N.Y., Nov. 10, 1882; s. Richard Levi and Alice Augusta (Bly) T.; ed. high sch., bus. schs. and pvt. tutoring; m. Lillian M. Bartlett, Nov. 14, 1901; children—Marjorie E. (Mrs. Alf E. Werolin), Dorothy T. (Mrs. Guy A. Loomis, Jr.). Accounting business Armour & Co., Albany, N.Y.; with F.B.I., Washington, 1911-18; Liberty Nat. Bank, N.Y. City, 1918-28, merged with N.Y. Trust Co., 1926; with Chatham Phenix Nat. Bank & Trust Co., N.Y. City, 1928-32; v.p. Mfrs. Trust Co., N.Y. City since 1932; dir. Gauley Mountain Coal Co., Oil Transfer Corp., Westchester Fire Ins. Co. (all of N.Y. City). Republican. Mason. Clubs: Union League, Bankers (N.Y. City). Home: N.Y.C. *

TRUOG, EMIL (TRU'OG), prof. of soils; b. Independence, Wis., Mar. 6, 1884; s. Thomas and Magdalena (Keller) T.; B.S.A., U. of Wis., 1909, M.S., 1912; m. Lucy Price Rayne, June 24, 1925; children—Nancy Price, John Rayne, Martha Rayne. With U. of Wis., dept. of soils, since 1909, as asst., 1909-12, instr., 1912-16, asst. prof., 1916-17, asso. prof., 1917-21, prof. since 1921, head of dept. since 1939. Fellow A.A.A.S., Am. Soc. Agronomy (pres. 1938); mem. Am. Chem. Soc., Soil Science Soc. of America, Internat. Soc. Soil Science, Wis. Acad. Sciences, Arts and Letters, Sigma Xi, Alpha Zeta, Alpha Chi Sigma, Phi Lambda Upsilon, Phi Sigma, Republican. Presbyterian. Club: University (Madison, Wis.). Associate editor, Jour. Am. Soc. Agronomy; consulting editor of Soil Science. Contbr. to prof. jours. Home: Madison, Wis. *

TRUPPNER, WILLIAM CHARLES, econs. cons. firm exec.; b. N.Y.C., Oct. 14, 1911; s. Ernest Frederick and Catherine (Schultz) T.; B.S., M.S. cum laude, CCNY, 1933; postgrad. George Washington U., 1936-39; m. Dorothy Virginia Burr, Feb. 15, 1939;

children—Carol (Mrs. Peter Julicher), Kathryn. Economist, Commerce Dept., Washington, 1935-41; asst. to vice chmn. WPB, 1941-44; chief bus. div. Census Bur., 1944-50; asst. adminstr. Nat. Prodn. Authority, 1950-53; dir. Office Indsl. Mblzn., 1953-61; def. economist Rand corp., 1961-63; head CD project Inst. Def. Analysis, 1963-67; asst. dir. resource analysis Office Emergency Preparedness, 1967-73; sr. asso. Robert R. Nathan Assos., Inc., Washington, 1973-76. Mem. Artus Soc., Phi Beta Kappa. Author: (with others) Wartime Production Controls, 1949. Home: Chevy Chase, Md. Died June 11, 1976.

TRUSLER, HARRY RAYMOND (TRUS'LER), dean law sch.; b. Berwick, Kan., Aug. 16, 1882; s. William Thomas and Matilda (Johnson) T.; student Ariz. Normal Sch., Tempe, Ariz., 1898-1902; LL.B., U. of Mich., 1906; hon. A.M., Oskaloosa Coll., 1911; m. Anna Decker, June 30, 1906; 1 dau., Susanna Jane. Admitted to Mich. and Okla. bars, 1906; practiced in Enid, 1906-08; prof. of law Stetson U., DeLand, Fla., 1908-09, U. of Fla., since 1909; dean of Coll. Law, 1915 to retirement. Mem. Am. Bar Assn., Fla. Bar Assn., Phi Kappa Phi, Phi Delta Phi, Alpha Phi Epsilon, Alpha Tau Omega. Democrat. Mem. Woodmen of the World. Author: Essentials of School Law, 1927. Contbr. to periodicals. Home: Gainesville, Fla. *

TRYON, CLARENCE HOWARD, newspaper exec.; b. Meridan, Conn., Oct. 27, 1881; s. Albert Chauncy and Thirza (Dayton) T.; Ph.B., Wesleyan Univ., 1905; m. Hazel Van Houten Crampton, June 17, 1908; children—Leigh Crampton, Robert Kenneth. Asso. with Record, Meriden, Conn., 1898-1906; with News, Springfield, Mass., 1906-07; with Traveler, Boston, Mass., 1907-08; sec. J. J. Niland Co., mfr. cut glass, Meriden, Conn., 1908-11; treas. Meriden Press & Drop Co., 1911-33; asst. editor Meriden Jour., 1915-16, advt. mgr., 1916-20, treas. and bus. mgr., 1920-45; pres. and treas. Jour. Pub. Co. and pub. Meriden Jour., 1945-49; trustee Meriden Savs. Bank. Mem. Beta Theta Pi. Republican. Methodist. Mason (K.T.). Club: Home (Meriden). Asso. editor of Wesleyan Alumnus. Home: Meriden, Conn. *

TRYTTEN, MERRIAM HARTWICK, physicist; b. Albert Lea, Minn., Jan. 17, 1894; s. Ole Christopher and Bertha (Ovrl) T.; A.B., Luther Coll., 1915, LL.D., 1950; M.S., U. Iowa, 1924, Ph.D., U. Pitts., 1928, D.Sc., 1962; LL.D., St. Olaf Coll., 1951; D.Sc., Wesleyan U. (Conn.), 1951, Carthage Coll., 1952, Drexel Inst. Tech., 1956; m. Hedvig Kathinka Forseth, June 17, 1920 (dec. Aug. 13, 1980); children—Martha K., George N. Supt. schs., Starkweather, N.D., 1916-17; instr. physics Luther Coll., 1917-18; head dept. physics, 1919-24; asst. prof. physics U. Pitts., 1928-41; physicist OSRD, 1941-42, War Manpower Commn., 1942-43; exec. officer Nat. Com. on Physicists, 1942-44, Sci. Personnel Com., Interdepartmental Com. on Sci. Research and Devel., 1950-56; dir. office sci. personnel Nat. Acad. Sci.-NRC, 1944-67, cons. to pres. Nat. Acad. Scis., 1967-70. Chmn. adv. com. on sci. personnel CSC, 1945-50; cons. USPHS and Research and Devel. Bd., 1947-53; chmn. Com. on Internat. Exchange of Persons; mem. Commn. on Human Resources and Advanced Tng., 1950-54, vice chmn., 1965-69; mem. Nat. Manpower Policy Task Force, 1967-71. Trustee, St. Mary's Coll., St. Mary's City, Md., 1971-77; bd. regents Luther Coll. Served with U.S. Army, 1918-19; AEF. Club: Cosmos. Home: Decorah, Iowa. Died Sept. 8, 1978.

TSALDARIS, M. CONSTANTINE, Greek govt. ofcl.; b. Alexandria, Egypt, 1884; grad. Law Sch., U. of Athens; student polit. sci. and law, Sorbonne (Paris), U. London, U. Berlin. Practiced law, Athens; elected dep. Greek Parliament; became leader Populist Party; minister fgn. affairs, 1947-50; now vice premier. Chmn. Greek delegation Paris Peace Conf., 1946; chmn. delegation to 2d, 3d, 4th gen. assemblies of U.N., 1947, 48, 49, rep. of Greece, 5th Gen. Assembly, 1950. Home: Athens, Greece. *

TSANOFF, RADOSLAV ANDREA, educator; b. Sofia, Bulgaria, Jan. 3, 1887; s. Andrea S. and Tana (Shivatcheva) T.; student Robert Coll., Constantinople, 1902-03; A.B., Oberlin Coll., 1906; Ph.D., Cornell, U., 1910; L.H.D., Oklahoma City U., 1966; m. Edith Corrinne Stephenson, June 24, 1912; children—Nevenna (Mrs. Don C. Travis, Jr.), Katherine (Mrs. H. Fletcher Brown). Came to U.S., 1903, naturalized, 1927. Instr. philosophy Clark U., 1912-14; asst. prof. philosophy Rice U., 1914-24, prof., 1924-56, prof., emeritus philosophy, 1956-76, Trustee Distinguished prof. humanities, 1961-71; McManis prof. philosophy, 1971-76; Anderson prof. philosophy U. Houston, 1959-61. Vis. prof. summer, Boston U., 1926, U. So. Cal., 1928-29, U. Tex. 1925, 1927, 34-36, 41, Johns Hopkins, 1948, 49, Shrivenham (Eng.) Am. U., 1945. Bd. dirs. Houston Symphony Soc., 1931-59, v.p., 1933-36; trustee Mus. Fine Arts Houston, 1928-34. Mem. Am. Philos. Assn. (v.p. Western div. 1940, pres. 1941), Philos. Soc. Tex., So. Soc. Philosophy and Psychology, Southwestern Philos. Soc. (pres. 1950), Am. Assn. U. Profs., Tex., Inst. Letters, Tex. Folklore Soc. (pres. 1939), Phi Beta Kappa. Author: Schopenhauer's Criticism of Kant's Theory of Experience, 1911; Pawns of Liberty (with Corrinne S. Tsanoff), 1914; The Problem of Immortality-Studies in Personality and Value, 1924; The Nature of Evil, 1931, reprinted, 1971; Religious Crossroads, 1942; The Moral Ideals of Our Civilization, 1942; Ethics, 1947, rev. edit., 1955; The Ways of Genius, 1949; The Great Philosophers, 1953, rev., 1964; Worlds to Know: A Philosophy of Cosmic Perspectives, 1962; Autobiographies of Ten Religious Leaders: Alternatives in Christian Experience, 1968; Civilization and Progress, 1971. Contbr. to Philosophical Essays in honor of James Edwin Creighton, 1917; Contemporary Idealism in America, 1932; Higher Education and Society, 1936; Texas Folk-Lore Soc. Publs., 1938, 39. Contbr. articles to philos., lit. jours. Home: Houston, Tex. Died May 29, 1976; buried Woodlawn Garden Cemetary, Houston.

TUCK, JAMES LESLIE, physicist; b. Manchester, Eng., Jan. 9, 1910; s. James Henry and Selina Jane (Reece) T.; B.Sc., Victoria U., Manchester, 1932, M.Sc., 1936; Salter fellow Clarendon Lab., U. Oxford, 1936-39, M.A., 1949; m. Elsie Mary Harper, Aug. 11, 1937; children—Sarah Catherine Mary (Mrs. Donald F. Pasicka), Peter Humphrey James. Came to U.S., 1949, naturalized, 1955. Chief sci. adviser to Lord Cherwell, mem. personal staff Winston Churchill, 1939-44; mem. Brit. mission to Manhattan Project, Los Alamos, 1944-46; supr. Inst. Advanced Studies, Clarendon Lab., Oxford U., 1946-49; mem. staff theoretical div. Los Alamos Sci. Lab., 1950-55, asso. physics div. leader, also head controlled thermonuclear research, 1955-73; Walker-Ames distinguished prof. U. Wash., 1974-80; vis. prof. U. Waikeato, New Zealand, 1974; Regents' lectr. U. Calif. at La Jolla, 1975. Guggenheim fellow, Paris, Rome, 1962; decorated Order Brit. Empire. Fellow Am. Phys. Soc. Contbr. numerous papers to profl. lit. Home: Los Alamos, N.M. Died Dec. 15, 1980.

TUCKER, DONALD SKEELE, economist; b. Peoria, Ill., Dec. 17, 1884; s. Frederic Sidney and Mary (Stehley) T.; student Dulwich Coll., London, England, 1896-1900, Colo. Springs (Colo.) High Sch., 1900-02; A.B., Colo. Coll., 1906; A.M., Williams Coll., 1912; Ph.D., Columbia U., 1922; m. Avis Sessions Jones, Sept. 13, 1919 (died, 1946); 1 son, Donald Asa; m. 2d, Edith M. Kingsbury, 1948. Engaged as teacher in high schs. in Colo., 1906-10; sec. Colo. Coll., Colorado Springs, 1910-11; lecturer Columbia U., 1914-16; asst. prof., Wellesley Coll., 1916-20; with Mass. Inst. Tech., since 1920, prof. economics, 1926-50, emeritus since 1950. Member American Economics Association, American Statis. Association, Am. Academy Arts and Sciences. Au-Statis. Assn., Am. Acad. Arts and Sciences. Author: Peoples Banks. Home: Cambridge, Mass. *

TUCKER, EVERETT BRACKIN, coll. pres.; b. Smyrna, Tenn., Apr. 12, 1881; s. John Fulton and Linnie (Cannon) T.; grad. Smyrna (Tenn.) Fitting Sch., 1898; A.B., Vanderbilt, 1905; grad. student George Peabody Coll. for Teachers, 1915; LL.D., Ark. Coll., 1925; m. Eva Rogers, Jan. 2, 1914. Teacher pub. and pvt. schs., 1899-1902; asso. prin. Haynes-McLean Sch., Lewisburg, Tenn., 1905-06; teacher Wallace's University Sch., Nashville, Tenn., 1906-08; founder and coprin. Peoples-Tucker Sch., Springfield, Tenn., 1908-10; farmer and stock raiser Smyrna, Tenn., 1910-13; supt. schs., Searcy, Ark., 1913-16, Helena, 1916-21; dir. Forward Edn. Movement, Little Rock, and business mgr. Ark. Edn. Assn., 1921-23; founder, and editor Jour. of Ark. Edn., 1922; pres. Ark. Coll., Batesville, Ark., 1923-31; pres. Austin Coll., Sherman, Tex., Feb. 1931 June, 1943; retired. Mem. faculty Webb Sch., since 1945, Mem. Gen. Assembly's Adv. Com. on Christian Edn., Assembly's Ad Interim Com. on Home Missions. Mem. N.E.A., Presbyn. Ednl. Assn. of South, Pi Gamma Mu, Sigma Chi. Democrat, Rotarian. Writer and speaker on ednl. and religioustopics. Address: Bell Buckle, Tenn. *

TUCKER, GLENN (IRVING), author, historian; b. Tampico, Ind., Nov. 30, 1892; s. William W. and Bertha (Clark) T.; A.B., DePauw U., 1914, D. Litt., 1960; B.Litt., Columbia, 1915; D.Litt., U. N.C., 1966; m. Dorothy Gail Thomas, Nov. 10, 1917; children—William Thomas, Richard C. White House corr. N.Y. World, then advt. account exec. Served as capt., inf. U.S. Army, World War I; AEF. Recipient Mayflower award for best nonfiction by N.C. author, 1956, 64, 66; Thomas Wolfe Meml. award for distinguished writing, 1956, 66; Distinguished Alumnus award DePauw U., 1958; Historians Cup award Western N.C. Hist. Assn., 1958; Fletcher Pratt award for best Civil War book N.Y. Civil War Round Table, 1962; Ann. Writers' Conf. award for best nonfiction book by Ind. author Ind. U., 1964; Jefferson Davis medal N.C. Daus. Confederacy, 1967; Harry S. Truman award for meritorious service in field of Civil War history, 1968; named Ky. col. Mem. N.C. (pres. 1965), Western N.C. (pres. 1965) lit. and hist. assn., Phi Beta Kappa, Sigma Delta Chi, Delta Kappa Epsilon. Methodist. Clubs: National Press (Washington); Civitan (hon. life). Author: Poltroons and Patriots, 1954; Tecumseh, 1956; High Tide at Gettysburg, 1958; Hancock the Superb, 1960; Chickamauga, 1961; Front Rank, 1962; Dawn Like Thunder, The Barbary Wars and the Birth of the U.S. Navy, 1963; Zeb Vance, Champion of Personal Freedom, 1966; Lee and Longstreet at Gettysburg, 1968; War of 1812-A Compact History (Naval Side), 1969; Mad Anthony Wayne and the New Nation-The Story of Washington's Front-Line General, 1973. Home: Fairview, N.C. Died Oct. 26, 1976.

TUCKER, IRWIN ST. JOHN, clergyman, editor; b. Mobile, Ala., Jan. 10, 1886; s. Gardiner C. and Melville Leigh (Eckford) T.; B.D., Gen. Theol. Sem., New York 1913; student, Columbia; m. Ellen Dorothy O'Reilly, July 14, 1914; children—Ernest Edward, John Irwin, Daniel Eugene. Ordained priest, Protestant Episcopal Ch., N.Y. Cathedral, 1913; pastor, St. Stephen's Episcopal Ch., Chicago, since 1927; asst. news editor and religion editor, Chicago Herald Am., since 1924. Pres., Patriarchal Council of Ch. of the East, since 1948, Aramaic Inst., since 1948. Author: History of Imperialism, 1920, Out of the Hellbox, 1946, Friar Tuck's Breviary, 1933, Army of the Faithful (series of religious instruction), 1946. Editor of Light from the East, since 1948. Lecturer, composer, sculptor. Home: Chicago. *

TUCKNER, HOWARD MELVIN, television corr.; b. N.Y.C., July 10, 1931; s. Irving and Jeanette Tuckner; B.A., Columbia Coll., 1956; M.S. (Univ. fellow), Columbia U., 1957. Staff and mag. writer New York Times, 1956-63; writer, fgn. corr. NBC-TV, N.Y.C., Vietnam, 1964-68; corr. ABC-TV Chgo. bur., fgn. corr. London bur., Vietnam, Laos, Cambodia, India, Pakistan, Bangledesh, bur. chief, Hong Kong, 1969-73, bur. chief, television-radio chief corr. So. Africa bur., Johannesburg, 1977-80. Served with USN, 1952-54. Recipient Emmy award nomination for reporting while wounded in Vietnam, 1968, award for Bangledesh documentary, 1971. Mem. Fgn. Corrs. Club S. Africa. Contbr. articles to anthologies. Home: New York, N.Y. Died June 4, 1980.

TUFTE, E(NGEBRET) T. (TUF'TE), coll. prof.; b. Hatton, N.D., April 5, 1884; s. Thorsten E. and Guri (Bry) T.; B.S., St. Olaf Coll., 1909; M.A., U. of N.D., 1911 (scholarship in biology); grad. student Columbia U., U. of Chicago; m. Olga Clarina Hanson, June 12, 1928. Mgr. farm, Hatton, N.D., 1901-03; supt. of schools, Gary, Minn., 1909-10; asst. biology dept., U. of N.D., 1910-12; biol. survey of N.D., 1910-12; proprietor drug store, Hatton, 1912-17; head biology dept. and dir. placement bureau, St. Olaf Coll., 1912-49. Served as 1st lt., San. Corps, 1918-19. Mem. conservation com. Nerstrand Woods, appointed by Gov. Benson. Fellow A.A.A.S.; Am. Assn. mem. Am. Forestry Assn., Nat. Assn. Biology Teachers, Nat. Assn. Placement Dirs., Minn. Edn. Assn., Minn. Acad. of Sci. (council, 1933-38, vice pres., 1938-39, council, 1939-41, pres., 1941-42), Am. Legion. Republican. Lutheran. Contbr. to Minn. State examination in biology, and articles to jours. Home: Northfield, Minn. *

TUFTS, C(LARENCE) ALBERT, organist, composer; b. Centralia, Ill., Aug. 1, 1883; s. George Demente and Ella Virginia (Gilbert) T.; ed. high sch., Belleville, Ill.; under pvt. teachers; B.Mus., Strassberger Conservatory, St. Louis, 1906; grad. Guilmant Organ Sch., New York, 1910; coached with Guilmant; studied summer schs., Chicago Music Coll., Cincinnati Coll. of Music. and Master Organ classes under Eddy, Dr. Heinroth, Courboin, Riemenschneider; m. 2d, Frances (Sarah) Allen, Aug. 7, 1934. Toured Eastern States, 1911, Western States, 1913, giving classical recitals; settled in Los Angeles, 1917; teacher voice, organ, piano and theory of music; was organist, Temple Bapt. Ch., Philharmonic Auditorium; organist Arlington Av. Christian Ch., Los Angeles. Former subdean and sec. Los Angeles Chapter of Am. Guild of Organists; ex-pres, Los Angeles Musicians Guild. Asso. Am. Guild of Organists. Writer on Anglo-Israel Theory. Mason. Author: Modern Organ Playing. *

TUGGLE, KENNETH HERNDON, govt. ofcl.; b. Barbourville, Ky., June 12, 1904; s. Jesse D. and Sue (Root) T.; A.B., U. Ky., 1926, law student, 1925-27; LL.D., Union Coll., 1947; m. Vivian Shifley, Aug. 20, 1938; children—Kenneth Jesse, Sarah Baldwin (Mrs. Andrew Johnson). Admitted to Ky. bar, 1926; pvt. practice, Barbourville, 1926-53; commr. ICC, 1953-75, chmn., 1959; chmn. bd. Union Nat. Bank of Barbourville, 1934-53; lt. gov. Ky., 1943-47; pres. Ky. State Senate, 1944-46; chmn Ky. Legis. Council, 1943-45, Ky. Com. of Interstate Corp., 1944-48. Mem. Council of State Govts., 1944-47; chmn. Ky. Disabled Ex-Service Men's Bd., 1943-47; mem. Ky. Com. Resources and Functions of State Govt., 1950-52. Mem. exec. com. Ky. Bookmobile Project 1952-54. Trustee Union Coll., World Safety Research Inst. Col., Ky. active militia, 1942-46. Named to U. Ky. Alumni Assn. Hall Distinguished Alumni, 1970. Mem. Am., Fed., Ky., Knox County (past pres.) bar assns., Am. Judicature Soc., Am. Soc. Traffic and Transp., Ky. Hist. Soc., Pi Kappa Alpha, Omicron Delta Kappa. Methodist. Home: Arlington, Va. Died Feb. 18, 1978.

TUGMAN, ORIN, prof. physics; b. Rockville, Ind., May 26, 1880; s. James R. and Harriet (Fisher) T.; A.B., Ind. Univ., 1903; Ph. D., Cornell U., 1909; m. Eupha Foley (Oct. 6, 1912) (died Aug. 8, 1944);

children—Robert F., Loretta. Asst. in physics, Purdue U., 1903-06, Cornell U., 1906-09; asst. physicist, U.S. Bureau of Standards, 1909-10; engr., Western Electric Co., 1910-12; asso. physicist, Eastman Kodak Co., 1912-15; asso. physics, U. of Utah, 1915-22, prof. and head dept. of physics and chmn. grad. council, 1922-47, retired. Mem. A.A.A.S., Am. Phys. Soc., Am. Physics Teachers Assn., Am. Assn. Univ. Profs., Phi Beta Kappa, Sigma Xi, Phi Kappa Phi. Home: Salt Lake City, Utah. *

TUGWELL, REXFORD GUY, author, polit. scientist; b. Sinclairville, N.Y., July 10, 1891; s. Charles Henry and Dessie (Rexford) T.; B.S. in Econs., Wharton Sch. Finance and Commerce, U. Pa., 1915, A.M., 1916, Ph.D., 1922; Litt.D., U. N.Mex., 1933; LL.D., U. P.R. 1953, U. Pa., 1971; m. Florence E. Arnold, June 7, 1914 (div. 1938); children—Tanis, Marcia; m. 2d, Grace Falke 1938; children—Tyler, Franklin. Instr. econs. U. Pa., 1915-17; asst. prof. econs. U. Wash., 1917-18; mgr. Am. Univ. Union, Europe, 1918; instr. econs. Columbia, 1920-22, asst. prof., 1922-26, asso. prof., 1926-31, prof. 1931-37; asst. sec. U.S. Dept. Agr., 1933, under sec. agr., 1934-36; adminstr. U.S. Resettlement Adminstrn., 1936-38; apptd. chmn. and head planning dept. N.Y.C. Planning Comm., 1938; chancellor U. P.R., 1941, devel. cons., 1961-64; appt. gov. P.R., 1941; mem. Caribbean Commn. 1942-47; dir. U. Chgo. Inst. Planning, 1946-52, prof. polit. sci., 1946-57, prof. emeritus, 1957. Vis. prof. polit. sci. London Sch. Econs., 1949-50; Hillman lectr. Howard U., 1959; cons. Center for Study Democratic Instns., 1964-65, sr. fellow polit. sci., 1966-78; research prof. polit. sci. U. So. Ill., Carbondale, 1965-66; prof. summer session Columbia, 1962-63. Recipient Woodrow Wilson Found. award, 1958; Silver medal Am. Assn. Planning Ofcls., 1967; Bancroft Prize, 1969. Mem. Am. Polit. Sci. Assn., Internat. Inst. Planners, Delta Upsilon. Club: Cosmos (Washington). Author: The Economic Basis of Public Interest, 1922; The Trend of Economics (with various economists, also editor), 1924; American Economic Life (with Thomas Munro, R.E. Stryker), 1925, Industry's Coming of Age, 1927; Soviet Russia in the Second Decade (with various economists, also editor), 1928; The Industrial Discipline, 1933; Battle for Democracy, 1935; Redirecting Education (with others), 1934-35; Puerto Rican Public Papers, 1945; The Stricken Land, 1946; The Place of Planning in Society, 1954; A Chronicle of Jeopardy, 1955; The Democratic Roosevelt, 1957; The Art of Politics, 1958; Early American Policy-Six Columbia Contributions, 1960; The Enlargement of the Presidency, 1960; The Light of Other Days, 1962; How They Became President: Thirty Five Ways to the White House, 1965; F.D.R.: Architect of an Era, 1967; Grover Cleveland, A Biography, 1968; The Brains Trust, 1968 (Bancroft award 1969); Off Course, 1970; In Search of Roosevelt, 1972; The Emerging Constitution, 1975; Tugwell's Thoughts on Planning, 1975; The Compromising of the Constitution, 1976; Roosevelt's Revolution, 1976; editor, contbr.: The Presidency Reappraised, 1974. Address: Santa Barbara, Calif. Died July 21, 1979; buried Sinclairville, N.Y.

TULLAR, CHARLES E. (TUL'ER), v.p. and mgr. patent dept. Gen. Elec. Co.; b. Neenah, Wis., Mar. 21, 1880; s. Charles A. and Delle L. (Conover) T.; E.E., U. of Minn., 1901; LL.B., Nat. U., Washington, D.C., 1914; m. Estella E. Burns, Dec. 11, 1911. Station operator St. Paul (Minn.) Gas Light Co.; then station operator St. Croix Power Co., Apple River, Wis., 1901-04; elec. engr. and draftsman supervising architect's office, Treasury Dept., Washington, 1904-05; examiner U.S. Patent Office, 1905-19; asst. atty. patent dept. Gen. Elec. Co., 1919-28, mgr. since 1928, v.p. since 1934; dir. Gen. Elec. X-Ray Corp. Republican. Presbyterian. Clubs: Mohawk, Mohwak Golf. Home: Schenectady. *

TULLY, RICHARD WILLIAM, mgmt. cons.; b. Beaver Dam, Wis., Aug. 11, 1917; s. William M. and Erma (Thiede) T.; B.S.C., Northwestern U., 1940, M.B.A., 1945; m. Helen M. Blidy, Sept. 21, 1940; 1 dau., Carolyn H. With Montgomery Ward & Co., 1941-43, Swift & Co., 1943-46; with Foote, Cone & Belding, 1946-70, sr. v.p., 1958-61, exec. v.p., 1961-66, chmn. bd., 1966-70; mgmt. cons., 1970-77; prin. R.W. Tully Co. Inc., Honolulu, 1977—. Lectr., Northwestern U. Sch. Bus., 1946-50. Served with AUS, 1944-45, 50-51. Club: Oahu Country (Honolulu). Home: Honolulu, Hawaii. Died May 30, 1980; buried Honolulu.

TUNNARD, CHRISTOPHER, educator, city planner; b. Victoria, B.C., Can., July 7, 1910; s. Christopher Coney and Madeliene (Kingscote) T.; ed. St. Michaels Sch., Victoria Coll., U. B.C., Westminster Tech. Inst., London Eng.; M.A., Yale, 1962; D.Fine Arts, Union Coll., 1964; LL.D., U. Victoria, 1970; m. Lydia Evans, June 9, 1945; 1 son, Christopher. Came to U.S., 1939, naturalized, 1949. Designer, P.S. Cane (site planners), 1932-34; condr. profl. office as designer, site planner, St. Ann's Hill, Surrey, Eng., 1934-37, London, 1937-39; lectr. landscape architecture, regional planning Grad. Sch. Design Harvard, 1939-42; Wheelwright fellow architecture Harvard, 1943-44; asst. prof. city planning Yale, 1945, asso. prof., 1948, prof., 1961-75, prof. city planning emeritus, 1975-79; dir. city planning studies, 1969-70, dir. grad. program in city planning, 1950-60, chmn. dept. city planning, 1966-69, mem. U.S. Adv. Council on Historic Preservation, 1967-69. Chmn., New Haven City Plan Commn., 1960; Guggenheim fellow, 1950; Fulbright fellow, 1956; Archtl. Forum (Time, Inc.), 1944-45. Served with Royal Canadian Engrs., 1942-43. Recipient spl. award for landscape design Paris Expn., 1937. Hon. sec. Inst. Landscape Architects, 1939; chmn. town planning com. Modern Archtl. Research Soc., London, 1938-39. Clubs: Century, Yale, Elizabethan. Author: Gardens in the Modern Landscape, 1938; The City of Man, 1953; American Skyline, 1955; Man-Made America: Chaos or Control?, 1963 (Nat. Book award 1964); The Modern American City, 1968; A World with a View, 1978. Contbr. numerous articles to periodicals; lectr. community planning. Address: New Haven, Conn. Died Feb. 13, 1979.

TUNNELL, JAMES MILLER, lawyer; born at Clarksville, Del., Aug. 2, 1879; s. Henry Maull and Rhoda Elizabeth (Bennett) T.; A.B., Franklin Coll. (now combined with Muskingum Coll., New Concord, O.), 1900; m. Sarah Ethel Dukes, Nov. 10, 1905; children—James Elisha (dec.), James Miller, Robert White. Began as teacher pub. sch., 1903, advancing to prin. Frankford and Ocean View schs.; admitted to Del. bar, 1907; member firm White & Tunnell, 1907-19; practiced alone, 1920-36; with James M. Tunnell, Jr., as Tunnell & Tunnell since 1936; director First National Bank of Frankford, Delaware. Chairman Democratic County Committee, Sussex County, 1910-12 and 1914-18; del. Dem. Nat. Conv., 1916; Dem. nominee for U.S. Senator, 1924; chmn. Dem. State Com. during campaigns of 1928 and 1930; mem. Dem. Nat. Com., 1931-48; elected U.S. senator, for term 1941-47. Pres. Bd. of Edn. Georgetown Spl. Sch., 1919-32. Mem. Del. State Bd. Edn. Trustee Muskingum Coll., New Corcord, O. Presbyn. Mason (32 deg.), Odd Fellow. Club: Rehoboth Beach (Del.) Country. Home: Georgetown,Del.*

TUNNEY, GENE (JAMES JOSEPH), corp. dir.; b. N.Y.C., May 25, 1897; s. John and Mary (Lydon) T.; grad. St. Veronica's Parochial Sch., N.Y.C., 1911, La Salle Acad., 1915; hon. degree Arnold Coll., 1942; LL.D., Ithaca Coll., Nasson Coll., Me., 1959; m. Mary J. Lauder, Oct. 3, 1928; children—Gene Lauder, John V., Jay R., Joan T. Cook. With Ocean S.S. Co., N.Y.C., 1912-17; won light heavyweight championship of AEF at Paris, Apr. 1919; began profl. career as boxer, 1919; won championship from Jack Dempsey, Sept. 23, 1926; return engagement at Chgo., 1927; ret. undefeated, 1928. Hon. dir. Bank of Commerce, N.Y.C., Pittston Co., N.Y.C. Served with USMC, 1918-19; apptd. lt. comdr. USNR to direct athletic and phys. fitness program for USN, 1940, comdr., 1942, capt., 1945. Roman Catholic. Club: Union League (N.Y.C.). Author: A Man Must Fight, 1932; Arms for Living, 1941. Contbr. articles to mags. Home: Stamford, Conn. Died Nov. 7, 1978.

TUOHY, EDWARD LEO (TOO'E), physician; b. Chatfield, Minn., Nov. 28, 1878; s. Edward and Margaret (Towey) T.; A.B., U. of Minn., 1902, M.D., 1905; m. Ida Margaret Boyce, June 25, 1907; children—Edward Boyce, Mary Catherine. Began as bacteriologist St. Mary's Hosp., Duluth, 1905, chief of medicine, The Duluth Clinic, since 1914, pres., 1915-35. Served as 1st lt. Med. Corps, Camp Dodge, Ia., 1918. Med. adviser to regional area Am. Red Cross, and dir. Red Cross blood bank in connection with St. Mary's Hospital laboratories. Mem. Duluth C. of C. Fellow Am. Coll. of Physicians; mem. Am. Heart Society, American and Minnesota State med. assns., St. Louis County Med. Soc. (past pres.), President, Minnesota State Medical Society, 1945. Interurban Acad. Medicine, Central Soc. for Clin. Research, Minn. Heart Soc. (past pres.), Minn. Soc. of Internal Medicine (past pres.), Nu Sigma Nu. Republican. Catholic. Clubs: Athletic Club, Rotary (past pres.; gov. 9th dist.). One of contbg. editors Journal Geriatrics. Author of series of arts. and pubs. dealing with the problems of age. Address: Duluth, Minn. *

TUOHY, JOHN JOSEPH, banker; b. Indpls., June 27, 1926; s. Joseph K. and Winifred (McMahan) T.; B.S. in Econs., Wharton Sch. U. Pa., 1949; m. Mary Virginia Koschnick, Apr. 16, 1955; children—Philip Gerard, Mary Virginia. In trust dept. Mchts. Nat. Bank & Trust Co., Indpls., 1949-58; investment counselor Scudder, Stevens & Clark, Cin., 1958-61; asst. v.p. investment dept. Am. Fletcher Nat. Bank & Trust Co., Indpls., 1961-62, v.p. investment dept., 1962-66, sr. v.p. trust dept., 1966-68, exec. v.p., 1969-70, pres., 1970-72, vice chmn., 1972-77, also dir.; v.p. Am. Fletcher Corp., 1968-71, pres. 1971, vice chmn., 1976-77, also dir.; dir. Am. Fletcher Leasing Corp., Indpls. Water Co. Bd. dirs. Community Hosp., Marian Coll., Goodwill Industries, Ind. Cath. Conf.; chmn. pres.'s council Brebeuf Preparatory Sch. Served with USNR, 1944-46. Mem. Ind. C. of C. (dir.), James Whitcomb Riley Meml. Assn. (gov.), Am. Mgmt. Assn., Indpls. Financial Analysts Soc. (past pres.), Sigma Chi. Clubs: Columbia, Ind. Athletic, Gyro Meridian Hills Country (Indpls.). Home: Indianapolis, Ind. Died Dec. 7, 1977.

TUREK, ROBERT JOSEPH, paper co. exec.; b. Green Bay, Wis., Apr. 9, 1919; s. Edward and Laura (Noel) T.; Ph.B., Marquette U., 1940; m. Doris J. Gehr, Oct. 18, 1941; children—Thomas, Patricia, Paul, Daniel, David, Robert Joseph, Peter, Christina. With advt. dept. No. Paper Mills, Green Bay, 1940-47, advt. mgr., 1947-53, merged with Marathon Corp., Rothschild, Wis., 1953, Am. Can Co., 1957; promotion, advt. merchandising mgr. No. Products div. Am. Can Co., 1962, marketing mgr. Marathon Home Products Marketing div., 1963, v.p. consumer sales Paper Products group Am. Can Co., 1964-69; pres. Riverside Paper Co., Appleton, Wis., 1969-76. Served to capt. AUS, 1942-45. Decorated Air medal with 2 clusters, Bronze Star. Home: Appleton, Wis. Died Feb. 15, 1976.

TUREMAN, HORACE ELDER (TOOR'MAN), orchestra Condr.; b. Virginia, Ill., June 5, 1878; s. Charles and Alice Cecilia (Elder) T.; prep. edn., high sch., W. Denver, Colo., study Am. Conservatory, Chicago, Ill., and Schola Cantorum, Paris, France; m. Isabella Webber, June 26, 1902; children—Herbert Hopkins (dec.). Ruth Hopkins. Formerly dean of Coll. of Music, U. of Denver, and head of theory dept., Conservatory of Music, Denver; now mem. faculty Denver U.; condr. Civic Symphony Soc. of Denver. Composer songs, symphonies, etc. Home: Denver. *

TURNBULL, GEORGE (STANLEY), educator; b. Newcastle-on-Tyne, Eng., Dec. 5, 1882; s. George and Annie Honoria (Beldon) T.; came to U.S., 1892, naturalized, 1904; B.A., U. of Wash., 1915, M.A., 1932; m. Mary Lou Burton, July 31, 1927; children—George Stanley, Sarah Louise (Mrs. Kenneth Everett Johnson). Employed as reporter, copy editor, mng. editor, Whatcom Reveille, Bellingham, Wash., 1902-05; reporter, copy editor, asst. city editor, telegraph editor, Seattle Post-Intelligencer, 1905-16; copy editor, Seattle Times, 1916-17; prof. of journalism, U. of Ore., 1917-48, acting dean, Sch. of Journalism, 1944-46, dean, 1946-48, 1948; acting prof. journalism Stanford U., 1948-49, 56, visiting prof. journalism, Univ. Neb., 1949-50, copy editor (summers) Seattle Times, 1917, Portland Oregonian, 1918, 19, 43, 44, 45, 49, 50 San Francisco Chronicle, 1920, 21; editorial writer Oregonian, 1951; asso. editor Albany Democrat-Herald, 1951-55; research journalism history, U. Ore., 1955—, acting professor of journalism, 1958—; mem. journalism faculty, U. of Cal., summers 1925, 26; visiting professor University of Florida, 1957. Member Association for Education in Journalism, Kappa Tau Alpha, Theta Chi, Phi Beta Kappa, Sigma Delta Chi, Quill and Scroll. Republican. Conglist. Club: Eugene Kiwanis. Author: History of Oregon Newspapers, 1939; An Oregon Editor's Battle for Freedom of the Press, 1952; An Oregon Crusader, 1955; Governors of Oregon, 1959; also numerous articles on journalism and journalistic history. Contributor to periodicals. Home: Eugene, Ore. *

TURNER, (HENRY) ARLIN, educator; b. Abilene, Tex., Nov. 25, 1909; s. John Henry and Verna Lee (Hatchell) T.; B.A., W. Tex. State Coll., 1927; M.A., U. Tex., 1930, Ph.D., 1934; L.H.D., Berea Coll., 1976; m. Thelma Elizabeth Sherrill, Aug. 7, 1937; children—Arline Elizabeth (Mrs. Richard W. Fonda), Jack Sherrill, Richard Arlin. Instr. English, U. Tex., 1933-36; from instr. to prof. La. State U., 1936-53; prof. Duke, 1953-74, James B. Duke prof., 1974-79, James B. Duke prof. emeritus, 1979-80, chmn. English dept., 1958-64; Lindsey prof. lit. S.W. Tex. State U., San Marcos, 1979-80. Staff summer sch. W. Tex. State Coll., 1934, E. Tex. State Coll., 1935, 36, N. Tex. State Coll., 1939, Duke, 1947-49, 53, U. Colo., 1951, U. Tex., 1957, U. Va., 1958, U. Ill., 1961, U. Iowa, 1963, N.Y. U., 1964, U. Pa., 1968; vis. prof. U. Montreal, 1951, U. Bombay, 1964, State U. N.Y., Albany, 1978; Fulbright lectr. U. Western Australia, 1952, U. Hull, 1966-67. Mem. Fulbright Screening Com., Am. Studies, 1956-60, 62, 67-68, chmn., 1957-60. Served from lt. (j.g.) to lt. comdr. USNR, 1942-46. Guggenheim fellow, 1947-48, 59-60; Nat. Endowment for Humanities sr. fellow, 1973-74, Huntington Library-Nat. Endowment for Humanities fellow, 1977; recipient ann. Nathaniel Hawthorne award, 1980. Mem. Modern Lang. Assn. Am. (sec. Am. lit. group 1949-53, chmn. 1966-67), Soc. for Study So. Lit. (v.p. 1971-73, pres. 1973-74), South Atlantic Modern Lang. Assn. (chmn. Am. lit. sect. 1956-57), Am. Studies Assn. (exec. council 1955-57, 67-69, exec. com. 1958-59, 67-68, v.p. 1969-70), Southeastern Am. Studies Assn. (pres. 1956-57, v.p. 1955-56, 68-70, pres. 1970-72), Coll. English Assn., So. Hist. Assn. (Sydnor award 1956-57); Soc. Am. Historians, Nat. Council Tchrs. English (dir. 1961-66), Am. Council Learned Socs. (asso. mem., former mem. fellowship selection com.), N.C. Lit. and Hist. Soc. (v.p. 1976-77), Nathaniel Hawthorne Soc. (pres. 1979-80), Poe Studies Assn. (hon.), Phi Beta Kappa (hon.), Alpha Chi, Phi Delta Kappa. Author: George W. Cable: A Biography, 1956; Nathaniel Hawthorne: An Introduction and Interpretation, 1961; Nathaniel Hawthorne: A Biography, 1980. Editor: Hawthorne as Editor, 1941; The Negro Question, 1958; Creoles and Cajuns, 1959; Southern Stories, 1960; Mark Twain and George W. Cable, 1960; Studies in The Scarlet Letter, 1970; Critical Essays on George W. Cable, 1980. Mng. editor Am. Lit., 1954-63, editor, 1969-78; mem.

editorial bd. South Atlantic Quar., 1956-80, So. Lit. Jour., 1968-80, Arlington Quar., 1967, Resources for Am. Lit. Study, 1970-80, Studies in American Humor, 1974-80, Ga. Rev., 1975-80. Home: Durham, N.C. Died Apr. 24, 1980; buried Austin, Tex.

TURNER, ARTHUR GORDON, editor; b. Baltimore, Md., Oct. 12, 1886; s. Charles and Rosalind (Flynn) T.; ed. various schs., Baltimore and Washington, D.C.; m. Florence Brainerd, of Chevy Chase, D.C., Mar. 20, 1920. With adv. dept. Baltimore News, 1906-9; New York Times, 1909-10; again with Baltimore News since 1910, mng. editor, 1917-23; advertising mgr. Daily American, 1923—. One of the originators and developers of church advertising on a large scale. Episcopalian. Clubs: City, Baltimore Country. Home: Mt. Washington, Baltimore. *

TURNER, BENJAMIN DICKINSON, III, lawyer; b. Healing Springs, Ala., Nov. 6, 1886; s. Benjamin Dickinson and Mary Binion (Cocke) T.; student Marion (Ala.) Mil. Inst., 1904-06; LL.B., U. Ala., 1908; m. Floride Garner Powell, June 30, 1913; children—Martha Andrews (Mrs. Paul Pirtle), Benjamin Dickinson, Julia Wilson (Mrs. John E. Wilson), Floride (Mrs. Chester A. Huff). Admitted to Ala. bar, 1908, practiced in St. Stephens, 1908-09; sr. mem. Turner, Wilson & Tucker, Chatom, 1909-15; judge circuit ct., First Jud. Circuit Ala., 1915-25; mem. Stevens, McCorvey, McLeod, Goode & Turner, Mobile, 1925-48, McCorvey, Turner, Rogers, Johnstone & Adams, 1948-53; dir. Coca-Cola Bottling Co., Inc., Mobile. Trustee Bellingrath-Morse Found. Mem. Mobile C. of C. (pres. 1941-44), Ala., Mobile Co. bar assns., Kappa Sigma. Democrat (past mem. state exec. com.). Methodist. Mason (Shriner, 32 deg.). Home: Spring Hill. *

TURNER, ETHEL LOUISE TOTMAN (MRS. CHARLES FLAVEL TURNER), clubwoman; b. Fairfield, Me., Marr. 11, 1880; d. Arthur Herman and Addie Viola (Jones-Thompson) Totman; A.B., Vassar Coll., 1901; m. Charles Flavel Turner, Dec. 30, 1903; children—Louise Bigelow (Mrs. Karl Raife), Barbara Flavel, Arthur Totman. Teacher high school, Fairfield, Maine, 1902-03; president Woman's Improvement Club, Calexico, Calif., 1913-14, Imperial County Fedn. Women's Clubs, 1915-16, Coll. Women's Club. Imperial Valley, 1916-18; an organizer, officer and dir. Southern Calif. Legal Aid Clinic Assn., 1927-32; dir. and sec. Southern Calif. Soc. for Mental Hygiene, 1927-46; preview chmn. Calif. Motion Picture Council, 1929-31; mem. and sec. Los Angeles Citizen's Traffic Safety Com., 1930-35; mem. Associated Women's Com. for Relief of Unemployed Women, 1930-35; became mem. Los Angeles NRA Gen. Compliance Bd., 1933; chmn. child welfare div. Los Angeles Council Social Agencies, 1939-41, also chmn. social planning com., 1941; sec. and chmn. Southern Calif. Com. for Mobilization of Trained Women to Care for Young Children, 1941-42; mem. Women's Residential Cabinet, Community Chest, 1931-33, speaker, 1931-32, chmn. speakers' placement com. 1932; dir. Calif. Hut (rehabilitation of vets.), 1927-32, treas., 1928-31; v.p. Los Angeles Children's Bureau; chmn. Los Angeles Co. Child Care Com. of Defense Council 1942-45. Mem. Vassar Alumnae Assn., Escholtzia chapter D.A.R., Am. Legion Auxiliary. Universalist. Clubs: Friday Morning (president, 1926-28), Women's City (president, 1931-32), Women's University (pres. 1923-25). Home: Altadena, Calif. *

TURNER, JOHN CLYDE, clergyman; b. near Statesville, N.C., Mar. 31, 1878; s. John Chapman and Nancy (Tuck) T.; A.B., Wake Forest (N.C.) Coll., 1899, D.D., 1920; Th.M., Southern Bapt. Theol. Sem., Louisville, Ky., 1905; m. Bertha Hicks, Mar. 5, 1908. Ordained Baptist ministry, 1903; pastor First Bapt. Ch., Newport, Ky., 1905-07, Tattnall Sq. Bapt. Ch., Macon, Ga., 1907-10, First Bapt. Ch., Greensboro, N.c., 1910-48. Pres. Bapt. State Conv., N.C., 1928-32. Pres. bd. of trustees. Southern Bapt. Theol. Sem. Author: A Truth in a Smile, The Gospel of the Grace of God,Soul winning Doctrines, Our Baptist Heritage. Home: Raleigh, N.C.*

TURNER, JUSTIN GEORGE, investment exec.; b. Chgo., Nov. 5, 1898; s. Oscar and Bessie (Taxey) T.; student U. Chgo., 1916-18; LL.B., DePaul U., 1920; LL.D., Lincoln Coll., 1956; L.H.D., U. Judaism, 1960; Lincoln diploma of honor Lincoln Meml. U., 1962; m. Gertrude Levin, July 27, 1932; children—Paul, Barbara. Admitted to Ill. bar; partner law firm Turner & Turner, Chgo., 1921-43; partner West End Investments, Los Angeles, 1942-50, Turner Investments, Los Angeles, 1950-76. Manuscript cons. U. Cal. Library, Los Angeles; v.p. Nat. Lincoln Civil War Council; chmn. library com. U. Judaism, Los Angeles Bd. dirs. Sci. and History Alliance of Los Angeles County Mus.; mem. Friends of Libraries, U. So. Cal.; past pres. Cal. Civil War Centennial Commn.; bd. dirs. Cal. Sch. Hebrew Union Coll.-Jewish Inst. Religion; fellow Pierpont Morgan Library, N.Y.; trustee Nat. Found. Jewish Culture, Jewish Publ. Soc. Served with U.S. Army, 1918. Mem. Am., Miss. Valley hist. assns., Hist. Soc. So. Cal. (past pres.), Ill., Pacific Coast hist. socs., Soc. Am. Archivists, Am. Assn. State and Local History, Mus. Assn., S.W. Mus., Book Club of Cal., Renaissance Soc. Am., Keats-Shelley Soc., Modern Lang. Assn. Am., Am. Studies Assn., Bibliog. Soc. Am., Alpha Epsilon Pi. Mason (Shriner); mem. B'nai B'rith (past pres. Chgo. council). Clubs: Hillcrest Country (Los Angeles); Covenant (Chgo.). Author: Mary Lincoln-Her Life and Letters; Mary Brooks-A Biography; The First Decade of Los Angeles Jewry; Noah Brooks. Mem. editorial bd. or publ. com. Hist. Soc. So. Cal., America: History and Life, Lincoln Sesquicentennial Assn. Contbr. articles to hist. jours., revs. Home: West Los Angeles, Calif. Died June 16, 1976.

TURNER, MABEL BASCOM, educator; b. Jersey City Heights, N.J., Dec. 13, 1886; d. William Fisher and Ettie A. (Davis) Turner; grad. Bergen Sch. for Girls, Jersey City Heights, 1904; A.B., Mount Holyoke Coll., 1908; A.M., Columbia, 1910. Teacher of history, Barnard Sch. for Girls, N.Y. City, 1914-20; city exec. under Nat. Bd. Y.W.C.A., Prague, Czechoslovakia, 1920-21; sec. finance dept., National Bd. of Y.W.C.A., 1922-24; head of high sch. dept. Birch Wathen Sch., N.Y. City, 1927-29; prin. Nat. Cathedral Sch., Washington, 1929-50. Episcopalian. Address:Tomkins Cove, N.Y.*

TURNER, ROBERT CLEMENS, economist, educator; b. Hiram, Ohio, Mar. 2, 1908; s. James Jesse and Bertha Irene (Clemens) T.; A.B., Hiram Coll., 1930; M.B.A., Northwestern U., 1932; Ph.D., Ohio State U., 1937; m. Lenora Adeline Habink, Dec. 29, 1932; children—Roderick Habink, Alice Carol. Dir. Warren (Ohio) br. Hiram Coll., 1932-35; instr., asst. prof. econs. Wayne U., Detroit, 1937-41; economist WPB, Washington, 1941-42, dep. dir., 1942-43, dir. fgn. div., 1943-45; dir. bur. internat. supply Civilian Prodn. Adminstrn., 1945-46; dep. U.S. mem. Combined Raw Materials Bd., 1945; adviser internat. operations Office War Mblzn. and Reconversion, 1946-47; econ. adviser to White House Staff, 1947-48; prof. bus. adminstrn. Ind. U., Bloomington, 1948-61, chmn. dept. bus. econs. and pub. policy, 1957-61, Distinguished prof. bus. econs. and pub. policy, 1961-78, vice chancellor Bloomington campus, 1969-73. Cons. comptroller gen. U.S., from 1969; vis. prof. bus. adminstrn. Notre Dame U., 1954-55; cons. White House Staff, 1948-52; asst. dir. Bur. Budget, 1961-62; vis. prof. U. Philippines, cons. Govt. Philippines, 1968-69. Mem. Pres.'s Council Econ. Advisers, 1952-53, Pres.'s Commn. Budget Concepts, 1967. Mem. Am., Midwest econ. assns., Ind. Acad. Social Sci. (pres. 1955-56), Beta Gamma Sigma. Author: Member Bank Borrowing, 1938; Export Control, 1947; An Economic Portrait of Indiana in 1970, 1956; (with J.P. Lewis) Business Conditions Analysis, 1967. Contbr. articles to profl. jours. Home: Bloomington, Ind. Died Dec. 5, 1978; buried Valhalla Memory Gardens, Bloomington.

TURNER, SOL, musician; b. Kobryn, Russia, Dec. 25, 1905; s. Charles and Lena (Roseman) T.; ed. DePaul Music Sch., Chgo., Chgo. Mus. Coll., Am. Conservatory; m. Evelyn Turner, Dec. 24, 1933; children—Carole (Mrs. Morton Malitz), Lynne (Mrs. Paul Singer), Richard. Violinist, Chgo. Civic Orch., 1925-28, concertmaster, 1928-29; concertmaster St. Louis Little Symphony, 1937-42; leader Sol Turner and His Continentals in leading St. Louis hotels, 1937-42; 1st violinist St. Louis Symphony, 1929-43, NBC Symphony Orch., 1949-65; 1st and 2d violinist Chgo. Symphony Orch., 1943-49, 65-77; also tchr. Home: Chicago, Ill. Died Oct. 8, 1979.

TURNER, W. B., mgmt. cons.; b. Dayton, O., 1888. Mem. Turner, Granzow, Spayd & Hollenkamp; gen. counsel, dir. emeritus, hon. chmn. Standard Register Co.; hon. dir. Third Nat. Bank & Trust Co. of Dayton. Address: Dayton, Ohio. Died Mar. 16, 1980.

TURRENTINE, JAMES LEWIS, mfg. co. exec.; b. Marionville, Mo., Dec. 15, 1917; s. Raymond Clifton and Alice (Davis) T.; student Mo. Valley Coll., Marshall, 1935-37; B.J., U. Mo., 1939; m. Elizabeth McNerney, Nov. 2, 1940 (dec. Jan. 1967); children—James Drake, John Paul, Alexander Thomas, Steven Calhoon; m. 2d, Julie P. Buhler, Feb. 22, 1968; stepchildren—Roman, Luis, Carlos. Reporter, Chattanooga Times, Louisville Courier-Jour., 1939-44; with overseas br. OWI, 1944-45, Hazard Advt. Co., N.Y.C., 1946; with Pitney-Bowes, Inc., Stamford, Conn., 1947-76, asst. to pres., 1950-59, asst. to chmn. bd., dir. pub. relations, 1959-63, dir. employee and pub. relations, 1963-66, v.p. employee and pub. relations, 1966-76; mem. bd. Liberty Nat. Bank, Stamford; dir. New Hope Corp. Pres., Family Service Assn. Am., 1961-63; mem. pub. affairs research council Conf. Bd., 1965-76, council execs. co. contbrs., 1954-76, chmn., 1970-71; mem. bd. Nat. Pub. Relations Council Health and Welfare Service, 1960-67; mem. commerce and industry council Nat. Urban League; chmn. adv. com. New Eng. Inst. Med. Research, Ridgefield, Conn., 1962-72; mem. Stamford Devel. Corp., Urban Redevl. Commn., Stamford, 1960-65. Bd. dirs. Stamford Equal Econ. Council. Mem. Pub. Relations Soc. Am. Clubs: Innis Arden Golf, Sankaty Head Golf, Landmark. Home: Stamford, Conn. Died Nov. 30, 1976.

TURRENTINE, JOHN WILLIAM, chemical engr.; b. Burlington, N.C., July 5, 1880; s. William Holt and Ella (Rea) T.; Ph.B., U. of N.C., 1901, M.S., 1902; Ph.D., Cornell, 1908; m. Katherine Whiting Bacon, July 2, 1926. Teacher chemistry, Lafayette Coll., 1902-05, Cornell, 1905-08, Wesleyan U., Conn., 1908-11; with U.S. Dept. Agr. as research chemist, investigation fertilizer resources, 1911-16, dir. exptl. plant for extraction of potash from kelp, at Summerland, Calif., 1916-22; in charge potash investigations, 1922-35; pres., chmn. Am. Potash Inst., Inc., 1935-49, emeritus. U.S. del. to 3d Internat. Congress Technology and Chem. in Agrl. Industries, 9th Internat. Congress Pure and Applied Chemistry, 11th Conf. Internat. Union Chemistry (councilor), 10th Internat. Congress of Chemistry. Awarded gold medal, Acad. of Agr., France. Fellow A.A.A.S.; mem. Am. Chem. Soc., Am. Inst. Chem. Engrs., Am. Soc. Agronomy, Am. Planning and Civic Assn., Gamma Alpha, Sigma Xi. Clubs: Comos, Chevy Chase Country Club (Washington, D.C.); Chemists (New York). Author: Potash, 1926; Potash Deficiency Symptoms (with Eckstein and Bruno), 1937; Potash in North America, 1943. Contbr. numerous articles on hydro-nitrogens, electro-chemistry, fixation of atmospheric nitrogen, fertilizer resources of U.S., Am potash industry, goiter eradication. Home: Washington, D.C. *

TUTTLE, CARL BYRON, sr. v.p. and treas. S.S. Kresge Co.; b. Corunna, Mich., Aug. 18, 1881; s. George R. and Lojena (Dutcher) T.; educated public schools; m. Alice E. Thomas, Dec. 21, 1935; 1 son by previous marriage. With S.S. Kresge Co. since 1899, buyer, 1909-16, treas. and dir. since 1916, sr. v.p., 1938; treas. and dir. S. S. Kresge Co., Ltd., Mount Clemens (Mich.) Pottery Co. Retired 1945. Rep. Protestant Clubs: Detroit Golf, Detroit Athletic, Turtle Lake, Rainbow, Florence Club of La. Home: Detroit, Mich. *

TUTTLE, CHARLES H(ENRY), lawyer; b. New York, N.Y., Apr. 21, 1879; s. Henry Croswell and Penelope (Cooke) T.; A.B., Columbia, 1899, LL.B., 1902; m. Hélène L. Wheeler; children—Evelyn, Charlotte, Croswell, Jasmine. Admitted to N.Y. bar, 1902, and began practice at N.Y. City; mem. firm Davies, Auerbach & Cornell, 1907-27; now mem. Breed, Abbott & Morgan. Chmn. Selective Service Bd. No. 145, N.Y. City, World War I. Chmn. of Appeal Bd., No. 4. N.Y. City World War II. U.S. atty., 1927-30. Mem. spl. com. Nat. Crime Commn. since 1927; mem. exec. com. N.Y. State Reorgn. Commn., 1926. Trustee Coll. City of New York; mem. bd. higher edn., City of New York. One of incorporators Religious Edn. Foundation; chmn. Christian edn. Protestant Council of New York; trustee International Council Religious Education. Delegate to Rep. Nat. Conv., 1928. Mem. Am. and N.Y. State bar assns., New York County Lawyers Assn., Assn. Bar City of New York, Trade and Commerce Bar Assn., Alumni Assn. Columbia College Alumni Assn. Columbia Law Sch., Lake George Assn. Episcopalian. Mason (33 deg., Shriner), Elk. Clubs: National Republican, Lawyers, Columbia University, Church. Home: New York. *

TUTTLE, HAROLD SAXE, educator; b. Worthington, Minn., Mar. 19, 1882; s. Amos Elliott and Frances Amelia (Worcester) T.; B.S., Coll. of the Pacific, San Jose, Calif., 1905, M.A., 1911; B.D., Pacific Sch. of Religion, 1911; Ph.D., Columbia, 1936; m. Pearl Dean, June 17, 1905; children—Lois Avalon, Harold Dean, Cecile. Ordained Congl. ministry, 1911; dir. edn., 1st Ch., Los Angeles, Calif., 1911-12; pastor Bethany Ch., San Francisco, 1913-15; prof. edn., Pacific U., 1920-26; asst. prof. edn., U. of Ore., 1926-33; asst. prof. edn., Coll. City of N.Y., 1934-47; prof. youth leadership, Lewis & Clark Coll. since 1947. Research in honesty trends of children, 1929-33; college agencies for social motivation, 1935; social attitude of freshmen, 1933-36; Social Attitudes of Junior High School Pupils, 1940; Causes of Emotion, 1940. Author or co-author books relating to field; contbr. to mags. Home: Portland, Ore. *

TUTTLE, WILBUR C., author; b. Glendive, Mont., Nov. 11, 1883; s. Henry Clay and Anna (Dineen) T.; student pub. schs.; m. Bertha M. Stutes, June 23, 1917; 1 adopted son, Gene Edward. Successivley cowpuncher, sheepherder, railroadman with Northern Pacific Ry., saddle and harness salesman, cigar salesman, expressman with Wells Fargo Express, forest ranger, miner, cook, reporter, cartoonist, camerman, motion picture script writer, baseball player and baseball club mgr., becoming pres. Pacific Coast Baseball League; has written fiction since 1915. Democrat. Christian Scientist. Has written 40 books and over 1,000 mag. stories. Author: Wolf Pack of Lobo Butte, 1946; Straws In the Wind, 1948. Address: Encino, Calif. *

TWOMBLY, WELLS, journalist; b. St. Johnsbury, Vt., Oct. 24, 1935; s. Albert F. and Dale (Wells) T.; B.A. in English and History, U. Conn., 1957; m. Margaret Zera, Nov. 30, 1955; children—Wells Albert, Scott A., Jason J., Dale Helen. Sports editor Willimantic (Conn.) Daily Chronicle, 1957-58; sports columnist Pasadena

Star-News, 1959, Hollywood Citizen-News and San Fernando Valley Times, 1959-62 (all Calif.), Houston Chronicle, 1962-68, Detroit Free Press, 1968-69, San Francisco Examiner, 1970-77, also Sporting News, St. Louis. Recipient U.P.I. awards, 1966, 67, 68, Best Sports Story award Nat. Newspaper Pubs. Assn., 1967; named Calif. Sportswriter of Year, 1971-74. Mem. Baseball Writers Am., Football Writers Am., Delta Chi. Democrat. Episcopalian. Author: Blanda; Fireworks and Fury; Shake Down the Thunder; also articles. Home: Burlingame, Calif. Died May 30, 1977.

TWYFORD, JAMES STANLEY (TWI'FORD), lawyer; b. Florence, Kan., June 17, 1883; s. Samuel Belt and Lucy Elizabeth (French) T.; LL.B., Washburn Coll., Topeka, Kan., 1906; m. Gladys Alida Frees, Sept. 22, 1912; 1 dau., Aileen Margret Fuller, Admitted to Okla. bar, 1906; admitted to practice before Supreme Court, U.S.; practiced in Oklahoma City since 1906; mem. firm Twyford, Smith & Crowe (formerly Twyford and Smith) since 1915; asst. county atty., 1907-09; city atty., 1909-11. Del. from Okla. to Rep. Nat. Conv., 1912, 28, 34. Spl. Lecturer State U. Law Sch. Mem. Am. Bar Assn., Okla. Bar Assn., Am. Arbitration Assn. Republican. Unitarian. Mason (32 deg., Shriner). Clubs: Beacon, Golf and Country (Oklahoma City). Author: Mr. Bailiff Call the Doctor. Home: Oklahoma City. *

TYLER, DAVID BERNARD, educator, physiologist, pharmacologist; b. N.Y.C., Jan. 13, 1905; s. Manuel Harry and Lena (Miller) T.; A.B., U. So. Calif., 1933, Ph.D., Sch. Medicine, 1937; m. Matilda Fischer, June 16, 1929, Lab. instr. U. So. Calif. Sch. Medicine, 1933-37, lectr., 1937-47; research asso. and Hixon Fund fellow Cal. Inst. Tech., 1940-46; asst. chief physiologist Army Chem. Center, 1947; staff dept. embryology Carnegie Inst. of Washington, 1947-50; prof., head dept. pharmacology U. P.R. Sch. Medicine and Dentistry, 1950-61; program dir., mem. panel regulatory biology NSF, 1961-63, head physiol. processes sect., 1964-72; prof. pharmacology, chmn. student affairs Coll. Medicine, U. South Fla., Tampa, from 1972, prof. emeritus, to 1977; vis. prof. Med. Coll., Trivandrum, India, 1959-60; fgn. service officer Tech. Coop. Mission, ICA, New Delhi, 1959-60. Investigator, OSRD, 1942-46, mem. panel on motion sickness, 1943-46. Mem. Am. Physiol. Soc., Soc. Exptl. Biology and Medicine, Am. Soc. Pharmacology and Exptl. Therapeutics, A.A.A.S., AAUP, Am. Acad. Neurology, Am. Assn. Med. Colls. Author sci. articles. Home: Tampa, Fla. Died Dec. 15, 1977.

TYLER, ERNEST FRANKLIN, decorator; b. New Haven, Conn., Apr. 13, 1879; s. Morris F. and Delia Talman (Audubon) T.; student Yale Sch. Fine Arts, 1899-1900, Columbia Sch. Arch., 1900-02, Paris, 1902-04; m. France Gregory, Dec. 16, 1911. Decorated Woolworth Bldg., Seaman's Bank for Savings, Standard Oil Co. Bldg., Columbia U. Dining Hall, Annex to Morgan Library (N.Y. City); Woolsey Hall, Yale (New Haven, Conn.); Acad. of Science, ceilings of various rooms and hallways in U.S. Supreme Court Bldg. (Washington, D.C.); Hall of Records and Essex County Courthouse (Newark, N.J.); Wis. State Capitol (Madison); Union Central Life Bldg. (Cincinnati); Sun Life Bldg., Houses of Parliament (Canada); Palmer House (Chicago); War Memorial (Nashville, Tenn., and Worcester, Mass.); churches, private homes and clubs; now painting portraits in water-color. Mem. Beaux-Arts Inst. of Design, Archtl. League of N.Y., Nat. Soc. of Mural Painters, Century Assn. Republican. Episcopalian. Clubs: Cooperstown (N.Y.) Country; Coffee House. Home: New York, N.Y. *

TYLER, MAX C., army officer; b. Sept. 25, 1880; B.S., U.S. Mil. Acad., 1903. Commd. 2d lt., June 11, 1903; promoted through grades to col., Oct. 1, 1934; brig. gen. and asst. to chief of engrs., 1936-39; pres. Mississippi River Gommn. 1939-45; retired with rank of maj. gen. Nowcons. engr. Address: Bradenton, Fla.*

TYLER, RICHARD GAINES, teacher, civ. engr.; b. Georgetown, Tex., Oct. 16, 1885; s. John Thomas and Emma P. (Ray) T.; C.E., U. of Tex., 1908; S.B. in C.E., Mass. Inst. Tech., 1910; married Willa Prée, June 3, 1924. Asst. engr., Tex. State Reclamation Dept., 1912-13; asst. city engr. Austin, Tex., 1914; city engr. Paris, Tex., 1915, 16, and 21; adj. prof. highway and sanitary engring., U. of Tex., 1917-19, asso. prof., 1920; dean of engring., Okla. Agrl. and Mech. Coll., 1922, 23, acting pres., Aug. and Sept. 1923; asso. prof. sanitary engring., Mass. Inst. Tech., 1923-25, prof., 1925-29; dean Coll. of Engring., U. of Wash., 1929-35, head of dept. of civil engring., 1929-37, prof. sanitary engring since 1929; research on industrial wastes, 1944-47, consultant on sanitary engring. problems. Chmn. King County Planning Commn., 1934-41. Capt., utilities branch of construction div., Q.M.C., U.S. Army, Aug. 1918-Mar. 1919; maj., Engrs. O.R.C., 1922-32. Mem. Am. Soc. C.E., Am. Water Works Assn., Fed. Sewage Works Assn., Am. Soc. Planning Officials, Sigma Xi, Tau Beta Pi, Sigma Tau, Acacia. Home: Seattle, Wash. *

TYLER, S. ROGER, JR., fgn. service officer; b. Hamilton, Va., June 16, 1908; s. S. Roger and Esther M. (Judkins) T.; B.A., U. Va., 1929; Rhodes scholar, Oxford U., 1929-30; M.A., Yale, 1934; m. Monique Portmann, June 3, 1950; children by previous marriage—Zora, Cheever. Instr. polit. sci. U. Del., 1934-36; joined U.S. fgn. service, 1935; vice consul, Toronto, Can., 1935-36, Mexico City, 1936-39; assigned Fgn. Service Sch., 1936; vice consul, 3d sec., San Jose, 1939-44; assigned Dept. State, 1944-45; vice consul, 2d sec., Moscow, 1945-46, consul, 1946, 1st sec., consul, 1946-47; consul, Geneva, Switzerland, 1947-50, Jerusalem, 1949-50, 51-54, Alexandria, Egypt, 1950-51; assigned Dept. State, 1954-56, supr. Fgn. Affairs Office, 1956-58, 58; assigned Fgn. Service Inst., 1957; consul. Nassau, Bahamas, 1958-59, consul gen., 1959-60; consul gen., Seville, Spain, 1960-64. Home: Huntington, W.Va. Died May 23, 1979.

TYNAN, KENNETH, writer; b. England, 1927; ed. Magdalen Coll., Oxford. Editor of Cherwell; pres. Exptl. Theatre Club, sec. of Union, Oxford; dir. Repertory Theatre, Lichfield, 1949; dir. plays in London, also on TV, 1950-51; drama critic The Spectator, 1951, Evening Standard, 1952-53, Daily Sketch, 1953-54, The Observer, 1954-63, New Yorker, 1958-60; script editor Ealing Films, 1956-58; TV producer, 1961-62, lIt. mgr. then cons. Nat. Theatre, 1930—; film critic The Observer, 1964-65. Author: He that Play the King, 1950; (with Cecil Beaton) Persona Grata, 1953; Alec Guiness, 1953; Bull Fever, 1955; (play for BBC, with Harold Lang) The Quest for Corbett, 1956; Curtains, 1961; Tynan Right andd Left, 1967. Devised and wrote (in part) revue Oh Calcutta, 1969. Contbr. to numerous mags., U.S. and Britain. Address: Santa Monica, Calif. Died July 26, 1980.

TYNES, BUFORD ACHILLES, tobacco co. exec.; b. Portsmouth, Ohio, May 6, 1934; s. Finley and Ann Elizabeth (Steiner) T.; A.B., Duke, 1961; M.B.A., Columbia, 1963; m. Mary Macklin, Oct. 10, 1964; 1 dau., Elizabeth Finley. Asst. v.p. 1st. Nat. City Bank, N.Y.C., 1963-70; asst. treas. Philip Morris Inc., N.Y.C., 1970-74, treas., 1974-75. Served to capt. USMCR, 1955-59. Mem. Anglers Club N.Y., Beta Theta Pi. Presbyn. (elder ch.). Club: University. Home: New York, N.Y. Died Dec. 15, 1975.

TYNG, FRANCIS EDMONDS (ED), writer, editor; b. Elizabeth, N.J., Nov. 25, 1896; s. Francis Edmonds and Margreta (Hyde) T.; student N.Y. chpt. Am. Inst. Banking, 1917-18; m. Julia Tabachuk, Oct. 14, 1935. With N.Y. Bank, 1914-18; reporter various N.Y. newspapers, 1919-25; financial reporter, travel and rod and gun editor N.Y. Sun, 1925-50; banking editor N.Y. Jour. Commerce, 1950-65, asst. editor, 1965-76. Served with M.C., U.S. Army, 1918-19. Mem. Hon. Tarheels of N.C. Mem. N.Y. Financial Writers Assn., Met. Rod and Gun Editors Assn. Greater N.Y. Author: Making a World's Fair, 1958. Contbr. articles financial, econ., sporting mags., also newspapers, N.Y.C., London. Home: Summit, N.J. Died Mar. 26, 1976; interred Cresthaven, Clifton, N.J.

TYRRELL, CECIL CLOUGH, coll. pres.; b. Crown Point, N.Y., Mar. 22, 1908; s. Orlin C. and Margaret (Clough) T.; B.S. in Mech. Engring., Purdue U., 1931, M.S., 1932; m. Lois Harrison, Sept. 8, 1928; children—David H., Margaret Ann (dec. Aug. 1966). Instr. U. Maine, 1934-37, Pratt Inst., 1937-42; asso. prof. Rutgers U., 1942-44; sr. mech. engr., Primos, Pa., 1944-46; dir. N.Y. State Inst. Applied Arts and Scis., Binghamton, 1946-53; pres. Broome Community Coll., Binghamton, 1953-72. Mem. adv. bd. Midland Trust Co. So. N.Y. Dir. Broome County Social Planning Council, pres., 1952-54; dir. Broome County United Fund, pres., 1959; chmn. bd. Sheltered Workshop Binghamton, Inc., Rehab. Services, Inc., Binghamton; dir., pres. Opportunities for Broome, Inc. Trustee Wyoming Sem., Kingston, Pa. Recipient James H. McGraw award Am. Soc. Engring. Edn., 1967. Mem. C. of C. (pres. 1962-63), Am. Soc. Engring. Edn. Clubs: Rotary, Torch. Home: Binghamton, N.Y. Died Feb. 26, 1976.

UHL, FREDERICK ELWOOD, army officer; b. Harrold, S.D., Mar. 30, 1886; s. George and Louisa Adline (Folkman) U.; B.S., U.S. Mil. Acad., West Point, 1910; grad. Inf. Sch., Ft. Benning, Ga., 1925, Command and Gen. Staff Sch., Ft. Leavenworth, Kan., 1928, Army War Coll., Washington, D.C., 1932; LL. D. (honorary), Muhlenberg College, 1948; married Julia Lathrop Ramsay, Oct. 13, 1920; children—Frederick Elwood, Jr. (dec.), Louise. Commd. 2d lt., inf., U.S. Army, 1910, advanced through ranks to major general, 1942; on duty in P.I., 1910-13, participating in operations against Moros; Dept. of Tactics, U.S. Mil. Acad., 1914-17; with 38th Inf., and with Hdqrs. 3d Div., Camp Greene, N.C., and France, 1917-18; mem. A.E.F. and War Dept. Gen. Staff, 1918-20; in Dept. Economics, Govt. and Polit. History, U.S. Mil. Acad., 1920-24; plans and training officer, The Inf. Sch., 1925-27; exec. officer and plans and training officer, 2d Brigade, 1928-31; in training and equipment sect., Office Chief of Inf., War Dept., 1932-35; with 65th Inf., Puerto Rico, 1935-37; mem. Inf. Bd., Ft. Benning, Ga., 1937-39; comdg. 38th Inf., Ft. Douglas, Utah, and Ft. Sam Houston, Tex., 1939-40; comdg. gen., Ft. Francis E. Warren, Wyo., 1940-41; comdg. gen., 7th Corps Area and 7th Service Command, Omaha, Neb., 1941-44; comdg. gen., 4th Service Command, Atlanta, Ga., 1944-45; comdg. gen., Replacement Command, United States Army Forces Western Pacific, 1945; retired with rank of major general, Aug. 31, 1946. Awarded Distinguished Service Medal, U.S.A., Purple Heart, Legion of Merit; Officer d' Academie (France), Philippine Campaign, Victory, American Defense Service, Army of Occupation of Germany, Am. Campaign, Asiatic-Pacific Theatre, Victory and Philippine Liberation medals, World War II; Order of Orange-Nassau (Netherlands). Mem. Mil. Order of the Carabo, Mil. Order of the World Wars, Am. Legion, Newcomen Soc. of England. Mason (K.T., Shriner). Club: Army and Navy (Washington). Address: Washington, D.C. Died June 26, 1976.

UHL, KENNETH PAUL, educator; b. Ames, Iowa, July 3, 1931; s. Edward G. and Caroline C. (Tweed) U.; B.S., U. Iowa, 1953, M.A., 1958, Ph.D., 1960; m. Eleanor Lock, Oct. 11, 1951; children—Jerrie R., Terrie R., Pamela K., Paul K., Robin A., Princetta. With Maytag Co., 1956-57; instr. U. Iowa, 1958-59, asst. prof., 1960-63, asst. dean, 1963-64, asso. prof. dept. bus., 1963-67, chmn. dept. bus., 1966-68, prof. dept. bus. adminstrn., 1967-72; asst. prof. U. Ariz., 1959-60; vis. prof. U. Wash., 1964-65; prof., head dept. bus. adminstrn. U. Ill., Urbana, 1972-81. Mktg. cons., 1960-81. Served to 1st lt. USAF, 1953-55. Research grantee U. Iowa, 1967-68, research award Consumers Research Inst., 1969-70, research prof. award U. Iowa, 1970. Ford Found. Mktg. Workshop fellow, 1963. Mem. Am. Inst. for Decision Scis. (v.p. membership 1970-71, 73-74, nat. program chmn. 1972-73, pres. 1975-76), Am. Mktg. Assn. (nat. program chmn. research tract 1972, nat. dir. 1975-81), Alpha Iota Delta. Author: (with J. Carman) Marketing: Principles and Methods, 7th edit., 1973; (with T. Pogue) Direct State Taxes on Advertising Services: Economic Implications, 1973; Marketing Today, 1975; (with B. Schoner) Marketing Research: Information Systems and Decision Making, 2d edit., 1975. Home: Champaign, Ill. Died Dec. 24, 1980.

UHL, MARSHALL MORTIMER, lawyer; b. Grand Rapids, Mich., Nov. 22, 1882; s. Edwin Fuller and Alice (Follett) U.; B.A., U. of Mich., 1906, LL.B. law sch., 1908; m. Ellen Birchard Howard, Oct. 1, 1912 (died, 1937); children—Alice Mortimer (Mrs. Lyman A. Spalding), John Howard, Edwin Fuller, Jane Ellen; m. 2d, Bernice Evans Pew, August 14, 1942. Admitted to Michigan bar, 1908; in practice with William P. Belden, Ishpeming, Mich., 1908-09; entered firm Kleinhans & Knappen, Grand Rapids, Mich., 1909, mem. firm Kleinhans, Knappen & Uhl. 1913-18; mem. Knappen, Uhl, Bryant & Snow, 1918-43; Uhl, Bryant, Snow & Slawson, Grand Rapids, 1942-47, Uhl, Bryant, Slawson and Wheeler since 1947. Mem. of the Michigan State Board Law Examiners, 1918-25. Hon. vice-pres. Grand Rapids Anti-Tuberculosis Soc. Mem. Grand Rapids Bar Assn. (pres. 1927-28), Am. and Mich. State Bar Assns., Alpha Delta Phi. Democrat. Episcopalian. Clubs: University, Grand Rapids Yacht, Kent Country (Grand Rapids); Pentwater (Mich.) Yacht. Home: Grand Rapids, Mich. *

UHL, PAUL EDGAR, banker; b. Holmes County, Ohio, July 31, 1914; s. Albert Allen and Grace Evangeline (Beall) U.; B.S., Ohio State U., 1936; J.D., John Marshall Law Sch., 1941; m. Dolores Imelda Riddell, Jan. 6, 1945; children—Michael Alan, Brian Paul. Mgr. municipal investments Continental Ill. Nat. Bank, Chgo., 1936-52; sec., asst. to pres. Golden State Co., Ltd., 1952-54; exec. v.p. investments and dealers United Calif. Bank, Los Angeles, 1954-78; advisor on debt mgmt. to sec. Treasury. Served with USNR, 1941-45, 50-52. Decorated Bronze Star (13). Mem. Investment Bankers Assn. (gov. 1968-70), Ill. Bar Assn., Ohio State U., John Marshall alumni assns., Securities Industry Assn., Chi Phi. Clubs: Stock Exchange (Los Angeles); Lake Arrowhead Country. Home: Arcadia, Calif. Died Sept. 21, 1978.

UIHLEIN, ROBERT AUGUST, JR., brewery exec.; b. Milw., Mar. 26, 1916; s. Robert A. and Mary (Isley) U.; grad. Phillips Acad., Andover, Mass., 1934; A.B., Harvard, 1938; LL.B., U. Wis., 1941; m. Lorraine Glaeser, Jan. 31, 1950; children—Robert August III, James I. With Jos. Schlitz Brewing Co., Milw., 1942-76, v.p., 1945-61, pres., 1961-76, chmn. bd., 1967-76; dir. Gateway Transp. Co., First Wis. Corp., Wehr Corp., First Wis. Nat. Bank, Wis. Elec. Power Co., Congoleum Corp.; trustee Northwestern Mut. Life Ins. Co. Mem. Business Com. for Arts. Trustee Milw. Art Center, Marquette U.; bd. dirs. Milw. unit Am. Cancer Soc., N.Y. Philharmonic, Boys Clubs Am.; bd. dirs., mem. exec. com. U.S. Brewers Assn.; bd. dirs. Greater Milw. Com., Milw. Boys' Club. Home: Milwaukee, Wis. Died Nov. 12, 1976.

ULLMAN, EDWARD L., geographer, educator; b. Chgo., July 24, 1912; s. B.L. and Mary Louise (Bates) U.; B.S., U. Chgo., 1934, Ph.D., 1942; A.M., Harvard, 1935; m. Doris E. Jackson Skenyon, Sept. 5, 1942 (div. 1958); children—Edward J., Anne B.; m. 2d, Joan Connelly, June 14, 1967. Asst. geography Harvard,

1934-35, 37-38, asst. prof. regional planning, 1946-49, asso. prof., 1949-51; instr. econ. geography Wash. State Coll., 1935-37, Ind. U., 1941-42; chief transport sect. OSS, 1942-43; dir. joint intelligence study pub. bd. Joint Chiefs of Staff, 1943-46; spl. estimates staff Dept. State, 1946; transp. economist U.S. Maritime Commn., 1946; prof. geography U. Wash., 1951-76, asso. dean Grad. Sch., 1962-65, dir. Center for Urban and Regional Research, 1968-69; Fulbright research prof. U. Rome, 1956-57; vis. prof. econ. geography, dir. Meramec Basin Research project Washington U., 1959-61; vis. prof., fall 1962; vis. prof. Salzburg Seminar in Am. Studies, 1965, Hebrew and Haifa univs., Israel, 1973; Dept. State Cultural Exchange vis. prof. U. Moscow, 1965; pres. Washington Center for Met. Studies, 1965-67. Transport cons. Stanford Research Inst. for ICA and Philippine Govt., Manila, 1956; cons. European Productivity Agy., OEEC, 1957, Asian Devel. Bank, Manila, 1968, 69; bd. dirs., exec. mgmt. com. Amtrak, 1974-76. Served as lt. USNR, 1943-46, Western Region econ. analysis com. Social Sci. Research Council, 1951-56. Mem. Assn. Am. Geographers (citation award 1958, council 1949, del. to Am. Council Learned Socs. 1950-54, Disting. Geographer 1972), New Eng. Geog. Conf. (pres. 1948-49), NRC (com. on geography Office Naval Research, com. econ., urban geography, mem. at large Behavioral Sci. div. 1968-71), Am. Geog. Soc., Regional Sci. Assn. (council 1958-60, pres. 1960-61, pres. Western sect. 1969-71), AAUP, Italian Geography Soc. (corr.; citation), Sigma Xi, Gamma Sigma Epsilon. Clubs: Cosmos (Washington); Faculty, Tennis (Seattle). Author: Mobile: Industrial Seaport and Trade Center, 1943; American Commodity Flow, 1957; An Economic Analysis of Philippine Domestic Transportation, 1957; The Meramec Basin, 1962; The Economic Base of American Cities, 1969, 71; Geography as Spatial Interaction. Essays by Edward L. Ullman, 1980. Subject of biography and bibliography: A Man for All Regions, 1978. Adv. editor Annals, Assn. Am. Geographers, 1951-57. Contbr. articles sci., profl. jours. Home: Seattle, Wash. Died Apr. 24, 1976.

ULMER, JACOB MORTON, lawyer; b. Shreve, O., Nov. 19, 1886; s. Solomon and Laura (Glueck) U.; LL.B., Western Res. U., 1908; m. Fan Berne, Oct. 14, 1912; children—Janet Louise, Susan Berne (Mrs. Adolph Reichenbach). Admitted to Ohio bar, 1908; sr. mem. firm Ulmer, Berne, Laronge, Glickman & Curtis, Cleve., 1908—. Mem. nat. com. Am. Constrn. Council, 1926-27; mem. inter-council com. all nat. pub. health insts. Dept. Health, Edn. and Welfare, 1950—; sec. Nat. Found. Eye Research, 1946—, mem. surgeon gen.'s adv. council Neurol. Diseases and Bindness Inst., USPHS, 1951-53; mem. nat. adv. research resources council NIH, USPHS, 1963-64; coordinator appeals bd. Ohio SSS, 1941-46. Recipient SSS medal, 1946; certificate of merit Rochester Eye Bank and Research Soc., 1960; Dean Andrews Outstanding Alumnus award Western Res. U. Sch. Law, 1966. Mem. Soc. Benchers, Western Res. U. Sch. Law Alumni Assn., Am., Ohio, Cleve. (chmn. fed. ct. com. 1954-56) bar assns., Assn. Research in Ophthalmology (hon.). Cleve. C. of C. Jewish religion. Clubs: City, Mid-Day, Oakwood (Cleve.). Home: Cleveland OH. *

ULP, CLIFFORD MCCORMICK, artists, educator; b. Olean, N.Y., Aug. 23, 1885; s. George Conrad and Cordelia Catherine (Brown) U.; grad. Sch. of Applied Art, Rochester Inst, of Tech., 1908; grad. Art Students League, New York, 1909; m. Ruth M. Huntley, Oct. 4, 1913; 1 dau., Justine Huntley. Prin. works: Allenby's Entrance into Damascus, Nat. Art Gallery, Washington, D.C.; Adoration of the Magi, St. Monica's Ch., Rochester; mural decorations Rochester Dental Dispensary; etc.; dir. Sch. of Applied Art, Rochester Institute of Technology, formerly Mechanics Institute, Rochester, since 1921. Fellow Rochester Museum Arts and Sciences, 1943. Member board dirs. Memorial Art Gallery, Rochester. Received Rochester Art Club award, 1939, 41, 42. Mem. Iroquois Art Assn., Henry Lomb Soc. (Rochester), Eastern Arts Assn. Christian Scientist. Clubs: Rochester Art, Kodak Camera (hon.). Home: 56 S. Washington St. (8). Address: Rochester, N.Y. *

UNDERHILL, RUTH MURRAY, anthropoligist; b. Ossining, N.Y., Aug. 22, 1884; d. Abram Sutton and Anna (Murray) U.; student Ossining Sch. for Girls, 1890-1901; A.B., Vassar Coll., 1905; student London Sch. Econs., 1907; Ph.D., Columbia University, 1934; LL.D., Denver U., 1962; D.Sc., U. Colo., 1965. Agt. Mass. Soc. Prevention Cruelty to Children, 1909-11, N.Y. Charity Orgn. Soc., 1911-12; with A.R.C. in Italy, 1917-20, charge Italian orphanages; field work Papago and Mohave Indians, Ariz., on fellowship from Columbia, also asst. anthropology Barnard Coll., 1930-34; cons. anthropologist U.S. Dept. Agr., 1936-37; supvr. Indian edn. U.S. Indian Service, 1937-49; prof. anthropology Denver U., 1949-52, professor emeritus; taught course on closed circuit TV, Denver, 1956; lectr. social anthropology Colo. Women's Coll., 1960-61; radio series on modern Indians. Fellow A.A.A.S.; mem. American Ethnological Society (president), American Anthrop. Assn., Am. (sec. 1930), Colo. (pres. 1954) folklore socs., New Mexico Historical Society, Delta Kappa Gamma (honorary member). Author: First Penthouse Dwellers of America, 1928; Singing for Power (songs of Papago Indians), 1938; Social Organization of the Papago Indians, 1939; Hawk Over Whirlpools (novel), 1940; Papago Indian Religion, 1946; Red Man's America, 1953; The Navajos, 1956; First Came the Family, 1958; Beaverbird, 1959; Antelope Singer, 1961; Red Man's Religion, 1966; also pamphlets on Am. Indians and articles children's encys. Home: Denver. *

UNDERWOOD, WALTER S(COTT), lawyer; b. Milwaukee, Dec. 15, 1884; s. Harold Green and Marie Lawson (Scott) U.; A.B., U. Wis., 1907; LL.B., Northwestern, 1909; Dr. Canon Law (hon.), Nashotah House (Wis.), 1962; m. Emily Caro Johnson, Sept. 8, 1915; children—Nancy (Mrs. George H. Adam), Sallie (Mrs. Robert M. Baker). Admitted to Ill. bar, 1909, practiced in Chgo. until retirement; sr. mem. firm Keck, Cushman, Mahlin & Cate; corp. counsel, Wheaton, Ill., 1927-31. Mem. Am., Ill., Chicago and DuPage Co. bar assns., Newcomen Soc., Alpha Delta Phi. Episcopalian (chancellor Diocese of Chicago, 1951-67). Clubs: University, Chicago Golf. Legal. Home: Chicago, Ill. Died Oct. 20, 1976.

UNGERMAN, IRVINE E., lawyer; b. Leavenworth, Kans., May 12, 1908; s. William and Rachel (Ettleman) U.; LL.B., Washburn U., 1930; m. Hanna Friedberg, Apr. 13, 1929; children—Maynard I., Rowena Mae (Mrs. David Galerston). Admitted to Okla. bar, 1930, since practiced in Tulsa; sr. mem. firm Ungerman, Conner, Little, Ungerman & Goodman, 1930-80. Gen. counsel, dir. Union Nat. Bank, Tulsa. Pres. Okla. Bd. Corrections, 1971-75, Tulsa Hebrew Sch., 1949-51, Congregation Bnai Emunah, 1951-53. Fellow Am. Coll. Trial Lawyers, Comml. Law Found. Am.; mem. Internat., Am., Okla. (bd. govs. 1978), Tulsa County bar assns., Am. Judicature Soc., Nat. Assn. Def. Counsel, Am., Okla. (pres. 1974-75) trial lawyers assns., Comml. Law League Am. Clubs: Meadowbrook Country (sec. 1952-65), University, Summit (Tulsa). Home: Tulsa, Okla. Died Oct. 16, 1980.

UNTERMEYER, JEAN STARR (UN'TER-MI-ER), author, b. Zanesville, O., May 13, 1886; d. Abram E. and Johanna (Shonfield) Starr; ed. Putnam's Sem. (Zanesville), Kohut Sch. for Girls (New York), and Columbia Extension Course; m. Louis Untermeyer, January 23, 1907 (div.). Made début as singer in Vienna and London, 1924, specializing in German songs. Club: P.E.N. Author: (poems) Growing Pains, 1918; Dreams Out of Darkness, 1921; Steep Ascent 1927; Winged Child. 1936; Love and Need, 1940. Was one of the original group to publish the biennials'. A Miscellany of American Poetry, 1920 and 1922. Translator Oscar Bie's Schubert, the Man, 1928 (chosen by Schubert Centennial Com. as the official biography). Lecturer and teacher, Olivet Writer's Conf., Olivet Coll., Mich., summers 1936, 37; teacher Writers Sch., League of Am. Writers, 1938-39; teacher, lectr. New Sch. Social Research since 1948. Translator of Hermann Broch's masterpiece The Death of Virgil, 1945. Recipient of Ford Madox Ford Chair of Creative Literature, Olivet Coll., Mich., 1940. Contbr. verse and criticism to mags. Author: Private Collection, a Memoir, 1965; Job's Daughter, 1967; Re-Creations, 1970. Mem. P.E.N. Home: N.Y.C. *

UNTERMEYER, LOUIS, author, editor; b. N.Y.C., Oct. 1, 1885; s. Emmanuel and Julia (Michael) U.; student De Witt Clinton High Sch.; D.H.L., Union Coll., 1967; m. Jean Starr, Jan. 23, 1907; m. 2d, Virginia Moore, Nov. 1926; m. 3d, Esther Antin, 1933; children—Richard Starr (dec.), John Moore, Lauren S., Joseph Louis; m. 4th, Bryna Ivens, 1948. In the mfg. jewelry bus. since age 17, with father's and uncle's firm (Untermeyer-Robbins Co. and Charles Keller & Co.); later v.p., mgr. chief factory, Newark; resigned, 1923, to devote time to study and writing; contbg. editor of The Liberator, and The Seven Arts; poetry editor of the Am. Mercury, 1934-37; occasional lectr. at various colls. and univs.; Honnold lectr. Knox Coll., 1937; Henry Ward Beecher lectr. Amherst Coll., 1937; poet-in-residence, U. Mich., 1939-40, U. Kansas City, 1939 Iowa State Coll., 1940; cons. in poetry Library of Congress, 1961-63. U.S. del. Internat. Cultural Conf., India, 1961, Japan, 1963. Author more than 100 works throughout field of lit., including Britannica Library of Great American Writing, 1960; Bygones, The Recollections of Louis Untermeyer, 1965. Translator or compiler poetry, stories. Editor misc. poetry stories and biographical items, later ones including Heritage American Poets Series (Longfellow to Emily Dickinson), Modern American and British Poetry (Mid-Century Edition, revised and enlarged), A Treasury of Great Poems, 1955, A Treasury of Ribaldry, 1956; Lives of the Poets (Chap-Book award Poetry Soc. Am.), 1959; The Golden Treasury of Poetry, 1959; Long Feud; Selected Poems, 1962; The Letters of Robert Frost to Louis Untermeyer, 1963; The World's Great Stories, 1964; Labyrinth of Love, 1965; Bygones: An Autobiography, 1965; The Firebringer and Other Stores, 1968; Tales From The Ballet, 1968; The Pursuit of Poetry, 1969; Cat O'Nine Tales, 1971; A Treasury of Great Humor, 1972; Fifty Modern American and British Poets, 1973; A Galaxy of Poetry (posthumous), 1978; prefaces various books. Mem. Nat. Inst. Arts and Letters. Publs. editor O. W.I. in Dec. 1942; editor Armed Services Editions, 1944. Phi Beta Kappa poet, Harvard, 1956. Recipient gold medal for services to poetry Poetry Society of America, 1956; Golden Rose, New Eng. Poetry Soc., 1966. Home: Newtown, Conn. Died Dec. 18, 1977.

UNTERMYER, IRWIN, lawyer; b. N.Y. City, Feb. 2, 1886; s. Samuel and Minnie (Carl) U.; B.S., Columbia, 1907, LL.B., 1910; m. Louise Fenchtwanger, of N.Y. City, Feb. 15, 1912. Practiced at N.Y. City since 1910; mem. firm Guggenheimer, Untermyer & Marshall; pres. United Boroughs Realty Co.; dir. Am. Lithographic Co., Bolivia Ry. Co., Central Petroleum Co., Ludlow Valve Mfg. Co., N.E. Brewing Co., Central Theatre Leasing & Constrn. Co., etc. Dem. candidate for justice Supreme Ct. of N.Y., 1919. Member Nat. Democratic Club, N.Y. Co. Lawyers' Assn. Home: New York, N.Y. *

UPDEGRAFF, ALLAN, author; b. Grinnell, Ia., Feb. 14, 1883; s. William Ross and Laura (Heberling) U.; student Drury Coll. (Springfield, Mo.) and Yale University (non-graduate). Reporter and city editor South Chicago (Ill.) Daily Calumet, 1901-02; editor Transatlantic Tales, 1908; editor Publishers Newspaper Syndicate, 1915; on editorial bd. Literary Digest, 1918-25. Author: Second Youth (novel), 1915; Strayed Revellers, 1918; Dancers in the Wind, 1925; Historical and Political Atlas of New Europe and the Far East. 1925; Whatever We Do (novel), 1927; Captain Jack (novel, pseudonymous, in collaboration), 1928; Native Soil (novel, 1929. Contbr. verse and fiction to Century, Harper's, Forum, Collier's Weekly, etc. Address: Paris, France. *

UPJOHN, EVERARD MILLER, educator; b. Scranton, Pa., Nov. 7, 1903; s. Hobart Brown and Margaret (Miller) U.; A.B., Harvard, 1925, M.Arch., 1929; m. Florence Davol, June 14, 1927; children—Richard Vassall, Amy Putnam. Asst. prof., founder dept. fine arts U. Minn., 1929-35; asst. prof. Columbia, 1935-42, asso. prof., 1942-51, prof. fine arts, 1951-70, prof. emeritus, 1970-78; cons. editor Rainbird, McLean, Ltd., London, 1962-64; Matthews lectr. Met. Mus. Art, N.Y.C., 1941-42, 59. Served to lt. USNR, 1942-45; lt. comdr. Res. Recipient Great Tchr. award, Soc. Older Grads. Columbia, 1969. Mem. Coll. Art Assn., Am. Soc. Archtl. Historians. Episcopalian. Author: Richard Upjohn, Architect and Churchman, 1939; (with Paul S. Wingert, Jane G. Mahler) History of World Art, rev. edit., 1958; (with John P. Sedgwick) Highlights: An Illustrated History of Art, 1963. Editorial adviser for art and architecture Grolier Ency., 1958, Richards Topical Ency., 1959, Ency. Americana, 1967. Contbr. articles, books revs. lit. jours., articles to encys. Home: Hightstown, N.J. Died Nov. 3, 1978.

UPLEGER, ARTHUR C(HRISTIAN), accountant; b. Mt. Clemens, Mich., Feb. 20, 1883; s. Joseph F. and Elizabeth (Ullrich) U.; B.C.S., N.Y.U., 1910; m. Leona Walthall, Dec. 7, 1915 (dec. 1965) m. 2d Mrs. Naida Barnes Patton. Accountant, 1907—, in Tex., 1911—. Chmn. Tex. Bd. Accountancy, 1924. Treas. St. Paul's House Bd., 1930-59, Waco Pub. Library Assn., 1955. C.P.A., Tex. Mem. Am. (pres. 1929), Tex. (pres. 1924) socs. C.P.A.'s, Am. Inst. C.P.A.'s (permanent council mem.), Civic Music Assn. Waco (treas.), So. States Accountants Conf. (exec. com.), Phi Delta Phi, Alpha Kappa Psi, Beta Alpha Psi. Republican. Episcopalian. Mason (Shriner, 33 deg.; imperial auditor 1949—). Clubs: Waco Philosophers, Rotary (Hall of Fame, Dist. 587 Conf. 1964). Home: Waco, Tex.

UPSON, ROBERT WILLIAM, chem. co. exec.; b. Odell, Nebr., Aug. 7, 1913; s. Robert Lyman and Frances (Hilder) U.; B.S., U. Nebr., 1937, M.S., 1938; Ph.D., U. Ill., 1941; m. Carol Umberger, Feb. 8, 1938; children—Barbara Ann Upson Gravely, Martha Jane Upson Moore, Donald Allen, James Robert. With E.I. DuPont de Nemours & Co., Inc., 1941-79, tech. mgr., then asst. dir. research and devel. div., Wilmington, Del., 1960-68, gen. dir. research and devel. div., photo products dept., 1968-79. Avery fellow, 1938; Rohm and Haas fellow, 1939-40; Eli Lilly fellow, 1941. Mem. Am. Chem. Soc., Soc. Photog. Scientists and Engrs., Am. Inst. Chemists, Soc. Chemistry Industry, Sigma Xi, Phi Lambda Upsilon, Alpha Chi Sigma. Republican. Presbyn. Club: Masons. Patentee in field. Home: Wilmington, Del. Died June 30, 1979; buried Wilmington, Del.

UREY, HAROLD CLAYTON, chemist; b. Walkerton, Ind., Apr. 29, 1893; s. Samuel Clayton and Cora Rebecca (Reinoehl) U.; B.S., U. Mont., 1917; Ph.D., U. Calif., 1923, LL.D., 1955; Am. Scandinavian Found. fellow, U. Copenhagen, 1923-24; D.Sc., U. Mont., Princeton, 1935, Rutgers U., 1939, Columbia, Oxford U., 1946, Washington and Lee U., 1948, U. Athens, 1951, McMaster U., 1951, Yale, 1951, Ind. U., 1953, Durham U., 1957, Birmingham U., 1957, U. Sask, 1960, Israeli Inst. Tech., 1962, Gustavus Adolphus Coll., 1963, U. Pitts., 1963, U. Chgo., 1963, U. Manchester (Eng.), 1966, U. Mich., 1967, Franklin and Marshall Coll., 1969, McGill U., 1970; LL.D., Wayne State U., 1958, U. Notre Dame, 1965; L.H.D., Hebrew Union Coll., 1959; m. Frieda Daum, June 12, 1926; children—Gertrude Elizabeth, Frieda Rebecca, Mary Alice, John Clayton. Tchr. rural schs., 1911-14; chemist

Barrett Chem. Co., Phila., 1917-19; inst. chemistry U. Mont., 1919-21; asso. in chemistry Johns Hopkins, 1924-29; asso. prof. chemistry Columbia, 1929-34, prof., 1934-45, exec. officer dept. chemistry, 1939-42, dir. research S.A.M. Labs., 1940-45; distinguished service prof. chemistry Inst. Nuclear Studies, U. Chgo., 1945-52, Martin A. Ryerson distinguished service prof. chemistry, 1952-58; prof. chemistry-at-large U. Calif., 1958-70, Univ. prof. emeritus chemistry, 1970-81; Bownocker lectr. Ohio State U., 1950; Silliman lectr. Yale, 1951; Montgomery lectr. U. Nebr., 1952; Hitchcock lectr. U. Calif., 1953; George Eastman vis. prof. Oxford U., 1956-57; Scott lectr. Cambridge U., 1957; Priestley lectr., 1963; Joseph Henry lectr., 1940, 70; John C. Lindsay lectr., 1970; vis. prof. univs. of U.K., 1971, others. Chmn. bd. Quadri-Sci., Inc.; dir. Deuterium Corp. Dir. Am. Scandinavian Found. Recipient Willard Gibbs medal Chgo. sect. Am. Chem. Soc., 1934; Nobel prize in chemistry, 1934; Davy medal Royal Soc. London, 1940; Franklin medal Franklin Inst., 1943; distinguished service award Phi Beta Kappa, 1950; Cordoza award, 1954; Honor Seroll award Chgo. chpt. Am. Inst. Chemists, 1954, gold medal award nat. soc., 1972; Priestley award, 1955; Alexander Hamilton award, 1961, J. Lawrence Smith medal, 1962; Remsen Meml. award, 1963; Medal of U. Paris, 1964; Nat. Medal Sci. award for astronomy, 1964, Gold Medal award Royal Astron. Soc. London, 1966; Am. Acad. Achievement award, 1966; Chem. Pioneer award Am. Inst. Chemists, 1969; Leonard medal Meteoritical Soc., 1969; Linus Pauling award Oreg. State U., 1970; Priestly medal Am. Chem. Soc., 1973; Exceptional Sci. Achievement award NASA, 1973; medallion, hon. mem. award Indiana Acad., 1974; V.M. Goldschmidt medal Geochem. Soc., 1975; Headliner award San Diego Press Club, 1974; medal, hon. council mem. Higher Council Sci. Research, Barcelona, Spain, 1973; Silver medal 50th Anniversary Internat. Fair Barcelona, 1973; 200th Anniversary plaque Am. Chem. Soc., 1976; named Knight of Malta, 1973. Fgn. mem. Royal Soc., Royal Swedish Acad. Scis., also other fgn. socs.; mem. A.A.A.S. (Johann Kepler medal 1971), Am. Chem. Soc., Nat. Acad. Scis., Am. Inst. Chemists (gold medal award 1972), Am. Philos Soc., Am. Phys. Soc., Am. Acad. Arts and Scis., Am. Geophys. Union, Geol. Soc. Am. (Arthur L. Day award 1969), Am. Astron. Soc., N.Y. Acad. Scis., Franklin Inst. (hon.), Geochim. Soc., Ill. Acad. Scis., Royal Irish Acad. (hon.), Royal Soc. Arts and Scis., Royal Astron. Soc. (asso.), French Chem. Soc. (hon.), Sigma Xi, Gamma Alpha, Phi Lambda Upsilon, Epsilon Chi, numerous others. Clubs: Quadrangle (Chgo.); Cosmos (Washington). Author: (with A.E. Ruark) Atoms, Molecules and Quanta, 1930; The Planets, 1952. Contbr. to Treatise on Physical Chemistry (edited by H.S. Taylor), 1931; chpt. in Physics and Astronomy of Moon (Z. Kopal), rev. edit., 1971. Editor Jour. Chem. Physics, 1933-40. Contbr. to sci. jours. Has specialized in structure of atoms and molecules, thermodynamic properties of gases, separation of isotopes, paleotemperatures, meteorites and the early solar system. Discoverer of hydrogen atom of atomic weight two; research for prodn. heavy water, and U235 for the atomic bomb. Home: La Jolla, Calif. Died Jan. 6, 1981.

UTLEY, FREDA, author, lectr.; b. London, Eng., Jan. 23, 1898; d. Willie Herbert and Emily (Williamson) Utley; B.A., first class honors in History, London U., 1923, M.A. with distinction, 1925; m. Arcadi Berdichevsky, 1928; 1 son, Jon Basil. Naturalized Am. citizen, 1950. Research fellow London Sch. Econs., 1926-28; spl. corr. Manchester Guardian Comml. in Japan, 1928-29; lived in Russia, 1930-36, working as sr. sci. worker Inst. of World Economy and Politics, Acad. Scis., Moscow; spl. corr. London News Chronicle, China war zone, 1938; resident in U.S., 1939-78; econ. adviser to Starr, Park, Freeman, Inc., N.Y.C., 1940-44; cons. to Chinese Supply Commn., 1944-45; accredited corr. Readers Digest in China, 1945-56, Germany, 1948. Adv. council dept. politics Princeton, 1941-47. Dir. Am.-China Policy Assn., Inc. Author: Lancashire and the Far East, 1931; Japan's Feet of Clay, 1936; Japan's Gamble in China, 1937; China at War, 1939; The Dream We Lost, 1940; Last Chance in China, 1946; Lost Illusion, 1948; The High Cost of Vengeance, 1949; The China Story, 1951; Will the Middle East Go West?, 1957; Odyssey of a Liberal, Memoirs, 1970. Home: Washington, D.C. Died Jan. 21, 1978.

UZZELL, THOMAS H. (UZ-ZEL), literary critic and adviser; b. Denver, Colo., Oct. 25, 1884; s. Charles and Stella (Alexander) U.; A.B., U. of Minn., 1909; student Harvard, 1909-10, Columbia, 1912-13; m. Camelia Waite, June 28, 1916; children—Mrs. Camelia Mary Berry, Sandra. Fiction editor Collier's Weekly, 1915-16; mng. editor The Nation's Business, 1917-18; spl. writer Everybody's Mag., 1919; confidential publicity investigator for Banker's Trust Co. of N.Y., in Eng. and France, 1920-21; editor and pub. The Blue Pencil, 1934-41; spl. lecturer, Columbia University Sch. of Journalism; former member faculty N.Y. University; former asso. prof. English dept., A. and M. Coll. of Okla.; professional adviser and instr. of Am. writers since 1920. Editor; Short story Hits, 1932, 33. Co-Author: The Psychology of Writing Success. Author: Narrative Technique, 1923; Writing As a Career, 1938; The Technique of the Novel, 1947; Compassionate Leave, produced by Martha's Vineyard Playhouse, 1946; also short stories and articles in mags. Home: Stillwater, Okla. *

VACCARO, ERNEST BEDFORD, reporter; b. Memphis, May 29, 1905; s. Vincent J. and Elizabeth (Wood) V.; ed. pub. schs. of Memphis and pvt. tutors; m. Lucille Poat, June 22, 1933. Reporter Memphis Commercial Appeal, 1925-29; White House corr. Asso. Press, Washington, 1945-53; gen. rep. of Asso. Press for midwest, Chgo., 1950, became exec. assistant to bureau chief, Washington, 1953, then AP Senate reporter. President White House Corr. Assn., 1948; mem. bd. govs., Nat. Press Club, 1949-51, v.p., 1953, pres., 1954. Mem. Sigma Delta Chi (Washington profl. chpt.). Home: Washington, D.C. Died Nov. 11, 1979.

VAGNOZZI, EGIDIO, clergyman, church ofcl.; b. Rome, Italy, Feb. 2, 1906; s. Francesco and Pasqua (Iachetti) V.; Ph.D., Lateran Pontifical Sem., 1924, S.T.D., 1928, J.C.D., 1930. Papal secretariat of state, Vatican City, 1930-32; sec., then auditor and counselor Apostolic Delegation, Washington, 1932-42; counselor Apostolic Nunciature, Paris, France, 1945-48; envoy extrordinary of Holy See to Ceylon, charge d'affaires, counselor Apostolic Internuntiature in India, 1948-49; apostolic del., then nuncio to P.I., 1949-58; 7th Apostolic Delegate to the U.S., 1958-67, created cardinal, 1967. Pres. Cardinal's Commn. for prefecture of econ. affairs of the Holy See, 1968-80. Decorated comdr. Legion of Honor (France); grand cross Order of Holy Sepulchre. Address: Rome, Italy. Died Dec. 27, 1980.

VAGTBORG, HAROLD, research adminstr.; b. Copenhagen, Sept. 17, 1904; s. Christian Peter V.; B.S., U. Ill., 1926; M.S., Armour Inst. Tech., 1934; D.Sc., Park Coll., 1947; LL.D., Mo. Valley Coll., 1950; m. Maurine Jones, June 3, 1926; children—Harold, Phyllis Maurine. Dir. Armour Research Found., Chgo., 1937-45, Inst. Gas. Tech., Chgo., 1942-44; pres., dir. Midwest Research Inst., Kansas City, Mo., 1945-48; pres. S.W. Research Inst.; dir. S.W. Found. Research and Edn., Inst. Inventive Research, San Antonio, 1948-59; pres. S.W. Research Center, 1950-76, S.W. Agrl. Inst., 1957-59; pres. S.W. Research Center comprising S.W. Research Inst., S.W. Agrl. Inst., S.W. Found. Research and Edn., San Antonio, 1959-76; mem. tech. adv. bd. Commerce Dept., 1965-69; dir. San Antonio br. Fed. Res. Bank. Mem. bd. San Antonio Med. Found., South Tex. Methodist Hosp.; vice chmn. bd. trustees Lady of Lake Coll.; chmn. bd. Cancer Therapy and Research Found.; bd. dirs. S.W. Heart and Lung Center; trustee St. Mary's U., Am. Inst. Character Edn.; nat. councilor U. Okla. Research Inst. Fellow A.A.A.S., ASME; mem. Chem. Soc. London, ASCE, Sci. Research Soc. Am., Soc. Chem. Industry of London, Am. Chem. Soc., Am. Phys. Soc. Methodist. Clubs: Oak Hills Country, San Antonio. Author: The Story of Southwest Research Center, 1974; Research and American Industrial Development, 1975. Home: San Antonio, Tex. Died Jan. 18, 1976; interred Mission Burial Park North.

VALENTINE, ALAN, univ. pres.; b. Glen Cove, N.Y., Feb. 23, 1901; s. Charles Post and Annie (Laurie) V.; B.A., Swarthmore Coll., 1921, LL.D., 1937; M.A., U. Pa., 1922; hon. B.A., Oxford (Eng.) U., 1925, M.A., 1928; hon. M.A., Yale, 1932; asso. fellow Pierson Coll., Yale, from 1936; LL.D., Syracuse U., Amherst Coll., Union U., 1935, Rutgers U., 1936, Denison U., 1940, Lake Forest Coll., 1942, Allegheny Coll., 1943, Colgate U., 1944; L.H.D. Hobart Coll., 1936, U. Rochester, 1966; Litt.D., Alfred U., 1937; m. Lucia Garrison Norton, Mar. 15, 1928; children—Garrison Norton, Anne Laurie (Mrs. John Buffinton), Sarah McKim. Instr. U. Pa., 1921-22; with Oxford U. Press in Eng. and U.S., 1925-28; asst. prof. English, dean of men Swarthmore Coll., also asst. Am. sec. to Rhodes Scholarship Trustees, 1928-32; prof. history arts and letters dept. Yale, also chmn. bd. admissions and master Pierson Coll., 1932-35; pres. U. Rochester, 1935-50; chief Netherlands Mission, ECA, 1948-49; adminstr. Econ. Stblzn. Agy., 1950-51; dir. various banks, railroads, corps., founds. Mem. Regents' Com. on Jr. Aviation 1942-80. Mng. dir. Nat. Com. Democrats for Wilkie, 1940. Served in O.T.C., Plattsburg, 1918. Decorated grand officer Orange-Nassau (Netherlands); recipient Gold medal Olympic Games, Paris, 1924. Fellow Internat. Order Artists and Writers; Intercontinental Biog. Assn.; mem. Assn. Am. Rhodes Scholars (dir. 1930-35). Newcomen Soc. Eng., Phi Beta Kappa, Delta Sigma Rho, Pi Delta Epsilon, Phi Kappa Psi. Mem. Soc. of Friends. Author: The English Novel, 1927; Biography, 1927; Dusty Answers, 1941; The Age of Conformity, 1954; Vigilante Justice, 1956; Trial Balance, 1956; Education of an American, 1958; Lord George Germain, 1962; 1913; Year of Transition, 1962; Fathers to Sons, 1963; Lord North, 2 vols., 1967; The British Establishment, 1760-84, 2 vols., 1968; Lord Stirling, 1968; (with Mrs. Valentine) The American Academy in Rome, 1973. Editor and compiler; Oxford of Today, 1928; editor American Oxonian, 1930-35; also articles and revs. Home: Princeton, N.J. Died July 14, 1980.

VALENTINE, J(OSEPH) ALFRED, raceway exec.; b. New Hyde Park, L.I., N.Y., July 22, 1894; s. Alfred and Louise (Davis) V.; student YMCA Bus. Adminstrn. Sch., N.Y.C.; m. Gulielma Robbins, Oct. 11, 1916; children—Barbara Jane (Mrs. Philip Ashley Rogers), Alfred Robbins, Richard Hewlett. Real estate and ins. exec. J. Alfred Valentine, Mineola, N.Y., from 1915; dir. First Nat. Bank of Mineola, N.Y., 1926-55, pres., 1951-55; pres. V. & B. Bldg. Corp., 1937-41; v.p., treas. Internal Surface Projector Corp., 1942-44; founder Roosevelt Raceway, Inc., chmn. bd., exec. v.p., gen. mgr., mem. exec. com., 1939-62; pres. L.I. Home, Ltd., Amityville, L.I., N.Y., from 1955. Organizer Red Cross Motor Corps, East Williston, N.Y.; dir. Nassau County Cerebral Palsy Assn; dir. adv. bd. Legal Aid. Soc. of Nassau County, City of Hope, L.I. Assn.; asso. trustee North Shore Hosp., Manhasset, L.I.; trustee, mem. exec. com. L.I. Fund; trustee Adelphi Coll., Garden City, New York. Recipient numerous awards for charity work. Mem. Agrl. Soc. of Queens Nassau and Suffolk Counties (pres. from 1938), N.Y. State Assn. Agrl. Fair Socs., L.I. Real Estate Bd., N.Y. State Assn. Real Estate Bds., N.Y. State Assn. Ins. Agts. (2d v.p. 1938), Nassau County Bar Assn., Mineola C. of C., Nassau County Grand Jurors' Assn., Shalimar Grotto of Garden City, Nassau County Extension Service Assn., U.S. Trotting Assn. Mason, Odd Fellow. Clubs: Sky (L.I.); Garden City Rotary; Mineola Republican; Wheatley Hills Golf (East Williston, L.I.); Ponte Vedra (Fla.) Club. Home: East Williston, L.I., N.Y. Died Nov. 19, 1976.

VALENTINE, P(ERCY) F(RIARS), educator; b. Boston, Mass., Dec. 1, 1884; s. Richard P. and Emma (Friars) V.; A.B., Stanford, 1909; M.L., Univ. of Calif. at Berkeley, 1915; Ed.D., 1927; m. Gladys Prestwood, Dec. 26, 1915; children—Virginia (Mrs. Robert H. Smith), Hope (Mrs. Milton A. Peterson), Edward. Instr. in history and govt., San Francisco State Normal Sch., 1910-17; prin. training sch. and instr. in psychology and logic, Fresno (Calif.) State Coll., 1918-24; prof. of psychology, San Francisco State Coll., 1924-50, dean, 1936-50, dean of gen. edn., 1945-50, dean emeritus since 1950; visiting prof., Univ. of N.D. summer sessions, 1928-29, University of Utah, summer 1931, San Diego State Coll., summer 1936; lecturer in edn., University of Calif. at Berkeley, 1939-40. Mem. Sigma Nu, Phi Delta Kappa, Alpha Phi Gamma. Democrat. Conglist. Author: California: The Story of Our State, 1915; The Psychology of Personality, 1927; The Art of the Teacher, 1931. Editor: Twentieth Century Education, 1946; The American College, 1949. Contbr. to various gen. and professional publs. Home: Berkeley. *

VAN ACKEREN, GERALD, educator, theologian; b. Cedar Rapids, Neb., Apr. 19, 1916; s. Edward M. and Frances (Leary) Van A.; A.B., St. Louis U., 1939, A.M. in Classics, 1941, A.M. in Philosophy, 1943, S.T.L., 1948; S.T.D., Gregorian U., Rome, 1951. Joined Soc. of Jesus, 1933, ordained priest Roman Cath. Ch., 1946; mem. faculty St. Louis U., 1951-78, dean Sch. Div., 1960-69, bd. dirs., mem. exec. com., 1968-75, prof. dogmatic and systematic theology, 1966, chmn. dept., 1970-74; editor Theology Digest, 1953-78. Mem. exec. com. St. Louis Theol. Consortium, 1971-75. Mem. Midwest Assn. Theol. Schs. (exec. com. 1969-74, v.p. 1973), Cath. Theol. Soc. Am. (pres. 1964-65, bd. dirs. 1958-61, 65-68, del. Council Study Religion 1969-75), Coll. Theology Soc. (charter), Am. Acad. Religion, Kansas City Soc. Theol. Studies, Inst. Theol. Encounter with Sci. and Tech. (bd. dirs. 1970-78). Author: Sacra Doctrina: The Subject of the First Question of the Summa Theologica of Saint Thomas Aquinas, 1952. Editor: The Church Teaches: Documents of the Church in English Translation, 1955. Editorial bd. Communio: Internat. Cath. Rev., 1974-78. Home: St. Louis, Mo. Died Jan. 10, 1978; interred Calvary Cemetery, St. Louis.

VAN ARSDALE, TALMAN WALKER, JR., banker; b. Buffalo, Sept. 10, 1915; s. Talman Walker and Hazel (Drake) Van A.; B.A., U. Buffalo, 1938, M.A., 1940, Ed.D., 1954; L.H.D., Canisius Coll., 1968; m. Nancy Elizabeth Collard, June 22, 1940; children—Janet Nancy (Mrs. John L. Marshall), Beth Ann (Mrs. Douglas Dean). Asst. dir. publicity U. Buffalo, 1938-39, dir. alumni relations, 1948-51, dir. devel., asso. prof. edn., 1952-56; head English dept. Park Sch., Buffalo, 1939-42, asst. headmaster, 1946-48; exec. v.p. Worcester Poly. Inst., 1956-61; pres. Bradley U., Peoria, Ill., 1961-71, chancellor, 1971-73; v.p. Comml. Nat. Bank, Peoria, 1973-77. Commr., Nat. Commn. on Accrediting; cons. U.S. Office Edn., 1959-61; mem. Peoria Bd. Med. Edn. Trustee Old Sturbridge Village; mem. bd. Sisters 3d Order St. Francis; bd. dirs. Lakeview Center Arts and Scis. Served from ensign to lt. comdr., USNR, 1942-46, from lt. comdr. to comdr., 1951-52. Mem. Assn. Urban Univs. (pres. 1965-66, sec.-treas. 1965-68), Assn. for Higher Edn., Ill. Conf. Higher Edn. (pres. 1965-69), Newcomen Soc., Fedn. Ind. Ill. Colls. and Univs. (pres. 1968-70), Zeta Pi, Phi Delta Kappa, Phi Kappa Psi, Phi Alpha Theta, Phi Eta Sigma, Omicron Delta Kappa, Alpha Kappa Psi. Episcopalian. Rotarian. Clubs: Peoria Country, Creve Coeur (Peoria). Author: Practical English Grammar, 1941; High School Vocabulary, 1942; Parodies of the Romantic Poets, 1944. Contbr. articles to profl. jours. Home: Peoria, Ill. Died Aug. 14, 1977; buried Cathedral of St. Paul Columbarium, Peoria.

VAN AUKEN, WILBUR RICE, naval officer; b. Utica, N.Y., Mar. 13, 1882; s. Myron W. and Caroline (Rice) Van Auken; B.S., M.S. U.S. Naval Acad., 1903; Naval War Coll., 1927; m. Pauline Thompson, June 16, 1909; 1 dau. Rosalie (wife of Comdr. Francis Blouin). Promoted through grades to captain, 1926; served as gunnery officer on Flagship Rhode Island (Mexican campaign, 1914) and later on Texas; in World War I, in charge fire control, Bureau Ordnance; naval ordnance observer on staff of Admiral W.S. Sims in Europe; command of Stribling in Mediterranean and Adriatic seas; head of Ordnance and Gunnery Dept. at U.S. Naval Acad., 1921-24; command of Aircraft Tender Aroostook, 1924-26; head Training Div., Bureau of Navigation, 1927-29; command of U.S.S. Vestal, 1929-31; staff of Naval War Coll., 1931-34; in command of Oklahoma, 1934-35; on Naval Examining Bd. Navy Dept., 1935-39; retired 1939; entered investment banking business, Washington, D.C; returned to active duty (on leave from Merrill Lynch Pierce Fenner & Beane) as chief of naval personnel, Bur. of Ordnance, Navy Dept., Jan. 1941-Sept. 1945. Retired, inactive duty, Navy 1941-Sept. 1945. Retired, inactive duty, Navy Dept., since Sept. 1, 1945. Awarded Mexican Campaign Victory, Army Occupation of Austria, 1918, National Emergency medals; World War II medals and Commendation Ribbon, citation from Sec. of Navy. Mem. Naval Hist. Foundn., Naval Inst., National Geographic Soc., Herkimer Co. (N.Y.) Hist. Soc., Fairfield Sem. Alumni Assn. Former pres. Washington Philateli Soc. Rep. Presbyterian. Mason. Clubs: Army and Navy, Country, Chevy Chase (Washington, Country,); N.Y. Yacht Club. Former mem. Bd. of Control. Naval Inst.; former mem. bd. of mgrs., Navy Relief Soc.; mem. bd. dirs. Navy Mutual Aid Assn., since 1942; chmn. restoration com. Fairfield Coll. and Sem. Chapel. Author: (textbooks) Technical Ordnance; Gunnery and Strategy Textbooks for Navy, Revised "Naval Ordnance," 1942 Edition Encyclopedia Britannica; "Notes on Half Century of U.S. Naval Ordnance, 1939"; Top of the Hill (with Thomas O'Durell) 1953. Contributor articles on naval subjects to mags. Speaker in colls. and Navy training schs., during World War II. Home: Herkimer County, N.Y. *

VAN BOMEL, LEROY ALLISON (VAN-BOM'EL), cons. Nat. Dairy Products Corp.; b. N.Y. City, Dec. 15, 1885; s. Isaac A. and Ida Gertrude (Slawson) VanB.; B.S.C.E., N.Y.U., 1908; 1 daughter, Charlotte. Salesman and bookkeeper, Sheffield Farms Company, New York City, from 1908 to 1909, plant operation, plant building, 1909-16, director, 1917, v.p. and mem. exec. com., 1924-26, pres., 1926-41; formed Sheffield Condensed Milk Co., N.Y.C., 1914, pres., 1914-27, dir., 1914-40; dir. Nat. Dairy Products Corp., N.Y.C., 1925-57, v.p., 1925, exec. v.p., 1935-41, pres., 1941-52, chmn. exec. com., chmn. bd. 1952-57.; trustee Am. Surety Co.; dir. Ryder System, Inc. Trustee N.Y. U. Mem. Am. Soc. M.E., St. Nicholas Soc., Phi Gamma Delta. Episcopalian. Mason. Clubs: Links, Turf and Field, South Side Sportsmen's, Twenty-Nine; Indian Creek (Fla.); Surf (Miami Beach). Home: N.Y.C. *

VANCE, JOSEPH ANDERSON, JR., lawyer, corp. exec.; b. Balt., Dec. 6, 1898; s. Joseph Anderson and Mary (Forman) V.; A.B., Dartmouth, 1921; J.D., Harvard, 1924; m. Jeanne Gilchrist, June 1931 (dec. Jan. 1943); m. 2d, Ruth Harper, Dec. 28, 1954; 1 dau., Jeanne (Mrs. Milton Dance). Admitted to Mich. bar, 1924, since practiced in Detroit; sr. partner firm Beaumont, Smith & Harris, 1961-69, counsel, 1969-78; treas., dir. Gilchrist Timber Co., 1936-78; pres., dir. Detroit & Windsor Ferry Co., also Boblo Steamers, Inc., 1936-41; dir. Massey Ferguson Inc., also Perkins Engines, Inc., 1962-68. Spl. legal counsel Surgeon Gen.'s Office, 1942-43; corp. counsel Village of Grosse Pointe Shores, 1948-64. Trustee Harper Hosp., (now Grace-Harper Hosp.), Detroit, 1944-78, trustee emeritus, 1978; bd. dirs. United Cerebral Palsy Assn. Detroit, 1960-74. Mem. Am., Mich., Detroit bar assns., Beta Theta Pi, Casque and Guantlet Sr. Soc. Presbyn. (past trustee, chmn. bd.). Clubs: Detroit Country, Hundred, Dartmouth, Harvard of Mich. (Detroit); Grosse Pointe (past chmn. bd.). Home: Grosse Pointe Shores, Mich. Died Jan. 28, 1978.

VANCE, LAWRENCE LEE, educator; b. St. Louis, Jan. 16, 1911; s. Archie Clifton and Myrtle (Lee) V.; B.B.A., U. Minn., 1932, M.A., 1933, Ph.D., 1947; m. Mary McLaury Gardner, Sept. 29, 1934; children—Lawrence Lee, Virginia McLaury (Mrs. Mark Braverman). Accountant, Peat, Marwick, Mitchell & Co., 1933-39; instr. accounting U. Kans., 1939-41; lectr., asso. prof., prof. accounting U. Calif. at Berkeley, 1941-78, asso. dean Grad. Sch. Bus. Adminstrn., 1965-69. Pres. Acalanes Community Concert Assn., Orchid Digest Corp. Mem. Am. Accounting Assn. (pres.), Am. Inst. C.P.A.'s, Calif. Soc. C.P.A.'s, Am. Orchid Soc. (Pres.), Phi Beta Kappa, Beta Gamma Sigma, Beta Alpha Psi, Delta Sigma Rho, Theta Chi. Democrat. Methodist. Author: Scientific Method for Auditing, 1950; Theory and Technique of Cost Accounting, 2d edit., 1958; (with John Neter) Statistical Sampling for Auditors and Accountants, 1956; (with Russell Taussig) Accounting Principles and Control, 3d edit., 1972; Tables for Estimating Error rates and Other Proportions, 1961 (with Wayne Boutell) Principles of Auditing, 1975. Home: Lafayette, Calif. Died June 4, 1978.

VAN COTT, HARRISON HORTON, educator; b. Bainbridge, N.Y., Sept. 23, 1884; s. Herman H. and Harriet N. (Westcott) Van C.; grad. N.Y. State Normal Sch., 1904; B.S., Columbia, 1906; A.M., N.Y. State Coll. Tchrs., 1919; Ph.D., N.Y.U., 1934; m. Mable G. Corbin, Aug. 29, 1906; 1 son, Harrison Corbin; m. 2d Edith V. Porter, Dec. 22, 1924; 1 son, Harold Porter. Instr. sci., asst. prin. high sch., Schenectady, N.Y., 1906-18, prin., 1918-26; state supervisor jr. high schs. N.Y. State, 1926-38; chief N.Y. State Bur. Instructional Supervision for Secondary Schs., 1938-47, dir. secondary edn. div. since 1947; instr. Chautauqua (N.Y.) Summer Sch., 1909-17, N.Y.U., 1949, 51, Alfred U., 1950, 52; asso. editor Jr. Sr. Clearing House, 1926-52. Mem. N.E.A. (dept. secondary sch. prins.), Nat., N.Y. State assns. secondary sch. prins., N.Y. State Tchrs. Assn., Phi Delta Kappa, Kappa Delta Phi. Mason. Club: Torch (Schenectady). Author ednl. articles. Home: Schenectady. *

VAN DEN BOSCH, ROBERT, educator; b. Martinez, Calif., Mar. 31, 1922; s. Pieter and Aline (Schulthess) van den B.; A.B., U. Calif. at Berkeley, 1943, Ph.D., 1950; m. Margaret Irene Bryant, Mar. 11, 1944. Asst. entomologist U. Hawaii, 1949-51, asst. entomologist U. Calif. at Riverside, 1951-57, asso. entomologist, 1957-63; asso. entomologist U. Calif. at Berkeley, 1963-64, entomologist, 1964-78, chmn. div. biol. control, 1969-78, prof. entomology, 1967-78. Guggenheim fellow, 1958-59. Fellow AAAS; mem. Entomol. Soc. Am., Ecol. Soc. Am., Pacific Coast Entomol. Soc., Am. Inst. Biol. Scis. Co-author text biol. control. Contbr. chpts. to books, articles to profl. jours. Research in biol. control of pest insects, ecology of parasitic insects, integrated control of agrl. pests. Home: Kensington, Calif. Died Nov. 19, 1978; buried Sunset View Cemetery, Berkeley, Calif.

VANDERBILT, HAROLD STIRLING, capitalist; b. Oakdale, N.Y., July 6, 1884; s. William Kissan and Alvia E. (Smith) V.; A.B., Harvard, 1907; Harvard U. Law Sch., 1907-10. Began active career with N.Y.C. R.R.; for many years dir. various ry. and other corps. Pres. bd. trust Vanderbilt U. Served from it. (j.g.) to lt. USNRF, 1917-18; comdg. officer Scout Patrol 56, later comdr. Block Island and New London sects., served with submarine chaser detachment 3, Queenstown, Ireland, 1918. Inventor contract bridge, 1925. Address: N.Y.C. *

VANDERHORST, ARIE, clergyman; b. at Leyden, The Netherlands, Aug. 24, 1883; s. Pieter and Gertrude (de Graaff) V.; A.B., U. of Leyden, 1904, A.M., 1908, Th.D., 1911; m. Amy Kamberg, Nov. 16, 1918; children—David Arie, Mary Alice, Daniel Paul, Philip John, Martha Anna, Benjamin Franklin, Elisabeth Ruth, Sarah Joy. Came to United States 1912, naturalized citizen, 1918. Ordained Presbyn. ministry, 1912; became pastor Netherland Ref. Ch., New York, 1912; with Bd. of Christian Edn., San Francisco, 1915; then prof. classics, Sheridan Coll., 1920, became pres., 1922; was made pres. Lincoln (Ill.) Coll. (junior coll.), 1928; now pastor Unity Church, Woodson, Ill. Engaged in lecturing. Army officer in The Netherlands, 1903. Mason. Rotarian. Author: The Philosophy of Spinoza, 1912; The Theology of Luther and Calvin Compared, 1913; Information and Defense, 1914; Christ and Culture, 1925. Home: Woodson,Ill.*

VANDERSALL, STANLEY BYRON (VAN'DER-SAWL), clergyman, editor; b. East Liberty, Summit County, O., Nov. 2, 1886; s. Elias Wesley and Myra Ethel (Kling) V.; A.B., Coll. of Wooster, 1907; M.A., N.Y. Univ., 1912; B.D., Drew Theol. Sem., 1912; hon. D.D., Albright Coll., 1935; m. Leah Mary Talbott, June 30, 1914; children—Dorothy Rena (deceased), Stanley Talbott, Elizabeth Ruth, Harold Wesley. Ordained in the Evangelical Church, 1908; pastor, Canton, O., 1906-07, Lorain, O., 1907-09; pastor, M.E. Ch., Sparrowbush, N.Y., 1909-12; field sec., gen. sec., Ohio Christian Endeavor Union, 1912-19; alumni sec., financial sec., vocations supt., Internat. Soc. of Christian Endeavor, 1919-34, asso. sec., 1934-46, exec. sec. program council, 1944-47, sec. ednl. committee since 1944, chairman topics committee, 1934-46 and since 1948; treasurer World's Christian Endeavor Union, 1919-41, general secretary, since 1938, trustee, member exec. com. since 1919; asso. editor Christian Endeavor World, 1934-37, editor, 1937-46; treas. and mem. exec. com. Lord's Day League of New England, 1940-47, dir. since 1930, gen. sec. since 1947; pres. New England Watch and Ward Society since 1946, dir. since 1936. Mason. Author: Christian Endeavor Essentials, 1938. Home: West Roxbury, Mass. *

VANDERSTUCKEN, EMILE FELIX, JR., lawyer; b. Sonora, Tex., Oct. 18, 1903; s. Emile Felix and Katherine Elizabeth (Wyatt) V.; B.A., U. Tex., 1923; B.S., Georgetown U., 1924; M.A., George Washington U., 1924; LL.B., Harvard, 1927; J.S.D., N.Y. U., 1939; m. Alice Frances Robinson, 1939; children—Emily Frances, Emile Felix. Admitted to Tex. bar, 1928, N.Y. bar, 1935, U.S. Supreme Ct., 1943, U.S. Patent Office, 1947; practice of law, San Angelo, Tex., 1928-34; atty. Tex. Gulf Sulphur Co. 1935-61, asst. sec., 1948-51, sec., 1951-61, vice president until 1961, then cons. atty.; adv. Conf. on German Indsl. Property, London, 1947; legal div. Office Mil. Govt., Berlin, 1947-48. Served as lt. comdr. U.S.N.R., 1943-45; legal div. Office Sec. Navy, also Office Research and Inventions. Mem. Fed., Am., Tex. bar assns., Am. Mining Congress, Am. Ordinance Assn., Am. Soc. Corp. Secs., Am. Soc. Internat. Law, Assn. Bar City N.Y., Internat. Law Assn., Delta Sigma Pi, Chi Phi. Episcopalian. Club: Harvard (N.Y.C.). Home: Princeton, N.J. Died Aug. 21, 1979; interred Trinity-All Saints Cemetery, Princeton.

VAN DERZEE, GOULD W(HITNEY) (VAN'DER-ZE), business exec.; b. Albany, N.Y., Jan. 8, 1886; s. Frank and Mabel Gould (Rugg) v.; B.S., U. of Wis., 1908; m. Margaret Brand, June 6, 1914 (dec. Dec. 8, 1921); children—Margaret (Mrs. Marvin C. Kramer), Karen (Mrs. Thomas E. Bogardus); m. 2d, Helen Lippka, Aug. 19, 1925. Director and member of the executive com. of Wis. Electric Power Co., Bucyrus-Erie Co., Marshall & Ilsley Bank, Milw.; dir. Wis.-Mich. Power Co., Wis. Natural Gas Co., Marshall & Ilsley Bank Stock Corp. Mem. Village Bd. Whitefish Bay, Wis., 1924-30, plan commn., 1930—. Past president Assn. Edison Illuminating Cos.; dir. Milw. War Chest, World War II; past dir. Edison Electric Inst.; mem. Greater Milw. Com.; dir. United Community Services. Received citation award U. Wis., 1948; Distinguished Service award Wis. Alumni Club 1964. Mem. Engrs. Soc. Milw., Delta Upsilon. Republican. Mason (33 deg.). Clubs: Milwaukee, Milwaukee Athletic, University, Gyro (past president). Home: Milw. *

VAN DER ZEE, JACOB (VAN-DER-ZE), prof. polit. science; b. The Netherlands, Feb. 9, 1884; s. Bauke and Janna (Van der Weg) Van der Z.; brought to U.S. in childhood; B.A., State U. of Ia., 1905; Rhodes scholar from Ia., 1905-08, B.A., Merton Coll., Oxford U., 1908, M.A., 1913; Harvard Law Sch., 1910-11; LL.B., State U. of Ia., 1913, J.D., 1924; admitted to the bar; m. Ethel A. McKnight, Sept. 6, 1913; children—John Jacob, Robert Willem. Instr. polit. science, 1913-15, asst. prof., 1915-20, asso. prof., 1920-29, prof., 1929-49, State U. of Ia. Asst. to Iowa Code Commn., 1919, 24. Mem. Am. Polit. Science Assn., Phi Delta Phi, Phi Beta Kappa. Presbyterian. Author: The Hollanders of Iowa (State Hist. Soc.), 1912; (with others) Statute Law-Making in Iowa, 1916; The British in Iowa (State Hist. Soc.), 1922. Contbr. to Ia. Jour. of History and Politics. Home: Iowa City, Ia. *

VAN DERZEE, JAMES, photographer; b. Lenox, Mass., 1886. Exhbns. of photographs include Met. Mus. Art. Recipient award Am. Soc. Magazine Photographers. *

VAN DEUSEN, GEORGE LANE, army officer; b. Passaic, N.J., Feb. 10, 1888; s. Clarence Richard and Mattie (Lane) Van D.; B.S., U.S. Mil. Acad., 1909; M.S., Yale, 1921; grad. Army Signal Sch., 1924, Command and Gen. Staff Sch., 1925, Army War Coll., 1936, Naval War Coll., 1937; m. Effie Baker, June 24, 1935. Commd. 2d lt., Inf., 1909, advanced through grades to maj. gen., May 24, 1944; comdr. 105th Field Signal Batn., 30th Div., France and Belgium, 1918; comdg. Eastern Signal Corps Training Center, Fort Monmouth, N.J., 1942-44; dir. Engring. and Tech. Service, Signal Corps, Washington, 1945-46; retired Aug. 1936. Awarded Distinguished Service Medal (Army). President RCA Institutes, N.Y. City, 1947-53. Mem. Holland Soc. of New York, Inst. Radio Engrs., N.Y. Soc. Mil. and Naval Officers World Wars. Clubs: Army and Navy (Washington); Military-Naval (New York). Home: Monmouth Beach, N.J. Died Jan. 12, 1977.

VANDIVER, HARRY SHULTZ (VAN'DI-VER), prof. of mathematics; b. Phila., Pa., Oct. 21, 1882; s. John Lyon and Ida Frances (Everett) V.; student University of Pennsylvania, 1904-05; Sc.D. (hon.) U. of Pa., 1945; m. Maude Folmsbee Everson, July 25, 1923; 1 son, Frank Everson. Asso. with John L. Vandiver as customs house broker, Phila., 1900-19; instr. in mathematics, Cornell U., 1919-24; asso. prof. of pure mathematics, U. of Tex., 1924-35, prof. since 1935, research prof., 1934-35, research fellow, 1939-40, 1946-47; vis. prof. math., U. of Chicago, summer 1922; Princeton, spring 1934; Univ. of Indiana, spring 1947, Notre Dame, summer 1947. Distinguished professor applied math., U. of Texas., 1947. Served with U.S.N.R.F., 1917-19. Chairman Com. on Algebraic Numbers, Nat. Research Council, 1923-28; colloquium lecturer Am. Math. Soc., 1935, v.p., 1935-37. Fellow Research Institute, U. of Texas, 1946, 1948. Member Am. Math. Soc., Math. Assn. of America, Am. Assn. Univ. Profs., Nat. Acad. Sciences. Awarded Cole prize of Am. Math. Soc., 1931; received Guggenheim Memorial Foundation grants, 1927, 30; received Am. Philos. Soc. grants, 1934, 40, four grants from Heckscher Research Foundation at Cornell U., 1920-23. Mem. Artisans Order of Mutual Protection.

Author: (with others) Report on Theory of Algebraic Numbers (Nat. Research Council), Part I, 1922, Part II, 1928. Contbr. numerous articles to math. jours. Home: Austin, Tex. *

VAN DORN, HORACE BISHOP, pencil mfr.; b. Red Bank, N.J., Sept. 23, 1883; s. Dr. Horace Bishop and Harriett Rebecca (Goff) Van Dorn; student Engring. Coll. Ohio State U., 1901-03; m. Mabel Wikoff, Oct. 12, 1909; children—Laura (Mrs. G. P. Bolsover), Horace Bishop 3d; m. 2d, Gertrude Kniering, Oct. 20, 1928; children—Daniel Kniering, Walter Goff. Draftsman Newport News Shipbuilding & Dry Dock Co., 1903-06; traveling salesman, stationery trade, 1906-08; successively pencil salesman, asst. sales mgr., sales mgr., v.p. and dir. Joseph Dixon Crucible Co., Jersey City, 1908—. Mem. Nat. Stationery and Office Equipment Assn. (chmn. mfrs. div. 1945-46), Am. Tariff League (bd. mgrs., exec. com. 1938—), Boston, Conn. Valley stationers assns. Mason (Shriner). Home: Maplewood, N.J. *

VAN DOUSER, ALTON MERIE, mfg. exec.; b. Ovid, Mich., May 19, 1885; s. Albert Henry and Emma E. (Munson) Van D.; student Ferris Inst., 1903-04; m. Laura I. Weiland, Sept. 18, 1911; 1 dau., Alice Marion (Mrs. W. D. Pickell). With Munising Paper Co., 1905-09, chief accountant, 1907-09; with Marathon Corp. (formerly Marathon Paper Mills Co.) since 1909, asst. treas., 1927-42, asst. sec., 1934-42, sec., treas. since 1942, dir. since 1951. Asso. organizer Paper Splty. Co., Wausau, 1915, pres. since 1920. Mem.-at-large Samoset council Boy Scouts Am. Mem. Wis. State C. of C. (past dist. v.p.; now dir.), Wausau C. of C. (past treas., pres., dir.), Marathon Co. Civic Corp. (pres., dir.). Republican. Presbyn. (elder). Mason. Club: Kiwanis. Home: Wausau. *

VAN DUSEN, WILLIAM, aviation historian; b. Toledo, Sept. 19, 1901; s. William Boyd and Rose Marie (Foley) Van D.; grad. Regis Acad., Denver, 1921; B.A., U. Denver, 1924; m. Katherine Lee Lohr, Apr. 14, 1945; children—William Babson, Michael Edlee, George William. With Doremus & Co., advt. agy., N.Y.C., 1925-28, Pan Am. Airways, 1928, N.Y., Rio & Buenos Aires Line (absorbed by Pan Am. Airways 1930), 1929; dir. pub. relations Pan Am. World Airways, 1930-47; spl. bus. cons. 1949-50; with Eastern Air Lines, Inc., N.Y.C., 1951-66, v.p. pub. relations and news bur., staff v.p., 1966-68. Assisted establishment first transcontinental air mail service, 1923-24; participated pioneer flights to Panama, C.Z., around S.A., 1928-34, first trans-Pacific flights, 1935-36, pioneer trans-Atlantic flights, 1939, South Pacific flights, 1940, South Atlantic-Africa, 1941; pioneered around-the-world airline, 1947. Served with the 32d Div., U.S. Army, World War I; as lt. condr. USNR, World War II; spl. mission Gen. Eisenhower's staff, Normandy Invasion. Mem. Inst. Aero. Scis., Nat. Aero. Assn., Aviation/Space Writers Assn., Sigma Delta Chi. Clubs: Explorers, Wings, N.Y. Athletic, Dutch Treat, Coffee House (N.Y.C.); Nat. Press (Washington). Author: Exploring the Maya with Lindbergh, 1932. Contbr. articles to popular mags. Home: Coral Gables, Fla. Died Mar. 2, 1976.

VAN ETTEN, EDWIN JAN, clergyman; b. Rhinebeck, N.Y., Apr. 28, 1884; s. Cornelius (M.D.) and Sarah Clarissa (Hill) Van E.; grad. Riverview Mil. Acad., 1901; B.A., Amherst, 1905; student Gen. Theol. Sem.; B.D., Episcopal Theol. Sch., Cambridge, Mass., 1911; D.D., U. of Pittsburgh, 1923, Allegheny Coll., 1923, Amherst (Mass.) Coll., 1935; unmarried. Deacon and priest P.E. Ch., 1911; asst. minister Trinity Ch., Boston, 1911-14; rector Christ Ch., New York, 1914-17, Calvary Ch., Pittsburgh, Pa., 1917-40; dean St. Paul's Cathedral, Boston, since 1940. Pres. Pa. Assn. for the Blind, 1923-25. Mem. Holland Soc., Alpha Delta Phi, Phi Beta Kappa. Club: Union. The pioneer (Jan. 1921) in broadcasting ch. services. Home: Boston, Mass. *

VAN EVERY, DALE, writer; b. Levering, Mich., July 23, 1896; s. Wilbert Maurice and Estella (Palmer) Van E.; A.B., Stanford, 1920; m. Ellen Calhoun, Apr. 7, 1922; children—David, Joan; m. 2d, Florence Mclaine Mason, Nov. 12, 1937; m. 3d, Frances R. Francis, Apr. 22, 1972. Corr., editor United Press, N.Y.C., Washington, 1920-28; writer, producer motion pictures, Hollywood, 1929-42. Author: A.E.F. in Battle, 1928; Westward the River, 1945; The Shining Mountains, 1948; Bridal Journey, 1950; The Captive Witch, 1951; The Trembling Earth, 1953; Men of the Western Waters, 1955; The Voyagers, 1957; Our Country Then, 1958; The Scarlet Feather, 1959; Forth to the Wilderness, 1961; A company of Heroes, 1962; Ark of Empire, 1963; The Final Challenge, 1964; The Disinherited, 1966; The Day the Sun Died, 1971. Home: Santa Barbara, Calif. Died May 28, 1976.

VAN HAERSMA DE WITH, HENRY MAURICE, diplomat; b. Utrecht, Netherlands, June 15, 1884; ed. Univ. of Utrecht; m. S.L. Van den Broek d'Obrenan, Sept.28, 1915; children—Nora, William, Ines. Sec. of The Netherlands legation at Petrograd, Bucharest, Belgrade and Berne, 1911-14, then at Vienna, 1914-18; counsellor of legation, Foreign Office, The Hague, 1918-22, Copenhagen, 1922-23; charge d'affaires, Oslo, Norway, 1923-24; minister to Portugal, 1925-30, Ethiopia, 1930, Prague, 1931-33; E.E. and M.P. from The Netherlands to U.S. since Jan. 1934. Sent on spl. mission to Ethiopia at coronation of emperor. 1930. Presbyn. Address: Washington, D.C. *

VAN HOOGSTRATEN, WILLEM, music conductor; b. Utrecht, Holland, Mar. 18, 1884; s. Samuel and Elizabeth (van Hoytema) van H.; ed. Conservatory, Cologne, Germany, 1901-08; m. Elly Ney, 1911; 1 dau., Eleonore. Began as violinist, 1911; formed own trio and traveled with it through Europe; municipal condr., Crefeld, Germany, 1914-18; guest condr. various European musical centers; came to U.S., 1920; condr. at Stadium, New York, since1922; condr. Philharmonic Orchestra, New York, 1923-24, Symphony Orchestra, Portland, Ore., since 1925. Home: Holland. *

VAN HOOK, CLIFFORD E(VANS), naval officer; b. Washington, D.C., Apr. 10, 1886; s. John Clifford and Carrie Evans Van Hook; B.S., U.S. Naval Acad., 1909; grad. Naval War Coll., 1923, Army War Coll., 1934; m. Helen Reid Evans, Sept. 24, 1912 (dec.); children—Helen (wife of Comdr. Hugh Wyman Howard, U.S. Navy), Margaret (wife of Lt. Eliot Hubbard, III, U.S.N.R.), Gordan; m. 2d Winifred Pigott Pendergast, Apr. 22, 1946. Entered Navy, 1909; promoted through grades to rear adm. 1942; served in Mexican Campaign, 1944, and World War I; aide to Adm. William Sims (pres. Naval War Coll.) and to his successor, Adm. G S. Williams, 1922-23; mem. U.S. Naval Mission to Brazil, 1927-30; on staff, Command and Gen. Staff Sch., 1931; prof. naval science and tactics, U. of Calif., 1937-40; comdg. officer, U.S.S. Portland, Pacific Fleet, 1940-42, comdr. Panama Sea Frontier and comdt. 15th Naval Dist. (Canal Zone), 1942-43; deputy comdr. 7th Fleet, 1943-45; comdr. U.S. Naval Forces Australia-New Guinea, 1945-46; gen. insp. Western Sea Frontier and Pacific Res. Fleet, 1946-47; retired May 1948. Decorations: (U.S. Navy) Mexican Campaign, Victory, Navy Cross, American Defense Service, Asiatic-Pacific Campaign, American Area Campaign; Legion of Merit, Distinguished Service, Distinguished Service (Army); Gran Oficial, Orden de Boyaca (Columbia); Presidential Medal of Merit (Nicaragua); Gran Oficial, Orden de Condor de los Andes (Bolivia); Orden de Abdon Calderon (Equador); Gran Oficial, Orden de Vasco Nuñez de Balboa (Panama); Gran Oficial, Orden Militar de Ayacucha (Peru). Clubs: Army and Navy Country (Washington); Faculty (U. of Calif.). Address: San Francisco. *

VAN HOVEN, PAUL HENRY, railway exec.; b. St. Paul, Minn., Oct. 24, 1886; s. Peter H. and Augusta (Zeigler) Van H.; ed. Central and Mechanics Arts High Sch., and St. John's U.; m. Ella L. Lysne; children—Jane (Mrs. Donald J. Mathers), Phyllis (Mrs. Richard P. Kepler), Robert P., Barbara, Rate clerk, Northern Pacific Railway Co., St. Paul, Minn., 1907-08; rate clerk, later chief clerk, accounting dept. Chicago, St. Paul, Minneapolis and Omaha Ry. Co., 1908-11; chief clerk to auditor, Duluth, Missabe & Northern Ry., 1911-19, federal auditor, 1919-20. asst. auditor, 1920-28, also wage schedule supervisor, 1923-28; asst. to gen. mgr. operating dept., 1928-30; asst. to pres. Duluth Missabe & Iron Range Ry. Co., 1930-34, first vice pres. 1934-44, pres. since 1944. Dir. and mem. exec. com. Minn. Arrowhead Assn., Duluth, Minn. Mem. finance com. Minn. Safety Council. Dir. St. Louis County Humane Soc.; vice pres. and dir. Tuberculosis and Health Assn. of St. Louis County; dir. Christmas Seal Sale, Duluth, Minn.; mem. C. of C. (Duluth) (mem. bd. dirs., mem. exec. com., dir. chmn. exec. safety, indsl. safety, pub. safety). Mason (K.T.). Clubs: Kitchi Gammi, Duluth Athletic, Northland Country, Rotary (Duluth). Home: Duluth. *

VAN KATWIJK, PAUL (VAN KAT'WIK), pianist condr.; b. Rotterdam, Netherlands, Dec. 7, 1885; s. Johannes and Catherina (Scholten) Van K.; studied piano under George Rijken, Rotterdam, and Carl Oberstadt, The Hague; grad. Royal Conservatory of Music, The Hague, 1904; studied composition under Wilhelm Klatte, Berlin, 1907-09; pupil of Leopold Godowsky, 1907-10; student Imperial Acad. Music, Vienna, 1909-10; hon. Mus.D., Drake Univ., Des Moines, Ia., 1931; m. Viola Edna Beck, June 15, 1922. Came to U.S., 1912, naturalized citizen, 1921. Head of piano dept., Neustadt-an-der-Hardt Conservatory, Germany, 1910-11, Nat. Conservatory, Helsingfors, Finland, 1911-12, Christian Coll., Columbia, Mo., 1912-13; mem. faculty Columbia Sch. of Music, Chicago, 1913-14; head of piano dept. Drake U., Des Moines, Ia., 1914-18; dean of music, Southern Meth. U., Dallas, Tex., 1919-49, resigned as dean, 1949, professor of piano, 1949-55; private teacher of piano, Dallas, Texas, 1955—. Conductor Des Moines Symphony Orchestra, 1915-18, Dallas Municipal Chorus, 1918-22, Dallas Symphony Orchestra, 1925-37. Mem. Dutch Ref. Ch. Mason. Composer songs, piano and orchestra compositions, transcriptions for 2 pianos, choruses for mixed voices, etc. Home: Dallas, Tex. *

VANNEMAN, HARRY WALTER, prof. of law; b. Sidell, Ill., July 23, 1882; s. Franklin Miller and Margaret (Canady) V.; A.B., U. of Ill., 1907, LL.B., 1909; LL.M., Yale, 1910; m. Winifred Campbell, June 22, 1912; 1 dau., Margaret (dec.). Admitted to Ill. bar, 1910, and practiced in Urbana, with firm of Franklin H. Boggs, 1910-11; asst. prof. of law, U. of S.D. Law Sch., 1911-12, prof., 1912-27; admitted to the S.D. bar, 1922, bar of Ohio, 1941; prof. of law, U. of Mo. Law Sch., 1927-28, Ohio State U. since 1928; acting dean 1946-47; prof. of law summers, univs. of Wis., 1928, Southern Calif., 1932, Mich., 1935, 36. George Washington Univ. 1945. Mem. Alpha Delta Phi, Phi Delta Phi, Order of Coif. Conglist. Clubs: Faculty, Saturday (Columbus). Contributor legal articles to law jours. Home: Columbus, O. *

VAN NUYS, FRANCIS, lawyer; b. Kansas City, Mo., Apr. 13, 1912; s. Dunlap W. and Rae (Wirthschaffer) Van N.; student Park Coll., 1929-31; A.B. magna cum laude, Harvard, 1933, LL.B. magna cum laude, 1936; m. Anna G. Chute, Dec. 20, 1935; children—Francis B., Peter. Admitted to N.Y. bar, 1939; mem. staff Cravath, de Gersdorff, Swaine & Wood, N.Y.C., 1936-40; mem. legal staff of trustees Asso. Gas & Electric Corp., 1940-42; with Bethlehem Steel Corp. (Pa.), 1942-80, asso. gen. counsel, 1963-67, dir. law dept., 1965-67, v.p. law and gen. counsel, 1967-80. Mem. Am., N.Y. State, Pa., Northampton County, bar assns., Am. Law Inst., Am. Iron and Steel Inst., Phi Beta Kappa. Clubs: Saucon Valley Country, Bethlehem (Bethlehem); Canadian (N.Y.C.). Editor Harvard Law Rev., 1935-36. Home: Bethlehem, Pa. Died Feb. 17, 1980.

VAN OOSTERHOUT, MARTIN D., U.S. judge; b. Orange City, Iowa, Oct. 10, 1900; s. Peter D. and Sara (Hospers) Van O.; B.A., U. Iowa, 1922, J.D., 1924; LL.D., Northwestern Coll., Orange City, 1970; m. Ethel Greenway, June 16, 1928; 1 son, Peter. Admitted to Iowa bar, 1924, practiced in Orange City, 1924-43; judge 21st Jud. Dist. Iowa, 1943-54; U.S. circuit judge 8th Circuit, 1954-79; chief judge U.S. Ct. Appeals, 8th Circuit, until 1970; mem. Temporary Emergency Ct. Appeals, 1972-77. Mem. Iowa Legislature, 1939-43, chmn. legis. interim com., 1941-43. Mem. Am., Iowa, Orange City, Sioux City bar assns., Am. Law Inst., Order of Coif, Phi Alpha Delta, Delta Tau Delta, Beta Gamma Sigma. Home: Orange City, Iowa. Died Jan. 28, 1979; buried West Lawn Cemetery, Orange City.

VAN PETTEN, GARRY ROBERT, univ. adminstr.; b. Camrose, Alta., Can., Nov. 9, 1936; s. William Stewart and Alice Louella (Pierce) Van P.; B.Sc., U. Alta., 1957, M.Sc., 1959; Ph.D. in Pharmacology, U. Glasgow, 1962; m. Betty Irene Converse, Aug. 26, 1957; children—Stewart, Deane, Wayne. Asso. prof. div. pharmacology and therapeutics Faculty of Medicine, U. Calgary (Alta.), 1970-75, prof., 1976-78, acting head div., 1974-76, head div., 1976-78, dir. med. vivarium, 1974-78; dean Faculty Pharmacy and Pharm. Scis., U. Alta., Edmonton, 1978-80. Recipient Harry Gold award Jour. Clin. Pharmacology, 1972. Mem. Pharm. Soc. Can. (pres.), Can. Soc. Toxicology, Western Pharm. Soc., Am. Soc. Clin. Pharmacology and Therapeutics. Contbr. articles to profl. jours. Home: Sherwood Park, Alta., Can. Died Feb. 11, 1980; buried Glenwood Meml. Gardens, Sherwood Park, Alta.

VAN PRAAG, ALEX, JR., cons. engr.; b. Little Falls, Minn., Jan. 29, 1896; s. Alexander and Rachel (Davis) Van P.; student James Millikin U., 1913-15; B.S. in Civil Engring., U. Ill., 1917; m. Bernice I. Metzger, Dec. 27, 1926; children—Roger C., James N. Asst. engr. Miller, Holbrook & Warren, Decatur, Ill., 1919-20; asst. to chief san. engr. Ill. Dept. Pub. Health, 1920-22; mem. firm Warren & Van Praag, Inc., cons. engrs., architects, Decatur, from 1922, pres., 1952-68, chmn. bd., from 1968; treas., dir. Midwest Computer Service, Decatur, 1958-64; dir. 1st Nat. Bank of Decatur. Mem. Ill. Bd. Pub. Health Advisers, Springfield, 1962-69; mem. Ill. Bldg. Authority, 1961-65. Mem. pres.'s citizens advisory com. U. Ill., 1961-79; mem. advisory com. St. Mary's Hosp., Decatur, 1963-68; trustee Millikin U., 1961-70; bd. dirs. United Fund of Decatur and Macon County, Ill., 1966-69. Served with U.S. Army, AEF, 1917-19. Recipient Loyalty award U. Ill. Alumni Assn., 1964; Alumni Merit Loyalty award Millikin U., 1973; Distinguished Alumnus award Civil Engring. Alumni Assn. U. Ill., 1975; registered profl. engr., Ill., Ind., Ohio, Ky., Mo., N.D., Iowa, Tenn., Wis. Fellow Am. Cons. Engrs. Council; mem. ASCE (life), Nat. (past pres.), Ill. (past pres., hon. mem.) socs. profl. engrs., Cons. Engrs. Council Ill., Ill. Registered Land Surveyors Assn., ASTM, Am. Rd. Builders Assn., Am. Water Works Assn., Water Pollution Control Assn. Central States, Decatur Assn. Commerce, Ill. C. of C. (chmn. water resources com. 1959-60), U. Ill. Alumni Assn., Am. Legion. Presbyterian. Clubs: Elks, Decatur. Home: Decatur, Ill. Died Feb. 6, 1979.

VAN REMOORTEL, EDOUARD, orch. condr.; b. Brussels, Belgium, May 30, 1926; s. William and Alice (Goldzieher) Van R.; student Conservatory of Music, Brussels, also Geneva, Switzerland, Acad. Chigiana,

Siena, Italy; m. Jeanne Kelly, May 18, 1962; 1 son, Patrick. Music dir. and permanent condr. St. Louis Symphony Orch., 1958-62; music counsellor Monte Carlo Nat. Opera Orch., 1965-69; music dir., chief condr. Chamber Orch. of Soloists, Vienna Symphony; guest condr. with 90 symphony orchestras in 6 continents. Decorated knight Order of Leopold, II, Knight Order of La Couronne (Belgium); officer French Merit Order, knight comdr. French Order Culture and Art. Club: Monte Carlo Yacht. Home: Monte Carlo, Principality of Monaco. Died May 26, 1977.

VAN RYSSELBERGHE, PIERRE, educator; b. Brussels, Belgium, May 18, 1905; s. François and Jeanne (Alvin) Van R.; Engr., U. Brussels, 1927; M.A., Stanford, 1928, Ph.D., 1929; m. Lily Laura Chloupek, Sept. 2, 1930; children—Jane, Pierre, Jacqueline. Came to U.S., 1927; naturalized, 1941. Instr. chemistry Stanford (Calif.), 1929-31, asst. prof., 1931-41, lectr., 1956-69, cons. prof., 1969—; asst. prof. chemistry U. Oreg., 1941-42, asso. prof., 1942-45, prof., 1945-56. Vis. lectr. Belgian Am. Ednl. Found., Belgian univs., 1935-36; supr. research project Office Naval Research, AEC: Fulbright lectr., Italy, 1950-51. Fellow Am. Inst. Chemists, AAAS, N.Y. Acad. Scis.; mem. Am. Chem. Soc., Electrochem. Soc., Internat. Com. Electrochem. Thermodynamics and Kinetics (pres. 1949-54), Internat. Union Pure Applied Chemistry (chmn. commn. electrochem. 1961-67), Assn. Engrs. U. Brussels, Sigma Xi. Author (with Th.De Donder) Affinity, 1936; Electrochemical Affinity, 1955; Thermodynamics of Irreversible Processes, 1963; also numerous articles. Home: Palo Alto, Calif. Died Aug. 21, 1977; buried Cyprus Lawn Cemetery, San Francisco.

VANS AGNEW, MARIAN FELL (MRS. PATRICK ALEXANDER VANS AGNEW), b. Cornwall-on-Hudson, N.Y., Sept. 28, 1886; d. E. Nelson and Anne Mumford (Palmer) Fell; ed. in London and Paris; m. Patrick Alexander Vans Agnew, of Winter Park, Fla., June 9, 1914; children—Anne Vaux, Patricia, Patrick Alexander, Marian Fell. Mem. Anglo-Russian Lit. Soc., London. Translator: Plays by Anton Tchekoff, 1912; Stories of Russian Life (by same) 1914; Russian Silhouettes (by same), 1915; Makar's Dream (by VladimirKorolenko), 1916. Home: Winter Park, Fla.*

VAN SCHAICK, GEORGE S. (VAN-SKOIK), lawyer; born at Cobleskill, New York, July 25, 1883; son of John and Frances Eliza (Shaver) Van Schaick; A.B., St. Lawrence U., 1905 (awarded nunc pro tunc, 1933); LL.B., magna cum laude, Yale, 1907; LL.D., U. of Rochester, 1938; m. Blanche A. Lefevre, Jan. 3, 1910; children—Frances, Sally (Cooley). Admitted to N.Y. bar and practicing atty. at Rochester, 1907-31, 1935-36, and since 1948; counsel to legal firm Oliver & Donnally, N.Y.C., and to legal firm Van Schaick, Woods, Strathman, Sturman & Costurza, Rochester, N.Y.; superintendent of insurance, State of N.Y., 1931-35; vice pres. N.Y. life Ins. Co. in charge real estate and mortgage loans 1936-48; trustee Bowery Savs. Bank; chmn. bd. Security Mut. Life Ins. Co. (Binghamton). Mem. New York State Housing Finance Agency, 1960-62. Dir. Regional Plan Assn., Citizen's Housing & Planning Council; v.p. Nat. Municipal League. Mem. Governor's Commn. on Unemployment, 1930-31; Governor's Commn. on Med. Problems of Workman's Compensation Act, 1931-32; Gov.'s. Com. on State aid to Municipalities, 1935-36; mem. special com. N.Y. State bar assn. to investigate adminstrn. of justice in Albany Co., N.Y., 1945; chmn. N.Y. State bar Assn. com. on legal aid, 1929-51, com. on Lawyers' Reference Service, 1950-51. Chmn. spl. com. of Citizens Union to study city mgr. plan for N.Y.C. Chmn. War Dept. Adv. Com. on Insurance, 1941-44. Regional dir. 2d Region, Office of Civilian Defense, 1942-43. Lecturer on Insurance Supervision, Yale Law School, 1938. Member N.Y. State Bar assn., Assn. Bar City of New York, Holland Soc. of New York, Alpha Tau Omega, Phi Delta Phi. Order of Coif. Democrat. Unitarian. Mason. Clubs: Anglers, Century (N.Y.C.). Mem. bd. editors Yale Law Jour., 1905-07. Address: Cobleskill, N.Y. *

VAN TUYL, ROBERT CORTLAND, stock broker; b. N.Y.C., Apr. 3, 1914; s. George H. and Anna M. (Stadich) Van T.; A.B., Colgate U., 1934; m. Irene A. Moriarty, June 12, 1937; 1 dau., Anna-marie. Br. mgr. IBM Corp., 1934; mng. partner Shearson, Hammill & Co., N.Y.C., 1946-78, chmn. bd. to 1978. Mayor Village of Brookville, N.Y. Bd. dirs. Budget Finance Plans; trustee Colgate U. Vice shmn. Am. Stock Exchange; mem. N.Y. Cotton Exchange, Los Angeles Stock Exchange, Canadian Stock Exchange, Chgo. Bd. Trade, Assn. Stock Exchange Firms (gov.), Phi Beta Kappa, Lambda Chi Alpha. Mem. Reformed Ch. Club: Meadowbrook (Westbury, N.Y.); Gardiners Bay Country (Shelter Island, N.Y.). Home: Brookville, N.Y. Died May 15, 1978.

VAN VLECK, JOHN HASBROUCK, physicist; b. Middletown, Conn., Mar. 13, 1899; s. Edward Burr and Hester Laurence (Raymond) Van V.; A.B., U. Wis., 1920, Sc.D., 1947; A.M., Harvard U., 1921, Ph.D., 1922, Sc.D., 1966; Sc.D., Wesleyan U., 1936, U. Md., 1955, Rockford Coll., 1961, U. Chgo., 1968, U. Nancy (France), 1961, U. Minn., 1971; Dr. honoris causa, U. Grenoble, 1950, U. Paris, 1960; Sc.D. honoris causa, Oxford (Eng.) U., 1958; m. Abigail June Pearson, June 10, 1927. Instr. physics Harvard U., 1922-23, asso. prof. math. physics, 1934-35, prof., 1935-69, chmn. physics dept., 1945-49, Hollis prof. math. and nat. philosophy, 1951-69, emeritus, 1969-80, dean engring. and applied physics, 1951-57; asst. prof. physics U. Minn., 1923-26, asso. prof., 1926-27, prof., 1927-28; prof. theoretical physics U. Wis., 1928-34. Vis. lectr. Stanford, 1927, 34, 41, U. Mich., 1933, Columbia, 1934, Princeton, 1937; Lorentz prof., Leiden, 1960; Eastman prof. Oxford (Eng.) U., 1961-62; head theory group Radio Research Lab., Harvard, 1943-45; cons. Radiation Lab., Mass. Inst. Tech., 1942-45; asso. editor various phys. jour. Guggenheim Meml. Found. fellow, 1930. Decorated chevalier Legion of Honor (France); recipient Albert A. Michelson award Case Inst. Tech., 1963; Irving Langmuir award in chem. physics Gen. Elec. Found., 1965; Nat. Medal of Sci., 1966; Distinguished Service award U. Wis. Alumni Assn., 1967, Cresson medal Franklin Inst., 1971; Lorentz medal Netherlands Acad., 1974; co-recipient Nobel prize in Physics, 1977. Fellow Am. Phys. Soc. (councillor 1932-35, pres. 1952-53), AAAS (v.p. 1960), Am. Acad. Arts and Scis. (v.p. 1956-57); mem. Nat. Acad. Sci., Am. Philos. Soc., Internat. Acad. Quantum Molecular Sci., Am. Math. Soc., Holland Soc. N.Y. (medal 1969), Netherlands Phys. Soc., Phi Beta Kappa, Sigma Xi; hon. mem. Societe Francaise de Physique; fgn. mem. Royal Netherlands Acad. Scis., Royal Acad. Sci. Uppsala, Royal Swedish Acad. Sci., Royal Soc. of London, Acad. des Sciences (France). Presbyn. Author: Quantum Principles and Line Spectra, 1926; The Theory of Electric and Magnetic Susceptibilities, 1932. Home: Cambridge, Mass. Died Oct. 27, 1980; buried Forest Hills Cemetery, Madison, Wis.

VAN WINKLE, MATTHEW, chem. engr., educator; b. Shelbyville, Ind., Nov. 18, 1910; s. William Shelley and Edith (Goodpasture) Van W.; B.S., Purdue U., 1933; M.S., U. Mich., 1945, postgrad., 1945-46; m. Mary Louise Angel, June 18, 1933; children—Susan Louise, John Shelley. Research chemist Cities Service Oil Co., 1933-40, Standard Oil Co. (Ind.) 1940-41; supr. petroleum and natural gas extension Pa. State Coll., 1941-43; instr. chem. engring. and cons. dept. engring. research U. Mich., 1943-47; asso. prof. to grad. prof. chem. engring. U. Tex., Austin, 1947-77, chmn. dept., 1951-53, Henry D. Beckman prof. chem. engring., 1971-77; indsl. cons. chem. engring., 1947-77; civilian, research and devel. project of fuels and lubricants, Ordnance Dept., U.S. Army, 1944-45. NSF grantee, 1954-56, 61-63, 63-65. Registered profl. engr., Tex. Fellow Am. Inst. Chem. Engrs. (5 publ. awards for best paper); mem. Am. Chem. Soc., Am. Soc. Engring. Edn., Sigma Xi, Phi Lambda Upsilon, Omega Chi Epsilon, Tau Beta Pi. Author: Aviation Gasoline Manufacture, 1944; Distillation, 1967; also sects. in books and articles in profl. jours. Home: Austin, Tex. Died Jan. 23, 1977.

VAN ZANDT, LYDIA, writer, lectr.; b. Boulder, Colo.; d. George Davis and Mary Abbey (Stevenson) Begole; student U. Chgo. 1918-19, Columbia, 1929-31; m. Arthur Edward Van Hagan, Oct. 7, 1921 (dec. June 1935); m. 2d, John Parker Van Zandt, July 10, 1937. Appeared N.Y. theatrical prodns. during 1920s; reviewed Books on World Affairs on radio, 1933-36; round the world tour, 1936-39; articles appeared in Washington Post, Los Angeles Times, also Washington Sunday Star, lectr. tour U.S., 1939; author radio scripts, lectr. for A.R.C. and world fellowship com. of YWCA, World War II; attended UN meetings in London, N.Y.C., Geneva, Beirut, also lectr. on subject, 1946-51; lived in Mexico City, 1951-52, in Paris, 1953-59, in Washington, 1960-76, in Santa Barbara, 1976-80. Author articles for Christian Sci. Monitor, 1946-80. Charter mem. Speakers Research Com. for UN, 1946—; U.S. del. pub. info. com. NATO, Paris, 1958. Bd. dirs. Capital area div. UN Assn. U.S., 1963-68. Mem. Soc. Woman Geographers (pres. 1963-66), YWCA (life D.C.), Assn. Am. Fgn. Service Women, Am. Newspaper Women's Club. Address: Montecito, Calif. Died Apr. 6, 1980; buried Denver, Colo.

VARDAMAN, JOHN WESLEY, lawyer; b. Montgomery, Ala., June 22, 1915; s. John Wesley and Nonie (Hobbie) V.; student Washington and Lee U., 1933-34; A.B. U. Ala., 1936, LL.B., 1938; children—John Wesley, Hugh Merrill. Admitted to Ala. bar, 1938; practice in Montgomery, 1938-39; asst. atty. gen. Ala., 1939-43; mem. firm Merrill, Merrill & Vardaman, and successor firms, Anniston, Ala., 1943-79; dir. Comml. Nat. Bank, Anniston. Chmn bd. Calhoun County Savs. Bond Com., 1951-79. Mem-at-large Calhoun County Democratic Exec. Com., 1958-79. Chmn. trustees Ala. Dist. 4 Tb Hosp., 1958-60. Mem. Am., Ala. (pres. jr. sec. 1945-46, Ala. pres. 1961-62), Calhoun County (pres. 1951) bar assns., Phi Delta Phi, Sigma Nu. Clubs: Anniston Country (chmn. trustees), Anniston Exchange (past pres.). Baptist (past pres. Baraca class). Contbr. articles to legal jours. Home: Anniston, Ala. Died May 4, 1979.

VARGAS, LESTER LAMBERT, surgeon, educator; b. Providence, May 20, 1921; A.B., Brown U., 1943; M.D. summa cum laude, George Washington U., 1945; m. Cynthia M. Baptist, Mar. 6, 1969; 1 dau., Leslie H. Intern, R.I. Hosp., Providence, 1945-46, dir. cardiac surgery and cardiovascular surgery research lab., 1956-71, pres. staff assn., 1967, surgeon-in-chief, 1961-70, asso. surgeon-in-chief, 1970—; intern, resident gen., thoracic, pediatric and cardiovascular surgery Columbia-Presbyn. Med. Center, N.Y.C., 1948-55; asst. resident thoracic surgeon Bellevue Hosp., N.Y.C., 1949; Lambert fellow in cardiovascular surgery Coll. Physicians and Surgeons, Columbia U., 1954-55, asst. in surgery, 1950-55; asst. clin. prof. surgery Tufts U. Sch. Medicine, 1959-62, lectr., 1963-80; prof. surgery R.I. Hosp. Brown U., 1963-67, prof. med. sci., 1968-80. Served from 1st lt. to capt., M.C., U.S. Army, 1946-48. Recipient Disting. Lectr. award Providence Coll., 1961. Diplomate Am. Bd. Surgery, Nat. Bd. Med. Examiners. Fellow Am. Coll. Cardiology (bd. govs. and gov. for R.I. 1963-66), Am. Coll. Chest Physicians, A.C.S., Am. Geriatrics Soc.; mem. Titulaire Société Internationale de Chirurgie, Internat. Soc. Cardiovascular Surgery, New Eng. Surg. Soc., New Eng. Soc. Vascular Surgery, AAAS, Am. Heart Assn. (pres. R.I. chpt. 1963-65, Disting. Service medal), N.Y. Acad. Scis., R.I. Med. Soc. (Fiske prize), Allen O. Whipple Soc., Sigma Xi. Contbr. articles to med. jours. and books; author, producer med. edn. films. Died Dec. 17, 1980; buried Riverside Cemetery, Pawtucket.

VARNEY, H(ARRY) R(OSS), diplomat; b. Bristol, Vermont, December 11, 1905; the son of Albert Edwin and Stella (Eseltine) V.; B.S. in Agr., U. Vt., 1926, M.S., 1932; Ph.D., Cornell U., 1935; m. Gladys Fuller, Sept. 17, 1927; 1 son, Harry Ross. Farmer, Bristol, Vt., 1926-28; country agrl. agent St. Johnsbury, Vt., 1928-32; extension asst. Cornell U., 1932-35; extension economist U. Vt., 1935-38; sr. mktg. specialist U.S. Dept. Agr., Washington, 1938-39; extension econ. and state rep. Bur. Agrl. Economics, U. of Vt., 1939-42, asst. dean agr., asst. dir. extension service and experiment sta., 1942-46, asso. dean, 1946-47; dean and dir. agr. N.Mex. Coll. of Agr. and Mech. Arts, 1947-50; dean coll. of agr., forestry and home econs. and dir. exptl. station W.Va. U., 1950-57; agrl. attache, F.A.S., U.S. Dept. Agr., 1957-71; chief of staff U.S. Senate Committee on Agriculture and Forestry, 1953-54. Fellow A.A.A.S.; mem. Soc. Internat. Devel., Alpha Zeta, Sigma Xi, Phi Kappa Phi, Epsilon Sigma Phi, Alpha Tau Alpha. Home: Charlotte, Vt. Died Oct. 26, 1979.

VARVARESSOS, KYRIAKOS, economist; b. Athens, Greece, Mar. 4, 1884; s. Charalambos and Hypatia V.; Dr. Law and Economics U. of Athens, 1906; student U. of Munich, Germany, 1908-09, U. of Berlin, 1909-11; hon. Ph.D., U. of Bonn, Germany, 1938; m. Mathilda Rakowitz, July 5, 1923; 1 dau., Yvonne. Chief sect., Ministry of Nat. Economy, Greece, 1911-13, dir. statistics, 1913-20; asst. prof. economics, Univ. of Athens, 1918-23, prof. since 1923; econ. adviser Greek Nat. Bank, 1924-33; minister of finance, 1932; dep. gov. Bank of Greece, 1933-39, gov., 1939-45; minister of finance, 1941-43 (with Greek govt. in exile, London); ambassador at large for econ. affairs representing Greece at U.N.R.R.A. Conf., Atlantic City, N.J., 1943, Bretton Woods, 1944, San Francisco, 1945), 1943-45; v.p. council of ministers, also minister of coordination for Greece, 1945; exec. dir. Internat. Bank for Reconstrn. and Development since May 1946. Decorated with various honors by Greece and other govts. Mem. Acad. of Athens. Greek Orthodox. Author (in Greek): Theory of Population, 1911; The Most-Favored Nation Clause in Commercial Treaties, 1923; The Economic Consequences of the Peace Treaties, 1923. Contbr. various articles to econ. periodicals. Home: Washington. *

VAUGHAN, BILL, columnist; b. St. Louis, Oct. 8, 1915; s. John R. and Sara (Thomas) V.; B.S. in Journalism, Washington U., St. Louis, 1936; m. Lenore Coates, Sept. 21, 1940; children—Kirk W., Ellen L. Mem. staff Leader and Press, Springfield, Mo., 1936-39; mem. staff Kansas City (Mo.) Star, 1939-77; writer Starbeams Column, 1945-77, asso. editor, 1965-77, writer syndicated columns Senator Soaper Says and Vaughan At Large. Served with USAAF, 1943-45. Recipient citation in journalism U. Mo., 1972. Mem. Sigma Nu. Presbyn. Author: Bird Thou Never Wert; Sorry I Stirred It; Half the Battle. Home: Kansas City, Mo. Died Feb. 26, 1977.

VAUGHAN, H. LELAND, retired educator, landscape architect; b. Alliance, O., Nov. 27, 1905; s. James E. and Frances (Harris) V.; student Mt. Union Coll., 1923-26; B. Landscape Architecture, Ohio State U., 1929; m. Adele Wharton, June 1934; children—Steven Wharton, Wharton Nicholas; m. 2d, Beulah Parker, Jan. 1954. With U. Cal. at Berkeley, 1930-74, successively instr., asst. prof., asso. prof., prof., 1949-69, emeritus, 1969-74, chmn. dept. landscape architecture, 1949-62, acting dean Coll. Agri., 1957-58, asst. dean Coll. Environmental Design, 1965-67, city planning commr. Richmond, Cal.; designer projects in San Francisco area; recreation and park commr., Richmond; U.S. del. to Internat. Fedn. Landscape Architects, 1966-69. Fellow Am. Soc. Landscape Architects; mem. Assn. Landscape Architects (past pres.), Am. Planning and Civic Assn. Club: Bohemian (San Francisco). Home: Richmond, Calif. Died 1974.

VAUGHAN, L(ILLIAM) L(EE), univ. prof.; b. near Franklin, Va., Apr. 5, 1884; s. James Buchanan and Ida Matilda (Rawles) V.; B.M.E., N.C. State Coll., 1906, M.S., 1909; M.E., Columbia, 1911; m. Lula Olive Brewer, Dec. 20, 1911. Instr. engring. drawing N.C. State Coll., 1906-09, instr. thermodynamics and mech. lab., N.C. State Coll., 1911-14, asst. prof. mech. engring., 1914-19, prof. exptl. engring., 1919-20, prof. mech. engring. and head dept., 1920-47, acting dean sch. engring., 1942-45, dir. instrn. Sch. of Engring., 1947-49. Spl. instr. for motor truck drivers and mechanics, N.C. State Coll., 1918. Taught under S.A.T.C. regulations and requirements N.C. State Coll., 1918-19; taught fuels, combustion and lubrication in diesel engring. program, sponsored by Bur. of Personnel, Navy Dept., N.C. State Coll., 1941-43. Mem. N.C. State Bd. Examiners of plumbing and heating contractors since 1939. Trustee Elon Coll. Mem. bd. dirs. State College Y.M.C.A., 1919-49; mem. adv. council, Consol. Univs. N.C. since 1945. Mem. Am. Soc. M.E. (active in orgn. Raleigh sect. 1925), Am. Soc. Heating, and Ventilating Engrs., Am. Soc. Engring. Edn. (past chmn. local br. 1936). N.C. Soc. Engrs. (chmn. com. prof. practice, 1935), Sigma Xi Kappa, Phi Kappa Phi (past treas. and pres.), Pi Tau Sigma, Tau Beta Pi (treas. N.C. Alpha chapter 1929-49), Sigma Chi (alumni mem.). Democrat. Christian. Club: Engineers (pres. 1940-41). Registered engr. in N.C. Inventor window lock (with Thomas), 1915. Owner and operator farm near Franklin, Va., since 1929. Home: Raleigh, N.C. *

VAUGHAN, RICHARD HENRY, banker; b. Mpls., Sept. 21, 1927; s. James A. and Katherine (Wyman) V.; grad. Deerfield (Mass.) Acad., 1945; B.A., Dartmouth, 1950, M.B.A., Amos Tuck Sch. Bus., 1951; grad. Stonier Grad. Sch. Banking, 1963; m. Mary Wurtele, Aug. 4, 1950; children—Peter Wurtele, Angus MacDonald, Charlotte Lindley, Carol Wyman. With Northwestern Nat. Bank, Mpls., 1951-71, exec. v.p., 1968-71, dir.; pres. Northwest Bancorp., 1971-79, also dir.; dir. N.W. Growth Fund, BancN.W. Mem. Fed. Adv. Council. Bd. dirs. United Fund, Mpls., 1967-73, chmn. spl. gifts, 1967-68; bd. dirs. Guthrie Theatre, Mpls., 1967-72, Minn. Orch., 1969, Upper Midwest Council; trustee Smith Coll., Carleton Coll., Blake Sch., Mpls., 1963-67, Minn. Outward Bound Sch., Mpls., 1964-68. Served with AUS, 1946-47. Republican. Clubs: Minneapolis; Woodhill Country (Wayzata). Home: Wayzata, Minn. Died June 16, 1979; buried Lakewood Cemetery, Mpls.

VAUGHAN, ROBERT CHARLES, ry. official; b. Toronto, Can., 1883; s. Robert Crawford and Blanchard (McCarthy) Vaughan; ed. Toronto pub. schs., Harbord Collegiate Inst. and Central Business Coll.; hon. Sc.D., Clarkson Coll., Potsdam, N.Y., 1946; married Rosalie Cheadle, Oct. 26, 1905; 4 children. Messenger boy, later clerk and stenographer, Railway Service, 1898-1902; with Grand Trunk Railway, 1902-03; joined Canadian Northern Ry., 1903, sec. to v.p. and gen. mgr., 1904-10, asst. to v.p. and gen. mgr., 1910-18; in charge operation Royal Line Steamers; asst. to pres. Canadian Nat. Ry. and asst. to pres. Canadian Govt. Merchant Marine, 1918-20; became v.p. in charge purchases, stores and steamships Canadian Nat. Rys., 1920, pres. since 1941, also chmn. since 1942. Dir. Trans-Canada Air Lines since 1941. Chmn. Defense Purchasing Bd. for Canadian Govt., 1939. Awarded Companion of the Most Distinguished Order of St. Michael and St. George, 1946. Gov. Montreal Gen. Hosp. Mason. Clubs: Granite, National (Toronto); St. James, Mount Bruno, Mount Royal (Montreal). Home: Montreal. *

VAUGHAN, THOMAS RAE, lawyer and bus. exec.; b. Little Rock, Aug. 28, 1908; s. Harry Brumby and Emeline (Prewitt) V.; LL.B., George Washington U., 1935; m. Elizabeth Leigh, Feb. 12, 1935; children—Thomas Rae, Cynthia Leigh. Admitted to N.Y. bar, 1938; officer Freeport Minerals Co., N.Y.C., 1942-60, v.p., gen. counsel, 1960-63, exec. v.p., gen. counsel, 1963-68, pres., 1968-69, chmn. bd., 1969-75, dir., mem. exec. com., 1961-75, chmn. exec. com., 1973-75; dir., pres., gen. counsel Nicaro Nickel Co., 1961-74; dir. Sulphur Export Corp. and various subsidiaries of Freeport Minerals Co.; chmn. bd. Freeport Indonesia, Inc., 1970-74, mem. exec. com., 1971-75; mem. nat. adv. bd. Comml. Nat. Bank, Little Rock, 1971-75. Bd. dirs., chmn. exec. com. Sulphur Inst., 1971, 75. Mem. Am., Ark., bar assns., Bar Assn. City of N.Y., Phi Delta Phi, Kappa Sigma. Clubs: Siwanoy Country, Am. Yacht. Home: Bronxville, N.Y. Died Dec. 12, 1979.

VAUGHAN, WILLIAM WASHINGTON, army officer; b. Farmville, Va., Sept. 7, 1886; s. George Tully (M.D.) and Maria Townsend (Venable) V.; student U. of Va., 1905-07; M.S. and M.D., Georgetown U., 1912; m. Mela Fairchild, July 13, 1917; children—Bradley William, Lydia; m. 2d, Frances Wade French, July 15, 1923; children—Harriet French, George Tully II. Commd. 1st lt., M.C., U.S. Army, 1913, and advanced through the grades to brig. gen., 1945; served in Philippine Islands, 1914-17; comd. Base Hosp. 14, A.E.F., France, 1918-19; qualified as flight surgeon, U.S. Army, 1919, airplane pilot, 1920; served in Hawaii, 1937-49; comd. Stark Gen. Hosp., Charleston, S.C., 1942-45; comdg. gen. Valley Forge Gen. Hosp., Phoenixville, Pa., 1945-46, ret. 1946. Received citation from gov. of S.C. for war work; cited by comdg. gen. Third Service Command for work performed at Valley Forge Gen. Hosp., 1945; received Legion of Merit, Army Commendation Ribbon (with oak leaf cluster), Mem. A.M.A., Assn. of Military Surgeons, Soc. of the Cincinnati, Soc. of Colonial Wars, Order of Washington, Lambda Pi, Delta Tau Delta, Phi Chi. Clubs: Cosmos, Army and Navy (Washington); Charleston (S.C.); Pickering Hunt (S.C.). Address:Bridgehampton, L.I., N.Y.*

VAWTER, WILLIAM ARTHUR II, business exec.; b. Danville, Ind., May 5, 1884; s. William Arthur and Alice Rebecca (Hadley) V.; student Northwestern U., 1900-01; A.B., Cornell U., 1905; m. Dorothy Rathbone Fuller, September 10, 1910 (dec. Oct. 1960); children—Dorothy (wife of Col. John E. Robb), Virginia (Mrs. Richard J. Storr), William Arthur III, Gordon; m. 2d, Mrs. Elizabeth Fogg Upton, May 5, 1962. Began as file clerk, Baker-Vawter Co., Benton Harbor, Mich., 1905. advanced to pres. and gen. mgr.; sec. Remington Rand, Inc., 1928; vice pres. Bonnar-Vawter, Inc., Kenne, N.H.; western Mich. mgr., Mich. Mutual Liability Co., 1933-34; v.p. Benton Harbor Abstract & Title Co. presdident Berrien Realty & Mortgage Co.; dir. Peoples Savings Association; pres. Berrien Community Found. Sec. Nat. Assn. Office Appliances Manufacturers. 1922-26. Mem. Berrien County (Michigan) Road Commn., 1931-53. Chmn. Berrien County chapter Am. Red Cross during World War I and World War II. Mem. Mich. state bd. YMCA, past nat. councillor. Member of Sigma Alpha Epsilon. Clubs: Point O'Woods Country; Sphinx Head (Cornell University); Berrien Hills Country; University (Chicago), Rotary (past pres.) (St. Joseph-Benton Harbor); Economics Club of Southwestern Michigan (dir.), St. Joseph River Yacht, Pickwick-Niles. Home: St. Joseph, Mich. *

VEATCH, JOHN C(URRIN) (VECH), lawyer; b. Cottage Grove, Ore., Dec. 13, 1883; s. Robert M. and Surphina (Currin) V.; A.B., U. of Ore., 1907, LL.B., 1911; m. Lillian Vredt, June 17, 1917; children—Lilyann, John C. II. Admitted to Ore. bar, 1911, and practiced since at Portland; mem. Raffety & Veatch, 1912-17; asst. U.S. atty., war work, 1917-21; mem. Joseph, Haney & Littlefield, 1921-29, Joseph, Haney and Veatch, 1929-35, Joseph Veatch and Bradshaw since 1943; Veatch and Bradshaw since 1944. Member Oregon State Tax Supervising and Conservation Commission, 1927-29; member State Sanitary Authority since 1939, State Fish Commn. since 1925, Pacific Marine Fisheries Commn. since 1947. Mem. Oregon and Am. bar assns.; American Judicature Soc.; pres. Oregon Hist. Soc.; dir. West Coast Life Ins. Co., San Francisco. Democrat. Club: University. Home: Portland, Ore. *

VEEDER, BORDEN SMITH (VE'DER), physician; b. Fonda, N.Y., Aug. 21, 1883; s. James Lansing and Jenny (Smith) V.; student Colgate Acad. and Coll.; M.D., U. of Pa., 1907; Sc.D., Colgate U., Hamilton, N.Y., 1929; studied Berlin, Germany; m. Vera Gianinni Angert, Sept. 15, 1930 (dec. 1959); m. 2d, Lilly deLeuw, Dec. 29, 1960. Was resident physician University Hosp., Phila.; prof. emeritus clin. pediatrics, Washington U. Med. Sch., St. Louis; cons. physician St. Louis Children's Hosp. and St. Luke's Hosp. Chmn. St. Louis chapter Am. Red Cross, 1942-45. Commd. lt. col., comdg. Base Hosp. 21, A.E.F. Med. O.R.C., U.S. Army. Decorated Companion Order of St. Michael and St. George, Mem. Am. Pediatric Soc. (pres. 1934), American Bd. of Pediatrics (pres. 1933-41), Nat. Bd. Med. Examiners, 1941-53 (pres. 1947-49), S.A.R., Sigma Xi, Delta Upsilon, Am. Acad. Pediatrics (pres. 1943), Am. Assn. Advancement Science. Clubs: University (president 1929-30), Round Table. Author: Preventive Pediatrics; The Adolescent (with S. I. Schwab); Pediatric Profiles. Editor Jour. of Pediatrics, 1931-60. Home: St. Louis. *

VEIHMEYER, FRANK J. (VE'MI-ER), irrigation engineer; b. Washington, D.C., Dec. 25, 1886; s. Jacob Oliver and Nellie Catherine (Leavy) V.; B.S., George Washington, U., 1912, C.E., 1913; Ph.D., Johns Hopkins U., 1927; m. Frances Kelly, Nov. 20, 1913; children—Kathryn, John Oliver, Donald Francis. Scientific asst. in mycology Bur. Plant Industry., U.S. Dept. Agr., 1909-13; asst. irrigation engr. Office of Expt. Stations, U.S. Dept. Agr., 1913-17, irrigation engr., 1917-18; asst. prof. of irrigation, Coll. of Agr., U. of Calif., 1918-30, asso. prof., 1930-35, prof. 1935-54, irrigation engr. Expt. Sta., 1931-54; head department, 1936-54; irrigation specialist University of California and Chilian government, 1955-56; consultant irrigationist, 1956—. Awarded Croix du Ouissam Alaouite Cherifien by his Majesty, the Sultan of Morocco, Feb. 9, 1932. Fellow A.A.A.S. Mem. Soc. Plant Physiologists, Western Society Soil Science, Soil Science Society of America, Am. Soc. Agrl. Engineers, Am. Geophysical Union (past pres. of the section of hydrology), Sigma Phi Epsilon, Gamma Alpha, Sigma Xi. Catholic. Club: Commonwealth of Calif. Author bulletins Agrl. Expt. Sta. and scientific papers on soil physicsand plant physiology. Home: Davis, Calif.*

VELDE, GAIL PATRICK, TV producer; b. Birmingham, Ala., June 20; d. Lawrence C. and La Valle (Smith) Fitzpatrick; A.B. with honors, Howard Coll. (now Samford U.); m. John E. Velde, Jr., Sept. 28, 1974; children by previous marriage—Jennifer Stanley Jackson, Thomas Cornwell Jackson, Jr. Actress in motion pictures including My Man Godfrey, Stage Door, My Favorite Wife, Up in Mabel's Room, Claudia and David; propr. Gail Patrick's Enchanted Cottage, children's shop, Beverly Hills, Calif., 1945-54, Gail Patrick's Enchanted Weavers, Beverly Hills, 1950-51; exec. producer Perry Mason Show, Paisano Prodns., Hollywood, Calif., 1957-66; mng. partner Paisano Prodns., 1957-80, pres., 1966-80; exec. cons. The New Perry Mason, 1973-74. Treas., Los Angeles County chpt. Freedoms Found. at Valley Forge, 1967-68; 1st v.p. The Muses, Mus. Sci. and Industry, Los Angeles, 1967-68, 1st vice-chmn. bd. dirs., 1979-80; co-chmn. Mayor's Celebrity Com., Los Angeles, 1966-80; nat. hon. chmn. Christmas Seal Campaign, 1970, Am. Lung Assn.; chmn. bd. dirs. Am. Diabetes Assn., 1973-74, bd. dirs., 1972-76, mem. nat. adv. council, 1979-80, chmn. public affairs com., 1972-76, bd. dirs. So. Calif. affiliate, 1977-80; mem. Nat. Commn. on Digestive Diseases, 1977-79; mem. bd. councilors Brain Research Inst., U. Calif. at Los Angeles, 1978-80; mem. nat. arthritis, metabolism and digestive diseases adv. council NIH, 1972-76; mem. adv. council U. Mid Am., 1974-80; regent Immaculate Heart Coll., Los Angeles, 1968-73; bd. dirs. Film Industries, Workshop, 1966-68; bd. dirs., co-chmn. bd. trustees Center for Ulcer Research and Edn. Found., 1977-80; bd. dirs., mem. fin. com. YMCA Met. Los Angeles, 1974-80; trustee Columbia Coll., 1963-80; v.p. bd. dirs. Digestive Diseases Info. Center, 1978-80. Named Woman of Year, Los Angeles Times, 1961. Businesswomen of Year, Nat. Assn. Accountants, 1962; recipient Muses award, 1966; Justica award Nat. Assn. Women Lawyers, 1960. Mem. Acad. TV Arts and Scis. (nat. trustee, bd. govs. 1959-63, chpt. pres. 1960-62, nat. v.p. 1960-62), Am. Women for Internat. Understanding, Les Dames de Champagne (Los Angeles), Delta Zeta (v.p. found. 1961-62, dir. 1961-65), Zeta Phi Eta. Home: Hollywood, Calif. Died July 6, 1980.

VELIKOVSKY, IMMANUEL, author, scientist; b. Vitebsk, Russia, June 10, 1895; s. Simon-Yehiel and Beila Rachel (Grodensky) V.; student Edinburgh U., Moscow Econ. Inst., Moscow U., Kharkov U.; M.D., U. Moscow, 1921; postgrad. Charité, Berlin, Monakow Brain Inst., Zürich; studied psychoanalysis under Wilhelm Stekel, Vienna, 1933; hon. doctorate in Arts and Sci., U. Lethbridge, 1974; m. Elisheva Kramer, Apr. 15, 1923; 2 daus. Practiced as M.D. then psychoanalyst, Palestine, 1924-39. Pub., organizer, editor Scripta Universitatis atque Bibliothecae Hierosolymitanarum, 1921-24. Author: Thirty Days and Nights of Diego Pires on the Bridge of Sant' Angelo, 1935; Worlds in Collision, 1950; Ages in Chaos, Vol. I, 1952; Earth in Upheaval, 1955; Oedipus and Akhnaton: Myth and History, 1960; Peoples of the Sea, 1977; Ramses II and His Time, 1978; Mankind in Amnesia, 1982; contbr. to sci. jours.; editorials on Middle East, New York Post, Observer, 1948-49. First to suggest characteristic brain waves in epileptics, 1930; cosmological postulations caused controversy in modern science: claimed Venus must be very hot, 1950, posited that Jupiter emits radio waves, 1953, suggested existence of terrestrial magnetosphere reaching to lunar orbit, 1956, claimed steep thermal gradient below lunar surface, predicted sun's magnetosphere reaches to Pluto. Address: Princeton, N.J. Died Nov. 17, 1979.

VENABLE, EDWARD CARRINGTON, author; b. Petersburg, Va., July 4, 1884; s. Edward Carrington and Helen Skipwith (Wilmer) V.; A.B., Princeton, 1906; m. Nancy Howard De Ford, of Baltimore, Md., Apr. 30, 1924. Began as contbr. to mags., 1908. Enlisted in Am. Ambulance Field Service, June 1917, and served in France; discharged because of physical disability; entered Air Service, U.S.A., Dec. 1917; commd. 2d lt., Apr. 1918; duty in office of chief signal officer; trans. to Flying Corps; hon. discharged, Feb. 1919. Episcopalian. Author: Pierre Vinton, 1914; Short Stories, 1915; The Wife of the Junior Partner, 1915; Lasca, 1916; Ali Babette, 1917; At Isham's, 1918. Home: Baltimore, Md. *

VENIOT, CLARENCE JOSEPH (VENIO), Canadian senator; b. Moncton, N.B., Can., Feb. 9, 1886; s. Hon. P. J. and Catherine (Melanson) V.; B.A., U. Sacred Heart, 1906; M.A., U. S.H. Bathurst, N.B., 1924, Ph.D., 1949; M.D., U. Montreal, 1910; m. Marie Leger, 1910; children—Louis Maurice, Corinne (Mrs. T. LeBlanc), Alberta (Mrs. R. I. Findlater), Irene (Mrs. J. H. Ferris). Physician, specialist in gen. surgery, Bathurst, N.B., 1910-50; pres., founder Veniot Pharmacy, 1917; mem. Parliament for Gloucester, 1916-48; mem. Senate of Can. since 1948. Pres. N.B. Union of Municipalities, 1935-36; mayor, Bathurst, N.B., 1933-35. Fellow Royal Coll. Phys. and Surg. Can. (certified in gen. surgery) mem. N.B. Med. Soc. (pres. 1929-30). Clubs: Rotary (past pres.), Golf (past pres.)(Bathurst). Home: Bathurst, N.B. *

VENN, GRANT, educator; b. Seattle, Mar. 1, 1919; s. Roy William and Vera Patience (Masters) V.; student U. Wash., 1937-38; B.S., B.Ed., Wash. State U., 1941, M.Ed., 1947, Ed.D., 1951; postgrad. U. Minn., summers 1949-50; m. Olga M. Tobia; children—Victoria Susan, John Jeffrey, Deborah Elizabeth; Tchr. vocational agr., Sedro Woolley, Wash., 1941-42; guidance dir. Pullman (Wash.) pub. schs., 1946-47; dir. guidance curriculum Yakami (Wash.) pub. schs., 1948-49; asst. supt. schs., Bellevue, Wash., 1949-51; asst prof. edn. Wash. State U., 1951-52; supt. schs., Othello, Wash., 1952-56, Corning, N.Y., 1956-60; pres. Western State Coll., Gunnison, Colo., 1960-62; dir. field tng. Peace Corps, 1962-63; cons. Am. Council on Edn., Washington, 1963; supt. Wood County Schs., Parkersburg, W.Va., 1963-66; asso. commr. edn. U.S. Office Edn., HEW, Washington 1966-70; dir. Nat. Acad. for Sch. execs., Washington 1970-72; Calloway prof. edn. Ga. State U., Atlanta, 1972—79. Pres. N.Y. State Council Econ. Edn., 1959-60; cons. N.Y. Citizens Com. Pub. Schs., 1957-60; panelist White House Conf. Edn., 1965; chmn. resolution com. Am. Assn. Sch. Adminstrs., 1965-66. Mem. Nat. Colo. edn. assns., Colo. Assn. Sch. Adminstrs., Phi Kappa Phi, Phi Delta Kappa, Alpha Zeta, Psi Chi. Rotarian. Author: Man, Education and work, 1964; Man, Education and Manpower, 1970. Editor: Man, Education and Society, 1976. Home: Roswell, Ga. Died May 14, 1979.

VENTURI, LIONELLO, critic, art juror; b. Modena, Italy, Arp. 25, 1885; s. Adolfo and Jenny (Zami) V.; student Rome U.; m. Ada Scaccioni, July 28, 1912; children—Franco, Rosabianca (Mrs. Skira), Lauro. Museum curator, Venice, Rome, Urbino, 1909-14; prof. history of art U. Turin, 1915-31; lectr., Paris, 1932-39, N.Y.C., 1939-45; prof. history art U. Rome, 1945—. Served as maj. Italian Army. Mem. Am. Philos. Soc., Institute of France (Paris), Academia delle Scieuze Turin. Address: Rome, Italy. *

VERBRYCKE, J. RUSSELL, JR. (ver-brik), physician; b. Preakness, N.J., June 12, 1885; s. Rev. J. Russell and Elizabeth Shortdean (Easton) V.; M.D., Georgetown U., 1906; m. Sophie English Barnes, Feb. 28, 1911; children—Helen Torrey, J. Russell III, Robert Barnes. Interne and resident hosps. Washington and New York, 1906-09; consultant gastro-intestinal surgery, Garfield Memorial Hospital; formerly attending physician Gallinger Hosp.; specialist in med. and surg. diseases of the digestive tract. Asso. med. dir. Potomac div. Am. Red Cross, World War. Fellow Am. Coll. Physicians, A.M.A.; Am. Gastro-Enterol. Assn; mem. Southern Med. Assn., Kappa Psi, Presbyterian. Clubs: Cosmos, West River Sailing, Bethesda Country. Contbr. articles on autopsy findings in tularemia, treatment of disease of the esophagus, gall bladder and peptic ulcers. Home: Washington. *

VERHULST, ALFRED, air force officer; b. Sheboygan Falls, Wis., Mar. 7, 1921; s. Leonard and Johanna (Roerdink) V.; student Sheboygan Bus. Coll., 1939; grad. Air War Coll., 1970; m. Hazel Mae Schatz, June 12, 1947; children—Jan K. Burns, Randal L. Enlisted U.S. Army AC, 1942, commd. 2d lt., 1943, advanced to capt., 1945; service in 5 major campaigns, PTO; breeder purebred Holsteins, Sheboygan Falls, Wis., 1946-55; commd. maj. USAF, 1955, advanced through grades to maj. gen., 1974; squadron comdr. 88th Fighter Bomber Squadron, 1955-56; group comdr. 438th Fighter Bomber Wing, 1956-58; wing comdr. operations 440th Tactical Airlift Wing, 1958-67; wing comdr. 434th Tactical Airlift Wing, 1967-69; vice comdr. Hdqrs. Air Force Res., Robin AFB, Ga., 1969-73; comdr. Eastern Air Force Res. Region, Dobbins AFB, Ga., 1973-75. Treas. Sheboygan County Agrl. Assn.; sponsor Sheboygan County Fair, 1948-55. Decorated Legion of Merit with oak leaf cluster, D.F.C., Air medal with oak leaf cluster, D.S.M. (posthumous). Mem. Res. Officers Assn. (pres. Wis. dept. 1967), Air Force Assn. (pres. Billy Mitchell chpt. Milw. 1966), Am. Legion (past post comdr.), Quiet Birdmen (Milw. chpt.). Rotarian. Home: Marietta, Ga. Died Dec. 23, 1975; interred Sheboygan Falls (Wis.) Cemetery.

VERNER, ELIZABETH O'NEILL, etcher, author, lecturer; b. Charleston, S.C., 1883; d. Henry and Mary Ann (Baker) O'Neill; grad. Ursuline Acad., Columbia, S.C., 1902; student Pa. Acad. Fine Arts, Phila., 1903-04, Central Sch. of Arts, London, 1930; D.H.L., U. N.C., 1947; Litt.D. U.S.C. 1947, Coll. of Charleston, 1969; m. E. Pettigrew Verner, Apr. 24, 1907 (dec. 1925); children—Elizabeth P., David Battle. Etchings and pastels of Charleston, pastels of Low Country, Negro men and women exhibited throughout U.S.; worked out new method of drawing pastels on silk; fellow Castle Hill Art Center, Ipswich, Mass., 1954; Collections of etchings in Boston Art Mus. Atlanta High Mus., Met. Mus., N.Y.C., Library of Congress, Gibbes Art Gallery, Charleston; one-man show Gibbes Gallery, 1963, Manila, Philippines, 1964, Spartanburg, S.C., 1970, Columbia, S.C., 1971, Sumter, S.C., 1971, Beaufort, S.C., 1972, Augusta, Ga., 1975, Mint Mus., Charlotte, N.C., 1976, Atlanta, 1977; Japanese series presented to Internat. Mus., Kyoto, by gov. of S.C., 1969; active in campaigns to retain historic landmarks in Charleston, Savannah, Ga., Fayetteville, N.C.; made pencil drawings of Williamsburg; apptd. to make drawings of Mt. Vernon for Mt. Vernon Ladies' Assn., drawings of N.Y. for Rockefeller Center; series of etchings of Savannah, 1928, Harvard Med. Sch., 1937, Japan, 1937; drawings of Fayetteville, 1935, West Point, 1944, Princeton, 1950, U. S.C., 1954. Founder, Preservation Soc. of Charleston. Episcopalian. Author: Prints and Impressions of Charleston, 1939; Mellowed by Time, 1941; Other Places, 1946; The Stonewall Ladies, 1963. Illustrator: Sullivan's Island edit. Goldbug (Poe), 1967; Charleston edit. Porgy (Heyward); also numerous books on S.C. history, guide books, others. Home: Charleston, S.C. Died Apr. 27, 1979; buried Churchyard of Scotch Presbyterian Ch., Charleston.

VERNEY, GILBERT, paper mfg. co. exec.; b. Lancashire, Eng., July 3, 1904; s. Harry Jewel and Elizabeth Ellen (Ingham) V.; student Royal Commercial Sch., London; Nautical Coll., Devonshire, Eng.; midshipman in Brit. Transport Service, 1919-23; m. Virginia Ruth Piggott, June 30, 1932 (dec. Nov. 1955); children—Dianne (Mrs. James C. Greenway III), Valerie (dec.), Richard, Edmund. Chmn. bd. Monadnock Paper Mills, Inc. Republican. Clubs: Nantucket Yacht; N.Y. Yacht; Royal Scandinavian Yacht; Algonquin; British Empire (Providence). Address: Bennington, N.H. Died Jan. 23, 1978.

VERNON, WESTON, JR., lawyer; b. Logan, Utah, July 29, 1904; s. Weston and Frances (Maughan) V.; B.S., Utah State Coll., Logan, 1925; LL.B., George Washington U. Law Sch., 1929; student U. Utah, 1921, U. of Mich. Law Sch., 1927; m. Adelaide Neilson, Sept. 21, 1926; children—Weston, 3d, Robert Gerard; m. 2d, Maude Congdon; children—William, James S.; m. 3d, Lillian Malley, Sept. 19, 1953. Admitted D.C. bar, 1928, N.Y. bar, 1938; with Dunnington, Walker and Gregg, Washington, D.C., 1928; with Davis, Polk, Wardwell, Gardiner & Reed, N.Y. City, 1930-38; partner Milbank, Tweed, Hadley & McCloy, from 1938, sr. partner until 1977. Chmn., Nat. Center for Automated Information Retrieval. Mem. Am. Law Inst., Am. (chmn. sect. on tax 1940-41, chmn. young lawyers sect. 1937-38, chmn. sect. sci. and tech.), N.Y. State (past pres.), N.Y.C. bar assns., Practicing Law Inst. (trustee), Fed., Internat., Inter-Am., bar assns., Bar Assn. D.C., Tax Forum of N.Y.C., Tax Inst. (past pres.). Clubs: Wall Street, Hemisphere (N.Y.C.); Metropolitan, Lawyers (Washington); Westhampton Beach Country. Home: New York, N.Y. Died Apr. 23, 1977.

VERSTEEG, JOHN MARINUS, clergyman; b. Den Helder, Holland, Sept. 9, 1888; s. Dirk Aren and Anna Petronella (Ollman) V.; B.D., Drew U., 1916, A.M., 1928; D.D., Allegheny Coll., 1931; D.D., Ohio Wesleyan U., 1942; S.T.D., Ohio No. U., 1945; Litt.D., Union Coll., 1946; m. Edna Catherine Ames, June 18, 1921; children—Sherwood Ames, Elaine Joan (Mrs. Ross May), Robert John, Virgil Neil. Came to U.S., 1900; naturalized citizen, 1909. Ordained ministry M.E. Ch., 1917; pastor West Side Church, Jersey City, 1920-21, Drew Church, Port Jervis, N.Y., 1922-25, Roseville Ch., Newark, 1926-28, South Ave. Ch., Wilkinsburg, Pa., 1929-31, Walnut Hills-Avondale Ch., Cin., 1932-46; superintendent Lima Dist., Meth. Church, 1945-51; pastor First Church, Athens, Ohio, 1951-57; dir. of libraries Meth. Theol. Sch., Ohio, 1957-60; editor Ohio Area Meth. Sesquicentennial, 1960-77. Pres. Council of Churches of Greater Cin., 1941-44; pres., Greater Cincinnati Writers League, 1942-44; chmn. Social Service Comm. of Ohio Annual Conf. Meth. Church, 1934-44; founder Cin. Sch. of Religion. Public (tripartite) mem., Regional War Labor Bd., 1943-45; lecturer in Bibl. lit., U. of Cincinnati, 1943-44; chmn. com. Field of Social Action, Meth. Ch. from 1948; mem. exec. com. Meth. Commn. on Ch. Union, 1944-56; mem. Gen. Conf., 1940, 48, 52; sec. mem. chs. of U.S.A. of World Meth. Council; mem. planning com., Protestant Commn. on Church Union. Mem. Am. Soc. of Church History, The Clergy Club, Torch Club, Kiwanis, Exec. Republican. Author: The Modern Meaning of Church Membership, 1919; The Deeper Meaning of Stewardship, 1923; Christ and the Problems of Youth, 1924; Christianity at Work, 1925; Perpetuating Pentecost, 1930; Save Money, 1939; Our Protestant Convictions, 1941; When Christ Controls, 1943; Protestant Prayer, 1947. Contr. to church mags. Home: Lakeside, Ohio. Died Jan. 14, 1977.

VERWEY, WILLARD FOSTER, microbiologist, educator; b. Walkill, N.Y., July 14, 1913; s. Daniel George and Delora (Zimmerman) V.; B.S., Rutgers U., 1934; Sc.D., Johns Hopkins Sch. Hygiene, 1937; m. Selma Louise Stoner, June 6, 1940; children—Delora (Mrs. James McWilliams), James R. Asst., instr. N.Y. U. Coll. Medicine, 1937-40; dir. bacteriological research Sharp & Dohme, 1940-53; dir. bacteriology Merck, Sharp & Dohme, 1953-57; prof. dept. microbiology U. Tex. Med. Br., Galveston, 1957-77, chmn. dept., 1957-74; dir. Cholera Research Lab., Dacca, Bangladesh, 1974-77. Mem. cholera panel U.S.-Japan Coop. Med. Sci. Program, 1965-72; mem. cholera adv. com. NIH, 1967-72; mem. com. Intersci. Conf. on Antimicrobial Agts. and Chemotherapy, 1964-68. Diplomate Am. Bd. Microbiology. Fellow Am. Acad. Microbiology; mem. Am. Soc. for Microbiology, A.A.A.S., Soc. for Exptl. Biology and Medicine, Sigma Xi. Mem. editorial bd. Antimicrobial Agts. and Chemotherapy, 1966-68. Contbr. articles to profl. jours. Home: West Sedona, Ariz. Died May 17, 1979; buried Sedona Meml. Park.

VEY, EBENEZER, educator; b. Grate's Cove, Newfoundland, Can., Nov. 13, 1913; s. Joshua and Henrietta (Snelgrove) V.; came to U.S., 1937, naturalized, 1950; B.S., Calif. Inst. Tech., 1941, M.S., 1942; D.Engring., Johns Hopkins, 1948; m. Georgiana G. Stacy, Feb. 14, 1947; 1 son, James E. Instr., Johns Hopkins, 1946-48; mem. faculty Ill. Inst. Tech., 1948-77, prof. civil engring., 1954-77, chmn. dept., 1969-75; asst. dir. IIT Research Inst., 1961-68; sci. adviser, 1968-69; cons. soil mechanics, found. engring., 1949-77. Mem. ASCE (dir. Ill. 1964-66, v.p. 1966-67, pres. 1967-68, nat. dir. 1974-77), Am. Soc. Engring. Edn., Am. Road Builders Assn., Sigma Xi, Tau Beta Pi, Chi Epsilon. Author tech. papers. Home: Evanston, Ill. Died Jan. 21, 1977.

VICKERS, HARRY FRANKLIN, business exec.; b. Red Lodge, Mont., Oct. 10, 1898; s. George Henry and Rose Mary (Baringer) V.; ed. pub. schs., Calif.; Sc. D., (honorary), U. So. Cal., 1956; m. Nell May Wilhite, Apr. 26, 1920; 1 dau., Dawn R. Organizer engring. and mfg. bus. H. F. Vickers Mfg. Co., Los Angeles, 1921, inc. in Calif. as Vickers, Inc., 1927; bus. moved to Detroit and inc. as Vickers, Inc., 1929, became pres., 1936; co. merged with Sperry Corp., 1937; continued as pres. Vickers, Inc., and became exec. v.p. operations Sperry Corp., 1947, pres., 1952-55, co. merged with Remington Rand, 1955, pres., chief exec. officer, dir. new company Sperry Rand Corp., 1955-65, chairman and chief executive officer, 1965-67, also officer and director of other Sperry Rand Divs.; dir. of the Flinkote Co. Served with Signal Corps, U.S. Army, 1917-19; overseas, France. Recipient American Society M.E. medal, 1956, American Soc. Tool Engrs. progress award, 1957. Member of the Society Automotive Engrs., Am. Soc. M.E., Inst. Aero Scis., Nat. Aero. Assn., Soc. Naval Architects and Marine Engrs., Am. Ordnance Assn., Nat. Security Indsl. Assn., Army Ordnance Assn., Engring. Soc. Detroit. Clubs: Detroit Golf; Creek (L.I., N.Y.); Everglades (Palm Beach, Fla.); Wings (N.Y.); Columbia Country, Burning Tree (Washington). Home: Princeton, Maine. Died Jan. 13, 1977.

VIETS, HOWARD T(HOMPSON) (VETS), univ. prof.; b. Lynn, Mass., Dec. 5, 1886; s. Frederick Henderson and Hattie Florence (Baldwin) V.; A.B., Harvard, 1909, A.M., 1914; m. Judith Delano Everett, Sept. 1914; children—Barbara, Priscilla. Clerk, Newton Trust Co., 1910-11; teacher of English, Marblehead (Mass.) High Sch., 1912-13; instr. in English, U. of Minn., 1914-20; asst. prof. English, Syracuse U., 1920-22, asso. prof., 1922-25, prof. of bus. writing since 1925. Mem. Am. Bus. Writing Assn., Alpha Delta Sigma, Phi Kappa Phi (pres. Syracuse U. chapter 1938-42). Republican. Unitarian. Author: A First Course in Practical Business English (with D. W. Morton), 1940. Editor: Readings in Modern Business Literature (with A.C. Babenroth), 1930. Home: Syracuse, N.Y. *

VIGDERMAN, ALFRED GREENFIELD, fgn. service officer; b. Phila., June 8, 1914; s. Samuel and Anna (Greenfield) V.; A.B., U. Pa., 1933, LL.B., 1936; m. Edythe Kathryn Auster, Oct. 17, 1937; children—Patricia, Linda Auster (Mrs. Bamber). Admitted to Pa. bar, 1937; practiced law, 1937-41; atty. OPA, 1941-47; research asst. to Senator Scott W. Lucas, 1947-49; sec. Democratic Policy Com., U.S. Senate, 1949 spl. asst. to sec. of state Dept. State, 1949, atty., 1950-52, asst. legal adviser for mut. security affairs, 1952, legal adviser, attache to U.S. del. to NATO, 1952-55. 1st sec. Am. embassy, Bonn, Germany, 1955-57; dep. dir. Office German Affairs, Dept. State, 1958-61; counselor of embassy for Mut. Security Affairs, Athens, Greece, 1961-65, polit. affairs, 1965-66; State Dept. sr. fellow, vis. prof. law and diplomacy Fletcher Sch. Law and Diplomacy, Medford, Mass., 1967; dep. asst. sec. for internat. affairs, Dept. Transp., 1967-69; country dir. for Greece, Dept. State, 1969-71, Am. consul gen., Palermo, Italy, 1971-73; research asso. Fletcher Sch. Law and Diplomacy, Medford, Mass., 1974-78; legal adv. and polit. analyst to Mass. League of Cities and Towns, 1976-78. Home: Lexington, Mass. Died Nov. 15, 1978; buried Rock Creek Cemetery, Washington.

VIGIER, HENRI, UN ofcl.; b. Lavalette, France, May 31, 1886; s. Jean and Louise (Joret) V.; student Ecole Normale Supérieure, Paris, France, Agrégé de l'Université, France; m. Francois Depuy, Jan. 21, 1918; children—Jean, Philippe, Francois. Formerly counsellor League of Nations Secretarist; prin. officer UN United Nations Secretariat, presently dir., also personal dep. to acting mediator for Palestine, 1948-49; chmn. armistice negotiations between Israel and Syria, Israel and Lebanon, 1949; advisor on armistice agreements Israel and adjacent Arab states. Office N.Y.C.; also Jerusalem. *

VINCENT, GEORGE CLARK, clergyman; b. Ligonier, Pa., Jan. 29, 1884; s. William Hanna and Martha Jeanette (Jamison) V.; B.A., Westminster Coll., New Wilmington, Pa., 1904, Rhodes scholar, Oxford U.,

Eng., 1904-07, B.A., 1907, M.A., 1923; Holwell exhibitioner, Queen's Coll., Oxford, 1908-09; studied Pittsburgh Theol. Sem., 1908; D.D., Monmouth (Ill.) Coll., 1925; m. Mary Aois McMichael, Mar. 25, 1913. Ordained ministry U.P. Ch., 1909; successively pastor Monmouth, Ill., Washington, Pa., South Park Presbyterian Ch., Newark, N.J., Shadyside Ch., Pittsburgh, Pa., until 1928, Union Congl. Ch. Upper Montclair, N.J., since 1928. Mem. Sigma Chi. Home: Upper Montclair, N.J.; (summer) Morristown, N.J. *

VINCENT, JOHN NATHANIEL, educator, composer; b. Birmingham, Ala., May 17, 1902; s. John Nathaniel and Mollie (Eager) V.; diploma N.E. Conservatory, 1926; B.S., George Peabody Coll., 1932, M.A., 1933; grad. study Harvard, 1933-35, Ecole Normale de Musique, 1935-37; Ph.D., Cornell, 1942; composition student of Chadwick, Piston, Copland, Boulanger, Harris; m. Amelia Bartlett, 1927 (div.); 1 son, Nathaniel Read; m. 2d, Ruth Kimball, Dec. 21, 1937 (div.); children—John Nathaniel, Helen Hancock; m. 3d, Margaret T. Alberstadt, 1967 (div.). Supr. instrumental music El Paso (Tex.) Schs., 1927-30; teaching fellow George Peabody, Coll., 1930-33; head music dept. Western Ky. State Coll., 1937-45; asso. prof. U. Cal. at Los Angeles, 1946-47, prof. music, 1947-69, chmn. dept., 1947-52; dir. Huntington Hartford Found. 1953-65; played flute Peoples Symphony, 1925-26, Boston Symphony Orch., 1926-27; guest condr. Atlanta, Bogota, Buenos Aires, Guatemala, Los Angeles, N.Y., Rio de Janeiro, Santiago, Seattle, Washington; fgn. music corr. Boston Transcript, 1935-37; mem. bd. Hollywood Bowl Assn. Elkan Naumberg fellow, 1934-35, John Knowles Paine traveling fellow, 1935-37; Guggenheim fellowship, 1962-63; recipient Specialist grantee State Dept., 1964. Mem. Nat. Assn. Am. Composers and Condrs. (pres. Los Angeles chpt. 1960-62, 71-75). Republican. Methodist. Compositions: Symphony in D, Symphonic Poem after Descartes, Rondo Rhapsody for Orch., Three Jacks (ballet), 2 string quartets, Symphony for Piano and String Orch., Primeval Void (opera), Stabat Mater for Soprano and Male Chorus, Suite for Percussion, many others. Author: Music for Sight-Reading, 1948; More Music for Sight-Reading, 1948; The Diatonic Modes in Modern Music 1951, rev., 1972. Home: Los Angeles, Calif. Died Jan. 21, 1977.

VINOGRAD, JEROME RUBIN, scientist, educator; b. Milw., Feb. 9, 1913; s. Oscar and Bertha (Bernstein) V.; student U. Minn., 1929-31, U. Berlin, 1931-33, Univ. Coll., London, 1933-35; M.A., UCLA, 1937; Ph.D., Stanford, 1940; m. Dorothy Colodny, Jan. 12, 1975; children by previous marriage—Julia Shalett, Deborah Shalett. Research asso. Stanford, 1939-41; research chemist Shell Devel. Co., 1941-51; mem. faculty Calif. Inst. Tech., 1951-76, prof. chemistry and biology, 1965-76, Bowles prof. chem. biology, 1975; cons. to govt. and industry, 1955-76; vis. prof. developmental biology and cancer Albert Einstein Coll. Medicine, 1967. Co-chmn. Gordon Conf. Nucleic Acids, 1969. Mem. adv. panel Cal. div. Am. Cancer Soc., 1967-72; adv. panel molecular biology NSF, 1963-64. Recipient Kendall Co. award in colloid and surface chemistry Am. Chem. Soc., 1970; T. Duckett Jones award Helen Hay Whitney Found., 1972; nat. lectr. ann. meeting Biophys. Soc., 1973. Mem. Nat. Acad. Sci., Am. Acad. Arts and Scis., Am. Soc. Biol. Chemists, Am. Chem. Soc., Faraday Soc., A.A.A.S., Am. Soc. Microbiology, Biophys. Soc. Author numerous articles in field. Mem. adv. editorial bd. Intervirology Advances Biol. and Med. Physics. Research theory and practice ultracentrifugation, structure and properties circular DNA in viruses and mitochondria. Died July 3, 1976. Home: La Jolla CA. *

VINSON, CARL, congressman; b. Baldwin County, near Milledgeville, Ga., Nov. 18, 1883; s. Edward S. and Anne (Morris) V.; grad. Ga. Mil. Coll., Milledgeville; LL.B., Mercer U., 1902; widower. Admitted to Ga. bar, 1902, and practiced in Milledgeville; mem. Hines & Vinson; county ct. solicitor, 2 terms, 1906-10; mem. Ga. Ho. of Rep., 1909-12; elected judge County Court, Baldwin County, term 1912-16; resigned Nov. 2, 1914; elected to 63d Congress, Nov. 3, 1914, to fill unexpired term; re-elected 64th to 72d Congresses, 10th Ga. Dist., and to 73d to 82d congresses, 6th Ga. Dist., 84th-88th congresses. Former chmn. Naval Affairs Com. Democrat. Methodist. Home: Milledgeville, Ga. Died June 1, 1981; buried Memory Hill Cemetery, Milledgeville.

VISHNIAK, MARK, writer, educator; b. Moscow, USSR, Jan. 15, 1883; s. Benjamin and Marie (Guinsburg) V.; grad. Law Sch., Moscow U., 1908; m. Marie Vishniak, Sept. 13, 1908 (dec. Oct. 1955). Came to U.S., 1940, naturalized, 1949. Prof. pub. law Moscow Pedagogical Inst., 1917; mem., sec. Russian Constituent Assembly, 1918; polit. emigre, 1919; prof. Slavonic Inst., Paris, France, 1920-40, Franco-Russian Inst., Paris, 1929-40; editor Russian Quar. Contemporary Annals, Paris, 1920-40; vis. prof. Acad. Internat. Law, The Hague, 1933; mem. area and lang. study curriculum ASPT Russian program Cornell U., 1943-44; prof. Navy Sch., U. Colo., 1944-46; cons. Russian affairs Time mag., from 1946. Grantee Social Sci. Research Council, 1943. Author 23 books and booklets, numerous articles. Home: New York, N.Y. Died Aug. 31, 1976.

VITZ, CARL (PETER PAUL) (VITS), librarian; b. St. Paul, Minn., June 3, 1883; s. Martin (D.D.) and Mary Ellen (Engeler) V.; B.L.S., N.Y. State Library Sch.; A.B., Adelbert Coll. (Western Reserve University), 1904; student Library School, Western Reserve University, 1905; grad. N.Y. State Library School, Albany, 1907; m. Ruth A. Van Aernam, Aug. 22, 1910 (died 1932); children—Howard E., Richard Van A. (dec.), Margaret E., Janet A., John S.; m. 2d, Alda Clayton, July 7, 1934; children—Paul Clayton, Martin Hibbert, Robert Carl, Donald Bradford. Asst. librarian of Public Library, Washington, D.C., 1907-09; director's assistant, State Library, Albany, 1909-12; 2d vice-librarian Public Library, Cleveland, O., 1912-19, vice-librarian, 1919-22; librarian Pub. Library, Toledo, O., 1922-37; librarian Minneapolis Pub. Library, 1937-46; librarian, Cincinnati Pub. Library since Jan. 1946. Lecturer New York State Library Sch., 1909-13, Sch. of Library Science, Western Reserve Univ., 1912-29, div. Library Instr., U. of Minn. 1937-46. Lippincott Award by American Library Assn., 1952. Fellow Am. Library Inst; mem. A.L.A. (mem. council 1925-29, 1937-41, mem. exec. bd., 1937-41, 1943-46, pres. July 1944-45, mem. bd. on library service to children and young people, 1933-36; mem. fed. relations com., chmn., 1946-47, member postwar planning com., president Public Library Division, 1946-47); member Ohio Library Assn. (pres. 1920-21, 1932-33). Am. Assn. for Adult Edn., Am. Inst. Graphic Arts, Literary Club, Ohio Philosophical and Historical Soc., Trustee Ohioana Library. Phi Beta Kappa. Ind. Democrat. Member Presbyterian Ch. Author: Circulation Work (3 edits.); A Federal Library Agency and Federal Library Aid, 1935. Editor; Current Problems in Public Library Finance, 1933. Home: Cincinnati. *

VODREY, JOSEPH KELLY, radio exec.; b. East Liverpool, O., Jan. 4, 1905; s. William Henry and Dorothy (Kelly) V.; grad. Mercersburg (Pa.) Acad., 1922; A.B. magna cum laude, Princeton, 1926; m. Mary W. Harris, June 7, 1930; children—Thompson Kelly, Cynthia Dodge. Started newspaper work Marion (O.) Star 1925; in mech. dept. Steubenville (O.) Herald-Star, 1926; successively reporter, asst. city editor, news editor, mng. editor Canton (O.) Repository, 1927-39, bus. mgr., 1939-46; mgr. Brush-Moore Newspapers, Inc., 1946-51, v.p., dir., 1951-68; v.p., dir. Beaverett Co., radio stas. WHBC, Canton, WFIR, Roanoke, Va., 1968-75; former v.p., dir. Canton Repository, East Liverpool Review, Marion (O.) Star, Portsmouth (O.) Times, Salem (O.) News, Steubenville Herald-Star, 1944-67; v.p., dir. Kohler Coating Machinery Corp., Canton, O. Mem. conservation com. Ohio Postwar Planning Commn., 1947-48, Ohio Agr. and Natural Resources Com., 1950-52; mem. bd. govs. Ohio Forestry Assn., 1952-54; mem. Canton Retail Mchts. Bd., 1940-46; dir. Canton Water Commn., 1935-36; chmn. Canton Civilian Navy Recruiting Com., 1942-44, Canton Council Navy League (past pres.); mem. Canton council Adv. Council Naval Affairs. Mem adv. bd. Mercy Hosp., Canton, 1946-75; bd. dirs. Canton chpt. A.R.C., 1954-56, 61-63; trustee Canton Safety Council (past pres.), Ohioana Library Assn., 1951-75, Stark County Hist. Soc.; mem. bd. advisers Walsh Coll. Mem. Am. Soc. Newspaper Editors, 1937-47, Asso. Press, Inland Daily Press Assn. (past dir.), Royal Dublin Soc. (Ireland), Arthur Machen Soc. U.S. (pres. 1957-63; pres. emeritus 1963-75), Soc. 5th Line (Chgo.), Navy League U.S. (life), Ohio Hist. Assn. (benefactor mem.), Phi Beta Kappa, Phi Beta Kappa Assos., Sigma Delta Chi. Republican. Episcopalian (vestryman 1953-55). Clubs: Terrace (Princeton); Nat. Press (Washington); Poor Richard (Phila.); Rowfant (Cleve.); Brookside (dir. 1958-60), Advertising, Woodchoppers (pres. 1957-58) (Canton); Press of Ohio (Columbus); Grolier (N.Y.C.); Chicago Athletic. Home: Canton, Ohio. Died Nov. 16, 1975.

VODREY, WILLIAM HENRY, lawyer; b. East Liverpool, Ohio, Sept. 23, 1903; s. William H. and Dorothy (Kelly) V.; grad. Mercersburg Acad., 1922; A.B., Princeton, 1926; J.D., Harvard, 1929; m. Evelyn Stroud, June 29, 1929; children—Barbara (Mrs. William K. Wamelink), Jackman S., Dorothy Grace (Mrs. John Stamat). Admitted to Ohio bar, 1929, practiced in East Liverpool; mem. firm Vodrey and Shay, 1929-79. Sec.-treas. Brush-Moore Newspapers, Inc., Canton, Ohio, 1955-67, Ohio Broadcasting Co., Canton, 1955-72; dir. First Nat. Bank East Liverpool, 1955-73; lectr. on East Liverpool pottery, Henry Ford Mus., Greenfield Village, 1964. Trustee East Liverpool YMCA, 1940-74. Decorated Order Queen Isabella (Spain). Mem. Columbiana County (pres. 1949-50), Ohio, Am. bar assns., East Liverpool (trustee treas. 1955-79, pres. 1977-79), Ohio (hon. life, trustee 1958-75, pres. 1965-67) hist. socs., Columbia County Law Library Assn. (sec.-treas. 1943-68), Phi Beta Kappa. Episcopalian (past vestryman and warden). Club: East Liverpool Country (trustee 1941-49, pres. 1943-45). Author: Pottery Industry in East Liverpool District, 1945; (with Max Gard) The Sandy and Beaver Canal, 1952; Record and Sources of Ohio Law, 1968; A.J. Poe, Artist, 1971. Home: East Liverpool, Ohio. Died Aug. 29, 1979; buried Riverview Cemetery, East Liverpool, Ohio.

VOGEL, CYRIL J., bishop; student Duquesne U., St. Vincent's Sem., Latrobe, Pa. Ordained priest Roman Catholic Ch., 1931; bishop of Salina (Kans.), 1965-79. Home: Salina, Kans. Died Oct. 4, 1979.

VOIGT, CARL EMIL, banker; b. James, S.D., May 6, 1895; s. Carl and Minnie (Affeldt) V.; B.S., Huron Coll., 1918, LL.D. (hon.), 1968; m. Eula Manwaring, July 3, 1920; children—Carl E., Robert S. Asst. cashier James Valley Bank, Huron, S.D., 1919-24; cashier Nat. Bank of Huron, 1924-35; mgr. Huron br. Northwest Security Nat. Bank of Sioux Falls, 1935-43, v.p., dir., 1951-56, pres., dir., 1956-79; with Northwest Bancorp., Mpls., 1943-79, v.p., 1946-51, chmn. bd., 1960. Chmn. War Bond drive, World War I; mem. S.S.S., World War II; pres. Sioux Falls Community Chest; pres., dir. Credit Bur. of Sioux Falls; v.p., dir. Sioux council Boy Scouts Am.; treas. Sioux Falls Traffic Bur.; del. Republican Nat. Conv., 1964; bd. dirs. United Fund, Sioux Falls Safety Council, Sioux Falls-Augustana Symphony Orch. Assn.; trustee Huron Coll., trustee emeritus, 1970-79. Served with 314th Engrs., 89th Div., U.S. Army, World War I. Mem. Zool. Soc. Sioux Falls (treas., dir.), Sioux Falls C. of C. (pres.), Greater S.D. Assn. (chmn. tax study com.), Am., S.D. bankers assns., Am. Legion, Navy League (v.p. council). Republican Presbyn. Elk, Mason (Shriner; grand master S.D. 1964, chmn. grand master's conf. N. Am. 1965). Clubs: Rotary (past pres., dist. gov. 1963), Minnehaha Country, Town, South Dakota Automobile (Sioux Falls). Home: Sioux Falls, S.D. Died Mar. 18, 1979; buried Sioux Falls.

VOLAVY, MARGUERITE, pianist; b. Brünn, Moravia, Bohemia, Dec. 28, 1886; grad. Vienna Conservatory, 1901 (1st prize); studied with E. Schütt and Leschetizky. Début with Prague Philharmonic Orchestra, 1902; toured Europe; New York début with Russian Symphony Orchestra, 1915; hasfrequently appeared in recitals and with orchestra.*

VOLD, LAWRENCE, prof. law; b. Dunlap, S.D., Apr. 11, 1886; s. Asbjorn and Bertha V.; holder Crowninshield Scholarship, 1906-10, Ricardo Prize Scholarship in Econs., 1909-10, Harvard U.; A.B. (cum laude), Harvard, 1910, LL.B., 1913, S.J.D., 1914; LL.D., U. N.D., 1949; m. Margaret Bryan, Dec. 25, 1909 (dec. 1947); children—Robert Donald, Gordon Arthur (foster son); m. 2d, Grace Johnson, Dec. 31, 1951 (dec. 1964). Instr. law U. N.D., 1914-15, asst. prof., 1915-20, asso. prof., 1920-21, prof., 1921-24, also chmn. law faculty. 1922-23; prof. law, U. Nebr., 1924-46; prof. law, Boston Univ. School of Law, 1946-48; prof. of law, Hastings Coll. Law, U. Calif., from 1948; vis. prof. U. Kansas, summer 1928, Univ. of So. Calif. summers 1947, 48, 49; principal atty. Land Div., Dept. Justice, Washington, 1942-46; asso. mem. Bd. Legal Examiners; practice law, San Francisco, 1964-78; part-time cons. Special counsel in litigation involving liability of broadcasting stations for defamation by radio, and involving crash of aircraft on homes; also counsel in litigation involving civil liabilities under Nebraska Antitrust Act; adviser Am. Law Inst., Comml. Law-Sales Group, 1942-43; labor arbitrator. Member Am., Calif. bar assns., Phi Beta Kappa, Phi Alpha Delta, Order of Coif. Republican. Presbyterian. Editor Vold's Cases on Sales; 3d edition, 1960, Woodward's Cases on Sales. Author: Vold on Sales, 1931, rev. edit. 1959; Acquisition of Property for War Purposes, 1944; also author numerous articles. Home: San Francisco, Calif. Died Nov. 7, 1978.

VOLD, ROBERT DONALD, educator, chemist; b. Boston, Dec. 11, 1910; s. Lawrence and Margaret (Bryan) V.; A.B., U. Neb., 1931, M.S., 1932; Ph.D., U. Cal. at Berkeley, 1935; m. Marjorie Jean Young, June 14, 1936; children—Mary Louise, Robert Lawrence, Wylda Bryan. Research chemist Procter & Gamble Co., 1935-37; research asso. Stanford, 1937-41; asst. prof. U. So. Cal., 1941-44, asso. prof., 1944-47, prof., 1947-74, emeritus, 1974-78, head dept. chemistry, 1950-53; sr. Fulbright research scholar U. Utrecht, Netherlands, 1953-54; prof. phys. chemistry Indian Inst. Sci., Bangalore, India, 1955-57; vis. research asso. Cal. Inst. Technology, 1963-64; cons. sci. inst. Jadavpur U., Calcutta, India, 1965. Fellow A.A.A.S.; mem. Am. Chem. Soc. (sec.-treas., vice chmn., chmn. div. colloid chemistry, 1944-45, 47, councilor So. Cal. sect. 1960-63, chmn. sect. 1967-68, recipient Tolman medal 1970, honoree Vold Symposium 1974), Internat. Union of Pure and Applied Chemistry (commn. on surface and colloid chemistry 1962), Chem. Soc. (London), Cal. Assn. Chemistry Tchrs. (chmn. 1960-61), Phi Beta Kappa, Sigma Xi, Phi Lambda Upsilon (editor The Register 1943-48), Alpha Chi Sigma. Presbyn. Mem. ed. bd. Jour. Colloid Sci., 1946-60. Contbr. sci. articles profl. publs. Home: San Diego, Calif. Died Oct. 28, 1978.

VOLK, LESTER DAVID, congressman; b. Brooklyn, N.Y., Sept. 17, 1884; s. Aron Barney and Esther (Topsky) V.; grad. Boys High Sch., Brooklyn, 1902; M.D., L.I. Med. Coll., 1906; LL.B., Brooklyn Law Sch., 1911; unmarried. Practiced medicine, 1906-13; coroner's phys., King's Co., N.Y., 1914; began practice of law, 1913; mem. N.Y. Assembly, 1913; elected mem. 66th Congress to fill unexpired term, and mem. 67th Congress (1921-23), 10th N.Y. Dist. Republican. Served as 1st lt. M.C., with A.E.F., 312th Remount Squadron, and 88th Aero Squadron, Army of Occupation. Mem. Vets. Fgn. Wars. Jewish religion. Mason. Odd Fellow, K.P., Elk. Address: Brooklyn, N.Y. *

VOLLMER, WILLIAM AUERBACH, editor; b. Brooklyn, N.Y., Oct. 26, 1886; s. Edward Richard and Mary J. (Auerbach) V.; grad. Polytechnic Prep. Sch., Brooklyn, 1905; B.A., Amherst, 1909; unmarried. With McBride, Nast & Co., since 1910; editor House and Garden (mag.). Mem. Chi Phi. Club: Crescent Athletic (Brooklyn). Editor: A Book of Distinctive Interiors, 1912. Author: A Book of Perennials, 1914. Contbr. to mags. Home: Brooklyn. *

VOLLMERS, HENRY EDWARD, investment banker; b. N.Y.C., Apr. 27, 1898; s. Henry Edward and Mathilda (Koch) V.; B.A., Columbia, 1920, Chem. Engr., 1922; m. Anne M. Henry, Nov. 20, 1924. Sales mgr., dir. W. N. Best Corp., N.Y.C., 1924-28; instl. salesman Halsey Stuart & Co., Inc., N.Y.C., 1928-42; engr. Am. Cyanamid Co., N.Y.C., 1942-45; with Morgan Stanley & Co., N.Y.C., 1945-76, partner, 1954-70, limited partner, 1970-75, mem. adv. council, 1975-76; dir. Bridgeport Hydraulic Co. Mem. finance com. Town of Newtown (Conn.), from 1958. Served with U.S. Army, 1918. Mem. Alpha Delta Phi, Tau Beta Pi. Episcopalian. Clubs: University, Recess, Bond (N.Y.C.), Mount Royal (Can.). Home: Newtown, Conn. Died Mar. 11, 1976.

VON BECKERATH, HERBERT (VON-BEK'ER-ËTH), univ. prof.; b. Crefeld, Germany, Apr. 4, 1886; s. Alvin Heinrich and Maria Hedwig (von der Leyen) von B.; student univs. of Freiburg, Berlin, and Bonn, Germany; Ph.D., 1911; m. Guelda Hillyard Elliott, July 17, 1937. Came to U.S., 1934; citizen since 1939. Economist with trade assns., Germany, 1912-13; instr. in economics, U. of Freiburg, 1914-15; with German army, 1915-16; mgr. German Nat. Silk Assn., 1916-19; instr. U. of Freiburg, 1919-20, prof. Tech. High Sch., Karlsruhe, 1920-21, Tubingen U., 1921-25, U. of Bonn, 1925-34; guest prof., Bowdoin Coll., 1934-35; prof. economics, joint appointment, Duke U. and Univ. of N.C., 1935-38; prof. econ. and polit. science, Duke U., since 1938. Mem. Am. Econ. Assn., Southern Econ. Assn. Protestant. Author: Modern Industrial Organization, 1931; In Defense of the West 1942. Author and editor of several books pub. in Germany. Contbr. articles to jours. and scientific periodicals. Home: Durham, N.C.*

VON BERGEN, HERBERT, beet sugar mfr.; b. Humphrey, Neb., Feb. 18, 1902; s. Albert and Louise (Schmidt) Von B.; student pub. schs., Neb.; m. Helen Winifred Looman, June 2, 1945; 1 dau., Gail Ann. With American Crystal Sugar Co., from 1925 beginning as clk., Grand Island Neb., successively storekeeper, chief clk., various depts. accounting and treasury offices, Denver, dir. purchases, asst. sec. and asst. treas., sec. and treas., v.p., sec. and treas., 1925-55, exec. v.p., 1955, pres., from 1956, also mem. exec. com., dir.; mem. adv. bd. Denver U.S. Nat. Bank. Mem. adv. council Jr. Achievement Met. Denver, Inc.; bd. dirs., Goodwill Industries, Denver, exec. com. Central City Opera House Assn., Denver; bd. dirs. Denver Symphony Soc.; adv. panel Denver Research Inst., U. Denver; trustee Denver Bot. Gardens. Mem. Sugar Assn. N.Y. (dir.), U.S. Beet Sugar Assn. (trustee), C. of C. (past dir.), Episcopalian. Clubs: Brown Palace, Denver Country, Mile High (Denver), Home: Denver, Colo. Died 1978.

VON BRAUN, WERNHER, engr.; b. Wirsitz, Eastern Germany, Mar. 23, 1912; s. Baron Magnus and Emmy (von Quistorp) Von B.; student Inst. Tech., Zurich, Switzerland, 1930; B.S., Inst. Tech., Berlin, 1932; Ph.D., U. Berlin, 1934; D.Sc., U. Ala., St. Louis U., U. Pitts., Canisius Coll., Clark U., Tech. U., Berlin, Nat. U., Cordoba, Argentina, Iowa Wesleyan Coll., Fla. Inst. Tech., Wagner Coll., Emory U., Butler U., Bradley U., U. S.D., Rollins Coll.; LL.D., U. Chattanooga, Pepperdine U., Pa. Mil. Coll., Adelphi Coll., Iona Coll., William Jewell Coll., Notre Dame U., m. Maria Von Quistorp, Mar. 1, 1947; children—Iris, Margrit, Peter. Came to U.S., 1945, naturalized, 1955. Asst. to Prof. Oberth, 1930, experimenting with small liquid fuel rocket motors, Berlin-Ploetzensee; founding mem. Rocket Field Berlin, small rocket exptl. sta., sponsored and financed by German Rocket Soc., 1930; liquid fuel rocket expert German Ordnance Dept., Kummersdorf, 1932-37; tech. dir. German Rocket Research Center, Peenemuende, Baltic Sea, 1937-45; responsible for devel. of V-2 Long Range Rocket and A.A. Guided Missile Wasserfall, 1937-45; with U.S. Dept. Def., Ordance Dept., as tech. adviser to White Sands Proving Grounds, also proj. dir. Ft. Bliss, Tex., 1945-50; chief Guided Missile Devel. Div., Redstone Arsenal, Huntsville, Ala., 1950-56; dir. Devel. Operations Div., Army Ballistic Missile Agy., Huntsville, 1956-60, dir. George C. Marshall Space Flight Center, NASA, 1960-70, responsible for devel. Saturn V rockets, Apollo lunar landing program and Skylab space sta., dep. asso. adminstr., Washington, 1970-72; v.p. engring. and devel. Fairchild Industries, 1972-77. Chmn. internat. sponsor com. Robert Goddard Library Program, Clark U. 1965-77; pres. Nat. Space Inst., Washington Recipient Distinguished Civilian Service award Dept. Def., 1957, Dr. Robert Goddard Meml. Trophy, 1958; award Aerospace Elec. Soc. and Am. Astron. Soc., 1965; Louis W. Hill Space Transp. award, 1965; Langley medal Smithsonian Instn., 1967; Man of of Year award ASME, 1967; numerous others. Fellow Brit. Interplanetary Soc. (hon.), AIAA, Am. Astron. Soc., Ind. Inst. Tech.; hon. mem. Norwegian Interplanetary Soc., Gesellschaft fuer Raketentechnik und Raumfahrt (Munich, Germany), Hermann Oberth Soc., Hellenic Astron. Soc.; mem. Rocket City Astron. Assn. (pres.), Internat. Acad. Astronautics (hon.), Nat. Acad. Engring., hon. mem. Tau Beta Pi, Pi Mu Epsilon, others. Author: The Mars Project, 1953; co-author: Physics and Medicine of the Upper Atmosphere, 1952; Space Medicine, 1952; Across the Space Frontier, 1952; Conquest of the Moon, 1953; The Exploration of Mars, 1956; Project Satellite, 1958; First Men to the Moon, 1960; A Journey Through Space and the Atom, 1962; History of Rocketry and Space Travel, 1967, rev. edit., 1973, 75; Space Frontier, 1967, rev. edit., 1971. Contbr. articles in field. Club: Explorer (N.Y.C.). Home: Alexandria, Va. Died June 16, 1977.

VON CANON, FRED, furniture mfr.; b. Troy, N.C., Apr. 16, 1903; s. James Bobbett and Amanda (Tysinger) Von C.; student Duke, 1921-24, Columbia, 1925-27; m. Mary Elizabeth Hogwood, Jan. 5, 1930; 1 son, Charles Alfred. Founder Sandhill Furniture Corp., West End, N.C., 1927, chmn. bd., 1943-64; founder Edinburg Industries, Inc., Washington, N.C., 1933, pres, to 1979; founder Sanford Furniture Co (N.C.), 1938, chmn., pres., until 1968; dir. Nat. Bank Sanford, Mem. nat. council Duke, 1949-55, exec. com., 1949-58, vice chmn., 1958-59, chmn., 1959, trustee, 1959-75, trustee emeritus, 1975-79, chmn. adv. com., 1960, chmn. bldg. and grounds com., 1965-75, mem. exec. com., 1965-75. Recipient U.S. Navy Certificate Achievement, World War II. Mem. So. Furniture Mfg. Assn. (dir.), Duke Alumni Assn. (pres. 1961-62), Sanford C. of C. (1st v.p. and dir. 1962), Omicron Delta Kappa (hon.). Episcopalian (sr. warden). Pioneer in devel. successful process to kiln dry black gum for use as cabinet wood. Home: Sanford, N.C. Died Dec. 9, 1979.

VON ERFFA, HELMUT HARTMANN, artist, educator; b. Lueneburg, Germany, Mar. 1, 1900; s. Gotthard Freiherr and Mathilde Frelin (von Künssberg) von E.; A.B., Harvard, 1931, M.A., 1933; M.F.A., Princeton, 1938; m. Eleanor Follansbee, July 25, 1931; children—Constance (dec.), Julie. Came to U.S., 1923, naturalized, 1938. Tutor, asst. dept. fine arts Harvard, 1930-33; research asst. Met. Museum of Art, 1934-35; lectr. Bryn Mawr Coll., 1935-36; instr. Northwestern U., 1938-43; asst. prof., chmn. dept. art Swarthmore Coll., 1943-46; asst. prof. Rutgers U., 1946-49, asso. prof., 1949-57, prof., 1957-64, prof. emeritus, 1964-79, chmn. dept., 1946-60; vis. prof. art U. N.Mex., Albuquerque, 1964-66; exhibited in group shows New Brunswick, N.J., 1970, Artisan Gallery, Princeton, N.J., 1970-75, Rutgers Mus., 1975, Bauhaus Archive, Berlin, 1976; one-man show Franklin, N.J., 1976; represented in permanent collections Rutgers U., Detroit Inst. Art, Seattle Mus. Art, Bauhaus Archive. Mem. Coll. Art Assn., Mus. Modern Art, Am. Archeol. Soc. Author catalog of the works of Benjamin West; author articles in field. Home: Piscataway, N.J. Died Feb. 17, 1979; buried Ahorn, West Germany.

VON ESCHEN, CLARENCE RAYMOND, educator; b. Shelby, Ia., July 21, 1904; s. Aaron Adolph and Jeannie (Smith) Von E.; A.B., Coe Coll., 1928; A.M., U. Ia., 1936; Ph.D., U. Wis., 1940; m. Charlotte Martha Kellogg, Aug. 1, 1929; 1 son, Donald Dean. High sch. prin., Lanesboro, Ia., 1925-27; supt. schs., Palmer, Ia., 1928-33, Ruthven, Ia., 1933-38; research asst. U. Wis., 1938-40, lectr. edn., summer 1948; mem. faculty Beloit (Wis.) Coll., from 1940, prof. edn. and chmn. dept., 1944-70, prof. edn., dir. tchr. placement chmn. Div. of Behavioral Sci., 1955-59, 62-64, vis. prof. edn., 1971-72; dean Beloit Community Coll., 1949-50; dir. Beloit Coll. Summer Sch., 1950-60; cons. ednl. instns. and orgns. Vis. prof. edn. U. So. Cal., 1970-71. Mem. Wis. Dept. Pub. Instrn. Com. on Proficiency Exams., from 1959; mem. NSF Inst. Panels, 1959-62, Mem. Bd. Edn., Beloit, 1947-50, v.p., 1948-50; staff mem. U. Wis. No. Nigeria Tchr. Edn. Project. Chmn. com. for self study Ford Found., 1953; mem. exec. com. Wis. Improvement Program. Mem. Nat. Instnl. Tchr. Placement Assn., N.E.A., Am. Assn. U. Profs., Am. Assn. Sch. Adminstrs., Nat. Assn. Coll. Tchrs. Edn., Wis. Edn. Assn. (chmn. tchr. edn. sect., 1955-56), Am. Edn. Research Assn., Midwest Collegiate Athletic Conf. (pres. 1963-64), Nat. Collegiate Athletic Assn., Am. Assn. Colls. for Tchr. Edn. (subcom. acad. and faund. discipline), Sigma Alpha Epsilon, Phi Delta Kappa, Omicron Delta Kappa. Rotarian. Author: The Measurement of Teaching Ability (with A.S. Barr), 1946. Home: Beloit, Wis. Died Oct. 11, 1976.

VON FRISCH, KARL, zoologist; b. Vienna, Austria, Nov. 20, 1886; s. Anton Ritter and Marie (Exner) von F.; several years of pvt. tutoring at home; attended a convent sch. of Piarist Fathers and Schottengymnasium, a Benedictine secondary sch., Vienna; Dr. Phil., U. Vienna, 1910; Dr. honoris causa, U. Bern (Switzerland), 1949, Eidgenossiche Technische Hochschule, Zurich, Switzerland, 1955, U. Graz (Austria), 1957, Harvard, 1963, Tubingen (Germany) U., 1964, U. Rostock (East Germany), 1969; m. Margarethe Mohr, July 20, 1917; children—Johanna (Mrs. Theodor Schreiner), Maria, Helen (Mrs. Eckehard Pfluger), Otto. Mem. faculty U. Munich (Germany), 1912-21, 25-46, 50-58; prof. zoology U. Rostock, 1921-23, U. Breslau (Poland), 1923-25, U. Graz, 1946-50. Recipient Magellanic prize Am. Philos. Soc., 1956, Kalinga prize for popularization of sci. UNESCO, 1959, Balzan prize for biology, 1963, Nobel prize for physiology or medicine (shared with Konrad Lorenz and Nikolaas Tinbergen) recognizing maj. contbns. to relatively new sci. sociobiology, 1973; Orden pour le merite fur Wissenschaften und Kunste, 1952. Mem. Royal Entomol. Soc. London (Eng.), Royal Soc., acads. sci. Washington, Stockholm (Sweden), Vienna, Munich, Copenhagen (Denmark), Uppsala (Sweden), Helsinki (Finland), Boston, Gottingen (Germany). Author: Aus dem Leben der Bienen, 1927; Du und das Leben, 1936; Bees, 1954; The Dancing Bees, 1954; Man and the Living World, 1963; The Dance Language and Orientation of Bees, 1967; A Biologist Remembers, 1967. Contbr. numerous articles to profl. jours. Research in lang. of bees, color sense in bees and fish, sense of smell and taste in bees, hearing in fish, perception of polarized light in bees. Address: Munich Federal Republic of Germany *

VON GONTARD, ADALBERT, executive; b. Hagen, Germany, July 20, 1900; s. Paul and Clara Hazel (Busch) von G.; came to U.S., 1923, naturalized, 1928; M.A. in Engring., Mech. Inst. Tech., Karlsruhe, Germany, 1922, Dr. Engring., 1938; m. Susanne Schilling von Constatt, July 31, 1924; children—Adalbert Etienne, Paul Victor, Clara Hazel. Asst. tech. engr., Anheuser-Busch, Inc., St. Louis, 1923-26, became chief engr., 1926, v.p., dir., from 1934, ret. as vice chmn. bd. and chmn. exec. com., 1955, now dir.; chmn. St. Louis & O'Fallen Coal Co., since 1936; 1st vice pres. and dir. Adolphus Hotel, Dallas, Tex., from 1926. Serving as lt. (s.g.), U.S.N.R., from 1942; on inactive duty for duration and 6 mos. thereafter, since Sept. 1944. Deputy sheriff of St. Louis County, from 1928; chief of police, Huntleigh Village, Mo., 1929-41; dir. St. Louis County Chamber of Commerce, 1930-42. Mem. Am. Soc. M.E., Soc. Am. Mil. Engrs. Lutheran. Clubs: Racquet (St. Louis); Bridlespur (Huntleigh Village, Mo.). Home: St. Louis, Mo. Died Apr. 30, 1976; buried Karlsruhe, Germany.

VON HEIMBURG, ERNEST H(ERMAN), naval officer; b. Cecil, Wis., June 19, 1896; s. Anno and Emma (Naber) von H.; student Univ. of Wis., Sept. 1914-Feb. 1915; B.S., U.S. Naval Acad., 1919; grad. Naval War Coll., 1931; m. Eleanor Phelps Glassford, May 6, 1931; children—Gretchen, Martha. Commd., ensign, U.S. Navy, June 6, 1918, and advanced through grades to rear admiral, Dec. 31, 1946. Served in World War I and II. Entire service afloat in destroyer, cruiser and staff duty; participated invasion of Salerno and Normandy, World War II and final phase of war against Japan; commanded cruiser div. eight, U.S. Atlantic Fleet, U.S.S. Manchester, Flagship; comdr. amphibious group 2, Atlantic Fleet, 1947; chief U.S. Naval Mission to Brazil, 1949-52; comdr. training command U.S. Atlantic Fleet, 1952-53; comdt. 4th Naval Dist., Naval-Base, Phila., 1953-56; comdr. Naval Reserve Tng. Command, Omaha, from 1956. Recipient Legion of Merit and 2 stars. B.S.M. with Combat V. Naval Order of Merit; Grand Officer, Brazil. Croix de Guerre (France). Clubs: Omaha; New York Yacht; Army-Navy Country. Address: Omaha, Nebr. Died June 18, 1976.

VON KIENBUSCH, CARL OTTO, civic leader; b. N.Y.C., Nov. 21, 1884; s. Gustav Carl and Clara Honora (Spitzner) von K.; B.A., Princeton, 1906, M.A. (hon.), 1952; L.H.D. (hon.), Wagner Coll., 1964; m. Mildred Clarke, Jan. 4, 1912 (dec. 1968); children—William Austin, Mildred (Mrs. Bayne Kelley), Juliana Patience (Mrs. John Watson Little II). With C. H. Spitzner & Son, Inc., wholesale leaf tobaccos, 1906-48, treas. 1921-48; propr. Badger State Tobacco Co. of Wis., also C. O. Kienbusch 1948-64; v.p. S. Ruppin, Inc., tobacco importers. Fellow Morgan Library, N.Y.C. Trustee Lenox Hill Hosp. Served from 1st lt. to capt. Ordnance Engrs., U.S. Army, 1918-19. Mem. N.Y. Leaf Tobacco Bd. of Trade (past pres.), U.S. C. of C., New York Historical Soc. (trustee). Lutheran. Clubs: The Union, Armor and Arms, Century Assn., Grolier, Downtown Assn., Union (N.Y.C.). Owner largest collection of ancient armor and arms in U.S. Home: New York, N.Y. Died Feb. 23, 1976.

VON KOERBER, HANS NORDEWIN FREIHERR (FON-KUR'-BER), prof. Asiatic studies; b. Treptow, Toll, Germany, July 23, 1886; s. Friedrich Theodor Joachim and Helene Elise (von Otto) von K.; grad. Orientalisches Seminar, U. of Berlin, 1905; student univs. of Bonn, Marburg and Cambridge; Ph.D., Marburg, 1920; m. Margarete Elisabeth (Brandenburg) von Boetticher, Nov. 13, 1922; 3 stepchildren. Came to U.S., 1928, naturalized, 1937. Ethnographical expdn. Central Africa, 1905-07, linguistic research Central and South Africa, 1907-08; research Siberia, Central Asia,

West China, Tibet, 1909-10, 1912-14, British India, 1914-20, Dutch Indies, 1921-22; lecturer Oriental linguistics, Godesberg Bonn, 1911-12, Marburg U., 1920-21; lecturer in comparative religion, Stralsund, Germany, 1923-24, U. of Amoy, China, 1924-25; prof. of Oriental linguistics, U. of Philippines, 1926-28; dir. Foundation of Asiatic Studies, 1930-40, prof. Asiatic studies, U. of So. Calif. since 1928; asso. in Oriental Culture, Los Angeles Museum History, Sciences and Art, since 1930; counselor to Chinese Consulate at Los Angeles, 1933-41. Mem. China Soc. of Southern Calif., Am. Oriental Soc., Royal Asiatic Soc. Great Britain and Ireland, Andhra Research Univ. of India, College Héraldique de France (corr.), Phi Beta Kappa (hon.), Pi Epsilon Theta, Alpha Pi Zeta, Mu Alpha Nu, Phi Alpha Theta, Delta Phi Alpha. Club: University (Los Angeles). Author: books relating to field; also articles and booklets on philology and philosophy; compiler and translator of Chinese, Japanese and German sects. in Lanz, Aviation Dictionary, 1944. Home: Redondo Beach, Calif. *

VON STORCH, SEARLE HENRY, architect; b. Scranton, Pa., Jan. 3, 1899; s. Charles Henry and Carrie (Mott) von S.; student U. Pa., 1917-20; B. Arch., Cornell, 1923; m. Helen Colegrove Nichols, May 2, 1925; children—Searle Kilmer, Gretchen (Mrs. Gordon Allen), Peter. Partner firm Morgan & von Storch, 1925-30; pvt. practice, 1930-45; partner von Storch & Pearce, 1945-50, von Storch & Burkavage, 1950-70; archtl. cons., 1970-76; projects include univ. and coll. bldgs., secondary schs., hosps., projects in radar communications and tracking for NASA, projects for armed services, also instnl. and indsl. bldgs. Served with USNR Force, World War I. Fellow AIA (v.p. 1947-48); mem. Pa. Assn. Architects (pres. 1942-45). Gargoyle Archtl. Soc., Delta Tau Delta, Rotarian. Republican. Presbyn. Home: Waverly, Pa. Died Mar. 6, 1976.

VON TRESS, EDWARD CAMPBELL, found. exec.; b. Monroe City, Ind., Sept. 4, 1899; s. Edward C. and Sada (Falls) Von T.; A.B., Ind. U., 1921; m. Elizabeth Smith, Mar. 14, 1927 (dec. May 1967); children—David E., Kathleen; m. 2d, Zelia Zigler McElroy, Nov. 3, 1969. Advt. mgr. Showers Bros. Co., Bloomington, Ind., 1921-22; sales mgr. Capitol Radio Supply Co., Indpls., 1923-24; alumni sec., editor alumni mags. Ind. U., 1924-26; travel advt. mgr. Chgo. Herald and Examiner, 1927-29; advt. solicitor Curtis Pub. Co., Chgo., 1929-44; chief mag. sect. W.P.B., 1944, dep. dir. printing and pub. div., 1945; sales mgr. Holiday mag., 1946-47, mgr., 1948-54, v.p. Phila., 1954-57, sr. v.p., 1957-63, dir. advt. Curtis Pub. Co., 1954-62; exec. asso. for spl. projects Ind. U. Found., Bloomington, from 1963, nat. chmn. ann. giving program, 1960. Served as 2d lt. Inf., U.S. Army, 1918-19. Recipient Ind. U. Distinguished Alumni Service award, 1958; Zora Clevenger award for outstanding contbn. to athletic program Ind. U., 1974. Mem. Ind. U. Alumni Assn. (pres. 1951-52, treas. 1969-75), Phi Kappa Psi. Republican. Presbyn. Rotarian. Clubs: Bloomington Country; Columbia (Indpls.). Home: Bloomington, Ind. Died July 4, 1976.

VOORHEES, ENDERS MCCLUMPHA, steel exec.; b. Amsterdam, N.Y., Apr. 28, 1891; s. James and Margaret (McClumpha) V.; B.S., Dartmouth, 1914; student Amos Tuck Sch. of Finance, 1914, Bentley Sch. of Accounting (Boston), 1914-16; D.C.S. (hon.), N.Y. U., 1950; m. Blanche Pauline Andrews, Sept. 15, 1923, Jr. accountant Hollis H. Sawyer & Co., 1914-15; with Pacific Commercial Co., Manila, 1915-16; asst. comptroller U.S. Rubber Co., 1918-20; gen. auditor and asst. to pres., Ajax Rubber Co., 1921-25; with Sanderson & Porter & W.A. Harriman & Co., 1926-27; gen. auditor, later sec.-treas. and v.p., Johns-Manville Corp., 1927-37; vice chmn. finance com. U.S. Steel Corp., 1937-38, chmn. finance com., mem. exec. com., dir., 1938-56, dir., mem. finance and exec. coms., 1956-65. Served lt. 73d F.A., Camp Jackson, 1917-18. Mem. Holland Soc., St. Nicholas Soc. Clubs: Links, Dartmouth, Seminole, Jupiter Island. Home: New York, N.Y. Died Apr. 12, 1980.

VOORHEES, TRACY S., lawyer; b. New Brunswick, N.J., June 30, 1890; s. John Schenck and Mary Hinman (Stebbins) V.; A.B., Rutgers U., 1911, A.M., 1914, LL.D., 1950; LL.B., Columbia Law Sch., 1915; m. Josephine Ludlow Palmer, Dec. 19, 1918; children—Mrs. Mary Van Wilson, John Schenck. Admitted to N.J. bar, 1915, N.Y. bar, 1918; asso. firm Satterlee, Canfield & Stone, N.Y., 1917; asst. to dir. Bur. of Imports, War Trade Bd., 1918; mem. firms Ewing, Alley & Voorhees and Ewing & Voorhees, 1919-28; mem. firm Blake & Voorhees 1929-42; spl. asst. to sec. war, 1946-47; Dept. War food adminstr. for occupied areas, 1947-48; asst. sec. army, 1948-49, under-sec., 1949-50; vice chmn. com. on present danger, 1951-53; L.I. Transit Authority, 1951-54; def. adv. to U.S. Mission to NATO with rank of minister and dir. offshore procurement in Europe for sec. of def., 1953-54; cons. to sec. of def., 1954-61; Pres.'s rep. Hungarian refugee affairs and chmn. Pres.'s Com. for Hungarian Refugee Relief, 1956-57; Pres.'s personal rep. for Cuban Refugees, 1960-61. Bd. regents L.I. Coll. Hosp., Bklyn., 1932-48, pres. bd., 1938-43, and 1945-48; trustee Rutgers U., 1942-43, 1947-74, bd. govs., 1957-65, vice chmn., 1959-65. Served as col. AUS, 1942-46. Recipient Rutgers U. award, 1941; Park Assn. (N.Y. City), Citation of Merit, 1942; D.S.M. (Army), 1946; Dept. Army Distinguished Civilian Service award, 1959; Dept. Def. award for Distinguished Pub. Service, 1960; Alumni Trustee award Rutgers U., 1971; papers in spl. collections dept. Rutgers U. Library; section of Rutgers U. Queens Campus designated Voorhees Campus, 1974. Mem. Beta Theta Pi, Phi Beta Kappa. Author: A Lawyer Among Army Doctors. Home: Brooklyn, N.Y. Died Sept. 25, 1974; interred Elm Ridge Cemetery, North Brunswick, N.J.

VOOYS, DANIEL WILLIAM, banker; b. Canajoharie, N.Y., July 22, 1914; s. Daniel Joseph and Matilda Patricia (Harlow) V.; grad. in accounting and finance, Bentley Coll., 1935; m. Grace Ellen Edick, Mar. 21, 1941; children—Daniel F., James D. With Nat. Spraker Bank, Canajoharie, 1936-40; asst. nat. bank examiner U.S. Treasury Dept., 1940-41, 46; auditor Central Nat. Bank, Canajoharie, 1947-49, asst. v.p., 1949-55, v.p., trust officer, 1955-57, pres., 1964-70, dir., 1964-71; v.p., cashier First Nat. Bank, Jamestown, N.Y., 1957-63, sr. v.p., cashier, 1963-64, dir., 1960-64; pres., chief exec. officer, dir. Bank of N.Y. at Albany (formerly Mechanics and Farmers Bank), Albany, 1970-74, chmn., chief exec. officer, 1974-78; dir. N.Y. Bus. Devel. Corp., 1967-70, treas., 1970-78. Co-founder, bd. dirs. Am. Philatelic Research Library, 1969-78, treas., 1969-71, v.p., 1973-75, pres., 1975-78; mem. philatelic adv. panel Am. Revolution Bicentennial Commn., 1971-74. Served to capt. AUS, 1941-45. Mem. Am. Philatelic Soc. (award 1956, dir. 1965-78, treas. 1965-69, pres. 1969-73), Fedn. Internationale de Philatelie (exec. com. 1969-72, dir. 1972—), Philatelic Lit. Assn. (founder 1942, editor Rev. 1942-56, 63-70, sec. 1963-70). Home: Albany, N.Y. Died Sept. 23, 1978; interred Canojoharie Falls Cemetery, Canojoharie, N.Y.

VORIS, HAROLD CORNELIUS, neurol. surgeon; b. Pleasant, Ind., Apr. 18, 1902; s. Cornelius and Molly (Vandever) V.; A.B., Hanover Coll., 1923, D.Sc., 1945; Ph.D., U. Chgo., 1929; M.D., Rush Med. Coll., 1930; M.S., U. Minn., 1934; m. Ila Knight, June 27, 1931; children—Elizabeth (Mrs. John Phillips), Judith Belle (Mrs. John Reppy), Mary Belle (Mrs. William Chen), Harold Knight. Intern Cook County Hosp., Chgo., 1930-31; fellow neurol. surgery Mayo Found., Mayo Clinic, Rochester, Minn., 1931-34; practice medicine specializing in neurol. surgery, Chgo., 1934-80; head sect. neurosurgery Mercy Hosp., 1934-72, cons., 1972-75; cons. neurosurgery Hines VA Hosp., 1954-67, 75-80; part time staff physician, chief neurosurgery 1967-75; cons. Presbyn.-St. Luke's Hosp., 1972-75; vol. attending surgeon Cook County Hosp., 1937-50, 75-80; clin. prof. neurol. surgery Stritch Sch. Medicine Loyola U., Chgo., 1936-64; clin. prof. neurol. surgery Med. Sch. U. Ill., Chgo., 1964-73, emeritus, 1973-80; emeritus prof. neurol. surgery Rush Med. Coll., 1972-80. Trustee Hanover Coll., 1956-75. Named Alumnus of Year Hanover Coll., 1956. Mem. AMA, Ill. Med. Soc., Chgo. Surg. Soc., A.C.S., Internat. Coll. Surgeons, Am. Assn. for Surgery Trauma, Chgo. Neurol. Soc., Assn. for Research Nervous and Mental Diseases, Am. Neurol. Assn., Soc. Neurol. Surgeons, Am. Assn. Neurol. Surgeons, Congress Neurol. Surgeons, Internat. Soc. for Research in Stereoencephalotomy, Sigma Xi, Alpha Omega Alpha, Beta Theta Pi, Phi Beta Pi. Contbr. articles to profl. jours. Home: Chicago, Ill. Died Mar. 13, 1980.

VORWALD, ARTHUR JOHN, physician, educator; b. Dubuque, Ia., Apr. 12, 1904; s. Dr. Theodore Francis and Rose (Wilkey) V.; B.A., Columbia Coll., Dubuque, Ia., 1925; M.D., U. Chgo., 1931, Ph.D. in Pathology, 1932, D.Sc. (hon.), Hobart and William Smith Colls., 1949; LL.D., Loras Coll., Dubuque, 1950; m. Madeleine Foeller, June 22, 1931. Asst. pathology U. Chgo., 1928-31, instr. pathology, 1931-32; intern Presbyn. Hosp., Chgo., 1932, Henry Ford Hosp., Detroit, 1932-33; fellow NRC, Cambridge U., Eng., 1933-34; lectr. and pathologist Trudeau Sch., 1934-42; dir. Edward L. Trudeau Found. and Saranac Lab., Saranac Lake, N.Y., 1947-54, dir. silicosis and beryllium symposia Saranac Lab., 1947-54; pathologist Trudeau (N.Y.) Sanatorium, 1934-42; pathologist active staff Gen. Hosp., Saranac Lake, 1947-54; asso. dept. pathology U. Rochester Med. Sch., 1936-42, 47-54; postgrad. Meml. Hosp., N.Y.C., 1938, Mallory Inst., Boston, 1939; asso. clin. prof. indsl. medicine N.Y. U. Postgrad. Med. Sch., 1949-54; prof., chmn. dept. occupational, environmental health Coll. Medicine, Wayne State U., 1954-72, prof. emeritus, 1972-74, dir. Summer Inst. Radiation Biology High Sch. Sci. Tchrs., AEC and Nat. Sci. Found., 1957-60. Served from lt. comdr. to capt. M.C., USNR, 1942-47. Recipient Howard Taylor Ricketts award bacteriology and pathology U. Chicago, 1930, distinguished service award U. of Chicago Medical Alumni, 1957; citation for excellence in medical authorship Indsl. Med. Assn., 1951; ann. award of honor, Am. Acad. Occupational Med., 1961; award Am. Cancer Soc., 1963. Diplomate Am. Bd. Clin. Pathology, Pathol. Anatomy, Am. Bd. Occupational Medicine. Fellow A.A.A.S., Am. Assn. Thoracic Surgery, Am. Coll. Chest Physicians, A.M.A., Indsl. Med. Assn., Royal Soc. Health, Am. Coll. Preventive Medicine; mem. Coll. Am. Pathologists, A.C.P., Am. Coll. Preventive Medicine, Royal Soc. Med. of Eng.; hon. mem. European and S.A. Med. and Tb Socs., Franklin County Med. Soc. (pres. 1938-39), Saranac Lake Med. Soc. N.Y. (pres. 1941-42), Pan Am. Med. Assn., Mich. and Detroit Med. Socs., Am. Assn. Pathologists and Bacteriologists, Am. Indsl. Hygiene Assn., Am. Pub. Health Assn., Am. Soc. Exptl. Pathology, Am. Thoracic Soc., Assn. Mil. Surgeons U.S., Nat. Tb Assn., N.Y. Acad. Medicine, Soc. Exptl. Biology and Medicine, Soc. Med. Jurisprudence, Am. Assn. Cancer Research, Internat. Assn. on Occupational Health (mem. permanent commn.), Am. Acad. Occupational Medicine, Internat. Acad. Pathology, Ramazzini Soc., Sigma Xi, Phi Beta Kappa. Clubs: Army-Navy, Cosmos (Washington); Oneida (Green Bay, Wis.). Contbr. med. articles profl. jours. Home: Green Bay, Wis. Died Nov. 29, 1974; buried Allouez Cemetery, Green Bay.

VRUWINK, HENRY ANDREW (VROO'WINK), clergyman; b. Grand Rapids, Mich., Apr. 29, 1886; s. Gerrit John and Minne (De Kraker) V.; student Hope Prep. School, Holland, Michigan, 1902-06, A.B., Hope College, 1910, M.A., 1913, D.D., 1942; student New Brunswick (N.J.) Theological Seminary, 1910-13; m. Jennie Pikaart, June 11, 1913; children—Ruth Elizabeth, Rev. John Henry, Lois Harriet. Ordained to ministry Reformed Church in America, 1913; missionary to Indians, 1913-17; pastor Second Church, Grand Haven, Mich., 1917-23, Herkimer Ch., Herkimer, N.Y., 1923-26, Madison Av. Ch., Albany, N.Y., 1926-37, Collegiate Ch. of New York in charge Ft. Washington Ch., 1938-46; Flatbush Reformed Ch., Brooklyn, since 1946; pres. General Synod Reformed Ch. in Am., 1950-51. Mason. Writer of religious pamphlets. Home: Brooklyn, N.Y. *

WAASDORP, LEONARD A(DRIAN), architect; b. Zaandam, Netherlands, Aug. 20, 1886; student Mus. Fine Arts, Utecht, Holland, 1904-05, Rochester Inst. Tech., 1907-08; m. 1911. Formerly with Kaelber & Waasdorp; with Waasdorp & Northrup, 1951-59; with Waasdorp, Northrup & Austin, Rochester, N.Y., 1959—; principal works include U. Rochester Hospital bldgs., med. sch., Atomic Energy Bldg. and Labs. U. Rochester, YWCA, Rochester. Recipient certificate of merit Rochester Soc. Architects. Fellow A.I.A. (v.p. central N.Y. chpt. 1942-43, pres. 1944-45); mem. Rochester C. of C. (pres. 1935-36), Rochester Engring. Soc. (pres. 1940-41). Clubs: Rotary, Commercial. Home: Rochester. *

WADE, EDWIN CARTER, real estate broker; born Farmville, Virginia, August 29, 1885; the son of Edwin George and Jane Cary (Vaughan) W.; Bachelor of Arts, Hampden-Sydney College, 1907; A.M., Columbia, 1912; m. Ernestine Barger, Oct. 11, 1922; children—Edwin Carter, Daisy Caldwell. Prin. Boydton (Va.) High Sch., 1907-09; instr. in history, Hoboken (N.J.) Acad., 1911-12; headmaster, Cedarcroft Sch., Kennett Square, Pa., 1912-17; supt. of schs., Bluefield, W.Va., 1917-21, 1923-34, Florence, S.C., 1921-23; instr. Winthrop Coll., Rock Hill, S.C., 1922-23, Concord Coll., Athens, W.Va., 1927-28; pres. Bluefield Coll., 1934-46; pres. Andrew-Crowell Co., Community Realty Co., Easley-Wilson Co.; dir. Bank of Matoaka; v.p. Community Savings & Loan Co., First Federal Bldg. & Loan Co. Member of Mercer County Real Estate Board. Commr. to general assembly Presbyn. Ch. in U.S.A., 1926-45. Pres. West Virginia Soc. of Crippled Children, 1947-48; dir. National Society for Crippled Children, 1948-49; del. Rotary Internat. Inst., Quebec, 1948. Mem. adv. bd. Salvation Army, 1924—, chmn., 1940-41; mem. bd. dirs. Blufield chpt., A.R.C., 1930—, chmn., 1948-49; bd. trustees Davis and Elkins Coll. Certificate Distinguished Citizenship, Am. Legion, 1948. Mem. Bluefield Chamber of Commerce (treasurer 1954), N.E.A., Kappa Sigma, Omicron Delta Kappa, Pi Gamma Mu, S.A.R. (pres. W.Va., soc. 1935-38). Democrat. Presbyn. (elder). Elk. Clubs: Rotary (gov. 24th Dist. Rotary Internat. 1932-33), Executives (pres.), University. Address: Bluefield, W.Va. *

WADE, H(ERBERT) WINDSOR, leprologist; b. Haddonfield, N.J., Nov. 23, 1886; s. Herbert and Anna (Mann) W.; student McGill U., 1908-09; M.D., Tulane, 1912; m. Dorothy Paul, Dec. 22, 1915. Instr. in pathology and bacteriology, Tulane, 1912-15; resident pathologist Charity Hosp., New Orleans, 1913-15; pathologist and bacteriologist Bur. of Science, Manila, P.I., 1916-18; prof. pathology and bacteriology, U. of the Philippines, 1918-22; chief pathologist Culion Leper Colony, 1922-31, acting chief physician, 1922-24; med. dir. Leonard Wood Memorial for the Eradication of Leprosy. Mem. A.M.A., Philippines Med. Assn., Culion Med. Soc., Internat. Leprosy Assn. (pres. since 1946), Am. Assn. Pathol. and Bacteriologists, Am. Soc. Trop. Medicine, Far Eastern Assn. of Tropical Medicine, Royal Society of Trop. Medicine, Société Belge de Médicine Tropicale (corr. mem.), A.A.A.S., Beta Theta Pi. Nu Sigma Nu. Republican. Clubs: University, Army and Navy Polo (Manila). Author: (with J. N. Rodriquez) A Description of Leprosy, 1927. Specialist in leprosy; closely identified with expansion of antileprosy activity in the Philippines, and editor

Internat. Jour. of Leprosy. Address: Palawan, Philippines. *

WADE, HARRY VAN NUYS, ins. co. exec.; b. Lafayette, Ind., Apr. 8, 1902; s. Harry and Anna E. (Fullenwider) W.; B.Arch., Cornell U., 1927; m. Agnes Throop Lester, June 16, 1928; children—Elizabeth Wade Freiberger, Harry V., Douglas M. Architect, Shreve, Lamb & Harmon, N.Y.C., 1927-31; asst. to pres. United Mut. Life Ins. Co., 1931-36; v.p. charge operations Am. United Life Ins. Co., 1936-41; pres. Standard Life Ins. Co. of Ind., 1941-67, chmn. bd., 1962-79; dir. Gen. Grain, Acme Evans Milling Co., Early Daniel Grain Co., Tidewater Grain Corp.; pres. Advisers Fund Mgmt. Corp. Chmn., Indpls. Housing Authority, 1948-50. Trustee Hanover Coll.; bd. dirs. Indpls. Symphony Orch., Civic Theatre. Mem. Cornell U. Alumni Assn. (past nat. pres.), Sigma Chi (past nat. pres.). Clubs: Masons, Shriners. Home: Indianapolis, Ind. Died June 23, 1979; buried Crownhill Cemetery, Indpls.

WADE, JAMES WILLIAM, mining engr.; b. Apr. 26, 1882; s. Henry C. and Janet (Byram) W.; brought by parents to U.S., 1884; B.S. in mining, U. of Utah, 1905; m. Caroline Atkins, Jan. 11, 1911; children—Lorna, James Atkins. With Honerine Mining & Milling Co., 1905-07, Annie Laurie Gold Mining Co., 1907-09, Mammoth Mining Co., 1909-13; now cons. mining engr.; became v.p. and gen. mgr. Tintic Standard Mining Co., 1918, now pres.; pres. and dir. Eureka Standard Mining Co., Colo. Consol. Mining Co., etc. Served as capt., Engr. Corps, U.S. Army, 1918-19. Regent U. of Utah. Mem. Am. Inst. Mining and Metall. Engrs. (chmn. Utah sect.), Am. Mining Congress (gov. Utah chapter), Beta Theta Pi, Phi Kappa Phi. Republican. Mason (32 deg.). Clubs: University, Alta. Home: Salt Lake City. *

WAGMAN, NICHOLAS EMORY, astronomer; b. Saratoga Springs, N.Y., Feb. 22, 1905; s. Nicholas and Minnie L. (Potter) W.; A.B., Wesleyan U., 1927, A.M., 1928; Ph.D., U. Pitts., 1937; m. Maria L. Taylor, Sept. 19, 1928; children—Maria-Louise, Sarah, Nicholas E., Jr., Lewis T. Astronomer U.S. Naval Obs., Washington, 1928-30; astronomer Allegheny Obs., U. Pitts., 1930-74, acting dir., 1941-54, dir., 1954-70, dir. emeritus, 1974-80; asso. prof. U. Pitts., 1941-54, prof., 1954-70, emeritus, 1974-80. Lectr., Buhl Planetarium, Pitts., 1939-74. Fellow AAAS; mem. Am. Astron. Soc., Internat. Astron. Union, Sigma Xi. Presbyn. Contbr. research articles to astron. jours. Home: Pittsburgh, Pa. Died Aug. 28, 1980; interred Greenridge Cemetery, Saratoga Springs, N.Y.

WAGNER, HERMAN BLOCK, educator; b. Balt., Dec. 25, 1923; s. Henry N. and Gertrude L. (Loane) W.; B.E., Johns Hopkins, 1944, M.A., 1946, Ph.D., 1948; m. Mary Louise Hagel, June 5, 1946. Asst. prof. chemistry Loyola Coll. at Balt., 1949-50; research chemist E.I. duPont Co., Phila., 1950-55; asso. research prof. Rutgers U., 1955-57; dir. chem. research TCA Research Center, Princeton, 1957-61; prof. chemistry Drexel U., Phila., from 1961; cons. Dow Chem. Co., TCA Research Center. Recipient research grants NSF, 1964-65, Dupont Co., 1962-64, Dow Chem. Co., 1963-77, Glycerin Research award for 1958; Tile Council Am. Herbert B. Wagner scholarship named in his honor, Drexel U., 1979. Mem. Am. Chem. Soc., A.A.A.S., Am. Inst. Chemists, Sigma Xi, Phi Lambda Upsilon. Patentee in field. Home: Perkasie, Pa. Died Oct. 16, 1979; buried Our Lady of the Sacred Heart Cemetery, Hilltown, Pa.

WAGNER, MYRON LEROY, educator, chemist; b. Oak Park, Ill., Nov. 11, 1923; s. Otto G. and Amy (Schultz) W.; A.B., Carthage Coll., 1948; M.S., State U. Ia., 1952, Ph.D., 1954; m. Adelaide Wagner, Dec. 21, 1947; children—Judith Ann, Amy Marie, Mark Myron. Postdoctoral research asso. Cornell U., 1954-56; instr. State U. Ia., 1956-57; mem. faculty U. Mo. at Kansas City, 1957-75, prof. chemistry, 1964-75, chmn. dept., 1960-71. Served with AUS, 1943-45. Mem. Am. Chem. Soc. (chmn. Kansas City sect. 1964), Sigma Xi. Contbr. profl. jours. Home: Kansas City, Mo. Died Mar. 3, 1975.

WAHL, HARRY ROSWELL (WAWL), pathology; b. Minnesota City, Minn., May 5, 1886; s. Henry and Clara (Waterman) W.; B.A., U. of Wis., M.A., 1910; M.D., Johns Hopkins, 1912; studied Western Reserve University Med. Sch. and University of Kansas; married Elizabeth Emery, Apr. 1, 1916; children—Marjorie, Nancy, Roswell; married 2d, Katharine Bell, June 15, 1940; 1 son, John Rupert. Served as Hanna research fellow and as instructor in pathology, Western Reserve University; with Med. Corps 19 mos., World War I; instr. in Yale Army Lab.; now prof. pathology, U. of Kan. Sch. of Medicine, dean 1924-48; pathologist U. of Kan. Hosps., Kansas City, Kan. Mem. A.M.A., Am. Assn. Pathologists and Bacteriologists, Alpha Omega Alpha. Member Unitarian Church. Mason. Clubs: Rotary (Kansas City, Kan.), University (Lawrence, Kan.). Home: Kansas City, Mo. *

WAHLSTROM, ERIC HERBERT, clergyman; b. Töreboda, Sweden, Mar. 28, 1892; s. John Eric and Augusta (Olson) W.; came to U.S., 1910, naturalized, 1924; A.B., Augustana Coll., Rock Island, Ill., 1919, B.D., Augustana Sem., 1924; student Yale, 1924-25, U. Chgo., summers 1932-36, Union Theol. Sem., 1936; D.D. Gustavus Adolphus Coll., 1944; m. Ruth Johnson, Aug. 22, 1925; children—Erica, Carl David. Teacher, Luther Coll., Wahoo, Neb., 1919-21; ordained to ministry of the Luth. Ch., 1924; pastor Meriden, Conn., 1924-25; missionary in China, 1925-27; pastor Warren, Ore., 1927-31; prof. New Testament Language and Literature, Augustana Theol. Sem., 1931-61, acting dean, 1944-48, v.p., 1949-60; guest prof. Pacific Luth. Theol. Sem., 1971, Augustana Theol. Sem., 1967; part-time prof. Three Hierarchs Sem., Eastern Orthodox Ch., Maitland, Fla., 1971-80. Del. Continuation Com. of Faith and Order, Switzerland, 1939. Mem. Bd. Fgn. Missions, Augustana Synod, 1941-80. Mem. Am. Theol. Com. of Faith and Order Movement, Soc. Bibl. Lit. and Exegesis. Author: My Father Worketh Hitherto: A brief outline of Christianity's expansion, 1945; The New Life in Christ, 1950; Let's Look at Paul, 1960; God Who Redeems, 1962. Home: Deland, Fla. Died Mar. 16, 1980.

WAINHOUSE, DAVID W., internat. lawyer and govt. cons.; b. Vilna, Lithuania, Sept. 15, 1900; s. Samuel and Ida (Steinberg) W.; brought to U.S., 1909, naturalized, 1923; A.B., Harvard, 1923, A.M., 1926, J.D., 1927; B.C.L., Oxford U., 1929; m. Katharine Cohen, Aug. 5, 1925; children—Austryn, Jonathan (dec.). Admitted to Me. bar, 1927; N.Y. State bar, 1934, D.C. bar, 1947, U.S. Supreme Ct. bar, 1945; lectr. Polit. sci. Fordham U., 1932-34; asst. U.S. atty, So. Dist. of N.Y., 1934-41; lectr. pub. law N.Y.U., 1934-41; became adviser Dept. of State, 1946, Dep. Asst. Sec. of State; former minister counsellor Am. Embassy, Vienna, Austria; now cons. Dept. of State; dir. Office UN Polit. Affairs, 1950-56; sr. adviser U.S. delegation to UN Gen Assembly, 1952, 53, spl. adv. 9th assembly; U.S. rep. to ILO Conf., Geneva, 1956, 57, 58, 61; U.S. rep to Law of the Sea Conf., 1960; sr. adviser U.S. delegation 1st Internat. Atomic Energy Conf., Vienna, 1957, Adj. prof. internat. law Am. U., 1962-63; lectr. Salzburg Seminar Am. Studies, 1965; vis. prof. Austrian Diplomatic Acad., 1968-69, Mem. Washington Center Fgn. Policy Research of Johns Hopkins U. Served as col. AUS, World War II; asst. chief staff Africa-Middle East Theatre, 1945-46. Decorated Legion of Merit. Mem. Assn. Bar City N.Y., Washington Inst. Fgn. Affairs. Clubs: Harvard (N.Y.C. and Wash.); Cosmos (Washington). Author: Foreign Relations of the U.S., 1930; History of American Foreign Policy, 1940; The Remnants of Empire, 1965; (with others) The Future Character and Role of Peace Observation Under the United Nations, 1966; Arms Control Agreements: Designs for Verification and Organization, 1968; International Peacekeeping at the Crossroads, 1973. Contbr. profl. mags. Home: Washington, D.C. Died Mar. 19, 1976.

WAITE, JOHN BARKER, educator; b. Toledo, O., Aug. 14, 1882; s. Richard and Alice Jane (Voris) W.; A.B., Yale, 1905; LL.B., U. of Mich., 1907; m. Harriet Ripley Williams, Aug. 4, 1915; 1 son, Richard Ripley. Admitted Ohio bar, 1907; practiced at Toledo 5 yrs.; prof. law, U. of Mich., since 1912; city alderman 1939-45; mem. U.S. Supreme Court com. to revise rules 1941-45. Compliance commr. War Prodn. Bd., Mich. region, since 1943. Mem. Research Club of U. of Mich. Mem. Am. Law Inst., Am. and Mich. State bar assns. (chmn. spl. coms.), Phi Beta Kappa, Phi Delta Phi, Order of the Coif. Author: Patent Law, 1920; The Law of Sales, 1921; Cases on the Law of Patents, 1924; Cases on Criminal Law and Procedure, 1931; Criminal Law in Action, 1934; Waite on Sales, 1938; The Prevention of Repeated Crime, 1943. Editor in chief Mich. Law Rev. (monthly), 1921-31. Contbr. to tech.and gen. mags. Home: 1909 Day St. Address: Hutchin's Hole, Omaha.*

WAITE, ROY ELLIS, coll. dean; b. Dexter, Mich., July 16, 1886; s. David Eliot and Ida May (Litchfield) W.; certificate, Mich. State Tchrs. Coll., 1907; A.B., U. Mich., 1913, M.S., 1928; student U. Cal., U. Chgo.; m. Nellie May Burt, July 9, 1913. High sch. prin. in Domondale, Mich., 1907-09, Lake Odessa, 1909-11, St. Johns, 1913-14, Marshfield, Ore., 1914-16, Mt. Clemens, Mich., 1916-17; asst. prin. Highland Park (Mich.) High Sch., 1917-46; instr. physics and mathematics Bob Jones U., 1946—, dean coll. arts and scis., 1953—. Ground sch. instr. Navy V5 program, 1943-44. Mem. N.E.A., S.C. Edn. Assn., S.C. Acad. Sci., Mich. Sch. Masters Club (life). Address: Greenville, S.C. *

WAKEMAN, ARTHUR G., paper mfr.; b. Oshkosh, Wis., Feb. 11, 1898; s. Charles A. and Frances (Norton) W.; B.S., Mass. Inst. Tech., 1921; m. Loraine Cheeseman, Sept. 19, 1928; 1 dau., Frances N. Asst. supt. Kimberly Mill, Kimberly Clark Corp., Neenah, Wis., 1922-25; gen. mgr. and dir., Fox River Paper Co., Appleton, Wis., 1925-42; mem. engring. dept. Kimberly Clark Corp., 1945-48, v.p., dir., 1956-80; pres. Coosa River Newsprint Co., 1948-60, chmn. bd., 1960-80; pres. Internat. Excelsior Machinery Co.; dir. Royal Crown Cola Co., Newsprint Service Bur. Chief, Pulp and Paper, W.P.B., 1942-43; mem. Mission of Econ. Affairs, London, 1944; surveyor of paper industry in Europe for U.S. Army, 1945. Served in U.S. Army, 1918-19. Mem. Tech. Assn. Pulp and Paper Industry, American Paper & Pulp Association Amateur Radio League, United States Power Squadron, Phi Delta Theta. Episcopalian. Clubs: University (Chicago); North Shore Golf (Neenah, Wis.); Mountain Brook (Birmingham). Contbr. articles to trade publs. Home: Neenah, Wis. Died Aug. 29, 1980; interred Oshkosh, Wis.

WAKUSUGI, KANAME (WĔ-KOO-SOO-GI), Japanese minister to U.S.; b. Tokyo, Japan, 1885; s. Keihichi and Mijiu Wakusigi; grad. Tung Wen Coll., Shanghai, China, 1907; LL.B., U. of Ore., 1912; M.A., New York U., 1914; m. Fumiko Mori, 1920; children—Takashi, Akira, Hiroshi. Began in foreign service of Japan as vice consul, 1916; now minister plenipotentiary to U.S. Address: Washington, D.C. *

WALB, WALTER WILDMAN, mfg. co. exec.; b. LaGrange, Ind., May 20, 1904; s. Clyde Allison and Vida (Wildman) W.; B.C.E., Purdue U., 1926; Dr.Engring., Tri-State Coll., 1966; m. Marjorie Heinrichs, May 17, 1930; 1 dau., Marsha (Mrs. Gerald D. Heller). Sec.-treas. Gen. Dredging Co., Inc., Ft. Wayne, Ind., 1930-35; sec.-treas., gen. mgr. Am. Steel Dredge Co., Inc., Ft. Wayne, 1935-45, pres., 1945-55; v.p., gen. mgr. Am. Hoist & Derrick Co., Ft. Wayne, 1955-67, chmn. bd., 1967-73, dir.; 1955-74; pres. Am. Steel Supply Corp., 1945-76; dir. Am. Steel Supply Corp., Gen. Dredging Co., Inc., Ft. Wayne Nat. Bank, No. Ind. Pub. Service Co., P & H Supply Co., Tokheim Corp. Vice pres., campaign mgr. Ft. Wayne Community Chest, 1947-49. Trustee Purdue U., Tri-State Coll. Mem. Ind. Soc. Chgo., Purdue Alumni Assn. (pres. 1951-53), Ind. (pres. 1964-66), Ft. Wayne (pres. 1945-46) chambers commerce, Sigma Alpha Epsilon. Republican. Methodist. Rotarian. Clubs: Ft. Wayne Country; Columbia (Indpls.). Home: Fort Wayne, Ind. Died Apr. 2, 1976; interred Lindenwood Cemetery, Fort Wayne.

WALDMAN, MILTON, author; b. Cleve., Oct. 4, 1895; s. Benjamin and Ida (Spira) W.; A.B., Yale, 1917; grad. work Sorbonne, Paris, 1922-23; m. Marguerite David, July 20, 1934. Newspaper reporter, 1917-19; asso. with law firm, 1919-20; editorial dept. New York Globe, 1922; asso. editor London Mercury, 1924-27; literary adviser William Collins Sons & Co., Ltd., pubs. Mem. U.S. Ednl. (Fulbright) Commn. U.K. Served as lt. inf., AUS, 1917-18. Club: Savile (London). Author: Americana, 1925; Sir Walter Raleigh, 1927; The Disinherited (novel), 1929; King, Queen, Jack, 1931; England's Elizabeth, 1933 Joan of Arc, 1935; Biography of a Family, 1936; Rod of Iron: The Absolute Rulers of England, 1941; Elizabeth and Leicester, 1945; Queen Elizabeth (in Brief Lives Series), 1952. Home: Rome, Italy. Died Mar. 6, 1976.

WALDO, DOROTHY, coll. prof.; b. New Haven, Conn., Nov. 18, 1885; d. Leonard and Dora (Fullerton) Waldo; A.B., Mt. Holyoke Coll., 1908, Ed.D., Harvard Univ., 1937. Teacher, Newton, Mass., 1908-10, Brookline, Mass., 1910-17; teacher and exec., Bennett Sch., Millbrook, N.Y., 1917-18; principal, Dana Hall Sch., Wellesley, Mass., 1918-38; prof. edn., N.J. Coll. for Women, New Brunswick, N.J., since 1938. Mem. N.E.A., Nat. Assn. of Principals of Pvt. Schs., N.J. Welfare Council, N.J. Ednl. Assn., Mt. Holyoke Alumnae Assn., Community Chest (trustee, chmn. budget com.). Plainfield Council of Social Agencies (past pres.), Pi Lambda Theta. Republican. Presbyterian. Clubs: Bus. and Professional Women's, Quota (hon.). Home: Plainfield, N.J. *

WALDO, TOMMY RUTH BLACKMON (MRS. SELDEN FENNELL WALDO), educator; b. Dallas, Jan. 14, 1916; d. Gulie Hargrove and Mary Lee (Craig) Blackmon; B.A., Agnes Scott Coll., 1938; M.A., U. Fla., 1955, Ph.D., 1961; m. Selden Fennell Waldo, Oct. 28, 1941 (dec. Nov. 1950); children—George Selden (dec.), Andrew Blackmon. Grad. asst. U. Fla., Gainesville, 1952-55, instr., 1955-61, asst. prof. English, 1961-68, asso. prof. English, 1968-76, prof., 1976-81; pvt. tchr. piano and organ, 1938-55. Mem. So. Atlantic Modern Lang. Assn., Modern Lang. Assn., Fla. Music Tchrs. Assn., Gainesville Music Tchrs. Assn., Southeastern Renaissance Conf., Phi Beta Kappa, Sigma Alpha Iota (patroness), Delta Kappa Gamma. Author book on Shakespeare. Contbr. articles to profl. jours. Home: Gainesville, Fla. Died Oct. 18, 1981.

WALKER, ALBERT LYELL, educator; b. Oklahoma City, Jan. 20, 1907; S. James Francis Docetti and Neva De France (Roberts) W.; A.B., Park Coll., 1929; M.A., U. Iowa, 1930, Ph.D., 1936; m. Jauvanta Maurine Young, Sept. 1, 1948; children by previous marriage—Judith Lyell, Anthony Lyell. Gen. Edn. Bd. fellow U. Chgo., 1941-42; faculty Ia. State U., Ames, 1935—, chmn. curriculum com. Coll. Scis. and Humanities, 1942-59, capital improvements com., 1963-72; prof. English, 1942-77, prof. emeritus, 1977-80, chmn. dept. English and speech, 1959-69, chmn. dept. English, 1959-72. Recipient Mu Phi Epsilon award in piano, 1928, Alumni-Faculty citation Iowa State U., 1974. Mem. Modern Lang. Assn., Nat., Iowa councils tchrs. English, Iowa Colls. Council English, Am. Assn. U. Profs., Lampos, Phi Kappa Phi.

Co-author: Minimum Essentials for Good Writing, 1952; Essentials of Good Writing, rev., 1959; The Range of Literature, 1960, rev., 1967, 73. Contbr. articles on edn., Shakespeare to profl. jours. Home: Ames, Iowa. Died Sept. 28, 1980.

WALKER, ARCHIE DEAN, lumber mfr.; b. Mpls., May 21, 1882; s. Thomas Barlow and Harriet Granger (Hulet) W.; student U. Minn., 1905, Cornell U., 1906; m. Bertha Willard Hudson, June 7, 1906; children—Hudson Dean, Stephen Archie, Walter Willard, Louise (Mrs. Malcolm A. McCannel), Philip Hulet, Archie Dean. Timber cruiser, surveyor Red River Lumber Co., Akeley, Minn., also timber lands No. Cal., 1899-08, sec. 1908-33, pres., 1933-45, now mem. timber coop. Shasta Forests Co., successor to Red River Lumber Co.; pres. Barlow Realty Co., 1933—; dir. Gamble-Skogmo, Inc., Gen. Securities, Inc. Mem. bd. Mpls. Pub. Library, 1928-55, pres., 1944-55; pres. T.B. Walker Found., 1929—, Archie D. and Bertha H. Walker Found., 1955—: pres. bd. Walker Meth. Home, 1959—; dir. Tyrone Guthrie Theatre Found.; mem. men's adv. com. Northwestern Hosp., 1951—. Mem. Psi Upsilon. Methodist (chmn. 1955-58). Clubs: Minneapolis; Woodhill Country. Home: Minneapolis. *

WALKER, BURNETT, business exec.; b. Anderson, Ind., Nov. 22, 1884; s. Edward B. and Minnie (Burnett) W.; A.B., De Pauw U., 1906; LL.B., N.Y.U., 1908; m. Jo Wallace, Oct. 17, 1936; children—Burnett Walker, John David. With Gebr. Stollwerck, Cologne, Germany, 1908-10, Harris, Forbes & Co., N.Y.C., 1910-20, Guaranty Trust Co. of N.Y. and Guaranty Co. of N.Y., 1920-34, partner Edward B. Smith & Co., 1934-37; partner Smith, Barney & Co., N.Y.C., 1938-61, ltd. partner, 1962-63; adv. bd. Smith, Barney & Co., Inc., 1964—. Decorated Comdr. Order of Crown (Belgium); Order of Sacred Treasure (Japan). Mem. Beta Theta Pi. Republican. Roman Catholic. Club: University (N.Y.C.); La Jolla Beach and Tennis; Sleepy Hollow Country (Scarborough-on-Hudson, N.Y.). Home: LaJolla, Cal. *

WALKER, DONALD GREGORY, educator; b. Rochester, N.Y., Feb. 17, 1925; s. Raymond Charles and Mary Ellen (Fenton) W.; A.B., U. Calif. at Berkeley, 1945, M.A., 1949, Ph.D., 1951; m. Shirley Loretta Rocha, Dec. 31, 1949; children—Victoria, Gregory, Chris, Donna, Brenda, Ben. Teaching asst. dept. anatomy U. Calif. at Berkeley, 1947-51; instr. dept. anatomy U. Ore., 1951-52, asst. prof., 1952-55; asst. prof. dept. anatomy Sch. Medicine, Johns Hopkins, 1955-59, asso. prof., 1959-66, prof., 1966-79; vis. research fellow arthritis research unit Mass. Gen. Hosp., Boston, 1963. Served with USNR, 1943-45. Recipient Med. Faculty award, 1958-61, Research Career Devel. award USPHS, 1962-67, Nicholas Andry award, W. Barry Wood, Jr. award; John Simon Guggenheim fellow, 1978. Mem. Am. Assn. Anatomists, Histochem. Soc., Orthopaedic Research Soc., Assn. Bone and Joint Surgeons, Sigma Xi. Research on cause and cure of osteopetrosis. Home: Glen Arm, Md. Died June 9, 1979.

WALKER, FRANK FISH, financial exec.; b. Berkeley, Calif., Mar. 20, 1896; s. David Henry and Nellie Emma (Fish) W.; A.B., Stanford, 1917; ensign U.S. Naval Acad., 1918; m. Ursula Coykendall, Apr. 24, 1926 (dec. Dec. 1974); 1 son, Frank Fish (dec.); m. Beatrice Matthews, June 2, 1976. Investment banking, v.p., dir. Blyth & Co., N.Y.C., 1919-34; gen. partner Eastman Dillon & Co., N.Y., 1934-39; trustee Stanford, 1939-40, fin. v.p., 1940-46; ltd. partner Dean Witter & Co.; dir. Calif. Water Service Co., Varian Assos., Kaiser Aluminum & Chem. Corp., Calif. Ink Co., Inc., San Jose Water Works. Trustee San Francisco Ladies' Protection and Relief Soc. Served as ensign USNRF, 1917-19. Clubs: Pacific Union, Bohemian (San Francisco), Union, Victoria Golf. Home: Menlo Park, Calif. Died July 28, 1978; buried Alta Mesa Cemetery, Mt. View, Calif.

WALKER, FRANKLIN DICKERSON, educator; b. Republic, Mich., Nov. 13, 1900; s. John Franklin and Lillian (Dickerson) W.; student U. of Ariz., 1918-20; A.B. (Rhodes scholar from Ariz., 1920-23), Oxford Univ., 1923; Ph.D., U. Cal., 1932; m. Dorothy Griffith, 1924; 1 son, Franklin Victor; m. 2d, Imogene Bishop, Aug. 15, 1933; 1 dau., Susan Imogene. Tchr., Francis Parker Sch., San Diego, 1924-26; instr. San Diego State Coll., 1926-28, 30-40; prof. English, U. Ore., 1940-43; Reinhardt prof. Am. lit. Mills Coll., Oakland, Cal., 1946-66, prof. emeritus, 1966-78; vis. lectr. in Am. lit. Uppsala (Sweden) U., 1949-50. Served as maj. USAAF, 1943-46. Rockefeller fellow Huntington Library, 1952-53; Guggenheim fellow, 1960-61. Mem. Modern Lang. Assn., Phi Beta Kappa, Sigma Chi. Author: Frank Norris, 1932; San Francisco's Literary Frontier, 1939; Ambrose Bierce, 1941; A Literary History of Southern California, 1950; The Seacoast of Bohemia, 1966; Jack London and the Klondike, 1966; Irreverent Pilgrims, 1974. Collected and edited: Prentice Mulford's California Sketches, 1935; The Washoe Giant in San Francisco, 1939; Mark Twain's Travels with Mr. Brown (with G. Ezra Dane), 1940; Mother of Felipe and Other Stories by Mary Austin, 1950; The Letters of Frank Norris, 1956; The Call of the Wild and Other Stories, 1960; The Sea-Wolf and Selected Stories, 1964; The Heart of Darkness and Secret Sharer, 1969. Address: Oakland, Calif. Died Dec. 29, 1978.

WALKER, HENRY ALEXANDER, corp. official; b. Honolulu, Hawaii, Feb. 19, 1885; s. John Smith and Jane (McIntyre) W.; student Harvard, 1903-07; m. Una Craig, Dec. 7, 1920; children—Henry Alexander, Mrs. Ann Burns. Chmn. bd. and dir. Am. Factors, Ltd.; director Kekaha Sugar Company, Limited, Hawaiian Canneries Company, Limited; director Grove Farms Ltd., Bank of Hawaii, Hawaiian Trust Co. Ltd., Pacific Chemical & Fertilizer Co.; trustee Oahu Cemetery Assn. Clubs: Chevy Chase (Maryland), Oahu Country (Honolulu). Home: Honolulu. *

WALKER, HENRY BABCOCK, lawyer; b. Evansville, Ind., Mar. 10, 1885; s. James Tyler and Lucy Alice (Babcock) W.; A.B., Princton, 1906; m. Dorothy Rachel Griffith, June 17, 1909; children—Ann G. (Mrs. John E. Early), Henry B., Jr., Lucy B. (Mrs. Richard R. McGinnis), Dorothy R. (Mrs. Lowry J. Bateman). Admitted to Indiana bar, 1906; in practice of law, Evansville, Indiana since 1906; now mem. firm Walker, Walker & Trockman; v.p. Curtis Radiocasting Corp., 1929-58, pres., 1958—; v.p. On The Air, Inc., 1929-58, pres., 1958—. Dir. Stapling Machines Co.; trustee Evansville (Ind.) College since 1949. Served as capt. U.S. Army, World War I; col. U.S. Army, World War II. Mem. Ind. State Bar Assn. (pres. 1929), Am. Judicature Soc. (vice pres. 1929-31), Fed. Ins. Counsel (pres. 1942-47), Am. Bar Assn., Internat. Assn. Ins. Counsel, Fed. Communications Bar Assn., Am. Counsel Assn., Am. Arbitration Assn., Internat. Bar Assn. Democrat. Presbyterian. Clubs: Princeton (N.J.) Quadrangle; Evansville (Ind.) Country. *

WALKER, HENRY POISON, judge; b. Indian Terr., Okla., Sept. 23, 1901; ed. pub. schs.; pvt. study law. Dep., county officer Delaware County, Okla., 1921-29; admitted to Okla. bar, 1928; practiced in Dealware County, 1929-32, Miami, Okla., 1932-66; county atty. Delaware County, 1934; asst. dist. atty.; spl. judge Dist. Ct. Okla. Dist. 13, 1969-75. Baptist. Home: Jay, Okla. Deceased.

WALKER, HUDSON DEAN, art specialist; b. Minneapolis, Minn., June 17, 1907; s. Archie Dean and Bertha Willard (Hudson) W.; student U. Minn., 1925-28, Harvard (Fogg Mus.), 1928-30; m. Ione Avery Gaul, June 13, 1936; children—Harriet (Mrs. Michael W. Heron), (twins) Berta, Louise (Mrs. Edgar Davy). Partner Goodman-Walker, Inc. Art Gallery, Boston, 1930-32; sec. Barlow Realty Co., Mpls., 1932-36; owner Hudson D. Walker Gallery, N.Y.C., 1936-40; pres., trustee Am. Fedn. Arts, 1945-48; asso. Walker & Ebeling, Jewelers, N.Y.C.; dir. The Red River Lumber Co., Westwood, Calif., 1940-44. With OWI, 1945. Dir. exhibn. of Marsden Hartley's paintings Mus. of Mod. Art, N.Y.C., 1944; exec. dir. Artists Equity Assn., 1947-51, Artists Equity Fund, 1948-59. Trustee T.B. Walker Found., Mpls. Mem. Nat. Council Am.-Soviet Friendship, 1944-48, Nat. Commn. for UNESCO, 1946-48. Mem. Municipal Art Soc., Friends of Whitney Mus. Am. Art, Psi Upsilon. Democrat. Clubs: Century, Minneapolis. Home: Forest Hills, N.Y. Died Sept. 20, 1976; interred at Provincetown, Mass.

WALKER, IRVING MILLER, lawyer; b. Louisville, Mar. 9, 1885; s. Walter and Mary Sydnor (Perkins) W.; B.A., University of Virginia, 1905; LL.D., Claremont College; m. Evangeline E. Duque, Oct. 6, 1914; 1 dau., Elita (Mrs. Fritz Caspari). Admitted to Cal. bar, 1906, since practiced in Los Angeles; mem. firm Loeb, Walker & Loeb, 1914-38, Walker, Adams, Duque & Smith, 1938-42, Walker, Adams & Duque, 1942-45, Walker, Wright, Tyler & Ward, 1956—. Hon. dir. United Cal. Bank; dir. Farmer Bros. Co., other corps. Adviser com. on adminstrv. justice State Bar of Cal. Active Community Chest, Welfare Planning Council, Legal Aid Found. Los Angeles; dir., hon. chmn. Travelers Aid Soc. Los Angeles; director National Travelers Aid Society. Director and trustee of Claremont Coll., Hosp. Good Samaritan, Scripps Coll., (pres.); hon. life bd. dirs. of Claremont U. Coll. Fellow Am. Bar Found.; mem. Am., Cal. (v.p.), Los Angeles County (pres., recipient first Shattuck-Price award) bar assns., Am. Judicature Soc., Am. Coll. Trial Lawyers, Phi Beta Kappa. Democrat. Episcopalian. Home: Los Angeles. *

WALKER, JOSEPH, lawyer, dept. store exec.; b. N.Y.C., Mar. 19, 1912; s. Benjamin and Celia (Margulies) W.; B.A., Coll. City N.Y., 1931; LL.B., Columbia, 1937; m. Eleanor Junger, Mar. 3, 1938; children—Mark, Robert. Admitted to N.Y. bar, 1937, since practiced in N.Y.C.; chief price atty. N.Y. dist. OPA, 1945-46; sec., gen. counsel S. Klein Dept. Stores, Inc., Grayson-Robinson Stores, Inc., 1953-60; v.p., counsel, sec., dir. S. Klein Dept. Stores, Inc., N.Y.C., 1960-80, exec. v.p., 1974-80; sr. v.p. McCrory Corp., 1975-80; dir. Lerner Stores Corp., 1971-73. Past chmn. Apparel Chain Store Credit Com. Mem. Mayor's Com. N.Y.C. Shakespeare Festival, 1966-70; co-chmn. lawyer's div. Anti-Defamation League, N.Y., 1967-69. Mem. Newcomen Soc., Phi Beta Kappa, Kappa Delta Pi. Home: New York, N.Y. Died Mar. 29, 1980.

WALKER, WILLIAM W., mfr., engineer; b. Lime Rock, Conn., May 1, 1883; s. Millidge and Jessie (Inches) W.; M.E. Stevens Inst. of Tech., 1906; E.D., 1946; m. Anna B. Gardiner, June 3, 1925; 1 dau., Marjorie. Dir. MacAndrews & Forbes Co., 1913—, former chmn. Republican. Episcopalian. Clubs: Union League, Merion Cricket. Home: Merion Station, Pa. *

WALL, NATHAN SANDERS, educator; b. Chgo., May 25, 1925; s. Peter and Sara (Melnick) W.; B.S., Rensselaer Poly. Inst., 1949; Ph.D., Mass. Inst. Tech., 1954; m. Charlotte Katz, Jan. 28, 1951; children—David, Johanna. Research asso. Ind. U., 1954; asst. prof. Mass. Inst. Tech., 1956-63; asst. prof. U. Rochester, 1955; prof. physics U. Md., 1963-79; vis. prof. Cath. U. Louvain (Belgium), 1978; cons. to bus., industry and govt. Bd. dirs. Montgomery County (Md.) chpt. ACLU. Served with AUS, 1943-45. Decorated Bronze Star. NSF sr. postdoctoral fellow, 1961; NATO fellow, 1971; Weizmann Inst. fellow, 1971. Fellow Am. Phys. Soc. Contbr. articles to profl. jours. Home: Silver Spring, Md. Died Sept. 2, 1979.

WALL, ZENO, clergyman; b. Mooresboro, N.C., Aug. 20, 1882; s. S. F. and Elora Jane (Robinson) W.; student of Mars Hill Coll., Southern Baptist Theol. Seminary; D.D., Miss Coll.; m. Ada Kate Ramsey, May 4, 1911; children—Zeno. Abbie Jane (Mrs. Harris), Yates, Woodrow, Ada Ramsey (Mrs. Fanning). Ordained to ministry of Baptist ch., July 8, 1908; pastor Marshall (N.C.) Baptist Church, 1908-09, Mt. Olive (Miss.) Baptist Church, 1911-14; enlistment sec. Home Mission Bd., 1914-15; pastor, First Baptist Church, Columbia, Miss., 1915-16, Clinton Baptist Church, Miss. Coll., 1916-21, First Baptist Church, Goldsboro, N.C., 1922-25, First Baptist Church, Shelby, N.C., 1925-48. Sec. bd. of trustees Miss. Coll., 1916-21; pres. Gardner-Webb Coll., Boiling Springs, N.C., 1930-32; vice pres. N.C. Baptist State Hosp., 1927; pres. N.C. Baptist State Conv. 1933-36; pres. bd. of trustees, Baptist Orphanage of N.C., Thomasville, N.C., gen. supt. since 1948; mem. Sunday Sch. Bd. on Southern Baptist Conv. Served as chaplain, U.S. Army, World War, 1917-18. Author: Heartening Messages; Verities of the Gospel; A Day For God-Called Men. Home: Thomasville, N.C. *

WALLACE, CHARLES LORING, ry. official; b. Banquo, Ind., Mar. 20, 1884; s. Leroy Samuel and Nellie (Charles) W.; studied engring. Purdue U.; m. Martha Jean Allen, of Greencastle, Ind., Nov. 4, 1907. Receiver and v.p. T.&P. Ry.; dir. Trans-Mississippi Terminal R.R. Co., Weatherford, Mineral Wells & Northern R.R. Mason (32 deg., Shriner), Elk. Republican. Clubs: Pickwick, Press, Chess, Checker and Whist, Country, Southern Yacht. Home: New Orleans. *

WALLACE, DEWITT, publisher; b. St. Paul, Nov. 12, 1889; s. James and Janet (Davis) W.; student Macalester Coll., 1907-09, U. Calif., 1909-11; m. Lila Bell Acheson, Oct. 15, 1921. With book dept. Webb Pub. Co., St. Paul, 1911-15, Brown & Bigelow, St. Paul, 1916; publicity dept. Westinghouse Electric & Mfg. Co., 1920-21; founder Reader's Digest Assn., Inc., 1921, ret., 1973. Served as sgt. 35th Div., U.S. Army, 1917-19. Home: Mount Kisco, N.Y. Died Mar. 30, 1981.

WALLACE, JAMES MURRAY, elec. corp. exec.; b. Pitts., Feb. 25, 1914; s. Guy DeYarmond and Laura (Schreiner) W.; B.S. in Physics and Engring., U. Pitts., 1935; grad. Advanced Mgmt. Program, Harvard, 1955; m. Mabel Elizabeth Lewis, May 23, 1940; children—Laura Richmond, Marilyn Lee. With Westinghouse Elec. Corp., 1935-77, mgr. East Pittsburgh divs., 1963-64, v.p. East Pittsburgh divs., 1964-69, v.p., asst. to pres., power systems, 1969-70, exec. v.p. Westinghouse Electric Europe N.V., Brussels, 1970-71, asst. to pres. Power Systems Co., 1971-73, v.p., gen. mgr. Power Systems Projects div., 1973-77. Chmn., Pa. Gov.'s Rev. of Govt. Mgmt., 1971. Registered profl. engr., Pa. Mem. I.E.E.E., Nat. Soc. Profl. Engrs., Eta Kappa Nu (Outstanding Young Elec. Engr. award 1945). Presbyn. Patentee circuit interrupters. Office: Pittsburgh, Pa. Died May 1, 1977; interred Homewood Cemetery, Pittsburgh.

WALLACE, WILLIAM KAY, historian; b. New York, N.Y., Nov. 10, 1886; s. John and Henriette (Clarn) W.; grad. Phillips Acad., Andover, Mass., 1904; B.A., Yale, 1908, M.A., 1911. Apptd. 3d sec. of Embassy, Tokyo, Japan, 1908, sec. Legation, Copenhagen, Denmark, 1909-11; chargé d'affaires Jan.-May 1910; sec. Legation, Havana, Cuba, 1911-13 (resigned); Spl. war corr. London Times, with French, British, Belgian and Italian armies, 1914-17; vol. for mil. service, Apr. 6, 1917; commd. capt. Gen. Staff, M.I.D., U.S. Army, June 1917; prepared daily and weekly survey of progress of World War issued by Gen. Staff for confidential information of President of U.S., the Chief of Staff and the Sec. of War; wrote weekly review of operations issued by Sec. of War to the press; prepared summary of operations and part played by Am. forces in the field, leading to the Armistice issued by Gen. Staff and submitted to Congress, Nov. 18, 1918; mem. Am. Commn. to Negotiate Peace at Paris, Nov. 1918; asst. mil. attaché Am. Embassy, Rome, Italy, 1919; maj. U.S.R., Mil. Intelligence Div., Gen. Staff, Dec. 1919. Observer at the 1st Internat. Econ. Conf., Geneva, 1927. Pres., Black Hills Keystone Corp., producers of Strategic beryl, lithium and mica ores. Decorated Knight Crown of Italy. Author: Greater Italy, 1917; The Trend of History, 1922; The Passing of Politics, 1924; Thirty Years of Modern History, 1926; The Scientific World View, 1928; Our Obsolete Constitution, 1932. Home: Ashwicken, Poundridge Rd., Bedford, N.Y. Address: New York, N.Y. *

WALLACE, WILLIAM LEWIS, shipbldg. exec.; b. Orange, N.J., Jan. 29, 1883; s. William Lewis and Emily T. (Hazard) W.; student Newark Acad., 1901, Princeton, 1901-02; M.E., Cornell U., 1906, M.M.E., 1907; m. May I. Recheygl, Aug. 29, 1911; children—Dorothy M. (Mrs. R. A. Derengoski), Helen M. (Mrs. H. V. Skatrud). With Manitowoc Shipbldg. and Drydock Co., now Manitowoc Shipbldg., Inc., 1907—, successively draftsman, sales engr., plant engr., works mgr., v.p. and gen. mgr., director, 1952, now pres. and dir. Manitowoc Shipbuilding Co., Inc.; director of The Manitowoc Company, Inc. Mem. Soc. Naval Architects and Marine Engrs., Am. Bur. Shipping and Sigma Xi. Presbyterian. Mason (Shriner). Club: Branch River Country. Home: Manitowac, Wisc. *

WALLACE, WILLIAM ROSS, lawyer; b. Salt Lake City, Aug. 14, 1898; s. William R. and Annie (McChrystal) W.; Harvard, 1920; m. Ina Claire, Mar. 16, 1939. Counsel, Hancock, Rothert & Bunshoft, San Francisco. Trustee Bothin Real Estate Co. Mem. Am., Calif., San Francisco (pres. 1946), bar assns., Assn. Bar City N.Y. Clubs: Pacific Union (San Francisco); Burlingame. Home: San Francisco, Calif. Died Feb. 28, 1976.

WALLACE, WILLIAM SWILLING, pub. co. exec., librerian, historian; b. Springfield, Ill., July 17, 1922; s. Jerry and Lenora (Swilling) W.; B.A., Western State Coll. Colo., 1945; M.A., U. Mont., 1948; M.A. in L.S., U. Denver, 1953; m. Almina Wiggins, Apr. 16, 1946. High sch. history tchr., Hot Springs, N.Mex., 1946-48, Douglas, Ariz., 1949-50; asst. librarian and archivist N.Mex. Highlands U., 1953- 59, head librarian and archivist, 1959-72; pres. Horn & Wallace Pub. Corp., 1973-76. Mem. Am., S.W., N.Mex. library assns., Soc. Am. Archivists, Am. Hist. Assn., Phi Alpha Theta. Democrat. Episcopalian. Elk. Clubs: Rounce and Coffin (Los Angeles); Westerners (Denver), Author: Antoine Robidoux, 1953; Journey Through New Mexico in 1864, 1956; Land Between 1957; also articles. Home: Albuquerque, N.Mex. Died July 26, 1976.

WALLACH, SIDNEY, pub. affairs cons., editor; b. Poland, July 4, 1905; s. Don Zevi and Bertha (Steinberg) W.; came to U.S., 1912, naturalized; A.B., Coll. City N.Y., 1925; postgrad. Columbia, 1925-26; m. Idalee Burrows, Aug. 17, 1929 (dec.); children—Roseanne (Mrs. Barry Stein), and Don H. (dec.); m. 2d, Dr. Pauline Rudnick, Feb. 5, 1967. Journalist, editor, fgn. corr., 1923-33; ednl. dir. later exec. dir. Am. Jewish Com., 1933-42; cons. to pub. orgns., assns., individuals, from 1942; lectr. civil rights, pub. relations, minority problems; founder, 1938, mag. now called Commentary; pub. Modern Mexico, 1945-51; editor City Coll. Alumnus, 1948-50; exec. v.p. Am. Inst. for Tropics, 1952-59; cons. Artists Equity Assn., N.Y.C. Exec. sec. Am. Com. for Study of War Documents; asst. dir. Theodore Roosevelt Centennial Commn., 1954-59; sec. Oscar S. Straus Meml. Assn.; sec. Am. Chess Found.; v.p. Am. Friends Tel Aviv Mus.; dir. Jewish Conciliation Bd. Am. Trustee, exec. officer Oliver Wendell Holmes Assn. Mem. Am. Arbitration Assn. (panel). Jewish. Author: Hitler, Menace to Mankind, 1933. Editor: Narrative of Commodore Perry's Expedition, 1952; The Theodore Roosevelt Round Up, 1958; (with Ronald B. Sobel) Justice, Justice, Shalt Thou Pursue, 1975. Home: New York, N.Y. Died June 24, 1979.

WALLER, C(ARL) RICHARD, engr.; b. Falun, Sweden, Feb. 7, 1882; s. Per Aron and Helena Elizabeth (Harling) W.; grad. Tech. Sch., Stockholm, 1903; m. Louise Buch, Jan. 21, 1913. Came to U.S., 1903, naturalized, 1910. Joined De Laval Steam Turbine Co., Trenton, N.J., 1903, chief engr., 1910, v.p., dir., 1934, dir. engring., 1949, retired 1950, continued as dir. engring., cons. engr.; dir. United Savs. & Loan Assn. since 1915, pres. since 1918. Mem. adv. com. bd. trustees Newark Coll. Engring. Awarded Certificate of Commendation for outstanding services (Navy), 1947; pres. award Soc. Naval Architects and Marine Engrs., 1948; David W. Taylor Gold medal, 1951. Fellow A.S.M.E. (life mem.); mem. Am. Soc. Swedish Engrs., Soc. Naval Architects and Marine Engrs., Am. Soc. Naval Engrs., U.S. Naval Inst., Inst. Marine Engrs. (Eng.), Trenton C. of C., Newcomen Soc. Eng. Elk. Clubs: Engrs. (pres. 1921), Torch, Country, Yardley Country (Trenton, N.J.). Author articles tech. jours. Holder patents. Home: Trenton, N.J. *

WALLER, CLIFFORD ELLISON, med. dir. (retired), U.S. Pub. Health Service; b. Bremond, Tex., Apr. 1, 1886; s. William Franklin and Sarah (Ellison) W.; M.D., George Washington U., 1910; m. Helen Stewart, 1910; children—Dorothy Stewart, William Franklin. Physician U.S. Indian Med. Service, 1910-13; asst. surgeon U.S. Pub. Health Service, 1914-18, passed asst. surgeon, 1918, surgeon. 1922, asst. surgeon gen., 1931; health officer Raleigh and Wake Counties, N.C., 1918-19, med. dir., 1940; state commissioner of health, N.M., 1919-21; dir. county health work, Georgia State Board of Health, 1922-25; chief Domestic Quarantine Div. (states relations div.), U.S. Public Health Service, 1931-39. Mem. A.M.A., Am. Pub. Health Assn.. Phi Sigma Kappa. Home: SilverSpring, Md. *

WALRATH, LAURENCE KAYE, lawyer, govt. ofcl.; b. Meadville, Pa., Aug. 16, 1909; s. Frank M. and Ina (Kaye) W.; A.B., U. Fla., 1931, J.D., 1934; m. 2d, Mildred Hoff, Oct. 28, 1950; children—Jean Camille (Mrs. E.K. Goethe), Shelby Ann (Mrs. Joseph F. Shad, Jr.), Laurence Kaye, Timothy Glass. Admitted to Fla. bar, 1934; asso. Albion W. Knight, Jacksonville, 1934-39, asso. Knight & Knight, 1939-41, partner, 1941-45, Knight, Knight, Walrath & Pegues, 1946-53, Knight, Walrath, Kincaid & Young, 1953-56; commr. ICC, 1956-72, chmn. commn., 1963, commn. div. 2, rates and practices, 1968-72; spl. cons. on comml. law. Dir. Legal Aid Assn., 1948-49; legal adviser N. Fla. council Boy Scouts Am., Jacksonville Lifesaving and Rescue Corps., 1949; disaster chmn., chpt. chmn. A.R.C., 1946-49, del. nat. conv., 1948, nat. A.R.C. nominating com., 1949; chmn. U.S. del. ECAFE Study Group, Tokyo, Japan, 1963; mem. U.S. del. Econ. Conf. European Nations, Geneva, 1968. Served from lt. (j.g.) to lt. comdr. USNR, 1942-45. Mem. Fla. (gov. 4th jud. circuit 1948-49), Jacksonville (pres. 1948) bar assns., Am. Legion, C. of C., Phi Delta Phi, Phi Kappa Phi, Pi Kappa Phi. Episcopalian. Mason, Elk. Club: Silver Lake Golf and Country (Leesburg, Fla.). Home: Leesburg, Fla. Died Apr. 5, 1976; interred St. James Episcopal Churchyard, Leesburg.

WALSH, CORNELIUS ROBERT, hosp. adminstr.; b. N.Y.C., July 20, 1928; s. Robert Emmett and Mary Ann (Brosnan) W.; B.B.A., Manhattan Coll., 1951; M.B.A. in Hosp. Administrn., Wagner Coll., 1974; m. Dorothy Edith MacMillan, June 7, 1952; children—Robert, Cornelius Robert, Kathleen, Dorothy, Gregory, Colleen. With N.Y. State Dept. Civil Service, Albany, 1951-54; personnel officer N.Y. State Dept. Mental Hygiene, Albany, 1954-58, Central Islip (N.Y.) State Hosp., 1958-65; bus. officer, then dep. dir. adminstrn. Suffolk State Sch., Melville, N.Y., 1965-70; dep. dir. adminstr. Letchworth Village State Sch., Thiells, N.Y., 1970-74; dir. Rome (N.Y.) Developmental Center, 1974-79; profl. adv. com. human services State Univ. Coll., Utica/Rome; trustee Rome Savs. Bank. Bd. dirs. Rome United Way. Recipient award honor Welfare League, Letchworth Village chpt. N.Y. State Assn. Retarded Children, 1973. Mem. Am. Assn. Mental Deficiency, Am. Hosp. Assn., Assn. Facility Dirs. N.Y. State Dept. Mental Hygiene, Rome C. of C. (dir.), Assn. Mental Health Administrs. Roman Catholic. Clubs: Rome, Rome Rotary (v.p.). Home: Rome, N.Y. Died July 20, 1979.

WALSH, LEONARD PATRICK, judge; b. Superior, Wis., Mar. 10, 1904; s. William Patrick and Margaret (Murphy) W.; student U. Minn.; LL.B., Nat. U., 1933; m. Dorothy Lloyd, Aug. 20, 1934 (dec. Sept. 1959); children—William Patrick, Dorothy Lynn; m. 2d, Bronia Kaczensky, Dec. 27, 1964; 1 son, Tobey Kaczensky. Admitted to D.C. bar, 1933, U.S. Supreme Ct. bar, 1943; pvt. practice law, Washington, 1933-53; chief judge Municipal Ct. for D.C., 1953-59; judge U.S. Dist. Ct. for D.C., 1959-71, sr. judge, 1971-80. Professorial lectr. Geo. Washington U., Sch. Law, 1956-64. Active-Met. Policy Boys Club; chmn. D.C. Armory Bd. Mem. Am. Bar Assn., Bar Assn. D.C. (pres. 1951-52), Phi Delta Phi, Delta Tau Delta, Omicron Delta Kappa. Home: Washington, D.C. Died Feb. 13, 1980; buried Washington, D.C.

WALSH, MATTHEW J., clergyman, educator; b. Chicago, Ill., May 14, 1882; s. David and Joanna (Clogm) W.; Litt. B. U. of Notre Dame, 1903; Ph.D., U., Catholic U., America, 1907; studied Johns Hopkins. Joined Congregation of the Holy Cross, 1903 priest. R.C. Ch., 1907; prof. history U. of Notre Dame, 1907-22, v.p., 1911-22 pres. 1922-28. Has specialized in European history. Chaplan 135th Machine Gun Batt., Camp Sheridan, Ala., Jan. 1917, May 1918 chaplain 30th Inf., 3d Div., A.E.F. Mem. Am. Catholic Hist. Assn., State Hist. Commn. of Ind. Home: Notre Dame, Ind.*

WALSH, TRAVIS WALTER, newspaper editor; b. Bishop, Tex., Jan. 7, 1924; s. Thomas Dewitt and Clyde (Gray) W.; B.J., U. Mo., 1948; m. Ann-Stelle Korff, Sept. 17, 1955 (dec. Apr. 1973); children—Amy Sue, Scott Martin. Reporter, Marietta (O.) Times, 1948-50, A.P., Columbus, Ohio, 1950-52, Corpus Christi (Tex.) Caller-Times, 1952-55; with Tulsa Daily World, from 1956, mng. editor, from 1969. Served with USNR, 1942-45. Mem. AP Mng. Editors Assn. (pres.), Sigma Delta Chi (dir., pres. Eastern Okla. chpt. 1974-75). Rotarian. Club: Tulsa Press. Address: Tulsa, Okla. Died Aug. 19, 1976.

WALSH, WARREN BARTLETT, educator; b. Brookfield, Mass., Dec. 21, 1909; s. William L. and Lucy P. (Bartlett) W.; A.B., Tufts Coll., 1930; A.M., Harvard, 1931, Ph.D., 1935; m. Elizabeth Jean Cantril, June 6, 1936; children—Lucy E., Elizabeth C., Sara B. Asst. history Tufts Coll., 1933-35; instr. to prof. Russian history Syracuse U., 1935-76, prof. emeritus, 1976-79, chmn. bd. Russian studies, 1944-63, chmn. dept. history, 1962-67, chairman spl. projects Research Inst., 1957-65; civilian faculty Nat. War Coll., 1952-55, dir. polit. affairs div., 1953-55, lectr. 1955-79, bd. consultants, 1962-65; lectr. Air War Coll., Army War Coll., NATO Def. Coll., Naval War Coll., Inter. Am. Def. Coll., Fgn. Service Inst.; vis. scholar N.Y. State U., 1962-65; cons. Am. Council on Edn., 1968-79; research asso. Dwight D. Eisenhower Inst. Hist. Research, Mus. History and Tech., Smithsonian Instn., 1977-79. Bd. dirs. Am. Unitarian Assn., 1947-53. Recipient commendation meritorious civilian service Dept. Def., 1953, Outstanding Civilian Service medal Dept. Army, 1973. Mem. Am. Assn. Advancement Slavic Studies, Am. Hist. Assn., Phi Alpha Theta, Phi Beta Kappa. Unitarian-Universalist. Author: Russia, A Handbook, 1948; Readings in Russian History, 4th edit., 1963; Russia and the Soviet Union, 1958, 2d edit., 1968; Perspective and Patterns, Discourses on History, 1962; International Conflict and Cooperation, 1964; Science and International Public Affairs, 1967. Asso. editor Russian Rev., 1948-79. Contbr. to various encyclopediae, profl. and other jours. Home: DeWitt, N.Y., also Southwest Harbor, Maine. Died June 9, 1979.

WALSH, WILLIAM ROBERT, lawyer, bus. exec.; born Port Huron, Mich., Feb. 18, 1886; s. Thomas and Mary (Fleming) W.; student Port Huron High Sch. LL.B., University of Michigan, 1908; married Rose O'Sullivan, November 29, 1917 (deceased March 27, 1952), children—Rosemary, Sister Rose Michaeleen, William Robert, Nan, Mary-Josephine, Joseph F.; married 2d, Marie Bourneuf, May 24, 1954. In practice of law in Port Huron since 1908; gen. counsel, dir. and v.p. Mueller Brass Co. since 1932; mem. firm Walsh, O'Sullivan, Stommel & Sharp; counsel Mich. Nat. Bank, Port Huron office, Louis Foster Lumber & Builders Supplies Co., Dunn Paper Co., F. Yeager Bridge & Culvert Company. Served as 2d lieutenant and 1st lt. and on detail as judge adv. of gen. and special courts, also as asst. to judge adv., 14th Div., Camp Custer, Mich., 1917-18. Republican. Roman Catholic. K.C., Elk. Club: Lawyers (U. of Mich.). Home: Port Huron, Mich. *

WALTER, ERICH ALBERT, former educator; b. Zanesville, Ohio, July 5, 1897; s. Waldemar Alexander and Selma (Gundert) W.; A.B., U. Mich., 1919, A.M., 1921; m. Meta Marie Henne, Aug. 24, 1922; children—Marie (Mrs. Howard R. Goodhew), Erich (dec.), Edward (dec.). Instr. rhetoric U. Mich., 1919, advancing to asso. prof. English, asso. dean coll. lit., sci. and arts, 1945; instr. rhetoric Mich. State Normal, summer 1921, asst. prof. summer 1923; chmn. acad. counselors, U. Mich., 1936-38, prof., 1947-67, dean students, 1947-53, asst. to pres. 1953-67, sec. regents, 1958-67, emeritus, 1967. Trustee Ann Arbor Pub. Schs., 1933-39, pres. 1938, 39; bd. dirs. Cranbrook Sch. for Boys, Bloomfield Hills, Mich., 1946-53, sec. 1949; bd. dirs. Ann Arbor Community Center. Chmn. planning com. Mich. Meml. Phoenix Project, 1946-47, represented U. Mich. installation Her Majesty The Queen Mother, as Chancellor U. London, 1955. Decorated Star of Italian Solidarity 2d class, 1962. Mem. Ann Arbor C. of C., Nat. Assn. Student Personnel Adminstrs., Modern Lang. Assn., Nat. Council Tchrs. English, Mich. Coll. Assn., AAUP, Schoolmasters Club, University Mus. Soc. (dir., sec. 1959-77). Phi Kappa Phi, Kiwanian (hon.). Clubs: Quadrangle, University; Dunworkin. Editor: (with C.D. Thorpe) University Readings, 1931; Bibliography of Contemporary Literature, 1932-37 (English Jour.); Essay Annual, yearly vols. from 1933-41; Toward Today, 1938; Religion and the State University, 1958; (with Harlan Hatcher) A Pictorial History of the Great Lakes, 1963; Our Michigan, 1966. Home: Ann Arbor, Mich. Died Apr. 27, 1977.

WALTERS, RICHARD J., printing co. exec.; b. Bklyn., Jan. 12, 1930; s. William H. and Mary C. (Savidge) W.; B.S., M.S., Georgetown U.; m. Wilma F. Ostergren, June 16, 1951; children—William, Norine, Mary, Richard J. With U.S. Printing & Lithograph Co. until 1959, v.p., 1950-59, exec. v.p., 1959; co. merged with Diamond Gardner Corp. to form Diamond Nat. Corp., 1959, name changed to Diamond Internat. Corp., 1969, v.p. Diamond Nat. Corp., N.Y.C., 1959-61, exec. v.p., 1961-65, pres., chief operating officer, 1965-78, chmn., chief exec. officer, 1970-78, also dir. Dir. Folding Paper Box Assn. Am., Lithographers and Printers Nat. Assn., Lithographic Tech. Found. Clubs: N.Y. Athletic; Wheatley Hills Golf (E. Williston, N.Y.); North Hempstead Country (Pt. Washington, N.Y.) Home: Manhasset, N.Y. Died June 28, 1978.

WALTON, J(OSEPH) BARNARD, sec. Friends General Conf.; b. Ercildoun, Pa., May 29, 1885; s. Joseph Solomon and Dora Elizabeth (Brosius) W.; student West Chester Normal Sch., 1896, 98; Friends Central Sch., Phila., 1898-1901: A.B., U. of Pa., 1905; A.M., Columbia U., 1908; student N.Y. Sch. of Philanthropy, 1907-08; m. Louise Elizabeth Haviland, Aug. 17, 1910; children—Joseph Haviland, Edward Haviland. Teacher Wilmington (Del.) Friends Sch., 1905-06, Friends Central Sch., Phila., 1906-07; sec. New York Friends Meeting, 1908-10; financial sec. Charity Orgn. Soc., New York, 1910-11; grad. sec. Student Y.M.C.A., New York City, 1911-14; sec. Friends Gen. Conf., 1915-51. Formerly director, now member of American Friends Service Com., Phila.; past chmn. Fellowship of Reconciliation, Phila. Dist.; formerly mem. bd. dirs. Swarthmore Cooperative Assn., mem. Phi Beta Kappa. Home: Swarthmore, Pa. *

WANGENSTEEN, OWEN H., surgeon; b. Lake Park, Minn., Sept. 21, 1898; s. Owen and Hannah (Hanson) W.; A.B., U. Minn., 1919, M.D., 1922, Ph.D. in Surgery, 1925; LL.D., U. Buffalo, 1946; D.Sc., U. Chgo., 1956, St. Olaf Coll., 1958, Temple U., 1961, Hamline U., 1963, Marquette U., 1970, U. Athens, 1978; Dr. h.c., U. Paris (Sorbonne), 1962; m. Helen Griffin, Jan. 6, 1923; children—Mary Helen (Brink), Owen Griffin, Stephen Lightner; m. 2d, Sarah Anne Davidson, Sept. 16, 1954. Fellow in medicine U. Minn., 1923; fellow in surgery Mayo Clinic, 1924; resident surgeon Univ. Hosp., 1925; faculty surgery U. Minn., 1926-67, prof. emeritus, 1967-81, Distinguished Service prof., 1960, Regents prof., 1966, dir. dept., 1930-67; asst. prof. F. de Quervain's Surg. Clinic and Physiol. Inst. Prof. Leon Asher, Berne, Switzerland, 1927-28. Bd. dirs. Am. Cancer Soc.; mem. O.S.R.D., 1940-45; mem. com. on research and devel. USPHS, 1940-45, com. on growth, 1947-49, NRC, chmn. gastric cancer com., 1948-51, mem. surgery study sect., 1949-53, mem. heart council, 1953-57, cons. to surgeon gen., 1956, mem. council research facility div., 1957-60; chmn. surgery study sect. NIH, 1952-53; mem. planning com. AAMC, 1958; pres. Minn. Med. Found., 1948-54. Served as pvt. S.A.T.C., World War I. Recipient Samuel D. Gross prize Phila. Acad. Surgery, 1935; John Scott award and medal Phila. Coll. Physicians, 1941, Alvarenza prize, 1949; Minn. div. award Am. Cancer Soc., 1949, Passano award, 1961, Lannelongue medal French Acad. Surgery, 1968; Distinguished Service award Minn. Acad. Sci., 1975; named 1st Minnesotan of 1969 by Gov.'s Com., 1969; Pembina Trail award Red River Valley Hist. Soc., 1973. Fellow Royal Coll. Surgeons Eng. (hon.), Hellenic Surg. Soc. Athens (hon.), A.C.S. (pres. 1959-60); mem. A.M.A. (Distinguished Service award 1968), Am. Surg. Assn. (pres. 1969). Minn. Acad. Medicine (pres. 1953), Internat. (pres. Am. chpt. 1969-72, v.p., del. internat. chpt. 1971-73), Minn., Mpls., Argentine (hon.), Halsted (pres. 1957-59) surg. socs., Soc. Exptl. Biology and Medicine, Soc. Exptl. Pathology, Am. Assn. Thoracic Surgery, A.A.A.S., Minn. Path. Soc., French Acad. Surgery, Norwegian (hon.), Nat. acad. scis., Royal Coll. Surgeons Edinburgh (hon.), German Surg. Congress (hon.), Royal Coll. Surgeons Ireland (hon.), Sigma Xi, Alpha Omega Alpha. Developed suction siphonage treatment of acute intestinal obstruction. Author: The Therapeutic Problem in Bowel Obstructions, 1937, 3d edit. 1955; Cancer, Esophagus and Stomach, 2d edit., 1956. Co-editor: Surgery, 1937-70. Contbr. to profl. jours. Home: Minneapolis, Minn. Died Jan. 13, 1981; buried Oakland Cemetery, St. Paul.

WAPLES, ROBERT M., bus. exec.; b. Phila., Feb. 11, 1894; s. Cornelius and Annie H. (Evans) W.; student Pierce Bus. Sch., 1911, Drexel Inst., 1913, Brown Prep. Sch., 1914-15; m. Ada C. Touchstone, Sept. 18, 1920; children—Robert M., Florence Elizabeth, James T. Mech. goods div. U.S. Rubber Co., 1920-22; v.p., mgr. Crandall Packing Co., 1922-23; with Garlock Packing Co., Phila. br., 1915-19, asst. to gen. mgr., Palmyra, N.Y., 1923-29, sec., 1929-48, v.p., 1948-52, exec. v.p., 1952-55, pres., 1955-59, chmn. bd., 1959-60, also dir.; bus. cons., 1960-76; dir. Garlock Packing Co. Can., Ltd., Mech. Leathers, Inc., Phila. Served as pvt., 319th Inf., U.S. Army, France, 1917-18. Mem. Mech. Packing Assn. (dir., past pres.), Am. Soc. Naval Engrs., VFW, Am. Legion, S.A.R., Rochester (N.Y.) C. of C. Mason. Clubs: Ontario Country; Rochester (N.Y.). Home: Palmyra, N.Y. Died May 7, 1976; buried Palmyra.

WARBURG, OTTO HEINRICH, scientist, biology; b. Freiburg, Baden, Oct. 8, 1883; s. Emil Warburg and Elizabeth Gertner; Dr. der Chemie, Berlin, 1906; Dr. der Medizin, Heidelberg U., 1911. Dir. Max Planck Inst. Zellphysiologie, Berlin-Dahlem, 1933—. Served with Prussian Horse Guards, 1914-18. Decorated Ordre pour le Merite, Great Cross Star and Shoulder Ribbon, Bunderrepublik; recipient Nobel prize for medicine. Fgn. mem. Royal Soc. Author: Freedom of West Berlin, 1963. Address: Berlin-Dahlem, Germany. *

WARD, CAMPBELL ALEXANDER, osteo. physician; b. Edmonton, Alta., Can., Jan. 11, 1903; s. Robert Campbell and Margaret Ann (Farley) W.; came to U.S., 1923, naturalized, 1942; student U. Man., 1921-22; pre. med. student, Des Moines Still Coll. Osteopathy, 1927; m. Iyla May Brown, Aug. 19, 1930; children—Robert Campbell, William Douglas, Mary Margaret Ward Yelton. Intern, Detroit Osteopathic Hosp., 1927-28; practice in Mt. Clemens, Mich., 1928-78. Mem. Mich. Hosp. Adv. Com.; sec. Children's Aid and Family Service, Macomb County, Mich. Trustee Mt. . Clemens Gen. Hosp., Nat. Osteopathic Found. Named Practitioner of the Year in Mich., 1963; tower at Mt. Clemens Gen. Hosp. named after him, 1980. Mem. Am. (trustee 1958-62, pres. elect 1963, pres. 1964; chmn. com. hosp. accreditation 1964-69), Macomb County (past pres.), Mich. (past pres.) osteopathic assns., Acad. Applied Osteopathy, Sigma Sigma Phi. Methodist. Mason. Club: Atlas (Des Moines). Home: Mount Clemens, Mich. Died Sept. 26, 1978; interred Clinton Grove Mausoleum, Mt. Clemens, Mich.

WARD, CLARENCE, college prof.; b. Brooklyn, N.Y., Mar. 11, 1884; s. Ferdinand and Ella Champion (Green) W.; A.B., Princeton, 1905, A.M., 1906, Ph.D., 1914; traveled and studied abroad, 1924-25; m. Helen Eshbaugh, July 15, 1907; children—Helen, Frederick Champion. Fellow in archaeology, 1905-08, lecturer in architecture, 1909-16, Princeton; asst. prof. architecture, later asso. prof., Rutgers Coll., 1908-16; prof. history and appreciation of art. Oberlin Coll. and dir. Dudley Peter Allen Memorial Art Mus., 1916-49, 1952-53; pastor East Oberlin Community Church, 1929-49, pastor emeritus since 1949; visiting lectr. fine arts Berea Coll., 1950; acting head dept. fine arts Johns Hopkins, 1950-51; John Hay Whitney Foundation visiting professor of fine arts University of the South, Sewanee, Tennessee, 1953-54; professor history of art, summers, 1925, 26, Univ. of Chicago; Mathews lecturer on Gothic architecture, Columbia Univ., 1940-41. Chairman celebration com., author and dir. of anniversary pageant, 150th Anniversary of the Founding of Rutgers Coll., 1916. Mem. Archaeol. Inst. America (formerly gen. sec. Charles Eliot Norton lecturer 1944-45), Coll. Art Assn., Mediaeval Acad. America, Ohio Academy of Science (fellow), American Soc. Archtl. Historians, Am. Assn. of Museums, Am. Assn. Univ. Profs., Am. Soc. for Aesthetics, Soc. for Promotion of Byzantine and Modern Greek Studies, Pi Gamma Mu, Phi Beta Kappa. Progressive Republican. Congregationalist. Author: Medieval Church Vaulting, 1915. Lecturer on art. Home: Oberlin, O. *

WARD, FRANCIS T., business exec.; b. Chgo., Nov. 11, 1893; s. Thomas W. and Anne J. W.; B.S., U. Chgo., 1915; m. Alice W., 1918; children—Francis T., Peter M., Lawrence W., Philip C. Partner Morgan Stanley & Co., N.Y.C. from 1943, adv. dir., to 1976. Home: Locust Valley, N.Y. Died Feb. 29, 1976.

WARD, HUGH CAMPBELL, exec.; b. Kansas City, Mo., Sept. 26, 1899; s. Hugh Campbell and Vassie (James) W.; A.B., Harvard, 1920; student Cambridge U., Eng., 1920-21; m. Grassie Bulkeley, June 14, 1923 (div. 1948); children—Virginia (Mrs. Samuel Cabot Jr.), Hugh Campbell, Mary Louise (Mrs. David D. Ryus), Ellen James, Peter Bulkeley; m. 2d, Frances Ebeling DuBois, Nov. 24, 1950. Various positions Westport Bank, Kansas City, Mo., Am. Red Cross Mission to Greece, N.Y. Trust Co.; staff First Nat. Bank of Boston, from 1923, asst. cashier, 1929, asst. v.p., 1930-32, v.p., 1932-64; asso. Clark, Dodge & Co., Inc., from 1964; dir. Moore Drop Forging Company, McCrory Corp., Boston Insulated Wire and Cable Co., trustee Eliot Savings Bank, Trustee U.S. Churchill Found. Served as 2d lt. C.A.C., U.S. Army, 1918-19. Decorated Silver Cross, Royal Order Savior (Greece) 1923. Down Town (Boston); Links (N.Y.C.); Maryland (Balt). Home: Cohasset, Mass. Died Apr. 15, 1976.

WARD, JESSE LYNN, univ. prof.; born Fountain County, Ind., Nov. 5, 1883; s. Benjamin Franklin and Mary Ann (Newkirk) W.; A.B., Ind. U., 1910, A.M., 1924; Ph.D., Ohio State U., 1933; m. Edith Lucetta Carmichael, March 2, 1912; children—Mary Ann (Mrs. Edwin Brady), Charlotte Eleanor, George Franklin, Edith Lucetta (Mrs. Harold Stahr). Pub. sch. administrator, 1910-27; prof. ednl. psychology, statistics, statis. research, U. of Toledo, since 1927, school adminstrn., head dept. secondary edn., since 1935, supervisor of secondary teacher training since 1946. Member Am. Statis. Soc., Ohio Edn. Assn. (mem. research div.). Democrat. Presbyterian. Mason. Club: Toledo Torch. Author: The Development of Faculty Personnel Forms for an Institution of Higher Learning, and the Calculation and Use of a Composite Index of Many Traits, 1934. Home: Toledo, O. *

WARD, MARY ALOYSIA, dean of women; b. San Francisco, Nov. 12, 1886; d. Daniel and Ellen (Toohey) Ward; A.B., Columbia, 1925; M.A., Stanford, 1932. Supervisor elementary edn., San Francisco Normal Sch., 1907-15, dean of women San Francisco State Coll., 1915-1948, acting pres., 1928, dir. summer sessions, 1929-35. Mem. Pi Lambda Theta, Kappa Delta Pi. Address: San Francisco.*

WARD, PAUL W., newspaperman; b. Lorain, Ohio, Oct. 9, 1905; s. Thomas Joseph and Dyma Nora (Hire) W.; student U. Akron, 1921-22, W.Va. U., 1922-23; A.B., Middlebury Coll., 1925; m. Dorothy I. Cate, Mar. 19, 1927; children—Kerry Dawson, Marren (Mrs. Thomas P. Meehan). With Powers Photo-Engraving Co., N.Y.C., 1925-26, New Bedford (Mass.) Standard, 1926-30; mem. local staff Balt. Sun. 1930-32, Washington bur., 1932-37, London bur., 1937-40, fgn. affairs specialist, Washington bur., 1940-70, bur. mgr., 1970-76; Washington corr. The Nation, 1936-37, Agence Francaise Independente, 1943-44, Le Pays (Paris), 1945. Recipient Pulitzer prize for distinguished reporting internat. affairs, 1948; decorated chevalier Legion of Honor. Mem. White House, State Dept. (pres. 1959-60) corrs. assns. Clubs: National Press (life), Overseas Writers (Washington); Fauteurs de Paix (Paris). Author: Life in the Soviet Union, 1947, Japanese edit., 1948. Home: Chevy Chase, Md. Died Nov. 24, 1976.

WARD, ROBERT ELWIN MCCRANER, naval officer; b. San Acacia, Colo., Feb. 2, 1914; s. Matthew and Minnie (Barnes) W.; student U. Cal., 1930-31; B.S., U.S. Naval Acad., 1935; grad. Nat. War Coll.; m. Frances Larco, Nov. 9, 1938; children—Robert Matthew, Spencer Rowan, Patricia Hope. Commd. ensign U.S. Navy, 1935, advanced through grades to rear adm., 1960; comdr. U.S.S. Sailfish, 1943-44, U.S.S. Sea Leopard, 1945-46, U.S.S. Chopper, 1946-48; tng. officer Anti-Submarine Sch. Pacific Fleet, 1949-50; comdr. Submarine Div. 52, 1951-52, Submarine Squadron 7, 1956-57; comdr. U.S.S. Washburn, 1957-58. U.S.S. Rochester, 1958-59; staff Office Chief Naval Operations, 1959-60; chief legislative affairs Office Sec. Navy, 1960-62, dir. material mgmt. rev. Dept. of Navy, 1962-63; comdr. Amphibious Group Two, 1963-64; Comdr. Naval Res. Tng. Command, Omaha, from 1964. Decorated Navy Cross with gold star, Silver Star with gold star, Presdl. Unit citation, Navy Unit citation. Home: Vigrinia Beach, Va. Died Apr. 9, 1980.

WARD, WALDRON M(ERRY), lawyer; b. Newark, N.J., June 27, 1886; s. Alexander Spencer and Julia Maria (Merry) W.; A.B., Princeton Univ., 1907; LL.B., New York Law Sch., 1909; m. Aline T. Coursen, Oct. 22, 1912; children—Lt. (j.g.) Waldron M. (dec. 1944), John S., Aileen, Roger C. Admitted to the bar of N.J., 1910; in gen. practice of law, Newark, 1914—, counsel to firm of Pitney, Hardin and Kipp and predecessor co., formerly asso., mem. firm and sr. mem. firm; former chmn. bd. Howard Savs. Inst., Newark; past dir. Nat. Newark & Essex Banking Co. (Newark). Fellow Am. Bar Assn. Found. Republican. Clubs: University, Princeton (N.Y.); Essex (Newark); Baltusrol Golf (Springfield, N.J.). Home: Summit, N.J. *

WARD, WALTER LEROY, JR., banker; b. Homer, La., Mar. 30, 1902; s. Walter Leroy and Virginia (Madden) W.; student Tulane U., Washington and Lee U.; m. Naomi Terry, Sept. 10, 1966; children (by previous marriage)—Walter Leroy III, Swan Sullivan. Chief clk. La. Banking Dept., 1923-27; engaged in bond and brokerage bus., also mem. New Orleans Cotton Exchange, 1928-31; bank examiner La., 1934-39; with Fidelity Nat. Bank Baton Rouge, 1939-80, pres., 1954-72, chmn. bd., 1960-78, chmn. emeritus, adv. dir., 1978-80. Mem. bd. Greater Baton Rouge Port Commn., 1962-80, Downtown Baton Rouge Assn., 1962-80, Baton Rouge Better Bus. Bur., 1942-80. Bd. dirs. Baton Rouge Little Theatre, Baton Rouge Parish Library, 1960-62; mem. La. State U. Found. Mem. Financial Pub. Relations Assn., Am., La. bankers assns., La. State Sr. Golf Assn. (dir.), Baton Rouge C. of C. (dir., exec. com. econ. devel. council). Clubs: Baton Rouge Country (past pres., dir.), Rotary, City, Boston (New Orleans). Home: Baton Rouge, La. Died Oct. 27, 1980.

WARDALL, WILLIAM JED (WOR-DEL'), business executive; born at Tuscola, Ill., Feb. 22, 1885; son of Xenophon Leonidas and Emma A. (Sawyer) W.; A.B., University of Illinois, 1908; married Mary Sherrill Burry, April 20, 1912 (died January 17, 1942); married 2d, Suzette F. Beavers, November 18, 1947. Bond salesman, 1909-16; western mgr. Bonbright & Co., Inc., 1916-32; pres. and dir. of Asso. Telephone Utilities Co. and various subsidiaries, New York, 1932-33; co-receiver Asso. Telephone Utilities Co., 1933-34, trustee in reorganization, 1934-35; pres. General Telephone Corp., successor, 1935-36; corporate reorganization work for various other corps., 1937-38; trustee in reorganization of Broad St. Hosp., New York, 1938-39; sole trustee in reorganization of McKesson & Robbins, Inc., 1938-41; chmn. bd. The Best Foods, Inc., 1942-50. Mem. Phi Gamma Delta, Beta Gamma Sigma. Republican. Presbyterian. Clubs: University (N.Y.C. and Chgo.). Home: Syosset, L.I., N.Y. *

WARDEN, JOHN A., army officer; b. July 31, 1886; B.S., Agrl. and Mech. Coll. of Tex., 1908. Commd. 2d lt. cavalry, Sept. 25, 1908; promoted through grades to rank of col., Nov. 1, 1937; temp. rank of brig. gen. since 1941; grad. Q.M. Sch., 1930; asst. comdt., Chicago Q.M. Depot, 1930-34; grad. Army War Coll., 1934; Naval War Coll., 1936; 4th Corps Area Q.M., Atlanta, Ga., 1938-41; Q.M. Replacement Center, Camp Lee,

1941; comdg. gen. Q.M. Replacement Training Center, Fort F. E. Warren, Wyo., Apr. 1941-43; assigned comdg. gen. Q.M. Sch., Camp Lee, Feb. 1943. Address: Camp Lee, Va. *

WARE, HOYT NICHOLAS, govt. ofcl.; b. Augusta, Ga., July 29, 1917; s. Hoyt and Lessie (Christie) W.; A.B., U. Ga., 1938; postgrad. Air War Coll., 1958-59, Fed. Exec. Inst. U. Va., 1971; m. Lillian Rose, Nov. 3, 1944; children—Catherine Rose, Nicholas Evans. With USIA, 1949-76, pub. affairs officer, Lima, Peru, 1971-73; bd. pub. affairs officer, Can Tho, 1973; dir. agy. press center, Washington, 1974-76. Address: Washington, D.C. Died Feb. 21, 1976.

WARE, ROMAINE BAKER, writer; b. Bridgeton, N.J., Apr. 18, 1886; grad. Bridgeton High Sch., 1904; student West Jersey Acad., 1905-06; m. Laura Rave, of Wilkes-Barre, Pa., 1911 (divorced, 1927); m. 2d, Stella St. Jacque, of Portland, Ore., Sept. 6, 1928; 1 son, William Romaine. Began writing on garden topics, 1923; writer for St. Paul Pioneer Press, 1923-26, Morning Oregonian, Portland, 1927-30; garden editor Nature Mag., 1933; owner Chart Pub. Co., New York, pubs. of garden charts, since 1935; pres. and gen. mgr. The Jelmeter Co., Bridgeton, since 1935; garden editor Ladies' Home Journal, 1935. Mem. Theosophical Soc. Republican. Contbr. on gardens and horticulture to mags. Home: Bridgeton, N.J. *

WARMACK, JOHN LEE, utility co. exec.; b. Hope, Ark., Jan. 19, 1928; s. Robert Lee and Birdie Jane (Huckabee) W.; B.S., La. State U., 1951; m. Mary Allen, Jan. 4, 1951; children—Patricia, John Lee, Mary Jane, Robert, Andrew. With Gulf States Utilities Co., Beaumont, Tex., 1952-67; with So. Ind. Gas & Electric Co., Evansville, 1967-81, exec. v.p., gen. mgr., 1975-76, pres., gen. mgr., 1976-81; dir. Nat. City Bank Bd. dirs. Vanderburgh County Soc. for Crippled Children and Adults, 1973-77, Jr. Achievement of Southwestern Ind., 1973-74, dist. chmn. Boy Scouts Am., 1976-81. Registered profl. engr., La., Tex. Mem. Ind. Electric Assn. (dir. 1970-74, pres. 1972-73), Constrn. Users Council, IEEE, Evansville C. of C. (dir. 1967-72) v.p. transp. and environ. mgmt. div. 1972-74). Clubs: Masons, Shriners, Petroleum (Evansville), Columbia (Indpls.). Home: Evansville, Ind. Died Feb. 3, 1981.

WARNER, GERTRUDE CHANDLER, teacher, author; b. Putnam, Conn., Apr. 16, 1890; d. Edgar Morris and Jane Elizabeth (Carpenter) Warner. Author stories for children, essays, mag. articles and articles in ednl. mags.; tchr., to 1950; author: Boxcar Children; Surprise Island; Yellow House Mystery; Mystery Ranch; Mike's Mystery; Blue Bay Mystery; Woodshed Mystery; Lighthouse Mystery; Mountain Top Mystery; Snowbound Mystery; Tree House Mystery; Bicycle Mystery; Mystery in the Sand; others. Named Woman of Year, 1965. Republican. Congregationalist. Home: Putnam, Conn. Deceased.

WARNER, HARRY PRESTON, lawyer; b. Des Arc, Ark., Oct. 18, 1885; s. Charles Edward and Harriet (Walsh) W.; ed. Center Coll., Danville, Ky., 1904-06; student U. of Va. (law dept.), 1907-08; m. Sydney Yantis, June 25, 1913; children—Lucy Yantis, Charles Edward. Admitted to Ark. bar, 1908, and since practiced at Ft. Smith; associated with father until his death, 1916, under title of Warner & Warner; with brother, Cecil R., under same firm name, since 1916. Pres. Ft. Smith C. of C., 1933-34, v.p., dir. Sparks Meml. Hosp. Mem. Am., Ark. State, Ft. Smith bar assns., Beta Theta Pi. Democrat. Presbyn. Club: Hardscrabble Country. Home: Ft. Smith, Ark. *

WARNER, JACK L., motion pictures exec.; b. London, Ont., Can.; s. Benjamin and Pearl (Eichelbaum) W.; student publ schs.; m. Ann Boyar. Early career as singer; pioneer with bros. in prodn., distbn., exhbn. motion pictures; in charge Warner Sunset Studios, Hollywood, Cal., 1918; pioneer with bros. in devel. talking pictures, 1926-28; co-founder Warner Bros. Pictures; pres. Jack Warner Prodns., Century City, Calif.; producer films 1776, Dirty Little Billy. Mem. Pres.'s Nat. Adv. Com. Jobs for Veterans, 1971. Trustee U. So. Calif. Served as lt. col. USAAF; organizer pioneer motion picture unit AAF. Decorated officer Legion of Honor (France), Order Aztec Eagle (Mexico), Order of Merit Carlos Manuel de Cespedes (Cuba); comdr. Order Brit. Empire; officer L'Ordre de la Couronne (Belgium); commendatore dell 'Ordine al Merito della Republica Italiana (Italy); Cross of Merit First Class (Germany); Diploma of Honor, Latin Am. Consular Assn.; Award of Recognition (China); Medal for Merit (U.S.); recipient Gold Distinguished Service medal D.A.V.; First World War Peace prize; Acad. award, Hollywood Fgn. Corrs. Assn. award for best prodn. for The Life of Emile Zola, 1937, Casablanca, 1943; Irving Thalberg award for consistent best prodn., 1958; Acad. award producer best picture My Fair Lady, 1964; David Di Donatella award for best picture, 1965; named hon. alumnus U. So. Calif. Mem. Com. Econ. Devel., Air Force Assn., So. Calif. Symphony Assn., Am. Inst. Cinematography (hon.), C. of C. Author: My First Hundred Yeard in Hollywood, 1965. Address: Century City, Calif. Died Sept. 9, 1978.

WARNER, ROGER SHERMAN, JR., corp. executive; b. Boston, June 12, 1907; s. Roger Sherman and Mary (Hooper) W.; A.B., Harvard, 1931; postgrad. Mass. Inst. Tech., 1933-34. Devel. engr. Kaysam Corp., 1936-38, B.F. Goodrich, 1938-42; tech. aide, project engr. OSRD, 1942-44; coordinating engr., div. head Manhattan project, Los Alamos, 1944-47; from staff mem. to gen. mgr. AEC, 1947, dir. engring., 1947-49; mem. engring. staff Arthur D. Little, Inc., 1949-51, v.p., dir. Cambridge Corp.; later mem. staff Advanced Research Projects Agy., Office Sec. Def., Washington; now v.p. Allied Research Assos., Inc. affiliate Boeing Aircraft Co., Boston; dir. research Inst. Naval Studies, Cambridge 1961-62, then acting dir.; mgr. advanced systems Astro Electronics Products div. RCA, from 1964. Recipient medal of merit for work performed with OSRD. Mem. Am. Chem. Soc. Club: Harvard (N.Y.C.). Home: Washington, D.C. Died Aug. 3, 1976.

WARREN, GORDON CHESTER, clergyman; b. North River, Prince Edward Island, Can., Nov. 5, 1884; s. William and Eliza (Harper) W.; student Prince of Wales Coll., Charlottetown, P.E. Island, 1899-1900; A.B., Acadia Univ., 1910, D.D. (hon.), 1927; B.D., Newton Theol. Inst., Newton Centre, Mass., 1912; m. Sadie M. Dyseman, July 8, 1914; 1 dau., Edith Gene (Mrs. J. Winston Miles). Ordained to ministry of Baptist Ch., 1911; pastor New Boston, New Hampshire, 1911-13, Bridgetown, N.S., 1913-17, Brunswick St. Baptist Ch., Fredericton, N.B., 1917-29; editor The Maritime Baptist, hdqrs., Wolfville, N.S., 1929-36; prof. practical theology, Acadia Univ., Wolfville, since 1936, acting prof. ch. history, 1936-38, dean sch. of theology since 1941. Mem. Baptist Fedn. of Can. (pres. 1944-47), Can. Baptist Fgn. Mission Bd. (chmn. 1941-47; chmn. Eastern sect., 1924-41); mem. exec. of Bapt. World Alliance since 1947. Home: Wolfville, Nova Scotia, Can. *

WARREN, KATHERINE, former univ. dean; b. Montgomery, Ala., Apr. 27, 1907; d. William Kennedy and Mary Eleanor (Greenwood) Warren; A.B., Fla. State Coll. for Women, 1933; M.A., Columbia Tchrs. Coll., 1939, postgrad., 1946-47; postgrad. U. N.C., 1945. Asst. to dean students Fla. State Coll. for Women, Tallahassee, 1935-38, asst. dean students, 1939-47; dean women Fla. State U. Tallahassee, 1947-67, dean women emerita. Mem. Gov.'s Commn. on Status of Women, Leon County-Tallahassee Planning Commn. Mem. Nat. Assn. Women Deans and Counselors (chmn. univ. sect. 1955-57, nat. rec. sec. 1959-61), Am. Assn. U. Women (pres. Fla. div. 1947-49), Fla. Assn. Deans and Counselors (pres. 1946-47), Mortar Bd., Alpha Lambda Delta (mem. at large nat. council 1949-54), Kappa Delta Pi, Delta Delta Delta. Address: Tallahassee, Fla. Died Oct. 22, 1974.

WARREN, LINDSAY CARTER, govt. official; b. Washington, N.C., Dec. 16, 1889; s. Charles Frederic and Elizabeth Mutter (Blount) W.; ed. Bingham Sch., Asheville, N.C., 1903-06; U. of N.C., 1906-08; studied law, same univ., 1911-12; LL.D., University of North Carolina, 1946; married Emily Harris, January 28, 1916; children—Emily Carter, Lindsay Carter, Charles. Admitted N.C. bar, 1912, began practice at Washington, N.C.; chmn. Dem. Exec. Com., Beaufort County, N.C., 1912-25; county atty. Beaufort County, 1912-25; mem. N.C. Senate, 1917, 19 (pres. pro tem. 1919); mem. Code Commn. of N.C., 1919; chmn. platform com. Dem. State Conv., N.C., 1920; chmn. spl. legislative com. on Workmen's Compensation Acts, N.C., 1920; mem. N.C. Ho. of Rep., 1923; mem. of 69th to 76th Congresses (1925-41), 1st N.C. Dist.; renominated to 77th Congress, but resigned, Nov. 1, 1940, to become comptroller gen. of U.S. Chmn. Dem. State Conv., 1930, 34; mem. Constl. Commn. N.C., 1931; del. at large Dem. Nat. Conv., 1932, 40; temporary chmn. Dem. State Conv., 1938. Trustee U. of N.C., 1921-25. Episcopalian. Died 1976.

WARREN, LOUIS AUSTIN, author, clergyman; b. Holden, Mass., Apr. 23, 1885; s. Joseph Austin and Flora Adell (Petts) W.; student Transylvania U., Lexington, Ky., 1909, B.P.T., Coll. of Bible, 1916; Litt.D., Lincoln Meml. U., 1929; m. Ellen Augusta Moore, Nov. 30, 1916; children—Eleanor Louise, Kenneth Austin, Lawrence Justin, Evelyn Adell, Lester Moore. Editor, La Rue County Herald, Hodgenville, 1918-19, Lincoln Kinsman, 1936-42. Dir. Lincoln Nat. Life Found., 1928-56, dir. emeritus, 1956. Mem. Ind. Library and Hist. Bd., 1941-56; adv. council U.S. Civil War Centennial Commn., 1958-65; hon. mem. U.S. Lincoln Sesquicentennial Commn., 1959. Recipient Alumni citation in history Transylvania Coll., 1954; Distinguished Biography award Ind. U. Writers Conf., 1959; Benjamin Barondess award for outstanding Lincolniana, 1965. Mem. Disciples of Christ Hist. Soc. (pres. 1957), Pi Kappa Alpha, Pi Gamma Mu. Club: Filson. Author: Lincoln's Parentage and Childhood, 1926; Slavery Atmosphere of Lincoln's Youth, 1933; Little Known Lincoln Episodes, 1934; Abraham Lincoln, a Concise Biography, 1934; Lincoln Bibliography Check List, 1942; Lincoln's Youth, Indiana Years, 1959; Lincoln's Gettysburg Declaration, 1964. Editor Lincoln Lore, 1929-55. Home: Fort Wayne IN. *

WARREN, NEWTON JOSEPH, college pres.; b. Carroll Co., Ga., Mar. 29, 1883; s. James W. and Rebecca (Turner) W.; A.B., Bowdon (Ga.) Coll., 1908; A.M., Mercer U., Macon, Ga., 1912; m. Eula Mae Simpson, of Tallapoosa, Ga., June 27, 1916. Supt. schs., Cave Springs, Ga., 1912-16; pres. Bowdon Coll. since 1915. Democrat. Baptist. Mason, Odd Fellow, Home: Bowdon, Ga.*

WARREN, SHIELDS, physician; b. Cambridge, Mass., Feb. 26, 1898; s. William Marshall and Sara Bainbridge (Shields) W.; A.B., Boston U., 1918; M.D., Harvard, 1923; S.D., Boston U., 1949; D.Sc., Western Res. U., 1952, Case Inst. Tech., 1956; LL.D., Tulane U., 1953; D.Sc. (hon.), Northwestern U., 1959; Dr. honoris causa, U. Brazil, 1964; D.M.S., Brown U., 1969; m. Alice Springfield, Aug. 11, 1923; children—A. Emilie (Mrs. Guy C. McLeod), Patricia (Mrs. David R. Palmer). Instr. in pathology Harvard Med. Sch., 1925-36, asst. prof., 1936-48, prof., 1948-65, prof. emeritus, 1965-80; pathologist New Eng. Deaconess Hosp., 1927-63, cons. pathology, 1963-80; dir. Mass. Tumor Diagnosis Service, 1928-55, cons., 1955-71; pathologist New Eng. Bapt. Hosp., to 1963; dir. Mallinckrodt, Inc.; dir. biology and medicine U.S. AEC, 1947-52, mem. adv. com., 1952-58; cons. Dept. Energy, 1959-80; spl. adviser, acting U.S. rep. to 2d Internat. Conf. on Peaceful Uses of Atomic Energy, Geneva, 1958; mem. sci. adv. bd. consultants Armed Forces Inst. Pathology, 1952-68; mem. Nat. Adv. Cancer Council, 1946-50; U.S. rep. UN Sci. Com. on Effects Atomic Radiation, 1955-63; sr. statesman, sci. adv. bd. USAF, 1961-62; chmn. life scis. com. NASA, 1971-74, mem. space program adv. council. Chmn. corp., trustee Boston U., 1953-69. Served as capt. USNR; res. cons. pathology USN. Recipient Ward Burdick award Am. Soc. Clin. Pathology, 1949; William Proctor award Sci. Research Soc. Am., 1952; Modern Medicine award, 1953; Banting medal Am. Diabetes Assn., 1953; Charles V. Chapin medal City of Providence, 1958; Order of So. Cross in degree of comdr. Brazilian govt., 1961; Albert Einstein medal and award, 1962; Enrico Fermi award AEC, 1972. Life trustee Am. Bd. Pathology. Mem. Nat. Acad. Scis., Am. Philos. Soc., Am. Cancer Soc. (medal 1950, Nat. award 1968, hon. life mem., dir., pres. Mass. div. 1958-60), AAAS, AMA, Am. Acad. Arts and Scis., Am. Assn. Pathologists (past pres.), Am. Soc. Exptl. Pathology (past pres.), Soc. Exptl. Biology and Medicine, Am. Assn. Cancer Research (ex-pres.); Phi Beta Kappa. Methodist. Clubs: Cosmos, Harvard, Waquoit Yacht. Author: Medical Science for Everyday Use, 1927; Pathology of Diabetes Mellitus, 1930, 3d edit., 1952; (with O. Gates) A Handbook for the Diagnosis of Cancer of the Uterus, 1947, 48, 49; (with S.P. Hicks) Introduction to Neuropathology; (with A.W. Oughterson) Medical Effects of the Atomic Bomb in Japan, 1956; The Pathology of Ionizing Radiation, 1961; (with P.M. LeCompte, M.A. Legg) Pathology of Diabetes Mellitus, 4th edit., 1966. Contbr. articles to profl. jours. Home: West Newton, Mass. Died July 1, 1980; buried Rochester, N.H.

WARREN, THONAS ALFRED, assn. exec.; b. Manchester, Eng., May 10, 1882; s. Alfred and Selina Warren; ed. Manchester Secondary School; m. Louisa Davidson, 1908; 1 son. Served as chief asst. for higher education and as supt. of evening schools, Manchester, as asst. edn. sec., Plymouth, and as dir. of edn., Wolverhampton. Pres. of Rotary in Great Britain and Ireland, 1937-39; vice pres. Rotary International, 1939-42, pres. since July 1, 1945. Comdr. Order of British Empire. Home: Wolverhampton, Eng. *

WARRINER, JESSE BOLLES, business exec.; b. Montrose, Pa., Dec. 1, 1883; s. Rev. Edward A. and Esther (Bolles) W.; B.S., Mining, Pa. State Coll., 1905; m. Louise Frederick, 1911; children—Lendall Pitts, John Sherman. Chief engr. The Lehigh Coal & Navigation Co., 1913-19, gen. mgr., 1921-27, vice-pres., 1927-30; pres. Lehigh Navigation Coal Co., Inc., 1930-48, chmn. bd. since 1948, sr. dir. since 1950; mgr. Cranberry Creek Coal Co., 1919-21; dir. Pa. Power & Light Co. Republican. Episcopalian. Clubs: Laurentian (Can.); Racquet, Rittenhouse. Contbr. articles on tech. subjects. Home: Bethlehem, Pa. *

WARRINGTON, ERNEST WILLIAM, educator; born Georgetown, Del., Dec. 16, 1883; s. William A. and Mary Emily (Marsh) W.; A.B., U. of Del., 1905; A.M., Princeton, 1907; grad. Princeton Theol. Sem., 1908; grad. work Columbia and Union Theol. Sem., 1926-28; D.D. (hon.), Lewis and Clark U., 1944; m. Laura Letty, July 22, 1912; children—William Rich, Letty Marsh (Mrs. Harry E. Faught). Ordained to ministry of Presbyn. Ch., 1908; pastor, Pilot Rock, Ore., 1908-14, Freewater, Ore., 1914-16, Roseburg, Ore., 1916-21; supply pastor Park Av. Presbyn. Ch., N.Y. City, 1926-27; interim preacher First Presbyn. Ch., Portland, Ore., 1933-34; Y.M.C.A. work with A.E.F. in France, 1918-19; gen. sec. student Y.M.C.A., Ore. State Coll., 1921-26; organizer depts. of religion and philosophy Ore. State Coll., 1928, and since head of depts., dir. interseminary movement, student dept.

Y.M.C.A., N.Y. City, 1927-28; lecturer in religion and character edn., U. of Ore., 1933-35. Mem. Nat. Religious Edn. Assn., N.E.A., Nat. Adult Edn. Assn., Ore. Council of Chs. (past pres.), Phi Kappa Phi, Kappa Delta Pi, Lambda Chi Alpha. Mason. Odd Fellow. Home: Corvallis, Ore. *

WASCHER, HOWARD GEORGE, business exec.; b. Frackville, Pa., Nov. 5, 1885; s. Charles Howard and Anna Elizabeth (Sanner) W.; student Bucknell U., 1903, Lehigh U., 1904-08; m. Ida May Richards, Sept. 24, 1913; children—Richard Paul, Howard Charles, Robert George, Elizabeth E. Began as draftsman and asst. to plant engr. Corn Products Refining Co., 1908, plant engr., Pekin, Ill., 1912-20, in charge of constrn. and operation of affiliated plants in Europe, 1920-40, in charge of foreign operations from N.Y., 1940-48, dir. since 1940, vice pres., 1944-47, exec. v.p., 1947-51, chmn. exec. com. since 1951; chmn. bd. Bedford Constrn. Co. since 1952; president Corn Industries Research Foundation since 1953; director Canada Starch Co., Ltd., Montreal, Bedford Constrn. Co., Chicago, Refinacoes de Milho, Sao Paulo Brazil. Trustee Whitehall Found. Home: Englewood, N.J. *

WASHBURN, HAROLD CONNETT, author; b. N.Y. City, Feb. 8, 1884; s. Jacob and Mary Belinda (Connett) W.; A.B., Harvard, 1906; m. Rosalie Thompson, of Louisville, Ky., Oct. 24, 1911. Apptd. instr. (later asst. prof.) English and history, U.S. Naval Acad., 1906; resigned, Oct. 1, 1919; assisted in revision of N.A. course in English and organized course in after-dinner speaking; with Blodgett, Hart & Co., investment securities, New York, since Jan. 1920. Field rep. Navy League of U.S., 1917; assisted in securing Harvard Endowment Fund, 1919. Republican. Episcopalian. Author: The American Blind Spot—The Failure of the Volunteer System as Shown in Our Military History, 1917. Recatalogued U.S. Navy collection of trophy flags (171 in number), 1912-13. Contbr. various articles to U.S. Naval Inst. Proc. Home: New York, N.Y. *

WASMUTH, THOMAS CALVIN, dept. store exec.; b. Andrews, Ind., Mar. 29, 1914; s. Arthur Denman and Hazel (Thomas) W.; B.S., Miami U., Oxford, Ohio, 1935; m. Ethel Miller, June 18, 1938; children—Thomas Calvin, Judith Ann. With Rike-Kumler Co., Dayton, O., 1935-65, chmn. profit-sharing plan com., 1944, v.p., dir., 1951-62, exec. v.p., 1962-65; pres. Burdine's, Miami, Fla., 1965-68, chmn. bd., chief exec. officer, 1968-75; dir. Asso. Merchandising Corp., N.Y.C., First Nat. Bank Miami. Campaign chmn. United Fund, 1957, pres., 1962-64; v.p. Orange Bowl Com. Bd. dirs. Dade Found.; chmn. bd. United Fund of Dade County; trustee U. Miami. Mem. Greater Miami C. of C. (dir., v.p.), Delta Kappa Epsilon, Eta Mu Pi, Delta Sigma Pi. Clubs: Met. (N.Y.C.); Miami Valley Hunt and Polo, Moraine Country (Dayton); Indian Creek Country, Bath (Miami Beach); Miami (pres.). Home: Miami Beach, Fla. Died Mar. 11, 1975.

WASSERMAN, WILLIAM STIX, b. Phila., Pa., Mar. 24, 1901.; s. Joseph and Edith (Stix) W., A.B., Princeton, 1922; m. Marion L. Fleisher, Dec. 4, 1923; children—Marie Blance, William Stix, Joseph, Steven Rice. Pres. Wm. Stix Wasserman & Co., N.Y.C.; pres., dir. Investment Corp of Phila.; pres. Skyline Ranch, Inc.; dir. Am. Busch Arma Corp., Nat. Patent Devel. Corp., Responsive Environments Corp., Alexander Stores, Inc.; spl. adviser Shearson; Hammil & Co.; N.Y.C. Past pres., chmn. Del. Fund Am. del. to World Econ. Congress, Berlin, 1931; adv. to Am. del. to Internat. Labor Conf., Geneva, 1937; chief U.S. Lend-Lease Mission to Australia, 1942; rep. the Office of Econ. Warfare, on two special missions to Eng., 1943; special adv. to chmn. Smaller War Plants Corp., 1944. Clubs: Princeton of N.Y.; Midday (Phila.). Contbr, articles on polit. and econ. subjects to mags. Home: New York, N.Y. Died Jan. 5, 1979.

WASSON, HOUSTON HUTCHINSON, lawyer; b. Songdo, Korea, June 29, 1911; s. Alfred Washington and Mabel (Sutton) W.; B.A., So. Meth. U., 1932; B.A. in Jurisprudence, Queen's Coll., Oxford, Eng., 1934, B.C.L., 1935, M.A., 1952; Sterling fellow, Yale, 1935-36; m. Linda Marion Wyckoff, Sept. 17, 1938; children—H. Reed, Linda M., Katherine R. (dec.), Ellen A., Elizabeth J, Alfred W. Admitted to N.Y. bar, 1937, since practiced in N.Y.C; asso. firm Sullivan & Cromwell, 1936-46; partner firm Lovejoy, Wasson, Lundgren & Ashton and predecessor firm, 1946-75, counsel to firm, 1975-77. Dir. Zapata Sea Services, Inc., Falcon Tankers, Inc. Trustee Mona Bismarck Found. Mem. Phi Beta Kappa, Kappa Alpha, Beta Pi Theta. Presbyn. Clubs: Circumnavigators, Yale (N.Y.C.); Waccabuc (N.Y.) Country; East Chop Beach, East Chop Tennis (Martha's Vineyard, Mass.); Shenorock Shore (Rye, N.Y.). Home: Waccabuc, N.Y. Died Jan. 26, 1977.

WASSON, SAMUEL CARSON, clergyman, life ins. co. exec.; b. Harford County, Md., Dec. 9, 1908; s. Samuel C. and Mary Lee (Archer) W.; student Balt. City Coll., 1922-26; A.B. (Adams Oratorical medal 1929), Johns Hopkins, 1930; Th.B. (Hugh Davies prize homiletics), Princeton Theol. Sem. 1935; spl. studies U. Edinburgh (Scotland), 1954, U. Pa., 1960-61; D.D. (hon.), Temple U., 1955, Coll. Ozarks, 1955; m. M. Elizabeth Ellis, Sept. 17, 1937; children—Samuel Carson, Diana, Ellis Archer. Br. mgr. B.F. Goodrich Rubber Co., 1930-32; ordained to ministry Presbyn. Ch., 1935; asst. minister in Phila., 1935-37; minister in Jeannette, Pa., 1937-40, Wayne, Pa., 1940-47, Rye, N.Y., 1947-60; exec. v.p. Presbyn. Ministers Fund, 1960-63, pres., 1963-73, also dir., ret., 1973. Pres., Friends of Old Pine St. Soc., 1968-76. Trustee U.P. Found., 1948-75, Conwell Sch. of Theology, Phila., 1966-71, U.P. Hist. Soc., 1966-71; alumni trustee Princeton Theol. Sem., 1954-57. Recipient Gold medal Freedoms Found., 1949. Mem. Alpha Tau Omega. Clubs: Athenaeum, Union League (Phila.); Canterbury Cleric. Author: Eleven O'Clock Sunday Morning, 1960. Home: Avalon, N.J. Died Mar. 26, 1976; interred Presbyterian Churchyard, Churchville, Md.

WATERHOUSE, FRANCIS ASBURY, college prof.; b. Newtonville, Mass., Jan. 30, 1883; s. Francis Asbury and Mary Isabelle (Hanson) W.; A.B., Harvard, 1905, A.M., 1906, Ph.D., 1918; studied U. of Berlin, Collège de France, Paris; m. Marie de Métivier, of Boston, Aug. 6, 1913. Mem. faculty, Dartmouth, 1910-14, Bowdoin, 1915, U. of Pa., 1915-18, U. of Tex., 1918-22, Hamilton Coll., 1922-3; chmn. dept. Romance langs., Kenyon Coll., Gambier, O., since 1923. Author: Random Studies in the Romantic Chaos, 1923. Address: Gambier, O.*

WATERMAN, HENRY SAMUEL, consular service; b. Port Townsend, Wash., Mar. 20, 1882; s. Sigmund and Sara (Kalisher) W.; B.S., U. of Calif., 1902; grad. student Mich. Coll. of Mines, 1902; m. Elsie Hess, June 6, 1919. Mining and civ. engr., 1902-09; bldg. contractor, Seattle, Wash., 1910-14; clk. Am. Consulate, Moscow, Russia, 1916-17, Bergen, Norway, 1917-18; vice consul Christiansand, Norway, 1918, Guatemala, 1919; consul at Corinto, Nicaragua, 1920, San Jose, Costa Rica, 1921-26, Shanghai, China, 1926-28, Saigon, French Indo China, 1928-33, Sheffield, Eng., 1933-35, Bombay, Ind., 1935-39, Bordeaux, France, 1939-41, Monterrey, Mexico, Sept. 18, 1941-45, consul gen., July 2, 1945-Nov. 30, 1946; retired. Mason (32 deg.). Clubs: Shanghai (China) Golf; Hallamshire (Sheffield); Royal Bombay Yacht; Casino de Monterrey. Address: San Francisco, Calif. *

WATERMAN, JEROME AARON, merchant; b. Hawkinsville, Ga., Nov. 6, 1883; s. Maurice and Henrietta (Maas) W.; student Mercer U., 1902; Dr. H. L. (hon.), U. Tampa, 1966; m. Daisy Guggenheim, Sept. 14, 1922 (dec. 1945); children—Cecile, Regina Lee. Chemist Tenn. Coal & Iron R. R., Bessemer, Ala., 1902-03, So. Paint & Turpentine Co., 1903-04; sec., treas. Standard Electric Co., 1904-07 (both Jacksonville, Fla.); office and advt. mgr. Maas Bros., Tampa, Fla., 1907-10, supt., mdse. mgr., 1910-15, sec.-treas., mdse. mgr., 1915-29, pres., gen. mgr., 1940-57, now chmn. bd. Maas Bros. of Tampa, St. Petersburg, Lakeland, Clearwater, Sarasota, Ft. Myers, Fla.; pres., dir. Maas Realty; v.p., dir. Founders Life Assurance Co., Tampa; dir. Chemex Industries, Inc., Nat. Airlines, Inc., also Tampa Bay Bank. Mem. Res. Officers Assn., Air Force Assn. (v.p. 1949), Aircraft Owners and Pilots Assn., Am. Legion, Army Ordnance Assn., 40 et 8, Mil. Order World Wars, Ret. Officers Assn., Fla., Tampa C.'s of C. Jewish religion. Elk, Mason (Shriner, Jester). Clubs: Wings, Marco Polo, (N.Y.C.); MacDill Field Officers, Tampa Yacht, Ye Mystic Krewe of Gasparilla, Palma Ceia Golf, Yacht, University (Tampa, Fla.); Nat. Aviation (Washington); Quiet Birdmen (N.Y.C.); River (Jacksonville); Palm Bay (Miami), Miami. Home: Tampa, FL. *

WATERMULDER, LOUIS F., bus. exec.; b. Chgo., Aug. 17, 1901; s. Gustave A. and Frances (Verbeck) W.; A.B., Yale, 1923, postgrad. law sch., 1923-24; m. Helen Dawes, May 23, 1936. With No. Trust Co., Chgo., 1924-39, asst. chasier, 1928-30, 2d v.p., 1930-39; asst. treas. Quaker Oats Co., 1939-42, treas., 1942-49; administrv. v.p., dir. Lever Bros., 1949-50; v.p., dir. W.R. Grace & Co., N.Y.C., 1951; chmn. bd. Electric Sprayit Co., Sheboygan, Wis., 1952; pres. L.F. Watermulder & Assos., Chgo.; chmn. Buckner Corp. Presbyn. Clubs: Onwentsia, Attic, Racquet (Chgo); Pinnacle (N.Y.C.). Died Nov. 20, 1975. Home: Chicago, Ill. Died Nov. 20, 1975.

WATERS, JOHN AUGUSTINE, JR., govt. ofcl.; b. Stamford, Conn., Nov. 12, 1897; s. John Augustine and Isabella (Devlin) W.; student Stevens Inst. Tech., 1916-17; B.S., U.S. Naval Acad., 1920; m. Elinor Veronica Barry, Oct. 21, 1923; 1 son, John Augustine III. Commd. ensign USN, 1920, advanced through grades to rear adm., 1950; exec. officer U.S.S. Milwaukee, 4th Fleet, 1941-43; comdg. officer U.S.S. Quincy, 3d Fleet, 1945-46; personnel officer U.S. Pacific Fleet, 1947-49, Bur. Naval Personnel Washington, 1949-50; retired, 1950; dir. div. security AEC, Washington, 1950-67. Decorated Bronze Star. Home: Arlington, Va. Died 1978.

WATERS, LEVIN LYTTLETON, physician, educator; b. Ruxton, Md., June 7, 1910; s. Arnold Elzey and Helen (Knight) W.; B.A. cum laude, Princeton, 1932; M.D., Yale, 1937; m. Priscilla Alden Hall-Warncke, Aug. 4, 1945; children—Levin Lyttleton V. Jonathan Barclay. From intern to instr. pathology Yale Sch. Medicine, 1938-40, asst. prof., 1943-49; tech. aide OSRD, 1941-45; assoc. prof. pathology Yale, 1949-57, prof., 1957-77. Bd. dirs. Jane Coffin Childs Meml. Fund for Med. Research, New Haven, 1950-77, chmn. bd. sci, advisers, 1970-77. Mem. Bus. and Profl. Mens Orch., New Haven. Mem. Am. Soc. Pathologists and Bacteriologists, Am. Heart Assn, (council arteriosclerosis, council high blood pressure research), A.A.A.S., Am. Soc. Cancer Research, Univs. Asso. for Research and Edn. in Pathology (dir.). Sigma Xi, Alpha Omega Alpha. Espicopalian. Home: Guilford, Conn. Died Nov. 14, 1977.

WATKINS, ARTHUR V., govt. official; b. Midway, Utah, Dec. 18, 1886; s. Arthur and Emily A. (Gerber) W.; student, Brigham Young Univ., 1903-06, N.Y. U., 1909-10; LL.B. Columbia University, 1912; LL.D., U. Utah, 1959; m. Andrea Rich, June 18, 1913; children—Nedra Reese, Arthur Rich, Don Rich, Venna Swalberg, Jeanene Scott, Nina Palmer. Dist. judge, 1928-33; asst. co. (Salt Lake) atty., 1914-17; commr. Utah State Bar; counsel Provo River Water Users Assn. since 1935. U.S. Senator from Utah, 1947-58, co-sponsor Colo. River Storage Project and numerous other reclamation projects; associate member of the Indian Claims Commission, 1959-60, became chmn., 1960, now chief commr. Pub. Orem-Geneva Times, Utah Valley News; fruit farmer; rancher. Mem. platform com., Rep. Nat. Conv., 1944, 56. Republican. Mem. Ch. of Latter Day Saints. Kiwanian (life mem.). Home: Arlington, Va. *

WATKINS, MYRON WEBSTER, economist; b. Milford, Mich., Apr. 2, 1893; s. John Taylor and Mary Sophia (Wells) W.; A.B., U. of Mich., 1914; grad. student U. of Mo., 1914-15; Ph.D., Cornell U., 1917; m. Elizabeth Hampton Brougher, Feb. 20, 1931; children—Peter, Stephen, Deryll Elizabeth. Instr. economics, Washington State Coll., Pullman, Wash., 1917-18; asst. prof., asso. prof., and prof. economics, U. of Mo., 1918-27; professor economics, New York University, 1927-46; director of anti-trust inquiry National Industrial Conference Bd., New York, N.Y., 1924-29; research asso. Brookings Instn., 1935-36, 1937-39. Chmn. Com. on Oil Prices, Conf. on Price Research, 1936-39; economist Anti-Trust Div., Dept. of Justice, 1941-44; co-director of survey of cartels and monopoly, Twentieth Century Fund, 1944-48; v.p. Boni, Watkins, Jason & Co., Inc. Fellow Royal Econ. Soc. Gt. Britain; mem. Am. Econ. Assn., Phi Beta Kappa. Presbyn. Author or co-author books relating to field, latest co-authorship: Monopoly and Free Enterprise, 1951; Make or Buy, 1956. Home: Stamford, Conn. Died Dec. 4, 1979.

WATKINS, THOMAS FRANKLIN, retired lawyer; b. Sandy Springs, B.C., Aug. 2, 1881; s. John C. and Elizabeth Jane (Smith) W.; A.B., Wofford Coll., 1902; LL.B., U. Va., 1904; m. Agnes D. Law, Nov. 14, 1906; 1 son, William Law. Admitted to S.C. bar, 1904, since in practice Anderson; now of counsel firm Watkins Vandiner, Kirven, Long & Gable; spl. judge S.C. Supreme Ct., 1934. Dir. Piedmont & No. Ry. Co., Ross Builders Supplies, Inc. Mem. S.C. Senate, 1919-23; chmn. bd. trustees Anderson Sch. Dist. 1941-57. Trustee Presbyn. Coll. S.C., Anderson Meml. Hosp. Mem. Am., S.C. (pres. 1935) bar assns., Cotton Mfrs. Assn. S.C. (gen. counsel 1928). Democrat (past pres. Anderson County Conv.; pres. S.C. Conv.). Home: Anderson SC. *

WATKINS, THOMAS WEBB, educator; b. Boston, Mass., Feb. 23, 1885; s. Rev. Thomas Corwin and Emma Dale (Hadley) W.; grad. Classical High Sch., Newton, Mass., 1902; A.B., Harvard, 1906 Ed.M., Harvard Grad. Sch. Edn., 1922; m. Mary Carlena Prescott, Aug. 24, 1911; children—Thomas Prescott, Barbara. Principal high sch., North Stratford, N.H., 1906-15; teacher, South High Sch., Youngstown, O., 1915-18; prin. Northeastern Prep. Sch., Boston, 1919-20; asst. headmaster Huntington Sch., Boston, 1920-23; prin. Kent's Hill (Me. Wesleyan) Sch., 1923-29; headmaster Tilton Sch., 1929-35; prin. Arms Acad., Shelburne Falls, Mass., since 1935. Served as 1st lt. F.A., U.S. Army, Camp Taylor, Ky., 1918. Mem. N.E.A., Nat. Assn. Secondary Sch. Prins., New Eng. Assn. Colls. and Secondary Schs., Mass. Secondary Sch. Principals Assn. (pres. 1950), Am. Legion, Phi Delta Kappa. Republican. Methodist. Mason. Club: Kiwanis. Home: ShelburneFalls, Mass.*

WATROUS, DAVID GAPEN, advt. and mktg. co. exec.; b. Madison, Wis., Apr. 11, 1915; s. Paul Jerome and Jane (Gapen) W.; student Northwestern U., 1933-35; m. Carol Roig, Aug. 18, 1945; children—Peter David, Matthew Gapen. Various advt., sales positions Chgo. Tribune, Parker Pen Co., Montgomery Ward & Co., Batten, Barton, Durstine & Osborn, Tatham-Laird, Inc., Dancer-Fitzgerald-Sample, Benton & Bowles, Inc., 1935-60; pres. Earle Ludgin & Co., Chgo., 1962-66,

David G. Watrous & Asso., Northfield, Ill., 1966-78, Marshall John & Assos., Northbrook, Ill.; dir. Parker Pen Co. Bd. dirs. Grant Hosp., Chgo. Served to lt. USNR, 1942-46. Episcopalian. Clubs: Chgo Economic; Glen View (Ill.). Author: Private Label versus Manufacturer Brands, 1974; How to Get More Value Out of Store-Redeemed Coupons of All Types, 1973; Consumer Views on Sampling, 1973; Consumer Views on Super Markets in Ad Coupons, 1973; (with Jervis J. Babb) The Unconditional Guarantee of Complete Satisfaction, 1976. Home: Winnetka, Ill. Died Aug. 15, 1978.

WATSON, BENJAMIN PHILP, gynecologist; b. Anstruther, Scotland, Jan. 4, 1880; s. David and Elizabeth (Philp) W.; M.B., Ch.B., U. of Edinburgh, 1902, M.D., 1905; m. Angele Hamenat, June 17, 1917; children—Monique, David. Prof. obstetrics and gynecology, U. of Toronto, Can., 1912-22; prof. same, Columbia, 1926-46, emeritus 1946-76; dir. Sloane Hosp. for Women; consultant. Served as capt. Med. Corps, Canadian Army, 1914-17. Fellow Am. Coll. Surgeons, Royal Coll. Surgeons; past pres. Am. Gynecol. Soc.; pres. N.Y. Academy of Medicine since 1949. Presbyterian. Clubs: University (New York); University (Edinburgh). Contributor numerous articles to med. jours. Home: New York, N.Y. Died Aug. 8, 1976.

WATSON, CLAUDE, A., lawyer; b. Wexford County, Mich., June 26, 1885; s. Joseph A. and Emma Jane (Dove) W.; student Alma (Mich.). Coll., 1906-07, Lincoln U., 1926-27; LL.B., LaSalle Extension U., 1920; J.D., Blackstone Coll. of Law; LL.D., Greenville Coll.; m. Maude L. Hagar, Dec. 27, 1911; children—Ralph Bradley, Claudia Jean, Robert Kendall. Ordained ministry Free Methodist Church of North A., 1911, dist. supt. S. Cal. Conf., 1923-33, 1940; admitted to Cal. bar and practicing atty., 1928—; sr. mem. firm Watson & Stewart Prohibition candidate for v.p. of the U.S., 1936; candidate for atty. gen., Cal., 1938, 42, 46; for pres. 1944, 48; chmn. and keynote speaker Nat. Prohibition Conv., 1940; past sec. Gen. Conf. Free Meth. Ch. Mem. Traitors to Am., Cal., Los Angeles bar assns., Lawyers Club. Clubs: Kiwanis (past pres.), Los Angeles Athletic (Los Angeles). Author: Fifth Columnists of America; God's Plan for Civil Government. Home: Los Angeles CA. *

WATSON, CONRAD ETHELBERT, communications co. exec.; b. Nevis, B.W.I., Apr. 21, 1896; s. George C. and Josephine (Rawlins) W.; student Munro Coll., Jamaica, 1907-15; B.Sc. in Civil Engring., McGill U., 1921; m. Gladys Mary C. Graves, Apr. 28, 1927; children—Conrad D., Patricia A. (Mrs. William J. Grier). With Bell Telephone Co. of Can., 1921—, beginning in traffic dept., successively with engring. dept., chief engr., gen. plant mgr., gen. mgr., 1921-56, v.p., gen. mgr., 1956—. Served as gunner, arty., Canadian Army, 1917-19. Mem. Engring. Inst. Can. Mem. Anglican Ch. Home: Toronta. *

WATSON, GOODWIN BARBOUR, educator; b. Whitewater, Wis.; July 9, 1899; s. Walter S. and Ellen D. (Goodwin) W.; A.B., U. Wis., 1920; student Union Theol. Sem., 1921-24; M.A., Columbia Tchrs. Coll., 1923, Ph.D., 1925; student U. Berlin, U. Vienna, 1931-32; m. Gladys M. Hipple, June 14, 1923 (div. 1946); children—Dorothy J., Walter W., Patricia R.; m. 2d, Barbara Bellow, 1946 (div. 1970); children—David G., Jonathan S., Robert N.; m. 3d, Doris. Prin. grade sch., Albion, Wis., 1916-17; asst. prin. Randall Jr. High Sch., Madison, Wis., 1917-18; asst. physics U. Wis., 1919-20; dir. religious edn., Denver and N.Y.C. chs., 1920-22; instr. religious edn. Union Theol. Sem., 1923-24; dir. research Nat. council YMCA, 1925-31; instr. psychology Columbia Tchrs. Coll., 1925-27, asst. prof., 1927-29, asso. prof., 1929-35, prof. edn. 1935-62, prof. emeritus, 1962-76, also co-chmn. grad. program in social psychology; prof. and dir. emeritus Union Grad. Sch., Union for Experimenting Colls. and Univs., 1970-76. Chief analyst fgn. intelligence service FCC, 1941-44; dir. World Studytours, Inc., from 1946; co-dir. Inst. Group Psychotherapy, N.Y.C., from 1954. Mgmt. cons. Glaser Snowden Assos., N.Y.C. Member A.A.A.S., N.E.A., Am. Psychol. Assn., Am. Sociol. Assn., Society Psychol. Study Social Issues (past pres.), Am. Orthopsychiat. Assn., Am. Group Psychotherapy Assn., Assn. Applied Psychoanalysis, Phi Beta Kappa, Sigma Xi, Delta Sigma Rho, Phi Delta Kappa, Kappa Delta Pi, Pi Gamma Mu. Author or co-author books relating to field. Editorial bd. Jour. Social Psychology. Home: Xenia, Ohio. Died Dec. 30, 1976.

WATSON, HERBERT L., business exec.; b. Terre Haute, Ind., Aug. 19, 1883; s. Joseph A. and Alice (Lockridge) W.; B.S., Rose Polytechnic Inst., 1905; m. Nelle B. Noland, Dec. 2, 1914; children—William J., John L. Student apprentice Allis Chalmers Mfg. Co., 1905-06, sales engr., 1906-13; gen. sales mgr. DeLaval Steam Turbine Co., 1913-34, exec. v.p., 1934-42, president, 1942-48, chmn. exec. com., 1948-50. Republican. Presbyterian. Clubs: Engineers, Bankers (New York); Trenton, Trenton Country (Trenton). Home: Trenton, N.J. *

WATSON, RUSSELL ELLSWORTH, lawyer; b. New Brunswick, N.J., Oct. 8, 1885; s. Frank Ellsworth and Elizabeth (Painter) W.; student Rutgers Coll., 1902-05, LL.D., Rutgers U., 1949; LL.B., N.Y. Law Sch., 1907; m. Beulah Fraleigh Fingar, Mar. 24, 1909; children—Russell Ellsworth, Malcolm (dec.), Jean (Mrs. William B. Moses, Jr.), Sarah Elizabeth (Mrs. Kendall B. DeBevoise). Admitted to N.J. bar, 1909, counsellor at law, 1912—; gen. practice of law, New Brunswick, 1909—; with firm R. E. & A. D. Watson, 1920—; asst. pros. of pleas. Middlesex County, N.J., 1909-12; asso. counsel in N.J., Port of N.Y. Authority. 1930—; dep. atty. gen., N.J., 1931-48. Counsel N.J. Legislative Com., 1928-30, 45; counsel to gov. N.J., 1947-50; counsel Rutgers U., 1944—, vice chmn., trustee, 1944-56. Fellow Am. Bar Found.; mem. Am. Bar. Assn., Chi Psi. Republican. Mem. Reformed Ch. Home: Belle Mead, N.J. *

WATT, GEORGE WILLARD, educator, chemist; b. Bellaire, Ohio, Jan. 8, 1911; s. Robert Whitefield and Grace (Korell) W.; B.A., Ohio State U., 1931, M.S., 1933, Ph.D., 1935; m. Pauline Ila Price, June 11, 1934; children—Susan Kathleen, George Winfield, Joseph Michael. Research chemist Goodyear Tire & Rubber Co., Akron, Ohio, 1935-37; asst., then asso. prof. chemistry U. Tex., Austin, 1937-43, prof., 1945-48, emeritus, 1948-80. With Manhattan Project, U. Chgo., 1943-45; cons. Gen. Electric Co., 1947-70, E.I. DuPont de Nemours & Co., from 1950, Exxon Nuclear Co., 1970-80; expert witness patent and product liability litigation. Recipient Renaud Found. award, 1961, Standard Oil of Ind. Found. award, 1968, S.W. regional award Am. Chem. Soc., 1974. Fellow Am. Inst. Chemists; mem. Am. Chem. Soc. (dir.-at-large 1969-73), Sigma Xi, Phi Lambda Upsilon, Phi Kappa Phi. Contbr. articles to profl. jours. Patentee in field. Home: Austin, Tex. Died Mar. 29, 1980; buried Austin Meml. Park.

WATT, JAMES ARTHUR, chem. co. exec.; b. Peoria, Ill., Oct. 6, 1925; s. Clarence Jay and Fern Ione (Wingate) W.; B.S., U. Calif., Berkeley, 1949; m. Mary Ruth Mobley, Mar. 30, 1947; children—Charles, Joan, Judith. Tech. sales rep. Martin Hoyt Milne, San Francisco, 1949-51; chemist H.B. Fuller, San Francisco, 1951-59, tech. dir., St. Paul, 1959-64, v.p., regional mgr., South San Francisco, 1964-72; exec. v.p., St. Paul, 1972-80, mem. exec. com., 1972-80, dir., 1969-80. Served with USNR, 1943-46. Mem. Adhesive Mfrs. Assn. Am. (pres. 1977-80). Mem. St. Paul Athletic, N. Oaks Golf. Home: Saint Paul, Minn. Died Mar. 28, 1980; buried Rose Hills, Calif.

WATTERSON, JOSEPH, architect; b. Cleve., Aug. 7, 1900; s. William Ruggles and Mary (Batchelor) W.; grad. Mt. Hermon (Mass.) Sch., 1920; student Sch. Architecture U. Pa., 1924; m. Kathleen T. Howes, June 6, 1923 (dec.); children—David S., Stephen W., Joseph; m. 2d, Gertrude Harris, Dec. 30, 1948. Draftsman, Abram Garfield, Cleve., 1922-24; with Frederick L. Ackerman, N.Y.C., 1924-27; travel study abroad, 1926: designer Schultze & Weaver, N.Y.C., 1927-30, Reinhard & Hoffmeister, 1931; head art dept. Nassau Collegiate Center, Garden City, L.I., 1932-36; instr. art appreciation Coll. City N.Y., 1936; propr. own office, Mineola, N.Y., 1936-56; chief engr. Dade Bros., Inc., Mineola, 1941-45. Cons. to sec. interior, 1965-66, spl. asst., 1966-67; chief div. historic architecture Office Archeology and Historic Preservation, Nat. Park Service, 1968-71, now ret.; lectr. univs. and confs. Fellow A.I.A. (editor Jour. 1957-65, past sec., v.p. L.I. chpt., Kemper award 1965); mem. Soc. Archtl. Historians (former dir.), Nat. Trust Historic Preservation, Archtl. League N.Y., Nassau County Hist. Soc. (hon. trustee), World Soc. for Ekistics, Am. Assn. State and Local History, Delta Kappa Epsilon. Episcopalian. Club: Cosmos (Washington). Author: Architecture—5000 Years of Building, 1950; Architecture A Short History, 1968; author-editor: The Growth of the Architect, 1971. Editor: Urban Design-The Planning of Towns and Cities, 1965; The Restoration Manual, 1966; (with others) with Heritage So Rich, 1966. Contbr. to Elementary School Self-Taught, 1940. Home: Titusville, Fla. Died May 30, 1971.

WATTLES, THOMAS IRVIN, lawyer; b. South Bend, Ind., Mar. 25, 1923; s. Charles Pierre and Carmen Eva (Irvin) W.; A.B., U. Mich., 1947, J.D., 1950; M. Martha Jean Frey, Oct. 6, 1945; children—David R., Jane C., John C. III. Admitted to Mich bar, 1951; Supreme Ct. Mich., U.S. Ct. of Appeals 6th Circuit, U.S. Dist. Ct. for Eastern Dist. Mich.; asso. firm Kerr, Wattles & Russell and predecessor firms, Detroit, 1951-58, partner, 1958-76. Franchised agt. Howard Johnson's Restaurant, Port Huron, Mich.; officer, dir. F. Joseph Lamb Co. and subsidiaries, Gt. Lakes Recreation Co. and subsidiaries, Central Detroit Warehouse Co., Terminal Sales Corp., Woodmont Corp. and subsidiary, Birmingham Enterprises Inc., All Am. Travel, Inc.; dir. DeVlieg Machine Co., Peoples Fed. Savs. & Loan Assn. of Detroit and subsidiary, Nat. Transit Corp., Mchts. Forwarding Co. Served to lt. (j.g.) USNR, 1944-46; PTO; Mem. Am., Mich., Detroit bar assns., Am. Judicature Soc., Phi Kappa Psi, Phi Alpha Delta. Presbyn. Clubs: Detroit; Orchard Lake (Mich.) Country; Ocean Reef (Key Largo, Fla.). Home: Bloomfield Hills, Mich. Died June 9, 1976.

WATTS, CLYDE JEFFERSON, lawyer; b. Wagoner, Okla., Dec. 30, 1907; s. Charles G. and Flora (Lindsey) W.; B.S., LL.B., Okla. U.; m. June Marian Alley, Nov. 21, 1938; children—Marian (Mrs. Kiker), Charles J., Bryan L., Gary E. Admitted to Okla. bar, 1931, since practiced in Oklahoma City; atty. for classmate Maj. Gen. Edwin A. Walker when wrongfully committed to prison hosp. and libelled by A.P. Lectr. on nat. security. Served to brig. gen. AUS, 1942-54; CBI. Decorated Bronze Star medal, Air medal, Yun Wei (Chinese). Mem. Am. Bar Assn. (v.p., fidelity and surety com.), Internat. Assn. Ins. Counsel, Lawyers Pilots Assn., Res. Officers Assn. (comdr. Okla.), Assn. U.S. Army (comdr. Okla.), Oklahoma City C. of C. (chmn. mil. affairs com.). Kiwanian. Home: Oklahoma City, Okla. Died Nov. 21, 1975.

WATTS, DAVID ALDEN, lawyer; b. Battle Creek, Mich., July 18, 1900; s. James T. and Edith L. (Swift) W.; A.B., U. Mich., 1921; J.D., Harvard, 1924; m. Margaret E. Beckett, Aug. 25, 1928; children—David Alden, Susan Elizabeth. Admitted to Ill. bar, 1924, since practiced in Chgo., mem. firm Bell, Boyd, Lloyd, Haddad & Burns, 1936-65, counsel, 1965-78. Charter mem. World Peace Through Law Center, 1963-, Mem. Am., Ill., Chgo. bar assns., Phi Beta Kappa, Delta Sigma Rho. Republican. Episcopalian. Clubs: Church, Union League, Law, Legal (Chgo.). Contbr. Author articles legal periodicals. Home: Glencoe, Ill. Died Dec. 16, 1978.

WATTS, FRANKLIN MOWRY, book publisher; b. Sioux City, Iowa, June 11, 1904; s. John F. and Amada (Mowry) W.; B.B.A., Boston U., 1925; m. Helen Hoke, May 25, 1945. Book buyer Geo. Innes Co., L.S. Ayres & Co., 1925-32; sales mgr. Vanguard Press, 1932-34, Julian Messner, 1934-50, Heritage Press, 1936-50; founder, pres. Franklin Watts, Inc., N.Y.C., 1942-70, vice chmn., 1970-78, mng. dir. Franklin Watts Ltd., 1970-76; founder, Frank Book Corp., 1977. Editor: Voices of History, 1942-45, The Pocket Book Mag., 1954-56; Complete Christmas Book, 1958. Mem. Am. Book Publishers Council; mem. Govt. Book Program Adv. Com. Unitarian. Club: Pubs, Luncheon. Address: New York, N.Y. Died May 21, 1978.

WAUCHOPE, ROBERT, anthropologist; b. Columbia, S.C., Dec. 10, 1909; s. George A. and Elizabeth (Bostedo) W.; A.B., U. S.C., 1931, LL.D., 1960; A.M., Harvard, 1933, Ph.D., 1943; m. Elizabeth Brown, Aug. 15, 1941; children—Elizabeth, Kenneth. Asst. prof. archaeology U. Ga., 1938-1940; asso. prof. anthropology U. N.C., 1940-42; dir. Middle Am. Research Inst., prof. anthropology Tulane U., 1942-75; with archaeol. expdn. to Pecos, N.M., for Phillips Acad., 1927, and also to Uaxactun, Guatemala for Carnegie Inst. Washington, 1932; with ethnographic and archaeol. surveys in Yucatan, Campeche, Quintana Roo and Guatemala for Carnegie Inst., 1933-36; archaeol. surveys of Ga. and N.C., 1938-42, Zacualpa, Utatlan, Jutiapa, Jalapa, Guatemala, for Tulane U., 1947, 74, 75. Served as lt. USNR, 1943-46; ETO. Decorated Bronze Star medal. Mem. Soc. Am. Archaeology (pres. 1954-55), Phi Beta Kappa, (vis. lectr. 1966-67), Omicron Delta Kappa, Sigma Nu. Author: House Mounds of Uaxactun, Guatemala, 1934; Modern Maya Houses, 1938; Excavations at Zacualpa, Guatemala, 1948; Lost Tribes and Sunken Continents, 1962; They Found the Buried Cities, 1965; Archaeological Survey of Northern Georgia, 1966; Protohistoric Pottery of the Guatemala Highlands, 1970; The Indian Background of Latin American History, 1970; Zacualpa, El Quiche, Guatemala, 1975. Contbr. chpts. in books, also articles and revs. on Maya archaeology and so. U.S. archaeology. Editor: Middle American Research publs. 11-42; contbg. editor Handbook Latin American Studies, vols. 14-21, adv. bd., 1959-68, chmn., 1965-68; gen. editor Handbook Middle American Indians, 16 vols., 1959-76. Home: New Orleans, La. Died Jan. 26, 1979.

WAXMAN, SAMUEL MONTEFIORE, univ. prof.; b. Boston, Mass., Oct. 22, 1885; s. Joseph and Simy (Benshimol) W.; A.B., summa cum laude, Harvard, 1907; student École des hautes etudes and École des chartes, U. of Paris, 1908-09; A.M., Harvard, 1910, Ph.D., 1912; m. Frances Burwell Sheafer, Sept. 23, 1910 (died May 5, 1938); m. 2d, Bashka Paeff, June 1, 1940. Instr. Romance langs., Syracuse U., 1907-08; John Harvard fellow and fellow Ministry of Pub. Instrn. of the French Republic, 1908-09; lecteur anglais adjoint, Faculte des Lettres, U. of Paris, 1908-09; instr. Romance langs., Harvard, 1910; instr. Romance langs., Boston U., 1910-13, asst. prof., 1913-20, prof. since 1920; also instr. in phonetics, Hartford Sch. of Missions, 1912-13, lecturer in contemporary French drama, Harvard, 1914. Stanwood Gray Wellington award, Roxbury Latin School, 1929. Mem. Am. Assn. Univ. Profs., Modern Language Assn. Am., New Eng. Modern Lang. Assn. (secretary, treas. and editor publications, 1914-16, president, 1948-49), American Association Teachers of Spanish, American Association

Teachers of French, Phi Beta Kappa (hon.). Club: Boston Authors. Author or editor books relating to field since 1916; also chpts. in other books and articles on lit. and langs. Home: Cambridge, Mass. *

WAYLAND, W. R., banker; b. New Franklin, Mo., Dec. 30, 1882; s. William Thornton and Elizabeth (Smith) W.; ed. high sch. and bus. sch.; m. Jane Addams, Feb. 13, 1908 (dec.); m. 2d, Mrs. Marie Tolleson Frey, July 10, 1948; step-children—Mrs. R. W. Linscott, Jr., Frank T. Frey, Jr. Hon. chmn. bd. Valley National Bank, Phoenix, Arizona; president Wayland's Prescription Pharmacy; vice president Read Mullan Motor Co., Lincoln-Mercury Motor Company; member partnership, Consolidated Motors; director and mem. exec. com. Arizona Public Service Company; mem. adv. bd., 12th Fed. Res. dist. R.F.C.; state mgr. Home Owners Loan Corp. Member of Civic Center Management Board; director Social Service Center; state chairman war memorial, University of Arizona. Democrat. Episcopalian. Mason (Shriner). Clubs: Phoenix Country, Arizona (life). Home: Phoenix. *

WAYNE, JOHN (MARION MICHAEL MORRISON), actor; b. Winterset, Iowa, May 26, 1907; s. Clyde L. and Mary (Brown) Morrison; student U. So. Calif., 1925-27, D.F.A., 1968; m. Josephine Saenz, June 24, 1933; children—Michael, Toni, Patrick, Melinda; m. 2d, Esperanza Baur, Jan. 17, 1946 (div. 1953); m. 3d, Pilar Palette, 1954; children—Aissa, John, Marisa. Prop boy, electrician, stunt man, asst. dir. motion pictures, 1926-28; starred in The Big Trail, 1929, successively under contract to Argosy Prodns., Warner Bros., Republic, 20 Century-Fox, R.K.O. and Paramount Studios; pictures include: Stagecoach, 1939; The Long Voyage Home, 1940; Reap the Wild Wind, 1942; A Lady Takes a Chance, 1943; Tall in the Saddle, 1944; They Were Expendable, 1945; Red River, 1946; Angel and the Badman, 1947; Wake of the Red Witch, 1948; Sands of Iwo Jima, 1949; Operation Pacific, 1950; The Quiet Man, Jet Pilot, Big Jim McLain, 1951-52; Fort Apache, Island in the Sky, Hondo, The High and the Mighty, The Searchers, Blood Alley; The Conqueror, 1955; Wings of Eagles, 1956; The Barbarian and the Geisha, 1958; Horse Soldiers, 1959; The Alamo (also producer, dir.), 1959; North to Alaska, 1960; Hatari, 1960; The Longest Day, 1961; Donovan's Reef, McLintock, 1962; Circus World, 1963; In Harm's Way, 1964; Sons of Katie Elder, Cast a Giant Shadow, 1965; El Dorado, The War Wagon, 1966; The Green Berets (also dir.), 1967; The Hellfighters, True Grit, 1968; The Undefeated Chisum, 1969; Rio Lobo, Big Jake, 1970; The Cowboys, 1972; Train Robbers, 1973. Hon. chmn. Am. Cancer Soc. Nominated for Acad. award in 1950 for performance as Sgt. Stryker in Sands of Iwo Jima, recipient Acad. award for True Grit, 1969; named Significant Sig. Sigma Chi Scopus award Am. Friends of Hebrew U., 1977. Mem. Skull and Dagger U. So. Calif., Acad. Motion Picture Arts and Scis. Mason (Shriner). Clubs: Newport Beach Yacht; Newport Harbor Yacht; Balboa Bay; Big Canyon Country; Irvine Country; John Wayne Tennis. Home: Newport Beach, Calif. Died June 11, 1979.

WAYSON, NEWTON EDWARD, U.S. Pub. Health Service; b. St. Inigoes, Md., Nov. 22, 1883; s. George Washington and Irene (Allen) W.; student McDonogh (Md.) Sch., 1897-1900; A.B., Johns Hopkins, 1904; student U. of Wis., 1905-07; M.D., Northwestern U., 1910; m. Anne Christina Ewing, Mar. 14, 1914; children—Allen Ewing (dec.), Edward Ewing, Margaret Helen (dec.). Commd. asst. surgeon U.S. P.H.S., 1914, passed asst. surgeon, 1918, surgeon, 1922, sr. surgeon, 1934, med. dir., 1940; assignments include charge of Plague Laboratory, San Francisco, Calif., 1914-15, 1922-27, 1941-47, ret.; dir. Leprosy Investigation Sta., Honolulu, Hawaii, 1927-35; engaged in cancer studies, 1938-41. Awarded Certificate of Merit by Northwestern U., 1931. Fellow Am. Med. Assn.; mem. A.A.A.S. Mem. Southern Presbyn. Ch. Contbr. articles on contagious diseases and plagues to med. jours. Address: San Francisco. *

WEAKLY, HAZEL BARNETT, educator; b. near Shelbyville, Ill., Feb. 4, 1912; d. Everett D. and Callie (Price) Barnett; B.S., Eastern Ill. State Teachers Coll., 1935; A.M., Northwestern U., 1937, Ph.D., 1940; m. Merlin Edson Weakly, Feb. 6, 1931 (dec. 1946); m. 2d, William F. Bowen, Mar. 22, 1947. Pub. sch. tchr. nr. Shelbyville, Ill., 1928-35, Evanston, Ill., 1935-40; grad. asst. Northwestern U., 1939-40, demonstration tchr., summer sessions, 1938, 39, 40; prof. edn., co-ordinator elementary edn. Drake U., 1940-76, dir. Summer Lab. Sch., 1941-76, also chmn. founds. dept. Dir. In-Service programs for teachers in various Ia. cities, 1942-76. Mem. N.E.A., Assn. Childhood Edn., Am. Edn. Fellowship, Assn. Supervision and Curriculum Development, Assn. Classroom Teachers, Iowa State Edn. Assn., Kappa Delta Pi. Home: Des Moines, Iowa. Died July 6, 1976; interred Resthaven Cemetery, West Des Moines, Iowa.

WEAN, RAYMOND JOHN, business exec.; b. Barto, Pa., May 1, 1895; s. Reuben Charles and Sarah M. (Fegley) W.; grad. Carnegie-Mellon U., 1917, D.Eng. (hon.), 1971; D.Sc. (hon.), Trinity Coll., Hartford, Conn., 1954; H.H.D., Youngstown U., 1963; m. Sara R. Boone, July 13, 1918; 1 son, Raymond John. Foundry supt. Union Switch & Signal Co. (Westinghouse Air Brake), 1919; sales engr. Lakewood Engring. Co., 1920-21, Aetna Foundry & Machine Co., 1922-25; v.p. Aetna-Standard Engring. Co., 1926-28; hon. chmn., dir. Wean United, Inc.; chmn. bd. emeritus, dir. 2d Nat. Bank, Warren. Trustee Community Chest, Palm Beach, Am. Inst. Econs., New Wilmington, Pa., Trinity Coll., Hartford, Conn.; life trustee Carnegie-Mellon U.; adv. bd. N.E. Inst. for Med. Research. Received award of merit Carnegie-Mellon U., also Distinguished Achievement award. Mem. Am. Iron and Steel Inst., ASME, Assn. Iron and Steel Engrs. N.A.M., Nat. Indsl. Conf. Bd., U.S., Warren (past pres.) chambers commerce, Newcomen Soc. Eng., Alpha Tau. Mason. Clubs: Duquesne (Pitts.); Union (Cleve.); Pepper Pike (Chagrin Falls); Trumbull Country (Warren); Everglades, Sailfish, Bath and Tennis (Palm Beach, Fla.). Collaborator: Romancing in Tin Pate, 1951. Inventor steel mill equipment. Home: Warren, Ohio. Died Sept. 23, 1980.

WEATHERFORD, HARRISON MARK, lawyer; b. Albany, Ore., Dec. 23, 1925; s. Mark Vern and Emmaline (Kuhn) W.; student Ore. State U., 1943, 46-48, Willamette U., 1948-50; J.D., Northwestern, 1952; m. Lillian Irene Odberg, July 24, 1952; children—Mark Harrison, Alice Vaughn, Joyce Verne. Wheat rancher, Arlington, Ore., 1944, 46-52; admitted to Ore. bar, 1952, since practiced in Albany; partner Weatherford, Thompson, Horton, Brickey & Powers, and predecessor firm, 1953-79; wheat and cattle rancher, Arlington and Condon, 1966-79. Chmn. Benton County Sch. Dist. reorgn. com., 1957-62; mem. Gov.'s Conf. on Edn., 1958; mem. Albany Zoning Commn., 1960-62; mem. adv. com. Intermediate Edn. Dist. Commn. of Ore. Legislature, 1967-69; dir. Rock Creek Water Control Dist., 1974-79. Pres., sec., bd. dirs. Albany Boys Club; pres., trustee McDowell-Catt Found.; v.p., bd. dirs. Willamette Osteo. Hosp. Served with AUS, 1944-46; PTO. Named Gilliam County and Ore. Co-Conservation Farmer of Year, 1962; Weatherford Indsl. Park named in his honor. Mem. Ore., Linn County bar assns., Air Force Assn., Ore. Wheat, Cattlemens and Rye grass Growers Assn., Aircraft Owners and Pilots Assn., Am. Legion, Phi Delta Theta. Democrat. Presbyn. (deacon, elder). Elk. Home: Albany, Oreg. Died Apr. 25, 1979; buried Albany Masonic Cemetery.

WEATHERFORD, WILLIS DUKE, educator; b. Weatherford, Tex., Dec. 1, 1875; s. Samuel L. and Margaret (Turner) W.; B.S., Weatherford Coll., 1895; B.A., Vanderbilt U., 1899, M.A., 1900, Ph.D., 1907; LL.D., Berea Coll., 1955, U. N.C., 1962; m. Julia McCrory Weatherford, May 27, 1915 (dec.); 1 son, Dr. Willis Duke. International student sec. YMCA, 1901-19, pres. YMCA Grad. Sch., Nashville, 1919-36; pres. Blue Ridge Coll., Inc., 1906-44; head dept. religion and philosophy Fisk U., 1936-46. Dir. Am. Cast Iron Pipe Co. Mem. bd. trustees Berea Coll., 1915-70, also vice pres. bd.; dir. adminstrn. So. Appalachian Studies, chmn. bd. Bd. dirs. Berea Coll. Mem. A.A.A.S., Am. Acad. Polit. and Social Sci., Tenn. Acad. Sci., Phi Beta Kappa, Pi Gamma Mu, Phi Kappa Phi, Alpha Tau Omega. Methodist. Author numerous books on lit., religion, race, 1909-25; later books: (with Charles S. Johnson) Race Relations, 1934; Life Sketch of James Brownson Dunwoody De Bow, 1935; The American Churches and the Negro, 1937; Analytical Index of De Bows Review, 1946; Pioneers of Destiny, 1955. Co-author, editor: Religion in the Appalachian Mountains, 1955; Educational Opportunities in the Appalachian Mountains, 1955; co-author: Life and Religion in Southern Appalachia. Home: Black Mountain, N.C. Died 1970.

WEATHERSPOON, WALTER HERBERT, business exec.; b. Durham County, N.C., 1884; ed. Wake Forest Coll., 1907. Vice pres., gen. counsel and dir. Carolina Power & Light Co.; dir. Atlantic Fire Ins. Co. Home: Raleigh, N.C. *

WEAVER, JOHN ERNST, botanist; b. Villisca, Ia., May 5, 1884; s. John and Amelia (Theroff) W.; B.Sc., U. of Neb., 1909, A.M., 1911; studied U. of Chicago, 1911; Ph.D., U. of Minn., 1916; m. Martha H. Hasse, Sept. 5, 1906; children—Cornelia Marcia, Robert John. Instr. botany, 1912-13, asst. prof., 1913-14, Wash. State Coll.; instr. botany, U. of Minn., 1914-15; asst. prof. botany, 1915-17, prof. plant ecology since 1917, U. of Neb. Research asso., ecology, Carnegie Instn., Washington, D.C., 1925-31; mem. Nat. Research Council Com. on Grasslands. Fellow A.A.A.S.; mem. Bot. Soc. America, Ecol. Soc. America (pres. 1930), Soc. Am. Physiologists, Neb. Acad. Science (pres. 1937). Phi Beta Kappa, Sigma Xi (past pres. Neb. chpt.), Phi Sigma. Author or co-author numerous publs. relating to field; latest: Stabilization of Midwestern Grassland, 1950. Home: Lincoln, Neb. *

WEAVER, PAUL, coll. pres., lectr., author; b. Ephrata, Pa., Mar. 15, 1907; s. John Lincoln and Gertrude Cerdula (Brenneman) W.; A.B., Franklin and Marshall Coll., 1928, D.D., 1950; M. Theology Yale, 1933; LL.D., Lake Erie Coll., 1971; m. Margaret Elizabeth Wurster, June 27, 1936; children—Paul David, Susan (Mrs. Robert Banta). Instr. philosophy Stephens Coll., 1934, prof., 1935-51, chmn. div. philosophy and religion, 1936-51; dir. The Burrall Class, 1934-51, dean religious life, 1948-51; pres. Lake Erie Coll., from 1951; dean faculty Internat. Seminar, Denmark, 1949; dir. Inter-U. Round Table, India, 1950; cons. on Germany to Fulbright Com. Mem. Cleve. Council World Affairs. Mem. Lake Erie Opera Theatre Bd.; trustee Ohio Found. Ind. Colls., Inc., from 1951, chmn., 1960-61; trustee Lake Erie Coll., from 1951, Cleve. Meml. Med. Found., Mus. Arts Assn., Family Planning Assn. Lake and Geauga Counties, Council for Youth Lake County; chmn. bd. regents Université Internacional, 1972-77. Mem. Bratenahl Place Assn., United Hunts Racing Assn., Newcomen Soc. N. Am., Phi Upsilon Kappa (hon.), Kappa Tau Alpha, Omicron Delta Kappa, Order Blue Gavel. Episcopalian. Clubs: Century Assn., Yale (N.Y.C.); Union, Cleve. Athletic, Rotary, Mentor Harbor Yacht, Chagrin Valley Hunt, Cotillion, Kirtland Country, Yachtsmen (Cleve.); Gulf Stream Bath and Tennis. Co-author (R.F. Davidson and K.K. Berry). Preface to Philosophy; Manual for U.S. Army Forces Inst.; also articles Editor: Introducing Students to the Field of Philosophy; proc. Mo. Acad. Science, Vol. 6, 1941; Youth and Religion, Annals of Am. Acad. Polit. and Social Sci., Nov. 1944; The Evolution of the Soul, Wm. F. Ayres Found, publn., 1946; Using Psychological Insights in the Religious Education, Sept.-Oct. 1946, The Turbulent Teens, 1964. Home: Debray Beach, Fla. Died Dec. 29, 1977.

WEAVER, WARREN, found, exec.; b. Reedsburg, Wis., July 17, 1894; s. Isaiah and Kittie Belle (Stupfell) W.; B.S., U. Wis., 1916, C.E., 1917, Ph.D., 1921, LL.D., 1948; Sc.D., U. Sao Paulo 1949, Drexel Inst. Tech., 1961, U. Pitts., 1964, N.Y.U., 1964; D.E., Rensselaer Polytech. Inst., 1962; L.H.D., U. Rochester, 1963; m. Mary Hemenway, Sept. 4, 1919; children—Warren, Helen Hemenway. Asst. prof. math. Throop Coll., 1917-18, Cal. Inst. Tech., 1919-20; asst. prof. math. U. Wis., 1920-25, asso. prof., 1925-28, prof., chmn. dept., 1928-32; lectr. U. Chgo., summer 1928; dir. div. natural scis. Gen. Edn. Bd., 1932-37; dir. div. natural scis. Rockefeller Found., 1932-55, v.p. for natural and med. scis., 1955-59. Chmn. basic research group Research and Devel. Bd., Dept. Def., 1952-53; chmn. Section D-2, 1940-42, chief applied math. panel nat. def. research com. OSRD, 1943-46; chmn., Naval Research Adv. Panel, 1946-47; mem. War Dept. Research Adv. Panel, 1946-47; mem. adv. com. on grants Research Corp., 1947-51; mem. bd. sci. consultants Sloan-Kettering Inst. on Cancer Research, 1951-54; trustee Sloan-Kettering Inst., 1954-67, chmn. com. on sci. policy, 1955-59, mem. exec. com. 1956-67, v.p., 1958-59; dir., pres. Pub. Health Research Inst., City N.Y., 1961-63; mem. nat. sci. bd. NSF, 1956-60; trustee Alfred P. Sloan Found., 1956-67, v.p., 1959-64, cons. sci. affairs, 1964-78, mem. exec. com., 1956-67, hon. trustee, 1967-78; nat. adv. cancer council USPHS, 1957-60; mem., vice chmn., mem. exec. com. Health Research Council N.Y.C., 1958-60; mem. Gov.'s Com. on Hosp. Costs, 1964-65; bd. mgrs. Meml. Center for Cancer and Allied Diseases, 1958-60; vice chmn. bd., chmn. com. sci. policy Meml. Sloan-Kettering Cancer Center, 1960-67; mem. exec. com., mgr. Meml. Hosp. Cancer and Allied Diseases, 1960-67. Asso. trustee U. Pa.; trustee, chmn. bd. non-resident fellow Salk Inst. Biol. Studies, San Diego; dir. Scientists' Inst. Pub. Information, 1963-67; hon. v.p. Acad. Religion and Mental Health. Served as 2d lt. Air Service, 1947-19. Awarded King's medal for Service Cuase of Freedom, 1948; U.S. medal for Merit; officer Legion of Honor (France), 1950; Pub. Welfare medal Nat. Acad. Scis., 1957; Kalinga prize, internat. literary award, 1965, Arches of Sci. award Pacific Sci. Center, 1965. Fellow Am. Acad. Arts and Scis. (past pres.), (pres., chmn. bd. 1955), Am. Phys. Soc.; mem. Am. Math. Soc., Math. Assn. Am., Am. Physiol. Soc. (councillor), Am. Soc. Naturalists, Am. Soc. Symbolic Logic, Council Library Resources (dir. 1956-59), Nat. Acad. Scis., Phi Kappa Sigma, Sigma Xi, Tau Beta Pi; corr. mem. Chr. Michelsens Institutt (Bergen, Norway). Presbyn. Clubs: Cosmos (Washington); Century (N.Y.C.). Author: The Electromagnetic Field (with Max Mason), 1929; Elementary Mathematical Analysis, 1925; The Mathematical Theory of Communication (with C.E. Shannon), 1949; Lady Luck-The Theory of Probability, 1963; Alice in Many Tongues, 1964; U.S. Philanthropic Foundations: Their History, Structure, Management and Record, 1967; Science and Imagination, 1967; (autobiography) Scene of Change, 1970. Editor: The Scientists Speak, 1947. Contbr. papers on math. research in sci. jours and on gen. aspects of sci. in gen. jours. Home: New Milford, Conn. Died Nov. 24, 1978.

WEBB, JOHN H(ENRY), clergyman; b. Elberton, Ga., Mar. 21, 1893; s. James William and Sarah (Cook) W.; A.B., Mercer U., 1914, D.D., 1929; B.D., Newton Theol. Sem., 1917; spl. courses Harvard U.; m. Lillie Inez Richardson, Aug. 28, 1917 (died Mar. 30, 1935); children—Willena June (Mrs. David G. Basile), Anne Judson (Mrs. Robert M. Basile), John Henry, Jean (Mrs. Wheeler Melton); m. 2d, Laura C. Lovell, July 5, 1936. Became minister Baptist Ch., 1913; pastor Hagerstown, Maryland, 1917-20, Monroe, Ga., 1920-26, First Bapt. Ch., Columbia, S.C., 1927-40 (new ch. bldg. erected during pastorate), Beech St. Baptist Ch., Texarkana,

Ark., 1940-43, S. Avondale Bapt. Ch., Birmingham, 1943-45; Cloverdale Bapt. Ch., Montgomery, Ala., 1945-48; pastor First Baptist Ch., Radford, Va., 1948-50, Allyn Ave. Bapt. Ch., Ontario, Calif., 1950-54; founder, pastor Calvary Bapt. Ch., Ontario, 1954-61; preacher conv. sermon, S.C. Baptist Conv., 1932; mem. Home Mission Bd., So. Bapt. Conv.; mem. exec. com. Baptist State Conv., Ark. and S.C. Democrat. Clubs: Rotary, Lions, Masons, Kiwanis. Author: At the Gates of Mercy. Home: Ontario, Calif. Died Dec. 3, 1979.

WEBB, LOUIE WINFIELD, univ. prof.; b.Texarkana, Ark., Sept. 8, 1883; s. Charles Wheeler and Bell (Hamilton) W.; grad. high sch., Texarkana; B.A., Ouachita Coll., Arkadelphia, Ar., 1906; Th.M., Southern Bapt. Theol. Sem., Louisville, Ky., 1909; M.A., U. of Chicago, 1913; Ph.D., 1916; m. Myrtle Anderson, Dec. 22, 1909; 1 dau., Frances (Mrs. F. J. Leishman). Prof. philosophy, Ouachita Coll., 1909-11; instr. in psychology and edn., Northwestern U., 1916-18, asst. prof. edn., 1919-21, asso. prof. of edn., 1922-32, prof. since 1932 vis. prof. U. of Colo., summer, 1927, U. of Wash., 1930, 33, U. of Pa., 1936; Fulbright prof., Bristol, Eng., 1949-50. Member Commission on research and service of North Central Assn. Colls. and secondary Schs., 1924-46, chmn., 1934-40. Fellow A.A.A.S.; mem. N.E.A., Am. Psychol. Assn., Sigma Xi, Phi Delta Kappa, A.A.U.P., Delta Sigma Pi. Baptist. Author: Transfer of Training and Retroaction, 1917; Standard Tests in the Elementary School, 1932; Testing in the Elementary school, 1939. Editor of volume, Reorgn. of Secondary Sch. Curricula. Home: Evanston, Ill. *

WEBB STUART WESTON, b. Worcester, Mass., Nov. 27, 1883; s. Stephen W. and Martha (Boyden) W.; A.B., Harvard, 1906; m. Marcia Sewall, July 9, 1910; children—Marcia S., Barbara, Elinor. Formerly pres. Eastern Mfg. Co., Boston; now pres. and dir. Pathé Exchange, Inc., New York; pres. and dir. Brightwater Paper Co., Adams, Mass.; dir. Dupont Film Mfg. Corpn., New York. Regional advisor for N.E. of War Industries Bd., World War. Republican. Episcopalian. Clubs: Racquet and Tennis, Harvard (New York); Country Club (Boston). Home: New York. *

WEBBER, ALBERT G., JR., lawyer, mfg. co. exec.; b. Decatur, Ill., Mar. 28, 1892; s. Albert G. and Alice M. (Roth) W.; student Millikin U., 1909-13; A.B., U. Ill., 1914, postgrad Coll. Law, 1914-1917; m. Elen Longley, May 8, 1920; children—Albert G. III, Richard L., Frederic L. Admitted to Ill. bar, 1918; gen. practice law, Decatur, 1919-71; pres. Mueller Co., Decatur, 1947-63, chmn., dir., 1944-71; pres. Mueller, Ltd., Sarnia, Ont., Can., 1961-63, dir., 1944-71. Mem. Adv. Council Naval Affairs, Decatur, 1947-69. Served with USNR, 1917-19. Mem. Delta Sigma Phi. Mason. Clubs: Decatur, Country of Decatur. Home: Decatur, Ill. Died Sept. 25, 1974.

WEBBER, CLYDE MAYO, labor union ofcl.; b. Siloam Springs, Ark., Dec. 9, 1919; s. E.E. and Virginia (Woodson) W.; m. Marie W. Klinke, Dec. 18, 1942; 1 son, Robert Alan. Nat. pres. Am. Fedn. Govt. Employees, Washington, 1972-76; v.p. exec. council AFL-CIO, 1975-76, treas. pub. employee dept., 1974-76. Home: Silver Sping, Md. Died June 15, 1976; buried Ogden, Utah.

WEBBER, LANE D(AVIS), pub. utilities exec.; b. Aurora, Ind., Aug. 25, 1885; s. Charles D. and Julia (Lane) W.; student bus. sch., Cincinnati, 1904-05; LL.B., George Washington U., 1911; m. Harriet A. Meck, Sept. 24, 1928. Court reporter, Ind., 1905-09; admitted to Calif. bar, 1912, and practiced in San Diego, 1912-22; v.p. and trust officer, 1st Nat. Trust & Savs. Bank, San Diego, 1922-35; dir. since 1922; with So. Calif. Edison Co., Los Angeles, since 1935, v.p. since 1941, dir. since 1945; v.p. dir. Edison Securities Co. since 1945. Dir. Panama-Calif. Internat. Expn., 1915-16, Cal-Pacific Internat. Expn., 1935-36. Trustee Tax Found. since 1948. Mem. Nat. Assn. Mfrs. (nat. v.p. 1951-53, dir., chmn. govt. spending com. 1947-49), Calif. Bankers Assn. (pres. 1930-31), Calif. State C. of C., Calif. Taxpayers Assn. (dir. since 1926, v.p.), Bldg. Owners and Mgrs. Assn. of Los Angeles (pres. 1945-48, dir. 1949-51), San Diego, Los Angeles C.'s of C., State Bar Cal., All Year Club of So. Cal. (dir.), S.R., Soc. of Colonial Wars, Beta Gamma Sigma (hon.). Republican. Mason (32 deg., K.T., Shrine, Past Potentate). Clubs: Cuyamaca; California, Lincoln. Home: Los Angeles. *

WEBER, CLEMENTS, corp. exec.; b. 1928; B.S. in Accounting, St. Peters Coll., 1953. With Peat, Marwick, Mitchell & Co., C.P.A.'s, 1953-55; with Metromedia Inc., 1955-80, treas., 1968-69, v.p., 1969-74, sr. v.p., 1974-75, exec. v.p. and chmn. bd., 1975-80. Served with USNR, 1946-48. Address: Saddle River, N.J. Died Mar. 25, 1980.

WEBER, FRANCIS JOHN, physician; b. Phila., Sept. 20, 1909; s. Frederick and Mary Theresa (Campbell) W.; A.B., U. Pa., 1932, M.D., 1936; M.P.H., Johns Hopkins, 1939, Dr. P.H., 1951; m. Margaret Chapman Favour, Sept. 20, 1938; children—John Rhinehardt, Dorothy Alice. NIH field studies poliomyelitis, 1939; asst. health officer Tri-County Health Unit, Brunswick, Ga., 1939-40; gen. health cons. Dist. 4, New Orleans, 1940; health officer Columbus, Ga., 1940-41; dir. div. venereal disease control Mich. Dept. Health, Lansing, 1941-44; gen. med. cons. Dist. 5, San Francisco, 1944; asst. chief tb control div. USPHS, Washington, 1944-46, chief, 1946-48, div. dir., Cleve., 1950-52, Denver, 1952-58, dir., chief radiol. health HEW, Washington, 1958-61; ret., 1962; cons. Environ. Control Adminstrn.; spl. cons. pub. health and med. mgmt., 1963-76; spl. cons. USPHS, Washington, WHO-UN, Geneva, 1967-76; former asst. clin. prof. medicine Georgetown U. Sch. Medicine, Washington; research asso. Johns Hopkins Sch. Hygiene and Pub. Health, 1950-51; former asst. clin. prof. preventive medicine and pub. health U. Colo.; asso. prof., chmn. div. environ. medicine dept. preventive medicine Coll. Medicine U. Utah, Salt Lake City, from 1967; chief div. health planning and resource devel. Ill. Dept. Pub. Health, Springfield, 1968-70; spl. cons. radiation WHO-UN, Geneva, Switzerland, 1965-66. USPHS fellow in psychiatry Johns Hopkins Hosp., Phipps Clinic, 1948-50. Diplomate Am. Bd. Preventive Medicine and Pub. Health. Recipient posthumous award Pres. Jimmy Carter, 1977. Fellow Am. Med. Writers Assn.; mem. Am. Assn. Pub. Health Physicians, Am. Coll. Preventive Medicine, Am. Psychiat. Assn., A.M.A., Nat. Tb Assn., Colo. Trudeau Soc., Am. Coll. Chest Physicians, Commd. Officers Assn. USPHS, Am. Pub. Health Assn., N.Y. Acad. Scis., World Med. Assn., Am. Med. Soc. Vienna, Am. Nat. Environ. Health Assn., Ill. Med. Soc., Med. Soc. D.C., Am. Thoracic Soc., A.A.U.P., Utah Acad. Arts and Scis., Phi Alpha Sigma. Contbr. articles to sci. jours. Home: Vacaville, Calif. Died Nov. 23, 1976; interred Elmira Cemetery, Vacaville.

WEBER, J. SHERWOOD, educator; b. Reading, Pa. Sept. 21, 1918; s. Milton K. and Florence (Madeira) W.; A.B., Temple U., 1939; M.A., 1940; Ph.D. U. Wis., 1947; m. Olga Svatik, Nov. 28, 1959; children—Mark Kenneth, J. Stephen. Teaching asst. English, U. Wis., 1940-44; instr. George Washington U., 1944-45, N.Y.U., 1945-47, Queens Coll., 1947-50; mem. faculty Pratt Inst., from 1950, prof. English and humanities, chmn. dept., 1963-74, provost, 1974-76; ednl. cons. New Am. Library, 1960-67; edn. commentator radio sta. WINS, N.Y.C., 1963-66. Mem. MLA, Coll. English Assn. Nat. Council Tchrs. English, Conf. Coll. Composition and Communication (exec. com. 1963-65, chmn. nat. conv. 1964), AAUP (chmn. local chpt. 1961-65). Author: Good Reading, 15th-20th edit., 1954-69, 21st edit., 1978; From Homer to Joyce, 1959; The Relevance of the Past, 1974; also articles, reviews. Home: Cragsmoor, N.Y. Died June 6, 1978.

WEBER, SHIRLEY HOWARD, library dir., educator; b. Petaluma, Calif., Apr. 14, 1883; s. Henry and Addie Marie (Petty) W., A.B., U. of Calif., 1907, A.M., 1914; Ph.D., Princeton U., 1917, m. Mrs. Elsa (Grant) Boughton, of St. Louis, Mo., June 8, 1918; stepchildren—Judson Grant Boughton, Isabel (Mrs. Alexander Capps). Instr. in classics, Washington U., 1917-18, asst. prof., 1918-19; asst. prof. of classics, Princeton U., 1919-25, asso. prof. since 1925 (on leave); dir. of Gennadius Library, Athens, Greece, since Aug. 1937; instr. U. of Calif., summer 1918; visiting prof., Rutgers Coll. and N.J. Coll. for Women, 1924-25. Hon. mem. bd. of trustees Athens Coll. since 1938. Mem. Am. Classical League (1920-24). Classical Assn. of Atlantic States (pres. 1936-37), Am. Philol. Soc., Am. Numismatic Soc., Archaeol. Inst. of America, Phi Beta Kappa. Episcopalian. Club: Peirasus Br. of Propeller of America (treas.). Editor: Latin Poetry (with J.W. Basore), 1924; Supplement to Latin Poetry (with J. W. Basore), 1936. Contbr. articles to jours. Address: Athens, Greece. *

WEBSTER, BRUCE PECK, physician; b. Lansdowne, Ont., Can., Nov. 1, 1901; s. Thomas Amos and Bertha (Peck) W.; M.D., C.M., McGill U., 1925. Came to U.S., 1927, naturalized, 1932. Intern, asst. resident medicine Montreal Gen. Hosp., 1925-27; asst. resident medicine, Jacques Loeb fellow Johns Hopkins Hosp. and U., 1927-29; fellow medicine NRC, 1929-31; asst. prof. medicine Tulane U., 1931-32; asst. prof. medicine Cornell U. Med. Sch., 1932-46, asso. prof. clin. medicine, 1946-66, clin. prof. medicine, 1966-76; pvt. practice medicine, 1946-76; attending physician N.Y. Hosp.; med. dir. Time, Inc., 1947-67. Past mem. pub. adv. com. to surgeon gen. USPHS; cons. Dept. Army; exec. com. Japanese Christian U. Found., St. Luke's Hosp., Tokyo; med. adv. bd. Am. Hosp., Paris; past pres. Internat. Union Against Trepanomatoses; past chmn. nat. commn. venereal disease HEW; cons. WHO. Served from lt. col. to col. AUS, 1942-46. Decorated Legion of Merit. Mem. Soc. Exptl. Biology and Medicine, Soc. Clin. Investigation Am. Inst. Nutrition, Harvey Soc. Soc. Research Child Devel., N.Y. Acad. Medicine, Am. Soc. Hygienne (past pres., chmn. internat. com.), Soc. Med. Consultants to Armed Forces (past pres.). Clubs: University, Century Assn., Nippon (N.Y.C.); Maidstone (Easthampton, N.Y.). Home: New York, N.Y. Died Jan 4, 1976.

WEBSTER, EDWARD MOUNT, Fed. Communications Commnr.; born Washington, D.C., Feb. 28, 1889; s. Edward and Emma Virginia (Mount) W.; ed. U.S. Coast Guard Acad., New London, Conn., 1909-12; m. Dorothy Richardson, Oct. 22, 1915; children—Edward, Dorothy Frances. Apptd. to staff engring. dept., Fed. Communications Commn., Washington, D.C., 1934, asst. chief engr., 1938-42; dir. Nat. Fedn. Am. Shipping's, Washington, D.C., Div. Telecommunications, 1946-47; apptd. mem. F.C.C., 1947. Attended 24 internat. telecommunication confs. Served as officer, U.S. Coast Guard, World War I, 1912-18; assigned communications duty, C.G. Hdqrs., 1919, chief communications officer, 1923, retired with rank of lt. comdr., 1934, recalled to active duty, Coast Guard, chief communications officer, capt., 1942, commodore, 1945, ret. 1946. Awarded Legion of Merit, 1945. Fellow Inst. Radio Engrs. (dir. 1946); mem. Vet. Wireless Operators Assn., N.Y.C. Mil. Order Loyal Legion, Mil. Order World Wars, Am. Vets. World War II, Armed Forces Communications Assn., U.S. Power Squadrons (govt. mem. governing bd.). Clubs: Propeller, Engineers. Home: Kensington, Md. Died July 27, 1976.

WECHSLER, DAVID, psychologist; b. Lespede, Romania, Jan. 12, 1896; s. Moses and Leah (Pascal) W.; A.B., Coll. City N.Y., 1916; M.A., Columbia, 1917, Ph.D., 1925; m. Ruth A. Halpern, July 21, 1939; children—Adam F., Leonard M. Chief psychologist Bellevue Psychiat. Hosp., 1932-67; clin. prof. N.Y. U. Coll. Medicine, 1942-70, prof., 1970-81; vis. prof. clin. psychology Hebrew U., Jerusalem, 1967. Spl. cons. sec. of war, 1941-43. Bd. govs. Hebrew U., 1965-81; v.p., dir. Am. Friends of Hebrew U. Fellow Gerontological Soc.; mem. A.A.A.S., Am. Psychol. Assn. (award of year clin. div. 1960, distinguished profl. contbn. award 1973), Am. Psychopath. Assn. (pres. 1959-60), N.Y. State Psychol. Assn., N.Y. Acad. Scis., Am. Assn. Mental Deficiency (spl. award 1972), Soc. Gen. Systems Research Child Devel., Sigma Xi. Author: Range of Human Capacities, 1935; Wechsler-Bellevue Intelligence Scale, 1939; The Measurements of Adult Intelligence, 1944; Wechsler Intelligence Scale for Children, 1949; Wechsler Preschool and Primary Scale of Intelligence, 1967; Selected Papers, 1974. Home: New York, N.Y. Died May 2, 1981.

WEED, OLIVER EUGENE, ins. exec.; b. Stamford,.Conn., Mar. 19, 1896; s. Frederick Eugene and Alice (Bell) W.; student pub. schs.; m. Gertrude S. Welton, Apr. 29, 1922; children—Shirley S. (Mrs. Robert F. Will), Phyllis E. (Mrs. William C. Murphy). With Johnson & Higgins, Ins., N.Y.C., 1916-22; placer marine dept. Rollins Burdick Hunter Co., Chgo., 1922-23, mgr. Kansas City, 1923-34, mgr. contact and prodn. dept. Chgo. office, 1934, dir., 1943-76, sec., 1944-76, v.p. 1945-52, exec. v.p., from 1952. Served as 1st lt. U.S. Army, World War I. Clubs: Chicago Athletic (Chgo.); Exmoor Country (Highland Park, Ill.). Home: Highland Park, Ill. Died Dec. 5, 1976.

WEEG, GERARD PAUL, educator; b. Davenport, Ia., Oct. 29, 1927; s. Edmund Anthony and Cecilia (Schebler) W.; B.S., St. Ambrose Coll., Davenport, 1949; M.S., Okla. State U., 1950; Ph.D., Ia. State U., 1955; m. Harriet I. Smith, Dec. 28, 1948; children—Judith, Carol, Joseph, Marla, John, Joyce, James, Catherine. Mathematician, Remington Rand Univac, St. Paul, 1954-56; prof. Mich. State U., 1956-63; vis. prof. Ia. State U., 1963-64; prof. computer sci. U. Ia., Iowa City, 1964-77. Mem. Am. Math. Soc., Math. Assn. Am., Assn. Computing Machinery, I.E.E.E. Author: (With G.B. Reed) Introduction to Numerical Analysis, 1966. Home: Iowa City, Iowa. Died Apr. 10, 1977; buried St. Joseph's Cemetery, Iowa City.

WEEKS, LEWIS GEORGE, geologist; b. Chilton, Wis., May 22, 1893; s. George T. and Katherine (Schneider) W.; B.A., U. Wis., 1917, D.Sc. (hon.), 1970; postgrad. Cornell U., 1919-20: D.Sc. (hon.), Tex. Tech. U., 1970; m. Una Austin, Oct. 12, 1921 (dec. May 1956); 1 son, Lewis Austin; m. 2d, Anne Sutton, Dec. 14, 1957. Geologist, mines engr., Mexico and Ariz., 1917-18, Mexico, 1919; instr. Cornell U., 1919-20; geologist Whitehall Petroleum Corp., Ltd., London and India, 1920-24; with Standard Oil Co. (N.J.), 1924-58, chief geologist, Argentina, 1933-38, pres. Standard Oil Co. Bolivia, 1933-38, chief research geologist parent co., 1938-53, chief geologist, 1953-58; cons. geologist, 1958-77; pres. Oil Basins, Ltd., Offshore Royalties, Inc.; chmn. Weeks Natural Resources Ltd.; adviser to UN, other govts. Mem. Am. Mus. Natural History. Mem. adv. com. Internat. Oil and Gas Ednl. Center, The Southwestern Legal Found., Dallas. Served with USN, 1918-19. Mem. Am. Assn. Petroleum Geologists (pres. 1959-60; Powers medal, Human Needs award), Am. Inst. Profl. Geologists, N.Y. Acad. Scis. (chmn. geol. scis. sect.), Soc. Exploration Geologists, A.A.A.S., Am. Geophys. Union, Am. Inst. Mining, Metall. and Petroleum Engrs., Geol. Soc. Am., Geol. Soc. Australia (hon.). Republican. Episcopalian. Club: Explorers (N.Y.C.). Editor, part author: Habitat of Oil, 1958; part author: Petroleum Exploration Handbook, Methods of Estimating Undiscovered Oil and Gas Resources, Geology of Continental Margins: author Basin Development and Oil Occurance, 1948; A Lifelong Love Affair, the memoirs of Lewis G. Weeks, geologist, 1978. Contbr. articles, sci. and tech. papers to profl. jours. Address: Westport, Conn. Died Mar. 4, 1977;

buried Churchyard of St. James the Less, Scarsdale, N.Y.

WEEKS, RUTH MARY, educator, author; b. Kansas City, Mo., Feb. 21, 1886; d. Edwin Rutbven and Mary (Harmon) Weeks; A.B., Vassar Coll., 1908; A.M., U. of Mich., 1913; student summers, U. of Chicago, 1916, 29, U. of Calif., 1923, Teachers Coll., Columbia, 1936, New York School of Philanthropy, 1908; unmarried; 1 foster son, Oliver Payne (lt. comdr., United States Navy). Teacher of English, Westport High School, Kansas City, Missouri, 1908-09, 1910-12; Borden European fellow from Vassar College, 1909-10; graduate fellow, University of Michigan, 1912-13; teacher Packer Collegiate Institute, 1913-14, Tudor Hall, 1914-15, Kansas City Junior College, 1916-26; teacher of English and head of department, Paseo High School, Kansas City, Missouri, since 1927; instructor, summers, Missouri State Teachers College, 1918, University of Pittsburgh, 1920, 21, Univ. of Calif., 1923, U. of Pa., 1931; lectures extensively to state and nat. ednl. assns. Pres. Kansas City Assn. High Sch. Women, 1942-43. Member Nat. Council of Teachers of English (pres. 1930), N.E.A., Am. Assn. Univ. Women, Phi Beta Kappa, Gamma Phi Beta. Club: Kansas City Women's City. Author or co-author books relating to field; latest publ.; Using Periodicals, 1950. Home: Kansas City, Mo. *

WEEMS, PHILIP V(AN) H(ORN), navigation specialist; b. Turbine, Tenn., Mar. 2, 1889; s. Joseph Burch and May Elizabeth (Rye) W.; student Branham and Hughes Sch., 1906-07; grad. U.S. Naval Acad., 1912; m. Margaret Thackray, Aug. 31, 1915; children—Philip (dec. 1943), Margaret Thackray, George Thackray (killed test plane, 1951). Founder, partner Weems System of Navigation, Annapolis, Md., from 1928; founder with others Inst. of Navigation, 1945. Served with U.S.N., active line duty, world wars I and II, 1908-33, 42-46; retired as capt.; active duty navy space navigation, 1961-62. Recipient Gold Medals. Fellow Inst. Aeronautical Scis. Author: Line of Position Book, 1927; Air Navigation, 1931; Marine Navigation, 1940; Star Altitude Curves, 1940. Contbr. tech. jours. Inventor: Second-Setting Watch; Mark II Aircraft Plotter. Home: Annapolis, Md. Died June 2, 1979; buried U.S. Naval Acad. Cemetery, Annapolis.

WEGNER, EARL EDWARD (WEG'NER), professor vet. surgery; b. Cheney, Wash., June 21, 1885; s. Ferdinand Christian and Amy Eleanor (Johnson) W.; student State Normal Sch., Cheney, 1902-03; D.V.S., State Coll. of Wash., 1908, B.S., 1915; m. Florence M. Wright, Dec. 21, 1913; children—Robert Edward (officer U.S. Army Air Corps Reserve), Glenn Wright. Began practice of veterinary medicine, 1908; inspector U.S. Bureau of Animal Industry, 1909; asst. prof. vet. surgery State Coll. of Wash., 1909-16, prof. since 1916, vice dean Coll. Vet. Medicine, 1919-21, dean, 1921-47; mayor of Pullman, 1926-30. Dir. National Board of Fur Farm Organizations; pres. Northwest Fur Breeders Regional Conference. Mem. Pullman Chamber Commerce (dir; ex-pres.). Mem. Am. Vet. Med. Assn. (exec. bd.), Wash. State Vet. Med. Assn. (ex-pres.), Internat. Veterinary Congress, Alpha Psi, Sigma Chi, Phi Kappa Phi, Crimson Circle. Studied and traveled in Europe, Aug. 1936 to Jan. 1937. Presbyterian. Elk (past Exalted Ruler). Home: Pullman, Wash. *

WEGNER, NICHOLAS H., clergyman; b. Humphrey, Nebr., July 6, 1898; s. Herman and Christina (Douan) W.; student, St. Joseph Coll., Teutopolis, Ill., 1912-18; St. Paul Seminary, Minn., 1918-20; S.T.D., Gregorian U., Rome, 1922-25; J.C.L., Cath. U. Washington, 1933-35; LL.D. Dir. Father Flanagan's Boys Home, Boys Town, 1948-76. Papal chamberlain, 1935, domestic prelate, 1945, protonotary apostolic, 1959. Mem. Canon Law Soc. Roman Catholic, K. of C., Moose, Elk. Club: Variety Internat. (Pitts.). Home: Boys Town, Nebr. Died Mar. 18, 1976.

WEHR, FREDERICK LEWIS, life ins. exec.; b. Balt., July 5, 1902; s. William Frederick and Bertha May (Lewis) W.; student Balt. Poly. Inst., 1917-21, Wharton Sch. Finance and Bus. Administrn., U. Pa., 1921-23; m. Nancy de Wolf Theobald, Oct. 21, 1924; children—Frederick T., Nancy de Wolf (Mrs. Nancy W. Smith), Asst. sec. Union Trust Co. of Md., 1926-34; with Monumental Life Ins. Co., Balt., 1934-75, successively asst. sec. sec., v.p., exec. v.p., 1953-60, pres., 1960-75, chmn. bd., 1962-75, chief exec. officer, 1964-75, chmn. exec. com., 1967-75, also dir.; dir. Monumental Corp., Title Guarantee Co., First Nat. Bank of Md., Monumental Life Ins. Co., Balt. Gas and Electric Co., Balt. Equitable Soc. Chmn. Joint fund com. United Appeal Central Md.; chmn. Balt. chpt. A.R.C.; mem. Vol. Council on Equal Opportunity, Baltimore County Revenue Authority. Trustee emeritus Goucher Coll.; past pres. bd. trustees Children's Hosp., Balt.; mem. bd. Eudowood Hosp. at Johns Hopkins; past mem. regional bd. NCCJ; sponsor Radio Free Europe. Mem. Am. Life Conv. (v.p., exec. com.), C. of C. Met. Balt. (dir., past pres.), Delta Phi Mem. Ch. of Good Shepherd. Clubs: Elkridge, Maryland, Bachelor's Cotilion, Rehoboth Beach Country. Home: Ruxton, Md. Died Dec. 2, 1975.

WEHR, PERRY NEAL., JR., diversified co. exec.; b. Youngstown, Ohio, Feb. 4, 1921; s. Perry Neal and Mary (Sprankle) W.; B.A., Allegheny Coll., 1943; M.A., U. Pitts, 1951; C.P.A., Pa., 1953; m. Margaret Louise Jones, May 29, 1952; 1 son, Roger Ellsworth. With Lybrand, Ross Bros. & Montgomery, C.P.A.'s, N.Y.C., 1953-58; comptroller, sec.-treas. Thatcher Glass Mfg. Co., 1958-65; exec. v.p. Seilon, Inc., 1965-68, pres., 1968-69; v.p. bus. devel. Electronics Capital Corp., 1970-71; v.p. Grow Chem. Corp., 1972-73; pres. Memhard & Co. Inc., Riverside, Conn., 1973-79. Club: Piping Rock (Locust Valley, L.I.). Home: Mill Neck, N.Y. Died Dec. 25, 1979.

WEIB, TAYLOR BLADEN, lawyer; b. Prince William County, Va., Mar. 23, 1883; s. Richard Mitchell and Fanny Elizabeth (Willcoxon) W.; LL.B., George Washington U., 1907; m. Anna Katherine Goodman, Aug. 10, 1910. Admitted to D.C. bar, 1907, Mont. bar, 1908, Supreme Court of U.S., 1916; practice in Helena, Mont., since 1908. Pres. Mont. Record Pub; Co.; dir. Mont. Power Co., First Nat. Bank and Trust Co. of Helena, Mont.; atty. for Mont., Great Northern Ry. Co. Mem. Am. and Mont. bar assns. Republican. Mason, Elk. Club: Montana (Helena). Home: Helena, Mont. *

WEIBLE, WALTER LEO, army ofcr.; b. Waterbu Waterbury, Conn., June 2, 1896; s. John Edward and Elizabeth (Walters) W.; grad. in elec. engring., Pratt Inst., Brooklyn, 1917, Coast Arty. Sch., 1927 and 1928, Chem. Warfare Sch., 1928, Command and Gen. Staff Sch., 1935, Army War Coll., 1938, Army Indsl. Coll., 1939; D.Sc., Washington and Jefferson College, 1944; LL.D., Pratt Inst., 1955; married Hazel Knight Bean, July 12, 1918; 1 daughter, Geraldine Madeline. Entered U.S. Army as private, Dec. 1917; commd. 2d lt. Coast Arty. Sect., O.R.C., June 1918; advanced through grades to lt. gen., 1953; served with 6th and 8th Armies, in command of logistical installations, Luzon and Japan, World War II; former dep. chief staff Ops. and Adminstrn., Dept. Army, ret. 1957; exec. v.p. Assn. U.S. Army, 1957-80; dir. State Nat. Bank, Bethesda, Md. Director of Arms of Friendship, Philadelphia. Decorated D.S.M. with Oak Leaf Cluster, Bronze Star Medal, Legion of Merit, World War I Victory Medal, World War II Victory Medal, Asiatic-Pacific Theater (with 2 battle stars), Army of Occupation medals, Philippine Liberation Medal with two bronze stars, Greek Higher Cross of Order Royal Batallion of Phoenix, UN Service Medal, Korean Service Medal. Member Mil. Order Carabao, Mil. Order World Wars, National Rifle Assn. (life), Omega Iota Pi. Clubs: Army and Navy, Columbia Country (Washington). Home: Rockville, Md. Died Feb. 19, 1980.

WEICKER, LOWELL PALMER, industrialist; s. Theodore and Florence (Palmer) W., B.S. Yale, 1926; m. Mary Hastings Bickford, Oct. 22, 1927 (div. 1951); children—T. Martin, Lowell Palmer, Mary Audrey, Harold H; m. 2d, Beverly Kraft Topping, June 6, 1953 (div. 1965); m. 3d, Antoinette Francois Littell, 1965. Former pres., dir. E.R. Squibb & Sons, v.p. dir. Jones Estate Corp.; chmn. dir. Lentheric, Inc., Lentheric of Can., Ltd., Lentheric Ltd. (Eng.); mng. dir. Parfums Lentheric, G.m. B.H.; vice chmn. bd., dir. Cia. Squibb De Formento, S.A., Lentherio, S.A. (France), E. R. Squibb & Sons, Ltd. (Eng.); asst. sec. gen. for production and logistics NATO, 1953-56; former Pres., chmn. bd. Bigelow-Sanford, Inc., N.Y.C., dir.; chmn. bd. Jesup and Lamont Internat. Ltd., London; pres., dir. Northco Corp., Panama; mem. exec. com., dir. Sperry and Hutchinson Co.; mem. Midtown adv., com. Chase Manhattan Bank. Decorated Legion Merit, Bronze Star, Legion d'Honneur, Croix de Guerre with Palm, order British Empire (Great Britain), Star of Solidarity; Grand 'Ufficiale al Merito Della Republica (Italy). Clubs: Union League, Univ. (N.Y.C.); Piping Rock, River, Seawanhaka Corinthian Yacht; Bucks (London). Home: Mill Neck, N.Y. Died Dec. 15, 1978.

WEIDA, FRANK MARK, ret. educator; b. Allentown, Pa., Sept. 28, 1891; s. Penrose John and Sarah Rebecca (Mark) W.; B.S., Kenyon Coll., 1913, student Johns Hopkins, 1913-14, U. Chgo., 1916-17; Ph.D., U. Ia., 1923; m. Opal Fern Dickson, Jan. 1, 1936; children—Charles Rietz, Mary Elizabeth. Head math. and sci. dept. St. Alban's Sch. Knoxville, Ill., 1914-16; asst. in math. U. Chgo., 1916-17; instr. math. U. Ia., 1917-24; asst. prof. math. Mont. State Coll., 1924-25, Lehigh U., 1925-30; asso. prof. math. George Washington U., 1930-35, prof. statistics, 1935-57, head dept. statistics, 1935-57, prof. emeritus in residence, 1957-62; research scientist, summer 1953; cons. Historic Records Project, 1954, Naval Logistics Research Project, 1954, 55, cons., prin. investigator Army Logistics Research Project, 1955-60; cons. in statistics and applied mathematics U.S. Army Engr. Research and Devel. Labs., Fort Belvoir, Va., 1958-63; cons. statistics NIH, 1940-44; dir. A.S.T.P. research statis. lab. George Washington U., 1944; expert cons. Office Chief of Engrs., War Dept. Washington, 1944-45, Office Sci. Personnel, NRC, Washington, 1948, 50, Eno Found. For Hwy. Traffic Control, Saugatuck, Conn., 1950; cons. math. statistics Hdqrs. Air Research and Devel. Command, Wright-Patterson AFB, Dayton, Ohio, 1951-52. Fellow A.A.A.S., Inst. Math. Statistics; mem. Am. Math. Soc., Math. Assn. Am., Econometric Soc., Am. Statis. Assn., Philos. Soc. Washington, Washington Acad. Scis., Washington Statis. Soc. (v.p. 1941), Square and Compass, Sigma Xi, Alpha Tau Omega, Gamma Alpha. Republican. Episcopalian. Mason (32, K.T., Shriner). Club: Cosmos. Co-author: Analytic Geometry and Elements of Calculus, 1930; Statistics and Their Applications to Highway Traffic Analysis, 1952. Asso. editor Am. Maths. Monthly, 1930-35. Contbr. numerous articles on research in math. and applied statistics to Annals of Math. Statistics, Annals of Maths., Am. Math. Monthly, Giornale di Matematica Finanziaria. Research in statistics, math. of finance, actuarial theory, theory of approximations, errors of correlations and probability, practical math. analysis. Home: Port Republic, Md. Died Sept. 13, 1977. Interred Christ Episcopal Churchyard, Port Republic, Md.

WEIGEL, JOHN C. (WI'GEL), govt. official; b. Joliet, Ill., Nov. 18, 1886; s. John G. and Margaret (Bauer) W.; grad. Joliet Township High Sch., 1905; B.A., Lombard Coll., 1908; grad. student Harvard, summer 1908, also various times U. of Chicago, 1909-19; travel and study in Europe, summers 1910, 11, 13, 14; unmarried. Reporter Joliet Daily News, 1904-05, summers 1906, 07; reporter Galesburg (Ill.) Mail, 1905-08; asst. in mathematics, Lombard Coll., 1905-08, asst. in physics, 1907-08, prof. of German, 1908-09; instr. in German, U. of Chicago, 1909-19; served in code and cipher sect., Div. Mil. Intelligence, Gen. Staff, Washington, D.C., 1918, later commd. 1st lt., O.R.C.; mem. exec. staff Sears, Roebuck & Co., Chicago, serving in office of mgr. of factory dept., as asst. to v.p. in charge of operations, asst. mgr. advertising and printing plant, 1919-24; asst. gen. supt., Philipsborn's, 1924; gen. mgr. and sec., Battle Ball Co. of America, 1925; administr. Div. of the Criminologist and Inst. for Juvenile Research, Chicago, 1926-33; adminstr. Behavior Research Fund, Chicago, 1926-33, sec. bd. trustees, 1931-48; fiscal supervisor Dept. of Pub. Welfare, State of Ill., 1933-37, administrative asst., 1937-41, acting supt. div. of old age assistance, 1937-40; regional adminstr. U.S. Office of Price Adminstrn., Chicago, Dec. 1941-Mar-1943; with Lend-Lease Adminstrn., Mar. 1943-Feb. 1944, assigned foreign service; member exec. staff United Nations Relief and Rehabilitation Adminstrn., 1944; chief administrative officer, UNRRA council, Montreal, Canada, Sept. 1944; assistant to director British Empire and Middle East branch. Foreign Economic Administration, 1945; function transferred to Office of Foreign Liquidation, Department of State, 1945; foreign affairs specialist, State Dept., 1948; pres. Ill. State Civil Service Commn. 1949-50. Lecturer Graduate School Social Service Adminstrn., U. Chgo., 1939-40. Established in his honor the John C. Weigel Fund and Prize at Knox Coll. Mem. Knox Coll. Fifty-Year Club (hon. president), Am. Acad. Polit. and Social Science, Academy of Polit. Sci., Ill. Conf. Social Welfare (past pres.), Cliff Dwellers, Phi Delta Theta. Author: A Manual of Business Methods for the Department of Public Welfare, 1941. Contbr. to Annual Reports of Ill. Pub. Welfare; also to professional jours. Address: Joliet, Ill. *

WEIGHTMAN, RICHARD HANSON, meterologist; b. Vicksburg, Miss., Aug. 26, 1882; s. Roger Chew and Meggie Hazlett (Maris) W.; prep. edn. high sch., Washington, D.C.; LL.B., Georgetown U., 1911; m. Emma Jane Honey, of Fredericksburg, Va., May 6, 1913. Entered Weather Bur., Washington, D.C., Jan. 1, 1901; asst. observer, Cleveland, O., 1904-5, Washington, D.C., 1905—, meteorologist, 1914—. Commd. 1st lt., Signal Corps U.S.A., Sept. 19, 1917-Mar. 1919, duty with A.E.F. in France. Episcopalian. Joint Author: The Types of Storms of the United States and Their Average Movements (Govt. Printing Office), 1915; The Types of Anti-cyclones of the U.S., and Their Average Movements (same), 1917. Home: West Chevy Chase, D.C. *

WEIGLE, CLIFFORD FRANCIS, educator; b. San Francisco, Sept. 17, 1906; s. Britton Day and Alice Carey (Van Reynegom) W.; A.B., Stanford, 1929, A.M., 1936; grad. work U. Cal. at Berkley, 1941, U. Minn., 1947-48; m. Margaret Sturrock, Oct. 4, 1930; 1 son, Charles Britton. Mem. editorial dept. San Francisco News, 1929-34; instr. journalism Stanford, 1934-36, asst. prof., 1937-42, asso. prof., 1943-48; dean, prof. journalism Sch. of Journalism, U. Ore., 1948-50; asso. dir., prof. journalism Inst. for Journalistic Studies, Stanford, 1950-56, asso. exec. head dept. communication and journalism, 1956, prof., 1956-71, exec. head dept. communication, 1961-68; faculty mem. U.S. Army Shrivenham (Eng.) Am. U., 1945-46. Mem. Am. Assn. U. Profs., Assn. Edn. in Journalism, Phi Beta Kappa, Sigma Delta Chi, Alpha Delta Sigma. Episcopalian. Clubs: Press, Commonwealth of California (San Francisco). Home: Stanford, Calif. Died Mar. 13, 1981.

WEIGLE, LUTHER ALLAN, educator; b. Littlestown, Pa., Sept. 11, 1880; s. Elias Daniel (D.D.) and Hannah (Bream) W.; B.A., Gettysburg Coll., 1900, M.A., 1903, LL.D., 1934; student Lutheran Theol. Sem. Gettysburg, 1900-02; Ph.D., Yale, 1905; D.D., Carleton Coll., 1916, Gettysburg Coll., 1917; Litt.D., Muhlenberg Coll., 1925; LL.D., Dickinson Coll., 1933, Wittenburg Coll.,

1949; S.T.D., Ohio U., 1934, Berkeley Div. Sch., 1950, J.U.D., Boston U., 1939, D.D., Queen's U., 1941, Princeton, 1946, Yale, 1950; L.H.D., Otterbein Coll., 1952., Lambuth Coll. 1960; m. Clara Boxrud, June 15, 1909; children—Richard Luther Allan, Margaret (Mrs. W. F. Quillian, Jr.), Ruth (Mrs. A.C. Guyton). Ordained to ministry Luth. Ch., 1903, pastor, Bridgeport, Conn., 1903-04, asst. in psychology, Yale, 1904-05, prof. philosophy Carleton Coll. Northfield, Minn. 1905-16, dean, 1910-15; Horace Bushnell prof. Christian nurture Yale, 1916-24. Sterling prof. religious edn. 1924-49, dean Div. Sch., 1928-49, now emeritus; lectureships at many sems. and univs. Pres. Conf. Theol. Sems., 1929, chmn. exec. com. 1930-49; chmn. administrv. com. Fed. Council Chs., 1929-32, pres., 1940-42; chmn. planning com. orgn. Nat. Council Chs. Christ, U.S.A., 1941-50; chmn. World Council Christian Edn. and Sunday Sch. Assn., 1928-58, chmn. com. which edited Revised Standard Version of the Bible, 1930-70; chmn. com. revising Apocrypha, 1953-70. Trustee Northfield Schs., Hazen Found., Yale-in China (pres. 1946-56). Decorated knight of St. Gregory the Great (Pope Paul VI); recipient citation distinguished service Congl. Chs., A.M.E. Zion Ch., Nat. Council Chs., Boy Scouts Am.; Gutenberg award, Chgo. Bible Soc., 1959; Wilbur Cross medal Yale, 1967. Author numerous books, latest being, The Living Word, 1956; The Bible Word Book (with Ronald Bridges), 1959; The New Octapla, Octapls, 1961: The Genesis Octapla, 1965. Home: New Haven, Conn. Died Sept 2, 1976.

WEIK, MARY HAYS, author; b. Greencastle, Ind.; d. Jesse W. and Allie (Hays) Weik; A.B., DePauw U., m. Joseph Grifalconi (div.); children—John W., Ann. Newspaper reporter, Chgo.; mag. editorial and community relations counselor schs. and social agys., N.Y.C.; UN Observer, 1956-62; founder, 1960, since editor Window on the World, N.Y.C. Founder, sec. Fellowship for World Citizens, 1954, Women's Com. to Stop Ravenswood Reactor, N.Y.C., 1962-64, Com. to End Radiol. Hazards, 1964—. Founding mem. Gesellscaft fur Biologische Sicherheit, Vienna, 1970. Author: (poetry) Adventure; The House at Cherry Hill; Jazz Man (A.L.A. Notable Books of 1966); A Parliament for Man: A Plan for UN Reform; The Scarlet Thread (plays), 1968; Nuclear Information Series, 1965-71. Address: New York City, Died Dec. 25, 1979.

WEIL, ARTHUR, neuropathologist; b. Brauschweig, Germany., Oct. 3, 1887; s. Abraham and Helene (Coblenzer) W.; grad. Oberrealschule, Hanover, 1906; studied medicine univs. of Munich, Halle and Berlin, 1907-14, M.D., 1914; unmarried. Began active career as asst. Univ. of Halle, 1912, continuing 2 years; capt. Med. Corps. German Army, World War, 1914-18; privatdozent of psysiology, U. of Halle, 1919-21. Came to U.S. 1922, naturalized citizen, 1929. Neuropathologist Montefiore Hosp., New York, 1924-28; asst. prof. neuropathology, Northwestern U. Med. Sch., Chicago, 1928-30, asso. prof. 1930-44. Consultant to Surgeon gen. Army Inst. Pathology, 1945; consultant U.S. Veterans Adminstrn., 1949-54. Fellow, N.Y., Acad. Medicine; member Am. Neurol. Assn., Sigma Xi., etc. Author: Internal Secretion (3 German edits., 1920-23; English, Spanish and Russian translations); Textbook of Neuropathology, 1933 (sec. ed. 1945). Contbr. to handbooks of physiology and biology. Editor: Jour. Neuropathology and Exptl. Neurology. Home: Kew Gardens, L.I., N.Y. *

WEIL, REUBEN W., dept. store exec.; b. N.Y.C., May 12, 1882; s. Nathan and Rosa (Haas) W.; ed. pub. schs.; m. Maude Foster, Sept. 11, 1913. Co-owner Weils Dept. Store, Hillsboro, Ore.; dir. U.S. Nat. Bank, Portland, Ore., Haley Foods, Inc. Past chmn. Wash. County Welfare; past chmn. and vice chmn. local A.R.C.; past chmn. SSS bd. I, World War II. Mem. Hillsboro C. of C. (past pres.). Jewish religion. Mason (Shriner), Elk; mem. B'nai B'rith, Woodmen of World. Clubs: Rotary, Toastmasters (Hillsboro).

WEILER, EMANUEL THORNTON, economist, A.M., U. Minn., 1939, Ph.D., 1942; m. Catherine Ann Reinoehl, May 5, 1934; children—Peter, Ann, Sarah, Susan. Instr., Sch. Bus. Adminstrn., U. Minn., 1939-43; sr. econ. analyst Dept. Commerce, 1943-44; economist Bd. Govs. of Fed. Res. System, 1944-45; prof., head dept. econs. Ohio Wesleyan U., 1945-48; prof. econs. Coll. Commerce and Bus Adminstrn., U. Ill., 1948-53; prof., head dept. econs. sch. sci. edn. and humanities Purdue U., 1953-56, head dept. indsl. mgmt., transp., Sch. Engring., 1956-58, dean Sch. Indsl. Mgmt., 1958-69, Krannert Grad. Sch. Indsl. Adminstrn., 1962-69, Herman C. Krannert distinguished prof. mgmt. and econs., 1969-79; dir. Central Soya Co., Inc., CTS Corp., Elkhart, Ind., Inland Container Corp. (Indpls.); trustee DePauw U., Greencastle, Ind.; chmn. bd. Ind. Mortgage and Realty Investors. Mem. Am. Econ. Assn., Am. Statis. Assn., Am. Finance Assn., Phi Gamma Delta. Episcopalian. Author: The Economic System, 1952; Economic Policy, rev. 1955; The American Economic System, 1957; Economics, 1976. Home: Lafayette, Ind. Died July 1, 1979.

WEILL, MICHEL DAVID, business exec.; b. Paris, France, Dec. 29, 1887; s. Jules and Louise (Caen) W.; student Coll. Rollin, Paris, 1899-1902, King's Coll. Sch., Wimbledon, Eng., 1902-03, King's Coll. Somerset House, London, 1903-04; m. Evelyn Palmer, July 18, 1921. Pres. Raphael Weil & Co., San Francisco, 1945, now chmn.; dir. Continental Opera Co., Californians, Inc. Chmn. San Francisco Planning Commn., 1942-46; mem. Mem. San Francisco Art's Commn., 1953—, Pres. bd. trustees DeYoung Meml. Mus., San Francisco; gov. San Francisco Symphony; v.p. French Hosp. Served from corp. to capt., French Army, 1914-19; gen. staff AEF, 1917-19; Decorated Croix de Guerre with Palm, Officer Legion of Honor (France); Merit Commercial; Stella della Solidarita (Italy). Mem. Alliance Francaise (pres.), San Francisco Planning and Housing Assn. (v.p.), Retail Dry Goods Assn. (dir.), San Francisco Retail Credit Assn. (dir.), Sigmund Stern Grove Musical Assn. (treas.). Home: San Francisco. *

WEIMER, ALOYSIUS GEORGE, educator; b. Chgo., Oct. 29, 1899; s. Jacob and Anna Maria (Schlitt) W.; student Art Inst. Chgo., 1916-20; B.F.A., Notre Dame du Lac (Ind.), 1934; A.M., N.Y. U., 1935; Ph.D. in Art History, U. Mich., 1940; m. Phyllis K. McKowen, Aug. 9, 1934; 1 son, Alois G. With John Crerar Library, Chgo., 1915-32, sr. asst., 1925-32; mem. faculty U. Detroit, 1936-80, prof. fine arts, 1945-70, chmn. dept., 1936-70; prof. emeritus, 1970-80. Mem. New Baltimore Library Commn., 1954—. Mem. Catholic, Coll. art assns. Home: New Baltimore, Mich. Died Aug. 2, 1980; interred St. Mary's Cemetery, New Baltimore.

WEINBERG, ABRAHAM JOSEPH, linen supply co. exec.; b. Poland, Dec. 25, 1886; s. Barnard and Kate (Goldstein) W.; brought to U.S., 1892, naturalized as minor; m. Lillian Silverman, Aug. 31, 1917; children—Harriet (Mrs. Elliott Goldstein), Sonia (Mrs. W. B. Schwartz, Jr.). With Weine Nat. Linen Service Corp., Atlanta, 1919—, vice chmn. bd., 1953—; chmn. bd. Citizens Nat. Bank, Sandy Springs, Ga.; pres. Weine Investment Corp., Atlanta. Treas. Jewish Children's Service, Simon Wolf Endowment Fund; mem. president's council Brandeis U. Mem. Nat. Conf. Christians and Jews (nat. bd.; Ga. co-chmn.). Mason (Shriner, 32 deg.). Home: *

WEINBERGER, BERNHARD WOLF, orthodontist; b. Idaho Springs, Colo., June 5, 1885; s. Simon and Betty (Rosenthal) W.; grad. high sch., East Denver, Colo., 1904; D.D.S., U. of Pa., 1908; grad. study Angle Sch. of Orthodontia, New York, 1909; m. Sylvia H. Goodman, Nov. 6, 1913 (died Feb. 7, 1924); m. 2d, Louise Haimes, Feb. 9, 1927; children—Suzanne, Bernhard Simon. Began practice N.Y. City, 1910; lecturer on dental history and lit., Coll. Dentistry, New York Univ., 1923-29, prof. dental history and lit., 1929-31; spl. lecturer on orthodontic history, U. of Pa. Dental Sch., 1927, Baltimore Coll. Dental Surgery, U. of Md., 1930. Dental librarian N.Y. Acad. Medicine, 1922-29, cons. librarian of dental lit. since 1929; sec-treas. Am. Dental Library and Mus. Assn., 1919-23. Pres. N.Y. Dental Centennial, 1934. Mem. bd. of trustees Pierre Fauchard Acad., 1938-44; nat. trustee Nat. Home for Jewish Children, Denver, Colo. Fellow A.A.A.S., N.Y. Acad. Sciences (life mem.), Internat. Coll. Dentists (mem. since 1929; a founder U.S. sect., 1930; mem. bd. regents, dist. 2, 1934-35; awarded Master degree, U.S. sect., 1941); asso. fellow N.Y. Acad. Medicine; mem. A.M.A., Am. Dental Assn. (chmn. com. on dental history 1935-42), Dental Soc. State of N.Y. (chmn. coms. dental history and dental mus. since 1934). 1st Dist. Dental Soc. (librarian 1913-46, dir. 1919-36; life mem.), Am. Assn. History of Medicine, N.Y. Soc. Dental History and Culture (pres. 1934-36), Bibliographical Soc. Am., Am. Assn. Orthodontists (mem. com. nomenclature), N.E. Soc. Orthodontists Pacific Coast Soc. Orthodontists (corr. mem.), N.Y. Soc. Med. History, Asociacion Mexicana de Ortodonica (hon. mem.), History of Science Soc., Am. Soc. Med. History, Fed. Dentaire Internationale (v.p., mem. com. on documentation from U.S., 1923-41); Alumni Soc. Angle Sch. Orthodontia Orthodontia (pres. 1926-27 and since 1938; sec. 1931), Delta Sigma Delta, Sigma Epsilon Delta (grand master, Orthodontia (pres. 1926-27 and since 1938; sec. 1931), Delta Sigma Delta, Sigma Epsilon Delta (grand master, 1919-21), Omicron Kappa Upsilon, Pi Gamma Mu. Vice pres., sect. history, 7th Internat. Dental Congress (Phila.), 1926; U.S. essayist, sect. 8th Internat. Dental Congress (Paris), 1931; U.S. reporter sect. 3, 9th Internat. Dental Congress (Vienna), 1936. Awarded illuminated testimonials, 1st Dist. Dental Society New York, 1929, New York Dental Centennial Commission, 1935; Benjamin Lord prize, 1st District Dental Society N.Y., 1931; N.Y. Dental Centennial medal, 1934; Sigma Epsilon Delta plaque, 1941. Served as mem. draft bd., N.Y., during World War I. Mem. nat. panel Am. Arbitration Assn. Jewish religion. Mason. (32 deg., Shriner), B'nai B'rith. Author books relating to field; contbr. to profl. jours. Home: N.Y. *

WEINBERGER, JACOB, judge; b. Czechoslovakia (formerly Austria-Hungary) Jan. 4, 1882; brought to U.S. 1889; s. Herman and Nettie (Flaster); LL.B., U. of Colo., 1904; Doctor of Laws (honorary), U. Arizona, 1959; married Blanche Ruth Solomon, June 11, 1907; children—Adrienne (Mrs. Herbert H. Hafter), Richard. Admitted to bar, Colo., 1904, Ariz., 1905, Calif., 1911. Practiced law, Denver, 1904, Gila Co., Ariz., 1905-11; asst. dist. atty., Gila Co., 1907-09; del. from Gila Co. to Ariz. constl. conv., 1910; practiced law, San Diego, Calif., 1911-41; city atty. San Diego, 1941-43; judge Superior Ct., San Diego Co., 1943-45; U.S. dist. judge, So. Dist. Cal., 1946—; sr. judge U.S. Dist. Court, 1958—. Member board of education, City of San Diego 21 years. Mason (32 deg. Shriner), Eagle, Lion. B'nai B'rith. Home: San Diego. *

WEINGARTEN, JOE (WINE GARTEN), retail food mcht.; b. Galicia, Poland, Oct. 8, 1884; s. Harris and Beili (Weidinger) W.; student pub. schs. and bus. coll.; m. Malvina Kessler, May 6, 1923; children—Bernard Louis, Eveta Lea (Mrs. Morris L. Levinson) (dec.), Jack. Started at early age in father's corner, service and charge-account grocery; opened first supermarket, 1920, now operating 66 supermarkets, also the supplying warehouse, bakery, ice-cream, fish, poultry and egg processing plants; chmn. bd. J. Weingarten, Inc.; dir. Burlington-Rock Island R.R., Topco Assos., Inc., Ampal-Am. Israel Corp. Mem. exec. bd. Sam Houston Area council Boy Scouts Am.; past trustee Baylor Med. Found., United Fund Houston and Harris County; mem. bd. Tex. Med. Center, Med. Research Found. Tex.; vice chmn. nat. planning com. Jewish Theol. Sem. Am; founder, pres. World Inst. for World Peace. Fellow Brandeis Univ., Waltham, Mass. Recipient Louis Marshall award, 1958; Brotherhood award Nat. Conf. Christians and Jews. Past pres. Super Market Inst. Am.; life mem. Houston Fat Stock Show. Jewish religion (mem. congregation adv. bd.), Mem. B'nai B'rith (life). Clubs: Houston, Westwood Country, Cork, International. Home: Houston. Died Feb. 26, 1967. *

WEINMAN, CARL ANDREW, fed. judge; b. Steubenville, Ohio, Jan. 27, 1903; s. Andrew G. and Dorothea (Becker) W.; A.B., U. Mich., 1924, J.D., 1926; postgrad. Hague Acad. Internat. Law, 1960-64; J.D. (hon.) Coll. Steubenville, 1968; m. Frances Glerum, Dec. 19, 1969. Admitted to Ohio bar, 1925; Common pleas judge, 1937-49; chief judge U.S. Dist. Ct. So. Ohio, from 1959, sr. dist. judge, to 1979. Mem. bd. commrs. for disbarment lawyers Supreme Ct. Ohio, 1956-59, chmn., 1959; chmn. Fed. Budget Com. Mem. Jud. Conf. U.S., Common Pleas Judges Assn. Ohio (past pres.), Am., Inter-Am., Ohio bar assns., Am. Soc. Internat. Law, Am. Bar Found., Delta Theta Phi. Kiwanian (bd. govs.), Mason (33 deg.). Contbr. articles to law jours. Home: Dayton, Ohio. Died Feb. 5, 1979.

WEINMANN, LOUIS RANDOLPH, lawyer; b. Benicia, Cal., May 28, 1884; s. Louis and Caroline Isabel (Laidley) W.; student Boones U. Acad.; A.B., Stanford, 1905; LL.B., U. Calif., 1908; m. Alice Louise Teller, June 1, 1910; children—Lois, Randolph, Teller. Admitted to Cal. bar, 1906; judge City of Alameda, Cal., 1914-24; atty. with L. R. Weinmann, Oakland, 1917-36, Weinmann Quayle & Berry, 1936-46, Weinmann, Rode, Burnhill & Moffitt, 1946-65; counsel Hardin, Cook, Lorber & Martin, 1965—; instr. law YMCA Law Sch., San Francisco. Mem. bd. of athletic control Stanford. Mem. Am., Cal., Alameda County bar assns., Phi Delta Phi, Delta Kappa Epsilon. Home: Oakland CA. *

WEINTRAUB, JOSEPH, state justice; b. Cranford, N.J., Mar. 5, 1908; s. Benjamin and Minnie (Nimaroff) W.; A.B., Cornell U., 1928, LL.B., 1930. Admitted to N.J. bar, 1930; practiced in Newark until 1956; spl. asst. to atty. gen. N.J., 1941-43; mem. for N.J., Waterfront Commn. N.Y. Harbor, also counsel gov. State of N.J., 1954-56; judge Superior Ct. N.J., 1956; asso. justice Supreme Ct. N.J., 1956-57, chief justice, 1957-73. Bd. govs. Rutgers, The State U. Served to capt. AUS, 1943-46. Mem. Am., N.J., Essex County bar assns., Judge Advocates Assn., Phi Beta Kappa, Order of Coif. Phi Kappa Phi, 1937; *

WEISBACH, HARRY, violinist; b. Odessa, Russia, Apr. 28, 1886; s. Israel and Sonia (Goniker) W.; ed. pub. schs.; studied with A. S. Volpe, New York, and Eugene Ysaye, in Brussels, Belgium; grad. Royal High Sch. of Music, Berlin, 1908; unmarried. Brought to America, 1890; first played in public, 1896; concert meister Chicago Symphony Orchestra (founded by Theodore Thomas), since June, 1912. Has appeared in concerts in leading cities of Europe and America. Jewish. Home: Chicago. *

WEISGERBER, CHARLES AUGUST, educator, clergyman; b. Cin., Sept. 11, 1912; s. August and Mary (Krieg) W.; student Xavier U., Cin., 1930-34; A.B., West Baden Coll., West Baden Springs, Ind., 1935, M.A., 1940, S.T.L., 1944; Ph.D., Loyola U., Chgo., 1949. Ordained priest Roman Cath. Ch., 1943; instr. St. Ignatius High Sch., Chgo., 1937-38, U. Detroit High Sch., 1938-40; psychologist Sarah Fisher Home for

Children, Detroit, 1950-53; instr. U. Detroit, 1949-51, asst. prof., 1951-53, asso. prof., 1953-60, prof., 1960-77, chmn. psychology dept., 1953-64, asst. dean Grad. Sch., 1955-56, acting dean; 1957-58. Mem. Insts. Religion and Health, Am. Psyol. Assn., Psychologists Interested in Religious Issues, A.A.A.S. Author: Psychological Assessment of Candidates for a Religious Order, 1969. Contbr. articles psychol. mags. Home: Detroit, Mich. Died Jan 9, 1977.

WEISIGER, GEORGE BATES (WIS'IG-ER), prof. law; b. Fairmount, Ill., Sept. 30, 1886; s. John W. and Mary Jane (Draper) W.; LL.B., U. of Ill., 1911, B.S., 1923; J.D., Yale, 1924; m. Hazel Terpening, Jan. 20, 1912; children—Benjamin Wilson, Gene David, James Richard. Admitted to Ill. Bar, 1911, and practiced in Danville; asst. prof. law, U. of Ill., 1924-26, asso., 1926-28, prof. since 1928. Mem. bd. dirs. U. of Ill. Athletic Assn., 1942-49. Mem. Am. and Ill. bar assns., Am. Jud. Soc., Order of Coif, Acacia, Phi Alpha Delta, Urbana Assn. of Commerce. Republican. Mason. Clubs: Rotary, Urbana Golf and Country; University (Urbana). Author: Manual for Use of Law Books, 1931, 3d edit., 1940. Contbr. to jours. Home: Urbana, Ill. *

WEISMAN, MILTON CHARLES, lawyer, business exec.; b. N.Y.C., Apr. 11, 1895; s. Karl and Rebecca (Hornstein) W.; A.B., Syracuse U., 1915; LL.B., Fordham U., 1917; m. Alleyne Sweig, June 29, 1920 (dec.); children—Margaret Helen (Mrs. Edison Rice), Patricia Alleyne (Mrs. Leonard Taylor). Admitted to N.Y. bar, 1917; mem. firm Weisman, Allan & Spett, 1932-34, Weisman, Quinn, Allan & Spott, 1934-47. Weisman, Celler, Quinn, Allan & Spett, 1937-53, Weisman, Celler, Allan, Spett & Sheinberg, 1953-73, Weisman, Celler, Spett, Modlin & Wertheimer, 1973-77; sec., dir. Fedders Corp.; dir. Trans-Lux Corp., N.Y., Susquehanna and Western R.R., Warner Communications, Inc., Am. Book-Stratford Press, Inc., Fedders Financial Corp. Pres. Daus, Jacob Geriatric Inst.; trustee Bertha and Abraham J. Dworsky Found., Touro Coll., Fedn. Jewish Philanthropies of N.Y. Mem. Am. Bar Assn., N.Y. County Lawyers Assn., Syracuse Alumni Assn., Fordham Alumni Assn. Mason. Clubs: Cavendish Bridge; Palm Beach Country. Home: New York, N.Y. Died Oct. 8, 1977.

WEISS, HERMAN LEONARD, elec. equipment mfg. co. exec.; b. Cleve., July 22, 1916; s. Herman Leonard and Elsie (Roth) W.; B.S. in Civil Engring., Case Inst. Tech., 1939; m. Pauline McCabe, Sept. 5, 1940; 1 son, Gregory Alan. With Gen. Electric Co., 1939-65, v.p. group exec. consumer products, 1962-67, exec. v.p., 1968, vice chmn. bd., exec. officer, 1968-76, also dir.; dir. Gen. Electric Overseas Capital Corp. Mem. bus. com. com. Brookings Instn.; trustee Case Western Res. U., Com. Econ. Devel.; mem. Pres.'s Commn. Personnel Interchange, 1970-76, chmn., 1972-74. Mem. Tau Beta Pi, Phi Delta Theta. Address: Fairfield, Conn. Died Sept. 6, 1976.

WEISS, JEROME SIDNEY, lawyer; b. Chgo., Feb. 7, 1909; s. Morris Henry and Fannie (Salamson) W.; Ph.B., U. Chgo., 1928, J.D. cum laude, 1930; m. Gertrude Levy, June 20, 1947; children—Marlene Weiss Plotkin, Stanton Henry Berlin. Admitted to Ill. bar, 1930, practiced in Chgo.; asso. firm Sonnenschein, Carlin, Nath & Rosenthal, 1930-42, sr. mem. firm, 1942—. Asst. sec. Cory Corp.; sec., dir. Unarco Industries, Inc., from 1945; v.p., asst. sec., dir. Don Beachcomber, Inc., 1940-75; sec., dir. Hokin Gallery, Inc.; asst. sec. B. Brody Seating Co.; dir. Goldblatt Bros. Inc. Chmn. character, fitness com. First Ill. Appellate Court Dist., 1956-58, commr., 1951-59; mem. mayor's coms. sch. bd. nominations, 1957-59, youth welfare, 1957-58; past chmn. correctional services advisory bd. Ill. Youth Commn. Past pres. and dir. Juvenile Protective Assn.; dir., past v.p. Welfare Council Met. Chgo. Past dir. Mt. Sinai Hosp.; past pres., hon. dir. Temple Sholom; gov., sec. Sarah Siddons Soc., Inc. Fellow Am. Bar Found.; mem. Am. (del. ho. dels. convs. 1956, 58-59, 69-72), Chgo. (pres. 1958-59, chmn. com. of past presidents 1968—) bar assns., Nat. Conf. Bar Pres., U. Chgo. Law Sch. Alumni Assn. (pres. 1958-61, dir.), Chgo. Law Inst., Order of Coif. Clubs: Standard (pres.), Mid-Day, Metropolitan, Carlton, Nat. Lawyers, Executives, City, Law (v.p. from 1978, exec. com.) (Chgo.). Died Sept. 11, 1979.

WEISS, SAMUEL ARTHUR, judge; b. Krotowicz (Warsaw), Poland, Apr. 15, 1902; s. Israel and Sadie (Golden) W.; brought to U.S., 1902; student U. Pitts., 1920-21; B.S. and E. Duquesne U., 1925, LL.B., 1927, LL.D., 1965; m. Jeannette E. Hoffman, June 29, 1930; children—Sandra Jacqueline (dec.), Joy (Mrs. S. R. Cohen), James. Admitted Pa. bar, 1927, private practice of law; mem. Pa. legislature, 1934-39; mem. 77th of 78th Congresses (1941-47), 33d Pa. Dist.; judge Common Pleas Court of Allegheny County, Pa., 1946-68. Dep. commr. Nat. Profl. Football League, also referee, 1942-62. Pres. Rosalia Foundling, Montefiore hosps., Pitts.; v.p. Nat. Jewish Hosp., Denver; pres. NCCJ; mem. athletic council Duquesne U. Outstanding Alumnus award, Duquesne U., 1949; Boys Club Outstanding Citizens award, 1950; B'nai B'rith Humanitarian award, 1960; named Sportsman of Year, Allen County Civic Sportsman's Assn., 1964. Mem. Am., Pa., Allegheny County bar assns., Am. Acad. Polit. Sci., Sigma Alpha Mu (awarded outstanding achievement award 1951). Democrat. Jewish religion. Mason, Elk, Eagle, Moose, K.P., Lion I.O.O.F., B'nai B'rith. Home: Pittsburgh, Pa. Died Feb. 1, 1977.

WEISSBERGER, L. ARNOLD, lawyer; b. N.Y.C., Jan. 16, 1907; s. Harry Arnold and Anna (Lenson) W.; grad. Ethical Cultural Sch., 1923; A.B. magna cum laude, Harvard, 1927, LL.B. cum laude, 1930. Admitted to N.Y. State bar, 1930, practiced in N.Y.C.; with firms Guggenheimer & Untermeyer, 1930-34, Riegelman, Hess & Hirsch, 1935-39; established own firm, 1939; partner Weissberger & Frosch, 1955-70, Weissberger & Harris, 1972-81. Chmn. Friends Theatre and Music Collection, Mus. City N.Y., also trustee mus.; chmn. New Dramatists; v.p., bd. dirs. Bronx House, 1936-50; trustee, chmn. Martha Graham Dance Center Contemporary Dance; trustee Fountain House Found., Am. Inst. Music, John Golden Fund, Inc., Dance Notations Bur., Inc., Actor's Studio, Inc., 1969-72, Fedn. Jewish Philanthropic Socs., 1940-50, Harlem Eye and Ear Hosp., Jose Greco Found. Hispanic Dance, Inc.; adviser Bedside Network; pres. Theatre Hall of Fame, Inc. Served with AUS, 1942-43. Mem. Bar Assn. City N.Y., Phi Beta Kappa. Author: Famous Faces, 1973; also articles in profl. jours. Home: New York, N.Y. Died Feb. 27, 1981.

WEISSMAN, ARTHUR, med. care adminstr.; b. N.Y.C., Mar. 26, 1913; s. Edward and Ray (Greenfield) W.; B.A., Coll. City N.Y., 1934; postgrad. in psychology Columbia, 1935; J.D., George Washington U., 1941; m. Louise Kay, Sept. 14, 1945; children—Ronald, David. Med. care and pub. health adminstrn. and research USPHS, 1937-41, 46-50; admitted to D.C. bar, 1938, Korean bar, 1946; research project dir. Calif. Dept. Pub. Health, 1950-53; dir. med. econs. Kaiser Found. Health Plan, Oakland, Calif., 1953-78, cons., 1978-80; sr. v.p. Kaiser Found. Health Plan and Kaiser Found. Hosps., 1971-78, bd. dirs., 1972-80; mem. nat. adv. council Leonard Davis Inst. Health Econs., Wharton Sch. Finance, U. Pa., 1967-80; panel advisers Nat. Center Health Statistics, HEW, 1969-80; mem. State of Calif. Adv. Com. on Health and Med. Care Services, 1977-80; mem. tech. cons. panel on statis. systems for nat. health ins. U.S. Nat. Com. on Vital and Health Statistics, 1977-80. Trustee Kaiser Community Health Found., Cleve., 1969-78; bd. dirs. Kaiser Found. Health Plan Colo., Denver, 1969-80, of Oreg., 1972-80, of Ohio, 1978-80, Kaiser-Permanente Adv. Service, 1977-80. Served from pvt. Q.M.C. to capt. Med. Adminstrv. Corps, AUS, 1942-46. Recipient Disting. Service award Group Health Assn. Am., 1980. Fellow Am. Pub. Health Assn. Editorial cons. Jour. Med. Care, 1968-80; mem. editorial panel Milbank Meml. Fund quar. Health and Society, 1977-80. Contbr. articles on med. care adminstrn., statistics and research pub. in med. and pub. health jours. Home: San Francisco, Calif. Died Oct. 12, 1980; interred Home of Peace Cemetery, San Francisco.

WELCH, CHARLES BUCKLEY, editor; b. Meriden, Conn., Nov. 16, 1883; s. George Fernando and Arletta Amanda (Short) W.; prep. edn., high sch., Meriden; student Yale, 1902; m. Marie Louise Douglass, Oct. 2, 1905; children—Charles Douglass; Stuart Wadsworth. Reporter Meriden Record, 1903; editor New Haven Palladium, 1904; editor Meriden Times, 1905; news editor Boston American, 1905-09; city editor Boston Herald, 1910; editor Boston Market Reporter, 1910-11; mng. editor Boston Traveller, 1911-13, Tacoma Tribune, 1913-18; editor Tacoma News Tribune 1918-56; dir. Tribune Pub. Co.; dir. Tacoma Savings and Loan Assn. Mem. Associated Press N.E. Editors, Mayflower Soc., S.A.R., Sigma Delta Chi. Republican Episcopalian. Mason (32 deg. Shriner). Author: Descendants, James Welch: Soldier in King Philips War. Clubs: Tacoma; C. of C., Internat. Rotary. Home: Tacomo, Wash. *

WELCH, ERNEST RIVERS, educator; b. Tuskegee, Ala., Oct. 9, 1904; s. William M. and Mamie (Rivers) W.; B.S. in elec. engring. cum laude, Howard U., 1926; M.S., U. Mich., 1931; grad. study U. Chicago, summer 1928, Cath. U., summer 1951, 52; grad. Inf. Sch., 1941, Command and Gen. Staff Sch., 1943; m. Margaret Ann Petway, Dec. 14, 1940. Instr., Howard U., Washington, 1926-35, head dept. elec. engring., 1935-66, asso. dean Sch. Engring. and Architecture, 1966-73, instr., 1935-38, asst, prof., 1938-40, asso. prof., 1940-45, prof. 1945-73, prof., asso. dean emeritus, 1973-78. Served from maj. to col. U.S. Army, 1941-46, bn. comdr. 366th Inf. Regt., 1941-44, staff mem. Inf. Sch., 1944-45, 1322d Engrs., P.I., 1945; now col. ret. Registered profl. engr. Mem. I.E.E.E. (sr.), Am. Soc. Engring. Edn. A.A.A.S., Nat. Tech. Assn., Res. Officers Assn., V.F.W., Am. Legion, Kappa Mu, Kappa Alpha Psi, Scabbard and Blade, Tau Beta Pi. Baptist (bd. deacons). Mason, Home: Washington, D.C. Died May 18, 1978.

WELCH, LEO DEWEY, former oil exec.; b. Rochester, N.Y., Apr. 22, 1898; s. William Frederick and Mary Elizabeth (Compton) W.; A.B., U. Rochester, 1919; LL.D., George Washington U., 1966; m. Veronica Purviance, Jan. 27, 1926 (dec. Nov. 1970); 1 dau., Dorothy. With Nat. City Bank of N.Y., 1919-44, v.p., 1943-44; dir. Central Bank of Argentina, 1936-40; pres. Argentine Trade Promotion Corp., 1941-43; treas. Standard Oil Co. (N.J.), 1944-54, dir., 1953-63, v.p., 1956-63, exec. v.p., 1957-63, chmn. bd., vice chmn. exec. com., until 1963; chmn. bd. Communications Satellite Corp., 1963-65; dir., 1963-77; dir. Scudder Duo-Vest, Inc., Scudder Duo-Vest Exchange Fund, Inc., Compania Ontario. Pres., U.S. C. of C. in Argentine, 1936-37; trustee, past vice chmn. U.S. council Internat. C. of C.; past bd. trustees Com. Econ. Devel., U.S. Inter-Am. Council; mem. dir. com. Internat. Assn. Promotion and Protection Fgn. Investments; mem. council fgn. relations, chmn. 1952 com. on Latin Am., Bus. Adv. Council, depts. Commerce and State; chmn. Nat. Arbitration Panel, 1971-76. Emeritus trustee Rochester U. Decorated comdr. Order of Merit (Chile); comdr. Order of Merit (Argentina). Mem. Pan Am. Soc., U.S. Inc., Theta Delta Chi. Clubs: University Links (N.Y.C.); Chevy Chase (Md.); Links Golf (Roslyn, N.Y.); Jockey (Buenos Aires, Argentina); Creek, Piping Rock (Locust Valley, L.I.). Home: Syosset, N.Y. Died Oct. 21, 1978.

WELCH, PAUL SMITH, univ. prof.; b. Oconee, Ill., Jan. 28, 1882; s. John Newton and Emma Louisa (Smith) W.; A.B., James Millikin U., 1910; M.A., U. of Ill., 1911, Ph.D., 1913; m. Eva Grace Miller, June 20, 1921; 1 dau., Anne Louise. Instr. of entomology, Kansas State Coll., 1913-14, asst. prof., 1914-16, asso. prof., 1916-18; asst. prof. zoölogy, U. of Mich., 1918-22, asso. prof., 1922-28, prof. since 1928; acting dir., U. of Mich. Biol. Sta., 1924-25, asst. dir., 1929-30. Mem. A.A.A.S., Am. Soc. Zoölogists, Limnological Soc. Am. Ecol. Soc. Am., Am. Soc. Naturalists, Entomol. Soc. Am., Am. Micros. Soc. Club: University (Ann Arbor, Mich.). Author: Textbook of Zoölogy (with T. W. Galloway), 1922; Limnology, 1935; Culture Methods for Invertebrate Animals (with others), 1937; Limnological Methods, 1948; also about 60 research papers in biol. jours. Home: Ann Arbor, Mich. *

WELD, LOUIS DWIGHT HARVELL, b. Hyde Park, Mass., Apr. 18, 1882; s. Stuart E. and Anna (Harvell) W.; A.B., Bowdoin, 1905; A.M., U. of Ill., 1907; Ph.D., Columbia, 1908; m. Barbara Applegate, of N.Y. City, Dec. 23, 1909; children—Dwight, Theodore Dwight. Instr. in economics, U. of Wash., 1908-09, U. of Pa., 1909-10, spl. aft. U.S. Census Bur., 1910-12; asst. prof. and chief of Div. Agrl. Economics, U. of Minn., 1912-15; prof. business administration, Sheffield Scientific Sch. (Yale), 1915-17; mgr. commercial research dept., Swift & Co., packers, Chicago, since 1917. Mem. Am. Economic Assn., Phi Beta Kappa, Theta Delta Chi. Republican. Unitarian. Author: Private Freight Cars and American Railways (thesis), 1908; Marketing of Farm Products, 1916. *

WELDON, FREDRIC EDWARD, diversified industry exec.; b. N.Y.C.; s. Albert B. and Carolyn L. (Roth) W.; student U.S. Naval Acad., 1936-37; B.S. in Engring., Rensselaer Poly. Inst., 1940; m. Nancy B. Conger, June 22, 1946; children—Nancy, Fredric Edward, Barbara. Vice pres. Gen. Controls Co., Des Plaines, Ill., 1954-64; dir. marketing, air conditioning group Internat. Tel. & Tel., N.Y.C., 1964-66, pres. environmental products div., 1966-68, group gen. mgr., v.p. Internat. Tel. & Tel., 1968-76. Bd. dirs. Civil Def. Glenview, Ill. Served to lt. comdr. USNR, 1943-46. Recipient Action award Nat. Elec. Mfrs. Assn. Mem. Am. Gas Assn., Instrument Soc. Am. Home: Greenwich, Conn. Died Apr. 27, 1976.

WELFLING, WELDON, economist, educator; b. Coudersport, Pa., June 18, 1912; s. Rudolph O. and Mary Emily (Erway) W.; A.B., Swarthmore Coll., 1933; A.M., Princeton, 1935, Ph.D., 1938; m. Elizabeth Stammelbach, Nov. 28, 1936; children—Elizabeth Watkins King, Mary Bowman. Instr., U. Minn., 1936; from instr. to asso. prof. econs. Duke, 1936-47; sect. chief, other positions, Washington, 1941-45; chmn. dept. econs. Simmons Coll., 1947-60, chmn. div. social studies, 1950-60, dir. Sch. Social Sci., 1953-60; prof., chmn. depts. banking, finance and econs. Western Res. U., 1960-67; chmn. banking and finance dept. Case Western Res. U., 1967-78; vis. prof. finance U. Mich., 1958; indsl. cons. Am. Inst. Banking, 1947-78. Am. Philos. Soc. research fellow, 1966. Mem. Am. Econ. Assn., Am. Finance Assn. Author: Savings Banking in New York State, 1939; Money and Banking, 1947: Money and Banking (Am. Inst. Banking), rev. edit., 1975; Financing Business Enterprise (Am. Inst. Banking), 1960; Bank Investments (Am. Inst. Banking), 1962; Mutual Savings Banks, 1968; Principles of Economics, 1971; Economics (Am. Inst. Banking), rev. edit., 1973. Contbr. articles to econ. jours. Home: Shaker Heights, Ohio. Died Sept. 16, 1978.

WELLES, JAMES BELL, educator; b. Utica, N.Y., July 6, 1886; s. Frank Ephraim and Cornelia B. (Bell) W.; student N.Y. State Normal School, Genesco, 1901-05; A.B., Union Coll., Schenectady, N.Y., 1909, L.H.D., 1934; A.M., Teachers Coll., Columbia, 1913, Ed.D., 1936; student N.Y. Univ., 1929-30; m. Grace E. Frazer, Aug. 20, 1914 (died May 30, 1940); children—Mary Eunice (Mrs. James Straton Bruce), Major James Bell, Jr.; married 2d Electa L. Foster, June 22, 1942. Principal of Morris High School, Otsego County, New York, 1909; teacher of Latin, Elmira Free Acad., 1910-12; supt. schs., Scotia, N.Y., 1914-17; asst.

dir. dept. of reference and research for Bd. of Edn., Cleveland, 1917-19, actg. dir., 1919-20; supt. schs., Roslyn, N.Y., 1920-34; prin. N.Y. State Normal Sch., 1934-42; pres. State Teachers Coll., 1942-46. Retired. Mem. Am. Eduational Research Assn., N.E.A., Phi Delta Kappa, Kappa Delta Pi, Phi Beta Kappa, Delta Phi. Republican. Presbyterian. Mason. Club: University (Winter Park, Fla.). Home: Webster, N.Y. *

WELLS, BARBARA JANE, coll. dean; b. Cleve., Aug. 2, 1918; d. Guy McNeill and Berlynn (Kramer) Wells; B.A., Oberlin Coll., 1940; M.A., N.Y.U., 1957; Ph.D., 1963. Sec. coll. council Douglass Coll., Rutgers U., 1956-60; asst. prof. govt. Skidmore Coll., 1960-64; asso. prof. govt. Mills Coll., 1964-68; dean Thomas More Coll., Fordham U., 1968-72; dean of the faculty, Vassar Coll., 1972-78; mem. N.Y. State-Middle Eastern seminar Columbia, summer 1963; instr. Peace Corps, Dartmouth, summer 1963, 64, 65. Bd. dirs. UN Assn. Alameda County, Calif., 1966-67; trustee St. Francis Hosp., Poughkeepsie, 1974-78. Recipient Founders Day award N.Y.U., 1964. Mem. A.C.L.U., Am. Polit. Sci. Assn., A.A.U.P., Internat. Studies Assn. Address: Poughkeepsie, N.Y. Died Oct. 25, 1978.

WELLS, CHARLES ARTHUR, editor, pub.; b. Greenfield, Ind.; s. Lindley Aaron and Lucinda (Jones) W.; A.B., Friends U., Wichita, Kan., 1920; grad. student U. Calif., 1926; m. Elizabeth M. Boykin; 1 son, Charles Arthur. Cartoonist, reporter Wichita (Kansas) Beacon, 1920; later cartoonist Central Press Assn., Cleve., N.Y., contbd. cartoons and editorials on religion and world affairs to religious periodicals and newspapers; publicity counselor, lectr. on world affairs for Nat. Bapt. bds.; has conducted the Conferences on Christ and World Need since 1938 (one week lecture confs. for churches, colls., etc.) since 1938; editor, pub. Between The Lines; frequent traveler in Europe and Asia. Mem. Fgn. Policy Assn., Council on Fgn. Relations, Acad. Political Sci., Am. Acad. Polit. and Social Sci., (Quaker coll. frat.), Alpha Phi Gamma. Mem. Soc. of Friends. Author: Pink-A Caricature of an American Revolutionary in Russia, 1935; Cancelled Crosses, 1937; Building a Better World (book of cartoons), 1939; The Great Alternative (illus. by author), 1950; Think of These Things, 1956; Journey into Light, 1958. Television analyst for various nat. stas. and affiliates. Address: Princeton, N.J. Died May 8, 1976.

WELLS, GEORGE ROSS (MAURICE), prof. psychology; b. Moose Jaw, Saskatchewan, Can., June 16, 1884; s. James Edward and Frances Barbara (Moule) W.; A.B., McMaster Univ., Toronto, 1906; A.M., Harvard, Univ., 1909; P.D., John Hopkins, 1912; m. Mildred Sayles Meader, Sept. 1, 1909; children—Barbara Alice, Charles Clifford, Lois Meader. Instr. psychology, Oberlin Coll., 1912-13, asso. prof., 1913-17; prof. psychology, Ohio Wesleyan U., 1917-20, Hartford Sem. Foundation since 1920, dean, Sch. of Religious Edn. since 1946; visiting prof. and chmn. Academic Dept. Julius Hart Musical Foundation, Naturalized 1917. Commd. 1st lt. San. Corps U.S. Army, Jan. 1918; capt., Apr. 1918; with Med. Research Laboratory Air Service; in charge Medical Research Laboratory, Selfridge Field, Mount Clemens, Michigan, later at School of Aeronautics, University of Illinois, and at Barron Field, Fort Worth, Tex.; honorably discharged, Dec. 1918. Mem. Sigma Xi. Congregationalist. Mason. Author: Influence of Stimulus Duration on Reaction Time, 1913; Youth and the Open Door, 1922; Individuality and Social Restraint, 1929; The Art of Being a Person, 1939.Columnist, Hartford Times. Home: Pleasant Valley, Conn.*

WELLS, HARRY H., lawyer; b. Washington County, Fla., June 14, 1884; s. Angus R. and Mary (Harrell) W.; student Fla. State Coll., 1903-05; LL.B., Grant U. (now U. of Chattanooga), 1907; m. Susye Belle Rollins, Sept. 20, 1917; 1 dau., Mary Sue (Mrs. Cameron McDavid). Admitted to the bar, State of Fla., 1907, and since in practice at Tallahassee, Fla. Served as capt., Co. H. 1st Fla. Inf., Nat. Guard, Mayor of Chipley, Fla., 1910; mem. Fla. State Senate, 1917, 1921, 1923, chmn. Fla. State Dem. Exec. Com., 1928-31; chmn. Fla. State Road Dept., 1932, Fla. Nat. Recovery Bd., 1933; Dem. Nat. Committeeman from Fla., 1936. Mem. Fla. Bar Assn., Kappa Alpha Theta Lambda Phi. Democrat. Baptist. Mason. (Shriner), Elk. I.P. Odd Fellow; Clubs Tallahassee Country. Also interested in farming, saw milling, naval stores and live stock. Home: Tallahassee. *

WELLS, HERBERT WILSON, banker, park and plan commr.; b. Spencer, Va., June 20, 1902; s. Gordon Taylor and Lillian Nevada (Grogan) W.; m. Evelyn O. Sims, Oct. 16, 1929; 1 son, Gordon Taylor II. Propr. G.T. Wells & Sons, fuel oil distbrs., College Park, Md.; v.p., dir. Citizens Bank of Md. Councilman, College Park; commr. Md.-Nat. Capital Park and Planning Commn., 1943-63, chmn., 1957-63; mem. Nat. Capitol Regional Planning Council, from 1951, chmn., from 1956; v.p. Citizens Bank Md., from 1952. Mem. Md. Ednl. Found. Mem. Md. Hist. Soc. (v.p. Prince George County chpt.), Prince George County C. of C. (past pres.). Democrat. Protestant. Mason. Club: Terrapin (College Park). Home: College Park, Md. Died Oct. 28, 1979.

WELLS, JOHN ASHLEY, lawyer; b. N.Y.C., Jan. 14, 1908; s. Lucien Roys and Maude (Suckert) W.; B.A. with high honors and high distinction, Wesleyan U., Middletown, Conn., 1932; B.A. Juris (Rhodes scholar), Oxford (Eng.) U., 1934, B.C.L., 1935, M.A., 1953; LL.M., Harvard U., 1936; m. Alicia Kenyon, June 22, 1935 (dec.); children—Michael Coolidge, Meredith Kenyon Wells Brownstein, Sharon Ashley Wells Quick, Jonathan Arnold; m. 2d, Pauline S. Montali, July 5, 1957; children—Antonie Lucienne, Gregory John. Admitted to N.Y. bar, 1937, D.C. bar, 1953, also U.S. Supreme Ct.; with firm Hughes, Schurman & Dwight, N.Y.C., 1936-37, Dwight, Harris, Koegel & Caskey, N.Y.C., 1937-41; A chief counsel OPA, 1942; chief asst. counsel N.Y. State Moreland Commn., 1943; asst. counsel Navy Price Adjustment Bd., 1944-45; partner, then sr. partner firm Rogers & Wells, and predecessors, N.Y.C. and Washington, 1947-80. Chmn. adv. com. on enforcement policies and practices SEC, 1972; mgr. Republican polit. campaigns, 1948-69. Served to lt. comdr. USNR, 1944-45. Decorated Commendation ribbon; named Distinguished Alumnus Wesleyan U., 1973. Mem. Phi Beta Kappa, Delta Kappa Epsilon. Republican. Episcopalian. Author: The Voter's Presidential Handbook, 1960. Editor: Thomas E. Dewey on the Two-Party System, 1966. Home: Rye, N.Y. Died Apr. 14, 1980.

WELLS, LINTON, ret. writer, traveler, aviator, broadcaster; b. Louisville, Apr. 1, 1893; s. Rufus Coleman and Minnie Belle (Tindel) W.; ed. Louisville and Denver pub. schs., also U.S. Naval Acad.; children—Barbara Jeanne, Patricia; m. 2d, Fay Gillis (traveler, aviatrix, writer, broadcaster), Apr. 1, 1935; 1 son, Linton II. Fgn. war corr. and staff writer for newspapers, syndicates and mags., 1911-76. Established circumnavigation of globe record, 28 days, 14 hours and 36 minutes, in 1926. Headed Govt. Mission Portuguese West Africa, 1942-46. Served with U.S. Navy, World War I; foreign deoorations. Mem. Radio and TV Analysts (founder). Clubs: Nat. Press, Internat., Georgetown (Washington); Overseas Press (N.Y.C.). Author: Around the World in 28 Days, 1926; Jumping Meridians, 1926; Blood on the Moon, 1937; Salute to Valor, 1942; (play) Second Guesses. Home: Washington, D.C. Died Jan. 30, 1976.

WELSH, MARTIN I., judge; b. San Jose, Calif., Oct. 1, 1882; student St. Vincent's Coll., Cape Girardeau, Missouri; married; children—Elynor, Mildred, Marie. Admitted to Calif. bar, 1912, to dist. U.S. Courts, Northern Calif., 1913, to Supreme Court, 1933; dep. dist. atty. Sacramento County, 1914; elected judge Superior Court of Sacramento County, 1914; U.S. commr. Northern Div., Northern Dist. Calif., 1914-19; city councilman, Sacramento, 1928-29, mayor, 1929; mem. Bd. Edn., 1931; appointed judge Superior Court, Sacramento County, 1932, elected to six year term, 1932, re-elected without opposition, 1938; apptd. by President, United States Dist. judge for Northern Calif., 1939; retired from the Federal Bench, Jan. 1, 1947. Sachem Sacremento Iroquois Club; grand sachem Calif. State Iroquois Clubs. Candidate for lt. gov., Dem. ticket, 1930; mem. Dem. State Central Com.; pres. Roosevelt for President Orgn. in Calif., 1936; County chmn. Roosevelt Birthday Ball Com. since 1928; pres. Sacramento Community Chest, 1938, 39, Sacramento Americanization Assembly, 1938, 39. Chmn. Calif. Nat. Bank Depositors Assn. during liquidation from 1933. Eagle, Native Sons of Golden West, Elks. Home: Sacramento, Calif. *

WELTON, THURSTON SCOTT, physician; b. Brooklyn, N.Y., July 14, 1885; s. Dr. Robert Bradlee and Henrietta Louise (Phillips) W.; M.D., Long Island Coll. of Medicine, 1908; m. Edith Roberts Schultz, June 12, 1912 (dec.); children—Robert Bradlee (dec.), Edith Jane (wife of Dr. E. Ellsworth Keet); m. 2d, Margaret Roberts, May 22, 1928. Began practice of medicine, 1908; attending gynecologist, Williamsburgh Hosp., 1917-23; attending obstetrician and gynecologist, L.I. Coll. Hosp., 1926-50, now cons.; clin. prof. obstetrics and gynecology L.I. Coll. Medicine, 1927-39, prof. clin. obstetrics and gynecology, 1939-50; emeritus prof. State U. N.Y. Coll. Medicine since 1950; dir. obstetrics and gynecology, Greenpoint Hosp., 1935, cons., 1946; cons. Southside Hosp., Mary Immaculate Hosp. Diplomate Am. Bd. Obstetrics and Gynecology. Fellow Am. Coll. Surgeons; emeritus fellow American Association of Obstetricians and Gynecologists; member of the Brooklyn Medical Society (pres. 1917), Brooklyn Gynecol. Soc. (pres. 1926), Med. Soc. of County of Kings (pres. 1927; trustee 1928-33; gold medalist, 1942). Theta Kappa Psi. Club: N. Hempstead Country (L.I.). Editor in chief Am. Jour. of Surgery since 1928. Editor: Practical Lecture Series (medical), 1923, 1935. Author: Modern Method of Birth Control, 1935. Contbr. sci. articles, biographies and editorials to med. pubs. Home: N.Y.C. *

WENDLAND, JOHN PRENTICE, physician, educator; b. Omaha, Nov. 16, 1917; s. Henry William and Janie Margaret (Pulver) W.; B.S., U. Nebr., 1939; M.D., 1941; M.S. in Ophthalmology, 1948; m. Louise Winholtz, June 17, 1942; children—Stanley Prentice, Nancy Denise. Intern, U. Nebr. Hosp., Omaha, 1941-42; resident U. Minn. Hosp., Mpls., 1942-46; practice medicine specializing in ophthalmology, Mpls., 1949-77; faculty U. Minn. Med. Sch., Mpls., 1949-77, prof. ophthalmology, 1957-77, cons. Health Service, 1957-77. Cons. VA., 1949-77. Served to maj. USAAF, 1943-46. Fellow A.C.S.; mem. Minn. Acad. Ophthalmology and Otolaryngology (pres. 1957-58), Am. Ophthal. Soc., Hennepin County Med. Soc., Pan Am. Assn. Ophtahlmology, Internat. Soc. Eye Surgeons, Contact Lense Assn. Ophthalmologists, Am. Acad. Ophthalmology and Otolaryngology. Club: Minneapolis Cine (pres. 1958-59). Home: Minneapolis, Minn. Died July 17, 1977.

WENDT, GEORGE RICHARD, psychologist, former educator; b. Rochester, N.Y., Jan. 27, 1906; s. George and Gertrude (Baker) W.; A.B., U. Rochester, 1927; A.M., Columbia, 1928, Ph.D., 1931; m. Ruth Frances Beecher, Aug. 8, 1928; children—Eleanor Beecher, Barbara Beecher, Peter Beecher. Fellow NRC, Yale Inst. Human Relations, 1930-32; instr. physiology Yale Sch. Medicine, 1932-35; instr. physiology and psychology Yale, 1935-36; asst. prof. psychology U. Va., 1936-37, U. Pa., 1937-39; asso. prof. psychology, chmn. dept. Wesleyan U., Middletown, Conn., 1939-45; prof. psychology U. Rochester, 1945-71, chmn. dept., 1945-60. Part time or summer tchr. Columbia, 1935-36, New Haven Women's Coll., 1935-36, Rutgers U., 1938-39, U. Cal. at Los Angeles, 1947; dir. various mil. research projects on selection of aircraft pilots, prevention of motion sickness et al, 1939-77; cons. USPHS, 1946-77. Mem. exec. subcom. NRC com. on selection and tng. of aircraft pilots, mem. and sec. subcom. on motion sickness com. on aviation medicine, World War II; mem. research study sect. Nat. Mental Health Council, 1946-52; mem. N.Y. adv. council in psychology, 1957-77; mem. VA area adv. council in psychology, 1957-77. Mem. Am. Assn. U. Profs., A.A.A.S., Am. Psychol. Assn., Nat. Inst. Psychology (sec.-treas.), Soc. Exptl. Psychologists, Eastern, N.Y. State psychol. assns., Sigma Xi, Delta Kappa Epsilon. Asso. editor Jour. Exptl. Psychology, 1946-50, Jour. Comparative and Physiol. Psychology, 1946-50. Contbr. article on hearing, conditioned reflexes, motion sickness and physiol. recording methods, effects of drugs on emotional and social behavior to psychol., physiol. jours. Home: Honeyoye, N.Y. Died Jan. 27, 1977.

WENGENROTH, STOW, artist; b. Bklyn., July 25, 1906; s. Frederic William and Isabelle (Stow) W.; student Art Students League, 1923-25, Grand Central Sch. Art, 1925-27; m. Edith Flack Ackley, Oct. 7, 1936; m. 2d, Harriet Knowlton Matson, July 1974. Rep. in Balt. Mus. Art, Whitney Mus. Am. Art, Congl. Library, Los Angeles Mus., Seattle Art Mus., Fogg Mus., Fine Arts Mus., Boston, Met. Museu. Awards: Eyre gold medal Phila. Water Color Club, 1933, Pennell Meml. medal, 1943; Silver medal Print Makers Cal., 1936; Mary Collins prize Print Club Phila., 1937, 39; Samuel Shaw prize Salmagundi Club, 1937; 2d print prize Artists for Victory Exhbn., 1942; Medal of Honor, Audubon Artists, 1945, John Tayler Arms Meml. medal, 1955; print prize Met. Mus., 1953; Samuel Finley Breese Morse medal N.A.D., 1968; medal of honor Rockport Art Assn., 1966. Mem. Pennell Fund com. Library of Congress, Washington, 1939-55; hon. mem. Smithsonian Fine Arts Commn. N.A. Mem. Soc. Am. Graphic Artists, Conn. Acad. Fine Arts, Albany Print Club, Nat. Inst. Arts and Letters. Clubs: Phila. Water Color; Water Color (Providence); Salmagundi (N.Y.C.). Author: Making a Lithograph; Stow Wengenroth's New England; the Lithographs of Stow Wengenroth. Address: Rockport, Mass. Died Jan. 22, 1978; buried Greenport, L.I., N.Y.

WENGER, ARTHUR DANIEL, coll. pres.; b. Aberdeen, Ida., Oct. 15, 1916; s. Frank Lewis and Anna (Toevs) W.; A.B., Bethel Coll., Kan., 1941; student San Francisco Theol. Sem., 1941-42; B.D., Tex. Christian U., 1948, LL.D., 1956; Litt.D., William Woods Coll., 1975; m. Doris Kellenbarger, May 29, 1944; children—Arthur Frank, Jon Michael, Mark Randolph. Ordained to ministry Mennonite Ch., 1942, Disciples of Christ Ch., 1946; minister First Mennonite Ch., Shafter, Cal., 1942-44, Central Christian Ch., Hamilton, Tex., 1946-47, First Christian Ch., Arlington, Tex., 1948-49; asso. minister First Christian Ch., New Castle, Pa., 1949-50; asst. to pres. Atlantic Christian Coll., Wilson, N.C., 1950-52, pres., 1956-77; dir. promotion Tex. Christian U., 1952-56. Pres. council Ch. Related Colls. N.C., 1959; chmn. Bd. of Higher Edn. Christian Chs., 1959, mem. Gen. Bd., 1969-71; N.C. del. to Edn. Commn. of the States, 1966; bd. dirs. N.C. State Ednl. Assistance Authority, 1966-71; pres. N.C. Assn. Colls. and Univs., 1965-66; pres. Wilson Arts Council, 1968-69; past mem. Wilson County Econ. Devel. Council; past bd. dirs. Wilson County United Fund; past mem. adv. bd. Salvation Army; past bd. dirs. Lexington Theol. Sem. Bd.; mem. Commn. on Brotherhood Restructure, Christian Chs. (Disciples of Christ); elder First Christian Ch., Wilson. Served as capt., Chaplains Corps, AUS, World War II. Recipient Disting. Alumnus award Tex. Christian U., 1960. Mem. Assn. Eastern N.C. Colls. (pres. 1969-70), N.C. Assn. Independent Colls. and Universities (pres. 1972-74), Wilson C. of C (past dir.), Delta Sigma Phi, Alpha Psi Omega. Club: Wilson Rotary (pres. 1962). Home: Wilson, N.C. Died Feb. 25, 1977; buried Maplewood Cemetery, Wilson.

WENTWORTH, EDWARD TUBBS, orthopedic surgeon; b. Dagus Mines, Pa., Dec. 24, 1884; s. Russell Allen and Elizabeth Atherton (Tubbs) W.; A.B., Harvard, 1909, M.D., 1913; m. Bertha Emily Pilsbury, Sept. 18, 1911; children—Ruth Pilsbury, Paul Roberts, Edward Tubbs. Practiced as orthopedic surgeon, Rochester, N.Y., SINCE 1920; chief of orthopedic service Rochester General Hospital, 1937-44; consultant in orthopedic surgery at University of Rochester School of Medicine and Dentistry and Rochester Gen. Hosp. Active in the formation of Rochester Hosp. insurance plan and med. service insurance for City of Rochester. Commd. 1st lt. Med. Reserve Corps, July 1916; served in active duty, U.S. Army, as orthopedist, at Camp Pike, Ark., and with A.E.F., Base Hosp. No. 19, 1917-19; disch. as maj.; commd. lt. col., Med. Corps, U.S. Army Reserve, 1924, col., 1939, ret.; active duty U.S. Army, comdg. officer Gen. Hosp. No. 19, July 1942-Oct. 1945 at four sites in Eng. and France. Diplomate of American Board of Orthopedic Surgery. Fellow American College Surgeons, American Academy Orthopedic Surgeons, A.M.A.; mem. Rochester Acad. of Medicine (past pres.); Monroe County Medical Soc. (past pres.), Rochester Pathol. Soc. (past pres.), N.Y. State Med. Soc. (pres. 1951-52). Delta Upsilon, Phi Rho Sigma, Alpha Omega Alpha. Catholic. Clubs: University (Rochester); Aesculapian (Boston); Monroe Golf (Pittsford, N.Y.); Harvard (N.Y. City). Contbr. to med. jours. Home: Pittsford, N.Y. *

WENTWORTH, REGINALD A., engr.; b. Boston, Mass., Nov. 23, 1882; s. William Hall and Annie L. (Locke) W.; B.S., Mass. Inst. Tech., 1904; m. Marianne Palmer, June 14, 1905; children—John, New York; 1910-15; supt. Saco-Lowell Shops, Lowell, Mass., 1915-18; in charge production, plant engring., construction and installation U.S. Cartridge Co., Lowell, Mass., 1918-19; works mgr. Union Carbide and Carbon Corp., New York, 1919-22; mfg. mgr. and v.p., The Barrett Co., New York, 1922-31; financial and exec. v.p. Sharp and Dohme, Phila., 1931-38; labor coordinator Calco Chemical Co., Bound Brook, N.J., 1938-40; partner Wallace Clark & Co., consultants in management, N.Y. City, 1940-43; in pvt. practice as management counsel since 1943. Trustee Lowell Textile Sch., 1916-19. Phila. Community Fund, 1933-38; dir. Wentworth Inst., Boston, since 1918. Mem. Am. Soc. Mech. Engrs. (chmn. management div.), Phila. Chamber of Commerce (industrial com. 1934-38), Am. Soc. Mech. Engrs. Clubs: Technology of Philadelphia (pres. 1937-38); The City Midday (New York). Home: Plainfield, N.J. *

WENTZ, ABDEL ROSS, clergyman, educator; b. Black Rock, York County, Pa., Oct. 8, 1883; s. John Valentine and Ellen Catharine (Tracy) W.; A.B., Gettysburg College, Pa., 1904; B.D., Luth. Theol. Sem., Gettysburg, 1907; univs. of Leipzig, Berlin, Tübingen, 1907-10; Ph.D., Geo. Washington, 1914; D.D., Gettysburg, 1921. Augustana College, 1939, LL.D., Gettysburg, 1940; Th.D., Sopron, Hungary, 1947; Litt.D., Wittenberg College, 1953; married Mary Edna Kuhlman, Aug. 15, 1917; children—Valentine (died 1936), Frederick Kuhlman, Mary Louise Beckstrand. Ordained to ministry of Lutheran Church, 1907; prof. hist. Gettsbury Coll., 1909-16; prof. ch. his., Lutheran Theol. Seminary, 1916-56, 1956-58; pres. Gettysburg Sem., 1940-51. Mem. exec. bd. of United Luth. Ch. in America, also member bd of foreign mission and pres.; sec. Am. Assn. Theol. Schools, 1934-36, treas., 1936-46; mem. American Bible Revision Committee; mem. exec. com. Lutheran World Fedn., 1935-52, v.p., 1946-52; mem. exec. com. World's Conf. on Faith and Order; member Com. of Fourteen to form World Council of Churches, Mem. Am. Soc. Church History (pres. 1931-32; sec. 1934-37). Lutheran Hist. Soc. (curator), Pa. German Soc., Phi Beta Kappa. Republican. Author or co-author books relating to field since 1916. Home: Gettysburg, Pa.*

WENTZEL, GREGOR, physicist; b. Dusseldorf, Germany, Feb. 17, 1898; s. Josef and Anna (Joesten) W.; Ph.D., U. Munchen, 1921; D.Sc. (hon.), Swiss Fed. Inst. Tech., 1966; m. to Anna Wielich, Dec. 5, 1929; 1 son, Donat G. Prof. physics U. Leipzig, 1926-28, U. Zurich, 1928-48, U. Chgo., 1948-69. Fellow Am. Phys. Soc.; mem. Schweizerische Naturforschende Gesellschaft, Schweizerische Physikalische Gesellschaft, Nat. Acad. Scis. Author: Quantentheorie der Wellenfelder, 1943, English translation (Quantum Theory of Fields), 1949. Home: Ascona, Ticino, Switzerland. Died Aug. 12, 1978; interred Ascona, Ticino, Switzerland.

WERNER, ALFRED, art critic; b. Vienna, Austria, Mar. 30, 1911; s. Ignatz and Frederika (Silberstein) W.; J.D., U. Vienna, 1934; student Inst. Fine Arts, N.Y. U., 1949-52; m. Lisa Tramm, Mar. 1975. Came to U.S., 1940, naturalized, 1945. Editor, Die Stimme mag., also Gerechtigkeit mag., Vienna, 1935-38; lectr. univ. extension, Vienna, 1935-38; editor Universal Jewish Ency., N.Y.C., 1941-45; cons. Office Jewish Affairs, Am. Jewish Congress, 1946-50; art cons. Theodor Herzl Inst., N.Y.C., 1956-79; contbg. editor Arts mag., 1956-79; U.S. corr. Pantheon Internat. Mag. Art, Munich, Germany, 1960-79; prof. honoris causa Austrian Ministry Edn., 1967; vis. prof. Rutgers U., 1974-79; art editor Ency. Judaica. Author: Modigliani the Sculptor, 1962; Jules Pascin, 1962; Ernst Barlach, 1966; Modigliani, 1967; Chagall, 1968: Degas Pastels, 1968; Inness Landscapes, 1973; Max Weber, 1975; Chaim Soutine, 1977; Edvard Munch, 1978. Home: NY. Died July 16, 1979.

WERNER, AUGUST ANTHONY, internist, endocrinologist; b. Newton, Kans., Jan. 30, 1883; s. Casper A. and Louisa (Loesser) W.; M.D., St. Louis U., 1911; m. Frances Carthaus, Aug. 16, 1928; 1 son, William Albert. Engaged in practice of medicine since 1911; asst. prof., internal med., St. Louis U. Med. Sch., since 1936; associate physician, St. Mary's Group Hospitals; staff member St. Louis City Sanitorium and Infirmary, Missouri State Hospital No. 4 (Farmington, Mo.), Missouri Baptist Hospital. Served as 1st lt., Med. Corps, U.S. Army, during World War I.. Mem. A.M.A., A.A.A.S., Am. Coll. Physicians, Southern Med. Assn., Soc for Study of Internal Secretions, Soc. for Exptl. Biology and Medicine, Mo. State Med. Assn., St. Louis Med. Soc., Phi Beta Pi, Sigma Xi, and Alpha Omega Alpha. Author: Endocrinology (textbook); Clinical research with sex hormones, menopause and climacteric phychoses. Frequent contbr. to tech. and sci. jours. Home: St. Louis. *

WERNER, WILLIAM G(EORGE), bus. exec.; b. Cin., July 15th, 1893; s. Gustav R. and Anna O. (Dupuis) W.; student U. Cin., 1911-14; m. Margaret Benninghofen, May 17, 1918; children—Margaret Anne Werner Fisher, William Thomas. With Procter and Gamble, 1911-17, 19-74, advt. dept., 1922-29, mgr. advt. dept., 1929-40, dir. pub. relations, 1941-53, dir. pub. and legal services, 1954-59, charge spl. services, 1959-74. Trustee, v.p. Procter & Gamble Fund, 1952-74; v.p. Hamilton Autographic Register Co., Ohio; bd. dirs. Greater Cin. TV Edn. Found., Mental Health Council Cin., Greater Cin. Hosp. Funds, Cin. Symphony Orch., Cin. Assn. Blind; bd. dirs., past chmn. Nat. Better Bus. Bur.; v.p. Bethesda Hosp. Assn.; mem. bd. Presbyn. Life mag. Served as 2d lt., Inf., AUS, 1917-18. Past pres. U.S. Trade Mark Assn., Pub. Relations Soc. Am. Clubs: Cincinnati, Queen City, Maketewah Country, Literary. Home: Cincinnati, Ohio. Died Mar. 17, 1974.

WERNETTE, NICODEMUS D. (WER-NET), lawyer; b. Remus, Mich., May 5, 1885; s. Jacob and Catherine (Bolz) W.; LL.B., U. of Mich., 1907; m. Ozalinda Blanchard, April 4, 1910; children—Frances C. Bernice E., Blanche M., Margaret M., Florence E., Thomas E., Mary C., Norma Dolores. Admitted to Ida. bar, 1907, in practice at Coeur d'Alene, 1907-33; pros. atty., Kootenai County, 1911-17; justice Supreme Court of Ida., 1933-35; practicing law, Spokane, Wash., since Feb. 1, 1935. Mem. Am., Ida. State and Wash. State bar assns. Democrat. Catholic. K.C., Elk. Home: 304 W. 18th St. Address: Spokane, Wash. *

WERWATH, KARL OSCAR, engring. sch. pres.; b. Milw., Mar. 1, 1909; s. Oscar and Johanna (Seelhorst) W.; B.S. in Elec. Engring., Milw. Sch. Engring., 1936; extension student Northwestern U., 1936-38; U. Wis., 1938; M.B.A. (hon.), Spencerian Coll., 1938; Sc.D. (hon.), Colby Coll., 1973; m. Charlotte Dorothea Becker, Sept. 1938 (dec.); 1 dau., Karlene Dorothea (Mrs. Robert Kaufmann); m. 2d, Marion A. Schmidt, Apr. 1977. Asst. registrar Milw. Sch. Engring., 1936-38, instr. pub. utilities, 1937-45, instr. commerce, 1939-45, registrar, 1938-47, v.p., 1947-48, pres., from 1948; dir. CAA civilian pilot tng. program, 1939-40, coordinator, 1940-41, job instr. tng. War Manpower Program, 1942-44; sec. Durner Co., 1945-64; dir. Equitable Savs. & Loan Assn. Vice pres. U.S. Jr. C. of C., 1940-43; mem. Pres.'s Com. Scientists and Engrs., chmn. working com. on supporting tech. personnel, 1956-58; cons. bd. visitors U.S. Army Ordnance Command; cons. sci. and tech. manpower panel Pres.'s Sci. Adv. Com., 1962—. Bd. dirs. Lutheran Manor, 1963, Kurtis R. Froedtert Meml. Luth. Hosp., 1965, Augustana Coll., 1962-64. Recipient James H. McGraw award in tech. inst. edn., 1958; Arthur L. Williston award Am. Soc. Engring. Edn., 1967; named Wis. Engr. of Year, 1968; Rotary citation, 1974. Registered profl. engr., Wis. Mem. Nat. Soc. Profl. Engrs. (nat. dir. 1964-79), Engrs. Council for Profl. Devel., Nat. Council Tech. Schs. (pres. 1950-51, sec.-treas. 1970-74), Am. Soc. for Engring. Edn. (chmn. tech. inst. council 1962-64, v.p. 1962-64), Am. Interprofl. Inst. (pres. 1955), Am. Assn. Sch. Adminstrs., Am. Soc. Heating, Refrigeration and Air Conditioning Engrs., Engrs. Soc. Milw. (Engr. of Year award 1971), Am. Welding Soc., Elec. League Milw., Illuminating Engring. Soc., Am. Assn. Jr. Colls., Midwest Coll. Placement Assn., Soc. for Coll. and Univ. Planning, N.E.A., A.A.A.S., Indsl. Relations Assn., Wis., Instrumentation Soc. Am., Assn. U.S. Army, Met. Milw. Assn. Commerce (chmn. industries com. 1962-68), Navy League U.S., Mil. Schoolmasters Club, Luth. Men. Am. (pres. 1975-76), Epsilon Rho Epsilon, Delta Phi Zeta, Kappa Gamma Phi, Sigma Pi Rho, Delta Alpha Epsilon, Kappa Eta Kappa. Lutheran (mem. found. bd.). Home: Milwaukee, Wis. Died Aug. 30, 1979; buried Forest Home Cemetery, Milwaukee, Wis.

WESLEY, EDGAR BRUCE, educator; b. Bethelridge, Ky., Dec. 5, 1891; s. Silas and Meania (Jones) W.; A.B., Baldwin-Wallace Coll., Berea, O., 1914, LL.D., 1945; student Yale, 1916-17, U. Wis., summer 1922; A.M., Washington U., 1925, Ph.D., 1929; Litt.D., Union Coll., Barbourville, Ky., 1943; m. Nannie Fay Medford, May 16, 1915; children—Silas Medford, Phyllis Margaret, Louis Wood, James Paul, Elaine; m. 2d, Helen Chase, July 1975. Successively tchr. rural sch. in Ky., high sch. prin. in Ohio, tchr. English and history in St. Louis, 1910-22; head social studies dept., University City (Mo.) High Sch., 1923-30; instr. history Washington U. extension dept. and summer sch., 1924-30; asst. prof. edn. U. Minn., 1931-34, asso. prof., 1934-37, became prof., 1937; vis. prof. Harvard, summer 1935, U. N.H., summer 1938, U. Cal., 1949, Stanford, 1952-55, U. Mich., 1957-58, U. Cal. at Los Angeles 1959; dir. Com. Am. Hist. in Schs. and Colls., summer 1943; vis. prof. social scis. Ball State Coll., fall 1959, 60, 61; Distinguished vis. prof. So. Ill. U., 1961, 63; vis. prof. University Texas, 1963, Ball State Teachers Coll., 1963-64, 64-70, John R. Emens Disting. prof. history, 1970. Fresno State College, summers 1964, and 1965. Member of Minnesota State Resources Commn., 1937-42; director Program of Information on World Affairs for Minnesota Star, 1946-49. Mem. Nat. Council Social Studies (pres. 1935, editorial com.), Am., Mississippi Valley hist. assns., Nat. Soc. Study Edn., N.E.A., Nat. Soc. Coll. Tchrs. Edn. Author or co-author of numerous books, from 1925, latest publs. including, American History in Schools and Colleges, 1944; Teaching Social Studies in Elementary Schools, 1946; Our United States: Its History in Maps, 1956; NEA: The First Hundred Years, 1957; Teaching the Social Studies, 5th edition, 1964; also work books in social studies. Editor: Wesley Social Study Maps, 1948; Our America Series. Contbr. to yearbook Nat. Council Social Studies. Address: Carmel, Calif. Died Nov. 26, 1980; interred Bethelridge (Ky.) Cemetery.

WEST, CARL JOSEPH, statistician; b. Martinsville, O., Feb. 25, 1885; s. James Frank and Elva (Leaf) W.; B.A., Ohio State U., 1908, M.A., 1909; Ph.D., Cornell, 1915; m. Edith Mitchell, of Columbus, O., Aug. 19, 1910; children—Elinor Josephine, Carl Joseph. Asst. prof. mathematics, Ohio State U., 1910-18, statistician, U.S. Dept. Agr., 1919—. Mem. Am. Statis. Assn. Coglist. Mason (K.T. Shriner). Mem. Phi Beta Kappa, Sigma Xi. Author: Introduction to Mathematical Statistics, 1918. Home: Columbus, O.*

WEST, EBEN MOREAU, univ. prof.; born Bay, La., Oct. 6, 1885; s. Elisha L. and Samantha (Estess) W.; A.B., La. State U., 1919, M.S., 1928; Ph.D., Ohio State U., 1934; m. Alma Kleinpeter, Mar. 14, 1915; children—Frances Kathleen (wife of Lt. Col. Robert Gordon Crandall), Barbara Louise (wife of Dr. John Allen Worley). Elementary sch. teacher, 1906-11; high sch. prin. and teacher, 1911-28; instr. and prof. La State U., 1928-42, prof. and asst. to dean of jr. div. since 1942. Mem. Ecol. Soc. of Am., Sigma Xi. Home: Baton Rouge, La. *

WEST, LOUIS CAULTON, assn. exec.; b. Milw., Oct. 15, 1882; s. John and Deborah (Caulton) W.; A.B., Northwestern, 1905, A.M., 1911; A.M., Harvard, 1912; D.Litt. (hon.), Western Res. U., 1931; m. Frances Bragdon, Nov. 13, 1920; 1 dau., Barbara. Mem. Harvard-Boston Mus. Expdn. to Egypt, 1912-14; Investment banking with Borton & Borton, 1915-19; partner Hayden Miller & Co., 1919-33; financial dir. City Cleve., 1933-35; research in ancient econs. and numismatics since 1935; lectr. dept. classics Princeton since 1946, curator coins and medals since 1944; dir. West Bros. Served as capt., M.I.D., U.S. Army, 1918-19. Awarded medal by Hispanic Soc. Am., 1952. Mem. Am. Numis. Soc. (pres. since 1948), Am. Philol. Assn., Commn. Internationale de Numismatique (hon.). Club: Nassau (Princeton). Author: Imperial Roman Spain, 1929; Roman Britain: The Objects of Trade, 1931; Roman Gaul: The Objects of Trade, 1935; Gold and Silver Standards in the Roman Empire, 1941; Currency in Roman and Byzantine Egypt, 1944; Economic Studies of Byzantine Egypt, 1950. Contbr. to bus. and classical publs. Home: Princeton, N.J. *

WEST, MAE, actress; b. Bklyn., Aug. 17, 1892; d. John Patrick and Matilda (Delker-Dolger) West; privately tutored; m. Frank Wallace, 1911 (dissolved 1943). Theatrical appearances include Little Nell the Marchioness, 1897, Mrs. Wiggs of The Cabbage Patch, Ten Nights in a Barroom, East Lynne, The Fatal Wedding (all 1897-1903), A la Broadway, 1911, Vera Violetta, 1911, A Winsome Widow, 1912, Such is Life, 1913, Sometime, 1918, Demi-Tasse, 1919, The Mimic World, 1921, Sex, 1926, The Wicked Age, 1927, Diamond Lil, 1928, The Constant Sinner, 1931, Catherine Was Great, 1944; on tour in Vaudeville's Youngest Headliner, 1913-18, Ring Twice Tonight, 1946, Diamond Lil, 1948, 49, 49-50, 1951, Come on Up . . . Ring Twice, 1952, Sextet, 1961; motion picture appearances include Night After Night, 1932, She Done Him Wrong, 1933, I'm No Angel, 1933, Bell of the Nighties, 1934, Goin' to Town, 1935, Klondike Annie,

1936, Go West, Young Man, 1936, Every Day's a Holiday, 1937, My Little Chickadee, 1940, The Heat's On, 1943, Myra Breckenridge, 1969, Sextette, 1978. Author: (play) Pleasure Man, 1928; The Drag, 1927; (autobiography) Goodness Had Nothing to Do With It, 1959; (novels) Diamond Lil, The Constant Sinner, LP rec. The Naked Ape. Home: Hollywood, Calif. Died Nov. 22, 1980; buried Bklyn.

WEST, ROGER BLAKE, Judge; b. New Orleans, May 10, 1928; s. William Alice and Marguerite Estelle (Flaspoller) W.; B.A., Tulane U., 1949, LL.B., 1951; m. Willey-Gayle Martin, Sept. 26, 1953; children—Melissa Gayle, Anne Estelle, Willey-Gayle Blake, George Sebastian. Admitted to La. Bar, 1951; practice in New Orleans, 1951-78; asso. firm Phelps, Dunbar, Marks, Claverie & Sims, New Orleans, 1951-56, partner, 1956-71; U.S. Dist. judge Eastern Dist. La., 1971-78. Bd. dirs. Bur. Govtl. Research, 1968-71, Met. New Orleans Crime Commn., 1970-71, So. Eye Bank, 1965-71. Mem. Am., Fed., La., New Orleans bar assns., Am. Judicature Soc., New Orleans C. of C. (dir. 1965-67), Order of Coif, Omicron Delta Kappa. Republican. Presbyterian. Clubs: La., Boston. Home: New Orleans, La. Died Jan. 24, 1978.

WEST, WILLIAM NELSON, lawyer; b. Wynnewood, Pa., July 1, 1903; s. William Nelson L. and Anna E. (West) W.; A.B., Haverford Coll., 1924; LL.B., U. Pa., 1927; m. Edith Thacher Harris, Aug. 27, 1928; children—William Nelson, Edith Thacher (Mrs. W. John Daub III). Admitted to Pa. bar, 1927, practiced in Phila.; partner firm Dechert, Price & Rhoads, and predecessor, 1954-73. Bd. mgrs. Haverford Coll., 1943-78, sec., 1944-78; bd. dirs. Pocono Lake Preserve, 1950-78, sec., 1951-78; bd. dirs. Methodist Home for Children, 1955-78, Mercer Meml. House, 1954-78; bd. dirs. Phila. Skating Club and Humane Soc., 1965-66, pres., 1966-68. Club: Merion Cricket (Haverford). Home: Bryn Mawr, Pa. Died Sept. 6, 1978; interred West Laurel Hill Cemetery, Philadelphia.

WESTCOTT, LINN HANSON, editor; b. Los Angeles, July 13, 1913; s. Linnaeus Hunt and Regina (Hanson) W.; student Comnock Coll., 1931-32, Pasadena Jr. Coll., 1932-33, Carleton Coll., 1933-35; m. Harriet Kron, July 15, 1939; children—Jane (Mrs. Geoffrey Mathews), Paul Arthur, Russell Linn. With Kalmbach Pub. Co., Milw., 1935-80, v.p., 1947-80, pub. Model Trains mag., 1956-64, Ships and the Sea mag., 1956-59, editor Model Railroader, 1960-80. Trustee Village of Elm Grove, Wis., 1958-61. Charter mem. Nat. Model R.R. Assn. Author books steam locomotives and model railroading. Home: Elm Grove, Wis. Died Sept. 8, 1980.

WESTERGAARD, WALDEMAR CHRISTIAN, prof. history; b. Buffalo, N.D., Feb. 4, 1882; s. Jacob and Kirstine (Andersen) W.; A.B., U. of N.D., 1906; M.L., U. of Calif., 1910, Ph.D., 1915; m. Viola Minor, Aug. 21, 1917 (died Jan. 7, 1919); m. 2d, Mabel Shride Pinger, Dec. 22, 1941. A. D. White fellow in Am. history, Cornell U., 1911-12; research student, Copenhagen, 1912-13; asst. in history, U. of Calif., 1913-14; head history dept. Santa Barbara (Calif.) High School and Jr. College, 1914-16; head dept. Calif., 1925-49, emeritus 1949, dept. chmn., 1937-39; lecturer European history, summers 1921, 33, 37; research work on Baltic problems, Stockholm, Copenhagen, Reval, under Am. Scandinavian Foundation, 1922-23; delivered series of 6 lectures on Am. problems before U. of Christiania, under auspices Carnegie Peace Foundation, Sept.-Oct. 1922; visited 14 European lands, 1922-23; lectured on Am. hist. themes, Copenhagen and Stockholm, 1923; participated in 5th Internat. Hist. Congress (Brussels), Apr. 1923, 6th Congress (Oslo), Aug. 1938, and 8th Congress (Zurich), July 1938; del. to Northern Historical Congress, Gothenburg, 1923, Stockholm,1935; lecturer at Stanford U., summer 1929. Research tours, visiting 9 Baltic archive centers, July 1930-Jan. 1931; and in Paris, London and Copenhagen, 1939-40. Cultural attaché, heading U.S. Information Service, U.S. legation, Copenhagen, Denmark, 1945-46. Life member American Historical Assn. (pres. Pacific Coast branch, 1941), Econ. Hist. Soc. (Gr. Brit.); fellow Royal Hist. Soc. (Gr. Brit.); mem. hist. socs. of Sweden, Denmark and Norway, Hanseatic Hist. Soc., Phi Beta Kappa, Phi Delta Theta, Pi Gamma Mu; hon. corr. mem. Institut Historique et Heraldique de France. Conference Histor. Societies U.S. and Canada. Unitarian. Club: Faculty (Berkeley, Calif.). Author: The Danish West Indies, 1917; Denmark and Slesvig, 1848-1864 (translated into Danish as Det slesvigske Spörgsmaal og Krigen), 1946; The First Triple Alliance, 1947; also many articles in hist. periodicals. Home: Los Angeles. *

WESTHEIMER, IRVIN FERDINAND, investment banker; b. Newark, Sept. 19, 1879; s. Fernidnand and Sarah (Flarsheim) W.; student Cornell U., 1898-1900; m. Duffie Freiberg Heinsheimer, Apr. 20, 1910; children—Charles, Robert. Partner Westheimer & Co., Cin., 1916-63; divisional dir. Hayden, Stone, Inc., 1963-70; past dir. several indsl. corps. Rep. of Manhattan Project in confs. with Anthony Eden, also Belgium re uranium; del. Great Lakes Conf.; past mem. N.Y. Stock Exchange; past vice consul of Paraguay in Cin. Founder Big Brother movement, 1903; co-founder Jr. Achievement Cin.; chmn. atomic energy exhibit Man and the Atom, 1948; mem. adv. com. for dean Grad. Sch. Arts and Scis., U. Cin.; chmn. War Savs. Stamp Com., Cin., World War I. Recipient Human Relations award Am. Jewish Com., 1960; Am. Honorarium citation, 1966; Great Living Cincinnatian award Cin. C. of C.; certificate perpetual membership St. Boniface Orphan Soc.; citation U. Cin.; Cin. plaque Am. Legion; Joint Brotherhood award for outstanding service in cause brotherhood; named Ky. col.; hon. mem. Kiwanis Club Cin. Clubs: Losantiville Country; Queen City, University (Cin.); Fraternity. Home: Cincinnati, Ohio. Died Dec. 31, 1980; buried United Jewish Cemetery, Cin.

WESTON, MELVILLE FULLER, lawyer; b. Bellows Falls, Vt., Feb. 9, 1899; s. George Ackley and Lettie Julia (Morgan) W.; A.B., Dartmouth, 1918; LL.B., Harvard, 1922; m. Marion Stone, Dec. 26, 1922; children—John, Nathan, Marion, Katharine Melville. Admitted to Mass. bar, 1922; asst. atty. gen. Mass., 1924-27; pvt. practice, Boston, from 1927; partner firm Powers & Hall, and predecessors, from 1931; pres. H & B Am. Machine Co., 1945-46; pres. C. E.Riley Co., 1956-74, also dir.; dir. Alves Photo Service, Inc., Boston Machine Works Co., Patterson, Wylde & Windeler, Inc., Standard Rivet Co., Groton Leatherboard Co., Certified Dry Mat Corp. Hon. trustee Lawrence Acad.; hon. trustee Worcester Found. Exptl. Biology; trustee Mabel Louise Riley Charitable Trust. Clubs: St. Botolph (Boston); Dedham (Mass.) Country and Polo. Home: Needham, Mass. Died Oct. 30.

WESTON, WILLARD GARFIELD, indsl. exec.; b. Toronto, Can., 1898; s. George and Emma Maude W.; Student Harbord Coll. Inst., Toronto; m. Reta Lila Howard; children—Miriam Louise, George Grainger, Barbara Elizabeth, Garfield Howard, Reta Nancy, Mary Dian Wendy, Gretchen Ann, Camilla Howard Wittington, Willard Galen; m. 2d, Marguerita Martin de Montoya. With George Weston, Ltd., Toronto, Ca., 1918-78, v.p., 1921-24, mgr., 1922-24, vice chmn. and pres., to 1978; organized Weston Biscuit Co., Passaic N.J., 1929; acquired Mitchell & Muil Ltd., Aberdeen, Scotland, 1933; organized Asso. Brit. Foods Ltd., London, U.K., now pres.; chmn. George Weston Holdings, Ltd., Eng., Fortnum & Mason Ltd., London, George Weston Inc.; dir. E.B. Eddy Co., Wittington Investments Ltd. Can., W. Garfield Weston Found., Can., George Weston Foods Ltd., Australia and New Zealand. Served with engrs. Can. Army, 1917-18; France; Officer of Order of Can. Conservative. Mem. United Church. Address: Toronto, Ont., Canada. Died Oct. 22, 1978.

WESTOVER, RUSSELL CHANNING, cartoonist; b. Los Angeles, Calif., Aug. 3, 1886; s. Channing Clisson and Alice (Aldrich) W.; grad. pub. schs., Oakland, Calif.; student Mark Hopkins Inst. of Art, San Francisco; m. Genesta Grace DeLancey, Aug. 2, 1908; children—Russell Channing, Alden DeLancey. Cartoonist San Francisco Bulletin, 1904-08, Oakland Herald, 1908-10, San Francisco Chronicle, 1910-14, San Francisco Post, 1914, later with New York Herald; contbr. to Life and Judge, 1918-21; cartoonist for King Features Syndicate since 1921; creator of comic series, "Tillie the Toiler," which appears in over 600 newspapers. Creator of the Strip "The Van Swaggers" which appears separately and in conjunction with "Tillie the Toiler" on Sundays—Song—"Tillie the Toiler" by Charles Tobias and Fred Coots. Republican. Conglist. Clubs: Press (San Francisco); New York Athletic. Author: Tillie the Toiler, 1925 (moving picture based on same; released 1927). Home: Ross, Calif. *

WETHERELL, CARL BRADLEE, educator; b. Boston, Mass., Aug. 13, 1886; s. Charles Bradlee and Alice Elizabeth (Dix) W.; grad. high sch., Brookline, Mass., 1904; A.B., Harvard, 1908; A.M., 1918; 1919-27; headmaster Proctor Acad., Andover, N.H., since 1927. mem. Delta Upsilon; Unitarian. Home: Andover, N.H.*

WETHERILL, SAMUEL PRICE, engring. exec.; b. Phila., May 13, 1880; s. Samuel P. and Christine (Northrop) W.; B.S., U. Pa., 1903; LL.D., Upsala Coll., East Orange, N.J., 1938; Sc.D. (hon.) Phila. Coll. of Pharmacy and Science; m. Edith Bucknell, June 7, 1902; m. 2d Alice Constable Jewett, Aug. 9, 1941. With Wetherill Engring. Co., Phila., president, 1927—; president of Hyper-Humus Company, 1915—, chairman of the board, 1965—. Grad. mem. Bus. Adv. Council, Dept. Commerce. Founder Regional Planning Fedn. (past pres.); former vice chmn. Phila. City Planning Commn.; bd. govs. Delaware Valley Council; pres. Interdependenence Council, Inc. Bd. dirs. West Phila. Corp. Served in Q.M., U.S. Army, World War I. Mem. U. Mus. Mem. Am. Planning & Civic Assn (dir.), City Parks Assn. (vice pres.) Phila. Art Alliance (hon. pres.), Fairmount Park Art Assn. (mem. bd.), Bur. Municipal Research, Nat. Econ. League, Nat. Bur. Econ. Research, Franklin Inst., Phila. Inst. Architects (hon.), S.A.E., Soc. for Preservation of Landmarks, Phila. Soc. Promoting Agr. (past president), The Business Council (hon.), Am. Acad. Polit, and Social Sci., Am. Philos. Soc., Mil. Order Fgn. Wars, Mil. Order Loyal Legion, Mil. Ord. World Wars, Soc. Colonial Wars, Wistar Assn., Sphinx Sr. Soc., Am. Swedish Hist. Found., S.R., Delta Psi, Gen. Alumni Soc. Pa. (past v.p.). Unitarian Church. Clubs: Union League, The Penn, Merion Cricket. Author: Interdependence, 1921; Public Guidance in Urban Land Utilization, 1930; Citizen Support for Planning, 1936; Counter-Gravity Die Casting of High Melting Point Metal, 1937; Criteria of Effective Citizenship, 1940; Early Swedish Influence in the Delaware Valley, 1946. Holder various patents. Chmn. bd. Phila. Coll. Pharmacy and Science. Home: Haverford, Pa. *

WETMORE, ALEXANDER, biologist; b. North Freedom, Wis., June 18, 1886; s. Nelson Franklin and Emma Amelia (Woodworth) W.; A.B., U. Kans., 1912; M.S., George Washington U., 1916. Ph.D., 1920, hon. Sc.D., 1932, alumni award, 1945; Sc.D., U. Wis., 1946; citation for distinguished service U. Kan., 1941; D.Sc., Centre Coll. (Ky.), 1947; D.Sc., Ripon Coll., 1959; m. Fay Holloway, Oct. 13, 1912 (dec. Feb. 1953); 1 dau., Margaret Fenwick Harlan; m. 2d, Beatrice Thielen, Dec. 16, 1953. Asst., U. Kan. Museum, 1905-08, 1910. Colo. Mus. Natural History, 1909; agt., Biol. Survey, U.S. Dept. Agr., 1910-12, asst. biologist, 1913-23, biologist 1924; supt. Nat. Zool. Park, Washington, Nov. 1924-Mar. 1925; asst. sec. Smithsonian Instn., in charge U.S. Nat. Museum, 1925-44, sec. Smithsonian Instn. 1945-52; research asso. 1953-78; head Tanager expdn. to Pacific, 1923. Trustee Textile Mus. Washington, George Washington U., Wildlife Inst.; dir. Gorgas Meml. Inst. Tropical Medicine; mem. adv. com. Internat. Wild Life Protection; mem. Internat. Commn. Bird Preservation, Joint Latin-American Study; rep. U.S. Inter-Am. com. Experts Nature Protection. Recipient Brewster medal Am. Ornithologists Union, 1959; Explorers Club medal, 1962. Fellow Rochester Museum Arts and Scis.; mem. Nat. Acad. Sci., A.A.A.S., Am. Philos. Soc., Nat. Geog. Soc. (trustee), many other nat., local scientific profl. orgns. and assns. has served as officer of several; also hon. or corr. mem. many fgn. profl. and scientific assns. Awarded Isidore Geoffroy St. Hilaire and Otto Herman medals; Hubbard medal Nat. Geographic Soc., 1975; medals; Order of Merit Carlos Manuel de Cespedes (Cuba). Clubs: Cosmos (Washington); Explorers, Boone and Crockett, Ends of the Earth (N.Y.C.). Author books relating to birds, papers on avian paleontology. Home: Washington, D.C. Died Dec. 7, 1978; interred at North Cohocton, N.Y.

WETMORE, HORACE ORTON, investment banker; b. Los Angeles, Feb. 17, 1902; s. Frank Orton and Marie Louise (Barlow) W.; student U. Wis., 1920-21; m. Lucia Pauline Ambrose, Sept. 8, 1923 (dec. June 1944); children—Horace Orton, Frank Orton II; m. 2d, Dorothy Kemper Spencer, July 27, 1945. Mgr. Wilson & Co., Inc., Chgo., 1922-29; with First Nat. Bank Chgo., 1930-35, 1939-67, v.p., 1941-63, sr. v.p., 1963-67; treas. Marshall Field & Co., Chgo., 1935-37; v.p., dir. mem. exec. com. Blyth & Co., Inc., Chgo., 1937-39; chmn., dir. Heinn Co., Milw. until 1968; pres., dir. Wetmore Corp., 1968-74. Clubs: Chicago, Chicago Golf, Racquet (Chgo.). Home: Wheaton, Ill. Died Sept. 30, 1974.

WETZLER, BENJAMIN, stock broker; b. Auburn, N.Y., Jan. 24, 1908; B.S., Syracuse U., 1930; m. Deborah Rabinowitz, Nov. 30, 1946; children—James Warren, Mark, Scott. With Hardy & Co., mem. N.Y. Stock Exchange, N.Y.C., 1957-78, mng. partner, 1968-78; partner Cowen & Co., mem. N.Y. Stock Exchange, N.Y.C., 1978-80. Sec. N.Y. State Democratic State Com., 1946-72. Served to col. 18th Airborne Corps, AUS, 1941-46. Decorated Bronze Star medal. Home: New York, N.Y. Died Apr. 26, 1980.

WEYBRIGHT, VICTOR, book publisher; b. Keymar, Md., Mar. 16, 1903; s. Samuel Royer and Lillie (Fogle) W.; student U. Pa., 1921-22, U. Chgo., 1924-26; L.H.D., Wagner Coll., 1961, Syracuse U., 1974; LL.D., U. Wyo., 1972; Litt.D., Western Md. Coll., 1976; m. Hildegarde Fillmore, May 30, 1928; m. 2d, Helen Talley, Feb. 28, 1950; step-children—Helen Haskell Sampson, Truman Talley. Sec. to Jane Addams, Chgo., 1924-26; traveling newspaper corr., 1926-27, 34; asso. editor Butterick Pub. Co., N.Y.C., 1927-34; free lance writer, 1934-35; mng. editor Survey Asso., 1935-42; cons. Readers Digest, 1935-42; exec. O.W.I., spl. asst. to U.S. Ambassador, Am. embassy, London, 1942-45; chmn. bd., editor-in-chief New Am. Library of World Lit., Inc., pub. Signet, Mentor books, N.Y.C., 1945-66, chmn. exec. com. 1960-63, chmn. pub. and editorial coms., 1962-64; chmn. Weybright & Talley, Inc., N.Y.C., 1966-70, Weybright & Talley, Ltd., London, Eng., 1966-70, sr. editorial adviser, 1970; v.p., dir. Carlyle House, Inc., 1971-75, pres., from 1975. Mem. exec. bd. P.E.N. Am. Center, from 1971, internat. rep. to People's Republic China, 1972; mem. bd. Am. Book Pubs. Council, 1954-57; life fellow Met. Mus. Art, N.Y.C.; v.p. Gypsy Lore Soc., from 1976; hon. trustee Western Md. Coll., from 1976. Recipient 1st pub. citation for distinctive service to internat. letters P.E.N., 1976. Dem. Episcopalian. Clubs: Cosmos (Washington); Overseas Press, Players, Century, National Beagle (N.Y.); Hamilton (Balt.); Timber Ridge Hunt (Md.); Savile (London). Author: Spangled Banner, 1935; The Americas: South and North, 1940; (with Henry B. Sell) Buffalo Bill and the Wild West, 1955; The Making of a Publisher, 1967. Contbr. to mags. Home: New York, N.Y. Deceased.

WEYERBACHER, ARTHUR FERDINAND, physician; b. Boonville, Ind., Nov. 7, 1883; s. Jacob and Caroline (Goerlitz) W.; M.D., Ind. U., 1909; postgrad. student U. of Vienna, 1926, 28. Clinical prof. urology Ind. U. since 1935; pres. of staff St. Vincent's Hosp., 1931-38; treas. Medical Mutual Ins. Co. of Ind. since 1946; mem. bd. dirs. Blue Cross, Ind. Mem. exec. com. and treas. Ind. State Med. Assn. since 1931. Commd. lt., M.C., U.S. Army, 1917; comd. Base Hosp. 52, France, late in war; discharged as maj., 1919; mem. com. for Selective Service med. officers; World War II. Mem. Am. Coll. Surgs., Am. Bd. Urology, Am. Urol. Assn., Sigma Chi. Phi Chi. Ind. Democrat. Clubs: Columbia, Indianapolis Literary. Home: Indianapolis. *

WEYL, WOLDEMAR ANATOL, educator; b. Darmstadt, Germany, June 13, 1901; s. Wladimir and Auguste (Blech) W.; Diploma Ingenieur, Tech. U., Darmstadt, 1926; Dr. Chem.E., Tech. U., Aachen, 1931; m. Ilse Rudow, Oct. 29, 1937; 1 dau., Karin Gisela. Came to U.S., 1936, naturalized, 1944. Head dept. glass tech. Kaiser Wilhelm Inst. Silicate Research, 1926-36; vis. prof. U.S., 1936-37; prof. glass tech. Pa. State U., 1938-75, chmn. div. mineral tech. Coll. Mineral Industries, 1948-59; research prof. Mineral Industries, 1959-75; Disting. vis. prof. Am. U., Cairo, 1966-67. Recipient key to city Toledo, 1968. Mem. Am. Chem. Soc., Am. Ceramics Soc., Brit., German socs. glass tech., Keramos. Editor: French jour. Verre et Refractaire. Home: State College, Pa. Died July 30, 1975; interred Graysville (Pa.) Cemetery.

WHALEN, WILL WILFRID, clergyman, author; b. near Mt. Carmel, Pa., May 7, 1882, s. Michael J. and Alice (Debo) W.; ed. St. Charles Sem., Overbrook, Pa., and Mt. St. Mary's Coll., Emmitsburg, Md. Served as singer and actor; writer and collaborator of plays; ordained priest R.C. Ch. 1911. Author: The Celibate Father, 1927; The Golden Squaw (the story of Mary Jemison), 3d edit., 1928; Give Me a Chance!, 1929; Co-Stars—Cecil Spooner and Oscar Wilde, 1930; also Twilight Talks to Tired Hearts; The Ex-Seminarian; The Girl from Mine Run; The Forbidden Man; The Girl Who Fought; The Ex-Nun; The Priest Who Vanished, 1942; (published plays) Scandal's Lash; What Priests Never Tell; The Irish Sparrow; (produced plays) The Virgin Queen's Daughter, War Wife, Ex-Nun! and Kit ofCockpit.*

WHALLEY, J. IRVING, congressman; b. Barnesboro, Pa.; s. James and Anna (Ashurst) W.; grad. Cambria Rowe Bus. Coll., Johnstown, Pa.; m. Ruth Anderson; children—John, Ruth. Mem. Pa. Ho. of Reps., 1951-55, Pa. Senate from 36th Dist., 1955-60; mem. 86th-87th congresses 18th Dist. Pa., 88th-92d Congresses 12th Dist. Pa., mem. fgn. affairs com.; U.S. del. to UN, fall 1969. Chmn. Somerset County (Pa.) Redevel. Authority, Windber (Pa.) Planning Commn.; mem. Windber Sch. Bd., 1935-47, pres., 1938-44. Mem. adv. bd. Johnstown Coll. of U. Pitts. Bd. dirs. Automotive Orgn. Team. Recipient Distinguished Service award Am. Legion; Dale Carnegie Internat. Good Human Relations award. Home: Windber, Pa. Died Mar. 7, 1980.

WHARTON, HUNTER POISAL, labor union exec.; b. Martinsburg, W.Va., Oct. 20, 1900; s. John Jacob and Anne Lee (Gordon) W.; student Carnegie Inst. Tech., 1920-22; LL.D. (hon.), Fordham U., 1966; m. Lydia Marie Koller, May 13, 1925. With Douglas of Pitts., contractors, 1922-30; with Internat. Union Operating Engrs., 1930-75, gen. sec.-treas., 1958-62, gen. pres., 1962-75; v.p. bldg. constrn. trade dept. AFL-CIO, from 1962, v.p. metal trades dept., from 1962, v.p. AFL-CIO, from 1965; dir. Union Labor Life Ins. Co. Vice pres. Nat. Safety Council, from 1963; mem. labor adv. bd. Office Emergency Planning, from 1965, Dept. Health, Edn. and Welfare, from 1965; bd. dirs. Nat. Com. Employment Youth Bd. dirs. Soc. Prevention Blindness, Big Bros. Am. Recipient several awards Nat. Safety Council. Elk, Eagle (pres. 1937-39; Murray-Greene award 1963, Eagles Hall of Fame award 1966). Knight of Malta (post comdr. 1925). Home: Rockville, Md. Died Nov. 14, 1980.

WHARTON, JOHN FRANKLIN, lawyer; b. Newark, July 28, 1894; s. Charles Adolphus and Lenna Irene (Lyon) W.; A.B., Williams Coll., 1915; student N.Y. Law Sch., 1915-17; LL.B., Columbia, 1920; m. Carolin Bumiller, Dec. 6, 1924 (div. 1949); children—Joan Franklin (dec.), Barry; m. 2d, Betty Ann Fisher, 1949. Admitted to N.Y. bar, 1920; law clk. McCarter & English, Newark, 1915-16, Rounds, Hatch, Dillingham & Debevoise, 1920-23; partner, then counsel firm Paul, Weiss, Rifkind, Wharton & Garrison and predecessor firms which included Adlai Stevenson, Willard Wirtz, Newton Minow, W.C. Blair, Arthur Goldberg, Ramsey Clark; former counsel, dir. Benson & Hedges, Tobacco & Allied Stocks, Inc., Field Enterprises, Inc. Chmn. Inst. Advanced Studies in Theatre Arts; former pres., dir. Theatre, Inc.; founder, counsel to Playwrights Producing Co., Inc.; past gen. counsel, dir. Am. Houses, Inc. Rep. Selznick Internat. Pictures, Inc., during prodn. in three color process Gone with the Wind; counsel, dir. Farnsworth TV & Radio Corp. during devel. electronic television; counsel Vitarama Corp., Cinerama Inc., developers cinerama motion picture process. Cons. Bd. Econ. Warfare, World War II. Cons., dir. Legitimate Theatre Exploratory Commn.; co-founder Citizens For Quieter City; chmn. bd. Hiroshima Peace Center Assos.; bd. dirs. Scherman Found.; an organizer, 1st chmn. Citizens for Clean Air, Inc.; counsel, past pres. Little Orch. Soc.; past counsel, officer Ballet Theatre Found. Trustee Cole Porter Songs. Enlisted in Naval Aviation in World War I, received medical discharge; worked with British Ministry of Shipping until conclusion of war. Recipient Kelcey Allen award, 1965; spl. Tony award, 1974; spl. New Dramatists award, 1974; N.Y.C. citation for distinguished service, 1975; named as man who did most for Theatre, Variety, 1966. Dir., one of organizers Council for Democracy, Home Front; former counsel, dir. ANTA. Mem. Bar Assn. City N.Y., Phi Beta Kappa, Theta Delta Chi. Author: This Road to Recovery, 1934; The Theory and Practice of Earning A Living 1945; The Explorations of George Burton, 1950; Life Among the Playwrights, 1974. Contbr. numerous articles on theatre and social problems to publs. Home: New York, N.Y. Died Nov. 24, 1977.

WHATLEY, BARNEY LEE, lawyer (ret.); b. Clay County, Ala., Oct. 23, 1885; s. Martin Wilburn and Anna Virginia (Smith) W.; student of law 1905-08; m. Gertrude H. Thielen, Dec. 25, 1920; children—Alfred Thielen, William James. Admitted to Ala. Bar, 1908; practiced law Birmingham, 1908-10, Breckenridge, Colo., 1911-18; Leadville, Colo., 1913-19, Denver, 1919-41; ret. 1941; dist. atty., 5th judicial dist., Colo., 1912-19. Elected Dem. State chmn., 1942; elected Dem. nat. committeeman for Colo., 1946, 48. Vice pres. trustees Colo. Women's Coll. since 1945. Home: Denver, Colo. *

WHEAT, HARRY G(ROVE), prof. edn.; b. Berkeley Springs, W.Va., April 8, 1890; s. Alfred Asbury and Tamson Bell (Shockey) W.; A.B., W.Va. U., 1912; A.M., U. of Chicago, 1917; Ph.D., Columbia, 1929; m. Florence Bodey, Aug. 20, 1919 (died Feb. 6, 1945); 1 dau., Mary Eleanor (Mrs. Harold Piggott). Teacher, high sch., Davis, W.Va., 1912-13; supt. schs., Williamstown, W.Va., 1913-16; instr. edn., State Normal Sch., Glenville, W.Va., 1917, 1919-24, State Teachers Coll., Milwaukee, 1924-25; prof. edn., Marshall Coll., Huntington, W.Va., 1925-35; prof. edn., W.Va. U., 1935-56, prof. emeritus, 1956-75; summer teacher, Duke U., 1940, U. of Alberta, 1947; spl. lecturer, U. of Pa., U. of Chicago, Temple U. Served in F.A., U.S. Army with A.E.F., 1918-19, grad. Saumur Arty. Sch., France, 1919. Mem. com. to prepare yearbooks on arithmetic in pub. schs. Nat. Council Teachers of Mathematics and Nat. Soc. for the Study of Edn. Mem. N.E.A., State Edn. Assn., Phi Beta Kappa, Phi Delta Kappa, Sigma Phi Epsilon. Republican. Methodist. Mason. Club: Kiwanis. Author: The Teaching of Reading, 1923; The Relative Merits of Arithmetic Problems, 1929; Psychology of the Elementary School, 1931; The Psychology and Teaching of Arithmetic, 1937; Practice Books for Arithmetic, 1936. Home: Morgantown, W.Va. Died Mar. 29, 1975.

WHEATLEY, ARCHER, lawyer; b. Du Quoin, Ill., Oct. 26, 1885; s. Rudolph Archer and Margaret Caroline (Kelly) W.; LL.B., Transylvania Coll. Law; 1907; m. Nelle A. Thaxton, Sept. 26, 1911 (dec. Dec. 29, 1957); children—Betty, Donald. Admitted to Ark. bar, 1909; chancellor 12th Chancery Circuit, 1917-23; mem. Ark. Gen. Assembly, 1929-32; mem. law firm Barrett, Wheatley, Smith & Deacon, and predecessors, Jonesboro, Ark., since 1943. Mem. Am., Ark., Craighead Co. bar assns., Pi Kappa Alpha. Democrat. Mem. Christian Ch. Home: Jonesboro, Ark. *

WHEATON, HARRISON HYLAS, b. Ottumwa, Ia., Sept. 2, 1884; s. William Morse and Sybil Mehitabel (Hatch) W.; student Grinnell (Ia.) Coll., 1903-07; Ph.B., U. of Chicago, 1910, J.D., 1911; m. Frances Elizabeth Eddy, of Chicago, Ill., July 20, 1909 (died Jan. 8, 1937); m. 2d, Dorothy Sommers, 1937. Began investigations into Americanization, Rochester, N.Y., 1911; supervising investigator N.Y. State Bur. Industries and Immigration, 1912-14; apptd. supervising investigator, Pa. State Dept. of Labor and Industry, 1914, also apptd. by U.S. commr. of edn. to investigate condition of immigrant edn.; chief div. of immigrant edn. in U.S., under Bur. of Edn., 1914-18; dir. bureau "America First" campaign, 1915; cons. expert Pa. Industrial Bd., 1914-18; drafted and secured passage of employment bills Pa. legislature, 1915; chmn. exec. com. of Nat. Com. of 100 apptd. by commr. of edn., 1916; director Conn. State Dept. Americanization, 1918; sec. and labor mgr. N.Y. Clothing Trade Assn., 1919; exec. mgr. Savings Banks Assn. State of N.Y., 1920-21; exec. mgr. N.Y. State Waterways Conf. Com., 1921-22. Pres. Harrison H. Wheaton, Inc., Continental Eastern Corpn. Mem. Institute of Am. Business (pres. 1933). *

WHEATON, WILLIAM LINDUS CODY, coll. dean; b. Cleve., Apr. 10, 1913; s. William Arthur and Gertrude (Cody) W.; A.B., Princeton, 1934; Wheelwright fellow, Harvard, 1945-46; Ph.D. (Hillman fellow), U. Chgo., 1953; m. Katherine Friend, Aug. 20, 1935; children—William Cody, Martha Hansen; m. 2d, Margaret Fry, Nov. 9, 1963, 1 son, Edward Fry. Asst. dir. parks, Cleve., 1937-40; orgn. officer Nat. Housing Agy., 1943-45; cons. city planner, 1946; spl. asst. adminstr. Housing and Home Finance Agy., 1946-48; asso. prof. regional planning Harvard, 1948-53, chmn. dept., 1951-53; prof. city planning U. Pa., 1953-63, dir. Inst. Urban Studies, 1954-63; prof. city planning U. Calif., Berkeley, 1963-78, dir. Inst. Urban and Regional Devel., 1963-68, dean Coll. Environ. Design, from 1967; cons. in field, 1960-78. Chmn., Calif. Council Intergovtl. Relations, 1967-68; U.S. rep. com. housing, bldg. and planning UN, 1963-65; UN sr. rep. Nagoya Devel. Center, 1968-71. Mem. Democratic Adv. Council, 1959-61. Bd. dirs. San Francisco Planning and Renewal, 1963-69, Calif. Tomorrow, from 1963, Regional Sci. Research Inst., 1965-78, Planning Found. Am., from 1965, Lasker Trust, from 1968, Nat. Assembly, 1968-74, Nat. Housing Conf., from 1948, Planning and Devel. Corp., 1965-74. Mem. Am. Inst. Planners (bd. dirs. 1952-60, Distinguished Service medal 1973), Nat. Assn. Housing and Renewal Ofcls. (bd. govs. 1953-55, Distinguished Service medal 1974), Am. Soc. Planning Ofcls. (bd. govs. 1970-74, recipient medal 1974). Author: (with others) Housing, People and Cities, 1961; (with others) Integration on Political Communities, 1964; also chpts. in books. Editor: (with others) Urban Housing, 1966. Mem. editorial bds. jours. in field. Home: Berkeley, Calif. Died Feb. 19, 1978.

WHEELER, DAN HUBERT, govt. official; b. Lake Wilson, Minn., Feb. 19, 1894; s. Anthony William and Sarah Elizabeth (Young) W.; LL.B., George Washington U., Washington, D.C., 1923; married Carolyn Faris, Oct. 1, 1928; children—Carol Elizabeth (Mrs. Ray C. Pittman), Robert Faris. Office boy, clerk, bookkeeper, 1909-17; entered Federal Govt. civil service as clerk, 1919, clerical supervisor, purchasing supervisor Vet.'s Bur., until 1923; admitted to D.C. bar, 1923; conducted research and drafted model legislation, U.S. Dept. of Commerce, 1923-33; atty., asso. div. director and div. dir. Fed. Emergency Adminstrn. of Pub. Works, 1933-39; asst. dir. Bituminous Coal Div., U.S. Dept. of Interior, 1939-41, acting director, 1941-42, director, Sept. 1942-Aug. 1943; assistant deputy solid fuels adminstr., U.S. Dept. of Interior, 1943-45, deputy solid fuels administrator, 1945-47; asst. dir. Program staff, Dept. of Interior, 1947-50, asst. dir. office of territories Dept. of Interior, 1950-53, pub. works advisor office territories, 1953-79; chairman Combined Coal Com. (U.S., Brit. and Can.) and chmn. of the asso. U.S. Operating Com., 1946-47. One of incorporators, dir. Health and Welfare Council Nat. Capitol Area, also mem. exec. com.; dir. United Givers Fund Nat. Capitol Area, also mem. exec. com. Served as pvt. to sergeant 1st class, U.S. Army, Sept., 1917 to Aug. 19, 1919. Mem. Federal Bar Association, National Lawyers Club, Sigma Chi, Phi Alpha Delta, Order of the Coif. Episcopalian. Mason. Asso. editor: Reports of President's Conference of Home Bldg. and Home Ownership (11 vols.), 1933. Home: Chevy Chase, Md. Died Mar. 2, 1979.

WHEELER, DONALD, prof., ret.; b. New Lebanon, Pa., Feb. 9, 1885; s. Lorenzo Dow and Eva Anette (Blatt) W.; A.B., Grove City Coll., 1905; Grad. Leland Powers Sch. of Dramatic Art, 1908; student U. of Paris, Univ. of Rome, Univ. of Berlin, Max Reinhardt's School of the Theatre; dir. Summer Theatre, Marthas Vineyard, Mass.; Litt.D., Grove City Coll., 1934. Lecture recitals under the Chautauqua Managers' Assn.; dir. plays, having directed more than 250 plays; actor, leading man; Murah Theatre, Ind.; leads in Shakespearean Co.; taught speech summers at McCormick Theol. Sem., Chicago, Grove City Bible School, Middlebury, College, noted for interpretative recital of Dickens' Christmas Carol, of which a recording has been made; master in Lawrenceville School, 1910-22; instructor, Princeton Univ. and Princeton Theol. Sem., 1924-29; prof. of speech, Princeton Theological Seminary, 1929-53; honorably retired in 1953; visiting professor of speech California Baptist Theol. Sem., Covina. Member Nat. Geor. Soc., Am. Acad. Polit. and Social Sciences, Nat. Speech Assn. Clubs: Nassau, Princeton; University. Republican. Presbyn. Contbr. articles to mags. Address: Tucson, Ret. *

WHEELER, GEORGE ALEXANDER, retired physician; b. Higgins, N.C., Mar. 10, 1885; s. John Bomar and Lovada (Higgins) W.; M.D., U. of Va., 1913; m. Agnes Elizabeth Kullgren, of Hartford, Conn., May 6, 1918; children—Charlotte, George, Alexander. Asst. surgeon, U.S.P.H.S., 1914-19, passed asst. surgeon, 1919-22, surgeon since 1922; engaged in researches on pellegra, 1915-28; in charge field investigations in nutrition, 1929-33; co-discoverer of the cause of pellagra and of vitamin G. Mem. Am. and Southern med. assns. Democrat. Presbyn. Home: Spartanburg, S.C.*

WHEELER, JOHN HERVEY, lawyer, banker; b. Kittrell, N.C., Jan. 1, 1908; s. John Leonadas and Margaret (Hervey) W.; A.B. summa cum laude, Morehouse Coll., 1929; LL.B., N.C. Coll., Durham, 1947; LL.D., Shaw U., 1954, Johnson C. Smith U., 1963, Tuskegee Inst., 1964; L.H.D., Morehouse Coll., 1968, Duke, 1970, N.C. Central U., 1971; m. Selena Warren, Dec. 25, 1935; children—Mrs. Julia W. Taylor, Warren H. Admitted to N.C. bar, 1947, practiced in

Durham; with Mechanics & Farmers Bank, Durham, 1929-78, pres., 1952-78, also dir.; dir., securities investment cons. N.C. Mut. Life Ins. Co.; dir. Mechanics & Farmers Bank, Durham, Raleigh and Charlotte, Mut. Savs. & Loan Assn., Durham; dir., exec. com. Nat. Corp. for Housing Partnership, Washington. Chmn. Durham Commn. on Negro Affairs, 1957-78; bd. dirs. Mut. Real Estate Investment Trust of N.Y.: apptd. by Pres. John F. Kennedy to U.S. EEO Commn., 1961; bd. dirs. U.S.-South Africa Leader Exchange Program, Inc., 1961-74; chmn. Durham Urban Redevel. Commn.; vice chmn. Durham City-County Library Bd.; mem. exec. com., past pres. So. Regional Council, Atlanta; v.p. United Fund, Inc., Durham, 1967-68; trustee Com. Econ. Devel. mem. legal staff NAACP, N.C.; vice chmn. Nat. Citizens' Com. for Community Relations; mem. Pres.'s Com. on Urban Housing. Chmn. bd. Atlanta U.; chmn. bd. trustees Atlanta U. Center, Inc.; trustee Morehouse Coll., John Avery Boys Club, Durham; mem. bd. Durham County Hosp. Corp. Mem. Nat. Negro Bankers Assn. (past pres.), Am. Bankers Assn.'s Minbac Capital Corp., Omega Psi Phi. African M.E. Ch. (gen. bd. 1956-60, 64-78). Mason (32 deg., Shriner). Home: Durham, N.C. Died July 6, 1978; buried Durham.

WHEELER, JOHN NEVILLE, newspaperman; b. Yonkers, N.Y., Apr. 11, 1886; s. Charles W. and Kate (Neville) W.; A.B., Columbia, 1908; m. Elizabeth Wood Thompson, Jan. 30, 1918; 1 dau., Elizabeth N. (Mrs. William McLaren Ellison) (dec.). With N.Y. Herald, 1908-12; est. Wheeler Syndicate, 1913, sold out, 1916; est. Bell Newspaper Syndicate, Inc., 1916, former pres., dir. The Bell Syndicate, Inc., N. Am. Newspaper Alliance, Inc.; now consultant to the United Feature Syndicate; pres. and director of Wheeler Development Corp.; was exec. editor Liberty Weekly. Served as 2d lt., later 1st lt. F.A., U.S. Army, Aug. 1917-Feb. 1919, with A.E.F. in France, May 1918-Feb. 1919. Mem. Sigma Chi. Episcopalian. Clubs: Maidstone Peachtree (Atlanta); University, Dutch Treat Club, Coffee House, National Golf Links of America, Artists and Writers. Author: I've Got News for You, 1961. Home: Ridgefield, Conn. *

WHEELER, MAYNARD C., business exec.; b. Terre Haute, Ind., Jan. 12, 1900; s. Conard Scott and Laura May (Echard) W.; B.S., Purdue U., 1923, D.Eng. (hon.), 1951; LL.D., Ind. State U., 1967; m. Mary Wibie McDaniel, June 9, 1923; children—Marilyn Pendergast, Maynard C. With Comml. Solvents Corp., Terre Haute, 1923-68, sr. v.p., 1957-58, pres., chief exec. officer, 1959-66, chmn. bd., 1966-68, now mem. bd. dirs.; dir. Grain Drying Equipment Co. Bd. dirs. Purdue Research Found., Nat. Plant Food Inst., Ind. State U. Found., Found. Am. Agr., Sheldon Swope Art Gallery, Terre Haute Com. Area Progress, Vigo County Extension Bd., Goodwil Industries, Terre Haute; bd. mgrs. Rose Poly. Inst. Mem. Am. Chem. Soc., Am. Inst. Chem. Engrs., N.A.M. (past dir., chmn. research com.), Newcomen Soc. N. Am., Tau Beta Pi, Delta Chi. Clubs: Columbia (Indpls.); Country (Terre Haute), Leland (Mich.) Country. Home: Terre Haute, Ind. Died Dec. 26, 1979.

WHEELER, RAYMOND ALBERT, army officer; b. Peoria, Ill., July 31, 1885; s. Stephen Andrew and Margaret (Maple) W.; B.S., U.S. Mil. Acad., 1911; grad. Engr. Sch. 1913, Command and Gen. Staff Sch., 1927, Army War Coll., 1937; m. Olive Keithley, June 29, 1912; 1 dau., Margaret Irene. Commd. 2d lt., 1911; promoted through grades to lt. gen., March 1944; construction engr. on Miss., Ohio, Kanawha, Monongahela and Alleghany Rivers, Panama Canal, 1911-12; Corps of Engrs. in Mexico, 1914, Hawaii, 1915-17, overseas, 1917-19; dist. engr. Newport, R.I., 1919-20, Wilmington, N.C., 1930-33, Rock Island, Ill., 1933-35; instr. engring., Inf. Sch., 1920-22; asst. engr. commr., D.C., 1922-26; asst. maintenance engr., Panama Canal, 1927-30; chief regional engr., W.P.A., Chicago, 1935-36; U.S. del. Permanent Internat. Assn. Navigation Congresses, Brussels, Belgium, 1936; resident mem. bd. engrs. for rivers and harbors, Washington, 1937-46, v.p., Panama R.R. Co., 1940-41 (dir. since 1940), engr. of maintenance since Oct. 1942. Deputy Supreme Allied Comdr., S.E.A.C., Feb. 1944; comdg. gen. India-Burma Theatre, June 1945; apptd. chief engrs., Army U.S., with rank of maj. gen. for period of 4 yrs., Sept. 1945. Decorated D.S.M. with two Oak Leaf Clusters, Silver Star with Oak Leaf Cluster. Mem. A.I.A., Soc. Am. Mil. Engrs. Presbyterian. Clubs: Army and Navy, Army and Navy Country (Washington); Gymkhana (New Delhi, India). Home: Washington, D.C. *

WHEELER, ROBERT WAYNE, lawyer; b. Columbus, Ohio, Dec. 10, 1901; s. Wayne B. and Ella Belle (Candy) W.; A.B., A.M., Oberlin Coll., 1923; J.D., Harvard, 1926; m. Grace Mary Strickland, Apr. 14, 1928. Admitted to Ohio bar, 1926, since practiced in Cleve.; partner firm McAfee, Hanning, Newcomer, Hazlett & Wheeler and predecessor, 1938-67, Squire, Sanders & Dempsey, 1967-77; dir. No. Ohio Lumber & Timber Co. Trustee Oberlin Coll., Cleve. Law Library Assn. Mem. Am., Ohio, Cleve. bar assns., Cleve. C. of C., Phi Beta Kappa. Clubs: Union, Mid-Day, Rowfant, Professional Men's, City (Cleve.). Home: Bratenahl, Ohio. Died Feb. 20, 1977; interred Lake View Cemetery, Cleve.

WHEELER, WALTER HALL, cons. engr.; b. Potsdam, N.Y., Apr. 15, 1883; s. Charles Hall and Frances Spencer (Knowles) W.; E.M., Sch. Mines, U. Minn., 1906; m. Eva M. Blasdell, Feb. 1, 1911; 1 son, Frank Knowles Blasdell (officer, USN ret.). Mining and constrn. engr. Colo. Fuel & Iron Co., Trinidad, Colo., 1906-07; chief engr. and supt. constrn. Dawson Fuel Co., N.M., 1907; partner Jones & Wheeler, Denver, 1907-08; sec., treas., chief engr. Jones-Wheeler-Cranmer Engring Co., 1908-12; mem. Charles H. Wheeler & Son, real estate, bldg. and investments, 1908-31; chmn. Walter H. Wheeler, Inc., structural engrs.; chmn. Wheeler & Tillitt, Inc., cons. engrs., 1969—; cons. practice, Mpls., 1912—, cons. on structural design approximately 860 buildings, bridges, grain elevators throughout U.S. and Can. Engr. for Hennepin County, Minn. in charge location design and constrn. of Ft. Snelling-Mendota bridge nr. Mpls (largest multiple rib-arch reinforced concrete bridge in the world), 1923-27; engr. and architect Cream of Wheat Co's factory and gen. office bldg. 2, Mpls., also of reinforced concrete and brick athletic stadium, Univ. N.D.; planned steel erection Shawneetown Bridge over Ohio River. Inventor smooth ceilings system of reinforced concrete; cons. structural engr. U.S. Treasury Dept., U.S. Appraisers' Stores Bldg., Balt.; adv. engr. RFC, 9th District, 1932-40; cons. architect, engr. Mpls. Armory Bldg. Mem. Standard Bldg. Code Com. and com. on design of reinforced concrete slabs of Am. Concrete Inst. In Red Cross and other campaigns, World War. Dir. and chmn. bldg. com. Ft. Snelling Chapel Assn. Awarded Gold medal and citation, Achievement award U. Minn.; award of merit D.A.R.; Engr. of Year award Minn. Soc. Profl. Engrs., 1964. Mem. Am. Soc. C.E., Nat., Minn. socs. profl. engrs., Mpls. Engrs. Club (mem. public affairs com.), Am. Soc. Mil. Engrs., Soc. Exptl. Stress Analysis, Am. Acad. Polit. and Social Scis., Mayflower Soc., S.A.R., Magna Charta Barons, Minn. Assn. Cons. Engrs., Alpha Delta Phi, Theta Tau. Republican. Presbyn. Contbr. on engring. and tech. subjects. Home: Minneapolis MN. *

WHEELER, WARREN ELWELL, educator, physician; b. Youngstown, Ohio, May 10, 1909; s. Harry E. and Ruth (Frederick) W.; B.S., Mt. Union Coll., 1929; M.D., Harvard, 1933; m. Margaret Spellmeyer, Nov. 25, 1939; children—Kenneth, James, Stephen. Pediatric residency Boston Children's Hosp., 1933-37; practice of pediatrics, Dayton, Ohio, 1937-39; cons. pediatrics Mich. Dept. Health, 1939-41; dir. labs. Children's Hosp. Mich., 1941-45; asso. prof. pediatrics Wayne U., 1941-45; former prof. pediatrics and bacteriology Ohio State U.; prof. emeritus, former chmn. dept. pediatrics U. Ky. Med. Sch., Lexington. Mem. Am. Acad. Pediatrics, Fayette County Med. Soc., Am. Pediatric Soc. (pres. 1972), So. Soc. Pediatric Research, Infectious Disease Soc. Chief editor Am. Jour. Diseases Children, 1959-62. Home: Lexington, Ky. Died Oct. 22, 1976.

WHEELOCK, JOHN HALL, author; b. Far Rockaway, L.I., N.Y., 1886; s. William Efner and Emily Charlotte (Hall) W.; A.B., Harvard, 1908; student U. Gottingen, 1909, U. Berlin, 1910; Dr. Humane Letters, Otterbein Coll., 1954; m. Phyllis E. de Kay, Aug. 25, 1940. With Charles Scribner's Sons, pubs., 1911-57, editor, 1926-57, dir., sec., 1932-42, treas., 1942-46, asst. treas., asst. sec., 1946-57; hon. fellow Acad. Am. Poets; v.p. Poetry Soc. Am., 1944-46; hon. cons. Am. letters Library of Congress. Recipient Golden Rose, New Eng. Poetry Soc., 1937; Ridgely Torrence Meml. award, 1956; Signet Soc. medal distinguished achievement in the arts, 1966; gold medal Poetry Soc. Am., 1972. Mem. Nat. Inst. Arts and Letters (v.p.), Am. Acad. Arts and Letters, Phi Beta Kappa. Author, co-author, translator or complier and editor numerous publs., 1905-78; author: Poems Old and New (Borestone Mountain Poetry award 1957), 1956; The Gardener and Other Poems (Bollingen prize for poetry 1962), 1961; What is Poetry?, 1963; Dear Men and Women; New Poems, 1966; By Daylight and In Dream; New and Collected Poems, 1904-70, 1970 (Gold medal for achievement Poetry Soc. Am. 1973); In Love and Song: Poems, 1971; selected and edited, with commentary and introduction: The Face of A Nation: Poetical Passages from the Writings of Thomas Wolfe, 1940; Editor to Author: The Letters of Maxwell E. Perkins, 1950. Editor ann., Poets of Today, 1954-61. Home: New York, N.Y. Died Mar. 22, 1978.

WHERRY, EDGAR (THEODORE), ecologist; b. Phila., Pa., Sept. 10, 1885; s. Albert C. and Elizabeth S. (Doll) W.; B.S., U. of Pa., 1906, Ph.D., 1909; m. E. G. Smith, 1914. Instructor in mineralogy, Lehigh U., 1908-10; asst. prof., 1910-13; asst. curator mineralogy, U.S. Nat. Museum, 1913-17; crystallographer, U.S. Bur. Chemistry, Washington, 1917-23; chemist in charge of crop chemistry, 1923-30; asso. prof. botany, Univ. of Pa., 1930-41; prof. since 1941; lecturer on chemistry, Wagner Free Inst., Phila., 1908-13. Fellow Geol. Soc. America, Mineral Soc. America (pres. 1923), A.A.A.S.; mem. Am. Chem. Soc. (pres. Washington sect., 1927), Pa. Acad. Science (pres. 1935), Phila. Mineral. Soc., Am. Fern Soc. (pres. 1934-38), Bot. Soc. Am. (chmn. Systematic Sect. 1940), Ecol. Soc. Am. Editor of Am. Mineralogist, 1919-21; Bulletin Am. Rock Garden Soc., 1943-47. Author: Wild Flowers of Mt. Desert Island; Guide to Eastern Ferns; Wild Flower Guide; also numerous tech. articles. Home: Philadelphia, Pa. *

WHITAKER, BENJAMIN PALMER, educator; b. Newburgh, N.Y., July 30, 1899; s. Lewis Samuel and Mary E. (Palmer) W.; A.B., Colgate U., 1921; student grad. Sch. Bus. Adminstrn., N.Y. U., 1921-23; M.A., Yale, 1925, Ph.D., 1931; L.H.D. (hon.), Union Coll., Schenectady, 1946; m. Helen Frances Johnson, Sept. 5, 1925; children—Jeanne Carol (dec.), Mary Ann (Mrs. James S. Dolliver), Benjamin Palmer, Robert Lewis. Instr. econs. Yale, 1925-29, vis. prof., 1930-31; tax cons. Brookings Instn., 1931-33; research dir. Conn. Spl. Tax Commn., 1933-35, Conn. Com. Reorgn. State Depts., 1935-37; budget dir. Conn., 1937-39; mem. faculty Union Coll., Schenectady, from 1939, chmn. social studies div., 1940-45, comptroller, 1943-45, acting pres., 1945-46, chmn. econs. dept., 1956-62, Armstrong prof. econs., from 1946. Sec. ways and means com. N.Y. State Assembly, 1949-50; research dir. Com. Fed. Tax Policy, 1953-54; financial cons. majority leader N.Y. State Senate, from 1958; Fulbright lectr. Keio and Sophia univs., Tokyo, 1957. Mgr. Ellis Hosp., Schenectady, 1946-72, treas., 1948-59, v.p., 1959-72; mem. exec. com. Schenectady Community Chest, 1952-53. Bd. dirs. Schenectady YMCA, trustee and treas., 1972-75; vestryman St. George's Episcopal Ch., to 1971. Mem. Nat. Tax Assn., Am. Econs. Assn., Am. Statis. Assn., Am. Finance Assn., Schenectady C. of C. (dir. 1946-49). Republican. Address: Schenectady, N.Y. Deceased.

WHITAKER, FREDERIC, artist, mfr.; b. Providence, Jan. 9, 1891; s. Edward Reginald and Ada (Hands) W.; ed. pub. schs., R.I.; m. Marie E. Tiedge, Sept. 20, 1912; children—Frederic H., Marion E. Whitaker Thurston; m. 2d, Eileen C. Monaghan, 1950. Mfr. religious articles, 1922-50; water color painter; represented in 35 museums, including Met. Mus. Art. Recipient 159 painting honors in nat. and regional exhbns. throughout U.S.; Horatio Alger award, 1974. Fellow Royal Soc. Arts; mem. NAD (council 1952-55, v.p. 1956-57), Internat. Assn. Plastic Arts (v.p. Am. div. 1953-60), Audubon Artists (dir., organizer 1943; pres. 1943-46), Am. Watercolor Soc. (pres. 1949-56), Calif., Phila., Boston, San Diego (hon.) watercolor socs., Nat. Soc. Mural Painters (hon.), Allied Artists Am., Watercolor West (hon.), Council Am. Artists Socs., Artists Fellowship. Clubs: Masons; Water Color (Phila.) (Providence); Nat. Arts, Salmagundi (N.Y.C.); Providence Art. Author: Whitaker on Watercolor, Guide to Painting Better Pictures; The Artist and The Real World; also 85 monographs on prominent artists; contbg. editor Am. Artist mag. Home: La Jolla, Calif. Died Mar. 9, 1980.

WHITAKER, HARRY EMERSON, engr.; b. Northborough, Mass., Aug. 11, 1886; s. Nathaniel Currier and Ella Catherine (Hawes) W.; S.B., Mass. Inst. Tech., 1909; m. Grace Lloyd Francis, May 29, 1914. Special asst. engr., testing and developing locomotives and locomotive superheaters, N.Y. Central Lines, 1909-10; engr. in exptl. and development lab., N.Y. Air Brake Co., Watertown, N.Y., 1910-11; engr. power betterment div., Stone & Webster Engring. Corp., 1911-16; engr., Westinghouse, Church, Kerr, Inc., N.Y. City, 1916-17; supt. power generation, Western Power & Light Co., Boulder, Colo., 1917-18; asst. to chief cons. engr., U.S. Govt. Explosives, New York, Nitro Smokeless Powder Plant, 1918; with Ford, Bacon & Davis, Inc., N.Y.C., 1918-51, chief engr., 1937-51, dir., 1941-51, sr. v.p., 1950-51, ret.; dir., v.p. Ford, Bacon & Davis, S.A., 1945-51; retired, 1951; mem. bd. govs., exec. com., ways and means com. chmn. plant com., v.p. Monmouth Medical Center, Long Branch, N.J., 1951—; chief engineer self-liquidating constrn. loans RFC, 1932-34; mem. adv. bd. on utilization of surplus indsl. facilities, War Dept., 1944. Registered profl. engr., N.Y., N.J., O., W. Va., Ky., Tex., Cal., Ill., Michigan and Massachusetts. Fellow Am. Soc. Mech. Engrs., Am. Geog. Society; mem. Engrs. Soc. of Western Pa., Soc. Am. Mil. Engrs. Army Ordnance Assn., Sigma Alpha Epsilon. Republican. Conglist. Clubs: Engineers, Technology, City Midday. Home: Sea Girt, N.J. *

WHITAKER, U. A., mfg. exec.; b. Lincoln, Kans., Mar. 22, 1900; s. Oliver Barr and Annetta Ruth (Boyle) W.; B.S. in Mech. Engring., M.I.T., 1923; B.S. in Elec. Engring., Carnegie Inst. Tech., 1929; J.D., Cleve. Law Sch., 1935; Sc.D., Elizabethtown Coll., 1954; LL.D., Gettysburg Coll., 1967; m. Helen Margaret Fisher, Sept. 26, 1944; children—Ruth (Holmes), Portia (Shumaker). Spl. engr. Westinghouse Air Brake Co., 1923-29; dir. devel. and design Hoover Co., 1929-38; dir. research and engring. Am. Machine & Foundry Co., 1938-41; founder, pres., dir. AMP Inc. (formerly Aircraft-Marine Products, Inc.), 1941-62, chmn. bd., 1962-75; chmn. bd. operating subsidiaries in France, Australia, Germany, Italy, Holland, Eng., Japan, Mexico, Spain, Sweden, Can., U.S., Argentina, Brazil, Siwtzerland, 1962-75; chmn. bd. affiliate Pamcor, Inc., Rio Piedras, P.R.,

1962-75. Life mem. corp. M.I.T., 1966-75; distinguished fellow Cleve. Clin. Found., 1972-75. Recipient Eli Whitney Meml. award Soc. Mfg. Engrs., 1970; Distinguished Achievement award Carnegie-Mellon U. Fellow I.E.E.E. (life mem.), ASME; mem. A.A.A.S. Clubs: N.Y. Yacht (N.Y.C.); Stamford Yacht; Key Largo Anglers; Ocean Reef; Port Royal Beach; Met. Home: Harrisburg, Pa. Died Sept. 16, 1975.

WHITBREAD, FRANK GEORGE, ins. exec.; b. Eng., June 30, 1904; s. Edward Jabez and Margaret Lowe (Thomson) W.; B.A., U. Manitoba, 1924; m. Ruth Groff, June 20, 1931; children—Edward Peter, Frances Rosalie (Mrs. Ed. Hamman). Came to U.S., 1947. Held various positions with Gt. W. Life Assurance Company, Winnipeg, Can., 1924-43, asso. actuary, 1943-47; v.p. Reliance Life Ins. Co., Pitts., 1947-69, dir., 1952-54; 2d v.p. Lincoln Nat. Life Ins. Co., Ft. Wayne, Ind., 1964-69. Fellow Soc. Actuaries; mem. Casualty Actuarial Soc., Canadian Assn. Actuaries. Author articles. Home: Fort Wayne, Ind. Died Dec. 8, 1979; buried Lindenwood Cemetery, Fort Wayne.

WHITCOMB, ERNEST MILLER, banker; b. Worcester, Mass., Feb. 28, 1882; s. George Henry and Abbie (Estabrook) W.; A.B., Amherst Coll., 1904, A.M., 1907; grad. study U. of Jena, Germany, 1904, Harvard Law Sch., 1904-05; m. Anna Gauntlett; children—Stephen, Jane; m. 2d, Catherine Carduff. Began in banking, Boston and Chicago, 1905; v.p. First Nat. Bank of Amherst (Mass.), 1910-16, president since 1916; president Wachusett Investment Co.; chmn. bd. and dir. United States Envelope Co. Mem. Mass. Vol. Militia, 1905, National Guard New York, 1907-11. Served with Am. Red Cross, Toul, France, 1918. Trustee and treas., Jones Library, Inc. Mem. Phi Beta Kappa, Psi Upsilon. Republican. Conglist. Clubs: Colony (Springfield, Mass.); Union League (New York); Laurentian (Canada); Monterey (Calif.) Peninsula Country; University (Chicago). *

WHITE, CARL FREDERICK, customs collector; b. nr. Warnock, Belmont Co., O., Apr. 20, 1884; s. Edwin and Mary (D'Ennis) W.; student Kan. State Tchrs. Coll., 1902-04, U. So. Cal., 1912-15; m. Verna Claire Thurston, Oct. 2, 1905; children—Carl Thurston, Olive Mary (Mrs. Russell H. Maddox). Formerly member of reportorial staff Kansas City Jour., Kansas City Star Times, Kansas Jour. Post; mng. editor Kansas City Kansan, Herald Express, Los Angeles, Glendale (Cal.) News Press; became mng. editor Santa Monica Evening Outlook, 1929; now U.S. collector of customs, 27th dist. Served as lt. and capt., U.S. Army, 1917-19, maj. Kan. N.G., 1920-24, lt. col., O.R.C., 1924-44. Mem. Asso. Press Mng. Editors Assn., Asso. Press. News Exec. Council Cal. and Nev., Am. Legion, Sigma Delta Chi. Mason (32 deg., Shriner). Presbyn. Club: Del Mar.*

WHITE, CAROLINA, operatic soprano, b. Dorchester, Mass., Dec. 2, 1886; d. James E. and Medora (Wallace) W.; grad. Brighton High Sch., 1902; studied singing with Weldon Hunt, Boston, 2 yrs., and prepared for opera 6 mos. under Frederick Roberti and Carlo Sebastiani, Naples, Italy; m. Paul Longone, of Naples, Italy, Sept. 1910 (divorced Apr. 1922). Début in Wagner's "Dusk of the Gods," in San Carlo Opera House, Naples, 1908, later appearing in "Aïda," "Cavalleria Rusticana" and "Mephistofele"; returned to America for further study; went abroad and appeared in winter of 1909-10, in chief opera houses of Italy, and sang leading parts in "La Wally," "Manon," "Aïda," "Iris," "Tosca," "Madame Butterfly," "Hérodiade," etc. Joined Chicago Opera Co., fall of 1910; created rôle of Minnie in "The Girl of the Golden West," and appeared in Boston in same rôle Feb. 24, 1911; also created part of Susanne in "Secret of Susanne," at Metropolitan Opera House, New York, same season; created part of Maliella in "The Jewels of the Madonna," singing in New York, Chicago and Philadelphia. Has a repertoire of 45operas. Address: New York, N.Y. *

WHITE, CHARLES MCELROY, steel co. exec.; b. Oakland, Md., June 13, 1891; s. Charles F. and Estella (Jarboe) W.; B.S., U. Md., 1913, D.Eng. (hon.), 1949; student Carnegie Inst. Tech., 1914-17, E.D. (hon.), Case Inst. Tech., 1955; LL.D., Harding Coll., 1956; H.H.D., Trinity Coll., 1957; D.Sc., John Carroll U. 1957; Dr. of Industry, Youngstown U., 1961; m. Helen Gordon Bradley, Sept. 4, 1918; 1 dau., Jean (Mrs. Robert L. Munger, Jr.). Millwright helper, Jones & Laughlin Steel Co., 1913-15, supt. sintering plant, 1915, asst. supt. blast furnace, 1916-17, master mechanic, 1917, asst. to gen. supt., 1919, supt. Monongahela Connecting R.R., 1920-27, asst. supt. Aliquippa (Pa.) works, 1927-29, gen. supt. Aliquippa works, 1929; asst. vice pres. Republic Steel Corp., 1930-35, v.p. ops., 1935-45; pres. Republic Steel Corporation, 1945-56, chief executive officer, 1955-60, chmn. bd., 1956-60, dir., hon. chmn., 1960-77; dir. Sherwin-Williams Co., Cleve. Trust Co. Mem. exec. bd. Greater Cleve. council Boy Scouts Am., nat. asso. Boys' Clubs Am. Trustee Fenn Coll., Bluecoats, Inc., Case Inst. Tech., Air Force Mus. Found., Automotive Safety Found., Freedoms Found. at Valley Forge; hon. v.p. Am. Iron and Steel Inst. Vice chmn. Rep. Nat. Finance Com. Decorated Am. Iron and Steel Inst. Medal, 1937; Crusade for Freedom medal, 1954; Am. Soc. Metals Research medal, 1956; Freedoms Found. medal; Silver Beaver award, Boy Scouts Am., 1959, Silver Buffalo award, 1961; Benjamin F. Fairless award, 1960; Gary Meml. Medal, Am. Iron and Steel Inst., 1961. Trustee Nat. Indsl. Conf. Bd., chmn., 1959-61, councillor, 1962-77. Mem. Sigma Nu. Clubs: Union, Pepper Pike Golf, Country, Chagrin Valley Hunt, The 50 (Cleve.); Links (N.Y.C.); Bath and Tennis, Everglades (Palm Beach, Fla.). Home: Shaker Heights, Ohio. Died Jan. 10, 1977.

WHITE, CHARLES WILBERT, artist; b. Chgo., Apr. 2, 1918; s. Charles and Ethel (Gary) W.; student (Inst. scholar), Art Inst., Chgo., 1937, Art Student's League, N.Y.C., 1942, Taller de Grafica and Esmeralda Sch. Painting and Sculpture, Mexico City, 1947; Dr. Art (hon.), Columbia Coll., Chgo., 1969, L.H.D., 1969; m. Frances Barrett, May 31, 1950; children—Jessica, Ian. Instr. Southside Art Center, Chgo., 1939-40; artist-in-residence Howard U., 1945; instr. Workshop Sch. Art, N.Y.C., 1950-53, Otis Art Inst., Los Angeles, 1965; exhibited in numerous one man shows including Heritage Gallery, Los Angeles, Forum Gallery, N.Y.C., Krannert Art Mus., High Mus. Art, Montgomery Mus. Art, Hunter Mus. Art, Palm Beach Art Inst., exhibited in numerous group shows U.S. and abroad, including Library of Congress, 1941, San Francisco Mus. Art, 1946, Whitney Mus., 1951, Am. Acad. Arts and Letters, 1952, Met. Mus. Art, 1952, Smithsonian Instn., 1954, Internat. Exhibit Art, Germany, 1959, Scripps Coll., 1966, Association pour la Racontre des Cultures, Paris, 1966, Fine Arts Gallery, San Diego, 1966, Howard U., Morgan State Coll., 1967, Fisk U., 1968, U. Dayton, 1968, Wilberforce Coll., 1968, Wright State U., 1968, Dayton Art Inst., 1968, Boston Mus. Fine Arts, 1968, Jackson State Coll., 1968, Nat. Center Afro-Am. Artists, 1970, Los Angeles County Mus., 1971, Monterey Peninsula Mus. Art, 1971, Los Angeles County Mus., 1976, High Mus. Art, 1977, Dallas Mus. Art, 1977, Bklyn. Mus. Art, 1977, Municipal Art Mus. Los Angeles, 1977, El Museo de Arte Moderne, Colombia, 1977; represented in permanent collections, including Wichita (Kans.) Art Mus., Met. Mus. Art, Whitney Mus. Art, Smithsonian Inst., Los Angeles County Mus. Art, Newark Mus. Art, Dresden Mus. Art; executed murals Hampton (Va.) Inst., Los Angeles Pub. Library, 1976. Exec. bd. Black Acad. Arts and Letters, Nat. Center Afro-Am. Artists, Los Angeles City Commn. on Art. Recipient numerous awards; honored by naming of Charles White Park, Altadena, Calif., 1980. Mem. N.A.D. Contbr. to art books, publs. Address: Los Angeles. Died Oct. 3, 1979.

WHITE, E(DWARD) LAURENCE, investment banker; b. Lowell, Mass., Aug. 11, 1884; s. Edward L. and Ida V. (Mosely) W.; grad. St. Paul's Sch., Concord, N.H., 1903; student Harvard, 1904-06; m. Harriet W. Lancashire, Apr. 29, 1911; children—E. Laurence, Sarah White (Mrs. William G. Robinson). Began as mining engr. and operator; entered banking business, 1919, and since engaged in banking as founder and partner firm of Watson & White, New York, N.Y.; pres. and dir. Investors and Traders, Inc., Watite Corp.; past dir. Internat. Utilities Corp. Clubs: Racquet and Tennis, Bankers (New York); Harvard (Boston). Home: Beverly Farms, Mass. *

WHITE, EDWARD C(LENDENNING), naval med. officer (ret.); b. Riverton, N.J., Oct. 1, 1883; s. Hugh Clendenning and Martha Austin (Pancoast) W.; M.D., Univ. of Pa., 1905; m. Gladys Alice Merritt, June 2, 1908; children—Gladys (Mrs. George W. Peterson), Edward Clendenning, Richard Pancoast, Robert, Kathleen (Mrs. Leo Smith Madlem). Commd. lt. j.g., U.S. Navy Med. Corps., 1905, and advanced through grades to rear adm., 1942; ret. from active service, 1946. Fellow A.C.S. and A.C.P. mem. A.M.A. Home: Long Beach, Calif. *

WHITE, FRANK KIGGINS, advertising exec.; b. Washington, Sept. 24, 1899; s. William W. and Mary (Kiggins) W.; ed. George Washington U.; m. Doris R. Booth, Apr. 21, 1928; children—Richard B., David L. Accountant, Lybrand, Ross Bros. & Montgomery, 1921-24; asst. to pres. Union News Co., 1924-29; treas. Literary Guild of America, 1929-35, Stage Publishing Co., 1935; treas. and bus. mgr. Newsweek, Inc., 1936-37; became treas. C.B.S., 1937, vice pres. and treas., 1942-47, president Columbia Records, Inc., 1947-49; pres., dir. Mutual Broadcasting System, 1949-52; v.p., gen. mgr. N.B.C., 1952, pres., dir., 1953; chmn. McCann-Erickson Corp. (Internat.) subs. McCann-Erickson, Inc., 1953-56; sr. v.p., treas., chmn. finance com. McCann-Erickson, Inc., 1957-59, sr. vice pres., vice chairman executive policy com., sr. mgmt. officer several major divs. co., 1959-60; vice chmn. bd. Interpublic, Inc., 1960-66; mktg. cons. Fgn. Agrl. Service, 1962-74; hon. dir. Advt. Council, Better Bus. Bur. of N.Y.; dir. Broadcast Music, Inc. Trustee, treas. N.Y. Housing Trust. Student flight ofcr., USN, 1918. Mem. Armed Forces Adv. Council for N.E. Area. Recipient citation Sec. Agr., 1968. Mem. Am. Assn. Advt. Agys. (dir.), Nat. Assn. Broadcasters (dir.), Sigma Nu. Republican. Clubs: Players (N.Y.); Larchmont Yacht; Goose Creek Country (Leesburg). Home: Leesburg, Va. Died Nov. 12, 1979.

WHITE, FRED RAY, civil engr.; b. Selma, Ia., May 21, 1884; s. Orin Ira and Matilda Ellen (Stephenson) W.; B.S. in civil engring., Ia. State Coll., 1907; m. Mary M. de Hart, Oct. 30, 1912; children—Margaret E., James W. Rodman Fla. East Coast Ry., 1907-08; instrumentman and party chief Morgan Engring. Co., Memphis, Tenn., 1910-11; bridge inspector Ia. State Highway Commn., 1908-10, field engr., 1011-16, road engr., 1916-19, chief engr., 1919-52; cons. engineer since September 15, 1952; director Ames Trust and Savings Bank. Member American Society of Civil Engrs., Am. Assn. State Highway Officials. Republican. *

WHITE, GEORGE PHILLIPS, lawyer; b. Centreville, Ala., Aug. 4, 1915; s. James Bailey and Berta (Jones) W.; LL.B., U. Ala., 1939; m. Betty Ann Poag, Nov. 28, 1952; children—George Phillips III, Allison, Rachel. Admitted to Ala. bar, 1939; with Employers Liability Assurance Corp., 1940-43; practice law, Centreville, 1946-77; dist. atty. Bibb County, 1965-77; Pres. Abstract Co., Inc.; sec. Centreville Oil Co., Inc., Belcher Motor Co., Inc. Past mem. Ala. Regional Bd. Library Trustees; past chmn. bd. Bibb County Hosp. Assn. Served to lt. USNR, 1943-46; PTO. Decorated Presdl. Unit citation, 5 battle stars. Mem. Am., 4th Jud. Circuit (past pres.), Ala. bar assns., U. Ala. Alumni Assn. (pres. Bibb County chpt. 1962). Presbyn. Home: Centreville, Ala. Died Mar. 4, 1977.

WHITE, JAMES ASA, minister; b. Quitman, Miss., Aug. 24, 1886; s. Thomas D. and Sallie K. (Boughan) W.; A.B., U. of Louisville, Ky., 1913, A.M., 1914; Th.M., Southern Bapt. Theol. Sem., 1914, Th.D., 1915; children—Mary Rosalind, James Asa, Charlotte Virginia, Ruth Helen. General Sec. Bapt. Young People's Union of America, 1915-23; pres. Colorado Woman's Coll., Denver, Sept. 1, 1923, to Aug. 1, 1925; minister Thousand Oaks Bapt. Ch., Berkeley, Calif., 1925-29; gen. sec. Northern Calif. Council Religious Edn. since 1929; exec. sec. Yosemite Nat. Park Ch. since 1929. Mem. Phi Delta Kappa, Pi Gamma Mu. Democrat. Author: B.Y.P.U. Handbook, 1917; our B.Y.P.U., 1921; The Junior Society in Action, 1923; Christian EducationObjectives, 1932. Home: Yosemite National Park, Calif.*

WHITE, JAMES CLARKE, neurosurgeon; b. Vienna, Austria, Feb. 6, 1895; s. Charles J. and Olivia (Richardson) W.; A.B., Harvard, 1917; M.D., 1923; m. Camilla Morgan, July 21, 1917 (dec. Apr. 17, 1981); children—Patricia (Mrs. P.M.W. Smith), Camilla (Mrs. C.W. Churchill), Michael M. Intern, resident Mass. Gen. Hosp., Boston, 1923-27, chief neurosurg. service, 1941-61, sr. cons. 1972-81; prof. surgery Harvard Med. Sch., 1955-61, emeritus, 1961-81; cons. Beth Israel Hosp., Boston, Capt., M.C., U.S. Navy, ret. Fellow A.C.S.; mem. Am. Surg. Assn., Am. Neurol. Assn., Am. Assn. Neurol. Surgeons, Soc. Neurol. Surgeons, Assn. Research Nervous and Mental Disease, Internat. Soc. Surgery, Academie de Chirurgie (Paris), Societe de Chirurgie de Lyon, Soc. de Neurochirurgie de Langue Francaise, American Acad. Arts and Sci. Author: (with Smithwick and Simeone) The Autonomic Nervous System, 1952; (with Sweet) Pain: Its Mechanisms and Neurosurgical Control, 1955; Pain and the Neurosurgeon: A Forty Year Experience, 1969. Home: Brookline, Mass. Died Jan. 7, 1981.

WHITE, JEROME BAKER, lawyer; b. San Francisco, Aug. 11, 1883; s. Harlow H. and Nellie S. (Brown) W.; A.B., U. Cal. at Berkeley, 1904; LL.B., Hastings Coll. of Law, 1906; m. Lucile O. Kaiser, July 10, 1906; children—Edna (wife of Lt. Comdr. Joseph Meredith, U.S. Navy), Robert J. Admitted to Cal. bar, 1936. Dir. Morris Plan Co. of San Francisco, Albert S. Samuels Co. Home: San Francisco. *

WHITE, JOHN WILLIAM, agrl. economist; b. Hamburg, Ark., Apr. 3, 1911; s. John Tyler and Willie Pearl (Bailey) W.; student Ark. A. & M. Coll., 1931-34; B.S.A., U. Ark., 1935; M.S., U. Minn., 1939, Ph.D., 1943; m. Trannye Mae Odom, June 24, 1939. Student clerk U. Ark., 1934, field agt., 1935, asst. county agt., 1935-37, co-op. research supr., 1938-39, instr., 1940-42, asst. prof., 1942, extension economist in marketing, 1942-44, supt. rice sta., 1944-47, prof., head dept. rural econs. and sociology, 1947-53; prof., asso. dir. Agrl. Exptl. Sta., 1953-59, v.p. agr., 1959-74; conducted agrl. market research study, Republic of Panama, summer 1952. Recipient Distinguished 4-H Alumni award, 1957, Man-of-Year in Ark. Agr., Progressive Farmer, 1957; award outstanding contbns. to Am. agr. Fed. Land Banks, 1967. Mem. Am. Farm Econs. Assn., Southwestern Social Sci. Assn. (pres. 1955-56), So. Agrl. Workers Assn. Baptist. Rotarian. Author expt. sta. bulls. Home: Fayetteville, Ark. Died Mar. 13, 1976.

WHITE, LELAND MARION, rubber co. exec.; b. Louisburg, Kan., Dec. 21, 1914; s. Levi D. and Myrtle (Cook) W.; Sc.B., Ottawa (Kan.) U., 1936; M.A., U. Kan., 1938, Ph.D., 1940; postgrad. Harvard, 1953; m. 2d, Grace Godfrey, Aug. 23, 1974; 1 dau., LeAnne (Mrs. Roy W. Ritchie). Chemist, Uniroyal, Inc., Wayne, N.J., 1940-48, research supr., 1948-53, asst. dir. research and devel. dept., 1953-58, dir. research and devel. dept., 1958-62, v.p., N.Y.C., 1962-66, v.p. research, 1966-74. Mem. Am. Chem. Soc., Am. Inst. Physics. Conglist. Club: Forest Hill Field (trustee) (Bloomfield, N.J.). Home: Clifton, N.J. Died Oct. 20, 1978; buried Louisburg, Kans.

WHITE, LEWIS CHARLES, govt. ofcl.; b. Morrison, Ill., Dec. 27, 1915; s. Lewis Woody and Reka (Laman) W.; ed. high sch., Holland, Mich.; m. Lillian May Ard, Nov. 26, 1936; children—Daniel Lyman, Paul Judson. Personnel officer, civilian personnel sect. Hdqrs. SCAP, Dept. Army, Tokyo, Japan, 1946-54; personnel officer U.S. Operations Mission, New Delhi, India, 1954-56; regional personnel officer ICA, Washington, 1956-58; exec. officer U.S. Operations Mission to Iran, Tehran, 1958-61; personnel office AID, Washington, 1961-73. Episcopalian. Mason. Club: American. Home: Alexandria, Va. Died Feb. 2, 1973; interred Pine Grove Cemetery, Sault Sainte Marie, Mich.

WHITE, LUCIEN WENDELL, librarian; b. Hillsdale, Ill., Nov. 16, 1914; s. Charles J. and Dora M. (Ellison) W.; A.B., Augustana Coll., 1935; student U. Ia., 1936, 40, Middlebury Coll., 1941, Sorbonne, 1947, U. Grenoble, 1949; A.M., U. Ill., 1944, Ph.D., 1947, M.S., 1954; m. Lois Samuelson, Aug. 6, 1949; children—David, Elizabeth. Tchr. modern langs. Augustana Coll., 1939-45, prof. French, 1945-53, librarian, 1954-58, editor library publs., 1954-58; vis. prof. library sci. U. Ill., summer 1957, prof. library adminstrn., 1958-75, library asso., dir. pub. service depts., 1958-65, dir. pub. service depts., 1965-68, asso. dean library adminstrn., 1968-71, univ. librarian, 1971-75. Mem. bd. Champaign Pub. Library, 1961-70, pres., 1969-70; mem. Ill. Library Adv. Council, 1965-71, Ill. Library Adv. Commn., 1971-75; chmn. council dirs. State U. Libraries Ill., 1972-73; bd. dirs. Center for Research Libraries, 1971-75. Mem. alumni bd. Augustana Coll., 1969-72. Mem. Am., Ill. (pres. 1949-50) assns. tchrs. French, Am. Assn. U. Profs. (pres. Augustana chpt. 1952-58), A.L.A., Am. Assn. Higher Edn., Assn. Coll. and Research Libraries (chmn. Eastern European resources com. 1972, mem. fgn. newspaper microfilm com. 1972-75), Ill. Library Assn. (pres. 1963-64, mem. legislative com. 1964-75), Modern Lang. Assn., Augustana Hist. Soc. (treas. 1956-58), Soc. Advancement Scandinavian study, Bibliog. Soc. Am., Am. Soc. Information Sci., Phi Beta Kappa (pres. Gamma chpt. 1962-63), Pi Delta Phi, Beta Phi Mu (pres. Alpha chpt. 1959-60). Contbr. articles to jours. Pub. bd. Library Trends, 1958-75. Home: Champaign, Ill. Died 1975.

WHITE, MARTIN MARSHALL, prof. psychology; b. Kyle, Tex., Sept. 23, 1904; s. Martin Mullins and Jean (Carpenter) W.; . A.B., U. Tex., 1925, M.A., 1926; Ph.D., U. Chicago, 1930; m. Dorritt Stumberg, Sept. 5, 1928; children—Dorritt Jean, Marshall Kurt. Tutor dept. psychology, U. Tex., 1924-25, instr., 1925-26; fellow dept. psychology, U. Chicago, 1926-28; asst. prof. psychology, U. Okla., 1928-30, U. Ky., 1930-31, asso. prof., 1931-33, prof., from 1934, acting personnel dir., 1942-45, acting asst. dean, Coll. Arts and Sciences, 1942-43, associate dean, 1944-47, dean, from 1947. Pres. Ky. Council for the Handicapped; mem. bd. dirs., Ky. State Mental Hygiene Assn.; chmn. Southern Academic Deans' Conference, 1949-50; chmn. div. arts and scis. Assn. Land-Grant Colls. and Univs., 1953-54. Mem. N.E.A., Fayette (Ky.) Co. Social Planning Council, Am. Psychol. Assn., Midwest Psychol. Assn., Phi Beta Kappa, Sigma Xi, Phi Eta Sigma. Meth. Democrat. Clubs: Kiwanis, Research. Author: (with Dorritt S. White) A Laboratory Manual for Beginning Psychology, 1932. Home: Lexington, Ky. Died Feb. 27, 1980.

WHITE, MILTON GRANDISON, sci. researcher, educator; b. Claremont, Calif., Jan. 12, 1910; s. Francis H. and Anna (Fairchild) W.; Ph.D., U. Calif. at Berkeley, 1935; NRC fellow Princeton, 1935-37; m. Elizabeth Ann Higley, Jan. 22, 1935 (dec. Oct. 1972); children—Ann Fairchild, Margaret Wynter, David Milton (dec.); m. 2d, Nancy C. Gryzbek, Jan. 1, 1973; 1 dau., Janice M. Gryzbek. Mem. faculty Princeton, 1937-40, prof. physics, 1945-49, Eugene Higgins prof. physics, 1949-79, dir. Princeton and Pa. Proton Synchroton Project, 1956-79; radar research Mass. Inst. Tech., 1940-45, head transmitter div. radiation lab., 1941-43, head airborne radar div., 1943-45; cons. Brookhaven Nat. Lab., 1947-79; vis. prof. Inst. for Advanced Study, 1971-73. Research elementary particles, nuclear physics and high energy accelerators, also high energy heavy ions for cancer therapy. Bd. dirs. Central N.J. Multiple Sclerosis Soc.; trustee Associated Univs., Inc., 1967-79; trustee, chmn. bd. Univ. Research Assn., 1975-79; pres. Univs. Research Assn., 1979. Recipient Certificate of Merit, 1946. Mem. Am. Phys. Soc., AAAS, AAUP, Phi Beta Kappa, Sigma Xi. Address: Princeton, N.J. Died Oct. 16, 1979.

WHITE, MINOR MARTIN, educator; b. Mpls., July 9, 1908; s. Charles Henry and Florence (Martin) W.; B.S., U. Minn., 1933. Instr. photography Calif. Sch. Fine Arts, San Francisco, 1946-52; courator, editor in photography George Eastman House, Rochester, N.Y., 1952-55; lectr. photography Rochester Inst. Tech., 1955-64; prof. photography M.I.T., Cambridge, 1965-76. Bd. dirs. Soc. of Photographic Edn., Friends of Photography; bd. advisers Imageworks-Sch. and Center of Photography. Served with inf., AUS, 1941-45. Decorated Bronze Star, Philippine Liberation medal with 2 Bronze Stars. Names Guggenheim fellow, 1970. Author: Mirrors, Messages, Manifestations, Apertures, 1969; Zone System Manual, 1956; New Zone System Manual, 1975. Editor: Aperture quar. photography, 1952-76. Contbr. articles to profl. jours. Home: Arlington, Mass. Died June 24, 1976.

WHITE, ORLAND EMILE, biologist; b. Sibley, Ia., April 25, 1885; s. Henry Clay and Margaret Belle (Rush) W.; B.S., S.D. State Coll., 1909, M.S., 1911; M.S., Harvard, 1912; Sc.D., Bussey Instn. of Harvard, 1913; m. Loto Rollinstall Underwood, July, 1913; children—Margaret Underwood (Mrs. Dean Winchester), Prudence Wayne (Mrs. James Quarles). Nurseryman, Yankton, S.D., 1904; research asst., S.D. State Coll. and experiment station, 1909-10, instr. in botany, 1910-11; lab. teaching asst. in botany, Radcliffe Coll., 1912, in genetics, 1913; asst. curator plant breeding Brooklyn Botanic Garden, 1913-15, curator, 1916-24, curator plant breeding and economic plants, 1924-27; collaborator U.S. Dept. of Agr., 1915-18, 1919-23, specialist, 1918-19; botanist Mulford Exploration of Amazon Basin Expedition, 1921-22; prof. agrl. biology and dir. Blandy Exptl. Farm, U. of Va., since 1927; research scholar, U.S. Ednl. Found., in Burma and vis. prof., Univ. Coll., Mandalay and U. of Rangoon, 1950-51. Fellow A.A.A.S.; mem. Nat. Research Council com. on fellowships in biology and agr., 1943-45, chmn. panel on botany, growth com., med. div., 1945-46; mem. Botanical Soc. of Am. (editorial bd., 1920-21, council mem. genetics sect., 1928, chmn. southeastern sect., 1943-45), Am. Naturalist, Am. Genetics Assn., Genetics Soc. of Am., Tenn. Acad. Science, Washington Acad. Science, Va. Acad. Science (chmn. biol. sect., 1931), Rock Garden Soc. of Am. (chmn. South Atlantic region, 1936-38, 1941-43), John Burroughs Memorial Assn. (2d vice pres., 1925-28, mem. bd. dirs. since 1928), Sigma Xi. Clubs: Genetics (pres. 1944-46), Harvard (Washington); Explorer's. Author numerous articles on plant genetics and cytology, origin of cultivated plants, cytogenetics of pisum, biology of fasciation, temperature tolerance in relation to mutation and geog. distbn. Mem. ed. bd. Am. Jour. of Botany, 1920-21; editor genetics sect. Bot. Abstracts, 1922-26, plant genetics sect., 1927-50. Sec. of round table conf. on agr. and population increase, Inst. of Politics, Williamstown, Mass., 1925; rep. Brooklyn Botanic Garden on Inst. for Research in Tropical Am., 1923-27. Address: Charlottesville, Va. *

WHITE, ORRIN AUGUSTINE, artist; b. Hanover, Ill., Dec. 5, 1883; s. Albert Brown and Martha (Reynolds) W.; B.S., U. of Notre Dame, 1902; grad. Phila. Sch. Applied Art, 1906; m. Margaret E. Fitschen, Nov. 27, 1923; children—Martha Ann, Margaret Eleanor. Silver medal, San Francisco Expn., 1915, San Diego Expn., 1915; Henry Huntington landscape prize, Calif. Art Club, 1921. Prin. works; Sierra Peaks, Los Angeles Museum; Sunset Glow, Cleveland Museum. Served as 2d lt. engrs., Camouflage, World War. Republican. Catholic. Clubs: California Art, Pasadena Fine Arts. Home: Pasadena, Calif. *

WHITE, ROBERT ARTHUR, lawyer; b. Fort Worth, Sept. 7, 1929; s. Robbie O. and Ethel Lois (Cole) W.; B.S. in Engring., Tex. A. and M. U., 1950; J.D., So. Meth. U., 1956; m. Nancy Elizabeth Whitten, Apr. 25, 1959; children—Kirkwood C., Nancy E., Mark H., John B. Instr. engring. So. Meth. U., 1955-56; admitted to Tex. bar, 1956; with firm Baker & Botts, Houston, 1956-69, firm Arnold, White & Durkee, Houston, 1969-77. Served to capt. C.E., AUS, 1951-53. Registered profl. engr., Tex.; Patent prize Patent Resources Group, 1977. Mem. Am. Bar Assn., State Bar Tex. (chmn. sect. patent, trademark and copyright 1974-75), Am., Houston patent law assns., Tex. Soc. Profl. Engrs. Club: University (Houston). Author: Patent Litigation: Procedure and Tactics, 1971. Home: Houston, Tex. Died Oct. 26, 1977; buried Meml. Oaks Cemetery, Houston.

WHITE, ROLLIE HOWARD, JR., fgn. service officer; b. Washington, Jan. 15, 1919; s. Rollie Howard and Minerva (Carr) W.; student U. Md., 1937-38; LL.B., National U., 1942; student Russian Inst., Columbia, 1954-55; m. Doris Jean Fitch, Oct. 18, 1952; children—Rollie Howard 3d, Thomas Freeman, Campbell Carlyle, Wesley Scot. Joined U.S. Fgn. Service 1942; vice consul, Mombasa, Kenya, 1942-44, Kabul, Afghanistan, 1944; asst. attache, Pretoria, S. Africa, 1948, Prague, Czechoslovakia, 1948-49; attache, Cairo, Egypt, 1949-51; 2d sec., consul, Moscow, USSR, 1955-57; consul, Frankfurt, W. Germany, 1958-62; assigned Officer Under Sec. Polit. Affairs, State Dept., 1962-66; polit. counselor, Vienna, 1966-68, dep. chief mission, 1968-77. Home: Washington, D.C. Deceased.

WHITE, THEO BALLOU, architect; b. Norfolk, Va., Nov. 26, 1903; s. Wilson and Patsey (Ballou) W.; B.Arch., U. Pa., 1925; m. Anne Wood Linn, Apr. 24, 1942. Asso. Paul P. Cret, Architect, Phila., 1926-39; partner Hatfield, Martin & White, Phila., 1939-78; works include Magee Meml. Hosp., Faculty Club of U. Pa. Dir. Phila. Art Alliance; trustee New Sch. Music (Phila.). Served to maj. C.E., AUS, 1942-45. Fellow in Am. Studies. Fellow A.I.A. Author: Colonial Mansions of Fairmount Park, 1932; Richmond, City on the James, 1933; History of Philadelphia Art Alliance, 1955. Editor: Nineteenth Century Architecture in Philadelphia, 1953; Paul Phillipe Cret, Architect and Teacher, 1973; Fairmount: Philadelphia's Park, 1975. Home: Villanova, Pa. Died Dec. 2, 1978.

WHITE, WILLIAM LINDSAY, newspaperman; b. Emporia, Kans., June 17, 1900; s. William Allen and Sallie (Lindsay) W.; student Kansas U., 1918-20; A.B., Harvard, 1924; m. Kathrine Klinkenberg, Apr. 29, 1931; 1 dau., Barbara. Reporter on Emporia Gazette, 1914, later circulation mgr., mng. editor, editorial writer, asso. editor pub., editor, 1944-73; staff Washington Post, 1935, Fortune Mag., 1937; war corr. for 40 Am. daily newspapers, also rep. CBS, European corr., 1939-40; Christmas, 1939, broadcast from Mannerheim Line in Finland; awarded first prize by Nat. Headliners Club as year's best European broadcast; went to England on one of 50 former Am. destroyers to represent North Am. Newspaper Alliance and Reader's Digest in London winter of 1940-41; became roving editor The Reader's Digest, 1942. Chmn. Rep. County Com., Lyon County, 1933-34; mem. Kansas State Legislature, 1931-32. Dir. Am. Friends of Middle East, Am. Com. for Liberation, Am. Assn. Indian Affairs. Overseer Harvard, 1950-56. Fellow Am. Numis. Soc.; mem. Am. Civil Liberties Union (past dir.), Theodore Roosevelt Meml. Assn. (dir.), Freedom House (dir.), Am. Soc. Newspaper Editors, Nat. Assn. Newspaper Editors, Internat. Press Inst., Inter-Am. Press Inst. Conglist. Clubs: Century Club, Harvard Club, Overseas Press Club, Coffee House (N.Y.C.); National Press (Washington). Author; What People Said (novel), 1938; co-author Zero Hour (fgn. affairs), 1940; author Journey for Margaret (war-time travel), 1941; They Were Expendable, 1942; Queens Die Proudly, 1943; Report on The Russians, 1945; Report of the Germans, 1947; Lost Boundaries, 1948; Land of Milk and Honey, 1949; Bernard Baruch, 1951; Back Down The Ridge, 1953; The Captives of Korea, 1957; The Little Toy Dog, 1962; Report on the Asians, 1969. Contbr. to Reader's Digest. Home: New York, N.Y. Died July 26, 1973.

WHITE, WILLIAM PATTERSON, author; b. St. Paul, Minn., Jan. 22, 1884; s. John Williamson and Louisa Ellmaker (Patterson) W.; ed. various schs. and academies in U.S., France and Switzerland; grad. New York Mil. Acad., Cornwall-on-Hudson, 1904; m. Olive Cornelia Scudder, of Huntington, L.I., N.Y., Aug. 30, 1919. Began as Western Union Telegraph messenger, later machinist, rodman, teamster, clerk, blacksmith's helper, car loader, electrician, draughtsman. Mem. Authors' League America, Alpha Chi Sigma. Republican. Episcopalian. Author: The Owner of the Lazy D, 1919; Lynch Lawyers, 1920; Hidden Trails, 1920; Paradise Bend, 1920; The Heart of the Range, 1921; The Rider of Golden Bar, 1922; The Wagon Wheel, 1923; Twisted Foot, 1924; Buster, 1926; Sweetwater Range, 1927; Cloudy in the West, 1928; Adobe Walls, 1933; Willow Canyon, 1933. Home: Tularosa, N. Mex.*

WHITE, WILLIAM RICHARDSON, church ofcl.; b. nr. Brownsboro, Tex., Dec. 2, 1892; s. Gibson and Kittie (Dorman) W.; A.B., Howard-Payne Coll., Brownwood, Tex., 1917, D.D., 1927; Th.M., Southwestern Bapt. Theol. Seminary, Fort Worth, 1922, Th.D., 1924; D.D., Baylor U., 1930, LL.D., 1970; Litt.D., Hardin-Simmons U., 1953; H.H.D., U. Ala., 1957; LL.D., Bishop Coll., 1958; m. Edna Woods, Jan. 17, 1916 (dec. Dec. 1948); m. 2d, Catherine W. Tarwater. June 20, 1950 (dec. Sept. 1970); m. 3d, Mrs. Hugo Mohr, Aug. 28, 1971. Ordained to ministry Missionary Bapt. Ch., 1911; pastor, Goldthwaite, Tex., 1917-19, Royce City, Tex., 1919-23; prof. missions Southwestern Bapt. Theol. Sem., 1923-27; pastor First Bapt. Ch., Greenville, Tex., 1927-28, First Ch., Lubbock, Tex., 1928-29; exec. sec. Bapt. Gen. Conv. Tex., 1929-1931; pastor Broadway Ch., Ft. Worth, 1931-35, 1st Ch., Oklahoma City, 1935-40; Flennikan lectr., Ouichita Coll., 1935; pres. Hardin-Simmons U., 1940-43; editorial sec. Sunday sch. bd. So. Bapt. Conv., 1943-45; pastor 1st Bapt. Ch., Austin, Tex., 1945-48; pres. Baylor U., 1948-61, chancellor, 1961-63, pres. emeritus, 1963-77. Attended Chaplain Tng. Sch., Louisville, 1918; dir. Bapt. Gen. Conv. of Tex. (mem. finance com. 3 yrs.); dir. fgn. mission bd. So. Bapt. Conv., Richmond, 1931-35; exec. sec. United Forces Against Liquor Traffic, 1932-35; dir. Okla. Bapt. U., 1935-40; bd. advisers Internat. Tech. Devel. Adminstrn., 1953-54; mem. Point-4 Com. Pres. Tex. Drys, 1949-77. Mem. Philos. Soc. Tex Democrat. Mason (33 deg., Shriner); Red Cross of Constantine. Contbr. Bapt. Standard, Bapt. Reflector, Bibl. Recorder, others. Author: The Royal Road to Life, 1938; Baptist Distinctives; Broadman Comments, 1946, '47, '48; A Manifesto of Faith, 1967. Home: Waco, Tex. Died Mar. 4, 1977.

WHITE, WILLYE ANDERSON, (MRS. FREDERICK HALL WHITE), b. Pueblo, Colo., Aug. 20, 1886; d. Horace Philip and Emma Belle (Kerby) Anderson; A.B., Wellesley Coll., 1909; m. Frederic Hall White, Feb. 14, 1910 (dec. 1920); children—Frederic

Hall, Horace Anderson, Willye (Mrs. Donald Charles Brockway). Dir. White and Bollard, Inc., 1920-27. Solicitor throughout U.S. for recreational equipment for armed forces under Civilian Def. and Red Cross, 1942-46. Co-founder Service Women's Club (Seattle) for enlisted women, 1942 (pres., 1944-45). Former mem. U.S.O. exec. council; mem. Council of Social Agencies of Settle and King County (com. services to armed forces, 1947-57); mem. of bd. English-Speaking Union, 1930-34, 1935-38. Seattle Symphony, 1938-41; co-chmn. U. of Wash. World Affairs Symposium, Inst. of Pub. Affairs, 1934-38; became mem. bd. Children's Orthopedic Hosp., 1921, now hon. mem. bd. trustees. Alumnae trustee Wellesley, 1946-52; trustee Allied Arts Seattle. Mem. UN Assn. (Washington state bd.), Nat. Soc. Colonial Dames of Am. (bd. dirs., bd. mgrs., 1950-53), Seattle Hist. Soc., Seattle Art Museum. Democrat. Presbyn. Clubs Sunset (incorp., 1913, mem. of bd., 1931-32). Women's University (co-founder, 1914, trustee, 1916-19, pres., 1924-25), Western Washington Wellesley (pres., 1944-46); Seattle Tennis, Garden (asso. mem.). Fortnightly Study. Address: Seattle WA also Bainbridge Island WA. *

WHITEHAIR, FRANCIS PRESTON, lawyer; b. Chapman, Kan., Oct. 1, 1900; s. Ira Andrew and Edna Shannon (Burns) W.; student So. Coll., 1918; LL.B., Stetson U., 1921, LL.D., 1952; grad. student, Columbia, 1942-43; m. Nina Louise Bizzelle, Apr. 2, 1924; children—Joan (Mrs. R. Spayd), Marilyn (Mrs. R. Gorman), Genevieve (Mrs. Dennison Williams). Admitted to Fla. bar, 1921; practice in DeLand, 1921-50, 53—; atty. Volusia Co. Bd. Pub. Instrn., 1929-36; atty. various municipalities, municipal dists., r.r. s. and utilities, 1926-42; atty. gen. Am. Samoa, 1943; spl. asst. Atty. Gen. Homer Cummings, 1934. Chmn. bd. dirs. Whitehair Co., 1936-77; owner Volusia Co. Mirror, 1940-43; pres. Seabreeze Properties, Inc., 1940-50; dir. Chgo., North Shore and Milw. Ry. Co., 1948-54, exec. v.p., 1949-54; owner, operator extensive citrus groves, 1929-46. Lectr. on law, Columbia Law Sch., 1942; gen. counsel Econ. Stblzh. Agy., 1950-51; under sec. navy, 1951-52. Pres. Charitable Trust created by late Judge Bert Fish, 1943-77; pres. Bert Fish Trustees, Inc., 1968-77; trustee, atty. Dick and Julie Pope Found., Inc., 1967—; bd. overseers Stetson U. Coll. Law; mem. bd. dirs. Fla. Cypress Gardens, Stetson Law Center Found. Citrus Exchange and chmn. finance com., 1934-36; mem. Fed. Citrus Control Com., 1933-39; Mem. bd. dirs. 7 bus. cos. in Wis.; dir. Beverly Hills (Calif.) Devel. Co. Mem. Circuit Ct. Commn. 7th Fla. Circuit, 1936-39; mem. Fla. Bd. Law Examiners, 1938-40, Fla. Rd. Bd., 1953-54. Chmn. bd. trustees Graham-Eckes Sch., Palm Beach, Fla., 1952-62. Served with U.S. Army, World War I, USNR, World War II; mem. Selective Bd. Appeals, 5th Congl. Dist., 1940; chmn. com. to draft manual for use in governing alien enemies in occupied countries. Decorated Commendation U.S. Army, World War I; commendation from comdr. Gilbert Isl. subarea, U.S. Navy, World War II; Bronze Star, Legion of Merit, Combat V and 4 combat stars, Congl. Selective Service medal, Certificate of Merit by Eric Johnston as adminstr. Econ. Stablzn. Agy., 1951. Mem. bars U.S. Dist. Court So. Dist. Fla., U.S. Supreme Ct., U.S. Circuit Ct. Appeals, FCC, U.S. Ct. Claims; mem. Am., Fla., Fed., Volusia Co. (pres. 1939-40) bar assns., Am. Judicature Soc., Fla., DeLand chambers commerce, Am. Legion, V.F.W., John B. Stetson U. Alumni Assn. (pres. 1934), Navy League, Stetson Lawyers Assn. Fla. (pres. 1955), Phi Alpha Delta, Sigma Nu. Democrat (candidate gov. Fla. 1939-40). Mem. Christian Church. Elk. Mason (Shriner, Jester). Clubs: Rotary; Nat. Capital Democratic (Washington). Home: DeLand, Fla. Died Mar. 20, 1977.

WHITEHEAD, DON, newspaperman; b. Inman, Va., Apr. 8, 1908; s. Harry Ford and Elizabeth (Bond) W.; student U. Ky., 1926-28, LL.D., 1948; m. Marie Patterson, Dec. 20, 1928; 1 dau., Ruth (Mrs. H.E. Graham). City editor Harlan (Ky.) Daily Enterprise, 1930-34; reporter Knoxville (Tenn.) Jour., 1934-35; joined Asso. Press, 1935, feature writer, N.Y.C., 1941-42, war corr., ETO and MTO, 1942-45, bur. chief, Hawaii, 1945-48, spl. corr., polit. reporter, Washington, 1948-56; chief Washington bur. N.Y. Herald Tribune, 1956-57; columnist Knoxville News-Sentinel, 1957-81; free lance writer. Recipient Medal of Freedom by Army as war corr., World War II; Pulitzer Prize for internat. reporting, 1950, for domestic reporting, 1952. Mem. Sigma Alpha Epsilon. Clubs: Cherokee Country (Knoxville); Gridiron (Washington). Author: The FBI Story, 1956; Journey into Crime, 1960; Border Guard, 1963; The FBI Story for Young Readers, 1964; The Dow Story, 1968; Attack on Terror: The FBI Against the Ku Klux Klan in Mississippi, 1970. Home: Knoxville, Tenn. Died Jan. 12, 1981.

WHITEHILL, WALTER MUIR, historian; b. Cambridge, Mass., Sept. 28, 1905; s. Walter Muir and Florence Marion (Williams) W.; A.B., Harvard U., 1926, A.M., 1929; Ph.D., U. London, 1934; Litt.D., U. N.B., 1959; LL.D., Washington and Jefferson Coll., 1959; L.H.D., Northeastern U., 1961, U. Del., 1967, Merrimack Coll., 1968, U. Mass., 1971, Coll. William and Mary, 1974; D. Humanities, Sulfolk U., 1970; D.C.L., Marlboro Coll., 1975; m. Jane Coolidge, June 5, 1930; children—Jane Whitehill Rotch, Diana Whitehill Laing. Tutor fine arts Harvard U., 1926-28; research medieval Spanish history and art, chiefly in Europe, 1928-36; asst. dir. Peabody Mus. of Salem, 1936-42; dir. librarian Boston Athenaeum, 1946-73; mem. faculty Peabody Mus., Harvard U., 1951-72, Allston Burr Sr. tutor in Lowell House, 1952-56, lectr. history Harvard U., 1956-57; Lowell Inst. lectr., 1958, 70. Pres. Merrimack Valley Textile Mus.; trustee Peabody Mus. of Salem, Fruitland Mus., John Greenleaf Whittier Homestead, Mus. of Fine Arts, Boston; pres. Historic Boston; hon. trustee Thomas Jefferson Meml. Found.; bd. dirs. U. Press of Va., Athenaeum of Phila.; trustee Eleutherian Mills-Hagley Found., Marlboro Coll. Served from lt. to comdr. USNR, 1942-46; with office Naval Records and Library, Navy Dept. Decorated Comdr. Order Alphonso X el Sabio (Spain), 1977. Fellow Soc. Antiquaries London, Am. Acad. Arts and Scis., Royal Soc. Arts; mem. AIA (hon.), Am. Antiquarian Soc., Medieval Acad., Art Workers Guild (London; hon.), Hispanic Soc. Am., Mass. Hist. Soc. (rec. sec.), Old South Assn. Boston (pres.), Phi Beta Kappa (pres. Harvard chpt. 1959-61). Republican. Episcopalian (mem. corp. Parish of Advent). Clubs: Somerset, Odd Volumes (past pres.), Tavern (Boston); Army and Navy (Washington); Century Assn. (N.Y.C.). Author: Spanish Romanesque Architecture of the Eleventh Century, 1941; The East India Marine Society and the Peabody Museum of Salem, a Sesquicentennial History, 1949; Fleet Admiral King, a Naval Record (with Fleet Adm. E. J. King, U.S.N.), 1952; Boston Public Library, A Centenary History, 1956; Boston: A Topographical History, 1959; Independent Historical Societies, 1962; Boston in the Age of John Fitzgerald Kennedy, 1966; Dumbarton Oaks, 1967; Museum of Fine Arts, Boston A Centennial History, 1970; Boston Statues, 1970, others; editor: Colonial Society Massachusetts, 1946; editorial bd. N.E. Quar.; adminstrv. bd. Adams Papers; The Papers of Benjamin Franklin. Home: North Andover, Mass. Died Mar. 5, 1978; buried Monticello Graveyard, Charlottesville, Va.

WHITEHOUSE, HAROLD CLARENCE, architect; b. Sommerville, Mass., Jan. 31, 1884; s. Arthur Thomas and Emily Dora (Chaney) W.; student Boston Art Club, 1902-03, Cornell U., 1911-13; European study, 1923; m. Catherine Cox Weston, June 2, 1909 (dec. July 1964); children—Helen M. (Mrs. Herbert M. Hamblen), Bruce T., Clare E. (Mrs. Fred W. Gilbert); m. 2d, Ruth Thompson, Sept. 1965. With various archtl. firms, Boston, also Butte, Mont. and Spokane, Wash., 1900-14; partner firm Whitehouse and Price, Spokane, 1914—; principal works include Hutton Settlement, Spokane, 1915, chemistry bldg. Wash. State U., Pullman, 1940, Cathedral St. John the Evangelist, Spokane, 1942, Naval Supply Depot, Spokane, Farragut Naval Tng. Sta., 1942, Epiphany Episcopal Parish, Seattle, 1945, Lincoln First Fed. Savs. & Loan Bldg., music and art bldgs. U. Wash. Campus, Seattle, 1948, Spokane Coliseum, 1954. Dir. Lincoln First Fed. Savs. & Loan Assn., Leland Trailer Co., Big West Oil Co., Spokane. Recipient Sands Meml. medal Coll. Architecture Cornell U., 1913. Certificate master craftsman in ecclesiastical metal work, 1954. Fellow A.I.A. (pres. Spokane 1950); mem. Spokane Art Assn. (past pres.), Church Archtl. Guild Am., Craftsman's Guild Wash. State, Asso. Engrs. Spokane, Wash. State Arts and Crafts Assn., Am. Craftsman's Council, S.A.R., Gargoyle Soc., Scarab. Episcopalian. Mason (32 deg., K.T.). Home: Spokane WA. *

WHITEHOUSE, SHELDON, diplomatic service; b. N.Y. City, Feb. 5, 1883; s. William Fitz Hugh and Frances (Sheldon) W.; student Eton Coll., Eng.; A.B., Yale, 1905; m. Mary Alexander, of N.Y., Oct. 14, 1920; children—Charles Sheldon, George Bruen, Sylvia. Pvt. sec. to Hon.Whitelaw Reid, ambassador to Gt. Britain, 1908; sec. Am. Legation at Caracas, Venezuela, 1909-11; 2d sec. Am. Embassy, Paris, France, 1911-14; sec. Am. Legation, Athens, Greece, 1914-16; 1st sec. Am. Embassy, Petograd, 1916-17; counselor Am. Legation, Stockholm, Sweden, 1918; attached to Am. Peace Commn., Paris, 1919; chief of near Eastern Div., Dept. of State, 1920-21; counselor Am. Embassy, Paris, 1921-28; counselor of Am. Embassy, Madrid, 1928-29; E.E. and M.P. to Guatemala, 1929-33, to Colombia, 1933-34, U.S. del. 6th Internat. Conference on Weights and Measures, 1921. Mem. Huguenot Soc., S.R. Episcopalian. Clubs: Metropolitan (Washington), Knickerbocker Brook, River (New York). Address: Newport, R.I. *

WHITELEATHER, MELVIN KERR, newspaper corr.; b. Damascus, O., June 15, 1903; s. William Ferdinand and Vinetta (Kerr) W.; B.S., Ohio State U., 1925; student Ecole Libre des Sciences Politiques, Paris, 1929-31, later U. Berlin; m. Eleanor Lindsay, April 26, 1929; 1 son, Alan Kerr; m. 2d, Estelle Oncken, July 25, 1941; children—Gerald Kerr, Christine. Mem. reportorial staff Youngtown Telegram, Pitts. Gazette-Times and Cleve. Times, 1925-26; contbr. Paris Times, 1927-28; wrote daily column for Paris edit. Chgo. Tribune, 1929-30; fgn. corr. Asso. Press, Paris Bur., 1930-34, Berlin Bur., 1934-37; chief of bureau, Rome, 1937-38; assigned as corr. at Young Plan Conf., Basel, 1931, Lausanne Reparations Conf., World Econ. Conf., London, 1933, 2 revolts in Spain, 1930, 34, Saar Territory Plebiscite, 1934-35, wedding of Ex-King Edward VIII to Wallis Simpson, Monts, France, 1937, German occupation of Austria and Sudetenland, 1938, German occupation of Bohemia-Moravia, 1939, and various meetings of assembly and council of League of Nations; war corr. on German front, 1939-40, war corr. in London, Algiers, Italy, Cairo, Moscow, radio commentator, lectr., from 1940. Mem. Sigma Delta Chi. Club: Franklin Inn (Philadelphia). Author: Main Street's New Neighbors; also chpt. in book. Home: Swarthmore, Pa. Died Nov. 21, 1976.

WHITESIDE, STANSELL EUGENE, lawyer; b. Oklahoma City, June 1, 1927; s. Stansell and Georgia (McMahan) W.; student Amherst Coll., 1946, U.S. Mil. Acad., 1946-47; B.A., U. Okla., 1950, LL.B., 1952; m. Bernice Phillips, Apr. 3, 1964; children—R. Scott, Georgia, John M., Brenda E. Admitted to Okla. bar, 1952, since practiced in Altus; mem. firm Harbison & Whiteside, 1952-62; pvt. practice, 1962-69; mem. firm Whiteside & Bowman, 1969-73, Whiteside & Watt, 1973-79, U.S. commr., 1957-79. Partner Pace Constrn. Co.; pres. Western Lease Finance Corp., Golden Triangle Corp.; sec., dir. Tri-W Corp., C & R Constrn. Co.; dir. Aerial Invironment Corp. Chmn. bd. Salvation Army. Served to 2d lt. AUS, 1945-46. Recipient Outstanding Service award Okla. Bar Assn., 1960; Commendation award Air Force Assn., 1968. Mem. Am., Okla., Jackson County bar assns., Am., Okla. trial lawyers assns., Am. Judicature Soc., Air Force Assn. (past chpt. pres.), Phi Alpha Delta, Sigma Alpha Epsilon. Democrat. Mason, Rotarian, Elk. Home: Altus, Okla. Died Mar. 14, 1979; buried Altus Cemetery.

WHITING, JOHN DOWNES, artist; b. Ridgefield, Conn., July 20, 1884; s. William Wallace and Catherine Jane (Downes) W.; grad. Yale Sch. of Fine Arts, 1910, B.F.A., 1915; studied under Clifton S. Carbee, of Boston, and Lucius W. Hitchcock, New Rochelle, N.Y.; m. Meredyth Gooch, May 10, 1913; children—Katherine Wyman, Elizabeth Coolidge. Actively engaged as illustrator sea stories, books on out-door life, etc., since 1911; has made illustrations for Met. Mag., Robert McBride & Co., E. P. Dutton & Co., G. P. Putnam's Sons, Doubleday, Page & Co., Houghton Mifflin Co., Harper Bros., etc. Mem. Co. F. 2d Regt. Conn. Nat. Guard, 1917-18; with Camouflage Corps, U.S. Navy, 2d District, June-Dec. 1918. Mem. Conn. Acad. of Fine Arts, Rockport (Mass.) Art Assn. Unitarian. Clubs: Paint and Clay (pres. 1938), New Haven, Chess (New Haven). Author: Practical Illustration, 1920; Storm Fighters, 1927; "S.O.S.," 1928; The Trail of Fire, 1930, Old New England Scenes (in color), 1939. His outstanding picture is "Old Ironsides" (pub. as art print, 24x30); picture "Dawn at Seicheprey" purchased for Conn. State Armory, 1935. Member World Federalists of Conn., 1946. *

WHITLOCK, E(RNEST) CLYDE, violinist, teacher; b. Leon, Kan., July 3, 1885; s. William Thomas and Adda Belle (Bevans) W.; grad. Carthage (Mo.) High Sch., 1903; studied violin with Ralph Wylie, Kansas City, Adolph Weidig, Am. Conservatory, Chicago, Issay Barmas, Berlin, Germany, Samuel Gardner, Inst. of Musical Art, New York; studied theory with Rossetter Cole, Chicago; m. Anna Waples, June 5, 1912 (divorced 1924); 1 dau., Elizabeth Belle (Mrs. Elizabeth Belle Hogan). Head violin dept., Poly. Coll., Ft. Worth, Tex., 1908-12, Southwestern Conservatory, Dallas, Tex., 1908-11, St. Mary's Coll., Dallas, 1908-20, Ft. Worth Conservatory since 1924, Our Lady of Victory Acad., Fort Worth, 1916-26, Tex. State Coll. for Women, 1933-37; mem. faculty, Texas Christian U., since 1943. Concert master Fort Worth Symphony Orchestra, 1915-36; music editor Fort Worth Star-Telegram since 1926; director Broadway Presbyn. Ch. choir., 1928-50. Member Tex. Music Teachers Assn. (dir.), Music Teachers Nat. Assn. Presbyterian. Mason. Co-author (with Cathinka Venth); My Memories, a biography of Carl Venth. Contbr. to musical periodicals. Home: Fort Worth. *

WHITMORE, GEORGE DEWEY, civil engr.; b. Hillman, Mich., Apr. 25, 1898; s. George Edward and Jenny (Ames) W.; student pub. schs., Mich.; m. Helen Fern O'Neill, June 26, 1918; children—Patricia, Richard (dec.), Robert, James (dec.), Jane, Margaret. With R.H. Randall & Co., geodetic and topographic engrs., 1917-33, v.p., Toledo, 1926-33; chief surveys, maps and surveys br. TVA, 1933-45; with topographic engr., 1957-68; mem. adv. com. photogrammetry Syracuse (N.Y.) U., 1945-50; adv. com. geodesy, cartography and photogrammetry Ohio State U., 1955-60; chmn. com. topographic maps and aerophotogrammetry, commn. cartography Pan Am. Inst. Geography and History, 1955-81; chmn. U.S. Govt. Tech. Adv. Com. Antarctica Mapping, 1957; U.S. Mem. sci. com. Antarctica research Internat. Council Sci. Union, 1959; chmn. com. internat. cartographic matters Nat. Acad. Scis.-NRC, 1960-61; mem. Am. editorial bd. Photogrammetria, 1960-68; chief U.S. rep. UN Tech. Conf. Internat. Map of World, 1962.

Recipient Distinguished Service award Dept. Interior, 1958; Carlos Struck award, 1968. Registered profl. engr., N.C., Va., Ind. Fellow ASCE (hon. mem.), Am. Geog. Soc., AAAS; mem. Am. Soc. Photogrammetry (pres. 1952), Am. Congress Surveying and Mapping (pres. 1943-45), Am. Geophys. Union, Soc. Am. Mil. Engrs., Am. Geol. Inst., Internat. Soc. Photogrammetry (gov. council 1960-64), Canadian Inst. Surveying, Wash. Soc. Engrs. Roman Cath. Club: Cosmos (Washington). Author textbooks, chpts. in books, articles. Address: Woodstock, Ill. Died Feb. 9, 1981; buried Woodland Cemetery, Jackson, Mich.

WHITNEY, GEORGE KIRKPATRICK, investment cons.; b. Concord, Mass., Nov. 9, 1907; s. Charles Hayden and Caroline (Patrick) W.; A.B., Harvard U., 1929, M.B.A., 1931; m. Donita Stahl, 1936 (dec.); children—Robert Hayden, Sarah Minot, Faith Thomas Newcomb; m. 2d, Una Rogers King, Sept. 6, 1951. With trust investment div., trust dept. First Nat. Bank Chgo., 1931-34; investment dept. Conn. Bank & Trust Co., 1934-43; investment research dept. Mass. Investors Trust, 1943-47, trustee, 1947-70; dir., mem. investment mgmt. com. Mass. Investors Growth Stock Fund, Inc., 1945-70, v.p., 1963-70; gov. Investment Co. Inst., 1960-63, mem. exec. com., 1960-62; sr. v.p., dir. Mass. Financial Services, 1969-70, cons., 1970-77, ltd. partner, 1977-80; dir. Pa. Co. Bd. dirs. Big Bros. Assn., Boston; corporator Emerson Hosp., Concord; chmn. Harvard Bus. Sch. Fund, 1963-66; mem. Harvard Overseers Com. to Visit Bus. Sch., 1968-74; bd. dirs. Harvard Bus. Sch. Assos., 1971-74, 75—. Mem. Boston C. of C., Mass. Hist. Soc. (fin. com.), Harvard Bus. Sch. Assn. (exec. council 1966-73, pres. 1967-68; Distinguished Service award 1969), Asso. Harvard Alumni (dir. 1968-70), World Affairs Council Boston (dir.), Nat. Trust Historic Preservation (life), Transp. Assn. Am. (dir. 1947-80, chmn. 1968-70, hon. chmn. 1970-74, chmn. bd. govs. 1976-77, Seley award 1974), Nat. Assn. Investment Cos. (pres. 1960-61), Am. Hist. Assn., Soc. Preservation of New Eng. Antiquities, Soc. Colonial Wars, New Eng. Historic Geneal. Soc., Bostonian Soc., Am. Forestry Assn., New Eng. Forestry Found. (founder). Republican. Episcopalian. Clubs: Econ., Union (Boston); Harvard (N.Y.C.); Country (Brookline, Mass.); Concord Country; Ekwanok Country (Manchester, Vt.); Harvard Varsity, Speakers' (Cambridge, Mass.); Met. (Washington); Mid-Ocean (Bermuda). Home: Concord, Mass. Died Dec. 30, 1980.

WHITTAKER, HUDSON (TAMPA RED), blues and folk singer. Home: Chicago, Ill. Died Mar. 19, 1981.

WHITTAKER, ROBERT HARDING, educator, ecologist; b. Wichita, Kans., Dec. 27, 1920; s. Clive Charles and Adeline (Harding) W.; A.B., Washburn Municipal U., 1942; Ph.D., U. Ill., 1948; m. Clara Caroline Buehl, Jan. 1, 1953 (dec. Dec. 1976); children—John Charles, Paul Louis, Carl Robert; m. 2d, Linda Susan Olsvig, Oct. 12, 1979. Instr. zoology Wash. State Coll., Pullman, 1948-50, asst. prof., 1950-51; sr. scientist biology Hanford Atomic Products Ops., 1951-54; instr. Bklyn. Coll., City U. N.Y., 1954-58, asst. prof., 1958-62, asso. prof., 1962-64; vis. scientist biology dept. Brookhaven Nat. Lab., Upton, N.Y., 1964-66; prof. biology U. Calif. at Irvine, 1966-68; prof. biology, ecology and systematics Cornell U., Ithaca, N.Y., 1968-76, Charles A. Alexander prof. biology, 1976-80. Served with USAAF, 1942-46. Mem. Ecol. Soc. Am. (Mercer award 1966), Am. Soc. Limnology and Oceanography, Brit. Ecol. Soc., Internat. Soc. Tropical Ecology, Internat. Assn. Phytosociology, Am. Soc. Naturalists (pres. 1980), Torrey Bot. Club, Swedish Plant Geographic Soc., AAAS, Am. Soc. Zoologists, Nat. Acad. Scis., Am. Acad. Arts and Scis., Brit. Ecol. Soc. (hon.), Swedish Plant Geog. Soc. (hon.), Phi Beta Kappa, Phi Sigma. Author: Communities and Ecosystems, 2d edit., 1975; Ordination and Classification of Communities, 2d edit., 1978; (with S.A. Levin) Niche: Theory and Application, 1975; (with H. Lieth) Primary Productivity of the Biosphere, 1975. Contbr. articles to profl. jours. Home: Ithaca, N.Y. Died Oct. 20, 1980.

WHITTEMORE, JOSEPH DAMON, banker and engr.; b. Somerville, Mass., May 14, 1885; s. John Murray and Mary Hewes (Damon) W.; B.S., Mass. Inst. of Tech., 1907; m. Katherine C. Noonan, Jan. 13, 1912; children—Joseph Damon, Jr., Margaret Damon (Mrs. Richard C. Wales). Exec. officer various utility companies, 1907-32; v.p. Chase Nat. Bank since 1934. Served in Office Coordinator Inter-Am. Relations, 1941-42; dep. chief Civil Communications Sect. Gen. Hdqrs., Supreme Comdr. for Allied Powers, Japan, 1946; consultant econ. cooperation adminstrn., China Div., 1948. Home: New York. *

WHITTEMORE, LEWIS BLISS, bishop; b. Hartford, Conn., June 17, 1885; s. William Emmons and Mary Bliss (Robinson) W.; A.B., Yale Univ., 1907; B.D., Episcopal Theol. Sch., 1915; D.D., Kenyon Coll. Gambier, O., 1939; m. Helen M. Crawford, Oct. 23, 1917; children—Virginia Crawford, James Robinson, Nancy. Ordained to ministry P.E. Ch., 1915; asst. minister Christ Ch., N.Y. City, 1915-17; asso. rector Calvary Ch., Pittsburgh, 1917-23; rector Trinity Ch., Detroit, 1923-27, Grace Ch., Grand Rapids, 1927-36; bishop co-adjutor diocese Western Mich., 1936-37, bishop since 1937. Teacher govt. service P.I., 1907-10; master Brent Sch., Baguio, 1910-12. Mem. Nat. Council of Episcopal Ch. Member Michigan Society for Mental Hygiene. Republican. Clubs: Rotary, University; president Yale Club of Western Michigan. Home: 442 Madison Av. Address: Grand Rapids, Mich. *

WHITTEMORE, WILFRED DOILOFF, banker; b. Bristol, N.H., Jan. 12, 1882; s. Frederick Austin and Ida May (Doloff) W.; B.A., Dartmouth Coll., 1904, M.C.S., 1905; m. Vilda Therese Anderson, Mar. 31, 1914; 1 dau., Nancy. Subaccountant, later accountant, branch mgr. Internat. Banking Corp. in the Far East, 1906-34; branch mgr. Nat. City Bank of N.Y., Dairen, South Manchuria, 1934-38; v.p. Export-Import Bank of Washington since 1938, v.p. and treas. 1946-56, sr. v.p., 1956—. Club: Metropolitan (Washington). Home: Washington. *

WICK, MYRON ARMS, corp. exec.; b. Youngstown, O., 1883; Ph.B., Yale (Sheffield Scientific Sch.), 1904; m. Lillian Schuttler, Mar. 2, 1910; children—Barbara Wick Ladd, Myron Arms. Chmn. Plastic Mfrs., Inc., Stamford, Conn.; pres. and dir. Jefferson Mining Co. Formerly v.p. and mem. exec. com. Republic Steel Corp.; formerly pres. Trucson Steel Co. Home: New York, N.Y. *

WICKWIRE, JERE RAYMOND, artist; b. Cortland, N.Y., July 3, 1883; s. Theodore H. and Emma V. (Woodmansee) W.; A.B., Yale, 1906; studied at Students League and with William M. Chase, N.Y. City; m. Constant Lounsbery Johnson, Apr. 21, 1908; children—Constant Jean, Bradley. Portraits of William Lyon Phelps and James M. Taylor, Vassar Coll.; Dr. Chevalier Jackson, Phila.; Alfred E. Stearns, Andover, Mass., exhibited in all large exbns. Asso. Nat. Acad. of Design; mem. Allied Artists of America, Alpha Delta Phi. Presbyterian. Clubs: Yale, Salmagundi (N.Y. City). Home: New York, N.Y. *

WIDDEMER, MARGARET, author; b. Doylestown, Pa.; d. Rev. Howard Taylor and Alice (De Witt) Widdemer; ed. at home; grad. Drexel Inst. Library Sch.; Litt.D., Bucknell U., 1931; M.A., Middlebury (Vt.) U., 1933; m. R. H. Schauffler (dec.). Began writing in childhood; first pub. poem entitled The Factories (a child-labor poem), was widely quoted; contbr. essays, reviews, poems and short stories to mags. Mem. Poetry Soc. Am. (past v.p.), mem. Sorosis (hon.), Pen and Brush P.E.N., Browning Soc. (hon.). Club: Query. Author many works, 1915-78; books since 1950 include: Red Cloak Flying, 1950; Lady of the Mohawks, 1951; Prince in Buckskin, 1952; Basic Techniques of Fiction, 1953; The Golden Wildcat, 1954; Collected Poems, 1957; Buckskin Baronet, 1960; Golden Friends I Had (reminiscences), 1964; The Red Castle Women, 1968. Recipient Trimmed Lamb prize for best lyric, 1916; Lit. Rev. prize for satire, 1922; Lyric prize for best lyric, 1923, and others. Shared with Carl Sandburg, Am. Poetry Soc. Pulitzer prize 1919, best book of poems for preceding year, Old Road to Paradise. Lectr. various confs. and orgn. meetings. Talks over NBC, Blue Network, Do You Want to Write?, 1936. Home: Gloversville, N.Y. Died July 13, 1978; buried Kensico, N.Y.

WIDDOES, HOWARD V(INCENT), corp. ofcl., assn. exec.; b. Burrelsville, R.I., Sept. 2, 1896; s. Andrew B. and Ella M. (Legg) W.; B.S., Wesleyan U., 1918; m. Natalie Peirce, Aug. 26, 1922; children—Peirce, Janet, Howard Vincent. Sales dept. Library Bur. Boston, 1919-22, asst. N.Y. mgr., 1922-25; with Remington Rand, Inc., N.Y.C., 1925-61, successively asst. mgr., mgr., gen. sales mgr. system div., gen. mgr. typewriter division, v.p., 1925-52, became v.p., gen. sales mgr., 1952; v.p. sales Univac-Systems div., Remington Rand div. Sperry Rand Corp., 1956-59, v.p. exec. staff Remington Rand div., 1959-61. Member Office Equipment Mfrs. Inst. (dir. 1948-76, pres. 1954-76; life), A.I.M., Am. Mgmt. Assn. Home: Winter Park, Fla. Died Sept. 5, 1976.

WIEDEFELD, MARY THERESA (WE'DÊ-FELD), former coll. pres.; b. Baltimore, Md., Feb. 2, 1886; d. William Jenkins and Frances (Johnston) W.; grad. Md. State Normal Sch., Baltimore, 1904; B.S., Johns Hopkins U., 1925, D.Ed., 1935. Engaged in teaching, elementary grades, Baltimore Co., Md., 1904-11, supervisor of primary grades, 1911-14; teacher of practice, Md. State Normal Sch., 1914-16, prin. training sch., 1916-19; supervisor elementary schs., Anne Arundel County, Md., 1919-24; state supervisor elementary schs., of Md., 1924-38; pres. State Teachers Coll., Towson, Md., 1938-47; retired 1947. Mem. Pi Lambda Theta, Kappa Delta Pi. Democrat. Roman Catholic. Home: Baltimore, Md. *

WIEMAN, HENRY NELSON, prof. philosophy of religion; b. Richhill, Mo., Aug. 19, 1884; s. William Henry and Alma (Morgan) W.; B.A., Park Coll., Parkville, Mo., 1907; student San Francisco Theol. Sem., 1910; univs. of Jena and Heidelberg, 1910-11; Ph.D., Harvard, 1917; D.D., Park Coll., 1929; Litt.D., Occidental Coll., 1930; m. Anna M. Orr, Jan. 15, 1912 (died in 1931); children—Florence Margaret, Nelson Orr, Marion Isabelle, Robert Morgan, Eleanor Brunhilda; married 2d, Regina H. Westcott, 1932 (divorced); married 3d, Laura Matlack. Professor of philosophy, Occidental Coll., Los Angeles, 1917-27; philosophy of religion Div. Sch., Un. of Chicago, 1927-47, emeritus; prof. philosophy, Univ. of Ore., 1949-51; prof. philosophy University of Houston since 1951. Lecturer McCormick Theol. Sem., 1926-27; delivered Nathaniel William Taylor lectures, Yale, 1930, Mendenhall lectures, De Pauw U., 1930, Swander lectures, Theol. Sem. of Ref. Ch., 1930; Carew lectures, Hartford Sem. Foundation, 1938; Earl Foundation lectures, Pacific Sch. of Religion, 1932; Ayer Lectures, 1947. Colgate-Rochester Seminary. Member Am. Philos. Assn., Am. Theol. Assn., Am. Assn. Univ. Profs., Quadrangle Club. Unitarian. Author or co-author books relating to field. Contbr. to Contemporary Am. Theology, New Nat. Ency., Ency. of Religion. *

WIENER, ALEXANDER S., physician, immunohematologist; b. Bklyn., Mar. 16, 1907; s. George and Mollie (Zuckerman) W.; A.B., Cornell U., 1926; M.D., State U. N.Y., 1930; Dr. honoris causa, U. Toulouse (France), 1969; m. Gertrude Rodman, June 15, 1932; children—Jane Helen (Mrs. Harold Einhorn), Barbara Rae (Mrs. Theodore Krevit). Intern Jewish Hosp., Bklyn., 1930-32; practice medicine, Bklyn.; head blood transfusion div. Bklyn. Jewish Hosp., 1932-76, attending immunohematologist, 1952-76; clin. pathologist, dir. Wiener Lab. 1935-76; serologist Office Chief Med. Examiner, mem. dept. forensic medicine N.Y. U. Med. Sch., 1938-76, adj. asso. prof., 1960-68, prof., 1968-76. Instrumental in passage N.Y. blood test bills for disputed paternity cases, 1935, N.Y. bills to compel blood tests in assault and homicide cases, 1952. Recipient Alvarenga prize Coll. Physicians Phila., 1945; Lasker award Am. Pub. Health Assn., 1947; Burdick award Am. Soc. Clin. Pathology, 1946; Passano Found. award, 1951; Modern Medicine award, 1953; Landsteiner award Am. Assn. Blood Banks, 1956; Joseph P. Kennedy, Jr., Found. internat. award research prevention mental retardation, 1966; others. Pioneer co-discoverer Rh blood factor, 1937-40; discoverer mechanism of heredity of Rh-Hr blood types, 1941-45; discoverer of blocking and conglutination tests for Rh sensitization, 1944-45; devised new method of treatment of erythroblastosis fetalis by exchange transfusion, 1944-46; discovered two new blood factors Ca and U, 1953, factor C of A-B-O System, 1952, I-i blood group system, 1956, factors RhA, RhB, RhC, RhD, 1957-59, Me, 1961, subgroup B3 of A-B-O System, 1973; V-A-B and C-E-F blood group systems and blood factors GC, HC, IC, KC, LC, MC and NC of chimpanzee blood, 1964-74, coding and nomenclature of blood groups, 1965-69, blood groups of apes, baboons and rhesus monkeys, from 1960, serological specificaties of serum gamma globulin of man, apes and monkeys, 1968-71. Diplomate Am. Bd. Pathology. Fellow Am. Soc. Clin. Pathologists, Am. Acad. Forensic Sci., A.M.A., A.A.A.S., A.C.P., N.Y. Acad. Scis., N.Y. Acad. Medicine, Coll. Am. Pathologists, Internat. Soc. Hematology, Am. Assn. Phys. Anthropology, Royal Coll. Physicians; mem. Am. Soc. Human Genetics, Kings County Med. Soc., Am. Assn. Immunologists, Am. Assn. Blood Banks, Blood Banks Assn. N.Y., Soc. Study Blood (organizer, 1st pres. 1945), Mystery Writers Am. (hon.), Acad. des Scis., Inscriptions et Belle Lattres (Toulouse, France), Deutsche Acad. der Naturforscher Leopoldina, Deutsche Gesellschaft fur gerichtliche und soziale Medizin (hon.), Phi Beta Kappa, Phi Beta Kappa Assos., Alpha Omega Alpha. Democrat. Editorial bds. Nouvelle Revue Francaise d'Hematologie, Acta Genet, Medica et Gemellol., Transfusion, Haematologia (Budapest), Jour. Forensic Sci., Lab. Digest. Author: Blood Groups and Transfusion, 3d edit., 1943, 62; The Rh-Hr Blood Types, 1954; Rh-Hr Syllabus, 2d edit., 1962; Heredity of the Blood Groups, 1958; Advances in Blood Grouping, 1961, Vol. 2, 1965, Vol. 3, 1970. Contbr. articles tech. jours. Home: Brodklyn, N.Y. Died Nov. 6, 1976.

WIENER, SAMUEL G., architect; b. Monroe, La., Dec. 26, 1896; s. Sam, Jr., and Tillie (Loeb) W.; B.Arch., U. Mich., 1920; student Atelier Corbett-Gugler, N.Y.C., 1921, Atelier Gromort, Paris, France, 1922-23; m. Marion Pfeifer, Apr. 15, 1926; children—Samuel G., Earl Louis. Engaged in practice of architecture, 1923-77; works exhibited Paris Internat. Exhbn., San Francisco Exhbn., European traveling exhibit Mus. Modern Art; plan. supervision pub. and comml. bldgs. Samuel G. Wiener & Asso., 1934-77. Mem. La. Bd. Architects, 1935-50. Served as ensign USNRF, World War I. Fellow A.I.A. (first pres. N. La. chpt.); mem. Tau Sigma Delta, Zeta Beta Tau. Author: Venetian Houses and Details, 1928. Home: Shreveport, La. Died June 24, 1977; cremated.

WIENPAHL, PAUL, philosopher, educator; b. Rock Springs, Wyo., Mar. 6, 1916; s. Paul and Constance Mary (DeVelin) W.; B.A., U. Calif. at Los Angeles, 1937, M.A., 1939, Ph.D., 1946; m. Janet Elizabeth Ward, June 9, 1942; children—Mark, Jan. Teaching asst. UCLA, 1937-42, instr. philosophy, 1947; instr. philosophy N.Y. U., 1947-48; asst. prof. U. Calif. at Santa Barbara 1948-54, asso. prof., 1954-62, prof.,

1962-80; chmn. dept. philosophy, 1960-64. Served with AUS, 1942-46; ETO. Ford Faculty fellow, Paris, France, 1954-55. Mem. Am. Philos Assn., Phi Beta Kappa. Author: The Matter of Zen, 1964; Zen Diary, 1970; The Radical Spinoza, 1979. Contbr. articles to profl. jours. Home: Santa Barbara, Calif. Died Mar. 1, 1980.

WIERSMA, CORNELIS ADRIANUS GERRIT, physiologist, educator; b. Naaldwyk, Holland, Oct. 10, 1905; s. Klaas and Cornelia (Rystenbil) W.; B.Sc., Leiden U., 1926; M.Sc., Utrecht U., 1929, Ph.D. (Dondersfonds research fellow), 1933; m. Jeanne J. Netten, Dec. 21, 1932. Came to U.S., 1934. Mem. faculty Utrecht U., Holland, 1929-34; mem. faculty Cal. Inst. Tech., Pasadena, 1934-79, prof. biology, 1947-79; vis. prof. Cambridge (Eng.) U., 1957-58. Guggenheim fellow, 1957-79. Mem. A.A.A.S., Am. Zool. Soc., Soc. Gen. Physiology. Contbr. articles profl. jours. Home: Pasadena, Calif. Died May 1979.

WIESE, AUGUSTO N., banker; b. Trujillo, Peru, Dec. 6, 1886; s. Guillermo and Sofia (Eslava) W.; student Sem. of San Carlos; m. Virginia de Osma, 1923; children—Augusto Felipe, Maria Virginia (wife Dr. Luis Ducassi), Guillermo, Clotilde (wife Dr. Gonzalo de la Puente), Sylvia (wife Dr. Diomedes Arias Schreiber). Pres. A. y F. Wiese S.A., Sindicato Wiese S.A., Gran Hotel Bolivar, Banco Wiese, Ltd.; dir. Cerro de Pasco Corp. N.Y. *

WIESINGER, FREDERICK P., educator, cons. engr.; b. Budapest, Hungary, July 11, 1922; s. Frigyes and Ildiko (Kádár) W.; student architecture, Royal Technol. U., Budapest, 1940-46; M.S. in Structural Engring., Northwestern U., 1959, Ph.D., 1961; m. Mary Jane Jensen, Jan. 28, 1956; children—Maja Ilde, Frederick Axel and Folmer Martin (twins). Came to U.S., 1949, naturalized, 1959. Designer, project engr. various cons. firms, Budapest, Paris, Chgo., 1945-54; pvt. practice cons. engr., Chgo., 1954-65; chmn. bd. Wiesinger-Holland, Ltd., Chgo., 1965-77; instr. dept. engring. U. Ill., Chgo., 1954-55, lectr., 1955-56, asst. prof., 1956-61, asso. prof., 1961-67, prof. structural engring., dept. architecture, 1967-77. Registered structural engr., Ill.; registered profl. engr. Ind., Mich., Ohio, Fla., Wis., Iowa, Pa., N.Y. Fellow Am. Soc. C.E. (chmn. structural div. 1963, dir. Ill. sect. 1968-70); mem. Nat. Soc. Profl. Engrs. (chmn. structural engring. sect. Ill. br. 1968-69), Am. Concrete Inst., Internat. Assn. Bridge and Structural Engring., Internat. Assn. Shell Structures, A.A.U.P., A.C.L.U., Ill. Engrs. Council (dir. 1971-74), Old Town Triangle Assn., Lincoln Park Conservation Assn. (dir. 1964-68), Ind. Voters Ill., Am. Arbitration Assn. (nat. panel arbitrators), Sigma Xi. Club: Cliff Dwellers, Lincoln Park Boat (Chgo.). Contbr. articles profl. jours. Home: Chicago, Ill. Died Dec. 27, 1977.

WIG, RUDOLPH JAMES, mfr.; b. Chgo., Oct. 3, 1883; s. Joseph and Emma Virginia (Gardner) W.; M.E., Ill. Inst. Tech., 1907; LL.D., Pomona College, 1953; m. Anna May Bartlett, Apr. 2, 1910 (deceased 1956); children—Helen Virginia (Mrs. James H. Elgin), Mary Bartlett (Mrs. J. Stanley Johnson), Winifred Celia (Mrs. Robert Beaton Smith). Mech. engr., engr. physicist Bur. Standards, Washington, 1910-17; coms. engr., Phila., 1918-20; head concrete ship div. U.S. Shipping Bd. Emergency Fleet Corp., Washington, 1917-19; v.p. Celite Co., Los Angeles, 1919-29; dir., spl. asst. Douglas Aircraft Corp., 1941-45; v.p., dir. Timm Aircraft Corp., 1942-45, Holly Mfg. Co., 1949-55; v.p. Kelco Co., 1930-48, dir. 1931—. Mem. profl. adv. com. Restudy Higher Edn. in Cal., 1953-55; chmn. Cal. Scholarship Commission, 1955-60. Mem. Gen. Assembly's Theol. Council of United Presbyn. Ch. of U.S.A., 1946-61; chmn. bd. ch. extension Los Angeles Presbytery; mem. bus. and finance com. Nat. Council Chs.; v.p., trustee Found. United Presbyn. Ch. U.S.A.; dir Westminster Gardens Corp., 1955—, Trustee Pomona Coll., 1929—, v.p. bd., 1961—, pres. bd., 1949-61; bd. dirs., chmn. finance com. Goodwill Industries of Los Angeles; trustee board fells. Claremont U. Coll.; trustee San Francisco Theol. Sem., Harvey Mudd Coll.; v.p., dir. Honnold Library Soc.; bd. dirs. So. Cal. Presbyn. Homes. Mem. Am. Soc. C.E., Assn. Ind. Cal. Colls. and Univs. Presbyn. Clubs: California (Los Angeles); Twilight (Pasadena). Home: Pasadena, Cal. *

WIGGINS, ARCHIBALD LEE MANNING, business exec.; b. Durham, N.C., Apr. 9, 1891; s. Archie Lee and Margaret London (Council) W.; A.B., U. N.C., 1913, LL.D., 1946; LL.D., U. S.C., 1944, Duke, 1958, Campbell Coll., 1969; m. Pauline Lawton, Apr. 28, 1915; children—Margaret Coker (Belding), Joseph Lawton, Lee Manning, Pauline Elizabeth (Bush). Chmn. bd. A.C.L.R.R., L.&N. R.R. and Atlantic Coast Line Co. of Conn., 1948-61; chmn. Bank of Hartsville, 1948-71; chmn. Pauline and Lee Wiggins Found., Inc., also Hartsville Pub. Co.; lectr. Grad. Sch. Banking, Rutgers U., 1941-57. Chmn. Fiscal Survey Commn. S.C., 1955-58, S.C. Tax Adv. Com., 1953-54, S.C. Reorgn. Com., 1948-50; under sec. U.S. Treasury Dept., 1947-48, spl. asst. sec., 1948-53; mem. regional adv. com. RFC, 1930-46; chmn. S.C. Deposit Liquidation Com., 1933-34; pres. So. Retail Merchants Conf., Richmond, 1922-23, S.C. Bankers Assn., 1931-32, S.C. Independent Merchants Assn., 1937-38, S.C. Fedn. Commerce, Agr. and Industry, 1938-39, S.C. Press Assn., 1942-43, Am. Bankers Assn., 1943-44; mem. fed. adv. council Fed. Res. System from 5th Fed. Res. Dist., 1946. Chmn. Darlington County Bd. Edn., 1934-42, Hartsville Meml. Library Commn., Hartsville Community Center Bldg. Commn., 1935-46, 59-66; treas. Nat. A.R.C., 1947-48. Trustee Coker Coll., 1938-67, treas. endowment fund, 1940-46; trustee S.C. Found. Ind. Colls., Inc., N. Greenville Jr. Coll., 1971-75; bd. mem. home mission bd. So. Bapt. Conv., 1964-70; past pres. bd. Baptist Found. S.C.; dir. Am. Cancer Soc., 1947-49; pres. Crippled Children Soc. S.C., 1953-56, S.C. Conf. Social Work, 1946. Recipient certificate of merit distinguished service agr. Clemson Agrl. Coll., 1940, Algernon Sydney Sullivan award Coker Coll., 1969; named to Wisdom Hall of Fame, 1971. Mem. So. Soc. N.Y., Sr. Order Golden Fleece (U. N.C.), Chi Psi, Omicron Delta Kappa, Sigma Upsilon. Baptist. Publisher autobiography, 1969. Clubs: Metropolitan, Nat. Press, Alfalfa (Washington); University (N.Y.C.); Palmetto (Columbia, S.C.); Home: Hartsville, S.C. Died July 7, 1980.

WIKEL, HOWARD HENRY (WI'KEL), univ. prof.; b. Fort Wayne, Ind., March 1, 1883; s. Samuel and Emily Anna Bowers (Bittenbender) W.; A.B., U. of Ind., 1905, A.M. (fellow in European history), 1906; studied in German, summer 1913, Paris, France, 1923-24. Prin. high sch., LaGrange, Ind., 1906-15, supt. of schs., 1915-16; instr., asst. prof. modern langs., Purdue U., 1916-25, asst. prof. European history, 1925-28, asso. prof., 1928-42, professor, since 1942. Chmn. com. on commencement, Purdue U., 1938-48. Mem. Am. Hist. Assn., Am. Assn. Univ. Profs., Ind. Hist. Assn., Tippecanoe County, Ind. Hist. Assn., Sigma Alpha Epsilon. Presbyterian. Mason. Conductor, private tours in Europe, 1925-31; author articles on Dutch hist. Home: West Lafayette, Ind. *

WILBER, CHARLES PARKER, state forester and dir.; b. New Brunswick, N.J., Oct. 23, 1883; s. Francis Augustus and Laura Birge (Parker) W.; grad. Rutgers Prep. Sch., New Brunswick, N.J., 1900; A.B., Rutgers U., 1905; M.A., 1908; M.F., Yale Forestry Sch., 1907; m. Evelyn Beer Beasley, June 10, 1918; step children—Frederick Bartling Beasley, Evelyn Beasley Faris; m. 2d, Ida Hutchinson MacNamara, Oct. 20, 1944. With William M. Ritter Lumber Co., Maben, W.Va., 1907-08; forest asst. U.S. Forest Service, Dist. IV, Ogden, Utah, 1908-10; asst. forester N.J. Forest Commn., Trenton, N.J., 1910-11, asst. forester and state firewarden, 1911-15; asst. forester and state firewarden N.J. Dept. Conservation and Development, Trenton, N.J., 1915-21, state forester and chief div. forests and parks, 1922-37, state forester and dir. since 1937. Mem. N.J. State Planning Bd. 1934-44, N.J. Council 1937-44, N.J. State Soil Conservation Com. since 1937, High Point State Park Commission, 1942-45. Deacon 2d Reformed Church, New Brunswick, N.J., 1914-18; elder 1st Presbyterian Ch., Trenton, N.J., 1919-39, leader Men's Bible Class 1920-22, pres. Men's Assn., 1921, supt. Sunday Sch., 1927-28; pres. Men's Bible Class Union, New Brunswick, 1917, Trenton Council of Chs., 1922-25; trustee New Brunswick Presbytery, Presbyn. Ch., U.S., 1929-49; commr. gen. assembly, Presbyn. Ch., U.S. 1926. Mem. Soc. of Am. Foresters (pres. Allegheny Sect., 1928), State Foresters Assn. (pres. 1930), Nat. Council State Parks (N.J. rep., 1928-38), Allegheny Forest Expt. Sta. (mem. advisory council since 1930), Trenton Hort. Soc., N.J. Advisory Com. on Pub. Recreation (pres. 1936-38), N.J. Parks and Recreation Assn. (exec. com. since 1938), Trenton Y.M.C.A. (dir.), pres. Fort Dix Y.M.C.A., 1940-47, American Forestry Asso. (dir. 1940-48), Nat. Geog. Soc., N.J. Fish and Game Conservation League, New Jersey Federation of Shade Tree Commissions. Delegate Valley Protection Assn. (dir. 1934), Rutgers Alumni Assn. (class sec. 1910-30), Rutgers Alumni Council (class rep. 1910-30), Yale Forest Sch. Alumni Assn. (pres. 1937-38), Alumni Assn. of Rutgers Coll. (trustee 1925-29), Yale Forest Sch. Robin Hood Soc., Chi Psi. Clubs: Rutgers (pres. 1922-25), Rotary (dir. 1931-33), Rutgers Varsity, Rutgers Outing (New Brunswick, N.J.); mem. Trenton Torch Club, 1925-26, Engineers Club, 1912-26 (dir. 1924-26, v.p. 1926). Author of numerous bulletins, leaflets, newspaper and mag. articles on forestry, forest fires, parks, land use and related subjects.

WILBUR, WILLIAM HALE, author, army officer; b. Palmer, Mass., Sept. 24, 1888; s. John and Edith B. (Smart) W.; student Haverford Coll., 1907-08; B.S., U.S. Mil. Acad., 1912; grad. Command and Gen. Staff Sch., 1932, Army War Coll., 1935; grad. Ecole Spéc. Militaire, St. Cyr, France, 1919-20, Ecole Superieure de Guerre, Paris, 1922-24; m. Laura Girard Schieffelin, Sept. 8, 1923; children—Mary S. (Mrs. L. H. Cummings), William H. (dec. 1950). Commd. 2d lt. inf. U.S. Army, 1912, advanced through grades to brig. gen., 1942; asst. chief of staff, G-1, personnel officer, Chgo., 1938-40; chief of staff 6th Corps Area, 1940-41; comdg. officer 60th Inf., Ft. Bragg, 1941-42; overseas duty with Allied Landing in N. Africa, 1942; dep. comdr. 36th div., participating in Salerno landing 1944. Apptd. warden Cook County Jail, Chgo., 1950. Mem. of Lake County Crime Commn., 1960-79; mem. radio panel, What's Best for America, from 1952; mem. Chicago Crime Commn., from 1954. Trustee Patriotic Edn., Inc., 1965-79. Decorated Congl. Medal of Honor by Pres. Roosevelt at Casablanca, Jan. 1943; Ouissam Alaouite medal by Moroccan Govt. (awarded by Sultan of Morocco) Jan. 1943; Legion of Merit with oak leaf cluster, Silver Star, Bronze Star, Combat Inf. badge (U.S.); knight comdr. SS. Maurice and Lazarus (Italy); named Illustrious Grad. U.S. Mil. Acad., 1967; recipient Nat. Collegiate Athletic Assn. award, 1971; Gold medal Nat. SAR, 1976. Mem. Am. Legion, West Point Soc. Chgo. (pres.), V.F.W., Am. Mil. Inst., Lafayette Soc. (dir.), Defenders Am. Liberties (dr.). Kiwanian, (hon.), Rotarian (hon.). Club: Army and Navy (Washington). Author: Koehler Method of Physical Drill, 1918; Guideposts to the Future, 1954; Russian Communism, A Challenge and a Fraud, 1964; Freedom Must Not Perish, 1964; The Making of George Washington, rev. edit., 1973; many articles for profl. jours. Speaker on internat., mil. and ednl. subjects. Home: Fort Myers, Fla. Died Dec. 27, 1979; buried West Point (N.Y.) Cemetery.

WILCOX, CHARLES SAXTON, lawyer; b. Rochester, N.Y., Nov. 22, 1901; s. Albert Henry and Ida Louise (Saxton) W.; A.B., Amherst Coll., 1923; LL.B., Harvard U., 1926; m. Frances Mary Greene, Apr. 16, 1928; children—Philip Andrew, Michael Craig, Susan Elizabeth. Admitted to N.Y. bar, 1927 thereafter practiced in Rochester; mem. firm Harris, Beach & Wilcox, Rochester, and predecessors, from 1929; asst. dist. atty. Monroe County, 1928-29; spl. asst. atty. gen. N.Y. State, 1949-50. Dir. Security Trust Co., Rochester. Past bd. dirs. Rochester YMCA, Rochester Bur. Municipal Research, A.R.C. Fellow Am. Bar Found.; mem. Am. Coll. Probate Counsel, Am. Coll. Trial Lawyers, Am., N.Y. State, Rochester (pres. 1940-50) bar assns., Am. Law Inst., Delta Upsilon. Club: Genesee Valley (Rochester). Home: Pittsford, N.Y. Died Feb. 18, 1980.

WILCOX, FLOYD CLEVELAND, educator; b. Mason, Mich., Mar. 17, 1886; s. Fred. R. and Emma (Cook) W.; B.A., Kalamazoo Coll., 1910; B.D., Union Theol. Sem., 1913; M.A., Teachers Coll. (Columbia), 1921; Ed.D., Stanford U., 1936; m. Emily C. Carder, Sept. 11, 1912; children—Robert Fraser, Carder, Dorothy Pratt, Winifred Cubberley. Teacher pub. schs., Mich., 1904; in China, 1915-28; prin. Ningpo Acad., 1915-20; dir. Ningpo Jr. Middle Sch., 1922-26; prof. edn., U. of Shanghai, 1926-28, dean of faculty, 1927-28; Cubberly fellow sch. adminstrn., Stanford U., 1929-30; president of Shimer College, Mount Carroll, Ill., 1930-35; prof. of education, dir. lower div., Linfield Coll., McMinnville, Ore., 1936-39; dir. of admissions and personnel, U. of Redlands, Calif., 1939-42, dean of administration since 1942, chmn. Administrative Com. in charge pres. office, 1944-45. Member American College Personnel Association California Council of Research and Guidance, Pacific Coast Assn. of Collegiate Registrars, Assn. Am. Colleges; mem. Academic Council, Western Personnel Inst.; mem. N.E.A., Am. Acad. of Polit. and Social Science, Phi Delta Kappa. Baptist, Kiwanian. Home: Redlands, Calif. *

WILCOX, GEORGE C., lawyer; b. Riga, N.Y., Oct. 5, 1884; LL.B., Syracuse U. Admitted to N.Y. bar, 1910; practice in Rochester; mem. firm Harris, Beach, Keating, Wilcox, Dale & Linowitz. Mem. N.Y. State, Monroe County bar assns., Phi Delta Phi. *

WILDE, LOUISE KATHLEEN, naval officer; b. Concord, N.H., July 18, 1910; d. George William and Jane Louise (O'Donoghue) Wilde; B.A., Mt. Holyoke Coll., 1931; M.A., Columbia, 1941; L.H.D., Rockford Coll., 1954; LL.D. (hon.), St. Joseph's College, 1959. Assistant dir. press bur. Mt. Holyoke College, 1931-34; reporter Springfield (Mass.) Union, 1934-35; dir. publicity Mt. Holyoke Coll., 1935-38; asst. to pres. and freshman dean Rockford Coll., 1938-40, 41-42; commnd. lt. (j.g.), USNR, 1942, advanced through grades to comdr., 1945; asst. to dir. WAVES and coordinator pub. relations, 1943-45; dist. dir. Women's Res., Hawaii, 1945-46; dep. dir. WAVES, 1946-52; trans. regular Navy, 1948; asst. dir. shipping control Western Sea Frontier, 1952-53; capt., USN, 1953-57; asst. chief Naval Personnel for Women, 1953-57; district public relations officer, special assistant to the Commandant 12th Naval District, 1958-62; staff officer, Office Asst. Sec. Def. (manpower), 1962-65. Alumnae trustee Mt. Holyoke Coll. Decorated B.S.M. Mem. Am. Assn. U. Women. Clubs: Mt. Holyoke Alumnae, Army and Navy (Washington). Home: Falls Church, Va. Died Dec. 6, 1979.

WILDENHAIN, FRANS, potter, painter, sculptor; b. Leipzig, Germany, June 5, 1905; s. Franz Emil and Frieda Marie (Starke) W.; studied Bauhaus, Weimar, Germany, 1925, Master of Craft deg., 1929; m. Lili Brockhardt-Rankin, 1969. Came to U.S., 1947, naturalized, 1950. Instr. pottery Folkwang Sch. Workshop, Margarethenhöhe, Essen-Ruhr, 1930; teaching staff State Sch., Halle-Saale, 1930-33; propr. workshop, Putten, Holland, 1933-40, Amsterdam,

1941-47, Pond Farm Workshops, Guerneville, Calif., 1947-50; mem. faculty Sch. Applied Arts, Amsterdam, St. Lioba, also Benedictine Convent, Noord-Holland, 1941-47; prof. ceramics Sch. Am. Craftsman, Rochester Inst. Tech., 1950; asso. with Shop One, Rochester, N.Y.; exhibited in one-man and group shows throughout U.S. and Europe including Cannes Internat., 1955, Ostend, 1959, Prague, 1962, World's Fair, Brussels, 1958, Seattle World's Fair, 1962; in collections of Boymans Mus., Rotterdam, Munson-Williams-Proctor Inst., Utica, N.Y. Stedelyk Mus., Amsterdam, Stoke-upon-Trent, Eng., Mons in Belgium, Faenza and Milan, Italy, Portland (Oreg.) Art Mus., Henry Gallery, Seattle, Scripps Coll., Claremont, Calif., Indpls. Art Mus., Chgo. Art Inst., Meml. Art Gallery, Rochester, St. Paul Gallery Art, Balt. Art Mus., U. Ill., U. So. Ill., U. Mich., others. Recipient numerous awards and prizes from Meml. Art Gallery, Rochester, U. of Rochester, Albright Art Gallery, St. Paul Gallery of Art, Miami Nat. Ceramic Exhbn., Everson Mus., Syracuse, others; Guggenheim fellow, 1958. Fellow Am. Crafts Council. Contbr. articles popular mags., profl. jours. Executed ceramic murals Stasenburgh Labs., Rochester, Nat. Library of Medicine, Washington, Overlook Hosp., Summit, N.J., Students Union, Rochester Inst. Tech., Lockhaven (Pa.) State Coll. Address: Pittsford, N.Y. Died Jan. 25, 1980.

WILDER, ALEC, composer; b. Rochester, N.Y., Feb. 16, 1907; student Lawrenceville (N.J.) Sch., St. Paul's Sch., Concord, N.H.; music edn. Eastman Sch. Music, Rochester, N.Y.; studied counterpoint with Herbert Inch, Edward Royce. Traveled Europe, resided in Italy, returned U.S., 1925; songs used Three's a Crowd, Thumbs Up; composer All the King's Horses, Soft as Spring, It's So Peaceful in the Country; writer arrangements various singers, composer original music for records; composer music Juke Box, ballet performed by Am. Ballet Co. in S.A.; selections performed by Alec Wilder Octet for Columbia Records; music for film The Sand Castle, 1961. Author: American Popular Song: The Great Innovators, 1900-1950. Died Dec. 25, 1980.

WILDER, MITCHELL ARMITAGE, museum ofcl.; b. Colorado Springs, Colo., Aug., 19, 1913; s. Charles Townsend and Maude (Mitchell) W.; B.A., McGill U., 1935; postgrad. U. Calif., Berkeley, 1939-40; m. Sally Duffeld, Dec. 25, 1964; children—Nicholas Forbes, Jennifer Redford. Curator, Tayor Mus., Colorado Springs, 1935-45; dir. Colorado Springs Fine Arts Center, 1945-53; v.p., dir. presentation Colonial Williamsburg (Va.), 1953-58; dir. Abby Aldrich Rockefeller Folk Art Collection, Williamsburg, 1956-58; dir. Chouinard Art Inst., Los Angeles, 1958-61, Amon Carter Mus., Fort Worth, from 1961; mem. adv. com. on environ. planning Bur. Reclamation, Dept. Interior, Washington from 1966, commr. Indian arts and crafts bd., 1967-70; mem. adv. com. to Vatican Mus., 1973-77; mem. adv. council Nat. Mus. Act, 1974-77; mem. Indo-U.S. Joint Com. on Museums of Indo-U.S. Subcommn. Edn. and Culture, 1975-77. Mem. Assn. Art Mus. Dirs. (pres. 1972-73). Club: Cosmos (Washington). Home: Fort Worth, Tex. Died Apr. 1, 1979.

WILDMAN, WILLIAM COOPER, educator; b. Oak Park, Ill., Mar. 20, 1923; s. William Y. and Pauline (Cooper) W.; A.B., DePauw U., 1943; M.S., U. Ill., 1947, Ph.D., 1949; m. Ruth Bowman, Aug. 21, 1947; children—William Young, C. Randall. Asst. prof. Princeton, 1950-53; chemist NIH, 1953-62; Guggenheim fellow Zurich, Switzerland, 1960-61; prof. chemistry Iowa State U., Ames, 1962-79. Served with USNR, 1944-46. Presbyn. Home: Ames, Iowa. Died Dec. 31, 1979.

WILDS, JOHN LAW, ins. exec.; b. Darlington, S.C., Aug. 31, 1883; s. Robert Ervin and Elizabeth Evans (Law) W.; B.S., U. of S.C., 1904; S.B., Mass. Inst. Tech., 1911; m. Mary McClellan Woodruff, Aug. 28, 1914; children—Ann Elizabeth (Mrs. Wilds Davidson), Charlotte Woodruff (Mrs. Gordon Eames Dale), Fire protection engr., N.E., Factory Mut. Cos., Boston, 1911-14; cons. engr. Protection Mut. Fire Ins. Co. (name changed to Protection Mut. Ins. Co.) (mem. Asso. Factory Mut. Fire Ins. Cos.), Chicago, 1914-18, v.p., dir. and gen. mgr., 1918-35, president, 1935-53, treasurer, 1938-53, chairman of the board, 1953—, director; director Firemen's Mut. Ins. Cos., Union Mutual Fire Ins. Co. (Providence), Mutual Boiler Ins. Co. (Boston), Am. Mutual Reins. Co., dir.and past pres., Nat. Fire Protection Assn. Mem. Theta Delta Chi, Omicron Delta Kappa. Presbyn. Clubs: Union League (Chicago); Sunset Ridge Country (Winnetka); Kenilworth (Kenilworth, Ill.); Country (Darlington, S.C.). Home: Darlington, S.C. *

WILDT, RUPERT, astrophysicist; b. Munich, Germany, June 25, 1905; s. Gero and Hertha Wildt; Ph.D., U. Berlin, 1927; m. Katherine Eldredge, Oct. 26, 1962. Came to U.S., 1935, naturalized, 1942. Mem. faculty Bonn U., 1928-29, U. Goettingen, 1930-34; Rockefeller fellow Mt. Wilson Obs., 1935-36; mem. Inst. for Advanced Study, Princeton, N.J., 1936-37; research asso. Princeton, 1937-42; asst. prof. U. Va., 1942-46; mem. faculty Yale, 1946-76, prof. astrophysics, 1958-73, prof. emeritus, 1973-76, chmn. astronomy dept., 1966-68; vis. prof. Basel U. (Switzerland), 1947, U. Calif., Berkeley, 1956, Nat. U. Mexico, 1963; cons. Goddard Inst. Space Studies, NASA, 1964-67. Recipient Bronze medal U. Liège (Belgium), 1962, Eddington Gold medal Royal Astron. Soc. (London), 1966; Scroll of Honor, Yale Sci. and Engring. Assn., 1973. Mem. Am., Royal Astron. socs., Internat. Astron. Union (pres. commn. 16), Assn. Univs. for Research in Astronomy (pres. 1965-68, 71-72, chmn. bd. 1972-74, dir. 1958-74, bd. cons. 1974—). Home: Orleans, Mass. Died Jan. 9, 1976.

WILEY, BELL IRVIN, educator, author; b. Halls, Tenn., Jan. 5, 1906; s. Ewing Baxter and Anna (Bass) W.; A.B., Asbury Coll., 1928, Litt.D., 1965; M.A., U. Ky., 1929, LL.D., 1968; Ph.D., Yale, 1933; Litt. D., Lincoln Coll., 1959; L.H.D., Jacksonville U., 1961; LL.D., Tulane U., 1961; M.A. (hon.), Oxford (Eng.) U., 1965; m. Mary Frances Harrison, Dec. 19, 1937; children—George Bell, John Francis. Asst. prof. history and debating Asbury Coll., 1938-31; prof. history, head dept. Miss. So. Coll., 1934-38, U. Miss., 1938-46; Julius Rosenwald fellow, 1941-42; prof. history, head dept. La. State U., 1946-48; prof. history Emory U., 1948-74, prof. emeritus, 1974-80; vis. prof. U. S.C., fall 1974; Mellon vis. prof. humanities Tulane U., fall 1975; vis. prof. U. Ky., fall 1977; historian in residence Agnes Scott Coll., 1975-77; vis. lectr. (under State Dept.), Europe, 1964-65, Australia and New Zealand, 1970; Harmsworth prof. Am. history Oxford U., 1965-66; Rockefeller Found. postwar fellow, 1948-49; vis. prof. Peabody Coll., summers 1935-38; lectr. Kyoto (Japan) summer seminar Am. studies, 1970. Served to lt. col., hist. officer, AUS, World War II; wrote preliminary history of 2d Army; asst. hist. officer Army Ground Forces, 1943-46. Decorated Legion of Merit, 1945. Mem. Nat. Civil War Centennial Commn., Am., So. (pres. 1955) hist. assns., Orgn. Am. Historians, Soc. Am. Historians, Nat. Hist. Soc. (chmn. bd. advisers), Phi Beta Kappa. Democrat. Episcopalian. Author: Southern Negroes, 1861-65, 1938; The Life of Johnny Reb: Common Soldier of the Confederacy, 1943; The Plain People of the Confederacy, 1943; The Organization of Ground Combat Troups (with K.R. Greenfield and R.R. Palmer), 1947; The Procurement and Training of Ground Combat Troops (with R.R. Palmer and W.R. Keast), 1948; The Life of Billy Yank: Common Soldier of the Union, 1952; The Road to Appomattox, 1956; (with H.D. Milhollen) They Who Fought Here, 1959. Editor: Sam R. Watkins Co. Aytch, 1953; William A. Fletcher, Rebel Private Front and Rear, 1954; Reminiscence of Big I (by W.N. Wood), 1956: Kentucky Cavaliers in Dixie (by George Dallas Mosgrove), 1957; Recollections of a Confederate Staff Officer (by G.M. Sorrel) 1958; Four Years on The Firing Line (by J.C. Nisbet), 1963; (with H.D. Milhollen) Embattled Confederates: An Illustrated History of Southerners at War, 1964; (with Allan Nevins and James I. Robertson) Civil War Books: A Critical Bibiolgraphy, 2 vols., 1967-69; Confederate Women, 1975; The Common Soldier of the Civil War, 1975; posthumously pub. books include: Slaves No More, Letters from Liberia, 1833-1869; Reminiscences of Confederate Service, 1861-1865. Home: Atlanta, Ga. Died Apr. 4, 1980.

WILEY, PAUL LUZON, educator; b. Seattle, July 13, 1914; s. Mont McDonald and Leah Rachel (Sully) W.; A.B., Pomona Coll., 1935; M.A., Claremont Coll., 1936; postgrad. U. Bonn (Germany), 1936-37; Ph.D., Stanford, 1941; m. Jean Pruett Giffen, Oct. 9, 1939; children—John M., Cynthia Sarah. Instr. English, U. Wis.-Madison, 1942, 45-46; asst. prof., 1946-49, prof., 1955-79; vis. prof. Pomona Coll., Claremont, Calif., 1950. Served with AUS, 1943. Internat. Exchange student, 1936-37; Huntington Library fellow, 1941. Mem. Modern Lang. Assn., Wis. Acad. Arts and Scis., Internat. Assn. U. Profs. English, U. Wis. Tennis Assn., Phi Beta Kappa. Author: Conrad's Measure of Man, 1954; Novelist of Three Worlds: Ford Madox Ford, 1962; British Poetry: 1880-21, 1969. Chmn. editorial bd. Contemporary Literature, 1965-79; reviewer Boston Herald Traveler, 1968-79. Home: Madison, Wis. Died Feb. 7, 1979.

WILEY, RALPH BENJAMIN, univ. prof.; b. Detroit, Mich., Mar. 5, 1884; s. John Dexter and Louise Sophia (Safford) W.; B.S. in Civ. Engring., U. of Mich., 1906; m. Agnes Kirkwood Mitchell, Apr. 10, 1909; children—John Safford, Ruth Mitchell (Mrs. James A. McClintock, Jr.). Draftsman, Columbus, O., 1906-08; instructor of sanitary engineering, Purdue University, 1908-10, assistant professor, 1910-16, asso. prof., 1916-19; prof. san. engring., 1919-37; prof. civil engring. and head Sch. of Civil Engring. since 1937; head Sch. Civil Enrgng. and Engring. Mechanics since 1944; dir. Materials Testing Lab. since 1937, Joint Highway Research Project since 1939. Chmn. Ind. Stream Pollution Control Board, mem. exec. com. Ind. Flood Control Commission, Am. Soc. C.E. (dir. 1941-43, v.p. 1947-48), Am. Water Works Assn., Am. Soc. for Engring. Edn., Scabbard and Blade, Sigma Xi, Tau Beta Pi, Theta Xi. Home: West Lafayette, Ind. *

WILFONG, ALBERT E., army officer; b. Virginia, Apr. 25, 1885; commd. 2d lt. Inf. Nat. Guard of Utah, Feb. 5, 1913, 1st lt. Cav., July 1916 in Fed. service for Mexican border crisis; 1st lieut. F. A., Mar. 1917, capt. F.A. Res. Corps. Apr. 1920, 2d lt. Cav. Nat. Guard Utah, Nov. 1921, 1st lt. F.A., June 1924, and advanced to brig. gen. of line, Feb. 1940; entered Fed. service, Mar. 1941, and now in command of 65th F.A.,Brigade, 40th Div. in training at Camp Merriam, San Luis Obispo, Calif.*

WILG, EDWIN ODDE, educator; b. Oslo, Norway, Aug. 14, 1899; s. Ove Edwin and Anna (Odde) W.; brought to U.S., 1904, naturalized, 1921; B.S., Rensselaer Poly. Inst., 1921; M.S., U. Wis., 1925, Ph.D., 1927; NRC fellow Princeton, Harvard, U. Berlin, U. Frankfurt, 1929-32; m. Gladys Mae Bagley, Sept. 18, 1923; children—Robert B., Donald E., Janet D. (Mrs. Russell Booth Bedford III). Chemist, Eastman Kodak Co., Rochester, N.Y., 1921-22, Rochester Gas & Electric Corp., 1922-23; instr. chemistry U. Wis., 1927-29; sr. research assoc. U. Rochester, 1932-35, asst. prof. chemistry, 1935-39, asso. prof., 1939-45, prof., 1945-65, chmn. dept., 1955-64, emeritus, 1965-78; vis. prof. U. Hawaii, 1961-62; Sloan vis. prof. U. Alaska. Ofcl. investigator NDRC, Rochester, 1941-45. Recipient Certificate of Merit, U.S. Army, 1946. Mem. Am. Chem. Soc. Author: (with others) Semimicro Qualitative Analysis, 1954; also sci. articles, lecture outlines and lab. manuals for chemistry. Home: San Diego, Calif. Died Nov. 13, 1978; buried San Diego.

WILKIE, HORACE W., state justice; b. 1917; B.A., U. Wis.; LL.B., George Washington U.; m. Marion Beardsley; 5 children. Admitted to bar, 1944; asso. justice Supreme Ct. Wis., 1962-76, chief justice, 1974-76. Fellow Am. Bar Found., Inst. Jud. Adminstrn.; mem. Am. Law Inst., Wis. Jud. Council, Am. Judicature Soc., Phi Beta Kappa. Address: Madison, Wis. Died May 23, 1976.

WILKINS, EDWIN STILES, soft drink co. exec.; b. E. Orange, N.J., June 30, 1929; s. Edwin Courtois and Marina (Stiles) W.; A.B., Princeton, 1951; LL.B., Harvard, 1957; m. Carol E. Sherman, Feb. 1958; children-Amy, Clay. Admitted to N.Y. bar, 1958; asso. firm Dorr, Hand, Whittaker & Watson, N.Y.C., 1957-59; asso. counsel Colgate-Palmolive Co., N.Y.C., 1960-66; sec., gen. counsel S.B. Penick & Co., N.Y.C., 1966-68; sec., gen. counsel Canada Dry Corp., 1968-78, v.p., 1969-78. Served to lt. (j.g.) USNR, 1951-54. Mem. N.Y. State Bar Assn., Assn. Bar City N.Y., Club: Princeton (N.Y.C.). Home: Chappaqua, N.Y. Died Dec. 1978.

WILKINS, JOHN ROBINSON, educator; b. Chgo., Aug. 15, 1925; s. J. Ernest and Lucile B. (Robinson) W.; B.A., U. Wis., 1944; J.D., Harvard, 1947; m. Constance Ednah Scruggs, Oct. 15, 1961; children—John Robinson, Mariah Constance. Admitted to Ill. bar, 1948, D.C. bar, 1956; teaching fellow U. Chgo. Law Sch., 1947-48; mem. firm Wilkins, Wilkins & Wilkins, Chgo., 1948-49; legal asst. U.S. Ct. Appeals for 3d Circuit, 1949-51; trial atty. Dept. Justice, 1951-54; atty.-adviser, asso. gen. counsel ICA, 1954-58, legal adviser U.S. econ. missions to S. Asia, 1958-60; asso. gen. counsel ICA, Washington, 1960-61; dep. gen. counsel AID, 1961-62, acting gen. counsel, 1962-63, gen. counsel, 1963-64; prof. law U. Calif., Berkeley, from 1964, prof. emeritus, to 1976. Recipient Arthur S. Flemming Award, 1962. Mem. Am. Soc. Internat. Law, N.A.A.C.P., Wis. Alumni Assn., Harvard Law Sch. Alumni Assn., Order of Coif, also Sigma Pi Phi, Kappa Alpha Psi. Club: The Committee (Washington). Editor Harvard Law Rev., 1945-47. Home: El Cerrito, Calif. Died Dec. 12, 1976.

WILKINS, ZORA PUTNAM, author; b. Middleton, Mass., Nov. 8, 1883; d. Fred H. and Susan E. (Killam) W.; B.A., Wellesley, 1904. Sec. to Prof. Hugo Munsterberg, 1908-16, and assisted in his psychol. experiments; research economist with Nat. Industrial Conf. Bd., 1917-20; editorial staff, Industrial Information Service, 1920-21; asst. sec. Bur. Commercial and Industrial Affairs, Boston Chamber of Commerce, 1921-27. Pres. Forewomen's Council of Boston, 1923-24. Author: Letters from a Business Woman, 1923. Home: Boston, Mass. *

WILKINSON, JOHN, educator, painter; b. Berkeley, Cal., July 2, 1913; s. James William and Amelia Catherine (Wyser) W.; student U. Oreg., 1932-34, Calif. Sch. Fine Arts, San Francisco, 1934-36, Acad. Ronson, Paris, 1938-39; m. Una McCann, Sept. 21, 1940; 1 dau., Catherine Marie. Exhbns. include Chgo. Art Inst., 1937, San Francisco Mus. Art, 1939-41, Portland Art Mus., 1945-59, other museums throughout U.S.; joined faculty U. Oreg., 1941, named prof. art, 1959, head dept. fine and applied arts, 1963-68; prof., head dept. fine arts La. State U., Baton Rouge, 1968-74. Fellow Royal Soc. Arts; mem. AAUP, Coll. Art Assn. Home: East Hampton, N.Y. Died Aug. 4, 1974.

WILKINSON, LAWRENCE, financial cons.; b. Evanston, Ill., Jan. 18, 1905; s. George L. and Adele (Enloe) W.; A.B., Yale, 1926; m. Gertrud Gleich, 1955. With N.Y. Trust Co., 1928-30; with Marine Midland Trust Co., 1930-31, 35, v.p., 1938; with Dillon, Read & Co., 1949-50; v.p. Continental Can Co., 1951-57, v.p. finance, 1952-54, group v.p. non-metal divs., 1954-56, exec. v.p., 1956-58, exec. v.p. finance and adminstrn.,

1958-65, exec. v.p. internat. operations, dir., 1966-67; cons. Phelps Dodge Corp., 1968-80; dir. Phelps Dodge Industries, Pantasote Inc., Naess & Thomas Spl. Fund, Adams Express Co., Consol. Aluminum Corp., Oremet Corp., Corp. Realty Consultants; trustee Corporate Property Investors. Econ. adviser to U.S. Mil. Govt., Berlin, Germany, 1946-49; dir. N.Y. State Civil Def. Commn., 1950-51, chmn., 1950-54. Served to col. Ordnance Dept., AUS, 1941-47. Home: New York, N.Y. Died May 10, 1980; buried East Haddam, Conn.

WILL, JOHN MYLIN, naval officer; b. Perth Amboy, N.J., Sept. 15, 1899; s. Otto W. and Jennie Franklin (Dally) W.; B.S., U.S. Naval Acad., 1923; M.S., Pa. State Coll., 1932; m. Louise Ley, Dec. 21, 1929 (dec.); 1 son, John Mylin Will. Commd. ensign U.S.N., 1923, advanced through grades to adm., 1959; comdg. officer U.S.S. S-35, 1934-35, U.S.S. Porpoise, 1937-39; comdr. Submarine Div. 202, also 62, Australia, 1942-44, Submarine Sqdn. 6, Midway Island, 1944, Sqdn. 28, Guam, 1944-45; mem. survey group to China, 1945-46; dir. tng. Bur. Naval Personnel, 1946-48; comdg. officer U.S.S. Columbus, 1948-50; comdr. Mil. Sea Transp. Service, Europe, 1950, Atlantic area, 1951, Amphibious Group Three, 1953-55; dir. personnel policy Office Sec. Def., 1955-56; comdr. Mil. Sea Transp. Service, 1956-59; ret., 1959; pres. Am. Export Isbrandtsen Lines, Inc., 1959-65, chief exec., chmn. bd., 1959-65, chmn. bd., 1965-71, vice chmn., 1971-72; past dir. George W. Rogers Constrn. Corp. Pres. N.Y. Shipping Assn.; pres. trustees N.Y. State Maritime Museum; past dir. West Side Assn. of N.Y.; pres. Italy-Am. C. of C., 1969-72, U.S.-Lebanese C. of C.; commr. of Pilots N.Y. State. Decorated Legion of Merit with 3 gold stars and combat V, Commendation ribbon (U.S.); Order of Yun Hui (China); comdr. Order House of Orange-Nassau (Holland); comdr. Order of Cedars (Lebanon); Order Al Merito Della (Italy); grand officiale del Ordeire al Merito della Republica Italiana. Clubs: Metropolitan Opera, Propeller, N.Y. Yacht, Metropolitan, Whitehall, India House (N.Y.C.); Army-Navy (Washington). Home: New York, N.Y. Died May 8, 1981.

WILLARD, CHARLOTTE, art critic; b. Miscolz, Hungary, 1914; d. Edmund and Hermina (Newman) Schwartz; came to U.S., 1916; B.A., N.Y.U.; grad. student Columbia, New Sch. Social Sci., Hunter Coll.; m. Howard W.-Willard, June 15, 1937. Mng. editor Seventeen mag., 1943-45; exec. editor Jr. Bazaar mag., 1945-46; asst. to Fluer Cowles at Look mag., 1951-55; art critic N.Y. Post, 1964-69; contbg. editor Art in Am., 1963-69. MacDowell fellow. Mem. Internat. Art Critics Assn. Author: Moses Seyer, 1962; What is a Masterpiece?, 1964; Cezanne to Op, 1971; Frank Lloyd Wright, American Architect, 1972; Adomas Goldikas, Color Odyssey, 1973. Home: New York, N.Y. Deceased.

WILLAUER, ARTHUR OSBORNE, architect; b. Rye, N.Y., Aug. 5, 1908; s. Arthur Ebbs and Katherine (Whiting) W.; grad. Phillips Exeter Acad.; B.S., Princeton, 1930, M.F.A., 1932; postgrad. Harvard, 1933; m. Alice Lowell Homer, Mar. 3, 1934; children—Peter O., Charles H., W. Bradford. Asso., Little & Russell, architects, Boston, 1935-39; partner Wirtz, Calhoun & Willauer, architects, Houston, 1939-41; archtl. coordinator Robert & Co., architects-engrs.-mgrs. Naval Air Sta., Corpus Christi, Tex., 1941-42; asst. to project mgr. Robert & Co. B-29 Bomber Plant, Marietta, Ga., 1942-45; dir. architecture Franzheim-Mills, architects, Washington, 1945-47; archtl. cons. New Eng. Mut. Life Ins. Co., Boston, 1946-71; architect, Captiva, Fla. and Prouts Neck, Maine, 1971-78; archtl. adviser to bldg. com. New Eng. Conservatory Music, 1956-59; dir., v.p., trustee, chmn. fin. com., chmn. bldg. com. Boston Archtl. Center, 1960-76. Mem. sch. bldg. com. Town of Dedham, 1958-60; mem. Town Hall Bldg. Com., 1960-61; mem. Police Sta. bldg. com., Dedham, 1961-62; chmn. zoning com. Captiva Civic Assn., 1975-78. Fellow AIA (treas. New Eng. Regional council 1961-64); mem. Mass. Assn. Architects (sec. 1953-54), Boston Soc. Architects (dir. 1952-56). Club: Prouts Neck Yacht. Important works include Willauer Residence, Dwinell Residence, Dedham, Hallward, Maynard, Rockefeller, Sprague, Smith and Talbot residences, Prouts Neck, Maine. Address: Captiva, Fla. Died Sept. 15, 1978; buried Prouts Neck, Maine.

WILLCOX, JOSEPH TANEY, ry. ofcl.; b. Glen Mills, Pa., Sept. 15, 1886; s. James Mark and Kate H. (Taney) W.; student St. Joseph's Prep. Sch., Notre Dame Acad.; m. Ruth Channing Odiorne, Oct. 3, 1923; children—Ruth Channing, Catherine Taney, Joseph Taney, Thomas Odiorne, Ann Louisa. Studied law in office Ex-Sen. George Wharton Pepper; admitted to Pa. bar, 1907; asso. Thomas DeWitt Cuyler, 1909-10; asst. to sec. Pa. R.R. Co., 1910-12, asst. sec., 1912-17, 1919-29, transfer agt., 1925-29, sec. since 1929; mgr. beneficial savs. fund soc., Elmira & Williamsport R.R. Co. Pres. Glen Mills (Pa.) Sch. Served as capt. Q.M.C. Embarkation Service, U.S. Army, 1917, sec. Am. Sect. Inter-Allied Transportation Council, A.E.F., 1918. Republican. Roman Catholic. Clubs: Rittenhouse (Phila.).Home: Wawa, Pa. Office: 1942 Suburban

WILLE, FRANK JOSEPH, naval officer; b. Omaha, Neb., July 30, 1886; s. Christian and Anna (Kratville) W.; B.S., U.S. Naval Acad., 1908; m. Anna ensign, U.S. Navy, 1910, and advanced through grades to rear admiral, 1944; served as senior engring. officer on battleships Arizona, Pennsylvania, California; duty at Navy Yards (Mare Island and Puget Sound); dir. contracts, Bur. of Ships, Navy Dept., Washington, since 1944. Awarded Mexican Service Medal, Dominican Campaign Medal, Victory Medal World War I; Am. Defense Service Medal, Am. Area Service Medal, African Service Medal, Letter of Commendation with ribbon for service in N. Africa, a second letter of Commendation with bronze star for inspection duty under Bur. of Ships, Legion of Merit, Victory Medal (World War II). Mem. Am. Soc. Naval Engrs. (mem. council), Newcomen Soc. of England. Home: Washington. *

WILLEMS, JOHN MURPHY, army officer; b. Leavenworth, Kan., Dec. 24, 1901; s. Leonard and Mary Ellen (Murphy) W.; B.S., U.S. Mil. Acad., 1925; grad. Field Arty. Sch., Cavalry Sch., Command and Gen. Staff Sch.; m. Louise Long (dec.); m. 2d, Aileen Hannaford Guy, May 30, 1936; children—John Carmody, Leonard Field. Commd. 2d lt., F.A., U.S. Army, 1925, advanced through grades to maj. gen., 1950; mem. Field Arty., Army horse show teams, 1932-36, U.S. Olympic Equestrian Team, Berlin, 1936; asst. arty. officer Western Task Force in invasion North Africa; arty. officer 7th Army, Sicilian campaign, chief staff, invasion Western Sicily and capture of Palermo; chief staff 2d Corps, Italian campaign, World War II; chief staff 7th Army of Occupation, Germany, 1945-46; mil. attache, Rome, Italy, 1946-49; mem. Army Gen. Staff, 1949-50, 52-55; comdg. gen. div. arty., 2d Armored Div., 1950-52; comdg. gen. 3d Armored Div., 1955; now asst. chief of staff for intelligence. Decorated D.S.M., Legion of Merit with cluster, Bronze Star Medal. Address: Arlington, Va. Died Sept. 14, 1976.

WILLENBUCHER, FRANZ OTTO, naval officer, lawyer; b. Jersey City, Aug. 23, 1897; s. Alfred Eugene and Dora Elizabeth (Schmidt) W.; B.S., U.S. Naval Acad., 1918; LL.B., N.Y. Law Sch., 1930; J.D., Georgetown U., 1937, postgrad., 1940-41; postgrad. Nat. U., 1946-47, Am. U., 1950; m. Amy Katherine Hart, Apr. 29, 1924; children—Dorothy Elizabeth (Mrs. Carl H. Imlay), Shirley Ann (Mrs. Murry Lee Randall) and Marshall Redfield. Commd. ensign USN, 1918, advanced through grades to capt., 1943; served in Austrian Field Party, Am. Commn. to Negotiate Peace, Vienna, 1918-19; participated in naval demonstration off Cuban ports, 1933-34, in nat. def. aspects Hull-Alfaro Treaty, 1935-36; comml. traffic supt. Office of Chief Naval Operations, 1935-37; exec. officer and comdg. officer U.S.S. Oglala, flagship mine force, U.S. Fleet, 1937-38; ret. as lt. comdr., 1938; editor legal, financial publs., 1938-39; in active Naval service, 1939-46; spl. asst. to chief Naval Communications for policy and legal matters, 1939-46; participated in establishing Def. Communications Bd., 1939-40; Navy dept. mem. coordinating and law coms. Bd. War Communications, 1941-46; coordinator comml. communications traffic during Normandy invasion, 1944. Admitted to N.Y. bar, 1934, D.C. bar, 1944, practiced in Washington, 1946-64. Decorated World War I Victory Medal with mine sweeping clasp, Am. Def. and Am. Theatre medals, Letter of commendation with ribbon bar, Legion of Merit. Mem. Ret. Officers Assn. (exec. v.p., legal counsel 1946-64), Pi Gamma Mu, Phi Delta Phi (vice chmn. com. for constl. integrity 1971-76). Mason. Club: Yacht (N.Y.C.). Author: The Robinson-Patman Anti-Price Discrimination Act, 1937. Home: Bethesda, Md. Died Sept. 5, 1976.

WILLETT, HUGH CAREY, archivist; b. nr. Rochester, Ont., Can., Apr. 23, 1886; s. Charles Carey and Flora Ann (MacDonald) W.; brought to U.S., 1887, naturalized, 1903; A.B., U. So. Calif., 1907, A.M., 1910; D.Sc. (hon.), U. Chicago, 1915, U. Ill., 1926; m. Annabelle Sasnett, Aug. 11, 1926; children—Hugh Carey, Flora Katherine. Instr., later asst. prof. Latin and mathematics U. So. Calif., Los Angeles, 1908-10, prin. U. high sch. and asso. prof., 1911-20, prof. mathematics, 1921-51, dir. admissions and registration, 1937-51, dir. univ. archives since 1951. Member Los Angeles Board of Education since 1952. Pres. Pacific Coast Intercollegiate Athletic Conf., 1933-38, Nat. Collegiate Athletic Assn., 1950-51. Served as 2d to 1st lt. F.A., U.S. Army, 1918-25. Mem. Phi Beta Kappa, Phi Kappa Phi, Kappa Alpha. Home: Los Angeles. *

WILLIAM, JAMES THOMAS JR., editor; b. Lincolnton, N.C., Aug. 10, 1881; s. James Thomas and Sarah (McBee) W.; A.B., Columbia, 1901; D.C.L., U. of South, 1921; LL.D., Norwich U., 1928. Washington corr. of The State, Columbia, S.C., 1901-02; mem. Washington staff Associated Press, 1902-06, and one of its representatives at the Republican and Democratic nat. convs., 1904, and at the Portsmouth Peace Conf., summer of 1905; Washington corr. Boston Eve. Transcript, 1906-08; U.S. Civil Service commr., 1909; editor Tucson Citizen, 1910-12, Boston Eve. Transcript, 1912-25, Boston Eve. American, 1925-27; Washington contbg. editor to nat. syndicates, 1925-37; Washington rep. Chgo. Daily News fgn. service, 1937-38. Mem. adv. council Civil War Centennial Commn.; mem. Sylvanus Thayer Hall Fame Com. Appointed by Pres. Coolidge mem. bd. visitors U.S. Naval Acad., 1924, U.S. Naval Inst. Decorated knight Order of Leopold (Belgium), 1920; comdr. Order of Crown of Italy, 1920. Mem. Anglican Soc. (exec. com.), Sigma Alpha Epsilon; hereditary mem. Soc. Cincinnati (S.C. br.). Episcopalian. Clubs: Metropolitan, Cosmos, Army and Navy (Washington); University (N.Y.C.). Lectr. nat. affairs, fgn. relations. Home: Lincolnton NC. *

WILLIAMS, ALBERT CALVIN, insurance rep.; b. near Cooper, Tex., Jan 23, 1886; s. John Martin Bittick and Eliza Virginia (Sissel) W.; ed. Tex. Christian U.; m. Alice Van Zandt, Sept. 28, 1910; children—Alice Virginia, Albert Calvin. With Neil P. Anderson Cotton Co., 1906-07; with Tex. and Southwestern Cattle Raisers' Assn., 1907-21; editor of The Cattleman, 1915-21; sec. of the Cattle Loan Agency of War Finance Corp. which as a war measure made direct loans to stockraisers of the southwest to conserve breeding herds, 1918-20; pres. and gen. mgr. Cattle Raisers Loan Co., 1921-23; examiner in charge Livestock Loan Dept. of War Finance Corp., Washington, D.C., 1923-24; mem. Federal Farm Loan Bd., Washington, D.C., Dec. 12, 1924-Mar. 15, 1933; gen. agent, of Federal Farm Credit Administration, 10th Federal Land Bank Dist. and pres. Federal Land Bank of Houston, 1933-40; now Texas ranch loan rep. Kansas City Life Ins. Co., Kansas City, Mo., farm loan commr., July 2, 1926-May 10, 1927; mem. President Coolidge's Cotton Com., 1926; mem. liquidating com. War Finance Corp., Washington, D.C., Sept. 1931-Mar. 15, 1933 and 1939-40; mem. Texas Farm Land Use Planning Com.; mem. State-wide Cotton Com. Mem. Tex. & Southwestern Cattle Raisers' Assn. Democrat. Mem. Christian (Disciples) Ch. Clubs: Congressional Country, Houston Country. Home: Fort Worth. *

WILLIAMS, ALBERT RHYS, author; b. Greenwich, O., Sept. 28, 1883; s. Rev. David Thomas and Esther (Rees) W.; B.A., Marietta (O.) Coll., 1904; B.D., Hartford Theol. Sem., 1907; fellow Cambridge U., Eng., and Marburg U., Germany, 1908; m. Lucita Squier, 1924. Ordained Congl. ministry, 1911; minister, Maverick Ch., Boston, Mass., 1907-14; was corr., The Outlook, 1914-15; Chautauqua lecturer, 1916; in Russia, 1917-18; asst. in Commissariat, Foreign Affairs, Soviet Govt. and prepared propaganda sent into Germany; organized Internat. Legion. In Russia gathering material on Russian folk-life and customs, 1922-28. Author: In the Claws of the German Eagle, 1917; Lenin, the Man and His Work, 1919; (pamphlet) 76 Questions and Answers; Through the Russian Revolution, 1921; The RussianLand, 1928. Address: New York, N.Y. *

WILLIAMS, ALFRED L. W., mfg. co. exec.; b. Buckingham, Eng., Sept. 24, 1898; s. A.E. and May (Roome) W.; student Royal Naval Coll., Dartmouth, Eng., 1911-14; m. Katherine Biays, Oct. 26, 1926; children—Clurie Williams Bennis, Leslie Williams Mills. Pres. Varley Pumps, Inc., 1927-31, The Brush Devel. Co. (now Clevite-Brush Devel. Co.), 1931-52; pres. Clevite Research Center, div. Clevite Corp., Cleve., 1952-58; v.p., dir. Clevite Corp., 1958-64, director and corporate consultant, 1964-76; orchid grower; dir. ARDAC, Inc., Medi-Comp, Inc. Trustee Cleve. Hearing and Speech Center, Coronary Club, Inc., 1969-76. Served to lt. comdr. Brit. Royal Navy, 1911-23. Recipient award of merit Royal Hort. Soc., Delia White Meml. medal Garden Center of Greater Cleve. Mem. Nat. Security Indsl. Assn. (ASW exec. com.). Patentee in field. Home: Cleveland, Ohio. Died July 7, 1976; buried Hancock, Md.

WILLIAMS, CHARL ORMOND, educator, b. Arlington, Tenn., Jan. 24, 1885. d. Crittenden and Minnie Lawrence (Thomas) Williams; grad. Arlington (Tenn.) Secondary School 1903; student Chautouqua, N.Y., 4 mos., U. of Colby Summer; hon. D. latt., Southwestern Memphis Tenn, 1925. Teaching confined to Shelby County, Tenn.; began at Millington, 1903; prin. secondary sch., Bartlett, 1904-06; teacher Germantown H.S., 1906-09; prin., 1909-12; asst. dept. of mathematics, W. Tenn. State Normal Sch., 1912-14; supt. of schs. Shelby County, Tenn, 1915-22. First Dem. Nat. committeewoman from Tenn., 1st woman v.chmn. Dem. Nat. Com.; del. Dem. Nat. Conv., San Francisco, 1920; mem. advisory ednl. group of Metropolitan Life Ins. Co.; mem. Com. on Internat. Relations, N.E.A., 1925-28; chmn. Ratification Com. when Tenn. ratified 19th Amendment to Constitution of U.S. Mem. N.E.A. (pres. 1921-22, past director of field service), Nat. Congress of Parents and Teachers (dir. dept. of edn. and 5th v.p. 1930-34; nat. chmn. sch. edn. 1923-30, 1934-42). Women's Joint Congt. Com., D.A.R., Nat. Fed. of Business and Professional Women's Clubs (1st v.p. 1933-35, pres. 1935-37); permanent guest mem. Am. Assn. Univ. Women, since 1923; mem. Internat. Fedn. Bus. and Prof. Women's Clubs (co-organizer); hon. Phi Beta Kappa, Chi Omega, Delta Kappa Gamma (hon. state founder). Delegate to World Federation of Education Assns., San Francisco, Calif., 1923, Edinburgh, 1925, Toronto, 1927, Denver, 1931.

Methodist. Club: Woman's Nat. Democratic. Home: Washington. *

WILLIAMS, CHARLES LAIDLAW, lawyer, banker; b. New York, N.Y., Feb. 9, 1884; s. Charles Eugene and Addie Bellenger (James) W.; A.B., Columbia Coll., 1906, A.M., 1908; LL.B., Columbia U. Law Sch., 1908; m. Gertrude E. Marshall, Aug. 14, 1915; 1 dau., Ariel. Admitted to N.J. bar, 1908; practiced at Newark, as mem. of firm Sommer, Colby & Whiting, 1908-13; founded Juvenile Court System of N.J., 1911-12; prof. of law, Cornell U. Law Sch., 1913-14; asso. with The Morris Plan Corp. of America, its predecessor and affiliated corps., N.Y. City, in pioneer development of indsl. banking in U.S. since 1915, dir. since 1923, v.p. since 1924, counsel since 1925; v.p., dir. and counsel The Morris Plan Corp. of Am. 1925-47, now dir.; pres. and dir. Indsl. Acceptance Co., Paris, France; former v.p. and dir. Indsl. Acceptance Corps. of S. America; v.p., counsel and dir. Collateral Discount Corp.; v.p., dir. and counsel Nat. Installment Credit Corp.; dir. Am. Installment Credit Corporation, Indsl. Insurance Corp.; ret. 1947, Bankers Security Life Insurance Society, Hamilton Fire Ins. Co. Chmn. Rep. Exec. Com., East Orange, N.J., 1908-11, mem. Essex County (N.J.) Rep. Com., 1909-11. Mem. Delta Tau Delta. Rep. Episcopalian. Club: Bronxville (N.Y.) Field. Contbr. poetry and prose to various mags. in Europe and U.S. Home: Bronxville, N.Y. *

WILLIAMS, CLANTON WARE, ednl. adminstr.; b. Montgomery, Ala., June 13, 1904; s. Clanton Ware and Tallulah Hart (McGehee) W.; A.B., Davidson Coll., 1927, LL.D.; A.M., U. Ala., 1928, L.H.D., 1974; postgrad. Ala. Poly. Inst., U. Chgo.; Ph.D., Vanderbilt U., 1938; m. Claudine Payne, July 25, 1936; children—Pamela McGehee (Mrs. Beeth), Eleanor Hart (Mrs. Densford). Tchr., Barnes Sch., Montgomery, 1922-23; with Asheville (N.C.) Sch. System, 1928-29; instr. to prof. history U. Ala., 1929-55; v.p. acad. affairs U. Houston, 1955-56, pres., 1956-61; ednl. cons. U.S. Air Force, Union of Burma, Dept. Health, Edn. and Welfare, NASA, AID, 1960-63; chief edn. adviser AID, India, 1963-67; resident coordinator Inst. Internat. Edn., Pakistan, 1967-69; exec. dir. Ala. Commn. on Higher Edn., Montgomery, 1970-73, exec. dir. emeritus, 1973-75; radio commentator, lectr., 1939-42, 47-51. Mem. Ala. Civilian Def. Council, 1942. Served from capt. to col. USAAF, 1942-46; chief historian USAAF, 1942-47; guest lectr. various U.S. and allied staff schs. and war colls.; faculty, staff Air War Coll., 1951-55. Decorated Legion of Merit, Army Commendation medal with clusters, others. Mem. Am., Mississippi Valley, Ala., So. hist. assns., Am. Mil. Inst., Am. Acad. Polit. and Social Sci., Air Force Assn., Air Res. Assn., Newcomen Soc., Am. Legion, S.A.R., English Speaking Union, Alpha Tau Omega, Phi Kappa Phi, Omicron Delta Kappa, Phi Delta Kappa, Phi Alpha Theta, others. Presbyn. Kiwanian. Clubs: Petroleum, River Oaks Country (Houston); Army-Navy, Cosmos (Washington). Author: Gist of English History, 1933 (revised as Topical History of Britain, 1936); Uncle Sam, A Short History of the U.S.A., 1943; Abner McGehee, rev. 1944; History of Montgomery, Alabama to 1846, rev. 1950; Ideologies in Conflict, 1950, 4th rev., 1955; Background of the News, 1939-51 (18 vols.); numerous vols. lectures, staff studies, histories in air force and internat. affairs; studies in Burmese, Indian, Pakistani, Tex. and Ala. higher edn. Home: Montgomery, Ala. Died Nov. 10, 1975; interred Oakwood Cemetery, Montgomery.

WILLIAMS, CLARA ANDREWS, author; b. Newark, N.J., Dec. 6, 1882; d. Arthur Picton and Bertha L. (Neiman) Andrews; grad. Miss Townsend's Sch., Newark, 1900; spl. pupil Wheaton Sem.; m. George Alfred Williams, Newark, Feb. 24, 1903; children—John Gardner (dec.), Bertha Elizabeth, Robert Havell, Marianna Olea, Rushforth. Author: Mammy's Li'l' Chilluns, 1904; The House That Glue Built, and 15 subsequent titles (Glue Book Series), 1905-10; The Surprise Book—The Advantures of Jack and Betty, 1911; The Magic Book, 1912; Jack and Betty's Magazine (serially in Woman's Home Companion, for 1915-16); The Indian Wigwam, 1915. Contbr. to mags. Home: Kennebunkport, Me.*

WILLIAMS, CLIFTON, ret. lawyer, artist; b. Richmond, Ind., July 1st, 1885; s. Isaac and Ruth Ann (Peacock) W.; LL.B., Ind. U., 1908; m. 2d, Baroness Ozelia Rach-Wolska, Dec. 28, 1942; children (by 1st marriage)—Conger, Jane Louise, Roger; m. 3d, Alma S. Harrington, February 25, 1946. Law librarian, Ind. U. Law Sch., 1906-08; began practice Chicago, 1908, as atty. for Wis. Central Ry.; moved to Milwaukee, Wis., 1909, asst. city atty., 1910-14, 1st asst., 1914-16, city atty., 1916-20; spl. counsel for Milwaukee, 1924-30; uniform law commr. of Wis., 1927-31; became mem. faculty Marquette U. Law Sch., 1911, dean 1927-33. Admitted to practice before Supreme Court of U.S. Mar. 1919, and handled many important matters there; handled 119 cases before Supreme Court of Wis., 1910-33; orange and lemon grower; artist; 19 oil paintings Bank of Am. Bldg., Oceanside, 1950; 3 oils Cassidy Med. Bldg.; self portrait purchases by law class 1931 for Marquette U. Law Library; one-man show Santa Barbara Mus. Art, May, 1956. Popularity and Best Oil prizes, Vista Art Show, 1949, 50. Life mem. Am. Bar Assn. (v.p. 1929) expbtg. mem. La Jolla Art Center; mem. Understandable Art Assn., Inc. of San Diego Co. (founder), Carmel Art Assn. (dir.), Kappa Sigma, Phi Delta Phi, Delta Sigma Rho. Mem. Soc. of Friends. Clubs: City Milwaukee Athletic, Blue Mound, Country (Milwaukee); Country Club (Oconomowoc, Wis.); Rancho Santa Fe Golf; La Jolla Beach. Now devoting time to oil Painting, chemistry of oils and other pigment carriers, research in canvas substitutes. Home: Santa Barbara CA. *

WILLIAMS, EDWARD FOSTER, JR., educator; b. Carroll County, Ga., Jan. 27, 1906; s. Edward Foster and Ila Idella (Alexander) W.; B.S. in Chem. Engring., Auburn U., 1925, M.S., 1929; Ph.D., U. Tenn., 1932; m. Ida Frances Richards, May 31, 1930; children—Edward Foster III, Paul Nash. Asst. research chemist Ala. Agrl. Expt. Sta., 1925-27; mem. faculty U. Tenn. Med. Units, 1927-32, 35-68, Goodman prof. biochemistry, 1968-72, emeritus, 1972-78; instr. N.Y. Postgrad. Med. Sch., 1932-33; research biochemist Killian Research Labs., N.Y.C., 1933-35; Fulbright lectr. Pahlavi U., Shiraz, Iran, 1960-61. Recipient Comer medal natural sci. Auburn U., 1925. Fellow Am. Assn. Clin. Chemists; mem. Am. Chem. Soc. (past chmn. sec. Memphis sect.), Sigma Xi (past pres. Med. Units chpt.), Sigma Phi Epsilon, Tau Beta Pi, Phi Kappa Phi, Phi Delta Chi, Gamma Sigma Epsilon. Home: Memphis, Tenn. Died Jan. 19, 1978.

WILLIAMS, ERIC EUSTACE, prime minister Trinidad; b. 1911; B.A., Queen's Royal Coll., Port of Spain; D.Phil., Oxford (Eng.) U., also hon. D.C.L.; LL.D., U. New Brunswick, 1965. Prof. social and polit. sci. Howard U., 1939; cons. British sect. Anglo-Am. Caribbean Commn., 1943-44, 46-48, sec. agrl. com., 1944-46, dep. chmn. research council, 1948-55; chief minister, minister finance, planning and devel., Trinidad, 1956-61, premier, minister external affairs, 1961-62; prime minister Trinidad and Tobago, from 1962, minister external affairs, 1962-64, minister of finance planning and devel., from 1967. Pro-chancellor U. West Indies, 1965. Named privy counsellor, 1964, companion of honour, 1969; decorated collar Order Liberator (Venezuela), 1970. Author: The Negro in the Caribbean, 1942; Capitalism and Slavery, 1944; Education in the West Indies, 1950. Editor: Caribbean Historical Rev.; Document on British West Indian History, 1807-1833, 1951; The British West Indies at Westminster, 1789-1823, 1953; A History of the People of Trinidad and Tobago, 1964; Captalism and Slavery, 1964; Inward Hunger, 1969. Home: Port of Spain, Trinidad. Died Mar. 31, 1981.

WILLIAMS, FRANKLIN P., business exec.; b. Frankfort, Ky., Jan. 5, 1894; s. Jesse P. and Annie L. (Jones) W.; student U. of Ky., 1912-15; m. Elizabeth B. Gaus, Aug. 9, 1916. Mgr., S.S. Kresge Co., Burlington, Ia., 1916-18, Bloomington, Ill., 1919, Louisville, Ky., 1928-32, Chicago, 1933-42, Detroit, 1943-45; dist. supt., hdqrs. Detroit, 1920-27, sales dir., Detroit, 1946-47, vice pres. in charge merchandising, Detroit, 1947-53, pres., gen. mgr. co., 1953-59, dir., 1947-64, chmn. exec. com.; pres. Mt. Clemens Pottery Co. Mem. Kappa Sigma. Clubs: Detroit Rotary, Detroit Athletic, Lochmoor Country. Home: Grosse Pointe Park, Mich. Died 1976.

WILLIAMS, HERMANN WARNER, JR., museum dir.; b. Boston, Mass., Nov. 2, 1908; s. Hermann Warner and Helen Chilton (French) W.; A.B., Harvard, 1931, A.M., 1933; Ph.D., Courtauld Inst. of Art, Univ. London, 1935. Student Inst. of Fine Arts, NeW York U., 1935-41; m. Alice Barrett Farley, Aug. 30, 1942; children—Susan, Penelope, Richard. Appt. interne Bklyn. Mus. grant of Rockefeller Found., 1935; asst., Dept. of Paintings, The Met. Mus. of Art, 1937, asst. curator, 1942; asst. dir. Corcoran Gallery of Art, Washington, 1946, dir., sec., 1947-68, dir. emeritus, 1968-74; cons. to bd. Lauren Rogers Mus. Art, Laurel, Miss., 1970-74. Served in U.S. Army, 1942-46, in part, as chief, hist. properties sect., War Dept.; returned to inactive duty as Major Corp. Engrs. Fellow Co. Mil. Historians; mem. Am. Assn. Museums (mem. adv. com.), Am. Art Research Council, Am. Soc. Arms Collectors, Civil War Round Table D.C. Unitarian. Clubs: Harvard, Armor and Arms, Century Association (N.Y.C.); Cosmos, Harvard (Washington). Author: (with Barrett Cowdrey) William Sidney Mount, 1944; The Civil War: The Artists' Record, 1961; Mirror to the American Past: A Survey of American Genre Painting 1750-1900, 1973. Contbr. articles on art subjects to art and ednl. pubs. Home: Washington, D.C. Died Nov. 3, 1974; interred Mt. Auburn Cemetery, Cambridge, Mass.

WILLIAMS, JACK G., advt. cons.; b. Detroit, Feb. 2, 1898; s. Frederick Miles and Margaret (Hutchings) W.; B.A., U. Mich., 1921; m. Gwen Burkard, July 7, 1934; 1 dau., Carole Ann. With circulation, advt. and cashier's depts. Detroit Free Press, 1915-23; creative staff Brooke, Smith, French & Dorrance, Inc., Detroit, 1921-23, account exec., 1923-40, account supr., v.p., 1940-60, chmn. exec. com., 1954-60; sr. v.p., chmn., exec. com. Ross Roy-B.S.F. & D., Inc., 1960-63; sr. v.p. Ross Roy, Inc., 1967-71; cons., from 1971. Mem. council planning commn., Village Grosse Pointe Shores, police commn., assessor, park commr., 1948-64, mayor, 1954-64. Republican. Presbyn. Clubs: Detroit Yacht; M Club of Mich. Home: St. Clair Shores, Mich. Deceased.

WILLIAMS, JAMES PETER, JR., corp. official; b. Henrico County, Va., April 13, 1884; s. James Peter and Anna Page (Kinckle) W.; student U. of Va., 1903-05; m. Virginia Watkins Carrington, Sept. 4, 1912; children—James Peter III, Nancy Carrington, Nell Baskerville. Mining and cons. engr. since 1905; dir. Koppers Co., Virginian Railway Co., Fidelity Trust Co., Flannery Bolt Co., trustee, Dollar Savings Bank, mem. Am. Inst. of Mining and Metall. Engrs. Democrat. Episcopalian. Clubs: Duquesne, Fox Chapel Golf (Pittsburgh); Pittsburgh Golf. Home: Berryville, Va. *

WILLIAMS, JESSE FEIRING, physical educator; b. Kenton, O., Feb. 12, 1886; s. Ora Otis and Ida May (Feiring) W.; A.B., Oberlin, 1909; diploma, Chautauqua Sch. Physical Edn., 1907; M.D., Coll. Phys. and Surg. (Columbia), 1915; Sc.D., Rollins Coll., 1939; m. Gertrude Carey Finney, Aug. 21, 1912. Prof. physical edn., Teachers' Coll. (Columbia), since 1919. Served as 1st lt. Med. Corps, U.S.A., 1918-19; maj. Red Cross, in charge recreation in hosps., Atlantic Div., 1919. Mem. N.E.A., Am. Physical Edn. Assn. (pres. 1932-33), Soc. Dirs. Physical Edn. in Colleges, N.Y. Soc. Physical Edn. (president), Nu Sigma Nu, Alpha Omega Alpha. Republican. Presbyterian. Clubs: Columbia Faculty. Author: Healthful Living, 1919, 34; Organization and Administration of Physical Education, 1922; Personal Hygiene Applied, 1922, 27, 31, 34, 35, 37, 39; Textbook Anatomy and Physiology, 1923, 28, 30, 32, 35, 39; Hygiene and Sanitation, 1927, 30, 35; Principles of Physical Education, 1927, 31, 38; The Business Man and his Health, 1933. Co-Author: Healthful Schools, 1916; Athletics and Education, 1929, 36; Health and Control, 1929; Industrial Hygiene, 1930; Health and Happiness, 1930; Health and Rules of the Game, 1930; Health and Service, 1930; Textbook of Physical Education, 1931, 39; Health and Physical Education for Public School Administrators, 2 vols., 1930, 31; the Administration of Health and Physical Education, 1935, 39. Methods and Materials in Health Education, 1935, 37. Home: New York, N.Y. *

WILLIAMS, JOHN FRED, cons.; b. Volga, Ky., Sept. 7, 1904; s. James Marion and Jennie (Vaughan) W.; A.B., U. Louisville, 1931; LL.D., Union Coll., Barbourville, Ky., 1945; m. Carrie Bennett Cecil, Mar. 29, 1929; children—John Marion, Jane Florence (Mrs. Howard Van Antwerp III). Tchr. rural sch., Johnson County, Ky., 1924-30, Louisville city schs., 1930-31, Johnson County High Sch., 1931-33, Paintsville (Ky.) High Sch., 1933-34; supt. Johnson County schs., 1934-43; supt. pub. instrn. Ky., 1944-48; v.p., personnel dir. Ashland (Ky.) Oil and Refining Co.; cons. Former sec. Ky. Textbook Commn.; former mem. Ky. com. Functions and Resources of State Govt.; chmn. Ky. Govs. Citizens Adv. Com. on Hwys; mem. Ky. State Fair Bd., Ky. Adv. Council for Vocational Edn. and Manpower Devel., Ky. Commn. on Pub. Edn.; former sec. State Textbook Commn., former chmn. Council on Pub. Higher Edn. Ky., Ky. Bd. Edn.; mem. planning bd. Ky. Edn. Assn. Bd. regents Ky. State Colls.; past chmn. bd. trustees Eastern State Tchrs. Coll., Western State Tchrs. Coll., Morehead State Tchrs. Coll., Murray State Tchrs. Coll.; former trustee U. Ky.; former trustee Ky. Tchrs. Retirement System. Designated hon. Ky. farmer, 1944; recipient award of merit for outstanding ednl. service Ky. Assn. Coll. and Secondary Schs., 1945. Mem. Ky. Hist. Soc. (pres.), Phi Delta Kappa. Methodist. Mason, Rotarian. Club: Filson (Louisville). Address: Ashland, Ky. Died Oct. 3, 1977.

WILLIAMS, JOHN HENRY, economist; b. Wales, June 21, 1887; son of John Hamer and Margaret (Hamer) W.; A.B., Brown Univ., 1912, hon. Sc.D., 1935; A.M., Harvard, 1916, Ph.D., 1919; m. Jessie Isabelle Monroe, Sept. 1, 1915 (dec. 1960); children—Margaret (Mrs. Margaret Woodman), Jane (Mrs. Calvert W. Watkins); m. second, Katherine R. McKinstry, Apr. 6, 1962. Instructor English Brown U., 1912-15; instr. econs. and asst. editor Rev. Econ. Statistics, Harvard, 1918-19; asst. prof. economics, Princeton, 1919-20; asso. prof. banking, Northwestern U., 1920-21; asst. prof. economics, Harvard University, 1921-25, asso. prof., 1925-29, prof., 1929-33, dean, Graduate School of Public Administration, 1937-47, Nathaniel Ropes professor of political economy, 1933-57, emeritus, 1957-80; William L. Clayton Prof. internat. econ. affairs, The Fletcher Sch. Law and Diplomacy, Tufts U., 1957-63; v.p. Fed. Res. Bank N.Y., 1936-47, econ. adv., 1933-52, econ. cons., 1952-64; Westinghouse prof., Italy, 1925-26. U.S. del. Preparatory Commn. World Monetary and Econ. Conf., 1932-33. Mem. E.C.A. adv. com., fiscal monetary problems, 1948-51. Contributing editor Rev. of Econ. Statistics, 1921-25. Former dir. Nat. Bur. Econ. Research, Inc. Mem. Am. Economic Assn. (pres. 1951), Am. Statis. Assn., American Philos. Soc., Phi Beta Kappa, Delta Sigma Rho, Theta Delta Chi. Author: Argentine International Trade Under Inconvertible Paper Money (Wells prize), 1920; Annual Studies of the Balance of Payments of the United States, 1919-23; Postwar Monetary Plans, 1944, 4th edition, 1949;

Economic Stability in a Changing World, 1953. Co-author Financing American Prosperity, 1945. Home: Cambridge, Mass. Died Dec. 24, 1980.

WILLIAMS, MARY LOU, composer, pianist; b. Pitts.; May 8, 1914; d. Mose and Virginia (Burley) Winn; ed. Western House High Sch.; m. John Williams; m. 2d, Harold Bake. Child prodigy; has perfect pitch; with Andy Kirk's orch. 12 years. yrs. (joined at age of 16) as pianist, arranger, condr. of rehearsals, composed, arranged recorded with band, Night Life and Overhand; appeared at Cafe Society Uptown and Downtown, 1942-47; with Duke Ellington's orchestra, 6 mos., 1943; a composer and arranger for Duke Ellington, Benny Goodman, Glen Gray, Earl Hines, Bob Crosby, Andy Kirk, Louie Armstrong and others; numerous night club appearances. Mem. Am. Soc. Composers and Publishers. Composer Zodiac Suite, (12 compositions based on astrology), played suite with N.Y. Symphony orchestra, 1946, introduced suite, Town Hall, Dec. 23, 1946. Composer: Lonely Moments, Whistle, Roll'Em, Walkin and Swingin, Fifth Dimension, The Juniper Tree, and over 100 others. Home: Durham, N.C. Died May 28, 1981.

WILLIAMS, MERTON YARWOOD, college prof.; b. Bloomfield, Ont., Can., June 21, 1883; s. Edwin Allison and Caroline Elizabeth (Bowerman) W.; student Westtown (Pa.) Boarding Sch., 1894-95; B.Sc., (Mining), Queen's Univ., Kingston, Ont., 1909; Ph.D., (Geology), Yale, 1912; m. Lula Maud Philp, Dec. 23, 1915; children—Edwin Philp, Marion Margaret, Kathleen Mavis. Teacher, public sch., Ont., 1903-05; with Victoria Mines, Ont., summer 1907; geol. survey of Can., 1908-12, asst. geologist, 1912-15, asso. geologist, 1915-24; asso. and prof. of stratigraphy and paleontology, Univ. of B.C., 1921-35, head dept. of geology and geography, 1936-50; chief of oil investigations for geol. survey of Can., 1920-21; commr. on Pacific Great Eastern Survey of resources for C.P.R., C.N.R. and B.C. govt., 1929-30; geologist to Hong Kong govt., 1924-25, geologist Northwest planning project, Alaskan Highway, 1943. Fellow Geol. Soc. of Am. (2d v.p. 1946), Paleontological Soc. of Am., Royal Soc. of Can. (past pres. sect. 4). Mem. Professional Engrs. of B.C. Adherent United Ch. of Can. Author 73 articles on geology in Geological Survey of Canada, Memoirs 47, 111 and 163; 12 articles on zoology, 2 on geog.; contbr. articles on fauna of James Bay, Mackenzie Valley, Yukon and elsewhere. Home: Vancouver, B.C., Can. *

WILLIAMS, PAUL REVERE, architect; b. Los Angeles, Feb. 18, 1896; s. C.S. and Lila A. (Wright) W.; student U. Soc. Cal., also Beaux Arts Inst. of Design; D.Arch., Howard U.; D.Sc., Lincoln U., 1941; D.F.A., Tuskegee Inst., 1956; m. Della M. Givens, June 27, 1922; children—Marilyn (Mrs. Elbert T. Hudson), Norma (Mrs. Frank Harvey). Designer, John Austin, architect, practice of architecture, 1923-80; asso. architect Los Angeles Internat. Airport, County of Los Angeles Ct. House, Fed. Customs and Office Bldg., Los Angeles; prin. works include Music Corp. of Am. office bldgs., N.Y.C., Beverly Hills, Saks Fifth Av., W.J. Sloan & Haggerty's, Beverly Hills, Franz Hall and Botany Bldg. at U. Cal. at Los Angeles; v.p., dir. Broadway Fed. Savs. & Loan Assn.; chmn. Internat. Opportunity Ins. Co. Mem. President's Adv. Com. Housing; mem. Cal. Civil Rights Com.; past mem. Cal. Redevel. Commn. and Cal. Housing Commn.; pres. Los Angeles Art Commn. Trustee Howard U. Recipient Man of Year award Omega Phi Psi, 1951; Spingarm medal, 1953; award for creative planning Los Angeles C. of C., 1955; award Wisdom mag., 1956. Fellow A.I.A.; mem. So. Cal. Heart Assn. (dir.). Mason (33 deg.). Author: Small Homes of Tomorrow; New Homes for Today. Home: Los Angeles, Calif. Died Jan. 23, 1980.

WILLIAMS, R(OBERT) R(OYCE), pres. S. S. Kresge Company; born Markeson, Wisconsin, 1882; son David D. and Louisa (Moore) Williams; married Edith Pickering, Sept. 1909 (died June 1942); children—David D., Donald A.; m. 2d, Maude V. Campbell, June 1943. With Franklin Life Ins. Co., Springfield, Ill., 1900-08; with S. S. Kresge Co. since 1908, as store mgr., 1909, buyer, 1910-20, v.p. of merchandising, 1920-38, pres., 1938-46, retired May 1946, still continues as dir. and chmn. exec. com.; dir. Nat. Bank of Detroit. Trustee and sec. Florence Crittenton Hospital. Presbyn. Mason (K.T., Shriner). Clubs: Detroit Athletic, Detroit Golf, Detroit Boat; Bloomfield Hills Country; Rotary (pres. 1925-26). Home: Detroit. *

WILLIAMS, T. HARRY, educator, author; b. Vinegar Hill, Ill., May 19, 1909; s. William D. and Emma (Necollins) W.; B.E., Platteville (Wis.) State Tchrs. Coll., 1931; Ph.M., U. Wis., 1932, Ph.D., 1937. Instr. extension div. U. Wis., 1936-38, W.Va. U., summer 1937; instr., asst. prof. U. Omaha, 1938-41; mem. faculty La. State U., Baton Rouge, 1941-79, prof. history, 1948-55, Boyd prof. history, 1953-79; Harmsworth prof. Am. history Queen's Coll., Oxford (Eng.) U., 1966-67. Mem. Hist. adv. com. Dept. Army, 1955-60. Recipient Lincoln Diploma of Honor, Lincoln Meml. U., 1956, Nat. Book award for Huey Long, 1969, Pulitzer prize, 1969. Guggenheim fellow, 1957. Mem. Am. Assn. U. Profs., Am. Mil. Inst., Civil War Centennial Assn. (dir.), Soc. Am. Historians, Am., So. (v.p. 1957-58, pres. 1958-59) hist. assns., Orgn. Am. Historians (v.p. 1971-72, pres. 1972-73). Author: Lincoln and the Radicals, 1941; Lincoln and His Generals, 1952; P.G.T. Beauregard, 1955; The Union Surrendered, 1963; The Union Restored, 1963. Editor: Selected Writings and Speeches of Abraham Lincoln, 1943; With Beauregard in Mexico, 1956; Abraham Lincoln—Selected Speeches, Messages and Letters, 1957; (with others) A History of the United States, 1959; Americans at War, 1960; Romance and Realism in Southern Politics, 1961; Military Memoirs of a Confederate by E. Porter Alexander, 1962; McClellan, Sherman and Grant, 1962; Every Man a King, 1964; Hayes: The Diary of a President, 1964; Hayes of the Twenty-third: The Civil War Volunteer Officer, 1965; Huey Long, 1969; The History of American Wars From Colonial Times to World War I, 1981. Home: Baton Rouge, La. Died July 6, 1979; buried Roselawn Cemetery, Baton Rouge.

WILLIAMS, WALKER ALONZO, automobile co. exec.; b. Wellington, Mo., June 8, 1901; s. Henry A. and Helen (Walker) W.; student U. Ill., 1922-23, Kansas City Sch. Law, evenings 1921, Kansas City Jr. Coll., evenings 1921; m. Evelyn Forrester, Sept. 25, 1926; children—Walker Forrester, John Haviland. With traffic dept. Armour Grain Co., Kansas City, Mo., 1920-22; with accounting dept. Am. Can Co., Kansas City, Mo., 1924-25; various positions up to wholesale mgr. Ford Motor Co., Kansas City, Mo., 1925-34, asst. br. mgr., Omaha, 1934-39, Kansas City, Mo., 1939-41, br. mgr., Salt Lake City, 1941-42, 44-45, Somerville, Mass., 1945-46, Ford sales mgr., Dearborn, Mich., 1946-48, gen. sales mgr. Ford div., 1948-50, v.p. sales and advt. for co., 1950-56, v.p., also vice chmn. dealer policy bd. for co., 1956-58, v.p., asst. gen. mgr. Lincoln-Mercury div., 1958-61, ret., 1961; bus. mgr. Kalunite Inc., Salt Lake City, 1942-44. Charter mem. Detroit Symphony Orch.; mem. Detroit Grand Opera Assn.; gen. chmn., bd. dirs. United Found. Detroit, 1958; chmn. Crusade for Freedom, State Mich., 1951-52; past bd. dirs. Automobile Safety Found., Washington. Past mem. Rapid Transit Commn., Detroit. Mem. Automotive Old Timers (life), DeMolay Legion of Honor, Fla. Atlantic Music Guild, Opera Guild Ft. Lauderdale, Founders Soc. of Detroit Inst. Arts English Speaking Union, Phi Gamma Delta. Clubs: Detroit Athletic; Boca Raton (Fla.), Boca Raton Hotel and Club; Vermilion Fairways Golf (Cook, Minn.). Home: Boca Raton, Fla. Died Jan. 14, 1981; interred Meditation Hall, Boca Raton Mausoleum.

WILLIAMS, WALTER ROBERTSON, JR., banker; b. N.Y.C., Sept. 15, 1911; B.S. in Indsl. Engring., Yale, 1932; grad. study Am. Inst. Banking, Columbia, N.Y. U.; m. Manie H. Connor, 1937; children—Stephanie Y., Elizabeth R. With Franklin Savs. Bank, 1932-41, auditor, 1935, asst. sec., 1936-41; exec. sec. Savs. Banks Assn. State N.Y., 1941-49; treas. Union Dime Savs. Bank, 1950, v.p., 1951-59, trustee, 1951-80, pres., 1959-67, chmn. bd., 1968-80; dir. Met. Life Ins. Co., Instl. Investors Mut. Fund; mem. lower midtown adv. bd. Chem. Bank N.Y. Trust Co. Vice chmn. Better Bus. Bur. Met. N.Y., Inc., 1966-80. Mem. N.Y. adv. bd. Salvation Army, 1961-80. Mem. Nat. Assn. Mut. Savs. Banks. Clubs: Yale (N.Y.C.); Baltusrol Golf. Home: Short Hills, N.J. Died Nov. 3, 1980.

WILLIAMSON, ADOLPH ANCRUM, consular service; b. Washington, D.C., Apr. 28, 1883; s. John Condy and Frances (Eilenberger) W.; grad. high sch. and business coll., Washington; m. Annie Pauline McKim, of Tokyo, Japan, Sept. 22, 1909. Student interpreter, Am. Embassy, Tokyo, Japan, 1906-8; v. and deputy consul at Dalny, 1908-11; consul at Antung, 1911-13, Tansui, 1913-14, Dalny, May 5, 1914, now at Dairen. Episcopalian. Clubs: Dairen, Twatutia Foreign (Taihoku, Formosa). Home: Washington, D.C. Address: Dairen, Manchuria.*

WILLIAMSON, ARTHUR PUTNAM, mfg. exec.; b. Norwalk, O., May 2, 1884; s. Rev. James DeLong and Edith Day (Ely) W.; B.A., Yale, 1907; m. Edna Wood, Oct. 12, 1912 (dec. 1945); 1 son, James Wood; m. 2d, Elizabeth M. Condict, 1947. Estimator Hill Clutch Co., Cleve., 1907-08; clk. Hubert H. Ward & Associates, 1908-09; treas. Dill Mfg. Co., tire valves, parts, 1909-35, pres., treas., 1935—; pres. Medical Mutual of Cleveland, Inc; chairman Society National Bank of Cleveland; trustee Blue Cross of North-East Ohio; mem. bd. of trustees Huron Rd. Hospital. Republican. Presbyterian. Clubs: Chagrin Valley Hunt, Union (Cleve.); Yale (N.Y. C.). Home: Chesterland, O. *

WILLIAMSON, EDISON B., mng. editor; b. Oxford, Pa., May 6, 1882; s. William T. and Amanda E (Harris) W.; LL.B., Dickinson Sch. of Law, 1903; m. Mayme A. Bubb, Aug. 15, 1911. Admitted to York County bar, 1904, and began in practice of law; became reporter York Daily, 1904; now mng. editor York Dispatch. Home: York, Pa. *

WILLIAMSON, JOE, JR., cons. engr.; b. St. Louis, Mar. 27, 1906; s. Joseph and Florence Emily (Burton) W.; B.S. in Civil Engring., U. Mo., Rolla, 1929; m. LaVerne Nimmo, May 28, 1952. Surveyman, Miss. River Commn., 1926-27; v.p. Russell & Axon, cons. engr., Mo. and Ill., 1929-39, Fla., 1939-51; owner, prin. engr. Williamson & Assos., cons. engrs., St. Louis, 1951-78; past pres. Fla. Soc. Profl. Engrs. Mem. exec. com. St. Louis Hills Home Owners Assn., 1975-78. Recipient Kenneth Allen award Fla. Sewage Works Assn., 1941, Service award, 1943; named Engr. of Year, St. Louis chpt. Mo. Soc. Profl. Engrs., 1975. Registered profl. engr., Mo., Ill., Fla., 10 other states. Mem. Am., Mo. (past pres.) cons. engrs. councils, Nat., Mo. socs. profl. engrs., ASCE (life), Am. Water Works Assn. (life), Water Pollution Control Assn., Am. Acad. Environ. Engrs., St. Louis Engrs. Club, Acad. Civil Engrs. U. Mo.-Rolla, St. Louis Astron. Soc., Theta Xi, Theta Tau. Democrat. Presbyn. Clubs: St. Louis Ambassadors, Shriners. Patentee water treatment processes, pneumatic sewage ejector. Home: St. Louis, Mo. Died Sept. 1978.

WILLIAMSON, RAYMOND FERRIS, lawyer; b. Oronoco, Minn., June 24, 1883; s. Nathan N. and Mary Elizabeth (Clason) W.; student Northwestern U. and U. of Minn.; m. May E. Madden. May 25, 1909; children—Marian Genevieve, Kenneth Raymond, Bernard Martin. Admitted to S.D. bar, 1909, and practiced since at Aberdeen; mem. Williamson & Williamson; state's atty. Brown County, S.D., 1919-23; mem. S.D. Ho. of Rep., 1923-29 (speaker of House, 1927-29). Mem. Am. Bar Assn., S.D. State Bar Assn. (past pres.), Aberdeen Civic Assn., Y.M.C.A. Republican. K.P., Elk. Club: Aberdeen Country. Home: Aberdeen, S.D. *

WILLIAMSON, ROBERT BYRON, judge, lawyer; b. Augusta, Me., Aug. 23, 1899; s. Joseph and Vallie Mary (Burleigh) W.; student Phillips Andover Acad., 1916; A.B., Harvard, 1920, J.D., 1923; LL.D., U. Me., 1956, Bowdoin Coll., 1961, Nasson Coll., 1971, New Eng. Coll., 1975; m. Grace Warren Whitney, June 2, 1925; children—Robert B., Martha C. Admitted to Me. bar, 1923; practiced in Augusta, 1923-45, 70-76; justice Superior Ct. Me., 1945-49, asso. justice Supreme Jud. Ct. Me., 1949-56, chief justice, 1956-70; U.S. commr. for Me., 1926-29, 31-35. Mem. Common Council, Augusta, 1923-24; mem. Me. Ho. of Reps., 1929-30. Served as 2d lt. inf., U.S. Army, 1918. Mem. Conf. Chief Justices (chmn. 1967-68), Am., Me. bar assns., Am. Legion, Phi Beta Kappa (hon.). Republican (del., mem. resolutions com. nat. conv. 1940). Congregational-Christian (pres. Conf. Me. 1950). Mason. Clubs: Augusta Country; Harvard (Boston). Address: Augusta, Maine. Died Dec. 27, 1976.

WILLIS, JOHN MITCHELL, army officer; b. King George, Va., Nov. 25, 1886; s. Andrew Johnston and Margaret Wilmot (Mitchell) W.; M.D., George Washington U., 1909; grad. Army Med. Sch., 1911, Med. Field Service Sch., 1928, Command and Gen. Staff Sch., 1931, Army War Coll., 1935; m. Anna Gibson, June 21, 1911; 1 son, John Mitchell. Commd. 1st lt., Med. Res. Corps, 1910, commd. 1st lt., 1911 and advanced through grades, U.S. Army, to maj. gen., 1948; comdg. gen. Brooke Army Med. Center, Fort Sam Houston, Tex., since 1946; ret. as maj. gen., 1948; apptd. dir. Hamot Hosp., Erie, Pa., 1948. Mem. A.M.A., Am. Coll., Physicians, Assn. Mil. Surgeons, Soc. of the Cincinnati of Va., Sigma Chi. Episcopalian. Mason. Address: Erie, Pa. *

WILLY, ROY EARLE, lawyer; b. Chgo., Dec. 2, 1889; s. Milo Ambrose and Mary Lincoln (Early) W.; LL.B., U. Mich., 1912, J.D., 1968; m. Josephine Amelia Lien, Jan. 11, 1920. Admitted to bars of Mich. and S.D., 1912; practiced at Platte, S.D., 1912-25, state's atty., Charles Mix County, 1919-24; spl. counsel State Banking Dept. of S.D., 1925-28; gen. practice, Sioux Falls, S.D., from 1928; partner Willy, Pruitt, Matthews & Jorgensen and predecessor firms; referee in bankruptcy for S.D., 1948-69; dir. Union Security Co., United Nat. Bank Sioux Falls. Mem. exec. bd. Sioux council Boy Scouts Am., 1928-54, commr. 1930-34; nat. council mem., 1935-50, v.p. 1939, pres. 1940-45; chief of civilian def., Sioux Falls, 1942-45, dir., 1950-58; civilian aide sec. Army, 1947-62. Served with inf. U.S. Army, 1918; 2d lt. inf., O.R.C., 1921. Recipient Silver Beaver award Boy Scouts Am., 1932, Outstanding Civilian Service medal Army, 1963. Pres. El Riad Trustees, Inc., from 1951. Fellow Am. Bar Found. (life mem.; recipient Disting. Service award 1968); mem. Am. Inst. of Jud. Adminstn. Am. Bar Assn. (state del. 1939-64, chmn. Ho. of Dels. 1950-52, chmn. state legislation com., 1955-56, mem. fed. judiciary com. 1957-68, mem. com. on expansion facilities 1962-69), Am. Law Inst. (life), State Bar S.D. (pres. 1939), Minnehaha County Bar Assn. (pres. 1950), Am. Legion, S.A.R. Presbyn. Mason (32 deg., Shriner, Jester), Elk. Club: Minnehaha Country. Mem. bd. editors Am. Bar Assn. Jours., 1950-67; chmn. editorial bd. S.D. Bar Jour., 1947-67. Home: Sioux Falls, S.D. Died Dec. 2, 1978.

WILSON, ALAN STAFFORD, internat. ednl. mgmt. cons.; b. Dayton, Ohio, March 8, 1905; s. Charles Clinton and Caroline (Stafford) W.; A.B., Ohio

Wesleyan U., Delaware, 1929; M.A., Wittenberg Coll., Springfield, Ohio, 1937; M.A., Yale, 1944; LL.D. (hon.), Nasson Coll., 1955; D.Sc., Portland U., 1956; m. Mary F. Seifert, Sept. 30, 1933; children—Mary Katherine, John Alan Thomas. Dir. training, Frigidaire Corp., 1929, materials control dept., 1930-32; tchr. White Chapel Elementary Sch., Xenia, Ohio, 1932-33; prin. Sinclair Coll. Evening High Sch., 1933-34, dean sch. commerce, finance, 1933-38, acting dir., 1937-38; dir. Hillyer Jr. Coll., Hartford, 1938-47; pres. Hillyer Coll., 1947-70, vice chancellor adminstrn. U. Hartford, 1960-77, treas., 1964, prof. edn., 1964-71, lectr. and curriculum cons., 1971-77; ednl. mgmt. cons. Govt. Malaysia and Republic of China, 1971-77. Adminstr., mem. faculty Land Reform Tng. Inst., Taiwan; lectr. Chines Cultural Coll., Taiwan; mem. Internat. Exec. Services Corps. Mem. Glastonbury Bd. Edn., 1945-51; co-founder Conn. Conf. Jr. and Community Colls. (past pres.); 1st pres., Conn. Chpt., Soc. Advancement of Mgmt.; hon. overseer Old Sturbridge Village; mem. exec. com. Conn. Council Higher Edn. 1955-56. Corporator U. Hartford, chmn. administrv. council, 1957-60; corporator Hartford Hosp.; regent Assn. Found. For Greece; mem. vis. com. edn. dept. Wadsworth Atheneum, 1962-77; corporator Mt. Sinai Hosp. Mem. Nat. Soc. Study of Edn., Nat. Assn. Biology Tchrs., A.A.A.S., Philosophy of Sci. Assn., Assn. Higher Edn., Conn. Acad. Arts and Scis., Phi Kappa Tau. Clubs: Civitan, University, Ind. Republican. Conglist. Home: Glastonbury, Conn. Died Mar. 24, 1977.

WILSON, ALLEN BARNUM, inventor, artist; b. Chgo., Apr. 8, 1898; s. Samuel Allen and Florence (Barnum) W.; student U. Wis., 1915-17, Sorbonne, Paris, France, 1919; Chgo. Acad. Fine Arts 1923-24; student of Frederic Tellander, 1935-39; m. Marion Gahan, Sept. 12, 1925; 1 son, Gahan. Dir. art gallery Carson Pirie Scott & Co., Chgo., 1923-26; exhibitor paintings galleries in U.S., 1926-27; with Acme Steel Co., Chgo., 1927-62, v.p., 1945-62, dir., ret. 1962; pres., chmn. bd. Breakwaters, Inc., Chgo., 1957-68; practicing artist until 1980. Inventor fibre drums, paper ice cream can, metal venetian blinds, breakwaters, wave diverting and dissipating means, bldg. materials. Address: Pompano Beach, Fla. Died Mar. 19, 1980; buried Pompano Beach.

WILSON, ARTHUR MCCANDLESS, educator; b. Rock Island County, Ill., July 29, 1902; s. Arthur McCandless and Clara (Zollinger) W.; A.B., Yankton (S.D.) Coll., 1922, L.H.D., 1942; B.A. (Rhodes scholar), Oxford U. (Eng.), 1926, B.Litt., 1927, M.A., 1931; A.M., Harvard, 1930, Ph.D., 1933; A.M. (hon.), Dartmouth, 1940, Litt.D. (hon.), 1973; m. Julia Mary Tolford, June 13, 1927. Tchr., Canova (S.D.) High Sch., 1922-23, Chippewa Falls (Wis.) High Sch., 1923-24; instr. history Grinnell Coll., 1927-29; asst., instr. and tutor, dept. history Harvard, 1929-33; instr. dept. biography Dartmouth, 1933-35, asst. prof., 1936-40, prof. biography, 1940-67, Daniel Webster prof., 1964-67, emeritus, 1967-79, chmn. dept. biography, 1942-47, 1951-55, also prof. govt., 1944-67, co-dir. Great Issues course, 1946-48; Vis. prof. history Columbia, N.Y.C., 1967-69, Univ. Seminar asso., 1969-79; vis. prof. govt. Dartmouth, 1976-77; instr. history U. Wash., summer 1931; asst. prof. history U. Mo., summer 1937; prof. biography Univ. Ia., summer 1948; Fulbright vis. prof. Kings Coll. U. London (Eng.), 1956; with OSS, Washington, 1943-45; cons. USAF Acad. Planning Bd., 1949; mem. steering com. Anglo-Am. Hist. Conf., London, 1956-59. Decorated chevalier de l'Ordre des Palmes Académiques (France). Recipient award Modern Lang. Assn.-Oxford U. Press, 1953. Guggenheim fellow 1939-40, 56-57. Fellow Royal Hist. Soc., Am. Acad. Arts Scis.; mem. Modern Lang. Assn. Am., Modern Humanities Research Assn. (British), Soc. French Hist. Studies, Am. Hist. Assn. (Herbert Baxter Adams prize 1938, 58), Am. Polit. Sci. Assn., Assn. Internationale des Etudes Francaises, A.A.U.P., Phi Beta Kappa. Mason. Author: French Foreign Policy under the Administration of Cardinal Fleury, 1726-1743, 1936; Diderot, the Testing Years, 1713-1759, 1957 (Italian transl. Diderot, gli anni decisivi 1971); Diderot, The Appeal to Posterity, 1759-1784, 1972 (Nat. Book award for arts and letters 1973 (Italian transl. Diderot, l'appello di posteri 1977). Editorial bd. Jour. Modern History, 1962-65, French Hist. Studies, 1969-72; contbg. editor Edition Nationale des Oeuvres de Diderot. Home: Norwich, Vt. Died June 12, 1979; buried Hillside Cemetery, Norwich.

WILSON, ASHER BOLDON, lawyer; b. Johnson, Neb., Apr. 7, 1882; s. Anthony P. and Mary Emeline (Boldon) W.; ed. high sch., Colby, Kan.; studied law in office of Clement L. Wilson, Colby, 2 yrs.; m. Harriet Smith, Dec. 24, 1907; children—Patricia, Asher Boldon. Admitted to Kan. bar, 1904, and began practice at Goodland; moved to Twin Falls, Ida., 1914; pres. Farmers Nat. Bank, Buhl, Ida., 1917-20; owner and mgr. 870-acre irrigated farm. Dem. candidate for gov. of Ida., 1926; mem. Dem. Nat. Com., term 1928-32. Mem. Bd. of Regents, U. of Ida. (pres. 1930 and 1942-47), State Bd. of Edn. (v.p. 1928-30; pres. 1930 and 1942-43, 1945-46; del. Idaho State Constitutional Conv. (elected pres. Oct. 17, 1933, presiding over convention); chmn. Democratic Congl. campaign, 2d District of Idaho, 1932. Del. Dem. Nat. Conv., Chicago (chmn. Ida. delegation). Presidential elector, State of Ida., 1940. Chmn. Twin Falls County Dem. Central Com., 1942-44, Twin Falls Co. Civilian Council of Defense, Twin Falls Co. Jefferson Club; delegate and chairman Idaho delegation Dem. National Conventions, 1944, 48 (platform com.) 52, 56; Idaho Presidential elector, 1948. Vice chairman Idaho War Fund, 1943-45; pres. Idaho State Reclamation Assn.; mem. and chmn. Idaho Edn. Survey Commn. (created by Idaho Legislature 1945); chmn. Idaho State Teacher Retirement Fund Commn. Apptd. mem. State Sch. Re-orgn. Com., 1948; chmn. Ida. Citizens Legislative Com. Mem. Am., Ida., Twin Falls Co. bar assns., Twin Falls Air Travel Assn. (chmn.). Odd Fellow, Elk. Clubs: Blue Lakes Country, Twin Falls Country. Address: Twin Falls, Ida. *

WILSON, DAVID C(OLE), psychiatrist; b. St. Elmo, Tenn., July 13, 1892; s. Henry B. and Nellie (Cole) W.; A.B., U. of Va., 1912, M.D., 1919; student Grad. Sch., U. of Pa., Dept. Neurology and Psychiatry, 1924; grad. student Phipps Clinic, Johns Hopkins, 1927-28; married Elizabeth Jackson, Sept. 14, 1922; children—Mary Frances (wife of Dr. Robert L. Reeves), David Cole, Betty Kearny, Patricia. Teacher and athletic coach, San Diego, Calif., 1912-13, Woodberry Forest Sch., Va., 1913-15; interne U. of Va. Hosp., Charlottesville, 1919; house officer, Peter Bent Brigham Hosp., Boston, 1919-21, Clifton Springs (N.Y.) Sanitarium, 1921-28; asso. prof., U. of Va., 1928-38, prof. neurology and psychiatry, 1938-60, prof. emeritus, dir. dept. of neurology and psychiatry U. Va. Hosp., 1938-56; on leave as chief profl. edn. Napa State Hosp., Imola, California, 1960; pvt. practice, Napa, Cal.; consultant to Vets.' Adminstrn.; mem. bd. of dirs. Children's Service Center, Charlottesville; vis. physician, Martha Jefferson Hosp., Charlottesville; chmn. Dean's Com. for Vets. Adminstrn. Hosp., Roanoke, Va., consultant for hosp.; med. advisor to Va. State Dir. of Selective Service. Fellow A.C.P., 1927; mem. Mental Hygiene Soc. of Charlottesville (sec.), A.M.A., Am. Neurol. Assn., Am. (past v.p.), So. (pres.) psychiatric associations, American Academy Neurology, Association Research Nervous and Mental Diseases, Southern Med. Assn., Mental Hygiene Soc. of Va., So. Psychiatric Assn., Phi Sigma Kappa, Phi Rho Sigma, Alpha Omega Alpha, Phi Beta Kappa, Sigma Xi. Democrat. Episcopalian. Home: Napa, Calif. Died Oct. 30, 1980.

WILSON, DAVID JOHN, judge; b. Midway, Utah, Oct. 27, 1887; s. James B. and Margaret (Powell) W.; A.B., Brigham Young U., 1914, LL.D., 1963; J.D., U. Cal., 1919; m. Mary Jacobs, May 31, 1916; children—Marian (Mrs. O.M. Wilson), D. Jay, L. Keith, Margaret (Mrs. Loren C. Barlow), Don B. Admitted to Utah bar, 1919, practiced in Ogden until 1954; atty. Weber County, 1921-25; dist. atty. 2d Utah Dist., 1929-33; judge U.S. Customs Ct., 1954-66; sr. judge, Salt Lake City, 1966-76; dir., v.p., gen. counsel Fed. Bldg. & Loan Assn., 1922-54, Asso. Investment Corp., 1930-54. Mem. Utah Bar Commn., 1953-54. Del. Republican Nat. Conv., 1932, 40; Rep. state chmn. for Utah 1936-44; candidate for U.S. Congress, 1st Utah Dist., 1946-48. Mem. Utah Salt Lake County bar assns., Sons Utah Pioneers. Mem. Ch. of Jesus Christ of Latter-day Saints. Clubs: Alta.; Bonneville Knife and Fork. Home: Salt Lake City, Utah. Died Apr. 23, 1976.

WILSON, DONALD GORDON, librarian; b. Culver City, Cal., June 7, 1931; s. Gordon Robinson and Irma (Street) W.; B.A., U. Redlands, 1952; M.A. in History, U. Cal. at Los Angeles, 1958; M.L.S., U. So. Cal., 1960; Ph.D. in History, State U. N.Y. at Albany, 1972; m. Mary M. Keogh, Apr. 30, 1954; 1 son, Thomas G. Supr. stack services research library U. Cal. at Los Angeles, 1956-59; asst. librarian tech. services Cal. State Coll. at Hayward, 1960-61; head librarian U. Hawaii, Hilo, 1961-64; head tech. services univ. library State U. N.Y. at Albany, 1964-67; acquisitions librarian U. Cal. at Riverside, 1967, asst. univ. librarian, 1967-69, univ. librarian, 1969-73; univ. librarian Humboldt State U., 1973-76. Mem. A.L.A., Am. Assn. U. Profs., Am. Hist. Assn., Orgn. Am. Historians, Beta Phi Mu. Home: Arcata, Calif. Died Apr. 2, 1976.

WILSON, DURWARD SAUNDERS, army officer; born Greenville, N.C., July 2, 1886; s. Walter Brown and Brittania Newberry (Saunders) W.; B.S., U.S. Mil. Acad., West Point, N.Y., 1910; grad. Advanced Course. Ft. Benning, Ga., 1926, Command and Gen. Staff Sch., 1927, Army War Coll., 1932, Naval War Coll., 1933; m. Olive Moye Morrill, Dec. 27, 1910; children—Olive (wife of Col. Charles Austin Kengla, U.S. Army), Durward Saunders, Jr. Commd. 2d lt. Inf., U.S. Army, 1910, advanced through ranks to major gen., 1942; post ordnance, finance, exchange officer, Forts McKinley and Mills, Corregidor, P.I., 1914-17; at Camp Forrest, Ga., Camp Wadsworth, S.C., comdg. 1st Replacement Batn., Camp Lee, Va., 1917-18; camp exec. officer Camp Lee, 1918-20; served as comdr., 2d Batn., 57th Inf., asst. G-3, Philippine Dept., acting G-2 and G-4, Philippine Div., 1920-23; instr Miss. Nat. Guard, Jackson, Miss., 1923-25; instr., Inf. Sch., Ft. Benning, 1927-31; post exchange officer, Ft. Meade, Md., 1933-34; exec. officer, 16th Brig. and Washington Provisional Brig., 1934-38; chief, 3d Sect., Acad. Dept., Inf. Sch., 1938-40; comdg. gen., 21st Inf. Brig., 1940-41; comdg. gen., 24th Inf. Div., Hawaii, Oct. 1, 1941-May 1942; comdg. 6th Motorized Div., Sept.-Nov., 1942; comdg. IRTC Camp Croft, S.C., Nov., 1942-May, 1944; comdg. S.E. Sector, E.D.C., 1944-45; ret. 1946. Address: Arlington, Va. *

WILSON, EDWARD ARTHUR, artist; b. Glasgow, Scotland, Mar. 4, 1886; s. Edward Joseph and Euphemia Evangeline (Murray) W.; came with parents to U.S., 1893; art edn., Art Inst. Chicago and under Howard Pyle, Wilmington, Del.; m. Dorothy Roe, Oct. 24, 1913; children—Jane, Mary Elizabeth. Painter and illustrator; prints are in Metropolitan Museum, New York Public Library, Library of Congress, and in private collection of H. H. Rogers and others. Awarded Art Director medal, 1926 and 1930; Isidor prize, 1927; Shaw prize, 1942; Soc. Illustrators Hall of Fame and medal, 1962. Fellow Royal Soc. Arts; mem. Guild of Free Lance Artists (pres. 1926), Am. Inst. Graphic Arts, Soc. Illustrators. Clubs: Dutch Treat, Players, Salmagundi, Century Assn. A.N.A., 1948. Illustrator and author numerous books; illustrator for mags. Home: Truro, Mass.*

WILSON, FADRA HOLMES, educator; b. Oxford, Miss., June 26, 1884; d. James Robert and Lucy Tennessee (Word) Holmes; grad. State Normal Sch., Natchitoches, La., 1902; A.B., Tulane U., 1923; A.M., U. Miss., 1924; grad. student Tex. U., 1930-31, Tchrs. Coll. Columbia, 1931-32, 52-53; m. Dr. Embry Pryor Wilson, Nov. 15, 1921 (dec. Jan. 1923); 1 dau., Embry Pryor (wife Lt. Col. Leo Bond Jones). Prin. primary sch., Lafayette, La., 1902-06; lectr., La. normal schs., summer of 1903, also 1906-10; critic tchr., State Normal, Natchitoches, La., 1906-10; tchr. Oliver Wendell Holmes Sch., Oak Park, Ill., 1912; critic and intermediate supr. So. Ill. U., 1912-21; lectr. Ill., O., Pa., Ind. and Eastern States, also Valley City (N.D.) State Tchrs. Coll., 1913-33; dean of women, Millsaps Coll., 1924-26; dean dept. edn., State Tchrs. Coll., California, Pa., 1926-32; prof. edn. and psychology, La. State U., 1933-54, emeritus, 1954—; summer instr., Tulane U., 1916, 23, 24, 25, 28, 30, 31, 33, 56, summer extension course, Pa. State Coll., Erie, Pa., 1927; Sunday chapel speaker, Girard Coll., intermittently, 1925-42; adult educator civic and professional clubs, churches and ednl. instns., in Ill., 1912-21, Ohio, 1917-30, Pa., 1920-33, La., 1933; adult edn. govt. E.R.A. program, Tex., summers, 1934-35. Special worker, rehabilitation of vets. of World War I; active in Am. Red Cross, 1921-22; asst. orgn. YWCA, Baton Rouge, 1943, bd. dirs., 1943-46. Mem. N.E.A., La. Tchrs. Assn., Progressive Edn., La. Acad. Sci., Am. Acad. Polit. and Social Sci., Nat. Assn. Tchrs. Colls., Am. Assn. U. Women, Am. Assn. U. Profs., D.A.R., Baton Rouge Civic Symphony, Community Concert Assn., P.T.A., Colonial Dames Early XVII Century, Pi Gamma Mu, Pi Lambda Theta, Kappa Delta Pi, Pi Omicron, Phi Beta (pres.), Psi Chi, Tri Delta. Democrat. Methodist. Clubs: Business and Professional Womens Quota, Faculty, Women's Faculty Baton Rouge Country. Home: Baton Rouge. *

WILSON, FRANCIS GRAHAM, ret. educator; b. Junction, Tex., Nov. 26, 1901; s. Horace Ernest and Stella Jane (Graham) W.; B.A., U. Tex., 1923; M.A., 1924; Ph.D., Stanford U., 1928; m. Millicent Rawdon, Dec. 20, 1924 (dec.); 1 son, Robert Rawdon. Newspaper reporter Austin (Tex.) American, 1922; teaching fellow U. Cal., 1924-25; instr. Fresno (Cal.) State Coll., 1925-26; instr. citizenship Stanford U., 1926-28; mem. faculty U. Wash., Seattle, 1928-39; mem. faculty U. Ill., 1939-67, chmn. dept. polit. sci., 1953-57; mem. staff C. W. Post Coll., L.I. Univ., 1967-70; vis. scholar Emory U., 1953. Chmn. Catholic Commn. on Intellectual and Cultural Affairs, 1956-57. Mem. task force on human rights and responsibilities Republican Nat. Com., 1965. Social Sci. Research Council fellow, 1931-32. Mem. Am. Polit. Sci. Assn. (mem. exec. council, 1937-40), Phi Beta Kappa, Pi Sigma Alpha. Clubs: University; Cosmos (Washington). Author: Labor in the League System, 1934; The Elements of Modern Politics, 1936; The American Political Mind, 1949; The Case for Conservatism, 1951; A Theory of Public Opinion, 1962; Political Thought in National Spain, 1967. Contbr. articles to polit. sci. publs. Home: Washington, D.C. Died May 24, 1976.

WILSON, GEORGE, profl. football coach; b. Chgo., Feb. 3, 1914; s. George and Vera (Hart) W.; student Northwestern U., 1936; m. Clare N. Moore, Nov. 26, 1938; children—Sue (Mrs. Arthur Burwick), Lynne (Mrs. Jim Wagner), Kathy, Laurie. Football player Chgo. Bears Profl. Football Team, 1937-47, asst. coach, 1947-48; asst. coach Detroit Lions Profl. Football Team, 1949-56, head coach, 1957-64; asst. coach Washington Red Skins Profl. Football Team, 1965-66; head coach Miami Dolphins Profl. Football Team, 1966-70. Named All Pro Player, 1942, Coach of Year, 1957. Chmn. Miami Cerebral Palsy Drive, 1967. Home: Coral Gables, Fla. Died Nov. 23, 1978.

WILSON, HARWELL, surgeon, educator; b. Lincoln, Ala., May 23, 1908; s. Joseph Harwell and Linda Louise (Harrison) W.; A.B., Vanderbilt U., 1928, M.D., 1932; m. Helen Cobb, Jan. 18, 1941; children—Linda Helen, Margaret Marie, William Harwell. Intern, research fellow in surgery U. Chgo. Clinics, 1932-33; research fellow surgery U. Chgo., 1933-34, asst. resident surgery,

1934-37, resident surg. pathology, 1937-38, chief resident, instr. surgery, 1938-39; mem. faculty U. Tenn., Memphis, 1939-77, prof. surgery, 1948-77, chmn. dept., 1948-74; surgeon in chief City of Memphis Hosps., 1948-74; sr. staff mem. Bapt. Meml. Hosp., also past pres. staff; cons Kennedy VA Hosp., Crippled Childrens Hosp., LeBonheur Childrens Hosp.; vis. staff Methodist and St. Joseph Hosp. Served to lt. col, M.C., AUS, World War II; MTO. Decorated Legion of Merit; recipient Distinguished Service award U. Chgo. Alumni Assn., 1952, Distinguished Service award Tenn. Med. Assn., 1975. Mem. A.C.S. (pres. Tenn. chpt. 1960, nat. treas. 1962-77), Am. Surg. Assn. (1st v.p. 1976), Southeastern Surg. Congress (pres. 1963), A.M.A., Am., So. (pres. 1970) surg. assns., Soc. Univ. Surgeons, Soc. Clin. Surgery, Soc. Vascular Surgery, Soc. Surgery Alimentary Tract (pres. 1964-65), Excelsior Surg. Soc., Internat. Soc. Surgery, Alpha Omega Alpha, Sigma Alpha Epsilon, Alpha Kappa Kappa. Contbr. numerous articles to profl. jours., chpts. in books. Producer surg. teaching motion pictures, surg. exhibits. Home: Memphis, Tenn. Died Oct. 10, 1977.

WILSON, JAMES TINLEY, geophysicist, educator; b. Claremont, Cal., Nov. 13, 1914; s. Raleigh and Mary T. (Brooks) W.; A.B., U. Cal. at Berkeley, 1935, Ph.D., 1939; m. Martha H. Wheeler, July 17, 1943; 1 dau., Deborah M. Research asst. Harvard, 1939-40; instr. U. Mich., Ann Arbor, 1940-43, from instr. to prof. geology and mineralogy, 1945-78, chmn. dept., 1956-61; from asso. dir. to dir. Inst. Sci. and Tech., 1960-78. Chmn. Nat. Acad. Sci.-NRC com. on remote sensing of environment, 1964-68, chmn. com. on seismology, 1960-65, mem. panel on strong-motion seismology, 1972-78; cons. AEC, 1967-75, Office Sci. and Tech., 1970, Nuclear Regulatory Commn., 1975-78, ERDA, 1975-78. Bd. govs. Cranbrook Inst. Sci.; trustee Univs. Space Research Assn., 1970-75. Fellow Am. Geophys. Union (pres. seismology sect. 1974-76), Earthquake Engring. Research Inst., Geol. Soc. Am., Royal Astron. Soc.; mem. Am. Inst. Mining, Metall. and Petroleum Engrs.; Seismol. Soc. Am. (dir., past pres.), Soc. Exploration Geophysicists. Home: Ann Arbor, Mich. Died May 25, 1978; buried St. Andrew's Episcopal Ch., Ann Arbor.

WILSON, JOHN ALBERT, educator, orientalist; b. Pawling, N.Y., Sept. 12, 1899; s. Warren H. and Pauline E. (Lane) W.; A.B., Princeton, 1920, Litt.D., 1961; A.M., Am. U. Beirut, Syria, 1923; Ph.D., U. Chgo., 1926; L.H.D., Loyola of Chgo., 1974; m. Mary W. Rouse, June 22, 1926; children—Margaret Lane, Frederick Thomas, Constance Waite. Instr. English, Am. U. Beirut, 1920-23; epigrapher epigraphic expdn. Oriental Inst. of U. Chgo., Luxor, Egypt, 1926-31, asst. prof. Egyptology, U. Chgo., 1931-35, asso. prof., 1935-36, prof., 1936-68, Andrew MacLeish Distinguished service prof., 1952-68, prof. emeritus, 1968-76, sci. sec. Oriental Inst., 1935, dir., 1936-46, 60-61, chmn. dept. Oriental lang., lit., 1936-46. Mem. Staff OSS, Washington, 1942-43; with Dept. States, 1943-44; mem. UNESCO Consultative Com. Preservation Nubian Monuments, 1960-72, dir. epigraphic expdn., Luxor, 1958-59; pres. Am. Research Center in Egypt, 1971-74. Fulbright research scholar, Egypt, 1952-53. Mem. Am. Philos. Soc., Am. Acad. Arts and Scis. Author: The Burden of Egypt, 1951; Signs and Wonders Upon Pharaoh, 1964; Thousands of Years, 1972. Home: Hightstown, N.J. Died Aug. 30, 1976.

WILSON, JOHN HENRY, advt. exec.; b. N.Y.C., Feb. 20, 1925; s. John Henry and Julia (Beck) W.; A.B., Iona Coll., New Rochelle, N.Y., 1946; m. Jean F. Burns, June 15, 1957; children—Karen, Lisa. With Ruthrauff & Ryan, N.Y.C., 1946-52, Ogilvy, Benson & Mather, 1952-55; eastern account exec. Grant Advt., 1955-57, merchandising and sales promotion dir., Detroit, 1957-59, v.p. retail marketing all domestic offices and supervising 30 U.S. Dodge dealer ad groups, 1959-60; nat. coordinator Dodge dealers, Batton, Barten, Durstine & Osborn, Detroit, 1960-62, account exec. Dodge cars, 1962-64, account supr., 1964-67, regional mgr., 1967-69, dir., 1969-75, sr. v.p., 1970-75. Chmn. promotion com. United Found. Torch drive, 1969, chmn. advt. com., 1970, overall campaign chmn. for promotion, 1971. Mem. Detroit Adcraft Club, Detroit C. of C., Detroit Advt. Assn. Clubs: Birmingham (Mich.) Country; Detroit Athletic; Hunters Creek (Metamora, Mich.). Advt.-promotion campaigns include Dodge Boys, Good Guys in White Hats, Dodge Rebellion, Dodge Fever and Dodge Material, Dodge Safety Sheriff characterization. Home: Bloomfield Hills, Mich. Died May 11, 1975.

WILSON, JOHN P., JR., lawyer; b. Chgo., Nov. 12, 1905; s. John P. and Eloise Babcock (Smith) W.; grad. St. Paul's Sch., Concord, N.H., 1924; B.S., Princeton, 1928; LL.B., U. Mich., 1932; m. Romayne Warren, June 23, 1928 (dec. June 1973); children—Warren, Gordon, Romayne (Mrs. Stewart Strawn Dixon). Admitted to Ill. bar, 1932; with Wilson & McIlvaine, Chgo., 1932-78, partner, 1941-78. Pres., Planned Parenthood Assn., Chgo. area, 1947-48, 49-52, 63-65, also bd. dirs.; bd. dirs. Children's Meml. Hosp., Chgo., Planned Parenthood Fedn. Am.; bd. dirs. Graceland Cemetery Co., pres., 1968-73. Served with USNR, 1942-46. Mem. Am., Ill., Chgo. bar assns., Phi Delta Phi. Republican. Episcopalian. Clubs: Commercial, Law, Legal, University, Attic, Chicago; Old Elm (Ft. Sheridan, Ill.); Onwentsia (Lake Forest, Ill.); Shoreacres (Lake Bluff, Ill.). Home: Lake Forest, Ill. Died Nov. 19, 1978.

WILSON, KARL MILLER, surgeon, univ. prof.; b. Madoc, Ont., Can., Sept. 27, 1885; s. Charles G. and Annie E. (Miller) W.; student Albert Coll., Belleville, Ont., 1900-03; M.D., McGill U., Montreal, Can., 1908; m. Mildred H. Bentley, June 1915; children—Charles B., Robert H., John G. Came to U.S., 1909; naturalized 1922. House surgeon Montreal Gen. Hosp., 1908-09; interne, asst. resident and resident obstetrician Johns Hopkins Hosp., 1909-12; resident gynecologist Royal Victoria Hosp., Montreal, 1912-13; practiced medicine in Baltimore, Md., 1913-23; successively instr., asso. and asso. prof. of obstetrics, Johns Hopkins U., 1913-24; prof. of obstetrics and gynecology, U. of Rochester, and obstetrician and gynecologist in chief Strong Memorial Hosp. and Rochester Municipal Hosp. since 1925; mem. cons. staff Rochester Gen., Genesee, Highland Hosps. Fellow Am. College of Surgeons; mem. Rochester Acad. Medicine, A.M.A., Am. Gynecol. Soc., Am. Soc. for Exptl. Pathology, A.A.A.S., Alpha Omega Alpha (hon.), Sigma Xi. Democrat. Club: Rochester Country. Home: Rochester, N.Y. *

WILSON, KENNETH LEON, Olympic official; b. Atwood, Ill., Mar. 27, 1896; s. Charles W. and Nelda (Gross) W.; B.S., U. of Ill., 1920; m. Dorothy Shade, Jan. 1, 1923; children—Nancy Ann, Suzanne. Asst. to dir. of athletics, U. of Ill., 1921; dir. of athletics, track coach and dir. of the Drake Relays, Drake U., Des Moines, Ia., 1922-25; dir. of athletics, Northwestern U., 1925-45; commr. of Western Intercollegiate Conference, Chicago, 1945-61; dir. Orrington Hotel (Evanston, Ill.); v.p., dir. Orrington Co. Mem. Pres.'s Council on Youth Fitness. Mem. Am. Council on Edn., Chgo. Recreation Commn., U.S. Olympic Com. (pres.), Delta Upsilon. Presbyn. Clubs: Glenview Country; Rotary, Executives, Chgo. Athletic, Chicago Farmers, (Chgo.). Home: Wilmette, Ill. Died 1979.

WILSON, LLOYD BENNETT, dir. Chesapeake and Potomac Telephone Cos.; b. Plattsmouth, Neb., May 27, 1883; s. Frank Hamburger and Carrie Louise (Bennett) W.; grad. Plattsmouth (Neb.) High Sch., 1900; m. Silence Howard Stewart, Dec. 22, 1906; children—Lloyd Bennett, Silence Margaret (Mrs. Karl Michelet), Martha Louise (Mrs. William H. Triplett). Began as night operator Northwestern Bell Telephone Co., Plattsmouth, 1899; now director of Chesapeake & Potomac Telephone Companies; dir. Riggs Nat. Bank, Security Storage Co., Acacia Mutual Life Insurance Co., U.S. Fidelity & Guaranty Co., Woodward & Lothron Dept. Store. Trustee, George Washington U., Nat. Geog. Soc., mem. Washington Cathedral Chapter; Treas., Protestant Episcopal Cathedral Foundation. Episcopalian. Clubs: Chevy Chase, Metropolitan, Alivi, Alfalfa (Washington, D.C.); Maryland (Baltimore); Omaha (Omaha, Neb.). Home: Bluemont, Va. *

WILSON, NORMAN W., paper mfr.; b. Erie, Pa., Jan. 31, 1885; ed. pub. sch. and high sch.; student A. Hamilton Inst.; LL.D., Lawrence College, Appleton, Wis., 1958; m. Flora Nick, Aug. 18, 1906. Asso. with Hammermill Paper Co., mfrs., Erie, Pa., 1901—, first v.p. and gen. mgr., 1929-40, pres., 1940-53, chmn. bd., 1953—; mem. bd. dirs. Hammermill Paper Co., First National Bank. Erie, Pa. Mem. governing bd., trustee Nat. Indsl. Conf. Bd., 1952-56. Mem. bd. corporator Hamot Hosp., St. Vincent's Hosp. Mem. Am. Paper and Pulp Assn. (pulp and paper industry council to Dept. Commerce 1944-51), U.S. Pulp Producers Assn. (regional dir. 1941-50), Inst. Paper Chemistry (trustee 1941-50), Writing Paper Mfrs. Assn. (pres. 1921-23), N.A.M. (dir. 1941-47). Republican. Episcopalian. Mem. St. Paul's Cathedral Chapter. Clubs: Kahkwa, Erie, Press (Erie); Princeton (N.Y.C.). Home: Erie, Pa.; (summer) Fairview, Pa. *

WILSON, PAUL WHITE, naval med. officer; b. Keokuk, Ia., Dec. 28, 1885; s. William George and Susan Jane (White) W.; B.S., Ia. Wesleyan Coll., 1906; M.D., U. of Minn., 1912; m. Alma Margaret von der Linden, May 20, 1939; 1 son, Joseph C. In gen. practice of medicine, Whittier, Calif., 1913-17; commd. officer in the Med. Corps, U.S. Navy, Feb. 1917, and advanced through the grades to capt.; has specialized in tropical medicine and parasitology since 1922; served 6 yrs. in Haiti, 3 yrs. at Gorgas Memorial Lab. in Panama, and 15 months in Am. Samoa; head dept. of tropical med., U.S. Naval Med. Sch., Washington, D.C., 1934-38, executive officer, 1941-42, in command, Sept. 1, 1942-Dec. 1944. Specializes on the variations in yaws as observed in different parts of the world. Mem. Haitian Pub. Health Service, 1922-25, 1926-29. Decorated Chevalier Honneur et Merite, Medal Honneur et Merite (Haiti). Diplomate, Board of Internal Medicine. Fellow Am. Coll. of Physicians; mem. A.M.A., Am. Soc. of Tropical Medicine, Am. Acad. of Tropical Medicine, Phi Delta Theta, Nu Sigma Nu. Club: Army and Navy (Washington). Contbr. articles on yaws to med. jours., on Ascariasis in Am. Samoa, in 1942. Address: Corvallis, Oregon. *

WILSON, PERRIN THACHER, osteo. physician; b. Middletown, Conn., Nov. 4, 1888; s. Edwin Horace and Jane Amelia (Bidwell) W.; student Harvard, 1909-13; D.O., Am. Sch. Osteopathy, 1918; m. Hilda Bruen, Oct. 12, 1920. Practiced osteo. medicine, Cambridge, Mass., from 1919. Trustee Mass. Osteo. Hosp. Served with U.S. Army, World War I. Perrin T. Wilson professorship established at Kirksville Coll. Osteo. Medicine, 1960. Mem. Am. Osteopathic Assn. (pres. 1933), Boston Osteo. Soc. (pres. 1922), Mass. Osteo. Soc. (pres. 1925). Republican. Conglist. Mason. Clubs: Faculty of Harvard U., Rotary (pres. 1943). Engaged in research on osteopathic lesion at Peter Bent Brigham Hosp., Boston, 1922-25. Contbr. articles to profl. jours. Mem. Mass. State Bd. of Registration in Medicine, Feb. 2, 1944-July 1, 1946; chmn. bd. trustees Kirksville Coll. Osteopathy and Surgery 1948. Home: Brookline, Mass. Died Dec. 13, 1977.

WILSON, RALPH LAWRENCE, engr.; b. Uhrichsville, Ohio, Sept. 19, 1899; s. Walter L. and Anna Elizabeth (Dickey) W.; Electrometallurgist, Lehigh U., 1921, H.H.D., 1968; m. Margretta Rawson Bockius, Nov. 28, 1953. Metallurgist United Alloy Steel Corp., 1922-26, Central Alloy Steel Corp., 1926-28, Timken Steel & Tube Co., 1928-33; metall. engr. Climax Molybdenum Co., 1938-44, Timken Roller Bearing Co., 1933-38, chief metall. engr., 1944-46, dir. metallurgy, 1946-79. Chief constructional steel section, metall. br., steel div. W.P.B., 1942-44; mem. industry adv. com. superalloys, leader on superalloys, metall. and operations com., Word War II; mem. panel on metals and minerals Research and Development Bd., Dept. of Def., 1952-53. Pres. Am. Soc. for Metals Found. for Edn. and Research, 1953-54; alumnus trustee Lehigh U., 1958-64, life trustee, 1973; trustee Canton Art Inst., 1972-77; fellow in perpetuity Cleve. Mus. Art, 1971. Recipient Citation, Ohio Soc. Profl. Engrs., 1960. Fellow Am. Soc. Metals (nat. trustee 1936-38, treas. 1949-51, v.p. 1951-52, pres. 1952-53), ASTM, Am. Petroleum Inst., Am. Welding Soc., Nat. Soc. Profl. Engrs., Am. Ordnance Assn., A.S.M.E., Engring. Soc. Detroit, AAAS, Am. Iron and Steel Institute, Newcomen Society Alumni Assn. Lehigh U. (pres., 1955-57), Sigma Phi Epsilon. Club: Chemists (N.Y.C.). Home: Canton, Ohio. Died July 2, 1979.

WILSON, RICHARD LAWSON, newspaper corr.; b. Galesburg, Ill., Sept. 3, 1905; s. Frank and Emily E. (McCord) W.; student Iowa State Coll., 1922-25, U. Ia., 1925-26; LL.D., Drake U., 1956; Litt.D. (hon.), Iowa Wesleyan Coll., 1958; L.H.D., Dakota Wesleyan U., 1967; m. Katherine Young Macy, Nov. 22, 1928; children—Susan Madge (Mrs. Seymour), Katherine Macy (Mrs. Lesses). Began as reporter on Des Moines (Iowa) Register, 1926; reporter St. Louis Globe-Democrat, 1928; covered city politics Des Moines Register, 1928-30, city editor, 1930-33; Washington corr. Des Moines Register and Tribune, from 1933; chief of Washington bur. Cowles Publs., 1938-70; pres. Nat. Press Bldg. Corp., Washington, 1962-72. Recipient Pulitzer Prize for distinguished reporting nat. affairs, 1954; Sigma Delta Chi award, 1954; Headliner Award, 1954; Golden Plate award Am. Acad. Achievements, 1966; others. Mem. White House Corrs. Assn., Theta Delta Chi, Sigma Delta Chi (exec. council; chmn. profl. awards com. 1941; sec. 1942). Clubs: National Press (pres. 1940), Gridiron (pres. 1948-49), Metropolitan, Alfalfa (Washington). Author: Setting the Course, 1970; A New Road for America, 1972; also numerous articles for mags., other periodicals, syndicated newspaper column. Home: Washington, D.C. Died Jan. 18, 1981.

WILSON, THEODORE HALBERT, univ. pres.; b. Middletown, Conn., Feb. 11, 1885; s. Edwin Horace and Jane Amelia (Bidwell) W.; grad. Cambridge (Mass.) Latin School, 1902; A.B., Harvard, 1907, A.M., 1908, Ed.M., 1928, Ed.D., 1935; B.D., Union Theol. Sem., 1911; married Faith Evelyn Harris, July 31, 1919 (died, 1941); children—Faith Evelyn, Theodore Halbert, Jr., and Carolyn Elise; m. 2d, Helen Estelle Wright, Oct. 19, 1946. Ordained to the ministry of the Congregational Church, 1910; assistant pastor Flatbush (N.Y.) Ch., 1909; asst. dir. Student Christian Work, Union Theol. Sem., 1908-11; prin. Union Sch. of Religion, N.Y. City, 1910-11; asso. pastor 1st Ch., Montclair, N.J., 1911-12; pastor Skowhegan, Me., 1912-15, Olivet, Mich., 1916-18; prof. religion, 1916-18, pres., 1918-19, Olivet Coll.; field representative Congl. Nat. Council Commn. on Pilgrim Memorial Fund, Sept.-Dec. 1919, also mem. of Council; surveyor of theol. seminaries and training schools for Interch. World Movement of N. America, Jan.-June 1920; prin. St. Johnsbury (Vt.) Acad., 1920-30; pres. Chevy Chase School, Washington, D.C., Aug. 1930-June 1932; dir. Nat. Park Sem., Forest Glen, Md., 1932-35; ednl. advisor McDonogh (Md.) Sch., 1935-40, U. Balt., 1937-40, pres., 1940—. Mem. Vt. Ednl. Survey Commn., 1928-30. Mem. of Nat. Ednl. Assn., Delta Upsilon, Phi Delta Kappa. Club: Harvard (Maryland), Rotary (fellowship and internat. student exchange com., 1956-58, internat. dir. 1960-62, 3d v.p. 1961-62). Home: Balt. *

WILSON, WILLIAM RALPH, educator; b. Rochester, N.Y., Nov. 18, 1924; s. Clair Van Deusen and Bertha (Gilfillan) W.; A.B., Hamtilon Coll., 1948; M.D., SUNY, Syracuse, 1952; m. Charlotte Ann York, June 24, 1950; 1 son, Jeffrey Scott. Intern, Ind. Med. Center, Indpls., 1952-53; resident U. Iowa Med. Center, Iowa City, 1953-56, research fellow, 1956-59, asst. prof. dept. medicine, 1959-63, asso. prof., 1963-68, prof., 1968-75; asso. prof. pharmacology Coll. Medicine, U. Ia., 1964-68, prof. pharmacology, 1968-75; research fellow medicine Johns Hopkins Hosp., 1961-62. Served with AUS, 1943-46; ETO. Burroughs Wellcome scholar in clin. pharmacology, 1965-70. Mem. Am. (dir. 1973-75), Iowa (pres. 1970-72) heart assns., Am. Soc. Clin. Investigation, A.C.P., Am. Soc. Pharmacology and Exptl. Therapeutics, Am. Fedn. Clin. Research, Central Soc. Clin. Research. Home: Iowa City, Iowa. Died May 1, 1975.

WIMBERLY, HARRINGTON, newspaper publisher; b. Hale Center, Tex., June 22, 1901; s. Joe Ed and Margaret (Wilson) W.; A.B., U. 1924; m. Myrth McCurley, Apr. 22, 1927; children—Janis Myrth, Mary Margaret. Editor, Altus (Okla.) Daily Times-Democrat, 1929-78, Duncan (Okla.) Dialy Banner; dir. Ark.-La. Gas Co. Chmn., Democratic State Com. of Okla., 1944-45; apptd. mem. Fed. Power Commn., 1945. Home: Duncan, Okla. Died Dec. 26, 1978.

WIMBERLY, JOHN HARRY, gas co. exec.; b. Houston, Dec. 6, 1904; s. Stonewall Jackson and Hallie (Holland) W.; student Rice Inst., 1922; B.B.A., U. Tex., 1927; m. Edith Cooney, Oct. 15, 1931; children—Bryan Holland, Lane Mayfield, Thomas Allan. Auditor, Houston Natural Gas Corp., 1931-40, treas., 1940-45, v.p., treas., 1945-47, exec. v.p., 1947-55, pres. corp. and subsidiaries, 1955-67, chmn. bd. corp. and subsidiaries, 1967-73, sr. chmn. bd. corp. and subsidiaries, 1973-75, hon. chmn., 1975-79, dir., 1940-79; dir. Port City State Bank, Houston. Pres., Houston Jr. C. of C., 1936. Trustee S.W. Research Inst., St. Luke's Episcopal Hosp. Mem. Am. (past dir., past pres.), So. (pres. 1952) gas assns., Tex. Bur. Econ. Understanding (past dir. v.p.), Tex. Research League (dir.), Tex. Mid-Continent Oil and Gas Assn. (past dir.). Episcopalian (pres. churchmen's assns. 1949). Clubs: Houston Country (past pres.), Tejas (Houston). Home: Houston, Tex. Died Jan. 1, 1979; buried Glenwood Cemetery, Houston.

WIMSATT, WILLIAM KURTZ, educator; b. Washington, Nov. 17, 1907; s. William K. and Bertha (McSherry) W.; B.A., Georgetown U., 1928, M.A., 1929; postgrad. Cath. U. Am., 1935-36; Ph.D., Yale, 1939; Litt.D., Villanova U., 1962, U. Notre Dame, 1963; LL.D., St. Louis U., 1964; Litt.D., Le Moyne Coll., 1965, Kenyon Coll., 1970; m. Margaret Elizabeth Hecht, Sept. 1944; children—William Alexander (dec. 1965), James Christopher. Head dept. English, Portsmouth (R.I.) Sch., 1930-35; instr. English, Yale, 1939-43, asst. prof., 1943-49, asso. prof., 1949-55, prof., 1955-75, Sterling prof., 1973-75. Guggenheim fellow, 1946-47; Fund for Advancement of Learning fellow, 1953-54. Mem. Modern Lang. Assn. Am. (exec. council 1955-58), English Inst. (chmn. 1954), Conn. Acad. Arts and Scis. (pres. 1969-70). Author: The Prose Style of Samuel Johnson, 1941; Philosophic Words, 1948; The Verbal Icon, 1954; (with Cleanth Brooks) Literary Criticism, A Short History, 1957; Hateful Contraries, 1965; The Portraits of Alexander Pope, 1965; The Day of the Leopards, 1975. Editor: The Idea of Comedy, 1969; Versification, Major Language Types, 1972; Literary Criticism, Idea and Act, 1974. Co-editor: Boswell for the Defence 1769-1774, 1959. Home: Hew Haven, Conn. Died Dec. 17, 1975; buried All Saints Cemetery, North Haven, Conn.

WINBORNE, JOHN WALLACE (WIN'BÔRN), justice; b. Chowan County, N.C., July 12, 1884; s. Dr. Robert H. and Annie F. (Parker) W.; prep. edn. Horner School, Oxford, N.C., 1900-02; A.B., U. of North Carolina, 1906; LL.D., 1946; m. Charlie May Blanton, March 30, 1910 (died Nov. 4, 1940); children—Charlotte (Mrs. Charles Milton Shaffer), John Wallace; married 2d, Lalage O. Rorison, June 14, 1947. Teacher Bingham Military School, Asheville, N.C., 1906-07; admitted to N.C. bar, 1906, and practiced in Marion, 1907-37; mem. Pless & Winborne, 1907-19, Pless, Winborne & Pless, 1919-26, Pless, Winborne, Pless & Proctor, 1926-27, Winborne & Proctor, 1928-37; atty. Marion and McDowell counties, 1918-37; associate justice of the Supreme Court of North Carolina, 1937-56, chief justice, 1956-62. Member board of aldermen, Marion, N.C., 1913-21; chmn. Democratic Exec. Com., McDowell County, N.C., 1910-12; mem. State Dem. Exec. Com., 1916-37; chmn., 1932-37; mem. Local Govt. commn. of N.C., 1931-33. Served on Selective Bd. during World War. Mem. N.C. Bar Assn. (hon.) N.C. Jud. Council (chmn.), Soc. of the Cincinnati, Delta Kappa Epsilon. Democrat. Episcopalian. Mason. Address: Marion, N.C. *

WINCH, ROBERT FRANCIS, educator, sociologist; b. Lakewood, O., Aug. 31, 1911; A.B., Western Res. U., 1935; A.M., U. Chgo., 1939, Ph.D., 1942; m. Martha Brashares, Sept. 3, 1938. Mem. faculty U. Chgo., 1941-42, Vanderbilt U., 1946-48; mem. faculty Northwestern U., 1948-77, prof. sociology, 1955-77, chmn. dept., 1967-70, Social Sci. Research Council fellow, 1945-46; Guggenheim fellow, 1955-56, 74-75; recipient Burgess award Nat. Council Family Relations, 1968. Served to lt. USNR, 1942-45. Fellow A.A.A.S., Am. Psycho;. Assn.; mem. Am. Sociol. Assn. (chmn. family sect. 1971-72), Sociol. Research Assn., Am. Statis. Assn., Midwest Sociol. Soc. (pres. 1972-73), Internat. Sociol. Assn., Soc. for Cross-Cultural Research. Author: The Modern Family, 3d edit., 1971; Mate-Selection: A Study of Complementary Needs, 1958; Identification and Its Familial Determinants, 1962; Familial Structure and Function As Influence, 1974; Familial Organization: A Quest for Determinants, 1977. Co-editor: Selected Studies in Marriage and the Family, 4th edit., 1974; asso. editor Sociometry, 1956-61, Jour. Marriage and Family, 1965-69, Sociol. Quar., 1970-77. Home: Highland Park, Ill. Died Apr. 19, 1977; buried Mt. Lebanon Cemetery, Pitts.

WINDELS, PAUL, lawyer; b. Brooklyn, N.Y., Dec. 7, 1885; John Henry and Pauline (Klink) W.; A.B., Columbia, 1908; LL.B., Brooklyn Law Sch., 1909, J.D., 1910; hon. LL.D., St. Lawrence U., 1937; m. Louise E. Gross, Feb. 22, 1919; children—Louise Margaret, Paul, Richard, Barbara. Admitted to N.Y. bar, 1910; began practice at Brooklyn, N.Y.; now partner firm Windels, Merritt & Ingraham; official referee Kings Co. Court, 1917-19; counsel N.Y. State Bridge and Tunnel Commn., 1918-30; asso. counsel Port of N.Y. Authority, 1930-33; corp. counsel City N.Y.,1934-37; spl. master U.S. District Ct., L.I. R.R. Reorgn. Consul New York City Housing Authority, Triborough Bridge Authority, 1934-37; mem. Bd. of Statutory Consolidation, City of N.Y., 1936; chmn. N.Y. City Traffic Commn., 1937. Officer Legion of Honor, France; awarded Distinguished Pub. Service medal, Columbia U., 1937. Del. Rep. Nat. Convs., 1920, 24, 28, 40; mem. com. on program Rep. National Com., 1937-39; Republican candidate for del. at large N.Y. State Constl. Conv., 1937; chmn. Brooklyn Housing Council, 1931-32; chmn. Committee of Fifteen 1940-50; mem. Mayor's Business Advisory Com., 1940-43; chmn. Citizens Transit Com., 1943-49; counsel, Joint Legislative Committee to Investigate Public Educational System, 1940, 1941. Pres. Regional Plan Assn. of New York, 1943-52, dir., 1943—. Mem. bd. dirs. Nat. War Fund, 1943-48, Downtown Brooklyn Association, Inc., 1946-48. Trustee Brooklyn Daily Eagle, 1934-37, Bowery Savings Bank since 1943, Brooklyn Public Library, 1940-49; v.p. Brooklyn Law Sch., 1952-58, trustee, 1952—; president Museum of French Art, French Institute in U.S., 1955—, trustee 1928—; trustee Lycée Francais de New York, 1945—; v.p., 1958—, chmn. bd., 1965. Member A.I.A. (honorary), Assn. of Bar of City of N.Y. (mem. exec. com. 1937-41; v.p. 1943-44, 59-60; chmn. com. on municipal affairs 1960-62), Am., N.Y. bar assns., L.I. Hist. Soc., Bklyn. Heights Assn. (pres., gov. 1962-65, adv. com. 1965), Phi Delta Phi, New Eng. Soc. Republican. Presbyn. Mason. Club: Down Town Assn. (N.Y.C.). Home: Maywood Rd., Darien, Conn.

WINDHAM, JAMES C., brewery exec.; b. Ala., Nov. 30, 1913; s. James Jefferson and Eula (Russell) W.; student East Miss. Jr. Coll.; B.C.S., M.C.S., Benjamin Franklin U.; student Nat. U. Law Sch., Washington; Loraine Eide, Sept. 2, 1941. Vice pres., treas. F.L. Jacobs Co., Detroit; treas. Grayson-Robinson Stores Inc., N.Y.C.; v.p., controller Schenley Industries, Inc., N.Y.C.; former pres. Blatz Brewing Co., Milw.; chief exec. officer, chmn. bd. Pabst Brewing Co., Milw. Served as maj. AUS, 1942-46. Clubs: Milwaukee Athletic, University (Milw.). Home: Macon, Miss. Died May 11, 1977.

WINDSOR, ANNE (MRS. ANNETTE B. DEWEY), writer; b. Carthage, N.C., Feb. 5, 1884; d. Jesse Samuel and Mary Jane (Wallace) Barrett; desc. of Gen. Sam Houston; ed. Campbell Coll. (N.C.) and N.C. Coll. for Women; studied voice and piano under masters; m. Henry B. Dewey, 1907; 1 son, Cooper. Formerly music teacher, soprano soloist, dir. church choirs, chorus clubs, etc.; writer since 1918, of stories, articles, verse, songs and book reviews, also courses in story writing, play writing, verse writing and journalism; asso. editor Internat. Poetry Mag., 1928-30; song, "Where'er You Go, My Heaven's There," awarded 1st honor of internat. contest, 1927; poems "Humanity," and "Waiting." Mem. Panhandle Pen Women (life), Internat. Writers League (v.p. 1930), and various other socs. Author: Mountain Tim, 1933; Laughter and Heart Cries (verse), 1934. Compiler and co-editor: North Carolina Poets, 1930. Editor of The Carthagenian. Also author various short stories and poems. Home: Carthage, N.C.*

WINGATE, FRANCIS ALFRED, univ. adminstr.; b. Hallowell, Me., Mar. 17, 1909; s. Frank S. and Annie (Laferriere) W.; A.B., Bowdoin Coll., 1931; M.B.A., Harvard, 1933, Ph.D., Ohio State U., 1950; m. Helen Abbot, June 27, 1937; children—Anthony A., George B. Asso. prof. Clarkson Coll., 1936-40, prof. marketing Syracuse U., 1946-73, comptroller, 1952-60, v.p., 1961-73, treas., 1960-73; v.p., treas. Onandaga Community Coll., Syracuse, 1973-77; dir. Unity Life Ins. Co. N.Y., First Fed. Savs. & Loan Assn. Syracuse. Served from 2d lt. to maj. AUS, 1941-46; col. Res. Universalist. Home: Syracuse, N.Y. Died Mar. 7, 1977.

WINGO, EFFIE GENE (MRS. OTIS WINGO), congresswoman; b. Lockesburg, Ark., Apr. 13, 1883; d. George Todd and Callie Blanche (Dooley) Locke; student Texarkana (Ark.) Coll. and Conservatory of Music, Union Female Coll., Oxford, Miss.; A.B., Maddox Sem., Little Rock, Ark., 1901; m. Otis Theodore Wingo, Oct. 15, 1902 (died Oct. 21, 1930); children—Janie Blanche (wife of Dr. Leroy Lee Sawyer, Jr.), Otis Theodore. Elected mem. 71st Congress to fill unexpired term of husband (congressman from Ark. 18 yrs.), Nov. 4, 1930-Mar. 4, 1931, and mem. 72d Congress (1931-33), 4th Ark. Dist. Mem. D.A.R., U.S. Daughters of 1812, P.E.O. Sisterhood. Democrat. Southern Methodist. Club: Congressional (Washington). Home: De Queen, Ark.*

WINIARSKI, BOHDAN, (VIN-YÄR'SKI), U.N. official; b. Bohdanowo, Poland; April 27, 1884, son of Stanislaw and Jadwiga (Mystkowska) W.; College of Lomza, LL.D., Warsaw, Cracow, Paris, Heidelberg; m. Wanda Markowska, April 5, 1913; children—Krystyna (Mrs. St. Byczewska), Mathew, Magdalena (Mrs. B. Gotowska). Lecturer at the Polish School of Political Science, Cracow, 1911-14; legal adviser for the Polish National Committee, Warsaw, Petrograd, Paris, 1914-19; legal adviser, Polish delegation, Peace Conf., Paris, 1919-20; del. internat. confs. League of Nations; v. pres. orgn. of communications and transit, League of Nations; pres. legal com. for inland navigation, League of Nations; Polish del. to Internat. Oder Commn., 1921-30; govt. commr. for liquidation of German properties, 1924-27; mem. Polish Diet (Nat. party opposition) 1928-35. Prof. internat. law, U. of Poznan since 1922, dean faculty of law, 1936-39. Pres. Bank of Poland, London, 1941-46. Judge Internat. Court of Justice, 1946-67, pres., 1961-64. Mem. Inst. Internat. Law, Am. Acad. Polit. and Social Sci. (Phila.). Roman Catholic. Author of books on constitutional, international law, i.e. Principes Genereaux Du Droit Fluvial International, Les Institutions politiques en Pologne au XIXieme S., and others. Home: Poznan, Poland. *

WINKLEMAN, ISADORE, clothing co. exec.; b. Manistique, Mich., Nov. 6, 1901; s. Moses Philip and Hattie Sarah (Friedman) W.; ed. in Mich.; m. Marian Freeman, Nov., 1939 (div. 1952); 1 dau., Margot P.; m. 2d Beryl Jacobs Zlatkin, Dec., 1953; 1 son, Eric D.; stepchildren—Jan, Ned, Harriet. With Winkelman's Dept. Store, Manistique, 1917-27; co-founder Winkelman Bros. Apparel, Inc. (co. name changed to Winkelman Stores, Inc.), Detroit, Mich., 1927, pres., dir., 1940-67, chmn., chief exec. officer, dir., 1967-79. Bd. dirs. Sinai Hosp., Detroit, Jewish Home for Aged, Detroit Mem. Nat. Retail Merchants Assn., Detroit Retail Merchants Assn. (dir. 1950-79), Detroit Central Bus. Dist. Assn. Home: Detroit, Mich. Died Oct. 20, 1979.

WINN, DEAN F., army officer; b. Ga., Feb. 6, 1886; M.D., Atlanta Sch. of Medicine, 1910. Commd. 1st lt., M.C., U.S. Army, 1917, and advanced through grades to brig. gen. Decorated Legion of Merit with oak leaf cluster. Address: Washington. *

WINNE, MARSHALL FRANCIS, clergyman, educator; b. Sacramento, Calif., December 5, 1886; s. Frank P. and Elizabeth (Rademacker) W.; A.B., St. Vincent's Coll., Los Angeles, Calif., 1907, A.M., 1909; studied theology, St. Mary's Sem., Perryville, Mo., 1908-13; Ph.D., U. of Dallas, Tex., 1913. Dean of discipline and prof. sociology, U. of Dallas, 1913-16; prof. ethics and natural theology, Kendrick Sem., Webster Groves, Mo., 1916-17, also treas.; v.p., 1917-18, and pres., 1918-22. U. of Dallas; pastor Holy Trinity Ch., Dallas, 1918-22; prof. ethics and natural theology, Kendrick Sem., 1922-24; prof. logic and psychology, dir. seminarians, St. Thomas Sem., prof. ethics, Loretto Heights Coll., Denver, Colo., 1924-25; prin. De Paul U. Acad., Chicago, 1925-26; pres. Los Angeles Coll., 1926-32; prin. St. Vincent's High Sch. and pastor St. Vincent's Ch., Kansas City, Mo., 1933-38; provincial Western Province Congregation of the Mission, 1938-50; rector Our Lady of the Miraculous Medal Ch., Montebello, Calif., since 1950. Address: Montebello, Calif. *

WINSHIP, NORTH, foreign service officer; b. Macon, Ga., Dec. 31, 1885; s. Nathaniel R. and Mary A. (North) W.; spl. courses, George Washington U., Washington, D.C.; B.L., Mercer, Macon, 1910; m. Catherine Colfelt Taylor, June 28, 1921. With Exchange Bank, Macon, 4 yrs.; admitted to Ga. bar, 1910; apptd. consul at Tahiti, June 24, 1910, at Owen Sound, July 14, 1913, at Petrograd, Apr. 24, 1914, Milan, July 17, 1917, Bombay, Dec. 27, 1921, Fiume, Mar. 30, 1923, Cairo, Egypt, Dec. 9, 1924; sec. of Legation, Cairo, Sept. 21, 1926; consul gen., Copenhagen, 1928; counselor Legation, Copenhagen, 1931; Class I, June 1, 1937; del. 6th Internat. Conf. for Standardization and Penal Law Copenhagen, 1937; counselor of Embassy, Warsaw, Poland, Aug. 7, 1937; chmn. Am. del. subcommn. of 3d World Conf. on

Radiotelegraph Experts for Aeronautics, Cracow, Poland, 1939; counselor of Legation, Pretoria, Oct. 7, 1939; consul gen., Toronto, Can., June 21, 1941; consul gen., Montreal, Can., Oct. 12, 1944; Envoy Extraordinary and Minister Plenipotentiary, Pretoria, Union of S. Africa, 1948; Ambassador Extraordinary and Plenipotentiary of U.S. to S. Africa, 1949. Episcopalian. Clubs: Metropolitan, University (Washington); Idle Hour Country (Macon, Ga.); York, Toronto (Toronto); St. James, Mount Royal (Montreal). Home: Macon, Ga. *

WINSLOW, CARLILE PATTERSON, b. Washington, D.C., Aug. 5, 1884; s. Francis and Harriet (Patterson) W.; student Trinity Coll., Conn., 1901-02; Ph.B. in M.E., Sheffield Scientific Sch. (Yale), 1905; unmarried. With Niagara Constrn. Co., and Ont. Power Co., until 1908; staff, Forest Products Lab., U.S. Forest Service, since 1910, asst. dir. of lab., Madison, Wis., 1912-17, dir., 1917-46; consultant to U.S. Forest Service, 1946-47; now agt. for Union Market Development Corp., Washington. Engaged in tech. work for war agencies during both world wars. Fel. Soc. Am. Foresters; mem. Soc. of Cincinnati in New Hampshire, (life) Am. Soc. C.E., Sigma Xi. Episcopalian. Clubs: Madison (Wis.); Metropolitan, Cosmos, Chevy Chase (Washington); Yale (New York), Address: Washington, D.C. *

WINSLOW, HORATIO GATES, author; b. Racine, Wis., May 5, 1882; s. John Bradley and Agnes (Clancy) W.; grad. high sch., Madison, Wis., 1900; student Georgetown College, 1900-01; B.A., University of Wis., 1904; m. Marie Madeleine Bellet, of Bourges, France, 1925; children—Jacqueline Emily Bellet, John Seymour. Asst. editor of Puck, 1909; editor Masses, 1910-11; contributor fiction to Saturday Evening Post, Liberty, Collier's, etc. Capt. of inf., U.S. Army, 1917-19; with North Russian Expdn., 1918-19. Decorated Croix de Guerre (French), May 5, 1919. Mem. Authors' League America, Phi Delta Theta. Author: Rhymes and Meters, 1906; Some Wander Songs and Other Verses, 1908; Spring's Banjo, 1927; (with Leslie Quirk) Into Thin Air, 1929. Address: Altadena, Calif.*

WINSLOW, OLA ELIZABETH, educator, author: b. Grant City, Mo.; d. William Delos and Hattie Elizabeth (Colby) Winslow; A.B., Stanford, 1906, A.M., 1914; Ph.D., U. Chgo., 1922. Tchr. English, Coll. of Pacific, San Jose, Cal., 1909-14, Goucher Coll., 1914-44, Wellesley Coll., 1944-50, Radcliffe Seminars, 1950-61. Recipient Pulitzer prize for biography, 1941. Author: Am. Broadside Verse, 1930; Jonathan Edwards, 1703-1758, 1940; Meetinghouse Hill, 1630-1783, 1952; Master Roger William, 1957; John Bunyan, 1961; Samuel Sewall of Boston, 1964; Portsmouth, The Life of a Town, 1966; Jonathan Edwards, Basic Writings, 1966; John Eliot Apostle to the Indians, 1968; A Destroying Angel, 1974; also articles and essays in mags. Home: Wiseassat, Maine. Died Sept. 27, 1977.

WINSLOW, WALTER C., lawyer; b. Salem, Ore., Oct. 29, 1882; s. Paris R. and Addie (Vandevort) W.; A.B., Univ. of Ore., 1906; LL.B., Willamette Univ., 1908; m. Lottie D. Deyoe, Nov. 30, 1910; children—Norman K., Gertrude (Mrs. W.A. Ayres), Genevieve (Mrs. Mervin Michenham). Admitted to Ore. State bar, 1908, and since practiced in Salem; asso. late Senator Charles L. McNary and late Judge John H. McNary, 1908-13, with S.M. Endicott, 1913-34, practiced under own name, 1934-Jan. 1947 and since Jan. 1948; interim asso. justice of Ore. Supreme Court, 1947; instr., Willamette Univ. Coll. of Law, 1908-18; dep. dist. atty. for Third Judicial Dist., 1908-13. Mem. Salem Sch. Bd. 1917-22, chmn., 1919, 22). Mem. Am., Ore. State and Marion County (pres. 1934) bar assns., Salem Bus. Men's League (sec., 1909-13), Univ. of Ore. Alumni Assn. (pres., 1917-18), Order of the "O", Council Fgn. Relations, Inc., Acad. Polit. Sci. Republican. Methodist (chmn. bd. trustees, 1937-47; lay rep. to Ore. Annual Conf., since 1939; lay rep. to Jurisdictional Conf., Western Jurisdiction from Ore. Annual Conf. since 1948). Mason (mem. bd. trustees, Masonic Grand Lodge of Ore., 1930-34, grand master, 1932-33, chmn. jurisprudence com. since 1946; pres. Masonic Temple Assn. since 1925; master, 1919, 1933-34). Club: Republican of New York City. Home:

WINSTON, HARRY, jewel mcht.; b. N.Y.C., Mar. 1, 1886; s. Jacob and Jeanette (Harivmen) W.; student pub. schs.; m. Edna Fleishman, Feb. 10, 1933; children—Ronald Harivmen, Bruce Harivmen. Individual owner jewel bus., 1916-78; pres. Harry Winston, Inc., N.Y.C., 1932-78; purchased and cut Jonker 726 carat diamond, Vargas 726.60 carats, Liberator 155 carats, Niarchos 426 carats, Winston 154.50 carats, Lesotho 601.25 carats, others; purchased famous estates and jewels, including 100 carat Indian Pearshape Diamonds, Star of East Diamond, Hope Diamond (contbd. Smithsonian Instn.), Catherine the Great Sapphire, Dudley emerald necklace, Lucky Baldwin estate, Huntington estate, Star of Sierra Leone, Star of Independence, Washington Diamond. Home: New York, N.Y. Died Dec. 8, 1978.

WINSTON, JAMES HORNER, lawyer; b. Oxford, N.C., Sept. 19, 1884; s. Robert W. and Sophronia (Horner) W.; B.A., U. of N.C., 1904; Rhodes Scholar at Oxford U., Eng., 1904-07, B.A. in Jurisprudence, 1907; studied law, U. of N.C., 1903-04; m. Laura Flanagan, Nov. 26, 1908 (deceased); children—Robert Watson III, Sara Virginia (Mrs. Herbert C. De Young), Albert Flanagan, Laura J. (Mrs. Robert B. Wilcox); married 2d. Carita Reiss Bachmann. Engaged in practice of law at Norfolk, Va., 1907-11; settled in Chicago, 1911; mem. Winston, Strawn & Shaw, 1914-47; was mem. Miller, Gorham, Westcott & Adams. Was mem. Civil Service Commn., Norfolk. Mem. Am., Ill. State and Chicago bar assns., Law Club, Legal Club, Phi Beta Kappa, Zeta Psi. Dem. Episcopalian. Clubs: Chicago, University (Chgo.); Indian Hill Golf. Home: Evanston, Ill. *

WINTER, TED, publishing co. exec.; b. Chgo., May 9, 1919; s. Irving E. and Florence (Regensteiner) W.; student U. Mich., 1937-40, Loyola U., Chgo., 1940-41; m. Joan Lee, July 1, 1941; children—John L., Thomas. Gen. mgr. Children's Press, Chgo., 1946-50, pres., 1950-80; pres. Regensteiner Pub. Enterprises, Inc., Chgo., 1961-80, chmn. bd., 1972-80; del. White House Conf. on Edn., 1960. Mem. Bd. Edn. Dist. 113, Highland Park, Ill., 1964-70; vice chmn. bd. dirs. Am. Jewish Com., 1960-64; bd. dirs. Duncan YMCA, 1971-75, West Central Assn., 1966-75, Bur. Jewish Employment Problems, 1968-75; bd. assos. Nat. Coll. Edn., 1964-75. Served to 1st lt. Signal Corps, AUS, 1941-46. Mem. Assn. Am. Pubs., Printing Industries Am., Zeta Beta Tau. Jewish. Clubs: Northmoor Country, Standard. Home: Highland Park, Ill. Died 1980.

WINTERBLE, WILLIAM F., ins. exec.; b. Primghar, Ia., Oct. 23, 1893; s. Charles Henry and Esther (Albright) W.; student, Pillsbury Acad., 1910-13, U. Minn., 1913-16; m. Kathryn McAdams, June 18, 1940; children—Martha Roberts, Jean Handley, William K., Peter G. Ins. agt., Bankers Life Co., Minn., Ia., Wis., 1913-23; agy. mgr., Madison, Wis., 1923-34, supt. agencies, Des Moines, Ia., 1934-38, dir. of agencies, 1938-44, agy. v.p. since 1944. Mem. Alpha Delta Phi. Mason. Home: Des Moines. *

WINTERKORN, HANS FRIEDRICH, educator, engr.; b. Mannheim, Germany, Nov. 24, 1905; s. Valentin Guénémé and Elisabeth Christine (de Gedde) W.; student Ruperto-Carola U., Heidelberg, Germany, 1924-31; D. Natural Philosophy, U. Heidelberg, 1931; postgrad. U. Mo., Mass. Inst. Tech., U. Mich.; m. Hazel Zumwalt, Oct. 13, 1940; children—Hans Friedrich Zumwalt, Erik Guinemer de Gedde. Came to U.S., 1931, naturalized, 1938. Head div. chemistry Sch. Adult Edn., Mannheim, 1929-31; research chemist, engr. Mo. Hwy. Dept., 1931-32, research cons., 1932-42; research asso. prof. soil mechanics U. Mo., 1940-42, asso. prof. civil engring., 1942-43; asso. prof. civil engring. Princeton, 1943-55, prof., 1955-74, prof. emeritus, 1974-79. Research cons. Vialidad Nacional Argentina, 1937-40; owner, mgr. Winterkorn Research Inst.; lectr., cons. in Europe, Near and Middle East, 1964-65, Nigeria, 1972, Japan, India, 1973; cons. Turkish Hwy. Engring. Mission to U.S., 1945, pvt. road improvement interests, Argentina, 1946, Bur. Yards and Docks, Navy Dept., 1947-52, U.S. Dept. Interior, 1954-79, Gen. Electric Co. (lunar soils), 1961-65, Jet Propulsion Lab. Calif. Inst. Tech., USAF, 1963-70. Decorated Officer's Cross, Order of Merit (Fed. Republic Germany), 1957. Fellow ASCE (life); mem. Soil Sci. Soc. Am. (chmn. soil tech. sect. 1943-45), Am. Rd. Builders Assn. (cons. Pan Am. div.), AAUP, Assn. Asphalt Paving Technologists (life), Hwy. Research Bd. (chmn. com. physico-chem. phenomena in soils 1936-66), Sigma Xi, Tau Beta Pi, Alpha Chi Sigma, Gamma Alpha. Author: Grundlagen Der Bodenstabilisierung, 1960. Editor-in-chief: Foundation Engineering Handbook; editorial bd. Quarternary Research, Iranian Jour. Sci. and Tech. Contbr. articles profl. jours. Developed soil stblzn. and water- proofing methods for fighter fields, also Navy method for stblzn. invasion beach heads, World War II; discovered thermo-electric effect in moist soils. Home: New, N.Y. Died Aug. 7, 1979; buried Columbia, Mo.

WINTERS, RHETT YOUMANS, agronomist; b. Society Hill, S.C., Mar. 9, 1886; s. David Lawrence and Dora (Sompayrac) W.; B.S., Clemson (S.C.) Agrl. Coll., 1906, D.Sc., 1937; M.S., U. of Fla., 1909; Ph.D., Cornell U., 1911; m. Elizabeth Washington Knox, June 17, 1917; children—Elsa Smedes, Rhett Youmans, Dora Sompayrac. Grad. asst. in botany, U. of Fla., 1906-09; grad. asst. in plant breeding, Cornell U., 1910-11, instr., 1911-12; plant breeding agronomist, N.C. Agrl. Expt. Sta., 1912-23, dir., 1924-37; prof. plant breeding, N.C. State Coll., 1923-24; prin. administrator agrl. research, Office of Expt. Stations, U.S. Dept. Agr., 1937-39; assistant dir. of research, U.S. Dept. Agr., 1939-42; research coordinator Agr. Research Adminstrn., U.S. Dept. Agr., since 1942. Member Institute for Social Research (member of bd.), Assn. of Land Grant Colls. and Univs., Assn. Southern Agri. Workers, Acacia, Alpha Zeta, Phi Kappa Phi, Sigma Xi. Democrat. Episcopalian. Clubs: Cosmos, Clemson (Washington, D.C.). Home: Washington, D.C. *

WINTON, HARRY NATHANIEL MCQUILLIAN, U.N. official; b. San Francisco, Calif., Dec. 10, 1907; s. Ulysses Nathaniel and Alice Bartley (McQuillian) W.; A.B., Stanford Univ., 1932, A.M., 1934; unmarried. Instr. in history, Stanford Univ., 1937-40; editorial asso. The Pacific Northwest Quarterly, Univ. of Wash., 1940-42; chief Documents Index Unit, United Nations, New York, 1945-50, librarian United Nations Collection, 1950-61, chief documents reference sect. Library UN, 1962-67. Served in Signal Corps, U.S. Army, 1942-46. Presbyn. Home: New York, N.Y. Deceased.

WINTON, KATE BARBER, vegetable histologist; b. Charlestown, R.I., Oct. 9, 1882; d. Herbert Lincoln and Evelyn Amelia (Gates) Barber; B.S., R.I. State Coll., 1903; Ph.D., Yale, 1906; D. Sc., University of Rhode Island, 1956; married Andrew Lincoln Winton, Dec. 16, 1911 (died Oct. 1946); 1 dau., Mary Gorham (Mrs. Robert C. Dickgiesser). Microscopist Conn. Agrl. Expt. Sta., New Haven, 1906-07; microanalyst Bur. Chem. U.S. Dept. Agr., Washington, D.C., 1907-11. Fellow A.A.A.S.; mem. Phi Kappa Phi. Republican. Author: (with husband) Structure and Composition of Foods: Vol. I, 1932; Vol. II, 1935, Vol. III, 1937; Vol. IV, 1939; Analysis of Foods, 1945. Home: Wilton, Conn. *

WINTON, WILL MCCLAIN, paleontologist; b. Santa Rosa, Calif., Apr. 21, 1885; s. George Beverly and Jessie (McClain) W.; B.S., Vanderbilt, 1908, M.S., 1908; research fellow Rice Inst., Houston, Tex., 1914; m. Hortense Tucker, Aug. 24, 1909. Prof. biology and geology, Epworth U., Oklahoma City, Okla., 1908-09; prof. biology, State Normal Sch., Edmond, Okla., 1909-11; instr. biology, Tex. Agrl. and Mech. Coll., 1911-13; prof. biology and geology, Tex. Christian U., Ft. Worth, 1913-30, prof. geology and chmn. natural science since 1930. Geologist Tex. State Bur. of Geology, summers 1919-22 and 1925-27; cons. geologist Trinity River Improvement District No. 1 since 1925, coordinator, Navy V-12 Program, 1943-45. Fellow A.A.A.S., mem. Paleontological Society America, Am. Assn. Petroleum Geologists, Soc. Econ. Paleontologists and Mineralogists, Am. Soc. Mammalogists, Société Géologique de France, Phi Kappa Sigma. Democrat. Methodist. Author: (with W. S. Adkins) Paleontological Correlation, 1919; geologic maps of following Texas counties—Tarrant, Denton, Johnson, Hood, Somervell and Upton; and brochures and papers on paleontol. and geol. topics. Address: Fort Worth, Tex.; (summer) Valley Ranch, N.M. *

WIRTZ, CABLE AMBROSE, lawyer; b. Honolulu, May 9, 1910; s. Ambrose J. and Mary Emma (Meyer) W.; A.B., Santa Clara U., 1932; LL.B., Harvard U., 1935, J.D, 1970; m. Margaret Virginia Hughes, June 17, 1937; children—Richard Paul, Sheila Marie. Admitted to Hawaii bar, 1935; with firm Smith, Wild, Beebe & Cades, Honolulu, 1935-39; dep. city and county atty., Honolulu, 1939-42, city and county atty., 1942-44; judge Circuit Ct. 2d Jud. Circuit, 1944-51, 56-59; dist. magistrate Hana, Maui, 1954-56; asso. justice Supreme Ct. of Hawaii, 1959-67; pvt. practice law, Wailuku, Maui, 1951-56, 68-79, Honolulu, 1968-73; mem. firm Wooddell Mukai, Wirtz Ichiki & Whitfield, 1968-73; of counsel to Mukal, Ichiki, Raffeto & MacMillan, 1974-79. Mem. Territorial Commn. on Children and Youth, 1949-54, Maui Commn. on Children and Youth, 1949-54, Territorial Loyalty Bd., 1951-57, Hawaii Aero. Commn., 1953-56; chmn. Maui Cath Bd. Edn., 1968-69; arbitrator labor disputes Del. Constl. Conv., 1950. Bd. dirs. Ka Lima O'Maui (Rehab. Center). Mem. Am. Judicature Soc., Inst. Jud. Adminstrn., Am., Hawaii, Maui County (pres. 1970-71, bd. ethics) bar assns., Maui C. of C. (dir. 1971-74). Harvard Law Sch. Assn., Santa Clara Alumni Assn., Maui County Fair and Racing Assn., Maui Hist. Soc., Polynesian Voyaging Soc., Hawaiian Ry. Soc. Clubs: Harvard (Hawaii); Maui Rotary. Home: Wailuku, Hawaii. Died Dec. 29, 1980.

WISE, EARL D., utility exec.; b. Greentown, O., Oct. 31, 1885; s. Milo D. and Mary E. (Long) W.; student Ohio Northern U.; m. Muriel D. Fisher, May 27, 1915; children—Marjorie M. (Mrs. Franklin A. Dick). Began as wire chief's clerk Sunset Telephone and Telegraph Co., 1907, becoming exchange mgr., engr., supt. of constrn., supt. bldgs., shops and motor vehicles, div. plant supt. and asst. to gen. mgr., became v.p. and gen. mgr. Ore. area, 1930, v.p., gen. mgr. Wash. Ida. area, 1940-50, ret. Served as lt., Army Signal Corps, 1918. Mem. Armed Forces Communications Assn. Republican. Clubs: University, Seattle Tennis, Rainier (Seattle). Home: Seattle. *

WISE, WALTER DENT, surgeon; b. Patuxent Beach, Md., May 18, 1885; s. Walter Hanson Briscoe Stone and Martha Jane (Dent) W.; ed. pvt. schs.; M.D., U. of Md., 1906; m. Agnes Gordon Whiting, Oct. 20, 1914 (died 1918); children—Marian Gordon Armistead (dec.), Agnes Whiting; m. 2d, Josephine Warfield McMillan, July 27, 1921. Practiced in Baltimore since 1906; prof. clin. surgery, U. of Md. 1931-37; prof. surgery, U. of Md. since 1937; lecturer Johns Hopkins Univ., chief surgeon Mercy Hosp.; visiting surgeon Union Memorial, Women's, Johns Hopkins Hosp., South

Baltimore General hospitals. Colonel, Med. Corps, 1943-45; surgical consultant 3d Service Command. Mem. Founders Group Am. Bd. of Surgery. Fellow Am. College Surgeons, American Surgical Assn., Southern Surg. Assn.; mem. Am., Md. State and Baltimore med. assns., Phi Beta Pi. Sec. Med. and Chirurg. Faculty Md., 1931-39, pres., 1951-52; Balt. City Medical Society, 1943. Democrat. Episcopalian. Clubs: Maryland, Gibson Island, Elkridge. Contbr. articles on surgery. Home: Baltimore. *

WISEMAN, SCOTT, composer; b. Ingalls, N.C., Nov. 8, 1908; s. Edward G. and Josie (Shields) W.; B.A., Fairmont State Tchrs. Coll., 1932; M.A., Northwestern U., 1958; m. Myrtle Eleanor Cooper, Dec. 13, 1935; children—Linda Lou, Steven Scott. Partner (with wife) team Lulubelle and Scotty, from 1934; announcer WMMN radio, Fairmont, W.Va., 1930-32; singer, WLS, Chgo., 1933-58; appearances in motion pictures Republic Studios, 1937-43, Paramount, 1943; composer songs Mountain Dew, Have I Told You Lately That I Love You?, Remember Me, Tenderly He Watches, others. Dir. Northwestern Bank, Spruce Pine, N.C. Mem. Avery County (N.C.) Bd. Edn., 1968-73. Trustee Spruce Pine Community Hosp., 1965-81. Mem. Nashville Songwriters Hall of Fame. Mem. Country Music Assn. Mason. Rec. artist for Conqueror, Bluebird, Mercury. Vocalion, Starday, Old Homestead. Home: Spruce Pine, N.C. Died Jan. 31, 1981.

WISHNICK, ROBERT ISIDORE, bus. exec.; b. Koltchina, Russia, Apr. 5, 1892; s. Eli and Minnie (Gendler) W.; B.S. in Chem. Engring., Armour Inst. Tech., 1914; LL.B., Kent Coll. Law, 1917; m. Freda Frankel, Nov. 29, 1919; children—Betty June (Mrs. Stanley Freeman), John Harrison, William. Naturalized, 1908. Pres., Witco Chem. Co., Inc., 1920-55, chmn. bd., 1955-64, chmn. exec. and finance coms., mng. dir. internat. div., 1964-80; organizer, 1935, then dir. Witco Chem. Co., Ltd., London; organizer Continental Carbon Co., 1936, pres., dir., 1936-63, dir., chmn. bd. 1959-61; pres., dir. Witco Chem. Italiana, S.R.L., pres. Witco Chem. Co. Inc. Found.; dir. Witco Chem. Bank Israel, Company, Can., Ltd., Indsl. Devel. Bank of Israel, Witco Chem. France, S.A., Adjubel, Witfield Chem. Corp., Ultra Chem. Co. Trustee Ill. Inst. Tech., Jewish Child Care Assn. N.Y., Hosp. for Joint Diseases, N.Y.C., Hebrew U., Israel, Weizmann Inst. Sci., Israel. Mem. A.A.A.S., Am. Inst. Chemists, Am. Inst. Chem. Engrs., Am. Chem. Soc., Am. Petroleum Inst., Am. Gas Assn., Mfg. Chemists Assn. (dir.), Fedn. Handicapped (dir.), N.Y. Paint, Varnish and Lacquer Assn., Soc. Chem. Industry. Republican. Jewish religion. Clubs: Chemists, Harmonie (N.Y.C.); Old Oaks Country (Purchase, N.Y.); Standard (Chgo.); Hillcrest Country (Beverly Hills, Cal.). Home: New York, N.Y. Died Feb. 14, 1980.

WISSEL, PETER E., petroleum co. exec.; b. Queens, N.Y., Feb. 12, 1922; s. Rudolph and Maria P. (Kohl) W.; B.A., Columbia, 1943, M.A., 1953. With Texaco Inc., 1947-77, asst. to v.p. charge finance and econs., 1970, gen. mgr. finance and econs., 1970-71, v.p. finance and econs., 1971-77. Home: Scarsdale, N.Y. Died May 8, 1977.

WISSINK, GERRIT MARTIN, coll. dean; b. Alton, Ia., May 4, 1903; s. Carl and Mina (Scholten) W.; A.B., Hope Coll., Holland, Mich., 1925; M.S., Ia. State U., 1927, Ph.D., 1933; m. Bess Molsberry, Aug. 24, 1931; children—Robert G., Mahlon K. Instr. physics Ia. State Coll., 1927-29, Burlington (Ia.) Jr. Coll., 1929-30; prof. physics Buena Vista Coll., Storm Lake, Ia., 1934-35; chief physicist Consol. Water Power & Paper Co., Wisconsin Rapids, Wis., 1944-46; mem. faculty Mankato (Minn.) Coll., 1935-76, dean instrn., 1955-59, prof. physics, 1944-71, prof. emeritus, 1971-76, adminstrv. dean, 1959-67. Mem. coms. grad. program, sci. curriculum guide Minn. Dept. Edn. Mem. Minn. Acad. Sci. (v.p. 1942, bd. dirs. 1940-42), Am. Phys. Soc., Am. Assn. Physics Tchrs., A.A.A.S., Nat., Minn. edn. assns., Sigma Xi, Sigma Zeta (nat. pres. 1952), Phi Delta Kappa. Presbyn. (elder). Kiwanian (dist. lt. gov. 1971-72). Co-author: Outlines in Physical Science, 1942. Home: Mankato, Minn. Died May 27, 1976; interred Glenwood Cemetery, Mankato.

WITHERS, ORVAL RAYMOND, physician; b. Medicine Lodge, Kans., Dec. 19, 1898; s. Frank A. and Katherine (Cunningham) W.; student Leland Stanford U., 1918-20, U. Kans., 1920-21; A.B., Northwestern U., 1924, M.D., 1926; m. Mary Louise Holdman, 1926; children—H. Theodore, William F.; m. 2d, Kathleen Goggan, 1952. Intern, Charity Hosp., New Orleans, 1926-28; established 1st free Allergy Clinic, in Greater Kansas City area, 1931; head allergy dept. Outpatient Clinic, U. Kans. Med. Center, 1931-56; asso. clin. prof. medicine Kans. U. Med. Sch., 1947-61, clin. prof., 1961-71, emeritus, 1972—; former staff U. Kans. Med. Center, Bapt. Meml. Hosp., St. Mary's Hosp., Kansas City, Mo.; regional cons. Children's Asthma Research Inst. and Hosp., Denver; cons. in medicine VA Hosp., Kansas City, Mo., 1954-61; bd. dirs. Nat. Asthmatic Children's Found., 1973-74. Recipient Selective Service medal U.S. Congress; cited by Pres. Franklin D. Roosevelt and Harry S. Truman, 1940-47. Fellow AMA, World Med. Assn., Am. Coll. Allergists (founder group, bd. regents 1951-55, v.p. 1944-45, pres. 1957-58), Internat. Assn. Allergolists (founder group, v.p. 1958-61), A.C.P., Am. Acad. Allergy, Am. Coll. Chest Physicians; mem. Am., Mo. socs. internal medicine, Am. Med. Assn. Vienna (life), West Coast Allergy Soc., S.W. Allergy Forum (founder group, pres. 1953), Royal Soc. Medicine London, Am. Assn. Micrological Investigations (founders group), Mexican Assn. Allergy, So., Mo. allergy assns., Jackson County Med. Soc. (treas. 1944-45), Nat. Cowboy Hall Fame and Western Heritage Center (life), SAR, Am. Legion, Phi Beta Pi, Alpha Omega Alpha. Clubs: Westerners, Carriage, Rotary; Last Man's (Kansas City, Mo.). Contbg. author: Allergy-Methods of Treatment, 6th-7th edits., 1956, 58; Current Therapy, 1953-58. Mem. editorial bd. Annals of Allergy, 1943-58. Contbr. articles to profl. jours. Home: Lee's Summit, Mo. Died Apr. 18, 1981; buried Pratt, Kans.

WITHERS, THOMAS, naval officer (ret.); b. South Platte, Colo., May 28, 1886; s. Thomas and Jenny (Barnes) W.; B.S., U.S. Naval Acad., 1906; grad. U.S. Naval War Coll., 1924; m. Helen Lorena LaBar, Nov. 25, 1914 (dec. 1937); 1 dau., Helen LaBar (wife of Comdr. Howard F. Stoner); m. 2d Helen Schuster Fuller, Sept. 30, 1940. Commd. ensign U.S. Navy, 1908, and advanced through grades to rear adm., 1940; served in all types of naval vessels; qualified submarine officer, 1914; comdr. submarines, Pacific, 1941-42; comdt. Navy Yard, Portsmouth, N.H., 1942-45; ret. from active duty, 1946. Episcopalian. Mason (K.T., Shriner). Home: Coronado, Calif. *

WITHINGTON, SIDNEY, elec. engr.; b. Roxbury (Boston), Mass., June 7, 1884; s. Charles Francis and Georgiana (Bowen) W.; grad. Roxbury Latin Sch., 1902; A.B., Harvard, 1906, S.B., 1907; m. Dorothea Barrows, Dec. 22, 1914; children—Virginia, Charles Francis. Began in elec. engring. dept. N.Y.,N.H.&H. R.R., New Haven, Conn., 1910; has since continued in design constrn. and electrical operation same rd., engineering assistant to exec. vice pres. Served as 1st lieutenant engrs., U.S. Army, 1918. V.p. Ry. and Locomotive Hist. Soc. (Boston); past chmn. com. on heavy elec. traction, Am. Elec. Ry. Assn., vice chmn. elec. standards com., Am. Standards Assn.; mem. U.S. nat. com. Internat. Electrotechnical Commn.; fellow Am. Inst. E.E. (past chmn. transportation com., also of Conn. sect.); past chmn. com. on electricity, Am. Ry. Engring Assn.; mem. Am. Soc. Me. Eng., Am. Ry. Assn. (past vice-chmn. engring. div.; past chmn. elec. sect.), Internat. Ry. Assn. (reporter for N. and S. America, Gt. Britain and colonies, China and Japan, 1932), Newcomen Society of England, The Acorn Club of Connecticut, Delegate to the World Power Conf., Sweden 1933, Vienna 1938. Conglist. Clubs: Graduate, Mory's Assn.; Harvard (N.Y. City). Author publs. relating to field; contbr. to ry., engring. and hist. publs. Home: New Haven, Conn. *

WITMAN, WILLIAM, II, govt. ofcl.; b. Harrisburg, Pa., Jan. 31, 1914; s. Horace Montgomery and Clara (Wallower) W.; student Harrisburg Acad., 1924-27, Coppet (Switzerland) College La Chataigneraie, 1927-29, Gunnery Sch., Washington, Conn., 1929-31; B.A., Yale, 1935; m. Melpomene Maria Fafalios, Sept. 24, 1947. Asst. trade commr., Caracas, Venezuela, 1935-39; vice consul, 3d sec. Am. Legation, Beirut, Lebanon, 1939-44; acting comml. attache, 3d sec. Am. embassy, Ankara, Turkey, 1944-45; asst. comml. attache, 2d sec., consul, Am. embassy, Athens, Greece, 1945-48; consul, Bombay, India, 1948-49; officer-in-charge India-Nepal-Ceylon affairs State Dept., Washington, 1949-52; adviser U.S. delegation 7th Session UN Assembly, N.Y., 1952; counselor legation, consul gen. Am. Legation, Tangier, Morocco, 1953-55; dep. dir. Office S. Asian affairs State Dept., 1955-57; acting dir. Office No. African affairs, 1957, dir., 1960-63; 1st sec. Am. embassy, Paris, 1957-60; mem. U.S. delegation 2d Internat. Law of Sea Conf., Geneva, 1960; U.S. ambassador to Togo, West Africa, 1964-67; mem. Policy Planning Council, Dept. State, 1967-69, dir. Inter-African affairs, 1969-71, spl. asst. to asst. sec. African affairs, 1971-73, acting dep. asst. sec. for African affairs, 1973-74; Cons. Dept. State, 1974-78. Mem. U.S. delegations UN Gen. Assembly, 1965, 66, 67, 72; personal rep. of Pres. with rank of spl. ambassador Algerian Independence Ceremonies, 1962. Recipient Superior Service award Dept. State, 1963. Mem. Fgn. Service Assn. Presbyn. Club: Yale (Washington). Home: Arlington, Va. Died Mar. 12, 1978; buried Rock Creek Cemetery, Washington.

WITT, JOSHUA CHITWOOD, engr.; b. Connersville, Ind., Aug. 5, 1884; s. Isaac Snyder and Amanda (Chitwood) W.; A.B., Butler U., 1908; B.S., U. of Chicago, 1909; M.S., U. of Pittsburgh, 1912, Ph.D., 1915; M.E., Armour Institute Technology (now Illinois Institute Technology), Chicago, 1935; m. Florence Ruth Oldham, Dec. 5, 1918. Testing and research asst. Swift & Co., Chicago, 1908-10; mgr. testing dept. R. W. Hunt Co., Pittsburgh, 1910-15; chief of sect. Bur. of Science, Manila, P.I., 1915-17; tech. dir. Rizal Cement Co., Manila, 1917-19; asst. prof. U. of Pittsburgh, and cons. engr., 1919-20; dir. chem. research Portland Cement Assn., Chicago, 1920-23; dir. research Universal Atlas Cement Co., Chicago, 1924-39; tech. dir. Marquette Cement Mfg. Co., 1939-48; cons. engr., 1948—. Cons. U.S. Bur. of Mines, 1922-23. Sect. editor Chemical Abstracts, 1924—; cons. editor, Concrete, 1933-48. Fellow Am. Soc. M.E., A.A.A.S., Am. Soc. C.E., Am. Inst. Chem. Engrs.; mem. Am. Inst. of Consulting Engineers, American Chem. Soc., Am. Concrete Inst., Am. Soc. Testing Materials, Ill. Acad. Sci., Sigma Xi, Phi Delta Theta, Tau Beta Pi. Rep. Presbyn. Mason (32 deg., K.T., Shriner). Clubs: Adventures, Engineers (Chgo.). Author of Portland Cement Technology (also in Spanish), second edition in English, 1966; also numerous science and tech. papers. Patentee in cement. Home: Lockport, Ill. *

WITTEN, GEORGE WALTER BOND, (GEORGE WITTEN, PEN NAME), writer, explorer, aviator; b. Bklyn., Jan. 23, 1885; s. Walter and Marian (Halsted) W.; grad. Columbia (Tenn.) Mil. Acad., 1909; student U. of South, 1909-10, Columbia, 1910-11; grad. U.S. Army Command and Gen. Staff Coll., 1929; grad. in chemistry, Loyola U., 1943; m. Bunty Azue, Oct. 20, 1915. Left home as a boy and traveled widely in U.S., Can., Cuba, Bahamas, Europe and Africa; with Imperial Light Horse, Boer War; served with Natal Mounted Police; reporter on Eastern and So. papers, U.S.; exposed plot of Cipriano Castro to overthrow Venezuela; lectr. N.Y. Bd. of Edn., 1910-14, also in many states; enlisted in 1st Canadian Contingent, Aug. 1914; officer Royal Field Arty.; wounded 4 times; advanced to maj., 1919; lt. col. U.S., ret.; recalled to active duty, 1941-45. Investigated fraudulent stock promotions for Mag. of Wall St.; conducted French trans-Atlantic fliers, Coste and Bellonte on 15,000 mile flight through U.S., 1930; commanded 8th Mobile Port, AUS, 1942; comd. 1st training regt., Camp Sibert, 1943-44; supr. tng. U.S. Flying Services, 1946-48. Awarded Army Commendation Ribbon for Outstanding Service. Holds U.S. Civil Aeros. Authority license as aeroplane pilot. Fellow Philos. Soc. of Eng.; mem. Authors League Am., Army and Navy Union, Am. Legion, Res. Officers Assn. Episcopalian. Mason. Clubs: Explorers, Army and Navy, Adventures (past pres.), Writers (past pres.), Sojourners, Military and Naval (New York). Author: Outlaw Trails, 1929; Mutiny, 1932, Contbr. about 700 stories and articles to mags. Has given over 500 radio broadcasts, chiefly on adventure and travel. Address: Madeira Beach FL. *

WITTER, DEAN, JR., former investment banker; b. San Francisco, May 19, 1922; s. Dean and Helen (Perkins) W.; A.B., Yale, 1944; m. Faith Atkins, July 20, 1946 (div. Apr. 1960); children—Dean, David Gordon, Helen C., Malcolm Guy; m. 2d, Faith van Chief, May 9, 1966. Exec. v.p., dir. Dean Witter & Co., Inc., 1968-70. Clubs: Pacific Union, Bohemian (San Francisco); Connetquot (Oakdale, L.I.); Links (N.Y.C.); Boone and Crockett. Home: Naples, Fla. Died July 13, 1976.

WITTLAKE, JESSE CLARKE, ins. co. exec.; b. McCook, Nebr., Sept. 15, 1910; s. Charles and Effie Maude (McCain) W.; student Rutgers U., 1929-30; B.S., U. Nebr., 1935; M.S., U. Iowa, 1936; m. Jamie Jewell Lewis, Aug. 20, 1935; 1 dau., Linda. With Bus. Men's Assurance Co., Kansas City, Mo., 1936-77, asst. actuary, 1946-47, asst. to pres., 1947-56, v.p. adminstrn., 1956-64, exec. v.p., 1964-71, exec. v.p., chief adminstr. officer, 1971-73, pres., 1973-77, ret., also dir. Vice pres., bd. dirs. United Campaign; bd. dirs. Kansas City Mus., United Community Services, Greater Kansas City Sports Commn., Civic Council; chmn. corp. div. United Way Campaign; bd. dirs. Community Service Broadcasting of Mid-Am., Inc. Served to maj. AUS, 1942-46. Mem. Casualty Actuarial Soc., Am. Acad. Actuaries, Am. Legion, Pi Mu Epsilon, Beta Gamma Sigma. Presbyterian. Clubs: Kansas City; Mission Hills. Home: Leawood, Kans. Died Oct. 11, 1980; interred Mt. Moriah Garden Mausoleum, Chapel of Hope, Kansas City, Mo.

WODEHOUSE, ERNEST HAY, bus. exec.; b Honolulu, T.H., July 13, 1868 (parents Brit. citizens); son James H. and Annette Fanny (Massie) W.; study of English French under tutors; m. May Augusta Ward 1893; 1 son, Cenric Nourse. Mng. dir. Theo. H. Davies & Co., Ltd., Honolulu, 1905-29; pres. Hawaii Consol. Ry. 1937-47; chmn. bd. Bishop Nat. Bank of Hawaii since 1945; dir. Hamakua Mill Co., Honolulu Iron Works, Hawaiian Trust Co., Ltd., Kukaiau Ranch Co., Oahu Sugar Co., Ltd. Chmn. Prison Inspectors, 1904-25; pres. territorial bd. Immigration, Labor and Statistics, 1910-16. Sr. Trustee Estate of S. M. Damon since 1931. Mem. Hawaiian Sugar Planters (past trustee, pres.). Home: Honolulu, *

WODSEDALEK, JERRY EDWARD (WOD'SE-DA-LEK), zoölogist; b. Kewaunee, Wis., Aug. 5, 1884; s. Frank and Marie (Posepney) W.; Ph.B., U. of Wis., 1910, Ph.M., 1911, Ph.D., 1913; grad. Oshkosh Normal Sch., 1908; m. Hazel Mae Phillips, Aug. 30, 1914 (died May 1946); children—Helen Marie, Lt. Stanley (killed in World War II). Assistant in zoölogy, University of Wisconsin, 1910-11; fellow in zoölogy, same, 1911-13; prof. zoölogy and head dept. zoölogy and entomology, U. of Idaho, 1913; dir.

premedical studies, same, 1915-28, head div. zoölogy and entomology. Expt. Sta., 1917-20, chmn. Univ. Research Com., 1919, dir. grad. study, 1924, dean Grad. Sch., 1925-28; sabbatical leave of absence, at U. of Minn., and professional lecturer, 1928-29; prof. zoölogy, U. of Minn., since 1929; visiting prof. zoölogy, Calif. Institute Tech. 1935-36. Fellow A.A.A.S.; mem. Am. Soc. Zoölogists, Am. Genetic Assn., Am. Micros. Soc., Minn. Acad. Sci., Am. Soc. Naturalists, Sigma Xi, Sigma Alpha Epsilon, Pi Gamma Mu. Republican. Mason. Author: General Zoology Laboratory Guide (illustrative method), 1938, rev., 1944, 1946; also Shortened Guide; General Biology Laboratory Guide (with H. L. Dean), 1947. Contbd. articles on cytology, genetics, insect physiology, econ. entomology.Address: Minneapolis, Minn. *

WOHLRAB, ALOYS H., mining engr.; b. Milwaukee, July 25, 1885; s. Sylvan W. and Rosa A. (Lindwurm) W.; student Univ. Wis., 2 1/2 years; B.S. and E.M., Mich. Coll. Mines and Tech., 1911; m. Jane E. Mulvihill, June 25, 1943. Efficiency engr. Superior and Allovez Mining Cos. (subsidiaries of Calumet and Hecla Copper Co.) 1911-13; underground supt. Isle Royale Copper Co. (subsidiary Calumet & Hecla), 1913-19; supt., 1919-34; asst. gen. mgr. Hollinger Cons. Gold Mines, Ltd., Timmins, Ont., 1934-45; became v.p. and gen. mgr. Calumet and Hecla Cons. Copper Co., 1945, now retired; formerly dir. Lake Chem. Co., Prosite Co., Torch Lake Canal Co. Mem. Am. Inst. Mining and Metall. Engrs., Canadian Inst. Mining and Metall., Assn. Profl. Engrs. of Province of Ont., Psi Upsilon. Republican. Club: Miscowaubik (dir.). Home: Calumet, Mich. Retired. *

WOITSCH, FREDERICK, chemist; b. Frystat, Czechoslovakia, Mar. 13, 1909; s. Josef and Victoria (Gwuzdz) W.; Dipl. Ing. Chem., Tech. U., Prague, Czechoslovakia, 1933; Dipl. Mth., 1943. Ph.D., 1944, M.S. in Quality Control, 1947; m. Herta Ella Korner, May 10, 1955. Came to U.S. 1951, naturalized, 1956. Chief chemist Pharma Remedia-Dunj, Prague, 1933-45, pres., chmn. dirs., dir. research, 1945-48; owner Frutta Food Processing Co., Benesov-Lovosice, Czechoslovakia, 1945-48; partner V. Chlistovsky & Co., Benesov by Prague, Czechoslovakia, 1948-50; dir. tng. instn. Tng. Sch. Internat. Refugee Orgn., Wartenberg-Obb., West Germany, 1951-55; research chemist Chgo. Carton Co. div. United Biscuit Co. of Am., Chgo., 1955-59; head research, process, prodn. Bexell Assos., Inc., Evanston, Ill., 1959-64; chief chemist, mgr. chem. process devel. sect. Hoffman Electronics Corp., Semiconductor div. sect. Hoffman Electronics Corp., Semiconductor div., El Monte, Calif., 1964-65; sr. tech. splst. in charge chem. process and devel. group Autonetics div. N.Am. Rockwell (formerly North Am. Aviation, Inc.), Anaheim, Calif., 1965-77; dir. electronics unit State of Calif., 1970-71; dir. research and devel., chem. engring. So. Calif. Chem. Co., Santa Fe Springs, 1971. Mem. Am. Chem. Soc. Electrochem. Soc., Am. Soc. Quality Control, Switzerland Chem. Soc., West German Chem. Soc., Council Higher Edn., Am. Ordnance Assn., AIME, Am. Czechoslovak Engrs. Soc. Patentee fields electronics, aviation. Contbr. articles to sci. jours. Home: Monrovia, Calif. Died Jan. 25, 1977; interred Oakdale Mortuary, Glendora, Calif.

WOJTUL, PETER PAUL, bus. exec.; b. Chgo., June 29, 1909; s. John Joseph and Veronica (Esko) W.; student Loyola U., 1926-30, Advanced Mgmt. Program, Harvard, 1953; m. Virginia Trull, Feb. 22, 1942. Asst. to v.p., comptroller Continental Can Co., Inc., N.Y.C., 1944-46, asst. to pres., 1946-47, dir. sales research and devel., 1947-50, gen. mgr. sales metal div., 1950-54, v.p. charge sales, 1954-57, v.p., gen. mgr. fiber drum and corrugated box div., 1957-61, folding carton and drum div., 1961-64, v.p., sec., treas., 1964-68, v.p., exec. asst. to chmn., 1968-74, ret., 1974. Home: Scarsdale, N.Y. Died Oct. 29, 1976.

WOLF, ALBERT G., mining engr.; b. Colorado Springs, Colo., Mar. 27, 1885; s. Harry J. and Emma Regina (Goldbeck) W.; E.M., Colo. Sch. Mines, 1907; m. Lora Walker, June 29, 1912. Various engring., supervisory positions Japan-Flora Mines & Tunnel Co., Smuggler-Union Mining Co., Liberty Bell Gold Mining Co., Telluride Leasing Co., Mary Murphy Gold Mining Co., Mason Valley Mines Co., 1907-18; with Tex. Gulf Sulphur Co. since 1919, mgr. exploration dept., 1951-52, v.p. since 1952. Mem. Am. Inst. Mining and Metall. Engrs., Mining and Metall Soc. Am., Am. Assn. Petroleum Geologists, Geol. Assn. Can., Houston Geol. Soc., Tex. Acad. Sci., Houston Trun Verein. Clubs: Houston, Petroleum. Contbr. tech. articles profl. jours. Home: Houston. *

WOLF, ARNOLD VERYL, physiologist, educ ; b. N.Y.C., Dec. 3, 1916; s. Paul and Anna E. (Greenfield) W.; S., Coll. City N.Y., 1938; Ph.D. in Physiology, U. Rochester, 1942; m. Orietta L. Behrens, May 18, 1944; children—Paula D., Robyn L., Rodney A. Asst., physiology expdn. in desert S.W. U.S., U. Rochester, 1942; from instr. to asso. prof. physiology Albany (N.Y.) Med. Coll., 1942-52; chief renal sect. dept. cardiorespiratory diseases Walter Reed Army Inst. Research, 1952-58; prof. physiology, head dept. U. Ill. Coll. Medicine, 1958-73, dean Grad. Coll., U. Ill. at Med. Center, Chgo., 1973-75. Cons. Am. Optical Co.; mem. adv. com. gen. medicine Office Surgeon Gen. Fellow A.A.A.S.; mem. Am. Physiol. Soc., Am. Soc. Artificial Internal Organs, Sigma Xi, Author: The Urinary Function of the Kidney, 1950, Thirst: Physiology of the Urge to Drink and Problems of Water Lack, 1958; (with N.A. Crowder) An Introduction to Body Fluid Metabolism, 1964; Aqueous Solutions and Body Fluids: Their Concentrative Properties and Conversion Tables, 1966; also papers in field water metabolism. A developer TS meter for refractometric determination of water and total solids content of body fluids. Home: Highland Park, Ill. Died Feb. 27, 1975.

WOLF, BERNARD SAUL, educator, radiologist; b. N.Y.C., Sept. 8, 1912; s. Alexander and Mildred (Levy) W.; B.S., N.Y. U., 1932, M.D., 1936; m. Isabel Masket, May 4, 1939; children—Ellen, Susan. Rotating intern Mt. Sinai Hosp., N.Y.C., 1937-40, resident radiology, 1940-42; med. dir. AEC, N.Y.C., 1947-49, cons., 1949-77; dir. dept. radiology Mt. Sinai Hosp., 1949-77, prof. radiology, chmn. dept. Sch. Medicine, 1965-77. Mem. Mayor N.Y.C. Tech. Adv. Com. Radiation, 1957-77, Mayor N.Y.C. Subcom. Human Applications of Radioactive Materials, 1963-77. Recipient Luigi Celano medal N.Y. U. Med. Coll., 1936. Fellow Am. Coll. Radiology, A.M.A.; mem. Am. Gastroent. Assn., Am., N.Y. (past pres.) Roentgen ray socs., Am. Soc. Neuroradiology, Radiol. Soc. N.Am. Contbr. articles to med. jours. Home: New York, N.Y. Died Sept. 16, 1977.

WOLF, FREDERICK ADOLPH, educator; b. Odell, Neb., June 25, 1885; s. August and Wilhelmina (Kracht) W.; A.B., U. Neb., 1907, A.M., 1908; student U. Tex., 1908-10; Ph.D., Cornell U., 1911; m. Wynnette Taylor, June 30, 1914. Tutor botany U. Tex., 1908-10; pathologist Dept. Agr., Washington, 1911; fruit disease investigator, 1925-27; plant pathologist Ala. Expt. Sta., 1911-15, N.C. Expt. Sta., 1916-25; prof. botany Duke U., from 1927; on leave to work in Venezuela under direction Rockefeller Found., 1947-48. Mem. A.A.A.S., Am. Phytopath. Soc., Bot. Soc. Am. Home: Durham, N.C. Died Nov. 7, 1975.

WOLF, MORRIS, lawyer; b. Phila., Aug. 20, 1883; s. Edwin and Miriam (Fleisher) W.; student Penn Charter Sch., 1893-99; grad. summa cum laude, U. Pn. 1903; m. Pauline Binswanger, 1914 (dec. 1916); children—Edwin II, Robert B.; m. Bessie Katzenberg, Aug. 18, 1952. Admitted to Pa. bar, 1903; since practiced in Phila.; partner Stern & Wolf, Phila., 1903-21, sr. counsel to Wolf, Block, Schorr & Solis-Cohen, Phila., 1921-53; gen. counsel FOA, Washington, 1953-54; dir. Superior Zinc Corp., Colonial Assurance Co., Am. Cement Corp., Consol. Sun Ray Corp. Exec. com. Rep. Pa. Finance Com. Dir. Art Mus., Phila.; trustee U. Pa. Home: Wyncote, Pa. *

WOLFE, BERTRAM DAVID, writer; b. Blkyn., Jan. 19, 1896; s. William D. and Ray (Samter) W.; B.A., CCNY, 1916; postgrad. U. Mexico, 1922-25; A.M., Columbia 1931; LL.D., U. Calif., 1962; m. Ella Goldberg, Apr. 18, 1917. Tchr. English, Boys High Sch., Bklyn., 1916-17, Miguel Lerdo High Sch., Mexico City, 1922-25; dir. Workers Sch., N.Y.C., 1925-29; free lance writer, 1931-77; chief idealogical adv. unit, internat. broadcasting div. Dept. State, 1951-54. Sr. fellow Slavic studies Hoover Library, Stanford, 1949-50, 65-68; sr. research fellow Hoover Instn. on War, Revolution and Peace, Stanford, 1966-77; sr. fellow Russian Inst., Columbia, 1950-51; Disting. vis. prof. Russian history U. Calif., 1961-62. A founder U.S. Communist Party, 1919; dir. Workers Sch. on Union Sq. Guggenheim fellow. Townsend Harris medalist C. of C. N.Y., 1964. Fellow Am. Acad. Arts and Scis.; mem. Phi Beta Kappa. Club: P.E.N. Author books including: Portrait of Mexico, 1937; Diego Rivera: His Life and Times, 1939; Three Who Made A Revolution, 1948; Six Keys to the Soviet System, 1956; Khrushchev and Stalin's Ghost, 1957; Communist Totalitarianism, 1961; Rosa Luxemburg and the Russian Revolution, 1961; The Fabulous Life of Diego Rivera, 1963; Marxism: 100 Years in the Life of a Doctrine, 1965; Strange Communists I Have Known, 1965; The Bridge and the Abyss: The Troubled Friendship of Maxim Gorky and V.I. Lenin, 1967; Lenin, The Architect of Twentieth Century Totalitarianism, 1967; An Ideology in Power: Reflections on the Russian Revolution, 1969; Revolution and Reality, 1980; Memoirs-A Life in Two Centuries, 1980; Lenin, 1981; Literary Essays, 1981; also articles on Russian and Hispanic culture, history. Home: Palo Alto, Calif. Died Feb. 21, 1977; interred Alta Mesa Park, Palo Alto.

WOLFE, CALEB WROE, educator; b. Washington, Oct. 22, 1908; s. Caleb Samuel and Irene (Belt) W.; B.S., River Falls State Tchrs. Coll., 1930; postgrad. Boston U., 1930-31; A.M., Harvard, 1935, Ph.D., 1940; m. Cornelia Ellen Cell, Sept. 5, 1936; children—Marilyn Roberta, Caleb Wroe, Arrola Lee (dec.); m. 2d, Nancy Paterson Hicks, Aug. 20, 1948; children—Colin, Nancy; m. 3d, Alice Pauline Caras, Dec. 21, 1957; children—Alice, Jeffrey. Faculty, Boston U., 1941-80, prof. geology, 1947-80, chmn. dept. 1947-62. Pres., Earth Sci. Inst., 1949-52; Fulbright lectr., Dacca, East Pakistan, 1963-64. Recipient Neil Miner award for outstanding teaching, 1974. Fellow Geol. Soc. Am., Mineral. Soc. Am.; mem. Am. Geophys. Union, Boston Geol. Soc. (pres. 1949-51, sec. 1951-53), Am. Meteorol. Soc., N.Y. Acad. Sci. Author: This Earth of Ours, 1949, 69; Earth Science (with Fletcher), 1952; Manual of Geometrical Crystallography, 1953; (with Fletcher) Laboratory Exercises in Earth Science, 1953; (with Battan, Flemming, Hawkins, Skornik) Earth and Space Science with Lab Manual, 1966, (with McCombs, Skornik, Hawkins, Battan, Flemming) 2d edit., 1971. Contbr. articles to profl. jours. Home: Andover, Mass. Died July 17, 1980.

WOLFE, DON MARION, educator; b. Parsons, W.Va., Oct. 24, 1902; s. George Don and Annie (Cunningham) W.; B.S., Davis-Elkins Coll., 1923, D.Litt., 1961; M.A., U. Pitts., 1927, Ph.D., 1930; postgrad. U. Chgo., 1929, Columbia, 1942; m. Mary Lytle Stormont, June 2, 1931; 1 dau., Sarah McIntyre Wolfe Notter. From asst. to asso. prof. Geneva Coll., Beaver Falls, Pa., 1930-37; instr. English, summer, evening sessions CCNY, 1939-45; instr. English, Bklyn. Poly. Inst., 1941-42, N.Y. U., 1942-45; asso. prof. English, chmn. dept. Am. U. Sch. Social Scis. and Pub. Affairs, 1945-46; instr. writing New Sch. Social Research, 1946-63; asst. prof. English, Bklyn. Coll., 1946-52, asso. prof., 1952-56, prof., 1957-72, prof. emeritus, 1972-76; mem. Inst. for Advanced Study, Princeton, 1957-58; Fulbright prof. Am. lit. U. Bordeaux, France, 1959-60. Lectr., Milton, various states, 1949-76. Recipient numerous research, publ. grants; Guggenheim fellow, 1971-72. Mem. Milton Soc. Am. (pres. 1956 1956-57; hon. scholar 1966), MLA. Author: Leveller Manifestoes of the Puritan Revolution, 1967; The Image of Man in America, 1970; Milton in the Puritan Revolution, 1963; Milton and His England, 1971. Gen. editor: Complete Prose Works of John Milton, 1953-74; Jour. Hist. Studies, 1967-70. Home: Hightstown, N.J. Died Apr. 21, 1976; interred Princeton (N.J.) Cemetery.

WOLFE, HENRY CUTLER, internat. relations cons., lectr.; b. Newcomerstown, O., Jan. 11, 1898; s. Albert Fletcher and Jane (Dever) W.; student Phillips-Andover (Mass.) Acad.; hon. A.M., Kenyon Coll., 1939; m. Ann Cecilia Fox, June 11, 1938. Officer, Am. Relief Adminstrn. in Samara Province, Russia, 1922, A.R.C. mission to Greece (Patras area), 1923; also with Am. Com. in Constantinople. Served with French Army in Res. Mallet, 1917, in Am. Ambulance Unit on Italian front, 1918. Fellow Am. Geog. Soc.; mem. Acad. Polit. Sci., Am. Acad. Polit. and Social Sci., Am. Soc. French Legion Honor, Am. Soc. Italian Legions Merit, S.R., Delta Kappa Epsilon. Decorated Medaille Commemorative (France), 1921; officer Order of George I (Greece), 1923, Order Acad. Palms France, 1933, officer Order of Crown (Rumania), 1934, officer Order of Polonia Restituta (Poland), 1935; chevalier Order of White Lion (Czechoslovakia), 1937; officer Order of St. Sava (Yugoslavia), 1937, nat. officer Order of Southern Cross (Brazil), 1946; chevalier Legion of Honor (France), 1951; commendatore Order of Star of Solidarity (Italy), 1955; Grand Medal of Honor (Austria), 1957; knight Order of Merit (Fed. Republic Germany), 1962; 10th Anniversary Commemorative medal Assembly Captive European Nations, 1966; George Washington Honor medal Freedoms Found. at Valley Forge, 1968, 73. Visited Dobrudja Province as guest Rumanian Govt. to observe minorities transplantation, July 1935. War corr. in ETO, 1943-44. Author: The German Octopus, 1938; Human Dynamite, 1939; The Imperial Soviets, 1940. Wrote regular feature European Scene, Columbus Sunday Dispatch to 1937. Writer, lectr. internat. relations; contbr. to mags., anthologies, book revs. Has interviewed Pres. Benes of Czechoslovakia, Chancellor Schuschnigg of Austria, Queen Marie of Rumania, Pres. Vargas of Brazil, Pres. Quezon of Philippines, Pierre Laval of France, others. Episcopalian. Mason. Clubs: University, Pilgrims (N.Y.C.). Address: New York, N.Y. Died Nov. 20, 1976.

WOLFE, OLIVER HOWARD, banker; b. Phila., Pa., Jan. 7, 1882; s. Oliver and Anna (Moyer) W.; ed. Radnor (Pa.) public schools; LL.D., Rutgers University, 1943; married Elizabeth Roehm, September 4, 1920; children—Marjorie Louise, Katharine Elizabeth. With Phila. National Bank, 1899-1911 cashier 1915-40; v.p. and cashier 1940-42; vice pres., 1942-47; with Am. Bankers Assn. 1911-15; mgr. Phila. loan agency. Reconstruction Finance Corp., Feb.-June, 1932. Chief, gen. office division, Phila. Ordnance Dist., U.S. Army, 1941-43; exec. mgr. Penna. War Finance Com., U.S. Treasury, 1944-45. With Y.M.C.A. in France, 1918-19; served with 1st Div., A.E.F., later chief of Bur. of Personnel, Paris hdqrs. Republican. Episcopalian. Mason. Clubs: Union League, Rotary (Phila.). Author of various textbooks on banking used by Am. Inst. Banking and by corr. schs. Member faculty Grad. Sch. of Banking, Rutgers Univ. Now retired. Home:Radnor, Pa.*

WOLFE, SAMUEL MARION, lawyer; b. Charlotte, N.C., Mar. 29, 1882; s. Samuel Columbus and Ida May (Mobley) W.; student Patrick Mil. Inst., Anderson, S.C., 1887-89; A.B., Furman U., Greenville, S.C., 1903; student law dept. U. of S.C., 1907-08; married: 1 son,

Samuel Marion. Teacher and prin. high schs., S.C., 3 yrs.; began practice at Anderson, 1909; mem. S.C. Ho. of Rep., 1914-16; atty. gen. of S.C., 3 terms, 1919-23; resumed practice at Anderson, 1925. Democrat. Baptist. Mem. Am., S.C. and Anderson bar assns., K.P., Elk, Red Man, Woodman. Author: Hand Book Onthe Law of The Road, 1925. Home: Anderson, S.C.*

WOLFF, ALFRED ANDREW, ins. co. exec.; b. Jersey City, Apr. 24, 1917; s. Frederick and Anna (Bott) W.; ed. in N.J., N.Y., Mass.; m. Gladys M. Kaufhold, Oct. 27, 1945; children—Janice (Mrs. Scott Estes), Andrew A. With Home Ins. Co., N.Y.C., 1936-78, spl. agt., Newark, 1941-52, asst. mgr., Boston, 1952-54, mgr., 1954-59, asst. sec., N.Y.C., 1959-62, sec., 1962-63, v.p., 1963-70, exec. v.p. ops., 1970-75, exec. v.p. adminstrn., 1975-78, dir., 1969-78; dir. Home Indemnity Co., Home Ins. of Ind., Home Ins. of Ill., Thico Plan Inc., City Ins. Co. Served with USAAF, World War II. Mason. Clubs: Bankers (N.Y.C.); Rock Spring. Home: Short Hills, N.J. Died Mar. 26, 1978.

WOLFF, HAROLD ARNOLD, bus. cons.; b. Boston, Mar. 29, 1909; s. David B. and Minna (Bonfeld) W.; student Boston Latin Sch., 1921-25; A.B., Harvard, 1929; postgrad., 1929-36; postgrad., New Sch. for Social Research, 1940-41; m. Selma Strauss, June 19, 1932; children—Peter, Anthony. Ednl. counselor, 1931-42; with OWI, overseas br., 1942-45; pub. relations dir. Anahist Corp., 1949-51, Harold Wolff & Assos., pub. relations, 1951-59; pres. Bus. Communication, Inc., 1961-80; dir. publ. services McKinsey & Co., 1961-64; cons. planning and devel. Booz, Allen & Hamilton, Inc., 1964-66. Lectr., Sloan Sch. Mgmt., Mass. Inst. Tech., 1966-69; adj. prof. Boston U. Coll. Bus. Adminstrn., 1966-70; lectr. mgmt. Grad. Sch. Bus. Adminstrn., N.Y. U., 1968-70; cons. to adminstr. NASA, 1966-69. Clubs: Nat. Press, Harvard. Author, editor publs. on Am. econs., bus., mgmt. tng. and devel. Home: New York, N.Y. Died Feb. 2, 1980.

WOLFF, JOSEPH SCOTT, ex-congressman; b. Westmoreland Co., Pa., June 14, 1878; s. Rev. Andrew Thompson and Sitiah Margarette (Young) W.; D.D.S., Washington U., 1905; LL.B., St. Louis Coll. of Law and Finance, 1923; m. Antonette Nengel, of Festus, Mo., July 31, 1905. Practiced dentistry and law, Festus, Mo., since 1905. Pres. Midget Oil & Gas Co. Mayor of Festus 3 terms; mem. Mo. Ho. of Rep., 1913-15; mem. 68th Congress (1923-25), 13th Mo. Dist. Mem. Mo. Dental Assn. Democrat. Odd Fellow, Red Man, Woodman, Elk. Home: Kansas City. *

WOLFF, LOUIS MICHAEL, architect; b. Allendale, S.C., Dec. 25, 1910; s. Henry and Ray (Pearlstine) W.; B.S., Clemson U., 1931; B.Arch., U. Pa., 1933; m. Elsie Benenson, Dec. 25, 1952; children—Terri Ray, Frances Ellen, Henry Michael, David Bruce. Archtl. designer Nat. Park Service, Myrtle Beach, S.C., 1934-36; draftsman Buckler & Fenhagen, architects, Balt., 1936-40; prin. Lyles, Bissett, Carlisle & Wolff, Columbia, S.C., 1948-77; chmn. bd., pres. LBC & W Asso. of S.C., architects, engrs., 1969-77. Mem. hosp. adv. council S.C. Bd. Health, 1960-77; chmn. S.C. Services Council, A.R.C., 1950-60. Served to col. C.E., AUS, 1940-46. Decorated Bronze Star medal, Polish Legion of Merit., Fellow A.I.A. (pres. S.C. chpt. 1957-58). Clubs: Columbia Country, Palmetto; Ft. Jackson Officers. Home: Columbia, S.C. died Oct. 30, 1977.

WOLFF, ROBERT JAY, artist; b. Chgo., July 27, 1905; s. Aaron Russell and Martha (Marks) W.; student Yale, 1923-26; ind. study N.Y., Eng., France, 1926-31; m. Elizabeth Crocker Leighton, Aug. 3, 1949. Exhibited group, one-man shows, N.Y.C., Chgo., San Francisco, also France, Germany, Switzerland, Italy; paintings in permanent collections Tate Gallery, London, Bklyn. Mus. Guggenheim Mus., N.Y.C., Wadsworth Atheneum, Hartford, Conn. Bauhaus Archiv Mus., West Berlin, Art Inst. Chgo. State supr. ease painting Fed. Art Project, Ill., 1937-38; dean, head painting and sculpture Sch. Design (now Inst. Design), Chgo., 1938-42; publs. designer Knoll Assos., N.Y.C., 1945-46; design cons. Gen. Electric Co., 1945-48; cons. dir. publs. design Boris Kroll Fabrics, Inc., N.Y.C., 1946-71; prof. art Bklyn. Coll. of City U. N.Y., 1946-71, prof. emeritus, 1971-77, chmn. dept., 1946-64, head grad. art program, 1964-69. Vis. Bemus prof. art Mass. Inst Tech., 1961; vis. lectr. Grad. Sch Design Harvard, 1961. Served as lt. USNR, 1943-45, head non-engring. graphics Naval Tgn. Aids Devel. Center, N.Y.C. Mem. Am. Abstract Artists (exhibiting), 1937-51. Author, designer: (ednl. portfolio) Elements of Design; author-illustrator 3 children's books on color, 1968: On Art and Learning, 1971. Contbr. articles on art to profl. publs. Home: New Preston, Conn. Died Dec. 29, 1977.

WOLFF, ROBERT LEE, educator, historian; b. N.Y.C., Dec. 22, 1915; s. Samuel Lee and Mathilde (Abraham) W.; A.B., Harvard, 1936, A.M., 1937, Ph.D., 1947; Litt.D., Williams Coll., 1961; m. Mary Andrews, Nov. 24, 1937; children—Rosamond Capen (Mrs. Dennis W. Purcell), Katharine, Robert Lee, James A. Teaching fellow history Harvard, 1937-41, asso. prof., 1950-55, prof., 1955-80, Coolidge prof. history, 1965-80, chmn. dept. history, 1960-63; asst. to dir., chief Balkan sect. Research and Analysis br. OSS, 1942-46; asst. prof., then asso. prof. history U. Wis., 1947-50. Harvard lectr. Yale, 1961; lectr. Ecole Universitaire des Hautes Etudes Internationales, Geneva, 1957. Trustee Brooks Sch., Radcliffe Coll. Fellow Am. Philos. Soc.; mem. Mediaeval Acad. Am. Clubs: Knickerbocker (N.Y.C.); Somerset, Tavern (Boston). Author: The Balkans in Our Time, 2d edit., 1974; The Golden Key, 1961; Strange Stories, 1971; Studies in the Latin Empire of Constantinople, 1976; Gains and Losses: Novels of Faith and Doubt in Victorian England, 1977; Sensational Victorian: The Life and Fiction of Mary Elizabeth Braddon, 1979; William Carlton, Irish Peasant Novelist: A Preface to his Fiction, 1980; co-author: A History of Civilization, 1955, 5th edit., 1975; History of the Crusades II, 1962, 2d edit., 1969. Home: Cambridge, Mass. Died Nov. 11, 1980.

WOLFLIN, HUGH MAUPIN (WOOLF'LIN), mining engr.; b. Canton, Mo., Aug. 12, 1886; B.S., U. of Ariz., 1907, B.S. in Mining Engring., 1908; M.A., Columbia, 1913; m. Dorothy MacBoyle, Apr. 30, 1919. Asst. engr. U.S. Bur. of Mines, 1910-13, dist. engr., 1914-15 and 1917-18, mine safety engr., 1916, head mining engr. and supervising engr., 1931-33; mining engr. Calif. Accident Commn., 1914-15 and 1917-18, supt. of safety, 1919-23; cons. engr. at San Francisco and Los Angeles, 1923-30; sr. engr. legal div. Met. Water Dist. of Southern Calif. from Nov. 1933, to Dec. 1936; in charge personnel and safety work for Idaho Maryland Mines Corp., Jan. 1937-Mar. 1938, asst. mgr., 1938-42; asst. mgr. Hercules Powder Co., Radford Ordnance Works, Radford, Va., 1942-45; now cons. engr. Mem. Am. Inst. Mining and Metall. Engrs., Delta Tau Delta. Republican. Mason. Club: Engineers (San Francisco). Address: El Monte, Calif. *

WOLKOMIR, NATHAN TULLY, labor union ofcl.; b. Baku, Russia, Oct. 12, 1909; s. Boris and Rose (Silver) W.; came to U.S., 1912, naturalized, 1917; B.S., N.Y. U., 1929, St. John's U., 1930, St. Francis Coll., N.Y.C., 1930; M.Ed., St. John's U., 1940; D.Ed., U. Ill., 1960; m. Louise Orthelia Schimmen, Mar. 10, 1944; 1 dau., Rhya Natalia. Tchr., N.Y.C., 1940-42; ednl. specialist, tng. command USAAF and USAF, 1942-64; mem. Nat. Fedn. Fed. Employees, 1942-76, pres. Ill., 1950-52, nat. pres., 1964-76. Chmn., Community Concerts, Rantoul, Ill., 1960, Rantoui Recreation Bd., 1961; pres. Chanute AFB Recreation and Welfare Orgn., 1962; mem. Pres.'s Com. on Hiring Handicapped, 1965, Eligibility Bd. for Administering Fed. Fund Raising Program, Employee Advisory Com. on Fed. Employers Health Benefits Program; mem. advisory council Nat. Wage Bd.; mem. Nat. Job Evaluation and Pay Rev. Task Force; mem. Wm. A. Jump award and selection com. Dept. Agr., 1978-79; mem. Nat. Council on Aging. Police commr., Rantoul, 1962. Mem. Soc. Personnel Adminstrn., Soc. Programmed Instruction, Am. Soc. Pub. Adminstrn., Pub. Personnel Assn., Am. Acad. Polit. and Social Scis., Nat. Civil Service League, Air Force Assn. Clubs: Masons (32 deg.), Shriners, Odd Fellows, Moose. Author: (with others), Modern Airmanship, 1957; editor Federal Employee, Report from Washington. Home: Silver Spring, Md. *

WOLLESON, E. A., dean; b. Belleville, Ill., Oct. 25, 1883; s. Anton Martin and Hanah Catherine (Hempelman) W.; B.S., U.S. Naval Acad., 1906; U.S. Naval War Coll., 1929-30; m. Daisy May Beech, Nov. 18, 1919; 1 dau., Katherine Mary. Appointed to U.S. Naval Acad., 1902 from 21st Congl. Dist. of Ill.; advanced through grades to capt., 1931; commanded destroyer squadron, U.S. Asiatic Fleet, 1932-34, U.S.S. Tennessee, 1937-38; chief of staff 9th Naval dist., 1935-37, 1939 to retirement date, July 1941; continued on active duty in command of naval training schs., Navy Pier, Chicago, 1942-46; dean of students, undergrad. div. Univ. of Ill., Navy Pier, Chicago, since inception, 1946. Awarded Navy Distinguished Service Medal, World War I; Letters of Commendation by Sec. of the Navy, World War II. Home: Chicago. *

WOLMAN, IRVING JACOB, physician, educator; b. Holyoke, Mass., Feb. 2, 1905; s. Benjamin and Pauline (Resnick) W.; A.B., Amherst Coll., 1925, D.Sc., 1975; M.D., Johns Hopkins, 1929; M.A. (hon.), U. Pa., 1970; m. Roslyn Stone, Apr. 12, 1935; children—Carol, James. Intern pediatrics Johns Hopkins Hosp., Balt., 1930-31; resident pathologist Pa. Hosp., Phila., 1929-30; resident pathologist Children's Meml. Hosp., Chgo., 1931-32; chief resident physician Children's Hosp., Phila., 1932-34, asst. pathologist, research fellow, attending physician, 1935-42, pathologist, dir. clin. labs., 1947-70 hematologist, 1954-70, cons., 1970-78; instr. to prof. pediatrics Medical Sch., U. Pa., 1932-73, emeritus, 1973-78, chmn. dept. pediatrics Grad. Sch. Medicine, 1959-70; pathologist St. Christopher's Hosp. for Children, Phila., 1946-47; pediatric cons. div. med. programs Pa. Dept. Welfare, 1974-78. Chmn., Phila. Milk Commn., 1936-71. Served as asst. surgeon, later surgeon Res. Corps, USPHS, active duty, 1942-46. Diplomate Am. Bd. Pediatrics, Am. Bd. Pathology (pathology, clin. pathology, hematology). Mem. A.M.A., Phila. Coll. Phys. Surgs., Phila. County Med. Soc., Phila. Pediatric Soc. (pres. 1952), Am. Acad. Pediatrics, Soc. Pediatric Research, Am. Pediatric Soc., Phi Beta Kappa, Sigma Xi, Alpha Omega Alpha, Club: Locust (Phila.). Author: Laboratory Applications in Clinical Pediatrics, 1957. Editor: Clin. Pediatrics. Address: Melrose Park, Pa. Died June 23, 1978.

WOLMAN, PAUL CARROLL, lawyer; b. Woodbine, Md., Mar. 17, 1896; s. Solomon and Esther (Schroeder) W.; grad. Balt. City Coll., 1915; LL.B., U. Md., 1920; Council of Legal Edn., London, 1919; m. Jeanette Rosner, Mar. 8, 1925; children—Paul Carroll, Benjamin Rosner. Admitted to Md. bar, practice 1920, since practiced in Balt.; dir. Woodbine Nat. Bank. Mem. Nat. Selective Service Appeal Bd., 1949-57; mem. Md. Bd. Parole and Probation, 1958-61, chmn., 1961—; dir. Md. Dept. Parole and Probation, 1961—. Md. chmn. armed services com. Nat. Jewish Welfare Bd.; mem. gen. and operations coms. Balt. USO; vice pres. East Balt. Boys Club; vice chmn. War Meml. Commn. of Md.; past pres. Jewish Big Brother League. Served with 313th Inf., U.S. Army, 1917-19. Mem. Am., Fed. (dir. Md. chpt.), Md., Balt. bar assns., Vets. Fgn. Wars (former nat. comdr.; recipient Distinguished Service medal, 1941), Am. Legion, Jewish War Vets. U.S., Sojourners, Phi Alpha. Mason (32 deg.). Home: Balt., Md. Died Oct. 23, 1978.

WOLSON, B. BERNARD, lawyer; b. Toledo, Nov. 17, 1912; s. Alex and Sophia (Brenner) W.; B.S. in Bus. Adminstrn., Ohio State U., 1934, J.D., 1936; m. Estelle Cronstine, Aug. 10, 1941; children—Alexa S., Rita. Admitted to Ohio bar 1936, since practiced in Toledo; asso. firm Rowe Williams & Dillon, 1936-39; partner firm Tuschman, Tuschman & Wolson, 1940-42; sr. mem firm Wolson, Kaplan, Shibley & Green, 1942-76. Tchr. law Biarritz Am. U., France, 1943-44. Bd. dirs. Lucas County (O.) Retarded Children's Program. Mem. Am., Ohio, Lucas County, Toledo bar assns. Jewish religion (pres. temple). Elk; mem. B'nai B'rith. Asso. editor Comml. Law Jour., 1945-76, Scribes. Contbr. articles to profl. jours. Home: Toledo, Ohio. Died Nov. 30, 1976.

WOLTER, ROY L., mfg. co. exec.; ed. U. Buffalo. With Automatic Transp. Co., 1918-33; company acquired by Yale & Towne Mfg. Co., 1933, gen. mgr. automatic div., 1955-78, v.p. company, 1962-78; pres. Indsl. Truck Assn., 1962-63. Mem. Am. Materials Handling Soc., Soc. Indsl. Packaging and Materials Handling Engrs.; asso. mem. Iron and Steel Engrs. Address: New York, N.Y. Died June 1978.

WOMACK, RICHARD ELWOOD (WOM'AK), coll. pres.; b. Centerton, Ark., Nov. 4, 1882; s. James Wilson and Elizabeth Jane (Gamble) W.; A.B., U. of Ark., 1909; grad. student, U. of Wis.; M.A., George Peabody College for Teachers, Nashville, Tenn., 1916; LL.D., Union Univ., 1926; m. Mamie Lee Boner, Jan. 1, 1904; children—Mamie Lucile, Elma Lee, Helen May, Hazel Belle, Richard Elwood, Edith Lynn, Robert Edward. Teacher rural schs., Ark., 1903-06; head of history dept. Ark. State Normal Sch., 1909-17; mem. summer faculty, Peabody Coll. for Teachers, 1915; supt. public schs., Conway, Ark., 1917-22; headmaster Hendrix Acad., Conway, 1922-24; president Lambuth College, Jackson, Tenn., 1924-52; trustee and treas. bd. of trustees Del. Gen. Conf. M.E. Ch., S., 1930, 34, 38, Methodist Uniting Conf., 1939, Southeastern Jurisdictional Conf., Meth. Ch., 1940, 1944, 48, Gen. Conf. Meth. Ch., 1948, 52. Pres. Tenn. Coll. Assn., 1936-37, pres. The Central Assn. of Colleges, 1943-47. Democrat. Home: Jackson, Tenn.*

WOMBLE, BUNYAN SNIPES, lawyer; b. Pittsboro, N.C., May 2, 1882; s. William Fletcher and Olivia Josephine (Snipes) W.; A.B., Trinity Coll. (now Duke), 1904, postgrad. Law Sch., 1904-06, LL.D., 1964; postgrad. Columbia Law Sch., 1907; m. Edith Willingham, Apr. 29, 1914; children—Lila (Mrs. F. Gaither Jenkins), William Fletcher, Olivia (Mrs. Charles Phillips), Edith (Mrs. Richard G. Chatham), Calder W., Ruth (Mrs. Laurence F. Lee, Jr.). Admitted to N.C. bar, 1906, since 1907 in practice at Winston-Salem; joined firm Manly, Hendren & Womble, 1911, name of firm changed to Womble, Carlyle, Martin & Sandridge, 1942, Womble, Carlyle, Sandridge & Rice, 1954; dir. emeritus Wachovia Bank & Trust Co., Security Life & Trust Co. (now Integon Corp.). Mem. N.C. Legislature, 1925, State Senate, 1927, 29, chmn. Senate Finance Com., 1929; mem. N.C. Adv. Budget Commn., 1929-31, N.C. Jud. Council, 1925-31. Chmn. bd. sch. commrs. Winston-Salem, 1933-43. Chmn. bd. trustees, exec. com. Duke, 1960-64, trustee, 1915-64, trustee emeritus; trustee Children's Home (Meth. Orphanage) 1930-59, Meth. Home for Aged. Mem. Am., N.C. (pres. 1936-37) bar assns., Soc. Cin., Order of Coif, Phi Delta Phi, Omicron Delta Kappa. Democrat. Methodist. Rotarian. Club: Forsyth Country. Home: Winston-Salem, N.C. Died May 17, 1976.

WONG, DICK YIN, fed. judge; b. Honolulu, Sept. 13, 1920; s. Lee Yau and Helen Kin (Dang) W.; B.A. in Accounting, U. Hawaii, 1942, M.A., 1944; J.D., Northwestern U., 1950; m. Lily Kwai Chan Yee, June 24, 1951; children—Diane Wai Inn, David Wing Keong, Lisa Mei Inn, Laurie Oi Inn, Steven Wing Hing. Jr. accountant Theodore Char, C.P.A., Honolulu,

1940-44; clk.-typist Navy Yard, Pearl Harbor, 1941-45; semi-sr. accountant Walton, Joplin, Langer & Co., C.P.A.'s, Chgo., 1947-49; admitted to Hawaii bar, 1951; asso. Peter A. Lee, Honolulu, 1950-51; partner firm Char & Wong, C.P.A.'s, Honolulu, 1951-54, Lau & Wong, C.P.A.'S, 1954-61, Wong, Lau & Lo, 1960-61; judge Hawaii Tax Appeal Ct., Honolulu, 1960-68; partner firm Wong & Lo, 1962-68, Wong & Kadowaki, C.P.A.'s, 1962-68; judge First Circuit Ct. Hawaii, Honolulu, 1968-73; partner firm Hong, Wong & Iwai, 1973-75; U.S. dist. judge Hawaii, Honolulu, 1975-78; chmn. bd. Wo Fat, Ltd., Mid-Pac Industries; dir. KDI Investments, Inc.; lectr. U. Hawaii, 1951-53. Pres., Wong Kong Har Tong, 1966-67; bd. dirs. Hawaii Youth Symphony Assn., 1966-74, Big Bros. of Hawaii, 1966-69, Honolulu Symphony Soc., 1973-75. Served with U.S. Army, 1945-47. Recipient Outstanding Alumni award U Hawaii, 1977. C.P.A., Hawaii. Mem. Am., Hawaii (pres. 1975) bar assns., Hawaii Soc. C.P.A.'s, Am. Judicature Soc., Am. Assn. Attys.-C.P.A.'s, Inc. Home: Honolulu, Hawaii. Died Dec. 1978.

WOOD, JOHN HOWLAND, JR., judge; b. Rockport, Tex., Mar. 31, 1916; s. John Howland and Cecilia (Browne) W.; grad. San Antonio Coll. and St. Marys U., 1935; J.D., U. Tex., 1938; m. Kathryn Wynter Holmes, Aug 17, 1941; children—Kathryn (Mrs. Chesley W. Johnston), Nancy (Mrs. Lewis J. Moorman III). Admitted to Tex. bar, 1938; sr. partner Beckmann, Stanard, Wood & Keene, San Antonio, 1938-70; U.S. dist. judge Western Dist. Tex., San Antonio, 1970-79. Instr. real estate law Trinity U., spring 1955, 56; mem. faculty Fed. Jud. Center. Charter mem. Greater San Antonio Devel. Commn. Del. Rep. Nat. Convs., 1952, 56, 60, 68. Bd. dirs. Guadalupe Community Center, San Antonio Research and Planning Council; bd. govs. St. Marys U. Served to ensign USNR, 1944-45; to lt., Res., 1945-54. Mem. Am. (sec. war work com. 5th Circuit 1942-43), San Antonio (past dir.) bar assns., State Bar Tex. (chmn. war work com. 1940-43, chmn. grievance com. 20th Dist. 1956-57, chmn. unauthorized practice of law com. 1968-73), Am. Judicature Soc., Tex. Assn. Def. Counsel (dir. 1968-70), San Antonio C. of C. (past dir.), Sons of Republic of Tex., S.A.R., Tex. Cavaliers, Order of the Alamo, Am. Legion, Mil. Order World Wars, Alpha Tau Omega. Clubs: Argyle, San Antonio, St. Anthony, San Antonio Country, San Antonio Gun, San Antonio. German. Lectures, publs. on fed. rules of evidence, procedure, prisoner petitions. Home: San Antonio, Tex. Died May 29, 1979.

WOOD, JOHN STEPHENS, ex-congressman; b. Cherokee Co., Ga., Feb. 8, 1885; ed. North Ga. Agrl. Coll.; LL.B., Mercer U. Formerly mem. Ga. Ho. of Rep.; was also solicitor gen. Blue Ridge Jud. Circuit of Ga.; later judge Superior Court, same circuit; mem. 72d and 73d Congresses (1931-35), 9th Ga. Dist. Democrat. Home: Canton, Ga.*

WOOD, L(ELAND) FOSTER, exec. secretary; b. Kendall Mills, N.Y., May 9, 1885; s. Benoni Ives and Effie May (Hill) W.; B.A., U. of Rochester, 1908, M.A., 1914; B.D., Rochester Theol. Sem., 1914; Ph.D., U. of Chicago, 1923; m. Georgia Ardelle Heaton, July 12, 1910; children—Katharine May (dec.), Georgia Dorothea. Ordained ministry Bapt. Ch., 1911; missionary Tshumbiri, Belgian Congo, under A.B.F.M.S., 1911-20; prof. religious edn., Bucknell U., 1923-25; prof. sociology and ethics, Rochester Theol. Sem., 1925-28; prof. social ethics, Colgate-Rochester Div. Sch., 1928-32; sec. Com. on Marriage and the Home, Fed. Council of Chs., 1932-50. Sec. Ch. Conf. Social Work, 1934-44. Member Am. Sociol. Society, Religious Edn. Assn., Nat. Council Parent Edn., Am. Social Hygiene Assn., Delta Upsilon, Pi Gamma Mu. Author or editor books relating to field. Contbr. to religious jours. Home: Flushing, L.I., N.Y. *

WOOD, REUBEN ESSELSTYN, educator, chemist; b. Lansing, Mich., Apr. 1, 1915; s. Frank Esler and Helen (Esselstyn) W.; B.S., Calif. Inst. Tech., 1936, Ph.D., 1939, postdoctoral fellow, 1939-43; M.S., U. Chgo., 1937; sr. research fellow Md. Research Labs., 1943-45; asst. prof. chemistry George Washington U., 1945-51, asso. prof., 1952-57, prof., 1958-80. Cons. Office of Saline Water, 1955-65; chemist Nat. Bur. Standards, 1955-70; pres. Med. & Tech. Summaries, Inc. Mem. Am. Chem. Soc., Electrochem. Soc., AAUP, AAAS, Washington, N.Y. acads. scis., Am. Inst. Chemists. Club: Cosmos (Washington). Author: (with Walter Hamer) Electrolytic Conductivity and Electrode Processes, rev. edit., 1967; Introduction to Chemical Thermodynamics, 1970. Contbr. articles to tech. jours. Research in electrochemistry, thermodynamics. Home: Arlington, Va. Died Mar. 24, 1980.

WOOD, RICHARDSON KING, bus. cons., coll. exec.; b. Irvington, N.Y., Nov. 26, 1903; s. Arthur King and Marguerite (Richardson) W.; student Harvard, 1921-22; B.A., King's Coll., Cambridge (Eng.) U., 1925, M.A., 1929; m. Mildred Carlisle Burgwin, Nov. 30, 1929; children—Nicholas Burgwin, Mary Burgwin. Press agt. authors Alfred A. Knopf, pubs., N.Y.C., 1926-29; mktg. surveyor J. Walter Thompson Co., advt., N.Y.C., 1929-33; partner firm Cherington, Roper & Wood, mktg. research, N.Y.C., 1934-36; writer, editor Fortune Mag., N.Y.C., 1937-45, mng. editor, 1940-41; cons. econ. devel. to numerous cities and regions U.S. and abroad, 1945-68; spl. asst. to pres. New Coll., Sarasota, Fla., 1969-72, dir. study of coll-based entrepreneurship, 1971-72; cons. in field; lectr. indsl. devel. Yale, 1967-68. Pres. Dalton Sch., N.Y.C., 1941-46; mem. City Planning Commn., Bradenton, Fla., 1974-76. Contbg. author Ency. Brit., 1952-60. Contbr. articles to profl. jours., popular mags. Prin. originator Fortune Survey of Pub. Opinion. Address: Bradenton, Fla. Died Oct. 24, 1976.

WOOD, WALDO EMERSON, educator; b. Columbus, Kan., Mar. 29, 1883; s. Peter and Alice (Shoemaker) W.; student Ind. State Teachers Coll., 1914; A.B., Central Normal Coll., Danville, Ind., 1915; A.M., U. of Wis., 1917; Ph.D., Indiana U., 1931; m. Adeline Bristow, Dec. 24, 1906. Teacher graded schs., Ind., 1903-08; prin. high schs. in various Ind. cities, 1910-28; v.p. Central Normal Coll., Danville, 1928-29, pres., 1929-36; helped survey schools of Santa Cruz County, Calif., and Sacramento City Schools; supt. schools, Frankfort, Ind., 1940-46. President, Clinton County Tuberculosis Society; member, Indiana Educational Review Committee. Member Indiana Schoolmen's Club, Ind. State Teachers Assn., N.E.A. (life), Am. Prison Assn., Am. Nat. Red Cross, Am. Acad. Polit. Science, American Academy Political and Social Science, American Geog. Society, Ind. Hist. Society, Nat. Instn. Teacher Placement, Izaak Walton League of America, Soc. Mental Hygiene, Phi Delta Kappa, Sigma Phi, Kappa Delta, Kappa Phi Beta, Pi Gamma Mu. Republican. Methodist: Mason (32 degree), Eastern Star. Club: Columbia (Indianapolis); Emerson, Chamber of Commerce (Frankfort, Ind.). Author: Minimum Essentials of Spelling, 1917; Correlation Between Habit Traits and Achievement and Correlation Between Intelligence and Achievement, 1929; Student Rating of College Professors, 1930; Study of Performance on the Graduate Level Based Upon Subject Marks and Intelligence Scores, Ages 20 to 60, 1931; Character Development in Supervised Teaching, 1934. Traveled extensively in all states and Mexico, and Canada. Home: Frankfort, Ind. *

WOODALL, ROBERT NEAL, ry. ofcl.; b. Lynchburg, Va., Aug. 11, 1904; s. Edgar Holcomb and Neal (Brown) W.; ed. pub. schs., Lynchburg; m. Catherine Harnsberger, Sept. 3, 1932; 1 dau., Nell. With So. Ry. System,'1922-58, successively messenger, stenographer, trace clk., rate clk., chief clk., Lynchburg, chief clk., Boston, dist. comml. agt., Lynchburg, freight and passenger agt., gen. Eastern freight agt., N.Y.C., gen. agt., Pitts., asst. freight traffic mgr., New Orleans, Eastern traffic mgr., N.Y.C., freight traffic mgr., Cin., 1922-53, asst. v.p., 1953-58; v.p. N. & W. Ry. Co., Roanoke, Va., 1958-73. Mem. Am. Soc. Traffic and Transp., N.Y. Southern Soc., N.Y.C., Washington traffic clubs, N.A.M., Va. State C. of C. (dir.), National Freight Traffic Assn. (exec. com.). Home: Charlottesville, Va. Died Dec. 30, 1979; buried Spring Hill Cemetery, Lynchburg.

WOODBRIDGE, PHILIP DUDLEY, physician; born Brookline, Mass., Nov. 11, 1895; s. S(amuel) Homer and Adele Reed (Taylor) W.; A.B. cum laude, Harvard, 1917, M.D., 1921; m. Marion Crane Maercklein, Mar. 15, 1924; 1 son, Dudley Hooker. Resident physician, Boston Consumptives Hosp., July-Oct. 1921; intern, Hartford (Conn.) Hosp., 1921-23; resident physician, dept. of contagious diseases, Boston City Hosp., 1923; gen. practice medicine, Portland, Conn., 1923-27; asst. in sect. anesthesia, Mayo Clinic, Rochester, Minn., 1927-28; mem. dept. of anesthesia, Lahey Clinic, Boston, Mass., 1928-40; engaged in practice of anesthesia, New Haven, 1941; prof. and head dept. anesthesiology, Temple U. Med. Sch. and Hosp., Phila., 1942-44; head dept. anesthesiology, Reading Hosp., Reading, Pa., 1945-49; chief of anesthesia Franklin County Pub. Hosp., 1950-64; then engaged in part-time practice of anesthesia, Greenfield, Massachusetts. Mem. permanent bd. New Eng. Yearly Meeting of Friends; treas., bd. dirs. Woolman Hill, Inc., Deerfield, Mass.; violist Pioneer Valley Symphony, Greenfield, Mass. Mem. United World Federalists, Fellowship of Reconciliation. Diplomate Am. Bd. Anesthesiology (mem. bd. 1938-49, pres. 1945-46. Mem. Am. Soc. Anesthesiologists (director 1958-61), N.E. Society Anesthesiology (pres. 1934, 36), Am. Coll. Anesthesiologists, AMA (chmn. sect. anesthesiology 1962-63). Contbr. numerous articles on clin. anesthesia to med. jours. and text books. Home: Greenfield, Mass. Died Dec. 11, 1978.

WOODBURY CHARLES G(OODRICH), conservationist, horticult.; b. Portland, Mich., Apr. 30, 1884; s. Chester Downer and May (Goodrich) W.; B.S., Mich. Agrl. Coll. (now Mich. State Coll.), 1904, M.S., 1906; D.Sc., Purdue U., 1937; m. Marion Benjamin, June 23, 1909; children—Barbara Ann (wife of Dr. Maylon H. Hepp), Richard Benjamin, Charles Benjamin. Asst. horticulturist, Purdue Agrl. Expt. Sta., 1906-08, asso. 1908; asst. prof. hort. Purdue, 1909-11, head of dept. 1911-17, dir. agri. expt. sta., 1917-20. dir. Bur. Raw Products Research. Nat. Canners Assn., Washington, 1920-42, spl. asst. to adminstr. Agrl. Research Adminstrn., U.S. Dept. Agr., 1942-44, dir. Raw Products Research Bur., 1944-46, retired June 30, 1946. Trustee. Nat. Parks Service Trust Fund Bd.; adv. bd. Nat. Parks, Historic Sites, Bldgs. and Monuments; nat. councilor Purdue Research Foundn. Fellow A.A.A.S.; mem. Am. Soc. Hort. Sci., Wash. Bot. Soc., Nat. Parks Assn. (v.p.), Wilderness Soc. (mem. council and exec. com.), Nat. Audubon Soc. (mem. bd. dirs.), Sigma Xi, Alpha Zeta. Clubs: Sierra (San Francisco); Cosmos (Washington). Home: Washington. *

WOODBURY, SIDNEY FRANK, indsl. supplies exec., b. Mt. Horeb. Wis., Aug. 30, 1883; s. Sidney Prescott and Sarah Jane (Brackenwagen) W.; student pub. schs. Wis.; extension, corr. night bus. coll. courses; m. Audrey Sue Welty, June 2, 1906; children—Sidney Frank (dec. 1940), Ralph (deceased). Operating dept. G.N. Ry., 1900-09, C.M.St. P.&P. R.R., 1914, Mt. Hood Ry. & Power Co., 1911, Portland (Ore.) Ry. Light & Power Co., 1912, Willamette Iron & Steel Works, Portland, 1913, 1916-21; established Woodbury & Company, 1922, becoming chmn., 1949, also chmn. Woodbury Hardware Co., 1939; now pres. Pine Street Company, Portland; dir. Portland Elec. Co., U.S. National Bank (both Portland), Western Air Lines (Los Angeles), Insurance Company of Oregon. Chairman of the advisory committee Oregon Planning and Development Commn.; vice president Portland Labor-Management Com. Past mem. Portland City Planning Commn.; past chmn. United War and Community Chests. Former trustee Lewis and Clark Coll.; dir. Good Samaritan Hosp. Mem. Portland (past pres.), U.S. C. of C., Purchasing Agts. Assn. of Ore. (hon.). Republican. Episcopalian. Mason (Shriner). Clubs: Rotary, Arlington, Multnomah Athletic (Portland); Mazamas. Home: Portland. *

WOODHAMS, BERTHOLD, ins. exec.; b. Aurora, Ill., Feb. 28, 1894; s. Herbert and Amelia (Degenhardt) W.; student pub. schs.; LL.D. (hon.), Ferris Inst., Big Rapids, Mich. m. Florence M. Legg, June 29, 1921; children—Carolyn W. (Mrs. Arthur L. Jones, Jr.), Frederick B. Claims adjuster Citizens' Mut. Automobile Ins. Co., Howell, Mich., 1920-26, v.p., 1926-50, dir., pres., 1950-63, chmn. bd., 1963-65, hon. chmn. bd., from 1965; chmn. bd. First Nat. Bank, Howell, from 1966, also dir. Pres., Conf. Mut. Casualty Cos., 1955. Past mem. Bd. Edn. Howell; mayor City of Howell, 1943-49. Gov., Mich. Ins. Info. Ser. Mason (past master, K.T., past comdr.), Rotarian (past pres.). Author: Man-to-Man and Dad-to-Daughter good driving agreements distributed by safety orgns., automobile clubs. Home: Howell, Mich. Died Feb. 9, 1980.

WOODHEAD, DANIEL, JR., elec. mfg.; b. Chgo., May 20, 1911; s. Daniel and Ellen Noyes (Chadwick) W.; B.A., Wesleyan U., Middletown, Conn., 1934; m. Elizabeth Cowperthwait Moon, May, 11, 1935; children—Daniel III, Ward Moon, Mary Caruth, Thomas Cowperthwait. With Donald Woodhead Co., Chgo., 1934-78, treas., 1949-78, pres., 1949-65, chmn. bd., 1966-78; also mem. bd. dirs.; dir. Central Rubber Co., Belvidere, Ill., 1952-78, pres., 1953-71, treas., 1953-78; dir., treas. Edmonds Engring. & Mfg. Co., Chgo., 1952-78, pres., 1958-62. Pres. Chgo. Wesleyan Club, 1953-54; chmn. nat. com. subfreshman cultivation Wesleyan U., 1953-55, chmn. com. which gave univ. ofcl. coat-of-arms, 1953, chmn. com. for alumni house, 1955-58, exec. com. alumni council, 1957-59, trustee univ., 1959-78. Mem. Beta Theta Pi. Clubs: University (Chgo.); Skokie Country (Glencoe, Ill.). Home: Winnetka, Ill. Died June 1978.

WOODHOUSE, EDWARD JAMES, univ. prof.; born near Norfolk, Va., Jan 19, 1884; s. Robert Woodside and Bettie Woodhouse (James) W.; student Randolph-Macon Acad., 1898-1900, A.B., Randolph-Macon Coll., 1903; LL.B., U.of Va., 1907; student U. of Wis., 1910-11. U. of Chicago, 1911-13, Yale, 1922-23; m. Chase Going, June 10, 1918; children—Noel Robert Seymour, Margaret Wark; m. 2d, Margaret Kinsman, Mar. 19, 1948. Teacher mathematics and chemistry, Randolph-Macon Acad., 1903-05; admitted to Va. bar 1907, and practiced in Norfolk, 1907-10; acting prof. history and polit. sci. Richmond Coll., 1912; instr. U.S. history Yale 1913-19; prof. polit. sci. Smith Coll., 1919-25; prof. polit. sci. U. of N.C., since 1925. Mayor of Northampton, Mass., 1924-25. Served as 1st lt., Inf., U.S. Army, 1917-18. Mem. Am. Polit. Sci. Assn. (mem. council, 1934-36), N.C. Municipal League (sec. 1925-29), Democrat (vice chmn. Mass. state com., 1924). Episcopalian. Mem. Phi Beta Kappa, Kappa Sigma. Author: Italy and the Yugoslavs (with Chase Going Woodhouse), 1920. Contbr. articles to various pubs. Home: Chapel Hill. N.C. *

WOODHOUSE, HENRY (ADOPTED NAME, LEGALIZED BY SUPREME COURT OF N.Y., FEB. 24, 1917; ORIGINAL NAME, MARIO TERENZIO ENRICO CASALEGNO), b. Turin, Italy, June 24, 1884; s. Lodovico and Carolyn (Garino) Casalegno; ed. high school, Turin, later studied in various cities of Europe and in N.Y. City; unmarried. Came to America in 1904, naturalized citizen, May 28, 1917. Founder, and pub., 1912-20, "Flying" (mag.), also

Aerial Age; pub. Air Power; pres. Woodhouse & Co., Inc., Scientific Age Corpn., pub. Scientific Age (mag.). Bought options, 1921-2, on claims to Turkish concessions of Rear Admiral Colby M. Chester, U.S.N., and formed syndicate which resulted in organization of Ottoman Am. Development Co., which obtained (1923) from the Govt. of Turkey the Chester concessions for constrn. and operation for 99 yrs. of 2,700 miles of railroads in Eastern Anatolia, two ports on Black Sea and one on Mediterranean Sea, exploitation of the oil fields of Mosul, etc.; owner one-sixth capital stock and dir. Ottoman Am. Development Co.; dir., sec. Turco-Am. Corpu.; bought option, 1923, to plan and build City of Angora, new capital of Turkey. Aeronautic advisor for and was associated with Peary, Amundsen, Bartlett, Shackleton and other Arctic and Antarctic explorers who planned to use aircraft for exploration; assisted Amundsen to organize the aviation sect. and to obtain aeroplanes and scientific instruments for the 1916 and 1922 Amundsen expdns. to North Pole; assisted Dept. of Justice, 1920-4, in investigation and preparation of actions on war frauds and in defense of civil actions by U.S. Govt. for recovery on claims; gave expert testimony, Mar. 1924, to Senate Pub. Lands and Surveys Com. on Teapot Dome and Calif. naval oil reserve lease investigations; defined and pub., 1921-24, 100 radio-elec. magnetic mysteries and possible solutions; organized, Jan, 1924, the 12 mos.' world radio check-up and Feb. 1924, the 12 mos.' aurora check-up, held by Aerial League of America; an organizer, dir. 1st, 2d and 3d Pan Am. aeronautic congresses and expns. Exec. sec. Advisory Com. on Aeronautics, by apptmt. of Navy Dept., Mar. 1917, to coöperate with comdt. 3d Naval Dist. to organize the Naval Aerial Reserves and Aerial Submarine Patrol; apptd., Mar. 1917, by French Govt., hon. dir. French Aerial Warfare Exhibit, which he directed in New York and other cities of U.S. Founder, 1915, Am. Soc. Aeronautic Engrs., combined, 1916, with Soc. Automotive Engrs.; mem. Aerial League America (trustee and pres. 1920-4), Franklin Inst. (life), A.A.A.S., U.S. Naval Inst. (life), etc. Awarded gold and silver medals, etc., by Aero Club of Italy, Aerial League America, Aero Club America, Am. Mus. Safety, etc. Clubs: Aero of England (hon.), Nat. Arts, Economic, Nat. Press. Author: Textbook of Naval Aeronautics, 1917; Textbook of Military Aeronautics, 1918; Aero Blue Book, 1919; Textbook of International and National Aerial Laws and Regulations for Air Traffic, 1920. Contbr. series articles on secret diplomacy of Near East, and U.S. problems in Latin America; mem. editorial bd. Nelson Ency. Home: New York. *

WOODIE, NORRIS BROWNING, educator; b. Welch, W.Va., Mar. 21, 1923; s. Walter Franklin and Linnie Olive (Browning) W.; B.A., Berea Coll., 1948; B.D., Yale, 1951, M.A., 1952, Ph.D., 1955; m. Hilda Mae Lane, Dec. 20, 1947; children—Rebecca, Scott, Ruth, Luke. Ordained to ministry Presbyn. Ch., 1953; dir. campus life Alderson-Broaddus Coll., Philippi, W.Va., 1953-55; alumni dir. Berea Coll., 1955-58, mem. faculty, 1958-76, prof. philosophy and religion, 1965-76. Mem. Berea City Council, 1960-64. Served with AUS, 1943-46. Danforth Asso., from 1962. Mem. Am. Acad. Religion, Phi Kappa Phi. Democrat. Editor Berea Alumnus, 1955-58; mem. book com. Bethany Press, 1960-68. Editorial bd. Mountain Life and Work, 1960-65. Author articles. Home: Berea, Ky. Died Jan. 14, 1976; interred Berea Cemetery.

WOODLE, JOSEPH CASS, lawyer; born in Logan, W.Va., Nov. 20, 1915; s. Bernon Tisdale and Anne Stevenson (Cass) W.; grad. Hotchkiss Sch., 1932; A.B., Princeton, 1937; LL.B., U. Va., 1942; m. Jessica Slocum, Dec. 21, 1940; children—Joanne, Peter. With Procter & Gamble Co., 1937-39; admitted to N.Y. bar; asso. Breed, Abbot & Morgan, N.Y.C., 1945-51; partner Nields & Woodle. White Plains, N.Y., 1954-56; staff SEC, Washington, 1956-63, dir. div. corp. regulation, 1957-61; pvt. practice of law, N.Y.C., 1963-80; partner firm Abberley, Koojman, Marcellino and Clay until 1980. Served to lt. (s.g.) with USNR, 1942-45. Mem. Raven Soc., Phi Delta Phi. Clubs: Charter (Princeton U.); Princeton, University (N.Y.C.); University (Washington); Home: New York, N.Y. Died Mar. 14, 1980.

WOODRUFF, HALE ASPACIO, artist, educator; b. Cairo, Ill., Aug. 26, 1900; student John Herron Art Inst., Indpls., Fogg Art Museum, Harvard, Academie Scandinave, Academie Moderne, Paris, France; studied fresco painting under Diego Rivera, Mexico; D.F.A., Morgan State Coll., 1968, Ind. U., 1978; L.H.D., Atlanta U., 1972; m. Theres A. Barker, June 14, 1934; 1 son, Roy H. One-man shows at Internat. Print Soc., N.Y.C., 1943, Bertha Schaefer Gallery, N.Y.C., State Mus. N.C., Raleigh, U. N.C., Chapel Hill, Greensboro, Eastern Mich. State Tchrs. Coll., U. So. Ill., Hampton (Va.) Inst., High Mus. Art, Atlanta, N.Y. U., N.Y.C., U. Mich., Tuskegee Inst.; exhibited in numerous group shows including Tex. Centennial Celebration, Dallas, Detroit Inst. Art, Los Angeles County Mus., Boston Mus., Kansas City (Mo.) Art Inst., Whitney Mus., N.Y.C., Va. Mus., Richmond, Balt. Mus., Raleigh Mus., Newark Mus., Grace Horne Gallery, Boston, Pyramid Club, Phila., Riverside Mus., N.Y.C., Bklyn. Mus.; represented in permanent collections including: Newark Mus., IBM Collection, Atlanta U., Howard U., Washington, Met. Mus. Art, N.Y.C., N.Y. U., Library of Congress, Lincoln U., Harmon Found., N.Y.C., Smithsonian Instn., Washington, Jackson Coll., Spelman Coll., Johnson Pub. Co., Chgo., Indpls. Mus. Art, Detroit Inst. Art; important works include murals: The Amistad Mutiny and Founding of Talladega, both at Talladega Coll., 1938-39, History of California for Golden State Mut. Life Ins. Co., Los Angeles, 1948-49, The Art of the Negro, at Atlanta U., 1950-51; dir. art Atlanta U.; asso. prof. art edn. to prof. N.Y. U., to 1968, prof. emeritus, 1968-80; lectr. in field. Mem. com. on art edn. Mus. Modern Art, N.Y.C.; mem. Art Commn. City N.Y., N.Y. State Council on Arts; lectr. Assn. Am. Colls; U.S. rep. at 1st Internat. Festival of Negro Arts, Dakar, Senegal, 1966. Recipient Bronze award Harmon Found., First award High Mus. Art, Second and Third awards Diamond Jubilee Expn., Chgo., Atlanta U. award, medal of Honor N.J. Soc. Artists, Great Tchr. award N.Y. U., 1966; Julius Rosenwald fellow, 1943-45. Home: New York, N.Y. Died Sept. 6, 1980.

WOODS, FRANK HENRY, business exec.; b. Lincoln, Nebr., May 2, 1905; s. Frank H. and Nelle S. (Cochrane) W., A.B., Yale, 1928; D.H.L., Lake Forest Coll., 1970; LL.D., U. Neb., 1975; m. Louise Hamilton Brewer, Feb. 16, 1935; children—Louise (Mrs. Theodore Levenson), Lucia (Mrs. Lindley), Brewer (dec. 1976), Amy (Mrs. Nelson Gore). Asso., Harris Trust & Savs. Bank, Chgo., 1928-33; asst. to pres. Sahara Coal Co., Chgo., 1933-38, sec.-treas., 1938-44, pres., treas., 1944-78, chmn. bd., 1978-80; dir. Lincoln Tel. & Tel. Co. (Nebr.), 1937-79, exec. com., from 1942, chmn. bd. dirs., 1958-79; dir., exec. com. Addressograph Multigraph Corp. (Cleve.), 1946, chmn. bd., 1958-76; dir. Harris Trust & Savs. Bank, Chgo., 1954-75. Chmn., Gov.'s Com. for Ill., Midcentury White House Conf. on Children and Youth 1949-51; mem. City of Lake Forest Plan Commn., 1954-58; mem. corp., gifts chmn. Community Fund of Chgo., 1947, dir., 1954-67, pres., 1957-59; pres. A.R.C. Joint Appeal of Chgo., 1957-58, North Side Boys' Clubs, 1940-47. Bd. dirs. United Community Funds and Councils Am., N.Y., 1958-64, v.p., 1960-61; pres. Welfare Council Met. Chgo., 1953-57, bd. dirs., 1947-66; treas., trustee Woods Charitable Fund, Chgo., 1941; life trustee, gov. mem. Chgo. Zool. Soc.; bd. dirs. Council on Founds., 1960-76, pres., 1964-65; bd. dirs. Hosp. Planning Council for Met. Chgo., 1957-66; trustee, life mem. gov. bd. Art Inst. Chgo., 1955-75, pres. 1966-70; life trustee U. Chgo., 1962-80. Mem. Ill. Mfrs. Assn. (dir. 1955-58), Nat. Soc. Prevention Blindness Inc. (dir. 1948-60), Ill. Soc. Prevention Blindness (pres. 1947-57, dir. 1946-62), Chgo. Hort. Soc. (trustee 1962, v.p. 1965, life trustee 1976-80), Taxpayers Fedn. Ill. (trustee 1948-58). Episcopalian. Clubs: Chicago, Comml., Casino, Onwentsia. Home: Lake Forest, Ill. Died Nov. 24, 1980; buried Lake Forest.

WOODS, HOWARD BURRELL, editor, publisher; b. Perry, Okla., Jan. 9, 1917; s. Frank and Mary E. (Howard) W.; m. Jane E. Gamble, June 22, 1965; children—Joanne M. (Mrs. Albert Austin), Judy Ann Matthews, Patricia Ann Matthews, Gail Margery. Asso. dir. USIA. Washington, 1965-67; editor-in-chief Sengstacke Newspapers, 1967-68; editor and publisher St. Louis Sentinel, 1968-81; newscaster, commentator current affairs KMOX-CBS Radio, St. Louis; St. Louis Bur. chief Chgo. Defender, various times; host The Black Experience show, KSD-TV, also St. Louis Forum, monthly; city editor St. Louis Argus, 1949, exec. editor, 1954. Mem. Pres. Kennedy's Com. on Equal Employment Opportunity, 1961-65; mem. Citizen's Adv. Com. to Community Relations Service, 1964-66; commr. Mo. Commn. Human Rights, 1957-65; chmn. bd. commrs. St. Louis Housing Authority; vice-chmn. bd. commrs. St. Louis Land Clearance Authority; mem. St. Louis Bicentennial Corp. Exec. bd. local A.R.C.; mem. pres.'s council St. Louis U.; v.p. St. Louis Family and Children's Service; bd. dirs. local council Boy scouts Am., Higher Edn. Coordinating Council, Race Relations Information Center; trustee Webster Coll. Recipient Outstanding Achievement Journalism award Lincoln U., 1965; Citizens Achievement award Nat. Shriners, 1964. Mem. St. Louis Advt. Club, St. Louis Met. Press Club. Chgo. Daily Defender's Round Table of Nat. Newspaper Pubs. Assn. (bd. dirs.; Merit award), Mound City Press Club (founder, past pres.; Newsmen's Newsman award), Internat. Soc. Weekly Newspaper Editors, Nat. Assn. Market Developers (dir.), East-West Gateway Coordinating Council (bd. dirs.), Regional Indsl. Devel. Corp. (bd. dirs.), Interracial Council for Bus. Opportunity (bd. dirs.), A.F.T.R.A., Sigma Delta Chi (Outstanding Contbn. Journalism award). Lutheran (elder). Home: St. Louis, Mo. Died Aug. 2, 1976.

WOODS, KATHERINE IRVIN, author, editor; born Philadelphia, Pennsylvania, March 29, 1886; daughter Reverend Matthew Cooper and Nannie Irvin (Shaw) Woods; graduate Blair Academy, Blairstown, N.J., 1902, Abbot Acad., Andover, Mass., 1905; student Mt. Holyoke Coll. Reporter and spl. writer Phila. Press, 1906-09; writer Sunday Mag., N.Y. Times, 1911-19, N.Y. Times Book Review, 1912-19, 1928-31 and 1935-42; editor Query Dept., N.Y. Times, 1914-17; writer with Nat. Lamp Works of Gen. Electric Co., 1919-26, and with Pa. R.R., 1926-27; staff writer, Collier Ency., 1930-31; consultant editor French Digest, 1939-40; literary editor, Tomorrow, also editor Creative Age Press, 1942-45; editor, L. B. Fischer Publishing Corp., 1945-46; head literature sect., Arts and Letters Div., UNESCO. Fellow Am. Geog. Soc.; mem. Authors League, League Woman Voters, Société Francaise d'Archéologie, Soc. of Woman Geographers. Presbyn. Clubs: Pen and Brush, Query. Author: The Other Chateau Country, 1931; Murder in a Walled Town, 1934; also series of booklets for workers' education, concerning economic questions and conditions, civics and citizenship, etc. Translator from the French Barrack 3, Room 12 (Marcel Haedrich), 1943; The Little Prince (Antoine de Saint-Exupéry), 1943; The Masterpiece (Émile Zola), 1946; Kingdom of the Rocks (Consuelo de Saint-Exupéry), 1946; Sirocco (Joseph Kessel), 1947. Contributor to magazines. Travel and historical study in France and Italy, 1927-35, Sweden, 1930. Address: Paris, France. *

WOODS, WILLIAM SLEDGE, educator; b. Chester, S.C., July 14, 1910; s. Harper Robert and Clara (Sledge) W.; A.B., U. S.C., 1931, M.A., 1932; postgrad. Johns Hopkins, 1934-35, Sorbonne, 1936; Ph.D., U. N.C., 1947. Instr. romance langs. U. S.C., 1935-40, asso. prof., 1947-48; instr. romance langs. U. N.C., 1946-47; asso. prof. Tulane U., 1948-51, prof., 1951-77, prof. emeritus, 1977-80, chmn. French and Italian, 1957-69. Served from pvt. to 2d lt., Signal Corps, AUS, 1942-45. Decorated Palmes Academiques (France). Mem. S. Central Modern Lang. Assn., Medieval Acad. Am., Renaissance Soc. Am., Modern Lang. Assn. Am., Phi Beta Kappa, Phi Sigma Iota, Omicron Delta Kappa. Address: New Orleans, La. Died Feb. 28, 1980.

WOODSMALL, RUTH FRANCES, born in Atlanta, Ga., on September 20, 1883; daughter of Harrison and Mary (Howes) Woodsmall; A.B., U. of Neb., 1905, LL.D., 1945; M.A., Winseley Coll., 1906; grad. work Columbia and Heidelberg. Began career as prin. Ouray (Colo.) High Sch., 1906. Teacher of German and English in high schs. Reno, Nev., Pueblo, Colorado Springs, Colo., to 1916; traveled in Orient, 1916-17; dir. Hostess House, Y.W.C.A., Camp Pike, Ark., 1917-18, in France, 1918-19, Coblentz, Germany, 1919; field surveys for Y.W.C.A. in Balkan and Baltic States, 1919-20; social survey of Constantinople, Y.W.C.A., exec. sec. in Turkey and Syria, sec. Eastern Mediterranean Fedn., 1920-23; engaged in study of "changing status of Moslem women" in the Near East, the Middle East and India, Rockefeller Foundation Fellowship, 1928-30; mem. Laymen's Foreign Missions Inquiry, fact finder on women's interests and activities in India and appraisal commn., 1930-32; also mem. Commn. on Christian Edn. in Japan, International Missionary Council, 1931; on nat. staff Y.W.C.A. in U.S., as interpreter in internat. relations, New York, 1932-35; gen. sec. World's Y.W.C.A. Council, Geneva, Switzerland, 1935-47; chief of women's affairs Office of Pub. Affairs, U.S. High Commn. for Germany since Feb. 1949. Member executive and research coms. Modern Missions Movement; mem. Nat. Council of Pacific Relations, Am. Assn. of Univ. Women, Kappa Alpha Theta, Phi Beta Kappa. Baptist. Author: Eastern Women Today and Tomorrow, 1933; Moslem Women Enter a New World, 1936. Collaborated on various books. Lecturer on international relations. Home: Silver Spring, Md. *

WOODUL, J(AMES) R(ICHMOND), business exec.; born Alma, Mo., Feb. 4, 1886; s. Richard Lynn and Minnie Lee (Young) W.; ed. pub. schs. of Tex.; m. Daisy Lee Lillie, Apr. 10, 1907; 1 adopted dau., Rosa Lee (Mrs. Manuel Munoz, Jr.). Traffic dept. Am. Smelting & Refining Co., 1906-17, asst. gen. mgr., 1917-24, gen. mgr., 1924-44, vice pres., Mexico, since 1944. Mem. Am. Inst. Mining and Metall. Engrs. Clubs: University, American, British, Chapultepec Golf. Home: Cuauhtemoc, Mexico. *

WOODWARD, HARPER, lawyer; b. Rochester, N.Y., Nov. 26, 1909; s. Roland B. and Anne (Murray) W.; grad. St. Paul's Sch., Concord, N.H., 1927; A.B., Harvard, 1931, LL.B., 1934; m. Ruth Keller, Aug. 1, 1942 (dec. July 1966); m. 2d, Edith M. Laird, Mar. 18, 1967; children—Bruce A., Belinda B. (Mrs. Glen R. Kendall), Edwin C. Laird III, Bonnie B. (Mrs. Stephane Y. Christen). Sec. to pres. Harvard U., 1934-35; admitted to N.Y. bar, 1936; mem. firm Barry, Wainwright, Thacher & Symmers, 1935-37, Woodward & Woodward, 1937-38, Spence, Windels, Walser, Hotchkiss & Angell, 1938-42, Spence, Hotchkiss, Parker & Duryee, 1946; asso. Laurance S. Rockefeller, N.Y.C., 1946-66; asso. Rockefeller Family & Assos., 1966-76, cons., 1976-81; dir., mem. exec. com., fin. and audit com. Eastern Air Lines; dir. Rockresorts, Inc., Caneel Bay Plantation, Wayfarer Ketch Corp. Trustee Meml. Sloan-Kettering Cancer Center; v.p., vice chmn. bd. mgrs. Meml. Hosp. Cancer and Allied Diseases, N.Y.C. Served with USAAF, 1942-45. Mem. Harvard Law Sch. Assn. Clubs: Wings (N.Y.C.); Am. Yacht. Home: Essex, Conn. Died Apr. 15, 1981.

WOODWARD, HELEN (MRS. WILLIAM E. WOODWARD), author; b. New York, N.Y., Mar. 19, 1882; d. Louis and Frederika (Sachs) Rosen; ed. Girls'

Latin Sch., Boston, Mass.; m. William E. Woodward, Dec. 15, 1913. In advertising business in N.Y. City, 1903-23; newspaper syndicate on Women and the Job 1930-31. Author: Through Many Windows, 1926; 200 Years Charleston Cooking, (in collaboration), 1931; (with Richard Boleslavski) Way of the Lancer, Lances Down, 1932; Queen's in the Parlor, 1933; Three Flights Up, 1935; It's an Art, 1938; Bowling Green Murders (with Frances Amherst) 1940; Money to Burn, 1945; lectures, mag. articles. Address: New York, N.Y. *

WOODWARD, ROBERT BURNS, educator; b. Boston, Apr. 10, 1917; s. Arthur Chester and Margaret (Burns) W.; B.S., Mass Inst. Tech., 1936, Ph.D., 1937; Sc.D. (hon.), Wesleyan U., Middletown, Conn., 1945, Victoria U., Manchester, Eng., 1954, Bucknell U., 1955, U. N.B. (Can.), 1956, Yale, 1956, Harvard, 1957, U. So. Calif., 1959, U. Chgo., 1961, New Eng. Coll. Pharmacy, 1961, Colby Coll., 1963, U. Cambridge (Eng.), 1964, Brandeis U., 1965, Stonehill Coll., 1966, U. Sheffield (Eng.), 1966; Israel Inst. Tech. (Haifa), 1966, Poly. Inst. Bklyn., 1967, U. Western Ont. (Can.), 1968, Columbia, 1969, U. Louvain (Belgium), 1970, U. Pierre et Marie Curie de Paris, 1975, U. St. Andrews (Scotland), 1976, U. London, 1976; LL.D., U. Glasgow, 1966; Dr. Tech. wiss., Eidg. Tech. Hochschule, Switzerland, 1967; A.M. (hon.), Harvard, 1946; m. Irja Pullman, JuLy 30, 1938; children—Siiri Anne, Jean Kirsten; m. 2d, Eudoxia M. M. Muller, Sept. 14, 1946; children—Crystal Elizabeth, Eric Richard Arthur. Post doctoral fellow Harvard, 1937-38, mem. soc. fellows, 1938-40, from instr. to prof., 1941-53, Morris Loeb prof. chemistry, 1953-60, Donner prof. sci., 1960-79; dir. Woodward Research Inst., Basel, Switzerland, 1963-79; cons. chem. mfrs., also Polaroid Corp., 1942-79, Chas. Pfizer & Co., Inc., 1951-70, also dir. Hon. lectr. many orgns.; Am. Swiss Found. lectr., 1948; Harrison Howe lectr., 1950; Centenary lectr. Chem. Soc. London, 1951; Stieglitz lectr., 1952; Edgar Fahs Smith Meml. lectr., 1959; Harvard lectr. at Yale, 1959; Morrell lectr. Cambridge U., 1959, Alexander Todd prof. Chemistry Christ's Coll., also fellow, 1973-74; lectr. Leermakers Symposium, Wesleyan U., 1972; synthesized quinine, 1944, patulin, 1950, cholesterol, 1951, cortisone, 1951, strychnine, 1954, lysergic acid, 1954, lanosterol, 1954, reserpine, 1956; deduced structure penicillin, 1945, strychnine, 1947, terramycin and aureomycin, 1952, ferrocene, 1952, cevine, 1954, magnamycin, 1956, oleandomycin, 1960, synthesized chlorophyll, 1960, tetracycline, 1962, Colchicine, 1963, cephalosporin C, 1965, vitamin B12, 1972, Prostaglandin F2a, 1973, streptonigrin, 1963, tetrodotoxin, 1964. Mem. corp. Mass. Inst. Tech., 1966-71. Decorated Order of Rising Sun (Japan), 1970; recipient John Scott medal, 1945, Baekeland medal, 1955; Ledlie prize, 1955; Research Corp. award, 1955; Nichols medal, 1956; Theodore William Richards medal, 1958; Synthetic Organic Chemistry award, 1957, Roger Adams award, 1961 (both Am. Chem. Soc.), Davy medal, 1959; Willard Gibbs medal Chgo. sect. Am. Chem. Soc., 1957; Pius XI gold medal Pontifical Acad. Scis., 1961; Dickinson Coll. Priestley medallion, 1962; Synthetic Organic Chem. Mfrs. Assn. medal for creative research in synthetic organic chemistry, 1962; Nat. Medal of Sci., 1964; Nobel prize in chemistry, 1965; Lavoisier medal Sociètè Chimique de France, 1968; Hanbury Meml. medal Pharm. Soc. Gt. Britain, 1970; Pierre Bruylant's medal U. Louvain, 1970; Sci. Achievement award A.M.A., 1971; Dr. B.C. Law Gold Medal Indian Assn. for Cultivation Sci., 1972; Arthur C. Cope award Am. Chem. Soc., 1973. Fellow The Chem. Soc. (hon.), Weizmann Inst. Sci. (hon.), Indian Nat. Sci. Acad. (fgn.) Indian Chem. Soc. (hon.), Am. Acad. Arts and Scis.; mem. German (hon.), Belgian (hon.), Swiss chem. socs., Royal Soc. (fgn.), Royal Irish Acad. (hon.), Austrian Acad. Scis. (corr.), Yugoslav Acad. Scis. and Arts (corr.), Am. Philos. Soc., Nat. Acad. Scis., Deutsche Akademie der Naturforscher (Leopoldina), Accademia Nazionale dei Lincei (fgn. mem.), Pharm, Soc. Japan (hon.), Pharm. Soc. Gt. Britain (hon.), Harvey Soc. N.Y. (hon.), Royal Instn. Gt. Britain (hon.), N.Y. Acad Scis. (hon. life), Acad. Scis. USSR (fgn.). Address: Cambridge, Mass. Died July 8, 1979.

WOODWARD, ROBERT M., state ofcl.; b. Nov. 25, 1898; grad. Phillips Sch. Oratory; LL.B., Northwestern 1920. Admitted to Ill. bar, 1920, since practiced in Chgo.; asst, corp. counsel, Chgo., also asst. state's atty., Cook Co.; lectr. law sch. Northwestern; elected mem. 29th dist., Ill. Ho. Reps., 1930-34, 1936; Ill. state dir. civil def. from 1953. Served as lt. col. judge adv. gen. dept., Ill. N.G.; maj., mil. govt. in Italy, U.S. Army; presided over war crime trials. Decorated Purple Heart, Bronze Star with oak leaf cluster; Cross of Cavaliers, Italy. Mem. Ill. Atomic Power Commn. Mem. Am., Ill. State, Chgo. bar assns., Am. Legion, Res. Officers Assn. U.S. Inf. Assn., Chgo. Field Mus. Soc., Northwestern U. Alumni Assn. Republican. Mason (Shriner). Elk, K.P. Home: Chicago, Ill. Died July 3, 1979.

WOODWARD, THOMAS MULLEN, lawyer; born in Philadelphia, Pennsylvania, Mar. 2, 1884; s. Winfield Scott and Katharine Carroll Dun (Mullen) W.; A.B., Princeton, 1906; LL.B., U. of Pa., 1910; m. Constance Goodnow Perry, June 2, 1917; children—Constance, Katharine Carroll, Anne Perry, Thomas Mullen, Jr. Admitted to Pa. bar. 1910. Supreme Court of U.S., 1921; in practice at Phila., 1910-14; atty. Interstate Commerce Commn., 1914-20; atty. for dir. gen. of railroads, 1920-24; in practice at Washington, 1924-33, and since 1946; atty. A.A.A., dept. of Agr., 1933; vice pres. U.S. Shipping Board Merchant Fleet Corp. and mem. advisory committee to Sec. Commerce, 1933-35; consumers' counsel of Nat. Bituminous Coal Commn., 1935-37; member U.S. Maritime Commn., Apr. 1937-45, vice chmn., 1938-42: chmn. Price Adjustment Bd. of Maritime Commn. Mem. Washington Lit. Soc. Club: Cosmos (Washington). Home: Grennsboro, Vt. *

WOODWORTH, LAURENCE NEAL, ofcl. Dept. Treasury; b. Loudenville, Ohio, Mar. 22, 1918; s. Alfred Ray and Nora (Sheldon) W.; A.B., Ohio No. U., 1940; M.S. in Govt. Mgmt., U. Denver, 1942; Ph.D., N.Y. U., 1960; m. Margaret Bretz, Sept. 1, 1940; children—Laurence, Joseph, Esther, Melissa. Research analyst Civic Research Inst., Kansas City, Mo., 1942-43, Tax Found., N.Y.C., 1943-44; economist Joint Com. on Internat. Revenue Taxation, Washington, 1944-64, chief of staff, 1964-76; asst. sec. for tax policy Dept. Treasury, Washington, 1977—. Pres., Md. Municipal League, 1964-65; councilman, Cheverly, Md., 1949-59, mayor, 1959-65. Recipient Alexander Hamilton award Dept. Treasury, posthumously 1977. Mem. Am. Econ. Assn., Nat. Tax Assn. (pres. 1975-76), Am. Soc. Pub. Adminstrn. Recipient Rockefeller Pub. Service award, 1972; Career Service award Nat. Civil Service League, 1972. Home: Cheverly, Md. Died Dec. 7, 1977.

WOODY, MCIVER, physician; b. Louisville, Ky., Mar. 16, 1886; s. Samuel Elisha and Emma Calmes (McIver) W.; A.B., University of Louisville, 1903, University of Richmond (Virginia), 1905, Harvard College, 1907 (cum laude); M.D., Harvard Medical School, 1912; married Regina Llewellyn Jones, May 1, 1918; children—McIver Wallace, Regina Llewellyn (Mrs. John Ben Butler, Jr.), Emma McIver (Mrs. J. M. Sowa). Asst. physician, Butler Hosp., Providence, 1912-13; surgical interne, Boston City Hospital, 1913-14; Austin teaching fellow, Harvard Med. Sch., 1914-19, James Jackson Cabot fellow, 1914-15, asst. in pathology, 1916-18, physician to students, 1917-18, sec. of the Faculty of Medicine, 1917-18; asst. out patient surgeon Boston City Hosp., 1920-21, Baylor U., 1921-22; physician Standard Oil Co., of N.J., 1922-44, medical director of the Esso Standard Oil Co., 1944-51; med. cons. Railroad Retirement Bd., 1951-65. Member medical advisory board American Petroleum Inst., 1945-51, chmn., 1945-46. Served as lieutenant, personnel and sanitation divisions Surg. General's Office, United States Army, 1918-19; maj., Med. Res. Corps, 1924-34. Fellow N.Y. Acad. of Med. Mass. Med. Soc., Indsl. Medical Association (president 1939-40), A.A.A.S., A.M.A., A.C.P.; member Med. Soc. State of N.Y., N.Y. Soc. Tropical Medicine (president 1941-43), Descs. of Colonial Clergy, Sons of Am. Revolution, Phi Beta Kappa, Kappa Alpha. Republican. Presbyterian. Clubs: Harvard (N.Y.C.). Address: Elizabeth, N.J. *

WOODYATT, JAMES BLAIN, utilities exec.; b. Brantford, Ont., July 2, 1886; s. Thomas and Mary (Kortum) W.; student Brantford Collegiate Inst., 1899-1903; B.Sc., McGill U., 1907; student elec. engring., Internat. Corr. Schs., 1907-08; m. Mary Davidson, May 10, 1911; 1 dau., Betty (Mrs. H. J. L. Petersson). Gen. supt. So. Canada Power Co., 1913-16, gen. mgr., 1916-20, v.p., gen. mgr., 1920-25, pres., gen. mgr., dir., 1925-52, pres., 1952-56, chmn., 1956-63; hon. dir. Power Corp. of Can.; pres., dir. Winisk Co., Ltd.; v.p., dir. Gt. Britain & Can. Investments Corp.; hon. dir. Bathurst Power & Paper Co. Mem. Engring. Inst. Can., Corp. Profl. Engrs. Que., Canadian Elec. Assn., Institute Electrical and Electronics Engrs., Delta Upsilon. Mason. Clubs: Montreal Amateur Athletic Assn., Royal Automobile, Royal Montreal Curling, Royal Montreal Golf, St. James, University, Montreal (Montreal); Hermitage (Magog); St. George's (Sherbrooke). Home: Westmount, Que.

WOOLLARD, GEORGE PRIOR, educator, scientist; b. Savannah, Ga., Dec. 20, 1908; s. Alfred and Anne (Jevons) Prior; adopted by Frank and Elizabeth Woollard, 1920; B.S. in Civil Engring., Ga. Inst. Tech., 1932, M.S., 1934; A.M., Princeton, 1935, Ph.D. in Geology, 1937; postdoctorate student (Am. Geophys. Union fellow 1938, NRC fellow 1939), Lehigh U., 1938-39; hon. doctorates U. Uppsala (Sweden), U. Wis.; m. Eleanore Monroe McClintock, May 7, 1937; children—Bruce, Monroe, Nancy Light, George, Harold, Matilda, Frank, Belinda, Elizabeth. Lectr. geophysics Rutgers U., 1941; research group leader underwater sound Woods Hole (Mass.) Oceanographic Inst., 1942-48; Field Meml. lectr. geophysics Princeton, 1948-49; asso. prof., then prof. geophysics and engring. geology U. Wis., 1949-63, dir. Geophys. and Polar Research Center, 1959-63; dir. Hawaii Inst. Geophysics, also prof. geophysics U. Hawaii, 1963-77; exchange prof. Inst. Geofisca, U. Nacional de Mexico, 1955. Chmn. coms. gravity, crust and core of earth U.S. nat. com. IGY, 1957-60; chmn. com. geodetic and navigational satellites, mem. space sci. bd. Nat. Acad. Scis., 1959-67, chmn. com. crust and core of earth, mem. polar bd., 1960-67, mem. Pacific sci. bd., 1963-67, mem. geophysics research bd., 1961-79; U.S. rep. for geophysics, sci. com. Antarctic research Internat. Council Sci. Unions, 1962-79; U.S. rep. for gravity on upper mantel commn. 1960-67, Internat. Union Geodesy and Geophysics, 1963-68; U.S. mem. Internat. Gravity Com., 1960-79, mem. spl. com. on standardization gravity, 1962-71, spl. com. on gravity-geophys. relations, 1967-79; mem. Pres.'s Commn. on Nat. Ocean Program, 1970; mem. exec. com., planning com. Joint Oceanographic Inst. Deep Earth Sampling, 1974-76; mem. Pan Am. Inst. Geology and Hist. Geophysics Commn., 1971-79; mem. Gov. Hawaii Adv. Com. Sci. and Tech., 1964—79; mem. Gov. Hawaii Task Force on Oceanographics, 1969-73; mem. Hawaii Dept. Transp. Harbor Task Force, 1967-70, Multi-Modal Task Force, 1973-79, Dept. Econ. Devel. Energy Task Force, 1974-76. Pres. Madison (Wis.) chpt. United World Federalists, 1957-60. Trustee Bermuda Biol. Sta. for Research, 1940-46. Served with F.A., U.S. Army, 1924-30. Recipient award for excellence in research U. Hawaii; Gov. Hawaii's award for distinguished service to state. Guggenheim fellow, 1941, 48. Fellow Am. Geophys. Union (chmn. spl. com. geol. and geophys. study continents 1948-63, nat. v.p. 1960-63, pres. 1963-65, Bowie medal), Geol. Soc. Am. (councillor 1958-61), Royal Astron. Soc.; mem. Am. Geol. Inst. (bd. dirs. 1956-59), Soc. Exploration Geophysicists, Am. Assn. Petroleum Geologists, European Assn. Exploration Geophysicists, Seismological Soc. Am., AAAS, Briarean Soc., Tau Beta Pi, Sigma Psi, Phi Kappa Phi, Omicron Delta Kappa. Episcopalian. Author: (with J.C. Rose) International Gravity Measurements, 1963; (with G. Hanson) Geophysical Methods Applied to Geological Problems in Wisconsin, 1957; also numerous articles. Home: Honolulu, Hawaii. Died Apr. 8, 1979.

WOOLLEN, HERBERT MILTON, physician and insurance executive; born in Indianapolis, Indiana on December 1, 1875; s. Milton Asbury and Ida (Baird) W.; student Purdue U., 1895-96; B.S., U. of Wis., 1900; M.D., Ind. U. Sch. of Medicine, 1903; certificate. N.Y. Polyclinic Eye and Ear Infirmary, 1904; m. Irma Wocher, Jan. 7, 1907. Began as asso. Dr. Greenly V. Woollen in practice of ear, nose and throat, 1905; lecturer in ear, nose and throat and bacteriology, Ind. U. Sch. of Medicine, 1904-07; asst. med. dir. Am. Central Life Ins. Co., Indianapolis, Ind., 1906-10, sec., 1910-11, pres., 1911-37; pres. and dir. Am. United Life Ins. Co., Indianapolis, Ind., 1937-40, dir., 1940—; dir. Merchants National Bank & Trust Co., Indpls. Dir. Ind. Symphony Soc. Mem. Academy Political Science, Life Insurance Assn. of America, Ind. Assn. Legal Res. Life Ins. Cos. (pres. 1916-19), Am. Life Conv. (exec. com., 1925, 1927; pres. 1926), Reinsurance Conf. (chmn. 1929), Life Ins. Sales Research Bur. (mem. bd. dirs. 1932). Mem. Indianapolis and U.S. chambers of commerce, Indianapolis Bd. of Trade; vice-chmn. Paderewski Testimonial Fund; pres. Les Cheneaux Club (Mich.). Mem. Ind. Med. Soc., A.A.A.S., Mil. Order Loyal Legion, Phi Rho Sigma, Phi Delta Theta. Republican. Mason, Elk. Clubs: University, Woodstock, Columbia, Traders Point Hunt (pres. 1943-46), Contemporary, Indianapolis Athletic, Indianapolis Dramatic (Indpls.); Indiana Society (Chgo.); Old Pueblo (Tucson). Address: Indpls. *

WOOSTER, HARVEY ALDEN, economist; b. Winsted, Conn., Feb. 16, 1886; s. Frederick Lewis and Ellen Elizabeth (Harvey) W.; A.B., Wesleyan U., Conn., 1909, A.M., 1910; Ph.D., Yale, 1916; m. Enola Ward, June 25, 1912; children—Enola Elizabeth, Alden Frederick, Ward Harvey. Asst. in exptl. psychology, Wesleyan U., 1909-10; instr. economics, DePauw U., 1911-12, Yale, 1912-16; asst. prof. economics U. of Missouri, 1916-19; prof. and head dept. of economics, Tufts Coll. 1919-23; prof. and head dept. of economics O Coll., 1923-51. Research specialist in econ. history with Ordinance Dept. U.S. Army, Washington, July-Aug. 1918; sp. expert in unemployment, U.S. Tariff Commn., July-Aug. 1921; visiting prof. economics, Tufts Coll., 1930-31; dir. Mass. Spl. Commn. on Stabilization of Employment, 1931-32; pres. social science sect., Ohio Coll. Assn., 1933-35. Fellow A.A.A.S.; member American Economic Association, Econ. Hist. Association, Am. Assn. Univ. Profs., Phi Beta Kappa. Ind. Democrat. Conglist. Author of Fluctuations in Employment in Cleveland and Cuyahoga County, 1923-28. Co-author: Toward International Organization. Contributor to economic and ednl. jours. Lecturer on econ. and allied topics. Home: Oberlin, Ohio. *

WOOSTER, LYMAN DWIGHT, educator; b. Greeley, Colo., July 15, 1884; s. Lyman Child and Ellen (Bassett) W.; A.B., Kan. State Teachers Coll., Emporia, 1911; Ph.M., U. of Wis., 1919; Ph.D., Stanford U., 1936; m. Mary Osburn Smith, May 27, 1913 (dec); children—Lyman Dwight, Martha Ellen, Mary Louise, Cynthia; m. 2d Velma Rippeteau, December 1948. Science teacher, Parsons (Kansas.) High School, 1906-07, W. Kan. Normal Sch., 1909-10, Kansas City (Kan.) High Sch., 1911-12; instr. Fort Hays Kan. State Coll., 1912-38, dean, 1939-41; pres. 1941-44. Mem. A.A.A.S., N.E.A., Kan. Acad. Science, Kan. State Teachers Assn., Kappa Delta Pi, Pi Kappa Delta,

Coronado Area Council of Boy Scouts of America, Hays (Kan.) Chamber of Commerce, Lions. Mason. Presbyterian. Author: Animal Studies, 1937. Home: Hays, Kan. *

WORDEN, RUTH, univ. prof.; b. Missoula, Mont., Aug. 31, 1886; d. Francis Lyman and Lucretia (Miller) Worden; A.B., Wellesley Coll. 1911; certificate in library science. U. of Wis., 1915; student U. of Chicago, 1930-31. Asst., open shelf dept., Buffalo (N.Y.) Pub. Library, 1915-16; asst. Missoula (Mont.) Pub. Library, 1916-17, Buffalo (N.Y.) Pub. Library, 1917-18; librarian, Missoula County Library, Missoula, Mont., 1918-26; instr. Sch. of Librarianship, U. of Wash., 1926-27, asst. prof., 1927-33, acting dean, 1931-33, asso. prof., 1933-35, dir., 1935-46, prof., 1937-46; asst., Am. Library Assn., Bd. of Edn. for Librarianship, summer 1929; ret. Mem. A.L.A., Special Libraries Assn., Pacific Northwest Library Assn., Kappa Kappa Gamma. Club: Womens University (Seattle). Home: Edmonds, Wash. *

WORK, HAROLD KNOWLTON, orgn. exec.; b. Hartford, Conn., May 21, 1901; s. Norman Porter and Hattie Simons (Lincoln) W.; A.B., Columbia, 1923, Chem. E., 1925; Ph.D., U. Pitts., 1929; m. Margaret Leal, Dec. 28, 1925; children—Mary Jane (Mrs. David Sanford Laity), Harriet Lincoln (Mrs. Robert Luce), Harold Knowlton, Virginia Leal (Mrs. John Foulke). Research fellow Mellon Inst., 1925-29; head research labs. div. Aluminum Co. Am., 1929-34, chem. engr. jobbing div., 1934-36; mgr. research devel. Jones & Laughlin Steel Corp., 1936-48, dir. research, 1948-49; dir. research div. Coll. Engring., N.Y.U., 1949-66, dir. Engring. Found., 1960, asso. dean Sch. Engring., 1957-66; secretary National Acad. of Engineering, 1966-76. Dir. R-N Corp. Trustee Univ. Corp. Atmospheric Research; pres. Indsl. Research Inst., 1944-45. Recipient Ilig medal Columbia, 1925; Robert W. Hunt prize Am. Inst. Mining and Metall. Engrs., 1942. Fellow A.A.A.S., Am. Inst. Chemists, N.Y. Acad. Sci.; mem. Am. Inst. Mining, Metall. and Petroleum Engrs., Am. Soc. Engring. Edn. (chmn. engring. coll. research council 1954-56), Am. Soc. Metals (pres. 1948-49), Am. Soc. Testing Materials, Am. Inst. Chem. Engrs., Am. Chemical Society, also Phi Beta Kappa, Sigma Xi, Phi Lambda Upsilon, Theta Tau, Epsilon Chi, Pi Tau Sigma (hon.), Chemists Club, Metals Science Club. Club: Cosmos. Home: Fairfax, Va. Died June 5, 1976.

WORK, JAMES, coll. adminstr.; b. Phila., Mar. 4, 1893; s. Robert Dickson and Elizabeth (Berry) W.; grad. Nat. Farm Sch., 1913; student Franklin Inst., 1916-18; D.Sc. (hon.), Delaware Valley Coll. Sci. and Agr., 1963, LL.D., 1971; m. Bertie Bishop, Sept. 22, 1921; children—Elizabeth Emilie (Mrs. Donald Meyer), Mary Louise (Mrs. Peter Glick, Jr.); m. 2d, Elizabeth Young, Sept. 9, 1936; 1 dau., Elizabeth Virginia Evans; m. 3d, Jean Hafley, Oct. 19, 1967. Farmer, 1913-16; supervising draftsman Navy Dept., 1917-21; asst. chief engr., chief draftsman U.S. Naval Air Sta., Lakehurst, N.J., 1921-26; asst. to mgr., aero. engr. U.S. Naval Aircraft Factory, 1926-28; v.p., gen. mgr. Detroit Aircraft Corp. and Lockheed Aircraft Co., 1928-32; pres., chmn. bd. Brewster Aero. Corp., 1932-46; pres. Work Engring. Corp., 1932-40; pres. Delaware Valley Coll. Sci. and Agr., Doylestown, Pa., 1946-73, chancellor, 1974-77. Head football coach Nat. Farm Sch., 1913-21, Naval Air Sta., Lakehurst, 1922-28. Served to lt., Aviation Corps, USNR, 1927-35. Republican. Episcopalian. Mason (32 deg.). Address: Doylestown, Pa. Died Nov. 6, 1977.

WORKMAN, ROBERT DUBOIS, naval chaplain; b. Zanesville, O., June 7, 1885; s. Rev. David R. and Sarah Gibson (McCullough) W.; student Pa. State Coll., 1903-04, Coll. of Wooster, 1909-12. Princeton Theol. Sem., 1912-15; hon. D.D., Coll. of Wooster, 1938; m. Elisabeth Margaret Stewart, Jan. 3, 1916; children—Elisabeth Jean, Patricia. Appointed chaplain with rank of lt., j.g., U.S. Navy, 1915; lt., 1920-24; lt.-comdr., 1924; capt. 1924; chief of naval chaplains since 1937; served in ships and stations throughout U.S. and abroad; rear admiral, Mar. 1945. Mem. Mil. Order World War (N.Y. chapter), Sigma Chi, Nat. Sojourners. Presbyterian. Mason. Home: New York, N.Y. *

WORLEY, JAMES F(RANCIS), U.S. Pub. Health Service; b. Abilene, Kan., Oct. 15, 1882; s. George F. and Carrie A.(Bolster) W.; A.B.,Washburn Coll., Topeka, Kan., 1903, A.M., 1904; M.D., U. of Pa., 1908; m. Theodora Bodwell, Oct. 27, 1909; children—Gilbert B. (dec.), George F., Catherine Virginia. Interne Delaware Hosp. Wilmington, 1908-09; practice of medicine, Emporia, Kan., 1909-14; commd. asst. surgeon U.S.P.H.S., 1914, passed asst. surgeon, 1920, surgeon, 1922, sr. surgeon, 1934, med. dir., 1940; dir. Alaskan Med. Service, Office of Indian Affairs, and regional consultant for Alaska, 1937-40; district med. dir., Office of Indian Affairs, Minneapolis (North Central States), 1940-46, transferred to San Francisco and retired Nov. 1946. Fellow A.M.A.; mem. Assn. of Mil. Surgeons, Am. Pub. Health Assn., Am. Inter-professional Inst., Calif. State Automobile Assn. Republican. Presbyterian. Mason (32deg). Clubs: Peter Pan Woodland (Big Bear City, Calif.). Home: San Francisco, Calif. *

WORTHAM, GUS SESSIONS, ins. co. exec.; b. Mexia, Tex., Feb., 1891; s. John Lee and Fanny Carter (Sessions) W.; student U. Tex., 1908-11; m. Lyndall Finley, Oct. 4, 1926; children—Lyndall (Mrs. Goss), Diana (Mrs. Skeens). Organized Am. Gen. Ins. Co., 1926, pres., 40 yrs., ret. as chmn. bd., chief exec. officer, dir. Am. Gen. Cos., 1972; dir. Am. Gen. Bond Fund, Inc., Am. Gen. Convertible Securities, Inc.; chmn. adv. bd. Tex. Commerce Bank; chmn. Longhorn Portland Cement Co., 1937-65; partner Houston Country Club Properties. Mem. adv. com. United Fund of Houston and Harris County (Tex.). Trustee DeBakey Med. Found., Tex. Safety Assn., Tex. Research League, Tex. Children's Hosp.; bd. dirs. Nat. Space Hall Fame; adv. com. Houston Symphony Soc.; exec. com. Soc. Performing Arts; mem. adv. bd. Houston Livestock Show and Rodeo; adv. trustee Mus. Fine Arts. Enlisted AS, U.S. Army, 1917; commd. 2d lt., 1918; comdg. officer 800th Aero Squadron, 1919. Recipient Ins. Man of Year award Fedn. Ins. Counsel, 1958, Distinguished Alumni award U. Tex., 1962, Coronat medal St. Edward's U., Austin, Tex., 1963, Distinguished Alumni award John Tarleton State Coll., 1966; named Key Houstonian Houston Bd. Realtors, 1968, hon. Eagle Scout, 1968. Mem. U.S. (dir. and chmn. policy com. 1953-59), Houston (pres. 1934-35) chambers commerce, Soc. Performing Arts (dir.) Newcomen Soc. N.Am., Philos. Soc. Tex., Tex. Safety Assn., Tex. Inst. Adv. Assn. (exec. com.), Beta Gamma Sigma, Sigma Nu, Theta Nu Epsilon. Democrat. Clubs: Houston, Houston Country, Ramada, Petroleum, Tejas, Coronado, Allegro (Houston); Metropolitan (N.Y.C.). Home: Houston, Tex. Died Sept. 1, 1976.

WORTHINGTON, ARTHUR (WHITTEMORE), ret. corp. exec.; born Steubenville, O., Apr. 26, 1885; s. Henry Daniel and Mary Florence (Hill) W.; B.S., Rose Polytech, Inst., 1906; C.E., 1913; married Elizabeth (Wood) Bunting, September 22, 1950. Asst. on engr. corps Pa. R.R., Pittsburgh, 1906-08, engr. in charge constrn., 1908-15; erecting engr. Koppers Co., Follansbee, W.Va., and Pittsburgh, 1915-17; cons. engr. Cleveland, 1920; asst. to gen. mgr. Pittsburgh Limestone Corp. (subsidiary of U.S. Steel Corp.), 1920-30, gen. mgr., 1930-32, vice pres. and gen. mgr. 1932-40, pres. since 1940, dir. since 1930. Served as 1st lt. engrs. to capt., U.S. Army, 1918-19; engr. maintenance of way, Am. Rys. Advance sect., A.E.F., France. Mem. Am. Inst. Mining and Metall. Engrs., Am. Iron and Steel Inst., Rose Polytech. Alumni Assn. (past v.p.). Republican. Episcopalian. Clubs: University (past pres.). Duquesne. Retired. Home: Jamestown, Pa. *

WORTHINGTON, EDWARD ARTHUR, chemist; b. New Orleans, Nov. 28, 1920; s. Roy Bowie and Winfred (Casey) W.; Ph.D., U. Pitts., 1948; m. Margaret Joyce Spear, June 4, 1946; children—Anne, Laurie, Edward. Instr., U. Pitts., 1946-48; sr. research chemist Allied Chem. Co., 1948-51; research supr., then mgr. research Kaiser Aluminum & Chem. Corp., 1951-69, adminstrv. dir. Center Tech., Pleasanton, Calif., 1969-78. City councilman, Palo Alto, Calif., 1965-67. Mem. Am. Chem. Soc. Home: Palo Alto, Calif. Died Nov. 5, 1979.

WORTHINGTON, MARJORIE, author; b. N.Y.C., 1899; d. Oscar and Rose (Samuels) Muir; m. Lyman Worthington, Mar. 10, 1923 (div. 1932); m. 2d, William B. Seabrook, Feb. 2, 1935 (div. 1941). Author books, 1930-76, including: The House on the Park, 1946; The Enchanted Heart, 1949; Miss Alcott of Concord, 1958; (biography) Abelard and Heloise, 1960; Bouboukar, 1962; The Strange World of Willie Seabrook, 1966; books pub. also in England, Germany, Italy. Contbr. nat. mags., encys. Story, Hunger, included in O'Henry Prize Stories of 1942, O'Brien Anthology of Best Short Stories, 1942. Letters and Manuscripts contained in collection at U. Oreg. Mem. Authors League, Nat. Audubon Soc., Defenders of Wildlife, Broward County Soc. Prevention Cruelty to Animals, Smithsonian Instn. Asso. editor: News of the Nation (Robert Hoffman), 1975. Home: Fort Lauderdale, Fla. Died Feb. 17, 1976.

WORTMAN, STERLING, scientist; b. Quinlan, Okla., Apr. 3, 1923; s. Leo Sterling and Gladys (Richwine) W.; B.S., Okla. State U., 1943, M.S., U. Minn., 1948, Ph.D., 1950; m. Ruth Eleanor Bolstad, June 17, 1949; children—Linda Susan, Steven Sterling, Mark Jeffry, David Eric. Geneticist charge corn breeding Rockefeller Found., 1950-54, dir. agrl. scis., 1966-70, v.p., 1970-80; pres. Internat. Agrl. Devel. Service 1975-80; asst. field dir. Internat. Rice Research Inst., 1960-64; head dept. plant breeding Pineapple Research Inst., Hawaii, 1955-59, dir., 1964-65; dir. Campbell Soup Co. Mem. agrl. bd. Nat. Acad. Scis.-NRC, 1967-71; chmn. Plant Studies Delegation to Peoples Republic of China, Nat. Acad. Scis., 1974, mem. bd. on sci. and tech. in internat. devel., 1974, mem. com. on scholarly communication with Peoples Republic of China, 1974-76; mem. steering com. Pres.'s Food and Nutrition Study, 1975-77; Coromandel lectr., India, 1977. Trustee Agronomic Sci. Found., 1967-81; bd. dirs. Agribus. Council, 1967-73, v.p., 1967-69; bd. dirs. Internat. Center Maize and Wheat Improvement, Mex., 1966-81, vice chmn. bd., 1968-74; mem. biol. and med. scis. adv. com. NSF, 1970-72, mem. research adv. com., 1972-74; trustee Internat. Rice Research Inst., Philippines, 1970, Internat. Inst. Tropical Agr., Nigeria, 1970; mem. vis. com. dept. nutrition Mass. Inst. Tech., 1971-74. Served to capt., inf., AUS, 1943-45; PTO. Decorated Medal of Merit (Philippines); recipient Outstanding Achievement award U. Minn., 1975, Joseph C. Wilson award for achievement in internat. affairs, 1975. Fellow AAAS; mem. Crop Sci. Soc., Am. Soc. Agronomy (Internat. Agronomy award 1975), Am. Inst. Biol. Scis., Sigma Xi. Home: Greenwich, Conn. Died May 26, 1981.

WRAGGE, SYDNEY, fashion designer; b. N.Y.C.; s. Joseph and Anna (Falber) W.; student N.Y. U., 1928, N.Y. Sch. Social Research, 1934; m. Phyllis Morse, Dec. 28, 1938; children—Ellen, Carla, Sara. Founder, B. H. Wragge, N.Y.C., 1935, pres., 1935-78. Recipient awards Coty, 1952, 57, Nieman-Marcus, 1961, Sports Illustrated, 1957. Home: Boca Raton, Fla. Died Mar. 23, 1978.

WREN, FRANK LYNWOOD, educator; b. Yorkville, Tenn., Sept. 28, 1894; s. Dr. Franklin and Susan Adelaide (Flowers) W.; A.B., U. of South, 1915; grad. work Johns Hopkins, 1917, 21; A.M., George Peabody Coll. Tchrs., 1925; Ph.D., U. Chgo., 1930; m. Sarah Alleyne Talley, June 25, 1921; children—Elizabeth Alleyne, Frances Virginia. Tchr. city high sch., Martin, Tenn., 1915-17, McFerrin School, Martin. 1919-21, McCallie Sch., Chattanooga, 1921-24; asso. prof. teaching math. Peabody Coll. Tchrs., 1927-30, prof. math., 1930-59. Julia A. Sears prof. emeritus, 1959-76; prof. math. Cal. State U., Northridge, 1959-75, prof. emeritus, 1975-76; vis. prof. math. U. Cal., 1958, others; instr., lectr. NSF Insts.; sch. cons. Mem. commn. on postwar plans, mem. joint com. on war needs. Nat. Council Tchrs. Math. and U.S. War Dept. Served from pvt. to sgt. U.S. Army, 1917-19; with AEF and Army Occupation. Fellow A.A.A.S.; mem. Tenn. Acad. Sci. (v.p. 1940-41, pres. 1941-42), Nat. Council Tchrs. Math. (v.p. 1940-42, pres., 1944-46; chmn. com. on election policies). Central Assn. Sci. and Math. Tchrs. (dir., chmn. com. on election policies, v.p. 1958-59), Tenn. Tchrs. Math., Math. Assn Am. (high sch. lectr.), Cal. Math. Council, Phi Beta Kappa, Sigma Xi (regional lectr. 1973-74). Phi Kappa Phi, Phi Delta Kappa, Kappa Delta Pi, Kappa Sigma. Democrat. Methodist. Author: Basic Mathematical Concepts, 1965, 2d edit., 1973; Practice Book: Mathematical Concepts, 1973; co-author Basic Algebraic Concepts, 1969; Teaching Secondary Mathematics, 5th edit., 1970. Contbr. to Ency. Ednl Research, Dictionary of Edn., Third Mental Measurements Yearbook. Editor: 23rd Yearbook of Nat. Council Tchrs Mathematics, 1957, also editor for the secondary sch. curriculum com., 1959-60. Co-author books relating to field; contbr. to ednl. and profl. jours. also to yearbooks Nat. Council Tchrs. Math. Home: Northridge, Calif. Died Oct. 20, 1976.

WREN, HAROLD ALOYSIUS, educator; b. Scranton, Pa., Feb. 16, 1907; s. Francis J. and Elizabeth (Hamm) W.; B.A., St. Thomas Coll., 1927; M.A., U. Buffalo, 1934; Ph.D., Columbia, 1941; m. Valerie Fite, Feb. 14, 1931; 1 son, Gregory. Tchr. pub. schs., Scranton, 1927-40; instr. Loyola U., Chgo., 1940-42; prof. Cooper Union, N.Y.C., 1946-50; prof. psychology, dir. Sch. Edn., grad. dean Our Lady of Lake Coll., San Antonio, 1950-72, emeritus, 1972-80. Pres., Archdioceesan Bd. Edn., San Antonio, 1966-69. Served to capt. USAAF, 1942-46. Mem. Am. Assn. Colls. for Tchr. Edn. (research com. 1961-66). Home: San Antonio, Tex. Died Nov. 15, 1980.

WREXE, ALEXANDER, writer; b. New Orleans, La., Dec. 7, 1882; s. Patrick Gardiner and Aloise (Duplis) W.; ed. pvt. schs., France and Eng.; m. Ethel King Life, of Paris, France, June 10, 1917 (died Mar. 13, 1926); 1 dau., Georgianne. Newspaper work, London, 1906-14; spl. corr., Paris, 1914-18; returned to U.S., 1926. Served with Boers in South African Boer War; deserted to Brit. when abandoned after being wounded; took part in relief of Ladysmith. Mem. Authors' League of America. Author: A Maid Among Men, 1927; The Love Wolf, 1928. Address: New York, N.Y. *

WRIGHT, AGNES FOSTER (MRS. RICHARDSON LITTLE WRIGHT), b. Boston, Mass., Jan. 29, 1882; d. Albert J. and Cornelia (Hull) Foster; ed. high sch., Boston; grad. New York Sch. of Fine Arts 1913; traveled and studied in Europe 5 yrs.; m. Richardson Little Wright, of New York, Sept. 19, 1914. In business in own name as interior decorator since 1914. Pres. Interior Decorators' League of New York, 1915-17. Clubs: Gamut, Pen and Brush (New York): Coin D'Or (Phila.). Author: Making Curtains and Hangings, 1915; Interior Decorating for Modern Needs, 1917. Home: New York, N.Y. *

WRIGHT, ALBERT BAYARD, economist; b. Wenona, Ill., Dec. 28, 1885; s. Frank and Charlotte Belle (Evans) W.; B.S., Ill. Wesleyan U., 1907; student law dept. same, 1907-08, 1909-10, M.A. in Economics, 1910; M.A. in Political Science, U. of Ill., 1914; Dr. Commercial Science, Duquesne U., 1927; m. Lucie Estabrook Newman, June 18, 1913 (died July 1, 1937); children—Charlotte Evans, Janet Estabrook, Albert Bayard, Priscilla Bromley. Teacher of science, high sch.,

Marysville, Mo., 1908-09; prof. chemistry, U. of Puget Sound, 1910-12; research asst. to dean of Grad. Sch., U. of Ill., 1912-14; instr. polit. science, U. of Pittsburgh, 1914, asst. prof., 1916, asso. prof. 1917, prof., 1918-20, prof. public and business administration, 1920-24, also dean Sch. of Economics, 1918-23 (leave of absence 1923-24); research asso. Sch. of Commerce, U. of Chicago, 1923-24; prof. economics, Sch. of Commerce, Duquesne U., since 1924, also dir. grad. div., 1927-31, head dept. of business administration since 1931, dean Sch. of Business Administration since 1932, also dir. Downtown Evening Div. since 1933; lecturer in social edn., Pa. State Coll., 1924-31. Mem. Nat. Econ. League, Sigma Chi, Phi Alpha Delta, Alpha Kappa Psi, Omicron Delta Kappa, Beta Gamma Sigma, Phi Kappa Phi. Home: Pittsburgh. *

WRIGHT, ARTHUR FREDERICK, educator; b. Portland, Ore., Dec. 3, 1913; s. Charles Frederick and Georgiana (Gwynne) W.; A.B., Stanford, 1935; B.Litt., Oxford (Eng.) U., 1937; A.M., Harvard, 1940, Ph.D., 1947; M.A. (hon.), Yale, 1959; m. Mary Oliver Clabaugh, July 6, 1940 (dec. June 1970); children—Charles Duncan, Jonathan Arthur; m. 2d, Marya Wankowicz Welch, Mar. 4, 1972. Fellow, Harvard Yenching Inst., 1939-40, 41-47; from asst. prof. history to prof. Stanford, 1947-59; prof. history Yale, 1959-76, Charles Seymour prof., 1962-76, chmn. council E. Asian studies, 1961-62, 68-69; exec. sec. univ. concilium on internat. studies, 1961-65. Chmn. com. studies Chinese civilization Am. Council Learned Socs., 1963-73; chmn. com. East Asian research Stanford, 1956-59. Bd. govs. Inst. Current World Affairs, 1961-66. Rockefeller fellow, 1937-39; Guggenheim fellow, 1953-54. Mem. Assn. Asian Studies (bd. dirs. 1951-58 v.p. 1963-64, pres. 1964-65, chmn. com. Chinese thought 1951-62), Soc. History Ideas, Am. Hist. Assn., Am. Assn. U. Profs. Author: Buddhism in Chinese History, 1959. Editor, contbr.; Studies in Chinese Thought, 1953; Confucianism in Action, 1959; The Confucian Persuasion, 1960; Confucian Personalities, 1962; Confucianism and Chinese Civilization, 1964; Perspectives on the T'ang, 1973. Editor Far Eastern Quar., 1951-55. Adv. editorial bd. Ency. Britannica, 1957-60. Home: Guilford, Conn. Died Aug. 11, 1976.

WRIGHT, ARTHUR WILLIAM, pathologist; b. Windsor Locks, Conn., July 20, 1894; s. Arthur and Elizabeth (Hayes) W.; A.B., Harvard, 1917, M.D., 1923; m. Henrietta S. Bratton, June 25, 1929 (dec. Jan. 1959); m. 2d, Janette R. Hollis, Nov. 23, 1963. House officer, asst. pathology Boston City Hosp., 1923-25; asst. prof. pathology Sch. Medicine, Vanderbilt U., Nashville, 1925-29; dir. Bender Hygienic Lab., 1929-34; lectr. pathology Albany Med. Coll., 1929-34, prof. of pathology and bacteriology, 1934-56, dept. chmn., 1934-60, prof. pathology, 1956-68, prof. emeritus, 1968-76; sec. N.Y. State Bd. for Medicine, 1961-64, acting sec., 1968-71, cons., 1971-76; chief pathologist, bacteriologist Albany Hosp., 1934-56, chief pathologist, 1956-60, sr. pathologist, 1960-73, hon. pathologist, 1973-76; adminstrv. asst. Albany Med. Coll., 1960-62; cons. pathology Greene County Meml. Hosp., Catskill, N.Y., 1947-60, V.A. Hosp., Albany, 1951-60; dir. Rensselaer County Pub. Health Lab., Troy, N.Y., 1948-65; pres. Albany County chpt. Am. Cancer Soc., 1967-69. Served with U.S. Army, 1917-19. Diplomate Am. Bd. Pathology, Nat. Bd. Med. Examiners (mem. bd. 1966-74). Fellow A.A.A.S., A.M.A., Am. Soc. Clin. Pathologists, Am. Pub. Health Assn., N.Y. Acad. Scis.; mem. Fedn. State Med. Bds. U.S., Soc. Exptl. Biology and Medicine, N.Y. State Med. Soc., N.Y. State Assn. Pub. Health Labs. (sec.-treas. 1960-72), Internat. Acad. Pathology, N.Y. State Soc. Pathologists, Research Soc. Am., Am. Assn. Cancer Research, Am. Assn. Pathologists and Bacteriologists, Am. Soc. Exptl. Pathology, Sigma Xi, Alpha Omega Alpha. Presbyn. Contbr. articles med. jours. Editor: Rypins' Medical Licensure Examinations. Home: Albany, N.Y. Died Sept. 8, 1976; interred Mt. Auburn Cemetery, Cambridge, Mass.

WRIGHT, BENJAMIN FLETCHER, educator; b. Austin, Tex., Feb. 8, 1900; s. Benjamin F. and Mary (Blandford) W.; A.B. and A.M., U. Tex., 1921; Ph.D., Harvard, 1925; LL.D., Amherst Coll., 1950, Mt. Holyoke Coll., 1958, U. Pitts., 1962; Litt.D., Am. Internat. Coll., 1958; m. Alexa Rhea, 1926 (dec. 1974); children—David, Janet (Mrs. Paul E. Jones, Jr.). Instr. govt. U. Tex., 1922-24, adj. prof., 1925-26; instr. govt. Harvard, 1926-28, asst. prof., 1928-40, asso. prof. 1940-45, prof. 1945-49, chmn. dept. govt., 1942-46, chmn. com. on gen. edn., 1946-49; pres. Smith Coll., 1949-59; fellow Center for Advanced Study in Behavioral Scis., 1959-60; prof. govt. U. Tex., 1960-76. Lowell lectr., Boston, 1947; mem. faculty Salzburg Seminar on Am. Studies, 1947, 49; Bacon lectr. Boston U., 1957; Jefferson Meml. lectr. U. Cal., Berkeley, 1964; vis. prof. govt. Harvard, 1966-67. Served with inf. U.S. Army, 1918. Mem. Am. Acad. Arts and Scis., Am Polit. Sci. Assn. Author: American Interpretations of Natural Law, 1931, The Contract Clause of the Constitution, 1938, The Growth of American Constitutional Law, 1942; (With others) General Education in a Free Society, 1945; Consensus and Continuity, 1776-1787, 1958; Five Public Philosophies of Walter Lippmann, 1973. Editor: Source Book of American Political Theory, 1929; The Federalist, 1961. Home: Austin, Tex. Died Nov. 28, 1976.

WRIGHT, EDWARD LEDWIDGE, lawyer; b. Little Rock, July 16, 1903; s. Benjamin B. and Katie (Ledwidge) W.; A.B., Little Rock Coll., 1923; LL.B., Georgetown U., 1928; LL.D., U. Scranton, William Mitchell Coll. Law, Suffolk U., U. Ark., Georgetown U., Loyola U., New Orleans; m. Rosemary Tuohey, Oct. 20, 1931; children—Edward Ledwidge, Rosemary, Bridget, Kathleen. Admitted to Ark. bar, 1925; practice in Little Rock, 1928-77; mem. law firm Wright, Lindsey & Jennings; co-draftsman Ark. Probate Code, 1948; dir. Pulaski Fed. Savs. & Loan Assn., Worthen Bank & Trust Co., Winburn Tile Mfg. Co.; trustee Ark. Blue Cross-Blue Shield. Chmn. Ark. Bd. Law Examiners, 1938-41; commr. Nat. Conf. Commrs. Uniform State Laws, 1945-57; mem. 2 Hoover Commn. Legal Task Force. Trustee Southwestern Legal Found. Fellow Am. Coll. Trial Lawyers (nat. pres. 1965-66); mem. Am. (state del. 1946-67, chmn. ho. dels. 1962-64, chmn. spl. com. on evaluation of ethical standards 1964, nat. pres. 1970-71), Ark. (pres. 1957), Pulaski County (pres. 1948) bar assns., Am. Judicature Soc., Am. Law Inst., Internat. Assn. Ins. Counsel. Roman Catholic. K.C. (4 deg.), Knight of Malta. Home: Little Rock, Ark. Died Feb. 1, 1977; interred Calvary Cemetery, Little Rock.

WRIGHT, F(REDERICK) WARREN, coll. prof.; born Middletown, R.I., Mar. 8, 1885; s. William Arter and Sarah Elizabeth (Longley) W.; student Chaffey Prep. Sch., Ontario, Calif. 1897-1901; A.B., Wesleyan U., Middletown, Conn., 1906; A.M., Harvard, 1908; Ph.D., Princeton, 1910; m. Louise Marion Fisher, July 2, 1915. Asst. prin. Portland (Conn.) High Sch., 1906-07; lecturer in Latin Bryn Mawr Coll., 1910-11; instr. Latin Smith Coll., 1911-14, asst. prof., 1914-20, asso. prof., 1920-37, prof. classics since 1937, chmn, dept. classical langs. and lit. since 1942. Marshal, Smith Coll., 1925-47, mem. bd. admission since 1934. Mem. Am. Philol. Assn., Archaeol. Inst. of Am., Am. Classical League, Classical Assn. of New Eng., Am. Assn. Univ. Profs., Classical Society of American Academy in Rome, Newcomen Society of London, Association of Guillaume Bude, Phi Nu Theta, Phi Beta Kappa. Clubs: Smith Faculty, Kiwanis (p.p., sec.), Touring Italiano. Author: Studies in Menander, 1911; Cicero and the Theater, 1931. Contbr. articles to profl. periodicals. European travel and study as asso., Am. Acad. in Rome, 1924-25, 1931-32. Home: Northampton, Mass. *

WRIGHT, HORACE WETHERILL, univ. prof.; born Philadelphia, Aug. 5, 1884; s. William Harry and Aubertine (Woodward) W.; student Boys Latin Sch., Baltimore, 1900-03, Wis. Acad., Madison. 1903-04; A.B., U. of Wis., 1908, grad. study, 1910-11; Ph.D., U. of Pa., 1917; fellow Am. Acad. in Rome, 1914-15. Teacher, Galahad Boys Sch., Hudson, Wis., 1908-10. St. Croix Falls (Wis.) High Sch., 1910; instr. U. of Mo., 1917-18; asst. prof. Oberlin Coll., 1918-19; asso. Bryn Mawr Coll., 1919-21; prof. and head dept. of Latin, Lehigh U., Bethlehem, Pa., 1921-50, emeritus since 1950. Founder Classical League of Lehigh Valley, 1922; lecturer Archaeol. Inst. of Am., 1929-33. Mem. Archeol. Inst. of Am. (recorder 1930-32; founder Bethlehem chapter 1925), Am. Philol. Assn., Classical Assn. of Atlantic States (v.p. 1928-31), Eta Sigma Phi (founder Lehigh chapter 1928; nat. trustee 1940-49), Am. Classical League (chmn. Horace Bimillenium Celebration in Schs.). Trinitarian. Author of articles on classical philology and archaeology. Home: Bethlehem, Pa. *

WRIGHT, JAMES ARLINGTON, poet; b. Martins Ferry, Ohio, 1927; B.A., Kenyon Coll., 1952; M.A., U. Wash., 1954, Ph.D., 1959; m. Ann Runk, 1967; children by previous marriage—Franz Paul, Marshall John. Formerly instr. English, U. Minn., Macalester Coll., St. Paul; poet translator; prof. English, Hunter Coll., N.Y.C., 1966-80. Served with AUS, World War II. Recipient Melville Cane award Poetry Soc. Am.; Pulitzer prize for poetry, 1972. Fellow Acad. Am. Poets. Author: The Green Wall, 1957; Saint Judas, 1959; The Lion's Tail and Eyes, 1962; The Branch Will Not Break, 1963; Shall We Gather at the River?, 1968; Collected Poems, 1971; Salt Mines and Such, 1971; Two Citizens, 1973; Moments of the Italian Summer, 1976; To a Blossoming Pear Tree, 1977. Translator: The Rider on the White Horse (Theodore Storm), 1964; Wandering: Notes and Sketches (Hermann Hesse), 1972; (with Robert Bly) Twenty Poems of George Frankl, 1961, Twenty Poems of César Vallejo, 1962, Twenty Poems of Pablo Neruda, 1962. Home: New York, N.Y. Died Mar. 25, 1980.

WRIGHT, JAMES FREDRICK, govt. ofcl.; b. Volga, S.D., Aug. 31, 1914; s. James Cady and Clara (Hymes) W.; student U. S.D., 1930-31; Asso. in Adminstrn., Am. U., 1952; m. Eula Page Hockett, Apr. 11, 1950; children—James Oliver, Clara Lynn. Various positions Naval Communications, Navy Dept., Washington, 1941-48; budget analyst, budget officer Office Navy Comptroller, 1948-53; dep. fiscal dir. Marine Corps, 1953-62, fiscal dir., 1962-73. Served with AUS, 1944-46. Mem. Am. Soc. Mil. Comptrollers, V.F.W. Presbyn. Home: Sterling, Va. Deceased.

WRIGHT, JOHN J., cardinal; b. Boston, July 18, 1909; s. John J. and Harriet L. (Cokely) W.; grad. Boston Latin Sch., 1927; A.B., Boston Coll., 1931; studied St. John's Sem., 1932; S.T.L., Gregorian U., Rome, 1936, S.T.D., 1939; hon. degrees from more than 20 Am. and Canadian colls. and univs. Ordained priest Roman Catholic Ch., 1935; prof. St. John's Sem., Boston, 1939-44; sec. to archbishop of Boston, 1943; apptd. papal chamberlain, 1945, domestic prelate 1946; consecrated titular bishop of Egea and aux. bishop of Boston, June 30, 1947; first bishop of Worcester, Mass., 1950-59; bishop of Pitts., 1959-69; elevated to cardinal, 1969; prefect Sacred Congregation of Clergy, Roman Curia, Vatican, 1969-79. Mem. numerous commns. and Am. coms. on intellectual and social questions. Decorated comdr. Knights of Holy Sepulchre; officer Legion of Honor (France); Order of Merit (Italy); named hon. citizen Chinon, France. Fellow Am. Acad. Arts and Scis.; mem. Harvard Mus. Soc., Am. Antiquarian Soc. K.C. Club: Odd Volumes, Athanaeum (Boston). Author: National Patriotism in Papal Teaching, 1939; The Pope and the War, 1944; The Christian and The Law, Words in Pain; The Church: the Hope of the World; also many articles on Cath. teaching. Home: Rome, Italy. Died Aug. 10, 1979; buried Boston, Mass.

WRIGHT, JOSEPH PURDON, lawyer; b. Colorado Springs, June 10, 1884; s. Richard William and Sarah Louise (Carter) W.; student Baltimore City Coll., 1905; A.B., Johns Hopkins, 1908; LL.B., U. Md., 1905; m. Lucy Agnes Wright, June 24, 1914 (dec. Mar. 1961); children—Margaret Louise (Mrs. J. A. Sader), Joseph Purdon, Richard Armstrong; m. second, Margaret Larrimore, August 24, 1963. Admitted to the Maryland bar, 1909, since practiced in Baltimore; assistant attorney general of Md., 1920-24; gen. counsel Pub. Service Commn. of Md., 1935-41; commr. Uniform Laws for Md., 1935-39; 1st supt. Md. State Police, 1935; dir., v.p., counsel Am. Nat. Bldg. & Loan Assn. Balt. City since 1920; dir. U.S. Fidelity & Guaranty Co. Trustee University of Baltimore, 1941—. Mem. Am., Maryland bar assns., American Law Institute, Commercial Law League Am. (past pres.), Hibernian Soc., Md. Hist. Soc., Phi Gamma Delta. Republican. Episcopalian. Mason (Shriner). Clubs: Terrapin (U. Md.); Merchants (Baltimore). Home: Balt. *

WRIGHT, RUSSEL, indsl. designer; b. Lebanon, Ohio, Apr. 3, 1904; s. Willard Jury and Harryet (Crigler) W.; ed. pub. schs., Lebanon; pupil Frank Duveneck, Cin. Art Acad., Kenneth Hayes Miller, Lentelli, Arts Students League, N.Y.C.; student Princeton, 1922-24, Columbia Sch. Architecture, 1923, N.Y. U. Sch. Architecture, 1938-39; m. Mary Einstein, Oct. 11, 1927 (dec. Aug. 1952); 1 dau., Eve Ann. Stage mgr., designer stage prodns., including work with Norman Bel Geddes, The Theatre Guild, Neighborhood Playhouse and the Group Theatre; established factory for prodn. first metal informal serving accesories, N.Y.C., 1930; became indsl. designer for mfrs., 1939; owner Russel Wright Assos., designer furniture, 1954-76. Assigned by ICA to develop native handicrafts, local and export use, Cambodia, Taiwan, Vietnam, 1956, craft survey, adviser on merchandising, Japan, 1957-58; designer dinnerware, glassware, Japan, 1964; designer Dragon Rock, exptl. home and arboretum using native materials on mountain Garrison-on-Hudson, 1960, donated with endowment to the Nature Conservancy for establishment Nature Center, Manitoga, 1975, dir. Nature Center, 1975-76; designer restaurant Shum Lee Dynasty, 1966; cons. master planning and programing of parks Nat. Park Service, 1967-74, author, dir. Summer in Parks program, Washington, 1968; cons. on devel. handcrafts to Govt. Barbados, 1970; cons. Palisades Interstate Park, N.Y., Carey Arboretum. Founding mem. bd. dirs. Harlem Sch. Arts. Recipient Trail Blazer award, Home Fashions League, 1951; numerous other awards Mayor Washington, Com. for More Beautiful Capitol; archives donated to George Arents Research Library, Syracuse U. Founding fellow Soc. Indsl. Designers (pres. 1951-52). Pioneer blond, modern, solid-maple furniture (American Modern), 1934, textured monotone glazed dinner-ware, 1938. Home furnishings designs exhibited and collected Met. Mus., Mus. of Modern Art, Cooper Hewitt Mus. Design; exhibited Good Design Show and others in U.S. and Europe; also designer of comml. interiors and N.Y. World's Fair exhibits. Author: (with Mary Wright) Easier Living, 1951. Address: Garrison, N.Y. Died Dec. 22, 1976; interred The Quadruple Oaks-Manitoga, Garrison-on-Hudson, N.Y.

WRIGHT, WYLLIS EATON, librarian; b. Jacksonville, Fla., Dec. 13, 1903; s. Arthur Andrew and Florence (Eaton) W.; A.B., Williams Coll., 1925, A.M., 1926; B.S., Columbia Library Sch., 1928; m. Helena Lawrence Kellogg, Sept. 21, 1929; children—Barbara, Lawrence Eaton. Cataloguer, N.Y. Pub. Library, 1927-30; librarian Am. Acad. in Rome, Italy, 1930-33; with N.Y. Pub. Library as chief classifier, 1933-36; chief cataloguer, 1936-45; asso. in library service Columbia U. Sch. Library Service, 1940-45; librarian Army Med. Library, 1945-46; librarian Williams Coll. Library, 1946-68; cataloger Stanford U. Library, 1969-73, acting chief spl. collections, 1973-74, catalog dept., summer 1979. Mem. A.L.A. (pres. div. cataloging and classification 1942-43, exec. bd. 1963-67), Assn. Coll. and Reference Libraries (pres. 1949-50), Bibliog. Soc. Am. Author: Colonel Ephraim Williams, 1970. Contbr. to library jours. Home: Portola Valley, Calif. Died Oct. 2, 1979; interred Williams Coll. Cemetery.

WRIGLEY, PHILIP KNIGHT, corp. exec.; b. Chgo., Dec. 5, 1894; s. William Jr. and Ada Elizabeth (Foote) W.; grad. Phillips Acad., Andover, Mass., 1914; m. Helen Blanche Atwater, Mar. 26, 1918; children—Blanche, Dorothy, William. With Wm. Wrigley Jr. Co., chewing gum mfrs., Melbourne, Australia, 1915; v.p. Wm. Wrigley Jr. Co., Chgo., 1920-25, pres., 1925-61, chmn. bd. dirs. 1961-77, dir., 1926-77; chmn. bd. Wm. Wrigley Jr. Co. Ltd., Can., 1932-77, also dir.; pres., dir. Wrigley Import Co., Chgo., 1937-77, pres., dir. Chgo. Nat. League Ball Club, Santa Catalina Island Co., Catalina Operations Co., Catalina Rock & Ranch Co., Wrigley Meml. Garden Found.; mgr. Deutsche Wrigley GmbH, West Germany; dir. Wrigley Italiana S.P.A., The Wrigley Co. Ltd., Eng., The Wrigley Co. Pty. Ltd., Australia, The Wrigley Co. (N.Z.) Ltd., New Zealand, Wrigley S.A., France, Wrigley Phillippines, Inc., Wrigley N.V., Netherlands. Mem. Nat. League Profl. Baseball Clubs (v.p. 1947-66). Served to lt. USNRF, in charge Sch. Aviation Mechanics, Great Lakes Naval Tr. Station, World War I. Mem. Chgo. Hist. Soc., Nat. Aero. Assn., Navy League U.S., Q.M. Assn., Am. Legion, Arab Horse Soc. (Eng.), Yachtsmen's Assn. Am., Arabian Horse Registry Am., Chgo. Acad. Scis., Art Inst. Chgo., Catalina Island Mus. Soc., Chgo. Urban League, Chgo. Zool. Soc., Field Mus. Natural History, Geneva Lake Civic Assn., Lincoln Park Zool. Soc., Naval Aviation Mus. Assn., Photog. Soc. Am., Shedd Aquarium. Moose. Clubs: Chicago Athletic Assn., Saddle and Cycle, Chicago, Mid-Am., Knollwood Country, Racquet, Chicago Yacht, Internat., Los Gringos Camp, Lake Geneva Country, Lake Geneva Yacht, Los Rancheros Vista Dores, Tavern, Catalina Island Yacht, Tuna (Catalina). Home: Chicago, Ill. Died Apr. 12, 1977.

WRIGLEY, THOMAS, publicity director, newspaperman; b. Elmira, N.Y., July 27, 1882; s. John and Mattie (de Graw) W.; ed. pub. schs. and Elmira Academy; m. Elsie M. Nagle, October 14, 1909 (deceased November 1961). Reporter for the Elmira Gazette, later Elmira Star-Gazette until 1909; mng. editor Elmira Herald, 1913-20; corr. Internat. News Service, 1920, chief of Kansas City Bur., 1921, Chicago Bur., 1922; mng. editor Elmira Advertiser and Elmira Sunday Telegram, 1923; city editor Boston Advertiser and Boston Sunday American, 1923-25; staff corr. Washington Bur. Universal Service, 1925-29, chief of Bur., 1929-32; news editor New York headquarters, Universal Service, 1933, Washington Bur., 1934-37; first publicized "March of Dimes" in 1938 as fund-raising plan for Nat. Foundation Infantile Paralysis campaigns, continuing as dir. publicity until 1943, resuming as publicity consultant, 1946-60; Washington columnist for Elk's Mag., 1950—. Emcee, publicity dir. Am. Banjo Fraternity. City historian Elmira, 1963—. Adv. bd. D.A.R., 1956-59. Mem. N.G.N.Y. 6 yrs. Democrat. Mason, Elk. Clubs: National Press; City (Elmira, N.Y.). Under auspices U.S. govt. conducted official tour, U.S. and Can., of five Turkish editors and journalists making study America's war effort by visiting munitions, armaments and other war plants, shipyards, airfields, and army and navy training camps, 1942. Home: Elmira, N.Y. *

WRISTON, HENRY MERRITT, educator; b. Laramie, Wyo., July 4, 1889; s. Henry Lincoln and Jennie Amelia (Atcheson) W.; A.B., Wesleyan U., Conn., 1911, A.M., 1912, LL.D., 1931, L.H.D., 1943; Ph.D., Harvard, 1922; recipient 34 hon. degrees Am. and fgn. colls. and univs., 1926—; m. Ruth Colton Bigelow, June 6, 1914 (dec.); children—Barbara, Walter Bigelow; m. 2d, Marguerite Woodworth, June 1947. Instr. history Wesleyan U., 1914-17, asso. prof., 1917-19, prof., 1919-25; pres. Lawrence Coll., 1925-37; dir. Inst. of Paper Chemistry, Appleton, Wis., 1929-37; pres. Brown U., 1937-55, now pres. emeritus; exec. dir. Am. Assembly, 1955-58, pres., 1958-62, chmn., 1962-65. Sometime officer numerous commns. and coms. ednl. and governmental fields, including; pub. gov. N.Y. Stock Exchange, 1950-52; trustee Ednl. Records Bur., 1939-54; trustee World Peace Found. 1939-52; del. to Internat. Studies Conf., Bergen, 1939; mem. bd. counselors Fletcher Sch. of Law and Diplomacy, 1939-44; dir. Diplomatic Affairs Found., 1939-44; trustee Carnegie Endowment for Internat. Peace, 1943-54. Fellow Am. Acad. Arts Sci.; mem. Am. Hist. Assn., Council Fgn. Relations (pres. 1953-64), Phi Beta Kappa, Delta Tau Delta, Delta Sigma Rho. Methodist. Club: Century (N.Y.). Author several books and reports. Latest: Diplomacy in a Democracy, 1956, Wriston Speaking, 1957; Academic Procession, 1959; Perspectives on Policy, 1963; also articles in jours., periodicals. Editorial adv. bd. Fgn. Affairs, 1943-67. Home: New York, N.Y. Died Mar. 7, 1978.

WULFECK, WALLACE HOWARD, psychologist; b. Cin., Sept. 6, 1900; s. Wallace Edward and Elizabeth (Panter) W.; A.B., Vanderbilt U., YMCA Grad. Sch., 1932; Ph.D., Yale, 1938; m. Katharine P. Ernst, Nov. 30, 1940; 1 son (by previous marriage), Joe Wallace. Sec. YMCA, Cin., Lexington and Bowling Green, Ky., Akron, Ohio, 1917-31; prof. psychology Larson Jr. Coll., New Haven, 1933-36; psychologist Neuropsychiat. Inst., Hartford, Conn., 1936-37; asso. psychologist div. indsl. hygiene USPHS, Washington, 1938-39; asso. dir. market research Psychol. Corp., N.Y.C., 1939-42, also res. asso. NDRC, 1940-42; v.p., sec., dir. research Fed. Advt. Agency, Inc., N.Y.C., 1942-50; chmn. exec. com. William Esty Co., Inc., N.Y.C., 1950-58, exec. v.p., 1958-60, vice chmn. bd., 1960-62; pres., dir. Palm Beach Shores Apts., Inc.; cons. psychologist, Stockton, N.J., from 1962; dir., sec.-treas. Vayco Products, Inc.; dir. Dunlap & Assos. Chmn. motivation com., vice chmn. Advt. Research Found., 1956, chmn., 1957-58, now dir. Fellow Am. Psychol. Assn., A.A.A.S., N.J. Acad. Scis.; mem. Am. Mktg. Assn., Market Research Council N.Y. (v.p. 1958, pres. 1959-60), Nat. Soc. Crippled Children and Adults (trustee 1957-62), Assn. Applied Psychology (past pres.), N.Y. Psychol. Assn. (past pres.), Copy Research Council (exec. com.), Sigma Xi. Republican. Conglist. Club: Union League (N.Y.C.). Contbr. articles profl. jours. Address: Palm Beach Shores, Fla. Died July 21, 1976; interred at Rosemont, N.J.

WUNSCH, WILLIAM FREDERIC, clergyman; b. Detroit, Mich., May 11, 1882; s. Henry and Elizabeth (Maul)) W.; LL.B., U. of Mich., 1906, A.B., 1908; grad. New Church Theol. Sch., Cambridge, Mass., 1909; m. Mary M. Gunn, Sept. 1, 1909; children—Gretchen, Henry, Barbara, Catherine (Mrs. Chas. L. Tuttle), Hilda (Mrs. George E. Worden). Ordained New Church (Swedenborgian) ministry, 1909; pastor Bath, Me., 1909-12, Roxbury, Mass., 1912-16; instr. New Ch. Theol. Sch., 1909-10 and 1911-14, prof. theology, 1914-30, prof. Bible lit. and langs., 1930-35, also principal, 1921-29; pastor Waltham, Mass., 1919-35; summer preacher at Little Harbor Chapel, Portsmouth, N.H., since 1927; pastor Ch. of the Neighbor, Brooklyn Heights, N.Y. City, 1935-43, Ch. of the Holy City, Washington, since 1943; chmn. bd. mgrs. New-Church Theol. Sch., 1945-50; has been a lecturer in Theology, same sch., since 1950. Author: An Outline of New-Church Teaching; The World within the Bible, 1929; A Practical Philosophy of Life, 1937. Editor New Church Review, 1917-34, The New Christianity, 1935-43, 47. Collaborator, The Gist of Swedenborg. Compiler; Swedenborg on Marriage, 1929; Swedenborg on the Bible; Marriage, Ideals and Realization, 1929. Translator: "Charity" (Swedenborg), 1931; Marital Love (Swedenborg), 1938. Editor: The Stairway of Life (Julian Kennedy Smyth, posthumous), 1939. Home: Washington. *

WURLITZER, FARNY R., pres. The Rudolph Wurlitzer Co.; b. Cincinnati, O., Dec. 7, 1883; s. Rudolph and Leonie (Farny) W. Vice-pres. and dir. The Rudolph Wurlitzer Co. prior to 1933, then pres. and chmn. exec. com., now chmn. bd., co. now named The Wurlitzer Co. Address: North Tonawanda, N.Y. *

WYCKOFF, HUBERT, lawyer; b. San Francisco, July 2, 1901; s. Hubert Coke and Anabel (McDonnell) W.; A.B., U. Calif., 1923; student Harvard Law Sch., 1923-25, Hastings Coll. Law, 1925-26; m. Florence Walton Richardson, Sept. 16, 1931. Admitted to Calif. bar, 1926; mem. firm Wyckoff, Gardner & Parker, Watsonville, Calif., 1926-28; asst. U.S. atty. No. Dist. Calif., 1928-31; pvt. practice San Francisco, 1932-42; asst. dep. adminstr. Maritime Labor Relations War Shipping Adminstrn., Washington, 1942-45; mem. firm Wyckoff, Parker, Boyle & Pope, Watsonville, 1946-79; arbitrator 1939-42, 46-79. Mem. Pajaro Valley Hist. Assn. (pres. 1963—), Delta Upsilon, Winged Helmet Soc., Big C Soc., Order Golden Bear. Clubs: Old Capital (Monterey, Calif.); University, Family (San Francisco); Pajaro Valley Domino (pres.) (Watsonville). Author arbitration awards in maritime, railroad, aviation, hotel, mfg., race track, newspaper, service industry and pub. employment areas. Home: Watsonville, Calif. Died Mar. 30, 1979; buried Pioneer Cemetery, Watsonville, Calif.

WYETH, OLA M., librarian; b. Newman, Ill., Nov. 25, 1882; d. George E. and Ina M. (Bills) Wyeth; graduate high school, Charleston, Illinois, 1900; A.B., Cornell University, 1904; B.L.S., University of Illinois Library School, 1906. Cataloger Northwestern University, 1906-08; librarian Modern Language Seminar, University of Illinois, 1910-18; war service with A.L.A., various camps until 1920; librarian A.L.A. Library for Am. Forces, Coblenz, Germany, 1920-21; asst. library supervisor, library unit, U.S.P.H.S. and Vets. Bur., 1921-23; acting supervisor library service, U.S. Vets. Bur., 1923-24; librarian Rockford (Ill.) Coll., Jan.-June 1924; librarian Pub. Library, Savannah, Georgia, 1924-51. Mem. A.L.A., Ga. Library Assn. (pres. 1925), South Eastern Library Assn. (pres. 1940-46, Ga. Hist. Soc. (dir.), Am. Assn. Univ. Women, Poetry Soc. Ga. (pres. 1936-37); Savannah Pan Hellenic Assn., Alpha Chi Omega. Home: Savannah, Ga. *

WYLAND, MARY JANE, univ. trustee; b. Shelby County, Ia., Dec. 19, 1883; d. Thomas Jefferson and Clara (Osborn) Wyland; Ph.B., Grinnell Coll., 1905; M.S., Columbia, 1944; student U. Wis., 1940, U. Chgo., 1938; D.D. (hon.), Juniata Coll., 1952. High sch. tchr., Brooklyn, Ia., 1905-08, Aberdeen, S.D., 1908-13; high sch. tchr., Harlan, Ia., 1913-15, supt. schs., 1915-26; mem. faculty Pa. State U., 1927-52, prof. edn., head dept. secondary edn., dir. summer workshop, 1935-52, mem. bd. trustees, 1957—. Mem. evaluating com. Pa. U., exec. dir. Coll. Christian Assn., 1952-53. Mem. Am. Assn. U. Women, Bus. and Profl. Womens Club, League Women Voters, Alumni Assn. Grinnell Coll., Pi Lambda Theta. Democrat. Club: Altrusa. Address: State College, Pa. *

WYLIE, CHARLES CLAYTON (WI'LÊ), astronomer; b. Idana, Kan., June 18, 1886; s. Oliver Moses and Mary Ida (Ritchie) W.; A.B., Park Coll., Parkville, Mo., 1908; A.M., U. of Mo., 1912; Ph.D., U. of Ill., 1922; m. Lirl Bunn, Dec. 25, 1918; children—Margaret Jean, Mary Louise, Elinor Martha, Miriam Jane. Prof. mathematics, Buena Vista Coll., Storm Lake, Ia., 1909-11; grad. asst. in astronomy, U. of Mo., 1911-13; at U.S. Naval Obs., 1913-19; with Ordnance Dept., U.S. Army, 1919-26; asst. in astronomy, U. of Ill. 1920-22, associate, 1922-25; asst. prof. astronomy, State U. of Ia., 1925-30, asso. prof., 1930-39, prof. since 1939. Mem. U.S. Naval Observatory Eclipse Expedition, 1918. Ednl. consultant Army Air Corps, 1942-43. Fellow Meteoritical Soc. (v.p., 1933-41; dir. meteor sect.), Ia. Acad. Scis., A.A.A.S. (sec. for astronomy, 1941-49); mem. Am. Astron. Soc., Math. Assn. America, Sigma Xi. Presbyterian. Mason. Author: Our Starland, 1938; Astronomy, Maps, and Weather, 1942; (with J. R. Naidem) Schiaparelli's Shooting Stars, 1943. Contbr. research articles, especially on meteors and meteorities. Announced the Paragould Meteorite, largest unbroken stone meteorite. Home: Iowa City, Ia. *

WYLIE, CRAIG, publisher; b. Washington, Mar. 11, 1908; s. Horace and Katharine V. (Hopkins) W.; A.B., Harvard, 1930; m. Angela Fowler, July 2, 1938; children—Moira Angela, Katharine Wylie Payne, Pamela Margaret, Andrew, Jennifer Ludlow. Master, St. Paul's Sch., Concord, N.H., 1930-42; field sec. Mass. Com. for World Fedn., Boston, 1946; editor Houghton Mifflin Co., Boston, 1946-58, mng. editor, 1958-64, exec. editor, 1964-67, editor-in-chief, 1967-69, v.p., dir. trade div., 1969-73. Chmn. disaster com. ARC, Concord, N.H., 1937-38. Mem. N.H. Ho. of Reps., 1935-39; chmn. Young Republicans, Concord, 1937-38. Trustee Boston Athenaeum. Served to lt. comdr. USNR, 1942-46. Mem. N.H., Mass. hist. socs. Episcopalian (vestryman, mem. ch. corp.). Clubs: Tavern, Badminton and Tennis, Odd Volumes (Boston); Century (N.Y.C.). Home: Cambridge, Mass. Died Dec. 6, 1976; interred Mt. Auburn Cemetery.

WYNIA, JESS EDWARD, motel exec.; b. St. Mary's, Idaho, Apr. 7, 1910; s. Daniel P. and Belle M. (Bottger) W.; B.A., Eastern Wash. State Coll., 1934; m. Lura Caudill, May 6, 1933; children—Tom, Lanny, Lynda, Terry. Ednl. adminstr., 1933-44; employed in retail food business, 1944-72; with Magic Key Inns of Am., Inc., Pasco, Wash., 1959-77, pres. Mem. Athletic Round Table. Clubs: Meadow Springs Country, Elks, Eagles. Office: Pasco, Wash. Died Nov. 19, 1977; buried Pasco.

WYNN, SPROESSER, lawyer; b. Dallas, Dec. 18, 1913; s. William Clement and Amy (Hirschfeld) W.; A.B., Tex. Christian U., 1933; LL.B., U. Tex., 1935; m. Mildred Patton, Apr. 11, 1936; children—Carol (Mrs. C. Harold Brown), Betty (Mrs. Larry Macy). Admitted to Tex. bar, 1935, then practiced in Ft. Worth; partner Wynn, Brown, Mack, Renfro & Thompson. Former dir. Council Adminstrn. Justice. Dir. 1st Nat. Bank Ft. Worth, State Automobile & Casualty Underwriters, Past pres. Tex. Social Welfare Assn.; pres. Duncan Found., Moslah Benefit Fund; past pres. Conf. S.W. Found. Republican nominee atty. gen. Tex., 1968; past chmn. Tower Senate Club Tex.; chmn. exec. com. S.W. Law Enforcement Inst. Past bd. dirs. Child Welfare League Am.; exec. com. Edna Gladney Home; sec. Tarrant County Hosp. Authority; trustee Tex. Scottish Rite Hosp.; mem. HEW panel on uniform laws on adoption of children. Fellow Tex. Bar Found.; mem. State Bar Tex. (past chmn. family law sect.), Am. Bar Assn. (chmn. adoption com.), Am. Social Health Assn. (dir.), Nat. Council Social Welfare (dir.), Am. Judicature Soc., Soc. Hosp. Attys. (charter), Masonic Temple Assn. (v.p.), Kappa Sigma. Mason (33 deg., Shriner). Home: Fort Worth, Tex. Died Jan. 28, 1980.

WYSZYNSKI, STEFAN, primate of Poland; b. Zuzela, nr. Nur, Poland, Aug. 3, 1901; s. Stanislaw and Julianna (Karp) W.; student schs. in Warsaw, Lomza and Wloclawek; student Spiritual Sem., Wloclawek, 1920-24, Lublin Cath. U., 1925-29. Ordained priest, 1924, canon, 1945; lectr. social economy, sociology, canonical law, Higher Spiritual Sem., Wloclawek, 1930-31; editor Ateneum Kaplanskie, 1932-39; resident Archdiocese of Warsaw, 1939-40, region of Lublin, 1940-42; staff Inst. for Blind, Laski, nr. Warsaw, 1943-45; founder, chief editor Lad Bozy. Cath. weekly, 1945; opened Spiritual Sem., Wloclawek, 1945;

nominated Bishop of Lublin, 1946; transferred to Capital of Primates of Poland in Gniezno and Capital of Archbishops in Warsaw, 1948; created cardinal, 1952; arrested and detained, 1953-56. Author: Principal Types of Catholic Action Outside Poland; Work of Cardinal Ferrari; Position of Spiritual Guidance Toward Present Social Movements, By the Light of the Millennium; The Great Novena of the Millennium; Work: The Wedding in Cana; The Sanctification of the Profession's Work; Mother of the Church; Un éveque au service du peuple de Dieu; The Deeds of Faith; A Strong Man Armed; Per la libertá la pace degli Uomini; The Letters to my Priests, others. Address: Warsaw, Poland. Died May 28, 1981.

XANDER, ENOS CLYDE (ZAN'DER), clergyman, educator; b. Lawrenceville, O., Mar. 21, 1885; s. Enos William and Anna Catharine (Ballentine) X.; A.B., Wittenberg Coll., 1906, D.D., 1927; B.D., Hamma Div. Sch., Springfield, 1912; grad. work Ohio State U.; m. Flossie Neff Turner. Sept. 12, 1912; children—Gordon William, Clyde Armstrong. Prin. German Twp. High Sch., 1907-09; ordained Luth. ministry, 1912; pastor North Riverdale Ch., Dayton, O., 1912-17, Indianola Ch., Columbus, Oh., 1917-25, also university pastor for Luth. students Ohio State U.; dean Midland Coll., Fremont, Neb., 1925-26; pres. Thiel Coll., Greenville, Pa., 1926-33; pastor First Luth. Ch., Springfield, O., 1933-42; missionary supt., Lutheran Ch., since 1942. Home: Columbus, O. *

YABLOKOFF, HERMAN, actor, composer, playwright, dir., producer; b. Grodno, Poland, 1903; come to U.S., 1924; m. Bella Mysell; children—Jack, Anita Yablokoff Willens. Active all phases of Yiddish theater, N.Y.C.; wrote and acted in musical prodns. in 1930's and 40's, including: Der Payatz, The King of Song, Godela Dem Bakers, Mein Veise Blum, Der Dishwasher, My Son and I; toured refugee camps in Germany, Austria, Italy, 1947, giving 104 performances in 94 camps; chmn. Yiddish Nat. Theater, N.Y.C. Recipient U.S. Army Cert of Merit for performances in refugee camps. Mem. Hebrew Actors Union (pres. numerous terms 1945-81), Yiddish Theatrical Alliance (pres.). Author: Around the World with Yiddish Theater (Zvi Kesel prize for Yiddish lit. 1970). Home: Brooklyn, N.Y. Died Apr. 3, 1981.

YANG, YOU CHAN, diplomat; b. Pusan, Korea; s. Dai Bong and Mary (Kim) Y.; grad. Kaahumanu Sch., Honolulu, T.H., 1912, McKinley H.S., 1916; student U. Hawaii, 1916-17; B.S., Boston U., 1920, B.Ch., 1921, M.D., 1922; m. Rita J. Waldron, June 21, 1924 (died 1936); 1 dau., Marguerite Joy (Mrs. Paul Dibell); m. 2d, Pauline Tai, Feb. 5, 1938; children—Sheila, Channing. Intern, N.Y. Lying-In Hosp., N.Y. Post Grad. Hosp., N.Y. City, 1929-30; active practice as physician and surgeon, Honolulu, 1923-51; Korean ambassador to U.S. 1951-60. Active in orgn. League of Friends of Korea, U.S., 1918-22, also Korean independence movement; leader Korean Community in Hawaii following departure of Dr. Syngman Rhee for U.S. mainland, 1939-51. Trustee and bd. mem. Korean Christian Inst.; trustee Korean Christian Student Movement of Hawaii (pres.). Mem. adv. bd. Dong Ji Hoi. Fellow A.M.A., Territorial and Honolulu Co. med. socs.; mem. Acad. Gen. Practitioners, Surg. Soc., Gyn. and Obs. Soc., Acad. Sci., Honolulu, Pan-Pacific Union (v.p.). Hon. chmn. American-Korean Found. Mem. Korean Christian Ch. (chmn.). Hon. mem. Barnum Tent Circus Saints & Sinners. Club: Metropolitan. Address: Washington, D.C. Died Oct. 19, 1975.

YARBROUGH, WILLIAM HENRY (YÄR'BRÔ), educator; b. Athens, Ala., May 1, 1885; s. James Archie and Martha Y.; student U. of Tex., 1912-14; B.S., Peabody Coll. for Teachers, Nashville, Tenn., 1918, M.A., 1923, Ph.D., 1932; m. Margaret Hite Allen, June 16, 1943; 1 dau., Elaine. Taught at Hagansport, Tex., 1908-10, Sulphur Bluff, 1910-12; superintendent schs., Rule, Tex., 1914-18; teacher at Fort Worth High Sch., 1918-22; prin. Peabody Coll. for Teachers Demonstration Sch., 1923-37; prin. West End High Sch. Mem. N.E.A. Author: History of United States for Senior High School, History of United States for Junior High School. Home: Nashville, Tenn. *

YARBROUGH, WILLIAM THOMAS (TOM), journalist; b. Chickasha, Okla., May 22, 1910; s. William Ambrus and Maude (Morton) Y.; student U. Okla., 1932; m. Julia Martha Fisher, Oct. 19, 1941; children—John, Julie, Mary. Reporter, Oklahoma City Times, 1932-35; reporter-editor A.P., 1935-50; adminstrv. asst. to U.S. Senator Hennings, 1951; spl. asst. to chmn. Nat. Security Resources Bd., 1951-52; reporter St. Louis Post-Dispatch, from 1953; book editor, 1965-69. Asst. dir. publicity Democratic Nat. Com., 1952-53. Mem. Phi Beta Kappa (hon.), Sigma Chi. Home: Webster Groves, Mo. Died Nov. 13, 1975.

YARDLEY, RICHARD QUINCY, cartoonist; b. Balt., Mar. 11, 1903; s. Richard Turner and Alice (Hall) Y.; student Md. Inst.; m. Margaret Bruening, Oct. 4, 1927; 1 dau., Susan. With news dept. The Evening Sun, 1923-34; news and polit. cartoonist The Morning Sun, 1934-49, editorial cartoonist, 1949-66; editorial cartoonist Balt. Sun, 1966-72; ret., 1972; author, artist, syndicated comic panel, Our Ancestors by Quincy. Mem. Nat. Cartoonists Soc., Nat. Editorial Cartoonists Soc., Navy League (historian Md. chpt.). Clubs: Nat. Press (Washington); University (Balt.). Contbr. cartoons to New Yorker, Reporter mags. Home: Baltimore, Md. Died Nov. 24, 1979; buried Green Mount Cemetery, Baltimore, Md.

YARNALL, CHARLTON, banker; b. Phila., Pa., Aug. 1, 1864; s. Ellis and Margaret (Harrison) Y.; student Harverford Coll., 1880-82; m. Anna Brinton Coxe, May 23, 1889; children—Alexander Coxe, Mrs. Margaret Newbold, Mrs. Sophia Jacobs, Mrs. Agnes LePage. Mem. Ellis, Yarnall & Son, mchts., Phila., 1885-1935; dir. Phila. Nat. Bank since 1910; dir. Buffalo & Susquehanna R.R. Corp.; dir. and chmn. Contributionship for Insurance of Houses from Loss by Fire; mgr. Philadelphia Saving Fund Soc.; dir. The Church Life Ins. Corp. The Church Properties Fire Insurance Corp. Trustee University of Pa., Ch. Pension Fund; trustee, v.p. Devon Horse Show and Country Fair Assn. Vice chairman Hospitals and Sanitation, Council National Defense, World War I. Member English-Speaking Union (vice-president and director). Republican, Episcopalian (president Corporation for Relief of Widows and Children of Clergymen in Pa.). Clubs: Philadelphia, Radnor Hunt; Everglades (v.p., dir.), Bath and Tennis, Gulf Stream (Palm Beach). Home: Devon, Pa. *

YATER, WALLACE MASON, diagnostician; b. Canton, N.Y., Sept. 26, 1895; s. Charles Baldwin and Stella Frances (Wallace) Y.; A.B., George Washington U., 1917; M.D., Georgetown U., 1921; M.S. in medicine, U. Minn., 1929; m. Ruth Millicent Becker, Dec. 22, 1932; children—Millicent Wallace, Stephanie Mason, Wallace Mason, Jr., Camille Frances. Intern, Garfield Meml. Hosp., 1921, Georgetown U. Hosp., 1922; pvt. practice at Washington, 1922-26; fellow in medicine Mayo Clinic, Rochester, 1926-29; asso. prof. medicine, Georgetown U., 1929-31, prof. medicine and chmn. dept., 1930-46; civilian cons. Surg. Gen. Army, WWII; formerly physician in chief Georgetown U. Hosp. and Gallinger Municipal Hosp.; dir. emeritus Yater Clinic, Washington. Cons. Clin. Center, NIH; past mem. nat. adv. health council USPHS; past mem. cardiovascular com. div. med. scis. NRC. Served with S.A.T.C., U.S. Army, World War I. Fellow A.C.P. (sec.-gen.); mem. A.M.A., Am. Assn. Med. Clinics (past pres.), Med. Soc. of D.C. (past pres.), Am. Soc. Clin. Investigation, Am., Washington heart assns., Washington Acad. Medicine (past pres.), So. Med. Assn., Am. Soc. Internal Medicine (past trustee), Sigma Xi. Author: Symptom Diagnosis, 1960; The Fundamentals of Internal Medicine, 1953; also numerous articles on medicine. Editor: Medical Annals of the District of Columbia; formerly asso. editor Circulation. Home: Washington, D.C. Died May 10, 1976.

YATES, CHARLES MOULDING, naval officer; b. Palmyra, Wis., Oct. 21, 1884; grad. U.S. Naval Acad., 1908. Commd. ensign, U.S. Navy, 1910, and advanced through the grades to commodore, 1943; served in U.S. ships, New Orleans, Barry, Mohican, Shark (comd.), U.S.S. F-2, 1910-15; navigator, U.S.S. Michigan, operating with Atlantic Fleet, 1918; comd. U.S.S. Arctic, 1934-36, U.S.S. San Francisco, 1939-41; on duty Office of Chief of Naval Operations, with additional duty, G.H.Q., U.S. Army Field Forces, Army War Coll., Washington, D.C., 1941-42; mem. staff of comdr. in chief U.S. Fleet (continuing additional duty), 1942; prof. naval science and tactics, Naval Res. Officers Training Corps Unit, Brown Univ., 1942-43; now comdt. Naval Operating Base, Oran, Algeria. Decorated Legion of Merit with gold star, Victory Medal with Atlantic Fleet clasp, Am. Defense Service Medal with fleet clasp, European-African-Middle Eastern Campaign Medal, Home: Vallejo, Calif. *

YATES, GERARD FRANCIS, educator; b. Staten Island, N.Y., Apr. 1, 1907; s. William Franklyn and Rose (Jennings) Y.; A.B., St. Andrew-on-Hudson and Woodstock Coll. 1929; A.M., Woodstock Coll., 1930, S.T.L., 1937; spl. student London Sch. Econs., 1938-39; A.M., Yale, 1943, Ph.D., 1947. Entered Soc. of Jesus, 1923, ordained priest, 1936; instr. classics Georgetown U., 1930-33, asst. prof. polit. sci., 1942-47, asso. prof., chmn. dept., 1947-49, prof. govt., 1949-72, professorial lectr., 1972-75, dean grad. sch., 1949-54, dean grad. sch. emeritus, 1954-79, dir. jr. year abroad program, 1954-71, chmn. univ. com. fgn. students, fgn. student adviser, 1960-71, dir. internat. student programs, 1965-71; vis. prof. U. Fribourg, Switzerland, summer 1952, 55-56, 57-58; scholar in residence, vis. prof. internat. studies Southwestern at Memphis, 1975-77; occasional cons. USAF; lectr. Air War Coll. Decorated gold cross Pro Piis Meritis, Sovereign Order Malta, also magistral chaplain, 1968; recipient Vicennial medal, 1959, Georgetown U., 175th Anniversary medal honor, 1964. Fellow Am. Geog. Soc.; mem. Am. Polit. Sci. Assn., Am. Soc. Internat. Law, Nat. Assn. Fgn. Students Advisers (hon. life; past dir. and regional chmn.), Georgetown U. Alumni Assn. (hon. life; Patrick Healy award 1970, spl. citation of merit 1972), Gold Key Soc., Chimes, Newcomen Soc. N. Am., English Speaking Union, Pi Sigma Alpha. Editor: Papal Thought on the State. Home: Washington, D.C. Died Sept. 13, 1979.

YATES, PETER BERTRAM, music educator; b. Toronto, Ont., Can., Nov. 30, 1909 (parents Am. citizens); s. Peter B. and Margery (Cochrane) Y.; B.A., Princeton, 1931; m. Frances Mullen, Nov. 26, 1932; children—Peter Barheidt, George E. Cochrane, John Stewart (dec.). With Calif. Dept. Employment, 1937-62; author, lectr., from 1962; became prof. music, chmn. dept. State U. Coll. N.Y. at Buffalo, 1968; critic music and other arts Arts and Architecture, 1940-67. Co-founder, coordinator Eves. on the Roof chamber concerts, Los Angeles, 1939-54; co-founder Poetry Los Angeles, 1956; mem. Salzburg Seminar Am. Studies, 1964; vol. broadcaster Pacifica Found., Sta. KPFK-FM. Los Angeles, 1959-67. Recipient Ford Found. award, 1964. Bd. dirs. So. Calif. Chamber Music Soc., from 1954. Author: A Smaller Poem Book, 1946; An Amateur at the Keyboard, 1964; Twentieth Century Music, 1967; (poetry) The Garden Prospect, 1981. Co-editor: Poetry Los Angeles, 1958; contbg. editor Arts in Socity. Home: Buffalo, N.Y. Died Feb. 25, 1976.

YAWKEY, THOMAS A., sports exec., conservationist; b. Detroit, Feb. 21, 1903; s. Thomas J. and Augusta L. (Yawkey) Austin; foster parents: William H. and Margaret (Draper) Yawkey; grad. Irving Sch., Tarrytown, N.Y., 1920; B.S., Yale, 1925; m. Elise Sparrow, June 18, 1925; m. 2d, Jean R. Hollander, Dec. 22, 1944. Directs the mgmt. of mines, mineral interests, timber lands, in U.S. and Can.; owner, pres. Boston Red Sox. Dir., v.p. Am. League Profl. Baseball Clubs, alternate mem. Maj. Leagues Exec. Council. Chmn. bd., mem. exec. com. Childrens Cancer Research Found. (Jimmy Fund), Boston. Mem. Phi Gamma Delta. Conglist. Clubs: Athletic, Yale (N.Y.C). Owner of 40,000—acre game preserve in coastal South Carolina where extensive devel. work is being carried on to provide feeding and resting grounds for migratory birds and other wild life; active in other movements for preservation and improvement of wild life, including cooperation with Fish and Wildlife Service, Ducks Unlimited, and Jack Miner Migratory Bird Found., Inc. Home: New York, N.Y. Died July 10, 1976.

YEAGER, W(ILLARD) HAYES, professor of speech; b. Lewistown, O., July 6, 1897; s. Lovinus Reed and Addie Caroline (Baker) Y.; A.B., Ohio State U., 1919, A.M., 1926; studied Columbia U., 1919-20, U. of Michigan, summer 1923, U. of Ill., 1927-28; LL.D., Morris Harvey College, 1956; married Clara Elizabeth Pritchard, Feb. 3, 1923; children—Hayes Pritchard, James Lee. Teacher high sch., Mingo Junction, O., 1922, Parkersburg, W.Va., 1922-23; instr. in English, Ohio State U., 1923-27; asso. in English, U. of Ill., 1927-29; Chauncey M. Depew prof. pub. speaking and exec. officer dept. of speech, George Washington U., 1929-45; prof. of speech and chmn. dept., Ohio State U., from 1945; Georgetown Univ. Summer Sch., 1942; chmn. exec. com. and nat. dir. Nat. Discussion Contest on Inter-Am. Affairs, sponsored by Office Coordinator of Inter-Am. Affairs, under auspices Am. Council on Edn., 1942-44; special consultant United States Office of Education, 1943; lectr. USAF, 1948-50, cons., 1952-56. Served in U.S. Navy, June-Dec. 1918. Mem. Speech Assn. of Am. (1st v.p., 1936, pres., 1941, exec. sec., 1944, exec. vice pres., 1945-48), Eastern Public Speaking Conf. (vice pres., 1937-39, pres., 1939-41), Am. Assn. U. Profs., Soc. Advancement Edn., del. Am. Council on Edn., 1944-48; mem. Delta Theta Phi, Phi Delta Gamma, Pi Gamma Mu, Omicron Delta Kappa, Acacia; hon. mem. Nat. Collegiate Players, Delta Sigma Rho. Presbyn. Club: Faculty. Co-author: (with William Phillips Sandford) Successful Speaking, 1927; Principles of Effective Speaking, 1928, rev. edit. 1930, 34, 42, 50, 63; Business and Profl. Speaking, 1929; Problems in Business and Professional Speaking, 1931; Problems for Debate Practice, 1933; Practical Business Speaking, 1937, revised edit., 1952; Effective Business Speech, 1960. Author: Chauncey Mitchell Depew, the Orator, 1934; Effective Speaking for Every Occasion, 1940, revised edition, 1951. Co-author: (with Kendall B. Taft, John Francis McDermott and Dana O. Jenson) English Communication, A Handbook of Writing and Speaking, 1943. Compiler: (with W. P. Sandford) Business Speeches by Business Men, 1930. Member editorial board and author of study of Wendell Phillips in History and Criticism of American Public Address, 1943. Contbr. World Book Ency. Lectr. Home: Columbus, Ohio. Died 1979.

YEATON, CHESTER HENRY, coll. prof.; born Richmond, Me., Nov. 1, 1886; s. Frank Marshall and Zelinda Ann (Litch) Y.; A.B., Bowdoin, 1908; A.M., Harvard, 1909, student (Thayer scholar), 1909-10; fellow, U. of Chicago, 1913-15, Ph.D., 1915; student Yerkes Obs., summer 1914; sr. participant. Advanced Instrn. and Research in Mechanics, Brown U., 1942-43; m. Ethel May Kitch, June 21, 1923 (dec. May 13, 1941); m. 2d Marie Mathilda Johnson, Oct. 27, 1943. Instr. engring. math., Union Coll., 1910-11; instr. math., Northwestern U., 1911-13 and 1915-16, asst. prof. math., 1916-17; instr. math., U. of Minn., 1919; prof. math. and head of dept., Coll. of Elec. Engring. of Milwaukee, 1919-21; asst. prof. math., Oberlin Coll., 1921-25, asso. prof. math., 1925-27, prof. math. since

1927. Served with Signal Corps and later as instr. math., F. A.C.O.T.S., U.S. Army, 1917-18. Fellow A.A.S.; mem. Am. Math. Soc., Math. Assn. of Am., Am. Assn. U. Profs., Phi Beta Kappa, Sigma Xi, Gamma Alpha. Conglist. Club: Rotary. Contbr. articles to math. jours. Home: Oberlin, O. *

YEOMAN, RAY CYRUS, civil engr.; b. Rensselaer, Ind., July 27, 1883; s. Andrew Knox and Amy Elizabeth (Brown) Y.; B.S. in C.E., Purdue U., 1907, C.E., 1909; m. Olive Gertrude Smith, of Knox, Ind., Dec. 2, 1911. Asst. instr. engring., 1907-9, prof., 1909-17, dean of engring., 1911-17, Valparaiso U.; asso. prof. highway engring., Purdue U., since Dec. 1, 1917. Insp. engr. Portland Cement Assn.; pres. University Cabinet Works; consulting practice, drainage and highways. Mem. Am. Assn. Engrs. (dir.), Western Soc. Engrs., Ind. Soc. Engrs. Presbyn. Home: West Lafayette, Ind.*

YEZIERSKA, ANZIA (YE-ZĚR'SKA), writer; b. Russia, 1885; d. Bernard and Pearl Yezierska; self ed.; unmarried. Came to U.S., 1901, naturalized, 1912; worked in factories, sweat shops and as cook in pvt. families; began writing short stories of East Side life (New York), 1918; "The Fat of the Land" pronounced by Edward J. O'Brien as the best short story of 1919. Author: Hungry Hearts, 1920 (motion picture, 1922); Salome of the Tenements, 1922; Children of Loneliness, 1923; Bread Givers, 1925; Arrogant Beggar, 1927; All I Could Never Be, 1932; Red Ribbon on a White Horse, 1951. Contbr. to mags. Home: N.Y.C. *

YLVISAKER, NILS MARTIN (IL'VI-SÄ-KER), ch. exec.; b. Sogndal, Norway, Mar. 23, 1882; s. Johannes (D.D.) and Kristi (Flugum) Y.; brought to U.S., 1882, naturalized, 1898; A.B., Luther College, 1902; C.T., Luther Theol. Sem., St. Paul, Minn., 1906; student U. of Minn. Grad. Sch., 1902-03, 1921-23, U. of Oslo, Norway, 1923-24; D.D., Augustana College Sioux Falls, S.D., 1934; Litt.D., Muhlenberg Coll. (Allentown, Pa.), 1945; m. Karine Elizabeth Magelssen, June 22, 1910; 1 son, Rolf Magelssen (Erik Rolf, present legal name). Ordained to ministry Lutheran Ch., July 22, 1906; pastor churches in Bottineau and Ward counties, N.D., Mohall, N.D., 1906-08, Christ and St. Stephen's Ch., St. Paul, Minn., 1908-10, Our Saviors Ch., Chicago, 1910-17; civilian chaplain, Camp Logan, Houston, Tex., 1917-19; exec. sec. Young Peoples Luth. League, 1919-41; chmn. Youth Commn., Lutheran World Fedn., 1939-46; pres. Chaplains Assn. of the Army and Navy of U.S., 1938-46; exec. dir. Service Commission, National Lutheran Council, 1941-47; mem. Joint Army and Navy Com. on Welfare and Recreation, 1943-45; dir. Am. Relief, French Zone, Germany, 1947-48; publicity dir., dept. edn., Evang. Luth. Ch., 1948-49. Pastor, College Lutheran Church, San Diego, Calif. Maj.-chaplain Reserves, U.S. Army since 1940. Received St. Olav's medal from King Haakon VII, of Norway, 1940. Fellow Am. Scandinavian Foundation to U. of Oslo, 1923-24. Mem. Am. Scandinavian Found., Norwegian Am. Hist. Soc. Republican. Club: Minneapolis Athletic. Author: The Glory Road, 1933; Faces Toward God, 1936; No Other Way, 1938; Service Prayer Book, 1940; Trumpets of God, 1945. Contbr. to religious jours. Home: San Diego, Calif. *

YLVISAKER, SIGURD CHRISTIAN, educator; b. Madison, Wis., June 15, 1884; s. Prof. Johannes (D.D.) and Kristi (Flugum) Y.; A.B., Luther Coll., Decorah, Ia., 1903; student U. of Minn., 1903-04; C.T., Luther Sem., St. Paul, Minn., 1907; Ph.D., U. of Leipzig, Germany, 1910; m. Norma M. Norem, Nov. 25, 1915; children—Elizabeth Norem (Mrs. Edw. E. Brush), John Richard, Paul Norman, Ruth Barbara, David Norem, Ordained to ministry Norwegian Luth. Ch., 1910; prof. Greek and Hebrew, Luther Coll., Decorah, 1911-19, Concordia Coll., St. Paul, 1919-23; pastor, Ch. of Our Savior, Madison, Wis., 1923-30; pres. Bethany Luth. Coll. and Theol. Sem., Mankato, Minn., 1930-50, now prof. Third v.p. Luth. Synod Conf., North America. Mem. Am. Oriental Soc., 1912-23. Author: Zur Babylonischen und Assyrischen Grammatik (Leipzig), 1912. Contbr. articles to religious ednl. jours. Chief editor, Grace for Grace, 1943. Home: Mankato, Minn.*

YOE, JOHN HOWE, chemist; b. Oxford, Ala., July 19, 1892; s. Alfred Moore and Tulliola May (Howe) Y.; student Birmingham Coll., 1908-10; B.S., Vanderbilt U., 1913, M.S., 1914; postgrad. U. Chgo., 1913; M.A., Princeton, 1917, Ph.D., 1923; m. Francoise Alexander Cheely, Aug. 18, 1919; children—Elizabeth Howe (Mrs. Richard W. Gordon), Francoise Cheely (Mrs. Charles F. Schneider), Jane Randolph Yoe Wood, Ann Everett (Mrs. Hinckley). Asst. chemistry Vanderbilt U., 1911-13, instr. biology, 1913-15; instr. George Peabody Coll. Tchrs., 1914, 15-17; asst. in chemistry Princeton, 1915-17; chem. engr. U.S. Bur. Mines Am. U. Expt. Sta., Washington, 1917-18; research chemist Pa. Trojan Powder Co., Allentown, 1919; mem. faculty U. Va., from 1919, asst. prof., then asso. prof., prof., 1919-63, prof. emeritus, 1963-75, chmn. dept., 1953-57; cons. in field. Sci. observer Atomic Bomb tests, Bikini, 1946; past mem. NRC. Served to 1st lt. U.S. Army, 1918-19. Recipient Research prize Va. Acad. Sci., 1928; Carnegie Corp. grantee, 1938; Jefferson award, 1940; Inter-acad. award, Jefferson gold Medal, 1944; Herty gold medal, 1943; Fisher award Am. Chem. Soc., 1957; named on Richmond (Va.) Times-Dispatch Honor Roll of 1943. Fellow A.A.A.S., Am. Inst. Chemists; mem Am. Chem. Soc. (editor bull. 1933-34; chpt. distinguished service award 1956), So. Assn. Sci. and Industry, Va. Acad. Sci., Am. Assn. U. Profs., Union Internationale de Chimie (com. analytical reactions), Phi Beta Kappa, Sigma Xi, Kappa Sigma, Sigma Upsilon, Alpha Chi Sigma. Democrat. Clubs: Farmington Country, Farmington Hunt (Charlotteville, Va.). Author 10 books, from 1920. Contbr. articles to profl. jours. Home: Charlottesville, Va. Died Nov. 25, 1975.

YORK, ROBERT, chem. engr., educator; b. Memphis, Dec. 21, 1912; s. Robert and Rosa (Knapp) Y.; B.S., U. Tenn., 1933, M.S., 1934; Sc.D., Mass. Inst. Tech., 1938. Mem. faculty Carnegie Inst. Tech., 1938-47, asso. prof. chem. engring., 1946-47; chem. engr., asst. dir. devel. dept. Monsanto Chem. Co., St. Louis, 1944-47, 47-56; Socony Mobil prof. chem. engring. Cornell U., 1956-78; cons. Inst. Francais du Petrole, Paris, France, 1963; cons. to chem. and petroleum industries. Bd. dirs., mem. exec. com Cornell Research Found., 1961-72. Registered profl. engr., Pa., Mo. Mem. Am. Inst. Chem. Engrs., Am. Chem. Soc. Republican. Episcopalian. Home: Ithaca, N.Y. Died Jan. 7, 1978.

YOST, DON MERLIN LEE, inorganic chemist, educator; b. Tedrow (Spring Hill), Ohio, Oct. 30, 1893; s. William Nicholas and Viola Lorena (Lee) Y., B.S., U. Calif., 1923; Ph.D., Calif. Inst. Tech., Pasadena, 1926; student U. Utah, 1923-24, U. Uppsala, Sweden, 1928-29, U. Berlin, Germany, 1929; m. Susie Marguerite Sims, Mar. 7, 1917; children—Helen Marguerite, Max Cayley. DuPont fellow Calif. Inst. Tech., 1924-25, teaching fellow, 1925-26, research fellow, 1926-27, instr., 1927-29, asst. prof., 1929-35, asso. prof., 1935-42, prof. inorganic chemistry, 1942-64, prof. emeritus, 1964-77; prof. Summer Sch., U. Calif., 1946. Julius Stieglitz Memorial lectr. U. Chgo., 1946; Arthur D. Little vis. prof. chemistry Mass. Inst. Tech., 1953. Served as Q.M. 1st class, U.S. Navy, 1917-18; lt. comdr. (retired), U.S.N.R. from 1936. Section chmn. and div. mem. Nat. Defense Research Com., Washington, 1942-43; mem. adv. com. to the dir. research AEC, 1949-51. Awarded Presidential Certificate of Merit, 1948. Fellow International Edn. Bd., Sweden and Germany, 1928-39. Fellow Am. Phys. Soc., A.A.A.S.; mem. Am. Acad. Arts and Scis., Nat. Acad. Scis., A.A.A.S., Sigma Xi, Lambda Chi Alpha (Mu Zeta chpt. Berkeley, Calif.). Roman Catholic. Club: Athenaeum (Pasadena). Author: Systematic Inorganic Chemistry (with Horace Russell, Jr.), 1944; The Rare Earth Elements and Their Compounds (with Horace Russell Jr. and C.S. Garner), 1947, Contbr. sci. articles to various publs. Home: Pasadena, Calif. Died Mar. 27, 1977.

YOUNG, ARIBERT LEE, lawyer; b. Terre Haute, Ind., Sept. 8, 1923; s. John D. and Birdie J. (Peak) Y.; student Okla. A. and M. U., 1942-43, Purdue U., 1946-47; LL.B., Ind. U., 1950; m. Mabel A. Cook, Sept. 7, 1946; children—Richard Alan, Deborah Jean, Douglas Edward. Admitted to Ind. bar, 1950, Supreme Ct. U.S., 7th Circuit Ct. of Appeals, Supreme Ct. Ind.; practiced in Indpls., 1950-80; sr. partner Kightlinger, Young, Gray & DeTrude; pres. Meridian Parking, Inc. Served with AC, USNR, 1942-46. Mem. Am., Ind., Indpls. bar assns., Fedn. Ins. Counsel (sec.-treas., dir.), Lawyers-Pilots Bar Assn., Phi Delta Phi. Methodist. Club: Columbia (Indpls.). Contbr. articles to profl. jours. Home: Indianapolis, Ind. Died June 5, 1980; buried Crown Hill Cemetery, Indpls.

YOUNG, BENJAMIN FRANKLIN, pub. utility exec.; b. Sarahsville, Ohio, May 8, 1886; s. Benjamin Franklin and Susan (Rucker) Y.; B.A., Ohio Wesleyan U., 1913; M.A., Columbia, 1915; m. Gwendolyn Farmer, Aug. 8, 1918; children—Robert Farmer, Richard Benjamin. Personnel statistician N.Y. Telephone Co., 1919-27, chief accountant, 1927-33, gen. auditor, 1933-38, v.p. and gen. auditor, 1938-44, v.p., comptroller, from 1944; v.p., gen. auditor Empire City Subway Co., Ltd., 1938-44, v.p., comptroller, from 1944; dir. Empire City Subway Co.; asst. dir. O.D.M., Exec. Office of the Pres., Washington, 1953-54. Served as Capt., statis. br., U.S. Army, 1918-19. Mem. Am. Acad. Polit. and Social Sci., Acad. Polit. Sci., Am. Sociol. Soc., Ohio Soc., Am. Statis. Assn., Am. Econ. Assn., Phi Beta Kappa, Alpha Sigma Phi, Delta Sigma Rho. Methodist. Clubs: Hudson River Country (Yonkers); Bankers, Ohio Society, Columbia University (N.Y.C.). Author: Statistics As Applied in Business, 1927. Home: San Francisco, Calif. Died Mar. 3, 1980.

YOUNG, DONALD RAMSEY, sociologist; b. Macungie, Pa., July 5, 1898; s. Jonas Francis and Mary Catherine (Rems) Y.; A.B., Lafayette Coll., 1919; A.M., U. Pa., 1920, Ph.D., 1922; L.H.D., Rutgers U., 1955; LL.D., Princeton, 1962, U. Denver, 1969; Litt.D. (hon.), Lafayette Coll., 1967; m. Ada Wise, Dec. 19, 1925; children—May, Robert Kaiser. Asst. instr. sociology Wharton School, U. Pa., 1919-20, instr., 1920-23, asst. prof., 1923-35, prof. 1935-47, chmn., 1943-45; vis. instr.; lectr. Drexel Inst., Phila., 1925-29; research sec. Social Sci. Research Council, 1932-45, exec. dir. 1945-47, pres., 1948; cons. Joint Army and Navy Com. Welfare and Recreation, 1942-45; gen. dir. Russell Sage Found., 1948-55, pres., 1955-63; vis. prof. Rockefeller Inst., N.Y.C., 1964-69; exec. cons. João Pinheiro Found., Brazil, 1972. Bd. dirs. Am. Council Nationalities Service. Seaman, 2d class, USNRF, 1918. Fellow Am. Sociol Assn. (pres. 1955), Royal Soc. Arts, A.A.A.S.; mem. Am. Philos. Soc., Sociol. Research Assn. (pres. 1937). Am. Acad. Polit. and Social Sci. (dir.), Phi Beta Kappa, Sigma Alpha Epsilon. Mason. Clubs: Cosmos (Washington); Century (N.Y.C.). Author: Motion Pictures, A Study in Social Legisln., 1922, American Minority Peoples, 1932, Minority Peoples in the Depression, 1937; (with W.E. Moore) Trusteeship and the Management of Foundations, 1970. Editor: The American Negro (vol. 90 of Annals of Am. Acad. Polit. and Social Sci.), 1928; The Modern American Family (vol. 160 of Annals), 1932; Minority Peoples in a Nation at War (vol. 223 of Annals); asso. editor same Annals, 1930-45. Contbr. articles to profl. jours. Home: Macungie, Pa. Died Apr. 17, 1977.

YOUNG, GIG (BYRON BARR), actor; b. St. Cloud, Minn., Nov. 4, 1917; s. John Earl and Emma (Dingham) Barr; student Pasadena Playhouse, 1937. In stock with Phil Hayden Players; played in Gay Sisters, 1941, also Old Acquaintance, Air Force; motion pictures include Woman in White, Wake of the Red Witch, Tell It to the Judge, Come Fill the Cup (Acad. Award nomination), Torch Song, Slaughter Trail, Holiday for Sinners, You for Me, Girl Who Had Everything, City That Never Sleeps, Arena, Young at Heart, 1955, Desperate Hours, 1955, Teacher's Pet (Acad. Award nomination), 1958, Tunnel of Love, Ask Any Girl, Story on Page One, 1960, Five Miles to Midnight, 1963, One Touch of Mink, For Love or Money, 1963, Strange Bedfellows, 1965, Ticklish Affair, 1963, The Shuttered Room, 1968, Midnight Patient, They Shoot Horses, Don't They? (Acad. award best supporting actor, Fgn. Press Globe award), 1969, Lovers and Other Strangers, 1970, Neon Ceiling, 1971, Bring Me the Head of Alfredo Garcia, 1974, Hindenberg. 1975, A Black Ribbon for Deborah, 1975; The Killer Elite, 1975; Broadway plays include Oh Men Oh Women, 1953, Under the Yum-Yum Tree, 1960, Teahouse of the August Moon, 1956, There's a Girl in My Soup, 1967; road tours: Nobody Loves an Albatross, September Tide, Music Man, 1965, Odd Couple, 1967, On a Clear Day You Can See Forever, Harvey, 1971, 73, 74, 75; starred TV series The Rogues; TV shows include The Great Ice Ripoff, 1974, Benjamin Franklin, 1974, Gibbsville, 1975. Served with USNR, 1942-45. Named Star of Tomorrow, 1943; recipient 2 Laurel awards The Film Buyers; 2 Ageis awards. Home: Los Angeles, Calif. Died Oct. 19, 1978.

YOUNG, HARRY JAMES, communications exec.; b. Oskloosa, Iowa, Sept. 28, 1911; s. John E. and Retta (Smith) Y.; ed. pub. schs., Iowa; m. Ruth E. Hurlbut, Aug. 10, 1938; children—Linda J. (Mrs. Robert Lala), Sandra L. (Mrs. Louis Baranello), Nancy J. (Mrs. Thomas C. C. Humick). Various Midwest field positions Western Union Telegraph Co., 1928-56, dist. mgr., Mpls., 1957-58, div. mgr. N.Y.C. and Eastern div., 1959-61, asst. treas., 1962-65, treas., 1965-71; treas. Western Union Corp., 1971-73, v.p., 1973-75; ret., 1975. Mem. Reformed Ch. Mason, Elk. Club: Bankers (N.Y.C.). Home: Oradell, N.J. Died Jan. 30, 1977; interred at Oskaloosa, Iowa.

YOUNG, IRVIN FREDERICK, educator; b. North Canton, Ohio, Dec. 18, 1900; s. Charles Henry and Pauline Juliana (Bremkamp) Y.; B.Sc., Capital U., 1926, LL.D., 1955; M.S., Ohio State U., 1930; m. Martha Ellen McAbee, Aug. 16, 1927. Sci. tchr. St. John's Acad., Petersburg, W.Va., 1926-30; sci. tchr. Columbus (Ohio) Pub. Schs., 1930-37, elementary sch. prin., 1937-40, jr. high sch. prin., 1940-43, sr. high sch. prin., 1943-45, jr.-sr. high sch. prin., 1945-54, coordinator tchr. personnel, 1954-56, asst. supt. personnel, 1956-75. Chmn. bd. regents Capital U.; trustee Columbus Town Meeting. Mem. North Central Assn. Secondary Schs. (mem. state com. from 1949), Ohio Edn. Assn., N.E.A., Ohio, Nat. high sch. prin. assns., Ohio Supts. Assn., Nat. Assn. Sch. Supts., Phi Delta Kappa. Lutheran. Clubs: Lions, Masons (33d degree) (Columbus). Home: Columbus, Ohio. Died Feb. 22, 1980.

YOUNG, JAMES BARCLAY, foreign service officer; b. Washington, D.C., Feb. 14, 1884; s. Hon. James Rankin and Mary (Barclay) Y.; B.S., U. of Pa., 1907; studied U. of Berlin; m. Kathryn Clifton, Apr. 21, 1920. Appointed consular asst., 1909; v. consul, Milan, Italy, 1909-11; served in Berlin, Breslau, Milan and Genoa until 1915; apptd. consul, 1915; served at Nish, Belgrade, and at Am. Embassy, Vienna, 1915-16; had charge of German and Austro-Hungarian interests in all of Serbia, 1915; apptd. consul at Fiume, July 1916, and had charge of British, French, Italian, Serbian, Russian, Roumanian, Japanese, Belgian, Montenegrin and San Marino interests there; detailed to Consular Bur., Washington, D.C., July 1917; consul, Venice, Italy, 1920-29, Southampton, Eng., 1929-33; promoted consul gen., Apr. 1933, assigned to Lima, Peru, 1933, Bucharest, Rumania, 1935; 1st sec. Legation and consul gen., Vienna, (counselor of legation), 1936-37; consul gen., Lisbon, 1937-41; Dept. of State, Washington, D.C., since Jan. 1941. Club: Chevy Chase (Md.). *

YOUNG, JAMES WEBB, advertising consultant; born at Covington, Kentucky, January 20, 1886; son of James Davidson and Susan Anna (Webb) Y.; educated public schools of Covington, Kentucky; LL.D., University of New Mexico, 1957; married Elizabeth Johnson, Sept. 18, 1907; children—James Philip, Richard Johnson, Webb. Successively office boy, stenographer, advertising business through departments and becoming v.p. of J. Walter Thompson Co., of New York, also dir.; later prof. bus. history and advertising, University of Chicago; dir. U.S. Bureau of Foreign and Domestic Commerce, Sept. 1939-Feb. 1941. Dir. Santa Fe National Bank. Founder, director, also past chairman of The Advertising Council; hon. trustee Com. Econ. Development; Devel.; hon. mem. The Business Council; Past pres. Am. Assn. Advtg. Agencies. Awarded Gold Medal for distinguished career in advertising, 1945. Clubs: Tavern, Chicago (Chgo.); Cosmos (Wash.), Author: Advertising Agy. Compensation, 1934; A Technique for Producing Ideas, 1940; The Diary of an Ad Man, 1944; A Footnote to History, 1950; A Story Still Untold, 1951; Pills for the Angels, 1952; The Compleat Angler, 1953; Mirror For a Lady, 1954; Ego-Biography, 1955; His Girl and His Dinner, 1956; The Itch for Orders, 1957; Hometown Boy Makes Good, 1958; Full Corn in the Ear, 1959; How To Become An Advertising Man, 1962. Address: Santa Fe, N.M. *

YOUNG, JOHN HOWARD, educator, archaeologist; b. Springfield, Mass., July 5, 1913; s. Lloyd Emerson and Grace (Conner) Y.; A.B., Brown U., 1936; A.M., Harvard, 1937, Ph.D., Johns Hopkins, 1942; m. Suzanne Halstead, July 14, 1938 (dec. Jan. 1971); 1 dau., Grace Halstead. Norton fellow from Harvard to Am. Sch. Classical Studies, Athens, Greece, 1937-38, research fellow, 1940-41; excavator Curium excavations, Cyprus, 1938-40, 46-48; mem. faculty Johns Hopkins, from 1948, W. H. Collins Vickers Found. prof. archaeology, from 1956; archaeologist Nemrud Dagh excavations, Turkey, 1954; field dir. Halieis excavations, Greece, 1962; research asso. U. Pa. Mus., from 1962. Asst. dir. Greek War Relief Assn., 1942-46. Mem. Archaeol. Inst. Am., German Archeol. Inst. (corr.). Author: (with wife) Terracotta Figurines from Kourion in Cyprus, 1953. Asso. editor Am. Jour. Philology. Home: Baltimore, Md. Died Jan. 17, 1978.

YOUNG, JOHN M., business exec.; b. Enid, Okla., Mar. 24, 1901; s. John McLain and Mary Elizabeth (Wittemeyer) Y.; B.S., Va. Mil. Inst., 1922; M.B.A., Harvard, 1924; m. Marian Hillyer Wolff, Nov. 28, 1933; children—Marian Meredith, Jonathan McLain, Hillyer McDowell. Student worker, J.P. Morgan & Co., N.Y.C., 1924, advancing to position as mgr. bond dept., resigned 1935; an original organizer, dir. Morgan Stanley & Co., Inc., underwriting and wholesaling investment securities, 1935-41, mng. dir., 1970-72, adv. dir., 1975-78; partner in successor firm Morgan Stanley & Co., 1941-75; dir. 825 Fifth Ave. Corp., others. Served to comdr. USNR, active duty Navy Dept. Washington, 1942-45; assigned to Joint Army and Navy Munitions Bd., 1942-43; dep. chief Indsl. Readjustment Br., Office Procurement and Material, Navy Dept., Washington, 1943-45. Mem. Am. Australian Assn. and C. of C. (dir.), The Pilgrims. Episcopalian. Clubs: Bedford Golf and Tennis (Bedford Village, N.Y.); Links. Home: New York, N.Y. Died Dec. 11, 1978; buried St. Matthews Churchyard, Bedford, N.Y.

YOUNG, JOHN ORR, advertising consultant; born Leon, Iowa, June 25, 1886; s. Maj. John Lewis and Elizabeth (Woodbury) Y.; student, Lake Forest College, 1906-08; m. Ethel Prague Butler, July 4, 1914 (dec.); children—Helen (Mrs. Andrew Jackson), John O. Jr., Raymond Butler; m. 2d, Lorna Holland Byrne, March 7, 1944 (div. May 1959); m. 3d, Bernice Foreman, May 16, 1959. Advt. dept. Salt Lake Herald Tribune, 1908-09; advt. writer Lord & Thomas, Chgo., 1910-12; advt. mgr. Crisco div. Procter & Gamble, Cincinnati, 1913-14; partner Young, Henri & Hurst, advt. agency, Chicago, 1914-15, John Orr Young Co., N.Y. City, 1916-18, F. Wallis Armstrong Co., Phila., 1918-20; N. W. Ayer & Son, 1921-22; co-founder Young & Rubicam, Phila. and N.Y.C., 1923; ret., 1935; mfr. toilet goods and farmer, Va., Vt., and Conn., 1937-43; cons. W.P. B., Washington, D.C., 1943-44; cons. N.A.M., 1944-45; advt. cons. and pres. John Orr Young Assos., Inc., N.Y.C., from 1945. Member of Phi Pi Epsilon. Club: Union League. Author: Adventures in Advertising. Home: Southbury, Conn. Died May 1, 1976.

YOUNG, JOHN SHAW, govt. ofcl.; b. Springfield, Mass., Aug. 3, 1901; s. Phillip Franklin and Anne (Shaw) Y.; student Yale, 1925-26, Cornell U. Coll. of Law, 1924-25, U. of Cambridge, England, 1926-28, Royal U. of Upsala, Sweden, 1937; LL.D., St. Benedicts Coll., Atchison, Kan., 1933; D.Sc., St. Bonaventure's, 1938; D.Sc., Suffolk U., 1939; unmarried. Announcer and dir. Westinghouse Mfg. Co., announcer and commentator on Internat. affairs, National Broadcasting Co., 1928-36; news commentator, Columbia Broadcasting Co., 1936-37; dir. gen. radio, broadcasting and television, N.Y. World's Fair, 1937-40; made tour of world, 1940-41; NBC corr. with Far East Command British Army, in Singapore, Java, Burma, India, late in 1941; lecturer on radio orientation, N.Y. Univ., 1932-37, lecturer on radio, Harvard University summer school, 1939. Director industrial exhibits New York World's Fair 1964-1965, Incorporated. Awarded gold trophy of radio (presented by Herbert Hoover), 1933; All-American announcer (award made by radio editors), 1929, 30, 31, 32; George Arents Pioneer Medal and Diploma, Syracuse U., 1939; first double award of Nat. Fed. of Press Women (gold trophy for distinguished service to radio; gold trophy for world peace through internation broadcasting 1939), 1939. Decorated Knight Comdr. Order of Crown of Yugoslavia, Knight Comdr. Order of Crown of Rumania, Officer Crown of Denmark (all 1939). Gold Cross of Order of Holy Land (Jerusalem), 1942; Asiatic, European and Am. campaign medals, Victory medal, Legion of Merit (U.S.). Commd. lt. comdr. U.S. Navy; assigned as naval attache U.S. embassy, Moscow, 1942; promoted comdr., Dec. 1942; assigned spl. asst. to Ambassador Adm. William H. Standley, Moscow, Jan. 1943; dir. pub. and cultural relations between U.S. and the Soviet Union, 1943; assigned office of under sec. of Navy, 1944; detailed to exec. office, sec. of Navy, 1944; mem. combined com. on North African affairs, 1944; mem. Brit.-Am. combined com. on French Empire economic affairs, Dept. of State, 1944; dep. to the Minister, Mission on Econ. Affairs, Am. Embassy, London, Eng., 1945. Apptd. asst. adminstr. Fgn. Econ. Adminstrn., Washington; inspector-gen., Lend-Lease Foreign Affairs and Missions, 1945; promoted to capt. U.S. Navy, Dec. 1945; spl. asst. to asst. sec. of State, in charge of pub. affairs, Dept. of State, Washington, D.C., 1945; U.S. commr. to Philippines for war damage and rehabilitation, 1946-47, rank rear admiral, naval aide to Governor Florida; U.S. commr. with rank of ambassador to Internat. Bicentennial Exposition, Republic of Haiti, 1949-50; now deputy chairman UN Committee of New York. Mem. Am. Assn. Univ. Profs., Am. Acad. Polit. Sci., Foreign Policy Assn., Nat. Geog. Soc., English-Speaking Union, Société Bibliotique Internationale, (Paris), Am. Hist. Assn., Pan-Am. Soc., Centre Assn. of Catholics (New York City; chmn. bd. govs.), Alpha Chi Rho. Democrat. Catholic. Clubs: Yale, Metropolitan, Centre, Terrace, Skating (N.Y.); University (Boston); Oxford-Cambridge Club of N.Y.; Army-Navy, Metropolitan (Washington). Home: New York, N.Y. Died Jan. 12, 1976.

YOUNG, RALPH AUBREY, economist; b. Cheyenne, Wyo., June 12, 1901; s. Benjamin and Virginia (Crawford) Y.; A.B., Ohio Wesleyan U., 1923, LL.D., 1969; M.B.A., Northwestern U., 1925; Ph.D., U. Pa., 1930; m. Louise Merwin, Sept. 5, 1925; children—Merwin Crawford, Anne Alexandra, Ralph Aubrey. Instr. U. Pa., 1925-28; research staff Nat. Indsl. Conf. Bd., 1928-29, 32-34; spl. bus. analyst Dept. of Commerce, 1929-30; Social Sci. Research Council fellow, 1930-31; asst. prof. U. Pa., 1931-37, asso. prof., 1937-40, prof., 1940-45; research staff and dir. financial research program, Nat. Bur. Econ. Research, 1938-45; asst. dir. div. research and statistics Bd. Govs. Fed. Res. System, 1946-47, asso. dir., 1947-48, dir., 1948-59, adviser to bd., 1960-66, chmn. com. to review regulatory activities, 1975-76, sec. Fed. Open Market Com., 1960-66, dir. bd.'s div. internat. finance, 1961-65; cons. div. central banking services IMF, 1966-76; dir. Independence Sq. Income Securities Fund, Temporary Investment Fund; trustee Trust for Short-Term Fed. Securities; dir. Westchester Corp.; lectr. Geo. Washington U., 1948-62. Mem. research adv. bd. Com. for Econ. Devel., 1944-56, asso. mem., 1956-66; com. on research in finance Nat. Bur. Econ. Research, 1938-58; mem. bd. Nat. Acad. Econs. and Polit. Sci., 1954-60; mem. Conf. Bus. Economists; trustee Joint Council Econ. Edn., 1962-65. Fellow Center for Advanced Study, Wesleyan U., 1968. Fellow Am. Statis. Assn.; mem. Beta Gamma Sigma, Phi Gamma Delta. Meth. Club: Cosmos (Washington). Author numerous books on banking and finance, latest being: Monetary Instruments in the United States: Role of the Federal Reserve System. Address: Washington, D.C. Died Apr. 2, 1980; buried Glenview Cemetery, East Palestine, Ohio.

YOUNG, ROBERT BUSBEY, mech. engr.; b. Los Angeles, Sept. 23, 1917; s. Lincoln A. and Mabel (Busbey) Y.; B.S., Calif. Inst. Tech., 1940; m. Ann Dickie, Oct. 5, 1940; children—Patricia Webster, Robert Busbey, Deborah Ann. With Aerojet-Gen. Corp., 1943-79, v.p. liquid rocket plant, 1957-63, v.p., gen. mgr. Sacramento plant, 1963-69, v.p. propulsion div., 1967-69, corporate v.p. engring. and quality assurance, 1969-79; dir. indsl. operations Marshall Space Flight Center NASA, Huntsville, Ala., 1963-64. Mem. sci. adv. bd. USAF; cons. adv. panel on aero. Office Sec. Def., Research and Engring., Washington; mem. subcom. on rocket engines NASA, Washington. Recipient Sci. Achievement award Calif. Wing, Air Force Assn., 1959-60; Propulsion award Am. Rocket Soc., 1961; Pub. Service award NASA, 1969; registered profl. engr., Calif. Fellow Am. Inst. Aeros. and Astronautics (aerospace tech. council 1969-79). Home: San Marino, Calif. Died Feb. 7, 1979.

YOUNG, RONALD JOHNSON, investment banking co. exec.; b. Orange, N.J., Apr. 15, 1926; s. Robert A. and Florence (Burger) Y.; B.S. in Bus. Adminstrn., Lehigh U., 1950; m. Jane Elizabeth Thomas, July 2, 1955; children—Stanford Thomas, Ronald Johnson, Elizabeth Baker. Br. mgr. Wood-Struthers & Winthrop, 1950-55; exec. v.p. Phila. Life Ins. Co., 1955-74; pres., dir. Pligrowth Fund, Inc., 1968-74, One Eleven Mgmt. Co., 1967-74; with Reynolds Securities Inc., investment bankers, Phila., 1975-76; dir. Cadence Industries, Inc. Bd. dirs. Children's Country Week Assn. Served with USNR, World War II. Mem. Phila. Securities Assn. Home: Haverford, Pa. Died Nov. 23, 1976; interred St. David's Episcopal Ch., Wayne, Pa.

YOUNG, SAMUEL ROLLO, ret. railroad exec.; b. Coatesville, Pa., Mar. 3, 1887; s. Samuel Scott and Sallie Pusey (Hammond) Y.; graduate State Normal Sch. (West Chester, Pa.), 1904; grad. Lehigh U. (Bethlehem, Pa.), 1909; m. Cidney Alta Young, Oct. 17, 1912; children—Samuel Richard, Robert George. Civil engr. Consolidation Coal Co., Van Leer, Ky., 1909-10; rodman Sunbury div. Pa. R.R., 1910-12; farmer, Coatesville, Pa., 1912-15; civil engr. Midvale Steel & Ordnance Co., 1915-16; asst. engr. Atlanta & West Point R.R.-The Western Ry. Ala.-Ga. R.R., 1916-17, div. engr., 1918, dist. engr., 1918-20, asst. chief engr., 1920-31, chief engr., 1931-44, asst. gen. mgr., 1944-47, pres. and gen. mgr., 1947-53, pres., chief exec. ofcr., 1953-56; past pres., dir. Augusta Union Sta. Co., Augusta & Summerville R.R., Savannah River Terminal Co.; past chmn. bd. control Atlanta Joint Terminals, now ret.; dir. Trust Co. of Georgia Assos. Pres. College Park Bd. Edn., 1927-29; mem. Atlanta-Fulton County Joint Planning Bd., 1948-72. Mem. Am. Soc. C.E., Soc. Am. Mil. Engrs., Georgia Engring. Soc., Newcomen Soc., Atlanta Hist. Soc., Pa.-Scotch Irish Soc., Alpha Tau Omega. Presbyn. Mason. Clubs: Kiwanis, Capital City (Atlanta). Home: College Park, Ga. Died Feb. 11, 1979; buried College Park Cemetery.

YOUNG, T(HEODORE) CUYLER, educator; b. Moosic, Pa., Aug. 16, 1900; s. Sylvester Wylie and Edna (McCune) Y.; A.B., Coll. of Wooster (Ohio), 1922, Litt.D., 1960; A.M., Princeton, 1925, Th.B., 1925; fellow Oriental Inst., U. Chgo., 1935-38; m. Helen Augusta Clarke, June 27, 1933; 1 son, Theodore Cuyler. Ordained to ministry Presbyn. Ch., 1925; asst. minister First Ch., Cortland, N.Y., 1925-27; tchr., pastor Bd. Fgn. Missions Presbyn. Ch. U.S.A., Resht, Iran, 1927-35; asst. minister First Ch., Chgo., 1936-38; lectr. Victoria Coll. U. Toronto, Can., 1938-39, asst. prof. semitics, 1939-42, asso. prof., 1942-47; asso. prof. Persian lang., history Princeton, 1947-53, Horatio Whitredge Garrett prof., 1953-69, prof. emeritus, 1969-76, chmn. dept. Oriental studies, 1954-69, dir. program Near Eastern studies, 1954-62; lectr. summer sessions Sch. Advanced Internat. Studies, Johns Hopkins, 1947-49, 53; vis. prof. history U. Nairobi (Kenya), 1969-71, U. Tex., 1975. Mem. com. Islamic culture Am. Council Learned Socs., 1949-74; chmn. Nr. East studies com. Social Sci. Research Council, 1950-59, Am. Council Learned Socs.-Social Sci. Research Council, 1959-62, mem. council bd., dir., 1960-62; bd. govs. Middle East Inst., 1962-76; spl. polit. attaché Am. Embassy, Tehran, Iran, 1951, spl. cons., 1952; research fellow Council Fgn. Relations, 1959-61. Sr. analyst, dep. chief Near East sect., research and analysis br. OSS, Washington, 1943-44; pub. affairs officer U.S. Embassy, Tehran, 1945-46. Decorated Knight of Holy Sepulcher, Orthodox Patriarch of Jerusalem, 1954. Mem. Am. Friends of Orthodox Patriarchate of Jerusalem (exec. bd. 1950-76, pres. 1953-63), Am. Oriental Soc., Am. Inst. Iranian Studies (pres. 1971-73), Am. Assn. for Middle East Studies, Council Fgn. Relations, Phi Beta Kappa, Delta Sigma Rho. Editor, contbr. to Near Eastern Culture and Soc., 1951; bd. adv. editors Middle East Jour., 1947-76. Contbr. articles profl. jours. Home: Princeton, N.J. Died Sept. 1, 1976.

YOUNG, VAILE GILBERT, dept. store exec.; b. Evansville, Ind., Feb. 14, 1907; s. William H. and Iva (Bedford) Y.; B.S. in Bus. Adminstrn., U. Cal. at Berkeley, 1930; m. Dorothy Barr, Feb. 15, 1936 (dec. 1950); children—Carol (Mrs. Robert W. Senske), Donald J.; m. 2d, Marjorie Wise, May 29, 1958. Buying and adminstrv. positions with Ransohoff's, San Francisco, 1934-35, Maison Mendessolle, San Francisco, 1935-37, Raphael Weill Co., San Francisco and N.Y.C., 1937-42; with Buffums Dept. Store, Long Beach, Cal., from 1942, gen. mdse. mgr., v.p., 1952-61; pres. gen. mgr., from 1961, later chmn., chief exec. officer, dir. Dir. mem. exec. com. Downtown Long Beach Assn., 1954-64, pres., 1954-56; 2d v.p. Long Beach C. of C., 1961, bd. dirs., 1959-61; dir. Cal. Mus. Sci. and Industry; mem. Long Beach Jr. League, 1961-64, Long Beach Assistance League, 1962-76, Long Beach Salvation Army, 1964, City of Hope, 1963-64; mem. merchants council N.Y. U. Sch. Retaling, 1962-76. Mem. Cal. Retailers Assn. (dir.), Theta Delta Chi. Clubs: Rotary (pres. 1956-57), Tuna, La Grulla Gun (Baja, Mexico); So. Cal. Tuna (Avalon, Santa Catalina Island). Home: Long Beach, Calif. Died Sept. 22, 1976; buried Long Beach.

YOUNG, WALKER ROLLO, engr.; b. Butler, Ind., May 7, 1885; s. Oscar and Jane (Walker) Y.; B.S. mining engring., U. of Ida., 1908, Dr. Engring., 1935; m. Marguerite Bush, Oct. 14, 1911; 1 dau., Jane (Mrs. William R. Ayers). Chainman, surveyor, summers 1902-09; surveying, mining and assaying, 1909-11; asst. engr. U.S. Reclamation Service, Arrowrock Dam, Ida.,

1911-16; asst. and engr. Chief Engr.'s Office, Denver, 1916-20; engr. in charge investigations Colo. River including Boulder dam site, 1921-24; engr. U.S. Bur. Reclamation, in charge investigations, San Francisco Bay, also Sacramento Valley, 1924-26; construction engr. in charge constrn. Kittitas div., Yakima Project, Wash., 1926-30; sr. engr. in gen. charge investigations of water resources of Calif., 1930; constrn. engr. U.S. Bur. Reclamation, in charge construction Boulder Dam, Power Plant and Appurtenant Works, 1930-35; constrn. engr. U.S. Bur. Reclamation, in charge Central Valley project, Calif., including Shasta Dam, Friant Dam and 350 miles of main canals, 1935-38; supervising engr., Central Valley Project, 1938-40; asst. chief engr., U.S. Bureau of Reclamation, Nov. 1940-Jan. 12, 1945; chief engr., U.S. Bureau of Reclamation, 1945-48; now pvt. practice as cons. engr.; pres. Thompson Pipe & Steel Co. Mem. Colorado Soc. Engrs., Am. Soc. C.E., Phi Delta Theta, Tau Beta Pi. Mem. Christian Ch. Home: Denver, Colo. *

YOUNG, WALTER ALBERT, educator; b. Marion, Ky., Apr. 2, 1882; s. Isaac Newton and Martha Ermina (Dowell) Y.; grad. Haviland (Kan.) Acad., 1901; A.B., Friends U., Wichita, Kan., 1905; A.B., Haverford (Pa.) Coll., 1906; A.M., U. of Chicago, 1912; student Harvard, summer 1908; diploma Institute Universitaire de Hautes Etudes Internationales, Geneva, Switzerland, 1930; m. Mary Edith Wilson, Aug. 16, 1916; children—Wilson Abron, Martha Lenore. Teacher Oak Grove Sem., 1906-11, Haviland Acad., 1912-13, Friends Univ. Prep. Sch., 1913-15, Wichita (Kan.) High Sch., 1915-21, Iowa State Teachers Coll., 1921-24, Wichita High Sch. East, 1924-25; with Friends Univ. since 1925, dean of coll., 1934-39, pres. of univ., 1939-47; prof. history, Baker Univ., Baldwin, Kan., since 1947. Won Haverford (Pa.) scholarship, 1905, Clement Biddle fellowship to Geneva, 1929. Mem. bd. of dirs. Wichita City Y.M.C.A., 1941. Clubs: Lions, Wichita Chamber of Commerce. Home: Baldwin, Kan.*

YOUNGDAHL, LUTHER W., judge; b. Mpls., May 29, 1896; s. John Carl and Elizabeth (Johnson) Y.; U. Minn., 1915-16; A.B., Gustavus Adolphus Coll., 1919; LL.B., Minn. Coll. Law, 1921; also numerous hon. degrees; m. Irene Annet Engdahl, June 23, 1923; children—Margaret Louise, Luther William Andrew, Paul David. Asst. city atty., Mpls., 1921-23; practiced law with Judge Tifft, 1923-30; judge Municipal Ct., Mpls., 1930-36; judge Dist. Ct., Hennepin County, Mpls., 1936-42; asso. justice of Minn. Surpreme Ct., 1942-46; gov. of Minn., 1947-51; judge U.S. Dist. Ct. for D.C., 1951-66, sr. judge, 1966-78. Served in World War I. Decorated Grand Cross Royal Order North Star (Sweden); Order of the Lion (Finland). Home: Washington, D.C. Died June 21, 1978; buried Arlington Nat. Cemetery.

YOUNGE, SHEILA FRANCES, editor; b. Oakland, Calif., Aug. 25, 1945; d. Fitzroy Edgerton and Winifred Tammseau (Abernathy) Younge; B.A. in English, San Jose State U., 1969. With Newsweek Mag., N.Y.C., 1969-70, N.J. Pub. Broadcasting Service Channel 52, 1970-71; editor Black Sports Mag., 1971-72; exec. editor Essence Mag., N.Y.C., 1971-76. Mem. Mag. Pubs. Assn. (internship winner 1969), Editor: Denise Nicholas Beauty Book; editor Unique N.Y. Mag., 1975-76. Author San Jose State U. proposal for Black studies dept.; first woman editor of nat. sports mag. Home: New York, N.Y. Died Oct. 20, 1977.

YOUNGER, EDWARD EUGENE, historian, educator; b. Pindall, Ark., June 29, 1909; s. William Randolph and Alma (Rainbolt) Y.; B.A., Ark. State Tchrs. Coll., 1933; M.A., Okla. State U., 1938; Ph.D., George Washington U., 1942; m. Barbara Ellen Badgett, June 29, 1936; 1 dau., Ellen Badgett. Tchr., prin., supt. pub. schs., Ark., Okla., 1928-36; lectr. internat. law Turner's Diplomatic Sch., Washington, 1940-42; asst. prof. Am. history U. Va., Charlottesville, 1946-49, asso. prof., 1949-56, prof., 1956-79, Alumni prof. history, 1974-79, maj. prof. for masters thesis, doctoral dissertions, 1946-79, dir. student aid, sec. com. scholarships, 1953-54, chmn. Page-Barbour and Richard lectr. com., 1954-58, fgn. student adviser, 1958-60, assn. dean, 1958-59, grad. history adviser, 1959-66, chmn. Wilson Gee Com. Faculty Research, 1959-62, chmn. Corcoran dept. history, 1962-66, dir. Spl. Master's Degree Program, from 1963, chmn. pub. occasions Com., 1962-67, dir. Asian Studies Inst. for Va. Coll. tchrs., summers 1964-65, dir. NDEA Inst. for Am. history tchrs., summer 1965, dean Grad. Sch. Arts and Scis., 1966-69; Fulbright lectr. Am. history Allahabad U. (India), 1957-58; Ernest J. King vis. prof. maritime history U.S. Naval War Coll., Newport, R.I., 1960-61; Am. specialist, India, Nepal, summer 1961; lectr. U.S. in World Affairs Series, Bangalore, Hyderabad, Madras and Trivandrum, India, 1958; Young lectures Memphis State U., 1965; lectr. NATO Def. Coll. (Paris), U.S. Naval War Coll., U.S. Air U. Served to lt. comdr. USNR, 1942-45. Mem. Am. (chmn. com. historian and fed. govt. 1956-58), Va. (hon.), Albemarle County (pres. 1975-76, editor Mag. History) hist. assns., So. Hist. Soc. (program com. chmn., mem. exec. council, editorial bd.), Orgn. Am. Historians (mem. exec. com.), Va. Social Sci. Assn. (pres. 1972), Raven Soc., Phi Beta Kappa. Democrat. Author: John A. Kasson: Diplomacy and Politics from Lincoln to McKinley (Phi Beta Kappa prize), 1955; Inside the Confederate Government: Diary of R.G.H. Kean (Civil War Book Club Selection), 1957. Home: Charlottesville, Va. Died June 23, 1979.

YUNG, VICTOR SEN, actor; b. San Francisco, Oct. 18, 1915; s. Sen Gam and Boy Soy (Chan) Y.; A.B., U. Calif., Berkeley, 1937; student Lipson Sch. Costume Design, 1946-47; grad. USAAF Statis. Sch., 1944, Harvard Sch. Bus. Adminstrn., 1944; 1 son, Brent Kee. Actor, # 2 Son, Charlie Chan series, 1938-49, Hop Sing, Bonanza TV series, 1958-73, Cousin Charlie, Bachelor Father series, 1950-55; character roles in over 300 motion picture, TV roles, 1936—; product mgr. Chinese Frozen Food Co., 1947-49; promoter food products, 1953-74; pres. Sen Yung Corp., 1975—. Served to capt. USAAF, 1943-47. Mem. Screen Actors Guild, AFTRA, Actors Equity. Democrat. Baptist. Author: Great Wok Cookbook, 1974. Died Nov. 1980.

ZACCARO, LUKE NICHOLAS, educator; b. Hartford, Conn., Feb. 10, 1924; s. John Francis and Anella (Jeverouskas) Z.; B.A., U. Conn., 1949, M.S., 1950; Ph.D., Syracuse U., 1957; m. Marilyn Lea Friel, Sept. 3, 1949; children—Richard, Edward, Lawrence, Nancy Daniel, Michael. Grad. asst. Syracuse U., 1951-55; instr. math. Georgetown U., 1955-57; asst. prof. math. U. R.I., 1957-59; asso. prof. math. Hiram Coll., 1959-63; prof. math. Worcester Poly. Inst., 1964-72; prof., chmn. dept. math. Youngstown (Ohio) State U., 1972-77. Mem. Northborough (Mass.) Appropriation Com., 1969-70; Northborough Sch. Com., 1970-72, Northborough Citizens Adv. Bd., Northborough Pub. Edn. Com. NSF Faculty fellow Mass. Inst. Tech., 1963-64. Served with AUS, 1942-46. Mem. A.A.U.P., Math. Assn. Am., Phi Mu Epsilon. Author (with Wendell Johnson): Modern Introductory Mathmatics, 1966. Home: Canfield, Ohio. Died Mar. 19, 1977; buried Rose Hill Meml. Park, Rocky Hill, Conn.

ZACHARIASEN, WILLIAM HOULDER (FREDRIK), educator; b. Langesund, Norway, Feb. 5, 1906; s. Zacharias and Louise (Bredesen) Z.; Ph.D., U. Oslo, 1928; m. Ragni Durban-Hansen, May 26, 1930; children—Fredrik, Ellen Houlder. Came to U.S., 1930, naturalized, 1941. Asst. prof. U. Oslo, 1928-30; asst. prof. physics U. Chgo., 1930-40, asso. prof., 1940-45, prof., 1945-79, chmn. dept. physics, 1945-50, 56-59, dean div. phys. sci., 1959-62, Ernest DeWitt Burton Distinguished prof. physics, 1962-74, now emeritus. Pres. Am. Soc. X-Ray and Electron Diffraction. Rockefeller Found. fellow, 1928, Guggenheim Found. fellow, 1935. Fellow Am. Physical Soc., Norwegian Acad. Scis.; mem. Nat. Acad. Scis., Am. Acad. Arts and Scis. Club: Quadrangle (Chgo.). Author: Theory of X-Ray Diffraction in Crystals, 1945. Contbr. articles to profl. jours. Home: Santa Fe, N.Mex. Died Dec. 24, 1979; cremated.

ZADOR, EUGENE, composer; b. Bataszek, Hungary, Nov. 5, 1894; s. Josef and Pauline (Boerman) Z.; came to U.S., 1939, naturalized, 1944; Ph.D., U. Halle (Germany) and Muenster (Germany), 1921; Mus.D. (hon.), N.Y. Coll. Music, 1935, Chgo. Conservatory-Coll., 1971; m. Maria Steiner, Nov. 9, 1946; children—Leslie, Margaret (Mrs. Schuyler Bassett). Prof. Vienna (Austria) Conservatory, 1921-38; chief orchestrator Metro-Goldwyn-Mayer Studios, Hollywood, Calif., 1940-41, 48-60. Performed in U.S. and abroad, including in Budapest, Hungary, Vienna, Berlin, Germany, Paris, France, London, Eng., N.Y.C., Chgo., Phila., San Francisco, Los Angeles. Recipient Hungarian Grand Prix, 1934, Benjamin prize, 1960. Mem. Motion Picture Acad. Arts and Scis., ASCAP. Composer 70 orchestral works, including Chamber Concerto, 1930, Divertimento for Strings, 1954, Elegie and Dance, 1954, Christmas Overture, 1961, Aria and Allegro for Strings and Brass, 1966, Hungarian Scherzo, 1977, Studies for Orchestra, 1971, Hungarian Caprice, 1921, Contrasts for Orchestra, 1969, Suite for Brass, 1961; composer 13 operas, including Christopher The Inspector General, 1935, Azra, 1936, Columbus, 1939, The Magic Chair, 1965, The Virgin and the Fawn, 1965, The Scarlet Mill, 1968, Yehu, 1974; composer chamber music including Suite for Brass, 1961, Suite for Woodwind Quintet, 1972, Brass Quintet, 1973. Home: Los Angeles, Calif. Died Apr. 4, 1977.

ZAIS, MELVIN, army officer; b. Fall River, Mass., May 8, 1916; s. A.R. and Jenny (Kauffman) Z.; B.A. in Polit. Sci., U. N.H., 1937; grad. various service schs.; m. Patricia Vachon Light, Aug. 6, 1967; children—Barrie E., Mitchell M.; stepchildren—David R. Light, John P. Light. Commd. 2d lt. U.S. Army, 1937, advanced through grades to gen., 1973; various assignments U.S. and Europe, 1940-52; assigned U.S. Army adv. group. Jammet, Turkey, 1952-53, 82d Airborne Div., 1953-54, Armed Forces Staff Coll., 1954-55, Spl. Weapons Project, Washington, 1955, office asst. chief staff G3, Dept. Army, 1955-56, 101st Airborne Div., 1956-57, Nat. War Coll., 1957-58; dep. asst. chief staff G1,Hdqrs. U.S. Army Europe, Germany, 1958-59; asst. chief staff G3, Hdqrs. 7th Army, 1959-62; assigned office asst. chief staff, J3, U.S. Army Element, U.S. Strike Command, MacDill AFB, Fla., 1962-63; dep. Dir. Plans, J5, U.S. Army Element, U.S. Strike Command, McDill AFB, Fla., 1963-64; dir. and dep. dir. enlisted personnel Office Personnel Operations, Dept. Army, 1964-66; dep. comdg. gen. I Field Force, Vietnam, 1966; asst. div. comdr. 1st Inf. Div., Vietnam, 1966; dir. individual tng. office dep. chief staff personnel Dept. Army, 1966-68; comdg. gen. 101st Airborne Div., Vietnam, 1968-69; comdg. gen. XXIV Corps, Vietnam, 1969-70; dir. J3, Operations Directorate office joint chiefs staff, 1970-72; comdg. gen. 3d Army, Ft. McPherson, Ga., 1972-73; comdg. gen. Allied Land Forces Southeastern Europe, Ismir, Turkey, 1973-76; ret., 1976. Decorated D.S.M. with four oak leaf clusters, Silver Star medal with oak leaf cluster, Legion of Merit with three oak leaf clusters, D.F.C. with oak leaf cluster, Bronze Star medal, Air medal with valor device, Army Commendation medal with oak leaf cluster, Purple Heart, also fgn. decorations. Home: Beaufort, S.C. Died May 6, 1981.

ZALLES, REGINALD HUGH, orgn. exec., writer; b. Washington, Dec. 20, 1910; s. Jorje and Arcadia (Calderon) Z.; A.B., William Coll., 1932; M.A. in Econs., Harvard, 1948. Faculty Henry George Sch. Social Scis., N.Y.C. and Boston, 1935-40; dir. Free Market Inst., Boston, 1939-40; dir. Mass. council CIO, 1949-51; exec. sec. Mass. chpt. Americans for Democratic Action, 1949-51, chmn. Boston chpt., 1950, Montgomery County, Md. chpt., 1955, Washington chpt., 1959, nat. exec. sec., 1951-54, sec. nat. bd., 1956-63, treas., 1963-68; free-lance writer, 1955-80. Democratic precinct chmn., Bethesda, Md.; vice chmn. Western Suburban Dem. Club Montgomery County; mem. Montgomery County Dem. Central Com., 1966—, treas., 1966-68; del. Dem. Nat. Conv., 1968. Trustee Montgomery County Art Center. Bd. dirs. Suburban Md. Fair Housing, Inc. Served to capt. inf., AUS, 1942-46. Decorated Bronze Star, Purple Heart. Mem. Ret. Officers Assn., Phi Beta Kappa, Delta Kappa Epsilon. Author: (play) Cristophe, 1959. Address: Bethesda, Md. Died Jan. 11, 1980.

ZANETTI, JOAQUIN ENRIQUE (ZA-NET'TE), professor chemistry; b. St. Domingo, Dominican Republic, Jan. 20, 1885; s. Enrique Lucas and Isabel (Hernandez) Z.; student Roxbury Latin Sch., Boston, Mass., 1901-02; A.B., magna cum laude, Harvard, 1906; A.M., 1907, Ph.D., 1909; m. Esperanza Conill, Apr. 23, 1913; 1 son, Juan Conill (died Apr. 24, 1915). Came to U.S., 1900 naturalized citizen, 1906. Instr. in chemistry, Columbia, 1909-12; dir. Inst. Industrial Chemistry, Montevideo, Uruguay, 1912-13; asst. prof. chemistry, Columbia, 1913-22, asso. prof., 1922-29, professor, 1929-53, professor emeritus since 1953, director of laboratories, 1939-53, associate provost 1948-50. Served as capt. Ordnance, A.U.S., 1917, captain, lt. col. C.W.S., 1918-19; lt. col. C.W. Res., U.S. Army, 1922-26, col. since 1926; called to active duty Washington, D.C., July 14, 1941, at Office of Chief Chemical Warfare Service; military observer, London, Aug. 1941; chief Incendiaries Branch, C.W.S., Sept. 1941-June 1942; asst. mil. attache, London, July 1942-Mar. 1944; chief, Special Projects Division, C.W.S., April-Sept. 1944; returned inactive status Nov. 10, 1944; retired June 28, 1948, Honorary Reserve, since 1948. Army War College, 1930; mem. Board Consulting Experts, C.W.S., U.S. Army. Liaison officer French C.W.S., 1917-18; sec. for U.S. of Inter-Allied Congress for Chem. Warfare, Paris, 1918; officer in charge C.W.S., Dist. of Paris 1919. Del. to Internat. Union Pure and Applied Chemistry, Paris, 1919, Cambridge, Eng., 1923, Copenhagen, 1924; cons. expert on chem. warfare to League of Nations, 1922-26. Mem. Am. Chem. Soc. Nat. Research Council (chmn. div. chemistry and chem. tech., 1923-24; exec. com. 1924-25). Decorated D.S.M. (U.S.), Legion Merit (U.S.) Distinguished Service Order, Order Brit. Empire (Eng.); Chevalier Legion d'Honneur (France); Officer Crown of Italy. Author: The Significance of Nitrogen, 1932; Fire from the Air, The ABC of Incendiaries, 1941; also tech. papers. Home: Germantown, N.Y. *

ZANUCK, DARRYL FRANCIS, motion picture producer; b. Wahoo, Nebr., Sept. 5, 1902; s. Frank and Liouse (Torpin) Z.; student Page Mil. Acad., Manual Tng. High Sch. and under pvt. tutors; m. Virginia Fox. Jan. 12, 1924; children—Darrylin, Susan Marie, Richard Darryl. Successively advt. and writer with Warner Bros. Pictures, Inc., producer motion pictures, supervisor prodn. Warner Bros. Studios and v.p. in charge 20th Century Pictures, Inc.,; pres. 20th Century Fox Film Corp., 1962-69, chmn., chief exec. officer, 1969-71, chmn. emeritus, 1971-79; producer numerous pictures including The Purple Heart, 1944, Wilson, 1944, Winged Victory, 1944, Dragonwyck, 1946, Anna and the King of Siam, 1946, The Razor's Edge, 1946, Gentleman's Agreement, 1947, Pinky, 1949, Twelve O'Clock High, 1949, No Way Out, 1950, All About Eve, 1950, David and Bathsheba, 1952, People Will Talk, 1951, Viva Zapata, 1952, Snows of Kilmanjaro, 1953, The Egyptian, 1954, Man in the Gray Flannel Suit, 1956, Island in the Sun, 1957, The Longest Day, 1962, others. Served with 37th Div., U.S. Army, with A.E.F.; apptd. lt. col. Signal Corps Res. and mem. adv. council to chief Signal Officer Jan. 1941, col., 1942. Decorated French Legion of Honor; recipient Irving Thalberg award, 1937, 44, 50. Clubs: Masons, Shriners. Home: Santa Monica, Calif. Died Dec. 22, 1979.

ZAPF, LACEY C. (ZAF), foreign service officer; b. Muncie, Ind., Oct. 11, 1882; student Hiron's Bus. Sch., Muncie, Ind.; Berlitz Sch. of Languages, 1910-12, DePauw Univ., Greencastle, Ind., 1901-02, George Washington Univ., Washington, D.C., 1908-10; LL.B., Georgetown Univ. Law Sch., Washington, D.C., 1913; m. Madeline A. Alexander, 1908; children—Lacey C. Jr., Betty A. Newspaper reporter, Muncie (Ind.) Star, 1902-04, Nashville (Tenn.) American, 1904-10; admitted to Dist. of Columbia bar, 1913; admitted to practice at the bar of the Supreme Court and Court of Appeals, Dist. of Columbia, 1913; Latin-Am. expert and spl. asst. to the dir. Bur. of Foreign and Domestic Commerce, 1911-14; spl. rep. Sec. of Commerce on the War Trade Bd., 1914-18; asst. mgr. Research Dept. Chamber of Commerce of the U.S., 1918-20; sec. Am. Sect. of the Internat. Chamber of Commerce, 1920-29; sec. Organization Com. Internat. Chamber of Commerce, Atlantic City, N.J., 1919, and served as sec. of American delegations to Congresses, in Paris, 1920, London, 1921, Paris, 1922, Rome, 1923, and Brussels, 1925; sec. Am. delegation of business men visiting European countries, Northern Africa, and Near East, 1925-27; chmn. advisory com. Bur. of Indsl. Research, 1929-32; financial expert, Reconstruction Finance Corp., 1932-33; dir. Field Service Bur. of Foreign and Domestic Commerce, 1933-37; asst. dir. Bur. of Foreign and Domestic Commerce, 1937-38; sec. Foreign Trade Com. of the Business Advisory Council Dept. of Commerce, 1933-38; sr. Am. Trade Commr. in Australia, 1938-39; consul and sec. Diplomatic Service in Australia, 1939-42; Am. commercial attache in Australia, Mar. 1942-Nov. 1946; retired. Mem. Kappa Alpha Phi, Delta Kappa Epsilon. Clubs: DKE (N.Y. City); Royal Canberra Golf (Canberra, Australia); Royal Sydney Golf (Sydney, Australia). Address: Washington, D.C. *

ZECKENDORF, WILLIAM, real estate consultant; b. Paris, Ill., June 20, 1905; s. Arthur William and Byrd (Rosefield) Z.; student N.Y. U., 1922-25; LL.D., L.I. U., Am. U.; L.H.D., Wilberforce U.; LL.D., Chung-ang U., Seoul; m. Irma Levy, Sept. 29, 1928; children—William Jr., Susan; m. 2d, Marion Griffin, Dec. 10, 1940 (dec. March 5, 1968); m. 3d, Alice K. Bacher, Dec. 21, 1972. Asst. purchasing agt. Samuel Bochard, real estate, 1925-26; asso. Leonard S. Gans, gen. real estate brokerage, 1926-39, partner, from 1930; v.p. Webb & Knapp, 1938, pres., 1947-61, chmn. bd., 1961-65; cons. Gen. Property Corp. (successor to Webb & Knapp), from 1965; dir. Am. Hydrofoil., Trizec, Webb & Knapp (Can.), Ltd.; chmn. bd. Colmar Surinam Oil Co.; dir. Gulf States Land & Industries, Inc., Roosevelt Field, Inc. Bd. dirs. The Children's Village, N.Y. Infirmary, Manhattan Eye, Ear and Throat Hosp., Am. Korean Found., World's Fair, 1964; trustee Am. Planning and Civic Assn; chmn. bd. trustees L.I. U., 1942-67, then trustee; hon. chmn. Realty Found. N.Y. Decorated chevalier Legion Honor (France), officer Order of Orange Nassau (Netherlands); officer Order of Merit (Italy). Mem. Navy League U.S. (life), Pi Lambda Phi. Jewish religion. Purchaser land of new UN site, N.Y. Author: Zeckendorf, 1970. Home: New York, N.Y. Died Oct. 1, 1976.

ZEHR, HOWARD JACOB, clergyman; b. Deer Creek, Ill., Mar. 24, 1916; s. Jacob and Elizabeth Ann (Wolber) Z.; student Goshen (Ind.) Coll., 1938-41, B.A., No. Baptist Sem., Chgo., 1942; B.A., Th.B. Goshen Coll. Bibl. Sem., 1962; m. Edna Good, June 21, 1942; children—Howard Jay, Edward Daniel, Ellen Elizabeth, Jonathan Philip. Ordained to ministry Mennonite Ch., 1942; pastor, Freeport, Ill., 1942-50, Peoria, Ill., 1950-52, Fisher, Ill., 1952-58, Elkhart, Ind., 1958-64; gen. sec. South Central Mennonite Conf., 1964-66; asst. moderator Mennonite Gen. Conf., 1955-57, mem. ministerial com., 1961-65, exec. sec. conf., 1966-72; asso. sec. Mennonite Bd. Congregational Ministries, 1972-77; mem. exec. com. Mennonite Bd. Edn., 1951-55, v.p., 1955-56; moderator Ill. Mennonite Conf., 1952-53, 55-56. Home: Elkhart, Ind. Died July 13, 1977; buried Prairie St. Cemetery, Elkhart.

ZELIGS, MEYER AARON, psychiatrist, author; b. Cin., Mar. 20, 1909; s. Joseph and Betty (Mirkin) Z.; B.A., U. Cin., 1928, B.M., 1931, M.D., 1932; grad. San Francisco Psychoanalytic Inst., 1955; m. Elizabeth Winifred Anderson, June 20, 1946; children—Betsy, Michael, Joseph, David. Intern, then resident physician Cin. Gen. Hosp., 1931-36; grad. study neurology Nat. Hosp. Nervous Diseases, London, Eng., 1936-37; practice medicine specializing in neurology-psychiatry, also tchr., Cin., 1937-42; asst. clin. prof. U. Calif. Med. Sch., San Francisco, 1946-52; practice medicine specializing in psychoanalysis, San Francisco, 1952-78. Mem. World Affairs Council San Francisco, 1960-78. Served to comdr., M.C., USNR, 1942-46; PTO. Mem. Am. Psychiat. Assn., Am. Psychoanalytic Assn., Phi Delta Epsilon. Clubs: Concordia-Argonaut, Calif. Tennis (San Francisco). Author: Friendship and Fratricide An Analysis of Whittaker Chambers and Alger Hiss, 1967; Loyalty and Betrayal: Nixon-Hiss-Chambers, 1978; also articles. Home: San Francisco, Calif. Died Mar. 20, 1978.

ZELLE, M(AX) R(OMAINE), lab. research adminstr.; b. Polk County, Iowa, Oct. 11, 1915; s. Guy C. and Clara (Ringgenberg) Z.; B.S., Iowa State U., 1937, Ph.D., 1940; m. Evelyn Hansen, Dec. 24, 1937; children—Claire Christine, Phillip Wayne. Asst. county agt., Audubon, Ia., 1935-36; asst. prof. genetics Purdue U., 1941-44; biologist NIH, Bethesda, Md., 1946-48; prof. bacteriology Cornell U., 1948-58; geneticist, div. biology and medicine AEC, 1950-51, 57-58, chief biology br., 1958-60, asst. dir. biol. scis., 1960-61; prof. genetics and dir. Center Radiol. Scis., U. Wash., 1961-62; dir. div. biol. and med. research Argonne Nat. Lab., 1962-69; prof., chmn. dept. radiology and radiation biology Colo. State U., Ft. Collins, 1969-80; cons. biology div. Oak Ridge Nat. Lab., 1947-49, 52-57, summer guest investigator, 1952, 54, 56. Mem. bd. advisers Phoenix project U. Mich., 1966. Adviser to U.S. delegation UN Sci. Com. on Effects Atomic Radiation, 1958-62; cons. Bur. Radiol. Health FDA, Dept. Health, Edn. and Welfare, 1969-73, Plowshare Programs Office AEC, 1972. Served to lt. (j.g.) USNR, 1944-46. Fellow A.A.A.S.; mem. Am. Inst. Biol. Scis., Genetics Soc. Am., Soc. Am. Microbiols., Am. Soc. Naturalists, Radiation Research Soc. (councilor 1960-63, sec.-treas. 1972-75), Health Physics Soc. (pres. Central Rocky Mountain chpt. 1975-76), Scabbard and Blade, Sigma Xi, Phi Kappa Phi, Alpha Zeta. Club: Cosmos (Washington). Home: Fort Collins, Colo. Died June 28, 1980; buried Fort Collins.

ZELLERBACH, HAROLD LIONEL, paper products exec.; b. San Francisco, Mar. 25, 1894; s. Isador and Jennie (Baruh) Z.; student U. Calif. 1913-15; B.S. in Econs., U. Pa., 1917; m. Doris Joseph, Apr. 19, 1917; children—Rolinde (Mrs. Stephen N. Loew, Jr.), William Joseph, Stephen Anthony. With Zellerback Paper Co., 1917-59, beginning as personnel mgr., dir., 1928-59, chmn. bd., 1957-59, then dir.; cons. dir. emeritus Crown Zellerback Corp. Bd. dirs. Asso. Council of Arts; v.p. bd. govs. San Francisco Symphony; bd. dirs. San Francisco Art Inst., Laguna Honda Home Aux. Crown Zellerbach Found., San Francisco Ballet Guild, San Francisco Opera Assn., Oakland Mus. Assn.; pres. Newhouse Found. San Francisco Art Commn.; bd. dirs., pres. Zellerbach Family Fund.; bd. dirs., pres. Harold and Doris Zellerbach Fund; trustee U. Pa., Cal. Palace Legion of Honor. Mason (Shriner). Clubs: St. Francis Yacht, San Francisco Commercial, Concordia, Commonwealth, Stock Exchange (San Francisco); Beach (Pebble Beach); Villa Taverna; Fifth Avenue (N.Y.C.). Home: San Francisco, Calif. Died Jan. 29, 1978.

ZELZER, HARRY, impressario, concert mgr.; b. Poland. Home: Chicago, Ill. Died June 14, 1979.

ZEMACH, HARVE (HARVEY FISCHTROM), author; b. Newark, Dec. 5, 1933; s. Mat and Ida (Rabinowitz) Fischtrom; B.A., Wesleyan U., Middlwtown, Conn., 1955; postgrad. (Fulbright scholar) U. Vienna (Austria), 1955-56; M.A. in History of Ideas, Brandeis U., 1959; m. Margot Zemach, Jan. 29, 1957; children—Kaethe, Heidi, Rachel. Instr. history and social sci. Boston U., 1960-65; instr. history and social sci. U. Mass., 1965-70. Recipient 1st prize Book Week Spring Children's Book Festival, 1965. Author: Small Boy Is Listening, 1958; A Hat with a Rose, 1960; Nail Soup, 1964; The Tricks of Master Dabble, 1965; Salt, A Russian Tale, 1965; The Speckled Hen, 1966; Mommy, Buy Me A China Doll, 1966; Judge (Caldecott honor book), 1969; Awake and Dreaming, 1970; Penny A Look, 1971; Duffy and the Devil, 1973; (with Kaethe Zemach) The Princess and the Froggie, 1975. Home: New York, N.Y. Died Nov. 1974.

ZEMKE, JOHN CLAUD, hosp. adminstr.; b. Portland, Mich., Sept. 12, 1913; s. Otto Albert and Anna Rosalie (Olsen) Z.; B.S., Ferris Inst., 1938; M.B.A., Rollins Coll., Winter Park, Fla., 1967; m. Madeline Mary Muck, Oct. 30, 1937; children—Ann Maureen (Mrs. Otis Graham, Jr.), Kathryn Mary (Mrs. Donald Wudtke), Margery Jean (Mrs. Dennis Enberg), Penny Sue, Jill Lakin. Comml. tchr., bus. mgr. athletic dept. Van Dyke (Mich.) pub. schs., 1938-41, asst. supt. schs., 1941-43; adminstr. Mt. Clemens (Mich.), Gen. Hosp., 1948-63; adminstr. Orlando (Fla.) Gen. Hosp., 1964-76. Cons. Gov's Study Com. on Blue Cross Rates; instr. gun safety Mich. Dept. Conservation. Pres. bd. edn., Armada Area Sch., 1944-59. Mem. Hosp. Financial Mgmt. Assn. (advanced mem.), Fla. (past pres.), Am. (pres., award of merit 1970), Mich. State (past pres.) osteo. hosp. assns., Am. Coll. Osteopathic Hosp. Adminstrs. (pres. 1974-75, fellow bd. examiners, Disting. Service award 1976), Am. Mgmt. Assn., Am. Acad. Med. Adminstrs. Conglist. (deacon). Mason (Shriner 32 deg.). Lion (past pres.). Home: Winter Park, Fla. Died Feb. 17, 1976; buried Armada, Mich.

ZIEGLER, SAMUEL GEORGE (ZEG'LER), church official; b. Hanover, Pa., Oct. 14, 1884; s. Daniel and Polly (Low) Z.; prep. edn., York (Pa.) Collegiate Inst.; A.B., Lebanon Valley Coll., Annville, Pa., 1911, D.D., 1922; B.D., Bonebrake Theol. Sem., Dayton, O., 1914; m. Georgia Ethel Redding, Oct. 10, 1911; children—Samuel Redding, Paul Fout, James Richard, Miriam Eileen. Ordained ministry U.B. Ch., 1911; pastor Duncannon, Pa., 1909-11, Otterbein Memorial Ch., Baltimore, Md., 1914-17, St. Paul's U.B. Ch., Hagerstown, Md., 1917-21; gen. sec. Fgn. Missionary Soc., U.B. Ch., 1921-46; associate sec. Dept. of World Missions, Evangelical United Brethren Church, since 1946. Member Board Christian Work in Santo Domingo (ex-pres.). Trustee Union Theol. Sem., Rio Piedras, P.R. Mason. Author: Preaching the Gospel Under Five Flags, 1924; Christian Movements in the Orient, 1927; The Fellowship in Action, 1930. Contbr. to Religious Telescope, Evangel. Home: Dayton. *

ZIEGLER, VICTOR, geologist; b. Beverungen, Germany, Nov. 2, 1886; s. Hermann and Frieda (Hess) Z.; came to U.S., 1901; student Cornell Coll., Mt. Vernon, Ia.; B.A., State U. of Ia., 1908; M.A., Columbia, 1910; Ph.D., U. of Denver, 1916; m. Mabel Irene Merrifield, of Iowa City, Ia., Sept. 16, 1908. Fellow in mining geology, Columbia, 1909-10; instr. in geology, Pa. State Coll., 1910-11; asst. prof. geology, S.D. State Sch. of Mines, 1911-14; asst. prof. geology, later prof. and head of dept. Colo. Sch. of Mines since 1914. Geologist, Wyo. State Geol. Survey, 1915; consulting work since 1915. Fellow Geol. Soc. America; mem. Am. Inst. Mining Engrs., Seismol. Soc. America, A.A.A.S., Sigma Xi, Tau Beta Pi, Theta Tau. Republican. Lutheran. Author: Poplar Oil Geology, 1918; also various articles and bulls. Home: Golden, Colo.*

ZIEGLER, VINCENT CHARLES, corp. exec.; b. Greenfield, Mich., Nov. 5, 1910; s. George and Catherine (Cavanaugh) Z.; student Coll. City of Detroit, 1927-29; LL.D. (hon.), Northeastern U., 1974; D.B.A. (hon.), Boston Coll., 1975; m. Marian Louise Hahn, Sept. 16, 1933; children—Mary Ann, Robert Earl. Asst. dir. sales Chrysler Corp., Detroit, 1927-34; exec. asst. Hiram Walker, Inc., Detroit, 1935-42; exec. asst. to v.p. Gillette Safety Razor Co., Boston, 1946-49, Eastern div. sales mgr., N.Y.C., 1949-51, asst. gen. sales mgr., Boston, 1951-52, gen. sales mgr., 1952-53, v.p. charge sales, 1953-58, pres. Gillette Razor Co. div. Gillette Co., 1958-65, exec. v.p. co., 1964-65, pres. co., 1965-66, chmn. bd. co., 1966-67, chmn. bd., pres. Gillette Co., 1967-71, chmn. bd., chief exec. officer, 1971-75, chmn. exec. com., dir., 1975-79; also dir.; dir. Nat. Shawmut Bank, New Eng. Mut. Life Ins. Co., Reed & Barton, Zayre Corp. Mem. adv. com. Simmons Coll. Bus. trustee Boston Coll.; mem. corp.; Northeastern U.; mem. corp., trustee Babson Coll.; bd. advisers Stonehill Coll. Served to maj., ordnance dept. AUS, 1942-46. Fellow Brandeis U. Mem. Nat. Sales Execs. Club, Knights of Malta. Clubs: Brae Burn Country (West Newton); Algonguin (Boston); Monterey Peninsula Country, Cypress Point (Pebble Beach, Calif.). Home: Wellesley Hills, Mass. Died Aug. 1, 1979.

ZIESING, HENRY HANNA, sales exec.; born Chicago, Mar. 31, 1886; s. August and Alice (Hanna) Z.; B.S. (Civ. Engring.), U. of Ill., 1908; m. Marybelle Peyton, June 28, 1916; children—Henry Hanna, Jr., Charlotte Anne, Robert August, Marybelle. Asst. plant mgr. Am. Bridge Co., 1912-16; supt. constrn. Midvale Steel & Ordnance Co., 1916-18; gen. sales mgr. The Midvale Co., 1925-44, vice pres. since 1944. Apptd. mem. steel adv. com. OPA Mem. Am. Soc. for Metals, Western Soc. Engrs., Am. Iron and Steel Inst. Republican. Presbyn. Mason. (Commandery, Scottish Rite). Clubs: University (Chicago); Racquet (Phila.); Merion Cricket (Haverford, Pa.), Merion Golf (Ardmore, Pa.). Home: Wayne, Pa. *

ZIMMER, HELEN ANNE POLLARD, bus. exec.; b. Newark; d. Edward and Delia (ONeill) Pollard; grad. Coleman Bus. Coll.; m. Almond F. Zimmer, Aug. 22, 1938 (dec. 1955). Sec. to sec., treas. Ellis Adding Typewriter Co., Newark, 1929-30, sec. to chief clk. engring. D., L. & W. R.R. Co., Hoboken, N.J., 1930-33; sec. to pres. Debow & Co., Newark, 1933-35; sec. law firm Riker, Danzig, Scherer & Hyland, Newark, 1935-56; sec. to chmn. exec. com., chmn. bd. Fidelity Union Trust Co., Newark, 1956-61, asst. sec., asst. treas., 1961-64, sec., 1964-70; asst. sec. Fidelity Union Bancorp., 1971-73, corporate sec., 1973-80. Service objective chmn. Soroptimist Club of Newark, 1965-66. Mem. Nat. Assn. Bank Women. Home: Newark, N.J. Died Apr. 29, 1980.

ZIMMERLY, GARNETT ALLAN, fgn. service officer; b. Hope, Ark., Dec. 21, 1928; s. Charles Peter and Louisa Freida (Steinkoenig) Z.; B.S.A., U. Mo., 1952; postgrad. George Washington U., 1963-64; m. Carol Mae Carpenter, Feb. 1, 1950, children—Janet, Richard, Denise, Alison. Mem. staff U. Mo., 1952-53, Kan. State U., 1953-58; program officer AID, Seoul, Korea and Washington, 1958-65; dep. asst. dir. program and econ. policy AID, Seoul, 1965-68; program and econ. affairs officer AID, Vientiane, Laos, 1968-69; sr. seminar in fgn. policy Dept. State, 1969-70; asso. dir. program AID, Saigon, Vietnam, 1970-71; dep. dir. Office Vietnam Affairs, Washington, 1971-72, dir., 1972-73; dep. asst. adminstr. supporting assistance bur. AID, Washington, 1973-74, acting asst. adminstr. East Asia Bur. AID, 1974-75; dir. AID/Philippines, Manila, 1975-76. Recipient Distinguished Honor award AID, 1975. Served with USNR, 1946-48. Lion. Home: San Francisco, Calif. Died Sept. 13, 1976; buried Winchester (Va.) Nat. Cemetery.

ZIMMERMAN, FREDERICK, clergyman; b. London, Eng., July 19, 1885; s. John and Elizabeth Louise (Wickert) Z.; student London Poly. Inst., 1907-10, Rutgers U., 1914-16; grad. N.B. Theol. Sem., 1919; D.D., Hope Coll., 1938; m. Sarah E. Rich, June 12, 1918; children—Dorothy E. (Mrs. Donald J. Kramer), Elizabeth L. (Mrs.William A. Peddie). Ordained to ministry, Reformed Ch., 1919, pastor Metuchen, N.H., 1919-37; Am. minister The Hauge English Ch., 1934; exec. sec. bd. domestic missions Reformed Ch. Am., 1937-48; became pastor 1st Ch. in Albany, 1948, Reformed Ch., Schoharie, N.Y., 1954-56, retired, 1956; pres. Gen. Synod, 1953-54; sometime lectr. N.B. Theol. Sem. Mem. Albany Ministers Assn. (pres. 1949). Rotarian. Address: Cambridge, N.Y. *

ZIMMERMAN, LEO M., educator, surgeon; b. Toluca, Ill., Oct. 27, 1898; s. Louis and Sara (Kahan) Z.; A.B., Ind. U., 1919; M.D., Rush Med. Coll., Chgo., 1922; m. Sara Radoff, Apr. 10, 1928; children—David, Judith. Intern Cook County Hosp., Chgo., 1922-24; practice medicine specializing in surgery, Chgo., 1924-80; mem. faculty Northwestern U. Med. Sch., Chgo., 1924-80, prof. surgery, 1948-80; prof. dept. surgery Chgo. Med. Sch., 1948-80, chmn. dept., 1954-62, 66-68, chmn. dept. history and philosophy of medicine, 1968-80; prof. surgery Cook County Grad. Sch. Medicine, 1950-65; attending surgeon Michael Reese Hosp., Chgo., 1928-80. Served with M.C. USNR, 1943-45. Fellow A.C.S., Royal Soc. Medicine (Eng.); mem. A.M.A., Soc. Med. History Chgo. (pres. from 1963), Ill., Chgo. med. socs., Chgo. Surg. Soc., Am. Thyroid Assn., Am. Assn. History Medicine, Sigma Xi, Alpha Omega Alpha. Author: Physiologic Principles of Surgery, 1957; Principles of Surgical Practice, 1960; History of American Medicine, 1967; Great Ideas in the History of Surgery, 1967; Anatomy and Surgery of Hernia, 1953. Contbr. to profl. jours. Home: Chicago, Ill. Died June 28, 1980; interred Chicago, Ill.

ZIMMERMAN, OTTO HERMAN, railroad exec.; b. Champaign, Ill., Apr. 10, 1914; s. Otto Herman and Anna G. (Donley) Z.; student Ill. Wesleyan U., U. Ill.; m. Martha J. White, May 3, 1940; children—Fredric W., Mary E. With Ill. Central Gulf R.R. Co., from 1936, beginning as switchman, successively asst. train master, train master, supt., asst. to v.p. operations, gen. supt. transp., gen. mgr., 1936-56, v.p. operations, 1956-68, sr. v.p. operations, 1968-72, exec. v.p. operations, 1972-74, also dir.; past v.p., dir. Chgo. & Ill. Western R.R., Chgo. Produce Terminal, Waterloo R.R. Co.; dir. Pullman Bank and Trust Co., Belt Ry. Co. Chgo., Peoria & Pekin Union R.R., Ill. Terminal R.R., Terminal R.R. Assn. St. Louis, Jefferson Southwestern R.R., Mut., Fire, Marine and Inland Ins. Co., Phila. Mem. gen. com. Assn. Am. Railroads; chmn. operating com. Ill. R.R. Assn. Mason (Shriner). Clubs: Chicago, Chicago Athletic Assn., Traffic, Western Railway (Chgo.); Flossmoor (Ill.) Country. Home: Flossmoor, Ill. Died Feb. 7, 1979.

ZIMMERMAN, WILLARD PAUL, glass mfr.; b. Washington Court House, Ohio, June 18, 1894; s. Samuel W. and Florence (Cockerill) Z.; A.B., Miami U., Oxford, Ohio, 1917, LL.D., 1973; LL.D., Toledo U., 1964; m. Ruth McCoy, Mar. 27, 1918; children—Doris Jean, Willard Paul. Sales mgr. Am. Seeding Machine Co., 1920-27; sec.treas. Hemingray Glass Co., 1927-33; plant mgr. Owens-Ill. Glass Co., 1933-36, gen. mgr. indsl. and structural div., Toledo 1936-38; exec. v.p. Owens-Corning Fiberglass Corp., 1946-56, cons., from 1956; dir. Ohio Citizens Trust Co. Trustee, Toledo Hosp., Inst. Med. Research, Miami U. Served as regt. adj., U.S. Army, World War I. Recipient Distinguished Service award Nat. Found. and Hall of Fame, 1963. Mem. AIM, U. S., Ohio chambers commerce, Res. Officers Assn., Am. Legion, 40 and 8, Ind. Soc. Chgo., Delta Kappa Epsilon, Sigma Delta Psi. Republican. Presbyn. Clubs: DKE (N.Y.C.); Toledo, Iverness (Toledo); Boca Raton, Royal Palm Yacht and Country (Boca Raton, Fla.). Mason (hon. 33 deg.). Home: Toledo, Ohio. Died Oct. 3, 1979.

ZIMMERMANN, FREDERICK JOHN, chemist; b. London, Eng., May 4, 1899; s. Frederick George and Louise (Stauffer) Z.; student schs., London, 1905-13, Real Gymnasium, Zurich, Switzerland, 1913-18; diploma Engineur Chemiker, Eidgenossische Technische Hochschule Zurich, 1922; m. Gertrude Lynds, Apr. 18, 1940; 1 dau., Katharine Louise. Came to U.S., 1929, naturalized, 1937. Cons. chemist, London, Eng., 1922-29; dir. devel. Burroughs Wellcome, N.Y., 1929-35; pres. Salvo Chem. div. Sterling Drug, Inc., Rothschild, Wis., 1942-67, Zimpro div., 1961-67, v.p. Sterling Drug, Inc., N.Y.C., 1961-67. Mem. Am., Brit. chem. socs. Author tech. articles. Patentee pharm. field, potash and waste disposal. Home: Naples, Fla. Died Mar. 6, 1976.

ZINN, ROLAND H., business exec.; born Milwaukee, Dec. 1, 1886; s. August and Marie (Schmidt) Z.; ed. pub. schs. of Milwaukee; m. Gertrude S. Harlowe, June 11, 1908; 1 son, Harlowe R. Began as clerk Wis. Central R.R. Co., 1904; with Allis Chalmers Co., 1906-11; Wis. sales rep. Sewell Clapp Mfg. Co., 1914, Thos. D. Murphy Co., 1915; in charge leather hides and shoes, Fed. Trade Commn., 1917-20; in charge cost accounting for industry, Tanners Council of Am., 1920-22; with U.S. Leather Co. since 1922. dir. Keystone Tanning and Glue Co., Keta Realty Co., U.S. Leather Co., Am. Hair and Felt Co. Mem. Commodity Exchange, Tanners Council of Am., Nat. Assn. Cost Accountants, Comtrollers Inst. Clubs: Bankers, Union League (Chicago); N.Y. Yacht, Manhasset Bay Yacht, Maplewood Country, Canoe Brook Country, Maplewood, Skytop. Author of books on cost accounting methods for industry, cost mannuals. Home: South Orange, N.J. *

ZINSMASTER, HARRY W., wholesale baker; b. Des Moines, May 15, 1885; s. William and Mary Ann (Kirkman) Z.; B.S., Amherst Coll., 1908; m. Josephine Van Dyne, Apr. 23, 1913 (dec. Sept. 1968); children—Jane (Mrs. Jose DeCastro), William; m. 2d, Dorothea Mae Elwell, Apr. 6, 1971. Advt. rep. J. Walter Thompson Co., N.Y.C., 1908-12; v.p., sales mgr. Des Moines Bakery Co., 1912-13; organizer Zins-master-Smith Bread Co. (named Zinmaster Bread Co., 1918), 1913, and served as pres.; organized Zinsmaster Baking Co., St. Paul, 1919, Mpls., 1929, pres. until 1959, chmn., 1959—; organized Zinsmaster Hol-Ry., Duluth 1931, and since served as pres.; dir. N.P. Ry., 1933-62, also mem. exec. comm.; dir. Interstate Bakeries Corp., Gamble Skogmo, Inc., First Am. Nat. Bank, Duluth. Mem. Pres. Truman's Citizens Food Com. following World War II. Dir., mem. exec. com., trustee Nutrition Found., Inc.; hon. mem. Bus. Council; regional chmn. 9th Fed. Dist., Com. for Econ. Devel., 1943-46, trustee, 1946—; mem. Minn. Postwar Council. Mem. N.A.M. (nat. v.p.), C. of C. (dir. 1939—), Am. Bakers Assn. (dir., past pres.), Minn. Golf Assn. (dir. 1946-47). Mason (32 deg., Shriner), Rotarian (pres. 1917-18). Clubs: Kitchi Gammi, Athletic (Duluth); Northland Country (pres. 1932- 33, dir. 1938—); Minneapolis Bakers, Minikahda Country (Mpls.); Town and Country, St. Paul Athletic, Minn. Athletic (St. Paul). Home: Minneapolis MN. * lis

ZINSSER, WILLIAM HERMAN, business exec.; b. New York, N.Y., Aug. 5, 1887; s. William H. and Frida (Scharman) Z.; A.B., Princeton, 1909; m. Joyce Knowlton, Jan. 6, 1917; children—Nancy (Walworth), Polly (Steinway), Joyce (Applewhite), William Knowlton. Asso. with William Zinsser and Co., New York and Chicago, shellac mfrs., pres., 1911-64. Former mayor Village Kings Point, N.Y.; mem. N.Y.C. Art Commn., 1960-79, N.Y.C. Landmarks Preservation Commn., 1962—. Trustee Lenox Hill Hosp., 1930-79, pres., 1941-53. Clubs: Century Assn. (N.Y.C.); University; Piping Rock; Yeamans Hall (Charleston, S.C.). Home: New York, N.Y. Died Feb. 20, 1979.

ZUCKERMAN, BEN, fashion designer; b. Romania, July 29, 1890; s. Michael and Ida (Goodman); student pub. schs., N.J. Head coat, suit mfg. Zuckerman & Hoffman, N.Y.C., 1911; organized Zuckerman & Kraus; founder Ben Zuckerman, 1950. Dir. N.Y. Indsl. Council. Recipient NiemanMarcus award, 1951, Am. Fashion Critics award, 1952. Home: New York, N.Y. Died Aug. 9, 1979.

ZUCKMAYER, CARL, author, playwright; b. Germany, Dec. 27, 1896; s. Carl and Amalie (Goldschmidt) Z.; ed. Gymnasium, Mainz, Germany, and U. Heidelberg; Litt.D., Dartmouth, 1955; Dr. phil. U. Bonn, 1956; Dr. h.c., U. Bonn, Dartmouth Coll., Hanover, N.H.; m. Alice von Herdan, June 26, 1925; 1 dau., Winnetou. First paly produced in Germany, "Kreuzweg", 1920; first great stage success Der Fröhliche Weinberg (comedy), 1925; Schinderhannes (drama), 1927; several plays including "Der Hauptmann von Kopenick", 1931. Received several prizes in Germany for literature and playwriting, recipient Goethe Prize, 1952, for collected works. Served as an officer in German Army during World War I. Member P.E.N. Club, Screen Writers Guild, and Authors League. Roman Catholic. Author: (translations from the German) The Captain of Kopenick, 1932; The Moons Over, 1936; Second Wind, 1940; The Devils General, 1945; Barbara Blomberg, 1948; Gesang im Feuerofen (drama), 1950; Die Erzaehlungen (short stories); Die Langen Wege (essay), 1952; Ulla Winblad, 1953; Das Kalte Licht (drama), 1955; Die Fastnachts beichte (novel), 1959; Collected Works 4 vols., 1960; Die Uhr schlaegt eins, 1961; Des Teufels General, 1962; The Life of Horace A. W. Tabor (drama), 1964; Als Wärs ein Stück von mir (Autobiographie), 1966. Home: Saas-Fee, Switzerland. Died Jan. 18, 1977.

ZUFALL, CHALMERS J(OSEPH) (ZOO-FAL), university prof., pharmacognosist; b. Frankfort, Ind., May 1, 1885; s. Elijah I. and Mary N. (Hill) Z.; B.S., Purdue U., 1907, M.S., 1914; Ph.D., U. of Wis., 1938; m. Eslie Lee Kirkpatrick, Sept. 10, 1908 (dec. 1919); children—Elizabeth Louise, Joseph Chalmers, David Philip; m. 2d, Lucy Wiebers, Nov. 23, 1921. Science teacher, Salem (O.) High Sch., 6 yrs.; pharmacognosist Eli Lilly & Co., Indianapolis, 4 yrs.; instr. in pharmacognosy, Phila. Coll. of Pharmacy and Science, 2 yrs.; pharmacognosist Food and Drug Adminstrn., Port of N.Y., 5 yrs.; prof. pharmacology and pharmacognosy, Purdue U., since 1921, acting dean sch. of pharmacy, 1926-27. Pres. Oakland Parent-Teacher Assn., Lafayette High Sch. Parent-Teacher Assn., Lafayette Council of Parent-Teacher Assns.; mem. Salem (O.) Bd. of Health; auxiliary mem. revision com., U.S. Pharmacopoeia. Mem. Am. Pharm. Assn., Ind. Acad. Sci., Optimist Internat. (pres., 1947), Internat. Assn. of Purdue U., Am. Inst. History of Pharmacy, Sigma Xi, Rho Chi, Kappa Psi. Presbyterian. Contbr. articles to Jour. of Am. Pharm. Assn.; research in discovery of plant constituents, scientific crime detection. Home: West Lafayette, Ind. *

ZUKOFSKY, LOUIS, poet; b. N.Y.C., Jan. 23, 1904; s. Paul and Chana (Pruss) Z.; M.A. in English, Columbia, 1924; Litt.D. (hon.), Bard Coll., 1977; m. Celia Thaew, Aug. 20, 1939 (dec. Nov. 18, 1980); 1 son, Paul. Instr. English and comparative lit. U. Wis-Madison, 1930-31, Queen's Coll., 1947, Colgate U., 1947, San Francisco State Coll., 1958; mem. faculty Poly. Inst. Bklyn., 1947-66, asso. prof. English, 1955-66; guest prof. Grad. Sch., U. Conn., Storrs, fall 1971. Recipient cash award Nat. Inst. Arts and Letters, 1976. Author: "A" 1-12, 1966; "A" 13-21, 1969; All the collected short poems 1923-1964, 1971; "A" 22 & 23, 1975; "A"-24, 1972; Autobiography, 1970; Bottom: on Shakespeare, 1963; Ferdinand, 1968; Arise, Arise, 1973; A test of Poetry, 1948; Little, 1970; Prepositions, 1967. Translator: (with Celia Zukofsky) Catullus, 1969. Home: Port Jefferson, N.Y. Died May 12, 1978.

ZUKOR, ADOLPH, motion picture exec.; b. Riese, Hungary, Jan. 7, 1873; s. Jacob and Hannah (Lieberman) Z.; ed. in Hungary, and evening schs., N.Y.; m. Lottie Kaufman, Jan. 10, 1897; children—Eugene James, Mrs. Mildred Loew. Came to U.S., 1888; engaged in hardware, upholstery and fur business N.Y., Chgo.; asso., 1904, with Mitchell Mark, who was owner of Strand Theatre, N.Y., and with Marcus Loew, presenting vaudeville and motion pictures; founder Famous Players Film Co., 1912; chmn. bd. emeritus Paramount Pictures Corp. Jewish. Clubs: Lambs, City Athletic (N.Y.), Masons. Home: Los Angeles, Calif. Died June 10, 1976.

ZWANCK, ALBERTO, physician; born Buenos Aires, Argentina, Apr. 26, 1884; s. Enrique and Isabel (Acosta) Z.; M.D., Nat. U. of Buenos Aires, 1908; m. Angela Galves, Apr. 26, 1909, Interne Hosp. Nacional de Clinicas, Universidad Nacional, Buenos Aires, 1909-10; health officer City Health Dept., 1910-18, sanitary inspector Nat. Dept. Health, 1920-31; asst. prof. pub. health, Universidad Nacional, Buenos Aires, 1920-30, prof. pub. health, 1931-46, founder and dir. sch. of social service and pub. health nursing, Buenos Aires, 1924-46; founder and dir. sch. of hygiene, Universidad National, 1940-46. Mem. Sanitary Interchanges Health div., League of Nations, 1925, 27, 37. Advisor on internat. pub. health relations Ministry of Health, Argentina, since 1946; Permanent rep. of Argentina at Internat. health orgns.: Pan Am. Sanitary Bur. and World Health Orgn. Advisor on pub. health to Argentine Del. to U.N. Catholic. Contbr. articles on public health, to tech. pubs. Home: Buenos Aires, Argentina. *